2022
Harris
Northern California
Business Directory and Buyers Guide

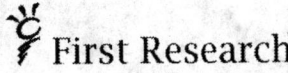

Published February 2022 next update February 2023

WARNING: Purchasers and users of this directory may not use this directory to compile mailing lists, other marketing aids and other types of data, which are sold or otherwise provided to third parties. Such use is wrongful, illegal and a violation of the federal copyright laws.

CAUTION: Because of the many thousands of establishment listings contained in this directory and the possibilities of both human and mechanical error in processing this information, Harris InfoSource cannot assume liability for the correctness of the listings or information on which they are based. Hence, no information contained in this work should be relied upon in any instance where there is a possibility of any loss or damage as a consequence of any error or omission in this volume.

Publisher

Mergent Inc.
444 Madison Ave
New York, NY 10022

©Mergent Inc All Rights Reserved
2022 Mergent Business Press
ISSN 1080-2614
ISBN 978-1-64972-633-9

TABLE OF CONTENTS

Summary of Contents & Explanatory Notes 4
User's Guide to Listings 6

PRODUCTS & SERVICES SECTION
Numerical SIC Index 9
Alphabetical SIC Section 13
Firms listed under primary SIC 17

Alphabetic Section
Firms listed alphabetically by company name 885

Geographic Section
Southern California county-city cross reference index 1127
Companies sorted alphabetically under their respective cities 1129

SUMMARY OF CONTENTS

Number of Companies 19,923
Number of Decision Makers 61,795
Minimum Number of Employees .... (Services) 35
Minimum Number of Employees .... (Manufacturers) 15

EXPLANATORY NOTES

How to Cross-Reference in This Directory

Sequential Entry Numbers. Each establishment in the Geographic Section is numbered sequentially (G-0000). The number assigned to each establishment is referred to as its "entry number." To make cross-referencing easier, each listing in the Geographic, SIC, Alphabetic and Product Sections includes the establishment's entry number. To facilitate locating an entry in the Geographic Section, the entry numbers for the first listing on the left page and the last listing on the right page are printed at the top of the page next to the city name.

Source Suggestions Welcome

Although all known sources were used to compile this directory, it is possible that companies were inadvertently omitted. Your assistance in calling attention to such omissions would be greatly appreciated. A special form on the facing page will help you in the reporting process.

Analysis

Every effort has been made to contact all firms to verify their information. The one exception to this rule is the annual sales figure, which is considered by many companies to be confidential information. Therefore, estimated sales have been calculated by multiplying the nationwide average sales per employee for the firm's major SIC/NAICS code by the firm's number of employees. Nationwide averages for sales per employee by SIC/NAICS codes are provided by the U.S. Department of Commerce and are updated annually. All sales—sales (est)—have been estimated by this method. The exceptions are parent companies (PA), division headquarters (DH) and headquarter locations (HQ) which may include an actual corporate sales figure—sales (corporate-wide) if available.

Types of Companies

Descriptive and statistical data are included for companies in the entire state. These comprise manufacturers, machine shops, fabricators, assemblers and printers. Also identified are corporate offices in the state.

Employment Data

The employment figure shown in the Products & Services Section includes male and female employees and embraces all levels of the company. This directory includes manufacturing companies with 15 or more employees and service companies with 35 or more employees. This figure is for the facility listed and does not include other plants or offices. It should be recognized that these figures represent an approximate year-round average. These employment figures are broken into codes A through F and used in the Product and SIC Sections to further help you in qualifying a company. Be sure to check the footnotes on the bottom right hand pages for the code breakdowns.

Standard Industrial Classification (SIC)

The Standard Industrial Classification (SIC) system used in this directory was developed by the federal government for use in classifying establishments by the type of activity they are engaged in. The SIC classifications used in this directory are from the 1987 edition published by the U.S. Government's Office of Management and Budget. The SIC system separates all activities into broad industrial divisions (e.g., manufacturing, mining, retail trade). It further subdivides each division. The range of manufacturing industry classes extends from two-digit codes (major industry group) to four-digit codes (product).

For example:

Industry Breakdown	Code	Industry, Product, etc.
*Major industry group	20	Food and kindred products
Industry group	203	Canned and frozen foods
*Industry	2033	Fruits and vegetables, etc.

*Classifications used in this directory

Only two-digit and four-digit codes are used in this directory.

Arrangement

1. The **Geographic Section** contains complete in-depth corporate data. This section is sorted by cities listed in alphabetical order and companies listed alphabetically within each city. A County/City Index for referencing cities within counties precedes this section.

> IMPORTANT NOTICE: It is a violation of both federal and state law to transmit an unsolicited advertisement to a facsimile machine. Any user of this product that violates such laws may be subject to civil and criminal penalties, which may exceed $500 for each transmission of an unsolicited facsimile. Harris InfoSource provides fax numbers for lawful purposes only and expressly forbids the use of these numbers in any unlawful manner.

2. The **Standard Industrial Classification (SIC) Section** lists companies under approximately 500 four-digit SIC codes. An alphabetical and a numerical index precedes this section. A company can be listed under several codes. The codes are in numerical order with companies listed alphabetically under each code.

3. The **Alphabetic Section** lists all companies with their full physical or mailing addresses and telephone number.

4. The **Product Section** lists companies under unique Harris categories. An index preceding this section lists all product categories in alphabetical order. Companies can be listed under several categories.

USER'S GUIDE TO LISTINGS

PRODUCT & SERVICES SECTION

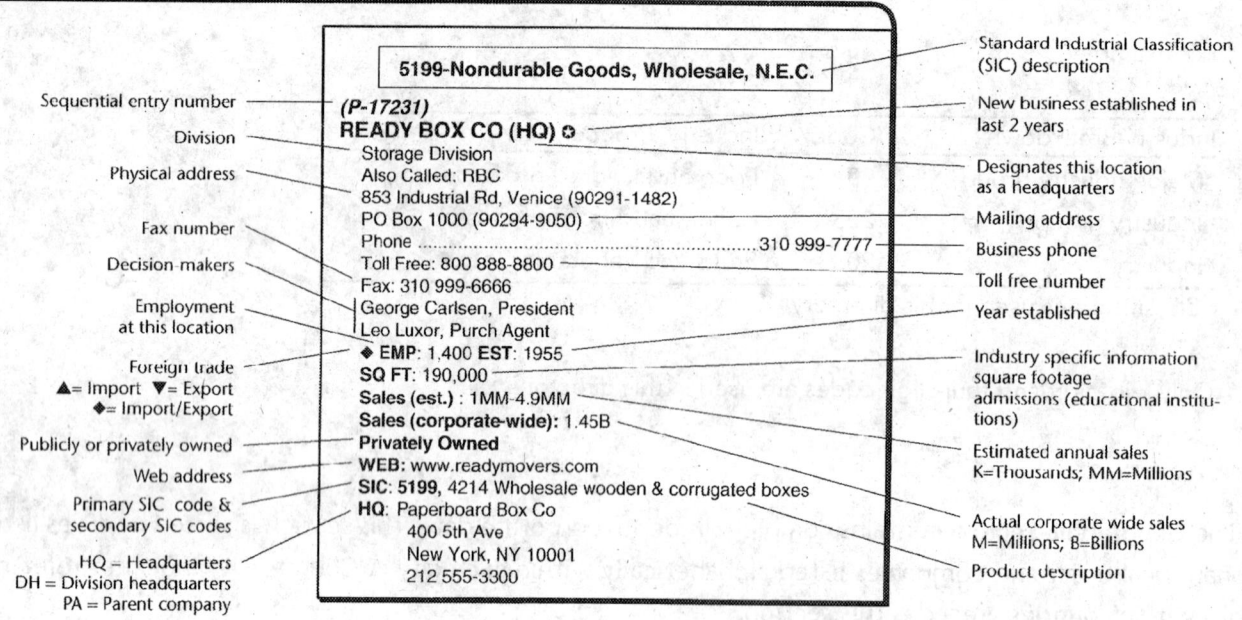

ALPHABETIC SECTION

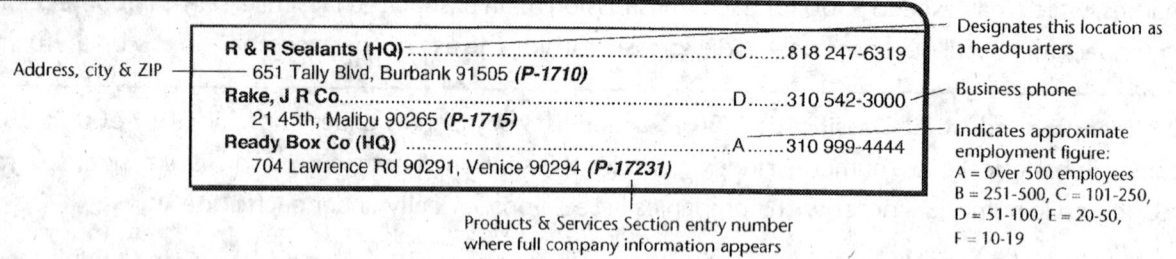

GEOGRAPHIC SECTION

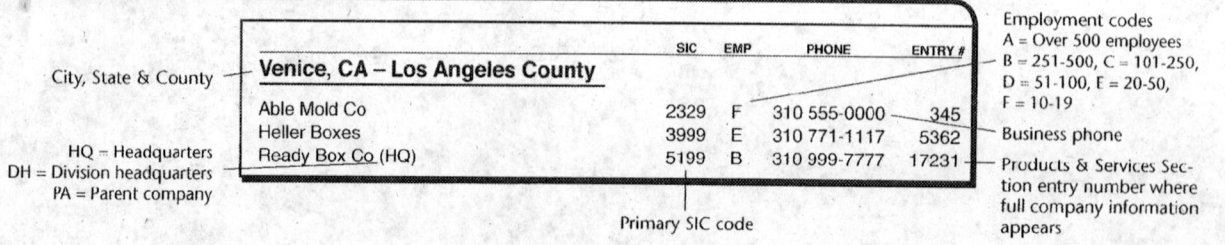

NUMERICAL INDEX of SIC DESCRIPTIONS
ALPHABETICAL INDEX of SIC DESCRIPTIONS

PRODUCT & SERVICES SECTION
Companies listed alphabetically under their primary SIC
In-depth company data listed

ALPHABETIC SECTION
Company listings in alphabetical order

GEOGRAPHIC SECTION
Companies sorted by city in alphabetical order

Northern California
County Map

SIC INDEX

Standard Industrial Classification Numerical Index

| SIC NO | PRODUCT |

01 agricultural production-crops
0111 Wheat
0112 Rice
0115 Corn
0119 Cash Grains, NEC
0131 Cotton
0133 Sugarcane & Sugar Beets
0139 Field Crops, Except Cash Grains, NEC
0161 Vegetables & Melons
0171 Berry Crops
0172 Grapes
0173 Tree Nuts
0174 Citrus Fruits
0175 Deciduous Tree Fruits
0179 Fruits & Tree Nuts, NEC
0181 Ornamental Floriculture & Nursery Prdts
0182 Food Crops Grown Under Cover
0191 Crop Farming, Misc

02 agricultural production-livestock and animal specialties
0211 Beef Cattle Feedlots
0212 Beef Cattle, Except Feedlots
0213 Hogs
0241 Dairy Farms
0251 Chicken & Poultry Farms
0252 Chicken Egg Farms
0253 Turkey & Turkey Egg Farms
0254 Poultry Hatcheries
0259 Poultry & Eggs Farms, NEC
0272 Horse & Other Equine Production
0279 Animal Specialties, NEC
0291 Animal Production, NEC

07 agricultural services
0711 Soil Preparation Svcs
0721 Soil Preparation, Planting & Cultivating Svc
0722 Crop Harvesting By Machine
0723 Crop Preparation, Except Cotton Ginning
0741 Veterinary Livestock Svcs
0742 Veterinary Animal Specialties
0751 Livestock Svcs, Except Veterinary
0752 Animal Specialty Svcs, Exc Veterinary
0761 Farm Labor Contractors & Crew Leaders
0762 Farm Management Svcs
0781 Landscape Counseling & Planning
0782 Lawn & Garden Svcs
0783 Ornamental Shrub & Tree Svc

08 forestry
0811 Timber Tracts
0851 Forestry Svcs

09 fishing, hunting, and trapping
0921 Finfish Farming & Fish Hatcheries
0971 Hunting & Trapping

10 metal mining
1011 Iron Ores
1021 Copper Ores
1041 Gold Ores
1061 Ferroalloy Ores, Except Vanadium
1081 Metal Mining Svcs

12 coal mining
1221 Bituminous Coal & Lignite: Surface Mining
1241 Coal Mining Svcs

13 oil and gas extraction
1311 Crude Petroleum & Natural Gas
1321 Natural Gas Liquids
1381 Drilling Oil & Gas Wells
1382 Oil & Gas Field Exploration Svcs
1389 Oil & Gas Field Svcs, NEC

14 mining and quarrying of nonmetallic minerals, except fuels
1411 Dimension Stone
1422 Crushed & Broken Limestone
1423 Crushed & Broken Granite
1429 Crushed & Broken Stone, NEC
1442 Construction Sand & Gravel
1446 Industrial Sand
1499 Miscellaneous Nonmetallic Mining

15 building construction-general contractors and operative builders
1521 General Contractors, Single Family Houses
1522 General Contractors, Residential Other Than Single Family
1531 Operative Builders
1541 General Contractors, Indl Bldgs & Warehouses
1542 General Contractors, Nonresidential & Non-indl Bldgs

16 heavy construction other than building construction-contractors
1611 Highway & Street Construction
1622 Bridge, Tunnel & Elevated Hwy Construction
1623 Water, Sewer & Utility Line Construction
1629 Heavy Construction, NEC

17 construction-special trade contractors
1711 Plumbing, Heating & Air Conditioning Contractors
1721 Painting & Paper Hanging Contractors
1731 Electrical Work
1741 Masonry & Other Stonework
1742 Plastering, Drywall, Acoustical & Insulation Work
1743 Terrazzo, Tile, Marble & Mosaic Work
1751 Carpentry Work
1752 Floor Laying & Other Floor Work, NEC
1761 Roofing, Siding & Sheet Metal Work
1771 Concrete Work
1781 Water Well Drilling
1791 Structural Steel Erection
1793 Glass & Glazing Work
1794 Excavating & Grading Work
1795 Wrecking & Demolition Work
1796 Installation Or Erection Of Bldg Eqpt & Machinery, NEC
1799 Special Trade Contractors, NEC

20 food and kindred products
2011 Meat Packing Plants
2013 Sausages & Meat Prdts
2015 Poultry Slaughtering, Dressing & Processing
2021 Butter
2022 Cheese
2023 Milk, Condensed & Evaporated
2024 Ice Cream
2026 Milk
2032 Canned Specialties
2033 Canned Fruits, Vegetables & Preserves
2034 Dried Fruits, Vegetables & Soup
2035 Pickled Fruits, Vegetables, Sauces & Dressings
2037 Frozen Fruits, Juices & Vegetables
2038 Frozen Specialties
2041 Flour, Grain Milling
2043 Cereal Breakfast Foods
2044 Rice Milling
2045 Flour, Blended & Prepared
2046 Wet Corn Milling
2047 Dog & Cat Food
2048 Prepared Feeds For Animals & Fowls
2051 Bread, Bakery Prdts Exc Cookies & Crackers
2052 Cookies & Crackers
2053 Frozen Bakery Prdts
2063 Sugar, Beet
2064 Candy & Confectionery Prdts
2066 Chocolate & Cocoa Prdts
2068 Salted & Roasted Nuts & Seeds
2076 Vegetable Oil Mills
2077 Animal, Marine Fats & Oils
2079 Shortening, Oils & Margarine
2082 Malt Beverages
2084 Wine & Brandy
2085 Liquors, Distilled, Rectified & Blended
2086 Soft Drinks
2087 Flavoring Extracts & Syrups
2091 Fish & Seafoods, Canned & Cured
2092 Fish & Seafoods, Fresh & Frozen
2095 Coffee
2096 Potato Chips & Similar Prdts
2097 Ice
2098 Macaroni, Spaghetti & Noodles
2099 Food Preparations, NEC

21 tobacco products
2131 Tobacco, Chewing & Snuff

22 textile mill products
2211 Cotton, Woven Fabric
2221 Silk & Man-Made Fiber
2231 Wool, Woven Fabric
2241 Fabric Mills, Cotton, Wool, Silk & Man-Made
2252 Hosiery, Except Women's
2253 Knit Outerwear Mills
2259 Knitting Mills, NEC
2261 Cotton Fabric Finishers
2273 Carpets & Rugs
2281 Yarn Spinning Mills
2296 Tire Cord & Fabric
2298 Cordage & Twine
2299 Textile Goods, NEC

23 apparel and other finished products made from fabrics and similar material
2311 Men's & Boys' Suits, Coats & Overcoats
2321 Men's & Boys' Shirts
2323 Men's & Boys' Neckwear
2325 Men's & Boys' Separate Trousers & Casual Slacks
2326 Men's & Boys' Work Clothing
2329 Men's & Boys' Clothing, NEC
2331 Women's & Misses' Blouses
2335 Women's & Misses' Dresses
2337 Women's & Misses' Suits, Coats & Skirts
2339 Women's & Misses' Outerwear, NEC
2353 Hats, Caps & Millinery
2361 Children's & Infants' Dresses & Blouses
2369 Girls' & Infants' Outerwear, NEC
2381 Dress & Work Gloves
2386 Leather & Sheep Lined Clothing
2387 Apparel Belts
2389 Apparel & Accessories, NEC
2391 Curtains & Draperies
2392 House furnishings: Textile
2393 Textile Bags
2394 Canvas Prdts
2395 Pleating & Stitching For The Trade
2396 Automotive Trimmings, Apparel Findings, Related Prdts
2399 Fabricated Textile Prdts, NEC

24 lumber and wood products, except furniture
2411 Logging
2421 Saw & Planing Mills
2426 Hardwood Dimension & Flooring Mills
2431 Millwork
2434 Wood Kitchen Cabinets
2435 Hardwood Veneer & Plywood
2436 Softwood Veneer & Plywood
2439 Structural Wood Members, NEC
2441 Wood Boxes
2448 Wood Pallets & Skids
2449 Wood Containers, NEC
2451 Mobile Homes
2452 Prefabricated Wood Buildings & Cmpnts
2491 Wood Preserving
2493 Reconstituted Wood Prdts
2499 Wood Prdts, NEC

25 furniture and fixtures
2511 Wood Household Furniture
2512 Wood Household Furniture, Upholstered
2514 Metal Household Furniture
2515 Mattresses & Bedsprings
2519 Household Furniture, NEC
2521 Wood Office Furniture
2522 Office Furniture, Except Wood
2531 Public Building & Related Furniture
2541 Wood, Office & Store Fixtures
2542 Partitions & Fixtures, Except Wood
2591 Drapery Hardware, Window Blinds & Shades
2599 Furniture & Fixtures, NEC

26 paper and allied products
2611 Pulp Mills
2621 Paper Mills
2631 Paperboard Mills
2652 Set-Up Paperboard Boxes
2653 Corrugated & Solid Fiber Boxes
2655 Fiber Cans, Tubes & Drums
2656 Sanitary Food Containers
2657 Folding Paperboard Boxes

SIC INDEX

SIC NO	PRODUCT
2671	Paper Coating & Laminating for Packaging
2672	Paper Coating & Laminating, Exc for Packaging
2673	Bags: Plastics, Laminated & Coated
2674	Bags: Uncoated Paper & Multiwall
2675	Die-Cut Paper & Board
2676	Sanitary Paper Prdts
2677	Envelopes
2678	Stationery Prdts
2679	Converted Paper Prdts, NEC

27 printing, publishing, and allied industries

SIC NO	PRODUCT
2711	Newspapers: Publishing & Printing
2721	Periodicals: Publishing & Printing
2731	Books: Publishing & Printing
2732	Book Printing, Not Publishing
2741	Misc Publishing
2752	Commercial Printing: Lithographic
2754	Commercial Printing: Gravure
2759	Commercial Printing
2761	Manifold Business Forms
2771	Greeting Card Publishing
2782	Blankbooks & Looseleaf Binders
2789	Bookbinding
2791	Typesetting
2796	Platemaking & Related Svcs

28 chemicals and allied products

SIC NO	PRODUCT
2812	Alkalies & Chlorine
2813	Industrial Gases
2819	Indl Inorganic Chemicals, NEC
2821	Plastics, Mtrls & Nonvulcanizable Elastomers
2822	Synthetic Rubber (Vulcanizable Elastomers)
2823	Cellulosic Man-Made Fibers
2824	Synthetic Organic Fibers, Exc Cellulosic
2833	Medicinal Chemicals & Botanical Prdts
2834	Pharmaceuticals
2835	Diagnostic Substances
2836	Biological Prdts, Exc Diagnostic Substances
2841	Soap & Detergents
2842	Spec Cleaning, Polishing & Sanitation Preparations
2844	Perfumes, Cosmetics & Toilet Preparations
2851	Paints, Varnishes, Lacquers, Enamels
2861	Gum & Wood Chemicals
2865	Cyclic-Crudes, Intermediates, Dyes & Org Pigments
2869	Industrial Organic Chemicals, NEC
2873	Nitrogenous Fertilizers
2874	Phosphatic Fertilizers
2875	Fertilizers, Mixing Only
2879	Pesticides & Agricultural Chemicals, NEC
2891	Adhesives & Sealants
2892	Explosives
2893	Printing Ink
2899	Chemical Preparations, NEC

29 petroleum refining and related industries

SIC NO	PRODUCT
2911	Petroleum Refining
2951	Paving Mixtures & Blocks
2952	Asphalt Felts & Coatings
2992	Lubricating Oils & Greases

30 rubber and miscellaneous plastics products

SIC NO	PRODUCT
3011	Tires & Inner Tubes
3021	Rubber & Plastic Footwear
3052	Rubber & Plastic Hose & Belting
3053	Gaskets, Packing & Sealing Devices
3061	Molded, Extruded & Lathe-Cut Rubber Mechanical Goods
3069	Fabricated Rubber Prdts, NEC
3081	Plastic Unsupported Sheet & Film
3082	Plastic Unsupported Profile Shapes
3083	Plastic Laminated Plate & Sheet
3084	Plastic Pipe
3085	Plastic Bottles
3086	Plastic Foam Prdts
3087	Custom Compounding Of Purchased Plastic Resins
3088	Plastic Plumbing Fixtures
3089	Plastic Prdts

31 leather and leather products

SIC NO	PRODUCT
3111	Leather Tanning & Finishing
3131	Boot & Shoe Cut Stock & Findings
3143	Men's Footwear, Exc Athletic
3144	Women's Footwear, Exc Athletic
3149	Footwear, NEC
3161	Luggage
3171	Handbags & Purses
3199	Leather Goods, NEC

32 stone, clay, glass, and concrete products

SIC NO	PRODUCT
3211	Flat Glass
3221	Glass Containers
3229	Pressed & Blown Glassware, NEC
3231	Glass Prdts Made Of Purchased Glass
3241	Cement, Hydraulic
3251	Brick & Structural Clay Tile
3253	Ceramic Tile
3255	Clay Refractories
3259	Structural Clay Prdts, NEC
3261	China Plumbing Fixtures & Fittings
3264	Porcelain Electrical Splys
3269	Pottery Prdts, NEC
3271	Concrete Block & Brick
3272	Concrete Prdts
3273	Ready-Mixed Concrete
3274	Lime
3275	Gypsum Prdts
3281	Cut Stone Prdts
3291	Abrasive Prdts
3292	Asbestos products
3295	Minerals & Earths: Ground Or Treated
3296	Mineral Wool
3297	Nonclay Refractories
3299	Nonmetallic Mineral Prdts, NEC

33 primary metal industries

SIC NO	PRODUCT
3312	Blast Furnaces, Coke Ovens, Steel & Rolling Mills
3315	Steel Wire Drawing & Nails & Spikes
3316	Cold Rolled Steel Sheet, Strip & Bars
3317	Steel Pipe & Tubes
3321	Gray Iron Foundries
3322	Malleable Iron Foundries
3324	Steel Investment Foundries
3325	Steel Foundries, NEC
3334	Primary Production Of Aluminum
3339	Primary Nonferrous Metals, NEC
3341	Secondary Smelting & Refining Of Nonferrous Metals
3351	Rolling, Drawing & Extruding Of Copper
3353	Aluminum Sheet, Plate & Foil
3354	Aluminum Extruded Prdts
3355	Aluminum Rolling & Drawing, NEC
3356	Rolling, Drawing-Extruding Of Nonferrous Metals
3357	Nonferrous Wire Drawing
3363	Aluminum Die Castings
3364	Nonferrous Die Castings, Exc Aluminum
3365	Aluminum Foundries
3366	Copper Foundries
3369	Nonferrous Foundries: Castings, NEC
3398	Metal Heat Treating
3399	Primary Metal Prdts, NEC

34 fabricated metal products, except machinery and transportation equipment

SIC NO	PRODUCT
3411	Metal Cans
3412	Metal Barrels, Drums, Kegs & Pails
3421	Cutlery
3423	Hand & Edge Tools
3425	Hand Saws & Saw Blades
3429	Hardware, NEC
3431	Enameled Iron & Metal Sanitary Ware
3432	Plumbing Fixture Fittings & Trim, Brass
3433	Heating Eqpt
3441	Fabricated Structural Steel
3442	Metal Doors, Sash, Frames, Molding & Trim
3443	Fabricated Plate Work
3444	Sheet Metal Work
3446	Architectural & Ornamental Metal Work
3448	Prefabricated Metal Buildings & Cmpnts
3449	Misc Structural Metal Work
3451	Screw Machine Prdts
3452	Bolts, Nuts, Screws, Rivets & Washers
3462	Iron & Steel Forgings
3463	Nonferrous Forgings
3465	Automotive Stampings
3466	Crowns & Closures
3469	Metal Stampings, NEC
3471	Electroplating, Plating, Polishing, Anodizing & Coloring
3479	Coating & Engraving, NEC
3482	Small Arms Ammunition
3483	Ammunition, Large
3489	Ordnance & Access, NEC
3491	Industrial Valves
3492	Fluid Power Valves & Hose Fittings
3493	Steel Springs, Except Wire
3494	Valves & Pipe Fittings, NEC
3495	Wire Springs
3496	Misc Fabricated Wire Prdts
3497	Metal Foil & Leaf
3498	Fabricated Pipe & Pipe Fittings
3499	Fabricated Metal Prdts, NEC

35 industrial and commercial machinery and computer equipment

SIC NO	PRODUCT
3511	Steam, Gas & Hydraulic Turbines & Engines
3519	Internal Combustion Engines, NEC
3523	Farm Machinery & Eqpt
3524	Garden, Lawn Tractors & Eqpt
3531	Construction Machinery & Eqpt
3532	Mining Machinery & Eqpt
3533	Oil Field Machinery & Eqpt
3534	Elevators & Moving Stairways
3535	Conveyors & Eqpt
3536	Hoists, Cranes & Monorails
3537	Indl Trucks, Tractors, Trailers & Stackers
3541	Machine Tools: Cutting
3542	Machine Tools: Forming
3543	Industrial Patterns
3544	Dies, Tools, Jigs, Fixtures & Indl Molds
3545	Machine Tool Access
3546	Power Hand Tools
3547	Rolling Mill Machinery & Eqpt
3548	Welding Apparatus
3549	Metalworking Machinery, NEC
3552	Textile Machinery
3553	Woodworking Machinery
3554	Paper Inds Machinery
3555	Printing Trades Machinery & Eqpt
3556	Food Prdts Machinery
3559	Special Ind Machinery, NEC
3561	Pumps & Pumping Eqpt
3562	Ball & Roller Bearings
3563	Air & Gas Compressors
3564	Blowers & Fans
3565	Packaging Machinery
3566	Speed Changers, Drives & Gears
3567	Indl Process Furnaces & Ovens
3568	Mechanical Power Transmission Eqpt, NEC
3569	Indl Machinery & Eqpt, NEC
3571	Electronic Computers
3572	Computer Storage Devices
3575	Computer Terminals
3577	Computer Peripheral Eqpt, NEC
3578	Calculating & Accounting Eqpt
3579	Office Machines, NEC
3581	Automatic Vending Machines
3582	Commercial Laundry, Dry Clean & Pressing Mchs
3585	Air Conditioning & Heating Eqpt
3589	Service Ind Machines, NEC
3592	Carburetors, Pistons, Rings & Valves
3593	Fluid Power Cylinders & Actuators
3594	Fluid Power Pumps & Motors
3596	Scales & Balances, Exc Laboratory
3599	Machinery & Eqpt, Indl & Commercial, NEC

36 electronic and other electrical equipment and components, except computer

SIC NO	PRODUCT
3612	Power, Distribution & Specialty Transformers
3613	Switchgear & Switchboard Apparatus
3621	Motors & Generators
3624	Carbon & Graphite Prdts
3625	Relays & Indl Controls
3629	Electrical Indl Apparatus, NEC
3631	Household Cooking Eqpt
3632	Household Refrigerators & Freezers
3634	Electric Household Appliances
3635	Household Vacuum Cleaners
3639	Household Appliances, NEC
3641	Electric Lamps
3643	Current-Carrying Wiring Devices
3644	Noncurrent-Carrying Wiring Devices
3645	Residential Lighting Fixtures
3646	Commercial, Indl & Institutional Lighting Fixtures
3647	Vehicular Lighting Eqpt
3648	Lighting Eqpt, NEC
3651	Household Audio & Video Eqpt
3652	Phonograph Records & Magnetic Tape
3661	Telephone & Telegraph Apparatus
3663	Radio & T V Communications, Systs & Eqpt, Broadcast/Studio
3669	Communications Eqpt, NEC
3671	Radio & T V Receiving Electron Tubes
3672	Printed Circuit Boards
3674	Semiconductors
3675	Electronic Capacitors
3676	Electronic Resistors
3677	Electronic Coils & Transformers
3678	Electronic Connectors
3679	Electronic Components, NEC
3691	Storage Batteries
3692	Primary Batteries: Dry & Wet

SIC INDEX

SIC NO	PRODUCT
3694	Electrical Eqpt For Internal Combustion Engines
3695	Recording Media
3699	Electrical Machinery, Eqpt & Splys, NEC

37 transportation equipment

3711 Motor Vehicles & Car Bodies
3713 Truck & Bus Bodies
3714 Motor Vehicle Parts & Access
3715 Truck Trailers
3716 Motor Homes
3721 Aircraft
3724 Aircraft Engines & Engine Parts
3728 Aircraft Parts & Eqpt, NEC
3731 Shipbuilding & Repairing
3732 Boat Building & Repairing
3743 Railroad Eqpt
3751 Motorcycles, Bicycles & Parts
3761 Guided Missiles & Space Vehicles
3764 Guided Missile/Space Vehicle Propulsion Units & parts
3769 Guided Missile/Space Vehicle Parts & Eqpt, NEC
3792 Travel Trailers & Campers
3795 Tanks & Tank Components
3799 Transportation Eqpt, NEC

38 measuring, analyzing and controlling instruments; photographic, medical an

3812 Search, Detection, Navigation & Guidance Systs & Instrs
3821 Laboratory Apparatus & Furniture
3822 Automatic Temperature Controls
3823 Indl Instruments For Meas, Display & Control
3824 Fluid Meters & Counters
3825 Instrs For Measuring & Testing Electricity
3826 Analytical Instruments
3827 Optical Instruments
3829 Measuring & Controlling Devices, NEC
3841 Surgical & Medical Instrs & Apparatus
3842 Orthopedic, Prosthetic & Surgical Appliances/Splys
3843 Dental Eqpt & Splys
3844 X-ray Apparatus & Tubes
3845 Electromedical & Electrotherapeutic Apparatus
3851 Ophthalmic Goods
3861 Photographic Eqpt & Splys
3873 Watch & Clock Devices & Parts

39 miscellaneous manufacturing industries

3911 Jewelry: Precious Metal
3914 Silverware, Plated & Stainless Steel Ware
3931 Musical Instruments
3942 Dolls & Stuffed Toys
3944 Games, Toys & Children's Vehicles
3949 Sporting & Athletic Goods, NEC
3952 Lead Pencils, Crayons & Artist's Mtrls
3953 Marking Devices
3955 Carbon Paper & Inked Ribbons
3961 Costume Jewelry & Novelties
3965 Fasteners, Buttons, Needles & Pins
3993 Signs & Advertising Displays
3995 Burial Caskets
3996 Linoleum & Hard Surface Floor Coverings, NEC
3999 Manufacturing Industries, NEC

40 railroad transportation

4011 Railroads, Line-Hauling Operations

41 local and suburban transit and interurban highway passenger transportation

4111 Local & Suburban Transit
4119 Local Passenger Transportation: NEC
4121 Taxi Cabs
4131 Intercity & Rural Bus Transportation
4141 Local Bus Charter Svc
4142 Bus Charter Service, Except Local
4151 School Buses
4173 Bus Terminal & Svc Facilities

42 motor freight transportation and warehousing

4212 Local Trucking Without Storage
4213 Trucking, Except Local
4214 Local Trucking With Storage
4215 Courier Svcs, Except Air
4221 Farm Product Warehousing & Storage
4222 Refrigerated Warehousing & Storage
4225 General Warehousing & Storage
4226 Special Warehousing & Storage, NEC
4231 Terminal & Joint Terminal Maint Facilities

44 water transportation

4412 Deep Sea Foreign Transportation Of Freight
4424 Deep Sea Domestic Transportation Of Freight
4449 Water Transportation Of Freight, NEC
4481 Deep Sea Transportation Of Passengers

SIC NO	PRODUCT
4482	Ferries
4489	Water Transport Of Passengers, NEC
4491	Marine Cargo Handling
4492	Towing & Tugboat Svcs
4493	Marinas
4499	Water Transportation Svcs, NEC

45 transportation by air

4512 Air Transportation, Scheduled
4513 Air Courier Svcs
4522 Air Transportation, Nonscheduled
4581 Airports, Flying Fields & Terminal Svcs

46 pipelines, except natural gas

4612 Crude Petroleum Pipelines
4613 Refined Petroleum Pipelines
4619 Pipelines, NEC

47 transportation services

4724 Travel Agencies
4725 Tour Operators
4729 Passenger Transportation Arrangement, NEC
4731 Freight Forwarding & Arrangement
4741 Railroad Car Rental
4783 Packing & Crating Svcs
4785 Fixed Facilities, Inspection, Weighing Svcs Transptn
4789 Transportation Svcs, NEC

48 communications

4812 Radiotelephone Communications
4813 Telephone Communications, Except Radio
4822 Telegraph & Other Message Communications
4832 Radio Broadcasting Stations
4833 Television Broadcasting Stations
4841 Cable & Other Pay TV Svcs
4899 Communication Svcs, NEC

49 electric, gas, and sanitary services

4911 Electric Svcs
4922 Natural Gas Transmission
4923 Natural Gas Transmission & Distribution
4924 Natural Gas Distribution
4931 Electric & Other Svcs Combined
4932 Gas & Other Svcs Combined
4939 Combination Utilities, NEC
4941 Water Sply
4952 Sewerage Systems
4953 Refuse Systems
4959 Sanitary Svcs, NEC
4971 Irrigation Systems

50 wholesale trade¨durable goods

5012 Automobiles & Other Motor Vehicles Wholesale
5013 Motor Vehicle Splys & New Parts Wholesale
5014 Tires & Tubes Wholesale
5015 Motor Vehicle Parts, Used Wholesale
5021 Furniture Wholesale
5023 Home Furnishings Wholesale
5031 Lumber, Plywood & Millwork Wholesale
5032 Brick, Stone & Related Construction Mtrls Wholesale
5033 Roofing, Siding & Insulation Mtrls Wholesale
5039 Construction Materials, NEC Wholesale
5043 Photographic Eqpt & Splys Wholesale
5044 Office Eqpt Wholesale
5045 Computers & Peripheral Eqpt & Software Wholesale
5046 Commercial Eqpt, NEC Wholesale
5047 Medical, Dental & Hospital Eqpt & Splys Wholesale
5048 Ophthalmic Goods Wholesale
5049 Professional Eqpt & Splys, NEC Wholesale
5051 Metals Service Centers
5063 Electrl Apparatus, Eqpt, Wiring Splys Wholesale
5064 Electrical Appliances, TV & Radios Wholesale
5065 Electronic Parts & Eqpt Wholesale
5072 Hardware Wholesale
5074 Plumbing & Heating Splys Wholesale
5075 Heating & Air Conditioning Eqpt & Splys Wholesale
5078 Refrigeration Eqpt & Splys Wholesale
5082 Construction & Mining Mach & Eqpt Wholesale
5083 Farm & Garden Mach & Eqpt Wholesale
5084 Industrial Mach & Eqpt Wholesale
5085 Industrial Splys Wholesale
5087 Service Establishment Eqpt & Splys Wholesale
5088 Transportation Eqpt & Splys, Except Motor Vehicles Wholesale
5091 Sporting & Recreational Goods & Splys Wholesale
5092 Toys & Hobby Goods & Splys Wholesale
5093 Scrap & Waste Materials Wholesale
5094 Jewelry, Watches, Precious Stones Wholesale
5099 Durable Goods: NEC Wholesale

SIC NO	PRODUCT

51 wholesale trade¨nondurable goods

5111 Printing & Writing Paper Wholesale
5112 Stationery & Office Splys Wholesale
5113 Indl & Personal Svc Paper Wholesale
5122 Drugs, Drug Proprietaries & Sundries Wholesale
5131 Piece Goods, Notions & Dry Goods Wholesale
5136 Men's & Boys' Clothing & Furnishings Wholesale
5137 Women's, Children's & Infants Clothing Wholesale
5139 Footwear Wholesale
5141 Groceries, General Line Wholesale
5142 Packaged Frozen Foods Wholesale
5143 Dairy Prdts, Except Dried Or Canned Wholesale
5144 Poultry & Poultry Prdts Wholesale
5145 Confectionery Wholesale
5146 Fish & Seafood Wholesale
5147 Meats & Meat Prdts Wholesale
5148 Fresh Fruits & Vegetables Wholesale
5149 Groceries & Related Prdts, NEC Wholesale
5153 Grain & Field Beans Wholesale
5154 Livestock Wholesale
5159 Farm-Prdt Raw Mtrls, NEC Wholesale
5162 Plastics Materials & Basic Shapes Wholesale
5169 Chemicals & Allied Prdts, NEC Wholesale
5171 Petroleum Bulk Stations & Terminals
5172 Petroleum & Petroleum Prdts Wholesale
5181 Beer & Ale Wholesale
5182 Wine & Distilled Alcoholic Beverages Wholesale
5191 Farm Splys Wholesale
5192 Books, Periodicals & Newspapers Wholesale
5193 Flowers, Nursery Stock & Florists' Splys Wholesale
5194 Tobacco & Tobacco Prdts Wholesale
5198 Paints, Varnishes & Splys Wholesale
5199 Nondurable Goods, NEC Wholesale

60 depository institutions

6021 National Commercial Banks
6022 State Commercial Banks
6029 Commercial Banks, NEC
6035 Federal Savings Institutions
6036 Savings Institutions, Except Federal
6061 Federal Credit Unions
6062 State Credit Unions
6081 Foreign Banks, Branches & Agencies
6082 Foreign Trade & Intl Banks
6091 Nondeposit Trust Facilities
6099 Functions Related To Deposit Banking, NEC

61 nondepository credit institutions

6111 Federal Credit Agencies
6141 Personal Credit Institutions
6153 Credit Institutions, Short-Term Business
6159 Credit Institutions, Misc Business
6162 Mortgage Bankers & Loan Correspondents
6163 Loan Brokers

62 security and commodity brokers, dealers, exchanges, and services

6211 Security Brokers & Dealers
6221 Commodity Contracts Brokers & Dealers
6231 Security & Commodity Exchanges
6282 Investment Advice

63 insurance carriers

6311 Life Insurance Carriers
6321 Accident & Health Insurance
6324 Hospital & Medical Svc Plans Carriers
6331 Fire, Marine & Casualty Insurance
6351 Surety Insurance Carriers
6361 Title Insurance
6371 Pension, Health & Welfare Funds
6399 Insurance Carriers, NEC

64 insurance agents, brokers, and service

6411 Insurance Agents, Brokers & Svc

65 real estate

6512 Operators Of Nonresidential Bldgs
6513 Operators Of Apartment Buildings
6514 Operators Of Dwellings, Except Apartments
6515 Operators of Residential Mobile Home Sites
6519 Lessors Of Real Estate, NEC
6531 Real Estate Agents & Managers
6541 Title Abstract Offices
6552 Land Subdividers & Developers
6553 Cemetery Subdividers & Developers

67 holding and other investment offices

6719 Offices Of Holding Co's, NEC
6722 Management Investment Offices
6726 Unit Investment Trusts, Face-Amount Certificate Offices
6732 Education, Religious & Charitable Trusts

SIC INDEX

SIC NO	PRODUCT
6733	Trusts Except Educational, Religious & Charitable
6792	Oil Royalty Traders
6794	Patent Owners & Lessors
6798	Real Estate Investment Trusts
6799	Investors, NEC

70 hotels, rooming houses, camps, and other lodging places

- 7011 Hotels, Motels & Tourist Courts
- 7021 Rooming & Boarding Houses
- 7032 Sporting & Recreational Camps
- 7033 Trailer Parks & Camp Sites
- 7041 Membership-Basis Hotels

72 personal services

- 7211 Power Laundries, Family & Commercial
- 7212 Garment Pressing & Cleaners' Agents
- 7213 Linen Sply
- 7215 Coin Operated Laundries & Cleaning
- 7216 Dry Cleaning Plants, Except Rug Cleaning
- 7217 Carpet & Upholstery Cleaning
- 7218 Industrial Launderers
- 7219 Laundry & Garment Svcs, NEC
- 7221 Photographic Studios, Portrait
- 7231 Beauty Shops
- 7241 Barber Shops
- 7251 Shoe Repair & Shoeshine Parlors
- 7261 Funeral Svcs & Crematories
- 7291 Tax Return Preparation Svcs
- 7299 Miscellaneous Personal Svcs, NEC

73 business services

- 7311 Advertising Agencies
- 7312 Outdoor Advertising Svcs
- 7313 Radio, TV & Publishers Adv Reps
- 7319 Advertising, NEC
- 7322 Adjustment & Collection Svcs
- 7323 Credit Reporting Svcs
- 7331 Direct Mail Advertising Svcs
- 7334 Photocopying & Duplicating Svcs
- 7335 Commercial Photography
- 7336 Commercial Art & Graphic Design
- 7338 Secretarial & Court Reporting Svcs
- 7342 Disinfecting & Pest Control Svcs
- 7349 Building Cleaning & Maintenance Svcs, NEC
- 7352 Medical Eqpt Rental & Leasing
- 7353 Heavy Construction Eqpt Rental & Leasing
- 7359 Equipment Rental & Leasing, NEC
- 7361 Employment Agencies
- 7363 Help Supply Svcs
- 7371 Custom Computer Programming Svcs
- 7372 Prepackaged Software
- 7373 Computer Integrated Systems Design
- 7374 Data & Computer Processing & Preparation
- 7375 Information Retrieval Svcs
- 7376 Computer Facilities Management Svcs
- 7378 Computer Maintenance & Repair
- 7379 Computer Related Svcs, NEC
- 7381 Detective & Armored Car Svcs
- 7382 Security Systems Svcs
- 7383 News Syndicates
- 7384 Photofinishing Labs
- 7389 Business Svcs, NEC

75 automotive repair, services, and parking

- 7513 Truck Rental & Leasing, Without Drivers
- 7514 Passenger Car Rental
- 7515 Passenger Car Leasing
- 7519 Utility Trailers & Recreational Vehicle Rental
- 7521 Automobile Parking Lots & Garages
- 7532 Top, Body & Upholstery Repair & Paint Shops
- 7534 Tire Retreading & Repair Shops
- 7537 Automotive Transmission Repair Shops
- 7538 General Automotive Repair Shop
- 7539 Automotive Repair Shops, NEC
- 7542 Car Washes
- 7549 Automotive Svcs, Except Repair & Car Washes

76 miscellaneous repair services

- 7622 Radio & TV Repair Shops
- 7623 Refrigeration & Air Conditioning Svc & Repair Shop
- 7629 Electrical & Elex Repair Shop, NEC
- 7631 Watch, Clock & Jewelry Repair
- 7641 Reupholstery & Furniture Repair
- 7692 Welding Repair
- 7694 Armature Rewinding Shops
- 7699 Repair Shop & Related Svcs, NEC

78 motion pictures

- 7812 Motion Picture & Video Tape Production
- 7819 Services Allied To Motion Picture Prdtn
- 7822 Motion Picture & Video Tape Distribution
- 7832 Motion Picture Theaters, Except Drive-In
- 7833 Drive-In Motion Picture Theaters
- 7841 Video Tape Rental

79 amusement and recreation services

- 7911 Dance Studios, Schools & Halls
- 7922 Theatrical Producers & Misc Theatrical Svcs
- 7929 Bands, Orchestras, Actors & Entertainers
- 7933 Bowling Centers
- 7941 Professional Sports Clubs & Promoters
- 7948 Racing & Track Operations
- 7991 Physical Fitness Facilities
- 7992 Public Golf Courses
- 7993 Coin-Operated Amusement Devices & Arcades
- 7996 Amusement Parks
- 7997 Membership Sports & Recreation Clubs
- 7999 Amusement & Recreation Svcs, NEC

80 health services

- 8011 Offices & Clinics Of Doctors Of Medicine
- 8021 Offices & Clinics Of Dentists
- 8031 Offices & Clinics Of Doctors Of Osteopathy
- 8041 Offices & Clinics Of Chiropractors
- 8042 Offices & Clinics Of Optometrists
- 8043 Offices & Clinics Of Podiatrists
- 8049 Offices & Clinics Of Health Practitioners, NEC
- 8051 Skilled Nursing Facilities
- 8052 Intermediate Care Facilities
- 8059 Nursing & Personal Care Facilities, NEC
- 8062 General Medical & Surgical Hospitals
- 8063 Psychiatric Hospitals
- 8069 Specialty Hospitals, Except Psychiatric
- 8071 Medical Laboratories
- 8072 Dental Laboratories
- 8082 Home Health Care Svcs
- 8092 Kidney Dialysis Centers
- 8093 Specialty Outpatient Facilities, NEC
- 8099 Health & Allied Svcs, NEC

81 legal services

- 8111 Legal Svcs

83 social services

- 8322 Individual & Family Social Svcs
- 8331 Job Training & Vocational Rehabilitation Svcs
- 8351 Child Day Care Svcs
- 8361 Residential Care
- 8399 Social Services, NEC

84 museums, art galleries, and botanical and zoological gardens

- 8412 Museums & Art Galleries
- 8422 Arboreta, Botanical & Zoological Gardens

86 membership organizations

- 8611 Business Associations
- 8621 Professional Membership Organizations
- 8631 Labor Unions & Similar Organizations
- 8641 Civic, Social & Fraternal Associations
- 8651 Political Organizations
- 8699 Membership Organizations, NEC

87 engineering, accounting, research, management, and related services

- 8711 Engineering Services
- 8712 Architectural Services
- 8713 Surveying Services
- 8721 Accounting, Auditing & Bookkeeping Svcs
- 8731 Commercial Physical & Biological Research
- 8732 Commercial Economic, Sociological & Educational Research
- 8733 Noncommercial Research Organizations
- 8734 Testing Laboratories
- 8741 Management Services
- 8742 Management Consulting Services
- 8743 Public Relations Svcs
- 8744 Facilities Support Mgmt Svcs
- 8748 Business Consulting Svcs, NEC

89 services, not elsewhere classified

- 8999 Services Not Elsewhere Classified

SIC INDEX

Standard Industrial Classification Alphabetical Index

SIC NO	PRODUCT

01 agricultural production-crops
0111 Wheat
0112 Rice
0115 Corn
0119 Cash Grains, NEC
0131 Cotton
0133 Sugarcane & Sugar Beets
0139 Field Crops, Except Cash Grains, NEC
0161 Vegetables & Melons
0171 Berry Crops
0172 Grapes
0173 Tree Nuts
0174 Citrus Fruits
0175 Deciduous Tree Fruits
0179 Fruits & Tree Nuts, NEC
0181 Ornamental Floriculture & Nursery Prdts
0182 Food Crops Grown Under Cover
0191 Crop Farming, Misc
02 agricultural production-livestock and animal specialties
0211 Beef Cattle Feedlots
0212 Beef Cattle, Except Feedlots
0213 Hogs
0241 Dairy Farms
0251 Chicken & Poultry Farms
0252 Chicken Egg Farms
0253 Turkey & Turkey Egg Farms
0254 Poultry Hatcheries
0259 Poultry & Eggs Farms, NEC
0272 Horse & Other Equine Production
0279 Animal Specialties, NEC
0291 Animal Production, NEC
07 agricultural services
0711 Soil Preparation Svcs
0721 Soil Preparation, Planting & Cultivating Svc
0722 Crop Harvesting By Machine
0723 Crop Preparation, Except Cotton Ginning
0741 Veterinary Livestock Svcs
0742 Veterinary Animal Specialties
0751 Livestock Svcs, Except Veterinary
0752 Animal Specialty Svcs, Exc Veterinary
0761 Farm Labor Contractors & Crew Leaders
0762 Farm Management Svcs
0781 Landscape Counseling & Planning
0782 Lawn & Garden Svcs
0783 Ornamental Shrub & Tree Svc
08 forestry
0811 Timber Tracts
0851 Forestry Svcs
09 fishing, hunting, and trapping
0921 Finfish Farming & Fish Hatcheries
0971 Hunting & Trapping
10 metal mining
1011 Iron Ores
1021 Copper Ores
1041 Gold Ores
1061 Ferroalloy Ores, Except Vanadium
1081 Metal Mining Svcs
12 coal mining
1221 Bituminous Coal & Lignite: Surface Mining
1241 Coal Mining Svcs
13 oil and gas extraction
1311 Crude Petroleum & Natural Gas
1321 Natural Gas Liquids
1381 Drilling Oil & Gas Wells
1382 Oil & Gas Field Exploration Svcs
1389 Oil & Gas Field Svcs, NEC
14 mining and quarrying of nonmetallic minerals, except fuels
1411 Dimension Stone
1422 Crushed & Broken Limestone
1423 Crushed & Broken Granite
1429 Crushed & Broken Stone, NEC
1442 Construction Sand & Gravel
1446 Industrial Sand
1499 Miscellaneous Nonmetallic Mining
15 building construction-general contractors and operative builders
1521 General Contractors, Single Family Houses
1522 General Contractors, Residential Other Than Single Family
1531 Operative Builders
1541 General Contractors, Indl Bldgs & Warehouses
1542 General Contractors, Nonresidential & Non-indl Bldgs

16 heavy construction other than building construction-contractors
1611 Highway & Street Construction
1622 Bridge, Tunnel & Elevated Hwy Construction
1623 Water, Sewer & Utility Line Construction
1629 Heavy Construction, NEC
17 construction-special trade contractors
1711 Plumbing, Heating & Air Conditioning Contractors
1721 Painting & Paper Hanging Contractors
1731 Electrical Work
1741 Masonry & Other Stonework
1742 Plastering, Drywall, Acoustical & Insulation Work
1743 Terrazzo, Tile, Marble & Mosaic Work
1751 Carpentry Work
1752 Floor Laying & Other Floor Work, NEC
1761 Roofing, Siding & Sheet Metal Work
1771 Concrete Work
1781 Water Well Drilling
1791 Structural Steel Erection
1793 Glass & Glazing Work
1794 Excavating & Grading Work
1795 Wrecking & Demolition Work
1796 Installation Or Erection Of Bldg Eqpt & Machinery, NEC
1799 Special Trade Contractors, NEC
20 food and kindred products
2011 Meat Packing Plants
2013 Sausages & Meat Prdts
2015 Poultry Slaughtering, Dressing & Processing
2021 Butter
2022 Cheese
2023 Milk, Condensed & Evaporated
2024 Ice Cream
2026 Milk
2032 Canned Specialties
2033 Canned Fruits, Vegetables & Preserves
2034 Dried Fruits, Vegetables & Soup
2035 Pickled Fruits, Vegetables, Sauces & Dressings
2037 Frozen Fruits, Juices & Vegetables
2038 Frozen Specialties
2041 Flour, Grain Milling
2043 Cereal Breakfast Foods
2044 Rice Milling
2045 Flour, Blended & Prepared
2046 Wet Corn Milling
2047 Dog & Cat Food
2048 Prepared Feeds For Animals & Fowls
2051 Bread, Bakery Prdts Exc Cookies & Crackers
2052 Cookies & Crackers
2053 Frozen Bakery Prdts
2063 Sugar, Beet
2064 Candy & Confectionery Prdts
2066 Chocolate & Cocoa Prdts
2068 Salted & Roasted Nuts & Seeds
2076 Vegetable Oil Mills
2077 Animal, Marine Fats & Oils
2079 Shortening, Oils & Margarine
2082 Malt Beverages
2084 Wine & Brandy
2085 Liquors, Distilled, Rectified & Blended
2086 Soft Drinks
2087 Flavoring Extracts & Syrups
2091 Fish & Seafoods, Canned & Cured
2092 Fish & Seafoods, Fresh & Frozen
2095 Coffee
2096 Potato Chips & Similar Prdts
2097 Ice
2098 Macaroni, Spaghetti & Noodles
2099 Food Preparations, NEC
21 tobacco products
2131 Tobacco, Chewing & Snuff
22 textile mill products
2211 Cotton, Woven Fabric
2221 Silk & Man-Made Fiber
2231 Wool, Woven Fabric
2241 Fabric Mills, Cotton, Wool, Silk & Man-Made
2252 Hosiery, Except Women's
2253 Knit Outerwear Mills
2259 Knitting Mills, NEC
2261 Cotton Fabric Finishers
2273 Carpets & Rugs
2281 Yarn Spinning Mills
2296 Tire Cord & Fabric
2298 Cordage & Twine

2299 Textile Goods, NEC
23 apparel and other finished products made from fabrics and similar material
2311 Men's & Boys' Suits, Coats & Overcoats
2321 Men's & Boys' Shirts
2323 Men's & Boys' Neckwear
2325 Men's & Boys' Separate Trousers & Casual Slacks
2326 Men's & Boys' Work Clothing
2329 Men's & Boys' Clothing, NEC
2331 Women's & Misses' Blouses
2335 Women's & Misses' Dresses
2337 Women's & Misses' Suits, Coats & Skirts
2339 Women's & Misses' Outerwear, NEC
2353 Hats, Caps & Millinery
2361 Children's & Infants' Dresses & Blouses
2369 Girls' & Infants' Outerwear, NEC
2381 Dress & Work Gloves
2386 Leather & Sheep Lined Clothing
2387 Apparel Belts
2389 Apparel & Accessories, NEC
2391 Curtains & Draperies
2392 House furnishings: Textile
2393 Textile Bags
2394 Canvas Prdts
2395 Pleating & Stitching For The Trade
2396 Automotive Trimmings, Apparel Findings, Related Prdts
2399 Fabricated Textile Prdts, NEC
24 lumber and wood products, except furniture
2411 Logging
2421 Saw & Planing Mills
2426 Hardwood Dimension & Flooring Mills
2431 Millwork
2434 Wood Kitchen Cabinets
2435 Hardwood Veneer & Plywood
2436 Softwood Veneer & Plywood
2439 Structural Wood Members, NEC
2441 Wood Boxes
2448 Wood Pallets & Skids
2449 Wood Containers, NEC
2451 Mobile Homes
2452 Prefabricated Wood Buildings & Cmpnts
2491 Wood Preserving
2493 Reconstituted Wood Prdts
2499 Wood Prdts, NEC
25 furniture and fixtures
2511 Wood Household Furniture
2512 Wood Household Furniture, Upholstered
2514 Metal Household Furniture
2515 Mattresses & Bedsprings
2519 Household Furniture, NEC
2521 Wood Office Furniture
2522 Office Furniture, Except Wood
2531 Public Building & Related Furniture
2541 Wood, Office & Store Fixtures
2542 Partitions & Fixtures, Except Wood
2591 Drapery Hardware, Window Blinds & Shades
2599 Furniture & Fixtures, NEC
26 paper and allied products
2611 Pulp Mills
2621 Paper Mills
2631 Paperboard Mills
2652 Set-Up Paperboard Boxes
2653 Corrugated & Solid Fiber Boxes
2655 Fiber Cans, Tubes & Drums
2656 Sanitary Food Containers
2657 Folding Paperboard Boxes
2671 Paper Coating & Laminating for Packaging
2672 Paper Coating & Laminating, Exc for Packaging
2673 Bags: Plastics, Laminated & Coated
2674 Bags: Uncoated Paper & Multiwall
2675 Die-Cut Paper & Board
2676 Sanitary Paper Prdts
2677 Envelopes
2678 Stationery Prdts
2679 Converted Paper Prdts, NEC
27 printing, publishing, and allied industries
2711 Newspapers: Publishing & Printing
2721 Periodicals: Publishing & Printing
2731 Books: Publishing & Printing
2732 Book Printing, Not Publishing
2741 Misc Publishing
2752 Commercial Printing: Lithographic
2754 Commercial Printing: Gravure

SIC INDEX

SIC NO	PRODUCT
2759	Commercial Printing
2761	Manifold Business Forms
2771	Greeting Card Publishing
2782	Blankbooks & Looseleaf Binders
2789	Bookbinding
2791	Typesetting
2796	Platemaking & Related Svcs
28	chemicals and allied products
2812	Alkalies & Chlorine
2813	Industrial Gases
2819	Indl Inorganic Chemicals, NEC
2821	Plastics, Mtrls & Nonvulcanizable Elastomers
2822	Synthetic Rubber (Vulcanizable Elastomers)
2823	Cellulosic Man-Made Fibers
2824	Synthetic Organic Fibers, Exc Cellulosic
2833	Medicinal Chemicals & Botanical Prdts
2834	Pharmaceuticals
2835	Diagnostic Substances
2836	Biological Prdts, Exc Diagnostic Substances
2841	Soap & Detergents
2842	Spec Cleaning, Polishing & Sanitation Preparations
2844	Perfumes, Cosmetics & Toilet Preparations
2851	Paints, Varnishes, Lacquers, Enamels
2861	Gum & Wood Chemicals
2865	Cyclic-Crudes, Intermediates, Dyes & Org Pigments
2869	Industrial Organic Chemicals, NEC
2873	Nitrogenous Fertilizers
2874	Phosphatic Fertilizers
2875	Fertilizers, Mixing Only
2879	Pesticides & Agricultural Chemicals, NEC
2891	Adhesives & Sealants
2892	Explosives
2893	Printing Ink
2899	Chemical Preparations, NEC
29	petroleum refining and related industries
2911	Petroleum Refining
2951	Paving Mixtures & Blocks
2952	Asphalt Felts & Coatings
2992	Lubricating Oils & Greases
30	rubber and miscellaneous plastics products
3011	Tires & Inner Tubes
3021	Rubber & Plastic Footwear
3052	Rubber & Plastic Hose & Belting
3053	Gaskets, Packing & Sealing Devices
3061	Molded, Extruded & Lathe-Cut Rubber Mechanical Goods
3069	Fabricated Rubber Prdts, NEC
3081	Plastic Unsupported Sheet & Film
3082	Plastic Unsupported Profile Shapes
3083	Plastic Laminated Plate & Sheet
3084	Plastic Pipe
3085	Plastic Bottles
3086	Plastic Foam Prdts
3087	Custom Compounding Of Purchased Plastic Resins
3088	Plastic Plumbing Fixtures
3089	Plastic Prdts
31	leather and leather products
3111	Leather Tanning & Finishing
3131	Boot & Shoe Cut Stock & Findings
3143	Men's Footwear, Exc Athletic
3144	Women's Footwear, Exc Athletic
3149	Footwear, NEC
3161	Luggage
3171	Handbags & Purses
3199	Leather Goods, NEC
32	stone, clay, glass, and concrete products
3211	Flat Glass
3221	Glass Containers
3229	Pressed & Blown Glassware, NEC
3231	Glass Prdts Made Of Purchased Glass
3241	Cement, Hydraulic
3251	Brick & Structural Clay Tile
3253	Ceramic Tile
3255	Clay Refractories
3259	Structural Clay Prdts, NEC
3261	China Plumbing Fixtures & Fittings
3264	Porcelain Electrical Splys
3269	Pottery Prdts, NEC
3271	Concrete Block & Brick
3272	Concrete Prdts
3273	Ready-Mixed Concrete
3274	Lime
3275	Gypsum Prdts
3281	Cut Stone Prdts
3291	Abrasive Prdts
3292	Asbestos products
3295	Minerals & Earths: Ground Or Treated
3296	Mineral Wool
3297	Nonclay Refractories

SIC NO	PRODUCT
3299	Nonmetallic Mineral Prdts, NEC
33	primary metal industries
3312	Blast Furnaces, Coke Ovens, Steel & Rolling Mills
3315	Steel Wire Drawing & Nails & Spikes
3316	Cold Rolled Steel Sheet, Strip & Bars
3317	Steel Pipe & Tubes
3321	Gray Iron Foundries
3322	Malleable Iron Foundries
3324	Steel Investment Foundries
3325	Steel Foundries, NEC
3334	Primary Production Of Aluminum
3339	Primary Nonferrous Metals, NEC
3341	Secondary Smelting & Refining Of Nonferrous Metals
3351	Rolling, Drawing & Extruding Of Copper
3353	Aluminum Sheet, Plate & Foil
3354	Aluminum Extruded Prdts
3355	Aluminum Rolling & Drawing, NEC
3356	Rolling, Drawing-Extruding Of Nonferrous Metals
3357	Nonferrous Wire Drawing
3363	Aluminum Die Castings
3364	Nonferrous Die Castings, Exc Aluminum
3365	Aluminum Foundries
3366	Copper Foundries
3369	Nonferrous Foundries: Castings, NEC
3398	Metal Heat Treating
3399	Primary Metal Prdts, NEC
34	fabricated metal products, except machinery and transportation equipment
3411	Metal Cans
3412	Metal Barrels, Drums, Kegs & Pails
3421	Cutlery
3423	Hand & Edge Tools
3425	Hand Saws & Saw Blades
3429	Hardware, NEC
3431	Enameled Iron & Metal Sanitary Ware
3432	Plumbing Fixture Fittings & Trim, Brass
3433	Heating Eqpt
3441	Fabricated Structural Steel
3442	Metal Doors, Sash, Frames, Molding & Trim
3443	Fabricated Plate Work
3444	Sheet Metal Work
3446	Architectural & Ornamental Metal Work
3448	Prefabricated Metal Buildings & Cmpnts
3449	Misc Structural Metal Work
3451	Screw Machine Prdts
3452	Bolts, Nuts, Screws, Rivets & Washers
3462	Iron & Steel Forgings
3463	Nonferrous Forgings
3465	Automotive Stampings
3466	Crowns & Closures
3469	Metal Stampings, NEC
3471	Electroplating, Plating, Polishing, Anodizing & Coloring
3479	Coating & Engraving, NEC
3482	Small Arms Ammunition
3483	Ammunition, Large
3489	Ordnance & Access, NEC
3491	Industrial Valves
3492	Fluid Power Valves & Hose Fittings
3493	Steel Springs, Except Wire
3494	Valves & Pipe Fittings, NEC
3495	Wire Springs
3496	Misc Fabricated Wire Prdts
3497	Metal Foil & Leaf
3498	Fabricated Pipe & Pipe Fittings
3499	Fabricated Metal Prdts, NEC
35	industrial and commercial machinery and computer equipment
3511	Steam, Gas & Hydraulic Turbines & Engines
3519	Internal Combustion Engines, NEC
3523	Farm Machinery & Eqpt
3524	Garden, Lawn Tractors & Eqpt
3531	Construction Machinery & Eqpt
3532	Mining Machinery & Eqpt
3533	Oil Field Machinery & Eqpt
3534	Elevators & Moving Stairways
3535	Conveyors & Eqpt
3536	Hoists, Cranes & Monorails
3537	Indl Trucks, Tractors, Trailers & Stackers
3541	Machine Tools: Cutting
3542	Machine Tools: Forming
3543	Industrial Patterns
3544	Dies, Tools, Jigs, Fixtures & Indl Molds
3545	Machine Tool Access
3546	Power Hand Tools
3547	Rolling Mill Machinery & Eqpt
3548	Welding Apparatus
3549	Metalworking Machinery, NEC
3552	Textile Machinery
3553	Woodworking Machinery

SIC NO	PRODUCT
3554	Paper Inds Machinery
3555	Printing Trades Machinery & Eqpt
3556	Food Prdts Machinery
3559	Special Ind Machinery, NEC
3561	Pumps & Pumping Eqpt
3562	Ball & Roller Bearings
3563	Air & Gas Compressors
3564	Blowers & Fans
3565	Packaging Machinery
3566	Speed Changers, Drives & Gears
3567	Indl Process Furnaces & Ovens
3568	Mechanical Power Transmission Eqpt, NEC
3569	Indl Machinery & Eqpt, NEC
3571	Electronic Computers
3572	Computer Storage Devices
3575	Computer Terminals
3577	Computer Peripheral Eqpt, NEC
3578	Calculating & Accounting Eqpt
3579	Office Machines, NEC
3581	Automatic Vending Machines
3582	Commercial Laundry, Dry Clean & Pressing Mchs
3585	Air Conditioning & Heating Eqpt
3589	Service Ind Machines, NEC
3592	Carburetors, Pistons, Rings & Valves
3593	Fluid Power Cylinders & Actuators
3594	Fluid Power Pumps & Motors
3596	Scales & Balances, Exc Laboratory
3599	Machinery & Eqpt, Indl & Commercial, NEC
36	electronic and other electrical equipment and components, except computer
3612	Power, Distribution & Specialty Transformers
3613	Switchgear & Switchboard Apparatus
3621	Motors & Generators
3624	Carbon & Graphite Prdts
3625	Relays & Indl Controls
3629	Electrical Indl Apparatus, NEC
3631	Household Cooking Eqpt
3632	Household Refrigerators & Freezers
3634	Electric Household Appliances
3635	Household Vacuum Cleaners
3639	Household Appliances, NEC
3641	Electric Lamps
3643	Current-Carrying Wiring Devices
3644	Noncurrent-Carrying Wiring Devices
3645	Residential Lighting Fixtures
3646	Commercial, Indl & Institutional Lighting Fixtures
3647	Vehicular Lighting Eqpt
3648	Lighting Eqpt, NEC
3651	Household Audio & Video Eqpt
3652	Phonograph Records & Magnetic Tape
3661	Telephone & Telegraph Apparatus
3663	Radio & T V Communications, Systs & Eqpt, Broadcast/Studio
3669	Communications Eqpt, NEC
3671	Radio & T V Receiving Electron Tubes
3672	Printed Circuit Boards
3674	Semiconductors
3675	Electronic Capacitors
3676	Electronic Resistors
3677	Electronic Coils & Transformers
3678	Electronic Connectors
3679	Electronic Components, NEC
3691	Storage Batteries
3692	Primary Batteries: Dry & Wet
3694	Electrical Eqpt For Internal Combustion Engines
3695	Recording Media
3699	Electrical Machinery, Eqpt & Splys, NEC
37	transportation equipment
3711	Motor Vehicles & Car Bodies
3713	Truck & Bus Bodies
3714	Motor Vehicle Parts & Access
3715	Truck Trailers
3716	Motor Homes
3721	Aircraft
3724	Aircraft Engines & Engine Parts
3728	Aircraft Parts & Eqpt, NEC
3731	Shipbuilding & Repairing
3732	Boat Building & Repairing
3743	Railroad Eqpt
3751	Motorcycles, Bicycles & Parts
3761	Guided Missiles & Space Vehicles
3764	Guided Missile/Space Vehicle Propulsion Units & parts
3769	Guided Missile/Space Vehicle Parts & Eqpt, NEC
3792	Travel Trailers & Campers
3795	Tanks & Tank Components
3799	Transportation Eqpt, NEC
38	measuring, analyzing and controlling instruments; photographic, medical an
3812	Search, Detection, Navigation & Guidance Systs & Instrs

SIC INDEX

SIC NO	PRODUCT
3821	Laboratory Apparatus & Furniture
3822	Automatic Temperature Controls
3823	Indl Instruments For Meas, Display & Control
3824	Fluid Meters & Counters
3825	Instrs For Measuring & Testing Electricity
3826	Analytical Instruments
3827	Optical Instruments
3829	Measuring & Controlling Devices, NEC
3841	Surgical & Medical Instrs & Apparatus
3842	Orthopedic, Prosthetic & Surgical Appliances/Splys
3843	Dental Eqpt & Splys
3844	X-ray Apparatus & Tubes
3845	Electromedical & Electrotherapeutic Apparatus
3851	Ophthalmic Goods
3861	Photographic Eqpt & Splys
3873	Watch & Clock Devices & Parts
39	miscellaneous manufacturing industries
3911	Jewelry: Precious Metal
3914	Silverware, Plated & Stainless Steel Ware
3931	Musical Instruments
3942	Dolls & Stuffed Toys
3944	Games, Toys & Children's Vehicles
3949	Sporting & Athletic Goods, NEC
3952	Lead Pencils, Crayons & Artist's Mtrls
3953	Marking Devices
3955	Carbon Paper & Inked Ribbons
3961	Costume Jewelry & Novelties
3965	Fasteners, Buttons, Needles & Pins
3993	Signs & Advertising Displays
3995	Burial Caskets
3996	Linoleum & Hard Surface Floor Coverings, NEC
3999	Manufacturing Industries, NEC
40	railroad transportation
4011	Railroads, Line-Hauling Operations
41	local and suburban transit and interurban highway passenger transportation
4111	Local & Suburban Transit
4119	Local Passenger Transportation: NEC
4121	Taxi Cabs
4131	Intercity & Rural Bus Transportation
4141	Local Bus Charter Svc
4142	Bus Charter Service, Except Local
4151	School Buses
4173	Bus Terminal & Svc Facilities
42	motor freight transportation and warehousing
4212	Local Trucking Without Storage
4213	Trucking, Except Local
4214	Local Trucking With Storage
4215	Courier Svcs, Except Air
4221	Farm Product Warehousing & Storage
4222	Refrigerated Warehousing & Storage
4225	General Warehousing & Storage
4226	Special Warehousing & Storage, NEC
4231	Terminal & Joint Terminal Maint Facilities
44	water transportation
4412	Deep Sea Foreign Transportation Of Freight
4424	Deep Sea Domestic Transportation Of Freight
4449	Water Transportation Of Freight, NEC
4481	Deep Sea Transportation Of Passengers
4482	Ferries
4489	Water Transport Of Passengers, NEC
4491	Marine Cargo Handling
4492	Towing & Tugboat Svcs
4493	Marinas
4499	Water Transportation Svcs, NEC
45	transportation by air
4512	Air Transportation, Scheduled
4513	Air Courier Svcs
4522	Air Transportation, Nonscheduled
4581	Airports, Flying Fields & Terminal Svcs
46	pipelines, except natural gas
4612	Crude Petroleum Pipelines
4613	Refined Petroleum Pipelines
4619	Pipelines, NEC
47	transportation services
4724	Travel Agencies
4725	Tour Operators
4729	Passenger Transportation Arrangement, NEC
4731	Freight Forwarding & Arrangement
4741	Railroad Car Rental
4783	Packing & Crating Svcs
4785	Fixed Facilities, Inspection, Weighing Svcs Transptn
4789	Transportation Svcs, NEC
48	communications
4812	Radiotelephone Communications
4813	Telephone Communications, Except Radio
4822	Telegraph & Other Message Communications
4832	Radio Broadcasting Stations
4833	Television Broadcasting Stations
4841	Cable & Other Pay TV Svcs
4899	Communication Svcs, NEC
49	electric, gas, and sanitary services
4911	Electric Svcs
4922	Natural Gas Transmission
4923	Natural Gas Transmission & Distribution
4924	Natural Gas Distribution
4931	Electric & Other Svcs Combined
4932	Gas & Other Svcs Combined
4939	Combination Utilities, NEC
4941	Water Sply
4952	Sewerage Systems
4953	Refuse Systems
4959	Sanitary Svcs, NEC
4971	Irrigation Systems
50	wholesale trade¨durable goods
5012	Automobiles & Other Motor Vehicles Wholesale
5013	Motor Vehicle Splys & New Parts Wholesale
5014	Tires & Tubes Wholesale
5015	Motor Vehicle Parts, Used Wholesale
5021	Furniture Wholesale
5023	Home Furnishings Wholesale
5031	Lumber, Plywood & Millwork Wholesale
5032	Brick, Stone & Related Construction Mtrls Wholesale
5033	Roofing, Siding & Insulation Mtrls Wholesale
5039	Construction Materials, NEC Wholesale
5043	Photographic Eqpt & Splys Wholesale
5044	Office Eqpt Wholesale
5045	Computers & Peripheral Eqpt & Software Wholesale
5046	Commercial Eqpt, NEC Wholesale
5047	Medical, Dental & Hospital Eqpt & Splys Wholesale
5048	Ophthalmic Goods Wholesale
5049	Professional Eqpt & Splys, NEC Wholesale
5051	Metals Service Centers
5063	Electrl Apparatus, Eqpt, Wiring Splys Wholesale
5064	Electrical Appliances, TV & Radios Wholesale
5065	Electronic Parts & Eqpt Wholesale
5072	Hardware Wholesale
5074	Plumbing & Heating Splys Wholesale
5075	Heating & Air Conditioning Eqpt & Splys Wholesale
5078	Refrigeration Eqpt & Splys Wholesale
5082	Construction & Mining Mach & Eqpt Wholesale
5083	Farm & Garden Mach & Eqpt Wholesale
5084	Industrial Mach & Eqpt Wholesale
5085	Industrial Splys Wholesale
5087	Service Establishment Eqpt & Splys Wholesale
5088	Transportation Eqpt & Splys, Except Motor Vehicles Wholesale
5091	Sporting & Recreational Goods & Splys Wholesale
5092	Toys & Hobby Goods & Splys Wholesale
5093	Scrap & Waste Materials Wholesale
5094	Jewelry, Watches, Precious Stones Wholesale
5099	Durable Goods: NEC Wholesale
51	wholesale trade¨nondurable goods
5111	Printing & Writing Paper Wholesale
5112	Stationery & Office Splys Wholesale
5113	Indl & Personal Svc Paper Wholesale
5122	Drugs, Drug Proprietaries & Sundries Wholesale
5131	Piece Goods, Notions & Dry Goods Wholesale
5136	Men's & Boys' Clothing & Furnishings Wholesale
5137	Women's, Children's & Infants Clothing Wholesale
5139	Footwear Wholesale
5141	Groceries, General Line Wholesale
5142	Packaged Frozen Foods Wholesale
5143	Dairy Prdts, Except Dried Or Canned Wholesale
5144	Poultry & Poultry Prdts Wholesale
5145	Confectionery Wholesale
5146	Fish & Seafood Wholesale
5147	Meats & Meat Prdts Wholesale
5148	Fresh Fruits & Vegetables Wholesale
5149	Groceries & Related Prdts, NEC Wholesale
5153	Grain & Field Beans Wholesale
5154	Livestock Wholesale
5159	Farm-Prdt Raw Mtrls, NEC Wholesale
5162	Plastics Materials & Basic Shapes Wholesale
5169	Chemicals & Allied Prdts, NEC Wholesale
5171	Petroleum Bulk Stations & Terminals
5172	Petroleum & Petroleum Prdts Wholesale
5181	Beer & Ale Wholesale
5182	Wine & Distilled Alcoholic Beverages Wholesale
5191	Farm Splys Wholesale
5192	Books, Periodicals & Newspapers Wholesale
5193	Flowers, Nursery Stock & Florists' Splys Wholesale
5194	Tobacco & Tobacco Prdts Wholesale
5198	Paints, Varnishes & Splys Wholesale
5199	Nondurable Goods, NEC Wholesale
60	depository institutions
6021	National Commercial Banks
6022	State Commercial Banks
6029	Commercial Banks, NEC
6035	Federal Savings Institutions
6036	Savings Institutions, Except Federal
6061	Federal Credit Unions
6062	State Credit Unions
6081	Foreign Banks, Branches & Agencies
6082	Foreign Trade & Intl Banks
6091	Nondeposit Trust Facilities
6099	Functions Related To Deposit Banking, NEC
61	nondepository credit institutions
6111	Federal Credit Agencies
6141	Personal Credit Institutions
6153	Credit Institutions, Short-Term Business
6159	Credit Institutions, Misc Business
6162	Mortgage Bankers & Loan Correspondents
6163	Loan Brokers
62	security and commodity brokers, dealers, exchanges, and services
6211	Security Brokers & Dealers
6221	Commodity Contracts Brokers & Dealers
6231	Security & Commodity Exchanges
6282	Investment Advice
63	insurance carriers
6311	Life Insurance Carriers
6321	Accident & Health Insurance
6324	Hospital & Medical Svc Plans Carriers
6331	Fire, Marine & Casualty Insurance
6351	Surety Insurance Carriers
6361	Title Insurance
6371	Pension, Health & Welfare Funds
6399	Insurance Carriers, NEC
64	insurance agents, brokers, and service
6411	Insurance Agents, Brokers & Svc
65	real estate
6512	Operators Of Nonresidential Bldgs
6513	Operators Of Apartment Buildings
6514	Operators Of Dwellings, Except Apartments
6515	Operators of Residential Mobile Home Sites
6519	Lessors Of Real Estate, NEC
6531	Real Estate Agents & Managers
6541	Title Abstract Offices
6552	Land Subdividers & Developers
6553	Cemetery Subdividers & Developers
67	holding and other investment offices
6719	Offices Of Holding Co's, NEC
6722	Management Investment Offices
6726	Unit Investment Trusts, Face-Amount Certificate Offices
6732	Education, Religious & Charitable Trusts
6733	Trusts Except Educational, Religious & Charitable
6792	Oil Royalty Traders
6794	Patent Owners & Lessors
6798	Real Estate Investment Trusts
6799	Investors, NEC
70	hotels, rooming houses, camps, and other lodging places
7011	Hotels, Motels & Tourist Courts
7021	Rooming & Boarding Houses
7032	Sporting & Recreational Camps
7033	Trailer Parks & Camp Sites
7041	Membership-Basis Hotels
72	personal services
7211	Power Laundries, Family & Commercial
7212	Garment Pressing & Cleaners' Agents
7213	Linen Sply
7215	Coin Operated Laundries & Cleaning
7216	Dry Cleaning Plants, Except Rug Cleaning
7217	Carpet & Upholstery Cleaning
7218	Industrial Launderers
7219	Laundry & Garment Svcs, NEC
7221	Photographic Studios, Portrait
7231	Beauty Shops
7241	Barber Shops
7251	Shoe Repair & Shoeshine Parlors
7261	Funeral Svcs & Crematories
7291	Tax Return Preparation Svcs
7299	Miscellaneous Personal Svcs, NEC
73	business services
7311	Advertising Agencies
7312	Outdoor Advertising Svcs
7313	Radio, TV & Publishers Adv Reps
7319	Advertising, NEC
7322	Adjustment & Collection Svcs
7323	Credit Reporting Svcs
7331	Direct Mail Advertising Svcs
7334	Photocopying & Duplicating Svcs
7335	Commercial Photography
7336	Commercial Art & Graphic Design
7338	Secretarial & Court Reporting Svcs

SIC INDEX

SIC NO	PRODUCT
7342	Disinfecting & Pest Control Svcs
7349	Building Cleaning & Maintenance Svcs, NEC
7352	Medical Eqpt Rental & Leasing
7353	Heavy Construction Eqpt Rental & Leasing
7359	Equipment Rental & Leasing, NEC
7361	Employment Agencies
7363	Help Supply Svcs
7371	Custom Computer Programming Svcs
7372	Prepackaged Software
7373	Computer Integrated Systems Design
7374	Data & Computer Processing & Preparation
7375	Information Retrieval Svcs
7376	Computer Facilities Management Svcs
7378	Computer Maintenance & Repair
7379	Computer Related Svcs, NEC
7381	Detective & Armored Car Svcs
7382	Security Systems Svcs
7383	News Syndicates
7384	Photofinishing Labs
7389	Business Svcs, NEC
75	automotive repair, services, and parking
7513	Truck Rental & Leasing, Without Drivers
7514	Passenger Car Rental
7515	Passenger Car Leasing
7519	Utility Trailers & Recreational Vehicle Rental
7521	Automobile Parking Lots & Garages
7532	Top, Body & Upholstery Repair & Paint Shops
7534	Tire Retreading & Repair Shops
7537	Automotive Transmission Repair Shops
7538	General Automotive Repair Shop
7539	Automotive Repair Shops, NEC
7542	Car Washes
7549	Automotive Svcs, Except Repair & Car Washes
76	miscellaneous repair services
7622	Radio & TV Repair Shops
7623	Refrigeration & Air Conditioning Svc & Repair Shop
7629	Electrical & Elex Repair Shop, NEC
7631	Watch, Clock & Jewelry Repair
7641	Reupholstery & Furniture Repair
7692	Welding Repair
7694	Armature Rewinding Shops
7699	Repair Shop & Related Svcs, NEC
78	motion pictures
7812	Motion Picture & Video Tape Production
7819	Services Allied To Motion Picture Prdtn
7822	Motion Picture & Video Tape Distribution
7832	Motion Picture Theaters, Except Drive-In
7833	Drive-In Motion Picture Theaters
7841	Video Tape Rental
79	amusement and recreation services
7911	Dance Studios, Schools & Halls
7922	Theatrical Producers & Misc Theatrical Svcs
7929	Bands, Orchestras, Actors & Entertainers
7933	Bowling Centers
7941	Professional Sports Clubs & Promoters
7948	Racing & Track Operations
7991	Physical Fitness Facilities
7992	Public Golf Courses
7993	Coin-Operated Amusement Devices & Arcades
7996	Amusement Parks
7997	Membership Sports & Recreation Clubs
7999	Amusement & Recreation Svcs, NEC
80	health services
8011	Offices & Clinics Of Doctors Of Medicine
8021	Offices & Clinics Of Dentists
8031	Offices & Clinics Of Doctors Of Osteopathy
8041	Offices & Clinics Of Chiropractors
8042	Offices & Clinics Of Optometrists
8043	Offices & Clinics Of Podiatrists
8049	Offices & Clinics Of Health Practitioners, NEC
8051	Skilled Nursing Facilities
8052	Intermediate Care Facilities
8059	Nursing & Personal Care Facilities, NEC
8062	General Medical & Surgical Hospitals
8063	Psychiatric Hospitals
8069	Specialty Hospitals, Except Psychiatric
8071	Medical Laboratories
8072	Dental Laboratories
8082	Home Health Care Svcs
8092	Kidney Dialysis Centers
8093	Specialty Outpatient Facilities, NEC
8099	Health & Allied Svcs, NEC
81	legal services
8111	Legal Svcs
83	social services
8322	Individual & Family Social Svcs
8331	Job Training & Vocational Rehabilitation Svcs
8351	Child Day Care Svcs
8361	Residential Care
8399	Social Services, NEC
84	museums, art galleries, and botanical and zoological gardens
8412	Museums & Art Galleries
8422	Arboreta, Botanical & Zoological Gardens
86	membership organizations
8611	Business Associations
8621	Professional Membership Organizations
8631	Labor Unions & Similar Organizations
8641	Civic, Social & Fraternal Associations
8651	Political Organizations
8699	Membership Organizations, NEC
87	engineering, accounting, research, management, and related services
8711	Engineering Services
8712	Architectural Services
8713	Surveying Services
8721	Accounting, Auditing & Bookkeeping Svcs
8731	Commercial Physical & Biological Research
8732	Commercial Economic, Sociological & Educational Research
8733	Noncommercial Research Organizations
8734	Testing Laboratories
8741	Management Services
8742	Management Consulting Services
8743	Public Relations Svcs
8744	Facilities Support Mgmt Svcs
8748	Business Consulting Svcs, NEC
89	services, not elsewhere classified
8999	Services Not Elsewhere Classified

PRODUCTS & SERVICES SECTION

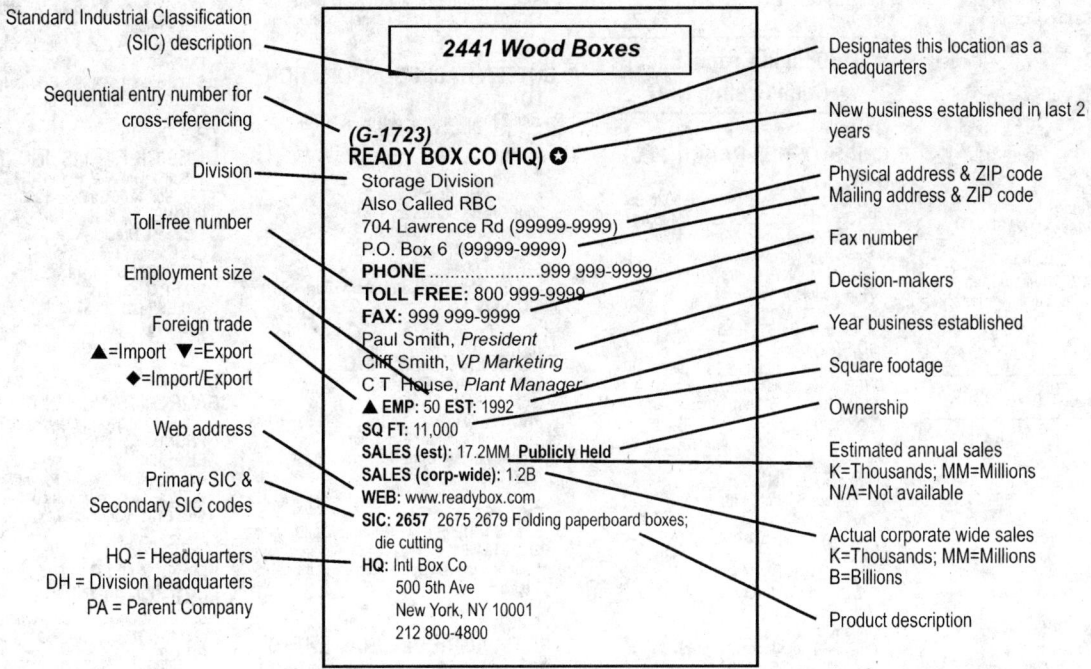

Sample entry diagram labels:
- Standard Industrial Classification (SIC) description
- Sequential entry number for cross-referencing
- Division
- Toll-free number
- Employment size
- Foreign trade ▲=Import ▼=Export ◆=Import/Export
- Web address
- Primary SIC & Secondary SIC codes
- HQ = Headquarters
- DH = Division headquarters
- PA = Parent Company
- Designates this location as a headquarters
- New business established in last 2 years
- Physical address & ZIP code
- Mailing address & ZIP code
- Fax number
- Decision-makers
- Year business established
- Square footage
- Ownership
- Estimated annual sales K=Thousands; MM=Millions N/A=Not available
- Actual corporate wide sales K=Thousands; MM=Millions B=Billions
- Product description

Sample entry:
2441 Wood Boxes

(G-1723)
READY BOX CO (HQ) ✪
Storage Division
Also Called RBC
704 Lawrence Rd (99999-9999)
P.O. Box 6 (99999-9999)
PHONE 999 999-9999
TOLL FREE: 800 999-9999
FAX: 999 999-9999
Paul Smith, *President*
Cliff Smith, *VP Marketing*
C T House, *Plant Manager*
▲ **EMP:** 50 **EST:** 1992
SQ FT: 11,000
SALES (est): 17.2MM **Publicly Held**
SALES (corp-wide): 1.2B
WEB: www.readybox.com
SIC: 2657 2675 2679 Folding paperboard boxes; die cutting
HQ: Intl Box Co
500 5th Ave
New York, NY 10001
212 800-4800

- Companies in this section are listed numerically under their primary SIC Companies are in alphabetical order under each code.
- A numerical and alphabetcal index precedes this section.
- **Sequential Entry Numbers.** Each establishment in this section is numbered sequentially. The number assigned to each establishment's Entry Number. To make cross-referencing easier, each listing in the Product's & Services, Alphabetic and Geographical Section includes the establishment's entry number. To facilitate locating an entry in this section, the entry numbers for the first listing on the left page and the last listing on the right page are printed at the top of the page next to the Standard Industrial Classification (SIC) description.
- Further information can be found in the Explanatory Notes starting on page 5.
- See the footnotes for symbols and abbreviations.

IMPORTANT NOTICE: It is a violation of both federal and state law to transmit an unsolicited advertisement to a facsimile machine. Any user of this product that violates such laws may be subject to civil and criminal penalties which may exceed $500 for each transmission of an unsolicited facsimile. Harris InfoSource provides fax numbers for lawful purposes only and expressly forbids the use of these numbers in any unlawful manner.

0111 Wheat

(P-1)
MULLER RANCH LLC
15810 County Road 95, Woodland (95695-9222)
PHONE 530 662-0105
Frank Muller, *Partner*
Thomas Muller, *Partner*
EMP: 85 **EST:** 1978
SALES (est): 9.6MM **Privately Held**
SIC: 0111 0115 0161 Wheat; corn; tomato farm

(P-2)
RIVER VISTA FARMS LLC
3536 State Highway 45, Colusa (95932-4006)
P.O. Box 209 (95932-0209)
PHONE 530 458-2550
Kathryn Yerxa,
Woodford Yerxa, *Officer*
EMP: 45 **EST:** 1984
SALES (est): 2.7MM **Privately Held**
WEB: www.rivervistafarms.com
SIC: 0111 0161 Wheat; watermelon farm; beet farm; cucumber farm; tomato farm

(P-3)
T & P FARMS
1241 Putnam Way, Arbuckle (95912-0738)
P.O. Box 83 (95912-0083)
PHONE 530 476-3038
Perry Charter, *Partner*
Tom Charter, *Partner*
Shelby Nation, *Bookkeeper*
EMP: 103 **EST:** 1976
SALES (est): 2.3MM **Privately Held**
SIC: 0111 0112 0181 0161 Wheat; rice; seeds, vegetable: growing of; tomato farm; general farms, primarily crop; food crops grown under cover

0112 Rice

(P-4)
CARRIERE FARMS LLC
1640 State Highway 45, Glenn (95943-9649)
PHONE 530 934-8200
William Carriere,
Jennifer Carriere-Laduke,
James Doyle,
Gary Enos,
Jason Enos,
◆ **EMP:** 35 **EST:** 2012
SALES (est): 2.8MM **Privately Held**
WEB: www.carrierefarms.com
SIC: 0112 0762 0173 Rice; orchard management & maintenance services; almond grove

(P-5)
HALF MOON FRUIT & PRODUCE CO (PA)
Also Called: Giovannetti Equipment Sales
403 Court St, Woodland (95695-3421)
PHONE 530 662-1727
John B Giovannetti, *President*
Harold Dickerson, *Corp Secy*
Ronald Giovannetti, *Vice Pres*
Eric Tenhunfeld, *General Mgr*
EMP: 50 **EST:** 1913
SQ FT: 60,000
SALES (est): 5MM **Privately Held**
SIC: 0112 0131 0111 0119 Rice; cotton; wheat; barley farm; alfalfa farm; lettuce farm

(P-6)
MCFADDEN FARM
16000 Powerhouse Rd, Potter Valley (95469-8771)
PHONE 707 743-1122
Eugene McFadden, *Owner*
Fontaine McFadden, *Opers Staff*
EMP: 28 **EST:** 1970
SQ FT: 1,000
SALES (est): 1.5MM **Privately Held**
WEB: www.mcfaddenfarm.com
SIC: 0112 0172 0139 2099 Rice; grapes; herb or spice farm; food preparations

0115 Corn

(P-7)
JOE HEIDRICK ENTERPRISES INC
36826 County Road 24, Woodland (95695-9355)
PHONE 530 662-2339
Joe Heidrick, *President*
EMP: 50 **EST:** 1990
SQ FT: 1,500
SALES (est): 6MM **Privately Held**
SIC: 0115 0111 0161 0139 Corn; wheat; tomato farm; alfalfa farm

0119 Cash Grains, NEC

(P-8)
FREDERICK L RICHTER & SON INC
707 Main St, Colusa (95932-2324)
PHONE 530 458-3180
Paul Richter, *Principal*
Nicole Garofalo, *Principal*

(PA)=Parent Co (HQ)=Headquarters (DH)=Div Headquarters
✪ = New Business established in last 2 years

0119 - Cash Grains, NEC County (P-9)   PRODUCTS & SERVICES SECTION

Kathryn Richter, *Principal*
Kurt Richter, *Principal*
EMP: 35 **EST:** 2001
SALES (est): 2.2MM **Privately Held**
SIC: 0119 0139 Cash grains; field crops, except cash grain

(P-9)
KNIGHT FARMS
7920 County Road 29, Glenn (95943-9618)
PHONE.................................530 934-9536
Ann M Knight, *Partner*
Craig M Knight, *Partner*
Jace G Knight, *Partner*
Peter D Knight, *Partner*
Peter A Knight, *Partner*
EMP: 48 **EST:** 2016
SALES (est): 2.8MM **Privately Held**
SIC: 0119 0139 0179 Sunflower farm; cereal crop farms; alfalfa farm; fruits & tree nuts

0131 Cotton

(P-10)
OLAM LLC
205 E Rver Pk Cir Ste 310, Fresno (93720)
PHONE.................................559 446-6420
Sandip Sharma, *President*
Tricia Ardissono, *Vice Pres*
Carl Askey, *Vice Pres*
Dave Defrank, *Vice Pres*
Ranjith Prabh Krishnamoorthy, *Vice Pres*
EMP: 50 **EST:** 2007
SALES (est): 9.6MM **Privately Held**
WEB: www.olamgroup.com
SIC: 0131 0722 0182 2281 Cotton; peanuts, machine harvesting services; tomatoes grown under cover; cotton yarn, spun

(P-11)
SAN ANDREAS FARMS CO
Also Called: Nunn Ranches
741 Sunset Rd, Brentwood (94513-5501)
PHONE.................................925 634-1717
Ronald E Nunn, *Partner*
Shirley A Nunn, *Partner*
EMP: 41 **EST:** 1975
SQ FT: 988
SALES (est): 2.1MM **Privately Held**
SIC: 0131 0161 0111 Cotton; tomato farm; lettuce farm; wheat

(P-12)
TEIXEIRA AND SONS LLC (PA)
22759 S Mercey Springs Rd, Los Banos (93635-9539)
PHONE.................................209 827-9800
John J Teixeira, *Partner*
Don Teixeira, *Partner*
Tom Teixeira, *Partner*
EMP: 121 **EST:** 1955
SALES (est): 3.7MM **Privately Held**
SIC: 0131 0133 0119 Cotton; sugar beet farm; safflower farm

(P-13)
TRIANGLE T RANCH INC
4408 Hays Dr, Chowchilla (93610-8929)
PHONE.................................559 665-2964
David Riley, *Manager*
EMP: 68
SALES (corp-wide): 3MM **Privately Held**
WEB: www.triangletranch.com
SIC: 0131 0115 Cottonseed farm; corn
PA: Triangle T Ranch, Inc.
1330 Broadway Ste 915
Oakland CA 94612
510 428-0428

(P-14)
WOLFSEN INCORPORATED
Sjr Farming
1269 W I St, Los Banos (93635-3930)
PHONE.................................209 827-7700
Albert Laguna, *Manager*
EMP: 157
SALES (corp-wide): 14.8MM **Privately Held**
WEB: www.wolfseninc.com
SIC: 0131 Cotton
PA: Wolfsen Incorporated
1269 W I St
Los Banos CA 93635
209 827-7700

0139 Field Crops, Except Cash Grains, NEC

(P-15)
CHRISTOPHER RANCH LLC (PA)
305 Bloomfield Ave, Gilroy (95020-9565)
PHONE.................................408 847-1100
William Christopher, *Mng Member*
Jaclyn Agnitsch, *Accountant*
Michael Mantelli, *Opers Mgr*
Jeffrey Stokes, *VP Sales*
Patsy Ross, *Mktg Dir*
▲ **EMP:** 170 **EST:** 1953
SQ FT: 220,000
SALES (est): 50.2MM **Privately Held**
SIC: 0139 0175 Herb or spice farm; cherry orchard

(P-16)
DAREGAL INC
Also Called: Superb Farms
300 Dianne Dr, Turlock (95380-9523)
P.O. Box 610 (95381-0610)
PHONE.................................209 633-3600
Charles Darbonne, *CEO*
Luc Darbonne, *CFO*
Matt Reid, *Admin Sec*
Chris Kaji, *Engineer*
Daniel Snider, *Accounting Mgr*
◆ **EMP:** 180 **EST:** 1992
SQ FT: 65,190
SALES (est): 46.5MM
SALES (corp-wide): 1.7MM **Privately Held**
WEB: www.superbfarms.com
SIC: 0139 2099 5149 Herb or spice farm; seasonings & spices; sauces: gravy, dressing & dip mixes; sauces
HQ: Daregal
6 Boulevard Du Marechal Joffre
Milly La Foret 91490
164 986-712

(P-17)
EDWARD SILVEIRA (PA)
Also Called: Silveira Ranch
4174 Sultana Ave, Atwater (95301-9605)
PHONE.................................209 394-8656
Edward Silveira, *Owner*
EMP: 38 **EST:** 1963
SALES (est): 192.1K **Privately Held**
SIC: 0139 Sweet potato farm

(P-18)
PAX LABS INC
660 Alabama St Ste 2, San Francisco (94110-2190)
PHONE.................................415 829-2336
Michael Murphy, *President*
Jill Agnello, *Partner*
Dominic O'brien, *Officer*
Nick Dor, *Vice Pres*
Campbell Smith, *Engineer*
EMP: 58 **EST:** 2017
SALES (est): 19.2MM **Privately Held**
WEB: www.pax.com
SIC: 0139 3999

(P-19)
QUAIL H FARMS LLC
5301 Robin Ave, Livingston (95334-9317)
P.O. Box 247 (95334-0247)
PHONE.................................209 394-8001
J Michael Hennigan, *Mng Member*
Darren Barfield, *COO*
Robbie Hamaguchi, *Controller*
Larelle Miller, *Sales Mgr*
Angie Maciel, *Sales Staff*
▼ **EMP:** 505 **EST:** 2005
SALES (est): 29.4MM **Privately Held**
WEB: www.quailhfarms.com
SIC: 0139 Sweet potato farm

(P-20)
RICHARD IEST DAIRY INC
13507 Road 17, Madera (93637-9040)
PHONE.................................559 673-2635
Richard C Iest, *President*
Marisela Macias, *General Mgr*
EMP: 99 **EST:** 2011
SALES (est): 9.1MM **Privately Held**
SIC: 0139 Field crops, except cash grain

(P-21)
SUTTER BASIN CORPORATION LTD
10982 Knights Rd, Robbins (95676)
P.O. Box 38 (95676-0038)
PHONE.................................530 738-4456
Janet Butler, *Ch of Bd*
Steven T Butler, *President*
Judy Bruce, *Corp Secy*
Edith Ramsey, *Vice Pres*
EMP: 37 **EST:** 1928
SQ FT: 1,000
SALES (est): 3MM **Privately Held**
SIC: 0139 Food crops

(P-22)
THOMSEN FARMS INC
2365 W Durham Ferry Rd, Tracy (95304-9318)
PHONE.................................209 835-5442
Kenneth Thomsen, *President*
Ruth Thomsen, *Corp Secy*
Allen Thomsen,
Thomas Thomsen,
EMP: 36 **EST:** 1973
SALES (est): 1.3MM **Privately Held**
SIC: 0139 0173 0161 0133 Alfalfa farm; almond grove; tomato farm; sugar beet farm

(P-23)
VIEIRA AGRICULTURAL ENTPS LLC
3978 Sultana Ave, Atwater (95301-9605)
P.O. Box 533, Livingston (95334-0533)
PHONE.................................209 394-2771
Manuel Vieira, *Principal*
EMP: 45 **EST:** 2014
SQ FT: 100
SALES (est): 1.2MM **Privately Held**
SIC: 0139 Sweet potato farm

0161 Vegetables & Melons

(P-24)
BALOIAN PACKING CO INC (PA)
Also Called: Baloian Farm
446 N Blythe Ave, Fresno (93706-1003)
P.O. Box 11337 (93772-1337)
PHONE.................................559 485-9200
Edward Baloian, *Ch of Bd*
Timothy Baloian, *President*
Peter Baloian, *Vice Pres*
Emily Baloian, *Admin Sec*
Pam Angulo, *Finance Dir*
▲ **EMP:** 147 **EST:** 1985
SQ FT: 35,000
SALES (est): 25.9MM **Privately Held**
WEB: www.baloianfarms.com
SIC: 0161 0723 Broccoli farm; vegetable packing services

(P-25)
DAN AVILA & SONS FARMS INC
2718 Roberts Rd, Ceres (95307-9627)
PHONE.................................209 495-3899
Daniel Avila, *Owner*
EMP: 60 **EST:** 2001
SALES (est): 16MM **Privately Held**
WEB: www.danavilaandsons.com
SIC: 0161 0139 Watermelon farm; sweet potato farm

(P-26)
DIMARE ENTERPRISES INC (PA)
Also Called: Dimare Company
1406 N St, Newman (95360-1309)
P.O. Box 517 (95360-0517)
PHONE.................................209 827-2900
Thomas F Dimare, *President*
Paul J Dimare, *Treasurer*
EMP: 250 **EST:** 1975
SQ FT: 20,000
SALES (est): 26.4MM **Privately Held**
WEB: www.dimarefresh.com
SIC: 0161 0174 Vegetables & melons; citrus fruits

(P-27)
DONALD W BEEMAN
Also Called: Don Beeman Farms
37190 County Road 24, Woodland (95695-9355)
PHONE.................................530 662-3012
EMP: 40
SALES (est): 3.4MM **Privately Held**
SIC: 0161 Tomato Farm

(P-28)
DRESICK FARMS INC (PA)
19536 Jayne Ave, Huron (93234)
P.O. Box 1260 (93234-1260)
PHONE.................................559 945-2513
Michael L Dresick, *CEO*
Jan Dresick, *Vice Pres*
EMP: 109 **EST:** 1974
SQ FT: 3,500
SALES (est): 20.8MM **Privately Held**
SIC: 0161 Lettuce farm; cantaloupe farm; tomato farm; rooted vegetable farms

(P-29)
FAUROT RANCH LLC
703 Hall Rd, Royal Oaks (95076-5712)
PHONE.................................831 722-1346
EMP: 40
SALES (est): 2.7MM **Privately Held**
WEB: www.faurotranch.com
SIC: 0161 Vegetable/Melon Farm

(P-30)
FRANK AND PATRICIA MAGGIORE (PA)
820 Quiet Gable Ct, Brentwood (94513-1913)
PHONE.................................925 634-4176
Frank Maggiore, *Partner*
Mark Maggiore, *Partner*
Marty Maggiore, *Partner*
Patricia Maggiore, *Partner*
Timmy Maggiore, *Partner*
EMP: 42 **EST:** 1953
SALES (est): 2.5MM **Privately Held**
SIC: 0161 0175 Tomato farm; cherry orchard; peach orchard

(P-31)
GEORGE CHIALA FARMS INC
Also Called: Chiala, George Packing
15500 Hill Rd, Morgan Hill (95037-9516)
PHONE.................................408 778-0562
George Chiala Sr, *President*
Alice Chiala, *CFO*
George Chiala Jr, *Vice Pres*
▲ **EMP:** 120 **EST:** 1972
SQ FT: 14,000
SALES (est): 41MM **Privately Held**
WEB: www.gcfarmsinc.com
SIC: 0161 0723 4783 Vegetables & melons; vegetable crops market preparation services; containerization of goods for shipping

(P-32)
ORO LOMA RANCH LLC (PA)
44474 W Nees Ave, Firebaugh (93622-9560)
PHONE.................................209 364-0070
Jason H Hall, *Mng Member*
◆ **EMP:** 45 **EST:** 2005
SALES (est): 3.3MM **Privately Held**
SIC: 0161 0173 0181 0175 Asparagus farm; almond grove; nursery stock, growing of; deciduous tree fruits

(P-33)
PAYNE BROTHERS RANCHES
13330 County Road 102, Woodland (95776-9119)
PHONE.................................530 662-2354
William A Payne, *Partner*
Robert B Payne, *Partner*
EMP: 66 **EST:** 1963
SALES (est): 1.4MM **Privately Held**
SIC: 0161 0191 Tomato farm; general farms, primarily crop

(P-34)
RICHTER BROS INC
22474 Karnak Rd, Knights Landing (95645-9405)
PHONE.................................530 735-6721
David Richter, *President*

PRODUCTS & SERVICES SECTION

0172 - Grapes County (P-61)

Amelia Richter, *Treasurer*
Mark Richter, *Admin Sec*
EMP: 49 **EST:** 1945
SQ FT: 2,300
SALES (est): 4.8MM **Privately Held**
SIC: 0161 0115 0112 Tomato farm; corn; rice

(P-35)
SEASHOLTZ JOHN
1355 M St, Firebaugh (93622-2338)
PHONE......................559 659-3805
EMP: 196
SALES (corp-wide): 11.2MM **Privately Held**
WEB: www.redroostertm.com
SIC: 0161 Vegetables & melons
PA: Seasholtz, John
  4965 N Crystal Ave Ste A
  Fresno CA 93705
  559 229-0453

(P-36)
VANN BROTHERS
365 Ruggieri Way, Williams (95987-5155)
PHONE......................530 473-2607
William B Vann, *Partner*
Garnett Vann Jr, *Partner*
Dprothy Murphy, *Asst Controller*
Bianca Salazar, *Clerk*
EMP: 123 **EST:** 1973
SQ FT: 4,500
SALES (est): 17.8MM **Privately Held**
WEB: www.vannfamilyorchards.com
SIC: 0161 0721 0131 0111 Tomato farm; orchard tree & vine services; cotton; wheat; seeds, vegetable: growing of

(P-37)
VICTORIA ISLAND LP
16021 W Highway 4, Holt (95234)
PHONE......................209 465-5600
Eileen Christin, *Partner*
EMP: 45 **EST:** 1994
SALES (est): 986K **Privately Held**
SIC: 0161 Tomato farm

(P-38)
WEBB RANCH INC
2720 Alpine Rd, Portola Valley (94028-6313)
PHONE......................650 854-6334
Nathan Hensley, *CFO*
Thomas Hubbard, *President*
Summer Hensley, *Admin Sec*
EMP: 48 **EST:** 1922
SALES (est): 1.2MM **Privately Held**
WEB: www.webbranchinc.com
SIC: 0161 0171 0272 0119 Tomato farm; berry crops; horse farm; bean (dry field & seed) farm; corn; boarding services, horses: racing & non-racing

0171 Berry Crops

(P-39)
CBS FARMS LLC
80 Sakata Ln, Watsonville (95076-5132)
P.O. Box 1825 (95077-1825)
PHONE......................831 724-0700
Ed Kelly, *Mng Member*
Brad Peterson, *Sales Staff*
Carl Hamona,
Bob Rigor,
EMP: 50 **EST:** 2009
SALES (est): 1MM **Privately Held**
WEB: www.cbsfarms.com
SIC: 0171 Strawberry farm

(P-40)
COLLEEN STRAWBERRIES INC (PA)
80 Sakata Ln, Watsonville (95076-5132)
P.O. Box 1825 (95077-1825)
PHONE......................831 724-0700
Ed Kelly, *Owner*
Charlie Staka, *Sales Staff*
EMP: 37 **EST:** 2008
SALES (est): 621.4K **Privately Held**
WEB: www.colleenstrawberries.com
SIC: 0171 Strawberry farm

(P-41)
RIO MESA FARMS LLC
75 Sakata Ln, Watsonville (95076-5132)
P.O. Box 1359 (95077-1359)
PHONE......................831 728-1965
Mary Gregg, *Administration*
EMP: 35 **EST:** 1996
SALES (est): 284.2K
SALES (corp-wide): 462.9K **Privately Held**
SIC: 0171 Strawberry farm
PA: California Giant, Inc.
  75 Sakata Ln
  Watsonville CA 95076
  831 728-1773

(P-42)
T T MIYASAKA INC (PA)
209 Riverside Rd, Watsonville (95076-3656)
PHONE......................831 722-3871
Tim Miyasaka, *President*
EMP: 232 **EST:** 1964
SQ FT: 500
SALES (est): 24.2MM **Privately Held**
SIC: 0171 Strawberry farm

0172 Grapes

(P-43)
BAKER FARMING
45499 W Panoche Rd, Firebaugh (93622-9780)
P.O. Box 867 (93622-0867)
PHONE......................559 659-3942
Byron Baker, *Partner*
Barry Baker, *Partner*
EMP: 37 **EST:** 1993
SQ FT: 350,000
SALES (est): 3MM **Privately Held**
SIC: 0172 0173 Grapes; almond grove

(P-44)
BELLAGRACE VINEYARDS (PA)
22715 Upton Rd, Plymouth (95669-9509)
PHONE......................209 681-2103
Charles Vennell Havill, *CEO*
Jess Havill, *Manager*
EMP: 41 **EST:** 2009
SALES (est): 961.3K **Privately Held**
WEB: www.bellagracevineyards.com
SIC: 0172 Grapes

(P-45)
BEVILL VINEYARD MANAGEMENT LLC
4724 Dry Creek Rd, Healdsburg (95448-9714)
PHONE......................707 433-1101
Duffern Bevill, *Mng Member*
Matt Vogensen,
EMP: 37 **EST:** 1998
SALES (est): 7.6MM **Privately Held**
WEB: www.bevillvineyard.com
SIC: 0172 Grapes

(P-46)
BOGLE VINEYARDS INC
Also Called: Bogle Winery
37783 County Road 144, Clarksburg (95612-5009)
PHONE......................916 744-1139
Warren W Bogle, *President*
Ryan Bogle, *Vice Pres*
Patty Bogle, *Admin Sec*
Eric Ariyoshi, *Marketing Staff*
Ginelle Cloar, *Marketing Staff*
▼ **EMP:** 40 **EST:** 1946
SALES (est): 15.1MM **Privately Held**
WEB: www.boglewinery.com
SIC: 0172 5813 Grapes; wine bar

(P-47)
BROCCHINI FARMS INC
27011 S Austin Rd, Ripon (95366-9627)
PHONE......................209 599-4229
Robert Brocchini, *President*
Steve Brocchini, *Principal*
EMP: 50 **EST:** 1948
SALES (est): 4.1MM **Privately Held**
SIC: 0172 0173 0139 Grapes; almond grove; alfalfa farm

(P-48)
CEDERLIND FARMS LP
2514 Kenney Ave, Winton (95388-9745)
PHONE......................209 606-8586
Jeff Cederlind, *Partner*
EMP: 99 **EST:** 1998
SALES (est): 3.3MM **Privately Held**
SIC: 0172 Grapes

(P-49)
DAVE J MENDRIN INC
4876 W Athens Ave, Fresno (93722-2119)
PHONE......................559 352-1700
Jack Mendrin, *President*
EMP: 18 **EST:** 1991
SALES (est): 700K **Privately Held**
SIC: 0172 2034 Grapes; raisins

(P-50)
DELU VINEYARDS INC
15175 N Devries Rd, Lodi (95242-9217)
PHONE......................209 334-6660
Alexander Delu, *President*
EMP: 80 **EST:** 1958
SALES (est): 1.4MM **Privately Held**
SIC: 0172 0722 Grapes; grapes, machine harvesting services

(P-51)
DOMAINE CARNEROS LTD
1240 Duhig Rd, NAPA (94559-9713)
P.O. Box 5420 (94581-0420)
PHONE......................707 257-0101
Eileen Crane, *Principal*
Kellie Hoppe, *Technician*
Kristen Guiducci, *Controller*
Fernanda Castro, *Hum Res Coord*
Nicole Hamill, *Buyer*
◆ **EMP:** 80
SQ FT: 50,000
SALES (est): 7.9MM **Privately Held**
WEB: www.domainecarneros.com
SIC: 0172 2084 Grapes; wines

(P-52)
ENTERPRISE VINEYARDS INC
16600 Norrbom Rd, Sonoma (95476-4780)
P.O. Box 233, Vineburg (95487-0233)
PHONE......................707 996-6513
Philip Coturri, *President*
Arden Kremer, *Vice Pres*
Jesse Apgar, *Director*
James Drummond, *Manager*
EMP: 35 **EST:** 1979
SALES (est): 2.8MM **Privately Held**
WEB: www.enterprisevineyards.com
SIC: 0172 Grapes

(P-53)
GROTH VINEYARDS AND WINERY
750 Oakville Cross Rd, Oakville (94562)
P.O. Box 390 (94562-0390)
PHONE......................707 944-0290
Dennis Groth, *Mng Member*
Judith Groth, *CFO*
Gayle Newman, *Administration*
Suzanne Groth, *Marketing Mgr*
Ken Uhl, *Sales Staff*
◆ **EMP:** 27 **EST:** 1982
SQ FT: 50,000
SALES (est): 3.1MM **Privately Held**
WEB: www.grothwines.com
SIC: 0172 2084 Grapes; wines

(P-54)
GUGLIELMO EMILO WINERY INC
Also Called: Emile's Table Wines
1480 E Main Ave, Morgan Hill (95037-3201)
PHONE......................408 779-2145
George E Guglielmo, *President*
Julie Bradford, *CFO*
Gary J Guglielmo, *Treasurer*
Madeline Guglielmo, *Vice Pres*
Gary Guglielmo, *General Mgr*
EMP: 15 **EST:** 1925
SQ FT: 56,000
SALES (est): 2.6MM **Privately Held**
WEB: www.gugliemowinery.com
SIC: 0172 2084 5921 7999 Grapes; wines; wine; recreation center

(P-55)
H & R GUNLUND RANCHES INC
3510 W Saginaw Ave, Caruthers (93609-9568)
PHONE......................559 864-8186
EMP: 220
SALES (est): 5.4MM **Privately Held**
SIC: 0172 Grape Vineyard

(P-56)
HONIG VINEYARD AND WINERY LLC
Also Called: Honig Cellars
850 Rutherford Rd, Rutherford (94573)
P.O. Box 406 (94573-0406)
PHONE......................707 963-5618
Louis Honig,
Chessa Moreno, *CIO*
Regina Weinstein, *Marketing Mgr*
Kim Villanueva, *Regl Sales Mgr*
Jon McPherson, *Facilities Mgr*
▲ **EMP:** 20 **EST:** 1982
SQ FT: 8,000
SALES (est): 3.1MM **Privately Held**
WEB: www.honigwine.com
SIC: 0172 2084 Grapes; wines

(P-57)
IRON HORSE RANCH & VINEYARD
9786 Ross Station Rd, Sebastopol (95472-2137)
PHONE......................707 887-1507
Audrey M Sterling, *Partner*
Barry Sterling, *Partner*
Joy Sterling, *Partner*
Lawrence Sterling, *Partner*
Lu Fraser, *Controller*
EMP: 22 **EST:** 1969
SALES (est): 1.3MM **Privately Held**
WEB: www.ironhorsevineyards.com
SIC: 0172 2084 Grapes; wines, brandy & brandy spirits

(P-58)
JACK NEAL & SON INC
360 Lafata St, Saint Helena (94574-1410)
PHONE......................707 963-7303
Mark J Neal, *President*
Tina Galambos, *Vice Pres*
EMP: 200 **EST:** 1968
SQ FT: 20,000
SALES (est): 10.5MM **Privately Held**
WEB: www.jacknealandson.com
SIC: 0172 Grapes

(P-59)
KANDARIAN AGRI ENTERPRISES
Also Called: Agrichem
116 W Adams Ave, Fowler (93625-9614)
P.O. Box 278 (93625-0278)
PHONE......................559 834-1501
Eugene Kandarian, *President*
Yvonne Kandarian, *Vice Pres*
EMP: 36 **EST:** 1966
SQ FT: 6,500
SALES (est): 1.2MM **Privately Held**
SIC: 0172 4213 5191 Grapes; contract haulers; chemicals, agricultural; fertilizer & fertilizer materials; pesticides

(P-60)
KAUTZ VINEYARDS INC (PA)
Also Called: Kautz Ironstone Vineyards
1894 6 Mile Rd, Murphys (95247-9543)
PHONE......................209 728-1251
John K Kautz, *CEO*
Stephen Kautz, *President*
Kurt Kautz, *Treasurer*
Gail Kautz, *Vice Pres*
Steve Millier, *Vice Pres*
◆ **EMP:** 100 **EST:** 1989
SQ FT: 75,000
SALES (est): 10MM **Privately Held**
WEB: www.ironstonevineyards.com
SIC: 0172 5812 Grapes; eating places

(P-61)
KLEIN FOODS INC
Also Called: Rodney Strong Vineyards
11455 Old Redwood Hwy, Healdsburg (95448-9523)
P.O. Box 6010 (95448-6010)
PHONE......................707 431-1533

0172 - Grapes County (P-62)

Thomas B Klein, *President*
Tobin Ginter, *CFO*
Carmen Castaldi, *Vice Pres*
Dan Wildermuth, *Vice Pres*
Christopher O'gorman, *Comms Dir*
◆ **EMP:** 100 **EST:** 1988
SQ FT: 20,000
SALES (est): 38.6MM **Privately Held**
WEB: www.rodneystrong.com
SIC: 0172 2084 5182 Grapes; wines; wine & distilled beverages

(P-62)
LAMANUZZI & PANTALEO LLC (PA)
11767 Road 27 1/2, Madera (93637-9108)
PHONE..................559 432-3170
Frank P Pantaleo,
Richard Barnes, *CIO*
Karol Ryals, *Accountant*
Gary Kalajian, *Sales Staff*
Tina Baer,
▲ **EMP:** 88 **EST:** 1937
SQ FT: 1,000
SALES (est): 16MM **Privately Held**
WEB: www.reginagrapejuice.com
SIC: 0172 4222 Grapes; warehousing, cold storage or refrigerated

(P-63)
LANZA VINEYARDS INC (PA)
Also Called: Wooden Valley Farms
4756 Suisun Valley Rd, Fairfield (94534-3114)
PHONE..................707 864-0730
Richard Lanza, *President*
Adrienne Lanza, *Corp Secy*
Kenneth Lee Lanza, *Vice Pres*
Lawrence Dean Lanza, *Vice Pres*
Mario Richard Lanza Jr, *Vice Pres*
EMP: 65 **EST:** 1955
SQ FT: 1,300
SALES (est): 7MM **Privately Held**
WEB: www.woodenvalley.com
SIC: 0172 2084 Grapes; wines

(P-64)
LODI FARMING INC
11292 N Alpine Rd, Stockton (95212-9325)
PHONE..................209 948-4022
Donald Lenz, *Corp Secy*
Jeffrey Colombini, *President*
Don Lenz, *Treasurer*
▲ **EMP:** 43 **EST:** 1989
SQ FT: 1,000
SALES (est): 2.8MM **Privately Held**
WEB: www.lodifarming.com
SIC: 0172 0175 Grapes; cherry orchard; apple orchard

(P-65)
MENDOCINO LAND COMPANY INC (DH)
383 4th St Ste 400, Oakland (94607-4104)
PHONE..................510 286-2000
Gregory Balogh, *President*
Jean Claude Rouzaud, *President*
▲ **EMP:** 62 **EST:** 1982
SALES (est): 25.3MM **Privately Held**
WEB: www.louis-roederer.com
SIC: 0172 2084 5182 Grapes; wines; wine
HQ: Champagne Louis Roederer
21 Boulevard Lundy
Reims 51100
326 404-211

(P-66)
NICKEL AND NICKEL INC
8164 St Helena Hwy, Oakville (94562)
P.O. Box 7 (94562-0007)
PHONE..................707 967-9600
Dirk Hampson, *President*
Reece Morrel, *Admin Sec*
Eric Kiser, *Facilities Mgr*
EMP: 16 **EST:** 1984
SALES (est): 2.6MM **Privately Held**
WEB: www.nickelandnickel.farniente.com
SIC: 0172 2084 Grapes; wine cellars, bonded: engaged in blending wines

(P-67)
ONEILL BEVERAGES CO LLC
Also Called: O'Neill Vintners & Distillers
8418 S Lac Jac Ave, Parlier (93648-9708)
PHONE..................559 638-3544

Marty Spate, *Vice Pres*
EMP: 200
SALES (corp-wide): 113.2MM **Privately Held**
WEB: www.oneillwine.com
SIC: 0172 2084 Grapes; wines; brandy
PA: O'neill Beverages Co. Llc
101 Larkspur Landing Cir
Larkspur CA 94939
844 825-6600

(P-68)
ONEILL BEVERAGES CO LLC (PA)
Also Called: O'Neill Vintners & Distillers
101 Larkspur Landing Cir, Larkspur (94939-1746)
PHONE..................844 825-6600
Jeffrey B O'Neill, *CEO*
Steve Lindsay, *Senior VP*
Ryan Davis, *Vice Pres*
Mike Drobnick, *Vice Pres*
Marty Spate, *Vice Pres*
◆ **EMP:** 63 **EST:** 2004
SQ FT: 5,000
SALES (est): 113.2MM **Privately Held**
WEB: www.oneillwine.com
SIC: 0172 2084 Grapes; wines

(P-69)
R & G SCHATZ FARMS INC
Also Called: Peltier Winery
22150 N Kennefick Rd, Acampo (95220-9242)
PHONE..................209 367-4881
Rodney Schatz, *President*
Gayla Schatz, *CFO*
Hanno Bezuidenhout, *General Mgr*
Faryn Schatz, *Manager*
▲ **EMP:** 15 **EST:** 1986
SQ FT: 6,802
SALES (est): 1.7MM **Privately Held**
WEB: www.peltierwinery.com
SIC: 0172 2084 Grapes; wines

(P-70)
R J M ENTERPRISES INC
Also Called: McManis Family Vineyards
18700 E River Rd, Ripon (95366-9711)
PHONE..................209 599-1186
Ronald W McManis, *President*
Jamie McManis, *Vice Pres*
Greg Cardey, *Controller*
◆ **EMP:** 49 **EST:** 1990
SQ FT: 1,600
SALES (est): 2.3MM **Privately Held**
SIC: 0172 Grapes

(P-71)
RAYMOND VINEYARD & CELLAR INC
849 Zinfandel Ln, Saint Helena (94574-1645)
PHONE..................707 963-3141
Alain Leonnet, *CEO*
Jean C Boisset, *President*
Phil Marquand, *CFO*
Mark Drake, *Sales Staff*
▲ **EMP:** 40 **EST:** 1971
SQ FT: 70,000
SALES (est): 11.1MM
SALES (corp-wide): 18.4MM **Privately Held**
WEB: www.raymondvineyards.com
SIC: 0172 2084 Grapes; wines
HQ: Jean-Claude Boisset Wines U.S.A., Inc.
849 Zinfandel Ln
Saint Helena CA 94574
707 967-7667

(P-72)
ROBERT ALVES FARMS INC
Also Called: Alves, Robert L
10642 E Dinuba Ave, Selma (93662-9783)
PHONE..................559 896-3309
EMP: 70
SALES (est): 2.1MM **Privately Held**
SIC: 0172 Grape Farmer

(P-73)
SCHEID VINEYARDS INC
373 Healdsburg Ave, Healdsburg (95448-4137)
PHONE..................707 433-1858
EMP: 107

SALES (corp-wide): 56.4MM **Publicly Held**
SIC: 0172 Grape Vineyard
PA: Scheid Vineyards Inc.
305 Hilltown Rd
Salinas CA 93908
310 301-1555

(P-74)
SCHRAMSBERG VINEYARDS COMPANY
1400 Schramsberg Rd, Calistoga (94515-9624)
PHONE..................707 942-4558
Hugh Davies, *President*
Katie Quinn, *Executive Asst*
Mara Ambrose, *Technician*
Lloyd Martin, *Business Mgr*
Douglas Francisco, *Controller*
▲ **EMP:** 50 **EST:** 1965
SQ FT: 20,000
SALES (est): 15.5MM **Privately Held**
WEB: www.schramsberg.com
SIC: 0172 2084 Grapes; wines

(P-75)
SONOMA-CUTRER VINEYARDS INC (HQ)
4401 Slusser Rd, Windsor (95492-7601)
P.O. Box 9, Fulton (95439-0009)
PHONE..................707 528-1181
David Perata, *Principal*
Steve Dorfman, *President*
Tori Underwood, *Technician*
Stephane Cantin, *Finance Mgr*
Daniel Dillon, *Manager*
◆ **EMP:** 126 **EST:** 1973
SALES (est): 24.2MM
SALES (corp-wide): 3.4B **Publicly Held**
WEB: www.sonomacutrer.com
SIC: 0172 2084 5921 Grapes; wines; liquor stores
PA: Brown-Forman Corporation
850 Dixie Hwy
Louisville KY 40210
502 585-1100

(P-76)
STOKES BROTHERS FARMS
7581 W Kile Rd, Lodi (95242-9300)
PHONE..................209 794-2380
William Stokes, *Partner*
Mike Stokes, *Partner*
Thomas Stokes, *Partner*
EMP: 70 **EST:** 2007
SQ FT: 3,550
SALES (est): 7.6MM **Privately Held**
SIC: 0172 Grapes

(P-77)
TOPOLOS AT RSSIAN RIVER VINYRD
Also Called: Russian River Vineyards
5700 Gravenstein Hwy N, Forestville (95436-9393)
P.O. Box 920 (95436-0920)
PHONE..................707 887-1575
Michael Topolos, *CEO*
Christine Topolos, *Partner*
Jerry Topolos, *Partner*
Giovanni Balistreri, *General Mgr*
EMP: 25 **EST:** 1978
SQ FT: 2,000
SALES (est): 2.7MM **Privately Held**
WEB: www.russianrivervineyards.com
SIC: 0172 2084 5813 5812 Grapes; wines; beer garden (drinking places); American restaurant

(P-78)
TWIN CREEKS VINEYARD COMPANY
Also Called: Brocap Vineyard Company
1000 Wooden Vly Cross Rd, NAPA (94558-8503)
PHONE..................707 224-4575
EMP: 40
SALES: 600K **Privately Held**
SIC: 0172 Grape Vineyard

(P-79)
TWIN TEAKS WINERY
Also Called: Cliff Lede Vineyards
1473 Yountville Cross Rd, Yountville (94599-9471)
PHONE..................707 944-8642
Cliff Lede, *Owner*
Kimberly Whistler, *Marketing Staff*
Sarah Delcampo, *Sales Staff*
Sherell Guyot, *Manager*
Bob Copeland, *Consultant*
▲ **EMP:** 23 **EST:** 1971
SALES (est): 4.8MM **Privately Held**
WEB: www.cliffledevineyards.com
SIC: 0172 2084 Grapes; wines

(P-80)
V SANGIACOMO & SONS
Also Called: Sangiacomo Vineyards
21543 Broadway, Sonoma (95476-8205)
PHONE..................707 938-5503
Victor F Sangiacomo, *Partner*
Angelo C Sangiacomo, *Partner*
Lorraine J Sangiacomo, *Partner*
Steve Sangciacomo,
EMP: 50 **EST:** 1927
SQ FT: 1,200
SALES (est): 5.2MM **Privately Held**
WEB: www.sangiacomo-vineyards.com
SIC: 0172 Grapes

(P-81)
VIRGINIA SARABIAN
Also Called: Sarabian Farms
2816 S Leonard Ave, Sanger (93657-9754)
PHONE..................559 493-2900
Virginia Sarabian, *Owner*
Michael Sarabian, *Owner*
Sarkis Sarabian, *Owner*
Jordan Sarabian, *Controller*
EMP: 50 **EST:** 1956
SQ FT: 1,200
SALES (est): 8.3MM **Privately Held**
WEB: www.sarabianfarms.com
SIC: 0172 4222 2033 0175 Grapes; warehousing, cold storage or refrigerated; fruits: packaged in cans, jars, etc.; nectarine orchard; farm management services

0173 Tree Nuts

(P-82)
BALDWIN-MINKLER FARMS
320 E South St, Orland (95963-9111)
P.O. Box 607 (95963-0607)
PHONE..................530 865-7676
Rod W Minkler, *President*
Peter Baldwin, *Shareholder*
Dan Soetaert, *Shareholder*
Holly I Salisbury, *CPA*
James St George, *CPA*
◆ **EMP:** 35 **EST:** 1993
SALES (est): 2.6MM **Privately Held**
SIC: 0173 Almond grove; walnut grove

(P-83)
BENTON ENTERPRISES LLC
Also Called: Elk Ridge Almonds
18252 Avenue 20, Madera (93637-9730)
P.O. Box 417 (93639-0417)
PHONE..................559 664-0800
William B Pitmann, *Mng Member*
Joan Rau,
Roger Rau,
Harry Stepanian,
Jeffrey Stepanian,
EMP: 30
SALES (est): 2.3MM **Privately Held**
WEB: www.elkridgealmonds.com
SIC: 0173 2068 5441 Tree nuts; salted & roasted nuts & seeds; nuts

(P-84)
CARRIERE FAMILY FARMS LLC
1640 State Highway 45, Glenn (95943-9649)
PHONE..................530 934-8200
William Carriere, *CEO*
Don Albright, *Admin Sec*
Blanca Palomino, *Sales Staff*
William David Carriere, *Mng Member*
EMP: 40 **EST:** 2016

PRODUCTS & SERVICES SECTION
0175 - Deciduous Tree Fruits County (P-111)

SALES (est): 4.5MM Privately Held
WEB: www.carrierefarms.com
SIC: 0173 2068 5145 Walnut grove; salted & roasted nuts & seeds; nuts, salted or roasted

(P-85)
CHARANJIT SINGH BATTH
Also Called: Batth Farms
5434 W Kamm Ave, Caruthers (93609-9400)
PHONE 559 864-9421
Charanjit Singh Batth, *Owner*
EMP: 90 **EST:** 1969
SQ FT: 1,200
SALES (est): 11MM Privately Held
WEB: www.batthfarms.com
SIC: 0173 0175 0172 2034 Almond grove; prune orchard; grapes; raisins

(P-86)
COSYNS FARMS
15310 Road 19, Madera (93637-9229)
PHONE 559 674-6283
Richard Cosyns, *Partner*
Allen Cosyns, *Partner*
EMP: 41 **EST:** 1959
SALES (est): 1.4MM Privately Held
SIC: 0173 0172 Almond grove; grapes

(P-87)
CRANE MILLS
22938 South Ave, Corning (96021)
P.O. Box 318 (96021-0318)
PHONE 530 824-5387
Robert Crane, *President*
Dan Mc Fall, *Treasurer*
Brian Crane, *Vice Pres*
EMP: 59 **EST:** 1946
SQ FT: 2,000
SALES (est): 1.8MM Privately Held
WEB: www.cranemills.com
SIC: 0173 0811 Almond grove; tree farm

(P-88)
FARMERS INTERNATIONAL INC
1260 Muir Ave, Chico (95973-8644)
PHONE 530 566-1405
Don Wada, *CEO*
Mohnish Seth, *Principal*
Chad Bales, *Accounting Mgr*
Mayra Feairbanks, *Manager*
◆ **EMP:** 50 **EST:** 2000
SALES (est): 8.3MM Privately Held
WEB: www.farmersinternational.com
SIC: 0173 Almond grove

(P-89)
FRAZIER NUT FARMS INC
10830 Yosemite Blvd, Waterford (95386-9637)
PHONE 209 522-1406
Jim Frazier Jr, *President*
Heidi Frazier-Slacks, *Corp Secy*
Steve Slacks, *Vice Pres*
◆ **EMP:** 50 **EST:** 1963
SALES (est): 4.8MM Privately Held
WEB: www.fraziernut.com
SIC: 0173 Walnut grove

(P-90)
RAJ SHARMA
Also Called: Sunrise Orchards
4750 Bear River Dr, Rio Oso (95674-9625)
P.O. Box 1107, Wheatland (95692-1107)
PHONE 530 633-2057
Raj Sharma, *Owner*
Cindy Cairnes, *Office Mgr*
EMP: 36 **EST:** 1989
SQ FT: 1,600
SALES (est): 1.7MM Privately Held
WEB: www.sunriseplants.com
SIC: 0173 0175 Walnut grove; peach orchard; prune orchard

(P-91)
RIDDLE RANCHES INC
Also Called: Waterford Almond Hller Sheller
12013 El Pomar Ave, Waterford (95386-9735)
PHONE 209 874-9784
Robert Riddle, *President*
Lane M Riddle, *Vice Pres*
Pamela Riddle Machado, *Admin Sec*
Gloria Riddle, *Clerk*
EMP: 27 **EST:** 1967

SALES (est): 1.8MM Privately Held
SIC: 0173 0175 2068 Almond grove; peach orchard; nuts: dried, dehydrated, salted or roasted

(P-92)
SALE FAMILY ORCHARDS LLC
425 Brearcliffe Dr, Red Bluff (96080-4332)
PHONE 530 527-4854
EMP: 36
SALES (est): 715.3K Privately Held
SIC: 0173 0175 Tree Nut Grove Fruit Tree Orchard

(P-93)
SIERRA VALLEY ALMONDS LLC
850 Commerce Dr, Madera (93637-5299)
PHONE 559 662-8900
Mark H Turmon, *Mng Member*
Dan Pronsolino, *General Mgr*
Adam Ellis, *Opers Mgr*
Kurt Friedenbach, *Sales Staff*
Dean K Nelson,
◆ **EMP:** 35 **EST:** 2006
SALES (est): 5.5MM Privately Held
WEB: www.svalmonds.com
SIC: 0173 Almond grove

(P-94)
TAYLOR BROTHERS FARMS INC (PA)
Also Called: Taylor Packing Co
182 Wilkie Ave, Yuba City (95991-9437)
PHONE 530 671-1505
Richard Taylor, *President*
John Taylor, *Vice Pres*
Barbara Brennan, *QA Dir*
Virgil Baker, *Controller*
Esther Curiel, *Plant Mgr*
◆ **EMP:** 49 **EST:** 1982
SQ FT: 26,000
SALES (est): 7.7MM Privately Held
WEB: www.taylorbrothersfarms.com
SIC: 0173 2034 0723 0175 Walnut grove; dried & dehydrated fruits; fruit crops market preparation services; apple orchard

0174 Citrus Fruits

(P-95)
AIRDROME ORCHARDS INC (PA)
111 E Alma Ave, San Jose (95112-2792)
PHONE 408 297-6461
Charles Fumia, *CEO*
John Fumia Jr, *CFO*
Anthony Buldo, *Vice Pres*
Paul Buldo, *Vice Pres*
Tony Buldo, *Vice Pres*
▼ **EMP:** 50 **EST:** 1977
SQ FT: 30,000
SALES (est): 8.5MM Privately Held
SIC: 0174 0175 Orange grove; pear orchard

0175 Deciduous Tree Fruits

(P-96)
BERTAGNA ORCHARDS INC
3329 Hegan Ln, Chico (95928-9589)
PHONE 530 343-8014
Ben N Bertagna, *President*
Mary Jane Bertagna, *Vice Pres*
EMP: 43 **EST:** 1946
SALES (est): 2.3MM Privately Held
WEB: www.bertagnaorchards.com
SIC: 0175 Apple orchard

(P-97)
BT HOLDINGS INC
Also Called: Quercus Ranch
4150 Soda Bay Rd, Kelseyville (95451)
P.O. Box 548 (95451-0548)
PHONE 707 279-4317
EMP: 50 **EST:** 1979
SQ FT: 120,000
SALES (est): 500K Privately Held
SIC: 0175 0172 Fruit Tree Orchard Grape Vineyard

(P-98)
CIRCLE K RANCH (PA)
8640 E Manning Ave, Selma (93662-9763)
PHONE 559 834-1571
Melvin Kazarian, *General Ptnr*
Ronald Kazarian, *Partner*
EMP: 68 **EST:** 1946
SQ FT: 25,000
SALES (est): 5.6MM Privately Held
WEB: www.circlekranch.com
SIC: 0175 Nectarine orchard; peach orchard; plum orchard

(P-99)
DUTTON RANCH CORP
10717 Graton Rd, Sebastopol (95472-9393)
P.O. Box 48, Graton (95444-0048)
PHONE 707 823-0448
Steve Dutton, *President*
Joe Dutton, *Vice Pres*
EMP: 52 **EST:** 1975
SALES (est): 3.7MM Privately Held
WEB: www.duttonranch.com
SIC: 0175 0172 Apple orchard; grapes

(P-100)
GERAWAN FARMING LLC
1467 E Dinuba Ave, Reedley (93654-3586)
PHONE 559 638-9281
Dan Gerawan, *Branch Mgr*
Josie Ramirez, *Executive*
Sara McNeely, *Asst Controller*
Nick Boos, *Purchasing*
Jason Ables, *Purch Agent*
EMP: 197
SALES (corp-wide): 455.3MM Privately Held
WEB: www.prima.com
SIC: 0175 0723 Apple orchard; fruit (fresh) packing services
HQ: Gerawan Farming Llc
 7108 N Fresno St Ste 450
 Fresno CA 93720
 559 787-8780

(P-101)
GERAWAN RANCHES (PA)
Also Called: Gerawan Enterprises
7108 N Fresno St Ste 450, Fresno (93720-2961)
P.O. Box 67, Sanger (93657-0067)
PHONE 559 787-8780
Raymond M Gerawan, *Owner*
EMP: 40 **EST:** 1950
SALES (est): 5.1MM Privately Held
WEB: www.prima.com
SIC: 0175 0172 Peach orchard; plum orchard; nectarine orchard; grapes

(P-102)
GERAWAN RANCHES
10045 W Lincoln Ave, Fresno (93706-9342)
PHONE 559 787-8780
EMP: 230
SALES (corp-wide): 5.1MM Privately Held
WEB: www.prima.com
SIC: 0175 0172 Peach orchard; plum orchard; nectarine orchard; grapes
PA: Gerawan Ranches
 7108 N Fresno St Ste 450
 Fresno CA 93720
 559 787-8780

(P-103)
J & R DEBENEDETTO ORCHARDS INC
Also Called: De Benedetto AG
26393 Road 22 1/2, Chowchilla (93610-9624)
PHONE 559 665-1712
Richard De Benedetto, *CEO*
EMP: 44 **EST:** 1984
SALES (est): 1.6MM Privately Held
SIC: 0175 Apple orchard

(P-104)
K DARPINIAN & SONS INC
5913 Coffee Rd, Modesto (95357-0820)
PHONE 209 524-4442
ARA Darpinian, *President*
Gary Darpinian, *Treasurer*
Ron Darpinian, *Vice Pres*
Nelson Hall, *Admin Sec*

EMP: 66 **EST:** 1952
SQ FT: 860
SALES (est): 1.9MM Privately Held
SIC: 0175 0173 Deciduous tree fruits; walnut grove

(P-105)
KAP LP
10363 Davis Ave, Kingsburg (93631-9539)
P.O. Box 456 (93631-0456)
PHONE 559 897-5132
Mike Jackson, *Partner*
Susan Jackson Diepersloot, *Ltd Ptnr*
Colleen Jackson, *Ltd Ptnr*
Brent Jackson, *Managing Prtnr*
▼ **EMP:** 61 **EST:** 1981
SQ FT: 140,000
SALES (est): 1.9MM Privately Held
WEB: www.kingsburgorchards.com
SIC: 0175 Apple orchard; pear orchard

(P-106)
KAY DIX INC
14400 Andrus Island Rd, Isleton (95641-9804)
P.O. Box 248, Walnut Grove (95690-0248)
PHONE 916 776-1701
Daniel M Wilson, *President*
Darrell Wilson, *Treasurer*
Daniel Wilson, *General Mgr*
Angela Gonzalez, *Office Mgr*
Chiles Wilson, *Admin Sec*
EMP: 50 **EST:** 1951
SQ FT: 1,000
SALES (est): 4.8MM Privately Held
WEB: www.kaydix.com
SIC: 0175 0115 0111 Pear orchard; corn; wheat

(P-107)
KOZUKI FARMING INC
16518 E Adams Ave, Parlier (93648-9718)
PHONE 559 646-2652
EMP: 60
SALES: 2.2MM Privately Held
SIC: 0175 0172 Deciduous Tree Fruit Orchard & Grape Vineyard

(P-108)
MICHELI FARMS INC
6005 Highway 99, Live Oak (95953-9749)
PHONE 530 695-9022
John Micheli, *President*
Justin Micheli, *Admin Sec*
EMP: 58 **EST:** 1946
SQ FT: 108,000
SALES (est): 3.8MM Privately Held
SIC: 0175 0173 Peach orchard; prune orchard; walnut grove

(P-109)
MIKE JENSEN FARMS LLC
13138 S Bethel Ave, Kingsburg (93631-9216)
PHONE 559 897-4192
Mike Jensen,
Justin Nunes, *Sales Mgr*
EMP: 200 **EST:** 1984
SQ FT: 14,000
SALES (est): 10.1MM Privately Held
SIC: 0175 2033 2099 Apricot orchard; fruits: packaged in cans, jars, etc.; food preparations

(P-110)
PACIFIC FARMS AND ORCHARDS INC
22880 Gerber Rd, Gerber (96035-9728)
P.O. Box 955 (96035-0955)
PHONE 530 385-1475
Sam Mudd, *President*
Brendon Flynn, *Corp Secy*
▲ **EMP:** 66 **EST:** 1971
SQ FT: 4,000
SALES (est): 2.4MM Privately Held
WEB: www.pacificfarms.com
SIC: 0175 0173 0119 0111 Prune orchard; walnut grove; almond grove; barley farm; wheat; tomato farm; general farms, primarily animals

(P-111)
PETERSON FAMILY INC
38694 Road 16, Kingsburg (93631-9106)
PHONE 559 897-5064
Vernon E Peterson, *Owner*

0175 - Deciduous Tree Fruits County (P-112) PRODUCTS & SERVICES SECTION

EMP: 100 EST: 1975
SALES (est): 6.4MM Privately Held
SIC: 0175 0174 Apple orchard; citrus fruits

(P-113)
RICH HARVEST INC
Also Called: Courtesy Moving and Storage
3515 N Sabre Dr, Fresno (93727-7817)
PHONE...................559 252-8000
Gerald Peters, President
EMP: 100 EST: 1998
SALES (est): 2.5MM Privately Held
WEB: www.richharvestfarms.com
SIC: 0175 4783 4221 Deciduous tree fruits; packing & crating; farm product warehousing & storage

(P-113)
RUSSELL WAYNE LESTER
Also Called: Dixon Ridge Farms
5430 Putah Creek Rd, Winters (95694-9612)
PHONE...................530 795-4619
Russell W Lester, Owner
Russ Lester, President
▼ EMP: 44 EST: 1979
SALES (est): 5.7MM Privately Held
WEB: www.dixonridgefarms.com
SIC: 0175 Deciduous tree fruits

(P-114)
VANN FAMILY LLC
Also Called: Vann Family Orchard
6141 Abel Rd, Williams (95987-5816)
PHONE...................530 473-3317
Bob Silveira, Sales Staff
Veronica Maldonado, Manager
EMP: 135
SALES (corp-wide): 6.3MM Privately Held
WEB: www.vannfamilyorchards.com
SIC: 0175 Deciduous tree fruits
PA: Vann Family, Llc
    365 Ruggieri Way
    Williams CA 95987
    530 473-2607

0181 Ornamental Floriculture & Nursery Prdts

(P-115)
3-WAY FARMS (PA)
428 Browns Valley Rd, Watsonville (95076-0330)
PHONE...................831 722-0748
Delbert Herschbach, President
Lorraine Stern, Treasurer
Rosemarie Herschbach, Admin Sec
EMP: 50 EST: 1976
SALES (est): 2.1MM Privately Held
SIC: 0181 3999 Ornamental nursery products; flowers, artificial & preserved

(P-116)
CALIFORNIA PAJAROSA FLORAL
133 Hughes Rd, Watsonville (95076-9458)
P.O. Box 684 (95077-0684)
PHONE...................831 722-6374
John Furman, President
Alan Mitchell, Vice Pres
▲ EMP: 43 EST: 1979
SQ FT: 10,000
SALES (est): 1.5MM Privately Held
WEB: www.pajarosa.com
SIC: 0181 Nursery stock, growing of

(P-117)
CSN WINDDOWN INC
Also Called: Color Spot Lodi
5400 E Harney Ln, Lodi (95240-6903)
PHONE...................209 369-3018
David Barrett, President
EMP: 188
SALES (corp-wide): 229.5MM Privately Held
SIC: 0181 5193 Plants, potted: growing of; flowers & florists' supplies
HQ: Csn Winddown, Inc.
    27368 Via Industria # 201
    Temecula CA 92590

(P-118)
DAVE WILSON NURSERY (PA)
Also Called: Dwn
19701 Lake Rd, Hickman (95323-9706)
P.O. Box 429 (95323-0429)
PHONE...................209 874-1821
Robert B Woolley, CEO
Dennis Tarry, President
Dave Wilson, Principal
EMP: 50 EST: 1938
SQ FT: 8,000
SALES (est): 20.2MM Privately Held
WEB: www.davewilson.com
SIC: 0181 Nursery stock, growing of

(P-119)
DUARTE NURSERY INC
23456 E Flood Rd, Linden (95236-9429)
PHONE...................209 887-3409
Jim Duarte, Manager
Stephen Krauss, Controller
EMP: 350
SQ FT: 1,558
SALES (corp-wide): 49.3MM Privately Held
WEB: www.duartenursery.com
SIC: 0181 Nursery stock, growing of
PA: Duarte Nursery, Inc.
    1555 Baldwin Rd
    Hughson CA 95326
    209 531-0351

(P-120)
DUARTE NURSERY INC (PA)
Also Called: Duarte Properties
1555 Baldwin Rd, Hughson (95326-9522)
PHONE...................209 531-0351
John Duarte, President
Anita Duarte, Treasurer
Jeff Duarte, Vice Pres
Brianna Perez, Administration
Frank Olide, Info Tech Mgr
EMP: 50 EST: 1989
SALES (est): 49.3MM Privately Held
WEB: www.duartenursery.com
SIC: 0181 Nursery stock, growing of

(P-121)
ERNST BENARY OF AMERICA INC
195 Paulsen Rd, Watsonville (95076-1320)
PHONE...................831 288-2803
Dr Matthias Redlefsen, CEO
Ann Robson, Admin Asst
Nancy Collins, Manager
Snow Maestas, Consultant
▲ EMP: 41 EST: 2009
SALES (est): 3.4MM Privately Held
WEB: www.benary.com
SIC: 0181 Seeds, flower: growing of

(P-122)
FRANTZ WHOLESALE NURSERY LLC
12161 Delaware Rd, Hickman (95323-9602)
PHONE...................209 874-1459
Michael Frantz,
Mitzi Frantz,
▲ EMP: 150 EST: 2001
SALES (est): 23.4MM Privately Held
WEB: www.frantznursery.com
SIC: 0181 Nursery stock, growing of

(P-123)
GADDIS NURSERY INC
3050 Piner Rd, Santa Rosa (95401-4082)
PHONE...................707 542-2202
William Gaddis, Principal
Karen Utley, Human Res Dir
EMP: 37 EST: 1941
SQ FT: 97,000
SALES (est): 1.1MM Privately Held
WEB: www.gaddisnursery.com
SIC: 0181 Nursery stock, growing of

(P-124)
GOLDMAN ENTERPRISES
Also Called: Sunborne Nursery
1150 Phelps St, San Francisco (94124-2170)
P.O. Box 472500 (94147-2500)
PHONE...................415 821-7726
Dan Goldman, CEO
Candice Goldman, CFO

Leslie Bacigalupi, Technology
Victor Esposto, Superintendent
▲ EMP: 43 EST: 1975
SQ FT: 40,000
SALES (est): 2.4MM Privately Held
WEB: www.sunborne.com
SIC: 0181 5261 Foliage, growing of; plants, potted: growing of; nurseries & garden centers

(P-125)
GROVER LANDSCAPE SERVICES INC
6224 Stoddard Rd, Modesto (95356-9198)
PHONE...................209 545-4401
Mark Grover, President
Lorraine Grover, Treasurer
Ruth Jupe, Accounting Mgr
Derek Schleth, Accounting Mgr
Cathy Welch, Purchasing
EMP: 100
SQ FT: 10,850
SALES: 16.5MM Privately Held
WEB: www.groverlandscapeservices.com
SIC: 0181 0782 0783 0781 Ornamental nursery products; landscape contractors; tree trimming services for public utility lines; landscape planning services

(P-126)
GROWERS TRANSPLANTING INC
27630 Carnation Rd, Gustine (95322-9511)
PHONE...................209 854-3702
Gloria Espinosa, Administration
EMP: 48 Privately Held
WEB: www.growerstrans.com
SIC: 0181 Nursery stock, growing of
HQ: Growers Transplanting, Inc.
    360 Espinosa Rd
    Salinas CA 93907
    831 449-3440

(P-127)
HMCLAUSE INC (DH)
260 Cousteau Pl Ste 210, Davis (95618-5490)
PHONE...................800 320-4672
Remi Bastien, CEO
Matthew M Johnston, President
Anne Azam, Vice Pres
James Brusca, Vice Pres
Andre Cariou, Vice Pres
◆ EMP: 133 EST: 1856
SQ FT: 200,000
SALES (est): 182.8MM
SALES (corp-wide): 159.3MM Privately Held
WEB: www.hmclause.com
SIC: 0181 Seeds, vegetable: growing of
HQ: Groupe Limagrain Holding
    Biopole Clermont Henri Moudor
    St Beauzire 63360
    475 828-101

(P-128)
HMCLAUSE INC
42 Glenshire Ln, Chico (95973-1093)
PHONE...................530 713-5838
EMP: 70
SALES (corp-wide): 159.3MM Privately Held
WEB: www.hmclause.com
SIC: 0181 Ornamental Nursery Products, Nsk
HQ: Hm.Clause, Inc.
    260 Cousteau Pl Ste 210
    Davis CA 95618
    800 320-4672

(P-129)
KAWAHARA NURSERY INC
698 Burnett Ave, Morgan Hill (95037-9022)
P.O. Box 1358 (95038-1358)
PHONE...................408 779-2400
David Kawahara, President
John Kawahara, CFO
Ken Portue, Vice Pres
Ashley Reid, Admin Asst
Michael Willson, CIO
▲ EMP: 240 EST: 1947
SALES (est): 21.8MM Privately Held
WEB: www.kawaharanursery.com
SIC: 0181 5193 Nursery stock, growing of; flowers & florists' supplies

(P-130)
MATSUDAS BY GREEN ACRES LLC
Also Called: Green Acres Nursery and Supply
10600 Florin Rd, Sacramento (95830-9404)
P.O. Box 6750, Folsom (95763-6750)
PHONE...................916 673-9290
Mark B Gill, Mng Member
Donna Casey, Human Resources
James Jessup, Merchandising
Ashley Gill, Mng Member
Mark Gill, Mng Member
EMP: 180 EST: 2013
SALES (est): 21.1MM Privately Held
WEB: www.matsudasnursery.com
SIC: 0181 Nursery stock, growing of

(P-131)
NAUMES INC
3792 Feather River Blvd, Olivehurst (95961-9688)
P.O. Box 2410, Marysville (95901-0086)
PHONE...................530 743-2055
Bob Cosey, General Mgr
EMP: 58
SQ FT: 66,646
SALES (corp-wide): 49.1MM Privately Held
WEB: www.naumesinc.com
SIC: 0181 0723 4731 Fruit stocks, growing of; fruit (farm-dried) packing services; agents, shipping
PA: Naumes, Inc.
    2 W Barnett Rd
    Medford OR 97501
    541 772-6268

(P-132)
PARK GREENHOUSES
12813 W Ripon Rd, Ripon (95366-9634)
PHONE...................209 599-7545
Gary Cover, President
Glenna Cover, Corp Secy
Dale Johnson, Vice Pres
EMP: 40 EST: 1974
SQ FT: 600
SALES (est): 3.4MM Privately Held
WEB: www.parkgreenhouse.net
SIC: 0181 Flowers: grown under cover (e.g. greenhouse production); foliage, growing of

(P-133)
ROCKET FARMS INC (PA)
2651 Cabrillo Hwy N, Half Moon Bay (94019-1357)
P.O. Box 3756, Salinas (93912-3756)
PHONE...................800 227-5229
Charles Kosmont, CEO
Steven Chan, Vice Pres
Gerald Cheng, Vice Pres
Mark Clark, Vice Pres
Jason Kamimoto, Vice Pres
▲ EMP: 112 EST: 1993
SQ FT: 1,500,000
SALES (est): 26.3MM Privately Held
WEB: www.rocketfarms.com
SIC: 0181 Flowers: grown under cover (e.g. greenhouse production)

(P-134)
SIERRA GOLD NURSERIES INC
5320 Garden Hwy, Yuba City (95991-9499)
PHONE...................530 674-1145
Jack Poukish, CEO
Brian Berg, Vice Pres
Ellen Berg, Vice Pres
Micah Stevens, Research
Stephen Allen, Finance
▲ EMP: 86 EST: 1952
SQ FT: 2,500
SALES (est): 10.9MM Privately Held
WEB: www.sierragoldtrees.com
SIC: 0181 Nursery stock, growing of

(P-135)
SIERRA-CASCADE NURSERY INC (PA)
472-715 Johnson Rd, Susanville (96130-8727)
PHONE...................530 254-6867
Steve Fortin, President
Randy Jertberg, COO
Robert Akeson, Vice Pres

▲ = Import ▼ = Export
◆ = Import/Export

PRODUCTS & SERVICES SECTION
0191 - Crop Farming, Misc County (P-160)

Robert Murie, *Vice Pres*
Susan Quale, *Human Res Dir*
▼ **EMP:** 400 **EST:** 1975
SQ FT: 2,600
SALES (est): 34.4MM **Privately Held**
WEB: www.sierracascadenursery.com
SIC: 0181 Nursery stock, growing of

(P-136)
SILVER TERRACE NURSERIES INC
501 North St, Pescadero (94060)
PHONE 650 879-2110
Richard Ruggeri, *President*
Robert Ruggeri, *Vice Pres*
EMP: 70 **EST:** 1934
SQ FT: 5,000
SALES (est): 2.2MM **Privately Held**
SIC: 0181 Florists' greens & flowers

(P-137)
SPEEDLING INCORPORATED
2640 San Juan Hwy, San Juan Bautista (95045-9783)
PHONE 813 645-3221
Victoria Rivera, *Project Mgr*
Lisa Touchton, *Controller*
EMP: 53 **Privately Held**
WEB: www.speedling.com
SIC: 0181 Bulbs & seeds
HQ: Speedling, Incorporated
   4447 Old Us 41 S
   Ruskin FL 33570
   813 645-3221

(P-138)
STUKE NURSERY CO INC
1463 State Highway 99, Gridley (95948-9701)
P.O. Box 1200 (95948-1200)
PHONE 530 846-2378
Joann S Diethrich, *President*
Joann Stuke Dietrich, *President*
James Diethrich, *Corp Secy*
Elias Carrasco, *Vice Pres*
EMP: 40 **EST:** 1924
SQ FT: 2,000
SALES (est): 1MM **Privately Held**
WEB: www.stukenursery.com
SIC: 0181 Nursery stock, growing of

(P-139)
SUN VALLEY GROUP INC (PA)
3160 Upper Bay Rd, Arcata (95521-9690)
PHONE 707 822-2885
Leendert De Vries, *President*
Kyle Sharp, *Administration*
Faith Borden, *Accountant*
Mary Bruhn, *Human Resources*
Ginny Wyche, *Production*
◆ **EMP:** 350 **EST:** 1991
SQ FT: 8,700
SALES (est): 46.5MM **Privately Held**
WEB: www.tsvg.com
SIC: 0181 Flowers: grown under cover (e.g. greenhouse production); flowers grown in field nurseries; bulbs, growing of

(P-140)
TAKAO NURSERY INC
2665 N Polk Ave, Fresno (93722-9761)
PHONE 559 275-3844
Danny Takao, *Partner*
Donald Kogi Takao, *Partner*
Renu Takao, *Partner*
Traci Nottingham, *Office Mgr*
Lisa Takao, *Opers Staff*
EMP: 45 **EST:** 1944
SQ FT: 200,000
SALES (est): 3.9MM **Privately Held**
WEB: www.californiabuffalograss.com
SIC: 0181 5193 Flowers: grown under cover (e.g. greenhouse production); plants, potted: growing of; nursery stock

(P-141)
TALLY ONE INC (PA)
Also Called: Bloom-Rite
2651 Cabrillo Hwy N, Half Moon Bay (94019-1357)
PHONE 650 726-6361
Jack Pearlstein, *President*
Gail Hollingsworth, *Corp Secy*
Clara Mello, *Purch Mgr*
John Susa, *Sales Mgr*
▲ **EMP:** 40 **EST:** 1941

SQ FT: 20,000
SALES (est): 15.8MM **Privately Held**
SIC: 0181 5191 Nursery stock, growing of; garden supplies

0182 Food Crops Grown Under Cover

(P-142)
COUNTRYSIDE MUSHROOMS INC
11300 Center Ave, Gilroy (95020-9257)
PHONE 408 683-2748
Donald W Hordness, *President*
Lewis Di Cecco, *Vice Pres*
EMP: 40 **EST:** 1987
SALES (est): 1.6MM **Privately Held**
SIC: 0182 Mushrooms grown under cover

(P-143)
FITZ FRESH INC
211 Lee Rd, Watsonville (95076-9447)
P.O. Box 1450, Freedom (95019-1450)
PHONE 831 763-4440
Patrick J Fitz, *President*
▲ **EMP:** 63 **EST:** 1947
SQ FT: 2,000
SALES (est): 5MM **Privately Held**
WEB: www.fitzfresh.com
SIC: 0182 Mushrooms grown under cover

(P-144)
MONTEREY MUSHROOMS INC (PA)
260 Westgate Dr, Watsonville (95076-2452)
PHONE 831 763-5300
Shah Kazemi, *President*
Robert V Jenkins, *CFO*
Kyon Kazemi, *Vice Pres*
Bharat Dewangan, *Software Dev*
Julie Williams, *Software Dev*
▲ **EMP:** 50 **EST:** 1972
SALES (est): 304.3MM **Privately Held**
WEB: www.montereymushrooms.com
SIC: 0182 Mushrooms grown under cover

0191 Crop Farming, Misc

(P-145)
ACEMIJ FARMS INC
3621 N Howard Ave, Kerman (93630-9619)
PHONE 559 842-7766
Alvaro L Garcia, *President*
EMP: 45 **EST:** 2018
SALES (est): 1.2MM **Privately Held**
SIC: 0191 General farms, primarily crop

(P-146)
ARNAUDO BROS TRANSPORT INC (PA)
Also Called: Arnaudo Bros Trucking
16505 S Tracy Blvd, Tracy (95304-9436)
PHONE 209 835-0406
Steve Arnaudo, *President*
Leo Arnaudo, *Vice Pres*
Ed Arnaudo, *Admin Sec*
EMP: 65 **EST:** 1947
SQ FT: 1,200
SALES (est): 7.2MM **Privately Held**
SIC: 0191 4212 General farms, primarily crop; local trucking, without storage

(P-147)
BELLA VIVA ORCHARDS INC
7030 Hughson Ave, Hughson (95326-8014)
P.O. Box 1014 (95326-1014)
PHONE 209 883-9015
Cristina Ribeiro, *Manager*
Mathias Garcia, *Director*
EMP: 19 **Privately Held**
WEB: www.bellaviva.com
SIC: 0191 2034 General farms, primarily crop; dehydrated fruits, vegetables, soups
PA: Viva Bella Orchards Inc
   3019 S Quincy Rd
   Denair CA 95316

(P-148)
BOWLES FARMING COMPANY INC
11609 Hereford Rd, Los Banos (93635-9514)
PHONE 209 827-3000
Phillip Bowles, *President*
Danny Royer, *Vice Pres*
Emery Silberman, *Vice Pres*
Fernando Banda, *Facilities Mgr*
Justin Metz, *Senior Mgr*
EMP: 56
SALES (corp-wide): 25MM **Privately Held**
WEB: www.bfarm.com
SIC: 0191 General farms, primarily crop
PA: Bowles Farming Company, Inc.
   545 Sansome St Ste 825
   San Francisco CA 94111
   415 421-4800

(P-149)
CAMPOS FAMILY FARMS LLC
4726 W Jacquelyn Ave, Fresno (93722-6406)
PHONE 559 275-3000
Fermin Campos,
Juan Campos, *Manager*
EMP: 60 **EST:** 2011
SALES (est): 5.8MM **Privately Held**
SIC: 0191 General farms, primarily crop

(P-150)
CARL J KRUPPA
Also Called: Kruppa Farms
9575 Walnut Ave, Winton (95388-9551)
PHONE 209 358-1759
Carl J Kruppa, *Owner*
EMP: 47 **EST:** 1986
SALES (est): 2.2MM **Privately Held**
SIC: 0191 General farms, primarily crop

(P-151)
CIRCLE G RANCH INC
30479 County Road 24, Woodland (95695-9327)
PHONE 530 666-0979
Joe Gnoss, *President*
Nancy Gnoss, *Admin Sec*
EMP: 58 **EST:** 1956
SALES (est): 2.7MM **Privately Held**
SIC: 0191 General farms, primarily crop

(P-152)
COELHO WEST CUSTOM FARMING
26979 S Butte Ave, Five Points (93624)
P.O. Box 434 (93624-0434)
PHONE 559 884-2566
Anthony P Coelho Jr, *President*
EMP: 58 **EST:** 1985
SALES (est): 4.1MM **Privately Held**
SIC: 0191 General farms, primarily crop

(P-153)
COX & PEREZ
Also Called: Cox & Perez Farms
5807 Highway 33, Westley (95387)
P.O. Box 155 (95387-0155)
PHONE 209 894-3741
James P Cox, *Partner*
Charles S Cox, *Partner*
John Stewart Cox, *Partner*
William Cox, *Partner*
Rusty Foster, *Treasurer*
EMP: 45 **EST:** 1952
SQ FT: 2,000
SALES (est): 5.1MM **Privately Held**
SIC: 0191 0182 General farms, primarily crop; vegetable crops grown under cover

(P-154)
DAN R COSTA INC
17239 Louise Ave, Escalon (95320-8732)
PHONE 209 234-2004
Dan R Costa, *President*
Shirley Costa, *Corp Secy*
EMP: 250 **EST:** 1983 **Privately Held**
WEB: www.dfd.dannysfalldecor.com
SIC: 0191 0115 0723 General farms, primarily crop; corn; vegetable packing services; fruit (fresh) packing services

(P-155)
DAVIS DRIER & ELEVATOR N F
9421 N Dos Palos Hwy, Firebaugh (93622)
P.O. Box 425 (93622-0425)
PHONE 559 659-3035
Joyce Davis, *Vice Pres*
William C Davis, *President*
▲ **EMP:** 47 **EST:** 1947
SQ FT: 20,000
SALES (est): 1MM **Privately Held**
SIC: 0191 0131 0112 0723 General farms, primarily crop; cotton; rice; rice drying services

(P-156)
DEL MAR FARMS PARTNERS LTD (PA)
Also Called: Del Mar Seed Processing
9843 Cox Rd, Patterson (95363-8509)
P.O. Box 97, Westley (95387-0097)
PHONE 209 894-5555
Jon Maring, *Owner*
Lee Del Don, *General Ptnr*
Katie Shotwell, *General Mgr*
Joel Ruiz, *Purch Dir*
Zach Maring, *Opers Staff*
◆ **EMP:** 45 **EST:** 1982
SQ FT: 25,000
SALES (est): 16.8MM **Privately Held**
WEB: www.delmarfarms.com
SIC: 0191 0723 General farms, primarily crop; vegetable packing services

(P-157)
DEVINE ORGANICS LLC (PA)
684 W Cromwell Ave # 107, Fresno (93711-5716)
PHONE 559 573-7500
Donald Devine, *Mng Member*
Kevin Dees, *Controller*
Rita Garcia, *Human Res Mgr*
Heidi Devine, *Purch Mgr*
Manuel Cabezas, *QC Mgr*
EMP: 41 **EST:** 2013
SQ FT: 6,000
SALES (est): 5MM **Privately Held**
WEB: www.doubledfarms.com
SIC: 0191 7389 4731 General farms, primarily crop; packaging & labeling services; freight transportation arrangement

(P-158)
DICK ANDERSON & SONS FARMING
Also Called: Vasto Valle Farms
15900 W Dorris Ave, Huron (93234)
P.O. Box 10 (93234-0010)
PHONE 559 945-2511
Richard Anderson, *President*
Robert Anderson, *Corp Secy*
Craig Anderson, *Vice Pres*
EMP: 135 **EST:** 1968
SQ FT: 1,000
SALES (est): 9.7MM **Privately Held**
SIC: 0191 General farms, primarily crop

(P-159)
DON GRAGNANI FARMS
Also Called: Universal Custom Farming Co
12910 S Napa Ave, Tranquillity (93668)
P.O. Box 128 (93668-0128)
PHONE 559 693-4352
Donald Gragnani, *Partner*
Irene Gragnani, *Partner*
Jerry Gragnani, *Partner*
Jeanne Gragnani-Lloyd, *Partner*
Martha Alejo, *Manager*
EMP: 63 **EST:** 1969
SQ FT: 3,000
SALES (est): 3.1MM **Privately Held**
WEB: www.gragnanifarms.com
SIC: 0191 General farms, primarily crop

(P-160)
DOUBLE D FARMS (PA)
29191 Fresno Coalinga Rd, Coalinga (93210-9514)
PHONE 559 573-7500
Steve Miller, *CEO*
Don Divine, *Partner*
Dave Wood, *Partner*
EMP: 48 **EST:** 1990
SQ FT: 43,000

0191 - Crop Farming, Misc County (P-161)

SALES (est): 7.1MM **Privately Held**
WEB: www.doubledfarms.com
SIC: 0191 General farms, primarily crop

(P-161)
ECO FARM HOLDINGS PBC
465 Stony Point Rd # 144, Santa Rosa (95401-5969)
PHONE.................707 485-3035
Devin Calloway, *CEO*
EMP: 40 **EST:** 2017
SALES (est): 1.1MM **Privately Held**
SIC: 0191 6719 General farms, primarily crop; investment holding companies, except banks

(P-162)
ELKHORN BERRY FARMS LLC
262 E Lake Ave, Watsonville (95076-4718)
PHONE.................831 722-2472
Thomas Amrhein, *General Mgr*
▲ **EMP:** 35 **EST:** 2011
SALES (est): 1.2MM **Privately Held**
SIC: 0191 0171 General farms, primarily crop; strawberry farm

(P-163)
EMERALD FARMS LLC
4599 Mcdermott Rd, Maxwell (95955-9100)
P.O. Box 658 (95955-0658)
PHONE.................530 438-2133
Frances Etchepare, *Partner*
Allen Etchepare, *Partner*
Jean Marie Etchepare, *Partner*
EMP: 40 **EST:** 1983
SALES (est): 3.3MM **Privately Held**
SIC: 0191 General farms, primarily crop

(P-164)
EMPRESAS DEL BOSQUE INC
51481 W Shields Ave, Firebaugh (93622-9579)
P.O. Box 2455, Los Banos (93635-2455)
PHONE.................209 364-6428
Joe L Del Bosque Jr, *President*
Krystal Del Bosque, *Director*
EMP: 325 **EST:** 2005
SQ FT: 1,600
SALES (est): 11MM **Privately Held**
WEB: www.delbosquefarms.com
SIC: 0191 General farms, primarily crop

(P-165)
ENSHER ALEXANDER & BARSOOM INC (PA)
926 J St Ste 503, Sacramento (95814-2703)
PHONE.................916 443-6875
Elliot Alexander, *President*
Steve Barsoom, *Manager*
EMP: 37 **EST:** 1914
SALES (est): 3MM **Privately Held**
SIC: 0191 General farms, primarily crop

(P-166)
ERROTABERE RANCHES
22895 S Dickenson Ave, Riverdale (93656-9640)
PHONE.................559 867-4461
Daniel Errotabere, *Owner*
Jean Errotabere, *Partner*
Remi Errotabere, *Partner*
EMP: 69 **EST:** 1935
SQ FT: 1,500
SALES (est): 3.4MM **Privately Held**
SIC: 0191 General farms, primarily crop

(P-167)
FARM FRESH TO YOU LLC (PA)
Also Called: Capay Organic
3880 Seaport Blvd, West Sacramento (95691-3449)
PHONE.................916 303-7145
Freeman Barsotti, *CEO*
Jeffrey Foreman, *CFO*
Brenda Phillips, *Vice Pres*
EMP: 180 **EST:** 1976
SALES (est): 51.4MM **Privately Held**
WEB: www.farmfreshtoyou.com
SIC: 0191 General farms, primarily crop

(P-168)
FOSTER FARMS
900 W Belgravia Ave, Fresno (93706-3909)
P.O. Box 306, Livingston (95334-0306)
PHONE.................559 265-2000
Tom Bower, *Vice Pres*
Ryan Schoenborn, *IT/INT Sup*
Bob Miller, *Project Engr*
Jeff Hayman, *Business Mgr*
Wanda Estep, *Analyst*
EMP: 51 **EST:** 2015
SALES (est): 24.2MM **Privately Held**
WEB: www.fosterfarms.com
SIC: 0191 General farms, primarily crop

(P-169)
HARRIS FARMS INC
Harris Ranch Inn & Restaurant
24505 W Dorris Ave, Coalinga (93210-9667)
PHONE.................559 935-0717
Jonathan Farrington, *General Mgr*
John Obermire, *Manager*
EMP: 340
SALES (corp-wide): 46.6MM **Privately Held**
WEB: www.harrisfarms.com
SIC: 0191 7011 5813 5812 General farms, primarily crop; hotels & motels; drinking places; eating places
PA: Harris Farms, Inc.
29475 Fresno Coalinga Rd
Coalinga CA 93210
559 884-2435

(P-170)
J CRECELIUS INC
Also Called: Montetisea Framing
5043 N Montpelier Rd, Denair (95316-9608)
P.O. Box 579 (95316-0579)
PHONE.................209 883-4826
EMP: 100
SALES (est): 2.4MM **Privately Held**
SIC: 0191 0173 General Crop Farm Tree Nut Grove

(P-171)
J H MEEK & SONS INC
22075 County Road 99, Woodland (95695-9313)
P.O. Box 299 (95776-0299)
PHONE.................530 662-1106
Steve Meek, *President*
John J Meek Jr, *President*
EMP: 50 **EST:** 1946
SALES (est): 3MM **Privately Held**
SIC: 0191 General farms, primarily crop

(P-172)
J MARCHINI & SON INC
12000 Le Grand Rd, Le Grand (95333-9708)
PHONE.................559 665-2944
EMP: 93 **Privately Held**
WEB: www.jmarchinifarms.com
SIC: 0191 General farms, primarily crop
PA: J. Marchini & Son, Inc.
8736 Minturn Rd
Le Grand CA 95333

(P-173)
JACOBS FARM/DEL CABO INC
Also Called: Jacob's Farm
1751 Coast Rd, Santa Cruz (95060-5602)
PHONE.................831 421-9171
Larry Jacobs, *Branch Mgr*
EMP: 55
SALES (corp-wide): 68.2MM **Privately Held**
WEB: www.jacobsfarmdelcabo.com
SIC: 0191 General farms, primarily crop
PA: Jacobs Farm/Del Cabo, Inc.
2450 Stage Rd
Pescadero CA 94060
650 879-0580

(P-174)
JACOBS FARM/DEL CABO INC
390 Swift Ave Ste 8, South San Francisco (94080-6221)
PHONE.................650 827-1133
Ted Witt, *Manager*
Jesse Vera, *General Mgr*
Michelle Terra, *Admin Asst*
Caroline Hogue, *Sales Staff*
Monica Jacobs, *Sales Staff*
EMP: 55
SALES (corp-wide): 68.2MM **Privately Held**
WEB: www.jacobsfarmdelcabo.com
SIC: 0191 General farms, primarily crop
PA: Jacobs Farm/Del Cabo, Inc.
2450 Stage Rd
Pescadero CA 94060
650 879-0580

(P-175)
JFB RANCH INC
Also Called: Bennett Ranch
51170 W Althea Ave, Firebaugh (93622-9533)
PHONE.................209 364-6149
John Bennett, *President*
Barbara Preimsberg, *Treasurer*
Sally Oldham, *Vice Pres*
Marguerite Bennett, *Admin Sec*
EMP: 41 **EST:** 1971
SQ FT: 1,300
SALES (est): 1.9MM **Privately Held**
WEB: www.jfbri.com
SIC: 0191 General farms, primarily crop

(P-176)
JOSE VRAMONTES
Also Called: V and V Farms
14445 N Highway 88, Lodi (95240-9312)
PHONE.................209 810-5384
EMP: 50
SALES: 700K **Privately Held**
SIC: 0191 General Crop Farm

(P-177)
KINGS RIVER PACKING LP
21083 E Trimmer Sprng Rd, Sanger (93657-9035)
PHONE.................559 787-2056
David Hines, *Partner*
Keith Gardner, *Ltd Ptnr*
Doug Hazelton, *Ltd Ptnr*
Kari Nale, *Human Res Mgr*
Dan Beeman, *Opers Mgr*
EMP: 45 **EST:** 2014
SALES (est): 1.7MM **Privately Held**
WEB: www.kingorange.com
SIC: 0191 General farms, primarily crop

(P-178)
KNOB HILL OIL & GAS CO
1143 Crane St Ste 200, Menlo Park (94025-4341)
PHONE.................650 328-0820
Henry N Kuechler IV, *President*
Henry Kuechler III, *President*
Carol Allen Wall, *Admin Sec*
EMP: 22 **EST:** 1996
SALES (est): 564.5K
SALES (corp-wide): 6.6MM **Privately Held**
SIC: 0191 1382 6799 General farms, primarily crop; oil & gas exploration services; venture capital companies
PA: Knob Hill Mines, Inc.
1143 Crane St Ste 200
Menlo Park CA 94025
650 328-0820

(P-179)
LION RAISINS INC
Also Called: Lion Brothers Farms-Newstone
12555 Road 9, Madera (93637-9089)
P.O. Box 1350, Selma (93662-1350)
PHONE.................559 662-8686
Jeff Bergeron, *Manager*
EMP: 180
SALES (corp-wide): 57.8MM **Privately Held**
WEB: www.lionraisins.com
SIC: 0191 General farms, primarily crop
PA: Lion Raisins, Inc.
9500 S De Wolf Ave
Selma CA 93662
559 834-6677

(P-180)
M NUNES INC
3990 Thrift Rd, Merced (95341-8985)
PHONE.................209 722-7943
Marvin Nunes, *President*
EMP: 40 **EST:** 1982
SALES (est): 1.7MM **Privately Held**
SIC: 0191 General farms, primarily crop

(P-181)
MADDOX FARMS LLC
12840 W Kamm Ave, Riverdale (93656-9761)
PHONE.................559 866-5308
Stephen Maddox Jr,
Brenda Maddox,
EMP: 95 **EST:** 1956
SALES (est): 14.9MM **Privately Held**
WEB: www.ruanngenetics.com
SIC: 0191 General farms, primarily crop

(P-182)
MATTEOLI BROTHERS
17580 Cranmore Rd, Knights Landing (95645-9516)
P.O. Box 226, Robbins (95676-0226)
PHONE.................530 738-4201
Lance Matteoli, *Partner*
Jon Matteoli, *Partner*
Richard Barnes, *CIO*
EMP: 45 **EST:** 1987
SQ FT: 1,200
SALES (est): 5.1MM **Privately Held**
WEB: www.matteoli-brothers.com
SIC: 0191 General farms, primarily crop

(P-183)
NARAGHI FARMS LLC
20001 Mchenry Ave, Escalon (95320-9614)
P.O. Box 602, Denair (95316-0602)
PHONE.................209 577-5777
◆ **EMP:** 38 **EST:** 1948
SALES (est): 1.1MM **Privately Held**
SIC: 0191 General farms, primarily crop

(P-184)
OLAM FARMING INC
205 E River Park Cir, Fresno (93720-1571)
PHONE.................559 446-6446
Leon Anthony, *Principal*
◆ **EMP:** 75 **EST:** 2009
SALES (est): 6.1MM **Privately Held**
WEB: www.olamgroup.com
SIC: 0191 General farms, primarily crop
HQ: Olam Americas, Inc.
205 E River Park Cir # 310
Fresno CA 93720
559 447-1390

(P-185)
PARROTT INVESTMENT COMPANY INC
Also Called: Llano Seco Rancho
8369 Hugh Baber Ln, Chico (95928-8928)
P.O. Box 1039 (95927-1039)
PHONE.................530 342-4505
Charlie Edgar, *Manager*
Jasmin Ramirez, *General Mgr*
EMP: 38
SALES (corp-wide): 5.5MM **Privately Held**
WEB: www.llanoseco.com
SIC: 0191 General farms, primarily crop
PA: Parrott Investment Company, Inc.
8369 Hugh Baber Ln
Chico CA 95928
530 342-0839

(P-186)
PLENTY UNLIMITED INC (PA)
570 Eccles Ave, South San Francisco (94080-1905)
PHONE.................650 735-3737
Matt Barnard, *CEO*
Nick Kalajian, *Senior VP*
Nate Storey, *Security Dir*
EMP: 175 **EST:** 2014
SQ FT: 200,000
SALES (est): 84.4MM **Privately Held**
WEB: www.plenty.ag
SIC: 0191 2099 General farms, primarily crop; salads, fresh or refrigerated

(P-187)
R MONTANEZ FARMS LLC
121 Hall Rd, Royal Oaks (95076-5618)
P.O. Box 1199, Watsonville (95077-1199)
PHONE.................831 761-5982
Jose Rocha Montanez,
EMP: 40 **EST:** 2016
SALES (est): 1.7MM **Privately Held**
SIC: 0191 General farms, primarily crop

▲ = Import ▼ = Export
◆ = Import/Export

PRODUCTS & SERVICES SECTION

0241 - Dairy Farms County (P-213)

(P-188)
RED ROCK RANCH INC
15671 W Oakland Ave, Five Points (93624-7322)
P.O. Box 97 (93624-0097)
PHONE..................559 884-4201
John Diener, *President*
Georgene Diener, *Admin Sec*
EMP: 47 **EST:** 1986
SQ FT: 1,000
SALES (est): 1.4MM **Privately Held**
WEB: www.redrockranchinc.com
SIC: 0191 General farms, primarily crop

(P-189)
SAN TOMO INC
11292 N Alpine Rd, Stockton (95212-9325)
P.O. Box 3951, Modesto (95352-3951)
PHONE..................209 948-0792
Robert E Graham, *Partner*
Dino A Cortopassi, *Principal*
▲ **EMP:** 52 **EST:** 1981
SQ FT: 3,000
SALES (est): 1MM **Privately Held**
WEB: www.santomo.com
SIC: 0191 General farms, primarily crop

(P-190)
SILLS FARMS INC
Also Called: Pleasant Grove Farms
5072 Pacific Ave, Pleasant Grove (95668-9719)
P.O. Box 636 (95668-0636)
PHONE..................916 655-3391
Edward M Sills, *President*
Thomas A Sills, *President*
Anna May Sills, *Corp Secy*
Wynette Sills, *Corp Secy*
Edward M Sills, *Vice Pres*
EMP: 55 **EST:** 1947
SQ FT: 4,000
SALES (est): 2.6MM **Privately Held**
WEB: www.pleasantgrovefarms.com
SIC: 0191 General farms, primarily crop

(P-191)
TERRANOVA RANCH INC
16729 W Floral Ave, Helm (93627-7705)
P.O. Box 130 (93627-0130)
PHONE..................559 866-5644
Diego Lissi, *President*
Don Cameron, *Vice Pres*
Don J Cameron, *Vice Pres*
Annette Bauer, *Info Tech Mgr*
Patrick Pinkard, *Asst Mgr*
EMP: 50 **EST:** 1987
SQ FT: 5,000
SALES (est): 5.7MM **Privately Held**
WEB: www.terranovaranch.com
SIC: 0191 0172 General farms, primarily crop; grapes

(P-192)
TRAVIS JAMES WATTS
646 Willowgreen Cir, Galt (95632-3314)
PHONE..................209 810-6159
Travis James Watts, *Owner*
EMP: 200 **EST:** 2013
SALES (est): 150K **Privately Held**
SIC: 0191 General farms, primarily crop

(P-193)
UNILEVER UNITED STATES INC
1400 Waterloo Rd, Stockton (95205-3743)
PHONE..................209 466-9580
Michael Pasquale, *Branch Mgr*
Joshua Green, *Software Dev*
Lauren Gardner, *QC Mgr*
Savita Yadav, *QC Mgr*
EMP: 673
SALES (corp-wide): 59.9B **Privately Held**
WEB: www.unileverusa.com
SIC: 0191 General farms, primarily crop
HQ: Unilever United States, Inc.
    800 Sylvan Ave
    Englewood Cliffs NJ 07632
    201 735-9661

(P-194)
VAN GRONINGEN & SONS INC
15100 Jack Tone Rd, Manteca (95336-9729)
PHONE..................209 982-5248
Robert Van Groningen, *President*
Monica Cisneros, *CFO*
Monica Kuil, *CFO*

Dan Groningen, *Vice Pres*
Daniel Groningen, *Vice Pres*
▼ **EMP:** 360 **EST:** 1971
SQ FT: 3,000
SALES (est): 50.3MM **Privately Held**
WEB: www.vgandsons.com
SIC: 0191 0762 General farms, primarily crop; farm management services

(P-195)
VAQUERO FARMS INC
43405 W Panoche Rd, Firebaugh (93622-9720)
PHONE..................559 659-2790
Havier Rodriquez, *Manager*
Larry Enos, *COO*
David Hanan, *Agent*
EMP: 60
SQ FT: 150
SALES (corp-wide): 5.5MM **Privately Held**
SIC: 0191 General farms, primarily crop
PA: Vaquero Farms, Inc.
    24591 Silver Cloud Ct # 100
    Monterey CA 93940
    209 476-0002

(P-196)
VINO FARMS INC
51375 S Netherlands Rd, Clarksburg (95612-5019)
PHONE..................916 775-4095
John Ledbetter, *Owner*
EMP: 130
SALES (corp-wide): 46.5MM **Privately Held**
WEB: www.vinofarms.com
SIC: 0191 General farms, primarily crop
PA: Vino Farms, Inc.
    1377 E Lodi Ave
    Lodi CA 95240
    209 334-6975

(P-197)
WOOLF FARMING CO CAL INC
Also Called: Lansing Farming Co
7041 N Van Ness Blvd, Fresno (93711-7169)
P.O. Box 219, Huron (93234-0219)
PHONE..................559 945-9292
Stuart P Woolf, *President*
John L Woolf III, *Chairman*
Michael T Woolf, *Treasurer*
Bernice Woolf, *Vice Pres*
Anne A Delaware, *Admin Sec*
EMP: 624 **EST:** 1974
SQ FT: 4,500
SALES (est): 33.8MM **Privately Held**
SIC: 0191 General farms, primarily crop

(P-198)
ZUCKERMAN-HERITAGE INC (PA)
Also Called: Delta Blue Grass
111 N Zuckerman Rd, Stockton (95206)
P.O. Box 487 (95201-0487)
PHONE..................209 444-1724
Alfred Zuckerman, *Ch of Bd*
Edward Zuckerman, *President*
Karen Lewis, *Vice Pres*
Mike Matuska, *Vice Pres*
Tony Ramirez, *Controller*
▼ **EMP:** 44 **EST:** 1947
SQ FT: 1,500
SALES (est): 11.9MM **Privately Held**
WEB: www.deltabluegrass.com
SIC: 0191 0161 0181 General farms, primarily crop; asparagus farm; sod farms

0211 Beef Cattle Feedlots

(P-199)
COALINGA FEED YARD INC
35244 Oil City Rd, Coalinga (93210-9221)
P.O. Box 835 (93210-0835)
PHONE..................559 935-0836
James Anderson, *President*
Christine Fisher, *Shareholder*
Leland Haun, *Corp Secy*
EMP: 65 **EST:** 1960
SQ FT: 1,000
SALES (est): 2.6MM **Privately Held**
SIC: 0211 Beef cattle feedlots

0212 Beef Cattle, Except Feedlots

(P-200)
AL LAMM RANCH INC
42902 Road 56, Reedley (93654-9006)
PHONE..................559 638-3204
Duane Lamm, *President*
EMP: 40 **EST:** 1976
SALES (est): 1.4MM **Privately Held**
SIC: 0212 Beef cattle except feedlots

(P-201)
JACK SPARROWK
Also Called: Sparrowk Livestock
18780 E Hwy 88, Clements (95227-7165)
P.O. Box 657 (95227-0657)
PHONE..................209 759-3530
Jack Sparrowk, *Owner*
EMP: 36 **EST:** 1963
SQ FT: 1,600
SALES (est): 1.4MM **Privately Held**
WEB: www.sparrowk.com
SIC: 0212 0752 Beef cattle except feedlots; animal specialty services

(P-202)
OLD ENGLISH RANCHO INC
461 N Piedra Rd, Sanger (93657-9527)
PHONE..................559 787-3020
Pete Hilvers, *Manager*
EMP: 45
SALES (corp-wide): 5.1MM **Privately Held**
WEB: www.oldenglishrancho.net
SIC: 0212 Beef cattle except feedlots
PA: Old English Rancho, Inc.
    1625 S Baker Ave
    Ontario CA 91761
    909 947-3911

(P-203)
REDFERN RANCHES
14664 Brannon Ave, Dos Palos (93620-9469)
P.O. Box 305 (93620-0305)
PHONE..................209 392-2426
Suzanne Redfern, *President*
John David Lecompte, *Treasurer*
Peter Lecompte, *Admin Sec*
EMP: 38 **EST:** 1926
SALES (est): 1.4MM **Privately Held**
WEB: www.redfernranches.com
SIC: 0212 0191 Beef cattle except feedlots; general farms, primarily crop

0213 Hogs

(P-204)
LINDA TERRA FARMS (PA)
5494 W Mount Whitney Ave, Riverdale (93656-9329)
P.O. Box 758 (93656-0758)
PHONE..................559 867-3473
John Coelho, *CEO*
EMP: 170 **EST:** 1974
SQ FT: 1,014
SALES (est): 21.5MM **Privately Held**
WEB: www.pickapig.com
SIC: 0213 0182 0172 Hogs; fruits grown under cover; grapes

0241 Dairy Farms

(P-205)
BAR 20 DAIRY LLC
25000 W Whitesbridge Ave, Kerman (93630-9499)
PHONE..................559 846-7095
Wally Armstrong, *Manager*
EMP: 56
SALES (corp-wide): 7.4MM **Privately Held**
WEB: www.producersdairy.com
SIC: 0241 Dairy farms
PA: Bar 20 Dairy, Llc
    250 E Belmont Ave
    Fresno CA 93701
    559 457-4653

(P-206)
BWC WESTSTEYN DAIRY LP
1763 S Hewitt Rd, Linden (95236-9727)
PHONE..................209 886-5334
Cheryl Weststeyn, *Partner*
Bert Weststeyn, *Partner*
EMP: 40 **EST:** 2014
SALES (est): 1MM **Privately Held**
SIC: 0241 Dairy farms

(P-207)
CASE VLOTT CATTLE
Also Called: Vlott Brothers
20330 Road 4, Chowchilla (93610-9489)
P.O. Box 309 (93610-0309)
PHONE..................559 665-7399
EMP: 50
SALES (est): 2MM **Privately Held**
SIC: 0241 Dairy Farm

(P-208)
CASTELANELLI BROTHERS
401 W Armstrong Rd, Lodi (95242-9335)
PHONE..................209 369-9218
Larry Castelanelli, *Partner*
Louise Castelanelli,
EMP: 22 **EST:** 1923
SALES (est): 1.2MM **Privately Held**
SIC: 0241 0191 7692 Milk production; general farms, primarily crop; welding repair

(P-209)
COSTA VIEW FARMS
Also Called: Costa View Farms Shop
16800 Road 15, Madera (93637-9445)
PHONE..................559 675-3131
Darryl Azevedo, *Partner*
Linda Azevedo, *Partner*
Teresa Carr, *Partner*
William Carr, *Partner*
▲ **EMP:** 50 **EST:** 1999
SALES (est): 10.1MM **Privately Held**
SIC: 0241 0115 0211 Milk production; corn; beef cattle feedlots

(P-210)
DOUBLE DIAMOND DAIRY & RANCH
729 E Jefferson Rd, El Nido (95317-9707)
PHONE..................209 722-8505
Wendy Vander Dussen, *Partner*
Michael Vander Dussen, *Partner*
EMP: 90 **EST:** 1999
SALES (est): 10MM **Privately Held**
SIC: 0241 Dairy farms

(P-211)
FRANK COELHO & SONS LP
12775 Anchor St, El Nido (95317-9750)
PHONE..................209 722-6843
Frank Coelho, *Partner*
Mark Coehlo, *Co-Owner*
Mary Coelho, *Partner*
Paul Coelho, *Partner*
EMP: 48 **EST:** 1999
SALES (est): 5.3MM **Privately Held**
SIC: 0241 Dairy farms

(P-212)
FRANK TOSTE
Also Called: Hill View Dairy Farm
11900 W Lincoln Ave, Fresno (93706-8924)
PHONE..................559 233-4329
EMP: 40
SALES (est): 3.9MM **Privately Held**
SIC: 0241 Dairy Farm

(P-213)
GALLO CATTLE CO A LTD PARTNR
Also Called: Joseph Farms Cheese
10561 State Highway 140, Atwater (95301-9309)
P.O. Box 775 (95301-0775)
PHONE..................209 394-7984
Michael Gallo, *CEO*
Micah Gallo, *Partner*
Tiffanie Gallo, *Partner*
Linda Jelacich, *Partner*
Mark Dahlstrom, *VP Bus Dvlpt*
EMP: 500 **EST:** 1941
SQ FT: 6,000

0241 - Dairy Farms County (P-214)

PRODUCTS & SERVICES SECTION

SALES (est): 54.5MM **Privately Held**
SIC: 0241 2022 Milk production; cheese, natural & processed

(P-214)
IEST FAMILY FARMS
Also Called: Richard Iest Dairy
14576 Avenue 14, Madera (93637-8922)
PHONE.................................559 674-9417
Richard Iest, *Partner*
Danny Iest, *Partner*
Gerrlyn Iest, *Partner*
Bryant Elkins, *CIO*
EMP: 70 EST: 1978
SALES (est): 9.1MM **Privately Held**
SIC: 0241 Dairy farms

(P-215)
JAMES J STEVINSON A CORP (PA)
Also Called: Anchor J Dairy
25079 River Rd, Stevinson (95374-9724)
P.O. Box 818, Newman (95360-0818)
PHONE.................................209 632-1681
Robert Kelley, *President*
Kevin F Kelley, *Treasurer*
George Kelley, *Vice Pres*
EMP: 50
SQ FT: 1,500
SALES (est): 7.5MM **Privately Held**
SIC: 0241 0191 Dairy farms; general farms, primarily crop

(P-216)
MADDOX DAIRY LLC
12863 W Kamm Ave Spc 2, Riverdale (93656-9200)
PHONE.................................559 866-5308
Stephen Maddox,
Julia Maddox Chow, *CFO*
EMP: 65 EST: 2015
SALES (est): 4.5MM **Privately Held**
WEB: www.ruanngenetics.com
SIC: 0241 Milk production

(P-217)
MADDOX DAIRY A LTD PARTNERSHIP (PA)
12863 W Kamm Ave Spc 2, Riverdale (93656-9200)
PHONE.................................559 867-3545
Steven Maddox, *Partner*
Douglas Maddox, *Partner*
Patrick Maddox, *Partner*
EMP: 60 EST: 1981
SALES (est): 4.6MM **Privately Held**
WEB: www.ruanngenetics.com
SIC: 0241 Milk production

(P-218)
P H RANCH INC
Also Called: Veldhuis Dairy
6335 Oakdale Rd, Winton (95388-9648)
PHONE.................................209 358-5111
Ray Veldhuis, *President*
Jeanette Veldhuis, *Corp Secy*
Ray Veldhuis Jr, *Vice Pres*
EMP: 50 EST: 1940
SALES (est): 1.2MM **Privately Held**
SIC: 0241 Milk production

(P-219)
RAW FARM LLC
7221 S Jameson Ave, Fresno (93706-9386)
PHONE.................................559 846-9732
Aaron McAfee, *President*
Marcy Oliver, *Mktg Coord*
ADM McAfee,
Eric McAfee,
Mark L McAfee, *Mng Member*
EMP: 50 EST: 1998
SALES (est): 8.5MM **Privately Held**
WEB: www.organicpastures.com
SIC: 0241 2021 2022 2026 Dairy farms; creamery butter; cheese, natural & processed; milk processing (pasteurizing, homogenizing, bottling)

(P-220)
REDWOOD HILL FARM & CRMRY INC (DH)
2064 Gravenstein Hwy N # 130, Sebastopol (95472-2630)
PHONE.................................707 823-8250
Jennifer Bice, *Principal*
Rich Martin, *Chief Mktg Ofcr*
Helen Lentze, *Comms Dir*
Christina Curry, *Accounting Mgr*
Andrew Malmanis, *Accounting Mgr*
EMP: 68 EST: 1968
SALES (est): 16.3MM
SALES (corp-wide): 280.1MM **Privately Held**
WEB: www.redwoodhill.com
SIC: 0241 Dairy farms
HQ: Emmi Holding (Usa) Inc.
5525 Nobel Dr Ste 100
Fitchburg WI 53711
608 285-9800

(P-221)
RICHIE IEST FARMS INC
14676 Avenue 14, Madera (93637-8731)
PHONE.................................559 675-8658
Richard R Iest, *President*
Tricia Iest, *Vice Pres*
Mike Hamelton, *Manager*
EMP: 41 EST: 1992
SALES (est): 1.4MM **Privately Held**
SIC: 0241 Dairy farms

(P-222)
RODONI DAIRY FARMS
Center & Copa De Ora, Los Banos (93635)
P.O. Box 942 (93635-0942)
PHONE.................................209 826-2978
Richard Rodoni, *Partner*
Lila J Rodoni, *Owner*
Brian Rodoni, *Partner*
EMP: 53 EST: 1936
SALES (est): 2.5MM **Privately Held**
SIC: 0241 Milk production

(P-223)
SOARES DAIRY FARMS INC
14515 Badger Flat Rd, Los Banos (93635-9779)
PHONE.................................209 826-3414
Albert Soares, *President*
Rosalyn Soares-Garcia, *Corp Secy*
David Soares, *Vice Pres*
EMP: 69 EST: 1958
SALES (est): 5.3MM **Privately Held**
SIC: 0241 Dairy farms

(P-224)
SWEET HAVEN DAIRY
Also Called: Rollin Valley Farm
10467 W Kamm Ave, Riverdale (93656-9740)
PHONE.................................559 866-5414
Paul A Rollin, *President*
Carol Rollin, *Corp Secy*
Andrew Rollin, *Vice Pres*
Don Rollin, *Principal*
EMP: 37 EST: 1934
SALES (est): 3.3MM **Privately Held**
SIC: 0241 Dairy farms

(P-225)
TEVELDE FARMS (PA)
8632 Meadow Dr, Winton (95388-9616)
PHONE.................................209 394-8008
Henry J Tevelde, *Owner*
EMP: 36 EST: 1976
SALES (est): 1.3MM **Privately Held**
SIC: 0241 Dairy heifer replacement farm

(P-226)
VALLEY MILK LLC
400 N Washington Rd, Turlock (95380-9550)
PHONE.................................209 410-6701
Donald A Machado, *Mng Member*
Jacob Schuelke, *CFO*
Kevin F Kelley,
Cassandra Johnstone, *Supervisor*
▼ EMP: 54 EST: 2016
SALES (est): 5.5MM **Privately Held**
WEB: www.valleymilkca.com
SIC: 0241 Milk production

(P-227)
VISTA LIVESTOCK CO NEW (PA)
22323 E Monte Vista Ave, Denair (95316-9614)
PHONE.................................209 874-9446
E C Burroughs, *General Ptnr*
Bruce Burroughs, *General Ptnr*
Ward Burroughs, *General Ptnr*
EMP: 40 EST: 1965
SALES (est): 6.4MM **Privately Held**
SIC: 0241 Dairy farms

(P-228)
WITHROW CATTLE
Also Called: Withrow Dairy
5301 Pleasant Grove Rd, Pleasant Grove (95668-9752)
PHONE.................................916 780-0364
Shane Johnson, *Manager*
EMP: 65
SALES (corp-wide): 2.6MM **Privately Held**
SIC: 0241 Dairy farms
PA: Withrow Cattle
5301 Pleasant Grove Rd
Pleasant Grove CA 95668
916 780-0364

(P-229)
ZONNEVELD DAIRIES INC
1560 Cerini Ave, Laton (93242-9700)
PHONE.................................559 923-4546
John Zonneveld Jr, *President*
Frank Zonneveld, *Corp Secy*
EMP: 44 EST: 1978
SALES (est): 2.7MM **Privately Held**
SIC: 0241 Dairy farms

0252 Chicken Egg Farms

(P-230)
GEMPERLE ENTERPRISES
Also Called: Gemperle Farms
10218 Lander Ave, Turlock (95380-9627)
PHONE.................................209 667-2651
Steve Gemperle, *Mng Member*
Louis Machado, *CFO*
◆ EMP: 90 EST: 1952
SQ FT: 8,000
SALES (est): 16.2MM **Privately Held**
WEB: www.gemperle.com
SIC: 0252 5144 2015 Chicken eggs; eggs; egg processing

(P-231)
PETALUMA FARMS INC
Also Called: Skippy's Wholesales
700 Cavanaugh Ln, Petaluma (94952-1251)
PHONE.................................707 763-0921
Steve Mahrt, *Owner*
▲ EMP: 35 EST: 1919
SQ FT: 5,000
SALES (est): 6.2MM **Privately Held**
WEB: www.tarafirmafarms.com
SIC: 0252 Chicken eggs

(P-232)
S K S ENTERPRISES INC (PA)
11830 French Camp Rd, Manteca (95336-9732)
PHONE.................................209 599-4095
Wen Chang Su, *President*
EMP: 30 EST: 1980
SALES (est): 7.2MM **Privately Held**
WEB: www.sksenterprisesinc.com
SIC: 0252 2015 Chicken eggs; poultry slaughtering & processing

(P-233)
VALLEY FRESH FOODS INC
Nest Best Egg Company
3600 E Linwood Ave, Turlock (95380-9109)
P.O. Box 370, Rochester WA (98579-0370)
PHONE.................................209 669-5600
Duane Olsen, *Branch Mgr*
EMP: 35
SALES (corp-wide): 48.9MM **Privately Held**
WEB: www.vffi.com
SIC: 0252 2048 Chicken eggs; prepared feeds
PA: Valley Fresh Foods, Inc.
3600 E Linwood Ave
Turlock CA 95380
209 669-5600

(P-234)
VALLEY FRESH FOODS INC
Also Called: Rainbow Farms
1220 Hall Rd, Denair (95316-9617)
P.O. Box 910, Turlock (95381-0910)
PHONE.................................209 669-5510
Danny O'Day, *Manager*
Raquel Bettencourt, *CFO*
David Bryson, *General Mgr*
Gail Campbell, *Admin Asst*
Curt Nelson, *Production*
EMP: 35
SQ FT: 1,216
SALES (corp-wide): 48.9MM **Privately Held**
WEB: www.vffi.com
SIC: 0252 2015 Started pullet farm; poultry slaughtering & processing
PA: Valley Fresh Foods, Inc.
3600 E Linwood Ave
Turlock CA 95380
209 669-5600

0253 Turkey & Turkey Egg Farms

(P-235)
DIESTEL TURKEY RANCH
14111 High Tech Dr C, Jamestown (95327)
P.O. Box 4314, Sonora (95370-1314)
PHONE.................................209 984-0826
Tim Diestel, *Owner*
Joan Diestel, *Co-Owner*
EMP: 21 EST: 1949
SALES (est): 2.1MM **Privately Held**
WEB: www.diestelturkey.com
SIC: 0253 2015 Turkey farm; poultry slaughtering & processing

(P-236)
DIESTEL TURKEY RANCH (PA)
Also Called: Distel Family Ranch
22200 Lyons Bald Mtn Rd, Sonora (95370-8772)
P.O. Box 4314 (95370-1314)
PHONE.................................209 532-4950
Timothy Diestel, *CEO*
David Harmer, *CFO*
Jared Orrock, *CFO*
Joan Diestel, *Vice Pres*
Heidi Diestel, *Principal*
EMP: 126 EST: 1949
SQ FT: 5,000
SALES (est): 31.3MM **Privately Held**
WEB: www.diestelturkey.com
SIC: 0253 Turkey farm

(P-237)
FOSTER TURKEY PRODUCTS
1000 Davis St, Livingston (95334-1526)
P.O. Box 457 (95334-0457)
PHONE.................................209 394-7901
Ron Foster, *President*
George Foster, *Ch of Bd*
Thomas Foster, *President*
Norma Foster Madig, *Vice Pres*
EMP: 3325 EST: 1982
SALES (est): 1.1MM
SALES (corp-wide): 1.2B **Privately Held**
WEB: www.fosterfarms.com
SIC: 0253 Turkeys & turkey eggs
PA: Foster Poultry Farms
1000 Davis St
Livingston CA 95334
209 394-7901

(P-238)
PITMAN FARMS (PA)
1075 North Ave, Sanger (93657-3539)
PHONE.................................559 875-9300
Richard G Pitman, *President*
Sheryl Morse, *CFO*
Mike Vance, *VP Opers*
EMP: 35 EST: 1973
SQ FT: 1,000
SALES (est): 207.5MM **Privately Held**
WEB: www.pitmanfarms.com
SIC: 0253 0251 Turkeys & turkey eggs; turkey farm; broiler, fryer & roaster chickens

(P-239)
SWANSON FARMS
5213 W Main St, Turlock (95380-9413)
P.O. Box 2367 (95381-2367)
PHONE.................................209 667-2002
Richard E Swanson, *President*
Larry Pickering, *Vice Pres*
EMP: 40 EST: 1942
SQ FT: 5,000

▲ = Import ▼ = Export
◆ = Import/Export

PRODUCTS & SERVICES SECTION
0722 - Crop Harvesting By Machine County (P-264)

SALES (est): 1.3MM **Privately Held**
SIC: 0253 0173 Turkey farm; almond grove

0254 Poultry Hatcheries

(P-240)
FOSTER POULTRY FARMS
834 Davis St, Livingston (95334)
P.O. Box 457 (95334-0457)
PHONE.............................209 394-7901
Chris Carter, *Branch Mgr*
EMP: 232
SALES (corp-wide): 1.2B **Privately Held**
WEB: www.fosterfarms.com
SIC: 0254 2015 Poultry hatcheries; poultry, processed
PA: Foster Poultry Farms
1000 Davis St
Livingston CA 95334
209 394-7901

0259 Poultry & Eggs Farms, NEC

(P-241)
REICHARDT DUCK FARM INC
3770 Middle Two Rock Rd, Petaluma (94952-4625)
PHONE.............................707 762-6314
John T Reichardt, *President*
Kathy Shaw, *CFO*
▼ EMP: 95 EST: 1901
SQ FT: 1,296
SALES (est): 4.6MM **Privately Held**
WEB: www.reichardtduckfarm.com
SIC: 0259 Duck farm

0279 Animal Specialties, NEC

(P-242)
BELCAMPO GROUP INC (PA)
65 Webster St, Oakland (94607-3720)
PHONE.............................510 250-7810
Anya Fernald, *CEO*
Nate Morr, *COO*
Nathan Morr, *COO*
Heather Cooper, *Senior VP*
Talia Dillman, *Project Mgr*
◆ EMP: 70 EST: 2011
SALES (est): 21.9MM **Privately Held**
WEB: www.belcampo.com
SIC: 0279 2011 2015 5812 Domestic animal farms; beef products from beef slaughtered on site; poultry slaughtering & processing; family restaurants; office management

(P-243)
OLIVAREZ HONEY BEES INC
6398 County Road 20, Orland (95963-9475)
P.O. Box 847 (95963-0847)
PHONE.............................530 865-0298
Ray A Olivarez Jr, *CEO*
EMP: 97 EST: 2002
SALES (est): 9MM **Privately Held**
WEB: www.ohbees.com
SIC: 0279 Apiary (bee & honey farm)

(P-244)
STRACHAN APIARIES INC
2522 Tierra Buena Rd, Yuba City (95993-7201)
PHONE.............................530 674-3881
Valeri A Severson, *President*
EMP: 37 EST: 1954
SQ FT: 600
SALES (est): 1.8MM **Privately Held**
WEB: www.strachanbees.com
SIC: 0279 Apiary (bee & honey farm)

0291 Animal Production, NEC

(P-245)
BARTON RANCH INC
22398 Mcbride Rd, Escalon (95320-9637)
PHONE.............................209 838-8930
Gerald L Barton, *President*
Brent Barton, *Vice Pres*
Gary Barton, *Vice Pres*
Donald Barton, *Principal*
Lisa Taylor, *Office Mgr*
EMP: 37 EST: 1979
SQ FT: 1,800
SALES (est): 3.1MM **Privately Held**
WEB: www.goldriverorchards.com
SIC: 0291 General farms, primarily animals

(P-246)
BOOTH RANCHES LLC (PA)
12201 Avenue 480, Orange Cove (93646-9507)
PHONE.............................559 626-4732
Otis Booth Jr, *Principal*
Franklin Booth, *Owner*
Loren Booth, *Owner*
Paul Adams, *CFO*
Izak Du Toit, *Vice Pres*
▲ EMP: 112 EST: 1957
SALES (est): 26.1MM **Privately Held**
WEB: www.boothranches.com
SIC: 0291 General farms, primarily animals

(P-247)
HAMMONDS RANCH INC
47375 W Dakota Ave, Firebaugh (93622-9516)
PHONE.............................209 364-6185
James M Hammonds, *President*
William E Hammond, *Chairman*
Mary Hicks, *Corp Secy*
EMP: 100 EST: 1929
SQ FT: 3,500
SALES (est): 12.2MM **Privately Held**
SIC: 0291 General farms, primarily animals

(P-248)
MISSION RANCHES COMPANY LLC
880 Lucy Brown Rd, San Juan Bautista (95045-9721)
PHONE.............................831 206-0535
EMP: 45
SALES (corp-wide): 11.8MM **Privately Held**
WEB: www.missionranches.com
SIC: 0291 General farms, primarily animals
PA: Mission Ranches Company, Llc
117 N 1st St
King City CA 93930
831 385-1263

0721 Soil Preparation, Planting & Cultivating Svc

(P-249)
BZ - BEE POLLINATION INC
24204 Rd 23, Esparto (95627)
P.O. Box 699 (95627-0699)
PHONE.............................530 787-3044
John Foster, *CEO*
EMP: 50 EST: 1975
SALES (est): 3.1MM **Privately Held**
SIC: 0721 Pollinating services

(P-250)
CALIFORNIA VALLEY LAND CO INC (PA)
Also Called: Woolf Enterprises
18036 Gale, Huron (93234)
P.O. Box 219 (93234-0219)
PHONE.............................559 945-9292
Stuart P Woolf, *President*
Michael T Woolf, *Treasurer*
John L Woolf, *Vice Ch Bd*
Susan Hornor, *Asst Controller*
Griselda Garcia, *Accountant*
EMP: 93 EST: 1960
SQ FT: 4,500
SALES (est): 38.8MM **Privately Held**
SIC: 0721 Planting services; crop cultivating services; crop protecting services

(P-251)
CHUCK JONES FLYING SERVICE (PA)
Also Called: Aerial Applicators
216 W Hamilton Rd, Biggs (95917-9793)
P.O. Box 497 (95917-0497)
PHONE.............................530 868-5798
Dale Jones, *President*
Lori A Jones, *Treasurer*
Alan Jones, *Vice Pres*
EMP: 50 EST: 1963
SQ FT: 25,000
SALES (est): 4.6MM **Privately Held**
SIC: 0721 Crop dusting services

(P-252)
CRINKLAW FARM SERVICES INC
13837 S Zediker Ave, Kingsburg (93631-9726)
PHONE.............................559 897-1077
David Crinklaw, *President*
Tami Crinklaw, *Corp Secy*
EMP: 40 EST: 1979
SQ FT: 5,000
SALES (est): 4.8MM **Privately Held**
WEB: www.crinklawfarmservice.com
SIC: 0721 Crop cultivating services

(P-253)
CROP CARE ASSOCIATES INC
851 Napa Vly Corp Way Ste, NAPA (94558)
PHONE.............................707 258-2998
Bob Gallagher, *President*
Thomas E Prentice, *Vice Pres*
Rachel Flynn, *Representative*
EMP: 44 EST: 1970
SALES (est): 5.6MM **Privately Held**
WEB: www.cropcareassociates.com
SIC: 0721 8748 Crop protecting services; agricultural consultant

(P-254)
GERAWAN FARMING PARTNERS INC
7108 N Fresno St Ste 450, Fresno (93720-2961)
P.O. Box 67, Sanger (93657-0067)
PHONE.............................559 787-8780
Dan Gerawan, *President*
David Hawe, *Project Mgr*
Juan Alba, *Maintence Staff*
Lori Faccinto, *Manager*
Jorge Leon, *Manager*
EMP: 94 EST: 1950
SALES (est): 4.5MM **Privately Held**
WEB: www.prima.com
SIC: 0721 0172 Tree orchards, cultivation of; grapes

(P-255)
JOHN H KAUTZ FARMS
5490 Bear Creek Rd, Lodi (95240-7213)
PHONE.............................209 334-4786
John H Kautz, *Co-Owner*
Gail Kautz, *Owner*
Corina Vasquez, *Manager*
EMP: 50 EST: 1952
SQ FT: 3,000
SALES (est): 5.4MM **Privately Held**
SIC: 0721 Orchard tree & vine services

(P-256)
ROBINSON AGSPRAY
Also Called: Pacific AG Services
915 10th St, Firebaugh (93622-2602)
P.O. Box 486 (93622-0486)
PHONE.............................559 659-3015
Thomas Cooke, *President*
Cynthia Cooke, *Corp Secy*
EMP: 42 EST: 1964
SALES (est): 1.6MM **Privately Held**
WEB: www.agspray.com
SIC: 0721 Crop dusting services

(P-257)
S & S RANCH INC
Also Called: Stamoules Produce Company
904 S Lyon Ave, Mendota (93640-9735)
PHONE.............................559 655-3491
Pagona Stefanopoulos, *CEO*
Athanasios Stefanopoulos, *Vice Pres*
▼ EMP: 85 EST: 1925
SQ FT: 500
SALES (est): 10.2MM **Privately Held**
WEB: www.stamoules.com
SIC: 0721 Planting services; crop cultivating services; crop protecting services

(P-258)
SEAMAN NURSERIES INC
336 Robertson Blvd Ste A, Chowchilla (93610-2867)
PHONE.............................559 665-1860
William Seaman, *President*
EMP: 70 EST: 1980
SALES (est): 3.9MM **Privately Held**
WEB: www.seamannurseries.com
SIC: 0721 0762 5261 Orchard tree & vine services; farm management services; nurseries

0722 Crop Harvesting By Machine

(P-259)
ACAMPO GRAPE HARVESTING LLC
2551 E Acampo Rd, Acampo (95220-9464)
P.O. Box 634 (95220-0634)
PHONE.............................209 333-7072
EMP: 36
SQ FT: 3,098
SALES (est): 2.1MM **Privately Held**
SIC: 0722 Crop Harvesting Services

(P-260)
ALPINE PACIFIC NUT CO INC
6413 E Keyes Rd, Hughson (95326-9552)
P.O. Box 999 (95326-0999)
PHONE.............................209 667-8688
John Mundt, *CEO*
Catherine Hendley-Mundt, *Vice Pres*
Kenny Dickens, *Plant Mgr*
Patrick Giffen, *QC Mgr*
Brock Middleton, *Mktg Dir*
◆ EMP: 40 EST: 2000
SQ FT: 90,000
SALES (est): 7MM **Privately Held**
WEB: www.alpinepacificnut.com
SIC: 0722 2099 5411 Tree nuts, machine harvesting services; food preparations; convenience stores; independent

(P-261)
CARNEROS VINTNERS INC
4202 Stage Gulch Rd, Sonoma (95476-9739)
PHONE.............................707 933-9349
Dennis Rippey, *President*
EMP: 17 EST: 2008
SALES (est): 1.1MM **Privately Held**
WEB: www.carnerosvintners.com
SIC: 0722 2084 Grapes, machine harvesting services; wines

(P-262)
I S A CONTRACTING SVCS INC
958 O St, Firebaugh (93622-2221)
PHONE.............................559 659-1080
Ileana Arvizu, *President*
EMP: 600 EST: 2006
SQ FT: 5,000
SALES (est): 10MM **Privately Held**
SIC: 0722 Crop harvesting

(P-263)
JACK KLEIN TRUST PARTNERSHIP
Also Called: Klein Family Farms
3101 W March Ln Ste B, Stockton (95219-2385)
P.O. Box 7424 (95267-0424)
PHONE.............................209 956-8800
Tom Klein, *Manager*
Jill Corkern, *Partner*
Kathy Jackson, *Partner*
Steve Klein, *Partner*
Jim Renney, *Partner*
EMP: 40 EST: 1950
SQ FT: 1,000
SALES (est): 3.3MM **Privately Held**
WEB: www.kleinbros.com
SIC: 0722 Crop harvesting

(P-264)
JAMES CAROLLO & CO
Also Called: High Quality Alfalfa Yields
1618 Redfern Ave, Dos Palos (93620-2426)
P.O. Box 536 (93620-0536)
PHONE.............................209 392-3737

0722 - Crop Harvesting By Machine County (P-265)

James Carollo, *Owner*
EMP: 15 **EST:** 1977
SQ FT: 2,400
SALES (est): 1.6MM **Privately Held**
SIC: 0722 2048 Hay, machine harvesting services; cereal-, grain-, & seed-based feeds

(P-265)
LA FOLLETTE ENTERPRISES INC
3312 S Blaker Rd, Turlock (95380-9320)
PHONE.....................................209 632-1385
Randy Lafollette, *President*
Kathy La Follette, *Treasurer*
Robert Tucker, *Vice Pres*
Marilyn Tucker, *Admin Sec*
EMP: 42 **EST:** 1951
SQ FT: 9,600
SALES (est): 3.4MM **Privately Held**
SIC: 0722 6519 Corn, machine harvesting services; farm land leasing

0723 Crop Preparation, Except Cotton Ginning

(P-266)
A RPAC LTD LIABILITY COMPANY
21490 Ortigalita Rd, Los Banos (93635-9793)
P.O. Box 2138 (93635-2138)
PHONE.....................................209 826-0272
Dennis P Soares, *Mng Member*
Dennis Soares, *Managing Prtnr*
David Parreira,
Paul Parreira,
Ned Ryan,
▼ **EMP:** 45 **EST:** 1986
SQ FT: 1,000
SALES (est): 7.7MM **Privately Held**
WEB: www.rpacalmonds.com
SIC: 0723 Tree nut crops market preparation services

(P-267)
AGRINOS INC (PA)
279 Cousteau Pl Ste 100, Davis (95618-7764)
P.O. Box 2368 (95617-2368)
PHONE.....................................888 706-9505
Kevin Helash, *CEO*
Jim Thompson, *CFO*
Keturah Pliska, *Opers Dir*
EMP: 63 **EST:** 2014
SALES (est): 7.1MM **Privately Held**
WEB: www.agrinos.com
SIC: 0723 Crop preparation services for market

(P-268)
ALLDRIN BROTHERS INC
Also Called: Alldrin Brothers Almonds
584 Hi Tech Pkwy, Oakdale (95361-9371)
PHONE.....................................855 667-4231
Gary Alldrin, *President*
Gary Alldrim, *Human Resources*
Grant Neil Alldrin, *Mktg Dir*
◆ **EMP:** 50 **EST:** 1994
SQ FT: 5,000
SALES (est): 4.9MM **Privately Held**
WEB: www.alldrinalmonds.com
SIC: 0723 Almond hulling & shelling services

(P-269)
ANDERSEN & SONS SHELLING INC
4530 Rowles Rd, Vina (96092)
P.O. Box 100 (96092-0100)
PHONE.....................................530 839-2236
Patrick Knudt Andersen, *President*
Franklin Andersen, *Vice Pres*
Michael Andersen, *Vice Pres*
Kristin Coley, *Administration*
Jeff West, *Controller*
◆ **EMP:** 100 **EST:** 2003
SALES (est): 22.4MM **Privately Held**
WEB: www.andersenshelling.com
SIC: 0723 0762 Walnut hulling & shelling services; farm management services

(P-270)
ANDERSEN NUT COMPANY
Also Called: Gustine Mini Storage
3050 S Hunt Rd, Gustine (95322-9810)
P.O. Box 445 (95322-0445)
PHONE.....................................209 854-6820
Brian Anderson, *Partner*
Dan Anderson, *Partner*
◆ **EMP:** 50 **EST:** 1971
SQ FT: 26,500
SALES (est): 5MM **Privately Held**
WEB: www.andersennut.com
SIC: 0723 Walnut hulling & shelling services

(P-271)
BLUE DIAMOND GROWERS
4800 Sisk Rd, Modesto (95356-8730)
PHONE.....................................209 545-6221
Bruce Mickelson, *Manager*
Eric Ingram, *Officer*
Ken Lehman, *Senior VP*
Steven Birgfeld, *Vice Pres*
Jereme Fromm, *Regional Mgr*
EMP: 200
SALES (corp-wide): 588.2MM **Privately Held**
WEB: www.bluediamond.com
SIC: 0723 2068 Almond hulling & shelling services; nuts: dried, dehydrated, salted or roasted
PA: Diamond Blue Growers
 1802 C St
 Sacramento CA 95811
 800 987-2329

(P-272)
BLUE DIAMOND GROWERS
10840 E Mckinley Ave, Sanger (93657-9480)
PHONE.....................................559 251-4044
Becky Davies, *Representative*
EMP: 110
SALES (corp-wide): 588.2MM **Privately Held**
WEB: www.bluediamond.com
SIC: 0723 Crop preparation services for market
PA: Diamond Blue Growers
 1802 C St
 Sacramento CA 95811
 800 987-2329

(P-273)
BOGHOSIAN RAISIN PKG CO INC
726 S 8th St, Fowler (93625-2506)
P.O. Box 338 (93625-0338)
PHONE.....................................559 834-5348
Phillip Boghosian, *President*
Philip Boghosian, *President*
Harold Myers, *CFO*
Peter Boghosian, *Corp Secy*
Cheryl Kennedy, *Vice Pres*
◆ **EMP:** 49 **EST:** 1972
SQ FT: 50,000
SALES (est): 34.2MM **Privately Held**
WEB: www.boghosianraisin.com
SIC: 0723 2034 Fruit (farm-dried) packing services; fruit drying services; dehydrated fruits, vegetables, soups

(P-274)
CALIFORNIA ROYALE LLC
Also Called: Monte Vista Farming Company
5043 N Montpelier Rd, Denair (95316-9608)
P.O. Box 579 (95316-0579)
PHONE.....................................209 874-1866
Jonathan Hoff, *Mng Member*
Elizabeth Nunez, *Treasurer*
Jim Crecelius,
▼ **EMP:** 27 **EST:** 2004
SQ FT: 60
SALES (est): 2.2MM **Privately Held**
WEB: www.californiaroyale.com
SIC: 0723 2068 Tree nut crops market preparation services; salted & roasted nuts & seeds

(P-275)
CENTRAL CAL ALMOND GRWERS ASSN (PA)
8325 S Madera Ave, Kerman (93630-8953)
P.O. Box 338 (93630-0338)
PHONE.....................................559 846-5377
Michael Kelley, *President*
Jeff McKinney, *Vice Chairman*
Bob Donnelly, *COO*
Jim Sears, *COO*
Geri Bartsch, *CFO*
EMP: 35 **EST:** 1963
SQ FT: 22,000
SALES (est): 17.4MM **Privately Held**
WEB: www.ccaga.com
SIC: 0723 2068 Almond hulling & shelling services; nuts: dried, dehydrated, salted or roasted

(P-276)
CENTRAL VALLEY AG GRINDING INC (PA)
Also Called: Cvag
5509 Langworth Rd, Oakdale (95361-7909)
PHONE.....................................209 869-1721
Michael Barry, *President*
Ryan Hogan, *CFO*
EMP: 29 **EST:** 1996
SQ FT: 80,000
SALES (est): 23.7MM **Privately Held**
WEB: www.cv-ag.com
SIC: 0723 2041 2048 Grain milling, custom services; flour & other grain mill products; prepared feeds

(P-277)
CENTRAL VALLEY AG TRNSPT INC
Also Called: Central Valley AG Transload
5509 Langworth Rd, Oakdale (95361-7909)
PHONE.....................................209 544-9246
Michael Barry, *President*
Ryan Hogan, *CFO*
Paul Konzen, *Admin Sec*
EMP: 93 **EST:** 2007
SALES (est): 8.1MM
SALES (corp-wide): 23.7MM **Privately Held**
WEB: www.cv-ag.com
SIC: 0723 1629 Field crops, except cash grains, market preparation services; railroad & railway roadbed construction
PA: Central Valley Ag Grinding, Inc.
 5509 Langworth Rd
 Oakdale CA 95361
 209 869-1721

(P-278)
CHINCHIOLO STEMILT CAL LLC
4799 N Jack Tone Rd, Stockton (95215-9144)
PHONE.....................................209 931-7000
Tom Chinchiolo,
Thomas Chinchiolo,
▲ **EMP:** 117 **EST:** 2003
SQ FT: 30,000
SALES (est): 5.8MM
SALES (corp-wide): 369.8MM **Privately Held**
WEB: www.stemilttrade.com
SIC: 0723 Fruit (farm-dried) packing services
PA: Stemilt Growers, Llc
 3135 Warehouse Rd
 Wenatchee WA 98801
 509 663-1451

(P-279)
CHOOLJIAN & SONS INC (PA)
Also Called: Del Rey Packing Co
5287 S Del Rey Ave, Del Rey (93616-9700)
P.O. Box 160 (93616-0160)
PHONE.....................................559 888-2031
Gerald Chooljian, *CEO*
Courtney Chooljian, *Corp Secy*
▼ **EMP:** 69 **EST:** 1929
SQ FT: 14,400
SALES (est): 12.5MM **Privately Held**
WEB: www.delreypacking.com
SIC: 0723 2034 Fruit (farm-dried) packing services; raisins

(P-280)
DE RUOSI GROUP LLC
Also Called: De Ruosi Nut
25055 Arthur Rd, Escalon (95320-9559)
PHONE.....................................209 838-8307
Michael Deruosi III, *Mng Member*
▼ **EMP:** 48 **EST:** 1947
SQ FT: 200,000
SALES (est): 4.5MM **Privately Held**
WEB: www.deruosinut.com
SIC: 0723 Crop preparation services for market

(P-281)
EARTHBOUND FARM LLC (PA)
Also Called: Taylor Farms
1721 San Juan Hwy, San Juan Bautista (95045-9780)
PHONE.....................................831 623-7880
Cristina Eisenhard,
Eric Tomkiewicz, *Business Mgr*
John Canoyer, *Controller*
Lucas Aguirre, *Human Resources*
Sonia Manzo, *Opers Staff*
◆ **EMP:** 995 **EST:** 1988
SQ FT: 15,000
SALES (est): 54.7MM **Privately Held**
WEB: www.earthboundfarm.com
SIC: 0723 2037 2099 Vegetable packing services; fruit crops market preparation services; frozen fruits & vegetables; food preparations

(P-282)
EB SAV INC
1721 San Juan Hwy, San Juan Bautista (95045-9780)
PHONE.....................................303 635-4500
Hesiquio Garcia, *President*
EMP: 35 **EST:** 2013
SALES (est): 2.6MM
SALES (corp-wide): 735.6MM **Privately Held**
WEB: www.danonenorthamerica.com
SIC: 0723 2099 Vegetable packing services; food preparations
HQ: Wwf Operating Company, Llc
 12002 Airport Way
 Broomfield CO 80021

(P-283)
FARMERS RICE COOPERATIVE
4937 Highway 45, Colusa (95932-4008)
P.O. Box 265, Princeton (95970-0265)
PHONE.....................................530 439-2244
Joseph Alves, *Director*
EMP: 70
SQ FT: 1,378
SALES (corp-wide): 71.8MM **Privately Held**
WEB: www.farmersrice.com
SIC: 0723 2044 Rice drying services; rice milling
PA: Rice Farmers' Cooperative
 2566 River Plaza Dr
 Sacramento CA 95833
 916 923-5100

(P-284)
FOWLER PACKING COMPANY INC
Also Called: Telemarketing
8570 S Cedar Ave, Fresno (93725-8905)
PHONE.....................................559 834-5911
Dennis Parnagian, *CEO*
Rigo Rios, *COO*
Randy Parnagian, *Treasurer*
Kenneth Parnagian, *Vice Pres*
Philip Parnagian, *Admin Sec*
◆ **EMP:** 125 **EST:** 1946
SQ FT: 6,300
SALES (est): 45.1MM **Privately Held**
WEB: www.fowlerpacking.com
SIC: 0723 4783 5148 Fruit (fresh) packing services; packing & crating; fresh fruits & vegetables

(P-285)
GLORIANN FARMS INC (PA)
4598 S Tracy Blvd Ste 160, Tracy (95377-8112)
P.O. Box 571 (95378-0571)
PHONE.....................................209 834-0010
Mark R Bacchetti, *President*
Jim Thoming, *CFO*

▲ = Import ▼ = Export
◆ = Import/Export

PRODUCTS & SERVICES SECTION

0723 - Crop Preparation, Except Cotton Ginning County (P-308)

Mark Bacchetti, *Branch Mgr*
Erica Gonzales, *Personnel Assit*
Katie Veenstra, *Mktg Dir*
EMP: 242 **EST:** 2001
SALES (est): 18.5MM **Privately Held**
WEB: www.gloriannfarms.com
SIC: 0723 Vegetable packing services

(P-286)
GROWER DIRECT NUT COMPANY INC
2288 Geer Rd, Hughson (95326-9614)
PHONE 209 883-4890
Aaron Martella, *President*
Kevin Chiesa, *COO*
Danny Jenkins, *Vice Pres*
Lucio Salazar, *Vice Pres*
Judith Gallardo, *Executive Asst*
◆ **EMP:** 50 **EST:** 2004
SALES (est): 22.1MM **Privately Held**
WEB: www.growerdirectnut.com
SIC: 0723 Walnut hulling & shelling services

(P-287)
GUERRA NUT SHELLING COMPANY
190 Hillcrest Rd, Hollister (95023-4944)
P.O. Box 1117 (95024-1117)
PHONE 831 637-4471
Frank Guerra, *President*
Jeff Guerra, *CFO*
▼ **EMP:** 55
SQ FT: 20,000
SALES (est): 8.1MM **Privately Held**
WEB: www.guerranut.com
SIC: 0723 Walnut hulling & shelling services

(P-288)
HARRIS WOOLF CAL ALMONDS LLC
26060 Colusa Ave, Coalinga (93210-9245)
P.O. Box 49, Ballico (95303-0049)
PHONE 559 884-2147
Joel Perkins, *Mng Member*
David Silva, *Info Tech Mgr*
Brian Staggs,
Stuart Woolf,
Yolanda Beaven, *Supervisor*
◆ **EMP:** 150 **EST:** 2014
SQ FT: 110,000
SALES (est): 39.4MM **Privately Held**
WEB: www.harriswoolfalmonds.com
SIC: 0723 Tree nut crops market preparation services; almond hulling & shelling services

(P-289)
HILLTOP RANCH INC
Also Called: Hilltop Trading
13890 Looney Rd, Ballico (95303-9710)
PHONE 209 874-1875
David Harrison Long, *CEO*
Brad Filbrun, *CFO*
Christine Long, *Vice Pres*
Dave Long Jr, *Vice Pres*
Dexter Long, *Vice Pres*
◆ **EMP:** 175 **EST:** 1980
SQ FT: 134,800
SALES (est): 25.4MM **Privately Held**
WEB: www.hilltopranch.com
SIC: 0723 5441 Almond hulling & shelling services; candy, nut & confectionary stores

(P-290)
HULLING COMPANY
2900 Airport Dr, Madera (93637-9288)
PHONE 559 674-1896
Russell Harris, *President*
EMP: 39 **EST:** 2002
SQ FT: 35,799
SALES (est): 3MM **Privately Held**
WEB: www.harrisfamilyenterprises.com
SIC: 0723 Almond hulling & shelling services

(P-291)
JUST TOMATOES INC
Also Called: Tomato Press
2103 W Hamilton Rd, Westley (95387)
P.O. Box 807 (95387-0807)
PHONE 209 894-5371
Bill Cox, *President*

Karen Cox, *President*
William Cox, *Admin Sec*
Stephanie Olson, *Sales Staff*
EMP: 56 **EST:** 1985
SALES (est): 5.1MM **Privately Held**
WEB: www.shopkarensnaturals.com
SIC: 0723 5961 2731 2771 Vegetable drying services; fruit drying services; fruit, mail order; book publishing; greeting cards; food preparations

(P-292)
MARIANI PACKING CO INC (PA)
500 Crocker Dr, Vacaville (95688-8706)
PHONE 707 452-2800
Mark A Mariani, *CEO*
George Sousa Jr, *President*
Carol Murphy, *CFO*
Marian Ciabattari, *Corp Secy*
Craig Mackley, *Exec VP*
◆ **EMP:** 275 **EST:** 1982
SALES (est): 114.7MM **Privately Held**
WEB: www.mariani.com
SIC: 0723 2034 5148 Fruit (farm-dried) packing services; fruit drying services; dried & dehydrated fruits; fresh fruits & vegetables

(P-293)
MID VALLEY NUT COMPANY INC (PA)
Also Called: California Valley Products
2065 Geer Rd, Hughson (95326-9614)
P.O. Box 987 (95326-0987)
PHONE 209 883-4491
John Casazza, *President*
Tina Cuiriz, *COO*
Suzanne Casazza, *Vice Pres*
Jim Monroe, *Finance*
Lilia Lujan, *Controller*
◆ **EMP:** 39 **EST:** 1969
SQ FT: 50,000
SALES (est): 5.3MM **Privately Held**
WEB: www.midvalleynut.com
SIC: 0723 Walnut hulling & shelling services

(P-294)
MONTPELIER NUT COMPANY INC
4931 S Montpelier Rd, Denair (95316-9663)
PHONE 209 874-5126
Kenfield Alldrin, *CEO*
EMP: 49
SALES (corp-wide): 9.8MM **Privately Held**
SIC: 0723 Almond hulling & shelling services
PA: Montpelier Nut Company, Inc.
1518 K St
Modesto CA 95354
209 566-9084

(P-295)
MOONEY FARMS
1220 Fortress St, Chico (95973-9029)
PHONE 530 899-2661
Mary Mooney, *President*
Steve Mooney, *Vice Pres*
▲ **EMP:** 50 **EST:** 1987
SQ FT: 100,000
SALES (est): 9.9MM **Privately Held**
WEB: www.bellasunluci.com
SIC: 0723 2034 2033 Fruit crops market preparation services; dried & dehydrated fruits; canned fruits & specialties

(P-296)
MOONLIGHT SALES CORPORATION
17719 E Huntsman Ave, Reedley (93654-9205)
P.O. Box 846 (93654-0846)
PHONE 559 637-7799
Brooks Russell Tavlan, *President*
Ty Tavlan, *Vice Pres*
Ben Clay, *Marketing Staff*
▲ **EMP:** 35 **EST:** 1999
SQ FT: 2,000
SALES (est): 4.5MM **Privately Held**
WEB: www.moonlightcompanies.com
SIC: 0723 Fruit (fresh) packing services

(P-297)
OLAM AMERICAS INC (DH)
Also Called: Olam Edible Nuts
205 E River Park Cir # 310, Fresno (93720-1571)
PHONE 559 447-1390
Gregory C Estep, *CEO*
Aditya Renjen, *Vice Pres*
Greg Estep, *Managing Dir*
Tejinder S Saraon, *Managing Dir*
Chow H Hoeng, *General Mgr*
◆ **EMP:** 1000 **EST:** 2006
SALES (est): 505.2MM **Privately Held**
WEB: www.olamgroup.com
SIC: 0723 Crop preparation services for market
HQ: Olam Us Holdings Inc
2077 Convention Ctr 150
College Park GA 30337
404 209-2676

(P-298)
OLAM SPICES & VEGETABLES INC (PA)
1350 Pacheco Pass Hwy, Gilroy (95020-9559)
PHONE 408 846-3200
Lester Karen, *Director*
Virginia Lowe, *Admin Asst*
Sherri Venegas, *Warehouse Mgr*
◆ **EMP:** 85 **EST:** 2010
SALES (est): 24.2MM **Privately Held**
WEB: www.actii.com
SIC: 0723 Crop preparation services for market

(P-299)
OLAM WEST COAST INC (DH)
Also Called: Olam Spces Vgtable Ingredients
205 E Rver Pk Cir Ste 310, Fresno (93720)
PHONE 559 256-6224
John Gibbons, *President*
James Fenn, *Vice Pres*
Yutaka Kyoya, *Exec Dir*
Sanjiv Misra, *Exec Dir*
George Verghese, *Exec Dir*
◆ **EMP:** 975 **EST:** 2008
SALES (est): 889.1MM **Privately Held**
WEB: www.olamgroup.com
SIC: 0723 Crop preparation services for market

(P-300)
OMEGA WALNUT INC
7233 County Road 24, Orland (95963-9777)
PHONE 530 865-0136
Todd J Southam, *CEO*
Marsha Squier, *Office Mgr*
Gerard Millen, *Manager*
◆ **EMP:** 50 **EST:** 2012
SALES (est): 4.2MM **Privately Held**
WEB: www.omegawalnut.com
SIC: 0723 Walnut hulling & shelling services

(P-301)
PEARL CROP INC (PA)
Also Called: Linden Nut
1550 Industrial Dr, Stockton (95206-3929)
PHONE 209 808-7575
Ulash Turkhan, *CEO*
Hulya Dayac, *Shareholder*
Halil Ulas Turkhan, *President*
Burak Baglar, *Vice Pres*
Scott Donald, *Vice Pres*
◆ **EMP:** 60
SQ FT: 126,000
SALES (est): 90MM **Privately Held**
WEB: www.pearlcrop.com
SIC: 0723 Crop preparation services for market

(P-302)
PHILON PAPPAS CO
181 Naples St, Mendota (93640-2030)
P.O. Box 963 (93640-0963)
PHONE 559 655-4282
Philon Pappas, *President*
George Pappas, *Vice Pres*
Stavorola Vergos, *Admin Sec*
EMP: 44 **EST:** 1930
SQ FT: 1,000
SALES (est): 786K **Privately Held**
SIC: 0723 Fruit (farm-dried) packing services; fruit (fresh) packing services

(P-303)
RED TOP RICE GROWERS
3200 8th St, Biggs (95917-9623)
P.O. Box 477 (95917-0477)
PHONE 530 868-5975
John Adams, *President*
Doug Rudd, *Corp Secy*
Steve Cribari, *Vice Pres*
Myron Leavell, *Administration*
EMP: 57 **EST:** 1958
SALES (est): 5.2MM **Privately Held**
SIC: 0723 Rice drying services

(P-304)
RIVER MAID LAND CO A CAL LI (PA)
6011 E Pine St, Lodi (95240-0815)
P.O. Box 350 (95241-0350)
PHONE 209 369-3586
Chiles Wilson, *President*
Patrick J Wilson, *Technology*
Marie Degalos, *Controller*
Brian Machado, *Marketing Staff*
Justin Bloss, *Sales Staff*
◆ **EMP:** 40 **EST:** 1992
SALES (est): 38.5MM **Privately Held**
WEB: www.rivermaid.com
SIC: 0723 Fruit (fresh) packing services; vegetable packing services

(P-305)
S & J RANCHES LLC
6715 N Palm Ave Ste 212, Fresno (93704-1073)
PHONE 559 437-2600
James M Burkhart,
Jim Burkhart,
Kevin Olsen,
EMP: 83 **EST:** 1950
SALES (est): 2.7MM
SALES (corp-wide): 2B **Privately Held**
WEB: www.sjranchmgmt.com
SIC: 0723 0762 Fruit (fresh) packing services; citrus grove management & maintenance services
HQ: Wonderful Citrus Packing Llc
1901 S Lexington St
Delano CA 93215

(P-306)
S STAMOULES INC
Also Called: Stamoules Produce Co
904 S Lyon Ave, Mendota (93640-9735)
PHONE 559 655-9777
Peggy Stefanopoulos, *President*
Chrispher S Stefanopoulos, *Treasurer*
Danny Stefanopoulos, *Vice Pres*
Tom Stefanopoulos, *Vice Pres*
Elena Stefanopoulos, *Admin Sec*
▼ **EMP:** 1000 **EST:** 1925
SQ FT: 40,000
SALES (est): 100MM **Privately Held**
WEB: www.stamoules.com
SIC: 0723 Fruit (fresh) packing services; vegetable packing services

(P-307)
SAN JOAQUIN FIGS INC
Also Called: Nutra-Figs
3564 N Hazel Ave, Fresno (93722-4912)
P.O. Box 9547 (93793-9547)
PHONE 559 224-4492
Keith Jura, *President*
Mary Jura, *Corp Secy*
◆ **EMP:** 50 **EST:** 1989
SQ FT: 18,000
SALES (est): 10.1MM **Privately Held**
WEB: www.nutrafig.com
SIC: 0723 Fruit (fresh) packing services

(P-308)
SIMONIAN BROTHERS INC (PA)
Also Called: Simonian Fruit
511 N 7th St, Fowler (93625-2331)
P.O. Box 340 (93625-0340)
PHONE 559 834-5921
David Simonian, *Ch of Bd*
Harold J Simonian, *President*
James P Simonian, *Treasurer*
Jeffery Simoninan, *Admin Sec*
▼ **EMP:** 171 **EST:** 1960
SQ FT: 70,000

0723 - Crop Preparation, Except Cotton Ginning County (P-309)

PRODUCTS & SERVICES SECTION

SALES (est): 22.7MM **Privately Held**
WEB: www.simonianfruit.com
SIC: 0723 7389 Fruit (fresh) packing services; packaging & labeling services

(P-309)
SKYLINE TREE ENTERPRISE INC
3650 Westhaven St, Cottonwood (96022-9435)
P.O. Box 811 (96022-0811)
PHONE.....................530 736-9327
Frank Fales, *President*
EMP: 35 **EST:** 2011
SALES (est): 2.9MM **Privately Held**
SIC: 0723 Tree nuts (general) hulling & shelling services

(P-310)
SUMA FRUIT INTL USA INC
1810 Academy Ave, Sanger (93657-3739)
PHONE.....................559 875-5000
Ralph Hackett, *CEO*
▼ **EMP:** 89 **EST:** 1989
SQ FT: 60,000
SALES (est): 9.4MM **Privately Held**
WEB: www.freshdelmonte.com
SIC: 0723 Fruit (fresh) packing services
HQ: Del Monte Fresh Produce N.A., Inc.
  241 Sevilla Ave
  Coral Gables FL 33134
  305 520-8400

(P-311)
SUNSHINE RAISIN CORPORATION (PA)
Also Called: National Raisin Company
626 S 5th St, Fowler (93625-9745)
P.O. Box 219 (93625-0219)
PHONE.....................559 834-5981
Lindakay Abdulian, *President*
May Firkus, *CFO*
Krikor Bedrosian, *Treasurer*
Bryan Bedrosian, *Vice Pres*
Michael Bedrosian, *Vice Pres*
◆ **EMP:** 249 **EST:** 1968
SQ FT: 400,000
SALES (est): 126.1MM **Privately Held**
WEB: www.nationalraisin.com
SIC: 0723 Crop preparation services for market

(P-312)
TELESIS ONION CO
21484 S Colusa, Five Points (93624)
P.O. Box 690 (93624-0690)
PHONE.....................559 884-2441
Dan Garcia, *Manager*
Danny Gracia, *Manager*
EMP: 115
SALES (corp-wide): 7.5MM **Privately Held**
SIC: 0723 Vegetable packing services
PA: Telesis Onion Co.
  3265 W Figarden Dr
  Fresno CA 93711
  559 884-2441

(P-313)
VALLEY FIG GROWERS
2028 S 3rd St, Fresno (93702-4156)
PHONE.....................559 349-1686
Gary Jue, *President*
Paul Mesple, *Chairman*
Linda Cain, *Vice Pres*
Michael N Emigh, *Principal*
Douglas D Parkhurst, *Controller*
◆ **EMP:** 50 **EST:** 1959
SQ FT: 100,000
SALES (est): 10.8MM **Privately Held**
WEB: www.valleyfig.com
SIC: 0723 2033 Fruit (fresh) packing services; fruits & fruit products in cans, jars, etc.

(P-314)
VAN DYKES RICE DRYER INC
4036 Pleasant Grove Rd, Pleasant Grove (95668-9727)
PHONE.....................916 655-3171
Donna Van Dyke, *President*
Jack L Cornelius Jr, *CFO*
James C Van Dyke, *Treasurer*
Dawn Cornelius, *Principal*
Connie L Jerome, *Principal*
EMP: 48 **EST:** 1940

SQ FT: 2,000
SALES (est): 3MM **Privately Held**
WEB: www.dryrice.com
SIC: 0723 Rice drying services

(P-315)
WILBUR PACKING COMPANY INC
1500 Eager Rd, Live Oak (95953)
P.O. Box 3730, Yuba City (95992-3730)
PHONE.....................530 671-4911
Richard G Wilbur, *President*
Richard R Wilbur, *COO*
Randy Baucom, *CFO*
Emily L Friend,
◆ **EMP:** 100
SQ FT: 60,650
SALES (est): 39.7MM **Privately Held**
WEB: www.wilburpacking.com
SIC: 0723 2034 Crop preparation services for market; dehydrated fruits, vegetables, soups

(P-316)
YOUNGSTOWN GRAPE DISTRS INC
1625 G St, Reedley (93654-3435)
P.O. Box 271 (93654-0271)
PHONE.....................559 638-2271
Michael J Forrest, *CEO*
Brian Forrest, *Sales Mgr*
Carlos Gonzales, *Manager*
▲ **EMP:** 206 **EST:** 1983
SQ FT: 100,000
SALES (est): 42.6MM **Privately Held**
WEB: www.youngstownd.com
SIC: 0723 Crop preparation services for market

0741 Veterinary Livestock Svcs

(P-317)
LOS BANOS VETERINARY CLINIC
1900 E Pacheco Blvd, Los Banos (93635-4935)
PHONE.....................209 826-5860
David Luces, *President*
David Simmons,
EMP: 35 **EST:** 1977
SQ FT: 2,500
SALES (est): 1MM **Privately Held**
WEB: www.losbanosveterinaryclinic.com
SIC: 0741 0742 Animal hospital services, livestock; animal hospital services, pets & other animal specialties

0742 Veterinary Animal Specialties

(P-318)
A PET EMRGNCY & SPECIALTY CTR
Also Called: Dana, Steven M Dvm
901 Francisco Blvd E, San Rafael (94901-4787)
PHONE.....................415 456-7372
Steve Dana, *Principal*
Mark Davis, *Administration*
Aarti Sabhlok, *Comp Spec*
Carla Robin,
Christopher Rodi,
EMP: 50 **EST:** 1999
SALES (est): 7.8MM **Privately Held**
WEB: www.pescm.ethosvet.com
SIC: 0742 Animal hospital services, pets & other animal specialties

(P-319)
ADOBE ANIMAL HOSPITAL
4470 El Camino Real, Los Altos (94022-1003)
PHONE.....................650 948-9661
Dave M Ross, *President*
Jerry Berg, *Vice Pres*
Denise Johnsen,
Deb Sell, *Chiropractor*
Summer Holmstrand, *Manager*
EMP: 100 **EST:** 1964
SQ FT: 6,577

SALES (est): 10.4MM **Privately Held**
WEB: www.adobe-animal.com
SIC: 0742 Animal hospital services, pets & other animal specialties

(P-320)
ANIMAL CLINIC OF SANTA CRUZ
815 Mission St, Santa Cruz (95060-3616)
PHONE.....................831 427-3345
Michael Shumate Dvm, *President*
Jay M Vick Dvm, *Admin Sec*
Laura Le,
Laura Ryle, *Med Doctor*
EMP: 43 **EST:** 1975
SQ FT: 4,000
SALES (est): 5.6MM
SALES (corp-wide): 42.8B **Privately Held**
WEB: www.santacruzveterinarian.com
SIC: 0742 Animal hospital services, pets & other animal specialties
HQ: Vca Inc.
  12401 W Olympic Blvd
  Los Angeles CA 90064
  310 571-6500

(P-321)
ARGUELLO PET HOSPITAL INC
Also Called: Ina, Michael T Dvm
530 Arguello Blvd, San Francisco (94118-3203)
PHONE.....................415 751-3242
Mike INA, *President*
Vicki INA, *Admin Sec*
Jamie INA, *Technician*
EMP: 37 **EST:** 1970
SQ FT: 2,000
SALES (est): 7.2MM **Privately Held**
WEB: www.arguellopet.com
SIC: 0742 Animal hospital services, pets & other animal specialties

(P-322)
ASSOCTED VTRNARY PRACTICES INC
Also Called: Brentwood Veterinary Hospital
4519 Ohara Ave, Brentwood (94513-2206)
PHONE.....................925 634-1177
Duane Schnittker Dvm, *Principal*
Shannon Cameron, *Top Exec*
EMP: 48 **EST:** 1979
SQ FT: 1,500
SALES (est): 9.6MM
SALES (corp-wide): 860MM **Privately Held**
WEB: www.brentwoodvet.net
SIC: 0742 Animal hospital services, pets & other animal specialties
HQ: National Veterinary Associates, Inc.
  29229 Canwood St Ste 100
  Agoura Hills CA 91301
  805 777-7722

(P-323)
BERKELEY DOG & CAT HOSP INC
2126 Haste St, Berkeley (94704-2019)
PHONE.....................510 848-5041
Allen G Shiro, *Partner*
Richard Benjamin, *Partner*
Natasha Fields, *Technician*
Sierra Holly, *Technician*
Leslie Silva Rvt, *Technician*
EMP: 60 **EST:** 1976
SQ FT: 3,000
SALES (est): 4.4MM **Privately Held**
WEB: www.berkeleydogandcat.com
SIC: 0742 Animal hospital services, pets & other animal specialties

(P-324)
BISHOP RANCH VETERINARY CENTER (PA)
2000 Bishop Dr, San Ramon (94583-2344)
PHONE.....................925 743-9300
James Delano, *Partner*
Jay Kerr, *Partner*
James Pogrel, *Partner*
Frank Utchen, *Partner*
Jordanna Ferreira, *Exec VP*
EMP: 83 **EST:** 2006
SALES (est): 5.2MM **Privately Held**
WEB: www.webvets.com
SIC: 0742 Animal hospital services, pets & other animal specialties

(P-325)
CITY SAN JOSE ANIMAL CARE CTR
2750 Monterey Hwy, San Jose (95111-3120)
PHONE.....................408 794-7297
John Cizirelli, *Director*
EMP: 50 **EST:** 2001
SALES (est): 1.1MM **Privately Held**
WEB: www.sanjoseca.gov
SIC: 0742 Veterinary services, specialties

(P-326)
HB ANIMAL CLINICS INC
Also Called: V C A Blossom Hill Animal Hosp
955 Blossom Hill Rd, San Jose (95123-1203)
PHONE.....................408 227-3717
Devona Brown, *Office Mgr*
Evans Erin,
Demarco Stephanie,
Terry Medinger, *Internal Med*
EMP: 50 **EST:** 1957
SALES (est): 3MM
SALES (corp-wide): 42.8B **Privately Held**
WEB: www.vcahospitals.com
SIC: 0742 Animal hospital services, pets & other animal specialties
HQ: Vca Inc.
  12401 W Olympic Blvd
  Los Angeles CA 90064
  310 571-6500

(P-327)
LOOMIS BSIN EQUINE MED CTR INC
2973 Penryn Rd, Penryn (95663-9684)
PHONE.....................916 652-7645
Bob Morgan Dvm, *Principal*
Diane Rhodes,
EMP: 38 **EST:** 2000
SALES (est): 5.5MM **Privately Held**
WEB: www.lbemc.com
SIC: 0742 Veterinarian, animal specialties

(P-328)
LOOMIS BSIN VTRNARY CLINIC INC
3901 Sierra College Blvd, Loomis (95650-7943)
P.O. Box 2059 (95650-2059)
PHONE.....................916 652-5816
Richard Frey, *President*
Marcia C Smith, *Vice Pres*
EMP: 47 **EST:** 1975
SQ FT: 15,500
SALES (est): 4.8MM **Privately Held**
WEB: www.loomisbasinvet.com
SIC: 0742 Animal hospital services, pets & other animal specialties

(P-329)
LOS GATOS DOG & CAT HOSPITAL
17480 Shelburne Way, Los Gatos (95030-3311)
PHONE.....................408 354-6474
Kyle Frandle, *Owner*
Megan Hanken,
EMP: 38 **EST:** 1990
SQ FT: 3,025
SALES (est): 5.6MM **Privately Held**
WEB: www.losgatosvet.com
SIC: 0742 Animal hospital services, pets & other animal specialties

(P-330)
MARINE MAMMAL CENTER (PA)
2000 Bunker Rd, Sausalito (94965-2697)
PHONE.....................415 339-0430
Jeffrey Roger Boehm, *CEO*
Marci Davis, *CFO*
Marvin Suchoff, *CFO*
Jason Barcelon, *Vice Pres*
Karen Takamoto, *Database Admin*
EMP: 49 **EST:** 1975
SQ FT: 25,000
SALES: 15.2MM **Privately Held**
WEB: www.marinemammalcenter.org
SIC: 0742 8299 8733 Animal hospital services, pets & other animal specialties; arts & crafts schools; noncommercial research organizations

▲ = Import ▼ = Export
◆ = Import/Export

PRODUCTS & SERVICES SECTION

0752 - Animal Specialty Svcs, Exc Veterinary County (P-354)

(P-331)
NORTHPINTE VETERINARY HOSP INC
1566 Springbrook Rd, Walnut Creek (94597-3935)
PHONE.................530 674-8670
Steven Sanders, *President*
EMP: 36 EST: 1982
SQ FT: 10,000
SALES (est): 3MM **Privately Held**
SIC: 0742 Animal hospital services, pets & other animal specialties

(P-332)
PET EMERGENCY TREATMENT SVC
1048 University Ave, Berkeley (94710-2135)
PHONE.................510 548-6684
Jean-Paul Cucuel, *President*
Christopher Rodi, *Managing Prtnr*
Lloyd Freitas, *Treasurer*
Richard Benjamin, *Admin Sec*
Regina Sanger, *Technician*
EMP: 50 EST: 1977
SQ FT: 3,000
SALES (est): 3MM **Privately Held**
WEB: www.petsreferralcenter.com
SIC: 0742 Animal hospital services, pets & other animal specialties; veterinarian, animal specialties

(P-333)
PROVIDENCE VETERINARY HOSPITAL
Also Called: Providence Veterinary Clinic W
2304 Pacific Ave, Alameda (94501-2999)
PHONE.................510 521-6608
Kent Rosenblum Dvm, *Partner*
Randall Miller S Dvm, *Partner*
Susan Phillips, *Practice Mgr*
Austin Hughes, *Technician*
EMP: 39 EST: 1968
SQ FT: 800
SALES (est): 3.3MM **Privately Held**
WEB: www.providencevethospital.com
SIC: 0742 Animal hospital services, pets & other animal specialties

(P-334)
SACRAMENTO ANIMAL HOSPITAL INC
5701 H St, Sacramento (95819-3331)
PHONE.................916 451-7213
Karen Mulvihill, *Partner*
Diana Portez DMD, *Partner*
Erin True DMD, *Partner*
EMP: 41 EST: 1994
SALES (est): 5.6MM **Privately Held**
WEB: www.mysacvet.com
SIC: 0742 Animal hospital services, pets & other animal specialties

(P-335)
SAGE VETERINARY CENTERS LP
1410 Monument Blvd, Concord (94520-4368)
PHONE.................925 288-4856
Gina Del Vecchio, *Managing Prtnr*
EMP: 461 EST: 1992
SALES (est): 45.7MM
SALES (corp-wide): 860MM **Privately Held**
WEB: www.sagecenters.com
SIC: 0742 Animal hospital services, pets & other animal specialties
HQ: National Veterinary Associates, Inc.
29229 Canwood St Ste 100
Agoura Hills CA 91301
805 777-7722

(P-336)
SHANDI INC
11536 Cleveland Ave, Oakdale (95361-7705)
PHONE.................209 847-5951
Jerry B Black, *President*
Hildaanne Baisel, *Med Doctor*
EMP: 55 EST: 1950
SQ FT: 20,184
SALES (est): 7.7MM **Privately Held**
WEB: www.pioneerequine.com
SIC: 0742 Animal hospital services, pets & other animal specialties

(P-337)
SILVERADO VETERINARY HOSP INC
2035 Silverado Trl, NAPA (94558-2048)
PHONE.................707 224-7953
Pete Morse, *President*
Karen Morse, *Corp Secy*
Dr Paul Hess, *Vice Pres*
EMP: 40 EST: 1977
SALES (est): 5.1MM **Privately Held**
WEB: www.silveradovet.com
SIC: 0742 Animal hospital services, pets & other animal specialties

(P-338)
SUNNYBRAE ANIMAL CLINIC INC
900 Buttermilk Ln, Arcata (95521-6799)
PHONE.................707 822-5124
Jay Hight, *President*
EMP: 45 EST: 1972
SALES (est): 2.7MM **Privately Held**
WEB: www.sunnybraeanimalclinic.com
SIC: 0742 Veterinarian, animal specialties

(P-339)
TONY LRSSAS ANMAL RSCUE FNDTIO
2890 Mitchell Dr, Walnut Creek (94598-1635)
PHONE.................925 256-1273
Elena Bicker, *Exec Dir*
Cheryl Mosby, *Hum Res Coord*
Stephanie Erickson, *Opers Staff*
Eon Newquist, *Education*
Debra Dangelo,
EMP: 70 EST: 1991
SQ FT: 37,000
SALES: 21.3MM **Privately Held**
WEB: www.arflife.org
SIC: 0742 8699 Veterinary services, specialties; animal humane society

(P-340)
UNITED EMRGNCY ANMAL CLNIC INC (PA)
905 Dell Ave, Campbell (95008-4120)
PHONE.................408 371-6252
Denise Shirey, *Director*
William Shirey, *President*
Mary Bradley, *Human Resources*
EMP: 35 EST: 1976
SQ FT: 4,000
SALES (est): 3.1MM **Privately Held**
WEB: www.medvetforpets.com
SIC: 0742 Animal hospital services, pets & other animal specialties

(P-341)
VCA ALMADEN VALLEY HOSPITAL
Also Called: V C A Almaden Vly Animal Hosp
15790 Almaden Expy, San Jose (95120-1502)
PHONE.................408 268-3550
Curtis Moran, *President*
Donald Jones, *Director*
EMP: 58 EST: 1979
SQ FT: 2,600
SALES (est): 3.8MM
SALES (corp-wide): 42.8B **Privately Held**
WEB: www.vcaalmadenvalley.com
SIC: 0742 Animal hospital services, pets & other animal specialties
HQ: Vca Inc.
12401 W Olympic Blvd
Los Angeles CA 90064
310 571-6500

(P-342)
VCA ANIMAL HOSPITALS INC
Also Called: VCA Holly Street
501 Laurel St, San Carlos (94070-2415)
PHONE.................650 631-7400
Barbara Beebe, *Office Mgr*
James Bower, *Director*
Josue Pereda, *Manager*
EMP: 50
SALES (corp-wide): 42.8B **Privately Held**
WEB: www.petschoice.com
SIC: 0742 Animal hospital services, pets & other animal specialties
HQ: Vca Animal Hospitals, Inc.
12401 W Olympic Blvd
Los Angeles CA 90064

(P-343)
VETERINARY EMERGENCY SERVICE
1639 N Fresno St, Fresno (93703-3029)
PHONE.................559 486-0520
Paul M Deauville, *President*
EMP: 41 EST: 1973
SALES (est): 1.7MM **Privately Held**
WEB: www.247petvets.com
SIC: 0742 Animal hospital services, pets & other animal specialties

(P-344)
VETERINARY INFORMATION NETWORK (PA)
Also Called: Vin
777 W Covell Blvd, Davis (95616-5916)
PHONE.................530 756-4881
Paul Pion, *President*
Ce Vin, *CFO*
Mike Thomas, *Vice Pres*
Jordan Benshea, *Exec Dir*
Monica Mastin, *Admin Sec*
EMP: 40 EST: 1991
SQ FT: 5,000
SALES (est): 10.7MM **Privately Held**
WEB: www.vin.com
SIC: 0742 Veterinarian, animal specialties

(P-345)
VETERINARY MEDICAL ASSOCIATES
204 W Granger Ave, Modesto (95350-4432)
PHONE.................209 527-5855
Jeff Kahler, *President*
EMP: 38 EST: 1971
SQ FT: 5,000
SALES (est): 3.1MM **Privately Held**
WEB: www.vmamodesto.com
SIC: 0742 Animal hospital services, pets & other animal specialties

(P-346)
VETERINARY SURGICAL ASSOCIATES (PA)
1410 Monu Blvd Ste 100, Concord (94520)
PHONE.................925 827-1777
Julie Smith, *Partner*
Elisabeth Richardson, *Partner*
Sharon Ullman, *Partner*
Charles Walls, *Partner*
Chuck Walls, *Partner*
EMP: 40 EST: 1993
SALES (est): 14.5MM **Privately Held**
WEB: www.sagecenters.com
SIC: 0742 Animal hospital services, pets & other animal specialties

(P-347)
WOODLAND VETERINARY HOSPITAL
445 Matmor Rd, Woodland (95776-5724)
PHONE.................530 666-2461
Dr Bruce Dennie, *Owner*
Marsha Torbert, *Technician*
EMP: 35 EST: 1974
SQ FT: 2,300
SALES (est): 6.1MM **Privately Held**
WEB: www.woodlandvethospital.com
SIC: 0742 Animal hospital services, pets & other animal specialties

0751 Livestock Svcs, Except Veterinary

(P-348)
J L G ENTERPRISES INC
11116 Sierra Rd, Oakdale (95361-8333)
P.O. Box 1375 (95361-1375)
PHONE.................209 847-4797
John Acebido, *President*
EMP: 43 EST: 1975
SQ FT: 6,000
SALES (est): 3.1MM **Privately Held**
WEB: www.jlgenterprises.com
SIC: 0751 Artificial insemination services, livestock

(P-349)
STANDARD CATTLE LLC
8105a S Lassen Ave, San Joaquin (93660-9728)
PHONE.................559 693-1977
Michael Vanderdussen, *Mng Member*
▲ EMP: 75 EST: 2005
SALES (est): 7.1MM **Privately Held**
WEB: www.standardcattlellc.com
SIC: 0751 Cattle services

0752 Animal Specialty Svcs, Exc Veterinary

(P-350)
ALPHA PET GROOMING SALON LLC
1325 Howard Ave, Burlingame (94010-4212)
PHONE.................650 271-4282
Carlos Chaves, *CEO*
EMP: 40 EST: 2012
SALES (est): 1.2MM **Privately Held**
WEB: www.alphagroomingpetsalon.com
SIC: 0752 Grooming services, pet & animal specialties

(P-351)
CANINE CMPNONS FOR INDPENDENCE (PA)
2965 Dutton Ave, Santa Rosa (95407-5711)
P.O. Box 446 (95402-0446)
PHONE.................707 577-1700
Paul Mundell, *CEO*
John D Miller, *Ch of Bd*
Alan Feinne, *CFO*
Todd Wurschmidt, *Officer*
Debbie Knatz, *Program Mgr*
EMP: 71 EST: 1975
SQ FT: 40,000
SALES: 31.9MM **Privately Held**
WEB: www.canine.org
SIC: 0752 Training services, pet & animal specialties (not horses)

(P-352)
CITY OF WOODLAND
Also Called: Yolo County Sherrfs Anml
140c Tony Diaz Way, Woodland (95776-5194)
PHONE.................530 668-5287
Vicky Fletcher, *Manager*
EMP: 67
SALES (corp-wide): 98.4MM **Privately Held**
WEB: www.cityofwoodland.org
SIC: 9229 0752 Public order & safety statistics centers; ; shelters, animal
PA: City Of Woodland
300 1st St
Woodland CA 95695
530 661-5830

(P-353)
CONFIDENTIAL CANINE SERVICES
Also Called: Team K9
8094 Langham Way, Sacramento (95829-6071)
P.O. Box 279311 (95827-9311)
PHONE.................800 574-5545
Tristan Murano, *CEO*
Joelyn Corrado, *Corp Secy*
Philip Corrado, *Co-CEO*
EMP: 43 EST: 2016
SALES (est): 1.5MM **Privately Held**
SIC: 0752 0751 Animal training services; livestock services, except veterinary

(P-354)
GUIDE DOGS FOR BLIND INC (PA)
Also Called: G D B
350 Los Ranchitos Rd, San Rafael (94903-3606)
P.O. Box 151200 (94915-1200)
PHONE.................415 499-4000
Chris Benninger, *CEO*
Amy Salger, *Vice Chairman*
Cathy Martin, *CFO*
Kenneth Stupi, *CFO*
Diana McQuarrie, *Bd of Directors*

0752 - Animal Specialty Svcs, Exc Veterinary County (P-355)

PRODUCTS & SERVICES SECTION

EMP: 170
SALES (est): 86.5MM **Privately Held**
WEB: www.guidedogs.com
SIC: **0752** 8299 Animal training services; educational service, nondegree granting; continuing educ.

(P-355)
HUMBOLDT DOG OBEDIENCE GROUP
Also Called: Humdog
P.O. Box 6733 (95502-6733)
PHONE.................707 444-3862
Marilyn Backman, *President*
Mark Nichols, *Treasurer*
EMP: 50 EST: 1978
SALES (est): 632.6K **Privately Held**
WEB: www.humdog.org
SIC: **0752** Training services, pet & animal specialties (not horses)

(P-356)
PRO-GROOM INC
935 Roseville Pkwy # 100, Roseville (95678-6062)
PHONE.................916 782-4172
Sally Randall, *Owner*
EMP: 36 EST: 1996
SQ FT: 2,400
SALES (est): 325.6K **Privately Held**
WEB: www.progroomroseville.com
SIC: **0752** 5999 Grooming services, pet & animal specialties; pet supplies

(P-357)
USA SELLER CO LLC
2840 Countryside Dr, Turlock (95380-8405)
PHONE.................209 656-7085
Diane Kline, *Branch Mgr*
EMP: 388 **Privately Held**
WEB: www.petsuppliesplus.com
SIC: **5999** 0752 Pets & pet supplies; dog pounds
HQ: Usa Seller Co., Llc
17197 N Laurel Park Dr
Livonia MI 48152
734 793-6600

0761 Farm Labor Contractors & Crew Leaders

(P-358)
GREEN VALLEY LABOR INC
1851 Freedom Ln Ste C, Atwater (95301-5210)
PHONE.................209 358-2851
Jose H Navarro Farias, *CEO*
Eleus Brown, *Bookkeeper*
EMP: 50 EST: 2014
SALES (est): 3.8MM **Privately Held**
SIC: **0761** Farm labor contractors

(P-359)
JJ RIOS FARM SERVICES INC
4890 E Acampo Rd, Acampo (95220-9601)
P.O. Box 550 (95220-0550)
PHONE.................209 333-7467
Fax: 209 333-3715
EMP: 80
SQ FT: 4,800
SALES (est): 2MM **Privately Held**
WEB: www.jjrios.com
SIC: **0761** Farm Labor Contractor

(P-360)
LABOR ONE INC
575 Minnewawa Ave Ste 3, Clovis (93612-6300)
PHONE.................559 430-4202
EMP: 70
SALES (est): 687.8K **Privately Held**
SIC: **0761** Farm Labor Contractor

(P-361)
OMAR OROZCO
Also Called: Omar Orozco's Contracting
816 Gibson Rd, Woodland (95695-4935)
PHONE.................530 723-0849
Omar Orozco, *Principal*
EMP: 55 EST: 2017
SALES (est): 648.5K **Privately Held**
SIC: **0761** Farm labor contractors

(P-362)
PACIFIC AG & VINEYARD INC
21282 N Ray Rd, Lodi (95242-9487)
P.O. Box 760, Woodbridge (95258-0760)
PHONE.................209 365-7222
Mack Worland, *President*
EMP: 45 EST: 2003
SQ FT: 4,000
SALES (est): 4.2MM **Privately Held**
WEB: www.pavdevelopment.com
SIC: **0761** Farm labor contractors

(P-363)
PALO ALTO VINEYARD MGT LLC
50 Adobe Canyon Rd, Kenwood (95452-9044)
P.O. Box 1399 (95452-1399)
PHONE.................707 996-7725
Beverly Ordaz,
Jesus Ordaz,
EMP: 90 EST: 1997
SQ FT: 1,000
SALES (est): 3.9MM **Privately Held**
SIC: **0761** Farm labor contractors

(P-364)
R AND R LABOR INC
710 Kirkpatric Ct Ste A, Hollister (95023-2808)
PHONE.................831 638-0290
Ramiro Rodriguez Jr, *President*
Jose Rodriguez, *Vice Pres*
Elda Garcia, *Executive*
EMP: 300 EST: 1980
SALES (est): 8.3MM **Privately Held**
SIC: **0761** Farm labor contractors

(P-365)
RODGZ FARM LABOR CONTG LLC
4422 College Way, Olivehurst (95961-4622)
PHONE.................530 329-8403
Fidel Rodriguez,
EMP: 80
SALES (est): 688.1K **Privately Held**
SIC: **0761** Crew leaders, farm labor: contracting services

0762 Farm Management Svcs

(P-366)
ADVANCED VITICULTURE INC
930 Shiloh Rd Bldg 44-E, Windsor (95492-9664)
P.O. Box 2236 (95492-2236)
PHONE.................707 838-3805
Mark Greenspan, *President*
Linda Greenspan, *Vice Pres*
Richard Barnes, *CIO*
EMP: 50
SALES (est): 3.5MM **Privately Held**
WEB: www.advancedvit.com
SIC: **0762** 0172 0721 8999 Vineyard management & maintenance services; grapes; orchard tree & vine services; scientific consulting

(P-367)
ARTHUR KUNDE & SONS INC
Also Called: Kunde Estate Winery
9825 Sonoma Hwy, Kenwood (95452)
P.O. Box 638 (95452-0638)
PHONE.................707 833-5501
Jim Mickelson, *President*
Arthur Kunde Jr, *President*
William Kunde, *Corp Secy*
▲ EMP: 20 EST: 1920
SQ FT: 2,000
SALES (est): 1.4MM **Privately Held**
WEB: www.kunde.com
SIC: **0762** 2084 Vineyard management & maintenance services; wines, brandy & brandy spirits

(P-368)
BLACKBURN FARMING COMPANY INC
43940 W North Ave, Firebaugh (93622-9773)
PHONE.................559 659-3753
Court Blackburn, *President*
EMP: 38 EST: 1964
SQ FT: 2,450

SALES (est): 3MM **Privately Held**
SIC: **0762** Farm management services

(P-369)
COLINAS FARMING COMPANY
990 Rutherford, Rutherford (94573)
PHONE.................707 963-2053
Paul Jackson, *President*
Derek Cronk, *Vice Pres*
Denise Jackson, *Vice Pres*
Chris Pedemonte, *Vice Pres*
EMP: 42 EST: 1975
SALES (est): 2.1MM **Privately Held**
WEB: www.colinasfarming.com
SIC: **0762** Vineyard management & maintenance services

(P-370)
CREEKSIDE FARMING COMPANY
30814 Avenue 9, Madera (93637-9154)
PHONE.................559 674-9999
Davindar Mahil, *CFO*
Tejpal Mahil, *Admin Sec*
Jay Mahill, *Admin Sec*
EMP: 40 EST: 2006
SALES (est): 3.9MM **Privately Held**
SIC: **0762** Farm management services

(P-371)
CUMMINGS-VIOLICH INC
Also Called: Cummings-Vlich Inc-Orchard MGT
1750 Dayton Rd, Chico (95928-6968)
P.O. Box 3157 (95927-3157)
PHONE.................530 894-5494
Dan Cummings, *President*
Paul Violich, *CFO*
EMP: 42 EST: 1989
SQ FT: 3,400
SALES (est): 1.1MM **Privately Held**
SIC: **0762** Farm management services

(P-372)
CYPRESS GREEN
5219 N Forestdale Cir, Dublin (94568-8754)
PHONE.................510 861-2214
Harpreet Kaur, *President*
EMP: 37 EST: 2018
SALES (est): 536.6K **Privately Held**
SIC: **0762** Farm management services

(P-373)
EASTSIDE MANAGEMENT CO INC
1131 12th St Ste C, Modesto (95354-0813)
PHONE.................209 578-9852
Steven Zeff, *President*
EMP: 148 **Privately Held**
SIC: **0762** Farm management services
PA: Eastside Management Company, Inc.
1518 K St
Modesto CA 95354

(P-374)
EASTSIDE MANAGEMENT CO INC (PA)
1518 K St, Modesto (95354-1108)
PHONE.................209 578-9852
Steven Zeff, *CEO*
Kenfield Aldrin, *President*
EMP: 174 EST: 1986
SQ FT: 2,650
SALES (est): 12.2MM **Privately Held**
SIC: **0762** Farm management services

(P-375)
FARMLAND MANAGEMENT SERVICES
17486 Road 23, Madera (93637-9253)
PHONE.................559 674-4305
EMP: 40
SALES (corp-wide): 27.9MM **Privately Held**
WEB: www.premierewinegrapes.com
SIC: **0762** Farm management services
PA: Farmland Management Services
301 E Main St
Turlock CA 95380
209 669-0742

(P-376)
FBN INPUTS LLC
Also Called: Farmers Business Network
388 El Camino Real, San Carlos (94070-2408)
PHONE.................844 200-3276
Amol Desphande, *Mng Member*
Dennis Kautz, *Sales Staff*
EMP: 57 EST: 2015
SALES (est): 10MM
SALES (corp-wide): 21.9MM **Privately Held**
WEB: www.fbn.com
SIC: **0762** Farm management services
PA: Farmer's Business Network, Inc.
388 El Camino Real
San Carlos CA 94070
844 200-3276

(P-377)
KAPCSANDY FAMILY LLC
Also Called: Kapcsandy Family Winery
1001 State Ln, Yountville (94599-9473)
PHONE.................707 948-3100
Louis E Kapscandy, *Mng Member*
Louis Kapcsandy Jr,
EMP: 17 EST: 2003
SQ FT: 2,738
SALES (est): 1.2MM **Privately Held**
WEB: www.kapcsandywines.com
SIC: **0762** 2084 Vineyard management & maintenance services; wines

(P-378)
KENDALL-JACKSON WINE CENTER
5007 Fulton Rd, Fulton (95439)
P.O. Box 296 (95439-0296)
PHONE.................707 571-7500
Jeff Jackson, *Owner*
Leeanne Edwards, *Vice Pres*
Jill Palmer, *Executive*
Mel Lamb, *Regional Mgr*
Ashley Szukalowski, *District Mgr*
EMP: 36 EST: 1984
SALES (est): 7.9MM **Privately Held**
WEB: www.kj.com
SIC: **0762** 5182 Vineyard management & maintenance services; wine & distilled beverages

(P-379)
KENZO ESTATE INC
3200 Monticello Rd, NAPA (94558-9655)
PHONE.................707 254-7572
Jude Radeski, *President*
Kenzo Tfujimoto, *CEO*
Atsushi Akahane, *Exec VP*
Hisako Sanjo, *Sales Staff*
Kenzo Estate, *Manager*
▲ EMP: 29 EST: 2000
SQ FT: 972
SALES (est): 6MM **Privately Held**
WEB: www.kenzoestate.com
SIC: **0762** 2084 Vineyard management & maintenance services; wine cellars, bonded: engaged in blending wines

(P-380)
KG VINEYARD MANAGEMENT LLC
9077 W Cotta Rd, Lodi (95242)
P.O. Box 688, Woodbridge (95258-0688)
PHONE.................209 367-8996
Benjamin Kolber,
Kris Gutierrez,
EMP: 40 EST: 2006
SALES (est): 3.1MM **Privately Held**
WEB: www.kgvm.net
SIC: **0762** Vineyard management & maintenance services

(P-381)
LENT BURDEN FARMING COMPANY
250 S Oak Ave Ste C1, Oakdale (95361-3572)
PHONE.................209 847-3276
Dennis L Wittchow, *Principal*
EMP: 36 EST: 2006
SALES (est): 2.8MM **Privately Held**
SIC: **0762** Farm management services

▲ = Import ▼ = Export
◆ = Import/Export

PRODUCTS & SERVICES SECTION
0781 - Landscape Counseling & Planning County (P-405)

(P-382)
MUM NAPA VALLEY
8445 Silverado Trl, NAPA (94558-9435)
PHONE.................................707 942-3425
Rob McNeil, *Manager*
Angelica Dupont, *Technician*
Bryn Wilson, *Technician*
Adam Soto, *Asst Broker*
James O 'shea, *Director*
▲ **EMP:** 130 **EST:** 1989
SALES (est): 6.3MM **Privately Held**
WEB: www.mummnapa.com
SIC: 0762 0172 Vineyard management & maintenance services; grapes

(P-383)
NOBLE VINEYARD MANAGEMENT INC
5350 Old River Rd, Ukiah (95482-9620)
P.O. Box 1030 (95482-1030)
PHONE.................................415 533-8642
Tyler Rodrigue, *President*
EMP: 50 **EST:** 2016
SALES (est): 2.8MM **Privately Held**
WEB: www.noblevm.com
SIC: 0762 Vineyard management & maintenance services

(P-384)
PATIN VINEYARD MANAGEMENT INC
Also Called: P V M
1601 Sanders Rd, Windsor (95492-9775)
P.O. Box 988, Healdsburg (95448-0988)
PHONE.................................707 838-6665
Mitchell Patin, *President*
EMP: 45 **EST:** 1976
SQ FT: 3,500
SALES (est): 1.3MM **Privately Held**
SIC: 0762 Vineyard management & maintenance services

(P-385)
PINA VINEYARD MANAGEMENT LLC
7960 Silverado Trl, NAPA (94558-9433)
P.O. Box 373, Oakville (94562-0373)
PHONE.................................707 944-2229
Davie Pina, *Owner*
Omar Cruz, *Human Resources*
EMP: 48 **EST:** 1960
SQ FT: 290
SALES (est): 6.4MM **Privately Held**
WEB: www.pinavineyards.com
SIC: 0762 0723 2084 Vineyard management & maintenance services; crop preparation services for market; wines, brandy & brandy spirits

(P-386)
REDWOOD EMPIRE VINYRD MGT INC
22000 Geyserville Ave, Geyserville (95441)
P.O. Box 729 (95441-0729)
PHONE.................................707 857-3401
Kevin W Barr, *President*
Nancy Barr, *Treasurer*
Linda Barr, *Corp Secy*
EMP: 100 **EST:** 1985
SALES (est): 11MM **Privately Held**
WEB: www.revm.net
SIC: 0762 0172 Vineyard management & maintenance services; grapes

(P-387)
RITA CHRISTIANA-SANTA FARMS
16035 Indiana Rd, Dos Palos (93620-9602)
PHONE.................................209 387-4578
Caroline C Baker, *General Ptnr*
Cynthia Nicoletti, *Partner*
EMP: 48 **EST:** 1965
SQ FT: 1,500
SALES (est): 1.8MM **Privately Held**
SIC: 0762 Farm management services

(P-388)
VIMARK INC
Also Called: Vimark Vineyards
19500 Geyserville Ave, Geyserville (95441-9310)
P.O. Box 576 (95441-0576)
PHONE.................................707 857-3588
Krishik Hicks, *Manager*
Denise T Hicks, *Sales Staff*
Kris Hicks, *Manager*
EMP: 85
SALES (corp-wide): 7.9MM **Privately Held**
WEB: www.vimarkvineyards.com
SIC: 0762 Vineyard management & maintenance services
PA: Vimark, Inc.
  101 D St Fl 2nd
  Santa Rosa CA
  707 542-3134

(P-389)
VINO FARMS INC (PA)
1377 E Lodi Ave, Lodi (95240-0840)
PHONE.................................209 334-6975
James D Ledbetter, *President*
John K Ledbetter, *Officer*
Kimberly Bronson, *Exec VP*
Craig Ledbetter, *Vice Pres*
Marissa Ledbetter, *Vice Pres*
EMP: 50 **EST:** 1976
SQ FT: 6,000
SALES (est): 46.5MM **Privately Held**
WEB: www.vinofarms.com
SIC: 0762 8748 2084 Vineyard management & maintenance services; agricultural consultant; wines

(P-390)
VINO FARMS INC
10651 Eastside Rd, Healdsburg (95448-9490)
PHONE.................................707 433-8241
Roy Davis, *Manager*
EMP: 130
SALES (corp-wide): 46.5MM **Privately Held**
WEB: www.vinofarms.com
SIC: 0762 Vineyard management & maintenance services
PA: Vino Farms, Inc.
  1377 E Lodi Ave
  Lodi CA 95240
  209 334-6975

(P-391)
WC AG SERVICES INC
800 E Keyes Rd, Ceres (95307-7539)
P.O. Box 488 (95307-0488)
PHONE.................................209 538-3131
Fred Franzia, *President*
John Franzia, *Vice Pres*
Joseph Franzia, *Admin Sec*
EMP: 2500 **EST:** 1987
SQ FT: 2,093
SALES (est): 69MM **Privately Held**
SIC: 0762 Farm management services

0781 Landscape Counseling & Planning

(P-392)
ABSHEAR LANDSCAPE DEVELOPMENT
3171b Rippey Rd, Loomis (95650-9504)
P.O. Box 1817 (95650-1817)
PHONE.................................916 660-1617
EMP: 50
SALES (est): 1.7MM **Privately Held**
WEB: www.abshearlandscapes.com
SIC: 0781 Landscape Counseling And Planning, Nsk

(P-393)
AMERINE SYSTEMS INCORPORATED
10866 Cleveland Ave, Oakdale (95361-9709)
PHONE.................................209 847-5968
Gary Amerine, *President*
Ronald Amerine, *Admin Sec*
EMP: 50 **EST:** 1975
SQ FT: 20,000
SALES (est): 6MM **Privately Held**
WEB: www.amerinesystems.com
SIC: 0781 5084 5083 Landscape services; pumps & pumping equipment; irrigation equipment

(P-394)
BANKSIA LANDSCAPE
1055 E Brokaw Rd 30-34, San Jose (95131-2318)
PHONE.................................408 617-7100
Kevin Pearson, *CFO*
Donald Defever, *CEO*
EMP: 50 **EST:** 2016
SALES (est): 1.3MM **Privately Held**
WEB: www.banksialandscape.com
SIC: 0781 Landscape services

(P-395)
BAYSCAPE MANAGEMENT INC
Also Called: Coast Landscape Management
1350 Pacific Ave, Alviso (95002)
P.O. Box 880 (95002-0880)
PHONE.................................408 288-2940
Thomas Ellington, *President*
Ali Kurth, *Accounting Mgr*
EMP: 70 **EST:** 2005
SALES (est): 7.1MM **Privately Held**
WEB: www.bayscape.net
SIC: 0781 Landscape services

(P-396)
BELLAVISTA LANDSCAPE SVCS INC (PA)
1165 Lincoln Ave Ste 200, San Jose (95125-3038)
PHONE.................................408 410-6000
Thomas Moore, *President*
Kimberly Taylor, *Vice Pres*
EMP: 60 **EST:** 2001
SALES (est): 6.5MM **Privately Held**
WEB: www.bvls.com
SIC: 0781 Landscape services

(P-397)
BRIGHTVIEW LANDSCAPE DEV INC
20 Business Pkwy Ste 200, Sacramento (95828)
PHONE.................................916 386-4875
Dan Harper, *Branch Mgr*
EMP: 105
SALES (corp-wide): 2.3B **Publicly Held**
WEB: www.brightview.com
SIC: 0781 Landscape services
HQ: Brightview Landscape Development, Inc.
  27001 Agoura Rd Ste 350
  Calabasas CA 91301
  818 223-8500

(P-398)
BRIGHTVIEW LANDSCAPE SVCS INC
20551b Corsair Blvd, Hayward (94545-1005)
PHONE.................................510 487-4826
Tom Stoutt, *Branch Mgr*
Tony Fargnoli, *Manager*
EMP: 120
SALES (corp-wide): 2.3B **Publicly Held**
WEB: www.brightview.com
SIC: 0781 Landscape services
HQ: Brightview Landscape Services, Inc.
  27001 Agoura Rd Ste 350
  Agoura Hills CA 91301
  818 223-8500

(P-399)
BRIGHTVIEW LANDSCAPE SVCS INC
4030 Alvis Ct, Rocklin (95677-4011)
PHONE.................................916 415-1004
EMP: 120
SALES (corp-wide): 2.3B **Publicly Held**
WEB: www.brightview.com
SIC: 0781 Landscape services
HQ: Brightview Landscape Services, Inc.
  27001 Agoura Rd Ste 350
  Agoura Hills CA 91301
  818 223-8500

(P-400)
BRIGHTVIEW LANDSCAPE SVCS INC
4677 Pacheco Blvd, Martinez (94553-3625)
PHONE.................................925 957-8831
Martin Becker, *Manager*
EMP: 120
SALES (corp-wide): 2.3B **Publicly Held**
WEB: www.brightview.com
SIC: 0781 Landscape services
HQ: Brightview Landscape Services, Inc.
  27001 Agoura Rd Ste 350
  Agoura Hills CA 91301
  818 223-8500

(P-401)
BRIGHTVIEW LANDSCAPE SVCS INC
4055 Bohannon Dr, Menlo Park (94025-1004)
PHONE.................................650 289-9324
Kyle G Sager, *Branch Mgr*
Ponciano Carmona, *Accounts Mgr*
EMP: 120
SQ FT: 3,000
SALES (corp-wide): 2.3B **Publicly Held**
WEB: www.brightview.com
SIC: 0781 Landscape services
HQ: Brightview Landscape Services, Inc.
  27001 Agoura Rd Ste 350
  Agoura Hills CA 91301
  818 223-8500

(P-402)
BRIGHTVIEW LANDSCAPE SVCS INC
5779 Preston Ave, Livermore (94551-9521)
PHONE.................................925 243-0288
EMP: 120
SALES (corp-wide): 2.3B **Publicly Held**
WEB: www.brightview.com
SIC: 0781 Landscape services
HQ: Brightview Landscape Services, Inc.
  27001 Agoura Rd Ste 350
  Agoura Hills CA 91301
  818 223-8500

(P-403)
BRIGHTVIEW LANDSCAPE SVCS INC
825 Mabury Rd, San Jose (95133-1024)
PHONE.................................408 453-5904
Nada Duna, *Manager*
Jeffrey Hillman, *Manager*
EMP: 120
SALES (corp-wide): 2.3B **Publicly Held**
WEB: www.brightview.com
SIC: 0781 0782 Landscape services; lawn & garden services
HQ: Brightview Landscape Services, Inc.
  27001 Agoura Rd Ste 350
  Agoura Hills CA 91301
  818 223-8500

(P-404)
BRIGHTVIEW LANDSCAPE SVCS INC
5745 Alder Ave, Sacramento (95828-1107)
PHONE.................................916 381-2800
John Bianco, *Manager*
Eric McClenahan, *Branch Mgr*
EMP: 120
SALES (corp-wide): 2.3B **Publicly Held**
WEB: www.brightview.com
SIC: 0781 Landscape services
HQ: Brightview Landscape Services, Inc.
  27001 Agoura Rd Ste 350
  Agoura Hills CA 91301
  818 223-8500

(P-405)
BRIGHTVIEW LANDSCAPE SVCS INC
7039 Commerce Cir Ste B, Pleasanton (94588-8006)
PHONE.................................925 924-8900
Doug Lape, *Manager*
Dave Kratt, *Project Mgr*
Marcos Manzano, *Production*
Daniel Sanchez, *Production*
Cesar Pardo, *Accounts Mgr*
EMP: 120
SALES (corp-wide): 2.3B **Publicly Held**
WEB: www.brightview.com
SIC: 0781 0782 Landscape services; lawn & garden services
HQ: Brightview Landscape Services, Inc.
  27001 Agoura Rd Ste 350
  Agoura Hills CA 91301
  818 223-8500

0781 - Landscape Counseling & Planning County (P-406)

PRODUCTS & SERVICES SECTION

(P-406)
BRIGHTVIEW TREE COMPANY
28915 E Funck Rd, Farmington (95230-9567)
PHONE...................209 886-5511
Gina Mortenson, *Executive*
EMP: 95
SQ FT: 784 Privately Held
WEB: www.brightview.com
SIC: 0781 Landscape services
HQ: Brightview Tree Company
24151 Ventura Blvd # 108
Calabasas CA 91302
818 223-8500

(P-407)
CLEARY BROS LANDSCAPE INC
4115 Blackhawk Plaza Cir, Danville (94506-4901)
P.O. Box B (94526)
PHONE...................925 838-2551
Martin Cleary, *Manager*
Karine Stuimer, *Maintence Staff*
David Kent, *Manager*
EMP: 155 Privately Held
WEB: www.brightview.com
SIC: 0781 0782 Landscape services; landscape counseling services; landscape architects; lawn & garden services
PA: Cleary Bros. Landscape, Inc.
4931 Pacheco Blvd
Martinez CA 94553

(P-408)
COAST LM INC (PA)
Also Called: Coast Landscape Management
4100 Paoli Loop Rd, American Canyon (94949-9725)
PHONE...................707 251-8872
Kelly Solomon, *CEO*
Robert Solomon, *Vice Pres*
Louren Kotow, *Area Mgr*
Larry WEI, *Branch Mgr*
Jamie Aranda, *Admin Asst*
EMP: 147 EST: 2005
SALES (est): 12MM Privately Held
WEB: www.brightview.com
SIC: 0781 Landscape services

(P-409)
COMET BUILDING MAINTENANCE INC
21 Commercial Blvd Ste 12, Novato (94949-6109)
P.O. Box 2163, San Rafael (94912-2163)
PHONE...................415 382-1150
Richard J Brasile, *CEO*
EMP: 70 EST: 1983
SQ FT: 1,800
SALES (est): 6.2MM Privately Held
WEB: www.cometps.com
SIC: 0781 7349 Landscape services; janitorial service, contract basis

(P-410)
CYNTHIA DUNLAP DUTRA
Also Called: Dutra's Dreamscape
5030 E Peach Ave, Manteca (95337-8543)
PHONE...................209 456-1531
Cynthia D Dutra, *Owner*
David M Dutra, *Manager*
EMP: 37 EST: 2001
SQ FT: 2,200
SALES (est): 1.6MM Privately Held
SIC: 0781 Landscape services

(P-411)
DAVID L GATES & ASSOCIATES INC
Also Called: Gates, David L & Associates
1655 N Main St Ste 365, Walnut Creek (94596-4641)
PHONE...................925 736-8176
David L Gates, *President*
Linda Gates, *Vice Pres*
BJ Jesse, *Executive Asst*
David Flack, *Software Dev*
Ana Dominguez, *Corp Comm Staff*
EMP: 68 EST: 1976
SALES (est): 8.2MM Privately Held
WEB: www.dgates.com
SIC: 0781 8712 0782 Landscape architects; architectural services; lawn & garden services

(P-412)
DEL CONTES LANDSCAPING INC
41900 Boscell Rd, Fremont (94538-3196)
PHONE...................510 353-6030
Tom Del Conte, *CEO*
Amy Pacheco, *CFO*
Mario Camacho, *Division Mgr*
John Soriano, *Facilities Mgr*
Ricardo Magana, *Manager*
EMP: 100 EST: 1972
SQ FT: 960
SALES (est): 12.2MM Privately Held
WEB: www.dclandscaping.com
SIC: 0781 Landscape services

(P-413)
ELS INVESTMENTS
Also Called: Environmental Ldscp Solutions
2701 Citrus Rd Ste A, Rancho Cordova (95742-6314)
PHONE...................916 388-0308
Darryl Alan Thompson Jr, *President*
Derek Broughton, *Vice Pres*
Shawna Thompson, *Vice Pres*
EMP: 110 EST: 2008
SALES (est): 16MM Privately Held
WEB: www.els-green.com
SIC: 0781 1771 Landscape services; concrete work

(P-414)
EMERALD LANDSCAPE COMPANY INC (HQ)
2265 Research Dr, Livermore (94550-3847)
PHONE...................925 449-4743
Stephen Jacobson, *President*
Juan Mata, *Area Mgr*
Marco Cisneros, *Opers Mgr*
EMP: 48 EST: 2001
SALES (est): 5.8MM
SALES (corp-wide): 2.3B Publicly Held
WEB: www.emeraldlandscapeco.com
SIC: 0781 Landscape services
PA: Brightview Holdings, Inc.
980 Jolly Rd Ste 300
Blue Bell PA 19422
484 567-7204

(P-415)
FRANK CARSON LDSCP & MAINT INC
Also Called: Carson Landscape Industries
9530 Elder Creek Rd, Sacramento (95829-9306)
PHONE...................916 856-5400
Frank M Carson, *CEO*
Kathy Pipis, *Admin Sec*
EMP: 200 EST: 1975
SQ FT: 36,000
SALES (est): 15.9MM Privately Held
WEB: www.carson1975.com
SIC: 0781 Landscape services

(P-416)
GACHINA LANDSCAPE MGT INC
1130 Obrien Dr, Menlo Park (94025-1411)
PHONE...................650 853-0400
Harumi Jacl Gachina, *CEO*
William Cruz, *Branch Mgr*
Lauren Galanes, *Branch Mgr*
Tyler Stocking, *Branch Mgr*
Sylvia Espinoza, *Administration*
EMP: 269 EST: 1988
SQ FT: 12,000
SALES (est): 22.6MM Privately Held
WEB: www.gachina.com
SIC: 0781 Landscape services

(P-417)
GOTHIC LANDSCAPING INC
29240 Pacific St, Hayward (94544-6016)
PHONE...................661 857-9020
EMP: 55
SALES (corp-wide): 51.6MM Privately Held
WEB: www.gothiclandscape.com
SIC: 0781 Landscape services
PA: Gothic Landscaping, Inc.
27413 Tourney Rd
Santa Clarita CA 91355
661 678-1400

(P-418)
GUZZARDO AND ASSOCIATES INC
836 Montgomery St, San Francisco (94133-5111)
PHONE...................510 923-1677
Gary Laymon, *President*
Paul Lettieri, *Vice Pres*
James Winstead, *Sr Associate*
EMP: 39 EST: 1960
SQ FT: 5,000
SALES (est): 3.5MM Privately Held
WEB: www.tgp-inc.com
SIC: 0781 Landscape architects

(P-419)
HART HOWERTON LTD (PA)
1 Union St Fl 3, San Francisco (94111-1223)
PHONE...................415 439-2200
Dave Howerton, *CEO*
Eron Ashley, *Partner*
Hart Howerton, *Bd of Directors*
Paul D Milton, *Bd of Directors*
Anne Haley Howerton, *Admin Sec*
EMP: 90 EST: 1982
SQ FT: 20,000
SALES (est): 13.2MM Privately Held
WEB: www.harthowerton.com
SIC: 0781 8712 Landscape architects; architectural services

(P-420)
HEAVENLY CONSTRUCTION INC
Also Called: Heavenly Greens
370 Umbarger Rd Ste A, San Jose (95111-2070)
PHONE...................408 723-4954
Daniel Theis, *President*
Kevin Cox, *Manager*
EMP: 73 EST: 2003
SQ FT: 75,000
SALES (est): 12.5MM Privately Held
WEB: www.heavenlygreens.com
SIC: 0781 Landscape services

(P-421)
HEMINGTON LANDSCAPE SVCS INC
4170 Business Dr, Cameron Park (95682-7230)
P.O. Box 1999, Shingle Springs (95682-1999)
PHONE...................530 677-9290
Mark E Hemington, *President*
Jill Hemington, *Corp Secy*
Marcus Hemington, *Vice Pres*
EMP: 100 EST: 1983
SALES (est): 7.3MM Privately Held
WEB: www.hemington.com
SIC: 0781 Landscape services

(P-422)
K & D LANDSCAPING INC
62-C Hngar Way Wtsonville, Watsonville (95076)
P.O. Box 2187, Freedom (95019-2187)
PHONE...................831 728-4018
Kendall White, *Owner*
Dawn White, *Co-Owner*
Kelsie White, *Vice Pres*
Nadene Snapp, *Finance*
Shane White, *Maintence Staff*
EMP: 57 EST: 1986
SALES (est): 5.8MM Privately Held
WEB: www.kndlandscaping.com
SIC: 0781 1629 Landscape services; irrigation system construction

(P-423)
LANDSCAPE & TREE COMPANY INC (HQ)
9350 Viking Pl, Roseville (95747-9713)
PHONE...................916 246-9987
Chris Huppe, *President*
Gina Huppe, *Admin Sec*
EMP: 68 EST: 1990
SQ FT: 215,000
SALES (est): 29.5MM
SALES (corp-wide): 49MM Privately Held
WEB: www.landscapetreeco.com
SIC: 0781 0782 Horticulture services; lawn & garden services
PA: Jensen Corporate Holdings, Inc.
1250 Ames Ave Ste 104
Milpitas CA 95035
408 446-1118

(P-424)
MANIGLIA LANDSCAPE INC
1655 Berryessa Rd Ste A, San Jose (95133-1082)
PHONE...................408 487-9620
Barry Cohen, *CEO*
Todd Bradrick, *Vice Pres*
Leo Maniglia, *Vice Pres*
EMP: 40 EST: 1974
SQ FT: 5,000
SALES (est): 3.1MM Privately Held
WEB: www.maniglialandscape.com
SIC: 0781 Landscape services

(P-425)
MEDALLION LANDSCAPE MGT INC (PA)
10 San Bruno Ave, Morgan Hill (95037-9214)
P.O. Box 1768 (95038-1768)
PHONE...................408 782-7500
John Gates, *CEO*
Joyce Dawson, *President*
Ildefonso Fonsie Bettencourt, *COO*
Robert Rosenberg, *CFO*
Tim Fitzgerald, *Branch Mgr*
EMP: 65 EST: 1995
SALES (est): 15.3MM Privately Held
WEB: www.mlmi.com
SIC: 0781 Landscape counseling services; landscape planning services

(P-426)
MONUMENT CONSTRUCTION INC
Also Called: Techcon
16200 Vineyard Blvd # 100, Morgan Hill (95037-7164)
PHONE...................408 778-1350
Paul Maxwell Swing, *President*
Diane Swing, *CFO*
Jackson Derler, *Exec VP*
Christine Ronayne, *Project Engr*
EMP: 90 EST: 2000
SQ FT: 6,000
SALES (est): 10.6MM Privately Held
WEB: www.monumentpoolsinc.com
SIC: 0781 Landscape services

(P-427)
NEW PATH LANDSCAPE SVCS INC
Also Called: Allied Landscape Services
16170 Vineyard Blvd # 180, Morgan Hill (95037-5498)
PHONE...................408 310-8476
Filiberto Fonseca, *President*
Gino Borello, *Vice Pres*
EMP: 65 EST: 2005
SALES (est): 8.8MM Privately Held
SIC: 0781 Landscape services

(P-428)
NORTH LANDSCAPING INC
Also Called: Creative Environments
1550 Gravenstein Hwy S, Sebastopol (95472-4835)
PHONE...................707 827-7980
Harry North, *President*
Deborah North, *Treasurer*
EMP: 43 EST: 1982
SQ FT: 1,500
SALES (est): 1.8MM Privately Held
WEB: www.creativeenvironments.biz
SIC: 0781 Landscape services

(P-429)
OPTIMA LDSCP SACRAMENTO INC
Also Called: Landscape Maintenance Services
9350 Eagle Springs Pl, Roseville (95767-6323)
PHONE...................916 541-5796

PRODUCTS & SERVICES SECTION

0782 - Lawn & Garden Svcs County (P-454)

Fidencio Rivera, *President*
Daniel Rivera, *Vice Pres*
Blanca Mendoza, *Office Mgr*
EMP: 40 **EST:** 2008
SQ FT: 500
SALES (est): 3.5MM **Privately Held**
WEB: www.optimalandscape.com
SIC: 0781 0782 Landscape services; garden maintenance services; highway lawn & garden maintenance services

(P-430)
OXBOW LANDSCAPE CONTRS INC
Also Called: Oxbow Pool & Landscape Contrs
2400 Oak St A, NAPA (94559-2229)
PHONE 707 339-6001
Chuck Haeuser, *President*
EMP: 36 **EST:** 2016
SALES (est): 2.7MM **Privately Held**
SIC: 0781 Landscape services

(P-431)
PACHECO BROTHERS GARDENING INC (PA)
20973 Cabot Blvd, Hayward (94545-1155)
PHONE 510 732-6330
George A Pacheco Jr, *CEO*
Lynn Pacheco, *Corp Secy*
Gary Pacheco, *Vice Pres*
EMP: 40 **EST:** 1979
SQ FT: 12,000
SALES (est): 6.7MM **Privately Held**
WEB: www.pachecobrothers.com
SIC: 0781 0782 Landscape services; landscape contractors

(P-432)
PACIFIC COAST LDSCP MGT INC
3960 Holway Dr, Byron (94514-1001)
P.O. Box 757 (94514-0757)
PHONE 925 513-2310
Alvaro Beltran, *President*
EMP: 60 **EST:** 1997
SALES (est): 7.5MM **Privately Held**
WEB: www.pacificcoastlandscape.net
SIC: 0781 0782 Landscape services; lawn & garden services; garden services; landscape contractors

(P-433)
PACIFIC LANDSCAPES INC (PA)
2833 Old Gravenstein Hwy, Sebastopol (95472-5209)
P.O. Box 481 (95473-0481)
PHONE 707 829-8064
David K Penry, *President*
Darryl G Orr, *Vice Pres*
EMP: 49 **EST:** 2000
SQ FT: 63,000
SALES (est): 4.1MM **Privately Held**
WEB: www.pacificlandscapes.com
SIC: 0781 Landscape services

(P-434)
PARKER LANDSCAPE DEV INC
6011 Franklin Blvd, Sacramento (95824-2517)
PHONE 916 383-4071
Timothy J Parker, *President*
Conney Parker, *Admin Sec*
Dan Rimmele, *Project Mgr*
EMP: 35 **EST:** 2005
SALES (est): 3.5MM **Privately Held**
WEB: www.parkerland.biz
SIC: 0781 Landscape services

(P-435)
PETALON LANDSCAPE MGT INC
1766 Rogers Ave, San Jose (95112-1109)
PHONE 408 453-3998
Rudy Sotelo, *CEO*
John Linn, *President*
Noreen Prado, *Office Mgr*
Brenda Monge, *Admin Asst*
Chris Hunger, *Accounts Mgr*
EMP: 65 **EST:** 2001
SQ FT: 5,000
SALES (est): 6.2MM **Privately Held**
WEB: www.petalon.com
SIC: 0781 Landscape services

(P-436)
PETER WLKER PRTNERS LDSCP ARCH
Also Called: Peter Walker & Partners
739 Allston Way, Berkeley (94710-2229)
PHONE 510 849-9494
Peter Walker, *Ch of Bd*
Douglas Findlay, *President*
Jeff Ulm, *CFO*
Monica Serve, *Administration*
Janet Beagle, *Associate*
EMP: 68 **EST:** 1984
SQ FT: 5,400
SALES (est): 5.7MM **Privately Held**
WEB: www.pwpla.com
SIC: 0781 Landscape architects

(P-437)
PROFESSNAL LDSCP SOLUTIONS INC
6108 27th St Ste C, Sacramento (95822-3711)
PHONE 916 424-3815
Michael E Parker, *President*
Chad Bush, *Vice Pres*
Penny Parker, *Admin Sec*
EMP: 36 **EST:** 2005
SQ FT: 11,000
SALES (est): 1.1MM **Privately Held**
WEB: www.prolandscapesolutions.com
SIC: 0781 Landscape services

(P-438)
SEQUOIA LANDSCAPE MGT INC
1071 N 13th St, San Jose (95112-2903)
PHONE 408 277-6390
George H Kaiser, *President*
EMP: 48 **EST:** 1988
SQ FT: 25,000
SALES (est): 2.8MM **Privately Held**
WEB: www.sequoialandscape.com
SIC: 0781 Landscape services

(P-439)
SERPICO LANDSCAPING INC
1764 National Ave, Hayward (94545-1722)
PHONE 510 293-0341
Sharon Serpico Hanson, *CEO*
Richard Hanson, *Admin Sec*
Mikaela Tran, *Relations*
EMP: 50 **EST:** 1988
SQ FT: 1,000
SALES (est): 6.8MM **Privately Held**
WEB: www.serpicolandscaping.com
SIC: 0781 Landscape services

(P-440)
SHOOTER & BUTTS INC
3768 Old Santa Rita Rd, Pleasanton (94588-3457)
PHONE 925 460-5155
James E Butts, *President*
Israel Deluna, *Project Mgr*
Richard Kusaba, *Project Mgr*
Megan Layman, *Asst Controller*
Jaime Hernandez, *Foreman/Supr*
EMP: 50 **EST:** 1977
SQ FT: 1,800
SALES (est): 9.1MM **Privately Held**
WEB: www.shooterandbutts.com
SIC: 0781 Landscape services

(P-441)
SIERRA LANDSCAPE & MAINT INC
546 Hickory St, Chico (95928-4811)
PHONE 530 895-0263
Catherine S Gurney, *Principal*
Maria Gomez, *Office Mgr*
Ashley Daniels, *Admin Asst*
Syndi Winter, *Administration*
EMP: 52 **EST:** 1982
SQ FT: 8,000
SALES (est): 4MM **Privately Held**
WEB: www.sierralm.com
SIC: 0781 Landscape services

(P-442)
SWA GROUP (PA)
2200 Bridgeway, Sausalito (94965-1750)
P.O. Box 5904 (94966-5904)
PHONE 415 332-5100
Gerdo Aquino, *CEO*
Kevin Shanley, *President*
John Reynolds, *Info Tech Dir*
James Vick, *Project Mgr*
Jeani Miles, *Engineer*
EMP: 60 **EST:** 1957
SQ FT: 12,000
SALES (est): 34.1MM **Privately Held**
WEB: www.swagroup.com
SIC: 0781 Landscape architects

(P-443)
VAN WINDEN LANDSCAPING INC
3101 California Blvd, NAPA (94558-3378)
PHONE 707 224-1367
Adrian J Van Winden, *President*
James Van Winden, *Vice Pres*
EMP: 37 **EST:** 1961
SQ FT: 5,000
SALES (est): 1.1MM **Privately Held**
WEB: www.vanwindenlandscaping.com
SIC: 0781 5087 Landscape architects; sprinkler systems

(P-444)
YARD & GARDEN LDSCP MAINT INC
802 N Cluff Ave, Lodi (95240-0707)
P.O. Box 1323 (95241-1323)
PHONE 209 369-9071
Anthony Cortez, *President*
Christine Cortez, *Principal*
EMP: 25 **EST:** 1990
SALES (est): 1.7MM **Privately Held**
WEB: www.yardandgardenlandscape.com
SIC: 0781 3271 0782 Landscape planning services; blocks, concrete: landscape or retaining wall; landscape contractors

0782 Lawn & Garden Svcs

(P-445)
ALL COMMERCIAL LANDSCAPE SVC
5213 E Pine Ave, Fresno (93727-2110)
PHONE 559 453-1670
Jack Murray, *President*
Carol Osborn, *Corp Secy*
Tom Delny, *Vice Pres*
EMP: 50 **EST:** 1992
SQ FT: 22,500
SALES (est): 5.8MM
SALES (corp-wide): 2.3B **Publicly Held**
WEB: www.brightview.com
SIC: 0782 Landscape contractors; lawn services
PA: Brightview Holdings, Inc.
980 Jolly Rd Ste 300
Blue Bell PA 19422
484 567-7204

(P-446)
ARAGON COMMERCIAL LDSCPG INC
2305 S Vasco Rd, Livermore (94550-9681)
PHONE 408 998-0600
Scott Tabler, *President*
Julie Tabler, *Office Mgr*
Sophie Martinez, *Controller*
EMP: 135 **EST:** 1974
SQ FT: 7,000
SALES (est): 7.9MM **Privately Held**
WEB: www.aragonlandscaping.com
SIC: 0782 Landscape contractors; landscape services

(P-447)
ARREOLAS COMPLETE LDSCP SVC
Also Called: Arreolas Complete Ldscp Svc
8671 Morrison Creek Dr, Sacramento (95828-1862)
PHONE 916 387-6777
Humberto Arreola, *Owner*
EMP: 52 **EST:** 1987
SQ FT: 10,000
SALES (est): 2.6MM **Privately Held**
WEB: www.arreolaslandscape.com
SIC: 0782 Landscape contractors

(P-448)
BIANCO LANDSCAPE MANAGEMENT
1524 Vista Ridge Way, Roseville (95661-4018)
PHONE 916 521-1314
John L Bianco III, *President*
EMP: 61 **EST:** 2005
SQ FT: 2,000
SALES (est): 1MM **Privately Held**
WEB: www.biancolandscape.com
SIC: 0782 Landscape contractors

(P-449)
BLOSSOM VALLEY CNSTR INC
1125 Mabury Rd, San Jose (95133-1029)
P.O. Box 611537 (95161-1537)
PHONE 408 993-0766
Mark Collishaw, *President*
Robert Jimenez, *CEO*
EMP: 60
SQ FT: 5,000
SALES (est): 5MM **Privately Held**
SIC: 0782 Landscape contractors

(P-450)
CARROLLCO INC
3104 N Miami Ave, Fresno (93727-8069)
P.O. Box 13039 (93794-3039)
PHONE 559 396-3939
Benjamin Carroll, *CEO*
Scott McHale, *Analyst*
Dawn Chen, *Director*
Elizabeth Hering, *Director*
Sean Connelly, *Manager*
EMP: 50
SQ FT: 5,000
SALES (est): 10.7MM **Privately Held**
WEB: www.carrollco.net
SIC: 0782 1711 1521 Warm air heating & air conditioning contractor; single-family home remodeling, additions & repairs

(P-451)
CHAMPAGNE LANDSCAPE NURS INC
3233 N Cornelia Ave, Fresno (93722-4606)
P.O. Box 9755 (93794-9755)
PHONE 559 277-8188
Robert Champagne, *President*
Gail Champagne, *Treasurer*
Robert N Champagne, *Vice Pres*
Courtney Woody, *Admin Sec*
EMP: 87 **EST:** 1971
SALES (est): 5.3MM **Privately Held**
WEB: www.champagnelandscaping.com
SIC: 0782 0781 Garden maintenance services; landscape architects

(P-452)
CIMAS LANDSCAPE & MAINT INC
3181 Luyung Dr Ste B, Rancho Cordova (95742-6881)
PHONE 916 635-2462
Frank M Cima, *President*
Tony Cima, *Vice Pres*
EMP: 45 **EST:** 1976
SALES (est): 5.1MM **Privately Held**
SIC: 0782 Landscape contractors

(P-453)
CITY II ENTERPRISES INC
Also Called: Flora Terra Landscape MGT
845 Earle Ave, San Jose (95126-3404)
PHONE 408 275-1200
Gene E Ebertowski, *President*
Kimberly Garcia, *Admin Sec*
EMP: 50 **EST:** 1997
SQ FT: 40,000
SALES (est): 3.4MM **Privately Held**
SIC: 0782 Landscape contractors

(P-454)
COLONY LANDSCAPE & MAINT INC
4911 Spreckles Ave, Alviso (95002)
P.O. Box 940 (95002-0940)
PHONE 408 941-1090
Edward Ott, *President*
Brian Hudson, *Manager*
▲ **EMP:** 45 **EST:** 1990
SQ FT: 1,000

0782 - Lawn & Garden Svcs County (P-455)

SALES (est): 5.7MM **Privately Held**
WEB: www.colonylandscape.com
SIC: **0782** Landscape contractors

(P-455)
COMMON GROUND LDSCP MGT INC
1127 Mockingbird Ct, San Jose (95120-3435)
PHONE..............................408 278-9807
William Jauch, *President*
Tris Jauch, *Treasurer*
EMP: 50 EST: 2001
SALES (est): 2MM **Privately Held**
WEB: www.commongroundlandscapeinc.com
SIC: **0782** Landscape contractors

(P-456)
DEAN MOON
Also Called: Nature Care Landscape Inds
9373 Elder Creek Rd, Sacramento (95829-9339)
P.O. Box 293480 (95829-3480)
PHONE..............................916 387-1339
Dean Moon, *Owner*
Caroline Smith, *Office Mgr*
EMP: 45 EST: 1977
SQ FT: 1,417
SALES (est): 3MM **Privately Held**
SIC: **0782** 0781 Landscape contractors; lawn services; landscape planning services

(P-457)
DECKER LANDSCAPING INC
13265 Bill Francis Dr, Auburn (95603-9022)
PHONE..............................916 652-1780
Christopher Decker, *President*
Dan McElvain, *COO*
Dan McElvin, *CFO*
Tom Decker, *Vice Pres*
Chris Mitchell, *Project Mgr*
EMP: 75 EST: 1993
SQ FT: 2,500
SALES (est): 10.3MM **Privately Held**
WEB: www.deckerlandscaping.com
SIC: **0782** 0781 Landscape contractors; landscape architects

(P-458)
DIABLO LANDSCAPE INC
1655 Berryessa Rd, San Jose (95133-1082)
PHONE..............................408 487-9620
Fax: 408 487-9621
EMP: 80
SQ FT: 38,000
SALES (est): 6.9MM
SALES (corp-wide): 32.2MM **Privately Held**
WEB: www.diablolandscape.com
SIC: **0782** Lawn And Garden Services
PA: The Celtis Group Inc
    1655 Berryessa Rd Ste A
    San Jose CA
    408 487-9620

(P-459)
DOMINGUEZ LANDSCAPE SVCS INC
8376 Rovana Cir, Sacramento (95828-2527)
P.O. Box 292727 (95829-2727)
PHONE..............................916 381-8855
Robert Dominguez, *President*
Bonnie J Dominguez, *Vice Pres*
EMP: 78 EST: 1980
SQ FT: 7,200
SALES (est): 5.1MM **Privately Held**
SIC: **0782** Landscape contractors

(P-460)
DULEYS LANDSCAPE INC
28876 Topaz Rd, Tollhouse (93667-9712)
P.O. Box 390, Prather (93651-0390)
PHONE..............................559 855-5090
Robert Duley, *President*
Debbie Duley, *Vice Pres*
EMP: 50 EST: 1991
SALES (est): 4.9MM **Privately Held**
SIC: **0782** Landscape contractors

(P-461)
ELITE LANDSCAPING INC
2972 Larkin Ave, Clovis (93612-3986)
PHONE..............................559 292-7760
Guy Stockbridge, *President*
Jill Stockbridge, *CFO*
EMP: 150 EST: 1987
SQ FT: 20,000
SALES (est): 15MM **Privately Held**
WEB: www.eliteteamoffices.com
SIC: **0782** Landscape contractors

(P-462)
ENGLISH GARDEN CARE INC
3294 Luyung Dr, Rancho Cordova (95742-6846)
PHONE..............................916 635-4275
Robert Munn, *President*
Jen Briggs, *Office Mgr*
Jaime Castillo, *Accounts Mgr*
EMP: 48 EST: 2011
SALES (est): 3.4MM **Privately Held**
WEB: www.englishgardencare.com
SIC: **0782** Landscape contractors

(P-463)
GARDELLE CNSTR & LDSCP INC
2625 Sinclair Ave, Concord (94519-2618)
PHONE..............................925 680-6425
Steve Gardelle, *President*
Illiana Fratus, *Office Mgr*
EMP: 35 EST: 1989
SQ FT: 750
SALES (est): 2.6MM **Privately Held**
WEB: www.gardelle.com
SIC: **0782** Landscape contractors

(P-464)
GARDENERS GUILD INC
2780 Goodrick Ave, Richmond (94801-1110)
PHONE..............................415 457-0400
Kevin Davis, *President*
Mike Davidson, *Vice Pres*
Dean Aquila, *Project Mgr*
Ginny Kuhel, *Director*
Paul Swanson, *Director*
EMP: 140 EST: 1972
SQ FT: 25,000
SALES (est): 13.5MM **Privately Held**
WEB: www.gardenersguild.com
SIC: **0782** Landscape contractors; lawn services; garden services

(P-465)
GARDENWORKS INC
20325 Geyserville Ave, Geyserville (95441-9533)
P.O. Box 326, Healdsburg (95448-0326)
PHONE..............................707 857-2050
Jay Tripathi, *President*
Peter Estournes, *Exec VP*
EMP: 54 EST: 1977
SQ FT: 4,500
SALES (est): 1.5MM **Privately Held**
WEB: www.gardenworks-inc.com
SIC: **0782** Landscape contractors

(P-466)
GATEWAY LANDSCAPE CNSTR INC
6735 Sierra Ct Ste A, Dublin (94568-2656)
PHONE..............................925 875-0000
Corey Pontrelli, *President*
David J Garcia, *Vice Pres*
Hali Pontrelli, *Purchasing*
EMP: 75 EST: 1984
SQ FT: 3,000
SALES (est): 5.1MM **Privately Held**
WEB: www.gatewaylci.com
SIC: **0782** 1711 Landscape contractors; irrigation sprinkler system installation

(P-467)
GOODLAND LANDSCAPE CNSTR INC
2455 Naglee Rd 402, Tracy (95304-7324)
PHONE..............................209 835-9956
Thomas Robert Wortham, *CEO*
Dena Wortham, *President*
EMP: 40 EST: 1995
SQ FT: 1,200
SALES (est): 4.8MM **Privately Held**
WEB: www.goodlandca.com
SIC: **0782** Landscape contractors

(P-468)
GROWING COMPANY INC
4 Wayne Ct Ste 3, Sacramento (95829-1305)
PHONE..............................916 379-9088
Bruno Sandoval, *President*
Jordan Paulsen, *Vice Pres*
Anne Sandoval, *Vice Pres*
Gualberto Cardenas, *Area Spvr*
Modesto Gonzalez, *Area Spvr*
EMP: 100 EST: 1987
SQ FT: 10,000
SALES (est): 10.8MM **Privately Held**
WEB: www.thegrowingcompany.com
SIC: **0782** Landscape contractors; garden maintenance services

(P-469)
H&GBYGISELLECO
Also Called: Laborer
626 Mssion Bay Blvd N Apt, San Francisco (94158)
PHONE..............................415 829-3867
Alston Sheppard Sr, *Owner*
EMP: 15 EST: 2019
SALES (est): 251.9K **Privately Held**
SIC: **0782** 7359 0781 1629 Landscape contractors; work zone traffic equipment (flags, cones, barrels, etc.); landscape architects; land clearing contractor; garden, patio, walkway & yard lighting fixtures: electric; painting & paper hanging

(P-470)
IKES LANDSCAPING & MAINTENANCE
2700 Tiber Ave, Davis (95616-2958)
PHONE..............................530 758-1698
Eric Aichwalder, *President*
Don Kearney, *Vice Pres*
Aletha Aichwalder, *Admin Sec*
EMP: 80 EST: 1974
SQ FT: 2,000
SALES (est): 4.8MM **Privately Held**
SIC: **0782** 5992 Landscape contractors; lawn care services; plants, potted

(P-471)
J REDFERN INC
Also Called: Golden State Landscaping
164 N L St, Livermore (94551-2118)
P.O. Box 2091 (94551-2091)
PHONE..............................925 371-3300
John E Redfern, *President*
Rashelle Redfern, *Vice Pres*
EMP: 71 EST: 1979
SALES (est): 5MM **Privately Held**
WEB: www.goldenstateinc.biz
SIC: **0782** Landscape contractors

(P-472)
JENSEN CORP LANDSCAPE CONTR
1983 Concourse Dr, San Jose (95131-1708)
PHONE..............................408 446-4811
John Vlay, *CEO*
Shamina Edwards, *Admin Sec*
EMP: 150
SALES (est): 10MM **Privately Held**
WEB: www.jensencorp.com
SIC: **0782** 1521 Landscape contractors; single-family housing construction

(P-473)
JENSEN CORPORATE HOLDINGS INC (PA)
1250 Ames Ave Ste 104, Milpitas (95035-6362)
PHONE..............................408 446-1118
John Vlay, *CEO*
Quang Trinh, *CFO*
Donald Defever, *Division Pres*
Glenn Berry, *Vice Pres*
Kirk Brown, *Vice Pres*
EMP: 117 EST: 1969
SQ FT: 13,000
SALES (est): 49MM **Privately Held**
WEB: www.jensencorp.com
SIC: **0782** Landscape contractors

(P-474)
JENSEN LANDSCAPE SERVICES INC
Also Called: Jensen Corp Landscape Contrs
1983 Concourse Dr, San Jose (95131-1708)
PHONE..............................408 446-1118
John Vlay, *CEO*
Anthony Whalls, *President*
Paul Johnson, *CFO*
Glenn Berry, *Vice Pres*
Darren Nosseck, *Regional Mgr*
EMP: 180 EST: 1988
SALES (est): 15.1MM
SALES (corp-wide): 49MM **Privately Held**
WEB: www.jensencorp.com
SIC: **0782** Landscape contractors
PA: Jensen Corporate Holdings, Inc.
    1250 Ames Ave Ste 104
    Milpitas CA 95035
    408 446-1118

(P-475)
JPA LANDSCAPE & CNSTR INC
256 Boeing Ct, Livermore (94551-9258)
P.O. Box 1292, Pleasanton (94566-0129)
PHONE..............................925 960-9602
Ed Morrissey, *President*
Jody Morrissey, *Treasurer*
Deanna Wallace, *Cust Mgr*
EMP: 75 EST: 1995
SQ FT: 9,000
SALES (est): 3.9MM **Privately Held**
WEB: www.jpalandscape.com
SIC: **0782** Landscape contractors

(P-476)
LANDCARE USA LLC
930 Shiloh Rd Bldg 44, Windsor (95492-9659)
PHONE..............................707 836-1460
Scott Hall, *Branch Mgr*
EMP: 52
SALES (corp-wide): 181.5MM **Privately Held**
WEB: www.landcare.com
SIC: **0782** Lawn care services
PA: Landcare Usa L.L.C.
    5295 Westview Dr Ste 100
    Frederick MD 21703
    301 874-3300

(P-477)
LANDCARE USA LLC
Also Called: Trugreen
3213 Fitzgerald Rd, Rancho Cordova (95742-6813)
PHONE..............................916 635-0936
Kevin Arnett, *Branch Mgr*
EMP: 52
SALES (corp-wide): 181.5MM **Privately Held**
WEB: www.landcare.com
SIC: **0782** Lawn care services
PA: Landcare Usa L.L.C.
    5295 Westview Dr Ste 100
    Frederick MD 21703
    301 874-3300

(P-478)
LANDCARE USA LLC
1064 Serpentine Ln Ste A, Pleasanton (94566-4810)
PHONE..............................925 462-2193
Jeff Ahrens, *Branch Mgr*
EMP: 52
SALES (corp-wide): 181.5MM **Privately Held**
WEB: www.landcare.com
SIC: **0782** Lawn care services
PA: Landcare Usa L.L.C.
    5295 Westview Dr Ste 100
    Frederick MD 21703
    301 874-3300

(P-479)
LANDCARE USA LLC
Also Called: Trugreen
85 Old Tully Rd, San Jose (95111-1910)
PHONE..............................408 727-4099
Jeff Kunkel, *Branch Mgr*
EMP: 52

PRODUCTS & SERVICES SECTION

0782 - Lawn & Garden Svcs County (P-505)

SALES (corp-wide): 181.5MM **Privately Held**
WEB: www.landcare.com
SIC: 0782 Lawn care services
PA: Landcare Usa L.L.C.
5295 Westview Dr Ste 100
Frederick MD 21703
301 874-3300

(P-480)
LOAYZAS LDSCPG POOLS SPAS INC
2096 Stone Ave Ste 1, San Jose (95125-1470)
P.O. Box 20608 (95160-0608)
PHONE 408 297-5555
Edmondo Loayza, *President*
Rosa Loayza, *CFO*
EMP: 39 **EST:** 1966
SQ FT: 5,000
SALES (est): 2.8MM **Privately Held**
WEB: www.loayzas.com
SIC: 0782 1799 1521 Landscape contractors; swimming pool construction; new construction, single-family houses

(P-481)
LONE STAR LANDSCAPE INC
1910 E San Martin Ave, San Martin (95046-9688)
P.O. Box 70 (95046-0070)
PHONE 408 682-0100
Robert Samaniego, *President*
Pedro Samaniego, *Manager*
EMP: 35 **EST:** 1978
SALES (est): 2.8MM **Privately Held**
WEB: www.lonestarland.net
SIC: 0782 Landscape contractors

(P-482)
LORAL LANDSCAPING
704 S Amphlett Blvd, San Mateo (94402-1401)
PHONE 650 340-6940
Allan Bergstrom, *President*
EMP: 45 **EST:** 1977
SQ FT: 8,000
SALES (est): 5.1MM **Privately Held**
WEB: www.lorallandscaping.com
SIC: 0782 0783 Garden services; lawn services; ornamental shrub & tree services

(P-483)
MARTIN RAGNO & ASSOCIATES INC
1303 Elmer St, Belmont (94002-4010)
PHONE 650 325-4996
Martin Ragno, *President*
Doug Ross, *Vice Pres*
EMP: 40 **EST:** 1980
SALES (est): 2.7MM **Privately Held**
SIC: 0782 1521 Landscape contractors; new construction, single-family houses

(P-484)
MARTINA LANDSCAPE INC
811 Camden Ave, Campbell (95008-4103)
PHONE 408 871-8800
Joe Martina, *President*
Robert Dobbins, *Vice Pres*
EMP: 80 **EST:** 1947
SQ FT: 2,000
SALES (est): 3.4MM **Privately Held**
WEB: www.martinalandscape.com
SIC: 0782 Landscape contractors

(P-485)
MCENTIRE LANDSCAPING INC
Also Called: Mc Entire Landscaping
4475 Tenaya Ct Ste B, Redding (96003-1486)
P.O. Box 492381 (96049-2381)
PHONE 530 245-4590
James L Mc Entire, *President*
Terry Pasero, *Supervisor*
EMP: 45 **EST:** 1978
SQ FT: 8,000
SALES (est): 3.9MM **Privately Held**
WEB: www.mcentirelandscaping.com
SIC: 0782

(P-486)
MIKE MCCALL LANDSCAPE INC
4749 Clayton Rd, Concord (94521-2936)
PHONE 925 363-8100
Mike McCall, *President*
Mark Tate, *COO*
Tamela Mosca, *CFO*
Mayra Rivas, *Office Mgr*
Cesar Arceo, *Project Mgr*
EMP: 140
SQ FT: 1,000
SALES (est): 14.8MM **Privately Held**
WEB: www.mmlinc.net
SIC: 0782 Landscape contractors

(P-487)
NAGEL LANDSCAPING
Also Called: Dale Road Nursery
5719 Mchenry Ave, Modesto (95356-8827)
PHONE 209 545-1696
Don Owens, *President*
Dale Nagel, *President*
Kimberly Davis, *Division Mgr*
Jeff Azevedo, *Director*
EMP: 44 **EST:** 1972
SQ FT: 2,000
SALES (est): 1.5MM **Privately Held**
WEB: www.nagellandscape.com
SIC: 0782 Landscape contractors

(P-488)
NATURESCAPES LANDSCAPING CORP
560 Newhall Dr, San Jose (95110-1109)
PHONE 408 294-4994
EMP: 35
SALES (est): 744K **Privately Held**
SIC: 0782 Lawn/Garden Services

(P-489)
NEW IMAGE LANDSCAPE COMPANY
3250 Darby Cmn, Fremont (94539-5601)
PHONE 510 226-9191
Brian Takehara, *President*
Irene Briggs, *Treasurer*
Gerardo Roque, *Opers Staff*
Donavan Agrella, *Manager*
Manuel Cabrera, *Manager*
EMP: 55 **EST:** 1996
SQ FT: 4,000
SALES (est): 7MM **Privately Held**
WEB: www.newimagelandscape.com
SIC: 0782 Landscape contractors

(P-490)
NISH-KO INC
713 N Valentine Ave, Fresno (93706-1041)
PHONE 559 275-6653
Konrad Nishikawa, *President*
Dean Nishikawa, *Vice Pres*
Karen Nishikawa, *Admin Sec*
EMP: 35 **EST:** 1989
SALES (est): 1.7MM **Privately Held**
SIC: 0782 Lawn & garden services

(P-491)
NORTH BAY LANDSCAPE MGT INC
444 Payran St, Petaluma (94952-5907)
PHONE 707 762-3850
Jeff Pottorff, *President*
Susan Pottorff, *Treasurer*
Erica Pottorff, *Office Mgr*
Raeme Kennedy, *Assistant*
EMP: 48 **EST:** 1996
SQ FT: 6,000
SALES (est): 4.7MM **Privately Held**
WEB: www.northbaylandscape.com
SIC: 0782 Landscape contractors

(P-492)
NORTHWEST LANDSCAPE MAINT CO
283 Kinney Dr, San Jose (95112-4433)
PHONE 408 298-6489
Warren Nakamura, *President*
Douglas Nakamura, *Corp Secy*
Paul Nakamura, *Vice Pres*
EMP: 42 **EST:** 1973
SQ FT: 4,808
SALES (est): 2.1MM **Privately Held**
WEB: www.northwestlandscape.com
SIC: 0782 Landscape contractors

(P-493)
PARK AVENUE TURF INC
3075 Old Gravenstein Hwy, Sebastopol (95472-5213)
P.O. Box 2198 (95473-2198)
PHONE 707 823-8899
Mike B Strunk, *President*
Marsha Wiedmann, *Controller*
Russ Clarke, *Sales Staff*
Billy Montesclaros, *Sales Staff*
Andy Bidia, *Manager*
EMP: 35 **EST:** 1985
SQ FT: 7,000
SALES (est): 2.5MM **Privately Held**
WEB: www.parkavenueturf.com
SIC: 0782 Lawn care services

(P-494)
PARK WEST LANDSCAPE INC
836 Jury Ct Ste 10, San Jose (95112-2827)
PHONE 925 560-9390
Keith Norman, *Manager*
Rick Jordan, *Maintence Staff*
EMP: 87
SALES (corp-wide): 85MM **Privately Held**
WEB: www.parkwestinc.com
SIC: 0782 Landscape contractors
HQ: Park West Landscape, Inc.
22421 Gilberto Ste A
Rcho Sta Marg CA 92688

(P-495)
PATRICK BAGINSKI
Also Called: Tahoe Outdoor Living
828 Eloise Ave, South Lake Tahoe (96150-6466)
PHONE 530 544-8873
Patrick Baginski, *Owner*
EMP: 35 **EST:** 1979
SQ FT: 320
SALES (est): 2MM **Privately Held**
WEB: www.tahoeoutdoorliving.com
SIC: 0782 Landscape contractors

(P-496)
PERENNIAL LANDSCAPE AND NURS
6891 N Lake Blvd, Tahoe Vista (96148-9803)
P.O. Box 193 (96148-0193)
PHONE 530 546-7383
Timothy McGowan, *President*
Holly McGowan, *Vice Pres*
EMP: 36 **EST:** 1972
SQ FT: 2,500
SALES (est): 1.7MM **Privately Held**
WEB: www.perenniallandscapeandnursery.com
SIC: 0782 0181 Landscape contractors; nursery stock, growing of

(P-497)
PROCIDA LANDSCAPE INC
8465 Specialty Cir, Sacramento (95828-2523)
PHONE 916 387-5296
John Procida Jr, *President*
Juan Garcia, *Opers Mgr*
Steve Detherage, *Opers Staff*
Mirta Aguilar, *Manager*
Seth Taylor, *Accounts Mgr*
EMP: 160 **EST:** 1980
SQ FT: 15,000
SALES (est): 10.2MM **Privately Held**
WEB: www.procidalandscape.com
SIC: 0782 Lawn care services; lawn services; garden planting services

(P-498)
RMT LANDSCAPE CONTRACTORS INC
421 Pendleton Way, Oakland (94621-2122)
PHONE 510 568-3208
Rick Deherrera, *President*
Julie Briggs, *Vice Pres*
Sally Lipska, *Admin Sec*
Lissette Eppler, *Administration*
Michael Laake, *Project Mgr*
EMP: 50 **EST:** 1977
SQ FT: 12,000
SALES (est): 5.7MM **Privately Held**
WEB: www.rmtlandscape.com
SIC: 0782 Landscape contractors

(P-499)
SANSEI GARDENS INC
3250 Darby Cmn, Fremont (94539-5601)
PHONE 510 226-9191
Brian Takehara, *President*
Matthew Dillingham, *Project Mgr*
Aracely Reyes, *Project Mgr*
Elodia Criado, *Manager*
EMP: 110 **EST:** 1973
SQ FT: 3,000
SALES (est): 10.5MM **Privately Held**
WEB: www.sanseigardens.com
SIC: 0782 Landscape contractors

(P-500)
SCAPES INC
12344 San Mateo Rd, Half Moon Bay (94019-7112)
PHONE 650 712-4460
Lane Poms, *President*
Scott Poms, *Vice Pres*
Jackie Nelson, *Marketing Staff*
Jackie Hodgdon, *Manager*
EMP: 35 **EST:** 1985
SQ FT: 9,700
SALES (est): 1.3MM **Privately Held**
WEB: www.scapes.org
SIC: 0782 Landscape contractors

(P-501)
SEVILLE MAINTENANCE INC
Also Called: Seville Landscape Construction
214 Commercial St, Sunnyvale (94085-4508)
PHONE 650 966-1091
Moses Guillardo, *President*
Jacob Guillardo, *Corp Secy*
Amanda Guillardo, *Managing Dir*
EMP: 35 **EST:** 1983
SQ FT: 3,600
SALES (est): 2.4MM **Privately Held**
WEB: www.sevillelandscape.com
SIC: 0782 Landscape contractors

(P-502)
SIERRA VIEW LANDSCAPE INC
Also Called: Restoration Resources
3888 Cincinnati Ave, Rocklin (95765-1312)
PHONE 916 408-2990
Fax: 916 408-2999
EMP: 50
SALES (est): 7MM **Privately Held**
SIC: 0782 Lawn/Garden Services

(P-503)
STEVENSON-SMITH ENTERPRISES
Also Called: Crystal Springs Landscape Co
426 Perrymont Ave, San Jose (95125-1444)
PHONE 408 286-9616
Brian Stevenson-Smith, *President*
Nancy Stevenson-Smith, *Treasurer*
Christine Alves, *Office Spvr*
EMP: 45 **EST:** 1997
SALES (est): 5.1MM **Privately Held**
WEB: www.csland.net
SIC: 0782 Garden maintenance services; lawn care services; landscape contractors

(P-504)
SUMA LANDSCAPING INC
2857 Chapman St, Oakland (94601-2128)
P.O. Box 550, Alameda (94501-9650)
PHONE 415 332-7862
Susan Frank, *President*
Gene Hacker, *Office Mgr*
EMP: 43 **EST:** 1977
SQ FT: 7,500
SALES (est): 5.8MM **Privately Held**
WEB: www.sumalandscaping.com
SIC: 0782 0781 Lawn services; garden maintenance services; landscape services

(P-505)
TREE SCULPTURE GROUP
Also Called: Tarra Landscape
642 Mccormick St, San Leandro (94577-1110)
PHONE 510 562-4000
Craig Lundin, *President*
Cassidy Lundin, *Vice Pres*
Dan Dachauer, *Division Mgr*
Paulette Roddy, *Office Mgr*
EMP: 60 **EST:** 1968

0782 - Lawn & Garden Svcs County (P-506)

PRODUCTS & SERVICES SECTION

SALES (est): 6.6MM Privately Held
WEB: www.treesculpture.com
SIC: 0782 Landscape contractors

(P-506)
TRIMACS MAINT LDSCP CNSTR INC
80 Hegenberger Loop, Oakland (94621-1324)
PHONE................510 569-9660
Stephen McAuliffe, *President*
Stephen Mc Auliffe, *President*
Janine F Mc Auliffe, *Vice Pres*
Jeffrey McAuliffe, *Vice Pres*
Denise Bacich, *Office Mgr*
EMP: 35 EST: 1972
SALES (est): 1.8MM Privately Held
WEB: www.trimacs.com
SIC: 0782 Landscape contractors

(P-507)
UNITED LANDSCAPE RESOURCE INC
Also Called: Botanica Landscapes
5411 Colusa Hwy, Yuba City (95993-9311)
P.O. Box 569 (95992-0569)
PHONE................530 671-1029
Bill Lucich, *President*
Edmund Clavel III, *President*
Tim Corey, *COO*
Candice Lucich, *Corp Secy*
Joe Turner, *Sr Project Mgr*
EMP: 45 EST: 1979
SQ FT: 2,000
SALES (est): 5.4MM Privately Held
SIC: 0782 Landscape contractors; lawn care services

(P-508)
VALLEY LANDSCAPING & MAINT INC
12900 N Lwer Scramento Rd, Lodi (95242)
PHONE................209 334-3659
Don Oliver, *President*
Lori Peck, *Treasurer*
Jed Phelps, *Vice Pres*
EMP: 120 EST: 1975
SQ FT: 5,000
SALES (est): 6.6MM Privately Held
WEB: www.valleylandscaping.net
SIC: 0782 Landscape contractors

(P-509)
WEST COAST ARBORISTS INC
3625 Stevenson Ave, Stockton (95205-2409)
PHONE................408 855-8660
EMP: 61
SALES (corp-wide): 44.5MM Privately Held
WEB: www.westcoastarborists.com
SIC: 0782 Landscape contractors
PA: West Coast Arborists, Inc.
2200 E Via Burton
Anaheim CA 92806
714 991-1900

(P-510)
ZUKES LANDSCAPE INC
3373 Luyung Dr, Rancho Cordova (95742-6860)
PHONE................916 635-6502
Dan Zuccaro, *President*
Pete Lisson, *Manager*
Sally Miller, *Manager*
Jose Morales, *Accounts Mgr*
Jennifer Zuccaro, *Contractor*
EMP: 48 EST: 1982
SQ FT: 18,000
SALES (est): 3.8MM Privately Held
WEB: www.enhancedlandscape.com
SIC: 0782 0781 Lawn services; landscape counseling & planning

---

0783 Ornamental Shrub & Tree Svc

(P-511)
A & E ARBORISTS TREE CARE INC
225 Butte Ave, Yuba City (95993-9367)
PHONE................530 790-5312
Andrew C Boger, *President*

EMP: 150 EST: 2018
SALES: 62.3MM Privately Held
WEB: www.aearborists.com
SIC: 0783 Planting, pruning & trimming services

(P-512)
ARBORICULTURAL SPECIALTIES INC
Also Called: Professional Tree Care
2828 8th St, Berkeley (94710-2707)
P.O. Box 2377 (94702-0377)
PHONE................510 549-3954
Brian Fenske, *President*
Kristen Klingen, *Controller*
Kris Bell, *Mktg Dir*
Charles Slesinger, *Mktg Dir*
EMP: 48 EST: 1980
SQ FT: 4,500
SALES (est): 5.2MM Privately Held
WEB: www.professionaltreecare.com
SIC: 0783 Planting, pruning & trimming services

(P-513)
ARBORWELL INC (PA)
2337 American Ave, Hayward (94545-1807)
PHONE................510 881-4260
Alvin Foye Sortwell, *President*
Brad Carson, *CFO*
Dennis Shanagher, *Corp Secy*
Matt Dickinson, *Vice Pres*
Ann B Sortwell, *Vice Pres*
▲ EMP: 141 EST: 1997
SQ FT: 5,000
SALES (est): 24.8MM Privately Held
WEB: www.arborwell.com
SIC: 0783 Planting, pruning & trimming services

(P-514)
ATLAS TREE SERVICE INC
Also Called: Atlas Pest Control
150 Medburn St, Concord (94520-1103)
P.O. Box 23343, Pleasant Hill (94523-0343)
PHONE................925 687-3631
William Lloyd, *President*
Pam Juarez, *Treasurer*
Patrick Stewart, *Exec VP*
EMP: 44 EST: 1964
SQ FT: 2,500
SALES (est): 1.9MM Privately Held
WEB: www.atlastreeservice.com
SIC: 0783 7342 Removal services, bush & tree; spraying services, ornamental bush; spraying services, ornamental tree; disinfecting & pest control services

(P-515)
COASTAL MOUNTAIN TIMBER INC
Also Called: Cmt
3737 Carson Rd Unit A, Camino (95709-9593)
P.O. Box 941 (95709-0941)
PHONE................530 303-3378
Todd Alter, *CEO*
Robin Lee, *Principal*
EMP: 60 EST: 2018
SQ FT: 1,800
SALES (est): 18.7MM Privately Held
SIC: 0783 Ornamental shrub & tree services

(P-516)
DAVEY TREE SURGERY COMPANY
6915 Eastside Rd Ste 94, Anderson (96007-9401)
PHONE................530 378-2674
EMP: 60
SALES (corp-wide): 1.1B Privately Held
SIC: 0783 Shrub/Tree Services
HQ: Davey Tree Surgery Company
2617 S Vasco Rd
Livermore CA 94550
925 443-1723

(P-517)
DAVEY TREE SURGERY COMPANY (HQ)
2617 S Vasco Rd, Livermore (94550-8322)
P.O. Box 5015 (94551-5015)
PHONE................925 443-1723
Karl J Warnke, *CEO*
R Douglas Cowan, *President*
David Adante, *CFO*
Howard Bowles, *Senior VP*
Rick Edson, *Admin Sec*
EMP: 873 EST: 1928
SQ FT: 5,000
SALES (est): 46.8MM
SALES (corp-wide): 1.1B Privately Held
WEB: www.davey.com
SIC: 0783 Tree trimming services for public utility lines
PA: The Davey Tree Expert Company
1500 N Mantua St
Kent OH 44240
330 673-9511

(P-518)
HAMILTON TREE SERVICE INC
4949 Pacheco Blvd, Martinez (94553-4324)
P.O. Box 5927, Concord (94524-0927)
PHONE................925 228-1010
Tolbert Dex Hamilton, *President*
Grant Hamilton, *Vice Pres*
EMP: 50 EST: 1976
SQ FT: 16,500
SALES (est): 2.3MM Privately Held
WEB: www.hamiltontree.com
SIC: 0783 Planting, pruning & trimming services

(P-519)
OLD DURHAM WOOD INC
1156 Oroville Chico Hwy, Durham (95938-9708)
PHONE................530 342-7381
Michael Randall McLaughlin, *CEO*
Sean Casey, *Office Mgr*
EMP: 33 EST: 1981
SQ FT: 1,800
SALES (est): 12MM Privately Held
SIC: 0783 2611 5099 Ornamental shrub & tree services; pulp manufactured from waste or recycled paper; wood & wood by-products; firewood

(P-520)
PACHECO BROTHERS GARDENING INC
6344 Bridgehead Rd, Oakley (94561-2945)
PHONE................510 487-3580
EMP: 50
SALES (corp-wide): 6.7MM Privately Held
WEB: www.pachecobrothers.com
SIC: 5261 0783 0782 Lawn & garden equipment; ornamental shrub & tree services; landscape contractors
PA: Pacheco Brothers Gardening, Inc.
20973 Cabot Blvd
Hayward CA 94545
510 732-6330

(P-521)
PROVIDENCE HORTICULTURE INC
Also Called: Tree Doctorx
6931 E Belmont Ave, Fresno (93727-2933)
P.O. Box 7735 (93747-7735)
PHONE................559 251-7907
John Pape, *President*
Lori Pape, *CFO*
David Kuhtz, *Vice Pres*
Delisa Kuhtz, *Vice Pres*
Tammy Hodgerney, *Admin Asst*
EMP: 52 EST: 1990
SQ FT: 217,800
SALES (est): 5.4MM Privately Held
WEB: www.provhort.com
SIC: 0783 Ornamental shrub & tree services

(P-522)
SP MCCLENAHAN CO
Also Called: McClenahan S P Co Tree Service
1 Arastradero Rd, Portola Valley (94028-8012)
PHONE................650 326-8781
James M Mc Clenahan, *President*
EMP: 56 EST: 1911
SQ FT: 5,000
SALES (est): 5.3MM Privately Held
WEB: www.spmcclenahan.com
SIC: 0783 Planting, pruning & trimming services

(P-523)
TREE TECHNOLOGY INC
Also Called: Tree Tech Services
8609 Weyand Ave, Sacramento (95828-2641)
P.O. Box 1207, Elk Grove (95759-1207)
PHONE................916 386-9416
Don McBride, *President*
Terry Stephens, *General Mgr*
EMP: 37 EST: 1990
SQ FT: 3,000
SALES (est): 3.9MM Privately Held
WEB: www.treetechservices.com
SIC: 0783 Planting, pruning & trimming services

(P-524)
TSU/TREE SERVICE UNLIMITED INC
5531 Silver Lode Dr, Placerville (95667-9725)
PHONE................530 626-8733
Ashley Harpine, *CEO*
Tammie Van Bebber, *President*
Dale Van Bebber, *Vice Pres*
EMP: 40 EST: 1979
SQ FT: 500
SALES (est): 3.8MM Privately Held
WEB: www.tsutrees.com
SIC: 0783 2411 Planting, pruning & trimming services; timber, cut at logging camp

(P-525)
UTILITY TREE SERVICE LLC (DH)
Also Called: Utility Tree Service, Inc.
1884 Keystone Ct Ste A, Redding (96003-4870)
PHONE................530 226-0330
Scott Asplundh, *President*
Joseph P Dwyer, *Corp Secy*
Brent D Asplundh, *Vice Pres*
Carl Asplundh III, *Vice Pres*
Gregg Asplundh, *Vice Pres*
EMP: 50 EST: 1993
SALES (est): 10.6MM
SALES (corp-wide): 1.1B Privately Held
WEB: www.utilitytreeservice.com
SIC: 0783 Tree trimming services for public utility lines

(P-526)
WEST COAST ARBORISTS INC
5424 N Barcus Ave, Fresno (93722-5067)
PHONE................559 275-2086
Patrick Mahoney, *Branch Mgr*
Richard Mahoney, *Vice Pres*
Brian Kirkegaard, *Area Mgr*
Herminio Padilla, *Area Mgr*
Gonzalo Regalado, *Area Mgr*
EMP: 122
SALES (corp-wide): 44.5MM Privately Held
WEB: www.westcoastarborists.com
SIC: 0783 Tree trimming services for public utility lines
PA: West Coast Arborists, Inc.
2200 E Via Burton
Anaheim CA 92806
714 991-1900

(P-527)
WEST COAST TREE CARE INC
2845 Moorpark Ave Ste 205, San Jose (95128-3158)
PHONE................408 260-2007
Chris Hall, *President*
Michael Callahan, *Vice Pres*
EMP: 42 EST: 1992
SQ FT: 800

▲ = Import ▼ = Export
◆ = Import/Export

PRODUCTS & SERVICES SECTION
1311 - Crude Petroleum & Natural Gas County (P-548)

SALES (est): 1MM **Privately Held**
WEB: www.westcoasttreecare.com
SIC: **0783** Planting, pruning & trimming services

0811 Timber Tracts

(P-528)
BOETHING TREELAND FARMS INC
2923 Alpine Rd, Portola Valley (94028-7546)
PHONE..................650 851-4770
Richard Hanley, *Branch Mgr*
EMP: 62
SALES (corp-wide): 29.8MM **Privately Held**
WEB: www.boethingtreeland.com
SIC: **0811** 5193 0181 Tree farm; nursery stock; nursery stock, growing of
PA: Boething Treeland Farms, Inc.
 23475 Long Valley Rd
 Woodland Hills CA 91367
 818 883-1222

(P-529)
BOETHING TREELAND FARMS INC
Also Called: Boething Treeland Nursery
20601 E Kettleman Ln, Lodi (95240-9756)
PHONE..................209 727-3741
Seilpe Gomez, *Branch Mgr*
Robert Fernandez, *Sales Staff*
Elliot Kozolchyk, *Sales Staff*
Paul Vanmiddlesworth, *Sales Staff*
Laura Matye, *Manager*
EMP: 62
SALES (corp-wide): 29.8MM **Privately Held**
WEB: www.boethingtreeland.com
SIC: **0811** Tree farm
PA: Boething Treeland Farms, Inc.
 23475 Long Valley Rd
 Woodland Hills CA 91367
 818 883-1222

(P-530)
BRIGHTVIEW TREE COMPANY
8501 Calaveras Rd, Sunol (94586-9434)
P.O. Box 289, Farmington (95230-0289)
PHONE..................925 862-2485
John Serviss, *Branch Mgr*
Dale Vanfossan, *Opers Mgr*
Glenn Hansen, *Sales Staff*
Manuel Cazares, *Manager*
EMP: 81 **Privately Held**
WEB: www.brightview.com
SIC: **0811** Tree farm
HQ: Brightview Tree Company
 24151 Ventura Blvd # 108
 Calabasas CA 91302
 818 223-8500

(P-531)
MARTINEZ RANCHES INC
8777 Halley Rd, Winters (95694-9643)
PHONE..................530 795-2957
Joseph Martinez, *President*
Brett Martinez, *Treasurer*
Michele Marnitez, *Vice Pres*
Jessica Lachapelle, *Office Mgr*
Ryan Martinez, *Admin Sec*
EMP: 47 EST: 1975
SQ FT: 1,000
SALES (est): 2.8MM **Privately Held**
WEB: www.martinezranches.com
SIC: **0811** 0173 Tree farm; tree nuts

(P-532)
WESTERN TREE NURSERY
3873 Hecker Pass Rd, Gilroy (95020-8805)
PHONE..................408 842-6800
James Blocker, *President*
EMP: 53 EST: 1968
SALES (est): 1.4MM **Privately Held**
WEB: www.westerntreenurseryinc.com
SIC: **0811** 0181 Tree farm; shrubberies grown in field nurseries

0851 Forestry Svcs

(P-533)
ALPINE LAND INFO SVCS INC (PA)
4451 Caterpillar Rd Ste 6, Redding (96003-1493)
P.O. Box 3579, Bend OR (97707-0579)
PHONE..................530 222-8100
Cinthia McCabe, *President*
Cindy McCabe, *Bookkeeper*
EMP: 44 EST: 1991 **Privately Held**
WEB: www.alpinelis.com
SIC: **0851** Forest management services

(P-534)
COURTNEY AVIATION INC
10747 Airport Rd, Columbia (95310-9727)
P.O. Box 1196 (95310-1196)
PHONE..................209 532-2345
Hart Drobish, *President*
Mark Zaller, *Senior Mgr*
EMP: 42 EST: 1967
SQ FT: 1,500
SALES (est): 1.8MM **Privately Held**
WEB: www.courtneyaviation.com
SIC: **0851** 7335 4522 Fire fighting services, forest; aerial photography, except mapmaking; air taxis

(P-535)
NORTH BAY FIRE
4500 Hessel Rd, Sebastopol (95472-6267)
PHONE..................707 823-1084
Mike Mickelson, *President*
Terri Bolduc, *Principal*
Bill Newman, *Principal*
Tiffanie Palmer, *Principal*
EMP: 85 EST: 1982 **Privately Held**
SIC: **9224** 0851 Fire protection; fire prevention services, forest

(P-536)
NORTH ZONE FALLERS INC (PA)
4705 Hartstrand Rd, Etna (96027-9743)
PHONE..................530 598-8518
Michelle Branson, *President*
Nik Branson, *Admin Sec*
EMP: 44 EST: 2004
SALES (est): 2.5MM **Privately Held**
WEB: www.northzonefallers.com
SIC: **0851** Forest management services

(P-537)
WATERSHED RES & TRAINING CTR
Also Called: WATERSHED CENTER
98 Clinic Ave Ste B, Hayfork (96041)
P.O. Box 356 (96041-0356)
PHONE..................530 628-4206
N Goulette, *Exec Dir*
Robert C Mountjoy, *President*
Sue Hayes, *Treasurer*
Nick Goulette, *Exec Dir*
Teckla Johnson, *Program Mgr*
EMP: 47 EST: 1993
SQ FT: 2,000
SALES (est): 3.3MM **Privately Held**
WEB: www.thewatershedcenter.com
SIC: **8299** 0851 Vocational counseling; forestry services

0921 Finfish Farming & Fish Hatcheries

(P-538)
MT LASSEN TROUT FARMS INC
20560 Lanes Valley Rd, Paynes Creek (96075-9604)
PHONE..................530 474-1900
Phil Mackey, *President*
Chris Lucero, *Controller*
EMP: 47 EST: 1949
SQ FT: 2,500
SALES (est): 1.4MM **Privately Held**
WEB: www.mtlassentrout.com
SIC: **0921** Fish hatcheries

0971 Hunting & Trapping

(P-539)
INFINITY SPORTS INC
Also Called: GUN ACCESSORY SUPPLY
900 Wakefield Dr, Oakdale (95361-7764)
P.O. Box 1228 (95361-1228)
PHONE..................209 845-3940
Ronald Day, *CEO*
▲ EMP: 45 EST: 1978
SQ FT: 30,000
SALES (est): 33.5MM **Privately Held**
WEB: www.gunaccessorysupply.com
SIC: **0971** 5091 Hunting services; sporting & recreation goods

(P-540)
WILDCARE TRWLLGER NTURE EDCATN
76 Albert Park Ln, San Rafael (94901-3929)
PHONE..................415 453-1000
Karen Wilson, *Exec Dir*
Tom O'Connell, *President*
Susan Rusche, *Treasurer*
Alison Hermance, *Comms Mgr*
Lacey Babnik, *Research*
EMP: 60 EST: 1953
SQ FT: 3,000
SALES: 2.8MM **Privately Held**
WEB: www.discoverwildcare.org
SIC: **0971** 0742 0752 Wildlife management; animal hospital services, pets & other animal specialties; animal specialty services

1041 Gold Ores

(P-541)
MERIDIAN GOLD INC
Also Called: Royal Mountain King
4461 Rock Creek Rd, Copperopolis (95228-7059)
PHONE..................209 785-3222
Edgar Smith, *Branch Mgr*
EMP: 474
SALES (corp-wide): 1.5B **Privately Held**
SIC: **1041** Gold ores
HQ: Meridian Gold Inc.
 4635 Longley Ln Ste 110
 Reno NV 89502

1081 Metal Mining Svcs

(P-542)
NATIONAL EWP INC
1961 Meeker Ave, Richmond (94804-6405)
PHONE..................510 236-6282
Chris Tatum, *Branch Mgr*
EMP: 15
SALES (corp-wide): 29.9MM **Privately Held**
WEB: www.nationalewp.com
SIC: **1081** Metal mining exploration & development services
PA: National Ewp, Inc.
 3707 Manzanita Ln
 Elko NV 89801
 775 753-7355

1221 Bituminous Coal & Lignite: Surface Mining

(P-543)
CUSTOM CRUSHING INDUSTRIES INC
2409 E Oberlin Rd, Yreka (96097-9577)
P.O. Box 357, Grenada (96038-0357)
PHONE..................530 842-5544
Clara Goodwin, *Treasurer*
Paul Goodwin, *President*
EMP: 37 EST: 2005
SALES (est): 9.5MM **Privately Held**
SIC: **1221** 3295 3281 1499 Strip mining, bituminous; minerals, ground or treated; stone, quarrying & processing of own stone products; peat mining & processing; excavation & grading, building construction; highway & street construction

1241 Coal Mining Svcs

(P-544)
METAMINING INC
1065 E Hillsdale Blvd, Foster City (94404-1613)
PHONE..................650 212-7900
Ling LI, *President*
Song Chen, *Shareholder*
George Wang, *Vice Pres*
EMP: 18 EST: 2010
SALES (est): 1MM **Privately Held**
WEB: www.metamininginc.com
SIC: **1241** 1011 1061 1021 Coal mining services; iron ore mining; manganese ores mining; copper ore milling & preparation

1311 Crude Petroleum & Natural Gas

(P-545)
BRIGHTMARK LLC (PA)
1725 Montgomery St Fl 3, San Francisco (94111-1018)
PHONE..................415 964-4411
Robert Powell, *CEO*
Andrew T Nekus, *COO*
Scott Healy, *CFO*
Rick Peterson, *Officer*
Zeina El-Azzi, *Senior VP*
EMP: 118 EST: 2016
SALES (est): 66.9MM **Privately Held**
WEB: www.brightmark.com
SIC: **1311** Natural gas production

(P-546)
CHEVRON MUNAIGAS INC (HQ)
6001 Bollinger Canyon Rd, San Ramon (94583-5737)
PHONE..................925 842-1000
EMP: 82 EST: 1995
SALES (est): 4.3MM
SALES (corp-wide): 94.6B **Publicly Held**
WEB: www.chevron.com
SIC: **5541** 1311 1382 1321 Filling stations, gasoline; crude petroleum production; oil & gas exploration services; natural gas liquids
PA: Chevron Corporation
 6001 Bollinger Canyon Rd
 San Ramon CA 94583
 925 842-1000

(P-547)
COMMERCIAL ENERGY MONTANA INC
Also Called: Commercial Energy California
7677 Oakport St Ste 525, Oakland (94621-1944)
PHONE..................510 567-2700
John Curry Stypula, *Branch Mgr*
Curry Stypula, *Vice Pres*
Patrick Vanbeek, *Opers Mgr*
Timothy Curtiss, *Opers Staff*
Alex Hersch, *Sales Staff*
EMP: 17
SALES (corp-wide): 15.8MM **Privately Held**
WEB: www.commercialenergy.net
SIC: **1311** Crude petroleum production
PA: Commercial Energy Of Montana Inc.
 118 E Main St
 Cut Bank MT 59427
 406 873-3300

(P-548)
PETROLEUM SALES INC
2066 Redwood Hwy, Greenbrae (94904-2467)
PHONE..................415 256-1600
Stephanie Shimk, *Branch Mgr*
EMP: 22

1311 - Crude Petroleum & Natural Gas County (P-549)

SALES (corp-wide): 13.5MM **Privately Held**
WEB: www.shineology.com
SIC: **1311** Crude petroleum & natural gas
PA: Petroleum Sales, Inc.
  1475 2nd St
  San Rafael CA 94901
  415 256-1600

(P-549)
SILURIA TECHNOLOGIES INC
409 Illinois St, San Francisco (94158-2509)
PHONE..................................415 978-2170
Robert Trout, *CEO*
Alex Tkachenko, *President*
Erik Scher, *COO*
Karl Kurz, *Chairman*
Richard Black, *Exec VP*
EMP: 30 EST: 2007
SALES (est): 13.1MM **Privately Held**
WEB: www.siluria.com
SIC: **1311** Natural gas production

(P-550)
TERRAPIN ENERGY LLC (PA)
897 Independence Ave 2g, Mountain View (94043-2341)
PHONE..................................650 386-6180
Tim Koltek, *CEO*
EMP: 42 EST: 2008
SALES (est): 1.5MM **Privately Held**
WEB: www.terrapinenergyservices.com
SIC: **1311** Crude petroleum & natural gas

(P-551)
TPG PARTNERS III LP (HQ)
Also Called: Tpg Growth
345 California St # 3300, San Francisco (94104-2606)
PHONE..................................415 743-1500
William E McGlashan, *Managing Prtnr*
David Bonderman, *Partner*
Fred Cohen, *Partner*
James G Coulter, *Partner*
Fred Paulenich, *Partner*
EMP: 40 EST: 1999
SALES (est): 294.9MM **Privately Held**
WEB: www.tpg.com
SIC: **1311 1389 4922 5082** Crude petroleum production; natural gas production; oil field services; natural gas transmission; oil field equipment

1321 Natural Gas Liquids

(P-552)
TEXACO INC (HQ)
6001 Bollinger Canyon Rd, San Ramon (94583-2324)
PHONE..................................925 842-1000
David O'Reilly, *Ch of Bd*
Kari H Endries, *CEO*
◆ EMP: 800 EST: 1902
SQ FT: 110,000
SALES (est): 1.7B
SALES (corp-wide): 94.6B **Publicly Held**
WEB: www.texaco.com
SIC: **5541 5511 1321 4612** Filling stations, gasoline; automobiles, new & used; natural gas liquids production; crude petroleum pipelines; refined petroleum pipelines; deep sea foreign transportation of freight
PA: Chevron Corporation
  6001 Bollinger Canyon Rd
  San Ramon CA 94583
  925 842-1000

1381 Drilling Oil & Gas Wells

(P-553)
AA PRODUCTION SERVICES INC
8032 County Road 61, Princeton (95970-9501)
PHONE..................................530 982-0123
EMP: 31
SALES (corp-wide): 4.5MM **Privately Held**
SIC: **1381** Drilling Oil And Gas Wells, Nsk

PA: Aa Production Services, Inc.
  433 2nd St Ste 103
  Woodland CA 95695
  530 668-7525

(P-554)
ASTA CONSTRUCTION CO INC (PA)
1090 Saint Francis Way, Rio Vista (94571-1200)
P.O. Box 758 (94571-0758)
PHONE..................................707 374-6472
Walt Koenig, *CEO*
Christien Koenig, *President*
Joan Brown, *Corp Secy*
Schmitt V Scott, *Vice Pres*
Scott Schmitt, *Marketing Staff*
▲ EMP: 31 EST: 1943
SQ FT: 1,200
SALES (est): 21.1MM **Privately Held**
WEB: www.astaconstruction.com
SIC: **1381 1611 5032** Drilling oil & gas wells; general contractor, highway & street construction; sand, construction

(P-555)
DICK BROWN TECHNICAL SERVICES
Also Called: Aera Energy
553 Airport Rd Ste B, Rio Vista (94571-1293)
P.O. Box 1035 (94571-3035)
PHONE..................................707 374-2133
Richard Brown, *President*
Richard Tucker, *Vice Pres*
EMP: 18 EST: 1984
SALES (est): 3.7MM **Privately Held**
SIC: **1381** Drilling oil & gas wells

(P-556)
PAUL GRAHAM DRILLING & SVC CO
2500 Airport Rd, Rio Vista (94571-1034)
P.O. Box 669 (94571-0669)
PHONE..................................707 374-5123
Kevin P Graham, *President*
Jill Graham, *CFO*
Clarence Santos, *Vice Pres*
Chris Clouser, *Technical Staff*
Alyssa Graham, *Graphic Designe*
EMP: 170 EST: 1968
SQ FT: 30,000
SALES (est): 33MM **Privately Held**
WEB: www.paulgrahamdrilling.com
SIC: **1381 7389 7359** Drilling oil & gas wells; crane & aerial lift service; industrial truck rental

(P-557)
WOODWARD DRILLING COMPANY INC
550 River Rd, Rio Vista (94571-1216)
P.O. Box 336 (94571-0336)
PHONE..................................707 374-4300
Concing Woodward, *President*
Wayne G Woodward, *Ch of Bd*
EMP: 28 EST: 1990
SQ FT: 40,000
SALES (est): 8.8MM **Privately Held**
WEB: www.woodwarddrilling.net
SIC: **1381 1781** Service well drilling; water well drilling

1382 Oil & Gas Field Exploration Svcs

(P-558)
ANTHONYS INDUSTRIAL RENTS
2999 Promenade St Ste 100, West Sacramento (95691-6418)
PHONE..................................916 373-5320
EMP: 17 EST: 1998
SALES (est): 2.4MM **Privately Held**
SIC: **1382** Oil & gas exploration services

(P-559)
LUCA INTERNATIONAL GROUP LLC (PA)
39650 Liberty St Ste 490, Fremont (94538-2261)
PHONE..................................510 498-8829
▲ EMP: 17

SALES (est): 3.4MM **Privately Held**
WEB: www.luca88.com
SIC: **1382** Oil/Gas Exploration Services

(P-560)
WICKLAND PIPELINES LLC (PA)
8950 Cal Center Dr # 125, Sacramento (95826-3262)
PHONE..................................916 978-2432
Roy L Wickland, *Principal*
EMP: 20 EST: 2010
SALES (est): 9.5MM **Privately Held**
WEB: www.wicklandpipelines.com
SIC: **1382** Oil & gas exploration services

1389 Oil & Gas Field Svcs, NEC

(P-561)
C CASE COMPANY INC
Also Called: Case's Oil
7010 W Cerini Ave, Riverdale (93656-9622)
PHONE..................................559 867-3912
Coofas Wayne Case Jr, *President*
Rodney Craig Case, *Vice Pres*
Sarah Dewey, *Admin Sec*
EMP: 23 EST: 1971
SALES (est): 6.5MM **Privately Held**
SIC: **1389 1311** Oil & gas wells: building, repairing & dismantling; crude petroleum production

(P-562)
CHARGING TREE CORPORATION
35788 Highway 41, Coarsegold (93614-9786)
PHONE..................................559 760-5473
Dean P Antoni, *President*
EMP: 19 EST: 2020
SALES (est): 1MM **Privately Held**
SIC: **1389** Construction, repair & dismantling services

(P-563)
DRI CLEAN & RESTORATION
2890 N Sunnyside Ave U114, Fresno (93727-1369)
PHONE..................................559 292-1100
Lee Dannie, *Principal*
EMP: 25 EST: 2012
SQ FT: 11,350
SALES (est): 3.4MM **Privately Held**
WEB: www.drirestoration.com
SIC: **1389 1521 7699** Construction, repair & dismantling services; single-family housing construction; cleaning services

(P-564)
DTE STOCKTON LLC
2526 W Washington St, Stockton (95203-2952)
PHONE..................................209 467-3838
Nelson Nail, *Mng Member*
Jay McCall, *Director*
Steven Henry, *Manager*
EMP: 34 EST: 2007
SALES (est): 18.9MM **Publicly Held**
WEB: www.dtepowerandindustrial.com
SIC: **1389** Construction, repair & dismantling services
HQ: Dte Energy Services, Inc.
  414 S Main St Ste 600
  Ann Arbor MI 48104

(P-565)
ELI KISELMAN ✪
Also Called: Dreamhome Remodeling and Bldrs
98 N 1st St Unit 725, San Jose (95113-1253)
PHONE..................................832 886-3743
Eli Kiselman, *Owner*
EMP: 31 EST: 2021
SALES (est): 748K **Privately Held**
SIC: **1389** Construction, repair & dismantling services

(P-566)
GLOBAL DIVING & SALVAGE INC
1280 Terminal St, West Sacramento (95691-3513)
PHONE..................................707 561-6810
Devon Grennan, *President*
Trinity Ng-Yeung, *Vice Pres*
Michael Langen, *Admin Sec*
Lara Mayer, *Marketing Staff*
Kristofer Lindberg, *Master*
EMP: 18 EST: 1980
SALES (est): 4.9MM **Privately Held**
WEB: www.gdiving.com
SIC: **1389 4959** Pipe testing, oil field service; sanitary services

(P-567)
KILGORE ENTERPRISES LLC
2005 San Jose Dr Unit 258, Antioch (94509-8607)
PHONE..................................925 885-8999
Detwan Kilgore, *CEO*
EMP: 27 EST: 2015
SALES (est): 1.3MM **Privately Held**
WEB: www.kilgore-enterprises-llc.business.site
SIC: **1389** Construction, repair & dismantling services

(P-568)
LINDEN STEEL & CNSTR INC
17863 Ideal Pkwy, Manteca (95336-9477)
PHONE..................................209 239-2160
Joe Orgon, *President*
EMP: 25 EST: 2004
SALES (est): 3.4MM **Privately Held**
SIC: **1389** Construction, repair & dismantling services

(P-569)
MUD PUPPY INC
38688 Kentucky Ave, Woodland (95695-5835)
PHONE..................................760 961-1160
Craig Henderson, *Principal*
EMP: 20 EST: 2017
SALES (est): 2MM **Privately Held**
SIC: **1389** Oil field services

(P-570)
RESOURCE CEMENTING LLC
2500 Airport Rd, Rio Vista (94571-1034)
P.O. Box 1027 (94571-3027)
PHONE..................................707 374-3350
Kevin P Graham, *Mng Member*
Marc Brennen, *Business Mgr*
Hamid Najafi, *Opers Mgr*
Paul Casavant, *Manager*
EMP: 23 EST: 2014
SALES (est): 30.5MM **Privately Held**
WEB: www.resourcecementing.com
SIC: **1389 1781** Cementing oil & gas well casings; geothermal drilling

(P-571)
SPORTON INTERNATIONAL USA INC
1175 Montague Expy, Milpitas (95035-6845)
PHONE..................................732 407-8718
Chih - Hsiang Yang, *CEO*
EMP: 15 EST: 2018
SALES (est): 3.8MM **Privately Held**
WEB: www.sporton.com.tw
SIC: **1389** Testing, measuring, surveying & analysis services
PA: Sporton International Inc.
  6f, No. 106, Xintai 5th Rd., Sec. 1
  New Taipei City TAP 22102

(P-572)
STRATEGIC INDUSTRY INC
1440 Draper St Ste C, Kingsburg (93631-1945)
P.O. Box 496 (93631-0496)
PHONE..................................559 419-9481
Charles Miller, *President*
Rick Arteaga, *Vice Pres*
Jason Miller, *Vice Pres*
Rudy Reyes, *Administration*
EMP: 20 EST: 2007

PRODUCTS & SERVICES SECTION
1442 - Construction Sand & Gravel County (P-593)

SALES (est): 4.6MM Privately Held
WEB: www.strategicindustry.us
SIC: 1389 1542 1541 Construction, repair & dismantling services; commercial & office building, new construction; factory construction; food products manufacturing or packing plant construction; industrial buildings, new construction

(P-573)
TEAM CASING
5073 Arboga Rd, Marysville (95901)
P.O. Box 1723 (95901-0050)
PHONE.................................530 743-5424
William W Cates, *President*
William Scheiber, *CFO*
Sandra Cates, *Admin Sec*
EMP: 20 EST: 1968
SQ FT: 700
SALES (est): 2.9MM Privately Held
SIC: 1389 Running, cutting & pulling casings, tubes & rods

(P-574)
TOTAL-WESTERN INC
3985 Teal Ct, Benicia (94510-1212)
PHONE.................................707 747-5506
EMP: 17
SALES (corp-wide): 489.5MM Privately Held
WEB: www.total-western.com
SIC: 1389 Oil field services
HQ: Total-Western, Inc.
    8049 Somerset Blvd
    Paramount CA 90723
    562 220-1450

1411 Dimension Stone

(P-575)
BO DEAN CO INC (PA)
1060 N Dutton Ave, Santa Rosa (95401-5011)
PHONE.................................707 576-8205
Dean N Soiland, *CEO*
Belinda Soiland, *Vice Pres*
Charlie Young, *Project Mgr*
Heather Hammerich, *Controller*
Josh Cleaver, *Sales Staff*
EMP: 26 EST: 1989
SQ FT: 5,000
SALES (est): 17.9MM Privately Held
WEB: www.bodeancompany.com
SIC: 1411 2951 Greenstone, dimension-quarrying; concrete, asphaltic (not from refineries)

(P-576)
TAKE IT FOR GRANITE INC
345 Phelan Ave, San Jose (95112-4104)
PHONE.................................408 790-2812
Jason Krulee, *President*
Kit Keahey, *Prdtn Mgr*
▲ EMP: 20 EST: 1997
SQ FT: 32,000
SALES (est): 4.8MM Privately Held
WEB: www.tifgranite.com
SIC: 1411 Dimension stone

1422 Crushed & Broken Limestone

(P-577)
NORTHERN AGGREGATES INC
500 Cropley Ln, Willits (95490-4140)
P.O. Box 1566 (95490-1566)
PHONE.................................707 459-3929
Frank Dutra, *President*
Randy Lucchetti, *Vice Pres*
Pat Allen, *Info Tech Mgr*
EMP: 25 EST: 1990
SQ FT: 10,000
SALES (est): 3.4MM Privately Held
SIC: 1422 Crushed & broken limestone

1429 Crushed & Broken Stone, NEC

(P-578)
CHILI BAR LLC
Also Called: Chili Bar Slate
11380 State Highway 193, Placerville (95667-9601)
PHONE.................................530 622-3325
Jacob Montazeri, *Principal*
EMP: 24 EST: 2012
SALES (est): 6.2MM Privately Held
WEB: www.chilibarslate.com
SIC: 1429 Slate, crushed & broken-quarrying

(P-579)
LANGLEY HILL QUARRY
12 Langley Hill Rd, Woodside (94062-4829)
P.O. Box 620626 (94062-0626)
PHONE.................................650 851-0179
Michael Dempsey, *Partner*
Patrick Dempsey, *Partner*
EMP: 43 EST: 1954
SALES (est): 6.3MM Privately Held
SIC: 1429 Igneous rock, crushed & broken-quarrying

(P-580)
OLIVER DE SILVA INC (PA)
Also Called: Gallagher & Burk
11555 Dublin Blvd, Dublin (94568-2854)
P.O. Box 2922 (94568-0922)
PHONE.................................925 829-9220
Edwin O De Silva, *Chairman*
Richard B Gates, *President*
David De Silva, *Exec VP*
J Scott Archibald, *Vice Pres*
Ernest Lampkin, *Vice Pres*
EMP: 20 EST: 1931
SQ FT: 60,000
SALES (est): 37.1MM Privately Held
WEB: www.desilvagates.com
SIC: 1429 Igneous rock, crushed & broken-quarrying

(P-581)
SAN RAFAEL ROCK QUARRY INC (HQ)
Also Called: Dutra Materials
2350 Kerner Blvd Ste 200, San Rafael (94901-5595)
PHONE.................................415 459-7740
Bill Toney Dutra, *CEO*
EMP: 70 EST: 1994
SALES (est): 58.6MM
SALES (corp-wide): 191.6MM Privately Held
WEB: www.sanrafaelrockquarry.com
SIC: 1429 1629 Basalt, crushed & broken-quarrying; marine construction
PA: The Dutra Group
    2350 Kerner Blvd Ste 200
    San Rafael CA 94901
    415 258-6876

1442 Construction Sand & Gravel

(P-582)
A TEICHERT & SON INC
Also Called: Teichert Aggregates
13879 Butterfield Dr, Truckee (96161-3331)
P.O. Box 447 (96160-0447)
PHONE.................................530 587-3811
Ed Herrnberger, *Plant Mgr*
EMP: 27
SALES (corp-wide): 842MM Privately Held
WEB: www.teichert.com
SIC: 1442 Construction sand & gravel
HQ: A. Teichert & Son, Inc.
    5200 Franklin Dr Ste 115
    Pleasanton CA 94588

(P-583)
A TEICHERT & SON INC
Also Called: Teichert Aggregates
36334 S Bird Rd, Tracy (95304-8678)
PHONE.................................209 832-4150
Jerry Hansen, *Plant Mgr*
Kevin Owen, *Supervisor*
EMP: 27
SALES (corp-wide): 842MM Privately Held
WEB: www.teichert.com
SIC: 1442 Construction sand & gravel
HQ: A. Teichert & Son, Inc.
    5200 Franklin Dr Ste 115
    Pleasanton CA 94588

(P-584)
A TEICHERT & SON INC
Also Called: Teichert Aggregates
27944 County Road 19a, Esparto (95627-2237)
PHONE.................................530 787-3468
Bill Cruickshank, *Plant Mgr*
EMP: 40
SALES (corp-wide): 842MM Privately Held
WEB: www.teichert.com
SIC: 1442 Construction sand & gravel
HQ: A. Teichert & Son, Inc.
    5200 Franklin Dr Ste 115
    Pleasanton CA 94588

(P-585)
A TEICHERT & SON INC
Also Called: Teichert Aggregates
2601 State Highway 49, Cool (95614-9528)
P.O. Box 280 (95614-0280)
PHONE.................................530 885-4244
Ed Herrnberger, *Plant Mgr*
EMP: 27
SALES (corp-wide): 842MM Privately Held
WEB: www.teichert.com
SIC: 1442 Construction sand & gravel
HQ: A. Teichert & Son, Inc.
    5200 Franklin Dr Ste 115
    Pleasanton CA 94588

(P-586)
A TEICHERT & SON INC
Also Called: Teichert Aggregates
3331 Walnut Ave, Marysville (95901-9421)
PHONE.................................530 749-1230
Brandon Stauffer, *Plant Mgr*
EMP: 27
SALES (corp-wide): 842MM Privately Held
WEB: www.teichert.com
SIC: 1442 Construction sand & gravel
HQ: A. Teichert & Son, Inc.
    5200 Franklin Dr Ste 115
    Pleasanton CA 94588

(P-587)
A TEICHERT & SON INC
Also Called: Teichert Aggregates
4249 Hmmnton Smrtville Rd, Marysville (95901)
PHONE.................................530 743-6111
Brandon Stauffer, *Plant Mgr*
EMP: 27
SALES (corp-wide): 842MM Privately Held
WEB: www.teichert.com
SIC: 1442 Construction sand & gravel
HQ: A. Teichert & Son, Inc.
    5200 Franklin Dr Ste 115
    Pleasanton CA 94588

(P-588)
A TEICHERT & SON INC
Also Called: Teichert Aggregates
3417 Grant Line Rd, Rancho Cordova (95742-7000)
P.O. Box 981, Folsom (95763-0981)
PHONE.................................916 351-0123
Mike Cunnigham, *Plant Mgr*
EMP: 27

SALES (corp-wide): 842MM Privately Held
WEB: www.teichert.com
SIC: 1442 Construction sand & gravel
HQ: A. Teichert & Son, Inc.
    5200 Franklin Dr Ste 115
    Pleasanton CA 94588

(P-589)
A TEICHERT & SON INC
Also Called: Teichert Aggregates
8760 Kiefer Blvd, Sacramento (95826-3917)
P.O. Box 15002 (95851-0002)
PHONE.................................916 386-6900
Mike Cunnigham, *Plant Mgr*
Chris Poyner, *Safety Mgr*
EMP: 27
SALES (corp-wide): 842MM Privately Held
WEB: www.teichert.com
SIC: 1442 Construction sand & gravel
HQ: A. Teichert & Son, Inc.
    5200 Franklin Dr Ste 115
    Pleasanton CA 94588

(P-590)
BALDWIN CONTRACTING CO INC
400 S Lincoln St, Stockton (95203-3312)
PHONE.................................209 460-3785
Kevin Smudrick, *Safety Mgr*
EMP: 15
SALES (corp-wide): 5.5B Publicly Held
SIC: 1442 Construction sand & gravel
HQ: Baldwin Contracting Company, Inc.
    1764 Skyway
    Chico CA 95928
    530 891-6555

(P-591)
BUTTE SAND AND GRAVEL
10373 S Butte Rd, Sutter (95982-9316)
P.O. Box 749 (95982-0749)
PHONE.................................530 755-0225
Darren Morehead, *President*
Martin Morehead, *CFO*
Joseph Morehead II, *Vice Pres*
EMP: 20 EST: 1963
SQ FT: 1,000
SALES (est): 5.1MM Privately Held
WEB: www.buttesand.com
SIC: 1442 5211 Gravel mining; sand & gravel

(P-592)
CANYON ROCK CO INC
Also Called: River Ready Mix
7525 Hwy 116, Forestville (95436-9227)
P.O. Box 639 (95436-0639)
PHONE.................................707 887-2207
Wendell Trappe, *President*
Gwen Trappe, *Vice Pres*
Wendel Trappe, *Opers Mgr*
Jeff Roades, *Opers Staff*
Jonathon Trappe, *Manager*
EMP: 20 EST: 1949
SQ FT: 3,000
SALES (est): 7MM Privately Held
WEB: www.canyonrockinc.com
SIC: 1442 3273 Construction sand & gravel; ready-mixed concrete

(P-593)
GRANITE ROCK CO (PA)
350 Technology Dr, Watsonville (95076-2488)
P.O. Box 50001 (95077-5001)
PHONE.................................831 768-2000
Thomas H Squeri, *CEO*
Bruce G Woolpert, *Vice Chairman*
Mary E Woolpert, *Chairman*
Shirley Ow, *Vice Pres*
Steve Snodgrass, *Vice Pres*
EMP: 100 EST: 1900
SQ FT: 10,000
SALES (est): 390.3MM Privately Held
WEB: www.graniterock.com
SIC: 1442 3273 5032 2951 Gravel mining; ready-mixed concrete; sand, construction; asphalt & asphaltic paving mixtures (not from refineries); highway & street paving contractor; concrete block & brick

1442 - Construction Sand & Gravel County (P-594)   PRODUCTS & SERVICES SECTION

(P-594)
HANSEN BROS ENTERPRISES (PA)
Also Called: Hbe Rental
11727 La Barr Meadows Rd, Grass Valley (95949-7722)
P.O. Box 1599 (95945-1599)
PHONE.................................530 273-3100
Orson Hansen, *President*
Frank Bennallack, *Treasurer*
Sue Peterson, *Vice Pres*
EMP: 70 **EST:** 1953
SQ FT: 20,000
SALES (est): 26.4MM **Privately Held**
WEB: www.gohbe.com
SIC: 1442 3273 1794 7359 Gravel mining; ready-mixed concrete; excavation work; equipment rental & leasing

(P-595)
KAUFMAN BUILDING & MGT INC
1834 Soscol Ave Ste C, NAPA (94559-1352)
PHONE.................................707 732-3770
Jeff Kaufman, *CEO*
EMP: 16 **EST:** 2016
SALES (est): 2.2MM **Privately Held**
WEB: www.kaufmanbuilding.com
SIC: 1442 Construction sand & gravel

(P-596)
NEVOCAL ENTERPRISES INC
Also Called: Kh Construction
5320 N Barcus Ave, Fresno (93722-5050)
PHONE.................................559 277-0700
Frank Cornell, *President*
EMP: 25 **EST:** 1997
SQ FT: 4,575
SALES (est): 2.4MM **Privately Held**
SIC: 1442 Construction sand & gravel

(P-597)
SANTA FE AGGREGATES INC (HQ)
11650 Shaffer Rd, Winton (95388-9604)
PHONE.................................209 358-3303
Ron C Turcotte, *President*
EMP: 19 **EST:** 1938
SALES (est): 25.4MM
SALES (corp-wide): 842MM **Privately Held**
WEB: www.teichert.com
SIC: 1442 Construction sand & gravel
PA: Teichert, Inc.
  5200 Franklin Dr Ste 115
  Pleasanton CA 94588
  916 484-3011

(P-598)
SIERRA CSCADE AGGRGATE ASP PDT
6600 Old Ski Rd, Chester (96020)
P.O. Box 1193 (96020-1193)
PHONE.................................530 258-4555
Kacie Holland, *President*
Caleb Holland, *Treasurer*
EMP: 21 **EST:** 2006
SALES (est): 5.9MM **Privately Held**
WEB: www.sierracascadeinc.com
SIC: 1442 Construction sand & gravel

(P-599)
THOMES CREEK ROCK CO INC
6069 99w, Corning (96021-9130)
PHONE.................................530 824-0191
Mary Belle Coulter, *President*
EMP: 22 **EST:** 1968
SQ FT: 1,000
SALES (est): 3.3MM **Privately Held**
WEB: www.thomascreek.com
SIC: 1442 Gravel & pebble mining

(P-600)
VULCAN CONSTRUCTION MTLS LLC
346 Mathew St, Santa Clara (95050-3114)
PHONE.................................408 213-4270
EMP: 21 **Publicly Held**
WEB: www.vulcanmaterials.com
SIC: 1442 Construction sand mining
HQ: Vulcan Construction Materials, Llc
  1200 Urban Center Dr
  Vestavia AL 35242
  205 298-3000

1446 Industrial Sand

(P-601)
BCJ SAND AND ROCK INC
3388 Regional Pkwy Ste A, Santa Rosa (95403-8219)
P.O. Box 440, Fulton (95439-0440)
PHONE.................................707 544-0303
J Brad Slender, *President*
EMP: 15 **EST:** 2002
SALES (est): 1.3MM **Privately Held**
WEB: www.bcj-co.com
SIC: 1446 Industrial sand

1499 Miscellaneous Nonmetallic Mining

(P-602)
H LIMA COMPANY INC
704 E Yosemite Ave, Manteca (95336-5827)
PHONE.................................209 239-6787
Michael Lima, *President*
Frank Lima, *Owner*
Debbie Enos, *Corp Secy*
Henry Frank Lima Jr, *Vice Pres*
Mark Lima, *Vice Pres*
EMP: 26 **EST:** 1962
SQ FT: 1,300
SALES (est): 6MM **Privately Held**
SIC: 1499 Gypsum mining

(P-603)
INDIAN HILL PROCESSING
2201 Michigan Bar Rd, Ione (95640-8505)
P.O. Box 218, Drytown (95699-0218)
PHONE.................................209 274-9164
Ron Matulich, *Administration*
EMP: 15 **EST:** 2013
SALES (est): 2MM **Privately Held**
SIC: 1499 Peat mining & processing

1521 General Contractors, Single Family Houses

(P-604)
ADVANCE CONSTRUCTION TECH INC
23575 Cabot Blvd Ste 206, Hayward (94545-1657)
P.O. Box 36221, San Jose (95158-6221)
PHONE.................................408 658-3682
Forest W Waldron III, *President*
EMP: 80 **EST:** 2009
SALES (est): 8.8MM **Privately Held**
WEB: www.actconstruction.net
SIC: 1521 Single-family home remodeling, additions & repairs

(P-605)
AIKEN UNDERGROUND INC
3000 Wilbur Ave Ste A, Antioch (94509-8569)
PHONE.................................925 776-4600
Mark Aiken, *President*
EMP: 42 **EST:** 2001
SQ FT: 2,500
SALES (est): 5.4MM **Privately Held**
SIC: 1521 Single-family housing construction

(P-606)
AIRPORT SPECIALTY PRODUCTS INC
2531 W Paul Ave, Fresno (93711-1145)
P.O. Box 5173 (93755-5173)
PHONE.................................559 439-9737
Timothy Bone, *President*
EMP: 40 **EST:** 1980
SQ FT: 2,000
SALES (est): 5MM **Privately Held**
SIC: 1521 1522 New construction, single-family houses; apartment building construction

(P-607)
ALBERT D SEENO CNSTR CO INC
4021 Port Chicago Hwy, Concord (94520-1122)
PHONE.................................925 671-7711
Albert D Seeno Jr, *CEO*
Colin Clements, *CFO*
Richard B Seeno, *Principal*
Thomas A Seeno, *Principal*
Steve Lichti, *Finance Dir*
EMP: 80 **EST:** 1959
SQ FT: 30,000
SALES (est): 36MM **Privately Held**
WEB: www.seenohomes.com
SIC: 1521 New construction, single-family houses

(P-608)
ALS INTERIORS INC
5710 Auburn Blvd Ste 14, Sacramento (95841-2945)
P.O. Box 41498 (95841-0498)
PHONE.................................916 344-2942
Ben Lillibridge, *President*
Alan Bodtker, *Vice Pres*
EMP: 40 **EST:** 2001
SQ FT: 3,000 **Privately Held**
SIC: 1521 1799 General remodeling, single-family houses; home/office interiors finishing, furnishing & remodeling

(P-609)
ALTEN CONSTRUCTION INC
1141 Marina Way S, Richmond (94804-3742)
PHONE.................................510 234-4200
Robert Andrew Alten, *CEO*
Shannon M Alten, *Vice Pres*
EMP: 80 **EST:** 1995
SQ FT: 14,000
SALES (est): 25.9MM **Privately Held**
WEB: www.altenconstruction.com
SIC: 1521 Single-family housing construction

(P-610)
ALWARD CONSTRUCTION COMPANY
1035 Carleton St, Berkeley (94710-2638)
PHONE.................................510 527-6498
Keith R Alward, *President*
Steve Boswell, *Project Mgr*
Stefan Carrieri, *Project Mgr*
Agustin Velasquez, *Maintence Staff*
Rick Patterson, *Master*
EMP: 35 **EST:** 1979
SALES (est): 6.3MM **Privately Held**
WEB: www.alwardconstruction.com
SIC: 1521 General remodeling, single-family houses; new construction, single-family houses

(P-611)
ANDREW CHEKENE ENTERPRISES INC
Also Called: AC Enterprises
21965 Meekland Ave, Hayward (94541-3862)
PHONE.................................650 588-1001
Andrew Chekene, *President*
Rafael Munoz, *Admin Sec*
Kim Lovell, *Administration*
Alex Halaj, *Superintendent*
EMP: 215 **EST:** 2007
SQ FT: 3,000
SALES (est): 48.5MM **Privately Held**
SIC: 1521 Single-family housing construction

(P-612)
APTIM FEDERAL SERVICES LLC
4005 Port Chicago Hwy, Concord (94520-1180)
PHONE.................................925 288-9898
Frank Hackett, *Branch Mgr*
Aimee Ransford, *Admin Asst*
EMP: 215
SALES (corp-wide): 2.3B **Privately Held**
WEB: www.aptim.com
SIC: 1521 Single-family housing construction
HQ: Aptim Federal Services, Llc
  4171 Essen Ln
  Baton Rouge LA 70809
  202 261-1900

(P-613)
AWT CONSTRUCTION GROUP INC
4740 E 2nd St Ste 22, Benicia (94510-1024)
PHONE.................................707 746-7500
James Kint, *President*
Gregory W Smith, *Vice Pres*
Shannon Brown, *Project Mgr*
Anthony Crumm, *Manager*
Julie Duggin, *Manager*
EMP: 65 **EST:** 2007
SQ FT: 3,000
SALES (est): 4MM **Privately Held**
WEB: www.awtconstructioninc.com
SIC: 1521 1542 Single-family housing construction; single-family home remodeling, additions & repairs; commercial & office building contractors

(P-614)
B C C S INC (PA)
Also Called: South Bay Construction Company
1711 Dell Ave, Campbell (95008-6904)
PHONE.................................408 379-5500
Richard Furtado, *Partner*
Chris Harris-Bolding, *Officer*
Luisa Samaha, *Admin Asst*
Carly Van Horn, *CIO*
Meghan Wilcox, *CIO*
EMP: 133 **EST:** 1993
SQ FT: 10,100
SALES (est): 59.1MM **Privately Held**
WEB: www.sbci.com
SIC: 1521 Single-family housing construction

(P-615)
BAINBRIDGE AND ASSOCIATES INC
Also Called: Chateau Construction
805 University Ave Ste I, Los Gatos (95032-7614)
PHONE.................................408 356-5040
Dan Bainbridge, *President*
Mary-Lynne Bainbridge, *Vice Pres*
EMP: 36 **EST:** 1977
SALES (est): 2.5MM **Privately Held**
SIC: 1521 New construction, single-family houses; general remodeling, single-family houses

(P-616)
BAY AREA BUILDERS INC
3360 De La Cruz Blvd, Santa Clara (95054-2606)
PHONE.................................408 648-4500
Kenneth E Rowell, *President*
Calvin Peterson, *Project Engr*
EMP: 40 **EST:** 2007 **Privately Held**
WEB: www.ba-builders.com
SIC: 1521 New construction, single-family houses

(P-617)
BETTER BUILDERS CNSTR INC
5263 Royal Oaks Dr, Oroville (95966-3878)
PHONE.................................530 589-2574
Jonathan J Starr, *President*
Belinda Starr, *Corp Secy*
EMP: 41 **EST:** 1975
SQ FT: 27,000
SALES (est): 2.4MM **Privately Held**
WEB: www.bbcoro.com
SIC: 1521 New construction, single-family houses; general remodeling, single-family houses

(P-618)
BIG-D PACIFIC BUILDERS LP
Also Called: Big-D Construction
6210 Stoneridge Mall Rd, Pleasanton (94588-3268)
PHONE.................................925 460-3232
Ken Mitchell, *Partner*
Darwin Morrison, *Project Mgr*
Jan De Jong, *Project Engr*
Randy Price, *Human Res Dir*
EMP: 77 **EST:** 2003

PRODUCTS & SERVICES SECTION
1521 - General Contractors, Single Family Houses County (P-643)

SALES (est): 12.4MM Privately Held
WEB: www.big-d.com
SIC: **1521** New construction, single-family houses

(P-619)
BILL BROWN CONSTRUCTION CO
242 Phelan Ave, San Jose (95112-6109)
PHONE.................................408 297-3738
William E Brown, *President*
EMP: 49 EST: 1978
SQ FT: 1,650
SALES (est): 5.6MM Privately Held
WEB: www.bbrownconstruction.com
SIC: **1521** 1794 1791 Single-family housing construction; excavation work; structural steel erection

(P-620)
BLU HOMES INC (PA)
1015 Walnut Ave, Vallejo (94592-1190)
PHONE.................................866 887-7997
William Haney, *President*
Gary Martell, *CFO*
Trevor Huffard, *Vice Pres*
Maura McCarthy, *Vice Pres*
Dennis Michaud, *Vice Pres*
EMP: 228 EST: 2007
SALES (est): 41.8MM Privately Held
WEB: www.bluhomes.com
SIC: **1521** New construction, single-family houses

(P-621)
BORGE CONSTRUCTION INC (PA)
Also Called: 5 Star Service
975 Fee Dr, Sacramento (95815-3907)
PHONE.................................916 927-4800
Thomas Burge, *CEO*
Glenn Pember, *Manager*
EMP: 48 EST: 2002
SALES (est): 5.7MM Privately Held
WEB: www.five-star-services.com
SIC: **1521** New construction, single-family houses

(P-622)
BRIDGE ECONOMIC DEV CORP (PA)
345 Spear St Ste 700, San Francisco (94105-6136)
PHONE.................................415 989-1111
Cynthia Parker, *CEO*
EMP: 59 EST: 1991
SALES (est): 2.7MM Privately Held
WEB: www.bridgehousing.com
SIC: **1521** Single-family housing construction

(P-623)
BRIGHT DEVELOPMENT
1620 N Carpenter Rd, Modesto (95351-1153)
PHONE.................................209 526-8242
Calvin E Bright, *President*
Carol Bright Tougas, *President*
Marjorie Bright, *Corp Secy*
Price Suzy, *Executive Asst*
David Butz, *Planning*
EMP: 40 EST: 1971
SQ FT: 7,000
SALES (est): 9.1MM Privately Held
WEB: www.bright-homes.com
SIC: **1521** New construction, single-family houses

(P-624)
BRITANNIA CONSTRUCTION INC
925 Terminal Way, San Carlos (94070-3224)
PHONE.................................650 742-6490
Gary Halpin, *President*
Tom Halpin, *Corp Secy*
Robert Halpin, *Vice Pres*
EMP: 40 EST: 1978
SALES (est): 5.5MM Privately Held
WEB: www.britanniarestoration.com
SIC: **1521** 1522 1531 1542 General remodeling, single-family houses; new construction, single-family houses; residential construction; operative builders; commercial & office buildings, renovation & repair

(P-625)
C & D CONTRACTORS INC
Also Called: C & D Construction
12803 Sneath Clay Rd, Nevada City (95959-3231)
P.O. Box 822 (95959-0822)
PHONE.................................530 264-7074
Charles Donald Faber, *CEO*
David Petty, *Exec VP*
Joel Shelton, *Manager*
EMP: 40 EST: 1988
SQ FT: 2,000
SALES (est): 17.9MM Privately Held
WEB: www.cdcontractors.squarespace.com
SIC: **1521** 1794 Single-family housing construction; excavation & grading, building construction

(P-626)
CENTRIX BUILDERS INC
160 S Linden Ave Ste 100, South San Francisco (94080-6435)
PHONE.................................650 876-9400
Joseph Cassidy, *CEO*
Sean Briody, *Supervisor*
EMP: 51 EST: 1995
SALES (est): 9.7MM Privately Held
WEB: www.centrixbuilders.com
SIC: **1521** New construction, single-family houses

(P-627)
CORNERSTONE SELECT BLDRS INC
5542 Brisa St Ste F, Livermore (94550-2524)
PHONE.................................510 490-7911
Juan Padilla, *President*
EMP: 43 EST: 2006 Privately Held
WEB: www.cornerstonesbi.com
SIC: **1521** New construction, single-family houses

(P-628)
CW HORTON GENERAL CONTR INC
3295 Depot Rd, Hayward (94545-2709)
PHONE.................................510 780-0949
Charles W Horton, *CEO*
Erinn Horton Kato, *Treasurer*
Erinn Kato, *Project Mgr*
Rick Leach, *Superintendent*
Ray Schubert, *Superintendent*
▲ EMP: 45 EST: 1982
SQ FT: 11,000
SALES (est): 9MM Privately Held
WEB: www.cwhortoninc.com
SIC: **1521** New construction, single-family houses

(P-629)
D CARLSON CONSTRUCTION INC (PA)
236 N Santa Cruz Ave # 244, Los Gatos (95030-7262)
PHONE.................................408 354-2893
Dennis Carlson, *President*
Libby Carlson, *Vice Pres*
EMP: 44 EST: 1990
SALES (est): 5.3MM Privately Held
WEB: www.dcarlsonconstructioninc.com
SIC: **1521** 1522 New construction, single-family houses; residential construction

(P-630)
DAVID SMITH
Also Called: Eagle Ridge Construction
7423 Winding Way, Fair Oaks (95628-6701)
PHONE.................................916 570-1460
David Smith, *Owner*
EMP: 50 EST: 2010
SALES (est): 4MM Privately Held
SIC: **1521** Single-family housing construction

(P-631)
DE MATTEI CONSTRUCTION INC
1794 The Alameda, San Jose (95126-1729)
PHONE.................................408 295-7516
Mark De Mattei, *President*
John Hinton, *CFO*
Travis Cotti, *Project Mgr*
Michael Ryan, *Project Mgr*
Holly Sweger, *Project Mgr*
▲ EMP: 60 EST: 1985
SQ FT: 5,000
SALES (est): 23.2MM Privately Held
WEB: www.demattei.com
SIC: **1521** 1542 New construction, single-family houses; commercial & office building contractors

(P-632)
DOMUS CONSTRUCTION & DESIGN
Also Called: Statewide
8864 Fruitridge Rd, Sacramento (95826-9708)
PHONE.................................916 381-7500
Maksim R Yurtsan, *CEO*
Alex Varabei, *Project Mgr*
Roman Cheglov, *Manager*
EMP: 50 EST: 1985
SALES (est): 10.2MM Privately Held
WEB: www.gostatewide.com
SIC: **1521** Repairing fire damage, single-family houses

(P-633)
DURDEN CONSTRUCTION INC
410 3rd St Ste A, San Juan Bautista (95045-3012)
P.O. Box 966 (95045-0966)
PHONE.................................831 623-1200
Judy Durden, *Principal*
Dennis Durden, *Principal*
Dodd Durden, *Principal*
Gregg Durden, *Principal*
Greg Durden, *Superintendent*
EMP: 48 EST: 2010
SALES (est): 7MM Privately Held
WEB: www.durdenconstruction.com
SIC: **1521** Single-family housing construction

(P-634)
E & E CO LTD
Also Called: Jla Home
2222 E Beamer St, Woodland (95776-6226)
PHONE.................................530 669-5991
Carys Lin, *Accountant*
EMP: 360 EST: 1994
WEB: www.ee1994.com
SIC: **1521** Single-family housing construction
PA: E & E Co., Ltd.
45875 Northport Loop E
Fremont CA 94538

(P-635)
ENERGY STAR CONSTRUCTION INC (PA)
2767 E Shaw Ave Ste 103, Fresno (93710-8231)
PHONE.................................559 231-5998
Hasham Ali, *CEO*
EMP: 37 EST: 2016
SALES (est): 577.7K Privately Held
WEB: www.energystarinc.com
SIC: **1521** Single-family housing construction

(P-636)
ERNST DEVELOPMENT INC
937 Lakeview Way, Emerald Hills (94062-3439)
PHONE.................................650 368-4539
Gary Ernst, *President*
EMP: 37 EST: 1981
SALES (est): 2.5MM Privately Held
SIC: **1521** 1522 6552 New construction, single-family houses; general remodeling, single-family houses; remodeling, multi-family dwellings; multi-family dwellings, new construction; land subdividers & developers, commercial

(P-637)
FAIRWEATHER & ASSOCIATES INC
140 Todd Rd, Santa Rosa (95407-8101)
PHONE.................................707 829-2922
Simon Fairweather, *Owner*
Galen Torneby, *COO*
Simonetta Baldwin, *Executive*
Sam Baldwin, *Office Mgr*
Justo Tapia, *Administration*
EMP: 40 EST: 1989
SQ FT: 600
SALES (est): 8.2MM Privately Held
WEB: www.fairweather-assoc.com
SIC: **1521** New construction, single-family houses

(P-638)
FJELLBO & SON CONSTRUCTION INC
1717 Solano Way Ste 20, Concord (94520-8302)
P.O. Box 476, Clayton (94517-0476)
PHONE.................................925 363-3000
Erik Scott Fjellbo, *Owner*
Linda Fjellbo, *Co-Owner*
EMP: 41 EST: 1965
SALES (est): 1MM Privately Held
WEB: www.fjellboson.com
SIC: **1521** General remodeling, single-family houses; new construction, single-family houses

(P-639)
FRONTIER LAND COMPANIES
Also Called: Frontrs-Frnters Land Companies
10100 Trinity Pkwy # 420, Stockton (95219-7238)
PHONE.................................209 957-8112
Thomas Doucette, *President*
George K Gibson, *Vice Pres*
EMP: 38 EST: 1991
SQ FT: 3,000
SALES (est): 4.1MM Privately Held
SIC: **1521** 8742 6552 Single-family housing construction; real estate consultant; subdividers & developers

(P-640)
FTG BUILDERS INC (PA)
384 Breen Rd, San Juan Bautista (95045-9710)
PHONE.................................408 564-1534
Matthew A Crosby, *Administration*
EMP: 38 EST: 2015
SALES (est): 5.1MM Privately Held
WEB: www.ftgbuilders.com
SIC: **1521** New construction, single-family houses

(P-641)
GALLAGHER INC
Also Called: Gallagher Construction
11198 Trails End Ct Ste 3, Truckee (96161-0272)
P.O. Box 2975 (96160-2975)
PHONE.................................530 414-0267
Seamus Gallagher, *President*
EMP: 45 EST: 2016
SALES (est): 7.2MM Privately Held
WEB: www.gallagherconstructiontahoe.com
SIC: **1521** New construction, single-family houses

(P-642)
GARY MCDONALD DEVELOPMENT CO
11326 N Glencastle Way, Fresno (93730-7003)
PHONE.................................559 436-1700
Gary McDonald, *CEO*
Jean Ishimoto, *Admin Asst*
Andrea McFadden, *Accounting Mgr*
Brad Hertel, *Prdtn Mgr*
Brian Hertel, *Sales Staff*
EMP: 37 EST: 1975
SALES (est): 7.4MM Privately Held
WEB: www.garymcdonaldhomes.com
SIC: **1521** New construction, single-family houses

(P-643)
GHILOTTI BROTHERS CNSTR INC
525 Jacoby St, San Rafael (94901-5305)
P.O. Box 10268 (94912-0268)
PHONE.................................415 454-7011
Eva R Ghilotti, *President*
Melissa Russo, *Assistant*
EMP: 56 EST: 1992

1521 - General Contractors, Single Family Houses County (P-644)

PRODUCTS & SERVICES SECTION

SALES (est): 10.3MM **Privately Held**
WEB: www.ghilotti.com
SIC: **1521** Single-family housing construction

(P-644)
GLA MORRIS CONSTRUCTION INC
10330 Donner Pass Rd A, Truckee (96161-2303)
PHONE.................................530 448-1613
Thomas Grossman, *President*
Richard Varela, *Business Dir*
Joseph Morris, *Principal*
Carl Harmon, *Project Mgr*
Jeremy Orenstein, *Opers Staff*
EMP: 42 EST: 1995
SALES (est): 9.2MM **Privately Held**
WEB: www.gla-morris.com
SIC: **1521** 1522 New construction, single-family houses; multi-family dwelling construction

(P-645)
GOLDEN COAST CNSTR RESTORATION
4811 Chippendale Dr # 301, Sacramento (95841-2555)
PHONE.................................916 955-7461
Alex Kotyakov, *President*
David Lewis, *General Mgr*
Don Trylovich, *Sales Staff*
Nick Terlouw, *Supervisor*
EMP: 68 EST: 2004
SALES (est): 10MM **Privately Held**
WEB: www.goldencoastco.com
SIC: **1521** 1542 1522 New construction, single-family houses; commercial & office buildings, renovation & repair; residential construction

(P-646)
GOODFELLOW BROS CALIFORNIA LLC
50 Contractors St, Livermore (94551-4863)
PHONE.................................925 245-2111
Brian Gates,
Ivan Eng, *Project Mgr*
Ryan Johnson, *Project Mgr*
Jeff Ramirez, *Project Mgr*
Brogan Cooper, *Project Engr*
EMP: 387 EST: 1921
SALES (est): 40MM **Privately Held**
WEB: www.goodfellowbros.com
SIC: **1521** Single-family housing construction

(P-647)
GRANITE CONSTRUCTION CO GUAM (DH)
585 W Beach St, Watsonville (95076-5123)
PHONE.................................831 724-1011
Tracy E Coppinger, *Ch of Bd*
Martin P Matheson, *President*
Darren S Beevor, *Vice Pres*
EMP: 63 EST: 2006
SALES (est): 10.5MM **Publicly Held**
WEB: www.graniteconstruction.com
SIC: **1521** New construction, single-family houses
HQ: Granite Construction Company
585 W Beach St
Watsonville CA 95076
831 724-1011

(P-648)
GRANVILLE HOMES INC
1396 W Herndon Ave # 101, Fresno (93711-7126)
PHONE.................................559 268-2000
Darius Assemi, *CEO*
Farid Assemi, *President*
Derek Hayashi, *CFO*
Jesse Buglione, *Creative Dir*
Cristina Lopez, *Executive Asst*
EMP: 60 EST: 1980
SQ FT: 5,000
SALES (est): 53.5MM **Privately Held**
WEB: www.gvhomes.com
SIC: **1521** New construction, single-family houses

(P-649)
GREEN VALLEY CORPORATION
Also Called: Barry Swenson Builders
740 Front St Ste 315, Santa Cruz (95060-4560)
PHONE.................................831 475-7100
Jennifer Cosby, *Manager*
Austin Johnson, *President*
Joshua Almazan, *Project Mgr*
James Brown, *Project Mgr*
Pat Deeton, *Project Mgr*
EMP: 70
SALES (corp-wide): 59MM **Privately Held**
WEB: www.swensonbuilders.com
SIC: **1521** New construction, single-family houses
PA: Green Valley Corporation
777 N 1st St Fl 5
San Jose CA 95112
408 287-0246

(P-650)
HAGGERTY CONSTRUCTION INC
2474 Wigwam Dr Ste A, Stockton (95205-2453)
PHONE.................................209 475-9898
Ryan Haggerty, *CEO*
Andrea Haggerty, *CFO*
Virginia Garcia, *Administration*
EMP: 49 EST: 2012
SALES (est): 25MM **Privately Held**
WEB: www.haggertybuilds.com
SIC: **1521** New construction, single-family houses

(P-651)
HARRELL REMODELING INC
944 Industrial Ave, Palo Alto (94303-4911)
PHONE.................................650 230-2900
Iris Harrell, *President*
Lisa Koutsky Sten, *General Mgr*
Olga Bazdyreva, *Administration*
Sinden Perren, *Administration*
Lisa Sten, *CIO*
EMP: 45 EST: 1985
SQ FT: 3,600
SALES (est): 15.6MM **Privately Held**
WEB: www.harrell-remodeling.com
SIC: **1521** 7389 General remodeling, single-family houses; interior designer

(P-652)
HUEY CONSTRUCTION MGT CO INC
Also Called: M H Construction
266 5th Ave Apt 1, San Francisco (94118-2394)
PHONE.................................415 558-9806
Elenita Dianela, *Principal*
Matthew Huey, *President*
EMP: 40 EST: 1979
SALES (est): 6.3MM **Privately Held**
SIC: **1521** General remodeling, single-family houses

(P-653)
IRON CONSTRUCTION INC
1955 The Alameda Fl 2, San Jose (95126-1445)
PHONE.................................408 282-1080
David Brian Edgar, *President*
Claudia Folzman, *COO*
William Klein, *CFO*
Mark Bendixen, *Executive*
Chris Branan, *Executive*
EMP: 40 EST: 2001
SQ FT: 11,832
SALES (est): 19.2MM **Privately Held**
WEB: www.ironconstruction.com
SIC: **1521** Single-family housing construction

(P-654)
ITSAGO BUILDERS INC
11928 Silver Cliff Way, Gold River (95670-8396)
PHONE.................................916 496-2316
Tad Rogers, *CEO*
EMP: 50 EST: 2015
SALES (est): 2.5MM **Privately Held**
SIC: **1521** New construction, single-family houses

(P-655)
JF SHEA CONSTRUCTION INC
17400 Clear Creek Rd, Redding (96001-5113)
P.O. Box 494519 (96049-4519)
PHONE.................................530 246-4292
Ed Kernaghan, *Vice Pres*
EMP: 60
SALES (corp-wide): 2.1B **Privately Held**
WEB: www.sheahomes.com
SIC: **1521** New construction, single-family houses
HQ: J.F. Shea Construction, Inc.
655 Brea Canyon Rd
Walnut CA 91789
909 594-9500

(P-656)
JKB HOMES CORP
2370 W Monte Vista Ave, Turlock (95382-9668)
P.O. Box 2998 (95381-2998)
PHONE.................................209 668-5303
James Konrad Brenda, *President*
Robert Martelly, *Vice Pres*
EMP: 36 EST: 1980
SQ FT: 4,500
SALES (est): 3.8MM **Privately Held**
WEB: www.jkbenergy.com
SIC: **1521** New construction, single-family houses

(P-657)
JOHN NAIMI INC
Also Called: New Horizon Mobile Homes
2410 Monterey Hwy, San Jose (95111-1919)
P.O. Box 3327 (95156-3327)
PHONE.................................408 280-7433
Faramarz Naimi, *President*
Ali Naimi, *Manager*
EMP: 40 EST: 1986
SALES (est): 2.4MM **Privately Held**
SIC: **5271** 1521 Mobile homes; single-family housing construction

(P-658)
JTS COMMUNITIES INC (PA)
11249 Gold Country Blvd # 180, Gold River (95670-3006)
P.O. Box 791, Browns Valley (95918-0791)
PHONE.................................916 487-3434
Jack T Sweigart, *CEO*
Tim Weir, *CFO*
Clara Surenkov, *Purch Mgr*
Kristen Sandahl, *Sales Staff*
Andrea Digini, *Mktg Coord*
EMP: 49 EST: 1973
SQ FT: 5,000
SALES (est): 44.2MM **Privately Held**
SIC: **1521** Single-family housing construction

(P-659)
JUNGSTEN CONSTRUCTION
495 Miller Ave, Mill Valley (94941-5837)
PHONE.................................415 381-3162
John C Caletti, *CEO*
Helen S Caletti, *Vice Pres*
▲ EMP: 47 EST: 1987
SALES (est): 10.3MM **Privately Held**
WEB: www.jungsten.com
SIC: **1521** 1542 New construction, single-family houses; nonresidential construction

(P-660)
KRUEGER BROS BUILDERS INC
535 Alabama St, San Francisco (94110-1348)
PHONE.................................415 863-5846
David Krueger, *President*
Catherine Krueger, *Vice Pres*
Chales Lewis, *Agent*
EMP: 40 EST: 1976
SQ FT: 12,300
SALES (est): 6.3MM **Privately Held**
WEB: www.kruegerbrosinc.com
SIC: **1521** 1542 General remodeling, single-family houses; new construction, single-family houses; commercial & office buildings, renovation & repair; commercial & office building, new construction

(P-661)
L & D CONSTRUCTION CO INC
255 W Julian St Ste 200, San Jose (95110-2444)
PHONE.................................408 292-0128
Michael A Lodoen, *President*
Gloria Chiang, *CFO*
Steve Davis, *Vice Pres*
Charles W Davidson, *Admin Sec*
Ted Lytle, *Superintendent*
EMP: 35 EST: 1979
SQ FT: 4,685
SALES (est): 8.9MM **Privately Held**
WEB: www.landd.com
SIC: **1521** 1522 New construction, single-family houses; apartment building construction

(P-662)
LAMPERTI ASSOCIATES
Also Called: Kitchencraft of Marin
1241 Andersen Dr Ste A, San Rafael (94901-5353)
PHONE.................................415 454-1623
Sean Kelly, *President*
EMP: 37 EST: 1987
SALES (est): 1.2MM **Privately Held**
WEB: www.lampertikitchens.com
SIC: **1521** General remodeling, single-family houses; new construction, single-family houses

(P-663)
LENCIONI CONSTRUCTION CO INC
420 Maple St, Redwood City (94063-1918)
PHONE.................................650 216-9900
Gary Lencioni, *President*
Geza Paulovits, *CFO*
Kathy Woods, *Corp Secy*
Jessica Garcia, *Office Mgr*
Cynthia Oatman, *Project Mgr*
EMP: 40 EST: 1974
SALES (est): 7.1MM **Privately Held**
WEB: www.lencioniconstruction.com
SIC: **1521** New construction, single-family houses; general remodeling, single-family houses

(P-664)
MACARTHUR TRNST CMNTY PRTNERS
345 Spear St Ste 700, San Francisco (94105-6136)
P.O. Box 190220 (94119-0220)
PHONE.................................415 989-1111
Susan Johnson, *Vice Pres*
EMP: 58 EST: 2004
SALES (est): 2.7MM **Privately Held**
WEB: www.bridgehousing.com
SIC: **1521** Single-family housing construction
PA: Bridge Economic Development Corporation
345 Spear St Ste 700
San Francisco CA 94105

(P-665)
MACHADO & SONS CNSTR INC
1000 S Kilroy Rd, Turlock (95380-9589)
PHONE.................................209 632-5260
Manuel B Machado, *President*
Jason Machado, *Vice Pres*
Mary E Machado, *Admin Sec*
Matt Machado, *Project Mgr*
EMP: 50 EST: 1985
SALES (est): 24.2MM **Privately Held**
WEB: www.machadoandsons.com
SIC: **1521** 1542 1771 1541 New construction, single-family houses; commercial & office building, new construction; patio construction, concrete; industrial buildings & warehouses

(P-666)
MAI CONSTRUCTION INC
50 Bonaventura Dr, San Jose (95134-2104)
PHONE.................................408 434-9880
Roger Mairose, *Ch of Bd*
Mike Mairose, *President*
Barry Paxton, *Vice Pres*
Joe Fabbri, *Project Mgr*
Dimitri Batalha, *Project Engr*

▲ = Import ▼ = Export
◆ = Import/Export

EMP: 109 **EST:** 1973
SQ FT: 38,036
SALES (est): 23.3MM **Privately Held**
WEB: www.maiconst.com
SIC: 1521 Single-family housing construction

(P-667)
MARK TANNER CONSTRUCTION INC
10603 E River St, Truckee (96161-0339)
PHONE..................530 587-4000
Mark Tanner, *President*
Kathy Tanner, *Admin Sec*
Rachel Dobronyi, *Project Mgr*
Rebecca Richstad, *Asst Controller*
Jen Weissenberg, *Manager*
EMP: 35 **EST:** 2004
SALES (est): 6.5MM **Privately Held**
WEB: www.marktannerconstruction.com
SIC: 1521 New construction, single-family houses

(P-668)
MARKETONE BUILDERS INC
Also Called: Market One Builders
1200 R St Ste 150, Sacramento (95811-5806)
PHONE..................916 928-7474
Tom Ford, *Principal*
Kayla Dehaven, *Executive Asst*
Tracy Price, *Administration*
Eric Bosley, *Project Mgr*
Mike Brown, *Project Mgr*
EMP: 49 **EST:** 1997
SQ FT: 3,000
SALES (est): 27MM **Privately Held**
WEB: www.m1b.com
SIC: 1521 New construction, single-family houses

(P-669)
MASON BPP INC
837 Arnold Dr Ste 4, Martinez (94553-6534)
PHONE..................925 256-1092
Lowell Mason, *Owner*
EMP: 35 **EST:** 1974
SALES (est): 3.8MM **Privately Held**
WEB: www.buildingperformanceprofessionals.com
SIC: 1521 1542 New construction, single-family houses; general remodeling, single-family houses; commercial & office building contractors

(P-670)
MATARZZI / PELSINGER BLDRS INC
355 11th St Ste 200, San Francisco (94103-4344)
PHONE..................415 285-6930
Daniel Pelsinger, *President*
David Samson, *COO*
Daniel Matarozzi, *Treasurer*
Shane Curnyn, *Dept Chairman*
James Kuhn, *Project Mgr*
EMP: 45 **EST:** 1982
SQ FT: 4,000
SALES (est): 19.2MM **Privately Held**
WEB: www.matpelbuilders.com
SIC: 1521 1522 1541 1542 New construction, single-family houses; multi-family dwellings, new construction; industrial buildings, new construction; commercial & office building, new construction

(P-671)
MCCLONE CONSTRUCTION COMPANY
4340 Product Dr, Cameron Park (95682-8492)
P.O. Box 939, Shingle Springs (95682-0939)
PHONE..................559 431-9411
Scott McClone, *Branch Mgr*
John Salluce, *Vice Pres*
Kim Wagner, *Office Mgr*
Chris Vassiliadis, *Info Tech Dir*
Nicanor Ceja, *Project Mgr*
EMP: 115 **Privately Held**
WEB: www.mcclone.net
SIC: 1521 Single-family housing construction

PA: Mcclone Construction Company
5170 Hillsdale Cir Ste B
El Dorado Hills CA 95762

(P-672)
MCCUTCHEON CONSTRUCTION CO INC
1280 6th St, Berkeley (94710-1402)
PHONE..................925 280-0083
Michael Mc Cutcheon, *President*
Leigh Genser, *Vice Pres*
Janet McCutcheon, *Admin Sec*
Vicente Contreras, *Project Leader*
Gary Whitehead, *Marketing Staff*
EMP: 42 **EST:** 1980
SQ FT: 6,000
SALES (est): 9.3MM **Privately Held**
WEB: www.mcbuild.com
SIC: 1521 New construction, single-family houses; general remodeling, single-family houses

(P-673)
MEHUS CONSTRUCTION INC
211 San Mateo Ave, Los Gatos (95030-4320)
PHONE..................408 395-2388
Paul Mehus, *President*
Jacqueline A Mehus, *Corp Secy*
Fernando Dacosta, *Vice Pres*
Milton Nicholas, *Vice Pres*
Mark Quale, *Director*
EMP: 45 **EST:** 1974
SQ FT: 800
SALES (est): 5.3MM **Privately Held**
WEB: www.mehus.com
SIC: 1521 New construction, single-family houses

(P-674)
MHP BUILDERS INC
3202 W March Ln, Stockton (95219-2351)
PHONE..................209 951-6190
Samantha Ann Matthews, *Principal*
Gary Mancebo, *CFO*
Richard Luck, *Vice Pres*
Marie Baretta, *Controller*
EMP: 35 **EST:** 2010
SALES (est): 2MM **Privately Held**
SIC: 1521 New construction, single-family houses

(P-675)
MIDSTATE CONSTRUCTION CORP
1180 Holm Rd Ste A, Petaluma (94954-7120)
PHONE..................707 762-3200
Roger Nelson, *President*
Jim Debolt, *CFO*
Wesley Barry II, *Vice Pres*
Patrick Draeger, *Vice Pres*
Richard Oberdorfer, *Vice Pres*
EMP: 80 **EST:** 1987
SQ FT: 18,928
SALES (est): 33.6MM **Privately Held**
WEB: www.midstateconstruction.com
SIC: 1521 1541 1542 New construction, single-family houses; general remodeling, single-family houses; industrial buildings, new construction; renovation, remodeling & repairs: industrial buildings; commercial & office building, new construction; commercial & office buildings, renovation & repair

(P-676)
MIGHTY BUILDINGS INC
610 85th Ave, Oakland (94621-1223)
PHONE..................415 583-5657
Vyacheslav Solonitsyn, *CEO*
Tim Barry, *Manager*
EMP: 35 **EST:** 2018
SALES (est): 5.2MM **Privately Held**
WEB: www.mightybuildings.com
SIC: 1521 Single-family housing construction

(P-677)
MIKE ROVNER CONSTRUCTION INC
1758 Junction Ave Ste C, San Jose (95112-1022)
PHONE..................408 453-6070

Mike Rovner, *President*
Dave Holland, *Vice Pres*
Skylar Jewett, *Executive Asst*
Kristen Abrams, *Administration*
Miguel Flores, *Contractor*
EMP: 157 **Privately Held**
WEB: www.rovnerconstruction.com
SIC: 1521 New construction, single-family houses
PA: Mike Rovner Construction, Inc.
5400 Tech Cir
Moorpark CA 93021

(P-678)
NORTH WIND CNSTR SVCS LLC
730 Howe Ave Ste 700, Sacramento (95825-4641)
PHONE..................916 333-3015
Brent Brooks,
EMP: 69 **EST:** 2011
SALES (est): 2.8MM **Privately Held**
WEB: www.northwindgrp.com
SIC: 1521 Single-family housing construction

(P-679)
OMNI MECHANICAL SOLUTION (PA)
6712 Preston Ave, Livermore (94551-5144)
PHONE..................925 784-4726
James Merver, *President*
EMP: 63 **EST:** 2017
SALES (est): 3.9MM **Privately Held**
SIC: 1521 Single-family housing construction

(P-680)
OPI COMMERCIAL BUILDERS INC (PA)
1202 Lincoln Ave Ste 10, San Jose (95125-3070)
PHONE..................408 377-4800
Jon Persing, *President*
David Beausoleil, *Project Mgr*
Aaron Cunningham, *Project Engr*
Adam Marrs, *Project Engr*
EMP: 66 **EST:** 2004
SALES (est): 10.2MM **Privately Held**
WEB: www.opibuilders.com
SIC: 1521 New construction, single-family houses

(P-681)
PAUL RYAN ASSOCIATES
200 Gate 5 Rd Ste 113, Sausalito (94965-1456)
PHONE..................415 861-3085
Paul Brill Ryan, *CEO*
Joseph Welsh, *CFO*
James Friedman, *Chairman*
▲ **EMP:** 66 **EST:** 1981
SALES (est): 50MM **Privately Held**
WEB: www.ryanassociates.com
SIC: 1521 New construction, single-family houses

(P-682)
PBC ENTERPRISES
Also Called: Petkus Brothers and Company
4760 Rocklin Rd, Rocklin (95677-4313)
PHONE..................916 415-9966
Kevin C Petkus, *President*
Daniel A Petkus, *Treasurer*
Kevin Petkus, *Vice Pres*
Keith Petkus, *Sales Staff*
EMP: 40 **EST:** 1983
SQ FT: 19,820
SALES (est): 8.5MM **Privately Held**
WEB: www.petkusbrothers.com
SIC: 1521 General remodeling, single-family houses; new construction, single-family houses; patio & deck construction & repair

(P-683)
PENINSULA CUSTOM HOMES INC
1401 Old County Rd, San Carlos (94070-5202)
PHONE..................650 574-0241
Richard L Breaux, *CEO*
Bryan Murphy, *President*
Dennis Neketin, *Project Mgr*
Courtney Roth, *Manager*

EMP: 60 **EST:** 1979
SALES (est): 11.8MM **Privately Held**
WEB: www.pchi.org
SIC: 1521 New construction, single-family houses

(P-684)
PEREIRA INDUS CNSTR MAINT INC
15355 W Grant Line Rd, Tracy (95304-9707)
PHONE..................209 835-2393
Thomas E Pereira, *President*
Carol Czupka, *Vice Pres*
Kim Christian, *Admin Mgr*
EMP: 46 **EST:** 1994
SALES (est): 1.4MM **Privately Held**
WEB: www.pereiraindustrialservices.com
SIC: 1521 Single-family housing construction

(P-685)
PETE MOFFAT CONSTRUCTION INC
947 Industrial Ave, Palo Alto (94303-4912)
PHONE..................650 493-8899
Pete Moffat, *President*
Brad Harris, *Officer*
Vanessa Liang, *Office Mgr*
Eric Aurandt, *Project Mgr*
Kurt Burnell, *Project Mgr*
EMP: 35
SQ FT: 1,000
SALES (est): 41.5MM **Privately Held**
WEB: www.petemoffat.com
SIC: 1521 New construction, single-family houses; general remodeling, single-family houses

(P-686)
PINNACLE BUILDERS INC
1911 Douglas Blvd Ste 85, Roseville (95661-3811)
PHONE..................916 372-5000
EMP: 300
SQ FT: 3,000
SALES (est): 11.5MM **Privately Held**
WEB: www.pinnaclebuildersinc.com
SIC: 1521 1542 1751 1522 Single-Family House Cnst Nonresidential Cnstn Carpentry Contractor Residential Construction

(P-687)
PLATINUM BUILDERS INC
948 N 8th St, San Jose (95112-2938)
PHONE..................408 456-0300
Donna De Avila, *CEO*
Nuno Deavila, *President*
Donna De, *CFO*
Donna Deavila, *CFO*
EMP: 35 **EST:** 2006
SALES (est): 4.9MM **Privately Held**
WEB: www.platinumbld.com
SIC: 1521 New construction, single-family houses

(P-688)
PRINCIPAL BUILDERS INC
616 Minna St, San Francisco (94103-2718)
PHONE..................415 434-1500
Scott Reay, *CEO*
Brandon Jones, *Principal*
Noel Morrison, *General Mgr*
Mike Tarrant, *General Mgr*
Caroline Burcham, *Project Mgr*
EMP: 35 **EST:** 2003
SQ FT: 6,400
SALES (est): 34.2MM **Privately Held**
WEB: www.principalbuilders.com
SIC: 1521 New construction, single-family houses

(P-689)
QUALITY FIRST HOME IMPRV INC (PA)
6545 Sunrise Blvd Ste 202, Citrus Heights (95610-5232)
PHONE..................877 663-6707
G C Anderson, *President*
Mike Wise, *COO*
Gary Kluck, *Vice Pres*
Tim Stapp, *Branch Mgr*
Deanna Richardson, *Admin Asst*
EMP: 103 **EST:** 2005

1521 - General Contractors, Single Family Houses County (P-690)

PRODUCTS & SERVICES SECTION

SALES (est): 22.5MM **Privately Held**
WEB: www.qualityfirsthome.com
SIC: **1521** General remodeling, single-family houses

(P-690)
QUALITY GROUP HOMES INC
Also Called: Consortium For Community Svcs
4928 E Clinton Way # 108, Fresno (93727-1526)
PHONE.....................................916 930-0066
EMP: 184 **Privately Held**
WEB: www.qualityfamilyservices.org
SIC: **1521** Single-Family House Construction
PA: Quality Group Homes, Inc.
4928 E Clinton Way # 108
Fresno CA 93727

(P-691)
R J DAILEY CONSTRUCTION CO
401 1st St, Los Altos (94022-3607)
PHONE.....................................650 948-5196
Robert J Dailey, *President*
Christine Dailey, *Corp Secy*
Dennis Davis, *Project Mgr*
Tracy Sinkinson, *Marketing Staff*
▲ EMP: 69 EST: 1976
SQ FT: 2,000
SALES (est): 12.2MM **Privately Held**
WEB: www.rjdailey.com
SIC: **1521** New construction, single-family houses; general remodeling, single-family houses

(P-692)
RAL BUILDERS
500 Giuseppe Ct Ste 1, Roseville (95678-6305)
PHONE.....................................916 960-4889
Phil Raynall, *President*
EMP: 47 EST: 1993
SALES (est): 1.3MM **Privately Held**
WEB: www.ralbuildersinc.com
SIC: **1521** 1541 New construction, single-family houses; single-family home remodeling, additions & repairs; industrial buildings & warehouses

(P-693)
REDHORSE CONSTRUCTORS INC
36 Professional Ctr Pkwy, San Rafael (94903-2703)
PHONE.....................................415 492-2020
David J Warner, *President*
Jay Blumenfeld, *General Mgr*
Majid Ghafary, *Administration*
Smith Craig, *Project Mgr*
Craig Smith, *Project Mgr*
▲ EMP: 75 EST: 1981
SQ FT: 3,500
SALES (est): 26.1MM **Privately Held**
WEB: www.redhorseconstructors.com
SIC: **1521** General remodeling, single-family houses; new construction, single-family houses

(P-694)
REDMONT CNSTR & INV CO INC
Also Called: Springs Jr Walter M Cnstr Co
881 Hurlingame Ave, Redwood City (94063-3519)
PHONE.....................................650 306-9344
Walter M Springs Jr, *President*
Zula Springs, *Corp Secy*
EMP: 53 EST: 1959
SQ FT: 2,200
SALES (est): 3MM **Privately Held**
WEB: www.springsconstruction.com
SIC: **1521** New construction, single-family houses; general remodeling, single-family houses; repairing fire damage, single-family houses

(P-695)
REGIONAL BUILDERS INC (PA)
3941 Park Dr Ste 20, El Dorado Hills (95762-4577)
PHONE.....................................916 717-2669
Austin Boling, *Manager*
EMP: 48 EST: 2010
SALES (est): 2.9MM **Privately Held**
SIC: **1521** New construction, single-family houses

(P-696)
REMICK ASSOCIATES DB INC
1230 Howard St 2, San Francisco (94103-2712)
PHONE.....................................415 896-9500
Nicolas J Ehr, *President*
Frederick Bicknell, *Treasurer*
Anna Wade, *Office Mgr*
John Kosich, *Admin Sec*
EMP: 45 EST: 1975
SQ FT: 1,600
SALES (est): 12.2MM **Privately Held**
WEB: www.remickassociates.com
SIC: **1521** 8712 New construction, single-family houses; architectural engineering

(P-697)
REYNEN & BARDIS CNSTR LLC (PA)
10630 Mather Blvd, Mather (95655-4125)
PHONE.....................................916 366-3665
Chris Bardis, *President*
John Reynen, *Admin Sec*
EMP: 120 EST: 1999
SALES (est): 39.3MM **Privately Held**
WEB: www.bardishomes.com
SIC: **1521** 6552 New construction, single-family houses; land subdividers & developers, residential

(P-698)
ROBERT L BROWN CNSTR INC
4878 Sunrise Dr, Martinez (94553-4346)
PHONE.....................................925 228-4944
Robert L Brown, *President*
David Brown, *Vice Pres*
Greg Cole, *Vice Pres*
Michael Phair, *Manager*
Ignacio Cambero, *Superintendent*
EMP: 35 EST: 1975
SQ FT: 6,500
SALES (est): 10.2MM **Privately Held**
WEB: www.rlbci.com
SIC: **1521** 1541 New construction, single-family houses; industrial buildings & warehouses

(P-699)
ROOFLINE BUILDERS INC
1807 Santa Rita Rd, Pleasanton (94566-4779)
PHONE.....................................925 201-1924
David Lander, *CEO*
EMP: 35 EST: 2015
SALES (est): 1.3MM **Privately Held**
WEB: www.rooflinebuilders.com
SIC: **1521** New construction, single-family houses

(P-700)
SAK CONSTRUCTION LLC
4253 Duluth Ave, Rocklin (95765-1400)
PHONE.....................................916 644-1400
Ryan Broyles, *Branch Mgr*
Chris Vogt, *Engineer*
EMP: 40
SALES (corp-wide): 140.9MM **Privately Held**
WEB: www.sakcon.com
SIC: **1521** Single-family housing construction
PA: Sak Construction, Llc
864 Hoff Rd
O Fallon MO 63366
636 674-9104

(P-701)
SANTOS LEGACY BUILDERS LLC
2829 Watt Ave 101, Sacramento (95821-6200)
PHONE.....................................916 439-2777
Ernesto David Santos, *Principal*
EMP: 99 EST: 2014
SALES (est): 3.4MM **Privately Held**
SIC: **1521** New construction, single-family houses

(P-702)
SCHALICH BROTHERS CNSTR INC
85 Galli Dr Ste J, Novato (94949-5716)
PHONE.....................................415 382-7733
John Schalich, *President*
Michael Schalich, *Corp Secy*
James Schalich, *Vice Pres*
EMP: 48 EST: 1980
SQ FT: 1,100
SALES (est): 2.5MM **Privately Held**
WEB: www.schalichbrosconstruction.com
SIC: **1521** New construction, single-family houses; general remodeling, single-family houses

(P-703)
SEARS HOME IMPRV PDTS INC
1155 Veterans Blvd, Redwood City (94063-2036)
PHONE.....................................650 645-9974
EMP: 139
SALES (corp-wide): 4.1B **Privately Held**
SIC: **1521** General remodeling, single-family houses
HQ: Sears Home Improvement Products, Inc.
1024 Florida Central Pkwy
Longwood FL 32750
407 767-0990

(P-704)
SEARS HOME IMPRV PDTS INC
491 Tres Pinos Rd, Hollister (95023-5592)
PHONE.....................................831 245-0062
EMP: 139
SALES (corp-wide): 4.1B **Privately Held**
SIC: **1521** General remodeling, single-family houses
HQ: Sears Home Improvement Products, Inc.
1024 Florida Central Pkwy
Longwood FL 32750
407 767-0990

(P-705)
SELIG CONSTRUCTION CORP
337 Huss Dr, Chico (95928-8209)
PHONE.....................................530 893-5898
M Scott Selig, *President*
William Brereton, *Mktg Dir*
Joyce Gulliver, *Sales Mgr*
▲ EMP: 50 EST: 1995
SALES (est): 7MM **Privately Held**
WEB: www.seligconstruction.com
SIC: **1521** General remodeling, single-family houses

(P-706)
SHEEHAN CONSTRUCTION INC
477 Devlin Rd Ste 108, NAPA (94558-7511)
PHONE.....................................707 603-2610
Steve Mosiman, *President*
Tom Sheehan, *Vice Pres*
Keith Mackey, *Planning*
Lori Scott, *Human Res Mgr*
EMP: 51 EST: 1983
SALES (est): 4.6MM **Privately Held**
WEB: www.sheehanconstruction.com
SIC: **1521** New construction, single-family houses

(P-707)
SIGNATURE HOMES INC
4670 Willow Rd Ste 200, Pleasanton (94588-8588)
PHONE.....................................925 463-1122
James C Ghielmetti, *CEO*
Gary L Galindo, *President*
John Ford, *CFO*
Jennifer Almeida, *Vice Pres*
Wendy Cohen, *Vice Pres*
EMP: 51 EST: 1987
SALES (est): 12.4MM **Privately Held**
WEB: www.sighomes.com
SIC: **1521** New construction, single-family houses

(P-708)
SILVERADO NAPA CORP (HQ)
1600 Atlas Peak Rd, NAPA (94558-1425)
PHONE.....................................707 226-1325
Isao Okawo, *President*
Takako Ogura, *Exec VP*
Setsuo Okawa, *Vice Pres*
Kaitlan Gaisor, *Manager*
EMP: 63 EST: 1977
SQ FT: 2,000
SALES (est): 28.9MM **Privately Held**
WEB: www.silveradoresort.com
SIC: **1521** 7997 Single-family housing construction; country club, membership

(P-709)
SST CONSTRUCTION LLC
2731 Citrus Rd Ste D, Rancho Cordova (95742-6303)
PHONE.....................................844 477-8787
Mehrad Saidi, *Principal*
EMP: 41 EST: 2015
SALES (est): 2.6MM **Privately Held**
WEB: www.sstsolar.com
SIC: **1521** Single-family housing construction

(P-710)
STEBBINS CONSTRUCTION CORP
1057 Wilmington Way, Emerald Hills (94062-4069)
PHONE.....................................650 299-1488
EMP: 40
SALES (est): 1.9MM **Privately Held**
SIC: **1521** Single-Family House Construction

(P-711)
SUAREZ & MUNOZ CNSTR INC
Also Called: S M C
2490 American Ave, Hayward (94545-1810)
PHONE.....................................510 782-6065
Eduardo Suarez, *President*
John Suarez, *Corp Secy*
Martin Munoz, *Vice Pres*
Jessica Munoz, *Admin Asst*
Efrain Ibarra, *Project Mgr*
EMP: 36 EST: 2005
SALES (est): 10.4MM **Privately Held**
WEB: www.suarezmunoz.com
SIC: **1521** Single-family housing construction

(P-712)
SUFFOLK CONSTRUCTION CO INC
525 Market St Ste 2850, San Francisco (94105-2772)
PHONE.....................................415 848-0500
Jason Cardamone, *Manager*
EMP: 161
SALES (corp-wide): 2.4B **Privately Held**
WEB: www.suffolk.com
SIC: **1521** Single-family housing construction
PA: Suffolk Construction Company, Inc.
65 Allerton St
Boston MA 02119
617 445-3500

(P-713)
SUMMERHILL CONSTRUCTION CO
Also Called: Summerhill Homes
3000 Executive Pkwy # 450, San Ramon (94583-4255)
PHONE.....................................925 244-7520
Roger Menard, *President*
Yvonne Sheets, *Vice Pres*
Tad Holland, *Marketing Staff*
Justin Shupp, *Director*
EMP: 35 EST: 1976
SQ FT: 45,000
SALES (est): 24.9MM
SALES (corp-wide): 201.9MM **Privately Held**
WEB: www.summerhillhomes.com
SIC: **1521** New construction, single-family houses
HQ: Summerhill Homes
3000 Executive Pkwy # 450
San Ramon CA 94583
925 244-7500

(P-714)
SUPPORT FOR HOME INC
1333 Howe Ave Ste 206, Sacramento (95825-3362)
PHONE.....................................530 792-8484
Bert Cave, *Principal*
Carlotta Sanchez, *Principal*
EMP: 50 EST: 2008
SALES (est): 8.1MM **Privately Held**
WEB: www.apexcare.com
SIC: **1521** Single-family housing construction

▲ = Import ▼ = Export ◆ = Import/Export

PRODUCTS & SERVICES SECTION — **1522 - General Contractors, Residential Other Than Single Family County (P-739)**

(P-715)
TALMADGE CONSTRUCTION INC
8070 Soquel Dr, Aptos (95003-3941)
PHONE 831 689-9133
Jeffrey H Talmadge, *President*
Sonia Swain, *Manager*
EMP: 43 **EST:** 1984
SALES (est): 11.3MM **Privately Held**
WEB: www.talmadgeconstruction.com
SIC: 1521 New construction, single-family houses

(P-716)
TARC CONSTRUCTION INC (PA)
3230 Darby Cmn Ste A, Fremont (94539-3225)
P.O. Box 4226, Santa Cruz (95063-4226)
PHONE 408 224-2154
Albert R Cavazos, *President*
Tamara Cavazos, *CFO*
Camara Cavazos, *Treasurer*
Raudel Perez, *Project Mgr*
Fernando Chavez, *Controller*
EMP: 45 **EST:** 2003
SALES (est): 30.9MM **Privately Held**
WEB: www.tarcinc.com
SIC: 1521 Single-family housing construction

(P-717)
TAYLOR MORRISON HOMES
81 Blue Ravine Rd Ste 220, Folsom (95630-4735)
PHONE 916 355-8900
Jennifer Besmer, *Vice Pres*
Andrew Bodary, *Vice Pres*
Kevin Huff, *Vice Pres*
Kathy Jensen, *Vice Pres*
Jodi Mosser, *Vice Pres*
EMP: 38 **EST:** 2010
SALES (est): 5.9MM **Privately Held**
SIC: 1521 New construction, single-family houses

(P-718)
THOMPSON BROOKS INC
151 Vermont St Ste 9, San Francisco (94103-5184)
PHONE 415 581-2600
Judith A Thompson, *CEO*
R Bruce Clymer, *President*
Clifton B Shoolroy, *CFO*
Greg Hall, *Vice Pres*
EMP: 50 **EST:** 1991
SQ FT: 5,000
SALES (est): 9.5MM **Privately Held**
WEB: www.thompsonbrooks.com
SIC: 1521 1542 1541 1531 New construction, single-family houses; general remodeling, single-family houses; nonresidential construction; industrial buildings & warehouses; operative builders

(P-719)
TIM LEWIS COMMUNITIES
3500 Douglas Blvd Ste 270, Roseville (95661-4280)
PHONE 916 783-2300
Jay Timothy Lewis, *CEO*
Ruth Mackwood, *Controller*
Ann Coombs, *Sales Associate*
Linda Sender, *Sales Associate*
Karen Ackerman, *Director*
EMP: 40 **EST:** 1986
SALES (est): 23.6MM **Privately Held**
WEB: www.timlewis.com
SIC: 1521 New construction, single-family houses

(P-720)
TIM MELLO CONSTRUCTION
464 Lamarque Ct, Grass Valley (95945-7061)
PHONE 530 205-8588
Timothy Mello, *Principal*
EMP: 50 **EST:** 2011
SALES (est): 2.3MM **Privately Held**
SIC: 1521 Single-family housing construction

(P-721)
TIMBERLINE WALL SYSTEMS
5276 Cold Springs Dr, Foresthill (95631-9740)
P.O. Box 8505, Woodland (95776-8505)
PHONE 530 613-8070
Casey Peoples, *President*
EMP: 49 **EST:** 2017
SALES (est): 3.4MM **Privately Held**
SIC: 1521 Single-family housing construction

(P-722)
TRILOGY AT RIO VISTA
1200 Clubhouse Dr, Rio Vista (94571-9801)
PHONE 707 374-6871
Steven Tindle, *Manager*
EMP: 170 **EST:** 1999
SALES (est): 5.2MM
SALES (corp-wide): 2.1B **Privately Held**
WEB: www.woodlistings.com
SIC: 1521 General remodeling, single-family houses
HQ: J.F. Shea Construction, Inc.
655 Brea Canyon Rd
Walnut CA 91789
909 594-9500

(P-723)
TRINITY CONSTRUCTION ENTPS INC
3604 W Gettysburg Ave, Fresno (93722-7816)
PHONE 559 313-9612
Jayson Emerian, *CEO*
EMP: 35 **EST:** 2005
SALES (est): 5.1MM **Privately Held**
WEB: www.trinitycei.com
SIC: 1521 1711 New construction, single-family houses; solar energy contractor

(P-724)
TUPAZ HOMES LLC
2038 Biarritz Pl, San Jose (95138-2259)
PHONE 408 377-1622
Rosario Tupaz, *Mng Member*
Beebe Tupaz, *CFO*
EMP: 100 **EST:** 1997
SALES (est): 8.6MM **Privately Held**
SIC: 1521 Single-family housing construction

(P-725)
VAN ACKER CNSTR ASSOC INC
1060 Rdwood Hwy Frntage R, Mill Valley (94941-1613)
PHONE 415 383-5589
Gary Van Acker, *President*
Heide Vasquez, *Administration*
Yun-Ju Cho, *Technology*
Wesley Lee, *Accountant*
Gregg Roos, *Opers Staff*
▲ **EMP:** 134 **EST:** 1976
SQ FT: 15,000
SALES (est): 27.3MM **Privately Held**
WEB: www.vanacker.com
SIC: 1521 New construction, single-family

(P-726)
VASONA MANAGEMENT INC
Also Called: Vasonic Construction
37390 Central Mont Pl, Fremont (94538)
PHONE 510 413-0091
Dan Scharnow, *Vice Pres*
Jackie Petrucci, *Manager*
EMP: 290
SALES (corp-wide): 29.8MM **Privately Held**
WEB: www.vasonamanagement.com
SIC: 1521 New construction, single-family houses
PA: Vasona Management, Inc.
1500 E Hamilton Ave # 210
Campbell CA 95008
408 354-4200

(P-727)
WATHEN-CASTANOS-MAZMANIAN INC
2505 Alluvial Ave, Clovis (93611-9505)
PHONE 559 432-8181
Kevin J Castanos, *President*
Robert Mazmanian, *CFO*
Richard G Wathen, *Vice Pres*
EMP: 40 **EST:** 1987
SALES (est): 12.6MM **Privately Held**
WEB: www.wchomes.com
SIC: 1521 1531 New construction, single-family houses; speculative builder, single-family houses

(P-728)
WDR RESTORATION INC
2450 Alvarado St Ste 1, San Leandro (94577-4316)
PHONE 800 886-1801
Maria Neumann, *CEO*
EMP: 45 **EST:** 2014
SALES (est): 5.1MM **Privately Held**
WEB: www.waterdamagerecovery.net
SIC: 1521 Repairing fire damage, single-family houses

(P-729)
WICKMAN DEVELOPMENT AND CNSTR
5616 Mission St, San Francisco (94112-4220)
PHONE 415 239-4500
Jonathan Wickman, *CEO*
Aidan Fahy, *COO*
EMP: 40 **EST:** 2012
SQ FT: 5,000
SALES (est): 4.8MM **Privately Held**
WEB: www.wickmandev.com
SIC: 1521 1522 1541 1542 Single-family housing construction; apartment building construction; industrial buildings, new construction; commercial & office building, new construction; restaurant construction; institutional building construction

(P-730)
WILKEYS CONSTRUCTION INC
4557 Skyway Dr, Olivehurst (95961-7473)
P.O. Box 671, Pleasant Grove (95668-0671)
PHONE 530 741-2233
Mark D Wilkey, *President*
Dale Adams, *Supervisor*
▲ **EMP:** 35 **EST:** 1989
SQ FT: 1,142
SALES (est): 3.6MM **Privately Held**
WEB: www.wilkeysconstruction.com
SIC: 1521 New construction, single-family houses

(P-731)
WL BUTLER INC
5666 La Ribera St Ste A, Livermore (94550-2501)
PHONE 650 361-1270
Frank York, *President*
EMP: 59 **EST:** 2017
SALES (est): 8.1MM **Privately Held**
WEB: www.wlbutler.com
SIC: 1521 Single-family housing construction
PA: W. L. Butler Construction, Inc.
1629 Main St
Redwood City CA 94063

(P-732)
XL CONSTRUCTION CORPORATION
1810 13th St Ste 110, Sacramento (95811-7149)
PHONE 916 282-2900
Eric Raff, *Branch Mgr*
Jerry Harmon, *Vice Pres*
Marcus Staniford, *Vice Pres*
Silas Nigam, *Executive*
Natalia Sanchez, *Executive Asst*
EMP: 75 **EST:** 2019
SALES (est): 7.9MM **Privately Held**
WEB: www.xlconstruction.com
SIC: 1521 Single-family housing construction
PA: Xl Construction Corporation
851 Buckeye Ct
Milpitas CA 95035

(P-733)
YOUNG & BURTON INC
1947 San Ramon Valley Blv, San Ramon (94583-1212)
PHONE 925 820-4953
Michael G Burton, *President*
Larry W Young, *Treasurer*
Samantha Burton, *Project Mgr*
Rob Kutscher, *Project Mgr*
Robert Kutscher, *Project Mgr*
EMP: 48 **EST:** 1985
SALES (est): 10.7MM **Privately Held**
WEB: www.youngandburton.com
SIC: 1521 New construction, single-family houses

1522 General Contractors, Residential Other Than Single Family

(P-734)
ADVANCED TI INC
Also Called: PSR West Coast Builders
1553 3rd Ave, Walnut Creek (94597-2604)
PHONE 925 299-0515
Stephen Bossert, *CEO*
EMP: 35 **EST:** 1999
SQ FT: 4,000
SALES (est): 12MM **Privately Held**
WEB: www.advancedti.com
SIC: 1522 1542 Residential construction; commercial & office building contractors

(P-735)
AG SPANOS COMPANIES (PA)
10100 Trinity Pkwy Fl 5, Stockton (95219-7242)
PHONE 209 478-7954
Dean A Spanos, *Principal*
Alexis Ruhl, *Bd of Directors*
Enrique Palacio, *VP*
Alexandros Economou, *Exec VP*
Anita Cornman, *Vice Pres*
▲ **EMP:** 62 **EST:** 2009
SALES (est): 103.4MM **Privately Held**
WEB: www.agspanos.com
SIC: 1522 Apartment building construction

(P-736)
ALDERSON CONSTRUCTION INC
2944 Elmwood Ct, Berkeley (94705-2326)
PHONE 510 841-7159
Thomas Alderson, *President*
Linda Alderson, *Treasurer*
EMP: 40 **EST:** 1979
SALES (est): 8.2MM **Privately Held**
WEB: www.aldersonconstruction.com
SIC: 1522 Residential construction

(P-737)
ASHWOOD CONSTRUCTION INC
5755 E Kings Canyon Rd # 11, Fresno (93727-4744)
PHONE 559 253-7240
Michael J Conway Jr, *President*
Daniel Rajewich, *Superintendent*
Brenden Baker, *Asst Supt*
EMP: 50 **EST:** 1988
SQ FT: 1,200
SALES (est): 10MM **Privately Held**
WEB: www.ashwoodco.com
SIC: 1522 Multi-family dwellings, new construction

(P-738)
AXIS SERVICES INC
Also Called: Axis Construction
2544 Barrington Ct, Hayward (94545-1133)
PHONE 510 732-6111
Bizhan Mahallati, *CEO*
Parisa Mahallati, *Vice Pres*
Conor Meyers, *Vice Pres*
Mario Flores, *Project Mgr*
Ren Anderson, *Controller*
EMP: 110 **EST:** 1991
SALES (est): 34.6MM **Privately Held**
WEB: www.axisconstruction.com
SIC: 1522 Residential construction

(P-739)
COMMUNITY RCNSTRCTION SLUTIONS
855 Hinckley Rd, Burlingame (94010-1502)
PHONE 650 692-3030
George Perrenod, *President*

1522 - General Contractors, Residential Other Than Single Family County (P-740)

PRODUCTS & SERVICES SECTION

Martin Romo, *Vice Pres*
Paula Estrada, *Business Mgr*
EMP: 43 **EST:** 2005
SQ FT: 2,800
SALES (est): 5.2MM **Privately Held**
WEB: www.crsbayarea.com
SIC: 1522 Residential construction

(P-740)
COUNTRY BUILDERS INC
Also Called: Country Builders Construction
5915 Graham Ct, Livermore (94550-9710)
PHONE.................................925 373-1020
Weldon Offill, *President*
Keith Offill, *CFO*
EMP: 150 **EST:** 1979
SQ FT: 5,000
SALES (est): 21.4MM **Privately Held**
WEB: www.countrybuilders.com
SIC: 1522 Apartment building construction; remodeling, multi-family dwellings

(P-741)
CP EMPLOYER INC (PA)
1000 Sansome St Fl 1, San Francisco (94111-1342)
PHONE.................................415 273-2900
Ron Zeff, *CEO*
Lee Bloch, *Partner*
Neils Cotter, *Partner*
Trey Hilberg, *Partner*
Michael Lahorgue, *Partner*
EMP: 120 **EST:** 1995
SALES: 69MM **Privately Held**
SIC: 1522 6531 6519 Multi-family dwellings, new construction; real estate agents & managers; real property lessors

(P-742)
CP MULTIFAMILY CNSTR CAL INC
1000 Sansome St Fl 1, San Francisco (94111-1342)
PHONE.................................415 273-2900
Ron Zeff, *CEO*
EMP: 250 **EST:** 2016
SALES (est): 8.9MM **Privately Held**
SIC: 1522 Multi-family dwellings, new construction

(P-743)
DANCO BUILDERS
5251 Ericson Way Ste A, Arcata (95521-9274)
PHONE.................................707 822-9000
Daniel J Johnson, *President*
Kendra Johnson, *Shareholder*
Kirk Heberly, *Vice Pres*
Dana Dominick, *Regional Mgr*
Camellia Preciado, *Technology*
EMP: 100 **EST:** 1985
SQ FT: 15,000
SALES (est): 32.9MM **Privately Held**
WEB: www.danco-group.com
SIC: 1522 1542 Apartment building construction; nonresidential construction; commercial & office building contractors

(P-744)
DOUGLAS ROSS CONSTRUCTION INC
900 E Hamilton Ave # 140, Campbell (95008-0665)
PHONE.................................408 429-7700
J Douglas Ross, *President*
Andrew Maurer, *CFO*
Jeff Jelniker, *Vice Pres*
Jeffrey Jelniker, *Vice Pres*
Gail Giolli, *Administration*
EMP: 55
SQ FT: 7,158
SALES: 71.9K **Privately Held**
WEB: www.palisadebuilders.com
SIC: 1522 Hotel/motel & multi-family home renovation & remodeling

(P-745)
DRYDEN CONSTRUCTION INC
72 Rickenbacker Cir Ste A, Livermore (94551-7203)
PHONE.................................925 243-8750
Dave Nelson, *President*
Dale Renton, *CFO*
James Lemming, *Vice Pres*
EMP: 49 **EST:** 1992
SQ FT: 2,000

SALES (est): 8.9MM **Privately Held**
SIC: 1522 Remodeling, multi-family dwellings

(P-746)
EDEN HOUSING INC (PA)
22645 Grand St, Hayward (94541-5031)
PHONE.................................510 582-1460
John Gaffney, *CEO*
Kasey Archey, *Owner*
Rudolph Johnson, *Vice Chairman*
Linda Mandolini, *President*
Jan Peters, *COO*
EMP: 143 **EST:** 1968
SQ FT: 10,000
SALES (est): 46.8MM **Privately Held**
WEB: www.edenhousing.org
SIC: 1522 Multi-family dwellings, new construction

(P-747)
G B GROUP INC (PA)
8921 Murray Ave, Gilroy (95020-3633)
PHONE.................................408 848-8118
Gregory D Brown, *CEO*
Mark Greening, *President*
Jeffery Dame, *CFO*
Regan L Brown, *Corp Secy*
Pat Falconio, *Exec VP*
EMP: 79 **EST:** 1992
SQ FT: 4,300
SALES (est): 47.4MM **Privately Held**
WEB: www.gbgroupinc.com
SIC: 1522 1542 8322 1541 Hotel/motel & multi-family home renovation & remodeling; condominium construction; nonresidential construction; rehabilitation services; renovation, remodeling & repairs: industrial buildings; construction management

(P-748)
HURLEY CONSTRUCTION INC
1801 I St Ste 200, Sacramento (95811-3000)
PHONE.................................916 446-7599
Peter H Geremia, *CEO*
Steven Eggert, *Vice Pres*
EMP: 80 **EST:** 1995
SQ FT: 2,500
SALES (est): 11.1MM **Privately Held**
SIC: 1522 Multi-family dwellings, new construction

(P-749)
INTERNATIONAL BUILDING INV INC
6117 Grant Ave, Carmichael (95608-3331)
P.O. Box 2022, Orangevale (95662-2022)
PHONE.................................916 716-9565
Roderick Brian Edwards, *CEO*
Chris Wojcik, *Opers Staff*
EMP: 75 **EST:** 1987
SALES (est): 10MM **Privately Held**
WEB: www.ibi-ca.com
SIC: 1522 7389 Remodeling, multi-family dwellings;

(P-750)
JAD CONSTRUCTION INC
1019 Nichols Ct, Rocklin (95765-1325)
PHONE.................................916 408-6850
James M Moore, *President*
Sherry Moore, *Corp Secy*
Dean E Rumberger, *Vice Pres*
EMP: 40 **EST:** 2002
SQ FT: 8,000
SALES (est): 8.6MM **Privately Held**
WEB: www.jadconstruction.net
SIC: 1522 Residential construction

(P-751)
JAMES E ROBERTS-OBAYASHI CORP
20 Oak Ct, Danville (94526-4006)
PHONE.................................925 820-0600
Larry R Smith, *CEO*
Obayashi Corporation, *Principal*
Brendan Radich, *Info Tech Dir*
Tim Clark, *Project Mgr*
Gary Fettke, *Project Mgr*
EMP: 110
SQ FT: 4,000

SALES (est): 30.7MM **Privately Held**
WEB: www.jerocorp.com
SIC: 1522 1542 Multi-family dwellings, new construction; commercial & office building, new construction

(P-752)
JS CONTRACTING SERVICES INC
3129 Swetzer Rd Ste E, Loomis (95650-9587)
PHONE.................................916 625-1690
James Moll, *President*
EMP: 45 **EST:** 1988
SQ FT: 10,000
SALES (est): 10MM **Privately Held**
SIC: 1522 1542 Renovation, hotel/motel; commercial & office buildings, renovation & repair

(P-753)
JUDSON ENTERPRISES INC (PA)
Also Called: K-Designers
2440 Gold River Rd # 100, Rancho Cordova (95670-6390)
PHONE.................................916 596-6721
Larry D Judson, *President*
Tony Tobia, *CFO*
Michael Burgess, *Vice Pres*
Brian Vidlock, *Vice Pres*
Michele Stone, *Office Mgr*
▲ **EMP:** 265 **EST:** 1978
SQ FT: 28,000
SALES (est): 76MM **Privately Held**
WEB: www.k-designers.com
SIC: 1522 Residential construction

(P-754)
KB HOME SOUTH BAY INC
5000 Executive Pkwy # 125, San Ramon (94583-4210)
PHONE.................................925 983-2500
Chris Apostolopoulos, *CEO*
Robert Freed, *President*
Joe Gregorich, *Vice Pres*
Andrew Kusnick, *Vice Pres*
Tony Dority, *Opers Staff*
EMP: 140 **EST:** 1985
SQ FT: 5,500
SALES (est): 36.1MM
SALES (corp-wide): 4.1B **Publicly Held**
SIC: 1522 1521 Residential construction; single-family housing construction
HQ: Kb Home Greater Los Angeles Inc.
 10990 Wilshire Blvd # 700
 Los Angeles CA 90024
 310 231-4000

(P-755)
LOBO SERVICES LTD
3298 Swetzer Rd, Loomis (95650-9515)
PHONE.................................916 660-9909
James Nolen, *President*
Leeann Keitt, *Assistant*
EMP: 35 **EST:** 1991
SALES (est): 3.3MM **Privately Held**
WEB: www.loboservices.com
SIC: 1522 Residential construction

(P-756)
LOWERY-PENA CNSTR CO INC
1509 W Yosemite Ave A1, Manteca (95337-5165)
PHONE.................................209 328-2050
Michael Lowery, *President*
Adam Owens, *CFO*
Nicole Lowery, *Vice Pres*
Trehvor Haff, *Superintendent*
Michael Morrow, *Superintendent*
EMP: 38 **EST:** 2015
SALES (est): 6.4MM **Privately Held**
WEB: www.lowerypena.com
SIC: 1522 1542 Hotel/motel & multi-family home construction; apartment building construction; commercial & office building, new construction

(P-757)
MARK SCOTT CONSTRUCTION INC
2250 Boynton Ave, Fairfield (94533-4320)
PHONE.................................707 864-8880
Dave Bergmini, *Manager*
EMP: 50 **Privately Held**

WEB: www.msconstruction.com
SIC: 1522 Residential construction
PA: Mark Scott Construction, Inc.
 2835 Contra Costa Blvd A
 Pleasant Hill CA 94523

(P-758)
MARK SCOTT CONSTRUCTION INC
2835 Contra Costa Blvd A, Pleasant Hill (94523-4221)
PHONE.................................209 982-0502
Mark Scott, *Principal*
EMP: 50 **Privately Held**
WEB: www.msconstruction.com
SIC: 1522 1521 Residential construction; single-family housing construction
PA: Mark Scott Construction, Inc.
 2835 Contra Costa Blvd A
 Pleasant Hill CA 94523

(P-759)
NIBBI BROS ASSOCIATES INC
Also Called: Nibbi Bros Concrete
1000 Brannan St Ste 102, San Francisco (94103-4888)
PHONE.................................415 863-1820
Robert L Nibbi, *President*
Larry Nibbi, *CEO*
Richard Fedick, *CFO*
Mike Nibbi, *Vice Pres*
Jeff Hartman, *Division Mgr*
EMP: 150 **EST:** 1998
SALES (est): 46.6MM **Privately Held**
WEB: www.nibbi.com
SIC: 1522 1542 Residential construction; custom builders, non-residential

(P-760)
NORTHERN CIR INDIAN HSING AUTH
694 Pinoleville Rd, Ukiah (95482-3165)
PHONE.................................707 468-1336
Darlene Tooley, *Exec Dir*
EMP: 47 **EST:** 1980
SQ FT: 3,300
SALES (est): 5.8MM **Privately Held**
WEB: www.nciha.org
SIC: 1522 6513 Residential construction; apartment building operators

(P-761)
PARKHURST TERRACE
100 Parkhurst Cir, Aptos (95003-9657)
PHONE.................................831 685-0800
Cheryl Digrazia, *Principal*
EMP: 53 **EST:** 2011
SALES (est): 423.5K **Privately Held**
WEB: www.midpen-housing.org
SIC: 1522 Apartment building construction
HQ: Midpen Property Management Corporation
 303 Vintage Park Dr # 250
 Foster City CA 94404
 650 356-2900

(P-762)
PROJECT FROG INC
99 Green St Ste 200, San Francisco (94111-1400)
PHONE.................................415 814-8500
Ann Hand, *CEO*
Mark Miller, *President*
Shirin Arnold, *Vice Pres*
Sam Rabinowitz, *Vice Pres*
Matthew Comber, *General Mgr*
▲ **EMP:** 132 **EST:** 2006
SALES (est): 23.7MM **Privately Held**
WEB: www.projectfrog.com
SIC: 1522 Residential construction

(P-763)
RDR BUILDERS LP
Also Called: Rdr Production Builders
1806 W Kettleman Ln Ste F, Lodi (95242-4316)
PHONE.................................209 368-7561
Ron Dos Reis, *Partner*
Mark Barbieri, *Partner*
Ed Dos Reis, *Partner*
Ron Dos-Reis, *President*
EMP: 85 **EST:** 1977
SQ FT: 1,400

▲ = Import ▼ = Export
◆ = Import/Export

PRODUCTS & SERVICES SECTION

1531 - Operative Builders County (P-785)

SALES (est): 17.9MM **Privately Held**
WEB: www.rdrbuilders.com
SIC: 1522 1542 Multi-family dwellings, new construction; hotel/motel & multi-family home renovation & remodeling; commercial & office building, new construction; commercial & office buildings, renovation & repair

(P-764)
REGENCY GENERAL CONTRS INC (PA)
4400 Auto Mall Pkwy, Fremont (94538-5989)
PHONE 408 946-7100
Kwang H Lee, *CEO*
David Lee, *President*
Kelly Lee, *CFO*
Daejong Lee, *Network Enginr*
Greg Witt, *Project Mgr*
EMP: 96 **EST:** 2002
SALES (est): 24.9MM **Privately Held**
WEB: www.regencygc.com
SIC: 1522 1542 Residential construction; nonresidential construction

(P-765)
RICK CARSEY TRUCKING & CNSTR
3181 E Manning Ave, Fowler (93625-9749)
P.O. Box 97 (93625-0097)
PHONE 559 834-5385
Rick Carsey, *President*
EMP: 48 **EST:** 1999
SALES (est): 2.7MM **Privately Held**
SIC: 1522 Residential construction

(P-766)
S & C SIDING INC
8733 Flute Cir, Elk Grove (95757-1742)
PHONE 916 491-0715
Jennifer Smith Floyd, *Principal*
Armando Chavez, *Principal*
EMP: 35 **EST:** 2020
SALES (est): 1.7MM **Privately Held**
SIC: 1522 Residential construction

(P-767)
SAARMAN CONSTRUCTION LTD
683 Mcallister St, San Francisco (94102-3111)
PHONE 415 749-2700
Jeffrey M Saarman, *President*
Bernabe Cardoso, *Partner*
Miguel Galvez, *Partner*
Venancio Luna, *Partner*
Steven P Saarman, *CEO*
EMP: 250 **EST:** 1977
SQ FT: 4,500
SALES (est): 64.1MM **Privately Held**
WEB: www.saarman.com
SIC: 1522 1521 Condominium construction; apartment building construction; general remodeling, single-family houses; new construction, single-family houses

(P-768)
SAUSALITO CONSTRUCTION INC
75 Pelican Way Ste B, San Rafael (94901-5564)
PHONE 415 889-5281
Gale Greisen, *President*
EMP: 45 **EST:** 2004
SALES (est): 10MM **Privately Held**
WEB: www.sausalitoconstruction.com
SIC: 1522 1542 Residential construction; nonresidential construction; commercial & office building, new construction; commercial & office buildings, renovation & repair; commercial & office building contractors

(P-769)
SBI BUILDERS INC (PA)
710 W Julian St, San Jose (95126-2713)
PHONE 408 549-1300
Paul Nuytten, *President*
Renato O'Neal, *COO*
Shiree Rothwein, *Office Mgr*
Trisha Van Lanen, *Controller*
Emun Davoodi, *Sr Project Mgr*
EMP: 35 **EST:** 2005

SALES (est): 26.4MM **Privately Held**
WEB: www.sbibuilders.com
SIC: 1522 1531 8741 Multi-family dwelling construction; operative builders; management services

(P-770)
SILICONSAGE CONSTRUCTION INC
560 S Mathilda Ave, Sunnyvale (94086-7607)
PHONE 408 916-3205
Sanjeev Acharya, *CEO*
Hassan Naboulsi, *Info Tech Mgr*
EMP: 200 **EST:** 2014
SALES (est): 50MM **Privately Held**
SIC: 1522 Multi-family dwellings, new construction

(P-771)
SPANOS CORPORATION (PA)
10100 Trinity Pkwy Fl 5, Stockton (95219-7242)
PHONE 209 955-2550
Steven L Cohen, *CEO*
Alexander G Spanos, *Ch of Bd*
Dean A Spanos, *President*
Jerry Murphy, *CFO*
Michael Spanos, *Vice Pres*
EMP: 40 **EST:** 1994
SALES (est): 20.9MM **Privately Held**
WEB: www.agspanos.com
SIC: 1522 Apartment building construction

(P-772)
SUNSERI CONSTRUCTION INC
48 Comanche Ct, Chico (95928-8898)
PHONE 530 891-6444
Donny Lieberman, *CEO*
Philip Sunseri, *Ch of Bd*
Cindy Lares, *CFO*
Cynthia Santulli, *CFO*
Greg Creighton, *Vice Pres*
EMP: 40 **EST:** 1979
SQ FT: 8,000
SALES (est): 41.7MM **Privately Held**
WEB: www.sunsericonstruction.com
SIC: 1522 1521 1541 1542 Residential construction; new construction, single-family houses; industrial buildings, new construction; commercial & office building, new construction

(P-773)
TEAMWRKX INC (PA)
Also Called: Teamwrkx Construction
1855 Park Ave, San Jose (95126-1635)
PHONE 408 287-2700
Eric J Venzon, *CEO*
Gary Wells, *President*
Joe Olla, *Vice Pres*
Timothy Talaugon, *VP Bus Dvlpt*
H John Aiassa Jr, *Principal*
EMP: 35 **EST:** 2004
SQ FT: 8,500
SALES (est): 29.2MM **Privately Held**
WEB: www.teamwrkx.com
SIC: 1522 1541 8711 7374 Residential construction; industrial buildings & warehouses; mechanical engineering; computer graphics service; plumbing, heating, air-conditioning contractors

(P-774)
THOMPSON BUILDERS CORPORATION
5400 Hanna Ranch Rd, Novato (94945)
PHONE 415 456-8972
Paul Thompson, *President*
F Joseph Hass, *Vice Pres*
Peter Hopkins, *Project Mgr*
James Sarkany, *Project Mgr*
Pat Chavez, *Project Engr*
▲ **EMP:** 170 **EST:** 1988
SQ FT: 6,000
SALES (est): 72.7MM **Privately Held**
WEB: www.tbcorp.com
SIC: 1522 1542 8711 7389 Multi-family dwelling construction; commercial & office building, new construction; construction & civil engineering; design services; general contractor, highway & street construction

(P-775)
TRI POINTE HOMES INC
2700 Camino Ramon Ste 130, San Ramon (94583-5004)
PHONE 925 804-2220
Jeffrey Frankel, *President*
Ken Hyland, *Vice Pres*
Doug Nazarenus, *Vice Pres*
Matt Roesch, *Vice Pres*
Mandy Briley, *Office Mgr*
EMP: 158
SALES (corp-wide): 3.2B **Publicly Held**
WEB: www.tripointehomes.com
SIC: 1522 Residential construction
HQ: Tri Pointe Homes, Inc.
19540 Jamboree Rd Ste 300
Irvine CA 92612

(P-776)
UPSCALE CONSTRUCTION INC
2151 Union St 1, San Francisco (94123-4003)
PHONE 415 563-7550
Danny J Bernardini, *CEO*
Tony Kelly, *President*
Grady Jackson, *Project Mgr*
Mary Kushman, *Accountant*
Melissa Carpenter, *Human Res Mgr*
EMP: 51 **EST:** 1998
SALES (est): 13.6MM **Privately Held**
WEB: www.upscaleconstruction.com
SIC: 1522 Remodeling, multi-family dwellings

(P-777)
WRIGHT CONTRACTING INC
3020 Dutton Ave, Santa Rosa (95407-7886)
P.O. Box 1270 (95402-1270)
PHONE 707 528-1172
Mark Davis, *CEO*
Jay V Wright, *Shareholder*
Michael J Wright, *Corp Secy*
Maureen Linde, *Office Mgr*
Louis Armanini, *Project Mgr*
EMP: 40
SQ FT: 8,500
SALES (est): 127MM **Privately Held**
WEB: www.wrightcontracting.com
SIC: 1522 1542 Apartment building construction; hospital construction

1531 Operative Builders

(P-778)
BRADDOCK LOGAN VENTR GROUP LP (PA)
Also Called: Diablo Lodge Partnership
4155 Blackhawk Plaza Cir, Danville (94506-4903)
P.O. Box 5300 (94526-1076)
PHONE 925 736-4000
Joseph Raphel, *Managing Prtnr*
David Lee, *Director*
EMP: 512 **EST:** 1947
SQ FT: 10,000
SALES (est): 38.7MM **Privately Held**
SIC: 1531 Speculative builder, single-family houses

(P-779)
ESAU CONCRETE INC DBA PCS CON
Also Called: Pcs Concrete & Masonry
101 Business Park Way, Atwater (95301-9483)
PHONE 209 357-7601
Veryl Esau, *President*
Michael Seay, *CEO*
Tim Esau, *Purchasing*
EMP: 100 **EST:** 1979
SALES (est): 16.6MM **Privately Held**
WEB: www.pcsconcrete.net
SIC: 1531 1541 1771 1791 ; dry cleaning plant construction; concrete work; concrete reinforcement, placing of

(P-780)
GRUPE DEV COMPANYNORTHERN CAL
3255 W March Ln Ste 400, Stockton (95219-2352)
P.O. Box 7576 (95267-0576)
PHONE 209 473-6000
Fritz Unruh, *CEO*
EMP: 67 **EST:** 1979
SQ FT: 7,000
SALES (est): 1.4MM
SALES (corp-wide): 65.6MM **Privately Held**
WEB: www.grupe.com
SIC: 1531 Speculative builder, single-family houses
PA: The Grupe Company
3255 W March Ln Ste 400
Stockton CA 95219
209 473-6000

(P-781)
HOFMANN CONSTRUCTION CO (PA)
Also Called: Hofmann Company
3000 Oak Rd Ste 300, Walnut Creek (94597-7775)
P.O. Box 907, Concord (94522-0907)
PHONE 925 478-2000
Thomas Whalen, *CEO*
Albert Shaw, *Ch of Bd*
John Amaral, *CEO*
Patrick S Simons, *Senior VP*
EMP: 40 **EST:** 1959
SQ FT: 12,000
SALES (est): 18.2MM **Privately Held**
SIC: 1531 2439 Speculative builder, single-family houses; speculative builder, multi-family dwellings; structural wood members; trusses, wooden roof

(P-782)
HOOPA MODULAR BUILDING ENTP (PA)
151 Cal Pac Rd, Hoopa (95546)
PHONE 530 625-4551
Len Mayor, *CEO*
EMP: 40 **EST:** 2000
SQ FT: 20,000
SALES (est): 3MM **Privately Held**
SIC: 1531 Operative builders

(P-783)
LENNAR MLTFMILY CMMUNITIES LLC
492 9th St Ste 300, Oakland (94607-4055)
PHONE 415 975-4980
Jim McCown, *Director*
EMP: 731
SALES (corp-wide): 22.4B **Publicly Held**
WEB: www.livelmc.com
SIC: 1531 Cooperative apartment developers
HQ: Lennar Multifamily Communities, Llc
500 E Morehead St Ste 300
Charlotte NC 28202
305 559-4000

(P-784)
PAN-CAL INVESTMENT COMPANY INC
Also Called: Greater Bay Construction
4125 Blackford Ave # 200, San Jose (95117-1700)
PHONE 408 248-6600
David K Chui, *President*
Benjamin Chui, *Vice Pres*
Joseph Chui, *Vice Pres*
Peter K Chui, *Vice Pres*
EMP: 42 **EST:** 1973
SQ FT: 2,000
SALES (est): 5.2MM **Privately Held**
WEB: www.pancal.com
SIC: 1531 Speculative builder, single-family houses

(P-785)
SOUTH COUNTY HOUSING CORP
Also Called: South County Property MGT
9015 Murray Ave Ste 100, Gilroy (95020-3675)
PHONE 408 842-9181
EMP: 80

1531 - Operative Builders County (P-786)

SALES (corp-wide): 113.4K Privately Held
SIC: 1531 Property Management For Low Income Housing
PA: South County Housing Corporation
16500 Monterey St Ste 120
Morgan Hill CA 95037
510 582-1460

(P-786)
WARMINGTON HOMES
Also Called: Warmington Residential
4160 Dublin Blvd Ste 130, Dublin (94568-7734)
PHONE.................................925 866-6700
Larry Riggs, *Exec VP*
EMP: 128
SALES (corp-wide): 94.3MM Privately Held
WEB: www.homesbywarmington.com
SIC: 1531 Speculative builder, single-family houses
PA: Warmington Homes
3090 Pullman St
Costa Mesa CA 92626
714 434-4435

1541 General Contractors, Indl Bldgs & Warehouses

(P-787)
ACME CONSTRUCTION COMPANY INC
1565 Cummins Dr, Modesto (95358-6401)
P.O. Box 4710 (95352-4710)
PHONE.................................209 523-2674
Nella Mastagni, *Treasurer*
Philip Mastagni, *President*
Judith Boydston, *CFO*
Ron Kettelman, *Vice Pres*
Greg Mastagni, *Vice Pres*
EMP: 49 EST: 1947
SQ FT: 12,000
SALES (est): 25.3MM Privately Held
WEB: www.acmeconstruction.com
SIC: 1541 1542 Industrial buildings, new construction; commercial & office building, new construction

(P-788)
ARNTZ BUILDERS INC
431 Payran St Ste A, Petaluma (94952-5935)
PHONE.................................415 382-1188
Donald M Arntz, *CEO*
Brian Proteau, *President*
Thomas Artz, *Corp Secy*
Dave Arntz, *Vice Pres*
Doug Clymer, *Project Mgr*
EMP: 50 EST: 1989
SALES (est): 25.4MM Privately Held
WEB: www.arntzbuilders.com
SIC: 1541 1542 Industrial buildings, new construction; renovation, remodeling & repairs: industrial buildings; commercial & office building, new construction; commercial & office buildings, renovation & repair

(P-789)
BCM CONSTRUCTION COMPANY INC
2990 California 32, Chico (95973)
PHONE.................................530 342-1722
Kurtis Carman, *President*
Nancy Chinn, *Treasurer*
Matt Bowman, *Vice Pres*
Scott January, *Vice Pres*
Ben Chung, *Administration*
EMP: 50 EST: 1997
SQ FT: 1,700
SALES (est): 26MM Privately Held
WEB: www.bcmconstruction.com
SIC: 1541 Industrial buildings, new construction

(P-790)
BLACH CONSTRUCTION COMPANY (PA)
2244 Blach Pl Ste 100, San Jose (95131-2041)
PHONE.................................408 244-7100
Mike Blach, *President*
Juan Barroso, *Vice Pres*
Gaye Landau, *Vice Pres*
Daniel Rogers, *Vice Pres*
Ken Treadwell, *Vice Pres*
EMP: 80 EST: 1973
SQ FT: 24,000
SALES (est): 64.6MM Privately Held
WEB: www.blach.com
SIC: 1541 1542 Industrial buildings & warehouses; commercial & office building, new construction

(P-791)
CALIFORNIA CUSTOM PROC LLC
3211 Aviation Dr, Madera (93637-8678)
PHONE.................................559 416-5122
Grant Willits, *Mng Member*
Allen Leighton, *CFO*
Derek Alexander, *Manager*
EMP: 24 EST: 2012
SALES (est): 5.6MM Privately Held
WEB: www.goldenvalleywine.com
SIC: 1541 3556 Food products manufacturing or packing plant construction; food products machinery

(P-792)
CMC REBAR WEST
1060 Kaiser Rd, NAPA (94558-6235)
PHONE.................................707 863-3933
Howard Bennion, *Branch Mgr*
EMP: 139 Privately Held
SIC: 1541 Steel building construction
HQ: Cmc Rebar West
3880 Murphy Canyon Rd # 100
San Diego CA 92123

(P-793)
DEES-HENNESSEY INC
200 Industrial Rd Ste 190, San Carlos (94070-6233)
PHONE.................................650 595-8933
Dan Evans, *Principal*
Jason Myers, *Vice Pres*
Matt Peterson, *Project Mgr*
Alaine Sankofa, *Accountant*
EMP: 49
SQ FT: 2,400
SALES (est): 11.7MM Privately Held
WEB: www.deeshenn.com
SIC: 1541 1542 Industrial buildings, new construction; commercial & office building, new construction

(P-794)
E-3 SYSTEMS
1220 Whipple Rd, Union City (94587-2026)
PHONE.................................510 487-9195
Kofi Tawiah, *President*
EMP: 42 EST: 1989
SQ FT: 7,500 Privately Held
WEB: www.e3systems.com
SIC: 1541 4813 1731 Industrial buildings, new construction; wire telephone; fiber optic cable installation

(P-795)
FLORY CONSTRUCTION INC
2325 Verna Ct, San Leandro (94577-4273)
PHONE.................................510 483-6860
David Flory, *President*
Beatrix Flory, *Admin Sec*
Lisa Towles, *Admin Asst*
George Saljian, *Manager*
Jonathan Jenkins, *Superintendent*
▲ EMP: 42 EST: 1965
SQ FT: 6,500
SALES (est): 4MM Privately Held
WEB: www.floryconstruction.com
SIC: 1541 Industrial buildings, new construction

(P-796)
HERRERO BUILDERS INCORPORATED (PA)
2100 Oakdale Ave, San Francisco (94124-1516)
PHONE.................................415 824-7675
Mark D Herrero, *Ch of Bd*
Rick Herrero, *President*
James Totoritis, *CFO*
Saptarshi Desai, *Executive*
Alejandro Cardenas, *Project Mgr*
▲ EMP: 128 EST: 1955

SQ FT: 10,000
SALES (est): 61.2MM Privately Held
WEB: www.herrero.com
SIC: 1541 Industrial buildings, new construction

(P-797)
HILLHOUSE CONSTRUCTION CO INC
140 Charcot Ave, San Jose (95131-1101)
PHONE.................................408 467-1000
Ken Huesby, *President*
Olivia Wood, *Admin Asst*
Doug Klein, *Project Mgr*
Jessica Reiswig, *Project Mgr*
Valerie Clark, *Project Engr*
EMP: 45 EST: 1987
SQ FT: 24,638
SALES (est): 46.6MM Privately Held
WEB: www.hillhouseconstruction.com
SIC: 1541 1542 Grain elevator construction; renovation, remodeling & repairs: industrial buildings; commercial & office building, new construction; commercial & office buildings, renovation & repair

(P-798)
J M ONEILL INC
354 Earhart Way, Livermore (94551-9309)
PHONE.................................925 225-1200
John Michael O'Neill, *President*
Tony McGuire, *Project Mgr*
Con McMahon, *Project Mgr*
Caitlin Grant, *Accounting Mgr*
Robert Sexton, *Superintendent*
EMP: 35 EST: 1983
SQ FT: 5,000
SALES (est): 9.5MM Privately Held
WEB: www.jmoneill.com
SIC: 1541 1542 Industrial buildings, new construction; commercial & office building, new construction

(P-799)
JACKSON CONSTRUCTION (PA)
155 Cadillac Dr, Sacramento (95825-5499)
PHONE.................................916 381-8113
John Jackson Jr, *President*
Lynda Jackson, *Treasurer*
Eric J Edelmayer, *Vice Pres*
Eric Edelmayer, *Vice Pres*
Brian Huddleston, *Vice Pres*
EMP: 39 EST: 1974
SQ FT: 10,000
SALES (est): 25.6MM Privately Held
WEB: www.jacksonprop.com
SIC: 1541 1542 6552 6531 Industrial buildings & warehouses; nonresidential construction; land subdividers & developers, residential; real estate agents & managers

(P-800)
KERNEN CONSTRUCTION
2350 Glendale Dr, McKinleyville (95519-9205)
P.O. Box 1340, Blue Lake (95525-1340)
PHONE.................................707 826-8686
Kurt Kernen, *Partner*
Scott Farley, *Partner*
EMP: 60 EST: 1983
SQ FT: 120
SALES (est): 19.2MM Privately Held
WEB: www.kernenconstruction.com
SIC: 1541 1542 Industrial buildings, new construction; renovation, remodeling & repairs: industrial buildings; commercial & office building, new construction; commercial & office buildings, renovation & repair

(P-801)
LRG BUILDER SERVICES INC
26 S 3rd St Ste E, Patterson (95363-2572)
P.O. Box 1685 (95363-1685)
PHONE.................................209 894-7100
Louis Gregoris, *President*
Nina Gregoris, *Admin Sec*
EMP: 42 EST: 2017
SQ FT: 500

SALES (est): 5MM Privately Held
SIC: 1541 1522 1521 1542 Industrial buildings, new construction; residential construction; multi-family dwelling construction; single-family housing construction; new construction, single-family houses; nonresidential construction

(P-802)
MA STEINER CONSTRUCTION INC
8854 Greenback Ln Ste 1, Orangevale (95662-4084)
PHONE.................................916 988-6300
Martin Steiner, *President*
EMP: 64 EST: 2011
SALES (est): 12.4MM Privately Held
WEB: www.masteinerconst.com
SIC: 1541 1794 1542 1611 Industrial buildings, new construction; excavation & grading, building construction; commercial & office building, new construction; highway & street construction; general contractor, highway & street construction

(P-803)
NORTH COAST FABRICATORS INC
4801 West End Rd, Arcata (95521-9242)
PHONE.................................707 822-4629
Paula E Crowley, *President*
Tim Crowley, *COO*
EMP: 50 EST: 1979
SQ FT: 12,000
SALES (est): 13.9MM Privately Held
WEB: www.northcoastfabricators.com
SIC: 1541 1542 7699 Prefabricated building erection, industrial; commercial & office buildings, prefabricated erection; industrial machinery & equipment repair

(P-804)
PERFORMANCE CONTRACTING INC
7085 Las Positas Rd Ste E, Livermore (94551-5116)
PHONE.................................925 273-3800
Mike Ligon, *Manager*
EMP: 50
SALES (corp-wide): 2.4B Privately Held
WEB: www.performancecontracting.com
SIC: 1541 Industrial buildings, new construction
HQ: Performance Contracting, Inc.
11145 Thompson Ave
Lenexa KS 66219
913 888-8600

(P-805)
RACKLEY COMPANY INC
3772 County Road 99w, Orland (95963-9785)
PHONE.................................530 865-9619
Bill Rackley, *President*
Jeffery Rackley, *CEO*
Scott Rackley, *Vice Pres*
EMP: 45 EST: 1974
SQ FT: 9,000
SALES (est): 21.2MM Privately Held
WEB: www.rackleyco.com
SIC: 1541 Steel building construction

(P-806)
RELIABLE CONCEPTS CORPORATION
636 Newhall Dr, San Jose (95110-1132)
P.O. Box 696, Santa Clara (95052-0696)
PHONE.................................408 271-6655
Daniel Montes, *President*
Marco Ferrel, *Vice Pres*
Alexis Salinas, *Project Mgr*
Iliana Torres, *Technology*
Antonio Martinez, *Supervisor*
EMP: 46 EST: 1992
SQ FT: 6,000
SALES (est): 6.8MM Privately Held
WEB: www.rcc-bgm.com
SIC: 1541 Industrial buildings & warehouses

(P-807)
RODAN BUILDERS INC
3486 Investment Blvd B, Hayward (94545-3811)
PHONE.................................650 508-1700

PRODUCTS & SERVICES SECTION **1542 - General Contractors, Nonresidential & Non-indl Bldgs County (P-829)**

Rory Morgan, *CEO*
Dan Oliver, *CFO*
James Graham, *Project Mgr*
Juan Herrera, *Project Mgr*
Keith Reynolds, *Project Mgr*
EMP: 40 **EST:** 2004
SALES: 94.5MM **Privately Held**
WEB: www.rodanbuilders.com
SIC: 1541 Industrial buildings & warehouses

(P-808)
ROLAND CONSTRUCTION INC
3269 Tomahawk Dr, Stockton (95205-2450)
P.O. Box 8670 (95208-0670)
PHONE 209 462-2687
Jim Hoagland, *President*
Glenna Matthews, *Corp Secy*
Tim Ramsey, *Project Mgr*
Mark Wilbur, *Controller*
John Blanco, *Opers Mgr*
EMP: 40 **EST:** 1986
SQ FT: 4,000
SALES (est): 8.6MM **Privately Held**
WEB: www.rolandconst.com
SIC: 1541 Prefabricated building erection, industrial

(P-809)
SHAWS STRCTURES UNLIMITED INC
Also Called: Shaw Construction
2435 N Grantland Ave, Fresno (93723-9234)
P.O. Box 9249 (93791-9249)
PHONE 559 275-3475
Paul W Shaw, *President*
Gloria Shaw, *Vice Pres*
Mildred Shaw, *Vice Pres*
EMP: 50 **EST:** 1951
SALES (est): 5.3MM **Privately Held**
WEB: www.shawstructures.com
SIC: 1541 1542 1791 Prefabricated building erection, industrial; commercial & office buildings, prefabricated erection; religious building construction; structural steel erection

(P-810)
SPENCER ENTERPRISES INC
5286 E Home Ave, Fresno (93727-1536)
PHONE 559 252-4043
Richard F Spencer, *CEO*
Karen Emery, *Admin Sec*
▲ **EMP:** 60 **EST:** 1966
SQ FT: 7,600
SALES (est): 4.1MM **Privately Held**
WEB: www.spencerenterprises.com
SIC: 1541 1542 1522 Industrial buildings, new construction; food products manufacturing or packing plant construction; commercial & office building, new construction; hospital construction; multi-family dwelling construction

(P-811)
SWINERTON BUILDERS INC (HQ)
Also Called: Swinerton MGT & Consulting
2001 Clayton Rd Ste 700, Concord (94520-2792)
PHONE 415 421-2980
Jeffrey C Hoopes, *Ch of Bd*
John T Capener, *President*
Gary J Rafferty, *President*
Linda G Schowalter, *CFO*
Frank Foellmer, *Exec VP*
▲ **EMP:** 200 **EST:** 1908
SQ FT: 300,353
SALES (est): 4.2B **Privately Held**
WEB: www.swinerton.com
SIC: 1541 1522 1542 Industrial buildings, new construction; steel building construction; hotel/motel, new construction; commercial & office building, new construction; commercial & office buildings, renovation & repair; specialized public building contractors

(P-812)
SWINERTON BUILDERS INC
1 Kaiser Plz Ste 701, Oakland (94612-3610)
PHONE 510 208-5800
Steve Johnson, *Manager*

James Watson, *Vice Pres*
Lauren Capriotti, *Admin Asst*
Harrison Snider, *Project Engr*
Alanna Dedek, *Engineer*
EMP: 51 **Privately Held**
WEB: www.swinerton.com
SIC: 1541 1542 Industrial buildings, new construction; nonresidential construction
HQ: Swinerton Builders, Inc.
2001 Clayton Rd Ste 700
Concord CA 94520
415 421-2980

(P-813)
SWINERTON BUILDERS INC
Scs
377 Oyster Point Blvd # 19, South San Francisco (94080-1976)
PHONE 415 984-1302
David Green, *Branch Mgr*
EMP: 51 **Privately Held**
WEB: www.swinerton.com
SIC: 1541 1542 Industrial buildings, new construction; commercial & office building, new construction; shopping center construction
HQ: Swinerton Builders, Inc.
2001 Clayton Rd Ste 700
Concord CA 94520
415 421-2980

(P-814)
TBI CONSTRUCTION CNSTR MGT INC
1960 The Alameda Ste 100, San Jose (95126-1441)
PHONE 408 246-3691
Tony Anthony Mirenda, *President*
Dan Breeding, *COO*
Sheila Breeding, *CFO*
Phil Wolz, *Manager*
EMP: 38 **EST:** 1983
SQ FT: 9,000
SALES (est): 6.8MM **Privately Held**
SIC: 1541 1542 Industrial buildings, new construction; commercial & office building contractors

(P-815)
TCB INDUSTRIAL INC (PA)
2955 Farrar Ave, Modesto (95354-4118)
PHONE 209 571-0569
Derek Todd Raybourn, *CEO*
Bruce Elliott, *CFO*
Casey Morrow, *Superintendent*
EMP: 55 **EST:** 1992
SALES (est): 15MM **Privately Held**
WEB: www.tcbindustrial.net
SIC: 1541 Industrial buildings, new construction

(P-816)
TLC FOODS LLC
4123 24th St, San Francisco (94114-3614)
PHONE 415 205-7111
Andrew Johnstone, *Principal*
EMP: 35 **EST:** 2010
SALES (est): 4.1MM **Privately Held**
SIC: 1541 5812 Food products manufacturing or packing plant construction; restaurant, family: independent

(P-817)
TRENT CONSTRUCTION INC
8270 Truckee Ave, Gerber (96035-9731)
PHONE 530 385-1778
Kendel Trent, *President*
Belinda Trent, *Corp Secy*
EMP: 40 **EST:** 1991
SQ FT: 1,700
SALES (est): 6.3MM **Privately Held**
WEB: www.trentconstructioninc.com
SIC: 1541 Industrial buildings & warehouses

(P-818)
VISIONARY NUTRITION LLC
9957 Medford Ave Ste 4, Oakland (94603-2360)
PHONE 510 567-1200
Scott Chaplan, *Mng Member*
EMP: 180 **EST:** 2020
SALES (est): 20.7MM **Privately Held**
WEB: www.visionarynutrition.net
SIC: 1541 Food products manufacturing or packing plant construction

---

1542 General Contractors, Nonresidential & Non-indl Bldgs

(P-819)
A RUIZ CNSTR CO & ASSOC INC
1601 Cortland Ave, San Francisco (94110-5716)
PHONE 415 647-4010
Antonio Ruiz, *President*
Thomas Cotter, *Executive*
Henrietta Ruiz, *General Mgr*
Juan Gomez, *Project Mgr*
Tony Ruiz, *Project Engr*
EMP: 50 **EST:** 1982
SQ FT: 10,000
SALES (est): 14.9MM **Privately Held**
WEB: www.aruizconstruction.com
SIC: 1542 Commercial & office building, new construction; commercial & office building contractors

(P-820)
ADVANTAGE FRAMING SOLUTIONS
1965 N Beale Rd, Marysville (95901-6914)
PHONE 530 742-7660
Joel Bueno, *CFO*
EMP: 50 **EST:** 2016
SALES (est): 9.1MM **Privately Held**
SIC: 1542 Nonresidential construction

(P-821)
ALPHA RSTORATION WATERPROOFING
218 Littlefield Ave, South San Francisco (94080-6902)
PHONE 650 875-7500
Emile Kishek, *President*
Taghreed Kishek, *Vice Pres*
Abe Sweis, *Project Mgr*
EMP: 35 **EST:** 1983
SQ FT: 20,000
SALES (est): 9.8MM **Privately Held**
WEB: www.alpharestoration.com
SIC: 1542 1799 Commercial & office buildings, renovation & repair; waterproofing

(P-822)
ALSTON CONSTRUCTION CO INC (PA)
8775 Folsom Blvd Ste 201, Sacramento (95826-3725)
PHONE 916 340-2400
Paul Little, *CEO*
Paul David Little, *CEO*
Adam Nickerson, *CFO*
Mike Bontrager, *Vice Pres*
Evan Hamilton, *Vice Pres*
EMP: 100 **EST:** 1998
SQ FT: 36,000
SALES (est): 1.2B **Privately Held**
WEB: www.alstonco.com
SIC: 1542 1541 Commercial & office building, new construction; industrial buildings & warehouses

(P-823)
AMES 1 LLC
2371 Washington Ave Ste G, Oroville (95966-5466)
PHONE 907 344-0067
John Mahler, *Principal*
EMP: 48 **EST:** 2016
SALES (est): 3MM **Privately Held**
SIC: 1542 Nonresidential construction

(P-824)
ANGOTTI & REILLY INC
2200 Jerrold Ave Ste E, San Francisco (94124-1036)
PHONE 415 575-3700
James Reilly, *President*
Eilleen Angotti, *Treasurer*
Michael Angotti, *Vice Pres*
Jovanne Reilly, *Admin Sec*
Jim Robertson, *Project Mgr*
EMP: 40

SALES: 5.2MM **Privately Held**
WEB: www.angotti-reilly.com
SIC: 1542 Commercial & office building, new construction

(P-825)
ASSOCIATED BUILDING ENTP INC
Also Called: Associated Builders
4026 3rd St, San Francisco (94124-2183)
PHONE 415 285-6200
John H Chung, *President*
Karen Chung, *Vice Pres*
EMP: 38 **EST:** 1981
SQ FT: 6,000
SALES (est): 3.5MM **Privately Held**
WEB: www.abei.net
SIC: 1542 1761 Commercial & office building, new construction; roofing contractor

(P-826)
BACKYARD UNLIMITED
5119 Quinn Rd, Vacaville (95688-9452)
PHONE 707 447-7433
Nathan Martin, *Branch Mgr*
EMP: 48 **Privately Held**
WEB: www.backyardunlimited.com
SIC: 5211 1542 Prefabricated buildings; agricultural building contractors
PA: Backyard Unlimited
4765 Pacific St
Rocklin CA 95677

(P-827)
BALLIET BROS CONSTRUCTION CORP
390 Swift Ave Ste 14, South San Francisco (94080-6221)
PHONE 650 871-9000
Robert F Balliet, *President*
Michael Warren, *Vice Pres*
Mareth Vedder, *Admin Sec*
Blanca Garache, *Bookkeeper*
EMP: 31 **EST:** 1947
SQ FT: 9,000
SALES (est): 2.8MM **Privately Held**
WEB: www.ballietbros.com
SIC: 1542 1522 2434 2431 Commercial & office buildings, renovation & repair; remodeling, multi-family dwellings; wood kitchen cabinets; trim, wood

(P-828)
BAYSIDE INSULATION & CNSTR INC
1635 Challenge Dr, Concord (94520-5206)
PHONE 925 288-8960
Shahram Ameli, *CEO*
Al Badakhshan, *Vice Pres*
EMP: 62 **EST:** 2001
SQ FT: 10,000
SALES (est): 27.3MM **Privately Held**
WEB: www.baysideinsulation.com
SIC: 1542 Commercial & office building, new construction

(P-829)
BCCI CONSTRUCTION LLC (HQ)
Also Called: Bcci Builders
1160 Battery St Ste 250, San Francisco (94111-1216)
PHONE 415 817-5100
Michael Scribner, *President*
Hisham Mushasha, *CFO*
Michael Dean, *Vice Pres*
Debbie Fleser, *Vice Pres*
William Groth, *Vice Pres*
EMP: 134 **EST:** 1986
SQ FT: 15,121
SALES: 103.7MM
SALES (corp-wide): 4.3B **Privately Held**
WEB: www.bcciconst.com
SIC: 1542 Commercial & office buildings, renovation & repair
PA: Sto Building Group Inc.
330 W 34th St
New York NY 10001
732 362-3472

1542 - General Contractors, Nonresidential & Non-indl Bldgs County (P-830)

PRODUCTS & SERVICES SECTION

(P-830)
BELMONT BRUNS CONSTRUCTION INC
1125 Mabury Rd, San Jose (95133-1029)
P.O. Box 1369, Lathrop (95330-1369)
PHONE 408 977-1708
Mark A Collishaw, *CEO*
Paul J Helvik, *Vice Pres*
Jack Collishaw, *Admin Sec*
EMP: 55 **EST:** 1986
SALES (est): 12.1MM **Privately Held**
SIC: 1542 1541 Commercial & office building, new construction; commercial & office buildings, renovation & repair; industrial buildings & warehouses

(P-831)
BENNATHON CORP (PA)
Also Called: Tudor Cnstr & Restoration
10278 Iron Rock Way, Elk Grove (95624-1355)
P.O. Box 5426, Stockton (95205-0426)
PHONE 916 405-2100
David Urman, *President*
Tony Huynh, *CFO*
Peter Jones, *Vice Pres*
EMP: 50 **EST:** 1979
SQ FT: 30,000
SALES (est): 11.3MM **Privately Held**
SIC: 1542 1541 1521 Commercial & office buildings, renovation & repair; renovation, remodeling & repairs: industrial buildings; repairing fire damage, single-family houses

(P-832)
BJORK CONSTRUCTION COMPANY INC (PA)
4420 Enterprise Pl, Fremont (94538-6344)
PHONE 510 656-4688
Jean Bjork, *President*
Don Bjork, *Vice Pres*
Jesica Bjork, *Vice Pres*
Jessica Madrigal, *Vice Pres*
Janet Maiden, *Vice Pres*
EMP: 111 **EST:** 1988
SQ FT: 6,500
SALES (est): 27.5MM **Privately Held**
WEB: www.bjorkconstruction.com
SIC: 1542 1522 1623 Nonresidential construction; multi-family dwelling construction; water, sewer & utility lines

(P-833)
BLAZONA CONCRETE CNSTR INC
525 Harbor Blvd Ste 10, West Sacramento (95691-2246)
PHONE 916 375-8337
J Dennis Blazona, *CEO*
Karen Blazona, *Vice Pres*
Rhett Havner, *General Mgr*
Randy Thayer, *General Mgr*
Terry Blazona, *Project Mgr*
EMP: 100
SALES (est): 24.3MM **Privately Held**
WEB: www.blazona.biz
SIC: 1542 Concrete work

(P-834)
BLUELINE ASSOCIATES INC
2134 Rheem Dr Ste 100, Pleasanton (94588-5601)
PHONE 925 462-2200
Kenneth M Larson, *President*
Michelle Dang, *Project Engr*
EMP: 37 **EST:** 2005
SALES (est): 12.6MM **Privately Held**
WEB: www.bluelinecompany.com
SIC: 1542 Commercial & office building, new construction

(P-835)
BOLDT COMPANY
375 Beale St Ste 500, San Francisco (94105-2177)
PHONE 415 762-8300
EMP: 168
SALES (corp-wide): 1B **Privately Held**
WEB: www.theboldtcompany.com
SIC: 1542 Specialized public building contractors

HQ: The Boldt Company
2525 N Roemer Rd
Appleton WI 54911
920 739-6321

(P-836)
BRADDOCK & LOGAN SERVICES INC
4155 Blackhawk Plaza Cir # 201, Danville (94506-4613)
P.O. Box 5300 (94526-1076)
PHONE 925 736-4000
Joseph E Raphel, *CEO*
Kari Cartner, *Administration*
EMP: 200 **EST:** 1947
SALES (est): 26.2MM **Privately Held**
SIC: 1542 1522 Nonresidential construction; residential construction

(P-837)
BROWARD BUILDERS INC
1200 E Kentucky Ave, Woodland (95776-5906)
PHONE 530 666-5635
Dennis Broward, *President*
Randy Cantrell, *Vice Pres*
Anne Jensen, *Office Mgr*
Chuck Klenzendorf, *Project Mgr*
Butch Powell, *Manager*
EMP: 100 **EST:** 1990
SQ FT: 7,000
SALES (est): 38.4MM **Privately Held**
WEB: www.browardbuilders.com
SIC: 1542 1531 School building construction; cooperative apartment developers

(P-838)
BROWN CONSTRUCTION INC
1465 Entp Blvd Ste 100, West Sacramento (95691)
P.O. Box 980700 (95798-0700)
PHONE 916 374-8616
Ron Brown, *President*
Ken Brown, *CFO*
Kenneth Brown, *CFO*
Diana Houston, *CFO*
Kathryn Mc Guire, *Treasurer*
EMP: 71
SQ FT: 11,000
SALES (est): 151.1MM **Privately Held**
WEB: www.brown-construction.com
SIC: 1542 1522 Commercial & office building, new construction; apartment building construction

(P-839)
BRUCE TUCKER CONSTRUCTION INC
2260 Brown St, NAPA (94558-4903)
PHONE 707 255-1587
Warren Bowers, *President*
Scot Johnson, *CFO*
Bruce Tucker, *Admin Sec*
EMP: 37 **EST:** 2005
SALES (est): 5.8MM **Privately Held**
WEB: www.brucetuckerconstruction.com
SIC: 1542 1521 Commercial & office building contractors; single-family housing construction

(P-840)
BUILD GROUP INC (PA)
160 S Van Ness Ave, San Francisco (94103-2519)
PHONE 415 367-9399
Ross Edwards, *President*
Eric Horn, *Ch of Bd*
Todd C Pennington, *President*
Ron Marano, *CFO*
Kenneth Jones, *Exec VP*
▲ **EMP:** 242 **EST:** 2006
SQ FT: 8,000
SALES (est): 696.6MM **Privately Held**
WEB: www.buildgc.com
SIC: 1542 Commercial & office building, new construction

(P-841)
BUILD GROUP INC
Also Called: Build Sjc
1210 Coleman Ave, Santa Clara (95050-4338)
PHONE 408 986-8711
Chris Whittell, *Business Mgr*
Leslie Williams-Hurt, *Corp Comm Staff*
Michael Fernandez, *Manager*

Alex Dorsey, *Superintendent*
EMP: 65
SALES (corp-wide): 696.6MM **Privately Held**
WEB: www.buildgc.com
SIC: 1542 Commercial & office building, new construction
PA: Build Group, Inc.
160 S Van Ness Ave
San Francisco CA 94103
415 367-9399

(P-842)
BUILDER INC
1445 Grange St, Redding (96001-3200)
P.O. Box 493370 (96049-3370)
PHONE 530 691-4354
Charles Ray Beard, *CEO*
Ronald H Stickney, *CFO*
EMP: 40 **EST:** 2010
SQ FT: 11,000
SALES (est): 12.5MM **Privately Held**
WEB: www.thebuildersolution.com
SIC: 1542 Commercial & office building contractors

(P-843)
BUILDING SRVCS/SYSTEM MINT INC
Also Called: Bsm
2575 Stanwell Dr, Concord (94520-4888)
PHONE 925 688-1234
Sam Martinovich III, *CEO*
EMP: 66 **EST:** 2008
SALES (est): 10.4MM **Privately Held**
WEB: www.bsminc.com
SIC: 1542 Commercial & office building, new construction

(P-844)
C & J CONTRACTING INC
331 Commercial St, San Jose (95112-4404)
PHONE 408 374-6025
Christopher S Reno, *President*
Arthur Javier, *CFO*
Jeff Long, *Project Mgr*
Smith Mark, *Project Mgr*
Vern Pitts, *Project Mgr*
EMP: 43 **EST:** 1982
SQ FT: 10,800
SALES (est): 12.4MM **Privately Held**
WEB: www.cnjcontr.com
SIC: 1542 1541 Commercial & office buildings, renovation & repair; renovation, remodeling & repairs: industrial buildings

(P-845)
C OVERAA & CO (PA)
Also Called: Overaa Construction
200 Parr Blvd, Richmond (94801-1191)
PHONE 510 234-0926
Jerry Overaa, *CEO*
Christopher Manning, *President*
Ellen Hoffman, *CFO*
Dale Jackson, *Vice Pres*
Jeff Naff, *Vice Pres*
EMP: 346 **EST:** 1907
SQ FT: 20,000
SALES (est): 413.5MM **Privately Held**
WEB: www.overaa.com
SIC: 1542 Commercial & office building, new construction

(P-846)
CAHILL CONTRACTORS INC (PA)
425 California St # 2200, San Francisco (94104-2207)
PHONE 415 986-0600
John E Cahill Jr, *CEO*
Chuck Palley, *President*
Darrell Diamond, *Corp Secy*
Steve Wellman, *Officer*
Arash Baradaran, *Vice Pres*
▲ **EMP:** 158 **EST:** 1974
SALES (est): 115.1MM **Privately Held**
WEB: www.cahill-sf.com
SIC: 1542 Commercial & office building, new construction

(P-847)
CAHILL CONTRACTORS LLC
425 California St # 2200, San Francisco (94104-2207)
PHONE 415 986-0600

Michael Grant, *CFO*
Trilce Farrugia, *Exec Sec*
EMP: 99 **EST:** 2016
SALES (est): 16.8MM **Privately Held**
WEB: www.cahill-sf.com
SIC: 1542 1522 Commercial & office building, new construction; residential construction

(P-848)
CAL INC
2040 Peabody Rd Ste 400, Vacaville (95687-6694)
P.O. Box 6327 (95696-6327)
PHONE 707 446-7996
David Esparza, *President*
Olivia Esparza, *Vice Pres*
Sandra Esparza, *Vice Pres*
Olivia Trudell, *Admin Sec*
Brandee Luegar, *Project Mgr*
EMP: 40 **EST:** 1983
SQ FT: 7,800
SALES (est): 29.7MM **Privately Held**
WEB: www.cal-inc.com
SIC: 1542 1611 8744 Nonresidential construction; general contractor, highway & street construction;

(P-849)
CAL-PACIFIC CONSTRUCTION INC
1009 Terra Nova Blvd, Pacifica (94044-4308)
PHONE 650 557-1238
John Wah Chan, *President*
Kennedy Chan, *CEO*
EMP: 50 **EST:** 2002
SQ FT: 4,500
SALES (est): 5.1MM **Privately Held**
WEB: www.pacific888.com
SIC: 1542 1521 Commercial & office building contractors; general remodeling, single-family houses

(P-850)
CALIFORNIA GOLD DEV CORP
133 Old Wards Ferry Rd G, Sonora (95370-7822)
PHONE 209 533-3333
Ronald Woodall, *CEO*
Scot Patterson, *President*
James D Todd, *COO*
Mark Patterson, *Vice Pres*
Michael Q Jones, *Admin Sec*
EMP: 35 **EST:** 1975
SQ FT: 6,500
SALES (est): 14.5MM **Privately Held**
WEB: www.calgolddevelopment.com
SIC: 1542 1541 1521 Commercial & office building, new construction; industrial buildings, new construction; new construction, single-family houses

(P-851)
CELLO & MAUDRU CNSTR CO INC
2505 Oak St, NAPA (94559-2226)
P.O. Box 10106 (94581-2106)
PHONE 707 257-0454
William F Maudru, *CEO*
Norman Meites, *Partner*
Michael Zatorski, *Partner*
Jody Dedulucca, *Executive*
David Northcutt, *Executive*
EMP: 50 **EST:** 1987
SQ FT: 2,000
SALES (est): 25.8MM **Privately Held**
WEB: www.cello-maudru.com
SIC: 1542 1521 Commercial & office building, new construction; new construction, single-family houses

(P-852)
CENTRAL CAL DAR CNSTR INC
2700 Lassiter Ln, Turlock (95380-9583)
P.O. Box 2935 (95381-2935)
PHONE 209 667-0381
Tony A Gregorio, *President*
Kathleen M Gregorio, *Admin Sec*
EMP: 101 **EST:** 1975
SQ FT: 7,500
SALES (est): 6.5MM **Privately Held**
WEB: www.californiadairies.com
SIC: 1542 Farm building construction

▲ = Import ▼=Export
◆ =Import/Export

PRODUCTS & SERVICES SECTION
1542 - General Contractors, Nonresidential & Non-indl Bldgs County (P-874)

(P-853)
CHARLES PNKOW BLDRS LTD A CAL
1111 Broadway Ste 200, Oakland (94607-4171)
PHONE..................510 893-5170
Scott Anderson, *Manager*
Jerman Valencia, *Engineer*
EMP: 450
SALES (corp-wide): 161.8MM **Privately Held**
WEB: www.pankow.com
SIC: **1542** Commercial & office building, new construction
PA: Charles Pankow Builders, Ltd., A California Limited Partnership
199 S Los Robles Ave # 3
Pasadena CA 91101
626 304-1190

(P-854)
CIRKS CONSTRUCTION INC
Also Called: Kdc Construction
3300 Industrial Blvd, West Sacramento (95691-5028)
PHONE..................916 362-5460
Ryan Ferris, *Branch Mgr*
Chad D 'angelo, *Project Mgr*
Corby Haas, *Project Mgr*
Jason Kelly, *Project Mgr*
Gary Wilder, *Project Mgr*
EMP: 124
SALES (corp-wide): 141.8MM **Privately Held**
WEB: www.kdcconstruction.com
SIC: **1542** Commercial & office building, new construction
PA: Cirks Construction Inc.
2570 E Cerritos Ave
Anaheim CA 92806
714 632-6717

(P-855)
CITY BUILDING INC
212 N San Mateo Dr, San Mateo (94401-2690)
PHONE..................415 285-1711
Wallace C Baldwin, *President*
Matt Ralls, *Executive*
Steven F Baldwin, *Principal*
Pat Fellowes, *Project Mgr*
Amy Gray, *Project Mgr*
▲ EMP: 40 EST: 1976
SQ FT: 2,400
SALES (est): 12.2MM **Privately Held**
WEB: www.citybuilding.com
SIC: **1542** Commercial & office building, new construction

(P-856)
CLARK & SULLIVAN CONSTRS INC
2024 Opportunity Dr # 150, Roseville (95678-3026)
PHONE..................916 338-7707
Ted Foor, *Branch Mgr*
Eric Jamison, *Project Mgr*
Amanda Frantz, *Project Engr*
Ying Lor, *Project Engr*
PO Thao, *Project Engr*
EMP: 120
SALES (corp-wide): 87.6MM **Privately Held**
WEB: www.clarksullivan.com
SIC: **1542** Commercial & office building, new construction
HQ: Clark & Sullivan Constructors Dba Clark/Sullivan Construction
905 Industrial Way
Sparks NV 89431
775 355-8500

(P-857)
CLARK SLLVAN BLDRS INC DBA CLR
1340 Blue Oaks Blvd Ste 1, Roseville (95678-7035)
P.O. Box 7100, Reno NV (89510-7100)
PHONE..................916 338-7707
Theodore Foor, *President*
B J Sullivan, *President*
Kevin Stroupe, *CFO*
Ted Foor, *Project Engr*
EMP: 150 EST: 2001
SALES (est): 25.1MM
SALES (corp-wide): 87.6MM **Privately Held**
WEB: www.clarksullivan.com
SIC: **1542** **1541** Commercial & office building, new construction; industrial buildings, new construction
PA: C.S. General, Inc.
905 Industrial Way
Sparks NV 89431
775 355-8500

(P-858)
CONSTRUCTION DEVELOPERS INC
Also Called: CDI
5755 W Barstow Ave # 103, Fresno (93722-5379)
PHONE..................559 277-4700
Williamfranklin Cornell IV, *CEO*
Joe Troncoso Jr, *CFO*
Leann Sehon, *Administration*
Stan Dobbs, *Project Mgr*
Ulysses Maravilla, *Project Engr*
EMP: 40 EST: 1995
SALES (est): 11.1MM **Privately Held**
WEB: www.cdi-ca.com
SIC: **1542** Commercial & office building, new construction

(P-859)
D A POPE INCORPORATED
1160 Chess Dr Ste 11, Foster City (94404-1163)
PHONE..................650 349-5086
Erik Redse, *President*
Ed Arnold, *CEO*
Robert M Bybee, *Vice Pres*
Carl Baughn, *Admin Sec*
Julio Escalante, *Project Mgr*
EMP: 47 EST: 1969
SQ FT: 8,500
SALES (est): 12.3MM **Privately Held**
WEB: www.dapope.com
SIC: **1542** Commercial & office building, new construction

(P-860)
D F P F CORPORATION
Also Called: Fine Line Construction
15 Brush Pl, San Francisco (94103-3967)
PHONE..................415 512-7677
Paolo Friedman, *CEO*
Emily Lin, *President*
Martin Imahori, *CFO*
Sally Lyle, *Opers Mgr*
EMP: 45 EST: 1979
SQ FT: 3,700
SALES (est): 81.2MM **Privately Held**
WEB: www.finelineconstruction.com
SIC: **1542** Commercial & office building, new construction

(P-861)
DESIGNED MBL SYSTEMS INDS INC
800 S State Highway 33, Patterson (95363-9148)
P.O. Box 367 (95363-0367)
PHONE..................209 892-6298
David W Smith, *President*
Edward Smith, *Vice Pres*
EMP: 17 EST: 1973
SQ FT: 100,000
SALES (est): 1.1MM **Privately Held**
WEB: www.dmsi-inc.com
SIC: **1542** **2451** **3448** **2452** Design & erection, combined: non-residential; mobile classrooms; prefabricated metal buildings; prefabricated wood buildings

(P-862)
DEVCON CONSTRUCTION INC (PA)
690 Gibraltar Dr, Milpitas (95035-6317)
PHONE..................408 942-8200
Gary Filizetti, *President*
Brett Sisney, *CFO*
Ken Sullivan, *Officer*
Jonathan Harvey, *Vice Pres*
Kinh Curotto, *Executive Asst*
EMP: 450 EST: 1976
SQ FT: 45,000
SALES (est): 309.7MM **Privately Held**
WEB: www.devcon-const.com
SIC: **1542** Commercial & office building, new construction

(P-863)
DIEDE CONSTRUCTION INC
12393 N Hwy 99, Lodi (95240-7269)
P.O. Box 1007, Woodbridge (95258-1007)
PHONE..................209 369-8255
Steven L Diede, *President*
Lillian Diede, *Corp Secy*
Bruce J Diede, *Vice Pres*
Wayne J Diede, *Vice Pres*
Shari Slover, *Accountant*
EMP: 100 EST: 1978
SQ FT: 23,000
SALES (est): 44.5MM **Privately Held**
WEB: www.diedeconstruction.com
SIC: **1542** **1771** **1761** Commercial & office buildings, renovation & repair; foundation & footing contractor; roof repair

(P-864)
DPR CONSTRUCTION INC (PA)
1450 Veterans Blvd, Redwood City (94063-2617)
PHONE..................650 474-1450
George Pfeffer, *President*
Alison Lyons, *President*
Michele Leiva, *CFO*
Ron J Davidowski, *Treasurer*
James Dolen, *Exec VP*
▲ EMP: 1200 EST: 1990
SQ FT: 36,300
SALES (est): 7B **Privately Held**
WEB: www.dpr.com
SIC: **1542** Commercial & office building contractors

(P-865)
DPR CONSTRUCTION A GEN PARTNR
1510 S Winchester Blvd, San Jose (95128-4334)
PHONE..................408 370-2322
Jim Carter, *Manager*
Jacob Hammon, *Engineer*
EMP: 141 **Privately Held**
SIC: **1542** Commercial & office building, new construction
HQ: Dpr Construction, A General Partnership
1450 Veterans Blvd
Redwood City CA 94063

(P-866)
DPR CONSTRUCTION A GEN PARTNR
1801 J St, Sacramento (95811-3009)
PHONE..................916 568-3434
Trish Timothy, *Manager*
Debbie Reed, *Executive*
David Lierly, *Project Engr*
Cassandra Dennis, *Accountant*
EMP: 141 **Privately Held**
WEB: www.dpr.com
SIC: **1542** Commercial & office building, new construction
HQ: Dpr Construction, A General Partnership
1450 Veterans Blvd
Redwood City CA 94063

(P-867)
DPR CONSTRUCTION A GEN PARTNR (HQ)
1450 Veterans Blvd, Redwood City (94063-2617)
PHONE..................650 474-1450
George Pfeffer, *President*
Michele Leiva, *CFO*
Devin Vigil, *Treasurer*
Ron J Davidowski, *Corp Secy*
James F Dolen, *Exec VP*
EMP: 2632 EST: 1990
SQ FT: 36,300
SALES (est): 7B **Privately Held**
WEB: www.dpr.com
SIC: **1542** Commercial & office building, new construction

(P-868)
DPR SKANSKA A JOINT VENTURE
1450 Veterans Blvd, Redwood City (94063-2617)
P.O. Box 5614 (94063-0614)
PHONE..................650 306-7671
Eric R Lamb, *Manager*
▲ EMP: 35 EST: 2011
SALES (est): 590.8K **Privately Held**
SIC: **1542** Commercial & office building, new construction

(P-869)
E A DAVIDOVITS & CO INC
555 Price Ave Ste 200, Redwood City (94061-1417)
PHONE..................650 366-6068
Edward Davidovits, *President*
EMP: 35 EST: 1989
SQ FT: 4,100
SALES (est): 8.6MM **Privately Held**
WEB: www.davidovitsco.com
SIC: **1542** Commercial & office building, new construction

(P-870)
F & H CONSTRUCTION (PA)
1115 E Lockeford St, Lodi (95240-0878)
P.O. Box 2329 (95241-2329)
PHONE..................209 931-3738
Charles Allen Ferrell, *President*
Dan Blackburn, *Partner*
Stephen Seibly, *Corp Secy*
Harold Erwin Jones, *Vice Pres*
Amy Billups, *Admin Asst*
EMP: 75 EST: 1972
SQ FT: 8,000
SALES: 81MM **Privately Held**
WEB: www.f-hconst.com
SIC: **1542** **1541** Commercial & office building, new construction; industrial buildings, new construction

(P-871)
FIELD CONSTRUCTION INC (PA)
490 2nd St Ste 100, San Francisco (94107-1419)
PHONE..................415 648-8140
John Garcina, *President*
Tracy Coletta, *Partner*
Tim Gibbons, *CFO*
Chris Przybysz, *Project Mgr*
Aileen Intara, *Bookkeeper*
EMP: 35 EST: 1973
SQ FT: 8,000
SALES (est): 50MM **Privately Held**
WEB: www.fieldgc.com
SIC: **1542** Nonresidential construction

(P-872)
FINE LINE GROUP INC
457 Minna St, San Francisco (94103-2914)
PHONE..................415 777-4070
John S Santori, *Ch of Bd*
Robert M Helmers, *Exec VP*
EMP: 36 EST: 1971
SQ FT: 7,000
SALES (est): 5.7MM **Privately Held**
WEB: www.finelinegroup.com
SIC: **1542** Commercial & office buildings, renovation & repair

(P-873)
FISHER DEVELOPMENT INC
Also Called: Fdi
601 California St Ste 300, San Francisco (94108-2808)
PHONE..................415 228-3060
Robert S Fisher, *CEO*
Alex Fisher, *President*
Rose Mitchell, *CFO*
Sidney Fisher-Bernier, *Vice Pres*
David Larson, *Vice Pres*
EMP: 40 EST: 1971
SALES (est): 19.1MM **Privately Held**
WEB: www.fisherinc.com
SIC: **1542** Commercial & office building, new construction; commercial & office buildings, renovation & repair

(P-874)
FLINT BUILDERS INC
401 Derek Pl, Roseville (95678-7153)
PHONE..................916 757-1000
John Stump, *President*

1542 - General Contractors, Nonresidential & Non-indl Bldgs County (P-875)

PRODUCTS & SERVICES SECTION

Cathy Robb, *CFO*
Kevin Mosher, *Vice Pres*
Jared Wright, *Principal*
David Garner, *Project Mgr*
EMP: 89 **EST:** 2013
SALES: 150MM **Privately Held**
WEB: www.flintbuilders.com
SIC: 1542 Commercial & office building, new construction; institutional building construction

(P-875)
GARDEN CITY CONSTRUCTION INC
1010 S 1st St, San Jose (95110-3129)
PHONE................................408 289-8807
James A Salata, *President*
EMP: 36 **EST:** 1989
SALES (est): 9.6MM **Privately Held**
WEB: www.gardencityconst.com
SIC: 1542 Commercial & office building, new construction

(P-876)
GCI INC
875 Battery St Fl 1, San Francisco (94111-1547)
PHONE................................415 978-2790
Jon Helman, *CFO*
Peter D Goldsmith, *Vice Pres*
Alex Docous, *Project Engr*
Vivienne Wen, *Accountant*
Star McAleese, *Controller*
▲ **EMP:** 48 **EST:** 1992
SALES: 222.6MM **Privately Held**
WEB: www.gcigc.com
SIC: 1542 Commercial & office buildings, renovation & repair

(P-877)
GENERAL SERVICES CAL DEPT
Also Called: Buildings & Grounds
625 Q St, Sacramento (95811-6310)
PHONE................................916 322-3880
Tim Bow, *CEO*
Richard Snyder, *Chief Engr*
EMP: 36 **Privately Held**
WEB: www.ca.gov
SIC: 9199 1542 1522 General government administration; ; commercial & office building contractors; residential construction
HQ: California Department Of General Services
707 3rd St
West Sacramento CA 95605

(P-878)
GIDEL & KOCAL CNSTR CO INC
574 Division St, Campbell (95008-6906)
PHONE................................408 370-0280
Lance Gidel, *President*
John Kocal, *Vice Pres*
Arlene Gidel, *Admin Sec*
Sean Bardes, *Project Mgr*
Mike Habing, *Project Mgr*
EMP: 43 **EST:** 1978
SQ FT: 5,000
SALES (est): 19.8MM **Privately Held**
WEB: www.gidelkocal.com
SIC: 1542 Commercial & office buildings, renovation & repair; commercial & office building, new construction

(P-879)
GORDON PRILL INC
310 E Caribbean Dr, Sunnyvale (94089-1148)
PHONE................................408 745-7164
Gopal K Aggarwal, *CEO*
Mike Valentine, *Project Mgr*
Leland Prior, *Project Engr*
Paul Otis, *Opers Staff*
Monique Ross, *Marketing Staff*
EMP: 45 **EST:** 1989
SQ FT: 24,000
SALES (est): 29.2MM **Privately Held**
WEB: www.gordonprill.com
SIC: 1542 8741 8712 8711 Commercial & office building contractors; construction management; architectural services; engineering services; industrial buildings, new construction

(P-880)
GREEN VALLEY CORPORATION (PA)
Also Called: Swenson, Barry Builder
777 N 1st St Fl 5, San Jose (95112-6350)
PHONE................................408 287-0246
C Barron Swenson, *Chairman*
Case Swenson, *President*
Lee Ann Woodard, *CFO*
Steven W Andrews, *Senior VP*
Ronald L Cot, *Senior VP*
▲ **EMP:** 50 **EST:** 1961
SQ FT: 12,000
SALES (est): 59MM **Privately Held**
WEB: www.swensonbuilders.com
SIC: 1542 1522 6512 Commercial & office building, new construction; multi-family dwelling construction; commercial & industrial building operation

(P-881)
GREENHOUSE SYSTEM USA
512 Casserly Rd, Watsonville (95076-9732)
P.O. Box 777 (95077-0777)
PHONE................................831 722-1188
Peter Fryn, *President*
James Fryn, *Supervisor*
◆ **EMP:** 45 **EST:** 1981
SQ FT: 30,000
SALES (est): 23.4MM **Privately Held**
WEB: www.systemusa.com
SIC: 1542 Greenhouse construction

(P-882)
GROUNDLVEL - OVRAA JOINT VENTR
5013 Forni Dr Ste C, Concord (94520-8524)
PHONE................................925 446-6084
Mark Rogelstad, *Principal*
Bryan Lee, *Principal*
EMP: 99 **EST:** 2018
SALES (est): 5MM **Privately Held**
WEB: www.groundlevelconstruction.com
SIC: 1542 Commercial & office building, new construction

(P-883)
HAGENSEN PACIFIC CNSTR INC
2033 Gateway Pl Ste 600, San Jose (95110-3712)
PHONE................................408 961-8656
Frank Nejat, *President*
EMP: 45 **EST:** 1986
SQ FT: 4,200
SALES (est): 16.7MM **Privately Held**
WEB: www.hagensenp.com
SIC: 1542 Commercial & office building contractors

(P-884)
HALSTEAD PARTNERSHIP
Also Called: Sundt Construction
2850 Gateway Oaks Dr # 450, Sacramento (95833-4347)
PHONE................................916 830-8000
John Wald, *Managing Prtnr*
Will Hill, *Bd of Directors*
Igor Ubryanov, *Engineer*
EMP: 60 **EST:** 1994
SALES (est): 25.2MM **Privately Held**
SIC: 1542 Commercial & office building, new construction

(P-885)
HARRIS CONSTRUCTION CO INC
5286 E Home Ave, Fresno (93727-2103)
PHONE................................559 251-0301
Mike Spencer, *President*
Ryan Diel, *COO*
Timothy Thornton, *CFO*
Richard F Spencer, *Chairman*
Courtney Miller, *Project Mgr*
▲ **EMP:** 150 **EST:** 1914
SQ FT: 6,000
SALES (est): 51.1MM **Privately Held**
WEB: www.harrisconstruction.com
SIC: 1542 1541 Hospital construction; commercial & office building, new construction; food products manufacturing or packing plant construction

(P-886)
HATHAWAY DINWIDDIE CNSTR CO
565 Laurelwood Rd, Santa Clara (95054-2419)
PHONE................................415 986-2718
Greg Cosko, *President*
David A Lee, *Senior VP*
Raul Valdez, *Foreman/Supr*
EMP: 100 **EST:** 1946
SQ FT: 7,000
SALES (est): 37.3MM **Privately Held**
WEB: www.hathawaydinwiddie.com
SIC: 1542 Commercial & office building, new construction

(P-887)
HATHAWAY DINWIDDIE CNSTR CO
275 Battery St Ste 300, San Francisco (94111-3378)
PHONE................................415 986-2718
Greg Cosko, *CEO*
Robin Byerly, *President*
Paul Gregory Cosko, *President*
Stephen W McCoid, *Exec VP*
Kevin O'riordan, *Exec VP*
▲ **EMP:** 400 **EST:** 1996
SQ FT: 21,000
SALES (est): 158.5MM **Privately Held**
WEB: www.hathawaydinwiddie.com
SIC: 1542 Commercial & office building, new construction
PA: Hathaway Dinwiddie Construction Group
275 Battery St Ste 300
San Francisco CA 94111

(P-888)
HATHAWAY DINWIDDIE CNSTR GROUP (PA)
275 Battery St Ste 300, San Francisco (94111-3378)
PHONE................................415 986-2718
Greg Cosko, *CEO*
David Miller, *CFO*
Stephen E Smith, *Senior VP*
Stephen W McCoid, *Vice Pres*
Steven Gabriel, *Engineer*
EMP: 60 **EST:** 1996
SQ FT: 18,000
SALES (est): 158.5MM **Privately Held**
WEB: www.hathawaydinwiddie.com
SIC: 1542 Commercial & office building, new construction

(P-889)
HELMER AND SONS INC (PA)
910 Howell Mountain Rd, Angwin (94508-9697)
P.O. Box 868 (94508-0868)
PHONE................................707 965-2425
Maurice Helmer, *President*
Curtis Helmer, *Treasurer*
Dennis S Helmer, *Vice Pres*
Douglas Helmer, *Admin Sec*
EMP: 39 **EST:** 1975
SQ FT: 2,880
SALES (est): 12MM **Privately Held**
WEB: www.helmers.net
SIC: 1542 1611 Commercial & office building, new construction; grading

(P-890)
HENSEL PHELPS CONSTRUCTION CO
4750 Willow Rd Ste 100, Pleasanton (94588-2963)
PHONE................................408 452-1800
Jon W Ball, *Vice Pres*
Tom Looby, *Regional Mgr*
Brad Jeanneret, *General Mgr*
Manal Boulos, *Office Mgr*
Maritza Dominguez, *Admin Asst*
EMP: 200
SALES (corp-wide): 5.6B **Privately Held**
WEB: www.henselphelps.com
SIC: 1542 1541 Commercial & office building, new construction; industrial buildings & warehouses
PA: Hensel Phelps Construction Co.
420 6th Ave
Greeley CO 80631
970 352-6565

(P-891)
HILBERS INC
Also Called: Hilbers Contractors & Engrg
770 N Walton Ave Ste 100, Yuba City (95993-9469)
PHONE................................530 673-2947
Kurt G Hilbers, *President*
Glenn Hilbers, *Treasurer*
Mary Hilbers, *Officer*
Larry E Hilbers, *Vice Pres*
Tom Jones, *Vice Pres*
EMP: 75 **EST:** 1988
SQ FT: 6,790
SALES: 121.7MM **Privately Held**
WEB: www.hilbersinc.com
SIC: 1542 1541 Commercial & office building, new construction; industrial buildings, new construction

(P-892)
HOLDER CORPORATION
2033 Gateway Pl Fl 6, San Jose (95110-3709)
PHONE................................408 516-4401
EMP: 62
SALES (corp-wide): 87.7MM **Privately Held**
WEB: www.holderconstruction.com
SIC: 1542 Commercial & office building, new construction
PA: Holder Corporation
3300 Cumberland Blvd Se
Atlanta GA 30339
770 988-3000

(P-893)
INTEGRITY CNSTR MAINT INC
3531 Gravenstein Hwy S, Sebastopol (95472-5258)
PHONE................................707 829-5300
Bennett White, *President*
EMP: 40 **EST:** 1997
SALES (est): 4MM **Privately Held**
WEB: www.icmconstruction.com
SIC: 1542 Commercial & office building, new construction

(P-894)
ISBELL CONSTRUCTION INC
11090 Trails End Ct, Truckee (96161-0203)
PHONE................................530 587-0230
Steven L Isbell, *President*
Lucy Isbell, *Corp Secy*
James Lebel, *Vice Pres*
EMP: 68 **EST:** 1977
SQ FT: 3,500
SALES (est): 5.2MM **Privately Held**
SIC: 1542 Commercial & office building, new construction

(P-895)
J B COMPANY
1825 Bell St Ste 100, Sacramento (95825-1020)
PHONE................................916 929-3003
EMP: 70
SQ FT: 24,000
SALES (est): 5.8MM **Privately Held**
SIC: 1542 1541 Nonresidential Construction Industrial Building Construction

(P-896)
J BENDER COMPANY
4491 Pacific St Ste B, Rocklin (95677-2051)
PHONE................................916 462-7900
Timothy Allen Bender, *CEO*
Ryanc Baird, *Vice Pres*
Braden McKenzie, *Manager*
EMP: 17 **EST:** 2017
SALES (est): 1MM **Privately Held**
WEB: www.bender-construction.com
SIC: 1542 1389 1541 1531 Commercial & office building contractors; commercial & office buildings, renovation & repair; construction, repair & dismantling services; renovation, remodeling & repairs: industrial buildings; ; commercial indusl & institutional electric lighting fixtures

(P-897)
J R ROBERTS CORP (HQ)
7745 Greenback Ln Ste 300, Citrus Heights (95610-5866)
PHONE................................916 729-5600
Robert Olsen, *CEO*

▲ = Import ▼ = Export
◆ = Import/Export

PRODUCTS & SERVICES SECTION
1542 - General Contractors, Nonresidential & Non-indl Bldgs County (P-920)

Robert C Hall Jr, *President*
Mike Vinks, *Vice Pres*
EMP: 100 **EST:** 1979
SQ FT: 9,000
SALES (est): 28.8MM
SALES (corp-wide): 391.5MM **Privately Held**
WEB: www.deacon.com
SIC: 1542 Commercial & office building, new construction
PA: Deacon Construction, Llc
901 Ne Glisan St Ste 100
Portland OR 97232
503 297-8791

(P-898)
J R ROBERTS ENTERPRISES INC
7745 Greenback Ln Ste 300, Citrus Heights (95610-5866)
PHONE 916 729-5600
Robert F Olsen, *Ch of Bd*
Robert C Hall Jr, *President*
James F Reilly, *Corp Secy*
EMP: 110 **EST:** 1984
SALES (est): 10.4MM **Privately Held**
SIC: 1542 1522 Commercial & office building contractors; multi-family dwellings, new construction; remodeling, multi-family dwellings

(P-899)
JIM WALTERS CONSTRUCTION INC (PA)
1042 Terminal Way, San Carlos (94070-3227)
PHONE 650 596-9751
James Lionel Walters, *CEO*
EMP: 72 **EST:** 2002
SALES (est): 5.7MM **Privately Held**
WEB: www.jimwaltersconstruction.com
SIC: 1542 1522 Commercial & office building contractors; residential construction

(P-900)
JL BRAY & SON INC
4501 Broadway, Salida (95368-9303)
P.O. Box L (95368-0607)
PHONE 209 545-2856
Jack E Bray, *President*
James W Bray, *Vice Pres*
EMP: 54 **EST:** 1948
SQ FT: 3,600
SALES (est): 2.2MM **Privately Held**
WEB: www.brayconstruction.com
SIC: 1542 Commercial & office building, new construction; school building construction

(P-901)
JL CONSTRUCTION INC
Also Called: J L C
70 Stony Point Rd Ste D, Santa Rosa (95401-4460)
PHONE 707 527-5788
Jeff Luchetti, *CEO*
Paul Gilles, *Vice Pres*
Nancy Luchetti, *Admin Sec*
Barbara Leuty, *Administration*
Tammy Sharp, *Administration*
EMP: 42 **EST:** 1999
SALES (est): 14.6MM **Privately Held**
WEB: www.jlcbuild.com
SIC: 1542 Commercial & office building, new construction

(P-902)
JM STREAMLINE INC
Also Called: Streamline Construction
154 Scandling Ave, Grass Valley (95945-5816)
PHONE 530 272-6806
Jesse McKenna, *President*
Robyn McCoy, *CFO*
Melody Buckley, *Executive Asst*
Andrew Ehlers, *Project Mgr*
Morgan Young, *Receptionist*
EMP: 55 **EST:** 2007
SALES (est): 10.3MM **Privately Held**
WEB: www.streamlineconstruction.net
SIC: 1542 Commercial & office building contractors

(P-903)
JMB CONSTRUCTION INC
132 S Maple Ave, South San Francisco (94080-6302)
PHONE 650 267-5300
Margaret P Burke, *President*
Ciaran Crossan, *Project Engr*
John Haughey, *Project Engr*
Adrian Power, *Project Engr*
Aidan Sullivan, *Opers Mgr*
▲ **EMP:** 100 **EST:** 1976
SALES (est): 35.4MM **Privately Held**
WEB: www.jmbconstruction.com
SIC: 1542 Commercial & office building, new construction

(P-904)
JOHN F OTTO INC
Also Called: OTTO CONSTRUCTION
1717 2nd St, Sacramento (95811-6214)
PHONE 916 441-6870
Carl Barrett, *President*
Preston Hatch, *CFO*
Carol Otto, *Corp Secy*
Allison Otto, *Exec VP*
Elease Terry, *IT/INT Sup*
EMP: 120
SQ FT: 10,000
SALES (est): 107.8MM **Privately Held**
WEB: www.ottoconstruction.com
SIC: 1542 1541 Commercial & office building, new construction; industrial buildings, new construction

(P-905)
JOHN PLANE CONSTRUCTION INC
661 Hayne Rd, Hillsborough (94010-7006)
PHONE 415 468-0555
EMP: 120
SQ FT: 4,500
SALES (est): 8.7MM **Privately Held**
WEB: www.johnplane.com
SIC: 1542 Nonresidential Construction

(P-906)
JOHN SIKKEMA CONSTRUCTION INC
26126 S Curtis Ave, Ripon (95366-9528)
PHONE 209 599-1573
John Sikkema, *CEO*
Melinda Sikkema, *Vice Pres*
EMP: 36 **EST:** 2000
SQ FT: 4,044
SALES (est): 8.8MM **Privately Held**
WEB: www.johnsikkemaconstruction.com
SIC: 1542 Agricultural building contractors

(P-907)
K G WALTERS CNSTR CO INC
195 Concourse Blvd Ste A, Santa Rosa (95403-8217)
P.O. Box 4359 (95402-4359)
PHONE 707 527-9968
Walt Johnson, *President*
David A Backman, *Senior VP*
Thomas Crotty, *Vice Pres*
Valerie Carmichael, *Admin Sec*
EMP: 55 **EST:** 1974
SQ FT: 4,000
SALES (est): 17.2MM **Privately Held**
WEB: www.kgwalters.com
SIC: 1542 Commercial & office building, new construction

(P-908)
KARSYN CONSTRUCTION INC
4697 W Jacquelyn Ave, Fresno (93722-6413)
PHONE 559 271-2900
Joseph C Parker, *President*
Judith Parnell, *CFO*
Kristin Parker, *Corp Secy*
EMP: 60 **EST:** 1995
SALES (est): 13.7MM **Privately Held**
WEB: www.karsyn.com
SIC: 1542 Commercial & office building, new construction

(P-909)
KIMMEL CONSTRUCTION INC
10 Main Ave Ste 2, Sacramento (95838-2042)
PHONE 916 927-3118
Michael A Kimmel, *President*

Bob Stevens, *Vice Pres*
EMP: 55 **EST:** 1946
SQ FT: 8,000
SALES (est): 5.7MM **Privately Held**
SIC: 1542 Commercial & office buildings, renovation & repair

(P-910)
KRW ENTERPRISES
Also Called: K W Construction
841 F St, West Sacramento (95605-2313)
PHONE 916 372-8600
Kevin Wong, *President*
Nikki Flores, *Human Resources*
Verna Bouie,
EMP: 39 **EST:** 1989
SQ FT: 20,000
SALES (est): 3.6MM **Privately Held**
WEB: www.kwconstruction.us
SIC: 1542 Commercial & office buildings, renovation & repair; commercial & office building, new construction

(P-911)
LAMON CONSTRUCTION COMPANY INC
871 Von Geldern Way, Yuba City (95991-4215)
P.O. Box 632 (95992-0632)
PHONE 530 671-1370
Henry S Lamon, *President*
Steve Ithururn, *Vice Pres*
Ken Northon, *Vice Pres*
EMP: 50 **EST:** 1952
SQ FT: 3,200
SALES (est): 20.9MM **Privately Held**
WEB: www.lamonconstruction.com
SIC: 1542 Commercial & office building, new construction

(P-912)
LATHROP CONSTRUCTION ASSOC INC (PA)
4001 Park Rd, Benicia (94510-1172)
P.O. Box 2005 (94510-0819)
PHONE 707 746-8000
Roy Van Pelt, *Chairman*
Ricky J Martellaro, *CEO*
Olav Lyssand, *Treasurer*
Anthony Reed, *Officer*
C Gary Kalian, *Exec VP*
EMP: 69 **EST:** 1981
SQ FT: 14,000
SALES (est): 24.4MM **Privately Held**
WEB: www.lathropconstruction.com
SIC: 1542 School building construction; hospital construction; commercial & office building, new construction

(P-913)
LEVEL 10 CONSTRUCTION LP
1050 Entp Way Ste 250, Sunnyvale (94089)
PHONE 408 747-5000
Dennis Giles, *President*
Casey Wend, *Partner*
Jim Evans, *CFO*
Kevin Fettig, *Vice Pres*
Joe Francini, *Vice Pres*
EMP: 220 **EST:** 2011
SQ FT: 12,000
SALES (est): 144.6MM **Privately Held**
WEB: www.level10gc.com
SIC: 1542 Commercial & office buildings, renovation & repair

(P-914)
LEVEL-IT INSTALLATIONS GROUP
3700 Yale Way, Fremont (94538-6183)
PHONE 604 942-2022
Colin Rimes, *President*
Todd Ifackson, *Vice Pres*
Natalie Mnconkey, *Finance*
EMP: 60 **EST:** 2019
SALES (est): 20MM **Privately Held**
SIC: 1542 Nonresidential construction

(P-915)
LEVEL-IT INSTALLATIONS LTD
2443 Fillmore St, San Francisco (94115-1814)
PHONE 604 942-2022
Colin Rimes, *CEO*
Todd Isackson, *Admin Sec*

Angie Marston, *Manager*
EMP: 50 **EST:** 2014
SQ FT: 15,000
SALES (est): 12MM
SALES (corp-wide): 10.2MM **Privately Held**
WEB: www.levelitgroup.com
SIC: 1542 Commercial & office building contractors
PA: Level It Installations Ltd
1515 Broadway St Unit 804
Port Coquitlam BC V3C 6
604 942-2022

(P-916)
LUSARDI CONSTRUCTION CO
6376 Clark Ave, Dublin (94568-3036)
PHONE 925 829-1114
Kurt Evans, *Manager*
Judy Freeman, *Receptionist*
EMP: 135
SALES (corp-wide): 84.7MM **Privately Held**
WEB: www.lusardi.com
SIC: 1542 Commercial & office building, new construction
PA: Lusardi Construction Co.
1570 Linda Vista Dr
San Marcos CA 92078
760 744-3133

(P-917)
LYON MEDICAL CONSTRUCTION INC
100 N Hill Dr Ste 52, Brisbane (94005-1014)
PHONE 415 508-1970
David A Lyon, *President*
Amy Rickert, *Office Mgr*
Dan Carter, *Sr Project Mgr*
EMP: 43 **EST:** 1970
SQ FT: 1,250
SALES (est): 4.4MM **Privately Held**
WEB: www.lyonmc.com
SIC: 1542 Commercial & office buildings, renovation & repair; specialized public building contractors

(P-918)
MARK SCOTT CONSTRUCTION INC (PA)
Also Called: M S
2835 Contra Costa Blvd A, Pleasant Hill (94523-4221)
P.O. Box 4658, Walnut Creek (94596-0658)
PHONE 925 944-0502
Mark A Scott, *CEO*
Antoinette Lewis, *Executive*
Dave Bergamini, *General Mgr*
Vickie Stubbles, *Office Admin*
Michael Barham, *Project Mgr*
EMP: 50 **EST:** 1991
SQ FT: 16,000
SALES (est): 65.9MM **Privately Held**
WEB: www.msconstruction.com
SIC: 1542 Commercial & office building, new construction

(P-919)
MATTHEW BURNS
Also Called: Act Associates
617 Flower Dr, Folsom (95630-4816)
PHONE 209 676-4940
EMP: 60
SALES (est): 6.2MM **Privately Held**
SIC: 1542 0851 Nonresidential Construction Forestry Services

(P-920)
MCCARTHY BLDG COMPANIES INC
Also Called: San Jose Office
3975 Freedom Cir Ste 950, Santa Clara (95054-1455)
PHONE 408 908-7005
Miles Murphy, *Manager*
EMP: 59
SALES (corp-wide): 4.7B **Privately Held**
WEB: www.mccarthybuildingcompanies.com
SIC: 1542 Commercial & office building, new construction

1542 - General Contractors, Nonresidential & Non-indl Bldgs County (P-921)

PRODUCTS & SERVICES SECTION

HQ: Mccarthy Building Companies, Inc.
12851 Manchester Rd
Saint Louis MO 63131
314 968-3300

(P-921)
MCLARNEY CONSTRUCTION INC
355 S Daniel Way, San Jose (95128-5120)
PHONE............................408 246-8600
Kevin M McLarney, *President*
Nicole Merriam, *CFO*
Brett McLarney, *Vice Pres*
Peter Jeziorske, *Project Mgr*
Kristen Sinnott, *Project Mgr*
EMP: 46 **EST:** 1987
SQ FT: 7,340
SALES (est): 97.4MM **Privately Held**
WEB: www.mclarney.com
SIC: 1542 Commercial & office building, new construction

(P-922)
MICHELS PACIFIC ENERGY INC
2200 Laurelwood Rd, Santa Clara (95054-1515)
PHONE............................920 924-8725
Robert Gitter, *Controller*
EMP: 100 **EST:** 2019
SALES (est): 13.2MM **Privately Held**
WEB: www.michelspacificenergy.us
SIC: 1542 Commercial & office building, new construction

(P-923)
MIDGLEN STUDIO ASSOCIATES
831 Midglen Way, Woodside (94062-4165)
PHONE............................650 366-0314
Akio Patrick, *President*
Henry Ehlers, *COO*
A Stevan Patrick, *Principal*
Ponch Robles, *Foreman/Supr*
Reza Javandel, *Associate*
EMP: 42 **EST:** 1977
SALES (est): 7MM **Privately Held**
WEB: www.midglen.net
SIC: 1542 1521 Commercial & office building, new construction; new construction, single-family houses

(P-924)
MISSION CONSTRUCTORS INC
195 Bay Shore Blvd, San Francisco (94124-1321)
PHONE............................415 282-8453
Jaime Maciel Gonzalez, *CEO*
Isabelle Concio, *Vice Pres*
EMP: 85 **EST:** 2012
SQ FT: 5,000
SALES (est): 8MM **Privately Held**
SIC: 1542 Specialized public building contractors

(P-925)
MONTGOMERY-SANSOME LP
161 El Camino Real, South San Francisco (94080-5900)
P.O. Box 2585 (94083-2585)
PHONE............................650 689-5622
Leonard A Nordeman, *Manager*
Leonard Nordeman, *General Ptnr*
Montgomery Sansome, *General Ptnr*
Catherine Diane Magee, *Partner*
EMP: 45 **EST:** 1997
SQ FT: 38,000
SALES (est): 10.5MM **Privately Held**
WEB: www.montgomerysansome.net
SIC: 1542 1522 Commercial & office building contractors; residential construction

(P-926)
MOOREFIELD CONSTRUCTION INC
4080 Truxel Rd Ste 200, Sacramento (95834-3774)
PHONE............................916 614-7888
Larry Moorefield, *Vice Pres*
Susan White, *Manager*
Randy Craven, *Superintendent*
EMP: 35
SALES (corp-wide): 234.5MM **Privately Held**
WEB: www.moorefieldconstruction.com
SIC: 1542 Commercial & office building, new construction

PA: Moorefield Construction, Inc.
600 N Tustin Ave Ste 210
Santa Ana CA 92705
714 972-0700

(P-927)
MORRIS GENERAL CONTRACTING INC
14451 W Whitesbridge Ave, Kerman (93630-9216)
PHONE............................559 842-9453
Robert Morris, *President*
Janet Ronspiez, *Office Mgr*
EMP: 44 **EST:** 1997
SALES (est): 5.7MM **Privately Held**
SIC: 1542 Commercial & office building, new construction

(P-928)
MURPHY-TRUE INC
Also Called: Jim Murphy & Associates
464 Kenwood Ct Ste B, Santa Rosa (95407-5709)
PHONE............................707 576-7337
Jim M Murphy, *CEO*
Leighton J True III, *Vice Pres*
Jay True, *Executive*
Tom Monroe, *Project Mgr*
Jill O'connor, *Manager*
EMP: 60 **EST:** 1968
SQ FT: 5,000
SALES (est): 35.1MM **Privately Held**
WEB: www.j-m-a.com
SIC: 1542 1521 Commercial & office building, new construction; new construction, single-family houses

(P-929)
NEVELL GROUP INC
179 Mason Cir, Concord (94520-1213)
PHONE............................714 579-7501
Michael Nevell, *CEO*
EMP: 375
SALES (corp-wide): 137.1MM **Privately Held**
WEB: www.nevellgroup.com
SIC: 1542 Commercial & office building, new construction
PA: The Nevell Group Inc
3001 Enterprise St # 200
Brea CA 92821
714 579-7501

(P-930)
NORDBY CONSTRUCTION CO
Also Called: Nordby Wine Caves
1550 Airport Blvd Ste 101, Santa Rosa (95403-1095)
PHONE............................707 526-4500
Wendell F Nordby Jr, *Ch of Bd*
Rick Shone, *President*
Jason Brown, *General Mgr*
Nancy C Nordby, *Admin Sec*
EMP: 43 **EST:** 1977
SQ FT: 8,000
SALES (est): 2.8MM **Privately Held**
WEB: www.winecaves.nordby.net
SIC: 1542 School building construction; commercial & office building, new construction; restaurant construction; shopping center construction

(P-931)
NORTH STAR CNSTR & ENGRG INC (PA)
1850 Lassen Blvd, Yuba City (95993-8906)
PHONE............................530 673-7080
Iqbal Basrai, *President*
Darlin Bugni, *Administration*
Zach Milner, *Project Dir*
Abraham Vang, *Project Engr*
Michelle Bouchard, *Marketing Staff*
EMP: 35 **EST:** 1990
SALES (est): 10.5MM **Privately Held**
WEB: www.northstarinc.com
SIC: 1542 1629 1622 Commercial & office building contractors; levee construction; tunnel construction

(P-932)
NOVO CONSTRUCTION INC (PA)
1460 Obrien Dr, Menlo Park (94025-1432)
PHONE............................650 701-1500
James C Fowler, *CEO*
Jim Fowler, *President*
Chris Fonseca, *CFO*

Mike Bank, *Vice Pres*
Russell Woods, *VP Bus Dvlpt*
EMP: 85 **EST:** 2000
SQ FT: 10,000
SALES (est): 872.5MM **Privately Held**
WEB: www.novoconstruction.com
SIC: 1542 Commercial & office building, new construction

(P-933)
OLIVER & COMPANY INC
1300 S 51st St, Richmond (94804-4628)
PHONE............................510 412-9090
Steven Henri Oliver, *CEO*
Josh Oliver, *Vice Pres*
Jeff Shields, *Vice Pres*
Nicole Sprague, *Executive Asst*
Mark Van Velzen, *Project Mgr*
▲ **EMP:** 90 **EST:** 1971
SQ FT: 6,302
SALES (est): 37MM **Privately Held**
WEB: www.oliverandco.net
SIC: 1542 Commercial & office building, new construction

(P-934)
PACATTE CONSTRUCTION CO INC
5560 Skylane Blvd Ste A, Santa Rosa (95403-9091)
PHONE............................707 527-5983
James L Pacatte, *President*
Rosemarie Pacatte, *Vice Pres*
Danielle Hagle, *Office Mgr*
EMP: 42 **EST:** 1980
SQ FT: 1,200
SALES (est): 2.7MM **Privately Held**
WEB: www.pacatteconstruction.com
SIC: 1542 Commercial & office building, new construction; commercial & office buildings, renovation & repair

(P-935)
PACIFIC RIDGE BUILDERS INC
1500 Wyatt Dr Ste 14, Santa Clara (95054-1522)
PHONE............................408 627-4765
Thomas Newman, *CEO*
Jason Livingstone, *Vice Pres*
John Meyers, *Vice Pres*
Nicole Gonzales, *Administration*
Ariana Hernandez, *Opers Staff*
EMP: 35 **EST:** 2015
SALES: 46.1MM **Privately Held**
WEB: www.pacificridgebuilders.com
SIC: 1542 1541 Commercial & office building contractors; industrial buildings, new construction

(P-936)
PACIFIC STTES ENVMTL CNTRS INC
11555 Dublin Blvd, Dublin (94568-2854)
P.O. Box 11357, Pleasanton (94588-1357)
PHONE............................925 803-4333
Robert E McCarrick, *CEO*
Ernie Lampkin, *Treasurer*
Debra Dillard, *Administration*
Austin Lewis, *Project Engr*
Chandan Singh, *Project Engr*
EMP: 50 **EST:** 1996
SQ FT: 2,000
SALES (est): 75.9MM **Privately Held**
WEB: www.pacificstates.net
SIC: 1542 1791 1794 8744 Nonresidential construction; storage tanks, metal: erection; excavation & grading, building construction;

(P-937)
PLATH & COMPANY INC
1575 Francisco Blvd E, San Rafael (94901-5503)
PHONE............................415 460-1575
Stephen Plath, *President*
Christopher Dailey, *Treasurer*
George Bill Ballas, *Vice Pres*
Deysi Ramos, *Administration*
Juanita Wayda, *Administration*
EMP: 38 **EST:** 1976
SQ FT: 9,000

SALES (est): 15.1MM **Privately Held**
WEB: www.plathco.com
SIC: 1542 1541 1521 Commercial & office buildings, renovation & repair; renovation, remodeling & repairs: industrial buildings; new construction, single-family houses

(P-938)
PRS/ROEBBELEN JV
4811 Tunis Rd, Sacramento (95835-1007)
PHONE............................916 641-0324
EMP: 50
SALES (est): 5.2MM **Privately Held**
SIC: 1542 Nonresidential Construction

(P-939)
QUIRING CORPORATION
5118 E Clinton Way # 201, Fresno (93727-2094)
PHONE............................559 432-2800
Paul K Quiring, *President*
Greg Quiring, *Treasurer*
Esther Cuevas, *Business Dir*
Carrie Rich, *Administration*
Kit Bedell, *Project Mgr*
EMP: 62 **EST:** 1947
SQ FT: 4,000
SALES (est): 26.9MM **Privately Held**
WEB: www.quiring.com
SIC: 1542 Commercial & office building, new construction

(P-940)
QUIRING GENERAL LLC
Also Called: Construction
5118 E Clinton Way # 201, Fresno (93727-2088)
PHONE............................559 432-2800
Greg A Quiring, *Mng Member*
Paul Quiring, *CEO*
John Wood, *CFO*
Dennis Lindner, *Project Mgr*
Thomas Dailey, *Project Engr*
EMP: 80 **EST:** 2011
SQ FT: 6,200
SALES (est): 46MM **Privately Held**
WEB: www.quiring.com
SIC: 1542 Commercial & office building, new construction

(P-941)
R & L BROSAMER INC (HQ)
1390 Willow Pass Rd # 95, Concord (94520-5200)
PHONE............................925 627-1700
Matthew M Walsh, *CEO*
Robert Brosamer, *President*
Cindy Lundquist, *CFO*
Linda Brosamer, *Vice Pres*
EMP: 40 **EST:** 1994
SQ FT: 16,000
SALES (est): 56.8MM
SALES (corp-wide): 3.5B **Privately Held**
WEB: www.brosamer.com
SIC: 1542 Commercial & office building, new construction
PA: The Walsh Group Ltd
929 W Adams St
Chicago IL 60607
312 563-5400

(P-942)
RANCHWOOD CONTRACTORS INC
923 E Pacheco Blvd, Los Banos (93635-4327)
PHONE............................209 826-6200
Greg Hostetler, *President*
Catherine Hostetler, *Corp Secy*
EMP: 57 **EST:** 1984
SQ FT: 3,500
SALES (est): 13.8MM **Privately Held**
WEB: www.ranchwood.com
SIC: 1542 1521 Commercial & office building, new construction; new construction, single-family houses

(P-943)
RANSOME COMPANY
1933 Williams St, San Leandro (94577-2303)
P.O. Box 2177 (94577-0217)
PHONE............................510 686-9900
Myles Oberto, *Ch of Bd*
Geoff Raaka, *President*

▲ = Import ▼ = Export
◆ = Import/Export

PRODUCTS & SERVICES SECTION
1542 - General Contractors, Nonresidential & Non-indl Bldgs County (P-964)

Peter Scott, *Vice Pres*
EMP: 50 **EST:** 1870
SALES (est): 21.6MM **Privately Held**
WEB: www.ransomeco.com
SIC: 1542 Nonresidential construction

(P-944)
RCP CONSTRUCTION INC
5180 Gldn Fthl Pkwy # 110, El Dorado Hills (95762-9346)
PHONE.....................916 358-9530
Richard Poipao, *CEO*
Cynthia Poipao, *CFO*
Tony Poipao, *Vice Pres*
Rob Matson, *Project Mgr*
Morgan Tempus, *Project Mgr*
EMP: 46 **EST:** 2011
SQ FT: 2,600
SALES (est): 10MM **Privately Held**
WEB: www.rcpconstructioninc.com
SIC: 1542 Commercial & office building, new construction

(P-945)
REEVE-KNIGHT CONSTRUCTION INC
128 Ascot Dr, Roseville (95661-3422)
PHONE.....................916 786-5112
Robert H Reeve, *CEO*
Joe E Knight, *President*
Cynthia Knight, *Treasurer*
M Kathy Reeve, *Admin Sec*
Christine Tadlock, *Admin Asst*
EMP: 75 **EST:** 1991
SQ FT: 9,200
SALES (est): 34MM **Privately Held**
WEB: www.reeve-knight.com
SIC: 1542 Commercial & office building, new construction; commercial & office buildings, renovation & repair

(P-946)
RMR CONSTRUCTION COMPANY
2424 Oakdale Ave, San Francisco (94124-1581)
PHONE.....................415 647-0884
Ray Reinertson Jr, *President*
Robert Reinertson, *Vice Pres*
Marie Reinertson, *Admin Sec*
EMP: 140 **EST:** 1979
SQ FT: 12,000
SALES (est): 36.2MM **Privately Held**
SIC: 1542 Commercial & office buildings, renovation & repair

(P-947)
ROBERTS MANAGING CONTRS INC
Also Called: RMC Constructors
5045 E Mckinley Ave, Fresno (93727-1964)
PHONE.....................559 252-6000
Cal Roberts, *CEO*
John Chan, *CFO*
M Peg Alvarez, *Vice Pres*
Richard Holtermann, *Vice Pres*
Dave Johnson, *Vice Pres*
EMP: 40 **EST:** 1983
SQ FT: 8,000
SALES (est): 23.7MM **Privately Held**
WEB: www.rmc-constructors.com
SIC: 1542 Commercial & office building, new construction

(P-948)
ROEBBELEN CONSTRUCTION INC
1241 Hawks Flight Ct, El Dorado Hills (95762-9648)
PHONE.....................916 939-4000
Hans J Roebbelen, *CEO*
Kenneth Roebbelen, *President*
Dennis Daniell, *CFO*
David Thuleen, *Exec VP*
Kenneth Debruhl, *Vice Pres*
EMP: 80 **EST:** 1989
SQ FT: 25,000
SALES (est): 26.9MM **Privately Held**
WEB: www.roebbelen.com
SIC: 1542 1541 Commercial & office building, new construction; industrial buildings & warehouses

(P-949)
ROEBBELEN CONTRACTING INC
1241 Hawks Flight Ct, El Dorado Hills (95762-9648)
PHONE.....................916 939-4000
Kenneth Wenham, *President*
Robert McLean, *COO*
Dennis Daniell, *CFO*
Bruce Stimson, *CFO*
Bob Kjome, *Officer*
EMP: 350 **EST:** 1959
SQ FT: 28,000
SALES (est): 248MM **Privately Held**
WEB: www.roebbelen.com
SIC: 1542 1541 8741 Commercial & office building, new construction; industrial buildings & warehouses; construction management

(P-950)
RUBECON GENERAL CONTG INC
Also Called: Rubecon Builders
3450 3rd St Ste 1b, San Francisco (94124-1444)
PHONE.....................415 206-7740
Ruben Santana, *President*
Sharon Santana, *Vice Pres*
Patrick Larose, *Project Mgr*
Zula Munkzuhl, *Sales Mgr*
Alex Tacussis, *Manager*
EMP: 35
SQ FT: 10,000
SALES (est): 8.7MM **Privately Held**
WEB: www.rubecon.com
SIC: 1542 Commercial & office building, new construction

(P-951)
RUDOLPH AND SLETTEN INC (HQ)
2 Circle Star Way Fl 4, San Carlos (94070-6200)
PHONE.....................650 216-3600
Jonathan Foad, *President*
Dan Dolinar, *Exec VP*
Michael P Mohrman, *Vice Pres*
Michael Mohrman, *Vice Pres*
Raymond Polidoro, *Vice Pres*
EMP: 100 **EST:** 1960
SQ FT: 27,000
SALES (est): 497.3MM
SALES (corp-wide): 5.3B **Publicly Held**
WEB: www.tutorperini.com
SIC: 1542 1541 Commercial & office building, new construction; industrial buildings & warehouses
PA: Tutor Perini Corporation
15901 Olden St
Sylmar CA 91342
818 362-8391

(P-952)
RUDOLPH AND SLETTEN INC
3614 Zephyr Ct, Stockton (95206-4207)
PHONE.....................209 941-1040
Gene Huffman, *Owner*
Patrick Krzyzosiak, *Director*
EMP: 48
SALES (corp-wide): 5.3B **Publicly Held**
SIC: 1542 Commercial & office building, new construction
HQ: Rudolph And Sletten, Inc.
2 Circle Star Way Fl 4
San Carlos CA 94070
650 216-3600

(P-953)
RUDOLPH AND SLETTEN INC
1504 Eureka Rd Ste 200, Roseville (95661-3058)
PHONE.....................916 781-8001
Dan Dolinar, *Branch Mgr*
Jon Foad, *Vice Pres*
Justin Jones, *Project Engr*
Robert Cervantes, *Superintendent*
John Davidson, *Superintendent*
EMP: 48
SALES (corp-wide): 5.3B **Publicly Held**
SIC: 1542 1541 Commercial & office building, new construction; industrial buildings & warehouses
HQ: Rudolph And Sletten, Inc.
2 Circle Star Way Fl 4
San Carlos CA 94070
650 216-3600

(P-954)
S J AMOROSO CNSTR CO LLC (PA)
390 Bridge Pkwy, Redwood City (94065-1061)
PHONE.....................650 654-1900
Dana McManus, *Ch of Bd*
Laura Heckenberg, *CFO*
Brian Dermatoian, *Vice Pres*
Robert Erskine, *Vice Pres*
Valerie L Frahm, *Executive Asst*
EMP: 330 **EST:** 1939
SQ FT: 22,500
SALES (est): 104.8MM **Privately Held**
WEB: www.sjamoroso.com
SIC: 1542 Commercial & office building, new construction

(P-955)
SANDERS CONTRACTING INC
P.O. Box 492 (94514-0492)
PHONE.....................925 308-7305
Kevin Garcia, *President*
Kari Garcia, *Vice Pres*
EMP: 60 **EST:** 2018
SALES (est): 7MM **Privately Held**
WEB: www.sanderscontracting.net
SIC: 1542 Commercial & office building contractors

(P-956)
SC BUILDERS INC (PA)
910 Thompson Pl, Sunnyvale (94085-4517)
PHONE.....................408 328-0688
Samuel B Abbey, *CEO*
Chris Smither, *Vice Pres*
Liz Bandalan, *Administration*
Tara Flores, *Administration*
Samantha Wueste, *Administration*
EMP: 88 **EST:** 1999
SALES (est): 28.4MM **Privately Held**
WEB: www.scbuildersinc.com
SIC: 1542 1611 8711 Custom builders, non-residential; general contractor, highway & street construction; building construction consultant

(P-957)
SCATES CONSTRUCTION INC
1769 Park Ave Ste 200, San Jose (95126-2025)
PHONE.....................408 293-9050
Lloyd Scates, *President*
Sandra Scates, *Corp Secy*
Lauren Pardini, *Administration*
EMP: 46 **EST:** 1995
SQ FT: 4,000
SALES (est): 4.2MM **Privately Held**
WEB: www.scatescon.com
SIC: 1542 Commercial & office building, new construction

(P-958)
SD DEACON CORP CALIFORNIA
7745 Greenback Ln Ste 250, Citrus Heights (95610-5865)
PHONE.....................916 969-0900
Richard G Smith, *President*
Robert K Aroyan, *Vice Pres*
Paul B Cunha, *Vice Pres*
Brett Mykrantz, *Vice Pres*
Brian Bentley, *Administration*
EMP: 70 **EST:** 1999
SALES (est): 18MM
SALES (corp-wide): 391.5MM **Privately Held**
WEB: www.deacon.com
SIC: 1542 Commercial & office building, new construction
PA: Deacon Construction, Llc
901 Ne Glisan St Ste 100
Portland OR 97232
503 297-8791

(P-959)
SHAMES CONSTRUCTION CO LTD
5826 Brisa St, Livermore (94550-2514)
PHONE.....................925 606-3000
Carolyn A Shames, *President*
Margarita Terrell, *CEO*
Michael Lundgren, *Officer*
Pete Panagopoulos, *Project Mgr*
Tricia Tom, *Controller*
EMP: 35 **EST:** 1981
SQ FT: 13,000
SALES (est): 77.1MM **Privately Held**
WEB: www.shames.com
SIC: 1542 Commercial & office building, new construction; commercial & office buildings, renovation & repair

(P-960)
SHASTA SERVICES INC
Also Called: Timber Works
624 S Mount Shasta Blvd, Mount Shasta (96067-2530)
P.O. Box 1240 (96067-1240)
PHONE.....................530 926-4093
Harold J Knight, *President*
Jennifer L Knight, *Treasurer*
Andrew T Gerdis, *Vice Pres*
Devin J Knight, *Vice Pres*
Richard T Knight, *Vice Pres*
EMP: 35 **EST:** 1983 **Privately Held**
WEB: www.bmccrillisphotography.com
SIC: 1542 1521 Nonresidential construction; new construction, single-family houses

(P-961)
SHIMMICK NICHOLSON CNSTR JV
8201 Edgewater Dr Ste 202, Oakland (94621-2023)
PHONE.....................510 777-5000
Mark Rawlinson, *Vice Pres*
EMP: 110 **EST:** 2020
SALES (est): 8.1MM **Privately Held**
WEB: www.shimmick.com
SIC: 1542 Nonresidential construction
PA: Shimmick Construction Company Incorporated
8201 Edgewater Dr Ste 202
Oakland CA 94621

(P-962)
SILMAN VENTURE CORPORATION (PA)
Also Called: Silman Construction
1600 Factor Ave, San Leandro (94577-5618)
PHONE.....................510 347-4800
Tom Mangin, *President*
Rick Silva, *COO*
Mikal Brevig, *Department Mgr*
Cynthia N Phifer, *Office Mgr*
Lindsey Donaldson, *Administration*
EMP: 125 **EST:** 2007
SQ FT: 17,000
SALES (est): 77.3MM **Privately Held**
WEB: www.silmanindustries.com
SIC: 1542 Commercial & office building, new construction

(P-963)
SKYLINE COMMERCIAL INTERIORS (PA)
Also Called: Skyline Construction
505 Sansome St Fl 7, San Francisco (94111-3108)
PHONE.....................415 908-1020
David Hayes, *CEO*
Rick Millitello, *President*
John Fara, *Bd of Directors*
Jeff Kuhn, *Bd of Directors*
Jack Selby, *Bd of Directors*
EMP: 75 **EST:** 1996
SQ FT: 9,000
SALES (est): 63.5MM **Privately Held**
WEB: www.skylineconstruction.build
SIC: 1542 Commercial & office buildings, renovation & repair

(P-964)
SLATTER CONSTRUCTION INC
126 Fern St, Santa Cruz (95060-2118)
PHONE.....................831 425-5425
Sid Slatter, *CEO*
Christine Slatter, *CFO*
Alexandra Slatter, *Accountant*
EMP: 35 **EST:** 1985
SQ FT: 4,400

1542 - General Contractors, Nonresidential & Non-indl Bldgs County (P-965)

PRODUCTS & SERVICES SECTION

SALES (est): 9.3MM **Privately Held**
WEB: www.slattcon.com
SIC: 1542 1521 Commercial & office building, new construction; commercial & office buildings, renovation & repair; general remodeling, single-family houses; new construction, single-family houses

(P-965)
SOUTH GATE BREWING COMPANY
40233 Enterprise Dr, Oakhurst (93644-8839)
PHONE...................559 692-2739
Steven Hawkins, *CEO*
EMP: 25 **EST:** 2013
SQ FT: 1,550
SALES (est): 3.8MM **Privately Held**
WEB: www.southgatebrewco.com
SIC: 1542 3589 5812 Restaurant construction; coffee brewing equipment; American restaurant

(P-966)
SOUTHWEST CNSTR & PROPERTY MGT
1213 San Mateo Ave, San Bruno (94066-1528)
P.O. Box 5410, South San Francisco (94083-5410)
PHONE...........\................650 877-0717
Yvette M Gardner, *President*
James T Gardner Sr, *Vice Pres*
EMP: 35 **EST:** 1998
SQ FT: 1,000
SALES (est): 10.6MM **Privately Held**
WEB: www.southwestcpm.com
SIC: 1542 School building construction

(P-967)
SPAN CONSTRUCTION & ENGRG INC (PA)
1841 Howard Rd, Madera (93637-5122)
PHONE...................559 661-1111
King F Husein, *CEO*
George Goddard, *President*
Firoz Mohamed Husein, *CEO*
Marilyn Clayton, *Executive Asst*
Douglas M Standing, *Admin Sec*
▼ **EMP:** 85 **EST:** 1979
SQ FT: 120,000
SALES (est): 45.1MM **Privately Held**
WEB: www.spanconstruction.com
SIC: 1542 1541 1791 Commercial & office buildings, prefabricated erection; agricultural building contractors; industrial buildings, new construction; structural steel erection

(P-968)
STURGEON CONSTRUCTION INC
Also Called: Michael Joseph Sturgeon Cnstr
8259 Alpine Ave, Sacramento (95826-4708)
PHONE...................916 452-6108
Michael J Sturgeon, *President*
EMP: 37 **EST:** 1966
SQ FT: 4,000
SALES (est): 3.6MM **Privately Held**
SIC: 1542 Commercial & office building, new construction

(P-969)
SWINERTON BUILDERS HC
Also Called: Hmh Builders
15 Business Park Way # 101, Sacramento (95828-0959)
PHONE...................916 383-4825
Gary J Rafferty, *Ch of Bd*
Eric M Foster, *President*
Leonard J Bischel, *CFO*
Frank Foellmer, *Exec VP*
Linda J Schowalter, *Senior VP*
EMP: 150 **EST:** 1957
SQ FT: 25,000
SALES (est): 33MM **Privately Held**
WEB: www.swinerton.com
SIC: 1542 Commercial & office building, new construction; hospital building construction; institutional building construction
PA: Swinerton Incorporated
2001 Clayton Rd Fl 7 Flr 7
San Francisco CA 94107

(P-970)
SWINERTON INCORPORATED (PA)
2001 Clayton Rd Fl 7 Flr 7, San Francisco (94107)
PHONE...................415 421-2980
Eric Foster, *CEO*
Gary J Rafferty, *President*
Eric M Foster, *CEO*
Michelle Smith, *COO*
Linda G Showalter, *CFO*
▲ **EMP:** 200 **EST:** 1888
SQ FT: 66,943
SALES (est): 4.3B **Privately Held**
WEB: www.swinerton.com
SIC: 1542 1541 6531 1522 Commercial & office building, new construction; industrial buildings & warehouses; real estate managers; residential construction

(P-971)
TCG BUILDERS INC
Also Called: Core Group, The
890 N Mccarthy Blvd # 100, Milpitas (95035-5127)
PHONE...................408 321-6450
Andrew W Meade, *CEO*
Timothy Tempel, *President*
Jillian Dressel, *Corp Secy*
Robert Wagle, *Vice Pres*
Dolores Manriquez, *Controller*
EMP: 50 **EST:** 2004
SQ FT: 6,000
SALES (est): 14.9MM **Privately Held**
WEB: www.tcgbuilders.com
SIC: 1542 Commercial & office building contractors; commercial & office building, new construction; commercial & office buildings, renovation & repair

(P-972)
TECHNICAL REPS INTL INC
Also Called: Scientific Hardware Systems
5770 Obata Way Ste B, Gilroy (95020-7064)
PHONE...................408 848-8868
Scott Jay Hagel, *President*
Tim Hagel, *Project Mgr*
EMP: 15 **EST:** 1981
SALES (est): 2.5MM **Privately Held**
SIC: 1542 3999 Nonresidential construction; atomizers, toiletry

(P-973)
TERRA NOVA INDUSTRIES
1607 Tice Valley Blvd, Walnut Creek (94595-1625)
PHONE...................925 934-6133
Ronald L Taylor, *President*
Mark Taylor, *General Mgr*
Katie Gatterer, *Executive Asst*
Ayako Wallace, *Administration*
Kevin Mulvey, *Project Mgr*
EMP: 44 **EST:** 1984
SQ FT: 2,600
SALES (est): 23MM **Privately Held**
WEB: www.terranova-ind.com
SIC: 1542 Restaurant construction

(P-974)
TICO CONSTRUCTION COMPANY INC (PA)
1585 Terminal Ave, San Jose (95112-4316)
PHONE...................408 487-0700
John Marmesh, *President*
Cybil Siler-Armstrong, *Shareholder*
Alexander V Hose, *President*
Ken Revizza, *Treasurer*
Leland Gerber, *Vice Pres*
EMP: 36 **EST:** 1988
SQ FT: 5,000
SALES (est): 16.1MM **Privately Held**
WEB: www.ticoinc.com
SIC: 1542 Commercial & office building, new construction

(P-975)
TRAINOR COMMERCIAL CNSTR INC (PA)
1925 Francisco Blvd E # 21, San Rafael (94901-5552)
PHONE...................415 259-0200
Brian A Trainor, *CEO*
Suzanne Trainor, *Vice Pres*
John Holmberg, *Project Mgr*

Richard Miller, *Project Engr*
Wendy Strait, *Engineer*
EMP: 37 **EST:** 2001
SALES (est): 14.2MM **Privately Held**
WEB: www.trainorconstruction.com
SIC: 1542 Commercial & office building, new construction

(P-976)
TRICORP GROUP INC (PA)
Also Called: Tricorp Hearn Construction
2540 Warren Dr Ste A, Rocklin (95677-2178)
PHONE...................916 779-8010
Assad M Moayed, *CEO*
Steve Hunter, *President*
Tony Moayed, *Vice Pres*
Jeannine H Long, *Business Dir*
Ken Cohen, *Principal*
EMP: 59 **EST:** 2014
SALES (est): 25.2MM **Privately Held**
WEB: www.tricorpconstruction.com
SIC: 1542 1521 Commercial & office building, new construction; single-family housing construction

(P-977)
TRUEBECK CONSTRUCTION INC (PA)
951 Mariners Island Blvd # 700, San Mateo (94404-1561)
PHONE...................650 227-1957
David C Becker, *President*
Brad Bastian, *Shareholder*
Jeff Nielson, *Shareholder*
Kathy Reiner, *CFO*
Mike Jackson, *Vice Pres*
EMP: 67 **EST:** 2007
SQ FT: 6,000
SALES (est): 28.1MM **Privately Held**
WEB: www.truebeck.com
SIC: 1542 Commercial & office building, new construction; custom builders, non-residential

(P-978)
TURNER CONSTRUCTION COMPANY
2500 Venture Oaks Way # 200, Sacramento (95833-4222)
PHONE...................916 444-4421
Donna Afflerdach, *Branch Mgr*
Adam Della Monica, *Project Engr*
William Carey, *Superintendent*
EMP: 75
SALES (corp-wide): 1B **Privately Held**
WEB: www.turnerconstruction.com
SIC: 1542 Commercial & office building, new construction
HQ: Turner Construction Company Inc
375 Hudson St Fl 6
New York NY 10014
212 229-6000

(P-979)
TURNER CONSTRUCTION COMPANY
300 Frank H Ogawa Plz # 510, Oakland (94612-2040)
PHONE...................510 267-8100
Danny Cooke, *Branch Mgr*
Kyleigh Haavisto, *Admin Asst*
Kelsey Lacour, *Marketing Staff*
EMP: 50
SALES (corp-wide): 1B **Privately Held**
WEB: www.turnerconstruction.com
SIC: 1542 8742 6531 Commercial & office building, new construction; management consulting services; real estate agents & managers
HQ: Turner Construction Company Inc
375 Hudson St Fl 6
New York NY 10014
212 229-6000

(P-980)
VANIR DEVELOPMENT COMPANY INC
4540 Duckhorn Dr Ste 100, Sacramento (95834-2679)
P.O. Box 1737 (95812-1737)
PHONE...................916 419-2400
Dorene Dominguez, *Chairman*
Ray Nez, *CFO*
Patricia Green, *Senior VP*

Amanda White, *Administration*
EMP: 37 **EST:** 2000
SALES (est): 2.9MM **Privately Held**
WEB: www.vanirdevelopment.com
SIC: 1542 Commercial & office building, new construction

(P-981)
VILA CONSTRUCTION CO
Also Called: Richard H Vila
590 S 33rd St, Richmond (94804-4108)
PHONE...................510 236-9111
Richard H Vila, *President*
Maria Elena Vila, *Office Mgr*
Sean Manion, *Project Mgr*
Bert Brendlinger, *Sr Project Mgr*
EMP: 75 **EST:** 1946
SQ FT: 8,000
SALES (est): 30MM **Privately Held**
WEB: www.vilacc.com
SIC: 1542 1751 1541 Commercial & office buildings, renovation & repair; carpentry work; industrial buildings & warehouses

(P-982)
W L BUTLER CONSTRUCTION INC (PA)
1629 Main St, Redwood City (94063-2121)
PHONE...................650 361-1270
William L Butler, *CEO*
Frank York, *President*
Dave Nevens, *COO*
Cole Hanley, *Officer*
Joel Butler, *Vice Pres*
EMP: 50 **EST:** 1994
SQ FT: 13,500
SALES: 272.4MM **Privately Held**
WEB: www.wlbutler.com
SIC: 1542 Commercial & office building, new construction; commercial & office buildings, renovation & repair

(P-983)
WALT OXLEY ENTERPRISES INC
Also Called: Ciarra Construction
663 Walnut St, San Jose (95110-2044)
PHONE...................408 278-0370
Walter M Oxley, *President*
Keith Penrod, *Opers Staff*
EMP: 40 **EST:** 1983
SQ FT: 1,700
SALES (est): 11.4MM **Privately Held**
WEB: www.ciarraconstruction.com
SIC: 1542 1521 Commercial & office building, new construction; new construction, single-family houses

(P-984)
WEBCOR BUILDERS INC
Also Called: Webcor Management Company
850 N El Camino Real, San Mateo (94401-5602)
PHONE...................650 591-7400
Rosser Edwards, *President*
Rosser B Edwards, *President*
David Fisher, *Treasurer*
Ryan Downey, *Technology*
Jordan Thrailkill, *Project Engr*
EMP: 57 **EST:** 1971
SALES (est): 10.9MM **Privately Held**
WEB: www.webcor.com
SIC: 1542 Commercial & office building, new construction

(P-985)
WEBCOR CONSTRUCTION LP (DH)
Also Called: Webcor Builders
207 King St Ste 300, San Francisco (94105-5499)
PHONE...................415 978-1000
Jes Pedersen, *CFO*
Margaret Austin, *President*
Matt Rossie, *COO*
Matt Reece, *CFO*
Vince Sarubbi, *Officer*
EMP: 71 **EST:** 2007
SALES (est): 2.2B **Privately Held**
WEB: www.webcor.com
SIC: 1542 Commercial & office building, new construction

▲ = Import ▼=Export
◆ =Import/Export

PRODUCTS & SERVICES SECTION   **1611 - Highway & Street Construction County (P-1007)**

HQ: Obayashi Usa, Llc
577 Airport Blvd Ste 600
Burlingame CA 94010
650 952-4910

(P-986)
WELLS CONSTRUCTION INC
10648 Industrial Ave, Roseville (95678-5902)
PHONE.................................916 257-6172
Glen Wells, *President*
Kathleen Wells, *Admin Sec*
Paul Gonzales, *Project Mgr*
Nicole Wencl, *Project Mgr*
Stephen Johnston, *Project Engr*
EMP: 48 **EST:** 1989
SQ FT: 12,000
SALES (est): 28.4MM **Privately Held**
WEB: www.wellsconstruction.com
SIC: 1542 Commercial & office building, new construction

(P-987)
WEST COAST CONTRACTORS INC
2320 Courage Dr Ste 111, Fairfield (94533-6743)
PHONE.................................214 281-3100
Alan Bond, *President*
Sharon Newcomer, *CFO*
Mark Dietlin, *Vice Pres*
Lonnie Kronsteiner, *Vice Pres*
James Latner, *Vice Pres*
EMP: 38 **EST:** 1983
SQ FT: 15,000
SALES (est): 4.6MM **Privately Held**
WEB: www.westcoastcontractors.com
SIC: 1542 Specialized public building contractors; school building construction; commercial & office buildings, renovation & repair

(P-988)
WESTERN CARE CNSTR CO INC
4020 Sierra College Blvd # 200, Rocklin (95677-3906)
PHONE.................................916 624-6200
Milton Harmon, *President*
Melanie Degrandmont, *Executive Asst*
Dean Arrington, *Project Mgr*
Rodger McDonald, *Controller*
Austin Murphy, *Manager*
EMP: 45 **EST:** 1984
SQ FT: 9,255
SALES (est): 10.6MM **Privately Held**
SIC: 1542 Commercial & office building, new construction

(P-989)
WESTGATE CNSTR & MAINT INC
5045 Fulton Dr Ste D, Fairfield (94534-1635)
PHONE.................................707 208-5763
Hilton Ham, *President*
EMP: 86 **EST:** 2001
SALES (est): 1.8MM **Privately Held**
SIC: 1542 Commercial & office building, new construction; commercial & office buildings, renovation & repair; restaurant construction; shopping center construction

(P-990)
WHITING-TURNER CONTRACTING CO
800 R St, Sacramento (95811-6411)
PHONE.................................916 355-1355
Jack Stackalis, *Vice Pres*
Carlee Corkery, *Project Engr*
Patrick Gallagher, *Project Engr*
Sean Kaford, *Project Engr*
Mason Pulcini, *Project Engr*
EMP: 106
SALES (corp-wide): 8.7B **Privately Held**
WEB: www.whiting-turner.com
SIC: 1542 Commercial & office building, new construction
PA: The Whiting-Turner Contracting Company
300 E Joppa Rd Ste 800
Baltimore MD 21286
410 821-1100

(P-991)
WL BUTLER INC
1629 Main St, Redwood City (94063-2121)
PHONE.................................650 361-1270
William Butler, *CEO*
Frank York, *President*
Dave Nevens, *COO*
David A Nevens Jr, *COO*
Gina Henson, *CFO*
EMP: 250
SALES (est): 37.7MM **Privately Held**
WEB: www.wlbutler.com
SIC: 1542 Commercial & office building, new construction

(P-992)
WOODYS POULTRY SUPPLY
2900 E Monte Vista Ave, Denair (95316-8540)
P.O. Box 1628, Turlock (95381-1628)
PHONE.................................209 634-2948
Richard Dias, *President*
Rita Dias, *Corp Secy*
EMP: 15 **EST:** 1947
SQ FT: 25,000
SALES (est): 4.7MM **Privately Held**
SIC: 1542 1541 3523 7699 Farm building construction; steel building construction; barn, silo, poultry, dairy & livestock machinery; recreational vehicle repair services

(P-993)
WRIGHT CONTRACTING LLC
Also Called: Wright Contracting EPA
3020 Dutton Ave, Santa Rosa (95407-7886)
P.O. Box 1270 (95402-1270)
PHONE.................................707 528-1172
Mark Davis, *President*
Stephen M Wright, *COO*
Bryan Wright, *Vice Pres*
Robert Chrzanowski, *Project Mgr*
Shane Magee, *Project Mgr*
EMP: 60 **EST:** 2016
SALES (est): 22MM **Privately Held**
WEB: www.wrightcontracting.com
SIC: 1542 Nonresidential construction

(P-994)
X7/24 CORPORATION
433 Airport Blvd Ste 219, Burlingame (94010-2011)
PHONE.................................650 401-2300
EMP: 37
SQ FT: 2,700
SALES: 33.4MM **Privately Held**
SIC: 1542 1522 Nonresidential Construction Residential Construction

(P-995)
XL CONSTRUCTION CORPORATION (PA)
851 Buckeye Ct, Milpitas (95035-7408)
PHONE.................................408 240-6000
Eric Raff, *President*
Richard Walker, *COO*
Tom Humbert, *CFO*
Dave Beck, *Exec VP*
Steve Winslow, *Exec VP*
EMP: 482 **EST:** 1992
SALES (est): 171.3MM **Privately Held**
WEB: www.xlconstruction.com
SIC: 1542 Commercial & office building, new construction

(P-996)
ZUMWALT CONSTRUCTION INC
5520 E Lamona Ave, Fresno (93727-2276)
PHONE.................................559 252-1000
Kurt E Zumwalt, *President*
Teri Zumwalt, *Admin Sec*
Pamela Lacone, *Admin Asst*
Dana Hester, *Project Mgr*
Tyson Peters, *Project Mgr*
EMP: 100 **EST:** 1995
SQ FT: 2,000
SALES (est): 52.2MM **Privately Held**
WEB: www.zumwaltconst.com
SIC: 1542 1522 Commercial & office building, new construction; residential construction

1611 Highway & Street Construction

(P-997)
A TEICHERT & SON INC
Also Called: Teichert Construction
265 Val Dervin Pkwy, Stockton (95206-4001)
P.O. Box 1118 (95201-1118)
PHONE.................................209 983-2300
Mark Nilsen, *District Mgr*
Chris McCaffree, *Treasurer*
Christine Jonas, *Executive Asst*
Brooks Taylor, *Administration*
Michael Boyle, *Project Mgr*
EMP: 38
SALES (corp-wide): 842MM **Privately Held**
WEB: www.teichert.com
SIC: 1611 5032 Highway & street construction; brick, stone & related material
HQ: A. Teichert & Son, Inc.
5200 Franklin Dr Ste 115
Pleasanton CA 94588

(P-998)
A TEICHERT & SON INC
Also Called: Teichert Construction
24207 County Road 100a, Davis (95616-9410)
P.O. Box 1890 (95617-1890)
PHONE.................................530 406-4200
Mark Stacy, *District Mgr*
EMP: 38
SALES (corp-wide): 842MM **Privately Held**
WEB: www.teichert.com
SIC: 1611 Highway & street construction
HQ: A. Teichert & Son, Inc.
5200 Franklin Dr Ste 115
Pleasanton CA 94588

(P-999)
A TEICHERT & SON INC
Also Called: Teichert Construction
4401 Duluth Ave, Roseville (95678-5999)
PHONE.................................916 645-4800
Dave Swartz, *District Mgr*
EMP: 38
SALES (corp-wide): 842MM **Privately Held**
WEB: www.teichert.com
SIC: 1611 5032 Highway & street construction; brick, stone & related material
HQ: A. Teichert & Son, Inc.
5200 Franklin Dr Ste 115
Pleasanton CA 94588

(P-1000)
A TEICHERT & SON INC
Also Called: Teichert Construction
5771 S Toyota Ave, Fresno (93725)
P.O. Box 520, Fowler (93625-0520)
PHONE.................................559 813-3100
Gordon Stout, *Principal*
Alejandro Suarez, *Manager*
Chase McElree, *Superintendent*
EMP: 38
SALES (corp-wide): 842MM **Privately Held**
WEB: www.teichert.com
SIC: 1611 5032 Highway & street construction; brick, stone & related material
HQ: A. Teichert & Son, Inc.
5200 Franklin Dr Ste 115
Pleasanton CA 94588

(P-1001)
A TEICHERT & SON INC
Also Called: Teichert Construction
1801 El Pinal Dr Ste B, Stockton (95205-2555)
PHONE.................................209 461-3700
Bill Quiroz, *District Mgr*
EMP: 40
SALES (corp-wide): 842MM **Privately Held**
WEB: www.teichert.com
SIC: 1611 5032 Highway & street construction; brick, stone & related material

HQ: A. Teichert & Son, Inc.
5200 Franklin Dr Ste 115
Pleasanton CA 94588

(P-1002)
A-1 ADVANTAGE ASPHALT INC
10308 Placer Ln Ste 100, Sacramento (95827-2553)
PHONE.................................916 388-2020
Melissa Mallo, *President*
Greg Mallo, *President*
Barbara Philpot, *Executive*
Shan Decker, *Superintendent*
EMP: 60 **EST:** 1999
SQ FT: 6,000
SALES (est): 10.8MM **Privately Held**
WEB: www.advantageasphalt.com
SIC: 1611 Surfacing & paving

(P-1003)
ABSL CONSTRUCTION
29393 Pacific St, Hayward (94544-6017)
PHONE.................................510 727-0900
Luis Allende, *President*
Mercedes Allende, *Vice Pres*
EMP: 48 **EST:** 1991
SQ FT: 78,000
SALES (est): 15MM **Privately Held**
WEB: www.abslconstruction.com
SIC: 1611 Highway & street construction

(P-1004)
ALANIZ CONSTRUCTION INC
7160 Stevenson Blvd, Fremont (94538-2485)
PHONE.................................510 770-5000
Jesse C Alaniz, *President*
Rosy Alaniz, *Corp Secy*
Zaira Alaniz, *Technology*
EMP: 44 **EST:** 1989
SALES (est): 11.6MM **Privately Held**
WEB: www.alanizpaving.com
SIC: 1611 Highway & street paving contractor; grading

(P-1005)
ALCCON GENERAL ENGINEERING
6060 Mortono St, Sacramento (95828-0929)
PHONE.................................916 381-4600
Juan Alcala,
EMP: 37 **EST:** 2010
SALES (est): 4.5MM **Privately Held**
WEB: www.alccongeneralengineering.com
SIC: 1611 Grading

(P-1006)
AMERICAN ASP REPR RSRFCING INC (PA)
24200 Clawiter Rd, Hayward (94545-2216)
P.O. Box 3367 (94540-3367)
PHONE.................................510 723-0280
Allan A Henderson, *CEO*
Steve Aguirre, *COO*
Kim Henschel, *Vice Pres*
Sofia Moral, *Mktg Coord*
Erica Ornelas, *Receptionist*
EMP: 99 **EST:** 1983
SALES (est): 23.1MM **Privately Held**
WEB: www.americanasphalt.com
SIC: 1611 Surfacing & paving

(P-1007)
AMERICAN CIVIL CONST
Also Called: ACC West Coast
2990 Bay Vista Ct Ste D, Benicia (94510-1195)
PHONE.................................707 746-8028
Jeffrey Foerste, *President*
Clifford Barber, *Vice Pres*
David Wilkerson, *Vice Pres*
EMP: 75 **EST:** 1987
SQ FT: 19,000
SALES (est): 14.9MM **Privately Held**
WEB: www.accbuilt.com
SIC: 1611 1622 Surfacing & paving; bridge construction
PA: American Civil Constructors Holdings, Inc.
4901 S Windermere St
Littleton CO 80120

1611 - Highway & Street Construction County (P-1008)

(P-1008)
AMERICAN PAVEMENT SYSTEMS INC
1012 11th St Ste 1000, Modesto (95354-0846)
PHONE 209 522-2277
Gregory B Reed, *President*
Marc Bertsch, *Vice Pres*
EMP: 35 EST: 2010
SALES (est): 10.4MM **Privately Held**
WEB: www.americanpavementsystems.com
SIC: 1611 Surfacing & paving; highway & street paving contractor; general contractor, highway & street construction

(P-1009)
AMERICAN PAVING CO
315 N Thorne Ave, Fresno (93706-1444)
P.O. Box 27587 (93729-7587)
PHONE 559 268-9886
Steve Poindexter, *President*
Ross Jenkins, *COO*
John Leonardo, *CFO*
Richard Murphy, *Admin Sec*
Jimmy Brager, *Manager*
EMP: 50 EST: 1958
SQ FT: 9,000
SALES (est): 17.2MM
SALES (corp-wide): 17.8MM **Privately Held**
WEB: www.americanpavingco.com
SIC: 1611 1771 Highway & street paving contractor; curb construction; sidewalk contractor
PA: Lyles Diversified, Inc.
   525 W Alluvial Ave
   Fresno CA 93711
   559 441-1900

(P-1010)
ANRAK CORPORATION
5820 Mayhew Rd, Sacramento (95827-9726)
PHONE 916 383-5030
Mark S Anderson, *President*
Lester Anderson, *President*
Jenny Saechao, *Manager*
Corey Wilson, *Superintendent*
EMP: 38 EST: 1956
SQ FT: 5,600
SALES (est): 196.9K **Privately Held**
WEB: www.anrak.com
SIC: 1611 Surfacing & paving

(P-1011)
ANVIL BUILDERS INC
1475 Donner Ave, San Francisco (94124-3614)
PHONE 415 285-5000
Alan Guy, *COO*
Ann Hauer, *Vice Pres*
Jeffrey Ward, *Executive*
Kevin Kilgore, *Adv Board Mem*
Richard Leider, *Admin Sec*
EMP: 125 EST: 2010
SQ FT: 4,000
SALES (est): 45.7MM **Privately Held**
WEB: www.anvilbuilders.com
SIC: 1611 1623 General contractor, highway & street construction; water, sewer & utility lines

(P-1012)
ARGONAUT CONSTRUCTORS INC
360 Sutton Pl, Santa Rosa (95407-8121)
P.O. Box 639 (95402-0639)
PHONE 707 542-4862
Michael D Smith, *CEO*
Michael A Smith, *Vice Pres*
Chris Hendricks, *Master*
Jim Huppert, *Superintendent*
EMP: 175 EST: 1957
SQ FT: 10,000
SALES (est): 33.7MM **Privately Held**
WEB: www.argonautconstructors.com
SIC: 1611 1623 Highway & street paving contractor; oil & gas pipeline construction

(P-1013)
BALDWIN CONTRACTING CO INC (DH)
Also Called: Knife River Construction
1764 Skyway, Chico (95928-8833)
PHONE 530 891-6555
David C Barney, *CEO*
Steve Essoyan, *President*
Rene' J Vercruyssen, *Exec VP*
Ben Carlson, *Sales Mgr*
EMP: 28 EST: 1946
SALES (est): 40.8MM
SALES (corp-wide): 5.5B **Publicly Held**
WEB: www.kniferiver.com
SIC: 1611 2951 5032 1442 Highway & street construction; concrete, asphaltic (not from refineries); sand, construction; gravel; construction sand & gravel
HQ: Knife River Corporation
   1150 W Century Ave
   Bismarck ND 58503
   701 530-1400

(P-1014)
BASIC RESOURCES INC (PA)
928 12th St Ste 700, Modesto (95354-2330)
P.O. Box 3191 (95353-3191)
PHONE 209 521-9771
Jeffrey Reed, *CEO*
Wendell Reed, *President*
Jeff Reed, *Vice Pres*
Jeff Roberts, *Vice Pres*
Leatha Wilson, *Admin Sec*
▲ EMP: 50 EST: 1973
SALES (est): 163.9MM **Privately Held**
WEB: www.basicresourcesinc.com
SIC: 1611 3273 2951 3532 Highway & street paving contractor; ready-mixed concrete; asphalt & asphaltic paving mixtures (not from refineries); mining machinery; construction machinery

(P-1015)
BAYVIEW GENERAL ENGRG INC
658 N L St, Livermore (94551-2810)
P.O. Box 2969 (94551-2969)
PHONE 925 447-6600
Donna Barton, *President*
Dan Woody, *Vice Pres*
Robert Barton, *Admin Sec*
EMP: 35 EST: 1997
SQ FT: 1,500
SALES (est): 4MM **Privately Held**
WEB: www.bayviewgeneral.com
SIC: 1611 Surfacing & paving

(P-1016)
BFL TRANSPORTATION LLC (PA)
29393 Pacific St, Hayward (94544-6017)
PHONE 510 727-0900
Luis Allende, *President*
Mercedes Allende, *Vice Pres*
Bill Surraco, *Sales Staff*
EMP: 35 EST: 1991
SQ FT: 78,000
SALES (est): 11.2MM **Privately Held**
WEB: www.abslconstruction.com
SIC: 1611 Surfacing & paving

(P-1017)
BRODERICK GENERAL ENGINEERING
21750 8th St E Ste B, Sonoma (95476-9803)
PHONE 707 996-7809
John Benward, *President*
Earl G Broderick, *Vice Pres*
Jesus Fernandez, *Project Mgr*
EMP: 50 EST: 1979
SQ FT: 6,400
SALES (est): 13.8MM **Privately Held**
WEB: www.broderickge.com
SIC: 1611 Surfacing & paving

(P-1018)
BRUCE CARONE GRADING & PAV INC
2294 Vista Del Rio St, Crockett (94525-1044)
P.O. Box 129 (94525-0129)
PHONE 510 787-4070
Bruce Carone, *President*
EMP: 53 EST: 1998
SALES (est): 3.3MM **Privately Held**
SIC: 1611 Highway & street paving contractor

(P-1019)
CALIFORNIA DEPARTMENT TRNSP
Also Called: Maintenance Department
611 Payran St, Petaluma (94952-5910)
PHONE 707 762-6641
John Peterson, *Manager*
EMP: 75 **Privately Held**
WEB: www.dot.ca.gov
SIC: 1611 9621 Highway & street maintenance; regulation, administration of transportation;
HQ: California, Department Of Transportation
   1120 N St
   Sacramento CA 95814

(P-1020)
CALIFORNIA DEPARTMENT TRNSP
Also Called: Caltrans
2019 W Texas St, Fairfield (94533-4461)
P.O. Box 8 (94533-0084)
PHONE 707 428-2031
E L Poplin, *Branch Mgr*
EMP: 75 **Privately Held**
WEB: www.dot.ca.gov
SIC: 1611 9621 Highway & street maintenance; regulation, administration of transportation;
HQ: California, Department Of Transportation
   1120 N St
   Sacramento CA 95814

(P-1021)
CALIFORNIA DEPARTMENT TRNSP
1745 S Main St, Yreka (96097-9518)
PHONE 530 842-2723
Kim Fitzpatrick, *Superintendent*
EMP: 75 **Privately Held**
WEB: www.dot.ca.gov
SIC: 1611 9621 Highway & street maintenance; bureau of public roads;
HQ: California, Department Of Transportation
   1120 N St
   Sacramento CA 95814

(P-1022)
CALIFORNIA PAVEMENT MAINT INC
Also Called: Rayner Equipment Systems
9390 Elder Creek Rd, Sacramento (95829-9326)
PHONE 916 381-8033
Gordon L Rayner, *CEO*
Richard Rayner, *President*
Mick Marchini, *Vice Pres*
Bruce Taylor, *Vice Pres*
Kristofer Hendren, *Info Tech Mgr*
EMP: 150 EST: 1979
SQ FT: 24,300
SALES (est): 15.2MM **Privately Held**
WEB: www.dryco.com
SIC: 1611 Highway & street paving contractor; surfacing & paving

(P-1023)
CALVAC INC
Also Called: Calvac Paving & Sealing
2645 Pacer Ln, San Jose (95111-2011)
PHONE 408 262-1162
James E Adam, *President*
Victor A Cantando, *Vice Pres*
Lindsay Lopez, *Office Mgr*
EMP: 45 EST: 1974
SQ FT: 28,000
SALES (est): 8.6MM **Privately Held**
WEB: www.calvacpaving.com
SIC: 1611 Highway & street paving contractor

(P-1024)
CCCS INC
Also Called: Corporate Construction Svcs
5061 24th St, Sacramento (95822-2201)
PHONE 916 457-6111
Daniel W Knight, *President*
Alfredo Hernandez, *Project Mgr*
Jeff Hogue, *Project Mgr*
Danny Lyttle, *Project Mgr*
Joe Berthelot, *Engineer*
EMP: 40 EST: 1995
SALES (est): 10.1MM **Privately Held**
WEB: www.ccselink.com
SIC: 1611 General contractor, highway & street construction

(P-1025)
CENTRAL STRIPING SERVICE INC
3489 Luyung Dr, Rancho Cordova (95742-6861)
PHONE 916 635-5175
James Lesniewski, *President*
Geri Leshiewski, *Vice Pres*
Geri Lesniewski, *Vice Pres*
Edgar Rodriguez, *Manager*
EMP: 35 EST: 1967
SQ FT: 12,000
SALES (est): 7.8MM **Privately Held**
WEB: www.centralstripingservice.com
SIC: 1611 1799 Highway & street maintenance; parking lot maintenance

(P-1026)
CENTRAL VALLEY ENGRG & ASP INC
216 Kenroy Ln, Roseville (95678-4202)
PHONE 916 791-1609
Warren Holt, *CEO*
James Castle, *CFO*
Bob Leppek, *Vice Pres*
Shannon Neill, *Project Mgr*
Shannon O' Neill, *Project Mgr*
EMP: 35 EST: 2000
SQ FT: 2,500
SALES (est): 9.4MM **Privately Held**
WEB: www.cenvalley.com
SIC: 1611 1771 Highway & street paving contractor; driveway, parking lot & blacktop contractors

(P-1027)
CHRISP COMPANY (PA)
43650 Osgood Rd, Fremont (94539-5631)
P.O. Box 1368 (94538-0136)
PHONE 510 656-2840
Robert P Chrisp, *CEO*
David Morris, *Vice Pres*
Roger Weisbrod, *Vice Pres*
Andy Cooper, *Administration*
Briana Laszlo, *Administration*
EMP: 167 EST: 1979
SQ FT: 8,000
SALES (est): 52MM **Privately Held**
WEB: www.chrispco.com
SIC: 1611 Highway signs & guardrails

(P-1028)
CITY OF BURLINGAME
Also Called: Public Works and Highway Dept
1361 N Carolan Ave, Burlingame (94010-2401)
PHONE 650 558-7670
Rob Mallick, *Branch Mgr*
Jim Brown, *Manager*
EMP: 50 **Privately Held**
WEB: www.burlingame.org
SIC: 1611 Surfacing & paving
PA: City Of Burlingame
   501 Primrose Rd
   Burlingame CA 94010
   650 558-7203

(P-1029)
CLY INCORPORATED
Also Called: Point Pacific Drilling
121 Lakeville St, Petaluma (94952-3126)
PHONE 707 763-5591
Richard Young, *President*
EMP: 40 EST: 1967
SALES (est): 8.5MM **Privately Held**
WEB: www.sonomamarinconstruction.com
SIC: 1611 1771 General contractor, highway & street construction; concrete pumping

PRODUCTS & SERVICES SECTION
1611 - Highway & Street Construction County (P-1052)

(P-1030)
D A MCCOSKER CONSTRUCTION CO
Also Called: Independent Construction Co
3911 Laura Alice Way, Concord (94520-8544)
PHONE..................925 686-1780
Brian Clay McCosker, *President*
David A McCosker, *Ch of Bd*
Mike Morris, *Treasurer*
Cindy Kolm, *Office Mgr*
Brian Cartmell, *Admin Sec*
EMP: 50 **EST:** 1910
SALES (est): 20.8MM **Privately Held**
SIC: 1611 Surfacing & paving; grading; highway & street paving contractor

(P-1031)
DESILVA GATES CONSTRUCTION LP (PA)
11555 Dublin Blvd, Dublin (94568-2854)
P.O. Box 2909 (94568-0909)
PHONE..................925 361-1380
Edwin O Desilva, *President*
David Desilva, *Exec VP*
Richard B Gates, *Exec VP*
J Scott Archibald, *Vice Pres*
Pete Davos, *Vice Pres*
EMP: 100 **EST:** 1932
SALES (est): 115.4MM **Privately Held**
WEB: www.desilvagates.com
SIC: 1611 1794 1542 General contractor, highway & street construction; excavation & grading, building construction; nonresidential construction

(P-1032)
DIRT DYNASTY INC
4110 Meadow Oaks Dr, Valley Springs (95252-8831)
P.O. Box 67, Farmington (95230-0067)
PHONE..................209 623-1141
Jason Alurcon, *CEO*
EMP: 35 **EST:** 2014
SALES (est): 3.9MM **Privately Held**
SIC: 1611 Grading

(P-1033)
DISNEY CONSTRUCTION INC
533 Airport Blvd Ste 120, Burlingame (94010-2007)
PHONE..................650 689-5149
Richard L Disney, *President*
Vincent Diep, *CIO*
Sharuk Khanna, *CIO*
Sean Lennan, *Project Engr*
Vickie Fierro, *Manager*
EMP: 60 **EST:** 2005
SALES (est): 24.6MM **Privately Held**
WEB: www.disneyconstruction.com
SIC: 1611 Highway & street construction

(P-1034)
DON BERRY CONSTRUCTION INC
13701 Golden State Blvd, Kingsburg (93631-9563)
P.O. Box 620, Selma (93662-0620)
PHONE..................559 896-5700
Janet Berry, *CEO*
Richard Berry, *President*
Don Berry, *CFO*
Dan Dorval, *Info Tech Mgr*
EMP: 56 **EST:** 1979
SQ FT: 400
SALES (est): 10.2MM **Privately Held**
WEB: www.donberryconstruction.com
SIC: 1611 1629 Highway & street paving contractor; earthmoving contractor

(P-1035)
DRYCO CONSTRUCTION INC (PA)
42745 Boscell Rd, Fremont (94538-3106)
PHONE..................510 438-6500
Daren R Young, *President*
David Henke, *CFO*
William McCrea, *Vice Pres*
Kevin Mitchell, *Vice Pres*
Ron Saisi, *Vice Pres*
EMP: 175 **EST:** 1978
SQ FT: 3,700
SALES (est): 80.5MM **Privately Held**
WEB: www.dryco.com
SIC: 1611 1721 5211 Highway & street paving contractor; pavement marking contractor; lumber & other building materials

(P-1036)
EAGLE PAVING & GRADING
2848 Tarmac Rd, Redding (96003-7320)
PHONE..................530 221-4194
Dave Ratcliffe, *Partner*
Michael Petraitis, *Partner*
EMP: 36 **EST:** 1984
SQ FT: 1,400
SALES (est): 3.1MM **Privately Held**
WEB: www.eaglepavingandgrading.com
SIC: 1611 Highway & street paving contractor; concrete construction: roads, highways, sidewalks, etc.

(P-1037)
ESQUIVEL GRADING & PAVING INC
918 Ingerson Ave, San Francisco (94124-3510)
PHONE..................415 822-5400
Ralph G Esquivel, *President*
Simar Esquivel, *Accountant*
EMP: 35 **EST:** 1984
SQ FT: 6,000
SALES (est): 6.3MM **Privately Held**
WEB: www.esquivelgradingpaving.thebluebook.com
SIC: 1611 Surfacing & paving

(P-1038)
FANFA INC
2401 Grant Ave, San Lorenzo (94580-1807)
PHONE..................510 278-8410
Joseph G Fanfa, *President*
Deborah Griffin, *Corp Secy*
Donald Fanfa, *Vice Pres*
EMP: 48 **EST:** 1942
SQ FT: 5,000
SALES (est): 4MM **Privately Held**
SIC: 1611 1794 Highway & street paving contractor; grading; excavation work

(P-1039)
FARWEST SAFETY INC
226 N Main St, Lodi (95240-2209)
PHONE..................209 339-8085
Ronald G Anderson, *President*
Dede A Anderson, *Vice Pres*
Dede Anderson, *Vice Pres*
Johnnie A Ashe, *Vice Pres*
Debbie Costa, *Controller*
EMP: 35 **EST:** 1985
SALES: 5.6MM **Privately Held**
SIC: 1611 Highway & street sign installation

(P-1040)
FONSECA/MCELROY GRINDING INC
Also Called: F M G Company
5225 Hellyer Ave Ste 220, San Jose (95138-1021)
PHONE..................408 573-9364
Michael McElroy, *President*
Frank Fonseca, *Vice Pres*
Lisa McElroy, *Admin Sec*
EMP: 38 **EST:** 1999
SQ FT: 1,000
SALES (est): 5.2MM **Privately Held**
WEB: www.graniterock.com
SIC: 1611 Highway & street construction

(P-1041)
FOUR TRIBES ENTERPRISES LLC
1516 Main St, Susanville (96130-4428)
PHONE..................530 317-2500
Dolye Lowry,
EMP: 45 **EST:** 2017
SALES (est): 2.6MM **Privately Held**
WEB: www.fourtribes.com
SIC: 1611 Highway & street construction

(P-1042)
FREMONT PAVING COMPANY INC
38370 Cedar Blvd, Newark (94560-4846)
PHONE..................510 797-3553
Ellen Marie Lebon, *President*
Joseph Lebon, *Corp Secy*
Donald Alan, *Vice Pres*
EMP: 55 **EST:** 1948
SQ FT: 600
SALES (est): 11.1MM **Privately Held**
WEB: www.fremontpaving.com
SIC: 1611 Highway & street paving contractor

(P-1043)
GALANTE BROTHERS GEN ENGRG INC
291 Barnard Ave, San Jose (95125-1302)
P.O. Box 41490 (95160-1490)
PHONE..................408 291-0100
Thomas F Galante, *President*
Donna Galante, *Treasurer*
Jack Galante, *Vice Pres*
Denise Galante, *Admin Sec*
EMP: 91 **EST:** 1969
SQ FT: 2,200
SALES (est): 3MM **Privately Held**
SIC: 1611 1623 8711 Grading; highway & street paving contractor; water & sewer line construction; sewer line construction; construction & civil engineering

(P-1044)
GOEBEL CONSTRUCTION INC
227 Howard St, Petaluma (94952-2761)
P.O. Box 2745 (94953-2745)
PHONE..................707 763-0088
Greg Goebel, *President*
Dj Goebel, *Vice Pres*
Duane D Goebel, *Vice Pres*
Joanne R Goebel, *Admin Sec*
Brandon Joyner, *Project Mgr*
EMP: 41 **EST:** 1977
SQ FT: 2,000
SALES (est): 11.7MM **Privately Held**
WEB: www.goebelconstructioninc.com
SIC: 1611 Surfacing & paving

(P-1045)
GRAHAM CONTRACTORS INC
860 Lonus St, San Jose (95126-3713)
P.O. Box 26770 (95159-6770)
PHONE..................408 293-9516
Gerald Graham Jr, *President*
Reed Graham, *Vice Pres*
John Waiters, *General Mgr*
Tony Gulbraa, *Administration*
Dave Maletta, *Purchasing*
EMP: 50 **EST:** 1976
SQ FT: 1,200
SALES (est): 10.8MM **Privately Held**
WEB: www.grahamcontractors.com
SIC: 1611 Highway & street paving contractor

(P-1046)
GRANIT-BAYASHI 3 A JOINT VENTR
585 W Beach St, Watsonville (95076-5123)
P.O. Box 50085 (95077-5085)
PHONE..................831 724-1011
Tobi Stonich, *Administration*
Rinkou Aki,
Jigisha Desai,
Mathew Tyler,
EMP: 50 **EST:** 2017
SALES (est): 3.8MM **Privately Held**
WEB: www.graniteconstruction.com
SIC: 1611 1542 General contractor, highway & street construction; nonresidential construction

(P-1047)
GRANITE CNSTR NORTHEAST INC
585 W Beach St, Watsonville (95076-5123)
PHONE..................831 724-1011
Michael F Donnino, *Senior VP*
EMP: 36 **Publicly Held**
WEB: www.graniteconstruction.com
SIC: 1611 General contractor, highway & street construction

HQ: Granite Construction Northeast, Inc.
1302 N 19th St Ste 300
Tampa FL 33605

(P-1048)
GRANITE CONSTRUCTION COMPANY (HQ)
585 W Beach St, Watsonville (95076-5123)
P.O. Box 50085 (95077-5085)
PHONE..................831 724-1011
Laurel Krzeminski, *Exec VP*
Christopher S Miller, *Exec VP*
Phil Decocco, *Vice Pres*
Richard A Watts, *Vice Pres*
Craig Hall, *Admin Sec*
▼ **EMP:** 200
SQ FT: 39,000
SALES (est): 696.7MM **Publicly Held**
WEB: www.graniteconstruction.com
SIC: 1611 1622 Highway & street construction; general contractor, highway & street construction; bridge construction; tunnel construction

(P-1049)
GRANITE CONSTRUCTION COMPANY
Also Called: Stockton
10500 S Harlan Rd, French Camp (95231-9603)
P.O. Box 151, Stockton (95201-0151)
PHONE..................209 982-4750
James Hopp Essick, *Engr R&D*
Carolyn Orgon, *Office Mgr*
Becka Schumacher, *Human Res Mgr*
Jerry Slavens, *Manager*
EMP: 200 **Publicly Held**
WEB: www.graniteconstruction.com
SIC: 1611 General contractor, highway & street construction
HQ: Granite Construction Company
585 W Beach St
Watsonville CA 95076
831 724-1011

(P-1050)
GRANITE ROCK CO
Also Called: Pavex Construction Company
355 Blomquist St, Redwood City (94063-2701)
PHONE..................650 869-3370
John Franich, *Manager*
Wayne Holman, *Vice Pres*
Angela Montes, *Admin Mgr*
Jason Alger, *Financial Analy*
EMP: 49
SALES (corp-wide): 390.3MM **Privately Held**
WEB: www.graniterock.com
SIC: 1611 Highway & street paving contractor
PA: Granite Rock Co.
350 Technology Dr
Watsonville CA 95076
831 768-2000

(P-1051)
INTERSTATE GRADING AND PAV INC
128 S Maple Ave, South San Francisco (94080-6302)
P.O. Box 389 (94083-0389)
PHONE..................650 952-7333
H Michael Pariani, *President*
Nancy Zammuto, *COO*
Kathleen Pariani, *Treasurer*
Jay Enbom, *Project Mgr*
Rudy Galli, *Maintence Staff*
EMP: 35 **EST:** 1978
SQ FT: 7,000
SALES (est): 11.3MM **Privately Held**
WEB: www.igpinc.com
SIC: 1611 Highway & street paving contractor; grading

(P-1052)
JIM CRAWFORD CNSTR CO INC
1189 Hoblitt Ave, Clovis (93612-2824)
PHONE..................559 299-0306
Jim D Crawford Jr, *President*
Joyce Crawford, *CFO*
Marshall W Crawford, *Vice Pres*
Marshall Crawford, *Vice Pres*
Shelly Crawford, *Admin Sec*
EMP: 40 **EST:** 1982

1611 - Highway & Street Construction County (P-1053)

PRODUCTS & SERVICES SECTION

SQ FT: 6,000
SALES (est): 9.4MM Privately Held
WEB: www.jcrawfordconst.com
SIC: **1611** Highway & street paving contractor; highway & street maintenance

(P-1053)
LEVEL 5 INC
1210 Coleman Ave, Santa Clara (95050-4338)
PHONE 669 263-6292
Dana Tirri, *Office Mgr*
EMP: 35 EST: 2017
SALES (est): 5.5MM Privately Held
WEB: www.level5inc.com
SIC: **1611** General contractor, highway & street construction

(P-1054)
MARK NICHOLSON INC
701 Mccray St, Hollister (95023-4033)
P.O. Box 58 (95024-0058)
PHONE 831 637-5728
Kurt Nicholson, *President*
Lawrence Nicholson, *President*
EMP: 64 EST: 1952
SQ FT: 3,000
SALES (est): 4.2MM Privately Held
WEB: www.marknicholsoninc.com
SIC: **1611** 1623 Surfacing & paving; grading; water, sewer & utility lines

(P-1055)
MARSHALL BROTHERS ENTPS INC
5783 Preston Ave, Livermore (94551-9521)
P.O. Box 2188 (94551-2188)
PHONE 925 449-4020
Phil Marshall, *President*
Phillip Marshall, *Info Tech Dir*
EMP: 45 EST: 2010
SALES (est): 10.1MM Privately Held
WEB: www.mbenterprises.com
SIC: **1611** Highway & street construction

(P-1056)
MARTIN BROTHERS CNSTR LLC (PA)
8801 Folsom Blvd Ste 260, Sacramento (95826-3250)
PHONE 916 386-1600
Felipe Martin, *CEO*
Mary Murano, *Manager*
Mike Fine, *Superintendent*
EMP: 60
SQ FT: 9,300
SALES (est): 36MM Privately Held
WEB: www.martinbrothers.net
SIC: **1611** 1794 1541 1795 General contractor, highway & street construction; surfacing & paving; highway & street paving contractor; excavation work; excavation & grading, building construction; industrial buildings, new construction; demolition, buildings & other structures

(P-1057)
MCCULLOUGH CONSTRUCTION INC
57 Aldergrove Rd, Arcata (95521-9276)
PHONE 707 825-1014
Jens Karlshoej, *Partner*
Dena McCullough, *Partner*
Hugh McCullough, *Partner*
Dan Schultz, *Partner*
Rachelle Hicks, *Vice Pres*
EMP: 80 EST: 2017
SALES (est): 6.2MM Privately Held
WEB: www.california8acontractor.com
SIC: **1611** 1622 Highway & street construction; tunnel construction

(P-1058)
MCE CORPORATION (PA)
4000 Industrial Way, Concord (94520-1289)
P.O. Box 508 (94522-0508)
PHONE 925 803-4111
Jeff Core, *President*
Stan Smalley, *Exec VP*
Justin Bray, *Vice Pres*
Dan Furtado, *Vice Pres*
Steve Loweree, *Vice Pres*
EMP: 65
SQ FT: 12,000
SALES (est): 45.4MM Privately Held
WEB: www.mce-corp.com
SIC: **1611** 0782 General contractor, highway & street construction; lawn & garden services

(P-1059)
MICHAEL TELFER (PA)
Also Called: Western Oil & Spreading
211 Foster St, Martinez (94553-1029)
P.O. Box 709 (94553-0151)
PHONE 925 228-1515
Michael Telfer, *Owner*
Eric Nielsen, *Technical Staff*
Cesar Lara, *Marketing Mgr*
Michelle Kydd, *Manager*
Trevor Dormire, *Superintendent*
EMP: 55 EST: 1992
SQ FT: 5,000
SALES (est): 22MM Privately Held
SIC: **1611** 2951 4213 4212 Highway & street paving contractor; resurfacing contractor; paving mixtures; liquid petroleum transport, non-local; local trucking, without storage

(P-1060)
MIDSTATE BARRIER INC
Also Called: MBI
3291 S Highway 99, Stockton (95215-8032)
P.O. Box 30550 (95213-0550)
PHONE 209 944-9565
Dale Breen, *CEO*
Clark Ebinger, *President*
Clark D Ebinger, *Vice Pres*
Chet Martin, *Superintendent*
Justin Slavich, *Superintendent*
EMP: 75 EST: 1987
SQ FT: 20,000
SALES (est): 22.2MM Privately Held
WEB: www.midstatebarrier.com
SIC: **1611** Highway signs & guardrails

(P-1061)
MOUNTAIN G ENTERPRISES INC
Also Called: Mountain G Engineering
950 Iron Point Rd Ste 190, Folsom (95630-8302)
P.O. Box 1040, Lotus (95651-1040)
PHONE 866 464-6351
Marcos Gomez, *CEO*
Juan Gomez, *President*
EMP: 250 EST: 2016
SQ FT: 3,000
SALES (est): 42MM Privately Held
WEB: www.mgeinc.com
SIC: **1611** 8711 8748 Grading; civil engineering; environmental consultant

(P-1062)
MUSE CONCRETE CONTRACTORS INC
8599 Commercial Way, Redding (96002-3902)
PHONE 530 226-5151
Boyce Muse, *President*
Joan Muse, *CFO*
Garrett Brown, *Vice Pres*
EMP: 94 EST: 1982
SALES (est): 19.5MM Privately Held
WEB: www.museconcrete.com
SIC: **1611** 1771 Concrete construction: roads, highways, sidewalks, etc.; concrete work; curb construction

(P-1063)
MYERS & SONS CONSTRUCTION LP (HQ)
4600 Northgate Blvd # 10, Sacramento (95834-1103)
PHONE 916 283-9950
Clinton C Myers, *Partner*
Michelle Dorenkamp, *Administration*
Sean Weddingfeld, *Project Mgr*
Jenna Carlson, *Human Res Mgr*
Brooke Torres, *Internal Med*
EMP: 242 EST: 2010
SALES (est): 181.5MM Publicly Held
WEB: www.myers-sons.com
SIC: **1611** Highway & street construction

(P-1064)
NEHEMIAH CONSTRUCTION INC
12150 Tributary Ln P, Rancho Cordova (95670)
PHONE 707 746-6815
EMP: 50
SQ FT: 2,500
SALES: 98.4K Privately Held
WEB: www.nehemiahconst.com
SIC: **1611** Highway/Street Construction

(P-1065)
NICHELINI GENERAL ENGRG CONTRS
4101 W Capitol Ave, West Sacramento (95691-2182)
PHONE 916 371-1300
Joseph Nichelini, *CEO*
Summer Dales, *General Mgr*
EMP: 38 EST: 2012
SALES (est): 6.2MM Privately Held
WEB: www.nichelinigec.com
SIC: **1611** Concrete construction: roads, highways, sidewalks, etc.

(P-1066)
O C JONES & SONS INC (PA)
1520 4th St, Berkeley (94710-1748)
PHONE 510 526-3424
Kelly Kolander, *President*
Robert Pelascini, *Ch of Bd*
Rob Layne, *CEO*
Beth Yoshida, *CFO*
Justin Cromwell, *Project Mgr*
EMP: 150 EST: 1924
SQ FT: 80,000
SALES (est): 58.3MM Privately Held
WEB: www.ocjones.com
SIC: **1611** Grading; highway & street paving contractor

(P-1067)
OBAYASHI CANADA LTD
577 Airport Blvd Ste 600, Burlingame (94010-2057)
PHONE 650 952-4910
Shirley A Carney, *Principal*
Rikako Murai, *Human Resources*
Jack Harper, *Manager*
Keisuke Mizutani, *Manager*
EMP: 35 EST: 2012
SALES (est): 14.7MM Privately Held
SIC: **1611** General contractor, highway & street construction
HQ: Obayashi Canada Holdings Ltd.
577 Airport Blvd Ste 600
Burlingame CA 94010
650 952-4910

(P-1068)
OGRADY PAVING INC
2513 Wyandotte St, Mountain View (94043-2311)
PHONE 650 966-1926
Thomas M O'Grady Jr, *President*
Craig Young, *COO*
Celine Duran, *Corp Secy*
Brett Hickman, *Manager*
Brett Kincaid, *Manager*
EMP: 110 EST: 1956
SQ FT: 3,200
SALES (est): 35.2MM Privately Held
WEB: www.ogradypavinginc.com
SIC: **1611** Highway & street paving contractor

(P-1069)
OUTBACK CONTRACTORS INC
13670 State Highway 36 E, Red Bluff (96080-7849)
P.O. Box 1035 (96080-1035)
PHONE 530 528-2225
Mattie Bunting, *CEO*
Megan Fox, *Admin Asst*
Daniel Ohara, *Sr Project Mgr*
Ray Walter, *Sr Project Mgr*
Ray Mueller, *Superintendent*
EMP: 150 EST: 2008
SQ FT: 625
SALES (est): 29MM Privately Held
WEB: www.outback-inc.com
SIC: **1611** Concrete construction: roads, highways, sidewalks, etc.; gravel or dirt road construction

(P-1070)
PERSSON INC
Also Called: California Paving Company
40077 Enterprise Dr, Oakhurst (93644-8947)
P.O. Box 1393 (93644-1393)
PHONE 559 683-3000
Bruce Persson, *President*
Eric Perrson, *Vice Pres*
EMP: 43 EST: 1986
SALES (est): 6.9MM Privately Held
SIC: **1611** Highway & street paving contractor

(P-1071)
REED GROUP (HQ)
Also Called: Munn & Perkins
928 12th St Ste 700, Modesto (95354-2330)
PHONE 209 521-7423
Wendell G Reed, *President*
John Shodun, *CFO*
EMP: 40 EST: 1944
SQ FT: 1,000
SALES (est): 33MM
SALES (corp-wide): 163.9MM Privately Held
WEB: www.georgereed.com
SIC: **1611** 3273 2951 5032 Highway & street paving contractor; ready-mixed concrete; asphalt & asphaltic paving mixtures (not from refineries); aggregate; concrete block & brick; construction sand & gravel
PA: Basic Resources, Inc.
928 12th St Ste 700
Modesto CA 95354
209 521-9771

(P-1072)
SILICON VALLEY PAVING INC
1050 Coml St Ste 101, San Jose (95112)
P.O. Box 26558 (95159-6558)
PHONE 408 286-9101
Todd Slyngstad, *President*
Jose Bizcaino, *Admin Sec*
Tom Meckenstock, *Sales Staff*
EMP: 40 EST: 1999
SALES (est): 10.3MM Privately Held
WEB: www.svpinc.com
SIC: **1611** Surfacing & paving

(P-1073)
SIMPSON & SIMPSON INC
10001 Ophir Rd, Newcastle (95658-9504)
P.O. Box 6746, Auburn (95604-6746)
PHONE 530 885-4354
Sher Simpson, *President*
Steve Simpson, *Vice Pres*
EMP: 36 EST: 1948
SQ FT: 2,500
SALES (est): 5.7MM Privately Held
WEB: www.simpsonpaving.com
SIC: **1611** Highway & street paving contractor

(P-1074)
STEVE MANNING CONSTRUCTION INC
5211 Churn Creek Rd, Redding (96002-3914)
P.O. Box 491660 (96049-1660)
PHONE 530 222-0810
Steve Manning, *President*
Arlene T Litsey, *Treasurer*
Bill Spoon, *Project Mgr*
Arlene Litsey, *Controller*
EMP: 54 EST: 1980
SQ FT: 2,200
SALES (est): 12.6MM Privately Held
WEB: www.smci-const.com
SIC: **1611** General contractor, highway & street construction

(P-1075)
STEVENS CREEK QUARRY INC (PA)
12100 Stevens Canyon Rd, Cupertino (95014-5443)
PHONE 408 253-2512
Richard A Voss, *President*
Richard Voss, *President*
Diana Voss, *Vice Pres*
Bob Romano, *Principal*
Mary Parson, *Webmaster*

PRODUCTS & SERVICES SECTION
1623 - Water, Sewer & Utility Line Construction

EMP: 60 **EST:** 1954
SALES (est): 15.5MM **Privately Held**
WEB: www.scqinc.com
SIC: 1611 7353 1442 General contractor, highway & street construction; heavy construction equipment rental; construction sand mining

(P-1076)
TALLEY OIL INC
12483 Road 29, Madera (93638-8401)
P.O. Box 568 (93639-0568)
PHONE 559 673-9011
Kenneth William Talley, *CEO*
EMP: 32 **EST:** 2004
SALES (est): 8.4MM **Privately Held**
WEB: www.talleyoil.com
SIC: 1611 2951 Highway & street maintenance; asphalt & asphaltic paving mixtures (not from refineries)

(P-1077)
TEAM GHILOTTI INC
2531 Petaluma Blvd S, Petaluma (94952-5523)
PHONE 707 763-8700
Glen Ghilotti, *President*
Glen C Ghilotti, *President*
Monica Bourdens, *Office Mgr*
Sean Durenberger, *Project Mgr*
Ed Ponte, *Manager*
EMP: 50 **EST:** 2007
SQ FT: 5,900
SALES (est): 10MM **Privately Held**
WEB: www.teamghilotti.com
SIC: 1611 General contractor, highway & street construction

(P-1078)
TRACY GRADING & PAVING INC
11 W 12th St, Tracy (95376-3501)
P.O. Box 444 (95378-0444)
PHONE 209 839-6590
Robert Rocha, *President*
Heather Dunlop, *Administration*
EMP: 39 **EST:** 2014
SALES (est): 4.6MM **Privately Held**
WEB: www.tracygradingandpaving.com
SIC: 1611 General contractor, highway & street construction; surfacing & paving

(P-1079)
VSS INTERNATIONAL INC (HQ)
Also Called: V S S
3785 Channel Dr, West Sacramento (95691-3421)
P.O. Box 981330 (95798-1330)
PHONE 916 373-1500
Jeffrey Reed, *President*
Ron Bolles, *Treasurer*
John Shoden, *Treasurer*
Alan Berger, *Vice Pres*
Diane Minor, *Admin Sec*
▲ **EMP:** 62 **EST:** 1974
SQ FT: 5,000
SALES (est): 55.8MM
SALES (corp-wide): 163.9MM **Privately Held**
WEB: www.slurry.com
SIC: 1611 3531 2951 Highway & street paving contractor; construction machinery; asphalt paving mixtures & blocks
PA: Basic Resources, Inc.
928 12th St Ste 700
Modesto CA 95354
209 521-9771

(P-1080)
WR FORDE ASSOCIATES INC
984 Hensley St, Richmond (94801-2117)
PHONE 510 215-9338
Donald Russell, *CEO*
Kathryn Massara, *General Mgr*
EMP: 55
SQ FT: 4,500
SALES: 17.6MM **Privately Held**
WEB: www.wrforde.net
SIC: 1611 1622 1794 Grading; bridge construction; excavation & grading, building construction

1622 Bridge, Tunnel & Elevated Hwy Construction

(P-1081)
COUNTY OF SACRAMENTO
Also Called: Municipal Svcs Agency
9700 Goethe Rd Ste D, Sacramento (95827-3558)
PHONE 916 875-2711
Thor Lude, *Chief*
EMP: 55
SALES (corp-wide): 3.1B **Privately Held**
WEB: www.saccounty.net
SIC: 1622 9199 Bridge, tunnel & elevated highway; general government administration;
PA: County Of Sacramento
700 H St Ste 7650
Sacramento CA 95814
916 874-8515

(P-1082)
FLATIRON WEST INC
2100 Goodyear Rd, Benicia (94510-1216)
PHONE 707 742-6000
Richard Tradinski, *Manager*
EMP: 150
SALES (corp-wide): 1B **Privately Held**
WEB: www.flatironcorp.com
SIC: 1622 1629 Bridge construction; industrial plant construction
HQ: Flatiron West, Inc.
16470 W Bernardo Dr 120
San Diego CA 92127

(P-1083)
GRANITE CONSTRUCTION INC (PA)
585 W Beach St, Watsonville (95076-5123)
P.O. Box 50085 (95077-5085)
PHONE 831 724-1011
Kyle T Larkin, *President*
Michael F McNally, *Ch of Bd*
James A Radich, *COO*
Elizabeth L Curtis, *CFO*
Jigisha Desai, *Exec VP*
EMP: 1652 **EST:** 1922
SALES (est): 3.5B **Publicly Held**
WEB: www.graniteconstruction.com
SIC: 1622 1629 1442 1611 Bridge construction; tunnel construction; dam construction; canal construction; land leveling; construction sand & gravel; general contractor, highway & street construction

(P-1084)
MCM CONSTRUCTION INC (PA)
6413 32nd St, North Highlands (95660-3001)
P.O. Box 620 (95660-0620)
PHONE 916 334-1221
Richard McCall, *President*
Harry D McGovern, *Vice Pres*
EMP: 70 **EST:** 1973
SQ FT: 5,000
SALES (est): 75.6MM **Privately Held**
WEB: www.mcmconstructioninc.com
SIC: 1622 Bridge construction

(P-1085)
R M HARRIS COMPANY INC
1000 Howe Rd Ste 200, Martinez (94553-3446)
PHONE 925 335-3000
David R Harris, *CEO*
Mark Snapp, *Admin Sec*
John Tymo, *Technology*
John Hoover, *Purch Mgr*
EMP: 100 **EST:** 1976
SQ FT: 4,500
SALES (est): 16.1MM **Privately Held**
WEB: www.rmhci.com
SIC: 1622 1611 Bridge, tunnel & elevated highway; highway & street construction

1623 Water, Sewer & Utility Line Construction

(P-1086)
3D DATA COM (PA)
Also Called: 3d Technology Services
11365 Sunrise Gold Cir, Rancho Cordova (95742-6512)
PHONE 916 573-3720
Mark Pedersen, *President*
Brian Boyle, *Treasurer*
Peter Pedersen, *Vice Pres*
Nick Bishop, *Technician*
Clint Brown, *Technician*
▲ **EMP:** 37 **EST:** 1998
SQ FT: 11,840
SALES (est): 26.4MM **Privately Held**
WEB: www.3dtsi.com
SIC: 1623 Cable laying construction

(P-1087)
ARROW DRILLERS INC (PA)
Also Called: Arrow Construction
1850 Diesel Dr, Sacramento (95838-2456)
PHONE 916 640-0600
Michael Wegener, *President*
Harry Barnes, *President*
Sal Rivera, *Vice Pres*
Jim Sams, *Executive*
Justin Bovolick, *Project Mgr*
EMP: 40 **EST:** 1995
SQ FT: 4,000
SALES (est): 13.7MM **Privately Held**
WEB: www.arrowcon.com
SIC: 1623 Underground utilities contractor

(P-1088)
BALCH PETRO CONTRS & BLDRS INC
930 Ames Ave, Milpitas (95035-6303)
P.O. Box 361230 (95036-1230)
PHONE 408 942-8686
Wilbur Balch, *President*
Tom Balch, *CFO*
Bill Balch, *Vice Pres*
EMP: 73 **EST:** 1976
SQ FT: 5,000
SALES (est): 9.9MM **Privately Held**
WEB: www.balchpetroleum.com
SIC: 1623 1799 Communication line & transmission tower construction; service station equipment installation, maintenance & repair

(P-1089)
BESS TESTLAB INC
2463 Tripaldi Way, Hayward (94545-5018)
PHONE 408 988-0101
Juan Jose Bohorquez, *President*
Diana Layseca, *Principal*
Brandy Molina, *Manager*
EMP: 50 **EST:** 1978
SALES (est): 10.8MM **Privately Held**
WEB: www.besstestlab.com
SIC: 1623 Water, sewer & utility lines

(P-1090)
BLACKWELL GENERAL ENGRG INC
1199 E Taylor St, San Jose (95133-1016)
P.O. Box 641150 (95164-1150)
PHONE 408 441-1120
Loran Blackwell, *CEO*
Mark Blackwell, *President*
Danny White, *CFO*
Dick Blackwell, *Engineer*
EMP: 40 **EST:** 1973
SALES (est): 10.7MM **Privately Held**
SIC: 1623 1794 Water main construction; sewer line construction; pipeline construction; excavation & grading, building construction

(P-1091)
CALIFORNIA TRENCHLESS INC
2315 Dunn Rd, Hayward (94545-2207)
P.O. Box 20817, Castro Valley (94546-8817)
PHONE 510 782-5335
Michael Jardin, *President*
Kathy Minerva, *Accountant*
Chris Asbury, *Superintendent*
EMP: 38 **EST:** 1997
SALES (est): 3MM **Privately Held**
WEB: www.californiatrenchless.com
SIC: 1623 Sewer line construction; pipeline construction

(P-1092)
CEDAR CREEK CORPORATION
15875 Jellys Ferry Rd, Red Bluff (96080-7964)
PHONE 530 364-2143
Katie Marie Gove, *CEO*
Nicholas Vona, *CFO*
John Kalapaca, *Treasurer*
Gary Gove, *Admin Sec*
EMP: 85 **EST:** 2017
SALES (est): 16.9MM **Privately Held**
WEB: www.cedarcreekcorp.com
SIC: 1623 Electric power line construction

(P-1093)
CLYDE WHEELER PIPELINE INC
Also Called: Wheeler Clyde Pipe Line
509 Hi Tech Pkwy, Oakdale (95361-9395)
P.O. Box 1500 (95361-1500)
PHONE 209 848-0809
Clyde Wheeler, *President*
Donna Wheeler, *Corp Secy*
EMP: 53 **EST:** 1981
SQ FT: 2,000
SALES (est): 2.3MM **Privately Held**
SIC: 1623 Water, sewer & utility lines

(P-1094)
COUNTY OF SAN JOAQUIN
Also Called: Sewer Maintenance
1702 E Scotts Ave, Stockton (95205-6240)
PHONE 209 468-3090
Ron Rall, *Branch Mgr*
Ben Guzman, *Asst Supt*
EMP: 64
SALES (corp-wide): 1.2B **Privately Held**
WEB: www.sjgov.org
SIC: 9111 1623 County supervisors' & executives' offices; water, sewer & utility lines
PA: County Of San Joaquin
44 N San Joaquin St # 640
Stockton CA 95202
209 468-3203

(P-1095)
COVENTINA-GSE JV LLC
6950 Preston Ave, Livermore (94551-9545)
PHONE 813 509-0669
John Coccaro, *Mng Member*
Dennis Gutierrez,
EMP: 50 **EST:** 2019
SALES (est): 1.3MM **Privately Held**
SIC: 1623 Water, sewer & utility lines

(P-1096)
COX & COX CONSTRUCTION INC
8837 Airport Rd Ste A, Redding (96002-9249)
P.O. Box 992588 (96099-2588)
PHONE 530 243-6016
Vernon R Cox Jr, *President*
EMP: 44 **EST:** 1977
SQ FT: 1,500
SALES (est): 11MM **Privately Held**
WEB: www.coxandcoxconstruction.com
SIC: 1623 1611 Pipeline construction; grading; surfacing & paving

(P-1097)
D W YOUNG CNSTR CO INC
333 Camille Ave, Alamo (94507-2411)
P.O. Box 130 (94507-0130)
PHONE 925 743-1536
Christian W Young, *President*
Barbara Young, *Corp Secy*
EMP: 57 **EST:** 1978
SQ FT: 1,800
SALES (est): 5.4MM **Privately Held**
WEB: www.dwyoung.com
SIC: 1623 1611 Underground utilities contractor; surfacing & paving; grading

(P-1098)
DALEO INC
550 E Luchessa Ave, Gilroy (95020-7068)
PHONE 408 846-9621
David A Levisay, *Principal*
Susan Levisay, *Corp Secy*
EMP: 54 **EST:** 1979

SALES (est): 9.8MM **Privately Held**
WEB: www.daleoinc.com
SIC: 1623 Cable television line construction

(P-1099)
DRESSER/AREIA CONSTRUCTION
3940 Valley Ave, Pleasanton (94566-4865)
PHONE 800 392-9891
Jody Areia, *President*
Dan Dresser, *Vice Pres*
EMP: 170 **EST:** 1989
SQ FT: 4,000
SALES (est): 1.7MM
SALES (corp-wide): 6.3B **Publicly Held**
SIC: 1623 Underground utilities contractor; pipeline construction
HQ: Mastec North America, Inc.
800 S Douglas Rd Ste 1200
Coral Gables FL 33134
305 599-1800

(P-1100)
ELECTRIC TECH CONSTRUCTION INC
1910 Mark Ct Ste 130, Concord (94520-1280)
PHONE 925 849-5324
Tim Pessin, *Principal*
Dean Balough, *Officer*
Kathryn Balough, *Admin Sec*
Jaime Gerardo, *Project Mgr*
EMP: 80 **EST:** 2007
SQ FT: 5,000
SALES (est): 22.8MM **Privately Held**
WEB: www.etech-inc.net
SIC: 1623 1731 Telephone & communication line construction; electrical work

(P-1101)
FLOYD JOHNSTON CNSTR CO INC
2301 Herndon Ave, Clovis (93611-8911)
PHONE 559 299-7373
Evelyn Johnston, *Vice Pres*
Steve Little, *Executive*
Suzi Prince, *Admin Asst*
EMP: 75 **EST:** 1969
SQ FT: 6,000
SALES (est): 15.8MM **Privately Held**
SIC: 1623 Water main construction; sewer line construction; pipeline construction

(P-1102)
GD NIELSON CONSTRUCTION INC
147 Camino Oruga, NAPA (94558-6215)
PHONE 707 253-8774
Diann Nielson, *President*
George S Nielson, *Corp Secy*
George Nielson, *Vice Pres*
Sean Larochelle, *Project Engr*
EMP: 60
SALES (est): 14.8MM **Privately Held**
WEB: www.nielsoninc.com
SIC: 1623 1629 1799 Sewer line construction; drainage system construction; boring for building construction

(P-1103)
GOLDEN STATE UTILITY CO
5275 Central Ave, Fremont (94536-6532)
PHONE 408 982-5420
Richard Santos, *Manager*
EMP: 43
SALES (corp-wide): 3.2B **Publicly Held**
WEB: www.gsuc.net
SIC: 1623 Underground utilities contractor
HQ: Golden State Utility Co.
16701 Se Mcgllvry Blvd
Vancouver WA 98683
209 579-3400

(P-1104)
GOLDEN STATE UTILITY CO
8766 Fruitridge Rd, Sacramento (95826-9740)
PHONE 916 387-6255
Mark Bohrer, *Manager*
EMP: 43
SALES (corp-wide): 3.2B **Publicly Held**
WEB: www.gsuc.net
SIC: 1623 Underground utilities contractor
HQ: Golden State Utility Co.
16701 Se Mcgllvry Blvd
Vancouver WA 98683
209 579-3400

(P-1105)
GOLDEN STATE UTILITY CO
10600 E Mountain View Ave, Selma (93662-9476)
PHONE 559 896-6690
Jason Snead, *Principal*
EMP: 43
SALES (corp-wide): 3.2B **Publicly Held**
WEB: www.gsuc.net
SIC: 1623 Telephone & communication line construction
HQ: Golden State Utility Co.
16701 Se Mcgllvry Blvd
Vancouver WA 98683
209 579-3400

(P-1106)
GSE CONSTRUCTION COMPANY INC (PA)
7633 Suthfront Rd Ste 160, Livermore (94551)
PHONE 925 447-0292
Dennis Gutierrez, *CEO*
Steve Mazza, *Vice Pres*
Sue Gutierrez, *Admin Sec*
Cynthia Gutierrez, *Marketing Staff*
Iris Sosa, *Accounts Mgr*
EMP: 138 **EST:** 1980
SQ FT: 23,400
SALES (est): 69MM **Privately Held**
WEB: www.gseconstruction.com
SIC: 1623 1542 Water & sewer line construction; pipe laying construction; pipeline construction; nonresidential construction

(P-1107)
HOWK WELL & EQUIPMENT CO INC
Also Called: Howk Systems
1825 Yosemite Blvd, Modesto (95354-2998)
PHONE 209 529-4110
Thomas R Weimer, *President*
EMP: 32 **EST:** 1985
SQ FT: 15,000
SALES (est): 7.3MM **Privately Held**
WEB: www.howksystems.com
SIC: 5999 1623 7699 5051 Farm equipment & supplies; pumping station construction; pumps & pumping equipment repair; pipe & tubing, steel; machine shop, jobbing & repair; water well drilling

(P-1108)
J & M INC
6700 National Dr, Livermore (94550-8804)
PHONE 925 724-0300
Manuel Marques III, *CEO*
John Cooper, *Opers Mgr*
EMP: 50 **EST:** 1958
SQ FT: 2,000
SALES (est): 13.7MM **Privately Held**
WEB: www.jminc.com
SIC: 1623 1629 Underground utilities contractor; drainage system construction

(P-1109)
J FLORES CONSTRUCTION CO INC
4229 Mission St, San Francisco (94112-1519)
PHONE 415 337-2934
Jesus Flores, *President*
J Brian Gleghorn, *Vice Pres*
EMP: 45 **EST:** 1995
SQ FT: 1,300
SALES (est): 5.8MM **Privately Held**
SIC: 1623 Pipe laying construction

(P-1110)
JERRYS TRENCHING SERVICE INC
3096 W Belmont Ave # 106, Fresno (93722-5960)
PHONE 559 275-1520
Jerry E Berlin Jr, *CEO*
Erin C Berlin, *CFO*
Erin Berlin, *CFO*
Don Simpson, *Technician*
Adam Buddell, *Project Mgr*
EMP: 46 **EST:** 2007
SQ FT: 10,000
SALES (est): 4.2MM **Privately Held**
WEB: www.jerrystrenching.com
SIC: 1623 1794 Underground utilities contractor; excavation & grading, building construction

(P-1111)
K J WOODS CONSTRUCTION INC
1485 Bay Shore Blvd # 149, San Francisco (94124-4001)
P.O. Box 947, South San Francisco (94083-0947)
PHONE 415 759-0506
Kieran Woods, *Principal*
EMP: 35 **EST:** 1994
SQ FT: 2,000
SALES (est): 29.1MM **Privately Held**
WEB: www.kjwoods.com
SIC: 1623 Underground utilities contractor

(P-1112)
K W EMERSON INC
413 W Saint Charles St, San Andreas (95249-9618)
P.O. Box 549 (95249-0549)
PHONE 209 754-3839
E Jean Emerson, *President*
Spencer Curran, *Officer*
Rusti Emerson, *Officer*
Dan Emerson, *Vice Pres*
Levi Emerson, *Foreman/Supr*
EMP: 44 **EST:** 1961
SQ FT: 2,550
SALES (est): 21MM **Privately Held**
WEB: www.kwemerson.com
SIC: 1623 1794 Underground utilities contractor; excavation & grading, building construction

(P-1113)
LASAR UNDERGROUND CNSTR INC
2929 N Burl Ave, Fresno (93727-0832)
PHONE 559 291-1024
Lorene Griswold, *President*
Dennis Gregory, *Vice Pres*
EMP: 43 **EST:** 1993
SALES (est): 7.8MM **Privately Held**
WEB: www.lasarunderground.com
SIC: 1623 Water, sewer & utility lines

(P-1114)
LINKUS ENTERPRISES LLC
Also Called: Honeywell Authorized Dealer
5595 W San Madele Ave, Fresno (93722-5068)
PHONE 559 256-6600
Horacio Guzman, *CEO*
Flavio Hernandez, *Technician*
Devin Hutchins, *Technician*
Gabriel Stovall, *Technician*
Montanna Mumma, *Marketing Staff*
EMP: 103 **Privately Held**
WEB: www.linkuscorp.com
SIC: 1623 Telephone & communication line construction
PA: Linkus Enterprises. Llc
18631 Lloyd Ln
Anderson CA 96007

(P-1115)
LINKUS ENTERPRISES LLC (PA)
Also Called: Honeywell Authorized Dealer
18631 Lloyd Ln, Anderson (96007-8459)
PHONE 530 229-9197
Horacio Guzman, *CEO*
John Daily, *COO*
Dant Morris, *Vice Pres*
Roger Fitzpatrick, *Technician*
Jon Warren, *VP Finance*
EMP: 524 **EST:** 2000
SQ FT: 3,200
SALES (est): 84.7MM **Privately Held**
WEB: www.linkuscorp.com
SIC: 1623 5731 4813 Telephone & communication line construction; antennas, satellite dish;

(P-1116)
M CONSTRUCTION & DESIGN INC
43126 Osgood Rd, Fremont (94539-5608)
PHONE 510 651-6981
Mark Martinez, *President*
EMP: 39 **EST:** 2002
SQ FT: 2,000
SALES (est): 5.4MM **Privately Held**
SIC: 1623 Electric power line construction

(P-1117)
MANUEL BROS INC
Also Called: Renaissance Construction
908 Taylorville Rd # 104, Grass Valley (95949-9632)
P.O. Box 995 (95945-0995)
PHONE 530 272-4213
Gary Smith, *President*
Robert Moen, *Corp Secy*
Mark Dykes, *Division Mgr*
Joseph Meidl, *Division Mgr*
Chowana Stumps, *Human Resources*
EMP: 83 **EST:** 1974
SQ FT: 3,000
SALES (est): 5.9MM
SALES (corp-wide): 11.2B **Publicly Held**
WEB: www.manuelbros.com
SIC: 1623 Telephone & communication line construction
PA: Quanta Services, Inc.
2800 Post Oak Blvd # 2600
Houston TX 77056
713 629-7600

(P-1118)
MCELVANY INC
13343 Johnson Rd, Los Banos (93635-9704)
PHONE 209 826-1102
Charles McElvany, *President*
Holli McElvany, *Treasurer*
Isaac McElvany, *Vice Pres*
Helen McElvany, *Principal*
EMP: 52 **EST:** 1950
SQ FT: 1,200
SALES (est): 12.2MM **Privately Held**
SIC: 1623 1629 Sewer line construction; land preparation construction

(P-1119)
MCGUIRE AND HESTER (PA)
2810 Harbor Bay Pkwy, Alameda (94502-3040)
PHONE 510 632-7676
Michael R Hester, *President*
Bruce Daseking, *Treasurer*
Robert Doud, *Exec VP*
David Koerber, *Vice Pres*
Andy Vasconi, *Vice Pres*
EMP: 290 **EST:** 1926
SQ FT: 22,000
SALES (est): 41.3K **Privately Held**
WEB: www.mcguireandhester.com
SIC: 1623 7353 1611 0782 Underground utilities contractor; heavy construction equipment rental; general contractor, highway & street construction; garden planting services

(P-1120)
MOUNTAIN CASCADE INC (PA)
555 Exchange Ct, Livermore (94550-2400)
P.O. Box 5050 (94551-5050)
PHONE 925 373-8370
Michael L Fuller, *CEO*
Michael Duke Fuller, *President*
Schelly Frades, *Treasurer*
David Hicks, *Vice Pres*
Roger Williamson, *Vice Pres*
EMP: 40 **EST:** 1982
SQ FT: 15,000
SALES (est): 116.7MM **Privately Held**
WEB: www.mountaincascade.com
SIC: 1623 Pipeline construction; water & sewer line construction

(P-1121)
MP NEXLEVEL CALIFORNIA INC
266 Industrial Rd Ste B, San Carlos (94070-6236)
PHONE 650 486-1359
Robbi Pribyl, *President*
EMP: 54 **EST:** 2007

PRODUCTS & SERVICES SECTION
1623 - Water, Sewer & Utility Line Construction County (P-1144)

SALES (est): 10.6MM
SALES (corp-wide): 3.5B **Publicly Held**
WEB: www.mpnexlevel.com
SIC: **1623** Gas main construction
HQ: Mp Nexlevel, Llc
500 County Road 37
Maple Lake MN 55358
320 963-2400

(P-1122)
MYERS & SONS CONSTRUCTION LLC
4600 Northgate Blvd # 10, Sacramento (95834-1103)
PHONE.................................916 283-9950
Clinton C Myers, *Principal*
Marlena Stockton, *Principal*
Jenna Carlson, *Info Tech Dir*
Brandon Beals, *Project Engr*
Bryan Decker, *Project Engr*
EMP: 149 EST: 2017
SALES (est): 154.7MM **Publicly Held**
WEB: www.myers-sons.com
SIC: **1623** 1622 Water, sewer & utility lines; bridge, tunnel & elevated highway
PA: Sterling Construction Company, Inc.
1800 Hughes Landing Blvd # 250
The Woodlands TX 77380

(P-1123)
N & T DIGMORE INC
1525 Tahoe Ct, Redding (96003-1429)
PHONE.................................530 241-2992
Thomas L Taylor, *President*
Joseph J Nadeker, *Corp Secy*
EMP: 51 EST: 1987
SQ FT: 1,500
SALES (est): 10.3MM **Privately Held**
WEB: www.ntdigmore.com
SIC: **1623** 1794 Underground utilities contractor; excavation work

(P-1124)
NEO POWER TECHNOLOGY INC
2330 W Covell Blvd, Davis (95616-5658)
PHONE.................................415 830-6167
Paul C Jonason, *Ch of Bd*
EMP: 65 EST: 2020
SALES (est): 2.9MM **Privately Held**
WEB: www.neopowertech.net
SIC: **1623** Electric power line construction

(P-1125)
NOR-CAL PIPELINE SERVICES
983 Reserve Dr, Roseville (95678-1340)
PHONE.................................916 442-5400
David Jaeger, *President*
David L Jaeger, *Vice Pres*
Max Page, *Area Mgr*
William Jaeger, *Admin Sec*
Manny Badyal, *Project Mgr*
EMP: 70 EST: 2009
SALES (est): 25.4MM **Privately Held**
WEB: www.norcalpipe.com
SIC: **1623** Pipeline construction

(P-1126)
NOVA GROUP INC (HQ)
185 Devlin Rd, NAPA (94558-6255)
P.O. Box 4050 (94558-0450)
PHONE.................................707 265-1100
Ronald M Fedrick, *Ch of Bd*
Scott R Victor, *President*
Scott Victor, *COO*
Carole Bionda, *Vice Pres*
Walter Birdsall, *Vice Pres*
◆ EMP: 189 EST: 1957
SQ FT: 15,000
SALES: 2.9MM
SALES (corp-wide): 11.2B **Publicly Held**
WEB: www.novagrp.com
SIC: **1623** Underground utilities contractor
PA: Quanta Services, Inc.
2800 Post Oak Blvd # 2600
Houston TX 77056
713 629-7600

(P-1127)
NOVA-CPF INC
7411 Napa Vallejo Hwy, NAPA (94558-7501)
P.O. Box 4050 (94558-0450)
PHONE.................................707 257-3200
Charles Fedrick, *President*
Elbert C Lewey, *Treasurer*
David W Fedrick, *Vice Pres*
Dee Fedrick, *Vice Pres*
Ronald Fredrick, *Principal*
EMP: 56 EST: 1992
SQ FT: 11,000
SALES (est): 2.3MM **Privately Held**
SIC: **1623** Underground utilities contractor

(P-1128)
NOVA/TIC GVRNMENT PRJCTS A JIN
185 Devlin Rd, NAPA (94558-6255)
P.O. Box 4050 (94558-0450)
PHONE.................................707 257-3200
Ronald M Fedrick, *President*
Scott R Victor, *President*
Carole L Bionda, *Vice Pres*
Walter M Birdsall, *Vice Pres*
Chris Mathies, *Vice Pres*
◆ EMP: 150 EST: 1999
SQ FT: 15,000
SALES (est): 15.2MM **Privately Held**
WEB: www.novagrp.com
SIC: **1623** Water, sewer & utility lines

(P-1129)
OUTBACK CONSTRUCTION INC
13660 State Highway 36 E, Red Bluff (96080-7849)
P.O. Box 1035 (96080-1035)
PHONE.................................530 528-2225
Mattie Bunting, *President*
EMP: 36 EST: 1999
SALES (est): 6.5MM **Privately Held**
WEB: www.outback-inc.com
SIC: **1623** Underground utilities contractor

(P-1130)
PACIFIC BORING INCORPORATED
1985 W Mountain View Ave, Caruthers (93609-9701)
P.O. Box 727 (93609-0727)
PHONE.................................559 864-9444
David Cline, *President*
James Gardner, *Vice Pres*
Calastro Terrasas, *Admin Sec*
Brad Gardner, *Foreman/Supr*
EMP: 50 EST: 1982
SQ FT: 750
SALES (est): 11.7MM **Privately Held**
WEB: www.pacificboring.com
SIC: **1623** Underground utilities contractor

(P-1131)
PRESTON PIPELINES INC (PA)
133 Bothelo Ave, Milpitas (95035-5325)
PHONE.................................408 262-1418
Michael D Preston, *President*
Ron Bianchini, *COO*
Dave Heslop, *Vice Pres*
David Heslop, *Vice Pres*
Rich Lewis, *Vice Pres*
EMP: 150 EST: 1970
SQ FT: 12,000
SALES (est): 110.7MM **Privately Held**
WEB: www.prestonco.com
SIC: **1623** Pipeline construction

(P-1132)
QUALITY TELECOM CONS INC (PA)
Also Called: Quality Techniques Engrg Cnstr
3740 Cincinnati Ave, Rocklin (95765-1204)
P.O. Box 807, Loomis (95650-0807)
PHONE.................................916 315-0500
Scott Duncan, *President*
Candice Northam, *Treasurer*
Jacob Duncan, *Vice Pres*
Osh Duncan, *Admin Sec*
Adam Lieb, *Project Mgr*
EMP: 89 EST: 2001
SALES (est): 18.4MM **Privately Held**
WEB: www.qualitytelecominc.com
SIC: **1623** 1731 4899 8748 Communication line & transmission tower construction; communications specialization; communication signal enhancement network system; telecommunications consultant

(P-1133)
RANGER PIPELINES INCORPORATED
1790 Yosemite Ave, San Francisco (94124-2622)
P.O. Box 24109 (94124-0109)
PHONE.................................415 822-3700
Thomas Hunt, *President*
Mary Shea-Hunt, *Corp Secy*
Peter Cuddihy, *Vice Pres*
Caroline Galle, *Administration*
Stephen McLaughlin, *Project Engr*
EMP: 101
SQ FT: 20,000
SALES (est): 35.8MM **Privately Held**
WEB: www.rangerpipelines.com
SIC: **1623** Pipeline construction

(P-1134)
SANCO PIPELINES INCORPORATED
727 University Ave, Los Gatos (95032-7610)
PHONE.................................408 377-2793
David R Schrader, *Principal*
Jim Sullivan, *Project Mgr*
EMP: 50 EST: 1956
SQ FT: 3,000
SALES (est): 21.3MM **Privately Held**
WEB: www.sancopipelines.com
SIC: **1623** Pipeline construction

(P-1135)
SOLCOM INC
Also Called: Solcom Communications Inc
24801 Huntwood Ave, Hayward (94544-1813)
PHONE.................................510 940-2490
Tony McMenamin, *President*
EMP: 500 EST: 2002
SALES (est): 50MM **Privately Held**
WEB: www.solcom.us
SIC: **1623** Telephone & communication line construction

(P-1136)
TALUS CONSTRUCTION INC
311 Oak St Apt 114, Oakland (94607-4602)
P.O. Box 208, Lathrop (95330-0208)
PHONE.................................925 406-4756
Sharon Alberts, *CEO*
Steve Alberts, *President*
EMP: 40 EST: 1987
SALES (est): 7.3MM **Privately Held**
WEB: www.talusconstruction.com
SIC: **1623** Underground utilities contractor; pipeline construction

(P-1137)
TDW CONSTRUCTION INC
101 Greenville Rd, Livermore (94551-5803)
P.O. Box 111 (94551-0111)
PHONE.................................925 455-5259
Edmundo M Alire, *President*
EMP: 49 EST: 1986
SQ FT: 1,200
SALES (est): 2.6MM **Privately Held**
WEB: www.tdwconstruction.com
SIC: **1623** Sewer line construction; water main construction

(P-1138)
TORO ENGINEERING INC
651 M St, Rio Linda (95673-2237)
P.O. Box 336 (95673-0336)
PHONE.................................916 238-4535
Eligio Toledo, *President*
Dan Risse, *Corp Secy*
Greg Risse, *Vice Pres*
Graham Finley, *General Mgr*
Laura Waterbury, *Office Mgr*
EMP: 35 EST: 2001
SALES (est): 3.7MM **Privately Held**
WEB: www.toroengineeringinc.com
SIC: **1623** Underground utilities contractor

(P-1139)
TRITON TOWER INC (PA)
3200 Jefferson Blvd, West Sacramento (95691-5418)
PHONE.................................916 375-8546
Kevin Wingard, *President*
Mike Monroe, *Treasurer*
Rex Avakian, *Admin Sec*
EMP: 54 EST: 2001
SALES (est): 11.1MM **Privately Held**
WEB: www.tritontower.com
SIC: **1623** Transmitting tower (telecommunication) construction

(P-1140)
VULCAN CNSTR & MAINT INC
1010 W Whites Bridge Ave, Fresno (93706-1328)
PHONE.................................559 443-1607
Robert Flores Jr, *CEO*
Cordelia Aldes, *Admin Sec*
Fred Dunigan, *Project Mgr*
EMP: 40 EST: 1981
SQ FT: 5,000
SALES (est): 7.3MM **Privately Held**
WEB: www.vulcan-construction.com
SIC: **1623** 7699 Pipeline construction; industrial equipment services; valve repair, industrial

(P-1141)
W M LYLES CO (HQ)
525 W Alluvial Ave, Fresno (93711-5521)
P.O. Box 28130 (93729-8130)
PHONE.................................559 441-1900
Stanley Simmons, *President*
David Dawson, *President*
Dave Dawson, *Vice Pres*
Grant Gourley, *Vice Pres*
Ken Strosnider, *Vice Pres*
EMP: 299 EST: 1945
SQ FT: 6,200
SALES (est): 190.6MM
SALES (corp-wide): 17.8MM **Privately Held**
WEB: www.wmlylesco.com
SIC: **1623** Pipeline construction; underground utilities contractor
PA: Lyles Diversified, Inc.
525 W Alluvial Ave
Fresno CA 93711
559 441-1900

(P-1142)
WEST VALLEY CNSTR CO INC (PA)
580 E Mcglincy Ln, Campbell (95008-4999)
PHONE.................................408 371-5510
Kevin Kelly, *CEO*
David Barnes, *CFO*
Jeff Azevedo, *Vice Pres*
Jeff Boss, *Vice Pres*
Jimm Vosburgh, *Vice Pres*
EMP: 150 EST: 1958
SQ FT: 9,000
SALES (est): 73.4MM **Privately Held**
WEB: www.westvalleyconstruction.com
SIC: **1623** Water main construction

(P-1143)
WEST VALLEY CNSTR CO INC
Also Called: West Valley Cnstr - Stockton
2655 E Miner Ave Ste A, Stockton (95205-4762)
PHONE.................................209 943-6812
EMP: 47
SALES (corp-wide): 73.4MM **Privately Held**
WEB: www.westvalleyconstruction.com
SIC: **1623** Telephone & communication line construction; water main construction
PA: West Valley Construction Company, Inc.
580 E Mcglincy Ln
Campbell CA 95008
408 371-5510

(P-1144)
WEST VALLEY CNSTR CO INC
809 Hurlingame Ave, Redwood City (94063-3519)
PHONE.................................650 364-9464
Mike Kelly, *Manager*
Darren Phelps, *President*
Michael Cadei, *Bd of Directors*
Darin Preisendorf, *Division Mgr*
Mike Renn, *Division Mgr*
EMP: 47
SALES (corp-wide): 73.4MM **Privately Held**
WEB: www.westvalleyconstruction.com
SIC: **1623** Water & sewer line construction

1629 - Heavy Construction, NEC County (P-1145)

PA: West Valley Construction Company, Inc.
580 E Mcglincy Ln
Campbell CA 95008
408 371-5510

1629 Heavy Construction, NEC

(P-1145)
AMERICAN CIVIL CONSTRS LLC
3701 Mallard Dr, Benicia (94510-1246)
PHONE.................707 746-8028
Pete Wells, *Manager*
Doug Silverwood, *Project Mgr*
EMP: 77
SALES (corp-wide): 1.7B **Publicly Held**
SIC: 1629 0783 0181 Land preparation construction; earthmoving contractor; golf course construction; dam construction; spraying services, ornamental bush; removal services, bush & tree; sod farms
HQ: American Civil Constructors Llc
4901 S Windermere St
Littleton CO 80120
303 795-2582

(P-1146)
ANDERSON PCF ENGRG CNSTR INC
1370 Norman Ave, Santa Clara (95054-2056)
PHONE.................408 970-9900
Peter E Anderson, *CEO*
Matthew Mirenda, *Vice Pres*
Ann Anderson, *Admin Sec*
Angela Schellenberg, *Project Engr*
Steve Haslam, *Manager*
EMP: 100 **EST:** 1966
SQ FT: 3,000
SALES (est): 39.8MM **Privately Held**
WEB: www.andpac.com
SIC: 1629 1623 Dams, waterways, docks & other marine construction; pumping station construction; underground utilities contractor

(P-1147)
AQUATIC ENVIRONMENTS INC
Also Called: Solitude Lake Management
345 Industrial Way, Benicia (94510-1119)
PHONE.................925 521-0400
Lance Dohman, *President*
Jose Botello, *Opers Mgr*
Benjamin Chen, *Manager*
EMP: 48 **EST:** 1998
SALES (est): 11.2MM **Privately Held**
WEB: www.solitudelakemanagement.com
SIC: 1629 Pond construction

(P-1148)
AUBURN CONSTRUCTORS LLC
730 W Stadium Ln, Sacramento (95834-1130)
PHONE.................916 924-0344
Dean Bailey, *President*
Bill Franceschini, *Treasurer*
Kevin Couper, *Vice Pres*
Barry Evans, *Division Mgr*
Karen Aziz, *Office Mgr*
EMP: 80
SQ FT: 5,500
SALES: 48.8MM **Privately Held**
WEB: www.auburnconstructors.com
SIC: 1629 Industrial plant construction; waste water & sewage treatment plant construction

(P-1149)
BARNARD BESSAC JOINT VENTURE
395 Shoreway Rd, Redwood City (94065-1601)
PHONE.................650 212-8957
EMP: 100 **EST:** 2018
SALES (est): 4.4MM **Privately Held**
SIC: 1629 Industrial plant construction

(P-1150)
BELLINGHAM MARINE INDS INC
8810 Sparling Ln, Dixon (95620-9605)
PHONE.................707 678-2385
James R Puder, *General Mgr*
Mark Secrest, *Project Mgr*
Craig Funston, *Manager*
Rob Rasmussen, *Manager*
Jay Varga, *Manager*
EMP: 45
SALES (corp-wide): 70.1MM **Privately Held**
WEB: www.bellingham-marine.com
SIC: 1629 3272 Marine construction; dock construction; concrete products, precast
HQ: Bellingham Marine Industries, Inc.
1323 Lincoln St Ste 101
Bellingham WA 98229
360 676-2800

(P-1151)
BRIGHTVIEW LANDSCAPE DEV INC
7039 Commerce Cir Ste A, Pleasanton (94588-8006)
PHONE.................925 463-0700
Jeffrey A Colton, *Branch Mgr*
Tammy Alameda, *Vice Pres*
Cindy V Oudheusden, *Office Mgr*
EMP: 90
SQ FT: 8,400
SALES (corp-wide): 2.3B **Publicly Held**
WEB: www.brightview.com
SIC: 1629 Irrigation system construction; land preparation construction
HQ: Brightview Landscape Development, Inc.
27001 Agoura Rd Ste 350
Calabasas CA 91301
818 223-8500

(P-1152)
CAL VALLEY CONSTRUCTION INC
Also Called: National Dispatching
5125 N Gates Ave Ste 102, Fresno (93722-6414)
PHONE.................559 274-0300
Michelle Avila, *President*
John G Avila, *Vice Pres*
Tony Storelli, *Admin Sec*
Lewis Schulze, *Manager*
Luis Garcia, *Superintendent*
EMP: 35 **EST:** 1988
SQ FT: 5,000
SALES (est): 17.4MM **Privately Held**
WEB: www.calvalleyconstruction.com
SIC: 1629 1611 Earthmoving contractor; grading

(P-1153)
CALIFORNIA ROCK CRUSHERS
Also Called: Cal Crush
339 Doak Blvd, Ripon (95366-2659)
P.O. Box 775 (95366-0775)
PHONE.................209 599-9941
Robert C Evans, *President*
Brian Evans, *Vice Pres*
Cheryl Evans, *Admin Sec*
▲ **EMP:** 35 **EST:** 2000
SQ FT: 1,200
SALES (est): 15MM **Privately Held**
WEB: www.calcrush.com
SIC: 1629 Rock removal

(P-1154)
DELTA GRINDING COMPANY INC
5131 Lone Tree Way, Antioch (94531-8484)
P.O. Box 2297 (94531-2297)
PHONE.................925 778-3939
Kenneth J Ferrante, *President*
EMP: 42 **EST:** 1987
SALES (est): 7MM **Privately Held**
WEB: www.deltagrinding.com
SIC: 1629 Trenching contractor

(P-1155)
DHR CONSTRUCTION INC
860 Green Island Rd, American Canyon (94503-9657)
PHONE.................707 552-6500
Daniel H Ramos, *President*
Joy Ramos, *Vice Pres*
▲ **EMP:** 40 **EST:** 1987
SQ FT: 1,600
SALES (est): 10.3MM **Privately Held**
WEB: www.dhrconstruction.com
SIC: 1629 Golf course construction

(P-1156)
DILLINGHAM CONSTRUCTION NA
1020 Serpentine Ln # 110, Pleasanton (94566-4758)
P.O. Box 1089 (94566-1089)
PHONE.................925 249-8850
John Capener, *President*
Dennis Haist, *Vice Pres*
Robert Schwab, *Vice Pres*
Jo Thielen, *Marketing Staff*
Lenore Thielen, *Manager*
EMP: 1677 **EST:** 1987
SQ FT: 70,000
SALES (est): 39.4MM **Privately Held**
SIC: 1629 1622 1542 1522 Waste water & sewage treatment plant construction; tunnel construction; commercial & office building, new construction; hotel/motel, new construction

(P-1157)
DUTRA CONSTRUCTION CO INC (HQ)
2350 Kerner Blvd Ste 200, San Rafael (94901-5595)
PHONE.................415 258-6876
Bill T Dutra, *President*
Cindy Zentner, *Administration*
EMP: 68 **EST:** 1994
SALES (est): 5.7MM
SALES (corp-wide): 191.6MM **Privately Held**
WEB: www.dutragroup.com
SIC: 1629 Marine construction
PA: The Dutra Group
2350 Kerner Blvd Ste 200
San Rafael CA 94901
415 258-6876

(P-1158)
DUTRA DREDGING COMPANY (HQ)
2350 Kerner Blvd Ste 200, San Rafael (94901-5595)
PHONE.................415 721-2131
Bill T Dutra, *CEO*
EMP: 60 **EST:** 1904
SQ FT: 2,000
SALES (est): 36.5MM
SALES (corp-wide): 191.6MM **Privately Held**
WEB: www.dutragroup.com
SIC: 1629 Marine construction
PA: The Dutra Group
2350 Kerner Blvd Ste 200
San Rafael CA 94901
415 258-6876

(P-1159)
DUTRA DREDGING COMPANY
615 River Rd, Rio Vista (94571-1217)
P.O. Box 338 (94571-0338)
PHONE.................707 374-5127
Steve Lee, *Manager*
EMP: 40
SALES (corp-wide): 191.6MM **Privately Held**
WEB: www.dutragroup.com
SIC: 1629 Dredging contractor; marine construction
HQ: Dutra Dredging Company
2350 Kerner Blvd Ste 200
San Rafael CA 94901
415 721-2131

(P-1160)
DUTRA GROUP (PA)
2350 Kerner Blvd Ste 200, San Rafael (94901-5595)
PHONE.................415 258-6876
Bill T Dutra, *CEO*
Harry Stewart, *COO*
James Hagood, *CFO*
Sheryl Dutra, *Officer*
JC Krause, *Division Mgr*
▲ **EMP:** 100 **EST:** 1973
SQ FT: 22,000
SALES (est): 191.6MM **Privately Held**
WEB: www.dutragroup.com
SIC: 1629 8711 1429 Marine construction; dredging contractor; earthmoving contractor; civil engineering; igneous rock, crushed & broken-quarrying

(P-1161)
FLAKE R RECYCLING
1710 W Pine Ave, Fresno (93728-1215)
PHONE.................559 233-9361
Rick Flake, *President*
Ron Flake, *Vice Pres*
EMP: 37 **EST:** 1953
SQ FT: 5,000
SALES (est): 1MM **Privately Held**
SIC: 1629 Land clearing contractor

(P-1162)
FORD CONSTRUCTION COMPANY INC
300 W Pine St, Lodi (95240-2022)
PHONE.................209 333-1116
Richard Piombo, *Treasurer*
Nicholas B Jones, *President*
Nicholas Jones, *Vice Pres*
Nick Jones, *Executive*
Jim Murray, *Info Tech Mgr*
EMP: 100 **EST:** 1979
SQ FT: 8,500
SALES (est): 24MM **Privately Held**
WEB: www.ford-construction.com
SIC: 1629 1623 Dam construction; earthmoving contractor; water & sewer line construction

(P-1163)
FOUNDATION CONSTRUCTORS INC (PA)
81 Big Break Rd, Oakley (94561-3081)
P.O. Box 97 (94561-0097)
PHONE.................925 754-6633
Derek Halecky, *President*
Pete Brandl, *President*
Nikki Sjoblom, *CFO*
Dermot Fallon, *Exec VP*
Don Hilton, *Vice Pres*
▲ **EMP:** 100 **EST:** 1971
SQ FT: 6,000
SALES (est): 55.4MM **Privately Held**
WEB: www.foundationpiledriving.com
SIC: 1629 Marine construction

(P-1164)
GHILOTTI CONSTRUCTION CO INC (PA)
Also Called: Gcc
246 Ghilotti Ave, Santa Rosa (95407-8152)
PHONE.................707 585-1221
Richard W Ghilotti, *CEO*
Matthew McDonald, *Project Mgr*
Frank Raya, *Project Engr*
Gregory Allen, *Manager*
Skyler Shearer, *Manager*
EMP: 263 **EST:** 1992
SQ FT: 9,000
SALES (est): 105.4MM **Privately Held**
WEB: www.ghilotti.com
SIC: 1629 Land preparation construction

(P-1165)
HAROLD SMITH & SON INC
800 Crane Ave, Saint Helena (94574)
PHONE.................707 963-7977
Pam Raybould, *President*
Irene Varozza, *Vice Pres*
Bob Abbott, *Sales Staff*
Tom Johnston, *Superintendent*
EMP: 25 **EST:** 1917
SQ FT: 800
SALES (est): 6.1MM **Privately Held**
WEB: www.hsandson.com
SIC: 1629 3273 1611 4212 Earthmoving contractor; irrigation system construction; ready-mixed concrete; highway & street paving contractor; dump truck haulage

(P-1166)
HAT CREEK CNSTR & MTLS INC (PA)
24339 State Highway 89, Burney (96013-9615)
PHONE.................530 335-5501
Robert Thompson, *President*
Perry Thompson, *Treasurer*
Weston Hutchings, *Vice Pres*
Howard A Lakey Jr, *Vice Pres*
Denise Williams, *Administration*
EMP: 50

PRODUCTS & SERVICES SECTION
1711 - Plumbing, Heating & Air Conditioning Contractors County (P-1189)

SALES (est): 17.3MM **Privately Held**
WEB: www.hatcreekconstruction.com
SIC: 1629 1771 1521 5032 Earthmoving contractor; concrete work; single-family housing construction; sand, construction; gravel; highway & street construction

(P-1167)
MANSON CONSTRUCTION CO
1401 Marina Way S F, Richmond (94804-3723)
PHONE 510 232-6319
Charlie Gibson, *Vice Pres*
Karissa Poitras, *Executive Asst*
Jeremy Cook, *Project Mgr*
Paul Horvath, *Project Mgr*
Bryan Haynes, *Project Engr*
EMP: 70
SQ FT: 1,500
SALES (corp-wide): 391.8MM **Privately Held**
WEB: www.mansonconstruction.com
SIC: 1629 Marine construction
HQ: Manson Construction Co.
5209 E Marginal Way S
Seattle WA 98134
206 762-0850

(P-1168)
MONTEREY MECHANICAL CO (PA)
Also Called: Contra Costa Metal Fabricators
8275 San Leandro St, Oakland (94621-1972)
PHONE 510 632-3173
Milton C Burleson, *CEO*
Jim Troup, *President*
Paul Moreira, *CFO*
Paul R Moreira, *CFO*
Vy Nguyen, *Executive*
▲ **EMP:** 50 **EST:** 1942
SQ FT: 40,000
SALES (est): 37.7MM **Privately Held**
WEB: www.montmech.com
SIC: 1629 1711 1761 3444 Waste disposal plant construction; waste water & sewage treatment plant construction; mechanical contractor; boiler setting contractor; boiler maintenance contractor; sheet metalwork; sheet metalwork; fabricated structural metal; nonresidential construction

(P-1169)
NATURNER MONT WIND ENRGY 2 LLC
394 Pacific Ave Ste 300, San Francisco (94111-1718)
PHONE 415 217-5508
EMP: 40 **EST:** 2010
SALES (est): 3.2MM **Privately Held**
SIC: 1629 Heavy Construction

(P-1170)
NEILS CONTROLLED BLASTING LP
490 Main St, Newcastle (95658-9358)
P.O. Box 749 (95658-0749)
PHONE 916 663-2500
Donald Belden, *Managing Prtnr*
EMP: 38 **EST:** 1982
SQ FT: 1,000
SALES (est): 9.1MM **Privately Held**
WEB: www.neils-controlled-blasting-lp-in-newcastle-ca.cityfos.com
SIC: 1629 Blasting contractor, except building demolition

(P-1171)
NORDIC INDUSTRIES INC
1437 Furneaux Rd, Olivehurst (95961-7404)
PHONE 530 742-7124
Jens Karlshoej, *President*
Inge Karlshoej, *Corp Secy*
Francisco Martins, *Principal*
Dale Martin, *Controller*
Brian Bushnell, *Superintendent*
EMP: 74 **EST:** 1990
SQ FT: 5,000
SALES (est): 30.3MM **Privately Held**
WEB: www.nordicind.com
SIC: 1629 4212 4213 Dam construction; levee construction; local trucking, without storage; trucking, except local

(P-1172)
NTK CONSTRUCTION INC
501 Cesar Chavez Ste 115, San Francisco (94124-1243)
PHONE 415 643-1900
Tin Tran, *CEO*
Martin Imahori, *CFO*
Sammy Kwok, *Vice Pres*
EMP: 45 **EST:** 2004
SQ FT: 1,500
SALES (est): 20.8MM **Privately Held**
WEB: www.ntkconstruction.com
SIC: 1629 1623 Railroad & subway construction; waste water & sewage treatment plant construction; water & sewer line construction; pumping station construction

(P-1173)
PATRICKS CONSTRUCTION CLEAN-UP
7851 14th Ave, Sacramento (95826-4301)
PHONE 916 452-5495
Patricio Mercado, *Owner*
Susan Mercado, *Vice Pres*
EMP: 100 **EST:** 2000
SALES (est): 9.6MM **Privately Held**
WEB: www.pccuinc.com
SIC: 1629 Land clearing contractor

(P-1174)
RE LA MESA LLC
300 California St Fl 8, San Francisco (94104-1416)
PHONE 415 675-1500
EMP: 100
SALES (est): 2.7MM **Privately Held**
SIC: 1629 Heavy Construction, Nec, Nsk

(P-1175)
SAVIANO COMPANY INC
1784 Smith Ave, San Jose (95112-4122)
PHONE 650 948-3274
John P Saviano, *President*
Monique Saviano, *Vice Pres*
Eric Hodges, *Project Mgr*
Anthony Saviano, *Project Mgr*
EMP: 40 **EST:** 1963
SQ FT: 1,500
SALES (est): 8.3MM **Privately Held**
WEB: www.saviano.com
SIC: 1629 Tennis court construction

(P-1176)
SB ENERGY DEVCO (US) INC
1 Circle Star Way, San Carlos (94070-6234)
PHONE 650 731-3262
Abhijeet Sathe, *President*
EMP: 46 **EST:** 2019
SALES (est): 3MM **Privately Held**
SIC: 1629 Power plant construction

(P-1177)
SCHWAGER DAVIS INC
198 Hillsdale Ave, San Jose (95136-1398)
PHONE 408 281-9300
Guido A Schwager, *President*
Michelle Haughey, *Project Mgr*
Josh McBride, *Project Mgr*
Keith McKenna, *Project Mgr*
Kelly Nguyen,
▲ **EMP:** 186 **EST:** 1986
SQ FT: 12,000
SALES (est): 27.7MM **Privately Held**
WEB: www.schwagerdavis.com
SIC: 1629 1622 Railroad & railway roadbed construction; bridge construction

(P-1178)
SHIMMICK CONSTRUCTION CO INC (PA)
8201 Edgewater Dr Ste 202, Oakland (94621-2023)
PHONE 510 777-5000
Steve Richards, *President*
Greg Dukellis, *Exec VP*
Christian Fassari, *Exec VP*
Jeff Lessman, *Exec VP*
Devin Nordhagen, *Exec VP*
EMP: 2454 **EST:** 1990
SQ FT: 30,000
SALES (est): 575.3MM **Privately Held**
WEB: www.shimmick.com
SIC: 1629 1623 Earthmoving contractor; sewer line construction

(P-1179)
SHIMMICK CONSTRUCTION/OBAYASH (PA)
24200 Clawiter Rd, Hayward (94545-2216)
PHONE 510 293-1100
Paul Cocotis, *President*
EMP: 100 **EST:** 1993
SALES (est): 16.9MM **Privately Held**
WEB: www.shimmick.com
SIC: 1629 Dam construction

(P-1180)
STROER & GRAFF INC
1830 Phillips Ln, Antioch (94509-7306)
PHONE 925 778-0200
David L Graff, *CEO*
Ralph Carter, *Admin Sec*
EMP: 40 **EST:** 1980
SQ FT: 2,000
SALES (est): 11.9MM **Privately Held**
WEB: www.stroer-graff-inc.hub.biz
SIC: 1629 Pile driving contractor

(P-1181)
T T S CONSTRUCTION CORPORATION
1220 E Pine St, Lodi (95240-0812)
PHONE 209 333-7788
Nathan Howard, *President*
Reinie Naeb, *Principal*
Rudge Wynn, *Admin Sec*
Dana Howard,
Wayne Cockream, *Superintendent*
EMP: 40 **EST:** 2004
SQ FT: 4,200
SALES (est): 8.4MM **Privately Held**
WEB: www.ttsconstruction.com
SIC: 1629 3589 Power plant construction; water treatment equipment, industrial

(P-1182)
TIMEC ACQUISITIONS INC (DH)
155 Corporate Pl, Vallejo (94590-6968)
PHONE 707 642-2222
Pat McMahon, *President*
Gary Green, *COO*
Dennis Turnipseed, *CFO*
Jeff Wood, *Treasurer*
EMP: 850 **EST:** 1998
SQ FT: 25,000
SALES (est): 152.8MM **Privately Held**
WEB: www.broadspectrum.com
SIC: 1629 Industrial plant construction

(P-1183)
TIMEC COMPANIES INC (DH)
155 Corporate Pl, Vallejo (94590-6968)
PHONE 707 642-2222
Denis Turnipseed, *President*
Justin Kissee, *Manager*
EMP: 350 **EST:** 1971
SQ FT: 80,000
SALES (est): 142.2MM **Privately Held**
SIC: 1629 1799 Industrial plant construction; chemical plant & refinery construction; oil refinery construction; welding on site
HQ: Timec Acquisitions Inc
155 Corporate Pl
Vallejo CA 94590
707 642-2222

(P-1184)
VORTEX MARINE CONSTRUCTION INC
1 Maritime Way, Antioch (94509-8500)
PHONE 510 261-2400
Blaise Fettig, *President*
Farshad Mazloom, *Vice Pres*
Matthew Fettig, *Project Mgr*
EMP: 40 **EST:** 1992
SQ FT: 15,000
SALES (est): 20.2MM **Privately Held**
WEB: www.vortex-sfb.com
SIC: 1629 7389 Marine construction; divers, commercial

1711 Plumbing, Heating & Air Conditioning Contractors

(P-1185)
8MINUTE SOLAR ENERGY LLC (PA)
Also Called: 8minuteenergy Renewables
4370 Town Center Blvd # 11, El Dorado Hills (95762-7140)
PHONE 916 608-9060
Martin Hermann, *CEO*
Tom Buttgenbach PHD, *President*
Josh Goldstein, *COO*
Todd Bruckel, *Vice Pres*
Tristan Cooke, *Vice Pres*
EMP: 36 **EST:** 2010
SALES (est): 23.1MM **Privately Held**
WEB: www.8minute.com
SIC: 1711 Solar energy contractor

(P-1186)
A & A AC HTG & SHTMTL
Also Called: A & A A/C Heating & Shtmtl
763 S Auburn St, Grass Valley (95945-4301)
P.O. Box 933 (95945-0933)
PHONE 530 273-1301
Ken Aguilar, *President*
Connie Aguilar, *Shareholder*
Joaquin Aguilar, *Shareholder*
Paul Aguilar, *Corp Secy*
Larry Aguilar, *Vice Pres*
EMP: 38 **EST:** 1960
SQ FT: 5,000
SALES (est): 2.3MM **Privately Held**
WEB: www.aaheating.com
SIC: 1711 Warm air heating & air conditioning contractor; ventilation & duct work contractor

(P-1187)
ACCO ENGINEERED SYSTEMS INC
1133 Aladdin Ave, San Leandro (94577-4311)
PHONE 510 346-4300
Ron Krassensky, *Manager*
Ken Westphal, *Officer*
Chuck Darway, *Exec VP*
John Boncich, *Vice Pres*
Gregg Holbrook, *Vice Pres*
EMP: 200
SALES (corp-wide): 1.4B **Privately Held**
WEB: www.accoes.com
SIC: 1711 7623 Process piping contractor; solar energy contractor; ventilation & duct work contractor; warm air heating & air conditioning contractor; air conditioning repair
PA: Acco Engineered Systems, Inc.
888 E Walnut St
Pasadena CA 91101
818 244-6571

(P-1188)
AEGIS FIRE SYSTEMS LLC
500 Boulder Ct Ste A, Pleasanton (94566-8311)
PHONE 925 417-5550
Matt Hammon, *CEO*
Kelly Sleek, *Accounting Mgr*
Kristen Quintana, *Payroll Mgr*
John Moreno, *Purch Mgr*
Dave Karrick, *Superintendent*
EMP: 100 **EST:** 2012
SALES (est): 23.2MM
SALES (corp-wide): 416.1MM **Privately Held**
WEB: www.aegisfire.com
SIC: 1711 Fire sprinkler system installation
HQ: Rapid Fire Protection, Inc.
1530 Samco Rd
Rapid City SD 57702

(P-1189)
AGC INC
745 Camden Ave Ste B, Campbell (95008-4146)
PHONE 408 369-6305
Jon Mohs, *President*
Randy Attaway, *President*
Beth Guinnane, *Vice Pres*
Tony Volpi, *Project Mgr*

1711 - Plumbing, Heating & Air Conditioning Contractors County (P-1190)

PRODUCTS & SERVICES SECTION

Keith Anderson, *Superintendent*
▼ **EMP:** 65 **EST:** 2000
SQ FT: 2,200
SALES: 34MM **Privately Held**
WEB: www.agcinc.com
SIC: 1711 Mechanical contractor

(P-1190)
AIR SYSTEMS INC
940 Remillard Ct Frnt, San Jose (95122-2684)
PHONE.................................408 280-1666
John W Davis, *President*
William D Wayker, *CFO*
Don Billups, *Vice Pres*
Eric Ensenal, *Vice Pres*
Jon Gundersen, *Vice Pres*
EMP: 500 **EST:** 2003
SALES (est): 158.5MM
SALES (corp-wide): 8.8B **Publicly Held**
WEB: www.airsystemsinc.com
SIC: 1711 7623 Plumbing contractors; refrigeration service & repair
PA: Emcor Group, Inc.
  301 Merritt 7 Fl 6
  Norwalk CT 06851
  203 849-7800

(P-1191)
AIR SYSTEMS SERVICE & CNSTR
10381 Old Placerville Rd # 100, Sacramento (95827-2558)
PHONE.................................916 368-0336
Garry Westover, *CEO*
Kathleen Westover, *President*
Craig Medley, *Vice Pres*
Jim Meurer, *Vice Pres*
Joe Vicochea, *Vice Pres*
EMP: 130 **EST:** 1996
SQ FT: 10,000
SALES (est): 27.9MM **Privately Held**
WEB: www.airsystems1.com
SIC: 1711 7623 Mechanical contractor; warm air heating & air conditioning contractor; ventilation & duct work contractor; plumbing contractors; refrigeration service & repair

(P-1192)
AIRCO COMMERCIAL SERVICES INC (HQ)
5725 Alder Ave, Sacramento (95828-1107)
PHONE.................................866 731-4458
Charles C Jones, *President*
EMP: 45 **EST:** 1988
SQ FT: 21,000
SALES (est): 12.3MM
SALES (corp-wide): 5.9B **Publicly Held**
WEB: www.abm.com
SIC: 1711 7623 8748 Heating systems repair & maintenance; warm air heating & air conditioning contractor; refrigerator repair service; air conditioning repair; energy conservation consultant
PA: Abm Industries Incorporated
  1 Liberty Plz Fl 7
  New York NY 10006
  212 297-0200

(P-1193)
AIRCO MECHANICAL INC (PA)
Also Called: AMI Manufacturing
8210 Demetre Ave, Sacramento (95828-0919)
PHONE.................................916 381-4523
Wyatt Jones, *CEO*
Joann Hillendrand, *CFO*
Molly Holder, *Administration*
Raymond Auble, *Project Mgr*
Tucker Caruso, *Engineer*
EMP: 245 **EST:** 1974
SQ FT: 105,000
SALES (est): 40MM **Privately Held**
WEB: www.aircomech.com
SIC: 1711 8711 Mechanical contractor; engineering services

(P-1194)
AIRE SHEET METAL INC
1973 E Bayshore Rd, Redwood City (94063-4149)
P.O. Box 5217 (94063-0217)
PHONE.................................650 364-8081
Eugene Bramlett, *CEO*
Bobby E Bramlett, *President*
Marlo Bramlett, *Exec VP*
Arsalan Khan, *Project Engr*
Ken McCoy, *Superintendent*
EMP: 40 **EST:** 1971
SALES (est): 9.7MM **Privately Held**
WEB: www.airesm.com
SIC: 1711 3444 1761 Warm air heating & air conditioning contractor; sheet metalwork; sheet metalwork

(P-1195)
ALBERT NAHMAN PLUMBING & HTG
3333 Mrtin Lther King Jr, Berkeley (94703-2720)
PHONE.................................510 843-6904
Albert Nahman, *Owner*
EMP: 36 **EST:** 1983
SQ FT: 3,700
SALES (est): 3.9MM **Privately Held**
WEB: www.albertnahmanplumbing.com
SIC: 1711 Plumbing contractors

(P-1196)
ALL BAY MECHANICAL INC
2033 Gateway Pl Ste 500, San Jose (95110-3712)
PHONE.................................408 280-5558
Jesus Martinez, *President*
Denise Martinez, *Vice Pres*
EMP: 39 **EST:** 2002
SALES (est): 1.3MM **Privately Held**
WEB: www.allbaymechanical.com
SIC: 1711 Mechanical contractor

(P-1197)
ALLIED FIRE PROTECTION
555 High St, Oakland (94601-3989)
PHONE.................................510 533-5516
Ted Vinther, *President*
Dave Alva-Hill, *CIO*
Fritz Descovich, *Project Mgr*
Scott Judy, *Controller*
Alfonso Gomez, *Manager*
EMP: 150 **EST:** 1965
SQ FT: 29,000
SALES (est): 20.7MM **Privately Held**
WEB: www.alliedfire.com
SIC: 1711 Fire sprinkler system installation

(P-1198)
ALTERNATIVE ENERGY SYSTEMS INC
Also Called: AES
13620 State Highway 99 N, Chico (95973-9481)
PHONE.................................530 345-6980
Lance McClung, *President*
Jason Grant, *Business Dir*
Tim Hamor, *Principal*
Debbie Nixon, *Office Admin*
Jenny Zimmerman, *Marketing Staff*
EMP: 70 **EST:** 2004
SALES (est): 10.8MM **Privately Held**
WEB: www.savingenergyforlife.com
SIC: 1711 Solar energy contractor

(P-1199)
AMERICAN MECHANICAL INC
1275 Boulevard Way, Walnut Creek (94595-1106)
PHONE.................................925 946-9101
Kyle S Blocker, *President*
Charles Knight, *Vice Pres*
Greg Thomas, *Vice Pres*
EMP: 35 **EST:** 1997
SALES (est): 7.6MM
SALES (corp-wide): 1.5B **Privately Held**
WEB: www.ami-hvac.com
SIC: 1711 Mechanical contractor; ventilation & duct work contractor; heating systems repair & maintenance
HQ: American Residential Services Of Indiana, Inc.
  10403 Baur Blvd Ste E
  Saint Louis MO 63132

(P-1200)
AMERICAN RSDNTIAL SVCS IND INC
Also Called: Rescue Rooter Bay East
1618 Doolittle Dr, San Leandro (94577-2230)
PHONE.................................650 409-1986
Chris Peterson, *General Mgr*
EMP: 165
SALES (corp-wide): 1.5B **Privately Held**
SIC: 1711 Plumbing contractors
HQ: American Residential Services Of Indiana, Inc.
  10403 Baur Blvd Ste E
  Saint Louis MO 63132

(P-1201)
AMOS & ANDREWS INC
1801 Walters Ct, Fairfield (94533-2758)
P.O. Box 250 (94533-0450)
PHONE.................................707 422-4844
Frank Andrews, *President*
Gary L Andrews, *Treasurer*
Bill Fong, *Vice Pres*
Dorothy Andrews, *Admin Sec*
EMP: 36 **EST:** 1964
SALES (est): 2.1MM
SALES (corp-wide): 7.3MM **Privately Held**
WEB: www.amosandandrews.com
SIC: 1711 Mechanical contractor
PA: The Andrews Group Inc
  1801 Walters Ct
  Fairfield CA 94533
  707 422-4844

(P-1202)
AMS HEATING INC
3602 Munford Ave, Stockton (95215-8121)
PHONE.................................209 466-6692
Arthur Sanders, *President*
Melissa Sanders, *CFO*
Giancarlo Rainone, *Project Engr*
Tami Fanning, *Manager*
Johnny Grissom, *Manager*
EMP: 40 **EST:** 1999
SALES (est): 8.1MM **Privately Held**
WEB: www.amsheatinginc.com
SIC: 1711 Warm air heating & air conditioning contractor

(P-1203)
ANDERSON ROWE & BUCKLEY INC
2833 3rd St, San Francisco (94107-3532)
PHONE.................................415 282-1625
Robert E Buckley III, *President*
Rosy Zucchiatti, *Treasurer*
Richard I Buckley Jr, *Vice Pres*
Rod Blackmon, *Foreman/Supr*
Maitexa Cuburu, *Manager*
EMP: 170 **EST:** 1921
SQ FT: 40,000
SALES (est): 27.1MM **Privately Held**
WEB: www.arbmechanical.com
SIC: 1711 Mechanical contractor

(P-1204)
AQUALINE PIPING INC
Also Called: Residential Plumbing
2108 Bering Dr Ste C, San Jose (95131-2029)
PHONE.................................408 745-7100
Joshua B Moores, *CEO*
Chrystal L Steele, *Vice Pres*
Chris Hjeltness, *Bookkeeper*
Edgar Lara, *Manager*
EMP: 75 **EST:** 2011
SALES (est): 15.1MM **Privately Held**
WEB: www.aqualinepiping.com
SIC: 1711 7389 Plumbing contractors;

(P-1205)
AQUAMATIC FIRE PROTECTION INC (PA)
540 Garcia Ave Ste A, Pittsburg (94565-4950)
PHONE.................................925 753-0420
Wes Bookout, *CEO*
James Mason, *Vice Pres*
Tony Reed, *Office Mgr*
Mary Bookout, *Admin Sec*
Tom Allen, *Project Mgr*
EMP: 49 **EST:** 1993
SQ FT: 11,000
SALES (est): 12.5MM **Privately Held**
WEB: www.aquamaticfire.com
SIC: 1711 Fire sprinkler system installation

(P-1206)
AQUATEK PLUMBING INC
1236 N 5th St, San Jose (95112-4417)
P.O. Box 23271 (95153-3271)
PHONE.................................408 354-5885
James Shepherd, *President*
Cynthia Johnson, *Admin Sec*
Wendy Shepherd, *Admin Asst*
EMP: 35 **EST:** 1985
SQ FT: 3,600
SALES (est): 7.1MM **Privately Held**
WEB: www.aquatek-plumbing.com
SIC: 1711 Plumbing contractors

(P-1207)
ARRAYCON INC
1143 Blumenfeld Dr # 200, Sacramento (95815-3921)
PHONE.................................916 925-0201
Dan Hubiak, *Principal*
Richard W Lavezzo, *CEO*
Nate Williams, *Warehouse Mgr*
Angela Lavezzo, *Director*
EMP: 51 **EST:** 2010
SALES (est): 6.8MM **Privately Held**
WEB: www.arraycon.com
SIC: 1711 Solar energy contractor

(P-1208)
ARRAYCON LLC (PA)
1143 Blumenfeld Dr # 200, Sacramento (95815-3921)
PHONE.................................916 925-0201
Rick Lavezzo, *Mng Member*
Jeff Calabro, *Exec VP*
Mathew Ricci, *Exec VP*
Dan Hubiak, *Principal*
Jason Endsley, *Project Mgr*
EMP: 50
SQ FT: 50,000
SALES: 31.1MM **Privately Held**
WEB: www.arraycon.com
SIC: 1711 8748 Solar energy contractor; business consulting

(P-1209)
ARTIC AIRE OF CHICO INC
2530 Zanella Way Ste A, Chico (95928-7152)
PHONE.................................530 895-3330
Royal D Hawkley, *General Mgr*
EMP: 39 **EST:** 1947
SALES (est): 2.9MM
SALES (corp-wide): 2.1B **Privately Held**
WEB: www.serviceexperts.com
SIC: 1711 Warm air heating & air conditioning contractor; refrigeration contractor
HQ: Service Experts Llc
  1840 N Grnvlle Ave Ste 12
  Richardson TX 75081

(P-1210)
AYOOB & PEERY PLUMBING CO INC
975 Indiana St, San Francisco (94107-3007)
PHONE.................................415 550-0975
Peter Vincent McHugh, *CEO*
Mylene Pabilona, *Admin Asst*
Harrison Sporrer, *Engineer*
EMP: 80
SQ FT: 20,000
SALES (est): 16MM **Privately Held**
WEB: www.ayoobpeery.com
SIC: 1711 Mechanical contractor

(P-1211)
B & L MECHANICAL INC
Also Called: Honeywell Authorized Dealer
3218 N Marks Ave 3220, Fresno (93722-4994)
P.O. Box 13189 (93794-3189)
PHONE.................................559 268-2727
Edmond G Lanfranco, *President*
Judy Lanfranco, *CFO*
Dale Hansen, *Sales Executive*
Brent Parkman, *Superintendent*
EMP: 50 **EST:** 1986
SQ FT: 27,000
SALES (est): 5.2MM **Privately Held**
WEB: www.blminc.com
SIC: 1711 Warm air heating & air conditioning contractor; ventilation & duct work contractor; mechanical contractor; refrigeration contractor

PRODUCTS & SERVICES SECTION
1711 - Plumbing, Heating & Air Conditioning Contractors County (P-1235)

(P-1212)
B J S HEATING & AC INC
1240 Wilson Way, Woodland (95776-6005)
PHONE.................................530 662-8601
Robert E Johnson, *President*
EMP: 35 **EST:** 1972
SQ FT: 16,000
SALES (est): 5MM **Privately Held**
SIC: 1711 Warm air heating & air conditioning contractor

(P-1213)
B Z PLUMBING COMPANY INC
1901 Aviation Blvd, Lincoln (95648-9557)
PHONE.................................916 645-1600
William J Zmrzel, *President*
Diane Zmrzel, *Treasurer*
Sara Ladeas, *Office Mgr*
Mark Nicodemus, *Planning*
Chuck Robertson, *Controller*
EMP: 40 **EST:** 1990
SQ FT: 12,000
SALES (est): 21.5MM **Privately Held**
WEB: www.bzplumbing.com
SIC: 1711 Plumbing contractors

(P-1214)
BAY CITY MECHANICAL INC (PA)
870 Harbour Way S, Richmond (94804-3613)
PHONE.................................510 233-7000
Helge Theiss-Nyland, *President*
Bobbie Amos, *CFO*
Joe Percia, *Vice Pres*
Theodore Garcia, *VP Bus Dvlpt*
Nadia Hamade, *VP Bus Dvlpt*
EMP: 250 **EST:** 1992
SQ FT: 85,000
SALES: 112.1MM **Privately Held**
WEB: www.baycitymech.com
SIC: 1711 Mechanical contractor

(P-1215)
BAYVIEW ENGRG & CNSTR CO INC
5040 Rbert J Mathews Pkwy, El Dorado Hills (95762-5702)
PHONE.................................916 939-8986
Robert Ellery, *CEO*
Pete Ellery, *Vice Pres*
Bart Wood, *Vice Pres*
EMP: 80 **EST:** 2009
SQ FT: 6,000
SALES (est): 9MM **Privately Held**
WEB: www.bayviewecci.com
SIC: 1711 8711 Boiler setting contractor; engineering services

(P-1216)
BDS PLUMBING INC
2125 Youngs Ct, Walnut Creek (94596-6319)
PHONE.................................925 939-1004
Brett M Stom, *President*
Dawn L Stom, *Corp Secy*
EMP: 38 **EST:** 1995
SQ FT: 400
SALES (est): 2.6MM **Privately Held**
SIC: 1711 Plumbing contractors

(P-1217)
BELL PRODUCTS INC
722 Soscol Ave, NAPA (94559-3014)
P.O. Box 396 (94559-0396)
PHONE.................................707 255-1811
Paul D Irwin, *President*
Stan Foltz, *Corp Secy*
Gina Massolo, *Administration*
Audrey Geitner, *Accounting Mgr*
Audrey L Geitner, *Accounting Mgr*
EMP: 74 **EST:** 1945
SQ FT: 24,400
SALES (est): 21.3MM **Privately Held**
WEB: www.bellproducts.com
SIC: 1711 Ventilation & duct work contractor; warm air heating & air conditioning contractor; mechanical contractor

(P-1218)
BENICIA PLUMBING INC
265 W Channel Rd, Benicia (94510-1146)
P.O. Box 1095 (94510-4095)
PHONE.................................707 745-2930
William J Cawley Jr, *CEO*
Doug Kuznik, *President*
Heidi Benjamin, *CFO*
Karen Ramey, *Corp Secy*
William J Cawley III, *Vice Pres*
EMP: 55
SQ FT: 10,000
SALES (est): 14MM **Privately Held**
WEB: www.beniciaplumbing.com
SIC: 1711 Plumbing contractors

(P-1219)
BFP FIRE PROTECTION INC
17 Janis Way, Scotts Valley (95066-3537)
PHONE.................................831 461-1100
Chris Amos, *President*
Rick Fischer, *CFO*
Rick L Fischer, *Officer*
EMP: 60 **EST:** 1989
SQ FT: 6,400
SALES (est): 7.6MM **Privately Held**
WEB: www.bfpfireprotection.com
SIC: 1711 8711 Fire sprinkler system installation; engineering services

(P-1220)
BLACKWELL SOLAR PARK LLC
1777 Borel Pl Ste 102, San Mateo (94402-3510)
PHONE.................................650 539-3380
EMP: 35
SALES (est): 2.5MM **Privately Held**
SIC: 1711 Plumbing/Heating/Air Cond Contractor

(P-1221)
BLOCKA CONSTRUCTION INC
445 Boulder Ct, Pleasanton (94566-8308)
PHONE.................................510 657-3686
Bob Blocka, *President*
Jean Blocka, *CFO*
Gregory Gazeley, *Admin Asst*
Chad Blocka, *Project Mgr*
Alex Boyd, *Project Mgr*
EMP: 70 **EST:** 1993
SQ FT: 7,300
SALES (est): 19.9MM **Privately Held**
WEB: www.blockainc.wordpress.com
SIC: 1711 1731 Mechanical contractor; general electrical contractor

(P-1222)
BLUE MOUNTAIN CNSTR SVCS INC
Also Called: Blue Mountain Air
707 Aldridge Rd, Vacaville (95688-9298)
PHONE.................................800 889-2085
Gregory S Owen, *President*
Doug Morse, *Vice Pres*
Brock Rose, *Vice Pres*
Michael Spier, *Vice Pres*
Angel Davila, *Administration*
▲ **EMP:** 200 **EST:** 2001
SQ FT: 37,000
SALES (est): 154.9MM **Privately Held**
WEB: www.bluemountainair.net
SIC: 1711 Heating & air conditioning contractors

(P-1223)
BOGNER SHEET METAL
142 Benito Ave, Santa Cruz (95062-2174)
PHONE.................................831 423-4322
Robert E Ciapponi, *President*
Gerald W Todd, *Chairman*
Jim Kennedy, *Vice Pres*
Katrina Ciapponi, *Office Mgr*
Janice Allegri, *Admin Sec*
EMP: 36 **EST:** 1947
SQ FT: 5,000
SALES (est): 5.2MM **Privately Held**
WEB: www.bognersheetmetal.com
SIC: 1711 1761 Warm air heating & air conditioning contractor; sheet metalwork

(P-1224)
BONETTI FRANK PLUMBING COMPANY
20878 Rutledge Rd, Castro Valley (94546-5419)
P.O. Box 2215 (94546-0215)
PHONE.................................510 582-0934
Mary Bonetti, *President*
Dan Bonetti, *Vice Pres*
Ray Bonetti, *Vice Pres*
EMP: 37 **EST:** 1955
SQ FT: 1,200
SALES (est): 1.5MM **Privately Held**
WEB: www.bonettiplumbing.com
SIC: 1711 Septic system construction

(P-1225)
BROADWAY MECH - CONTRS INC
873 81st Ave, Oakland (94621-2509)
PHONE.................................510 746-4000
Fred Nurisso, *President*
Michael Guglielmo, *Project Mgr*
Jacky Tran, *Accountant*
Chris Tobin, *Foreman/Supr*
Elin Lupo, *Manager*
EMP: 150 **EST:** 1971
SALES (est): 30.3MM **Privately Held**
WEB: www.broadwaymechanical.com
SIC: 1711 Mechanical contractor

(P-1226)
CALIFORNIA COML SOLAR INC
Also Called: Calcom Energy
9479 N Fort Washington Rd # 105, Fresno (93730-5939)
PHONE.................................559 667-9200
Dylan Dupre, *CEO*
Rob Burkholder, *CFO*
Dave Williams, *Officer*
Ali Baird, *Vice Pres*
Jordan Collins, *Vice Pres*
EMP: 56 **EST:** 2012
SALES (est): 14.7MM **Privately Held**
WEB: www.calcomenergy.com
SIC: 1711 Solar energy contractor

(P-1227)
CALIFORNIA UNITED MECH INC (PA)
2185 Oakland Rd, San Jose (95131-1574)
PHONE.................................408 232-9000
Tom Sosine, *CEO*
Jon Gundersen, *President*
Blaine Flickner, *Vice Pres*
Frank Nascimento, *Vice Pres*
Christopher Daniel, *Executive*
EMP: 330 **EST:** 2003
SQ FT: 40,000
SALES (est): 104.9MM **Privately Held**
WEB: www.umi1.com
SIC: 1711 Mechanical contractor

(P-1228)
CALIFRNIA SOLAR INNOVATORS INC
Also Called: PV SOLAR CONTRACTOR
580 N Wilma Ave Ste H, Ripon (95366-9514)
PHONE.................................209 596-0350
Jordan Jones, *President*
Jonathan Jones, *Vice Pres*
EMP: 35 **EST:** 2010
SQ FT: 1,200
SALES (est): 7.8MM **Privately Held**
WEB: www.calsolar.com
SIC: 1711 Solar energy contractor

(P-1229)
CAN-AM PLUMBING INC
151 Wyoming St, Pleasanton (94566-6277)
PHONE.................................925 846-1833
Ronald Capilla, *President*
Martin Ogara, *CFO*
Michael Capilla, *Vice Pres*
Rebecca Jose, *Human Res Mgr*
Ron Dovichi, *Purch Mgr*
EMP: 250 **EST:** 1972
SQ FT: 16,000
SALES (est): 24.5MM **Privately Held**
WEB: www.canamplumbing.com
SIC: 1711 Plumbing contractors

(P-1230)
CASCADE COMFORT SERVICE INC
5203 Industrial Way, Anderson (96007-4954)
PHONE.................................530 365-5350
Randy Downey, *President*
Richard Boudro, *Corp Secy*
Andrew Dempsey, *Vice Pres*
EMP: 22 **EST:** 1984
SQ FT: 12,800
SALES (est): 2.1MM **Privately Held**
WEB: www.cascadecomfort.com
SIC: 1711 3444 Warm air heating & air conditioning contractor; sheet metalwork

(P-1231)
CEN-CAL FIRE SYSTEMS INC
1615 S Stockton St, Lodi (95240-6353)
P.O. Box 1284 (95241-1284)
PHONE.................................209 334-9166
Wayne Weisz, *President*
Byron Weisz, *Admin Sec*
EMP: 40
SALES: 26.9MM **Privately Held**
WEB: www.cen-calfire.com
SIC: 1711 Fire sprinkler system installation

(P-1232)
CENTRAL VALLEY CONCRETE INC
4200 Lester Rd, Denair (95316-9411)
PHONE.................................209 667-0161
Don Klikna, *Manager*
Stacy Neal, *Vice Pres*
EMP: 68
SALES (corp-wide): 34.4MM **Privately Held**
WEB: www.centralvalleyconcrete.com
SIC: 1711 3273 5032 7699 Septic system construction; ready-mixed concrete; brick, stone & related material; waste cleaning services; landscaping equipment; lumber & other building materials
PA: Central Valley Concrete, Inc.
3823 N State Highway 59
Merced CA 95348
209 723-8846

(P-1233)
CHAMPION INDUSTRIAL CONTRS INC (PA)
1420 Coldwell Ave, Modesto (95350-5704)
P.O. Box 4399 (95352-4399)
PHONE.................................209 524-6601
Darrell Frederick Champion, *CEO*
James C Champion, *Ch of Bd*
John E L Walter, *COO*
Charles Vanwey, *President*
Eulala Jo Champion, *Treasurer*
EMP: 38 **EST:** 1933
SQ FT: 62,000
SALES (est): 19.6MM **Privately Held**
WEB: www.championindustrial.com
SIC: 1711 1761 3444 Mechanical contractor; plumbing contractors; warm air heating & air conditioning contractor; sheet metalwork; sheet metalwork

(P-1234)
CHAMPION INDUSTRIAL CONTRS INC
451 Tully Rd, Modesto (95350-5856)
PHONE.................................209 579-5478
Charles Vanwey, *Manager*
EMP: 42
SALES (corp-wide): 19.6MM **Privately Held**
WEB: www.championindustrial.com
SIC: 1711 1761 3444 Mechanical contractor; plumbing contractors; warm air heating & air conditioning contractor; sheet metalwork; sheet metalwork
PA: Champion Industrial Contractors, Inc.
1420 Coldwell Ave
Modesto CA 95350
209 524-6601

(P-1235)
CLARK HARRY PLUMBING & HEATING
Also Called: Harry Clark Sewers
3026 Broadway, Oakland (94611-5713)
PHONE.................................510 444-1776
Brad Marshall, *President*
Don Marshall, *CFO*
Kathleen Marshall, *Vice Pres*
Laura Marshall, *Vice Pres*
EMP: 46 **EST:** 1952
SALES (est): 4.4MM **Privately Held**
WEB: www.hcplumbing.com
SIC: 1711 Plumbing contractors; warm air heating & air conditioning contractor

1711 - Plumbing, Heating & Air Conditioning Contractors County (P-1236) — PRODUCTS & SERVICES SECTION

(P-1236)
CLI-METRICS INC
Also Called: Cli-Metrics Service Company
382 Martin Ave, Santa Clara (95050-3112)
PHONE................................408 886-3800
Kevin Colin, *CEO*
Rick Thompson, *Sr Project Mgr*
EMP: 49 **EST:** 2009
SALES (est): 3.3MM **Privately Held**
WEB: www.cli-metrics.com
SIC: 1711 Mechanical contractor

(P-1237)
COBALT POWER SYSTEMS INC
2557 Wyandotte St, Mountain View (94043-2314)
PHONE................................650 938-9574
Mark Byington, *President*
Natasha Sherbaf, *Admin Asst*
Vince Valencia, *Project Mgr*
Evan Haskins, *Opers Staff*
▼ **EMP:** 45
SQ FT: 3,300
SALES (est): 5.4MM **Privately Held**
WEB: www.cobaltpower.com
SIC: 1711 Solar energy contractor

(P-1238)
COMFORT AIR INC
1607 French Camp Tpke, Stockton (95206-1960)
P.O. Box 1969 (95201-1969)
PHONE................................209 466-4601
Steven J Evans, *President*
Gregory A Gaut, *Vice Pres*
Paulette Gaut, *Admin Sec*
EMP: 75
SQ FT: 7,000
SALES (est): 11MM **Privately Held**
WEB: www.comfortairstocktonca.com
SIC: 1711 Warm air heating & air conditioning contractor

(P-1239)
COMFORT ENERGY INC
Also Called: Comfort Zone Mechanical Air
1465 N Milpitas Blvd, Milpitas (95035-3160)
PHONE................................408 263-3100
Yuka Abbott, *President*
Craig Hall, *Officer*
Harold Abbott, *Vice Pres*
Harry Abbott, *Vice Pres*
▲ **EMP:** 39 **EST:** 2005
SALES (est): 8.9MM **Privately Held**
WEB: www.comfortenergy.com
SIC: 1711 Warm air heating & air conditioning contractor; solar energy contractor

(P-1240)
CONFORTI PLUMBING INC
6080 Pleasant Valley Rd C, El Dorado (95623-4257)
PHONE................................530 622-0202
Marvin Collins, *President*
Jan Zygalinski, *CFO*
EMP: 50 **EST:** 1977
SALES (est): 8.9MM **Privately Held**
WEB: www.confortiplumbingonline.com
SIC: 1711 Plumbing contractors

(P-1241)
CONTROL AIR NORTH INC
30655 San Clemente St, Hayward (94544-7133)
PHONE................................510 441-1800
Greg Ellis, *President*
Darrell Griffith, *Vice Pres*
Mike Pence, *Vice Pres*
Ken Ellis, *Principal*
Stan Ellis, *Principal*
EMP: 100 **EST:** 1995
SALES (est): 46.9MM **Privately Held**
WEB: www.controlac.com
SIC: 1711 Warm air heating & air conditioning contractor

(P-1242)
COSCO FIRE PROTECTION INC
4320 Anthony Ct Ste 8, Rocklin (95677-2139)
PHONE................................916 652-2210
Rory Low, *Manager*
EMP: 37 **Privately Held**
WEB: www.coscofire.com
SIC: 1711 Fire sprinkler system installation
HQ: Cosco Fire Protection, Inc.
29222 Rancho Viejo Rd # 205
San Juan Capistrano CA 92675

(P-1243)
COSCO FIRE PROTECTION INC
4223 W Srra Mdre Ave # 108, Fresno (93722-3933)
PHONE................................559 275-3795
Lisa Dean, *Branch Mgr*
Michael Cunnien, *Sales Staff*
Robert Alves, *Manager*
Gene Janecko, *Manager*
Diane Medlin, *Manager*
EMP: 37 **Privately Held**
WEB: www.coscofire.com
SIC: 1711 Fire sprinkler system installation
HQ: Cosco Fire Protection, Inc.
29222 Rancho Viejo Rd # 205
San Juan Capistrano CA 92675

(P-1244)
CRITCHFIELD MECHANICAL INC
4085 Campbell Ave, Menlo Park (94025-1939)
PHONE................................650 321-7801
Joe Critchfield, *Chairman*
Steve Gustafson, *Vice Pres*
Angie Espinosa, *Office Mgr*
Euft Kruithof, *Engineer*
Jolynn Boice, *Mktg Coord*
EMP: 394
SALES (corp-wide): 162.2MM **Privately Held**
WEB: www.cmihvac.com
SIC: 1711 Mechanical contractor
PA: Critchfield Mechanical, Inc.
1901 Junction Ave
San Jose CA 95131
408 437-7000

(P-1245)
D & J PLUMBING INC
4341 Winters St, Sacramento (95838-3031)
PHONE................................916 922-4888
Steve Waldron, *President*
Geri Richards, *Shareholder*
John Richards, *Shareholder*
Randy Golden, *Vice Pres*
EMP: 37 **EST:** 1982
SQ FT: 5,000
SALES (est): 3.3MM **Privately Held**
SIC: 1711 Plumbing contractors

(P-1246)
D W NICHOLSON CORPORATION (PA)
24747 Clawiter Rd, Hayward (94545-2225)
P.O. Box 4197 (94540-4197)
PHONE................................510 887-0900
John L Nicholson, *Principal*
Melinda Silva, *COO*
Gonzalo Alliende, *Vice Pres*
Mari Duncan, *Accountant*
Tom Reed Jr, *Safety Mgr*
EMP: 249 **EST:** 1935
SQ FT: 12,000
SALES: 23.2MM **Privately Held**
WEB: www.dwnicholson.com
SIC: 1711 1731 8711 1796 Mechanical contractor; general electrical contractor; engineering services; millwright; residential construction; industrial buildings & warehouses

(P-1247)
DAGGETT SOLAR POWER 3 LLC
100 California St Ste 400, San Francisco (94111-4509)
PHONE................................415 627-1600
EMP: 167 **EST:** 2016
SALES (est): 1.6MM
SALES (corp-wide): 330.4MM **Privately Held**
WEB: www.nrg.com
SIC: 1711 Solar energy contractor
PA: Clearway Energy Group Llc
100 California St Ste 400
San Francisco CA 94111
415 627-1600

(P-1248)
DANIEL LARRATT PLUMBING INC
Also Called: Dli Mechanical
944 Terminal Way, San Carlos (94070-3225)
PHONE................................415 553-6011
John Gregory Doran, *President*
Daniel Larratt, *Vice Pres*
Renee Sanchez, *Project Mgr*
EMP: 39 **EST:** 1999
SALES (est): 3.9MM **Privately Held**
SIC: 1711 Plumbing contractors

(P-1249)
DEPENDABLE SHEET METAL
Also Called: Dependable Heating & AC
1855 N 1st St Unit A, Dixon (95620-9758)
PHONE................................707 678-9600
Helen Hansen, *President*
Brad Hansen, *Vice Pres*
EMP: 40 **EST:** 1968
SQ FT: 49,600
SALES (est): 8.3MM **Privately Held**
WEB: www.dependableair.com
SIC: 1711 Warm air heating & air conditioning contractor; ventilation & duct work contractor

(P-1250)
DLIGHT DESIGN INC
2100 Geng Rd Ste 210, Palo Alto (94303-3307)
PHONE................................415 872-6136
Ned Tozun, *CEO*
Sam Goldman, *President*
Marco Galfre, *Engineer*
Jacob Okoth, *Director*
Ramesh Tuli, *Director*
▲ **EMP:** 800 **EST:** 2007
SALES (est): 45.4MM **Privately Held**
WEB: www.dlight.com
SIC: 1711 5074 Solar energy contractor; heating equipment & panels, solar

(P-1251)
DONALD P DICK AC INC (PA)
Also Called: Mr Cool
1444 N Whitney Ave, Fresno (93703-4513)
PHONE................................559 255-1644
James B Dick, *President*
David B Dick, *Vice Pres*
David Dick, *Vice Pres*
Nick Scott, *Vice Pres*
Jeffrey Dick, *Admin Sec*
EMP: 50
SQ FT: 30,000
SALES (est): 12.8MM **Privately Held**
WEB: www.mrcool4ac.com
SIC: 1711 Warm air heating & air conditioning contractor

(P-1252)
DPW INC
203 E Harris Ave, South San Francisco (94080-6807)
PHONE................................650 588-8482
Don Pheil, *President*
Don Wood, *Vice Pres*
Jorge Gordils, *Controller*
Paul Vian, *Manager*
EMP: 35 **EST:** 1994
SALES (est): 10MM **Privately Held**
WEB: www.dpwinc.com
SIC: 1711 Heating systems repair & maintenance; fire sprinkler system installation

(P-1253)
EAGLE SYSTEMS INTL INC
Also Called: Synergy Companies
28436 Satellite St, Hayward (94545-4863)
PHONE................................510 259-1700
Steven R Shallenberger, *President*
Russell Jacobsen, *CFO*
EMP: 375 **EST:** 2002
SQ FT: 6,962
SALES (est): 28.8MM **Privately Held**
WEB: www.synergycompanies.com
SIC: 1711 1731 1742 1793 Warm air heating & air conditioning contractor; general electrical contractor; plastering, drywall & insulation; glass & glazing work

(P-1254)
EJ PLUMBING
1170 Martin Ave, Santa Clara (95050-2607)
PHONE................................650 520-8718
Emanuel Jimenez, *President*
EMP: 48 **EST:** 2017
SALES (est): 3.1MM **Privately Held**
WEB: www.ejplumbing.com
SIC: 1711 Plumbing contractors

(P-1255)
ENERGY SAVING PROS LLC
3334 Swetzer Rd, Loomis (95650-9584)
PHONE................................916 259-2501
Brian Pierce, *Principal*
EMP: 36 **EST:** 2011
SALES (est): 3.5MM **Privately Held**
WEB: www.energysavingpros.com
SIC: 1711 Solar energy contractor

(P-1256)
ENVIRNMNTAL SYSTEMS INC NTHRN (PA)
Also Called: Honeywell Authorized Dealer
3353 De La Cruz Blvd, Santa Clara (95054-2633)
PHONE................................408 980-1711
V C Enfantino, *President*
Lisa Enfantino, *Office Mgr*
Eugene L Enfantino, *Admin Sec*
Patti Maletta, *Admin Asst*
Ron Hillman, *Prgrmr*
EMP: 83 **EST:** 1975
SQ FT: 13,800
SALES: 40.6MM **Privately Held**
WEB: www.esite.net
SIC: 1711 7623 3444 Mechanical contractor; refrigeration service & repair; sheet metalwork

(P-1257)
ENVISE
33333 Western Ave, Union City (94587-2210)
PHONE................................510 447-3300
Annie Jackman, *Principal*
Ronan O 'mahony, *General Mgr*
Annabelle Caberte, *Admin Asst*
Leandro Miguez, *Technician*
Jay Barthel, *Project Mgr*
EMP: 181
SALES (corp-wide): 940.1MM **Privately Held**
WEB: www.enviseco.com
SIC: 1711 Plumbing, heating, air-conditioning contractors
HQ: Envise
12131 Western Ave
Garden Grove CA 92841
800 613-6240

(P-1258)
ERNEST ONGARO & SONS INC
2995 Dutton Ave, Santa Rosa (95407-5711)
PHONE................................707 579-3511
Ernest Joseph Ongaro, *President*
Mitchell Allen Ongaro, *Treasurer*
Dean Mathew Ongaro, *Vice Pres*
Rick Chandler, *General Mgr*
David Langdale, *General Mgr*
EMP: 35 **EST:** 1931
SQ FT: 7,000
SALES (est): 7.3MM **Privately Held**
WEB: www.ongaroandsons.com
SIC: 1711 Plumbing contractors; warm air heating & air conditioning contractor

(P-1259)
F W SPENCER & SON INC
Also Called: Brisbane Mechanical
99 S Hill Dr, Brisbane (94005-1274)
PHONE................................415 468-5000
William D Spencer, *President*
Dan Everett, *Vice Pres*
Joe Meyer, *Division Mgr*
John Hohman, *Project Mgr*
Chia Kwong, *Personnel*
EMP: 200 **EST:** 1903
SQ FT: 140,000
SALES (est): 25.6MM **Privately Held**
WEB: www.harriscompany.com
SIC: 1711 Plumbing contractors; warm air heating & air conditioning contractor

▲ = Import ▼ = Export
◆ = Import/Export

PRODUCTS & SERVICES SECTION
1711 - Plumbing, Heating & Air Conditioning Contractors County (P-1283)

(P-1260)
FAMAND INC
1604 Airport Blvd, Santa Rosa (95403-8204)
PHONE....................707 255-9295
Charlie Butts, *Branch Mgr*
Stan Butts, *President*
Charlie Oliver, *Design Engr*
Jeff Walling, *Project Mgr*
Vincent Carpenter, *Engineer*
EMP: 96
SALES (corp-wide): 59.8MM **Privately Held**
SIC: 1711 Plumbing, heating, air-conditioning contractors
PA: Famand, Inc.
1512 Silica Ave
Sacramento CA 95815
916 988-8808

(P-1261)
FAMAND INC (PA)
Also Called: Indoor Environmental Services
1512 Silica Ave, Sacramento (95815-3312)
PHONE....................916 988-8808
Michael Andress, *CEO*
John Anderson, *CFO*
Kathleen Thompson, *Vice Pres*
Deborah Amberg, *Admin Sec*
Roxy Kugler, *Administration*
EMP: 44 **EST:** 1988
SQ FT: 26,000
SALES (est): 59.8MM **Privately Held**
SIC: 1711 Warm air heating & air conditioning contractor

(P-1262)
FAULT LINE PLUMBING INC
7640 National Dr, Livermore (94550-8809)
PHONE....................925 443-6450
Sean Collins, *President*
Karrie Collins, *Treasurer*
Melanie Lindgren, *Accounting Mgr*
Kari Collins, *Payroll Mgr*
Josh Elsbernd, *Opers Mgr*
EMP: 50 **EST:** 1997
SALES (est): 10.3MM **Privately Held**
WEB: www.faultlineplumbing.com
SIC: 1711 Plumbing contractors

(P-1263)
FLETCHER PLUMBING INC
3237 Rippey Rd Ste 150, Loomis (95650-7662)
PHONE....................916 652-9769
Carl Fletcher, *President*
EMP: 35 **EST:** 1996
SALES (est): 5.5MM **Privately Held**
SIC: 1711 Plumbing contractors

(P-1264)
FLETCHERS PLUMBING & CONTG INC (PA)
219 Burns Dr Unit 2, Yuba City (95991-7235)
PHONE....................530 673-2489
Carl Fletcher, *President*
Adam Fletcher, *CFO*
EMP: 41 **EST:** 1973
SQ FT: 23,000
SALES (est): 8.2MM **Privately Held**
WEB: www.fletchersplumbing.net
SIC: 1711 5211 Plumbing contractors; bathroom fixtures, equipment & supplies

(P-1265)
FOOTHILL FIRE PROTECTION INC (PA)
4000 Alvis Ct, Rocklin (95677-4011)
PHONE....................916 663-3582
William Gray, *CEO*
Carrie Gray, *Vice Pres*
Chris Kohler, *General Mgr*
Justin Harrison, *Project Mgr*
Bill Gray, *Financial Exec*
EMP: 40 **EST:** 1993
SQ FT: 12,500
SALES (est): 9.9MM **Privately Held**
WEB: www.ffprotection.com
SIC: 1711 Fire sprinkler system installation

(P-1266)
FRANK M BOOTH INC (PA)
Also Called: Valley Sheet Metal Co
222 3rd St, Marysville (95901-5948)
P.O. Box 5 (95901-0001)
PHONE....................530 742-7134
Lawrence R Booth, *President*
Richard Gabel, *CFO*
Jodye Porter, *CFO*
Woody Bradford, *Project Mgr*
Ryan Delariva, *Project Mgr*
EMP: 40 **EST:** 1912
SQ FT: 75,000
SALES (est): 110MM **Privately Held**
WEB: www.frankbooth.com
SIC: 1711 Mechanical contractor

(P-1267)
FRANK M BOOTH INC
Also Called: Valley Sheet Metal
251 Michelle Ct, South San Francisco (94080-6202)
PHONE....................650 871-8292
F Martin Booth, *CEO*
Martin Booth, *Vice Pres*
Dave Radicali, *Project Mgr*
EMP: 116
SQ FT: 70,000
SALES (corp-wide): 110MM **Privately Held**
WEB: www.frankbooth.com
SIC: 1711 8712 3444 1761 Mechanical contractor; architectural services; sheet metalwork; sheet metalwork
PA: Frank M. Booth, Inc.
222 3rd St
Marysville CA 95901
530 742-7134

(P-1268)
FRESCHI AIR SYSTEMS INC
Also Called: Freschi Service Experts
715 Fulton Shipyard Rd, Antioch (94509-7557)
PHONE....................925 827-9761
John R Freschi Jr, *President*
EMP: 55 **EST:** 1980
SQ FT: 5,000
SALES (est): 9.8MM
SALES (corp-wide): 2.1B **Privately Held**
WEB: www.freschiserviceexperts.com
SIC: 1711 3444 Warm air heating & air conditioning contractor; sheet metalwork
HQ: Service Experts Llc
1840 N Grnvlle Ave Ste 12
Richardson TX 75081

(P-1269)
FRESNO PLUMBING & HEATING INC (PA)
Also Called: Ace Hardware
2585 N Larkin Ave, Fresno (93727-1357)
PHONE....................559 294-0200
Larry Kumpe, *CEO*
Dean Kumpe, *Corp Secy*
Debbie Kumpe, *CIO*
Laura Mayfield, *Human Resources*
EMP: 180
SQ FT: 20,000
SALES (est): 27MM **Privately Held**
WEB: www.fresnoplumbinginc.com
SIC: 1711 5251 Plumbing contractors; hardware; door locks & lock sets; tools, hand; tools, power

(P-1270)
GCL SOLAR ENERGY INC
1 Market Er 00 Steuart Tow, San Francisco (94105-1596)
PHONE....................415 362-2601
Peng Fang, *CEO*
Emma Ye, *Admin Sec*
Quan Wang, *Info Tech Mgr*
Ashish Sharma, *Engineer*
Esther Clayson, *Human Res Dir*
▲ **EMP:** 54 **EST:** 2009
SALES (est): 18.5MM **Privately Held**
WEB: www.gcl-poly.com.hk
SIC: 1711 Solar energy contractor
HQ: Gcl Solar Energy Technology Holdings Limited
Rm 1703b-06 17/F International Commerce Ctr
Yau Ma Tei KLN

(P-1271)
GEORGE M ROBINSON & CO (PA)
1461 Atteberry Ln, San Jose (95131-1409)
PHONE....................510 632-7017
John P Joyce, *President*
Ned Raudsep, *Treasurer*
EMP: 26 **EST:** 1932
SQ FT: 20,000
SALES (est): 4.5MM **Privately Held**
SIC: 1711 3498 Fire sprinkler system installation; fabricated pipe & fittings

(P-1272)
GOLD RUSH ENERGY SOLUTIONS
4911 Windplay Dr Ste 4, El Dorado Hills (95762-9643)
PHONE....................530 334-0676
Jordan Lykins, *CEO*
EMP: 38 **EST:** 2016
SALES (est): 6MM **Privately Held**
WEB: www.goldrushenergy.com
SIC: 1711 Solar energy contractor

(P-1273)
GRAVES 6 INC (PA)
Also Called: Preferred Plumbing & Drain
3437 Myrtle Ave Ste 440, North Highlands (95660-5147)
PHONE....................916 348-3098
Kathy Graves, *CEO*
Brian Graves, *Principal*
EMP: 77 **EST:** 2004
SALES (est): 2.8MM **Privately Held**
SIC: 1711 1799 Heating & air conditioning contractors; plumbing contractors; insulation of pipes & boilers

(P-1274)
GREINER HTG - A - SLAR ENRGY I
Also Called: Greiner Heating & AC
8235 Pedrick Rd, Dixon (95620-9606)
PHONE....................707 678-1784
Patricia Greiner, *CEO*
David Krueger, *President*
EMP: 37 **EST:** 1991
SQ FT: 10,000
SALES (est): 6.2MM **Privately Held**
WEB: www.ghac.com
SIC: 1711 3444 Warm air heating & air conditioning contractor; ducts, sheet metal

(P-1275)
GRID ALTERNATIVE
1171 Ocean Ave Ste 200, Emeryville (94608-1147)
PHONE....................510 731-1310
Tim Sears, *Principal*
Erica Mackie, *Principal*
EMP: 300 **EST:** 2009
SALES (est): 5.7MM **Privately Held**
SIC: 1711 Solar energy contractor

(P-1276)
GUY PLUMBING & HEATING INC
1265 El Camino Real, Menlo Park (94025-4208)
PHONE....................650 323-8415
Roger Guy, *President*
David Guy, *Vice Pres*
Alan Guy, *Admin Sec*
EMP: 41 **EST:** 1948
SQ FT: 4,000
SALES (est): 2.2MM **Privately Held**
WEB: www.guyplumbing.com
SIC: 1711 Plumbing contractors; heating & air conditioning contractors

(P-1277)
HEATHORN & ASSOC CONTRS INC
Also Called: American Air Conditioning Co
2799 Miller St, San Leandro (94577-5619)
PHONE....................510 351-7578
Norman T R Heathorn Jr, *President*
Mark Defranco, *Vice Pres*
Lisa Heathorn, *Admin Sec*
EMP: 20 **EST:** 1992
SQ FT: 6,800

SALES: 5MM **Privately Held**
WEB: www.aacph.com
SIC: 1711 3444 Warm air heating & air conditioning contractor; ventilation & duct work contractor; mechanical contractor; sheet metalwork

(P-1278)
HENRY MECHANICAL INC
Also Called: Honeywell Authorized Dealer
7656 Bell Rd, Windsor (95492-8998)
PHONE....................707 838-3311
Doug Henry, *President*
Joe Henry, *Vice Pres*
Jarrett Martin, *Purchasing*
EMP: 41 **EST:** 1992
SQ FT: 23,040
SALES (est): 2.5MM **Privately Held**
WEB: www.henrymechanical.com
SIC: 1711 Warm air heating & air conditioning contractor

(P-1279)
HOMEENERGY INC
2930 Domingo Ave, Berkeley (94705-2454)
PHONE....................707 200-8287
Thomas Enzendorfer, *CEO*
EMP: 80 **EST:** 2018
SALES (est): 4.5MM **Privately Held**
WEB: www.he.solar
SIC: 1711 Solar energy contractor

(P-1280)
HUMPHREY PLUMBING INC
880 S Kilroy Rd, Turlock (95380-9570)
PHONE....................209 634-4626
Justin Humphrey, *President*
Robin Humphrey, *Corp Secy*
EMP: 75 **EST:** 1985
SQ FT: 7,500
SALES (est): 8.7MM **Privately Held**
WEB: www.humphreyplumbing.business.site
SIC: 1711 Plumbing contractors

(P-1281)
I C REFRIGERATION SVC INC
2216 Rockefeller Dr, Ceres (95307-7201)
PHONE....................209 538-8271
Richard J Imfeld Jr, *CEO*
Kevin Silva, *Vice Pres*
Ryan Floyd, *CIO*
Eric Buchanan, *Technician*
Tracey Buck, *Controller*
EMP: 35 **EST:** 1940
SQ FT: 12,000
SALES (est): 11.6MM **Privately Held**
WEB: www.icceres.com
SIC: 1711 Refrigeration contractor; warm air heating & air conditioning contractor

(P-1282)
ICOM MECHANICAL INC
477 Burke St, San Jose (95112-4101)
P.O. Box 975 (95108-0975)
PHONE....................408 292-4968
Donald George Isaacson, *CEO*
Dane Littleton, *President*
Elizabeth Wozniak, *CFO*
Alan Glace, *Vice Pres*
Thomas Radich, *Vice Pres*
EMP: 225 **EST:** 1981
SQ FT: 24,000
SALES (est): 42.3MM **Privately Held**
WEB: www.icominc.com
SIC: 1711 Mechanical contractor

(P-1283)
INCOM MECHANICAL INC
975 Transport Way Ste 5, Petaluma (94954-6860)
PHONE....................707 586-0511
Charles J Lacoti, *President*
Gabrielle Candrian, *Treasurer*
Jeff Lacoti, *Vice Pres*
Phil Lacoti, *Vice Pres*
Leavell Jennifer, *Administration*
EMP: 65 **EST:** 1987
SQ FT: 7,000
SALES (est): 10MM **Privately Held**
WEB: www.incommechanical.com
SIC: 1711 Plumbing contractors

1711 - Plumbing, Heating & Air Conditioning Contractors County (P-1284)

PRODUCTS & SERVICES SECTION

(P-1284)
INFINITY ENERGY INC
3825 Atherton Rd Ste 101, Rocklin (95765-3704)
PHONE..................916 474-4723
Mark Stacy, *CEO*
Jon Lapray, *COO*
Bryson Solomon, *COO*
Cory Gilbert, *CFO*
Cameron Kelly, *Security Dir*
EMP: 150 **EST:** 2014
SALES (est): 63.6MM **Privately Held**
WEB: www.infinityenergy.com
SIC: 1711 Solar energy contractor

(P-1285)
INTECH MECHANICAL COMPANY LLC
7501 Galilee Rd, Roseville (95678-6905)
PHONE..................916 797-4900
Richard B Chowdry,
Dena Randall, *CFO*
Julie Chowdry, *Corp Secy*
Mike Friesen, *Vice Pres*
Joshua Ackenheil, *Technician*
EMP: 150 **EST:** 2014
SQ FT: 39,775
SALES (est): 32.3MM **Privately Held**
WEB: www.intech-mech.com
SIC: 1711 8711 Plumbing contractors; heating & air conditioning contractors; mechanical contractor; process piping contractor; heating & ventilation engineering

(P-1286)
IRON MECHANICAL INC (PA)
721 N B St Ste 100, Sacramento (95811-0347)
PHONE..................916 341-3530
Terrance Risse, *President*
Taylor Wilson, *Asst Controller*
Marissa Ayala, *Human Res Mgr*
Jeremy Marchi, *Foreman/Supr*
EMP: 95 **EST:** 2009
SQ FT: 3,000
SALES (est): 24MM **Privately Held**
WEB: www.ironmechanical.com
SIC: 1711 Mechanical contractor

(P-1287)
IRON OAK PLUMBING INC
3825 Cincinnati Ave Ste A, Rocklin (95765-1316)
P.O. Box 2811 (95677-8473)
PHONE..................916 782-9565
Gary Ferrari, *President*
EMP: 40 **EST:** 2011
SALES (est): 3.1MM **Privately Held**
WEB: www.ironoakplumbing.com
SIC: 1711 Plumbing contractors

(P-1288)
J & J AIR CONDITIONING INC
Also Called: Honeywell Authorized Dealer
1086 N 11th St, San Jose (95112-2927)
PHONE..................408 920-0662
Jerry Hurwitz, *Owner*
Susan Borkin, *Treasurer*
Connie Shoffner, *Executive Asst*
Pam York, *Admin Asst*
Rhonda Yee, *Administration*
EMP: 60 **EST:** 1978
SQ FT: 10,000
SALES (est): 13.7MM **Privately Held**
WEB: www.jjair.com
SIC: 1711 Warm air heating & air conditioning contractor; ventilation & duct work contractor

(P-1289)
J H SIMPSON COMPANY INC
Also Called: Simpson, J H Co
4025 Coronado Ave, Stockton (95204-2311)
P.O. Box 8640 (95208-0640)
PHONE..................209 466-1477
William J Relf, *CEO*
Marvin G Rosato, *Vice Pres*
Michael Lawson, *Principal*
EMP: 54 **EST:** 1944
SQ FT: 10,000
SALES (est): 2.5MM **Privately Held**
WEB: www.honeywell.com
SIC: 1711 1761 Warm air heating & air conditioning contractor; sheet metalwork

(P-1290)
J R PIERCE PLUMBING COMPANY
14481 Wicks Blvd, San Leandro (94577-6711)
PHONE..................510 483-5473
Richard Pierce, *President*
Mike Bobosky, *Vice Pres*
Dave Barich, *General Mgr*
Antonio Estrada, *Purchasing*
Matt EXT, *Purchasing*
EMP: 49 **EST:** 1927
SQ FT: 4,000
SALES (est): 5.3MM **Privately Held**
WEB: www.jrpierceplumbing.com
SIC: 1711 Plumbing contractors

(P-1291)
JASON MECHANICAL INC
1379 Fitzgerald Rd, Rancho Cordova (95742)
PHONE..................916 638-8763
Jason Gerald Voll, *CEO*
EMP: 50 **EST:** 2015
SALES (est): 3.5MM **Privately Held**
WEB: www.jasonmech.net
SIC: 1711 Mechanical contractor

(P-1292)
JC HEATING & AC INC (PA)
Also Called: J C Heating & Air Conditioning
1900 Commercial Way Ste E, Santa Cruz (95065-1844)
P.O. Box 1078, Soquel (95073-1078)
PHONE..................831 475-6538
John Hadley Sr, *President*
Carol Hadley, *Corp Secy*
EMP: 35 **EST:** 1977
SQ FT: 2,000
SALES (est): 8MM **Privately Held**
WEB: www.jcheatingairconditioning.com
SIC: 1711 Warm air heating & air conditioning contractor

(P-1293)
JERICO FIRE PROTECTION CO INC
1380 N Hulbert Ave, Fresno (93728-1137)
PHONE..................559 255-6446
Jerry L Miller, *President*
Peggy Miller, *Corp Secy*
Gloria Magdalena, *Administration*
Kevin Clay, *Manager*
Jory Rothenfluh, *Manager*
EMP: 46 **EST:** 1986
SQ FT: 5,000
SALES (est): 7.9MM **Privately Held**
WEB: www.jericofire.com
SIC: 1711 Fire sprinkler system installation

(P-1294)
JESSEE HEATING & AC
3025 Southgate Ln, Chico (95928-7427)
PHONE..................530 891-4926
John Gray Jr, *President*
Mike S Gray, *Vice Pres*
Mike Gray, *Opers Mgr*
EMP: 40 **EST:** 1981
SQ FT: 10,000
SALES (est): 7.6MM **Privately Held**
WEB: www.jesseeheatingandair.com
SIC: 1711 1761 Warm air heating & air conditioning contractor; sheet metalwork

(P-1295)
JINKOSOLAR (US) HOLDING INC (PA)
595 Market St Ste 2200, San Francisco (94105-2834)
PHONE..................415 402-0502
Kangping Chen, *CEO*
Xiande LI, *Ch of Bd*
Longgen Zhang, *CFO*
Allen Guo, *Vice Pres*
Xianhua LI, *Vice Pres*
▲ **EMP:** 181 **EST:** 2011
SALES (est): 20.1MM **Privately Held**
SIC: 1711 Solar energy contractor

(P-1296)
JR PERCE PLBG INC SACRAMENTO
3610 Cincinnati Ave, Rocklin (95765-1203)
PHONE..................916 434-9554
Dennis Pierce, *President*
Jeremy McKellar, *Superintendent*
EMP: 150
SQ FT: 11,000
SALES (est): 38.3MM **Privately Held**
WEB: www.onlinejrp.com
SIC: 1711 Plumbing contractors

(P-1297)
KINETICS MECHANICAL SVC INC
6336 Patterson Pass Rd H, Livermore (94550-9577)
PHONE..................925 245-6200
Ralph E Dorotinsky, *President*
Craig Kirk, *Vice Pres*
Minh Le, *General Mgr*
Sean McIntyre, *Project Mgr*
John Zhang, *Manager*
EMP: 100 **EST:** 1997
SQ FT: 10,000
SALES (est): 14.3MM **Privately Held**
WEB: www.kms-inc.com
SIC: 1711 Mechanical contractor

(P-1298)
KUYKENDALL SOLAR CORPORATION
2840 Yosemite Spgs, Coarsegold (93614)
PHONE..................559 658-2525
Brian Eric Kuykendall, *President*
Brian Kuykendall, *Bd of Directors*
Elizabeth Kuykendall, *Vice Pres*
Brian Mathewso, *Manager*
EMP: 46 **EST:** 2010
SALES (est): 5.5MM **Privately Held**
WEB: www.kuykendallsolar.com
SIC: 1711 Solar energy contractor

(P-1299)
L J KRUSE CO
Also Called: Honeywell Authorized Dealer
920 Pardee St, Berkeley (94710-2626)
P.O. Box 2900 (94702-0900)
PHONE..................510 644-0260
David J Kruse, *President*
Karen Lown, *CFO*
Andrew S Kruse, *Exec VP*
Nate Kruse, *Vice Pres*
Nathan Kruse, *Vice Pres*
EMP: 60
SQ FT: 14,000
SALES (est): 12.5MM **Privately Held**
WEB: www.ljkruse.com
SIC: 1711 Plumbing contractors

(P-1300)
LADELL INC
Also Called: Johnson Air
605 N Halifax Ave, Clovis (93611-7270)
PHONE..................559 650-2000
Steve Johnson, *President*
Ryan Calvert, *Consultant*
EMP: 50 **EST:** 1947
SQ FT: 38,000
SALES (est): 5.9MM **Privately Held**
WEB: www.johnsonair.net
SIC: 1711 Warm air heating & air conditioning contractor

(P-1301)
LANDMARK CAPITAL INC
Also Called: Solar Energy Collective
2311 W Alpine Ave, Stockton (95204-2701)
PHONE..................209 242-8880
EMP: 41
SALES (est): 4.1MM **Privately Held**
WEB: www.collective.solar
SIC: 1711 Plumbing/Heating/Air Cond Contractor

(P-1302)
LAWSON MECHANICAL CONTRACTORS (PA)
6090 S Watt Ave, Sacramento (95829-1302)
P.O. Box 15224 (95851-0224)
PHONE..................916 381-5000
Rodney Lawson, *President*
David Lawson, *Corp Secy*
Rod Barbour, *Vice Pres*
Rodney Barbour, *Vice Pres*
Keith Velasquez, *Executive*
EMP: 98 **EST:** 1947
SQ FT: 31,000
SALES (est): 38.9MM **Privately Held**
WEB: www.lawsonmechanical.com
SIC: 1711 Plumbing contractors; heating & air conditioning contractors; mechanical contractor

(P-1303)
LEGACY MECH & ENRGY SVCS INC
3130 Crow Canyon Pl # 410, San Ramon (94583-1346)
PHONE..................925 820-6938
Bill Longbotham, *Vice Pres*
Charles Barnes, *Vice Pres*
Chip Eskildsen, *Vice Pres*
Jack Larkin, *Vice Pres*
Mary Castello, *Admin Asst*
EMP: 100
SQ FT: 4,000
SALES (est): 25.2MM **Privately Held**
WEB: www.legacymechanical.com
SIC: 1711 Mechanical contractor

(P-1304)
LEK ENTERPRISES INC
Also Called: Plumbing Enterprises
12175 Folsom Blvd Ste B, Rancho Cordova (95742-6312)
P.O. Box 921, Folsom (95763-0921)
PHONE..................916 985-4102
Leon Kelly, *President*
Kate Gadberry, *Controller*
EMP: 48 **EST:** 1999
SQ FT: 1,400
SALES (est): 9.1MM **Privately Held**
WEB: www.lekenterprises.com
SIC: 1711 Plumbing contractors

(P-1305)
LESCURE COMPANY INC
2301 Arnold Industrial Wa, Concord (94520-5376)
P.O. Box 968, Lafayette (94549-0968)
PHONE..................925 283-2528
Michael Lescure, *President*
Allen Lescure, *Vice Pres*
Brian Lescure, *Vice Pres*
Conrad Chin, *Sales Mgr*
Donna Burpee, *Receptionist*
EMP: 70 **EST:** 1947
SQ FT: 10,000
SALES (est): 10.4MM **Privately Held**
WEB: www.lescurecompany.com
SIC: 1711 Plumbing contractors

(P-1306)
LINDSTROM CO
1121 Bayswater Ave, San Mateo (94401-1196)
PHONE..................650 343-4542
Donald R Lindstrom, *President*
Nancy M Lindstrom, *Corp Secy*
Adan Gomez, *Opers Staff*
Bruce Quittenton, *Sales Staff*
EMP: 41 **EST:** 1936
SQ FT: 2,200
SALES (est): 3.4MM **Privately Held**
WEB: www.lindstromfasteners.com
SIC: 1711 Plumbing contractors

(P-1307)
LIVE ACTION GENERAL ENGRG INC
2972 Larkin Ave, Clovis (93612-3986)
PHONE..................559 564-3444
Bobby Tracy, *President*
Carl Mackey, *Project Mgr*
EMP: 30 **EST:** 2014
SALES (est): 9MM **Privately Held**
WEB: www.eliteteamoffices.com
SIC: 1711 1771 1611 3531 Solar energy contractor; concrete work; surfacing & paving; plows: construction, excavating & grading; general electrical contractor

(P-1308)
LOVAZZANO MECHANICAL INC
189 Constitution Dr, Menlo Park (94025-1106)
PHONE..................650 367-6216
Bruce Lovazzano Sr, *CEO*
Ed Mariano, *Purch Mgr*
EMP: 70 **EST:** 1991
SQ FT: 3,100

PRODUCTS & SERVICES SECTION
1711 - Plumbing, Heating & Air Conditioning Contractors County (P-1331)

SALES (est): 9.5MM **Privately Held**
WEB: www.lovazzano.com
SIC: **1711** Plumbing contractors

(P-1309)
MARCUCCI HEATING AND AC INC
Also Called: R & R Marcuccia/C Htg & Shtmtl
2400 Bay Rd, Redwood City (94063-3013)
PHONE.................650 556-1882
Roy Huhn, *Partner*
Ralph Schletter, *Partner*
Jon McLaughlin, *Advisor*
EMP: 33 EST: 1952
SQ FT: 8,888
SALES (est): 1.2MM **Privately Held**
WEB: www.marcuccihvac.pro
SIC: **1711** 3444 Warm air heating & air conditioning contractor; sheet metalwork

(P-1310)
MARELICH MECHANICAL CO INC (HQ)
24041 Amador St, Hayward (94544-1201)
PHONE.................510 785-5500
Keith R Atteberry, *President*
Chad Johnston, *Vice Pres*
Terry J Kvochak, *Vice Pres*
Andrew Ostrowski, *Vice Pres*
John Powell, *Vice Pres*
EMP: 65 EST: 1946
SQ FT: 40,000
SALES (est): 67.3MM
SALES (corp-wide): 8.8B **Publicly Held**
WEB: www.marelich.com
SIC: **1711** 1623 3822 Mechanical contractor; pipeline construction; auto controls regulating residntl & coml environmt & applncs
PA: Emcor Group, Inc.
 301 Merritt 7 Fl 6
 Norwalk CT 06851
 203 849-7800

(P-1311)
MARQUEE FIRE PROTECTION LLC (PA)
710 W Stadium Ln, Sacramento (95834-1130)
PHONE.................916 641-7997
Donna Awtrey, *Principal*
Jeff Awtrey, *Vice Pres*
Rick Awtrey, *Vice Pres*
Kimberly Reed, *Vice Pres*
EMP: 41 EST: 1989
SQ FT: 5,400
SALES (est): 14MM **Privately Held**
WEB: www.marqueefire.com
SIC: **1711** Fire sprinkler system installation

(P-1312)
MONSTER MEP INC
1521 Terminal Ave, San Jose (95112-4316)
P.O. Box 6, Los Gatos (95031-0006)
PHONE.................408 727-8362
Jeffery Miller, *President*
EMP: 60 EST: 1997
SQ FT: 10,000
SALES (est): 7.8MM **Privately Held**
WEB: www.monstermechanical.com
SIC: **1711** Plumbing contractors

(P-1313)
MOUNTING SYSTEMS INC
180 Promenade Cir Ste 300, Sacramento (95834-2952)
PHONE.................916 374-8872
Kasim Ersoy, *President*
◆ EMP: 51 EST: 2010
SALES (est): 14.1MM
SALES (corp-wide): 479.2MM **Privately Held**
WEB: www.mounting-systems.com
SIC: **1711** Mechanical contractor
HQ: Mounting Systems Gmbh
 Mittenwalder Str. 9a
 Rangsdorf BB 15834
 337 085-2910

(P-1314)
N V HEATHORN INC
Also Called: N V H
1980 Olivera Rd Ste C, Concord (94520-5454)
PHONE.................510 569-9100
Edward W Heathorn, *President*
David A Heathorn, *CFO*
Norman T R Heathorn, *Principal*
Scott Heathorn, *Project Engr*
Melissa Hassler, *Manager*
EMP: 70 EST: 1932
SALES (est): 12.8MM **Privately Held**
WEB: www.nvheathorn.com
SIC: **1711** 1629 Warm air heating & air conditioning contractor; waste water & sewage treatment plant construction

(P-1315)
NEW ENGLAND SHTMTL & MECH CO
2731 S Cherry Ave, Fresno (93706-5423)
P.O. Box 27409 (93729-7409)
PHONE.................559 268-7375
John Sloan, *CEO*
Laura Marchese, *Vice Pres*
Joshua Wilkinson, *Vice Pres*
EMP: 220 EST: 2008
SALES: 63.6MM
SALES (corp-wide): 17.8MM **Privately Held**
WEB: www.nesm.com
SIC: **1711** Mechanical contractor
PA: Lyles Diversified, Inc.
 525 W Alluvial Ave
 Fresno CA 93711
 559 441-1900

(P-1316)
NEXUS ENERGY SYSTEMS INC
4025 S Golden State Blvd, Fresno (93725-9242)
PHONE.................866 334-6639
Michael Rietkerk, *CEO*
EMP: 47 **Privately Held**
WEB: www.nexussolar.net
SIC: **1711** Solar energy contractor
PA: Nexus Energy Systems Inc.
 2810 Harbor Blvd Ste 201
 Oxnard CA 93035

(P-1317)
NOR-CAL CLIMATE CONTROL INC (PA)
3963 Apple Blossom Way, Carmichael (95608-2347)
PHONE.................916 439-6534
Nikolay P Petrashishin, *Owner*
EMP: 37 EST: 2013
SALES (est): 495.4K **Privately Held**
SIC: **1711** Heating & air conditioning contractors

(P-1318)
NORTHERN CAL FIRE PRTCTION SVC
Also Called: Nor-Cal Fire Protection
16840 Joleen Way Ste A, Morgan Hill (95037-4606)
PHONE.................408 776-1580
Matt Cetani, *President*
Paul Cetani, *Vice Pres*
EMP: 38 EST: 1995
SQ FT: 6,000
SALES (est): 5.1MM **Privately Held**
WEB: www.norcalfire.com
SIC: **1711** 5999 Fire sprinkler system installation; alarm & safety equipment stores; fire extinguishers; safety supplies & equipment

(P-1319)
O C MCDONALD CO INC
1150 W San Carlos St, San Jose (95126-3440)
P.O. Box 26560 (95159-6560)
PHONE.................408 295-2182
James Mc Donald, *President*
Heidi Dunn, *Admin Asst*
Melissa Allison, *CTO*
Matthew McDonald, *Engineer*
J Brennan, *Controller*
EMP: 150
SQ FT: 10,500
SALES (est): 50MM **Privately Held**
WEB: www.ocmcdonald.com
SIC: **1711** 3585 3541 3444 Mechanical contractor; refrigeration & heating equipment; machine tools, metal cutting type; sheet metalwork; plumbing fixture fittings & trim

(P-1320)
OAKVILLE PUMP SERVICE INC
2310 Laurel St Ste 1, NAPA (94559-3155)
PHONE.................707 944-2471
Roger Lutz Jr, *President*
Marlys Lutz, *CFO*
Nik Lutz, *General Mgr*
Aaron Garcia, *Opers Staff*
Jean Butala, *Director*
▲ EMP: 44 EST: 1983
SALES (est): 9.9MM **Privately Held**
WEB: www.oakvillepump.com
SIC: **1711** 3594 5084 Plumbing contractors; pumps, hydraulic power transfer; pumps & pumping equipment

(P-1321)
OBRIEN MECHANICAL INC
1515 Galvez Ave, San Francisco (94124-1707)
PHONE.................415 695-1800
John O'Brien, *President*
Armand Kilijian, *Vice Pres*
EMP: 45 EST: 1972
SQ FT: 16,000
SALES (est): 10.1MM **Privately Held**
WEB: www.obmi2.com
SIC: **1711** Mechanical contractor

(P-1322)
OHAGIN MANUFACTURING LLC
210 Classic Ct Ste 100, Rohnert Park (94928-1660)
PHONE.................707 872-3620
Greg Daniels, *President*
Mark Marquez, *COO*
Carl Forman, *Sales Staff*
Danielle Kinney, *Mktg Coord*
Crissy Mansfield, *Manager*
EMP: 50 EST: 2013
SALES (est): 4.2MM **Privately Held**
WEB: www.ohagin.com
SIC: **1711** Ventilation & duct work contractor

(P-1323)
OHAGINS INC
210 Classic Ct Ste 100, Rohnert Park (94928-1660)
PHONE.................707 303-3660
Carolina O'Hagin, *CEO*
Greg Daniels, *CEO*
Mark Marquez, *COO*
Mike Fulton, *Technical Staff*
▲ EMP: 60 EST: 1969
SQ FT: 57,000
SALES (est): 7.8MM **Privately Held**
WEB: www.ohagin.com
SIC: **1711** Ventilation & duct work contractor

(P-1324)
ON-TIME AC & HTG LLC
Also Called: Service Champions
4430 Yankee Hill Rd, Rocklin (95677-1629)
PHONE.................916 229-6370
Kevin Comerford, *Branch Mgr*
Stephen Gilchrist, *Advisor*
EMP: 39
SALES (corp-wide): 154.8MM **Privately Held**
WEB: www.servicechampions.net
SIC: **1711** Warm air heating & air conditioning contractor
HQ: On-Time Air Conditioning & Heating, Llc
 7020 Commerce Dr
 Pleasanton CA 94588
 925 598-1911

(P-1325)
ON-TIME AC & HTG LLC
Also Called: Service Champions
2161 Del Franco St, San Jose (95131-1570)
PHONE.................408 279-5843
EMP: 52
SALES (corp-wide): 154.8MM **Privately Held**
WEB: www.servicechampions.net
SIC: **1711** Warm air heating & air conditioning contractor
HQ: On-Time Air Conditioning & Heating, Llc
 7020 Commerce Dr
 Pleasanton CA 94588
 925 598-1911

(P-1326)
ON-TIME AC & HTG LLC
Also Called: Service Champions
200 Mason Cir Ste 200 # 200, Concord (94520-1249)
PHONE.................925 566-2422
Osag Temple, *Technician*
Scott Self, *Advisor*
EMP: 62
SALES (corp-wide): 154.8MM **Privately Held**
WEB: www.servicechampions.net
SIC: **1711** Septic system construction
HQ: On-Time Air Conditioning & Heating, Llc
 7020 Commerce Dr
 Pleasanton CA 94588
 925 598-1911

(P-1327)
ON-TIME AC & HTG LLC
Also Called: Service Champions
96 Rickenbacker Cir, Livermore (94551-7211)
PHONE.................925 800-5804
EMP: 71
SALES (corp-wide): 154.8MM **Privately Held**
WEB: www.servicechampions.net
SIC: **1711** Warm air heating & air conditioning contractor
HQ: On-Time Air Conditioning & Heating, Llc
 7020 Commerce Dr
 Pleasanton CA 94588
 925 598-1911

(P-1328)
ON-TIME AC & HTG LLC (HQ)
Also Called: Service Champions
7020 Commerce Dr, Pleasanton (94588-8021)
PHONE.................925 598-1911
Keviin J Comerford, *CEO*
Ray Dias, *Vice Pres*
Mark Stewart, *General Mgr*
Stephanie Schumacher, *Human Resources*
Lyndy Rose, *Prdtn Mgr*
EMP: 88 EST: 2002
SALES (est): 59.3MM
SALES (corp-wide): 154.8MM **Privately Held**
WEB: www.servicechampions.net
SIC: **1711** Warm air heating & air conditioning contractor
PA: Wrench Group, Llc
 1787 Williams Dr
 Marietta GA 30066
 678 784-2260

(P-1329)
ORCA HEATING AND RFRGN INC
Also Called: Franks Heating & Refrigeration
250 Michigan Rd, Crescent City (95531-9262)
PHONE.................707 464-9529
Frank Ormonde, *CEO*
EMP: 40 EST: 1989
SQ FT: 10,000
SALES (est): 5.5MM **Privately Held**
WEB: www.bestheatinginfo.com
SIC: **1711** Refrigeration contractor

(P-1330)
OXYPOWER INC (PA)
Also Called: Occidental Power Solar Co.
5982 Mission St, San Francisco (94112-4036)
PHONE.................415 681-8861
Gregory J Kennedy, *CEO*
EMP: 65 EST: 2007
SALES (est): 7.2MM **Privately Held**
WEB: www.oxypower.com
SIC: **1711** 8711 Solar energy contractor; electrical or electronic engineering

(P-1331)
PACIFIC COAST FIRE INC
470 Division St, Campbell (95008-6923)
PHONE.................408 370-1234

1711 - Plumbing, Heating & Air Conditioning Contractors County (P-1332)

PRODUCTS & SERVICES SECTION

Bradley J Smith, *President*
Gabrielle Fidiam-Smith, *Vice Pres*
Jason Buelle-Corbin, *Engineer*
EMP: 37 **EST:** 1997
SQ FT: 5,000
SALES (est): 2.3MM **Privately Held**
WEB: www.pacificcoastfire.ca
SIC: 1711 Fire sprinkler system installation

(P-1332)
PACIFIC RIM PLUMBING
2283 Research Dr, Livermore (94550-3847)
PHONE.................................925 443-3333
Lucinda Borovick, *Principal*
Donna Griffith, *Vice Pres*
Jim Ellison, *General Mgr*
Jacob Rezac, *Purch Mgr*
Jose Torres, *Purch Mgr*
EMP: 39 **EST:** 2005
SALES (est): 5.5MM **Privately Held**
WEB: www.pacrimplumbing.com
SIC: 1711 Plumbing contractors

(P-1333)
PAN-PACIFIC MECHANICAL LLC
48363 Fremont Blvd, Fremont (94538-6580)
PHONE.................................650 561-8810
Tom Sakurai, *Manager*
Ryan Cavanaugh, *COO*
Mario Santilli, *Executive*
Jason Tendler, *Executive*
Reed McMackin, *General Mgr*
EMP: 425
SALES (corp-wide): 367.1MM **Privately Held**
WEB: www.ppmechanical.com
SIC: 1711 Plumbing contractors
PA: Pan-Pacific Mechanical Llc
18250 Euclid St
Fountain Valley CA 92708
949 474-9170

(P-1334)
PANELIZED SOLAR INC
5731 Stoddard Rd, Modesto (95356-9000)
PHONE.................................209 343-8600
EMP: 41 **EST:** 2014
SALES (est): 494.4K **Privately Held**
WEB: www.panelizedsolar.com
SIC: 1711 Solar energy contractor
PA: Panelized Structures, Inc.
5731 Stoddard Rd
Modesto CA 95356

(P-1335)
PARAGON VENTURES INC
Also Called: Paragon Heating & AC
1722 E Flora St, Stockton (95205-4262)
PHONE.................................209 466-3530
Harry H Shuler Jr, *President*
William D Brewer, *Vice Pres*
EMP: 35 **EST:** 1984
SQ FT: 12,000
SALES (est): 3.8MM **Privately Held**
SIC: 1711 Warm air heating & air conditioning contractor; plumbing contractors

(P-1336)
PATTERN RENEWABLES 2 LP (DH)
1088 Sansome St, San Francisco (94111-1308)
PHONE.................................415 283-4000
EMP: 129 **EST:** 2016
SALES (est): 2MM
SALES (corp-wide): 220.9K **Privately Held**
WEB: www.patternenergy.com
SIC: 1711 Solar energy contractor
HQ: Pattern Energy Group Inc.
1088 Sansome St
San Francisco CA 94111
415 283-4000

(P-1337)
PINASCO PLUMBING & HEATING INC
Also Called: Pinasco Mechinical
2145 E Taylor St, Stockton (95205-6337)
P.O. Box 55287 (95205-8787)
PHONE.................................209 463-7793
Tom Pinasco, *President*
John Pinasco, *Treasurer*

Joseph Pinasco, *Admin Sec*
EMP: 51 **EST:** 1957
SQ FT: 1,000
SALES (est): 1MM **Privately Held**
WEB: www.pinascoplumbing.com
SIC: 1711 Plumbing contractors; fire sprinkler system installation; warm air heating & air conditioning contractor

(P-1338)
PRO-TECH FIRE PRTCTION SYSTEMS
8880 Cal Center Dr # 400, Sacramento (95826-3222)
PHONE.................................916 388-0255
Michael Walsh, *Principal*
EMP: 100 **Privately Held**
WEB: www.pro-techfire.com
SIC: 1711 Fire sprinkler system installation
HQ: Pro-Tech Fire Protection Systems Corp.
8540 Younger Creek Dr # 2
Sacramento CA 95828

(P-1339)
PROMISE ENERGY INC
3558 Round Barn Blvd # 200, Santa Rosa (95403-0991)
PHONE.................................707 938-7207
Adam Boucher, *President*
Derek Huntington, *CFO*
Richard Barnes, *Vice Pres*
Michael Boucher, *Vice Pres*
Andy Mannle, *Vice Pres*
EMP: 40 **EST:** 2011
SQ FT: 1,500
SALES (est): 5MM **Privately Held**
WEB: www.promiseenergy.com
SIC: 1711 Solar energy contractor

(P-1340)
PURLS SHEET METAL & AC
232 S Schnoor Ave, Madera (93637-5189)
PHONE.................................559 674-2774
Michael Purl, *President*
Billee Michelle Purl, *Vice Pres*
Pat Reese, *Technician*
Omar Tinajero, *Technician*
EMP: 35 **EST:** 1952
SQ FT: 5,000
SALES (est): 6.2MM **Privately Held**
WEB: www.purlsheetmetal.com
SIC: 1711 1761 Warm air heating & air conditioning contractor; sheet metalwork

(P-1341)
R B SPENCER INC
Also Called: Honeywell Authorized Dealer
1188 Hassett Ave, Yuba City (95991-7212)
PHONE.................................530 674-8307
Robert B Spencer, *President*
Brigit Spencer, *CFO*
Kayce Wolcott, *Admin Asst*
Rich Bogdonoff, *Sales Staff*
EMP: 52 **EST:** 1992
SQ FT: 8,000
SALES (est): 10.2MM **Privately Held**
WEB: www.rbspencerinc.com
SIC: 1711 Warm air heating & air conditioning contractor

(P-1342)
RAM MECHANICAL INC
3506 Moore Rd, Ceres (95307-9402)
PHONE.................................209 531-9155
Neil Hodgson, *President*
Marcus Pollard, *Project Mgr*
Kevin Caine, *Engineer*
Rob Stevenson, *Controller*
Frank Muniain, *Foreman/Supr*
EMP: 60
SQ FT: 22,500
SALES (est): 25.1MM **Privately Held**
WEB: www.ram-mechanical.com
SIC: 1711 8711 3599 3535 Mechanical contractor; engineering services; custom machinery; conveyors & conveying equipment

(P-1343)
RANDO AAA HVAC INC
Also Called: A A A Furnace Company
1712 Stone Ave Ste 1, San Jose (95125-1309)
PHONE.................................408 293-4717

Jim Rando, *President*
Marrissa Rando, *Principal*
EMP: 50 **EST:** 1951
SQ FT: 5,000
SALES (est): 6.1MM **Privately Held**
WEB: www.aaa-furnace.com
SIC: 1711 3444 3433 Warm air heating & air conditioning contractor; ventilation & duct work contractor; sheet metalwork; heating equipment, except electric

(P-1344)
RE MILANO PLUMBING CORP
280 Arthur Rd B, Martinez (94553-2208)
P.O. Box 1383 (94553-7383)
PHONE.................................925 500-1372
Leigha M Ramirez, *CEO*
Robert Romeo, *President*
EMP: 50 **EST:** 2014
SALES (est): 4MM **Privately Held**
SIC: 1711 Plumbing contractors

(P-1345)
RECURRENT ENERGY LLC (HQ)
123 Mission St Ste 1800, San Francisco (94105-5134)
PHONE.................................415 956-3168
David Brochu, *CEO*
Mitchell Randall, *President*
EMP: 95 **EST:** 2006
SALES (est): 46.9MM
SALES (corp-wide): 3.4B **Privately Held**
WEB: www.recurrentenergy.com
SIC: 1711 Solar energy contractor
PA: Canadian Solar Inc
545 Speedvale Ave W
Guelph ON N1K 1
519 837-1881

(P-1346)
RIGHT NOW AIR
821 Eubanks Dr Ste C, Vacaville (95688-9356)
PHONE.................................707 447-3063
John Neuman, *President*
Renee Neuman, *Admin Sec*
EMP: 42 **EST:** 2004
SALES (est): 5.5MM **Privately Held**
WEB: www.rightnowairandsolar.com
SIC: 1711 Warm air heating & air conditioning contractor; heating & air conditioning contractors

(P-1347)
RISSE CONSTRUCTION INC
Also Called: Rci Plumbing
651 M St, Rio Linda (95673-2237)
P.O. Box 10 (95673-0010)
PHONE.................................916 991-2700
Dana M Risse, *President*
Greg Risse, *Vice Pres*
EMP: 40 **EST:** 1988
SALES (est): 12.8MM **Privately Held**
WEB: www.rciplumbingcontractors.com
SIC: 1711 1542 Plumbing contractors; commercial & office building, new construction

(P-1348)
RL FULLER INC
Also Called: Superior Mechanical
5130 Fulton Dr Ste K, Fairfield (94534-4223)
PHONE.................................707 207-0100
Ricky Lee Fuller, *President*
Bonnie Fuller, *Admin Sec*
EMP: 39 **EST:** 1997
SALES (est): 7.5MM **Privately Held**
WEB: www.mysuperiormechanical.com
SIC: 1711 Warm air heating & air conditioning contractor

(P-1349)
ROSS & SONS RFRGN & CNSTR INC
Also Called: Ross & Christopher
7828 S Maple Ave, Fresno (93725-9787)
PHONE.................................559 834-5947
Rick L Ross, *CEO*
Jack Farnesi, *CFO*
Adam Ross, *Vice Pres*
EMP: 40 **EST:** 2000
SQ FT: 20,000
SALES (est): 8.4MM **Privately Held**
SIC: 1711 Refrigeration contractor

(P-1350)
ROUNTREE PLUMBING AND HTG INC
1624 Santa Clara Dr # 120, Roseville (95661-3553)
PHONE.................................650 298-0300
Stephen Singewald, *President*
Pat Singewald, *Corp Secy*
Sean Singewald, *Vice Pres*
Scott Strombom, *Sr Project Mgr*
EMP: 60 **EST:** 1961
SQ FT: 10,000
SALES (est): 11.4MM **Privately Held**
WEB: www.rountreeinc.com
SIC: 1711 Plumbing contractors; warm air heating & air conditioning contractor

(P-1351)
ROV ENTERPRISES INC
Also Called: Rapid First Plumbing
5013 Roberts Ave Ste B, McClellan (95652-2623)
PHONE.................................916 448-2672
Sharon Blomquist, *President*
Michael Carter, *Vice Pres*
Wendy Challberg, *Admin Sec*
EMP: 48 **EST:** 1974
SQ FT: 13,000
SALES (est): 1.7MM **Privately Held**
WEB: www.rapidfirstplumbing.com
SIC: 1711 Plumbing contractors

(P-1352)
RUSSELL MECHANICAL INC
3251 Monier Cir Ste A, Rancho Cordova (95742-6812)
PHONE.................................916 635-2522
Danny L Russell, *President*
Steve Russell, *Vice Pres*
Karen Russell, *Principal*
Patrick Wanner, *Director*
Rod Hammond, *Superintendent*
EMP: 90 **EST:** 1982
SQ FT: 22,000
SALES (est): 18.9MM **Privately Held**
WEB: www.russellmechanical.com
SIC: 1711 1799 7389 3441 Mechanical contractor; welding on site; design services; fabricated structural metal

(P-1353)
SAN BENITO HTG & SHTMTL INC
Also Called: Honeywell Authorized Dealer
1771 San Felipe Rd, Hollister (95023-2543)
P.O. Box 321 (95024-0321)
PHONE.................................831 637-1112
Robert Rodriguez, *President*
Enrique T Rodriguez, *Treasurer*
Araceli Rodriguez, *Vice Pres*
Priscilla Rodriguez, *Vice Pres*
EMP: 85 **EST:** 1985
SQ FT: 12,000
SALES (est): 11.1MM **Privately Held**
WEB: www.sanbenitoheating.com
SIC: 1711 1761 Warm air heating & air conditioning contractor; sheet metalwork; roofing contractor

(P-1354)
SAN JOSE AIR CONDITIONING INC
5725 Winfield Blvd Ste 5, San Jose (95123-2430)
PHONE.................................408 457-7936
EMP: 35
SALES (est): 2MM **Privately Held**
WEB: www.hvac-sanjose.com
SIC: 1711 Plumbing/Heating/Air Cond Contractor

(P-1355)
SANTA CRUZ WESTSIDE ELC INC
Also Called: Sandbar Solar and Electric
2656 Mission St, Santa Cruz (95060-5703)
PHONE.................................831 469-8888
Scott Laskey, *President*
Denny Mosher, *Vice Pres*
Dave Brill, *Project Mgr*
Ramey White, *Sales Staff*
Sven Brown, *Director*
EMP: 55 **EST:** 2004

PRODUCTS & SERVICES SECTION
1711 - Plumbing, Heating & Air Conditioning Contractors County (P-1379)

SALES (est): 8.4MM Privately Held
WEB: www.sandbarsc.com
SIC: 1711 Solar energy contractor

(P-1356)
SERVI-TECH CONTROLS INC (PA)
470 W Warwick Ave, Clovis (93619-0405)
PHONE..................559 264-6679
Glenn L Johnson, *President*
Janelle R Silva, *Treasurer*
Nick Johnson, *Project Mgr*
Esther Gregory, *Controller*
Debra Brittsan, *Opers Staff*
EMP: 53 EST: 1975
SALES (est): 8.7MM Privately Held
WEB: www.servi-techcontrols.com
SIC: 1711 Warm air heating & air conditioning contractor; ventilation & duct work contractor

(P-1357)
SILICON VALLEY MECHANICAL INC
2115 Ringwood Ave, San Jose (95131-1725)
P.O. Box 10415, Southport NC (28461-0415)
PHONE..................408 943-0380
Blaine Flickner, *CEO*
Dania Amireh-Baker, *CFO*
Hannah Pettinichio, *Admin Mgr*
Monica Sanchez, *Administration*
Otto Ruano, *IT Specialist*
EMP: 255 EST: 2014
SALES (est): 35MM Privately Held
WEB: www.svminc.com
SIC: 1711 Mechanical contractor

(P-1358)
SILRAY INC
1245 S Winchester Blvd # 301, San Jose (95128-3908)
PHONE..................650 331-1117
April Zhong, *President*
Lee Askelson, *Vice Pres*
Collin Ackerman, *Director*
▲ EMP: 48 EST: 2007
SALES (est): 50MM Privately Held
WEB: www.silray.com
SIC: 1711 Solar energy contractor

(P-1359)
SIMPSON SHEET METAL INC
2833 Dowd Dr Ste C, Santa Rosa (95407-7898)
P.O. Box 2834 (95405-0834)
PHONE..................707 576-1500
Barbara Richardson, *President*
Nancy Simpson, *Treasurer*
Barbara Young, *Web Dvlpr*
EMP: 45 EST: 1977
SQ FT: 88,000
SALES (est): 10.2MM Privately Held
WEB: www.simpsonsheetmetal.com
SIC: 1711 Warm air heating & air conditioning contractor

(P-1360)
SKI AIR CONDITIONING COMPANY
5528 Merchant Cir, Placerville (95667-8625)
P.O. Box 1054, El Dorado (95623-1054)
PHONE..................530 626-4010
Michael Lubinski, *President*
Nannette Lubinski, *Admin Sec*
EMP: 20 EST: 1978
SQ FT: 6,000
SALES (est): 4.3MM Privately Held
WEB: www.skiair.com
SIC: 1711 3443 Warm air heating & air conditioning contractor; sheet metalwork

(P-1361)
SMITS SHEET METAL INC
Also Called: Smit's Heating & AC
6205 Enterprise Dr Ste A, Diamond Springs (95619-9439)
PHONE..................530 622-8446
Toll Free:..................877
Russell Smit, *President*
Janice Smit, *Corp Secy*
EMP: 35 EST: 1972
SQ FT: 3,000
SALES (est): 1.7MM Privately Held
WEB: www.smitssolutions.com
SIC: 1711 Warm air heating & air conditioning contractor; ventilation & duct work contractor

(P-1362)
SOLAR COMPANY INC
20861 Wilbeam Ave Ste 1, Castro Valley (94546-5832)
PHONE..................510 888-9488
Mark Danenhower, *President*
Duane Redman, *CFO*
Nicole Gant, *Consultant*
Misty Wales, *Representative*
EMP: 90
SQ FT: 4,000
SALES (est): 28MM Privately Held
WEB: www.ilovemysolar.com
SIC: 1711 Solar energy contractor

(P-1363)
SOLECON INDUSTRIAL CONTRS INC
1401 Mcwilliams Way, Modesto (95351-1125)
PHONE..................209 572-7390
Jeffrey Grover, *President*
Allen Layman, *Treasurer*
Elaine Grover, *Vice Pres*
Will Grover, *Vice Pres*
Dave Hedrick, *Vice Pres*
EMP: 70 EST: 1981
SQ FT: 15,000
SALES (est): 16.3MM Privately Held
SIC: 1711 Plumbing contractors

(P-1364)
SOLEEVA ENERGY INC
1938 Junction Ave, San Jose (95131-2102)
PHONE..................408 396-4954
Ahmad Qazi, *CEO*
Ralph Ahlgren, *President*
Klaus Petry, *Vice Pres*
Michele Miranda, *Project Mgr*
▲ EMP: 55 EST: 2010
SQ FT: 17,000
SALES (est): 5.1MM Privately Held
WEB: www.soleeva.com
SIC: 1711 Solar energy contractor

(P-1365)
SONNIKSON AND STORDAHL CNSTR
4858 Sunrise Dr, Martinez (94553-4346)
PHONE..................925 229-4028
Michael Sonnikson, *CEO*
Pat Stordahl, *Vice Pres*
Joe Griego, *Manager*
Brad McNabb, *Manager*
Mary Robbins, *Manager*
EMP: 40 EST: 1992
SQ FT: 9,000
SALES (est): 9.1MM Privately Held
WEB: www.sonstor.com
SIC: 1711 1771 Mechanical contractor; foundation & footing contractor

(P-1366)
STEVE SILVA PLUMBING INC
Also Called: Steve Silva Plumbing Showroom
901a Enterprise Way, NAPA (94558-6209)
P.O. Box 6137 (94581-1137)
PHONE..................707 252-3941
Stephen Silva, *President*
Laurie McCord, *Top Exec*
Kathy Silva, *Principal*
Paul Sieber, *Warehouse Mgr*
Chris Delacy, *Manager*
EMP: 38 EST: 1983
SALES (est): 5MM Privately Held
WEB: www.stevesilvaplumbing.com
SIC: 1711 Plumbing contractors; fire sprinkler system installation

(P-1367)
STRATEGIC MECHANICAL INC
4661 E Commerce Ave, Fresno (93725-2204)
PHONE..................559 291-1952
Lonnie F Petty, *President*
Donn Petty, *Treasurer*
Chad Petty, *Exec VP*
Ken McNeal, *Vice Pres*
Katherine Aldrich, *Controller*
EMP: 120 EST: 2004
SQ FT: 60,000
SALES (est): 30.4MM Privately Held
WEB: www.strategicmechanical.com
SIC: 1711 3444 3441 Mechanical contractor; awnings & canopies; fabricated structural metal

(P-1368)
SUNPOWER CORPORATION SYSTEMS (DH)
Also Called: Powerlight
1414 Hrbour Way S Ste 190, Richmond (94804)
P.O. Box 3821, Sunnyvale (94088-3821)
PHONE..................510 260-8200
Thomas L Dinwoodie, *CEO*
Daniel S Shugar, *President*
Peter Aschenbrenner, *Exec VP*
Lisa Bodensteiner, *Exec VP*
Charles D Boynton, *Exec VP*
◆ EMP: 100 EST: 2007
SQ FT: 5,000
SALES (est): 128.1MM
SALES (corp-wide): 4.6B Publicly Held
WEB: www.us.sunpower.com
SIC: 1711 Solar energy contractor
HQ: Sunpower Corporation
  51 Rio Robles
  San Jose CA 95134
  408 240-5500

(P-1369)
SUNRUN CLLSTO ISSUER 2015-1 LL
595 Market St Fl 29, San Francisco (94105-2802)
PHONE..................415 580-6900
EMP: 36 EST: 2015
SALES (est): 1.4MM Publicly Held
WEB: www.sunrun.com
SIC: 1711 Solar energy contractor
PA: Sunrun Inc.
  225 Bush St Ste 1400
  San Francisco CA 94104

(P-1370)
SUNRUN INSTALLATION SVCS INC
575 Dado St, San Jose (95131-1207)
PHONE..................408 746-3062
Dan Alcombright, *Vice Pres*
Billy Heidt, *Director*
EMP: 270 Publicly Held
SIC: 1711 Solar energy contractor
HQ: Sunrun Installation Services Inc.
  775 Fiero Ln Ste 200
  San Luis Obispo CA 93401
  415 580-6900

(P-1371)
SUNRUN INSTALLATION SVCS INC
595 Market St Fl 29, San Francisco (94105-2802)
PHONE..................415 580-6900
Lynn Jurich, *CEO*
EMP: 270 Publicly Held
SIC: 1711 Solar energy contractor
HQ: Sunrun Installation Services Inc.
  775 Fiero Ln Ste 200
  San Luis Obispo CA 93401
  415 580-6900

(P-1372)
SUNRUN INSTALLATION SVCS INC
4933 W Jennifer Ave # 101, Fresno (93722-5087)
PHONE..................559 298-7652
Debbie Aguilar, *Branch Mgr*
EMP: 270 Publicly Held
SIC: 1711 5074 5999 Solar energy contractor; plumbing & hydronic heating supplies; alcoholic beverage making equipment & supplies
HQ: Sunrun Installation Services Inc.
  775 Fiero Ln Ste 200
  San Luis Obispo CA 93401
  415 580-6900

(P-1373)
SUNWORKS UNITED INC (HQ)
2270 Douglas Blvd Ste 216, Roseville (95661-4239)
PHONE..................916 409-6900
James Nelson, *Ch of Bd*
Abe Emard, *COO*
Paul McDonnel, *CFO*
Scott Bowden, *Vice Pres*
Aspen Locken, *Opers Mgr*
EMP: 98 EST: 2010
SALES (est): 20MM
SALES (corp-wide): 37.9MM Publicly Held
WEB: www.sunworksusa.com
SIC: 1711 Solar energy contractor
PA: Sunworks, Inc.
  2270 Douglas Blvd Ste 216
  Roseville CA 95661
  916 409-6900

(P-1374)
SUPERIOR AUTOMATIC SPRNKLR CO
4378 Enterprise St, Fremont (94538-6305)
PHONE..................408 946-7272
Bob Lawson, *President*
Peter Hulin, *President*
Marci Kearney, *Vice Pres*
EMP: 100
SQ FT: 15,000
SALES (est): 24.5MM Privately Held
WEB: www.superior-fire.com
SIC: 1711 Fire sprinkler system installation

(P-1375)
SURE FIRE PROTECTION CO INC
4141 Pestana Pl, Fremont (94538-6325)
PHONE..................510 490-7873
Charlie F Quickert, *CEO*
Thomas Smallen, *Shareholder*
Robert Alonzo, *Sales Staff*
EMP: 40 EST: 1998
SQ FT: 1,000
SALES (est): 6MM Privately Held
WEB: www.surefireprotection.com
SIC: 1711 Fire sprinkler system installation

(P-1376)
TANCO INC
Also Called: Tenney A Norquist
2310 N Walnut Rd, Turlock (95382-8910)
P.O. Box 4776, Modesto (95352-4776)
PHONE..................209 523-8365
Richard Norquist, *President*
Thomas Norquist, *Vice Pres*
Doug Campbell, *Manager*
EMP: 26 EST: 1957
SQ FT: 10,000
SALES (est): 3.5MM Privately Held
WEB: www.tenneyanorquist.com
SIC: 1711 3444 Warm air heating & air conditioning contractor; sheet metalwork

(P-1377)
TAO MECHANICAL LTD
136 Wright Brothers Ave, Livermore (94551-9240)
PHONE..................925 447-5220
Mitchell Ibsen, *President*
EMP: 50 EST: 1989
SQ FT: 16,250
SALES (est): 8.2MM Privately Held
WEB: www.taoltd.us
SIC: 1711 Plumbing contractors

(P-1378)
TERRY MECHANICAL INC
6541 Via Del Oro Ste C, San Jose (95119-1207)
PHONE..................408 629-7822
Donald Terry, *President*
EMP: 47 EST: 1994
SQ FT: 3,500
SALES (est): 5.6MM Privately Held
SIC: 1711 Plumbing contractors

(P-1379)
TESLA ENERGY OPERATIONS INC (HQ)
3055 Clearview Way, San Mateo (94402-3709)
PHONE..................888 765-2489
Elon Musk, *Ch of Bd*

1711 - Plumbing, Heating & Air Conditioning Contractors County (P-1380)   PRODUCTS & SERVICES SECTION

Erin Theriault, *Partner*
John Germain, *Vice Pres*
Jiunn Heng, *Vice Pres*
Anurag Malik, *Vice Pres*
▲ **EMP:** 616 **EST:** 2006
SQ FT: 68,025
SALES (est): 1.2B
SALES (corp-wide): 31.5B **Publicly Held**
WEB: www.solarcity.com
SIC: 1711 Solar energy contractor
PA: Tesla, Inc.
3500 Deer Creek Rd
Palo Alto CA 94304
650 681-5000

(P-1380)
TF WELCH ENTERPRISES INC
Also Called: Commercial Restaurant Service
10556 Combie Rd 6528, Auburn (95602-8908)
PHONE 916 645-4277
Frank R Welch, *President*
Teresa Welch, *Vice Pres*
EMP: 15 **EST:** 2002
SALES (est): 461.8K **Privately Held**
SIC: 1711 3443 3444 Refrigeration contractor; hoods, industrial: metal plate; hoods, range: sheet metal

(P-1381)
THERMAL MECHANICAL
425 Aldo Ave, Santa Clara (95054-2322)
P.O. Box 4730 (95056-4730)
PHONE 408 988-8744
Richard Rood, *CEO*
David Rood, *President*
Martin Burke, *Department Mgr*
Rob Moyer, *Project Mgr*
Dave Steadman, *Project Mgr*
EMP: 77 **EST:** 1969
SQ FT: 30,000
SALES (est): 23.6MM **Privately Held**
WEB: www.thermalmech.com
SIC: 1711 Mechanical contractor

(P-1382)
THORPE DESIGN INC
410 Beatrice St Ct Ste A, Brentwood (94513)
P.O. Box 1149 (94513-3149)
PHONE 925 634-0787
James Thorpe, *President*
Renee Thorpe, *Treasurer*
Scott Burke, *Department Mgr*
Eric Gonzales, *Department Mgr*
Jose Gonzalez, *Department Mgr*
EMP: 60 **EST:** 1986
SQ FT: 500
SALES (est): 12MM **Privately Held**
WEB: www.thorpedesign.com
SIC: 1711 Fire sprinkler system installation

(P-1383)
TOPDOT SOLAR LLC
30930 Huntwood Ave, Hayward (94544-7006)
PHONE 800 731-5104
Britney Perkins, *Mng Member*
EMP: 50 **EST:** 2020
SALES (est): 2.3MM **Privately Held**
SIC: 1711 Solar energy contractor

(P-1384)
TRENDSETTER SOLAR PRODUCTS INC
818 Broadway, Eureka (95501-0122)
PHONE 707 443-5652
Dirk Atkinson, *CEO*
Brian Fretter, *CFO*
Norman Ehrlich, *Vice Pres*
▲ **EMP:** 17 **EST:** 1980
SQ FT: 2,000
SALES (est): 2.9MM **Privately Held**
WEB: www.trendsetterindustries.com
SIC: 1711 3433 5074 Solar energy contractor; solar heaters & collectors; heating equipment & panels, solar

(P-1385)
TRINA SOLAR (US) INC
7100 Stevenson Blvd, Fremont (94538-2485)
PHONE 800 696-7114
Jifan Gao, *CEO*
Shilian Wang, *CFO*
Merry Xu, *CFO*

Yang Shao, *Vice Pres*
Gary Yu, *Vice Pres*
◆ **EMP:** 41 **EST:** 2009
SQ FT: 7,000
SALES (est): 41.8MM **Privately Held**
WEB: www.trinasolar.com
SIC: 1711 Solar energy contractor
PA: Trina Solar Co., Ltd.
No.2, Tianhe Road, Tianhe Guangfu Industrial Park, Xinbei Distri
Changzhou 21300

(P-1386)
TUBULAR FLOW INC
Also Called: Preferred Plumbing
317 W Beach St, Watsonville (95076-4508)
P.O. Box 1270 (95077-1270)
PHONE 831 761-0644
Jeffrey Rodriguez, *CEO*
Jeff Rodriguez, *President*
Regina Rodriguez, *Corp Secy*
Ryan Rodriguez, *Project Mgr*
Kyla Rodriguez, *Business Mgr*
EMP: 51 **EST:** 1986
SQ FT: 3,000
SALES (est): 1.2MM **Privately Held**
WEB: www.preferredplumbing.com
SIC: 1711 Plumbing contractors

(P-1387)
TUCK AIRE HEATING & AC CORP
Also Called: Atlas Heating
407 Cabot Rd, South San Francisco (94080-4819)
PHONE 650 873-7000
Geoffrey S Tuck, *President*
Christopher Tuck, *CFO*
Hope Goblirsch, *Vice Pres*
Khalaf Almasarweh, *Sr Project Mgr*
EMP: 51 **EST:** 2004
SQ FT: 9,000
SALES (est): 5.2MM **Privately Held**
WEB: www.tuckaire.net
SIC: 1711 Heating systems repair & maintenance; warm air heating & air conditioning contractor

(P-1388)
UNBOUND RENEWABLE ENERGY INC
412 N Mount Shasta Blvd, Mount Shasta (96067-2232)
P.O. Box 124 (96067-0124)
PHONE 800 472-1142
Wil J Vandewiel, *CEO*
Charles Hirsh, *COO*
Michael Murray, *CFO*
Judith Roda, *Officer*
Bonnie Graham, *Admin Asst*
▼ **EMP:** 52 **EST:** 2004
SQ FT: 5,000
SALES (est): 21.6MM **Privately Held**
WEB: www.unboundsolar.com
SIC: 1711 Solar energy contractor

(P-1389)
VALLEY AC & REPR INC
1350 F St, Fresno (93706-1607)
PHONE 559 237-3188
Tobbie Biglione, *CEO*
Steve Mendrin, *Consultant*
EMP: 37 **EST:** 1971
SQ FT: 7,527
SALES (est): 3.2MM **Privately Held**
WEB: www.valleyairrepair.com
SIC: 1711 7623 Warm air heating & air conditioning contractor; air conditioning repair

(P-1390)
VALLEY AC ENGRG INC
1313 Lone Palm Ave, Modesto (95351-1536)
PHONE 209 524-7756
Mike Eyerly Sr, *President*
Patricia Eyerly, *Corp Secy*
Richard Utz, *Vice Pres*
Alissa Ahlswede, *Admin Asst*
Mario Franco, *Technician*
EMP: 41 **EST:** 1995

SALES (est): 5.4MM **Privately Held**
WEB: www.valleyairconditioning.com
SIC: 1711 Warm air heating & air conditioning contractor; heating & air conditioning contractors

(P-1391)
VILLARA CORPORATION (PA)
Also Called: Walk Through Video
4700 Lang Ave, McClellan (95652-2023)
PHONE 916 646-2700
Calvin Rick Wylie, *Principal*
Gary Beutler, *CEO*
Tom Beutler, *Vice Pres*
Rob Penrod, *Vice Pres*
Jeffrey Starsky, *Vice Pres*
▲ **EMP:** 482 **EST:** 1947
SALES (est): 147.2MM **Privately Held**
WEB: www.villara.com
SIC: 1711 Warm air heating & air conditioning contractor

(P-1392)
VILLARA CORPORATION
Also Called: Beutler Heating & AC
332 E Wetmore St, Manteca (95337-5741)
PHONE 209 824-1082
Glen Hartsough, *General Mgr*
Scot Williams, *Vice Pres*
Andre Coetser, *Info Tech Mgr*
Scott Eagle, *Opers Staff*
Jeff Davies, *Manager*
EMP: 44
SALES (corp-wide): 147.2MM **Privately Held**
WEB: www.villara.com
SIC: 1711 Mechanical contractor
PA: Villara Corporation
4700 Lang Ave
Mcclellan CA 95652
916 646-2700

(P-1393)
W L HICKEY SONS INC
930 E California Ave, Sunnyvale (94085-4502)
P.O. Box 61209 (94088-1209)
PHONE 408 736-4938
Adam Hickey, *President*
Edward Hickey, *CFO*
Deborah Lopez, *Controller*
Jody Ruiz, *Assistant*
EMP: 150 **EST:** 1904
SQ FT: 10,000
SALES (est): 25.1MM **Privately Held**
WEB: www.wlhs.com
SIC: 1711 Plumbing contractors

(P-1394)
WALSCHON FIRE PROTECTION INC
2178 Rheem Dr Ste A, Pleasanton (94588-2894)
PHONE 650 594-1588
George Walschon, *President*
Brandon Day, *CEO*
Jaimie Littlefield, *Vice Pres*
Dolores Walschon, *Vice Pres*
EMP: 40 **EST:** 1989
SQ FT: 6,000
SALES (est): 6.5MM **Privately Held**
WEB: www.walschon.com
SIC: 1711 Fire sprinkler system installation

(P-1395)
WATER HEATER SPECIALISTS INC
23 28th Ave, San Mateo (94403-2426)
PHONE 415 775-5100
EMP: 43
SALES (corp-wide): 361.3K **Privately Held**
SIC: 1711 Plumbing contractors
PA: Water Heater Specialists Inc
1163 Chess Dr Ste K
Foster City CA 94404
925 803-8003

(P-1396)
WAYNE MAPLES PLUMBING & HTG
317 W Cedar St, Eureka (95501-1698)
PHONE 707 445-2500
Rodney Maples, *Partner*
Dale Maples, *Partner*

Mike Maples, *Partner*
Roger Maples, *Partner*
EMP: 55 **EST:** 1960
SQ FT: 7,000
SALES (est): 7MM **Privately Held**
SIC: 1711 1623 Plumbing contractors; warm air heating & air conditioning contractor; underground utilities contractor

(P-1397)
WEEKS DRILLING AND PUMP CO (PA)
6100 Sebastopol Ave, Sebastopol (95472-3821)
PHONE 707 823-3184
Chris A Thompson, *CEO*
Charles Judson, *President*
Kathryn Daniels, *Human Res Dir*
Renee Thompson, *Human Resources*
EMP: 45 **EST:** 1906
SQ FT: 13,000
SALES (est): 12.7MM **Privately Held**
WEB: www.weeksdrilling.com
SIC: 1711 5251 5084 3589 Plumbing, heating, air-conditioning contractors; pumps & pumping equipment; pumps & pumping equipment; water treatment equipment, industrial; water well servicing

(P-1398)
WENCON DEVELOPMENT INC
Also Called: Quick Mount Pv
2700 Mitchell Dr Ste 2, Walnut Creek (94598-1602)
PHONE 925 478-8269
Claudia Wentworth, *President*
Jeff Spies, *President*
Sam Cast, *Vice Pres*
Marshall Green, *Vice Pres*
Jeanna Bauer, *Surgery Dir*
▲ **EMP:** 88 **EST:** 1993
SQ FT: 1,700
SALES (est): 20.5MM
SALES (corp-wide): 288.5MM **Privately Held**
SIC: 1711 Solar energy contractor
HQ: Esdec, Inc.
976 Brady Ave Nw Ste 100
Atlanta GA 30318
404 512-0716

(P-1399)
WESTATES MECHANICAL CORP INC
2566 Barrington Ct, Hayward (94545-1133)
PHONE 510 635-9830
Nigel Cowan, *CEO*
Daniel Loeffler, *Senior VP*
William Bird, *Director*
EMP: 60 **EST:** 2003
SALES (est): 17.1MM **Privately Held**
WEB: www.westatesmechanical.com
SIC: 1711 Mechanical contractor

(P-1400)
WESTERN ALLIED MECHANICAL INC
1180 Obrien Dr, Menlo Park (94025-1411)
PHONE 650 326-8290
Angela Simon, *CEO*
Robert Dills, *Shareholder*
Peter Kelly, *Shareholder*
Richard Taipale, *Shareholder*
James A Muscarella, *President*
EMP: 175 **EST:** 2003
SALES (est): 85.9MM **Privately Held**
WEB: www.westernallied.com
SIC: 1711 3444 Mechanical contractor; sheet metalwork

(P-1401)
WILMOR & SONS PLUMBING & CNSTR
8510 Thys Ct, Sacramento (95828-1007)
PHONE 916 381-9114
Terry Wilson, *President*
Gary Morrissette, *CEO*
Elliott Wilson, *Purch Mgr*
EMP: 49 **EST:** 1983
SQ FT: 6,000
SALES (est): 3.8MM **Privately Held**
SIC: 1711 Plumbing contractors

PRODUCTS & SERVICES SECTION
1721 - Painting & Paper Hanging Contractors County (P-1424)

(P-1402)
YOUR WARM FRIEND INC
Also Called: Atlas Heating and AC Co
1451 32nd St, Oakland (94608-4117)
P.O. Box 8467 (94662-0467)
PHONE..............................510 893-1343
Robert Tuck, *President*
Elizabeth Tuck, *Corp Secy*
Mike Piasente, *Vice Pres*
EMP: 35 **EST:** 1908
SQ FT: 15,167
SALES (est): 1.4MM **Privately Held**
WEB: www.atlasheating.com
SIC: 1711 5075 Warm air heating & air conditioning contractor; furnaces, warm air

1721 Painting & Paper Hanging Contractors

(P-1403)
ARMSTRONG INSTLLTION SVC A CAL
Also Called: Armstrong Construction Company
4575 San Pablo Ave, Emeryville (94608-3325)
PHONE..............................408 777-1234
Mitchell Fine, *CEO*
Arthur Levine, *CFO*
Andrew Landies, *Consultant*
EMP: 130 **EST:** 1966
SQ FT: 8,000
SALES (est): 10.5MM **Privately Held**
WEB: www.armstrong1234.com
SIC: 1721 1761 1793 Exterior residential painting contractor; interior residential painting contractor; exterior commercial painting contractor; interior commercial painting contractor; roofing, siding & sheet metal work; glass & glazing work

(P-1404)
BM LYNN PAINTING INC
4324 Pinell St, Sacramento (95838-2928)
PHONE..............................916 920-4000
Bradley Lynn, *President*
Karen Lynn, *Treasurer*
Myrna Arreola, *Office Mgr*
EMP: 35 **EST:** 2012
SALES (est): 2.3MM **Privately Held**
WEB: www.bmlynnpainting.com
SIC: 1721 Residential painting

(P-1405)
C & O PAINTING INC
1500 N 4th St, San Jose (95112-4606)
PHONE..............................408 279-8011
Rick Ohlund, *President*
Paul Rood, *Officer*
Richard Middleton, *Manager*
Chanel Ohlund, *Manager*
EMP: 50 **EST:** 1987
SQ FT: 6,000
SALES (est): 5.8MM **Privately Held**
WEB: www.candopainting.com
SIC: 1721 Exterior commercial painting contractor; commercial wallcovering contractor

(P-1406)
CABRERA PAINTING INC
1262 Shortridge Ave, San Jose (95116-2349)
PHONE..............................408 998-4789
Joe M Cabrera, *President*
Martha Cabrera, *Vice Pres*
Karen Martinez, *Admin Sec*
Patti Y Nowak, *Admin Sec*
EMP: 40 **EST:** 1971
SQ FT: 1,500
SALES (est): 1.8MM **Privately Held**
WEB: www.cabrerapainting.com
SIC: 1721 Residential painting; commercial painting

(P-1407)
CERTIFIED COATINGS COMPANY
2320 Cordelia Rd, Fairfield (94534-1600)
PHONE..............................707 639-4414
David Joseph Brockman, *CEO*
Rachele Pereira, *General Mgr*
Pamela Langan, *Admin Sec*
EMP: 100 **EST:** 2006
SQ FT: 8,000
SALES (est): 22.2MM
SALES (corp-wide): 307.9MM **Privately Held**
WEB: www.certifiedcoatings.com
SIC: 1721 Industrial painting
PA: Muehlhan Ag
Schlinckstr. 3
Hamburg HH 21107
407 527-10

(P-1408)
CHAY & HARRIS PNTG CONTRS INC
2520 Wyandotte St Ste E, Mountain View (94043-2381)
PHONE..............................650 966-1472
Ron L Harris, *President*
Thomas E Chay, *Treasurer*
Blanca Garcia, *Office Mgr*
EMP: 30 **EST:** 1974
SQ FT: 5,000
SALES (est): 2.7MM **Privately Held**
WEB: www.chayharris.com
SIC: 1721 3479 Commercial painting; coating of metals & formed products

(P-1409)
CROWN PAINTING INC
4210 Kiernan Ave, Modesto (95356-9758)
P.O. Box 1845, Oakdale (95361-1845)
PHONE..............................209 322-3725
Gretchen Arbini, *President*
Ronald G Anderson, *CEO*
Toby Kitchens, *Project Mgr*
EMP: 80 **EST:** 2012
SALES (est): 6.6MM **Privately Held**
WEB: www.crownpaintinginc.com
SIC: 1721 2519 Residential painting; furniture, household: glass, fiberglass & plastic

(P-1410)
D C VIENT INC (PA)
1556 Cummins Dr, Modesto (95358-6412)
P.O. Box D (95352-3668)
PHONE..............................209 578-1224
Darlene Vient, *President*
Danielle Bell, *Shareholder*
Douglas J Vient Jr, *Corp Secy*
Douglas C Vient, *Vice Pres*
Louis Melvin, *Info Tech Mgr*
EMP: 100 **EST:** 1954
SQ FT: 12,000
SALES (est): 14.6MM **Privately Held**
WEB: www.dcvient.com
SIC: 1721 Residential painting

(P-1411)
D ZELINSKY & SONS INC
5301 Adeline St, Oakland (94608-3107)
PHONE..............................510 215-5253
James G McCloskey, *President*
Richard B McCloskey, *CFO*
Kathleen McCloskey, *Admin Sec*
EMP: 50 **EST:** 1884
SQ FT: 11,800
SALES (est): 5.5MM
SALES (corp-wide): 2.7B **Privately Held**
WEB: www.dzelinskyandsons.com
SIC: 1721 1799 2391 Exterior commercial painting contractor; interior commercial painting contractor; window treatment installation; draperies, plastic & textile: from purchased materials
HQ: F. D. Thomas, Inc.
217 Bateman Dr
Central Point OR 97502
541 664-3010

(P-1412)
EUROPEAN PAVING DESIGNS INC
1474 Berger Dr, San Jose (95112-2701)
PHONE..............................408 283-5230
Randy Hays, *CEO*
Robyn Cerutti, *COO*
Liz Schooler, *Administration*
Javier Licea, *Project Engr*
Urvi Oza, *Engineer*
EMP: 55 **EST:** 1980
SQ FT: 3,000
SALES (est): 6.7MM **Privately Held**
WEB: www.europeanpavingdesigns.com
SIC: 1721 Pavement marking contractor

(P-1413)
GENERAL COATINGS CORPORATION
1220 E North Ave, Fresno (93725-1930)
PHONE..............................559 495-4004
Lee Morrison, *Principal*
EMP: 83
SALES (corp-wide): 35.9MM **Privately Held**
WEB: www.gencoat.com
SIC: 1721 1799 Painting & paper hanging; coating of concrete structures with plastic
PA: General Coatings Corporation
6711 Nancy Ridge Dr
San Diego CA 92121
858 587-1277

(P-1414)
GEORGE E MASKER INC
Also Called: Masker Painting
7699 Edgewater Dr, Oakland (94621-3028)
PHONE..............................510 568-1206
Alan Bjerke, *President*
Stefanie Mitchell, *Admin Asst*
Richard Barnes, *CIO*
Matt Johnson, *Project Mgr*
Newt Millward, *Project Mgr*
EMP: 100 **EST:** 1963
SQ FT: 18,000
SALES (est): 22.6MM **Privately Held**
WEB: www.maskerpainting.com
SIC: 1721 Exterior commercial painting contractor; interior commercial painting contractor

(P-1415)
GIAMPOLINI & CO
Also Called: Giampolini/Courtney
1482 67th St, Emeryville (94608-1016)
PHONE..............................415 673-1236
Greg Quilici, *President*
Patrick Roland, *CFO*
Tom Quilici, *Vice Pres*
James Patrick Roland, *Principal*
Michael Kwan, *Accountant*
EMP: 225 **EST:** 1912
SQ FT: 9,720
SALES (est): 33.7MM **Privately Held**
WEB: www.giampolini.com
SIC: 1721 1542 1742 Exterior commercial painting contractor; interior commercial painting contractor; commercial & office buildings, renovation & repair; plastering, drywall & insulation

(P-1416)
HERMSMEYER PAINTING CO INC (PA)
19005 Hwy 89, Hat Creek (96040)
P.O. Box 907, Sagle ID (83860-0907)
PHONE..............................707 575-4549
Craig Hermsmeyer, *President*
Rebecca Hermsmeyer, *Vice Pres*
EMP: 43 **EST:** 1977
SALES (est): 2.2MM **Privately Held**
WEB: www.hermsmeyer.com
SIC: 1721 Exterior residential painting contractor; interior residential painting contractor; exterior commercial painting contractor; interior commercial painting contractor

(P-1417)
JEFFCO PAINTING & COATING INC
1260 Railroad Ave, Vallejo (94592-1012)
P.O. Box 1888 (94590-0655)
PHONE..............................707 562-1900
Steve Jeffress, *President*
Gene Glockner, *CFO*
Todd Anderson, *Vice Pres*
Paul Schoep, *Project Mgr*
Mike Maldonado, *Manager*
EMP: 100 **EST:** 1978
SALES (est): 12.6MM **Privately Held**
WEB: www.jeffcoptg.com
SIC: 1721 3471 Industrial painting; sand blasting of metal parts

(P-1418)
JERRY THOMPSON & SONS PNTG INC
3 Simms St, San Rafael (94901-5414)
PHONE..............................415 454-1500
Stephen G Thompson, *President*
Dennis J Thompson, *Corp Secy*
Amaya Ben, *Project Mgr*
Dalit Miller, *Accountant*
Bob Williams, *Opers Mgr*
EMP: 140 **EST:** 1993
SALES (est): 14.7MM **Privately Held**
WEB: www.jtspainting.com
SIC: 1721 Residential painting

(P-1419)
KBI PAINTING INC
866 Palm Ave, Penngrove (94951-8800)
P.O. Box 750397, Petaluma (94975-0397)
PHONE..............................707 795-4955
James Damian Koreen, *President*
Todd Guidi, *Safety Mgr*
Rich Robles, *Sr Project Mgr*
Nickie Benjamson, *Director*
EMP: 35 **EST:** 2010
SALES (est): 6MM **Privately Held**
WEB: www.kbipaint.com
SIC: 1721 Residential painting

(P-1420)
LB FORD PAINTING INC
Also Called: California Paint Company
4325 Abernathy Rd, Fairfield (94534-9717)
PHONE..............................707 447-5274
Leonard Brad Ford, *President*
EMP: 40 **EST:** 2013
SQ FT: 800
SALES (est): 3.1MM **Privately Held**
SIC: 1721 Residential painting; commercial painting

(P-1421)
MOLINAS PNTG WALLCOVERING INC
4285 Pacheco Blvd, Martinez (94553-2227)
PHONE..............................925 228-7487
Oscar Molina, *CEO*
Oscar M Molina, *CFO*
Vanessa Molina, *Admin Sec*
Marissa Molina, *Bookkeeper*
EMP: 75 **EST:** 2003
SQ FT: 3,750
SALES (est): 4.8MM **Privately Held**
SIC: 1721 Wallcovering contractors

(P-1422)
N J KANN PAINTING
662 Giguere Ct Ste B, San Jose (95133-1744)
PHONE..............................408 437-0220
Nancy Kann, *Executive*
EMP: 50 **EST:** 2000
SALES (est): 1.5MM **Privately Held**
WEB: www.njkannpainting.com
SIC: 1721 Residential painting

(P-1423)
PETERSON PAINTING INC
5750 La Ribera St, Livermore (94550-9204)
PHONE..............................925 455-5864
Raymond Peterson, *President*
John Peterson, *Vice Pres*
EMP: 350 **EST:** 1970
SQ FT: 10,000
SALES (est): 11.4MM **Privately Held**
SIC: 1721 Residential painting

(P-1424)
PYRAMID PAINTING INC
2925 Bayview Dr, Fremont (94538-6520)
PHONE..............................650 903-9791
Craig Ruybalid, *President*
EMP: 50 **EST:** 1956
SQ FT: 6,240
SALES (est): 5.8MM **Privately Held**
SIC: 1721 Exterior commercial painting contractor; interior commercial painting contractor

1721 - Painting & Paper Hanging Contractors County (P-1425) PRODUCTS & SERVICES SECTION

(P-1425)
R & A PAINTING INC
11730 Sheldon Lake Dr, Elk Grove (95624-9649)
P.O. Box 292730, Sacramento (95829-2730)
PHONE..................................916 688-3955
Antonio Rodrigues, *President*
Cidalia Rodrigues, *Corp Secy*
EMP: 60 **EST:** 1990
SALES (est): 2.6MM **Privately Held**
WEB: www.rapainting.com
SIC: 1721 Commercial painting; residential painting

(P-1426)
R & M PAINTING INC
Also Called: Gold Star Painting
2928 Yosemite Blvd, Modesto (95354-4138)
PHONE..................................209 576-2576
Robert E Wright, *President*
EMP: 16 **EST:** 1977
SQ FT: 10,000
SALES: 1.9MM **Privately Held**
WEB: www.goldstarmodesto.com
SIC: 1721 3479 Commercial painting; painting, coating & hot dipping

(P-1427)
R&B PROTECTIVE COATINGS INC
19968 E Highway 26, Linden (95236-9483)
P.O. Box 652 (95236-0652)
PHONE..................................209 887-2030
Richard Joaquin, *President*
EMP: 37 **EST:** 1973
SQ FT: 20,000
SALES (est): 2.9MM **Privately Held**
WEB: www.rb-protectivecoatings.com
SIC: 1721 1799 Industrial painting; sandblasting of building exteriors

(P-1428)
R-BROS PAINTING INC
707 W Hedding St, San Jose (95110-1533)
PHONE..................................408 291-6820
Rod Rodriquez, *President*
Elias Cisneros, *Foreman/Supr*
▲ **EMP:** 50 **EST:** 1985
SQ FT: 3,000
SALES (est): 9.4MM **Privately Held**
WEB: www.rbrothers.com
SIC: 1721 Residential painting

(P-1429)
REDWOOD PAINTING CO INC
620 W 10th St, Pittsburg (94565-1806)
P.O. Box 1269 (94565-0126)
PHONE..................................925 432-4500
Charles Del Monte, *CEO*
Charles Duke Del Monte, *CEO*
George Del Monte, *Exec VP*
Paul Loustaunau, *Executive*
Tracy Glynn, *Admin Asst*
EMP: 110 **EST:** 1947
SQ FT: 19,000
SALES: 20.1MM **Privately Held**
WEB: www.redwoodptg.com
SIC: 1721 Commercial painting; industrial painting

(P-1430)
RYSAW PAINTING INC
1713 Stone Canyon Dr, Roseville (95661-4041)
PHONE..................................916 817-2393
Tim Flood, *President*
EMP: 35 **EST:** 2002
SALES (est): 1.7MM **Privately Held**
WEB: www.rysaw.com
SIC: 1721 Commercial painting

(P-1431)
SCHAPER CONSTRUCTION INC (PA)
1177 N 15th St, San Jose (95112-1422)
PHONE..................................408 437-0337
Leon Schaper, *CEO*
Greg Sipe, *General Mgr*
Travis Selway, *Office Mgr*
Jina Duncan, *Executive Asst*
Chantelle Somerville, *Administration*
EMP: 90 **EST:** 1985
SQ FT: 8,400
SALES (est): 28MM **Privately Held**
WEB: www.schaperco.com
SIC: 1721 1611 1542 Exterior residential painting contractor; interior residential painting contractor; general contractor, highway & street construction; nonresidential construction

(P-1432)
SIGNATURE PAINTING & CNSTR INC
1559 3rd Ave, Walnut Creek (94597-2604)
PHONE..................................925 287-0444
Brian Mitchell, *President*
Erik Oller, *Vice Pres*
Christian Cupolo, *Project Mgr*
Christian D Cupolo, *Project Mgr*
Charlie Johnson, *Superintendent*
EMP: 50 **EST:** 2010
SALES (est): 9.1MM **Privately Held**
WEB: www.signatureservices.us
SIC: 1721 Painting & paper hanging

(P-1433)
SIPCO SURFACE PROTECTION INC (DH)
Also Called: Muehlhan Marine
2320 Cordelia Rd, Fairfield (94534-1600)
PHONE..................................707 639-4414
William C Legrande, *President*
Paul Oatman, *CFO*
Pamela Langan, *Treasurer*
◆ **EMP:** 68 **EST:** 1994
SQ FT: 13,000
SALES (est): 5.5MM
SALES (corp-wide): 307.9MM **Privately Held**
WEB: www.muehlhan.com
SIC: 1721 Industrial painting
HQ: Muehlhan Surface Protection Inc.
2320 Cordelia Rd
Fairfield CA 94534
707 639-4421

(P-1434)
TRUJILLO ORLANDO PNTG CONTR
6 S Amphlett Blvd, San Mateo (94401-2940)
PHONE..................................650 579-0707
Orlando Trujillo Sr, *President*
Joseph Trujillo, *Vice Pres*
Orlando Trujillo Jr, *Vice Pres*
EMP: 40 **EST:** 1976
SQ FT: 3,000
SALES (est): 1.3MM **Privately Held**
WEB: www.orlandotrujillopainting.com
SIC: 1721 Interior commercial painting contractor; exterior commercial painting contractor; interior residential painting contractor; exterior residential painting contractor

(P-1435)
UNIVERSAL PLASTICS INC
Also Called: M & M Materials
1020 Winding Creek Rd, Roseville (95678-7041)
PHONE..................................916 787-0541
Steve Tullgren, *President*
Kara Trammel, *Administration*
EMP: 35 **EST:** 1977
SQ FT: 5,000
SALES (est): 5.4MM **Privately Held**
WEB: www.uniplastics.com
SIC: 5211 1721 Wallboard (composition) & paneling; wallcovering contractors

(P-1436)
URBAN PAINTING INC
40 Lisbon St, San Rafael (94901-4709)
PHONE..................................415 485-1730
Michael James Urban, *President*
Robert S Urban, *Shareholder*
James De Martini, *Vice Pres*
Chris Urban, *Vice Pres*
Marshall Johnson, *Technology*
EMP: 60 **EST:** 1983
SQ FT: 6,000
SALES (est): 10.3MM **Privately Held**
WEB: www.urbanco.com
SIC: 1721 Commercial painting; residential painting

(P-1437)
WHITS PAINTING INC (PA)
150 Mason Cir Ste K, Concord (94520-1261)
PHONE..................................925 429-2669
D Kathleen Whitney, *President*
Diane Kathleen Whitney, *President*
Kassie Giampapa, *Office Mgr*
Kelly Whitney, *Admin Sec*
Shane Whitney, *Foreman/Supr*
EMP: 45 **EST:** 2002
SALES (est): 5.2MM **Privately Held**
WEB: www.whitspaintinginc.com
SIC: 1721 Residential painting

(P-1438)
WM B SALEH CO
1364 N Jackson Ave, Fresno (93703-4624)
PHONE..................................559 255-2046
Mark Saleh, *President*
Katherine Brusellas, *Corp Secy*
William B Saleh, *Vice Pres*
Richard Purcell, *Manager*
EMP: 75 **EST:** 1959
SQ FT: 6,800
SALES (est): 12.7MM **Privately Held**
WEB: www.salehcompany.com
SIC: 1721 Commercial painting; industrial painting; commercial wallcovering contractor

1731 Electrical Work

(P-1439)
3S COMMUNICATIONS INC
105 Serra Way 312, Milpitas (95035-5206)
PHONE..................................408 505-9517
Maria Darilay, *CEO*
EMP: 35 **EST:** 2001
SALES (est): 1.6MM **Privately Held**
SIC: 1731 Electrical work

(P-1440)
A-C ELECTRIC COMPANY
A-C Electric, Co Div F
2560 S East Ave, Fresno (93706-5103)
P.O. Box 81977, Bakersfield (93380-1977)
PHONE..................................559 233-2208
Jim McGurk, *Sales/Mktg Mgr*
EMP: 73
SQ FT: 5,096
SALES (corp-wide): 66.6MM **Privately Held**
WEB: www.a-celectric.com
SIC: 1731 8711 General electrical contractor; electrical or electronic engineering
PA: A-C Electric Company
2921 Hanger Way
Bakersfield CA 93308
661 410-0000

(P-1441)
AA/ACME LOCKSMITHS INC
1660 Factor Ave, San Leandro (94577-5618)
PHONE..................................510 483-6584
Timothy J Whall, *CEO*
Jim Devries, *President*
Donald Young, *COO*
Jeff Likosar, *CFO*
Jamie Rosand Haenggi, *Officer*
EMP: 95 **EST:** 1974
SQ FT: 20,000
SALES (est): 23.4MM
SALES (corp-wide): 5.3B **Publicly Held**
WEB: www.adt.com
SIC: 1731 5999 Fire detection & burglar alarm systems specialization; alarm signal systems
PA: Adt Inc.
1501 W Yamato Rd
Boca Raton FL 33431
561 988-3600

(P-1442)
ABBETT ELECTRIC CORPORATION
1850 Bryant St, San Francisco (94110-1407)
PHONE..................................415 864-7500
Jeffrey B Abbett, *President*
Gregory W Abbett, *Vice Pres*
EMP: 40 **EST:** 1933
SQ FT: 15,000
SALES (est): 10.9MM **Privately Held**
SIC: 1731 General electrical contractor

(P-1443)
ACCESS TELECOMM SYSTEMS INC
Also Called: Access Communications
976 Rincon Cir, San Jose (95131-1313)
PHONE..................................800 342-4439
David J Duarte Jr, *CEO*
Dave Duarte Sr, *Principal*
Jordan Bolla, *Accounts Exec*
EMP: 40 **EST:** 1997
SQ FT: 7,200
SALES (est): 8.8MM **Privately Held**
WEB: www.access-comm.net
SIC: 1731 Telephone & telephone equipment installation

(P-1444)
ACCESS TO POWER INC
Also Called: Access Electric
1990 Foundry Ct, Ceres (95307-9223)
P.O. Box 3447, Modesto (95353-3447)
PHONE..................................209 577-1491
Walter Resendes, *President*
Pon Phimmachack, *Vice Pres*
John Pires, *Admin Asst*
Eric Eyerly, *Project Mgr*
Andy Meneses, *Project Mgr*
EMP: 45 **EST:** 2002
SQ FT: 9,000
SALES (est): 11.4MM **Privately Held**
WEB: www.accesstopower.com
SIC: 1731 General electrical contractor

(P-1445)
AECO SYSTEMS INC
3512 Breakwater Ct, Hayward (94545-3611)
PHONE..................................510 342-0008
Jim Millerick, *President*
Randall Wold, *Treasurer*
Brent Hensley, *Admin Sec*
Mike Batteate, *Info Tech Mgr*
Matt Anthony, *Opers Mgr*
EMP: 42 **EST:** 1989
SQ FT: 3,500
SALES (est): 5.2MM **Privately Held**
WEB: www.aeco-systems.com
SIC: 1731 Electrical work

(P-1446)
ALESSANDRO ELECTRIC INC
11335 Sunrise Gold Cir, Rancho Cordova (95742-6512)
PHONE..................................916 283-6966
Clint Alessandro, *President*
Clinton Lee Alessandro, *President*
Larry Neff, *Project Mgr*
Meghan Goodwin, *Human Resources*
EMP: 75 **EST:** 2005
SALES (est): 17.2MM **Privately Held**
WEB: www.alessandroelectric.com
SIC: 1731 7389 General electrical contractor;

(P-1447)
ALL GUARD ALARM SYSTEMS INC (PA)
Also Called: GRAND CENTRAL STATION
1306 Stealth St, Livermore (94551-9356)
PHONE..................................800 255-4273
Denis Cooke, *Ch of Bd*
Michael Cooke, *Corp Secy*
Patricia Cooke, *Vice Pres*
Ben Martinez, *Business Mgr*
Jodie L Osborne, *Controller*
EMP: 66 **EST:** 1980
SQ FT: 12,600
SALES: 11MM **Privately Held**
WEB: www.allguardsystems.com
SIC: 1731 7382 Fire detection & burglar alarm systems specialization; burglar alarm maintenance & monitoring

(P-1448)
ALVAH CONTRACTORS INC
263 S Maple Ave, South San Francisco (94080-6305)
PHONE..................................650 741-6785
Cameron Hale, *President*
Tom Henkels, *COO*
Dennis Mueller, *CFO*
Lisa Bladecki, *Project Mgr*
Maureen Horn, *Controller*

▲ = Import ▼ = Export
◆ = Import/Export

PRODUCTS & SERVICES SECTION

1731 - Electrical Work County (P-1472)

EMP: 346 EST: 2008
SALES (est): 104.8MM Privately Held
WEB: www.alvahgroup.com
SIC: 1731 General electrical contractor

(P-1449)
AMERICAN ENGRG CONTRS INC
Also Called: Budget Electric
25445 S Schulte Rd, Tracy (95377-9709)
PHONE..............................209 229-1591
Larry Walling, *President*
Patricia Walling, *Corp Secy*
Don Collins, *Finance Mgr*
Joe Lorusso, *Superintendent*
EMP: 180 EST: 1979
SQ FT: 4,000
SALES (est): 12.2MM Privately Held
WEB: www.budget-e.com
SIC: 1731 General electrical contractor

(P-1450)
AMERICAN HI SECURITY INC
8156 S El Dorado St, French Camp (95231-9752)
PHONE..............................209 518-9207
Taljit Singh, *President*
EMP: 35 EST: 2013
SALES (est): 2MM Privately Held
SIC: 1731 Safety & security specialization

(P-1451)
AMERICAN PWR & COMMUNICATIONS
1416 Mariani Ct Ste 130, Tracy (95376-2849)
PHONE..............................209 833-1369
Dustin Wortham, *President*
Tiffany Wortham, *Vice Pres*
EMP: 40 EST: 2004
SQ FT: 2,000
SALES (est): 7MM Privately Held
WEB: www.americanpowercomm.net
SIC: 1731 General electrical contractor

(P-1452)
AMS ELECTRIC INC
6905 Sierra Ct Ste A, Dublin (94568-2708)
PHONE..............................925 961-1600
William Breyton, *Principal*
John Modica, *Vice Pres*
Craig Ayers, *Executive*
Rick Bellmer, *Project Mgr*
Owen Kishaba, *Project Mgr*
EMP: 75 EST: 2003
SQ FT: 25,000
SALES (est): 8.9MM Privately Held
WEB: www.ams-electric.com
SIC: 1731 General electrical contractor

(P-1453)
ANDRADE ELECTRIC INC
3245 Fitzgerald Rd Ste A, Rancho Cordova (95742-6885)
PHONE..............................916 635-4082
Ralph J Andrade, *CEO*
Ralph Andrade, *President*
Sotero Andrade, *CEO*
Juanita Andrade, *Vice Pres*
EMP: 37 EST: 1981
SQ FT: 9,600
SALES (est): 2.4MM Privately Held
SIC: 1731 General electrical contractor

(P-1454)
B F C INC
Also Called: Cbf Electric & Data
675 Davis St, San Francisco (94111-1903)
PHONE..............................415 495-3085
John M Walsh, *President*
Novelynn Tejada, *CFO*
Leanne Goff, *Admin Sec*
Miles Luquingan, *Admin Asst*
Lindsay Rosecrans, *Admin Asst*
EMP: 110 EST: 1951
SQ FT: 6,300
SALES (est): 53.8MM Privately Held
WEB: www.cbfelectric.com
SIC: 1731 General electrical contractor

(P-1455)
BANISTER ELECTRICAL INC
2532 Verne Roberts Cir, Antioch (94509-7904)
PHONE..............................925 778-7801
Daniel T Pauline, *President*
Shovawn Barrera, *Controller*
John Hammett, *Purch Mgr*
EMP: 70 EST: 2006
SALES (est): 7.1MM Privately Held
SIC: 1731 General electrical contractor

(P-1456)
BARNUM & CELILLO ELECTRIC INC (PA)
135 Main Ave, Sacramento (95838-2089)
PHONE..............................916 646-4661
Fred Troy Barnum, *CEO*
Lee Sanders, *Trustee*
Paul Celillo, *Vice Pres*
John Aspling, *Project Mgr*
Matthew Evans, *Project Mgr*
EMP: 149 EST: 1990
SQ FT: 3,000
SALES: 50.5MM Privately Held
WEB: www.barnumcelillo.com
SIC: 1731 General electrical contractor

(P-1457)
BARRI ELECTRIC COMPANY INC
61 Napoleon St, San Francisco (94124-1110)
PHONE..............................415 468-6477
Ernie Ulibarri, *President*
Joan Ulibarri, *Corp Secy*
Yolanda Cazessus, *Finance*
Monica La Russa, *Purch Agent*
EMP: 45 EST: 1987
SQ FT: 22,000
SALES (est): 5.8MM Privately Held
WEB: www.barrielectric.com
SIC: 1731 General electrical contractor

(P-1458)
BAY ALARM COMPANY (PA)
Also Called: S A S
5130 Commercial Cir, Concord (94520-8522)
P.O. Box 8140, Walnut Creek (94596-8140)
PHONE..............................925 935-1100
Bruce A Westphal, *Ch of Bd*
Roger L Westphal, *CEO*
Graham Westphal, *Co-President*
Matt Westphal, *Co-President*
Porchia Freeman, *Officer*
◆ EMP: 70
SQ FT: 12,000
SALES (est): 137MM Privately Held
WEB: www.bayalarm.com
SIC: 1731 7382 5063 Fire detection & burglar alarm systems specialization; burglar alarm maintenance & monitoring; fire alarm maintenance & monitoring; electrical apparatus & equipment

(P-1459)
BAY ALARM COMPANY
3819 Duck Creek Dr, Stockton (95215-7956)
PHONE..............................209 465-1986
Margaret Blair, *Manager*
Bill Metzinger, *Branch Mgr*
Celia Vazquez, *Sales Staff*
Cyndee Doyle, *Manager*
Butch Guinn, *Manager*
EMP: 44
SQ FT: 2,000
SALES (corp-wide): 137MM Privately Held
WEB: www.bayalarm.com
SIC: 1731 Fire detection & burglar alarm systems specialization
PA: Bay Alarm Company
  5130 Commercial Cir
  Concord CA 94520
  925 935-1100

(P-1460)
BAY AREA SYSTEMS SOLUTIONS INC
Also Called: Bass Electric
390 Swift Ave Ste 12, South San Francisco (94080-6221)
PHONE..............................650 295-1600
Jeffrey Yee, *CEO*
Jennifer Trevino, *COO*
Jennifer Mitchell, *Vice Pres*
Jawaad Mitchell, *Project Mgr*
Mike Marinus, *Opers Mgr*
▲ EMP: 43 EST: 1996
SQ FT: 5,000
SALES (est): 27.5MM Privately Held
WEB: www.basselectric.net
SIC: 1731 General electrical contractor

(P-1461)
BEAM VACUUMS CALIFORNIA INC
Also Called: Beam "easy Living" Center
422 Henderson St, Grass Valley (95945-7311)
P.O. Box 1803 (95945-1803)
PHONE..............................916 564-3279
Robert Medlyn, *President*
Brian Obrien, *Vice Pres*
Ryan Hendrick, *Technician*
Brian O"brien, *Sales Executive*
Justin Anthney, *Sales Staff*
EMP: 50 EST: 1980
SQ FT: 13,000
SALES (est): 7MM Privately Held
WEB: www.beameasy.com
SIC: 1731 1799 5722 5731 Environmental system control installation; sound equipment specialization; voice, data & video wiring contractor; closet organizers, installation & design; vacuum cleaners; high fidelity stereo equipment; communication equipment; closet organizers & shelving units

(P-1462)
BERGELECTRIC CORP
11333 Sunrise Park Dr, Rancho Cordova (95742-6532)
PHONE..............................916 636-1880
Matt Ordway, *Branch Mgr*
Robert Trabert, *Sr Project Mgr*
Peter Casazza, *Manager*
Stephan Varnell, *Supervisor*
EMP: 84
SALES (corp-wide): 483.1MM Privately Held
WEB: www.bergelectric.com
SIC: 1731 General electrical contractor
PA: Bergelectric Corp.
  3182 Lionshead Ave
  Carlsbad CA 92010
  760 638-2374

(P-1463)
BESTCO ELECTRIC INC (PA)
1322 7th St, Modesto (95354-2213)
PHONE..............................209 569-0120
Dimitri Guzman, *President*
Leanne Guzman, *Corp Secy*
EMP: 42
SQ FT: 2,400
SALES (est): 12.3MM Privately Held
WEB: www.bestelectric.us
SIC: 1731 General electrical contractor

(P-1464)
BESTCO ELECTRIC INC
Also Called: Best Electric
2160 Wardrobe Ave, Merced (95341-6400)
PHONE..............................209 723-2061
Jason Paper, *Manager*
Don Seward, *Manager*
EMP: 48
SALES (corp-wide): 12.3MM Privately Held
WEB: www.bestelectric.us
SIC: 1731 General electrical contractor
PA: Bestco Electric, Inc.
  1322 7th St
  Modesto CA 95354
  209 569-0120

(P-1465)
BI-JAMAR INC
Also Called: Quality Sound
2010 E Fremont St, Stockton (95205-5057)
P.O. Box 5501 (95205-0501)
PHONE..............................209 948-2104
James Bryan, *President*
Sonia Langford, *Treasurer*
Marvin Langford, *Vice Pres*
Marv Langford, *Executive*
Bianca Tapia, *Admin Asst*
EMP: 45 EST: 1948
SQ FT: 27,000
SALES (est): 13.8MM Privately Held
SIC: 1731 Sound equipment specialization

(P-1466)
BILL SHARP ELECTRICAL CONTR
5136 Caterpillar Rd, Redding (96003-2048)
P.O. Box 2187, Weaverville (96093-2187)
PHONE..............................530 338-1735
EMP: 48 Privately Held
WEB: www.sharpelectric.us
SIC: 1731 General electrical contractor
PA: Bill Sharp Electrical Contractor
  1101 Oregon St
  Weaverville CA 96093

(P-1467)
BLACK DIAMOND ELECTRIC INC
2595 W 10th St, Antioch (94509-1374)
PHONE..............................925 777-3440
Jason C Pauline, *CEO*
Carey Neely, *Officer*
Glenn Patrick, *Vice Pres*
Dan James, *Office Mgr*
Tim Pauline, *Project Mgr*
EMP: 100
SQ FT: 9,000
SALES (est): 23.2MM Privately Held
WEB: www.blackdiamondelectric.com
SIC: 1731 General electrical contractor

(P-1468)
BME ELECTRICAL CONSTRUCTION
1281 30th St, Oakland (94608-4437)
PHONE..............................510 208-1967
Barry McGraw, *President*
EMP: 35 EST: 2006
SALES (est): 3.7MM Privately Held
WEB: www.bmeconstruction.com
SIC: 1731 Electrical work; fire detection & burglar alarm systems specialization

(P-1469)
BOCKMON & WOODY ELC CO INC
1528 El Pinal Dr, Stockton (95205-2643)
P.O. Box 1018 (95201-1018)
PHONE..............................209 464-4878
Gary E Woody, *President*
Nick Woody, *Treasurer*
Jeff Bockmon, *Vice Pres*
Gary M Woody, *Vice Pres*
Clyde Carter, *Project Mgr*
EMP: 190 EST: 1990
SQ FT: 36,000
SALES (est): 40MM Privately Held
WEB: www.bockmonwoody.com
SIC: 1731 General electrical contractor

(P-1470)
BUTTERFIELD ELECTRIC INC
2101 Freeway Dr Ste A, Woodland (95776-9510)
P.O. Box 25 (95776-0025)
PHONE..............................530 666-2116
Rick Butterfield, *President*
Rorie Butterfield, *Vice Pres*
Dan Granillo, *Manager*
Lea Redfearn, *Manager*
EMP: 165 EST: 1985
SQ FT: 14,000
SALES (est): 37.9MM Privately Held
WEB: www.butterfieldelectric.com
SIC: 1731 General electrical contractor

(P-1471)
C H REYNOLDS ELECTRIC INC
Also Called: Ch Reynolds
1281 Wayne Ave, San Jose (95131-3599)
PHONE..............................408 436-9280
Charles Reynolds, *President*
Jason Bright, *COO*
Paul J Derania, *CFO*
John Anderson, *Senior VP*
Will Swick, *Senior VP*
EMP: 400 EST: 1983
SQ FT: 25,000
SALES (est): 86.3MM Privately Held
WEB: www.chreynolds.com
SIC: 1731 General electrical contractor

(P-1472)
CAPITOL COMMUNICATIONS INC
480 9th St, San Francisco (94103-4411)
PHONE..............................415 861-1727

1731 - Electrical Work County (P-1473)
PRODUCTS & SERVICES SECTION

Parnell Pollinioni, *President*
Ron Burgess, *Vice Pres*
Brian Hidalgo, *Representative*
EMP: 35 **EST:** 1995
SALES (est): 3.6MM **Privately Held**
WEB: www.capitolcommunications.com
SIC: 1731 Telephone & telephone equipment installation; general electrical contractor

(P-1473)
CAPITOL VALLEY ELECTRIC INC
8550 Thys Ct, Sacramento (95828-1007)
PHONE 916 686-3244
David Lee Reis, *President*
David Derek, *Vice Pres*
Dave Derick, *Vice Pres*
Willa Vega, *General Mgr*
Jim Hospitalier, *Project Mgr*
EMP: 48 **EST:** 2004
SQ FT: 11,000
SALES (est): 14MM **Privately Held**
WEB: www.capitolvalleyelectric.com
SIC: 1731 General electrical contractor

(P-1474)
CENTRAL VALLEY ELECTRIC INC
24 Frazine Rd Ste A, Modesto (95357-0310)
PHONE 209 531-2470
Troy Wells, *CEO*
Craig Days, *Vice Pres*
Craig Dyas, *Project Dir*
Todd Crawford, *Project Mgr*
Mike Jack, *Project Mgr*
EMP: 38 **EST:** 1990
SALES (est): 11.1MM **Privately Held**
WEB: www.centralvalleyelectric.com
SIC: 1731 General electrical contractor

(P-1475)
CES ELECTRIC INC
632 Entler Ave, Chico (95928-9503)
PHONE 530 636-4257
Russell D Boyd, *Principal*
EMP: 49 **EST:** 2017
SALES (est): 1.2MM **Privately Held**
WEB: www.ceschico.com
SIC: 1731 Electrical work

(P-1476)
CHICO ELECTRIC INC
36 W Eaton Rd, Chico (95973-0160)
PHONE 530 891-1933
Norman Nielsen, *CEO*
Charlene Bellante, *Vice Pres*
Jake Albertson, *Project Mgr*
Kevin Pierce, *Project Mgr*
Sharon Young, *Human Resources*
EMP: 60
SQ FT: 8,500
SALES: 12MM **Privately Held**
WEB: www.chicoelectric.com
SIC: 1731 General electrical contractor

(P-1477)
CIRIMELE ELECTRICAL WORKS INC
607 Marina Way S, Richmond (94804-3732)
PHONE 510 620-1150
EMP: 35
SQ FT: 15,000
SALES (est): 3MM **Privately Held**
WEB: www.cirimeleelectric.com
SIC: 1731 General Electrical Contractor

(P-1478)
CITIZEN CORPORATION
Also Called: Citizen Electric
340 Spenker Ave, Modesto (95354-3922)
PHONE 209 537-6334
Paige Spradling, *President*
Stacey Letts, *Office Mgr*
Steve Golambos, *Sr Project Mgr*
Francisco Guzman, *Manager*
EMP: 41 **EST:** 2005
SALES (est): 10MM **Privately Held**
WEB: www.citizenelectric.com
SIC: 1731 General electrical contractor

(P-1479)
COLLINS ELECTRICAL COMPANY INC (PA)
3412 Metro Dr, Stockton (95215-9440)
PHONE 209 466-3691
Eugene C Gini, *President*
Phil Asborno, *COO*
Brian Gini, *Vice Pres*
Craig Gini, *Vice Pres*
Dianne R Gini, *Vice Pres*
EMP: 200 **EST:** 1928
SQ FT: 80,000
SALES (est): 76.6MM **Privately Held**
WEB: www.collinselectric.com
SIC: 1731 General electrical contractor

(P-1480)
COLLINS ELECTRICAL COMPANY INC
1902 Channel Dr, West Sacramento (95691-3441)
PHONE 209 466-3691
Kevin Gini, *Branch Mgr*
Joe Moreno, *Executive*
Rick Henry, *Branch Mgr*
Kelly Bergquist, *Office Mgr*
John Bangert, *Project Mgr*
EMP: 37
SALES (corp-wide): 76.6MM **Privately Held**
WEB: www.collinselectric.com
SIC: 1731 General electrical contractor
PA: Collins Electrical Company, Inc.
3412 Metro Dr
Stockton CA 95215
209 466-3691

(P-1481)
COLLINS ELECTRICAL COMPANY INC
1809 N Helm Ave Ste 7, Fresno (93727-1629)
PHONE 559 454-8164
Dave Helsel, *Manager*
EMP: 37
SALES (corp-wide): 76.6MM **Privately Held**
WEB: www.collinselectric.com
SIC: 1731 General electrical contractor
PA: Collins Electrical Company, Inc.
3412 Metro Dr
Stockton CA 95215
209 466-3691

(P-1482)
COLUMBIA ELECTRIC INC
1980 Davis St, San Leandro (94577-1209)
PHONE 510 430-9505
Joann Scruggs, *CEO*
Kim Scruggs, *Treasurer*
Gerrod Scruggs, *Vice Pres*
Nick Scruggs, *Vice Pres*
Denille Robinson, *Supervisor*
EMP: 40 **EST:** 1999
SQ FT: 4,000
SALES (est): 10.4MM **Privately Held**
WEB: www.columbia-elec.com
SIC: 1731 General electrical contractor

(P-1483)
COMTEL SYSTEMS TECHNOLOGY INC
1292 Hammerwood Ave, Sunnyvale (94089-2232)
PHONE 408 543-5600
Richard Nielsen, *President*
Andrea Nielsen, *Vice Pres*
Steve Albarran, *Technician*
Corey Oliver, *Technician*
Keith McWilliams, *Project Mgr*
EMP: 70 **EST:** 1972
SQ FT: 10,760
SALES (est): 13.8MM **Privately Held**
WEB: www.comtelsys.com
SIC: 1731 Communications specialization; access control systems specialization; fire detection & burglar alarm systems specialization

(P-1484)
CON J FRANKE ELECTRIC INC
317 N Grant St, Stockton (95202-2633)
PHONE 209 462-0717
Barry Frain, *President*
James A Ratner, *Chairman*
Diana Frain, *Corp Secy*
Lewis Frain, *Vice Pres*
Larry Woolstrum, *Vice Pres*
EMP: 100 **EST:** 1925
SQ FT: 7,000
SALES (est): 25.5MM **Privately Held**
WEB: www.cjfranke.com
SIC: 1731 General electrical contractor

(P-1485)
CONTRA COSTA ELECTRIC INC (DH)
825 Howe Rd, Martinez (94553-3441)
P.O. Box 2523 (94553-0317)
PHONE 925 229-4250
Michael Dias, *President*
Dave Galli, *CFO*
Charlie Hadsell, *Vice Pres*
Carla Palmer, *Vice Pres*
Joey Ramirez, *Vice Pres*
EMP: 300 **EST:** 1946
SALES (est): 148.7MM
SALES (corp-wide): 8.8B **Publicly Held**
WEB: www.ccelectric.com
SIC: 1731 General electrical contractor

(P-1486)
COSCO FIRE PROTECTION INC
7455 Longard Rd, Livermore (94551-8238)
PHONE 925 455-2751
Phil Raya, *Manager*
Jamie Duncan, *Administration*
EMP: 52 **Privately Held**
WEB: www.coscofire.com
SIC: 1731 3494 8711 7382 General electrical contractor; sprinkler systems; field engineering services; security systems services; plumbing, heating, air-conditioning contractors
HQ: Cosco Fire Protection, Inc.
29222 Rancho Viejo Rd # 205
San Juan Capistrano CA 92675

(P-1487)
CREATION NETWORKS INC
1001 Shary Cir Ste 1, Concord (94518-2419)
PHONE 925 446-4332
Lisa Benson, *Mng Member*
Eric Benson, *CEO*
Kathryn Altman, *Sales Staff*
EMP: 19 **EST:** 2006
SALES (est): 3.2MM **Privately Held**
WEB: www.creationnetworks.net
SIC: 5999 1731 5065 5099 Audio-visual equipment & supplies; computerized controls installation; voice, data & video wiring contractor; video equipment, electronic; video & audio equipment; audio electronic systems

(P-1488)
CROWN ELECTRIC INC (PA)
85 Columbia Sq, San Francisco (94103-4015)
P.O. Box 4277, San Mateo (94404-0277)
PHONE 415 559-7432
Christopher Powell, *President*
Alvin Mesita, *Vice Pres*
EMP: 37 **EST:** 1907
SQ FT: 3,000
SALES (est): 3MM **Privately Held**
SIC: 1731 General electrical contractor

(P-1489)
CSC CORPORATION
Also Called: Electrical Services Company
9835 Kitty Ln, Oakland (94603-1071)
PHONE 510 430-0399
Cathy Simpson, *President*
Christopher Asturias, *COO*
Scott Williams, *Admin Sec*
EMP: 35 **EST:** 1979
SQ FT: 5,264
SALES (est): 8MM **Privately Held**
SIC: 1731 General electrical contractor

(P-1490)
CUPERTINO ELECTRIC INC
350 Lenore Way, Felton (95018-8973)
P.O. Box 1517 (95018-1517)
PHONE 408 808-8260
EMP: 698
SALES (corp-wide): 490.5MM **Privately Held**
WEB: www.cei.com
SIC: 1731 General electrical contractor
PA: Cupertino Electric, Inc.
1132 N 7th St
San Jose CA 95112
408 808-8000

(P-1491)
CUPERTINO ELECTRIC INC (PA)
Also Called: Cei
1132 N 7th St, San Jose (95112-4438)
PHONE 408 808-8000
Tom Schott, *President*
Brett Boncher, *COO*
Bill Slakey, *CFO*
Estrella Parker, *Officer*
Rob Thorne, *Vice Pres*
▲ **EMP:** 400 **EST:** 2000
SQ FT: 90,000
SALES (est): 490.5MM **Privately Held**
WEB: www.cei.com
SIC: 1731 General electrical contractor

(P-1492)
CUPERTINO ELECTRIC INC
1740 Cesar Chavez Fl 2, San Francisco (94124-1134)
PHONE 415 970-3400
Adam Spillane, *Branch Mgr*
Rudy Bergthold, *Senior VP*
Kurt Freitas, *Executive*
John Jennings, *Executive*
Ageno Lori, *Executive Asst*
EMP: 698
SALES (corp-wide): 490.5MM **Privately Held**
WEB: www.cei.com
SIC: 1731 General electrical contractor
PA: Cupertino Electric, Inc.
1132 N 7th St
San Jose CA 95112
408 808-8000

(P-1493)
D M JEPSEN INC
Also Called: Jepsen Electric
295 Boeing Ct, Livermore (94551-9258)
PHONE 925 455-0872
Moira Jepsen, *President*
David Jepsen, *Vice Pres*
Marla Raber, *HR Admin*
Chris Morrison, *Manager*
Stacy Pardini, *Receptionist*
EMP: 45 **EST:** 1984
SQ FT: 7,600
SALES (est): 7.1MM **Privately Held**
WEB: www.jepsenelectric.com
SIC: 1731 General electrical contractor

(P-1494)
DATALOGIX TEXAS INC
33250 Central Ave, Union City (94587-2010)
PHONE 510 475-8787
EMP: 43
SALES (corp-wide): 6MM **Privately Held**
SIC: 1731 4899 7373 7371 Electrical Contractor Communication Services Computer Systems Design Computer Programming Svc Electrical Repair
PA: Datalogix Texas, Inc.
8315 Navisota Dr Ste 100
Lantana TX 76226
940 728-0152

(P-1495)
DEL MONTE ELECTRIC CO INC (PA)
6998 Sierra Ct Ste A, Dublin (94568-2655)
PHONE 925 829-6000
John Hunter, *President*
Cynthia Hunter, *Admin Sec*
Chris Walker, *Project Mgr*
Joseph Fong, *Project Engr*
Matt Hutchison, *Project Engr*
EMP: 35 **EST:** 1938
SQ FT: 10,000
SALES (est): 22.7MM **Privately Held**
WEB: www.delmonteelectricco.com
SIC: 1731 General electrical contractor

▲ = Import ▼ = Export
◆ = Import/Export

PRODUCTS & SERVICES SECTION
1731 - Electrical Work County (P-1522)

(P-1496)
DILIGENCE SECURITY GROUP
66 Franklin St Ste 300, Oakland (94607-3734)
PHONE..................510 710-5806
Joy Baucom, *CEO*
Kenton Barnes, *COO*
EMP: 200 **EST:** 2020
SALES (est): 7.7MM **Privately Held**
SIC: 1731 Safety & security specialization

(P-1497)
EJ WEBER ELECTRIC CO INC
895 Innes Ave, San Francisco (94124-2902)
PHONE..................415 641-9300
Daniel J Vogl, *President*
Laura Coffman, *Corp Secy*
Richard Barnes, *CIO*
Jim Brown, *Sr Project Mgr*
EMP: 35 **EST:** 1997
SQ FT: 7,500
SALES (est): 10.9MM **Privately Held**
WEB: www.ejweber.com
SIC: 1731 General electrical contractor

(P-1498)
ELCOR ELECTRIC INC
3310 Bassett St, Santa Clara (95054-2702)
PHONE..................408 986-1320
George Woodley, *General Mgr*
Clint Woodley, *Vice Pres*
EMP: 120 **EST:** 1989
SQ FT: 5,000
SALES (est): 36.9MM **Privately Held**
WEB: www.elcorelectric.com
SIC: 1731 General electrical contractor

(P-1499)
ELECTRIC INNOVATIONS INC
3711 Meadow View Dr # 100, Redding (96002-9795)
PHONE..................530 222-3366
Theodore Paul Thompson, *CEO*
EMP: 51 **EST:** 2013
SQ FT: 2,000
SALES (est): 9MM **Privately Held**
WEB: www.electricinnovations.com
SIC: 1731 3511 General electrical contractor; steam turbine generator set units, complete

(P-1500)
ELECTRIC USA
480 Aldo Ave, Santa Clara (95054-2304)
PHONE..................800 921-1151
EMP: 50
SALES (est): 1.4MM **Privately Held**
SIC: 1731 1711 Electrical Work, Nsk

(P-1501)
ELITE POWER INC
6530 Asher Ln, Sacramento (95828-1832)
PHONE..................916 739-1580
Walt Zacharias, *President*
Shannon Allen, *Accounting Mgr*
Chris Bissing, *Foreman/Supr*
Keith Diffey, *Foreman/Supr*
Chris Garduno, *Foreman/Supr*
EMP: 54 **EST:** 2001
SQ FT: 15,000
SALES (est): 9.7MM **Privately Held**
WEB: www.elitepower.com
SIC: 1731 General electrical contractor

(P-1502)
ELSON ELECTRIC HOLDINGS INC
3440 Vincent Rd, Pleasant Hill (94523-4338)
PHONE..................925 464-7461
Robert W Elson, *CEO*
Rachel Moreno, *Principal*
EMP: 42 **EST:** 2014
SALES (est): 3.9MM **Privately Held**
WEB: www.elsonelectric.com
SIC: 1731 General electrical contractor

(P-1503)
FERGUSON FAMILY ENTPS INC
Also Called: Gray Electric Company
12911 Loma Rica Dr, Grass Valley (95945-9061)
PHONE..................530 273-0686
Dave Ferguson, *President*
Kerry Ferguson, *Vice Pres*
Rob Sorum, *Project Mgr*
▲ **EMP:** 36 **EST:** 1995
SQ FT: 10,000
SALES (est): 9.6MM **Privately Held**
WEB: www.grayelectricco.com
SIC: 1731 General electrical contractor; safety & security specialization

(P-1504)
FERN ELECTRIC & CONTROL INC
6 S Linden Ave Ste 2, South San Francisco (94080-6422)
PHONE..................650 952-3203
Joyce Fernandez, *President*
EMP: 20 **EST:** 1978
SQ FT: 2,800
SALES (est): 1.9MM **Privately Held**
SIC: 1731 3823 General electrical contractor; electrolytic conductivity instruments, industrial process

(P-1505)
FISHEL COMPANY
Also Called: Team Fishel
5431 W Grant Line Rd, Tracy (95304-9343)
PHONE..................209 207-9068
EMP: 36
SALES (corp-wide): 540MM **Privately Held**
WEB: www.teamfishel.com
SIC: 1731 8711 1623 General electrical contractor; engineering services; gas main construction; cable television line construction; telephone & communication line construction; electric power line construction
PA: The Fishel Company
1366 Dublin Rd
Columbus OH 43215
614 274-8100

(P-1506)
FONEXPERTS INC
Also Called: Telecommunications Designs
1650 Northpoint Pkwy F, Santa Rosa (95407-5043)
PHONE..................707 303-8200
Robert Butler, *President*
Bryan Cates, *Vice Pres*
Donna Cates, *Vice Pres*
Charlie Swanson, *Supervisor*
EMP: 45 **EST:** 1993
SQ FT: 1,500
SALES (est): 5.8MM **Privately Held**
SIC: 1731 Telephone & telephone equipment installation

(P-1507)
GD LONG ELECTRIC COMPANY
450 Technology Way, NAPA (94558-7564)
PHONE..................707 252-3512
Greg Long, *Owner*
Patti Long, *Admin Sec*
Thomas Long, *Project Mgr*
EMP: 40 **EST:** 1990
SQ FT: 5,000
SALES (est): 10.7MM **Privately Held**
WEB: www.longelectric.com
SIC: 1731 1799 General electrical contractor; fireproofing buildings

(P-1508)
GILL GROVE ELECTRIC COMPANY
909 7th St, Oakland (94607-3101)
PHONE..................510 451-2929
Brad Gill, *President*
Nancy Gill, *Corp Secy*
Greg Carey, *Vice Pres*
EMP: 40
SQ FT: 26,000
SALES (est): 7.2MM **Privately Held**
WEB: www.gillselectric.com
SIC: 1731 General electrical contractor

(P-1509)
GRUENDL INC
Also Called: Ray's Electric
411 Pendleton Way Ste B, Oakland (94621-2115)
PHONE..................510 577-7700
Greg Gruendl, *President*
Raymond E Gruendl, *Vice Pres*
Charlotte Gruendl, *Admin Sec*
EMP: 48 **EST:** 1960
SQ FT: 3,000
SALES (est): 9.6MM **Privately Held**
SIC: 1731 General electrical contractor

(P-1510)
H & D ELECTRIC
5237 Walnut Ave Ste 100, Sacramento (95841-2694)
P.O. Box 41360 (95841-0360)
PHONE..................916 332-0794
Mark E Cooper, *President*
Jack Headley, *Division Mgr*
Kristin Strand, *Admin Sec*
EMP: 360 **EST:** 1957
SQ FT: 14,400
SALES (est): 27.4MM **Privately Held**
WEB: www.hdelectric.com
SIC: 1731 General electrical contractor

(P-1511)
H A BOWEN ELECTRIC INC
2055 Williams St, San Leandro (94577-2305)
P.O. Box 2153 (94577-0329)
PHONE..................510 483-0500
Herbert A Bowen, *President*
Jason Kaneko, *Manager*
Felix Sifuentes, *Manager*
EMP: 60
SQ FT: 9,000
SALES (est): 30.3MM **Privately Held**
WEB: www.bowenelectric.com
SIC: 1731 General electrical contractor

(P-1512)
HAMILTON AND DILLON ELC INC
1128 Reno Ave, Modesto (95351-1128)
P.O. Box 581890 (95358-0033)
PHONE..................209 529-6292
Bobby Hamilton, *President*
John Dillon, *Vice Pres*
EMP: 60 **EST:** 1998
SQ FT: 5,000
SALES (est): 7.4MM **Privately Held**
WEB: www.hamdill.com
SIC: 1731 General electrical contractor

(P-1513)
HAROLD E NUTTER INC
5934 Rosebud Ln, Sacramento (95841-2914)
PHONE..................916 334-4343
Norman Nutter, *Manager*
EMP: 50
SALES (corp-wide): 7.2MM **Privately Held**
WEB: www.henutter.net
SIC: 1731 General electrical contractor
PA: Harold E. Nutter, Inc.
5930 Rosebud Ln
Sacramento CA 95841
916 334-4343

(P-1514)
HGH ELECTRIC INC
3032 Market St, Oakland (94608-4336)
PHONE..................510 923-1859
Doug Hicks, *President*
Ronald Hammer, *Corp Secy*
EMP: 35 **EST:** 1999
SALES (est): 2.7MM **Privately Held**
SIC: 1731 General electrical contractor

(P-1515)
HODGES ELECTRIC INC
1239 Hoblitt Ave, Clovis (93612-2807)
PHONE..................559 298-5533
Roger L Hidy, *President*
Janel M Hidy, *CFO*
EMP: 50 **EST:** 1979
SQ FT: 5,000
SALES (est): 5.2MM **Privately Held**
SIC: 1731 General electrical contractor

(P-1516)
HORN ELECTRIC
1008 Black Diamond Way A, Lodi (95240-0727)
P.O. Box 2059 (95241-2059)
PHONE..................209 339-4278
EMP: 40
SQ FT: 1,600
SALES (est): 3.3MM **Privately Held**
SIC: 1731 Electrical Contractor

(P-1517)
HOT LINE CONSTRUCTION INC
9020 Brentwood Blvd Ste H, Brentwood (94513-4049)
PHONE..................925 634-9333
Carol G Bade, *CEO*
Troy D Myers, *President*
Kelly G Kutchera, *CFO*
Kelly Kutchera, *CFO*
Troy Myers, *Vice Pres*
EMP: 584 **EST:** 1986
SQ FT: 4,000
SALES (est): 264.5MM **Privately Held**
WEB: www.hotlineconstructioninc.com
SIC: 1731 1799 Electric power systems contractors; cable splicing service

(P-1518)
HOWE ELECTRIC INC (PA)
4682 E Olive Ave, Fresno (93702-1689)
PHONE..................559 255-8992
Clinton Howe, *CEO*
Harry S Truman, *President*
Clifford J Howe, *Vice Pres*
Boon Tee, *Vice Pres*
Marjorie Montes, *Info Tech Mgr*
EMP: 40 **EST:** 1949
SQ FT: 8,500
SALES (est): 30.4MM **Privately Held**
WEB: www.howe-electric.com
SIC: 1731 General electrical contractor

(P-1519)
HOWE ELECTRIC INC
4690 E Olive Ave, Fresno (93702-1636)
PHONE..................559 255-8992
Clinton Howe, *President*
EMP: 145
SQ FT: 12,502
SALES (corp-wide): 30.4MM **Privately Held**
WEB: www.howe-electric.com
SIC: 1731 General electrical contractor
PA: Howe Electric, Inc.
4682 E Olive Ave
Fresno CA 93702
559 255-8992

(P-1520)
HOWE ELECTRIC CONSTRUCTION INC
4682 E Olive Ave, Fresno (93702-1689)
PHONE..................559 255-8992
Todd Howe, *President*
Marjorie Montes, *Treasurer*
Ty Howe, *Vice Pres*
Monica Teare, *Admin Sec*
Bianca Chu, *Administration*
EMP: 140 **EST:** 2007
SALES (est): 18.6MM **Privately Held**
WEB: www.howe-electric.com
SIC: 1731 General electrical contractor

(P-1521)
ICS INTEGRATED COMM SYSTEMS
6680 Via Del Oro, San Jose (95119-1392)
PHONE..................408 491-6000
Aaron Colton, *CEO*
Don Haygood, *Admin Sec*
Carolyn Brown, *Administration*
Jason Meyer, *Prgrmr*
Vince Lacorte, *Project Mgr*
▲ **EMP:** 65 **EST:** 2002
SQ FT: 18,000
SALES: 17MM **Privately Held**
WEB: www.ics-integration.com
SIC: 1731 Fire detection & burglar alarm systems specialization; access control systems specialization; cable television installation; voice, data & video wiring contractor

(P-1522)
IDEX GLOBAL SERVICES INC
2301 Kerner Blvd Ste D, San Rafael (94901-5554)
PHONE..................415 482-4242
Dominic Dimare, *Manager*
Sean Canon, *Vice Pres*
David Holcomb, *Supervisor*
EMP: 165 **Privately Held**
WEB: www.idexgs.com

1731 - Electrical Work County (P-1523)

PRODUCTS & SERVICES SECTION

SIC: 1731 Communications specialization
HQ: Idex Global Services, Inc.
851 Van Ness Ave Fl 2
San Francisco CA 94109
415 249-3400

(P-1523)
INDUSTRIAL ELEC SYSTEMS INC (PA)
3250 Monier Cir Ste F, Rancho Cordova (95742-6839)
PHONE.............................916 638-1000
Edward L Lane, *President*
Alan Steele, *Vice Pres*
Scott Athey, *Project Mgr*
Jonathan Hiltner, *Technology*
David McCoy, *Librarian*
EMP: 35 EST: 1980
SQ FT: 3,000
SALES (est): 11.7MM **Privately Held**
WEB: www.iesi.net
SIC: 1731 3699 Fire detection & burglar alarm systems specialization; security control equipment & systems

(P-1524)
INTERMOUNTAIN ELECTRIC COMPANY
947 Washington St, San Carlos (94070-5316)
PHONE.............................650 591-7118
David Signorello, *CEO*
Stacy Signorello, *Admin Sec*
EMP: 35 EST: 1982
SQ FT: 5,000
SALES (est): 8.3MM **Privately Held**
WEB: www.im-electric.com
SIC: 1731 General electrical contractor

(P-1525)
JAROTH INC
Also Called: Pacific Telemanagement Svcs
2001 Crow Canyon Rd # 200, San Ramon (94583-5368)
PHONE.............................925 553-3650
Thomas R Keane, *CEO*
Michael R Zumbo, *President*
Nancy Rossi, *CFO*
EMP: 130 EST: 1986
SALES (est): 21.7MM **Privately Held**
WEB: www.ptsservices.net
SIC: 1731 7349 Telephone & telephone equipment installation; telephone booth cleaning & maintenance

(P-1526)
JFC ELECTRIC INC
7451 Galilee Rd Ste 130, Roseville (95678-6999)
PHONE.............................916 789-9311
Joseph F Clark, *President*
Nichola Clark, *CFO*
Nick Larson, *Project Mgr*
EMP: 45 EST: 2004
SQ FT: 3,500
SALES (est): 6.8MM **Privately Held**
WEB: www.jfcelectric.com
SIC: 1731 General electrical contractor

(P-1527)
JOE LUNARDI ELECTRIC INC
5334 Sebastopol Rd, Santa Rosa (95407-6423)
P.O. Box 120, Sebastopol (95473-0120)
PHONE.............................707 545-4755
Joseph I Lunardi, *Ch of Bd*
Jolene A Corcoran, *President*
Ronald J Lunardi, *Corp Secy*
Raymond J Lunardi, *Vice Pres*
Howie Fenton, *Marketing Staff*
EMP: 52 EST: 1946
SQ FT: 12,000
SALES (est): 10.5MM **Privately Held**
WEB: www.lunardielectric.com
SIC: 1731 General electrical contractor

(P-1528)
JUPITER INTELLIGENCE INC
181 2nd Ave Ste 300, San Mateo (94401-3815)
PHONE.............................650 255-7122
Rich Sorkin, *CEO*
Eric Wun, *COO*
Darren Weber, *Research*
Ramana Lokavarapu, *Engineer*
Gail Pomerantz, *Marketing Staff*
EMP: 44 EST: 2017
SALES (est): 5.8MM **Privately Held**
WEB: www.jupiterintel.com
SIC: 1731 Energy management controls

(P-1529)
KAIAM CORP
39677 Eureka Dr, Newark (94560-4806)
PHONE.............................650 344-2231
Bardia Pezeshki, *CEO*
Art Stein, *CFO*
John Heanue, *Vice Pres*
Karen Liu, *Vice Pres*
Thomas Schrans, *Vice Pres*
▲ EMP: 54 EST: 2009
SALES (est): 8.2MM **Privately Held**
WEB: www.kaiamcorp.com
SIC: 1731 Communications specialization

(P-1530)
KERTEL COMMUNICATIONS INC (HQ)
Also Called: Sebastian
7600 N Palm Ave Ste 101, Fresno (93711-5520)
PHONE.............................559 432-5800
William S Barcus, *CEO*
Thomas Lentz, *President*
Barbara Douglas, *Bd of Directors*
Ruth Barcus, *Vice Pres*
Ron Cato, *Vice Pres*
EMP: 91 EST: 1987
SQ FT: 9,436
SALES: 23.4MM
SALES (corp-wide): 65.3MM **Privately Held**
WEB: www.sebastiancorp.com
SIC: 1731 Telephone & telephone equipment installation
PA: Sebastian Enterprises, Inc.
811 S Madera Ave
Kerman CA 93630
559 946-4954

(P-1531)
KNIGHTS ELECTRIC INCORPORATED
11410 Old Redwood Hwy, Windsor (95492-9523)
PHONE.............................707 433-6931
Robert A Knight, *President*
Barbara Ragsdale, *CFO*
Arthur Knight, *Vice Pres*
Elizabeth Knight, *Vice Pres*
Rhoda Hauth, *Office Mgr*
EMP: 54 EST: 1976
SQ FT: 1,000
SALES (est): 6.5MM **Privately Held**
WEB: www.knightselectric.com
SIC: 1731 General electrical contractor

(P-1532)
KOSITCH ENTERPRISES INC
Also Called: Mission Electric Company
5700 Boscell Cmn, Fremont (94538-5111)
PHONE.............................510 657-4460
Jeffrey Kositch, *CEO*
Rui Gomes, *Purch Agent*
Patrick Macones, *Manager*
Loren Olk, *Manager*
EMP: 80
SQ FT: 9,000
SALES: 29.7MM **Privately Held**
WEB: www.mission-elec.com
SIC: 1731 General electrical contractor

(P-1533)
KRUG ASSOCIATES INC
Also Called: Kbl Associates
26269 Research Pl, Hayward (94545-3725)
PHONE.............................510 887-1117
Jeffrey P Krug, *CEO*
Bill Bixby, *Vice Pres*
William Bixby, *Vice Pres*
Andy Ly, *Principal*
Maureen Krug, *Office Mgr*
▲ EMP: 64 EST: 1987
SQ FT: 16,800
SALES (est): 10.4MM **Privately Held**
WEB: www.kblassociates.com
SIC: 1731 Electronic controls installation

(P-1534)
LUMEWAVE INC (DH)
550 Meridian Ave, San Jose (95126-3422)
PHONE.............................916 400-3535
Mark Keating, *President*
EMP: 120 EST: 2010
SALES (est): 522.7K
SALES (corp-wide): 1.3B **Privately Held**
WEB: www.dialog-semiconductor.com
SIC: 1731 3648 Lighting contractor; street lighting fixtures
HQ: Echelon Corporation
3600 Peterson Way
Santa Clara CA 95054
408 938-5200

(P-1535)
MARK III CONSTRUCTION INC (PA)
Also Called: Mark III Dvlpers Dsgn/Builders
5101 Florin Perkins Rd, Sacramento (95826-4817)
PHONE.............................916 381-8080
Daniel Carlton, *CEO*
Mike O'brien, *Partner*
Jennifer O'Brien Cooley, *President*
Michael O'Brien, *Treasurer*
Jeff Olsen, *Officer*
EMP: 72 EST: 1975
SQ FT: 11,000
SALES (est): 77.6MM **Privately Held**
WEB: www.mark-three.com
SIC: 1731 1542 1711 General electrical contractor; electronic controls installation; commercial & office building, new construction; plumbing contractors; fire sprinkler system installation

(P-1536)
MARTICUS ELECTRIC INC
9266 Beatty Dr Ste D, Sacramento (95826-9732)
PHONE.............................916 368-2186
Art Munoz, *President*
Susan Munoz, *Corp Secy*
David Munoz, *Vice Pres*
Tim Collins, *Opers Spvr*
Mark Green, *Commercial*
EMP: 45 EST: 1984
SQ FT: 14,000
SALES (est): 3.1MM **Privately Held**
WEB: www.marticus.com
SIC: 1731 General electrical contractor

(P-1537)
MAY-HAN ELECTRIC INC
Also Called: M & M Electric
1600 Auburn Blvd, Sacramento (95815-1906)
PHONE.............................916 929-0150
Cecilia J Hanson, *CEO*
Audrey Daugherty, *President*
Connie Gisler, *Corp Secy*
EMP: 65
SQ FT: 16,000
SALES: 12.7MM **Privately Held**
SIC: 1731 Lighting contractor

(P-1538)
MBKT CORP
2372 Qume Dr Ste A, San Jose (95131-1843)
PHONE.............................408 212-0230
EMP: 40 EST: 2018
SALES (est): 3.1MM **Privately Held**
SIC: 1731 1711 Electrical work; plumbing, heating, air-conditioning contractors

(P-1539)
MCH ELECTRIC INC (PA)
7693 Longard Rd, Livermore (94551-8208)
PHONE.............................925 453-5041
James Humphrey, *President*
Christine Morris, *CFO*
Gary Tennyson, *Vice Pres*
Steven Corsaro, *Project Mgr*
Tom Golembeck, *Project Mgr*
EMP: 138 EST: 1999
SQ FT: 2,600
SALES (est): 50.3MM **Privately Held**
WEB: www.mchelectric.com
SIC: 1731 General electrical contractor

(P-1540)
MCKEE AND COMPANY ELECTRIC
594 Monterey Blvd, San Francisco (94127-2416)
PHONE.............................415 724-2738
Steven McKee, *CEO*
EMP: 73
SALES: 9.7MM **Privately Held**
WEB: www.mckeeselectric.com
SIC: 1731 General electrical contractor

(P-1541)
MCMILLAN DATA CMMNICATIONS INC
1823 Egbert Ave, San Francisco (94124-2519)
P.O. Box 880307 (94188-0307)
PHONE.............................415 992-6582
James Patrick Murray, *CEO*
Mark Andrew Mahoney, *CFO*
David Auch, *Vice Pres*
Ryan Mahoney, *Vice Pres*
Patrick John McMillan, *Admin Sec*
EMP: 55 EST: 2008
SALES (est): 9.5MM **Privately Held**
WEB: www.mcmillanco.com
SIC: 1731 Electrical work

(P-1542)
MCMILLAN ELECTRIC
1950 Cesar Chavez, San Francisco (94124-1132)
PHONE.............................415 826-5100
William Musgrave, *President*
Russell Schmittou, *CFO*
David Auch, *Vice Pres*
Ryan Mahoney, *Vice Pres*
Michael McAlister, *Vice Pres*
EMP: 280 EST: 1965
SQ FT: 30,000
SALES (est): 118.5MM **Privately Held**
WEB: www.mcmillanco.com
SIC: 1731 General electrical contractor

(P-1543)
MDE ELECTRIC COMPANY INC
Also Called: MDE Electric
152 Commercial St, Sunnyvale (94086-5201)
PHONE.............................408 738-8600
Marshall Goldman, *CEO*
Harry Goldman, *Corp Secy*
Larry Sever, *Business Mgr*
Ranfis Villatoro, *Purch Agent*
Rudy Cervantes, *Foreman/Supr*
EMP: 50 EST: 1973
SQ FT: 5,000
SALES (est): 15.3MM **Privately Held**
WEB: www.mde-services.com
SIC: 1731 General electrical contractor

(P-1544)
METROPOLITAN ELEC CNSTR INC
2400 3rd St, San Francisco (94107-3111)
PHONE.............................415 642-3000
Nick Dutto, *Principal*
Mark Friedeberg, *CFO*
Manuel Cruz, *Project Mgr*
Devin Wright, *Project Mgr*
Conor Brummer, *Project Engr*
EMP: 210 EST: 1981
SQ FT: 23,000
SALES: 63MM **Privately Held**
WEB: www.metroelectric.com
SIC: 1731 General electrical contractor

(P-1545)
MGH ENTERPRISES INC
2540 Cactus Ave, Chico (95973-7607)
PHONE.............................530 894-2537
Ginger M Hook, *President*
Mark S Hook, *Vice Pres*
Tiffany Garcia, *Project Mgr*
Rich Myers, *Foreman/Supr*
EMP: 36 EST: 1989
SQ FT: 1,250
SALES (est): 3.5MM **Privately Held**
WEB: www.mghenterprises.com
SIC: 1731 Electrical work

▲ = Import ▼ = Export
◆ = Import/Export

PRODUCTS & SERVICES SECTION

1731 - Electrical Work County (P-1571)

(P-1546)
MIKE BROWN ELECTRIC CO
561a Mercantile Dr, Cotati (94931-3040)
PHONE.................707 792-8100
James Brown, *President*
James G Brown, *President*
Tiffany Howe, *Vice Pres*
Gregg Mills, *Project Mgr*
Austin Smith, *Project Mgr*
EMP: 120 EST: 1979
SQ FT: 14,000
SALES (est): 53.8MM **Privately Held**
WEB: www.mbelectric.com
SIC: 1731 General electrical contractor

(P-1547)
NELSON & SONS ELECTRIC INC
401 N Walnut Rd, Turlock (95380-9426)
PHONE.................209 667-4343
Keith Nelson, *President*
Shelly Nelson, *Treasurer*
David Nelson, *Vice Pres*
Travis Nelson, *Vice Pres*
EMP: 50 EST: 2007
SALES (est): 7.7MM **Privately Held**
WEB: www.nelsonselectric.com
SIC: 1731 General electrical contractor

(P-1548)
NETRONIX INTEGRATION INC (PA)
2170 Paragon Dr, San Jose (95131-1305)
PHONE.................408 573-1444
Craig E Jarrett, *President*
Steve Piechota, *CFO*
Eric Ryan, *Executive*
Dean Scoggins, *Branch Mgr*
Kimberly Jarrett, *Office Mgr*
EMP: 92 EST: 2007
SQ FT: 13,500
SALES (est): 28MM **Privately Held**
WEB: www.netronixint.com
SIC: 1731 General electrical contractor

(P-1549)
NEVADA REPUBLIC ELECTRIC N INC
11855 White Rock Rd, Rancho Cordova (95742-6603)
PHONE.................916 294-0140
Eric Stafford, *President*
Jeff Stafford, *Treasurer*
Jerry Stafford, *Director*
Linda Stafford, *Director*
EMP: 41 EST: 1999
SQ FT: 14,000
SALES (est): 1MM **Privately Held**
SIC: 1731 General electrical contractor

(P-1550)
NEW AGE ELECTRIC INC
1085 N 11th St, San Jose (95112-2928)
PHONE.................408 279-8787
Kurt Rocklage, *President*
Nick Hughly, *Project Mgr*
Alan Pumphrey, *Finance Mgr*
Muhamed Hantalasevic, *Foreman/Supr*
Jani Youhanapour, *Foreman/Supr*
EMP: 60 EST: 1989
SQ FT: 8,500
SALES (est): 28.4MM **Privately Held**
WEB: www.newageelectric.com
SIC: 1731 General electrical contractor

(P-1551)
NEW SOLAR ELECTRIC INC (PA)
200 Brown Rd Ste 114, Fremont (94539-7984)
PHONE.................888 886-0103
Charles Ng, *Director*
Slavko Micic, *Director*
Porter Wong, *Director*
EMP: 56 EST: 2015
SALES (est): 225.9K **Privately Held**
WEB: www.newsolarelectric.com
SIC: 1731 General electrical contractor

(P-1552)
NORTH STATE ELEC CONTRS INC
11101 White Rock Rd, Rancho Cordova (95670-6996)
PHONE.................916 572-0571
Rodney Bingaman, *President*
Lori Kirk, *CFO*
Jason Alexander, *Project Mgr*
Eric Wymore, *Manager*
EMP: 80 EST: 2007
SQ FT: 24,000
SALES (est): 26.8MM **Privately Held**
WEB: www.northstate-eci.com
SIC: 1731 General electrical contractor

(P-1553)
OEG INC
602 Charcot Ave, San Jose (95131-2204)
PHONE.................408 909-9399
EMP: 77
SALES (corp-wide): 5.5B **Publicly Held**
WEB: www.oeg.us.com
SIC: 1731 General electrical contractor
HQ: Oeg, Inc.
3200 Nw Yeon Ave
Portland OR 97210
503 234-9900

(P-1554)
OFFICE AUTOMATION GROUP
6910 Santa Teresa Blvd, San Jose (95119-1339)
PHONE.................408 292-0308
Michael Dyer, *Principal*
Heath Wright, *General Mgr*
Marny Dyer, *Admin Sec*
EMP: 37
SALES (corp-wide): 6.8MM **Privately Held**
WEB: www.oagi.com
SIC: 1731 Electrical work
PA: Office Automation Group
1066 Elm St
San Jose CA 95126
408 554-6244

(P-1555)
OFFICE AUTOMATION GROUP (PA)
Also Called: Oagi Suntelco
1066 Elm St, San Jose (95126-1014)
PHONE.................408 554-6244
Michael W Dyer, *President*
Tara Walsh, *Opers Staff*
Heath Wright, *Sales Executive*
EMP: 37 EST: 2001
SQ FT: 2,400
SALES (est): 6.8MM **Privately Held**
WEB: www.oagi.com
SIC: 1731 Fiber optic cable installation

(P-1556)
OLIVEIRA-LUCAS ENTERPRISES INC
Also Called: Acme Electric Co
1025 S Kilroy Rd, Turlock (95380-9589)
P.O. Box 766 (95381-0766)
PHONE.................209 667-2851
Frank Lucas, *President*
Fred Zumstein, *Project Mgr*
EMP: 35 EST: 1971
SQ FT: 5,000
SALES (est): 5.9MM **Privately Held**
WEB: www.acme-electric.net
SIC: 1731 General electrical contractor

(P-1557)
OROURKE ELECTRIC INC
3347 Industrial Dr Ste 4, Santa Rosa (95403-2025)
PHONE.................707 528-8539
Daniel D Orourke, *President*
Daniel T O'Rourke, *President*
Paul Swallow, *Project Mgr*
EMP: 38 EST: 1977
SQ FT: 2,000
SALES (est): 2.2MM **Privately Held**
WEB: www.orourke-electric.com
SIC: 1731 General electrical contractor

(P-1558)
PACIFIC GAS AND ELECTRIC CO
4400 E State Highway 140, Merced (95340-9388)
PHONE.................209 726-7623
Wayne Pouncey, *Consultant*
EMP: 169 **Publicly Held**
WEB: www.pge.com
SIC: 1731 Electrical work
HQ: Pacific Gas And Electric Company
77 Beale St
San Francisco CA 94105
415 973-7000

(P-1559)
PACIFIC METRO ELECTRIC INC
3150 E Fremont St, Stockton (95205-3918)
P.O. Box 127 (95201-0127)
PHONE.................209 939-3222
Glen Rigsbee, *President*
Krista Rigsbee, *Project Mgr*
EMP: 60 EST: 1995
SALES (est): 10MM **Privately Held**
WEB: www.pacificmetroelectric.com
SIC: 1731 General electrical contractor

(P-1560)
PACIFIC POWER & SYSTEMS INC
4970 Peabody Rd, Fairfield (94533-6552)
PHONE.................707 437-2300
Wally Budgell, *President*
Linda Messer, *Treasurer*
EMP: 38 EST: 1999
SQ FT: 16,000
SALES (est): 5MM
SALES (corp-wide): 20.5MM **Privately Held**
WEB: www.rbigroup.net
SIC: 1731 General electrical contractor; communications specialization; fire detection & burglar alarm systems specialization
HQ: Robertson Bright Industries Llc
5125 S Vly View Blvd
Las Vegas NV 89118

(P-1561)
PAGANINI ELECTRIC CORPORATION
Also Called: Paganini Companies
190 Hubbell St Ste 200, San Francisco (94107-2240)
PHONE.................415 575-3900
Kenneth A Paganini, *CEO*
Michael K Paganini, *President*
Eva Wong, *Executive*
Kristi Dougherty, *Info Tech Dir*
Benson Lee, *Info Tech Dir*
EMP: 115
SQ FT: 20,000
SALES (est): 28.4MM **Privately Held**
WEB: www.pagcos.com
SIC: 1731 General electrical contractor

(P-1562)
PEI PLACER ELECTRIC INC (PA)
5439 Stationers Way, Sacramento (95842-1900)
PHONE.................916 338-4400
Lynne Harker, *CEO*
Richard Nogleberg, *President*
Heather Kravchen, *CFO*
Kelly Krick, *Purchasing*
Ray Evans, *Foreman/Supr*
EMP: 35
SQ FT: 7,000
SALES (est): 5MM **Privately Held**
WEB: www.placerelectric.com
SIC: 1731 General electrical contractor

(P-1563)
PFEIFFER ELECTRIC CO INC
448 Queens Ln, San Jose (95112-4394)
PHONE.................408 436-8523
William J Pfeiffer, *President*
Victor C Pfeiffer Jr, *Shareholder*
Patric Pfeiffer, *Vice Pres*
Vanesa Calderon, *Office Mgr*
Kyle Laine, *Foreman/Supr*
EMP: 35 EST: 1926
SQ FT: 9,000
SALES (est): 17.9MM **Privately Held**
WEB: www.pfefferelectric.com
SIC: 1731 General electrical contractor

(P-1564)
PHASE 3 COMMUNICATIONS INC (PA)
1355 Felipe Ave, San Jose (95122-2602)
PHONE.................408 946-9011
Nicolas Dezubiria, *CEO*
Ruben N Yusi, *CFO*
Ruben Yusi, *CFO*
Juan Dezubiria, *Vice Pres*
Kenneth Harris, *Office Mgr*
EMP: 97 EST: 1994
SALES (est): 18.7MM **Privately Held**
WEB: www.p3com.net
SIC: 1731 1799 Fiber optic cable installation; cable splicing service

(P-1565)
PIONEER ELECTRIC & TELECOM INC
Also Called: Pioneer Electric and Telcom
7975 Cameron Dr Ste 1500, Windsor (95492-8573)
PHONE.................707 838-4057
Darryl Kirchner, *President*
Gerri Kirchner, *CFO*
Warren Yuers, *Office Mgr*
John Graham, *Project Mgr*
EMP: 37 EST: 1971
SALES (est): 1MM **Privately Held**
WEB: www.pioneer-electric.com
SIC: 1731 General electrical contractor

(P-1566)
PMN DESIGN ELECTRIC INC (PA)
39 Wyoming St, Pleasanton (94566-6277)
PHONE.................925 846-0650
Peter Nowak, *President*
Mike Price, *Vice Pres*
Mikel Price, *Vice Pres*
Steve Farro, *Project Mgr*
Jennifer Scholting, *Marketing Mgr*
EMP: 79 EST: 1976
SQ FT: 4,430
SALES (est): 33MM **Privately Held**
WEB: www.designelectriccompany.com
SIC: 1731 General electrical contractor

(P-1567)
POINT ONE ELEC SYSTEMS INC
6751 Southfront Rd, Livermore (94551-8218)
PHONE.................925 667-2935
Michael G Curran, *President*
Thomas F Curran, *Vice Pres*
Ken Miller, *Vice Pres*
Sean Bithell, *Maintence Staff*
EMP: 60 EST: 1998
SQ FT: 30,000
SALES (est): 15MM **Privately Held**
WEB: www.point1.com
SIC: 1731 General electrical contractor

(P-1568)
POWER FACTOR ELECTRIC INC
4011 Alvis Ct Ste 4, Rocklin (95677-4030)
PHONE.................916 435-8838
Marc Purscell, *President*
Jasmine Purscell, *Vice Pres*
EMP: 37 EST: 1996
SALES (est): 5MM **Privately Held**
SIC: 1731 General electrical contractor

(P-1569)
PRESIDIO SYSTEMS INC (PA)
159 Wright Brothers Ave, Livermore (94551-9466)
P.O. Box 886 (94551-0886)
PHONE.................925 362-8400
Joe Schratz, *President*
Kris Schratz, *Vice Pres*
Christine Lane, *Manager*
EMP: 21 EST: 2002
SALES (est): 5MM **Privately Held**
WEB: www.presidiosystemsinc.com
SIC: 1731 3589 Electrical work; sewer cleaning equipment, power

(P-1570)
PRIMETEK FIELD SOLUTIONS INC
605 Rialto Dr, Vacaville (95687-5450)
PHONE.................619 271-4555
Kimberly Ringler, *President*
Kimberly Y Ringler, *President*
EMP: 40 EST: 2014
SALES (est): 4.9MM **Privately Held**
WEB: www.primetekfieldsolutions.com
SIC: 1731 Cable television installation

(P-1571)
PTS COMMUNICATIONS INC
2001 Crow Canyon Rd # 200, San Ramon (94583-5368)
PHONE.................925 553-3609
Thomas Keane, *CEO*

1731 - Electrical Work County (P-1572)

PRODUCTS & SERVICES SECTION

Leif Kalberg, *CFO*
EMP: 35 **EST:** 2017
SALES (est): 3.4MM **Privately Held**
SIC: 1731 Telephone & telephone equipment installation

(P-1572)
R F I SECURITY INC (HQ)
360 Turtle Creek Ct, San Jose (95125-1389)
PHONE.................408 298-5400
Lawrence Reece, *President*
Brad Wilson, *President*
Marilyn Duell, *CFO*
EMP: 68 **EST:** 1983
SQ FT: 3,000
SALES (est): 13.7MM
SALES (corp-wide): 63.2MM **Privately Held**
WEB: www.rfi.com
SIC: 1731 7382 Access control systems specialization; security systems services
PA: Rfi Enterprises, Inc.
  360 Turtle Creek Ct
  San Jose CA 95125
  408 298-5400

(P-1573)
RADONICH CORP
Also Called: Cal Coast Telecom
886 Faulstich Ct, San Jose (95112-1361)
PHONE.................408 275-8888
Rick M Radonich, *CEO*
David S Miguel, *Corp Secy*
William L Radonich Jr, *Vice Pres*
Shanon Baker, *Project Mgr*
Bob Sanchez, *Project Mgr*
EMP: 50 **EST:** 1966
SQ FT: 5,000
SALES (est): 22.2MM **Privately Held**
WEB: www.cctcom.net
SIC: 1731 Fiber optic cable installation

(P-1574)
RANDELL C TOWNE
Also Called: Towne Electric Company
14558 Wicks Blvd, San Leandro (94577-6714)
PHONE.................510 483-1635
Randell C Towne, *Owner*
EMP: 66 **EST:** 2003
SQ FT: 7,917
SALES (est): 1.7MM **Privately Held**
SIC: 1731 General electrical contractor

(P-1575)
RAY SCHEIDTS ELECTRIC INC
1055 N 7th St, San Jose (95112-4426)
PHONE.................408 292-8715
Steve Morin, *CEO*
Richard A Morin II, *CEO*
Rick Morin, *Treasurer*
Richard Morin, *Corp Secy*
EMP: 35 **EST:** 1961
SQ FT: 6,000
SALES (est): 6.1MM **Privately Held**
WEB: www.rayscheidtselectric.com
SIC: 1731 General electrical contractor

(P-1576)
REDWOOD ELECTRIC GROUP INC (PA)
2775 Northwestern Pkwy, Santa Clara (95051-0947)
PHONE.................707 451-7348
Victor Castello, *President*
Jeff Tarzwell, *CFO*
Gordon Armstrong, *Vice Pres*
Bruce Kelly, *Vice Pres*
Eric Kelly, *Project Engr*
EMP: 680 **EST:** 1974
SQ FT: 35,000
SALES (est): 124.8MM **Privately Held**
WEB: www.redwoodeg.com
SIC: 1731 General electrical contractor

(P-1577)
REDWOOD SECURITY SYSTEMS INC
160 Almonte Blvd, Mill Valley (94941-3558)
P.O. Box 1809 (94942-1809)
PHONE.................415 388-5355
Richard Rider, *President*
Robert Nagy, *Vice Pres*
Declan Grant, *Executive*
Sarah Clark, *Executive Asst*
EMP: 39 **EST:** 1977
SQ FT: 2,200
SALES (est): 4.9MM **Privately Held**
WEB: www.redwoodsecurity.com
SIC: 1731 7382 Fire detection & burglar alarm systems specialization; fire alarm maintenance & monitoring; burglar alarm maintenance & monitoring

(P-1578)
REECES FANTASIES INC (HQ)
360 Turtle Creek Ct, San Jose (95125-1315)
PHONE.................408 298-5400
Lawrence Reece, *President*
Marilyn Duell, *CFO*
EMP: 68 **EST:** 1979
SQ FT: 30,000
SALES (est): 6.7MM
SALES (corp-wide): 63.2MM **Privately Held**
WEB: www.rfi.com
SIC: 1731 7382 7378 Communications specialization; safety & security specialization; security systems services; computer maintenance & repair
PA: Rfi Enterprises, Inc.
  360 Turtle Creek Ct
  San Jose CA 95125
  408 298-5400

(P-1579)
REFFICIENCY HOLDINGS LLC
1601 Las Plumas Ave, San Jose (95133-1613)
PHONE.................408 347-3400
Jeff Sprau, *Mng Member*
Steve Hansen, *COO*
Phillip Le Bris, *CFO*
EMP: 3000 **EST:** 2020
SALES (est): 700MM **Privately Held**
SIC: 1731 Energy management controls

(P-1580)
REPUBLIC ELECTRIC INC
3820 Happy Ln, Sacramento (95827-9721)
PHONE.................916 294-0140
Eric Stafford, *Manager*
Willy Perez, *Officer*
Scott Stewardson, *Officer*
Ron Bloom, *General Mgr*
Cindy Findley, *Office Mgr*
EMP: 115 **Privately Held**
WEB: www.nvrepublic.com
SIC: 1731 General electrical contractor
PA: Republic Electric, Inc.
  3985 N Pecos Rd
  Las Vegas NV 89115

(P-1581)
REPUBLIC ELECTRIC WEST INC
3820 Happy Ln, Sacramento (95827-9721)
PHONE.................916 294-0140
Eric J Stafford, *President*
Gerald Stafford, *CFO*
Rachel Staples, *Chief Mktg Ofcr*
Skip Harvey, *General Mgr*
Jerry Stafford, *Admin Sec*
EMP: 70 **EST:** 1999
SALES (est): 10.3MM **Privately Held**
WEB: www.republicelectricwest.com
SIC: 1731 General electrical contractor

(P-1582)
REPUBLIC INTELLIGENT
1513 Sports Dr Ste 250, Sacramento (95834-1904)
PHONE.................916 515-0855
Andrew Poster, *President*
EMP: 52 **Privately Held**
SIC: 1731 Electrical work
PA: Republic Intelligent Transportation Services, Inc.
  371 Bel Marin Blvd
  Novato CA 94949

(P-1583)
REX MOORE GROUP INC
6001 Outfall Cir, Sacramento (95828-1066)
PHONE.................916 372-1300
David Rex Moore, *President*
Doug Cuthbert, *President*
J Brock Littlejohn, *CFO*
James Brock Littlejohn, *CFO*
Jason Blum, *Bd of Directors*
EMP: 450
SQ FT: 36,000
SALES (est): 121.2MM **Privately Held**
WEB: www.rexmoore.com
SIC: 1731 8711 General electrical contractor; engineering services

(P-1584)
REX MORE ELEC CNTRS ENGNERS IN (PA)
6001 Outfall Cir, Sacramento (95828-1066)
PHONE.................916 372-1300
David R Moore, *CEO*
William C Hubbard, *Partner*
James B Littlejohn, *Partner*
Steven R Moore, *Partner*
David Morandi, *Branch Mgr*
EMP: 350
SQ FT: 36,000
SALES (est): 55.5MM **Privately Held**
WEB: www.rexmoore.com
SIC: 1731 General electrical contractor

(P-1585)
REX MORE ELEC CNTRS ENGNERS IN
5803 E Harvard Ave, Fresno (93727-1366)
P.O. Box 7677 (93747-7677)
PHONE.................559 294-1300
John Abele, *Opers Staff*
Daniel Costilla, *Project Engr*
Dave Ramos, *Advisor*
EMP: 200
SALES (corp-wide): 55.5MM **Privately Held**
WEB: www.rexmoore.com
SIC: 1731 General electrical contractor
PA: Rex Moore Electrical Contractors & Engineers, Inc.
  6001 Outfall Cir
  Sacramento CA 95828
  916 372-1300

(P-1586)
RFI ENTERPRISES INC (PA)
Also Called: RFI Communications SEC Systems
360 Turtle Creek Ct, San Jose (95125-1389)
PHONE.................408 298-5400
Dee Ann Harn, *CEO*
Brandon Wilson, *COO*
Michelle Brooks, *Vice Pres*
Dale Mac McComb, *Vice Pres*
Dale Mc Comb, *Vice Pres*
EMP: 54 **EST:** 1983
SQ FT: 30,000
SALES (est): 63.2MM **Privately Held**
WEB: www.rfi.com
SIC: 1731 7382 Fire detection & burglar alarm systems specialization; communications specialization; security systems services

(P-1587)
RIIVOS INC
101 California St # 1500, San Francisco (94111-5888)
PHONE.................415 813-1840
Michele Wardell McGovern, *CEO*
Jeffrey Axelrod, *Executive*
Sarah Boles, *Human Resources*
Crystal Balandran, *Marketing Staff*
Randall Crail, *Sales Staff*
EMP: 60 **EST:** 2015
SALES (est): 17.7MM **Privately Held**
WEB: www.riivos.com
SIC: 1731 Electrical work

(P-1588)
RK ELECTRIC INC
49211 Milmont Dr, Fremont (94538-7349)
PHONE.................510 772-4125
Lonnie Robinson, *President*
Raul Real, *Vice Pres*
Dale Swanson, *Vice Pres*
Dan Yeggy, *Vice Pres*
Michael Wonderlin, *Info Tech Mgr*
EMP: 130 **EST:** 1985
SQ FT: 11,500
SALES (est): 27MM **Privately Held**
WEB: www.rkelectric.com
SIC: 1731 General electrical contractor

(P-1589)
ROBERTS ELECTRIC CO INC
480 23rd St, Oakland (94612-2322)
PHONE.................510 834-6161
Danel S Pitcock, *President*
▲ **EMP:** 35 **EST:** 1960
SQ FT: 2,000
SALES (est): 900.2K **Privately Held**
WEB: www.robertselectric.com
SIC: 1731 General electrical contractor

(P-1590)
RODDA ELECTRIC INC (PA)
380 Carrol Ct Ste L, Brentwood (94513-7353)
PHONE.................925 240-6024
Raymond Rodda, *CEO*
Nathan King, *Project Mgr*
Jim Morgan, *Project Mgr*
Rob Roy, *Purch Mgr*
Tom Jamison, *Foreman/Supr*
EMP: 109 **EST:** 1998
SQ FT: 21,000
SALES (est): 27.6MM **Privately Held**
WEB: www.roddaelectric.com
SIC: 1731 General electrical contractor

(P-1591)
ROSENDIN ELECTRIC INC (PA)
880 Mabury Rd, San Jose (95133-1021)
P.O. Box 49070 (95161-9070)
PHONE.................408 286-2800
Mike Greenawalt, *CEO*
Tom Sorley, *Ch of Bd*
Paolo Degrassi, *President*
Keith Douglas, *COO*
Matt Englert, *COO*
EMP: 3000 **EST:** 1919
SQ FT: 45,000
SALES: 1.8B **Privately Held**
WEB: www.rosendin.com
SIC: 1731 General electrical contractor

(P-1592)
ROSENDIN ELECTRIC INC
2698 Orchard Pkwy, San Jose (95134-2020)
PHONE.................408 321-2200
Mary Marshall, *Principal*
EMP: 668
SALES (corp-wide): 1.8B **Privately Held**
WEB: www.rosendin.com
SIC: 1731 General electrical contractor
PA: Rosendin Electric, Inc.
  880 Mabury Rd
  San Jose CA 95133
  408 286-2800

(P-1593)
ROSEVILLE ROCKLIN ELECTRIC INC
910 Pleasant Grove Blvd, Roseville (95678-6193)
PHONE.................916 772-2698
Jennifer Carrasco, *CEO*
Kevin Amaral, *President*
EMP: 36 **EST:** 2018
SALES (est): 6.4MM **Privately Held**
WEB: www.rocklinelectric.com
SIC: 1731 General electrical contractor

(P-1594)
RPD ELECTRICAL SERVICE CO INC
Also Called: Electrical Service Company
3550 Charter Park Dr, San Jose (95136-1380)
P.O. Box 33021, Los Gatos (95031-3021)
PHONE.................408 265-2850
Fax: 408 265-1262
EMP: 44
SALES (est): 3.4MM **Privately Held**
SIC: 1731 Electrical Contractor

(P-1595)
SABAH INTERNATIONAL INC (HQ)
5925 Stoneridge Dr, Pleasanton (94588-2705)
PHONE.................925 463-0431
Michele Sabah, *CEO*
Stan Kain, *Project Mgr*
Derrick Tillman, *Technical Staff*
Rick Lewis, *Engineer*
Sherry Rapp, *Controller*

▲ = Import ▼ = Export
◆ = Import/Export

PRODUCTS & SERVICES SECTION
1731 - Electrical Work County (P-1617)

EMP: 51 **EST:** 1979
SQ FT: 13,000
SALES (est): 15.2MM
SALES (corp-wide): 110.1MM **Privately Held**
WEB: www.sciensbuildingsolutions.com
SIC: 1731 7382 Fire detection & burglar alarm systems specialization; protective devices, security
PA: Sciens Building Solutions, Llc
541 29th St
San Francisco CA 94131
925 249-7700

(P-1596)
SACRAMENTO COOLING SYSTEMS INC (PA)
Also Called: L & H Airco
2530 Warren Dr, Rocklin (95677-2167)
PHONE.................................916 677-1000
Frank L Wegener, *President*
John Harris, *Vice Pres*
Richard Racette, *Vice Pres*
Richard Racetti, *Vice Pres*
Cheryl Bacon, *Human Res Mgr*
▲ **EMP:** 40 **EST:** 1983
SQ FT: 12,500
SALES (est): 11.9MM **Privately Held**
WEB: www.lhairco.com
SIC: 1731 5075 Electronic controls installation; air conditioning & ventilation equipment & supplies

(P-1597)
SACRAMNTO VLY ALARM SEC SYS IN
5933 Folsom Blvd, Sacramento (95819-4611)
PHONE.................................916 452-1481
Gregory Nibbelink, *CEO*
Diane Goulding, *Treasurer*
Laura Nibbelink, *Admin Sec*
Tina Williams, *Manager*
EMP: 35 **EST:** 1972
SQ FT: 1,500
SALES (est): 2.2MM **Privately Held**
WEB: www.sacalarm.com
SIC: 1731 7382 Fire detection & burglar alarm systems specialization; security systems services

(P-1598)
SAN JOAQUIN ELECTRIC INC
2342 Teepee Dr, Stockton (95205-2447)
P.O. Box 30068 (95213-0068)
PHONE.................................209 952-9980
Douglas Talbert, *President*
Roger Schrum, *Vice Pres*
Kari Schoch, *Administration*
Fran Jarvis, *Comptroller*
Ken Everitt, *Purchasing*
EMP: 35 **EST:** 1981
SQ FT: 10,500
SALES (est): 13.3MM **Privately Held**
WEB: www.sanjoaquinelectric.com
SIC: 1731 General electrical contractor

(P-1599)
SASCO ELECTRIC INC
Also Called: Sasco Valley Electric
598 Gibraltar Dr, Milpitas (95035-6315)
PHONE.................................408 970-8300
Tim Bott, *Branch Mgr*
Nikki Gruel, *Office Mgr*
Lisa Nguyen, *Executive Asst*
Janette Lynch, *Administration*
Ricky Rivetti, *CIO*
EMP: 271
SALES (corp-wide): 519.2MM **Privately Held**
WEB: www.sasco.com
SIC: 1731 7373 General electrical contractor; computer integrated systems design
HQ: Sasco Electric Inc.
2750 Moore Ave
Fullerton CA 92833
714 870-0217

(P-1600)
SCHETTER ELECTRIC INC (PA)
471 Bannon St, Sacramento (95811-0296)
P.O. Box 1377 (95812-1377)
PHONE.................................916 446-2521
Frank E Schetter, *President*
Linda Schetter, *Shareholder*
Vince Bernacchi, *Vice Pres*
Marlin Cole, *Vice Pres*
Brett Nogleberg, *Vice Pres*
EMP: 90 **EST:** 1959
SQ FT: 7,800
SALES (est): 50.9MM **Privately Held**
WEB: www.schetter.com
SIC: 1731 General electrical contractor

(P-1601)
SCHETTER ELECTRIC INC
737 Arnold Dr Ste D, Martinez (94553-6859)
PHONE.................................925 228-2424
Tom Stucker, *Branch Mgr*
Ryan Clement, *Project Mgr*
Brad Whitney, *Project Mgr*
EMP: 120
SALES (corp-wide): 50.9MM **Privately Held**
WEB: www.schetter.com
SIC: 1731 General electrical contractor
PA: Schetter Electric, Inc.
471 Bannon St
Sacramento CA 95811
916 446-2521

(P-1602)
SCHETTER ELECTRIC LLC
471 Bannon St, Sacramento (95811-0296)
P.O. Box 1377 (95812-1377)
PHONE.................................916 446-2521
Frank Schetter, *CEO*
Vince Bernacchi, *President*
Marlin Cole, *Vice Pres*
Brett Nogleberg, *Vice Pres*
Christy Johnston, *Administration*
EMP: 90 **EST:** 2018
SALES (est): 24MM
SALES (corp-wide): 50.9MM **Privately Held**
WEB: www.schetter.com
SIC: 1731 General electrical contractor
PA: Schetter Electric, Inc.
471 Bannon St
Sacramento CA 95811
916 446-2521

(P-1603)
SECURECOM INC
4822 Gldn Fthl Pkwy # 4, El Dorado Hills (95762-9829)
PHONE.................................916 638-2855
Kevin McElwee, *President*
EMP: 61 **Privately Held**
WEB: www.securecom.net
SIC: 1731 Fire detection & burglar alarm systems specialization
PA: Securecom, Inc.
1940 Don St Ste 100
Springfield OR 97477

(P-1604)
SERRANO ELECTRIC INC
15920 Concord Cir, Morgan Hill (95037-5451)
PHONE.................................408 986-1570
Daniel Serrano, *President*
Harry Serrano, *Executive*
Leslie Nakamura, *Admin Sec*
David Haney, *Project Mgr*
Damon Paras, *Foreman/Supr*
EMP: 50 **EST:** 1986
SQ FT: 8,000
SALES (est): 15.3MM **Privately Held**
WEB: www.serranoelectric.com
SIC: 1731 General electrical contractor

(P-1605)
SF SIERRA CO INC
Also Called: Sierra Electric Co
3112 Geary Blvd, San Francisco (94118-3317)
PHONE.................................415 752-2850
Rose Stadtner, *President*
David Stadtner, *Vice Pres*
Larry Stadtner, *Vice Pres*
EMP: 50 **EST:** 1953
SQ FT: 2,500
SALES (est): 11.7MM **Privately Held**
WEB: www.sierraelectric.com
SIC: 1731 General electrical contractor

(P-1606)
SJ CIMINO ELECTRIC INC
3267 Dutton Ave, Santa Rosa (95407-7891)
PHONE.................................707 542-6231
Salvatore J Cimino, *President*
EMP: 45 **EST:** 1974
SALES (est): 5.3MM **Privately Held**
WEB: www.ciminoelectric.com
SIC: 1731 General electrical contractor

(P-1607)
SKYWALKER SOUND
1110 Gorgas Ave, San Francisco (94129-1406)
P.O. Box 3000, San Rafael (94912-3000)
PHONE.................................415 662-1000
Rollin Feld, *COO*
Glenn Kiser, *Vice Pres*
Cameron Wiggins, *Executive Asst*
Steve Morris, *Info Tech Dir*
Francis Aitken, *Info Tech Mgr*
EMP: 49 **EST:** 2008
SALES (est): 5.6MM **Privately Held**
WEB: www.skysound.com
SIC: 1731 8299 Sound equipment specialization; music school

(P-1608)
SOLARCRAFT SERVICES INC (PA)
8 Digital Dr Ste 101, Novato (94949-5759)
PHONE.................................415 382-7717
Galen Torneby, *CEO*
Phil Alwitt, *COO*
Bruce King, *CFO*
Kate Laughlin, *Vice Pres*
John Maloney, *Vice Pres*
EMP: 40 **EST:** 1984
SQ FT: 7,000
SALES (est): 11.2MM **Privately Held**
WEB: www.solarcraft.com
SIC: 1731 5211 Electrical work; solar heating equipment

(P-1609)
SPRIG ELECTRIC CO (HQ)
1860 S 10th St, San Jose (95112-4108)
PHONE.................................408 298-3134
Pepper Snyder, *CEO*
Mark Mandarelli, *President*
Clint Ramsey, *CFO*
Laura Lacomble, *Officer*
Hossein Tofangsazan, *Officer*
EMP: 228 **EST:** 1970
SQ FT: 24,100
SALES (est): 105MM
SALES (corp-wide): 1B **Privately Held**
WEB: www.sprigelectric.com
SIC: 1731 General electrical contractor
PA: Archkey Solutions Llc
1572 Larkin Williams Rd
Fenton MO 63026
636 492-7500

(P-1610)
ST FRANCIS ELECTRIC INC
975 Carden St, San Leandro (94577-1102)
P.O. Box 2057 (94577-0317)
PHONE.................................510 639-0639
Robert Spinardi, *President*
Joey Medeiros, *Vice Pres*
Joseph Medeiros, *Vice Pres*
Guy Smith, *Vice Pres*
Ivana Gery, *Manager*
EMP: 250 **EST:** 1947
SQ FT: 32,500
SALES (est): 48.6MM **Privately Held**
WEB: www.stfrancislectric.com
SIC: 1731 General electrical contractor

(P-1611)
ST FRANCIS ELECTRIC LLC
975 Carden St, San Leandro (94577-1102)
P.O. Box 2057 (94577-0317)
PHONE.................................510 639-0639
Guy Smith, *CEO*
EMP: 250 **EST:** 2014
SALES (est): 70MM **Privately Held**
WEB: www.stfrancislectric.com
SIC: 1731 General electrical contractor

(P-1612)
STAR ENERGY MANAGEMENT INC
6120 Lincoln Blvd Ste G, Oroville (95966-9665)
PHONE.................................530 532-9250
Robert Allan Birkholz, *President*
Heather Baker, *CFO*
EMP: 40 **EST:** 2008
SQ FT: 3,000
SALES (est): 2.5MM **Privately Held**
WEB: www.starenergyinc.com
SIC: 1731 General electrical contractor

(P-1613)
STARLITE ELECTRIC INC
1465 Carroll Ave, San Francisco (94124-3604)
P.O. Box 882283 (94188-2283)
PHONE.................................415 648-8888
William Lee, *President*
EMP: 42 **EST:** 1994
SQ FT: 12,000
SALES (est): 1.5MM **Privately Held**
WEB: www.starliteinc.com
SIC: 1731 1711 1623 General electrical contractor; fire sprinkler system installation; telephone & communication line construction

(P-1614)
STOMMEL INC (PA)
Also Called: Lehr
631 N Market Blvd Ste N, Sacramento (95834-1212)
PHONE.................................916 646-6626
Jim Stommel, *President*
Linda Stommel, *Vice Pres*
Kathryn Deering, *Office Mgr*
Mark Matthews, *Sales Associate*
Mike McGee, *Sales Staff*
EMP: 50 **EST:** 1945
SALES (est): 16.2MM **Privately Held**
WEB: www.lehrauto.com
SIC: 1731 7539 5531 Safety & security specialization; electrical services; automotive parts

(P-1615)
STUDEBAKER BROWN ELECTRIC INC
3237 Rippey Rd Ste 100, Loomis (95650-7665)
PHONE.................................916 678-4660
David Studebaker, *CEO*
Shane Brown, *Vice Pres*
EMP: 50 **EST:** 2006
SALES (est): 10.1MM **Privately Held**
WEB: www.sbec.biz
SIC: 1731 General electrical contractor

(P-1616)
SUMMIT ELECTRIC INC (PA)
2450 Bluebell Dr Ste C, Santa Rosa (95403-2546)
PHONE.................................707 542-4773
Laurence W Dashiell, *President*
Antonio Carreno, *Vice Pres*
Kenny Cotton, *General Mgr*
John Monahan, *Manager*
Jason Booth, *Supervisor*
EMP: 47 **EST:** 1968
SQ FT: 5,000
SALES (est): 5MM **Privately Held**
WEB: www.summit-e.com
SIC: 1731 General electrical contractor

(P-1617)
SUMMIT TECHNOLOGY GROUP INC
Also Called: Summit Electric
2450c Bluebell Dr Ste C, Santa Rosa (95403-2509)
PHONE.................................707 542-4773
Laurence W Dashiell, *President*
Jeff Anderson, *Project Mgr*
EMP: 50 **EST:** 2005
SALES (est): 5.7MM **Privately Held**
WEB: www.summit-e.com
SIC: 1731 General electrical contractor

1731 - Electrical Work County (P-1618)

(P-1618)
SYNCHRONOSS TECHNOLOGIES INC
60 S Market St Ste 700, San Jose (95113-2370)
PHONE..........................800 575-7606
EMP: 316 Publicly Held
WEB: www.synchronoss.com
SIC: 1731 7379 7371 Computerized controls installation; access control systems specialization; cogeneration specialization; electronic controls installation; ; computer software development & applications
PA: Synchronoss Technologies, Inc.
200 Crossing Blvd Fl 8
Bridgewater NJ 08807

(P-1619)
TELECMMNCTONS MGT SLUTIONS INC
Also Called: T M S
570 Division St, Campbell (95008-6906)
PHONE..........................408 866-5495
Bruce Jaftok, President
Gitta Turelinckx, CFO
Michael Finn, Vice Pres
Robert Bargas, Technician
Jesus Castrejon, Technician
EMP: 57 EST: 1982
SALES (est): 10.2MM Privately Held
WEB: www.yru.com
SIC: 1731 Voice, data & video wiring contractor

(P-1620)
TELSTAR INSTRUMENTS (PA)
1717 Solano Way Ste 34, Concord (94520-5478)
PHONE..........................925 671-2888
Robert S Marston Jr, CEO
John Gardiner, Vice Pres
Alan D Strong, Branch Mgr
Kyle Johnsen, Project Engr
Paul Berson, Engineer
EMP: 48 EST: 1981
SQ FT: 4,000
SALES (est): 28.5MM Privately Held
WEB: www.telstarinc.com
SIC: 1731 7629 General electrical contractor; electrical repair shops

(P-1621)
TENNYSON ELECTRIC INC
7275 National Dr, Livermore (94550-8869)
PHONE..........................925 606-1038
Michael A Tennyson, CEO
Cathleen Tennyson, Treasurer
EMP: 50
SQ FT: 26,000
SALES (est): 18.5MM Privately Held
WEB: www.tennysonelec.com
SIC: 1731 General electrical contractor

(P-1622)
THERMA HOLDINGS LLC (PA)
1601 Las Plumas Ave, San Jose (95133-1613)
PHONE..........................408 347-3400
Jeffrey Sprau, CEO
Phillip Le Bris, CFO
Scott Carstairs, Exec VP
Mike Delgado, Exec VP
Francis Wong, Exec VP
EMP: 525 EST: 2017
SALES (est): 402.3MM Privately Held
WEB: www.therma.com
SIC: 1731 General electrical contractor

(P-1623)
TRI-SIGNAL INTEGRATION INC
5007 Windplay Dr Ste 1, El Dorado Hills (95762-9359)
PHONE..........................916 933-3155
Robert Brady, Manager
Mike Swisher, COO
Eric Neesmith, Vice Pres
Jayme Doyle, Technical Mgr
Brian Hennings, Technician
EMP: 78
SALES (corp-wide): 50.9MM Privately Held
WEB: www.tri-signal.com
SIC: 1731 Fire detection & burglar alarm systems specialization
PA: Tri-Signal Integration Inc.
28110 Avenue Stanford D
Santa Clarita CA 91355
818 566-8558

(P-1624)
TRI-SIGNAL INTEGRATION INC
4277 W Richert Ave # 105, Fresno (93722-6337)
PHONE..........................559 274-1299
Ben Moore, Vice Pres
Ken Brade, Business Dir
EMP: 78
SALES (corp-wide): 50.9MM Privately Held
WEB: www.tri-signal.com
SIC: 1731 Fire detection & burglar alarm systems specialization
PA: Tri-Signal Integration Inc.
28110 Avenue Stanford D
Santa Clarita CA 91355
818 566-8558

(P-1625)
TUCKER TECHNOLOGY INC (PA)
300 Frank H Ogawa Plz, Oakland (94612-2037)
PHONE..........................510 836-0422
Frank Tucker, President
Conchita Tucker, Senior VP
Rodney Stanley, Vice Pres
Hernan Camacho, General Mgr
Tony Fletcher, Project Mgr
EMP: 47 EST: 1995
SQ FT: 5,000
SALES (est): 10.3MM Privately Held
WEB: www.tti-usa.co
SIC: 1731 Communications specialization

(P-1626)
UNITED STATES INFO SYSTEMS INC
7621 Galilee Rd, Roseville (95678-6972)
PHONE..........................845 353-9224
EMP: 140 Privately Held
WEB: www.usis.net
SIC: 1731 Communications specialization
PA: United States Information Systems Inc.
35 W Jefferson Ave
Pearl River NY 10965

(P-1627)
VALLEY COMMUNICATIONS INC (PA)
6921 Roseville Rd, Sacramento (95842-1660)
PHONE..........................916 349-7300
Ken Hurst, President
Kate Dewitt, Vice Pres
Jeff Frydenlund, Vice Pres
Leeann Kress, Office Mgr
Jared Carpenter, Administration
EMP: 60 EST: 1983
SQ FT: 12,000
SALES (est): 11.8MM Privately Held
WEB: www.valley-com.com
SIC: 1731 3699 Voice, data & video wiring contractor; closed circuit television installation; security control equipment & systems

(P-1628)
VALLEY UNIQUE ELECTRIC INC
75 Park Creek Dr Ste 101, Clovis (93611-4432)
PHONE..........................559 237-4795
Mark Worthington, Director
Hogi Selling III, CFO
Andrea Watterson, General Mgr
Walt Worthington, Admin Sec
Tom Moore, Project Mgr
EMP: 100 EST: 1979
SALES (est): 10.4MM Privately Held
WEB: www.valleyunique.com
SIC: 1731 5719 5063 General electrical contractor; lighting fixtures; lamps & lamp shades; lighting fixtures, residential

(P-1629)
VASKO ELECTRIC INC
4300 Astoria St, Sacramento (95838-3004)
PHONE..........................916 568-7700
Darryl A Vasko, President
Ron Gracik, Vice Pres
Bob Bramer, Purch Mgr
Sam Tenbrink, Foreman/Supr
EMP: 80 EST: 1982
SQ FT: 8,500
SALES (est): 20.9MM Privately Held
WEB: www.vasko.com
SIC: 1731 General electrical contractor

(P-1630)
VEXILLUM INC (PA)
Also Called: E Z Electric
1250 Birchwood Dr, Sunnyvale (94089-2205)
PHONE..........................408 541-4245
Clifford Anthony Zachman, CEO
Scott Zachman, President
William Gearing, CFO
Robert Mathews, Vice Pres
Terry Shouse, Accounts Mgr
EMP: 178 EST: 1986
SQ FT: 4,000
SALES (est): 24.7MM Privately Held
WEB: www.ez-electric.com
SIC: 1731 General electrical contractor

(P-1631)
W BRADLEY ELECTRIC INC
501 Seaport Ct Ste 103a, Redwood City (94063-2776)
PHONE..........................650 701-1502
EMP: 125
SALES (corp-wide): 61.4MM Privately Held
SIC: 1731 Electrical Contractor
PA: W. Bradley Electric, Inc.
90 Hill Rd
Novato CA 94945
415 898-1400

(P-1632)
W BRADLEY ELECTRIC INC (PA)
90 Hill Rd, Novato (94945-4506)
PHONE..........................415 898-1400
Leslie Bradley, CEO
Mike Murphy, COO
Ralph Greenwood, CFO
Bob Bourdet, Vice Pres
Michelle Coleman, Executive Asst
▲ EMP: 50 EST: 1977
SQ FT: 24,000
SALES (est): 56.7MM Privately Held
WEB: www.wbeinc.com
SIC: 1731 General electrical contractor; communications specialization

(P-1633)
WALKER COMMUNICATIONS INC
521 Railroad Ave, Suisun City (94585-4244)
PHONE..........................707 421-1300
Gary Walker, President
EMP: 23 EST: 1996
SQ FT: 2,200
SALES (est): 1.2MM Privately Held
SIC: 1731 3669 4812 Communications specialization; emergency alarms; radio telephone communication

(P-1634)
WB ELECTRIC INC
6790 Monterey Rd, Gilroy (95020-6643)
P.O. Box 319, Coarsegold (93614-0319)
PHONE..........................408 842-7911
Randy Walker, CEO
Susan Walker, CFO
Arnold Monaco, Project Mgr
Nick Skarvelis, Technical Staff
Omar Gonzales, Project Engr
EMP: 60 EST: 1987
SALES (est): 10.4MM Privately Held
WEB: www.wbelectric.com
SIC: 1731 General electrical contractor

(P-1635)
WESTECH SYSTEMS INC
827 Jefferson Ave, Clovis (93612-2260)
PHONE..........................559 455-1720
Helder Domingos, President
Larry Troglin, President
Matt James, Vice Pres
Darin Culbertson, Project Mgr
Jon Hardamon, Project Mgr
EMP: 60 EST: 1997
SQ FT: 10,000
SALES (est): 41.3MM Privately Held
WEB: www.westechsys.com
SIC: 1731 1711 Electrical work; solar energy contractor

(P-1636)
WESTERN SUN ENTERPRISES INC
Also Called: Three D Electric
4690 E 2nd St Ste 4, Benicia (94510-1008)
PHONE..........................707 748-2542
David Alan Whitt, President
Laura Whitt, Corp Secy
EMP: 45 EST: 1989
SQ FT: 4,700
SALES (est): 10.7MM Privately Held
SIC: 1731 General electrical contractor

(P-1637)
WIGGINS ENTERPRISES LLC (PA)
Also Called: J F Lighting & Design
1370 Airport Blvd, Santa Rosa (95403-1009)
P.O. Box 11688 (95406-1688)
PHONE..........................707 545-7869
Floyd Wiggins,
Julie Wiggins,
Mike Cox, Manager
EMP: 45 EST: 1972
SQ FT: 15,000
SALES (est): 7.3MM Privately Held
SIC: 1731 5719 General electrical contractor; lighting contractor; lighting fixtures

(P-1638)
WILD ELECTRIC INCORPORATED
4626 E Olive Ave, Fresno (93702-1660)
PHONE..........................559 251-7770
Fred Merlo, President
Jan Merlo, Vice Pres
Craig Mull, Project Mgr
Jackie Bacorn, Controller
Russ Westerman, Superintendent
EMP: 55 EST: 1973
SQ FT: 3,750
SALES (est): 17.1MM Privately Held
WEB: www.wildelectric.com
SIC: 1731 General electrical contractor

(P-1639)
WILLIAM D WHITE CO INC
3505 Magnolia St, Oakland (94608-4127)
PHONE..........................510 658-8167
Aria White, Treasurer
EMP: 17 EST: 1950
SQ FT: 8,900
SALES (est): 806.1K Privately Held
WEB: www.wmdwhiteco.com
SIC: 1731 3448 Safety & security specialization; prefabricated metal buildings

(P-1640)
WOLTCOM INC
Also Called: W C I
2300 Tech Pkwy Ste 8, Hollister (95023)
PHONE..........................831 638-4900
Mona K Wolters, President
Lisa Scheufler, Shareholder
Pat Scheufler, CFO
Kimberly A Morgan, Exec VP
EMP: 64 EST: 1966
SQ FT: 2,250
SALES (est): 339.7K Privately Held
WEB: www.woltcom.com
SIC: 1731 Communications specialization

(P-1641)
WONG ELECTRIC INC
4067 Transport St Ste A, Palo Alto (94303-4914)
PHONE..........................650 813-9999
Steve L Wong, President
Lester Wong, Vice Pres
Raymond Fung, Administration
Sam Peppas, Manager
Don Yarber, Manager
EMP: 35 EST: 1978

PRODUCTS & SERVICES SECTION **1742 - Plastering, Drywall, Acoustical & Insulation Work County (P-1667)**

SALES (est): 6.9MM **Privately Held**
WEB: www.wongelectric.com
SIC: 1731 General electrical contractor

(P-1642)
WPCS INTRNTIONAL-SUISUN CY INC
2208 Srra Madows Dr Ste B, Rocklin (95677)
PHONE.................................916 624-1300
EMP: 60
SALES (corp-wide): 24.4MM **Publicly Held**
SIC: 1731 Communications Specialization
HQ: Wpcs International-Suisun City, Inc.
  521 Railroad Ave
  Suisun City CA 94585
  707 398-3421

(P-1643)
XIPHOS CORPORATION
2951 Sunrise Blvd Ste 150, Rancho Cordova (95742-7203)
PHONE.................................719 963-3948
Aaron Brandenburg, *CFO*
Christopher Weatherly, *CFO*
EMP: 43 EST: 2018
SALES (est): 4.9MM **Privately Held**
WEB: www.xiphoscorp.com
SIC: 1731 Safety & security specialization

(P-1644)
YOUNG ELECTRIC CO
Also Called: Young Communications
195 Erie St, San Francisco (94103-2416)
PHONE.................................415 648-3355
James P Young, *President*
Wayne Huie, *President*
James Young, *Treasurer*
Richard Green, *Corp Secy*
Len Beatie, *Vice Pres*
EMP: 120 EST: 1977
SQ FT: 5,000
SALES (est): 28.4MM **Privately Held**
WEB: www.youngelec.com
SIC: 1731 General electrical contractor

1741 Masonry & Other Stonework

(P-1645)
E J MASONRY INC
3195 Luyung Dr, Rancho Cordova (95742-6899)
PHONE.................................916 941-8760
Guy Jashinsky, *President*
EMP: 36 EST: 1974
SQ FT: 3,600
SALES (est): 7MM **Privately Held**
WEB: www.ejmasonry.com
SIC: 1741 Masonry & other stonework

(P-1646)
ENGINEERED SOIL REPAIRS INC (PA)
1267 Springbrook Rd, Walnut Creek (94597-3916)
PHONE.................................408 297-2150
Steve O'Connor, *President*
Mark Wilhite, *Treasurer*
Morgan Anderson, *Vice Pres*
Bill Gibson, *Vice Pres*
William Gibson, *Vice Pres*
EMP: 54 EST: 1992
SQ FT: 3,000
SALES (est): 7.9MM **Privately Held**
WEB: www.esrweb.com
SIC: 1741 1771 Foundation building; foundation & footing contractor

(P-1647)
GEORGE BIANCHI CNSTR INC
Also Called: Bianchi-Amaker
775a Mabury Rd, San Jose (95133-1023)
PHONE.................................408 453-3037
George J Bianchi Jr, *President*
Travis Bianchi, *Vice Pres*
Diane Bradbury, *Admin Sec*
EMP: 37 EST: 1945
SQ FT: 3,000
SALES (est): 1MM **Privately Held**
SIC: 1741 Masonry & other stonework

(P-1648)
J GINGER MASONRY LP
9850 Hillview Rd B, Newcastle (95658-9590)
PHONE.................................209 229-1581
Carlos Alonso, *Superintendent*
EMP: 35 **Privately Held**
WEB: www.jgingermasonry.com
SIC: 1741 Stone masonry
PA: J Ginger Masonry, L.P.
  8188 Lincoln Ave Ste 100
  Riverside CA 92504

(P-1649)
JOHN JACKSON MASONRY
5691 Power Inn Rd Ste B, Sacramento (95824-2361)
PHONE.................................916 381-8021
Tom Sneed, *President*
Matt Carlson, *Vice Pres*
Robert Prater, *Vice Pres*
EMP: 60 EST: 1963
SQ FT: 6,200
SALES (est): 19MM **Privately Held**
WEB: www.johnjacksonmasonry.com
SIC: 1741 Bricklaying

(P-1650)
KEMPER & SONS MASONRY INC
2083 James Ave Unit A, South Lake Tahoe (96150-4376)
PHONE.................................530 600-3697
Kemper Hendrick, *CEO*
EMP: 41 EST: 2020
SALES (est): 2.2MM **Privately Held**
WEB: www.kempermasonry.com
SIC: 1741 Masonry & other stonework

(P-1651)
KLEARY MASONRY INC
4612 Auburn Blvd Ste 2, Sacramento (95841-4275)
PHONE.................................916 869-6835
Nick Kleary, *President*
Athena Kleary, *Manager*
EMP: 230 EST: 1960
SQ FT: 700
SALES (est): 16.6MM
SALES (corp-wide): 4.6B **Publicly Held**
WEB: www.cornerstonebuildingbrands.com
SIC: 1741 Masonry & other stonework
PA: Cornerstone Building Brands, Inc.
  5020 Weston Pkwy
  Cary NC 27513
  281 897-7788

(P-1652)
R H KIGGINS CONSTRUCTION INC
4735 E Floradora Ave, Fresno (93703-4506)
PHONE.................................559 251-8661
Ronnie H Kiggins, *President*
Marjeane Kiggins, *Treasurer*
Warren D Kiggins Sr, *Vice Pres*
Cynthia Kiggins, *Admin Sec*
EMP: 40 EST: 1982
SQ FT: 11,200
SALES (est): 5.3MM **Privately Held**
SIC: 1741 Masonry & other stonework

(P-1653)
SPANGLER CONCRETE & ENGRG INC
830 W Evelyn Ave, Sunnyvale (94086-5929)
PHONE.................................408 830-0400
Mel Spangler, *President*
Dan Spangler, *Director*
EMP: 39 EST: 2004
SQ FT: 2,000 **Privately Held**
WEB: www.spanglerconcrete.com
SIC: 1741 Concrete block masonry laying

(P-1654)
TOWNSEND & SCHMIDT MASONRY
8788 Elder Creek Rd, Sacramento (95828-1804)
PHONE.................................916 383-5354
Kevin Macdonald, *President*
Bruce Mann, *Treasurer*
Bruce M Mann, *Vice Pres*
Robin Tuyul, *Office Mgr*
Robert Bishop, *Foreman/Supr*
EMP: 35 EST: 1957
SQ FT: 2,600
SALES (est): 2.9MM **Privately Held**
WEB: www.townsendschmidt.com
SIC: 1741 Tuckpointing or restoration

1742 Plastering, Drywall, Acoustical & Insulation Work

(P-1655)
AD-IN INCORPORATED
42200 Boscell Rd, Fremont (94538-5100)
PHONE.................................510 656-6700
James E Thompson, *President*
Bill Thompson, *Vice Pres*
Gracie Uchida, *Controller*
Chris Francis, *Superintendent*
EMP: 40 EST: 1978
SQ FT: 10,000
SALES (est): 4.2MM **Privately Held**
WEB: www.ad-ininc.vpweb.com
SIC: 1742 Acoustical & ceiling work

(P-1656)
ADCO/GRIER INC
11242 Pyrites Way, Gold River (95670-4481)
PHONE.................................916 631-7010
Kenneth Roy Grier, *CEO*
Bob Hurdle, *COO*
Layne Row, *Manager*
EMP: 43 EST: 2011
SALES (est): 5.4MM **Privately Held**
WEB: www.adcodrywall.com
SIC: 1742 Drywall

(P-1657)
ALL PRO DRYWALL
22148 Buckeye Pl, Cottonwood (96022-7701)
PHONE.................................530 722-5182
EMP: 50
SALES (est): 3MM **Privately Held**
SIC: 1742 Drywall/Steel Stud Frame Contractor

(P-1658)
ALLEN DRYWALL & ASSOCIATES
380 Lang Rd, Burlingame (94010-2003)
PHONE.................................650 579-0664
Richard Allen, *President*
Julie Allen, *Corp Secy*
Nick Allen, *Project Mgr*
Katie Lawton, *Art Dir*
EMP: 60 EST: 1989
SALES (est): 7.9MM **Privately Held**
WEB: www.allendrywall.com
SIC: 1742 Drywall

(P-1659)
ANNING-JOHNSON COMPANY
22955 Kidder St, Hayward (94545-1670)
PHONE.................................510 670-0100
R Todd Fearon, *Vice Pres*
Nicole Linscott, *Project Mgr*
Rafael Luna, *Project Mgr*
Michael Bean, *Purchasing*
Dewayne Grant, *Foreman/Supr*
EMP: 140
SQ FT: 16,000
SALES (corp-wide): 461.9MM **Privately Held**
WEB: www.anningjohnson.com
SIC: 1742 Drywall; acoustical & ceiling work
HQ: Anning-Johnson Company
  1959 Anson Dr
  Melrose Park IL 60160
  708 681-1300

(P-1660)
B12 DRYWALL INC
11467 Sunrise Gold Cir # 8, Rancho Cordova (95742-6579)
PHONE.................................916 635-3600
Bryan Carl Lebaron, *President*
David Lebaron, *CFO*
EMP: 49 EST: 2015
SALES (est): 850K **Privately Held**
WEB: www.b12drywall.com
SIC: 1742 Drywall

(P-1661)
BAYSIDE INTERIORS INC (PA)
3220 Darby Cmn, Fremont (94539-5601)
PHONE.................................510 438-9171
Steven A Rivera, *CEO*
Tim Hogan, *President*
Michael Nicholson, *COO*
Jon Braden, *CFO*
Norma Nicholson, *Treasurer*
▲ EMP: 143 EST: 1984
SQ FT: 20,000
SALES (est): 29.8MM **Privately Held**
WEB: www.baysideinteriors.com
SIC: 1742 Drywall

(P-1662)
BOYETT CONSTRUCTION INC (PA)
2404 Tripaldi Way, Hayward (94545-5017)
PHONE.................................510 264-9100
Vernon H Boyett, *President*
James Roberts, *Officer*
Kim Wodarczyk, *Office Mgr*
Julie Mah, *Accountant*
Matt Arntz, *Foreman/Supr*
EMP: 78 EST: 1988
SQ FT: 2,600
SALES (est): 26.1MM **Privately Held**
WEB: www.boyettconstruction.com
SIC: 1742 1751 Drywall; acoustical & ceiling work; window & door installation & erection

(P-1663)
C R S DRYWALL INC
Also Called: Cr Drywall
135 San Jose Ave, San Jose (95125-1018)
PHONE.................................408 998-4360
Carlos Silveria, *President*
EMP: 80 EST: 1996
SQ FT: 4,000
SALES (est): 4MM **Privately Held**
WEB: www.crdrywall.com
SIC: 1742 Drywall

(P-1664)
CALIFORNIA DRYWALL CO (PA)
2290 S 10th St, San Jose (95112-4114)
PHONE.................................408 292-7500
Greg Eckstrom, *Vice Pres*
Kent Bowles, *President*
David Garrett, *COO*
Stephen Eckstrom, *Vice Pres*
Jaime Garcia, *Vice Pres*
EMP: 247 EST: 1946
SQ FT: 15,000
SALES (est): 64MM **Privately Held**
WEB: www.caldrywall.com
SIC: 1742 Drywall

(P-1665)
CAPITAL CITY DRYWALL INC
6525 32nd St Ste B1, North Highlands (95660-3028)
PHONE.................................916 331-9200
John Beers, *President*
Andrew Sellers, *Vice Pres*
Sal Villalpando, *Supervisor*
EMP: 100 EST: 2000
SQ FT: 2,500
SALES (est): 12.4MM **Privately Held**
WEB: www.capitalcitydrywall.com
SIC: 1742 Drywall

(P-1666)
CEN CAL PLASTERING INC (PA)
1256 W Lathrop Rd, Manteca (95336-9671)
P.O. Box 307 (95336-1125)
PHONE.................................209 858-1045
Jeffery F Gann, *President*
Jeffrey F Gann, *President*
Sandra Brown, *Manager*
EMP: 383 EST: 2010
SALES (est): 40.9MM **Privately Held**
WEB: www.cencalplastering.com
SIC: 1742 Plastering, plain or ornamental

(P-1667)
CEN CAL PLASTERING INC
15300 E Wyman Rd, Lathrop (95330)
PHONE.................................209 981-5265
EMP: 67

1742 - Plastering, Drywall, Acoustical & Insulation Work County (P-1668)

SALES (corp-wide): 40.9MM **Privately Held**
WEB: www.cencalplastering.com
SIC: **1742** Plastering, plain or ornamental
PA: Cen Cal Plastering, Inc.
1256 W Lathrop Rd
Manteca CA 95336
209 858-1045

(P-1668)
CHARLES CULBERSON INC
Also Called: Culberson Drywall
1084 Allen Way, Campbell (95008-4509)
P.O. Box 1954, Chester (96020-1954)
PHONE.................................650 335-4730
Fax: 650 335-4736
EMP: 150
SQ FT: 8,000
SALES (est): 7.3MM **Privately Held**
SIC: **1742** Drywall/Insulating Contractor

(P-1669)
CUSTOM DRYWALL INC
1570 Gladding Ct, Milpitas (95035-6814)
PHONE.................................408 263-1616
Gene Cox, *President*
Artemio Bautista, *Manager*
Christine Cox, *Manager*
Craig Lammers, *Manager*
EMP: 90 EST: 1961
SQ FT: 10,000
SALES (est): 7.7MM **Privately Held**
WEB: www.custom-drywall-inc.com
SIC: **1742** Drywall

(P-1670)
DALEYS DRYWALL AND TAPING INC
960 Camden Ave, Campbell (95008-4104)
PHONE.................................408 378-9500
Craig Spencer Daley, *President*
Brittni Daley, *CFO*
Chris Daley, *Vice Pres*
Steve Spangenberg, *Division Mgr*
Kerie Ireland, *Project Mgr*
EMP: 381 EST: 1963
SQ FT: 20,000
SALES (est): 84MM **Privately Held**
WEB: www.daleysdrywall.com
SIC: **1742** Drywall

(P-1671)
DANA KITCHENS & ASSOCIATES INC
5464 Skylane Blvd, Santa Rosa (95403-1004)
PHONE.................................707 571-8326
Dana Kitchens, *President*
Summer Kitchens, *Officer*
Debra Sue Kitchens, *Vice Pres*
Gary Joseph Markarian, *Vice Pres*
EMP: 50 EST: 1991
SALES (est): 7.7MM **Privately Held**
WEB: www.danakitchens.com.au
SIC: **1742** Acoustical & ceiling work

(P-1672)
DH SMITH COMPANY INC
6000 Hellyer Ave Ste 150, San Jose (95138-1031)
P.O. Box 730189 (95173-0189)
PHONE.................................408 532-7617
Daniel Smith III, *President*
Cheryl Smith, *Treasurer*
Steven Smith, *Vice Pres*
EMP: 85 EST: 1996
SQ FT: 20,000
SALES (est): 6.8MM **Privately Held**
SIC: **1742** Plastering, plain or ornamental

(P-1673)
ERIC STARK INTERIORS INC
2284 Paragon Dr, San Jose (95131-1306)
PHONE.................................408 441-6136
Eric Stark, *President*
Dan Lilly, *Vice Pres*
Dora Stanich, *Technology*
EMP: 100 EST: 1992
SQ FT: 10,000
SALES (est): 8.5MM **Privately Held**
WEB: www.ericstarkinteriors.com
SIC: **1742** Drywall

(P-1674)
F C BICKERT COMPANY INC
1315 Vista Way, Red Bluff (96080-4508)
PHONE.................................530 529-3575
Fred Bickert Jr, *President*
William Groom, *CFO*
EMP: 35 EST: 1988
SALES (est): 3.7MM **Privately Held**
WEB: www.fcbickert.com
SIC: **1742** Drywall

(P-1675)
FUTURE ENERGY CORPORATION (PA)
Also Called: Future Energy Savers
8980 Grant Line Rd, Elk Grove (95624-1415)
P.O. Box 87, Wilton (95693-0087)
PHONE.................................800 985-0733
Jeffrey Adkins, *CEO*
Trevor Fisher, *Controller*
Rob Heckendorn, *Prdtn Mgr*
Anil Kumar, *Manager*
EMP: 204 EST: 1982
SQ FT: 6,800
SALES (est): 28.3MM **Privately Held**
WEB: www.energysavers.com
SIC: **1742** Insulation, buildings

(P-1676)
GEORGE FAMILY ENTERPRISES
32 Pamaron Way Ste A, Novato (94949-6221)
PHONE.................................415 884-0399
Debi George, *President*
Aaron Elliott, *Vice Pres*
Debra George, *Vice Pres*
Sierra Smith, *Executive Asst*
John Haugen, *Admin Sec*
▲ EMP: 60 EST: 1979
SALES (est): 7MM **Privately Held**
WEB: www.gfeinc.com
SIC: **1742** Drywall

(P-1677)
GOLDEN BAY INSULATION INC (PA)
652 Scofield Ave, E Palo Alto (94303-2346)
PHONE.................................650 743-1628
Marco Antonio Rocha, *Principal*
EMP: 35 EST: 2014
SALES (est): 403K **Privately Held**
SIC: **1742** Insulation, buildings

(P-1678)
GREEN WALL TECH INC
2020 Warm Springs Ct # 2, Fremont (94539-6744)
P.O. Box 15134 (94539-2234)
PHONE.................................510 252-1170
Phillip Leon, *President*
EMP: 40 EST: 2011
SALES (est): 3.8MM **Privately Held**
WEB: www.greenwalltech.com
SIC: **1742** Drywall

(P-1679)
HANSON DRYWALL
7180 Forest St, Gilroy (95020-6612)
PHONE.................................831 297-4581
Joshua K Hanson, *Principal*
EMP: 80 EST: 2018
SALES (est): 4.9MM **Privately Held**
WEB: www.hansondrywallinc.com
SIC: **1742** Drywall

(P-1680)
HARRISON DRYWALL INC
447 10th St, San Francisco (94103-4303)
P.O. Box 508, Cotati (94931-0508)
PHONE.................................415 821-9584
Jeff Harrison, *President*
Matt Richardson, *Project Engr*
Sasha Brady, *Controller*
Fred Denno, *Foreman/Supr*
Jeffrey Thomas, *Superintendent*
EMP: 50 EST: 1991
SQ FT: 5,000
SALES (est): 10.2MM **Privately Held**
WEB: www.harrisondrywallinc.com
SIC: **1742** Drywall

(P-1681)
J & J ACOUSTICS INC
2260 De La Cruz Blvd, Santa Clara (95050-3008)
PHONE.................................408 275-9255
James Jean, *President*
James Hansell, *Vice Pres*
Joseph Jean, *Vice Pres*
Marge Meide, *Admin Sec*
Mark Hidde, *Project Mgr*
EMP: 140 EST: 1975
SALES (est): 20MM **Privately Held**
WEB: www.jjacoustics.com
SIC: **1742** Drywall; acoustical & ceiling work

(P-1682)
KENYON CONSTRUCTION INC
Also Called: Kenyon Plastering
63 Trevarno Rd, Livermore (94551-4931)
PHONE.................................800 949-4319
EMP: 42
SALES (corp-wide): 88.1MM **Privately Held**
WEB: www.kenyonweb.com
SIC: **1742** Plastering, plain or ornamental
PA: Kenyon Construction, Inc.
4001 W Indian School Rd
Phoenix AZ 85019
602 484-0080

(P-1683)
KENYON CONSTRUCTION INC
4667 N Blythe Ave, Fresno (93722-3908)
PHONE.................................559 277-5645
Jose Valenzuela, *Manager*
EMP: 42
SQ FT: 9,182
SALES (corp-wide): 88.1MM **Privately Held**
WEB: www.kenyonweb.com
SIC: **1742** Plastering, plain or ornamental
PA: Kenyon Construction, Inc.
4001 W Indian School Rd
Phoenix AZ 85019
602 484-0080

(P-1684)
KENYON CONSTRUCTION INC
Also Called: Kenyon Plastering
3223 E St, North Highlands (95660-4606)
P.O. Box 2077 (95660-8077)
PHONE.................................916 514-9502
Carl Schmidt, *Principal*
EMP: 42
SALES (corp-wide): 88.1MM **Privately Held**
WEB: www.kenyonweb.com
SIC: **1742** Plastering, plain or ornamental
PA: Kenyon Construction, Inc.
4001 W Indian School Rd
Phoenix AZ 85019
602 484-0080

(P-1685)
KENYON CONSTRUCTION INC
Also Called: Kenyon Plastering
1286 N Broadway Ave, Stockton (95205-3039)
PHONE.................................209 462-4060
Don Bee, *General Mgr*
EMP: 42
SALES (corp-wide): 88.1MM **Privately Held**
WEB: www.kenyonweb.com
SIC: **1742** Plastering, plain or ornamental
PA: Kenyon Construction, Inc.
4001 W Indian School Rd
Phoenix AZ 85019
602 484-0080

(P-1686)
KURT MEISWINKEL INC
1407 E 3rd Ave, San Mateo (94401-2109)
PHONE.................................650 344-7200
Kurt Meiswinkel, *President*
EMP: 50 EST: 2004
SQ FT: 25,000 **Privately Held**
WEB: www.kurtmeiswinkel.com
SIC: **1742** Drywall

(P-1687)
LANCASTER BURNS CNSTR INC
Also Called: L B Construction
8655 Washington Blvd, Roseville (95678-5945)
PHONE.................................916 624-8404
Jordan Edward Burns, *President*
Christine Lancaster, *CFO*
Vance Lancaster, *Vice Pres*
Gayle Capik, *Admin Asst*
Barbara Brogdon, *Purch Mgr*
EMP: 150 EST: 1992
SQ FT: 43,000
SALES (est): 36.1MM **Privately Held**
WEB: www.lbconstructioninc.com
SIC: **1742** 1751 1791 3449 Drywall; framing contractor; building front installation metal; bars, concrete reinforcing: fabricated steel

(P-1688)
LEEMAN BROTHERS DRYWALL INC
3851 Taylor Rd, Loomis (95650-9221)
P.O. Box 631 (95650-0631)
PHONE.................................916 652-9019
Alan Leeman, *President*
EMP: 37 EST: 1990
SQ FT: 900
SALES (est): 1.2MM **Privately Held**
WEB: www.leeman-brothers-drywall-inc.hub.biz
SIC: **1742** Drywall

(P-1689)
LEVEL 5 DRYWALL INC
70 Glenn Way Ste 4, San Carlos (94070-6220)
PHONE.................................650 486-1657
Alan Amirteymour, *CEO*
EMP: 80 EST: 2015
SALES (est): 4.6MM **Privately Held**
WEB: www.levelfivedrywall.com
SIC: **1742** 1751 Drywall; lightweight steel framing (metal stud) installation

(P-1690)
MAGNUM DRYWALL INC
42027 Boscell Rd, Fremont (94538-3106)
PHONE.................................510 979-0420
Gary Robinson, *CEO*
John Kreitzer, *Project Engr*
Steve Tietsort, *Foreman/Supr*
EMP: 72 EST: 1991
SQ FT: 3,200
SALES (est): 26.6MM **Privately Held**
WEB: www.magnumdrywall.com
SIC: **1742** 1721 1751 Plastering, drywall & insulation; plaster & drywall work; drywall; acoustical & ceiling work; painting & paper hanging; carpentry work

(P-1691)
MGM DRYWALL INC
1050 Coml St Ste 102, San Jose (95112)
PHONE.................................408 292-4085
Miguel Guillen, *President*
Martina Guillen, *CFO*
Gonzalo Guillen, *Vice Pres*
Maggie Jacquez, *Office Mgr*
William Guillen, *Project Engr*
EMP: 100 EST: 2000
SALES (est): 18.9MM **Privately Held**
WEB: www.mgmdrywall.com
SIC: **1742** 1721 3446 Drywall; acoustical & insulation work; acoustical & ceiling work; residential painting; commercial painting; acoustical suspension systems, metal

(P-1692)
MID VALLEY PLASTERING INC
15300 Mckinley Ave, Lathrop (95330-8782)
PHONE.................................209 858-9766
Jeff Gann, *President*
Kevin Gann, *Corp Secy*
Jeremy Gann, *Vice Pres*
EMP: 400 EST: 1998
SQ FT: 5,000
SALES (est): 30.9MM **Privately Held**
WEB: www.midvalleymasonry.com
SIC: **1742** Plastering, plain or ornamental

PRODUCTS & SERVICES SECTION

1743 - Terrazzo, Tile, Marble & Mosaic Work County (P-1717)

(P-1693)
NEW WEST PARTITIONS
2550 Sutterville Rd, Sacramento (95820-1020)
PHONE.................................916 456-8365
Kem P Modellas, *CEO*
Mark Modellas, *Admin Sec*
EMP: 120 **EST:** 1994
SQ FT: 3,000
SALES (est): 28.9MM **Privately Held**
WEB: www.nwpsac.com
SIC: 1742 Drywall

(P-1694)
NEWMAT NORCAL INC
32 Pamaron Way Ste A, Novato (94949-6221)
PHONE.................................415 884-4421
Laurence George, *President*
Kira George, *Treasurer*
John Haugen, *Vice Pres*
Newmat Norcal, *Project Mgr*
Ryan Zebroski, *Project Engr*
▲ **EMP:** 38 **EST:** 2008
SALES (est): 2.3MM **Privately Held**
WEB: www.newmatnorcal.com
SIC: 1742 Acoustical & ceiling work

(P-1695)
NOROGACHI CONSTRUCTION INC/CA
600 Industrial Dr Ste 100, Galt (95632-8164)
PHONE.................................916 236-4201
Anival Guerrero, *CEO*
Laura Guerrero, *Vice Pres*
Gustavo Loya, *General Mgr*
Gerardo Guerrero, *Office Mgr*
Juan Sanchez, *Project Mgr*
EMP: 100 **EST:** 2005
SALES (est): 15.6MM **Privately Held**
WEB: www.norogachiconstruction.com
SIC: 1742 1542 Drywall; acoustical & insulation work; acoustical & ceiling work; institutional building construction

(P-1696)
NORTH COUNTIES DRYWALL INC
20563 Broadway, Sonoma (95476-7590)
P.O. Box 260 (95476-0260)
PHONE.................................707 996-0198
Diane Merlo, *President*
Richard Merlo, *President*
Olivia Acevedo, *Administration*
Dennis Thomas, *Project Mgr*
Fred Burbage, *Manager*
EMP: 50 **EST:** 1986
SQ FT: 2,000
SALES (est): 13.8MM **Privately Held**
WEB: www.ncdinc.net
SIC: 1742 1542 1521 Drywall; commercial & office building, new construction; new construction, single-family houses

(P-1697)
PATRICK J RUANE INC
283 Wattis Way, South San Francisco (94080-6715)
PHONE.................................650 616-7676
James Ruane, *President*
Norene Ruane, *Corp Secy*
Keith Currier, *Controller*
EMP: 56 **EST:** 1941
SQ FT: 7,000
SALES (est): 4MM **Privately Held**
WEB: www.pjruane.com
SIC: 1742 Plastering, plain or ornamental; drywall

(P-1698)
PERFORMANCE CONTRACTING INC
Also Called: PCI Bay Area Interior
1080 Marina Village Pkwy # 300, Alameda (94501-6440)
PHONE.................................510 214-1444
David Link, *General Mgr*
Laura Spears, *Administration*
Kevin Ullrich, *Project Mgr*
EMP: 40
SQ FT: 25,000
SALES (corp-wide): 2.4B **Privately Held**
WEB: www.performancecontracting.com
SIC: 1742 Insulation, buildings
HQ: Performance Contracting, Inc.
11145 Thompson Ave
Lenexa KS 66219
913 888-8600

(P-1699)
PETRO-CHEM INDUSTRIES INC
Also Called: Petro-Chem Insulation
2300 Clayton Rd, Concord (94520-2100)
PHONE.................................707 644-7455
Greg Johnson, *President*
Robert Case, *Vice Pres*
Erich Freudenthaler, *Vice Pres*
Chad Denning, *Division Mgr*
Vicki Adams, *Admin Asst*
EMP: 87 **EST:** 1989
SALES (est): 7.2MM **Privately Held**
WEB: www.petrocheminc.com
SIC: 1742 Insulation, buildings

(P-1700)
PETROCHEM INSULATION INC
945 Teal Dr, Benicia (94510-1210)
PHONE.................................707 645-1121
EMP: 64
SALES (corp-wide): 2.7B **Privately Held**
WEB: www.petrocheminc.com
SIC: 1742 Insulation, buildings
HQ: Petrochem Insulation, Inc.
1501 W Ftnhead Pkwy # 550
Tempe AZ 85282
707 644-7455

(P-1701)
RAYMOND - NORTHERN CAL INC
Also Called: Raymond Interior Systems
4589 Pacheco Blvd, Martinez (94553-2233)
PHONE.................................925 602-4910
Travis Winsor, *CEO*
Tom O'Brien, *CEO*
David Shedd, *COO*
Kristen Potter, *Corp Secy*
Michael Potter, *Exec VP*
EMP: 72 **EST:** 1963
SQ FT: 10,400
SALES (est): 12.1MM **Privately Held**
WEB: www.raymondgroup.com
SIC: 1742 Drywall; acoustical & ceiling work; plastering, plain or ornamental

(P-1702)
RFJ CORPORATION
Also Called: Rfj Meiswinkel
930 Innes Ave, San Francisco (94124-2905)
PHONE.................................415 824-6890
Joseph Meiswinkel, *President*
Guy Cross, *Controller*
EMP: 60 **EST:** 1983
SQ FT: 15,000
SALES (est): 9.5MM **Privately Held**
WEB: www.rfjmeiswinkel.com
SIC: 1742 Plastering, plain or ornamental; drywall

(P-1703)
ROCHAS DRYWALL INC
575 Southside Dr Ste C, Gilroy (95020-7031)
PHONE.................................408 842-4188
Joe Rocha, *President*
Claudia Rocha, *Vice Pres*
EMP: 46 **EST:** 1981
SQ FT: 3,250
SALES (est): 1.3MM **Privately Held**
WEB: www.rochadrywall.com
SIC: 1742 Drywall

(P-1704)
S & S DRYWALL INC (PA)
202 N 27th St, San Jose (95116-1120)
PHONE.................................408 294-4393
Gabriel Silveira, *President*
Maria Silveira, *Treasurer*
EMP: 199 **EST:** 1987
SALES (est): 16.9MM **Privately Held**
WEB: www.ssdrywall.net
SIC: 1742 Drywall

(P-1705)
SPACETONE ACOUSTICS INC
1051 Serpentine Ln # 300, Pleasanton (94566-8451)
PHONE.................................925 931-0749
Robert A Libby, *President*
Joan Libby, *Vice Pres*
Robert Libby, *Vice Pres*
Katie Chan, *Payroll Mgr*
Dominic Sanchez, *Manager*
EMP: 50 **EST:** 1976
SQ FT: 3,500
SALES (est): 11.4MM **Privately Held**
WEB: www.spacetoneacousticsinc.com
SIC: 1742 Drywall

(P-1706)
TRUTEAM OF CALIFORNIA INC
2400 Rockefeller Dr, Ceres (95307-9285)
PHONE.................................916 826-3194
Jeff Curtain, *Credit Mgr*
Robert Buck, *CEO*
EMP: 51
SALES (corp-wide): 2.7B **Publicly Held**
WEB: www.truteam.com
SIC: 1742 Insulation, buildings
HQ: Truteam Of California, Inc.
260 Jimmy Ann Dr
Daytona Beach FL 32114

(P-1707)
WESTERN BUILDING MATERIALS CO (PA)
4620 E Olive Ave, Fresno (93702-1660)
PHONE.................................559 454-8500
Peter Hastrup, *President*
Vitaliy Gorbachev, *Director*
EMP: 60 **EST:** 1967
SQ FT: 32,000
SALES (est): 12.8MM **Privately Held**
SIC: 1742 5211 Acoustical & ceiling work; millwork & lumber

(P-1708)
WESTERN DRYWALL INC
4971 Salida Blvd, Salida (95368-9420)
P.O. Box 11130, Oakdale (95361-1025)
PHONE.................................209 543-9361
Cecil Shatswell, *President*
John Shatswell, *Vice Pres*
Kevin Shatswell, *Vice Pres*
Tim Ribeiro, *Manager*
EMP: 70 **EST:** 1977
SALES (est): 7.3MM **Privately Held**
WEB: www.westerndrywall.com
SIC: 1742 Drywall

(P-1709)
WINEGARD ENERGY INC
2885 S Chestnut Ave, Fresno (93725-2211)
PHONE.................................559 441-0243
Wallas Winegard, *Owner*
EMP: 42 **Privately Held**
WEB: www.winegardenergy.com
SIC: 1742 Insulation, buildings
PA: Winegard Energy, Inc.
5354 Irwindale Ave Ste B
Irwindale CA 91706

(P-1710)
WM ONEILL LATH AND PLST CORP
1261 Birchwood Dr, Sunnyvale (94089-2206)
P.O. Box 60352 (94088-0352)
PHONE.................................408 329-1413
William O'Neill, *President*
Sandra O'Neill, *Admin Sec*
EMP: 50 **EST:** 2009
SALES (est): 5.2MM **Privately Held**
WEB: www.wmoneilllath.thebluebook.com
SIC: 1742 Drywall

1743 Terrazzo, Tile, Marble & Mosaic Work

(P-1711)
CAL CUSTOM TILE
1300 Commerce Way, Sanger (93657-8731)
PHONE.................................559 875-1460
Rick Berry, *President*
Michele Berry, *Vice Pres*
Gerson Cruz, *Supervisor*
EMP: 95 **EST:** 1981
SQ FT: 10,000
SALES (est): 9MM **Privately Held**
WEB: www.calcustomtile.com
SIC: 1743 Tile installation, ceramic

(P-1712)
D & J TILE COMPANY INC
1045 Terminal Way, San Carlos (94070-3226)
PHONE.................................650 632-4000
David Newman, *Principal*
John Reich, *Admin Sec*
Brian Lanier, *Technology*
Lincoln Williams, *Comptroller*
Rena Fregosi, *Bookkeeper*
◆ **EMP:** 100 **EST:** 1990
SALES (est): 12.6MM **Privately Held**
WEB: www.djtile.com
SIC: 1743 Tile installation, ceramic

(P-1713)
DELLA MAGGIORE TILE INC
87 N 30th St, San Jose (95116-1124)
PHONE.................................408 286-3991
Nick D Maggiore, *President*
Julie D Maggiore, *Admin Sec*
▲ **EMP:** 80
SQ FT: 20,000
SALES (est): 7.4MM **Privately Held**
WEB: www.dellamaggiore.com
SIC: 1743 Tile installation, ceramic

(P-1714)
FISCHER TILE AND MARBLE INC
1800 23rd St, Sacramento (95816-7112)
PHONE.................................916 452-1426
Jay H Fischer, *President*
Matthew Beauchamp, *Opers Mgr*
▲ **EMP:** 150
SQ FT: 22,000
SALES (est): 17.2MM **Privately Held**
WEB: www.fischertile.com
SIC: 1743 Tile installation, ceramic; marble installation, interior

(P-1715)
GINO RINALDI INC
Also Called: Rinaldi Tile & Marble
51 Fremont St, Royal Oaks (95076-5213)
PHONE.................................831 761-0195
Gino Rinaldi, *President*
Yvonne Rinaldi, *Corp Secy*
Rick Rinaldi, *General Mgr*
Sue McGhee, *Office Mgr*
Paul Rosewall, *Opers Staff*
▲ **EMP:** 80 **EST:** 1973
SQ FT: 10,000
SALES (est): 11.2MM **Privately Held**
WEB: www.rinalditileandmarble.com
SIC: 1743 Tile installation, ceramic

(P-1716)
NORTH CAST TILE STONE DSIGN IN
3854 Santa Rosa Ave, Santa Rosa (95407-8221)
PHONE.................................707 586-2064
Tom Bodell, *President*
Chris Daniels, *Vice Pres*
Stacy Morris, *Manager*
EMP: 37 **EST:** 1990
SALES (est): 5MM **Privately Held**
WEB: www.nctile.com
SIC: 1743 Tile installation, ceramic

(P-1717)
PACIFIC STONE INC
1375 Franquette Ave Ste F, Concord (94520-7932)
PHONE.................................925 680-8741
Bert Sandy, *President*
Christine Wolfinger,
▲ **EMP:** 43 **EST:** 1996
SQ FT: 6,000
SALES (est): 1.7MM **Privately Held**
WEB: www.pacificstone.com
SIC: 1743 5999 5032 1799 Tile installation, ceramic; monuments & tombstones; marble building stone; counter top installation

1743 - Terrazzo, Tile, Marble & Mosaic Work County (P-1718)

PRODUCTS & SERVICES SECTION

(P-1718)
PENNACCHIO TILE INC
655 Carlson Ct, Rohnert Park (94928-2038)
PHONE..................707 586-8858
Leo Pennacchio, *President*
Leo Pennacchio, *President*
Wendy Pennacchio, *Vice Pres*
EMP: 57 **EST:** 1980
SQ FT: 4,000
SALES (est): 7.8MM **Privately Held**
WEB: www.pennacchiotile.com
SIC: 1743 Tile installation, ceramic

(P-1719)
SHANE ALXANDER CSTM TILE STONE
1415 Nichols Dr, Rocklin (95765-1306)
PHONE..................916 652-0250
Jean H Marchbanks, *President*
EMP: 35 **EST:** 2012
SALES (est): 1.9MM **Privately Held**
WEB: www.sactile.com
SIC: 1743 Tile installation, ceramic

(P-1720)
SHERMN-LEHR CSTM TILE WRKS INC
5691 Power Inn Rd Ste A, Sacramento (95824-2361)
PHONE..................916 386-0417
James P Loehr, *President*
Jane Sherman, *Treasurer*
Eber T Sherman, *Vice Pres*
Joyce Loehr, *Admin Sec*
Heather Loehr, *Project Mgr*
EMP: 100 **EST:** 1979
SQ FT: 3,400
SALES (est): 11.6MM **Privately Held**
WEB: www.shermanloehr.com
SIC: 1743 Tile installation, ceramic

(P-1721)
SONOMA TILEMAKERS INC (DH)
7750 Bell Rd, Windsor (95492-8518)
PHONE..................707 837-8177
Jon Gray, *President*
Lisa Dannecker, *Partner*
Kenneth E Wiedemann, *CEO*
Sergio Garcia, *Training Dir*
Randall Ray, *Opers Mgr*
▲ **EMP:** 99 **EST:** 1994
SQ FT: 22,000
SALES (est): 12.1MM
SALES (corp-wide): 46.3MM **Privately Held**
WEB: www.sonomatilemakers.com
SIC: 1743 Tile installation, ceramic
HQ: United Tile Corp.
750 S Michigan St
Seattle WA 98108
425 251-5290

(P-1722)
SOSA GRANITE & MARBLE INC
Also Called: Sosa Tile Co
7701 Marathon Dr, Livermore (94550-9550)
PHONE..................925 373-7675
Mario Sosa, *President*
Arlene Contreras, *Technology*
▲ **EMP:** 50 **EST:** 1986
SQ FT: 16,000
SALES (est): 5.4MM **Privately Held**
WEB: www.sosagranite.com
SIC: 1743 Tile installation, ceramic

(P-1723)
STOCKTON CERAMIC TILE INC
420 N Harrison St, Stockton (95203-2804)
PHONE..................209 464-1291
Manuel Sanchez, *President*
Mary Sanchez, *Treasurer*
EMP: 40 **EST:** 1977
SQ FT: 5,000
SALES (est): 4.8MM **Privately Held**
WEB: www.stocktonceramictile.com
SIC: 1743 Tile installation, ceramic

(P-1724)
SUPERIOR TILE & MARBLE INC (PA)
2300 Polvorosa Ave, San Leandro (94577-2218)
P.O. Box 2106, Oakland (94621-0006)
PHONE..................510 895-2700
Robert F Herman, *President*
Bob Herman, *CFO*
Steve Scolari, *Vice Pres*
Jerry Sue, *Vice Pres*
Rod J Riggs, *Admin Sec*
▲ **EMP:** 46 **EST:** 1995
SALES (est): 9.8MM **Privately Held**
WEB: www.superiortileandmarble.com
SIC: 1743 5999 Tile installation, ceramic; marble installation, interior; monuments & tombstones

(P-1725)
TILE WEST INC (PA)
11 Hamilton Dr, Novato (94949-5602)
P.O. Box 5789 (94948-5789)
PHONE..................415 382-7550
Carl E Jacobson, *President*
Julia M Ratto, *Corp Secy*
Cliff E Jacobson, *Vice Pres*
Wayne Jackson, *Project Mgr*
▲ **EMP:** 37 **EST:** 1963
SQ FT: 5,000
SALES (est): 7.5MM **Privately Held**
WEB: www.tilewestinc.com
SIC: 1743 Tile installation, ceramic

(P-1726)
TRM CORPORATION (PA)
Also Called: Superior Tile Co
2378 Polvorosa Ave, San Leandro (94577-2218)
P.O. Box 2106, Oakland (94621-0006)
PHONE..................510 895-2700
Tommy Conner, *CEO*
Robert Herman, *President*
Jerry T Sue, *CFO*
Jon Pitcher, *Officer*
Bob Herman, *Vice Pres*
▲ **EMP:** 65 **EST:** 1975
SQ FT: 12,000
SALES (est): 28.1MM **Privately Held**
SIC: 1743 Tile installation, ceramic; marble installation, interior

(P-1727)
U S PERMA INC
Also Called: California Tile Installers
1696 Rogers Ave, San Jose (95112-1105)
PHONE..................408 436-0600
Jack O'Brien, *President*
Randall Sundberg, *Vice Pres*
Donald K O'Brien, *Admin Sec*
Summer Martinez, *Administration*
▲ **EMP:** 50 **EST:** 1962
SQ FT: 9,000
SALES (est): 9.4MM **Privately Held**
SIC: 1743 Tile installation, ceramic

1751 Carpentry Work

(P-1728)
ADM GARAGE DOORS (PA)
4185 69th St, Sacramento (95820-3415)
PHONE..................916 595-5355
Andre Marshall, *Principal*
EMP: 35 **EST:** 2007
SALES (est): 521.3K **Privately Held**
WEB: www.admgaragedoors.com
SIC: 1751 Garage door, installation or erection

(P-1729)
ALLIED FRAMERS INC
4990 Allison Pkwy, Vacaville (95688-9346)
PHONE..................707 452-7050
Jakki Kutz, *President*
Dave Burrell, *Vice Pres*
Mark Johnson, *Vice Pres*
Dawn Richardson, *Administration*
Danielle Gregorich, *Controller*
EMP: 130 **EST:** 1995
SQ FT: 6,000
SALES (est): 12.3MM **Privately Held**
WEB: www.alliedframers.com
SIC: 1751 Framing contractor

(P-1730)
BARTON OVERHEAD DOOR INC
1132 N Carpenter Rd, Modesto (95351-1140)
PHONE..................209 571-3667
Michael L Barton, *CEO*
Michael Barton Sr, *President*
Ichael Barton Jr, *CEO*
Naomi Barton, *Corp Secy*
Lee Brubaker, *Safety Mgr*
EMP: 39 **EST:** 1973
SQ FT: 20,000
SALES (est): 7.1MM **Privately Held**
WEB: www.bartondoor.com
SIC: 1751 Garage door, installation or erection

(P-1731)
BAY AREA CNSTR FRAMERS INC
1150 W Center St Ste 105, Manteca (95337-4313)
PHONE..................925 454-8514
Fax: 925 454-0507
EMP: 175
SQ FT: 6,700
SALES (est): 14MM **Privately Held**
SIC: 1751 1521 Carpentry Contractor Single-Family House Construction

(P-1732)
CAPITOL BUILDERS HARDWARE INC (HQ)
Also Called: Capitol Door Service
4699 24th St, Sacramento (95822-1412)
PHONE..................916 451-2821
David Karaczozoff, *CEO*
Chris Matheny, *CFO*
Kirk Karacozoff, *Vice Pres*
Nestor Saducos, *Info Tech Mgr*
Donna Bellingham, *Project Mgr*
EMP: 68 **EST:** 1957
SQ FT: 25,000
SALES (est): 10MM
SALES (corp-wide): 10.1B **Privately Held**
WEB: www.capitolbh.com
SIC: 1751 5031 5072 Finish & trim carpentry; window & door (prefabricated) installation; metal doors, sash & trim; door frames, all materials; builders' hardware
PA: Assa Abloy Ab
Klarabergsviadukten 90
Stockholm 111 6
850 648-500

(P-1733)
CHI DOORS HOLDINGS INC
3748 Zephyr Ct, Stockton (95206-4213)
PHONE..................209 229-5663
EMP: 124 **Publicly Held**
WEB: www.chiohd.com
SIC: 1751 Garage door, installation or erection
HQ: C.H.I Doors Holdings, Inc.
1485 Sunrise Dr
Arthur IL 61911
217 543-2135

(P-1734)
CONTRA COSTA DOOR CO
145 Mason Cir, Concord (94520-1213)
PHONE..................925 671-7888
Dale Brooks, *President*
Gary Brooks, *Treasurer*
Lucille Brooks, *Admin Sec*
EMP: 35 **EST:** 1951
SALES (est): 7.4MM **Privately Held**
WEB: www.contracostadoor.com
SIC: 1751 Garage door, installation or erection

(P-1735)
COOK CABINETS INC
6428 Capitol Ave, Diamond Springs (95619-9521)
PHONE..................530 621-0851
Richard Gularte, *President*
Steve Gularte, *Vice Pres*
EMP: 20 **EST:** 1976
SQ FT: 35,000
SALES (est): 1.5MM **Privately Held**
WEB: www.cccabinetryinc.com
SIC: 1751 5031 2434 Cabinet building & installation; cabinet work, custom; lumber, plywood & millwork; wood kitchen cabinets

(P-1736)
FEIST CABINETS & WOODWORKS INC
9930 Kent St, Elk Grove (95624-9400)
PHONE..................916 686-8230
Randall C Feist, *President*
Al Clark, *COO*
Barbara Feist, *Treasurer*
Charles Feist, *Vice Pres*
Frank Feist, *Admin Sec*
EMP: 20 **EST:** 1987
SQ FT: 20,000
SALES (est): 2.4MM **Privately Held**
WEB: www.feistcabinets.com
SIC: 5712 1751 2434 2431 Cabinet work, custom; cabinet & finish carpentry; wood kitchen cabinets; millwork

(P-1737)
FIXTURE-PRO INC
2344 Bluebell Dr Ste A, Santa Rosa (95403-2517)
PHONE..................707 545-3901
Toll Free:..................888 -
Richard Key, *President*
Kara Key, *Admin Sec*
EMP: 40 **EST:** 1998
SALES (est): 2.5MM **Privately Held**
WEB: www.fixture-pro.com
SIC: 1751 Store fixture installation

(P-1738)
GARAGE CABINET WAREHOUSE INC (PA)
Also Called: We're Organized Northern Cal
2700 Merc Dr Ste 800, Rancho Cordova (95742)
P.O. Box 428 (95741-0428)
PHONE..................916 638-0123
Joseph Rawlings, *Owner*
EMP: 22 **EST:** 1987
SQ FT: 10,000
SALES (est): 4MM **Privately Held**
WEB: www.wereorganized.net
SIC: 1751 2434 Cabinet building & installation; wood kitchen cabinets

(P-1739)
GOLDFIRE CORPORATION
Also Called: Metro Caseworks
4882 Davenport Pl, Fremont (94538-6304)
PHONE..................510 354-3666
Arthur Howard Amon, *President*
Chris Flanders, *Project Mgr*
EMP: 15 **EST:** 2008
SQ FT: 22,000
SALES: 5.5MM **Privately Held**
SIC: 1751 2431 Cabinet building & installation; millwork

(P-1740)
HERITAGE INTERESTS LLC (PA)
4300 Jetway Ct, North Highlands (95660-5702)
P.O. Box 214609, Sacramento (95821-0609)
PHONE..................916 481-5030
Edward Zuckerman, *President*
Dennis Gardemeyer, *CFO*
Charlie Gardemeyer, *Vice Pres*
Cecily Keating, *Accounts Mgr*
EMP: 90 **EST:** 2011
SQ FT: 80,000
SALES (est): 51.2MM **Privately Held**
WEB: www.buildwithbmc.com
SIC: 1751 5031 2431 Cabinet & finish carpentry; finish & trim carpentry; lumber, plywood & millwork; windows & window parts & trim, wood; louver windows, glass, wood frame

(P-1741)
ISEC INCORPORATED
395 Oyster Point Blvd # 21, South San Francisco (94080-1928)
PHONE..................650 872-1391
Zeeshan Haiter, *Branch Mgr*
EMP: 75

▲ = Import ▼ = Export
◆ = Import/Export

PRODUCTS & SERVICES SECTION
1752 - Floor Laying & Other Floor Work, NEC County (P-1764)

SALES (corp-wide): 317.2MM **Privately Held**
WEB: www.isecinc.com
SIC: **1751** Cabinet & finish carpentry
PA: Isec, Incorporated
6000 Greenwood Plaza Blvd # 200
Greenwood Village CO 80111
303 790-1444

(P-1742)
ISEC INCORPORATED
7077 Koll Center Pkwy # 200, Pleasanton (94566-3142)
PHONE...................510 490-1333
Mike Polanchyck, *Sales & Mktg St*
Marie Laquian, *Project Mgr*
Bryan Ove, *Project Mgr*
Zeeshan Haider, *Opers Staff*
Phil Rittenmeyer, *Sr Project Mgr*
EMP: 40
SQ FT: 2,000
SALES (corp-wide): 317.2MM **Privately Held**
WEB: www.isecinc.com
SIC: **1751** Cabinet & finish carpentry
PA: Isec, Incorporated
6000 Greenwood Plaza Blvd # 200
Greenwood Village CO 80111
303 790-1444

(P-1743)
ISEC INCORPORATED
1855 N 1st St Unit D, Dixon (95620-9758)
P.O. Box 6849, Englewood CO (80155-6849)
PHONE...................707 693-6555
Ed Miller, *Branch Mgr*
EMP: 75
SALES (corp-wide): 317.2MM **Privately Held**
WEB: www.isecinc.com
SIC: **1751** Cabinet & finish carpentry
PA: Isec, Incorporated
6000 Greenwood Plaza Blvd # 200
Greenwood Village CO 80111
303 790-1444

(P-1744)
J J J & K INC
Also Called: Alexander Company
1322 Marsten Rd, Burlingame (94010-2406)
PHONE...................650 373-3900
John W Alexander, *President*
Jeffrey J Alexander, *Vice Pres*
EMP: 36 EST: 1973
SQ FT: 8,000
SALES (est): 1.4MM **Privately Held**
WEB: www.alexanderco.com
SIC: **1751** Window & door (prefabricated) installation

(P-1745)
KEYSTONE DOOR & BLDG SUP INC
1037 N Market Blvd Ste 9, Sacramento (95834-1917)
PHONE...................916 623-8100
Dale Winchester, *CEO*
Thaddeus Carpenter, *President*
David Herron, *Vice Pres*
Craig Forsyth, *Sales Staff*
EMP: 40 EST: 2013
SQ FT: 35,000
SALES (est): 4.1MM **Privately Held**
WEB: www.keystonedoor.com
SIC: **1751** **3429** Carpentry work; furniture builders' & other household hardware; builders' hardware

(P-1746)
NORTHWEST EXTERIORS INC
4404 N Knoll Ave, Fresno (93722-7825)
PHONE...................559 456-1632
Jimmy Brown, *Branch Mgr*
EMP: 64 **Privately Held**
WEB: www.northwestexteriors.com
SIC: **1751** **5211** **5031** Window & door (prefabricated) installation; cabinets, kitchen; metal doors, sash & trim
PA: Northwest Exteriors, Inc.
11200 Sun Center Dr
Rancho Cordova CA 95670

(P-1747)
NORTHWEST EXTERIORS INC (PA)
Also Called: Windows Hawaii
11200 Sun Center Dr, Rancho Cordova (95670-6145)
PHONE...................916 851-1632
Thomas Orr, *President*
Thomas Marvin Orr, *President*
Todd McKinstry, *Exec VP*
Mario Garcia, *General Mgr*
Skip Hunter, *Finance Mgr*
EMP: 45 EST: 1996
SQ FT: 5,000
SALES (est): 16.1MM **Privately Held**
WEB: www.northwestexteriors.com
SIC: **1751** **5074** **1761** **2434** Window & door (prefabricated) installation; heating equipment & panels, solar; roofing, siding & sheet metal work; wood kitchen cabinets

(P-1748)
OVERHEAD DOOR SNTA CLARA VLY I
Also Called: Overhead Door Santa Clara Vly
1266 Lawrence Station Rd, Sunnyvale (94089-2282)
PHONE...................408 734-8010
Robert Hurkmans, *President*
Linda Hurkmans, *Treasurer*
Alan Cullumber, *Vice Pres*
William Cullumber, *Vice Pres*
Michelle Cooke, *Regional Mgr*
EMP: 21 EST: 1921
SQ FT: 6,800
SALES (est): 4.7MM **Privately Held**
WEB: www.odcsantaclara.com
SIC: **1751** **3442** Garage door, installation or erection; metal doors, sash & trim

(P-1749)
PACIFIC DOOR PRODUCTS INC
470 Aaron St, Cotati (94931-3025)
PHONE...................707 795-7777
Jim Granados, *President*
EMP: 27 EST: 1982
SQ FT: 6,000
SALES (est): 1.1MM **Privately Held**
WEB: www.pacificdoorproducts.com
SIC: **1751** **5251** **5211** **2431** Window & door (prefabricated) installation; door locks & lock sets; doors, storm: wood or metal; garage doors, overhead: wood

(P-1750)
PRODUCTION FRAMING SYSTEMS INC (PA)
2000 Opportunity Dr # 140, Roseville (95678-3020)
PHONE...................916 978-2888
Steve J Benjamin, *President*
Kerry Palmer, *Vice Pres*
EMP: 150 EST: 1993
SALES (est): 15.9MM **Privately Held**
WEB: www.productionframing.com
SIC: **1751** Framing contractor

(P-1751)
R & S ERECTION N PENINSULA INC
133 S Linden Ave, South San Francisco (94080-6410)
PHONE...................415 467-5630
David Arrighi, *President*
William Lawrence, *Treasurer*
Garth Grotemeyer, *Vice Pres*
EMP: 35 EST: 1976
SQ FT: 5,000
SALES (est): 1.7MM **Privately Held**
WEB: www.rsdoorandgate.com
SIC: **1751** Garage door, installation or erection

(P-1752)
RICHARD HANCOCK INC
Also Called: Rhi
1029 3rd St, Santa Rosa (95404-6635)
PHONE...................707 528-4900
Bruce Lamar, *President*
Dan Lamar, *Project Mgr*
EMP: 50 EST: 1984
SQ FT: 1,600
SALES (est): 10MM **Privately Held**
WEB: www.rhiframing.com
SIC: **1751** Carpentry work

(P-1753)
RJ LOCICERO CORP
503 Giuseppe Ct Ste 3, Roseville (95678-6307)
PHONE...................916 781-2004
Bradley Locicero, *President*
Richard J Locicero, *CEO*
Eugene Monday, *Vice Pres*
EMP: 40 EST: 1983
SQ FT: 5,400
SALES (est): 4.7MM **Privately Held**
WEB: www.rjlocicero.com
SIC: **1751** **1742** Framing contractor; drywall; acoustical & ceiling work

(P-1754)
RJP FRAMING INC
1139 Sibley St Ste 100, Folsom (95630-3572)
P.O. Box 5057, El Dorado Hills (95762-0001)
PHONE...................916 941-3934
Laurie Payne, *President*
Robert Payne, *Vice Pres*
Curtis Linsley, *Controller*
EMP: 180 EST: 2004
SALES (est): 22.5MM **Privately Held**
WEB: www.rjpframing.com
SIC: **1751** Framing contractor

(P-1755)
SEGALE BROS WOOD PRODUCTS INC
1705 Sabre St, Hayward (94545-1015)
PHONE...................510 300-1170
Donald A Segale, *CEO*
Christine Segale, *Admin Sec*
Michael Fitzgerald, *Sales Staff*
Libby Sandoval, *Manager*
EMP: 28 EST: 1976
SQ FT: 40,000
SALES (est): 6.1MM **Privately Held**
WEB: www.segalebros.com
SIC: **1751** **2434** Cabinet building & installation; wood kitchen cabinets

(P-1756)
SHOOK & WALLER CNSTR INC
7677 Bell Rd Ste 101, Windsor (95492-7432)
PHONE...................707 578-3933
Eddie Waller, *President*
Shawn Dolan, *CFO*
Steven Shook, *Corp Secy*
Daryl Shook, *Project Mgr*
Candy Wigton, *Accounting Mgr*
EMP: 64 EST: 1980
SQ FT: 8,000
SALES (est): 8.7MM **Privately Held**
WEB: www.shookandwallerbuilders.com
SIC: **1751** **1521** **1542** Framing contractor; new construction, single-family houses; nonresidential construction

(P-1757)
SIERRA LUMBER CO
Also Called: Sierra Lumber & Decking
1711 Senter Rd, San Jose (95112-2598)
PHONE...................408 286-7071
Roger Burch, *President*
James Moblad, *Vice Pres*
EMP: 102 EST: 1974
SQ FT: 22,000
SALES (est): 3.1MM
SALES (corp-wide): 141.1MM **Privately Held**
WEB: www.sierrafence.com
SIC: **1751** **5211** Carpentry work; lumber products
PA: Pacific States Industries, Incorporated
10 Madrone Ave
Morgan Hill CA 95037
408 779-7354

(P-1758)
SIERRA TRIM INC
Also Called: Construction
3137 Swetzer Rd Ste B, Loomis (95650-7611)
PHONE...................916 259-2966
William D Snow, *CEO*
EMP: 25 EST: 2009

SALES (est): 1.8MM **Privately Held**
SIC: **1751** **2431** Finish & trim carpentry; door frames, wood

(P-1759)
SINGLEY ENTERPRISES (PA)
Also Called: Garage Door Specialists
2901 Duluth St, West Sacramento (95691-2205)
P.O. Box 572 (95691-0572)
PHONE...................916 375-0575
Jennifer Merica, *President*
Jane Cheek, *Manager*
Luke McIntosh, *Manager*
Steve Serrano, *Manager*
▲ EMP: 47 EST: 1997
SALES (est): 9.9MM **Privately Held**
SIC: **1751** Garage door, installation or erection

(P-1760)
SR FREEMAN INC
2380 S Bascom Ave Ste 200, Campbell (95008-4389)
PHONE...................408 364-2200
Shone Freeman, *President*
Josie Freeman, *Admin Sec*
EMP: 60 EST: 1992
SALES (est): 35.3MM **Privately Held**
WEB: www.srfreemaninc.com
SIC: **1751** Framing contractor

(P-1761)
STOCKHAM CONSTRUCTION INC
475 Portal St, Cotati (94931-3006)
PHONE...................707 664-0945
Boyd L Stockham, *President*
Dani Stockham, *Treasurer*
Denise Dunlap, *Admin Asst*
Shani Cavazos, *Controller*
EMP: 450 EST: 1991
SQ FT: 15,301
SALES: 149.2MM **Privately Held**
WEB: www.stockhamconstruction.com
SIC: **1751** **1742** Lightweight steel framing (metal stud) installation; drywall; acoustical & ceiling work

(P-1762)
WALTERS & WOLF INTERIORS (PA)
41450 Boscell Rd, Fremont (94538-3103)
PHONE...................415 243-9400
Randall Alan Wolf, *CEO*
Michael Wolf, *President*
Jeff Belzer, *CFO*
▲ EMP: 80 EST: 1980
SQ FT: 30,000
SALES (est): 9.3MM **Privately Held**
WEB: www.interiors.waltersandwolf.com
SIC: **1751** Carpentry work

1752 Floor Laying & Other Floor Work, NEC

(P-1763)
ALPINE CARPETS CORPORATION (PA)
Also Called: Alpine Carpet One Floor & Home
2212 Lake Tahoe Blvd, South Lake Tahoe (96150-6406)
PHONE...................530 541-6171
Peter Friederici, *President*
Rochelle Friederici, *Corp Secy*
Paul Friederici, *Vice Pres*
EMP: 67 EST: 1970
SQ FT: 3,000
SALES (est): 2.9MM **Privately Held**
WEB: www.alpinecarpetonesouthlaketahoe.com
SIC: **5713** **1752** Carpets; floor laying & floor work

(P-1764)
ANTHONY TREVINO
Also Called: A&S Floors
938 Adams St Ste A, Benicia (94510-2948)
PHONE...................707 747-4776
Anthony Trevino, *Owner*
EMP: 52 EST: 1993
SALES (est): 3.8MM **Privately Held**
SIC: **1752** Carpet laying

1752 - Floor Laying & Other Floor Work, NEC County (P-1765)

(P-1765)
B T MANCINI CO INC (PA)
Also Called: B.T. Mancini Company
876 S Milpitas Blvd, Milpitas (95035-6311)
P.O. Box 361930 (95036-1930)
PHONE..................................408 942-7900
Brooks T Mancini Jr, *President*
Jim Evans, *Vice Pres*
Greg Hartwick, *Vice Pres*
Brooks T Mancini Sr, *Vice Pres*
Tom McGovern, *Vice Pres*
▲ **EMP:** 100
SQ FT: 36,000
SALES (est): 58.2MM **Privately Held**
WEB: www.btmancini.com
SIC: 1752 1761 Wood floor installation & refinishing; roofing, siding & sheet metal work; siding contractor

(P-1766)
BIG OAK HARDWOOD FLOOR CO INC
1731 Leslie St, San Mateo (94402-2409)
PHONE..................................650 591-8651
Richard Mack, *President*
Robert Connor, *Treasurer*
EMP: 58 **EST:** 1991
SQ FT: 7,500
SALES (est): 3.8MM **Privately Held**
SIC: 1752 Wood floor installation & refinishing

(P-1767)
CREATIVE DESIGN INTERIORS INC (PA)
Also Called: C D I
737 Del Paso Rd, Sacramento (95834-1106)
PHONE..................................916 641-1121
Ronald Lapp, *President*
Kathy Lapp, *Vice Pres*
Ron Lewis, *Branch Mgr*
Jeff Barth, *General Mgr*
Brenda Mansur, *Finance*
EMP: 100 **EST:** 1991
SQ FT: 10,000
SALES (est): 53MM **Privately Held**
SIC: 1752 Ceramic floor tile installation

(P-1768)
DS BAXLEY INC
6571 Las Positas Rd, Livermore (94551-5157)
PHONE..................................925 371-3950
Daniel S Baxley, *President*
Remonda Gorgis, *Administration*
Dianne Huynh, *Administration*
Veronica Merchant, *Administration*
Josh Brewer, *Project Mgr*
EMP: 40 **EST:** 1997
SQ FT: 11,000
SALES (est): 16.3MM **Privately Held**
WEB: www.dsb-plus.com
SIC: 1752 1771 Carpet laying; flooring contractor

(P-1769)
FIRST LAST & ALWAYS INC
1311 22nd St, San Francisco (94107-3433)
P.O. Box 31776 (94131-0776)
PHONE..................................415 541-7978
Deven Gadula, *President*
▲ **EMP:** 35 **EST:** 2000
SQ FT: 9,501
SALES (est): 3.8MM **Privately Held**
WEB: www.first-last-always.com
SIC: 1752 Wood floor installation & refinishing

(P-1770)
FLOOR SEAL TECHNOLOGY INC (PA)
1005 Ames Ave, Milpitas (95035-6305)
PHONE..................................408 436-8181
William Clyne, *CEO*
Theresa Luu, *CFO*
William Terry Ireland, *CTO*
EMP: 50 **EST:** 1980
SALES (est): 20.3MM **Privately Held**
WEB: www.floorseal.com
SIC: 1752 2891 3829 Wood floor installation & refinishing; carpet laying; sealants; measuring & controlling devices

(P-1771)
H V WELKER CO INC
Also Called: Welker Bros
970 S Milpitas Blvd, Milpitas (95035-6323)
PHONE..................................408 263-4400
Stuart Welker, *President*
Chuck Gulan, *Shareholder*
Stuart H Welker, *President*
Jack Sanguiniti, *Exec VP*
Vincent A Grana, *Vice Pres*
EMP: 65
SQ FT: 18,375
SALES (est): 33.8MM **Privately Held**
WEB: www.welkers.com
SIC: 1752 Floor laying & floor work

(P-1772)
HANES FLOOR INCORPORATED
870 Commerce St, Redding (96002-0614)
PHONE..................................530 221-6544
Mark Todd, *President*
Chester Todd, *Corp Secy*
Delbert Wellock, *Vice Pres*
EMP: 47 **EST:** 1947
SQ FT: 8,500
SALES (est): 1.6MM **Privately Held**
SIC: 1752 5713 Carpet laying; wood floor installation & refinishing; ceramic floor tile installation; linoleum installation; floor covering stores

(P-1773)
HOEM & ASSOCIATES INC
951 Linden Ave, South San Francisco (94080-1753)
PHONE..................................650 871-5194
Russell William Hoem, *CEO*
Sean Hogan, *President*
Mike Valerio, *Vice Pres*
Mike N Valerio, *Vice Pres*
Jackie Morino, *Sales Associate*
EMP: 115 **EST:** 1937
SQ FT: 24,000
SALES (est): 38MM **Privately Held**
WEB: www.hoemassociates.com
SIC: 1752 Carpet laying; vinyl floor tile & sheet installation; wood floor installation & refinishing

(P-1774)
JUSTIN CAREY ENTERPRISES INC
703 N Abby St, Fresno (93701-1001)
PHONE..................................559 213-4731
Justin Carey, *CEO*
EMP: 35 **EST:** 2011
SQ FT: 5,000
SALES (est): 5MM **Privately Held**
SIC: 1752 1721 Floor laying & floor work; industrial painting

(P-1775)
ROSEVILLE FLOORING INC
Also Called: Roseville Carpet One
1109 Smith Ln, Roseville (95661-4103)
PHONE..................................916 945-2015
Earl Mann, *CEO*
EMP: 40 **EST:** 1987
SQ FT: 5,000
SALES (est): 14.1MM **Privately Held**
WEB: www.californiarenovation.com
SIC: 5713 5211 1752 5031 Carpets; flooring, wood; carpet laying; kitchen cabinets

(P-1776)
SIMAS FLOOR CO INC (PA)
Also Called: Simas Floor Co Design Center
3550 Power Inn Rd, Sacramento (95826-3892)
PHONE..................................916 452-4933
Ken Simas, *President*
David G Simas, *Vice Pres*
John U Simas, *Vice Pres*
David Highfill, *Sales Staff*
Jan Madison, *Manager*
EMP: 180 **EST:** 1951
SQ FT: 10,000
SALES (est): 31.3MM **Privately Held**
WEB: www.simasfloleranddesign.com
SIC: 1752 5713 Floor laying & floor work; floor covering stores

(P-1777)
TERA-LITE INC
Also Called: Revolan Systems
1631 S 10th St, San Jose (95112-2594)
PHONE..................................408 288-8655
David Palomino, *President*
EMP: 35 **EST:** 1964
SQ FT: 10,000
SALES (est): 5.3MM **Privately Held**
WEB: www.tera-lite.com
SIC: 1752 5023 2851 Floor laying & floor work; floor coverings; paints & allied products

(P-1778)
WEST VALLEY CARPET SERVICE
1291 Pintail Ct, San Jose (95118-2041)
PHONE..................................408 946-2447
EMP: 43
SQ FT: 5,000
SALES (est): 4.9MM **Privately Held**
WEB: www.wvcs.net
SIC: 1752 Floor Laying Contractor

1761 Roofing, Siding & Sheet Metal Work

(P-1779)
ABSOLUTE URETHANE
Also Called: Absolute Roofing CA
6614 S Elm Ave, Fresno (93706-9213)
PHONE..................................877 471-3626
Eric Plaza, *CEO*
Carolyn Plaza, *CFO*
EMP: 50 **EST:** 2006
SALES (est): 1MM **Privately Held**
WEB: www.absoluteurethane.com
SIC: 1761 1721 1742 7389 Roofing contractor; painting & paper hanging; insulation, buildings;

(P-1780)
ADVANCED ROOF DESIGN INC (PA)
4 Wayne Ct Ste 10, Sacramento (95829-1305)
PHONE..................................916 381-2266
Timothy Balbi, *President*
Ann M Balbi, *Admin Sec*
EMP: 35 **EST:** 2002
SQ FT: 5,000
SALES (est): 5.6MM **Privately Held**
WEB: www.ardroofing.com
SIC: 1761 Roofing contractor

(P-1781)
AEP SPAN INC
2110 Enterprise Blvd, West Sacramento (95691-3428)
PHONE..................................916 372-0933
Al Price, *Manager*
EMP: 184 **EST:** 2001
SQ FT: 16,000
SALES (est): 818.3K **Privately Held**
WEB: www.ascprofiles.com
SIC: 1761 3448 3444 3443 Roofing contractor; prefabricated metal buildings; sheet metalwork; fabricated plate work (boiler shop)
HQ: Asc Profiles Llc
2110 Enterprise Blvd
West Sacramento CA 95691
916 376-2800

(P-1782)
ALCAL SPECIALTY CONTG INC (DH)
946 N Market Blvd, Sacramento (95834-1268)
PHONE..................................916 929-3100
Darren C Morris, *President*
Sonny Kooner, *CFO*
Arthur R Gardner, *Exec VP*
Richard Bledsoe, *Vice Pres*
Robert Colla, *Vice Pres*
EMP: 470 **EST:** 1971
SALES (est): 103.1MM
SALES (corp-wide): 1.1B **Privately Held**
WEB: www.alcal.com
SIC: 1761 1793 1742 1799 Roofing contractor; glass & glazing work; plastering, drywall & insulation; coating, caulking & weather, water & fireproofing; garage door, installation or erection

(P-1783)
ALL FAB PRCSION SHEETMETAL INC
1015 Timothy Dr, San Jose (95133-1050)
PHONE..................................408 279-1099
Son P Ho, *CEO*
Kelly T Ho, *CFO*
▲ **EMP:** 100 **EST:** 2000
SQ FT: 58,000
SALES (est): 26.9MM **Privately Held**
WEB: www.allfabprecision.com
SIC: 1761 3444 Sheet metalwork; sheet metalwork

(P-1784)
ALLIANCE ROOFING COMPANY INC
630 Martin Ave, Santa Clara (95050-2914)
PHONE..................................800 579-2595
Roderick Miller, *CEO*
Donna Miller, *Admin Sec*
Robert Strohmaier, *Project Mgr*
Pauru Sorabji, *Asst Controller*
Arturo Guerrero, *Superintendent*
EMP: 50 **EST:** 1986
SQ FT: 2,800
SALES (est): 17.1MM **Privately Held**
WEB: www.allianceroofingcal.com
SIC: 1761 1799 Roofing contractor; waterproofing

(P-1785)
AMD METAL WORKS INC
8155 Belvedere Ave # 100, Sacramento (95826-4764)
PHONE..................................916 465-8185
Rocco Di Giovanni, *CEO*
EMP: 21 **EST:** 2016
SALES (est): 1.3MM **Privately Held**
WEB: www.amdmetalworks.com
SIC: 1761 3441 Sheet metalwork; fabricated structural metal

(P-1786)
ANDYS ROOFING CO INC
2161 Adams Ave, San Leandro (94577-1023)
PHONE..................................510 777-1100
Jonathan W Engquist, *President*
Therese Engquist, *Officer*
EMP: 40
SQ FT: 4,000
SALES (est): 6MM **Privately Held**
WEB: www.andysroofing.com
SIC: 1761 Roofing contractor

(P-1787)
BARRIER SPCLTY ROFG CTINGS INC
2671 S Cherry Ave, Fresno (93706-5450)
PHONE..................................559 233-1680
Blair Cunnings, *President*
▲ **EMP:** 35 **EST:** 1999
SALES (est): 9.3MM **Privately Held**
WEB: www.barrierroofing.com
SIC: 1761 Roofing contractor

(P-1788)
BEST CONTRACTING SERVICES INC
4301 Bettencourt Way, Union City (94587-1519)
PHONE..................................510 886-7240
Mohmmad Beigi, *Branch Mgr*
Christiano Ramos, *Managing Prtnr*
Kayhan Fatemi, *Exec VP*
Peyvand Tehrani, *Administration*
Angel Aviles, *Project Mgr*
EMP: 100
SALES (corp-wide): 87.2MM **Privately Held**
WEB: www.bestcontracting.com
SIC: 1761 Roofing contractor

PRODUCTS & SERVICES SECTION

1771 - Concrete Work County (P-1915)

(P-1889)
M F MAHER INC
Also Called: Maher M F Concrete Cnstr
490 Ryder St, Vallejo (94590-7217)
PHONE.................................707 552-2774
Malcolm F Maher, *President*
Janice K Maher, *Corp Secy*
Ronald Maher, *Vice Pres*
Steve Maher, *Executive*
Mike Maher, *Office Mgr*
EMP: 70 **EST:** 1970
SQ FT: 4,000
SALES (est): 9.3MM **Privately Held**
WEB: www.mfmaher.com
SIC: 1771 Concrete work

(P-1890)
M4 CONCRETE AND DRYWALL INC (PA)
2930 Geer Rd, Turlock (95382-1142)
PHONE.................................209 850-9250
Jose Mendoza, *Vice Pres*
EMP: 53 **EST:** 2018
SQ FT: 5,000
SALES (est): 2.7MM **Privately Held**
WEB: www.m4concreteanddrywall.com
SIC: 1771 1742 5031 1751 Concrete work; drywall; plywood; lightweight steel framing (metal stud) installation

(P-1891)
M4 CONCRETE AND DRYWALL INC
11380 Early Dawn Rd, Turlock (95380-9649)
PHONE.................................209 850-9250
Jose Antonio Mendoza, *Branch Mgr*
EMP: 35
SALES (corp-wide): 2.7MM **Privately Held**
WEB: www.m4concreteanddrywall.com
SIC: 1771 Concrete work
PA: M4 Concrete And Drywall Incorporated
2930 Geer Rd
Turlock CA 95382
209 850-9250

(P-1892)
MARR B OLSEN INC
320 1st St, Petaluma (94952-4225)
PHONE.................................707 763-9707
Marr B Olsen, *President*
Kim Olsen, *Vice Pres*
EMP: 45 **EST:** 1985
SQ FT: 4,000
SALES (est): 10.1MM **Privately Held**
WEB: www.marrbolsen.com
SIC: 1771 1521 Foundation & footing contractor; new construction, single-family houses; general remodeling, single-family houses

(P-1893)
MCCLONE CONSTRUCTION COMPANY
3880 El Dorado Hills Blvd, El Dorado Hills (95762-4566)
PHONE.................................916 358-5495
William R Patterson, *Branch Mgr*
EMP: 115 **Privately Held**
WEB: www.mcclone.net
SIC: 1771 Concrete work
PA: Mcclone Construction Company
5170 Hillsdale Cir Ste B
El Dorado Hills CA 95762

(P-1894)
MITCHELL JONES CONCRETE INC
Also Called: Mitchell Concrete
3187 Fitzgerald Rd, Rancho Cordova (95742-6801)
PHONE.................................916 638-6870
Mitchell L Jones, *President*
Peggy Jones, *Vice Pres*
EMP: 43 **EST:** 1986
SALES (est): 6.7MM **Privately Held**
WEB: www.mitchellconcrete.com
SIC: 1771 Concrete work

(P-1895)
MURGA STRANGE & CHALMERS INC
924 Lemon St, Vallejo (94590-7248)
PHONE.................................707 643-9075
Harold Strange, *President*
Kim Stahnke, *CFO*
Harry Chalmers, *Vice Pres*
Shane Chalmers, *Vice Pres*
Sharon REA, *Admin Sec*
EMP: 39 **EST:** 1986
SQ FT: 1,750
SALES (est): 3.3MM **Privately Held**
SIC: 1771 Curb construction

(P-1896)
NMN CONSTRUCTION INC
1077 Lakeville St, Petaluma (94952-3331)
P.O. Box 110244, Campbell (95011-0244)
PHONE.................................707 763-6981
Fax: 408 874-2574
EMP: 100
SALES (est): 4.5MM **Privately Held**
SIC: 1771 Concrete Contractor

(P-1897)
NOAH CONCRETE CORPORATION
5900 Rossi Ln, Gilroy (95020-7013)
PHONE.................................408 842-7211
Don Alvarez, *CEO*
Christine Morales, *Office Mgr*
Noah Alvarez, *Opers Staff*
▲ **EMP:** 60 **EST:** 1996
SALES (est): 11.3MM **Privately Held**
WEB: www.noahconcretecorporation.com
SIC: 1771 Concrete work

(P-1898)
ODYSSEY LANDSCAPING CO INC
Also Called: Odyssey Environmental Services
5400 W Highway 12, Lodi (95242-9170)
PHONE.................................209 369-6197
Martin Gates, *President*
Jason Arambula, *Division Mgr*
Brian Zanni, *Division Mgr*
Richard Barnes, *CIO*
Anthony Martinez, *Supervisor*
EMP: 80 **EST:** 1982
SQ FT: 2,400
SALES (est): 12.7MM **Privately Held**
WEB: www.odysseylandscape.com
SIC: 1771 0781 Concrete work; landscape architects

(P-1899)
PACIFIC STRUCTURES SC INC (PA)
457 Minna St, San Francisco (94103-2914)
PHONE.................................415 970-5434
Ross Edwards, *Ch of Bd*
David E Williams, *President*
Ron Marano, *CFO*
Eric Horn, *Treasurer*
Kris Fahrion, *Vice Pres*
EMP: 249 **EST:** 2008
SALES (est): 275.7MM **Privately Held**
WEB: www.pacific-structures.com
SIC: 1771 Concrete work

(P-1900)
PACIFIC SURFACING
2066 Warm Springs Ct, Fremont (94539-6744)
PHONE.................................510 440-9494
Clay Laucella, *President*
Michael Walitsch, *Vice Pres*
Ross Livingston, *Project Mgr*
Jason Wellman, *Accountant*
Carol Elias, *Controller*
EMP: 40 **EST:** 1992
SQ FT: 3,000
SALES (est): 6.1MM **Privately Held**
WEB: www.pacificsurfacing.chiefmall.com
SIC: 1771 Curb & sidewalk contractors; driveway, parking lot & blacktop contractors

(P-1901)
PECK & HILLER COMPANY
870 Napa Vly Corp Way Ste, NAPA (94558)
PHONE.................................707 258-8800
Russell B Peck, *Principal*
Ben Kerr, *Vice Pres*
Tom H O'Connor, *Vice Pres*
Cindy Joy Westerberg, *Controller*
Serafin Espinoza, *Superintendent*
EMP: 100 **EST:** 1949
SQ FT: 8,680
SALES (est): 20.5MM **Privately Held**
WEB: www.peckandhiller.com
SIC: 1771 Foundation & footing contractor

(P-1902)
PRECISION EMPRISE LLC
417 Harrison St, Oakland (94607-4117)
PHONE.................................866 792-8006
Marc Cussenot
EMP: 48 **EST:** 2017
SALES (est): 1.7MM **Privately Held**
SIC: 1771 Concrete repair

(P-1903)
R & R MAHER CONSTRUCTION CO
1324 Lemon St, Vallejo (94590-7250)
PHONE.................................707 552-0330
Brad Maher, *President*
Bradley V Maher, *Vice Pres*
Bradley Maher, *Vice Pres*
Richard D Maher, *Vice Pres*
Ken Scolavino, *Vice Pres*
EMP: 50 **EST:** 1970
SQ FT: 1,600
SALES (est): 10.1MM **Privately Held**
WEB: www.maherconcrete.com
SIC: 1771 Concrete work

(P-1904)
R E MAHER INC
4545 Hess Rd, American Canyon (94503-9727)
PHONE.................................707 642-3907
Rod E Maher, *CEO*
Rod Maher, *Executive*
Linda Green, *Controller*
EMP: 95 **EST:** 1997
SQ FT: 1,000
SALES (est): 15.1MM **Privately Held**
WEB: www.remaherinc.com
SIC: 1771 Foundation & footing contractor

(P-1905)
RESCUE CONCRETE INC
9275 Beatty Dr, Sacramento (95826-9702)
P.O. Box 276812 (95827-6812)
PHONE.................................916 852-2400
David Winn, *President*
EMP: 60 **EST:** 1995
SALES (est): 4.8MM **Privately Held**
SIC: 1771 Concrete work

(P-1906)
RJS & ASSOCIATES INC
1675 Sabre St, Hayward (94545-1013)
PHONE.................................510 670-9111
Robert J Simmons, *President*
EMP: 225 **EST:** 1994
SQ FT: 10,000
SALES (est): 41.5MM **Privately Held**
WEB: www.rjsandassociates.net
SIC: 1771 1521 Foundation & footing contractor; single-family housing construction

(P-1907)
ROBERT A BOTHMAN INC (PA)
Also Called: B & B Concrete
2690 Scott Blvd, Santa Clara (95050-2511)
PHONE.................................408 279-2277
Robert A Bothman, *CEO*
Saeed Yousuf, *COO*
Andy Bothman, *Vice Pres*
Brian Bothman, *Vice Pres*
Jim Brogoitti, *Vice Pres*
EMP: 128 **EST:** 1978
SQ FT: 20,000
SALES (est): 51.5MM **Privately Held**
WEB: www.bothman.com
SIC: 1771 0782 Concrete work; landscape contractors

(P-1908)
RON NURSS INC
Also Called: Blueline Construction
11290 Sunrise Park Dr B, Rancho Cordova (95742-6895)
PHONE.................................916 631-9761
Ron Nurss, *President*
Cecily Sorenson, *Office Mgr*
Darcy Nurss, *Admin Sec*
EMP: 65 **EST:** 1985
SQ FT: 6,400
SALES (est): 11.1MM **Privately Held**
WEB: www.blueline-construction.com
SIC: 1771 Concrete work

(P-1909)
SINCLAIR CONCRETE
7205 Church St, Penryn (95663-9411)
PHONE.................................916 663-0303
Keith Sinclair, *Admin Sec*
Karin Sinclair, *Admin Sec*
EMP: 85 **EST:** 1982
SALES (est): 11MM **Privately Held**
WEB: www.sinclairconcreteinc.com
SIC: 1771 Foundation & footing contractor

(P-1910)
STROUSS BROS CONSTRUCTION INC
700 Comstock St, Santa Clara (95054-3402)
PHONE.................................408 267-3222
David C Strouss, *President*
William Strouss, *Treasurer*
Tim Valdivieso, *Project Mgr*
EMP: 40 **EST:** 1969
SQ FT: 2,800
SALES (est): 6.2MM **Privately Held**
WEB: www.stroussbrothers.com
SIC: 1771 Foundation & footing contractor

(P-1911)
SUNSTONE CONSTRUCTION INC
176 Gilman Ave, Campbell (95008-3006)
PHONE.................................408 379-0592
Richard L Fuller, *President*
Debra Fuller, *Treasurer*
William Robowski, *Vice Pres*
EMP: 54 **EST:** 1978
SQ FT: 6,400
SALES (est): 3.8MM **Privately Held**
WEB: www.sunstoneconstructioninc.com
SIC: 1771 Foundation & footing contractor

(P-1912)
TERRY TUELL CONCRETE INC
287 W Fllbrook Ave Ste 10, Fresno (93711)
P.O. Box 3933 (93650-3933)
PHONE.................................559 431-0812
Terry Tuell, *President*
Matthew Tuell, *Treasurer*
EMP: 90 **EST:** 1974
SQ FT: 3,000
SALES (est): 9.4MM **Privately Held**
WEB: www.terrytuell.com
SIC: 1771 Concrete work

(P-1913)
TOM COREA CONSTRUCTION INC
2696 Nfordham Ave, Fresno (93727)
PHONE.................................559 292-9224
Tom Corea, *President*
EMP: 43 **EST:** 1993
SQ FT: 7,410
SALES (est): 4.7MM **Privately Held**
WEB: www.meconstruction.net
SIC: 1771 Concrete work

(P-1914)
URATA & SONS CONCRETE INC
3430 Luyung Dr, Rancho Cordova (95742-6871)
PHONE.................................916 638-5364
Charles Urata, *President*
Kelly Urata, *Corp Secy*
John Bell, *Vice Pres*
David Acrell, *Sr Project Mgr*
Rick Rice, *Sr Project Mgr*
EMP: 125 **EST:** 1972
SQ FT: 10,000
SALES (est): 71MM **Privately Held**
WEB: www.urataconcrete.com
SIC: 1771 Foundation & footing contractor

(P-1915)
URATA & SONS CONCRETE LLC
3430 Luyung Dr, Rancho Cordova (95742-6871)
PHONE.................................916 638-5364
Charles A Urata, *Mng Member*
EMP: 99 **EST:** 2018

1771 - Concrete Work County (P-1916)

SALES (est): 6.9MM **Privately Held**
WEB: www.urataconcrete.com
SIC: **1771** Concrete work

(P-1916)
VAN MIDDE & SON CONCRETE
490 B St, San Rafael (94901-3818)
PHONE.................................415 459-2530
Ted Van Midde, *President*
Jennifer Van Midde, *Admin Sec*
EMP: 58 EST: 1991
SQ FT: 6,000
SALES (est): 6.4MM **Privately Held**
WEB: www.vanmiddeconcrete.com
SIC: **1771** Concrete work

(P-1917)
WAYNE E SWISHER CEM CONTR INC
2620 E 18th St, Antioch (94509-7229)
PHONE.................................925 757-3660
Wayne Swisher, *President*
Elma Swisher, *Vice Pres*
EMP: 75 EST: 1970
SQ FT: 4,000
SALES (est): 12.6MM **Privately Held**
WEB: www.swishercement.com
SIC: **1771** Foundation & footing contractor

(P-1918)
WHITESIDE CONSTRUCTION CORP
1151 Hensley St, Richmond (94801-2162)
PHONE.................................510 234-6681
David Whiteside, *President*
Michelle Jacobsen, *CFO*
Richard James Whiteside, *Corp Secy*
Margaret Birmingham, *Administration*
EMP: 49 EST: 1986
SQ FT: 3,000
SALES (est): 8MM **Privately Held**
WEB: www.whitesideconstruction.com
SIC: **1771** Concrete work

1781 Water Well Drilling

(P-1919)
EATON DRILLING CO INC
20 W Kentucky Ave, Woodland (95695-5837)
PHONE.................................530 402-1143
Thomas Edward Eaton, *CEO*
Mark Cobey, *Vice Pres*
EMP: 43 EST: 1928
SQ FT: 4,800
SALES (est): 10.2MM **Privately Held**
WEB: www.eatondrilling.com
SIC: **1781** Water well drilling

(P-1920)
MAGGIORA BROS DRILLING INC (PA)
595 Airport Blvd, Watsonville (95076-2094)
PHONE.................................831 724-1338
David T Maggiora, *CEO*
Mark Maggiora, *Treasurer*
Joanne Maggiora, *Vice Pres*
Michael Maggiora, *Admin Sec*
EMP: 50
SQ FT: 5,000
SALES (est): 11.2MM **Privately Held**
WEB: www.maggiorabros.com
SIC: **1781** 1711 Water well drilling; plumbing contractors

1791 Structural Steel Erection

(P-1921)
BAJA CONSTRUCTION CO INC (PA)
223 Foster St, Martinez (94553-1029)
P.O. Box 3080 (94553-8080)
PHONE.................................925 229-0732
Robert Hayworth, *Chairman*
Laura Daum, *President*
Brandon Morford, *CEO*
Robert J Hayworth, *Chairman*
Luis Fabian, *Vice Pres*
EMP: 90 EST: 1981
SQ FT: 7,200
SALES (est): 25.3MM **Privately Held**
WEB: www.bajacarports.com
SIC: **1791** Structural steel erection

(P-1922)
C&N REINFORCING INC
2194 Gibralter Dr, Manteca (95337-8409)
PHONE.................................209 399-2022
Juan Perez, *President*
EMP: 35 EST: 2018
SALES (est): 1.6MM **Privately Held**
SIC: **1791** Concrete reinforcement, placing of

(P-1923)
CALIFRNIA ERCTORS BAY AREA INC
4500 California Ct, Benicia (94510-1021)
PHONE.................................707 746-1990
David W McEuen, *CEO*
Dennis Mc Euen, *Ch of Bd*
Galen Jaeger, *Vice Pres*
Matt McEuen, *Vice Pres*
EMP: 115 EST: 1964
SQ FT: 16,000
SALES (est): 13.3MM **Privately Held**
WEB: www.calerectors.com
SIC: **1791** Iron work, structural

(P-1924)
HARRIS REBAR NORTHERN CAL INC
355 S Vasco Rd, Livermore (94550-5300)
P.O. Box 73549, Puyallup WA (98373-0549)
PHONE.................................925 373-0733
Tyler Keith, *President*
Connie Caisse, *CFO*
Brady Buckley, *Vice Pres*
Ed Mize, *Vice Pres*
Lyle Sieg, *Vice Pres*
▲ EMP: 250 EST: 1985
SQ FT: 4,000
SALES (est): 28.3MM **Privately Held**
SIC: **1791** Structural steel erection

(P-1925)
KWAN WO IRONWORKS INC
31628 Hayman St, Hayward (94544-7122)
PHONE.................................415 822-9628
Florence Kong, *President*
Kanger Shum, *General Mgr*
Ada Tang, *Office Mgr*
Fay Chu, *Admin Asst*
Sammy Huang, *Admin Asst*
▲ EMP: 120 EST: 1992
SQ FT: 32,000
SALES (est): 29.8MM **Privately Held**
WEB: www.kwanwo.com
SIC: **1791** 5051 Iron work, structural; metals service centers & offices

(P-1926)
LHL CONSTRUCTION INC
Also Called: Rankin and Rankin
1370 Furneaux Rd, Olivehurst (95961-7466)
PHONE.................................916 782-9001
Len Lewis Jr, *President*
Lenond B Lewis Jr, *President*
Dave Coder, *Production*
Chris Koski, *VP Sales*
EMP: 30 EST: 1984
SALES (est): 3.9MM **Privately Held**
WEB: www.lhlconstruction.com
SIC: **1791** 3448 2394 Structural steel erection; prefabricated metal buildings; canvas & related products

(P-1927)
MID STATE STEEL ERECTION (PA)
1916 Cherokee Rd, Stockton (95205-2721)
PHONE.................................209 464-9497
Jerry Shipman, *President*
Patty Shipman, *Corp Secy*
Glenda Roe, *Technology*
Jeff Benge,
EMP: 70 EST: 1978
SALES (est): 9.5MM **Privately Held**
WEB: www.midstatesteelerectors.com
SIC: **1791** Structural steel erection

(P-1928)
NEHEMIAH REBAR SERVICES INC
4110 Business Dr Ste B, Cameron Park (95682-7268)
P.O. Box 2149, Shingle Springs (95682-2149)
PHONE.................................530 676-6310
Kevin W Rhodes, *CEO*
EMP: 150 EST: 2004
SALES: 20.5MM **Privately Held**
WEB: www.nehemiahrebar.com
SIC: **1791** Structural steel erection

(P-1929)
PJS LUMBER INC
Also Called: P.J.'s Rebar
250 D St, Turlock (95380-5431)
PHONE.................................209 850-9444
Shane McMillan, *Principal*
EMP: 60 EST: 2017
SALES (est): 2.1MM **Privately Held**
SIC: **1791** Structural steel erection

(P-1930)
QUALITY ERECTORS CNSTR CO INC
3130 Bayshore Rd, Benicia (94510-1232)
PHONE.................................707 746-1233
Jesse Esquivel, *President*
Bill Wells, *Vice Pres*
Steve Law, *Executive*
Karen Anne Esquivel, *Admin Sec*
Bruce Cox, *Sr Project Mgr*
EMP: 60 EST: 1980
SALES (est): 17.2MM **Privately Held**
WEB: www.qec-inc.com
SIC: **1791** 1761 Structural steel erection; sheet metalwork

(P-1931)
SACRAMENTO REBAR INC (PA)
6415 Hedge Ave, Sacramento (95829-9316)
PHONE.................................916 447-9700
Stanley Rhodes, *CEO*
Janet Rhodes, *CFO*
Stacy Bonney, *Office Mgr*
Mike Wimmer, *Admin Asst*
EMP: 40 EST: 1987
SQ FT: 5,000
SALES (est): 11.4MM **Privately Held**
WEB: www.sacramentorebar.com
SIC: **1791** Structural steel erection

(P-1932)
SCHUFF STEEL COMPANY
10100 Trinity Pkwy # 400, Stockton (95219-7240)
PHONE.................................209 938-0869
Chase Abbott, *Branch Mgr*
EMP: 94 **Publicly Held**
WEB: www.schuff.com
SIC: **1791** 3441 Structural steel erection; fabricated structural metal
HQ: Schuff Steel Company
    3003 N Central Ave # 700
    Phoenix AZ 85012
    623 386-2432

(P-1933)
VALLEY IRON WORKS INC
127 E Harney Ln, Lodi (95240-8836)
PHONE.................................209 368-7037
Joseph M Coubal, *President*
Sherry Campbell, *Office Mgr*
Deborah Coubal, *Admin Sec*
EMP: 30 EST: 1979
SQ FT: 20,000
SALES (est): 6MM **Privately Held**
WEB: www.valleyironworks.com
SIC: **1791** 3449 Iron work, structural; miscellaneous metalwork

1793 Glass & Glazing Work

(P-1934)
AAC GLASS INC
31044 San Antonio St, Hayward (94544-7904)
PHONE.................................909 214-4049
Ali Missaghi, *CEO*
EMP: 40 EST: 2017
SALES (est): 14.9MM **Privately Held**
SIC: **1793** Glass & glazing work

(P-1935)
BAGATELOS GLASS SYSTEMS INC (PA)
Also Called: Bagatlos Archtctral GL Systems
2750 Redding Ave, Sacramento (95820-2156)
PHONE.................................916 364-3600
Nick Bagatelos, *CEO*
Dave Ferret, *Vice Pres*
Chris Anderson, *Executive*
Chris Bagatelos, *Admin Sec*
John Papagna, *Project Mgr*
▲ EMP: 79 EST: 1999
SQ FT: 50,000
SALES (est): 23.1MM **Privately Held**
WEB: www.bagatelos.com
SIC: **1793** Glass & glazing work

(P-1936)
DELTA SPECIALTIES INC
1250 S Wilson Way Ste C1, Stockton (95205-7057)
PHONE.................................209 937-9650
Tanya Watters, *President*
Robert Couillard, *Treasurer*
Gene Watters, *Vice Pres*
EMP: 15 EST: 2008
SALES (est): 3.6MM **Privately Held**
WEB: www.deltaspecialties.net
SIC: **1793** 2452 Glass & glazing work; prefabricated wood buildings

(P-1937)
HORIZON CONTRACT GLAZING INC
Also Called: Horizon Glass Company
1200 Triangle Ct, West Sacramento (95605-2343)
PHONE.................................916 373-9900
John Shurnas, *President*
Michelle Klein, *Corp Secy*
Debbie Shurnas, *Vice Pres*
Justin Tinsley, *Superintendent*
EMP: 45 EST: 1978
SQ FT: 21,000
SALES (est): 8.3MM **Privately Held**
WEB: www.horizonglass.com
SIC: **1793** Glass & glazing work

(P-1938)
MONTEZ GLASS INC
7571 14th Ave, Sacramento (95820-3555)
PHONE.................................916 452-1288
Tony Montez, *Principal*
Sue Montez, *Vice Pres*
▲ EMP: 42 EST: 1992
SQ FT: 13,000
SALES (est): 3.2MM **Privately Held**
WEB: www.montezglass.com
SIC: **1793** Glass & glazing work

(P-1939)
NATIONAL GLASS SYSTEMS INC
Also Called: Architctral Coml Glzing Alum P
4778 Gertrude Dr, Fremont (94536-7321)
PHONE.................................408 835-5124
Octavio Martinez, *CEO*
EMP: 23 EST: 2019
SALES (est): 3.3MM **Privately Held**
SIC: **1793** 1761 1799 3446 Glass & glazing work; skylight installation; architectural sheet metal work; glass tinting, architectural or automotive; architectural metalwork

(P-1940)
PROGRESS GLASS CO INC (PA)
25 Patterson St, San Francisco (94124-1377)
PHONE.................................415 824-7040
Tom Burkard, *CEO*
Chuck Burkard, *President*
Thomas C Burkard III, *President*
Shirley Wallace, *Treasurer*
Jim Holmberg, *Senior VP*
▲ EMP: 105 EST: 1956
SQ FT: 16,250
SALES (est): 17.9MM **Privately Held**
WEB: www.progressglass.com
SIC: **1793** Glass & glazing work

PRODUCTS & SERVICES SECTION
1794 - Excavating & Grading Work County (P-1964)

(P-1941)
ROYAL GLASS COMPANY INC
3200 De La Cruz Blvd, Santa Clara (95054-2602)
PHONE..................408 969-0444
John Maggiore, *CEO*
Chris Gerber, *COO*
James Maggiore, *Vice Pres*
Julius Esposito, *Project Mgr*
Steve Kilekas, *Sr Project Mgr*
▲ **EMP:** 80
SALES (est): 22.6MM **Privately Held**
WEB: www.royalglassinc.com
SIC: 1793 Glass & glazing work

(P-1942)
SAFECO DOOR & HARDWARE INC
Also Called: Safeco Glass
31054 San Antonio St, Hayward (94544-7904)
PHONE..................510 429-4768
Mahboubeh Ahmadi, *President*
Sina Ahmadi, *COO*
Milagors Missaghi, *Treasurer*
Ali Missaghi Akoub, *Vice Pres*
Hamid Ahmadi, *Admin Sec*
EMP: 65 **EST:** 2001
SQ FT: 13,000
SALES (est): 8.2MM **Privately Held**
SIC: 1793 Glass & glazing work

(P-1943)
SAN JOAQUIN GLASS INC
2150 E Mckinley Ave, Fresno (93703-3089)
PHONE..................559 268-7646
Steven M Salcedo, *President*
Wanda Salcedo, *CFO*
EMP: 40 **EST:** 2007
SQ FT: 15,000
SALES (est): 3.9MM **Privately Held**
WEB: www.sjglass.com
SIC: 1793 Glass & glazing work

(P-1944)
SILICON VALLEY GLASS INC (PA)
18695 Madrone Pkwy, Morgan Hill (95037-2868)
PHONE..................408 778-7786
Linda Goyette, *CEO*
Gregg Goyette, *President*
Audrey Morse, *Project Mgr*
Anthony Centeno, *Project Engr*
▲ **EMP:** 47 **EST:** 1997
SALES (est): 12.6MM **Privately Held**
WEB: www.siliconvalleyglass.com
SIC: 1793 Glass & glazing work

(P-1945)
SOUTH BAY SHOWERS INC
Also Called: Shower Glass & Mirror Co
540 Martin Ave, Santa Clara (95050-2954)
PHONE..................408 988-3484
Ron Ebel, *President*
Susan Ebel, *Treasurer*
Bob Sutton, *Vice Pres*
Helen Sutton, *Admin Sec*
▲ **EMP:** 25 **EST:** 1970
SQ FT: 15,800
SALES (est): 4.8MM **Privately Held**
WEB: www.southbayshowers.com
SIC: 1793 5039 5231 3231 Glass & glazing work; glass construction materials; glass; products of purchased glass

(P-1946)
US GLASS INC
Also Called: USG
1745 Enterprise Blvd, West Sacramento (95691-3457)
PHONE..................916 376-8801
Mark R Dutrow, *CEO*
Alex Dorokhin, *Project Engr*
EMP: 36 **EST:** 2004
SALES (est): 5MM **Privately Held**
WEB: www.usglassco.com
SIC: 1793 Glass & glazing work

(P-1947)
V B GLASS CO INC
Also Called: Banks Glass
10002 Victoria Way, Jamestown (95327-9700)
P.O. Box 657 (95327-0657)
PHONE..................209 984-4111
Mark Banks, *President*
John Banks, *Admin Sec*
Hause Banks, *Project Mgr*
Kathi Banks, *Human Res Mgr*
Nikki Hiemstra, *Consultant*
EMP: 40 **EST:** 1963
SQ FT: 15,000
SALES (est): 5.3MM **Privately Held**
WEB: www.banksglass.com
SIC: 1793 Glass & glazing work

(P-1948)
WALTERS & WOLF GLASS COMPANY (PA)
Also Called: Walter & Wolf
41450 Boscell Rd, Fremont (94538-3103)
PHONE..................510 490-1115
Randall A Wolf, *President*
Tom Black, *COO*
Nick Koselj, *COO*
Jeff Belzer, *CFO*
Nick Kocelj, *Vice Pres*
▲ **EMP:** 135 **EST:** 1977
SALES (est): 85.1MM **Privately Held**
WEB: www.waltersandwolf.com
SIC: 1793 Glass & glazing work

1794 Excavating & Grading Work

(P-1949)
A J EXCAVATION INC
Also Called: American Fencing
514 N Brawley Ave, Fresno (93706-1014)
PHONE..................559 408-5908
Alisa Emmett, *President*
Greg Stenger, *Manager*
EMP: 150 **EST:** 2009
SALES (est): 20.2MM **Privately Held**
WEB: www.movendirt.com
SIC: 1794 Excavation work

(P-1950)
ANDREW M JORDAN INC
Also Called: A & B Construction
1350 4th St, Berkeley (94710-1349)
PHONE..................510 999-6000
Andrew M Jordan, *President*
Rami Khoury, *Project Mgr*
Alan Sau, *Project Engr*
Oswaldo Torres, *Foreman/Supr*
Christopher Conner, *Sr Project Mgr*
EMP: 90 **EST:** 1991
SQ FT: 1,000
SALES (est): 30MM **Privately Held**
WEB: www.a-bconstruction.net
SIC: 1794 Excavation & grading, building construction

(P-1951)
BAY CITIES PAV & GRADING INC
1450 Civic Ct Ste 400, Concord (94520-7950)
PHONE..................925 687-6666
Ben L Rodriguez, *CEO*
Marlo Manqueros, *Vice Pres*
Kim Rodriguez, *Admin Sec*
Adrian Calderon, *Project Engr*
Saul Gonzaga, *Project Engr*
EMP: 250
SQ FT: 4,000
SALES (est): 61.7MM **Privately Held**
WEB: www.baycities.us
SIC: 1794 1611 7353 Excavation work; highway & street construction; earth moving equipment, rental or leasing

(P-1952)
CARONE & COMPANY INC
Also Called: Diablo Valley Rock
5009 Forni Dr Ste A, Concord (94520-8525)
PHONE..................925 602-8800
Richard Lloyd Carone, *President*
EMP: 60 **EST:** 1998
SQ FT: 48,000
SALES (est): 13.1MM **Privately Held**
WEB: www.caroneandcompany.com
SIC: 1794 Excavation work

(P-1953)
CLYDE NED CONSTRUCTION INC
159 Mason Cir, Concord (94520-1213)
PHONE..................925 689-5411
Myron Hagen, *Ch of Bd*
Sally Baer, *Treasurer*
Carolee Broby, *Vice Pres*
Jon Hagen, *Project Engr*
Dwight Hansen, *Supervisor*
EMP: 38 **EST:** 1981
SQ FT: 10,080 **Privately Held**
WEB: www.nedclydeconstruction.com
SIC: 1794 Excavation work

(P-1954)
COOK GENERAL ENGINEERING INC
Also Called: Cook Engineering
3203 Fitzgerald Rd, Rancho Cordova (95742-6813)
PHONE..................916 631-1365
Sean P Cook, *President*
Michelle Cook, *Admin Sec*
Shawn Scott, *Project Mgr*
Shellie Cook, *Marketing Staff*
Lester Gustafson, *Manager*
EMP: 35 **EST:** 2002
SQ FT: 4,800
SALES (est): 25.9MM **Privately Held**
WEB: www.cookengineeringinc.com
SIC: 1794 Excavation & grading, building construction

(P-1955)
DIRT MOVERS
1930 W Fremont St, Stockton (95203-2041)
PHONE..................209 461-7111
John McDaniel, *Owner*
EMP: 47 **EST:** 1991
SALES (est): 1.7MM **Privately Held**
WEB: www.dirtmoversca.com
SIC: 1794 Excavation & grading, building construction

(P-1956)
DUDLEYS EXCAVATING INC
209 San Benito Ave, Gerber (96035-2135)
P.O. Box 901 (96035-0901)
PHONE..................530 385-1445
Mike Dudley, *President*
Scott Dudley, *Vice Pres*
Kammi Reynolds, *Admin Sec*
Kenneth Dudley, *Director*
EMP: 35
SQ FT: 10,000
SALES: 5.3MM **Privately Held**
WEB: www.dudleysexcavatinginc.com
SIC: 1794 Excavation & grading, building construction

(P-1957)
DURAN & VENABLES INC
748 S Hillview Dr, Milpitas (95035-5455)
PHONE..................408 741-9883
Marchand D B Venables, *President*
Mark Petersen, *Corp Secy*
Mark Peterson, *Vice Pres*
Mike Stogner, *Project Mgr*
Todd Truong, *Project Mgr*
EMP: 45 **EST:** 1978
SQ FT: 2,000
SALES (est): 12.3MM **Privately Held**
WEB: www.duran-venables.com
SIC: 1794 1611 Excavation & grading, building construction; surfacing & paving

(P-1958)
EMERALD SITE SERVICES INC
9190 Jackson Rd, Sacramento (95826-9709)
PHONE..................916 685-7211
Kaycie Edwards, *President*
Mark Edwards, *Treasurer*
Austin Edwards, *Admin Sec*
Coleen Cortiz, *Controller*
Art Estrada, *Superintendent*
EMP: 55 **EST:** 2011
SALES (est): 9.5MM **Privately Held**
WEB: www.emeraldss.com
SIC: 1794 1796 0782 Excavation & grading, building construction; pollution control equipment installation; garden maintenance services; turf installation services, except artificial; highway lawn & garden maintenance services

(P-1959)
G AND L BROCK CNSTR CO INC
4145 Calloway Ct, Stockton (95215-2400)
PHONE..................209 931-3626
Lynne Brock, *President*
Gary Brock, *Vice Pres*
EMP: 50 **EST:** 1979
SQ FT: 5,800
SALES (est): 8.4MM **Privately Held**
WEB: www.brockconstruction.com
SIC: 1794 Excavation & grading, building construction

(P-1960)
GALLAGHER PROPERTIES INC (PA)
344 High St, Oakland (94601-3902)
P.O. Box 779, Lafayette (94549-0779)
PHONE..................510 261-0466
Allen McKeen, *Vice Pres*
Denise Barger, *Admin Sec*
EMP: 25 **EST:** 1946
SQ FT: 20,000
SALES (est): 7.5MM **Privately Held**
WEB: www.gallagherandburk.com
SIC: 1794 1611 2951 1771 Excavation & grading, building construction; highway & street construction; asphalt paving mixtures & blocks; concrete work

(P-1961)
GHILOTTI BROS INC
Also Called: Concrete Craft
525 Jacoby St, San Rafael (94901-5370)
PHONE..................415 454-7011
Michael Ghilotti, *CEO*
Michael M Ghilotti, *President*
Dante W Ghilotti, *CEO*
Daniel Y Chin, *CFO*
Thomas G Barr, *Vice Pres*
▲ **EMP:** 290 **EST:** 1914
SQ FT: 86,249
SALES (est): 67.9MM **Privately Held**
WEB: www.ghilottibros.com
SIC: 1794 1623 1771 1611 Excavation work; water, sewer & utility lines; concrete work; highway & street construction

(P-1962)
HUDSON EXCAVATION INC
570 Valdry Ct Ste C10, Brentwood (94513-4053)
P.O. Box 1208 (94513-3208)
PHONE..................925 250-1990
Steve Hudson, *President*
EMP: 40 **EST:** 2014
SALES (est): 5.2MM **Privately Held**
SIC: 1794 Excavation work

(P-1963)
LUPTON EXCAVATION INC
8467 Florin Rd, Sacramento (95828-2512)
PHONE..................916 387-1104
Kenneth Lupton Jr, *President*
EMP: 75 **EST:** 1987
SQ FT: 4,000
SALES (est): 11MM **Privately Held**
WEB: www.luptonexcavation.com
SIC: 1794 Excavation & grading, building construction

(P-1964)
MACHADO BACKHOE INC
22332 Third Ave, Stevinson (95374-9745)
PHONE..................209 634-4836
Daniel Machado, *President*
Natalie Pires, *CFO*
Corinne Machado, *Vice Pres*
Natalie Machado, *Manager*
EMP: 25 **EST:** 1971
SQ FT: 1,100
SALES (est): 4.8MM **Privately Held**
WEB: www.machadobackhoe.com
SIC: 1794 3272 Excavation & grading, building construction; solid containing units, concrete; meter boxes, concrete

1794 - Excavating & Grading Work

(P-1965)
MEYERS EARTHWORK INC
4150 Fig Tree Ln, Redding (96002-9315)
P.O. Box 493730 (96049-3730)
PHONE.................530 365-8858
Jacob Meyers, *President*
Charleen Meyers, *Vice Pres*
▼ **EMP:** 55 **EST:** 1990
SQ FT: 2,000
SALES (est): 8.8MM Privately Held
WEB: www.titanmeyers.com
SIC: 1794 Excavation & grading, building construction

(P-1966)
MITCHELL ENGINEERING
1395 Evans Ave, San Francisco (94124-1703)
P.O. Box 880308 (94188-0308)
PHONE.................415 227-1040
Michael A Silva, *President*
Curtis F Mitchell, *Vice Pres*
Thelma Welch, *Manager*
▲ **EMP:** 50 **EST:** 1998
SQ FT: 2,000
SALES (est): 14.2MM Privately Held
WEB: www.mitchell-engineering.com
SIC: 1794 1623 1622 1629 Excavation & grading, building construction; water main construction; pipeline construction; bridge, tunnel & elevated highway; railroad & subway construction

(P-1967)
MOZINGO CONSTRUCTION INC
751 Wakefield Ct, Oakdale (95361-7761)
PHONE.................209 848-0160
Kurtis Mozingo, *CEO*
Doni Mozingo, *President*
Michael Freeman, *Vice Pres*
Mike Freeman, *Vice Pres*
Phil Gianfortone, *Vice Pres*
EMP: 50 **EST:** 1990
SALES (est): 25.2MM Privately Held
WEB: www.mozingoconstruction.com
SIC: 1794 Excavation work

(P-1968)
NORTHWEST GENERAL ENGINEERING
5492 Old Redwood Hwy, Santa Rosa (95403-1231)
P.O. Box 11099 (95406-1099)
PHONE.................707 579-1163
Kevin Holtzinger, *President*
Janelle H Holtzinger, *Purch Mgr*
Jason Holtzinger, *Opers Mgr*
Ted Couture, *Manager*
EMP: 83 **EST:** 2000
SALES (est): 12.5MM Privately Held
WEB: www.nwgen.com
SIC: 1794 Excavation & grading, building construction

(P-1969)
O NELSON & SON INC
Also Called: O Nelson & Son
3345 Tripp Rd, Woodside (94062-3631)
PHONE.................650 851-3600
Harold Nelson, *CEO*
EMP: 36 **EST:** 1950
SQ FT: 2,000
SALES (est): 2.5MM Privately Held
SIC: 1794 Excavation & grading, building construction

(P-1970)
PACIFIC GOLD MARKETING INC
745 Broadway St, Fresno (93721-2807)
PHONE.................559 272-8168
Sarah Woolf, *CEO*
Lawrence Clark, *Treasurer*
Andrew Clark, *Admin Sec*
Molly Jones, *Admin Sec*
Tish Hopkins, *Administration*
EMP: 35 **EST:** 1990
SQ FT: 9,400
SALES: 10.5MM Privately Held
WEB: www.pgmpower.com
SIC: 1794 1623 8711 3271 Excavation & grading, building construction; water & sewer line construction; pumping station construction; civil engineering; paving blocks, concrete

(P-1971)
PARMETER LOGGING AND EXCAV INC
6040 Cazadero Hwy, Cazadero (95421-9513)
P.O. Box 128 (95421-0128)
PHONE.................707 632-5610
Steven Parmeter, *President*
Dana Radtkey, *Treasurer*
Kenneth Parmeter, *Vice Pres*
Harriet Parmeter, *Admin Sec*
EMP: 29 **EST:** 1979
SQ FT: 5,400
SALES (est): 2.4MM Privately Held
WEB: www.parmeterlogging.com
SIC: 1794 2411 Excavation & grading, building construction; logging

(P-1972)
R & J JOY INC
Also Called: Joy Engineering
190 Industrial Way, Portola (96129-1070)
PHONE.................530 832-4435
Richard L Joy Jr, *President*
EMP: 42 **EST:** 1979
SQ FT: 1,500
SALES (est): 3.3MM Privately Held
SIC: 1794 1611 Excavation work; highway & street paving contractor

(P-1973)
R V STICH CONSTRUCTION INC
769 S 13th St, Richmond (94804-3706)
P.O. Box 1707 (94802-0707)
PHONE.................510 412-9070
Rocky J G Stich, *President*
Angela Stich, *Corp Secy*
Ana Carvalho, *Accountant*
EMP: 40 **EST:** 1973
SQ FT: 3,000
SALES (est): 9.3MM Privately Held
WEB: www.rvstich.com
SIC: 1794 1542 Excavation & grading, building construction; commercial & office building, new construction

(P-1974)
SCHNABEL FOUNDATION COMPANY
3075 Citrus Cir Ste 150, Walnut Creek (94598-2670)
PHONE.................925 947-1881
Ronald K Chapman, *Branch Mgr*
John Macy, *Superintendent*
EMP: 81
SALES (corp-wide): 75.9MM Privately Held
WEB: www.schnabel.com
SIC: 1794 1771 1741 Excavation & grading, building construction; foundation & footing contractor; foundation building
PA: Schnabel Foundation Company Inc
45240 Business Ct Ste 250
Sterling VA 20166
703 742-0020

(P-1975)
SWAN ENGINEERING INC
4470 Yankee Hill Rd # 130, Rocklin (95677-1630)
PHONE.................916 474-5299
Justin Swanson, *President*
Anna Aslin, *Project Mgr*
Michael Niederhuth, *Controller*
Jon Fulton, *Foreman/Supr*
John Bravo, *Superintendent*
EMP: 54 **EST:** 2010
SALES (est): 9.8MM Privately Held
WEB: www.swaneng inc.com
SIC: 1794 1623 1611 Excavation & grading, building construction; water & sewer line construction; telephone & communication line construction; gravel or dirt road construction

(P-1976)
WC MALONEY INC
4020 Newton Rd, Stockton (95205-2425)
P.O. Box 30326 (95213-0326)
PHONE.................209 942-1129
Curt Maloney, *President*
Amy Campbell, *Office Mgr*
Glenn Sweesy, *Admin Sec*
Eric Edsberg, *Safety Mgr*
EMP: 40 **EST:** 1995
SALES (est): 9.1MM Privately Held
WEB: www.wcmaloney.com
SIC: 1794 Excavation & grading, building construction

1795 Wrecking & Demolition Work

(P-1977)
ALARCON BOHM CORP
5301 Adeline St, Oakland (94608-3107)
P.O. Box 24301 (94623-1301)
PHONE.................510 893-4405
Kevin J Bohm, *President*
Patty Chu, *CFO*
Denise McGuire, *Office Mgr*
EMP: 60 **EST:** 1993
SQ FT: 15,000
SALES (est): 8.6MM Privately Held
WEB: www.alarconbohm.com
SIC: 1795 Wrecking & demolition work

(P-1978)
ALW ENTERPRISES INC
8727 W Herndon Ave, Fresno (93723-9303)
P.O. Box 12163 (93776-2163)
PHONE.................559 275-2828
Timothy H Weaver, *CEO*
EMP: 35
SALES (est): 5.3MM Privately Held
WEB: www.alwenterprisesinc.com
SIC: 1795 Demolition, buildings & other structures

(P-1979)
BAYVIEW DEMOLITION SVCS INC
6925 San Leandro St, Oakland (94621-3320)
PHONE.................510 544-5270
Marvin Henderson, *CEO*
Richard Cleveland, *Principal*
John McCarthy, *Opers Staff*
Dave Davis, *Manager*
EMP: 40 **EST:** 1999
SALES: 17.7MM Privately Held
WEB: www.bayviewservices.com
SIC: 1795 Demolition, buildings & other structures
PA: Bayview Services, Inc.
6925 San Leandro St
Oakland CA 94621

(P-1980)
BAYVIEW SERVICES INC (PA)
6925 San Leandro St, Oakland (94621-3320)
PHONE.................510 562-6181
Marvin Henderson, *CEO*
Lance Cleveland, *CFO*
Richard Cleveland, *Treasurer*
Kayla Knight, *Admin Mgr*
Austin Viramontes, *Admin Sec*
EMP: 50 **EST:** 1996
SALES: 56.7MM Privately Held
WEB: www.bayviewservices.com
SIC: 1795 1542 4959 1799 Demolition, buildings & other structures; commercial & office building contractors; toxic or hazardous waste cleanup; asbestos removal & encapsulation

(P-1981)
BLUEWATER ENVMTL SVCS INC
2075 Williams St, San Leandro (94577-2305)
PHONE.................510 346-8800
Chris J Kirschenheuter, *CEO*
Todd Kirschenheuter, *Vice Pres*
Kelly Mestas-Boot, *Administration*
Humberto Navarro, *Project Mgr*
Ron Drummond, *Purchasing*
EMP: 100 **EST:** 1991
SQ FT: 15,000
SALES (est): 16.7MM Privately Held
WEB: www.bwserv.com
SIC: 1795 Demolition, buildings & other structures

(P-1982)
CAMPANELLA CORPORATION
2216 Dunn Rd, Hayward (94545-2206)
PHONE.................510 536-4800
Mike Campanella, *President*
Mike Littlefield, *Vice Pres*
Dan Ray, *Manager*
▲ **EMP:** 40 **EST:** 1997
SALES (est): 7.1MM Privately Held
WEB: www.campanellacorporation.com
SIC: 1795 Demolition, buildings & other structures

(P-1983)
CLEVELAND WRECKING COMPANY
1580 Chabot Ct, Hayward (94545-2423)
PHONE.................510 674-2600
EMP: 2099
SALES (corp-wide): 13.2B Publicly Held
SIC: 1795 Demolition, buildings & other structures
HQ: Cleveland Wrecking Company
999 W Town And Country Rd
Orange CA 92868
626 967-4287

(P-1984)
DAVID KNOTT INC
Also Called: Dki
4711 N Blythe Ave, Fresno (93722-3976)
PHONE.................559 449-8935
EMP: 35
SALES (est): 533.3K Privately Held
WEB: www.davidknottinc.com
SIC: 1795 Wrecking/Demolition Contractor

(P-1985)
FERMA CORPORATION
6655 Smith Ave Ste A, Newark (94560-4219)
PHONE.................510 794-0414
Rob Verga, *Manager*
Kris Bradshaw, *Accounting Mgr*
Linda Ells, *Accounting Mgr*
Mike Duffy, *Business Mgr*
Dan Silverman, *Purch Mgr*
EMP: 180
SALES (corp-wide): 40MM Privately Held
WEB: www.fermacorp.com
SIC: 1795 Demolition, buildings & other structures
PA: Ferma Corporation
6639 Smith Ave
Newark CA 94560
650 961-2742

(P-1986)
FISK DEMOLITION INC (PA)
8507 Goggin St, Valley Springs (95252-9116)
P.O. Box 802 (95252-0802)
PHONE.................209 323-8999
Harold J Fisk, *President*
EMP: 38 **EST:** 2007
SALES (est): 1MM Privately Held
WEB: www.parked.nichebuilder.com
SIC: 1795 Wrecking & demolition work

(P-1987)
KROEKER INC
4627 S Chestnut Ave, Fresno (93725-9238)
PHONE.................559 237-3764
Joyce Kroeker, *President*
Jeff Kroeker, *Corp Secy*
Ed Kroeker, *Vice Pres*
Rodney Ainsworth, *General Mgr*
John Ramirez, *Office Mgr*
EMP: 120 **EST:** 1991
SQ FT: 9,000
SALES (est): 47.8MM Privately Held
WEB: www.kroekerinc.com
SIC: 1795 1629 4953 Demolition, buildings & other structures; land reclamation; earthmoving contractor; recycling, waste materials

(P-1988)
SILVERADO CONTRACTORS INC (PA)
2855 Mandela Pkwy Fl 2, Oakland (94608-4050)
PHONE.................510 658-9960

Joseph M Capriola, *President*
Sue Capriola, *Treasurer*
Peter Knutch, *Vice Pres*
Richard Riggs, *Vice Pres*
EMP: 64 **EST:** 2000
SALES (est): 26.4MM **Privately Held**
WEB: www.silveradocontractors.com
SIC: 1795 Demolition, buildings & other structures

(P-1989)
STOMPER CO INC
3135 Diablo Ave, Hayward (94545-2701)
PHONE....................510 574-0570
Donna R Rehrmann, *President*
George Rehrmann, *Vice Pres*
EMP: 60 **EST:** 1968
SQ FT: 15,000
SALES (est): 8.9MM **Privately Held**
WEB: www.stompercompany.com
SIC: 1795 Demolition, buildings & other structures

(P-1990)
TWO RIVERS DEMOLITION INC
2620 Mercantile Dr 100, Rancho Cordova (95742-6519)
PHONE....................916 638-6775
W Roderick Palon, *President*
EMP: 55 **EST:** 1996
SALES (est): 10.6MM **Privately Held**
WEB: www.demolition.global
SIC: 1795 Demolition, buildings & other structures; concrete breaking for streets & highways

1796 Installation Or Erection Of Bldg Eqpt & Machinery, NEC

(P-1991)
CASCADE FILTRATION INC
Also Called: Pneumatic Conveying & Mfg Pcm
205 Kimball Rd, Red Bluff (96080-4458)
P.O. Box 1068 (96080-1068)
PHONE....................530 529-1212
Brian Spina, *President*
Katheen Axtelo, *Admin Sec*
EMP: 38 **EST:** 1997
SQ FT: 6,000
SALES (est): 1.7MM **Privately Held**
SIC: 1796 Installing building equipment

(P-1992)
HMI INDUSTRIAL CONTRACTORS INC
3899 Security Park Dr, Rancho Cordova (95742-6920)
PHONE....................916 386-2586
Ruth Gilman, *CEO*
Don Gilman, *Vice Pres*
Jonathan Reimer, *Foreman/Supr*
Dion Henke, *Superintendent*
EMP: 62 **EST:** 1992
SQ FT: 37,000
SALES (est): 15MM **Privately Held**
WEB: www.hmiindustrial.com
SIC: 1796 Millwright

(P-1993)
S & J ROYAL INC
2599 Reed Rd, Yuba City (95993-9244)
P.O. Box 3537 (95992-3537)
PHONE....................530 682-5861
Harmon Thiara, *CEO*
Sarbjit Thiara, *President*
EMP: 42 **EST:** 2005
SALES (est): 3.2MM **Privately Held**
SIC: 1796 Installing building equipment

(P-1994)
TK ELEVATOR CORPORATION
940 Riverside Pkwy Ste 20, West Sacramento (95605-1513)
PHONE....................916 376-8700
Guy Buckman, *Branch Mgr*
Scott Hopkinson, *Manager*
EMP: 40

SALES (corp-wide): 1B **Privately Held**
WEB: www.tkelevator.com
SIC: 1796 7699 Elevator installation & conversion; elevators: inspection, service & repair
HQ: Tk Elevator Corporation
11605 Haynes Bridge Rd
Alpharetta GA 30009
678 319-3240

(P-1995)
TRANSBAY FIRE PROTECTION INC (PA)
2182 Rheem Dr, Pleasanton (94588-2796)
PHONE....................925 846-9484
Charlie Marlin, *President*
Julie Schmidt, *CFO*
Nicholas Balaban, *Design Engr*
William Haley, *Design Engr*
Linda Bozsum, *Technology*
▲ **EMP:** 50 **EST:** 1988
SQ FT: 17,000
SALES (est): 9.7MM **Privately Held**
WEB: www.transbayfire.com
SIC: 1796 7389 Installing building equipment; safety inspection service

1799 Special Trade Contractors, NEC

(P-1996)
1ST LIGHT ENERGY INC (PA)
1869 Moffat Blvd, Manteca (95336-8944)
PHONE....................209 824-5500
Justin Krum, *CEO*
Gregory Smith, *CFO*
Zhen Han, *Officer*
Jaime Robles, *CIO*
Nikki Mendoza, *Project Mgr*
EMP: 50 **EST:** 2005
SQ FT: 6,300
SALES (est): 36.8MM **Privately Held**
WEB: www.1stle.com
SIC: 1799 1711 Hydraulic equipment, installation & service; solar energy contractor

(P-1997)
AHLBORN FENCE & STEEL INC (PA)
Also Called: Ahlborn Companies
1230 Century Ct, Santa Rosa (95403-1042)
PHONE....................707 573-0742
Thomas C Ahlborn, *CEO*
Cathy Ahlborn, *Admin Sec*
Jim Ahlborn, *Project Mgr*
Pete Wilhelmsen, *Project Mgr*
Bruce Ahlgren, *Opers Staff*
EMP: 22 **EST:** 1991
SQ FT: 20,000
SALES (est): 6MM **Privately Held**
WEB: www.ahlbornfence.com
SIC: 1799 3449 3493 Fence construction; miscellaneous metalwork; steel springs, except wire

(P-1998)
AIR & LUBE SYSTEMS INC (PA)
8353 Demetre Ave, Sacramento (95828-0920)
PHONE....................916 381-5588
Michael Bewsey, *President*
Dennis Thomsen, *Vice Pres*
Penny Hartnett, *Administration*
Roman Fursov, *Technology*
Lisa Greene, *Controller*
▲ **EMP:** 40 **EST:** 1997
SQ FT: 24,000
SALES (est): 10MM **Privately Held**
WEB: www.airandlube.com
SIC: 1799 Service station equipment installation & maintenance

(P-1999)
AIR BLOWN CONCRETE
Also Called: Air Blown Concrete & Ready Mix
601 W Delano St, Elverta (95626-9221)
P.O. Box 99 (95626-0099)
PHONE....................916 991-1738
Paul Richard Holzmeister, *President*
Sandi Holzmeister, *Admin Sec*
EMP: 40 **EST:** 1960
SQ FT: 9,000

SALES (est): 4.8MM **Privately Held**
SIC: 1799 Swimming pool construction

(P-2000)
ALL AMERICAN FENCE CORPORATION
568 Mcgraw Ave, Livermore (94551-9665)
P.O. Box 3057, Danville (94526-8057)
PHONE....................925 275-5110
Fran Myers, *President*
Bill Myers, *Vice Pres*
EMP: 40 **EST:** 1988
SQ FT: 1,500
SALES (est): 5.9MM **Privately Held**
WEB: www.allamericanfencecorp.com
SIC: 1799 Fence construction

(P-2001)
ALL FENCE COMPANY INC
1900 Spring St, Redwood City (94063-2410)
PHONE....................650 369-4556
Martin A Webster, *President*
Charles Soulard, *Corp Secy*
Peter Kaine, *Vice Pres*
EMP: 35 **EST:** 1994
SQ FT: 10,000 **Privately Held**
WEB: www.buildallfences.com
SIC: 1799 Fence construction

(P-2002)
AMERICAN SYNRGY ASB RMVAL SVCS
Also Called: Synergy Environmental
28436 Satellite St, Hayward (94545-4863)
PHONE....................510 444-2333
David C Clark, *President*
Price Doug, *Manager*
Douglas Price, *Manager*
EMP: 37 **EST:** 1987
SQ FT: 6,000
SALES (est): 2.5MM **Privately Held**
WEB: www.synergycompanies.com
SIC: 1799 Asbestos removal & encapsulation

(P-2003)
ANDRIAN
Also Called: Stations
1935 Lundy Ave, San Jose (95131-1848)
PHONE....................408 434-0730
Andrew Lanier, *President*
Brian Fajardo, *CEO*
Flo Pacheco, *Office Mgr*
Steven Garnica, *Supervisor*
EMP: 50 **EST:** 1997
SQ FT: 11,000
SALES (est): 19.8MM **Privately Held**
WEB: www.gostations.com
SIC: 1799 Office furniture installation

(P-2004)
APEX FENCE CO INC
19896 Alexander Ave, Anderson (96007-4900)
P.O. Box 545 (96007-0545)
PHONE....................530 365-3316
David Parmer, *President*
EMP: 35 **EST:** 1970
SQ FT: 1,500
SALES: 8.9MM **Privately Held**
WEB: www.apexfencecompany.com
SIC: 1799 Fence construction

(P-2005)
AQUA GUNITE INC
5830 S Naylor Rd, Livermore (94551-8308)
PHONE....................408 271-2782
Jose G Aguayo, *CEO*
Fargio Garcia, *Vice Pres*
EMP: 50 **EST:** 2006
SQ FT: 2,120
SALES (est): 9.8MM **Privately Held**
WEB: www.aquagunite.com
SIC: 1799 Swimming pool construction

(P-2006)
ASBESTOS MGT GROUP OF CAL
3438 Helen St, Oakland (94608-4030)
PHONE....................510 654-8441
Brent Bates, *President*
Michelle Fong, *Human Res Mgr*
Jennifer Bates, *Marketing Mgr*
EMP: 35 **EST:** 1989

SALES (est): 5.7MM **Privately Held**
WEB: www.amgofca.com
SIC: 1799 1795 Asbestos removal & encapsulation; wrecking & demolition work

(P-2007)
ATI RESTORATION LLC
Also Called: American Restoration Services
25000 Industrial Blvd, Hayward (94545-2349)
PHONE....................510 429-5000
Toll Free:....................888 -
Kyle Picket, *Manager*
Bianca Mollo, *Partner*
Grant Wassall, *Vice Pres*
Brittany Deboer, *Executive*
Julie Marcus, *Office Mgr*
EMP: 60 **Privately Held**
WEB: www.atirestoration.com
SIC: 1799 Antenna installation
PA: Ati Restoration, Llc
3360 E La Palma Ave
Anaheim CA 92806

(P-2008)
BAILEY FENCE COMPANY INC
3205 Baumberg Ct, Hayward (94545-4400)
PHONE....................510 538-1175
Karrick Bailey, *President*
Benjamin Gleichner, *CFO*
Kent Bailey, *Vice Pres*
EMP: 35 **EST:** 1984
SQ FT: 100,000
SALES (est): 6.8MM **Privately Held**
WEB: www.baileyfenceco.com
SIC: 1799 5211 5039 Fence construction; fencing; wire fence, gates & accessories

(P-2009)
BAY AREA INSTALLATIONS INC (PA)
2481 Verna Ct, San Leandro (94577-4222)
PHONE....................510 895-8196
Thomas Clark Mohamed, *President*
Herman B Chibnick, *Vice Pres*
Alta Clark, *Admin Sec*
Tom Mohamed, *Accounting Mgr*
▲ **EMP:** 53 **EST:** 1983
SQ FT: 25,000
SALES (est): 8.7MM **Privately Held**
WEB: www.baiinc.com
SIC: 1799 4212 Demountable partition installation; office furniture installation; delivery service, vehicular

(P-2010)
BAYVIEW ENVIRONMENTAL SVCS INC
6925 San Leandro St, Oakland (94621-3320)
PHONE....................510 562-6181
Marvin Henderson, *CEO*
Lance Cleveland, *CFO*
Richard Cleveland, *Treasurer*
Austin Viramontes, *Admin Sec*
Darrell Dj Knight, *Manager*
EMP: 225 **EST:** 1993
SQ FT: 12,000
SALES: 38.1MM **Privately Held**
WEB: www.bayviewservices.com
SIC: 1799 4212 4959 Asbestos removal & encapsulation; hazardous waste transport; toxic or hazardous waste cleanup
PA: Bayview Services, Inc.
6925 San Leandro St
Oakland CA 94621

(P-2011)
BRETT LEE WOMACK (PA)
Also Called: Almanor Dock Supply
461 Firehouse Rd, Westwood (96137-9521)
PHONE....................530 596-3358
Brett Lee Womack, *Owner*
EMP: 35 **EST:** 1967
SQ FT: 1,000
SALES (est): 4.2MM **Privately Held**
SIC: 1799 1521 Dock equipment installation, industrial; single-family housing construction

1799 - Special Trade Contractors, NEC County (P-2012)

(P-2012)
BURDICK PAINTING
705 Nuttman St, Santa Clara (95054-2623)
PHONE...............................408 567-1330
John C Cintas, *CEO*
Robbie Starks, *Project Mgr*
EMP: 67 **EST:** 1967
SQ FT: 8,000
SALES (est): 14MM **Privately Held**
WEB: www.burdickpainting.com
SIC: 1799 1721 Paint & wallpaper stripping; coating, caulking & weather, water & fireproofing; coating of concrete structures with plastic; coating of metal structures at construction site; commercial painting

(P-2013)
C E TOLAND & SON
5300 Industrial Way, Benicia (94510-1025)
PHONE...............................707 747-1000
Clyde E Toland Jr, *Ch of Bd*
Blake Toland, *President*
Jeanette Vaiana, *Executive*
Ted Toland, *General Mgr*
Lisa Castro, *Human Res Mgr*
▲ **EMP:** 120 **EST:** 1942
SQ FT: 90,000
SALES (est): 25.2MM **Privately Held**
WEB: www.cetoland.com
SIC: 1799 Ornamental metal work

(P-2014)
CALIFORNIA CLOSET COMPANY INC (DH)
1414 Harbour Way S, Richmond (94804-3694)
PHONE...............................510 763-2033
Bill Barton, *CEO*
Jonathan Louie, *CFO*
Samara Toole, *Chief Mktg Ofcr*
Carol Summersgill, *Senior VP*
Jill Larue, *Vice Pres*
EMP: 40 **EST:** 1978
SQ FT: 4,830
SALES (est): 103.2MM
SALES (corp-wide): 2.4B **Privately Held**
WEB: www.californiaclosets.com
SIC: 1799 5023 2499 Closet organizers, installation & design; home furnishings; applicators, wood
HQ: Franchise Company Inc, The
5397 Eglinton Ave W Suite 108
Etobicoke ON
416 620-4700

(P-2015)
CALIFORNIA LUMBER COMPANY INC
Also Called: A & J Fencing
2336 Bates Ave, Concord (94520-1244)
PHONE...............................925 939-2105
Justin Lena, *CEO*
Jim Bogert, *Vice Pres*
EMP: 40 **EST:** 2010
SQ FT: 5,000
SALES (est): 8MM **Privately Held**
SIC: 1799 Fence construction

(P-2016)
CALIFRNIA CSTM SNROMS PTIO CVE
Also Called: California Sun Rooms
3160 Gold Valley Dr # 300, Rancho Cordova (95742-6577)
PHONE...............................800 834-3211
Abe Alvi, *President*
EMP: 19 **EST:** 1991
SALES (est): 2.4MM **Privately Held**
WEB: www.californiasunrooms.com
SIC: 1799 3448 Spa or hot tub installation or construction; sunrooms, prefabricated metal; panels for prefabricated metal buildings; docks: prefabricated metal

(P-2017)
CALIFRNIAS GNITE POOL PLST INC
510 Greenville Rd, Livermore (94550-9297)
PHONE...............................925 960-9500
Manuel Rodriguez, *President*
Jose Arellano, *Vice Pres*
Alvaro Lando, *Vice Pres*
Monroe Rodriguez, *Vice Pres*
Luz Rodriguez, *Accounts Mgr*
EMP: 60 **EST:** 1992
SQ FT: 15,625
SALES (est): 7.6MM **Privately Held**
WEB: www.californiasgunite.com
SIC: 1799 Swimming pool construction

(P-2018)
CHAMPION SCAFFOLD SERVICES INC
112 Railroad Ave, Richmond (94801-3924)
PHONE...............................510 788-4731
Art Cruz, *President*
Jessica Smith, *Principal*
EMP: 60 **EST:** 2009
SALES (est): 3.5MM **Privately Held**
WEB: www.championscaffcld.com
SIC: 1799 Scaffolding construction

(P-2019)
CLEAN HRBORS ES INDUS SVCS INC
3789 Spinnaker Ct, Fremont (94538-6537)
PHONE...............................510 979-9210
Nancy Evans, *Branch Mgr*
EMP: 50
SALES (corp-wide): 3.1B **Publicly Held**
SIC: 1799 Steam cleaning of building exteriors
HQ: Clean Harbors Es Industrial Services, Inc.
4760 World Hstn Pkwy
Houston TX 77032
713 672-8004

(P-2020)
CLOSET DIMENSION (PA)
23768 Eichler St Ste A, Hayward (94545-2798)
PHONE...............................650 594-1155
Keith McKay, *Owner*
Doug Bui, *Webmaster*
Paul Pavon, *Manager*
EMP: 43 **EST:** 1987
SQ FT: 14,000
SALES (est): 1.9MM **Privately Held**
SIC: 1799 Closet organizers, installation & design

(P-2021)
CLOSET INNOVATION INC
Also Called: California Closet Co
2956 Treat Blvd Ste D, Concord (94518-3612)
PHONE...............................925 687-5033
Fax: 925 687-0273
EMP: 40
SQ FT: 2,000
SALES (est): 4.8MM **Privately Held**
SIC: 1799 5211 Trade Contractor Ret Lumber/Building Materials

(P-2022)
COASTWIDE ENVMTL TECH INC
170 2nd St, Watsonville (95076-4922)
PHONE...............................831 761-5511
Stewart Peterson, *President*
Scott Lovell, *Manager*
EMP: 35 **EST:** 1986
SQ FT: 5,200
SALES (est): 5.7MM **Privately Held**
WEB: www.coastwide.net
SIC: 1799 Asbestos removal & encapsulation

(P-2023)
CONTRCTOR CMPLIANCE MONITORING (PA)
635 Mariners Island Blvd, San Mateo (94404-1044)
PHONE...............................650 522-4403
Deborah Wilder, *President*
Steven Noguera, *Officer*
Ida Brooker, *Consultant*
EMP: 36 **EST:** 2005
SALES (est): 2.2MM **Privately Held**
WEB: www.ccmilcp.com
SIC: 1799 Special trade contractors

(P-2024)
CORPORATE INTERIOR SOLUTIONS
25546 Seaboard Ln, Hayward (94545-3210)
PHONE...............................510 670-8800
Jesus Silva, *President*
Gail Siordia, *Office Mgr*
Horatio Hernandez, *Admin Sec*
Angelica Hollins,
Matthew Harder, *Manager*
EMP: 40 **EST:** 1999
SQ FT: 1,500
SALES (est): 8.6MM **Privately Held**
WEB: www.corporateinteriorsolutions.websitepro.hosting
SIC: 1799 Demountable partition installation

(P-2025)
COUNTERTOP DESIGNS INC
1522 Silica Ave, Sacramento (95815-3312)
PHONE...............................916 929-4562
Sam A Hall, *President*
Jennifer Ginn, *Manager*
EMP: 53 **EST:** 1976
SQ FT: 3,600
SALES (est): 5.4MM **Privately Held**
WEB: www.countertopdesigns.net
SIC: 1799 Counter top installation

(P-2026)
CRUSADER FENCE COMPANY INC
3115 Gold Valley Dr Ste B, Rancho Cordova (95742-6588)
PHONE...............................916 631-9191
Brent Henderson, *CEO*
Robert Raker, *President*
Irene Henderson, *Treasurer*
Brayton Statham, *General Mgr*
Nathan Boek, *Project Mgr*
EMP: 48 **EST:** 1993
SQ FT: 12,000
SALES (est): 17.1MM **Privately Held**
WEB: www.crusaderfence.com
SIC: 1799 Fence construction

(P-2027)
CUSTOM EXTERIORS INC
Also Called: Custom Exteriors Windors Door
2142 Rheem Dr Ste E, Pleasanton (94588-5600)
PHONE...............................925 249-2280
Toll Free:...............................888 -
Jeff Kendall, *President*
Kevin Gundry, *CFO*
EMP: 35 **EST:** 1997
SQ FT: 8,500
SALES (est): 7MM **Privately Held**
WEB: www.custom-exteriors.com
SIC: 1799 1771 Window treatment installation; exterior concrete stucco contractor

(P-2028)
DAVE GROSS ENTERPRISES INC
Also Called: Adams Pool Specialties
7 Wayne Ct, Sacramento (95829-1300)
PHONE...............................916 388-2000
David William Gross, *CEO*
Michel McDonnell, *Vice Pres*
Klayette Evans, *Administration*
Richard Barnes, *CIO*
Barbara Hall, *Controller*
EMP: 65 **EST:** 1998
SQ FT: 25,000 **Privately Held**
WEB: www.adamspoolsac.com
SIC: 1799 Swimming pool construction

(P-2029)
ERNIE & SONS SCAFFOLDING
Also Called: Unique Scaffold
1960 Olivera Rd, Concord (94520-5425)
PHONE...............................925 446-4442
Ernesto Negrete Jr, *CEO*
Joe Garcia, *CFO*
John Soto, *Vice Pres*
Gilbert Soto, *Project Mgr*
▲ **EMP:** 180
SQ FT: 47,000
SALES (est): 21MM **Privately Held**
WEB: www.uniquescaffoldca.com
SIC: 1799 Scaffolding construction

(P-2030)
ESCUE AND ASSOCIATES INC
Also Called: On The Move
745 85th Ave Ste M-N, Oakland (94621-1212)
PHONE...............................510 924-7422
Logan Escue, *President*
Kristin Escue, *Vice Pres*
EMP: 40 **EST:** 2011
SQ FT: 10,000
SALES (est): 4.5MM **Privately Held**
SIC: 1799 Office furniture installation

(P-2031)
FENCECORP INC
6837 Power Inn Rd, Sacramento (95828-2401)
PHONE...............................916 388-0887
EMP: 85
SALES (corp-wide): 69.2MM **Privately Held**
WEB: www.fencecorp.us
SIC: 1799 Fence construction
HQ: Fencecorp, Inc.
18440 Van Buren Blvd
Riverside CA 92508

(P-2032)
FRIANT & ASSOCIATES LLC (PA)
1980 W Avenue 140th, San Leandro (94577-5608)
P.O. Box 2399, Oakland (94614-0399)
PHONE...............................510 535-5113
Paul W Friant,
Karen Edwards, *Vice Pres*
Eric Larson, *Administration*
Andrea Amondson, *Sales Staff*
Jeri Lee, *Sales Staff*
◆ **EMP:** 97 **EST:** 1990
SQ FT: 150,000
SALES (est): 25.7MM **Privately Held**
WEB: www.friant.com
SIC: 5932 1799 7641 Office furniture, secondhand; office furniture installation; office furniture repair & maintenance

(P-2033)
GCI GENERAL CONTRACTORS
875 Battery St Fl 1, San Francisco (94111-1547)
PHONE...............................415 978-2790
James Jenkins, *President*
James Buresh, *Vice Pres*
Jon Helman, *Vice Pres*
Fernando Iniguez, *Vice Pres*
Seth Berling, *Executive*
EMP: 65 **EST:** 2014
SALES (est): 10.2MM **Privately Held**
WEB: www.gcigc.com
SIC: 1799 Athletic & recreation facilities construction

(P-2034)
GETTLER-RYAN INC (PA)
6805 Sierra Ct Ste G, Dublin (94568-2694)
PHONE...............................925 551-7555
Jeffrey M Ryan, *CEO*
Dave Byron, *Vice Pres*
Janice Grant, *Admin Sec*
Jan Grant, *Administration*
Liddy McKenzie, *Design Engr*
EMP: 65 **EST:** 1963
SQ FT: 20,000
SALES (est): 26MM **Privately Held**
WEB: www.grinc.com
SIC: 1799 Petroleum storage tanks, pumping & draining; service station equipment installation, maintenance & repair

(P-2035)
GUITONS POOL CENTER INC
2305 Larkspur Ln, Redding (96002-0611)
PHONE...............................530 221-6656
Richard Guiton, *Ch of Bd*
Dale Simpson, *President*
Mark Mitchell, *CFO*
Peggy Mc Clary, *Corp Secy*
Peggy McClary, *Vice Pres*
EMP: 35 **EST:** 1962
SALES (est): 8.3MM **Privately Held**
WEB: www.guitons.com
SIC: 1799 5999 7389 Swimming pool construction; swimming pool chemicals, equipment & supplies; swimming pool & hot tub service & maintenance

(P-2036)
HIGH END DEVELOPMENT INC
665 Stone Rd, Benicia (94510-1141)
PHONE...............................925 687-2540
James Metzger, *President*
Larry V Harmen, *CFO*

▲ = Import ▼ = Export
◆ = Import/Export

PRODUCTS & SERVICES SECTION
1799 - Special Trade Contractors, NEC County (P-2059)

Anthony Froyd, *Admin Sec*
Kym Surani, *Marketing Staff*
EMP: 143 **EST:** 2006
SALES (est): 26.5MM **Privately Held**
WEB: www.highenddevelopment.com
SIC: 1799 Waterproofing

(P-2037)
INNOVATIVE INSTALLERS INC (PA)
43134 Osgood Rd, Fremont (94539-5608)
PHONE..................................510 651-9890
Mirzett Evans, *President*
Glenda Heldris, *CFO*
EMP: 45 **EST:** 1992
SQ FT: 16,000 **Privately Held**
SIC: 1799 Office furniture installation

(P-2038)
INSTALLTION DGTAL TRNSMSSONS I
Also Called: Idt Telecomm Data
517 Jacoby St Ste C, San Rafael (94901-5343)
PHONE..................................415 226-0020
Theresa Benecchi, *President*
James McGowan, *Vice Pres*
Frank Hernandez, *Principal*
Pamela Hopper, *Sales Staff*
EMP: 15 **EST:** 2008
SALES (est): 1.3MM **Privately Held**
SIC: 1799 3612 Special trade contractors; line voltage regulators

(P-2039)
JANUS CORPORATION (PA)
1081 Shary Cir, Concord (94518-2407)
PHONE..................................925 969-9200
Mike Ely, *CEO*
Sean Tavernier, *President*
Craig M Uhle, *Vice Pres*
Juana Bailey, *Executive*
Barbara Eaves, *Executive*
EMP: 177 **EST:** 1989
SQ FT: 15,000
SALES (est): 30.1MM **Privately Held**
WEB: www.januscorp.com
SIC: 1799 Asbestos removal & encapsulation; decontamination services

(P-2040)
JARKA ENTERPRISES INC (PA)
Also Called: Jei Corporate Services
675 Brennan St, San Jose (95131-1205)
PHONE..................................408 325-5700
David Wayne Jarka, *President*
Laura Rivas, *Administration*
Jacquie Jahn, *Controller*
Robert Hoffman, *Supervisor*
Kyle Kortz, *Supervisor*
EMP: 84 **EST:** 2003
SQ FT: 75,000
SALES (est): 14.1MM **Privately Held**
WEB: www.jei-cs.com
SIC: 1799 Office furniture installation

(P-2041)
KARCHER ENVIRONMENTAL INC
1718 Fairway Dr, San Leandro (94577-5628)
PHONE..................................510 297-0180
Steve Bramlett, *Manager*
Mark Kavanaugh, *Sales Staff*
EMP: 70
SALES (corp-wide): 10.5MM **Privately Held**
WEB: www.karcherenv.com
SIC: 1799 Asbestos removal & encapsulation
PA: Karcher Environmental, Inc.
2300 E Orangewood Ave
Anaheim CA 92806
714 385-1490

(P-2042)
LD STROBEL CO INC
1022 Shary Cir Ste 9, Concord (94518-2463)
PHONE..................................925 686-3241
Richard Gillilan, *CEO*
Larry Strobel, *President*
Betty Nelson, *Sales Staff*
Jeff Giese, *Manager*
EMP: 35 **EST:** 1987
SQ FT: 24,000
SALES: 8.7MM **Privately Held**
WEB: www.ldstrobel.com
SIC: 1799 1623 8712 Antenna installation; transmitting tower (telecommunication) construction; architectural engineering

(P-2043)
MAK ASSOCIATES INC
Also Called: Playgrounds Unlimited
980 Memorex Dr, Santa Clara (95050-2810)
PHONE..................................408 244-9848
Joe T Mendes, *President*
Mike Kelly, *Admin Sec*
◆ **EMP:** 40
SQ FT: 3,000
SALES (est): 5.8MM **Privately Held**
WEB: www.playgroundsunlimited.com
SIC: 1799 Playground construction & equipment installation

(P-2044)
MALCOLM DRILLING COMPANY INC (PA)
92 Natoma St Ste 400, San Francisco (94105-2685)
PHONE..................................415 901-4400
John M Malcolm, *CEO*
Jerry Riggs, *President*
Terry Tucker, *President*
Clint McFarlane, *Officer*
Rob Jameson, *Exec VP*
▲ **EMP:** 3729 **EST:** 1968
SQ FT: 7,500
SALES (est): 49.9K **Privately Held**
WEB: www.malcolmdrilling.com
SIC: 1799 Building site preparation; boring for building construction

(P-2045)
MUEHLHAN CERTIFED COATINGS INC
2320 Cordelia Rd, Fairfield (94534-1600)
PHONE..................................707 639-4414
David Brockman, *President*
Dieter Niehues, *Managing Dir*
Goran Skopljak, *Sales Mgr*
EMP: 50 **EST:** 2007
SQ FT: 18,000
SALES (est): 5.9MM
SALES (corp-wide): 307.9MM **Privately Held**
WEB: www.muehlhan.com
SIC: 1799 Coating, caulking & weather, water & fireproofing
HQ: Muehlhan Surface Protection Inc.
2320 Cordelia Rd
Fairfield CA 94534
707 639-4421

(P-2046)
NORTHLAND CONTROL SYSTEMS INC (PA)
1533 California Cir, Milpitas (95035-3023)
PHONE..................................833 811-4185
Pierre Trapanese, *CEO*
Jim Conley, *CFO*
Patricia Trapanese, *CFO*
Terry Browne, *Managing Dir*
James Choi, *Program Mgr*
EMP: 136 **EST:** 1982
SALES (est): 93MM **Privately Held**
WEB: www.northlandcontrols.com
SIC: 1799 1731 Athletic & recreation facilities construction; access control systems specialization; fire detection & burglar alarm systems specialization

(P-2047)
NORTHSTAR CONTG GROUP INC
2616 Barrington Ct, Hayward (94545-1100)
PHONE..................................510 491-1330
Trip Turner, *President*
EMP: 107
SALES (corp-wide): 640.1MM **Privately Held**
SIC: 1799 Asbestos removal & encapsulation
HQ: Northstar Contracting Group, Inc.
2614-20 Barrington Ct
Hayward CA 94545

(P-2048)
NORTHSTAR CONTG GROUP INC (DH)
2614-20 Barrington Ct, Hayward (94545)
PHONE..................................510 491-1330
John Leonard, *President*
Jeffrey P Adix, *Treasurer*
Bryan Diloreto, *Co-President*
Gregory G Dicarlo, *Vice Pres*
Ramon Rivera, *Vice Pres*
EMP: 59 **EST:** 1987
SALES (est): 45.6MM
SALES (corp-wide): 640.1MM **Privately Held**
SIC: 1799 1795 Asbestos removal & encapsulation; wrecking & demolition work
HQ: Northstar Group Services, Inc.
370 7th Ave Ste 1803
New York NY 10001
212 951-3660

(P-2049)
ONE WORKPLACE L FERRARI LLC
1780 N Market Blvd, Sacramento (95834-1997)
PHONE..................................916 553-5900
Graham Wallace, *General Mgr*
EMP: 40
SALES (corp-wide): 329.1MM **Privately Held**
WEB: www.oneworkplace.com
SIC: 5712 1799 Office furniture; office furniture installation
PA: One Workplace L. Ferrari, Llc
2500 De La Cruz Blvd
Santa Clara CA 95050
669 800-2500

(P-2050)
PACIFIC HOUSING GROUP LLC
1356 S Buttonwillow Ave, Reedley (93654-9333)
PHONE..................................559 651-1133
George Bravante Jr, *Partner*
EMP: 70 **EST:** 1997
SALES (est): 2.6MM **Privately Held**
SIC: 5271 1799 Mobile homes; mobile home site setup & tie down

(P-2051)
PARADISO MECHANICAL INC
2600 Williams St, San Leandro (94577-3153)
PHONE..................................510 614-8390
Angelo Paradiso, *President*
Paul Paradiso, *Treasurer*
Eric Montesano, *Vice Pres*
Randa Khan, *Admin Sec*
EMP: 43 **EST:** 1947
SQ FT: 8,000
SALES (est): 1.1MM **Privately Held**
WEB: www.pminc.net
SIC: 1799 Service station equipment installation, maintenance & repair

(P-2052)
PARC SPECIALTY CONTRACTORS
1400 Vinci Ave, Sacramento (95838-1716)
PHONE..................................916 992-5405
Greg Johnson, *President*
John Kimmel, *Vice Pres*
Eddie Hagedorn, *Division Mgr*
Paul Lane, *Admin Sec*
Stuart Webb, *Project Mgr*
EMP: 85 **EST:** 1997
SQ FT: 10,000
SALES (est): 17.3MM **Privately Held**
WEB: www.parcspecialty.com
SIC: 1799 Asbestos removal & encapsulation

(P-2053)
PENHALL COMPANY
Also Called: Penhall Santa Clara 152
696 Walsh Ave, Santa Clara (95050-2628)
PHONE..................................408 970-9494
Josh Heath, *Branch Mgr*
EMP: 35 **Privately Held**
WEB: www.penhall.com
SIC: 1799 1741 1795 Building site preparation; masonry & other stonework; wrecking & demolition work
HQ: Penhall Company
7501 Esters Blvd Ste 150
Irving TX 75063

(P-2054)
PENHALL COMPANY
Also Called: Penhall Sacramento 151
8416 Specialty Cir, Sacramento (95828-2504)
PHONE..................................916 386-1589
Toll Free:..................................888 -
Ron Lerossignol, *Manager*
EMP: 35 **Privately Held**
WEB: www.penhall.com
SIC: 1799 1741 1795 Building site preparation; masonry & other stonework; wrecking & demolition work
HQ: Penhall Company
7501 Esters Blvd Ste 150
Irving TX 75063

(P-2055)
PERFORMANCE ABATEMENT SVCS INC
Also Called: Pas Livermore
1943 Rutan Dr, Livermore (94551-7646)
PHONE..................................925 273-3800
Todd Forbush, *General Mgr*
EMP: 43
SALES (corp-wide): 2.4B **Privately Held**
WEB: www.performancecontracting.com
SIC: 1799 Asbestos removal & encapsulation
HQ: Performance Abatement Services, Inc.
11145 Thompson Ave
Lenexa KS 66219
913 888-8600

(P-2056)
PREMIER POOLS AND SPAS LP (PA)
11250 Pyrites Way, Gold River (95670-4481)
PHONE..................................916 852-0223
Keith H Harbeck, *General Ptnr*
Paul Porter, *General Ptnr*
Greg Hopper, *CFO*
Michael Carson, *Vice Pres*
Aaron Gurley, *Vice Pres*
EMP: 90 **EST:** 1988
SQ FT: 3,500
SALES (est): 23.2MM **Privately Held**
WEB: www.premierpoolsandspas.com
SIC: 1799 Spa or hot tub installation or construction; swimming pool construction

(P-2057)
PROJECT GO INCORPORATED
801 Vernon St, Roseville (95678-3149)
PHONE..................................916 782-3443
Linda Timbers, *Exec Dir*
Lynda Timbers, *Exec Dir*
Kandace Rickard-Lohner, *Admin Asst*
EMP: 50
SQ FT: 3,000
SALES: 3.8MM **Privately Held**
WEB: www.projectgoinc.org
SIC: 1799 Waterproofing

(P-2058)
PSG FENCING CORPORATION (PA)
Also Called: Soares Lumber Company
6630 Monterey Rd, Gilroy (95020-6644)
PHONE..................................831 726-2002
Frank Soares, *President*
EMP: 164 **EST:** 1986
SQ FT: 5,000
SALES (est): 9.7MM **Privately Held**
WEB: www.psgfencinginc.com
SIC: 1799 5031 5211 Fence construction; lumber, plywood & millwork; lumber products

(P-2059)
QUALITY SYSTEMS INSTLLTONS LTD
Also Called: Q S I
212 Shaw Rd Ste 3, South San Francisco (94080-6613)
PHONE..................................650 875-9000
Jon Chase, *President*
Daniel Castillo, *Vice Pres*

1799 - Special Trade Contractors, NEC County (P-2060)

PRODUCTS & SERVICES SECTION

Robert W Lindstrom, *Vice Pres*
EMP: 60 **EST:** 1986
SQ FT: 40,000
SALES (est): 6.7MM **Privately Held**
WEB: www.qsiltd.com
SIC: 1799 Office furniture installation

(P-2060)
RAINBOW WTRPROFING RESTORATION
600 Treat Ave, San Francisco (94110-2016)
PHONE 415 641-1578
Christopher Abel, *President*
Rob Browne, *Corp Secy*
Barb Powers, *Office Mgr*
Leticia Ramirez, *Admin Asst*
Jessica Walitt, *Project Mgr*
EMP: 124 **EST:** 1927
SALES (est): 21.3MM **Privately Held**
WEB: www.rainbow415.com
SIC: 1799 Waterproofing

(P-2061)
RESTEC CONTRACTORS INC
22955 Kidder St, Hayward (94545-1670)
PHONE 510 670-0100
John Andrzejewski, *President*
Freeman Boyett, *Treasurer*
R Todd Fearon, *Vice Pres*
Joe Defigueiredo, *Sales Staff*
David Brueggen, *Asst Sec*
EMP: 100 **EST:** 1985
SALES (est): 19MM
SALES (corp-wide): 461.9MM **Privately Held**
WEB: www.resteccontractors.com
SIC: 1799 Asbestos removal & encapsulation
HQ: Vertecs Corporation
  14700 Ne 95th St Ste 201
  Redmond WA
  425 885-1990

(P-2062)
REUBEN J BORG
Also Called: Reuben Borg Fence
3300 Busch Rd, Pleasanton (94566-8455)
PHONE 925 931-0570
Reuben Borg, *Owner*
EMP: 40
SALES (corp-wide): 6.8MM **Privately Held**
WEB: www.reubenborgfence.com
SIC: 1799 Fence construction
PA: Reuben J Borg
  2415 San Ramon Vly Blvd
  San Ramon CA 94583
  925 931-0570

(P-2063)
ROWAR CORPORATION
Also Called: Arrow Fence Co
4025 Cincinnatti Ave, Sacramento (94203-0001)
PHONE 916 626-3030
Alan Harris, *President*
Kim Harris, *Vice Pres*
EMP: 20 **EST:** 1978
SQ FT: 2,200
SALES (est): 1.4MM **Privately Held**
SIC: 1799 3699 3446 Fence construction; security devices; architectural metalwork

(P-2064)
RT WESTERN INC
Also Called: Rt Western Construction Svcs
160 Mendell St, San Francisco (94124-1740)
PHONE 415 677-9202
Thomas P Pua, *CEO*
Jacob Luera, *Project Mgr*
James McMillan, *Sr Project Mgr*
Ralph Vargas, *Sr Project Mgr*
Roberto Garcia, *Director*
EMP: 40 **EST:** 2006
SALES (est): 6.6MM **Privately Held**
WEB: www.rtwestern.com
SIC: 1799 1751 2431 Cleaning new buildings after construction; construction site cleanup; cabinet & finish carpentry; doors & door parts & trim, wood; doors, wood

(P-2065)
SANTA CLARA COUNTY OF
15555 Sanborn Rd, Saratoga (95070-9709)
PHONE 408 573-3050
Edith Mourtos, *Branch Mgr*
EMP: 41 **Privately Held**
WEB: www.sccgov.org
SIC: 1799 Playground construction & equipment installation
PA: County Of Santa Clara
  70 W Hedding St 2wing
  San Jose CA 95110
  408 299-5200

(P-2066)
SELEX INC (PA)
Also Called: Borg Redwood Fences
442 Longfellow St, Livermore (94550-7122)
P.O. Box 5430, Pleasanton (94566-1430)
PHONE 707 836-8836
Julie Borg, *CEO*
Reuben Borg, *President*
Dave Lamarre, *Vice Pres*
EMP: 90 **EST:** 1995
SALES (est): 8.3MM **Privately Held**
SIC: 1799 Fence construction

(P-2067)
SERVICE STATION SYSTEMS INC
680 Quinn Ave, San Jose (95112-2635)
PHONE 408 971-2445
Mark Able, *CEO*
Colleen Able, *Corp Secy*
Randy Mello, *Technician*
Ryan Brownlee, *Project Mgr*
Kristy Jennings, *Human Res Mgr*
EMP: 42 **EST:** 1985
SQ FT: 20,000
SALES (est): 10MM **Privately Held**
WEB: www.servicestationsystems.com
SIC: 1799 Service station equipment installation, maintenance & repair

(P-2068)
SIERRA LUMBER AND FENCE PSI
Also Called: Sierra Lumber and Fence Co
1711 Senter Rd, San Jose (95112-2598)
PHONE 707 769-0345
Mike Seibold, *Manager*
EMP: 38
SALES (corp-wide): 141.1MM **Privately Held**
WEB: www.sierrafence.com
SIC: 1799 Fence construction
HQ: Sierra Lumber And Fence Psi
  1711 Senter Rd
  San Jose CA 95112

(P-2069)
SIERRA LUMBER AND FENCE PSI (HQ)
1711 Senter Rd, San Jose (95112-2598)
PHONE 408 286-7071
Roger Burch, *President*
Austin Vanderhoof, *Vice Pres*
EMP: 40 **EST:** 1970
SQ FT: 1,200
SALES (est): 8.8MM
SALES (corp-wide): 141.1MM **Privately Held**
WEB: www.sierrafence.com
SIC: 1799 Fence construction
PA: Pacific States Industries, Incorporated
  10 Madrone Ave
  Morgan Hill CA 95037
  408 779-7354

(P-2070)
SKYLINE SCAFFOLD INC
3131 52nd Ave, Sacramento (95823-1022)
PHONE 916 391-8929
Amy Johnson, *CEO*
David Johnson, *COO*
Frank Towse, *Project Mgr*
Carissa Bradley, *Opers Staff*
Michael McCurdy, *Director*
EMP: 98

SALES (est): 20MM **Privately Held**
WEB: www.skylinescaffold.com
SIC: 1799 Scaffolding construction; shoring & underpinning work; erection & dismantling of forms for poured concrete

(P-2071)
SOUTHWEST FENCE AND SUP CO INC (PA)
18042 Sycamore Ave, Patterson (95363-9751)
P.O. Box 1156, Oakdale (95361-1156)
PHONE 209 892-9205
Christopher Hanneken, *President*
Thomas Simmons, *Exec VP*
Helene Hanneken, *Vice Pres*
EMP: 38 **EST:** 1985
SQ FT: 5,000
SALES (est): 5.2MM **Privately Held**
WEB: www.southwestfenceandsupply.com
SIC: 1799 5031 Fence construction; fencing, wood

(P-2072)
SUTTER BUTTES MFG LLC
Also Called: Sutter Buttes Mfg
1221 Independence Pl, Gridley (95948-9341)
PHONE 530 846-9960
EMP: 20 **EST:** 2015
SALES (est): 1.5MM **Privately Held**
WEB: www.sutterbuttesmfg.com
SIC: 1799 3999 Athletic & recreation facilities construction; atomizers, toiletry

(P-2073)
TAILORED LIVING CHOICES LLC
1957 Sierra Ave, NAPA (94558-2840)
PHONE 707 259-0526
Vicki Robinson, *Mng Member*
Miranda Hatchell, *Office Mgr*
Glenda Thomas, *Office Mgr*
Samantha Larot, *Human Resources*
Stacy Perez,
EMP: 112 **EST:** 2006
SALES (est): 7.7MM **Privately Held**
WEB: www.tailoredlivingchoices.com
SIC: 1799 Home/office interiors finishing, furnishing & remodeling

(P-2074)
TATA AMERICA INTL CORP
3115 Java Ct, West Sacramento (95691-5880)
PHONE 916 803-5441
Anthony Camarena, *Branch Mgr*
EMP: 70 **Privately Held**
WEB: www.ex-ngn.com
SIC: 1799 Artificial turf installation
HQ: Tata America International Corporation
  101 Park Ave Fl 26
  New York NY 10178
  212 557-8038

(P-2075)
THUNDER MOUNTAIN ENTPS INC (PA)
9335 Elder Creek Rd, Sacramento (95829-9339)
P.O. Box 292667 (95829-2667)
PHONE 916 381-3400
Dave Smiley, *President*
Beth Smiley, *Corp Secy*
Nicole Smiley, *Sales Staff*
EMP: 60 **EST:** 2000
SQ FT: 5,000
SALES (est): 7MM **Privately Held**
WEB: www.tme1.com
SIC: 1799 Corrosion control installation

(P-2076)
TOPBUILD SERVICES GROUP CORP
Also Called: Masco
1341 Old Oakland Rd, San Jose (95112-1317)
PHONE 408 882-0411
Bob Colla, *Branch Mgr*
EMP: 1896
SALES (corp-wide): 2.7B **Publicly Held**
WEB: www.topbuild.com
SIC: 1799 Prefabricated fireplace installation

HQ: Topbuild Services Group Corp.
  475 N Williamson Blvd
  Daytona Beach FL 32114
  386 304-2200

(P-2077)
TORRES FENCE CO INC
2357 S Orange Ave, Fresno (93725-1021)
P.O. Box 10137 (93745-0137)
PHONE 559 237-4141
Ralph Torres, *President*
Rebecca Torres, *Corp Secy*
Ralph Torres Jr, *Vice Pres*
Rene J Torres, *Vice Pres*
Rene Torres, *Vice Pres*
▲ **EMP:** 50 **EST:** 1963
SQ FT: 6,000
SALES (est): 6.3MM **Privately Held**
WEB: www.torresfence.com
SIC: 1799 3315 3496 Fence construction; chain link fencing; barbed wire, made from purchased wire

(P-2078)
TOURNESOL SITEWORKS LLC (PA)
2930 Faber St, Union City (94587-1214)
PHONE 800 542-2282
Christopher J Lyon, *Owner*
Michelle Cheung, *Engineer*
Tony Rizzo, *Engineer*
Jinky Arevalo, *Buyer*
Cathy Flaherty, *Plant Mgr*
▲ **EMP:** 55 **EST:** 1979
SQ FT: 10,000
SALES (est): 18.7MM **Privately Held**
WEB: www.tournesol.com
SIC: 1799 5023 3444 1521 Fiberglass work; home furnishings, wicker, rattan or reed; metal roofing & roof drainage equipment; patio & deck construction & repair; retaining wall construction; fountain repair

(P-2079)
TREASTER MILES & ASSOCIATES
1810 13th St, Sacramento (95811-7149)
PHONE 916 373-1800
Therese Kingsbury, *CEO*
Ken Dinsmore, *Vice Pres*
Joseanna TSE, *Vice Pres*
Patricia Beckman, *Project Mgr*
Chris Flanders, *Marketing Staff*
EMP: 75 **EST:** 1958
SQ FT: 16,500
SALES (est): 24.3MM **Privately Held**
WEB: www.mtaoffice.com
SIC: 5712 1799 Office furniture; office furniture installation

(P-2080)
TURNER MANUFACTURING COMPANY
2677 S Chestnut Ave, Fresno (93725-2113)
PHONE 559 251-1918
Jose L Turner, *President*
EMP: 16 **EST:** 1972
SQ FT: 5,000
SALES (est): 2.3MM **Privately Held**
WEB: www.tmfginc.com
SIC: 1799 3446 Ornamental metal work; grillwork, ornamental metal

(P-2081)
UNITED FENCE CONTRACTORS INC (PA)
Also Called: Thomson and Thomson Fence Co
515 23rd Ave, Oakland (94606-5306)
PHONE 510 276-8350
Gary Thompson, *CEO*
Robert Marshall, *Vice Pres*
EMP: 35 **EST:** 2002
SALES (est): 9.1MM **Privately Held**
SIC: 1799 Fence construction

(P-2082)
UNITED MARBLE & GRANITE INC
2163 Martin Ave, Santa Clara (95050-2701)
PHONE 408 347-3300
Manuel De Oliveira, *President*
Velma De Oliveira, *Executive*

PRODUCTS & SERVICES SECTION

2011 - Meat Packing Plants County (P-2104)

Connie Silveira, *Office Admin*
Joseph Enos, *Purchasing*
Greg Tompkins, *Manager*
▲ **EMP:** 80 **EST:** 1998
SALES (est): 6.9MM **Privately Held**
WEB: www.unitedmarbleusa.com
SIC: 1799 Counter top installation

(P-2083)
VALENTINE CORPORATION
111 Pelican Way, San Rafael (94901-5519)
P.O. Box 9337 (94912-9337)
PHONE.................................415 453-3732
Toll Free:...............................877 -
Robert O Valentine, *CEO*
Robert Valentine Jr, *President*
Alan Hanley, *CFO*
Madeline Valentine, *Corp Secy*
David Levine, *Vice Pres*
EMP: 50 **EST:** 1964
SQ FT: 3,000
SALES (est): 14.9MM **Privately Held**
WEB: www.valentinecorp.com
SIC: 1799 8711 1622 Waterproofing; building construction consultant; bridge construction

(P-2084)
VALLEY WATERPROOFING INC
825 Civic Center Dr Ste 6, Santa Clara (95050-3961)
P.O. Box 20003, San Jose (95160-0003)
PHONE.................................408 985-7701
Donna O'Brien, *President*
Michael O'Brien, *Vice Pres*
Jay Perez, *Project Mgr*
Kathy Clark, *Manager*
EMP: 80 **EST:** 1981
SQ FT: 1,000
SALES (est): 6.4MM **Privately Held**
WEB: www.valleywaterproofing.com
SIC: 1799 Waterproofing

(P-2085)
W BANKS MOORE INC
Also Called: Banks & Co
2403 E Belmont Ave, Fresno (93701-2299)
P.O. Box 6543 (93703-6543)
PHONE.................................559 485-3456
Johnny W Moore, *President*
Patricia J Moore, *CFO*
Patricia Moore, *CFO*
Eric Katen, *Administration*
Leroy Griffin, *Purchasing*
EMP: 43 **EST:** 1926
SQ FT: 10,000
SALES (est): 11.9MM **Privately Held**
WEB: www.banks-co.com
SIC: 1799 5084 4212 Service station equipment installation, maintenance & repair; pumps & pumping equipment; hazardous waste transport

(P-2086)
WALTON ENGINEERING INC
3900 Commerce Dr, West Sacramento (95691-2157)
P.O. Box 1025 (95691-1025)
PHONE.................................916 372-1888
Michael Walton, *President*
Richard Walton, *Vice Pres*
Sheryl Mortenson, *Controller*
Chris Huntington, *Manager*
EMP: 65 **EST:** 1988
SQ FT: 13,000
SALES (est): 13.4MM **Privately Held**
WEB: www.waltonengineering.com
SIC: 1799 1542 7389 Service station equipment installation, maintenance & repair; service station construction; drafting service, except temporary help

(P-2087)
WESTERN WATER FEATURES INC
5088 Hillsdale Cir Ste A, El Dorado Hills (95762-5779)
PHONE.................................916 939-1600
Daniel K Parkes, *President*
Laura Parkes, *Corp Secy*
Michael Leja, *Vice Pres*
Richard Barnes, *CIO*
Dave Schultz, *Project Mgr*
▲ **EMP:** 35 **EST:** 1994
SQ FT: 2,000

SALES (est): 7.2MM **Privately Held**
WEB: www.westernwaterfeatures.com
SIC: 1799 Swimming pool construction

(P-2088)
WESTERN WATERPROOFING CO INC
15061 Wicks Blvd, San Leandro (94577-6621)
PHONE.................................510 875-2109
Tony Lieder Jr, *Branch Mgr*
Jon Carden, *Superintendent*
EMP: 42
SALES (corp-wide): 226.2MM **Privately Held**
WEB: www.westernspecialtycontractors.com
SIC: 1799 1761 1741 1771 Waterproofing; roofing contractor; masonry & other stonework; concrete work
HQ: Western Waterproofing Company, Inc.
  1637 N Warson Rd
  Saint Louis MO 63132
  314 427-1637

(P-2089)
WLMD
Also Called: Wellmade Products
1715 Kibby Rd, Merced (95341-9301)
PHONE.................................209 723-9120
Mark R Riley, *CEO*
Doug Bartman, *CFO*
Donna Wickham, *Asst Controller*
Jerry Yon, *Controller*
▲ **EMP:** 130 **EST:** 1992
SQ FT: 120,000
SALES (est): 15.8MM **Privately Held**
WEB: www.wlmd.com
SIC: 1799 1761 Lightning conductor erection; roofing, siding & sheet metal work

---

2011 Meat Packing Plants

(P-2090)
CARGILL MEAT SOLUTIONS CORP
2350 Academy Ave, Sanger (93657-9559)
PHONE.................................559 875-2232
Robert Case, *Branch Mgr*
EMP: 391
SALES (corp-wide): 113.4B **Privately Held**
WEB: www.cargill.com
SIC: 2011 Meat packing plants
HQ: Cargill Meat Solutions Corp
  151 N Main St Ste 900
  Wichita KS 67202
  316 291-2500

(P-2091)
CARGILL MEAT SOLUTIONS CORP
3115 S Fig Ave, Fresno (93706-5647)
P.O. Box 12503 (93778-2503)
PHONE.................................559 268-5586
Tod Ventura, *Manager*
EMP: 391
SALES (corp-wide): 113.4B **Privately Held**
WEB: www.cargill.com
SIC: 2011 Beef products from beef slaughtered on site
HQ: Cargill Meat Solutions Corp
  151 N Main St Ste 900
  Wichita KS 67202
  316 291-2500

(P-2092)
CERTIFIED MEAT PRODUCTS INC
4586 E Commerce Ave, Fresno (93725-2203)
P.O. Box 12502 (93778-2502)
PHONE.................................559 256-1433
Cassi Maxey, *CEO*
Rob Maxey, *Executive*
Matthew Lloyd, *Prdtn Mgr*
EMP: 75 **EST:** 2005
SALES (est): 15.7MM **Privately Held**
WEB: www.certifiedmeatproducts.com
SIC: 2011 Meat packing plants

(P-2093)
CLAUSEN MEAT COMPANY INC
19455 W Clausen Rd, Turlock (95380)
P.O. Box 1826 (95381-1826)
PHONE.................................209 667-8690
Ping Lau, *CEO*
Ying Hung Vinh, *CFO*
Kenneth Khoo, *Vice Pres*
▲ **EMP:** 40 **EST:** 1983
SQ FT: 15,000
SALES (est): 4.5MM **Privately Held**
WEB: www.clausenmeat.com
SIC: 2011 Meat packing plants

(P-2094)
COLUMBUS FOODS LLC
30977 San Antonio St, Hayward (94544-7109)
PHONE.................................510 921-3400
Ralph Denisco, *CEO*
John Piccetti, *Ch of Bd*
Adam Ferrif, *CFO*
Jeannea Enriquez, *Cust Mgr*
▲ **EMP:** 345 **EST:** 1917
SALES (est): 41.4MM **Privately Held**
WEB: www.columbuscraftmeats.com
SIC: 2011 5143 5147 Luncheon meat from meat slaughtered on site; cheese; meats & meat products

(P-2095)
ELLENSBURG LAMB COMPANY INC
Also Called: Superior Packing Co
7390 Rio Dixon Rd, Dixon (95620-9665)
P.O. Box 940 (95620-0940)
PHONE.................................707 678-3091
Martin Ducken, *Manager*
Patricia Galvez, *Office Mgr*
Hector Rivera, *Human Resources*
Victor Ortega, *Purchasing*
Jerry Ruhland, *Plant Engr*
EMP: 80 **Privately Held**
SIC: 2011 Meat packing plants
HQ: Ellensburg Lamb Company, Inc.
  2530 River Plaza Dr # 200
  Sacramento CA 95833

(P-2096)
ELLENSBURG LAMB COMPANY INC (HQ)
Also Called: Superior Farms
2530 River Plaza Dr # 200, Sacramento (95833-3674)
PHONE.................................530 758-3091
Les Oestereich, *President*
Carlos Barba, *COO*
Jeff Evanson, *CFO*
Gary Pfeiffer, *Exec VP*
Karen Ellis, *Vice Pres*
▼ **EMP:** 18 **EST:** 1996
SQ FT: 7,500
SALES (est): 49.9MM **Privately Held**
SIC: 2011 Lamb products from lamb slaughtered on site

(P-2097)
GOLDEN VALLEY INDUSTRIES INC
960 Lone Palm Ave, Modesto (95351-1533)
PHONE.................................209 939-3370
Mike Sullivan, *President*
Linda Diaz, *Controller*
EMP: 40 **EST:** 1997
SQ FT: 40,000
SALES (est): 11.5MM **Privately Held**
WEB: www.goldenvalleyindustries.com
SIC: 2011 Meat packing plants

(P-2098)
HARRIS RANCH BEEF COMPANY
16277 S Mccall Ave, Selma (93662-9458)
P.O. Box 220 (93662-0220)
PHONE.................................559 896-3081
John Harris, *Ch of Bd*
Randy Dehart, *Info Tech Mgr*
Louis Ontiveros, *Maintence Staff*
▼ **EMP:** 700
SALES (est): 168.8MM **Privately Held**
WEB: www.harrisranchbeef.com
SIC: 2011 2013 Meat packing plants; sausages & other prepared meats

PA: Central Valley Meat Co., Inc.
  10431 8 3/4 Ave
  Hanford CA 93230

(P-2099)
LA PACHANGA FOODS INC
708 L St, Modesto (95354-2240)
PHONE.................................209 522-2222
Gabriel Villa, *CEO*
EMP: 34 **EST:** 2013
SALES (est): 3.2MM **Privately Held**
SIC: 2011 Meat packing plants

(P-2100)
LOS BANOS ABATTOIR CO
1312 W Pacheco Blvd, Los Banos (93635-7807)
P.O. Box 949 (93635-0949)
PHONE.................................209 826-2212
Steven La Salvia, *President*
Laura La Salvia, *Vice Pres*
EMP: 35 **EST:** 1920
SQ FT: 7,500
SALES (est): 5.4MM **Privately Held**
WEB: www.losbanos.com
SIC: 2011 5147 Beef products from beef slaughtered on site; meats & meat products

(P-2101)
MOHAWK LAND & CATTLE CO INC
1660 Old Bayshore Hwy, San Jose (95112-4304)
P.O. Box 601 (95106-0601)
PHONE.................................408 436-1800
Steve Tognoli, *President*
▼ **EMP:** 64 **EST:** 1957
SQ FT: 50,000
SALES (est): 9.3MM **Privately Held**
WEB: www.johnmorrell.com
SIC: 2011 Meat packing plants
HQ: Smithfield Packaged Meats Corp.
  805 E Kemper Rd
  Cincinnati OH 45246
  513 782-3800

(P-2102)
OBERTI WHOLESALES FOODS INC
14471 Griffith St, San Leandro (94577-6701)
PHONE.................................510 357-8600
Gary Oberti, *President*
EMP: 15 **EST:** 1986
SQ FT: 4,500
SALES (est): 597.3K **Privately Held**
WEB: www.oberti.com
SIC: 2011 Meat packing plants

(P-2103)
OLSON MEAT COMPANY
7301 Cutler Ave, Orland (95963-9601)
PHONE.................................530 865-8111
James Olson, *CEO*
Fred Olson, *Principal*
EMP: 35 **EST:** 1969
SALES (est): 4.3MM **Privately Held**
WEB: www.olson-meat-company.business.site
SIC: 2011 Meat packing plants

(P-2104)
RICHWOOD MEAT COMPANY INC
2751 N Santa Fe Ave, Merced (95348-4109)
P.O. Box 2599 (95344-0599)
PHONE.................................209 722-8171
Michael J Wood, *President*
Carol J Wood, *Shareholder*
Hellen Diane Inks-Fragie, *CFO*
Steve Wood, *Vice Pres*
Steven J Wood, *Vice Pres*
EMP: 100 **EST:** 1964
SQ FT: 43,000
SALES: 57.7MM **Privately Held**
WEB: www.richwoodmeat.com
SIC: 2011 5147 5421 Meat packing plants; meats, fresh; meats, cured or smoked; meat & fish markets

2011 - Meat Packing Plants

(P-2105)
TRANSHUMANCE HOLDING CO INC
Also Called: Superior Farms
7390 Rio Dixon Rd, Dixon (95620-9665)
P.O. Box 940 (95620-0940)
PHONE..................707 693-2303
Julie Angel, *Manager*
Anders Hemphill, *Vice Pres*
Nita Baggett, *Administration*
Justin Smith, *Accountant*
Arnie Ellis, *Opers Staff*
EMP: 200 **Privately Held**
SIC: 2011 Lamb products from lamb slaughtered on site
PA: Transhumance Holding Company, Inc.
2530 River Plaza Dr # 200
Sacramento CA 95833

(P-2106)
TRANSHUMANCE HOLDING CO INC (PA)
2530 River Plaza Dr # 200, Sacramento (95833-3674)
PHONE..................530 758-3091
Rick Stott, *President*
David Waggoner, *President*
Jeff Evanson, *CFO*
Gary Pfeiffer, *Exec VP*
Anders Hemphill, *Vice Pres*
◆ **EMP:** 50 **EST:** 1997
SQ FT: 16,000
SALES (est): 118.5MM **Privately Held**
SIC: 2011 Meat packing plants

(P-2107)
WO HING LLC
78 4th St, Oakland (94607-4604)
PHONE..................510 922-8778
Ethan Cheung, *Mng Member*
Nhi Mui Le Truong,
EMP: 16 **EST:** 2005
SALES (est): 1.4MM **Privately Held**
SIC: 2011 Meat by-products from meat slaughtered on site

(P-2108)
YOSEMITE VLY BEEF PKG CO INC
970 E Sandy Mush Rd, Merced (95341-7903)
P.O. Box 1828, Duarte (91009-4828)
PHONE..................626 435-0170
Michael Ban, *President*
E K Ban, *Controller*
Ek Ban, *Manager*
EMP: 28 **EST:** 1965
SQ FT: 5,000
SALES (est): 4.9MM **Privately Held**
SIC: 2011 Meat packing plants

2013 Sausages & Meat Prdts

(P-2109)
AIDELLS SAUSAGE COMPANY INC
2411 Baumann Ave, San Lorenzo (94580-1801)
PHONE..................510 614-5450
Ernie Gabiati, *President*
Yvette Abreu, *Office Mgr*
Tony Kwan, *Controller*
Donna Soares, *Cust Svc Dir*
Dan Vuletich, *Manager*
EMP: 900 **EST:** 2007
SQ FT: 15,000
SALES (est): 186.3MM
SALES (corp-wide): 47B **Publicly Held**
WEB: www.aidells.com
SIC: 2013 5147 Sausages from purchased meat; meats & meat products
HQ: The Hillshire Brands Company
400 S Jefferson St Ste 1n
Chicago IL 60607
312 614-6000

(P-2110)
ALPINE MEATS INC
9850 Lower Sacramento Rd, Stockton (95210-3915)
PHONE..................209 477-2691
Rick Martin, *CEO*
Fernando Estrada, *Production*
Luis Rodriguez, *Maintence Staff*
Robby Jaynes, *Manager*
Dean Wickett, *Manager*
EMP: 50 **EST:** 2009
SALES (est): 8.3MM **Privately Held**
WEB: www.alpinemeats.com
SIC: 2013 Smoked meats from purchased meat

(P-2111)
AMERICAN CUSTOM MEATS LLC
4276 N Tracy Blvd, Tracy (95304-1501)
PHONE..................209 839-8800
Neil Kinney, *President*
Ryan Varni, *Technician*
Kathy Miller, *Controller*
EMP: 88 **EST:** 2011
SQ FT: 75,000
SALES (est): 39.3MM **Privately Held**
WEB: www.acmeats.com
SIC: 2013 2015 2032 Prepared beef products from purchased beef; poultry slaughtering & processing; puddings, except meat: packaged in cans, jars, etc.

(P-2112)
BAR-S FOODS CO
392 Railroad Ct, Milpitas (95035-4339)
PHONE..................408 941-9958
Olga Vasquez, *Branch Mgr*
EMP: 92 **Privately Held**
WEB: www.bar-s.com
SIC: 2013 Sausages & other prepared meats
HQ: Bar-S Foods Co.
5090 N 40th St Ste 300
Phoenix AZ 85018
602 264-7272

(P-2113)
BUCKHORN CAFE INC (PA)
Also Called: Putah Creek Cafe
2 Main St, Winters (95694-1723)
PHONE..................530 795-1319
John Pickerel, *President*
Laura Lucero,
EMP: 70 **EST:** 1954
SQ FT: 7,000
SALES (est): 8MM **Privately Held**
SIC: 5812 5813 2013 Cafe; caterers; bar (drinking places); smoked meats from purchased meat

(P-2114)
CHOICE FOOD PRODUCTS INC
Also Called: Saladino Sausage Company
1822 W Hedges Ave, Fresno (93728-1140)
PHONE..................559 266-1674
Ty Kenny, *President*
Ty Kinney, *President*
Marlese Kinney, *Treasurer*
EMP: 20 **EST:** 2000
SQ FT: 3,048
SALES (est): 2.4MM **Privately Held**
WEB: www.choicefoodproducts.com
SIC: 2013 Sausages & other prepared meats

(P-2115)
COLUMBUS MANUFACTURING INC (HQ)
30977 San Antonio St, Hayward (94544-7109)
PHONE..................510 921-3423
Joe Ennen, *CEO*
Randy Sieve, *CFO*
▲ **EMP:** 100 **EST:** 2006
SQ FT: 121,000
SALES (est): 79.8MM
SALES (corp-wide): 9.6B **Publicly Held**
WEB: www.columbuscraftmeats.com
SIC: 2013 Sausages & related products, from purchased meat
PA: Hormel Foods Corporation
1 Hormel Pl
Austin MN 55912
507 437-5611

(P-2116)
CORRALITOS MARKET & SAUSAGE CO
569 Corralitos Rd, Watsonville (95076-0596)
PHONE..................831 722-2633
Dave Peterson, *President*
Ken Wong, *Vice Pres*
Jo Ellen Tartala, *Admin Sec*
EMP: 23 **EST:** 1957
SQ FT: 5,000
SALES (est): 1.4MM **Privately Held**
WEB: www.corralitosmarketsausagecompany.com
SIC: 2013 5411 Sausages & other prepared meats; grocery stores

(P-2117)
COURAGE PRODUCTION LLC
2475 Courage Dr, Fairfield (94533-6723)
PHONE..................707 422-6300
Philip Gatto, *Mng Member*
Peter Keim, *General Mgr*
Tom Ziegler, *Research*
Kevin Zaccardi, *Controller*
Dorothy Dominguez-Phr, *Human Res Dir*
EMP: 100
SALES (est): 25.4MM **Privately Held**
WEB: www.courageproduction.com
SIC: 2013 Sausages from purchased meat

(P-2118)
FUSION RANCH INC
405 S Airport Blvd, South San Francisco (94080-6909)
PHONE..................650 589-8899
Kaiyen MAI, *President*
EMP: 50 **EST:** 2011
SALES (est): 3.3MM **Privately Held**
WEB: www.fusionranch.com
SIC: 2013 Snack sticks, including jerky: from purchased meat; sausages & related products, from purchased meat; ham, smoked: from purchased meat

(P-2119)
KRAVE PURE FOODS INC
Also Called: Krave Jerky
117 W Napa St Ste A, Sonoma (95476-6691)
PHONE..................707 939-9176
Jonathan A Sebastiani, *CEO*
Katie Toka, *Human Res Dir*
Frank Zampardi, *Sales Dir*
Chris Davis, *Marketing Mgr*
Jake Lastrina, *Marketing Staff*
EMP: 58 **EST:** 2009
SALES (est): 9.7MM **Privately Held**
WEB: www.kravejerky.com
SIC: 2013 5147 Snack sticks, including jerky: from purchased meat; meats & meat products

(P-2120)
MILLER PACKING COMPANY
Also Called: Miller Hot Dogs
1122 Industrial Way, Lodi (95240-3119)
P.O. Box 1390 (95241-1390)
PHONE..................209 339-2310
Michael A De Benedetti, *President*
Staige P Debenedetti, *CEO*
Juan Munguia, *Opers Mgr*
Les Wilson, *Director*
EMP: 50 **EST:** 1965
SQ FT: 40,000
SALES (est): 7.4MM **Privately Held**
WEB: www.millerhotdogs.com
SIC: 2013 Sausages & other prepared meats

(P-2121)
PROVENA FOODS INC
Swiss-American Sausage
251 Darcy Pkwy, Lathrop (95330-8756)
PHONE..................209 858-5555
Theodore Arena, *Branch Mgr*
EMP: 188
SQ FT: 49,000
SALES (corp-wide): 9.6B **Publicly Held**
SIC: 2013 Sausages & other prepared meats
HQ: Provena Foods Inc.
5010 Eucalyptus Ave
Chino CA 91710
909 627-1082

(P-2122)
RSJ VENTURES LLC
Also Called: Chef's Cut Real Jerky
117 W Napa St Ste A, Sonoma (95476-6691)
P.O. Box 110871, Naples FL (34108-0115)
PHONE..................212 905-8666
Dennis Riedel,
Rohan Oza,
Blair Swiler,
EMP: 25 **EST:** 2009
SALES (est): 1.5MM
SALES (corp-wide): 1.8MM **Privately Held**
WEB: www.sonomabrands.com
SIC: 2013 5149 Snack sticks, including jerky: from purchased meat; dried or canned foods
PA: Sonoma Brands Llc
117 W Napa St Ste C
Sonoma CA 95476
707 656-2015

(P-2123)
SAAGS PRODUCTS LLC
1799 Factor Ave, San Leandro (94577-5617)
P.O. Box 2078 (94577-0207)
PHONE..................510 678-3412
Jim Mosle, *CEO*
Timothy Dam, *President*
Peter Turcotte, *Technology*
John Ling, *Safety Mgr*
Brenda Kemp, *Supervisor*
▲ **EMP:** 52 **EST:** 2006
SQ FT: 40,000
SALES (est): 7.1MM
SALES (corp-wide): 9.6B **Publicly Held**
WEB: www.saags.com
SIC: 2013 Sausages from purchased meat; spiced meats from purchased meat
PA: Hormel Foods Corporation
1 Hormel Pl
Austin MN 55912
507 437-5611

(P-2124)
SAPAR USA INC (HQ)
Also Called: Fabrique Delices
1610 Delta Ct Unit 1, Hayward (94544-7043)
PHONE..................510 441-9500
Marc Poinsignon, *President*
Antonio Pinheiro, *Vice Pres*
David Kemp, *Principal*
Vanessa Sanchez, *Office Mgr*
Manuel Navarro, *QC Mgr*
EMP: 25 **EST:** 1985
SQ FT: 20,000
SALES (est): 11.5MM
SALES (corp-wide): 40.6MM **Privately Held**
WEB: www.fabriquedelices.com
SIC: 2013 Spreads, sandwich: meat from purchased meat
PA: Village Gourmet Holdco, Llc
32 W 39th St Ph 17
New York NY 10018
212 219-1230

(P-2125)
SPAR SAUSAGE CO
Also Called: Caspers
688 Williams St, San Leandro (94577-2624)
PHONE..................510 614-8100
Jack Dorian, *Manager*
EMP: 19
SQ FT: 9,750
SALES (corp-wide): 3.1MM **Privately Held**
WEB: www.sparsausage.com
SIC: 2013 Sausages from purchased meat
PA: Spar Sausage Co.
3508 Mt Diablo Blvd Ste J
Lafayette CA 94549
925 283-6877

(P-2126)
SUNNYVALLEY SMOKED MEATS INC
2475 W Yosemite Ave, Manteca (95337-9641)
P.O. Box 2158 (95336-1159)
PHONE..................209 825-0288
William Andreetta, *President*

PRODUCTS & SERVICES SECTION 2022 - Cheese County (P-2146)

Treva Andreetta, *Vice Pres*
Dominic Marquez, *Controller*
Heather Grandstaff, *Human Res Dir*
Debi Hawkes, *QC Mgr*
▲ **EMP:** 250 **EST:** 1990
SQ FT: 41,000
SALES: 147.8MM **Privately Held**
WEB: www.sunnyvalleysmokedmeats.com
SIC: 2013 Bacon, side & sliced: from purchased meat; ham, smoked: from purchased meat; smoked meats from purchased meat

(P-2127)
VALLEY PROTEIN LLC
1828 E Hedges Ave, Fresno (93703-3633)
PHONE.............................559 498-7115
Robert Coyle, *Mng Member*
Angela Sanchez, *Controller*
Nate Coyle, *Purchasing*
EMP: 95 **EST:** 2010
SALES (est): 9.6MM **Privately Held**
WEB: www.valleyproteinfresno.com
SIC: 2013 Prepared beef products from purchased beef

(P-2128)
WYCEN FOODS INC (PA)
560 Estabrook St, San Leandro (94577-3512)
PHONE.............................510 351-1987
Arthur Leong, *President*
Nancy Leong, *Treasurer*
Cynthia Wong, *Opers Staff*
▲ **EMP:** 17 **EST:** 1981
SQ FT: 25,000
SALES (est): 2.9MM **Privately Held**
WEB: www.wycenfoods.com
SIC: 2013 2038 Sausages from purchased meat; ethnic foods, frozen

2015 Poultry Slaughtering, Dressing & Processing

(P-2129)
FOSTER FARMS LLC
1900 Kern St, Kingsburg (93631-9687)
PHONE.............................559 897-1081
Donald Jones, *Branch Mgr*
EMP: 60 **Privately Held**
WEB: www.fosterfarms.com
SIC: 2015 Poultry slaughtering & processing
PA: Foster Farms, Llc
    1000 Davis St
    Livingston CA 95334

(P-2130)
FOSTER POULTRY FARMS (PA)
1000 Davis St, Livingston (95334-1526)
P.O. Box 457 (95334-0457)
PHONE.............................209 394-7901
Dan Huber, *CEO*
Ron M Foster, *President*
Donald Jackson, *President*
Caryn Doyle, *CFO*
Analuisa Reynoso, *CFO*
◆ **EMP:** 250
SQ FT: 40,000
SALES (est): 3B **Privately Held**
WEB: www.fosterfarms.com
SIC: 2015 Poultry slaughtering & processing

(P-2131)
FOSTER POULTRY FARMS
Also Called: Foster Farms
1307 Ellenwood Rd, Waterford (95386-8702)
PHONE.............................209 394-7901
Jay Husman, *Manager*
Janice Cardoza, *Supervisor*
EMP: 464
SQ FT: 68,316
SALES (corp-wide): 1.2B **Privately Held**
WEB: www.fosterfarms.com
SIC: 2015 Poultry slaughtering & processing
PA: Foster Poultry Farms
    1000 Davis St
    Livingston CA 95334
    209 394-7901

(P-2132)
FOSTER POULTRY FARMS
Also Called: Foster Farms
1333 Swan St, Livingston (95334-1559)
P.O. Box 457 (95334-0457)
PHONE.............................209 394-7901
Brent Allen, *Branch Mgr*
Gene Runca, *Executive*
Donna Machado, *Creative Dir*
Jeremy Handy, *Programmer Anys*
Robert Miles, *Research*
EMP: 464
SALES (corp-wide): 1.2B **Privately Held**
WEB: www.fosterfarms.com
SIC: 2015 Poultry slaughtering & processing
PA: Foster Poultry Farms
    1000 Davis St
    Livingston CA 95334
    209 394-7901

(P-2133)
FOSTER POULTRY FARMS
Also Called: Foster Turkey Live Haul
1033 S Center St, Turlock (95380-5568)
PHONE.............................209 668-5922
Steve Page, *Manager*
Tim Baker, *Maintence Staff*
EMP: 100
SALES (corp-wide): 1.2B **Privately Held**
WEB: www.fosterfarms.com
SIC: 2015 Poultry slaughtering & processing
PA: Foster Poultry Farms
    1000 Davis St
    Livingston CA 95334
    209 394-7901

(P-2134)
FOSTER POULTRY FARMS
900 W Belgravia Ave, Fresno (93706-3909)
PHONE.............................559 265-2000
Jessi Amezcua, *Branch Mgr*
Andy Rutherford, *Foreman/Supr*
Eric Baker, *Marketing Staff*
Sheryl Morse, *Manager*
EMP: 464
SALES (corp-wide): 1.2B **Privately Held**
WEB: www.fosterfarms.com
SIC: 2015 5812 0173 5191 Chicken slaughtering & processing; turkey processing & slaughtering; chicken restaurant; almond grove; animal feeds; local trucking, without storage; chicken hatchery
PA: Foster Poultry Farms
    1000 Davis St
    Livingston CA 95334
    209 394-7901

(P-2135)
FOSTER POULTRY FARMS
Also Called: Foster Farms
2960 S Cherry Ave, Fresno (93706-5445)
PHONE.............................559 442-3771
Bob Hansen, *Manager*
Tracy Bianchi, *Controller*
Rebeca Reyes, *Human Res Mgr*
Scott Shows, *Plant Mgr*
Michael Montero, *Maint Spvr*
EMP: 464
SALES (corp-wide): 1.2B **Privately Held**
WEB: www.fosterfarms.com
SIC: 2015 Poultry slaughtering & processing
PA: Foster Poultry Farms
    1000 Davis St
    Livingston CA 95334
    209 394-7901

(P-2136)
GRIMAUD FARMS CALIFORNIA INC (DH)
1320 S Aurora Ave Ste A, Stockton (95206-1616)
PHONE.............................209 466-3200
Rheal Cayer, *President*
Fricrick Grimaud, *Ch of Bd*
▲ **EMP:** 20 **EST:** 1985
SQ FT: 42,000
SALES (est): 12.1MM
SALES (corp-wide): 355.8K **Privately Held**
WEB: www.grimaudfarms.com
SIC: 2015 Poultry slaughtering & processing
HQ: Groupe Grimaud La Corbiere
    Grimaud
    Sevremoine 49450
    964 435-509

(P-2137)
OLIVERA EGG RANCH LLC
Also Called: Olivera Foods
3315 Sierra Rd, San Jose (95132-3099)
P.O. Box 32126 (95152-2126)
PHONE.............................408 258-8074
Edward F Olivera,
▲ **EMP:** 60 **EST:** 1949
SQ FT: 35,000
SALES (est): 8.8MM **Privately Held**
WEB: www.oliveraeggranch.com
SIC: 2015 5143 5142 5144 Egg processing; cheese; butter; packaged frozen goods; eggs

(P-2138)
PETALUMA ACQUISITIONS LLC
2700 Lakeville Hwy, Petaluma (94954-5606)
PHONE.............................707 763-1904
George N Gillett Jr,
Darrel Freitas,
Jeffrey J Joyce,
EMP: 849 **EST:** 2001
SALES (est): 6.4MM
SALES (corp-wide): 1.2B **Privately Held**
WEB: www.cityofpetaluma.org
SIC: 2015 Chicken slaughtering & processing
PA: Perdue Farms Inc.
    31149 Old Ocean City Rd
    Salisbury MD 21804
    410 543-3000

(P-2139)
VALLEY FRESH INC (HQ)
1404 S Fresno Ave, Stockton (95206-1174)
PHONE.............................209 943-5411
Ronald W Fielding, *CEO*
Eugene Carney, *Vice Pres*
EMP: 50 **EST:** 1956
SQ FT: 120,000
SALES (est): 66.9MM
SALES (corp-wide): 9.6B **Publicly Held**
WEB: www.hormel.com
SIC: 2015 Poultry, processed: canned; poultry, processed: frozen
PA: Hormel Foods Corporation
    1 Hormel Pl
    Austin MN 55912
    507 437-5611

(P-2140)
ZACKY & SONS POULTRY LLC (PA)
Also Called: Zacky Farms
2020 S East Ave, Fresno (93721-3328)
P.O. Box 12556 (93778-2556)
PHONE.............................559 443-2700
Lillian Zacky,
Kirk Vandergeest, *CFO*
EMP: 629 **EST:** 2013
SALES (est): 119.6MM **Privately Held**
WEB: www.zacky.com
SIC: 2015 Poultry slaughtering & processing

2021 Butter

(P-2141)
CALIFORNIA DAIRIES INC
Also Called: San Joaquin Valley Dairymen
475 S Tegner Rd, Turlock (95380-9406)
PHONE.............................209 656-1942
Tamara Staggs, *Branch Mgr*
Tom Baldwin, *Manager*
EMP: 143
SALES (corp-wide): 3.3B **Privately Held**
WEB: www.californiadairies.com
SIC: 2021 2023 2026 Creamery butter; dry, condensed, evaporated dairy products; fluid milk
PA: California Dairies, Inc.
    2000 N Plaza Dr
    Visalia CA 93291
    559 625-2200

(P-2142)
MIYOKOS KITCHEN
Also Called: Miyoko's Creamery
2086 Marina Ave, Petaluma (94954-6714)
PHONE.............................415 521-5313
Miyoko Schinner, *CEO*
John Breen, *CFO*
Tom Shonn, *CFO*
Shonn Tom, *CFO*
Dan Rauch, *Vice Pres*
◆ **EMP:** 50 **EST:** 2013
SQ FT: 30,000
SALES (est): 14MM **Privately Held**
WEB: www.miyokos.com
SIC: 2021 2022 Creamery butter; cheese, natural & processed; cheese spreads, dips, pastes & other cheese products

(P-2143)
STRAUS FAMILY CREAMERY INC
1105 Industrial Ave # 200, Petaluma (94952-1141)
PHONE.............................707 776-2887
Albert Straus, *CEO*
Deborah Parrish, *CFO*
Michael Scheu, *Vice Pres*
Juan Gomez, *Opers Staff*
Shereen Mahnami, *Corp Comm Staff*
EMP: 64 **EST:** 1994
SQ FT: 40,000
SALES (est): 28.7MM **Privately Held**
WEB: www.strausfamilycreamery.com
SIC: 2021 2023 2026 Creamery butter; ice cream mix, unfrozen: liquid or dry; yogurt

2022 Cheese

(P-2144)
CHEESE ADMINISTRATIVE CORP INC
429 H St, Los Banos (93635-4113)
PHONE.............................209 826-3744
Frank Peluso, *CEO*
EMP: 26 **EST:** 1980
SQ FT: 3,000
SALES (est): 3.8MM **Privately Held**
SIC: 2022 Natural cheese

(P-2145)
CYPRESS GROVE CHEVRE INC
1330 Q St, Arcata (95521-5740)
PHONE.............................707 825-1100
Pamela Dressler, *President*
Jack Ridlon, *Technician*
Lynne Sandstrom, *Finance*
Robert Kohrt, *Sales Staff*
Bob McCall, *Director*
▲ **EMP:** 52 **EST:** 2000
SQ FT: 12,500
SALES (est): 16.6MM
SALES (corp-wide): 280.1MM **Privately Held**
WEB: www.cypressgrovecheese.com
SIC: 2022 Natural cheese
HQ: Emmi Ag
    Landenbergstrasse 1
    Luzern LU 6005
    582 272-727

(P-2146)
DAIRY FARMERS AMERICA INC
600 Trade Way, Turlock (95380-9433)
PHONE.............................209 667-9627
Thomas Baker, *Manager*
Kristin Naranjo, *Administration*
Mark Rollins, *Engineer*
Sara Santos, *Marketing Staff*
EMP: 87
SQ FT: 63,976
SALES (corp-wide): 17.8B **Privately Held**
WEB: www.dfamilk.com
SIC: 2022 2026 Natural cheese; fluid milk
PA: Dairy Farmers Of America, Inc.
    1405 N 98th St
    Kansas City KS 66111
    816 801-6455

2022 - Cheese County (P-2147)   **PRODUCTS & SERVICES SECTION**

(P-2147)
EINSTEIN NOAH REST GROUP INC
Also Called: Noah's
15996 Los Gatos Blvd, Los Gatos (95032-3424)
PHONE..................................408 358-5895
Susan Asef, *Manager*
EMP: 180 Privately Held
WEB: www.bagelbrands.com
SIC: 2022 5812 Spreads, cheese; cafe
PA: Einstein Noah Restaurant Group, Inc.
 555 Zang St Ste 300
 Lakewood CO 80228

(P-2148)
GALLO GLOBAL NUTRITION LLC
Also Called: Joseph Farms
10561 Highway 140, Atwater (95301-9309)
P.O. Box 775 (95301-0775)
PHONE..................................209 394-7984
Michael Gallo, *CEO*
Peter Lundrigan, *Info Tech Dir*
Jenny Cargill, *Human Res Dir*
EMP: 105 EST: 2003
SQ FT: 5,000
SALES (est): 14.4MM Privately Held
WEB: www.josephfarms.com
SIC: 2022 8099 0241 Cheese spreads, dips, pastes & other cheese products; nutrition services; dairy farms

(P-2149)
HILMAR CHEESE COMPANY INC
3600 W Canal Dr, Turlock (95380-8507)
P.O. Box 910, Hilmar (95324-0910)
PHONE..................................209 667-6076
David Ahlem, *CEO*
EMP: 83
SALES (corp-wide): 264.3MM Privately Held
WEB: www.hilmarcheese.com
SIC: 2022 Natural cheese
PA: Hilmar Cheese Company, Inc.
 8901 Lander Ave
 Hilmar CA 95324
 209 667-6076

(P-2150)
HILMAR CHEESE COMPANY INC (PA)
Also Called: Hilmar Ingredients
8901 Lander Ave, Hilmar (95324-8355)
P.O. Box 910 (95324-0910)
PHONE..................................209 667-6076
John J Jeter, *President*
Donald Jay Hicks, *CFO*
Frank Cortez, *Officer*
Lisa Sahlman, *Executive Asst*
Rodolfo Rojo, *Administration*
◆ EMP: 1244 EST: 1984
SALES (est): 264.3MM Privately Held
WEB: www.hilmarcheese.com
SIC: 2022 Natural cheese

(P-2151)
LAND OLAKES INC
3601 County Road C, Orland (95963-9117)
PHONE..................................530 865-7626
EMP: 29
SALES (corp-wide): 6.8B Privately Held
SIC: 2022 Cheese; Natural And Processed, Nsk
PA: Land O'lakes, Inc.
 4001 Lexington Ave N
 Arden Hills MN 55126
 651 375-2222

(P-2152)
LEPRINO FOODS COMPANY
2401 N Macarthur Dr, Tracy (95376-2095)
PHONE..................................209 835-8340
Joel Crane, *General Mgr*
Catherine Cardenas, *Analyst*
Gabriela Frausto, *Human Res Mgr*
Michael Lopez, *Purchasing*
Mike Lopez, *Purch Agent*
EMP: 253
SALES (corp-wide): 1.9B Privately Held
WEB: www.leprinofoods.com
SIC: 2022 Natural cheese
PA: Leprino Foods Company
 1830 W 38th Ave
 Denver CO 80211
 303 480-2600

(P-2153)
RIZO LOPEZ FOODS INC
Also Called: Don Francisco Cheese
201 S Mcclure Rd, Modesto (95357-0519)
P.O. Box 1689, Empire (95319-1689)
PHONE..................................800 626-5587
Edwin Rizo, *President*
Ivan Rizo, *CEO*
Stefan Edh, *Controller*
Sergio Vaca, *Controller*
Juan Luis De La Torre, *Plant Mgr*
▲ EMP: 298 EST: 1990
SQ FT: 3,800
SALES (est): 65.8MM Privately Held
WEB: www.donfranciscocheese.com
SIC: 2022 5143 2023 5141 Natural cheese; whey, raw or liquid; processed cheese; dairy products, except dried or canned; dry, condensed, evaporated dairy products; yogurt mix; groceries, general line

(P-2154)
RUMIANO CHEESE CO (PA)
1629 County Road E, Willows (95988-9642)
P.O. Box 863 (95988-0863)
PHONE..................................530 934-5438
Baird Rumiano, *President*
John F Rumiano, *Vice Pres*
Aaron Michaels, *Info Tech Mgr*
Kevin Muno, *Software Dev*
Anthony Rumiano, *Controller*
▲ EMP: 106 EST: 1921
SQ FT: 30,000
SALES (est): 32MM Privately Held
WEB: www.rumianocheese.com
SIC: 2022 Natural cheese

(P-2155)
RUMIANO CHEESE CO
511 9th St, Crescent City (95531-3408)
P.O. Box 305 (95531-0305)
PHONE..................................707 465-1535
Baird Rumiano, *Manager*
Jill Whipple, *Technology*
Patrick Henson, *Opers Staff*
Kirk Olesen, *Sales Executive*
Michel Bray, *Sales Staff*
EMP: 44
SALES (corp-wide): 32MM Privately Held
WEB: www.rumianocheese.com
SIC: 2022 Natural cheese
PA: Rumiano Cheese Co.
 1629 County Road E
 Willows CA 95988
 530 934-5438

(P-2156)
SAPUTO CHEESE USA INC
691 Inyo Ave, Newman (95360-1403)
PHONE..................................262 307-6738
Evan Sikma, *Branch Mgr*
EMP: 100 Privately Held
WEB: www.saputousafoodservice.com
SIC: 2022 Natural cheese
HQ: Saputo Cheese Usa Inc.
 1 Overlook Pt Ste 300
 Lincolnshire IL 60069

(P-2157)
SIERRA NEVADA CHEESE CO INC
6505 County Road 39, Willows (95988-9709)
PHONE..................................530 934-8660
Ben Gregersen, *President*
John Dundon, *Vice Pres*
Kathleen McJunkin, *Human Resources*
Adrienne Ramos, *Marketing Staff*
Meghan Curry, *Mktg Coord*
EMP: 58 EST: 1997
SQ FT: 27,000
SALES (est): 15.6MM Privately Held
WEB: www.sierranevadacheese.com
SIC: 2022 Natural cheese

2023 Milk, Condensed & Evaporated

(P-2158)
CYTOSPORT INC
1340 Treat Blvd Ste 350, Walnut Creek (94597-7581)
PHONE..................................707 751-3942
Rahul Pinto, *CEO*
Scott Silberman, *COO*
Ada Cheng, *CFO*
Nikki Brown, *Chief Mktg Ofcr*
Kirk Connors, *Vice Pres*
▲ EMP: 190 EST: 1997
SALES (est): 37.4MM
SALES (corp-wide): 70.3B Publicly Held
WEB: www.musclemilk.com
SIC: 2023 2086 Dry, condensed, evaporated dairy products; soft drinks: packaged in cans, bottles, etc.
PA: Pepsico, Inc.
 700 Anderson Hill Rd
 Purchase NY 10577
 914 253-2000

(P-2159)
FIVE FLAVORS HERBS INC
344 40th St, Oakland (94609-2609)
PHONE..................................510 923-0178
Benjamin Zappin, *Partner*
Vincent Frascello, *Mfg Staff*
Meghan Elizabeth, *Opers Staff*
EMP: 18 EST: 2012
SALES (est): 2.1MM Privately Held
WEB: www.fiveflavorsherbs.com
SIC: 2023 Dietary supplements, dairy & non-dairy based

(P-2160)
FOSTER DAIRY FARMS
572 State Highway 1, Fortuna (95540-9705)
PHONE..................................707 725-6182
Rich Gilladuci, *Manager*
EMP: 19
SALES (corp-wide): 374.1MM Privately Held
WEB: www.crystalcreamery.com
SIC: 2023 Powdered milk
PA: Foster Dairy Farms
 529 Kansas Ave
 Modesto CA 95351
 209 576-3400

(P-2161)
FREAL FOODS LLC
6121 Hollis St Ste 500, Emeryville (94608-2078)
PHONE..................................800 483-3218
Dinsh Guzdar, *President*
John Steel, *Engineer*
Diane Garvin, *Opers Staff*
Steven Casey, *Marketing Staff*
Leah Dixon, *Marketing Staff*
◆ EMP: 100 EST: 1997
SALES (est): 25.1MM
SALES (corp-wide): 4B Privately Held
WEB: www.freal.com
SIC: 2023 Milkshake mix
PA: Rich Products Corporation
 1 Robert Rich Way
 Buffalo NY 14213
 716 878-8000

(P-2162)
GMP MANUFACTURING INC
Also Called: Cytosport
1340 Treat Blvd Ste 350, Walnut Creek (94597-7581)
PHONE..................................707 751-3942
Gregory Pickett, *President*
EMP: 35 EST: 1998
SQ FT: 67,000
SALES (est): 8.3MM
SALES (corp-wide): 70.3B Publicly Held
WEB: www.pepsico.com
SIC: 2023 Dietary supplements, dairy & non-dairy based
PA: Pepsico, Inc.
 700 Anderson Hill Rd
 Purchase NY 10577
 914 253-2000

(P-2163)
HILMAR WHEY PROTEIN INC (PA)
9001 Lander Ave, Hilmar (95324-8320)
P.O. Box 910 (95324-0910)
PHONE..................................209 667-6076
John J Jeter, *President*
EMP: 399 EST: 1991
SALES (est): 32.7MM Privately Held
WEB: www.hilmaringredients.com
SIC: 2023 Concentrated whey

(P-2164)
MISSION AG RESOURCES LLC
Also Called: Sierra Feeds
6801 Avenue 430 Unit A, Reedley (93654-9002)
PHONE..................................559 591-3333
Al Cumin, *Mng Member*
Therald Benevedo, *Mng Member*
Michelle Bonce, *Assistant*
EMP: 20 EST: 2005
SALES (est): 3.3MM Privately Held
WEB: www.techag.com
SIC: 2023 Dietary supplements, dairy & non-dairy based

(P-2165)
NESTLE USA INC
Also Called: Nestle Dsd
4065 E Therese Ave, Fresno (93725-8920)
PHONE..................................559 834-2554
Miguel Alvarez, *Branch Mgr*
EMP: 208
SALES (corp-wide): 92.3B Privately Held
WEB: www.nestleusa.com
SIC: 2023 Evaporated milk
HQ: Nestle Usa, Inc.
 1812 N Moore St Ste 118
 Rosslyn VA 22209
 440 264-7249

(P-2166)
NESTLE USA INC
Also Called: Nestle Confections Factory
736 Garner Rd, Modesto (95357-0515)
PHONE..................................209 574-2000
Stephanie Hart, *Branch Mgr*
Courtney Archibald, *Manager*
Becky Kemplin, *Representative*
EMP: 208
SALES (corp-wide): 92.3B Privately Held
WEB: www.nestleusa.com
SIC: 2023 2033 2064 2099 Evaporated milk; canned milk, whole; cream substitutes; fruits: packaged in cans, jars, etc.; tomato paste: packaged in cans, jars, etc.; tomato sauce: packaged in cans, jars, etc.; candy & other confectionery products; breakfast bars; pasta, uncooked: packaged with other ingredients
HQ: Nestle Usa, Inc.
 1812 N Moore St Ste 118
 Rosslyn VA 22209
 440 264-7249

(P-2167)
SANTINI FOODS INC
Also Called: Santini Fine Wines
16505 Worthley Dr, San Lorenzo (94580-1811)
PHONE..................................510 317-8888
Bruce Liu, *President*
Alyssia Smith, *Admin Asst*
Punit Dave, *Research*
Lisa Medina, *Finance Mgr*
Rohit Vaidya, *Analyst*
◆ EMP: 133 EST: 1987
SQ FT: 105,000
SALES (est): 54.3MM Privately Held
WEB: www.santinifoods.com
SIC: 2023 2026 2032 2087 Condensed, concentrated & evaporated milk products; milk processing (pasteurizing, homogenizing, bottling); ethnic foods: canned, jarred, etc.; beverage bases, concentrates, syrups, powders & mixes

(P-2168)
WAYNE
Also Called: Molaniki Distributor
640 W California Ave, Sunnyvale (94086-3624)
PHONE..................................669 206-2179
EMP: 30 EST: 2020

▲ = Import ▼ = Export
◆ = Import/Export

PRODUCTS & SERVICES SECTION   2026 - Milk County (P-2192)

SALES (est): 1.6MM Privately Held
SIC: 2023 Baby formulas

2024 Ice Cream

(P-2169)
B44 CATALAN BISTRO
44 Belden Pl, San Francisco (94104-2802)
PHONE...................................415 986-6287
Daniel Olivella, *Principal*
EMP: 20 EST: 1999
SALES (est): 108.5K Privately Held
WEB: www.b44sf.com
SIC: 5812 5813 2024 Seafood restaurants; wine bar; ice cream & frozen desserts

(P-2170)
CYGNUS HOME SERVICE LLC
Also Called: Schwan's Home Service
9919 Kent St, Elk Grove (95624-1401)
PHONE...................................916 686-8662
Marvin Schwan, *President*
EMP: 17
SALES (corp-wide): 462.5MM Privately Held
WEB: www.schwans.com
SIC: 5963 2024 2037 Food services, direct sales; lingerie sales, house-to-house; ice cream, packaged: molded, on sticks, etc.; ice milk, packaged: molded, on sticks, etc.; fruit juice concentrates, frozen
PA: Cygnus Home Service, Llc
  115 W College Dr
  Marshall MN 56258
  507 532-3274

(P-2171)
DREYERS GRAND ICE CREAM INC (DH)
Also Called: Haagen-Dazs
5929 College Ave, Oakland (94618-1325)
PHONE...................................510 594-9466
Michael Mitchell, *CEO*
Steven P Barbour, *CFO*
Tony Fernandez, *Business Anlyst*
Dan Kilgore, *Business Mgr*
Jessie Sanchez, *Business Mgr*
◆ EMP: 230 EST: 1928
SQ FT: 64,000
SALES (est): 644.6MM
SALES (corp-wide): 177.9K Privately Held
WEB: www.haagendazs.us
SIC: 5812 2024 Ice cream stands or dairy bars; ice cream & frozen desserts
HQ: Dreyer's Grand Ice Cream Holdings, Inc.
  5929 College Ave
  Oakland CA 94618
  510 652-8187

(P-2172)
DREYERS GRAND ICE CREAM INC
5929 College Ave, Oakland (94618-1325)
PHONE...................................510 652-8187
Scott Brooks, *Controller*
Kim Peddle-Rguem, *CEO*
Dale Brockmeyer, *CFO*
Heidi Zuber, *Officer*
EMP: 2500 EST: 1985
SALES (est): 2.8B Privately Held
WEB: www.dreyersgrandicecream.com
SIC: 2024 5143 Ice cream & frozen desserts; dairy products, except dried or canned

(P-2173)
FONO UNLIMITED (PA)
Also Called: Bravo Fono
99 Stanford Shopping Ctr, Palo Alto (94304-1424)
PHONE...................................650 322-4664
Paulette Fono, *President*
Laslo Fono, *Vice Pres*
EMP: 30 EST: 1972
SALES (est): 3.2MM Privately Held
SIC: 2024 5812 5813 Ice cream, bulk; Italian restaurant; drinking places

(P-2174)
GLASS JAR INC
Also Called: Picnic Basket, The
125 Beach St, Santa Cruz (95060-5412)
PHONE...................................831 427-9946
Zachary Davis, *CEO*
EMP: 17
SALES (corp-wide): 7MM Privately Held
WEB: www.theglassjar.com
SIC: 2024 Ice cream & frozen desserts
PA: The Glass Jar Inc
  913 Cedar St
  Santa Cruz CA 95060
  831 227-2247

(P-2175)
GLASS JAR INC (PA)
Also Called: Penny Ice Creamery, The
913 Cedar St, Santa Cruz (95060-3801)
PHONE...................................831 227-2247
Zachary Davis, *CEO*
EMP: 83 EST: 2010
SALES (est): 7MM Privately Held
WEB: www.theglassjar.com
SIC: 2024 5812 Ice cream & frozen desserts; ice cream stands or dairy bars

(P-2176)
HELADOS LA TAPATIA INC
4495 W Shaw Ave, Fresno (93722-6206)
PHONE...................................559 441-1105
Emilio Sandoval, *Principal*
Sergio Sandoval, *CFO*
EMP: 40 EST: 1984
SQ FT: 8,800
SALES (est): 9.1MM Privately Held
WEB: www.heladoslatapatia.com
SIC: 2024 5143 Ice cream & frozen desserts; ice cream & ices

(P-2177)
LOCO VENTURES INC
Also Called: Loard's Ice Cream and Candies
2000 Wayne Ave, San Leandro (94577-3333)
PHONE...................................510 351-0405
Steven Cohen, *President*
Scott Cohen, *Vice Pres*
EMP: 21 EST: 1950
SQ FT: 16,000
SALES (est): 735.4K Privately Held
WEB: www.loards.com
SIC: 2024 2064 5812 5441 Ice cream, bulk; candy & other confectionery products; ice cream stands or dairy bars; candy

(P-2178)
MARIANNES ICE CREAM LLC (PA)
2100 Delaware Ave Ste B, Santa Cruz (95060-6362)
PHONE...................................831 457-1447
Charles Wilcox, *Mng Member*
Kelly Dillon,
▲ EMP: 47 EST: 1993
SALES (est): 5.1MM Privately Held
WEB: www.mariannesicecream.com
SIC: 2024 5812 Ice cream & frozen desserts; ice cream stands or dairy bars

(P-2179)
MATTERHORN ICE CREAM INC
1221 66th St, Sacramento (95819-4323)
PHONE...................................208 287-8916
Thomas Nist, *President*
Todd Wilson, *CFO*
EMP: 19 EST: 1982
SQ FT: 24,000
SALES (est): 917.4K Privately Held
SIC: 2024 Ice cream & ice milk

(P-2180)
MAVENS CREAMERY LLC
1701 S 7th St Ste 7, San Jose (95112-6024)
PHONE...................................408 216-9270
Kim Lam, *Mng Member*
Tony Lam, *Mng Member*
EMP: 30 EST: 2015
SQ FT: 5,000
SALES (est): 3.6MM Privately Held
WEB: www.mavenscreamery.com
SIC: 2024 Ice cream & frozen desserts

(P-2181)
NAIA INC
Also Called: Gelateria Naia
736 Alfred Nobel Dr, Hercules (94547-1805)
PHONE...................................510 724-2479
Christopher Tan, *President*
Mark Bagnall, *COO*
Christopher C Tan, *Principal*
EMP: 21 EST: 2002
SALES (est): 5.4MM Privately Held
WEB: www.gelaterianaia.com
SIC: 2024 Ice cream, bulk

(P-2182)
RAMAR INTERNATIONAL CORP (PA)
Also Called: Orientex Foods
1101 Railroad Ave, Pittsburg (94565-2641)
P.O. Box 111 (94565-0011)
PHONE...................................925 439-9009
Susan Quesada, *CEO*
Edmund Pascual, *Branch Mgr*
Grace Cruz, *Office Mgr*
Primo Quesada, *CIO*
Reginald Mendoza, *Info Tech Dir*
◆ EMP: 40 EST: 1968
SALES (est): 44.5MM Privately Held
WEB: www.ramarfoods.com
SIC: 2024 2013 5141 Ice cream & frozen desserts; sausages & other prepared meats; groceries, general line

(P-2183)
SUPER STORE INDUSTRIES
Also Called: Mid Valley Dairy
2600 Spengler Way, Turlock (95380-8591)
PHONE...................................209 668-2100
Joe Mc Gill, *Manager*
Yancy Hopper, *Engineer*
Joseph Lui, *Controller*
Mark Hujdic, *Manager*
Don Warren, *Manager*
EMP: 100 Privately Held
WEB: www.ssica.com
SIC: 2024 5143 Ice cream & frozen desserts; ice cream & ices
PA: Super Store Industries
  16888 Mckinley Ave
  Lathrop CA 95330

(P-2184)
THREE TWINS ORGANIC INC (PA)
Also Called: Three Twins Organic Ice Cream
600 California St Fl 6, San Francisco (94108-2733)
PHONE...................................707 763-8946
Neal H Gottlieb, *CEO*
Scott Sowry, *Vice Pres*
Debbie Lee, *Finance*
Edith Jimenez, *Assistant*
EMP: 21 EST: 2005
SALES (est): 3.4MM Privately Held
WEB: www.threetwinsicecream.com
SIC: 2024 5199 5812 Ice cream, bulk; ice, manufactured or natural; ice cream stands or dairy bars

(P-2185)
VAMPIRE PENGUIN LLC (PA)
907 K St, Sacramento (95814-3511)
PHONE...................................916 553-4197
Leo Alejandro San Luis, *Mng Member*
EMP: 19 EST: 2013
SALES (est): 1.9MM Privately Held
WEB: www.vampirepenguin.com
SIC: 2024 Ice cream, bulk

2026 Milk

(P-2186)
CALIFORNIA DAIRIES INC
755 F St, Fresno (93706-3416)
P.O. Box 11865 (93775-1865)
PHONE...................................559 233-5154
Robert Ray, *Branch Mgr*
Bill Twist, *Branch Mgr*
EMP: 179
SALES (corp-wide): 3.3B Privately Held
WEB: www.californiadairies.com
SIC: 2026 2021 2023 Fluid milk; creamery butter; dried milk
PA: California Dairies, Inc.
  2000 N Plaza Dr
  Visalia CA 93291
  559 625-2200

(P-2187)
CRYSTAL CREAM & BUTTER CO (HQ)
8340 Belvedere Ave, Sacramento (95826-5902)
PHONE...................................916 444-7200
Donald K Hansen, *Chairman*
Michael J Newell, *President*
Dan Kosewski, *Vice Pres*
EMP: 100 EST: 1901
SQ FT: 100,000
SALES (est): 51.3MM
SALES (corp-wide): 2.2B Privately Held
WEB: www.crystalcreamery.com
SIC: 2026 2021 2023 Milk processing (pasteurizing, homogenizing, bottling); cottage cheese; yogurt; creamery butter; ice cream & ice milk
PA: Hp Hood Llc
  6 Kimball Ln Ste 400
  Lynnfield MA 01940
  617 887-8441

(P-2188)
FISCALINI CHEESE COMPANY LP
7206 Kiernan Ave, Modesto (95358-8974)
PHONE...................................209 346-0384
John Fiscalini, *Partner*
EMP: 17 EST: 2000
SALES (est): 1.2MM Privately Held
WEB: www.fiscalinifarmstead.com
SIC: 2026 Bakers' cheese

(P-2189)
FOSTER DAIRY FARMS
Also Called: Foster Farms Dairy
415 Kansas Ave, Modesto (95351-1515)
PHONE...................................209 576-2300
Cliff Oilar, *Manager*
EMP: 19
SALES (corp-wide): 374.1MM Privately Held
WEB: www.crystalcreamery.com
SIC: 5451 2026 2022 2021 Dairy products stores; fluid milk; cheese, natural & processed; creamery butter
PA: Foster Dairy Farms
  529 Kansas Ave
  Modesto CA 95351
  209 576-3400

(P-2190)
GOLDEN STATE MIXING INC
415 D St, Turlock (95380-5452)
P.O. Box 3046 (95381-3046)
PHONE...................................209 632-3656
Tim D Brewster, *President*
Brant Enoch, *Vice Pres*
EMP: 30 EST: 2009
SALES (est): 4.6MM Privately Held
WEB: www.goldenstatemixing.com
SIC: 2026 Fluid milk

(P-2191)
HP HOOD LLC
8340 Belvedere Ave, Sacramento (95826-5902)
PHONE...................................916 379-9266
Gary Saavedra, *Branch Mgr*
Aaron Nickens, *Technician*
Jeremy Banko, *Analyst*
Karen Tobin, *QC Mgr*
Maria Yepez-Cuevas, *Senior Mgr*
EMP: 296
SALES (corp-wide): 2.2B Privately Held
WEB: www.hood.com
SIC: 2026 Fluid milk
PA: Hp Hood Llc
  6 Kimball Ln Ste 400
  Lynnfield MA 01940
  617 887-8441

(P-2192)
JACKSON-MITCHELL INC (PA)
Also Called: Meyenburg Goat Milk Products
1240 South Ave, Turlock (95380-5113)
P.O. Box 934 (95381-0934)
PHONE...................................209 667-0786
Robert Jackson, *Ch of Bd*
Doug Buehrle, *CFO*

2026 - Milk County (P-2193)

Carol Jackson, *Treasurer*
Frank Fillman, *Executive*
Jonathan Mitchell, *Admin Sec*
EMP: 22 **EST:** 1934
SQ FT: 11,200
SALES (est): 14.1MM **Privately Held**
WEB: www.meyenberg.com
SIC: 2026 2023 Milk, ultra-high temperature (longlife); evaporated milk; powdered milk

(P-2193)
PERFECT DAY INC
1485 Park Ave, Emeryville (94608-3559)
PHONE....................203 848-8633
Ryan Pandya, *CEO*
Sharisse Huie, *Admin Mgr*
EMP: 50 **EST:** 2014
SALES (est): 6.6MM **Privately Held**
WEB: www.perfectdayfoods.com
SIC: 2026 2023 Fluid milk; powdered milk

(P-2194)
SAPUTO DAIRY FOODS USA LLC
Also Called: Morningstar Foods
299 5th Ave, Gustine (95322-1202)
PHONE....................209 854-6461
Richard Rosemire, *Manager*
Lisa Crist, *Human Res Mgr*
Jody Ahlstrom, *Sales Staff*
Charles Rodriguez, *Manager*
EMP: 175
SQ FT: 5,000 **Privately Held**
WEB: www.saputo.com
SIC: 2026 Milk processing (pasteurizing, homogenizing, bottling)
HQ: Saputo Dairy Foods Usa, Llc
2711 N Haskell Ave # 370
Dallas TX 75204
214 863-2300

(P-2195)
VONS COMPANIES INC (DH)
Also Called: Pavilions
5918 Stoneridge Mall Rd, Pleasanton (94588-3229)
PHONE....................925 467-3000
Tom Keller, *President*
Larree Renda, *President*
Bruce Everette, *Exec VP*
David Bond, *Senior VP*
Melissa Plaisance, *Senior VP*
EMP: 900 **EST:** 1906
SQ FT: 244,000
SALES (est): 2B
SALES (corp-wide): 69.6B **Publicly Held**
WEB: www.safeway.com
SIC: 5411 2026 2024 Supermarkets, chain; supermarkets; fluid milk; ice cream, packaged; molded, on sticks, etc.
HQ: Safeway Inc.
5918 Stoneridge Mall Rd
Pleasanton CA 94588
925 226-5000

2032 Canned Specialties

(P-2196)
BIEN PADRE FOODS INC
1459 Railroad St, Eureka (95501-2147)
P.O. Box 3748 (95502-3748)
PHONE....................707 442-4585
Benito Lim, *President*
Rosita Lim, *Treasurer*
Bob McCall, *Vice Pres*
Domingo Bernardo Jr, *Admin Sec*
▲ **EMP:** 18 **EST:** 1974
SQ FT: 14,000
SALES (est): 1.1MM **Privately Held**
WEB: www.bienpadre.com
SIC: 2032 5149 2099 2096 Ethnic foods: canned, jarred, etc.; canned goods: fruit, vegetables, seafood, meats, etc.; spices & seasonings; tortillas, fresh or refrigerated; potato chips & similar snacks

(P-2197)
BOBBY SLZARS MXCAN FD PDTS INC (PA)
Also Called: Bobby Salazar Corporate
2810 San Antonio Dr, Fowler (93625-9799)
PHONE....................559 834-4787
Robert Salazar, *CEO*
Bobby Salazar, *President*
Charles Gamoian, *Vice Pres*
Sheila Martinez, *Sales Staff*
Wendy Ledestich, *Director*
EMP: 25
SQ FT: 16,375
SALES (est): 5MM **Privately Held**
WEB: www.bobbysalazar.com
SIC: 2032 5812 Mexican foods: packaged in cans, jars, etc.; Mexican restaurant

(P-2198)
CALI FOOD COMPANY INC (PA)
45401 Research Ave, Fremont (94539-6111)
PHONE....................408 515-3178
Pankaj Ansal, *CEO*
EMP: 15 **EST:** 2017
SALES (est): 508.8K **Privately Held**
WEB: www.califoodco.com
SIC: 2032 Italian foods: packaged in cans, jars, etc.

(P-2199)
GIORGIOS RESTAURANT ITALIANO
99 Rock Rd, Greenbrae (94904-2644)
PHONE....................415 925-0808
George Dexter, *Owner*
EMP: 30 **EST:** 2002
SALES (est): 1.3MM **Privately Held**
WEB: www.giorgiosrestaurant.com
SIC: 2032 Italian foods: packaged in cans, jars, etc.

(P-2200)
HOMESTEAD RAVIOLI COMPANY
Also Called: Homestead Fine Foods
315 S Maple Ave Ste 106, South San Francisco (94080-6335)
PHONE....................910 755-6802
Terry Hall, *President*
Charles Osborne, *Treasurer*
Christopher Osborne, *Admin Sec*
EMP: 17 **EST:** 1904
SQ FT: 19,000
SALES (est): 508.4K **Privately Held**
WEB: www.brunswickprimarycare.org
SIC: 2032 3058 5149 2096 Ravioli: packaged in cans, jars, etc.; frozen specialties; sauces; macaroni & spaghetti; pickles, sauces & salad dressings

(P-2201)
IF COPACK LLC
Also Called: Initiative Foods
1912 Industrial Way, Sanger (93657-9508)
PHONE....................559 875-3354
John Ypma, *President*
Jeff Jankovic, *CFO*
EMP: 42 **EST:** 2017
SQ FT: 51,348
SALES (est): 2.8MM **Privately Held**
WEB: www.initiativefoods.com
SIC: 2032 Baby foods, including meats: packaged in cans, jars, etc.

(P-2202)
INITIATIVE FOODS LLC
1912 Industrial Way, Sanger (93657-9508)
PHONE....................559 875-3354
John Ypma,
Richard Turner,
EMP: 130 **EST:** 2007
SALES (est): 30.1MM **Privately Held**
WEB: www.initiativefoods.com
SIC: 2032 Baby foods, including meats: packaged in cans, jars, etc.
PA: If Holding, Inc.
1912 Industrial Way
Sanger CA 93657
559 875-3354

(P-2203)
KINGS ASIAN GOURMET INC
683 Brannan St Unit 304, San Francisco (94107-1592)
PHONE....................415 222-6100
Inja Wang, *President*
Jane Park, *Executive*
Walter Wang, *Manager*
▲ **EMP:** 37 **EST:** 1963
SQ FT: 25,000
SALES (est): 2.5MM **Privately Held**
WEB: www.kingsasian.com
SIC: 2032 Ethnic foods: canned, jarred, etc.

(P-2204)
LA CASCADA INC
1940 Union St Ste 10, Oakland (94607-2352)
PHONE....................510 452-3663
Mohammad Bahrani, *President*
Mohsen Bahrani, *CFO*
Asad Bahrani, *Admin Sec*
EMP: 19 **EST:** 2018
SQ FT: 2,500
SALES (est): 1.5MM **Privately Held**
SIC: 2032 Mexican foods: packaged in cans, jars, etc.

(P-2205)
MARIN FOOD SPECIALTIES INC
14800 Byron Hwy, Byron (94514-0017)
P.O. Box 609 (94514-0609)
PHONE....................925 634-6126
Fred J Vuylsteke, *President*
Larry Brucia, *Corp Secy*
◆ **EMP:** 35 **EST:** 1974
SQ FT: 27,000
SALES (est): 7.7MM **Privately Held**
WEB: www.marinfoods.com
SIC: 2032 Canned specialties

(P-2206)
S & W FINE FOODS INC
P.O. Box 193575 (94119-3575)
PHONE....................800 252-7033
David Meyers, *CEO*
EMP: 24 **EST:** 2001
SALES (est): 74.1K **Privately Held**
WEB: www.delmontefoods.com
SIC: 2032 2033 Beans & bean sprouts, canned, jarred, etc.; canned fruits & specialties

(P-2207)
SAMS ITALIAN DELI & MKT INC
Also Called: Sam's Super Market
2415 N 1st St, Fresno (93703-1202)
PHONE....................559 229-9333
Sam Mazeleano, *President*
Angelinas Mazeleano, *Partner*
Darcy Barrett, *Manager*
EMP: 24 **EST:** 1979
SQ FT: 4,000
SALES (est): 1.6MM **Privately Held**
WEB: www.samsitaliandeli.com
SIC: 5411 5921 2032 5812 Delicatessens; wine & beer; Italian foods: packaged in cans, jars, etc.; delicatessen (eating places)

(P-2208)
SANCHEZ BUSINESS INC
Also Called: Casa Sanchez
250 Napoleon St Ste M, San Francisco (94124-1040)
PHONE....................415 282-2400
James Sanchez, *President*
Elizabeth Sanchez, *Treasurer*
George Sanchez, *Vice Pres*
Martha Sanchez, *Admin Sec*
Marta Sanchez, *Director*
EMP: 32 **EST:** 1986
SQ FT: 2,500
SALES (est): 3MM **Privately Held**
WEB: www.casasanchezsf.com
SIC: 5812 2032 Mexican restaurant; tortillas: packaged in cans, jars etc.

(P-2209)
WEI LABORATORIES INC
3002 Scott Blvd, Santa Clara (95054-3323)
PHONE....................408 970-8700
Jeffery WEI, *CEO*
Jeffrey Horan, *President*
Sarah LI, *Vice Pres*
Nathan Kent, *Accounts Mgr*
EMP: 25 **EST:** 2002
SALES (est): 3.2MM **Privately Held**
WEB: www.weilab.com
SIC: 2032 Chinese foods: packaged in cans, jars, etc.

2033 Canned Fruits, Vegetables & Preserves

(P-2210)
ABSINTHE GROUP INC
2043 Airpark Ct Ste 30, Auburn (95602-9009)
PHONE....................530 823-8527
Kim Sullivan, *Director*
EMP: 25
SALES (corp-wide): 17.5MM **Privately Held**
WEB: www.absinthe.com
SIC: 2033 2099 8742 2035 Barbecue sauce: packaged in cans, jars, etc.; food preparations; food & beverage consultant; pickles, sauces & salad dressings
PA: The Absinthe Group Inc
368 Hayes St
San Francisco CA 94102
415 864-2693

(P-2211)
AMAZON PRSRVATION PARTNERS INC
Also Called: Zola Acai
1550 Leigh Ave, San Jose (95125-5301)
PHONE....................415 775-6355
Chris Cuvelier, *CEO*
Devin Cardoza, *Manager*
▲ **EMP:** 24 **EST:** 2002
SALES (est): 4MM **Privately Held**
WEB: www.livezola.com
SIC: 2033 Fruit juices: fresh

(P-2212)
BELL-CARTER FOODS INC
Also Called: Bell-Carter Packaging
4207 Finch Rd, Modesto (95357-4101)
PHONE....................209 549-5939
Bill Floyd, *Manager*
Joseph Khanona, *Vice Pres*
Patrick McGovern, *Director*
Theresa Nielsen, *Manager*
Catherine Sabor, *Assistant*
EMP: 20
SALES (corp-wide): 122.6MM **Privately Held**
WEB: www.bellcarter.com
SIC: 2033 Olives: packaged in cans, jars, etc.
PA: Bell-Carter Foods, Llc
590 Ygnacio Valley Rd # 300
Walnut Creek CA 94596
209 549-5939

(P-2213)
BELL-CARTER FOODS LLC (PA)
Also Called: Bell-Carter Olive Company
590 Ygnacio Valley Rd # 300, Walnut Creek (94596-3807)
PHONE....................209 549-5939
Timothy T Carter, *CEO*
Timothy Carter, *COO*
Paul Adcock, *CFO*
John Toth, *CFO*
Doug Reifsteck, *Exec VP*
◆ **EMP:** 368 **EST:** 1912
SQ FT: 9,000
SALES (est): 122.6MM **Privately Held**
WEB: www.bellcarter.com
SIC: 2033 Olives: packaged in cans, jars, etc.

(P-2214)
DEL MAR FOOD PRODUCTS CORP
1720 Beach Rd, Watsonville (95076-9536)
P.O. Box 891 (95077-0891)
PHONE....................831 722-3516
Paul Joseph Mecozzi, *CEO*
Wayne Jordan, *CFO*
Paul Wendt, *CFO*
Carolyn Mecozzi, *Treasurer*
Roger Wyant, *Vice Pres*
◆ **EMP:** 500 **EST:** 1955
SQ FT: 53,408
SALES (est): 108.7MM **Privately Held**
WEB: www.delmarfoods.com
SIC: 2033 2099 Canned fruits & specialties; food preparations

▲ = Import ▼ = Export
◆ = Import/Export

2033 - Canned Fruits, Vegetables & Preserves County (P-2235)

(P-2215)
G L MEZZETTA INC
105 Mezzetta Ct, American Canyon (94503-9604)
PHONE..................707 648-1050
Jeffery Mezzetta, CEO
Ronald J Mezzetta, President
◆ EMP: 80 EST: 1957
SQ FT: 35,000
SALES (est): 32.1MM Privately Held
WEB: www.mezzetta.com
SIC: 2033 Pizza sauce: packaged in cans, jars, etc.

(P-2216)
INGOMAR PACKING COMPANY LLC (PA)
9950 S Ingomar Grade, Los Banos (93635)
P.O. Box 1448 (93635-1448)
PHONE..................209 826-9494
Gregory Pruett, President
Danny Green, CFO
Musa Mustafa, CFO
William B Cahill Jr, Vice Pres
Mark Medeiros, General Mgr
◆ EMP: 100
SQ FT: 10,000
SALES (est): 66.9MM Privately Held
WEB: www.ingomarpacking.com
SIC: 2033 Tomato paste: packaged in cans, jars, etc.

(P-2217)
KAGOME INC (HQ)
333 Johnson Rd, Los Banos (93635-9768)
PHONE..................209 826-8850
Luis De Oliveira, President
Luis De Oliveira, Officer
Ann Hall, Vice Pres
Molly Cassidy, Executive
Ignacio Carrillo, Technician
◆ EMP: 215 EST: 1998
SQ FT: 175,000
SALES (est): 105.5MM Privately Held
WEB: www.kagomeusa.com
SIC: 2033 Tomato products: packaged in cans, jars, etc.

(P-2218)
KOZLOWSKI FARMS A CORPORATION
5566 Hwy 116, Forestville (95436-9697)
PHONE..................707 887-1587
Cindy Kozlowski Hayworth, CEO
Carol Kozlowski Every, Vice Pres
Kyle Hayworth, General Mgr
EMP: 50 EST: 1949
SQ FT: 8,000
SALES (est): 2.3MM Privately Held
SIC: 2033 5149 2035 2099 Jams, jellies & preserves: packaged in cans, jars, etc.; fruit butters; condiments; sauces; pickles, sauces & salad dressings; vinegar

(P-2219)
KRAFT HEINZ FOODS COMPANY
2603 Camino Ramon Ste 180, San Ramon (94583-9127)
PHONE..................925 242-4504
EMP: 15
SALES (corp-wide): 18.3B Publicly Held
SIC: 2033 Mfg Canned Fruits/Vegetables
HQ: Heinz Kraft Foods Company
1 Ppg Pl Ste 3200
Pittsburgh PA 15222
412 456-5700

(P-2220)
LANDEC CORPORATION (PA)
5201 Great America Pkwy # 232, Santa Clara (95054-1126)
PHONE..................650 306-1650
Albert D Bolles, President
Andrew Powell, Ch of Bd
Ronald L Midyett, COO
Brian McLaughlin, CFO
John D Morberg, CFO
EMP: 198 EST: 1986
SQ FT: 3,657
SALES: 544.1MM Publicly Held
WEB: www.landec.com
SIC: 2033 5148 5999 Fruits: packaged in cans, jars, etc.; vegetables: packaged in cans, jars, etc.; fresh fruits & vegetables; medical apparatus & supplies

(P-2221)
LIDESTRI FOODS INC
Also Called: International Co-Packing Co
568 S Temperance Ave, Fresno (93727-6601)
PHONE..................559 251-1000
Willie Bynum, Branch Mgr
Charlotte Harper, Admin Asst
Ron Benedicto, CIO
Anitha Balakrishnan, Software Dev
Henry Hernandez, Technician
EMP: 58
SALES (corp-wide): 504.7MM Privately Held
WEB: www.lidestrifoods.com
SIC: 2033 Spaghetti & other pasta sauce: packaged in cans, jars, etc.; tomato products: packaged in cans, jars, etc.
PA: Lidestri Foods, Inc.
815 Whitney Rd W
Fairport NY 14450
585 377-7700

(P-2222)
LLC LYONS MAGNUS (PA)
3158 E Hamilton Ave, Fresno (93702-4163)
PHONE..................559 268-5966
Ed Carolan, CEO
Rod Wright, Vice Pres
Simranjeet Gill, Admin Asst
Alan Burrows, Technical Staff
Jeremy Avery, Graphic Designe
◆ EMP: 285 EST: 1967
SQ FT: 63,000
SALES (est): 219.6MM Privately Held
WEB: www.lyonsmagnus.com
SIC: 2033 2026 2087 Jams, including imitation: packaged in cans, jars, etc.; yogurt; syrups, flavoring (except drink)

(P-2223)
LLC LYONS MAGNUS
1636 S 2nd St, Fresno (93702-4143)
PHONE..................559 268-5966
Robert E Smittcamp, Branch Mgr
Jim Davis, Executive
Parnavi Kande, Research
Lauren Millard, Asst Controller
Rebecca Just, Opers Staff
EMP: 16
SALES (corp-wide): 219.6MM Privately Held
WEB: www.lyonsmagnus.com
SIC: 2033 2026 2087 Jams, including imitation: packaged in cans, jars, etc.; jellies, edible, including imitation: in cans, jars, etc.; preserves, including imitation: in cans, jars, etc.; fruit pie mixes & fillings: packaged in cans, jars, etc.; yogurt; syrups, flavoring (except drink); extracts, flavoring
PA: Lyons Magnus, Llc
3158 E Hamilton Ave
Fresno CA 93702
559 268-5966

(P-2224)
LOS GATOS TOMATO PRODUCTS LLC (PA)
7041 N Van Ness Blvd, Fresno (93711-7169)
P.O. Box 429, Huron (93234-0429)
PHONE..................559 945-2700
Reuben Peterson, Mng Member
Steven Sesock, Opers Mgr
Isaac Solis, Manager
◆ EMP: 19 EST: 1990
SQ FT: 35,000
SALES (est): 12.4MM Privately Held
WEB: www.losgatostomato.com
SIC: 2033 Tomato paste: packaged in cans, jars, etc.

(P-2225)
MANZANA PRODUCTS CO INC
9141 Green Valley Rd, Sebastopol (95472-2245)
P.O. Box 209 (95473-0209)
PHONE..................707 823-5313
Jean-Jacques Ducom, CEO
Suzanne C Kaido, President
Richard H Norton, Treasurer
Ralph E Sandborn, Vice Pres
Edith Norton, Admin Sec
◆ EMP: 40 EST: 1920
SQ FT: 91,000
SALES (est): 12.7MM Privately Held
WEB: www.manzanaproductsco.com
SIC: 2033 2099 Apple sauce: packaged in cans, jars, etc.; fruit juices: packaged in cans, jars, etc.; vinegar

(P-2226)
MORNING STAR COMPANY
Also Called: Morning Star Packing
13448 Volta Rd, Los Banos (93635-9785)
P.O. Box 2238 (93635-2238)
PHONE..................209 827-2724
Chris Rufer, President
EMP: 447
SALES (corp-wide): 481.1K Privately Held
WEB: www.morningstarco.com
SIC: 2033 Tomato paste: packaged in cans, jars, etc.
PA: The Morning Star Company
724 Main St Ste 202
Woodland CA 95695
530 666-6600

(P-2227)
MORNING STAR PACKING CO LP
12045 Ingomar Grade, Los Banos (93635-9796)
PHONE..................209 826-8000
EMP: 45 Privately Held
WEB: www.morningstarco.com
SIC: 2033 Tomato paste: packaged in cans, jars, etc.
PA: The Morning Star Packing Company L P
13448 Volta Rd
Los Banos CA 93635

(P-2228)
MORNING STAR PACKING CO LP
2211 Old Highway 99, Williams (95987)
PHONE..................530 473-3642
Rich Rostomily, Branch Mgr
Ashley Areia, Manager
EMP: 30 Privately Held
WEB: www.morningstarco.com
SIC: 2033 Tomato paste: packaged in cans, jars, etc.
PA: The Morning Star Packing Company L P
13448 Volta Rd
Los Banos CA 93635

(P-2229)
NEIL JONES FOOD COMPANY
San Benito Foods
711 Sally St, Hollister (95023-3934)
P.O. Box 100 (95024-0100)
PHONE..................831 637-0573
Steven Arnoldy, Manager
George Micha, IT/INT Sup
Mary Haro, Finance
Krysta Johnson, Analyst
Ana Jimenez, Human Resources
EMP: 27
SALES (corp-wide): 78.3MM Privately Held
WEB: www.neiljonesfoodcompany.com
SIC: 2033 Canned fruits & specialties
PA: The Neil Jones Food Company
1701 W 16th St
Vancouver WA 98660
360 696-4356

(P-2230)
NEIL JONES FOOD COMPANY
Also Called: Toma Tek
2502 N St, Firebaugh (93622-2456)
P.O. Box 8 (93622-0008)
PHONE..................559 659-5100
Steve Arnoldy, Vice Pres
Glen Morelli, Business Mgr
David Birts, Purchasing
Dennis Lea, Regl Sales Mgr
Agustin Mota, Director
EMP: 25
SALES (corp-wide): 78.3MM Privately Held
WEB: www.neiljonesfoodcompany.com
SIC: 2033 Tomato products: packaged in cans, jars, etc.
PA: The Neil Jones Food Company
1701 W 16th St
Vancouver WA 98660
360 696-4356

(P-2231)
OASIS FOODS INC
10881 Toews Ave, Le Grand (95333-9754)
PHONE..................209 382-0263
Eric Stephen Bocks, President
Lorraine Bocks, Corp Secy
EMP: 15 EST: 1975
SQ FT: 3,367
SALES (est): 1MM Privately Held
SIC: 2033 Fruits & fruit products in cans, jars, etc.

(P-2232)
OLAM TOMATO PROCESSORS INC (DH)
205 E River Park Cir # 310, Fresno (93720-1571)
P.O. Box 160, Lemoore (93245-0160)
PHONE..................559 447-1390
Sunny Verghese, CEO
Greg Estep, President
John Gibbons, Principal
◆ EMP: 65 EST: 2009
SALES (est): 9.4MM Privately Held
WEB: www.olamus.com
SIC: 2033 0723 Tomato sauce: packaged in cans, jars, etc.; crop preparation services for market
HQ: Olam Americas, Inc.
205 E River Park Cir # 310
Fresno CA 93720
559 447-1390

(P-2233)
OLAM WEST COAST INC
Also Called: Olam Spices and Vegetables
1400 Churchill Downs Ave, Woodland (95776-6146)
PHONE..................530 473-4290
Rich Freidas, Branch Mgr
EMP: 25 Privately Held
WEB: www.olamgroup.com
SIC: 2033 Tomato products: packaged in cans, jars, etc.
HQ: Olam West Coast, Inc.
205 E Rver Pk Cir Ste 310
Fresno CA 93720
559 256-6224

(P-2234)
OLIVE MUSCO PRODUCTS INC (PA)
Also Called: Musco Family Olive Co
17950 Via Nicolo, Tracy (95377-9767)
PHONE..................209 836-4600
Nicholas Musco, CEO
Felix Musco, CEO
Scott Hamilton, CFO
John Hamilton, CFO
Todd Humphery, Administration
▲ EMP: 180
SQ FT: 350,000
SALES (est): 78.4MM Privately Held
WEB: www.olives.com
SIC: 2033 2035 Canned fruits & specialties; olives, brined: bulk

(P-2235)
OLIVE PIT LLC
2156 Solano St, Corning (96021-2713)
PHONE..................530 824-4667
Ron Craig, President
Ronald Craig, General Mgr

2033 - Canned Fruits, Vegetables & Preserves

Bonnie Jackson, *Admin Sec*
EMP: 15 **EST:** 1967
SQ FT: 2,500
SALES (est): 2.7MM Privately Held
WEB: www.olivepit.com
SIC: 5499 5812 2033 Gourmet food stores; delicatessen (eating places); cafe; fruit juices: packaged in cans, jars, etc.

(P-2236)
PACIFIC COAST PRODUCERS
741 S Stockton St, Lodi (95240-4809)
P.O. Box 880 (95241-0880)
PHONE 209 334-3352
Mike Van Gundy, *Branch Mgr*
Andrew Russick, *Vice Pres*
EMP: 58
SALES (corp-wide): 864.2MM Privately Held
WEB: www.pacificcoastproducers.com
SIC: 2033 Vegetables: packaged in cans, jars, etc.; fruits: packaged in cans, jars, etc.
PA: Pacific Coast Producers
  631 N Cluff Ave
  Lodi CA 95240
  209 367-8800

(P-2237)
PACIFIC COAST PRODUCERS (PA)
631 N Cluff Ave, Lodi (95240-0756)
P.O. Box 1600 (95241-1600)
PHONE 209 367-8800
Daniel L Vincent, *CEO*
Dale Waldschmitt, *COO*
Matt Strong, *CFO*
Matthew Strong, *CFO*
Zeb Rocha, *Treasurer*
◆ **EMP:** 300 **EST:** 1971
SQ FT: 20,000
SALES: 864.2MM Privately Held
WEB: www.pacificcoastproducers.com
SIC: 2033 Fruits: packaged in cans, jars, etc.; vegetables: packaged in cans, jars, etc.

(P-2238)
PACIFIC COAST PRODUCERS
1601 Mitchell Ave, Oroville (95965-5863)
P.O. Box 311 (95965-0311)
PHONE 530 533-4311
Niraj Raj, *Principal*
Julie Gomez, *Personnel Assit*
EMP: 58
SQ FT: 60,000
SALES (corp-wide): 864.2MM Privately Held
WEB: www.pacificcoastproducers.com
SIC: 2033 Fruits: packaged in cans, jars, etc.; vegetables: packaged in cans, jars, etc.
PA: Pacific Coast Producers
  631 N Cluff Ave
  Lodi CA 95240
  209 367-8800

(P-2239)
PACIFIC COAST PRODUCERS
Also Called: Contadina Foods
1376 Lemen Ave, Woodland (95776-3369)
PHONE 530 662-8661
Craig Powell, *Branch Mgr*
Steve Freeman, *Vice Pres*
EMP: 58
SALES (corp-wide): 864.2MM Privately Held
WEB: www.pacificcoastproducers.com
SIC: 2033 Canned fruits & specialties
PA: Pacific Coast Producers
  631 N Cluff Ave
  Lodi CA 95240
  209 367-8800

(P-2240)
PACIFIC COAST PRODUCERS
6005 Highway 99, Live Oak (95953-9749)
PHONE 530 695-1126
EMP: 58
SALES (corp-wide): 864.2MM Privately Held
WEB: www.pacificcoastproducers.com
SIC: 2033 Canned fruits & specialties

PA: Pacific Coast Producers
  631 N Cluff Ave
  Lodi CA 95240
  209 367-8800

(P-2241)
PURVEYORS KITCHEN
2043 Airpark Ct Ste 30, Auburn (95602-9009)
PHONE 530 823-8527
Karen Foley, *CEO*
John Foley, *Principal*
Terry Downey, *Prdtn Mgr*
EMP: 20 **EST:** 2012
SALES (est): 4.8MM
SALES (corp-wide): 17.5MM Privately Held
WEB: www.absinthegroup.com
SIC: 2033 2099 8742 2035 Barbecue sauce: packaged in cans, jars, etc.; food preparations; food & beverage consultant; pickles, sauces & salad dressings
PA: The Absinthe Group Inc
  368 Hayes St
  San Francisco CA 94102
  415 864-2693

(P-2242)
RIO PLUMA COMPANY LLC (HQ)
1900 Highway 99, Gridley (95948-9401)
P.O. Box 948 (95948-0948)
PHONE 530 846-5200
Brad Stapleton, *President*
Eric Heitman,
Gavin Heitman,
◆ **EMP:** 32 **EST:** 1978
SQ FT: 100,000
SALES (est): 12.1MM
SALES (corp-wide): 25.2MM Privately Held
WEB: www.stapleton-spence.com
SIC: 2033 2034 2068 0723 Fruits & fruit products in cans, jars, etc.; dried & dehydrated fruits; nuts: dried, dehydrated, salted or roasted; fruit crops market preparation services
PA: Stapleton - Spence Packing Co.
  1900 State Highway 99
  Gridley CA 95948
  408 297-8815

(P-2243)
STANISLAUS FOOD PRODUCTS CO (PA)
1202 D St, Modesto (95354-2407)
P.O. Box 3951 (95352-3951)
PHONE 209 548-3537
Thomas A Cortopassi, *CEO*
William D Butler, *Exec VP*
Rick Serpa, *Senior VP*
Chris Lehikainen, *Vice Pres*
Grant Linhares, *Analyst*
▲ **EMP:** 104 **EST:** 1942
SQ FT: 50,000
SALES (est): 56MM Privately Held
WEB: www.stanislaus.com
SIC: 2033 Tomato paste: packaged in cans, jars, etc.

(P-2244)
STAPLETON - SPENCE PACKING CO (PA)
1900 State Highway 99, Gridley (95948-9401)
P.O. Box 948 (95948-0948)
PHONE 408 297-8815
Martin Bradley Stapleton, *CEO*
Tom Thornton, *Vice Pres*
Gavin Heitman, *Admin Sec*
Jerry Lavin, *QC Mgr*
◆ **EMP:** 79 **EST:** 1951
SQ FT: 105,000
SALES (est): 25.2MM Privately Held
WEB: www.stapleton-spence.com
SIC: 2033 5085 Fruits & fruit products in cans, jars, etc.; cans for fruits & vegetables

(P-2245)
TEASDALE QUALITY FOODS INC
901 Packers St, Atwater (95301-4614)
P.O. Box 814 (95301-0814)
PHONE 209 356-5616
Jerry Cook, *Ch Credit Ofcr*
Ann Bell, *Research*

Barbara Bauer, *Controller*
Raman Tull, *Director*
EMP: 5074
SALES (est): 11.3MM
SALES (corp-wide): 355.7MM Privately Held
WEB: www.teasdalelatinfoods.com
SIC: 2033 Tomato products: packaged in cans, jars, etc.
PA: Palladium Equity Partners Iii, L.P.
  1270 Ave Of T Flr 31
  New York NY 10020
  212 218-5150

(P-2246)
VALLEY VIEW FOODS INC
7547 Sawtelle Ave, Yuba City (95991-9514)
PHONE 530 673-7356
Jaswant Bains, *President*
Satwant Bains, *Admin Sec*
Anneke Amiga, *Administration*
EMP: 70 **EST:** 2016
SQ FT: 80,000
SALES (est): 10MM Privately Held
WEB: www.valleyviewfoods.com
SIC: 2033 Fruit juices: fresh

(P-2247)
VIE-DEL COMPANY (PA)
11903 S Chestnut Ave, Fresno (93725-9618)
P.O. Box 2908 (93745-2908)
PHONE 559 834-2525
Dianne S Nury, *President*
Richard Watson, *CFO*
Richard D Watson, *Treasurer*
Janice Terry, *Executive Asst*
Massud S Nury, *Admin Sec*
▲ **EMP:** 75 **EST:** 1946
SQ FT: 500,000
SALES (est): 24.9MM Privately Held
WEB: www.vie-delequipmentsales.com
SIC: 2033 2084 Fruit juices: concentrated, hot pack; brandy

(P-2248)
VITA-PAKT CITRUS PRODUCTS CO
8898 E Central Ave, Del Rey (93616-9769)
PHONE 559 233-4452
EMP: 17
SALES (corp-wide): 32.5MM Privately Held
WEB: www.vita-pakt.com
SIC: 2033 2037 Canned fruits & specialties; frozen fruits & vegetables
PA: Vita-Pakt Citrus Products Co.
  4825 Calloway Dr Ste 102
  Bakersfield CA 93312
  626 332-1101

(P-2249)
WILDBRINE LLC (PA)
322 Bellevue Ave, Santa Rosa (95407-7711)
PHONE 707 657-7607
Chris Glab, *Mng Member*
Bobby Anderson, *Prdtn Mgr*
Richard Goldberg,
EMP: 39 **EST:** 2012
SQ FT: 9,000
SALES (est): 5.5MM Privately Held
WEB: www.wildbrine.com
SIC: 2033 5149 Sauerkraut: packaged in cans, jars, etc.; beverages, except coffee & tea

2034 Dried Fruits, Vegetables & Soup

(P-2250)
B & R FARMS LLC
5280 Fairview Rd, Hollister (95023-9009)
PHONE 831 637-9168
Jim Rossey, *Principal*
Mari Rossi, *Principal*
▲ **EMP:** 23 **EST:** 1979
SALES (est): 3.8MM Privately Held
WEB: www.brfarms.com
SIC: 2034 0191 Dried & dehydrated fruits; general farms, primarily crop

(P-2251)
BASIC AMERICAN INC (PA)
Also Called: Basic American Foods
2999 Oak Rd Ste 800, Walnut Creek (94597-2054)
PHONE 925 472-4438
Bryan Reese, *President*
James Collins, *CFO*
Jim Collins, *CFO*
John Barnecut, *Admin Sec*
Brenda Auten, *Admin Asst*
▼ **EMP:** 60 **EST:** 1986
SALES (est): 354MM Privately Held
WEB: www.baf.com
SIC: 2034 2099 Potato products, dried & dehydrated; potatoes, peeled for the trade

(P-2252)
BATTH DEHYDRATOR LLC
4624 W Nebraska Ave, Caruthers (93609-9566)
P.O. Box 309 (93609-0309)
PHONE 559 864-3501
Charanjit S Batth,
Kanwarjit S Batth,
▲ **EMP:** 28 **EST:** 2005
SQ FT: 217,800
SALES (est): 1.6MM Privately Held
WEB: www.batthfarms.com
SIC: 2034 Raisins

(P-2253)
BROTHERS PRIDE PRODUCE INC (PA)
Also Called: Sigona's Farmers Market
2345 Middlefield Rd, Redwood City (94063-2834)
PHONE 650 368-6993
Carmelo Sigona, *CEO*
Paul Sigona, *Treasurer*
Liliana Solorio, *Office Mgr*
John Sigona Jr, *Admin Sec*
Debbie Sigona, *Admin Asst*
EMP: 30 **EST:** 1976
SQ FT: 10,000
SALES (est): 21.5MM Privately Held
WEB: www.sigonas.com
SIC: 5431 5411 5963 2034 Fruit stands or markets; grocery stores, independent; food services, direct sales; fruits, dried or dehydrated, except freeze-dried

(P-2254)
CAL RANCH INC (PA)
2628 Concord Blvd, Concord (94519-2605)
P.O. Box 608, Clayton (94517-0608)
PHONE 925 429-2900
Juliana Colline, *President*
Charles Deng, *Executive*
Paul Rebelo, *Sales Staff*
Juliana Zhang, *Sales Staff*
◆ **EMP:** 79 **EST:** 1998 Privately Held
WEB: www.calranchfood.com
SIC: 2034 2084 5146 Dried & dehydrated fruits; wine cellars, bonded: engaged in blending wines; seafoods

(P-2255)
CARO NUT COMPANY
2885 S Cherry Ave, Fresno (93706-5406)
PHONE 559 475-5400
David Mahaffy, *CEO*
▲ **EMP:** 50 **EST:** 2008
SALES (est): 46.3MM
SALES (corp-wide): 75.5MM Privately Held
WEB: www.caro-nut.com
SIC: 2034 Dried & dehydrated fruits
PA: Candor-Ags, Inc.
  2885 S Cherry Ave
  Fresno CA 93706
  559 439-2365

(P-2256)
CARUTHERS RAISIN PKG CO INC (PA)
12797 S Elm Ave, Caruthers (93609-9711)
PHONE 559 864-9448
Donald Kizirian, *President*
Don Kizirian, *President*
Gina Elsea, *CFO*
Dennis Housepian, *Exec VP*
Gregg Weaver, *Regional Mgr*
◆ **EMP:** 68

2035 - Pickled Fruits, Vegetables, Sauces & Dressings County (P-2280)

SQ FT: 4,000
SALES (est): 12.3MM **Privately Held**
WEB: www.caruthersraisinpacking.com
SIC: **2034** Dehydrated fruits, vegetables, soups

(P-2257)
CLARA FOODS CO
1 Tower Pl Fl 8, South San Francisco (94080-1828)
PHONE.................................415 570-1535
David Anchel, *Co-Founder*
Bobby Carouthers, *Business Anlyst*
Weixi Zhong, *Engineer*
Farnoosh Ayoughi, *Associate*
EMP: 40 EST: 2015
SALES (est): 3.7MM **Privately Held**
WEB: www.clarafoods.com
SIC: **2034** Dehydrated fruits, vegetables, soups

(P-2258)
CULINARY FARMS INC
1244 E Beamer St, Woodland (95776-6002)
PHONE.................................916 375-3000
Kirk Bewley, *President*
Bal Pattar, *CFO*
Sukhchan Gill, *Admin Asst*
Kathy Rogers, *Administration*
Jazmin Velasquez, *Technician*
▲ EMP: 50 EST: 1994
SALES (est): 7.6MM **Privately Held**
WEB: www.culinaryfarms.com
SIC: **2034** Dried & dehydrated vegetables

(P-2259)
DOLE FOOD COMPANY INC
12840 W Shields Ave, Kerman (93630-9618)
PHONE.................................559 843-2504
Thomas Gularte, *Branch Mgr*
EMP: 160 **Privately Held**
WEB: www.dole.com
SIC: **2034** Raisins
HQ: Dole Food Company, Inc.
1 Dole Dr
Westlake Village CA 91362
818 874-4000

(P-2260)
JAIN FARM FRESH FOODS INC (DH)
Also Called: White Oak Frozen Foods
2525 Cooper Ave, Merced (95348-4313)
PHONE.................................541 481-2522
Jack Sollazzo, *President*
Suvan Sharma, *CEO*
John Donovan, *CFO*
Narinder Gupta, *Admin Sec*
John Boufford, *Analyst*
◆ EMP: 45 EST: 1993
SQ FT: 75,000
SALES (est): 26.4MM **Privately Held**
WEB: www.jainfarmfresh.us
SIC: **2034** Dried & dehydrated vegetables

(P-2261)
LION RAISINS INC (PA)
Also Called: Lion Packing Co
9500 S De Wolf Ave, Selma (93662-9534)
P.O. Box 1350 (93662-1350)
PHONE.................................559 834-6677
Alfred Lion Jr, *President*
Bruce Lion, *Vice Pres*
Isabel Lion, *Principal*
Larry Lion, *Principal*
Raul Gomez, *Safety Mgr*
◆ EMP: 220 EST: 1903
SQ FT: 130,000
SALES (est): 57.8MM **Privately Held**
WEB: www.lionraisins.com
SIC: **2034** Raisins

(P-2262)
MARIANI PACKING CO INC
Also Called: Mariani Bros
9281 Highway 70, Marysville (95901-3064)
PHONE.................................530 749-6565
Mark Kettmann, *Manager*
Kim Judkins, *Senior Mgr*
Izzie Ali, *Manager*
EMP: 43

SALES (corp-wide): 114.7MM **Privately Held**
WEB: www.mariani.com
SIC: **2034** Prunes, dried
PA: Mariani Packing Co., Inc.
500 Crocker Dr
Vacaville CA 95688
707 452-2800

(P-2263)
MELKONIAN ENTERPRISES INC
Also Called: California Fruit Basket
2730 S De Wolf Ave, Sanger (93657-9770)
PHONE.................................559 217-0749
Mark Melkonian, *CEO*
Dennis Melkonian, *Vice Pres*
Douglas Melkonian, *Vice Pres*
EMP: 20 EST: 1951
SQ FT: 160,000
SALES (est): 6.2MM **Privately Held**
WEB: www.cal-fruit.com
SIC: **2034** 0172 5431 Raisins; fruits, dried or dehydrated, except freeze-dried; grapes; fruit stands or markets

(P-2264)
MERCER FOODS LLC (HQ)
1836 Lapham Dr, Modesto (95354-3900)
PHONE.................................209 529-0150
David A Noland, *CEO*
Clark Driftmier, *Exec VP*
Mike Alaga, *Vice Pres*
Pam Denney, *Vice Pres*
Doug Dobbs, *Vice Pres*
▲ EMP: 15 EST: 2011
SQ FT: 160,000
SALES (est): 10.4MM **Privately Held**
WEB: www.mercerfoods.com
SIC: **2034** Dehydrated fruits, vegetables, soups

(P-2265)
RAY MOLES FARMS INC
9503 S Hughes Ave, Fresno (93706-9731)
PHONE.................................559 444-0324
Ray Moles, *President*
EMP: 65 EST: 1975
SALES (est): 8.3MM **Privately Held**
SIC: **2034** Raisins

(P-2266)
RIVER RANCH RAISINS INC
4087 N Howard Ave, Kerman (93630-9674)
P.O. Box 27, Biola (93606-0027)
PHONE.................................559 843-2294
Troy Gillespie, *President*
Barbara Gillespie, *Vice Pres*
Amy Burgess, *General Mgr*
Linda Kay Abdulian,
EMP: 46 EST: 2015
SALES (est): 7.7MM **Privately Held**
WEB: www.rrraisins.com
SIC: **2034** Raisins

(P-2267)
SACRAMENTO PACKING INC
833 Tudor Rd, Yuba City (95991-9532)
P.O. Box 3540 (95992-3540)
PHONE.................................530 671-4488
Jaswant S Bains, *President*
◆ EMP: 300 EST: 1991
SQ FT: 80,000
SALES (est): 25.4MM **Privately Held**
WEB: www.sacramentopacking.com
SIC: **2034** Dehydrated fruits, vegetables, soups

(P-2268)
SUNRISE FRESH LLC
Also Called: Sunrise Fresh Dried Fruit Co
237 N Golden Gate Ave, Stockton (95205-4768)
P.O. Box 128, Linden (95236-0128)
PHONE.................................209 932-0192
Jane Samuel,
Luis Acevedo, *Office Mgr*
Jake Samuel, *Opers Staff*
James Samuel,
EMP: 50 EST: 2003
SQ FT: 42,000
SALES (est): 6.2MM **Privately Held**
WEB: www.sunrisefresh.com
SIC: **2034** Dehydrated fruits, vegetables, soups

(P-2269)
SUNSWEET DRYERS
23760 Loleta Ave, Corning (96021-9699)
P.O. Box 201 (96021-0201)
PHONE.................................530 824-5854
Dan Lima, *Manager*
EMP: 238
SALES (corp-wide): 244.8MM **Privately Held**
SIC: **2034** Prunes, dried
HQ: Sunsweet Dryers
901 N Walton Ave
Yuba City CA 95993
530 846-5578

(P-2270)
SUNSWEET DRYERS
26 E Evans Reimer Rd, Gridley (95948-9544)
PHONE.................................530 846-5578
Jeff Wilson, *Manager*
EMP: 238
SALES (corp-wide): 244.8MM **Privately Held**
SIC: **2034** Prunes, dried
HQ: Sunsweet Dryers
901 N Walton Ave
Yuba City CA 95993
530 846-5578

(P-2271)
SUNSWEET GROWERS INC (PA)
901 N Walton Ave, Yuba City (95993-9370)
PHONE.................................800 417-2253
Dane Lance, *President*
Brendon S Flynn, *Ch of Bd*
Ana Klein, *CEO*
Don Wood, *CFO*
Sharon Braun, *Vice Pres*
◆ EMP: 600
SQ FT: 1,200,000
SALES: 244.8MM **Privately Held**
WEB: www.sunsweet.com
SIC: **2034** 2037 2086 Dried & dehydrated fruits; fruit juices; fruit drinks (less than 100% juice): packaged in cans, etc.

(P-2272)
TRUE LEAF FARMS LLC
1275 San Justo Rd, San Juan Bautista (95045-9733)
P.O. Box 509, Salinas (93902-0509)
PHONE.................................831 623-4667
Rio Farms, *Mng Member*
Francis Adenuga, *Vice Pres*
Pradeep Hadavale, *Vice Pres*
Timothy McAfee, *General Mgr*
Allison Coelho, *Controller*
EMP: 500 EST: 2002
SALES (est): 118.4MM **Privately Held**
WEB: www.trueleaffarms.com
SIC: **2034** Vegetables, dried or dehydrated (except freeze-dried)

(P-2273)
VACAVILLE FRUIT CO INC (PA)
2055 Cessna Dr Ste 200, Vacaville (95688-8838)
P.O. Box 1537 (95696-1537)
PHONE.................................707 448-5292
Nicole Ciarabellini, *Principal*
Sonia Nunez, *Accountant*
◆ EMP: 40
SQ FT: 15,000
SALES (est): 5.3MM **Privately Held**
WEB: www.vacavillefruit.com
SIC: **2034** Prunes, dried; fruits, dried or dehydrated, except freeze-dried

(P-2274)
VICTOR PACKING INC
11687 Road 27 1/2, Madera (93637-9440)
PHONE.................................559 673-5908
Victor Sahatdjian, *President*
Margaret Sahatdjian, *Vice Pres*
Freda Rixman, *Executive Asst*
Bill Sahatdjian, *Admin Sec*
Jennifer Williams, *Accountant*
◆ EMP: 50 EST: 1963
SQ FT: 150,000
SALES (est): 11.1MM **Privately Held**
WEB: www.victorpacking.com
SIC: **2034** Raisins

(P-2275)
VSP PRODUCTS INC
3324 Orestimba Rd, Newman (95360-9628)
PHONE.................................209 862-1200
Chris J Rufer, *President*
Robert Benech, *President*
▲ EMP: 53 EST: 2007
SQ FT: 27,000
SALES (est): 44.7K
SALES (corp-wide): 481.1MM **Privately Held**
WEB: www.valleysun.com
SIC: **2034** Dehydrated fruits, vegetables, soups
PA: The Morning Star Company
724 Main St Ste 202
Woodland CA 95695
530 666-6600

2035 Pickled Fruits, Vegetables, Sauces & Dressings

(P-2276)
BELL-CARTER FOODS LLC
Also Called: Bell-Carter Olive Packing Co
1012 2nd St, Corning (96021-3248)
PHONE.................................530 528-4820
Steve Henderson, *Branch Mgr*
Jennifer N Robertson, *Comms Dir*
Marcy Cromwell, *General Mgr*
Kevin McKinzie, *Business Anlyst*
Jasmine Asuncion, *Project Mgr*
EMP: 300
SALES (corp-wide): 122.6MM **Privately Held**
WEB: www.bellcarter.com
SIC: **2035** 2033 Olives, brined: bulk; canned fruits & specialties
PA: Bell-Carter Foods, Llc
590 Ygnacio Valley Rd # 300
Walnut Creek CA 94596
209 549-5939

(P-2277)
CALCHEF FOODS LLC
4221 E Mariposa Rd Ste B, Stockton (95215-8139)
PHONE.................................888 638-7083
Dan Costa,
EMP: 28 EST: 2012
SALES (est): 5.9MM **Privately Held**
SIC: **2035** 2032 5142 Pickles, sauces & salad dressings; ethnic foods: canned, jarred, etc.; dinners, frozen

(P-2278)
COLLETTE FOODS LLC
Also Called: Kona Prince Food
7251 Galilee Rd Ste 180, Roseville (95678-7218)
PHONE.................................209 487-1260
Joseph Collette,
EMP: 100 EST: 2017
SQ FT: 55,000
SALES (est): 10.1MM **Privately Held**
SIC: **2035** 2087 Seasonings & sauces, except tomato & dry; extracts, flavoring

(P-2279)
EAT JUST INC (PA)
2000 Folsom St, San Francisco (94110-1318)
PHONE.................................844 423-6637
Joshua Tetrick, *CEO*
Beth Lawrence, *Partner*
Alexandra Dallago, *President*
Erez Simha, *COO*
Lee Chae, *Vice Pres*
EMP: 55 EST: 2011
SQ FT: 2,300
SALES (est): 123.2MM **Privately Held**
WEB: www.ju.st
SIC: **2035** 2052 5147 Mayonnaise; cookies; meats & meat products

(P-2280)
H V FOOD PRODUCTS COMPANY
1221 Broadway, Oakland (94612-1837)
PHONE.................................510 271-7612
George C Roeth, *President*

2035 - Pickled Fruits, Vegetables, Sauces & Dressings County (P-2281)

Pamela Fletcher, *Vice Pres*
EMP: 481 **EST:** 1972
SQ FT: 218,000
SALES (est): 5.3MM
SALES (corp-wide): 7.3B **Publicly Held**
SIC: 2035 Pickles, sauces & salad dressings
HQ: The Kingsford Products Company Llc
1221 Broadway Ste 1300
Oakland CA 94612
510 271-7000

(P-2281)
KRUGER FOODS INC
18362 E Highway 4, Stockton (95215-9433)
P.O. Box 220, Farmington (95230-0220)
PHONE 209 941-8518
Kara Kruger, *CEO*
Leslie Kruger, *COO*
Carolyn Sasser, *Accountant*
Eric Kruger, *VP Opers*
Gilbert Olmos, *Production*
▼ **EMP:** 155 **EST:** 1930
SQ FT: 80,000
SALES (est): 61.1MM **Privately Held**
WEB: www.krugerfoods.com
SIC: 2035 Pickles, vinegar; vegetables, pickled

(P-2282)
LEE BROTHERS INC
Also Called: Four In One Company
1011 Timothy Dr, San Jose (95133-1043)
PHONE 650 964-9650
Gene Lee, *President*
Jay Lee, *Corp Secy*
Jim Lee, *Vice Pres*
EMP: 30 **EST:** 1974
SQ FT: 46,000
SALES (est): 9.3MM **Privately Held**
WEB: www.leebros.com
SIC: 2035 Dressings, salad: raw & cooked (except dry mixes); soy sauce

(P-2283)
OLIVE MUSCO PRODUCTS INC
Swift & 5th St # 5, Orland (95963)
P.O. Box 368 (95963-0368)
PHONE 530 865-4111
Dennis Burreson, *Plant Mgr*
EMP: 42
SALES (corp-wide): 78.4MM **Privately Held**
WEB: www.olives.com
SIC: 2035 2033 Pickles, sauces & salad dressings; olives: packaged in cans, jars, etc.
PA: Olive Musco Products Inc
17950 Via Nicolo
Tracy CA 95377
209 836-4600

(P-2284)
PACIFIC CHOICE BRANDS INC (PA)
4652 E Date Ave, Fresno (93725-2123)
PHONE 559 892-5365
Allan R Andrews, *CEO*
Orlando Carranza, *Prdtn Mgr*
Gary Guelce, *Opers Staff*
◆ **EMP:** 200 **EST:** 1930
SQ FT: 225,000
SALES (est): 50.6MM **Privately Held**
WEB: www.pcbrands.com
SIC: 2035 Pickled fruits & vegetables

(P-2285)
S M S BRINERS INC
17750 E Highway 4, Stockton (95215-9721)
PHONE 209 941-8515
Kara Kruger, *CEO*
Frances Sousa, *President*
Laurie Flatter, *Corp Secy*
Arnold Sousa, *Vice Pres*
EMP: 36 **EST:** 1966
SQ FT: 5,000
SALES (est): 2.9MM **Privately Held**
WEB: www.s-m-s-briners-inc.hub.biz
SIC: 2035 Vegetables, brined

(P-2286)
SONOMA GOURMET INC
21684 8th St E Ste 100, Sonoma (95476-2816)
PHONE 707 939-3700
William K Weber, *President*
Rodger C Declercq, *Vice Pres*
Kristina Kemp, *Vice Pres*
EMP: 37 **EST:** 1990
SQ FT: 50,000
SALES (est): 5.6MM **Privately Held**
WEB: www.sonomagourmet.com
SIC: 2035 Pickles, sauces & salad dressings

(P-2287)
SUNOPTA GLOBL ORGNIC INGRDNTS (DH)
Also Called: Sunopta Food Solutions
100 Enterprise Way B10, Scotts Valley (95066-3248)
PHONE 831 685-6506
Joseph Stern, *President*
David Largey, *Vice Pres*
Loren Morr, *Vice Pres*
Gabriel Gebregiorgis, *Technician*
Ruth Updegraff, *Controller*
◆ **EMP:** 20 **EST:** 1996
SQ FT: 2,800
SALES (est): 19.8MM
SALES (corp-wide): 789.2MM **Privately Held**
WEB: www.sunopta.com
SIC: 2035 2033 Relishes, vinegar; fruit nectars: packaged in cans, jars, etc.

(P-2288)
U S ENTERPRISE CORPORATION
Also Called: Wing Nien Company
30560 San Antonio St, Hayward (94544-7102)
PHONE 510 487-8877
David H Hall, *President*
Ken Jue MD, *Vice Pres*
Gregory Hall, *Admin Sec*
▲ **EMP:** 35 **EST:** 1942
SQ FT: 40,000
SALES (est): 4.6MM **Privately Held**
WEB: www.wingnien.wordpress.com
SIC: 2035 5141 Seasonings & sauces, except tomato & dry; groceries, general line

(P-2289)
VALLEY GARLIC INC
500 Enterprise Pkwy, Coalinga (93210-9513)
PHONE 559 934-1763
Gary Caneza, *President*
EMP: 20 **EST:** 2002
SALES (est): 2.2MM **Privately Held**
SIC: 2035 Spreads, garlic

2037 Frozen Fruits, Juices & Vegetables

(P-2290)
CALIFORNIA CONCENTRATE COMPANY
Also Called: KIMBERLEY WINE VINEGARS
18678 N Highway 99, Acampo (95220-9557)
PHONE 209 334-9112
Thomas Alexander, *President*
Dennis Alexander, *President*
Kim Roberts, *CFO*
Andy Alexander, *Vice Pres*
Thomas P Alexander, *Vice Pres*
◆ **EMP:** 24 **EST:** 1969
SQ FT: 17,000
SALES: 20.6MM **Privately Held**
WEB: www.californiaconcentrate.com
SIC: 2037 2082 Fruit juice concentrates, frozen; malt extract

(P-2291)
DEL REY JUICE CO
Also Called: Paramount Food Processing
5286 S Del Rey Ave, Del Rey (93616)
PHONE 559 888-8533
EMP: 99

SALES (est): 8.1MM **Privately Held**
SIC: 2037 Frozen Fruits And Vegetables, Nsk

(P-2292)
DOLE PACKAGED FOODS LLC
Also Called: Glacier Foods Division
1117 K St, Sanger (93657-3200)
PHONE 559 875-3354
Alvin Mc Avoy, *Manager*
Nicholas Barker, *Production*
Jim Berry, *Sales Staff*
EMP: 272 **Privately Held**
WEB: www.dolesunshine.com
SIC: 2037 2033 2095 2032 Fruits, quick frozen & cold pack (frozen); canned fruits & specialties; roasted coffee; canned specialties; frozen specialties
HQ: Dole Packaged Foods, Llc
3059 Townsgate Rd
Westlake Village CA 91361
805 601-5500

(P-2293)
FORAGER PROJECT LLC (PA)
235 Montgomery St Ste 420, San Francisco (94104-2921)
PHONE 855 729-5253
Stephen Williamson, *CEO*
John Charles Hanley, *President*
Alexis Hager, *CFO*
Matt Collins, *Officer*
Maude Manoukian, *Officer*
◆ **EMP:** 73 **EST:** 2014
SALES (est): 35MM **Privately Held**
WEB: www.foragerproject.com
SIC: 2037 Fruit juices

(P-2294)
HAYWARD ENTERPRISES INC
2700 Napa Valley Corp Dr, NAPA (94558)
PHONE 707 261-5100
Tracy Collier Hayward, *President*
Medhane Kidane, *CFO*
Tracy Hayward, *Info Tech Dir*
Kevin Zeigler, *Controller*
Jerry Benjamin, *Human Res Mgr*
▼ **EMP:** 42 **EST:** 1988
SQ FT: 8,166
SALES (est): 5MM **Privately Held**
WEB: www.perfectpuree.com
SIC: 2037 Frozen fruits & vegetables

(P-2295)
PATTERSON FROZEN FOODS INC
10 S 3rd St, Patterson (95363-2509)
P.O. Box 487 (95363-0487)
PHONE 209 892-5060
Angelo Ielmini, *President*
Susan Scheuber, *CFO*
◆ **EMP:** 35 **EST:** 1946
SQ FT: 600,000
SALES (est): 1.2MM **Privately Held**
SIC: 2037 Fruits, quick frozen & cold pack (frozen); vegetables, quick frozen & cold pack, excl potato products

(P-2296)
PERFECT PUREE OF NAPA VLY LLC
2700 Napa Valley Corp Dr, NAPA (94558)
PHONE 707 261-5100
Kevin Zeigler, *President*
Medhane Kidane, *CFO*
Meuy Saechao, *Controller*
Jason Whaley, *Production*
Liza Cheng, *Natl Sales Mgr*
▲ **EMP:** 19 **EST:** 2006
SALES (est): 10.6MM **Privately Held**
WEB: www.perfectpuree.com
SIC: 2037 Frozen fruits & vegetables

(P-2297)
PURITY ORGANIC LLC
405 14th St Ste 1000, Oakland (94612-2706)
PHONE 415 440-7777
EMP: 25
SALES (est): 133.7K **Privately Held**
WEB: www.purityorganic.com
SIC: 2037 Mfg Frozen Fruits/Vegetables

(P-2298)
SMOOTHIE OPERATOR INC
8690 Sierra College Blvd, Roseville (95661-5961)
PHONE 916 773-9541
Ritchie Labate, *Principal*
Leslie Sue Broadland, *Principal*
EMP: 16 **EST:** 2015
SALES (est): 2.4MM **Privately Held**
SIC: 2037 Frozen fruits & vegetables

(P-2299)
SONOMA BEVERAGE COMPANY LLC (PA)
2710 Giffen Ave, Santa Rosa (95407-7331)
PHONE 707 431-1099
David Langer, *Mng Member*
Bruce Langer,
▲ **EMP:** 19 **EST:** 2008
SALES (est): 2MM **Privately Held**
SIC: 2037 Fruit juices

(P-2300)
SUN TROPICS INC
2420 Camino Ramon Ste 101, San Ramon (94583-4207)
P.O. Box 407 (94583-0407)
PHONE 925 202-2221
Ashley Lao, *CEO*
Sharon Sy, *Vice Pres*
Jennifer Tan, *Marketing Staff*
Benny San Andres, *Sales Staff*
Christine McDonald, *Mktg Coord*
◆ **EMP:** 16 **EST:** 2002
SALES (est): 2.5MM **Privately Held**
WEB: www.suntropics.com
SIC: 2037 Fruit juices

2038 Frozen Specialties

(P-2301)
AJINOMOTO FOODS NORTH AMER INC
Also Called: Windsor Foods
2395 American Ave, Hayward (94545-1807)
PHONE 510 293-1838
Venita Darien, *Branch Mgr*
Janet Zhou, *Accountant*
EMP: 193 **Privately Held**
WEB: www.ajinomotofoods.com
SIC: 2038 2037 Frozen specialties; frozen fruits & vegetables
HQ: Ajinomoto Foods North America, Inc.
4200 Concours Ste 100
Ontario CA 91764

(P-2302)
AMYS KITCHEN INC (PA)
1650 Corporate Cir, Petaluma (94954-6950)
P.O. Box 4759 (94955-4759)
PHONE 707 578-7188
Xavier Unkovic, *President*
Andrew Koprel, *CFO*
Scott Reed, *Exec VP*
Rachel Berliner, *Vice Pres*
Sandeep Bhandari, *Vice Pres*
◆ **EMP:** 800 **EST:** 1988
SQ FT: 100,000
SALES (est): 372.2MM **Privately Held**
WEB: www.amyskitchen.com
SIC: 2038 2053 Dinners, frozen & packaged; frozen bakery products, except bread

(P-2303)
ARMANINO FOODS DISTINCTION INC
30588 San Antonio St, Hayward (94544-7102)
PHONE 510 441-9300
Edmond J Pera, *CEO*
Edgar Estonina, *CFO*
Katherene Negrete, *Analyst*
Georgianne Stephen, *Opers Mgr*
Deborah Armanino, *Sales Staff*
▼ **EMP:** 41 **EST:** 1978
SQ FT: 31,783
SALES (est): 11.8MM **Privately Held**
WEB: www.armaninofoods.com
SIC: 2038 2099 Frozen specialties; sauces: gravy, dressing & dip mixes

PRODUCTS & SERVICES SECTION

2044 - Rice Milling County (P-2327)

(P-2304)
NATES FINE FOODS LLC
8880 Industrial Ave # 100, Roseville (95678-5946)
PHONE.................................310 897-2690
Nathan Barker, COO
EMP: 39 EST: 2012
SQ FT: 50,000
SALES (est): 5.4MM Privately Held
WEB: www.natesfinefood.com
SIC: 2038 Ethnic foods, frozen; lunches, frozen & packaged

(P-2305)
NIPPON INDUSTRIES INC
2430 S Watney Way, Fairfield (94533-6730)
PHONE.................................707 427-3127
Eric D Wong, President
David Marcus, Natl Sales Mgr
Arlene Quintanilla, Assistant
◆ EMP: 31
SQ FT: 30,000
SALES (est): 8.9MM Privately Held
WEB: www.nipponindustries.com
SIC: 2038 Dinners, frozen & packaged

(P-2306)
SAN FRANCISCO FOODS INC
14054 Catalina St, San Leandro (94577-5508)
PHONE.................................510 357-7343
Hamad M Malak, CEO
Robert F Steel, President
John Sim, Engineer
Charley Luckhard, Marketing Staff
Bernard K Ludwig, Asst Sec
▲ EMP: 55 EST: 1998
SQ FT: 12,000
SALES (est): 9.8MM Privately Held
WEB: www.sanfranciscofoods.com
SIC: 2038 Pizza, frozen

(P-2307)
WESTECH INV ADVISORS LLC (PA)
104 La Mesa Dr 102, Portola Valley (94028-7510)
PHONE.................................650 234-4300
Jay Cohan, Mng Member
David Wanek, Partner
Ronald W Swenson, Ch of Bd
Meher Haider, Director
EMP: 28 EST: 1980
SQ FT: 1,500
SALES (est): 3.7MM Privately Held
SIC: 2038 7359 6141 Frozen specialties; equipment rental & leasing; personal credit institutions

2041 Flour, Grain Milling

(P-2308)
ARDENT MILLS LLC
3939 Producers Dr, Stockton (95206-4204)
PHONE.................................209 983-6551
EMP: 16
SALES (corp-wide): 571.3MM Privately Held
WEB: www.ardentmills.com
SIC: 2041 Flour & other grain mill products
PA: Ardent Mills, Llc
    1875 Lawrence St Ste 1400
    Denver CO 80202
    800 851-9618

(P-2309)
BAY STATE MILLING COMPANY
360 Hanson Way, Woodland (95776-6212)
PHONE.................................530 666-6565
Vanderliet Joseph, Owner
EMP: 26
SALES (corp-wide): 131.8MM Privately Held
WEB: www.baystatemilling.com
SIC: 2041 Flour
PA: Bay State Milling Company
    100 Congress St Ste 2
    Quincy MA 02169
    617 328-4423

(P-2310)
CERTIFIED FOODS INC
41890 E Main St, Woodland (95776-9508)
PHONE.................................530 666-6565
Joseph A Vanderliet, President
▲ EMP: 64 EST: 1992
SQ FT: 32,000
SALES (est): 816.4K Privately Held
WEB: www.baystatemilling.com
SIC: 2041 Flour & other grain mill products

(P-2311)
GIUSTOS SPECIALTY FOODS LLC (PA)
344 Littlefield Ave, South San Francisco (94080-6103)
PHONE.................................650 873-6566
Craig A Moore, Mng Member
Jarjeet Bahia, COO
Ann Moore, CFO
Dan Weggenman, Executive
Michael Giusto, Purchasing
▲ EMP: 43 EST: 1940
SQ FT: 5,000
SALES (est): 12MM Privately Held
WEB: www.giustos.com
SIC: 2041 Flour mills, cereal (except rice); grain mills (except rice)

(P-2312)
VALLEY FINE FOODS COMPANY INC (PA)
Also Called: Pasta Prima
3909 Park Rd Ste H, Benicia (94510-1167)
PHONE.................................707 746-6888
Todd Nettleton, CEO
Ryan Tu, Ch of Bd
Mike Defabio, President
Wayne Tu, COO
David Weber, CFO
▲ EMP: 100 EST: 1992
SQ FT: 83,598
SALES (est): 99.1MM Privately Held
WEB: www.valleyfine.com
SIC: 2041 2038 Doughs, frozen or refrigerated; frozen specialties; snacks, including onion rings, cheese sticks, etc.

(P-2313)
VICOLO WHOLESALE LLC (PA)
Also Called: Vicolo Pizza
31112 San Clemente St, Hayward (94544-7802)
PHONE.................................510 475-6019
Eric Mount, Partner
Richard Sander, Partner
EMP: 49 EST: 1998
SQ FT: 1,400
SALES (est): 7.8MM Privately Held
WEB: www.vicolopizza.com
SIC: 2041 Flour & other grain mill products

2043 Cereal Breakfast Foods

(P-2314)
GENERAL MILLS INC
2000 W Turner Rd, Lodi (95242-2239)
P.O. Box 3002 (95241-1906)
PHONE.................................209 334-7061
Fax: 209 333-2949
EMP: 50
SALES (corp-wide): 17.6B Publicly Held
SIC: 2043 2045 Mfg Packaged Cereals & Prepared Packaged Food Mixes
PA: General Mills, Inc.
    1 General Mills Blvd
    Minneapolis MN 55426
    763 764-7600

2044 Rice Milling

(P-2315)
AMERICAN RICE INC
Comet Rice Division
1 Comet Ln, Maxwell (95955)
PHONE.................................530 438-2265
EMP: 60 Privately Held
SIC: 2044 Rice Milling, Nsk
HQ: American Rice Inc.
    10700 North Fwy Ste 800
    Houston TX 77037
    281 272-8800

(P-2316)
CALIFORNIA FAMILY FOODS LLC
6550 Struckmeyer Rd, Arbuckle (95912)
PHONE.................................530 476-3326
David Myers, President
Perry Charter,
Tom Charter, Mng Member
Bruce Meyers, Mng Member
Laura Cobb, Manager
▼ EMP: 75 EST: 1995
SQ FT: 75,000
SALES (est): 20MM Privately Held
WEB: www.californiafamilyfoods.com
SIC: 2044 0723 Rice milling; rice drying services

(P-2317)
CALIFORNIA HERITAGE MILLS INC
1 Comet Ln, Maxwell (95955-8062)
P.O. Box 152 (95955-0152)
PHONE.................................530 438-2100
Paul Richter, President
Steven Sutter, CEO
Kathryn Richter, Admin Sec
Alyssa Ramirez, Technician
Peggy Koch, Controller
◆ EMP: 30 EST: 2011
SALES (est): 4.8MM Privately Held
WEB: www.chmrice.com
SIC: 2044 Rice milling

(P-2318)
CALIFRNIA PCF RICE MIL A CA LP
194 W Main St, Woodland (95695-2999)
P.O. Box 8729 (95776-8729)
PHONE.................................530 661-1923
Grant F Chappell, Partner
Joe Westover, Partner
EMP: 23 EST: 1985
SQ FT: 10,000
SALES (est): 411.3K Privately Held
WEB: www.calrice.org
SIC: 2044 Rice milling

(P-2319)
FAR WEST RICE INC
3455 Nelson Rd, Nelson (95958)
P.O. Box 370, Durham (95938-0370)
PHONE.................................530 891-1339
C W Johnson, CEO
Gregory Johnson, President
Charles Schwab, Treasurer
Bill Short, Maintence Staff
Paul Browning, Director
◆ EMP: 35 EST: 1985
SQ FT: 3,000
SALES (est): 4.3MM Privately Held
WEB: www.farwestrice.com
SIC: 2044 5141 2099 Rice milling; groceries, general line; food preparations

(P-2320)
FARMERS RICE COOPERATIVE (PA)
Also Called: Frc
2566 River Plaza Dr, Sacramento (95833-3673)
P.O. Box 15223 (95851-0223)
PHONE.................................916 923-5100
Frank Bragg, CEO
Bill Tanimoto, CFO
H Kirk Messick, Senior VP
Keith Hargrove, Vice Pres
Rob Paschoal, Vice Pres
◆ EMP: 35 EST: 1944
SQ FT: 12,000
SALES (est): 71.8MM Privately Held
WEB: www.farmersrice.com
SIC: 2044 Rice milling

(P-2321)
FARMERS RICE COOPERATIVE
1800 Terminal Rd, Sacramento (95820)
PHONE.................................916 373-5549
Bill Tanimoto, CFO
Anthony Coronas, Info Tech Dir
Kristina Chavez, Marketing Staff
Isaac Cuevas, Supervisor
EMP: 56
SALES (corp-wide): 71.8MM Privately Held
WEB: www.farmersrice.com
SIC: 2044 Rice milling
PA: Rice Farmers' Cooperative
    2566 River Plaza Dr
    Sacramento CA 95833
    916 923-5100

(P-2322)
FARMERS RICE COOPERATIVE
845 Kentucky Ave, Woodland (95695-2744)
PHONE.................................530 666-1691
EMP: 56
SALES (corp-wide): 71.8MM Privately Held
WEB: www.farmersrice.com
SIC: 2044 Rice milling
PA: Rice Farmers' Cooperative
    2566 River Plaza Dr
    Sacramento CA 95833
    916 923-5100

(P-2323)
FARMERS RICE COOPERATIVE
2224 Industrial Blvd, West Sacramento (95691-3429)
P.O. Box 15223, Sacramento (95851-0223)
PHONE.................................916 373-5500
Keith Hargrove, Manager
EMP: 56
SALES (corp-wide): 71.8MM Privately Held
WEB: www.farmersrice.com
SIC: 2044 Rice milling
PA: Rice Farmers' Cooperative
    2566 River Plaza Dr
    Sacramento CA 95833
    916 923-5100

(P-2324)
GOLD RIVER MILLS LLC (PA)
1620 E Kentucky Ave, Woodland (95776-6110)
P.O. Box 8729 (95776-8729)
PHONE.................................530 661-1923
Thomas S Atkinson II,
Timothy R Magil,
John Perry,
▲ EMP: 41 EST: 2001
SALES (est): 5.8MM Privately Held
SIC: 2044 Rice milling

(P-2325)
KODA FARMS INC
22540 Russell Ave, South Dos Palos (93665)
P.O. Box 10 (93665-0010)
PHONE.................................209 392-2191
Edward K Koda, President
Laura Koda, Vice Pres
Robin Koda, Vice Pres
Ross Koda, Vice Pres
Tama T Koda, Vice Pres
▲ EMP: 36 EST: 1946
SQ FT: 20,000
SALES (est): 7.7MM Privately Held
WEB: www.kodafarms.com
SIC: 2044 0112 Rice milling; rice

(P-2326)
RICE CORPORATION (PA)
Also Called: Krohn Division
11140 Fair Oaks Blvd, Fair Oaks (95628-5126)
PHONE.................................916 784-7745
Jay Kapila, President
Xavier Verspieren, CFO
Praveen K Kaps, Vice Pres
Praveen Kaps, Vice Pres
Javier Molins, Vice Pres
◆ EMP: 20
SQ FT: 7,000
SALES (est): 500MM Privately Held
WEB: www.riceco.com
SIC: 2044 Rice milling

(P-2327)
RIVERBEND RICE MILL INC
234 Main St, Colusa (95932)
P.O. Box 830 (95932-0830)
PHONE.................................530 458-8561
Fax: 530 458-8569
EMP: 17

2044 - Rice Milling County (P-2328)

PRODUCTS & SERVICES SECTION

SALES (est): 2.2MM Privately Held
SIC: 2044 Rice Milling, Nsk

(P-2328)
SUN VALLEY RICE COMPANY LLC
7050 Eddy Rd, Arbuckle (95912-9789)
P.O. Box 8, Dunnigan (95937-0008)
PHONE..................530 476-3000
Kenneth M Lagrande, *Mng Member*
Steve Vargas, *Vice Pres*
Chris Fantl, *Administration*
Brett Lagrande, *Accountant*
Marta Stegall, *Human Res Dir*
◆ EMP: 98 EST: 1999
SQ FT: 20,000
SALES (est): 25.7MM Privately Held
WEB: www.sunvalleyrice.com
SIC: 2044 Rice milling

(P-2329)
TAMAKI RICE CORPORATION
1701 Abel Rd, Williams (95987-5156)
PHONE..................530 473-2862
Masami Kitagawa, *President*
Kurt Barrett, *General Mgr*
◆ EMP: 20 EST: 1989
SQ FT: 14,000
SALES (est): 2.7MM Privately Held
WEB: www.tamakimai.com
SIC: 2044 Rice milling
PA: Hombo Shoten Co.,Ltd.
  8-56, Kinkocho
  Kagoshima KGM 892-0

(P-2330)
WEHAH FARM INC
Also Called: Lundberg Family Farms
5311 Midway, Richvale (95974)
P.O. Box 369 (95974-0369)
PHONE..................530 538-3500
Grant Lundberg, *CEO*
Jeff Trailer, *Treasurer*
Mike Denny, *Vice Pres*
Jessica Wilhite, *Planning*
Krista Cooprider, *Engineer*
EMP: 255
SALES (est): 69.5MM Privately Held
WEB: www.lundberg.com
SIC: 2044 Rice milling

2046 Wet Corn Milling

(P-2331)
CORN PRODUCTS DEVELOPMENT INC (HQ)
1021 Industrial Dr, Stockton (95206-3928)
P.O. Box 6129 (95206-0129)
PHONE..................209 982-1920
Samuel Scott, *Principal*
EMP: 560 EST: 2011
SALES (est): 1.1MM
SALES (corp-wide): 5.9B Publicly Held
WEB: www.ingredion.com
SIC: 2046 Wet corn milling
PA: Ingredion Incorporated
  5 Westbrook Corporate Ctr
  Westchester IL 60154
  708 551-2600

2047 Dog & Cat Food

(P-2332)
ARCHEYY & FRIENDS LLC
3630 Andrews Dr Apt 114, Pleasanton (94588-3015)
PHONE..................703 579-7649
Sean Marler,
EMP: 20
SALES (est): 671.8K Privately Held
SIC: 2047 0752 Dog food; animal boarding services

(P-2333)
BIG HEART PET BRANDS INC (HQ)
1 Maritime Plz Fl 2, San Francisco (94111-3407)
P.O. Box 193575 (94119-3575)
PHONE..................415 247-3000
Richard K Smucker, *CEO*
David J West, *President*
Mark R Belgya, *CFO*
Barry C Dunaway, *Senior VP*
Jill Penrose, *Vice Pres*
◆ EMP: 300 EST: 2002
SALES (est): 1.2B
SALES (corp-wide): 8B Publicly Held
WEB: www.jmsmucker.com
SIC: 2047 Dog food
PA: The J M Smucker Company
  1 Strawberry Ln
  Orrville OH 44667
  330 682-3000

(P-2334)
DIAMOND PET FD PRCSSORS CAL LL
250 Roth Rd, Lathrop (95330-9724)
PHONE..................209 983-4900
Michael Kampeter, *Mng Member*
Richard Kampeter,
Gary Schell,
Mark Schell,
◆ EMP: 27 EST: 1998
SALES (est): 5.8MM Privately Held
SIC: 2047 Dog & cat food

(P-2335)
PRIMAL PET FOODS INC
535 Watt Dr Ste B, Fairfield (94534-1790)
PHONE..................415 642-7400
Matthew Koss, *CEO*
Alanna Abbott, *Executive*
Nicole Kramlich, *Regional Mgr*
David Hendrickson, *Finance*
Patricia Diaz, *Human Res Dir*
▲ EMP: 97 EST: 2001
SQ FT: 5,000
SALES (est): 33.3MM Privately Held
WEB: www.primalpetfoods.com
SIC: 2047 Dog food

(P-2336)
SCHELL & KAMPETER INC
250 Roth Rd, Lathrop (95330-9724)
PHONE..................209 983-4900
Gary Schell, *Branch Mgr*
Stephen Hansen, *Regl Sales Mgr*
Jon Lowe, *Warehouse Mgr*
EMP: 128
SALES (corp-wide): 85.6MM Privately Held
WEB: www.tasteofthewildpetfood.com
SIC: 2047 Dog food
PA: Schell & Kampeter, Inc.
  103 N Olive St
  Meta MO 65058
  573 229-4203

2048 Prepared Feeds For Animals & Fowls

(P-2337)
A L GILBERT COMPANY
Also Called: Lockwood Seed & Grain
504 S Tehama St, Willows (95988-3469)
PHONE..................530 934-2157
Ken Lohse, *Principal*
EMP: 18
SALES (corp-wide): 345.3MM Privately Held
WEB: www.farmerswarehouse.com
SIC: 2048 Alfalfa or alfalfa meal, prepared as animal feed
PA: A. L. Gilbert Company
  4367 Jessup Rd
  Oakdale CA 95361
  209 847-1721

(P-2338)
CALVA PRODUCTS LLC (PA)
4351 E Winery Rd, Acampo (95220-9506)
PHONE..................800 328-9680
Beth Ford, *CEO*
EMP: 24 EST: 2016
SALES (est): 2.6MM Privately Held
WEB: www.calvaproducts.com
SIC: 2048 Prepared feeds

(P-2339)
CALVA PRODUCTS CO INC
4351 E Winery Rd, Acampo (95220-9506)
P.O. Box 126 (95220-0126)
PHONE..................209 339-1516
Jim Cook Sr, *CEO*
Bill Cook, *Vice Pres*
◆ EMP: 39 EST: 1975
SQ FT: 62,000
SALES (est): 11.1MM
SALES (corp-wide): 2.8B Privately Held
WEB: www.calvaproducts.com
SIC: 2048 Prepared feeds
HQ: Purina Animal Nutrition Llc
  100 Danforth Dr
  Gray Summit MO 63039

(P-2340)
ECONOMY STOCK FEED COMPANY INC
10508 E Central Ave, Del Rey (93616-9711)
PHONE..................559 888-2187
Rod Kramer, *President*
Judy Kramer, *Vice Pres*
EMP: 32 EST: 1948
SQ FT: 1,200
SALES (est): 5.1MM Privately Held
SIC: 2048 Prepared feeds

(P-2341)
ELK GROVE MILLING INC
8320 Eschinger Rd, Elk Grove (95757-9739)
PHONE..................916 684-2056
Robert Lent, *President*
Jerry Mayberry, *General Mgr*
Simone Keyawa, *Admin Asst*
Richard Barnes, *CIO*
Sally Stincelli, *Controller*
▲ EMP: 25 EST: 1985
SQ FT: 400,000
SALES (est): 7.6MM Privately Held
WEB: www.elkgrovemilling.com
SIC: 2048 3541 5191 Livestock feeds; shell crushing, for feed; machine tools, metal cutting type; animal feeds

(P-2342)
FOSTER COMMODITIES
Also Called: Foster Farms
1900 Kern St, Kingsburg (93631-9687)
P.O. Box 457, Livingston (95334-0457)
PHONE..................559 897-1081
Todd Elrod, *Manager*
John Rocha, *Opers Mgr*
Nikita Tipnis, *Manager*
EMP: 25 EST: 1978
SALES (est): 2.5MM Privately Held
WEB: www.fosterfarms.com
SIC: 2048 Prepared feeds

(P-2343)
FOSTER POULTRY FARMS
221 Stefani Ave, Livingston (95334-1543)
PHONE..................209 394-7950
Jeremiah Nord, *Manager*
Arnesh Raj, *Technician*
EMP: 232
SALES (corp-wide): 1.2B Privately Held
WEB: www.fosterfarms.com
SIC: 2048 Poultry feeds
PA: Foster Poultry Farms
  1000 Davis St
  Livingston CA 95334
  209 394-7901

(P-2344)
FRONTIER AG CO INC (PA)
46735 County Road 32b, Davis (95618-9501)
PHONE..................530 297-1020
John Pereira, *President*
Matthew S Labriola, *Shareholder*
Mathew Labriola, *Admin Sec*
Susanne Brager, *Export Mgr*
Matthew Labriola, *Manager*
EMP: 40 EST: 2004
SALES (est): 10.5MM Privately Held
WEB: www.frontieragco.com
SIC: 2048 0723 Livestock feeds; rice drying services

(P-2345)
J S WEST MILLING CO INC
501 9th St, Modesto (95354-3420)
PHONE..................209 529-4232
D Gary West, *President*
Robert J Benson, *Ch of Bd*
Bob Metz, *CFO*
Amanda Silva, *CFO*
Eric Benson, *Vice Pres*
EMP: 26 EST: 1909
SQ FT: 1,692
SALES (est): 4.4MM Privately Held
WEB: www.jswest.com
SIC: 2048 0252 5999 5191 Livestock feeds; started pullet farm; pets & pet supplies; animal feeds

(P-2346)
LAWLEYS INC
Also Called: Lawley's Trucking
4554 Qantas Ln, Stockton (95206-4919)
P.O. Box 31447 (95213-1447)
PHONE..................209 337-1170
Casey Lawley, *CEO*
Desirea Hernandez, *CFO*
Carly Pavia, *Admin Mgr*
Kevin Dewark, *Plant Mgr*
Scott Dickerman, *Natl Sales Mgr*
EMP: 37 EST: 1984
SQ FT: 40,000
SALES (est): 16.3MM Privately Held
WEB: www.lawleys.com
SIC: 2048 Feed premixes

(P-2347)
LIND MARINE INC (PA)
100 E D St, Petaluma (94952-3109)
PHONE..................707 762-7251
Mike Lind, *President*
Aaron Lind, *Vice Pres*
Christian Lind, *Vice Pres*
Jeanine Andrus, *Opers Mgr*
Skyler Coleman, *Manager*
EMP: 22 EST: 1920
SQ FT: 18,500
SALES (est): 9.8MM Privately Held
WEB: www.lindmarine.com
SIC: 2048 1629 Oyster shells, ground; prepared as animal feed; dredging contractor

(P-2348)
MENEZES HAY CO
5030 Dwight Way, Livingston (95334-9604)
PHONE..................209 394-3111
Jeremy Menezes, *President*
EMP: 16 EST: 2005
SALES (est): 1.7MM Privately Held
WEB: www.menezeshaycompany.weebly.com
SIC: 2048 Hay, cubed

(P-2349)
NEXSTEPPE INC
400 E Jamie Ct Ste 202, South San Francisco (94080-6230)
P.O. Box 1561, Hereford TX (79045-1561)
PHONE..................650 887-5700
Anna Rath, *CEO*
EMP: 16 EST: 2010
SALES (est): 710K Privately Held
SIC: 2048 Livestock feeds

(P-2350)
NUTRA-BLEND LLC
Also Called: Thomas Products
2140 W Industrial Ave, Madera (93637-5210)
PHONE..................559 661-6161
Mike Osborne, *Branch Mgr*
Scott Cooper, *CFO*
Andrea Martinez, *Analyst*
John Silva, *Plant Mgr*
Dustin Kibler, *Production*
EMP: 40
SALES (corp-wide): 2.8B Privately Held
WEB: www.nutrablend.com
SIC: 2048 5191 Pulverized oats, prepared as animal feed; animal feeds
HQ: Nutra-Blend, L.L.C.
  3200 2nd St
  Neosho MO 64850
  417 451-6111

(P-2351)
NUTRIUS LLC
39494 Clarkson Dr, Kingsburg (93631-9100)
PHONE..................559 897-5862
Jim Hansen,
Michael Bizik, *Plant Mgr*
Chris McCormick, *Plant Mgr*
Bob Van Der Schaaf, *Sales Staff*

▲ = Import ▼ = Export
◆ = Import/Export

PRODUCTS & SERVICES SECTION
2051 - Bread, Bakery Prdts Exc Cookies & Crackers County (P-2375)

Russell Dutra, *Manager*
▲ **EMP:** 45 **EST:** 2005
SALES (est): 8.9MM **Privately Held**
WEB: www.nutrius.com
SIC: 2048 Prepared feeds

(P-2352)
NUWEST MILLING LLC
4636 Geer Rd, Hughson (95326-9403)
P.O. Box 1031 (95326-1031)
PHONE 209 883-1163
Gary West, *Mng Member*
John Machado, *CFO*
Eric H Benson, *CFO*
◆ **EMP:** 16 **EST:** 1998
SQ FT: 1,250
SALES (est): 5.1MM **Privately Held**
WEB: www.nuwestmilling.com
SIC: 2048 Prepared feeds

(P-2353)
PACIFIC CATCH INC
770 Tamalpais Dr Ste 210, Corte Madera (94925-1736)
PHONE 415 504-6905
Keith M Cox, *President*
Tom Hanson, *COO*
Warren Gambell, *General Mgr*
Mary Christensen, *Marketing Mgr*
Jack Basilotta, *Manager*
EMP: 36 **EST:** 2011
SALES (est): 10.9MM **Privately Held**
WEB: www.pacificcatch.com
SIC: 2048 Prepared feeds

(P-2354)
REED MARICULTURE INC
Also Called: Instant Algae
900 E Hamilton Ave # 100, Campbell (95008-0664)
P.O. Box 1049, Freedom (95019-1049)
PHONE 408 377-1065
Timothy Allen Reed, *CEO*
Lyn Reed, *COO*
Shawn Neverve, *Vice Pres*
Edwin Reed, *Admin Sec*
◆ **EMP:** 18 **EST:** 1995
SQ FT: 217,800
SALES (est): 8.4MM **Privately Held**
WEB: www.reedmariculture.com
SIC: 2048 Fish food

(P-2355)
RIPON MILLING LLC
30636 E Carter Rd, Farmington (95230-9633)
PHONE 209 599-4269
George E Jenkins, *President*
Arie E Den Dulk III, *Vice Pres*
Walter Den Dulk, *Vice Pres*
Ronald Den Dulk,
EMP: 20 **EST:** 1966
SQ FT: 8,000
SALES (est): 7.2MM **Privately Held**
SIC: 2048 Poultry feeds

(P-2356)
ROBINSON FARMS FEED COMPANY
7000 S Inland Dr, Stockton (95206-9688)
PHONE 209 466-7915
Michael S Robinson, *President*
Dale L Drury, *Corp Secy*
Jerry N Robinson, *Vice Pres*
EMP: 30 **EST:** 1943
SQ FT: 10,000
SALES (est): 2.3MM **Privately Held**
WEB: www.robinsonfarmsfeedco.com
SIC: 2048 0139 0119 0115 Feed premixes; stock feeds, dry; alfalfa or alfalfa meal, prepared as animal feed; alfalfa farm; safflower farm; corn; wheat

(P-2357)
SAN FRANCISCO BAY BRAND INC (PA)
8239 Enterprise Dr, Newark (94560-3305)
PHONE 510 792-7200
Andreas Schmidt, *President*
Anthony Schmidt, *Exec VP*
Kearny Wong, *Technology*
John Huynh, *Sales Staff*
Paul Wong, *Manager*
◆ **EMP:** 35 **EST:** 1969
SQ FT: 30,000
SALES (est): 6.9MM **Privately Held**
WEB: www.sfbb.com
SIC: 2048 Fish food

(P-2358)
SEED FACTORY NORTHWEST INC (PA)
4319 Jessup Rd, Ceres (95307-9604)
P.O. Box 245 (95307-0245)
PHONE 209 634-8522
Randall Steele, *President*
Lynda Blakemore, *Admin Sec*
David Block, *Marketing Staff*
▲ **EMP:** 20 **EST:** 2000
SQ FT: 30,000
SALES (est): 5.1MM **Privately Held**
SIC: 2048 Bird food, prepared

2051 Bread, Bakery Prdts Exc Cookies & Crackers

(P-2359)
ACME BREAD CO
362 E Grand Ave, South San Francisco (94080-6210)
PHONE 650 938-2978
Drew Wescott, *Principal*
EMP: 19 **EST:** 2004
SALES (est): 1.2MM **Privately Held**
WEB: www.acmebread.com
SIC: 2051 Bakery: wholesale or wholesale/retail combined

(P-2360)
ALBECO INC
Also Called: Mollie Stone Market
270 Bon Air Ctr, Greenbrae (94904-2416)
PHONE 415 461-1164
Jeffrey Lane, *Manager*
EMP: 68
SALES (corp-wide): 163.4MM **Privately Held**
WEB: www.molliestones.com
SIC: 5411 5921 5421 5431 Grocery stores, independent; liquor stores; meat markets, including freezer provisioners; fruit stands or markets; vegetable stands or markets; florists; bread, cake & related products
PA: Albeco, Inc.
150 Shoreline Hwy Bldg D
Mill Valley CA 94941
415 289-5720

(P-2361)
ANDRE-BOUDIN BAKERIES INC
67 Broadwalk Ln, Walnut Creek (94596)
PHONE 925 935-4375
Andrew Friedman, *Manager*
EMP: 23 **Privately Held**
WEB: www.boudinbakery.com
SIC: 2051 5812 Bread, cake & related products; cafe
HQ: Andre-Boudin Bakeries, Inc.
50 Francisco St Ste 200
San Francisco CA 94133
415 882-1849

(P-2362)
ANDRE-BOUDIN BAKERIES INC
619 Market St, San Francisco (94105-3301)
PHONE 415 283-1230
Stephen Floyd, *Manager*
Caroline Creer-Saldua, *Supervisor*
EMP: 20 **Privately Held**
WEB: www.boudinbakery.com
SIC: 5461 2051 5812 Cakes; bread, cake & related products; sandwiches & submarines shop
HQ: Andre-Boudin Bakeries, Inc.
50 Francisco St Ste 200
San Francisco CA 94133
415 882-1849

(P-2363)
ASPIRE BAKERIES LLC
Also Called: Fresh Start Bakeries
920 Shaw Rd, Stockton (95215-4014)
PHONE 209 469-4920
Dan Bailey, *Mng Officer*
Jeffrey Harrigan, *Division VP*
Christopher Woo, *Division VP*
Suzanne Wooley, *Division VP*
Jason Buntin, *Vice Pres*
EMP: 91
SALES (corp-wide): 1.7B **Privately Held**
WEB: www.aryzta.com
SIC: 2051 Bakery: wholesale or wholesale/retail combined
HQ: Aspire Bakeries Llc
350 N Orleans St 3001n
Chicago IL 60654
855 427-9982

(P-2364)
BAGELRY INC (PA)
320 Cedar St Ste A, Santa Cruz (95060-4362)
PHONE 831 429-8049
John Hamstra, *President*
Laurie Rivin, *Vice Pres*
EMP: 35 **EST:** 1977
SQ FT: 3,000
SALES (est): 1.9MM **Privately Held**
WEB: www.bagelrysantacruz.com
SIC: 2051 5812 2052 Bakery: wholesale or wholesale/retail combined; eating places; cookies & crackers

(P-2365)
BECKMANNS OLD WORLD BAKERY LTD
Also Called: Beckmann's Bakery
1053 17th Ave, Santa Cruz (95062-3053)
PHONE 831 423-9242
Beth Holland, *CEO*
Peter Beckmann, *President*
Sharon May, *Vice Pres*
▲ **EMP:** 100 **EST:** 1985
SQ FT: 17,000
SALES (est): 19.8MM **Privately Held**
WEB: www.beckmannsbakery.com
SIC: 2051 5461 Bakery: wholesale or wholesale/retail combined; bakeries

(P-2366)
BEL AIR MART
Also Called: Bel Air Market 509
1039 Sunrise Ave, Roseville (95661-7008)
PHONE 916 786-6101
EMP: 106
SALES (corp-wide): 2.1B **Privately Held**
WEB: www.raleys.com
SIC: 5411 5992 5912 2051 Supermarkets, chain; florists; drug stores & proprietary stores; bread, cake & related products
HQ: Bel Air Mart
500 W Capitol Ave
West Sacramento CA

(P-2367)
BEL AIR MART
Also Called: Bel Air Market 501
6231 Fruitridge Rd, Sacramento (95820-5844)
PHONE 916 739-8647
Allen Kamura, *Manager*
EMP: 106
SALES (corp-wide): 2.1B **Privately Held**
WEB: www.raleys.com
SIC: 5411 2051 5461 Supermarkets, chain; bread, cake & related products; bakeries
HQ: Bel Air Mart
500 W Capitol Ave
West Sacramento CA

(P-2368)
BEL AIR MART
Also Called: Bel Air Market 510
1540 W El Camino Ave, Sacramento (95833-1946)
PHONE 916 920-2493
Phil Canaday, *Manager*
EMP: 106
SALES (corp-wide): 2.1B **Privately Held**
WEB: www.raleys.com
SIC: 5411 5992 5912 2051 Supermarkets, chain; florists; drug stores & proprietary stores; bread, cake & related products
HQ: Bel Air Mart
500 W Capitol Ave
West Sacramento CA

(P-2369)
BEST EXPRESS FOODS INC
1718 Boeing Way Ste 100, Stockton (95206-4995)
PHONE 209 490-2612
Jesus Mendoza, *President*
Daniel Mendoza, *Vice Pres*
EMP: 270 **EST:** 1989
SALES (est): 65.9MM **Privately Held**
WEB: www.bestxfoods.com
SIC: 2051 Breads, rolls & buns

(P-2370)
BIMBO BAKERIES USA INC
2007 N Main St, Manteca (95336-9629)
PHONE 209 825-8647
Jesus Mendoza, *President*
Daniel Mendoza, *Branch Mgr*
EMP: 16 **Privately Held**
WEB: www.arnoldbread.com
SIC: 2051 Bread, cake & related products
HQ: Bimbo Bakeries Usa, Inc
255 Business Center Dr # 200
Horsham PA 19044
215 347-5500

(P-2371)
BIMBO BAKERIES USA INC
1836 G St, Fresno (93706-1617)
PHONE 559 498-3632
EMP: 18
SALES (corp-wide): 13.7B **Privately Held**
SIC: 2051 Mfg Bread/Related Products
HQ: Bimbo Bakeries Usa, Inc
255 Business Center Dr # 200
Horsham PA 19044
215 347-5500

(P-2372)
CARAVAN BAKERY INC
33300 Western Ave, Union City (94587-2211)
PHONE 510 487-2600
Joseph Maroun Sr, *President*
Gabriel Hernanadez, *Superintendent*
EMP: 19 **EST:** 1975
SALES (est): 681.7K **Privately Held**
WEB: www.caravantrd.com
SIC: 2051 Bakery: wholesale or wholesale/retail combined

(P-2373)
CITY BAKING COMPANY
1373 Lowrie Ave, South San Francisco (94080-6403)
PHONE 650 332-8730
Alex Bulazo, *President*
Richard Barnes, *CIO*
Judie Gee, *Cust Mgr*
EMP: 55 **EST:** 1991
SALES (est): 4.8MM **Privately Held**
WEB: www.citybaking.com
SIC: 2051 Bread, cake & related products

(P-2374)
DESSERTS ON US INC
57 Belle Falor Ct, Arcata (95521-9234)
PHONE 707 822-0160
Emran Essa, *CEO*
Kathleen Essa, *Admin Sec*
▲ **EMP:** 15 **EST:** 1990
SQ FT: 20,000
SALES (est): 3MM **Privately Held**
WEB: www.dessertsonus.com
SIC: 2051 2099 2052 Pastries, e.g. danish: except frozen; dessert mixes & fillings; cookies

(P-2375)
DLA COLMENA INC
129 W Lake Ave, Watsonville (95076-4511)
PHONE 831 724-4544
Manuel Gonzales, *President*
Andrean Gonzales, *Vice Pres*
Connie Gonzales, *Admin Sec*
EMP: 50 **EST:** 1978
SQ FT: 6,100
SALES (est): 6.5MM **Privately Held**
WEB: www.dlacolmenacatering.com
SIC: 5411 2051 5812 Grocery stores, independent; pastries, e.g. danish: except frozen; delicatessen (eating places)

2051 - Bread, Bakery Prdts Exc Cookies & Crackers County (P-2376)

(P-2376)
DOMINICS ORGNAL GNOVA DELI INC
Also Called: Ravioli Factory
1550 Trancas St, NAPA (94558-2916)
PHONE..................707 253-8686
Dominic De Vincenzi, *President*
David De Vincenzi, *Vice Pres*
Al Ferrer, *Manager*
EMP: 65 EST: 1966
SQ FT: 1,500
SALES (est): 5.3MM **Privately Held**
WEB: www.genovadelinapa.com
SIC: 5411 2051 5921 Delicatessens; bread, all types (white, wheat, rye, etc): fresh or frozen; beer (packaged); wine

(P-2377)
DOUGHTRONICS INC (PA)
Also Called: Acme Bread Company
1601 San Pablo Ave, Berkeley (94702-1317)
PHONE..................510 524-1327
Steven Sullivan, *President*
Susan Sullivan, *Vice Pres*
Doug Volkmer, *Vice Pres*
EMP: 30 EST: 1983
SALES (est): 15.7MM **Privately Held**
WEB: www.acmebread.com
SIC: 2051 5461 Bakery: wholesale or wholesale/retail combined; bread

(P-2378)
DOUGHTRONICS INC
Also Called: Acme Bread Co Div II
2730 9th St, Berkeley (94710-2633)
PHONE..................510 843-2978
Rick Kirkby, *Manager*
EMP: 43
SQ FT: 4,372
SALES (corp-wide): 15.7MM **Privately Held**
WEB: www.acmebread.com
SIC: 2051 Bakery: wholesale or wholesale/retail combined
PA: Doughtronics, Inc.
1601 San Pablo Ave
Berkeley CA 94702
510 524-1327

(P-2379)
EINSTEIN NOAH REST GROUP INC
Also Called: Noah's
1521 Sloat Blvd, San Francisco (94132-1222)
PHONE..................415 731-1700
Albert Puzon, *General Mgr*
EMP: 54 **Privately Held**
WEB: www.bagelbrands.com
SIC: 5461 2051 2022 Bagels; bagels, fresh or frozen; spreads, cheese
PA: Einstein Noah Restaurant Group, Inc.
555 Zang St Ste 300
Lakewood CO 80228

(P-2380)
EINSTEIN NOAH REST GROUP INC
Also Called: Noah's Bagels
1067 El Camino Real, Redwood City (94063-1632)
PHONE..................650 299-9050
Antelop Tran, *Manager*
EMP: 54 **Privately Held**
WEB: www.bagelbrands.com
SIC: 5461 2051 2022 Bagels; bagels, fresh or frozen; spreads, cheese
PA: Einstein Noah Restaurant Group, Inc.
555 Zang St Ste 300
Lakewood CO 80228

(P-2381)
EINSTEIN NOAH REST GROUP INC
Also Called: Einstein Brothers Bagels
170 Bon Air Ctr, Greenbrae (94904-2417)
PHONE..................415 925-9971
Astid Ludlow, *Manager*
EMP: 135 **Privately Held**
WEB: www.bagelbrands.com
SIC: 5812 2051 2022 Cafe; bagels, fresh or frozen; spreads, cheese
PA: Einstein Noah Restaurant Group, Inc.
555 Zang St Ste 300
Lakewood CO 80228

(P-2382)
FLOWERS BAKING CO MODESTO LLC (HQ)
736 Mariposa Rd, Modesto (95354-4133)
PHONE..................209 857-4600
Paul Holshouser,
EMP: 59 EST: 2013
SQ FT: 250,000
SALES (est): 16.3MM
SALES (corp-wide): 4.3B **Publicly Held**
WEB: www.flowersfoods.com
SIC: 2051 Breads, rolls & buns
PA: Flowers Foods, Inc.
1919 Flowers Cir
Thomasville GA 31757
912 226-9110

(P-2383)
FREEPORT BAKERY INC
2966 Freeport Blvd, Sacramento (95818-3855)
PHONE..................916 442-4256
Marlene Goetzeler, *President*
Walter Goetzeler, *Principal*
EMP: 18 EST: 1982
SALES (est): 1.1MM **Privately Held**
WEB: www.freeportbakery.com
SIC: 2051 5461 5812 Bread, cake & related products; bakeries; eating places

(P-2384)
FRESNO FRENCH BREAD BAKERY INC
Also Called: Basque French Bakery
2625 Inyo St, Fresno (93721-2732)
PHONE..................559 268-7088
Al Lewis, *President*
Rita Ingmire, *Vice Pres*
EMP: 34 EST: 1963
SQ FT: 32,000
SALES (est): 3.7MM **Privately Held**
WEB: www.fresnobread.com
SIC: 2051 Bakery: wholesale or wholesale/retail combined

(P-2385)
FULLBLOOM BAKING COMPANY INC
6500 Overlake Pl, Newark (94560-1083)
PHONE..................510 456-3638
Karen Trilevsky, *CEO*
Leo Carpio, *Engineer*
Javier Urenda, *Manager*
▲ EMP: 2207 EST: 1989
SQ FT: 95,000
SALES (est): 12.5MM
SALES (corp-wide): 1.7B **Privately Held**
WEB: www.fullbloom.com
SIC: 2051 Bread, cake & related products
HQ: Aspire Bakeries Llc
350 N Orleans St 300'n
Chicago IL 60654
855 427-9982

(P-2386)
GALAXY DESSERTS
1100 Marina Way S Ste D, Richmond (94804-3727)
PHONE..................510 439-3160
Paul Levitan, *CEO*
Jean-Yves Charon, *Vice Pres*
John Mitchell, *Info Tech Mgr*
Rohana Stone Rice, *Controller*
Seck Rokhaya, *Purchasing*
▲ EMP: 160 EST: 1991
SQ FT: 56,000
SALES (est): 26.4MM
SALES (corp-wide): 6.2MM **Privately Held**
WEB: www.galaxydesserts.com
SIC: 2051 Bread, cake & related products
HQ: Brioche Pasquier Cerqueux
Pitch
Les Cerqueux 49360
241 637-541

(P-2387)
GOLDILOCKS CORPORATION CALIF (PA)
Also Called: Goldilocks Bakeshop and Rest
30865 San Clemente St, Hayward (94544-7136)
PHONE..................510 476-0700
Mendrei Leelin, *President*
Menard Leelin, *President*
Cecilia Leelin, *Treasurer*
EMP: 50 EST: 2000
SQ FT: 12,000
SALES (est): 8.8MM **Privately Held**
SIC: 2051 Bread, cake & related products

(P-2388)
HOUSE OF BAGELS INC (PA)
1007 Washington St, San Carlos (94070-5318)
PHONE..................650 595-4700
Larry Chassy, *President*
EMP: 15 EST: 1962
SALES (est): 5.8MM **Privately Held**
SIC: 2051 5461 Bread, cake & related products; bakeries

(P-2389)
JORODA INC (PA)
Also Called: Sunrise Bistro
1559 Botelho Dr, Walnut Creek (94596-5102)
PHONE..................925 930-0122
Cindy Gershen, *President*
EMP: 30 EST: 1980
SQ FT: 5,000
SALES (est): 3.6MM **Privately Held**
WEB: www.sunrisebistrocatering.com
SIC: 5812 2051 Caterers; bakery: wholesale or wholesale/retail combined

(P-2390)
LA BOULANGERIE FRENCH BKY CAFE
730 W Shaw Ave, Fresno (93704-2301)
PHONE..................559 222-0555
Patrick Bourrel, *Owner*
EMP: 20 EST: 2007
SALES (est): 2.2MM **Privately Held**
WEB: www.laboufresno.com
SIC: 2051 Bagels, fresh or frozen

(P-2391)
LOS BAGELS INC (PA)
1061 I St Ste 101, Arcata (95521-5517)
PHONE..................707 822-3150
Dennis Rael, *President*
Peter Jermyn, *Treasurer*
Paul Hebb Jr, *Vice Pres*
Kate Monahan,
EMP: 21 EST: 1984
SQ FT: 1,500
SALES (est): 1.2MM **Privately Held**
WEB: www.losbagels.com
SIC: 5461 2051 5149 Bagels; bread; bagels, fresh or frozen; bread, all types (white, wheat, rye, etc): fresh or frozen; groceries & related products

(P-2392)
LY BROTHERS CORPORATION (PA)
Also Called: Sugar Bowl Bakery
1963 Sabre St, Hayward (94545-1021)
PHONE..................510 782-2118
Andrew A Ly, *President*
Tom Ly, *Chairman*
Paul Ly, *Treasurer*
Sam Ly, *Exec VP*
Binh Ly, *Vice Pres*
◆ EMP: 238 EST: 1954
SQ FT: 100,000
SALES (est): 79.5MM **Privately Held**
WEB: www.sugarbowlbakery.com
SIC: 2051 Bakery: wholesale or wholesale/retail combined

(P-2393)
M & M BAKERY PRODUCTS INC
Also Called: Maggiora Baking Co
1900 Garden Tract Rd, Richmond (94801-1219)
PHONE..................510 235-0274
Dennis Maggiora, *President*
Margaret Maggiora, *Ch of Bd*
Lisa Wilde, *Treasurer*
Scott Krumland, *QC Mgr*
EMP: 80 EST: 1985
SQ FT: 35,000 **Privately Held**
WEB: www.maggiorabaking.com
SIC: 5812 2051 Eating places: bread, all types (white, wheat, rye, etc): fresh or frozen

(P-2394)
MARY ANNS BAKING CO INC
8371 Carbide Ct, Sacramento (95828-5636)
PHONE..................916 681-7444
George A Demas, *President*
Robert Burzinski, *CFO*
John Demas, *Admin Sec*
Shelley Wert, *Controller*
Rafael Barajas, *Manager*
EMP: 200 EST: 1961
SQ FT: 75,000
SALES (est): 33MM **Privately Held**
WEB: www.maryannsbaking.com
SIC: 2051 Doughnuts, except frozen; rolls, sweet: except frozen; rolls, bread type: fresh or frozen

(P-2395)
MIDDLE EAST BAKING CO
1380 Marsten Rd, Burlingame (94010-2406)
PHONE..................650 348-7200
Isaac Cohen, *Owner*
▲ EMP: 17 EST: 1977
SALES (est): 999.9K **Privately Held**
SIC: 2051 Bakery: wholesale or wholesale/retail combined

(P-2396)
OVEN FRESH BAKERY INCORPORATED
23188 Foley St, Hayward (94545-1602)
PHONE..................650 366-9201
Juanita Casillas, *President*
Jorge A Alfonso, *Treasurer*
Andrea Casillas, *Marketing Staff*
EMP: 15 EST: 1951
SQ FT: 18,000
SALES (est): 1.9MM **Privately Held**
WEB: www.ovenfresh-bakery.com
SIC: 2051 2053 Bakery: wholesale or wholesale/retail combined; frozen bakery products, except bread

(P-2397)
PAMELAS PRODUCT INC
1924 4th St, San Rafael (94901-2697)
PHONE..................707 462-6605
Pamela Giusto-Sorells, *Principal*
EMP: 20 EST: 1989
SALES (est): 621.2K **Privately Held**
WEB: www.pamelasproducts.com
SIC: 2051 Bread, cake & related products

(P-2398)
PAN-O-RAMA BAKING INC
500 Florida St, San Francisco (94110-1415)
PHONE..................415 522-5500
Bill Upson, *President*
Alicia Zuniga, *Opers Staff*
Bob Mannion, *Sales Executive*
EMP: 25 EST: 1993
SALES (est): 918.7K **Privately Held**
WEB: www.panoramabaking.com
SIC: 2051 Bakery: wholesale or wholesale/retail combined

(P-2399)
PETITS PAINS & CO LP
1730 Gilbreth Rd, Burlingame (94010-1305)
PHONE..................650 692-6000
Alain Bourgade, *Principal*
Richard Barnes, *CIO*
Matt Booth, *Sales Mgr*
Pamela Davis, *Supervisor*
Lynn Knott, *Supervisor*
EMP: 19 EST: 2013
SALES (est): 4.6MM **Privately Held**
WEB: www.petitspains.com
SIC: 2051 Bakery: wholesale or wholesale/retail combined

PRODUCTS & SERVICES SECTION
2063 - Sugar, Beet County (P-2423)

(P-2400)
QUINOA CORPORATION
Also Called: Ancient Harvest
1 Carousel Ln Ste D, Ukiah (95482-9509)
PHONE......................707 462-6605
Dave Schnorr, *Branch Mgr*
EMP: 44
SALES (corp-wide): 38.9MM **Privately Held**
WEB: www.ancientharvest.com
SIC: 2051 2052 Bakery products, partially cooked (except frozen); cookies & crackers
HQ: Quinoa Corporation
4653 Tbl Muntian Dr Ste 1
Golden CO 80403
303 957-5907

(P-2401)
ROMA BAKERY INC
655 S Almaden Ave, San Jose (95110-2999)
P.O. Box 348 (95103-0348)
PHONE......................408 294-0123
Robert Pera, *President*
Mario Pera II, *Vice Pres*
Steven Pera, *Admin Sec*
EMP: 60 **EST:** 1907
SQ FT: 15,000
SALES (est): 5.1MM **Privately Held**
SIC: 2051 Bakery: wholesale or wholesale/retail combined; rolls, bread type: fresh or frozen

(P-2402)
SACRAMENTO BAKING CO INC
9221 Beatty Dr, Sacramento (95826-9702)
PHONE......................916 361-2000
Samir Elajou, *CEO*
Juma Al Ajon, *President*
Juma Elajou, *President*
Samira Al Ajon, *CEO*
EMP: 25 **EST:** 1984
SQ FT: 10,000
SALES (est): 1.6MM **Privately Held**
SIC: 2051 5812 Bread, all types (white, wheat, rye, etc): fresh or frozen; pastries, e.g. danish: except frozen; cafe

(P-2403)
SAVE MART SUPERMARKETS
Also Called: Foodmaxx
8065 Watt Ave, Antelope (95843-9102)
PHONE......................916 348-3425
EMP: 100
SALES (corp-wide): 2.8B **Privately Held**
WEB: www.thesavemartcompanies.com
SIC: 5411 2051 Grocery Stores, Nsk
PA: Save Mart Supermarkets Disc
1800 Standiford Ave
Modesto CA 95350
209 577-1600

(P-2404)
SAVE MART SUPERMARKETS DISC
Also Called: Foodmaxx
1330 Churn Creek Rd, Redding (96003-4087)
PHONE......................530 222-6740
Ray Prigmore, *Director*
Matt Wigham, *Manager*
EMP: 85
SALES (corp-wide): 414.7K **Privately Held**
WEB: www.thesavemartcompanies.com
SIC: 5411 5992 2051 Supermarkets, chain; florists; bread, cake & related products
PA: Save Mart Supermarkets Disc
1800 Standiford Ave
Modesto CA 95350
209 577-1600

(P-2405)
SWEETIE PIES LLC
520 Main St, NAPA (94559-3353)
PHONE......................707 257-7280
Toni M Chiappetta,
EMP: 19 **EST:** 1994
SQ FT: 600
SALES (est): 2.1MM **Privately Held**
SIC: 2051 5812 Bakery: wholesale or wholesale/retail combined; eating places

(P-2406)
TAHOE HOUSE INC
625 W Lake Blvd, Tahoe City (96145-2295)
P.O. Box 1899 (96145-1899)
PHONE......................530 583-1377
Barbara Vogt, *President*
Caroline Vogt, *Treasurer*
Helen Vogt, *Vice Pres*
▲ **EMP:** 15 **EST:** 1977
SQ FT: 6,800
SALES (est): 1MM **Privately Held**
WEB: www.tahoe-house.com
SIC: 2051 Bakery: wholesale or wholesale/retail combined

(P-2407)
TARTINE LP
Also Called: Tartine Bakery & Cafe
600 Guerrero St, San Francisco (94110-1528)
PHONE......................415 487-2600
Frederic Soulies, *CEO*
Matija Blazic, *Comms Mgr*
Elisabeth Prueitt, *Principal*
Chad Robertson, *Principal*
Robin Rodriguez, *General Mgr*
EMP: 45 **EST:** 2002
SALES (est): 5.6MM **Privately Held**
WEB: www.tartinebakery.com
SIC: 2051 5812 5921 Breads, rolls & buns; cakes, pies & pastries; cafe; wine & beer

(P-2408)
THIRD CULTURE FOOD GROUP INC
2701 8th St, Berkeley (94710-2675)
PHONE......................650 479-4585
EMP: 26 **EST:** 2017
SALES (est): 1.3MM **Privately Held**
SIC: 2051 Bakery: wholesale or wholesale/retail combined

(P-2409)
VALLEY LAHVOSH BAKING CO INC
502 M St, Fresno (93721-3013)
PHONE......................559 485-2700
Janet F Saghatelian, *President*
Agnes Wilson, *Vice Pres*
Rebecca Cline, *Administration*
Danny Giosa, *Opers Mgr*
▲ **EMP:** 30 **EST:** 1922
SQ FT: 27,000
SALES (est): 7.6MM **Privately Held**
WEB: www.valleylahvosh.com
SIC: 2051 5461 Bread, all types (white, wheat, rye, etc): fresh or frozen; breads, rolls & buns; bread

(P-2410)
VITAL VITTLES BAKERY INC
Also Called: Schwin and Tran Mill & Bakery
2810 San Pablo Ave, Berkeley (94702-2204)
PHONE......................510 644-2022
Binh Tran, *President*
EMP: 20 **EST:** 1976
SQ FT: 2,424
SALES (est): 1.7MM **Privately Held**
SIC: 2051 2052 5461 Bakery: wholesale or wholesale/retail combined; cookies & crackers; bakeries

(P-2411)
WESTLAKE BAKERY INC
Also Called: Bread Basket
7099 Mission St, Daly City (94014-2253)
PHONE......................650 994-7741
Jaime Cavan, *President*
Nelly Cavan, *Vice Pres*
EMP: 15 **EST:** 1977
SQ FT: 5,000
SALES (est): 1.1MM **Privately Held**
SIC: 2051 5461 Bakery: wholesale or wholesale/retail combined; bakeries

(P-2412)
WINDMILL CORPORATION
Also Called: Wedemeyer Bakery
314 Harbor Way, South San Francisco (94080-6900)
PHONE......................650 873-1000
Larry Strain, *President*
EMP: 19 **EST:** 2004

SALES (est): 1.2MM **Privately Held**
SIC: 2051 5461 5149 Bread, all types (white, wheat, rye, etc): fresh or frozen; rolls, bread type: fresh or frozen; bakeries; groceries & related products

2052 Cookies & Crackers

(P-2413)
BEL AIR MART
Also Called: Bel Air Market 502
4320 Arden Way, Sacramento (95864-3103)
PHONE......................916 972-0555
Gary Spencer, *Manager*
EMP: 106
SALES (corp-wide): 2.1B **Privately Held**
WEB: www.raleys.com
SIC: 5411 5912 2052 2051 Supermarkets, chain; drug stores & proprietary stores; cookies & crackers; bread, cake & related products
HQ: Bel Air Mart
500 W Capitol Ave
West Sacramento CA

(P-2414)
BROWNIE BAKER INC
4870 W Jacquelyn Ave, Fresno (93722-5027)
PHONE......................559 277-7070
Dennis Perkins, *CEO*
Villy Bergquam, *Admin Asst*
Janea Marks, *Human Res Dir*
Mike Collins, *Opers Staff*
Ken Morgan, *Sales Staff*
▲ **EMP:** 70 **EST:** 1979
SQ FT: 30,000
SALES (est): 16.7MM **Privately Held**
WEB: www.browniebaker.com
SIC: 2052 2051 Cookies; bread, cake & related products

(P-2415)
HYE QUALITY BAKERY INC
2222 Santa Clara St, Fresno (93721-2921)
P.O. Box 25395 (93729-5395)
PHONE......................559 445-1511
Sammy Ganimian, *President*
Sammy E Ganimian, *President*
Paula Ganimian, *Treasurer*
EMP: 24 **EST:** 1957
SQ FT: 10,000
SALES (est): 550.2K **Privately Held**
WEB: www.hyequalitybakery.com
SIC: 5461 2052 Bakeries; crackers, dry

(P-2416)
KEEBLER COMPANY
1550 N Chrisman Rd, Tracy (95304-9396)
PHONE......................209 836-0302
EMP: 112
SALES (corp-wide): 13.7B **Publicly Held**
WEB: www.keebler.com
SIC: 2052 Cookies
HQ: Keebler Company
1 Kellogg Sq
Battle Creek MI 49017
269 961-2000

(P-2417)
MURRAY BISCUIT COMPANY LLC
Also Called: Famous Amos Chclat Chip Cookie
5250 Claremont Ave, Stockton (95207-5700)
PHONE......................209 472-3718
Chris Lopes, *Branch Mgr*
EMP: 109
SALES (corp-wide): 13.7B **Publicly Held**
SIC: 2052 Cookies
HQ: Murray Biscuit Company, L.L.C.
1550 Marvin Griffin Rd
Augusta GA 30906
706 798-8600

(P-2418)
SOOJIANS INC
Also Called: AK Mak Bakeries Division
89 Academy Ave, Sanger (93657-2104)
PHONE......................559 875-5511
Manoog Soojian, *President*

Hagop Soojian, *Vice Pres*
EMP: 35 **EST:** 1936
SQ FT: 8,000
SALES (est): 3.2MM **Privately Held**
WEB: www.akmakbakeries.com
SIC: 2052 5046 Crackers, dry; bakery equipment & supplies

(P-2419)
TRIPLE C FOODS INC
Also Called: Golden Phoenix Bakery
1465 Factor Ave, San Leandro (94577-5615)
PHONE......................510 357-8880
Tom Chua, *President*
Kim Chua, *Vice Pres*
Aaron Chua, *Office Mgr*
EMP: 21 **EST:** 1981
SQ FT: 65,000
SALES (est): 1.3MM **Privately Held**
WEB: www.bakerystreet.com
SIC: 2052 Cookies

2053 Frozen Bakery Prdts

(P-2420)
BENNETTS BAKING COMPANY
Also Called: Bennett's Bakery
2530 Tesla Way, Sacramento (95825-1912)
PHONE......................916 481-3349
Michael Bennett, *President*
EMP: 15 **EST:** 1993
SQ FT: 3,000
SALES (est): 2MM **Privately Held**
WEB: www.bennettsbakery.com
SIC: 2053 Frozen bakery products, except bread

(P-2421)
CARAVAN FOODS II INC
Also Called: Caravan Trading
33300 Western Ave, Union City (94587-2211)
PHONE......................510 487-2600
John Likovich, *Chairman*
EMP: 15 **EST:** 2016
SALES (est): 384.7K **Privately Held**
SIC: 2053 2051 Croissants, frozen; bagels, fresh or frozen

(P-2422)
HORIZON SNACK FOODS INC
Also Called: Cutie Pie Snack Pies
197 Darcy Pkwy, Lathrop (95330-9222)
PHONE......................925 373-7700
William D Reynolds, *President*
Andrew Kunkler, *CFO*
Lee Rucker, *CFO*
Colleen Planting, *Executive*
Betty Blakely, *Manager*
EMP: 62 **EST:** 1957
SQ FT: 9,000
SALES (est): 14.9MM **Privately Held**
WEB: www.getcutiepie.com
SIC: 2053 Pies, bakery: frozen
PA: Horizon Holdings, Llc
1 Bush St Ste 650
San Francisco CA 94104

2063 Sugar, Beet

(P-2423)
C&H SUGAR COMPANY INC
Also Called: C&H Sugar
830 Loring Ave, Crockett (94525-1104)
PHONE......................510 787-2121
Antonio L Contreras, *CEO*
Luis J Fernandez, *President*
Gregory H Smith, *CFO*
Gregory A Maitner, *Treasurer*
Antonio Contreras, *Co-President*
▲ **EMP:** 550 **EST:** 1998
SQ FT: 385,000
SALES (est): 100.4MM
SALES (corp-wide): 2.1B **Privately Held**
WEB: www.candhsugarcompany.com
SIC: 2063 Beet sugar
HQ: American Sugar Refining, Inc.
1 N Clematis St Ste 200
West Palm Beach FL 33401
561 366-5100

2064 - Candy & Confectionery Prdts County (P-2424)

2064 Candy & Confectionery Prdts

(P-2424)
18 RABBITS INC (PA)
995 Market St Fl 2, San Francisco (94103-1732)
P.O. Box 411142 (94141-1142)
PHONE...............................415 922-6006
Alison Vercruysse, *CEO*
Josephine Nguyen, *Opers Mgr*
Craig Vercruysse, *Director*
EMP: 15 **EST:** 2014
SALES (est): 2.8MM **Privately Held**
SIC: 2064 Granola & muesli, bars & clusters

(P-2425)
AMERICAN LICORICE COMPANY
2477 Liston Way, Union City (94587-1979)
P.O. Box 826 (94587-0826)
PHONE...............................510 487-5500
John Sullivan, *Principal*
James Kretchmer, *President*
Clifford Walsh, *COO*
Suresh Kumar, *CIO*
Joaquin Almaguer, *Prdtn Mgr*
EMP: 350
SALES (corp-wide): 156.1MM **Privately Held**
WEB: www.americanlicorice.com
SIC: 2064 Licorice candy
PA: American Licorice Company
1914 Happiness Way
La Porte IN 46350
219 324-1400

(P-2426)
CHIODO CANDY CO
2923 Adeline St, Oakland (94608-4422)
P.O. Box 8155 (94662-0155)
PHONE...............................510 464-2977
Louis J Chiodo, *President*
EMP: 18 **EST:** 1955
SALES (est): 491.5K **Privately Held**
SIC: 2064 Candy & other confectionery products

(P-2427)
CLIF BAR & COMPANY (PA)
1451 66th St, Emeryville (94608-1004)
PHONE...............................510 596-6300
Sally Grimes, *CEO*
Kevin Cleary, *CEO*
Corey Fujioka, *COO*
Hari Avula, *CFO*
Kit Crawform, *Co-CEO*
▲ **EMP:** 641 **EST:** 1986
SQ FT: 120,000
SALES (est): 337.8MM **Privately Held**
WEB: www.clifbar.com
SIC: 2064 5149 Candy bars, including chocolate covered bars; specialty food items

(P-2428)
GOLD RUSH KETTLE KORN LLC
Also Called: Kettle Pop
4690 E 2nd St Ste 9, Benicia (94510-1008)
PHONE...............................707 747-6773
Jeff Schletewitz, *Mng Member*
Rovner Steve, *VP Sales*
William Baker Jr,
Aaron Reimer, *Manager*
▲ **EMP:** 31 **EST:** 2002
SQ FT: 1,596
SALES (est): 3.4MM **Privately Held**
SIC: 2064 Popcorn balls or other treated popcorn products

(P-2429)
INTERNATIONAL GLACE INC (PA)
4067 W Shaw Ave, Fresno (93722-6214)
PHONE...............................559 385-7675
Allen Sipole, *President*
EMP: 24 **EST:** 2017
SALES (est): 2.6MM **Privately Held**
SIC: 2064 Nuts, glace

(P-2430)
LE BELGE CHOCOLATIER INC
761 Skyway Ct, NAPA (94558-7510)
PHONE...............................707 258-9200
David Grunhut, *CEO*
Debby Kelly, *Vice Pres*
◆ **EMP:** 25 **EST:** 1984
SQ FT: 15,000
SALES (est): 5.4MM
SALES (corp-wide): 82.1MM **Privately Held**
WEB: www.lebelgechocolatier.com
SIC: 2064 2066 Chocolate candy, except solid chocolate; chocolate candy, solid
PA: Astor Chocolate Corp.
651 New Hampshire Ave
Lakewood NJ 08701
732 901-1000

(P-2431)
MARICH CONFECTIONERY CO INC
2101 Bert Dr, Hollister (95023-2562)
PHONE...............................831 634-4700
Bradley M Van Dam, *President*
Von Packard, *Shareholder*
Troy Van Dam, *COO*
Steve Mangelsen, *CFO*
Ronald B Packard, *Chairman*
▲ **EMP:** 150 **EST:** 1983
SQ FT: 60,000
SALES (est): 33.3MM **Privately Held**
WEB: www.marich.com
SIC: 2064 2099 2068 Candy & other confectionery products; food preparations; salted & roasted nuts & seeds

(P-2432)
SCONZA CANDY COMPANY
1 Sconza Candy Ln, Oakdale (95361-7899)
PHONE...............................209 845-3700
James R Sconza, *President*
Janet Angers, *Vice Pres*
Ronald J Sconza, *Vice Pres*
Virginia Gaxiola, *Technician*
James Brackman, *Controller*
▲ **EMP:** 100
SQ FT: 40,000
SALES (est): 28.2MM **Privately Held**
WEB: www.sconza.com
SIC: 2064 Lollipops & other hard candy

(P-2433)
SEES CANDY SHOPS INCORPORATED (HQ)
Also Called: See's Candies
210 El Camino Real, South San Francisco (94080-5968)
PHONE...............................650 761-2490
Daryl Wollenburg, *Treasurer*
John Jee, *Vice Pres*
Mary Taylor, *Vice Pres*
Tupper Marcia, *Office Mgr*
Kamlesh Jethani, *Administration*
▲ **EMP:** 40 **EST:** 1921
SQ FT: 250,000
SALES (est): 630.7MM
SALES (corp-wide): 245.5B **Publicly Held**
WEB: www.chocolateshops.sees.com
SIC: 2064 5441 Candy & other confectionery products; candy
PA: Berkshire Hathaway Inc.
3555 Farnam St Ste 1140
Omaha NE 68131
402 346-1400

(P-2434)
TORN RANCH INC (PA)
2198 S Mcdowell Blvd Ext, Petaluma (94954-6902)
PHONE...............................415 506-3000
Su Morrow, *CEO*
Dean Morrow, *President*
Kimberly Delasantos, *Controller*
Nick Kay, *Opers Staff*
Michelle Chodor, *Natl Sales Mgr*
◆ **EMP:** 78 **EST:** 1991
SALES (est): 12.9MM **Privately Held**
WEB: www.tornranch.com
SIC: 2064 Candy & other confectionery products

2066 Chocolate & Cocoa Prdts

(P-2435)
BARRY CALLEBAUT USA LLC
1175 Commerce Blvd Ste D, American Canyon (94503-9626)
PHONE...............................707 642-8200
Peter Dell,
Barry Callebaut, *Director*
Imelda Gutierrez, *Manager*
EMP: 167
SALES (corp-wide): 7.4B **Privately Held**
WEB: www.barry-callebaut.com
SIC: 2066 Chocolate
HQ: Barry Callebaut U.S.A. Llc
600 W Chicago Ave Ste 860
Chicago IL 60654

(P-2436)
BLOMMER CHOCOLATE COMPANY CAL
1515 Pacific St, Union City (94587-2041)
PHONE...............................510 471-4300
Henry J Blommer Jr, *CEO*
Joseph W Blommer, *President*
Peter W Blommer, *Vice Pres*
Martin Krueger, *Vice Pres*
Jack S Larsen, *Vice Pres*
◆ **EMP:** 200 **EST:** 1902
SQ FT: 142,000
SALES (est): 51.7MM **Privately Held**
WEB: www.blommer.com
SIC: 2066 Chocolate coatings & syrup; powdered cocoa; cocoa butter
HQ: The Blommer Chocolate Company
1101 Blommer Dr
East Greenville PA 18041
800 825-8181

(P-2437)
GHIRARDELLI CHOCOLATE CO (DH)
1111 139th Ave, San Leandro (94578-2616)
PHONE...............................510 483-6970
Martin Thompson, *CEO*
Dan Brown, *Vice Pres*
Rob Budowski, *Vice Pres*
Andrew Curran, *Vice Pres*
Raffael Payer, *Vice Pres*
◆ **EMP:** 375 **EST:** 1852
SQ FT: 210,000
SALES (est): 137.9MM
SALES (corp-wide): 4.4B **Privately Held**
WEB: www.ghirardelli.com
SIC: 5441 2066 5812 5149 Candy; chocolate; soda fountain; chocolate
HQ: Lindt & Sprungli (Usa) Inc.
1 Fine Chocolate Pl
Stratham NH 03885
603 778-8100

(P-2438)
GUITTARD CHOCOLATE HOLDINGS CO
10 Guittard Rd, Burlingame (94010-2203)
P.O. Box 4308 (94011-4308)
PHONE...............................650 697-4427
Gary W Guittard, *President*
Gerry Allen, *COO*
Kathy Perotti, *Exec VP*
Brad Newcombe, *Executive*
Daniel Lim, *CIO*
◆ **EMP:** 240 **EST:** 1868
SALES (est): 86.8MM **Privately Held**
WEB: www.guittard.com
SIC: 2066 2064 Chocolate; cocoa & cocoa products; candy & other confectionery products

(P-2439)
POCO DOLCE CHOCOLATES
2419 3rd St, San Francisco (94107-3110)
PHONE...............................415 255-1443
Kathy Wiley, *President*
EMP: 15 **EST:** 2007
SALES (est): 2.2MM **Privately Held**
WEB: www.pocodolce.com
SIC: 2066 Chocolate & cocoa products; chocolate

(P-2440)
SSI G DEBBAS CHOCOLATIER LLC
2794 N Larkin Ave, Fresno (93727-1315)
PHONE...............................559 294-2071
Bret Lorenc, *President*
Maria Gutierrez, *QC Mgr*
EMP: 37 **EST:** 2015
SALES (est): 2.5MM **Privately Held**
WEB: www.debbasgourmet.com
SIC: 2066 Chocolate & cocoa products

2068 Salted & Roasted Nuts & Seeds

(P-2441)
AHARONI & STEELE INC
Also Called: Sante Specialty Foods
1855 Norman Ave, Santa Clara (95054-2029)
PHONE...............................408 451-9585
Sara Tidhar, *President*
Phil Aufricht, *Sales Staff*
Michael Del Rosario, *Manager*
Martha Medina, *Manager*
EMP: 18 **EST:** 2004
SALES (est): 3.6MM **Privately Held**
WEB: www.santenuts.com
SIC: 5499 2068 Dried fruit; salted & roasted nuts & seeds

(P-2442)
ALMOND COMPANY
22782 Road 9, Chowchilla (93610-8967)
PHONE...............................559 665-4405
Russell Harris, *President*
Dave Bazar, *Sales Executive*
▼ **EMP:** 27 **EST:** 1997
SALES (est): 5.2MM **Privately Held**
WEB: www.harrisfamilyenterprises.com
SIC: 2068 Nuts: dried, dehydrated, salted or roasted

(P-2443)
DIAMOND FOODS LLC (PA)
Also Called: Diamond of California
1050 Diamond St, Stockton (95205-7020)
PHONE...............................209 467-6000
Gary Ford, *CEO*
David Colo, *COO*
Ray Silcock, *CFO*
Lloyd J Johnson, *Officer*
Isobel Jones, *Exec VP*
◆ **EMP:** 575 **EST:** 2005
SALES (est): 605MM **Privately Held**
WEB: www.diamondnuts.com
SIC: 2068 2096 Salted & roasted nuts & seeds; potato chips & similar snacks

(P-2444)
DSD MERCHANDISERS INC
Also Called: Sweet Factory Express
6226 Industrial Way Ste A, Livermore (94551-9280)
P.O. Box 10008, Pleasanton (94588-0008)
PHONE...............................925 449-2044
Urvesh Kotecha, *President*
EMP: 40 **EST:** 1996
SQ FT: 28,000
SALES (est): 6.9MM **Privately Held**
WEB: www.dsdmerchandisers.com
SIC: 5441 2068 2066 5153 Candy; salted & roasted nuts & seeds; chocolate & cocoa products; grains; beans, dry: bulk; dried & dehydrated fruits

(P-2445)
HUGHSON NUT INC (HQ)
1825 Verduga Rd, Hughson (95326-9675)
P.O. Box 1150 (95326-1150)
PHONE...............................209 883-0403
Martin Pohl, *President*
◆ **EMP:** 360 **EST:** 1985
SQ FT: 40,000
SALES (est): 58.1MM **Privately Held**
WEB: www.hughsonnut.com
SIC: 2068 Salted & roasted nuts & seeds

(P-2446)
JOHN B SANFILIPPO & SON INC
29241 Cottonwood Rd, Gustine (95322-9574)
PHONE...............................209 854-2455

▲ = Import ▼ = Export
◆ = Import/Export

PRODUCTS & SERVICES SECTION
2082 - Malt Beverages County (P-2470)

Isidro Cortez, *Manager*
Mike Cannon, *Vice Pres*
Tom Fordonski, *Vice Pres*
Angelina Roberts, *Project Mgr*
David Caldera, *Business Mgr*
EMP: 242
SQ FT: 1,286
SALES (corp-wide): 858.4MM **Publicly Held**
WEB: www.jbssinc.com
SIC: 2068 Nuts: dried, dehydrated, salted or roasted
PA: John B. Sanfilippo & Son, Inc.
1703 N Randall Rd
Elgin IL 60123
847 289-1800

(P-2447)
KLEIN BROS HOLDINGS LTD
Also Called: Klein Bros Snacks
3101 W March Ln Ste B, Stockton (95219-2385)
PHONE..................209 465-5033
Thomas B Klein, *Ch of Bd*
Robert J Corkern, *CEO*
EMP: 41 **EST:** 1977
SALES (est): 1.4MM **Privately Held**
WEB: www.kleinbroswhse.com
SIC: 2068 4783 5141 Seeds: dried, dehydrated, salted or roasted; packing & crating; groceries, general line

(P-2448)
LAKE COUNTY WALNUT INC
4545 Loasa Dr, Kelseyville (95451)
P.O. Box 308 (95451-0308)
PHONE..................707 279-1200
EMP: 18
SALES (est): 1.9MM **Privately Held**
SIC: 2068 Mfg Salted/Roasted Nuts/Seeds

(P-2449)
MERIDIAN GROWERS PROC INC
1625 Howard Rd, Madera (93637-5128)
PHONE..................559 458-7272
Jim Zion, *President*
EMP: 16 **EST:** 2020
SALES (est): 1.3MM **Privately Held**
SIC: 2068 Nuts: dried, dehydrated, salted or roasted

(P-2450)
PADDACK ENTERPRISES
Also Called: Paddack Almond Hlling Shelling
27052 State Highway 120, Escalon (95320-9502)
PHONE..................209 838-1536
Vernon Paddack, *President*
Pauline Paddack, *Treasurer*
EMP: 16 **EST:** 1972
SQ FT: 3,000
SALES (est): 547.1K **Privately Held**
SIC: 2068 Nuts: dried, dehydrated, salted or roasted

(P-2451)
STEWART & JASPER MARKETING INC (PA)
Also Called: Stewart & Jasper Orchards
3500 Shiells Rd, Newman (95360-9798)
PHONE..................209 862-9600
Jim Jasper, *President*
Susan Dompe, *Corp Secy*
Jason Jasper, *Vice Pres*
Mike Gorrasi, *General Mgr*
Zach William, *Marketing Staff*
◆ **EMP:** 175 **EST:** 1993
SQ FT: 225,000
SALES (est): 40.2MM **Privately Held**
WEB: www.stewartandjasper.com
SIC: 2068 0723 0173 5148 Nuts: dried, dehydrated, salted or roasted; crop preparation services for market; tree nuts; fresh fruits & vegetables; food preparations

(P-2452)
WIZARD MANUFACTURING INC
2244 Ivy St, Chico (95928-7172)
PHONE..................530 342-1861
Alan Reiff, *CEO*
Sheridan Hankinse, *Engineer*
Bruce Clements, *Purchasing*
EMP: 29 **EST:** 2007

SALES (est): 5.4MM **Privately Held**
WEB: www.wizardmanufacturing.com
SIC: 2068 Nuts: dried, dehydrated, salted or roasted

(P-2453)
YOSEMITE FARMS
2341 N St, Merced (95340-3616)
PHONE..................209 383-3411
Coleen Slacter, *Owner*
Fred Slacter, *Co-Owner*
Vincent Kaehler, *Loan Officer*
EMP: 22 **EST:** 1992
SALES (est): 534.7K **Privately Held**
WEB: www.yosemitefarmcredit.com
SIC: 5441 2068 Nuts; nuts: dried, dehydrated, salted or roasted

2076 Vegetable Oil Mills

(P-2454)
PEARL CROP INC
Also Called: Turkhan Nuts
17641 French Camp Rd, Ripon (95366-9799)
PHONE..................209 982-9933
EMP: 26
SALES (corp-wide): 90MM **Privately Held**
WEB: www.pearlcrop.com
SIC: 2076 Walnut oil; tung oil
PA: Pearl Crop, Inc.
1550 Industrial Dr
Stockton CA 95206
209 808-7575

(P-2455)
PETALUMA BY PRODUCTS
84 Corona Rd, Petaluma (94952-1315)
PHONE..................707 763-9181
Manuel Brazil, *Principal*
EMP: 24 **EST:** 1996
SALES (est): 405.7K **Privately Held**
WEB: www.petalumapoultry.com
SIC: 2076 Vegetable oil mills

(P-2456)
WILMAR OILS FATS STOCKTON LLC
2008 Port Road B, Stockton (95203-2923)
PHONE..................925 627-1600
Thomas Lim, *Mng Member*
Anayeli Morales, *Sales Staff*
SNG Miow Ching,
Mike Fargas,
Nathan Shan, *Manager*
▲ **EMP:** 25
SALES (est): 136MM **Privately Held**
SIC: 2076 Palm kernel oil

2077 Animal, Marine Fats & Oils

(P-2457)
BAKER COMMODITIES INC
16801 W Jensen Ave, Kerman (93630-9194)
P.O. Box 416 (93630-0416)
PHONE..................559 237-4320
Manuel Ponte, *Director*
EMP: 32
SQ FT: 28,690
SALES (corp-wide): 153.6MM **Privately Held**
WEB: www.bakercommodities.com
SIC: 2077 Tallow rendering, inedible
PA: Baker Commodities, Inc.
4020 Bandini Blvd
Vernon CA 90058
323 268-2801

(P-2458)
NORDIC NATURALS INC (PA)
Also Called: Westport Scandinavia
111 Jennings Way, Watsonville (95076-2054)
PHONE..................800 662-2544
Joar A Opheim, *CEO*
Michele Opheim, *Vice Pres*
Geri Zerbini, *Administration*
Michelle Hughes, *Info Tech Dir*
Tristan Gruener, *Software Dev*

▲ **EMP:** 145 **EST:** 1995
SALES (est): 64.5MM **Privately Held**
WEB: www.nordic.com
SIC: 2077 Fish oil

(P-2459)
NORTH STATE RENDERING CO INC
15 Shippee Rd, Oroville (95965-9297)
P.O. Box 239, Durham (95938-0239)
PHONE..................530 343-6076
Chris Ottone, *President*
Patrick Ottone, *Vice Pres*
William Ottone, *Admin Sec*
EMP: 23 **EST:** 1969
SQ FT: 15,000
SALES (est): 2.2MM **Privately Held**
WEB: www.rendering.com
SIC: 2077 Tallow rendering, inedible

(P-2460)
SRC MILLING CO LLC
Also Called: Sacramento Rendering Co
11350 Kiefer Blvd, Sacramento (95830-9405)
PHONE..................916 363-4821
Jim Walsh, *Mng Member*
A Michael Koewler,
Michael Patrick Koewler,
Timothy D Koewler,
Richard Wilbur,
▲ **EMP:** 20 **EST:** 1996
SALES (est): 1.8MM **Privately Held**
WEB: www.srccompanies.com
SIC: 2077 Rendering

2079 Shortening, Oils & Margarine

(P-2461)
BOUNDARY BEND INC
Also Called: Boundary Bend Olives
455 Harter Ave, Woodland (95776-6105)
PHONE..................844 626-2726
Adam Englehardt, *CEO*
Taylor Bock, *CFO*
▲ **EMP:** 20 **EST:** 2014
SALES (est): 7.1MM **Privately Held**
WEB: www.cobramestate.com
SIC: 2079 Olive oil
PA: Cobram Estate Olives Limited
151 Broderick Rd
Lara VIC 3212

(P-2462)
BUNGE OILS INC
Also Called: Bunge North America
436 S Mcclure Rd, Modesto (95357-0519)
PHONE..................209 574-9981
Dale Casky, *Manager*
EMP: 75
SQ FT: 76,824 **Privately Held**
WEB: www.bungenorthamerica.com
SIC: 2079 Cooking oils, except corn: vegetable refined
HQ: Bunge Oils, Inc.
1391 Tmbarlake Manor Pkwy
Chesterfield MO 63017
314 292-2000

(P-2463)
CALIFORNIA OLIVE AND VINE LLC
Also Called: Sutter Buttes Olive Oil
1670 Poole Blvd, Yuba City (95993-2610)
PHONE..................530 763-7921
Alka Kumar, *President*
EMP: 15 **EST:** 2011
SQ FT: 10,000
SALES (est): 2MM **Privately Held**
WEB: www.sutterbuttesoliveoil.com
SIC: 2079 5921 Olive oil; liquor stores

(P-2464)
CALIFORNIA OLIVE RANCH INC (PA)
265 Airpark Blvd Ste 200, Chico (95973-9518)
PHONE..................530 846-8000
Gregory B Kelly, *CEO*
Pedro Olabrria, *Ch of Bd*
Mike Forbes, *Vice Pres*

Jim Lipman, *Vice Pres*
Antonio Valla, *Vice Pres*
◆ **EMP:** 41 **EST:** 1998
SALES (est): 28.3MM **Privately Held**
WEB: www.californiaoliveranch.com
SIC: 2079 Olive oil

(P-2465)
MCEVOY OF MARIN LLC
Also Called: McEvoy Ranch
5935 Red Hill Rd, Petaluma (94952-9437)
P.O. Box 341 (94953-0341)
PHONE..................707 778-2307
Nion McEvoy,
Monique Spaulding, *Purchasing*
Ria D 'aversa, *Opers Staff*
Sherry Paragee, *Opers Staff*
Nan Tucker McEvoy,
◆ **EMP:** 100 **EST:** 1998
SALES (est): 17.3MM **Privately Held**
WEB: www.mcevoyranch.com
SIC: 2079 Olive oil

(P-2466)
NICK SCIABICA & SONS A CORP
Also Called: Sciabica's
2150 Yosemite Blvd, Modesto (95354-3931)
PHONE..................209 577-5067
Gemma Sciabica, *CEO*
Joseph N Sciabica, *President*
Daniel Sciabica, *Treasurer*
Daniel R Sciabica, *Corp Secy*
Jonathan Sciabica, *Vice Pres*
▲ **EMP:** 20 **EST:** 1925
SQ FT: 68,728
SALES (est): 7.8MM **Privately Held**
WEB: www.sunshineinabottle.com
SIC: 2079 5149 Olive oil; cooking oils

(P-2467)
OLIVE CORTO L P
10201 Live Oak Rd, Stockton (95212-9319)
P.O. Box 1706, Lodi (95241-1706)
PHONE..................209 888-8100
Brady Whitlow, *President*
David Garci-Aguirre, *Vice Pres*
Chris Martinez, *Opers Spvr*
Paul Busalacchi, *Opers Staff*
Grant Linhares, *Manager*
▲ **EMP:** 15 **EST:** 2006
SALES (est): 3.6MM **Privately Held**
WEB: www.corto-olive.com
SIC: 2079 Olive oil

(P-2468)
OLIVE OIL FACTORY LLC
770 Chadbourne Rd, Fairfield (94534-9643)
PHONE..................707 426-3400
Francine Brossier, *Mng Member*
Katie Bishop, *Research*
Michael Brossier,
▲ **EMP:** 43 **EST:** 2004
SALES (est): 14MM **Privately Held**
WEB: www.theoofactory.com
SIC: 2079 Olive oil

(P-2469)
VERONICA FOODS COMPANY
1991 Dennison St, Oakland (94606-5225)
P.O. Box 2225 (94621-0125)
PHONE..................510 535-6833
Michael Bradley, *President*
Veronica Bradley, *Vice Pres*
◆ **EMP:** 50 **EST:** 1940
SALES (est): 12.1MM **Privately Held**
WEB: www.evoliveoil.com
SIC: 2079 5149 Cooking oils, except corn: vegetable refined; olive oil; salad oils, except corn: vegetable refined; cooking oils & shortenings; dried or canned foods

2082 Malt Beverages

(P-2470)
ANCHOR BREWERS & DISTLRS LLC (HQ)
4 Rebelo Ln, Novato (94947-3629)
PHONE..................415 892-4569
Keith Greggor, *CEO*
Anthony P Foglio, *Mng Member*
Martin Geraghty, *Advisor*

2082 - Malt Beverages County (P-2471)

PRODUCTS & SERVICES SECTION

EMP: 59 EST: 2010
SALES (est): 23.4MM **Privately Held**
WEB: www.tgg.us.com
SIC: 2082 Malt beverages
PA: The Griffin Group Llc
 4 Rebelo Ln Ste D
 Novato CA 94947
 415 892-4569

(P-2471)
ANDERSON VALLEY BREWING INC
Also Called: Anderson Valley Brewing Co
17700 Hwy 253, Boonville (95415)
P.O. Box 505 (95415-0505)
PHONE..............................707 895-2337
Kenneth D Allen, *President*
Lauren Payne, *Sales Staff*
Brian Jette, *Cust Mgr*
Roxanne Barnes, *Manager*
Ian McCarten, *Manager*
◆ EMP: 45 EST: 1987
SQ FT: 5,000
SALES (est): 16.2MM **Privately Held**
WEB: www.avbc.com
SIC: 2082 5812 Ale (alcoholic beverage); porter (alcoholic beverage); stout (alcoholic beverage); cafe

(P-2472)
ANHEUSER-BUSCH LLC
3101 Busch Dr, Fairfield (94534-9726)
PHONE..............................707 429-7595
Kevin Finger, *Manager*
Corry Smith, *Engineer*
Andrew Knowles, *Manager*
Alonzo Peterson, *Manager*
EMP: 450
SALES (corp-wide): 1.2B **Privately Held**
WEB: www.budweisertours.com
SIC: 2082 Beer (alcoholic beverage)
HQ: Anheuser-Busch, Llc
 1 Busch Pl
 Saint Louis MO 63118
 800 342-5283

(P-2473)
ARTISAN BREWERS LLC
Also Called: Drake's Brewing Company
1933 Davis St Ste 177, San Leandro (94577-1256)
PHONE..............................510 567-4926
John Martin,
John Gittins, *Vice Pres*
Dow Tunis, *VP Bus Dvlpt*
Jeanne Young, *Human Resources*
Anthony Raggio, *Opers Staff*
◆ EMP: 44 EST: 2008
SALES (est): 4.5MM **Privately Held**
SIC: 2082 Beer (alcoholic beverage)

(P-2474)
BAREBOTTLE BREWING COMPANY INC
1525 Cortland Ave, San Francisco (94110-5714)
PHONE..............................415 926-8617
Michael Seitz, *CEO*
Ben Sterling, *Principal*
Lester Koga, *Admin Sec*
EMP: 19 EST: 2011
SQ FT: 17,000
SALES (est): 550K **Privately Held**
WEB: www.barebottle.com
SIC: 2082 Ale (alcoholic beverage)

(P-2475)
BREWERY ON HALF MOON BAY INC
Also Called: Half Moon Bay Brewing Company
390 Capistrano Rd, Half Moon Bay (94019)
P.O. Box 879, El Granada (94018-0879)
PHONE..............................650 728-2739
Michael Laffen, *President*
Christine Mendonca, *Corp Secy*
EMP: 140 EST: 2000
SQ FT: 12,000
SALES (est): 4MM **Privately Held**
WEB: www.hmbbrewingco.com
SIC: 5812 2082 Chicken restaurant; brewers' grain

(P-2476)
COORS BREWING COMPANY
3001 Douglas Blvd Ste 200, Roseville (95661-3809)
PHONE..............................916 786-2666
Fax: 916 786-9396
EMP: 20
SALES (corp-wide): 3.5B **Publicly Held**
SIC: 2082 5181 Mfg Malt Beverages Whol Beer/Ale
HQ: Coors Brewing Company
 17735 W 32nd Ave
 Golden CO 80401
 303 279-6565

(P-2477)
EEL RIVER BREWING CO INC (PA)
1777 Alamar Way, Fortuna (95540-9548)
PHONE..............................707 725-2739
Ted Vivatson, *President*
Margaret Vivatson, *CFO*
Vivatson Matt, *General Mgr*
Marissa Vivatson, *Sales Mgr*
EMP: 36 EST: 1995
SQ FT: 5,000
SALES (est): 3.6MM **Privately Held**
WEB: www.eelriverbrewing.com
SIC: 5813 5812 2082 Bars & lounges; family restaurants; beer (alcoholic beverage)

(P-2478)
FORT POINT BEER COMPANY (PA)
644 Mason St, San Francisco (94129-1600)
PHONE..............................415 336-3596
Justin Catalana, *CEO*
Ben Sanders, *Technician*
Alex Blunk, *Sales Staff*
Steve Boatright, *Sales Staff*
Felipe Bravo, *Manager*
EMP: 101 EST: 2016
SALES (est): 10.8MM **Privately Held**
WEB: www.fortpointbeer.com
SIC: 5921 2082 Liquor stores; ale (alcoholic beverage)

(P-2479)
FULL CIRCLE BREWING CO LTD LLC
Also Called: Los Californias Winery
620 F St, Fresno (93706-3413)
P.O. Box 1163 (93715-1163)
PHONE..............................559 264-6323
Jeff Haak, *Mng Member*
EMP: 18 EST: 1998
SALES (est): 3.1MM **Privately Held**
WEB: www.fullcirclebrewing.com
SIC: 2082 Beer (alcoholic beverage)

(P-2480)
GORDON BIERSCH BREWING COMPANY
357 E Taylor St, San Jose (95112-3105)
PHONE..............................408 792-1546
William Bullard, *Manager*
Joshua Anderson, *General Mgr*
EMP: 93
SALES (corp-wide): 71.1MM **Privately Held**
WEB: www.gordonbierschbrewing.com
SIC: 2082 Beer (alcoholic beverage)
PA: Gordon Biersch Brewing Company
 357 E Taylor St
 San Jose CA 95112
 408 278-1008

(P-2481)
GORDON BIERSCH BREWING COMPANY (PA)
357 E Taylor St, San Jose (95112-3105)
PHONE..............................408 278-1008
Daniel Gordon, *CEO*
William Bullard, *CFO*
Paul Michels, *CFO*
Michelle Orlina, *Controller*
Frank Fertitta III, *Director*
▲ EMP: 15 EST: 1987
SQ FT: 1,500
SALES (est): 71.1MM **Privately Held**
WEB: www.gordonbierschbrewing.com
SIC: 2082 Malt beverages; beer (alcoholic beverage)

(P-2482)
JOES DWNTWN BREWRY & REST INC
Also Called: Downtown Joe's
902 Main St, NAPA (94559-3045)
PHONE..............................707 258-2337
Joe Peatman, *President*
EMP: 40 EST: 1994
SQ FT: 6,000
SALES (est): 3.3MM **Privately Held**
WEB: www.downtownjoes.com
SIC: 5812 5813 2082 American restaurant; drinking places; malt beverages

(P-2483)
JUNE SF LLC
Also Called: Fort Point Beer Company
644 Old Mason St, San Francisco (94129-1613)
PHONE..............................415 906-4021
Dina Dobkin, *Creative Dir*
Mike Schnebeck, *Admin Sec*
Steve Boatright, *Sales Staff*
Jonathan Esparza, *Sales Staff*
Justin Catalana,
EMP: 20 EST: 2013
SALES (est): 7.2MM **Privately Held**
SIC: 2082 5181 Beer (alcoholic beverage); beer & ale

(P-2484)
MAD RIVER BREWING COMPANY INC
101 Taylor Way, Blue Lake (95525-9724)
P.O. Box 767 (95525-0767)
PHONE..............................707 668-4151
Robert W Smith Jr, *President*
James Crowell, *CEO*
Charlie Jordan, *CEO*
Kelly Elliott, *CFO*
Nanda Mayo, *Human Resources*
▼ EMP: 30 EST: 1988
SQ FT: 11,400
SALES (est): 69.9K **Privately Held**
WEB: www.madriverbrewing.com
SIC: 5813 2082 Bar (drinking places); beer (alcoholic beverage)

(P-2485)
MARIN BREWING CO INC
1809 Larkspur Landing Cir, Larkspur (94939-1801)
PHONE..............................415 461-4677
Brendon Moylan, *General Ptnr*
Jeff Brooks, *Vice Pres*
Jen Procopio, *General Mgr*
Jenn Procopio, *Marketing Staff*
Phillip Agren, *Manager*
EMP: 66 EST: 1988
SQ FT: 6,200
SALES (est): 4.2MM **Privately Held**
WEB: www.marinbrewing.com
SIC: 5812 2082 American restaurant; beer (alcoholic beverage)

(P-2486)
MENDOCINO BREWING COMPANY INC (HQ)
1601 Airport Rd, Ukiah (95482-6456)
PHONE..............................707 463-2627
Yashpal Singh, *President*
Vijay Mallya, *Ch of Bd*
Mahadevan Narayanan, *CFO*
▲ EMP: 80 EST: 1983 **Publicly Held**
WEB: www.mendobrew.com
SIC: 2082 Beer (alcoholic beverage); brewers' grain

(P-2487)
NORTH COAST BREWING CO INC
444 N Main St, Fort Bragg (95437-3216)
PHONE..............................707 964-3400
EMP: 25
SALES (corp-wide): 14.6MM **Privately Held**
WEB: www.northcoastbrewing.com
SIC: 2082 Beer (alcoholic beverage)
PA: North Coast Brewing Co., Inc.
 455 N Main St
 Fort Bragg CA 95437
 707 964-2739

(P-2488)
NORTH COAST BREWING CO INC (PA)
Also Called: Brew Building
455 N Main St, Fort Bragg (95437-3215)
PHONE..............................707 964-2739
Jeffrey Ottoboni, *CEO*
Mark E Ruedrich, *President*
Tom Allen, *Vice Pres*
Marten Compton, *Vice Pres*
Sheila Martins, *Vice Pres*
▲ EMP: 50 EST: 1988
SQ FT: 3,000
SALES (est): 14.6MM **Privately Held**
WEB: www.northcoastbrewing.com
SIC: 2082 5812 5813 Beer (alcoholic beverage); eating places; bars & lounges

(P-2489)
OUTLAW BEVERAGE INC
3945 Freedom Cir Ste 560, Santa Clara (95054-1269)
PHONE..............................310 424-5077
Douglas Weekes, *CEO*
Lance Collins, *Founder*
Jamie Ciolino, *Marketing Staff*
Julia Weekes, *Director*
Cindy Johnson, *Manager*
EMP: 18 EST: 2015
SALES (est): 2.3MM **Privately Held**
SIC: 2082 Malt beverages

(P-2490)
RARE BARREL LLC
940 Parker St, Berkeley (94710-2524)
PHONE..............................510 984-6585
Brad Goodwin, *Mng Member*
Danielle Byers, *COO*
Alex Wallash, *Sales Staff*
Jay Goodwin,
▲ EMP: 23 EST: 2012
SALES (est): 2.6MM **Privately Held**
WEB: www.therarebarrel.com
SIC: 2082 Beer (alcoholic beverage)

(P-2491)
SIERRA NEVADA BREWING CO (PA)
1075 E 20th St, Chico (95928-6722)
PHONE..............................530 893-3520
Jeff White, *CEO*
Kenneth Grossman, *President*
Paul Janicki, *CFO*
Mike Bennett, *Officer*
Megan Andrews, *Social Dir*
◆ EMP: 475 EST: 1979
SALES (est): 300MM **Privately Held**
WEB: www.sierranevada.com
SIC: 2082 5812 Beer (alcoholic beverage); eating places

(P-2492)
SINGHA NORTH AMERICA INC
303 Twin Dolphin Dr # 600, Redwood City (94065-1422)
PHONE..............................714 206-5097
Palit Bbhakdi, *CEO*
Soravij B Bhakdi, *President*
Mario Ylanan, *Treasurer*
▲ EMP: 19 EST: 2002
SALES (est): 15.4MM **Privately Held**
WEB: www.singhabeerusa.com
SIC: 2082 Beer (alcoholic beverage)
PA: Boonrawd Brewery Company Limited
 999 Samsen Road
 Dusit 10300

(P-2493)
SNOWSHOE BREWING CO LLC (PA)
2050 Hwy 4, Arnold (95223-9420)
P.O. Box 936 (95223-0936)
PHONE..............................209 795-2272
Jeff Yarnell,
Gregory Allen Obrien,
Jeannine Yarnell,
EMP: 30 EST: 1995
SQ FT: 6,000
SALES (est): 2.5MM **Privately Held**
WEB: www.snowshoebrewing.com
SIC: 5812 2082 5813 Chicken restaurant; malt beverages; drinking places

▲ = Import ▼ = Export
◆ = Import/Export

PRODUCTS & SERVICES SECTION
2084 - Wine & Brandy County (P-2519)

(P-2494)
STEINBECK BREWING COMPANY
Also Called: Buffalo Bills Brewery
1082 B St, Hayward (94541-4108)
PHONE.................510 886-9823
Geoffrey A Harries, *President*
Jim Crudo, *Sales Staff*
EMP: 84 **EST:** 1994
SQ FT: 4,000
SALES (est): 8.4MM Privately Held
SIC: 2082 5812 Beer (alcoholic beverage)

(P-2495)
SUDWERK PRIVATBRAUEREI HUBSCH
2001 2nd St, Davis (95618-5474)
PHONE.................530 756-2739
Fax: 530 753-0590
EMP: 65
SQ FT: 27,000
SALES (est): 2.5MM Privately Held
WEB: www.sudwerk.com
SIC: 5812 5813 2082 5181 American & German Restaurant & Brewery Producing & Whol Malt Beverages

(P-2496)
TABLE BLUFF BREWING INC (PA)
Also Called: Lost Coast Brewery & Cafe
617 4th St, Eureka (95501-1013)
PHONE.................707 445-4480
Barbara Groom, *CEO*
Wendy Pound, *Corp Secy*
Kurt Kovacs, *Vice Pres*
Amanda Sabolish, *Admin Asst*
◆ **EMP:** 30 **EST:** 1989
SALES (est): 10.2MM Privately Held
WEB: www.tablebluff.openfos.com
SIC: 2082 5812 5813 Beer (alcoholic beverage); eating places; bar (drinking places)

(P-2497)
THIRSTY BEAR BREWING CO LLC
661 Howard St, San Francisco (94105-3915)
PHONE.................415 974-0905
Ronald Silberstein, *Director*
Ragnhild Lorentzen,
Brenden Brewer, *Brewer*
Aleksandra Grozdanic, *Manager*
EMP: 25 **EST:** 1996
SQ FT: 18,000
SALES (est): 5.4MM Privately Held
WEB: www.thirstybear.com
SIC: 2082 5812 7299 Beer (alcoholic beverage); eating places; banquet hall facilities

(P-2498)
TOWER BREW CO LLC
Also Called: Tower Brewing
1210 66th St, Sacramento (95819-4327)
PHONE.................916 606-3373
Jeff Howes, *Mng Member*
EMP: 16 **EST:** 2015
SALES (est): 2.4MM Privately Held
SIC: 2082 Malt beverages

(P-2499)
WANDERLUST LLC (PA)
2401 E Orangeburg Ave # 6, Modesto (95355-3351)
PHONE.................209 404-0716
Ronald Olcott, *Principal*
EMP: 19 **EST:** 2014
SALES (est): 212.3K Privately Held
SIC: 2082 Malt beverages

2084 Wine & Brandy

(P-2500)
3 BADGE BEVERAGE CORPORATION
32 Patten St, Sonoma (95476-6727)
PHONE.................707 343-1167
Richard Zeller, *President*
August David Sebastiani, *CEO*
Keith Casale, *COO*
Harvard Gates, *Vice Pres*
Donald Morse, *Regional Mgr*
EMP: 15 **EST:** 2009
SALES (est): 4MM Privately Held
WEB: www.3badge.com
SIC: 2084 5182 Wine cellars, bonded: engaged in blending wines; bottling wines & liquors

(P-2501)
ADAMS WINERY LLC (PA)
9711 W Dr Creek Rd, Healdsburg (95448)
PHONE.................707 395-6126
Timothy Nordvedt,
Lynn Adams,
Scott Adams,
Adams Ridge Vineyards LLC,
EMP: 20 **EST:** 1999
SALES (est): 3.3MM Privately Held
SIC: 2084 Wines

(P-2502)
ADAMS WINERY LLC
9711 W Dry Creek Rd, Healdsburg (95448-8113)
PHONE.................508 648-2505
Timothy Nordvedt, *Branch Mgr*
EMP: 30
SALES (corp-wide): 3.3MM Privately Held
SIC: 2084 Wines
PA: Adams Winery, Llc
9711 W Dr Creek Rd
Healdsburg CA 95448
707 395-6126

(P-2503)
AH WINES INC
Also Called: Winery Direct Distributors
27 E Vine St, Lodi (95240-4854)
PHONE.................209 625-8170
Jeffery W Hansen, *President*
Richard Gerlach, *CFO*
Jeri White, *Executive Asst*
Brandon Casella, *Natl Sales Mgr*
Lita Castor, *Associate*
◆ **EMP:** 17 **EST:** 2008
SQ FT: 5,000
SALES (est): 5MM Privately Held
WEB: www.ahwines.com
SIC: 2084 5182 Wines; wine

(P-2504)
ANCHOR DISTILLING COMPANY
1705 Mariposa St, San Francisco (94107-2334)
PHONE.................415 863-8350
Charles Keith Greggor, *President*
Dennis Carr, *Vice Pres*
Lynn Lackey, *VP Mktg*
John Spicer, *Manager*
▲ **EMP:** 23 **EST:** 1988
SALES (est): 4.5MM Privately Held
WEB: www.hotalingandco.com
SIC: 2084 Wine cellars, bonded: engaged in blending wines

(P-2505)
ANTINORI CALIFORNIA
Also Called: Antica NAPA Valley
3149 Soda Canyon Rd, NAPA (94558-9448)
PHONE.................707 265-8866
Marchase P Antinori, *President*
Glenn Salva, *Manager*
Kim Wiss, *Manager*
▲ **EMP:** 22 **EST:** 1993
SALES (est): 2.9MM Privately Held
WEB: www.anticanapavalley.com
SIC: 2084 5921 Wines; wine

(P-2506)
APRIORI CELLAR LLC (PA)
1432 Main St, Saint Helena (94574-1848)
PHONE.................707 512-0606
Betsy Potter, *Opers Staff*
EMP: 18 **EST:** 2015
SALES (est): 284.3K Privately Held
WEB: www.aprioricellar.com
SIC: 2084 Wines

(P-2507)
AVV WINERY CO LLC
Also Called: Alexander Valley Vineyards
8644 Highway 128, Healdsburg (95448-9021)
P.O. Box 175 (95448-0175)
PHONE.................707 433-7209
Harry H Wetzel, *Opers Staff*
Katie Wetzel, *Managing Prtnr*
Linda Wetzel, *COO*
Kevin Hall, *Lab Dir*
Arnold Gilberg, *Regional Mgr*
▲ **EMP:** 25 **EST:** 1975
SQ FT: 32,000
SALES (est): 5.5MM Privately Held
WEB: www.avvwine.com
SIC: 2084 Wines

(P-2508)
BARBOUR VINEYARDS LLC
104 Camino Dorado, NAPA (94558-6212)
PHONE.................707 257-1829
Jim Barbour, *Mng Member*
EMP: 21 **EST:** 1990
SALES (est): 2.9MM Privately Held
WEB: www.barbourwines.com
SIC: 2084 Wines

(P-2509)
BARREL TEN QARTER CIR LAND INC
33 Harlow Ct, NAPA (94558-7520)
P.O. Box 789, Ceres (95307-0789)
PHONE.................209 538-3131
Fred T Franzia, *Principal*
EMP: 15
SALES (corp-wide): 196.9MM Privately Held
SIC: 2084 Wines
HQ: Barrel Ten Quarter Circle Land Company, Inc.
6342 Bystrum Rd
Ceres CA 95307
707 258-0550

(P-2510)
BAYWOOD CELLARS INC
Also Called: Hook or Crook Cellars
5573 W Woodbridge Rd, Lodi (95242-9497)
PHONE.................415 606-4640
William Stokes, *CEO*
John Healy, *Partner*
Allen Lambardi, *Partner*
EMP: 30 **EST:** 2012
SALES (est): 30MM Privately Held
WEB: www.hookorcrookcellars.com
SIC: 2084 Wines

(P-2511)
BFW ASSOCIATES LLC (HQ)
Also Called: Benziger Family Winery
1883 London Ranch Rd, Glen Ellen (95442-9728)
PHONE.................707 935-3000
Michael Benziger,
Bill Thompson, *Controller*
Gerard Benziger,
Jospeh Benziger Jr,
Robert Benziger,
▲ **EMP:** 30 **EST:** 1980
SQ FT: 6,000
SALES (est): 13.5MM Privately Held
WEB: www.benziger.com
SIC: 2084 5921 Wines; wine

(P-2512)
BOEGER WINERY INC
1709 Carson Rd, Placerville (95667-5195)
PHONE.................530 622-8094
Greg Boeger, *President*
Susan Boeger, *Treasurer*
Jim Schmitgal, *Natl Sales Mgr*
Byron Elmendorf, *Assistant*
EMP: 50 **EST:** 1972
SQ FT: 8,000
SALES (est): 5.2MM Privately Held
WEB: www.boegerwinery.com
SIC: 2084 0172 Wines; grapes

(P-2513)
BONNY DOON VINEYARD (PA)
328 Ingalls St, Santa Cruz (95060-5882)
P.O. Box 1242 (95061-1242)
PHONE.................831 425-3625
Lisa Kohrf, *Owner*
Sara Rossini, *Executive Asst*
Abbey Chrystal, *Technician*
Alex Krause, *Export Mgr*
Nicole Walsh, *Production*
EMP: 22 **EST:** 2007
SALES (est): 4.9MM Privately Held
WEB: www.bonnydoonvineyard.com
SIC: 2084 Wines

(P-2514)
BONNY DOON WINERY INC
328 Ingalls St, Santa Cruz (95060-5882)
PHONE.................831 425-3625
Randall Grahm, *President*
Lisa Kohrs, *CFO*
Barbara Smith, *Natl Sales Mgr*
◆ **EMP:** 19 **EST:** 1983
SQ FT: 20,000
SALES (est): 889K Privately Held
WEB: www.bonnydoonvineyard.com
SIC: 2084 Wines

(P-2515)
BOUCHAINE VINEYARDS INC
Also Called: Bouchaine Wineary
1075 Buchli Station Rd, NAPA (94559-9716)
PHONE.................707 252-9065
Tatiana Copeland, *President*
Gerret Copeland, *Chairman*
Chris Kajani, *General Mgr*
Annie Trimpe, *Office Mgr*
Kristina Whitten, *Accounting Mgr*
EMP: 18 **EST:** 1980
SQ FT: 35,000 Privately Held
WEB: www.bouchaine.com
SIC: 2084 5812 Wines; eating places

(P-2516)
BROWN ESTATE VINEYARDS LLC (PA)
3233 Sage Canyon Rd, Saint Helena (94574-9642)
PHONE.................707 963-2435
David Brown,
Eric Molinatti, *Sales Mgr*
Coral Brown,
Deann Brown,
EMP: 24 **EST:** 1998
SALES (est): 3.2MM Privately Held
WEB: www.brownestate.com
SIC: 2084 Wines

(P-2517)
BRUTOCAO VINEYARDS
Also Called: Brutocaosellers.com
1400 Highway 175, Hopland (95449-9754)
PHONE.................707 744-1320
Leonard Brutocao Jr, *Partner*
Daniel Brutocao, *Partner*
David Brutocao, *Partner*
Steven Brutocao, *Partner*
Renee Ortiz, *Partner*
EMP: 25 **EST:** 1976
SQ FT: 5,000
SALES (est): 1.6MM Privately Held
WEB: www.brutocaocellars.com
SIC: 2084 Wines

(P-2518)
BRYANT ESTATE
1567 Sage Canyon Rd, Saint Helena (94574-9628)
PHONE.................707 963-0483
Bettina Bryant, *President*
EMP: 24 **EST:** 2006
SALES (est): 1.5MM Privately Held
WEB: www.bryant.estate
SIC: 2084 Wines

(P-2519)
BUONCRISTIANI WINE CO LLC
2275 Soda Canyon Rd, NAPA (94558-9201)
P.O. Box 6946 (94581-1946)
PHONE.................707 259-1681
Matthew Buoncristiani,
Aaron Buoncristiani,
Jason Buoncristiani,
EMP: 15 **EST:** 2002
SALES (est): 1.3MM Privately Held
WEB: www.buonwine.com
SIC: 2084 Wines

2084 - Wine & Brandy County (P-2520) — PRODUCTS & SERVICES SECTION

(P-2520)
BURGESS CELLARS INC
1108 Deer Park Rd, Saint Helena (94574-9728)
P.O. Box 282 (94574-0282)
PHONE.....................707 963-4766
Thomas E Burgess, *President*
Tom Burgess, *Manager*
EMP: 23 EST: 1972
SQ FT: 20,000
SALES (est): 4.4MM **Privately Held**
WEB: www.burgesscellars.com
SIC: **2084** 0172 Wines; grapes

(P-2521)
C AND C WINE SERVICES INC
Also Called: Hook & Ladder Winery
2134 Olivet Rd, Santa Rosa (95401-3819)
PHONE.....................707 546-5712
Cecil Deloach, *President*
Jeff Cummins, *CFO*
Maureen Faulk, *Manager*
Lisa Snider, *Manager*
▲ EMP: 20 EST: 1984
SALES (est): 2.2MM **Privately Held**
WEB: www.hookandladderwinery.com
SIC: **2084**

(P-2522)
C MONDAVI & FAMILY (PA)
Also Called: Charles Krug Winery
2800 Main St, Saint Helena (94574-9502)
P.O. Box 191 (94574-0191)
PHONE.....................707 967-2200
John Lennon, *President*
Peter Mondavi Jr, *Treasurer*
David Brown, *Vice Pres*
Mark Mondavi, *Admin Sec*
Sam Stamey, *Info Tech Mgr*
▲ EMP: 85
SQ FT: 175,000
SALES (est): 13.4MM **Privately Held**
WEB: www.ckmondavi.com
SIC: **2084** 0172 Wine cellars, bonded: engaged in blending wines; grapes

(P-2523)
CAKEBREAD CELLARS
Also Called: Cakebread Cellar Vineyards
8300 Saint Helena Hwy, Rutherford (94573)
P.O. Box 216 (94573-0216)
PHONE.....................707 963-5221
Jack E Cakebread, *CEO*
Bruce Cakebread, *President*
Josef Wally, *CFO*
Dolores Cakebread, *Senior VP*
Dennis Cakebread, *Vice Pres*
▲ EMP: 60 EST: 1973
SQ FT: 100,000
SALES (est): 21.3MM **Privately Held**
WEB: www.cakebread.com
SIC: **2084** Wines

(P-2524)
CALDWELL VINEYARD LLC
169 Kreuzer Ln, NAPA (94559-3604)
PHONE.....................707 255-1294
John Caldwell, *Owner*
▲ EMP: 15 EST: 1988
SALES (est): 2.4MM **Privately Held**
WEB: www.caldwellvineyard.com
SIC: **2084** Wines

(P-2525)
CARNEROS RANCHING INC
1134 Dealy Ln, NAPA (94559-9706)
PHONE.....................707 253-9464
Francis Mahoney, *President*
EMP: 15 EST: 2010
SALES (est): 499.1K **Privately Held**
WEB: www.carneroswinecompany.com
SIC: **2084** Wines

(P-2526)
CATHERINE-ELIZABETH INC (PA)
4707 Vine Hill Rd, Sebastopol (95472-2236)
P.O. Box 317, Bodega (94922-0317)
PHONE.....................707 827-1655
Stephen W Kistler, *Principal*
EMP: 21 EST: 2008
SALES (est): 957.8K **Privately Held**
WEB: www.headiedesigns.com
SIC: **2084**

(P-2527)
CEDAR KNOLL VINEYARDS INC
Also Called: Palmaz Vineyards
4029 Hagen Rd, NAPA (94558-3818)
PHONE.....................707 226-5587
Amalia Palmaze, *President*
Pablo Diaz, *Manager*
Barbara Packham, *Associate*
▲ EMP: 30 EST: 1998
SALES (est): 5.2MM **Privately Held**
WEB: www.palmazvineyards.com
SIC: **2084** Wines

(P-2528)
CHAPPELLET VINEYARD
1581 Sage Canyon Rd, Saint Helena (94574-9628)
PHONE.....................707 286-4219
Donn Chappellet,
Andrew Opatz,
Laura Engle, *Manager*
Ry Richards, *Associate*
EMP: 26 EST: 2009
SALES (est): 1.7MM **Privately Held**
WEB: www.chappellet.com
SIC: **2084** Wines

(P-2529)
CHAPPELLET WINERY INC (PA)
1581 Sage Canyon Rd, Saint Helena (94574-9628)
PHONE.....................707 286-4268
Cyril Donn Chappellet, *CEO*
Devonna Smith, *CFO*
David Francke, *Managing Dir*
Mary Alice Chappellet, *Admin Sec*
Daniel Docher, *Engineer*
▲ EMP: 34 EST: 1967
SQ FT: 22,472
SALES (est): 5.1MM **Privately Held**
WEB: www.chappellet.com
SIC: **2084** Wines

(P-2530)
CHATEAU DIANA LLC (PA)
6195 Dry Creek Rd, Healdsburg (95448-8100)
P.O. Box 1013 (95448-1013)
PHONE.....................707 433-6992
Corey Manning, *Mng Member*
Danna Gibson, *CFO*
Kristin Gummer, *Opers Staff*
Adam Toomire, *Production*
Ed Hajeian, *VP Sales*
▲ EMP: 15 EST: 1978
SQ FT: 8,000
SALES (est): 4.3MM **Privately Held**
WEB: www.chateaud.com
SIC: **2084** Wines

(P-2531)
CHATEAU MASSON LLC
Also Called: Mountain Winery
14831 Pierce Rd, Saratoga (95070-9724)
PHONE.....................408 741-7002
William Hirschman,
Jennifer Perkins, *General Mgr*
Kristina Schmidt, *Opers Staff*
Donovan Haney, *Production*
Marty Barker, *Marketing Staff*
EMP: 25 EST: 1999
SQ FT: 1,500
SALES (est): 5.5MM **Privately Held**
WEB: www.mountainwinery.com
SIC: **2084** Wines

(P-2532)
CHATEAU MONTELENA LLC
Also Called: Chateau Montelena Winery
1429 Tubbs Ln, Calistoga (94515-9726)
PHONE.....................707 942-5105
Bo Barrett, *Mng Member*
Amy Biege, *Sales Staff*
Matt Crafton,
Cameron Parry,
Dave Vella,
▲ EMP: 30 EST: 2015
SQ FT: 22,000
SALES (est): 6.5MM **Privately Held**
WEB: www.montelena.com
SIC: **2084** 0172 Wines; grapes

(P-2533)
CLOS DU BOIS WINES INC
Also Called: Constltion Brnds US Oprations
19410 Geyserville Ave, Geyserville (95441-9603)
PHONE.....................707 857-1651
Jon Moramarco, *President*
Tom Hobart, *Vice Pres*
Mike Jellison, *Vice Pres*
▲ EMP: 27 EST: 1982
SALES (est): 11.5MM **Privately Held**
WEB: www.closdubois.com
SIC: **2084** Wines
HQ: Beam Suntory Inc.
   222 Mdse Mart Plz # 1600
   Chicago IL 60654
   312 964-6999

(P-2534)
CLOS DU VAL WINE COMPANY LTD
Also Called: Golet Wine Estates
5330 Silverado Trl, NAPA (94558-9410)
PHONE.....................707 259-2200
Bernard Portet, *Chairman*
Jon-Mark Chappellet, *President*
Adam Torpy, *CEO*
Stephen Kirschenmann, *Analyst*
Stacy Spring, *Human Res Mgr*
◆ EMP: 50
SQ FT: 32,000
SALES (est): 10.3MM **Privately Held**
WEB: www.closduval.com
SIC: **2084** Wines

(P-2535)
CLOS LA CHANCE WINES INC
1 Hummingbird Ln, San Martin (95046-9473)
PHONE.....................408 686-1050
Bill Murphy, *Ch of Bd*
Brenda Murphy, *President*
Bob Dunnett, *Corp Secy*
Michaelangelo Kallman, *Sales Staff*
▲ EMP: 45 EST: 1992
SQ FT: 25,000
SALES (est): 7.2MM **Privately Held**
WEB: www.clos.com
SIC: **2084** Wines

(P-2536)
CLOS PEGASE WINERY INC
1060 Dunaweal Ln, Calistoga (94515-9642)
P.O. Box 305 (94515-0305)
PHONE.....................707 942-4981
Jan Isaac Shrem, *President*
Richard Sowalsky, *Principal*
▲ EMP: 26 EST: 1986
SALES (est): 3.1MM **Privately Held**
WEB: www.clospegase.com
SIC: **2084** Wines

(P-2537)
CODORNIU NAPA INC
Also Called: Artesa Winery
1345 Henry Rd, NAPA (94559-9705)
PHONE.....................707 254-2148
Xavier Pages, *CEO*
Arthur O'Connor, *President*
Michael Kenton, *Principal*
David Gilbreath, *Admin Sec*
Tim O 'leary, *Finance Dir*
▲ EMP: 89 EST: 1988
SQ FT: 120,000
SALES (est): 23.2MM
SALES (corp-wide): 2.3MM **Privately Held**
WEB: www.artesawinery.com
SIC: **2084** Wines
HQ: Codorniu Sa
   Avenida Jaume De Codorniu, S/N
   Sant Sadurni D Anoia 08770
   938 194-600

(P-2538)
CONETECH CUSTOM SERVICES LLC
Also Called: Martini Prati Winery
2191 Laguna Rd, Santa Rosa (95401-3705)
PHONE.....................707 823-2404
Wayne Salk, *Principal*
EMP: 16 EST: 2000
SQ FT: 1,280
SALES (est): 256.7K **Privately Held**
WEB: www.martinrraywinery.com
SIC: **2084** Wines

(P-2539)
COSENTINO SIGNATURE WINERIES
Also Called: Cosentino Winery
7415 St Helena Hwy, Yountville (94599)
P.O. Box 2818 (94599-2818)
PHONE.....................707 921-2809
Mitch Cosentino, *President*
Larry J Soldinger, *Ch of Bd*
▲ EMP: 25 EST: 1981
SQ FT: 7,000
SALES (est): 3.2MM **Privately Held**
WEB: www.cosentinowinery.com
SIC: **2084** Wines

(P-2540)
CRIMSON WINE GROUP LTD (PA)
5901 Silverado Trl, NAPA (94558-9417)
PHONE.....................800 486-0503
Jennifer L Locke, *CEO*
John D Cumming, *Ch of Bd*
Karen L Diepholz, *CFO*
Mike S Cekay, *Senior VP*
Kimberly Benson, *Vice Pres*
▲ EMP: 116 EST: 1991
SQ FT: 13,200
SALES (est): 64.1MM **Publicly Held**
WEB: www.crimsonwinegroup.com
SIC: **2084** 5182 Wines, brandy & brandy spirits; wines; wine & distilled beverages; wine

(P-2541)
CRYSTAL BASIN CELLARS
3550 Carson Rd, Camino (95709-9330)
PHONE.....................530 303-3749
Mike Owen, *Owner*
Jack Wohler, *Technology*
Todd Smith, *Engineer*
EMP: 15 EST: 2006
SALES (est): 632.1K **Privately Held**
WEB: www.crystalbasin.com
SIC: **2084** Wines

(P-2542)
DANA ESTATES INC (PA)
1500 Whitehall Ln, Saint Helena (94574-9685)
P.O. Box 153, Rutherford (94573-0153)
PHONE.....................707 963-4365
HI Sang Lee, *President*
Brigid Babb, *Sales Staff*
▲ EMP: 49 EST: 2005
SALES (est): 6MM **Privately Held**
WEB: www.danaestates.com
SIC: **2084** Wines

(P-2543)
DARCIE KENT VINEYARDS
4590 Tesla Rd, Livermore (94550-9002)
PHONE.....................925 243-9040
Darcie Kent, *Principal*
Andrew Lauer, *Officer*
David Harrell, *Area Mgr*
Dana Welker, *CIO*
Evan Field, *Sales Staff*
▲ EMP: 25 EST: 2011
SALES (est): 2.5MM **Privately Held**
WEB: www.darciekentvineyards.com
SIC: **2084** Wines

(P-2544)
DARIOUSH KHALEDI WINERY LLC
4240 Silverado Trl, NAPA (94558-1117)
PHONE.....................707 257-2345
Darioush Khaledi, *Mng Member*
Ryan Ruhl, *General Mgr*
Yvette Sherer, *Executive Asst*
Viktoriya Kobzar, *Accounting Mgr*
Rob Deocampo, *Controller*
▲ EMP: 21
SALES (est): 4.3MM **Privately Held**
WEB: www.darioush.com
SIC: **2084** Wines

PRODUCTS & SERVICES SECTION
2084 - Wine & Brandy County (P-2567)

(P-2545)
DAVID BRUCE WINERY INC
21439 Bear Creek Rd, Los Gatos (95033-9429)
PHONE 408 354-4214
David Bruce, *Ch of Bd*
EMP: 15 **EST:** 1963
SQ FT: 12,000
SALES (est): 2.5MM **Privately Held**
WEB: www.davidbrucewinery.com
SIC: 2084 0172 Wines; grapes

(P-2546)
DELEGAT USA INC
555 Mission St Ste 2625, San Francisco (94105-0922)
PHONE 415 538-7988
Jakov Nikola Delegat, *Ch of Bd*
Alexandria Kimsey, *Principal*
▲ **EMP:** 53 **EST:** 2008
SALES (est): 6.9MM **Privately Held**
WEB: www.delegat.com
SIC: 5921 2084 Wine; wines
HQ: Delegat Limited
L 6, 10 Viaduct Harbour Avenue
Auckland 1010

(P-2547)
DELICATO VINEYARDS
455 Devlin Rd Ste 201, NAPA (94558-7562)
PHONE 707 265-1700
Chris Indelicato, *Manager*
Juan Valdes, *CFO*
Riccardo Mora, *Exec VP*
Paul Bourget, *Vice Pres*
David De Boer, *Vice Pres*
EMP: 42
SALES (corp-wide): 260.8MM **Privately Held**
WEB: www.delicato.com
SIC: 2084 Wines
PA: Delicato Vineyards, Llc
12001 S Highway 99
Manteca CA 95336
209 824-3600

(P-2548)
DELICATO VINEYARDS LLC (PA)
Also Called: Costal Brands
12001 S Highway 99, Manteca (95336-8499)
PHONE 209 824-3600
Christopher Indelicato, *Mng Member*
Roberto Reyes, *COO*
Emily Ingram, *Exec VP*
Mark Merrion, *Exec VP*
Riccardo Mora, *Exec VP*
◆ **EMP:** 150 **EST:** 1924
SQ FT: 12,000
SALES (est): 260.8MM **Privately Held**
WEB: www.delicato.com
SIC: 2084 Wines

(P-2549)
DIAGEO NORTH AMERICA INC
Also Called: Glen Ellen Carneros Winery
21468 8th St E Ste 1, Sonoma (95476-9782)
P.O. Box 1636 (95476-1636)
PHONE 707 939-6200
Fax: 707 938-2592
EMP: 75
SALES (corp-wide): 16.6B **Privately Held**
SIC: 2084 0172 Winery & Vineyard
HQ: Diageo North America Inc.
801 Main Ave
Norwalk CT 10007
203 229-2100

(P-2550)
DIAGEO NORTH AMERICA INC
Also Called: United Distlrs Vintners N Amer
1160 Battery St Ste 30, San Francisco (94111-1215)
PHONE 415 835-7300
Karen Cass, *Branch Mgr*
Joanna Kardinal, *Human Res Dir*
Jennifer Batinich, *Marketing Staff*
Jessie Ward, *Manager*
EMP: 25
SALES (corp-wide): 18B **Privately Held**
SIC: 2084 2082 Wines, brandy & brandy spirits; malt beverages
HQ: Diageo North America Inc.
3 World Trade Ctr
New York NY 10007
212 202-1800

(P-2551)
DOMAINE CHANDON INC (DH)
1 California Dr, Yountville (94599-1426)
PHONE 707 944-8844
Matthew Wood, *CEO*
Greg Godchaux, *Vice Pres*
Lisa Meyer, *Executive*
Nicolas Berton, *Human Resources*
Chas McEwan, *Opers Staff*
◆ **EMP:** 100 **EST:** 1973
SQ FT: 240,000
SALES (est): 63.3MM
SALES (corp-wide): 419.1MM **Privately Held**
WEB: www.chandon.com
SIC: 2084 5812 0762 5813 Wines; eating places; vineyard management & maintenance services; drinking places
HQ: Moet Hennessy Usa, Inc.
7 World Trade Ctr At250
New York NY 10007
212 251-8200

(P-2552)
DOMINUS ESTATE CORPORATION
2570 Napa Nook Rd, Yountville (94599-1455)
PHONE 707 944-8954
Christian Moueix, *President*
Regina Feiner, *Administration*
Julie Levitan, *Finance Mgr*
Guillaume Eicholz, *Manager*
Carmel Greenberg, *Manager*
▲ **EMP:** 18 **EST:** 1982
SQ FT: 4,000
SALES (est): 4.4MM **Privately Held**
WEB: www.dominusestate.com
SIC: 2084 Wines

(P-2553)
DON SBSTANI SONS INTL WINE NGC
520 Airpark Rd, NAPA (94558-7535)
PHONE 707 337-1961
John Nicolette, *Branch Mgr*
Matt Seifert, *Division VP*
Alice Castorena, *Office Mgr*
Ashley Andrews, *Administration*
Allison Brewer, *Merchandising*
EMP: 40
SALES (corp-wide): 28MM **Privately Held**
WEB: www.donsebastianiandsons.com
SIC: 2084 Wines
PA: Don Sebastiani & Sons International Wine Negociants
19150 Sonoma Hwy 12
Sonoma CA 95476
707 224-0410

(P-2554)
DRY CREEK VINEYARD INC
3770 Lambert Bridge Rd, Healdsburg (95448-9713)
P.O. Box T (95448-0107)
PHONE 707 433-1000
Don Wallace,
Jerry Smith, *General Mgr*
Amanda Barber, *Administration*
Joseph Czesnakowicz, *Regl Sales Mgr*
Randall Pettit, *Regl Sales Mgr*
▲ **EMP:** 35 **EST:** 1972
SQ FT: 11,000
SALES (est): 6.9MM **Privately Held**
WEB: www.drycreekvineyard.com
SIC: 2084 0172 Wines; grapes

(P-2555)
DRY FARM WINES INC (PA)
3149 California Blvd C, NAPA (94558-3335)
PHONE 707 944-1500
David Allred, *CEO*
Mark Moschel, *President*
EMP: 57 **EST:** 2015
SALES (est): 8.5MM **Privately Held**
WEB: www.dryfarmwines.com
SIC: 2084 Wines

(P-2556)
DUCKHORN PORTFOLIO INC (HQ)
1201 Dowdell Ln, Saint Helena (94574-1416)
PHONE 707 302-2658
Alex Ryan, *Ch of Bd*
Zach Rasmuson, *COO*
Lori Beaudoin, *CFO*
Pete Przybylinski, *Exec VP*
Carol Reber, *Exec VP*
EMP: 200 **EST:** 1976
SQ FT: 12,000
SALES: 336.6MM **Privately Held**
WEB: www.duckhornportfolio.com
SIC: 2084 Wines, brandy & brandy spirits
PA: Mallard Holdco, Llc
1201 Dowdell Ln
Saint Helena CA 94574
707 302-2658

(P-2557)
DUCKHORN WINE COMPANY (HQ)
Also Called: Goldeneye
1000 Lodi Ln, Saint Helena (94574-9410)
PHONE 707 963-7108
Alex Ryan, *CEO*
Lori Beaudoin, *CFO*
Alicia Martin, *Officer*
Ashley O'Leary, *Vice Pres*
Caitlin Hartwigsen, *District Mgr*
▲ **EMP:** 40 **EST:** 1976
SALES (est): 68.2MM
SALES (corp-wide): 133.9MM **Privately Held**
WEB: www.duckhorn.com
SIC: 2084 0172 Wines; grapes
PA: Tsg Consumer Partners Llc
4 Orinda Way
Orinda CA 94563
415 217-2300

(P-2558)
E & J GALLO WINERY (PA)
Also Called: California Natural Color
600 Yosemite Blvd, Modesto (95354-2760)
P.O. Box 1130 (95353-1130)
PHONE 209 341-3111
Joseph E Gallo, *CEO*
Herb Smith, *Vice Pres*
Bruce Defrees, *Creative Dir*
Samantha Christensen, *Admin Asst*
Jayna Plante, *Business Anlyst*
◆ **EMP:** 2500 **EST:** 1942
SALES (est): 2.1B **Privately Held**
WEB: www.gallo.com
SIC: 2084 0172 Wines; grapes

(P-2559)
E & J GALLO WINERY
Also Called: Louis M. Martini Winery
254 Saint Helena Hwy S, Saint Helena (94574-2203)
PHONE 707 963-2736
EMP: 50
SALES (corp-wide): 2.1B **Privately Held**
WEB: www.gallo.com
SIC: 2084 0172 Mfg Varietal Wines & Vineyard Operations
PA: E. & J. Gallo Winery
600 Yosemite Blvd
Modesto CA 95354
209 341-3111

(P-2560)
EHREN JORDAN WINE CELLARS LLC
Also Called: Failla Wines
3530 Silverado Trl N, Saint Helena (94574-9663)
PHONE 707 963-0530
Ehren Jordan,
Cat Fairchild, *Sales Staff*
Jane Drummond, *Manager*
EMP: 15 **EST:** 2008
SALES (est): 4.4MM **Privately Held**
SIC: 2084 Wines

(P-2561)
ELLISTON VINEYARDS INC
463 Kilkare Rd, Sunol (94586-9415)
PHONE 925 862-2377
Donna Flavetta, *President*
Madeline Maita, *Officer*
EMP: 55 **EST:** 1983
SQ FT: 1,000
SALES (est): 5.5MM **Privately Held**
WEB: www.elliston.com
SIC: 2084 Wines; wine cellars, bonded: engaged in blending wines

(P-2562)
EMILIO GUGLIELMO WINERY INC
1480 E Main Ave, Morgan Hill (95037-3201)
PHONE 408 779-2145
EMP: 17 **EST:** 1973
SALES (est): 1.1MM **Privately Held**
WEB: www.guglielmowinery.com
SIC: 2084 Wines

(P-2563)
ETUDE WINES INC
1250 Cuttings Wharf Rd, NAPA (94559-9738)
P.O. Box 3382 (94558-0338)
PHONE 707 299-3057
Jon Priest, *Manager*
David Cone, *Sales Staff*
Melanie Edwards, *Manager*
Greg Gerow, *Supervisor*
EMP: 22 **EST:** 1982
SQ FT: 6,000
SALES (est): 3.1MM **Privately Held**
WEB: www.etudewines.com
SIC: 2084 Wines

(P-2564)
EVEHRTAY LLC (PA)
421 1st St W, Sonoma (95476-6608)
PHONE 707 293-3033
James Hahn, *Principal*
EMP: 22 **EST:** 2008
SALES (est): 430.5K **Privately Held**
SIC: 2084 Wines

(P-2565)
F KORBEL & BROS (PA)
Also Called: Korbel Champagne Cellers
13250 River Rd, Guerneville (95446-9593)
PHONE 707 824-7000
Gary B Heck, *President*
David Faris, *Treasurer*
Brian McClusky, *Treasurer*
Andrew Matthias, *Officer*
Dan Baker, *Exec VP*
◆ **EMP:** 200 **EST:** 1882
SQ FT: 66,000
SALES (est): 103.8MM **Privately Held**
WEB: www.korbel.com
SIC: 2084 0172 Wines; grapes

(P-2566)
FAR NIENTE WINERY INC
Also Called: Far Niente Wine Estates
1350 Acacia Dr, Oakville (94562)
P.O. Box 327 (94562-0327)
PHONE 707 944-2861
Larry Maguire, *CEO*
Jeremy Nickel, *Partner*
Laura Harwood, *CFO*
Donna Blevins, *Admin Asst*
June Wong, *Accountant*
▲ **EMP:** 100
SQ FT: 30,000
SALES (est): 24.1MM **Privately Held**
WEB: www.farniente.com
SIC: 2084 Wines

(P-2567)
FERRAR-CRANO VNYRDS WINERY LLC (PA)
Also Called: Ferrari-Carano Winery
8761 Dry Creek Rd, Healdsburg (95448-9133)
P.O. Box 1549 (95448-1549)
PHONE 707 433-6700
Rhonda Carano, *CEO*
Jeff Smith, *Prdtn Mgr*
Cheryl McMillan, *Marketing Staff*
Jim Boswell, *Manager*
Teri Rolleri, *Manager*
▲ **EMP:** 119 **EST:** 1981
SQ FT: 46,000
SALES (est): 35.4MM **Privately Held**
WEB: www.ferrari-carano.com
SIC: 2084 0172 Wines; grapes

2084 - Wine & Brandy County (P-2568) — PRODUCTS & SERVICES SECTION

(P-2568)
FETZER VINEYARDS (HQ)
12901 Old River Rd, Hopland (95449-9813)
P.O. Box 611 (95449-0611)
PHONE....................707 744-1250
Eduardo Guilisasti Gana, *CEO*
Wade Grote, *President*
Chris McFerran, *Senior VP*
Brian Dorn, *Vice Pres*
Sid Goldstein, *Vice Pres*
◆ **EMP:** 242 **EST:** 1960
SALES (est): 65.2MM **Privately Held**
WEB: www.fetzer.com
SIC: 2084 Wines

(P-2569)
FIELD STONE WINERY VINYRD INC
10075 Highway 128, Healdsburg (95448-9025)
PHONE....................707 433-7266
John C Staten, *President*
Ben Staten, *Corp Secy*
Staten Katrina J, *Vice Pres*
Katrina J Staten, *Vice Pres*
EMP: 15 **EST:** 1986
SQ FT: 4,000
SALES (est): 711.3K **Privately Held**
SIC: 2084 5921 Wines; wine

(P-2570)
FIOR DI SOLE LLC
2511 Napa Valley Corp Dr, NAPA (94558)
P.O. Box 6829 (94581-1829)
PHONE....................707 259-1477
Dario De Conti,
Lana Lobao, *Project Mgr*
Tony Ramos, *Production*
Fabiola Watson, *Marketing Mgr*
Robert Lockhart, *Sales Mgr*
EMP: 225 **EST:** 2012
SQ FT: 52,118
SALES: 82.5MM **Privately Held**
WEB: www.fiordisole.com
SIC: 2084 Wines

(P-2571)
FIOR DI SOLE LLC
2511 Napa Valley Corp Dr, NAPA (94558)
PHONE....................707 259-1477
EMP: 39
SALES (corp-wide): 9.9MM **Privately Held**
SIC: 2084 Mfg Wines/Brandy/Spirits
PA: Fior Di Sole, Llc
   2515 Napa Valley Corp Dr
   Napa CA 94558
   707 259-1477

(P-2572)
FLORA SPRINGS WINE COMPANY
677 Saint Helena Hwy S, Saint Helena (94574-2209)
PHONE....................707 963-5711
John Komes, *President*
Martha Komes, *Treasurer*
Julie Garvey, *Vice Pres*
Patrick Garvey, *Vice Pres*
Margaret Meraz, *Vice Pres*
▲ **EMP:** 19 **EST:** 1978
SALES (est): 3.2MM **Privately Held**
WEB: www.florasprings.com
SIC: 2084 Wines

(P-2573)
FLOWERS VINEYARD & WINERY LLC
28500 Seaview Rd, Cazadero (95421-9767)
PHONE....................707 847-3661
Jason Jardine, *President*
▲ **EMP:** 15 **EST:** 1989
SALES (est): 2.3MM **Privately Held**
WEB: www.flowerswinery.com
SIC: 2084 Wines

(P-2574)
FOLEY FAMILY WINES INC (HQ)
Also Called: Foley Wine Group
200 Concourse Blvd, Santa Rosa (95403-8210)
PHONE....................707 708-7600
William Patrick Foley II, *CEO*
Shawn Schiffer, *President*
Ryan Martin, *Vice Pres*
Al Losardo, *Regional Mgr*
Jennifer Darcy, *Admin Asst*
◆ **EMP:** 89 **EST:** 2007
SALES (est): 63.4MM
SALES (corp-wide): 81.2MM **Privately Held**
WEB: www.foleyfoodandwinesociety.com
SIC: 2084 0172 Wines; grapes
PA: Foley Family Wines Holdings, Inc.
   200 Concourse Blvd
   Santa Rosa CA 95403
   707 708-7600

(P-2575)
FOLEY FMLY WINES HOLDINGS INC (PA)
200 Concourse Blvd, Santa Rosa (95403-8210)
PHONE....................707 708-7600
William Patrick Foley II, *CEO*
Shawn Schiffer, *President*
Marty Peterson, *COO*
David Smith, *CFO*
Gerard Thoukis, *Chief Mktg Ofcr*
EMP: 60 **EST:** 2009
SALES (est): 81.2MM **Privately Held**
WEB: www.foleyfoodandwinesociety.com
SIC: 2084 Wines

(P-2576)
FOWLES WINE (USA) INC
230 Colfax Ave Ste A, Grass Valley (95945-6818)
PHONE....................703 975-8093
Matt Fowles, *CEO*
Victor Nash, *Principal*
Tom Pollock, *Principal*
Jeanmarie Miller, *Administration*
Chris Armstrong, *Regl Sales Mgr*
EMP: 17 **EST:** 2012
SALES (est): 1.2MM **Privately Held**
WEB: www.fowleswine.com
SIC: 2084 5182 Wines; wine coolers (beverages); wine & distilled beverages
PA: Fowles Wine Pty Ltd
   1175 Lambing Gully Road
   Avenel VIC 3664

(P-2577)
FOX BARREL CIDER COMPANY INC
1213 S Auburn St Ste A, Colfax (95713-9773)
P.O. Box 753 (95713-0753)
PHONE....................530 346-9699
Bruce Nissen, *President*
Sean Deorsey, *CFO*
EMP: 50 **EST:** 2004
SALES (est): 1.1MM
SALES (corp-wide): 9.6B **Publicly Held**
WEB: www.molsoncoors.com
SIC: 2084 Wines
HQ: Crispin Cider Company
   3939 W Highland Blvd
   Milwaukee WI 53208
   530 346-9699

(P-2578)
FRANCIS COPPOLA WINERY LLC
300 Via Archimedes, Geyserville (95441-9325)
PHONE....................707 857-1400
Francis Coppola, *Mng Member*
Kristin Thwaites, *Marketing Staff*
Christine Gaudenzi, *Sales Staff*
James Luchini, *Sales Staff*
Yolanda Basurto, *Manager*
▲ **EMP:** 35 **EST:** 2006
SALES (est): 7.2MM **Privately Held**
WEB: www.thefamilycoppola.com
SIC: 2084 Wines

(P-2579)
FRANCIS FORD CPPOLA PRSNTS LLC
Also Called: Francis Ford Coppola Winery
300 Via Archimedes, Geyserville (95441-9325)
PHONE....................707 251-3200
Francis Coppola, *Mng Member*
Brian Condon, *Vice Pres*
Stephan Micallef, *Vice Pres*
Ken Minami, *Vice Pres*
Allison Westhoven, *Vice Pres*
◆ **EMP:** 20 **EST:** 2006 **Privately Held**
WEB: www.thefamilycoppola.com
SIC: 2084 Wines

(P-2580)
FRANCISCAN VINEYARDS INC
Also Called: Ravenswood Winery
18701 Gehricke Rd, Sonoma (95476-4710)
PHONE....................707 933-2332
Joel Peterson, *Branch Mgr*
Ellis Chrystal, *Human Res Dir*
Kelly Exner, *Corp Comm Staff*
David Yale, *Teacher*
EMP: 94
SALES (corp-wide): 8.6B **Publicly Held**
WEB: www.franciscan.com
SIC: 2084 5921 Wines; wine
HQ: Franciscan Vineyards Inc.
   1178 Galleron Rd
   Saint Helena CA 94574
   707 963-7111

(P-2581)
FRANCISCAN VINEYARDS INC
Also Called: Woodbridge Winery
5950 E Woodbridge Rd, Acampo (95220-9429)
P.O. Box 1260, Woodbridge (95258-1260)
PHONE....................209 369-5861
Mark Garbrielli, *Manager*
EMP: 94
SQ FT: 2,450
SALES (corp-wide): 8.6B **Publicly Held**
WEB: www.franciscan.com
SIC: 2084 Wines
HQ: Franciscan Vineyards Inc.
   1178 Galleron Rd
   Saint Helena CA 94574
   707 963-7111

(P-2582)
FRANCISCAN VINEYARDS INC (HQ)
1178 Galleron Rd, Saint Helena (94574-9790)
PHONE....................707 963-7111
Agustin Francisco Huneeus, *President*
Bill Skowronski, *CFO*
▲ **EMP:** 75 **EST:** 1971
SQ FT: 110,000
SALES (est): 51.2MM
SALES (corp-wide): 8.6B **Publicly Held**
WEB: www.franciscan.com
SIC: 2084 Wines
PA: Constellation Brands, Inc.
   207 High Point Dr # 100
   Victor NY 14564
   585 678-7100

(P-2583)
FRANCISCAN VINYARDS INC
Also Called: Simi Winery
16275 Healdsburg Ave, Healdsburg (95448-9075)
P.O. Box 698 (95448-0698)
PHONE....................707 433-6981
Hustin Huneeus, *President*
▲ **EMP:** 27 **EST:** 1876
SALES (est): 4.4MM
SALES (corp-wide): 8.6B **Publicly Held**
WEB: www.cbrands.com
SIC: 2084 0172 5812 Wines; grapes; eating places
PA: Constellation Brands, Inc.
   207 High Point Dr # 100
   Victor NY 14564
   585 678-7100

(P-2584)
FRANZIA WINERY LP
17000 E State Highway 120, Ripon (95366-9412)
P.O. Box 897 (95366-0897)
PHONE....................209 599-4111
Chris Metzger, *Principal*
▲ **EMP:** 16 **EST:** 2013
SALES (est): 1.6MM **Privately Held**
WEB: www.franzia.com
SIC: 2084 Wines

(P-2585)
FRANZIA WINERY LLC
Also Called: Wine Group, The
17000 E State Highway 120, Ripon (95366-9412)
PHONE....................209 599-4111
Lou Dambrosio, *Plant Mgr*
▲ **EMP:** 27 **EST:** 2004
SALES (est): 596K **Privately Held**
WEB: www.franzia.com
SIC: 2084 Wines

(P-2586)
FRANZIA/SANGER WINERY
Also Called: Franzia Winery
17000 E State Highway 120, Ripon (95366-9412)
PHONE....................209 599-4111
Arthur Ciocca, *Partner*
F Lynn Bates, *Partner*
▲ **EMP:** 100 **EST:** 1933
SQ FT: 160,000
SALES (est): 3.1MM **Privately Held**
SIC: 2084 Wines

(P-2587)
FREEMARK ABBEY WNERY LTD PRTNR
3022 Saint Helena Hwy N, Saint Helena (94574-9652)
P.O. Box 410 (94574-0410)
PHONE....................707 963-9694
John Bryan,
Kimberly Rupp, *Marketing Staff*
Reed Kimberly, *Director*
Barry Dodds, *Manager*
Russell Flood, *Manager*
EMP: 25 **EST:** 1967
SQ FT: 4,500
SALES (est): 1.9MM **Privately Held**
WEB: www.freemarkabbey.com
SIC: 2084 0172 Wines; grapes

(P-2588)
FREIXENET SONOMA CAVES INC
Also Called: Gloria Ferrer Winery
23555 Arnold Dr, Sonoma (95476-9285)
P.O. Box 1949 (95476-1949)
PHONE....................707 996-4981
Jose M Ferrer, *CEO*
Diego Jimenez, *President*
Gloria Caves, *Manager*
▲ **EMP:** 40 **EST:** 1982
SQ FT: 4,000
SALES: 9MM
SALES (corp-wide): 176.2MM **Privately Held**
WEB: www.gloriaferrer.com
SIC: 2084 5812 Wines; eating places
PA: Freixenet Sa
   Plaza Joan Sala 2
   Sant Sadurni D Anoia 08770
   938 917-000

(P-2589)
FREY VINEYARDS LTD
14000 Tomki Rd, Redwood Valley (95470-6135)
PHONE....................707 485-5177
Paul Frey, *President*
Marguerite Frey, *Corp Secy*
Tamara Frey, *Corp Secy*
Adam Frey, *Vice Pres*
John Frey, *Vice Pres*
EMP: 15 **EST:** 1980
SQ FT: 6,000
SALES (est): 1MM **Privately Held**
WEB: www.freywine.com
SIC: 2084 Wines

(P-2590)
FROGS LEAP WINERY
8815 Conn Creek Rd, Rutherford (94573)
P.O. Box 189 (94573-0189)
PHONE....................707 963-4704
John T Williams, *President*
Frank Leeds, *Vice Pres*
Leah S White, *Executive Asst*
Brad Lusk, *Engineer*
Edibel Deibert, *Human Res Mgr*
◆ **EMP:** 36 **EST:** 1981
SQ FT: 8,000

▲ = Import ▼ = Export ◆ = Import/Export

PRODUCTS & SERVICES SECTION

2084 - Wine & Brandy County (P-2615)

SALES (est): 6.1MM Privately Held
WEB: www.frogsleap.com
SIC: 2084 Wines

(P-2591)
GALLO SALES COMPANY INC (DH)
30825 Wiegman Rd, Hayward (94564-7893)
P.O. Box 1266, Union City (94587-6266)
PHONE 510 476-5000
Joseph E Gallo, *President*
Stewart Fine, *District Mgr*
Michelle Mendoza, *Admin Asst*
George Agra, *Sales Staff*
Justin Anderson, *Sales Staff*
▲ EMP: 225 EST: 1952
SQ FT: 59,000
SALES (est): 45.7MM
SALES (corp-wide): 2.1B Privately Held
WEB: www.gallocareers.com
SIC: 2084 Wines
HQ: Gallo Glass Company
605 S Santa Cruz Ave
Modesto CA 95354
209 341-3710

(P-2592)
GEKKEIKAN SAKE USA INC
1136 Sibley St, Folsom (95630-3223)
PHONE 916 985-3111
Masahiro Namise, *CEO*
Yu Hyodo, *Admin Sec*
Philip Maher, *Controller*
◆ EMP: 25 EST: 1989
SQ FT: 390,000
SALES (est): 11.1MM Privately Held
WEB: www.gekkeikan.com
SIC: 2084 Wines
PA: Gekkeikan Sake Company, Ltd.
247, Minamihamacho, Fushimi-Ku
Kyoto KYO 612-8

(P-2593)
GEYSER PEAK WINERY
Also Called: Canyon Road Winery
1300 1st St Ste 368, NAPA (94559-2956)
PHONE 707 857-9463
Stephen Brower, *President*
Tim Matz, *Director*
▲ EMP: 20 EST: 1989
SALES (est): 3.1MM Privately Held
WEB: www.geyserpeakwinery.com
SIC: 2084 Wines

(P-2594)
GIBSON WINE COMPANY
1720 Academy Ave, Sanger (93657-3704)
PHONE 559 875-2505
Wayne Albrecht, *CEO*
Donald Weber, *Treasurer*
Kim Spruance, *Admin Sec*
▲ EMP: 25 EST: 1939
SQ FT: 2,000
SALES (est): 8.9MM
SALES (corp-wide): 196.9MM Privately Held
WEB: www.gibsonwinecompany.com
SIC: 2084 Wines
PA: Bronco Wine Company
6342 Bystrum Rd
Ceres CA 95307
209 538-3131

(P-2595)
GLOBAL WINE GROUP
Also Called: Triad Global Group
3750 E Woodbridge Rd, Acampo (95220-8700)
PHONE 209 340-8500
Jeffery Hansen, *President*
James R Grant III, *CFO*
Rod Moniz, *Vice Pres*
Jim O'Connor, *Vice Pres*
Tom Bonomi, *Managing Dir*
▼ EMP: 22 EST: 2000
SQ FT: 50,000
SALES (est): 2.7MM Privately Held
SIC: 2084 Wine cellars, bonded: engaged in blending wines

(P-2596)
GNEKOW FAMILY WINERY LLC
17347 E Gawne Rd, Stockton (95215-9646)
PHONE 209 463-0697
Sean Gnekow,
David Brown, *General Mgr*
Rudy Gnekow,
▲ EMP: 26 EST: 1996
SQ FT: 18,000
SALES (est): 3.2MM Privately Held
WEB: www.campusoakswines.com
SIC: 2084 Wines

(P-2597)
GOLDEN CELLARS LLC
14251 Old River Rd, Hopland (95449-9618)
P.O. Box 340 (95449-0340)
PHONE 707 528-8500
Catherine Julie Golden,
▲ EMP: 25 EST: 2004
SALES (est): 1.1MM Privately Held
SIC: 2084 Wines

(P-2598)
GOLDEN STATE VINTNERS (PA)
4596 S Tracy Blvd, Tracy (95377-8106)
PHONE 707 254-4900
Brian Jay Vos, *CEO*
John Oliver Sutton, *CFO*
▼ EMP: 15 EST: 1995
SQ FT: 8,000
SALES (est): 79K Privately Held
WEB: www.vinarium-usa.com
SIC: 2084 Wines; brandy

(P-2599)
GOLDEN STATE VINTNERS
1075 Golden Gate Dr, NAPA (94558-6187)
PHONE 707 254-1985
Mike Blom,
EMP: 31
SALES (corp-wide): 79K Privately Held
WEB: www.vinarium-usa.com
SIC: 2084 Wine cellars, bonded: engaged in blending wines
PA: Golden State Vintners
4596 S Tracy Blvd
Tracy CA 95377
707 254-4900

(P-2600)
GOLDEN STATE VINTNERS
1175 Commmerce Blvd, Vallejo (94503)
PHONE 707 553-6480
Jeff Neil, *Branch Mgr*
EMP: 31
SALES (corp-wide): 79K Privately Held
WEB: www.vinarium-usa.com
SIC: 2084 Wines
PA: Golden State Vintners
4596 S Tracy Blvd
Tracy CA 95377
707 254-4900

(P-2601)
GOLDEN VLY GRAPE JICE WINE LLC (PA)
11770 Road 27 1/2, Madera (93637-9108)
PHONE 559 661-4657
Gerard Pantaleo, *Mng Member*
Rodger Williams, *Technical Staff*
Frank Pantaleo,
Jerry Pantaleo,
Nicholas Pantaleo,
▲ EMP: 39 EST: 1997
SALES (est): 19.9MM Privately Held
WEB: www.goldenvalleywine.com
SIC: 2084 Wines

(P-2602)
GOLDSTONE LAND COMPANY LLC
Also Called: Bear Creek Winery
11900 Furry Rd, Lodi (95240-7201)
PHONE 209 368-3113
Joan M Kautz, *Mng Member*
Lisa Gibson, *Accounting Mgr*
D'nell Parker, *Opers Staff*
Stephen J Kautz, *Mng Member*
D'Nell Parker, *Manager*
◆ EMP: 30 EST: 1995
SALES (est): 5.9MM Privately Held

(P-2603)
GOOSECROSS CELLARS A CAL CORP
1119 State Ln, Yountville (94599-9407)
PHONE 707 944-1986
David Topper, *CEO*
Geoffrey Gorsuch, *Vice Pres*
EMP: 23 EST: 1985
SALES (est): 497.1K Privately Held
WEB: www.goosecross.com
SIC: 2084 Wine cellars, bonded: engaged in blending wines

(P-2604)
GRAPE LINKS INC
Also Called: Barefoot Cellars
420 Aviation Blvd Ste 106, Santa Rosa (95403-1039)
P.O. Box 1130, Modesto (95353-1130)
PHONE 707 524-8000
Michael C Houlihan, *President*
Martin A Jones, *Exec VP*
Bonnie Harvey, *Vice Pres*
Jennifer Wall, *Admin Sec*
Aaron J Fein, *Sales Staff*
EMP: 35 EST: 1986
SQ FT: 4,200
SALES (est): 6.2MM
SALES (corp-wide): 2.1B Privately Held
WEB: www.gallo.com
SIC: 2084 Wines
PA: E. & J. Gallo Winery
600 Yosemite Blvd
Modesto CA 95354
209 341-3111

(P-2605)
GRGICH HILLS CELLAR
Also Called: G and H Vineyards
1829 St Helena Hwy, Rutherford (94573)
P.O. Box 450 (94573-0450)
PHONE 707 963-2784
Miljenko Mike Grgich, *President*
Austin E Hills, *Shareholder*
Violet Grgich, *Corp Secy*
Paul Hayashi, *Exec VP*
Ivo Jeramaz, *Vice Pres*
▲ EMP: 35 EST: 1977
SQ FT: 43,000
SALES (est): 7.4MM Privately Held
WEB: www.grgich.com
SIC: 2084 5812 0172 Wines; eating places; grapes

(P-2606)
GRINDSTONE WINES LLC
130 Cortina School Rd, Arbuckle (95912)
PHONE 530 393-2162
Michael Doherty, *Partner*
EMP: 20 EST: 2019
SALES (est): 789.8K Privately Held
WEB: www.grindstonewines.com
SIC: 2084 Wines

(P-2607)
GROSKOPF WAREHOUSE & LOGISTICS
20580 8th St E, Sonoma (95476-9590)
P.O. Box 128, Vineburg (95487-0128)
PHONE 707 939-3100
Alec Merriam, *Owner*
Charlene Groskopf, *General Mgr*
Shelly Levin, *Human Res Dir*
Todd Finch, *Opers Staff*
Shannon Gibson, *Supervisor*
▲ EMP: 41 EST: 2001
SALES (est): 5.9MM Privately Held
WEB: www.groskopf.com
SIC: 2084 Wines

(P-2608)
H DE V LLC
588 Trancas St, NAPA (94558-3013)
PHONE 541 386-9119
Rick Hyde, *Principal*
EMP: 20
SALES (corp-wide): 559K Privately Held
WEB: www.hdvwines.com
SIC: 2084 Wines
PA: H De V, Llc
1101 Sherman Ave
Hood River OR 97031
541 386-9119

(P-2609)
HAGAFEN CELLARS INC
4160 Silverado Trl, NAPA (94558-1118)
PHONE 707 252-0781
Ernie Weir, *President*
Irit Weir, *Vice Pres*
Michael Gelven, *Sales Staff*
Marissa Napierski, *Manager*
▲ EMP: 17 EST: 1979
SQ FT: 6,000
SALES (est): 2.9MM Privately Held
WEB: www.hagafen.com
SIC: 2084 Wines

(P-2610)
HALL WINES LLC
401 Saint Helena Hwy S, Saint Helena (94574-2200)
P.O. Box 25, Rutherford (94573-0025)
PHONE 707 967-2626
Mike Reynolds,
Dominique Alexander, *Partner*
Kathleen Fidler, *Vice Pres*
Emily Harrison, *Vice Pres*
Whitney Jacobson, *Vice Pres*
▲ EMP: 50 EST: 2003
SQ FT: 20,000
SALES (est): 22.8MM Privately Held
WEB: www.hallwines.com
SIC: 2084 Wines

(P-2611)
HANDLEY CELLARS LTD
Also Called: Handley Cellars Winery
3151 Highway 128, Philo (95466)
P.O. Box 66 (95466-0066)
PHONE 707 895-3876
Milla Handley, *General Ptnr*
Raymond Handley, *Partner*
Colleen Bassett, *Sales Staff*
EMP: 26 EST: 1982
SQ FT: 10,000
SALES (est): 7MM Privately Held
WEB: www.handleycellars.com
SIC: 2084 Wines

(P-2612)
HANZELL VINEYARDS
18596 Lomita Ave, Sonoma (95476-4619)
PHONE 707 996-3860
Jean L Arnold, *President*
Alexander De Brye, *Treasurer*
Lauren Hortum, *Asst Controller*
Judy Martinez, *Opers Staff*
Ayn McDonald,
EMP: 16 EST: 1958
SALES (est): 3.1MM Privately Held
WEB: www.hanzell.com
SIC: 2084 Wines

(P-2613)
HARTFORD JACKSON LLC
Also Called: Hartford Family Winery
8075 Martinelli Rd, Forestville (95436-9255)
P.O. Box 1459 (95436-1459)
PHONE 707 887-1756
Don Hartford,
Tiaan Lordan, *Associate*
EMP: 23 EST: 1982
SQ FT: 40,000
SALES (est): 5.7MM Privately Held
WEB: www.hartfordwines.com
SIC: 2084 Wines

(P-2614)
HAUS BEVERAGE INC
1377 Grove St Ste D, Healdsburg (95448-4774)
PHONE 503 939-5298
EMP: 30 EST: 2019
SALES (est): 5.8MM Privately Held
SIC: 2084 Wines

(P-2615)
HEDGESIDE VINTNERS
Also Called: Del Dotto
540 Technology Way, NAPA (94558-7513)
PHONE 707 963-2134
Dave Del Dotto, *Owner*
Desiree Del Dotto, *COO*
Michelle Aldous, *Admin Asst*
Kristen Cadwallader, *Sales Associate*
Michelle Clark, *Sales Staff*
▲ EMP: 38 EST: 2000

2084 - Wine & Brandy County (P-2616)

(P-2616)
HESS COLLECTION WINERY
1166 Commerce Blvd, American Canyon (94503-9621)
PHONE.................707 255-1144
John Bulleri, *Manager*
Brian Batridge, *Vice Pres*
Michael Murphy, *Vice Pres*
Marcia Passavant, *Regional Mgr*
Ryan Jones, *Division Mgr*
EMP: 95 **Privately Held**
WEB: www.hessperssonestates.com
SIC: 2084 Wines
HQ: The Hess Collection Winery
4411 Redwood Rd
Napa CA 94558
707 255-1144

(P-2617)
HESS COLLECTION WINERY (DH)
Also Called: Hess Collection Import Co
4411 Redwood Rd, NAPA (94558-9708)
P.O. Box 4140 (94558-0565)
PHONE.................707 255-1144
Timothy Persson, *CEO*
Clement J Firko, *President*
Tom Selfridge, *President*
John Grant, *COO*
Mary Lawler, *COO*
◆ EMP: 25 EST: 1978
SQ FT: 100,000
SALES (est): 57.5MM **Privately Held**
WEB: www.hessperssonestates.com
SIC: 2084 Wines
HQ: Colome Holding Ag
Hohle Gasse 4
Liebefeld BE 3097
319 703-131

(P-2618)
HUNEEUS VINTNERS LLC (PA)
Also Called: Quintessa Vinyards
1040 Main St Ste 204, NAPA (94559-2605)
P.O. Box 505, Rutherford (94573-0505)
PHONE.................707 286-2724
Agustin Huneeus, *Mng Member*
Agustin Huneeus, *Managing Prtnr*
Michael Alter, *COO*
Casey Wilmot, *Controller*
Erica Presser, *Sales Executive*
▲ EMP: 23 EST: 1999
SQ FT: 40,000
SALES (est): 9.7MM **Privately Held**
WEB: www.huneeuswines.com
SIC: 2084 Wines

(P-2619)
HUSCH VINEYARDS INC (PA)
4400 Highway 128, Philo (95466-9476)
P.O. Box 189, Talmage (95481-0189)
PHONE.................707 895-3216
Zac Robinson, *President*
Richard Robinson, *President*
Al White, *Finance Mgr*
Chris Baral, *Natl Sales Mgr*
Margaret Pickens, *Sales Staff*
EMP: 30 EST: 1979
SALES (est): 5.5MM **Privately Held**
WEB: www.huschvineyards.com
SIC: 2084 0172 Wines; grapes

(P-2620)
INGLENOOK
1991 St Helena Hwy, Rutherford (94573)
PHONE.................707 968-1100
Francis Ford Coppola, *Principal*
Norma Villegas, *Human Res Mgr*
Cher Engelstad, *Sales Staff*
James Graves, *Maintence Staff*
Ken Wallin, *Maintence Staff*
▲ EMP: 25 EST: 2011
SALES (est): 5.2MM **Privately Held**
WEB: www.inglenook.com
SIC: 2084 Wines

(P-2621)
IRON HORSE VINEYARDS
Also Called: Vineyards and Winery
9786 Ross Station Rd, Sebastopol (95472-2179)
PHONE.................707 887-1909
Joy Sterling, *Partner*
Barry H Sterling, *Partner*
Laurence Sterling, *Partner*
Eileen Vasko, *Controller*
Munksgard David, *Plant Mgr*
▲ EMP: 35 EST: 1979
SQ FT: 19,000
SALES (est): 4.7MM **Privately Held**
WEB: www.ironhorsevineyards.com
SIC: 2084 Wines

(P-2622)
J LOHR WINERY CORPORATION (PA)
Also Called: J Lohr Viney
1000 Lenzen Ave, San Jose (95126-2739)
PHONE.................408 288-5057
Steven W Lohr, *CEO*
Jerome J Lohr, *President*
Bruce Arkley, *President*
Steve Doyle, *Vice Pres*
Craig Miller, *Vice Pres*
▲ EMP: 50 EST: 1974
SQ FT: 47,000
SALES (est): 42MM **Privately Held**
WEB: www.jlohr.com
SIC: 2084 Wines

(P-2623)
J LOHR WINERY CORPORATION
Also Called: J Lohr Warehouse
1935 S 10th St, San Jose (95112-4111)
PHONE.................408 293-1345
Albert Perez, *Branch Mgr*
EMP: 47
SALES (corp-wide): 42MM **Privately Held**
WEB: www.jlohr.com
SIC: 2084 Wines
PA: J. Lohr Winery Corporation
1000 Lenzen Ave
San Jose CA 95126
408 288-5057

(P-2624)
J PEDRONCELLI WINERY
1220 Canyon Rd, Geyserville (95441-9639)
PHONE.................707 857-3531
John A Pedroncelli, *President*
James A Pedroncelli, *Treasurer*
EMP: 33 EST: 1927
SQ FT: 25,000
SALES (est): 4.1MM **Privately Held**
WEB: www.pedroncelli.com
SIC: 2084 0172 Wine cellars, bonded: engaged in blending wines; grapes

(P-2625)
JACKSON FAMILY FARMS LLC (PA)
425 Aviation Blvd, Santa Rosa (95403-1069)
PHONE.................707 837-1000
Don Hartford,
Carolyn Wasem, *Vice Pres*
EMP: 102 EST: 1999
SALES (est): 16.4MM **Privately Held**
WEB: www.jacksonfamilywines.com
SIC: 2084 Wines

(P-2626)
JACKSON FAMILY FARMS LLC
5660 Skylane Blvd, Santa Rosa (95403-1086)
PHONE.................707 836-2047
Jeff Jackson, *Manager*
EMP: 54
SALES (corp-wide): 16.4MM **Privately Held**
WEB: www.jacksonfamilywines.com
SIC: 2084 Wines
PA: Jackson Family Farms Llc
425 Aviation Blvd
Santa Rosa CA 95403
707 837-1000

(P-2627)
JACKSON FAMILY WINES INC
1190 Kittyhawk Blvd, Santa Rosa (95403-1013)
PHONE.................707 836-2035
Barbara Banke, *President*
Leona Penning, *Executive Asst*
Ingrid Canelo, *Purchasing*
Ed Robbins, *Maintence Staff*
Denise Horn, *Director*
EMP: 21 **Privately Held**
WEB: www.kj.com
SIC: 2084 Wines
PA: Jackson Family Wines, Inc.
421 And 425 Aviation Blvd
Santa Rosa CA 95403

(P-2628)
JACKSON FAMILY WINES INC (PA)
Also Called: Vineyards of Monterey
421 And 425 Aviation Blvd, Santa Rosa (95403)
PHONE.................707 544-4000
Barbara Banke, *Director*
Don Hartford, *Vice Chairman*
Jill Palmer, *CFO*
Bill O'connor, *Exec VP*
Gayle Bartscherer, *Senior VP*
▲ EMP: 100 EST: 1987
SQ FT: 25,000
SALES (est): 280.9MM **Privately Held**
WEB: www.lacrema.com
SIC: 2084 0172 5813 Wines; grapes; wine bar

(P-2629)
JACUZZI FAMILY VINEYARDS LLC
24724 Arnold Dr, Sonoma (95476-2814)
PHONE.................707 931-7500
Frederick T Cline, *Vice Pres*
Mark Marinozzi, *Vice Pres*
Robert Hawk, *Regional Mgr*
Sarah Pons, *Admin Asst*
Chris Merino, *Planning*
▲ EMP: 25 EST: 2008
SALES (est): 5.3MM **Privately Held**
WEB: www.jacuzziwines.com
SIC: 2084 Wines

(P-2630)
JARVIS
Also Called: Jarvis Winery
2970 Monticello Rd, NAPA (94558-9615)
PHONE.................707 255-5280
William R Jarvis, *President*
William E Jarvis, *Ch of Bd*
Deanna Martinez, *CFO*
Leticia Jarvis, *Vice Pres*
David Crane, *Sales Mgr*
EMP: 30 EST: 1991
SQ FT: 45,000
SALES (est): 6.7MM **Privately Held**
WEB: www.jarviswines.com
SIC: 2084 Wines

(P-2631)
JEPSON VINEYARD LTD
Also Called: Jepson Vnyrds-Wnery-Distillery
10400 S Highway 101, Ukiah (95482)
PHONE.................707 468-8936
Robert S Jepson Jr, *Ch of Bd*
Scott Jepson, *Manager*
EMP: 15 EST: 1985
SQ FT: 13,000
SALES (est): 953.5K **Privately Held**
WEB: www.jepsonwine.com
SIC: 2084 0172 Wines; grapes

(P-2632)
JERICHO CANYON VINEYARDS LLC
3292 Old Lawley Toll Rd, Calistoga (94515-9744)
P.O. Box 996 (94515-0996)
PHONE.................707 942-9665
Dale Bleecher, *President*
Marla Bleecher, *CFO*
Nicholas Bleecher, *General Mgr*
Paul Toti, *Maintence Staff*
▲ EMP: 20 EST: 1989
SALES (est): 2.7MM **Privately Held**
WEB: www.jerichocanyonvineyard.com
SIC: 2084 Wines

(P-2633)
JESSIES GROVE WINERY
1973 W Turner Rd, Lodi (95242-9677)
P.O. Box 1406, Woodbridge (95258-1406)
PHONE.................209 368-0880
Greg Burns, *President*
Wanda Bechthold, *Vice Pres*
Lisa Brand, *Manager*
Sarah Williams, *Manager*
EMP: 22 EST: 1998
SALES (est): 3.8MM **Privately Held**
WEB: www.jessiesgrovewinery.com
SIC: 2084 Wines

(P-2634)
JORDAN VINEYARD & WINERY LP
1474 Alexander Valley Rd, Healdsburg (95448-9003)
PHONE.................707 431-5250
Jordan John, *President*
Terri Murphy, *CTO*
Lisa Mattson, *Graphic Designe*
Julie Parrish, *Controller*
Darin Kane, *Maint Spvr*
▲ EMP: 25 EST: 2011
SALES (est): 7.1MM **Privately Held**
WEB: www.jordanwinery.com
SIC: 2084 Wines

(P-2635)
JOSEPH PHELPS VINEYARDS LLC
200 Taplin Rd, Saint Helena (94574-9544)
PHONE.................707 963-2745
Bill Phelps, *Mng Member*
Kim Beto, *Vice Pres*
Jay James, *VP Sales*
Michael Lamb, *Master*
Joseph Phelps, *Mng Member*
EMP: 70 EST: 1983
SQ FT: 50,000
SALES (est): 9.2MM
SALES (corp-wide): 20MM **Privately Held**
WEB: www.josephphelps.com
SIC: 2084 Wines
PA: Stone Bridge Cellars, Inc.
200 Taplin Rd
Saint Helena CA 94574
707 963-2745

(P-2636)
JVW CORPORATION
Also Called: Jordan Vineyard & Winery
1474 Alexander Valley Rd, Healdsburg (95448-9003)
P.O. Box 878 (95448-0878)
PHONE.................707 431-5250
John Jordan, *CEO*
Thomas N Jordan Jr, *President*
◆ EMP: 75
SQ FT: 50,000
SALES (est): 19.4MM **Privately Held**
WEB: www.jordanwinery.com
SIC: 2084 0172 Wines; grapes

(P-2637)
KAUTZ VINEYARDS INC
6111 E Armstrong Rd, Lodi (95240-7224)
PHONE.................209 369-1911
John Kautz, *Owner*
Andy Tonetti, *Foreman/Supr*
EMP: 20
SQ FT: 2,062 **Privately Held**
WEB: www.ironstonevineyards.com
SIC: 2084 Wines
PA: Kautz Vineyards, Inc.
1894 6 Mile Rd
Murphys CA 95247

(P-2638)
KENDALL-JACKSON WINE ESTATES (HQ)
425 Aviation Blvd, Santa Rosa (95403-1069)
PHONE.................707 544-4000
Edward Pitlik, *CEO*
Jonathan Hollister, *President*
Jess Jackson, *President*
Jill Bartley, *CEO*
Tyler Comstock, *Treasurer*
EMP: 275 EST: 1995
SQ FT: 10,000
SALES (est): 148.6MM **Privately Held**
WEB: www.jacksonfamilywines.com
SIC: 2084 Wines

▲ = Import ▼ = Export
◆ = Import/Export

(P-2639)
KENEFICK RANCHES LLC
2200 Pickett Rd, Calistoga (94515-1805)
PHONE...................707 942-6175
Thomas Kenefick, *Mng Member*
Chris Kenefick, *Vice Pres*
Rosalie McDonough, *Marketing Staff*
EMP: 25 **EST:** 1981
SALES (est): 5MM **Privately Held**
WEB: www.kenefickranch.com
SIC: 2084 7389 Wines;

(P-2640)
KIEU HOANG WINERY LLC
1285 Dealy Ln, NAPA (94559-9706)
PHONE...................707 253-1615
Kieu Hoang,
Tommy Hoang, *Vice Pres*
Ian Scally, *General Mgr*
Al Ho, *Purch Mgr*
Taryn Imrie, *Sales Associate*
EMP: 19 **EST:** 2014
SALES (est): 9.5MM **Privately Held**
WEB: www.kieuhoangwinery.com
SIC: 2084 Wines

(P-2641)
KOSTA BROWNE WINES LLC
Also Called: Kosta Browne Winery
220 Morris St, Sebastopol (95472-3801)
P.O. Box 1959 (95473-1959)
PHONE...................707 823-7430
Kosta Browne, *Office Mgr*
Britt Clyde, *Marketing Mgr*
Kate Noble, *Sales Staff*
Regina Sanz, *Director*
Ben Diaz, *Associate*
▲ **EMP:** 29 **EST:** 2001
SALES (est): 2.9MM **Privately Held**
WEB: www.kostabrowne.com
SIC: 2084 Wines

(P-2642)
KUNDE ENTERPRISES INC
Also Called: Kunde Estate Winery
9825 Sonoma Hwy, Kenwood (95452)
P.O. Box 639 (95452-0639)
PHONE...................707 833-5501
Don Chase, *President*
▲ **EMP:** 60 **EST:** 1989
SQ FT: 15,000
SALES (est): 6.8MM **Privately Held**
WEB: www.kunde.com
SIC: 2084 Wines

(P-2643)
L FOPPIANO WINE CO
Also Called: Foppiano Vineyards
12707 Old Redwood Hwy, Healdsburg (95448-9241)
P.O. Box 606 (95448-0606)
PHONE...................707 433-2736
Louis J Foppiano, *President*
Joseph Naujokas, *Executive*
Kourtney Nieblas, *Office Mgr*
Katie Burwell, *Office Admin*
Heidi Numainville, *Finance Mgr*
▲ **EMP:** 35 **EST:** 1896
SQ FT: 140,000
SALES (est): 5.7MM **Privately Held**
WEB: www.foppiano.com
SIC: 2084 Wines

(P-2644)
LADERA VINEYARDS LLC
150 White Cottage Rd S, Angwin (94508-9615)
P.O. Box 313, Saint Helena (94574-0313)
PHONE...................707 965-2445
Patrick L Stotesbery,
Chris Artley, *COO*
Carolyn Stotesbery, *Lab Dir*
Gordon Waggoner, *Technician*
Dan Stotesbery, *Natl Sales Mgr*
▲ **EMP:** 51 **EST:** 1998
SALES (est): 3.4MM **Privately Held**
WEB: www.laderavineyards.com
SIC: 2084 Wines

(P-2645)
LADERA WINERY LLC
Also Called: Chateau Woltner
150 White Cottage Rd S, Angwin (94508-9615)
P.O. Box 313, Saint Helena (94574-0313)
PHONE...................707 965-2445
Patrick L Stotesbery, *Mng Member*
Brenda Bullington, *Vice Pres*
Christopher Rye,
▲ **EMP:** 30 **EST:** 1998
SALES (est): 3.6MM **Privately Held**
WEB: www.laderavineyards.com
SIC: 2084 Wines

(P-2646)
LAGUNA OAKS VNYARDS WINERY INC
Also Called: Balletto Vineyards
5700 Occidental Rd, Santa Rosa (95401-5533)
P.O. Box 2579, Sebastopol (95473-2579)
PHONE...................707 568-2455
John G Balletto, *President*
Teresa M Balleto, *Vice Pres*
Debbie Donaldson, *Sales Staff*
Ashley Kikenny, *Sales Staff*
Monica Hunter, *Manager*
▲ **EMP:** 42 **EST:** 1999
SQ FT: 9,600
SALES (est): 7.8MM **Privately Held**
WEB: www.ballettovineyards.com
SIC: 2084 Wines

(P-2647)
LAIRD FAMILY ESTATE LLC (PA)
5055 Solano Ave, NAPA (94558-1326)
PHONE...................707 257-0360
Rebecca A Laird, *Mng Member*
Pamela Ford, *Sales Staff*
Gail Laird,
Ken Laird, *Mng Member*
Chris Andrews, *Director*
▲ **EMP:** 20 **EST:** 1998
SQ FT: 64,000
SALES (est): 14.1MM **Privately Held**
WEB: www.lairdfamilyestate.com
SIC: 2084 Wines

(P-2648)
LANGETWINS INC
1298 E Jahant Rd, Acampo (95220)
PHONE...................209 339-4055
Randy Lange, *President*
Brad Lange, *CFO*
Charlene Lange, *Vice Pres*
Susan Lange, *Admin Sec*
Alyssa Drake, *Business Mgr*
EMP: 36 **EST:** 1970
SALES (est): 3MM **Privately Held**
WEB: www.langetwins.com
SIC: 2084 Wines

(P-2649)
LANGETWINS WINE COMPANY INC
Also Called: Langetwins Winery & Vineyards
1525 E Jahant Rd, Acampo (95220-9187)
PHONE...................209 334-9780
Marissa Lange, *President*
Aaron Lange, *CFO*
Kendra Altnow, *Vice Pres*
Philip Lange, *Admin Sec*
Joseph Lange, *Asst Sec*
EMP: 22 **EST:** 2005
SALES (est): 20MM **Privately Held**
WEB: www.langetwins.com
SIC: 2084 Wines

(P-2650)
LANGTRY FARMS LLC
21000 Butts Canyon Rd, Middletown (95461-9606)
PHONE...................707 987-2772
Eason Manson, *Mng Member*
Chuck Doty, *President*
EMP: 15 **EST:** 2007
SALES (est): 3MM **Privately Held**
WEB: www.langtryfarms.com
SIC: 2084 Wines, brandy & brandy spirits

(P-2651)
LAVA SPRINGS INC
Also Called: Lava Cap Winery
2221 Fruitridge Rd, Placerville (95667-3700)
PHONE...................530 621-0175
Thomas D Jones, *President*
Jeanne H Jones, *Chairman*
Kevin Jones, *Mktg Dir*
Danny Mantle, *Sales Staff*
Kassidy Kosmata,
▲ **EMP:** 30 **EST:** 1981
SQ FT: 18,000
SALES (est): 4.4MM **Privately Held**
WEB: www.lavacap.com
SIC: 2084 Wines

(P-2652)
MACCHIA INC
7099 E Peltier Rd, Acampo (95220-9605)
PHONE...................209 333-2600
Tim Holdener, *President*
Tanya McMahan, *General Mgr*
EMP: 15 **EST:** 2007
SALES (est): 1.6MM **Privately Held**
WEB: www.macchiawines.com
SIC: 2084 Wines

(P-2653)
MAGITO & COMPANY LLC
1446 Industrial Ave, Sebastopol (95472-4848)
PHONE...................707 567-1521
Tom Meadowcroft,
▼ **EMP:** 17 **EST:** 2004
SALES (est): 1.2MM **Privately Held**
SIC: 2084 Wines

(P-2654)
MALLARD HOLDCO LLC (PA)
1201 Dowdell Ln, Saint Helena (94574-1416)
PHONE...................707 302-2658
Alex Ryan, *Ch of Bd*
EMP: 33 **EST:** 2016
SALES (est): 336.6MM **Privately Held**
SIC: 2084 Wines, brandy & brandy spirits

(P-2655)
MATANZAS CREEK WINERY
6097 Bennett Valley Rd, Santa Rosa (95404-8570)
PHONE...................707 528-6464
Jeff Jackson, *President*
▲ **EMP:** 16 **EST:** 1977
SQ FT: 20,000
SALES (est): 1.3MM **Privately Held**
WEB: www.matanzascreek.com
SIC: 2084 0172 Wine cellars, bonded: engaged in blending wines; grapes

(P-2656)
MCMANIS FAMILY VINEYARDS INC
18700 E River Rd, Ripon (95366-9711)
PHONE...................209 599-1186
Ronald W McManis, *Administration*
Tary Salinger, *CIO*
Ed Bianchi, *Opers Mgr*
▲ **EMP:** 21 **EST:** 2014
SALES (est): 5.4MM **Privately Held**
WEB: www.mcmanisfamilyvineyards.com
SIC: 2084 Wines

(P-2657)
MCNAB RIDGE WINERY LLC
2350 Mcnab Ranch Rd, Ukiah (95482-9350)
PHONE...................707 462-2423
John A Parducci, *Mng Member*
Willard A Carle,
Richard M Lawson,
EMP: 19 **EST:** 1999
SALES (est): 1.9MM **Privately Held**
WEB: www.mcnabridge.com
SIC: 2084 Wines

(P-2658)
MEREDITH VINEYARD ESTATE INC
Also Called: Merry Edwards Wines
636 Gold Ridge Rd, Sebastopol (95472-3932)
PHONE...................707 823-7466
Merideth Edwards, *CEO*
Richard Privet, *Ch of Bd*
Einer Sunde, *Treasurer*
Nick Abudi, *Technician*
Ken Lerch, *Associate*
EMP: 15 **EST:** 1997
SALES (est): 2.5MM **Privately Held**
WEB: www.merryedwards.com
SIC: 2084 Wines

(P-2659)
MERRYVALE VINEYARDS LLC
Also Called: Starmont Winery
1000 Main St, Saint Helena (94574-2011)
PHONE...................707 963-2225
Rene Schlatter, *President*
Mark Evans, *COO*
Kevin Bersofsky, *CFO*
Glenn Ochsner, *CPA*
Craig Cooper, *Facilities Mgr*
◆ **EMP:** 40 **EST:** 1983
SQ FT: 30,850
SALES (est): 9.9MM **Privately Held**
WEB: www.merryvale.com
SIC: 2084 0172 Wines; grapes

(P-2660)
MICHEL-SCHLMBERGER PARTNERS LP
Also Called: Michel-Schlmbrger Fine Wine Es
4155 Wine Creek Rd, Healdsburg (95448-9112)
PHONE...................707 433-7427
Jacques Schlumberger, *General Ptnr*
Hana Michaelson, *Sales Staff*
William Kissel, *Manager*
◆ **EMP:** 17 **EST:** 1979
SQ FT: 20,000
SALES (est): 1.7MM **Privately Held**
WEB: www.michelschlumberger.com
SIC: 2084 Wines

(P-2661)
MPL BRANDS INC (PA)
71 Liberty Ship Way, Sausalito (94965-1731)
PHONE...................888 513-3022
Michael Patane, *CEO*
EMP: 40 **EST:** 2016
SQ FT: 5,000
SALES (est): 8.7MM **Privately Held**
WEB: www.mplbrands.com
SIC: 2084 Wines, brandy & brandy spirits

(P-2662)
MUNSELLE VINEYARDS LLC
3660 Highway 128, Geyserville (95441-9432)
P.O. Box 617 (95441-0617)
PHONE...................707 857-9988
Reta Munselle, *Mng Member*
Gretchen Crebs, *Marketing Staff*
Bret Munselle, *Manager*
EMP: 15 **EST:** 2011
SALES (est): 1MM **Privately Held**
WEB: www.munsellevineyards.com
SIC: 2084 Wines

(P-2663)
NAPA SELECT VINEYARD SERVI
5 Financial Plz Ste 200, NAPA (94558-6419)
PHONE...................707 294-2637
Jason Ray, *President*
EMP: 17 **EST:** 2017
SALES (est): 2.4MM **Privately Held**
WEB: www.sterlingvineyards.com
SIC: 2084 Wines

(P-2664)
NAPA WINE COMPANY LLC
7830 St Helena Hwy 40, Oakville (94562-9200)
P.O. Box 434 (94562-0434)
PHONE...................707 944-8669
Rob Lawson,
Russ Joy, *General Mgr*
Kendall Hoxsey, *Business Mgr*
Kendall Hoxsey-Onysko, *Business Mgr*
Mark Solorio, *Opers Staff*
▲ **EMP:** 35 **EST:** 1993
SQ FT: 100,000
SALES (est): 5.7MM **Privately Held**
WEB: www.napawineco.com
SIC: 2084 Wines; wine cellars, bonded: engaged in blending wines

(P-2665)
NAVARRO WINERY
Also Called: Navarro Vineyard
5601 Highway 128, Philo (95466-9513)
P.O. Box 47 (95466-0047)
PHONE...................707 895-3686
Edward T Bennett, *Partner*
Deborah S Cahn, *Partner*
Ted Bennett, *CFO*

2084 - Wine & Brandy County (P-2666)

PRODUCTS & SERVICES SECTION

Martel Duvigneaud, *Sr Software Eng*
Val Doran, *Manager*
▲ **EMP:** 31 **EST:** 1974
SQ FT: 10,000
SALES (est): 5.7MM **Privately Held**
WEB: www.navarrowine.com
SIC: 2084 0172 5921 Wine cellars, bonded: engaged in blending wines; grapes; wine

(P-2666)
NELSON & SONS INC
Also Called: Nelson Family Vineyard
550 Nelson Ranch Rd, Ukiah (95482-9316)
PHONE................................707 462-3755
Gregory Nelson, *President*
Christopher Nelson, *Vice Pres*
Tyler Nelson, *Vice Pres*
EMP: 34 **EST:** 1932
SALES (est): 3MM **Privately Held**
WEB: www.nelsonfamilyvineyards.com
SIC: 2084 0172 Wines; grapes

(P-2667)
NEW VAVIN INC
Also Called: Ehlers Estate
3222 Ehlers Ln, Saint Helena (94574-9657)
PHONE................................707 963-5972
Kelly McElearney, *General Mgr*
Matt Alfaro, *Sales Associate*
Andy Bartee, *Sales Staff*
Rebecca Martin, *Director*
Maureen Key, *Receptionist*
▲ **EMP:** 20 **EST:** 1980
SALES (est): 2.9MM **Privately Held**
SIC: 2084 Wines

(P-2668)
NEWTON VINEYARD LLC (DH)
1040 Main St Ste 204, NAPA (94559-2605)
P.O. Box 540, Saint Helena (94574-5040)
PHONE................................707 204-7423
Peter L Newton,
Rosa Sandoval, *Personnel*
Russell J Bollman,
Dr Su Hua Newton,
▲ **EMP:** 40 **EST:** 1979
SALES (est): 21.2MM
SALES (corp-wide): 419.1MM **Privately Held**
WEB: www.newtonvineyard.com
SIC: 2084 0172 Wines; grapes
HQ: Moet Hennessy
Moet Hennessy Estates & Wines 24 A 32
Paris 75008
144 132-222

(P-2669)
NIEBAM-CPPOLA ESTATE WINERY LP
Also Called: Cafe Niebaum Coppola
916 Kearny St, San Francisco (94133-5107)
PHONE................................415 291-1700
Krista Voisin, *Manager*
EMP: 50 **Privately Held**
WEB: www.inglenook.com
SIC: 2084 Wines
PA: Niebaum-Coppola Estate Winery, L.P.
1991 St Helena Hwy
Rutherford CA 94573

(P-2670)
NIEBAM-CPPOLA ESTATE WINERY LP (PA)
1991 St Helena Hwy, Rutherford (94573)
P.O. Box 208 (94573-0208)
PHONE................................707 968-1100
Gordon Wang, *CFO*
Niebaum-Coppola Estate Winery, *General Ptnr*
The Coppola Family Trust, *Ltd Ptnr*
American Zoetrope, *Ltd Ptnr*
Earl Martin, *President*
◆ **EMP:** 150 **EST:** 1992
SALES (est): 26MM **Privately Held**
WEB: www.inglenook.com
SIC: 2084 Wines

(P-2671)
NZ WINERY DIRECT LLC (PA)
235 Montgomery St Fl 30, San Francisco (94104-3117)
PHONE................................844 569-9463
EMP: 21 **EST:** 2018
SALES (est): 286.8K **Privately Held**
SIC: 2084 Wines

(P-2672)
OAK RIDGE WINERY LLC
6100 E Hwy 12 Victor Rd, Lodi (95240)
PHONE................................209 369-4768
Rudy Maggio,
Heather Casity, *CFO*
Raquel Casity, *CFO*
Jason Allen, *Officer*
Stephen Merritt, *Vice Pres*
◆ **EMP:** 50 **EST:** 2002
SALES (est): 10.9MM **Privately Held**
WEB: www.oakridgewinery.com
SIC: 2084 Wines

(P-2673)
ONE TRUE VINE LLC (PA)
Also Called: Cherry Pie
1050 Adams St Ste A, Saint Helena (94574-1103)
PHONE................................707-967-9398
Jayson B Woodbridge,
Christopher V Radomski, *Mng Member*
▲ **EMP:** 26 **EST:** 2003
SALES (est): 1.2MM **Privately Held**
WEB: www.onetruevine.com
SIC: 2084 Wines, brandy & brandy spirits

(P-2674)
OPAL MOON WINERY LLC
21660 8th St E Ste A, Sonoma (95476-2828)
PHONE................................707 996-0420
John Bambury,
EMP: 15 **EST:** 2011
SQ FT: 30,000
SALES (est): 1.2MM **Privately Held**
WEB: www.opalmooncrush.com
SIC: 2084 Wines

(P-2675)
OPUS ONE WINERY LLC (PA)
7900 St Helena Hwy, Oakville (94562)
P.O. Box 6 (94562-0006)
PHONE................................707-944-9442
Christopher Lynch, *CEO*
David Pearson, *CEO*
Robert Fowles, *CFO*
Roger Asleson, *Vice Pres*
Christopher Barefoot, *Vice Pres*
◆ **EMP:** 75 **EST:** 1979
SQ FT: 85,000
SALES (est): 24.5MM **Privately Held**
WEB: www.opusonewinery.com
SIC: 2084 Wines

(P-2676)
OZEKI SAKE (USA) INC (HQ)
249 Hillcrest Rd, Hollister (95023-4921)
PHONE................................831 637-9217
Bunjiro Osabe, *Ch of Bd*
Norio Sumomogi, *Treasurer*
Masaru Ogihara, *Vice Pres*
Ruth Reid, *Office Mgr*
Daisaku Tsubota, *Marketing Mgr*
▲ **EMP:** 25 **EST:** 1979
SQ FT: 22,000
SALES (est): 13.9MM **Privately Held**
WEB: www.ozekisake.com
SIC: 2084 Wines

(P-2677)
PAN MAGNA GROUP
Also Called: Domaine St George Winery
1141 Grant Ave, Healdsburg (95448-9570)
P.O. Box 548 (95448-0548)
PHONE................................707 433-5508
Somchai Likitprakong, *Principal*
EMP: 30
SQ FT: 1,237
SALES (corp-wide): 3.3MM **Privately Held**
SIC: 2084 0172 Wines; grapes
PA: Pan Magna Group
350 Sansome St Ste 1010
San Francisco CA
415 394-7244

(P-2678)
PARDUCCI WINE ESTATES LLC
Also Called: Mendicino Wine Company
501 Parducci Rd, Ukiah (95482-3015)
PHONE................................707 463-5350
Carl Thoma,
Thomas Thornhill, *Managing Prtnr*
Tom Thornhill, *Managing Prtnr*
Brendan Jin, *District Mgr*
Lisa Lambertus, *Division Mgr*
▲ **EMP:** 35 **EST:** 1986
SALES (est): 5.4MM **Privately Held**
WEB: www.mendocinowineco.com
SIC: 2084 Wines

(P-2679)
PEJU PROVINCE WINERY A CA LTD
8466 Saint Helena Hwy, Rutherford (94573)
P.O. Box 478 (94573-0478)
PHONE................................800 446-7358
Anthony Peju, *Partner*
Herta Peju, *Partner*
Oren Lewin, *General Mgr*
Oma Hackett, *Office Admin*
Christine Lilienthal, *Marketing Staff*
▲ **EMP:** 95 **EST:** 1983
SQ FT: 50,000
SALES (est): 20.7MM **Privately Held**
WEB: www.peju.com
SIC: 5921 2084 Wine; wines

(P-2680)
PERNOD RICARD USA LLC
Also Called: Kenwood Vineyards
9592 Sonoma Hwy, Kenwood (95452-8028)
P.O. Box 669 (95452-0669)
PHONE................................707 833-5891
EMP: 75
SQ FT: 1,414
SALES (corp-wide): 224.6MM **Privately Held**
WEB: www.pernod-ricard-usa.com
SIC: 2084 0172 Wines; grapes
HQ: Pernod Ricard Usa, Llc
250 Park Ave Ste 17a
New York NY 10177
212 372-5400

(P-2681)
PERNOD RICARD USA LLC
Also Called: Mumm NAPA Valley
8445 Silverado Trl, Rutherford (94573)
PHONE................................707 967-7770
Samuel Bronfman II, *Branch Mgr*
Ronald Lee, *Manager*
EMP: 65
SALES (corp-wide): 224.6MM **Privately Held**
WEB: www.pernod-ricard-usa.com
SIC: 2084 Wines
HQ: Pernod Ricard Usa, Llc
250 Park Ave Ste 17a
New York NY 10177
212 372-5400

(P-2682)
PETALUMAIDENCE OPCO LLC
Also Called: Vineyard Post Acute
101 Monroe St, Petaluma (94954-2328)
PHONE................................707 763-4109
Jason Murray, *Principal*
Mark Hancock, *Principal*
Lisa Laborte, *Human Res Dir*
EMP: 124 **EST:** 2016
SALES (est): 11.7MM **Privately Held**
WEB: www.vineyardpostacute.com
SIC: 2084 8051 Wines; skilled nursing care facilities

(P-2683)
PINE RIDGE WINERY LLC (HQ)
Also Called: Pine Ridge Vineyards
5901 Silverado Trl, NAPA (94558-9417)
P.O. Box 2508, Yountville (94599-2508)
PHONE................................707 253-7500
Michael Beaulac,
Winnie St John, *Controller*
Ian M Cumming,
Joseph A Orlando,
Joseph S Stienbert,
◆ **EMP:** 78 **EST:** 1978
SQ FT: 17,000
SALES (est): 13MM
SALES (corp-wide): 64.1MM **Publicly Held**
WEB: www.pineridgevineyards.com
SIC: 2084 5812 0172 Wines; eating places; grapes
PA: Crimson Wine Group, Ltd.
5901 Silverado Trl
Napa CA 94558
800 486-0503

(P-2684)
PINE RIDGE WINERY LLC
Also Called: Seghesio Family Vineyards
700 Grove St, Healdsburg (95448-4753)
PHONE................................707 260-0330
EMP: 22
SALES (corp-wide): 64.1MM **Publicly Held**
WEB: www.pineridgevineyards.com
SIC: 2084 Wines
HQ: Pine Ridge Winery, Llc
5901 Silverado Trl
Napa CA 94558
707 253-7500

(P-2685)
PJK WINERY LLC
Also Called: Quivira Vineyards
4900 W Dry Creek Rd, Healdsburg (95448-9721)
PHONE................................707 431-8333
Pete Kight, *Mng Member*
Vikki Tola, *Manager*
EMP: 25 **EST:** 1981
SQ FT: 5,400
SALES (est): 2.8MM **Privately Held**
SIC: 2084 Wines

(P-2686)
PLC LLC
Also Called: McNab Ridge Winery
2350 Mcnab Ranch Rd, Ukiah (95482-9350)
PHONE................................707 462-2423
John Parducci, *Mng Member*
Jen Petrey, *Marketing Staff*
Bill Carle,
EMP: 19 **EST:** 1999
SQ FT: 30,000
SALES (est): 1.2MM **Privately Held**
WEB: www.mcnabridge.com
SIC: 2084 Wines

(P-2687)
PRESTON VINEYARDS INC
Also Called: Preston Vineyards & Winery
9282 W Dry Creek Rd, Healdsburg (95448-9134)
PHONE................................707 433-3372
Louis Preston, *President*
Susan Preston, *Vice Pres*
Ken Blair, *Sales Dir*
Matthew Wells, *Director*
Matt Norelli, *Manager*
EMP: 15 **EST:** 1973
SALES (est): 1.8MM **Privately Held**
WEB: www.prestonfarmandwinery.com
SIC: 2084 5812 5182 Wines; eating places; wine

(P-2688)
PROVENANCE VINEYARDS
1695 Saint Helena Hwy S, Saint Helena (94574-9777)
P.O. Box 688, Rutherford (94573-0688)
PHONE................................707 968-3633
Tom Rinaldi, *Owner*
Chad Hathaway, *Maintence Staff*
▲ **EMP:** 24 **EST:** 1999
SALES (est): 5.6MM **Privately Held**
WEB: www.provenancevineyards.com
SIC: 2084 Wines
HQ: Treasury Wine Estates Americas Company
555 Gateway Dr
Napa CA 94558
707 259-4500

(P-2689)
PURPLE WINE COMPANY
Also Called: Purple Wines
625 2nd St, Petaluma (94952-5119)
P.O. Box 390, Graton (95444-0390)
PHONE................................707 829-6100
Derek Benham, *Mng Member*

▲ = Import ▼=Export
◆ =Import/Export

PRODUCTS & SERVICES SECTION
2084 - Wine & Brandy County (P-2713)

John Gause, *Info Tech Mgr*
Robin Nehasil, *Controller*
Jim Reed, *Opers Staff*
David Seide, *VP Sales*
▲ **EMP:** 160 **EST:** 2004
SALES (est): 18.9MM **Privately Held**
SIC: 2084 Wine cellars, bonded: engaged in blending wines; wines

(P-2690)
QUADY LLC (PA)
13181 Road 24, Madera (93637-9087)
P.O. Box 728 (93639-0728)
PHONE.................559 673-8068
Andrew Quady, *CEO*
Laurel Quady, *CFO*
EMP: 21 **EST:** 2011
SQ FT: 16,000
SALES (est): 5.7MM **Privately Held**
WEB: www.quadywinery.com
SIC: 2084 Wines

(P-2691)
QUADY WINERY INC
13181 Road 24, Madera (93637-9087)
P.O. Box 728 (93639-0728)
PHONE.................559 673-8068
Andrew K Quady, *President*
Andrew Quady, *President*
Laurel Quady, *Vice Pres*
Dave Glover, *Info Tech Mgr*
Dan Mejia, *Prdtn Mgr*
EMP: 16 **EST:** 1979
SQ FT: 16,000
SALES (est): 3.3MM **Privately Held**
WEB: www.quadywinery.com
SIC: 2084 Wines

(P-2692)
RAMS GATE WINERY LLC
28700 Arnold Dr, Sonoma (95476-9700)
PHONE.................707 721-8700
Jeffrey O'Neill, *Mng Member*
Michael J John,
Peter Mullin,
Paul Violich,
Shannon Rosenberg, *Manager*
▲ **EMP:** 38 **EST:** 2006
SALES (est): 4.2MM **Privately Held**
WEB: www.ramsgatewinery.com
SIC: 2084 Wines

(P-2693)
RB WINE ASSOCIATES LLC
Also Called: Rack & Riddle
499 Moore Ln, Healdsburg (95448-4825)
P.O. Box 2400 (95448-2400)
PHONE.................707 433-8400
Bruce Lundquist,
Mark Garaventa, *Managing Prtnr*
Kathy Dogali, *Admin Asst*
Penny Gadd-Coster, *CIO*
Manveer Sandhu, *CIO*
EMP: 80 **EST:** 2007
SQ FT: 100,000
SALES (est): 11MM **Privately Held**
WEB: www.rackandriddle.com
SIC: 2084 Wines

(P-2694)
REGUSCI VINEYARD MGT INC
Also Called: Regusci Winery
5584 Silverado Trl, NAPA (94558-9411)
PHONE.................707 254-0403
James Regusci, *President*
Randy Kingsford, *CFO*
Diana Regusci, *Vice Pres*
EMP: 30 **EST:** 1995
SALES (est): 6MM **Privately Held**
WEB: www.regusciwinery.com
SIC: 2084 0762 Wines; vineyard management & maintenance services

(P-2695)
RHYS VINEYARDS LLC
11715 Skyline Blvd, Los Gatos (95033-9588)
PHONE.................650 419-2050
Kevin Harvey,
Eric Sothern, *Sales Dir*
Javier Meza,
Efrocino Mendoza, *Manager*
▲ **EMP:** 34 **EST:** 2010
SALES (est): 3.5MM **Privately Held**
WEB: www.rhysvineyards.com
SIC: 2084 Wines

(P-2696)
RIOS-LOVELL ESTATE WINERY
Also Called: Rios-Lovell Winery
6500 Tesla Rd, Livermore (94550-9123)
PHONE.................925 443-0434
Max Rios, *Partner*
Katie Lovell, *Partner*
EMP: 20 **EST:** 1994
SALES (est): 2.2MM **Privately Held**
WEB: www.rioslovellwinery.com
SIC: 2084 Wines

(P-2697)
ROBERT MONDAVI CORPORATION (HQ)
166 Gateway Rd E, NAPA (94558-7576)
P.O. Box 407, Rutherford (94573-0407)
PHONE.................707 967-2100
Gregory Evans, *President*
Gregory M Evans, *President*
Henry J Salvo Jr, *CFO*
Timothy J Mondavi, *Vice Ch Bd*
▲ **EMP:** 75 **EST:** 1966
SQ FT: 5,000
SALES (est): 65MM
SALES (corp-wide): 8.6B **Publicly Held**
WEB: www.robertmondaviwinery.com
SIC: 2084 Wines
PA: Constellation Brands, Inc.
207 High Point Dr # 100
Victor NY 14564
585 678-7100

(P-2698)
ROBERT MONDAVI CORPORATION
770 N Guild Ave, Lodi (95240-0861)
PHONE.................209 365-2995
Rick Anderson, *Manager*
EMP: 844
SALES (corp-wide): 8.6B **Publicly Held**
WEB: www.robertmondaviwinery.com
SIC: 2084 Wines
HQ: The Robert Mondavi Corporation
166 Gateway Rd E
Napa CA 94558
707 967-2100

(P-2699)
ROBERT MONDAVI WINERY
7801 St Helena Hwy, Oakville (94562)
PHONE.................707 738-5727
EMP: 23 **EST:** 2017
SALES (est): 3.8MM **Privately Held**
WEB: www.robertmondaviwinery.com
SIC: 2084 Wines

(P-2700)
ROBERT YOUNG FAMILY LTD PARTNR
Also Called: Robert Young Vineyards
4950 Red Winery Rd, Geyserville (95441-9573)
PHONE.................707 433-3228
Robert Young, *Partner*
Susan Sheehy, *Partner*
Fred Young, *Partner*
James Young, *Partner*
Joann Young, *Partner*
EMP: 20 **EST:** 1997
SQ FT: 5,078
SALES (est): 2.6MM **Privately Held**
WEB: www.ryew.com
SIC: 2084 Wines

(P-2701)
ROCK WALL WINE COMPANY INC
2301 Monarch St, Alameda (94501-7554)
PHONE.................510 522-5700
Kent Rosenblum, *CEO*
Jessica Sanders, *Accountant*
Angela Lemcke, *Controller*
EMP: 20 **EST:** 2008
SQ FT: 200
SALES (est): 3.2MM **Privately Held**
WEB: www.rockwallwines.com
SIC: 2084 Wines

(P-2702)
ROMBAUER VINEYARDS INC (PA)
3522 Silverado Trl N, Saint Helena (94574-9663)
PHONE.................707 963-5170
Koerner Rombauer, *President*
Matthew Owings, *COO*
Lynn Sletto, *Vice Pres*
Roberta Flinn, *Finance*
Alan Cannon, *Natl Sales Mgr*
◆ **EMP:** 52 **EST:** 1980
SQ FT: 25,000
SALES (est): 35.9MM **Privately Held**
WEB: www.rombauer.com
SIC: 2084 Wines

(P-2703)
ROUND HILL CELLARS
Also Called: Rutherford Wine Company
1680 Silverado Trl S, Saint Helena (94574-9542)
P.O. Box 387, Rutherford (94573-0387)
PHONE.................707 968-3200
Marko B Zaninovich, *President*
Theo Zaninovich, *Principal*
Keith Lavine, *General Mgr*
Sierra Macintyre, *Marketing Staff*
Bob Browne, *Sales Staff*
▼ **EMP:** 55 **EST:** 1978
SQ FT: 31,000
SALES (est): 10.5MM **Privately Held**
WEB: www.rutherfordranch.com
SIC: 2084 Wines

(P-2704)
RUDD WINES INC (PA)
Also Called: Rudd Winery
500 Oakville Xrd, Oakville (94562)
P.O. Box 105 (94562-0105)
PHONE.................707 944-8577
Leslei Rudd, *President*
Mason Garrity, *COO*
Karen Trippe, *Director*
Brian Hong-Yee, *Manager*
Erica Kincaid, *Manager*
▲ **EMP:** 20 **EST:** 1996
SALES (est): 3.5MM **Privately Held**
WEB: www.ruddwines.com
SIC: 2084 Wines

(P-2705)
RUSSIAN RIVER WINERY INC
2191 Laguna Rd, Santa Rosa (95401-3705)
PHONE.................707 824-2005
Courtney M Benham, *CEO*
EMP: 26 **EST:** 2003
SQ FT: 76,000
SALES (est): 1.4MM **Privately Held**
WEB: www.martinraywinery.com
SIC: 2084 Wines

(P-2706)
SAINT FRNCIS WINERY TASTING RM
Also Called: Saint Frncis Winery Tasting Rm
500 Pythian Rd, Santa Rosa (95409-6545)
PHONE.................707 833-4666
EMP: 41
SALES (corp-wide): 437K **Privately Held**
WEB: www.stfranciswinery.com
SIC: 2084 Wines
PA: Saint Francis Winery Tasting Room
100 Pythian Rd
Camarillo CA 93012
707 833-4668

(P-2707)
SAINTSBURY LLC
1500 Los Carneros Ave, NAPA (94559-9742)
PHONE.................707 252-0592
Richard Ward, *General Mgr*
Dick Ward, *Info Tech Mgr*
Heather Vance, *Accountant*
Lisa Stuijvenberg, *Controller*
Lisa Van Stuijvenberg, *Controller*
EMP: 18 **EST:** 1981
SQ FT: 32,500
SALES (est): 2.4MM **Privately Held**
WEB: www.saintsbury.com
SIC: 2084 Wines

(P-2708)
SAN BERNABE VINEYARDS LLC
12001 S Highway 99, Manteca (95336-8499)
PHONE.................209 824-3501
Delicato Vineyards, *Principal*
▼ **EMP:** 16 **EST:** 2001
SALES (est): 760.2K **Privately Held**
WEB: www.dfvtastingroom.com
SIC: 2084 Wines

(P-2709)
SAVANNAH CHANELLE VINEYARDS
Also Called: Mariani Winery
23600 Big Basin Way, Saratoga (95070-9755)
PHONE.................301 758-2338
Michael Ballard, *President*
Kellie Ballard, *CFO*
EMP: 20 **EST:** 1992
SALES (est): 2.8MM **Privately Held**
WEB: www.savannahchanelle.com
SIC: 2084 5812 0172 Wines; eating places; grapes

(P-2710)
SBRAGIA FAMILY VINEYARDS LLC
9990 Dry Creek Rd, Geyserville (95441-9686)
PHONE.................707 473-2992
Edward Sbargia, *Mng Member*
Adam Sbragia, *Director*
Peggy Lord, *Manager*
EMP: 25 **EST:** 2006
SALES (est): 5.1MM **Privately Held**
WEB: www.sbragia.com
SIC: 2084 Wines

(P-2711)
SEBASTIANI VINEYARDS INC
Also Called: Sebastiani Vineyards & Winery
389 4th St E, Sonoma (95476-5790)
PHONE.................707 933-3200
Mary Ann Sebastiani Cuneo, *CEO*
Richard Cuneo, *Ch of Bd*
Emma Swain, *COO*
Paul Bergena, *Exec VP*
Omar Percich, *Controller*
◆ **EMP:** 100 **EST:** 1972
SQ FT: 2,000
SALES (est): 16.3MM
SALES (corp-wide): 81.2MM **Privately Held**
WEB: www.sebastiani.com
SIC: 2084 Wines
HQ: Foley Family Wines, Inc.
200 Concourse Blvd
Santa Rosa CA 95403

(P-2712)
SEGHESIO WINERIES INC
Also Called: Seghesio Winery
700 Grove St, Healdsburg (95448-4753)
PHONE.................707 433-3579
Eugene Peter Seghesio, *CEO*
Amy Seghesio, *Treasurer*
Raymond Seghesio, *Vice Pres*
Edward H Seghesio Jr, *Admin Sec*
Stephanie Friedman, *Director*
▼ **EMP:** 20 **EST:** 1942
SQ FT: 6,000
SALES (est): 2.6MM **Privately Held**
WEB: www.seghesio.com
SIC: 2084 0172 Wines; grapes

(P-2713)
SHAFER VINEYARDS
6154 Silverado Trl, NAPA (94558-9748)
PHONE.................707 944-2877
John Shafer, *Chairman*
Elizabeth S Cafaro, *Shareholder*
Bradford J Shafer, *Shareholder*
Douglas S Shafer, *President*
Marykay Schatz, *Office Mgr*
◆ **EMP:** 17 **EST:** 1979
SQ FT: 2,000
SALES (est): 2.6MM **Privately Held**
WEB: www.shafervineyards.com
SIC: 2084 Wines

2084 - Wine & Brandy County (P-2714)

(P-2714)
SHANNON RIDGE INC
13888 Point Lakeview Rd, Lower Lake (95457-9617)
P.O. Box 279, Kelseyville (95451-0279)
PHONE..................................707 994-9656
Clay Shannon, *President*
Mark Altrecht, *CFO*
Amber Lee, *Regional Mgr*
Sheila Lapoint, *Controller*
Brian Altomari, *Natl Sales Mgr*
EMP: 20 **EST:** 2003
SALES (est): 14MM Privately Held
WEB: www.shannonfamilyofwines.com
SIC: 2084 5921 Wines; wine

(P-2715)
SIERRA SUNRISE VINEYARD INC
Also Called: Montevina Winery
20680 Shenandoah Schl Rd, Plymouth (95669-9511)
P.O. Box 248, Saint Helena (94574-0248)
PHONE..................................209 245-6942
Louis Trinchero, *Ch of Bd*
Robery Tortelson, *President*
Roger Trinchero, *CEO*
Jeff Meyers, *Vice Pres*
Vera Trinchero Torres, *Admin Sec*
EMP: 29 **EST:** 1970
SQ FT: 52,000
SALES (est): 2.3MM
SALES (corp-wide): 188.1MM Privately Held
WEB: www.montevina.com
SIC: 2084 0172 Wines; grapes
PA: Sutter Home Winery, Inc.
100 Saint Helena Hwy S
Saint Helena CA 94574
707 963-3104

(P-2716)
SILENUS VINTNERS
5225 Solano Ave, NAPA (94558-1019)
PHONE..................................707 299-3930
Bob Williamson, *Owner*
▲ **EMP:** 17 **EST:** 2010
SALES (est): 2.5MM Privately Held
WEB: www.silenuswinery.com
SIC: 2084 Wines
HQ: Henan Meijing Group Co., Ltd.
Room 1601, Torch Building B, Hi-Tech Industrial Development Area
Zhengzhou 45004
371 569-9502

(P-2717)
SILVER OAK WINE CELLARS LLC
Also Called: Alexander Valley Winery
7300 Highway 128, Healdsburg (95448-8018)
PHONE..................................707 942-7082
Timothy E Duncan, *Principal*
EMP: 26 **EST:** 2019
SALES (est): 1.3MM Privately Held
SIC: 2084 Wines

(P-2718)
SILVER OAK WINE CELLARS LLC (PA)
915 Oakville Cross Rd, Oakville (94562)
P.O. Box 414 (94562-0414)
PHONE..................................707 942-7022
David R Duncan, *Partner*
Raymond Duncan, *Partner*
Tony Leblanc, *General Mgr*
Laureen Stambaugh, *Sales Staff*
Carissa Wendt, *Sales Staff*
EMP: 15 **EST:** 1972
SALES (est): 37.9MM Privately Held
WEB: www.silveroak.com
SIC: 2084 Wines

(P-2719)
SILVERADO VINEYARDS
6121 Silverado Trl, NAPA (94558-9415)
PHONE..................................707 257-1770
Ronald W Miller, *CEO*
Ron Miller, *Owner*
Kimberli Rogers, *Partner*
Tersilla Gregory, *CFO*
Russell Weis, *Treasurer*
▲ **EMP:** 23 **EST:** 1980
SALES (est): 10.7MM
SALES (corp-wide): 14.1MM Privately Held
WEB: www.silveradovineyards.com
SIC: 2084 Wines
PA: Laird Family Estate Llc
5055 Solano Ave
Napa CA 94558
707 257-0360

(P-2720)
SINSKEY VINEYARDS INC
Also Called: Robert Sinskey Vineyards
6320 Silverado Trl, NAPA (94558-9747)
PHONE..................................707 944-9090
Robert M Sinskey MD, *Chairman*
Robert Sinskey Jr, *President*
Jennifer Gallagher, *Controller*
Ruben Moreno, *Sales Mgr*
Kyle Shepanek, *Sales Staff*
▲ **EMP:** 20 **EST:** 1987
SQ FT: 2,000
SALES (est): 4.6MM Privately Held
WEB: www.robertsinskey.com
SIC: 5921 2084 0172 Wine; wines; grapes

(P-2721)
SONOMA WINE HARDWARE INC
360 Swift Ave Ste 34, South San Francisco (94080-6220)
PHONE..................................650 866-3020
James Mackey, *President*
EMP: 20 **EST:** 2005
SALES (est): 893.3K Privately Held
SIC: 2084 Wines, brandy & brandy spirits

(P-2722)
ST GEORGE SPIRITS INC
2601 Monarch St, Alameda (94501-7541)
PHONE..................................510 769-1601
Jorg Rupf, *Principal*
Lance Winters, *President*
Rob Ortiz, *Vice Pres*
Meysa Budzinski, *Admin Asst*
James Lee, *Production*
▲ **EMP:** 25 **EST:** 1982
SQ FT: 65,000
SALES (est): 5.6MM Privately Held
WEB: www.stgeorgespirits.com
SIC: 2084 2085 Brandy spirits; distilled & blended liquors

(P-2723)
ST SUPERY INC (DH)
Also Called: Skalli Vineyards
8440 St Helena Hwy, Rutherford (94573)
P.O. Box 38 (94573-0038)
PHONE..................................707 963-4507
Emma Swain, *CEO*
◆ **EMP:** 50 **EST:** 1982
SQ FT: 20,000
SALES (est): 14.3MM Privately Held
WEB: www.stsupery.com
SIC: 2084 Wines
HQ: Chanel, Inc.
9 W 57th St Bsmt 2b
New York NY 10019
212 688-5055

(P-2724)
STAGS LEAP WINE CELLARS
Also Called: Hawk Crest
5766 Silverado Trl, NAPA (94558-9413)
PHONE..................................707 944-2020
Warren Winiarski, *Principal*
Sara Martinez, *Treasurer*
Bertha Rodriguez, *Executive*
Tom Davis, *Controller*
Karla Jensen, *Sales Staff*
▲ **EMP:** 110 **EST:** 1973
SQ FT: 40,000
SALES (est): 14.1MM Privately Held
WEB: www.stagsleapwinecellars.com
SIC: 2084 Wines

(P-2725)
STEELE WINES INC
4350 Thomas Dr, Kelseyville (95451)
P.O. Box 190 (95451-0190)
PHONE..................................707 279-9475
Jedediah T Steele, *President*
Naomi Key, *Admin Sec*
Drew Procaccini, *Marketing Staff*
EMP: 25 **EST:** 1989
SALES (est): 3.2MM Privately Held
WEB: www.shannonfamilyofwines.com
SIC: 2084 Wines

(P-2726)
STERLING VINEYARDS INC (PA)
1111 Dunaweal Ln, Calistoga (94515-9799)
P.O. Box 365 (94515-0365)
PHONE..................................707 942-3300
Samuel Bronfman II, *Ch of Bd*
Ron Lilly, *Vice Pres*
Mike Westrick, *Vice Pres*
▲ **EMP:** 50 **EST:** 1969
SQ FT: 80,000
SALES (est): 25.1MM Privately Held
WEB: www.sterlingvineyards.com
SIC: 2084 0172 Wine cellars, bonded: engaged in blending wines; grapes

(P-2727)
STERLING VINEYARDS INC
1105 Oak Knoll Ave, NAPA (94558-1304)
P.O. Box 365, Calistoga (94515-0365)
PHONE..................................707 252-7410
Vincent Vinnodo, *Manager*
EMP: 103
SALES (corp-wide): 25.1MM Privately Held
WEB: www.sterlingvineyards.com
SIC: 2084 0172 Wines; grapes
PA: Sterling Vineyards, Inc.
1111 Dunaweal Ln
Calistoga CA 94515
707 942-3300

(P-2728)
STEVEN KENT LLC
Also Called: La- Rochelle
5443 Tesla Rd, Livermore (94550-9621)
PHONE..................................925 243-6442
Steven Mirassou, *Mng Member*
Michael Ghielmetti,
▲ **EMP:** 19 **EST:** 2001
SALES (est): 3.3MM Privately Held
WEB: www.stevenkent.com
SIC: 2084 Wines

(P-2729)
STEVENOT WINERY & IMPORTS INC (PA)
2690 San Domingo Rd, Murphys (95247-9646)
PHONE..................................209 728-0638
Barden Stevenot, *President*
Jack Munar, *Principal*
▲ **EMP:** 24 **EST:** 2000
SALES (est): 2.9MM Privately Held
WEB: www.stevenotwinery.com
SIC: 2084 Wines

(P-2730)
STONE BRIDGE CELLARS INC (PA)
Also Called: Joseph Phelps Vineyards
200 Taplin Rd, Saint Helena (94574-9544)
P.O. Box 1031 (94574-0531)
PHONE..................................707 963-2745
Joseph Phelps, *Ch of Bd*
Robert Boyd, *President*
Clarice Turner, *President*
William H Phelps, *CEO*
AMI Iadarola, *CFO*
▲ **EMP:** 50 **EST:** 1984
SQ FT: 50,000
SALES (est): 20MM Privately Held
WEB: www.josephphelps.com
SIC: 2084 Wines

(P-2731)
STONE EDGE WINERY LLC
Also Called: Stone Edge Farm
19330 Carriger Rd, Sonoma (95476-6229)
P.O. Box 487 (95476-0487)
PHONE..................................707 935-6520
John A McQuown,
Whitney Reese, *Administration*
Richard Barnes, *CIO*
Kim Bandel, *Opers Mgr*
EMP: 19 **EST:** 2005
SQ FT: 1,500
SALES (est): 2.9MM Privately Held
WEB: www.stoneedgefarm.com
SIC: 2084 Wines

(P-2732)
STONECUSHION INC (PA)
Also Called: Wilson Artisan Wineries
1400 Lytton Springs Rd, Healdsburg (95448-9695)
P.O. Box 487, Geyserville (95441-0487)
PHONE..................................707 433-1911
Kenneth C Wilson, *President*
Jon Pelleriti, *CFO*
Sydney Wilson, *Marketing Staff*
EMP: 24 **EST:** 2005
SALES (est): 4.3MM Privately Held
WEB: www.mazzocco.com
SIC: 2084 Wines

(P-2733)
SUGARLOAF FARMING CORPORATION
Also Called: Peter Michael Winery
12400 Ida Clayton Rd, Calistoga (94515-9507)
PHONE..................................707 942-4459
Scott Rodde, *CEO*
Bill Vyenielo, *Vice Pres*
Stuart Bockman, *General Mgr*
◆ **EMP:** 25 **EST:** 1982
SQ FT: 1,000
SALES (est): 6.7MM
SALES (corp-wide): 34MM Privately Held
WEB: www.petermichaelwinery.com
SIC: 2084 Wines
PA: Stockford Limited
Sheet Street
Windsor BERKS

(P-2734)
SUTTER HOME WINERY INC (PA)
Also Called: Trinchero Family Estates
100 Saint Helena Hwy S, Saint Helena (94574-2204)
P.O. Box 248 (94574-0248)
PHONE..................................707 963-3104
Bob Torkelson, *President*
Brie Wohld, *Vice Pres*
Dave Harrington, *District Mgr*
Courtney Pask, *Technician*
Cyndi Chong, *Analyst*
◆ **EMP:** 200 **EST:** 1946
SQ FT: 17,000
SALES (est): 188.1MM Privately Held
WEB: www.sutterhome.com
SIC: 2084 0172 Wines; grapes

(P-2735)
SUTTER HOME WINERY INC
18667 Jacob Brack Rd, Lodi (95242-9185)
PHONE..................................209 368-4357
EMP: 105
SQ FT: 1,500
SALES (corp-wide): 188.1MM Privately Held
WEB: www.tfewines.com
SIC: 2084 Wines
PA: Sutter Home Winery, Inc.
100 Saint Helena Hwy S
Saint Helena CA 94574
707 963-3104

(P-2736)
SWANSON VINEYARDS AND WINERY (DH)
1271 Manley Ln, Rutherford (94573)
P.O. Box 148, Oakville (94562-0148)
PHONE..................................707 754-4018
Clarke Swanson Jr, *CEO*
Michael Jellison, *President*
Bill Cole, *CFO*
▲ **EMP:** 25 **EST:** 1987
SQ FT: 3,500
SALES (est): 5.5MM
SALES (corp-wide): 220.7MM Publicly Held
WEB: www.swansonvineyards.com
SIC: 2084 Wines

(P-2737)
TAFT STREET INC
Also Called: Taft Street Winery
2030 Barlow Ln, Sebastopol (95472-2555)
PHONE..................................707 823-2049
Michael Tierney, *President*
Mike Martini, *CFO*

PRODUCTS & SERVICES SECTION
2084 - Wine & Brandy County (P-2761)

Martin Tierney Jr, *Vice Pres*
Laurie Keith, *Sales Mgr*
Bruce Walker, *Sales Staff*
EMP: 20 **EST:** 1982
SQ FT: 30,000
SALES (est): 2.6MM Privately Held
WEB: www.taftstreetwinery.com
SIC: 2084 Wines

(P-2738)
TESLA VINEYARDS LP
Also Called: Concannon Vineyard
4590 Tesla Rd, Livermore (94550-9002)
PHONE 925 456-2500
Eric Wente, *Partner*
Edward Lanphier, *Partner*
Henry Wilder, *Partner*
Dennis Wood, *Partner*
Michael Wood, *Partner*
▲ **EMP:** 35 **EST:** 1883
SALES (est): 2.5MM Privately Held
WEB: www.concannonvineyard.com
SIC: 2084 0721 Wines; vines, cultivation of

(P-2739)
TESTAROSSA VINEYARDS LLC
Also Called: Testarossa Winery
300 College Ave Ste A, Los Gatos (95030-7066)
P.O. Box 969 (95031-0969)
PHONE 408 354-6150
Diana Jensen, *Production*
Gavin Binz, *Production*
Matt Clasen, *Natl Sales Mgr*
Robert Jensen, *Director*
Bill Brosseau, *Director*
▲ **EMP:** 25 **EST:** 1994
SQ FT: 10,000
SALES (est): 6.6MM Privately Held
WEB: www.testarossa.com
SIC: 2084 Wines

(P-2740)
THOMAS DEHLINGER
Also Called: Dehlinger Winery
4101 Ginehill Rd, Sebastopol (95472)
PHONE 707 823-2378
Thomas Dehlinger, *Owner*
Carmen Dehlinger, *Sales Staff*
EMP: 20 **EST:** 1973
SQ FT: 18,000
SALES (est): 1.2MM Privately Held
WEB: www.dehlingerwinery.com
SIC: 2084 0172 Wines; grapes

(P-2741)
THOMAS FOGARTY WINERY LLC (PA)
3130 Alpine Rd, Portola Valley (94028-7549)
PHONE 650 851-6777
Thomas J Fogarty MD,
Melissa Baker, *Office Admin*
▲ **EMP:** 23 **EST:** 1979
SQ FT: 4,000 Privately Held
WEB: www.fogartywinery.com
SIC: 2084 0172 7299 Wines; grapes; facility rental & party planning services

(P-2742)
THOMAS LEONARDINI
Also Called: Whitehall Lane Winery
1563 Saint Helena Hwy S, Saint Helena (94574-9775)
PHONE 707 963-9454
Thomas Leonardini, *Owner*
▲ **EMP:** 15 **EST:** 1988
SQ FT: 24,000
SALES (est): 3.7MM Privately Held
WEB: www.whitehalllane.com
SIC: 2084 0172 Wines; grapes

(P-2743)
THREE STICKS WINES LLC
21692 8th St E Ste 280, Sonoma (95476-2804)
P.O. Box 1869 (95476-1869)
PHONE 707 996-3328
Bill Price, *Owner*
Tricia O'brien, *Marketing Staff*
Maral Papakhian, *Marketing Staff*
Hayden Schmidter, *Sales Staff*
Rob Harris, *Director*
EMP: 21 **EST:** 2006

SALES (est): 1.7MM Privately Held
WEB: www.threestickswines.com
SIC: 2084 Wines

(P-2744)
TMR WINE COMPANY LLC
Also Called: Continuum Estate Winery Co
1677 Sage Canyon Rd, Saint Helena (94574-9809)
PHONE 707 944-8100
Tim Mondalvi, *Owner*
Marcia Mandalvi, *Principal*
Chiara Mondavi, *Technician*
David Bantly, *Sales Dir*
Carissa Mondavi, *Marketing Staff*
EMP: 25 **EST:** 2009
SALES (est): 2.4MM Privately Held
WEB: www.continuumestate.com
SIC: 2084 Wines

(P-2745)
TREASURY WINE ESTATES AMERICAS (HQ)
555 Gateway Dr, NAPA (94558-6291)
PHONE 707 259-4500
Michael Clarke, *CEO*
Robert Foye, *President*
Don McCall, *President*
Bob Spooner, *President*
Noel Meehan, *CFO*
◆ **EMP:** 400 **EST:** 1973
SQ FT: 26,000
SALES (est): 454.6MM Privately Held
WEB: www.treasurywineestates.com
SIC: 2084 Wines

(P-2746)
TREASURY WINE ESTATES AMERICAS
2000 Saint Helena Hwy N, Saint Helena (94574)
PHONE 707 963-7115
EMP: 81 Privately Held
SIC: 2084 Mfg Wines/Brandy/Spirits
HQ: Treasury Wine Estates Americas Company
555 Gateway Dr
Napa CA 94558
707 259-4500

(P-2747)
TREFETHEN VINEYARDS WINERY INC
Also Called: Trefethen Family Vineyards
1160 Oak Knoll Ave, NAPA (94558-1398)
P.O. Box 2460 (94558-0291)
PHONE 707 255-7700
Jon Ruel, *President*
Carla Trefethen, *Shareholder*
Robert Helmer, *CFO*
David Whitehouse, *Officer*
Janet Trefethen, *Principal*
▲ **EMP:** 50 **EST:** 1973
SQ FT: 4,000
SALES (est): 12.4MM Privately Held
WEB: www.trefethen.com
SIC: 2084 5921 Wines; wine

(P-2748)
TRUETT-HURST INC (PA)
125 Foss Creek Cir, Healdsburg (95448-4288)
P.O. Box 1532 (95448-1532)
PHONE 707 431-4423
Philip L Hurst, *Ch of Bd*
Karen Weaver, *CFO*
Jason Strobbe, *Exec VP*
▲ **EMP:** 32 **EST:** 2007
SQ FT: 2,500
SALES: 6.4MM Publicly Held
WEB: www.truetthurstwinery.com
SIC: 2084 Wine cellars, bonded: engaged in blending wines

(P-2749)
TURLEY WINE CELLARS INC
Also Called: Pesenti Winery
3358 Saint Helena Hwy N, Saint Helena (94574-9660)
PHONE 707 968-2700
Larry Turley, *President*
Tegan Passalacqua, *Director*
Allison Caruso, *Manager*
Brennan Stover, *Manager*
EMP: 54 **EST:** 1994

SALES (est): 9.7MM Privately Held
WEB: www.turleywinecellars.com
SIC: 2084 Wines

(P-2750)
TWIN PEAKS WINERY INC
1473 Yountville Cross Rd, Yountville (94599-9471)
PHONE 707 945-0855
Cliff Lede, *Principal*
EMP: 24 **EST:** 2005
SALES (est): 1.7MM Privately Held
SIC: 2084 Wines

(P-2751)
TWISTED OAK WINERY LLC (PA)
4280 Red Hill Rd, Vallecito (95251)
P.O. Box 2385, Murphys (95247-2385)
PHONE 209 728-3000
Jeffrey Stai,
Jeff Stai, *Manager*
EMP: 15 **EST:** 2001
SQ FT: 1,000
SALES (est): 2.8MM Privately Held
WEB: www.twistedoak.com
SIC: 2084 Wine cellars, bonded: engaged in blending wines; wines

(P-2752)
V SATTUI WINERY
1111 White Ln, Saint Helena (94574-1599)
PHONE 707 963-7774
Tom Davies, *President*
Daryl Sattui, *CEO*
Roumen Gadelev, *CFO*
Rick Rosenbrand, *Vice Pres*
Gordon Rickmart, *Admin Sec*
▲ **EMP:** 65 **EST:** 1975
SQ FT: 20,000
SALES (est): 21.3MM Privately Held
WEB: www.vsattui.com
SIC: 5921 5451 5947 5961 Wine; cheese; gift shop; general merchandise, mail order; wines, brandy & brandy spirits

(P-2753)
VALLEY OF MOON WINERY
134 Church St, Sonoma (95476-6612)
P.O. Box 1951, Glen Ellen (95442-1951)
PHONE 707 939-4500
Gary Heck, *President*
◆ **EMP:** 19 **EST:** 1945
SALES (est): 1.6MM
SALES (corp-wide): 103.8MM Privately Held
WEB: www.valleyofthemoonwinery.com
SIC: 2084 0172 Wines; grapes
PA: F. Korbel & Bros.
13250 River Rd
Guerneville CA 95446
707 824-7000

(P-2754)
VIE-DEL COMPANY
13363 S Indianola Ave, Kingsburg (93631-9268)
PHONE 559 896-3065
Richard Watson, *Principal*
EMP: 24
SALES (corp-wide): 24.9MM Privately Held
WEB: www.vie-delequipmentsales.com
SIC: 2084 2037 Brandy; wines; frozen fruits & vegetables
PA: Vie-Del Company
11903 S Chestnut Ave
Fresno CA 93725
559 834-2525

(P-2755)
VIGNETTE WINERY LLC (PA)
Also Called: Wine Foundry
45 Enterprise Ct, NAPA (94558-7586)
PHONE 707 637-8821
Steve Ryan, *General Mgr*
Stuart Ake, *Vice Pres*
Alexandria Disbrow, *Finance Mgr*
Ben Jones, *Finance Mgr*
Jeremy Weiss, *Prdtn Mgr*
▲ **EMP:** 43 **EST:** 2012
SALES (est): 10.6MM Privately Held
WEB: www.thewinefoundry.com
SIC: 5921 2084 Wine; wines

(P-2756)
VILLA AMOROSA
Also Called: Castello Diamorosa
4045 Saint Helena Hwy, Calistoga (94515-9609)
PHONE 707 942-8200
Georg Falzner, *President*
Antoinette Freeman, *Director*
▲ **EMP:** 100 **EST:** 1994
SALES (est): 15MM Privately Held
WEB: www.castellodiamorosa.com
SIC: 2084 Wines

(P-2757)
VILLA TOSCANO WINERY
10600 Shenandoah Rd, Plymouth (95669-9513)
P.O. Box 1029 (95669-1029)
PHONE 209 245-3800
Jerry Wright, *Owner*
▲ **EMP:** 21 **EST:** 1996
SQ FT: 18,000
SALES (est): 4.9MM Privately Held
WEB: www.villatoscano.com
SIC: 2084 Wines

(P-2758)
VINEBURG WINE COMPANY INC (PA)
Also Called: Bartholomew Park Winery
2000 Denmark St, Sonoma (95476-9615)
P.O. Box 1, Vineburg (95487-0001)
PHONE 707 938-5277
Jim Bundschu, *CEO*
Nancy Bundschu, *President*
Lisa Dencklau, *Executive*
Jasmin Hinton, *Accounting Mgr*
Jennifer Sahouria-Pangle, *Asst Controller*
▲ **EMP:** 25 **EST:** 1858
SQ FT: 4,000
SALES (est): 5.9MM Privately Held
WEB: www.gunbun.com
SIC: 2084 0172 Wines; grapes

(P-2759)
WEIBEL INCORPORATED
Also Called: Weibel Champagne Vineyards
1 Winemaster Way Ste D, Lodi (95240-0860)
P.O. Box 87, Woodbridge (95258-0087)
PHONE 209 365-9463
Fred E Weibel Jr, *President*
Suzanne Cruz-Y-Corro, *Treasurer*
Gary Habluetzel, *Vice Pres*
Doug Richards, *Vice Pres*
▲ **EMP:** 35 **EST:** 1943
SALES (est): 6.7MM Privately Held
WEB: www.weibel.com
SIC: 2084 Wines

(P-2760)
WENTE BROS (PA)
Also Called: Wente Vineyards
5565 Tesla Rd, Livermore (94550-9149)
PHONE 925 456-2300
Carolyn Wente, *Ch of Bd*
Jean Wente, *Ch of Bd*
Philip Wente, *Vice Chairman*
Eric P Wente, *CEO*
Karl Wente, *COO*
◆ **EMP:** 100 **EST:** 1900
SQ FT: 168,000
SALES (est): 92.4MM Privately Held
WEB: www.wentevineyards.com
SIC: 2084 8742 Wines; restaurant & food services consultants

(P-2761)
WENTE BROS
Also Called: Wente Vineyard Restaurant
5050 Arroyo Rd, Livermore (94550-9645)
PHONE 925 456-2450
Monte Jenson, *Branch Mgr*
Amy Hoopes, *Officer*
Arthur Jeannet, *Exec VP*
Christine Wente, *Vice Pres*
Adrian Knotter, *Area Mgr*
EMP: 22
SQ FT: 6,282
SALES (corp-wide): 92.4MM Privately Held
WEB: www.wentevineyards.com
SIC: 5812 2084 Eating places; wines

2084 - Wine & Brandy County (P-2762)

PA: Wente Bros.
5565 Tesla Rd
Livermore CA 94550
925 456-2300

(P-2762)
WHEELER WINERY INC
9000 Windsor Rd, Windsor (95492-9701)
PHONE..............................415 979-0630
Jean Boisset, *President*
Alain Leonnet, *Vice Pres*
EMP: 21 **EST:** 1972
SQ FT: 50,000
SALES (est): 855.1K
SALES (corp-wide): 18.4MM **Privately Held**
WEB: www.wheelerfarmswine.com
SIC: 2084 Wines
HQ: Jean-Claude Boisset Wines U.S.A., Inc.
849 Zinfandel Ln
Saint Helena CA 94574
707 967-7667

(P-2763)
WHISPERKOOL CORPORATION
Also Called: Whisperkoll
1738 E Alpine Ave, Stockton (95205-2505)
PHONE..............................800 343-9463
Thomas R Schneider, *CEO*
Doug Smith, *Sales Dir*
EMP: 15 **EST:** 2010
SQ FT: 32,000
SALES (est): 2.9MM **Privately Held**
WEB: www.whisperkool.com
SIC: 2084 Wine coolers (beverages)

(P-2764)
WINDSOR OAKS VINEYARDS LLP
10810 Hillview Rd, Windsor (95492-7519)
P.O. Box 883 (95492-0883)
PHONE..............................707 433-4050
Windsor Oaks, *Partner*
Trish Moyer, *Bookkeeper*
Ralph Hoag, *Manager*
Douglas Lumgair, *Manager*
◆ **EMP:** 32 **EST:** 1992
SALES (est): 5.1MM **Privately Held**
WEB: www.windsoroaks.com
SIC: 2084 Wines

(P-2765)
WINE GROUP INC (HQ)
Also Called: Mogan David Wine
17000 E State Highway 120, Ripon (95366-9412)
PHONE..............................209 599-4111
Brian Jay Vos, *CEO*
Arthur Ciocca, *Ch of Bd*
Morris Ball, *Vice Pres*
Stephen Hughes, *Vice Pres*
Katie McConville, *Vice Pres*
◆ **EMP:** 200 **EST:** 1933
SQ FT: 3,000
SALES (est): 114.7MM **Privately Held**
WEB: www.thewinegroup.com
SIC: 2084 Wines

(P-2766)
WINE MART GROUPS LLC ⊙
766 Harrison St Unit 312, San Francisco (94107-1279)
PHONE..............................866 583-2312
Paul Chan, *Principal*
EMP: 15 **EST:** 2021
SALES (est): 528.5K **Privately Held**
SIC: 2084 Wines, brandy & brandy spirits

(P-2767)
WISE VILLA WINERY LLC
4226 Wise Rd, Lincoln (95648-8528)
PHONE..............................916 543-0323
Grover Cleveland Lee, *Mng Member*
Sarah Lemberg, *Sales Staff*
EMP: 17 **EST:** 2008
SALES (est): 6.1MM **Privately Held**
WEB: www.wisevillawinery.com
SIC: 2084 Wines

2085 Liquors, Distilled, Rectified & Blended

(P-2768)
DIAGEO NORTH AMERICA INC
Also Called: Beaulieu Vineyard
1960 Saint Helena Hwy, Rutherford (94573)
P.O. Box 219 (94573-0219)
PHONE..............................707 967-5200
Armond Rist, *Dir Ops-Prd-Mfg*
EMP: 54
SALES (corp-wide): 18B **Privately Held**
SIC: 2085 2084 0172 Distilled & blended liquors; wines, brandy & brandy spirits; grapes
HQ: Diageo North America Inc.
3 World Trade Ctr
New York NY 10007
212 202-1800

(P-2769)
DIAGEO NORTH AMERICA INC
6130 Stoneridge Mall Rd, Pleasanton (94588-3279)
PHONE..............................925 520-3116
Lisa Buell, *Manager*
EMP: 20
SALES (corp-wide): 18B **Privately Held**
SIC: 2085 Distilled & blended liquors
HQ: Diageo North America Inc.
3 World Trade Ctr
New York NY 10007
212 202-1800

(P-2770)
DIAGEO NORTH AMERICA INC
151 Commonwealth Dr, Menlo Park (94025-1105)
PHONE..............................650 329-3220
Del Kruse, *Branch Mgr*
Phil Stefaniak, *Project Mgr*
Fabian Nodal, *Engineer*
Ed Wong, *Buyer*
EMP: 42
SALES (corp-wide): 18B **Privately Held**
SIC: 2085 2084 Distilled & blended liquors; wines, brandy & brandy spirits
HQ: Diageo North America Inc.
3 World Trade Ctr
New York NY 10007
212 202-1800

(P-2771)
GRATON SPIRITS COMPANY LLC (PA)
Also Called: Purple Spirits
617 2nd St Ste C, Petaluma (94952-5160)
PHONE..............................707 829-6100
Derek Benham, *Mng Member*
EMP: 33 **EST:** 2013
SALES (est): 722.5K **Privately Held**
WEB: www.purplebrands.com
SIC: 2085 Distilled & blended liquors

(P-2772)
HOPPY BREWING CO INC
2425 24th St Ste B, Sacramento (95818-2552)
PHONE..............................916 451-4677
Troy Paski, *President*
Scott Patterson, *Marketing Staff*
EMP: 32 **EST:** 1991
SQ FT: 10,000
SALES (est): 2.5MM **Privately Held**
WEB: www.hoppy.com
SIC: 5812 2085 Chicken restaurant; grain alcohol for beverage purposes

(P-2773)
HOTALING & CO LLC (PA)
550 Montgomery St Ste 300, San Francisco (94111-6508)
PHONE..............................415 630-5910
Dan Leese, *President*
Brian Radics, *Chief Mktg Ofcr*
Kelly McCarthy, *District Mgr*
Chloe Davidson, *Analyst*
Brandon Foglio, *Export Mgr*
EMP: 47 **EST:** 2018
SALES (est): 13.7MM **Privately Held**
WEB: www.hotalingandco.com
SIC: 2085 5182 Distilled & blended liquors; bottling wines & liquors

(P-2774)
JJ PFISTER DISTILLING CO LLC
9819 Business Park Dr # 3, Sacramento (95827-1735)
PHONE..............................503 939-9535
Kevin Keck, *Branch Mgr*
EMP: 18
SALES (corp-wide): 520.9K **Privately Held**
WEB: www.jjpfister.com
SIC: 2085 Distilled & blended liquors
PA: Jj Pfister Distilling Company Llc
1059 Wilhaggin Park Ln
Sacramento CA 95864
916 500-2914

(P-2775)
LIN FRANK DISTILLERS
2455 Huntington Dr, Fairfield (94533-9734)
PHONE..............................707 437-1092
Frank Lin, *Principal*
Debbie Callsen, *Accountant*
EMP: 41 **EST:** 2010
SALES (est): 10.6MM **Privately Held**
WEB: www.frank-lin.com
SIC: 2085 Distilled & blended liquors

(P-2776)
RARE BREED DISTILLING LLC (DH)
Also Called: Wild Turkey Distillery
55 Francisco St Ste 100, San Francisco (94133-2136)
PHONE..............................415 315-8060
Francesca Mazzoleni, *Principal*
▼ **EMP:** 20 **EST:** 2009
SALES (est): 17.8MM
SALES (corp-wide): 177.9K **Privately Held**
WEB: www.campari.com
SIC: 2085 Distilled & blended liquors
HQ: Davide Campari Milano N.V.
Via Franco Sacchetti 20
Sesto San Giovanni MI 20099
026 225-1

(P-2777)
SANTA CROCE LLC
Also Called: Savage & Cooke
1097 Nimitz Ave, Vallejo (94592-1025)
P.O. Box 2020, Saint Helena (94574-2018)
PHONE..............................707 227-7834
EMP: 15
SALES (corp-wide): 2.6MM **Privately Held**
SIC: 2085 Distilled & blended liquors
PA: Santa Croce Llc
1352 Main St
Saint Helena CA 94574
707 967-9179

(P-2778)
SELTZER REVOLUTIONS INC
Also Called: Mexi
2911 Branciforte Dr, Santa Cruz (95065-9774)
PHONE..............................604 765-9966
Alice Chen, *CEO*
Kevin Finkas, *COO*
EMP: 15 **EST:** 2020
SALES (est): 821.2K **Privately Held**
SIC: 2085 7389 Distilled & blended liquors;

(P-2779)
TAKARA SAKE USA INC (DH)
Also Called: Numano Sake Company
708 Addison St, Berkeley (94710-1925)
PHONE..............................510 540-8250
Yoshihiro Naka, *CEO*
Yoichiro Miyakuni, *President*
Atsushi Himeno, *Officer*
Jim Zhang, *Area Mgr*
Izumi Motai, *Marketing Mgr*
◆ **EMP:** 28 **EST:** 1977
SQ FT: 15,000
SALES (est): 6.7MM **Privately Held**
WEB: www.takarasake.com
SIC: 2085 5182 Grain alcohol for beverage purposes; wine

(P-2780)
TEQUILAS PREMIUM INC
470 Columbus Ave Ste 210, San Francisco (94133-3930)
PHONE..............................415 399-0496

▲ **EMP:** 17
SALES (est): 1.5MM **Privately Held**
SIC: 2085 Mfg Distilled/Blended Liquor

2086 Soft Drinks

(P-2781)
AMCAN BEVERAGES INC
Also Called: Pokka Beverages
1201 Commerce Blvd, American Canyon (94503-9611)
PHONE..............................707 557-0500
Don Soetaert, *President*
EMP: 252 **EST:** 1976
SQ FT: 250,000
SALES (est): 5.3MM
SALES (corp-wide): 33B **Publicly Held**
WEB: www.coca-colacompany.com
SIC: 2086 Iced tea & fruit drinks, bottled & canned
PA: The Coca-Cola Company
1 Coca Cola Plz Nw
Atlanta GA 30313
404 676-2121

(P-2782)
ANOMALIES INTERNATIONAL INC
Also Called: Partyaid
2833 Mission St, Santa Cruz (95060-5755)
P.O. Box 761 (95061-0761)
PHONE..............................800 855-1113
Orion Melehan, *CEO*
Aaron Hinde, *COO*
Erik Gundersen, *Creative Dir*
Chelsey Sittner, *Executive Asst*
Jordan Costa, *Marketing Mgr*
▲ **EMP:** 55 **EST:** 2011
SQ FT: 9,105
SALES (est): 19.8MM **Privately Held**
WEB: www.lifeaidbevco.com
SIC: 2086 Bottled & canned soft drinks

(P-2783)
BOTTLING GROUP LLC
1150 E North Ave, Fresno (93725-1929)
PHONE..............................559 485-5050
EMP: 1463
SALES (corp-wide): 70.3B **Publicly Held**
WEB: www.pepsico.com
SIC: 2086 Bottled & canned soft drinks
HQ: Bottling Group, Llc
1111 Westchester Ave
White Plains NY 10604
914 253-2000

(P-2784)
BOTTLING GROUP LLC
3440 S East Ave, Fresno (93725-9481)
PHONE..............................914 767-6000
EMP: 1463
SALES (corp-wide): 70.3B **Publicly Held**
WEB: www.pepsico.com
SIC: 2086 Bottled & canned soft drinks; carbonated soft drinks, bottled & canned; carbonated beverages, nonalcoholic: bottled & canned
HQ: Bottling Group, Llc
1111 Westchester Ave
White Plains NY 10604
914 253-2000

(P-2785)
CAPITOL BEVERAGE PACKERS
Also Called: Seven Up Bottling
2670 Land Ave, Sacramento (95815-2380)
PHONE..............................916 929-7777
Millard C Tonkin, *President*
Millard Tonkin, *Shareholder*
▲ **EMP:** 39 **EST:** 1958
SQ FT: 110,360
SALES (est): 2MM **Privately Held**
WEB: www.7up.com
SIC: 2086 5078 Bottled & canned soft drinks; refrigerated beverage dispensers

(P-2786)
CASTLE ROCK SPRING WATER CO
4121 Dunsmuir Ave, Dunsmuir (96025-1704)
PHONE..............................530 678-4444
Ed Lauth, *President*
Scott Lidster, *Vice Pres*

▲ = Import ▼=Export
◆ =Import/Export

PRODUCTS & SERVICES SECTION

2086 - Soft Drinks County (P-2809)

Clark Wright, *Vice Pres*
EMP: 23 **EST:** 1990
SQ FT: 42,000
SALES (est): 1.3MM **Privately Held**
WEB: www.castlerockwatercompany.com
SIC: 2086 Water, pasteurized: packaged in cans, bottles, etc.

(P-2787) CG ROXANE LLC
10 Pimentel Ct, Novato (94949-8604)
PHONE 415 339-9521
EMP: 22 **Privately Held**
WEB: www.crystalgeyserplease.com
SIC: 2086 Water, pasteurized: packaged in cans, bottles, etc.
PA: Cg Roxane Llc
2330 Marinship Way # 190
Sausalito CA 94965

(P-2788) COCA-COLA COMPANY AMERICAN CYN
1201 Commerce Blvd, American Canyon (94503-9611)
PHONE 707 556-1220
EMP: 18 **EST:** 2014
SALES (est): 3.4MM **Privately Held**
WEB: www.careers.coca-colacompany.com
SIC: 2086 Bottled & canned soft drinks

(P-2789) CRYSTAL GEYSER WATER COMPANY
5001 Fermi Dr, Fairfield (94534-6894)
PHONE 707 647-4410
Ernesto Olivarez, *Branch Mgr*
EMP: 44 **Privately Held**
WEB: www.crystalgeyser.com
SIC: 2086 Water, pasteurized: packaged in cans, bottles, etc.
HQ: Crystal Geyser Water Company
501 Washington St
Calistoga CA 94515
707 265-3900

(P-2790) DR PEPPER/SEVEN UP INC
1901 Russell Ave, Santa Rosa (95403-2646)
PHONE 707 545-7797
Ray Gutendorf, *Principal*
EMP: 17 **Publicly Held**
WEB: www.drpepper.com
SIC: 2086 Soft drinks: packaged in cans, bottles, etc.
HQ: Dr Pepper/Seven Up, Inc.
6425 Hall Of Fame Ln
Frisco TX 75034
972 673-7000

(P-2791) HA RIDER & SONS INC
2482 Freedom Blvd, Watsonville (95076-1099)
PHONE 831 722-3882
George C Rider, *Partner*
Thomas Rider, *Partner*
Dassie Hernandez, *Technology*
Rosario Lopez, *Manager*
▲ **EMP:** 45 **EST:** 1940
SQ FT: 168,000
SALES (est): 5.6MM **Privately Held**
WEB: www.hariderandsons.com
SIC: 2086 Soft drinks: packaged in cans, bottles, etc.

(P-2792) HINT INC
2124 Union St Ste D, San Francisco (94123-4044)
P.O. Box 29078 (94129-0078)
PHONE 415 513-4051
Kara Goldin, *CEO*
Theodore Goldin, *COO*
Terrence Sweeney, *Chief Mktg Ofcr*
Brian Cramer, *Vice Pres*
Blair Owens, *Vice Pres*
EMP: 44 **EST:** 2005

SALES (est): 18.3MM **Privately Held**
WEB: www.drinkhint.com
SIC: 2086 Mineral water, carbonated: packaged in cans, bottles, etc.; fruit drinks (less than 100% juice): packaged in cans, etc.; carbonated beverages, nonalcoholic: bottled & canned

(P-2793) HUMBOLDT BOTTLING LLC
Also Called: Humboldt Bottling Co.
517 7th St, Fortuna (95540-1901)
PHONE 707 725-4119
Nathan Leavitt,
Trevor Barcelos, *Manager*
EMP: 15 **EST:** 2012
SALES (est): 1.1MM **Privately Held**
WEB: www.humboldtcountysown.com
SIC: 2086 Soft drinks: packaged in cans, bottles, etc.

(P-2794) JOHN FITZPATRICK & SONS
Also Called: Pepsico
1480 Beltline Rd, Redding (96003-1410)
PHONE 530 241-3216
John Fitzpatrick Jr, *CEO*
Jerome Fitzpatrick, *Vice Pres*
EMP: 29 **EST:** 1958
SQ FT: 2,000
SALES (est): 942.9K **Privately Held**
WEB: www.pepsico.com
SIC: 2086 Carbonated soft drinks, bottled & canned

(P-2795) LIFEAID BEVERAGE COMPANY LLC (PA)
2833 Mission St, Santa Cruz (95060-5755)
PHONE 888 558-1113
Orion Melehan,
Aaron Hinde, *COO*
Emily Sommariva, *Chief Mktg Ofcr*
Dan Leja, *Vice Pres*
Graham Katie, *Mfg Staff*
EMP: 66 **EST:** 2015
SALES (est): 8.6MM **Privately Held**
WEB: www.lifeaidbevco.com
SIC: 2086 Bottled & canned soft drinks

(P-2796) NOR-CAL BEVERAGE CO INC
1375 Terminal St, West Sacramento (95691-3514)
PHONE 916 372-1700
Larry Buban, *Manager*
EMP: 59
SALES (corp-wide): 231.7MM **Privately Held**
WEB: www.ncbev.com
SIC: 2086 5181 Carbonated beverages, nonalcoholic: bottled & canned; beer & ale
PA: Nor-Cal Beverage Co., Inc.
2150 Stone Blvd
West Sacramento CA 95691
916 372-0600

(P-2797) PATHWATER INC
44137 Fremont Blvd, Fremont (94538-6044)
PHONE 510 518-0014
Shadi Bakour, *CEO*
Amer Orabi, *President*
EMP: 40 **EST:** 2015
SALES (est): 5.6MM **Privately Held**
SIC: 2086 Pasteurized & mineral waters, bottled & canned

(P-2798) RAINBOW ORCHARDS INC
2569 Larsen Dr, Camino (95709-9704)
PHONE 530 644-1594
Tom Heflin, *Partner*
Christa Campbell, *Partner*
EMP: 19 **EST:** 1977
SALES (est): 1.5MM **Privately Held**
WEB: www.rainboworchards.net
SIC: 2086 0175 Fruit drinks (less than 100% juice): packaged in cans, etc.; apple orchard

(P-2799) REYES COCA-COLA BOTTLING LLC
1555 Old Bayshore Hwy, San Jose (95112-4303)
PHONE 408 436-3700
Larry Loeffer, *Manager*
EMP: 57
SALES (corp-wide): 850.1MM **Privately Held**
WEB: www.coca-cola.com
SIC: 2086 Bottled & canned soft drinks
PA: Reyes Coca-Cola Bottling, L.L.C.
3 Park Plz Ste 600
Irvine CA 92614
213 744-8616

(P-2800) REYES COCA-COLA BOTTLING LLC
2025 Pike Ave, San Leandro (94577-6708)
PHONE 510 476-7000
Andy Darren, *Branch Mgr*
EMP: 57
SALES (corp-wide): 850.1MM **Privately Held**
WEB: www.coca-cola.com
SIC: 2086 5149 Bottled & canned soft drinks; groceries & related products
PA: Reyes Coca-Cola Bottling, L.L.C.
3 Park Plz Ste 600
Irvine CA 92614
213 744-8616

(P-2801) REYES COCA-COLA BOTTLING LLC
14655 Wicks Blvd, San Leandro (94577-6715)
PHONE 510 667-6300
Ron King, *Branch Mgr*
EMP: 110
SALES (corp-wide): 850.1MM **Privately Held**
WEB: www.coca-cola.com
SIC: 2086 2087 2037 2095 Bottled & canned soft drinks; syrups, drink; fruit juice concentrates, frozen; roasted coffee; tea blending; wines
PA: Reyes Coca-Cola Bottling, L.L.C.
3 Park Plz Ste 600
Irvine CA 92614
213 744-8616

(P-2802) REYES COCA-COLA BOTTLING LLC
3220 E Malaga Ave, Fresno (93725-9353)
PHONE 559 264-4631
Mike Lozier, *Branch Mgr*
Kayla Castaneda, *Manager*
EMP: 57
SQ FT: 62,365
SALES (corp-wide): 850.1MM **Privately Held**
WEB: www.coca-cola.com
SIC: 2086 Bottled & canned soft drinks
PA: Reyes Coca-Cola Bottling, L.L.C.
3 Park Plz Ste 600
Irvine CA 92614
213 744-8616

(P-2803) REYES COCA-COLA BOTTLING LLC
1467 El Pinal Dr, Stockton (95205-2672)
PHONE 209 466-9501
Clay Frenzel, *Manager*
EMP: 57
SALES (corp-wide): 850.1MM **Privately Held**
WEB: www.coca-cola.com
SIC: 2086 Bottled & canned soft drinks
PA: Reyes Coca-Cola Bottling, L.L.C.
3 Park Plz Ste 600
Irvine CA 92614
213 744-8616

(P-2804) REYES COCA-COLA BOTTLING LLC
1510 Rollins Rd, Burlingame (94010-2306)
PHONE 408 483-4259
Larry Loeffler, *Branch Mgr*

EMP: 57
SALES (corp-wide): 850.1MM **Privately Held**
WEB: www.coca-cola.com
SIC: 2086 Bottled & canned soft drinks
PA: Reyes Coca-Cola Bottling, L.L.C.
3 Park Plz Ste 600
Irvine CA 92614
213 744-8616

(P-2805) REYES COCA-COLA BOTTLING LLC
1580 Beltline Rd, Redding (96003-1408)
PHONE 530 241-4315
David Hallagan, *Manager*
EMP: 57
SQ FT: 75,000
SALES (corp-wide): 850.1MM **Privately Held**
WEB: www.coca-cola.com
SIC: 2086 Bottled & canned soft drinks
PA: Reyes Coca-Cola Bottling, L.L.C.
3 Park Plz Ste 600
Irvine CA 92614
213 744-8616

(P-2806) REYES COCA-COLA BOTTLING LLC
1430 Melody Rd, Marysville (95901)
PHONE 530 743-6533
Tom Quilty, *Manager*
EMP: 57
SALES (corp-wide): 850.1MM **Privately Held**
WEB: www.coca-cola.com
SIC: 2086 Bottled & canned soft drinks
PA: Reyes Coca-Cola Bottling, L.L.C.
3 Park Plz Ste 600
Irvine CA 92614
213 744-8616

(P-2807) REYES COCA-COLA BOTTLING LLC
530 Getty Ct, Benicia (94510-1139)
PHONE 707 747-2000
Gerold Henderickson, *Manager*
EMP: 57
SALES (corp-wide): 850.1MM **Privately Held**
WEB: www.coca-cola.com
SIC: 2086 Bottled & canned soft drinks
PA: Reyes Coca-Cola Bottling, L.L.C.
3 Park Plz Ste 600
Irvine CA 92614
213 744-8616

(P-2808) REYES COCA-COLA BOTTLING LLC
2633 Camino Ramon Ste 300, San Ramon (94583-2570)
PHONE 925 830-6500
Jim Hegenbart, *Manager*
EMP: 57
SALES (corp-wide): 850.1MM **Privately Held**
WEB: www.coca-cola.com
SIC: 2086 Bottled & canned soft drinks
PA: Reyes Coca-Cola Bottling, L.L.C.
3 Park Plz Ste 600
Irvine CA 92614
213 744-8616

(P-2809) ROGER ENRICO
Also Called: Pepsi-Cola
1150 E North Ave, Fresno (93725-1929)
PHONE 559 485-5050
Eric Foss, *CEO*
Craig Weatherup, *Ch of Bd*
Robert King, *President*
Terri Scherer, *Analyst*
Corinne Rogers, *Human Res Dir*
EMP: 109 **EST:** 1900
SQ FT: 250,000
SALES (est): 11.7MM **Privately Held**
WEB: www.pepsico.com
SIC: 2086 Soft drinks: packaged in cans, bottles, etc.; carbonated beverages, non-alcoholic: bottled & canned

2086 Soft Drinks

(P-2810)
SACRAMENTO COCA-COLA BTLG INC (HQ)
4101 Gateway Park Blvd, Sacramento (95834-1951)
PHONE..................916 928-2300
Steven A Cahillane, *CEO*
David Etheridge, *President*
EMP: 365 **EST:** 1927
SQ FT: 260,000
SALES (est): 38.2MM
SALES (corp-wide): 850.1MM **Privately Held**
WEB: www.previewsaccoke.weebly.com
SIC: 2086 Bottled & canned soft drinks
PA: Reyes Coca-Cola Bottling, L.L.C.
3 Park Plz Ste 600
Irvine CA 92614
213 744-8616

(P-2811)
SACRAMENTO COCA-COLA BTLG INC
1733 Morgan Rd Ste 200, Modesto (95358-5841)
PHONE..................209 541-3200
Rex McGowen, *Principal*
EMP: 78
SALES (corp-wide): 850.1MM **Privately Held**
WEB: www.coca-cola.com
SIC: 2086 Bottled & canned soft drinks
HQ: Sacramento Coca-Cola Bottling Co., Inc.
4101 Gateway Park Blvd
Sacramento CA 95834
916 928-2300

(P-2812)
SEVEN UP BTLG CO SAN FRANCISCO (HQ)
Also Called: Seven-Up Bottling
2875 Prune Ave, Fremont (94539-6731)
PHONE..................925 938-8777
Roger Easley, *Ch of Bd*
Linda Orsi, *Vice Pres*
EMP: 175 **EST:** 1935
SALES (est): 61.4MM **Publicly Held**
WEB: www.7up.com
SIC: 2086 5149 4225 Soft drinks: packaged in cans, bottles, etc.; groceries & related products; general warehousing & storage

(P-2813)
SEVEN UP BTLG CO SAN FRANCISCO
Also Called: Seven-Up Bottling
2670 Land Ave, Sacramento (95815-2380)
P.O. Box 15820 (95852-0820)
PHONE..................916 929-7777
Tom Tontes, *Manager*
Wayne Buffington, *Production*
Kelly Dixon, *Manager*
EMP: 166 **Publicly Held**
WEB: www.drpepper.com
SIC: 2086 5078 Soft drinks: packaged in cans, bottles, etc.; refrigerated beverage dispensers
HQ: Seven Up Bottling Company Of San Francisco
2875 Prune Ave
Fremont CA 94539
925 938-8777

(P-2814)
SHASTA BEVERAGES INC (DH)
Also Called: National Bevpak
26901 Indl Blvd, Hayward (94545)
PHONE..................954 581-0922
Joseph G Caporella, *CEO*
John Minton, *President*
Dean McCoy, *Vice Pres*
Nick Caporella, *Principal*
Jerry House, *Plant Supt*
◆ **EMP:** 80 **EST:** 1889
SQ FT: 156,000
SALES (est): 141.7MM
SALES (corp-wide): 1B **Publicly Held**
WEB: www.shastapop.com
SIC: 2086 Soft drinks: packaged in cans, bottles, etc.; carbonated beverages, nonalcoholic: bottled & canned

(P-2815)
SMUCKER NATURAL FOODS INC (HQ)
37 Speedway Ave, Chico (95928-9554)
PHONE..................530 899-5000
Richard K Smucker, *CEO*
Timothy P Smucker, *President*
Julia Sabin, *Vice Pres*
Tricia Rollman, *Project Leader*
Kim Dietz, *Human Res Dir*
◆ **EMP:** 130 **EST:** 1971
SQ FT: 85,000
SALES (est): 602.2MM
SALES (corp-wide): 8B **Publicly Held**
WEB: www.jmsmucker.com
SIC: 2086 2033 2087 Iced tea & fruit drinks, bottled & canned; carbonated beverages, nonalcoholic: bottled & canned; canned fruits & specialties; syrups, drink
PA: The J M Smucker Company
1 Strawberry Ln
Orrville OH 44667
330 682-3000

(P-2816)
SVC MFG INC A CORP
Also Called: Pepsi Co
5625 International Blvd, Oakland (94621-4403)
PHONE..................510 261-5800
David Chu, *Principal*
▲ **EMP:** 16 **EST:** 2005
SALES (est): 1.9MM **Privately Held**
WEB: www.pepsico.com
SIC: 2086 Carbonated soft drinks, bottled & canned

(P-2817)
VARNI BROTHERS CORPORATION
Also Called: 7 Up
1109 W Anderson St, Stockton (95206-1158)
PHONE..................209 464-7778
Larry Varni, *Manager*
EMP: 93
SALES (corp-wide): 80.1MM **Privately Held**
WEB: www.7up.com
SIC: 2086 Bottled & canned soft drinks
PA: Varni Brothers Corporation
400 Hosmer Ave
Modesto CA 95351
209 521-1777

(P-2818)
WIT GROUP
1822 Buenaventura Blvd # 101, Redding (96001-6313)
PHONE..................530 243-4447
Paul A Kassis, *President*
James Akers, *Vice Pres*
Jim Akers, *Marketing Staff*
▼ **EMP:** 35 **EST:** 2001
SQ FT: 1,100
SALES (est): 7.5MM **Privately Held**
SIC: 2086 Water, pasteurized: packaged in cans, bottles, etc.

2087 Flavoring Extracts & Syrups

(P-2819)
BLOSSOM VALLEY FOODS INC
Also Called: Pepper Plant, The
20 Casey Ln, Gilroy (95020-4539)
PHONE..................408 848-5520
Robert M Wagner, *President*
Virginia Ponce, *Cust Mgr*
Phil Quintero, *Manager*
EMP: 25 **EST:** 1933
SQ FT: 27,000
SALES (est): 3.9MM **Privately Held**
WEB: www.blossomvalleyfoods.com
SIC: 2087 2099 Cocktail mixes, nonalcoholic; food preparations; vinegar

(P-2820)
PACIFIC COAST INGREDIENTS (PA)
Also Called: Perfumer's Apprentice
170 Technology Cir, Scotts Valley (95066-3520)
PHONE..................831 316-7137
Linda Andrews, *CEO*
Travis McIntosh, *Opers Mgr*
EMP: 15 **EST:** 2004
SQ FT: 50,000
SALES (est): 9.8MM **Privately Held**
WEB: www.shop.perfumersapprentice.com
SIC: 2087 5141 8741 Extracts, flavoring; food brokers; administrative management

(P-2821)
PACIFIC COAST PRODUCTS LLC
Also Called: Perfumer's Apprentice
200 Technology Cir, Scotts Valley (95066-3500)
PHONE..................831 316-7137
David Hertzberg, *Prdtn Mgr*
EMP: 32
SQ FT: 26,000
SALES (corp-wide): 9.8MM **Privately Held**
WEB: www.shop.perfumersapprentice.com
SIC: 2087 2844 Extracts, flavoring; concentrates, perfume
PA: Pacific Coast Ingredients
170 Technology Cir
Scotts Valley CA 95066
831 316-7137

(P-2822)
QUAKER OATS COMPANY
5625 International Blvd, Oakland (94621-4403)
PHONE..................510 261-5800
Joan Parrott Sheffer, *Branch Mgr*
EMP: 106
SALES (corp-wide): 70.3B **Publicly Held**
WEB: www.quakeroats.com
SIC: 2087 2086 Beverage bases, concentrates, syrups, powders & mixes; bottled & canned soft drinks
HQ: The Quaker Oats Company
555 W Monroe St Fl 1
Chicago IL 60661
312 821-1000

(P-2823)
R TORRE & COMPANY INC (PA)
Also Called: Torani Syrups & Flavors
2000 Marina Blvd, San Leandro (94577-3208)
PHONE..................800 775-1925
Melanie Dulbecco, *CEO*
Doug Reifsteck, *COO*
Lisa Lucheta, *Principal*
Paul Lucheta, *Principal*
Pruthvi Varshu, *General Mgr*
◆ **EMP:** 158 **EST:** 1925
SQ FT: 110,000
SALES (est): 75.9MM **Privately Held**
WEB: www.torani.com
SIC: 2087 Syrups, drink

(P-2824)
R TORRE & COMPANY INC
2000 Marina Ct, San Leandro (94577-3125)
PHONE..................650 624-2830
Steve Schultz, *Surgery Dir*
EMP: 35
SALES (corp-wide): 75.9MM **Privately Held**
WEB: www.torani.com
SIC: 2087 Syrups, drink
PA: R. Torre & Company, Inc.
2000 Marina Blvd
San Leandro CA 94577
800 775-1925

(P-2825)
SAFEWAY INC
1200 Irving St Ste 2, San Francisco (94122-2121)
PHONE..................415 661-3220
John Bacho, *Manager*
EMP: 3512
SQ FT: 36,999
SALES (corp-wide): 69.6B **Publicly Held**
WEB: www.safeway.com
SIC: 5411 5912 2087 2051 Frozen food & freezer plans, except meat; drug stores & proprietary stores; flavoring extracts & syrups; bread, cake & related products; eating places; bakeries
HQ: Safeway Inc.
5918 Stoneridge Mall Rd
Pleasanton CA 94588
925 226-5000

(P-2826)
STILL ROOM LLC
Also Called: Small Hand Foods
2624 Barrington Ct, Hayward (94545-1100)
PHONE..................510 847-1930
Jennifer Colliau,
John Monetta, *CFO*
EMP: 33 **EST:** 2018
SALES (est): 2.7MM **Privately Held**
SIC: 2087 Beverage bases, concentrates, syrups, powders & mixes; syrups, drink

2091 Fish & Seafoods, Canned & Cured

(P-2827)
OCEAN FRESH LLC (PA)
Also Called: Ocean Fresh Seafood Products
344 N Franklin St, Fort Bragg (95437-3402)
PHONE..................707 964-1389
Robert S Juntz, *Mng Member*
Susan Juntz,
▲ **EMP:** 36 **EST:** 1981
SALES (est): 4.7MM **Privately Held**
WEB: www.of.mcn.org
SIC: 2091 Fish, canned & cured

(P-2828)
PACIFIC PLAZA IMPORTS INC (PA)
Also Called: Plaze De Caviar
3018 Willow Pass Rd # 102, Concord (94519-2543)
PHONE..................925 349-4000
Mark Bolourchi, *President*
Ali Bolourchi, *Vice Pres*
Sharon Bolourchi, *Vice Pres*
◆ **EMP:** 17 **EST:** 1985
SQ FT: 24,000
SALES (est): 5MM **Privately Held**
WEB: www.plazadecaviar.com
SIC: 2091 Caviar: packaged in cans, jars, etc.

2092 Fish & Seafoods, Fresh & Frozen

(P-2829)
AZUMA FOODS INTL INC USA (HQ)
Also Called: Azuma Foods Intl Inc USA
20201 Mack St, Hayward (94545-1224)
PHONE..................510 782-1112
Takahiro Tamura, *CEO*
Toshie Azuma, *CFO*
Toshinobu Azuma, *Chairman*
◆ **EMP:** 72 **EST:** 1990
SQ FT: 70,000
SALES (est): 21.2MM **Privately Held**
WEB: www.azumafoods.com
SIC: 2092 5146 Fresh or frozen packaged fish; seafoods

(P-2830)
EAGLE CANYON CAPITAL LLC (PA)
Also Called: My Goods Market
3130 Crow Canyon Pl # 240, San Ramon (94583-1346)
PHONE..................925 884-0800
Sam Hirbod,
EMP: 1641 **EST:** 2007
SQ FT: 20,000 **Privately Held**
WEB: www.circlek.com
SIC: 5411 5499 2092 Convenience stores; beverage stores; coffee; crab meat, fresh: packaged in nonsealed containers

PRODUCTS & SERVICES SECTION
2096 - Potato Chips & Similar Prdts County (P-2855)

(P-2831)
MS INTERTRADE INC (PA)
Also Called: Sonoma Foods
2221 Bluebell Dr Ste A, Santa Rosa (95403-2545)
P.O. Box 6083 (95406-0083)
PHONE..................707 837-8057
Matthew J Mariani, *CEO*
Scott A Gray, *President*
Charles Hansen, *Vice Pres*
EMP: 44 **EST:** 1993
SQ FT: 8,000
SALES (est): 5.1MM **Privately Held**
WEB: www.sonomaseafoods.com
SIC: 2092 Fresh or frozen fish or seafood chowders, soups & stews

(P-2832)
TARDIO ENTERPRISES INC
Also Called: Newport Fish
457 S Canal St, South San Francisco (94080-4607)
PHONE..................650 877-7200
Andrew Tardio, *President*
EMP: 25
SALES (est): 4.8MM **Privately Held**
SIC: 2092 5421 Fresh or frozen packaged fish; fish & seafood markets

(P-2833)
WILD TYPE INC
Also Called: Wildtype
2325 3rd St Ste 209, San Francisco (94107-3196)
PHONE..................408 669-5207
Justin Kolbeck, *CEO*
Arye Elfenbein, *Principal*
John Melas-Kyriazi, *Principal*
EMP: 19 **EST:** 2016
SALES (est): 2.1MM **Privately Held**
WEB: www.wildtypefoods.com
SIC: 2092 Seafoods, fresh: prepared; seafoods, frozen: prepared

2095 Coffee

(P-2834)
AMERICAS BEST BEVERAGE INC
600 50th Ave, Oakland (94601-5004)
PHONE..................800 723-8808
Hovik Azadkhanian, *CEO*
EMP: 25 **EST:** 2018
SALES (est): 10MM **Privately Held**
WEB: www.americasbestbeverage.com
SIC: 2095 2086 Roasted coffee; tea, iced: packaged in cans, bottles, etc.

(P-2835)
ANDYTOWN LLC (PA)
Also Called: Andytown Coffee Roasters
3016 Taraval St, San Francisco (94116-2105)
PHONE..................415 702-9859
Lauren Crabbe, *Mng Member*
Corazon Padilla, *QC Dir*
Michael McCrory,
EMP: 46 **EST:** 2017
SALES (est): 4.3MM **Privately Held**
WEB: www.andytownsf.com
SIC: 5812 2095 Coffee shop; coffee roasting (except by wholesale grocers)

(P-2836)
BORESHA INTERNATIONAL INC
7041 Koll Center Pkwy # 100, Pleasanton (94566-3175)
PHONE..................925 676-1400
Tony Drexel Smith, *President*
George Najjar, *President*
EMP: 25 **EST:** 2007
SALES (est): 3.3MM **Privately Held**
WEB: www.boreshainternational.com
SIC: 2095 Coffee extracts

(P-2837)
CAFE CHROMATIC
460 Lincoln Ave Ste 10, San Jose (95126-3888)
PHONE..................510 220-1341
EMP: 63

SALES (corp-wide): 583.7K **Privately Held**
WEB: www.chromaticcoffee.com
SIC: 5812 2095 Coffee shop; coffee extracts
PA: Cafe Chromatic
5237 Stevens Creek Blvd
Santa Clara CA 95051
408 248-4500

(P-2838)
COFFEE WORKS INC
3418 Folsom Blvd, Sacramento (95816-5312)
PHONE..................916 452-1086
John Shahabian, *Owner*
David Casavantes, *Engineer*
Brenn Paterson, *Business Mgr*
EMP: 16 **EST:** 1982
SQ FT: 4,000
SALES (est): 3.1MM **Privately Held**
WEB: www.coffeeworks.com
SIC: 2095 5499 Coffee roasting (except by wholesale grocers); coffee

(P-2839)
JEREMIAHS PICK COFFEE COMPANY
1495 Evans Ave, San Francisco (94124-1706)
PHONE..................415 206-9900
Jeremiah Pick, *President*
Mike Ahmadi, *Shareholder*
Krislyn Asagra, *Webmaster*
▲ **EMP:** 19 **EST:** 1993
SQ FT: 11,000
SALES (est): 3MM **Privately Held**
WEB: www.jeremiahspick.com
SIC: 2095 5149 Coffee roasting (except by wholesale grocers); coffee, green or roasted

(P-2840)
NOBLE BREWER BEER COMPANY
Also Called: Office Libations
4721 Tidewater Ave Ste C, Oakland (94601-4917)
PHONE..................301 536-1934
Claude Burns, *CEO*
EMP: 25 **EST:** 2014
SQ FT: 3,500
SALES (est): 3.4MM **Privately Held**
WEB: www.noblebrewer.com
SIC: 5963 2095 5149 Direct selling establishments; food services, direct sales; food service, coffee-cart; food service, mobile, except coffee-cart; coffee roasting (except by wholesale grocers); coffee & tea

(P-2841)
PEERLESS COFFEE COMPANY INC
Also Called: Peerles Coffee and Tea
260 Oak St, Oakland (94607-4512)
PHONE..................510 763-1763
George J Vukasin Jr, *CEO*
Mike Pine, *CFO*
Kristina V Brouhard, *Exec VP*
John Ziglar, *Vice Pres*
Rene Finney, *VP Finance*
EMP: 85 **EST:** 1924
SQ FT: 65,000
SALES (est): 17.3MM **Privately Held**
WEB: www.peerlesscoffee.com
SIC: 2095 5149 Coffee roasting (except by wholesale grocers); tea; spices & seasonings

(P-2842)
PEETS COFFEE INC (DH)
1400 Park Ave, Emeryville (94608-3520)
P.O. Box 12509, Berkeley (94712-3509)
PHONE..................510 594-2100
David Burwick, *President*
Gerald Baldwin, *Ch of Bd*
Patrick Odea, *President*
Hennine Anderson, *CFO*
John Coletta, *CFO*
EMP: 75 **EST:** 1966
SQ FT: 60,000

SALES (est): 132.2MM
SALES (corp-wide): 177.9K **Privately Held**
WEB: www.peets.com
SIC: 5499 2095 5149 Coffee; roasted coffee; cat food
HQ: Peet's Coffee & Tea, Llc
1400 Park Ave
Emeryville CA 94608
510 594-2100

(P-2843)
PEETS COFFEE & TEA LLC (DH)
1400 Park Ave, Emeryville (94608-3520)
PHONE..................510 594-2100
David Burwick, *CEO*
Paul Clayton, *President*
Shawn Conway, *Vice Pres*
Jason Fatta, *General Mgr*
Ann Renneker, *Planning*
▲ **EMP:** 859 **EST:** 1971
SQ FT: 60,000
SALES (est): 1.5B
SALES (corp-wide): 177.9K **Privately Held**
WEB: www.peets.com
SIC: 2095 5149 Roasted coffee; coffee, green or roasted

(P-2844)
PEETS COFFEE & TEA LLC
1875 S Bascom Ave, Campbell (95008-2310)
PHONE..................408 558-9535
EMP: 22
SALES (corp-wide): 177.9K **Privately Held**
WEB: www.peets.com
SIC: 2095 5499 Roasted coffee; beverage stores
HQ: Peet's Coffee & Tea, Llc
1400 Park Ave
Emeryville CA 94608
510 594-2100

(P-2845)
QUETZAL GROUP INC
1234 Polk St, San Francisco (94109-5542)
PHONE..................415 673-4181
Frederick L Charron, *CEO*
Wayne R Newman, *CFO*
EMP: 23 **EST:** 1997
SQ FT: 3,000
SALES (est): 750.3K **Privately Held**
SIC: 5812 2095 5499 5149 Coffee shop; roasted coffee; coffee; cocoa

(P-2846)
RED BAY COFFEE COMPANY INC
3098 E 10th St, Oakland (94601-2960)
PHONE..................510 409-1076
Keba Konte, *CEO*
EMP: 50 **EST:** 2020
SALES (est): 5.5MM **Privately Held**
WEB: www.redbaycoffee.com
SIC: 2095 Coffee roasting (except by wholesale grocers)

(P-2847)
TAYLOR MAID FARMS LLC
6790 Mckinley Ave, Sebastopol (95472-3496)
PHONE..................707 824-9110
Christ Martin,
Michael Presley,
EMP: 30 **EST:** 2000
SALES (est): 3.5MM **Privately Held**
WEB: www.taylorlane.com
SIC: 2095 Roasted coffee

(P-2848)
TULLYS COFFEE CO INC (HQ)
2455 Fillmore St, San Francisco (94115-1814)
PHONE..................415 929-8808
Tom O' Keefe, *President*
Steve Griffin, *CFO*
EMP: 25 **EST:** 1983
SQ FT: 8,000
SALES (est): 7.4MM **Privately Held**
WEB: www.tullys.com
SIC: 2095 5149 5499 5812 Coffee, ground: mixed with grain or chicory; coffee, green or roasted; coffee; coffee shop

(P-2849)
TULLYS COFFEE CO INC
1509 Sloat Blvd, San Francisco (94132-1222)
PHONE..................415 213-8791
Jen Wong, *Manager*
EMP: 24 **Privately Held**
SIC: 2095 5499 Coffee roasting (except by wholesale grocers); coffee
HQ: Tully's Coffee Co Inc
2455 Fillmore St
San Francisco CA 94115
415 929-8808

(P-2850)
ZOCALO COFFEE HOUSE
659 Broadmoor Blvd, San Leandro (94577-1951)
PHONE..................510 569-0102
Timothy Holmes, *Principal*
EMP: 18 **EST:** 2002
SALES (est): 286.6K **Privately Held**
WEB: www.zocalocoffee.com
SIC: 5812 2095 Coffee shop; roasted coffee

2096 Potato Chips & Similar Prdts

(P-2851)
4505 MEATS INC
548 Market St, San Francisco (94104-5401)
PHONE..................415 255-3094
Ryan Farr, *CEO*
Bob Ziegler, *Sales Staff*
Greg Lagios, *Director*
EMP: 20 **EST:** 2017
SALES (est): 394K **Privately Held**
WEB: www.4505meats.com
SIC: 2096 Pork rinds

(P-2852)
CALIFORNIA NUGGETS INC
23073 S Frederick Rd, Ripon (95366-9616)
PHONE..................209 599-7131
Steve Gikas, *CEO*
Richard Piercefield, *CFO*
Barbara Bain, *Corp Secy*
Lori Gikas, *Vice Pres*
Chris Ben Groningen, *Controller*
◆ **EMP:** 40 **EST:** 1998
SQ FT: 50,000
SALES (est): 8.2MM **Privately Held**
WEB: www.californianuggets.com
SIC: 2096 2068 Potato chips & similar snacks; nuts: dried, dehydrated, salted or roasted

(P-2853)
CUP4CUP LLC (PA)
840 Latour Ct Ste B, NAPA (94558-6286)
PHONE..................707 754-4263
Thomas Keller,
Brett Lanford, *COO*
EMP: 34 **EST:** 2015
SALES (est): 1.1MM **Privately Held**
WEB: www.cup4cup.com
SIC: 2096 Potato chips & other potato-based snacks

(P-2854)
DON VITO OZUNA FOODS CORP
180 Cochrane Cir, Morgan Hill (95037-2807)
PHONE..................408 465-2010
Cevero Ozuna, *President*
EMP: 22 **EST:** 2009
SQ FT: 12,000
SALES (est): 2.3MM **Privately Held**
WEB: www.ozunatortillafactory.com
SIC: 2096 Tortilla chips

(P-2855)
FANTE INC (PA)
Also Called: Casa Sanchez Foods
2898 W Winton Ave, Hayward (94545-1122)
P.O. Box 12582, San Francisco (94112-0582)
PHONE..................650 697-7525
Robert C Sanchez, *President*
Robert Sanchez, *President*
Juliana Gallon, *Manager*

2096 - Potato Chips & Similar Prdts County (P-2856)

Rosemarie Ramos, *Manager*
▲ **EMP:** 30
SALES (est): 16MM **Privately Held**
WEB: www.casasanchezfoods.com
SIC: 2096 2099 Tortilla chips; dips, except cheese & sour cream based

(P-2856)
FRITO-LAY NORTH AMERICA INC
600 Garner Rd, Modesto (95357-0514)
PHONE......................209 544-5400
Bob Schreck, *Manager*
EMP: 450
SALES (corp-wide): 70.3B **Publicly Held**
WEB: www.fritolay.com
SIC: 2096 2099 Potato chips & similar snacks; food preparations
HQ: Frito-Lay North America, Inc.
  7701 Legacy Dr
  Plano TX 75024

(P-2857)
MINTURN NUT CO INC
8800 Minturn Rd, Le Grand (95333-9711)
PHONE......................559 665-8500
Jeff Marchini, *CEO*
Kitt Kahl, *President*
Henry Kelsey, *Treasurer*
Brad Schnoor, *Vice Pres*
Dave Hudgins, *Department Mgr*
◆ **EMP:** 20 **EST:** 1996
SQ FT: 75,000
SALES (est): 4.9MM **Privately Held**
WEB: www.minturnnut.com
SIC: 5441 2096 Nuts; cheese curls & puffs

(P-2858)
PURE NATURE FOODS LLC
700 Santa Anita Dr Ste A, Woodland (95776-6102)
P.O. Box 2387 (95776-2387)
PHONE......................530 723-5269
Miguel Reyna, *President*
Shan Staka, *CFO*
Dan Miller, *VP Opers*
EMP: 30 **EST:** 2016
SQ FT: 60,000
SALES (est): 1.8MM **Privately Held**
WEB: www.purenaturefoodsco.com
SIC: 2096 Rice chips

(P-2859)
WARNOCK FOOD PRODUCTS INC
20237 Masa St, Madera (93638-9457)
PHONE......................559 661-4845
Donald Warnock, *Principal*
Cathryn Warnock, *Admin Sec*
Kraig Rawls, *Purch Mgr*
Mario Sanchez, *Plant Mgr*
Trish Blankenship, *Director*
▲ **EMP:** 98
SQ FT: 25,000
SALES (est): 32.2MM **Privately Held**
WEB: www.warnockfoods.com
SIC: 2096 2099 2033 Tortilla chips; food preparations; canned fruits & specialties
HQ: Calbee America Incorporated
  2600 Maxwell Way
  Fairfield CA 94534
  707 427-2500

2097 Ice

(P-2860)
GLACIER VALLEY ICE COMPANY LP (PA)
Also Called: Glacier Ice Company
8580 Laguna Station Rd, Elk Grove (95758-9550)
PHONE......................916 394-2939
Sarah Demartini, *Principal*
Angela Aistrup, *Systems Mgr*
Karen Anderson, *Human Resources*
Bob Sikes, *Sales Executive*
EMP: 40 **EST:** 1972
SQ FT: 72,000
SALES (est): 3.9MM **Privately Held**
SIC: 2097 5199 Manufactured ice; ice, manufactured or natural

(P-2861)
PELTON-SHEPHERD INDUSTRIES INC (PA)
812 W Luce St Ste B, Stockton (95203-4937)
P.O. Box 30218 (95213-0218)
PHONE......................209 460-0893
Alicia M Shepherd, *President*
Pat Shepherd, *Sales Staff*
▲ **EMP:** 35
SQ FT: 30,000
SALES (est): 14.4MM **Privately Held**
WEB: www.peltonshepherd.com
SIC: 2097 Manufactured ice

(P-2862)
UNITED STATES COLD STORAGE INC
3936 Dudley Blvd, McClellan (95652-2317)
PHONE......................916 640-2800
EMP: 28
SALES (corp-wide): 14.2B **Privately Held**
WEB: www.uscold.com
SIC: 2097 4222 Manufactured ice; warehousing, cold storage or refrigerated
HQ: United States Cold Storage, Inc.
  2 Aquarium Dr Ste 400
  Camden NJ 08103
  856 354-8181

(P-2863)
UNITED STATES COLD STORAGE INC
4233 Rosecrest Way, Sacramento (95826-5634)
PHONE......................916 392-9160
Coy Brumley, *Branch Mgr*
EMP: 28
SALES (corp-wide): 14.2B **Privately Held**
WEB: www.uscold.com
SIC: 2097 Manufactured ice
HQ: United States Cold Storage, Inc.
  2 Aquarium Dr Ste 400
  Camden NJ 08103
  856 354-8181

2098 Macaroni, Spaghetti & Noodles

(P-2864)
NEW HONG KONG NOODLE CO INC
360 Swift Ave Ste 22, South San Francisco (94080-6220)
PHONE......................650 588-6425
Steven Lum, *President*
Wai-Kui England Lum, *Treasurer*
Richard Lum, *Vice Pres*
Lam Wai Lum, *Admin Sec*
◆ **EMP:** 40
SQ FT: 26,000
SALES (est): 7.4MM **Privately Held**
WEB: www.nhknoodle.com
SIC: 2098 Food preparations

(P-2865)
PASTA SONOMA LLC
640 Martin Ave Ste 1, Rohnert Park (94928-7994)
PHONE......................707 584-0800
Don Luber,
▲ **EMP:** 20 **EST:** 1983
SQ FT: 6,500
SALES (est): 1MM **Privately Held**
WEB: www.pastasonoma.com
SIC: 2098 5812 Macaroni & spaghetti; eating places

2099 Food Preparations, NEC

(P-2866)
ALEXANDER VALLEY GOURMET LLC
140 Grove Ct B, Healdsburg (95448-4780)
PHONE......................707 473-0116
David Ehreth,
EMP: 20 **EST:** 2013
SALES (est): 1.7MM **Privately Held**
SIC: 2099 Food preparations

(P-2867)
ANNIES INC (HQ)
Also Called: Homegrown Naturals
1610 5th St, Berkeley (94710-1715)
PHONE......................510 558-7500
John Foraker, *CEO*
Molly F Ashby, *Ch of Bd*
Kelly J Kennedy, *CFO*
Amanda K Martinez, *Exec VP*
Mark Mortimer, *Exec VP*
EMP: 125 **EST:** 2004
SQ FT: 33,500
SALES (est): 91.4MM
SALES (corp-wide): 18.1B **Publicly Held**
WEB: www.annies.com
SIC: 2099 Food preparations
PA: General Mills, Inc.
  1 General Mills Blvd
  Minneapolis MN 55426
  763 764-7600

(P-2868)
ARANDAS TORTILLA COMPANY INC
1318 E Scotts Ave, Stockton (95205-6152)
PHONE......................209 464-8675
Victor Aranda, *CEO*
Javier Aranda, *Treasurer*
Vicent Aranda, *Vice Pres*
EMP: 48 **EST:** 1982
SQ FT: 20,000
SALES (est): 9.6MM **Privately Held**
WEB: www.arandastortillacompany.com
SIC: 2099 Tortillas, fresh or refrigerated

(P-2869)
BARNEY & CO CALIFORNIA LLC
2925 S Elm Ave Ste 101, Fresno (93706-5465)
PHONE......................559 442-1752
Dawn Kelley, *President*
Steve Kelley, *COO*
Steven J Luttrell,
EMP: 18 **EST:** 2006
SQ FT: 37,000
SALES (est): 6.4MM **Privately Held**
WEB: www.barneybutter.com
SIC: 2099 Almond pastes

(P-2870)
BERBER FOOD MANUFACTURING INC
Also Called: MI Rancho Tortilla Factory
10115 Iron Rock Way Ste 1, Elk Grove (95624-2795)
PHONE......................510 553-0444
Manuel Berber, *President*
Robert Berber Jr, *Corp Secy*
Joe Santana, *Vice Pres*
Alexa Lavere, *Sales Staff*
Suzie Lister, *Sales Staff*
▼ **EMP:** 150 **EST:** 1994
SALES (est): 36.9MM **Privately Held**
WEB: www.miranchoretail.com
SIC: 2099 Tortillas, fresh or refrigerated

(P-2871)
BLUE DIAMOND GROWERS
1701 C St, Sacramento (95811-1029)
PHONE......................916 446-8464
EMP: 154
SALES (corp-wide): 588.2MM **Privately Held**
WEB: www.bluediamond.com
SIC: 2099 Food preparations
PA: Diamond Blue Growers
  1802 C St
  Sacramento CA 95811
  800 987-2329

(P-2872)
BLUE DIAMOND GROWERS
Also Called: Blue Diamond
1300 N Washington Rd, Turlock (95380-9506)
PHONE......................209 604-1501
EMP: 154
SALES (corp-wide): 588.2MM **Privately Held**
WEB: www.bdingredients.com
SIC: 2099 Food preparations
PA: Diamond Blue Growers
  1802 C St
  Sacramento CA 95811
  800 987-2329

(P-2873)
BREWER BREWER LOFGREN LLP (PA)
650 University Ave # 220, Sacramento (95825-6726)
PHONE......................916 550-1482
Roy E Brewer, *Principal*
EMP: 22 **EST:** 2014
SALES (est): 406.9K **Privately Held**
WEB: www.brewerlofgren.com
SIC: 2099 Almond pastes

(P-2874)
BRIGHT PEOPLE FOODS INC (PA)
Also Called: Dr McDougall's Right Foods
1640 Tide Ct, Woodland (95776-6210)
P.O. Box 2205 (95776-2205)
PHONE......................530 669-6870
Michael L Vinnicombe, *President*
Carolyn Vinnicombe, *Vice Pres*
▼ **EMP:** 24 **EST:** 1953
SQ FT: 30,000
SALES (est): 14.2MM **Privately Held**
WEB: www.rightfoods.com
SIC: 2099 Spices, including grinding

(P-2875)
BUSSETO FOODS INC (PA)
1351 N Crystal Ave, Fresno (93728-1142)
P.O. Box 12403 (93777-2403)
PHONE......................559 485-9882
G Michael Grazier, *President*
Randy Hergenroeder, *CFO*
Ed Fanucchi, *Admin Sec*
James Freeny, *Purchasing*
▲ **EMP:** 147 **EST:** 1981
SQ FT: 40,000
SALES (est): 58.1MM **Privately Held**
WEB: www.busseto.com
SIC: 2099 Food preparations

(P-2876)
C&S GLOBAL FOODS INC
Also Called: Ojo De Agua Produce
1651 Reynolds Ave, Dos Palos (93620)
P.O. Box 1209, Los Banos (93635-1209)
PHONE......................209 392-2223
Reuben Castaneda, *Owner*
EMP: 19 **EST:** 2004
SALES (est): 553.3K **Privately Held**
SIC: 2099 4789 Food preparations; freight car loading & unloading

(P-2877)
CACHE CREEK FOODS LLC
411 N Pioneer Ave, Woodland (95776-6122)
P.O. Box 180 (95776-0180)
PHONE......................530 662-1764
Matthew Morehart,
Connie Stephens, *Office Mgr*
▲ **EMP:** 19 **EST:** 1993
SQ FT: 40,000
SALES (est): 5.9MM **Privately Held**
WEB: www.cachecreekfoods.com
SIC: 2099 2064 Almond pastes; nuts, glace

(P-2878)
CALIFORNIA NATURAL PRODUCTS
Also Called: Power Automation Systems
1250 Lathrop Rd, Lathrop (95330-9709)
P.O. Box 1219 (95330-1219)
PHONE......................209 858-2525
Craig Lemieux, *CEO*
Timothy Preuninger, *CFO*
David Stott, *Admin Sec*
David Tigerino, *Administration*
Janet Walther, *Planning*
◆ **EMP:** 375 **EST:** 1976
SQ FT: 220,000
SALES (est): 128.2MM
SALES (corp-wide): 310MM **Privately Held**
WEB: www.gehlfoodandbeverage.com
SIC: 2099 7389 Food preparations; packaging & labeling services

▲ = Import ▼ = Export
◆ = Import/Export

PRODUCTS & SERVICES SECTION
2099 - Food Preparations, NEC County (P-2903)

PA: Gehl Foods, Llc
W185 N 11300 Whitney Way W 185 N
Germantown WI 53022
262 251-8570

(P-2879)
CASA LUPE INC (PA)
Also Called: Casa Lupe Market & Restaurants
130 Magnolia St, Gridley (95948-2618)
P.O. Box 1230 (95948-1230)
PHONE 530 846-3218
Esther De La Torre, *President*
Luz Maria De La Torre, *Treasurer*
Lupe De La Torre, *Admin Sec*
EMP: 55 **EST:** 1968
SQ FT: 11,000
SALES (est): 13MM **Privately Held**
WEB: www.casalupe.com
SIC: 5812 5411 2099 Mexican restaurant; grocery stores, independent; tortillas, fresh or refrigerated

(P-2880)
CEDARLANE NATURAL FOODS NORTH
Also Called: Cedar Lane North
150 Airport Blvd, South San Francisco (94080-4739)
PHONE 650 742-0444
EMP: 25
SALES (est): 4.1MM **Privately Held**
SIC: 2099 Mfg Food Preparations

(P-2881)
CFARMS INC
1244 E Beamer St, Woodland (95776-6002)
PHONE 916 375-3000
Baljit Pattar, *Branch Mgr*
EMP: 28
SALES (corp-wide): 9.2MM **Privately Held**
WEB: www.culinaryfarms.com
SIC: 2099 5149 Food preparations; flavourings & fragrances
PA: Cfarms, Inc.
1330 N Dutton Ave Ste 100
Santa Rosa CA 95401
916 375-3000

(P-2882)
CFARMS INC (PA)
Also Called: Culinary Farms
1330 N Dutton Ave Ste 100, Santa Rosa (95401-4646)
PHONE 916 375-3000
Adam Lee, *CEO*
Baljit Pattar, *General Mgr*
EMP: 28 **EST:** 2017
SALES (est): 9.2MM **Privately Held**
SIC: 2099 5149 Food preparations; flavourings & fragrances

(P-2883)
CLARMIL MANUFACTURING CORP (PA)
Also Called: Goldilocks
30865 San Clemente St, Hayward (94544-7136)
PHONE 510 476-0700
Mary-Ann Yee Ortiz-Luis, *President*
Mary Ann Yee Ortiz Luis, *President*
Freddie L Go Jr, *COO*
Mannette Roxas, *Treasurer*
Maryann Ortizluis, *Bd of Directors*
▲ **EMP:** 95 **EST:** 1991
SQ FT: 57,000
SALES (est): 19.6MM **Privately Held**
WEB: www.goldilocks-usa.com
SIC: 2099 5149 2051 Food preparations; bakery products; bread, cake & related products

(P-2884)
CLASSIC SALADS LLC
100 Harrington Rd, Royal Oaks (95076-5604)
P.O. Box 3800, Salinas (93912-3800)
PHONE 831 763-4520
Lance Batistich, *Mng Member*
Gene Stoffey, *Enginer*
Jill Lenz, *Sales Mgr*
Dale Chase, *Sales Staff*
Richard Diaz, *Sales Staff*
▲ **EMP:** 44 **EST:** 2000
SALES (est): 8.4MM **Privately Held**
SIC: 2099 Salads, fresh or refrigerated

(P-2885)
CNC NOODLE CORPORATION
325 Fallon St, Oakland (94607-4611)
PHONE 510 835-2269
Betty Lim, *President*
▲ **EMP:** 18 **EST:** 1984
SQ FT: 12,000
SALES (est): 1MM **Privately Held**
SIC: 2099 Noodles, fried (Chinese)

(P-2886)
CORBION BIOTECH INC (HQ)
1 Tower Pl Ste 600, South San Francisco (94080-1832)
PHONE 650 780-4777
Tjerk De Ruiter, *CEO*
EMP: 33 **EST:** 2017
SALES (est): 17.4MM
SALES (corp-wide): 1B **Privately Held**
WEB: www.corbion.com
SIC: 2099 Emulsifiers, food
PA: Corbion N.V.
Piet Heinkade 127
Amsterdam
205 906-911

(P-2887)
DAN ON & ASSOCIATES (USA) LTD (PA)
Also Called: Cashew Farm
2628 S Cherry Ave, Fresno (93706-5420)
PHONE 559 233-2828
Dan On, *CEO*
Li-Ting Chang, *President*
◆ **EMP:** 27 **EST:** 1994
SALES (est): 8.2MM **Privately Held**
WEB: www.dan-d-pak.com
SIC: 2099 Food preparations

(P-2888)
DEL CASTILLO FOODS INC
Also Called: La Campana Tortilla Factory
2346 Maggio Cir, Lodi (95240-8812)
PHONE 209 369-2877
Marciano Del Castillo, *President*
Rosario Del Castillo, *Treasurer*
Bertha Del Castillo, *Vice Pres*
EMP: 40 **EST:** 1981
SQ FT: 16,200
SALES (est): 2.9MM **Privately Held**
SIC: 2099 5461 5411 2096 Tortillas, fresh or refrigerated; bakeries; grocery stores; potato chips & similar snacks

(P-2889)
DEL MONTE CORPORATION (PA)
1 Maritime Plz Ste 700, San Francisco (94111-3410)
P.O. Box 193575 (94119-3575)
PHONE 415 247-3000
David West, *CEO*
Nathan Huffine, *Adv Board Mem*
Danny Bolstad, *Technical Staff*
Kristin Garcia, *Business Mgr*
Louis Sekula, *Safety Mgr*
EMP: 233 **EST:** 2016
SALES (est): 913.5K **Privately Held**
WEB: www.delmontefoods.com
SIC: 2099 Food preparations

(P-2890)
EVOLVA NUTRITION INC
101 Larkspur Landing Cir # 222, Larkspur (94939-1746)
PHONE 415 374-0785
Simon Waddington, *CEO*
Carol Snyder, *Vice Pres*
Rachelle Gonzales, *Sales Mgr*
Kim Greenbaum, *Director*
EMP: 18 **EST:** 2008
SALES (est): 1MM
SALES (corp-wide): 8.2MM **Privately Held**
WEB: www.evolva.com
SIC: 2099 Food preparations
PA: Evolva Holding Sa
Duggingerstrasse 23
Reinach BL 4153
614 852-000

(P-2891)
FALCON TRADING COMPANY (PA)
Also Called: Sunridge Farms
423 Salinas Rd, Royal Oaks (95076-5232)
PHONE 831 786-7000
Morty Cohen, *CEO*
Rebecca Cohen, *Vice Pres*
Ann Slaydon, *Executive*
Robin Van Soest, *Executive*
Ron Giannini, *General Mgr*
◆ **EMP:** 150 **EST:** 1977
SQ FT: 24,500
SALES (est): 50.8MM **Privately Held**
WEB: www.shopsunridgefarms.com
SIC: 2099 Food preparations

(P-2892)
FIORE DI PASTA INC
4776 E Jensen Ave, Fresno (93725-1704)
PHONE 559 457-0431
Bernadatta Primavera, *President*
Anthony Primavera, *CFO*
Martin Flores, *Plant Supt*
Anna Dicicco, *Sales Staff*
Brad Lowe, *Director*
▲ **EMP:** 67 **EST:** 1994
SQ FT: 59,000
SALES (est): 16.5MM **Privately Held**
WEB: www.fioredipasta.com
SIC: 2099 Pasta, uncooked: packaged with other ingredients

(P-2893)
FISHER NUT COMPANY
137 N Hart Rd, Modesto (95358-9537)
PHONE 209 527-0108
Ronald Fisher, *President*
Kevin Weber, *Manager*
◆ **EMP:** 15 **EST:** 1980
SALES (est): 3.2MM **Privately Held**
WEB: www.fishernut.com
SIC: 2099 Food preparations

(P-2894)
FOREVER YOUNG
Also Called: Supernutrition
208 Palmetto Ave, Pacifica (94044-1374)
PHONE 650 355-5481
EMP: 24
SQ FT: 12,000
SALES (est): 2.9MM **Privately Held**
SIC: 2099 2834 Mfg Food Preparations Mfg Pharmaceutical Preparations

(P-2895)
GH FOODS CA LLC (DH)
8425 Carbide Ct, Sacramento (95828-5609)
PHONE 916 844-1140
Jim Gibson,
Brianne Goree, *QA Dir*
EMP: 330 **EST:** 2007
SQ FT: 60,000
SALES (est): 135.4MM
SALES (corp-wide): 1B **Publicly Held**
WEB: www.rgfoods.com
SIC: 2099 Salads, fresh or refrigerated
HQ: Renaissance Food Group, Llc
11020 White Rock Rd Ste 1
Rancho Cordova CA 95670
916 638-8825

(P-2896)
GHIRINGHLLI SPCIALTY FOODS INC
101 Benicia Rd, Vallejo (94590-7003)
PHONE 707 561-7670
Mike Ghiringhelli, *President*
Ed Ferrero, *Vice Pres*
Tiffany Ho, *Manager*
Matt Kyne, *Manager*
EMP: 145 **EST:** 1984
SQ FT: 55,000
SALES (est): 26.2MM **Privately Held**
WEB: www.gfoods.net
SIC: 2099 Ready-to-eat meals, salads & sandwiches; salads, fresh or refrigerated

(P-2897)
GOBBLE INC
282 2nd St Ste 300, San Francisco (94105-3128)
PHONE 650 847-1258
Ooshma Garg, *CEO*
Robyn Risso, *Vice Pres*
Will Medford, *Buyer*
EMP: 170 **EST:** 2010
SALES (est): 30.1MM **Privately Held**
WEB: www.gobble.com
SIC: 2099 Food preparations

(P-2898)
GOOD VIEW FUTURE GROUP INC
277 S B St, San Mateo (94401-4017)
PHONE 408 834-5698
William Jiang, *CEO*
EMP: 18 **EST:** 2019
SALES (est): 1MM **Privately Held**
SIC: 2099 Desserts, ready-to-mix

(P-2899)
HAIGS DELICACIES LLC
25673 Nickel Pl, Hayward (94545-3221)
PHONE 510 782-6285
Rita Takvorian, *Mng Member*
Mark Takvorian, *COO*
David Casida, *Plant Mgr*
Steven Cherezian, *VP Sales*
Nadine Takvorian,
EMP: 20 **EST:** 1958
SQ FT: 1,200
SALES (est): 8.7MM **Privately Held**
WEB: www.haigs.com
SIC: 2099 Dips, except cheese & sour cream based

(P-2900)
HARMLESS HARVEST INC (PA)
1814 Franklin St Ste 1000, Oakland (94612-3461)
PHONE 347 688-6286
Ben Mand, *CEO*
Justin Guilbert, *President*
Giannella Alvarez, *CEO*
Brad Paris, *COO*
Sara-Scott Smith, *Admin Sec*
▲ **EMP:** 44 **EST:** 2010
SALES (est): 14.9MM **Privately Held**
WEB: www.harmlessharvest.com
SIC: 2099 Coconut, desiccated & shredded

(P-2901)
HARVEST FOOD PRODUCTS CO INC
710 Sandoval Way, Hayward (94544-7111)
PHONE 510 675-0383
Danny Kha, *President*
Peter Kha, *Purch Mgr*
Connie Kha, *Manager*
◆ **EMP:** 100 **EST:** 1981
SQ FT: 30,000
SALES (est): 17.7MM **Privately Held**
WEB: www.harvestfoodproducts.com
SIC: 5812 2099 2038 Eating places; food preparations; ethnic foods, frozen

(P-2902)
HUGHSON NUT INC
11173 Mercedes Ave, Livingston (95334-9707)
PHONE 209 394-6005
Luis MA, *Principal*
EMP: 15 **Privately Held**
WEB: www.hughsonnut.com
SIC: 2099 Food preparations
HQ: Hughson Nut, Inc.
1825 Verduga Rd
Hughson CA 95326
209 883-0403

(P-2903)
IF HOLDING INC (PA)
Also Called: Initiative Food Company
1912 Industrial Way, Sanger (93657-9508)
PHONE 559 875-3354
John Ypma, *President*
John P Mulvaney, *Vice Pres*
David F Markle, *Admin Sec*
James Ypma, *Project Mgr*
Holly Haydostian, *Controller*
EMP: 125 **EST:** 2002
SQ FT: 200,094
SALES (est): 30.1MM **Privately Held**
WEB: www.initiativefoods.com
SIC: 2099 Food preparations

2099 - Food Preparations, NEC County (P-2904) — PRODUCTS & SERVICES SECTION

(P-2904)
IMPERFECT FOODS INC (PA)
Also Called: Imperfect Produce
1616 Donner Ave, San Francisco (94124-3220)
PHONE.....................415 829-2262
Ben Simon, *CEO*
Tony Masco, *Vice Pres*
Edward O'malley, *Vice Pres*
Emily Carter, *Comms Mgr*
Scott Mowrey, *General Mgr*
EMP: 1453 EST: 2017
SALES (est): 402.3MM **Privately Held**
WEB: www.imperfectfoods.com
SIC: 2099 Vegetables, peeled for the trade

(P-2905)
IMPOSSIBLE FOODS INC (PA)
400 Saginaw Dr, Redwood City (94063-4749)
PHONE.....................650 461-4385
Patrick Brown, *CEO*
Dennis Woodside, *President*
David Borecky, *CFO*
Dana Wagner,
Nick Halla, *Officer*
▲ EMP: 340 EST: 2011
SALES (est): 173.7MM **Privately Held**
WEB: www.impossiblefoods.com
SIC: 2099 Food preparations

(P-2906)
J W FLOOR COVERING INC
3401 Enterprise Ave, Hayward (94545-3201)
PHONE.....................858 444-1214
Decklan Donohue, *Manager*
Victor Melena, *Branch Mgr*
EMP: 134
SALES (corp-wide): 39.6MM **Privately Held**
WEB: www.schedule.jwfloors.com
SIC: 2099 Food preparations
PA: J. W. Floor Covering, Inc.
9881 Carroll Centre Rd
San Diego CA 92126
858 536-8565

(P-2907)
JBR INC (PA)
Also Called: San Francisco Bay Coffee Co
1731 Aviation Blvd, Lincoln (95648-9317)
PHONE.....................916 258-8000
Peter Rogers, *CEO*
Albert Troutman, *CFO*
Mark Vincenzini, *CFO*
Barbara Rogers, *Vice Pres*
Julie Strickland, *Vice Pres*
◆ EMP: 226 EST: 1979
SQ FT: 400,000
SALES (est): 55.4MM **Privately Held**
WEB: www.sfbaycoffee.com
SIC: 2099 2095 Tea blending; coffee roasting (except by wholesale grocers)

(P-2908)
LA ESTRELLITA TIZAPAN MERCADO (PA)
Also Called: La Estrellita Restaurant
2205 Middlefield Rd, Redwood City (94063-2833)
PHONE.....................650 369-3877
Hector Cornelio, *Owner*
EMP: 20 EST: 1990
SQ FT: 10,000
SALES (est): 3.2MM **Privately Held**
WEB: www.laestrellitarestaurant.com
SIC: 2099 5411 5812 Tortillas, fresh or refrigerated; grocery stores, independent; Mexican restaurant

(P-2909)
LA ROSA TORTILLA FACTORY INC
26 Menker St, Watsonville (95076-4915)
PHONE.....................831 728-5332
Alfonso Solorio, *Owner*
Richard Barnes, *CIO*
EMP: 118 **Privately Held**
WEB: www.larosatortillafactory.com
SIC: 2099 Tortillas, fresh or refrigerated
PA: La Rosa Tortilla Factory, Inc.
142 2nd St
Watsonville CA 95076

(P-2910)
LA TAPATIA - NORCAL INC
23423 Cabot Blvd, Hayward (94545-1665)
PHONE.....................510 783-2045
Antonio Chavez, *President*
EMP: 19 EST: 1987
SQ FT: 35,000
SALES (est): 604.5K **Privately Held**
SIC: 2099 2096 Tortillas, fresh or refrigerated; tortilla chips

(P-2911)
LA TAPATIA TORTILLERIA INC
104 E Belmont Ave, Fresno (93701-1403)
PHONE.....................559 441-1030
Helen Chavez-Hansen, *Principal*
John Hansen, *Senior VP*
EMP: 170 EST: 1944
SQ FT: 40,000
SALES (est): 27.6MM **Privately Held**
WEB: www.tortillas4u.com
SIC: 2099 Tortillas, fresh or refrigerated

(P-2912)
LA TERRA FINA USA INC
1300 Atlantic St, Union City (94587-2004)
PHONE.....................510 404-5888
Peter Molloy, *President*
Stephen Cottrell, *CFO*
Henri Madaj, *Engineer*
PHI Tran, *Financial Analy*
Scott Byrnes, *Controller*
EMP: 70 EST: 1994
SQ FT: 24,000
SALES (est): 28.7MM **Privately Held**
WEB: www.laterrafina.com
SIC: 2099 Seasonings & spices

(P-2913)
LA TORTILLA FACTORY INC
3645 Standish Ave, Santa Rosa (95407-8142)
PHONE.....................707 586-4000
Carlos Tamayo, *President*
Dave Davis, *COO*
Clarke Katz, *Info Tech Mgr*
Piero Di Manno, *Network Analyst*
Sheryl Garcia, *Purch Mgr*
EMP: 30
SALES (corp-wide): 79MM **Privately Held**
WEB: www.latortillafactory.com
SIC: 2099 Tortillas, fresh or refrigerated
PA: La Tortilla Factory Inc.
3300 Westwind Blvd
Santa Rosa CA 95403
707 586-4000

(P-2914)
LASELVA BEACH SPICE CO INC
453 Mcquaide Dr, Watsonville (95076-1908)
PHONE.....................831 724-4500
Floyd W Brady, *CEO*
Nick Brady, *Director*
EMP: 18 EST: 2018
SALES (est): 2.2MM **Privately Held**
WEB: www.laselvabeachspice.com
SIC: 2099 Seasonings & spices

(P-2915)
LAURENT CULINARY SERVICE
Also Called: Jessie A Laurent
1945 Francisco Blvd E # 4, San Rafael (94901-5525)
PHONE.....................415 485-1122
Jessie Laurent Boucher, *Partner*
EMP: 15 EST: 1998
SALES (est): 573.7K **Privately Held**
WEB: www.jessieetlaurent.com
SIC: 2099 5812 Ready-to-eat meals, salads & sandwiches; eating places

(P-2916)
LIBERTY FRESH FOODS LLC
11020 White Rock Rd # 100, Rancho Cordova (95670-6402)
PHONE.....................916 638-8825
Kenneth J Catchot,
James E Gibson, *Mng Member*
EMP: 22 EST: 2002
SALES (est): 437.3K **Privately Held**
WEB: www.rfgfoods.com
SIC: 2099 Food preparations

(P-2917)
LOUIE FOODS INTERNATIONAL
471 S Teilman Ave, Fresno (93706-1315)
PHONE.....................559 264-2745
Jay Louie, *President*
Stephanie Louie, *Admin Sec*
EMP: 24 EST: 1950
SALES (est): 989.5K **Privately Held**
SIC: 2099 0182 5199 Noodles, fried (Chinese); tofu, except frozen desserts; bean sprouts grown under cover; packaging materials

(P-2918)
LUCERNE FOODS INC
5918 Stoneridge Mall Rd, Pleasanton (94588-3229)
PHONE.....................925 951-4724
Kenneth Gott, *President*
Peggy Han, *Senior VP*
▼ EMP: 5031 EST: 1979
SALES (est): 4.5MM
SALES (corp-wide): 69.6B **Publicly Held**
WEB: www.lucernefoods.com
SIC: 2099 Food preparations
HQ: Safeway Inc.
5918 Stoneridge Mall Rd
Pleasanton CA 94588
925 226-5000

(P-2919)
LUKES LOCAL INC (PA)
960 Cole St, San Francisco (94117-4316)
PHONE.....................415 643-4510
Luke Chappell, *CEO*
Toms Gutierrez, *CTO*
Kayleigh Kahn, *Associate*
EMP: 81 EST: 2009
SALES (est): 7MM **Privately Held**
WEB: www.lukeslocal.com
SIC: 2099 5141 Ready-to-eat meals, salads & sandwiches; groceries, general line

(P-2920)
LYRICAL FOODS INC
Also Called: Kite Hill
3180 Corporate Pl, Hayward (94545-3916)
PHONE.....................510 784-0955
John Haugen, *CEO*
Jean Prebot, *COO*
Susan McDonald, *CFO*
David Bauer, *Vice Pres*
Stephanie Gilbreath, *Vice Pres*
▲ EMP: 108 EST: 2012
SQ FT: 20,000
SALES (est): 24.4MM **Privately Held**
WEB: www.kite-hill.com
SIC: 2099 Food preparations

(P-2921)
MARTINLLI ORCHRD OPRATIONS LLC
227 E Beach St, Watsonville (95076-4808)
P.O. Box 1868 (95077-1868)
PHONE.....................831 724-1126
Amy Sierra, *Sales Staff*
EMP: 21 EST: 2016
SALES (est): 325.7K **Privately Held**
WEB: www.martinellis.com
SIC: 2099 Food preparations

(P-2922)
MEXICO TORTILLA FACTORY & DELI
7015 Thornton Ave, Newark (94560-3640)
PHONE.....................510 792-9909
Roger Collazo, *President*
Gloria Megrette, *Shareholder*
Ercilia M Collazo, *Treasurer*
Maria Collazo, *Admin Sec*
EMP: 19 EST: 1972
SALES (est): 2.5MM **Privately Held**
WEB: www.mexicotortillafactory.com
SIC: 5411 2099 Delicatessens; tortillas, fresh or refrigerated

(P-2923)
MI RANCHO TORTILLA INC
801 Purvis Ave, Clovis (93612-2892)
PHONE.....................559 299-3183
Criss K Cruz, *CEO*
Dorothy Cruz, *President*
EMP: 56 EST: 1948
SQ FT: 6,000
SALES (est): 9.8MM **Privately Held**
SIC: 2099 Tortillas, fresh or refrigerated

(P-2924)
MIZKAN AMERICA INC
46 Walker St, Watsonville (95076-4925)
PHONE.....................831 728-2061
David Shields, *Manager*
EMP: 51 **Privately Held**
WEB: www.mizkan.com
SIC: 2099 Vinegar
HQ: Mizkan America, Inc.
1661 Feehanville Dr 100a
Mount Prospect IL 60056
847 590-0059

(P-2925)
NANCYS SPECIALTY FOODS
2400 Olympic Blvd Ste 8, Lafayette (94595-1500)
PHONE.....................510 494-1100
Adam Ferrif, *COO*
Nancy S Mueller, *President*
R Larry Booth, *Vice Pres*
David M Joiner, *Vice Pres*
EMP: 375 EST: 1977
SQ FT: 86,000
SALES (est): 32.7MM
SALES (corp-wide): 26.1B **Publicly Held**
WEB: www.nancys.com
SIC: 2099 Food preparations
HQ: Kraft Heinz Foods Company
1 Ppg Pl Ste 3400
Pittsburgh PA 15222
412 456-5700

(P-2926)
NEW HORIZON FOODS INC
33440 Western Ave, Union City (94587-3202)
PHONE.....................510 489-8600
Kenneth Crawford, *President*
Elieser Pedroza, *Prdtn Mgr*
EMP: 25 EST: 1998
SQ FT: 20,000
SALES (est): 4.2MM **Privately Held**
WEB: www.newhorizonfoodsinc.com
SIC: 2099 Food preparations

(P-2927)
NIPPON TRENDS FOOD SERVICE INC
631 Giguere Ct Ste A1, San Jose (95133-1745)
PHONE.....................408 479-0558
Hideyuki Yamashita, *President*
Tomoko Yamashita, *Vice Pres*
Kristi Yamashita, *Admin Sec*
▲ EMP: 60 EST: 2000
SQ FT: 5,000
SALES (est): 7.7MM **Privately Held**
WEB: www.yamachanramen.com
SIC: 2099 Noodles, uncooked: packaged with other ingredients

(P-2928)
NOODLES FRESH LLC
48 Rincon Rd, Kensington (94707-1047)
PHONE.....................510 898-1710
Wenyan Petersen, *Principal*
EMP: 15 EST: 2014
SALES (est): 153.1K **Privately Held**
WEB: www.noodlesfresh.com
SIC: 5812 2099 Family restaurants; tea blending

(P-2929)
NUTIVA
213 W Cutting Blvd, Richmond (94804-2015)
PHONE.....................510 255-2700
John Roulac, *Ch of Bd*
Steven Naccarato, *CEO*
Christian Amsler, *Senior VP*
Lei Gong, *Executive*
Pam Zahedani, *Executive Asst*
◆ EMP: 115 EST: 1999
SQ FT: 1,300
SALES (est): 49.9MM **Privately Held**
WEB: www.nutiva.com
SIC: 2099 Vegetables, peeled for the trade

▲ = Import ▼ = Export ◆ = Import/Export

PRODUCTS & SERVICES SECTION — 2099 - Food Preparations, NEC County

(P-2930)
ORGANIC SPICES (PA)
4180 Business Center Dr, Fremont (94538-6354)
PHONE..................510 440-1044
Bijan Chansari, CEO
Clara Bonner, CEO
Chris Cole, General Mgr
Jimmy Evans, Account Dir
◆ EMP: 28 EST: 2002
SQ FT: 27,000
SALES (est): 10.4MM Privately Held
WEB: www.organicspices.com
SIC: 2099 Seasonings & spices

(P-2931)
PAPPYS MEAT COMPANY INC
Also Called: Pappy's Fine Foods
5663 E Fountain Way, Fresno (93727-7813)
P.O. Box 5257 (93755-5257)
PHONE..................559 291-0218
Marie Papulias, President
Edward Papulias, CEO
Patricia Papulias, Corp Secy
EMP: 23 EST: 1964
SQ FT: 10,000
SALES (est): 3.5MM Privately Held
WEB: www.pappysfinefoods.com
SIC: 2099 Seasonings & spices; seasonings: dry mixes

(P-2932)
PEARL CROP INC
Also Called: Linden Nut
8452 Demartini Ln, Linden (95236-9446)
PHONE..................209 887-3731
Halil Ulas Turkhan, President
EMP: 26
SALES (corp-wide): 90MM Privately Held
WEB: www.pearlcrop.com
SIC: 2099 2068 Food preparations; salted & roasted nuts & seeds
PA: Pearl Crop, Inc.
1550 Industrial Dr
Stockton CA 95206
209 808-7575

(P-2933)
PETIT POT INC
4221 Horton St, Emeryville (94608-3533)
PHONE..................650 488-7432
Maxime Pouvreau, CEO
Emma Bouvier, Opers Staff
Jonathan Neves, Sales Mgr
Anne Lesgourgues, Director
EMP: 20 EST: 2015
SQ FT: 20,000
SALES (est): 2.7MM Privately Held
WEB: www.petitpot.com
SIC: 2099 Dessert mixes & fillings

(P-2934)
PGP INTERNATIONAL INC (DH)
351 Hanson Way, Woodland (95776-6224)
P.O. Box 2060 (95776-2060)
PHONE..................530 662-5056
Nicolas J Hanson, CEO
Carmen Sciackitano, Admin Sec
◆ EMP: 180 EST: 1998
SALES (est): 70.3MM
SALES (corp-wide): 18.2B Privately Held
WEB: www.pgpint.com
SIC: 2099 Almond pastes

(P-2935)
PRE-PEELED POTATO CO INC
1585 S Union St, Stockton (95206-2269)
P.O. Box 111 (95201-0111)
PHONE..................209 469-6911
Bart Birt, President
EMP: 20 EST: 1965
SQ FT: 10,000
SALES (est): 1.1MM Privately Held
SIC: 2099 Potatoes, peeled for the trade; vegetables, peeled for the trade

(P-2936)
PRODUCE WORLD INC
30611 San Antonio St, Hayward (94544-7103)
PHONE..................510 441-1449
Joseph Fereira, President
Dennis Dahlin, Vice Pres
EMP: 75 EST: 1979
SQ FT: 20,000
SALES (est): 6.8MM Privately Held
SIC: 2099 Vegetables, peeled for the trade

(P-2937)
RENAISSANCE FOOD GROUP LLC (HQ)
Also Called: Garden Highway
11020 White Rock Rd Ste 1, Rancho Cordova (95670-6402)
PHONE..................916 638-8825
James S Catchot, President
Donald Ochoa, President
Jim Gibson, COO
Ken Catchot, CFO
Mark Lodge, Exec VP
▲ EMP: 48 EST: 2002
SQ FT: 12,000
SALES (est): 173.2MM
SALES (corp-wide): 1B Publicly Held
WEB: www.rfgfoods.com
SIC: 2099 Salads, fresh or refrigerated
PA: Calavo Growers, Inc.
1141 Cummings Rd Ste A
Santa Paula CA 93060
805 525-1245

(P-2938)
RESERS FINE FOODS INC
15100 Jack Tone Rd, Manteca (95336-9729)
PHONE..................503 643-6431
Mark Reser, CEO
EMP: 30
SALES (corp-wide): 1.5B Privately Held
WEB: www.resers.com
SIC: 2099 Salads, fresh or refrigerated
PA: Reser's Fine Foods, Inc.
15570 Sw Jenkins Rd
Beaverton OR 97006
503 643-6431

(P-2939)
ROBLES BROS INC (PA)
Also Called: La Colonial
1700 Rogers Ave, San Jose (95112-1107)
PHONE..................408 436-5551
George Robles, President
Claudia Robles, Corp Secy
Hector Robles, Vice Pres
EMP: 34 EST: 1976
SQ FT: 7,000
SALES (est): 3MM Privately Held
WEB: www.lacolonial.com
SIC: 2099 Tortillas, fresh or refrigerated

(P-2940)
S MARTINELLI & COMPANY (PA)
735 W Beach St, Watsonville (95076-5141)
P.O. Box 1868 (95077-1868)
PHONE..................831 724-1126
Stephen C Martinelli, Chairman
Stephen John Martinelli, President
Rick Swanson, COO
Gun Ruder, CFO
Doris M Brown, Vice Pres
▲ EMP: 189 EST: 1868
SALES (est): 59.6MM Privately Held
WEB: www.martinellis.com
SIC: 2099 Food preparations

(P-2941)
SALAD COSMO USA CORP
5944 Dixon Ave W, Dixon (95620-9730)
PHONE..................707 678-6633
Masahiro Nakada, President
Isaura Nakada, Admin Sec
Kyudai Nishio, Manager
Peter Saeteurn, Manager
▲ EMP: 20 EST: 1995
SQ FT: 50,000
SALES (est): 3.6MM Privately Held
WEB: www.saladcosmo.com
SIC: 2099 Food preparations

(P-2942)
SENSIENT NTRAL INGREDIENTS LLC (HQ)
Also Called: Sensient Dehydrated Flavors
151 S Walnut Rd, Turlock (95380-5127)
P.O. Box 1524 (95381-1524)
PHONE..................209 667-2777
Craig Mitchel, President
Danielle Trovao, IT/INT Sup
Mike Hagood, Plant Mgr
Hugh Williams, Plant Mgr
EMP: 47 EST: 2007
SALES (est): 15.3MM
SALES (corp-wide): 1.3B Publicly Held
WEB: www.sensientnaturalingredients.com
SIC: 2099 Food preparations
PA: Sensient Technologies Corporation
777 E Wisconsin Ave # 1100
Milwaukee WI 53202
414 271-6755

(P-2943)
SIMPLY ASIA FOODS LLC
Also Called: Thai Kitchen
2342 Shattuck Ave, Berkeley (94704-1517)
PHONE..................800 967-8424
Alan D Wilson,
▲ EMP: 41 EST: 2009
SALES (est): 2.4MM
SALES (corp-wide): 5.6B Publicly Held
WEB: www.mccormick.com
SIC: 2099 Spices, including grinding
PA: Mccormick & Company Incorporated
24 Schilling Rd Ste 1
Hunt Valley MD 21031
410 771-7301

(P-2944)
SUN BASKET INC
1 Clarence Pl Unit 14, San Francisco (94107-2577)
PHONE..................408 669-4418
Justin Eckhart, Engineer
Erik Phillips, Train & Dev Mgr
Ebru Brown, Recruiter
Denis Duello, Buyer
Nicholas Rico, Buyer
EMP: 118
SALES (corp-wide): 106.8MM Privately Held
WEB: www.sunbasket.com
SIC: 2099 Almond pastes
PA: Sun Basket, Inc.
1170 Olinder Ct
San Jose CA 95122
408 669-4418

(P-2945)
SUN BASKET INC (PA)
1170 Olinder Ct, San Jose (95122-2619)
PHONE..................408 669-4418
Adam Zbar, CEO
Don Barnett, COO
Marc Friend, CFO
Jessica Jensen, Chief Mktg Ofcr
Sam Faillace, Vice Pres
EMP: 200 EST: 2012
SALES (corp-wide): 106.8MM Privately Held
WEB: www.sunbasket.com
SIC: 2099 Food preparations

(P-2946)
THISTLE HEALTH INC
1000 Van Ness Ave Ste 100, San Francisco (94109-6971)
PHONE..................917 587-2341
Ashwin Ninan Cheriyan, CEO
Shiri Avnery, COO
Sheel Mohnot, CFO
Christopher Haas, Opers Staff
Sydney Deal, Production
EMP: 400 EST: 2013
SALES (est): 41.1MM Privately Held
WEB: www.thistle.co
SIC: 2099 Food preparations

(P-2947)
TOFU SHOP SPECIALTY FOODS INC
65 Frank Martin Ct, Arcata (95521-8930)
PHONE..................707 822-7401
Matthew Schmit, President
Pam Olson, Data Proc Dir
EMP: 17 EST: 1980
SQ FT: 4,400
SALES (est): 681.7K Privately Held
WEB: www.tofushop.com
SIC: 2099 Tofu, except frozen desserts

(P-2948)
TRADIN ORGANICS USA LLC
Also Called: Big Basin Foods
100 Enterprise Way B10, Scotts Valley (95066-3248)
PHONE..................831 685-6565
Gerard Versteegh, CEO
Hendrik Rabbie, Vice Pres
Roy Overwijn, Asst Controller
Lee Malaspina, Controller
Sandra Schmid, Human Res Mgr
◆ EMP: 30 EST: 2000
SALES (est): 23.8MM
SALES (corp-wide): 836.5MM Privately Held
WEB: www.tradinorganic.com
SIC: 2099 Food preparations
PA: Amsterdam Commodities N.V.
Beursplein 37 21e Etage
Rotterdam
104 051-195

(P-2949)
TRADITIONAL MEDICINALS INC (PA)
4515 Ross Rd, Sebastopol (95472-2250)
P.O. Box 239, Cotati (94931-0239)
PHONE..................707 823-8911
Drake Sadler, Chairman
Blair Kellison, CEO
Teal Tasso, COO
Jane C Howard, CFO
Kevin Haslebacher, Officer
▲ EMP: 131 EST: 1979
SQ FT: 20,000
SALES (est): 63.1MM Privately Held
WEB: www.traditionalmedicinals.com
SIC: 2099 Tea blending

(P-2950)
TRADITIONAL MEDICINALS INC
1400 Valley House Dr # 120, Rohnert Park (94928-4935)
PHONE..................707 664-5801
Jeffrey Flasher, Vice Pres
Daniella Allam, Manager
EMP: 19
SALES (corp-wide): 63.1MM Privately Held
WEB: www.traditionalmedicinals.com
SIC: 2099 Tea blending
PA: Traditional Medicinals, Inc.
4515 Ross Rd
Sebastopol CA 95472
707 823-8911

(P-2951)
TRUROOTS INC (HQ)
Also Called: Enray Inc.
6999 Southfront Rd, Livermore (94551-8221)
PHONE..................925 218-2205
Nimesh Ray, CEO
Esha Ray, President
▲ EMP: 46 EST: 2006
SQ FT: 20,000
SALES (est): 18.2MM
SALES (corp-wide): 8B Publicly Held
WEB: www.truroots.com
SIC: 2099 Rice, uncooked: packaged with other ingredients
PA: The J M Smucker Company
1 Strawberry Ln
Orrville OH 44667
330 682-3000

(P-2952)
UNITED FOODS INTL USA INC (HQ)
23447 Cabot Blvd, Hayward (94545-1665)
PHONE..................510 264-5850
Takeo Shimura, President
Kaz Kaneko, Project Mgr
Tadashi Isahai, Sales Staff
Miki Kakutani, Manager
◆ EMP: 39 EST: 1988
SQ FT: 24,000
SALES (est): 14.3MM Privately Held
WEB: www.ufiusa.com
SIC: 2099 Seasonings: dry mixes

(P-2953)
UPSIDE FOODS INC
804 Heinz Ave Ste 200, Berkeley (94710-2755)
PHONE..................510 746-1198
Uma Valeti, CEO
Amy Chen, COO
Roshan Patel, Research
Jill Schriewer, Research
Brett Gellman, Opers Staff
EMP: 45 EST: 2016

(PA)=Parent Co (HQ)=Headquarters (DH)=Div Headquarters
✪ = New Business established in last 2 years

2099 - Food Preparations, NEC County (P-2954)

SALES (est): 6MM **Privately Held**
WEB: www.upsidefoods.com
SIC: 5421 2099 Meat markets, including freezer provisioners; food preparations

(P-2954)
VALLEY FINE FOODS COMPANY INC
300 Epley Dr, Yuba City (95991-7221)
PHONE.....................530 671-7200
Amanpreet Brar, *Vice Pres*
Sing Cheng, *Info Tech Mgr*
Mike Patrick, *Plant Mgr*
Vee Caragay, *Marketing Staff*
Mitzi Moskovitz, *Manager*
EMP: 84 **Privately Held**
WEB: www.valleyfine.com
SIC: 2099 Food preparations
PA: Valley Fine Foods Company, Inc.
3909 Park Rd Ste H
Benicia CA 94510

(P-2955)
VALLEY SUN PRODUCTS OF CALI
3324 Orestimba Rd, Newman (95360-9628)
PHONE.....................209 862-1200
Cynthia Apodaca, *Principal*
EMP: 23 **EST:** 2017
SALES (est): 2.2MM **Privately Held**
WEB: www.valleysun.com
SIC: 2099 Food preparations

(P-2956)
VANNELLI FOODS LLC
4031 Alvis Ct, Rocklin (95677-4011)
PHONE.....................916 412-1204
Jerry Moore,
EMP: 17 **EST:** 2006
SALES (est): 954.7K **Privately Held**
WEB: www.vannellibrands.com
SIC: 2099 Pasta, uncooked: packaged with other ingredients

(P-2957)
WAWONA FROZEN FOODS (PA)
100 W Alluvial Ave, Clovis (93611-9176)
PHONE.....................559 299-2901
William Smittcamp, *President*
Earl Smittcamp, *Ch of Bd*
Julie Olsen, *CFO*
Muriel Smittcamp, *Corp Secy*
Kristi Losson, *Executive Asst*
▲ **EMP:** 123
SQ FT: 125,000
SALES (est): 419.5MM **Privately Held**
WEB: www.wawona.com
SIC: 2099 Food preparations

(P-2958)
WESTERN FOODS LLC (DH)
420 N Pioneer Ave, Woodland (95776-6122)
P.O. Box 115 (95776-0115)
PHONE.....................530 601-5991
Miguel Reyna, *Mng Member*
Shan Staka, *CFO*
Tom Andringa, *Vice Pres*
Jennifer Nielson, *Executive Asst*
Colin Garner, *Marketing Staff*
▲ **EMP:** 105 **EST:** 2010
SQ FT: 87,000
SALES (est): 39.3MM
SALES (corp-wide): 587.3MM **Privately Held**
WEB: www.westernfoodsco.com
SIC: 2099 Food preparations
HQ: Western Milling, Llc
31120 W St
Goshen CA 93227
559 302-1000

(P-2959)
WIN FOODS CORPORATION
Also Called: Wing Nien Foods
30560 San Antonio St, Hayward (94544-7102)
PHONE.....................510 487-8877
Gregory D Hall, *President*
Novita Teng, *QC Mgr*
Nicholas Sienkiewicz, *Manager*
▲ **EMP:** 87 **EST:** 2001

SALES (est): 16.3MM **Privately Held**
WEB: www.wingnien.wordpress.com
SIC: 2099 Food preparations

(P-2960)
WOOLERY ENTERPRISES INC
Also Called: Will's Fresh Foods
1991 Republic Ave, San Leandro (94577-4220)
PHONE.....................510 357-5700
Daniel C Woolery, *CEO*
Susan Woolery, *Admin Sec*
EMP: 43 **EST:** 1935
SQ FT: 23,000
SALES (est): 7.5MM **Privately Held**
WEB: www.willsfreshfoods.com
SIC: 2099 Salads, fresh or refrigerated

(P-2961)
YBP HOLDINGS LLC
Also Called: Yagi Brothers Produce LLC
5614 Lincoln Blvd, Livingston (95334-9642)
PHONE.....................209 394-7311
EMP: 45 **EST:** 2019
SALES (est): 3.2MM **Privately Held**
WEB: www.yagibros.com
SIC: 2099 Potatoes, dried: packaged with other ingredients

2131 Tobacco, Chewing & Snuff

(P-2962)
MOD ZOMBIE LLC (PA)
3499 E Bayshore Rd Spc 30, Redwood City (94063-4622)
PHONE.....................650 346-2047
Dustin Springman, *Principal*
EMP: 30 **EST:** 2015
SALES (est): 137.3K **Privately Held**
SIC: 2131 Chewing & smoking tobacco

2211 Cotton, Woven Fabric

(P-2963)
APPLIED SEWING RESOURCES INC
Also Called: Kiva Designs
6440 Goodyear Rd, Benicia (94510-1219)
PHONE.....................707 748-1614
EMP: 25
SALES: 3MM **Privately Held**
SIC: 2211 2393 Mfg Textile Bags And Soft Sided Luggage

(P-2964)
PAIGE LLC
Also Called: Paige Denim
2237 Fillmore St, San Francisco (94115-2221)
PHONE.....................415 660-2970
EMP: 21
SALES (corp-wide): 51.5MM **Privately Held**
WEB: www.paigeusa.net
SIC: 2211 Denims
HQ: Paige, Llc
10119 Jefferson Blvd
Culver City CA 90232

(P-2965)
SOUTHPNTE CHRSTN CTR SCRMNTO C
7520 Stockton Blvd, Sacramento (95823-3915)
PHONE.....................916 504-3370
Brent Sorlien, *Pastor*
Kevin Allen, *Pastor*
Kim Boyd, *Pastor*
Kathy Trenton, *Pastor*
Mike Trenton, *Pastor*
EMP: 22 **EST:** 1963
SQ FT: 29,000
SALES (est): 1.2MM **Privately Held**
WEB: www.southpointecc.net
SIC: 8661 2211 Assembly of God Church; madras, cotton

2221 Silk & Man-Made Fiber

(P-2966)
3 INK PRODUCTIONS INC
4790 W Jacquelyn Ave, Fresno (93722-6406)
PHONE.....................559 275-4565
Craig Stidham, *President*
Dianne Stidham, *Partner*
EMP: 23 **EST:** 1996
SALES (est): 1.3MM **Privately Held**
WEB: www.3inkpro.com
SIC: 2221 5023 Textile warping, on a contract basis; sheets, textile

(P-2967)
AGRICULTURE BAG MFG USA INC (PA)
Also Called: Agriculture Bag Manufacturing
960 98th Ave, Oakland (94603-2347)
PHONE.....................510 632-5637
Jeff C Kuo, *CEO*
▲ **EMP:** 44 **EST:** 1984
SALES (est): 6.1MM **Privately Held**
SIC: 2221 2673 2393 Polypropylene broadwoven fabrics; plastic & pliofilm bags; textile bags

2231 Wool, Woven Fabric

(P-2968)
ICON APPAREL GROUP LLC
2989 Promenade St Ste 100, West Sacramento (95691-6419)
PHONE.....................916 372-4266
Juan Carlos Ceja, *CEO*
Alberto Rivera, *Controller*
Araceli Sanchez, *Prdtn Mgr*
Ronald Leavitt, *Sales Executive*
Jerrad Fiore,
EMP: 35 **EST:** 2002
SQ FT: 10,000
SALES: 2.1MM **Privately Held**
WEB: www.iconapparel.com
SIC: 2231 7389 2759 Apparel & outerwear broadwoven fabrics; apparel designers, commercial; screen printing

2241 Fabric Mills, Cotton, Wool, Silk & Man-Made

(P-2969)
HILMAR OAKS LLC
23546 American Ave, Hilmar (95324-9627)
PHONE.....................209 668-0867
Mark K Ahlem,
EMP: 20 **EST:** 2010
SALES (est): 1.1MM **Privately Held**
WEB: www.hilmar.k12.ca.us
SIC: 2241 Rubber & elastic yarns & fabrics

(P-2970)
HORVATH HOLDINGS INC
Also Called: Clayborn Lab
40173 Trk Arpt Rd, Truckee (96161-4115)
PHONE.....................530 587-4700
Justin Horvath, *President*
Amy Horvath, *CFO*
Maureen Horvath, *Purchasing*
Nick Oneill, *Sales Engr*
EMP: 15 **EST:** 2019
SQ FT: 4,500
SALES (est): 3MM **Privately Held**
WEB: www.claybornlab.com
SIC: 2241 Electric insulating tapes & braids, except plastic

(P-2971)
INDUSTRIAL WIPER & SUPPLY INC
1025 98th Ave A, Oakland (94603-2356)
PHONE.....................408 286-4752
Mitchell Tobin, *CEO*
Robert Tobin, *President*
▲ **EMP:** 16 **EST:** 1958
SQ FT: 10,000
SALES (est): 683.6K **Privately Held**
WEB: www.industrialwiper.com
SIC: 2241 Narrow fabric mills

2252 Hosiery, Except Women's

(P-2972)
SOCKSMITH DESIGN INC (PA)
1515 Pacific Ave, Santa Cruz (95060-3911)
PHONE.....................831 426-6416
Eric Gil, *President*
Cassandra Aaron, *Principal*
Ellen Gil, *Principal*
Ryan Dineen, *Sales Staff*
Sean Jimenez, *Sales Staff*
▲ **EMP:** 24 **EST:** 2009
SQ FT: 10,000
SALES (est): 8.5MM **Privately Held**
WEB: www.socksmith.com
SIC: 2252 Socks

2253 Knit Outerwear Mills

(P-2973)
SNOWFLAKE DESIGNS
2893 Larkin Ave, Clovis (93612-3908)
PHONE.....................559 291-6234
Ladonna Snow, *Co-Owner*
Richard L Snow, *Co-Owner*
Rick Snow, *Vice Pres*
Kindra Snow-Walker, *Vice Pres*
EMP: 22 **EST:** 1995
SQ FT: 7,100
SALES (est): 2.2MM **Privately Held**
WEB: www.snowflakedesigns.com
SIC: 2253 5632 Leotards, knit; dancewear

(P-2974)
TRIPLE AUGHT DESIGN LLC
660 22nd St, San Francisco (94107-3119)
PHONE.....................415 318-8252
Brett Eisenberg, *Mng Member*
Christopher Powers, *Analyst*
Whitley Seamus, *Controller*
Gianni Donati, *Prdtn Mgr*
Connor Moynihan, *Marketing Mgr*
▲ **EMP:** 28 **EST:** 2010
SALES (est): 3.1MM **Privately Held**
WEB: www.tripleaughtdesign.com
SIC: 5699 2253 5941 3161 Sports apparel; jerseys, knit; scarves & mufflers, knit; sweaters & weather coats, knit; camping & backpacking equipment; backpacking equipment; traveling bags

2259 Knitting Mills, NEC

(P-2975)
SW SAFETY SOLUTIONS INC
33278 Central Ave Ste 102, Union City (94587-2016)
PHONE.....................510 429-8692
Belle Chou, *CEO*
Bob Gaither, *Officer*
Mike Kimberley, *Regional Mgr*
Ted Tsaltas, *Regional Mgr*
Richard Barnes, *CIO*
EMP: 26 **EST:** 2010
SALES (est): 9.5MM **Privately Held**
WEB: www.swsafety.com
SIC: 2259 Gloves & mittens, knit

2261 Cotton Fabric Finishers

(P-2976)
MANDEGO INC
Also Called: Mandego Apparel
2300 Tech Pkwy Ste 2, Hollister (95023)
PHONE.....................831 637-5241
Dean Machado, *President*
Marianne Obertello, *Office Mgr*
Kelly Machado, *Admin Sec*
EMP: 16 **EST:** 1984
SQ FT: 4,000
SALES (est): 1MM **Privately Held**
WEB: www.mandego.com
SIC: 2261 Screen printing of cotton broadwoven fabrics

▲ = Import ▼=Export
◆ =Import/Export

PRODUCTS & SERVICES SECTION

2329 - Men's & Boys' Clothing, NEC County (P-2996)

(P-2977)
MISHI APPAREL INC (PA)
Also Called: Mishi Apparel Retail Store
201 Western Ave, Petaluma (94952-2909)
PHONE..................707 525-1075
EMP: 44
SQ FT: 16,500
SALES (est): 3.1MM Privately Held
SIC: 5621 2261 2339 2335 Ret Women's Clothing Cotton Finishing Plant Mfg Women/Miss Outerwear Mfg Women/Misses Dresses

(P-2978)
SRL APPAREL INC
Also Called: Printed Image, The
2209 Park Ave, Chico (95928-6704)
PHONE..................530 898-9525
Scott Laursen, *President*
Marie Halvorsen, *Shareholder*
Chris Urbach, *Prdtn Mgr*
David Bryant, *Accounts Exec*
EMP: 26 EST: 1980
SQ FT: 14,130
SALES (est): 4.7MM Privately Held
WEB: www.printedimagechico.com
SIC: 2261 5137 5136 2396 Screen printing of cotton broadwoven fabrics; women's & children's sportswear & swimsuits; men's & boys' sportswear & work clothing; automotive & apparel trimmings

2273 Carpets & Rugs

(P-2979)
SAVNIK & COMPANY
21698 Gail Dr, Castro Valley (94546-6810)
PHONE..................510 568-4628
Berry Savnik, *General Mgr*
Kathryn Savnik, *Treasurer*
Kurt Savnik, *Manager*
EMP: 17 EST: 1963
SALES (est): 651.4K Privately Held
WEB: www.savnik.com
SIC: 2273 Carpets, hand & machine made; rugs, tufted

2296 Tire Cord & Fabric

(P-2980)
BEBOP SENSORS INC (PA)
970 Miller Ave, Berkeley (94708-1406)
PHONE..................503 875-4990
Keith A McMillen, *CEO*
Conner Lacy, *Vice Pres*
Michelle Cook, *Admin Sec*
EMP: 23 EST: 2014
SALES (est): 1.9MM Privately Held
WEB: www.bebopsensors.com
SIC: 2296 Tire cord & fabrics

2298 Cordage & Twine

(P-2981)
BAY ASSOCIATES WIRE TECH CORP (DH)
46840 Lakeview Blvd, Fremont (94538-6543)
PHONE..................510 988-3800
Harry Avonti, *CEO*
Jack Sanford, *Treasurer*
Mark Rotner, *Admin Sec*
Ernie Drinkmann, *Info Tech Dir*
Strato Han, *Engineer*
◆ EMP: 575 EST: 2008
SQ FT: 45,000
SALES (est): 63MM
SALES (corp-wide): 150MM Privately Held
WEB: www.baycable.com
SIC: 2298 3351 3357 Cable, fiber; copper rolling & drawing; nonferrous wiredrawing & insulating
HQ: New England Wire Technologies Corporation
130 N Main St
Lisbon NH 03585
603 838-6624

(P-2982)
RIP-TIE INC
883 San Leandro Blvd, San Leandro (94577-1530)
P.O. Box 549 (94577-0549)
PHONE..................510 577-0200
Michael Paul Fennell, *President*
Bin MEI, *General Mgr*
Marsha Duffie, *Marketing Staff*
▲ EMP: 18 EST: 1985
SQ FT: 45,000
SALES (est): 3MM Privately Held
WEB: www.riptie.com
SIC: 2298 Cordage & twine

2299 Textile Goods, NEC

(P-2983)
AGRIBAG INC
3925 Alameda Ave, Oakland (94601-3931)
PHONE..................510 533-2388
Hsieh Liang, *President*
Wen-Ping Liang, *Vice Pres*
Annie Chang, *General Mgr*
Belle Chang, *Graphic Designe*
Robert Clark, *Sales Staff*
▲ EMP: 25 EST: 1987
SQ FT: 20,000
SALES (est): 3.7MM Privately Held
WEB: www.agribag.com
SIC: 2299 2673 Bagging, jute; bags: plastic, laminated & coated

2311 Men's & Boys' Suits, Coats & Overcoats

(P-2984)
FIRST TACTICAL LLC
4300 Spyres Way, Modesto (95356-9259)
PHONE..................855 665-3410
Dan J Costa, *President*
Christopher White, *Business Mgr*
Denise Schmidt, *Opers Staff*
John Crist, *Marketing Staff*
Denise L Costa, *President*
EMP: 901 EST: 2015
SALES (est): 44.8MM Privately Held
WEB: www.firsttactical.com
SIC: 2311 Military uniforms, men's & youths': purchased materials

(P-2985)
TRUMAKER INC
Also Called: Trumaker & Co.
228 Grant Ave Fl 2, San Francisco (94108-4647)
PHONE..................415 662-3836
Mark Lovas, *CEO*
Michael Zhang, *President*
Adam Sidney, *Vice Pres*
Blair Golden, *Sales Staff*
Kerriann Forester, *Director*
▲ EMP: 50 EST: 2011
SALES (est): 8.6MM Privately Held
WEB: www.trumaker.com
SIC: 2311 2321 2325 Men's & boys' suits & coats; men's & boys' furnishings; men's & boys' trousers & slacks

2323 Men's & Boys' Neckwear

(P-2986)
ADAPTIVE INSIGHTS LLC
14 W Central Ave, Los Gatos (95030-7121)
PHONE..................408 656-4229
EMP: 55 Publicly Held
WEB: www.adaptiveplanning.com
SIC: 2323 Men's & boys' neckwear
HQ: Adaptive Insights Llc
2300 Geng Rd Ste 100
Palo Alto CA 94303
650 528-7500

2325 Men's & Boys' Separate Trousers & Casual Slacks

(P-2987)
LEVI STRAUSS & CO (PA)
1155 Battery St, San Francisco (94111-1264)
PHONE..................415 501-6000
Charles V Bergh, *President*
Stephen C Neal, *Ch of Bd*
Marc Rosen, *President*
Harmit Singh, *CFO*
Seth Ellison, *Ch Credit Ofcr*
◆ EMP: 1600 EST: 1853
SALES (est): 4.4B Publicly Held
WEB: www.levistrauss.com
SIC: 2325 2339 2321 2331 Jeans: men's, youths & boys'; slacks, dress: men's, youths & boys'; jeans: women's, misses & juniors'; slacks: women's, misses & juniors'; athletic clothing: women's, misses & juniors'; men's & boys' furnishings; shirts, women's & juniors': made from purchased materials; T-shirts & tops, women's: made from purchased materials; skirts, separate: women's, misses & juniors'; jackets (suede, leatherette, etc.), sport: men's & boys'; athletic (warmup, sweat & jogging) suits: men's & boys'

(P-2988)
UNSPUN INC
371 10th St, San Francisco (94103-3832)
PHONE..................207 577-8745
Elizabeth Faith Esponnette, *CEO*
EMP: 22 EST: 2018
SALES (est): 2.5MM Privately Held
WEB: www.unspun.io
SIC: 2325 Jeans: men's, youths & boys'

2326 Men's & Boys' Work Clothing

(P-2989)
MENS WEARHOUSE
6100 Stevenson Blvd, Fremont (94538-2490)
PHONE..................510 657-9821
EMP: 48
SALES (est): 9MM Privately Held
SIC: 2326 Mfg Men's/Boy's Work Clothing

(P-2990)
WEST COAST GARMENT MFG INC
70 Elmira St, San Francisco (94124-1911)
PHONE..................415 896-1772
Katherine Ng, *President*
Erica Ku, *Admin Sec*
▲ EMP: 19 EST: 1996
SQ FT: 10,000
SALES (est): 1.5MM Privately Held
SIC: 2326 2369 2339 Industrial garments, men's & boys'; girls' & children's outerwear; women's & misses' outerwear

2329 Men's & Boys' Clothing, NEC

(P-2991)
ATHLETA LLC
1 Harrison St Lbby, San Francisco (94105-6131)
PHONE..................707 559-2200
Nancy Green, *CEO*
Sarah Wallis, *Vice Pres*
Natalie Rosen, *Analyst*
Emily Bois, *Production*
Michelle Kresser, *Production*
▲ EMP: 37 EST: 2010
SALES (est): 1.5MM
SALES (corp-wide): 13.8B Publicly Held
WEB: www.gapinc.com
SIC: 2329 Athletic (warmup, sweat & jogging) suits: men's & boys'
PA: The Gap Inc
2 Folsom St
San Francisco CA 94105
415 427-0100

(P-2992)
FIVE KEYS INC
Also Called: Mount Seven
152 E Broadway Ave, Atwater (95301-4562)
PHONE..................209 358-7971
Mohan Johal, *President*
Bob Johal, *Controller*
EMP: 15 EST: 1990
SALES (est): 542.5K Privately Held
WEB: www.mountseven.com
SIC: 2329 5632 7389 Men's & boys' sportswear & athletic clothing; women's accessory & specialty stores; sewing contractor

(P-2993)
KOKATAT INC
5350 Ericson Way, Arcata (95521-9277)
PHONE..................707 822-7621
Stephen O Meara, *President*
Kit Mann, *Vice Pres*
Aaron McVanner, *Technology*
Michele Bisgrove, *Human Res Mgr*
Krista Nero, *Purchasing*
▲ EMP: 100
SQ FT: 30,000
SALES (est): 10.7MM Privately Held
WEB: www.kokatat.com
SIC: 2329 2339 Men's & boys' sportswear & athletic clothing; women's & misses' athletic clothing & sportswear

(P-2994)
MAD APPAREL INC
Also Called: Athos
201 Arch St, Redwood City (94062-1305)
PHONE..................650 503-3386
Dhananja Jayalath, *CEO*
Chris Wiebe, *CTO*
Ryan Matsumura, *Software Dev*
Matt McLaughlin, *Software Engr*
Guido Gioberto, *Engineer*
EMP: 38 EST: 2012
SALES (est): 4.1MM Privately Held
WEB: www.shop.liveathos.com
SIC: 2329 2339 Men's & boys' sportswear & athletic clothing; women's & misses' athletic clothing & sportswear

(P-2995)
QOR LLC
775 Baywood Dr Ste 312, Petaluma (94954-5500)
P.O. Box 1020 (94953-1020)
PHONE..................707 658-1941
Joe Teno, *Mng Member*
Lori Overton, *Info Tech Dir*
▲ EMP: 16 EST: 2013
SALES (est): 2MM Privately Held
WEB: www.qorkit.com
SIC: 2329 Athletic (warmup, sweat & jogging) suits: men's & boys'

(P-2996)
VF OUTDOOR LLC (HQ)
Also Called: North Face, The
2701 Harbor Bay Pkwy, Alameda (94502-3041)
P.O. Box 372670, Denver CO (80237-6670)
PHONE..................855 500-8639
Scott Baxter, *President*
Christine Reuss, *Partner*
Jim Gerson, *Vice Pres*
Douglas L Hassman, *Vice Pres*
Becky Avila, *Store Mgr*
▲ EMP: 250 EST: 1994
SQ FT: 151,085
SALES (est): 887.7MM
SALES (corp-wide): 9.2B Publicly Held
WEB: www.vfc.com
SIC: 2329 2339 3949 2394 Men's & boys' leather, wool & down-filled outerwear; ski & snow clothing: men's & boys'; women's & misses' outerwear; camping equipment & supplies; tents: made from purchased materials; sleeping bags; camping & backpacking equipment; skiing equipment
PA: V.F. Corporation
1551 Wewatta St
Denver CO 80202
720 778-4000

(PA)=Parent Co (HQ)=Headquarters (DH)=Div Headquarters
✿ = New Business established in last 2 years

2331 Women's & Misses' Blouses

(P-2997)
BYER CALIFORNIA (PA)
66 Potrero Ave, San Francisco (94103-4800)
PHONE 415 626-7844
Allan G Byer, *CEO*
Ed Manburg, *CFO*
Marian Byer, *Corp Secy*
Barbara Berling, *Vice Pres*
Janis Byer, *Vice Pres*
▲ **EMP:** 575 **EST:** 1964
SQ FT: 230,000
SALES (est): 289MM **Privately Held**
WEB: www.byerca.com
SIC: 2331 Women's & misses' blouses & shirts

(P-2998)
BYER CALIFORNIA
3740 Livermore Outlets Dr, Livermore (94551-4215)
PHONE 925 245-0184
EMP: 67
SALES (corp-wide): 372.3MM **Privately Held**
SIC: 2331 Mfg Women's/Misses' Blouses
PA: Byer California
66 Potrero Ave
San Francisco CA 94103
415 626-7844

(P-2999)
MAKING IT BIG INC
1375 Corp Ctr Pkwy Ste A, Santa Rosa (95407-5432)
PHONE 707 795-1995
Tracy Amiral, *President*
Kristina Chan, *Marketing Staff*
EMP: 17 **EST:** 1984
SALES (est): 2.1MM **Privately Held**
WEB: www.ontheplusside.com
SIC: 2331 2335 2337 2339 Women's & misses' blouses & shirts; women's, juniors' & misses' dresses; women's & misses' suits & coats; women's & misses' outerwear; women's apparel, mail order; women's clothing stores

2335 Women's & Misses' Dresses

(P-3000)
AZAZIE INC
148 E Brokaw Rd, San Jose (95112-4203)
PHONE 650 963-9420
Qi Zhong, *CEO*
Ranu Coleman, *Manager*
Rachel Hogue, *Manager*
EMP: 33 **EST:** 2015
SALES (est): 8.4MM **Privately Held**
WEB: www.azazie.com
SIC: 2335 Gowns, formal

(P-3001)
DAVIDS BRIDAL INC
1515 Springfield Dr # 100, Chico (95928-5996)
PHONE 530 342-5914
Andrea McKellips, *Branch Mgr*
EMP: 15 **Privately Held**
WEB: www.davidsbridal.com
SIC: 5621 2335 Bridal shops; wedding gowns & dresses
PA: David's Bridal, Inc.
1001 Washington St
Conshohocken PA 19428

(P-3002)
L Y Z LTD (PA)
Also Called: Lily Samii Collection
210 Post St, San Francisco (94108-5102)
PHONE 415 445-9505
Lily Samii, *President*
Laleh Eskandari, *Treasurer*
EMP: 17 **EST:** 1969
SQ FT: 7,200
SALES (est): 2.7MM **Privately Held**
WEB: www.lilysamii.com
SIC: 2335 5621 Women's, juniors' & misses' dresses; dress shops

(P-3003)
TONY MARTERIE & ASSOCIATES INC
Also Called: North Coast Industries
28 Liberty Ship Way Fl 2, Sausalito (94965-3320)
P.O. Box 2018 (94966-2018)
PHONE 415 331-7150
Tony Marterie, *President*
Roxanne Marterie, *Vice Pres*
Robert Ghiorci, *Manager*
▲ **EMP:** 25 **EST:** 1965
SQ FT: 27,000
SALES (est): 2.5MM **Privately Held**
WEB: www.blast-usa.com
SIC: 2335 2339 Women's, juniors' & misses' dresses; women's & misses' outerwear

2337 Women's & Misses' Suits, Coats & Skirts

(P-3004)
ANN LILLI CORP (PA)
1010 B St Ste 333, San Rafael (94901-2920)
PHONE 415 482-9444
Don Kamler, *Principal*
Jo Schuman, *Principal*
EMP: 63 **EST:** 1969
SALES (est): 5.8MM **Privately Held**
SIC: 2337 Women's & misses' suits & coats

(P-3005)
DANOC MANUFACTURING CORP INC
Also Called: Danoc Embroidery
6015 Power Inn Rd Ste A, Sacramento (95824-2336)
PHONE 916 455-2876
Tom Land, *President*
Dirk Ross, *Manager*
EMP: 16 **EST:** 1910
SQ FT: 1,500
SALES (est): 1.5MM **Privately Held**
WEB: www.motowear.com
SIC: 2337 2326 Uniforms, except athletic: women's, misses' & juniors'; industrial garments, men's & boys'; work garments, except raincoats: waterproof

(P-3006)
SCHOOL APPAREL INC (PA)
Also Called: A Career Apparel
838 Mitten Rd, Burlingame (94010-1304)
PHONE 650 777-4500
Kenneth Knoss, *CEO*
Ryan Knoss, *Ch of Bd*
Dave Weil, *CFO*
Bernice B Knoss, *Treasurer*
Marty Crowley, *Vice Pres*
◆ **EMP:** 164 **EST:** 1976
SALES (est): 25.9MM **Privately Held**
WEB: www.schoolapparel.com
SIC: 2337 2311 2326 Uniforms, except athletic: women's, misses' & juniors'; men's & boys' uniforms; work uniforms

2339 Women's & Misses' Outerwear, NEC

(P-3007)
BABETTE (PA)
867 Newton Carey Jr Way, Oakland (94607-1596)
PHONE 510 625-8500
Babette Pinsky, *President*
Steven Pinsky, *CFO*
Elfriede Griffey, *Admin Sec*
▲ **EMP:** 37 **EST:** 1968
SQ FT: 28,000
SALES (est): 4.9MM **Privately Held**
WEB: www.shopbabette.com
SIC: 2339 2369 Sportswear, women's; girls' & children's outerwear

(P-3008)
C P SHADES INC (PA)
403 Coloma St, Sausalito (94965-2827)
PHONE 415 331-4581
David Weinstein, *President*
Denise Weinstein, *Treasurer*
Alison Pownall, *Vice Pres*
Cyndi Pettibone, *Office Mgr*
Kyrrha Martin, *Opers Staff*
▲ **EMP:** 17 **EST:** 1973
SQ FT: 40,405
SALES (est): 29.1MM **Privately Held**
WEB: www.cpshades.com
SIC: 2335 5621 Women's & misses' athletic clothing & sportswear; women's; women's sportswear

(P-3009)
CUT LOOSE (PA)
101 Williams Ave, San Francisco (94124-2619)
PHONE 415 822-2031
Will Wenham, *President*
Rosemarie Ovian, *Vice Pres*
◆ **EMP:** 55 **EST:** 1984
SQ FT: 17,000
SALES (est): 10MM **Privately Held**
WEB: www.cutloose.com
SIC: 2339 5621 2331 Sportswear, women's; women's clothing stores; women's & misses' blouses & shirts

(P-3010)
FIFTH SUN LLC
495 Ryan Ave, Chico (95973-8846)
P.O. Box 6744 (95927-6744)
PHONE 530 343-8725
Dawn Gonzales, *Mng Member*
Christine McAdams, *Vice Pres*
Svetlana Reardon, *Planning*
Richard Barnes, *CIO*
Robert Brockman, *Software Dev*
EMP: 61 **EST:** 1999
SALES (est): 10.9MM **Privately Held**
WEB: www.5sun.com
SIC: 2339 Athletic clothing: women's, misses' & juniors'

(P-3011)
JAPANESE WEEKEND INC (PA)
496 S Airport Blvd, South San Francisco (94080-6911)
PHONE 415 621-0555
Barbara White, *President*
▲ **EMP:** 25 **EST:** 1979
SQ FT: 6,000
SALES (est): 7.1MM **Privately Held**
SIC: 2339 5621 Maternity clothing; maternity wear

(P-3012)
MARGARET OLEARY INC (PA)
50 Dorman Ave, San Francisco (94124-1807)
PHONE 415 354-6663
Margaret O'Leary, *CEO*
Joanna King, *Vice Pres*
Joya Choudhuri, *Production*
▲ **EMP:** 70 **EST:** 1991
SQ FT: 16,000
SALES (est): 17.6MM **Privately Held**
WEB: www.margaretoleary.com
SIC: 2339 2253 Sportswear, women's; knit outerwear mills

(P-3013)
SFO APPAREL
41 Park Pl 43, Brisbane (94005-1306)
PHONE 415 468-8816
Peter Mou, *President*
▲ **EMP:** 140 **EST:** 1994
SQ FT: 20,000
SALES (est): 8.7MM **Privately Held**
SIC: 2339 Women's & misses' athletic clothing & sportswear; beachwear; women's, misses' & juniors'

2353 Hats, Caps & Millinery

(P-3014)
ONE HAT ONE HAND LLC
1335 Yosemite Ave, San Francisco (94124-3319)
PHONE 415 822-2020
Chrisray Collins,
James Manus, *Technician*
Joe Martin, *Engineer*
Jenn Fawcett, *Finance*
Marcus Guillard,
EMP: 42 **EST:** 2008
SQ FT: 19,000
SALES (est): 4.1MM **Privately Held**
WEB: www.onehatonehand.com
SIC: 2353 Hats, caps & millinery

2361 Children's & Infants' Dresses & Blouses

(P-3015)
JESSICA MCCLINTOCK INC (PA)
2307 Broadway St, San Francisco (94115-1291)
PHONE 415 553-8200
Jessica Mc Clintock, *President*
▲ **EMP:** 150 **EST:** 1970
SQ FT: 120,000
SALES (est): 49.2MM **Privately Held**
WEB: www.jessicamcclintock.com
SIC: 2361 2335 2844 Dresses: girls', children's & infants'; women's, juniors' & misses' dresses; perfumes, natural or synthetic

2369 Girls' & Infants' Outerwear, NEC

(P-3016)
MACK & REISS INC
Also Called: Biscotti and Kate Mack
5601 San Leandro St Ste 3, Oakland (94621-4433)
PHONE 510 434-9122
Bernadette Reiss, *President*
Robert Mack, *Corp Secy*
▲ **EMP:** 85 **EST:** 1986
SQ FT: 75,000
SALES (est): 9.5MM **Privately Held**
WEB: www.biscottiinc.com
SIC: 2369 Girls' & children's outerwear

2386 Leather & Sheep Lined Clothing

(P-3017)
GB SPORT SF LLC
Also Called: Golden Bear Sportswear
200 Potrero Ave, San Francisco (94103-4815)
PHONE 415 863-6171
Ronald Gilmere, *Mng Member*
Clare Bouey, *Credit Mgr*
EMP: 20 **EST:** 2018
SALES (est): 1.7MM **Privately Held**
WEB: www.goldenbearsportswear.com
SIC: 2386 Leather & sheep-lined clothing

(P-3018)
MR S LEATHER
Also Called: Fetters U.S.A.
385 8th St, San Francisco (94103-4423)
PHONE 415 863-7764
Richard Hunter, *President*
Tchukon Hunter, *Vice Pres*
Jonathan Schroder, *General Mgr*
Santiago Salsido, *Opers Staff*
▲ **EMP:** 45 **EST:** 1979
SQ FT: 15,000
SALES (est): 6.9MM **Privately Held**
WEB: www.mr-s-leather.com
SIC: 2386 5699 5136 Garments, leather; leather garments; men's & boys' clothing; men's & boys' furnishings

2387 Apparel Belts

(P-3019)
ARCADE BELTS INC (PA)
150 Alpine Meadows Rd, Alpine Meadows (96146-9880)
P.O. Box 2728, Olympic Valley (96146-2728)
PHONE 530 580-8089

▲ = Import ▼ = Export
◆ = Import/Export

PRODUCTS & SERVICES SECTION

2394 - Canvas Prdts County (P-3042)

Tristan Queen, *President*
David Bronkie, *Corp Secy*
Amanda Kimmey, *Sales Mgr*
EMP: 93 **EST:** 2011
SALES (est): 6.4MM **Privately Held**
WEB: www.arcadebelts.com
SIC: 2387 Apparel belts

2389 Apparel & Accessories, NEC

(P-3020)
SUSPENDER FACTORY INC
Also Called: Suspender Factory of S F
1425 63rd St, Emeryville (94608-2188)
PHONE 510 547-5400
John Nemec, *President*
▲ **EMP:** 35
SQ FT: 6,000
SALES (est): 4MM **Privately Held**
WEB: www.suspenderfactory.com
SIC: 2389 2387 Suspenders; apparel belts

2391 Curtains & Draperies

(P-3021)
AMERICAN BLINDS AND DRAP INC
30776 Huntwood Ave, Hayward (94544-7002)
P.O. Box 56267 (94545-6267)
PHONE 510 487-3500
Paul Russo, *President*
EMP: 40 **EST:** 1961
SQ FT: 30,000
SALES (est): 796.1K **Privately Held**
SIC: 2391 2591 Draperies, plastic & textile: from purchased materials; mini blinds

(P-3022)
SANDYS DRAPERY INC (PA)
48374 Milmont Dr Bldg A, Fremont (94538-7324)
PHONE 510 445-0112
Donald L Yauger, *President*
Harry Yauger, *Treasurer*
Cindy Yauger, *Admin Sec*
EMP: 22 **EST:** 1955
SQ FT: 27,500
SALES (est): 1.6MM **Privately Held**
WEB: www.sandysdrapery.net
SIC: 2391 2591 2211 Draperies, plastic & textile: from purchased materials; drapery hardware & blinds & shades; draperies & drapery fabrics, cotton

---

2392 House furnishings: Textile

(P-3023)
DREAMS DUVETS & BED LINENS INC
Also Called: Dreams Duvets & Linens
921 Howard St, San Francisco (94103-4108)
PHONE 415 543-1800
Kusum Jain, *President*
EMP: 15 **EST:** 1993
SQ FT: 17,000
SALES (est): 455.8K **Privately Held**
SIC: 2392 5719 7699 Comforters & quilts: made from purchased materials; beddings & linens; general household repair services

(P-3024)
DV KAP INC
Also Called: Canaan Company
426 W Bedford Ave, Fresno (93711-6858)
PHONE 559 435-5575
Dan Sivas, *CEO*
Khach Sivas, *Manager*
◆ **EMP:** 50 **EST:** 2002
SQ FT: 25,000
SALES (est): 11.8MM **Privately Held**
WEB: www.dvkap.com
SIC: 2392 Cushions & pillows

(P-3025)
FARALLON BRANDS INC (PA)
Also Called: Peanut Shell
33300 Central Ave, Union City (94587-2044)
PHONE 510 550-4299
Michael Roach, *CEO*
William T Tauscher, *Ch of Bd*
Laura Tauscher, *COO*
Yvonne Ortiz, *Vice Pres*
Teresa Skinner, *Director*
◆ **EMP:** 17 **EST:** 2007
SQ FT: 27,000
SALES (est): 2.7MM **Privately Held**
WEB: www.farallonbrands.com
SIC: 2392 3944 Blankets, comforters & beddings; baby carriages & restraint seats

(P-3026)
HUDSON & COMPANY LLC
Also Called: Spirit Throws
100 Irene Ave, Roseville (95678-3226)
P.O. Box 968 (95678-0968)
PHONE 916 774-6465
Shannon Hudson, *Mng Member*
Richard Barnes, *CIO*
▼ **EMP:** 16 **EST:** 1997
SQ FT: 984
SALES (est): 463.3K **Privately Held**
WEB: www.hudsonthrows.com
SIC: 2392 Blankets, comforters & beddings

(P-3027)
JR WATKINS LLC
101 Mission St, San Francisco (94105-1705)
PHONE 415 477-8500
Michael Fox, *CEO*
Dan Swander, *Partner*
Chris Folena, *CFO*
Heather Fraser, *CFO*
EMP: 22 **EST:** 2017
SALES (est): 1.4MM **Privately Held**
SIC: 2392 5963 Household furnishings; home related products, direct sales

(P-3028)
MAGNOLIA LANE SOFT HM FURN INC
Also Called: Designs With Fabric
187 Utah Ave, South San Francisco (94080-6712)
PHONE 650 624-0700
Kathleen Redmond, *President*
Mary McWilliams, *CFO*
Judy Powers, *Marketing Staff*
EMP: 24 **EST:** 1983
SQ FT: 5,000
SALES (est): 1.1MM **Privately Held**
WEB: www.magnolialane.com
SIC: 2392 2391 Cushions & pillows; blankets, comforters & beddings; draperies, plastic & textile: from purchased materials

(P-3029)
ONE BELLA CASA INC
Also Called: Artehouse
101 Lucas Valley Rd # 130, San Rafael (94903-1791)
PHONE 707 746-8300
Gary Sattin, *CEO*
Cindy Harris, *Manager*
▲ **EMP:** 24 **EST:** 2013
SQ FT: 10,000
SALES (est): 1.3MM **Privately Held**
WEB: www.onebellacasa.com
SIC: 2392 3952 Pillows, bed: made from purchased materials; canvas, prepared on frames: artists'

(P-3030)
THOMAS WEST INC (PA)
Also Called: T W I
470 Mercury Dr, Sunnyvale (94085-4706)
PHONE 408 481-3850
Tom West, *CEO*
Dr Steve Kirtley, *COO*
Suli Holani, *Prdtn Mgr*
▲ **EMP:** 26 **EST:** 1981
SQ FT: 43,000
SALES (est): 8.6MM **Privately Held**
WEB: www.twimaterials.com
SIC: 2392 Towels, dishcloths & dust cloths

2393 Textile Bags

(P-3031)
CHICOECO INC
Also Called: Chicobag
747 Fortress St, Chico (95973-9012)
PHONE 530 342-4426
Andrew Keller, *President*
Ben Doney, *Administration*
Martha Mathern, *CIO*
CAM Smeltzer, *Production*
Chrystal Tunnell, *Sales Mgr*
▲ **EMP:** 30 **EST:** 2005
SALES (est): 3.9MM **Privately Held**
WEB: www.chicobag.com
SIC: 2393 Textile bags

(P-3032)
RICKSHAW BAGWORKS INC
904 22nd St, San Francisco (94107-3427)
PHONE 415 904-8368
Mark Dwight, *CEO*
Shalee LI, *Prdtn Mgr*
Joseph Montana, *Marketing Staff*
▲ **EMP:** 18 **EST:** 2007
SALES (est): 1.2MM **Privately Held**
WEB: www.rickshawbags.com
SIC: 2393 Textile bags

(P-3033)
TIMBUK2 DESIGNS INC
2031 Cessna Dr, Vacaville (95688-8903)
PHONE 800 865-2513
Chris Garcia, *Manager*
EMP: 25 **Privately Held**
WEB: www.timbuk2.com
SIC: 2393 Canvas bags
PA: Timbuk2 Designs, Inc.
400 Alabama St 201
San Francisco CA 94110

(P-3034)
TIMBUK2 DESIGNS INC (PA)
400 Alabama St 201, San Francisco (94110-1315)
PHONE 415 252-4300
Paul Devries, *CEO*
Chris Brown, *Executive*
Jesse Gillingham, *Business Mgr*
Matt Fisher, *Opers Mgr*
Carlos Esqueda, *Marketing Staff*
◆ **EMP:** 192 **EST:** 2016
SALES (est): 20.4MM **Privately Held**
WEB: www.timbuk2.com
SIC: 2393 Canvas bags

(P-3035)
WORLD TEXTILE AND BAG INC
4680 Pell Dr Ste B, Sacramento (95838-2082)
PHONE 916 922-9222
Richard Quinley, *CEO*
Bud Sciscio, *Opers Staff*
EMP: 25 **EST:** 2010
SALES (est): 4MM **Privately Held**
WEB: www.wtbinc.net
SIC: 2393 Textile bags

2394 Canvas Prdts

(P-3036)
AIRCRAFT COVERS INC
Also Called: Bruce's Custom Covers
18850 Adams Ct, Morgan Hill (95037-2816)
PHONE 408 738-3959
Bruce Perlitch, *President*
Ivan Uranga, *Purchasing*
Tom Blaine, *Sales Mgr*
EMP: 31
SQ FT: 21,909
SALES (corp-wide): 9.9MM **Privately Held**
WEB: www.aircraftcovers.com
SIC: 2394 Canvas & related products
PA: Aircraft Covers, Inc.
18850 Adams Ct
Morgan Hill CA 95037
408 738-3959

(P-3037)
BRAMPTON MTHESEN FABR PDTS INC
Also Called: Sullivan & Brampton
1688 Abram Ct, San Leandro (94577-3227)
PHONE 510 483-7771
Fax: 510 483-7723
EMP: 20
SQ FT: 40,000
SALES (est): 1.9MM **Privately Held**
WEB: www.sullivanandbrampton.com
SIC: 2394 2519 2393 Mfg Canvas/Related Prdts Mfg Household Furniture Mfg Textile Bags

(P-3038)
CITY CANVAS
1381 N 10th St, San Jose (95112-2804)
PHONE 408 287-2688
John M Cerrito, *President*
EMP: 20 **EST:** 1978
SQ FT: 10,000
SALES (est): 1.5MM **Privately Held**
WEB: www.citycanvas.com
SIC: 2394 7699 Awnings, fabric: made from purchased materials; awning repair shop

(P-3039)
LARSENS INC
1041 17th Ave Ste A, Santa Cruz (95062-3070)
PHONE 831 476-3009
Kurt W Larsen, *President*
Susan Larsen, *Vice Pres*
Karen Tracey, *Vice Pres*
EMP: 15 **EST:** 1972
SQ FT: 6,000
SALES (est): 2.2MM **Privately Held**
WEB: www.larsensinc.com
SIC: 2394 Sails: made from purchased materials

(P-3040)
MODESTO TENT AND AWNING INC
Also Called: Mid-Valley Tarp Service
4448 Sisk Rd, Modesto (95356-8729)
PHONE 209 545-1607
Robert Valk, *President*
Leonard Rigg, *Corp Secy*
▲ **EMP:** 30 **EST:** 1930
SQ FT: 26,000
SALES (est): 1.1MM **Privately Held**
WEB: www.midvalleytarp.com
SIC: 2394 2399 7359 5999 Awnings, fabric: made from purchased materials; banners, made from fabric; tent & tarpaulin rental; tents; signs, not made in custom sign painting shops; truck equipment & parts

(P-3041)
PHILIP A STITT AGENCY
Also Called: Capitol Tarpaulin Co
3900 Stockton Blvd, Sacramento (95820-2913)
PHONE 916 451-2801
Martin Stitt, *President*
Philip L Stitt, *Corp Secy*
Richard Pechal, *Vice Pres*
EMP: 24 **EST:** 1947
SQ FT: 13,000
SALES (est): 1.1MM **Privately Held**
SIC: 2394 Tarpaulins, fabric: made from purchased materials; tents: made from purchased materials; awnings, fabric: made from purchased materials

(P-3042)
SAN JOSE AWNING COMPANY INC
755 Chestnut St Ste E, San Jose (95110-1832)
PHONE 408 350-7000
Michael Yaholkovsky, *President*
Tracie Ho, *Admin Asst*
Evelyn Trang, *Production*
EMP: 27 **EST:** 1983
SQ FT: 8,800
SALES (est): 3MM **Privately Held**
WEB: www.sanjoseawning.com
SIC: 2394 Awnings, fabric: made from purchased materials

2395 Pleating & Stitching For The Trade

(P-3043)
SAN FRANSTITCHCO INC
624 Portal St, Cotati (94931-3069)
PHONE 707 795-6891
Darrel Kolse, *President*
EMP: 19 EST: 1978
SALES (est): 1.2MM **Privately Held**
SIC: 2395 Embroidery products, except schiffli machine

2396 Automotive Trimmings, Apparel Findings, Related Prdts

(P-3044)
AD SPCIAL TS EMB SCRNPRNTING I
202 Bella Vista Rd Ste B, Vacaville (95687-5412)
PHONE 707 452-7272
Mike Anderson, *President*
Donald McKimmy, *Vice Pres*
Lela Anderson, *Admin Sec*
EMP: 16 EST: 1972
SQ FT: 6,300
SALES (est): 1.4MM **Privately Held**
WEB: www.adspecialts.com
SIC: 2396 2395 5941 5699 Screen printing on fabric articles; embroidery & art needlework; sporting goods & bicycle shops; sports apparel

(P-3045)
BANDMERCH LLC
3945 Freedom Cir Ste 560, Santa Clara (95054-1269)
PHONE 818 736-4800
Joseph Bongiovi, *President*
Rafael Sanchez, *Prdtn Mgr*
Rachel Verber, *Marketing Staff*
Nicole Caughey,
Kyle Barber, *Art Dir*
▲ EMP: 33 EST: 2003
SALES (est): 13.1MM **Privately Held**
WEB: www.bandmerch.com
SIC: 2396 Fabric printing & stamping
HQ: Aeg Presents Llc
425 W 11th St
Los Angeles CA 90015
323 930-5700

(P-3046)
MONICA BRUCE DESIGNS INC
Also Called: Inmotion
28913 Arnold Dr, Sonoma (95476-9738)
PHONE 707 938-0277
T Michael Fellows, *President*
Nick Castro, *Art Dir*
Norma Rosas, *Manager*
EMP: 17 EST: 1974
SQ FT: 9,000
SALES (est): 1.1MM **Privately Held**
SIC: 2396 2395 Screen printing on fabric articles; embroidery & art needlework

(P-3047)
PARTSFLEX INC
1775 Park St Ste 77, Selma (93662-3659)
PHONE 408 677-7121
Max Alsedda, *President*
EMP: 25 EST: 2017
SALES (est): 8MM **Privately Held**
SIC: 2396 5013 Automotive & apparel trimmings; automotive supplies & parts

(P-3048)
TSHIRTGUYSCOM (PA)
11264 Chula Vista Ave, San Jose (95127-1316)
PHONE 619 793-4635
Frank De La Cruz,
Marcela Loaiza, *Admin Mgr*
Maria Rodriguez, *Sales Staff*
Maria Rodriguez,
EMP: 53 EST: 2000
SALES (est): 4.9MM **Privately Held**
WEB: www.tshirtguys.com
SIC: 5699 2396 T-shirts, custom printed; screen printing on fabric articles

(P-3049)
WESTSIDE RESEARCH INC
4293 County Road 99w, Orland (95963-9153)
PHONE 530 330-0085
Tim Dexter, *President*
Karen Dexter, *Vice Pres*
Richard Barnes, *CIO*
◆ EMP: 16 EST: 2003
SALES (est): 946.6K **Privately Held**
WEB: www.westsideresearch.com
SIC: 2396 Automotive & apparel trimmings

2399 Fabricated Textile Prdts, NEC

(P-3050)
DRAKE ENTERPRISES INCORPORATED
Also Called: Big D Products
490 Watt Dr, Fairfield (94534-1663)
P.O. Box 820, Millsap TX (76066-0820)
PHONE 707 864-3077
Glenn Drake, *President*
Pilar Pena, *Bookkeeper*
▲ EMP: 67 EST: 1958
SQ FT: 55,000
SALES (est): 6.9MM **Privately Held**
WEB: www.bigdblankets.com
SIC: 2399 Horse blankets; horse & pet accessories, textile

(P-3051)
JESSIE STEELE INC
1020 The Alameda, San Jose (95126-3139)
PHONE 510 204-0991
Helena J Steele, *President*
Larry Philipps, *COO*
◆ EMP: 17 EST: 2003
SALES (est): 1.4MM **Privately Held**
WEB: www.jessiesteele.com
SIC: 2399 Aprons, breast (harness)

(P-3052)
NORTH BAY RHBLITATION SVCS INC (PA)
Also Called: North Bay Industries
649 Martin Ave, Rohnert Park (94928-2050)
PHONE 707 585-1991
Robert Hutt, *CEO*
William Stewart, *Ch of Bd*
Bella Hutt, *CFO*
Liz Sutton, *Exec VP*
Bob Hutt, *Vice Pres*
EMP: 229 EST: 1968
SQ FT: 18,000
SALES: 16.2MM **Privately Held**
WEB: www.nbrs.org
SIC: 2399 0782 8331 Banners, pennants & flags; lawn services; community service employment training program

(P-3053)
SEVENTH HEAVEN INC
Also Called: Western Mountaineering
1025 S 5th St, San Jose (95112-3927)
PHONE 408 287-8945
Gary Schaezlein, *Sales Mgr*
Gary Peterson, *Prdtn Mgr*
Patrica Madsen, *Assistant*
▲ EMP: 30 EST: 1970
SQ FT: 12,000
SALES (est): 3.7MM **Privately Held**
WEB: www.westernmountaineering.com
SIC: 2399 2392 2329 Sleeping bags; comforters & quilts; made from purchased materials; down-filled clothing: men's & boys'

2411 Logging

(P-3054)
ALDERMAN TIMBER COMPANY INC
Also Called: Alderman Logging
17180 Alderman Rd, Sonora (95370-8909)
P.O. Box 127, Soulsbyville (95372-0127)
PHONE 209 532-9636
Keith Alderman, *President*
Linda Alderman, *Corp Secy*
Roger Alderman, *Vice Pres*
EMP: 24 EST: 1949
SALES (est): 1.1MM **Privately Held**
SIC: 2411 Logging camps & contractors

(P-3055)
ANDERSON LOGGING INC
1296 N Main St, Fort Bragg (95437-8407)
P.O. Box 1266 (95437-1266)
PHONE 707 964-2770
Michael Anderson, *President*
Joseph Anderson, *Vice Pres*
Mike Anderson, *Executive*
Maribelle Anderson, *Admin Sec*
Joye Fereira, *Manager*
EMP: 100 EST: 1977
SQ FT: 3,000
SALES (est): 8MM **Privately Held**
WEB: www.andersonlogging.com
SIC: 2411 4212 Logging camps & contractors; lumber (log) trucking, local

(P-3056)
BIG HILL LOGGING & RD BUILDING (PA)
680 Sutter St, Yuba City (95991-4218)
PHONE 530 673-4155
Macarthur Siller, *President*
McArthur Siller, *President*
Janet Siller, *Vice Pres*
Dane Siller, *Admin Sec*
EMP: 25 EST: 1986
SQ FT: 1,726
SALES (est): 5MM **Privately Held**
SIC: 2411 1611 Logging camps & contractors; highway & street construction

(P-3057)
BUNDY AND SONS INC
15196 Mountain Shadows Dr, Redding (96001-9544)
PHONE 530 246-3868
William J Bundy, *President*
Terrice Bundy, *Vice Pres*
EMP: 17 EST: 1985
SQ FT: 2,000
SALES (est): 1MM **Privately Held**
SIC: 2411 Logging camps & contractors

(P-3058)
DEL LOGGING INC
101 Punkin Center Rd, Bieber (96009)
P.O. Box 246 (96009-0246)
PHONE 530 294-5492
Russ Hawkins, *President*
Helen Hawkins, *Corp Secy*
EMP: 19 EST: 1971
SQ FT: 450
SALES (est): 1.5MM **Privately Held**
SIC: 2411 Logging camps & contractors

(P-3059)
ELIZABETH HEADRICK
Also Called: Headrick Logging
7194 Bridge St, Anderson (96007-9496)
PHONE 530 247-8000
Elizabeth Headrick, *Owner*
EMP: 22 EST: 1986
SQ FT: 4,500
SALES (est): 2MM **Privately Held**
SIC: 2411 Logging camps & contractors

(P-3060)
FORD LOGGING INC
Also Called: Pacific Earthscape
1225 Central Ave Ste 11, McKinleyville (95519-5301)
PHONE 707 840-9442
Delman Ford, *President*
Heath Ford, *Treasurer*
Glenn Ford, *Vice Pres*
Derek Ford, *Admin Sec*
EMP: 37 EST: 1995
SALES (est): 2.6MM **Privately Held**
WEB: www.pacificearthscape.com
SIC: 2411 1611 Logging camps & contractors; gravel or dirt road construction

(P-3061)
FRANKLIN LOGGING INC
11906 Wilson Way, Redding (96003-7589)
PHONE 530 549-4924
Dianne Franklin, *Branch Mgr*
EMP: 56
SALES (corp-wide): 1.9MM **Privately Held**
SIC: 2411 Logging camps & contractors
PA: Franklin Logging Inc.
1300 West St Ste A
Redding CA

(P-3062)
FRAY LOGGING
10619 Jim Brady Rd, Jamestown (95327-9518)
PHONE 209 984-5968
Richard N Fray, *President*
Susan Fray, *Treasurer*
EMP: 29 EST: 1963
SALES (est): 2.1MM **Privately Held**
SIC: 2411 Logging camps & contractors

(P-3063)
HOOPA FOREST INDUSTRIES
778 Marshall Ln, Hoopa (95546-9762)
P.O. Box 759 (95546-0759)
PHONE 530 625-4281
Merwin Clark, *CEO*
EMP: 29 EST: 2014
SALES (est): 2.5MM **Privately Held**
WEB: www.hoopaforestry.com
SIC: 2411 Logging
PA: Hoopa Valley Tribal Council
11860 State Highway 96
Hoopa CA 95546
530 625-4211

(P-3064)
HUFFMAN LOGGING CO INC
1155 Huffman Dr, Fortuna (95540-3337)
PHONE 707 725-4335
EMP: 45
SALES (est): 2.9MM **Privately Held**
SIC: 2411 Logging

(P-3065)
J & R LOGGING INC
9252 Bush St, Plymouth (95669-9008)
P.O. Box 485 (95669-0485)
PHONE 209 245-5540
EMP: 18 EST: 2009
SALES (est): 2.4MM **Privately Held**
SIC: 2411 Logging camps & contractors

(P-3066)
J W BAMFORD INC
Also Called: Bamford Equipment
4288 State Highway 70, Oroville (95965-8340)
PHONE 530 533-0732
Joel Bamford, *President*
James Bamford, *Vice Pres*
Lori Curtis, *Vice Pres*
Nathan Bamford, *Admin Sec*
Kelly McDaniels, *Bookkeeper*
EMP: 16 EST: 1980
SQ FT: 8,000
SALES (est): 5MM **Privately Held**
SIC: 2411 Logging

(P-3067)
JOHN WHEELER LOGGING INC
13570 State Highway 36 E, Red Bluff (96080-8878)
P.O. Box 339 (96080-0339)
PHONE 530 527-2993
Dave Holder, *President*
Vern Mc Coshum, *Vice Pres*
EMP: 105 EST: 1966
SQ FT: 3,500
SALES (est): 9.3MM **Privately Held**
SIC: 2411 4212 Logging camps & contractors; local trucking, without storage

▲ = Import ▼ = Export
◆ = Import/Export

PRODUCTS & SERVICES SECTION

2421 - Saw & Planing Mills County (P-3094)

(P-3068)
LEONARDO LOGGING AND CNSTR INC
Also Called: Anthony Leonardo Logging
604 L St, Fortuna (95540-1900)
P.O. Box 875 (95540-0875)
PHONE.................................707 725-1809
Anthony Leonardo, *CEO*
Janice Leonardo, *CFO*
Shannon Leonardo, *Vice Pres*
EMP: 40 **EST:** 1993
SALES (est): 5.3MM **Privately Held**
SIC: 2411 4212 Logging camps & contractors; lumber & timber trucking

(P-3069)
LEWIS LOGGING
3897 Rohnerville Rd, Fortuna (95540-3121)
P.O. Box 96, Redcrest (95569-0096)
PHONE.................................707 722-1975
Ed B Lewis, *President*
Patricia Fountain, *Corp Secy*
Dean Lewis, *Vice Pres*
Vicki McCutchen, *Principal*
EMP: 25 **EST:** 1965
SQ FT: 1,100
SALES (est): 1MM **Privately Held**
SIC: 2411 Logging camps & contractors

(P-3070)
MARTIN FISCHER LOGGING CO INC
1165 Skull Flat Rd, West Point (95255-7053)
P.O. Box 146 (95255-0146)
PHONE.................................209 293-4847
Martin M Fischer, *President*
Lillian Fischer, *Admin Sec*
EMP: 19 **EST:** 1956
SALES (est): 1MM **Privately Held**
SIC: 2411 Logging camps & contractors

(P-3071)
MATTHEWS SKYLINE LOGGING INC
10100 East Rd, Potter Valley (95469-9773)
P.O. Box 419, Calpella (95418-0419)
PHONE.................................707 743-2890
Cecil Matthews, *President*
Betty Matthews, *Admin Sec*
EMP: 27 **EST:** 1977
SQ FT: 20,000
SALES (est): 2.6MM **Privately Held**
SIC: 2411 Logging camps & contractors

(P-3072)
MESSER LOGGING INC
32111 Rock Hill Ln, Auberry (93602-9771)
PHONE.................................559 855-3160
Timothy Messer, *President*
Tery Messer, *CFO*
Hayley Ferguson, *Corp Secy*
EMP: 34 **EST:** 1948
SALES (est): 2.6MM **Privately Held**
WEB: www.timmesserconstruction.com
SIC: 2411 Logging camps & contractors

(P-3073)
MOUNTAIN F ENTERPRISES INC
Also Called: Tree Service
950 Iron Point Rd Ste 210, Folsom (95630-8338)
P.O. Box 1040, Lotus (95651-1040)
PHONE.................................530 626-4127
Raul Gomez, *President*
Marcos A Gomez, *CEO*
Jake Wolf, *CFO*
EMP: 40 **EST:** 1989
SQ FT: 4,000
SALES (est): 15MM **Privately Held**
WEB: www.mtfent.com
SIC: 2411 0851 0783 5099 Logging; forestry services; tree trimming services for public utility lines; arborist services; firewood; flagging service (traffic control)

(P-3074)
PHILBRICK INC
Also Called: Philbrick Logging & Trucking
32180 Airport Rd, Fort Bragg (95437-9509)
P.O. Box 1288 (95437-1288)
PHONE.................................707 964-2277
Jerry D Philbrick, *President*
EMP: 22 **EST:** 1961

SQ FT: 500
SALES (est): 618.7K **Privately Held**
SIC: 2411 Logging camps & contractors

(P-3075)
ROACH BROS INC
23550 Shady Ln, Fort Bragg (95437-8421)
PHONE.................................707 964-9240
Leroy Roach, *President*
Sybil Roach, *Treasurer*
Gary Roach, *Vice Pres*
Sally Roach, *Admin Sec*
EMP: 70 **EST:** 1968
SALES (est): 5.2MM **Privately Held**
SIC: 2411 Logging camps & contractors

(P-3076)
ROUNDS LOGGING COMPANY
4350 Lynbrook Loop Apt 1, Redding (96003-6853)
PHONE.................................530 247-0517
Roger Rounds, *President*
Stacie Rounds, *Admin Sec*
EMP: 24 **EST:** 1951
SQ FT: 1,200
SALES (est): 1.9MM **Privately Held**
SIC: 2411 Logging camps & contractors

(P-3077)
SANDERS PRCSION TMBER FLLING I (PA)
9509 N Old Stage Rd, Weed (96094-9516)
PHONE.................................530 938-4120
Ross Sanders, *Owner*
Bernard Cilione, *Treasurer*
Forest Sanders, *Vice Pres*
Tom Midget, *Admin Sec*
EMP: 20 **EST:** 1981
SALES (est): 1.4MM **Privately Held**
SIC: 2411 Timber, cut at logging camp

(P-3078)
SHASTA GREEN INC
Also Called: Franklin Logging
35586a State Hwy 299 E, Burney (96013-4048)
PHONE.................................530 335-4924
Diane Franklin, *President*
Keith Tiner, *Vice Pres*
EMP: 50 **EST:** 2002
SQ FT: 1,500
SALES (est): 10.2MM **Privately Held**
SIC: 2411 Logging camps & contractors

(P-3079)
SHUSTERS LOGGING INC
750 E Valley St, Willits (95490-9749)
PHONE.................................707 459-4131
Steve Shuster, *President*
Marv Lawrence, *Corp Secy*
Phillip L Shuster, *Vice Pres*
EMP: 22 **EST:** 1979
SQ FT: 2,300
SALES (est): 1MM **Privately Held**
SIC: 2411 Logging

(P-3080)
SIERRA RESOURCE MANAGEMENT INC
12015 La Grange Rd, Jamestown (95327-9724)
PHONE.................................209 984-1146
Mike Albrecht, *President*
Stacy Dodge, *Vice Pres*
EMP: 34 **EST:** 1993
SQ FT: 4,500
SALES (est): 3MM **Privately Held**
WEB: www.sierraresourcemanagement.com
SIC: 2411 Logging camps & contractors

(P-3081)
SILLER BROTHERS INC (PA)
Also Called: Siller Aviation
1250 Smith Rd, Yuba City (95991-6948)
P.O. Box 1585 (95992-1585)
PHONE.................................530 673-0734
Tom Siller, *President*
Hunt Norris, *CFO*
Jack Parnell, *Chairman*
Andrew Jansen, *Vice Pres*
Rod Glassford, *Maintence Staff*
EMP: 99 **EST:** 1943

SALES (est): 9.3MM **Privately Held**
WEB: www.sillerhelicopters.com
SIC: 2411 Logging camps & contractors; sawmills & planing mills, general

(P-3082)
SKYLINE ALTERATIONS INC (PA)
10771 Cheshire Way, Palo Cedro (96073-9777)
PHONE.................................530 549-4010
Dawn Sherman, *President*
Jody Sherman, *Vice Pres*
Brian Parnell, *Admin Sec*
EMP: 25 **EST:** 2003
SALES (est): 3.6MM **Privately Held**
SIC: 2411 Logging

(P-3083)
SOPER-WHEELER COMPANY LLC (PA)
100 N Pine St Unit B, Nevada City (95959-2531)
PHONE.................................530 675-2343
David Westcott, *CEO*
William Morrison, *Records Dir*
Daniel Krueger, *President*
Paul Violet, *Vice Pres*
Paul Violett, *Vice Pres*
EMP: 37 **EST:** 1904
SALES (est): 4.8MM **Privately Held**
WEB: www.soperwheeler.com
SIC: 2411 Logging camps & contractors

(P-3084)
TS LOGGING
18121 Rays Rd, Philo (95466-9533)
P.O. Box 31 (95466-0031)
PHONE.................................707 895-3751
Timothy Slotte, *Owner*
EMP: 20 **EST:** 1991
SALES (est): 1.1MM **Privately Held**
SIC: 2411 Logging camps & contractors

(P-3085)
TUBIT ENTERPRISES INC
21640 S Vallejo St, Burney (96013-9778)
P.O. Box 1019 (96013-1019)
PHONE.................................530 335-5085
Douglas Lindgren, *CEO*
Richard Lindgren, *President*
EMP: 40 **EST:** 1995
SQ FT: 3,000
SALES (est): 6.9MM **Privately Held**
WEB: www.tubit-enterprises-inc.business.site
SIC: 2411 Logging camps & contractors

(P-3086)
WARNER ENTERPRISES INC
1577 Beltline Rd, Redding (96003-1407)
PHONE.................................530 241-4000
Paul Warner, *President*
Gary Warner, *Vice Pres*
EMP: 30 **EST:** 1978
SQ FT: 9,000
SALES (est): 4.6MM **Privately Held**
SIC: 2411 Wood chips, produced in the field; logging camps & contractors

(P-3087)
WILLIAM R SCHMITT
Also Called: Schmitt Superior Classics
18135 Clear Creek Rd, Redding (96001-5233)
PHONE.................................530 243-3069
William R Schmitt, *Owner*
Sylvia Schmitt, *Co-Owner*
Ken Rice, *Manager*
EMP: 20 **EST:** 1950
SALES (est): 1.5MM **Privately Held**
WEB: www.superiorclassics.com
SIC: 2411 4212 5521 Logging; lumber (log) trucking, local; automobiles, used cars only; antique automobiles

(P-3088)
WYLATTI RESOURCE MGT INC
23601 Cemetery Ln, Covelo (95428-9773)
P.O. Box 575 (95428-0575)
PHONE.................................707 983-8135
Brian K Hurt, *President*
EMP: 20 **EST:** 1999

SALES (est): 2.7MM **Privately Held**
SIC: 2411 1611 1622 1442 Logging; general contractor, highway & street construction; bridge construction; construction sand & gravel; dump truck haulage; heavy machinery transport, local

(P-3089)
Z LOGGING LLC
403 Old State Hwy, Orick (95555)
PHONE.................................707 488-2151
Albert Zuber,
Cheryl Zuber,
EMP: 15 **EST:** 1952
SALES (est): 2MM **Privately Held**
SIC: 2411 Logging camps & contractors

2421 Saw & Planing Mills

(P-3090)
BERRYS SAWMILL INC
405 Cazadero Hwy, Cazadero (95421-9712)
P.O. Box 106 (95421-0106)
PHONE.................................707 865-2365
Loren M Berry, *President*
Beatrice Berry, *Corp Secy*
EMP: 32 **EST:** 1941
SQ FT: 1,000
SALES (est): 3.5MM **Privately Held**
WEB: www.berrysmill.com
SIC: 5211 2421 Planing mill products & lumber; custom sawmill; lumber: rough, sawed or planed

(P-3091)
BIG CREEK LUMBER COMPANY (PA)
3564 Highway 1, Davenport (95017-9706)
PHONE.................................831 457-5015
Janet Webb, *President*
Dave Renkens, *CFO*
Homer McCrary, *Vice Pres*
Frank McCrary Jr, *Principal*
David Williams, *Branch Mgr*
EMP: 100 **EST:** 1946
SQ FT: 3,000
SALES (est): 51.9MM **Privately Held**
WEB: www.bigcreeklumber.com
SIC: 5211 2421 Millwork & lumber; sawmills & planing mills, general

(P-3092)
BRACUT INTERNATIONAL CORP
Also Called: Mill Yard
4949 West End Rd, Arcata (95521-9243)
PHONE.................................707 826-9850
Laurie Mark, *President*
Tanka Chase, *Vice Pres*
EMP: 32 **EST:** 1972
SALES (est): 4.9MM **Privately Held**
WEB: www.themillyard.biz
SIC: 5211 2421 Lumber products; sawmills & planing mills, general; resawing lumber into smaller dimensions

(P-3093)
BURGESS LUMBER (PA)
3610 Copperhill Ln, Santa Rosa (95403-1090)
PHONE.................................707 542-5091
Orin Burgess, *CEO*
Andrew Lee Burgess, *Corp Secy*
Warren A Burgess, *Vice Pres*
Michael Douglass, *General Mgr*
EMP: 15 **EST:** 1972
SQ FT: 1,500
SALES (est): 5.3MM **Privately Held**
WEB: www.burgesslumber.com
SIC: 5211 2421 Millwork & lumber; resawing lumber into smaller dimensions

(P-3094)
BURGESS LUMBER
8800 West Rd, Redwood Valley (95470-6199)
PHONE.................................707 485-8072
Bobby Puga, *Manager*
EMP: 26
SALES (corp-wide): 5.3MM **Privately Held**
WEB: www.burgesslumber.com
SIC: 2421 Resawing lumber into smaller dimensions

2421 - Saw & Planing Mills County (P-3095)

PA: Burgess Lumber
3610 Copperhill Ln
Santa Rosa CA 95403
707 542-5091

(P-3095)
COLLINS PINE COMPANY
500 Main St, Chester (96020)
P.O. Box 796 (96020-0796)
PHONE 530 258-2111
Chris Verderber, *Branch Mgr*
Steve Ackley, *Manager*
EMP: 26
SALES (corp-wide): 87MM **Privately Held**
WEB: www.doitbest.com
SIC: 2421 Sawmills & planing mills, general
PA: Collins Pine Company
29100 Sw Town Ctr Loop W
Wilsonville OR 97070
503 227-1219

(P-3096)
COLLINS PINE COMPANY
Builders Sup Div Collinspine
540 Main St, Chester (96020)
P.O. Box 990 (96020-0990)
PHONE 530 258-2131
Mike Stelzriede, *Manager*
Dean Johnson, *Sales Mgr*
EMP: 26
SALES (corp-wide): 87MM **Privately Held**
WEB: www.doitbest.com
SIC: 2421 Sawmills & planing mills, general
PA: Collins Pine Company
29100 Sw Town Ctr Loop W
Wilsonville OR 97070
503 227-1219

(P-3097)
I & E LATH MILL
8701 Philo School Rd, Philo (95466-9555)
P.O. Box 9 (95466-0009)
PHONE 707 895-3380
Gary Island, *President*
Rodney Island, *President*
Virginia Island, *Corp Secy*
EMP: 46 **EST:** 1955
SQ FT: 40,000
SALES (est): 1.2MM **Privately Held**
WEB: www.ielath.com
SIC: 2421 2411 Lumber: rough, sawed or planed; snow fence lath; logging

(P-3098)
LARSON PACKAGING COMPANY LLC
1000 Yosemite Dr, Milpitas (95035-5410)
PHONE 408 946-4971
Mark A Hoffman, *Mng Member*
Ray Horner, *COO*
Tom Moore, *Design Engr*
Arnold Hoffman,
Gold Hoffman,
EMP: 48 **EST:** 1967
SQ FT: 30,000
SALES (est): 14.2MM **Privately Held**
WEB: www.larsonpkg.com
SIC: 2421 2441 2448 Sawmills & planing mills, general; nailed wood boxes & shook; pallets, wood

(P-3099)
NORTH CAL WOOD PRODUCTS INC
700 Kunzler Ranch Rd, Ukiah (95482-3264)
P.O. Box 1534 (95482-1534)
PHONE 707 462-0686
Frank Van Vranken, *President*
Tony Fernandez, *Vice Pres*
Charles Currey, *Admin Sec*
EMP: 50 **EST:** 1984
SQ FT: 8,000
SALES (est): 8.5MM **Privately Held**
WEB: www.northcal.com
SIC: 2421 2431 2435 Lumber: rough, sawed or planed; panel work, wood; hardwood veneer & plywood

(P-3100)
PLUM VALLEY INC
Also Called: Pacwood
3308 Cyclone Ct, Cottonwood (96022)
P.O. Box 1485 (96022-1485)
PHONE 530 262-6262
Clinton Heiss, *CEO*
Donald E Frank, *CEO*
Jackie Tonner, *Manager*
Mary Victor, *Manager*
EMP: 20 **EST:** 2003
SQ FT: 5,000
SALES (est): 3MM **Privately Held**
SIC: 2421 Lumber: rough, sawed or planed

(P-3101)
RAFAEL SANDOVAL
Also Called: Lathrop Woodworks
16175 Mckinley Ave, Lathrop (95330-9703)
PHONE 209 858-4173
Rafael Sandoval, *Owner*
▲ **EMP:** 45 **EST:** 1984
SQ FT: 1,000
SALES (est): 5.5MM **Privately Held**
SIC: 2421 Outdoor wood structural products; specialty sawmill products

(P-3102)
REUSER INC
370 Santana Dr, Cloverdale (95425-4224)
PHONE 707 894-4224
Bruce Reuser, *President*
John Reuser, *Vice Pres*
Tina Reuser, *Manager*
EMP: 15 **EST:** 1978
SQ FT: 5,000
SALES (est): 2.6MM **Privately Held**
WEB: www.reuserinc.com
SIC: 2421 2875 Sawdust & shavings; wood chips, produced at mill; fertilizers, mixing only

(P-3103)
SCHMIDBAUER LUMBER INC (PA)
Also Called: Pacific Clears
1099 W Waterfront Dr, Eureka (95501)
P.O. Box 152 (95502-0152)
PHONE 707 443-7024
Frank Schmidbauer, *Vice Pres*
Arvid Lacy, *CFO*
Duane Martin, *Treasurer*
Mary Schmidbauer, *Vice Pres*
▲ **EMP:** 110 **EST:** 1972
SQ FT: 200,000
SALES (est): 25.3MM **Privately Held**
WEB: www.schmidbauerlumber.com
SIC: 2421 5211 Sawmills & planing mills, general; lumber & other building materials

(P-3104)
SCHMIDBAUER LUMBER INC
Pacific Clears
1017 Samoa Blvd, Arcata (95521-6605)
P.O. Box 1141 (95518-1141)
PHONE 707 822-7607
Lee Iorg, *Sales/Mktg Mgr*
Lee Liorg, *Plant Mgr*
EMP: 100
SQ FT: 3,000
SALES (corp-wide): 25.3MM **Privately Held**
WEB: www.schmidbauerlumber.com
SIC: 2421 5211 Resawing lumber into smaller dimensions; planing mill products & lumber
PA: Schmidbauer Lumber, Inc.
1099 W Waterfront Dr
Eureka CA 95501
707 443-7024

(P-3105)
SETZER FOREST PRODUCTS INC
Also Called: Millwork Div
1980 Kusel Rd, Oroville (95966-9528)
PHONE 530 534-8100
Terry Dunn, *Vice Pres*
Alexander Distefano, *Engineer*
Brian Hoyle, *Purchasing*
Don May, *Manager*
EMP: 118
SALES (corp-wide): 49.5MM **Privately Held**
WEB: www.setzerforest.com
SIC: 2421 2431 Cut stock, softwood; millwork
PA: Forest Setzer Products Inc
2555 3rd St Ste 200
Sacramento CA 95818
916 442-2555

(P-3106)
SIERRA PACIFIC INDUSTRIES
2771 Bechelli Ln, Redding (96002-1924)
PHONE 530 226-5181
Sheri Dunmoyer, *Admin Asst*
Becky Riley, *Administration*
Jerome Daguio, *IT/INT Sup*
David Kiff, *Accountant*
Greg Thom, *Plant Mgr*
EMP: 46
SALES (corp-wide): 1.2B **Privately Held**
WEB: www.spi-ind.com
SIC: 2421 Lumber: rough, sawed or planed
PA: Sierra Pacific Industries
19794 Riverside Ave
Anderson CA 96007
530 378-8000

(P-3107)
SIERRA PACIFIC INDUSTRIES
1538 Lee Rd, Quincy (95971-9687)
PHONE 530 283-2820
Randy Lilburn, *Branch Mgr*
Jane Hume, *Executive*
Steve Roberts, *District Mgr*
Tim Tate, *General Mgr*
David Miesbauer, *Analyst*
EMP: 225
SQ FT: 216
SALES (corp-wide): 1.2B **Privately Held**
WEB: www.spi-ind.com
SIC: 2421 4939 Sawmills & planing mills, general; combination utilities
PA: Sierra Pacific Industries
19794 Riverside Ave
Anderson CA 96007
530 378-8000

(P-3108)
SIERRA PACIFIC INDUSTRIES (PA)
19794 Riverside Ave, Anderson (96007-4908)
P.O. Box 496028, Redding (96049-6028)
PHONE 530 378-8000
George Emmerson, *President*
Mark Emmerson, *Chairman*
Howard Hughes, *Officer*
Dominic Truniger, *Vice Pres*
Len Lindstrand, *Program Mgr*
◆ **EMP:** 100 **EST:** 1949
SQ FT: 37,000
SALES (est): 1.2B **Privately Held**
WEB: www.spi-ind.com
SIC: 2421 2431 Lumber: rough, sawed or planed; millwork; windows, wood

(P-3109)
SIERRA PACIFIC INDUSTRIES
14980 Camage Ave, Sonora (95370-9287)
P.O. Box 247, Standard (95373-0247)
PHONE 530 378-8301
Rod Johnson, *Opers-Prdtn-Mfg*
Jon Gartman, *Admin Sec*
Tammy Weir, *Analyst*
Chris Hubbard, *Manager*
Mark Luster, *Manager*
EMP: 46
SALES (corp-wide): 1.2B **Privately Held**
WEB: www.spi-ind.com
SIC: 2421 Lumber: rough, sawed or planed
PA: Sierra Pacific Industries
19794 Riverside Ave
Anderson CA 96007
530 378-8000

(P-3110)
SIERRA PACIFIC INDUSTRIES
36336 Hwy 299 E, Burney (96013)
PHONE 530 378-8301
Ed Fischer, *Branch Mgr*
EMP: 46
SALES (corp-wide): 1.2B **Privately Held**
WEB: www.spi-ind.com
SIC: 2421 Sawmills & planing mills, general
PA: Sierra Pacific Industries
19794 Riverside Ave
Anderson CA 96007
530 378-8000

(P-3111)
SIERRA PACIFIC INDUSTRIES
Hwy 299 E, Burney (96013)
P.O. Box 2677 (96013-2677)
PHONE 530 335-3681
Ed Fisher, *Branch Mgr*
Nadine Raymond, *Safety Mgr*
Robert Terras, *Manager*
EMP: 46
SQ FT: 1,000
SALES (corp-wide): 1.2B **Privately Held**
WEB: www.spi-ind.com
SIC: 2421 Lumber: rough, sawed or planed
PA: Sierra Pacific Industries
19794 Riverside Ave
Anderson CA 96007
530 378-8000

(P-3112)
SIERRA PACIFIC INDUSTRIES
3735 El Cajon Ave, Shasta Lake (96019-9211)
PHONE 530 275-8851
Darrell Dearman, *Branch Mgr*
Chip Brittain, *Sales Staff*
Brent Gerard, *Manager*
EMP: 46
SALES (corp-wide): 1.2B **Privately Held**
WEB: www.spi-ind.com
SIC: 2421 2426 Lumber: rough, sawed or planed; hardwood dimension & flooring mills
PA: Sierra Pacific Industries
19794 Riverside Ave
Anderson CA 96007
530 378-8000

(P-3113)
SIERRA PACIFIC INDUSTRIES
19758 Riverside Ave, Anderson (96007-4908)
P.O. Box 10939 (96007-1939)
PHONE 530 365-3721
Shane Young, *Manager*
EMP: 46
SALES (corp-wide): 1.2B **Privately Held**
WEB: www.spi-ind.com
SIC: 2421 Lumber: rough, sawed or planed
PA: Sierra Pacific Industries
19794 Riverside Ave
Anderson CA 96007
530 378-8000

(P-3114)
SIERRA PACIFIC INDUSTRIES
3950 Carson Rd, Camino (95709-9347)
P.O. Box 680 (95709-0680)
PHONE 530 644-2311
Brian Coyle, *Branch Mgr*
EMP: 46
SALES (corp-wide): 1.2B **Privately Held**
WEB: www.spi-ind.com
SIC: 2421 Lumber: rough, sawed or planed
PA: Sierra Pacific Industries
19794 Riverside Ave
Anderson CA 96007
530 378-8000

(P-3115)
SIERRA PACIFIC INDUSTRIES
1440 Lincoln Blvd, Lincoln (95648-9105)
P.O. Box 670 (95648-0670)
PHONE 916 645-1631
Dan Quarton, *Branch Mgr*
Alan Gulko, *Executive*
Mike Hess, *Supervisor*
EMP: 46
SALES (corp-wide): 1.2B **Privately Held**
WEB: www.spi-ind.com
SIC: 2421 Lumber: rough, sawed or planed
PA: Sierra Pacific Industries
19794 Riverside Ave
Anderson CA 96007
530 378-8000

(P-3116)
SIERRA PACIFIC INDUSTRIES
Window Division
11605 Reading Rd, Red Bluff (96080-6702)
P.O. Box 8489 (96080-8489)
PHONE 530 527-9620

▲ = Import ▼ = Export
◆ = Import/Export

PRODUCTS & SERVICES SECTION

2431 - Millwork County (P-3140)

Bob Taylor, *Manager*
Patricia Carlson, *Managing Prtnr*
Bud Tomacheski, *Vice Pres*
Rob Macdonald, *Admin Sec*
Marilyn Robrahn, *CIO*
EMP: 500
SALES (corp-wide): 1.2B **Privately Held**
WEB: www.spi-ind.com
SIC: 2421 Sawmills & planing mills, general
PA: Sierra Pacific Industries
19794 Riverside Ave
Anderson CA 96007
530 378-8000

(P-3117)
SUNSET MOULDING CO (PA)
2231 Paseo Rd, Live Oak (95953-9721)
P.O. Box 326, Yuba City (95992-0326)
PHONE 530 790-2700
John A Morrison, *CEO*
Wendy Forren, *CFO*
Michel Morrison, *Vice Pres*
Mark Westlake, *Vice Pres*
Krissy Putland, *Sales Staff*
▲ **EMP:** 50 **EST:** 1946
SALES (est): 25.1MM **Privately Held**
WEB: www.sunsetmoulding.com
SIC: 2421 2431 Cut stock, softwood; moldings, wood: unfinished & prefinished

(P-3118)
TERRAMAI
1104 Firenze St, McCloud (96057-8123)
P.O. Box 1744, Medford OR (97501-0136)
PHONE 530 964-2740
▲ **EMP:** 20
SALES (est): 291.2K **Privately Held**
WEB: www.terramai.com
SIC: 2421 Sawmill/Planing Mill

(P-3119)
WILLITS REDWOOD COMPANY INC
220 Franklin Ave, Willits (95490-4132)
PHONE 707 459-4549
Bruce Burton, *President*
Chris Baldo, *Vice Pres*
EMP: 45 **EST:** 1975
SQ FT: 500
SALES (est): 5.3MM **Privately Held**
WEB: www.willitsredwood.com
SIC: 2421 Sawmills & planing mills, general

2426 Hardwood Dimension & Flooring Mills

(P-3120)
CALICO HARDWOODS INC
3580 Westwind Blvd, Santa Rosa (95403-8239)
PHONE 707 546-4045
John T Skeuse, *President*
Stephen T Finney, *Treasurer*
Brian Skeuse, *Vice Pres*
Kathryn M Rasmussen, *Controller*
◆ **EMP:** 95 **EST:** 1960
SQ FT: 30,000
SALES (est): 2.6MM
SALES (corp-wide): 517MM **Privately Held**
WEB: www.calicohardwoods.com
SIC: 2426 Gun stocks, wood
PA: Reagent Chemical & Research, Inc.
115 Rte 202
Ringoes NJ 08551
908 284-2800

2431 Millwork

(P-3121)
A & R DOORS INC
Also Called: A & R Pre-Hung Door
41 5th St Frnt, Hollister (95023-3975)
PHONE 831 637-8139
Ruben L Rodriguez, *President*
Albert Rodriguez, *Vice Pres*
EMP: 24 **EST:** 1980
SQ FT: 8,000
SALES (est): 2.2MM **Privately Held**
WEB: www.aandrdoors.com
SIC: 2431 Doors, wood

(P-3122)
ANLIN INDUSTRIES
Also Called: Anlin Window Systems
1665 Tollhouse Rd, Clovis (93611-0523)
PHONE 800 287-7996
Thomas Anton Vidmar, *Principal*
Harry Parisi, *CFO*
Eric Vidmar, *Corp Secy*
Chris Gillette, *Exec VP*
Stan Fikes, *Vice Pres*
EMP: 250 **EST:** 1990
SQ FT: 188,000
SALES (est): 57.3MM **Privately Held**
WEB: www.anlin.com
SIC: 2431 Windows & window parts & trim, wood

(P-3123)
CALIFORNIA CAB & STORE FIX
8472 Carbide Ct, Sacramento (95828-5609)
PHONE 916 386-1340
Bruce D Nicolson, *President*
EMP: 30 **EST:** 1989
SQ FT: 20,640
SALES (est): 590.8K **Privately Held**
SIC: 2431 2541 Millwork; table or counter tops, plastic laminated

(P-3124)
CALIFRNIA MANTEL FIREPLACE INC (PA)
4141 N Freeway Blvd, Sacramento (95834-1209)
P.O. Box 340037 (95834-0037)
PHONE 916 925-5775
Stephen Casey, *President*
Jonathan Medina, *Division Mgr*
Melanie Casey, *Office Mgr*
EMP: 38 **EST:** 1988
SQ FT: 7,000
SALES (est): 7.5MM **Privately Held**
WEB: www.calmantel.com
SIC: 2431 3272 Mantels, wood; mantels, concrete

(P-3125)
COMMERCIAL CASEWORK INC (PA)
Also Called: Madera Fina
41780 Christy St, Fremont (94538-5106)
PHONE 510 657-7933
William M Palmer, *CEO*
Ben Castellon, *Project Mgr*
Jason Starbird, *Project Mgr*
Richard Topete, *Engineer*
Randall Williams, *Engineer*
EMP: 72 **EST:** 1976
SQ FT: 35,000
SALES (est): 16.3MM **Privately Held**
WEB: www.commercialcasework.com
SIC: 2431 2541 Millwork; office fixtures, wood

(P-3126)
COMPOSITE TECHNOLOGY INTL INC
Also Called: Composite Technology Intl
1730 I St Ste 100, Sacramento (95811-3015)
PHONE 916 551-1850
J Griffin Reid, *CEO*
Cynthia Reid, *Corp Secy*
Griffin Reid, *Vice Pres*
Joseph Falmer, *VP Finance*
▲ **EMP:** 46 **EST:** 2004
SQ FT: 3,000
SALES (est): 12.8MM **Privately Held**
WEB: www.cti-web.com
SIC: 2431 5023 8711 3999 Moldings, wood: unfinished & prefinished; frames & framing, picture & mirror; sanitary engineers; barber & beauty shop equipment

(P-3127)
CRESTMARK MILLWORK INC
5640 West End Rd, Arcata (95521-9202)
PHONE 707 822-4034
Scott D Olsen, *CEO*
Ian Hall, *Engineer*
Dottie Shieman, *Manager*
EMP: 35 **EST:** 1997
SALES (est): 4.6MM **Privately Held**
WEB: www.crestmarkmillwork.com
SIC: 2431 Millwork

(P-3128)
DECORE-ATIVE SPC NC LLC
104 Gate Eats Stock Blvd, Elk Grove (95624)
PHONE 916 686-4700
Jack Albright, *Manager*
Jeff Hahn, *Vice Pres*
EMP: 111
SALES (corp-wide): 202.6MM **Privately Held**
WEB: www.decore.com
SIC: 2431 Doors, wood
PA: Decore-Ative Specialties Nc Llc
2772 Peck Rd
Monrovia CA 91016
626 254-9191

(P-3129)
DESIGN WOODWORKING INC (PA)
709 N Sacramento St, Lodi (95240-1255)
PHONE 209 334-6674
David Worfolk, *President*
Stefan I Sekula, *Admin Sec*
EMP: 20 **EST:** 1976
SQ FT: 22,000
SALES (est): 3MM **Privately Held**
WEB: www.deswood.com
SIC: 2431 Millwork

(P-3130)
DORRIS LUMBER AND MOULDING CO (PA)
3453 Ramona Ave Ste 5, Sacramento (95826-3828)
PHONE 916 452-7531
Joshua Tyler, *President*
Nels Israelson, *Shareholder*
E Chase Israelson, *Ch of Bd*
Dennis Murcko, *CFO*
Larry White, *Vice Pres*
▲ **EMP:** 75 **EST:** 1924
SALES (est): 10.2MM **Privately Held**
WEB: www.dorrismoulding.com
SIC: 2431 Moldings, wood: unfinished & prefinished

(P-3131)
ECMD INC
4722 Skyway Dr, Marysville (95901)
PHONE 530 741-0769
Don Mays, *Manager*
EMP: 37
SQ FT: 85,960
SALES (corp-wide): 186.4MM **Privately Held**
WEB: www.ecmd.com
SIC: 2431 Millwork
PA: Ecmd, Inc.
2 Grandview St
North Wilkesboro NC 28659
336 667-5976

(P-3132)
FLETCHER DORS WINDOWS TRIM INC
1720 Paulson Rd, Turlock (95380-9709)
PHONE 209 632-3610
Josh Fletcher, *President*
EMP: 17 **EST:** 2016
SQ FT: 1,000
SALES (est): 1.6MM **Privately Held**
WEB: www.fletcherdoors.com
SIC: 2431 3442 Doors, wood; screen & storm doors & windows

(P-3133)
GARAGE DOORS INCORPORATED
147 Martha St, San Jose (95112-5814)
PHONE 408 293-7443
Scott Jensen, *President*
Nancy Jensen, *Treasurer*
EMP: 31 **EST:** 1987
SQ FT: 45,000
SALES (est): 1.8MM **Privately Held**
WEB: www.garagedoorsinc.com
SIC: 2431 5031 Garage doors, overhead: wood; doors, garage

(P-3134)
HAND CRFTED DUTCHMAN DOORS INC
770 Stonebridge Dr, Tracy (95376-2812)
PHONE 209 833-7378
Larry B Vis, *President*
Donna Vis, *CFO*
EMP: 40 **EST:** 1982
SQ FT: 16,000
SALES (est): 5.2MM **Privately Held**
WEB: www.dutchmandoors.com
SIC: 2431 2434 Doors, wood; wood kitchen cabinets

(P-3135)
HARWOOD PRODUCTS
Branscomb Rd, Branscomb (95417)
P.O. Box 224 (95417-0224)
PHONE 707 984-1601
Art Harwood, *CEO*
EMP: 230 **EST:** 2000
SALES (est): 24.4MM **Privately Held**
WEB: www.harwoodproducts.com
SIC: 2431 Millwork

(P-3136)
HEALDSBURG LUMBER COMPANY INC
Also Called: Hlc
359 Hudson St, Healdsburg (95448-4415)
P.O. Box 970 (95448-0970)
PHONE 707 431-9663
Eric A Ziedrich, *CEO*
Jeff Pescar, *CFO*
Janet Ziedrich, *Corp Secy*
Neal Geils, *Opers Mgr*
Karen Graves, *Marketing Staff*
EMP: 90 **EST:** 1973
SQ FT: 11,000
SALES (est): 29.1MM **Privately Held**
WEB: www.hlc-inc.com
SIC: 5251 5211 2431 Hardware; lumber & other building materials; millwork

(P-3137)
J & J QUALITY DOOR INC
Also Called: Quality Door & Trim
741 S Airport Way, Stockton (95205-6126)
PHONE 209 948-5013
Jeffery Dean Cannon, *CEO*
Steve Cantrell, *President*
Debbie Sue Cantrell, *CFO*
Jeff JC, *General Mgr*
EMP: 35
SALES (est): 6.8MM **Privately Held**
WEB: www.jandjqualitydoor.com
SIC: 2431 Doors, wood

(P-3138)
LAZESTAR INC
6956 Preston Ave, Livermore (94551-9545)
PHONE 925 443-5293
Michael Hartman, *CEO*
Daniel P Schwertfeger, *President*
Karmin Schwertfeger, *Accountant*
EMP: 25 **EST:** 2002
SALES (est): 3.8MM **Privately Held**
WEB: www.lazestar.com
SIC: 2431 3699 Millwork; laser welding, drilling & cutting equipment

(P-3139)
LLC MERRITT WEST
709 N Sacramento St, Lodi (95240-1255)
PHONE 209 334-6674
Stefan Sekula, *Vice Pres*
EMP: 15 **EST:** 2018
SALES (est): 3.8MM **Privately Held**
WEB: www.merrittwoodwork.com
SIC: 2431 Millwork

(P-3140)
LLOYDS CUSTOM WOODWORK INC
1012 Shary Cir, Concord (94518-2408)
PHONE 925 680-6600
David Lloyd, *President*
Jeff Cronk, *Vice Pres*
EMP: 23 **EST:** 2005
SALES (est): 1.2MM **Privately Held**
WEB: www.lcwoodwork.com
SIC: 2431 Millwork

2431 - Millwork County (P-3141)   PRODUCTS & SERVICES SECTION

(P-3141)
LOWPENSKY MOULDING
900 Palou Ave, San Francisco (94124-3429)
PHONE....................415 822-7422
Theodore M Lowpensky, *Owner*
Todd Lowpensky, *Office Mgr*
EMP: 15 **EST:** 1949
SQ FT: 13,000
SALES (est): 1.8MM Privately Held
WEB: www.lowpenskymoulding.com
SIC: 2431 Moldings, wood: unfinished & prefinished

(P-3142)
MABREY PRODUCTS INC
200 Ryan Ave, Chico (95973-9032)
P.O. Box 1345 (95927-1345)
PHONE....................530 895-3799
Douglas Tobey, *President*
EMP: 15 **EST:** 1984
SQ FT: 5,000
SALES (est): 1.2MM Privately Held
WEB: www.mabreyproducts.com
SIC: 2431 Woodwork, interior & ornamental

(P-3143)
NORTH BAY PLYWOOD INC
510 Northbay Dr, NAPA (94559-1426)
P.O. Box 2338 (94558-0518)
PHONE....................707 224-7849
Thomas H Lowenstein, *President*
Janice Leann Lowenstein, *Treasurer*
John Claudino, *Sales Staff*
EMP: 23 **EST:** 1958
SQ FT: 24,000
SALES (est): 6.6MM Privately Held
WEB: www.northbayplywood.com
SIC: 2431 2599 5211 2434 Doors, wood; cabinets, factory; cabinets, kitchen; doors, wood or metal, except storm; wood kitchen cabinets

(P-3144)
PACIFIC DOOR & CABINET COMPANY
7050 N Harrison Ave, Pinedale (93650-1008)
PHONE....................559 439-3822
Duane Failla, *President*
Janet Failla, *Human Resources*
Terry Freeman, *Sales Executive*
Gail Baker, *Manager*
EMP: 30 **EST:** 1968
SQ FT: 16,000
SALES (est): 3.3MM Privately Held
WEB: www.pacificdoorinc.com
SIC: 2431 3442 Doors, wood; windows, wood; metal doors, sash & trim

(P-3145)
PACIFIC MDF PRODUCTS INC (PA)
Also Called: Pac Trim
4312 Anthony Ct Ste A, Rocklin (95677-2174)
PHONE....................916 660-1882
Clifford Stokes, *President*
Geri Grommett, *General Mgr*
Scott Clapp, *Controller*
Karen Sanders, *Human Res Dir*
Randall Smith, *Plant Mgr*
▲ **EMP:** 41 **EST:** 1992
SQ FT: 55,000
SALES (est): 21.9MM Privately Held
WEB: www.pactrim.com
SIC: 2431 Moldings, wood: unfinished & prefinished

(P-3146)
PLANT/ALLISON CORPORATION
300 Newhall St, San Francisco (94124-1498)
PHONE....................415 285-0500
David G Plant, *General Ptnr*
Greg Bonderud, *Vice Pres*
Harvinder Matharu, *Executive*
John Wilson, *General Mgr*
James Byers, *Project Mgr*
EMP: 19 **EST:** 2016
SALES (est): 1MM Privately Held
WEB: www.plantconstruction.com
SIC: 2431 Millwork

(P-3147)
PREMIER WOODWORKING LLC
Also Called: Cabinetry
2290 Dale Ave, Sacramento (95815-2924)
PHONE....................916 289-4058
Robert Griffith, *CEO*
EMP: 41 **EST:** 2016
SALES (est): 1.6MM Privately Held
WEB: www.premierwoodworkingusa.com
SIC: 2431 Millwork

(P-3148)
RITESCREEN INC
33444 Western Ave, Union City (94587-3202)
P.O. Box 965. (94587-0965)
PHONE....................800 949-4174
Art Lucero, *General Mgr*
EMP: 15 **EST:** 1942
SALES (est): 155.7K Privately Held
WEB: www.ritescreen.com
SIC: 2431 Door screens; wood frame

(P-3149)
RIVER CITY MILLWORK INC
3045 Fite Cir, Sacramento (95827-1814)
PHONE....................916 364-8981
Paul Parks, *President*
Valerie Parks, *Corp Secy*
Doug Parker, *General Mgr*
Scott Penley, *Project Mgr*
Josh Wyatt, *Project Mgr*
EMP: 33 **EST:** 1984
SQ FT: 24,000
SALES (est): 6.7MM Privately Held
WEB: www.rcmill.com
SIC: 2431 2434 Moldings, wood: unfinished & prefinished; wood kitchen cabinets

(P-3150)
SETZER FOREST PRODUCTS INC (PA)
2555 3rd St Ste 200, Sacramento (95818-1196)
PHONE....................916 442-2555
D Mark Kable, *CEO*
Hardie Setzer, *Shareholder*
Garner Setzer, *President*
Laura Trussell, *CFO*
Jeff Setzer, *Vice Pres*
▲ **EMP:** 160 **EST:** 1927
SALES (est): 49.5MM Privately Held
WEB: www.setzerforest.com
SIC: 2431 2441 Moldings, wood: unfinished & prefinished; box shook, wood

(P-3151)
SIERRA PACIFIC INDUSTRIES
Alameda Rd, Corning (96021)
PHONE....................530 824-2474
Kendall Pierson, *Vice Pres*
EMP: 57
SALES (corp-wide): 1.2B Privately Held
WEB: www.spi-ind.com
SIC: 2431 2426 2421 Millwork; hardwood dimension & flooring mills; sawmills & planing mills, general
PA: Sierra Pacific Industries
19794 Riverside Ave
Anderson CA 96007
530 378-8000

(P-3152)
SIMMONS STAIRWAYS INC
Also Called: Stair Service
255 Apollo Way B, Hollister (95023-2507)
PHONE....................408 920-0105
Howard Simmons, *CEO*
Charles Simmons, *Vice Pres*
Nichole Montrouil, *Accounting Mgr*
EMP: 20 **EST:** 1995
SQ FT: 15,000
SALES (est): 3.3MM Privately Held
WEB: www.simmonsstairways.com
SIC: 2431 Millwork

(P-3153)
SISKIYOU FOREST PRODUCTS (PA)
6275 State Highway 273, Anderson (96007-9418)
PHONE....................530 378-6980
Fred Duchi, *President*
Angel Havens, *COO*
Bill Duchi, *Vice Pres*
▲ **EMP:** 48 **EST:** 1974
SQ FT: 2,280
SALES (est): 8.4MM Privately Held
WEB: www.siskiyouforestproducts.com
SIC: 2431 5031 Millwork; lumber, plywood & millwork

(P-3154)
SUN MOUNTAIN INC
2 Henry Adams St Ste 150, San Francisco (94103-5045)
PHONE....................415 852-2320
EMP: 25
SALES (corp-wide): 11.9MM Privately Held
WEB: www.sunmountaindoor.com
SIC: 2431 Millwork
PA: Sun Mountain, Inc.
140 Commerce Rd
Berthoud CO 80513
970 532-2105

(P-3155)
SUNSET MOULDING CO
Also Called: Morrison Building Materials
1856 Skyway, Chico (95928-8833)
P.O. Box 7120 (95927-7120)
PHONE....................530 695-1000
Tom Maclean, *Principal*
EMP: 38
SALES (corp-wide): 25.1MM Privately Held
WEB: www.sunsetmoulding.com
SIC: 5211 2431 Lumber & other building materials; millwork
PA: Sunset Moulding Co.
2231 Paseo Rd
Live Oak CA 95953
530 790-2700

(P-3156)
T M COBB COMPANY
Also Called: Haley Brothers
2651 E Roosevelt St, Stockton (95205-3825)
PHONE....................209 948-5358
John Jenkins, *Branch Mgr*
Katrina O'Boyle, *Office Mgr*
David Kung, *Purch Mgr*
Brad Lamountain, *Purchasing*
Carlos Vizcarra, *Purchasing*
EMP: 55
SQ FT: 1,200
SALES (corp-wide): 111.9MM Privately Held
WEB: www.tmcobb.com
SIC: 2431 Doors, wood
PA: T. M. Cobb Company
500 Palmyrita Ave
Riverside CA 92507
951 248-2400

(P-3157)
TMR EXECUTIVE INTERIORS INC
1287 W Nielsen Ave, Fresno (93706-1395)
PHONE....................559 346-0631
Jamie Russell, *President*
Timothy Russell, *Vice Pres*
Nick Pauls, *Engineer*
David Andrade, *Purch Agent*
Brendan Russell, *Production*
EMP: 21 **EST:** 2016
SQ FT: 21,000
SALES (est): 2.4MM Privately Held
WEB: www.executiveinteriorsinc.com
SIC: 2431 1751 Millwork; cabinet & finish carpentry

(P-3158)
UNITY FOREST PRODUCTS INC
1162 Putman Ave, Yuba City (95991-7216)
P.O. Box 1849 (95992-1849)
PHONE....................530 671-7152
Enita Elphick, *President*
Ryan Smith, *Treasurer*
Michael Smith, *Vice Pres*
Shawn Nelson, *Admin Sec*
Ken Smith, *Sales Dir*
EMP: 48 **EST:** 1988
SQ FT: 4,200
SALES (est): 11MM Privately Held
WEB: www.unityforest.com
SIC: 2431 Millwork

(P-3159)
WESTGATE HARDWOODS INC (PA)
9296 Midway, Durham (95938-9779)
PHONE....................530 892-0300
Ivan Hoath, *President*
Becky Hoath, *Treasurer*
Ivan Hoath III, *Vice Pres*
Craig Jones, *Draft/Design*
Alex Hoath, *Production*
EMP: 22 **EST:** 1986
SQ FT: 10,000
SALES (est): 6.6MM Privately Held
WEB: www.westgatehardwoods.com
SIC: 2431 5031 Millwork; lumber: rough, dressed & finished

(P-3160)
WINDSOR WILLITS COMPANY (PA)
Also Called: Windsor One
737 Southpoint Blvd Ste H, Petaluma (94954-7462)
PHONE....................707 665-9663
Craig Flynn, *President*
Douglas Sherer, *CFO*
Kevin Platte, *General Mgr*
Alrene Flynn, *Admin Sec*
Janda Mueller, *Administration*
◆ **EMP:** 29 **EST:** 1976
SQ FT: 50,000
SALES (est): 12.9MM Privately Held
WEB: www.windsorone.com
SIC: 2431 Moldings, wood: unfinished & prefinished

(P-3161)
WINDSOR WILLITS COMPANY
Also Called: Windsor Mill
661 Railroad Ave, Willits (95490-3942)
PHONE....................707 459-8568
John Hankins, *Opers-Prdtn-Mfg*
Beth Green, *Manager*
Paul Rebich, *Supervisor*
EMP: 59
SALES (corp-wide): 12.9MM Privately Held
WEB: www.windsorone.com
SIC: 2431 2439 Moldings, wood: unfinished & prefinished; structural wood members
PA: Windsor Willits Company
737 Southpoint Blvd Ste H
Petaluma CA 94954
707 665-9663

(P-3162)
WOOD CONNECTION INC
4701 N Star Way, Modesto (95356-9567)
PHONE....................209 577-1044
William W Fenstermacher, *President*
Aimee Menera, *Office Admin*
Judy L Fenstermacher, *Admin Sec*
Johnny Cagle, *Project Mgr*
William Fenstermacher, *Marketing Staff*
EMP: 33 **EST:** 1982
SQ FT: 11,400
SALES (est): 3.9MM Privately Held
WEB: www.inthepinklink.com
SIC: 2431 2434 Millwork; wood kitchen cabinets

(P-3163)
WOODEN WINDOW INC
849 29th St, Oakland (94608-4507)
PHONE....................510 893-1157
William P Essert, *President*
Priscilla Call Essert, *Vice Pres*
Robert D Essert, *Vice Pres*
Mark Christiansen, *Principal*
EMP: 30 **EST:** 1980
SALES (est): 3.7MM Privately Held
WEB: www.kinneywoodworks.com
SIC: 2431 Millwork

(P-3164)
YOUNG & FAMILY INC
Also Called: Quality Doors & Trim
64 Soda Bay Rd, Lakeport (95453-5609)
P.O. Box 897 (95453-0897)
PHONE....................707 263-8877
Hilary Young, *President*
Andrew Young, *Vice Pres*
EMP: 25 **EST:** 1988
SQ FT: 11,400

PRODUCTS & SERVICES SECTION
2434 - Wood Kitchen Cabinets County (P-3190)

SALES (est): 2.9MM **Privately Held**
SIC: 2431 2434 Doors, wood; wood kitchen cabinets

(P-3165)
YUBA RVER MLDING MILL WORK INC (PA)
Also Called: Cal Yuba Investments
3757 Feather River Blvd, Olivehurst (95961-9615)
P.O. Box 1078, Yuba City (95992-1078)
PHONE.................................530 742-2168
Thomas C Williams Sr, *Ch of Bd*
Thomas C Williams Jr, *President*
Jolyne Williams, *Treasurer*
Damon Munsee, *Vice Pres*
Andrea Watson, *Department Mgr*
▲ **EMP**: 40 **EST**: 1977
SQ FT: 200,000
SALES (est): 8.7MM **Privately Held**
WEB: www.yubarivermoulding.com
SIC: 2431 6512 Moldings, wood: unfinished & prefinished; commercial & industrial building operation

2434 Wood Kitchen Cabinets

(P-3166)
AMERICAN WOODMARK CORPORATION
Also Called: Timberlake Cabinet
3146 Gold Camp Dr, Rancho Cordova (95670-6035)
PHONE.................................916 851-7400
John Eldredge, *Manager*
EMP: 191
SALES (corp-wide): 1.7B **Publicly Held**
WEB: www.americanwoodmark.com
SIC: 2434 Wood kitchen cabinets
PA: American Woodmark Corporation
561 Shady Elm Rd
Winchester VA 22602
540 665-9100

(P-3167)
ARCHITECTURAL WOOD DESIGN INC
Also Called: Carpentry Millwork
5672 E Dayton Ave, Fresno (93727-7801)
PHONE.................................559 292-9104
Phillip D Farnsworth, *President*
Riley Farnsworth, *COO*
Corey Farnsworth, *Vice Pres*
Jason Terry, *Engineer*
Gus Gonzalez, *Purchasing*
EMP: 40
SQ FT: 16,000
SALES (est): 8MM **Privately Held**
WEB: www.awdfresno.com
SIC: 2434 Wood kitchen cabinets

(P-3168)
BAKER CUSTOM CABINETS INC
455 S Pine St Ste 2, Madera (93637-5242)
PHONE.................................559 675-1395
Larry Baker, *President*
Grace Aranda, *Office Mgr*
EMP: 19 **EST**: 1998
SALES (est): 1MM **Privately Held**
WEB: www.bakercustomcabinetsinc.com
SIC: 5712 2434 Cabinet work, custom; wood kitchen cabinets

(P-3169)
BARBOSA CABINETS INC
2020 E Grant Line Rd, Tracy (95304-8525)
PHONE.................................209 836-2501
Edward Barbosa, *President*
Ron Barbosa, *Exec VP*
Jonathan Adams, *Vice Pres*
Christina Sena, *Administration*
Johnny Horton, *Project Mgr*
▲ **EMP**: 346
SQ FT: 300,000
SALES (est): 57.1MM **Privately Held**
WEB: www.barcab.com
SIC: 2434 Wood kitchen cabinets

(P-3170)
BURNETT SONS PLANING MILL LBR
214 11th St, Sacramento (95814-0893)
P.O. Box 1646 (95812-1646)
PHONE.................................916 442-0493
James Miller, *Ch of Bd*
Simone Miller, *Corp Secy*
Fitz Miller, *Vice Pres*
Katie Daniels, *Project Mgr*
Bob Beeston, *Technology*
EMP: 50
SQ FT: 12,000
SALES (est): 9.9MM **Privately Held**
WEB: www.burnett-sons.com
SIC: 5211 2434 2431 2421 Lumber & other building materials; wood kitchen cabinets; millwork; sawmills & planing mills, general

(P-3171)
CABINETS BY ANDY INC
2411 Central Ave, McKinleyville (95519-3615)
PHONE.................................707 839-0220
Andy Dickey, *President*
EMP: 16 **EST**: 1980
SQ FT: 10,000
SALES (est): 1.2MM **Privately Held**
WEB: www.cabinetsbyandy.com
SIC: 2434 Wood kitchen cabinets

(P-3172)
CALIFORNIA CABINET & STR FIXS
Also Called: California Cabinet & Storage
8472 Carbide Ct, Sacramento (95828-5609)
PHONE.................................916 681-0901
Bruce Nichols, *President*
EMP: 20 **EST**: 1985
SALES (est): 2.3MM **Privately Held**
WEB: www.californiacabinets.net
SIC: 2434 Wood kitchen cabinets

(P-3173)
CALIFORNIA KIT CAB DOOR CORP (PA)
Also Called: California Door
400 Cochrane Cir, Morgan Hill (95037-2859)
PHONE.................................408 782-5700
Edward Joseph Rossi, *Principal*
Ed Rossi, *CFO*
Beth Mosson, *Executive*
Melissa Naranjo, *Executive*
Troy Vu, *Info Tech Dir*
◆ **EMP**: 278 **EST**: 1988
SQ FT: 260,000
SALES (est): 51.2MM **Privately Held**
SIC: 2434 2431 Wood kitchen cabinets; millwork

(P-3174)
CHAMPION INSTALLS INC
9631 Elk Grove Florin Rd, Elk Grove (95624-2225)
PHONE.................................916 627-0929
Brock Rhodes, *Principal*
Stephanie Rodriguez, *Manager*
EMP: 25 **EST**: 2014
SALES (est): 2.8MM **Privately Held**
WEB: www.championinstalls.com
SIC: 2434 Wood kitchen cabinets

(P-3175)
CLASSIC MILL & CABINET LLC
Also Called: Classic Innovations
590 Santana Dr, Cloverdale (95425-4296)
PHONE.................................707 894-9800
Tony Mertes, *President*
Ms Billie Siemsen, *Manager*
Michael Siemsen, *Manager*
▲ **EMP**: 37 **EST**: 1967
SQ FT: 35,000
SALES (est): 4.3MM **Privately Held**
WEB: www.classicmill.com
SIC: 2434 Wood kitchen cabinets

(P-3176)
CUSTOM FURNITURE DESIGN INC
Also Called: Entertainment Centers Plus
3340 Sunrise Blvd Ste F, Rancho Cordova (95742-7316)
PHONE.................................916 631-6300
Dan Gwiazdon, *President*
EMP: 17 **EST**: 1997
SQ FT: 13,000
SALES (est): 726.1K **Privately Held**
WEB: www.cfdsacto.com
SIC: 2434 Wood kitchen cabinets

(P-3177)
D & D CBNETS - SVAGE DSGNS INC
1478 Sky Harbor Dr, Olivehurst (95961-7418)
PHONE.................................530 634-9713
Peter D Giordano, *President*
EMP: 29 **EST**: 2006
SALES (est): 1.3MM **Privately Held**
WEB: www.savagecabinets.com
SIC: 2434 Wood kitchen cabinets

(P-3178)
DAVID BEARD
Also Called: Beards Custom Cabinets
821 Twin View Blvd, Redding (96003-2002)
PHONE.................................530 244-1248
David Beard, *Owner*
EMP: 15 **EST**: 1983
SQ FT: 8,550
SALES (est): 905.2K **Privately Held**
WEB: www.beardscustomcabinets.com
SIC: 2434 2521 2541 Wood kitchen cabinets; cabinets, office: wood; lockers & shelving

(P-3179)
FINELINE CARPENTRY INC
1297 Old County Rd, Belmont (94002-3920)
PHONE.................................650 592-2442
Mac Bean, *President*
Cheryl Bean, *Vice Pres*
EMP: 25
SQ FT: 15,000
SALES (est): 4MM **Privately Held**
WEB: www.finelinecarpentry.com
SIC: 2434 Wood kitchen cabinets

(P-3180)
GRAND CABINETS AND STONE INC (PA)
10368 Hite Cir, Elk Grove (95757-3522)
PHONE.................................916 270-7207
Yong Luo, *Principal*
EMP: 19 **EST**: 2017
SALES (est): 177.5K **Privately Held**
SIC: 2434 Wood kitchen cabinets

(P-3181)
HEART WOOD MANUFACTURING INC
Also Called: Heartwood Cabinets
5860 Obata Way, Gilroy (95020-7038)
P.O. Box 2552 (95021-2552)
PHONE.................................408 848-9750
David Boll, *President*
Eileen Boll, *Vice Pres*
EMP: 19 **EST**: 1974
SQ FT: 25,000
SALES (est): 1MM **Privately Held**
SIC: 2434 2511 2431 Wood kitchen cabinets; wood household furniture; millwork

(P-3182)
JOHN C DESTEFANO
Also Called: Destefano Design Group
7325 Reese Rd, Sacramento (95828-3704)
PHONE.................................916 276-4056
John Destefano, *Owner*
Parris Reed, *Agent*
EMP: 30 **EST**: 1982
SQ FT: 1,500
SALES (est): 400K **Privately Held**
SIC: 2434 Wood kitchen cabinets

(P-3183)
JR STEPHENS COMPANY
5208 Boyd Rd, Arcata (95521-4410)
PHONE.................................707 825-0100
Jim Stephens, *President*
Bryan Stephens, *CFO*
Josh Stephens, *Vice Pres*
Rosalie Stephens, *Admin Sec*
EMP: 23 **EST**: 1978
SALES (est): 2.8MM **Privately Held**
SIC: 2434 Wood kitchen cabinets

(P-3184)
KENEY MANUFACTURING CO (PA)
Also Called: Keney's Cabinets
586 Broadway Ave, Atwater (95301-4408)
P.O. Box 518 (95301-0518)
PHONE.................................209 358-6474
Robert Hernandez, *Partner*
Rodney Haygood, *Partner*
EMP: 16 **EST**: 1952
SALES (est): 1.4MM **Privately Held**
SIC: 2434 Wood kitchen cabinets

(P-3185)
KITCHENS NOW INC
20 Blue Sky Ct, Sacramento (95828-1015)
PHONE.................................916 229-8222
Douglas Carl Schubert, *CEO*
Kevin Sexton, *COO*
EMP: 33 **EST**: 2007
SALES (est): 6.3MM **Privately Held**
WEB: www.kitchensnow.com
SIC: 2434 Wood kitchen cabinets

(P-3186)
LACKEY WOODWORKING INC
2730 Chanticleer Ave, Santa Cruz (95065-1812)
PHONE.................................831 462-0528
John E Lackey, *President*
Kathy Lackey, *Principal*
EMP: 20 **EST**: 1974
SQ FT: 6,000
SALES (est): 750K **Privately Held**
WEB: www.lackeywoodworking.com
SIC: 2434 2541 2431 2511 Wood kitchen cabinets; cabinets, except refrigerated: show, display, etc.: wood; doors, wood; wood household furniture; signboards, wood

(P-3187)
R A JENSON MANUFACTURING CO
102 Heather Dr, Atherton (94027-2120)
PHONE.................................415 822-2732
EMP: 15
SALES (est): 1.9MM **Privately Held**
WEB: www.jensonvanities.com
SIC: 2434 Wood Kitchen Cabinets

(P-3188)
RAWSON CUSTOM CABINETS INC
1115 Holly Oak Cir, San Jose (95120-1542)
PHONE.................................408 779-9838
Dennis Rawson, *President*
Patricia Rawson, *Admin Sec*
Luke Nervig, *Design Engr*
Fred Agustinez, *Prdtn Mgr*
EMP: 24 **EST**: 1975
SALES (est): 1.5MM **Privately Held**
WEB: www.rawson-cabinets.com
SIC: 2434 Wood kitchen cabinets

(P-3189)
RDI FINISHING
Also Called: Rhyne Design Cabinets Showroom
350 Morris St Ste F, Sebastopol (95472-3871)
PHONE.................................707 829-1226
Richard Geernaert, *President*
Christy Geernaert, *Vice Pres*
EMP: 30 **EST**: 1977
SQ FT: 10,000
SALES (est): 2.3MM **Privately Held**
WEB: www.rhynedesign.com
SIC: 2434 Wood kitchen cabinets

(P-3190)
RUCKER MILL & CAB WORKS INC
5828 Mother Lode Dr, Placerville (95667-8233)
PHONE.................................530 621-0236
John Rucker, *President*
Janice Rucker, *Admin Sec*
EMP: 19 **EST**: 1979
SQ FT: 8,800
SALES (est): 1.3MM **Privately Held**
SIC: 2434 2431 1751 Wood kitchen cabinets; millwork; cabinet & finish carpentry

---

(PA)=Parent Co (HQ)=Headquarters (DH)=Div Headquarters
✪ = New Business established in last 2 years

2434 - Wood Kitchen Cabinets County (P-3191)

PRODUCTS & SERVICES SECTION

(P-3191)
SHAKER CABINET CO (PA)
535 Palms Dr, Martinez (94553-1433)
PHONE.....................925 286-6066
Mehrdad Hazratizadeh, *Principal*
EMP: 23 **EST:** 2018
SALES (est): 372.5K **Privately Held**
WEB: www.pittsburgcacabinetrycontractor.com
SIC: 2434 Wood kitchen cabinets

(P-3192)
SUPERIOR KITCHEN CABINETS INC
1703 Voumard Ranch Dr, Turlock (95382-7426)
PHONE.....................209 247-0097
Noah Ramirez, *President*
EMP: 20 **EST:** 2011
SALES (est): 1.3MM **Privately Held**
SIC: 2434 Wood kitchen cabinets

(P-3193)
TAMALPAIS COML CABINETRY INC
200 9th St, Richmond (94801-3146)
P.O. Box 2169 (94802-1169)
PHONE.....................510 231-6800
John Kenner, *President*
EMP: 30 **EST:** 1985
SQ FT: 23,000
SALES (est): 4.3MM **Privately Held**
WEB: www.tamcab.com
SIC: 2434 Wood kitchen cabinets

(P-3194)
UNITED GRANITE & CABINETS LLC
Also Called: United Gran Cab Ctr Cbnets Cnt
5225 Central Ave, Richmond (94804-5805)
PHONE.....................510 558-8999
Paul Yu, *Owner*
Simon Yu CHI Ao, *Principal*
▲ **EMP:** 16 **EST:** 2005
SALES (est): 993.4K **Privately Held**
SIC: 2434 Wood kitchen cabinets

(P-3195)
WOODLINE PARTNERS INC
Also Called: Woodline Cabinets
5165 Fulton Dr, Fairfield (94534-1638)
PHONE.....................707 864-5445
Grant Paxton, *President*
Paul McKay, *CFO*
Lloyd Alexander, *Opers Mgr*
EMP: 49 **EST:** 1982
SQ FT: 37,500
SALES (est): 6.9MM **Privately Held**
SIC: 2434 Wood kitchen cabinets

2435 Hardwood Veneer & Plywood

(P-3196)
TIMBER PRODUCTS CO LTD PARTNR
Also Called: Yreka Division
130 N Phillipe Ln, Yreka (96097-9014)
P.O. Box 766 (96097-0766)
PHONE.....................530 842-2310
Pete Himmel, *Branch Mgr*
Mike Williamson, *Plant Supt*
EMP: 15
SALES (corp-wide): 376.2MM **Privately Held**
WEB: www.timberproducts.com
SIC: 2435 2436 Veneer stock, hardwood; softwood veneer & plywood
PA: Timber Products Co. Limited Partnership
305 S 4th St
Springfield OR 97477
541 747-4577

2436 Softwood Veneer & Plywood

(P-3197)
AMPINE LLC (HQ)
11300 Ridge Rd, Martell (95654)
PHONE.....................209 223-6091
Joseph Gonyea III, *CEO*
EMP: 17 **EST:** 2015
SALES (est): 44.6MM
SALES (corp-wide): 376.2MM **Privately Held**
WEB: www.timberproducts.com
SIC: 2436 2435 5031 2493 Plywood, softwood; plywood, hardwood or hardwood faced; lumber: rough, dressed & finished; particleboard products
PA: Timber Products Co. Limited Partnership
305 S 4th St
Springfield OR 97477
541 747-4577

2439 Structural Wood Members, NEC

(P-3198)
ADVANTAGE TRUSS COMPANY LLC
Also Called: Manufacturer
2025 San Juan Rd, Hollister (95023-9601)
PHONE.....................831 635-0377
Jennifer Pfeiffer, *CEO*
EMP: 35 **EST:** 2000
SALES (est): 3.7MM **Privately Held**
WEB: www.advantagetruss.com
SIC: 2439 1522 Trusses, wooden roof; residential construction

(P-3199)
ALL-TRUSS INC
22700 Broadway, Sonoma (95476-8233)
PHONE.....................707 938-5595
Robert L Biggs, *President*
EMP: 20 **EST:** 1992
SALES (est): 3MM **Privately Held**
WEB: www.trusscalifornia.com
SIC: 2439 Trusses, wooden roof

(P-3200)
AUTOMATED BLDG COMPONENTS INC
2853 S Orange Ave, Fresno (93725-1921)
PHONE.....................559 485-8232
David Cervantes, *President*
Violet Cervantes, *Treasurer*
Gabriel Cervantes, *Vice Pres*
EMP: 25 **EST:** 1991
SQ FT: 15,669
SALES (est): 5.6MM **Privately Held**
SIC: 2439 Trusses, wooden roof

(P-3201)
BETTER BUILT TRUSS INC
251 E 4th St, Ripon (95366-2774)
P.O. Box 1319 (95366-1319)
PHONE.....................209 869-4545
Jeff Qualle, *CEO*
David Sanders, *President*
Andrea Baer, *Planning*
Marcus Munoz, *Accounts Mgr*
EMP: 50 **EST:** 2010
SALES (est): 8.3MM **Privately Held**
WEB: www.betterbuilttruss.com
SIC: 2439 Trusses, wooden roof

(P-3202)
CAL-ASIA TRUSS INC
10547 E Stockton Blvd, Elk Grove (95624-9743)
PHONE.....................916 685-5648
Richard Avery, *Manager*
EMP: 47 **Privately Held**
SIC: 2439 Trusses, wooden roof
PA: Cal-Asia Truss, Inc.
2300 Clayton Rd Ste 1400
Concord CA 94520

(P-3203)
COMPU TECH LUMBER PRODUCTS
1980 Huntington Ct, Fairfield (94533-9753)
PHONE.....................707 437-6683
Walter L Young, *President*
Michael Blazer, *CFO*
Greg Young, *Vice Pres*
EMP: 41 **EST:** 1995
SQ FT: 94,657
SALES (est): 9.9MM **Privately Held**
SIC: 2439 2431 1742 Trusses, wooden roof; doors & door parts & trim, wood; plastering, plain or ornamental

(P-3204)
CY TRUSS
10715 E American Ave, Del Rey (93616-9703)
P.O. Box 188 (93616-0188)
PHONE.....................559 888-2160
Dave Campos, *Owner*
EMP: 30 **EST:** 2012
SALES (est): 4.8MM **Privately Held**
SIC: 2439 Trusses, wooden roof

(P-3205)
EL DORADO TRUSS CO INC
300 Industrial Dr, Placerville (95667-6828)
PHONE.....................530 622-1264
Steve Stewart, *President*
Edith Stewart, *Corp Secy*
EMP: 45 **EST:** 1978
SQ FT: 15,000
SALES (est): 6MM **Privately Held**
WEB: www.eldoradotruss.com
SIC: 2439 Trusses, wooden roof

(P-3206)
HAISCH CONSTRUCTION CO INC
Also Called: Systems Plus Lumber
1800 S Barney Rd, Anderson (96007-9703)
PHONE.....................530 378-6800
Matthew C Haisch, *CEO*
Bill Ivey, *Corp Secy*
Douglas C Haisch, *Principal*
Tony Lobue, *Program Mgr*
EMP: 18
SQ FT: 10,000
SALES (est): 3.2MM **Privately Held**
WEB: www.systplus.com
SIC: 2439 3441 Trusses, wooden roof; fabricated structural metal

(P-3207)
HANSON TRUSS COMPONENTS INC
4476 Skyway Dr, Olivehurst (95961-7477)
P.O. Box 31, Marysville (95901-0001)
PHONE.....................530 740-7750
Steven L Hanson, *President*
EMP: 60 **EST:** 2012
SALES (est): 6.3MM **Privately Held**
SIC: 2439 Trusses, wooden roof

(P-3208)
HOLT LUMBER INC (PA)
1916 S Cherry Ave, Fresno (93721-3398)
P.O. Box 1008 (93714-1008)
PHONE.....................559 233-3291
John W Holt Jr, *President*
Jack Holt, *President*
Tom Powers, *Admin Sec*
EMP: 25 **EST:** 1960
SQ FT: 25,000
SALES (est): 7.3MM **Privately Held**
WEB: www.holtlumber.com
SIC: 5211 2439 Lumber & other building materials; trusses, wooden roof

(P-3209)
HOMEWOOD COMPONENTS INC
Also Called: Homewood Truss
5033 Feather River Blvd, Marysville (95901)
P.O. Box 5010 (95901-8501)
PHONE.....................530 743-8855
Hamid Noorani, *President*
Lain Moss, *Treasurer*
Adam Noorani, *Director*
EMP: 34 **EST:** 1990
SQ FT: 120,000
SALES (est): 1.3MM **Privately Held**
WEB: www.hbs-lbm.com
SIC: 2439 Trusses, wooden roof; trusses, except roof: laminated lumber

(P-3210)
INLAND VALLEY TRUSS INC
150 N Sinclair Ave, Stockton (95215-5132)
PHONE.....................209 943-4710
Daniel Irwin, *President*
Dan Irwin, *President*
EMP: 16 **EST:** 2000
SALES (est): 1.8MM **Privately Held**
WEB: www.inlandtruss.com
SIC: 2439 Trusses, wooden roof
PA: Inland Empire Truss, Inc.
275 W Rider St
Perris CA 92571

(P-3211)
INTER-MUNTAIN TRUSS GIRDER INC
9604 Allende Ln, Oakdale (95361-9250)
PHONE.....................209 847-9184
Paul Girard, *President*
Lance B Lester, *Treasurer*
EMP: 27 **EST:** 1979
SALES (est): 3.9MM **Privately Held**
WEB: www.intermountaintruss.com
SIC: 2439 Trusses, wooden roof

(P-3212)
LASSEN FOREST PRODUCTS INC
22829 Casale Rd, Red Bluff (96080)
P.O. Box 8520 (96080-8520)
PHONE.....................530 527-7677
Peter Brunello Jr, *President*
EMP: 42 **EST:** 1960
SQ FT: 30,000
SALES (est): 4.5MM **Privately Held**
WEB: www.lassenforestproducts.com
SIC: 2439 5031 Structural wood members; lumber, plywood & millwork

(P-3213)
PACIFIC COAST SUPPLY LLC
Also Called: Pacific Supply
5550 Roseville Rd, North Highlands (95660-5038)
PHONE.....................916 339-8100
Lisa Cirullo, *Executive*
Stephanie Reddaway, *Branch Mgr*
Brenda Granger, *Administration*
Heather Miller, *Administration*
Alan Hatch, *CIO*
EMP: 15
SALES (corp-wide): 1.1B **Privately Held**
WEB: www.paccoastsupply.com
SIC: 2439 Trusses, wooden roof
HQ: Pacific Coast Supply, Llc
4290 Roseville Rd
North Highlands CA 95660
916 971-2301

(P-3214)
TRUSS ENGINEERING INC
477 Zeff Rd, Modesto (95351-3943)
P.O. Box 580210 (95358-0005)
PHONE.....................209 527-6387
Lawrence O Brien, *President*
Lawrence Obrien, *Vice Pres*
EMP: 20 **EST:** 1978
SQ FT: 14,000
SALES (est): 2.3MM **Privately Held**
SIC: 2439 Trusses, wooden roof

(P-3215)
VOLUMETRIC BLDG COMPANIES LLC
2302 Paradise Rd, Tracy (95304-8530)
PHONE.....................623 236-5322
Matt Ryan, *Branch Mgr*
Aravind Prakash, *Engineer*
Reema Kakkar, *Analyst*
Terri Merjano, *Receptionist*
EMP: 29
SALES (corp-wide): 5.4MM **Privately Held**
WEB: www.cases.primeclerk.com
SIC: 2439 2421 2434 Trusses, wooden roof; lumber: rough, sawed or planed; wood kitchen cabinets

▲ = Import ▼ = Export
◆ = Import/Export

PA: Volumetric Building Companies Llc
6128 Ridge Ave
Philadelphia PA 19128
800 674-9340

2441 Wood Boxes

(P-3216)
NEFAB PACKAGING INC
8477 Central Ave, Newark (94560-3431)
PHONE.....................408 678-2500
Ana Gonzales, *Branch Mgr*
Rui Garrido, *Exec VP*
Andreas Pihl, *Exec VP*
Ken Wilson, *Vice Pres*
Patrick Antrobus, *Project Mgr*
EMP: 98
SALES (corp-wide): 585.7MM **Privately Held**
WEB: www.nefab.com
SIC: 2441 5113 5199 Shipping cases, wood: nailed or lock corner; cardboard & products; packaging materials
HQ: Nefab Packaging, Inc.
204 Airline Dr Ste 100
Coppell TX 75019
469 444-5268

2448 Wood Pallets & Skids

(P-3217)
ALL BAY PALLET COMPANY INC (PA)
24993 Tarman Ave, Hayward (94544-2119)
PHONE.....................510 636-4131
Eladio Garcia Padilla, *President*
EMP: 36
SQ FT: 50,000
SALES (est): 2.1MM **Privately Held**
SIC: 2448 2449 Pallets, wood; wood containers

(P-3218)
ALL GOOD PALLETS INC
1055 Diamond St, Stockton (95205-7020)
PHONE.....................209 467-7000
Jasbir Nagra, *President*
Jagdev Singh, *Treasurer*
Jack Singh Nagra, *Vice Pres*
EMP: 40 **EST:** 1995
SALES (est): 4.3MM **Privately Held**
WEB: www.allgoodpallets.com
SIC: 2448 7699 Pallets, wood & metal combination; pallet repair

(P-3219)
CUTTER LUMBER PRODUCTS
4004 S El Dorado St, Stockton (95206-3759)
PHONE.....................209 982-4477
Tony Palma, *Manager*
EMP: 38
SALES (corp-wide): 7.3MM **Privately Held**
WEB: www.cutterlumber.com
SIC: 2448 Pallets, wood
PA: Cutter Lumber Products
10 Rickenbacker Cir
Livermore CA 94551
925 443-5959

(P-3220)
DEL RIO WEST PALLETS
3845 S El Dorado St, Stockton (95206-3760)
PHONE.....................209 983-8215
Candy Villalobos, *Owner*
EMP: 27 **EST:** 1992
SALES (est): 1.2MM **Privately Held**
SIC: 2448 Pallets, wood

(P-3221)
FIVE STAR LUMBER COMPANY LLC (PA)
Also Called: Five Star Pallet Co
6899 Smith Ave, Newark (94560-4223)
PHONE.....................510 795-7204
Marco Beretta, *President*
Bruce Beretta
David Beretta
Sandra Beretta
▲ **EMP:** 25 **EST:** 1981
SQ FT: 20,000
SALES (est): 4.5MM **Privately Held**
WEB: www.fivestarpallet.com
SIC: 2448 5031 Pallets, wood; lumber: rough, dressed & finished

(P-3222)
G PALLETS INC
2200 Hoover Ave, Modesto (95354-3906)
P.O. Box 1565, Patterson (95363-1565)
PHONE.....................209 814-2250
Margarita Garza, *Principal*
EMP: 31 **EST:** 2003
SQ FT: 16,000
SALES (est): 1.5MM **Privately Held**
SIC: 2448 Wood pallets & skids

(P-3223)
GARCIAS PALLETS INC
Also Called: Garcia Pallet
4125 S Golden State Blvd, Fresno (93725-9356)
PHONE.....................559 485-8182
Guadalupe Garcia, *CEO*
EMP: 31 **EST:** 1997
SQ FT: 19,600
SALES (est): 3.8MM **Privately Held**
SIC: 2448 Pallets, wood

(P-3224)
GONZALEZ PALLETS INC (PA)
1261 Yard Ct, San Jose (95133-1048)
PHONE.....................408 999-0280
Rafael Gomez, *CEO*
Jaime Silva, *Treasurer*
Rafael Gomez Jr, *Admin Sec*
EMP: 35 **EST:** 1994
SQ FT: 85,000
SALES (est): 12MM **Privately Held**
WEB: www.gonzalezpallets.com
SIC: 2448 Pallets, wood

(P-3225)
MARTINEZ PALLETS INC
6541 26th St, Rio Linda (95673-3810)
PHONE.....................916 238-4548
Miguel Cruz, *Administration*
EMP: 15 **EST:** 2016
SALES (est): 584.4K **Privately Held**
WEB: www.martinezpalletsinc.business.site
SIC: 2448 Pallets, wood

(P-3226)
MPT INC
10842 Road 28 1/2, Madera (93637-8504)
P.O. Box 602 (93639-0602)
PHONE.....................559 673-1552
John Gonzales, *President*
Beatrice Gonzales, *Admin Sec*
EMP: 34 **EST:** 1987
SALES (est): 1.1MM **Privately Held**
SIC: 2448 7699 Pallets, wood; pallet repair

(P-3227)
PALLETS UNLIMITED INC
2390 Athens Ave, Lincoln (95648-9508)
P.O. Box 1656 (95648-1443)
PHONE.....................916 408-1914
Nick Mehalakis, *President*
EMP: 18 **EST:** 2010
SALES (est): 3MM **Privately Held**
SIC: 2448 Pallets, wood

(P-3228)
RM PALLETS INC
2512 Paulson Rd, Turlock (95380-9757)
PHONE.....................209 632-9887
Georgina Ceja, *CEO*
EMP: 15 **EST:** 2015
SALES (est): 1MM **Privately Held**
SIC: 2448 Pallets, wood

(P-3229)
SELMA PALLET INC
1651 Pacific St, Selma (93662-9336)
P.O. Box 615 (93662-0615)
PHONE.....................559 896-7171
Lupe Romero, *President*
Vera Romero, *Vice Pres*
Lynette Romero Wilson, *Admin Sec*
EMP: 50 **EST:** 1988
SQ FT: 1,000
SALES (est): 8.1MM **Privately Held**
WEB: www.selmapallet.com
SIC: 2448 Pallets, wood; skids, wood

(P-3230)
TRANPAK INC
1209 Victory Ln, Madera (93637-5059)
PHONE.....................800 827-2474
Martin Ueland, *President*
Christian Ueland, *COO*
Donna Ueland, *Treasurer*
Lucie Colmenero, *Office Mgr*
Lucy Colmero, *Office Mgr*
◆ **EMP:** 21 **EST:** 1994
SQ FT: 80,000
SALES (est): 9.3MM **Privately Held**
WEB: www.tranpak.com
SIC: 2448 Pallets, wood

(P-3231)
TRIPLE A PALLETS INC
Also Called: Ayala and Son Pallets
3555 S Academy Ave, Sanger (93657-9566)
P.O. Box 1380 (93657-1380)
PHONE.....................559 313-7636
Arturo Ayala, *Principal*
EMP: 15 **EST:** 2014
SALES (est): 1MM **Privately Held**
WEB: www.tripleapallets.com
SIC: 2448 Pallets, wood

(P-3232)
UNITED PALLET SERVICES INC
4043 Crows Landing Rd, Modesto (95358-9404)
PHONE.....................209 538-5844
Wayne Randall, *President*
Darrel Roberson, *Vice Pres*
Amber McMahon, *Admin Sec*
Callen Cochran, *Business Mgr*
Ryan Roberson, *Sales Staff*
EMP: 150
SQ FT: 46,884
SALES (est): 22.6MM **Privately Held**
WEB: www.unitedpalletservices.com
SIC: 2448 7699 Pallets, wood; pallet repair

(P-3233)
WESTSIDE PALLET INC
2138 L St, Newman (95360-9765)
P.O. Box 786 (95360-0786)
PHONE.....................209 862-3941
Bernadine Rocha, *President*
Carolyn Beach, *Vice Pres*
EMP: 35 **EST:** 1994
SQ FT: 10,000
SALES (est): 3.4MM **Privately Held**
WEB: www.westsidepallet.net
SIC: 2448 Pallets, wood; skids, wood

2449 Wood Containers, NEC

(P-3234)
COUNTRY CONNECTION INC (PA)
2805 Richter Ave, Oroville (95966-5917)
P.O. Box 1115, Berry Creek (95916-1115)
PHONE.....................530 589-5176
Marc Hillier, *President*
Jessica Holliday, *Business Mgr*
◆ **EMP:** 15 **EST:** 2007
SQ FT: 20,000
SALES (est): 5.7MM **Privately Held**
WEB: www.countryconnection.biz
SIC: 5999 Alcoholic beverage making equipment & supplies; planters & window boxes, wood

(P-3235)
DEMPTOS NAPA COOPERAGE (HQ)
1050 Soscol Ferry Rd, NAPA (94558-6228)
PHONE.....................707 257-2628
Jerome Francois, *President*
William Jamieson, *Vice Pres*
Craig Colagrossi, *Sales Staff*
◆ **EMP:** 28 **EST:** 1982
SQ FT: 27,500
SALES (est): 14.1MM
SALES (corp-wide): 40.9MM **Privately Held**
WEB: www.demptos.fr
SIC: 2449 5085 Barrels, wood: coopered; barrels, new or reconditioned

PA: Tonnellerie Francois Freres
Tonnellerie Daniel Chapelle
St Romain 21190
380 212-333

(P-3236)
INNERSTAVE LLC
Also Called: Custom Cooperage Innerstave
21660 8th St E Ste B, Sonoma (95476-2828)
PHONE.....................707 996-8781
Brian Daw, *Facilities Mgr*
Rob Mirante, *Admin Mgr*
Carl Dillon, *General Mgr*
Alicia McBride, *General Mgr*
Candy Hemert, *Controller*
◆ **EMP:** 28 **EST:** 1980
SALES (est): 2.7MM **Privately Held**
WEB: www.innerstave.com
SIC: 2449 5085 5182 Wood containers; commercial containers; wine & distilled beverages

(P-3237)
JOHN DANIEL GONZALEZ
Also Called: Custom Wood Products
13458 E Industrial Dr, Parlier (93648-9678)
P.O. Box 783 (93648-0783)
PHONE.....................559 646-6621
John Daniel Gonzalez, *Owner*
Jennifer Gonzalez, *Co-Owner*
EMP: 43 **EST:** 2005
SQ FT: 14,000
SALES (est): 2.9MM **Privately Held**
SIC: 2449 Wood containers

(P-3238)
JOHNSTONS TRADING POST INC
11 N Pioneer Ave, Woodland (95776-5907)
PHONE.....................530 661-6152
James B Johnston, *CEO*
Cary Johnston, *Vice Pres*
Gloria Johnston, *Admin Sec*
EMP: 50 **EST:** 1980
SQ FT: 112,000
SALES (est): 7.8MM **Privately Held**
WEB: www.johnstontrading.com
SIC: 2449 4225 Wood containers; general warehousing & storage

(P-3239)
RED RIVER LUMBER CO
Also Called: Barrel Merchants
2959 Saint Helena Hwy N, Saint Helena (94574-9703)
PHONE.....................707 963-1251
EMP: 20
SQ FT: 1,200
SALES (est): 1.6MM **Privately Held**
SIC: 2449 Mfg Decorative Water Fountains With Cast Iron Pumps

(P-3240)
SEGUIN MOREAU USA HOLDINGS INC (HQ)
Also Called: Seguin Moreau NAPA Cooperage
151 Camino Dorado, NAPA (94558-6213)
PHONE.....................707 252-3408
Lance Spears, *CEO*
John Foster, *Vice Pres*
▲ **EMP:** 37 **EST:** 1992
SQ FT: 40,000
SALES (est): 7.1MM **Privately Held**
WEB: www.seguinmoreaunapa.com
SIC: 2449 Barrels, wood: coopered

(P-3241)
SPECILIZED PACKG SOLUTIONS INC
Also Called: Specilized Packg Solutions-Wood
38505 Cherry St Ste H, Newark (94560-4700)
P.O. Box 3042, Fremont (94539-0304)
PHONE.....................510 494-5670
Karen Besso, *CEO*
Terrence Besso, *Vice Pres*
Lisa Matthews, *Executive*
Steve Lobrovich, *Sales Staff*
OH Jay, *Manager*
▲ **EMP:** 50 **EST:** 1994
SQ FT: 63,000

2449 - Wood Containers, NEC County (P-3242) — PRODUCTS & SERVICES SECTION

SALES (est): 7.7MM Privately Held
WEB: www.specializedpackagingsolutions.com
SIC: 2449 2653 5113 3086 Rectangular boxes & crates, wood; sheets, corrugated: made from purchased materials; corrugated & solid fiber boxes; plastics foam products

(P-3242)
TONNELLERIE FRANCAISE FRENCH C
Also Called: Nadalie USA
1401 Tubbs Ln, Calistoga (94515-9726)
P.O. Box 798 (94515-0798)
PHONE 707 942-9301
Jean Jacques Nadalie, *CEO*
Alain Poisson, *Vice Pres*
Frederic Pavon, *Production*
Emmanuel Mathe, *Sales Mgr*
Kevin Andre, *Sales Staff*
▲ **EMP:** 18 **EST:** 1980
SQ FT: 12,000
SALES (est): 9.6MM
SALES (corp-wide): 32.4MM Privately Held
WEB: www.nadalie.com
SIC: 2449 Barrels, wood: coopered
PA: Tonnelerie Nadalie
  99 Rue Lafont
  Ludon Medoc 33290
  557 100-200

(P-3243)
TONNELLERIE RADOUX USA INC
480 Aviation Blvd, Santa Rosa (95403-1069)
PHONE 707 284-2888
Christen Liarg, *President*
Phillip Doray, *Corp Secy*
Maria Vigil, *Admin Asst*
Andrea Chappell, *Regl Sales Mgr*
Robert Crandell, *Regl Sales Mgr*
▲ **EMP:** 17 **EST:** 1994
SQ FT: 25,000
SALES (est): 4.2MM
SALES (corp-wide): 40.9MM Privately Held
WEB: www.tonnellerieradoux.com
SIC: 2449 Vats, wood: coopered
HQ: Tonnelerie Radoux
  Avenue Faidherbe
  Jonzac 17500
  546 480-065

(P-3244)
WINE COUNTRY CASES INC
621 Airpark Rd, NAPA (94558-6272)
PHONE 707 967-4805
Dan C Pina, *President*
Ignacio Delgadillo, *Manager*
EMP: 87 **EST:** 1988
SQ FT: 5,500
SALES (est): 8.2MM Privately Held
WEB: www.winecountrycases.com
SIC: 2449 2657 Butter crates, wood: wirebound; folding paperboard boxes

(P-3245)
WOOD-N-WOOD PRODUCTS CAL INC (PA)
2247 W Birch Ave, Fresno (93711-0442)
PHONE 559 896-3636
Rodney Allen Scary, *CEO*
Susan Scarry, *Treasurer*
EMP: 20 **EST:** 1982
SQ FT: 15,000
SALES (est): 3.8MM Privately Held
SIC: 2449 Wood containers

(P-3246)
WOOD-N-WOOD PRODUCTS CAL INC
13598 S Golden State Blvd, Selma (93662)
PHONE 559 896-3636
Rick Murillo, *Manager*
EMP: 15
SALES (corp-wide): 3.8MM Privately Held
SIC: 2449 Containers, plywood & veneer wood

PA: Wood-N-Wood Products Of California, Inc.
  2247 W Birch Ave
  Fresno CA 93711
  559 896-3636

2451 Mobile Homes

(P-3247)
CALIFORNIA TINY HOUSE INC
3337 W Sussex Way, Fresno (93722-4993)
PHONE 559 316-4500
Nicholas A Mosley, *Owner*
Bell Lisa, *Sales Staff*
EMP: 15 **EST:** 2017
SALES (est): 1.1MM Privately Held
WEB: www.californiatinyhouse.com
SIC: 2451 2452 Mobile buildings: for commercial use; prefabricated wood buildings

---

2452 Prefabricated Wood Buildings & Cmpnts

(P-3248)
AMERICAN MODULAR SYSTEMS INC
Also Called: AMS
787 Spreckels Ave, Manteca (95336-6002)
PHONE 209 825-1921
Daniel Sarich, *President*
Tony Sarich, *Vice Pres*
Carmen Ocampo, *Director*
Jose Arevalo, *Manager*
EMP: 100 **EST:** 1982
SQ FT: 85,000
SALES (est): 12.5MM Privately Held
WEB: www.americanmodular.com
SIC: 2452 1542 Modular homes, prefabricated, wood; nonresidential construction

(P-3249)
ENTEKRA LLC
945 E Whitmore Ave, Modesto (95358-9408)
PHONE 209 624-1630
Gerard McCaughey,
Alan Fannin, *Vice Pres*
Bran Keogh,
Meredith Cramer, *Manager*
EMP: 31 **EST:** 2018
SQ FT: 200,000
SALES (est): 12.3MM Privately Held
WEB: www.entekra.com
SIC: 2452 Prefabricated wood buildings

(P-3250)
GARY DOUPNIK MANUFACTURING INC
3237 Rippey Rd, Loomis (95650-7654)
P.O. Box 527 (95650-0527)
PHONE 916 652-9291
Sherie Edgar, *President*
Gary Doupnik Sr, *Treasurer*
Gary Doupnik Jr, *Vice Pres*
Jt Doupnik, *Vice Pres*
Kirtus Doupnik, *Vice Pres*
EMP: 33 **EST:** 1976
SQ FT: 4,000
SALES (est): 756.3K Privately Held
SIC: 2452 3448 Prefabricated buildings, wood; prefabricated metal buildings

(P-3251)
GLOBAL DIVERSIFIED INDS INC (PA)
1200 Airport Dr, Chowchilla (93610-9344)
P.O. Box 32, Atwater (95301-0032)
PHONE 559 665-5800
Phillip Hamilton, *President*
Adam N Debard, *Corp Secy*
Jeff Chan-Lugay, *Engineer*
Jeffrey Chan-Lugay, *Engineer*
EMP: 32 **EST:** 1990
SQ FT: 100,000
SALES (est): 9.6MM Privately Held
WEB: www.gdvi.net
SIC: 2452 Modular homes, prefabricated, wood

(P-3252)
GLOBAL MODULAR INC (HQ)
1120 Commerce Ave, Atwater (95301-5216)
P.O. Box 369, Chowchilla (93610-0369)
PHONE 209 676-8029
Adam De Bard, *President*
Milo King, *Admin Sec*
Robert Cronin, *Opers Mgr*
EMP: 44 **EST:** 2001
SALES (est): 5.7MM
SALES (corp-wide): 9.6MM Privately Held
WEB: www.gdvi.net
SIC: 2452 Prefabricated wood buildings
PA: Global Diversified Industries, Inc.
  1200 Airport Dr
  Chowchilla CA 93610
  559 665-5800

(P-3253)
MCCARTHY RANCH
15425 Los Gatos Blvd # 102, Los Gatos (95032-2541)
PHONE 408 356-2300
Joe McCarthy, *Owner*
EMP: 19 **EST:** 2006
SALES (est): 643.3K Privately Held
WEB: www.mccarthyranch.com
SIC: 2452 Farm & agricultural buildings, prefabricated wood

(P-3254)
NEW AVENUE INC
36 Panoramic Way, Berkeley (94704-1828)
PHONE 510 621-8679
Evan Schwimmer, *Branch Mgr*
EMP: 27 Privately Held
WEB: www.newavenuehomes.com
SIC: 2452 Prefabricated wood buildings
PA: New Avenue, Inc.
  1135 Centre Dr
  Walnut CA

2491 Wood Preserving

(P-3255)
AARDVARK WOODCRAFT INC (PA)
8283 Branchoak Ct, Elk Grove (95758-7929)
PHONE 916 230-3518
David O'Boyle, *Principal*
EMP: 35 **EST:** 2009
SALES (est): 281.4K Privately Held
SIC: 2491 Structural lumber & timber, treated wood

(P-3256)
CALIFORNIA CASCADE INDUSTRIES
7512 14th Ave, Sacramento (95820-3539)
P.O. Box 130026 (95853-0026)
PHONE 916 736-3353
Stuart D Heath, *President*
Stu Heath, *President*
Richard Rose, *CFO*
Kyle Keaton, *Corp Secy*
Joshua Coyne, *Admin Sec*
EMP: 200 **EST:** 1975
SQ FT: 6,500
SALES (est): 49.4MM
SALES (corp-wide): 1.2B Privately Held
WEB: www.californiacascade.com
SIC: 2491 2421 Wood preserving; sawmills & planing mills, general
PA: Doman Building Materials Group Ltd
  1100 Melville St Suite 1600
  Vancouver BC V6E 4
  604 432-1400

(P-3257)
CALIFORNIA CASCADE-WOODLAND
Also Called: Western Wood Treating
1492 Churchill Downs Ave, Woodland (95776-6113)
P.O. Box 1443 (95776-1443)
PHONE 530 666-1261
Henry Feenstra, *President*
EMP: 38 **EST:** 1978
SQ FT: 1,000

SALES (est): 6.6MM Privately Held
WEB: www.westernwoodtreating.com
SIC: 2491 Structural lumber & timber, treated wood

(P-3258)
CONRAD WOOD PRESERVING CO
7085 Eddy Rd Unit C, Arbuckle (95912-9789)
PHONE 530 476-2894
Fred Noah, *Branch Mgr*
Don Bratcher, *Vice Pres*
Jennifer Carter, *Accounts Mgr*
EMP: 19
SALES (corp-wide): 20.3MM Privately Held
WEB: www.conradfp.com
SIC: 2491 Wood preserving
PA: Conrad Wood Preserving Co.
  68765 Wildwood Rd
  North Bend OR 97459
  800 356-7146

(P-3259)
EAST BAY FIXTURE COMPANY
941 Aileen St, Oakland (94608-2805)
PHONE 510 652-4421
Richard Laible, *President*
Frances Laible, *Corp Secy*
Jenny Laible, *Supervisor*
EMP: 50 **EST:** 1923
SQ FT: 32,000
SALES (est): 7.6MM Privately Held
WEB: www.eastbayfixture.com
SIC: 2491 2541 Millwork, treated wood; office fixtures, wood

(P-3260)
JJ CHARLES INC
Also Called: Used Pellet Co
4115 S Orange Ave, Fresno (93725-9367)
PHONE 559 264-6664
Jeffrey Seib, *President*
EMP: 40 **EST:** 1998
SALES (est): 4.4MM Privately Held
SIC: 2491 Wood preserving

(P-3261)
THUNDERBOLT SALES INC
3400 Patterson Rd, Riverbank (95367-2998)
P.O. Box 890 (95367-0890)
PHONE 209 869-4561
T W Ted Seybold, *President*
T W Seybold, *President*
Don De Vries, *Vice Pres*
Leonard Lovalvo, *Vice Pres*
EMP: 17 **EST:** 1982
SALES (est): 2.4MM
SALES (corp-wide): 4.5MM Privately Held
WEB: www.thunderboltwoodtreating.com
SIC: 2491 Wood preserving
PA: Thunderbolt Wood Treating Co., Inc.
  3400 Patterson Rd
  Riverbank CA 95367
  209 869-4561

2493 Reconstituted Wood Prdts

(P-3262)
CALPLANT I LLC
Also Called: Eureka
6101 State Highway 162, Willows (95988-9774)
P.O. Box 1338 (95988-1338)
PHONE 530 361-0003
Jeffrey N Wagner, *Mng Member*
Christopher Motley, *CFO*
Les Younie, *Vice Pres*
Jeff Ward, *Maintence Staff*
Jason Bernzweig,
EMP: 23 **EST:** 2008
SALES (est): 13.5MM Privately Held
WEB: www.eurekamdf.com
SIC: 2493 Reconstituted wood products
PA: Calplant I Holdco, Llc
  6101 State Highway 162
  Willows CA 95988
  530 570-0542

PRODUCTS & SERVICES SECTION 2512 - Wood Household Furniture, Upholstered County (P-3288)

(P-3263)
CALPLANT I HOLDCO LLC (PA)
6101 State Highway 162, Willows (95988-9774)
P.O. Box 1338 (95988-1338)
PHONE..................................530 570-0542
Jeffrey N Wagner,
Gerald Uhland, *CEO*
Chris Motley, *CFO*
EMP: 23 **EST:** 2017
SALES (est): 13.5MM Privately Held
WEB: www.eurekamdf.com
SIC: 2493 Reconstituted wood products

2499 Wood Prdts, NEC

(P-3264)
APPLIED SILVER INC
26254 Eden Landing Rd, Hayward (94545-3717)
PHONE..................................888 939-4747
Sean Morham, *CEO*
Elizabeth Hutt Pollard, *Ch of Bd*
Priya Balachandran, *COO*
Paul McCabe, *CFO*
Keith Copenhagen, *Engineer*
EMP: 15 **EST:** 2011
SALES (est): 2.6MM Privately Held
WEB: www.appliedsilver.com
SIC: 2499 5719 Laundry products, wood; linens

(P-3265)
CALIFORNIA CEDAR PRODUCTS CO (PA)
2385 Arch Airport Rd # 50, Stockton (95206-4403)
PHONE..................................209 932-5002
Charles Berolzheimer, *President*
Susan Macintyre, *CFO*
Vincent Bricka, *Vice Pres*
Dave Morgali, *Info Tech Mgr*
Troy White, *VP Finance*
◆ **EMP:** 50 **EST:** 1920
SQ FT: 10,000
SALES (est): 34MM Privately Held
WEB: www.calcedar.com
SIC: 2499 Pencil slats, wood

(P-3266)
CARRIS REELS CALIFORNIA INC (HQ)
2100 W Almond Ave, Madera (93637-5203)
P.O. Box 88 (93639-0088)
PHONE..................................802 733-9111
William Carris, *Ch of Bd*
Dave Ferraro, *President*
David Fitzgerald, *CFO*
David Ferraro, *Vice Pres*
Shelly Hunt, *Office Mgr*
▲ **EMP:** 30 **EST:** 1966
SALES (est): 10MM Privately Held
WEB: www.carris.com
SIC: 2499 2448 Spools, reels & pulleys: wood; reels, plywood; pallets, wood

(P-3267)
COOLING TOWER RESOURCES INC (PA)
Also Called: C T R
1470 Grove St, Healdsburg (95448-4700)
P.O. Box 159 (95448-0159)
PHONE..................................707 433-3900
Gordon Martin, *CEO*
Terri Martin, *Treasurer*
Brad Pirrung, *Sales Executive*
Justin Davis, *Marketing Staff*
Rachelle Jackson, *Manager*
◆ **EMP:** 20 **EST:** 1997
SQ FT: 1,200
SALES (est): 4.4MM Privately Held
WEB: www.cooltower.com
SIC: 2499 Cooling towers, wood or wood & sheet metal combination

(P-3268)
HANDLE INC
251 Tennyson Ave, Palo Alto (94301-3737)
PHONE..................................650 863-6113
Yvette MA, *Principal*
EMP: 20 **EST:** 2011
SALES (est): 657.2K Privately Held
WEB: www.handle.today
SIC: 2499 Handles, wood

(P-3269)
J & S STAKES INC
3157 Greenwood Heights Dr, Kneeland (95549-8912)
PHONE..................................707 668-5647
EMP: 18
SQ FT: 21,000
SALES: 2MM Privately Held
SIC: 2499 Mfg Wood Fencing And Stakes

(P-3270)
LUTHIERS MERCANTILE INTL INC
Also Called: LMI
7975 Cameron Dr Ste 1600, Windsor (95492-8574)
PHONE..................................707 433-1823
Duane Waterman, *President*
Natalie Swango, *CFO*
▲ **EMP:** 18 **EST:** 1994
SQ FT: 10,000
SALES (est): 2.4MM Privately Held
WEB: www.lmii.com
SIC: 5961 2499 7389 Mail order house; books, mail order (except book clubs); tools & hardware, mail order; carved & turned wood; hand tool designers

(P-3271)
SHASTA FOREST PRODUCTS INC
1423 Montague Rd, Yreka (96097-9659)
P.O. Box 777 (96097-0777)
PHONE..................................530 842-2787
Bill Hall, *Manager*
EMP: 38
SALES (corp-wide): 10.7MM Privately Held
WEB: www.shastabark.com
SIC: 2499 2421 Mulch, wood & bark; sawmills & planing mills, general
PA: Shasta Forest Products, Inc.
1412 Montague Rd
Yreka CA 96097
530 842-0527

(P-3272)
WHOLESALE ART AND FRAMING INC
3068 Sunrise Blvd Ste E, Rancho Cordova (95742-6525)
PHONE..................................916 851-0770
Ranell Carpenter, *Branch Mgr*
EMP: 17 Privately Held
WEB: www.wholesaleartandframing.com
SIC: 2499 Picture frame molding, finished
PA: Wholesale Art And Framing Inc
1774 Broadway
Placerville CA

2511 Wood Household Furniture

(P-3273)
ART OF MUSE LLC
Also Called: Oly
2222 5th St, Berkeley (94710-2217)
PHONE..................................510 644-2100
Brad Huntzinger, *President*
Kate McIntyre, *Vice Pres*
▲ **EMP:** 20 **EST:** 1989
SALES (est): 1.5MM Privately Held
SIC: 2511 2521 Wood household furniture; wood office furniture

(P-3274)
BEAUTY CRAFT FURNITURE CORP
Also Called: California House
3316 51st Ave, Sacramento (95823-1089)
PHONE..................................916 428-2238
Steven Start, *President*
Dee Start, *Ch of Bd*
▲ **EMP:** 44 **EST:** 1953
SQ FT: 65,000
SALES (est): 6.1MM Privately Held
WEB: www.californiahouse.com
SIC: 2511 Wood game room furniture

(P-3275)
BERKELEY MLLWK & FURN CO INC
Also Called: Berkeley Mills
2830 7th St, Berkeley (94710-2703)
PHONE..................................510 549-2854
Eugene Agress, *President*
Luong Lee Dinh, *Vice Pres*
Scott Pew, *Vice Pres*
EMP: 43 **EST:** 1989
SQ FT: 18,000
SALES (est): 3.3MM Privately Held
WEB: www.berkeleymills.com
SIC: 2511 2541 2434 Wood household furniture; wood partitions & fixtures; wood kitchen cabinets

(P-3276)
CB MILL INC
1232 Connecticut St, San Francisco (94107-3352)
PHONE..................................415 386-5309
EMP: 19 **EST:** 2001
SQ FT: 16,000
SALES: 2.2MM Privately Held
WEB: www.cbmill.net
SIC: 2511 Mfg Wood Household Furniture

(P-3277)
ELEMENTS BY GRAPEVINE INC
18251 N Highway 88, Lockeford (95237-9716)
P.O. Box 1458 (95237-1458)
PHONE..................................209 727-3711
Isaac Kubryk, *President*
Renee Kubryk, *Vice Pres*
◆ **EMP:** 16 **EST:** 1979
SQ FT: 60,000
SALES (est): 15MM Privately Held
SIC: 2511 2519 Tables, household: wood; lawn & garden furniture, except wood & metal

(P-3278)
JM CUSTOM CABINETS & FURNITURE
Also Called: J M Custom Cabinets
3848 N Winery Ave, Fresno (93726-4703)
PHONE..................................559 291-6638
Joseph J Marzullo II, *President*
Joseph J Marzullo III, *President*
EMP: 21 **EST:** 1974
SQ FT: 6,000
SALES (est): 1MM Privately Held
SIC: 5712 2511 Cabinet work, custom; tables, household: wood; chairs, household, except upholstered: wood

(P-3279)
KERROCK COUNTERTOPS INC (PA)
Also Called: Lisac Construction
1450 Dell Ave Ste C, Campbell (95008-6600)
PHONE..................................510 441-2300
William G Lisac, *President*
▲ **EMP:** 17 **EST:** 1996
SALES (est): 1.7MM Privately Held
WEB: www.kerrock.com
SIC: 2511 5211 1799 Wood household furniture; cabinets, kitchen; counter top installation

(P-3280)
KINWAI USA INC
2951 Whipple Rd, Union City (94587-1207)
PHONE..................................510 780-9388
Chongwei Zhao, *President*
Alexis Chang, *Sales Staff*
▲ **EMP:** 30 **EST:** 2001
SALES (est): 1.2MM Privately Held
WEB: www.kinwaiusa.info
SIC: 2511 5021 Wood household furniture; household furniture

(P-3281)
LOTUS BED SOLUTIONS LLC ✪
4600 Greenholme Dr Apt 3, Sacramento (95842-3473)
PHONE..................................415 756-5099
Katrina Smith, *Principal*
EMP: 19 **EST:** 2021
SALES (est): 551.4K Privately Held
SIC: 2511 Wood household furniture

(P-3282)
MICHAELS FURNITURE COMPANY INC
15 Koch Rd Ste J, Corte Madera (94925-1231)
PHONE..................................916 381-9086
Gary Friedman, *CEO*
Mike Bollum, *General Mgr*
▲ **EMP:** 157 **EST:** 1974
SQ FT: 150,000
SALES (est): 6.2MM
SALES (corp-wide): 2.8B Publicly Held
SIC: 2511 Wood household furniture
HQ: Restoration Hardware, Inc.
15 Koch Rd Ste K
Corte Madera CA 94925
415 965-7628

(P-3283)
MIWA INC
5733 San Leandro St Ofc, Oakland (94621-4426)
PHONE..................................510 261-5999
Thomas Yan, *President*
Sandra Yan, *Vice Pres*
▲ **EMP:** 17 **EST:** 1992
SQ FT: 45,000
SALES (est): 542.2K Privately Held
SIC: 2511 2512 3496 5719 Screens, privacy: wood; couches, sofas & davenports: upholstered on wood frames; mats & matting; lighting, lamps & accessories

(P-3284)
WESTCOTT DESIGNS INC
4455 Park Rd, Benicia (94510-1124)
PHONE..................................510 367-7229
Michael Westcott Isheim, *CEO*
Sheryl Isheim, *Vice Pres*
▲ **EMP:** 20 **EST:** 1990
SQ FT: 40,000
SALES (est): 2.4MM Privately Held
SIC: 2511 Wood household furniture

(P-3285)
WESTERN DOVETAIL INCORPORATED
1101 Nimitz Ave Ste 209, Vallejo (94592-1034)
P.O. Box 1592 (94590-0159)
PHONE..................................707 556-3683
Maxfield Hunter, *Principal*
Joshua Hunter, *Director*
EMP: 22 **EST:** 1993
SQ FT: 1,000
SALES (est): 5.1MM Privately Held
WEB: www.drawer.com
SIC: 2511 Wood household furniture

(P-3286)
WOOD TECH INC
4611 Malat St, Oakland (94601-4903)
PHONE..................................510 534-4930
Juan D Figueroa, *CEO*
EMP: 70 **EST:** 1993
SQ FT: 92,000
SALES (est): 10MM Privately Held
WEB: www.woodtechonline.com
SIC: 2511 2521 Wood household furniture; wood office furniture

2512 Wood Household Furniture, Upholstered

(P-3287)
GUY CHADDOCK & COMPANY (PA)
1100 La Avenida St, Mountain View (94043-1452)
PHONE..................................408 907-9200
EMP: 230
SQ FT: 75,000
SALES (est): 21.9MM Privately Held
SIC: 2512 2521 2511 Mfg Upholstered Household Furniture Mfg Wood Office Furniture Mfg Wood Household Furniture

(P-3288)
J F FITZGERALD COMPANY INC
Also Called: Fitzgerald Designers & Mfrs
429 Cabot Rd, South San Francisco (94080-4819)
PHONE..................................415 648-6161

2512 - Wood Household Furniture, Upholstered County (P-3289)

PRODUCTS & SERVICES SECTION

Charles James Willin Jr, *President*
Michael Willin, *Vice Pres*
EMP: 28 **EST:** 1953
SALES (est): 1MM **Privately Held**
WEB: www.fitzgeraldcompany.com
SIC: 2512 Upholstered household furniture

(P-3289)
KAY CHESTERFIELD INC
6365 Coliseum Way, Oakland (94621-3719)
PHONE 510 533-5565
Kriss Kokoefer, *President*
Joanne H Jones, *Vice Pres*
Michelle Soto, *Office Mgr*
Kevelynne Ely, *Engineer*
EMP: 24 **EST:** 1921
SQ FT: 10,000
SALES (est): 2.6MM **Privately Held**
WEB: www.kaychesterfield.com
SIC: 2512 7641 Upholstered household furniture; upholstery work

(P-3290)
MARCO FINE FURNITURE INC
650 Potrero Ave, San Francisco (94110-2117)
P.O. Box 590659 (94159-0659)
PHONE 415 285-3235
◆ **EMP:** 20
SQ FT: 23,000
SALES (est): 1.9MM **Privately Held**
WEB: www.marcofinefurniture.com
SIC: 2512 Mfg Upholstered Furniture

(P-3291)
MULHOLLAND BROTHERS (PA)
1710 4th St, Berkeley (94710-1711)
PHONE 415 824-5995
Jay Holland, *President*
Guy Holland, *Vice Pres*
▲ **EMP:** 87 **EST:** 1996
SALES (est): 8.1MM **Privately Held**
WEB: www.shopmulholland.com
SIC: 2512 5199 3161 Upholstered household furniture; leather, leather goods & furs; cases, carrying

(P-3292)
STANFORD FURNITURE MFG INC
3170 Orange Grove Ave, North Highlands (95660-5706)
PHONE 916 387-5300
Alireza Angha, *President*
EMP: 17 **EST:** 1997
SALES (est): 1.3MM **Privately Held**
WEB: www.stanfordmfg.com
SIC: 2512 Upholstered household furniture

(P-3293)
VAN SARK INC (PA)
Also Called: Dependable Furniture Mfg Co
410 Harriet St, San Francisco (94103-4915)
PHONE 510 635-1111
Kevin Sarkisian, *President*
Eniko Sarkisian, *Treasurer*
Baltazar Garcia, *Prdtn Mgr*
▲ **EMP:** 111 **EST:** 1991
SQ FT: 75,000
SALES (est): 13.4MM **Privately Held**
WEB: www.dependablefm.com
SIC: 2512 Wood upholstered chairs & couches

2514 Metal Household Furniture

(P-3294)
COSMO IMPORT & EXPORT LLC
3771 Channel Dr, West Sacramento (95691-3421)
PHONE 916 209-5500
Jennifer Hayes, *CEO*
EMP: 20 **EST:** 2013
SQ FT: 100,000
SALES (est): 60MM **Privately Held**
SIC: 2514 Garden furniture, metal

(P-3295)
THOMAS LUNDBERG
Also Called: Lundberg Designs
2620 3rd St, San Francisco (94107-3115)
PHONE 415 695-0110
Thomas Lundberg, *Owner*
Michael Bernard, *Managing Dir*
Emily Pearl, *Manager*
Debra Sassenrath, *Manager*
EMP: 21 **EST:** 1987
SQ FT: 5,000
SALES (est): 2.9MM **Privately Held**
WEB: www.lundbergdesign.com
SIC: 2514 Metal household furniture

(P-3296)
TK CLASSICS LLC
3771 Channel Dr Ste 100, West Sacramento (95691-3421)
PHONE 916 209-5500
Jennifer Hayes, *Mng Member*
EMP: 20 **EST:** 2017
SQ FT: 100,000
SALES (est): 7.4MM
SALES (corp-wide): 67.4MM **Privately Held**
WEB: www.twinstarhome.com
SIC: 2514 5712 Garden furniture, metal; outdoor & garden furniture
PA: Twin-Star International, Inc.
1690 S Congress Ave # 210
Delray Beach FL 33445
866 661-1218

2515 Mattresses & Bedsprings

(P-3297)
SQUARE DEAL MATTRESS FACTORY
Also Called: Square Deal Mat Fctry & Uphl
1354 Humboldt Ave, Chico (95928-5952)
PHONE 530 342-2510
Lois Lash, *President*
Richard Lash, *President*
EMP: 24 **EST:** 1920
SQ FT: 6,000
SALES (est): 2.3MM **Privately Held**
WEB: www.squaredealmattress.com
SIC: 2515 5712 Mattresses & bedsprings; furniture stores

(P-3298)
ZINUS INC (HQ)
1951 Fairway Dr Ste A, San Leandro (94577-5643)
PHONE 925 417-2100
Youn Jae Lee, *President*
Sungjin Kim, *Engineer*
Jiyun Jeong, *Accounting Mgr*
Soojin Lee, *Accounting Mgr*
Stephanie TSO, *Accountant*
▲ **EMP:** 70 **EST:** 1987
SQ FT: 155,000
SALES (est): 52.1MM **Privately Held**
WEB: www.zinus.com
SIC: 2515 Chair & couch springs, assembled

2519 Household Furniture, NEC

(P-3299)
RECYCLED SPACES INC
Also Called: High Camp Home
10191 Donner Pass Rd # 1, Truckee (96161-0408)
P.O. Box 10358 (96162-0358)
PHONE 530 587-3394
Diana Vincent, *CEO*
Teresa Mersky, *President*
Amy Trehal, *Opers Mgr*
▲ **EMP:** 15 **EST:** 1997
SALES (est): 2.8MM **Privately Held**
WEB: www.highcamphome.com
SIC: 2519 5712 Lawn & garden furniture, except wood & metal; furniture stores

2521 Wood Office Furniture

(P-3300)
AMPINE LLC
11610 Ampine Fibreform Rd, Sutter Creek (95685-9686)
PHONE 209 223-1690
Terry Velasco, *General Mgr*
EMP: 56
SALES (corp-wide): 376.2MM **Privately Held**
SIC: 2521 Wood office furniture
HQ: Ampine, Llc
11300 Ridge Rd
Martell CA 95654
209 223-6091

(P-3301)
CAPITOL STORE FIXTURES
Also Called: Capitol Components
4220 Pell Dr Ste C, Sacramento (95838-2575)
PHONE 916 646-9096
Toll Free: .... 888 -
Jim Pelc, *President*
Vicki Pelc, *Vice Pres*
EMP: 25 **EST:** 1985
SQ FT: 24,000
SALES (est): 3.6MM **Privately Held**
WEB: www.csfixtures.com
SIC: 2521 5046 Cabinets, office: wood; shelving, commercial & industrial

(P-3302)
CREATIVE WOOD PRODUCTS INC
900 77th Ave, Oakland (94621-2573)
PHONE 510 635-5399
Jose Mendes, *President*
Polly Peggs Mendes, *CFO*
Diana Barragan, *Info Tech Dir*
Kevin Bento, *Engineer*
Josh Halsey, *Sales Staff*
▲ **EMP:** 120 **EST:** 1964
SQ FT: 85,000
SALES (est): 19.8MM **Privately Held**
WEB: www.creativewood.net
SIC: 2521 Desks, office: wood

(P-3303)
HPL CONTRACT INC
525 Baldwin Rd, Patterson (95363-8859)
PHONE 209 892-1717
Frank Stratiotis, *President*
Jim Robertson, *Vice Pres*
EMP: 17 **EST:** 1997
SQ FT: 7,200
SALES (est): 4.7MM **Privately Held**
WEB: www.hplcontract.com
SIC: 2521 Wood office furniture

(P-3304)
ICON DESIGN AND DISPLAY INC
17740 Shideler Pkwy, Lathrop (95330-9356)
PHONE 707 416-0230
EMP: 26 **EST:** 2016
SALES (est): 2.4MM **Privately Held**
WEB: www.icondisplay.com
SIC: 2521 Wood office furniture

(P-3305)
IRONIES
2200 Central St Ste D, Richmond (94801-1213)
PHONE 510 644-2100
Kathleen McIntyre, *President*
Ambar Aguayo, *Manager*
Jenny Ambrosio, *Accounts Mgr*
EMP: 35 **EST:** 1989
SALES (est): 5.1MM **Privately Held**
WEB: www.ironies.com
SIC: 2521 Wood office furniture

(P-3306)
J & C CUSTOM CABINETS INC
11451 Elks Cir, Rancho Cordova (95742-7355)
PHONE 916 638-3400
Chris Christie, *Ch of Bd*
James E Farrell, *President*
EMP: 16 **EST:** 2011
SQ FT: 20,000
SALES (est): 3.7MM **Privately Held**
WEB: www.jandccustomcabinets.com
SIC: 2521 2434 Cabinets, office: wood; wood kitchen cabinets

(P-3307)
LUXER CORPORATION
Also Called: Luxer One
5040 Dudley Blvd, McClellan (95652-1029)
PHONE 415 390-0123
Arik Levy, *CEO*
Jaelin Williams, *Executive*
Joshua Grosser, *Business Dir*
Kelsey Ciupak, *Project Mgr*
Gabe Matteucci, *Project Mgr*
EMP: 130 **EST:** 2014
SALES (est): 26.5MM
SALES (corp-wide): 10.1B **Privately Held**
WEB: www.luxerone.com
SIC: 2521 5712 Wood office furniture; furniture stores
PA: Assa Abloy Ab
Klarabergsviadukten 90
Stockholm 111 6
850 648-500

(P-3308)
NORTHWOOD DESIGN PARTNERS INC
1550 Atlantic St, Union City (94587-2006)
PHONE 510 731-6505
Michael Hayes, *CEO*
Josh Michael Hayes, *President*
Sonny Im, *Director*
EMP: 38 **EST:** 2010
SQ FT: 2,000
SALES (est): 4.9MM **Privately Held**
WEB: www.northwooddp.com
SIC: 2521 2431 Wood office furniture; millwork

(P-3309)
OHIO INC
630 Treat Ave, San Francisco (94110-2016)
PHONE 415 647-6446
David Pierce, *President*
Penny Gates, *Officer*
Beth Clark, *Finance Mgr*
Helen Wardeh, *Professor*
EMP: 46 **EST:** 1996
SQ FT: 7,000
SALES (est): 4.7MM **Privately Held**
WEB: www.ohiodesign.com
SIC: 2521 Wood office furniture

(P-3310)
ZENBOOTH INC
650 University Ave # 10, Berkeley (94710-1946)
PHONE 510 646-8368
Sam Johnson, *CEO*
Mischa Szymanski, *Mktg Coord*
EMP: 21 **EST:** 2016
SALES (est): 2.9MM **Privately Held**
WEB: www.zenbooth.net
SIC: 2521 Wood office furniture

2522 Office Furniture, Except Wood

(P-3311)
RDM INDUSTRIAL PRODUCTS INC
1652 Watson Ct, Milpitas (95035-6822)
PHONE 408 945-8400
Ricky Vigil, *President*
Kristi Cubillo, *Info Tech Mgr*
Kristi Ehrhorn, *Manager*
Lynn Tweedie, *Assistant*
EMP: 18 **EST:** 1976
SQ FT: 17,000
SALES (est): 6.4MM **Privately Held**
WEB: www.rdm-ind.com
SIC: 2522 5712 Cabinets, office: except wood; cabinet work, custom; custom made furniture, except cabinets; office furniture; cabinets, office: wood

▲ = Import ▼ = Export
◆ = Import/Export

PRODUCTS & SERVICES SECTION
2599 - Furniture & Fixtures, NEC County (P-3333)

2531 Public Building & Related Furniture

(P-3312)
KINGS RIVER CASTING INC
1350 North Ave, Sanger (93657-3742)
PHONE...................................559 875-8250
Patrick Henry, *President*
Merry Henry, *Corp Secy*
▼ EMP: 31 EST: 1978
SQ FT: 30,000
SALES (est): 2.3MM Privately Held
WEB: www.kingsrivercasting.com
SIC: 2531 3648 2599 Benches for public buildings; street lighting fixtures; bar furniture

2541 Wood, Office & Store Fixtures

(P-3313)
ELEMENTS MANUFACTURING INC
115 Harvey West Blvd C, Santa Cruz (95060-2168)
PHONE...................................831 421-9440
Ken Ketch, *President*
Kristy Stormes, *Partner*
Alan Stormes, *Admin Sec*
David Wright, *Opers Staff*
EMP: 20 EST: 1995
SQ FT: 15,000
SALES (est): 2.8MM Privately Held
WEB: www.elementsmfg.com
SIC: 2541 Cabinets, lockers & shelving; counter & sink tops

(P-3314)
EMERZIAN WOODWORKING INC
2555 N Argyle Ave, Fresno (93727-1378)
PHONE...................................559 292-2448
Tom Emerzian, *Owner*
Gus Gonzalez, *Purchasing*
EMP: 40 EST: 1984
SQ FT: 46,000
SALES (est): 8.4MM Privately Held
WEB: www.emerzianwoodworking.com
SIC: 2541 2434 Showcases, except refrigerated: wood; wood kitchen cabinets

(P-3315)
JBE INC
Also Called: Dimensions Unlimited
1080 Nimitz Ave Ste 400, Vallejo (94592-1009)
PHONE...................................707 552-6800
John Ewer, *President*
Jane Ewer, *Admin Sec*
EMP: 15 EST: 1971
SQ FT: 9,300
SALES (est): 1.6MM Privately Held
WEB: www.ducabinetry.com
SIC: 2541 1751 5712 Cabinets, except refrigerated: show, display, etc.: wood; lockers, except refrigerated: wood; cabinet & finish carpentry; customized furniture & cabinets

(P-3316)
LIMITLESS KITCHEN AND BATH INC
1201 Auto Center Dr, Antioch (94509-1381)
PHONE...................................925 238-0046
Lou Mathew Hellman, *CEO*
EMP: 15 EST: 2015
SALES (est): 1.4MM Privately Held
WEB: www.limitlesskitchenandbath.com
SIC: 2541 5251 2434 Counter & sink tops; hardware; vanities, bathroom: wood

(P-3317)
OLDE WORLD CORPORATION
Also Called: Great Spaces USA
360 Grogan Ave, Merced (95341-6446)
PHONE...................................209 384-1337
Richard T Conas, *President*
Jan Conas, *Vice Pres*
EMP: 20 EST: 1979
SQ FT: 35,000
SALES (est): 3.3MM Privately Held
WEB: www.greatspacesusa.com
SIC: 2541 Store & office display cases & fixtures

(P-3318)
PG EMMINGER INC
4036 Pacheco Blvd A, Martinez (94553-2224)
PHONE...................................925 313-5830
Philip G Emminger, *President*
William Clark, *Vice Pres*
EMP: 22 EST: 1971
SQ FT: 10,000
SALES (est): 3.4MM Privately Held
WEB: www.emminger.com
SIC: 2541 Wood partitions & fixtures

(P-3319)
PLANET ONE PRODUCTS INC (PA)
Also Called: Cellarpro Cooling Systems
1445 N Mcdowell Blvd, Petaluma (94954-6516)
PHONE...................................707 794-8000
Ben Z Argov, *President*
Bruce Kirsten, *Treasurer*
Keith Sedwick, *Vice Pres*
Doug McAlpine, *Engineer*
▲ EMP: 23 EST: 2004
SQ FT: 18,000
SALES (est): 9.7MM Privately Held
WEB: www.lecachewinecabinets.com
SIC: 2541 Cabinets, except refrigerated: show, display, etc.: wood

(P-3320)
SUBA MFG INC
921 Bayshore Rd, Benicia (94510-2990)
P.O. Box 394, Diablo (94528-0394)
PHONE...................................707 745-0358
Jack Bell, *President*
Sue Bell, *Admin Sec*
Scott Cody, *Marketing Staff*
EMP: 15 EST: 1964
SQ FT: 40,000
SALES (est): 976.9K Privately Held
WEB: www.subatech.com
SIC: 2541 3083 Table or counter tops, plastic laminated; laminated plastics plate & sheet

(P-3321)
SULLIVAN COUNTER TOPS INC
1189 65th St, Oakland (94608-1108)
PHONE...................................510 652-2337
Thomas C Sullivan, *President*
Stacey Steele, *Opers Mgr*
EMP: 27 EST: 1977
SQ FT: 10,000
SALES (est): 1.2MM Privately Held
WEB: www.sullivancountertops.com
SIC: 2541 2821 Counter & sink tops; table or counter tops, plastic laminated; plastics materials & resins

(P-3322)
SURFACE TECHNIQUES CORPORATION (PA)
Also Called: Surface Technology
25673 Nickel Pl, Hayward (94545-3221)
PHONE...................................510 887-6000
Howard Berger, *President*
EMP: 30 EST: 1986
SQ FT: 13,000
SALES (est): 21.7MM Privately Held
SIC: 2541 Counters or counter display cases, wood

(P-3323)
VIEW RITE MANUFACTURING
455 Allan St, Daly City (94014-1627)
PHONE...................................415 468-3856
Brad Somberg, *President*
Nha Nguyen, *Vice Pres*
EMP: 43 EST: 1969
SQ FT: 78,000
SALES (est): 2.9MM Privately Held
SIC: 2541 2542 Store fixtures, wood; fixtures, store: except wood

2542 Partitions & Fixtures, Except Wood

(P-3324)
EVOLV SURFACES INC
Also Called: Fox Marble & Granite
825 Potter St, Berkeley (94710-2745)
PHONE...................................415 767-4600
Charles McLaughlin, *President*
Bob Booth, *CFO*
Peter Wazna-Blank, *Vice Pres*
Debbie Smyser, *Executive Asst*
Jennifer Sexton, *Project Mgr*
▲ EMP: 122 EST: 1986
SALES (est): 19.6MM Privately Held
SIC: 2542 5032 Counters or counter display cases: except wood; marble building stone

(P-3325)
GALINDO INSTLLTION MVG SVCS IN
Also Called: G.I.M.S.
2901 Mariposa St Ste 3, San Francisco (94110-1339)
PHONE...................................415 861-4230
Wilfredo Galindo, *Owner*
Marjorie Lovell, *CEO*
Isaac Rios, *Manager*
EMP: 19 EST: 1995
SQ FT: 3,000
SALES (est): 2.8MM Privately Held
WEB: www.gims-sf.com
SIC: 2542 1799 7641 7389 Partitions for floor attachment, prefabricated: except wood; office furniture installation; office furniture repair & maintenance; relocation service; moving services

(P-3326)
GLOBAL STEEL PRODUCTS CORP
Also Called: Global Specialties Direct
936 61st St, Oakland (94608-1307)
PHONE...................................510 652-2060
Steve Allen, *Manager*
Kevin Ashbey, *General Mgr*
Dustin Lippincott, *General Mgr*
Stephanie Contreras, *Project Mgr*
Mario Hernandez, *Project Mgr*
EMP: 37
SQ FT: 13,600
SALES (corp-wide): 232.6MM Privately Held
WEB: www.specialtiesdirect.com
SIC: 2542 5023 5021 5046 Partitions for floor attachment, prefabricated: except wood; home furnishings; furniture; partitions
HQ: Global Steel Products Corp
95 Marcus Blvd
Deer Park NY 11729
631 586-3455

(P-3327)
JOHNS FORMICA INC
Also Called: John's Formica Shop
2439 Piner Rd, Santa Rosa (95403-2356)
PHONE...................................707 544-8585
John Deas, *President*
Ellen Deas, *Vice Pres*
EMP: 29 EST: 1966
SQ FT: 4,500
SALES (est): 5.6MM Privately Held
WEB: www.johnsformicashop.com
SIC: 2542 2434 Counters or counter display cases: except wood; wood kitchen cabinets

(P-3328)
ONQ SOLUTIONS INC (PA)
24540 Clawiter Rd, Hayward (94545-2222)
PHONE...................................650 262-4150
Paul Chapuis, *President*
Alan Garrison, *CFO*
Jack Lester, *CFO*
Laura Metz, *Vice Pres*
Andrew Purchase, *Creative Dir*
EMP: 28 EST: 2007
SQ FT: 1,700
SALES (est): 8.1MM Privately Held
WEB: www.onqsolutions.com
SIC: 2542 Stands, merchandise display: except wood

(P-3329)
TEAMMATE BUILDERS INC
Also Called: Formatop
281 E Mcglincy Ln Frnt, Campbell (95008-4946)
P.O. Box 901 (95009-0901)
PHONE...................................408 377-9000
Toll Free:...888 -
Gary Eagan, *President*
EMP: 16 EST: 1976
SQ FT: 12,000
SALES (est): 3.1MM Privately Held
SIC: 2542 Counters or counter display cases: except wood

2591 Drapery Hardware, Window Blinds & Shades

(P-3330)
BYTHEWAYS MANUFACTURING INC
Also Called: B T W
2080 Enterprise Blvd, West Sacramento (95691-5051)
PHONE...................................916 453-1212
Mervin Bytheway Jr, *President*
Jann Bytheway, *Corp Secy*
EMP: 88 EST: 1958
SALES (est): 17.4MM Privately Held
WEB: www.hunterdouglasgroup.com
SIC: 2591 Drapery hardware & blinds & shades
HQ: Hunter Douglas N.V.
Piekstraat 2
Rotterdam 3071
104 869-911

(P-3331)
HUNTER DOUGLAS FABRICATIONS
Also Called: Win-Glo Window Coverings
842 Charcot Ave, San Jose (95131-2210)
PHONE...................................408 435-8844
Jerry Fuchs, *President*
Ajit Mehra, *Treasurer*
Steve Pirylis, *Vice Pres*
Tom Hill, *Admin Sec*
Chand Amit, *Administration*
EMP: 203 EST: 1930
SQ FT: 76,000
SALES (est): 12.1MM Privately Held
WEB: www.hunterdouglasgroup.com
SIC: 2591 Window blinds; blinds vertical; venetian blinds; window shades
HQ: Hunter Douglas N.V.
Piekstraat 2
Rotterdam 3071
104 869-911

(P-3332)
MILLERTON BUILDERS INC
Also Called: Vinyl Specialties
4714 E Home Ave, Fresno (93703-4509)
PHONE...................................559 252-0490
Frank Spencer, *President*
Matthew Carlton, *Treasurer*
Matt Carlton, *Corp Secy*
EMP: 18 EST: 2001
SQ FT: 20,000
SALES (est): 2.7MM Privately Held
WEB: www.pandjwindowcoverings.com
SIC: 2591 Drapery hardware & blinds & shades

2599 Furniture & Fixtures, NEC

(P-3333)
ACCENT MANUFACTURING INC
105 Leavesley Rd Bldg 3d, Gilroy (95020-3688)
PHONE...................................408 846-9993
Joe Catanzaro, *President*
Esther Catanzaro, *Corp Secy*
Frank Catanzaro, *Vice Pres*
EMP: 37 EST: 1963
SQ FT: 30,000

2599 - Furniture & Fixtures, NEC County (P-3334)

PRODUCTS & SERVICES SECTION

SALES (est): 1.1MM **Privately Held**
WEB: www.accentmfg.com
SIC: **2599** 2431 5031 2434 Cabinets, factory; doors & door parts & trim, wood; lumber, plywood & millwork; wood kitchen cabinets

(P-3334)
AFN SERVICES LLC
Also Called: Socialight, The
368 E Campbell Ave, Campbell (95008-2029)
PHONE..................................408 364-1564
EMP: 40
SQ FT: 2,200
SALES: 250K **Privately Held**
SIC: **2599** 5813 7929 Mfg Furniture/Fixtures Drinking Place Entertainer/Entertainment Group

(P-3335)
DIVISADERO 500 LLC
Also Called: Madrone Art Bar
502 Divisadero St, San Francisco (94117-2213)
PHONE..................................415 572-6062
Michael J Krouse, *President*
EMP: 16 EST: 2009
SALES (est): 403K **Privately Held**
WEB: www.madroneartbar.com
SIC: **2599** Bar, restaurant & cafeteria furniture

(P-3336)
ELB US INC
Also Called: Elb Global
415 Boulder Ct Ste 500, Pleasanton (94566-8322)
PHONE..................................925 400-6175
Damian Bolton, *President*
Allison Bolton, *Vice Pres*
Jeff Schultz, *Vice Pres*
Denese Callen, *Office Mgr*
Leticia Magdaleno, *Project Mgr*
▲ EMP: 42 EST: 2012
SALES: 24MM **Privately Held**
WEB: www.elb.com.au
SIC: **5999** 2599 3651 8742 Audio-visual equipment & supplies; factory furniture & fixtures; audio electronic systems; construction project management consultant

(P-3337)
MAD OAK BAR AND YARD
Also Called: Mad Oak
135 12th St, Oakland (94607-4905)
PHONE..................................510 924-2047
EMP: 19 EST: 2015
SALES (est): 370.1K **Privately Held**
WEB: www.madoakbar.com
SIC: **2599** Bar, restaurant & cafeteria furniture

(P-3338)
RIVER CITY
Also Called: River City Restaurant
505 Lincoln Ave, NAPA (94558-3610)
P.O. Box 2553 (94558-0255)
PHONE..................................707 253-1111
Assaad Barazi, *President*
Cordia Losh, *Vice Pres*
EMP: 20 EST: 1983
SQ FT: 6,000
SALES (est): 1.3MM **Privately Held**
SIC: **2599** 5812 Bar, restaurant & cafeteria furniture; eating places

(P-3339)
ROTH WOOD PRODUCTS LTD
2260 Canoas Garden Ave, San Jose (95125-2007)
PHONE..................................408 723-8888
Robert E Roth, *CEO*
Marilyn Roth, *Treasurer*
EMP: 33 EST: 1974
SQ FT: 12,800
SALES (est): 3.6MM **Privately Held**
WEB: www.rothwoodproducts.com
SIC: **2599** 2434 Cabinets, factory; wood kitchen cabinets

2611 Pulp Mills

(P-3340)
CENCAL RECYCLING LLC
501 Port Road 22, Stockton (95203-2909)
PHONE..................................209 546-8000
Steve Sutta, *Mng Member*
EMP: 16 EST: 2004
SQ FT: 104,400
SALES (est): 2.2MM **Privately Held**
WEB: www.cencalrecycling.com
SIC: **2611** Pulp mills, mechanical & recycling processing

(P-3341)
EVERGREEN PAPER AND ENERGY LLC (PA)
Also Called: Evergreen-Energy
353 Rio Del Oro Ln, Sacramento (95825-6311)
PHONE..................................802 357-1003
Ronald J Morgan,
JD McBride, *Vice Pres*
EMP: 64
SALES (est): 3.7MM **Privately Held**
SIC: **2611** 2621 Pulp mills; paper mills

2621 Paper Mills

(P-3342)
BOISE CASCADE COMPANY
12030 S Harlan Rd, Lathrop (95330-8768)
PHONE..................................209 983-4114
Brad Terrell, *Branch Mgr*
Kim Jackson, *Consultant*
EMP: 49
SALES (corp-wide): 5.4B **Publicly Held**
WEB: www.bc.com
SIC: **2621** 2679 Paper mills; building paper, laminated; made from purchased material
PA: Boise Cascade Company
1111 W Jefferson St # 100
Boise ID 83702
208 384-6161

(P-3343)
DOCUMENT PROC SOLUTIONS INC
535 Main St Ste 317, Martinez (94553-1102)
PHONE..................................925 839-1182
EMP: 44
SALES (corp-wide): 9.5MM **Privately Held**
WEB: www.dpsx.com
SIC: **2621** Paper mills
PA: Document Processing Solutions, Inc.
590 W Lambert Rd
Brea CA 92821
714 482-2060

(P-3344)
ENVELOPE PRODUCTS CO
Also Called: Epco
2882 W Cromwell Ave, Fresno (93711-0353)
PHONE..................................925 939-5173
Alex Macdonald, *Chairman*
Darlene Macdonald, *President*
Janine Eldred, *Vice Pres*
EMP: 26 EST: 1967
SQ FT: 23,000
SALES (est): 2.1MM **Privately Held**
SIC: **2621** 2761 Envelope paper; manifold business forms

(P-3345)
METHOD HOME PRODUCTS
631 Howard St Fl 5, San Francisco (94105-3934)
PHONE..................................415 568-4600
Steve Jurvetson, *Owner*
Jeremy Bruno, *Vice Pres*
Garry Embleton, *Vice Pres*
Hank Mercier, *Vice Pres*
Justin Penrod, *Vice Pres*
EMP: 15 EST: 2011
SALES (est): 1.6MM **Privately Held**
SIC: **2621** Cleansing paper

(P-3346)
NAKAGAWA MANUFACTURING USA INC
8652 Thornton Ave, Newark (94560-3330)
PHONE..................................510 782-0197
Yuzuru Isshiki, *CEO*
Shinji Aoki, *President*
Tetsuya Isshiki, *President*
Teppei Tokura, *Controller*
Azusa Imai, *Sales Mgr*
◆ EMP: 40 EST: 1987
SQ FT: 40,000
SALES (est): 10.1MM **Privately Held**
WEB: www.nakagawa-usa.com
SIC: **2621** Specialty papers
HQ: Nakagawa Mfg.Co., Ltd.
2-5-21, Nishikicho
Warabi STM 335-0

(P-3347)
NOVACART (DH)
Also Called: Novacart USA
512 W Ohio Ave, Richmond (94804-2040)
P.O. Box 70579 (94807-0579)
PHONE..................................510 215-8999
Toll Free:..................................877
Giorgio Angahileri, *President*
Jennifer Bleasdale, *Admin Asst*
Guadalupe Gonzalez, *Accounting Mgr*
Joe Miglia, *Human Res Mgr*
Terry Schepper, *Prdtn Mgr*
◆ EMP: 33 EST: 1985
SQ FT: 35,000
SALES (est): 7MM
SALES (corp-wide): 116.4K **Privately Held**
WEB: www.novacartusa.com
SIC: **2621** Molded pulp products
HQ: Novacart Spa
Via Europa 1
Garbagnate Monastero LC
031 858-611

(P-3348)
PPS PACKAGING COMPANY
Also Called: Continental Enterprises
3189 E Manning Ave, Fowler (93625-9749)
P.O. Box 427 (93625-0427)
PHONE..................................559 834-1641
▲ EMP: 75
SQ FT: 108,000
SALES (est): 18.9MM **Privately Held**
WEB: www.ppspackaging.com
SIC: **2621** Paper Mill Mfg Pharmaceutical Preparations

(P-3349)
PRATT INDUSTRIES INC
2131 E Louise Ave, Lathrop (95330-9607)
PHONE..................................770 922-0117
Ron McComas, *General Mgr*
Renita Culp, *Controller*
EMP: 110 **Privately Held**
WEB: www.prattindustries.com
SIC: **2621** Packaging paper
PA: Pratt Industries, Inc.
1800 Sarasot Bus Pkwy Ne S
Conyers GA 30013

2631 Paperboard Mills

(P-3350)
BUZZ CONVERTING INC
4343 E Fremont St, Stockton (95215-4032)
PHONE..................................209 948-1341
Merlin Davis Jr, *President*
Jeff Vandan Baum, *General Mgr*
EMP: 38 EST: 2001
SQ FT: 35,000
SALES (est): 677.2K **Privately Held**
WEB: www.pacificpapertube.com
SIC: **2631** Chip board

(P-3351)
MAXCO SUPPLY INC
2059 E Olsen Ave, Reedley (93654)
P.O. Box 814, Parlier (93648-0814)
PHONE..................................559 638-8449
Roy Ortega, *Manager*
EMP: 65
SQ FT: 50,550
SALES (corp-wide): 72.1MM **Privately Held**
WEB: www.maxcopackaging.com
SIC: **2631** Cardboard
PA: Maxco Supply, Inc.
605 S Zediker Ave
Parlier CA 93648
559 646-8449

2652 Set-Up Paperboard Boxes

(P-3352)
CUSTOM PAPER PRODUCTS LP
2360 Teagarden St, San Leandro (94577-4341)
PHONE..................................510 352-6880
Robert W Field Jr, *President*
Frank Leyva, *COO*
Blake Field, *Vice Pres*
Joseph Hurst, *Sales Mgr*
Cameron Field, *Sales Staff*
EMP: 70 EST: 1950
SQ FT: 100,000
SALES (est): 8.1MM **Privately Held**
WEB: www.custompaperproducts.com
SIC: **2652** 3089 Filing boxes, paperboard: made from purchased materials; boxes, plastic

2653 Corrugated & Solid Fiber Boxes

(P-3353)
BAYCORR PACKAGING LLC (PA)
Also Called: Heritage Paper Co
6850 Brisa St, Livermore (94550-2521)
P.O. Box 44441, San Francisco (94144-0001)
PHONE..................................925 449-1148
John Tatum, *CEO*
Richard Heinz, *President*
Iris Romero, *Human Res Mgr*
▲ EMP: 130 EST: 1986
SQ FT: 129,000
SALES (est): 31.6MM **Privately Held**
WEB: www.heritagesolutions.com
SIC: **2653** 5113 Boxes, corrugated: made from purchased materials; corrugated & solid fiber boxes

(P-3354)
CAL SHEETS LLC
1212 Performance Dr, Stockton (95206-4925)
P.O. Box 30370 (95213-0370)
PHONE..................................209 234-3300
Rick Goddard, *CEO*
Scott Sherman, *President*
Pete Brodie, *CFO*
Joe Escobar, *Mng Member*
◆ EMP: 68 EST: 1998
SQ FT: 203,000
SALES (est): 17.4MM
SALES (corp-wide): 317.1MM **Privately Held**
WEB: www.calsheets.com
SIC: **2653** Boxes, corrugated: made from purchased materials
PA: Golden West Packaging Group Llc
15400 Don Julian Rd
City Of Industry CA 91745
888 501-5893

(P-3355)
CAPITAL CORRUGATED LLC
Also Called: Capital Corrugated and Carton
8333 24th Ave, Sacramento (95826-4809)
P.O. Box 278060 (95827-8060)
PHONE..................................916 388-7848
Dennis D Watson, *President*
Jackson Angle, *Vice Pres*
Tom Wynne, *General Mgr*
Robert Lawson, *Technician*
John Dabney, *Sales Staff*
▲ EMP: 80 EST: 1995
SQ FT: 124,000

▲ = Import ▼=Export
◆ =Import/Export

PRODUCTS & SERVICES SECTION

2671 - Paper Coating & Laminating for Packaging County (P-3376)

SALES (est): 25.2MM
SALES (corp-wide): 317.1MM **Privately Held**
WEB: www.capitalcorrugated.com
SIC: 2653 Boxes, corrugated: made from purchased materials; display items, corrugated: made from purchased materials; sheets, corrugated: made from purchased materials; partitions, corrugated: made from purchased materials
PA: Golden West Packaging Group Llc
15400 Don Julian Rd
City Of Industry CA 91745
888 501-5893

(P-3356)
COMPRO PACKAGING LLC
Also Called: Bayline
1600 Atlantic St, Union City (94587-2017)
PHONE 510 475-0118
Michael Ramelot, *President*
John Roberts, *Ch of Bd*
Donald Cook, *Vice Pres*
EMP: 21 EST: 1998
SQ FT: 75,000
SALES (est): 425.2K **Privately Held**
SIC: 2653 2679 5113 Boxes, corrugated: made from purchased materials; corrugated paper: made from purchased material; industrial & personal service paper

(P-3357)
CORRUGATED PACKAGING PDTS INC
21615 Hesperian Blvd B, Hayward (94541-7026)
PHONE 650 615-9180
Christopher Grandov, *President*
Linda Grandov, *Admin Sec*
EMP: 38 EST: 1960
SALES (est): 11.2MM **Privately Held**
SIC: 2653 2631 Corrugated & solid fiber boxes; paperboard mills

(P-3358)
CUSTOM PAD AND PARTITION INC
1100 Richard Ave, Santa Clara (95050-2800)
PHONE 408 970-9711
James L Jones, *CEO*
Janice Jones, *Treasurer*
Gil Pesqueira, *Vice Pres*
Gina Bence, *Cust Mgr*
EMP: 65
SQ FT: 60,000
SALES (est): 21.4MM **Privately Held**
WEB: www.custompad.com
SIC: 2653 Boxes, corrugated: made from purchased materials; partitions, corrugated: made from purchased materials

(P-3359)
MENASHA PACKAGING COMPANY LLC
1550 N Chrisman Rd, Tracy (95304-9396)
PHONE 951 660-5361
Esther Martinez, *Branch Mgr*
EMP: 20
SALES (corp-wide): 1.9B **Privately Held**
WEB: www.menasha.com
SIC: 2653 Boxes, corrugated: made from purchased materials
HQ: Menasha Packaging Company, Llc
1645 Bergstrom Rd
Neenah WI 54956
920 751-1000

(P-3360)
NEXGEN CONTAINER LLC
10576 N Old Course Dr, Fresno (93730-3581)
PHONE 916 716-8962
Bobby Marina, *CEO*
Christie Marina, *CFO*
EMP: 40 EST: 2019
SALES (est): 5.4MM **Privately Held**
WEB: www.ngcontainer.com
SIC: 2653 Corrugated & solid fiber boxes

(P-3361)
PACKAGEONE INC (PA)
Also Called: All West Container
401 S Granada Dr Ste 100, Madera (93637-5055)
P.O. Box 27095, San Francisco (94127-0095)
PHONE 559 662-1910
Richard Pfaff, *President*
Christopher Grandov, *Vice Pres*
▼ EMP: 43 EST: 1958
SQ FT: 129,000
SALES (est): 3.3MM **Privately Held**
SIC: 2653 Boxes, corrugated: made from purchased materials

(P-3362)
PACKAGING PLUS
3816 S Willow Ave Ste 102, Fresno (93725-9241)
PHONE 209 858-9200
Robert Crossman, *President*
Alecia Crossman, *Vice Pres*
Michelle Reid, *Opers Staff*
Tom Franz, *Sales Associate*
▲ EMP: 27 EST: 2001
SQ FT: 60,000
SALES (est): 3.9MM **Privately Held**
SIC: 2653 Sheets, corrugated: made from purchased materials

(P-3363)
PCA CENTRAL CAL CORRUGATED LLC
Also Called: Packaging America - Sacramento
4841 Urbani Ave, McClellan (95652-2025)
PHONE 916 614-0580
Bob Bruna, *General Mgr*
Machel Leroy, *Supervisor*
EMP: 29
SALES (corp-wide): 6.6B **Publicly Held**
WEB: www.packagingcorp.com
SIC: 2653 Boxes, corrugated: made from purchased materials
HQ: Pca Central California Corrugated, Llc
1955 W Field Ct
Lake Forest IL 60045
847 482-3000

(P-3364)
PK1 INC (HQ)
Also Called: American River Packaging
4225 Pell Dr, Sacramento (95838-2533)
PHONE 916 858-1300
Thomas Kandris, *CEO*
Ronald Frederick, *CFO*
Shanthe Hernandez, *Executive Asst*
Kelly Husted, *Credit Mgr*
Steve Farinelli, *Opers Mgr*
▲ EMP: 100 EST: 1980
SQ FT: 240,000
SALES (est): 31.1MM
SALES (corp-wide): 317.1MM **Privately Held**
WEB: www.package1.com
SIC: 2653 5113 4783 Boxes, corrugated: made from purchased materials; industrial & personal service paper; packing goods for shipping
PA: Golden West Packaging Group Llc
15400 Don Julian Rd
City Of Industry CA 91745
888 501-5893

(P-3365)
PRATT LATHROP CORRUGATING LLC
2131 E Louise Ave, Lathrop (95330-9607)
PHONE 209 670-0900
Brian McPheely, *CEO*
▲ EMP: 27 EST: 2017
SALES (est): 3.7MM **Privately Held**
SIC: 2653 Corrugated & solid fiber boxes

(P-3366)
SONOCO PRTECTIVE SOLUTIONS INC
3466 Enterprise Ave, Hayward (94545-3219)
PHONE 510 785-0220
Rob Hazelton, *Manager*
Dolores Odgers, *Executive*
Sanjay Maharaj, *Materials Mgr*
EMP: 60
SQ FT: 125,975
SALES (corp-wide): 5.2B **Publicly Held**
WEB: www.sonoco.com
SIC: 2653 3086 Boxes, corrugated: made from purchased materials; plastics foam products
HQ: Sonoco Protective Solutions, Inc.
1 N 2nd St
Hartsville SC 29550
843 383-7000

2655 Fiber Cans, Tubes & Drums

(P-3367)
ADMAIL WEST INC
800 N 10th St Ste F, Sacramento (95811-0342)
PHONE 916 554-5755
Mike Mc Bride, *Manager*
EMP: 95
SALES (corp-wide): 14.1MM **Privately Held**
WEB: www.admailwest.com
SIC: 2655 Fiber shipping & mailing containers
PA: Admail West, Inc.
4130 S Market Ct
Sacramento CA 95834
916 442-3613

(P-3368)
PACIFIC PAPER TUBE INC (PA)
4343 E Fremont St, Stockton (95215-4032)
PHONE 510 562-8823
Toll Free: .... 888 -
Patrick Wallace, *President*
Colleen Wallace, *Vice Pres*
Nancy Wallace, *Executive*
Todd Abram, *Sales Staff*
▲ EMP: 50 EST: 1989
SQ FT: 85,000
SALES (est): 38.9MM **Privately Held**
WEB: www.pacificpapertube.com
SIC: 2655 Tubes, fiber or paper: made from purchased material

2656 Sanitary Food Containers

(P-3369)
PACKAGING EQUITY HOLDINGS LLC
2334 M St Ste 2893, Merced (95340-9921)
PHONE 209 404-9553
Alex Millar, *CEO*
David Lawrence, *Manager*
EMP: 285
SALES (est): 75MM **Privately Held**
SIC: 2656 Sanitary food containers

2657 Folding Paperboard Boxes

(P-3370)
CRAFTON CARTON
31790 Hayman St, Hayward (94544-7934)
P.O. Box 3644 (94540-3644)
PHONE 510 441-5985
Glenn Boatley, *President*
Diane Boatley, *Vice Pres*
EMP: 25 EST: 1987
SQ FT: 20,000
SALES (est): 1.2MM **Privately Held**
WEB: www.sierrapack.com
SIC: 2657 Folding paperboard boxes

(P-3371)
EVERETT GRAPHICS INC
7300 Edgewater Dr, Oakland (94621-3006)
PHONE 510 577-6777
Munson Wittman Everett, *President*
Mark Carlson, *CFO*
John F Everett, *Vice Pres*
John Schikora, *Executive*
Alicia Bass, *Planning*
▲ EMP: 75 EST: 1980
SQ FT: 100,000
SALES (est): 25.6MM **Privately Held**
WEB: www.everettgraphics.com
SIC: 2657 Folding paperboard boxes

(P-3372)
GOLDEN W PPR CONVERTING CORP
2480 Grant Ave, San Lorenzo (94580-1808)
PHONE 510 317-0646
Shirley Hooi, *President*
David Hooi, *Vice Pres*
Henry Hooi, *Principal*
Kevin Miller, *Technology*
Michelle Walker, *Manager*
▼ EMP: 26 EST: 1984
SQ FT: 42,000
SALES (est): 9.1MM **Privately Held**
SIC: 2657 3565 Folding paperboard boxes; carton packing machines

2671 Paper Coating & Laminating for Packaging

(P-3373)
AIRVAPOR LLC
Also Called: Air Vapor System
200 Mason Cir, Concord (94520-1249)
PHONE 925 405-5582
Peter Hackett, *Principal*
EMP: 19 EST: 2016
SQ FT: 4,500
SALES (est): 5.6MM **Privately Held**
WEB: www.airvapor.com
SIC: 2671 5999 Packaging paper & plastics film, coated & laminated; electronic parts & equipment

(P-3374)
AMCOR FLEXIBLES LLC
5425 Broadway St, American Canyon (94503-9678)
PHONE 707 257-6481
Richard Evans, *Branch Mgr*
Rito Delgadillo, *General Mgr*
Brad Philip, *Engineer*
Hector N Nunez, *Accountant*
Alphonsine Viry, *Human Res Mgr*
EMP: 135
SALES (corp-wide): 12.4B **Privately Held**
SIC: 2671 2621 2821 3081 Plastic film, coated or laminated for packaging; packaging paper; plastics materials & resins; packing materials, plastic sheet; closures, stamped metal
HQ: Amcor Flexibles Llc
2150 E Lake Cook Rd
Buffalo Grove IL 60089
224 313-7000

(P-3375)
MARIANI PACKING PARTNERSHIP LP
500 Crocker Dr, Vacaville (95688-8706)
PHONE 707 452-2864
Mark A Mariani, *President*
EMP: 22 EST: 2002
SALES (est): 558.4K **Privately Held**
WEB: www.mariani.com
SIC: 2671 Packaging paper & plastics film, coated & laminated

(P-3376)
MICHELSEN PACKAGING CO CAL
Also Called: Michelsen Packaging California
4165 S Cherry Ave, Fresno (93706-5709)
P.O. Box 10109 (93745-0109)
PHONE 559 237-3819
Dan Keck, *President*
Chad Gregerson, *General Mgr*
Jason Cline, *Plant Mgr*
EMP: 31
SALES (corp-wide): 74.6MM **Privately Held**
WEB: www.michelsenpackaging.com
SIC: 2671 2674 Packaging paper & plastics film, coated & laminated; paper bags: made from purchased materials

2671 - Paper Coating & Laminating for Packaging County (P-3377)

PA: Michelsen Packaging Company Of California
202 N 2nd Ave
Yakima WA 98902
509 248-6270

(P-3377)
PACIFIC SOUTHWEST CONT LLC (PA)
4530 Leckron Rd, Modesto (95357-0517)
PHONE.................................209 526-0444
John W Mayol, *Mng Member*
Lester H Mangold, *CFO*
Darin Jones, *Exec VP*
Bryan Smith, *Exec VP*
Troy Carroll, *Planning*
▲ **EMP:** 347
SQ FT: 129,600
SALES (est): 143.5MM Privately Held
WEB: www.teampsc.com
SIC: 2671 2657 3086 2653 Packaging paper & plastics film, coated & laminated; folding paperboard boxes; packaging & shipping materials, foamed plastic; boxes, corrugated: made from purchased materials; commercial printing, lithographic

(P-3378)
PACIFIC SOUTHWEST CONT LLC
671 Mariposa Rd, Modesto (95354-4145)
PHONE.................................209 526-0444
EMP: 44
SALES (corp-wide): 143.5MM Privately Held
WEB: www.teampsc
SIC: 2671 2657 3086 2653 Packaging paper & plastics film, coated & laminated; folding paperboard boxes; packaging & shipping materials, foamed plastic; boxes, corrugated: made from purchased materials; commercial printing, lithographic
PA: Pacific Southwest Container, Llc
4530 Leckron Rd
Modesto CA 95357
209 526-0444

(P-3379)
SHIP SMART INC
783 Rio Del Mar Blvd Frnt # 9, Aptos (95003-4702)
PHONE.................................831 661-4841
John Kessler, *President*
Carole-Anne Kessler, *Treasurer*
Matt Jarrell, *Sales Mgr*
Mitchell Lardie,
Nick Rivera,
EMP: 25 **EST:** 1999
SQ FT: 1,200
SALES (est): 13.4MM Privately Held
WEB: www.shipsmart.com
SIC: 2671 4783 Packaging paper & plastics film, coated & laminated; packing goods for shipping

(P-3380)
TAN PACKAGING LLC
3527 Mt Diablo Blvd Ste 2, Lafayette (94549-3815)
PHONE.................................800 237-1009
Joseph Tulley II,
EMP: 32 **EST:** 2019
SALES (est): 1.5MM Privately Held
SIC: 2671 2679 3086 3544 Packaging paper & plastics film, coated & laminated; resinous impregnated paper for packaging; thermoplastic coated paper for packaging; paper coated or laminated for packaging; building, insulating & packaging paper; building, insulating & packaging paperboard; packaging & shipping materials, foamed plastic; dies, plastics forming; packing materials, plastic sheet; packaging materials

2672 Paper Coating & Laminating, Exc for Packaging

(P-3381)
NITTO AMERICAS INC (HQ)
Also Called: Permacel-Automotive
101 Metro Dr, San Jose (95110-1314)
PHONE.................................510 445-5400
Toru Takeuchi, *Ch of Bd*
Yoichiro Sakuma, *President*
Steve Evans, *CFO*
William Stowell, *CFO*
Bob Vath, *Info Tech Dir*
◆ **EMP:** 125 **EST:** 2018
SALES (est): 627MM Privately Held
WEB: www.nitto.co.jp
SIC: 2672 3589 5162 5065 Tape, pressure sensitive: made from purchased materials; water treatment equipment, industrial; plastics products; electronic parts

(P-3382)
VINTAGE 99 LABEL MFG INC (PA)
611 Enterprise Ct, Livermore (94550-5200)
PHONE.................................925 294-5270
Mark Gonzales, *CEO*
James Courtney, *President*
Kathy Gonzales, *President*
Gary Cane, *Vice Pres*
Samantha Gomez, *Creative Dir*
EMP: 20 **EST:** 1998
SALES (est): 6.9MM Privately Held
WEB: www.vintage99.com
SIC: 2672 2752 Labels (unprinted), gummed: made from purchased materials; commercial printing, lithographic

2673 Bags: Plastics, Laminated & Coated

(P-3383)
CLEAR IMAGE INC (PA)
Also Called: Clearbags
4949 Windplay Dr Ste 100, El Dorado Hills (95762-9318)
PHONE.................................916 933-4700
Benny Dyal Wilkins, *President*
Laura Wilkins, *Admin Sec*
Aaron Johnson, *Administration*
Kirsten Westvik, *Technology*
Ben Wilkins, *Controller*
◆ **EMP:** 40 **EST:** 1992
SQ FT: 35,000
SALES (est): 14.3MM Privately Held
WEB: www.clearbags.com
SIC: 2673 5112 Bags: plastic, laminated & coated; envelopes

(P-3384)
HIGH TEK USA INC
12420 Gold Flake Ct, Rancho Cordova (95742-6900)
PHONE.................................800 504-7120
Jason Sigman, *President*
Teresa Moody, *Office Mgr*
EMP: 16 **EST:** 2004
SALES (est): 10.1MM Privately Held
WEB: www.hightekusa.com
SIC: 2673 Food storage & frozen food bags, plastic

(P-3385)
METRO POLY CORPORATION
1651 Aurora Dr, San Leandro (94577-3101)
PHONE.................................510 357-9898
Peter Kung, *Principal*
Jean Lo, *Office Mgr*
Julie MA, *Representative*
▲ **EMP:** 48 **EST:** 1990
SQ FT: 40,000
SALES: 17.6MM Privately Held
WEB: www.metropolybag.com
SIC: 2673 Plastic bags: made from purchased materials

(P-3386)
PRINTPACK INC
5870 Stnrdge Mall Rd Ste, Pleasanton (94588)
PHONE.................................925 469-0601
Doug Brow, *Manager*
Terri Moss, *Planning*
Abelino Gonzalez, *Business Mgr*
Bill Roper, *Plant Mgr*
EMP: 62
SALES (corp-wide): 1.3B Privately Held
WEB: www.printpack.com
SIC: 2673 3081 Bags: plastic, laminated & coated; plastic film & sheet
HQ: Printpack, Inc.
2800 Overlook Pkwy Ne
Atlanta GA 30339
404 460-7000

(P-3387)
ROPLAST INDUSTRIES INC
3155 S 5th Ave, Oroville (95965-5858)
PHONE.................................530 532-9500
Robert Berman, *Chairman*
Robert Bateman, *President*
Roxanne Spiekerman, *Exec VP*
Tommy Briggs, *Executive*
Douglas Smith, *Engineer*
◆ **EMP:** 164 **EST:** 1989
SQ FT: 160,000
SALES (est): 12.1MM
SALES (corp-wide): 502.7MM Privately Held
WEB: www.prezero.us
SIC: 2673 5199 Plastic bags: made from purchased materials; packaging materials
HQ: Prezero Us, Inc.
2301 E 7th St Ste A337
Los Angeles CA 90023
858 677-0884

(P-3388)
SIUS PRODUCTS AND DISTR INC (PA)
700 Kevin Ct, Oakland (94621-4040)
PHONE.................................510 382-1700
Kuai Cheong Siu, *CEO*
Peter Siu, *Vice Pres*
▲ **EMP:** 15 **EST:** 1980
SQ FT: 45,000
SALES (est): 2.8MM Privately Held
SIC: 2673 Plastic bags: made from purchased materials

(P-3389)
UNI POLY INC
2040 Williams St, San Leandro (94577-2306)
PHONE.................................510 357-9898
Alex Eduardo, *Manager*
EMP: 18
SALES (corp-wide): 8.7MM Privately Held
WEB: www.metropolybag.com
SIC: 2673 Plastic & pliofilm bags
PA: Uni Poly, Inc.
1651 Aurora Dr
San Leandro CA 94577
510 357-9898

2674 Bags: Uncoated Paper & Multiwall

(P-3390)
ACME BAG CO INC (PA)
Also Called: California Bag
440 N Pioneer Ave Ste 300, Woodland (95776-6139)
PHONE.................................530 662-6130
David Rosenberg, *CEO*
Paresh Shah, *General Mgr*
Gary Malkin, *Sales Mgr*
◆ **EMP:** 15 **EST:** 1923
SQ FT: 40,000
SALES (est): 1.6MM Privately Held
SIC: 2674 5199 5191 2673 Bags: uncoated paper & multiwall; bags, textile; greenhouse equipment & supplies; bags: plastic, laminated & coated; textile bags; broadwoven fabric mills, cotton

(P-3391)
PETER
Also Called: Shlbao Distributors
2850 Gateway Oaks Dr, Sacramento (95833-4347)
PHONE.................................916 588-9954
EMP: 30 **EST:** 2020
SALES (est): 1.2MM Privately Held
SIC: 2674 Shipping & shopping bags or sacks

(P-3392)
ROMEO PACKING COMPANY
106 Princeton Ave, Half Moon Bay (94019-4035)
PHONE.................................650 728-3393
Charles Romeo, *President*
Frank Romeo, *Treasurer*
Joey Romeo, *Vice Pres*
Constance Romeo, *Admin Sec*
EMP: 22 **EST:** 1947
SQ FT: 40,000
SALES (est): 6.6MM Privately Held
WEB: www.romeopacking.com
SIC: 2674 2873 Paper bags: made from purchased materials; fertilizers: natural (organic), except compost

2675 Die-Cut Paper & Board

(P-3393)
APEX DIE CORPORATION
840 Cherry Ln, San Carlos (94070-3394)
PHONE.................................650 592-6350
Thomas J Cullen, *Chairman*
Kevin Cullen, *President*
Eva Cummings, *CFO*
Chris J Cullen, *Vice Pres*
Judy Grilli, *Accountant*
EMP: 55 **EST:** 1956
SQ FT: 33,800
SALES (est): 6.8MM Privately Held
WEB: www.apexdie.com
SIC: 2675 2759 2672 Die-cut paper & board; embossing on paper; coated & laminated paper

(P-3394)
IMPERIAL DIE CUTTING INC
300 N 12th St, Sacramento (95811-0510)
PHONE.................................916 443-6142
Brent Rabe, *President*
Jennifer Rabe, *Vice Pres*
EMP: 35 **EST:** 1991
SALES (est): 4.7MM Privately Held
WEB: www.imperialtradebindery.com
SIC: 2675 3469 2759 Die-cut paper & board; metal stampings; commercial printing

2676 Sanitary Paper Prdts

(P-3395)
JOHNSON & JOHNSON
3509 Langdon Cmn, Fremont (94538-5403)
PHONE.................................650 237-4878
Phil Palin, *Principal*
Diane Panos, *Project Mgr*
Beth Hill, *Research*
EMP: 80
SALES (corp-wide): 82.5B Publicly Held
WEB: www.jnj.com
SIC: 2676 Feminine hygiene paper products
PA: Johnson & Johnson
1 Johnson And Johnson Plz
New Brunswick NJ 08933
732 524-0400

(P-3396)
KAS DIRECT LLC
Also Called: Babyganics
637 Commercial St Fl 3, San Francisco (94111-6515)
PHONE.................................516 934-0541
Kevin Schwartz, *CEO*
Mark Ellis, *CFO*
Robin Forbes, *Vice Pres*
EMP: 50 **EST:** 2008

PRODUCTS & SERVICES SECTION   **2711 - Newspapers: Publishing & Printing County (P-3418)**

SALES (est): 16MM
SALES (corp-wide): 1.1B **Privately Held**
WEB: www.babyganics.com
SIC: 2676 Infant & baby paper products
PA: S. C. Johnson & Son, Inc.
1525 Howe St
Racine WI 53403
262 260-2000

2677 Envelopes

(P-3397)
CLEANSMART SOLUTIONS INC
Also Called: San Francisco Envelope
47422 Kato Rd, Fremont (94538-7319)
PHONE.................................650 871-9123
Don Clark, *Branch Mgr*
EMP: 25
SALES (corp-wide): 1.3B **Privately Held**
WEB: www.kellyspicers.com
SIC: 2677 Envelopes
HQ: Cleansmart Solutions Inc.
47422 Kato Rd
Fremont CA 94538
510 413-4700

(P-3398)
GOLDEN WEST ENVELOPE CORP
1009 Morton St, Alameda (94501-3904)
PHONE.................................510 452-5419
Raymond Mazur, *President*
Gert Mazur, *Vice Pres*
EMP: 25
SQ FT: 17,000
SALES (est): 1MM **Privately Held**
WEB: www.goldenwestenvelope.com
SIC: 2677 2752 Envelopes; commercial printing, offset

2678 Stationery Prdts

(P-3399)
MRS GROSSMANS PAPER COMPANY
Also Called: Paragon Label
3810 Cypress Dr, Petaluma (94954-5613)
PHONE.................................707 763-1700
Fax: 707 763-7121
▲ EMP: 100 EST: 1975
SQ FT: 11,000
SALES (est): 22.9MM **Privately Held**
WEB: www.paragonlabel.com
SIC: 2678 2679 2759 2752 Mfg Stationery Products Mfg Converted Paper Prdt Commercial Printing Lithographic Coml Print

2679 Converted Paper Prdts, NEC

(P-3400)
A A LABEL INC (PA)
Also Called: All American Label
6958 Sierra Ct, Dublin (94568-2641)
PHONE.................................925 803-5709
Bradley Brown, *CEO*
Cynthia Brown, *Vice Pres*
Kristina Garrett, *Business Dir*
Marci Hector, *Sales Staff*
Dionne Henderson, *Manager*
▲ EMP: 22 EST: 1995
SQ FT: 25,000
SALES (est): 16.5MM **Privately Held**
WEB: www.allamericanlabel.net
SIC: 2679 Labels, paper: made from purchased material

(P-3401)
FLEENOR COMPANY INC (PA)
Also Called: Fleenor Paper Company
2225 Harbor Bay Pkwy, Alameda (94502-3026)
P.O. Box 14438, Oakland (94614-2438)
PHONE.................................800 433-2531
Rebecca Fleenor, *President*
Ramon Cazares, *COO*
Janine Rochex, *CFO*
Corina Rochex, *Vice Pres*
Kirk Kahler, *Area Mgr*
◆ EMP: 40 EST: 1962
SALES (est): 41.5MM **Privately Held**
WEB: www.fleenorpaper.com
SIC: 2679 Paper products, converted; paperboard products, converted

(P-3402)
LABEL TECHNOLOGY INC
2050 Wardrobe Ave, Merced (95341-6409)
PHONE.................................209 384-1000
Dennis Deisenroth, *Vice Pres*
Dale Reschenberg, *VP Mfg*
Ginger Ikeda, *Sales Staff*
Levi Roberts, *Sales Staff*
Richard Sanchez, *Manager*
EMP: 31 EST: 2019
SALES (est): 9.5MM **Privately Held**
WEB: www.fortissolutionsgroup.com
SIC: 2679 Labels, paper: made from purchased material

(P-3403)
NATIONAL RECYCLING CORPORATION
1312 Kirkham St, Oakland (94607-2257)
PHONE.................................510 268-1022
Richard Wang, *President*
▼ EMP: 30 EST: 1985
SQ FT: 80,000
SALES (est): 1.9MM **Privately Held**
WEB: www.nationalrecycle.com
SIC: 2679 4953 Paper products, converted; recycling, waste materials

(P-3404)
PAPER PULP & FILM
Also Called: Fresno Paper Express
2822 S Maple Ave, Fresno (93725-2207)
PHONE.................................559 233-1151
G Carol Jones, *CEO*
Tal Cloud, *President*
Meredith Orman, *Admin Sec*
▲ EMP: 40 EST: 1986
SQ FT: 120,000
SALES (est): 10K **Privately Held**
WEB: www.paperconverter.com
SIC: 2679 4213 Wrappers, paper (unprinted): made from purchased material; heavy hauling

(P-3405)
SACHS INDUSTRIES INC
Also Called: Custom Label
801 Kate Ln, Woodland (95776-5733)
PHONE.................................631 242-9000
EMP: 18
SQ FT: 12,000
SALES (est): 2.3MM **Privately Held**
SIC: 2679 5113 Mfg Converted Paper Products Whol Industrial/Service Paper

(P-3406)
SUNRISE MFG INC (PA)
2665 Mercantile Dr, Rancho Cordova (95742-6521)
PHONE.................................916 635-6262
James Sewell, *CEO*
Matt Sewell, *Vice Pres*
Jessica Morris, *Office Mgr*
Teri Bradley, *CTO*
Susan Wilson, *Bookkeeper*
◆ EMP: 25 EST: 1981
SQ FT: 72,000
SALES (est): 15.1MM **Privately Held**
WEB: www.sunrisemfg.com
SIC: 2679 Building, insulating & packaging paper

(P-3407)
TAB LABEL INC
21 Hegenberger Ct, Oakland (94621-1321)
P.O. Box 6266 (94603-0266)
PHONE.................................510 638-4411
EMP: 17
SQ FT: 11,000
SALES (est): 223.8K **Privately Held**
WEB: www.tablabel.com
SIC: 2679 Mfg Pressure Sensitive Labels

(P-3408)
TAPP LABEL INC (HQ)
161 S Vasco Rd L, Livermore (94551-5130)
PHONE.................................707 252-8300
John Attayek, *CEO*
Jeff Licht, *Vice Pres*
Brooks Denny, *Business Dir*
Natalie Morrell, *Business Dir*
Doug Smith, *Business Dir*
EMP: 26 EST: 2012
SALES (est): 8.4MM
SALES (corp-wide): 18MM **Privately Held**
WEB: www.tapptech.com
SIC: 2679 Labels, paper: made from purchased material

(P-3409)
WINFIELD DESIGN INTERNATIONAL
Also Called: Winfield International
3000 23rd St, San Francisco (94110-3385)
PHONE.................................415 216-3169
Thomas T S Shuen, *President*
Milton J Gaines, *Vice Pres*
Nelson Shum, *Controller*
EMP: 19 EST: 1953
SQ FT: 20,000
SALES (est): 1.3MM **Privately Held**
SIC: 2679 5199 Wallpaper; general merchandise, non-durable

(P-3410)
WORLD CENTRIC
1400 Valley House Dr # 220, Rohnert Park (94928-4940)
PHONE.................................707 241-9190
Aseem Das, *CEO*
Mark Marinozzi, *Vice Pres*
Mark Stephany, *Vice Pres*
Brandon Lourenzo, *Planning*
Xing Jin, *Research*
◆ EMP: 17 EST: 2004
SALES (est): 10.5MM **Privately Held**
WEB: www.worldcentric.com
SIC: 2679 2675 5113 Plates, pressed & molded pulp: from purchased material; die-cut paper & board; industrial & personal service paper

2711 Newspapers: Publishing & Printing

(P-3411)
ALAMEDA NEWSPAPERS INC (DH)
Also Called: Times Herald
22533 Foothill Blvd, Hayward (94541-4109)
PHONE.................................510 783-6111
Joh Schueler, *President*
P Scott McKibben, *President*
EMP: 250 EST: 1985
SQ FT: 50,000
SALES (est): 114.3MM
SALES (corp-wide): 1.8B **Privately Held**
WEB: www.medianewsgroup.com
SIC: 2711 Newspapers, publishing & printing

(P-3412)
ALAMEDA NEWSPAPERS INC
Also Called: San Mateo Times
1080 S Amphlett Blvd, San Mateo (94402-1802)
PHONE.................................650 348-4321
Dan Cruey, *Manager*
EMP: 195
SALES (corp-wide): 1.8B **Privately Held**
SIC: 2711 Newspapers: publishing only, not printed on site; newspapers, publishing & printing
HQ: Alameda Newspapers, Inc
22533 Foothill Blvd
Hayward CA 94541
510 783-6111

(P-3413)
AUBURN JOURNAL INC (HQ)
1030 High St, Auburn (95603-4707)
P.O. Box 5910 (95604-5910)
PHONE.................................530 885-5656
Craig Dennis, *President*
Tony Hazarian, *Owner*
Martin Cody, *President*
William J Brehm Sr, *Vice Pres*
Moana Brehm, *Admin Sec*
EMP: 110 EST: 1852
SQ FT: 18,000
SALES (est): 33.5MM
SALES (corp-wide): 228.3MM **Privately Held**
WEB: www.goldcountrymedia.com
SIC: 2711 Commercial printing & newspaper publishing combined; newspapers, publishing & printing
PA: Brehm Communications, Inc.
16644 W Bernardo Dr # 300
San Diego CA 92127
858 451-6200

(P-3414)
AUBURN TRADER INC (DH)
1115 Grass Valley Hwy, Auburn (95603-3439)
P.O. Box 5910 (95604-5910)
PHONE.................................530 888-7653
Bill Brehm, *President*
Kim Christen, *Manager*
EMP: 20 EST: 1981
SALES (est): 33.5MM
SALES (corp-wide): 228.3MM **Privately Held**
WEB: www.goldcountrymedia.com
SIC: 2711 Newspapers, publishing & printing
HQ: Auburn Journal Inc
1030 High St
Auburn CA 95603
530 885-5656

(P-3415)
BAR MEDIA INC
Also Called: Bay Area Reporter
44 Gough St Ste 204, San Francisco (94103-5424)
PHONE.................................415 861-5019
Michael Yamashita, *President*
Thomas E Horn, *Ch of Bd*
Patrick Brown, *CFO*
Mike Yamashita, *General Mgr*
Todd Vogt, *Admin Sec*
EMP: 15 EST: 2013
SQ FT: 1,258
SALES (est): 1.4MM **Privately Held**
WEB: www.ebar.com
SIC: 2711 Newspapers, publishing & printing

(P-3416)
BAY GUARDIAN COMPANY
Also Called: San Francisco Bay Guardian
135 Micaicaippi St, San Francisco (94107)
PHONE.................................415 255-3100
Bruce Brugman, *President*
Jean Brugman, *President*
EMP: 23 EST: 1966
SQ FT: 28,000
SALES (est): 792.6K **Privately Held**
WEB: www.sfbg.com
SIC: 2711 Newspapers, publishing & printing

(P-3417)
BERKELEYSIDE LLC
2120 University Ave, Berkeley (94704-1026)
PHONE.................................510 671-0380
Wendy Cohen,
EMP: 15 EST: 2012
SALES (est): 429.9K **Privately Held**
WEB: www.berkeleyside.org
SIC: 2711 Newspapers, publishing & printing

(P-3418)
BIOCENTURY INC (PA)
1235 Radio Rd Ste 100, Redwood City (94065-1315)
P.O. Box 1246, San Carlos (94070-1246)
PHONE.................................650 595-5333
David Flores, *President*
Adam Gordon, *Vice Pres*
Selina Koch, *Senior Editor*
Michael Schuppenhauer PH, *Senior Editor*
EMP: 26 EST: 1992
SALES (est): 8MM **Privately Held**
WEB: www.biocentury.com
SIC: 2711 2721 Newspapers; periodicals

(PA)=Parent Co (HQ)=Headquarters (DH)=Div Headquarters
✿ = New Business established in last 2 years

2022 Northern California Business Directory and Buyers Guide

2711 - Newspapers: Publishing & Printing County (P-3419)

PRODUCTS & SERVICES SECTION

(P-3419)
BRENTWOOD PRESS & PUBG CO LLC
Also Called: Brentwood Yellow Pages
248 Oak St, Brentwood (94513-1337)
PHONE..............................925 516-4757
Jimmy Chamores Mg Mem, *Principal*
Eric Kinnaird, *Production*
Rhonda Duran, *Sales Staff*
Jimmy Chamores, *Mng Member*
Greg Robinson, *Editor*
EMP: 45 **EST:** 1997
SQ FT: 3,500
SALES (est): 7.2MM **Privately Held**
WEB: www.thepress.net
SIC: 2711 Newspapers: publishing only, not printed on site

(P-3420)
BULLDOG REPORTER
124 Linden St, Oakland (94607-2538)
PHONE..............................510 596-9300
EMP: 16
SALES (est): 3MM **Privately Held**
SIC: 2711 Newspapers-Publishing/Printing

(P-3421)
BUSINESS JRNL PUBLICATIONS INC
125 S Market St 11, San Jose (95113-2292)
PHONE..............................408 295-3800
Italo Jimenez, *Manager*
EMP: 370
SALES (corp-wide): 2.8B **Privately Held**
SIC: 2711 Newspapers: publishing only, not printed on site
HQ: Business Journal Publications, Inc.
4350 W Cypress St Ste 800
Tampa FL 33607

(P-3422)
CALAVERAS FIRST CO INC
Also Called: Calaveras Enterprise
15 Main St, San Andreas (95249-7725)
P.O. Box 1197 (95249-1197)
PHONE..............................209 754-3861
Ralph Alldredge, *President*
Talibah Al-Rafiq, *General Mgr*
Buz Engleton, *General Mgr*
Jeremy Malamed, *Editor*
EMP: 20 **EST:** 1998
SQ FT: 8,000
SALES (est): 2.8MM **Privately Held**
WEB: www.calaverasenterprise.com
SIC: 2711 Newspapers: publishing only, not printed on site

(P-3423)
CALIFORNIA NEWSPAPERS INC
Also Called: Marin Independent Journal
150 Alameda Del Prado, Novato (94949-6665)
PHONE..............................415 883-8600
Roger Grossman, *President*
Mario Bendingan, *President*
Carolyn Ware, *Executive*
EMP: 2129 **EST:** 1861
SQ FT: 60,000
SALES (est): 15.1MM
SALES (corp-wide): 1.8B **Privately Held**
SIC: 2711 Commercial printing & newspaper publishing combined
HQ: California Newspapers Limited Partnership
605 E Huntington Dr # 100
Monrovia CA 91016
626 962-8811

(P-3424)
CALIFORNIA NEWSPAPERS PARTNR (PA)
Also Called: Mng Newspapers
4 N 2nd St Ste 700, San Jose (95113-1308)
PHONE..............................408 920-5333
Steven B Rossi, *President*
Jennifer Belton, *Advt Staff*
Marie Chavarria, *Sales Staff*
Randall Keith, *Manager*
Rick Raker, *Manager*
EMP: 50 **EST:** 2004

SALES (est): 17.6MM **Privately Held**
SIC: 2711 Newspapers, publishing & printing

(P-3425)
CALIFRNIA NWSPAPERS LTD PARTNR
Also Called: Media News
5399 Clark Rd, Paradise (95969-6325)
P.O. Box 70 (95967-0070)
PHONE..............................530 877-4413
Steve McCormick, *Controller*
EMP: 106
SALES (corp-wide): 1.8B **Privately Held**
SIC: 2711 2796 2791 2789 Newspapers: publishing only, not printed on site; platemaking services; typesetting; bookbinding & related work; commercial printing, lithographic
HQ: California Newspapers Limited Partnership
605 E Huntington Dr # 100
Monrovia CA 91016
626 962-8811

(P-3426)
CHICKEN RNCH ECONOMIC DEV CORP ◆
Also Called: Cred-Corp
16929 Chicken Ranch Rd, Jamestown (95327-9779)
PHONE..............................209 984-9066
Michael J Roberts,
Lloyd Mathiesen,
EMP: 25 **EST:** 2021
SALES (est): 988.1K **Privately Held**
SIC: 2711 Newspapers

(P-3427)
CHICO COMMUNITY PUBLISHING (PA)
Also Called: Reno News & Review
353 E 2nd St, Chico (95928-5469)
P.O. Box 56 (95927-0056)
PHONE..............................530 894-2300
Jeff Von Kaenel, *CEO*
Jeff Vonkaenel, *President*
Charles Marcks, *CFO*
Valentina Flynn, *Vice Pres*
Deborah Redmond, *Admin Sec*
EMP: 40 **EST:** 1977
SQ FT: 7,200
SALES (est): 19.9MM **Privately Held**
WEB: www.chicoer.com
SIC: 2711 Newspapers, publishing & printing

(P-3428)
CHICO COMMUNITY PUBLISHING
Also Called: Sacramento News & Review
1124 Del Paso Blvd, Sacramento (95815-3607)
P.O. Box 13370 (95813-3370)
PHONE..............................916 498-1234
Angela Hanson, *Manager*
Sarah Hansel, *Graphic Designe*
Angel De La O, *Advt Staff*
Adam Lew, *Advt Staff*
Vincent Marchese, *Advt Staff*
EMP: 101
SALES (corp-wide): 19.9MM **Privately Held**
WEB: www.chicoer.com
SIC: 2711 Newspapers, publishing & printing
PA: Chico Community Publishing Inc
353 E 2nd St
Chico CA 95928
530 894-2300

(P-3429)
CONTRA COSTA NEWSPAPERS INC (DH)
Also Called: Contra Costa Times
175 Lennon Ln Ste 100, Walnut Creek (94598-2466)
PHONE..............................925 935-2525
George Riggs, *CEO*
John Armstrong, *President*
Chris Boisvert, *Info Tech Dir*
Mike Lefkow, *Editor*
EMP: 1000 **EST:** 1947
SQ FT: 180,000

SALES (est): 158.1MM
SALES (corp-wide): 1.8B **Privately Held**
WEB: www.medianewsgroup.com
SIC: 2711 Newspapers, publishing & printing

(P-3430)
CONTRA COSTA NEWSPAPERS INC
4301 Lakeside Dr, San Pablo (94806-5281)
PHONE..............................510 758-8400
Kathy Edwards, *Principal*
Pat Toliver, *Sales/Mktg Mgr*
EMP: 100
SQ FT: 8,000
SALES (corp-wide): 1.8B **Privately Held**
WEB: www.eastbaytimes.com
SIC: 2711 Newspapers, publishing & printing
HQ: Contra Costa Newspapers, Inc.
175 Lennon Ln Ste 100
Walnut Creek CA 94598
925 935-2525

(P-3431)
DAILY REVIEW
Also Called: A and G News Papers
3317 Arden Rd, Hayward (94545-3903)
PHONE..............................510 783-6111
Steve Cressoub, *CFO*
Pam Hornung, *Advt Staff*
Dawn Hibbert, *Sales Staff*
Amber Zurn, *Sales Staff*
Gordon Campbell, *Supervisor*
EMP: 19 **EST:** 2001
SALES (est): 566.2K **Privately Held**
WEB: www.eastbaytimes.com
SIC: 2711 Newspapers, publishing & printing

(P-3432)
DISPATCHER NEWSPAPER
1188 Franklin St Fl 4, San Francisco (94109-6800)
PHONE..............................415 775-0533
Robert McEllreth, *President*
John Barton, *Exec Dir*
Sam Alvarado, *Director*
Joe Cabrales, *Director*
Hunny Powell, *Representative*
EMP: 16 **EST:** 1994
SALES (est): 300.3K **Privately Held**
SIC: 2711 Newspapers, publishing & printing

(P-3433)
DOW JONES LMG STOCKTON INC
Also Called: Record The
530 E Market St, Stockton (95202-3009)
P.O. Box 900 (95201-0900)
PHONE..............................209 943-6397
Deitra Kenoly, *President*
Roger Coover, *President*
Dave Kelso, *Finance Dir*
Paula Allard, *Supervisor*
EMP: 1032 **EST:** 2003
SALES (est): 12.6MM
SALES (corp-wide): 3.4B **Publicly Held**
WEB: www.recordnet.com
SIC: 2711 Newspapers, publishing & printing
HQ: Local Media Group, Inc.
90 Crystal Run Rd Ste 310
Middletown NY 10941
845 341-1100

(P-3434)
EL DORADO NEWSPAPERS (DH)
Also Called: Clovis Independent
2100 Q St, Sacramento (95816-6816)
P.O. Box 15779 (95852-0779)
PHONE..............................916 321-1826
Karole Morgan-Prager, *Admin Sec*
Bill Gutierrez, *Adv Mgr*
EMP: 200 **EST:** 1979
SALES (est): 45.8MM
SALES (corp-wide): 709.5MM **Privately Held**
WEB: www.mcclatchy.com
SIC: 2711 Commercial printing & newspaper publishing combined

HQ: Mcclatchy Newspapers, Inc.
1601 Alhambra Blvd # 100
Sacramento CA 95816
916 321-1855

(P-3435)
EMBARCADERO PUBLISHING COMPANY (PA)
Also Called: Country Almanac
450 Cambridge Ave, Palo Alto (94306-1507)
P.O. Box 1610 (94302-1610)
PHONE..............................650 964-6300
William Johnson, *President*
Mike Naar, *Treasurer*
Tom Zahiralis, *Vice Pres*
Frank A Bravo, *Info Tech Dir*
Chris Planessi, *Technology*
EMP: 100 **EST:** 1979
SQ FT: 4,500
SALES (est): 15.1MM **Privately Held**
WEB: www.embarcaderomediagroup.com
SIC: 2711 Commercial printing & newspaper publishing combined; newspapers, publishing & printing

(P-3436)
EXIN LLC
1213 Evans Ave, San Francisco (94124-1717)
PHONE..............................415 359-2600
Ted Fang, *President*
Florence Fang, *Ch of Bd*
James Fang, *Treasurer*
Suzanne Galletly, *Portfolio Mgr*
EMP: 15 **EST:** 2000
SQ FT: 27,526
SALES (est): 360.2K **Privately Held**
SIC: 2711 Newspapers: publishing only, not printed on site

(P-3437)
FEATHER PUBLISHING COMPANY INC (PA)
Also Called: Feather River Bulletin
287 Lawrence St, Quincy (95971-9477)
P.O. Box B (95971-3586)
PHONE..............................530 283-0800
Michael C Taborski, *President*
Keri B Taborski, *Vice Pres*
Marc Marino, *Sales Associate*
Keith Brown, *Manager*
EMP: 30 **EST:** 1866
SALES (est): 8.5MM **Privately Held**
WEB: www.plumasnews.com
SIC: 2711 2752 Newspapers, publishing & printing; lithographing on metal

(P-3438)
GATEHOUSE MEDIA LLC
Also Called: Fort Bragg Advocate-News
617 S State St, Ukiah (95482-4912)
P.O. Box 1188, Fort Bragg (95437-1188)
PHONE..............................707 964-5642
Stan Anderson, *Enginr/R&D Mgr*
EMP: 25
SALES (corp-wide): 3.4B **Publicly Held**
WEB: www.gannett.com
SIC: 2711 Newspapers, publishing & printing
HQ: Gatehouse Media, Llc
175 Sullys Trl Fl 3
Pittsford NY 14534
585 598-0030

(P-3439)
GATEHOUSE MEDIA LLC
Also Called: Siskiyou Daily News
309 S Broadway St, Yreka (96097-2905)
P.O. Box 127, Mount Shasta (96067-0127)
PHONE..............................530 842-5777
Rod Ows, *Branch Mgr*
EMP: 25
SALES (corp-wide): 3.4B **Publicly Held**
WEB: www.gannett.com
SIC: 2711 Newspapers, publishing & printing
HQ: Gatehouse Media, Llc
175 Sullys Trl Fl 3
Pittsford NY 14534
585 598-0030

PRODUCTS & SERVICES SECTION

2711 - Newspapers: Publishing & Printing County (P-3461)

(P-3440)
GATEHOUSE MEDIA LLC
Also Called: Chico Enterprise Record
400 E Park Ave, Chico (95928-7127)
P.O. Box 9 (95927-0009)
PHONE...................................530 891-1234
Wolf Rosenburg, *Branch Mgr*
EMP: 25
SALES (corp-wide): 3.4B **Publicly Held**
WEB: www.gannett.com
SIC: 2711 Newspapers, publishing & printing
HQ: Gatehouse Media, Llc
   175 Sullys Trl Fl 3
   Pittsford NY 14534
   585 598-0030

(P-3441)
GIBSON PRINTING & PUBG INC
Also Called: Benicia Herald
820 1st St, Benicia (94510-3216)
P.O. Box 65 (94510-0065)
PHONE...................................707 745-0733
Pam Poppee, *Manager*
EMP: 25
SALES (corp-wide): 4.6MM **Privately Held**
SIC: 2711 7313 Newspapers: publishing only, not printed on site; newspaper advertising representative
PA: Gibson Printing & Publishing, Inc.
   544 Curtola Pkwy
   Vallejo CA

(P-3442)
GILROY DISPATCH
6400 Monterey Rd, Gilroy (95020-6663)
P.O. Box 516 (95021-0516)
PHONE...................................408 842-6400
Anthony Allegretti, *President*
EMP: 15 EST: 2010
SALES (est): 471.8K **Privately Held**
WEB: www.gilroydispatch.com
SIC: 2711 Commercial printing & newspaper publishing combined; newspapers, publishing & printing

(P-3443)
GREAT NORTHERN WHEELS DEALS
Also Called: Wheels and Deals
810 Lake Blvd Ste C, Redding (96003-2200)
PHONE...................................530 533-2134
Fax: 530 533-1531
EMP: 33
SQ FT: 2,400
SALES: 2MM **Privately Held**
WEB: www.wheelsanddeals.com
SIC: 2711 7313 Newspapers-Publishing/Printing Advertising Representative

(P-3444)
GUM SUN TIMES INC (PA)
Also Called: Chinese Times
625 Kearny St, San Francisco (94108-1849)
PHONE...................................415 379-6788
Michael Lamm, *President*
See B Hom, *President*
Harrison Lim, *President*
EMP: 28 EST: 1920
SQ FT: 9,000
SALES (est): 1.3MM **Privately Held**
SIC: 2711 Newspapers: publishing only, not printed on site

(P-3445)
HERBURGER PUBLICATIONS INC (PA)
Also Called: Galt Herald
604 N Lincoln Way, Galt (95632-8601)
P.O. Box 307 (95632-0307)
PHONE...................................916 685-5533
Roy Herburger, *President*
David Herburger, *Vice Pres*
Diana Jacobson, *Advt Staff*
EMP: 60 EST: 1903
SQ FT: 10,000
SALES (est): 5MM **Privately Held**
WEB: www.herburger.net
SIC: 2711 Commercial printing & newspaper publishing combined

(P-3446)
HORIZON CAL PUBLICATIONS INC
Also Called: Mammoth Times
452 Old Mammoth Rd, Mammoth Lakes (93546-2013)
P.O. Box 3929 (93546-3929)
PHONE...................................760 934-3929
David J Radler, *President*
EMP: 32 EST: 1999
SQ FT: 2,100
SALES (est): 4.6MM **Privately Held**
SIC: 2711 Newspapers

(P-3447)
HUMBOLDT NEWSPAPER INC
Also Called: Times-Standard
930 6th St, Eureka (95501-1112)
P.O. Box 3580 (95502-3580)
PHONE...................................707 442-1711
Stephan J Sosinski, *Publisher*
John Richmond, *General Mgr*
Jacob Woodford, *Advt Staff*
Mike Maloney, *Director*
Ruth Schneider, *Editor*
EMP: 51 EST: 1854
SQ FT: 49,872
SALES (est): 4.1MM **Privately Held**
WEB: www.times-standard.com
SIC: 2711 Newspapers, publishing & printing

(P-3448)
INDEPNDENT BRKLEY STDNT PUBG I
Also Called: DAILY CALIFORNIAN
2483 Hearst Ave, Berkeley (94709-1320)
P.O. Box 1949 (94701-1949)
PHONE...................................510 548-8300
Karim Doumar, *President*
Bryan Wang, *Chief Mktg Ofcr*
Alexander Hong, *Creative Dir*
Emily Denny, *Research*
Sherdil Niyaz, *Research*
EMP: 86 EST: 1871
SQ FT: 4,100
SALES (est): 237.6K **Privately Held**
WEB: www.dailycal.org
SIC: 2711 7372 Newspapers: publishing only, not printed on site; application computer software

(P-3449)
INDIA-WEST PUBLICATIONS INC (PA)
933 Macarthur Blvd, San Leandro (94577-3062)
PHONE...................................510 383-1140
Ramesh Murarka, *President*
Bina Murarka, *Corp Secy*
Dyana Bhandari, *Advt Staff*
EMP: 21 EST: 1975
SQ FT: 7,000
SALES (est): 3.8MM **Privately Held**
WEB: www.indiawest.com
SIC: 2711 Newspapers, publishing & printing

(P-3450)
INLAND VALLEY PUBLISHING CO
Also Called: Independent, The
2250 1st St, Livermore (94550-3143)
P.O. Box 1198 (94551-1198)
PHONE...................................925 243-8000
Joan Seppala, *President*
Virginia Hoato, *Office Mgr*
Jorge Carmona, *Webmaster*
EMP: 28 EST: 1963
SQ FT: 5,000
SALES (est): 850K **Privately Held**
SIC: 2711 Newspapers: publishing only, not printed on site

(P-3451)
JCK LEGACY COMPANY (HQ)
1601 Alhambra Blvd # 100, Sacramento (95816-7164)
P.O. Box 15779 (95852-0779)
PHONE...................................916 321-1844
Tony Hunter, *CEO*
Tony Berg, *Senior VP*
Jeffrey Dorsey, *Senior VP*
Don Macgregor, *Vice Pres*
Joseph Ramirez, *Vice Pres*
EMP: 220 EST: 1857
SALES: 709.5MM **Privately Held**
WEB: www.mcclatchy.com
SIC: 2711 Newspapers, publishing & printing

(P-3452)
JOONG-ANG DAILY NEWS CAL INC
23575 Cabot Blvd Ste 201, Hayward (94545-1657)
PHONE...................................510 487-3333
Joung Sihn, *Branch Mgr*
Gwang Shin, *General Mgr*
Yul Lee, *Sr Software Eng*
Jaehwang Shim, *Info Tech Mgr*
Sulgi Choi, *Advt Staff*
EMP: 46 **Privately Held**
SIC: 2711 Commercial printing & newspaper publishing combined
HQ: The Joong-Ang Daily News California Inc
   690 Wilshire Pl
   Los Angeles CA 90005
   213 368-2500

(P-3453)
LAKE COUNTY PUBLISHING CO INC (DH)
Also Called: Lake County Record-Bee
617 S State St, Ukiah (95482-4912)
P.O. Box 849, Lakeport (95453-0849)
PHONE...................................707 263-5636
Edward Mead, *President*
EMP: 69 EST: 1981
SALES (est): 12.3MM
SALES (corp-wide): 1.8B **Privately Held**
WEB: www.record-bee.com
SIC: 2711 Newspapers, publishing & printing

(P-3454)
LIVE JOURNAL INC
6363 Skyline Blvd, Oakland (94611-1042)
PHONE...................................415 230-3600
Andrew Paulson, *President*
Steffenie Gravelle, *CFO*
Tony Stucker, *Vice Pres*
Brenden Delzer, *Editor*
EMP: 33 EST: 1999
SALES (est): 3.9MM **Privately Held**
WEB: www.livejournal.com
SIC: 2711 Newspapers, publishing & printing

(P-3455)
LODI NEWS SENTINEL
Also Called: Lodi Mail Express
125 N Church St, Lodi (95240-2197)
P.O. Box 1360 (95241-1360)
PHONE...................................209 369-2761
Frederick E Weybret, *Ch of Bd*
Alcyon Weybret, *Shareholder*
James Weybret, *Shareholder*
Martin Weybret, *President*
Mike Schafer, *Vice Pres*
◆ EMP: 47 EST: 1881
SQ FT: 19,000
SALES (est): 4.8MM **Privately Held**
WEB: www.lodinews.com
SIC: 2711 Commercial printing & newspaper publishing combined; newspapers, publishing & printing

(P-3456)
MCCLATCHY NEWSPAPERS INC (DH)
Also Called: Sacramento Bee
1601 Alhambra Blvd # 100, Sacramento (95816-7164)
P.O. Box 15779 (95852-0779)
PHONE...................................916 321-1855
R Elaine Lintecum, *Vice Pres*
Erwin Potts, *Ch of Bd*
James P Smith, *Treasurer*
Guy Harrison, *Analyst*
Jamileh Smith, *Controller*
◆ EMP: 2500 EST: 1857
SALES: 709.5MM **Privately Held**
WEB: www.mcclatchy.com
SIC: 2711 2759 7375 Newspapers, publishing & printing; commercial printing; online data base information retrieval

(P-3457)
MCNAUGHTON NEWSPAPERS
Also Called: D Davis Enterprise
315 G St, Davis (95616-4119)
P.O. Box 1470 (95617-1470)
PHONE...................................530 756-0800
Foy McNaughton, *Owner*
Richard B Mc Naughton, *Admin Sec*
Shelley Butler, *Human Resources*
Linda Dubois, *Assoc Editor*
Sebastian Onate, *Assoc Editor*
EMP: 66 EST: 1966
SALES (est): 4.2MM **Privately Held**
WEB: www.davisenterprise.com
SIC: 2711 Commercial printing & newspaper publishing combined; newspapers, publishing & printing

(P-3458)
MCNAUGHTON NEWSPAPERS INC (PA)
Also Called: Daily Republic
1250 Texas St, Fairfield (94533-5748)
P.O. Box 47 (94533-0747)
PHONE...................................707 425-4646
Foy Mc Naughton, *President*
R Burt Mc Naughton, *Corp Secy*
▲ EMP: 99 EST: 1855
SQ FT: 35,000
SALES (est): 13MM **Privately Held**
SIC: 2711 Commercial printing & newspaper publishing combined; newspapers, publishing & printing

(P-3459)
MEDIANEWS GROUP INC
Also Called: Convertly
4 N 2nd St Ste 800, San Jose (95113-1317)
PHONE...................................408 920-5713
Michael Koren, *CFO*
EMP: 500
SALES (corp-wide): 1.8B **Privately Held**
WEB: www.medianewsgroup.com
SIC: 2711 Newspapers, publishing & printing
HQ: Medianews Group, Inc.
   101 W Colfax Ave Ste 1100
   Denver CO 80202

(P-3460)
METRO PUBLISHING INC
Also Called: Metrosa
445 Center St, Healdsburg (95448-3807)
PHONE...................................707 527-1200
Rosemary Olson, *Manager*
Daedalus Howell, *Editor*
Jennifer Wadsworth, *Editor*
EMP: 32
SALES (corp-wide): 10MM **Privately Held**
WEB: www.metronews.com
SIC: 2711 8611 Newspapers, publishing & printing; business associations
PA: Metro Publishing, Inc.
   380 S 1st St
   San Jose CA
   408 298-8000

(P-3461)
MOONSHINE INK LLC
10137 Riverside Dr, Truckee (96161-0303)
P.O. Box 4003 (96160-4403)
PHONE...................................530 587-3607
Mayumi Elegado, *Owner*
Nina Miller, *Advt Staff*
Juliana Demarest, *Assoc Editor*
Kara Fox, *Associate*
EMP: 15 EST: 2008
SALES (est): 587.2K **Privately Held**
WEB: www.moonshineink.com
SIC: 2711 Newspapers: publishing only, not printed on site

2711 - Newspapers: Publishing & Printing County (P-3462)

(P-3462)
MORRIS NEWSPAPER CORP CAL (HQ)
Also Called: Manteca Bulletin
531 E Yosemite Ave, Manteca (95336-5806)
P.O. Box 1958 (95336-1156)
PHONE.................................209 249-3500
Jennifer Merrick, *Director*
Jennifer Webber, *Advt Staff*
Dennis Wyatt, *Director*
EMP: 65 **EST:** 1972
SQ FT: 8,000
SALES (est): 5.5MM
SALES (corp-wide): 285.7MM **Privately Held**
WEB: www.mantecabulletin.com
SIC: 2711 6531 Newspapers, publishing & printing; real estate agents & managers
PA: Morris Multimedia, Inc.
27 Abercorn St
Savannah GA 31401
912 233-1281

(P-3463)
MORRIS PUBLICATIONS (PA)
Also Called: Advertiser, The
122 S 3rd Ave, Oakdale (95361-3935)
P.O. Box 278 (95361-0278)
PHONE.................................209 847-3021
Drew Savage, *General Mgr*
EMP: 40 **EST:** 1888
SQ FT: 5,000
SALES (est): 3.4MM **Privately Held**
SIC: 2711 2752 8999 Commercial printing & newspaper publishing combined; photo-offset printing; newspaper column writing

(P-3464)
MOTHER LODE PRTG & PUBG CO INC
Also Called: Mountain Democrat
2889 Ray Lawyer Dr, Placerville (95667-3914)
P.O. Box 1088 (95667-1088)
PHONE.................................530 344-5030
James Webb, *Principal*
Richard Esposito, *General Mgr*
Ruth Pietrowski, *Business Mgr*
Susie Graunstadt, *Advt Staff*
Krysten Kellum, *Editor*
EMP: 28 **EST:** 1851
SQ FT: 19,400
SALES (est): 4.1MM **Privately Held**
WEB: www.mtdemocrat.com
SIC: 2711 Commercial printing & newspaper publishing combined

(P-3465)
MOUNTAIN VIEW VOICE
450 Cambridge Ave, Palo Alto (94306-1507)
P.O. Box 405, Mountain View (94042-0405)
PHONE.................................650 326-8210
William Johnson, *President*
EMP: 18 **EST:** 1992
SALES (est): 166.8K **Privately Held**
WEB: www.mv-voice.com
SIC: 2711 Newspapers, publishing & printing

(P-3466)
NAPA VALLEY PUBLISHING CO
Also Called: NAPA Valley Register
1615 Soscol Ave, NAPA (94559-1901)
P.O. Box 150 (94559-0050)
PHONE.................................707 226-3711
Carson Pierce, *Director*
Marialena Flamini, *Administration*
Luis Roldan, *Administration*
Tracy Hardee, *Data Proc Staff*
Betzaida Fernandez, *Asst Controller*
EMP: 74
SALES (corp-wide): 6.9MM **Privately Held**
WEB: www.napavalleyregister.com
SIC: 2711 Newspapers: publishing only, not printed on site
PA: Napa Valley Publishing Co
1615 Soscol Ave
Napa CA 94559
707 226-3711

(P-3467)
NAPA VALLEY PUBLISHING CO (PA)
Also Called: NAPA Register
1615 Soscol Ave, NAPA (94559-1901)
PHONE.................................707 226-3711
E W Scripps, *Ch of Bd*
Betty Knight Scripps, *Vice Chairman*
Randy Dowis, *Mktg Dir*
Sean Scully, *Editor*
EMP: 26 **EST:** 1958
SALES (est): 6.9MM **Privately Held**
WEB: www.napavalleyregister.com
SIC: 2711 Newspapers: publishing only, not printed on site

(P-3468)
NORTH AREA NEWS (PA)
2612 El Camino Ave, Sacramento (95821-5937)
P.O. Box 214245 (95821-0245)
PHONE.................................916 486-1248
Tom Hoey, *President*
Joanne Hoey, *Corp Secy*
John Hoey, *Vice Pres*
EMP: 39 **EST:** 1961
SQ FT: 2,400
SALES (est): 2.6MM **Privately Held**
WEB: www.north-area-news.hub.biz
SIC: 2711 Newspapers, publishing & printing

(P-3469)
OAKLAND TRIBUNE INC
Also Called: Tribune, The
600 Grand Ave 308, Oakland (94610-3548)
PHONE.................................510 208-6300
John Armstrong, *President*
Doug Van Sant, *Producer*
◆ **EMP:** 21 **EST:** 1983
SALES (est): 1.8MM
SALES (corp-wide): 1.8B **Privately Held**
WEB: www.medianewsgroup.com
SIC: 2711 Newspapers, publishing & printing
HQ: Medianews Group, Inc.
101 W Colfax Ave Ste 1100
Denver CO 80202

(P-3470)
OLYMPIC CASCADE PUBLISHING (DH)
Also Called: Puyallup Herald
2100 Q St, Sacramento (95816-6816)
P.O. Box 15779 (95852-0779)
PHONE.................................916 321-1000
R Elaine Lintecum, *Vice Pres*
Marion Dodd, *Corp Secy*
Steven Robinson, *Vice Pres*
EMP: 110 **EST:** 1965
SQ FT: 5,100
SALES (est): 3.9MM
SALES (corp-wide): 709.5MM **Privately Held**
WEB: www.thenewstribune.com
SIC: 2711 Commercial printing & newspaper publishing combined; newspapers, publishing & printing
HQ: Mcclatchy Newspapers, Inc.
1601 Alhambra Blvd # 100
Sacramento CA 95816
916 321-1855

(P-3471)
PACIFIC NORTHWEST PUBG CO INC
Also Called: Tallahassee Democrat, Inc
2100 Q St, Sacramento (95816-6816)
PHONE.................................916 321-1828
R Elaine Lintecum, *Vice Pres*
Patrick Talmantes, *Director*
EMP: 365 **EST:** 1905
SQ FT: 100,000
SALES (est): 8.7MM
SALES (corp-wide): 3.4B **Publicly Held**
WEB: www.gannett.com
SIC: 2711 Newspapers, publishing & printing
HQ: Gannett River States Publishing Corporation
7950 Jones Branch Dr
Mc Lean VA 22102
703 284-6000

(P-3472)
PACIFIC PRESS CORPORATION
Also Called: Viet Nam Daily Newspaper
2350 S 10th St, San Jose (95112-4109)
PHONE.................................408 292-3422
Can Nguyen, *President*
Giang Nguyen, *Corp Secy*
EMP: 19 **EST:** 1986
SQ FT: 10,000
SALES (est): 456K **Privately Held**
WEB: www.vietnamdaily.com
SIC: 2711 2752 Newspapers: publishing only, not printed on site; commercial printing, lithographic

(P-3473)
PASADENA NEWSPAPERS INC
Also Called: Eureka Times-Standard
930 6th St, Eureka (95501-1112)
P.O. Box 3580 (95502-3580)
PHONE.................................707 442-1711
Gerry Adolph, *Manager*
EMP: 160
SQ FT: 49,872 **Privately Held**
WEB: www.pasadenastarnews.com
SIC: 2711 2752 Newspapers: publishing only, not printed on site; commercial printing, lithographic
PA: Pasadena Newspapers Inc
2 N Lake Ave Ste 150
Pasadena CA 91101

(P-3474)
PHILIPPINES TODAY LLC
6454 Mission St, Daly City (94014-2013)
PHONE.................................650 872-3200
Meyrick Camilosa, *Principal*
Marilyn King, *Vice Pres*
EMP: 15 **EST:** 2008
SALES (est): 1.3MM **Privately Held**
WEB: www.philippinestodayus.com
SIC: 2711 Newspapers, publishing & printing

(P-3475)
REPORTER
Also Called: Media News Groups
916 Cotting Ln, Vacaville (95688-9338)
PHONE.................................707 448-6401
Jody Lodevick, *President*
Kelly Spadorcio, *Sales Mgr*
Candy Gray, *Manager*
Matt Meredith, *Manager*
Stevie Gomez, *Consultant*
EMP: 100 **EST:** 1883
SQ FT: 40,000
SALES (est): 2.7MM **Privately Held**
WEB: www.thereporter.com
SIC: 2711 Commercial printing & newspaper publishing combined; newspapers, publishing & printing

(P-3476)
SAN JOSE MERCURY-NEWS LLC (DH)
Also Called: DIGITAL FIRST MEDIA
4 N 2nd St Fl 8, San Jose (95113-1308)
P.O. Box 65190, Colorado Springs CO (80962-5190)
PHONE.................................408 920-5000
Michael Hopkins,
Astrid Garcia, *Principal*
Mindy Kiernan, *Principal*
Joseph T Natoli, *Principal*
Dennis Ryerson, *Principal*
EMP: 1000 **EST:** 2006
SQ FT: 400,000
SALES: 683.4K
SALES (corp-wide): 1.8B **Privately Held**
WEB: www.mercurynews.com
SIC: 2711 Commercial printing & newspaper publishing combined; newspapers, publishing & printing

(P-3477)
SANTA ROSA PRESS DEMOCRAT INC (HQ)
Also Called: Press Democrat, The
427 Mendocino Ave, Santa Rosa (95401-5391)
P.O. Box 569 (95402-0569)
PHONE.................................707 546-2020
Michael J Parman, *President*
Jill Lyman, *Accountant*
Steve Schneiderman, *Advt Staff*
Rebecca Pate, *Marketing Staff*
Mark Flaviani, *Director*
EMP: 270 **EST:** 1998
SALES (est): 75MM **Privately Held**
WEB: www.pressdemocrat.com
SIC: 2711 Newspapers, publishing & printing
PA: Sonoma Media Investments, Llc
427 Mendocino Ave
Santa Rosa CA 95401
707 526-8563

(P-3478)
SCALABLE PRESS
41454 Christy St, Fremont (94538-5105)
PHONE.................................877 752-9060
Joe Orminski, *General Mgr*
Joe Huff, *Info Tech Mgr*
Simon Chen, *Software Dev*
Rui Jiang, *Software Engr*
Ryan McGill, *Software Engr*
EMP: 17 **EST:** 2015
SALES (est): 2.7MM **Privately Held**
WEB: www.scalablepress.com
SIC: 2711 Newspapers

(P-3479)
SING TAO NEWSPAPERS (HQ)
Also Called: Sing Tao Daily
1818 Gilbreth Rd Ste 108, Burlingame (94010-1217)
PHONE.................................650 808-8800
Robin Mui, *CEO*
Charles Fu, *CFO*
Teresa Mau, *Officer*
Joel Leung, *General Mgr*
Florence TSO, *General Mgr*
▲ **EMP:** 75 **EST:** 1977
SQ FT: 22,000
SALES (est): 14.8MM **Privately Held**
WEB: www.singtaousa.com
SIC: 2711 Commercial printing & newspaper publishing combined

(P-3480)
SONOMA INDEX-TRIBUNE
Also Called: Sonoma Valley Publishing
117 W Napa St Ste A, Sonoma (95476-6691)
P.O. Box C (95476-0209)
PHONE.................................707 938-2111
William Lynch, *President*
James Lynch, *Corp Secy*
Jean Lynch, *Vice Pres*
EMP: 25 **EST:** 1879
SQ FT: 17,000
SALES (est): 1.7MM **Privately Held**
WEB: www.sonomanews.com
SIC: 2711 Commercial printing & newspaper publishing combined

(P-3481)
SONOMA MEDIA INVESTMENTS LLC (PA)
427 Mendocino Ave, Santa Rosa (95401-5391)
PHONE.................................707 526-8563
Steven B Falk, *Manager*
Stephen Daniels, *CFO*
Gary Nelson,
EMP: 78 **EST:** 2012
SALES (est): 75MM **Privately Held**
WEB: www.sonomamediainvestments.com
SIC: 2711 Newspapers

(P-3482)
ST LOUIS POST-DISPATCH LLC
Also Called: Novato Advance Newspaper
1068 Machin Ave, Novato (94945-2458)
P.O. Box 8 (94948-0008)
PHONE.................................415 892-1516
William C Haigwood, *Manager*
Maureen Tomczak, *Office Mgr*
Josh Renaud, *Software Dev*
Cathy Hensley, *Production*
EMP: 93
SALES (corp-wide): 618MM **Publicly Held**
WEB: www.stltoday.com
SIC: 2711 Newspapers, publishing & printing
HQ: St. Louis Post-Dispatch Llc
900 N Tucker Blvd
Saint Louis MO 63101
314 340-8000

▲ = Import ▼=Export
◆ =Import/Export

PRODUCTS & SERVICES SECTION
2721 - Periodicals: Publishing & Printing County (P-3504)

(P-3483)
ST LOUIS POST-DISPATCH LLC
Also Called: Argus Courier
830 Petaluma Blvd N, Petaluma (94952-2109)
P.O. Box 1091 (94953-1091)
PHONE..................707 762-4541
John Burnes, *Branch Mgr*
EMP: 93
SQ FT: 10,000
SALES (corp-wide): 618MM **Publicly Held**
WEB: www.stltoday.com
SIC: 2711 Newspapers, publishing & printing
HQ: St. Louis Post-Dispatch Llc
 900 N Tucker Blvd
 Saint Louis MO 63101
 314 340-8000

(P-3484)
STATE HORNET
6000 J St, Sacramento (95819-2605)
PHONE..................916 278-6583
Claire Morgan, *Chief*
Margherita Beale, *Manager*
EMP: 118 **EST:** 1949
SALES (est): 6.4MM **Privately Held**
WEB: www.statehornet.com
SIC: 2711 Newspapers, publishing & printing
HQ: California State University, Sacramento
 6000 J St Ste 2200
 Sacramento CA 95819

(P-3485)
TAMARACK SPRINGS MUTUAL WTR CO (PA)
125 N Church St, Lodi (95240-2102)
P.O. Box 1360 (95241-1360)
PHONE..................209 369-2761
Melissa Harris, *Business Mgr*
EMP: 19 **EST:** 1967
SALES (est): 2.4MM **Privately Held**
SIC: 2711 Newspapers, publishing & printing

(P-3486)
TRACY PRESS INC
145 W 10th St, Tracy (95376-3952)
P.O. Box 419 (95378-0419)
PHONE..................209 835-3030
Robert S Matthews, *President*
Tom Matthews, *Vice Pres*
Maggie Jauregui, *Graphic Designe*
Michael Langley, *Editor*
EMP: 38 **EST:** 1896
SQ FT: 20,000
SALES (est): 4.8MM **Privately Held**
WEB: www.ttownmedia.com
SIC: 2711 Commercial printing & newspaper publishing combined; newspapers, publishing & printing

(P-3487)
VIETNAM DAILY NEWS LLC
510 Parrott St Ste 1, San Jose (95112-4117)
PHONE..................408 292-3422
Can T Nguyen, *Principal*
Nguyen Can, *Vice Pres*
Can Nguyen, *Principal*
Quynh T Nguyen, *Publisher*
EMP: 17 **EST:** 2011
SALES (est): 437.9K **Privately Held**
WEB: www.vietnamdaily.com
SIC: 2711 Newspapers: publishing only, not printed on site

(P-3488)
VILLAGE VOICE MEDIA
Also Called: Eastbay Express
537 Crofton Ave, Oakland (94610-1520)
PHONE..................510 879-3700
Josh Fromson, *Principal*
Israel Brown, *Director*
EMP: 26 **EST:** 1978
SALES (est): 1.1MM **Privately Held**
WEB: www.eastbayexpress.com
SIC: 2711 5812 Newspapers, publishing & printing; eating places

(P-3489)
WICK COMMUNICATIONS CO
714 Kelly St, Half Moon Bay (94019-1919)
P.O. Box 68 (94019-0068)
PHONE..................650 726-4424
Debra Godshall, *Principal*
EMP: 24
SALES (corp-wide): 87.6MM **Privately Held**
WEB: www.wickcommunications.com
SIC: 2711 6531 Newspapers, publishing & printing; real estate agents & managers
HQ: Wick Communications Co.
 333 W Wilcox Dr Ste 302
 Sierra Vista AZ 85635
 520 458-0200

(P-3490)
WORLD JOURNAL INC (PA)
231 Adrian Rd, Millbrae (94030-3102)
PHONE..................650 692-9936
Pl Ly Wang, *President*
Shiun Yi Hsia, *CEO*
Cary Cheng, *Executive*
Joe Hung, *Executive*
Max Wu, *Editor*
▲ **EMP:** 98 **EST:** 1975
SQ FT: 15,000
SALES (est): 14.6MM **Privately Held**
SIC: 2711 Newspapers, publishing & printing

2721 Periodicals: Publishing & Printing

(P-3491)
A-1 RUIZ & SONS INC
Also Called: El Avisador Magazine
460 W Taylor St, San Jose (95110-1928)
PHONE..................408 293-0909
Orlando Ruiz, *President*
Jose Alarcon, *Sales Executive*
EMP: 25 **EST:** 1986
SALES (est): 1MM **Privately Held**
WEB: www.autoventamagazine.com
SIC: 2721 Magazines: publishing only, not printed on site

(P-3492)
BUSINESS EXTENSION BUREAU LTD
Also Called: Western Real Estate News
500 S Airport Blvd, South San Francisco (94080-6912)
PHONE..................650 737-5700
Gil Chin, *President*
Steven Hufford, *Technical Staff*
Osama Mostafa, *Accountant*
EMP: 43 **EST:** 1927
SQ FT: 7,000
SALES (est): 1MM **Privately Held**
SIC: 2721 7331 2752 Trade journals: publishing & printing; direct mail advertising services; commercial printing, lithographic

(P-3493)
BUSINESS JOURNAL
Also Called: Fresno Business Journal
1315 Van Ness Ave Ste 200, Fresno (93721-1729)
P.O. Box 126 (93707-0126)
PHONE..................559 490-3400
Gordon M Webster Jr, *President*
Brandie Carpenter, *Marketing Staff*
Ashley Webster, *Manager*
EMP: 24 **EST:** 1886
SALES (est): 2.5MM **Privately Held**
WEB: www.thebusinessjournal.com
SIC: 2721 2711 Trade journals: publishing only, not printed on site; newspapers

(P-3494)
COMSTOCK PUBLISHING INC
Also Called: Comstock's Magazine
2335 Amrcn Rver Dr Ste 30, Sacramento (95825)
PHONE..................916 364-1000
Comstockca Exc, *Vice Pres*
Winnie Comstockcarlson, *Exec VP*
Clayton Blakley, *Vice Pres*
Ryan Montoya, *Vice Pres*
Sara Bogovich, *Graphic Designe*
EMP: 15 **EST:** 1989
SQ FT: 1,600
SALES (est): 2.4MM **Privately Held**
WEB: www.comstocksmag.com
SIC: 2721 Magazines: publishing only, not printed on site

(P-3495)
COYNE & BLANCHARD INC
Also Called: Communication Arts
110 Constitution Dr, Menlo Park (94025-1107)
P.O. Box 889, Belmont (94002-0889)
PHONE..................650 326-6040
Patrick Coyne, *President*
Martha Coyne, *Corp Secy*
Eric Coyne, *Vice Pres*
Marti Coyne, *Admin Sec*
Jiping Hu, *Sr Software Eng*
EMP: 56 **EST:** 1958
SQ FT: 7,500
SALES (est): 5.1MM **Privately Held**
WEB: www.commarts.com
SIC: 2721 Magazines: publishing only, not printed on site

(P-3496)
DIABLO COUNTRY MAGAZINE INC
Also Called: Diablo Custom Publishing
2520 Camino Diablo, Walnut Creek (94597-3939)
PHONE..................925 943-1111
Steven J Rivera, *President*
Eileen Cunningham, *COO*
Steven Rivera, *Vice Pres*
Sylvia Bajjaliya, *Executive*
Dave Bergeron, *Creative Dir*
▲ **EMP:** 40 **EST:** 1979
SQ FT: 7,640
SALES (est): 5.7MM **Privately Held**
WEB: www.diablomag.com
SIC: 2721 2741 Magazines: publishing only, not printed on site; miscellaneous publishing

(P-3497)
DWELL LIFE INC (PA)
595 Pacific Ave Fl 4, San Francisco (94133-4685)
P.O. Box 40608 (94140-0608)
PHONE..................415 373-5100
Michela Abrams, *CEO*
Amy Lloyd, *Partner*
Jenna Page, *Marketing Mgr*
Lara H Deam,
David Morin,
▲ **EMP:** 40 **EST:** 2002
SALES (est): 20MM **Privately Held**
WEB: www.dwell.com
SIC: 2721 7389 Magazines: publishing & printing; advertising, promotional & trade show services

(P-3498)
EXCELLENCE MAGAZINE INC
Also Called: Ross Periodicals
42 Digital Dr Ste 5, Novato (94949-5762)
PHONE..................415 382-0582
Tom Toldrian, *President*
Greg Hudock, *Editor*
EMP: 17 **EST:** 1986
SQ FT: 2,850
SALES (est): 268.2K **Privately Held**
WEB: www.excellence-mag.com
SIC: 2721 Magazines: publishing only, not printed on site

(P-3499)
FOUNDATION FOR NAT PROGRESS
Also Called: MOTHER JONES MAGAZINE
222 Sutter St Ste 600, San Francisco (94108-4457)
PHONE..................415 321-1700
Madeleine Buckingham, *CFO*
Matt Cohen, *Officer*
Tommy Craggs, *CIO*
Daniel Moattar, *Research*
Emily Harris, *Business Mgr*
EMP: 39 **EST:** 1975
SQ FT: 13,500
SALES: 16.5MM **Privately Held**
WEB: www.motherjones.com
SIC: 2721 Magazines: publishing & printing

(P-3500)
FRANCHISE UPDATE INC
Also Called: Franchise Update Media Group
6489 Camden Ave Ste 204, San Jose (95120-2851)
P.O. Box 20547 (95160-0547)
PHONE..................408 402-5681
Therese Thilgen, *CEO*
Jamie N Hage, *Partner*
Andrew P Loewinger, *Partner*
Carolyn G Nussbaum, *Partner*
Arthur L Pressman, *Partner*
EMP: 15 **EST:** 1988
SALES (est): 4.1MM **Privately Held**
WEB: www.franchising.com
SIC: 2721 Magazines: publishing only, not printed on site

(P-3501)
FREEDOM OF PRESS FOUNDATION
601 Van Ness Ave Ste E731, San Francisco (94102-3200)
PHONE..................510 995-0780
Trevor Timm, *Exec Dir*
Camille Squires, *Fellow*
EMP: 16 **EST:** 2012
SALES: 3MM **Privately Held**
WEB: www.freedom.press
SIC: 2721 Periodicals

(P-3502)
HARTLE MEDIA VENTURES LLC
Also Called: 7x7
680 2nd St, San Francisco (94107-2015)
PHONE..................415 362-7797
Tom Hartle,
Heather Hartle,
Jason Oronzi, *Assoc Editor*
EMP: 22 **EST:** 2000
SQ FT: 2,000
SALES (est): 2.1MM **Privately Held**
WEB: www.7x7.com
SIC: 2721 Magazines: publishing only, not printed on site

(P-3503)
IDG CONSUMER & SMB INC (DH)
Also Called: PC World Online
501 2nd St, San Francisco (94107-1469)
PHONE..................415 243-0500
Colin Crawford, *President*
Michael Kisseberth, *President*
Edward B Bloom, *Vice Pres*
Kevin C Krull, *Vice Pres*
Jason Fleckles, *Executive*
EMP: 116 **EST:** 1982
SQ FT: 21,000
SALES (est): 50.5MM
SALES (corp-wide): 1.8MM **Privately Held**
WEB: www.idg.com
SIC: 2721 Magazines: publishing only, not printed on site; periodicals: publishing only
HQ: Idg Communications, Inc.
 140 Kendrick St Bldg B
 Needham MA 02494
 508 872-8200

(P-3504)
INFOWORLD MEDIA GROUP INC (DH)
501 2nd St Ste 500, San Francisco (94107-4133)
PHONE..................415 243-4344
Robert Ostrow, *CEO*
Patrick J Mc Govern, *Ch of Bd*
William P Murphy, *Treasurer*
Virginia Hines, *Vice Pres*
Derek Butcher, *Engineer*
▲ **EMP:** 75 **EST:** 1979
SQ FT: 50,000
SALES (est): 18.5MM
SALES (corp-wide): 1.8MM **Privately Held**
WEB: www.idg.com
SIC: 2721 2741 7389 Magazines: publishing only, not printed on site; newsletter publishing; trade show arrangement
HQ: Idg Communications, Inc.
 140 Kendrick St Bldg B
 Needham MA 02494
 508 872-8200

2721 - Periodicals: Publishing & Printing County (P-3505)

(P-3505)
MAC PUBLISHING LLC (DH)
Also Called: Macworld Magazine
501 2nd St Ste 600, San Francisco
(94107-4133)
PHONE..................................415 243-0505
Colin Crawford, *President*
Stephen Daniels, *President*
Roman Loyola, *Senior Editor*
EMP: 20 **EST:** 1997
SALES (est): 10.9MM
SALES (corp-wide): 1.8MM **Privately Held**
WEB: www.macworld.com
SIC: 2721 Magazines: publishing only, not printed on site
HQ: International Data Group, Inc.
140 Kendrick St Ste C110b
Needham MA 02494
508 875-5000

(P-3506)
MAKE COMMUNITY LLC
150 Todd Rd Ste 100, Santa Rosa
(95407-8412)
P.O. Box 239, Sebastopol (95473-0239)
PHONE..................................707 200-3714
Dale Dougherty, *President*
EMP: 20 **EST:** 2019
SALES (est): 1MM **Privately Held**
WEB: www.make.co
SIC: 2721 Magazines: publishing only, not printed on site

(P-3507)
MARIN MAGAZINE INC
1 Harbor Dr Ste 208, Sausalito
(94965-1434)
PHONE..................................415 332-4800
Nikki Wood, *President*
Hazel Jaramillo, *Office Mgr*
Peter Thomas, *Technology*
Maeve Walsh, *Controller*
Michele Johnson, *Adv Dir*
EMP: 28 **EST:** 2017
SQ FT: 2,500
SALES (est): 6.2MM **Privately Held**
WEB: www.marinmagazine.com
SIC: 2721 7313 Magazines: publishing only, not printed on site; printed media advertising representatives

(P-3508)
MHB GROUP INC
Also Called: Mobile Home Park Magazines
1240 Mtn View Alviso Rd S, Sunnyvale
(94089-2252)
PHONE..................................408 744-1011
Elizabeth Tripp, *President*
Clifford Shores, *Shareholder*
Dana Sketchley, *Shareholder*
Rosemary Walsh, *Shareholder*
EMP: 18 **EST:** 1974
SQ FT: 3,500
SALES (est): 1.3MM **Privately Held**
SIC: 2721 6531 Trade journals: publishing & printing; real estate listing services

(P-3509)
MODERN LUXURY MEDIA LLC (HQ)
Also Called: Angeleno Magazine
243 Vallejo St, San Francisco (94111-1511)
PHONE..................................404 443-0004
Michael B Kong, *Mng Member*
John Carroll, *President*
Michael Dickey, *President*
Leslie Wolfson, *President*
Doreen Olsen, *Executive*
▲ **EMP:** 40 **EST:** 1993
SALES (est): 13MM
SALES (corp-wide): 26MM **Privately Held**
WEB: www.jezebelmagazine.com
SIC: 2721 Magazines: publishing only, not printed on site
PA: Dickey Publishing, Inc.
3280 Peachtree Rd Ne # 23
Atlanta GA 30305
404 949-0700

(P-3510)
OMICS GROUP INC
731 Gull Ave, Foster City (94404-1329)
PHONE..................................650 268-9744
Srinu B Gedela, *Branch Mgr*
EMP: 460
SALES (corp-wide): 109.6MM **Privately Held**
WEB: www.omicsonline.org
SIC: 2721 Trade journals: publishing & printing
PA: Omics Group Inc
2360 Corp Cir Ste 400
Henderson NV 89074
888 843-8169

(P-3511)
PACIFIC SUN
445 Center St, Healdsburg (95448-3807)
PHONE..................................415 488-8100
Gina Channell-Allen, *Principal*
Marianne Misz, *Legal Staff*
EMP: 15 **EST:** 2007
SALES (est): 363.6K **Privately Held**
WEB: www.pacificsun.com
SIC: 2721 Periodicals

(P-3512)
REFINITIV US LLC
50 California St, San Francisco (94111-4624)
PHONE..................................415 344-6000
Andrea Lavoie, *Principal*
Akhil Chandoke, *Sales Staff*
John Kalehua, *Sales Staff*
John Brack, *Director*
Stephen Chung, *Manager*
EMP: 192
SALES (corp-wide): 3.2B **Privately Held**
WEB: www.thomsonreuters.com
SIC: 2721 Periodicals
HQ: Refinitiv Us Llc
3 Times Sq
New York NY 10036
646 223-4000

(P-3513)
SAINT GERMAIN FOUNDATION (PA)
Also Called: I AM Activity
1120 Stonehedge Dr, Dunsmuir (96025)
PHONE..................................530 235-2994
Barbara Arden, *Director*
EMP: 15 **EST:** 1938
SQ FT: 7,500
SALES (est): 2.4MM **Privately Held**
WEB: www.saintgermainfoundation.org
SIC: 8661 2721 2731 Non-church religious organizations; magazines: publishing, not printed on site; books: publishing only

(P-3514)
SELECT COMMUNICATIONS INC
Also Called: Los Altos Town Crier
138 Main St, Los Altos (94022-2905)
PHONE..................................650 948-9000
Paul D Nyberg, *President*
Elizabeth Nyberg, *Vice Pres*
Mary Watanabe, *Production*
Kathy Lera, *Advt Staff*
Zoe Morgan, *Education*
EMP: 27 **EST:** 1984
SQ FT: 3,600
SALES (est): 1.5MM **Privately Held**
WEB: www.losaltosonline.com
SIC: 2721 2711 Magazines: publishing only, not printed on site; newspapers, publishing & printing

(P-3515)
STYLE MEDIA GROUP INC
909 Mormon St, Folsom (95630-2412)
P.O. Box 925 (95763-0925)
PHONE..................................916 988-9888
Terence Carroll, *CEO*
Wendy Sipple, *COO*
Emily Peter, *Assoc Editor*
Tom Gherini, *Accounts Mgr*
Bettie Grijalva, *Accounts Mgr*
EMP: 24 **EST:** 2003
SALES (est): 4.4MM **Privately Held**
WEB: www.stylemg.com
SIC: 2721 Magazines: publishing only, not printed on site

(P-3516)
SUBDIRECT LLC (PA)
Also Called: 360 Media Direct
653 W Fllbrook Ave Ste 10, Fresno (93711)
PHONE..................................559 321-0449
Kelly Vucovich,
Melissa Storti, *Vice Pres*
Scott Porterfield, *Division Mgr*
Jonathan Eropkin, *CTO*
Clyde Wauchope, *Finance*
EMP: 119 **EST:** 2009
SQ FT: 10,000
SALES (est): 6.3MM **Privately Held**
WEB: www.360mediadirect.com
SIC: 2721 Magazines: publishing & printing

(P-3517)
SUNSET PUBLISHING CORPORATION (HQ)
Also Called: Sunset Magazine
55 Harrison St Ste 200, Oakland (94607-3790)
PHONE..................................800 777-0117
Kevin Lynch, *Vice Pres*
Doug Neiman, *Partner*
Christopher Kevorkian, *Vice Pres*
Mark Okean, *Vice Pres*
Christina Olsen, *Vice Pres*
EMP: 150 **EST:** 1928
SQ FT: 56,000
SALES (est): 45.6MM
SALES (corp-wide): 206.5MM **Privately Held**
WEB: www.sunset.com
SIC: 2721 2731 Magazines: publishing only, not printed on site; books: publishing only
PA: Regent, Lp
9720 Wilshire Blvd
Beverly Hills CA 90212
310 299-4100

(P-3518)
VIDEOMAKER INC
Also Called: Smart TV & Sound
645 Mangrove Ave, Chico (95926-3946)
P.O. Box 4591 (95927-4591)
PHONE..................................530 891-8410
Matthew York, *President*
Patrice York, *Treasurer*
Issac York, *Admin Sec*
Katz Rosal, *Web Dvlpr*
Mike Wilhelm, *Chief*
EMP: 36 **EST:** 1985
SQ FT: 8,000
SALES (est): 4.1MM **Privately Held**
WEB: www.videomaker.com
SIC: 2721 7812 Magazines: publishing only, not printed on site; motion picture & video production

(P-3519)
VIZ MEDIA LLC
Also Called: Viz Media Music
1355 Market St Ste 200, San Francisco (94103-1460)
P.O. Box 77010 (94107-0010)
PHONE..................................415 546-7073
Hidemi Fukuhara, *CEO*
Brad Woods, *Chief Mktg Ofcr*
Leyla Aker, *Vice Pres*
Akane Matsuo, *Vice Pres*
Diana Chan, *Planning*
▲ **EMP:** 153 **EST:** 1986
SALES (est): 64.8MM **Privately Held**
WEB: www.viz.com
SIC: 2721 2731 7819 6794 Comic books: publishing only, not printed on site; books: publishing only; video tape or disk reproduction; copyright buying & licensing; pre-recorded records & tapes
PA: Shogakukan Inc.
2-3-1, Hitotsubashi
Chiyoda-Ku TKY 101-0

(P-3520)
WINE COMMUNICATIONS GROUP
Also Called: Wine Business Monthly
584 1st St E, Sonoma (95476-6753)
PHONE..................................707 939-0822
Eric Jorgensen, *President*
Jacki Kardum, *Office Mgr*
EMP: 15 **EST:** 2001 **Privately Held**
WEB: www.winebusiness.com
SIC: 2721 Magazines: publishing only, not printed on site

(P-3521)
ZIMBIO INC (PA)
990 Industrial Rd Ste 204, San Carlos (94070-4120)
PHONE..................................650 594-1723
Tony Mamone, *CEO*
Danny Khatib, *President*
Thomas Ream, *CFO*
Bruce Martin, *CTO*
EMP: 82 **EST:** 2005
SALES (est): 1.1MM **Privately Held**
WEB: www.zimbio.com
SIC: 2721 Magazines: publishing only, not printed on site

2731 Books: Publishing & Printing

(P-3522)
ANANDA CHURCH OF SELF-REALZTN (PA)
Also Called: EXPANDING LIGHT, THE
14618 Tyler Foote Rd, Nevada City (95959-9316)
PHONE..................................530 478-7560
John Novak, *President*
Cathy Parojinog, *Corp Secy*
Latika Parojinog, *General Mgr*
Robert Stolzman, *Administration*
Suzanne Ilgun, *Human Res Dir*
EMP: 80 **EST:** 1968
SQ FT: 25,000
SALES (est): 9.2MM **Privately Held**
WEB: www.ananda.org
SIC: 8661 8299 5942 2731 Religious organizations; religious school; books, religious; books: publishing only

(P-3523)
BERRETT-KOEHLER PUBLISHERS INC (PA)
1333 Broadway Ste 1000, Oakland (94612-1926)
PHONE..................................510 817-2277
Steven Piersanti, *President*
Nina Thompson, *Finance*
Valerie Caldwell, *Production*
Tryn Brown, *Sales Staff*
Jason Van Den Eng, *Manager*
▲ **EMP:** 16 **EST:** 1991
SQ FT: 5,400
SALES (est): 2.5MM **Privately Held**
WEB: www.bkconnection.com
SIC: 2731 Books: publishing only

(P-3524)
BLUE MTN CTR OF MEDITATION INC
Also Called: Nilgiri Press
3600 Tomales Rd, Tomales (94971)
P.O. Box 256 (94971-0256)
PHONE..................................707 878-2369
Christine Easwaran, *President*
Debbie McMurray, *President*
Joan Barnicle, *Executive*
Lisa Bishop, *Director*
John Suerstedt, *Manager*
EMP: 31 **EST:** 1961
SQ FT: 1,800
SALES (est): 2.7MM **Privately Held**
WEB: www.bmcm.org
SIC: 2731 8661 Books: publishing & printing; religious organizations

(P-3525)
BLURB INC
580 California St Fl 3, San Francisco (94104-1024)
PHONE..................................415 364-6300
Eileen Gittins, *CEO*
Kelly Leach, *COO*
Elizabeth Allen, *Chief Mktg Ofcr*
Jacob Waddles, *Vice Pres*
Bruce Watermann, *Vice Pres*
EMP: 88 **EST:** 2004
SALES (est): 9.7MM **Privately Held**
WEB: www.blurb.com
SIC: 2731 Books: publishing only

PRODUCTS & SERVICES SECTION

2731 - Books: Publishing & Printing County (P-3548)

(P-3526)
CALLISTO MEDIA INC
1955 Broadway 400, Oakland
(94612-2205)
PHONE.....................510 253-0500
Benjamin Wayne, *CEO*
Mary Amicucci, *COO*
Brian Cooper, *CFO*
Timothy Musgrove, *CTO*
Laurens Drost,
EMP: 65 **EST:** 2011
SALES (est): 5.5MM **Privately Held**
WEB: www.callistomedia.com
SIC: 2731 Books: publishing only

(P-3527)
CENTER FOR CLLBRTIVE CLASSROOM
1001 Marina Village Pkwy # 1, Alameda
(94501-1091)
PHONE.....................510 533-0213
Roger King, *CEO*
Wendy Sadd, *Partner*
Victor Young, *President*
Brent Welling, *CFO*
Peter Brunn, *Vice Pres*
▲ **EMP:** 99 **EST:** 1975
SQ FT: 15,000
SALES (est): 17.6MM **Privately Held**
WEB: www.support.ccclearningportal.org
SIC: 2731 8299 Book publishing; personal development school

(P-3528)
CHRONICLE BOOKS LLC (HQ)
680 2nd St, San Francisco (94107-2015)
PHONE.....................415 537-4200
Nion McEvoy,
Emily Malter, *COO*
Lynn N Schroeder, *Vice Pres*
Sarah Billingsley, *Executive*
Evelyn Liang, *Executive*
◆ **EMP:** 159 **EST:** 1999
SALES (est): 73.9MM
SALES (corp-wide): 81.2MM **Privately Held**
WEB: www.chroniclebooks.com
SIC: 2731 Books: publishing only
PA: The Mcevoy Group Llc
   680 2nd St
   San Francisco CA 94107
   415 537-4200

(P-3529)
CITY LIGHTS BOOKS
Also Called: Book Sellers & Publishers
261 Columbus Ave, San Francisco
(94133-4586)
PHONE.....................415 362-8193
Andrew Bellows, *Principal*
Lawrence Ferlinghetti, *President*
Andy Bellows, *Bd of Directors*
Nancy Peters, *Vice Pres*
▲ **EMP:** 41 **EST:** 1953
SQ FT: 1,500
SALES (est): 5.4MM **Privately Held**
WEB: www.citylights.com
SIC: 5942 2731 Book stores; books: publishing only

(P-3530)
CLP APG LLC
1700 4th St, Berkeley (94710-1711)
PHONE.....................510 528-1444
Charles B Winton, *Ch of Bd*
Susan Reich, *President*
EMP: 214 **EST:** 1994
SQ FT: 14,000
SALES (est): 2MM
SALES (corp-wide): 99.6MM **Privately Held**
SIC: 2731 Books: publishing only
PA: Clp Pb, Llc
   1290 Ave Of The Amrcas Fl
   New York NY 10104
   212 340-8100

(P-3531)
CPP INC
185 N Wolfe Rd, Sunnyvale (94086-5212)
PHONE.....................650 969-8901
Elizabeth Connolly, *Vice Pres*
Thaddeus G Stephens, *Vice Pres*
Nimesh Mistry, *Software Dev*
Priya Nagarajan, *Analyst*
Martin Boult, *Director*
EMP: 19 **EST:** 2020
SALES (est): 1MM **Privately Held**
WEB: www.themyersbriggs.com
SIC: 2731 Book publishing

(P-3532)
DHARMA MUDRANALAYA (PA)
Also Called: DHARMA PUBLISHING
35788 Hauser Bridge Rd, Cazadero
(95421-9611)
PHONE.....................707 847-3380
Arnaud Maitland, *CEO*
Tarthang Tulku, *President*
Debbie Black, *Vice Pres*
▲ **EMP:** 21 **EST:** 1971
SQ FT: 16,000
SALES: 92.5K **Privately Held**
WEB: www.arnaudmaitland.com
SIC: 2731 7336 Books: publishing & printing; commercial art & graphic design

(P-3533)
EDUCATION TRAINING & RES ASSOC (PA)
Also Called: ETR
5619 Scotts Valley Dr # 140, Scotts Valley (95066-3453)
PHONE.....................831 438-4060
Vignetta Charles, *CEO*
Robert Keet, *Ch of Bd*
Robert Christensen, *Treasurer*
John Casken, *Vice Pres*
Rosalind Alexander-Kasperik, *Admin Sec*
EMP: 51 **EST:** 1981
SALES (est): 17.1MM **Privately Held**
WEB: www.etr.org
SIC: 8299 2731 2741 Educational services; pamphlets: publishing & printing; miscellaneous publishing

(P-3534)
HESPERIAN HEALTH GUIDES (PA)
1919 Addison St Ste 304, Berkeley
(94704-1143)
PHONE.....................510 845-1447
Sarah Shannon, *Exec Dir*
Rick Solomon, *Administration*
Mary A Buckley, *Business Mgr*
Sherry Nadworny, *Manager*
Rachel Grinstein, *Representative*
EMP: 20 **EST:** 1962
SQ FT: 1,600
SALES (est): 2.9MM **Privately Held**
WEB: www.hesperian.org
SIC: 2731 2741 8399 8641 Books: publishing only; miscellaneous publishing; community development groups; civic social & fraternal associations

(P-3535)
INSIGHT EDITIONS LP
800 A St, San Rafael (94901-3011)
P.O. Box 3088 (94912-3088)
PHONE.....................415 526-1370
Raoul Goff, *Partner*
Michael Madden, *Partner*
Callum Davenport, *Technology*
Jason Smalridge, *Accounting Mgr*
Thomas Chung, *Production*
▲ **EMP:** 70 **EST:** 2005
SALES (est): 14.5MM **Privately Held**
WEB: www.insighteditions.com
SIC: 2731 2721 Books: publishing only; comic books: publishing only, not printed on site

(P-3536)
KLUTZ
1450 Veterans Blvd, Redwood City (94063-2617)
PHONE.....................650 687-2650
Kelly Shasfer, *Branch Mgr*
EMP: 21
SALES (corp-wide): 1.3B **Publicly Held**
SIC: 2731 5092 Book publishing; toys
HQ: Klutz
   568 Broadway Rm 503
   New York NY 10012
   650 687-2600

(P-3537)
MCEVOY PROPERTIES LLC
680 2nd St, San Francisco (94107-2015)
PHONE.....................415 537-4200
Nion McEvoy,
EMP: 15 **EST:** 1999
SALES (est): 1.1MM **Privately Held**
WEB: www.mcevoygroup.com
SIC: 2731 Book publishing

(P-3538)
MEREDITH CORPORATION
Also Called: Meredith Publishing
201 Mission St Fl 12, San Francisco
(94105-1888)
PHONE.....................415 249-2362
Tamara Marcsisak, *Manager*
Julie Carp, *Marketing Staff*
April Rim, *Sales Staff*
Alyssa Roush, *Sales Staff*
Albert Murillo, *Accounts Exec*
EMP: 80
SALES (corp-wide): 2.9B **Publicly Held**
WEB: www.meredith.com
SIC: 2731 2721 Book publishing; periodicals
PA: Meredith Corporation
   1716 Locust St
   Des Moines IA 50309
   515 284-3000

(P-3539)
MIKE MURACH & ASSOCIATES
3730 W Swift Ave, Fresno (93722-6350)
PHONE.....................559 440-9071
Michael Murach, *President*
EMP: 22 **EST:** 1972
SALES (est): 3.5MM **Privately Held**
WEB: www.murach.com
SIC: 2731 Textbooks: publishing only, not printed on site

(P-3540)
NATIONAL DIRECTORY SERVICES
19698 View Forever Ln, Grass Valley (95945-8883)
PHONE.....................530 268-8636
EMP: 20 **EST:** 1989
SALES (est): 1.4MM **Privately Held**
WEB: www.lucchesivineyards.com
SIC: 2731 2741 Books-Publishing/Printing Misc Publishing

(P-3541)
NATURAL STD RES COLLABORATION
3120 W March Ln Fl 1, Stockton (95219-2368)
PHONE.....................617 591-3300
EMP: 20
SQ FT: 2,000
SALES (est): 2.5MM **Privately Held**
SIC: 2731 Books-Publishing/Printing

(P-3542)
NEW HARBINGER PUBLICATIONS INC (PA)
5674 Shattuck Ave, Oakland (94609-1662)
PHONE.....................510 652-0215
Matt McKay, *President*
Heather Garnos, *Vice Pres*
Rebekah Ayers, *Executive*
Minoo Irvani, *Executive*
Neocles Serafimidis, *Technology*
▲ **EMP:** 33 **EST:** 1975
SQ FT: 6,500 **Privately Held**
WEB: www.newharbinger.com
SIC: 2731 3652 Books: publishing only; master records or tapes, preparation of

(P-3543)
NOLO
6801 Koll Center Pkwy # 300, Pleasanton (94566-7095)
PHONE.....................510 549-1976
Bob Dubow, *CEO*
Laurence Nathanson, *Vice Pres*
John Plessas, *Vice Pres*
Mark Stuhr, *Vice Pres*
Jackie Thompson, *Vice Pres*
EMP: 120 **EST:** 1981
SALES (est): 10.3MM
SALES (corp-wide): 188.1MM **Privately Held**
WEB: www.nolo.com
SIC: 2731 8111 8742 Books: publishing only; legal services; marketing consulting services

PA: Autodata Solutions Group, Inc.
   909 N Pacific Coast Hwy # 11
   El Segundo CA 90245
   310 280-4000

(P-3544)
ROBERT W CAMERON & CO INC
Also Called: Cameroncompany
149 Kentucky St Ste 7, Petaluma
(94952-2940)
PHONE.....................707 769-1617
Robert Cameron, *Ch of Bd*
Christopher Roger Gruener, *CEO*
Tracy Davis, *Treasurer*
Iain Morris, *Vice Pres*
Linda Henry, *Admin Sec*
▲ **EMP:** 20 **EST:** 1965
SQ FT: 8,000
SALES (est): 1.3MM **Privately Held**
WEB: www.cameronbooks.com
SIC: 2731 Books: publishing only

(P-3545)
SOCIETY FOR THE STUDY NTIV ART
Also Called: North Atlantic Books
2526 Mrtin Lther King Jr, Berkeley
(94704-2607)
PHONE.....................510 549-4270
Douglas Reil, *CEO*
Lindy Hough, *Treasurer*
Richard Grossinger, *Exec Dir*
Alla Spector, *Finance Dir*
Bryan Lovitz, *Purch Dir*
▲ **EMP:** 25 **EST:** 1964
SQ FT: 6,000
SALES (est): 4.9MM **Privately Held**
WEB: www.northatlanticbooks.com
SIC: 2731 Books: publishing only

(P-3546)
TEACHERS CURRICULUM INST LLC (PA)
2440 W El Cmino Real Ste, Mountain View (94040)
P.O. Box 1327, Rancho Cordova (95741-1327)
PHONE.....................800 497-6138
Bert Bower, *Mng Member*
Kathy Peasley, *Admin Sec*
Nathan Wellborne, *Software Dev*
Marsha Ifurung, *Opers Mgr*
Jodi Forrest, *Prdtn Mgr*
▲ **EMP:** 24 **EST:** 1989
SQ FT: 7,994
SALES (est): 28MM **Privately Held**
WEB: www.teachtci.com
SIC: 2731 8748 Books: publishing only; educational consultant

(P-3547)
UNIVERSITY CAL PRESS FUNDATION (PA)
155 Grand Ave Ste 400, Oakland
(94612-3764)
PHONE.....................510 642-4247
Lynne Withey, *President*
Richard C Atkinson, *President*
Tim Sullivan, *Exec Dir*
Alma Yee, *Accounting Mgr*
Armine Hacoupian, *Accountant*
▲ **EMP:** 100 **EST:** 1893
SALES (est): 15.7MM **Privately Held**
WEB: www.ucpress.edu
SIC: 2731 Books: publishing only

(P-3548)
UNIVERSITY CAL PRESS FUNDATION
2000 Center St Ste 303, Berkeley
(94704-1200)
PHONE.....................510 642-4247
EMP: 25
SALES (corp-wide): 7MM **Privately Held**
WEB: www.ucpress.edu
SIC: 2731 Books-Publishing/Printing
PA: University Of California Press Foundation
   155 Grand Ave Ste 400
   Oakland CA 94612
   510 642-4247

2731 - Books: Publishing & Printing

(P-3549)
UNIVERSITY CALIFORNIA BERKELEY
Also Called: University of California Press
155 Grand Ave Ste 400, Oakland (94612-3764)
PHONE 510 642-4247
EMP: 20
SALES (corp-wide): 300.1MM Privately Held
WEB: www.berkeley.edu
SIC: 2731 8221 9411 Books-Publishing/Printing
HQ: The University California Berkeley
200 Clfrnia Hall Spc 1500
Berkeley CA 94720
510 642-6000

(P-3550)
WHATEVER PUBLISHING INC
Also Called: New World Library
14 Pamaron Way Ste 1, Novato (94949-6215)
PHONE 415 884-2100
Marc Allen, President
Victoria Clarke, CEO
▲ EMP: 18 EST: 1977
SQ FT: 6,000
SALES (est): 2.6MM Privately Held
WEB: www.whatever-publishing-inc.hub.biz
SIC: 2731 Books: publishing only

2732 Book Printing, Not Publishing

(P-3551)
CONSOLIDATED PRINTERS INC
2630 8th St, Berkeley (94710-2588)
PHONE 510 843-8524
Lawrence A Hawkins, CEO
Jim Fassett, Vice Pres
Paula Dudley, Human Res Dir
Ken Thorsen, VP Mfg
Mike Fave, Mktg Dir
EMP: 50 EST: 1952
SQ FT: 60,000
SALES (est): 8.6MM Privately Held
WEB: www.consoprinters.com
SIC: 2732 2752 Books: printing & binding; commercial printing, lithographic

2741 Misc Publishing

(P-3552)
ADOBE
601 Townsend St Fl 1, San Francisco (94103-5248)
PHONE 415 832-7791
Robert Hardy, Executive
Kashka Pregowska, Creative Dir
Rhona Pau, Executive Asst
Tammy Leamons, Administration
Rahul Biswas, Engineer
EMP: 32 EST: 2017
SALES (est): 1.1MM Privately Held
WEB: www.adobeintelapplab.com
SIC: 2741 Miscellaneous publishing

(P-3553)
AIRCRAFT TECHNICAL PUBLISHERS (PA)
Also Called: Atp
2000 Sierra Point Pkwy # 501, Brisbane (94005-1874)
PHONE 415 330-9500
Rick Noble, CEO
Stephen Gray, CFO
Mark Culpepper,
Ted Haugner, Vice Pres
Victor Sanchez, Vice Pres
EMP: 50 EST: 1973
SQ FT: 28,000
SALES (est): 23.8MM Privately Held
WEB: www.atp.com
SIC: 2741 Miscellaneous publishing

(P-3554)
AMERICAN MEDIA CORP
Also Called: Digital Media Publishing
150 Harbor Dr 2442, Sausalito (94965-9900)
PHONE 800 652-0778
Cliff Fortune, CEO
Kian Ali, President
Janice Aurelio, CFO
Juvy Daclison, Director
EMP: 15 EST: 2020
SALES (est): 40MM Privately Held
SIC: 2741

(P-3555)
ARENA PRESS
Also Called: Academic Therapy Publications
20 Leveroni Ct, Novato (94949-5746)
PHONE 415 883-3314
Anna Arena, Administration
Jenica Wilson, Officer
Jim Arena, Production
Jill Inglish, Manager
Ellen Thomsen, Assistant
EMP: 15 EST: 1980
SALES (est): 544K Privately Held
SIC: 2741 Miscellaneous publishing

(P-3556)
ART BRAND STUDIOS LLC (PA)
18715 Madrone Pkwy, Morgan Hill (95037-2876)
PHONE 408 201-5000
Steve Loveless,
Kristen Barthelman, Vice Pres
Lisa Nixon, Vice Pres
Lonnie Tsai, VP Finance
Karen Batista, Marketing Staff
EMP: 50 EST: 2014
SQ FT: 40,000
SALES (est): 12.9MM Privately Held
WEB: www.artbrandstudios.com
SIC: 2741 6794 Art copy & poster publishing; copyright buying & licensing

(P-3557)
ASK MEDIA GROUP LLC
555 12th St Ste 500, Oakland (94607-3699)
PHONE 510 985-7400
Joanne Hawkins, Mng Member
Gregg Winiarski,
EMP: 15 EST: 2016
SALES (est): 762.2K Privately Held
WEB: www.askmediagroup.com
SIC: 2741

(P-3558)
ASSOCTED STDNTS OF THE UNIV CA
Also Called: Bsr
112 Hearst Gym Rm 4520, Berkeley (94720-3611)
P.O. Box 40140 (94704-4140)
PHONE 510 590-7874
Omotara Oloye, Vice Chairman
EMP: 100
SALES (corp-wide): 1.9MM Privately Held
WEB: www.asuc.org
SIC: 2741 8299 Miscellaneous publishing; educational services
PA: Associated Students Of The University Of California
Bancroft Way 400 Eshleman St Bancroft W
Berkeley CA 94704
510 642-5420

(P-3559)
BEST VALUE TEXTBOOKS LLC
Also Called: BVT Publishing
410 Hemsted Dr Ste 100, Redding (96002-0164)
P.O. Box 492831 (96049-2831)
PHONE 800 646-7782
Jason James, Mng Member
Richard Schofield, Business Dir
Shannon Conley, Business Mgr
Christine Davies, Sales Staff
EMP: 27 EST: 2004
SQ FT: 2,000
SALES (est): 4.6MM Privately Held
WEB: www.bvtpublishing.com
SIC: 2741 Miscellaneous publishing

(P-3560)
BIRDEYE INC (PA)
2479 E Byshore Rd Ste 175, Palo Alto (94303)
PHONE 800 561-3357
Navee Gupta, CEO
Ajay Chopra, General Ptnr
Phillip Long, Partner
Evan Manning, Partner
Dave Lehman, President
EMP: 107 EST: 2012
SALES (est): 11.6MM Privately Held
WEB: www.birdeye.com
SIC: 2741

(P-3561)
C&T PUBLISHING INC
1651 Challenge Dr, Concord (94520-5206)
PHONE 925 677-0377
J Todd Hensley, CEO
Tony Hensley, CFO
Gailen Runge, Creative Dir
Sue Astroth, Project Mgr
Tristan Gallagher, Marketing Staff
▲ EMP: 43 EST: 1983
SQ FT: 12,250
SALES (est): 6.2MM Privately Held
WEB: www.ctpub.com
SIC: 2741 Miscellaneous publishing

(P-3562)
CHINESE OVERSEAS MKTG SVC CORP
33420 Alvarado Niles Rd, Union City (94587-3110)
PHONE 510 476-0880
Alan KAO, President
EMP: 20
SALES (corp-wide): 1.5MM Privately Held
WEB: www.ccyp.com
SIC: 2741 7389 Directories, telephone: publishing only, not printed on site; trade show arrangement
PA: Chinese Overseas Marketing Service Corporation
3940 Rosemead Blvd
Rosemead CA 91770
626 280-8588

(P-3563)
CHINESE OVERSEAS MKTG SVC CORP
Also Called: Chinese Consumer Yellow Pages
46292 Warm Springs Blvd, Fremont (94539-7997)
PHONE 626 280-8588
Gorden KAO, Branch Mgr
EMP: 20
SALES (corp-wide): 1.5MM Privately Held
WEB: www.ccyp.com
SIC: 2741 7389 8742 Directories, telephone: publishing only, not printed on site; trade show arrangement; marketing consulting services
PA: Chinese Overseas Marketing Service Corporation
3940 Rosemead Blvd
Rosemead CA 91770
626 280-8588

(P-3564)
CRAZY MAPLE STUDIO INC (PA)
1277 Borregas Ave Ste A, Sunnyvale (94089-1311)
PHONE 972 757-1283
Yi Jia, President
EMP: 33 EST: 2016
SALES (est): 1MM Privately Held
WEB: www.crazymaplestudios.com
SIC: 2741

(P-3565)
CRITTENDEN PUBLISHING INC (HQ)
45 Leveroni Ct Ste 204, Novato (94949-5721)
P.O. Box 1150 (94948-1150)
PHONE 415 475-1522
Alan Crittenden, CEO
Allen Crittenden, President
David Berger, Principal
Teresa Moody, Principal
EMP: 100 EST: 1980
SQ FT: 9,500
SALES (est): 2MM
SALES (corp-wide): 6.2MM Privately Held
WEB: www.crittendenonline.com
SIC: 2741 2721 Newsletter publishing; periodicals
PA: Crittenden Research, Inc.
45 Leveroni Ct
Novato CA
415 475-1576

(P-3566)
DLIVE INC
3390 Octavius Dr Apt 438, Santa Clara (95054-3165)
PHONE 650 491-9555
Charles Wayn, CEO
EMP: 20 EST: 2018
SALES (est): 749.3K Privately Held
SIC: 2741

(P-3567)
DWELL LIFE INC
Also Called: Dwell Store The
548 Market St, San Francisco (94104-5401)
P.O. Box 160171, Brooklyn NY (11216-0171)
PHONE 212,382-2010
Regina Flynn, Office Mgr
Camille Rankin, Manager
Samantha Daly, Assistant
EMP: 17
SALES (corp-wide): 20MM Privately Held
WEB: www.dwell.com
SIC: 2741 Miscellaneous publishing
PA: Dwell Life, Inc.
595 Pacific Ave Fl 4
San Francisco CA 94133
415 373-5100

(P-3568)
ECONODAY INC
3730 Mt Diablo Blvd # 340, Lafayette (94549-3641)
P.O. Box 954 (94549-0954)
PHONE 925 299-5350
Cynthia Parker, President
June Moberg, Admin Sec
Alana Kleinberger, Director
EMP: 17 EST: 1990
SQ FT: 1,200
SALES (est): 1.7MM Privately Held
WEB: www.econoday.com
SIC: 2741 Miscellaneous publishing

(P-3569)
EMPLOYERWARE LLC
Also Called: Poster Compliance Center
350 N Wiget Ln Ste 200, Walnut Creek (94598-2448)
P.O. Box 188, Hopkinton MA (01748-0188)
PHONE 925 283-9735
Maurice Levich,
Jacqueline Smith, Research
Crystal Soto, Marketing Staff
Elizabeth Gilbertson, Manager
Angel Tims, Manager
EMP: 33 EST: 1996
SALES (est): 2.6MM Privately Held
WEB: www.postercompliance.com
SIC: 2741 8748 Miscellaneous publishing; publishing consultant

(P-3570)
EP EXECUTIVE PRESS INC
201 Stonewall Rd, Berkeley (94705-1418)
PHONE 925 685-5111
Jesse M Brill, Principal
EMP: 15 EST: 2001
SALES (est): 290.6K Privately Held
WEB: www.ccrcorp.com
SIC: 2741 Miscellaneous publishing

(P-3571)
FIRST DATABANK INC (DH)
Also Called: First Data Bank
701 Gateway Blvd Ste 600, South San Francisco (94080-7084)
PHONE 800 633-3453
Gregory H Dorn, President
Don Nielsen, President
James Schultz, Treasurer
Bob Katter, Exec VP
Clifton Louie, Exec VP

PRODUCTS & SERVICES SECTION

2741 - Misc Publishing County (P-3596)

EMP: 100 **EST:** 1977
SALES (est): 64.4MM
SALES (corp-wide): 4.2B **Privately Held**
WEB: www.fdbhealth.com
SIC: 2741 7375 Technical manuals: publishing only, not printed on site; micropublishing; information retrieval services; data base information retrieval
HQ: Hearst Business Media Corp
2620 Barrett Rd
Gainesville GA 30507
770 532-4111

(P-3572)
FUNDX INVESTMENT GROUP LLC
Also Called: Fundex Investment Group
235 Montgomery St # 1049, San Francisco (94104-2902)
PHONE 415 986-7979
Janet Brown, *President*
Jeffrey Smith, *Principal*
Dannielle Kimpel, *Executive Asst*
Bernard Burke, *Portfolio Mgr*
Avani Desai, *Portfolio Mgr*
EMP: 18 **EST:** 1969
SQ FT: 2,000
SALES (est): 1.9MM **Privately Held**
WEB: www.fundx.com
SIC: 2741 6282 Newsletter publishing; investment advisory service

(P-3573)
GOFF INVESTMENT GROUP LLC
Also Called: Global Printing Sourcing & Dev
135 3rd St Ste 150, San Rafael (94901-3531)
PHONE 415 456-2934
Steven Goff, *Managing Dir*
▲ **EMP:** 21 **EST:** 2004
SQ FT: 3,000
SALES (est): 1.7MM **Privately Held**
WEB: www.touchstoneeditions.com
SIC: 2741 Miscellaneous publishing

(P-3574)
GUADALUPE ASSOCIATES INC (PA)
Also Called: Ignatius Press
1348 10th Ave, San Francisco (94122-2304)
PHONE 415 387-2324
Mark Brumley, *CEO*
Vanessa Dekkers, *VP Finance*
Jack Gergurich, *Accountant*
Carolyn Lemon, *Production*
Lisa Becerra, *Sales Staff*
◆ **EMP:** 15
SQ FT: 1,500
SALES (est): 2.9MM **Privately Held**
WEB: www.ignatius.com
SIC: 2741 2731 Miscellaneous publishing; books: publishing only

(P-3575)
HAGADONE DIRECTORIES INC
555 H St Ste E, Eureka (95501-1045)
PHONE 707 444-0255
Jim Hail, *President*
EMP: 219
SALES (corp-wide): 290.9MM **Privately Held**
WEB: www.blackphonebook.com
SIC: 2741 Directories: publishing & printing
HQ: Hagadone Directories Inc
201 N 2nd St
Coeur D Alene ID 83814
208 667-8744

(P-3576)
HEALTHLINE MEDIA INC (PA)
660 3rd St, San Francisco (94107-1927)
PHONE 415 281-3100
David Kopp, *CEO*
Cheryl Kim, *CFO*
Laurie Dewan, *Vice Pres*
Steve Swasey, *Vice Pres*
Matthew Urbanos, *Vice Pres*
EMP: 270 **EST:** 2015
SALES (est): 79.9MM **Privately Held**
WEB: www.healthline.com
SIC: 2741

(P-3577)
INSTITUTIONAL REAL ESTATE INC (PA)
1475 N Broadway Ste 300, Walnut Creek (94596-4643)
PHONE 925 933-4040
Geoffrey Dohrmann, *CEO*
Nyia Dohrman, *President*
Erika Cohen, *COO*
Jonathan A Schein, *Senior VP*
Randy Schein, *Info Tech Mgr*
EMP: 20 **EST:** 1986
SQ FT: 3,000
SALES (est): 4MM **Privately Held**
WEB: www.irei.com
SIC: 2741 8742 8748 2721 Newsletter publishing; real estate consultant; business consulting; periodicals

(P-3578)
ISSUU INC (PA)
131 Lytton Ave, Palo Alto (94301-1045)
PHONE 844 477-8800
Joseph Hyrkin, *CEO*
Erika Fogarty, *Vice Pres*
EMP: 59 **EST:** 2007
SALES (est): 11MM **Privately Held**
WEB: www.issuu.com
SIC: 2741 Miscellaneous publishing

(P-3579)
JIGSAW DATA CORPORATION
900 Concar Dr, San Mateo (94402-2600)
PHONE 650 235-8400
James Fowler, *President*
Barry Friefield, *Partner*
Steven Klei, *CFO*
Garth Moulton, *Vice Pres*
EMP: 45 **EST:** 2004
SALES (est): 2.9MM
SALES (corp-wide): 17.1B **Publicly Held**
WEB: www.salesforce.com
SIC: 2741 Telephone & other directory publishing
PA: Salesforce.Com, Inc.
415 Mission St Fl 3
San Francisco CA 94105
415 901-7000

(P-3580)
JOURNEYWORKS PUBLISHING
763 Chestnut St, Santa Cruz (95060-3751)
P.O. Box 8466 (95061-8466)
PHONE 831 423-1400
Steven Bignell, *President*
Judith Carey, *Vice Pres*
Mary Bignell, *Admin Sec*
Daniel Dowell,
Paul Forsyth, *Manager*
EMP: 16 **EST:** 1995
SQ FT: 5,200
SALES (est): 2.4MM **Privately Held**
WEB: www.journeyworks.com
SIC: 2741 Miscellaneous publishing

(P-3581)
KUDOS&CO INC
470 Ramona St, Palo Alto (94301-1707)
PHONE 650 799-9104
Ole Vidar Hestaas, *CEO*
EMP: 15 **EST:** 2018
SALES (est): 9MM **Privately Held**
WEB: www.kudos.com
SIC: 2741

(P-3582)
MIND GARDEN INC
707 Menlo Ave Ste 120, Menlo Park (94025-4737)
PHONE 650 322-6300
Robert Most, *President*
Valorie Keller, *Marketing Staff*
EMP: 16 **EST:** 1994 **Privately Held**
WEB: www.mindgarden.com
SIC: 2741 Miscellaneous publishing

(P-3583)
MONGABAYORG CORPORATION
37 W Summit Dr, Emerald Hills (94062-3340)
PHONE 209 315-5573
Rhett Butler, *President*
David Martin, *Director*
Erik Hoffner, *Editor*
EMP: 15 **EST:** 2011
SALES: 2.9MM **Privately Held**
WEB: www.mongabay.org
SIC: 2741

(P-3584)
MOTHERLY INC
1725 Oakdell Dr, Menlo Park (94025-5735)
PHONE 917 860-9926
Jill Kozio, *CEO*
Christina Cubeta, *COO*
Liz Tenety, *Officer*
Allie Litwak, *Business Dir*
Lynn Egan, *General Mgr*
EMP: 24 **EST:** 2018
SALES (est): 1.3MM **Privately Held**
WEB: www.mother.ly
SIC: 2741

(P-3585)
NEXTAG INC (PA)
555 Twin Dolphin Dr # 370, Redwood City (94065-2133)
PHONE 650 645-4700
EMP: 81
SALES (est): 68.7MM **Privately Held**
WEB: www.nextag.co.uk
SIC: 2741 Misc Publishing

(P-3586)
NEXTLESSON INC
28 2nd St Ste 501, San Francisco (94105-3461)
P.O. Box 11543, Oakland (94611-0543)
PHONE 415 968-9655
Dion Lim, *CEO*
Michelle Labelle-Fisch, *Principal*
Duy Tran, *Software Engr*
Michael Escalante, *Professor*
Erin Carson, *Manager*
EMP: 17 **EST:** 2015
SALES (est): 545K **Privately Held**
WEB: www.nextlesson.org
SIC: 2741 Miscellaneous publishing

(P-3587)
OREILLY MEDIA INC (PA)
1005 Gravenstein Hwy N, Sebastopol (95472-2811)
PHONE 707 827-7000
Timothy O'Reilly, *President*
Maria Manrique, *CFO*
Vicky Dutkiewicz, *Vice Pres*
Michael Williams, *Vice Pres*
John Bennett, *Creative Dir*
▲ **EMP:** 150 **EST:** 1983
SQ FT: 90,000
SALES (est): 191.5MM **Privately Held**
WEB: www.oreilly.com
SIC: 2741 2731 8231 ; books: publishing only; libraries

(P-3588)
PEACHPIT PRESS
1301 Sansome St, San Francisco (94111-1122)
PHONE 415 336-6831
M Carreiro, *Director*
Lupe Edgar, *Production*
Lisa McClain, *Editor*
EMP: 15 **EST:** 2013
SALES (est): 625.7K **Privately Held**
WEB: www.peachpit.com
SIC: 2741 Miscellaneous publishing

(P-3589)
PENROSE STUDIOS INC
223 Mississippi St Ste 3, San Francisco (94107-2501)
P.O. Box 2507, Windermere FL (34786-2507)
PHONE 703 354-1801
Eugene Chung, *CEO*
Terry Kaleas, *Technical Staff*
EMP: 15 **EST:** 2015
SALES (est): 891.9K **Privately Held**
WEB: www.penrosestudios.com
SIC: 2741

(P-3590)
PEOPLEFINDERS NGT POR PRIOF
1915 21st St, Sacramento (95811-6813)
PHONE 916 341-0227
Rob Miller, *Principal*
Joseph Nocerino, *Vice Pres*
Jeremy Cheung, *Administration*
Emil Grigoryan, *Sr Software Eng*
Shawn Britton, *CTO*
EMP: 19 **EST:** 2014
SALES (est): 2.8MM **Privately Held**
WEB: www.peoplefinders.com
SIC: 2741 Miscellaneous publishing

(P-3591)
POPSUGAR INC (PA)
111 Sutter St Fl 16, San Francisco (94104-4541)
P.O. Box 560 (94104-0560)
PHONE 415 391-7576
Brian Sugar, *CEO*
Lexie McCarthy, *Partner*
Angelica Marden, *President*
Sean Macnew, *CFO*
Alex McNealey, *Exec VP*
▲ **EMP:** 134 **EST:** 2002
SALES (est): 70.7MM **Privately Held**
WEB: www.groupninemedia.com
SIC: 2741 Miscellaneous publishing

(P-3592)
PROVIDENCE PUBLICATIONS LLC
1620 Santa, Roseville (95661)
P.O. Box 2610, Granite Bay (95746-2610)
PHONE 916 774-4000
J Dale Debber, *Managing Dir*
Dwight T Lovan, *Commissioner*
Janet M Debber,
EMP: 30 **EST:** 1998
SQ FT: 7,904
SALES (est): 2.1MM **Privately Held**
WEB: www.wcexec.com
SIC: 2741 Miscellaneous publishing

(P-3593)
PUBLIC LIBRARY OF SCIENCE
1265 Battery St Ste 200, San Francisco (94111-6216)
PHONE 415 624-1200
Alison Mudditt, *CEO*
Elizabeth Marincola, *President*
Kristina Martin, *Officer*
Allison Rozema, *Admin Asst*
Carmen Melatti, *CIO*
EMP: 180 **EST:** 2001
SALES (est): 36.1MM **Privately Held**
WEB: www.plos.org
SIC: 8231 2741 Public library; miscellaneous publishing

(P-3594)
RANGEME USA LLC
821 Folsom St, San Francisco (94107-1190)
PHONE 510 688-0995
Nicky Jackson, *CEO*
Brandon Leong, *Vice Pres*
Darryl Jackson, *Admin Sec*
Josh Male, *Software Dev*
Phil Zarganis, *Opers Staff*
EMP: 17 **EST:** 2016
SALES (est): 672.4K **Privately Held**
WEB: www.rangeme.com
SIC: 2741 Miscellaneous publishing

(P-3595)
REDDIT INC (PA)
548 Market St Ste 16093, San Francisco (94104-5401)
PHONE 415 666-2330
Steve Huffman, *Founder*
Paula Klein, *Partner*
Julian Williams, *Partner*
Jen Wong, *COO*
Drew Vollero, *CFO*
EMP: 192 **EST:** 2011
SALES (est): 86.4MM **Privately Held**
WEB: www.reddit.com
SIC: 2741

(P-3596)
RETAIL CONTENT SERVICE INC
440 N Wolfe Rd, Sunnyvale (94085-3869)
PHONE 415 890-2097
Zakhar Dikhtyar, *CEO*
EMP: 45 **EST:** 2017
SALES (est): 968.8K **Privately Held**
SIC: 2741

2741 - Misc Publishing County (P-3597)

(P-3597)
SAFARI BOOKS ONLINE LLC (PA)
1003 Gravenstein Hwy N, Sebastopol (95472-2811)
PHONE..................707 827-7000
Kathy Lanterman,
Sonia Bobadilla, *Vice Pres*
Becki Valente, *Vice Pres*
Stuart Silcox, *Executive*
Chris Henley, *Senior Engr*
EMP: 70 **EST:** 2001
SALES (est): 11.3MM **Privately Held**
WEB: www.oreilly.com
SIC: 8231 2741 2731 Libraries; ; books: publishing only

(P-3598)
SERVICE EXPRESS INC
Also Called: Logistics
3619 S Fowler Ave, Fresno (93725-9327)
P.O. Box 565, Fowler (93625-0565)
PHONE..................559 495-4790
Harninder S Gill, *President*
EMP: 20 **EST:** 1996
SALES (est): 1.5MM **Privately Held**
SIC: 2741 Miscellaneous publishing

(P-3599)
SILICONINDIA INC
46560 Fremont Blvd # 413, Fremont (94538-6482)
PHONE..................510 440-8249
Harvi Sachar, *Principal*
Sunil Kolar, *Research*
Livya Leela, *Analyst*
Shashi Ranjan, *Marketing Staff*
Ashok Kumar, *Art Dir*
EMP: 89 **EST:** 2011
SALES (est): 570.2K **Privately Held**
WEB: www.siliconindia.com
SIC: 2741 Miscellaneous publishing

(P-3600)
SPARKCENTRAL INC (HQ)
535 Mission St Fl 14, San Francisco (94105-3253)
PHONE..................866 559-6229
Tom Keiser, *CEO*
Jess Hazlett, *Manager*
EMP: 57 **EST:** 2012
SQ FT: 1,400
SALES (est): 10.4MM
SALES (corp-wide): 207.8MM **Privately Held**
WEB: www.hootsuite.com
SIC: 2741 4899 Miscellaneous publishing; data communication services
PA: Hootsuite Inc
111 5th Ave E Suite 300
Vancouver BC V5T 4
604 681-4668

(P-3601)
STAFFING INDUSTRY ANALYSTS INC
Also Called: Staffing Industry Report
1975 W El Cmino Real Ste, Mountain View (94040)
PHONE..................650 390-6200
Ron Mester, *CEO*
Barry Asin, *CEO*
Tony Gregoire, *Research*
Lynn Dunn, *Technology*
Rohan Verma, *Marketing Mgr*
EMP: 68 **EST:** 1990
SQ FT: 4,307
SALES (est): 2.6MM
SALES (corp-wide): 249.1MM **Privately Held**
WEB: www.staffingindustry.com
SIC: 2741 Newsletter publishing
PA: Crain Communications, Inc.
1155 Gratiot Ave
Detroit MI 48207
313 446-6000

(P-3602)
STONE PUBLISHING INC (PA)
Also Called: Almaden
2549 Scott Blvd, Santa Clara (95050-2508)
PHONE..................408 450-7910
Eric Stern, *Ch of Bd*
Manny Cuevas, *President*
Chris Siebert, *CEO*

Aida Buljubasic, *Project Mgr*
Charlotta Gallo, *Project Mgr*
EMP: 110 **EST:** 1998
SQ FT: 100,000
SALES (est): 30MM **Privately Held**
WEB: www.almadenglobal.com
SIC: 2741 Miscellaneous publishing

(P-3603)
STRING LETTER PUBLISHING INC
Also Called: Acoustic Guitar Magazine
941 Marina Way S Ste E, Richmond (94804-3768)
PHONE..................510 215-0010
David Lusterman, *President*
Anita Evans, *Officer*
Amy-Lynn Fischer, *Sales Mgr*
Kevin Owens, *Manager*
Phil Hood, *Publisher*
EMP: 25 **EST:** 2013
SALES (est): 3.1MM **Privately Held**
WEB: www.stringletter.com
SIC: 2741 Miscellaneous publishing

(P-3604)
TELLME NETWORKS INC
1065 La Avenida St, Mountain View (94043-1421)
PHONE..................650 693-1009
John Lamacchia, *Chairman*
Robert Komin, *CFO*
▲ **EMP:** 330 **EST:** 1999
SALES (est): 72.9MM
SALES (corp-wide): 168B **Publicly Held**
WEB: www.247.ai
SIC: 2741 4812 Telephone & other directory publishing; radio telephone communication
PA: Microsoft Corporation
1 Microsoft Way
Redmond WA 98052
425 882-8080

(P-3605)
THINK SOCIAL PUBLISHING INC
404 Saratoga Ave Ste 200, Santa Clara (95050-7000)
PHONE..................408 557-8595
Michelle Winner, *CEO*
Pamela Crooke, *Officer*
Cathy Hart, *Office Mgr*
Veronica Zysk, *Manager*
▲ **EMP:** 20 **EST:** 2006
SALES (est): 3MM **Privately Held**
WEB: www.socialthinking.com
SIC: 2741 Miscellaneous publishing

(P-3606)
TOUCANED INC
1716 Brommer St, Santa Cruz (95062-3002)
PHONE..................831 464-0508
Kathleen Middleton, *President*
Jack Suitor, *Info Tech Dir*
EMP: 25 **EST:** 2002
SALES (est): 3.2MM **Privately Held**
WEB: www.toucaned.com
SIC: 2741 8742 Miscellaneous publishing; hospital & health services consultant

(P-3607)
TWITCH INTERACTIVE INC
350 Bush St Fl 2, San Francisco (94104-2879)
PHONE..................415 919-5000
Emmett Shear, *CEO*
Tyler Nosenzo, *Partner*
Kevin Lin, *COO*
John Sutton, *CFO*
Doug Scott, *Chief Mktg Ofcr*
EMP: 1146 **EST:** 2006
SALES (est): 228MM **Publicly Held**
WEB: www.justin.tv
SIC: 2741
PA: Amazon.Com, Inc.
410 Terry Ave N
Seattle WA 98109

(P-3608)
TWO LINES A JOURNAL
582 Market St Ste 700, San Francisco (94104-5308)
PHONE..................415 512-8812
Olivia Sears, *Principal*

Olivia E Sears, *Principal*
EMP: 18 **EST:** 1998
SALES (est): 167.4K **Privately Held**
WEB: www.catranslation.org
SIC: 2741 Miscellaneous publishing

(P-3609)
UCC GUIDE INC
Also Called: Ernst Publishing Co
225 Cabrillo Hwy S 200c, Half Moon Bay (94019-7200)
PHONE..................800 345-3822
Gregory E Teal, *Branch Mgr*
EMP: 15
SALES (corp-wide): 1.2B **Publicly Held**
SIC: 2741 Miscellaneous publishing
HQ: The Ucc Guide Inc
99 Washngton Ave Ste 309
Albany NY 12210

(P-3610)
UNITED REPORTING PUBG CORP
1835 Iron Point Rd # 100, Folsom (95630-8770)
P.O. Box 41037, Sacramento (95841-0037)
PHONE..................916 542-7501
Paul Curry, *CEO*
Christopher M Thompson, *President*
EMP: 17 **EST:** 1995
SQ FT: 3,399
SALES (est): 1.2MM **Privately Held**
WEB: www.unitedreporting.com
SIC: 2741 Miscellaneous publishing

(P-3611)
VISION PUBLICATIONS INC
Also Called: Vision Design Studio
109 Wappo Ave, Calistoga (94515-1136)
PHONE..................562 597-4000
Carl Patrick Dene, *President*
Beverly Wurth, *Director*
EMP: 28 **EST:** 2000
SALES (est): 3.4MM **Privately Held**
SIC: 2741 7311 Miscellaneous publishing; advertising agencies

(P-3612)
YB MEDIA LLC
1534 Plaza Ln 146, Burlingame (94010-3204)
PHONE..................310 467-5804
Benjamin Maggin, *CEO*
EMP: 20 **EST:** 2017
SALES (est): 523.8K **Privately Held**
WEB: www.yardbarker.com
SIC: 2741

2752 Commercial Printing: Lithographic

(P-3613)
ABC PRINTING INC
1090 S Milpitas Blvd, Milpitas (95035-6307)
PHONE..................408 263-1118
Danny Luong, *President*
Diana Wong, *Treasurer*
EMP: 15 **EST:** 1986
SQ FT: 8,000 **Privately Held**
SIC: 2752 Commercial printing, offset

(P-3614)
ACME PRESS INC
Also Called: California Lithographers
2312 Stanwell Dr, Concord (94520-4809)
P.O. Box 5698 (94524-0698)
PHONE..................925 682-1111
Mardjan Taheripour, *CEO*
Bahman Taheripour, *Vice Pres*
Randy Waterhouse, *Executive*
Kenneth Vonberg, *Info Tech Dir*
Kari Wasson, *Technology*
EMP: 87 **EST:** 1976
SQ FT: 36,000
SALES (est): 21.2MM **Privately Held**
WEB: www.calitho.com
SIC: 2752 Commercial printing, offset

(P-3615)
ACP VENTURES
Also Called: Allegro Copy & Print
3340 Mt Diablo Blvd Ste B, Lafayette (94549-4076)
PHONE..................925 297-0100
Peter Smyth, *President*
Karen Smyth, *Vice Pres*
William Slovick, *Technical Staff*
EMP: 19 **EST:** 1987
SQ FT: 6,300
SALES (est): 2.1MM **Privately Held**
SIC: 2752 2791 2789 7331 Commercial printing, offset; typesetting; bookbinding & related work; mailing service

(P-3616)
ADMAIL-EXPRESS INC
31640 Hayman St, Hayward (94544-7122)
PHONE..................510 471-6200
Brian M Schott, *CEO*
EMP: 45 **EST:** 1973
SQ FT: 55,000
SALES (est): 7.5MM **Privately Held**
WEB: www.admail.com
SIC: 2752 Commercial printing, offset

(P-3617)
AKIDO PRINTING INC
Also Called: Promotion Xpress Prtg Graphics
2096 Merced St, San Leandro (94577-3230)
PHONE..................510 357-0238
Thanh Do, *President*
Stella Phan, *CFO*
EMP: 15 **EST:** 1992
SQ FT: 12,000
SALES (est): 873.9K **Privately Held**
WEB: www.proxprint.com
SIC: 2752 Commercial printing, offset

(P-3618)
ALLYN JAMES INC
6575 Trinity Ct Ste B, Dublin (94568-2643)
PHONE..................925 828-5530
Mark Cady, *President*
Mark W Cady, *President*
Curtis J Mc Carthy, *Vice Pres*
Curtis McCarthy, *Vice Pres*
Cindy McInnis, *Production*
EMP: 16 **EST:** 2001
SALES (est): 3.7MM **Privately Held**
WEB: www.jamesallyn.com
SIC: 2752 Commercial printing, offset

(P-3619)
AMERICAN LITHOGRAPHERS INC
Also Called: Pacific Standard Print
1281 National Dr, Sacramento (95834-1902)
PHONE..................916 441-5392
Joe R Davis, *CEO*
Tom Mueller, *President*
Peter Bachelor, *Executive*
Ian Redmond, *Sales Executive*
Phil Degaa, *Sales Staff*
EMP: 70 **EST:** 2001
SALES (est): 15.1MM
SALES (corp-wide): 4.7B **Publicly Held**
WEB: www.rrd.com
SIC: 2752 2759 Commercial printing, offset; commercial printing
HQ: Consolidated Graphics, Inc.
5858 Westheimer Rd # 200
Houston TX 77057
713 787-0977

(P-3620)
API MARKETING
Also Called: Auburn Printers and Mfg
13020 Earhart Ave, Auburn (95602-9536)
PHONE..................916 632-1946
Merrill Kagan-Weston, *President*
Brad Weston, *Vice Pres*
Richard Neal, *Network Mgr*
Kelley Buxton, *Opers Mgr*
Steve Reynolds, *Sales Staff*
EMP: 17 **EST:** 1946
SQ FT: 10,000 **Privately Held**
WEB: www.api-marketing.com
SIC: 2752 Commercial printing, offset; catalogs, lithographed; circulars, lithographed

▲ = Import ▼=Export
◆ =Import/Export

PRODUCTS & SERVICES SECTION
2752 - Commercial Printing: Lithographic County (P-3646)

(P-3621)
ASIA AMERICA ENTERPRISE INC
Also Called: America Printing
1321 N Carolan Ave, Burlingame (94010-2401)
PHONE..................................650 348-2333
Macy Mak, *CEO*
Ryan Mak, *Corp Secy*
Wistaria Sum, *Manager*
EMP: 20 **EST:** 1980
SQ FT: 27,000
SALES (est): 3.4MM Privately Held
WEB: www.americanspeedy.com
SIC: 2752 Commercial printing, offset

(P-3622)
ASL PRINT FX
871 Latour Ct, NAPA (94558-6258)
PHONE..................................707 927-3096
EMP: 16 **EST:** 2017
SALES (est): 3.4MM Privately Held
WEB: www.aslprintfx.com
SIC: 2752 Commercial printing, lithographic

(P-3623)
AUTUMN PRESS INC
945 Camelia St, Berkeley (94710-1437)
PHONE..................................510 654-4545
Miguel Alson, *President*
Theresa Thornton, *Vice Pres*
EMP: 27 **EST:** 1978
SQ FT: 15,000
SALES (est): 5.3MM Privately Held
WEB: www.autumnpress.com
SIC: 2752 Commercial printing, offset

(P-3624)
AVOY CORP
114 Greenbank Ave, Piedmont (94611-4336)
PHONE..................................510 295-8055
Sedrick A Tydus, *Branch Mgr*
EMP: 44 Privately Held
WEB: www.chanhassen-mn.minutemanpress.com
SIC: 2752 Commercial printing, offset
PA: Avoy Corp.
2633 Telg Ave Ste 103
Oakland CA 94612

(P-3625)
B R PRINTERS INC (PA)
665 Lenfest Rd, San Jose (95133-1615)
PHONE..................................408 278-7711
Adam Demaestri, *President*
Richard Brown, *President*
Derek Giulianelli, *Vice Pres*
Chris Rooney, *Vice Pres*
Carlee Harder-Brown, *Admin Sec*
EMP: 68 **EST:** 1992
SQ FT: 90,000
SALES (est): 51.3MM Privately Held
WEB: www.brprinters.com
SIC: 2752 Commercial printing, offset

(P-3626)
BABYLON PRINTING INC
Also Called: Medius
15850 Concord Cir Ste B, Morgan Hill (95037-7143)
PHONE..................................408 519-5000
Daisy Zaia, *CEO*
George Zaia, *Vice Pres*
Gene Joudy, *Exec Dir*
Miruna Williams, *Marketing Staff*
Dena Toma, *Director*
◆ **EMP:** 43
SALES: 14.7MM Privately Held
WEB: www.mediuscorp.com
SIC: 2752 Commercial printing, offset

(P-3627)
BACCHUS PRESS INC (PA)
1287 66th St, Emeryville (94608-1198)
PHONE..................................510 420-5800
Monsoor Assadi, *President*
Jerry Blueford, *Supervisor*
EMP: 20 **EST:** 1975
SQ FT: 10,000
SALES (est): 7.4MM Privately Held
WEB: www.bacchuspress.com
SIC: 2752 Commercial printing, offset

(P-3628)
BARLOW AND SONS PRINTING INC
Also Called: Barlow Printing
481 Aaron St, Cotati (94931-3081)
PHONE..................................707 664-9773
Patrick Barlow, *President*
Ken Reed, *Vice Pres*
EMP: 15 **EST:** 1961
SQ FT: 20,000
SALES (est): 3.2MM Privately Held
WEB: www.barlowprinting.com
SIC: 2752 Letters, circular or form: lithographed; commercial printing, offset

(P-3629)
BATCHLDER BUS CMMNICATIONS INC
Also Called: AlphaGraphics
2900 Standiford Ave Ste 5, Modesto (95350-6575)
PHONE..................................209 577-2222
Ardern Batchelder, *President*
EMP: 21 **EST:** 1999
SALES (est): 1.4MM Privately Held
WEB: www.alphagraphics.com
SIC: 2752 7331 Commercial printing, lithographic; mailing list compilers

(P-3630)
BAY PRINT SOLUTIONS INC
161 W San Fernando St, San Jose (95113-2108)
PHONE..................................408 579-6640
John Peters, *Administration*
EMP: 17 **EST:** 2015
SALES (est): 651.7K Privately Held
WEB: www.bayprint.com
SIC: 2752 Commercial printing, offset

(P-3631)
BIBBERO SYSTEMS INC (HQ)
1425 N Mcdowell Blvd # 211, Petaluma (94954-1180)
PHONE..................................800 242-2376
Michael Buckley, *President*
Joan Buckley, *Corp Secy*
EMP: 23 **EST:** 1953
SALES (est): 1.7MM
SALES (corp-wide): 31.5MM Privately Held
WEB: www.bibbero.com
SIC: 2752 2759 Commercial printing, offset; business forms: printing
PA: Professional Filing Systems, Inc.
5076 Winters Chapel Rd # 200
Atlanta GA 30360
770 396-4994

(P-3632)
CALIFRNIA INTEGRATED MEDIA INC
Also Called: AlphaGraphics
14 Avila St, San Francisco (94123-2008)
PHONE..................................415 627-8310
Manuel Torres, *CEO*
EMP: 16 **EST:** 2015
SALES (est): 1.5MM Privately Held
WEB: www.alphagraphics.com
SIC: 2752 Commercial printing, lithographic

(P-3633)
CENTRAL BUSINESS FORMS INC
Also Called: Central Printing Group
289 Foster City Blvd B, Foster City (94404-1100)
PHONE..................................650 548-0918
Jeanine M Morgan, *President*
Michelle L Cabral, *Corp Secy*
EMP: 29 **EST:** 1982
SQ FT: 22,800
SALES (est): 3.5MM Privately Held
WEB: www.cpgusa.com
SIC: 2752 Commercial printing, offset

(P-3634)
CENVEO WORLDWIDE LIMITED
665 3rd St Ste 505, San Francisco (94107-1956)
PHONE..................................415 821-7171
Coleen Schoenatide, *Branch Mgr*
James Stafford, *Vice Pres*
Karen Vaughn, *Production*
Mark Gustafson, *Sales Staff*
Jose Jimenez, *Maintence Staff*
EMP: 152
SALES (corp-wide): 1B Privately Held
WEB: www.cenveo.com
SIC: 2752 Commercial printing, offset
HQ: Cenveo Worldwide Limited
200 First Stamford Pl
Stamford CT 06902
203 595-3000

(P-3635)
CHECCHI ENTERPRISES INC
Also Called: Harvest Printing Company
19849 Riverside Ave, Anderson (96007-4909)
PHONE..................................530 378-1207
Tom Watega, *President*
Diana Watega, *Bookkeeper*
Joni Sargent, *Manager*
EMP: 15 **EST:** 1976
SQ FT: 10,200
SALES (est): 1.8MM Privately Held
WEB: www.harvestprinting.com
SIC: 2752 Commercial printing, offset

(P-3636)
CLIC LLC
Also Called: Andresen
396 Forbes Blvd Ste D, South San Francisco (94080-2025)
PHONE..................................415 421-2900
Michael Hicks, *Mng Member*
Cynthia Pinkney, *Broker*
John Franco, *Prdtn Mgr*
Andresen Family Trust, *Mng Member*
EMP: 24 **EST:** 2004
SALES (est): 4.9MM Privately Held
SIC: 2752 7374 Commercial printing, lithographic; computer graphics service

(P-3637)
CMY IMAGE CORPORATION
Also Called: Compandsave
33268 Central Ave, Union City (94587-2010)
PHONE..................................510 516-6668
Andrew Yeung, *CEO*
EMP: 15 **EST:** 2013
SALES (est): 6MM Privately Held
WEB: www.cmyimage.com
SIC: 2752 Photo-offset printing

(P-3638)
COMMUNITY PRINTERS INC
1827 Soquel Ave, Santa Cruz (95062-1385)
PHONE..................................831 426-4682
Joe Chavez, *President*
Shelly D'Amour, *CFO*
Mischa Kandinksy, *Treasurer*
Andy Bacon, *Project Mgr*
Shelly D 'amour, *CPA*
EMP: 32 **EST:** 1977
SQ FT: 10,000
SALES: 4.9MM
SALES (corp-wide): 316.3K Privately Held
WEB: www.comprinters.com
SIC: 2752 Commercial printing, offset
PA: Eschaton Foundation
612 Ocean St
Santa Cruz CA 95060
831 423-1626

(P-3639)
DAKOTA PRESS INC
14400 Doolittle Dr, San Leandro (94577-5546)
PHONE..................................510 895-1300
Mary Reid, *President*
Gary Reid, *Vice Pres*
EMP: 15 **EST:** 2010
SALES (est): 2.4MM Privately Held
WEB: www.dakotapress.com
SIC: 2752 Commercial printing, offset

(P-3640)
DIGITAL MANIA INC
Also Called: Copymat
455 Market St Ste 180, San Francisco (94105-2476)
PHONE..................................415 896-0500
Darius Meykadah, *President*
EMP: 20 **EST:** 1994
SALES (est): 4.5MM Privately Held
WEB: www.copymat1.com
SIC: 2752 Commercial printing, offset

(P-3641)
DUMONT PRINTING INC
Also Called: Dumont Printing & Mailing
1333 G St, Fresno (93706-1634)
P.O. Box 12726 (93779-2726)
PHONE..................................559 485-6311
Susan Denise Moore, *CEO*
Susan Moore, *President*
▼ **EMP:** 42
SQ FT: 21,000
SALES (est): 9.7MM Privately Held
WEB: www.dumontprinting.com
SIC: 2752 2759 7331 7334 Commercial printing, offset; commercial printing; direct mail advertising services; photocopying & duplicating services; signs & advertising specialties; subscription fulfillment services: magazine, newspaper, etc.

(P-3642)
EDELSTEIN PRINTING CO
Also Called: Service Printing Co
2725 Miller St, San Leandro (94577-5619)
PHONE..................................510 352-7890
Jerome Edelstein, *Ch of Bd*
James Edelstein, *President*
EMP: 35 **EST:** 1925
SQ FT: 24,000
SALES (est): 2MM Privately Held
SIC: 2752 Lithographing on metal

(P-3643)
EPAC TECHNOLOGIES INC (PA)
2561 Grant Ave, San Leandro (94579-2501)
PHONE..................................510 317-7979
Sasha Dobrovolsky, *CEO*
James Gentilcore, *President*
Jose Perez, *President*
Cathy Mack, *Vice Pres*
Bob McDowell, *Vice Pres*
▲ **EMP:** 131 **EST:** 1998
SALES (est): 26.8MM Privately Held
WEB: www.epac.com
SIC: 2752 Commercial printing, lithographic

(P-3644)
ESSENCE PRINTING INC (PA)
270 Oyster Point Blvd, South San Francisco (94080-1911)
PHONE..................................650 952-5072
Sue WEI, *President*
Herbert WEI, *CEO*
Edwin WEI Jr, *Vice Pres*
Sean Foley, *Sales Staff*
EMP: 83 **EST:** 1988
SQ FT: 40,000
SALES (est): 12.2MM Privately Held
WEB: www.essenceprinting.com
SIC: 2752 Commercial printing, offset

(P-3645)
FINGERPRINT DIGITAL INC
4220 Shelter Bay Ave, Mill Valley (94941-6016)
PHONE..................................415 497-2611
Nancy Macintyre, *CEO*
Johanns Gregorian, *Vice Pres*
Hye Lee, *Business Dir*
Bobby Michael, *Project Mgr*
Adam Blumberg, *QC Mgr*
EMP: 32 **EST:** 2011
SALES (est): 544.8K Privately Held
WEB: www.fingerprintplay.com
SIC: 2752 Commercial printing, lithographic

(P-3646)
FIRST IMPRESSIONS PRINTING INC
25030 Viking St, Hayward (94545-2704)
PHONE..................................510 784-0811
Gary E Stang, *President*
Nancy Stang, *Treasurer*
Jennifer Stang, *Admin Sec*
EMP: 28 **EST:** 1988
SQ FT: 10,000
SALES (est): 3.4MM Privately Held
WEB: www.firstimpressionsprinting.com
SIC: 2752 Commercial printing, offset

(PA)=Parent Co (HQ)=Headquarters (DH)=Div Headquarters
✪ = New Business established in last 2 years

2752 - Commercial Printing: Lithographic County (P-3647)

(P-3647)
FONG BROTHERS PRINTING INC (PA)
320 Valley Dr, Brisbane (94005-1208)
PHONE..................................415 467-1050
Tony D Fong, *President*
Susie Woo, *CFO*
Eugene Fong, *Vice Pres*
Paul Fong, *Vice Pres*
Peter Fong, *Vice Pres*
▲ EMP: 150
SQ FT: 105,000
SALES (est): 49.1MM **Privately Held**
WEB: www.fbp.com
SIC: 2752 Commercial printing, offset

(P-3648)
FONG FONG PRTRS LTHGRPHERS INC
3009 65th St, Sacramento (95820-2021)
PHONE..................................916 739-1313
Karen Cotton, *CEO*
Marsha Fong, *Corp Secy*
May L Fong, *Vice Pres*
Rex Barr, *Sales Staff*
EMP: 43 EST: 1958
SQ FT: 50,000
SALES (est): 8MM **Privately Held**
WEB: www.fongprinters.com
SIC: 2752 Commercial printing, offset

(P-3649)
FOREST INVESTMENT GROUP INC
Also Called: Unicorn Group
83 Hamilton Dr Ste 100, Novato (94949-5674)
PHONE..................................415 459-2330
David A Brooks, *CEO*
Mark Schmidt, *Vice Pres*
EMP: 15 EST: 2003
SQ FT: 8,000
SALES (est): 2.3MM **Privately Held**
SIC: 2752 2791 2789 7334 Commercial printing, offset; typesetting; bookbinding & related work; photocopying & duplicating services

(P-3650)
FRICKE-PARKS PRESS INC
Also Called: F-P Press
33250 Transit Ave, Union City (94587-2035)
PHONE..................................510 489-6543
Robert C Parks, *Ch of Bd*
David Brown, *President*
Patti Parks, *Vice Pres*
EMP: 41 EST: 1972
SQ FT: 50,000
SALES (est): 7.7MM **Privately Held**
WEB: www.fricke-parks.com
SIC: 2752 Commercial printing, offset

(P-3651)
FRUITRIDGE PRTG LITHOGRAPH INC (PA)
3258 Stockton Blvd, Sacramento (95820-1418)
PHONE..................................916 452-9213
Susan Hausmann, *President*
Karen Young, *Vice Pres*
EMP: 39 EST: 1965
SQ FT: 28,500
SALES (est): 4MM **Privately Held**
WEB: www.fruitridge.com
SIC: 2752 2796 Color lithography; platemaking services

(P-3652)
GIANT HORSE PRINTING INC
1336 San Mateo Ave, South San Francisco (94080-6501)
PHONE..................................650 875-7137
Steve MA, *President*
Jeanie MA, *General Mgr*
EMP: 17 EST: 1970
SQ FT: 15,000
SALES (est): 1.8MM **Privately Held**
WEB: www.gianthorse.com
SIC: 2752 2732 2791 Commercial printing, offset; books: printing only; typographic composition, for the printing trade

(P-3653)
GSL FINE LITHOGRAPHERS
1281 National Dr, Sacramento (95834-1902)
PHONE..................................916 231-1410
Joe R Davis, *Ch of Bd*
Darian Koberl, *President*
Chanel Decker, *Principal*
Alan Flippo, *Manager*
Charrizza Ventanilla, *Assistant*
EMP: 38 EST: 1985
SALES (est): 5.7MM
SALES (corp-wide): 4.7B **Publicly Held**
WEB: www.rrd.com
SIC: 2752 Commercial printing, offset
HQ: Consolidated Graphics, Inc.
5858 Westheimer Rd # 200
Houston TX 77057
713 787-0977

(P-3654)
HERDELL PRTG & LITHOGRAPHY INC
340 Mccormick St, Saint Helena (94574-1419)
P.O. Box 72 (94574-0072)
PHONE..................................707 963-3634
Michael Herdell, *President*
Patricia A Herdell, *Admin Sec*
Patty Ditomaso, *Controller*
EMP: 41 EST: 1951
SQ FT: 22,200
SALES (est): 4.9MM **Privately Held**
WEB: www.herdellprinting.com
SIC: 2752 Commercial printing, offset; lithographing on metal

(P-3655)
HNC PRINTING SERVICES LLC
Also Called: Business Point Impressions
5125 Port Chicago Hwy, Concord (94520-1216)
PHONE..................................925 771-2080
Cynthia Yee,
EMP: 17 EST: 2006
SALES (est): 1.7MM **Privately Held**
WEB: www.bpiprinting.com
SIC: 2752 Commercial printing, offset

(P-3656)
HUNTFORD PRINTING
Also Called: Huntford Printing & Graphics
275 Dempsey Rd, Milpitas (95035-5556)
PHONE..................................408 957-5000
George Loughborough, *President*
Charles H Loughborough, *Vice Pres*
Larry Nadeau, *Admin Sec*
Wagner Chiang, *Art Dir*
EMP: 30 EST: 1969
SQ FT: 10,000
SALES (est): 3.5MM **Privately Held**
WEB: www.huntford.com
SIC: 2752 Commercial printing, offset

(P-3657)
IMAGEX INC
5990 Stoneridge Dr # 112, Pleasanton (94588-4517)
PHONE..................................925 474-8100
Stan Poitras, *President*
Kay Smith, *Executive*
Richard Barnes, *CIO*
Tiffany Foronda, *Marketing Staff*
EMP: 17 EST: 1986
SALES (est): 3.3MM **Privately Held**
WEB: www.imagexprint.com
SIC: 2752 Commercial printing, offset; advertising posters, lithographed; business form & card printing, lithographic

(P-3658)
INAUDR LLC (PA)
Also Called: O'Dell Printing Company
5460 State Farm Dr, Rohnert Park (94928-1642)
PHONE..................................707 585-2718
Nicolas Ammar, *Mng Member*
Irene Ammar,
Andrew Gehres, *Manager*
Trish Jackson, *Manager*
Charlotte Zelaya, *Manager*
EMP: 42 EST: 2017
SALES (est): 6.8MM **Privately Held**
WEB: www.odellprinting.com
SIC: 2752 Commercial printing, offset

(P-3659)
INTEGRATED DIGITAL MEDIA (PA)
Also Called: AlphaGraphics
840 Sansome St, San Francisco (94111-1508)
PHONE..................................415 986-4091
Manuel Torres, *Principal*
EMP: 56 EST: 2010
SALES (est): 4.3MM **Privately Held**
WEB: www.alphagraphics.com
SIC: 2752 Commercial printing, lithographic

(P-3660)
INTER-CITY PRINTING CO INC
Also Called: Madison Street Press
614 Madison St, Oakland (94607-4726)
PHONE..................................510 451-4775
Paul Murai, *President*
Miok Murai, *Admin Sec*
David Gallagher, *Production*
Christopher Dougherty, *Marketing Mgr*
Diane Duppman, *Manager*
EMP: 17 EST: 1909
SQ FT: 6,500
SALES (est): 2.4MM **Privately Held**
WEB: www.madisonstreetpress.com
SIC: 2752 Commercial printing, offset

(P-3661)
IPS PRINTING INC
1730 Lathrop Way, Sacramento (95815-4206)
PHONE..................................916 442-8961
Richard Peterson, *President*
Ken Peterson, *Vice Pres*
Steve Bralley, *Executive*
Chris Semkiw, *Manager*
Tim Stults, *Manager*
EMP: 18 EST: 1966
SALES (est): 1.1MM **Privately Held**
WEB: www.ipsprints.com
SIC: 2752 2791 Photolithographic printing; typesetting

(P-3662)
J P GRAPHICS INC
Also Called: JP
3310 Woodward Ave, Santa Clara (95054-2627)
PHONE..................................408 235-8821
Joan Escover, *CEO*
Nick Brevik, *General Mgr*
Michael Iburg, *General Mgr*
Suean Shank, *Admin Asst*
Barbara Gasman, *Graphic Designe*
▲ EMP: 40 EST: 1998
SQ FT: 14,000
SALES (est): 7.7MM **Privately Held**
WEB: www.jp-graphics.com
SIC: 2752 Commercial printing, offset

(P-3663)
JSL PARTNERS INC
Also Called: AlphaGraphics
1294 Anvilwood Ct, Sunnyvale (94089-2200)
PHONE..................................408 747-9000
Jeff Lerner, *President*
Jill Learner, *Vice Pres*
Chris Kelsey, *Project Mgr*
EMP: 27 EST: 1997
SQ FT: 7,500
SALES (est): 794.3K **Privately Held**
WEB: www.jslpartners.com
SIC: 2752 Commercial printing, lithographic

(P-3664)
KKP - ROSEVILLE INC
Also Called: Avalon Graphics
106 N Sunrise Ave Ste B2, Roseville (95661-2915)
PHONE..................................916 786-8573
Kenneth Frank, *President*
Sandra Frank, *Vice Pres*
EMP: 22 EST: 1991
SQ FT: 4,500
SALES (est): 2.6MM **Privately Held**
SIC: 2752 Commercial printing, offset

(P-3665)
KP LLC (PA)
13951 Washington Ave, San Leandro (94578-3220)
PHONE..................................510 346-0729
Joe Atturio, *CEO*
Brett Birky, *Officer*
Jill Gardner, *Vice Pres*
Joe Hollandsworth, *Vice Pres*
Tracy Wreden, *Program Mgr*
▲ EMP: 80
SQ FT: 12,000
SALES (est): 100MM **Privately Held**
WEB: www.kpcorp.com
SIC: 2752 7334 7331 7374 Commercial printing, offset; photocopying & duplicating services; direct mail advertising services; computer graphics service; subscription fulfillment services: magazine, newspaper, etc.; marketing consulting services

(P-3666)
KP LLC
K/P Graphics-Salem Division
13951 Washington Ave, San Leandro (94578-3220)
PHONE..................................510 346-0729
Keith Whittier, *Manager*
David Gibson, *Systems Admin*
Amee Adair, *Accounting Mgr*
EMP: 21
SALES (corp-wide): 100MM **Privately Held**
WEB: www.kpcorp.com
SIC: 2752 8742 7331 2796 Commercial printing, offset; management consulting services; direct mail advertising services; platemaking services; partitions & fixtures, except wood
PA: Kp Llc
13951 Washington Ave
San Leandro CA 94578
510 346-0729

(P-3667)
KP LLC
Also Called: K P Graphics
1134 Enterprise St, Stockton (95204-2316)
P.O. Box 8900 (95208-0900)
PHONE..................................209 466-6761
Roberta Morris, *Manager*
EMP: 21
SQ FT: 10,000
SALES (corp-wide): 100MM **Privately Held**
WEB: www.kpcorp.com
SIC: 2752 Commercial printing, offset
PA: Kp Llc
13951 Washington Ave
San Leandro CA 94578
510 346-0729

(P-3668)
LA BROTHERS ENTERPRISE INC
Also Called: Oscar Printing
57 Columbia Sq, San Francisco (94103-4015)
PHONE..................................415 626-8818
Jeffrey La, *President*
Steve La, *Corp Secy*
Marco Rodriguez, *Accounts Exec*
▲ EMP: 21 EST: 1984
SQ FT: 8,000
SALES (est): 1.5MM **Privately Held**
SIC: 2752 2759 Commercial printing, offset; letterpress printing

(P-3669)
LABEL ART - HM ES-E STIK LBELS
Also Called: Label Art of California
290 27th St, Oakland (94612-3821)
PHONE..................................510 465-1125
David S Masri, *President*
Daniel Masri, *Vice Pres*
Elizabeth Masri, *Admin Sec*
EMP: 25 EST: 1964
SALES (est): 3MM **Privately Held**
WEB: www.allamericanlabel.net
SIC: 2752 Commercial printing, offset
PA: A A Label, Inc.
6958 Sierra Ct
Dublin CA 94568

▲ = Import ▼=Export
◆ =Import/Export

PRODUCTS & SERVICES SECTION
2752 - Commercial Printing: Lithographic County (P-3695)

(P-3670)
LAHLOUH INC
1649 Adrian Rd, Burlingame (94010-2103)
P.O. Box 4345 (94011-4345)
PHONE.................................650 692-6600
John Lahlouh, *President*
Fadi Lahlouh, *Vice Pres*
Michael Lahlouh, *Admin Sec*
▲ **EMP:** 185 **EST:** 1981
SALES (est): 53.9MM **Privately Held**
WEB: www.lahlouh.com
SIC: 2752 Commercial printing, offset

(P-3671)
LEEWOOD PRESS INC
1407 Indiana St, San Francisco (94107-3515)
PHONE.................................415 896-0513
Tom W Lee, *President*
Lina Woo, *COO*
John Frisch, *Manager*
EMP: 24 **EST:** 1992
SQ FT: 19,000
SALES (est): 3MM **Privately Held**
WEB: www.leewoodpress.com
SIC: 2752 Commercial printing, offset

(P-3672)
LEO LAM INC
Also Called: A & M Printing
3589 Nevada St Ste A, Pleasanton (94566-6323)
PHONE.................................925 484-3690
Leo Lam, *President*
Amy Chan, *CEO*
Maria Johnston, *Graphic Designe*
EMP: 30 **EST:** 1983
SQ FT: 13,000
SALES (est): 4MM **Privately Held**
SIC: 2752 7331 2789 Commercial printing, offset; direct mail advertising services; bookbinding & related work

(P-3673)
LIGHTS FANTASTIC
Also Called: Screen Machine
2408 Lincoln Village Dr, San Jose (95125-2741)
PHONE.................................408 266-2787
Clay Wescott, *President*
EMP: 18 **EST:** 2003
SQ FT: 1,200
SALES (est): 175K **Privately Held**
WEB: www.screenmachine.com
SIC: 2752 1799 7389 Offset & photolithographic printing; screening contractor: window, door, etc.; business services

(P-3674)
LITHOS ENERGY INC
1281 Andersen Dr Ste A, San Rafael (94901-5335)
PHONE.................................415 944-5482
James Meredith, *CEO*
Timothy Coogan, *Vice Pres*
EMP: 23 **EST:** 2015
SALES (est): 7.2MM **Privately Held**
WEB: www.lithosenergy.com
SIC: 2752 Commercial printing, lithographic

(P-3675)
LITHOTYPE COMPANY INC (PA)
333 Point San Bruno Blvd, South San Francisco (94080-4917)
PHONE.................................650 871-1750
Aphos Ikonomou, *President*
Kevin Staranowicz, *President*
Penelope Rich, *CEO*
Linda Sartori, *CFO*
Dan Gitter, *Vice Pres*
▲ **EMP:** 65 **EST:** 1940
SQ FT: 41,000
SALES (est): 25.2MM **Privately Held**
WEB: www.lithotype.com
SIC: 2752 Wrappers, lithographed

(P-3676)
MERILIZ INCORPORATED
Also Called: Dome Printing and Lithograph
2031 Dome Ln, McClellan (95652-2033)
PHONE.................................916 923-3663
Tim Poole, *President*
Robert Poole, *Partner*
Timothy M Poole, *President*
Cathy Nau, *CFO*

Bob Poole, *Chief Mktg Ofcr*
EMP: 200 **EST:** 1947
SQ FT: 340,000
SALES (est): 63.9MM **Privately Held**
WEB: www.domeprinting.com
SIC: 2752 Commercial printing, offset

(P-3677)
MITZU PRINTING INC
434 9th St, San Francisco (94103-4411)
PHONE.................................650 922-0500
Takashi Yoshimatsu, *Principal*
Lyudmila Shukhat, *Controller*
EMP: 15 **EST:** 2008
SALES (est): 329.2K **Privately Held**
WEB: www.allegramarketingprint.com
SIC: 2752 Commercial printing, offset

(P-3678)
MOQUIN PRESS INC
555 Harbor Blvd, Belmont (94002-4020)
PHONE.................................650 592-0575
Gregory A Mocquin, *Founder*
Garret Liang, *Manager*
EMP: 60 **EST:** 1985
SQ FT: 22,000
SALES (est): 13.1MM **Privately Held**
WEB: www.moquinpress.com
SIC: 2752 Commercial printing, offset

(P-3679)
NSS ENTERPRISES
Also Called: Cyber Press
3380 Viso Ct, Santa Clara (95054-2625)
PHONE.................................408 970-9200
Chuck Nijmeh, *President*
Adam Zeno, *Vice Pres*
Mark Jones, *Prgrmr*
EMP: 22 **EST:** 1996
SALES (est): 3.6MM **Privately Held**
WEB: www.cyberpress.net
SIC: 2752 Commercial printing, offset

(P-3680)
OAKMEAD PRTG REPRODUCTION INC
233 E Weddell Dr Ste G, Sunnyvale (94089-1659)
PHONE.................................408 734-5505
Toll Free:.................................888 -
Tony Ngo, *President*
EMP: 50 **EST:** 1978
SQ FT: 2,000
SALES (est): 5.4MM **Privately Held**
WEB: www.oakmead.com
SIC: 2752 2791 Commercial printing, offset; typesetting, computer controlled

(P-3681)
PATSONS PRESS
Also Called: Patsons Media Group
3000 Scott Blvd Ste 101, Santa Clara (95054-3321)
PHONE.................................408 567-0911
Patricia Dellamano, *President*
Joseph Dellamano, *Treasurer*
Mark Dellamano, *Vice Pres*
George Crawford, *Office Mgr*
Veronica Smoot, *Sales Staff*
EMP: 50 **EST:** 1968
SALES (est): 8.7MM **Privately Held**
WEB: www.advantageinc.com
SIC: 2752 Commercial printing, offset

(P-3682)
PAUL BAKER PRINTING INC
4251 Gateway Park Blvd, Sacramento (95834-1975)
PHONE.................................916 969-8317
Kasey Cotulla, *President*
James Davis, *Vice Pres*
Bonnie Townsend, *Admin Asst*
Maggie Soderman, *Sales Staff*
EMP: 32 **EST:** 1990
SALES (est): 6.9MM **Privately Held**
WEB: www.pbaker.com
SIC: 2752 Commercial printing, offset

(P-3683)
PERAZZA PRINTS LLC (PA)
25 Crescent Dr Ste A349, Pleasant Hill (94523-5508)
PHONE.................................925 681-2458
Michael Perillo, *Principal*
EMP: 26 **EST:** 2009

SALES (est): 1.2MM **Privately Held**
WEB: www.perazzaprints.com
SIC: 2752 Commercial printing, lithographic

(P-3684)
PINNACLE DIVERSIFIED INC
Also Called: Pinnacle Press
1248 San Luis Obispo St, Hayward (94544-7916)
PHONE.................................510 400-7929
Jason Kim, *President*
Rui Wang, *Vice Pres*
EMP: 17 **EST:** 1994
SQ FT: 13,000
SALES (est): 1.3MM **Privately Held**
SIC: 2752 Commercial printing, offset

(P-3685)
POPPYCOLOR LLC
4028 Adelheid Way, Sacramento (95821-2807)
PHONE.................................916 549-6209
Connie B Moody, *Branch Mgr*
EMP: 21
SALES (corp-wide): 94.4K **Privately Held**
SIC: 2752 Commercial printing, lithographic
PA: Poppycolor Llc
1410 Georgia St
Vallejo CA

(P-3686)
PROFESSIONAL PRINT & MAIL INC
2818 E Hamilton Ave, Fresno (93721-3209)
PHONE.................................559 237-7468
Doug Carlile, *President*
Rorberta Carlile, *CFO*
Mike Carlile, *Vice Pres*
Laurie Wax, *General Mgr*
Roberta L Carlile, *Admin Sec*
EMP: 30 **EST:** 1985
SQ FT: 20,000
SALES (est): 5.5MM **Privately Held**
WEB: www.printfresno.com
SIC: 2752 7331 5999 Commercial printing, offset; mailing service; banners, flags, decals & posters

(P-3687)
PYRAMID GRAPHICS
Also Called: Pyramid Printing and Graphics
325 Harbor Way, South San Francisco (94080-6919)
PHONE.................................650 871-0290
Kingman Leung, *President*
Nancy Tam, *Treasurer*
Larry Phan, *General Mgr*
Jay Leung, *Administration*
EMP: 23 **EST:** 1988
SQ FT: 4,000
SALES (est): 3.1MM **Privately Held**
WEB: www.pyramidgraphics.net
SIC: 2752 7374 7336 Commercial printing, offset; data processing & preparation; commercial art & graphic design

(P-3688)
QG LLC
Worldcolor Merced
2201 Cooper Ave, Merced (95348-4307)
PHONE.................................209 384-0444
EMP: 62
SALES (corp-wide): 2.9B **Publicly Held**
SIC: 2752 Commercial printing, offset
HQ: Qg, Llc
N61w23044 Harrys Way
Sussex WI 53089

(P-3689)
QUADCO PRINTING INC
2535 Zanella Way, Chico (95928-7146)
PHONE.................................530 894-4061
Richard Braak, *President*
Sherryl Garcia Braak, *CFO*
EMP: 18 **EST:** 1978
SQ FT: 15,000
SALES (est): 2.5MM **Privately Held**
WEB: www.quadcoprinting.com
SIC: 2752 Commercial printing, offset

(P-3690)
RAYMONDS LITTLE PRINT SHOP INC
Also Called: Jim Little Raymonds Print Shop
41454 Christy St, Fremont (94538-5105)
PHONE.................................510 353-3608
Raymond Lei, *President*
EMP: 450 **EST:** 2012
SQ FT: 100,000
SALES (est): 10MM
SALES (corp-wide): 75.4MM **Privately Held**
WEB: www.ooshirts.com
SIC: 2752 Commercial printing, lithographic
PA: Ooshirts Inc.
39899 Balentine Dr # 220
Newark CA 94560
866 660-8667

(P-3691)
REDDING PRINTING CO INC (PA)
1130 Continental St, Redding (96001-0799)
PHONE.................................530 243-0525
Ken Peterson, *President*
Richard Peterson, *Treasurer*
Mel Phelps, *Graphic Designe*
EMP: 30 **EST:** 1937
SQ FT: 14,000
SALES (est): 2.6MM **Privately Held**
WEB: www.reddingprinting.com
SIC: 2752 Commercial printing, offset

(P-3692)
REDSTONE PRINT & MAIL INC
2830 Howe Rd Ste B, Martinez (94553-4000)
PHONE.................................925 335-9090
Andy Cody, *CEO*
Scott Giessman, *Controller*
EMP: 108 **EST:** 2015
SALES (est): 8.9MM **Privately Held**
SIC: 2752 Commercial printing, lithographic

(P-3693)
REGULUS INTGRTED SOLUTIONS LLC
860 Latour Ct, NAPA (94558-6258)
PHONE.................................707 254-4000
EMP: 28
SALES (corp-wide): 1.2B **Publicly Held**
SIC: 2752 7389 3861 2759 Lithographic Coml Print Business Services Mfg Photo Equip/Supplies Commercial Printing
HQ: Regulus Integrated Solutions Llc
9645-L Part Blvd
Charlotte NC 28216
704 904-8759

(P-3694)
RIVER CITY PRINTERS LLC
4251 Gateway Park Blvd, Sacramento (95834-1975)
PHONE.................................916 638-8400
Kasey Cotulla, *Mng Member*
Eric Fields, *Vice Pres*
Tony Higuera, *Vice Pres*
Jim Davis,
EMP: 35 **EST:** 2011
SALES (est): 4.1MM **Privately Held**
WEB: www.rcprint.net
SIC: 2752 Commercial printing, offset

(P-3695)
SAN FRANCISCO PRINT MEDIA CO (PA)
835 Market St Ste 550, San Francisco (94103-1906)
PHONE.................................415 487-2594
David Black, *CEO*
Jay Curran, *Officer*
Curran Jay, *Officer*
Aaron Barber, *Vice Pres*
Emma MAI, *Executive*
EMP: 81 **EST:** 2004
SALES (est): 11.5MM **Privately Held**
WEB: www.sfexaminer.com
SIC: 2752 Commercial printing, lithographic

2752 - Commercial Printing: Lithographic County (P-3696)

(P-3696)
SEEGERS INDUSTRIES INC
Also Called: Seeger's Printing
210 N Center St, Turlock (95380-4003)
PHONE..................209 667-2750
Arthur W Seeger, *President*
Richard Berger, *Treasurer*
Toni Jevert,
Nancy Wallen, *Manager*
EMP: 26 **EST:** 1974
SQ FT: 7,100
SALES (est): 2.7MM **Privately Held**
WEB: www.seegersprinting.com
SIC: 2752 Photo-offset printing; commercial printing, offset

(P-3697)
SIERRA OFFICE SYSTEMS PDTS INC (PA)
Also Called: Sierra Office Supply & Prtg
9950 Horn Rd Ste 5, Sacramento (95827-1905)
PHONE..................916 369-0491
Michael Kipp, *CEO*
Jason Gallivan, *COO*
Tom Mini, *Vice Pres*
Rick Holmes, *Executive*
Suzie Schuenemann, *Executive*
EMP: 100 **EST:** 1981
SQ FT: 28,000
SALES (est): 28.1MM **Privately Held**
WEB: www.sierrabg.com
SIC: 2752 5712 5943 Commercial printing, offset; office furniture; office forms & supplies

(P-3698)
SOCIAL IMPRINTS LLC
2500 Marin St, San Francisco (94124-1015)
PHONE..................510 610-6511
Aisha Leach, *Human Resources*
Alexa Golden, *Purchasing*
EMP: 22 **EST:** 2018
SALES (est): 5.9MM **Privately Held**
WEB: www.socialimprints.com
SIC: 2752 Commercial printing, lithographic

(P-3699)
SOURCING GROUP LLC
1672 Delta Ct, Hayward (94544-7043)
PHONE..................510 471-4749
EMP: 30
SALES (corp-wide): 60MM **Privately Held**
SIC: 2752 2761 Lithographic Commercial Printing Mfg Manifold Business Forms
PA: Sourcing Group The Llc
77 Water St Ste 902
New York NY 10005
646 572-7520

(P-3700)
SPECTRUM LITHOGRAPH INC
4300 Business Center Dr, Fremont (94538-6358)
PHONE..................510 438-9192
Fernandino Pereira, *President*
Fernanda Pereira, *CFO*
Shawn Pereira, *Vice Pres*
Tim Freeman, *Sales Staff*
EMP: 27 **EST:** 2006
SQ FT: 46,000
SALES (est): 8.6MM **Privately Held**
WEB: www.spectrumlithograph.com
SIC: 2752 Commercial printing, offset

(P-3701)
STRAHMCOLOR
3000 Kerner Blvd, San Rafael (94901-5413)
P.O. Box 9445 (94912-9445)
PHONE..................415 459-5409
Jason Strahm, *President*
EMP: 16 **EST:** 1980
SQ FT: 10,000
SALES (est): 562.2K **Privately Held**
WEB: www.strahmcom.com
SIC: 2752 Commercial printing, offset

(P-3702)
TACKETT VOLUME PRESS INC
1348 Terminal St, West Sacramento (95691-3515)
PHONE..................916 374-8991
Ron Tackett, *Officer*
EMP: 28 **EST:** 1998
SQ FT: 45,000
SALES (est): 4.4MM **Privately Held**
SIC: 2752 Commercial printing, offset

(P-3703)
THERMCRAFT INC
3762 Bradview Dr, Sacramento (95827-9702)
PHONE..................916 363-9411
Ray Summers, *President*
Maurine Summers, *Vice Pres*
Johnny Bowman, *Plant Mgr*
EMP: 16 **EST:** 1988
SQ FT: 4,600
SALES (est): 2.4MM **Privately Held**
WEB: www.thermcraft.com
SIC: 2752 Commercial printing, offset

(P-3704)
TRADE LITHO INC
Also Called: Trade Lithography
720 Harbour Way S Ste A, Richmond (94804-3631)
PHONE..................510 965-6501
John Lompa, *Owner*
EMP: 15 **EST:** 1998
SQ FT: 14,000
SALES (est): 2.8MM **Privately Held**
WEB: www.tradelitho.us
SIC: 2752 Commercial printing, offset

(P-3705)
TULIP PUBG & GRAPHICS INC
Also Called: Greener Printer
1003 Canal Blvd, Richmond (94804-3549)
PHONE..................510 898-0000
Mario Assadi, *Principal*
Andrea Larson, *Accounting Mgr*
David Grant, *Opers Mgr*
Michael Chipman, *Production*
EMP: 28 **EST:** 1986
SQ FT: 40,000
SALES (est): 6.1MM **Privately Held**
WEB: www.greenerprinter.com
SIC: 2752 Commercial printing, offset

(P-3706)
TYT LLC (HQ)
Also Called: PS Print, LLC
2861 Mandela Pkwy, Oakland (94608-4011)
PHONE..................510 444-3933
Andy Comly, *Mng Member*
Carol Leung, *Accountant*
Luis Arteaga, *Sales Staff*
Randy Kmieciak, *Sales Staff*
Chris Strabley, *Maintence Staff*
▼ **EMP:** 110 **EST:** 2003
SQ FT: 55,000
SALES (est): 19.5MM
SALES (corp-wide): 1.7B **Publicly Held**
WEB: www.psprint.com
SIC: 2752 Commercial printing, offset
PA: Deluxe Corporation
3680 Victoria St N
Shoreview MN 55126
651 483-7111

(P-3707)
UNITED CRAFTSMEN PRINITING
Also Called: Craftsman Printing
2526 Qume Dr Ste 20, San Jose (95131-1870)
PHONE..................408 224-6464
Joan Falkenstein, *President*
EMP: 23 **EST:** 1979
SALES (est): 1.4MM **Privately Held**
SIC: 2752 Commercial printing, offset

(P-3708)
UTAP PRINTING CO INC
1423 San Mateo Ave, South San Francisco (94080-6504)
PHONE..................650 588-2818
Patrick Y Chin, *President*
Kyi Khin, *Controller*
EMP: 21 **EST:** 1986
SQ FT: 5,200
SALES (est): 2MM **Privately Held**
WEB: www.utap.com
SIC: 2752 Commercial printing, offset

(P-3709)
VILLAGE INSTANT PRINTING INC
Also Called: Park's Prtg & Lithographic Co
1515 10th St, Modesto (95354-0726)
PHONE..................209 576-2568
Austin E Parks, *President*
Michelle Neilsen, *Corp Secy*
Frank Parks, *Vice Pres*
Patricia Parks Minnix, *Director*
EMP: 40 **EST:** 1974
SQ FT: 10,000
SALES (est): 6.7MM **Privately Held**
SIC: 2752 Commercial printing, offset

(P-3710)
VISTA WAY CORPORATION
472 Vista Way, Milpitas (95035-5406)
PHONE..................408 586-8107
Jim Dibona, *President*
David Hinds, *Vice Pres*
Maryann Dibona, *Admin Sec*
Robb Pratt, *Graphic Designe*
Catherine Chiaro, *Cust Mgr*
EMP: 25 **EST:** 2003
SALES (est): 4.9MM **Privately Held**
WEB: www.teklabel.com
SIC: 2752 Commercial printing, lithographic

(P-3711)
W B MASON CO INC
4100 Whipple Rd, Union City (94587-1522)
PHONE..................888 926-2766
EMP: 30
SALES (corp-wide): 1B **Privately Held**
WEB: www.wbmason.com
SIC: 5943 5712 2752 Office forms & supplies; office furniture; commercial printing, lithographic
PA: W. B. Mason Co., Inc.
59 Ctr St
Brockton MA 02301
508 586-3434

(P-3712)
WALKER LITHOGRAPH
Also Called: Walker Printing
20869 Walnut St, Red Bluff (96080-9704)
PHONE..................530 527-2142
Neal Gagliano, *Partner*
Chris Gagliano, *Partner*
Mike Walker, *Vice Pres*
EMP: 27 **EST:** 1996
SQ FT: 5,000
SALES (est): 5.2MM **Privately Held**
WEB: www.walkerlitho.com
SIC: 2752 Commercial printing, offset

(P-3713)
WALMART INC
1601 S Lwer Sacramento Rd, Lodi (95242)
PHONE..................209 368-6658
EMP: 15
SALES (corp-wide): 559.1B **Publicly Held**
WEB: www.corporate.walmart.com
SIC: 5311 2752 Department stores, discount; commercial printing, lithographic
PA: Walmart Inc.
702 Sw 8th St
Bentonville AR 72716
479 273-4000

(P-3714)
WESTERN WEB INC
1900 Bendixsen St Ste 2, Samoa (95564-9525)
P.O. Box 278 (95564-0278)
PHONE..................707 444-6236
Stephen Jackson, *President*
Michael Morris, *Vice Pres*
Patricia Cornwell, *Office Mgr*
EMP: 21 **EST:** 2010
SQ FT: 25,400
SALES (est): 3MM **Privately Held**
WEB: www.western-web.net
SIC: 2752 Commercial printing, offset

(P-3715)
WILLEY PRINTING COMPANY (PA)
1405 10th St, Modesto (95354-0724)
P.O. Box 886 (95353-0886)
PHONE..................209 524-4811
Jerry Sauls, *President*
Mary Alice Willey, *Vice Pres*
Barbara Haynes, *Bookkeeper*
EMP: 29 **EST:** 1946
SQ FT: 20,000
SALES (est): 2.8MM **Privately Held**
WEB: www.willeyprinting.com
SIC: 2752 Commercial printing, offset

2754 Commercial Printing: Gravure

(P-3716)
FERNQVIST RETAIL SYSTEMS INC (HQ)
Also Called: Fernqvist Labeling Solutions
2544 Leghorn St, Mountain View (94043-1614)
PHONE..................650 428-0330
Tom Vargas, *CEO*
Jim Clark, *President*
Teresa Caputo, *Officer*
EMP: 16 **EST:** 1989
SQ FT: 6,100
SALES (est): 3.8MM **Privately Held**
WEB: www.fernqvist.com
SIC: 2754 5734 Labels: gravure printing; printers & plotters: computers
PA: Epic Labeling Solutions, Inc.
2544 Leghorn St
Mountain View CA 94043
650 428-0330

2759 Commercial Printing

(P-3717)
A-MARK T-SHIRTS INC
3 E Shields Ave, Fresno (93704-4547)
PHONE..................559 227-6370
Thomas M Machado, *President*
Erin Homen, *Sales Staff*
EMP: 23 **EST:** 1978
SQ FT: 5,000
SALES (est): 2.1MM **Privately Held**
WEB: www.amarkshirts.com
SIC: 2759 Screen printing

(P-3718)
ABC IMAGING OF WASHINGTON
2327 Union St, Oakland (94607-2320)
PHONE..................202 429-8870
Michael Weisend, *Manager*
EMP: 17
SALES (corp-wide): 124.9MM **Privately Held**
WEB: www.abcimaging.com
SIC: 2759 Commercial printing
PA: Abc Imaging Of Washington, Inc
5290 Shawnee Rd Ste 300
Alexandria VA 22312
202 429-8870

(P-3719)
ABC IMAGING OF WASHINGTON
832 Folsom St, San Francisco (94107-4502)
PHONE..................415 525-3874
EMP: 17
SALES (corp-wide): 124.9MM **Privately Held**
WEB: www.abcimaging.com
SIC: 2759 Advertising literature: printing
PA: Abc Imaging Of Washington, Inc
5290 Shawnee Rd Ste 300
Alexandria VA 22312
202 429-8870

(P-3720)
ADAMS LABEL COMPANY LLC (PA)
6052 Industrial Way Ste G, Livermore (94551-9711)
PHONE..................925 371-5393
David Bowyer, *CEO*
EMP: 20 **EST:** 2014
SALES (est): 147.1K **Privately Held**
SIC: 2759 3565 Labels & seals: printing; labeling machines, industrial

PRODUCTS & SERVICES SECTION
2759 - Commercial Printing County (P-3743)

(P-3721)
AMCOR FLEXIBLES LLC
800 N Walton Ave, Yuba City (95993-9352)
P.O. Box 3057 (95992-3057)
PHONE.................530 671-9000
Donna Steele, *Purchasing*
EMP: 85
SALES (corp-wide): 12.4B **Privately Held**
SIC: 2759 3497 2823 2752 Flexographic printing; metal foil & leaf; cellulosic man-made fibers; commercial printing, lithographic; coated & laminated paper
HQ: Amcor Flexibles Llc
2150 E Lake Cook Rd
Buffalo Grove IL 60089
224 313-7000

(P-3722)
BORDEN DECAL COMPANY INC
11760 San Pablo Ave Ste B, El Cerrito (94530-1791)
PHONE.................415 431-1587
Richard Parmelee, *President*
Sharon Parmelee, *Treasurer*
Mark Flagg, *Vice Pres*
EMP: 17 EST: 1923
SALES (est): 582.9K **Privately Held**
WEB: www.bordendecal.com
SIC: 2759 2396 Decals; printing; automotive & apparel trimmings

(P-3723)
BY QUEST LLC
Also Called: Quest Inds - Stockton Plant
2518 Boeing Way, Stockton (95206-3937)
PHONE.................209 234-0202
Ryan Reid, *Branch Mgr*
Dennis Sones, *Vice Pres*
Matthew Trisch, *Vice Pres*
Benny Garcia, *Chief Engr*
Kodie Zimmerman, *Accountant*
EMP: 18
SALES (corp-wide): 21.6MM **Privately Held**
WEB: www.questllc.com
SIC: 2759 Labels & seals: printing
PA: By Quest, Llc
900 W Park Rd
Elizabethtown KY 42701
908 851-9070

(P-3724)
CAMEO CRAFTS
Also Called: York Label
4995 Hillsdale Rd, El Dorado Hills (95762-5707)
PHONE.................513 381-1480
John McKernan, *CEO*
Scott Grigsby, *VP Opers*
Kevin Grigsby, *VP Sales*
EMP: 53 EST: 1975
SQ FT: 30,000
SALES (est): 399K **Privately Held**
SIC: 2759 Labels & seals: printing

(P-3725)
COLLOTYPE LABELS USA INC (DH)
Also Called: Multi-Color Napa/Sonoma
21 Executive Way, NAPA (94558-6271)
PHONE.................707 603-2500
Nigel Vinecombe, *CEO*
David Buse, *President*
Mike Huntsinger, *Vice Pres*
Ken Gumiran, *Technician*
Angel Galvez, *Human Res Mgr*
▲ EMP: 100 EST: 1997
SQ FT: 14,500
SALES (est): 33.5MM **Privately Held**
WEB: www.mcclabel.com
SIC: 2759 Labels & seals: printing
HQ: Multi-Color Corporation
4053 Clough Woods Dr
Batavia OH 45103
513 381-1480

(P-3726)
CONTENT MANAGEMENT CORPORATION
Also Called: C M C
4287 Technology Dr, Fremont (94538-6339)
PHONE.................510 505-1100
Tom Pipkin, *CEO*
Zack Tsuji, *President*
Chris Gomes, *Info Tech Mgr*
Lenny Yee,
Charles Price, *Project Leader*
EMP: 17 EST: 1994
SQ FT: 8,000
SALES (est): 4MM **Privately Held**
WEB: www.cmcondemand.com
SIC: 2759 Commercial printing

(P-3727)
CUSTOM LABEL & DECAL LLC
3392 Investment Blvd, Hayward (94545-3809)
PHONE.................510 876-0000
Colin Ho-Tseung Jr, *Mng Member*
Connie Gouveia, *Vice Pres*
Travis Gilkey, *Sales Mgr*
Wade Ignacio, *Sales Mgr*
Scott Dickes,
EMP: 20 EST: 1976
SQ FT: 25,000
SALES (est): 3.1MM **Privately Held**
WEB: www.customlabel.com
SIC: 2759 2752 2672 Labels & seals: printing; commercial printing, lithographic; coated & laminated paper

(P-3728)
CYMMETRIK USA INC
62 Bonaventura Dr, San Jose (95134-2123)
PHONE.................408 205-1114
Kuo Hui Isai, *Principal*
EMP: 21 EST: 2010
SALES (est): 1MM **Privately Held**
WEB: www.cymmetrik.com
SIC: 2759 Screen printing
HQ: Cymmetrik Enterprise Co., Ltd.
No. 31, Lane. 50, Sec. 3, Nangang Rd.,
Taipei City TAP 11510

(P-3729)
DELTA WEB PRINTING INC
Also Called: Delta Web Printing & Bindery
4251 Gateway Park Blvd, Sacramento (95834-1975)
PHONE.................916 375-0044
James Davis, *President*
Kasey Cotulla, *Vice Pres*
Linda Gould, *Bookkeeper*
Peggy Foley, *Plant Mgr*
EMP: 22 EST: 1992
SALES (est): 4.3MM **Privately Held**
WEB: www.deltawebprinting.com
SIC: 2759 2789 Screen printing; binding & repair of books, magazines & pamphlets

(P-3730)
EAST PRIVATE HOLDINGS II LLC (PA)
6750 Dumbarton Cir, Fremont (94555-3616)
PHONE.................650 357-3500
Kris Franchini, *Partner*
Josef Coetsee, *Vice Pres*
Diane Spera, *Administration*
Kevin Farrell, *Planning*
Vicki Atkins, *IT/INT Sup*
EMP: 40 EST: 2019
SALES (est): 1B **Privately Held**
SIC: 2759 Commercial printing

(P-3731)
ELECTRONICS FOR IMAGING INC (HQ)
Also Called: Efi
6453 Kaiser Dr, Fremont (94555-3610)
PHONE.................650 357-3500
Jeff Jacobson, *CEO*
Scott Schinlever, *COO*
Grant Fitz, *CFO*
Thomas Georgens, *Bd of Directors*
Richard Kashnow, *Bd of Directors*
▲ EMP: 50 EST: 1988
SALES (est): 1B **Privately Held**
WEB: www.efi.com
SIC: 2759 3955 Commercial printing; print cartridges for laser & other computer printers
PA: East Private Holdings Ii, Llc
6750 Dumbarton Cir
Fremont CA 94555
650 357-3500

(P-3732)
FORTIS SOLUTIONS GROUP LLC
535 Airpark Rd, NAPA (94558-7514)
PHONE.................707 256-6343
Nicole Hardy, *Supervisor*
EMP: 32 **Privately Held**
WEB: www.fortissolutionsgroup.com
SIC: 2759 Labels & seals: printing
PA: Fortis Solutions Group, Llc
2505 Hawkeye Ct
Virginia Beach VA 23452

(P-3733)
FORTIS SOLUTIONS GROUP LLC
1870 Wardrobe Ave, Merced (95341-6407)
PHONE.................800 388-1990
Greg McLain, *Research*
Edward Peek, *Technical Staff*
Susan Rozier, *Technical Staff*
Roger Vorse, *Controller*
Marygrace Quigley, *Marketing Staff*
EMP: 32 **Privately Held**
WEB: www.fortissolutionsgroup.com
SIC: 2759 Labels & seals: printing
PA: Fortis Solutions Group, Llc
2505 Hawkeye Ct
Virginia Beach VA 23452

(P-3734)
GRAPHIC PACKAGING INTL LLC
Also Called: Sierra Pacific Packaging
525 Airport Pkwy, Oroville (95965-9248)
PHONE.................530 533-1058
Allen Ennis, *Branch Mgr*
Russell Chitwood, *Engineer*
Stefanie Garcia, *Human Resources*
EMP: 160 **Publicly Held**
WEB: www.graphicpkg.com
SIC: 2759 2752 2671 2631 Commercial printing; commercial printing, lithographic; packaging paper & plastics film, coated & laminated; paperboard mills
HQ: Graphic Packaging International, Llc
1500 Riveredge Pkwy # 100
Atlanta GA 30328

(P-3735)
GRAPHIC SPORTSWEAR LLC
173 Utah Ave, South San Francisco (94080-6712)
P.O. Box 77193, San Francisco (94107-0193)
PHONE.................415 206-7200
Ken Watson,
Mike Smith, *Sales Mgr*
Pat McCune,
EMP: 52 EST: 1976
SQ FT: 20,000
SALES (est): 6.2MM **Privately Held**
WEB: www.graphicsportswear.com
SIC: 2759 Screen printing

(P-3736)
HIRONAKA PROMOTIONS LLC
Also Called: Garage Champs
2608 R St, Sacramento (95816-6915)
PHONE.................916 631-8470
Derek Hironaka,
Andrew Nguyen,
Jami Sparano, *Manager*
EMP: 20 EST: 2018
SALES (est): 1.3MM **Privately Held**
WEB: www.garagechamps.com
SIC: 2759 Screen printing

(P-3737)
IC INK IMAGE CO INC
Also Called: Legends Apparel & I C Ink
4627 E Fremont St, Stockton (95215-4010)
P.O. Box 4487 (95204-0487)
PHONE.................209 931-3040
Tom Sousa, *President*
Debbie Dolin, *Purchasing*
Dixie Costa, *Sales Staff*
EMP: 20 EST: 1991
SQ FT: 25,000
SALES (est): 3.6MM **Privately Held**
WEB: www.icink.com
SIC: 2759 2396 2395 Screen printing; automotive & apparel trimmings; pleating & stitching

(P-3738)
IGRAPHICS (PA)
Also Called: Precision Printers
165 Spring Hill Dr, Grass Valley (95945-5936)
PHONE.................530 273-2200
James G Clay, *Owner*
Patrick Keown, *COO*
David Clay, *Mng Member*
EMP: 24 EST: 1981
SQ FT: 15,000
SALES (est): 2.2MM **Privately Held**
WEB: www.igraphicspp.com
SIC: 2759 7389 3993 2671 Screen printing; printing broker; signs & advertising specialties; packaging paper & plastics film, coated & laminated; automotive & apparel trimmings

(P-3739)
INFOIMAGE OF CALIFORNIA INC (PA)
175 S Hill Dr, Brisbane (94005-1203)
PHONE.................650 473-6388
Howard Lee, *President*
Rose Lee, *COO*
Lilly Fong, *CFO*
Lenora Lee, *CFO*
Tomas Lee, *Officer*
EMP: 75 EST: 1984
SALES (est): 28.4MM **Privately Held**
WEB: www.infoimageinc.com
SIC: 2759 7331 7374 Laser printing; mailing service; data processing service

(P-3740)
LUSTRE-CAL LLC
715 S Guild Ave, Lodi (95240-3153)
PHONE.................206 370-1600
Heather Chartrand, *Principal*
Chris Colbert, *Principal*
Avinash Pathak, *Principal*
Maxwell Smith, *Principal*
EMP: 65 EST: 2020
SALES (est): 3.3MM **Privately Held**
SIC: 2759 Commercial printing

(P-3741)
LUSTRE-CAL NAMEPLATE CORP
715 S Guild Ave, Lodi (95240-3153)
P.O. Box 439 (95241-0439)
PHONE.................209 370-1600
Clydene Hohenrieder, *CEO*
Joseph Hohenrieder, *President*
Heather Chartrand, *COO*
Chris Colbert, *Vice Pres*
Claudine Hohenrieder, *Vice Pres*
▲ EMP: 65 EST: 1964
SQ FT: 50,000
SALES (est): 9.6MM **Privately Held**
WEB: www.lustrecal.com
SIC: 2759 Labels & seals: printing

(P-3742)
MEPCO LABEL SYSTEMS
1313 S Stockton St, Lodi (95240-5942)
PHONE.................209 946-0201
Jennifer Tracy, *CEO*
Tom Gassner, *President*
Alfred M Gassner, *CEO*
Carol Gassner, *CEO*
Karl Gassner, *Exec VP*
EMP: 96
SQ FT: 83,000
SALES (est): 17.6MM **Privately Held**
WEB: www.mepcolabel.com
SIC: 2759 Labels & seals: printing

(P-3743)
OKI GRAPHICS INC
2148 Zanker Rd, San Jose (95131-2113)
PHONE.................408 451-9294
Yoon OH Kim, *President*
Matthew Cho, *Sales Staff*
EMP: 17 EST: 2001
SALES (est): 2.1MM **Privately Held**
WEB: www.okigraphics.com
SIC: 2759 Commercial printing

2759 - Commercial Printing County (P-3744)

PRODUCTS & SERVICES SECTION

(P-3744)
OOSHIRTS INC (PA)
39899 Balentine Dr # 220, Newark (94560-5358)
PHONE...................................866 660-8667
Raymond Lei, *President*
Rick Barger, *Facilities Mgr*
◆ **EMP:** 304 **EST:** 2011
SALES (est): 75.4MM **Privately Held**
WEB: www.ooshirts.com
SIC: 2759 Screen printing

(P-3745)
PREMIER PRINT & MAIL INC
Also Called: Tri-City Print & Mail
2615 Del Monte St, West Sacramento (95691-3809)
PHONE...................................916 503-5300
Charles F Sievers Jr, *President*
EMP: 18 **EST:** 1993
SQ FT: 10,000
SALES (est): 1.5MM **Privately Held**
WEB: www.premierprint-mail.com
SIC: 2759 7331 Advertising literature: printing; direct mail advertising services

(P-3746)
PRINT INK INC
Also Called: Build Your Own Garment
6918 Sierra Ct, Dublin (94568-2641)
PHONE...................................925 829-3950
Cathileen Marchese, *President*
Jacqui Peters, *Sales Staff*
Michelle Johnson,
EMP: 25 **EST:** 1993
SALES (est): 5.7MM **Privately Held**
WEB:
SIC: 2759 Screen printing

(P-3747)
RESOURCE LABEL GROUP LLC
Also Called: Spectrum Label
39611 Eureka Dr, Newark (94560-4806)
PHONE...................................510 477-0707
Linda Hayashi, *Accountant*
Tony King, *Cust Mgr*
EMP: 49 **Privately Held**
WEB: www.resourcelabel.com
SIC: 2759 Labels & seals: printing
PA: Resource Label Group, Llc
147 Seaboard Ln
Franklin TN 37067

(P-3748)
ROBERT R WIX INC (PA)
Also Called: Valley Printing
2140 Pine St, Ceres (95307-3620)
P.O. Box 2671 (95307-7871)
PHONE...................................209 537-4561
Robert R Wix, *President*
Linny Goodrich, *Vice Pres*
Tom Mink, *Vice Pres*
EMP: 32 **EST:** 1959
SQ FT: 31,000
SALES (est): 7.1MM **Privately Held**
SIC: 2759 2752 2672 2671 Letterpress printing; flexographic printing; commercial printing, offset; coated & laminated paper; packaging paper & plastics film, coated & laminated

(P-3749)
SONOMA PINS ETC CORPORATION
Also Called: Sonoma Promotional Solutions
841 W Napa St, Sonoma (95476-6414)
PHONE...................................707 996-9956
Bernard Friedman, *President*
Judy Friedman, *Exec VP*
Arthur Battaglia, *Executive*
Ken Tymula, *CIO*
Jacob Powell, *Business Mgr*
▲ **EMP:** 33 **EST:** 1997
SQ FT: 600
SALES (est): 5.1MM **Privately Held**
WEB: www.sonomapromo.com
SIC: 2759 Promotional printing

(P-3750)
SPECTRAPRINT INC
24 Moody Ct, San Rafael (94901-1029)
PHONE...................................415 460-1228
EMP: 16
SQ FT: 12,800
SALES (est): 1.8MM **Privately Held**
WEB: www.spectaprintinc.com
SIC: 2759 Commercial Printing

(P-3751)
THERAPEUTIC RES FACULTY LLC
3120 W March Ln, Stockton (95219-2368)
PHONE...................................209 472-2240
Wes Crews, *CEO*
EMP: 200 **EST:** 2013
SALES (est): 5.3MM **Privately Held**
SIC: 2759 Publication printing

(P-3752)
TRANSCONTINENTAL NRTHERN CA 20
47540 Kato Rd, Fremont (94538-7303)
PHONE...................................510 580-7700
Brian Reid, *CEO*
Francois Olivier, *Principal*
Vivian Marzin McKay, *Finance*
▲ **EMP:** 200 **EST:** 2006
SALES (est): 48.6MM
SALES (corp-wide): 1.9B **Privately Held**
WEB: www.tctranscontinental.com
SIC: 2759 Magazines: printing
PA: Transcontinental Inc
1 Place Ville-Marie Bureau 3240
Montreal QC H3B 0
514 954-4000

(P-3753)
US1COM INC
715 Southpoint Blvd Ste D, Petaluma (94954-6836)
P.O. Box 3303, Santa Fe Springs (90670-1303)
PHONE...................................707 781-2560
EMP: 17
SQ FT: 5,417
SALES: 614.2K **Privately Held**
WEB: www.us1com.com
SIC: 2759 Credit Card Printer
PA: A F E Industries Inc.
13233 Barton Cir
Whittier CA 90605

(P-3754)
VALLEY IMAGES LLC
1925 Kyle Park Ct, San Jose (95125-1029)
PHONE...................................408 279-6777
Carlo Strangis, *Partner*
Robert Malik, *Partner*
Cindy Smith, *Accounts Mgr*
EMP: 17 **EST:** 1990
SQ FT: 10,201
SALES (est): 2.4MM **Privately Held**
WEB: www.valleyimages.com
SIC: 2759 Screen printing

(P-3755)
WESTERN ROTO ENGRAVERS INC
Also Called: W R E Colortech
1225 6th St, Berkeley (94710-1401)
PHONE...................................510 525-2950
Bill Mackay, *Manager*
Kathleen Harrelson, *CFO*
John Comerford, *VP Bus Dvlpt*
Chris Stramaglia, *Technician*
Dan Comerford, *VP Opers*
EMP: 43
SALES (corp-wide): 12.9MM **Privately Held**
WEB: www.wrecolor.com
SIC: 2759 2796 Engraving; plates & cylinders for rotogravure printing
PA: Western Roto Engravers, Incorporated
533 Banner Ave
Greensboro NC 27401
336 275-9821

(P-3756)
XYZ GRAPHICS INC (PA)
190 Lombard St, San Francisco (94111-1111)
PHONE...................................415 227-9972
Steven Waterloo, *President*
Sean McGlynn, *Exec VP*
Sean Mc Glynn, *Vice Pres*
M C Pfeiffer, *Managing Dir*
John Gatewood, *Project Mgr*
EMP: 28 **EST:** 2001
SQ FT: 8,500
SALES (est): 9.6MM **Privately Held**
WEB: www.wearexyz.com
SIC: 2759 Commercial printing

2761 Manifold Business Forms

(P-3757)
TAYLOR COMMUNICATIONS INC
1300 Ethan Way Ste 675, Sacramento (95825-2295)
P.O. Box 255366 (95865-5366)
PHONE...................................916 927-1891
Pegge Kiszely, *Branch Mgr*
EMP: 17
SALES (corp-wide): 3.6B **Privately Held**
WEB: www.taylor.com
SIC: 2761 Manifold business forms
HQ: Taylor Communications, Inc.
1725 Roe Crest Dr
North Mankato MN 56003
866 541-0937

(P-3758)
TAYLOR COMMUNICATIONS INC
3885 Seaport Blvd Ste 40, West Sacramento (95691-3527)
PHONE...................................916 340-0200
John Joyce, *Branch Mgr*
Inna Uskova, *Buyer*
EMP: 17
SALES (corp-wide): 3.6B **Privately Held**
WEB: www.taylor.com
SIC: 2761 Manifold business forms
HQ: Taylor Communications, Inc.
1725 Roe Crest Dr
North Mankato MN 56003
866 541-0937

(P-3759)
TAYLOR COMMUNICATIONS INC
10390 Coloma Rd Ste 7, Rancho Cordova (95670-2152)
PHONE...................................916 368-1200
John Miller, *Manager*
EMP: 17
SALES (corp-wide): 3.6B **Privately Held**
WEB: www.taylor.com
SIC: 2761 Manifold business forms
HQ: Taylor Communications, Inc.
1725 Roe Crest Dr
North Mankato MN 56003
866 541-0937

2782 Blankbooks & Looseleaf Binders

(P-3760)
CHAMELEON LIKE INC
Also Called: Chameleon Books & Journals
345 Kishimura Dr, Gilroy (95020-3653)
PHONE...................................408 847-3661
Pierre Martichoux, *President*
Bradley Boggs, *COO*
Mark Strauss, *Executive*
Amanda Gil, *Admin Asst*
Micah Robertson, *Technical Staff*
▲ **EMP:** 80
SQ FT: 12,000
SALES (est): 10MM **Privately Held**
WEB: www.chameleonlike.com
SIC: 2782 Blankbooks & looseleaf binders

2789 Bookbinding

(P-3761)
JS TRADE BINDERY SERVICES INC
209 Oxford Way, Belmont (94002-2565)
PHONE...................................650 486-1475
Jai Kumar, *President*
Puente Armando, *Production*
Debbie Carter, *Cust Mgr*
EMP: 20 **EST:** 1989
SALES (est): 1.2MM **Privately Held**
WEB: www.jsbindery.com
SIC: 2789 Trade binding services

(P-3762)
SPECIALTY GRAPHICS INC
18686 Walnut Rd, Castro Valley (94546-2146)
PHONE...................................510 351-7705
Angela Plowman, *President*
Deborah Waltmire, *Admin Sec*
EMP: 18 **EST:** 1978
SALES (est): 2.2MM **Privately Held**
WEB: www.sgica.com
SIC: 2789 2732 Trade binding services; books: printing only

2791 Typesetting

(P-3763)
BARKERBLUE INC
363 N Amphlett Blvd, San Mateo (94401-1806)
PHONE...................................650 696-2100
Eugene A Klein, *CEO*
Michael Callaghan, *CFO*
Konstantin Koshelev, *Senior VP*
Sandra Asuncion, *Principal*
Susan Phegley, *CIO*
EMP: 35 **EST:** 1961
SALES (est): 5MM **Privately Held**
WEB: www.barkerblue.com
SIC: 2791 7334 Typesetting; blueprinting service

(P-3764)
FOLGERGRAPHICS INC
21093 Forbes Ave, Hayward (94545-1115)
PHONE...................................510 293-2294
Richard L Folger, *CEO*
Patricia A Folger, *Vice Pres*
Brianna Parker, *Project Mgr*
Robby Alberto, *Sales Staff*
EMP: 40 **EST:** 1958
SQ FT: 16,000
SALES (est): 6MM **Privately Held**
WEB: www.folgergraphics.com
SIC: 2791 2752 Typesetting; commercial printing, offset

(P-3765)
NORCO PRINTING INC
4588 Grenadier Pl, Castro Valley (94546-1275)
PHONE...................................510 569-2200
Ricky C Damiani, *President*
Rick C Damiani, *President*
Rose Damiani, *Vice Pres*
EMP: 15 **EST:** 1973
SALES (est): 2.1MM **Privately Held**
WEB: www.norcoprint.com
SIC: 2791 2759 2752 2789 Typesetting; letterpress & screen printing; commercial printing, offset; bookbinding & related work; manifold business forms

(P-3766)
RAPID LASERGRAPHICS (HQ)
836 Harrison St, San Francisco (94107-1125)
PHONE...................................415 957-5840
Bent Kjolby, *President*
John Perkins, *Vice Pres*
EMP: 32 **EST:** 1992
SALES (est): 1.2MM
SALES (corp-wide): 5.1MM **Privately Held**
WEB: www.rapidgraphics.com
SIC: 2791 2752 7336 Typesetting; color lithography; graphic arts & related design
PA: Rapid Typographers Company Inc
836 Harrison St
San Francisco CA 94107
415 957-5840

(P-3767)
RAPID TYPOGRAPHERS COMPANY (PA)
Also Called: Rapid Lasergraphics
836 Harrison St, San Francisco (94107-1125)
PHONE...................................415 957-5840
Bent Kjolby, *President*
John Perkins, *Vice Pres*
EMP: 15 **EST:** 1964
SQ FT: 12,000

PRODUCTS & SERVICES SECTION

2819 - Indl Inorganic Chemicals, NEC County (P-3790)

SALES (est): 5.1MM **Privately Held**
WEB: www.rapidgraphics.com
SIC: **2791** 2752 7336 2759 Typesetting; color lithography; graphic arts & related design; commercial printing

2796 Platemaking & Related Svcs

(P-3768)
COAST ENGRAVING COMPANIES INC
Also Called: Coast Creative Nameplates
1097 N 5th St, San Jose (95112-4449)
PHONE 408 297-2555
Ida Wool, *President*
Fred A Wool Jr, *CFO*
Matt Wool, *Director*
EMP: 40 EST: 1970
SQ FT: 10,000
SALES (est): 4MM **Privately Held**
WEB: www.coastengraving.com
SIC: **2796** 2752 2759 Engraving on copper, steel, wood or rubber; printing plates; lithographic plates, positives or negatives; commercial printing, lithographic; commercial printing

2812 Alkalies & Chlorine

(P-3769)
CLOROX MANUFACTURING COMPANY
11950 S Harlan Rd, Lathrop (95330-8767)
PHONE 925 425-6040
▲ EMP: 37
SALES (corp-wide): 7.3B **Publicly Held**
WEB: www.thecloroxcompany.com
SIC: **2812** Chlorine, compressed or liquefied
HQ: Clorox Manufacturing Company
 1221 Broadway
 Oakland CA 94612
 -

2813 Industrial Gases

(P-3770)
AMERICAN AIR LIQUIDE INC (DH)
46409 Landing Pkwy, Fremont (94538-6496)
PHONE 510 624-4000
Benoit Potier, *Chairman*
Pierre Dufour, *President*
Scott Krapf, *CFO*
Gregory Alexander, *Treasurer*
Jean-Pierre Duprieu, *Exec VP*
◆ EMP: 90 EST: 1940
SQ FT: 40,000
SALES (est): 314.8MM
SALES (corp-wide): 102.6MM **Privately Held**
WEB: www.industry.airliquide.us
SIC: **2813** 5084 3533 4931 Industrial gases; welding machinery & equipment; oil & gas drilling rigs & equipment; electric & other services combined
HQ: Air Liquide International
 75 Quai D Orsay
 Paris 75007
 140 625-555

(P-3771)
HORNBLOWER ENERGY LLC
The Embarcadero Pier 3 St Pier, San Francisco (94211)
PHONE 415 788-7020
Kevin Rabbitt, *Mng Member*
Cameron Clark, *Vice Pres*
Nick Monroe, *Vice Pres*
EMP: 15 EST: 2019
SALES (est): 1.1MM **Privately Held**
SIC: **2813** Industrial gases

(P-3772)
LINDE GAS & EQUIPMENT INC
Also Called: Praxair
203 Golden State Blvd, Turlock (95380)
PHONE 800 225-8247
EMP: 23 **Privately Held**
WEB: www.praxair.com
SIC: **2813** Industrial gases
HQ: Linde Gas & Equipment Inc.
 10 Riverview Dr
 Danbury CT 06810
 203 837-2000

(P-3773)
LINDE INC
Also Called: Praxair
901 Embarcadero, Oakland (94606-5120)
PHONE 510 451-4100
Mike Tyler, *Principal*
Ryan Robertson, *CIO*
EMP: 150 **Privately Held**
WEB: www.praxair.com
SIC: **2813** Carbon dioxide
HQ: Linde Inc.
 10 Riverview Dr
 Danbury CT 06810
 203 837-2000

(P-3774)
LINDE INC
Also Called: Praxair
2995 Atlas Rd, San Pablo (94806-1167)
PHONE 510 223-9593
Bill Holland, *Branch Mgr*
EMP: 20 **Privately Held**
WEB: www.praxair.com
SIC: **2813** Industrial gases
HQ: Linde Inc.
 10 Riverview Dr
 Danbury CT 06810
 203 837-2000

(P-3775)
MESSER LLC
5858 88th St, Sacramento (95828-1104)
PHONE 916 381-1606
Steve Morgan, *Branch Mgr*
EMP: 16
SALES (corp-wide): 1.3B **Privately Held**
WEB: www.messeramericas.com
SIC: **2813** Nitrogen; oxygen, compressed or liquefied
HQ: Messer Llc
 200 Smrst Corp Blvd # 7000
 Bridgewater NJ 08807
 800 755-9277

(P-3776)
NEL HYDROGEN INC
2371 Verna Ct, San Leandro (94577-4205)
PHONE 650 543-3180
Joseph Aranda, *Technician*
Kyle McKeown, *Engineer*
EMP: 25 EST: 2017
SALES (est): 11.8MM **Privately Held**
WEB: www.nelhydrogen.com
SIC: **2813** Hydrogen

2819 Indl Inorganic Chemicals, NEC

(P-3777)
AIR LIQUIDE ELECTRONICS US LP
Also Called: Aloha
46401 Landing Pkwy, Fremont (94538-6496)
PHONE 510 624-4338
Yun Liu, *Program Mgr*
EMP: 5003
SALES (corp-wide): 102.6MM **Privately Held**
WEB: www.airliquide.com
SIC: **2819** Industrial inorganic chemicals
HQ: Air Liquide Electronics U.S. Lp
 9101 Lyndon B Johnson Fwy # 800
 Dallas TX 75243
 972 301-5200

(P-3778)
AMCOR MANUFACTURING INC
500 Winmoore Way, Modesto (95358-5750)
PHONE 209 581-9687
Michael Harvey, *President*
Michael Archibald, *Vice Pres*
EMP: 15 EST: 1996
SQ FT: 36,000
SALES (est): 1.2MM **Privately Held**
WEB: www.amcormfg.com
SIC: **2819** Industrial inorganic chemicals

(P-3779)
AMPAC FINE CHEMICALS LLC (HQ)
Hwy 50 Hzel Ave Bldg 0501, Rancho Cordova (95741)
P.O. Box 1718 (95741-1718)
PHONE 916 357-6880
Aslam Malik, *CEO*
Jeff Butler, *President*
Joe Warchol, *CFO*
Christopher Conley, *Vice Pres*
William Dubay, *Vice Pres*
▲ EMP: 369 EST: 1998
SQ FT: 235,000
SALES (est): 167.9MM **Privately Held**
WEB: www.ampacfinechemicals.com
SIC: **2819** Industrial inorganic chemicals

(P-3780)
AMPAC FINE CHEMICALS LLC
12295 Hartford St, Rancho Cordova (95742-6444)
PHONE 916 357-6221
Jary Xiong, *Controller*
EMP: 30 **Privately Held**
WEB: www.ampacfinechemicals.com
SIC: **2819** Industrial inorganic chemicals
HQ: Ampac Fine Chemicals Llc
 Hwy 50 Hzel Ave Bldg 0501
 Rancho Cordova CA 95741
 916 357-6880

(P-3781)
BD BISCNCES SYSTEMS RGENTS INC
2350 Qume Dr, San Jose (95131-1812)
PHONE 408 518-5024
EMP: 103
SALES (corp-wide): 1.2MM **Privately Held**
SIC: **2819** Mfg Industrial Inorganic Chemicals
PA: Bd Biosciences, Systems And Reagents, Inc.
 1 Becton Dr
 Franklin Lakes NJ 07417
 201 847-6800

(P-3782)
CODEXIS INC (PA)
200 Penobscot Dr, Redwood City (94063-4718)
PHONE 650 421-8100
John J Nicols, *President*
Bernard J Kelley, *Ch of Bd*
Ross Taylor, *CFO*
Laurie Heilmann, *Senior VP*
Hicham Alaoui, *Vice Pres*
EMP: 177 EST: 2002
SQ FT: 77,300
SALES (est): 69MM **Publicly Held**
WEB: www.codexis.com
SIC: **2819** 2869 8731 Catalysts, chemical; industrial organic chemicals; commercial research laboratory

(P-3783)
ECO SERVICES OPERATIONS CORP
100 Mococo Rd, Martinez (94553-1314)
PHONE 925 313-8224
Darrel Hodge, *Plant Mgr*
James Jordan, *Engineer*
Jim Cesen, *Opers Mgr*
EMP: 42
SALES (corp-wide): 1.1B **Publicly Held**
SIC: **2819** Sulfuric acid, oleum
HQ: Eco Services Operations Corp.
 300 Lindenwood Dr
 Malvern PA 19355
 610 251-9118

(P-3784)
EKC TECHNOLOGY INC (HQ)
Also Called: E K C Technology/Burmar Chem
2520 Barrington Ct, Hayward (94545-1163)
PHONE 510 784-9105
Douglas J Holmes, *CEO*
Seng Wui Lim, *President*
John Odom, *President*
Thomas M Connelly Jr, *Exec VP*
David G Bills, *Senior VP*
◆ EMP: 115 EST: 1963
SQ FT: 65,000
SALES (est): 50.7MM
SALES (corp-wide): 20.4B **Publicly Held**
WEB: www.dupont.com
SIC: **2819** Industrial inorganic chemicals
PA: Dupont De Nemours, Inc.
 974 Centre Rd Bldg 730
 Wilmington DE 19805
 302 774-3034

(P-3785)
ELEMENT SIX TECH US CORP
3901 Burton Dr, Santa Clara (95054-1583)
PHONE 408 986-8184
Adrian Wilson, *President*
EMP: 17 EST: 2011
SALES (est): 4.8MM **Privately Held**
WEB: www.e6cvd.com
SIC: **2819** Industrial inorganic chemicals

(P-3786)
ENKI TECHNOLOGY INC
1035 Walsh Ave, Santa Clara (95050-2645)
PHONE 408 383-9034
Kevin Kopczynski, *CEO*
Tom Colson, *COO*
Paul Kidman, *Vice Pres*
Brenor Brophy, *CTO*
▲ EMP: 46 EST: 2009
SQ FT: 8,000
SALES (est): 2.4MM **Privately Held**
WEB: www.firstsolar.com
SIC: **2819** Silica compounds

(P-3787)
ERG AEROSPACE CORPORATION
Also Called: Erg Materials and Aerospace
964 Stanford Ave, Oakland (94608-2323)
PHONE 510 658-9785
Mitchell Hall, *CEO*
Brian Rothwell, *General Mgr*
Jessica Hills, *IT/INT Sup*
Stephen Brewer, *Finance*
Lee Hughes, *Opers Staff*
EMP: 70 EST: 1967
SQ FT: 60,000
SALES (est): 22.2MM **Privately Held**
WEB: www.ergaerospace.com
SIC: **2819** Aluminum compounds

(P-3788)
GE-HITACHI NUCLEAR ENERGY
Also Called: GE Vallecitos Nuclear Center
6705 Vallecitos Rd, Sunol (94586-9524)
PHONE 925 862-4382
David Turner, *Manager*
EMP: 72
SALES (corp-wide): 79.6B **Publicly Held**
WEB: www.nuclear.gepower.com
SIC: **2819** Nuclear fuel & cores, inorganic
HQ: Ge-Hitachi Nuclear Energy Americas Llc
 3901 Castle Hayne Rd
 Castle Hayne NC 28429
 -

(P-3789)
GREEN CATALYSTS INC (PA)
870 Market St Ste 659, San Francisco (94102-3020)
PHONE 415 271-0675
Santosh Alexander, *President*
▲ EMP: 78 EST: 2005
SALES (est): 173.2K **Privately Held**
SIC: **2819** Catalysts, chemical

(P-3790)
JM HUBER CORPORATION
700 Kiernan Ave Ste D, Modesto (95356-9329)
PHONE 209 549-9771
Aaron Bolinger, *Manager*
Michael Darsillo, *Director*
EMP: 87
SALES (corp-wide): 1.1B **Privately Held**
WEB: www.huber.com
SIC: **2819** Industrial inorganic chemicals
PA: J.M. Huber Corporation
 499 Thornall St Ste 8
 Edison NJ 08837
 732 549-8600

2819 - Indl Inorganic Chemicals, NEC County (P-3791)

(P-3791)
LICAP TECHNOLOGIES INC
9795 Business Park Dr A, Sacramento (95827-1708)
PHONE.................................916 329-8099
Linda Zhong, *CEO*
Martin M Zea, *Principal*
EMP: 67 **EST:** 2016
SALES (est): 10.1MM **Privately Held**
WEB: www.licaptech.com
SIC: 2819 Elements

(P-3792)
MISSION PARK HOTEL LP
Also Called: Element Santa Clara
1950 Wyatt Dr, Santa Clara (95054-1544)
PHONE.................................408 809-3838
Mona Rigdon, *Principal*
Brent Lower, *Principal*
EMP: 38 **EST:** 2019
SALES (est): 2.6MM **Privately Held**
SIC: 2819 Elements

(P-3793)
MONOLITH MATERIALS INC
662 Laurel St Ste 201, San Carlos (94070-3103)
PHONE.................................650 933-4957
Rob Hanson, *CEO*
Bill Brady, *Chairman*
Roscoe Taylor, *Vice Pres*
Tommy Allen, *Project Engr*
Aaron Bush, *Engineer*
EMP: 26 **EST:** 2012
SQ FT: 3,500
SALES (est): 8.7MM **Privately Held**
WEB: www.monolith-corp.com
SIC: 2819 Chemicals, high purity: refined from technical grade

(P-3794)
MORGAN ADVANCED CERAMICS INC
13079 Earhart Ave, Auburn (95602-9536)
PHONE.................................530 823-3401
John Stang, *CEO*
James A West, *President*
Chester Chiu, *Info Tech Mgr*
▲ **EMP:** 201 **EST:** 1986
SQ FT: 80,000
SALES (est): 15.5MM
SALES (corp-wide): 1.2B **Privately Held**
SIC: 2819 3356 3264 Aluminum oxide; zirconium & zirconium alloy bars, sheets, strip, etc.; porcelain electrical supplies
HQ: Morganite Industries Inc.
4000 Westchase Blvd # 170
Raleigh NC 27607
919 821-1253

(P-3795)
PICKERING LABORATORIES INC
1280 Space Park Way, Mountain View (94043-1434)
PHONE.................................650 694-6700
Michael Pickering, *President*
John Mariscal, *Officer*
Jim Murphy, *Vice Pres*
Mike Gottschalk, *Principal*
David Mazawa, *Principal*
EMP: 22 **EST:** 1979
SQ FT: 17,000
SALES (est): 5.7MM **Privately Held**
WEB: www.pickeringlabs.com
SIC: 2819 3826 2899 Chemicals, reagent grade: refined from technical grade; liquid chromatographic instruments; chemical preparations

(P-3796)
SIGNA CHEMISTRY INC
720 Olive Dr Ste Cd, Davis (95616-4740)
PHONE.................................212 933-4101
EMP: 25
SALES (corp-wide): 8.9MM **Privately Held**
SIC: 2819 3511 Mfg Industrial Inorganic Chemicals Mfg Turbines/Generator Sets
PA: Signa Chemistry, Inc.
445 Park Ave Ste 937
New York NY 10017
212 933-4101

(P-3797)
TIGER-SUL PRODUCTS LLC
61 Stork Rd, Stockton (95203-8200)
PHONE.................................209 451-2725
EMP: 15 **EST:** 2008
SALES (est): 3.2MM **Privately Held**
WEB: www.tigersul.com
SIC: 2819 Industrial inorganic chemicals

(P-3798)
TOKYO OHKA KOGYO AMERICA INC
Also Called: Tok America
190 Topaz St, Milpitas (95035-5429)
PHONE.................................408 956-9901
Yoshi Arai, *Manager*
Kazumasa Wakiya, *Vice Pres*
Takahiro Niwa, *General Mgr*
Tamlin Bley-Dawson, *Technician*
Chris Carlson, *Human Res Mgr*
EMP: 42
SQ FT: 12,560 **Privately Held**
WEB: www.tokamerica.com
SIC: 2819 3674 Industrial inorganic chemicals; semiconductors & related devices
HQ: Tokyo Ohka Kogyo America, Inc.
4600 Ne Brookwood Pkwy
Hillsboro OR 97124

(P-3799)
VACUUM ENGRG & MTLS CO INC
390 Reed St, Santa Clara (95050-3108)
PHONE.................................408 871-9900
John S Kavanaugh Jr, *Ch of Bd*
Robert T Kavanaugh, *President*
Stephanie McConnell, *CFO*
Melvin Hirata, *Vice Pres*
Kelli Rivers, *Business Mgr*
EMP: 50 **EST:** 1986
SQ FT: 16,500
SALES (est): 36.8MM **Privately Held**
WEB: www.vem-co.com
SIC: 2819 3399 3499 Chemicals, high purity: refined from technical grade; powder, metal; friction material, made from powdered metal

(P-3800)
W R GRACE & CO
252 W Larch Rd Ste H, Tracy (95304-1638)
PHONE.................................209 839-2800
EMP: 164
SALES (corp-wide): 3.1B **Publicly Held**
SIC: 2819 Mfg Industrial Inorganic Chemicals
PA: W. R. Grace & Co.
7500 Grace Dr
Columbia MD 21044
410 531-4000

2821 Plastics, Mtrls & Nonvulcanizable Elastomers

(P-3801)
EEZER PRODUCTS INC
4734 E Home Ave, Fresno (93703-4509)
PHONE.................................559 255-4140
Leighton Sjostrand, *President*
Cyndi Alcoser, *Vice Pres*
◆ **EMP:** 21 **EST:** 1964
SQ FT: 20,000
SALES: 2MM **Privately Held**
WEB: www.eezer.com
SIC: 2821 Plastics materials & resins

(P-3802)
ENVIRONMENTAL TECHNOLOGY INC
Also Called: Eti
300 S Bay Depot Rd, Fields Landing (95537)
P.O. Box 365 (95537-0365)
PHONE.................................707 443-9323
David C Fonsen, *President*
◆ **EMP:** 25 **EST:** 1969
SQ FT: 3,000
SALES (est): 6.1MM
SALES (corp-wide): 49.5MM **Privately Held**
WEB: www.eti-usa.com
SIC: 2821 Thermoplastic materials
PA: Polytek Development Corp.
55 Hilton St
Easton PA 18042
610 559-8620

(P-3803)
GLASFORMS INC
271 Barnard Ave, San Jose (95125-1302)
PHONE.................................408 297-9300
EMP: 17 **EST:** 2019
SALES (est): 511.5K **Privately Held**
WEB: www.avient.com
SIC: 2821 Plastics materials & resins

(P-3804)
INDUSPAC CALIFORNIA INC (HQ)
Also Called: Western Foam
6818 Patterson Pass Rd A, Livermore (94550-4231)
PHONE.................................510 324-3626
John McAuslan, *CEO*
Owen Sylvester, *Managing Dir*
EMP: 33 **EST:** 1999
SALES (est): 10.1MM **Privately Held**
WEB: www.induspac.com.mx
SIC: 2821 Polyethylene resins

(P-3805)
MANGO MATERIALS INC
800 Buchanan St, Berkeley (94710-1105)
P.O. Box 11, Palo Alto (94302-0011)
PHONE.................................650 440-0430
Molly Morse, *CEO*
Anne Schauer-Gimenez, *Vice Pres*
Brian Grubbs, *Research*
EMP: 19 **EST:** 2010
SALES (est): 2.6MM **Privately Held**
WEB: www.mangomaterials.com
SIC: 2821 Plastics materials & resins

(P-3806)
MITSUBSHI CHEM ADVNCED MTLS IN
3837 Imperial Way, Stockton (95215-9691)
PHONE.................................209 464-2701
EMP: 22 **Privately Held**
WEB: www.mcam.com
SIC: 2821 Plastics materials & resins
HQ: Mitsubishi Chemical Advanced Materials Inc.
2120 Fairmont Ave
Reading PA 19605
610 320-6600

(P-3807)
NORTH AMRCN SPECIALTY PDTS LLC
300 S Beckman Rd, Lodi (95240-3103)
PHONE.................................209 365-7500
Joseph Bondi,
Sasda Uma, *Supervisor*
EMP: 159 **Publicly Held**
WEB: www.westlake.com
SIC: 2821 Plastics materials & resins
HQ: North American Specialty Products Llc
993 Old Eagle School Rd
Wayne PA 19087
484 253-4545

(P-3808)
POLY PROCESSING COMPANY LLC
8055 Ash St, French Camp (95231-9667)
P.O. Box 80 (95231-0080)
PHONE.................................209 982-4904
Dixon Abell, *Mng Member*
Jeff Simonich, *Sales Staff*
EMP: 90 **EST:** 1995
SQ FT: 75,000
SALES (est): 8.4MM
SALES (corp-wide): 276.8MM **Privately Held**
WEB: www.polyprocessing.com
SIC: 2821 3443 Molding compounds, plastics; fabricated plate work (boiler shop)
PA: Abell Corporation
2500 Sterlington Rd
Monroe LA 71203
318 343-7565

(P-3809)
SOUTHWALL TECHNOLOGIES INC (DH)
3788 Fabian Way, Palo Alto (94303-4601)
PHONE.................................650 798-1285
B Travis Smith, *CEO*
Mallorie Burak,
Michael Vargas, *VP Admin*
◆ **EMP:** 101 **EST:** 1979
SQ FT: 30,174
SALES (est): 47.3MM **Publicly Held**
WEB: www.eastman.com
SIC: 2821 Plastics materials & resins
HQ: Solutia Inc.
575 Maryville Centre Dr
Saint Louis MO 63141
423 229-2000

(P-3810)
TAP PLASTICS INC A CAL CORP (PA)
3011 Alvarado St Ste A, San Leandro (94577-5707)
PHONE.................................510 357-3755
David Freeberg, *President*
Carole L Bremer, *CFO*
Robert J Wilson, *Vice Pres*
EMP: 15 **EST:** 1952
SQ FT: 4,000
SALES (est): 29.8MM **Privately Held**
WEB: www.tapplastics.com
SIC: 2821 5162 Acrylic resins; resins, synthetic

(P-3811)
TAP PLASTICS INC A CAL CORP
3011 Alvarado St, San Leandro (94577-5707)
PHONE.................................510 357-3755
Russ Miller, *Branch Mgr*
EMP: 36
SALES (corp-wide): 29.8MM **Privately Held**
WEB: www.tapplastics.com
SIC: 2821 Plastics materials & resins
PA: Tap Plastics, Inc., A California Corporation
3011 Alvarado St Ste A
San Leandro CA 94577
510 357-3755

(P-3812)
TORAY ADVNCED CMPSITES ADS LLC
2450 Cordelia Rd, Fairfield (94534-1651)
PHONE.................................707 359-3400
Buddy Berry, *Manager*
EMP: 46 **EST:** 2019
SALES (est): 17.9MM **Privately Held**
WEB: www.toraytac.com
SIC: 2821 2891 Thermoplastic materials; adhesives & sealants

2822 Synthetic Rubber (Vulcanizable Elastomers)

(P-3813)
CALIFORNIA INDUSTRIAL RBR CO
1690 Sierra Ave, Yuba City (95993-8981)
PHONE.................................530 674-2444
Andy Campos, *Branch Mgr*
Jake Jennings, *Purchasing*
Brad Greminger, *Sales Staff*
Tommy Hoyle, *Sales Staff*
Hugh Powell, *Manager*
EMP: 15
SQ FT: 4,800
SALES (corp-wide): 74.8MM **Privately Held**
WEB: www.californiaindustrialrubber.net
SIC: 2822 2891 3496 3241 Synthetic rubber; adhesives; conveyor belts; cement, hydraulic; agricultural chemicals
PA: California Industrial Rubber Co, Inc
2539 S Cherry Ave
Fresno CA 93706
559 268-7321

PRODUCTS & SERVICES SECTION

2834 - Pharmaceuticals County (P-3837)

(P-3814)
LTI HOLDINGS INC (PA)
Also Called: Boyd
5960 Inglewood Dr Ste 115, Pleasanton (94588-8611)
PHONE.................................925 271-8041
Doug Britt, *CEO*
Michael Sutsko, *Officer*
Adriana Druma, *Engineer*
▲ **EMP:** 15 **EST:** 1991
SALES (est): 661.7MM **Privately Held**
SIC: 2822 3069 Synthetic rubber; hard rubber & molded rubber products; rubber automotive products

---

2824 Synthetic Organic Fibers, Exc Cellulosic

(P-3815)
ARCLINE INVESTMENT MGT LP (PA)
4 Embarcadero Ctr # 3460, San Francisco (94111-4151)
PHONE.................................415 801-4570
Rajeev Amara, *CEO*
Shyam Ravindran, *President*
Gib Efird, *CFO*
Kim Deremo, *Project Mgr*
Hope Islas, *Director*
EMP: 15 **EST:** 2018
SALES (est): 653.4MM **Privately Held**
WEB: www.arcline.com
SIC: 2824 6211 Elastomeric fibers; investment firm, general brokerage

---

2833 Medicinal Chemicals & Botanical Prdts

(P-3816)
GLOBALRIDGE LLC
Also Called: Nutribiotic
865 Parallel Dr, Lakeport (95453-5707)
PHONE.................................800 225-4345
Kenneth Ridgeway, *CEO*
Lori Herren, *Production*
EMP: 19 **EST:** 2019
SALES (est): 1.9MM **Privately Held**
WEB: www.nutribiotic.com
SIC: 2833 Medicinals & botanicals

(P-3817)
MEGA HERBAL PRODUCTS INC
2f Ocean Ave, San Francisco (94112-2627)
PHONE.................................516 996-7770
Shikher Singla, *Branch Mgr*
EMP: 37
SALES (corp-wide): 97.8K **Privately Held**
SIC: 2833 Drugs & herbs: grading, grinding & milling
PA: Mega Herbal Products Inc.
3790 Brigadoon Way
San Jose CA 95121
516 996-7770

(P-3818)
MULTIVITAMIN DIRECT INC
2178 Paragon Dr, San Jose (95131-1305)
PHONE.................................408 573-7292
Paul Huang, *CEO*
▲ **EMP:** 30 **EST:** 2010
SQ FT: 5,000
SALES (est): 1.3MM **Privately Held**
SIC: 2833 Vitamins, natural or synthetic: bulk, uncompounded

(P-3819)
NOAH PHARMACEUTICALS INC
1380 San Andreas Rd, Watsonville (95076-9636)
PHONE.................................707 631-0921
Joshua Atiba, *CEO*
EMP: 20 **EST:** 2018
SALES (est): 1.3MM **Privately Held**
SIC: 2833 Drugs & herbs: grading, grinding & milling

(P-3820)
PROTHENA CORP PUB LTD CO ✪
331 Oyster Point Blvd, South San Francisco (94080-1913)
PHONE.................................650 837-8550
Karin L Walker, *Officer*
Wagner Zago, *Officer*
Keith Lui, *Vice Pres*
Ray Devyani, *Associate Dir*
Caroline Garrido, *Associate Dir*
EMP: 27 **EST:** 2021
SALES (est): 1MM **Privately Held**
WEB: www.prothena.com
SIC: 2833 Medicinals & botanicals

(P-3821)
RAINBOW LIGHT
125 Mcpherson St, Santa Cruz (95060-5883)
PHONE.................................831 429-9089
Linda Kahler, *Manager*
Scott Dunn, *Creative Dir*
Michael Murphey, *Planning*
Bill Klein, *Controller*
Mark Keller, *Mfg Spvr*
EMP: 45
SALES (corp-wide): 7.3B **Publicly Held**
WEB: www.rainbowlight.com
SIC: 2833 2834 Vitamins, natural or synthetic: bulk, uncompounded; pharmaceutical preparations
HQ: Rainbow Light Nutritional Systems, Inc.
1301 Sawgrs Corp Pkwy
Sunrise FL 33323
954 233-3300

(P-3822)
THRESHOLD ENTERPRISES LTD (PA)
Also Called: Vanguard Marketing
23 Janis Way, Scotts Valley (95066-3546)
PHONE.................................831 438-6851
Ira L Goldberg, *CEO*
Tom Grillea, *CEO*
Thomas Grillea, *COO*
Daniel Goldberg, *Managing Dir*
Jessica Cohen, *Executive Asst*
◆ **EMP:** 463 **EST:** 1978
SQ FT: 100,000
SALES (est): 121.1MM **Privately Held**
WEB: www.thresholdenterprises.com
SIC: 2833 Vitamins, natural or synthetic: bulk, uncompounded

2834 Pharmaceuticals

(P-3823)
89BIO INC
142 Sansome St Fl 2, San Francisco (94104-3702)
PHONE.................................415 500-4614
Rohan Palekar, *CEO*
Steven M Altschuler, *Ch of Bd*
Ram Waisbourd, *COO*
Ryan Martins, *CFO*
Hank Mansbach, *Chief Mktg Ofcr*
EMP: 27 **EST:** 2018
SQ FT: 3,600 **Privately Held**
WEB: www.89bio.com
SIC: 2834 Pharmaceutical preparations

(P-3824)
ABBOTT DIABETES CARE SLS CORP
1360 S Loop Rd, Alameda (94502-7000)
PHONE.................................510 749-5400
Robert Ford, *CEO*
Nevin Miller, *Regional*
EMP: 64 **EST:** 2007
SALES (est): 31.9MM
SALES (corp-wide): 34.6B **Publicly Held**
WEB: www.abbott.com
SIC: 2834 Pharmaceutical preparations
PA: Abbott Laboratories
100 Abbott Park Rd
Abbott Park IL 60064
224 667-6100

(P-3825)
ABBOTT NUTRITION
2302 Courage Dr, Fairfield (94533-6713)
PHONE.................................707 399-1100

EMP: 15 **EST:** 2014
SALES (est): 3.7MM **Privately Held**
SIC: 2834 Pharmaceutical preparations

(P-3826)
ABBOTT NUTRITION MFG INC (HQ)
2351 N Watney Way Ste C, Fairfield (94533-6726)
PHONE.................................707 399-1100
Mark Shaffar, *Vice Pres*
Mel Williamson, *Principal*
▼ **EMP:** 183 **EST:** 2004
SALES (est): 311.6MM
SALES (corp-wide): 34.6B **Publicly Held**
WEB: www.abbottnutrition.com
SIC: 2834 Vitamin, nutrient & hematinic preparations for human use
PA: Abbott Laboratories
100 Abbott Park Rd
Abbott Park IL 60064
224 667-6100

(P-3827)
ABBVIE BIOTHERAPEUTICS INC
1500 Seaport Blvd, Redwood City (94063-5540)
PHONE.................................650 454-1000
Faheem Hasnain, *President*
Andrew Guggenhime, *CFO*
Ted Llana PHD, *Senior VP*
Julie Badillo, *Vice Pres*
Ligia Gandia, *Vice Pres*
EMP: 98 **EST:** 2008
SQ FT: 450,000
SALES (est): 17.2MM
SALES (corp-wide): 45.8B **Publicly Held**
WEB: www.abbvie.com
SIC: 2834 Pharmaceutical preparations
PA: Abbvie Inc.
1 N Waukegan Rd
North Chicago IL 60064
847 932-7900

(P-3828)
ABCO LABORATORIES INC (PA)
Also Called: Baron Brand Spices
2450 S Watney Way, Fairfield (94533-6730)
P.O. Box 2519 (94533-0251)
PHONE.................................707 432-2200
Allen Baron, *President*
Greg Northam, *President*
Adrian Cesana, *CIO*
Conor Emberley, *Technician*
Hamed Malekan, *Research*
▲ **EMP:** 99 **EST:** 1964
SQ FT: 29,000
SALES (est): 21.3MM **Privately Held**
WEB: www.abcolabs.com
SIC: 2834 2099 Vitamin preparations; spices, including grinding

(P-3829)
ABGENIX INC (PA)
6701 Kaiser Dr, Fremont (94555-3659)
PHONE.................................510 608-6500
EMP: 101 **EST:** 2017
SALES (est): 1.3MM **Privately Held**
SIC: 2834 Pharmaceutical preparations

(P-3830)
ACELRX PHARMACEUTICALS INC (PA)
25821 Industrial Blvd # 400, Hayward (94545-2919)
PHONE.................................650 216-3500
Vincent J Angotti, *CEO*
Adrian Adams, *Ch of Bd*
Raffi Asadorian, *CFO*
Pamela P Palmer, *Chief Mktg Ofcr*
Badri Dasu, *Officer*
EMP: 27 **EST:** 2005
SQ FT: 25,893
SALES (est): 5.4MM **Publicly Held**
WEB: www.acelrx.com
SIC: 2834 Pharmaceutical preparations

(P-3831)
ACHAOGEN INC
1 Tower Pl Ste 300, South San Francisco (94080-1835)
PHONE.................................650 800-3636
EMP: 200
SQ FT: 16,000

SALES: 11.1MM **Privately Held**
WEB: www.achaogen.com
SIC: 2834 Pharmaceutical Preparations

(P-3832)
ADAMAS PHARMACEUTICALS INC (PA)
1900 Powell St Ste 1000, Emeryville (94608-1839)
PHONE.................................510 450-3500
Neil McFarlane, *CEO*
David L Mahoney, *Ch of Bd*
Neil F McFarlane, *CEO*
Chris Prentiss, *CFO*
Christopher B Prentiss, *CFO*
EMP: 134 **EST:** 2000
SQ FT: 37,626
SALES (est): 54.6MM **Publicly Held**
WEB: www.adamaspharma.com
SIC: 2834 Drugs acting on the central nervous system & sense organs

(P-3833)
ADIANA INC
1240 Elko Dr, Sunnyvale (94089-2212)
PHONE.................................650 421-2900
Paul Goeld, *CEO*
EMP: 415 **EST:** 1997
SQ FT: 12,000
SALES (est): 1.6MM
SALES (corp-wide): 5.6B **Publicly Held**
WEB: www.hologic.com
SIC: 2834 8731 Pharmaceutical preparations; commercial physical research
HQ: Cytyc Corporation
250 Campus Dr
Marlborough MA 01752
-

(P-3834)
ADURO GVAX INC
740 Heinz Ave, Berkeley (94710-2748)
PHONE.................................510 848-4400
Jennifer Lew, *CFO*
EMP: 37 **EST:** 2018
SALES (est): 291.4K **Publicly Held**
WEB: www.aduro.com
SIC: 2834 Pharmaceutical preparations
PA: Chinook Therapeutics, Inc.
1600 Frview Ave E Ste 100
Seattle WA 98102

(P-3835)
AEA PHARMACEUTICALS INC
351 Galveston Dr, Redwood City (94063-4736)
PHONE.................................650 996-5895
Mark Wan, *Bd of Directors*
Christy Sweet, *Business Dir*
Monica Mazziotti, *Exec Dir*
Lars Larson, *Technology*
Casidy Domingo, *Engineer*
EMP: 23 **EST:** 2017
SALES (est): 6.3MM **Privately Held**
SIC: 2834 Pharmaceutical preparations

(P-3836)
AGRAQUEST INC (DH)
Also Called: Bayer Cropscience
890 Embarcadero Dr, West Sacramento (95605-1503)
PHONE.................................866 992-2937
James Blome, *CEO*
Michael Mille, *COO*
Joel R Jung, *CFO*
Jonathan Margolis, *Senior VP*
Ashish Malik, *Vice Pres*
▲ **EMP:** 249 **EST:** 1995
SQ FT: 28,000
SALES (est): 53.1MM
SALES (corp-wide): 48.9B **Privately Held**
WEB: www.cropscience.bayer.us
SIC: 2834 Pharmaceutical preparations
HQ: Bayer Cropscience Ag
Kaiser-Wilhelm-Allee 20
Leverkusen NW 51373
214 301-

(P-3837)
AIMMUNE THERAPEUTICS INC
8000 Marina Blvd Ste 300, Brisbane (94005-1884)
PHONE.................................650 614-5220
Jayson Dallas, *CEO*
Mark D McDade, *Ch of Bd*

2834 - Pharmaceuticals County (P-3838)

Tracy Lash, *COO*
Eric H Bjerkholt, *CFO*
Andrew Oxtoby, *Ch Credit Ofcr*
EMP: 131 **EST:** 2011
SQ FT: 53,000
SALES (corp-wide): 92.3B **Privately Held**
WEB: www.aimmune.com
SIC: 2834 Pharmaceutical preparations
HQ: Societe Des Produits Nestle S.A.
Avenue Nestle 55
Vevey VD 1800
219 245-111

(P-3838)
AKERO THERAPEUTICS INC (PA)
601 Gateway Blvd Ste 350, South San Francisco (94080-7030)
PHONE 650 487-6488
Andrew Cheng, *President*
Mark T Iwicki, *Ch of Bd*
Jonathan Young, *COO*
William White, *CFO*
Timothy Rolph, *Security Dir*
EMP: 19 **EST:** 2017
SQ FT: 6,647 **Publicly Held**
WEB: www.akerotx.com
SIC: 2834 Pharmaceutical preparations

(P-3839)
ALEXZA PHARMACEUTICALS INC (HQ)
2091 Stierlin Ct, Mountain View (94043-4655)
PHONE 650 944-7000
Tatjana Naranda, *President*
Stacy Palermini, *Senior VP*
Lawrence Carter, *Vice Pres*
David Hasegawa, *Vice Pres*
Edwin Kamemoto, *Vice Pres*
EMP: 47 **EST:** 2000
SQ FT: 65,604
SALES (est): 35.2MM **Privately Held**
WEB: www.alexza.com
SIC: 2834 Pharmaceutical preparations

(P-3840)
ALLSTRIPES RESEARCH INC
121 2nd St Ste 700, San Francisco (94105-3608)
PHONE 415 404-9287
Nancy Yu, *CEO*
EMP: 15 **EST:** 2018
SALES (est): 3.1MM **Privately Held**
WEB: www.allstripes.com
SIC: 2834 Medicines, capsuled or ampuled

(P-3841)
ALTRUBIO INC (PA)
455 Margarita Ave, Palo Alto (94306-2827)
PHONE 650 453-3462
EMP: 38
SALES (est): 443.7K **Privately Held**
SIC: 2834 Pharmaceutical preparations

(P-3842)
ALX ONCOLOGY HOLDINGS INC (PA)
323 Allerton Ave, South San Francisco (94080-4816)
PHONE 650 466-7125
Jaume Pons, *President*
Corey Goodman, *Ch of Bd*
Peter Garcia, *CFO*
Sophia Randolph, *Chief Mktg Ofcr*
Shelly Pinto, *Vice Pres*
EMP: 22 **EST:** 2015
SALES (est): 1.1MM **Publicly Held**
WEB: www.alxoncology.com
SIC: 2834 Pharmaceutical preparations

(P-3843)
ALZA CORPORATION (HQ)
Also Called: Alza Pharmaceuticals
700 Eubanks Dr, Vacaville (95688-9470)
PHONE 707 453-6400
Katie Fitz Chaddock, *President*
Meena Desai, *Technical Staff*
Earl Born, *Engineer*
Steve Yeh, *Engineer*
Brian Putney, *Mfg Staff*
▲ **EMP:** 800 **EST:** 1987
SQ FT: 74,200

SALES (est): 286.6MM
SALES (corp-wide): 82.5B **Publicly Held**
WEB: www.alza.com
SIC: 2834 Pharmaceutical preparations
PA: Johnson & Johnson
1 Johnson And Johnson Plz
New Brunswick NJ 08933
732 524-0400

(P-3844)
AMGEN INC
1120 Veterans Blvd, South San Francisco (94080-1985)
PHONE 650 244-2000
David V Goeddel, *Site Mgr*
Steven K Galson, *Vice Pres*
Erin Denny, *Executive*
Paulina Ogagan, *Executive*
Adam Elinoff, *Exec Dir*
EMP: 25
SALES (corp-wide): 25.4B **Publicly Held**
WEB: www.amgen.com
SIC: 2834 Pharmaceutical preparations
PA: Amgen Inc.
1 Amgen Center Dr
Thousand Oaks CA 91320
805 447-1000

(P-3845)
AMPAC FINE CHEMICALS LLC
Also Called: Ampac Analytical
1100 Windfield Way, El Dorado Hills (95762-9622)
PHONE 916 245-6500
Renato Murrer, *Branch Mgr*
EMP: 40 **Privately Held**
WEB: www.ampacfinechemicals.com
SIC: 2834 Digitalis pharmaceutical preparations
HQ: Ampac Fine Chemicals Llc
Hwy 50 Hzel Ave Bldg 0501
Rancho Cordova CA 95741
916 357-6880

(P-3846)
ANACOR PHARMACEUTICALS INC
1020 E Meadow Cir, Palo Alto (94303-4230)
PHONE 650 543-7500
EMP: 20
SALES (corp-wide): 20.6MM **Publicly Held**
SIC: 2834 Mfg Pharmaceutical Preparations
PA: Anacor Pharmaceuticals, Inc.
1020 E Meadow Cir
Palo Alto CA 10017
650 543-7500

(P-3847)
ANNEXON INC (PA)
180 Kimball Way Ste 200, South San Francisco (94080-6218)
PHONE 650 822-5500
Douglas Love, *President*
Thomas G Wiggans, *Ch of Bd*
Jennifer Lew, *CFO*
Sanjay Keswani, *Chief Mktg Ofcr*
Michael Overdorf, *Exec VP*
EMP: 47 **EST:** 2011
SQ FT: 12,300 **Publicly Held**
WEB: www.annexonbio.com
SIC: 2834 8731 Pharmaceutical preparations; biotechnical research, commercial

(P-3848)
ANTIPODEAN PHARMACEUTICALS INC (PA)
1700 Montgomery St # 209, San Francisco (94111-1021)
P.O. Box 776, Menlo Park (94026-0776)
PHONE 866 749-3338
Ken Taylor, *Principal*
EMP: 64 **EST:** 2008
SALES (est): 111.2K **Privately Held**
WEB: www.antipodeanpharma.com
SIC: 2834 Pharmaceutical preparations

(P-3849)
APELLIS PHARMACEUTICALS INC
720 Market St Fl 5, San Francisco (94102-2511)
PHONE 415 872-9970

Najib Maslouh, *Vice Pres*
EMP: 23 **Publicly Held**
WEB: www.apellis.com
SIC: 2834 Pharmaceutical preparations
PA: Apellis Pharmaceuticals, Inc.
100 5th Ave Fl 3
Waltham MA 02451

(P-3850)
APEXIGEN INC
75 Shoreway Rd Ste C, San Carlos (94070-2727)
PHONE 650 931-6236
Xiaodong Yang, *President*
Linda Rubinstein, *CFO*
Frank J Hsu, *Chief Mktg Ofcr*
Frances Rena Bahjat, *Vice Pres*
Thomas Jahn, *Vice Pres*
EMP: 29 **EST:** 2010
SALES (est): 7.1MM **Privately Held**
WEB: www.apexigen.com
SIC: 2834 Pharmaceutical preparations

(P-3851)
APPLIED MOLECULAR TRNSPT INC
450 E Jamie Ct, South San Francisco (94080-6205)
PHONE 650 392-0420
Tahir Mahmood, *CEO*
Helen S Kim, *Ch of Bd*
Shawn Cross, *CFO*
Bittoo Kanwar, *Chief Mktg Ofcr*
Elizabeth Bhatt, *Officer*
EMP: 80 **EST:** 2010
SQ FT: 19,000 **Privately Held**
WEB: www.appliedmt.com
SIC: 2834 Pharmaceutical preparations

(P-3852)
ARADIGM CORPORATION
1613 Lyon St, San Francisco (94115-2414)
PHONE 510 265-9000
Adia Jackson, *Research*
Lisa Thomas, *Controller*
Francis Dayton, *Director*
Adrienne Ste Marie, *Director*
Charles Herst, *Consultant*
EMP: 23 **EST:** 1991
SALES (est): 14.4MM **Privately Held**
WEB: www.aradigm.com
SIC: 2834 Drugs acting on the respiratory system

(P-3853)
ARDELYX INC
34175 Ardenwood Blvd, Fremont (94555-3653)
PHONE 510 745-1700
Michael Raab, *President*
David Mott, *Ch of Bd*
Justin Renz, *CFO*
Jeff Jacobs, *Officer*
Susan Rodriguez, *Officer*
EMP: 129 **EST:** 2007
SQ FT: 72,500
SALES (est): 7.5MM **Privately Held**
WEB: www.ardelyx.com
SIC: 2834 8731 Pharmaceutical preparations; biotechnical research, commercial

(P-3854)
ARIDIS PHARMACEUTICALS INC
983 University Ave Bldg B, Los Gatos (95032-7637)
PHONE 408 385-1742
Vu Truong, *CEO*
Eric Patzer, *Ch of Bd*
Fred Kurland, *CFO*
Michael A Nazak, *CFO*
Michael Nazak, *CFO*
EMP: 31 **EST:** 2003
SQ FT: 4,500
SALES (est): 1MM **Privately Held**
WEB: www.aridispharma.com
SIC: 2834 Pharmaceutical preparations

(P-3855)
ARMO BIOSCIENCES INC
575 Chesapeake Dr, Redwood City (94063-4724)
PHONE 650 779-5075
Peter Van Vlasselaer, *President*
Herb Cross, *CFO*

Joseph Leveque, *Chief Mktg Ofcr*
Russell Kawahata, *Vice Pres*
Clinton Musil, *Vice Pres*
EMP: 21 **EST:** 2010
SQ FT: 11,388
SALES (corp-wide): 24.5B **Publicly Held**
WEB: www.armobio.com
SIC: 2834 Pharmaceutical preparations
PA: Eli Lilly And Company
Lilly Corporate Ctr
Indianapolis IN 46285
317 276-2000

(P-3856)
ASCENDIS PHARMA INC
1000 Page Mill Rd, Palo Alto (94304-1019)
PHONE 650 352-8389
Jan Mller Mikkelsen, *President*
Flemming Steen Jensen, *President*
Scott T Smith, *CFO*
Michael Wolff Jensen, *Chairman*
Jonathan Leff MD, *Officer*
EMP: 16 **EST:** 2013
SALES (est): 8.6MM
SALES (corp-wide): 8.2MM **Privately Held**
WEB: www.ascendispharma.com
SIC: 2834 Pharmaceutical preparations
PA: Ascendis Pharma A/S
Tuborg Boulevard 12
Hellerup 2900
702 222-44

(P-3857)
ASSEMBLY BIOSCIENCES INC (PA)
331 Oyster Point Blvd # 4, South San Francisco (94080-1913)
PHONE 833 509-4583
John McHutchison, *President*
William R Ringo Jr, *Ch of Bd*
Graham Cooper, *COO*
Jason Okazaki, *COO*
Thomas J Russo, *CFO*
EMP: 94 **EST:** 2005
SALES (est): 79.1MM **Publicly Held**
WEB: www.assemblybio.com
SIC: 2834 Pharmaceutical preparations

(P-3858)
ASTEX PHARMACEUTICALS INC (DH)
4420 Rosewood Dr Ste 200, Pleasanton (94588-3008)
PHONE 925 560-0100
James Manuso, *President*
Michael Molkentin, *CFO*
Mohammad Azab, *Chief Mktg Ofcr*
Martin Buckland, *Officer*
Nipun Davar, *Vice Pres*
EMP: 116 **EST:** 2011
SQ FT: 37,000
SALES (est): 50.4MM **Privately Held**
WEB: www.astx.com
SIC: 2834 Pharmaceutical preparations

(P-3859)
ASTRAZENECA LP
121 Oyster Point Blvd, South San Francisco (94080-2040)
PHONE 650 634-0103
David Fredrickson, *Exec VP*
Leon Cuevas, *Technician*
Imara Kassam, *Project Mgr*
Joshua Bradley, *Opers Staff*
Brett Hellman, *Sales Staff*
EMP: 20 **EST:** 1998
SALES (est): 3.3MM **Privately Held**
WEB: www.astrazeneca-us.com
SIC: 2834 Pharmaceutical preparations

(P-3860)
ASTRAZENECA PHARMACEUTICALS LP
200 Cardinal Way, Redwood City (94063-4702)
PHONE 650 305-2600
Ed Louie, *Branch Mgr*
EMP: 26
SALES (corp-wide): 26.6B **Privately Held**
WEB: www.astrazeneca.com
SIC: 2834 Druggists' preparations (pharmaceuticals)

PRODUCTS & SERVICES SECTION

2834 - Pharmaceuticals County (P-3884)

HQ: Astrazeneca Pharmaceuticals Lp
1800 Concord Pike
Wilmington DE 19850

(P-3861)
BAUSCH HEALTH AMERICAS INC
1330 Redwood Way Ste C, Petaluma (94954-7122)
PHONE...........................707 793-2600
EMP: 140
SALES (corp-wide): 8.6B Privately Held
WEB: www.bauschhealth.com
SIC: 2834 Pharmaceutical preparations
HQ: Bausch Health Americas, Inc.
400 Somerset Corp Blvd
Bridgewater NJ 08807
908 927-1400

(P-3862)
BAYER HEALTHCARE LLC
5885 Hollis St, Emeryville (94608-2404)
PHONE...........................510 597-6150
Anita Bawa, Branch Mgr
EMP: 104
SALES (corp-wide): 48.9B Privately Held
WEB: www.bayer.us
SIC: 2834 Pharmaceutical preparations
HQ: Bayer Healthcare Llc
100 Bayer Blvd
Whippany NJ 07981
862 404-3000

(P-3863)
BAYER HEALTHCARE LLC
800 Dwight Way, Berkeley (94710-2428)
PHONE...........................510 705-7545
Paul Heiden, Branch Mgr
Christine Di Toro, Officer
Melissa Armstrong, Associate Dir
Shachi Sharma, Associate Dir
Priya Murali, General Mgr
EMP: 134
SALES (corp-wide): 48.9B Privately Held
WEB: www.bayer.us
SIC: 2834 Pharmaceutical preparations
HQ: Bayer Healthcare Llc
100 Bayer Blvd
Whippany NJ 07981
862 404-3000

(P-3864)
BEIGENE USA INC
2955 Campus Dr Fl 2, San Mateo (94403-2500)
PHONE...........................877 828-5568
Michael Musante, Associate Dir
Amy Wong, Office Mgr
Yasser Ali, CIO
Lilian Kee, CIO
Tracy Tan, CIO
EMP: 85 Privately Held
WEB: www.beigene.com
SIC: 2834 5122 8731 Pharmaceutical preparations; pharmaceuticals; commercial research laboratory
HQ: Beigene Usa, Inc.
55 Cambrdge Pkwy Ste 700w
Cambridge MA 02142
781 801-1887

(P-3865)
BETTER THERAPEUTICS INC
548 Market St 49404, San Francisco (94104-5401)
PHONE...........................415 887-2311
Kevin Appelbaum, CEO
David Perry, Ch of Bd
Mark Heinen, CFO
Justin Zamirowski, Ch Credit Ofcr
Mark Berman, Chief Mktg Ofcr
EMP: 36 EST: 2020
SALES (est): 2.8MM Privately Held
WEB: www.mcacquisition.com
SIC: 2834 Pharmaceutical preparations

(P-3866)
BIOELECTRON TECHNOLOGY CORP (PA)
350 Bernardo Ave, Mountain View (94043-5207)
PHONE...........................650 641-9200
Guy Miller, CEO
James Gibson, CFO
Peter Heinecke, Officer

Sarah Nemec, Executive
Yuko Kosaka, Research
EMP: 19 EST: 2005
SALES (est): 8.6MM Privately Held
WEB: www.ptcbio.com
SIC: 2834 Pharmaceutical preparations

(P-3867)
BIOKEY INC
44370 Old Warm Springs Bl, Fremont (94538-6148)
PHONE...........................510 668-0881
San-Laung Chow, President
George Lee, President
Paul Dickinson, QC Mgr
Wen Wu, Supervisor
▼ EMP: 34 EST: 2000
SQ FT: 28,000
SALES (est): 4.3MM Privately Held
WEB: www.biokeyinc.com
SIC: 2834 Pharmaceutical preparations

(P-3868)
BIOMARIN PHARMACEUTICAL INC (PA)
770 Lindaro St, San Rafael (94901-3991)
PHONE...........................415 506-6700
Jean-Jacques Bienaime, Ch of Bd
Robert A Baffi, President
Henry J Fuchs, President
Brian R Mueller, CFO
Jeff Ajer, Ch Credit Ofcr
EMP: 350 EST: 1997
SQ FT: 407,300
SALES (est): 1.8B Publicly Held
WEB: www.biomarin.com
SIC: 2834 2835 Pharmaceutical preparations; enzyme & isoenzyme diagnostic agents

(P-3869)
BIOQ PHARMA INCORPORATED (PA)
1325 Howard St, San Francisco (94103-2612)
PHONE...........................415 336-6496
Josh Kriesel, CEO
Walter Clerymans, COO
Ronald Pauli, CFO
Doug Cullum, Vice Pres
Serena Joshi, Vice Pres
EMP: 18 EST: 2003
SALES (est): 4.4MM Privately Held
WEB: www.bioqpharma.com
SIC: 2834 Pharmaceutical preparations

(P-3870)
BLACKTHORN THERAPEUTICS INC
780 Brannan St, San Francisco (94103-4919)
PHONE...........................415 548-5401
William J Martin, CEO
Paul L Berns, Ch of Bd
Jane Tiller, Chief Mktg Ofcr
Monique Levy, Officer
Annette Madrid, Officer
EMP: 35 EST: 2013
SALES (est): 4.2MM Privately Held
WEB: www.blackthornrx.com
SIC: 2834 Pharmaceutical preparations

(P-3871)
BLADE THERAPEUTICS INC
442 Littlefield Ave, South San Francisco (94080-6105)
PHONE...........................650 334-2079
Wendye Robbins, CEO
Jean-Frdric Viret, CFO
Lloyd Klickstein, Officer
Jeff Evans, Opers Staff
EMP: 21 EST: 2015
SQ FT: 65,000
SALES (est): 3.7MM Privately Held
WEB: www.blademed.com
SIC: 2834 Pharmaceutical preparations

(P-3872)
BOLT BIOTHERAPEUTICS INC
900 Chesapeake Dr, Redwood City (94063-4727)
PHONE...........................650 260-9295
Randall C Schatzman, CEO
Peter Moldt, Ch of Bd
William P Quinn, CFO

Edith A Perez, Chief Mktg Ofcr
Nathan Ihle, Vice Pres
EMP: 63 EST: 2015
SQ FT: 80,500
SALES (est): 231K Privately Held
WEB: www.boltbio.com
SIC: 2834 Pharmaceutical preparations

(P-3873)
BRIDGEBIO PHARMA INC (PA)
421 Kipling St, Palo Alto (94301-1530)
PHONE...........................650 391-9740
Neil Kumar, CEO
Brian C Stephenson, CFO
Michael Henderson, Vice Pres
Andy Whitney, Vice Pres
Hannah Shen, Associate Dir
EMP: 186 EST: 2015
SQ FT: 3,900
SALES (est): 8.2MM Publicly Held
WEB: www.bridgebio.com
SIC: 2834 8731 Pharmaceutical preparations; biotechnical research, commercial

(P-3874)
BRIDGENE BIOSCIENCES INC ✪
75 Nicholson Ln, San Jose (95134-1366)
PHONE...........................626 632-3188
Ping Cao, CEO
Irene Yuan, Exec VP
Hang Chen, Vice Pres
EMP: 16 EST: 2021
SALES (est): 6.3MM Privately Held
WEB: www.bridgenebio.com
SIC: 2834 Pharmaceutical preparations

(P-3875)
BRISTOL-MYERS SQUIBB COMPANY
700 Bay Rd, Redwood City (94063-2477)
PHONE...........................800 332-2056
EMP: 57
SALES (corp-wide): 42.5B Publicly Held
WEB: www.bms.com
SIC: 2834 Pharmaceutical preparations
PA: Bristol-Myers Squibb Company
430 E 29th St Fl 14
New York NY 10016
212 546-4000

(P-3876)
CALITHERA BIOSCIENCES INC
343 Oyster Point Blvd # 20, South San Francisco (94080-1913)
PHONE...........................650 870-1000
Susan M Molineaux, President
Stephanie Wong, CFO
Sumita Ray, Ch Credit Ofcr
Emil T Kuriakose, Chief Mktg Ofcr
Christopher J Molineaux, Senior VP
EMP: 94 EST: 2010
SQ FT: 34,000 Privately Held
WEB: www.calithera.com
SIC: 2834 8731 Pharmaceutical preparations; biotechnical research, commercial

(P-3877)
CAPNIA INC (PA)
1101 Chess Dr, Foster City (94404-1102)
PHONE...........................650 213-8444
Anish Bhatnagar MD, CEO
David D O Toole, CFO
Ann Rich, Vice Pres
Anthony Wondka, Vice Pres
Kristen Yen, Vice Pres
EMP: 53 EST: 2006
SALES (est): 5.3MM Privately Held
WEB: www.capnia.com
SIC: 2834 Pharmaceutical preparations

(P-3878)
CATALYST BIO INC (HQ)
611 Gateway Blvd Ste 710, South San Francisco (94080-7029)
PHONE...........................650 871-0761
Nassim Usman PHD, President
Fletcher Payne, CFO
Edwin Madison PHD, Security Dir
EMP: 16 EST: 2002
SALES (est): 14.2MM Publicly Held
WEB: www.catalystbiosciences.com
SIC: 2834 Pharmaceutical preparations

(P-3879)
CATALYST BIOSCIENCES INC (PA)
611 Gateway Blvd Ste 710, South San Francisco (94080-7029)
PHONE...........................650 871-0761
Nassim Usman, President
Augustine Lawlor, Ch of Bd
Clinton Musil, CFO
Howard Levy, Chief Mktg Ofcr
Grant Blouse, Security Dir
EMP: 51 EST: 2002
SQ FT: 16,208
SALES (est): 20.9MM Publicly Held
WEB: www.catalystbiosciences.com
SIC: 2834 Pharmaceutical preparations

(P-3880)
CELL DESIGN LABS INC
5858 Horton St Ste 240, Emeryville (94608-2018)
PHONE...........................510 398-0501
Brian Atwood, CEO
Peter Emtage, Officer
Roger Sidhu, Officer
EMP: 50 EST: 2015
SQ FT: 19,000
SALES (est): 1MM
SALES (corp-wide): 24.6B Publicly Held
WEB: www.gilead.com
SIC: 2834 Pharmaceutical preparations
PA: Gilead Sciences, Inc.
333 Lakeside Dr
Foster City CA 94404
650 574-3000

(P-3881)
CELLTHEON CORPORATION
32980 Alvarado Niles Rd, Union City (94587-8104)
PHONE...........................650 743-3672
Amita S Goel, CEO
Anura Goel, CFO
Divya Goel, Vice Pres
EMP: 17 EST: 2012
SQ FT: 4,000
SALES (est): 3MM Privately Held
WEB: www.celltheon.com
SIC: 2834 Pharmaceutical preparations

(P-3882)
CHEMOCENTRYX INC (PA)
835 Industrial Rd Ste 600, San Carlos (94070-3312)
PHONE...........................650 210-2900
Thomas J Schall, Ch of Bd
Tausif Butt, COO
Markus J Cappel, Treasurer
Thomas Schall, Bd of Directors
Rita I Jain, Chief Mktg Ofcr
EMP: 64 EST: 1997
SQ FT: 35,755
SALES (est): 64.8MM Publicly Held
WEB: www.chemocentryx.com
SIC: 2834 Drugs affecting parasitic & infective diseases

(P-3883)
CHIRON CORPORATION
4560 Horton St, Emeryville (94608-2916)
PHONE...........................510 655-8730
Edward E Penhoet, President
EMP: 4245 EST: 1981
SALES (est): 10.9MM
SALES (corp-wide): 45.3B Privately Held
SIC: 2834 Pharmaceutical preparations
HQ: Novartis Vaccines And Diagnostics, Inc.
475 Green Oaks Pkwy
Holly Springs NC 27540
617 871-7000

(P-3884)
CITRAGEN PHARMACEUTICALS INC
3789 Spinnaker Ct, Fremont (94538-6537)
PHONE...........................510 249-9066
Ravichandran Mahalingam, CEO
Ravi Jayapal, Vice Pres
EMP: 17 EST: 2014
SALES (est): 3.1MM Privately Held
WEB: www.citragenpharma.com
SIC: 2834 Pharmaceutical preparations

(PA)=Parent Co (HQ)=Headquarters (DH)=Div Headquarters
✪ = New Business established in last 2 years

2834 - Pharmaceuticals County (P-3885)

PRODUCTS & SERVICES SECTION

(P-3885)
CORCEPT THERAPEUTICS INC
149 Commonwealth Dr, Menlo Park (94025-1133)
PHONE 650 327-3270
Joseph K Belanoff, *President*
James N Wilson, *Ch of Bd*
Ted Kummert, *President*
Atabak Mokari, *CFO*
Amy Flood, *Ch Credit Ofcr*
EMP: 136 **EST:** 1998
SQ FT: 23,473
SALES (est): 353.8MM **Privately Held**
WEB: www.corcept.com
SIC: 2834 Pharmaceutical preparations

(P-3886)
CORVUS PHARMACEUTICALS INC
863 Mitten Rd Ste 102, Burlingame (94010-1311)
PHONE 650 900-4520
Richard A Miller, *Ch of Bd*
Katherine Woodworth, *CEO*
Leiv Lea, *CFO*
Ian Clark, *Bd of Directors*
Steve Krognes, *Bd of Directors*
EMP: 55 **EST:** 2014
SQ FT: 28,633 **Privately Held**
WEB: www.corvuspharma.com
SIC: 2834 Pharmaceutical preparations

(P-3887)
COTHERA BIOPHARMA INC
1960 Noel Dr, Los Altos (94024-7060)
PHONE 510 364-1930
Yue Alexander Wu, *CEO*
EMP: 30 **EST:** 2018
SALES (est): 100K **Privately Held**
SIC: 2834 7389 Pharmaceutical preparations; business services

(P-3888)
CYMABAY THERAPEUTICS INC (PA)
7575 Gateway Blvd Ste 110, Newark (94560-1194)
PHONE 510 293-8800
Sujal Shah, *President*
Robert J Wills, *Ch of Bd*
Paul Quinlan, *Ch Credit Ofcr*
Charles McWherter, *Senior VP*
Daniel Menold, *VP Finance*
EMP: 42 **EST:** 1988 **Publicly Held**
WEB: www.cymabay.com
SIC: 2834 Druggists' preparations (pharmaceuticals)

(P-3889)
CYTOKINETICS INCORPORATED (PA)
280 E Grand Ave, South San Francisco (94080-4808)
PHONE 650 624-3000
Robert I Blum, *President*
L Patrick Gage, *Ch of Bd*
Ching Jaw, *CFO*
Erik Atkisson, *Officer*
David Cragg, *Officer*
EMP: 136 **EST:** 1997
SQ FT: 81,587
SALES (est): 55.8MM **Publicly Held**
WEB: www.cytokinetics.com
SIC: 2834 8731 Pharmaceutical preparations; biotechnical research, commercial

(P-3890)
CYTOMX THERAPEUTICS INC
151 Oyster Point Blvd # 40, South San Francisco (94080-1840)
PHONE 650 515-3185
Sean A McCarthy, *Ch of Bd*
Carlos Campoy, *CFO*
Alison L Hannah, *Chief Mktg Ofcr*
Rachel W Humphrey, *Chief Mktg Ofcr*
Rachel Humphrey, *Chief Mktg Ofcr*
EMP: 139 **EST:** 2008
SQ FT: 76,000
SALES (est): 57.4MM **Privately Held**
WEB: www.cytomx.com
SIC: 2834 Pharmaceutical preparations

(P-3891)
DERMIRA INC
275 Middlefield Rd # 150, Menlo Park (94025-4008)
PHONE 650 421-7200
Heather Wasserman, *President*
Philip L Johnson, *Treasurer*
Andrew Guggenhime, *Officer*
Ray Bassi, *Vice Pres*
Becky Chaitesipaseut, *Vice Pres*
EMP: 333 **EST:** 2010
SALES: 42.3MM
SALES (corp-wide): 24.5B **Publicly Held**
WEB: www.dermira.com
SIC: 2834 Pharmaceutical preparations
PA: Eli Lilly And Company
Lilly Corporate Ctr
Indianapolis IN 46285
317 276-2000

(P-3892)
DIABLO CLINICAL RESEARCH INC
2255 Ygnacio Valley Rd M, Walnut Creek (94598-3347)
PHONE 925 930-7267
Richard Weinstein, *President*
Leonard H Chuck, *Director*
EMP: 22 **EST:** 1995
SQ FT: 2,200
SALES (est): 600K **Privately Held**
WEB: www.diabloclinical.com
SIC: 2834 8011 Pharmaceutical preparations; offices & clinics of medical doctors

(P-3893)
DICE MOLECULES SV INC
279 E Grand Ave Ste 300, South San Francisco (94080-4804)
PHONE 650 566-1402
Kevin Judice, *CEO*
EMP: 18 **EST:** 2014
SALES (est): 435K **Privately Held**
WEB: www.dicetherapeutics.com
SIC: 2834 Pharmaceutical preparations

(P-3894)
DURECT CORPORATION (PA)
10260 Bubb Rd, Cupertino (95014-4166)
PHONE 408 777-1417
James E Brown, *President*
Felix Theeuwes, *Ch of Bd*
Matthew J Hogan, *CFO*
Norman Sussman, *Chief Mktg Ofcr*
Weiqi Lin, *Exec VP*
EMP: 83 **EST:** 1998
SALES (est): 30.1MM **Publicly Held**
WEB: www.durect.com
SIC: 2834 Drugs acting on the central nervous system & sense organs

(P-3895)
EXELIXIS INC
169 Harbor Way, South San Francisco (94080-6109)
PHONE 650 837-8254
EMP: 200 **Publicly Held**
SIC: 2834 Pharmaceutical Products
PA: Exelixis, Inc.
210 E Grand Ave
South San Francisco CA 94502

(P-3896)
EXELIXIS INC
1851 Harbor Bay Pkwy, Alameda (94502-3016)
PHONE 650 837-7000
EMP: 129 **Publicly Held**
SIC: 2834 Mfg Pharmaceutical Preparations
PA: Exelixis, Inc.
210 E Grand Ave
South San Francisco CA 94502

(P-3897)
FIBROGEN INC (PA)
409 Illinois St, San Francisco (94158-2509)
PHONE 415 978-1200
Enrique Conterno, *CEO*
James A Schoeneck, *Ch of Bd*
Pat Cotroneo, *CEO*
Thane Wettig, *Ch Credit Ofcr*
Mark Eisner, *Chief Mktg Ofcr*
EMP: 597 **EST:** 1993

SQ FT: 234,000
SALES (est): 176.3MM **Publicly Held**
WEB: www.fibrogen.com
SIC: 2834 Pharmaceutical preparations

(P-3898)
FIVE PRIME THERAPEUTICS INC
111 Oyster Point Blvd, South San Francisco (94080-2037)
PHONE 415 365-5600
Thomas Civik, *President*
William Ringo, *CEO*
Linda Rubinstein, *CFO*
David V Smith, *CFO*
Helen Collins, *Chief Mktg Ofcr*
EMP: 87 **EST:** 2001
SQ FT: 115,466
SALES: 13.1MM
SALES (corp-wide): 25.4B **Publicly Held**
WEB: www.amgen.com
SIC: 2834 8733 Pharmaceutical preparations; biotechnical research, noncommercial
PA: Amgen Inc.
1 Amgen Center Dr
Thousand Oaks CA 91320
805 447-1000

(P-3899)
FORMULATION TECHNOLOGY INC
571 Armstrong Way, Oakdale (95361-9367)
P.O. Box 1895 (95361-1895)
PHONE 209 847-0331
Keith W Hensley, *President*
Mary G Hangley, *Shareholder*
April Houck, *Shareholder*
Celia Meese, *Corp Secy*
Jed Meese, *Vice Pres*
▲ **EMP:** 49 **EST:** 1981
SQ FT: 15,000
SALES (est): 14.4MM **Privately Held**
WEB: www.formulationtech.com
SIC: 2834 Vitamin preparations

(P-3900)
FORTY SEVEN INC (HQ)
333 Lakeside Dr, Foster City (94404-1147)
PHONE 650 352-4150
Mark A McCamish, *CEO*
Andrew D Dickinson, *President*
Ann D Rhoads, *CFO*
Chris H Takimoto, *Chief Mktg Ofcr*
Chris Takimoto, *Chief Mktg Ofcr*
EMP: 67 **EST:** 2014
SALES (est): 15.6MM
SALES (corp-wide): 24.6B **Publicly Held**
WEB: www.gilead.com
SIC: 2834 8731 Pharmaceutical preparations; biotechnical research, commercial
PA: Gilead Sciences, Inc.
333 Lakeside Dr
Foster City CA 94404
650 574-3000

(P-3901)
FREMONT AMGEN INC (HQ)
6397 Kaiser Dr, Fremont (94555-3602)
PHONE 510 284-6500
Kevin Sharer, *President*
R Scott Greer, *Ch of Bd*
H Ward Wolff, *CFO*
Gisela M Schwab, *Officer*
Kristen M Anderson, *Senior VP*
▲ **EMP:** 225 **EST:** 1996
SQ FT: 516,000
SALES (est): 25.1MM
SALES (corp-wide): 25.4B **Publicly Held**
WEB: www.amgen.com
SIC: 2834 Extracts of botanicals: powdered, pilular, solid or fluid; antibiotics, packaged
PA: Amgen Inc.
1 Amgen Center Dr
Thousand Oaks CA 91320
805 447-1000

(P-3902)
FRONTAGE LABORATORIES INC
3825 Bay Center Pl, Hayward (94545-3619)
PHONE 510 626-9993
EMP: 34 **Privately Held**

WEB: www.frontagelab.com
SIC: 2834 8731 Pharmaceutical preparations; biological research
HQ: Frontage Laboratories, Inc.
700 Pennsylvania Dr
Exton PA 19341
610 232-0100

(P-3903)
FRONTIER MEDICINES
151 Oyster Point Blvd # 200, South San Francisco (94080-1841)
PHONE 650 457-1005
Chris Varma, *CEO*
Gregory Chow, *CFO*
EMP: 50 **EST:** 2018
SALES (est): 7.4MM **Privately Held**
WEB: www.frontiermeds.com
SIC: 2834 Medicines, capsuled or ampuled

(P-3904)
GENELABS TECHNOLOGIES INC (HQ)
505 Penobscot Dr, Redwood City (94063-4737)
P.O. Box 13398, Durham NC (27709-3398)
PHONE 415 297-2901
Frederick W Driscoll, *President*
Gerald Suh, *Owner*
Irene A Chow, *Ch of Bd*
Ronald C Griffith PHD, *Officer*
Heather Criss Keller, *Vice Pres*
EMP: 64 **EST:** 1985
SQ FT: 50,000
SALES (est): 4.7MM
SALES (corp-wide): 45.3B **Privately Held**
WEB: www.genelabs.com
SIC: 2834 Proprietary drug products
PA: Glaxosmithkline Plc
G S K House
Brentford MIDDX TW8 9
208 047-5000

(P-3905)
GENENTECH INC
1000 New Horizons Way, Vacaville (95688-9431)
PHONE 707 454-1000
Frank Jackson, *General Mgr*
Ekaterine Kortkhonjia, *Officer*
Jane Pyle, *Executive*
Kim Balchios, *Admin Asst*
Thomas Glenn, *Administration*
EMP: 25
SALES (corp-wide): 69.8B **Privately Held**
WEB: www.gene.com
SIC: 2834 Pharmaceutical preparations
HQ: Genentech, Inc.
1 Dna Way
South San Francisco CA 94080
650 225-1000

(P-3906)
GENENTECH INC
530 Forbes Blvd, South San Francisco (94080-2018)
PHONE 650 225-2791
Tyng Loh, *Counsel*
Kristi Griffin, *Consultant*
EMP: 173
SALES (corp-wide): 69.8B **Privately Held**
WEB: www.gene.com
SIC: 2834 Pharmaceutical preparations
HQ: Genentech, Inc.
1 Dna Way
South San Francisco CA 94080
650 225-1000

(P-3907)
GENENTECH INC (DH)
1 Dna Way, South San Francisco (94080-4990)
P.O. Box 4354, Portland OR (97208-4354)
PHONE 650 225-1000
Ian Clark, *CEO*
Pascal Soriot, *COO*
Steve Krognes, *CFO*
Hal Barron, *Chief Mktg Ofcr*
Rick Kentz, *Officer*
◆ **EMP:** 2000 **EST:** 1986
SQ FT: 140,000
SALES (est): 689.1MM
SALES (corp-wide): 69.8B **Privately Held**
WEB: www.gene.com
SIC: 2834 Hormone preparations

▲ = Import ▼ =Export
◆ =Import/Export

PRODUCTS & SERVICES SECTION

2834 - Pharmaceuticals County (P-3930)

HQ: Roche Holdings, Inc.
1 Dna Way
South San Francisco CA 94080
650 225-1000

(P-3908)
GENENTECH INC
465 E Grand Ave Ms432, South San Francisco (94080-6225)
PHONE.................................408 963-8759
Bhe Hundel, *Prgrmr*
Jocelyn Martinez, *Manager*
EMP: 173
SALES (corp-wide): 69.8B **Privately Held**
WEB: www.gene.com
SIC: 2834 Pharmaceutical preparations
HQ: Genentech, Inc.
1 Dna Way
South San Francisco CA 94080
650 225-1000

(P-3909)
GENENTECH INC
550 Broadway St, Redwood City (94063-3115)
PHONE.................................650 216-2900
Jay Edwards, *Corp Comm Staff*
Ellen Armijo, *Senior Mgr*
Martin Majchrowicz, *Director*
EMP: 173
SALES (corp-wide): 69.8B **Privately Held**
WEB: www.gene.com
SIC: 2834 Pharmaceutical preparations
HQ: Genentech, Inc.
1 Dna Way
South San Francisco CA 94080
650 225-1000

(P-3910)
GENENTECH INC
431 Grandview Dr Bldg 2, South San Francisco (94080-4905)
PHONE.................................650 225-3214
Rick Rouleau, *Manager*
Stephanie Mendelsohn, *Litigation*
EMP: 173
SALES (corp-wide): 69.8B **Privately Held**
WEB: www.gene.com
SIC: 2834 Pharmaceutical preparations
HQ: Genentech, Inc.
1 Dna Way
South San Francisco CA 94080
650 225-1000

(P-3911)
GENENTECH INC
1 Dna Way, South San Francisco (94080-4990)
PHONE.................................650 225-1000
Severin Schwan, *Branch Mgr*
Natasha Coyle, *Marketing Staff*
EMP: 173
SALES (corp-wide): 69.8B **Privately Held**
WEB: www.gene.com
SIC: 2834 Pharmaceutical preparations
HQ: Genentech, Inc.
1 Dna Way
South San Francisco CA 94080
650 225-1000

(P-3912)
GENENTECH INC
220 Miramontes Ave, Half Moon Bay (94019-1889)
PHONE.................................650 438-7573
Stuart Bunting, *Principal*
EMP: 15 **EST:** 2010
SALES (est): 403.7K **Privately Held**
WEB: www.gene.com
SIC: 2834 Pharmaceutical preparations

(P-3913)
GENENTECH USA INC
1 Dna Way, South San Francisco (94080-4990)
PHONE.................................650 225-1000
Ian T Clark, *Principal*
Leonard Kanavy, *Principal*
Frederick C Kentz III, *Principal*
Steve Krognes, *Principal*
Antoinette Domingues, *Oncology*
▲ **EMP:** 4764 **EST:** 2007
SALES (est): 110.9MM
SALES (corp-wide): 69.8B **Privately Held**
WEB: www.gene.com
SIC: 2834 Hormone preparations

HQ: Genentech, Inc.
1 Dna Way
South San Francisco CA 94080
650 225-1000

(P-3914)
GERON CORPORATION (PA)
919 E Hillsdale Blvd # 250, Foster City (94404-3296)
PHONE.................................650 473-7700
John A Scarlett, *Ch of Bd*
Andrew J Grethlein, *COO*
Olivia K Bloom, *CFO*
Susan M Molineaux, *Bd of Directors*
Aleksandra Rizo, *Chief Mktg Ofcr*
EMP: 51 **EST:** 1990
SALES (est): 253K **Publicly Held**
WEB: www.geron.com
SIC: 2834 Pharmaceutical preparations

(P-3915)
GILEAD COLORADO INC
333 Lakeside Dr, Foster City (94404-1394)
PHONE.................................650 574-3000
J William Freytag, *President*
John Milligan, *President*
Joseph L Turner, *CFO*
Michael R Bristow, *Officer*
Richard J Gorczynski, *Senior VP*
EMP: 58 **EST:** 1996
SQ FT: 40,000
SALES (est): 15.3MM
SALES (corp-wide): 24.6B **Publicly Held**
WEB: www.gilead.com
SIC: 2834 Pharmaceutical preparations
PA: Gilead Sciences, Inc.
333 Lakeside Dr
Foster City CA 94404
650 574-3000

(P-3916)
GILEAD PALO ALTO INC (HQ)
333 Lakeside Dr, Foster City (94404-1394)
PHONE.................................650 384-8500
John C Martin, *Chairman*
Louis Lange PHD, *Ch of Bd*
John F Milligan, *President*
Daniel K Spiegelman, *CFO*
Brent K Blackburn PHD, *Senior VP*
EMP: 401 **EST:** 1987
SALES (est): 91.2MM
SALES (corp-wide): 24.6B **Publicly Held**
WEB: www.gilead.com
SIC: 2834 8731 Drugs acting on the cardiovascular system, except diagnostic; commercial physical research
PA: Gilead Sciences, Inc.
333 Lakeside Dr
Foster City CA 94404
650 574-3000

(P-3917)
GILEAD SCIENCES INC (PA)
333 Lakeside Dr, Foster City (94404-1394)
PHONE.................................650 574-3000
Daniel P O'Day, *Ch of Bd*
Andrew D Dickinson, *CFO*
Johanna Mercier, *Ch Credit Ofcr*
Merdad V Parsey, *Chief Mktg Ofcr*
Brett A Pletcher, *Exec VP*
▲ **EMP:** 289 **EST:** 1987
SALES (est): 24.6B **Publicly Held**
WEB: www.gilead.com
SIC: 2834 2836 Pharmaceutical preparations; biological products, except diagnostic

(P-3918)
GLAXOSMTHKLINE CNSMR HLTHCARE
2020 E Vine Ave, Fresno (93706-5458)
PHONE.................................559 650-1550
Mark Bullard, *Branch Mgr*
EMP: 101
SALES (corp-wide): 45.3B **Privately Held**
WEB: www.gsk-answers.com
SIC: 2834 Pharmaceutical preparations
HQ: Glaxosmithkline Consumer Healthcare, L.P.
184 Libery Corner Rd
Warren NJ 07059

(P-3919)
GLOBAL BLOOD THERAPEUTICS INC (PA)
Also Called: GBT
181 Oyster Point Blvd, South Francisco (94080-2044)
PHONE.................................650 741-7700
Ted W Love, *President*
Jeffrey Farrow, *CFO*
David L Johnson, *Ch Credit Ofcr*
Tricia Suvari,
Jung E Choi, *Officer*
EMP: 355 **EST:** 2012
SALES (est): 123.8MM **Publicly Held**
WEB: www.gbt.com
SIC: 2834 8731 Pharmaceutical preparations; biological research

(P-3920)
GRAIL LLC (HQ)
1525a Obrien Dr, Menlo Park (94025-1463)
PHONE.................................833 694-2553
Bob Ragusa, *CEO*
Matthew Young, *COO*
Marissa Song, *Ch Credit Ofcr*
Joshua Ofman, *Chief Mktg Ofcr*
Gautam Kollu, *Officer*
EMP: 335 **EST:** 2011
SALES (est): 210.9MM
SALES (corp-wide): 3.2B **Publicly Held**
WEB: www.grail.com
SIC: 2834 8731 Pharmaceutical preparations; biotechnical research, commercial
PA: Illumina, Inc.
5200 Illumina Way
San Diego CA 92122
858 202-4500

(P-3921)
GRAYBUG VISION INC (PA)
275 Shoreline Dr Ste 450, Redwood City (94065-1491)
PHONE.................................650 487-2800
Frederic Guerard, *President*
Christy Shaffer, *Ch of Bd*
Robert S Breuil, *CFO*
Parisa Zamiri, *Chief Mktg Ofcr*
Daniel Domingues, *Research*
EMP: 23 **EST:** 2011
SQ FT: 6,000 **Publicly Held**
WEB: www.graybug.vision
SIC: 2834 8731 Pharmaceutical preparations; biotechnical research, commercial

(P-3922)
GU
1204 10th St, Berkeley (94710-1509)
PHONE.................................510 527-4664
Bill Vaughn, *Owner*
EMP: 17 **EST:** 1994
SALES (est): 1.3MM **Privately Held**
WEB: www.guenergy.com
SIC: 2834 Vitamin, nutrient & hematinic preparations for human use

(P-3923)
HIMS & HERS HEALTH INC (PA)
2269 Chestnut St 523, San Francisco (94123-2600)
PHONE.................................415 851-0195
Andrew Dudum, *Ch of Bd*
Melissa Baird, *COO*
Spencer Lee, *CFO*
Patrick Carroll, *Chief Mktg Ofcr*
Soleil Boughton,
EMP: 33 **EST:** 2013 **Publicly Held**
WEB: www.forhims.com
SIC: 2834 5912 5122 8742 Pharmaceutical preparations; proprietary (non-prescription medicine) stores; cosmetics, perfumes & hair products; hospital & health services consultant

(P-3924)
HYPERION THERAPEUTICS INC
2000 Sierra Point Pkwy # 400, Brisbane (94005-1845)
PHONE.................................650 492-1385
Don Santel, *CEO*
Michael Abraham, *Manager*
EMP: 27 **EST:** 2016
SALES (est): 848.1K **Privately Held**
SIC: 2834 Pharmaceutical preparations

(P-3925)
IDEAYA BIOSCIENCES INC
7000 Shoreline Ct Ste 350, South San Francisco (94080-7604)
PHONE.................................650 443-6209
Yujiro Hata, *President*
John Diekman, *Ch of Bd*
Julie Hambleton, *Chief Mktg Ofcr*
Michael Dillon, *Senior VP*
Jeffrey Hager, *Senior VP*
EMP: 58 **EST:** 2015
SALES (est): 19.5MM **Privately Held**
WEB: www.ideayabio.com
SIC: 2834 Pharmaceutical preparations

(P-3926)
IGNYTA INC (HQ)
1 Dna Way, South San Francisco (94080-4918)
PHONE.................................858 255-5959
Jonathan E Lim, *Ch of Bd*
Zachary Hornby, *COO*
Jacob Chacko, *CFO*
James Freddo, *Bd of Directors*
Pratik Multani, *Chief Mktg Ofcr*
EMP: 105 **EST:** 2011
SALES (corp-wide): 69.8B **Privately Held**
WEB: www.roche.com
SIC: 2834 Pharmaceutical preparations
PA: Roche Holding Ag
Grenzacherstrasse 124
Basel BS 4058
616 881-111

(P-3927)
IMIDOMICS INC ✪
541 Jefferson Ave Ste 100, Redwood City (94063-1700)
PHONE.................................415 652-4963
Juan Harrison, *CEO*
Manuel Lopez-Figueroa, *COO*
Susan Vuong, *CFO*
EMP: 18 **EST:** 2021
SALES (est): 775.6K **Privately Held**
SIC: 2834 Proprietary drug products

(P-3928)
INCARDA THERAPEUTICS INC
39899 Balentine Dr # 185, Newark (94560-5355)
PHONE.................................510 422-5522
Grace Colon, *President*
Carlos Schuler, *COO*
Luiz Belardinelli, *Chief Mktg Ofcr*
Jeff Ho, *Vice Pres*
Anna Popovici, *Vice Pres*
EMP: 20 **EST:** 2009
SALES (est): 2.9MM **Privately Held**
WEB: www.incardatherapeutics.com
SIC: 2834 Pharmaceutical preparations

(P-3929)
INCLINE THERAPEUTICS INC
900 Saginaw Dr Ste 200, Redwood City (94063-4701)
PHONE.................................650 241-6800
Alan Levy, *CEO*
David Socks, *President*
John Tucker, *Officer*
Patti Oto, *Senior VP*
Brad Phipps, *Senior VP*
EMP: 17 **EST:** 2009
SALES (est): 555K
SALES (corp-wide): 6.1MM **Privately Held**
WEB: www.novartis.com
SIC: 2834 Pharmaceutical preparations
PA: The Medicines Company
8 Sylvan Way
Parsippany NJ 07054
973 290-6000

(P-3930)
INTERMUNE INC (DH)
1 Dna Way, South San Francisco (94080-4918)
PHONE.................................415 466-4383
Daniel G Welch, *President*
John C Hodgman, *CFO*
Jonathan A Leff, *Exec VP*
Sean P Nolan, *Exec VP*
Andrew Powell, *Exec VP*
EMP: 215 **EST:** 1998
SQ FT: 56,000

(PA)=Parent Co (HQ)=Headquarters (DH)=Div Headquarters
✪ = New Business established in last 2 years

2834 - Pharmaceuticals County (P-3931)   PRODUCTS & SERVICES SECTION

SALES (est): 90.4MM
SALES (corp-wide): 69.8B **Privately Held**
WEB: www.gene.com
SIC: 2834 8731 Pharmaceutical preparations; medical research, commercial
HQ: Roche Holdings, Inc.
    1 Dna Way
    South San Francisco CA 94080
    650 225-1000

(P-3931)
IOVANCE BIOTHERAPEUTICS INC (PA)
999 Skyway Rd Ste 150, San Carlos (94070-2724)
PHONE.................................650 260-7120
Frederick G Vogt, *President*
Iain Dukes, *Ch of Bd*
Igor Bilinsky, *COO*
Jean-Marc Bellemin, *CFO*
Friedrich Graf Finckenstein, *Chief Mktg Ofcr*
EMP: 222 EST: 2011
SQ FT: 8,733 **Publicly Held**
WEB: www.iovance.com
SIC: 2834 Pharmaceutical preparations

(P-3932)
JAGUAR HEALTH INC (PA)
Also Called: JAGUAR ANIMAL HEALTH
200 Pine St Fl 4, San Francisco (94104-2710)
PHONE.................................415 371-8300
James J Bochnowski, *Ch of Bd*
Lisa A Conte, *President*
Carol Lizak, *CFO*
Karen S Wright, *CFO*
Jonathan Wolin, *Ch Credit Ofcr*
EMP: 23 EST: 2013
SQ FT: 6,008
SALES (est): 9.3MM **Publicly Held**
WEB: www.jaguar.health
SIC: 2834 0752 Veterinary pharmaceutical preparations; animal specialty services

(P-3933)
JANSSEN BIOPHARMA INC
260 E Grand Ave, South San Francisco (94080-4811)
PHONE.................................650 635-5500
Lawrence Blatt MD, *President*
Leonid Beigelman MD, *Security Dir*
Derrick De Leon, *Info Tech Dir*
Abbie Oey, *Manager*
EMP: 26 EST: 2006
SALES (est): 10.1MM
SALES (corp-wide): 82.5B **Publicly Held**
WEB: www.jnj.com
SIC: 2834 Pharmaceutical preparations
PA: Johnson & Johnson
    1 Johnson And Johnson Plz
    New Brunswick NJ 08933
    732 524-0400

(P-3934)
JAZZ PHARMACEUTICALS INC (HQ)
3170 Porter Dr, Palo Alto (94304-1212)
PHONE.................................650 496-3777
Bruce C Cozadd, *Ch of Bd*
Kathryn E Falberg, *CFO*
Russell J Cox, *Exec VP*
Jeffrey Tobias, *Exec VP*
Jed Black, *Vice Pres*
▲ EMP: 507 EST: 2003
SALES: 1.6B **Privately Held**
WEB: www.jazzpharma.com
SIC: 2834 Drugs acting on the central nervous system & sense organs

(P-3935)
KEZAR LIFE SCIENCES INC
4000 Shoreline Ct Ste 300, South San Francisco (94080-2005)
PHONE.................................650 822-5600
John Fowler, *CEO*
Jean-Pierre Sommadossi, *Ch of Bd*
Christopher Kirk, *President*
Marc L Belsky, *CFO*
Niti Goel, *Chief Mktg Ofcr*
EMP: 20 EST: 2015
SQ FT: 24,357 **Privately Held**
WEB: www.kezarlifesciences.com
SIC: 2834 8731 Pharmaceutical preparations; biotechnical research, commercial

(P-3936)
KINDRED BIOSCIENCES INC (HQ)
1555 Bayshore Hwy Ste 200, Burlingame (94010-1617)
PHONE.................................650 701-7901
Katja Buhrer, *Vice Pres*
Wendy Wee, *CFO*
Hangjun Zhan, *Officer*
Normand Brown, *Vice Pres*
Russell Radefeld, *Vice Pres*
EMP: 125 EST: 2012
SALES (est): 42.1MM
SALES (corp-wide): 3.2B **Publicly Held**
WEB: www.kindredbio.com
SIC: 2834 Veterinary pharmaceutical preparations
PA: Elanco Animal Health Incorporated
    2500 Innovation Way N
    Greenfield IN 46140
    877 352-6261

(P-3937)
KINTARA THERAPEUTICS INC
3475 Edison Way Ste R, Menlo Park (94025-1821)
PHONE.................................650 269-1984
Saiid Zarrabian, *President*
Jeffrey Bacha, *President*
Scott Praill, *CFO*
Erich Mohr, *Chairman*
Dennis M Brown, *Officer*
EMP: 15 EST: 2011
SALES (est): 592.5K **Privately Held**
WEB: www.kintara.com
SIC: 2834 Druggists' preparations (pharmaceuticals)

(P-3938)
KOSAN BIOSCIENCES INCORPORATED
3832 Bay Center Pl, Hayward (94545-3619)
P.O. Box 4000, Princeton NJ (08543-4000)
PHONE.................................650 995-7356
Helen S Kim, *President*
Peter Davis PHD, *Ch of Bd*
Gary S Titus, *CFO*
Peter J Licari PHD, *Senior VP*
Jonathan K Wright, *Senior VP*
EMP: 86 EST: 1996
SALES (est): 13.6MM
SALES (corp-wide): 42.5B **Publicly Held**
WEB: www.bms.com
SIC: 2834 8731 Pharmaceutical preparations; commercial research laboratory
PA: Bristol-Myers Squibb Company
    430 E 29th St Fl 14
    New York NY 10016
    212 546-4000

(P-3939)
KRONOS BIO INC (PA)
1300 S El Cmino Real Ste, San Mateo (94402)
PHONE.................................650 781-5200
Norbert Bischofberger, *President*
Arie S Belldegrun, *Ch of Bd*
Barbara Kosacz, *COO*
Yasir Al-Wakeel, *CFO*
Jorge Dimartino, *Chief Mktg Ofcr*
EMP: 54 EST: 2017
SQ FT: 8,075 **Publicly Held**
WEB: www.kronosbio.com
SIC: 2834 Pharmaceutical preparations

(P-3940)
LIGAND PHARMACEUTICALS INC (PA)
5980 Horton St Ste 405, Emeryville (94608-2059)
PHONE.................................858 550-7500
John L Higgins, *CEO*
John W Kozarich, *Ch of Bd*
Matthew W Foehr, *President*
Matthew Korenberg, *CFO*
Sarah Boyce, *Bd of Directors*
EMP: 32 EST: 1987
SALES (est): 186.4MM **Publicly Held**
WEB: www.ligand.com
SIC: 2834 Pharmaceutical preparations

(P-3941)
LOBOB LABORATORIES INC
1440 Atteberry Ln, San Jose (95131-1410)
PHONE.................................408 324-0381
Robert M Lohr, *President*
EMP: 19 EST: 1964
SQ FT: 20,000
SALES (est): 4MM **Privately Held**
WEB: www.loboblabs.com
SIC: 2834 3851 2841 Solutions, pharmaceutical; ophthalmic goods; soap & other detergents

(P-3942)
LOGICBIO THERAPEUTICS INC
815 Perseus Ln, Foster City (94404-2817)
PHONE.................................415 710-8265
Leszek Lisowski, *CEO*
Sandra Poole, *COO*
EMP: 17 EST: 2016
SALES (est): 381.8K **Privately Held**
WEB: www.logicbio.com
SIC: 2834 Pharmaceutical preparations

(P-3943)
LONZA BIOLOGICS INC
1978 W Winton Ave, Hayward (94545-1206)
PHONE.................................510 731-3500
Alexander Hoy, *CEO*
EMP: 53 EST: 2018
SALES (est): 9.4MM **Privately Held**
WEB: www.lonza.com
SIC: 2834 Pharmaceutical preparations

(P-3944)
MACROGENICS WEST INC
3280 Byshore Blvd Ste 200, Brisbane (94005)
PHONE.................................650 624-2600
Scott Koenig, *President*
Ezio Bonvini, *President*
Jeff Hooley, *Manager*
EMP: 20 EST: 2010
SALES (est): 3.6MM **Privately Held**
WEB: www.macrogenics.com
SIC: 2834 Druggists' preparations (pharmaceuticals)

(P-3945)
MAVERICK THERAPEUTICS INC
3260 Bayshore Blvd, Brisbane (94005-1021)
PHONE.................................650 684-7140
James J Scibetta, *CEO*
David Ross, *Partner*
Robert Dubridge, *Exec VP*
Bob Dubridge, *Senior VP*
Chulani Karunatilake, *Senior VP*
EMP: 45 EST: 2017
SALES (est): 5.1MM **Privately Held**
SIC: 2834 Pharmaceutical preparations

(P-3946)
MEDIVATION INC
499 Illinois St, San Francisco (94158-2518)
PHONE.................................415 812-6345
EMP: 15
SALES (corp-wide): 41.9B **Publicly Held**
WEB: www.pfizer.com
SIC: 2834 Pharmaceutical preparations
HQ: Medivation, Inc.
    525 Market St Ste 2800
    San Francisco CA 94105
    415 543-3470

(P-3947)
MEDIVATION INC (HQ)
Also Called: Xtandi
525 Market St Ste 2800, San Francisco (94105-2736)
PHONE.................................415 543-3470
David T Hung, *President*
Marion McCourt, *COO*
Jennifer Jarrett, *CFO*
Mohammad Hirmand, *Chief Mktg Ofcr*
Joseph Lobacki, *Officer*
EMP: 534 EST: 2004
SQ FT: 143,000
SALES (est): 263.9MM
SALES (corp-wide): 41.9B **Publicly Held**
WEB: www.pfizer.com
SIC: 2834 Adrenal pharmaceutical preparations

PA: Pfizer Inc.
    235 E 42nd St Rm 107
    New York NY 10017
    212 733-2323

(P-3948)
MEREO BIOPHARMA 5 INC
800 Chesapeake Dr, Redwood City (94063-4748)
PHONE.................................650 995-8200
Denise Scots-Knight, *CEO*
Robert Stagg, *Vice Pres*
Lee Baker, *Counsel*
Kelley Corley, *Director*
Andrew Alcantara, *Manager*
EMP: 56 EST: 2004
SQ FT: 45,690
SALES: 44.4MM
SALES (corp-wide): 4.8MM **Privately Held**
WEB: www.mereobiopharma.com
SIC: 2834 Pharmaceutical preparations
HQ: Mereo Us Holdings Inc.
    800 Chesapeake Dr
    Redwood City CA 94063
    650 995-8200

(P-3949)
MIRUM PHARMACEUTICALS INC (PA)
950 Tower Ln Ste 1050, Foster City (94404-4251)
PHONE.................................650 667-4085
Christopher Peetz, *President*
Michael Grey, *Ch of Bd*
Peter Radovich, *COO*
Ian Clements, *CFO*
Edwin J Tucker, *Chief Mktg Ofcr*
EMP: 67 EST: 2018
SQ FT: 11,200 **Publicly Held**
WEB: www.mirumpharma.com
SIC: 2834 Pharmaceutical preparations

(P-3950)
MOM ENTERPRISES LLC
1003 W Cutting Blvd # 110, Richmond (94804-2092)
P.O. Box 6524, San Rafael (94903-0524)
PHONE.................................415 694-3799
Yasmin Kaderali, *CEO*
Shiraz Kaderali, *President*
Roshan Kaderali, *CFO*
Caroline Lloyd, *Vice Pres*
Stephanie O 'brien, *Marketing Staff*
EMP: 45 EST: 1999
SQ FT: 3,000
SALES (est): 8.3MM **Privately Held**
WEB: www.mommysbliss.com
SIC: 2834 Antacids; extracts of botanicals: powdered, pilular, solid or fluid

(P-3951)
MYOKARDIA INC
1000 Sierra Point Pkwy, Brisbane (94005-1804)
PHONE.................................650 741-0900
Tassos Gianakakos, *President*
Taylor C Harris, *CFO*
William Fairey, *Ch Credit Ofcr*
June Lee, *Exec VP*
Lisa Alaimo, *Vice Pres*
EMP: 235 EST: 2012
SQ FT: 34,400
SALES (est): 33.5MM
SALES (corp-wide): 42.5B **Publicly Held**
WEB: www.bms.com
SIC: 2834 Drugs acting on the cardiovascular system, except diagnostic
PA: Bristol-Myers Squibb Company
    430 E 29th St Fl 14
    New York NY 10016
    212 546-4000

(P-3952)
NEILMED PHARMACEUTICALS INC
601 Aviation Blvd, Santa Rosa (95403-1025)
PHONE.................................707 525-3784
Kaetan Mehta MD, *CEO*
Nina Mehta, *President*
Rekha Upendra, *President*
Dinesh Patel, *Vice Pres*
Ajit Mehta, *VP Bus Dvlpt*
▲ EMP: 300 EST: 2001

PRODUCTS & SERVICES SECTION
2834 - Pharmaceuticals County (P-3975)

SALES (est): 80.8MM **Privately Held**
WEB: www.neilmed.com
SIC: 2834 Pharmaceutical preparations

(P-3953)
NEKTAR THERAPEUTICS (PA)
455 Mssion Bay Blvd S Ste, San Francisco (94158)
PHONE.................................415 482-5300
Howard W Robin, *President*
Robert B Chess, *Ch of Bd*
Gil M Labrucherie, *COO*
John Northcott, *Officer*
Dimitry SA Nuyten, *Officer*
EMP: 280 EST: 1990
SQ FT: 134,356
SALES (est): 152.9MM **Publicly Held**
WEB: www.nektar.com
SIC: 2834 Pharmaceutical preparations

(P-3954)
NGM BIOPHARMACEUTICALS INC (PA)
Also Called: Ngmbio
333 Oyster Point Blvd, South San Francisco (94080-1978)
PHONE.................................650 243-5555
David J Woodhouse, *CEO*
William J Rieflin, *Ch of Bd*
Siobhan Nolan Mangini, *CFO*
Valerie Pierce, *Ch Credit Ofcr*
Hsiao D Lieu, *Chief Mktg Ofcr*
EMP: 209 EST: 2008
SQ FT: 122,000
SALES (est): 87.3MM **Publicly Held**
WEB: www.ngmbio.com
SIC: 2834 Pharmaceutical preparations

(P-3955)
NIVAGEN PHARMACEUTICALS INC (PA)
3050 Fite Cir Ste 100, Sacramento (95827-1818)
PHONE.................................916 364-1662
Jwalant S Shukla, *CEO*
Robert Miller, *CFO*
Dasaradhi Lakkaraju, *Officer*
Ray Walker, *Exec VP*
Thomas Henry, *Vice Pres*
EMP: 21 EST: 2009
SALES (est): 4.9MM **Privately Held**
WEB: www.nivagen.com
SIC: 2834 Pharmaceutical preparations

(P-3956)
NKARTA INC
6000 Shoreline Ct Ste 102, South San Francisco (94080-7606)
PHONE.................................415 582-4923
Paul Hastings, *President*
Ali Behbahani, *Ch of Bd*
Nadir Mahmood, *CFO*
Kanya Rajangam, *Chief Mktg Ofcr*
Ralph Brandenberger, *Vice Pres*
EMP: 70 EST: 2015
SQ FT: 28,469 **Privately Held**
WEB: www.nkartatx.com
SIC: 2834 Pharmaceutical preparations

(P-3957)
NOVABAY PHARMACEUTICALS INC
2000 Powell St Ste 1150, Emeryville (94608-1866)
PHONE.................................510 899-8800
Justin M Hall, *CEO*
Paul E Freiman, *Ch of Bd*
Andrew D Jones, *CFO*
▲ EMP: 25 EST: 2000
SQ FT: 7,799
SALES (est): 9.9MM **Privately Held**
WEB: www.novabay.com
SIC: 2834 Pharmaceutical preparations; drugs acting on the central nervous system & sense organs

(P-3958)
OCULEVE INC
4410 Rosewood Dr, Pleasanton (94588-3050)
PHONE.................................415 745-3784
Michael D Ackermann, *President*
EMP: 15 EST: 2011

SALES (est): 3.9MM **Privately Held**
WEB: www.allergan.com
SIC: 2834 Pharmaceutical preparations
PA: Allergan Limited
    Clonshaugh Business & Technology Park
    Dublin

(P-3959)
ORIC PHARMACEUTICALS INC
240 E Grand Ave Fl 2, South San Francisco (94080-4811)
PHONE.................................650 388-5600
Jacob M Chacko, *President*
Richard Heyman, *Ch of Bd*
Dominic Piscitelli, *CFO*
Pratik Multani, *Chief Mktg Ofcr*
Lori Friedman, *Officer*
EMP: 57 EST: 2014
SQ FT: 33,322 **Privately Held**
WEB: www.oricpharma.com
SIC: 2834 Pharmaceutical preparations

(P-3960)
ORPHAN MEDICAL INC
3180 Porter Dr, Palo Alto (94304-1287)
PHONE.................................650 496-3777
Matthew Fust, *CFO*
Sharon Erwin, *Assistant*
EMP: 80 EST: 1994
SQ FT: 15,000
SALES (est): 17.2MM **Privately Held**
WEB: www.jazzpharma.com
SIC: 2834 8731 Pharmaceutical preparations; commercial physical research
HQ: Jazz Pharmaceuticals, Inc.
    3170 Porter Dr
    Palo Alto CA 94304
    650 496-3777

(P-3961)
PEREZ DISTRIBUTING FRESNO INC (PA)
103 S Academy Ave, Sanger (93657-2428)
P.O. Box 579 (93657-0579)
PHONE.................................800 638-3512
Emeterio P Perez, *President*
Alma Perez, *Vice Pres*
▲ EMP: 26 EST: 2002
SQ FT: 16,000
SALES (est): 6.6MM **Privately Held**
WEB: www.perezdistfresno.com
SIC: 2834 Druggists' preparations (pharmaceuticals)

(P-3962)
PHARMACYCLICS LLC (HQ)
1000 Gateway Blvd, South San Francisco (94080-7028)
PHONE.................................408 215-3000
Wulff-Erik Von Borcke,
John Northcott, *Officer*
Fong Clow, *Vice Pres*
Thorsten Graef MD, *Vice Pres*
Karen L Hale, *Vice Pres*
EMP: 899 EST: 2015
SALES (est): 301.8MM
SALES (corp-wide): 45.8B **Publicly Held**
WEB: www.pharmacyclics.com
SIC: 2834 Pharmaceutical preparations
PA: Abbvie Inc.
    1 N Waukegan Rd
    North Chicago IL 60064
    847 932-7900

(P-3963)
PHOENIX PHARMACEUTICALS INC
330 Beach Rd, Burlingame (94010-2004)
PHONE.................................650 558-8898
Jaw-Kang Chang, *President*
Chang Jaw, *Info Tech Dir*
Crystal Chang, *Technical Staff*
Chentao Wang, *Marketing Staff*
Robert Lyu, *Senior Mgr*
EMP: 20 EST: 1994
SQ FT: 5,000
SALES (est): 3.4MM **Privately Held**
WEB: www.phoenixpeptide.com
SIC: 2834 8731 Pharmaceutical preparations; commercial physical research

(P-3964)
PIONYR IMMUNOTHERAPEUTICS INC
2 Tower Pl 8, South San Francisco (94080-1826)
PHONE.................................415 226-7503
Steven P James, *President*
Alicia Levey, *Officer*
Kevin Baker, *Senior VP*
Monte Montgomery, *Senior VP*
Leonard Reyno, *Senior VP*
EMP: 49 EST: 2017
SALES (est): 5.5MM **Privately Held**
WEB: www.pionyrtx.com
SIC: 2834 Pharmaceutical preparations

(P-3965)
PLEXXIKON INC
329 Oyster Point Blvd, South San Francisco (94080-1913)
PHONE.................................510 647-4000
Gideon Bollag, *CEO*
Paul Lin, *COO*
Joseph Young, *Treasurer*
Keith B Nolop MD, *Chief Mktg Ofcr*
Chao Zhang, *Officer*
EMP: 44 EST: 2000
SQ FT: 10,000
SALES (est): 12MM **Privately Held**
WEB: www.plexxikon.com
SIC: 2834 Tablets, pharmaceutical
PA: Daiichi Sankyo Company, Limited
    3-5-1, Nihombashihoncho
    Chuo-Ku TKY 103-0

(P-3966)
PRINCIPIA BIOPHARMA INC (HQ)
220 E Grand Ave, South San Francisco (94080-4811)
PHONE.................................650 416-7700
Martin Babler, *President*
Alan B Colowick, *Ch of Bd*
Christopher Y Chai, *CFO*
Dolca Thomas, *Chief Mktg Ofcr*
Roy Hardiman, *Officer*
EMP: 68 EST: 2011
SQ FT: 47,500
SALES (est): 35.1MM **Privately Held**
WEB: www.principiabio.com
SIC: 2834 Pharmaceutical preparations

(P-3967)
PROTAGONIST THERAPEUTICS INC
7707 Gateway Blvd Ste 140, Newark (94560-1160)
PHONE.................................510 474-0170
Dinesh V Patel, *President*
Harold E Selick, *Ch of Bd*
Donald Kalkofen, *CFO*
Scott Plevy, *Exec VP*
Abha Bommireddi, *Vice Pres*
EMP: 79 EST: 2006
SQ FT: 42,877
SALES (est): 28.6MM **Privately Held**
WEB: www.protagonist-inc.com
SIC: 2834 8731 Pharmaceutical preparations; commercial physical research

(P-3968)
QUARK PHARMACEUTICALS INC (DH)
495 N Whisman Rd Ste 100, Mountain View (94043-5725)
PHONE.................................510 402-4020
Daniel Zurr, *President*
Philip B Simon, *Ch of Bd*
Rami Skaliter, *COO*
Joseph Rubinfeld, *Vice Ch Bd*
Elena Feinstein, *Officer*
EMP: 25 EST: 1991
SALES (est): 10.2MM **Privately Held**
WEB: www.quarkpharma.com
SIC: 2834 Pharmaceutical preparations

(P-3969)
RANDAL OPTIMAL NUTRIENTS LLC
Also Called: Vimco
1595 Hampton Way, Santa Rosa (95407-6844)
P.O. Box 7328 (95407-0328)
PHONE.................................707 528-1800

William A Robotham, *President*
Lynn J Brinker, *Corp Secy*
Donna Coats, *Vice Pres*
EMP: 32
SQ FT: 22,500
SALES (est): 8.3MM **Privately Held**
WEB: www.randaloptimal.com
SIC: 2834 5122 Vitamin preparations; drugs, proprietaries & sundries

(P-3970)
RANI THERAPEUTICS LLC
2051 Ringwood Ave, San Jose (95131-1703)
PHONE.................................408 457-3700
Talat Imran, *CEO*
Svai Sanford, *CFO*
Mohsen Shirazi, *Vice Pres*
Rudi Ruffy, *Director*
EMP: 71 EST: 2012
SQ FT: 22,000
SALES (est): 462K
SALES (corp-wide): 9MM **Publicly Held**
WEB: www.ranitherapeutics.com
SIC: 2834 Pharmaceutical preparations
PA: Rani Therapeutics Holdings, Inc.
    2051 Ringwood Ave
    San Jose CA 95131
    408 457-3700

(P-3971)
RANI THERAPEUTICS HOLDINGS INC (PA)
2051 Ringwood Ave, San Jose (95131-1703)
PHONE.................................408 457-3700
Talat Imran, *CEO*
Mir Imran, *Ch of Bd*
Svai Sanford, *CFO*
Mir Hashim, *Security Dir*
EMP: 18 EST: 2012
SQ FT: 22,000
SALES (est): 9MM **Publicly Held**
SIC: 2834 Pharmaceutical preparations

(P-3972)
RAPT THERAPEUTICS INC
561 Eccles Ave, South San Francisco (94080-1906)
PHONE.................................650 489-9000
Brian Wong, *President*
William Rieflin, *Ch of Bd*
Eric Hall, *CFO*
Rodney Young, *CFO*
William Ho, *Chief Mktg Ofcr*
EMP: 62 EST: 2015
SQ FT: 36,754
SALES (est): 5MM **Privately Held**
WEB: www.rapt.com
SIC: 2834 8731 Pharmaceutical preparations; biotechnical research, commercial

(P-3973)
RASCAL THERAPEUTICS INC
3000 El Cmino Real Bldg 4, Palo Alto (94306)
PHONE.................................650 770-0192
Michael Mann, *CEO*
EMP: 20 EST: 2011
SALES (est): 1.7MM **Privately Held**
WEB: www.rascaltherapeutics.com
SIC: 2834 Drugs affecting neoplasms & endocrine systems

(P-3974)
REVANCE THERAPEUTICS INC
7555 Gateway Blvd, Newark (94560-1152)
PHONE.................................615 724-7755
EMP: 65
SALES (corp-wide): 15.3MM **Publicly Held**
WEB: www.revance.com
SIC: 2834 Pharmaceutical preparations
PA: Revance Therapeutics, Inc.
    1222 Demonbreun St # 1001
    Nashville TN 37203
    615 724-7755

(P-3975)
REZOLUTE INC (PA)
201 Rdwood Shres Pkwy Ste, Redwood City (94065)
PHONE.................................650 206-4507
Nevan C Elam, *CEO*
Young-Jin Kim, *Ch of Bd*
Keith Vendola, *Officer*

2834 - Pharmaceuticals County (P-3976)

PRODUCTS & SERVICES SECTION

Loredie Lugos, *Associate Dir*
Sankaram Mantripragada, *Security Dir*
EMP: 21 **EST:** 2010
SQ FT: 3,500 **Publicly Held**
WEB: www.rezolutebio.com
SIC: 2834 Pharmaceutical preparations

(P-3976)
RIGEL PHARMACEUTICALS INC (PA)
1180 Veterans Blvd, South San Francisco (94080-1985)
PHONE..................650 624-1100
Raul R Rodriguez, *President*
Gary A Lyons, *Ch of Bd*
Dean L Schorno, *CFO*
David A Santos, *Ch Credit Ofcr*
Wolfgang Dummer, *Chief Mktg Ofcr*
EMP: 167 **EST:** 1996
SQ FT: 147,000
SALES (est): 108.6MM **Publicly Held**
WEB: www.rigel.com
SIC: 2834 8733 Pharmaceutical preparations; medical research

(P-3977)
RINAT NEUROSCIENCE CORP
230 E Grand Ave, South San Francisco (94080-4811)
PHONE..................650 615-7300
Patrick Lynn, *President*
Arnon Rosenthal, *CTO*
C Fletcher Payne, *Finance*
EMP: 48 **EST:** 2000
SALES (est): 12MM
SALES (corp-wide): 41.9B **Publicly Held**
WEB: www.mpmcapital.com
SIC: 2834 Druggists' preparations (pharmaceuticals)
PA: Pfizer Inc.
  235 E 42nd St Rm 107
  New York NY 10017
  212 733-2323

(P-3978)
ROCHE DIAGNOSTICS CORPORATION
1 Dna Way, South San Francisco (94080-4918)
PHONE..................650 491-7251
Peter Macbride, *Associate Dir*
Mateusz Szewczyk, *Sr Software Eng*
Stacy Pullen, *Comp Spec*
Lakesha Miller, *Technician*
Clara Bermejo, *Research*
EMP: 157
SALES (corp-wide): 69.8B **Privately Held**
WEB: www.roche.com
SIC: 2834 Pharmaceutical preparations
HQ: Roche Diagnostics Corporation
  9115 Hague Rd
  Indianapolis IN 46256
  800 428-5076

(P-3979)
ROCHE PHARMACEUTICALS
4300 Hacienda Dr, Pleasanton (94588-2722)
PHONE..................908 635-5692
Fidel Fampo, *Principal*
Christoph Franz, *Bd of Directors*
Terri Johnson, *Vice Pres*
Stefanos Tsamousis, *General Mgr*
Lucienne Goetz, *Technician*
EMP: 17 **EST:** 2017
SALES (est): 5.8MM **Privately Held**
SIC: 2834 Pharmaceutical preparations

(P-3980)
RXD NOVA PHARMACEUTICALS INC
2010 Cessna Dr, Vacaville (95688-8712)
PHONE..................610 952-7242
Jianning Liu, *CEO*
Matt Mitchell, *Director*
EMP: 18 **EST:** 2017
SALES (est): 5MM **Privately Held**
SIC: 2834 Pharmaceutical preparations

(P-3981)
SANOFI US SERVICES INC
185 Berry St, San Francisco (94107-5705)
PHONE..................415 856-5000
EMP: 136
SALES (corp-wide): 609.6MM **Privately Held**
SIC: 2834 Mfg Pharmaceutical Preps
HQ: Sanofi Us Services Inc.
  55 Corporate Dr
  Bridgewater NJ 08807
  336 407-4994

(P-3982)
SANTA CRUZ NUTRITIONALS (PA)
2200 Delaware Ave, Santa Cruz (95060-5707)
PHONE..................831 457-3200
Michael Westhusing, *CEO*
Randy Bridges, *COO*
Doug Hopkinson, *Exec VP*
Merit Herman, *Info Tech Dir*
Anthony Romaine, *Info Tech Mgr*
▲ **EMP:** 399 **EST:** 2002
SQ FT: 200,000
SALES (est): 125.4MM **Privately Held**
WEB: www.santacruznutritionals.com
SIC: 2834 2064 Vitamin, nutrient & hematinic preparations for human use; candy & other confectionery products

(P-3983)
SCILEX PHARMACEUTICALS INC
960 San Antonio Rd, Palo Alto (94303-4922)
PHONE..................650 430-3238
Dmitri Lissin, *Vice Pres*
Jasim Shah, *CEO*
Beth Stannard, *Opers Staff*
EMP: 30
SALES (corp-wide): 39.9MM **Publicly Held**
WEB: www.scilexpharma.com
SIC: 2834 Pharmaceutical preparations
HQ: Scilex Pharmaceuticals Inc.
  4955 Directors Pl Ste 100
  San Diego CA 92121
  949 441-2270

(P-3984)
SIERRA ONCOLOGY INC (PA)
1820 Gateway Dr Ste 110, San Mateo (94404-4059)
PHONE..................650 376-8679
Stephen G Dilly, *President*
Robert Pelzer, *Ch of Bd*
Sukhi Jagpal, *CFO*
Mark Kowalski, *Chief Mktg Ofcr*
EMP: 21 **EST:** 2003
SQ FT: 3,800
SALES (est): 300K **Privately Held**
SIC: 2834 Pharmaceutical preparations

(P-3985)
SIRNA THERAPEUTICS INC
1700 Owens St, San Francisco (94158-0004)
PHONE..................415 512-7200
Howard W Robin, *President*
Gregory L Weaver, *CFO*
Roberto Guerciolini, *Chief Mktg Ofcr*
Barry Polisky, *Senior VP*
J Michael French, *Development*
EMP: 51 **EST:** 1992
SALES (est): 6.2MM
SALES (corp-wide): 492.8MM **Publicly Held**
WEB: www.alnylam.com
SIC: 2834 Pharmaceutical preparations
PA: Alnylam Pharmaceuticals, Inc.
  675 W Kendall St
  Cambridge MA 02142
  617 551-8200

(P-3986)
SK PHARMTECO INC
12460 Akron St Ste 100, Rancho Cordova (95742-6447)
PHONE..................888 330-2232
Aslam Malik, *CEO*
EMP: 32 **EST:** 2019
SALES (est): 2.5MM **Privately Held**
WEB: www.skpharmteco.com
SIC: 2834 Pharmaceutical preparations

(P-3987)
SPRUCE BIOSCIENCES INC
2001 Junipero Serra Blvd # 640, Daly City (94014-3891)
PHONE..................415 294-1687
Richard King, *CEO*
Michael Grey, *Ch of Bd*
Samir Gharib, *CFO*
Rosh Dias, *Chief Mktg Ofcr*
Sangita Ghosh, *Vice Pres*
EMP: 15 **EST:** 2014
SQ FT: 8,267 **Privately Held**
WEB: www.sprucebiosciences.com
SIC: 2834 Pharmaceutical preparations

(P-3988)
STAIDSON BIOPHARMA INC
2600 Hilltop Dr Bldg A, San Pablo (94806-1971)
PHONE..................800 345-1899
Zhiwen Zhou, *President*
EMP: 18 **EST:** 2014
SALES (est): 4.7MM **Privately Held**
WEB: www.staidsonbio.com
SIC: 2834 Pharmaceutical preparations
PA: Staidson(Beijing) Biopharmaceuticals Co.,Ltd.
  No.36, Jinghai 2nd Road, Beijing Economic Technology Development
  Beijing 10017

(P-3989)
SURROZEN OPERATING INC
171 Oyster Point Blvd, South San Francisco (94080-1936)
PHONE..................650 918-8818
Craig Parker, *CEO*
Charles Williams, *CFO*
Tim Kutzkey, *Chairman*
Reza Afkhami, *Vice Pres*
Sheela Mohan-Peterson, *Vice Pres*
EMP: 46 **EST:** 2015
SALES (est): 6.9MM
SALES (corp-wide): 10.4MM **Publicly Held**
WEB: www.surrozen.com
SIC: 2834 Adrenal pharmaceutical preparations
PA: Surrozen, Inc.
  171 Oyster Point Blvd # 30
  South San Francisco CA 94080
  650 489-9000

(P-3990)
TANOX INC (DH)
1 Dna Way, South San Francisco (94080-4918)
PHONE..................650 851-1607
Stephen G Juelsgaard, *President*
Zhengbin Yao, *Vice Pres*
Robert C Bast,
▲ **EMP:** 124 **EST:** 1986
SQ FT: 111,000
SALES (est): 41.1MM
SALES (corp-wide): 69.8B **Privately Held**
WEB: www.gene.com
SIC: 2834 Pharmaceutical preparations
HQ: Genentech, Inc.
  1 Dna Way
  South San Francisco CA 94080
  650 225-1000

(P-3991)
TEIKOKU PHARMA USA INC (HQ)
1718 Ringwood Ave, San Jose (95131-1711)
PHONE..................408 501-1800
Masahisa Kitagawa, *President*
Ichiro Mori, *COO*
Atsumu Matsushita, *CFO*
Tetsuto Nagata, *Exec VP*
Larry Caldwell, *Vice Pres*
▲ **EMP:** 59 **EST:** 1997
SALES (est): 16.2MM **Privately Held**
WEB: www.teikokuusa.com
SIC: 2834 Pharmaceutical preparations

(P-3992)
TERNS PHARMACEUTICALS INC (PA)
1065 E Hillsdale Blvd # 100, Foster City (94404-1688)
PHONE..................650 525-5535

Senthil Sundaram, *CEO*
Weidong Zhong, *Ch of Bd*
Bryan Yoon, *COO*
Mark Vignola, *CFO*
Erin Quirk, *Chief Mktg Ofcr*
EMP: 29 **EST:** 2016
SQ FT: 9,750 **Publicly Held**
WEB: www.ternspharma.com
SIC: 2834 Pharmaceutical preparations

(P-3993)
THERAVANCE BIOPHARMA US INC
901 Gateway Blvd, South San Francisco (94080-7024)
PHONE..................650 808-6000
Rick Winningham, *CEO*
Rhonda F Farnum, *Vice Pres*
Srikanth Pendyala, *Vice Pres*
Scott Saywell, *Vice Pres*
Whedy Wang, *Vice Pres*
EMP: 244 **EST:** 2013
SALES (est): 76.1MM **Privately Held**
WEB: www.theravance.com
SIC: 2834 Pharmaceutical preparations
PA: Theravance Biopharma Inc
  C/O Maples Corporate Services Ltd
  George Town GR CAYMAN

(P-3994)
THERAVNCE BPHRMA ANTBOTICS INC
901 Gateway Blvd, South San Francisco (94080-7024)
PHONE..................877 275-6930
Rick Winningham, *CEO*
EMP: 20 **EST:** 2013
SALES (est): 3.1MM **Privately Held**
WEB: www.theravance.com
SIC: 2834 Pharmaceutical preparations
PA: Theravance Biopharma Inc
  C/O Maples Corporate Services Ltd
  George Town GR CAYMAN

(P-3995)
THORX LABORATORIES INC
30831 Huntwood Ave, Hayward (94544-7003)
PHONE..................510 240-6000
Frederick Wilkinson, *Principal*
EMP: 19 **EST:** 2013
SALES (est): 1.4MM
SALES (corp-wide): 1.6B **Publicly Held**
WEB: www.impaxlabs.com
SIC: 2834 Pharmaceutical preparations
HQ: Impax Laboratories, Llc
  30831 Huntwood Ave
  Hayward CA 94544

(P-3996)
TITAN PHARMACEUTICALS INC (PA)
400 Oyster Point Blvd # 505, South San Francisco (94080-1958)
PHONE..................650 244-4990
Sunil Bhonsle, *President*
Marc Rubin, *Ch of Bd*
Dane Hallberg, *Ch Credit Ofcr*
Katherine Beebe Devarney, *Exec VP*
Raj Patel, *Vice Pres*
EMP: 22 **EST:** 1992
SQ FT: 9,255
SALES (est): 4.8MM **Publicly Held**
WEB: www.titanpharm.com
SIC: 2834 Pharmaceutical preparations; drugs acting on the central nervous system & sense organs

(P-3997)
TOWER HOLDINGS INC (DH)
30831 Huntwood Ave, Hayward (94544-7003)
PHONE..................510 240-6000
Admir Talic, *President*
Mirsa Talic, *Admin Sec*
EMP: 100 **EST:** 2007
SALES (est): 9.4MM
SALES (corp-wide): 1.6B **Publicly Held**
WEB: www.impaxlabs.com
SIC: 2834 Pharmaceutical preparations

▲ = Import ▼ = Export
◆ = Import/Export

PRODUCTS & SERVICES SECTION

2835 - Diagnostic Substances County (P-4019)

(P-3998)
TRICIDA INC
7000 Shoreline Ct Ste 201, South San Francisco (94080-7603)
PHONE 415 429-7800
Gerrit Klaerner, *President*
Klaus R Veitinger, *Ch of Bd*
Geoffrey M Parker, *CFO*
Susannah Cantrell, *Ch Credit Ofcr*
Dawn Parsell, *Officer*
EMP: 76 **EST:** 2013
SQ FT: 26,987 **Privately Held**
WEB: www.tricida.com
SIC: 2834 Pharmaceutical preparations

(P-3999)
TRUEPILL INC (PA)
1720 S Amphlett Blvd, San Mateo (94402-2702)
PHONE 510 388-0406
EMP: 100 **EST:** 2019
SALES (est): 41.7MM **Privately Held**
WEB: www.truepill.com
SIC: 2834 Pharmaceutical preparations

(P-4000)
ULTRAGENYX PHARMACEUTICAL INC (PA)
60 Leveroni Ct, Novato (94949-5746)
PHONE 415 483-8800
Emil D Kakkis, *President*
Daniel G Welch, *Ch of Bd*
Mardi C Dier, *CFO*
Camille L Bedrosian, *Officer*
Erik Harris, *Officer*
EMP: 676 **EST:** 2010
SALES (est): 271MM **Publicly Held**
WEB: www.ultragenyx.com
SIC: 2834 Pharmaceutical preparations

(P-4001)
VALOR COMPOUNDING PHARMACY INC
2461 Shattuck Ave, Berkeley (94704-2030)
PHONE 510 548-8777
Rick Niemi, *CEO*
Richard Niemi, *President*
Andrew Beyers, *CEO*
Ann Olaguer, *Project Mgr*
EMP: 21 **EST:** 2016
SALES (est): 2.9MM **Privately Held**
WEB: www.valorcompounding.com
SIC: 2834 5961 Syrups, pharmaceutical; druggists' preparations (pharmaceuticals); pharmaceuticals, mail order

(P-4002)
VERSEON CORPORATION (PA)
47071 Bayside Pkwy, Fremont (94538-6517)
PHONE 510 225-9000
Adityo Prakash, *President*
Eniko Fodor, *COO*
David Kita, *Vice Pres*
Kevin Short, *Director*
David Williams, *Director*
EMP: 28 **EST:** 2002
SQ FT: 8,000
SALES (est): 6.7MM **Privately Held**
WEB: www.verseon.com
SIC: 2834 Druggists' preparations (pharmaceuticals)

(P-4003)
VIBRANT CARE PHARMACY INC
7400 Macarthur Blvd Ste B, Oakland (94605-2939)
PHONE 510 638-9851
Kalpesh Patel, *CEO*
Phil Black, *Vice Pres*
EMP: 21 **EST:** 2015
SALES (est): 2.9MM **Privately Held**
WEB: www.vibrantcarepharmacy.com
SIC: 2834 5912 Chlorination tablets & kits (water purification); drug stores

(P-4004)
VIFOR PHARMA INC
200 Cardinal Way 200-B, Redwood City (94063-4703)
PHONE 650 421-9500
Greg Oaks, *CEO*
Todd Ungard, *Ch Credit Ofcr*
Deborah Sim, *Senior VP*
Laurie Hastings, *Vice Pres*
William Leschensky, *Vice Pres*
EMP: 329 **EST:** 2007
SQ FT: 93,904
SALES (est): 94.8MM
SALES (corp-wide): 214.4MM **Privately Held**
WEB: www.viforpharma.com
SIC: 2834 Pharmaceutical preparations
PA: Vifor Pharma Ag
Rechenstrasse 37
St. Gallen SG 9014
588 518-484

(P-4005)
VINCERX PHARMA INC (PA)
260 Sheridan Ave Ste 400, Palo Alto (94306-2011)
PHONE 650 800-6676
Ahmed M Hamdy, *Ch of Bd*
Raquel E Izumi, *President*
Alexander A Seelenberger, *CFO*
Hermes D Garban, *Chief Mktg Ofcr*
Tom C Thomas,
EMP: 43 **EST:** 2020 **Publicly Held**
WEB: www.vincerx.com
SIC: 2834 Pharmaceutical preparations

(P-4006)
VIVUS INC (PA)
900 E Hamilton Ave # 550, Campbell (95008-0643)
PHONE 650 934-5200
John P Amos, *CEO*
David Y Norton, *Ch of Bd*
Mark K Oki, *CFO*
Santosh T Varghese, *Chief Mktg Ofcr*
Deborah Larsen, *Officer*
EMP: 49 **EST:** 1991
SQ FT: 13,981
SALES (est): 65MM **Privately Held**
WEB: www.vivus.com
SIC: 2834 Druggists' preparations (pharmaceuticals); proprietary drug products

(P-4007)
WEDGEWOOD CONNECT
Also Called: Leiter's Compounding
17 Great Oaks Blvd, San Jose (95119-1359)
PHONE 855 321-3477
Paul Yamamoto, *Mng Member*
Jim Cunniff, *CEO*
Charles Leiter, *Vice Pres*
Dj Michina, *Exec Dir*
EMP: 50 **EST:** 2020
SALES (est): 11.3MM **Privately Held**
SIC: 2834 Druggists' preparations (pharmaceuticals)

(P-4008)
WRIGHT PHARMA INC
700 Kiernan Ave Ste A, Modesto (95356-9329)
PHONE 209 549-9771
Eric Fogleman, *Branch Mgr*
Ken Abramowitz, *Technical Staff*
Martin Morales, *Manager*
EMP: 20
SALES (corp-wide): 6.9MM **Privately Held**
WEB: www.thewrightgroup.net
SIC: 2834 2023 Pharmaceutical preparations; dietary supplements, dairy & non-dairy based
PA: Wright Pharma, Inc.
201 Energy Pkwy Ste 400
Lafayette LA 70508
337 783-3096

(P-4009)
X-37 LLC
400 Oyster Point Blvd # 20, South San Francisco (94080-1904)
PHONE 650 273-5748
David Collier, *Mng Member*
Antoine Blondeau,
EMP: 18 **EST:** 2018
SALES (est): 2.9MM **Privately Held**
WEB: www.x37.ai
SIC: 2834 Pharmaceutical preparations

(P-4010)
ZOGENIX INC (PA)
5959 Horton St Ste 500, Emeryville (94608-2120)
PHONE 510 550-8300
Stephen J Farr, *President*
CAM L Garner, *Ch of Bd*
Leslie Simpson, *CFO*
Michael P Smith, *CFO*
Ashish M Sagrolikar, *Ch Credit Ofcr*
EMP: 23 **EST:** 2006
SQ FT: 37,307
SALES (est): 13.6MM **Publicly Held**
WEB: www.zogenix.com
SIC: 2834 Pharmaceutical preparations; drugs acting on the central nervous system & sense organs

(P-4011)
ZOSANO PHARMA CORPORATION (PA)
34790 Ardentech Ct, Fremont (94555-3657)
PHONE 510 745-1200
Steven Lo, *President*
John P Walker, *Ch of Bd*
Christine Matthews, *CFO*
Joseph Hagan, *Bd of Directors*
Kleanthis Xanthopoulos, *Bd of Directors*
EMP: 36 **EST:** 2012
SALES (est): 224K **Publicly Held**
WEB: www.zosanopharma.com
SIC: 2834 Pharmaceutical preparations

(P-4012)
ZP OPCO INC
Also Called: Zosano
34790 Ardentech Ct, Fremont (94555-3657)
PHONE 510 745-1200
Konstantinos Alataris, *President*
Daniel Hunt, *President*
Winnie W TSO, *CFO*
Don Kellerman, *Vice Pres*
Hayley Lewis, *Vice Pres*
EMP: 32 **EST:** 2006
SALES (est): 128K
SALES (corp-wide): 224K **Publicly Held**
WEB: www.zosanopharma
SIC: 2834 Pharmaceutical preparations
PA: Zosano Pharma Corporation
34790 Ardentech Ct
Fremont CA 94555
510 745-1200

(P-4013)
ZS PHARMA INC
1100 Park Pl Fl 3, San Mateo (94403-1599)
PHONE 650 753-1823
Mae Lai, *Director*
EMP: 24 **EST:** 2017
SALES (est): 4.5MM
SALES (corp-wide): 26.6B **Privately Held**
WEB: www.astrazeneca.com
SIC: 2834 Pharmaceutical preparations
PA: Astrazeneca Plc
1 Francis Crick Avenue
Cambridge CAMBS CB2 0
203 749-5000

2835 Diagnostic Substances

(P-4014)
ABBOTT DIABETES CARE INC (HQ)
Also Called: Medisense
1420 Harbor Bay Pkwy, Alameda (94502-7080)
PHONE 510 749-5400
Lawrence W Huffman, *Vice Pres*
Mark C Tatro, *Vice Pres*
Robert D Brownell, *Principal*
Adam Heller, *Principal*
Charles T Liamos, *Principal*
▲ **EMP:** 250 **EST:** 1995
SQ FT: 54,500
SALES (est): 131.8MM
SALES (corp-wide): 34.6B **Publicly Held**
WEB: www.diabetescare.abbott
SIC: 2835 3845 3823 In vitro diagnostics; electromedical equipment; industrial instrmnts msrmnt display/control process variable
PA: Abbott Laboratories
100 Abbott Park Rd
Abbott Park IL 60064
224 667-6100

(P-4015)
ADEZA BIOMEDICAL CORPORATION
1240 Elko Dr, Sunnyvale (94089-2212)
PHONE 408 745-6491
Emory V Anderson, *President*
Andrew E Senyei, *CFO*
Mark D Fischer Colbrie, *CFO*
Durlin E Hickok, *Vice Pres*
Robert O Hussa, *Vice Pres*
EMP: 579 **EST:** 1985
SQ FT: 22,600
SALES (est): 3MM
SALES (corp-wide): 5.6B **Publicly Held**
WEB: www.eftymarket.com
SIC: 2835 Pregnancy test kits
HQ: Cytyc Corporation
250 Campus Dr
Marlborough MA 01752

(P-4016)
ANTIBODIES INCORPORATED
25242 County Road 95, Davis (95616-9405)
P.O. Box 1560 (95617-1560)
PHONE 800 824-8540
Richard Krogsrud, *President*
Janis Stafford, *CFO*
Melissa Zeltner, *Manager*
EMP: 18 **EST:** 1962
SQ FT: 23,000
SALES (est): 8.3MM **Privately Held**
WEB: www.antibodiesinc.com
SIC: 2836 In vitro & in vivo diagnostic substances; serums

(P-4017)
CELL MARQUE CORPORATION
6600 Sierra College Blvd, Rocklin (95677-4306)
PHONE 916 746-8900
Nora Lacey, *President*
David Zembo, *CFO*
Paul Ardi, *Vice Pres*
Anh Ngo, *Vice Pres*
Veronica Runyan, *Vice Pres*
EMP: 42 **EST:** 1994
SALES (est): 12.8MM
SALES (corp-wide): 20.7B **Privately Held**
WEB: www.cellmarque.com
SIC: 2835 In vitro & in vivo diagnostic substances
HQ: Sigma-Aldrich Corporation
3050 Spruce St
Saint Louis MO 63103
314 771-5765

(P-4018)
CEPHEID
632 E Caribbean Dr, Sunnyvale (94089-1108)
PHONE 408 548-9104
Sarah Parker, *Executive*
Jessamae Caluag, *Analyst*
Manjit Bhullar, *Buyer*
Kate Baer, *Sales Staff*
Shobana Raghunath, *Infectious Dis*
EMP: 17 **EST:** 2017
SALES (est): 3.5MM **Privately Held**
WEB: www.cepheid.com
SIC: 2835 In vitro & in vivo diagnostic substances

(P-4019)
CORE DIAGNOSTICS INC
3535 Breakwater Ave, Hayward (94545-3610)
PHONE 650 561-4176
Krishnamurthy Balachandran, *CEO*
Sankar Mohan, *Director*
EMP: 18 **EST:** 2009
SALES (est): 16.1MM
SALES (corp-wide): 1.9B **Publicly Held**
WEB: www.corediagnostics.net
SIC: 2835 In vitro & in vivo diagnostic substances
HQ: Canopy Biosciences, Llc
4340 Duncan Ave Ste 220
Saint Louis MO 63110
618 580-4653

2835 - Diagnostic Substances

(P-4020)
DANISCO US INC (HQ)
Also Called: Genencor International
925 Page Mill Rd, Palo Alto (94304-1013)
PHONE 650 846-7500
James C Collins, *CEO*
Mark A Goldsmith, *Senior VP*
Michael Arbige, *Vice Pres*
Karl Sanford, *Vice Pres*
Xing Xia, *Administration*
◆ EMP: 200 EST: 1989
SQ FT: 128,000
SALES (est): 532.4MM
SALES (corp-wide): 5B Publicly Held
WEB: www.dupont.com
SIC: 2835 8731 2899 2869 In vitro & in vivo diagnostic substances; commercial physical research; chemical preparations; industrial organic chemicals
PA: International Flavors & Fragrances Inc.
    521 W 57th St
    New York NY 10019
    212 765-5500

(P-4021)
EPIBIOME INC (HQ)
201 Gateway Blvd Ste 2061, South San Francisco (94080-7019)
PHONE 650 825-1600
Nick Conley, *CEO*
Aeron Tynes Hammack, *COO*
Lucia Mokres, *Chief Mktg Ofcr*
EMP: 17 EST: 2013
SALES (est): 3.3MM
SALES (corp-wide): 3.4MM Privately Held
WEB: www.locus-bio.com
SIC: 2835 Microbiology & virology diagnostic products
PA: Locus Biosciences, Inc.
    523 Davis Dr Ste 350
    Morrisville NC 27560
    919 495-4510

(P-4022)
FREENOME HOLDINGS INC
279 E Grand Ave, South San Francisco (94080-4804)
PHONE 650 446-6630
Gabriel Otte, *President*
Riley Ennis, *COO*
Jimmy Lin, *Officer*
Jennifer Harrison, *Office Mgr*
Anna Cunningham, *Software Engr*
EMP: 230 EST: 2015
SALES (est): 54.5MM Privately Held
WEB: www.freenome.com
SIC: 2835 Blood derivative diagnostic agents

(P-4023)
LUCIRA HEALTH INC
1412 62nd St, Emeryville (94608-2036)
PHONE 510 350-8071
Erik T Engelson, *President*
Tony Allen, *COO*
Daniel George, *CFO*
Tamanna Prashar, *Vice Pres*
Kevin Collins, *Risk Mgmt Dir*
EMP: 57 EST: 2013
SQ FT: 6,353
SALES (est): 269K Privately Held
WEB: www.lucirahealth.com
SIC: 2835 In vitro & in vivo diagnostic substances

(P-4024)
METRA BIOSYSTEMS INC (HQ)
2981 Copper Rd, Santa Clara (95051-0716)
PHONE 408 616-4300
John Tamerius, *Manager*
Bill Sommer, *Asst Controller*
EMP: 50 EST: 1990
SQ FT: 24,000
SALES (est): 35.9MM
SALES (corp-wide): 1.6B Publicly Held
WEB: www.quidel.com
SIC: 2835 In vitro & in vivo diagnostic substances
PA: Quidel Corporation
    9975 Summers Ridge Rd
    San Diego CA 92121
    858 552-1100

(P-4025)
MICROPOINT BIOSCIENCE INC
3521 Leonard Ct, Santa Clara (95054-2043)
PHONE 408 588-1682
Nan Zhang, *CEO*
Michael Huang, *COO*
Jenny Jiang, *Controller*
David Longwell, *Manager*
▲ EMP: 30 EST: 2007
SALES (est): 8.2MM Privately Held
WEB: www.micropointbio.com
SIC: 2835 In vitro & in vivo diagnostic substances
PA: Micropoint Biotechnologies,Co.,Ltd.
    Floor ,6, Floor ,3, Floor 2, Taiping Baojian Building, No.3, She
    Shenzhen 51806

(P-4026)
MINDRAY DS USA INC
Also Called: Mindray Innvtion Ctr Slcon Vly
2100 Gold St, San Jose (95002-3700)
PHONE 650 230-2800
Catherine Chen, *Sales Staff*
EMP: 323 Privately Held
WEB: www.mindraynorthamerica.com
SIC: 2835 3841 3845 In vitro diagnostics; surgical & medical instruments; patient monitoring apparatus
HQ: Mindray Ds Usa, Inc.
    800 Macarthur Blvd
    Mahwah NJ 07430

(P-4027)
MONOGRAM BIOSCIENCES INC
345 Oyster Point Blvd, South San Francisco (94080-1913)
PHONE 650 635-1100
Floyd S Eberts III, *CEO*
Alfred G Merriweather, *CFO*
Michael J Dunn, *Officer*
Sarah Irwin, *Assoc VP*
Chuck Walworth, *Assoc VP*
EMP: 382
SQ FT: 41,000
SALES (est): 60.1MM Publicly Held
WEB: www.monogrambio.com
SIC: 2835 In vitro & in vivo diagnostic substances
PA: Laboratory Corporation Of America Holdings
    358 S Main St
    Burlington NC 27215

(P-4028)
NOVARTIS PHARMACEUTICALS CORP
Also Called: Novartis Bphrmctcal Oprtons -
2010 Cessna Dr, Vacaville (95688-8712)
PHONE 707 452-8081
Chris Busstioneau, *Manager*
Justin Stone, *Analyst*
Adam Feire, *Director*
David Tully, *Director*
EMP: 286
SALES (corp-wide): 53.2B Privately Held
WEB: www.novartis.com
SIC: 2835 2834 In vitro & in vivo diagnostic substances; pharmaceutical preparations
HQ: Novartis Pharmaceuticals Corporation
    1 Health Plz
    East Hanover NJ 07936
    862 778-8300

(P-4029)
SEQUENTA LLC
329 Oyster Point Blvd, South San Francisco (94080-1913)
PHONE 650 243-3900
Tom Willis, *CEO*
Malek Faham, *Security Dir*
EMP: 30 EST: 2008
SALES (est): 7MM Publicly Held
WEB: www.adaptivebiotech.com
SIC: 2835 2836 In vitro & in vivo diagnostic substances; biological products, except diagnostic
PA: Adaptive Biotechnologies Corporation
    1551 Estlake Ave E Ste 20
    Seattle WA 98102

(P-4030)
VERGE GENOMICS
2 Tower Pl Ste 950, South San Francisco (94080-1808)
PHONE 312 489-7455
Alice Zhang, *CEO*
Ben Jackson, *Vice Pres*
Michelle Mighdoll, *Director*
EMP: 21 EST: 2017
SALES (est): 2.7MM Privately Held
WEB: www.vergegenomics.com
SIC: 2835 Microbiology & virology diagnostic products

2836 Biological Prdts, Exc Diagnostic Substances

(P-4031)
ADVERUM BIOTECHNOLOGIES INC
800 Saginaw Dr, Redwood City (94063-4740)
PHONE 650 656-9323
Laurent Fischer, *CEO*
Paul B Cleveland, *Ch of Bd*
Patrick Machado, *Ch of Bd*
Thomas Leung, *CFO*
Linda Neuman, *Chief Mktg Ofcr*
EMP: 78 EST: 2006
SQ FT: 36,000
SALES (est): 250K Privately Held
WEB: www.adverum.com
SIC: 2836 8731 Biological products, except diagnostic; biotechnical research, commercial

(P-4032)
AGENUS WEST LLC
793 Heinz Ave, Berkeley (94710-2732)
PHONE 781 674-4400
Garo H Armen, *Ch of Bd*
Alfred Dadson, *Officer*
Archivald Cruz, *Mfg Staff*
James Pagsolingan, *Mfg Staff*
Jeffrey Bettencourt, *Director*
EMP: 21 EST: 2015
SALES (est): 13MM
SALES (corp-wide): 88.1MM Publicly Held
WEB: www.agenusbio.com
SIC: 2836 Biological products, except diagnostic
PA: Agenus Inc.
    3 Forbes Rd
    Lexington MA 02421
    781 674-4400

(P-4033)
ALIGOS THERAPEUTICS INC (PA)
1 Corporate Dr Fl 2, South San Francisco (94080-7043)
PHONE 800 466-6059
Lawrence M Blatt, *CEO*
Jack B Nielsen, *Ch of Bd*
Leonid Beigelman, *President*
Lesley Ann Calhoun, *CFO*
Matthew W McClure, *Officer*
EMP: 66 EST: 2018
SQ FT: 39,000 Publicly Held
WEB: www.aligos.com
SIC: 2836 2834 Biological products, except diagnostic; pharmaceutical preparations

(P-4034)
ALPHA TEKNOVA INC
2290 Bert Dr, Hollister (95023-2567)
PHONE 831 637-1100
Stephen Gunstream, *President*
Paul Grossman, *Ch of Bd*
Matthew Lowell, *CFO*
Damon Terrill, *Ch Credit Ofcr*
Lisa Hood,
EMP: 194 EST: 1996
SQ FT: 114,000
SALES (est): 31.3MM Privately Held
WEB: www.teknova.com
SIC: 2836 Biological products, except diagnostic

(P-4035)
APPLIED EXTRACTS INC
1027 S Claremont St, San Mateo (94402-1835)
PHONE 415 260-9786
James R White, *Owner*
EMP: 17 EST: 2017
SALES (est): 4.5MM Privately Held
WEB: www.aeextract.com
SIC: 2836 Extracts

(P-4036)
ATARA BIOTHERAPEUTICS INC (PA)
611 Gateway Blvd Ste 900, South San Francisco (94080-7029)
PHONE 650 278-8930
Pascal Touchon, *President*
Utpal Koppikar, *CFO*
Eric Dobmeier, *Bd of Directors*
Amie Krause,
Mitchall G Clark, *Officer*
EMP: 140 EST: 2012
SQ FT: 13,670 Publicly Held
WEB: www.atarabio.com
SIC: 2836 8731 Biological products, except diagnostic; biotechnical research, commercial; medical research, commercial

(P-4037)
ATRECA INC
835 Industrial Rd Ste 400, San Carlos (94070-3312)
PHONE 650 595-2595
Brian Atwood, *Ch of Bd*
John A Orwin, *President*
Herbert Cross, *CFO*
Norman Michael Greenberg, *Officer*
Tito A Serafini, *Officer*
EMP: 85 EST: 2010
SQ FT: 41,124 Privately Held
WEB: www.atreca.com
SIC: 2836 Biological products, except diagnostic

(P-4038)
AUDENTES THERAPEUTICS INC (DH)
600 California St Fl 17, San Francisco (94108-2725)
PHONE 415 818-1001
Matthew Patterson, *Ch of Bd*
Natalie Holles, *President*
Thomas Soloway, *CFO*
Eric B Mosbrooker, *Ch Credit Ofcr*
Edward R Conner, *Chief Mktg Ofcr*
EMP: 164 EST: 2012
SQ FT: 29,496 Privately Held
WEB: www.astellasgenetherapies.com
SIC: 2836 Biological products, except diagnostic

(P-4039)
AUDENTES THERAPEUTICS INC
201 Gateway Blvd, South San Francisco (94080-7019)
PHONE 415 818-1001
Jonathan Silverstein, *Ch of Bd*
EMP: 41 Privately Held
WEB: www.astellasgenetherapies.com
SIC: 2836 Biological products, except diagnostic
HQ: Audentes Therapeutics, Inc.
    600 California St Fl 17
    San Francisco CA 94108
    415 818-1001

(P-4040)
BIOSEARCH TECHNOLOGIES INC (DH)
Also Called: Lgc Biosearch Technologies
2199 S Mcdowell Blvd, Petaluma (94954-6904)
PHONE 415 883-8400
Ronald M Cook, *CEO*
Daren Dick, *COO*
Ebin Koenig, *Network Enginr*
Marco Guerrero, *Comp Spec*
Bernard Slack, *IT/INT Sup*
EMP: 118 EST: 1993
SQ FT: 121,000

▲ = Import ▼ = Export
◆ = Import/Export

PRODUCTS & SERVICES SECTION

2841 - Soap & Detergents County (P-4063)

SALES (est): 62.5MM **Publicly Held**
WEB: www.biosearchtech.com
SIC: **2836** 2899 2835 2869 Biological products, except diagnostic; chemical preparations; in vitro diagnostics; industrial organic chemicals
HQ: Lgc Science Group Limited
Queens Road
Teddington MIDDX TW11
208 943-7000

(P-4041)
CARIBOU BIOSCIENCES INC
2929 7th St Ste 105, Berkeley (94710-2753)
PHONE.................510 982-6030
Rachel E Haurwitz, *President*
Jason V O'Byrne, *CFO*
Barbara G McClung,
Chris Fuller, *Vice Pres*
Steven B Kanner, *Security Dir*
EMP: 76 EST: 2011
SQ FT: 61,735
SALES (est): 12.3MM **Privately Held**
WEB: www.cariboubio.com
SIC: **2836** Biological products, except diagnostic

(P-4042)
CERUS CORPORATION (PA)
1220 Concord Ave Ste 600, Concord (94520-4906)
PHONE.................925 288-6000
William M Greenman, *President*
Daniel N Swisher Jr, *Ch of Bd*
Vivek Jayaraman, *COO*
Kevin D Green, *CFO*
Chrystal N Menard,
▲ EMP: 265 EST: 1991
SQ FT: 84,631
SALES (est): 91.9MM **Publicly Held**
WEB: www.cerus.com
SIC: **2836** Biological products, except diagnostic

(P-4043)
CORTEXYME INC (PA)
269 E Grand Ave, South San Francisco (94080-4804)
PHONE.................415 910-5717
Casey C Lynch, *Ch of Bd*
Christopher Lowe, *CFO*
Michael Detke, *Chief Mktg Ofcr*
Stephen Dominy, *Officer*
Leslie Holsinger, *Exec VP*
EMP: 18 EST: 2014
SQ FT: 3,185 **Publicly Held**
WEB: www.cortexyme.com
SIC: **2836** Biological products, except diagnostic

(P-4044)
DENALI THERAPEUTICS INC (PA)
161 Oyster Point Blvd, South San Francisco (94080-2042)
PHONE.................650 866-8548
Ryan J Watts, *President*
Vicki Sato, *Ch of Bd*
Alexander O Schuth, *COO*
Steve E Krognes, *CFO*
Carole Ho, *Chief Mktg Ofcr*
EMP: 214 EST: 2015
SALES (est): 335.6MM **Publicly Held**
WEB: www.denalitherapeutics.com
SIC: **2836** 2834 Biological products, except diagnostic; pharmaceutical preparations

(P-4045)
DYNAVAX TECHNOLOGIES CORP (PA)
2100 Powell St Ste 900, Emeryville (94608-1844)
PHONE.................510 848-5100
Ryan Spencer, *CEO*
Scott Myers, *Ch of Bd*
Victoria House, *President*
David F Novack, *President*
Kelly Macdonald, *CFO*
EMP: 82 EST: 1996
SQ FT: 23,976

SALES (est): 46.5MM **Publicly Held**
WEB: www.dynavax.com
SIC: **2836** Biological products, except diagnostic; biological research; commercial physical research

(P-4046)
EIGER BIOPHARMACEUTICALS INC (PA)
2155 Park Blvd, Palo Alto (94306-1543)
PHONE.................650 272-6138
David Cory, *President*
Thomas J Dietz, *Ch of Bd*
Sriram Ryali, *CFO*
Erik Atkisson, *Ch Credit Ofcr*
Eldon Mayer III, *Ch Credit Ofcr*
EMP: 24 EST: 2000
SQ FT: 8,029 **Publicly Held**
WEB: www.eigerbio.com
SIC: **2836** 3845 Biological products, except diagnostic; cardiographs

(P-4047)
EXELIXIS INC (PA)
1851 Harbor Bay Pkwy, Alameda (94502-3010)
PHONE.................650 837-7000
Michael M Morrissey, *President*
Stelios Papadopoulos, *Ch of Bd*
Christopher J Senner, *CFO*
Patrick J Haley, *Exec VP*
Jeffrey J Hessekiel, *Exec VP*
EMP: 57 EST: 1994
SQ FT: 228,941
SALES (est): 987.5MM **Publicly Held**
WEB: www.exelixis.com
SIC: **2836** Biological products, except diagnostic

(P-4048)
EXPRESSION SYSTEMS LLC (PA)
2537 2nd St, Davis (95618-5475)
PHONE.................877 877-7421
David Hedin, *Owner*
Thera Mulvania, *COO*
Kareem Anderson, *Manager*
Paul Bailey, *Manager*
EMP: 34 EST: 1997
SQ FT: 27,000
SALES (est): 5.1MM **Privately Held**
WEB: www.expressionsystems.com
SIC: **2836** Culture media

(P-4049)
GRITSTONE BIO INC (PA)
5959 Horton St Ste 300, Emeryville (94608-2120)
PHONE.................510 871-6100
Andrew Allen, *CEO*
Elaine V Jones, *Ch of Bd*
Erin Jones, *COO*
Jean-Marc Bellemin, *CFO*
Raphael Rousseau, *Chief Mktg Ofcr*
EMP: 150 EST: 2015
SQ FT: 13,100
SALES (est): 4MM **Publicly Held**
WEB: www.gritstonebio.com
SIC: **2836** Biological products, except diagnostic

(P-4050)
HEMOSTAT LABORATORIES INC (PA)
515 Industrial Way, Dixon (95620-9779)
P.O. Box 790 (95620-0790)
PHONE.................707 678-9594
Jim Mc Elligott, *President*
Gordon Murphy, *Vice Pres*
EMP: 20 EST: 1980
SQ FT: 9,500
SALES (est): 3.5MM **Privately Held**
WEB: www.hemostat.com
SIC: **2836** 2673 Blood derivatives; plastic & pliofilm bags

(P-4051)
HYGIEIA BIOLOGICAL LABS
1240 Commerce Ave Ste B, Woodland (95776-5923)
PHONE.................530 661-1442
James L Wallis, *Manager*
EMP: 20 **Privately Held**
WEB: www.hygieialabs.com

SIC: **2836** Biological products, except diagnostic
PA: Hygieia Biological Laboratories
1785 E Main St Ste 4
Woodland CA 95776

(P-4052)
KRIYA THERAPEUTICS INC
1100 Island Dr Ste 203, Redwood City (94065-5187)
PHONE.................833 574-9289
Shankar Ramaswamy, *CEO*
Ilise Lombardo, *Chief Mktg Ofcr*
EMP: 20 EST: 2020
SALES (est): 2.7MM **Privately Held**
SIC: **2836** Biological products, except diagnostic

(P-4053)
LIST BIOLOGICAL LABS INC
Also Called: List Labs
540 Division St, Campbell (95008-6906)
PHONE.................408 866-6363
Karen Crawford, *President*
Maggie Tam, *CFO*
Linda Eaton, *Bd of Directors*
Debra Booth, *Vice Pres*
Gary Henderson, *Business Dir*
▼ EMP: 25 EST: 1978
SQ FT: 11,000
SALES (est): 5.1MM **Privately Held**
WEB: www.listlabs.com
SIC: **2836** Biological products, except diagnostic

(P-4054)
MICROMIDAS INC
930 Riverside Pkwy Ste 10, West Sacramento (95605-1511)
PHONE.................916 231-9329
John Bissell, *CEO*
Chloe Grinberg, *Technician*
Makoto Masuno, *Research*
Nolan Nicholson, *Engineer*
EMP: 36 EST: 2008
SALES (est): 9.9MM
SALES (corp-wide): 10.1MM **Publicly Held**
WEB: www.originmaterials.com
SIC: **2836** Biological products, except diagnostic
PA: Origin Materials, Inc.
930 Riverside Pkwy Ste 10
West Sacramento CA 95605
916 231-9329

(P-4055)
PROTEUS DIGITAL HEALTH INC (PA)
2600 Bridge Pkwy, Redwood City (94065-6136)
PHONE.................650 632-4031
Lawrence Perkins, *CEO*
Jonathan Symonds, *Ch of Bd*
Steven Fieler, *CFO*
Uneek Mehra, *CFO*
Molly O'Neill, *Officer*
▲ EMP: 237 EST: 2001
SALES (est): 62.7MM **Privately Held**
WEB: www.proteus.com
SIC: **2836** Biological products, except diagnostic

(P-4056)
SANGAMO THERAPEUTICS INC (PA)
7000 Marina Blvd, Brisbane (94005-1815)
PHONE.................510 970-6000
Alexander D Macrae, *President*
H Stewart Parker, *Ch of Bd*
Prathyusha Duraibabu, *Officer*
Gary H Loeb, *Exec VP*
D Mark McClung, *Exec VP*
EMP: 374 EST: 1995
SQ FT: 87,700
SALES (est): 118.1MM **Publicly Held**
WEB: www.sangamo.com
SIC: **2836** Biological products, except diagnostic

(P-4057)
SURROZEN INC (PA)
171 Oyster Point Blvd # 30, South San Francisco (94080-1936)
PHONE.................650 489-9000

Craig Parker, *President*
Tim Kutzkey, *Ch of Bd*
Charles Williams, *CFO*
Geertrui Vanhove, *Chief Mktg Ofcr*
Elizabeth Nguyen, *Vice Pres*
EMP: 20 EST: 2020
SALES (est): 10.4MM **Publicly Held**
SIC: **2836** Biological products, except diagnostic

(P-4058)
SUTRO BIOPHARMA INC (PA)
310 Utah Ave Ste 150, South San Francisco (94080-6803)
PHONE.................650 392-8412
William J Newell, *CEO*
Connie Matsui, *Ch of Bd*
Edward Albini, *CFO*
Arturo Molina, *Chief Mktg Ofcr*
Linda Fitzpatrick, *Officer*
EMP: 155 EST: 2003
SQ FT: 52,200
SALES (est): 42.7MM **Publicly Held**
WEB: www.sutrobio.com
SIC: **2836** Biological products, except diagnostic

(P-4059)
VAXCYTE INC (PA)
353 Hatch Dr, Foster City (94404-1162)
PHONE.................650 837-0111
Grant Pickering, *CEO*
Kurt Von Emster, *Ch of Bd*
Andrew Guggenhime, *President*
Jim Wassil, *COO*
Jane Wright-Mitchell, *Ch Credit Ofcr*
EMP: 56 EST: 2013
SQ FT: 22,000 **Publicly Held**
WEB: www.vaxcyte.com
SIC: **2836** Biological products, except diagnostic; vaccines

(P-4060)
VECTOR LABORATORIES INC (HQ)
30 Ingold Rd, Burlingame (94010-2206)
PHONE.................650 697-3600
James S Whitehead, *President*
Kevin Thompson, *CFO*
William Cahalan, *Vice Pres*
Brian Kanagy, *Research*
Jonathan Milbourne, *Production*
◆ EMP: 52 EST: 1976
SQ FT: 65,000
SALES (est): 12.7MM
SALES (corp-wide): 284.1MM **Publicly Held**
WEB: www.vectorlabs.com
SIC: **2836** 2899 Biological products, except diagnostic; chemical preparations
PA: Maravai Lifesciences Holdings, Inc.
10770 Wtridge Cir Ste 200
San Diego CA 92121
858 546-0004

(P-4061)
VISIT HEALTHCARE INC
20 S Santa Cruz Ave # 30, Los Gatos (95030-6830)
PHONE.................408 890-6648
Olympia Bliss, *CEO*
EMP: 28 EST: 2020
SALES (est): 1.8MM **Privately Held**
SIC: **2836** Vaccines

2841 Soap & Detergents

(P-4062)
ECOLAB
640 Lenfest Rd, San Jose (95133-1614)
PHONE.................408 928-8100
Donald Valsvik, *Accounts Mgr*
EMP: 15 EST: 2019
SALES (est): 2.4MM **Privately Held**
WEB: www.ceoecolab.com
SIC: **2841** Soap & other detergents

(P-4063)
LIFEKIND PRODUCTS INC
333 Crown Point Cir # 225, Grass Valley (95945-9538)
P.O. Box 1774 (95945-1774)
PHONE.................530 477-5395
Walter Bader, *President*

2841 - Soap & Detergents County (P-4064)

EMP: 16 EST: 1996
SALES (est): 1.4MM **Privately Held**
WEB: www.lifekind.com
SIC: **2841** 2515 Detergents, synthetic organic or inorganic alkaline; mattresses & bedsprings

(P-4064)
PROCTER & GAMBLE MFG CO
8201 Fruitridge Rd, Sacramento (95826-4716)
PHONE 916 383-3800
Bob Randall, *Branch Mgr*
EMP: 206
SALES (corp-wide): 76.1B **Publicly Held**
WEB: www.pg.com
SIC: **2841** Detergents, synthetic organic or inorganic alkaline
HQ: The Procter & Gamble Manufacturing Company
   1 Procter And Gamble Plz
   Cincinnati OH 45202
   513 983-1100

(P-4065)
VALUE PRODUCTS INC
Also Called: Pride Line Products
2128 Industrial Dr, Stockton (95206-4936)
PHONE 209 345-3817
Douglas Hall, *President*
Erica Hall, *Corp Secy*
June Guanzon, *Technician*
Steve Dufort, *Sales Mgr*
Mark Hall, *Products*
EMP: 25 EST: 1969
SQ FT: 34,000
SALES (est): 4.5MM **Privately Held**
WEB: www.valueproductsinc.com
SIC: **2841** Detergents, synthetic organic or inorganic alkaline

2842 Spec Cleaning, Polishing & Sanitation Preparations

(P-4066)
BEST SANITIZERS INC
310 Prvdnce Mine Rd # 120, Nevada City (95959-2981)
P.O. Box 1360, Penn Valley (95946-1360)
PHONE 530 265-1800
Hillard T Witt, *President*
Ed Hay, *Vice Pres*
Ryan Witt, *Vice Pres*
Jasmine Mobley, *Enginr/R&D Asst*
Deborah Bilz, *Controller*
◆ EMP: 52 EST: 1995
SQ FT: 10,000
SALES (est): 11.7MM **Privately Held**
WEB: www.bestsanitizers.com
SIC: **2842** Sanitation preparations

(P-4067)
CHEMETALL US INC
Also Called: Chemetall Oakite
46716 Lakeview Blvd, Fremont (94538-6529)
PHONE 408 387-5340
Daryl Burnett, *Manager*
EMP: 50
SALES (corp-wide): 69.9B **Privately Held**
WEB: www.chemetallna.com
SIC: **2842** Automobile polish
HQ: Chemetall U.S., Inc.
   675 Central Ave
   New Providence NJ 07974

(P-4068)
CLOROX COMPANY (PA)
1221 Broadway Ste 1300, Oakland (94612-1871)
PHONE 510 271-7000
Linda Rendle, *CEO*
Kathleen Yellin, *Partner*
Benno Dorer, *Ch of Bd*
Kevin B Jacobsen, *CFO*
Eric Reynolds, *Chief Mktg Ofcr*
▼ EMP: 2914 EST: 1913
SALES: 7.3B **Publicly Held**
WEB: www.theclroxcompany.com
SIC: **2842** 2673 2035 2844 Laundry cleaning preparations; polishing preparations & related products; food storage & frozen food bags, plastic; seasonings & sauces, except tomato & dry; dressings, salad: raw & cooked (except dry mixes); seasonings, meat sauces (except tomato & dry); cosmetic preparations; insecticides & pesticides

(P-4069)
CLOROX COMPANY
4900 Johnson Dr, Pleasanton (94588-3308)
PHONE 925 368-6000
Wayne L Delker, *President*
Matt Plum, *Research*
Stephanie Lorino, *Consultant*
EMP: 19
SALES (corp-wide): 7.3B **Publicly Held**
WEB: www.theclroxcompany.com
SIC: **2842** Specialty cleaning, polishes & sanitation goods
PA: The Clorox Company
   1221 Broadway Ste 1300
   Oakland CA 94612
   510 271-7000

(P-4070)
CLOROX MANUFACTURING COMPANY
2600 Huntington Dr, Fairfield (94533-9736)
PHONE 707 437-1051
Scott Johnston, *Manager*
Dan Dahlgren, *Vice Pres*
Dave Iacobelli, *Vice Pres*
Theo Razzouk, *Vice Pres*
Dwan Armstrong, *Executive*
EMP: 73
SALES (corp-wide): 7.3B **Publicly Held**
WEB: www.theclroxcompany.com
SIC: **2842** Bleaches, household: dry or liquid
HQ: Clorox Manufacturing Company
   1221 Broadway
   Oakland CA 94612

(P-4071)
CLOROX MANUFACTURING COMPANY (HQ)
1221 Broadway, Oakland (94612-1837)
P.O. Box 3429, Torrance (90510-3429)
PHONE 510 271-7000
T E Bailey, *CEO*
Karen M Rose, *Treasurer*
Suzanne Thompson, *Vice Pres*
Roland Castro, *Senior Mgr*
◆ EMP: 180 EST: 1996
SALES (est): 500.8MM
SALES (corp-wide): 7.3B **Publicly Held**
WEB: www.theclroxcompany.com
SIC: **2842** Specialty cleaning, polishes & sanitation goods
PA: The Clorox Company
   1221 Broadway Ste 1300
   Oakland CA 94612
   510 271-7000

(P-4072)
CLOROX SERVICES COMPANY (HQ)
1221 Broadway, Oakland (94612-1837)
P.O. Box 3429, Torrance (90510-3429)
PHONE 510 271-7000
Benno Dorer, *Ch of Bd*
Kevin Jacobsen, *CFO*
Margaret Gomez, *Admin Asst*
Michelle Landers, *Senior Engr*
Ben Kimberley, *Counsel*
EMP: 100 EST: 1996
SALES (est): 154.3MM
SALES (corp-wide): 7.3B **Publicly Held**
WEB: www.theclroxcompany.com
SIC: **2842** 5169 Specialty cleaning, polishes & sanitation goods; laundry cleaning preparations; specialty cleaning & sanitation preparations
PA: The Clorox Company
   1221 Broadway Ste 1300
   Oakland CA 94612
   510 271-7000

(P-4073)
ENVIRNMNTAL CMPLIANCE PROS INC ☉
2701 Del Paso Rd Ste 130, Sacramento (95835-2306)
PHONE 916 953-9006
Joy Brown, *CEO*
EMP: 31 EST: 2021
SALES (est): 1.8MM **Privately Held**
SIC: **2842** Sanitation preparations

(P-4074)
GEA FARM TECHNOLOGIES INC
Also Called: W S West
2717 S 4th St, Fresno (93725-1938)
PHONE 559 497-5074
Warren Dorathy, *Manager*
EMP: 40
SALES (corp-wide): 5.4B **Privately Held**
SIC: **2842** Specialty cleaning, polishes & sanitation goods
HQ: Gea Farm Technologies, Inc.
   1880 Country Farm Dr
   Naperville IL 60563
   630 548-8200

(P-4075)
KINGSFORD MANUFACTURING CO
1221 Broadway Ste 1300, Oakland (94612-2072)
PHONE 510 271-7000
Josh Nash, *Site Mgr*
EMP: 17 EST: 2019
SALES (est): 5.2MM
SALES (corp-wide): 7.3B **Publicly Held**
WEB: www.kingsford.com
SIC: **2842** Laundry cleaning preparations
PA: The Clorox Company
   1221 Broadway Ste 1300
   Oakland CA 94612
   510 271-7000

(P-4076)
OMEGA INDUSTRIAL SUPPLY INC
101 Grobric Ct, Fairfield (94534-1673)
PHONE 707 864-8164
Adam Brady, *CEO*
Lori Rehn, *President*
Pam Wilcox, *Purchasing*
Erica Mann Pearson, *Manager*
Allan Baker, *Accounts Mgr*
EMP: 35 EST: 1997
SQ FT: 10,000
SALES (est): 6.2MM **Privately Held**
WEB: www.onlyomega.com
SIC: **2842** 5169 Sanitation preparations; chemicals & allied products

(P-4077)
QUANTUM GLOBAL TECH LLC (HQ)
Also Called: Quantumclean
26462 Corporate Ave, Hayward (94545-3914)
P.O. Box 1000, Dublin PA (18917-1000)
PHONE 215 892-9300
Scott Nicholas, *CEO*
David Zuck, *COO*
Stephen Dirugeris, *CFO*
Dave Zuck, *Vice Pres*
Margaret Cox, *Program Mgr*
▲ EMP: 105 EST: 2004
SALES (est): 60.6MM
SALES (corp-wide): 1.4B **Publicly Held**
WEB: www.quantumclean.com
SIC: **2842** Specialty cleaning preparations
PA: Ultra Clean Holdings, Inc.
   26462 Corporate Ave
   Hayward CA 94545
   510 576-4400

(P-4078)
SURTEC INC
Also Called: Surtec System, The
1880 N Macarthur Dr, Tracy (95376-2841)
PHONE 209 820-3700
William A Fields, *President*
Don C Fromm, *Treasurer*
Carol Newman, *Technical Staff*
Mary O'Neil, *Marketing Staff*
Brian Fields, *Manager*
◆ EMP: 50 EST: 1975
SQ FT: 87,000
SALES (est): 14.7MM **Privately Held**
SIC: **2842** 5087 Specialty cleaning preparations; floor machinery, maintenance

2844 Perfumes, Cosmetics & Toilet Preparations

(P-4079)
ALLURE LABS INC
30901 Wiegman Ct, Hayward (94544-7809)
PHONE 510 489-8896
Sam Dhatt, *CEO*
Renu Dhatt, *Vice Pres*
Harry Kalkat, *General Mgr*
Sumeet Dhatt, *Info Tech Dir*
Aakansha Gambhir, *Research*
▲ EMP: 30 EST: 1995
SQ FT: 50,000
SALES (est): 5.1MM **Privately Held**
WEB: www.allurelabs.com
SIC: **2844** Cosmetic preparations

(P-4080)
AMYRIS CLEAN BEAUTY INC
Also Called: Biossance
5885 Hollis St Ste 100, Emeryville (94608-2405)
PHONE 510 450-0761
John Melo, *CEO*
EMP: 24 EST: 2019
SALES (est): 1.3MM
SALES (corp-wide): 173.1MM **Publicly Held**
WEB: www.amyris.com
SIC: **2844** Toilet preparations
PA: Amyris, Inc.
   5885 Hollis St Ste 100
   Emeryville CA 94608
   510 450-0761

(P-4081)
COLUMBIA COSMETICS MFRS INC (PA)
1661 Timothy Dr, San Leandro (94577-2311)
PHONE 510 562-5900
Rachel Rendel, *CEO*
Limei Meyar, *Office Mgr*
Paul Northam, *Info Tech Mgr*
Haley Burris, *Purch Agent*
Melissa Ramos, *Purch Agent*
▲ EMP: 75 EST: 1972
SQ FT: 31,000
SALES (est): 14.1MM **Privately Held**
WEB: www.columbiacosmetics.com
SIC: **2844** Cosmetic preparations

(P-4082)
ELF BEAUTY INC (PA)
570 10th St, Oakland (94607-4038)
PHONE 510 210-8602
Tarang Amin, *President*
Mandy Fields, *CFO*
Rich Baruch, *Ch Credit Ofcr*
Scott Milsten,
Kory Marchisotto, *Officer*
EMP: 192 EST: 2004
SALES: 318.1MM **Publicly Held**
WEB: www.elfcosmetics.com
SIC: **2844** 5122 5999 Cosmetic preparations; cosmetics; cosmetics

(P-4083)
GS COSMECEUTICAL USA INC
131 Pullman St, Livermore (94551-5128)
PHONE 925 371-5000
Gurpreet Sangha, *CEO*
Gurkirpal Sandhu, *COO*
Varinder Sangha, *CFO*
Norman Poon, *Info Tech Mgr*
Fredalyn Rivera, *Materials Mgr*
▲ EMP: 68 EST: 1998
SQ FT: 60,000
SALES (est): 18MM **Privately Held**
WEB: www.gscos.com
SIC: **2844** Face creams or lotions; cosmetic preparations

▲ = Import ▼ = Export
◆ = Import/Export

PRODUCTS & SERVICES SECTION
2851 - Paints, Varnishes, Lacquers, Enamels County (P-4106)

(P-4084)
H2O PLUS LLC (PA)
111 Sutter St Fl 22, San Francisco (94104-4540)
PHONE..................800 242-2284
Joy Chen, *President*
Robert Seidl, *Vice Pres*
◆ **EMP:** 90 **EST:** 1993
SQ FT: 82,000
SALES (est): 14.9MM **Privately Held**
WEB: www.h2oplus.com
SIC: 2844 5999 5122 Toilet preparations; cosmetics; cosmetics

(P-4085)
HIMS INC (HQ)
2269 Chestnut St 523, San Francisco (94123-2600)
PHONE..................415 851-0195
Andrew Dudum, *CEO*
Spencer Lee, *CFO*
Arash Mostaghimi, *Dermatology*
EMP: 156 **EST:** 2013
SALES (est): 48.6MM **Publicly Held**
WEB: www.forhims.com
SIC: 2844 2329 2211 3143 Toilet preparations; sweaters & sweater jackets: men's & boys'; corduroys, cotton; boots, dress or casual: men's; boots, canvas or leather: women's; candles
PA: Hims & Hers Health, Inc.
 2269 Chestnut St 523
 San Francisco CA 94123
 415 851-0195

(P-4086)
JAPONESQUE LLC
12647 Alcosta Blvd # 375, San Ramon (94583-4774)
PHONE..................925 866-6670
Rich Conti, *CEO*
Christine CHI, *Director*
Heather Hinton, *Director*
▲ **EMP:** 16 **EST:** 2002
SALES (est): 5.3MM **Privately Held**
WEB: www.japonesque.com
SIC: 2844 5122 Cosmetic preparations; cosmetics

(P-4087)
LIBBY LABORATORIES INC
1700 6th St, Berkeley (94710-1806)
PHONE..................510 527-5400
Susan Libby, *President*
Gordon Libby, *Treasurer*
Charles Mendoza, *Info Tech Mgr*
George Pieri, *Plant Engr*
EMP: 23 **EST:** 1959
SQ FT: 25,000
SALES (est): 2.9MM **Privately Held**
WEB: www.libbylabs.com
SIC: 2844 2834 2899 Cosmetic preparations; pharmaceutical preparations; solutions, pharmaceutical; chemical preparations

(P-4088)
LLC BAKER CUMMINS
580 Garcia Ave, Pittsburg (94565-4901)
PHONE..................925 732-9338
Evan Warshawsky, *President*
EMP: 75 **EST:** 2017
SALES (est): 2.5MM **Privately Held**
WEB: www.bakercummins.com
SIC: 2844 2834 Cosmetic preparations; pharmaceutical preparations

(P-4089)
MADISON REED INC
430 Shotwell St, San Francisco (94110-1914)
PHONE..................415 225-0872
Amy Erriatt, *CEO*
Brian Bouma, *CFO*
Eric Hutchinson, *COO*
Carrie Kalinowski, *CFO*
Heidi Doros, *Chief Mktg Ofcr*
▲ **EMP:** 31
SALES (est): 5.8MM **Privately Held**
WEB: www.madison-reed.com
SIC: 5999 2844 Hair care products; hair coloring preparations

(P-4090)
MEGA CREATION INC
Also Called: Protec
228 Linus Pauling Dr, Hercules (94547-1823)
PHONE..................510 741-9998
Newton Lun, *CEO*
EMP: 30 **EST:** 2006
SALES (est): 3.1MM **Privately Held**
SIC: 2844 Cosmetic preparations

(P-4091)
NATIVE
201 California St Ste 450, San Francisco (94111-5032)
PHONE..................562 217-9338
Katie Weltz, *Principal*
Mia De Andrade, *Executive Asst*
EMP: 20 **EST:** 2019
SALES (est): 7.9MM **Privately Held**
WEB: www.nativecos.com
SIC: 2844 Suntan lotions & oils

(P-4092)
PEACE OUT INC
666 Natoma St, San Francisco (94103-2720)
PHONE..................305 297-8017
Enrico Frezza, *CEO*
EMP: 25 **EST:** 2016
SQ FT: 1,800
SALES (est): 11.8MM **Privately Held**
WEB: www.peaceoutskincare.com
SIC: 2844 Cosmetic preparations

(P-4093)
PRIMA FLEUR BOTANICALS INC
84 Galli Dr, Novato (94949-5706)
PHONE..................415 455-0957
Marianne Griffeth, *President*
Ron Griffeth, *Corp Secy*
Christina Mitaine, *Purch Mgr*
Stacy Huang, *Sales Staff*
▲ **EMP:** 16 **EST:** 1993
SQ FT: 5,000
SALES (est): 4MM **Privately Held**
WEB: www.primafleur.com
SIC: 2844 5169 Suntan lotions & oils; essential oils

(P-4094)
RMF SALT HOLDINGS LLC
Also Called: San Francisco Bath Salt Co
2217 S Shore Ctr 200, Alameda (94501-8073)
PHONE..................510 477-9600
Lee J Williamson, *President*
Steve Tracy, *Senior VP*
Michele Emmerling, *CIO*
Joy Coleman, *Sales Staff*
Savannah Downey, *Director*
◆ **EMP:** 16 **EST:** 2002
SALES (est): 4.1MM
SALES (corp-wide): 56.1MM **Privately Held**
WEB: www.sfbsc.com
SIC: 2844 5149 Bath salts; salt, edible
PA: Red Monkey Foods, Inc.
 6751 W Kings St
 Springfield MO 65802
 417 319-7300

(P-4095)
SUN DEEP INC
Also Called: Sun Deep Cosmetics
31285 San Clemente St, Hayward (94544-7814)
P.O. Box 2814, Danville (94526-7814)
PHONE..................510 441-2525
Sundeep Gill, *Exec Dir*
Prabhleen S Gill, *President*
Jay Gill, *CEO*
Ravi Gill, *Corp Secy*
◆ **EMP:** 200 **EST:** 1987
SQ FT: 40,000
SALES (est): 26.3MM **Privately Held**
WEB: www.sundeepinc.com
SIC: 2844 5122 Cosmetic preparations; toilet preparations; cosmetics, perfumes & hair products

(P-4096)
TENDER LOVING THINGS INC
Also Called: Happy Company, The
26203 Prod Ave Ste 4, Hayward (94545)
PHONE..................510 300-1260
Mark Juarez, *CEO*
Alan Widdoss, *CFO*
Ray Campbell, *Business Dir*
Alan Chen, *Business Dir*
EMP: 15 **EST:** 1992
SQ FT: 20,000
SALES (est): 1.6MM **Privately Held**
SIC: 2844 2499 5122 Toilet preparations; novelties, wood fiber; drugs, proprietaries & sundries

(P-4097)
TRANS-INDIA PRODUCTS INC
Also Called: Shikai Products
3330 Coffey Ln Ste A&B, Santa Rosa (95403-1917)
P.O. Box 2866 (95405-0866)
PHONE..................707 544-0298
Dennis Sepp, *President*
Jason Sepp, *CEO*
Carol Sepp, *Corp Secy*
Vasant Telang, *Vice Pres*
◆ **EMP:** 25 **EST:** 1970
SQ FT: 30,000
SALES (est): 5.9MM **Privately Held**
WEB: www.shikai.com
SIC: 2844 Face creams or lotions; cosmetic preparations

(P-4098)
TRUE BOTANICALS INC
1 Lovell Ave, Mill Valley (94941-1848)
PHONE..................415 420-0403
Hillary Peterson, *CEO*
EMP: 19 **EST:** 2016
SALES (est): 251.9K **Privately Held**
SIC: 2844 5961 Toilet preparations; cosmetics & perfumes, mail order

(P-4099)
W3LL PEOPLE INC
570 10th St 3, Oakland (94607-4038)
PHONE..................800 790-1563
Tarang P Amin, *CEO*
James Walker, *Master*
▲ **EMP:** 15 **EST:** 2017
SALES (est): 2.7MM
SALES (corp-wide): 318.1MM **Publicly Held**
WEB: www.w3llpeople.com
SIC: 2844 Cosmetic preparations
PA: E.L.F. Beauty, Inc.
 570 10th St
 Oakland CA 94607
 510 210-8602

(P-4100)
ZENLEN INC
Also Called: Native Deodorants
201 California St, San Francisco (94111-5002)
PHONE..................415 834-8238
Tyler Myhan, *CEO*
Moiz Ali, *CEO*
EMP: 25 **EST:** 2016
SALES (est): 5.6MM
SALES (corp-wide): 76.1B **Publicly Held**
WEB: www.nativecos.com
SIC: 2844 Deodorants, personal
PA: The Procter & Gamble Company
 1 Procter And Gamble Plz
 Cincinnati OH 45202
 513 983-1100

2851 Paints, Varnishes, Lacquers, Enamels

(P-4101)
AKZO NOBEL COATINGS INC
2100 Adams Ave, San Leandro (94577-1010)
PHONE..................510 562-8812
Greg Decker, *President*
EMP: 34
SALES (corp-wide): 10B **Privately Held**
SIC: 2851 Paints & allied products
HQ: Akzo Nobel Coatings Inc.
 8220 Mohawk Dr
 Strongsville OH 44136
 440 297-5100

(P-4102)
CARDINAL PAINT AND POWDER INC
890 Commercial St, San Jose (95112-1410)
PHONE..................408 452-8522
Tom Cross, *Manager*
EMP: 96
SALES (corp-wide): 70MM **Privately Held**
WEB: www.cardinalpaint.com
SIC: 2851 Paints & allied products
PA: Cardinal Paint And Powder, Inc.
 1900 Aerojet Way
 North Las Vegas NV 89030
 702 852-2333

(P-4103)
DUNCAN ENTERPRISES (HQ)
Also Called: Ilovetocreate A Duncan Entps
5673 E Shields Ave, Fresno (93727-7819)
PHONE..................559 291-4444
Larry Duncan, *CEO*
Larry Hermansen, *President*
Larry R Duncan, *CEO*
Valerie Marderosian, *Vice Pres*
Bruce Sharp, *Vice Pres*
◆ **EMP:** 170 **EST:** 1944
SQ FT: 260,000
SALES (est): 54.2MM **Privately Held**
WEB: www.ilovetocreate.com
SIC: 2851 3299 3952 3944 Colors in oil, except artists'; ceramic fiber; lead pencils & art goods; games, toys & children's vehicles
PA: Duncan Financial Corporation
 5673 E Shields Ave
 Fresno CA 93727
 559 291-4444

(P-4104)
INTEGRATED OPTICAL SVCS CORP
Also Called: Ios Optics
3270 Keller St Ste 102, Santa Clara (95054-2615)
PHONE..................408 982-9510
Douglas Fitzpatrick, *President*
Elmer Valencia, *Treasurer*
Maria Flores, *QC Mgr*
Cynthia Norwood, *Director*
▲ **EMP:** 35 **EST:** 1978
SALES (est): 3.9MM **Privately Held**
WEB: www.iosoptics.com
SIC: 2851 3827 Paints & allied products; prisms, optical

(P-4105)
JANCO CHEMICAL CORPORATION
Also Called: Janco Airless Center
1235 5th St, Berkeley (94710-1395)
PHONE..................510 527-9770
Kevin Glenn Kjelstrom, *President*
Janice S Kjelstrom, *Vice Pres*
EMP: 33 **EST:** 1962
SQ FT: 12,000
SALES (est): 5.5MM **Privately Held**
WEB: www.jancopaintsupplies.com
SIC: 2851 5198 Wood stains; paint brushes, rollers, sprayers

(P-4106)
KELLY-MOORE PAINT COMPANY INC (PA)
Also Called: Kelly-Moore Paints
1390 El Cmino Real Ste 30, San Carlos (94070)
P.O. Box 3016 (94070-1316)
PHONE..................650 592-8337
Steve De Voe, *CEO*
James Alberts, *Vice Pres*
Todd Wirdzek, *Vice Pres*
Shawn Lawrence, *General Mgr*
Curt Skinner, *General Mgr*
◆ **EMP:** 250 **EST:** 1946
SALES (est): 507.8MM **Privately Held**
WEB: www.kellymoore.com
SIC: 2851 Paints: oil or alkyd vehicle or water thinned; lacquers, varnishes, enamels & other coatings; removers & cleaners

2851 - Paints, Varnishes, Lacquers, Enamels County (P-4107)

(P-4107)
MALLAR INDUSTRIAL FINSHG INC
4500 Enterprise St, Fremont (94538-6315)
PHONE...................510 651-6694
Joseph C Simpson, *CEO*
EMP: 15 **EST:** 2018
SALES (est): 2.9MM **Privately Held**
WEB: www.centralfloridacommissary.com
SIC: 2851 Shellac (protective coating)

(P-4108)
PERFORMANCE COATINGS INC
360 Lake Mendocino Dr, Ukiah (95482-9497)
P.O. Box 1569 (95482-1569)
PHONE...................707 462-3023
Barbara Newell, *Ch of Bd*
◆ **EMP:** 20
SQ FT: 4,300
SALES (est): 7.3MM **Privately Held**
WEB: www.penofin.com
SIC: 2851 Wood stains

(P-4109)
R J MCGLENNON COMPANY INC (PA)
Also Called: Maclac Co
198 Utah St, San Francisco (94103-4826)
PHONE...................415 552-0311
Michael McGlennon, *President*
Michael Mc Glennon, *President*
EMP: 22 **EST:** 1961
SQ FT: 30,000
SALES (est): 3.3MM **Privately Held**
WEB: www.maclac.com
SIC: 2851 Lacquer: bases, dopes, thinner; enamels

(P-4110)
RUPERT GIBBON & SPIDER INC
Also Called: Jacquard Products
1147 Healdsburg Ave, Healdsburg (95448-3405)
P.O. Box 425 (95448-0425)
PHONE...................800 442-0455
Asher Katz, *President*
Devon Scrivner, *Treasurer*
EMP: 35 **EST:** 2013
SQ FT: 24,570
SALES (est): 3.7MM **Privately Held**
WEB: www.jacquardproducts.com
SIC: 2851 8742 5169 Paints & allied products; merchandising consultant; waxes, except petroleum

(P-4111)
SIMPSON COATINGS GROUP INC
401 S Canal St A, South San Francisco (94080-4606)
P.O. Box 2265 (94083-2265)
PHONE...................650 873-5990
EMP: 25
SQ FT: 35,000
SALES (est): 4.6MM
SALES (corp-wide): 5MM **Privately Held**
SIC: 2851 Mfg Paints/Allied Products
PA: D J Simpson Company
401 S Canal St A
South San Francisco CA
650 225-9404

(P-4112)
TRESCO PAINT CO
21595 Curtis St, Hayward (94545-1307)
PHONE...................510 887-7254
Khosrow M Sohrabi, *President*
Behrooz Sohrabi, *Vice Pres*
EMP: 22 **EST:** 1945
SQ FT: 18,000
SALES (est): 763.7K **Privately Held**
WEB: www.roofguardcoatings.com
SIC: 2851 Paints & allied products

(P-4113)
VIVID INC
180 E Sunnyoaks Ave, Campbell (95008-6631)
P.O. Box 320486, Los Gatos (95032-0108)
PHONE...................408 982-9101
John Comeau, *CEO*
Kurt Nielsen, *Engineer*
Stephanie Comeau,
▲ **EMP:** 35 **EST:** 1989
SQ FT: 38,800
SALES (est): 6.7MM **Privately Held**
WEB: www.vividinc.com
SIC: 2851 Paints & allied products

(P-4114)
WALTON INDUSTRIES INC
Also Called: General Coatings
1220 E North Ave, Fresno (93725-1930)
P.O. Box 11127 (93771-1127)
PHONE...................559 495-4004
Lee Walton, *President*
Will Lorenz, *Vice Pres*
Lance Bennett, *Opers Staff*
Steve Goold, *Sales Staff*
EMP: 26 **EST:** 1987
SQ FT: 40,000
SALES (est): 7.8MM **Privately Held**
WEB: www.generalcoatings.net
SIC: 2851 3086 Paints & allied products; insulation or cushioning material, foamed plastic

2861 Gum & Wood Chemicals

(P-4115)
KINGSFORD PRODUCTS COMPANY LLC (HQ)
1221 Broadway Ste 1300, Oakland (94612-2072)
PHONE...................510 271-7000
Richard T Conti, *President*
A W Biebl, *President*
Karen Rose, *CFO*
L L Hoover, *Treasurer*
B C Blewett, *Vice Pres*
▲ **EMP:** 75 **EST:** 1971
SQ FT: 506,000
SALES (est): 106.9MM
SALES (corp-wide): 7.3B **Publicly Held**
WEB: www.thecloroxcompany.com
SIC: 2861 2099 2035 2033 Charcoal, except activated; dressings, salad: dry mixes; dressings, salad: raw & cooked (except dry mixes); barbecue sauce: packaged in cans, jars, etc.; insecticides, agricultural or household
PA: The Clorox Company
1221 Broadway Ste 1300
Oakland CA 94612
510 271-7000

2865 Cyclic-Crudes, Intermediates, Dyes & Org Pigments

(P-4116)
HAZTECH SYSTEMS INC
4996 Gold Leaf Dr, Mariposa (95338-8510)
P.O. Box 929 (95338-0929)
PHONE...................209 966-8088
Thomas Archibald, *CEO*
Dawn Plunkett, *Executive*
Brenda Archibald, *Admin Sec*
Will Johnson, *Marketing Staff*
EMP: 20 **EST:** 1986 **Privately Held**
WEB: www.hazcat.com
SIC: 2865 Chemical indicators

2869 Industrial Organic Chemicals, NEC

(P-4117)
AEMETIS INC (PA)
20400 Stevns Crk Blvd # 700, Cupertino (95014-2296)
PHONE...................408 213-0940
Eric A McAfee, *Ch of Bd*
Andrew B Foster, *COO*
Todd A Waltz, *CFO*
EMP: 15 **EST:** 1983
SQ FT: 9,238
SALES (est): 165.5MM **Publicly Held**
WEB: www.aemetis.com
SIC: 2869 2911 5172 Fuels; diesel fuels; fuel oil

(P-4118)
AEMETIS ADVNCED FELS KEYES INC
4209 Jessup Rd, Ceres (95307-9604)
P.O. Box 879, Keyes (95328-0879)
PHONE...................209 632-4511
Eric McAfee, *CEO*
Andy Foster, *COO*
Todd Waltz, *CFO*
Lydia Beebe, *Bd of Directors*
Adam McAfee, *VP Finance*
EMP: 47 **EST:** 2009
SALES (est): 29.7MM **Publicly Held**
WEB: www.aemetis.com
SIC: 2869 Ethyl alcohol, ethanol
PA: Aemetis, Inc.
20400 Stevns Crk Blvd # 700
Cupertino CA 95014

(P-4119)
AMERICAN BIODIESEL INC
Also Called: Community Fuels
809 Snedeker Ave Ste C, Stockton (95203-4923)
PHONE...................209 466-4823
Chris Young, *Principal*
Patrick Samson, *Manager*
EMP: 17
SALES (corp-wide): 8.6MM **Privately Held**
WEB: www.communityfuels.com
SIC: 2869 Fuels
PA: American Biodiesel, Inc.
809c Snedeker Ave
Stockton CA 95203
760 942-9306

(P-4120)
AMYRIS INC (PA)
5885 Hollis St Ste 100, Emeryville (94608-2405)
PHONE...................510 450-0761
John Melo, *President*
Geoffrey Duyk, *Ch of Bd*
Eduardo Alvarez, *COO*
Han Kieftenbeld, *Officer*
Jim Iacoponi, *Vice Pres*
◆ **EMP:** 504 **EST:** 2003
SQ FT: 136,000
SALES (est): 173.1MM **Publicly Held**
WEB: www.amyris.com
SIC: 2869 Industrial organic chemicals

(P-4121)
BASF VENTURE CAPITAL AMER INC
46820 Fremont Blvd, Fremont (94538-6571)
PHONE...................510 445-6140
Hans Ulrich Engel, *President*
Sanjeev Gandhi,
Wayne T Smith,
EMP: 26 **EST:** 2003
SALES (est): 6.1MM
SALES (corp-wide): 69.9B **Privately Held**
WEB: www.basf.com
SIC: 2869 Industrial organic chemicals
HQ: Basfin Corporation
100 Park Ave
Florham Park NJ 07932
973 245-6000

(P-4122)
BEARS FOR HUMANITY INC
Also Called: Futurama
841 Ocean View Ave, San Mateo (94401-3139)
PHONE...................866 325-1668
Renju Prathap, *President*
EMP: 50 **EST:** 2016
SQ FT: 10,000
SALES (est): 6.4MM **Privately Held**
WEB: www.bearsforhumanity.com
SIC: 2869 Industrial organic chemicals

(P-4123)
CALYSTA INC (PA)
1900 Alameda De Las Pulga, San Mateo (94403-1295)
PHONE...................650 492-6880
Alan Shaw, *CEO*
Keysha Bailey, *CFO*
Ted Hull, *CFO*
Lynsey Wenger, *CFO*
Craig Barratt, *Vice Pres*
EMP: 19 **EST:** 2011
SALES (est): 6.8MM **Privately Held**
WEB: www.calystaenergy.com
SIC: 2869 Industrial organic chemicals

(P-4124)
JSR MICRO INC (HQ)
Also Called: Materials Innovation
1280 N Mathilda Ave, Sunnyvale (94089-1213)
PHONE...................408 543-8800
Eric R Johnson, *President*
Hitoshi Inoue, *Treasurer*
Eiichi Kobayashi, *Treasurer*
Andy Cohen, *Vice Pres*
Isao Katayama, *Vice Pres*
◆ **EMP:** 140 **EST:** 1990
SQ FT: 12,125
SALES (est): 98.9MM **Privately Held**
WEB: www.jsrmicro.com
SIC: 2869 2899 Industrial organic chemicals; chemical preparations

(P-4125)
MOLECULE LABS INC
524 Stone Rd Ste A, Benicia (94510-1169)
PHONE...................925 473-8200
Michael Guasch, *CEO*
Paul Wold, *Director*
Nestor Vargas, *Manager*
EMP: 50 **EST:** 2006
SALES (est): 7.4MM **Privately Held**
WEB: www.moleculelabs.com
SIC: 2869 Laboratory chemicals, organic

(P-4126)
NEXSTEPPE SEEDS INC
400 E Jamie Ct Ste 202, South San Francisco (94080-6230)
PHONE...................650 887-5700
EMP: 35 **EST:** 2013
SALES (est): 3.4MM **Privately Held**
SIC: 2869 Mfg Industrial Organic Chemicals

(P-4127)
OAKBIO INC
Also Called: Novonutrients
1292 Anvilwood Ct, Sunnyvale (94089-2200)
PHONE...................888 591-9413
Rusell J Howard, *CEO*
Brian Sefton, *President*
Pierre Pujoi, *CFO*
Chris Oakes, *VP Business*
Kumiko Yoshinari, *VP Finance*
EMP: 17 **EST:** 2010
SQ FT: 3,000
SALES (est): 2.5MM **Privately Held**
WEB: www.oakbio.com
SIC: 2869 5172 2821 8731 Industrial organic chemicals; engine fuels & oils; thermoplastic materials; biological research; biotechnical research, commercial

2873 Nitrogenous Fertilizers

(P-4128)
AGRI TECHNOVATION INC
516 Villa Ave, Clovis (93612-7605)
PHONE...................559 931-3332
Dirk Cornelis Barnard, *Director*
Ian Bay, *Sales Staff*
EMP: 200 **EST:** 2018
SALES (est): 12.4MM **Privately Held**
WEB: www.agritechnovation.com
SIC: 2873 Plant foods, mixed: from plants making nitrog. fertilizers

(P-4129)
BOYER INC
105 Thompson Rd, Watsonville (95076-8658)
P.O. Box 82 (95077-0082)
PHONE...................831 724-0123
Fred Willoughby, *CEO*
▲ **EMP:** 22 **EST:** 1925
SALES (est): 4.3MM
SALES (corp-wide): 4.9MM **Privately Held**
WEB: www.boyerfertilizer.com
SIC: 2873 2874 Nitrogenous fertilizers; phosphatic fertilizers

PRODUCTS & SERVICES SECTION

2892 - Explosives County (P-4153)

PA: Willoughby Farms, Inc.
261 Coward Rd
Watsonville CA
831 722-7763

(P-4130)
DR EARTH INC
4021 Devon Ct, Vacaville (95688-8730)
P.O. Box 460, Winters (95694-0460)
PHONE.....................707 448-4676
Milad Shammas, CEO
Ray Sidey, President
Debra White, COO
Joseph Gallo, Vice Pres
Tyler Vinyard, Vice Pres
▲ EMP: 15 EST: 1992
SQ FT: 958,320
SALES (est): 3.5MM Privately Held
WEB: www.drearth.com
SIC: 2873 5191 Fertilizers: natural (organic), except compost; fertilizer & fertilizer materials

(P-4131)
HAWTHORNE HYDROPONICS LLC
2877 Giffen Ave, Santa Rosa (95407-5064)
PHONE.....................800 221-1760
Chris Hagedorn, Mng Member
EMP: 23
SALES (corp-wide): 4.1B Publicly Held
SIC: 2873 Fertilizers: natural (organic), except compost
HQ: Hawthorne Hydroponics Llc
14111 Scottslawn Rd
Marysville OH 43040
888 478-6544

(P-4132)
HYPONEX CORPORATION
Also Called: Scotts- Hyponex
23390 E Flood Rd, Linden (95236-9488)
P.O. Box 479 (95236-0479)
PHONE.....................209 887-3845
Aaron Teach, Manager
EMP: 45
SALES (corp-wide): 4.1B Publicly Held
WEB: www.scotts.com
SIC: 2873 Plant foods, mixed: from plants making nitrog. fertilizers
HQ: Hyponex Corporation
14111 Scottslawn Rd
Marysville OH 43040
937 644-0011

(P-4133)
KELLOGG SUPPLY INC
Also Called: Kellogg Garden Product
12686 Locke Rd, Lockeford (95237-9701)
PHONE.....................209 727-3130
Clayton De Bie, Principal
Todd Yeager, Opers Staff
Jeff Beck, Manager
Kerri Gardner, Manager
Jose Vargas, Supervisor
EMP: 35
SALES (corp-wide): 80MM Privately Held
WEB: www.kelloggarden.com
SIC: 2873 5191 2875 Nitrogenous fertilizers; fertilizer & fertilizer materials; fertilizers, mixing only
PA: Kellogg Supply, Inc.
350 W Sepulveda Blvd
Carson CA 90745
310 830-2200

(P-4134)
MINERAL KING MINERALS INC (PA)
7600 N Ingram Ave Ste 105, Fresno (93711-5824)
PHONE.....................559 582-9228
EMP: 18
SQ FT: 2,000
SALES (est): 1.5MM Privately Held
SIC: 2873 Fertilizer Manufacturer

(P-4135)
OMEX AGRIFLUIDS INC
1675 Dockery Ave, Selma (93662-9785)
PHONE.....................559 661-6138
David Featherstone, President
Alastair Rubie, Treasurer
S A Dekock, Admin Sec
Chris Gipp, Opers Mgr

Andrew Butler, Sales Mgr
▲ EMP: 18 EST: 1976
SQ FT: 10,000
SALES (est): 3.1MM Privately Held
WEB: www.omex.com
SIC: 2873 Fertilizers: natural (organic), except compost

(P-4136)
UNITED COMPOST & ORGANICS INC
1900 Bendixsen St, Samoa (95564-9526)
PHONE.....................707 443-4369
EMP: 49 Privately Held
SIC: 2873 Nitrogenous fertilizers
PA: United Compost And Organics
8601 N Scottsdale Rd # 309
Scottsdale AZ 85253

2875 Fertilizers, Mixing Only

(P-4137)
BAYLANDS SOIL PROCESSING LLC (PA)
712 Sansome St, San Francisco (94111-1704)
PHONE.....................415 956-4157
Alan Varela,
William Gilmartin III,
EMP: 21 EST: 2009
SALES (est): 661.3K Privately Held
SIC: 2875 3255 2611 Fertilizers, mixing only; clay refractories; pulp mills

(P-4138)
COLD CREEK COMPOST INC
6000 Potter Valley Rd, Ukiah (95482-9260)
PHONE.....................707 485-5966
Martin Mileck, President
Mari Mileck, Admin Sec
Sam Todd, Architect
EMP: 20 EST: 1983
SALES (est): 2.9MM Privately Held
WEB: www.coldcreekcompost.com
SIC: 2875 5261 Compost; fertilizer

(P-4139)
HELENA INDUSTRIES LLC
1075 S Vineland Ave, Kerman (93630-9246)
P.O. Box 305 (93630-0305)
PHONE.....................559 846-5303
Randy Alvarado, Branch Mgr
Paul Grayson, Sales Mgr
EMP: 107 Privately Held
WEB: www.helenaindustries.com
SIC: 5261 2875 Fertilizer; compost
HQ: Helena Industries, Llc
225 Schilling Blvd # 100
Collierville TN 38017

(P-4140)
MALIBU COMPOST LLC (PA)
1442a Walnut St Ste 80, Berkeley (94709-1405)
PHONE.....................800 282-6676
Colum Riley, Mng Member
Randy Ritchie,
EMP: 21 EST: 2009
SALES (est): 2.7MM Privately Held
WEB: www.malibucompost.com
SIC: 2875 Compost

2879 Pesticides & Agricultural Chemicals, NEC

(P-4141)
CENTEN AG LLC
901 Loveridge Rd, Pittsburg (94565-2811)
PHONE.....................925 432-5000
EMP: 19
SALES (corp-wide): 38.5B Publicly Held
SIC: 2879 Agricultural chemicals
HQ: Centen Ag Llc
2030 Dow Ctr
Midland MI 48674
989 636-1000

(P-4142)
CLOROX INTERNATIONAL COMPANY (HQ)
1221 Broadway Fl 13, Oakland (94612-1837)
P.O. Box 24305 (94623-1305)
PHONE.....................510 271-7000
Benno Dorer, Principal
Warwick Every-Burns, President
Larry Peirof, CEO
William F Ausfahl, Vice Pres
Edward A Cutter, Admin Sec
◆ EMP: 75 EST: 1972
SALES (est): 361.3MM
SALES (corp-wide): 7.3B Publicly Held
WEB: www.thecloroxcompany.com
SIC: 2879 2842 Insecticides, agricultural or household; bleaches, household: dry or liquid
PA: The Clorox Company
1221 Broadway Ste 1300
Oakland CA 94612
510 271-7000

(P-4143)
MARRONE BIO INNOVATIONS INC (PA)
1540 Drew Ave, Davis (95618-6320)
PHONE.....................530 750-2800
Kevin Helash, CEO
Robert A Woods, Ch of Bd
Suping Liu Cheung, CFO
Linda V Moore, Ch Credit Ofcr
Keith J Pitts, Senior VP
▲ EMP: 139 EST: 2006
SQ FT: 27,300
SALES (est): 38.3MM Publicly Held
WEB: www.marronebio.com
SIC: 2879 Agricultural chemicals

(P-4144)
NOVARTIS CORPORATION
5300 Chiron Way, Emeryville (94608-2966)
PHONE.....................510 879-9500
EMP: 58
SALES (corp-wide): 53.2B Privately Held
SIC: 2879 0181 2032 2865 Mfg Agricultural Chemcl Ornamental Nursery
HQ: Novartis Corporation
1 S Ridgedale Ave Ste 1 # 1
East Hanover NJ 07936
212 307-1122

(P-4145)
TRICAL INC (PA)
8100 Arroyo Cir, Gilroy (95020-7305)
P.O. Box 1327, Hollister (95024-1327)
PHONE.....................831 637-0195
Dean Storkan, CEO
Brett Jones, CFO
Hank Maze, CFO
Joanne Vargas, Corp Secy
Chuck Edmunds, VP Admin
▲ EMP: 30 EST: 1961
SQ FT: 6,000
SALES (est): 39.5MM Privately Held
WEB: www.trical.com
SIC: 2879 Agricultural chemicals

(P-4146)
TRICAL INC
8770 Hwy 25, Hollister (95023)
PHONE.....................831 637-0195
Dean Storkan, CEO
EMP: 22
SALES (corp-wide): 39.5MM Privately Held
WEB: www.trical.com
SIC: 2879 Agricultural chemicals
PA: Trical, Inc.
8100 Arroyo Cir
Gilroy CA 95020
831 637-0195

(P-4147)
VALENT USA LLC
Also Called: Valent Dublin Laboratories
4600 Norris Canyon Rd, San Ramon (94583-1320)
P.O. Box 5075 (94583-0975)
PHONE.....................925 256-2700
EMP: 20 Privately Held
WEB: www.valent.com
SIC: 2879 Mfg Agricultural Chemicals

HQ: Valent U.S.A. Llc
1600 Riviera Ave Ste 200
Walnut Creek CA 94583
925 256-2700

(P-4148)
YARA NORTH AMERICA INC
3961 Channel Dr, West Sacramento (95691-3431)
PHONE.....................916 375-1109
David Johnson, Manager
EMP: 22
SQ FT: 2,000 Privately Held
WEB: www.yara.us
SIC: 2879 Agricultural chemicals
HQ: Yara North America, Inc
100 N Tampa St Ste 3200
Tampa FL 33602

2891 Adhesives & Sealants

(P-4149)
BONDLINE ELCTRNIC ADHSIVE CORP
777 N Pastoria Ave, Sunnyvale (94085-2918)
PHONE.....................408 830-9200
Erik Olson, CEO
Erik V Olson, President
Neal Olson, CEO
EMP: 70 EST: 1989
SQ FT: 12,000
SALES (est): 5.5MM Privately Held
WEB: www.bondline.net
SIC: 2891 Adhesives

(P-4150)
BOYD CORPORATION (HQ)
5960 Inglewood Dr Ste 115, Pleasanton (94588-8611)
PHONE.....................209 236-1111
Mitchell Aiello, President
Daniel Goodwin, Vice Pres
Damian Wellesley-Winte, Vice Pres
Amanda Turner, Administration
Michael Beliveau, Engineer
EMP: 618 EST: 1934
SALES (est): 570.8MM Privately Held
WEB: www.boydcorp.com
SIC: 2891 Adhesives & sealants

(P-4151)
KWIK BOND POLYMERS LLC
923 Teal Dr Ste A, Benicia (94510-1225)
PHONE.....................866 434-1772
Randy Slezak, President
Sheila Cherry, Regional Mgr
Traci Tessier, Project Mgr
Meghan Wingard, Project Mgr
Daniel Tikusis, Technical Staff
▲ EMP: 20 EST: 2001
SALES (est): 7.7MM Privately Held
WEB: www.kwikbondpolymers.com
SIC: 2891 Adhesives

2892 Explosives

(P-4152)
MP ASSOCIATES INC
Also Called: M P A
6555 Jackson Valley Rd, Ione (95640-9630)
P.O. Box 546 (95640-0546)
PHONE.....................209 274-4715
Thaine Morris, President
David Pier, Treasurer
Joel Baechle, Director
▲ EMP: 170
SQ FT: 3,112
SALES (est): 30.4MM Privately Held
WEB: www.mpassociates.com
SIC: 2892 2899 Explosives; pyrotechnic ammunition: flares, signals, rockets, etc.

(P-4153)
TELEDYNE RISI INC (HQ)
32727 S Corral Hollow Rd, Tracy (95377)
P.O. Box 359 (95378-0359)
PHONE.....................925 456-9700
Al Pichelli, CEO
James Varosh, Marketing Staff
EMP: 21 EST: 1984

SQ FT: 5,000
SALES (est): 22MM
SALES (corp-wide): 3B Publicly Held
WEB: www.teledynedefenseelectronics.com
SIC: 2892 Explosives
PA: Teledyne Technologies Inc
    1049 Camino Dos Rios
    Thousand Oaks CA 91360
    805 373-4545

2893 Printing Ink

(P-4154)
KUPRION INC
4425 Fortran Dr, San Jose (95134-2300)
PHONE.................................650 223-1600
Nicholas Antonopoulos, *CEO*
Alfred Zinn, *President*
EMP: 32 EST: 2016
SALES (est): 3MM Privately Held
WEB: www.kuprioninc.com
SIC: 2893 Printing ink

(P-4155)
WATER INK TECHNOLOGY
Also Called: Actega Wit
2350 S Watney Way Ste G, Fairfield (94533-6738)
PHONE.................................707 426-9420
Roland Gapasen, *Manager*
EMP: 15 EST: 2001
SALES (est): 256.7K Privately Held
SIC: 2893 Printing ink

2899 Chemical Preparations, NEC

(P-4156)
CADE CORPORATION
100 Lewis St, San Jose (95112-5853)
PHONE.................................310 539-2508
Norman Angell, *President*
Rozann Stenshoel, *CFO*
Ken Keeth, *Technical Staff*
Natalie Sanchez, *Purch Agent*
EMP: 61 EST: 1984
SQ FT: 25,000
SALES (est): 8MM Privately Held
SIC: 2899 Waterproofing compounds

(P-4157)
CHEVRON ORONITE COMPANY LLC (DH)
6001 Bollinger Canyon Rd, San Ramon (94583-5737)
PHONE.................................925 842-1000
Desmond King, *President*
Rich Conway, *CFO*
Andrew Busby, *Design Engr*
B A Claar, *Mng Member*
K Endries, *Mng Member*
◆ EMP: 50 EST: 2000
SALES (est): 560.3M
SALES (corp-wide): 94.6B Publicly Held
WEB: www.oronite.com
SIC: 2899 2869 1311 2821 Chemical preparations; industrial organic chemicals; crude petroleum & natural gas; polystyrene resins
HQ: Chevron U.S.A. Inc.
    6001 Bollinger Canyon Rd D1248
    San Ramon CA 94583
    925 842-1000

(P-4158)
COPPER HARBOR COMPANY INC
2300 Davis St, San Leandro (94577-2206)
PHONE.................................510 639-4670
Daniel Walters, *President*
EMP: 16 EST: 1997
SQ FT: 18,000
SALES (est): 2MM Privately Held
WEB: www.ehevk.chdzo.servertrust.com
SIC: 2899 2865 2911 Chemical supplies for foundries; solvent naphtha; solvents

(P-4159)
DURA CHEMICALS INC (PA)
1901 Harrison St Ste 1100, Oakland (94612-3648)
PHONE.................................510 658-1987
Raghu Santhanam, *CEO*
Reena Patel, *Controller*
Rakesh Kalra, *Purchasing*
Jack Jones, *Manager*
Josephine Togia, *Manager*
◆ EMP: 23 EST: 1991
SALES (est): 14.7MM Privately Held
WEB: www.durachem.com
SIC: 2899 Chemical preparations

(P-4160)
GARRATT-CALLAHAN COMPANY (PA)
50 Ingold Rd, Burlingame (94010-2206)
PHONE.................................650 697-5811
Jeffrey L Garratt, *CEO*
Matthew Colvin, *CFO*
Matthew R Garratt, *Exec VP*
Jim Gamlen, *Vice Pres*
Maggie Scott, *Lab Dir*
EMP: 64 EST: 1904
SQ FT: 60,000
SALES (est): 106.7MM Privately Held
WEB: www.g-c.com
SIC: 2899 2911 Water treating compounds; oils, lubricating

(P-4161)
HELIX RE INC (PA)
4055 Happy Valley Rd, Lafayette (94549-2424)
PHONE.................................415 254-2724
James Roche, *CEO*
Mariana Paolucci, *Project Mgr*
EMP: 93 EST: 2017
SALES (est): 3.4MM Privately Held
WEB: www.helixre.com
SIC: 2899 Fluxes: brazing, soldering, galvanizing & welding

(P-4162)
IL HELTH BUTY NATURAL OILS INC
Also Called: Hbno
2644 Hegan Ln, Chico (95928-9572)
PHONE.................................530 358-0222
Josef Demangeat, *CEO*
Hussam Bdour, *Senior Mgr*
EMP: 50 EST: 2013
SALES (est): 22MM Privately Held
WEB: www.essentialnaturaloils.com
SIC: 2899 2836 Essential oils; extracts

(P-4163)
K2 PURE SLUTIONS NOCAL SALT LP
950 Loveridge Rd, Pittsburg (94565-2808)
PHONE.................................925 297-4901
Howard Brodie, *CEO*
David Cynamon, *Chairman*
EMP: 16 EST: 2008
SALES (est): 712.9K Privately Held
WEB: www.k2pure.com
SIC: 2899 Chemical preparations

(P-4164)
MCGRAYEL COMPANY
Also Called: Eascare Products USA
5361 S Villa Ave, Fresno (93725-8903)
P.O. Box 12362 (93777-2362)
PHONE.................................559 299-7660
Marvin J Rezac Jr, *CEO*
Evangelina Serrano, *President*
Todd Wilson, *Treasurer*
Tiffany Rolofson, *General Mgr*
Joseph Mendez, *Mfg Mgr*
EMP: 25 EST: 1978
SQ FT: 10,000
SALES (est): 4.9MM Privately Held
WEB: www.easycarewater.com
SIC: 2899 Water treating compounds

(P-4165)
NUGENERATION TECHNOLOGIES LLC (PA)
Also Called: Nugentec
1155 Park Ave, Emeryville (94608-3631)
P.O. Box 30428, Stockton (95213-0428)
PHONE.................................707 820-4080
Donato Polignone,
Dino Polignone, *Vice Pres*
Bruce Winn, *VP Bus Dvlpt*
Stephen Utschig-Samuels, *Research*
Shoeb Moiyadi, *Business Mgr*
◆ EMP: 17
SQ FT: 11,000
SALES (est): 7.6MM Privately Held
WEB: www.nugentec.com
SIC: 2899 2841 1389 Chemical preparations; soap & other detergents; lease tanks, oil field: erecting, cleaning & repairing; chemically treating wells; oil field services; servicing oil & gas wells

(P-4166)
PACIFIC SCIENTIFIC ENERGETIC (HQ)
3601 Union Rd, Hollister (95023-9635)
PHONE.................................831 637-3731
Gregory Scaven, *President*
John Collins, *CFO*
John Davis, *Vice Pres*
Michael Haley, *Vice Pres*
Kathryn Macdonald, *Vice Pres*
EMP: 300 EST: 1945
SQ FT: 65,000
SALES (est): 200MM
SALES (corp-wide): 4.6B Publicly Held
WEB: www.psemc.com
SIC: 2899 3489 3483 3699 Igniter grains, boron potassium nitrate; projectors: depth charge, grenade, rocket, etc.; arming & fusing devices for missiles; high-energy particle physics equipment; armament, except guns; fuses, safety
PA: Fortive Corporation
    6920 Seaway Blvd
    Everett WA 98203
    425 446-5000

(P-4167)
RICHARD K GOULD INC
Also Called: Sierra Chemical Company
788 Northport Dr, West Sacramento (95691-2145)
PHONE.................................916 371-5943
Robert Gould, *CEO*
Steve Gould, *President*
Karen Silva, *Treasurer*
EMP: 37 EST: 1978
SQ FT: 18,500
SALES (est): 9.8MM Privately Held
WEB: www.sierrachemicalcompany.com
SIC: 2899 5999 Oils & essential oils; cleaning equipment & supplies

(P-4168)
TUMELO INC
420 Tesconi Cir Ste B, Santa Rosa (95401-4681)
PHONE.................................707 523-4411
Scott Maddock, *Principal*
EMP: 25 EST: 2017
SALES (est): 1.4MM Privately Held
SIC: 2899 2841 Oils & essential oils; soap & other detergents

(P-4169)
VULPINE INC
Also Called: Shape Products
1127 57th Ave, Oakland (94621-4427)
PHONE.................................510 534-1186
Dan Daniel, *President*
Tony Weiler, *Vice Pres*
▲ EMP: 42 EST: 1979
SQ FT: 22,000
SALES (est): 2.3MM Privately Held
WEB: www.transene.com
SIC: 2899 5169 Chemical preparations; chemicals & allied products

2911 Petroleum Refining

(P-4170)
CHEVRON CORPORATION (PA)
6001 Bollinger Canyon Rd, San Ramon (94583-5737)
PHONE.................................925 842-1000
Michael K Wirth, *Ch of Bd*
Pierre R Breber, *CFO*
Rhonda J Morris, *Officer*
Joseph C Geagea, *Exec VP*
James W Johnson, *Exec VP*
EMP: 14390 EST: 1926
SALES (est): 94.6B Publicly Held
WEB: www.chevron.com
SIC: 2911 1311 1382 1321 Petroleum refining; crude petroleum production; oil & gas exploration services; natural gas liquids; filling stations, gasoline

(P-4171)
CHEVRON GLOBAL ENERGY INC (HQ)
Also Called: Chevron Global Lubricants
6001 Bollinger Canyon Rd, San Ramon (94583-5737)
P.O. Box 6046 (94583-0746)
PHONE.................................925 842-1000
Jock D McKenzie, *Ch of Bd*
John S Watson, *Ch of Bd*
Richard J Guiltinan, *CFO*
Malcolm J McAuley, *Treasurer*
Pierre R Breber, *Exec VP*
EMP: 100 EST: 1936
SQ FT: 200,000
SALES (est): 706MM
SALES (corp-wide): 94.6B Publicly Held
WEB: www.chevron.com
SIC: 2911 4731 5172 Petroleum refining; freight transportation arrangement; petroleum products
PA: Chevron Corporation
    6001 Bollinger Canyon Rd
    San Ramon CA 94583
    925 842-1000

(P-4172)
CHEVRON USA INC
841 Chevron Way, Richmond (94801-2007)
P.O. Box 4107 (94804-0107)
PHONE.................................510 242-3000
Gary Masada, *Branch Mgr*
Thad Sauvain, *Design Engr Mgr*
Bradlee Petzak, *Project Mgr*
Russell Rosete, *Technology*
Kristin Phillips, *Financial Analy*
EMP: 100
SALES (corp-wide): 94.6B Publicly Held
WEB: www.chevron.com
SIC: 2911 Gasoline blending plants
HQ: Chevron U.S.A. Inc.
    6001 Bollinger Canyon Rd D1248
    San Ramon CA 94583
    925 842-1000

(P-4173)
CHEVRON USA INC
6001 Bollinger Canyon Rd, San Ramon (94583-5737)
P.O. Box 6017 (94583-0717)
PHONE.................................925 842-0855
Kim Smith, *Branch Mgr*
Bruce Lincoln, *Supervisor*
EMP: 100
SALES (corp-wide): 94.6B Publicly Held
WEB: www.chevron.com
SIC: 5541 2911 Filling stations, gasoline; petroleum refining
HQ: Chevron U.S.A. Inc.
    6001 Bollinger Canyon Rd D1248
    San Ramon CA 94583
    925 842-1000

(P-4174)
CLEAIRE ADVANCED EMISSION (PA)
1001 42nd St, Emeryville (94608-3620)
PHONE.................................510 347-6103
Michael J Doherty,
EMP: 34 EST: 2004
SALES (est): 2.8MM Privately Held
SIC: 2911 Diesel fuels

(P-4175)
INTERNATIONAL GROUP INC
102 Cutting Blvd, Richmond (94804-2126)
PHONE.................................510 232-8704
EMP: 108
SALES (corp-wide): 419.3K Privately Held
WEB: www.igiwax.com
SIC: 2911 Paraffin wax
HQ: The International Group Inc
    1007 E Spring St
    Titusville PA 16354
    814 827-4900

PRODUCTS & SERVICES SECTION **3011 - Tires & Inner Tubes County (P-4197)**

(P-4176)
MASTERANK WAX INCORPORATED (PA)
2221 Carion Ct, Pittsburg (94565-4029)
PHONE 925 998-2186
Siu Ling Chan, *CEO*
EMP: 18 **EST:** 2012
SALES (est): 64.8MM **Privately Held**
WEB: www.masterank.com
SIC: 2911 Mineral waxes, natural

(P-4177)
NOVVI LLC (PA)
1600 Harbor Bay Pkwy # 200, Alameda (94502-3035)
PHONE 281 488-0833
Jeffrey Brown, *CEO*
Alan Kominek, *Vice Pres*
Willbe Ho, *Research*
Liwenny Ho, *Engineer*
Rachael Butler, *Production*
EMP: 60 **EST:** 2012
SALES (est): 8.1MM **Privately Held**
WEB: www.novvi.com
SIC: 2911 Oils, lubricating

(P-4178)
REED & GRAHAM INC (PA)
690 Sunol St, San Jose (95126-3751)
P.O. Box 5940 (95150-5940)
PHONE 408 287-1400
Gerald R Graham Jr, *President*
Gerald R Graham Sr, *Ch of Bd*
Gerald Gaham, *Senior VP*
Steven Reed Graham, *Senior VP*
David Smiley, *Vice Pres*
▲ **EMP:** 50 **EST:** 1923
SQ FT: 8,000
SALES (est): 72.3MM **Privately Held**
WEB: www.rginc.com
SIC: 2911 2952 8731 5032 Asphalt or asphaltic materials, made in refineries; road oils; coating compounds, tar; commercial research laboratory; brick, stone & related material

(P-4179)
ROCK ENGINEERED MCHY CO INC
Also Called: Remco
1627 Army Ct Ste 1, Stockton (95206-4100)
PHONE 925 447-0805
Kevin Cadwalader, *President*
Chalin Luizinho, *Marketing Staff*
Lupe Chin, *Sales Staff*
Daniel Ramirez, *Sales Staff*
Mike Starnes, *Sales Staff*
◆ **EMP:** 19 **EST:** 1983
SALES (est): 5.9MM **Privately Held**
WEB: www.remcovsi.com
SIC: 2911 5084 Heavy distillates; crushing machinery & equipment

(P-4180)
SINCLAIR COMPANIES
5792 N Palm Ave, Fresno (93704-1844)
PHONE 559 997-3617
EMP: 70
SALES (corp-wide): 4.4B **Privately Held**
WEB: www.sinclairoil.com
SIC: 2911 Petroleum refining
PA: The Sinclair Companies
550 E South Temple
Salt Lake City UT 84102
801 524-2700

(P-4181)
SINCLAIR COMPANIES
1703 W Olive Ave, Fresno (93728-2617)
PHONE 559 351-1916
EMP: 70
SALES (corp-wide): 4.4B **Privately Held**
WEB: www.sinclairoil.com
SIC: 2911 Petroleum refining
PA: The Sinclair Companies
550 E South Temple
Salt Lake City UT 84102
801 524-2700

(P-4182)
TEXACO OVERSEAS HOLDINGS INC (DH)
6001 Bollinger Canyon Rd, San Ramon (94583-2324)
PHONE 510 242-5357
John J O'Connor, *President*
Ira D Hall, *Treasurer*
Glen F Tilton, *Senior VP*
William M Wicker, *Senior VP*
Michael H Rudy, *Admin Sec*
▼ **EMP:** 15 **EST:** 1984
SALES (est): 41.1MM
SALES (corp-wide): 94.6B **Publicly Held**
WEB: www.texaco.com
SIC: 5541 2911 Filling stations, gasoline; petroleum refining
HQ: Texaco Inc.
6001 Bollinger Canyon Rd
San Ramon CA 94583
925 842-1000

(P-4183)
TURLOCK PETROLEUM INC
2219 Lander Ave, Turlock (95380-6230)
PHONE 209 634-8432
Prabhjot Singh, *CEO*
Nirmal Singh, *Administration*
EMP: 17 **EST:** 2010
SALES (est): 2.8MM **Privately Held**
SIC: 2911 Fractionation products of crude petroleum, hydrocarbons

(P-4184)
VALERO ENERGY CORPORATION
3400 E 2nd St, Benicia (94510-1005)
PHONE 707 745-7011
Don Wilson, *Manager*
David Thackrey, *Planning*
Mathew Troncao, *Planning*
Ben Lafountain, *Engineer*
Ray Quain, *Human Resources*
EMP: 450
SALES (corp-wide): 64.9B **Publicly Held**
WEB: www.valero.com
SIC: 5541 2911 Filling stations, gasoline; gasoline
PA: Valero Energy Corporation
1 Valero Way
San Antonio TX 78249
210 345-2000

(P-4185)
VALERO REF COMPANY-CALIFORNIA
3400 E 2nd St, Benicia (94510-1005)
PHONE 707 745-7011
Dough Comeau, *Branch Mgr*
Seymour Battle, *Vice Pres*
Dora Bazan, *Vice Pres*
John Locke, *Vice Pres*
Martin Parrish, *Vice Pres*
EMP: 1194
SALES (corp-wide): 64.9B **Publicly Held**
WEB: www.valero.com
SIC: 2911 Petroleum refining
HQ: Valero Refining Company-California
1 Valero Way
San Antonio TX 78249
210 345-2000

2951 Paving Mixtures & Blocks

(P-4186)
AJW CONSTRUCTION
966 81st Ave, Oakland (94621-2512)
PHONE 510 568-2300
Ed Webster, *Principal*
Alfonso Quintor, *Principal*
Juan Quintor, *Principal*
EMP: 42 **EST:** 1996
SALES (est): 6.3MM **Privately Held**
WEB: www.brooksconsultingservices.com
SIC: 2951 Asphalt paving mixtures & blocks

(P-4187)
GRANITE ROCK CO
365 Blomquist St, Redwood City (94063-2701)
PHONE 650 482-3800
Rich Sacher, *Manager*
EMP: 28
SQ FT: 2,500
SALES (corp-wide): 390.3MM **Privately Held**
WEB: www.graniterock.com
SIC: 2951 2992 5032 Asphalt & asphaltic paving mixtures (not from refineries); lubricating oils & greases; brick, stone & related material
PA: Granite Rock Co.
350 Technology Dr
Watsonville CA 95076
831 768-2000

(P-4188)
MAXIM EQUIPMENT INC
339 Doak Blvd, Ripon (95366-2659)
P.O. Box 630 (95366-0630)
PHONE 209 649-7225
Robert Charles Evans, *President*
EMP: 18 **EST:** 2008
SALES (est): 2.8MM **Privately Held**
WEB: www.maximequipment.com
SIC: 2951 Asphalt paving mixtures & blocks

(P-4189)
REED & GRAHAM INC
26 Light Sky Ct, Sacramento (95828-1016)
PHONE 888 381-0800
Bruce Adams, *Branch Mgr*
Johnny Perez, *Plant Mgr*
EMP: 44
SALES (corp-wide): 72.3MM **Privately Held**
WEB: www.rginc.com
SIC: 2951 Paving mixtures
PA: Reed & Graham, Inc.
690 Sunol St
San Jose CA 95126
408 287-1400

(P-4190)
SAN RAFAEL ROCK QUARRY INC
Also Called: Dutra Materials
961 Western Dr, Richmond (94801-3756)
PHONE 510 970-7700
Erin Johnson, *Manager*
EMP: 36
SALES (corp-wide): 191.6MM **Privately Held**
WEB: www.sanrafaelrockquarry.com
SIC: 2951 Asphalt paving mixtures & blocks
HQ: San Rafael Rock Quarry, Inc.
2350 Kerner Blvd Ste 200
San Rafael CA 94901

2952 Asphalt Felts & Coatings

(P-4191)
MBTECHNOLOGY
188 S Teilman Ave, Fresno (93706-1334)
PHONE 559 233-2181
Bahman Behbehani, *President*
Denise Jaqua, *CFO*
Charlotte Behbehani, *Exec VP*
Rostam Felfeli, *Vice Pres*
Koriney Kgolane, *Exec Dir*
◆ **EMP:** 31 **EST:** 1981
SQ FT: 54,000
SALES (est): 8.2MM **Privately Held**
WEB: www.mbtechnology.com
SIC: 2952 Roofing materials

(P-4192)
MIDWESTERN PIPELINE SVCS INC (PA)
160 Klamath Ct, American Canyon (94503-9700)
PHONE 707 557-6633
T Michael Harrison, *President*
John L Poyas, *Senior VP*
Stan Brady, *Vice Pres*
Chris M Harrison, *Vice Pres*
Michael T Wilhite, *Vice Pres*
EMP: 15 **EST:** 1940
SQ FT: 20,000
SALES (est): 2.3MM **Privately Held**
SIC: 2952 1799 Asphalt felts & coatings; welding on site

(P-4193)
RGM PRODUCTS INC
Also Called: Ridgeline
3301 Navone Rd, Stockton (95215-9312)
PHONE 559 499-2222
Clay Crum, *President*
Gus Freshwater, *Exec VP*
▲ **EMP:** 426 **EST:** 1993
SALES (est): 16MM
SALES (corp-wide): 4.4B **Privately Held**
SIC: 2952 Asphalt felts & coatings
HQ: Elk Premium Building Products, Inc
14911 Quorum Dr Ste 600
Dallas TX 75254

2992 Lubricating Oils & Greases

(P-4194)
INTERNTNAL PTRO PDTS ADDTVES I
Also Called: Ipac
7600 Dublin Blvd Ste 240, Dublin (94568-2908)
PHONE 925 556-5530
Brian Cereghino, *CEO*
Gordon Dillaman, *Manager*
▲ **EMP:** 17 **EST:** 1999
SQ FT: 7,500
SALES (est): 6.2MM **Privately Held**
WEB: www.ipac-inc.com
SIC: 2992 5172 Lubricating oils & greases; petroleum products

(P-4195)
IPAC INC
7600 Dublin Blvd Ste 240, Dublin (94568-2908)
PHONE 925 556-5530
Brian Cereghino, *President*
Neil Olsen, *Project Mgr*
Jeff Melendez, *Sales Staff*
EMP: 18 **EST:** 2011
SALES (est): 4.4MM **Privately Held**
WEB: www.ipac-inc.com
SIC: 2992 Lubricating oils & greases

(P-4196)
PHILLIPS 66 SPECTRUM CORP
Also Called: Red Line Synthetic Oil
6100 Egret Ct, Benicia (94510-1269)
PHONE 707 745-6100
Ann M Oglesby, *Principal*
Marcie Johnson, *CIO*
Michael Andrew, *Opers Staff*
Timothy Decesaro, *Sales Staff*
Roy Howell, *Manager*
EMP: 58
SALES (corp-wide): 131.2MM **Privately Held**
WEB: www.phillips66.com
SIC: 2992 Lubricating oils; brake fluid (hydraulic): made from purchased materials; transmission fluid: made from purchased materials
PA: Phillips 66 Spectrum Corporation
3010 Briarpark Dr
Houston TX 77042
281 293-6600

3011 Tires & Inner Tubes

(P-4197)
CONTINNTAL INTLLGENT TRNSP SYS
3901 N 1st St, San Jose (95134-1506)
PHONE 408 391-9008
Seval Oza, *Mng Member*
Eileen Riorden, *Executive Asst*
Tammer Zein-El-Abedein, *Administration*
Tejas Desai,
Seval Oz, *Mng Member*
EMP: 33 **EST:** 2014
SALES (est): 8.5MM
SALES (corp-wide): 44.6B **Privately Held**
WEB: www.continental.com
SIC: 3011 Tires & inner tubes

3011 - Tires & Inner Tubes County (P-4198)

PA: Continental Ag
Vahrenwalder Str. 9
Hannover NI 30165
511 938-01

(P-4198)
EAST BAY TIRE CO
4961 Park Rd, Benicia (94510-1190)
PHONE 707 747-5613
Neil Larimer, *Branch Mgr*
EMP: 15
SALES (corp-wide): 110.5MM **Privately Held**
WEB: www.eastbaytire.com
SIC: 3011 5014 Tires & inner tubes; tires & tubes
PA: East Bay Tire Co.
2200 Huntington Dr Unit C
Fairfield CA 94533
707 437-4700

3021 Rubber & Plastic Footwear

(P-4199)
IMPLUS LLC
1610 Dell Ave Ste S, Campbell (95008-6914)
PHONE 408 796-7739
Olivia Colman, *Marketing Staff*
Sean Cope, *Marketing Staff*
EMP: 123
SALES (corp-wide): 300MM **Privately Held**
WEB: www.implus.com
SIC: 3021 Rubber & plastics footwear; protective footwear, rubber or plastic
HQ: Implus, Llc
2001 Tw Alexander Dr
Durham NC 27709
919 544-7900

3052 Rubber & Plastic Hose & Belting

(P-4200)
PRICE RUBBER COMPANY INC
17760 Ideal Pkwy, Manteca (95336-8992)
P.O. Box 100, French Camp (95231-0100)
PHONE 209 239-7478
Donna J Sprouse, *President*
Shurene Rehmke, *Vice Pres*
Christen A Lewis-Griffin, *Admin Sec*
EMP: 30 **EST:** 1977
SQ FT: 15,000
SALES (est): 1.7MM **Privately Held**
WEB: www.pricerubber.net
SIC: 3052 3053 Rubber & plastics hose & beltings; gaskets, packing & sealing devices

3053 Gaskets, Packing & Sealing Devices

(P-4201)
A & D RUBBER PRODUCTS CO INC (PA)
1438 Bourbon St, Stockton (95204-2404)
PHONE 209 941-0100
Dale W Wolford, *President*
Ann Wolford, *CFO*
Katherine Turner, *Admin Asst*
Dale Wolford, *Products*
▲ **EMP:** 26 **EST:** 1991
SQ FT: 20,000
SALES (est): 4.1MM **Privately Held**
WEB: www.adrubber.com
SIC: 3053 5085 2822 5169 Gaskets, packing & sealing devices; industrial supplies; synthetic rubber; synthetic resins; rubber & plastic materials

(P-4202)
LTI FLEXIBLE PRODUCTS INC
Also Called: Boyd
5960 Inglewood Dr Ste 115, Pleasanton (94588-8611)
PHONE 209 491-4797
Mitch Aiello, *CEO*

EMP: 28 **EST:** 1996
SALES (est): 226.1K **Privately Held**
SIC: 3053 Gaskets, packing & sealing devices

(P-4203)
MCMILLAN - HENDRYX INC
Also Called: American Seals West
3924 Starlite Dr Ste B, Ceres (95307-9766)
P.O. Box 1104 (95307-1104)
PHONE 209 538-2300
Gary Hendryx, *President*
EMP: 18 **EST:** 1988
SQ FT: 10,000
SALES (est): 1.3MM **Privately Held**
WEB: www.americansealswest.com
SIC: 3053 Gaskets & sealing devices

(P-4204)
PACIFIC DIE CUT INDUSTRIES
3399 Arden Rd, Hayward (94545-3924)
PHONE 510 732-8103
Mohammed M Behnam, *CEO*
Ronald Tripp, *QC Mgr*
Jei Chang, *Marketing Staff*
Koichi Aizawa, *Manager*
▲ **EMP:** 73 **EST:** 1989
SQ FT: 30,000
SALES (est): 16.2MM **Privately Held**
WEB: www.pacificdiecut.com
SIC: 3053 Gaskets, all materials

(P-4205)
PACIFIC STATES FELT MFG CO INC
23850 Clawiter Rd Ste 20, Hayward (94545-1723)
P.O. Box 5024 (94540-5024)
PHONE 510 783-2357
Walter L Perscheid Jr, *CEO*
Kristin Gudjohnsen, *General Mgr*
Robert Perscheid, *General Mgr*
EMP: 16 **EST:** 1920
SQ FT: 23,000
SALES (est): 2.1MM **Privately Held**
WEB: www.pacificstatesfelt.net
SIC: 3053 5085 Gaskets, all materials; industrial supplies

(P-4206)
ROCKYS GASKET SHOP INC
Also Called: Rgs Industries
445 Laurelwood Rd, Santa Clara (95054-2416)
PHONE 408 980-9190
Heraclio Caballero, *President*
Lisa Southard, *Treasurer*
EMP: 32 **EST:** 1980
SALES (est): 2.5MM **Privately Held**
WEB: www.rgsindustries.com
SIC: 3053 Gaskets, all materials

(P-4207)
TILLEY MANUFACTURING CO INC (PA)
Also Called: Precision Graphics
2734 Spring St, Redwood City (94063-3524)
P.O. Box 5766 (94063-0766)
PHONE 650 365-3598
Owen Conley, *President*
Tommy Conley, *Vice Pres*
Judy Meer, *VP Finance*
Aya Lanzarin, *Prdtn Mgr*
▲ **EMP:** 51 **EST:** 1958
SQ FT: 35,000
SALES (est): 4.9MM **Privately Held**
WEB: www.tilleymfg.com
SIC: 3053 3411 3634 3312 Gaskets, all materials; food containers, metal; beverage cans, metal: except beer; urns, electric: household; tool & die steel & alloys; metal stampings; pressed & blown glass

3061 Molded, Extruded & Lathe-Cut Rubber Mechanical Goods

(P-4208)
DYNATECT RO-LAB INC
8830 W Linne Rd, Tracy (95304-9109)
P.O. Box 450 (95378-0450)
PHONE 262 786-1500

Henry Wright, *General Mgr*
Marina Wright, *Corp Secy*
John Dodge, *Vice Pres*
▲ **EMP:** 50 **EST:** 1971
SQ FT: 65,000
SALES (est): 16.7MM
SALES (corp-wide): 1.2B **Privately Held**
WEB: www.dynatect.com
SIC: 3061 3052 3069 3089 Mechanical rubber goods; rubber & plastics hose & beltings; hard rubber & molded rubber products; plastic hardware & building products
HQ: Dynatect Manufacturing, Inc.
2300 S Calhoun Rd
New Berlin WI 53151
262 786-1500

(P-4209)
PERFORMANCE POLYMER TECH LLC
8801 Washington Blvd # 109, Roseville (95678-6200)
PHONE 916 677-1414
Lonnie Wimberly, *President*
Ken Marshall, *COO*
Paul Parenti, *CFO*
Ian Macauley, *Vice Pres*
Martha Wimberly, *Vice Pres*
EMP: 35 **EST:** 1995
SQ FT: 37,000
SALES (est): 6MM **Privately Held**
WEB: www.pptech.com
SIC: 3061 3069 Mechanical rubber goods; molded rubber products

(P-4210)
WESTLAND TECHNOLOGIES INC
107 S Riverside Dr, Modesto (95354-4004)
PHONE 800 877-7734
John Grizzard, *President*
Jennifer Stanford, *General Mgr*
Yolanda Wiggs, *Exec Sec*
Benjamin Banta, *Director*
Denny Zadra, *Consultant*
EMP: 60 **EST:** 1991
SQ FT: 117,000
SALES (est): 26.8MM **Publicly Held**
WEB: www.westlandtech.com
SIC: 3061 3069 Mechanical rubber goods; flooring, rubber: tile or sheet
PA: Esco Technologies Inc.
9900 Clayton Rd Ste A
Saint Louis MO 63124

3069 Fabricated Rubber Prdts, NEC

(P-4211)
A B BOYD CO (PA)
5960 Inglewood Dr Ste 115, Pleasanton (94588-8611)
PHONE 888 244-6931
Mitchell Aiello, *President*
Eric Struik, *CFO*
Gerardo Sandoval, *Maintence Staff*
▲ **EMP:** 1993 **EST:** 1949
SALES (est): 175.7MM **Privately Held**
WEB: www.boydcorp.com
SIC: 3069 2822 Hard rubber & molded rubber products; rubber automotive products; synthetic rubber

(P-4212)
ALASCO RUBBER & PLASTICS CORP
1250 Enos Ave, Sebastopol (95472-4454)
PHONE 707 823-5270
EMP: 17
SALES (est): 982.2K
SALES (corp-wide): 1.8MM **Privately Held**
SIC: 3069 Mfg Fabricated Rubber Products
PA: Alasco Rubber & Plastic Corp
3432 Roberto Ct
San Luis Obispo CA 93401
805 543-3008

(P-4213)
BURKE INDUSTRIES DELAWARE INC (HQ)
2250 S 10th St, San Jose (95112-4197)
PHONE 408 297-3500
Robert Pitman, *President*
Edward Reginelli, *CFO*
Bob Heathcoate, *Info Tech Mgr*
Dan Garrison, *Technical Mgr*
Bob Pitman, *Technology*
◆ **EMP:** 160 **EST:** 1976
SQ FT: 115,930
SALES (est): 40.8MM
SALES (corp-wide): 686.3MM **Privately Held**
WEB: www.burkeindustries.com
SIC: 3069 2822 2821 3061 Flooring, rubber: tile or sheet; molded rubber products; polyethylene, chlorosulfonated (hypalon); silicone rubbers; plastics materials & resins; silicone resins; mechanical rubber goods
PA: Mannington Mills Inc.
75 Mannington Mills Rd
Salem NJ 08079
856 935-3000

(P-4214)
CRICKET COMPANY LLC
68 Leveroni Ct Ste 200, Novato (94949-5769)
PHONE 415 475-4150
Wayne Clark, *Mng Member*
Michael Chidlowsky, *Purch Mgr*
Jeff Schwartz, *VP Sales*
Christin Bosque, *Marketing Mgr*
▲ **EMP:** 25 **EST:** 2003
SALES (est): 5.7MM **Privately Held**
WEB: www.cricketco.com
SIC: 3069 Capes, vulcanized rubber or rubberized fabric

(P-4215)
GIBBS PLASTIC & RUBBER LLC
Also Called: Mint Grips
3959 Teal Ct, Benicia (94510-1212)
PHONE 707 746-7300
Lee Michels, *Partner*
Waunell Michels, *Accountant*
EMP: 15 **EST:** 1926
SQ FT: 14,000 **Privately Held**
WEB: www.gibbsrubber.com
SIC: 3069 3061 Molded rubber products; mechanical rubber goods

(P-4216)
HOLZ RUBBER COMPANY INC
Also Called: Hr
1129 S Sacramento St, Lodi (95240-5701)
PHONE 209 368-7171
James R Dryburgh, *President*
David Smith, *President*
Ben Tannler, *Vice Pres*
Ruben O 'campo, *CIO*
Alyson Origone, *Asst Controller*
▲ **EMP:** 120 **EST:** 1935
SQ FT: 144,000
SALES (est): 18.7MM **Privately Held**
WEB: www.holzrubber.com
SIC: 3069 3441 3061 Molded rubber products; fabricated structural metal; mechanical rubber goods

(P-4217)
MEDCONX INC
2901 Tasman Dr Ste 211, Santa Clara (95054-1138)
PHONE 408 330-0003
Hal Kent, *President*
William Deihl, *CFO*
Mary Starling, *Sales Staff*
EMP: 55 **EST:** 1996
SALES (est): 4.8MM **Privately Held**
WEB: www.atltechnology.com
SIC: 3069 Medical & laboratory rubber sundries & related products
PA: Atl Technology, Llc
1335 W 1650 N
Springville UT 84663

(P-4218)
MODUS ADVANCED INC
1575 Greenville Rd, Livermore (94550-9713)
PHONE 925 960-8700

▲ = Import ▼ = Export
◆ = Import/Export

PRODUCTS & SERVICES SECTION

3089 - Plastic Prdts County (P-4286)

(P-4263)
BAYVIEW PLASTIC SOLUTIONS INC
43651 S Grimmer Blvd, Fremont (94538-6347)
PHONE.....................510 360-0001
Martin Hernandez, *President*
Laurie Couto, *Vice Pres*
Terri Hernandez, *General Mgr*
EMP: 28 **EST:** 2007
SALES (est) 6.1MM **Privately Held**
WEB: www.bayviewplasticsolutions.com
SIC: 3089 Injection molding of plastics

(P-4264)
CAPTIVE PLASTICS LLC
601 Tesla Dr, Lathrop (95330-9263)
PHONE.....................209 858-9188
Jim Campbell, *Branch Mgr*
Bill Ventresca, *Engineer*
EMP: 82 **Publicly Held**
WEB: www.captiveplastics.com
SIC: 3089 Plastic containers, except foam
HQ: Captive Plastics, Llc
 101 Oakley St
 Evansville IN 47710
 812 424-2904

(P-4265)
CENTRAL CALIFORNIA CONT MFG
Also Called: Synder California Container
800 Commerce Dr, Chowchilla (93610-9395)
P.O. Box 848 (93610-0848)
PHONE.....................559 665-7611
Tom O'Connell, *CEO*
Shelli Humphries, *Controller*
EMP: 31 **EST:** 1989
SQ FT: 2,500
SALES (est): 2.2MM **Privately Held**
WEB: www.snydernet.com
SIC: 3089 Plastic containers, except foam

(P-4266)
CHAWK TECHNOLOGY INTL INC (PA)
31033 Huntwood Ave, Hayward (94544-7007)
PHONE.....................510 330-5299
Jonathan Chang, *CEO*
Dan Echternkamp, *Sales Staff*
▲ **EMP:** 155 **EST:** 2006
SALES (est) 28.9MM **Privately Held**
WEB: www.chawktechnology.com
SIC: 3089 Injection molding of plastics

(P-4267)
CHEMICAL SAFETY TECHNOLOGY INC
Also Called: C S T I
2461 Autumnvale Dr, San Jose (95131-1802)
PHONE.....................408 263-0984
Lincoln Bejan, *President*
Jackie Bejan, *Vice Pres*
Quan Nguyen, *Electrical Engi*
Christopher Bejan, *Production*
EMP: 26 **EST:** 1986
SQ FT: 14,000
SALES (est) 7MM **Privately Held**
WEB: www.kemsafe.com
SIC: 3089 Injection molding of plastics

(P-4268)
CHINA CUSTOM MANUFACTURING LTD
44843 Fremont Blvd, Fremont (94538-6318)
PHONE.....................510 979-1920
George Huang, *President*
Robin Lee, *Vice Pres*
◆ **EMP:** 860 **EST:** 2002
SALES (est) 45.5MM **Privately Held**
WEB: www.pacificbusinessco.com
SIC: 3089 Injection molded finished plastic products; injection molding of plastics

(P-4269)
COLVIN-FRIEDMAN LLC
1311 Commerce St, Petaluma (94954-1426)
PHONE.....................707 769-4488
Mitchell Friedman, *President*
EMP: 25 **EST:** 1949
SQ FT: 10,000
SALES (est) 4.3MM **Privately Held**
WEB: www.colvin-friedman.com
SIC: 3089 5162 3544 Injection molding of plastics; plastics materials; dies, plastics forming

(P-4270)
COMMERCIAL PATTERNS INC
260 Bridgehead Ln, Hayward (94544-6646)
PHONE.....................510 784-1014
Donald Loobey Sr, *President*
Mildred Loobey, *Treasurer*
Don Loobey Jr, *Vice Pres*
Mark Loobey, *Vice Pres*
EMP: 15 **EST:** 1976
SALES (est) 1.2MM **Privately Held**
WEB: www.commpattern.com
SIC: 3089 2821 Molding primary plastic; polyurethane resins

(P-4271)
CROWN MFG CO INC
37625 Sycamore St, Newark (94560-3946)
PHONE.....................510 742-8800
Aziz Shariat, *CEO*
Angie Pham, *Pub Rel Mgr*
▲ **EMP:** 40 **EST:** 1959
SQ FT: 60,000
SALES (est) 5.6MM **Privately Held**
WEB: www.crown-plastics.com
SIC: 3089 Injection molding of plastics

(P-4272)
D & T FIBERGLASS INC
8900 Osage Ave, Sacramento (95828-1124)
P.O. Box 293330 (95829-3330)
PHONE.....................916 383-9012
Donald R Stommel, *CEO*
EMP: 37 **EST:** 1987
SQ FT: 35,000
SALES (est) 8.5MM **Privately Held**
WEB: www.dtfiberglass.com
SIC: 3089 Plastic & fiberglass tanks

(P-4273)
DCO ENVIRONMENTAL & RECYCL LLC
300 Montgomery St Ste 421, San Francisco (94104-1903)
P.O. Box 330562 (94133-0562)
PHONE.....................573 204-3844
Claudine Osipow, *Mng Member*
◆ **EMP:** 16 **EST:** 2007
SALES (est) 16.5MM **Privately Held**
WEB: www.dcointl.com
SIC: 3089 Plastic processing
PA: Dco International Trading Inc.
 300 Montgomery St Ste 421
 San Francisco CA 94104

(P-4274)
DELPHON INDUSTRIES LLC (PA)
Also Called: Touchmark
31398 Huntwood Ave, Hayward (94544-7818)
PHONE.....................510 576-2220
Jeanne Beacham, *Mng Member*
Diana Morgan, *CFO*
Richard Barnes, *CIO*
Eric Kreipe, *CIO*
Margarette Comes, *Technician*
▲ **EMP:** 123 **EST:** 1972
SQ FT: 40,000
SALES: 25.8MM **Privately Held**
WEB: www.delphon.com
SIC: 3089 Injection molding of plastics

(P-4275)
DELTA YIMIN TECHNOLOGIES INC
Also Called: Delta Pacific Products
33170 Central Ave, Union City (94587-2042)
PHONE.....................510 487-4411
Fred Betke, *President*
Edward Van De Krol, *Exec VP*
Yi Wang, *Project Mgr*
Linda Arcaina, *Human Resources*
Leonard Garza, *Prdtn Mgr*
◆ **EMP:** 48 **EST:** 1988
SQ FT: 34,000
SALES (est): 27.1MM
SALES (corp-wide): 170MM **Privately Held**
WEB: www.westfalltechnik.com
SIC: 3089 Injection molded finished plastic products; injection molding of plastics
PA: Westfall Technik, Inc.
 3883 Howard Hughes Pkwy # 590
 Las Vegas NV 89169
 702 829-8681

(P-4276)
DEMTECH SERVICES INC
6414 Capitol Ave, Diamond Springs (95619-9393)
PHONE.....................530 621-3200
Dave McLaury, *President*
Thomas Metzger, *General Mgr*
Jerry Collins, *Controller*
Jeff Loyd, *Purch Agent*
Gus Fauci, *Prdtn Mgr*
▲ **EMP:** 24 **EST:** 1999
SQ FT: 8,000
SALES (est) 6.1MM **Privately Held**
WEB: www.demtech.com
SIC: 3089 Thermoformed finished plastic products

(P-4277)
DEPENDABLE PLAS & PATTERN INC
4900 Fulton Dr, Fairfield (94534-1641)
PHONE.....................707 863-4900
Harry Marquez, *President*
Emil Eger, *Vice Pres*
EMP: 50 **EST:** 1983
SQ FT: 50,000
SALES (est) 10.5MM **Privately Held**
WEB: www.dependableplastics.com
SIC: 3089 Injection molding of plastics

(P-4278)
DESIGN OCTAVES
2701 Research Park Dr, Soquel (95073-2090)
PHONE.....................831 464-8500
Norman Weiss, *CEO*
Dan McCabe, *Vice Pres*
Nancie Newby, *Office Admin*
Eliseo Valencia, *Technology*
EMP: 30 **EST:** 1979
SQ FT: 21,000
SALES (est) 5.6MM **Privately Held**
WEB: www.designoctaves.com
SIC: 3089 3469 Cases, plastic; metal stampings

(P-4279)
EMPIRE WEST INC
Also Called: Empire West Plastics
9270 Graton Rd, Graton (95444-9375)
P.O. Box 511 (95444-0511)
PHONE.....................707 823-1190
Richard F Yonash, *CEO*
Edward J Davis, *President*
Donna Yonash, *Vice Pres*
Liz Faolain, *Project Mgr*
Glenn Kerbein, *Technology*
EMP: 28 **EST:** 1973
SQ FT: 30,000
SALES (est) 4.7MM **Privately Held**
WEB: www.empirewest.com
SIC: 3089 Injection molding of plastics

(P-4280)
ENVIRONMENTAL SAMPLING SUP INC
640 143rd Ave, San Leandro (94578-3304)
PHONE.....................510 465-4988
William Levey, *Branch Mgr*
EMP: 105
SALES (corp-wide): 367.9K **Privately Held**
WEB: www.essvial.com
SIC: 3089 3231 Plastic containers, except foam; products of purchased glass
HQ: Environmental Sampling Supply, Inc.
 4101 Shuffel St Nw
 North Canton OH 44720
 330 497-9396

(P-4281)
FABRICATED EXTRUSION CO LLC (PA)
2331 Hoover Ave, Modesto (95354-3907)
PHONE.....................209 529-9200
Jeffrey S Aichele, *Mng Member*
Allison Aichele, *CFO*
Tom Peot, *Vice Pres*
Jeffrey Aichele, *CTO*
Brian Indelicato, *QA Dir*
EMP: 34 **EST:** 1988
SQ FT: 36,000
SALES (est) 10.2MM **Privately Held**
WEB: www.fabexco.com
SIC: 3089 Injection molding of plastics

(P-4282)
FORTUNE BRANDS WINDOWS INC
Also Called: Simonton Windows
2019 E Monte Vista Ave, Vacaville (95688-3100)
PHONE.....................707 446-7600
Tom Riseili, *General Mgr*
James Candelario, *Technician*
Colvin Heeren, *Technician*
Eric Lozier, *Engineer*
Tina Jenkins, *Analyst*
EMP: 129
SALES (corp-wide): 4.6B **Publicly Held**
SIC: 3089 3442 Window frames & sash, plastic; sash, door or window: metal
HQ: Fortune Brands Windows, Inc
 3948 Townsfair Way # 200
 Columbus OH 43219
 614 532-3500

(P-4283)
FRESNO PRECISION PLASTICS INC
8456 Carbide Ct, Sacramento (95828-5609)
PHONE.....................916 689-5284
David Frericks, *Manager*
EMP: 58
SALES (corp-wide): 12.7MM **Privately Held**
WEB: www.precisionplasticsinc.com
SIC: 3089 Injection molding of plastics
PA: Fresno Precision Plastics, Inc.
 998 N Temperance Ave
 Clovis CA 93611
 559 323-9595

(P-4284)
GLOVEFIT INTERNATIONAL CORP
4705 N Sonora Ave Ste 108, Fresno (93722-3947)
PHONE.....................559 243-1110
Bill Burgess, *Vice Pres*
▲ **EMP:** 17 **EST:** 1997
SQ FT: 10,000
SALES (est) 686.8K **Privately Held**
WEB: www.glovefit.com
SIC: 3089 Work gloves, plastic

(P-4285)
GOLDEN PLASTICS CORPORATION
8465 Baldwin St, Oakland (94621-1924)
PHONE.....................510 569-6465
Ron Pardee, *President*
Stewart Pardee, *President*
Ruth Pardee, *Corp Secy*
Daniel K Pardee, *Vice Pres*
Ronald S Pardee, *Vice Pres*
▲ **EMP:** 32 **EST:** 1945
SQ FT: 9,500
SALES (est) 1.6MM **Privately Held**
WEB: www.goldenplasticscorp.com
SIC: 3089 Plastic hardware & building products; ducting, plastic; plastic processing

(P-4286)
GREENWASTE RECOVERY INC
610 E Gish Rd, San Jose (95112-2707)
PHONE.....................408 283-4800
Richard Anthony Cristina, *Branch Mgr*
Tracy Adams, *Officer*
Emily Hanson, *Officer*
Murray Hall, *Vice Pres*
Adolfo Aldana, *Administration*
EMP: 21 **Privately Held**

3089 - Plastic Prdts County (P-4287)

WEB: www.greenwaste.com
SIC: 3089 Garbage containers, plastic
PA: Greenwaste Recovery, Inc.
1500 Berger Dr
Watsonville CA 95077

(P-4287)
H N LOCKWOOD INC
880 Sweeney Ave, Redwood City (94063-3024)
PHONE.................650 366-9557
Daniel A Lockwood, *President*
Dan Lockwood, *Vice Pres*
Raoul Jeanneret, *Office Mgr*
Maggie Moreno, *Office Mgr*
EMP: 21 EST: 1972
SQ FT: 1,030
SALES (est): 4.1MM **Privately Held**
WEB: www.hnlockwood.com
SIC: 3089 2759 Plastic processing; commercial printing

(P-4288)
HENRY PLASTIC MOLDING INC
Also Called: Hpmi
41703 Albrae St, Fremont (94538-3120)
PHONE.................510 490-7993
Edwin Henry, *CEO*
Edwin L Henry Sr, *Shareholder*
Helen Henry, *Corp Secy*
Linda Henry, *Vice Pres*
Don Kattenhorn, *Engineer*
▲ EMP: 165 EST: 1972
SQ FT: 45,000
SALES (est): 17.8MM **Privately Held**
WEB: www.ksplastic.com
SIC: 3089 Injection molding of plastics

(P-4289)
HUMANGEAR INC
2962 Fillmore St, San Francisco (94123-4024)
PHONE.................415 580-7553
Chris Miksovsky, *President*
Scott Cook, *Design Engr*
Jordan Hurder, *Opers Staff*
▲ EMP: 15 EST: 2009
SALES (est): 2.6MM **Privately Held**
WEB: www.humangear.com
SIC: 3089 Tubs, plastic (containers)

(P-4290)
INNOVATIVE MOLDING (HQ)
1200 Valley House Dr # 100, Rohnert Park (94928-4902)
PHONE.................707 238-9250
Grahame W Reid, *CEO*
Lynn Brooks, *CEO*
Alan Williams, *CFO*
Robert T Stenson, *Corp Secy*
Rodger Moody, *Vice Pres*
EMP: 65 EST: 1982
SQ FT: 27,000
SALES (est): 18.3MM
SALES (corp-wide): 769.9MM **Publicly Held**
WEB: www.trimascorp.com
SIC: 3089 Injection molding of plastics
PA: Trimas Corporation
38505 Woodward Ave # 200
Bloomfield Hills MI 48304
248 631-5450

(P-4291)
INNOVTIVE RTTIONAL MOLDING INC
Also Called: IRM
2300 W Pecan Ave, Madera (93637-5056)
PHONE.................559 673-4764
Daniel Humphries, *President*
Shellie Humphries, *Vice Pres*
EMP: 35 EST: 2007
SALES (est): 4.6MM **Privately Held**
WEB: www.irm-corp.com
SIC: 3089 Injection molding of plastics

(P-4292)
ITOUCHLESS HOUSEWARES PDTS INC
777 Mariners Island Blvd, San Mateo (94404-5008)
PHONE.................650 578-0578
Fong Chan, *President*
Vivian Jin, *Analyst*
Winnie Lei, *Analyst*

Michael Shek, *Marketing Staff*
Curtis Stimson, *Marketing Staff*
◆ EMP: 50 EST: 1994
SALES (est): 6.2MM **Privately Held**
WEB: www.itouchless.com
SIC: 3089 Plastic kitchenware, tableware & houseware

(P-4293)
JUNOPACIFIC INC
2840 Res Pk Dr Ste 160, Soquel (95073)
PHONE.................831 462-1141
Jeff Wollerman, *Manager*
Jeff Reeves, *Program Mgr*
Shiqin Chen, *Project Mgr*
Mark Wollschlager, *Project Mgr*
Jim Biggs, *Engineer*
EMP: 150
SALES (corp-wide): 596.9MM **Privately Held**
WEB: www.junopacific.com
SIC: 3089 Injection molding of plastics
HQ: Junopacific, Inc.
1040 Lund Blvd
Anoka MN 55303
763 703-5000

(P-4294)
KENNERLEY-SPRATLING INC (PA)
2116 Farallon Dr, San Leandro (94577-6604)
PHONE.................510 351-8230
Richard Spratling, *CEO*
Bill Roure, *CFO*
Paul Hoefler, *Principal*
Tom Bridgeman, *General Mgr*
Nathan Chandler, *CIO*
▲ EMP: 250
SQ FT: 60,000
SALES (est): 148.7MM **Privately Held**
WEB: www.ksplastic.com
SIC: 3089 3082 Injection molding of plastics; unsupported plastics profile shapes

(P-4295)
KENNERLEY-SPRATLING INC
Also Called: M O S Plastics
2308 Zanker Rd, San Jose (95131-1115)
PHONE.................408 944-9407
Douglas Cullum, *Principal*
Youhan Khosravi, *Engineer*
Mike Rawlings, *Engineer*
EMP: 134
SALES (corp-wide): 148.7MM **Privately Held**
WEB: www.ksplastic.com
SIC: 3089 Injection molding of plastics
PA: Kennerley-Spratling, Inc.
2116 Farallon Dr
San Leandro CA 94577
510 351-8230

(P-4296)
KNIGHTSBRIDGE PLASTICS INC
Also Called: K P I
3075 Osgood Ct, Fremont (94539-5612)
PHONE.................510 440-8444
Jean Nagra, *CEO*
Dave Platt, *President*
Dave Terry, *Treasurer*
Sean Tregear, *Vice Pres*
Omar Blancarte, *Production*
▲ EMP: 58 EST: 1995
SQ FT: 19,000
SALES (est): 12.5MM **Privately Held**
WEB: www.kpi.net
SIC: 3089 3423 Injection molding of plastics; hand & edge tools

(P-4297)
LABCON NORTH AMERICA
3700 Lakeville Hwy # 200, Petaluma (94954-7611)
PHONE.................707 766-2100
James A Happ, *President*
Connie Hansen, *CFO*
Mike Ford, *General Mgr*
Lily Remennik, *Administration*
Dan Cuenca, *Technician*
◆ EMP: 200 EST: 1959
SQ FT: 120,000

SALES (est): 55.3MM
SALES (corp-wide): 221.1MM **Privately Held**
WEB: www.labcon.com
SIC: 3089 Injection molding of plastics
PA: Helena Laboratories Corporation
1530 Lindbergh Dr
Beaumont TX 77707
409 842-3714

(P-4298)
MACRO PLASTICS INC (PA)
2250 Huntington Dr, Fairfield (94533-9732)
PHONE.................707 437-1200
Alan Walsh, *CEO*
Steve Moya, *CFO*
Shane Revlett, *IT/INT Sup*
Jonathan Cody, *Controller*
Christine Harris, *Purchasing*
▲ EMP: 40 EST: 1991
SQ FT: 28,000
SALES (est): 37.4MM **Privately Held**
WEB: www.macroplastics.com
SIC: 3089 Injection molding of plastics

(P-4299)
MASTER PLASTICS INCORPORATED
820 Eubanks Dr Ste I, Vacaville (95688-8837)
PHONE.................707 451-3168
Ravi Mirchandani, *Principal*
Frank Ortiz, *QC Mgr*
▲ EMP: 25 EST: 1990
SQ FT: 35,000
SALES (est): 5.7MM **Privately Held**
WEB: www.masterplastics.com
SIC: 3089 Injection molding of plastics

(P-4300)
MCNEAL ENTERPRISES INC
2031 Ringwood Ave, San Jose (95131-1703)
PHONE.................408 922-7290
De Anna McNeal-Mirzadegan, *CEO*
Deanna Godfrey, *Vice Pres*
Robert McNeal, *Admin Sec*
EMP: 100 EST: 1976
SQ FT: 62,000
SALES (est): 15.8MM **Privately Held**
WEB: www.mcnealplasticmachining.com
SIC: 3089 3498 3559 Injection molding of plastics; tube fabricating (contract bending & shaping); semiconductor manufacturing machinery

(P-4301)
MOLDING SOLUTIONS INC
3225 Regional Pkwy, Santa Rosa (95403-8214)
PHONE.................707 575-1218
Barbara F Roberts, *President*
EMP: 61 EST: 1970
SQ FT: 22,000
SALES (est): 5MM **Privately Held**
SIC: 3089 Plastic hardware & building products

(P-4302)
MORGAN HILL PLASTICS INC
8118 Arroyo Cir, Gilroy (95020-7305)
PHONE.................408 842-1322
Chet Hudson, *President*
EMP: 24 EST: 1972
SQ FT: 26,000
SALES (est): 1.2MM **Privately Held**
WEB: www.morganhillplastics.net
SIC: 3089 Injection molding of plastics; plastic processing

(P-4303)
MOSPLASTICS INC
2308 Zanker Rd, San Jose (95131-1115)
PHONE.................408 944-9407
Douglas Cullum, *CEO*
Dan Flamen, *Shareholder*
Tom Howard, *Shareholder*
Werner Schultz, *President*
EMP: 15 EST: 1977
SQ FT: 60,000
SALES (est): 5.8MM
SALES (corp-wide): 148.7MM **Privately Held**
WEB: www.ksplastic.com
SIC: 3089 Injection molding of plastics

PA: Kennerley-Spratling, Inc.
2116 Farallon Dr
San Leandro CA 94577
510 351-8230

(P-4304)
MOTHER LODE PLAS MOLDING INC
Also Called: Central Plastics and Mfg
1905 N Macarthur Dr # 100, Tracy (95376-2845)
PHONE.................209 532-5146
Chand Shyani, *President*
Hiren Patel, *Vice Pres*
▲ EMP: 27 EST: 1972
SQ FT: 30,000
SALES (est): 3.5MM **Privately Held**
WEB: www.centplasticmfg.com
SIC: 3089 2671 Injection molding of plastics; thermoplastic coated paper for packaging

(P-4305)
MTECH INC
Also Called: Blackline Manufacturing
1072 Marauder St Ste 210, Chico (95973-9001)
PHONE.................530 894-5091
Jason Black, *President*
Bernadette Black, *CFO*
Thomas E Black Sr, *Vice Pres*
EMP: 19 EST: 1996
SQ FT: 3,000
SALES (est): 3.2MM **Privately Held**
WEB: www.mtechincorporated.com
SIC: 3089 3569 3552 3523 Injection molding of plastics; firefighting apparatus; printing machinery, textile; sprayers & spraying machines, agricultural

(P-4306)
NEODORA LLC
Also Called: Espe Machine Work / Ver Mfg
1545 Berger Dr, San Jose (95112-2704)
PHONE.................650 283-3319
Madhumathi Rupakukla,
EMP: 20 EST: 2014
SQ FT: 12,000
SALES (est): 3.5MM **Privately Held**
WEB: www.neodorallc.com
SIC: 3089 Injection molding of plastics

(P-4307)
NORTON PACKAGING INC (PA)
Also Called: Norpak
20670 Corsair Blvd, Hayward (94545-1008)
PHONE.................510 786-1922
Scott Norton, *Co-President*
Greg Norton, *Co-President*
Mark Norton, *Vice Pres*
Patrick Lambertson, *Purch Mgr*
Jim Skinner, *Plant Mgr*
◆ EMP: 60 EST: 1901
SQ FT: 7,200
SALES (est): 55.5MM **Privately Held**
WEB: www.nortonpackaging.com
SIC: 3089 Plastic containers, except foam

(P-4308)
P S C MANUFACTURING INC
Also Called: Plastic Service Center
3424 De La Cruz Blvd, Santa Clara (95054-2610)
PHONE.................408 988-5115
Howard Roetken, *President*
Dreena Roetken, *Vice Pres*
EMP: 25 EST: 1974
SQ FT: 26,000
SALES (est): 1.1MM **Privately Held**
SIC: 3089 Injection molding of plastics

(P-4309)
PAN PACIFIC PLASTICS MFG INC
26551 Danti Ct, Hayward (94545-3917)
PHONE.................510 785-6888
Ying Wang, *President*
Robert Lin, *CFO*
Mike Tan, *Vice Pres*
Maurice Wang, *Vice Pres*
Mark Shih, *Purch Mgr*
◆ EMP: 44 EST: 1981
SQ FT: 46,080

PRODUCTS & SERVICES SECTION

3089 - Plastic Prdts County (P-4334)

SALES (est): 6.8MM **Privately Held**
WEB: www.pppmi.com
SIC: 3089 2673 Plastic processing; bags: plastic, laminated & coated

(P-4310)
PARKER PLASTICS INC
12762 Highway 29, Lower Lake (95457-9872)
P.O. Box 459 (95457-0459)
PHONE.................................707 994-6363
▲ EMP: 25
SQ FT: 3,200
SALES (est): 4.1MM **Privately Held**
WEB: www.parkerplastics.com
SIC: 3089 Mfg Thermoformed & Rotational Molded Prdts

(P-4311)
PIONETICS CORPORATION
151 Old County Rd Ste H, San Carlos (94070-6247)
PHONE.................................650 551-0250
Gordon Mitchard, *President*
▲ EMP: 18 EST: 1995
SALES (est): 2.7MM **Privately Held**
WEB: www.linxwater.com
SIC: 3089 Extruded finished plastic products

(P-4312)
PLASTIKON INDUSTRIES (PA)
688 Sandoval Way, Hayward (94544-7129)
PHONE.................................510 400-1010
Fred Soofer, *Ch of Bd*
Fereydoon Soofer, *CEO*
Paul Gutwald, *CFO*
Michele Shaw, *Officer*
Mark Petri, *Vice Pres*
▲ EMP: 418 EST: 1979
SQ FT: 90,000
SALES (est): 151.6MM **Privately Held**
WEB: www.plastikon.com
SIC: 3089 Injection molded finished plastic products; automotive parts, plastic

(P-4313)
PRE/PLASTICS INC
Also Called: Preplastics
12600 Locksley Ln Ste 100, Auburn (95602-2070)
PHONE.................................530 823-1820
Richard L Miller, *CEO*
Linda Miller, *Corp Secy*
Kazumi Edwards, *Accounting Mgr*
Rich Ulmer, *Marketing Staff*
Brian Miller, *Director*
▲ EMP: 30 EST: 1986
SQ FT: 20,000
SALES (est): 10.8MM **Privately Held**
WEB: www.preplastics.com
SIC: 3089 Injection molding of plastics

(P-4314)
RAPID ACCU-FORM INC
3825 Sprig Dr, Benicia (94510-1248)
P.O. Box 699 (94510-0699)
PHONE.................................707 745-1879
George L Brown, *President*
Linda Brown, *Vice Pres*
EMP: 15 EST: 1976
SQ FT: 29,000
SALES (est): 2.8MM **Privately Held**
WEB: www.rapidaccuform.com
SIC: 3089 3545 Plastic processing; tools & accessories for machine tools

(P-4315)
RAPIDWERKS INCORPORATED
1257 Quarry Ln Ste 140, Pleasanton (94566-8483)
PHONE.................................925 417-0124
Scott Herbert, *President*
EMP: 15 EST: 2004
SQ FT: 15,000
SALES (est): 2.5MM **Privately Held**
WEB: www.rapidwerks.com
SIC: 3089 Injection molding of plastics

(P-4316)
RATERMANN MANUFACTURING INC (PA)
Also Called: Rmi
601 Pinnacle Pl, Livermore (94550-9705)
PHONE.................................800 264-7793
George Ratermann, *President*
Doug Griffith, *CFO*
Brent Lockhart, *Vice Pres*
Melissa Adams, *Accounting Mgr*
Mary Ratermann, *Marketing Staff*
◆ EMP: 35 EST: 1995
SQ FT: 20,000
SALES (est): 7.4MM **Privately Held**
WEB: www.rmiorder.com
SIC: 3089 3081 3679 Plastic processing; packing materials, plastic sheet; cryogenic cooling devices for infrared detectors, masers

(P-4317)
REPSCO INC
5300 Claus Rd Ste 3, Modesto (95357-1665)
P.O. Box 2809, Parker CO (80134-1424)
PHONE.................................303 294-0364
Paul Bennett Jr, *President*
John Shedd, *Shareholder*
Bob Flynn, *Vice Pres*
Shawn Byrne, *Sales Staff*
◆ EMP: 25 EST: 1971
SALES (est): 6MM **Privately Held**
WEB: www.repsco.com
SIC: 3089 Injection molding of plastics

(P-4318)
RIMNETICS INC
Also Called: R I M
3445 De La Cruz Blvd, Santa Clara (95054-2110)
PHONE.................................650 969-6590
David L Chew, *President*
Gary Quigley, *Principal*
Siegfried Waaga, *General Mgr*
Marjorie Chew, *Admin Sec*
Al Sanchez, *Production*
EMP: 17 EST: 1985
SQ FT: 20,000
SALES (est): 10MM
SALES (corp-wide): 10.8MM **Privately Held**
WEB: www.rimnetics.com
SIC: 3089 Injection molding of plastics
PA: Minimatics, Inc.
    3445 De La Cruz Blvd
    Santa Clara CA 95054
    650 969-5630

(P-4319)
SCHOLLE IPN PACKAGING INC
2500 Cooper Ave, Merced (95348-4312)
PHONE.................................209 384-3100
Esmeralda Gutierrez, *Human Res Mgr*
EMP: 35
SALES (corp-wide): 279.6MM **Privately Held**
WEB: www.scholleipn.com
SIC: 3089 Plastic processing
HQ: Scholle Ipn Packaging, Inc.
    200 W North Ave
    Northlake IL 60164

(P-4320)
SCIENTIFIC MOLDING CORP LTD
3250 Brickway Blvd, Santa Rosa (95403-8235)
PHONE.................................707 303-3041
EMP: 72
SALES (corp-wide): 601.9MM **Privately Held**
SIC: 3089 Mfg Plastic Products
PA: Scientific Molding Corporation, Ltd.
    330 Smc Dr
    Somerset WI 54025
    715 247-3500

(P-4321)
SCRIBNER ENGINEERING INC
11455 Hydraulics Dr, Rancho Cordova (95742-6870)
PHONE.................................916 638-1515
Richard L Scribner, *President*
Janet Scribner, *Corp Secy*
Linda Beisner, *General Mgr*
EMP: 23 EST: 1985
SQ FT: 30,000
SALES (est): 5.2MM **Privately Held**
WEB: www.scribnerplastics.com
SIC: 3089 Injection molding of plastics

(P-4322)
SCRIBNER PLASTICS
11455 Hydraulics Dr, Rancho Cordova (95742-6870)
PHONE.................................916 638-1515
Rick Scribner, *Owner*
Linda Beisner, *General Mgr*
EMP: 15 EST: 2001
SALES (est): 1.8MM **Privately Held**
WEB: www.scribnerplastics.com
SIC: 3089 Molding primary plastic; injection molding of plastics

(P-4323)
SISTEMA US INC
775 Southpoint Blvd, Petaluma (94954-6870)
P.O. Box 5068, Novato (94948-5068)
PHONE.................................707 773-2200
Simon Kirby, *President*
Peter Carter, *CFO*
Brendan Lindsay, *Managing Dir*
▲ EMP: 30 EST: 2007
SQ FT: 42,500
SALES (est): 3MM **Privately Held**
WEB: www.sistemaplastics.com
SIC: 3089 Plastic kitchenware, tableware & houseware

(P-4324)
SNYDER INDUSTRIES LLC
800 Commerce Dr, Chowchilla (93610-9395)
P.O. Box 848 (93610-0848)
PHONE.................................559 665-7611
Reyes Morales, *CEO*
EMP: 55 **Privately Held**
WEB: www.snydernet.com
SIC: 3089 Pallets, plastic
HQ: Snyder Industries, Llc
    6940 O St Ste 100
    Lincoln NE 68510
    402 467-5221

(P-4325)
SPLAY INC
2116 Farallon Dr, San Leandro (94577-6604)
PHONE.................................510 351-8230
EMP: 16 EST: 2017
SALES (est): 1.4MM **Privately Held**
WEB: www.ksplastic.com
SIC: 3089 Injection molding of plastics

(P-4326)
STACK PLASTICS INC
3525 Haven Ave, Menlo Park (94025-1009)
PHONE.................................650 361-8600
Mark Rackley, *President*
Michael Mendonca, *Vice Pres*
David Diaz, *Engineer*
▲ EMP: 30 EST: 1995
SQ FT: 9,000
SALES (est): 7.2MM **Privately Held**
WEB: www.stackplastics.com
SIC: 3089 Injection molding of plastics

(P-4327)
TRIAD TOOL & ENGINEERING INC
Also Called: Engineered Plastic Division
1750 Rogers Ave, San Jose (95112-1109)
P.O. Box 8168 (95155-8168)
PHONE.................................408 436-8411
William Bartlett, *President*
David C Bartlett, *Vice Pres*
James S Bartlett, *Vice Pres*
Mildred Carvelho, *Admin Sec*
EMP: 28 EST: 1978
SQ FT: 39,960
SALES (est): 3MM **Privately Held**
SIC: 3089 3599 3364 3363 Injection molded finished plastic products; machine shop, jobbing & repair; zinc & zinc-base alloy die-castings; aluminum die-castings

(P-4328)
TRIFORMIX INC
487 Aviation Blvd Ste 100, Santa Rosa (95403-1069)
P.O. Box 2865 (95405-0865)
PHONE.................................707 545-7645
Joseph Michael Adam, *CEO*
Dave Whitney, *President*
▲ EMP: 27 EST: 2000
SQ FT: 15,000
SALES (est): 3.3MM **Privately Held**
SIC: 3089 Injection molding of plastics

(P-4329)
VALLEY DECORATING COMPANY
2829 E Hamilton Ave, Fresno (93721-3208)
PHONE.................................559 495-1100
James Offen, *President*
Sharron Cotton, *Controller*
Rebecca Karmann, *Controller*
Terry Rickards, *Opers Staff*
▼ EMP: 28 EST: 1946
SQ FT: 25,000
SALES (est): 2.5MM **Privately Held**
WEB: www.valleydecorating.com
SIC: 3089 Novelties, plastic

(P-4330)
VIANT MEDICAL LLC
45581 Northport Loop W, Fremont (94538-6462)
PHONE.................................510 657-5800
Bill Tarajos, *Branch Mgr*
Gaynell Mays, *Human Res Mgr*
Robert Mondore, *Opers Staff*
Angeles Torres, *Director*
Sam Amirikia, *Manager*
EMP: 54
SALES (corp-wide): 1.1B **Privately Held**
WEB: www.viantmedical.com
SIC: 3089 Injection molding of plastics
HQ: Viant Medical, Llc
    2 Hampshire St
    Foxborough MA 02035

(P-4331)
VOLEX INC (HQ)
Also Called: Powercords
3110 Coronado Dr, Santa Clara (95054-3205)
PHONE.................................669 444-1740
Christoph Eisenhardt, *CEO*
James Stuart, *President*
Nick Parker, *CFO*
Phil Stevens, *Project Mgr*
Veronica Corral, *Buyer*
▲ EMP: 30 EST: 1979
SQ FT: 10,000
SALES (est): 349.9MM
SALES (corp-wide): 443.3MM **Privately Held**
WEB: www.volex.com
SIC: 3089 Injection molded finished plastic products
PA: Volex Plc
    Unit C1
    Basingstoke HANTS RG24
    203 370-8830

(P-4332)
WILLIAM KREYSLER & ASSOC INC
501 Green Island Rd, American Canyon (94503-9649)
PHONE.................................707 552-3500
William Bartley Kreysler, *CEO*
Pat Sorensen, *Purch Agent*
Jacque Giuffre, *Art Dir*
Joshua Zabel, *Director*
▼ EMP: 26 EST: 1982
SALES (est): 5.2MM **Privately Held**
WEB: www.kreysler.com
SIC: 3089 Panels, building: plastic

(P-4333)
WINDOW HARDWARE SUPPLY
1717 Kirkham St, Oakland (94607-2214)
PHONE.................................510 463-0301
Kevin Kemble, *Principal*
▲ EMP: 16 EST: 2007
SALES (est): 434.1K **Privately Held**
WEB: www.windowhardwaresupply.com
SIC: 3089 Window frames & sash, plastic

(P-4334)
WING INFLATABLES INC (HQ)
Also Called: MTI Adventurewear
1220 5th St, Arcata (95521-6155)
P.O. Box 279 (95518-0279)
PHONE.................................707 826-2887
Andrew Branagh, *CEO*
Mark French, *CFO*
Mark Lougheed, *Vice Pres*

3089 - Plastic Prdts County (P-4335)

Mark Talbert, *Vice Pres*
Michael Dunaway, *Principal*
◆ **EMP:** 106 **EST:** 1990
SQ FT: 80,000
SALES (est): 25MM **Privately Held**
WEB: www.inflatablesolutions.com
SIC: 3089 Plastic boats & other marine equipment; life rafts, nonrigid: plastic

(P-4335)
WREX PRODUCTS INC CHICO
25 Wrex Ct, Chico (95928-7176)
PHONE 530 895-3838
Wrex A Howard, *Ch of Bd*
Jim Barnett, *President*
James Barnett, *CEO*
Dennis Rupp, *Engineer*
Victor Morales, *Controller*
▲ **EMP:** 66
SQ FT: 70,000
SALES (est): 17.5MM **Privately Held**
WEB: www.wrexproducts.com
SIC: 3089 3363 3544 3599 Injection molding of plastics; aluminum die-castings; special dies, tools, jigs & fixtures; machine & other job shop work; sandblasting equipment

(P-4336)
WUNDER-MOLD INC
790 Eubanks Dr, Vacaville (95688-9470)
PHONE 707 448-2349
Richard A Martindale, *CEO*
William Martindale, *Principal*
Calvin Swesey, *General Mgr*
Paramjit Singh, *Manager*
▲ **EMP:** 22 **EST:** 1996
SQ FT: 56,000
SALES (est): 5.7MM **Privately Held**
WEB: www.wundermold.com
SIC: 3089 Injection molding of plastics; injection molded finished plastic products; plastic processing

(P-4337)
XTIME INC
1400 Bridge Pkwy Ste 200, Redwood City (94065-6130)
PHONE 650 508-4300
Neal East, *President*
Jim Doehrman, *CFO*
Dennis Zwaschka, *Surgery Dir*
Marjorie Cristobal, *Administration*
Leigh Hayes, *Administration*
EMP: 32 **EST:** 1999
SQ FT: 6,000
SALES (est): 13.9MM
SALES (corp-wide): 1.6MM **Privately Held**
WEB: www.xtime.com
SIC: 3089 Automotive parts, plastic
HQ: Ccx Automotive, Inc.
3003 Summit Blvd Fl 200
Brookhaven GA 30319
855 449-0010

3111 Leather Tanning & Finishing

(P-4338)
WILDLIFE FUR DRESSING INC
3415 Harold St, Ceres (95307-3614)
PHONE 209 538-2901
Armando Navas, *President*
▲ **EMP:** 17 **EST:** 1984
SQ FT: 10,000
SALES (est): 1.1MM **Privately Held**
WEB: www.wildlifefurdressing.com
SIC: 3111 Leather tanning & finishing

3131 Boot & Shoe Cut Stock & Findings

(P-4339)
1919 INVESTMENT COUNSEL LLC
49 Stevenson St Ste 1075, San Francisco (94105-2945)
PHONE 415 500-6707
Warwick M Carter, *Managing Dir*
Lawrence Zartarian, *Portfolio Mgr*
Meredith A Mowen, *Director*
EMP: 23
SALES (corp-wide): 3.7B **Publicly Held**
WEB: www.1919ic.com
SIC: 3131 Rands
HQ: 1919 Investment Counsel, Llc
1 South St Ste 2500
Baltimore MD 21202

3143 Men's Footwear, Exc Athletic

(P-4340)
ALLBIRDS INC
730 Montgomery St, San Francisco (94111-2104)
PHONE 628 225-4848
Joseph Zwillinger, *President*
Joe Vernachio, *COO*
Michael Bufano, *CFO*
Timothy Brown, *Co-CEO*
EMP: 546 **EST:** 2015
SQ FT: 6,000
SALES (est): 219.3MM **Privately Held**
WEB: www.allbirds.com
SIC: 3143 3144 Men's footwear, except athletic; women's footwear, except athletic

(P-4341)
LANE INTERNATIONAL TRADING INC (PA)
33155 Transit Ave, Union City (94587-2091)
P.O. Box 2223 (94587-7223)
PHONE 510 489-7364
Lane Shay, *President*
▲ **EMP:** 100 **EST:** 1987
SQ FT: 2,500
SALES (est): 5.6MM **Privately Held**
SIC: 3143 3144 Men's footwear, except athletic; women's footwear, except athletic

(P-4342)
SUNRISE SHS PEDORTHIC SVC CORP
3127 Fite Cir Ste G, Sacramento (95827-1803)
P.O. Box 124, Roseville (95661-0124)
PHONE 916 368-7700
Peter Wong, *President*
CHI Tu, *CFO*
Jay Chen, *Admin Sec*
▲ **EMP:** 18 **EST:** 1986
SQ FT: 10,000
SALES (est): 2.6MM **Privately Held**
WEB: www.sunriseshoes.com
SIC: 5661 3143 3144 3149 Shoes, orthopedic; shoes, custom; men's footwear, except athletic; orthopedic shoes, men's; women's footwear, except athletic; orthopedic shoes, women's; athletic shoes, except rubber or plastic; footwear, custom made; medical services organization

(P-4343)
VIONIC GROUP LLC
Also Called: Orthaheel
4040 Civic Center Dr # 430, San Rafael (94903-4150)
PHONE 415 526-6932
Chris Gallagher, *CEO*
Connie X Rishwain, *President*
Bruce Campbell, *COO*
Steve Furtado, *CFO*
Tom Nelson, *Bd of Directors*
▲ **EMP:** 84 **EST:** 2006
SQ FT: 16,000
SALES (est): 16.2MM
SALES (corp-wide): 2.1B **Publicly Held**
WEB: www.vionicgroup.com
SIC: 3143 3144 3149 Orthopedic shoes, men's; orthopedic shoes, women's; orthopedic shoes, children's
PA: Caleres, Inc.
8300 Maryland Ave
Saint Louis MO 63105
314 854-4000

(P-4344)
VIONIC INTERNATIONAL LLC (HQ)
4040 Civic Center Dr # 430, San Rafael (94903-4150)
PHONE 888 882-7954
Christopher Gallagher, *Mng Member*
EMP: 100 **EST:** 2012
SALES (est): 896.5K
SALES (corp-wide): 2.1B **Publicly Held**
WEB: www.vionicshoes.com
SIC: 3143 3144 3149 Orthopedic shoes, men's; orthopedic shoes, women's; orthopedic shoes, children's
PA: Caleres, Inc.
8300 Maryland Ave
Saint Louis MO 63105
314 854-4000

3149 Footwear, NEC

(P-4345)
FOOT LOCKER RETAIL INC
Also Called: Champs Sports
2059 Newpark Mall Fl 2, Newark (94560-5249)
PHONE 510 797-5750
Arthur Cervantes, *Manager*
EMP: 21 **Publicly Held**
WEB: www.footlocker.com
SIC: 3149 5661 Athletic shoes, except rubber or plastic; footwear, athletic
HQ: Foot Locker Retail, Inc.
330 W 34th St
New York NY 10001
212 720-3700

3161 Luggage

(P-4346)
ACE PRODUCTS ENTERPRISES INC
Also Called: Ace Products Group
3920 Cypress Dr Ste B, Petaluma (94954-7603)
PHONE 707 765-1500
Allen R Poster, *President*
Charlie Kiesser, *Controller*
Jesse Grossmann, *Sales Mgr*
Alex Bailetti, *Marketing Staff*
Leah Murphy, *Marketing Staff*
◆ **EMP:** 23 **EST:** 1984
SALES (est): 3.4MM **Privately Held**
WEB: www.aceproducts.com
SIC: 3161 3931 Musical instrument cases; drums, parts & accessories (musical instruments)

(P-4347)
B & B TRAVELWARE LLC
5700 Stnrdge Mall Rd Ste, Pleasanton (94588)
PHONE 408 564-7569
Kiran Pathak, *Mng Member*
EMP: 15 **EST:** 2014
SALES (est): 2.3MM **Privately Held**
SIC: 3161 Attache cases

(P-4348)
GOYARD MIAMI LLC
Also Called: Maison Goyard
345 Powell St, San Francisco (94102-1804)
PHONE 415 398-1110
Rogelio Ortega, *Branch Mgr*
EMP: 32
SALES (corp-wide): 55.2MM **Privately Held**
WEB: www.catalogue.goyard.us
SIC: 3161 Wardrobe bags (luggage)
HQ: Goyard Miami, Llc
20 E 63rd St
New York NY 10065
212 813-0005

(P-4349)
SPECULATIVE PRODUCT DESIGN LLC (DH)
Also Called: Speck Products
177 Bovet Rd Ste 200, San Mateo (94402-3118)
PHONE 650 462-2040
Robert Hales, *President*
Donald Walden, *CFO*
Eric Shambaugh, *Marketing Staff*
Paul Solis, *Master*
Bill De Dufour, *Director*
▲ **EMP:** 61 **EST:** 2001
SQ FT: 5,000
SALES (est): 49.1MM
SALES (corp-wide): 177.9K **Privately Held**
WEB: www.speckproducts.com
SIC: 3161 Cases, carrying
HQ: Samsonite Llc
575 West St Ste 110
Mansfield MA 02048
508 851-1400

(P-4350)
WALKER/DUNHAM CORP
Also Called: Walker Bags
445 Barneveld Ave, San Francisco (94124-1501)
PHONE 415 821-3070
Eveline Dunham, *President*
Emily Hughes, *Vice Pres*
Marion Dunham, *Asst Sec*
EMP: 20 **EST:** 1978
SQ FT: 10,000
SALES (est): 1.2MM **Privately Held**
WEB: www.walkerbagswholesale.com
SIC: 3161 Cases, carrying

(P-4351)
ZUCA INC
320 S Milpitas Blvd, Milpitas (95035-5421)
PHONE 408 377-9822
Bruce Kinnee, *President*
Meraf Gedlu, *Accounting Mgr*
Shannon Petros, *Accountant*
Tariku Sintayehu, *Accountant*
Marcail Joakimson, *Opers Staff*
◆ **EMP:** 20 **EST:** 2003
SALES (est): 4.2MM **Privately Held**
WEB: www.zuca.com
SIC: 3161 5099 Luggage; luggage

3199 Leather Goods, NEC

(P-4352)
ARIAT INTERNATIONAL INC (PA)
3242 Whipple Rd, Union City (94587-1217)
PHONE 510 477-7000
Elizabeth Cross, *CEO*
Pankaj Gupta, *CFO*
Nahal Namdjoo, *Chairman*
Maria Merino, *Vice Pres*
Brian Mignano, *Vice Pres*
◆ **EMP:** 200 **EST:** 1991
SALES (est): 198.2MM **Privately Held**
WEB: www.ariat.com
SIC: 3199 5139 5137 5136 Equestrian related leather articles; boots, horse; leather garments; footwear; women's & children's clothing; men's & boys' clothing

(P-4353)
OXBASE INC
3500 N Laughlin Rd 100, Santa Rosa (95403-9098)
PHONE 707 824-2560
Darryl G Thurner, *President*
Marc Dewey, *Engineer*
Susan Alberts, *Sales Mgr*
EMP: 48 **EST:** 1980
SALES (est): 9.3MM **Privately Held**
SIC: 3199 Leather garments

(P-4354)
YATES GEAR INC
2608 Hartnell Ave Ste 6, Redding (96002-2347)
PHONE 530 222-4606
John Yates, *President*
Karen Yates, *Vice Pres*
▲ **EMP:** 55 **EST:** 1986
SALES (est): 8.5MM **Privately Held**
WEB: www.yatesgear.com
SIC: 3199 3842 Safety belts, leather; personal safety equipment

PRODUCTS & SERVICES SECTION

3211 Flat Glass

(P-4355)
CARDINAL GLASS INDUSTRIES INC
Also Called: Cardinal Cg Company
680 Industrial Dr, Galt (95632-1598)
PHONE 209 744-8940
Michael Potter, *Manager*
Robyn Wegner, *Vice Pres*
James Stevens, *Executive*
Richard Barnes, *CIO*
Richard Gliha, *Info Tech Mgr*
EMP: 150
SALES (corp-wide): 1B **Privately Held**
WEB: www.cardinalcorp.com
SIC: 3211 Flat glass
PA: Cardinal Glass Industries Inc
775 Pririe Ctr Dr Ste 200
Eden Prairie MN 55344
952 229-2600

(P-4356)
GUARDIAN INDUSTRIES LLC
Also Called: Guardian-Kingsburg
11535 E Mountain View Ave, Kingsburg (93631-9233)
PHONE 559 891-8867
Jeffery Booey, *Manager*
Drew Kirk, *Engineer*
Alvin Perez, *Production*
Mitchell Sanchez, *Production*
Samer Abughazaleh, *Regl Sales Mgr*
EMP: 275
SQ FT: 486,000
SALES (corp-wide): 36.9B **Privately Held**
WEB: www.guardian.com
SIC: 3211 3231 Sheet glass; tempered glass; products of purchased glass
HQ: Guardian Industries, Llc
2300 Harmon Rd
Auburn Hills MI 48326
248 340-1800

(P-4357)
GUARDIAN INDUSTRIES CORP
11535 E Mountain View Ave, Kingsburg (93631-9233)
PHONE 559 891-8867
Fax: 714 525-3529
EMP: 60
SALES (corp-wide): 27.6B **Privately Held**
SIC: 3211 5231 Mfg Flat Glass Ret Paint/Glass/Wallpaper
HQ: Guardian Industries Corp.
2300 Harmon Rd
Auburn Hills MI 48326
248 340-1800

(P-4358)
GUARDIAN INDUSTRIES CORP
11535 E Mountain View Ave, Kingsburg (93631-9233)
PHONE 559 638-3588
EMP: 90
SALES (corp-wide): 27.6B **Privately Held**
SIC: 3211 3231 Mfg Flat Glass Mfg Products-Purchased Glass
HQ: Guardian Industries Corp.
2300 Harmon Rd
Auburn Hills MI 48326
248 340-1800

(P-4359)
HELIOTROPE TECHNOLOGIES INC
850 Marina Village Pkwy # 10, Alameda (94501-1007)
PHONE 510 871-3980
Peter Green, *CEO*
David England, *Consultant*
EMP: 32 EST: 2013
SALES (est): 4.3MM **Privately Held**
WEB: www.heliotropetech.com
SIC: 3211 Insulating glass, sealed units

(P-4360)
I G S INC
Also Called: Industrial Glass Service
916 E California Ave, Sunnyvale (94085-4505)
PHONE 408 733-4621
John R Gracia, *President*
▲ EMP: 23 EST: 1976
SQ FT: 15,000
SALES (est): 3.8MM **Privately Held**
WEB: www.iglobalsol.com
SIC: 3211 Optical glass, flat

(P-4361)
LINOLEUM SALES CO INC (PA)
Also Called: Anderson's Carpet & Linoleum
1000 W Grand Ave, Oakland (94607-2933)
PHONE 510 652-1032
Don Christophe, *CEO*
Tom Christophe, *President*
Bob Mullarkey, *CFO*
Vince Lopez, *Vice Pres*
Andrei Wallace, *Vice Pres*
EMP: 138 EST: 1954
SQ FT: 3,500
SALES (est): 26.6MM **Privately Held**
WEB: www.andersoncf.com
SIC: 3211 5713 Flat glass; floor covering stores

(P-4362)
VIEW INC (PA)
195 S Milpitas Blvd, Milpitas (95035-5425)
PHONE 408 263-9200
RAO Mulpuri, *CEO*
Harold Hughes, *Ch of Bd*
Amy S Reeves, *CFO*
Bill Krause, *Senior VP*
Martin Neumann, *Senior VP*
EMP: 424 EST: 2019
SALES (est): 251.8MM **Privately Held**
SIC: 3211 Flat glass

(P-4363)
VIEW OPERATING CORPORATION (HQ)
Also Called: Soladigm
195 S Milpitas Blvd, Milpitas (95035-5425)
PHONE 408 263-9200
RAO Mulpuri, *CEO*
Martin Neumann, *COO*
Vidul Prakash, *CFO*
Jim Pape, *Ch Credit Ofcr*
Rahul Bammi, *Officer*
▲ EMP: 87 EST: 2007
SALES (est): 247.4MM
SALES (corp-wide): 251.8MM **Privately Held**
WEB: www.view.com
SIC: 3211 Window glass, clear & colored
PA: View, Inc.
195 S Milpitas Blvd
Milpitas CA 95035
408 263-9200

(P-4364)
VITRO FLAT GLASS LLC
Also Called: Fresno Glass Plant
3333 S Peach Ave, Fresno (93725-9220)
P.O. Box 2748 (93745-2748)
PHONE 559 485-4660
Henry Good, *Manager*
EMP: 140 **Privately Held**
WEB: www.vitroglazings.com
SIC: 3211 Window glass, clear & colored
HQ: Vitro Flat Glass Llc
400 Guys Run Rd
Cheswick PA 15024
412 820-8500

(P-4365)
WSGLASS HOLDINGS INC (HQ)
Also Called: Western States Glass
3241 Darby Cmn, Fremont (94539-5601)
P.O. Box 6058 (94538-0658)
PHONE 510 623-5000
Michael A Smith, *President*
Michael S Foss, *Vice Pres*
Donald E Post, *Vice Pres*
Jonathan M Witkin, *Vice Pres*
▲ EMP: 120 EST: 1991
SQ FT: 107,000
SALES (est): 6.6MM **Privately Held**
WEB: www.trulite.com
SIC: 3211 3231 Transparent optical glass, except lenses; insulating glass, sealed units; mirrored glass

3221 Glass Containers

(P-4366)
GALLO GLASS COMPANY (HQ)
605 S Santa Cruz Ave, Modesto (95354-4299)
P.O. Box 1230 (95353-1230)
PHONE 209 341-3710
Robert J Gallo, *President*
Craig Beck, *Info Tech Mgr*
Kevin Grossman, *Project Mgr*
Steve Blattler, *Technical Staff*
Marcos Moreno, *Technical Staff*
▲ EMP: 1000 EST: 1957
SALES (est): 223.9MM
SALES (corp-wide): 2.1B **Privately Held**
WEB: www.galloglass.com
SIC: 3221 Glass containers
PA: E. & J. Gallo Winery
600 Yosemite Blvd
Modesto CA 95354
209 341-3111

(P-4367)
O-I OWENS ILLINOIS INC
3600 Alameda Ave, Oakland (94601-3329)
PHONE 510 436-2000
Steve Springer, *Sales Executive*
Pam Fernandez, *Human Res Mgr*
Lisa Grundhoffer, *Sales Staff*
Boscacci Bill, *Manager*
EMP: 15 EST: 2013
SALES (est): 3.5MM **Privately Held**
SIC: 3221 Glass containers

3229 Pressed & Blown Glassware, NEC

(P-4368)
ALLIANCE FIBER OPTIC PDTS INC
445 Lakeside Dr, Sunnyvale (94085-4704)
PHONE 408 736-6900
Peter C Chang, *Ch of Bd*
Anita K Ho, *CFO*
David A Hubbard, *Exec VP*
▲ EMP: 1576 EST: 1995
SQ FT: 18,088
SALES (est): 215.2MM
SALES (corp-wide): 11.3B **Publicly Held**
WEB: www.corning.com
SIC: 3229 3661 Fiber optics strands; fiber optics communications equipment
PA: Corning Incorporated
1 Riverfront Plz
Corning NY 14831
607 974-9000

(P-4369)
ANNIEGLASS INC (PA)
310 Harvest Dr, Watsonville (95076-5103)
P.O. Box 2610 (95077-2610)
PHONE 831 761-2041
Annie Morhauser, *President*
Kristin Wilsey, *Vice Pres*
Biagio Scarpello, *Prdtn Mgr*
EMP: 19 EST: 1982
SQ FT: 16,000
SALES (est): 3.5MM **Privately Held**
WEB: www.annieglass.com
SIC: 3229 Tableware, glass or glass ceramic

(P-4370)
CLEAREDGE SOLUTIONS INC
1020 Rock Ave, San Jose (95131-1610)
PHONE 408 262-2800
Alan Truong, *CEO*
Nathan Cho, *Controller*
EMP: 30 EST: 2018
SALES (est): 2.8MM **Privately Held**
SIC: 3229 Fiber optics strands

(P-4371)
FARLOWS SCNTFIC GLSSBLWING INC
Also Called: Farlows Scentific Glassblowing
200 Litton Dr Ste 234, Grass Valley (95945-5040)
PHONE 530 477-5513
Carol Conley, *President*
Charolette Farlow, *Vice Pres*
EMP: 23 EST: 1980
SQ FT: 5,250
SALES (est): 1.3MM **Privately Held**
WEB: www.farlowsci.com
SIC: 3229 Scientific glassware

(P-4372)
FUJITSU TECH & BUS AMER INC
1250 E Arques Ave, Sunnyvale (94085-5401)
PHONE 408 746-6000
Hiroshi Haruki, *CEO*
Annie Bogue, *Finance*
Catherine Nice, *Controller*
EMP: 49 EST: 2013
SALES (est): 9.4MM **Privately Held**
WEB: www.fujitsu.com
SIC: 3229 Optical glass
PA: Fujitsu Limited
1-5-2, Higashishimbashi
Minato-Ku TKY 105-0

(P-4373)
LEWIS JOHN GLASS STUDIO
10229 Pearmain St, Oakland (94603-3023)
PHONE 510 635-4607
John C Lewis, *Owner*
Lynn Zboyovsky, *Admin Asst*
EMP: 20 EST: 1969
SQ FT: 17,000
SALES (est): 1.4MM **Privately Held**
WEB: www.johnlewisglass.com
SIC: 3229 5947 Pressed & blown glass; gift, novelty & souvenir shop

(P-4374)
LIFI LABS INC (PA)
Also Called: Lifx
350 Townsend St Ste 830, San Francisco (94107-0009)
PHONE 650 739-5563
Mac Alexander, *CEO*
John Cameron, *Vice Pres*
Kyle Guo, *Vice Pres*
Rachel Wilson, *Director*
EMP: 40 EST: 2012
SALES (est): 382.4K **Privately Held**
WEB: www.lifx.com
SIC: 3229 3641 Bulbs for electric lights; electric light bulbs, complete

(P-4375)
MODERN CERAMICS MFG INC
2240 Lundy Ave, San Jose (95131-1816)
PHONE 408 383-0554
Christina Hoang, *CEO*
Tuan Le, *Purch Agent*
Frank Kramer, *Opers Mgr*
Kevin Ly, *Sales Staff*
▲ EMP: 20 EST: 1999
SQ FT: 3,087
SALES (est): 3MM **Privately Held**
WEB: www.modernceramics.com
SIC: 3229 Tableware, glass or glass ceramic

(P-4376)
NEPTEC OPTICAL SOLUTIONS INC
48603 Warm Springs Blvd, Fremont (94539-7782)
PHONE 510 687-1101
David Cheng, *President*
Eugene Lin, *Vice Pres*
Jianxun Fang, *CTO*
Sylvia Bustamante, *Purch Mgr*
Sharon Lu, *Purch Mgr*
▲ EMP: 25 EST: 2010
SALES (est): 950K **Privately Held**
WEB: www.neptecos.com
SIC: 3229 Pressed & blown glass

(P-4377)
OPTIWORKS INC (PA)
47211 Bayside Pkwy, Fremont (94538-6517)
PHONE 510 438-4560
Roger Liang, *CEO*
Annie Kuo, *Vice Pres*
Steve Kuo, *Vice Pres*
Dennis MA, *Vice Pres*
Elizabeth Rueda, *Engineer*
EMP: 65 EST: 2000

3229 - Pressed & Blown Glassware, NEC County

SALES (est): 13.5MM **Privately Held**
WEB: www.optiworks.com
SIC: 3229 Fiber optics strands

(P-4378)
ORIENT & FLUME ART GLASS
2161 Park Ave, Chico (95928-6702)
P.O. Box 3298 (95927-3298)
PHONE 530 893-0373
Douglas Boyd, *President*
John A Fowell, *CFO*
EMP: 17 EST: 1970
SQ FT: 20,000
SALES (est): 1.1MM **Privately Held**
WEB: www.orientandflume.com
SIC: 3229 8412 Glassware, art or decorative; museums & art galleries

(P-4379)
PLEXUS OPTIX INC
3333 Quality Dr, Rancho Cordova (95670-7985)
PHONE 800 852-7600
Don Oakley, *President*
EMP: 118 EST: 2009
SALES (est): 824.2K
SALES (corp-wide): 34.2MM **Privately Held**
WEB: www.vspoptics.com
SIC: 3229 Optical glass
PA: Vsp Optical Group, Inc.
3333 Quality Dr
Rancho Cordova CA 95670
916 851-4682

(P-4380)
TE CONNECTIVITY MOG INC (HQ)
501 Oakside Ave, Redwood City (94063-3800)
PHONE 650 361-5292
Craig Newell, *Principal*
EMP: 2431 EST: 2014
SALES (est): 617.4MM
SALES (corp-wide): 12.1B **Privately Held**
WEB: www.te.com
SIC: 3229 Fiber optics strands
PA: Te Connectivity Ltd.
Muhlenstrasse 26
Schaffhausen SH 8200
526 336-677

(P-4381)
VITRICO CORP
Also Called: Firelight Glass
2181 Williams St, San Leandro (94577-3224)
PHONE 510 652-6731
Karen Boss, *CEO*
James Maslach, *President*
EMP: 21 EST: 1975
SALES (est): 1.5MM **Privately Held**
WEB: www.firelight.com
SIC: 3229 Glassware, art or decorative; glassware, industrial

(P-4382)
WEST COAST QUARTZ CORPORATION (HQ)
Also Called: WCQ
1000 Corporate Way, Fremont (94539-6105)
PHONE 510 249-2160
Johng Bae, *CEO*
Dave Lopes, *President*
Howard Cho, *COO*
Jun Hyung Kim, *CFO*
Michele Graff, *Controller*
▲ EMP: 97 EST: 1981
SQ FT: 60,000
SALES (est): 32.5MM **Privately Held**
WEB: www.wcq.com
SIC: 3229 3679 3674 5065 Glassware, industrial; quartz crystals, for electronic application; semiconductors & related devices; semiconductor devices

3231 Glass Prdts Made Of Purchased Glass

(P-4383)
ATLAS SPECIALTIES CORPORATION (PA)
Also Called: Atlas Shower Door Co
4337 Astoria St, Sacramento (95838-3001)
PHONE 503 636-8182
Edwin A Lindquist, *President*
Fred Ferri, *CFO*
Roger Lindquist, *Vice Pres*
EMP: 28 EST: 1955
SQ FT: 5,000
SALES (est): 5MM **Privately Held**
WEB: www.atlasshowerdoor.com
SIC: 3231 5039 Doors, glass: made from purchased glass; glass construction materials

(P-4384)
BEVELED EDGE INC
Also Called: Original Glass Design
1740 Junction Ave Ste D, San Jose (95112-1035)
PHONE 408 467-9900
Mark Idzal, *President*
Allan Jaffe, *Opers Staff*
▲ EMP: 16 EST: 1988
SQ FT: 8,500
SALES (est): 1.9MM **Privately Held**
SIC: 3231 Products of purchased glass

(P-4385)
EMPIRE SHOWER DOORS INC
1217 N Mcdowell Blvd, Petaluma (94954-1112)
PHONE 707 773-2898
Roy German, *President*
Marylou German, *Admin Sec*
EMP: 26 EST: 1989
SQ FT: 5,000
SALES (est): 1MM **Privately Held**
WEB: www.empireshowerdoors.com
SIC: 3231 5031 1793 Doors, glass: made from purchased glass; doors; glass & glazing work

(P-4386)
FABRICATED GLASS SPC INC
2350 S Watney Way Ste E, Fairfield (94533-6738)
PHONE 707 429-6160
Harvey Holtz, *President*
EMP: 32
SALES (corp-wide): 23.3MM **Privately Held**
WEB: www.fabglass.com
SIC: 3231 Mirrored glass
PA: Fabricated Glass Specialties, Inc.
101 E Rapp Rd
Talent OR 97540
541 535-1582

(P-4387)
FLYLEAF WINDOWS INC
11040 Bollinger Canyon Rd # 40, San Ramon (94582-4969)
PHONE 925 344-1181
Billy Alcantara, *President*
EMP: 40 EST: 2018
SALES (est): 500K **Privately Held**
SIC: 3231 3211 Doors, glass: made from purchased glass; window glass, clear & colored

(P-4388)
FORETHOUGHT TECHNOLOGIES INC
150 Spear St Ste 350, San Francisco (94105-1747)
PHONE 415 994-9706
Deon Nicholas, *CEO*
EMP: 50 EST: 2017
SALES (est): 5.2MM **Privately Held**
WEB: www.forethought.ai
SIC: 3231 Scientific & technical glassware: from purchased glass

(P-4389)
HALIO INC (PA)
3955 Trust Way, Hayward (94545-3723)
PHONE 650 416-5200
Bruce Sohn, *CEO*
Anna Brunelle, *CFO*
Alok Gupta, *CFO*
Hal Hawthorne, *Vice Pres*
Gregg Higashi, *Vice Pres*
▲ EMP: 127 EST: 2010
SQ FT: 1,000
SALES (est): 28.3MM **Privately Held**
WEB: www.halioinc.com
SIC: 3231 Products of purchased glass

(P-4390)
LARRY MTHVIN INSTALLATIONS INC
Also Called: LMI
128 N Cluff Ave, Lodi (95240-3104)
PHONE 209 368-2105
Christy Puerta, *Vice Pres*
Michelle Dantuono, *Human Res Mgr*
EMP: 73
SALES (corp-wide): 2.4B **Publicly Held**
WEB: www.larrymethvin.com
SIC: 3231 3088 Framed mirrors; shower stalls, fiberglass & plastic
HQ: Larry Methvin Installations, Inc.
501 Kettering Dr
Ontario CA 91761
909 563-1700

(P-4391)
MAC THIN FILMS INC
2721 Giffen Ave, Santa Rosa (95407-5063)
PHONE 707 791-1656
Mark Madigan, *CEO*
Julie Leonhard, *CFO*
Gary Hyer, *Admin Asst*
David Rummel, *Technician*
Connie Sisson, *QC Mgr*
▲ EMP: 50 EST: 2014
SALES (est): 5.7MM **Privately Held**
WEB: www.macthinfilms.com
SIC: 3231 Products of purchased glass

(P-4392)
RESEARCH DEV GL PDTS & EQP INC
Also Called: Research & Dev GL Pdts & Eqp Inc
1808 Harmon St, Berkeley (94703-2416)
PHONE 510 547-6464
Doug Dobson, *President*
EMP: 16 EST: 1967
SQ FT: 10,000
SALES (est): 800K **Privately Held**
SIC: 3231 3229 Scientific & technical glassware: from purchased glass; ornamental glass: cut, engraved or otherwise decorated; pressed & blown glass

(P-4393)
ULTRA GLASS
4001 Vista Park Ct Ste 1, Sacramento (95834-2975)
PHONE 916 338-3911
Kurtis Ryder, *President*
EMP: 15 EST: 1990
SQ FT: 10,000
SALES (est): 4MM **Privately Held**
SIC: 3231 Doors, glass: made from purchased glass; insulating glass: made from purchased glass

3241 Cement, Hydraulic

(P-4394)
CEMEX CALIFORNIA CEMENT LLC
8251 Power Ridge Rd, Sacramento (95826-4723)
PHONE 760 381-7616
Clarance C Comer,
Julia Bonser, *Accountant*
Don Wilkey, *Manager*
▲ EMP: 260 EST: 1998
SALES (est): 57.7MM **Privately Held**
WEB: www.cemex.com
SIC: 3241 Portland cement
HQ: Cemex, Inc.
10100 Katy Fwy Ste 300
Houston TX 77043
713 650-6200

(P-4395)
LEHIGH SOUTHWEST CEMENT CO
24001 Stevens Creek Blvd, Cupertino (95014-5659)
PHONE 408 996-4271
W Lee, *Branch Mgr*
Neil McDermott, *Administration*
Gregg Hilliker, *Electrical Engi*
Scott Turner, *Production*
Richard Beatty, *VP Sales*
EMP: 15
SALES (corp-wide): 20.8B **Privately Held**
WEB: www.lehighhanson.com
SIC: 3241 2891 5032 5211 Portland cement; cement, except linoleum & tile; cement; cement
HQ: Lehigh Southwest Cement Company
2300 Clayton Rd Ste 300
Concord CA 94520
972 653-5500

(P-4396)
LEHIGH SOUTHWEST CEMENT CO (DH)
2300 Clayton Rd Ste 300, Concord (94520-2175)
PHONE 972 653-5500
Dan Harrington, *CEO*
Bill Boughton, *Vice Pres*
John Moquin, *Vice Pres*
▲ EMP: 15 EST: 1925
SQ FT: 10,000
SALES (est): 100.4MM
SALES (corp-wide): 20.8B **Privately Held**
WEB: www.lehighhanson.com
SIC: 3241 2891 5032 5211 Portland cement; masonry cement; pozzolana cement; cement, except linoleum & tile; cement; cement

(P-4397)
RMC PACIFIC MATERIALS LLC (PA)
Also Called: Cemex
6601 Koll Center Pkwy # 30, Pleasanton (94566-3112)
P.O. Box 5252 (94566-0252)
PHONE 925 426-8787
Eric F Woodhouse, *President*
Rodrigo Trevia O, *CFO*
◆ EMP: 200 EST: 1998
SQ FT: 30,000
SALES (est): 49.1MM **Privately Held**
WEB: www.cemex.com
SIC: 3241 3273 3273 1442 Cement, hydraulic; ready-mixed concrete; asphalt plant, including gravel-mix type; sand mining; gravel & pebble mining; abrasive products

3251 Brick & Structural Clay Tile

(P-4398)
CALSTAR PRODUCTS INC
3945 Freedom Cir Ste 560, Santa Clara (95054-1269)
PHONE 262 752-9131
Joel Rood, *CEO*
Mike Lemberg, *CFO*
EMP: 17 EST: 2006
SALES (est): 539.1K **Privately Held**
SIC: 3251 Paving brick, clay

(P-4399)
PABCO CLAY PRODUCTS LLC
Also Called: Gladding McBean
601 7th St, Lincoln (95648-1828)
PHONE 916 645-3341
Bill Padavona, *Branch Mgr*
Sarah Bradshaw, *Administration*
Patrice Duran, *Engineer*
Joe Parker, *Opers Mgr*
Jamie Farnham, *Natl Sales Mgr*
EMP: 250
SALES (corp-wide): 1.1B **Privately Held**
SIC: 3251 3253 3259 3269 Ceramic glazed brick, clay; ceramic wall & floor tile; clay sewer & drainage pipe & tile; roofing tile, clay; vases, pottery

PRODUCTS & SERVICES SECTION

3272 - Concrete Prdts County (P-4422)

HQ: Pabco Clay Products, Llc
605 Industrial Way
Dixon CA 95620

(P-4400)
PABCO CLAY PRODUCTS LLC
Also Called: H C Muddox
4875 Bradshaw Rd, Sacramento
(95827-9727)
PHONE..................................916 859-6300
Greg Morrison, *Branch Mgr*
Rocky Turner, *Safety Mgr*
EMP: 46
SALES (corp-wide): 1.1B **Privately Held**
WEB: www.hcmuddox.com
SIC: 3251 Brick & structural clay tile
HQ: Pabco Clay Products, Llc
605 Industrial Way
Dixon CA 95620

3253 Ceramic Tile

(P-4401)
ORTECH INC
Also Called: Ortech Advanced Ceramics
6760 Folsom Blvd 100, Sacramento
(95819-4626)
PHONE..................................916 549-9696
Oded Morgenshtern, *President*
▲ **EMP:** 15 **EST:** 2002
SALES (est): 1.1MM **Privately Held**
WEB: www.ortechceramics.com
SIC: 3253 Ceramic wall & floor tile

(P-4402)
PACIFIC CERAMICS INC
3524 Bassett St, Santa Clara (95054-2704)
PHONE..................................408 747-4600
Dennis J Fleming, *CEO*
EMP: 37 **EST:** 1994
SALES (est): 6.3MM **Privately Held**
WEB: www.pceramics.com
SIC: 3253 Ceramic wall & floor tile

(P-4403)
PROGRESSIVE TECHNOLOGY INC
4130 Citrus Ave Ste 17, Rocklin
(95677-4006)
PHONE..................................916 632-6715
Shannon Rogers, *President*
Carol Rogers, *Vice Pres*
EMP: 47 **EST:** 1989
SQ FT: 23,000
SALES (est): 2.3MM **Privately Held**
WEB: www.prgtech.com
SIC: 3253 Ceramic wall & floor tile

(P-4404)
STRATAMET ADVANCED MTLS CORP
2718 Prune Ave, Fremont (94539-6780)
PHONE..................................510 440-1697
EMP: 16
SALES (est): 1.7MM **Privately Held**
SIC: 3253 Mfg Ceramic Wall/Floor Tile

3259 Structural Clay Prdts, NEC

(P-4405)
PABCO BUILDING PRODUCTS LLC
Also Called: Gladding McBean
601 7th St, Lincoln (95648-1828)
P.O. Box 97 (95648-0097)
PHONE..................................916 645-3341
Erik Absalon, *General Mgr*
Jason Nilges, *Branch Mgr*
Stephen Ensley, *Accounting Mgr*
Jess Ouwerkerk, *Manager*
EMP: 53
SQ FT: 952
SALES (corp-wide): 1.1B **Privately Held**
WEB: www.pabcogypsum.com
SIC: 3259 Architectural terra cotta
HQ: Pabco Building Products, Llc
10600 White Rock Rd Ste 1
Rancho Cordova CA 95670
510 792-1577

3261 China Plumbing Fixtures & Fittings

(P-4406)
WESTINGHOUSE A BRAKE TECH CORP
Microphor
452 E Hill Rd, Willits (95490-9721)
PHONE..................................707 459-5563
EMP: 35 **Publicly Held**
WEB: www.wabteccorp.com
SIC: 3261 3589 Toilet fixtures, vitreous china; sewage treatment equipment
PA: Westinghouse Air Brake Technologies Corporation
30 Isabella St
Pittsburgh PA 15212

3264 Porcelain Electrical Splys

(P-4407)
COUNTIS INDUSTRIES INC
Also Called: Orbit Industries
12295 Charles Dr, Grass Valley
(95945-9371)
PHONE..................................530 272-8334
EMP: 20 **EST:** 1956
SQ FT: 10,000
SALES (est): 10MM **Privately Held**
WEB: www.countis.com
SIC: 3264 3423 Mfg Ceramic Magnetic Ferrite Material

(P-4408)
SAN JOSE DELTA ASSOCIATES INC
482 Sapena Ct, Santa Clara (95054-2442)
PHONE..................................408 727-1448
Scott J Budde, *CEO*
Joe Perez, *Production*
Rosemary Chavez, *Sales Executive*
James Farmer, *Manager*
EMP: 50 **EST:** 1971
SQ FT: 12,500
SALES (est): 6.3MM **Privately Held**
WEB: www.sanjosedelta.com
SIC: 3264 Magnets, permanent: ceramic or ferrite; porcelain parts for electrical devices, molded

---

3269 Pottery Prdts, NEC

(P-4409)
HEATH CERAMICS LTD
2900 18th St, San Francisco (94110-2005)
PHONE..................................415 361-5552
Robin Petravic, *Manager*
EMP: 20
SALES (corp-wide): 22.7MM **Privately Held**
WEB: www.heathceramics.com
SIC: 3269 Stoneware pottery products
PA: Heath Ceramics, Ltd.
400 Gate 5 Rd
Sausalito CA 94965
415 332-3732

3271 Concrete Block & Brick

(P-4410)
CALSTONE COMPANY
13755 Llagas Ave, San Martin
(95046-9563)
PHONE..................................408 686-9627
Joe Young, *Manager*
Lupe Naranjo, *Train & Dev Mgr*
EMP: 32
SQ FT: 23,262
SALES (corp-wide): 13.2MM **Privately Held**
WEB: www.calstone.com
SIC: 3271 Blocks, concrete or cinder: standard
PA: Calstone Company
5787 Obata Way
Gilroy CA 95020
408 984-8800

(P-4411)
CALSTONE COMPANY
421 Crystal Way, Galt (95682-8418)
PHONE..................................209 745-2981
Ted Schimdt, *Manager*
Ted Schimdt, *Safety Dir*
EMP: 32
SALES (corp-wide): 13.2MM **Privately Held**
WEB: www.calstone.com
SIC: 3271 3272 Blocks, concrete or cinder: standard; concrete products
PA: Calstone Company
5787 Obata Way
Gilroy CA 95020
408 984-8800

(P-4412)
CASTLELITE BLOCK LLC (PA)
8615 Robben Rd, Dixon (95620-9608)
PHONE..................................707 678-3465
John Espinoza,
John Urquidez, *Sales Staff*
EMP: 29 **EST:** 2006
SALES (est): 4MM **Privately Held**
WEB: www.castleliteblock.com
SIC: 3271 Blocks, concrete or cinder: standard

(P-4413)
EARTHPRO INC
2010 El Camino Real, Santa Clara
(95050-4051)
PHONE..................................408 294-1920
EMP: 28
SALES (est): 1.8MM **Privately Held**
SIC: 3271 Mfg Concrete Block/Brick

(P-4414)
L P MCNEAR BRICK CO INC
Also Called: McNear Brick & Block
1 Mcnear Brickyard Rd, San Rafael
(94901-8310)
P.O. Box 151380 (94915-1380)
PHONE..................................415 453-7702
John E McNear, *CEO*
Jeffrey McNear, *President*
Dan Mc Near, *CFO*
Daniel McNear, *CFO*
Daniel M Near, *Treasurer*
◆ **EMP:** 70
SALES (est): 11.9MM **Privately Held**
WEB: www.mcnear.com
SIC: 3271 3251 Brick, concrete; brick clay: common face, glazed, vitrified or hollow

(P-4415)
VALLEY ROCK LNDSCPE MATERIAL
4018 Taylor Rd, Loomis (95650-9004)
PHONE..................................916 652-7209
Kurtis D Nixon, *President*
Don Clark, *CFO*
Kelly Nixon, *Vice Pres*
EMP: 20 **EST:** 1990
SQ FT: 300
SALES (est): 4.1MM **Privately Held**
WEB: www.valleyrock.com
SIC: 3271 5261 Blocks, concrete: landscape or retaining wall; nurseries & garden centers

---

3272 Concrete Prdts

(P-4416)
A & A STEPPING STONE MFG INC (PA)
10291 Ophir Rd, Newcastle (95658-9504)
PHONE..................................530 885-7481
Keith S Arellano, *President*
Diane Arellano, *Vice Pres*
Liz Serven, *Site Mgr*
Jamie Jacinto, *Manager*
EMP: 25 **EST:** 1974
SQ FT: 3,740
SALES (est): 22.2MM **Privately Held**
SIC: 5211 3272 Concrete & cinder block; precast terrazo or concrete products

(P-4417)
ARCHITCTRAL FCDES UNLMITED INC
600 E Luchessa Ave, Gilroy (95020-7068)
PHONE..................................408 846-5350
Mary Alice Kinzler Bracken, *CEO*
Francis X Bracken, *Vice Pres*
Maurice Lafayette, *Project Mgr*
Robert Bianco, *Sales Staff*
EMP: 75 **EST:** 1986
SQ FT: 35,000
SALES (est): 8.1MM **Privately Held**
WEB: www.afuinc.com
SIC: 3272 Concrete products, precast

(P-4418)
BASALITE BUILDING PRODUCTS LLC (HQ)
2150 Douglas Blvd Ste 260, Roseville
(95661-3873)
PHONE..................................707 678-1901
Scott Weber, *President*
Dallas Barrett, *CFO*
Richard Blickensderfer, *Bd of Directors*
Alfred Mueller, *Bd of Directors*
Fredrick Nelson, *Bd of Directors*
◆ **EMP:** 37 **EST:** 1979
SALES (est): 185.3MM
SALES (corp-wide): 1.1B **Privately Held**
WEB: www.basalite.com
SIC: 3272 Concrete products, precast
PA: Pacific Coast Building Products, Inc.
10600 White Rock Rd # 100
Rancho Cordova CA 95670
916 631-6500

(P-4419)
BESCAL INC
Also Called: Bes Concrete Products
10304 W Linne Rd, Tracy (95377-9128)
PHONE..................................209 836-3492
EMP: 48
SALES (est): 6.7MM **Privately Held**
WEB: www.bescal.com
SIC: 3272 Mfg Concrete Products

(P-4420)
BLACKS IRRIGATIONS SYSTEMS
Also Called: Black's Irrigation Systems
144 N Chowchilla Blvd, Chowchilla (93610)
P.O. Box 357 (93610-0357)
PHONE..................................559 665-4891
James Black, *President*
Cheryl Black, *Corp Secy*
EMP: 46 **EST:** 1900
SQ FT: 1,500
SALES (est): 5.9MM **Privately Held**
SIC: 3272 Irrigation pipe, concrete

(P-4421)
BOND MANUFACTURING CO INC (PA)
2516 Verne Roberts Cir H3, Antioch
(94509-7918)
PHONE..................................866 771-2663
Daryl Merritt, *CEO*
Ronald Merritt, *Ch of Bd*
Pete Carpentier, *Vice Pres*
Doug Scheer, *Vice Pres*
Cameron Jenkins, *Principal*
◆ **EMP:** 98 **EST:** 1946
SQ FT: 250,000
SALES (est): 125MM **Privately Held**
WEB: www.bondmfg.com
SIC: 3272 5083 Fireplaces, concrete; lawn & garden machinery & equipment; garden machinery & equipment

(P-4422)
CALIFORNIA CONCRETE PIPE CORP
2960 S Highway 99, Stockton
(95215-8047)
PHONE..................................209 466-4212
James B Schack, *Ch of Bd*
Cy Thomson III, *Vice Pres*
Michael Lynch, *Admin Sec*
Robert Quinn, *Asst Sec*
EMP: 76 **EST:** 1980
SQ FT: 2,440
SALES (est): 3.5MM
SALES (corp-wide): 27.5B **Privately Held**
WEB: www.oldcastleinfrastructure.com
SIC: 3272 Sewer pipe, concrete

3272 - Concrete Prdts County (P-4423)

HQ: Oldcastle Infrastructure, Inc.
7000 Central Pkwy Ste 800
Atlanta GA 30328
770 270-5000

(P-4423)
CEMEX CNSTR MTLS PCF LLC
Also Called: Readymix - Cordelia R/M
4132 Cordelia Rd, Suisun City (94585)
PHONE.................................800 992-3639
EMP: 23 **Privately Held**
SIC: 3272 Concrete products
HQ: Cemex Construction Materials Pacific, Llc
1501 Belvedere Rd
West Palm Beach FL 33406
561 833-5555

(P-4424)
CENTRAL PRECAST CONCRETE INC
Also Called: Western Concrete Products
3500 Boulder St, Pleasanton (94566-4700)
P.O. Box 727 (94566-0868)
PHONE.................................925 417-6854
Don Hmphreys, *President*
Vince Bormolini, *Corp Secy*
Charles Bormolini, *Vice Pres*
EMP: 74 **EST:** 1979
SQ FT: 3,000
SALES (est): 2.8MM **Publicly Held**
WEB: www.us-concrete.com
SIC: 3272 1442 Manhole covers or frames, concrete; culvert pipe, concrete; sewer pipe, concrete; construction sand & gravel
HQ: U.S. Concrete, Inc.
331 N Main St
Euless TX 76039
817 835-4105

(P-4425)
CHANNEL SYSTEMS INC
74 98th Ave, Oakland (94603-1002)
PHONE.................................510 568-7170
Lauren Bockmiller, *President*
Douglas Bockmiller, *Treasurer*
▲ **EMP:** 27 **EST:** 1988
SQ FT: 20,000
SALES (est): 1.3MM **Privately Held**
WEB: www.channelsystems.com
SIC: 3272 5031 1542 1541 Building materials, except block or brick: concrete; building materials, interior; nonresidential construction; industrial buildings & warehouses

(P-4426)
CHRISTY VAULT COMPANY (PA)
1000 Collins Ave, Colma (94014-3299)
PHONE.................................650 994-1378
Robert B Christensen, *Ch of Bd*
Gregg Christensen, *Vice Pres*
EMP: 28 **EST:** 1930
SQ FT: 16,500
SALES (est): 5.4MM **Privately Held**
WEB: www.christyvault.com
SIC: 3272 Burial vaults, concrete or precast terrazzo; concrete products, precast

(P-4427)
CON-FAB CALIFORNIA CORPORATION (PA)
Also Called: Confab
1910 Lathrop Rd, Lathrop (95330-9708)
PHONE.................................209 249-4700
Philip French, *President*
Miaja French, *Shareholder*
Katy Young, *Executive*
Brent Koch, *Chief Engr*
EMP: 17 **EST:** 1977
SQ FT: 2,400
SALES (est): 6.6MM **Privately Held**
WEB: www.ccnfabca.com
SIC: 3272 Concrete products, precast

(P-4428)
COOK CONCRETE PRODUCTS INC
5461 Eastside Rd, Redding (96001-4533)
P.O. Box 720280 (96099-7280)
PHONE.................................530 243-2562
L Edward Shaw, *President*
Ken Shaw, *Prdtn Mgr*
Debbie Byrd, *Manager*
EMP: 35 **EST:** 1956
SQ FT: 1,000
SALES (est): 5.7MM **Privately Held**
WEB: www.cookconcreteproducts.com
SIC: 3272 Concrete products, precast

(P-4429)
CULTURED STONE CORPORATION (PA)
Hwy 29 & Tower Rd, NAPA (94559)
PHONE.................................707 255-1727
Stephen Nowak, *CEO*
▼ **EMP:** 739 **EST:** 1967
SQ FT: 17,000
SALES (est): 44.3MM **Privately Held**
SIC: 3272 3281 Cast stone, concrete; cut stone & stone products

(P-4430)
DESIGN INDUSTRIES INC
17918 Brook Dr W, Madera (93638-9624)
P.O. Box 26386, Fresno (93729-6386)
PHONE.................................559 675-3535
Robert Cisco, *President*
James Cisco, *Vice Pres*
EMP: 52 **EST:** 1987
SQ FT: 8,283
SALES (est): 7MM **Privately Held**
WEB: www.designindustriesinc.com
SIC: 3272 1791 Concrete stuctural support & building material; concrete reinforcement, placing of

(P-4431)
DYNAMIC PRE-CAST CO INC
5300 Sebastopol Rd, Santa Rosa (95407-6423)
PHONE.................................707 573-1110
Guenter Meiburg, *President*
Elaine Meiburg, *Vice Pres*
EMP: 34 **EST:** 1984
SQ FT: 2,500
SALES (est): 5.9MM **Privately Held**
WEB: www.dynamicprecast.com
SIC: 3272 1771 Concrete products, precast; concrete work

(P-4432)
FLORENCE & NEW ITLN ART CO INC
27735 Industrial Blvd, Hayward (94545-4045)
PHONE.................................510 785-9674
Mariano Fontana, *CEO*
Gerard Fontana, *CFO*
Marc Fontana, *Vice Pres*
▲ **EMP:** 40 **EST:** 1914
SQ FT: 30,000
SALES (est): 5.2MM **Privately Held**
WEB: www.florenceartcompany.com
SIC: 3272 Concrete products

(P-4433)
FORTERRA PIPE & PRECAST LLC
7020 Tokay Ave, Sacramento (95828-2418)
PHONE.................................916 379-9695
Drew Black, *Manager*
Robert Moots, *Administration*
Jim Andon, *Plant Mgr*
Mike Garcia, *Sales Staff*
EMP: 37
SALES (corp-wide): 1.5B **Publicly Held**
WEB: www.forterrabp.com
SIC: 3272 Pipe, concrete or lined with concrete
HQ: Forterra Pipe & Precast, Llc
511 E John Carpenter Fwy
Irving TX 75062
469 458-7973

(P-4434)
GC PRODUCTS INC
601 7th St, Lincoln (95648-1828)
PHONE.................................916 645-3870
John Coburn, *President*
Michael Coburn, *Vice Pres*
EMP: 43 **EST:** 2003
SQ FT: 4,000
SALES (est): 5.3MM **Privately Held**
WEB: www.gcproductsinc.com
SIC: 3272 Concrete products

(P-4435)
GEORGETOWN PRE-CAST INC
2420 Georgia Slide Rd, Georgetown (95634-2201)
P.O. Box 65 (95634-0065)
PHONE.................................530 333-4404
Ronny R Beam, *President*
EMP: 17 **EST:** 1974
SQ FT: 2,600
SALES (est): 1MM **Privately Held**
WEB: www.georgetownprecast.com
SIC: 3272 3273 5039 Septic tanks, concrete; tanks, concrete; manhole covers or frames, concrete; ready-mixed concrete; septic tanks

(P-4436)
GIANNINI GARDEN ORNAMENTS INC
225 Shaw Rd, South San Francisco (94080-6605)
PHONE.................................650 873-4493
Piera Giannini, *President*
Alessandro Giannini, *Sales Staff*
Joan Chiorato, *Manager*
▲ **EMP:** 30 **EST:** 1993
SALES (est): 4.6MM **Privately Held**
WEB: www.gianninigarden.com
SIC: 3272 Concrete products

(P-4437)
HILFIKER PIPE CO
Also Called: Hilfiker Retaining Walls
1902 Hilfiker Ln, Eureka (95503-5711)
PHONE.................................707 443-5091
Harold Hilfiker, *President*
Brenda Peterson, *Treasurer*
Bill Hilfiker, *Vice Pres*
William K Hilfiker, *Vice Pres*
William Hilfiker, *Vice Pres*
EMP: 30 **EST:** 1900
SQ FT: 14,400
SALES (est): 6.5MM **Privately Held**
WEB: www.hilfiker.com
SIC: 3272 3315 5051 5074 Concrete products, precast; wall & ceiling squares, concrete; welded steel wire fabric; pipe & tubing, steel; pipes & fittings, plastic

(P-4438)
INDEPNDENT FLR TSTG INSPTN INC
1390 Willow Pass Rd # 1010, Concord (94520-5200)
PHONE.................................925 676-7682
Lee Eliseian, *President*
David Gotz, *Technician*
Danee Lumbre, *Project Mgr*
Kristina Cullen, *Manager*
EMP: 16 **EST:** 1997
SALES (est): 2.2MM **Privately Held**
WEB: www.ifti.com
SIC: 3272 8611 Floor slabs & tiles, precast concrete; business associations

(P-4439)
JENSEN ENTERPRISES INC
7210 State Highway 32, Orland (95963-9790)
PHONE.................................530 865-4277
Don Jensen, *Branch Mgr*
EMP: 26
SALES (corp-wide): 237.2MM **Privately Held**
WEB: www.jensenprecast.com
SIC: 3272 5039 Concrete products, precast; septic tanks
PA: Jensen Enterprises, Inc.
9895 Double R Blvd
Reno NV 89521
775 352-2700

(P-4440)
KIE-CON INC
3551 Wilbur Ave, Antioch (94509-8530)
PHONE.................................925 754-9494
Eric Scott, *President*
EMP: 90 **EST:** 2010
SALES (est): 17.7MM
SALES (corp-wide): 10.2B **Privately Held**
WEB: www.kiecon.com
SIC: 3272 Concrete products

HQ: Kiewit Corporation
1550 Mike Fahey St
Omaha NE 68102
402 342-2052

(P-4441)
KRISTICH-MONTEREY PIPE CO INC
225 Salinas Rd Ste B, Royal Oaks (95076-5253)
P.O. Box 606, Watsonville (95077-0606)
PHONE.................................831 724-4186
Chris Kristich, *President*
EMP: 31 **EST:** 1966
SQ FT: 2,000
SALES (est): 6.9MM **Privately Held**
SIC: 3272 Pipe, concrete or lined with concrete

(P-4442)
LEGACY VULCAN LLC
Also Called: Gustine Ready Mix
28525 Bambouer Rd, Gustine (95322-9570)
PHONE.................................209 854-3088
EMP: 16
SALES (corp-wide): 3.5B **Publicly Held**
SIC: 3272 Mfg Concrete Products
HQ: Legacy Vulcan, Llc
1200 Urban Center Dr
Vestavia AL 35242
205 298-3000

(P-4443)
MONUMENTAL NUTRITION LLC
2349 Stratford Dr, San Jose (95124-2638)
PHONE.................................408 410-0890
Doan Tran, *Branch Mgr*
EMP: 27
SALES (corp-wide): 256.4K **Privately Held**
SIC: 3272 Monuments & grave markers, except terrazo
PA: Monumental Nutrition Llc
2059 Camden Ave
San Jose CA

(P-4444)
N V CAST STONE LLC
Also Called: NAPA Valley Cast Stone
2003 Seville Dr, NAPA (94559-4318)
PHONE.................................707 261-6615
Mark Akey, *Mng Member*
Tom Brown,
Jeff Latreille,
Bill Tough,
EMP: 24 **EST:** 1991
SALES (est): 4.6MM **Privately Held**
WEB: www.californiastonecraft.com
SIC: 3272 3281 Concrete products, precast; cut stone & stone products

(P-4445)
PACIFIC CORRUGATED PIPE CO LLC
5999 Power Inn Rd, Sacramento (95824-2318)
PHONE.................................916 383-4891
Rob Roles, *Branch Mgr*
EMP: 29
SALES (corp-wide): 13.4MM **Privately Held**
SIC: 3272 Culvert pipe, concrete
HQ: Pacific Corrugated Pipe Company, Llc
471 Old Newport Blvd # 205
Newport Beach CA 92663
949 650-4555

(P-4446)
PACIFIC INTRLOCK PVNGSTONE INC (PA)
1895 San Felipe Rd, Hollister (95023-2541)
PHONE.................................831 637-9163
Dean Richardt Tonder, *CEO*
John Tonder, *Principal*
Tim Donovan, *Mktg Dir*
EMP: 16 **EST:** 1990
SALES (est): 2.6MM **Privately Held**
WEB: www.pacinterlock.com
SIC: 3272 Concrete products, precast

PRODUCTS & SERVICES SECTION

3273 - Ready-Mixed Concrete County (P-4470)

(P-4447)
PIRANHA PIPE & PRECAST INC
16000 Avenue 25, Chowchilla (93610-9353)
P.O. Box 820 (93610-0820)
PHONE...................................559 665-7473
Anita Simpson, *President*
▲ EMP: 28 EST: 2000
SALES (est): 6.5MM Privately Held
WEB: www.piranhapipe.com
SIC: 3272 Precast terrazo or concrete products

(P-4448)
PRECAST CON TECH UNLIMITED LLC
Also Called: Ctu Precast
1260 Furneaux Rd, Olivehurst (95961-7415)
PHONE...................................530 749-6501
Rez Moulla,
Robert Roesner, *Officer*
Todd Whitney, *Officer*
Aditya Jamwal, *Engineer*
Kevin Steinkraus, *Opers Mgr*
EMP: 80 EST: 2008
SQ FT: 160,000
SALES (est): 13.1MM Privately Held
WEB: www.ctuprecast.com
SIC: 3272 Concrete products, precast

(P-4449)
REDWOOD VALLEY GRAVEL PDTS INC
11200 East Rd, Redwood Valley (95470-6108)
PHONE...................................707 485-8585
David Ford, *President*
Melvin Ford, *Vice Pres*
EMP: 28 EST: 1972
SQ FT: 1,280
SALES (est): 5.2MM Privately Held
WEB: www.redwoodvalleygravel.com
SIC: 3272 Septic tanks, concrete

(P-4450)
SAN BENITO SUPPLY (PA)
1060 Nash Rd, Hollister (95023-5303)
PHONE...................................831 637-5526
Mark Schipper, *President*
Ted Schipper, *Admin Sec*
Mason Otta, *Sales Mgr*
EMP: 129 EST: 1978
SQ FT: 1,870
SALES (est): 19.5MM Privately Held
WEB: www.sbs-cas.com
SIC: 3272 5032 Concrete products; brick, stone & related material

(P-4451)
SANDMAN INC (PA)
Also Called: Star Concrete
1404 S 7th St, San Jose (95112-5927)
PHONE...................................408 947-0669
Gerald Ray Blatt, *CEO*
Nicole Candelaria, *CFO*
Jody Vasquez, *Administration*
Lucy Crawford, *Credit Mgr*
Jerry Blatt, *Director*
EMP: 88 EST: 1969
SQ FT: 14,000
SALES (est): 23.1MM Privately Held
WEB: www.starqualityconcrete.com
SIC: 3272 3273 Dry mixture concrete; ready-mixed concrete

(P-4452)
SIERRA PRECAST INC
Also Called: U.S. Concrete Precast Group
1 Live Oak Ave, Morgan Hill (95037-9245)
PHONE...................................408 779-1000
Eric Scholz, *President*
EMP: 173 EST: 1974
SQ FT: 4,000
SALES (est): 5.1MM Publicly Held
WEB: www.us-concrete.com
SIC: 3272 1771 Panels & sections, prefabricated concrete; columns, concrete; concrete work
HQ: U.S. Concrete, Inc.
331 N Main St
Euless TX 76039
817 835-4105

(P-4453)
WALTERS & WOLF GLASS COMPANY
41450 Cowbell Rd, Fremont (94538)
PHONE...................................510 226-9800
Jody Vegas, *Branch Mgr*
Juan Martinez, *Project Engr*
EMP: 20
SALES (corp-wide): 85.1MM Privately Held
WEB: www.waltersandwolf.com
SIC: 3272 Precast terrazo or concrete products
PA: Walters & Wolf Glass Company
41450 Boscell Rd
Fremont CA 94538
510 490-1115

(P-4454)
WALTERS & WOLF PRECAST
41450 Boscell Rd, Fremont (94538-3103)
PHONE...................................510 226-9800
Randy A Wolf, *President*
Jeff B Belzer, *CFO*
Doug Frost, *Vice Pres*
Ed Knowles, *Vice Pres*
Juliusz Knuzynkski, *Vice Pres*
▲ EMP: 160 EST: 1996
SALES (est): 19.6MM Privately Held
WEB: www.waltersandwolf.com
SIC: 3272 Concrete products, precast

(P-4455)
WILLIS CONSTRUCTION CO INC
2261 San Juan Hwy, San Juan Bautista (95045-9565)
PHONE...................................831 623-2900
Lawrence M Willis, *CEO*
Mark Hildebrand, *President*
Tom Yezek, *CFO*
Roger Ely, *Vice Pres*
Scott Sarria, *Manager*
◆ EMP: 120 EST: 1976
SQ FT: 4,000
SALES (est): 30.6MM Privately Held
WEB: www.willisconstruction.com
SIC: 3272 1791 Concrete products, precast; precast concrete structural framing or panels, placing of

3273 Ready-Mixed Concrete

(P-4456)
A TEICHERT & SON INC
Also Called: Teichert Readymix
8609 Jackson Rd, Sacramento (95826-9731)
PHONE...................................916 386-6974
Dave Bearden, *Division Mgr*
EMP: 22
SALES (corp-wide): 842MM Privately Held
WEB: www.teichert.com
SIC: 3273 Ready-mixed concrete
HQ: A. Teichert & Son, Inc.
5200 Franklin Dr Ste 115
Pleasanton CA 94588

(P-4457)
A TEICHERT & SON INC
Also Called: Teichert Readymix
721 Berry St, Roseville (95678-1307)
PHONE...................................916 783-7132
Dave Bearden, *Division Mgr*
EMP: 22
SALES (corp-wide): 842MM Privately Held
WEB: www.teichert.com
SIC: 3273 Ready-mixed concrete
HQ: A. Teichert & Son, Inc.
5200 Franklin Dr Ste 115
Pleasanton CA 94588

(P-4458)
ALLIED CONCRETE AND SUPPLY CO
440 Mitchell Rd Ste B, Modesto (95354-3915)
P.O. Box 1022 (95353-1022)
PHONE...................................209 524-3177
Michael G Ruddy Sr, *President*
Martin J Ruddy III, *Treasurer*
James M Ruddy, *Vice Pres*
Martin Ruddy Jr, *Vice Pres*
Sally Ruddy, *Vice Pres*
EMP: 20 EST: 1952
SQ FT: 3,500
SALES (est): 2.7MM Privately Held
WEB: www.allied-concrete-supply.com
SIC: 3273 Ready-mixed concrete

(P-4459)
AZUSA ROCK LLC
Also Called: Los Banos Rock and Ready Mix
22101 Sunset Dr, Los Banos (93635)
P.O. Box 1111 (93635-1111)
PHONE...................................209 826-5066
Wayne Stoughton, *Manager*
EMP: 37 Publicly Held
SIC: 3273 Ready-mixed concrete
HQ: Azusa Rock, Llc
3901 Fish Canyon Rd
Azusa CA 91702
858 530-9444

(P-4460)
BOHAN CNLIS - ASTIN CREEK RDYM
Also Called: Austn Creek Materials
1528 Copperhill Pkwy F, Santa Rosa (95403-8200)
P.O. Box 317, Cazadero (95421-0317)
PHONE...................................707 632-5296
Timothy Canelis, *President*
Homer Canelis, *Treasurer*
EMP: 67 EST: 1946
SQ FT: 800
SALES (est): 7.4MM Privately Held
WEB: www.canyonrockinc.com
SIC: 3273 Ready-mixed concrete

(P-4461)
BUILDERS CONCRETE INC (DH)
3664 W Ashlan Ave, Fresno (93722-4499)
P.O. Box 9129 (93790-9129)
PHONE...................................559 225-3667
Charlie Wensley, *President*
Don Unmacht, *President*
Dominique Bidet, *Corp Secy*
Mark Mitzel, *Vice Pres*
David Street, *Sales Staff*
EMP: 50 EST: 1953
SQ FT: 2,500
SALES (est): 17MM
SALES (corp-wide): 521.8MM Privately Held
WEB: www.nationalcement.com
SIC: 3273 Ready-mixed concrete
HQ: National Cement Company Of California, Inc.
15821 Ventura Blvd # 475
Encino CA 91436
818 728-5200

(P-4462)
BUILDERS CONCRETE INC (DH)
Also Called: Builders Concrete - Merced
3169 Beachwood Dr, Merced (95348-3620)
P.O. Box 9129, Fresno (93790-9129)
PHONE...................................209 388-0183
Donald Unmacht, *President*
EMP: 15 EST: 1996
SALES (est): 9.3MM
SALES (corp-wide): 521.8MM Privately Held
WEB: www.buildersconcrete.com
SIC: 3273 Ready-mixed concrete
HQ: Builders Concrete, Inc.
3664 W Ashlan Ave
Fresno CA 93722
559 225-3667

(P-4463)
BUILDERS CONCRETE INC
17041 E Kings Canyon Rd, Sanger (93657-9604)
PHONE...................................559 787-3117
John Gills, *Manager*
EMP: 50
SALES (corp-wide): 521.8MM Privately Held
WEB: www.buildersconcrete.com
SIC: 3273 Ready-mixed concrete
HQ: Builders Concrete, Inc.
3169 Beachwood Dr
Merced CA 95348
209 388-0183

(P-4464)
CALAVERAS MATERIALS INC (DH)
Also Called: CMI
1100 Lowe Rd, Hughson (95326-9178)
P.O. Box 26240, Fresno (93729-6240)
PHONE...................................209 883-0448
David Vickers, *President*
EMP: 20 EST: 1984
SQ FT: 8,000
SALES (est): 80.7MM
SALES (corp-wide): 20.8B Privately Held
WEB: www.lehighhanson.com
SIC: 3273 5032 3272 2951 Ready-mixed concrete; sand, construction; gravel; concrete products; asphalt paving mixtures & blocks; construction sand & gravel

(P-4465)
CEMEX CNSTR MTLS PCF LLC
Also Called: Aggregate -Eliot Quarry
1544 Stanley Blvd, Pleasanton (94566-6308)
P.O. Box 697 (94566-0866)
PHONE...................................925 846-2824
Gordon Brown, *Branch Mgr*
EMP: 45 Privately Held
SIC: 3273 Ready-mixed concrete
HQ: Cemex Construction Materials Pacific, Llc
1501 Belvedere Rd
West Palm Beach FL 33406
561 833-5555

(P-4466)
CEMEX CNSTR MTLS PCF LLC
Also Called: Shop -Ncal Rmx Fixed Maint Sho
1601 Cement Hill Rd, Fairfield (94533-2659)
PHONE...................................707 422-2520
Graham Dubois, *Branch Mgr*
Hector Avalos, *Area Mgr*
Randy Farmer, *Manager*
EMP: 33 Privately Held
SIC: 3273 Ready-mixed concrete
HQ: Cemex Construction Materials Pacific, Llc
1501 Belvedere Rd
West Palm Beach FL 33406
561 833-5555

(P-4467)
CEMEX CNSTR MTLS PCF LLC
Also Called: Readymix -Newman Rm
3407 W Stuhr Rd, Newman (95360-9774)
PHONE...................................209 862-0182
EMP: 23
SALES (corp-wide): 15.4B Privately Held
SIC: 3273 Mfg Ready-Mixed Concrete
HQ: Cemex Construction Materials Pacific, Llc
1501 Belvedere Rd
West Palm Beach FL 33406
561 833-5555

(P-4468)
CEMEX CNSTR MTLS PCF LLC
Also Called: Readymix - Union City Rm
900 Whipple Rd, Union City (94587-1347)
PHONE...................................855 292-8453
EMP: 23 Privately Held
SIC: 3273 Ready-mixed concrete
HQ: Cemex Construction Materials Pacific, Llc
1501 Belvedere Rd
West Palm Beach FL 33406
561 833-5555

(P-4469)
CEMEX CNSTR MTLS PCF LLC
Also Called: Readymix- Lodi Rm
1290 E Turner Rd, Lodi (95240-0749)
PHONE...................................855 292-8453
EMP: 23 Privately Held
SIC: 3273 Ready-mixed concrete
HQ: Cemex Construction Materials Pacific, Llc
1501 Belvedere Rd
West Palm Beach FL 33406
561 833-5555

(P-4470)
CEMEX MATERIALS LLC
7059 Tremont Rd, Dixon (95620-9609)
PHONE...................................707 678-4311

3273 - Ready-Mixed Concrete County (P-4471)

Ed Ozbun, *Branch Mgr*
EMP: 95 **Privately Held**
SIC: 3273 Ready-mixed concrete
HQ: Cemex Materials Llc
1501 Belvedere Rd
West Palm Beach FL 33406
561 833-5555

(P-4471)
CEMEX MATERIALS LLC
1645 Stanley Blvd, Pleasanton (94566-6309)
PHONE 855 292-8453
Joe Sostaric, *Branch Mgr*
Kevin Hoy, *Opers Mgr*
Jack Shade, *Sales Mgr*
Bob Stacy, *Superintendent*
EMP: 33 **Privately Held**
SIC: 3273 Ready-mixed concrete
HQ: Cemex Materials Llc
1501 Belvedere Rd
West Palm Beach FL 33406
561 833-5555

(P-4472)
CEMEX MATERIALS LLC
401 Wright Ave, Richmond (94804-3508)
PHONE 510 234-3616
Karl H Watson Jr, *Branch Mgr*
EMP: 95 **Privately Held**
SIC: 3273 Ready-mixed concrete
HQ: Cemex Materials Llc
1501 Belvedere Rd
West Palm Beach FL 33406
561 833-5555

(P-4473)
CEMEX MATERIALS LLC
385 Tower Rd, NAPA (94558)
P.O. Box 3508 (94558-0553)
PHONE 707 255-3035
George Kerr, *Manager*
EMP: 95
SQ FT: 30,000 **Privately Held**
SIC: 3273 Ready-mixed concrete
HQ: Cemex Materials Llc
1501 Belvedere Rd
West Palm Beach FL 33406
561 833-5555

(P-4474)
CEMEX MATERIALS LLC
4150 N Brawley Ave, Fresno (93722-3914)
PHONE 559 275-2241
EMP: 95 **Privately Held**
SIC: 3273 Ready-mixed concrete
HQ: Cemex Materials Llc
1501 Belvedere Rd
West Palm Beach FL 33406
561 833-5555

(P-4475)
CENTRAL CONCRETE SUPPLY CO INC (DH)
Also Called: Westside Building Materials
755 Stockton Ave, San Jose (95126-1839)
PHONE 408 293-6272
William T Albanese, *CEO*
Scott Perrine, *President*
Laurie Cerrito, *Vice Pres*
Jeff Davis, *Vice Pres*
David Perry, *Vice Pres*
EMP: 60 **EST:** 1951
SQ FT: 2,000
SALES (est): 56.4MM **Publicly Held**
WEB: www.centralconcrete.com
SIC: 3273 Ready-mixed concrete
HQ: U.S. Concrete, Inc.
331 N Main St
Euless TX 76039
817 835-4105

(P-4476)
CLAY MIX LLC (PA)
1003 N Abby St, Fresno (93701-1007)
PHONE 559 485-0065
Ritsuko Miyazaki, *Principal*
EMP: 22 **EST:** 2008
SALES (est): 1.6MM **Privately Held**
WEB: www.clay-mix.com
SIC: 3273 Ready-mixed concrete

(P-4477)
CONCRETE INC (DH)
400 S Lincoln St, Stockton (95203-3312)
P.O. Box 66001 (95206-0901)
PHONE 209 933-6999
David C Barney, *CEO*
Terry D Hildestad, *CEO*
Larry Hansen, *CFO*
Mary Ann Johnson, *Vice Pres*
Lester H Loble II, *Admin Sec*
EMP: 55 **EST:** 1986
SALES (est): 24.2MM
SALES (corp-wide): 5.5B **Publicly Held**
WEB: www.con-inc.com
SIC: 3273 5032 Ready-mixed concrete; brick, stone & related material
HQ: Knife River Corporation
1150 W Century Ave
Bismarck ND 58503
701 530-1400

(P-4478)
CONCRETE READY MIX INC
33 Hillsdale Ave, San Jose (95136-1308)
P.O. Box 50006 (95150-0006)
PHONE 408 224-2452
Ron Minnis, *President*
EMP: 35 **EST:** 1983
SALES (est): 5.1MM **Privately Held**
WEB: www.concretecrm.com
SIC: 3273 Ready-mixed concrete

(P-4479)
E-Z HAUL READY MIX INC
Also Called: Star Building Products
1538 N Blackstone Ave, Fresno (93703-3612)
PHONE 559 233-6603
Calvin Coley, *President*
Pat Coley, *Treasurer*
Donald Crawford, *Vice Pres*
EMP: 30 **EST:** 1969
SQ FT: 1,500
SALES (est): 3.2MM **Privately Held**
WEB: www.starbuildingsupplies.com
SIC: 3273 5211 Ready-mixed concrete; cement

(P-4480)
ELITE READY-MIX LLC
6790 Bradshaw Rd, Sacramento (95829-9303)
PHONE 916 366-4627
Dominic Sposeto,
Mike Camello, *Business Mgr*
Kyle Bridges, *Sales Staff*
Billie Sposeto,
EMP: 35 **EST:** 2008
SALES (est): 6MM **Privately Held**
WEB: www.elitereadymix.net
SIC: 3273 Ready-mixed concrete

(P-4481)
FOLSOM READY MIX INC (PA)
3401 Fitzgerald Rd, Rancho Cordova (95742-6815)
PHONE 916 851-8300
Scott Silva, *CEO*
Randy Barnes, *Vice Pres*
Joshua Neff, *Vice Pres*
Jon Jackson, *QC Mgr*
EMP: 28 **EST:** 1999
SALES (est): 10MM **Privately Held**
WEB: www.folsomreadymix.com
SIC: 3273 Ready-mixed concrete

(P-4482)
FOOTHILL READY MIX INC
11415 State Highway 99w, Red Bluff (96080-7716)
PHONE 530 527-2565
Kevin Brunnemer, *President*
Cathy Brunnemer, *Admin Sec*
EMP: 19 **EST:** 1979
SQ FT: 1,000
SALES (est): 2.2MM **Privately Held**
WEB: www.foothillreadymix.com
SIC: 3273 Ready-mixed concrete

(P-4483)
GAMBREL COMPANIES INC
Also Called: Gold & Sons Ready Mix
6780 Martin Ln, Ione (95640-9190)
PHONE 209 274-0150
Ryan Gold, *CEO*
EMP: 17 **EST:** 2018
SALES (est): 3.4MM **Privately Held**
SIC: 3273 Ready-mixed concrete

(P-4484)
HANFORD READY-MIX INC
9800 Kent St, Elk Grove (95624-9483)
PHONE 916 405-1918
Preston Hanford Jr, *CEO*
Diane Hanford-Butz, *Vice Pres*
EMP: 30 **EST:** 1981
SQ FT: 3,500
SALES (est): 3.5MM **Privately Held**
WEB: www.hanfordsandandgravel.com
SIC: 3273 Ready-mixed concrete

(P-4485)
HANSON AGGRGTES MD-PACIFIC INC
7999 Athenour Way, Sunol (94586-9454)
PHONE 925 862-2236
Tom Jackson, *Branch Mgr*
Rick Beatty, *Sales Executive*
Antonio Fuentes, *Manager*
EMP: 15
SALES (corp-wide): 20.8B **Privately Held**
WEB: www.sunolaggregates.com
SIC: 3273 Ready-mixed concrete
HQ: Hanson Aggregates Mid-Pacific, Inc.
12667 Alcosta Blvd # 400
San Ramon CA

(P-4486)
HANSON AGGRGTES MD-PACIFIC INC
699 Virginia St, Berkeley (94710-1727)
PHONE 510 526-1811
Seth Watkins, *Branch Mgr*
EMP: 15
SALES (corp-wide): 20.8B **Privately Held**
SIC: 3273 Ready-mixed concrete
HQ: Hanson Aggregates Mid-Pacific, Inc.
12667 Alcosta Blvd # 400
San Ramon CA

(P-4487)
HANSON LEHIGH INC
3000 Executive Pkwy # 240, San Ramon (94583-4255)
PHONE 972 653-5603
Blake Hall, *Branch Mgr*
Solomon Figueroa, *Business Anlyst*
Kenneth Moore, *Regl Sales Mgr*
EMP: 30
SALES (corp-wide): 20.8B **Privately Held**
WEB: www.lehighhanson.com
SIC: 3273 Ready-mixed concrete
HQ: Lehigh Hanson, Inc.
100 N Loop 336 W
Conroe TX 77301

(P-4488)
HOLLISTER LANDSCAPE SUPPLY INC
2410 San Juan Rd, Hollister (95023-9107)
PHONE 831 636-8750
Barabara A Chaplin, *President*
Janet Snodderly, *Manager*
EMP: 55 **Privately Held**
WEB: www.hollisterlandscapesupply.com
SIC: 3273 Ready-mixed concrete
HQ: Hollister Landscape Supply, Inc.
520 Crazy Horse Canyon Rd A
Salinas CA 93907
831 443-8644

(P-4489)
KYLES ROCK & REDI-MIX INC
1221 San Simeon Dr, Roseville (95661-5364)
PHONE 916 681-4848
Kyle Rosburg, *CEO*
Patti Rosburg, *CFO*
EMP: 15 **EST:** 1976
SQ FT: 1,700
SALES (est): 1.2MM **Privately Held**
SIC: 3273 Ready-mixed concrete

(P-4490)
L K LEHMAN TRUCKING
Also Called: A & L Ready Mix
19333 Industrial Dr, Sonora (95370-9232)
P.O. Box 9, Standard (95373-0009)
PHONE 209 532-5586
Lowell K Lehman, *President*
Darlene Lehman, *Corp Secy*
EMP: 35 **EST:** 1976
SQ FT: 1,500
SALES (est): 3.4MM **Privately Held**
WEB: www.lklehmantrucking.com
SIC: 3273 4214 Ready-mixed concrete; local trucking with storage

(P-4491)
LAS ANIMAS CON & BLDG SUP INC
146 Encinal St, Santa Cruz (95060-2111)
P.O. Box 507 (95061-0507)
PHONE 831 425-4084
Scott French, *President*
EMP: 20 **EST:** 1965
SALES (est): 4.8MM **Privately Held**
WEB: www.lasanimasconcrete.com
SIC: 3273 Ready-mixed concrete

(P-4492)
LEES CONCRETE MATERIALS INC
200 S Pine St, Madera (93637-5206)
P.O. Box 509 (93639-0509)
PHONE 559 486-2440
Tom Da Silva, *President*
Deidre Da Silva, *Treasurer*
EMP: 55 **EST:** 1963
SQ FT: 7,000
SALES (est): 10.7MM **Privately Held**
SIC: 3273 Ready-mixed concrete

(P-4493)
LIVINGSTONS CONCRETE SVC INC (PA)
5416 Roseville Rd, North Highlands (95660-5097)
PHONE 916 334-4313
Patricia Henley, *President*
Edith Livingston, *Corp Secy*
Ted Henley, *Vice Pres*
Joe Russi, *Vice Pres*
Larry Livingston, *Principal*
EMP: 24
SALES (est): 15MM **Privately Held**
WEB: www.livingstonsconcrete.com
SIC: 3273 Ready-mixed concrete

(P-4494)
LIVINGSTONS CONCRETE SVC INC
Also Called: Plant 1
5416 Roseville Rd, North Highlands (95660-5097)
PHONE 916 334-4313
Terry Regan, *Branch Mgr*
EMP: 25
SALES (corp-wide): 15MM **Privately Held**
WEB: www.livingstonsconcrete.com
SIC: 3273 Ready-mixed concrete
PA: Livingston's Concrete Service, Inc.
5416 Roseville Rd
North Highlands CA 95660
916 334-4313

(P-4495)
LIVINGSTONS CONCRETE SVC INC
Also Called: Plant 3
2915 Lesvos Ct, Lincoln (95648-9341)
PHONE 916 334-4313
Bill Redden, *Branch Mgr*
EMP: 25
SALES (corp-wide): 15MM **Privately Held**
WEB: www.livingstonsconcrete.com
SIC: 3273 Ready-mixed concrete
PA: Livingston's Concrete Service, Inc.
5416 Roseville Rd
North Highlands CA 95660
916 334-4313

PRODUCTS & SERVICES SECTION

3281 - Cut Stone Prdts County (P-4519)

(P-4496)
M B I READY-MIX L L C
44 Central St, Colfax (95713-9006)
PHONE...................530 346-2432
Paul Manuel, *Principal*
Kellye Manuel,
Matthew Melugin,
James Milhous,
Gary Smith,
EMP: 16 **EST:** 1997
SALES (est): 412.1K **Privately Held**
WEB: www.gohbe.com
SIC: 3273 Ready-mixed concrete

(P-4497)
MATHEWS READY MIX LLC
1619 Skyway, Chico (95928-8833)
PHONE...................530 893-8856
Chad Christee, *Branch Mgr*
EMP: 22
SQ FT: 4,780
SALES (corp-wide): 1.6B **Publicly Held**
WEB: www.mathewsreadymixllc.com
SIC: 3273 Ready-mixed concrete
HQ: Mathews Ready Mix Llc
4711 Hammonton Rd
Marysville CA 95901
530 749-6525

(P-4498)
MATHEWS READY MIX LLC
Also Called: Mathews Readymix
249 Lamon St, Yuba City (95991-4200)
P.O. Box 749, Marysville (95901-0020)
PHONE...................530 671-2400
Lee Cooper, *Manager*
EMP: 22
SALES (corp-wide): 1.6B **Publicly Held**
WEB: www.mathewsreadymixllc.com
SIC: 3273 Ready-mixed concrete
HQ: Mathews Ready Mix Llc
4711 Hammonton Rd
Marysville CA 95901
530 749-6525

(P-4499)
NORCAL MATERIALS INC
Also Called: Harbor Ready Mix
941 Bransten Rd, San Carlos (94070-4021)
PHONE...................650 365-4811
EMP: 20 **Publicly Held**
WEB: www.us-concrete.com
SIC: 3273 Ready-mixed concrete
HQ: Norcal Materials, Inc.
331 N Main St
Euless TX 76039
817 835-4105

(P-4500)
NORTHERN CAL BLDG MTLS INC (PA)
Also Called: Norcal Building Materials
1534 Copperhill Pkwy, Santa Rosa (95403-8200)
P.O. Box 751222, Petaluma (94975-1222)
PHONE...................707 546-9422
James B Hill, *President*
EMP: 20 **EST:** 1982
SALES (est): 5.4MM **Privately Held**
WEB: www.shamrockmaterials.com
SIC: 5211 3273 Lumber & other building materials; ready-mixed concrete

(P-4501)
P & L CONCRETE PRODUCTS INC
1900 Roosevelt Ave, Escalon (95320-1763)
PHONE...................209 838-1448
Jeff Francis, *President*
Arlene Francis, *Vice Pres*
EMP: 22 **EST:** 1972
SQ FT: 1,500
SALES (est): 3.7MM **Privately Held**
WEB: www.plconcrete.net
SIC: 3273 Ready-mixed concrete

(P-4502)
PLEASANTON READY MIX CON INC
Also Called: Pleasanton Readymix Concrete
3400 Boulder St, Pleasanton (94566-4769)
P.O. Box 879 (94566-0874)
PHONE...................925 846-3226
Albert Riebli, *President*
John Santos, *Treasurer*
EMP: 15 **EST:** 1966
SQ FT: 1,000
SALES (est): 2.7MM **Privately Held**
WEB: www.pleasantonreadymix.com
SIC: 3273 Ready-mixed concrete

(P-4503)
RC READYMIX CO INC
1227 Greenville Rd, Livermore (94550-9299)
PHONE...................925 449-7785
Rob Costa, *President*
Rob C0sta, *President*
EMP: 24 **EST:** 1998
SALES (est): 4.4MM **Privately Held**
WEB: www.rcreadymixco.com
SIC: 3273 Ready-mixed concrete

(P-4504)
RIGHT AWAY CONCRETE PMPG INC
401 Kennedy St, Oakland (94606-5321)
PHONE...................510 536-1900
David Filipek, *Manager*
Jose Chacon, *Supervisor*
EMP: 30
SQ FT: 3,328 **Publicly Held**
WEB: www.rightawayredymix.com
SIC: 3273 1771 Ready-mixed concrete; concrete pumping
HQ: Right Away Concrete Pumping, Inc.
725 Julie Ann Way
Oakland CA 94621

(P-4505)
SHAMROCK MATERIALS INC (PA)
181 Lynch Creek Way # 201, Petaluma (94954-2388)
P.O. Box 751300 (94975-1300)
PHONE...................707 781-9000
Eugene B Ceccotti, *CEO*
Robert Bowen, *CFO*
Joe Webb, *Technology*
Joe Enes, *Sales Staff*
▲ **EMP:** 25 **EST:** 1945
SQ FT: 5,000
SALES (est): 15.3MM **Privately Held**
WEB: www.shamrockmaterials.com
SIC: 3273 5211 Ready-mixed concrete; lumber & other building materials

(P-4506)
SHAMROCK MATERIALS OF NOVATO
7552 Redwood Blvd, Novato (94945-2425)
P.O. Box 808044, Petaluma (94975-8044)
PHONE...................415 892-1571
Eugene B Ceccotti, *CEO*
EMP: 66 **EST:** 1961
SALES (est): 871.9K
SALES (corp-wide): 15.3MM **Privately Held**
WEB: www.novato.org
SIC: 3273 Ready-mixed concrete
PA: Shamrock Materials, Inc.
181 Lynch Creek Way # 201
Petaluma CA 94954
707 781-9000

(P-4507)
SIERRA-TAHOE READY MIX INC
1526 Emerald Bay Rd, South Lake Tahoe (96150-6112)
PHONE...................530 541-1877
Donald Wallace, *President*
William Santos, *Treasurer*
EMP: 22 **EST:** 1970
SQ FT: 2,000
SALES (est): 2.8MM **Privately Held**
SIC: 3273 Ready-mixed concrete

(P-4508)
SOUSA READY MIX LLC
Also Called: Siskiyou County Family Plng R
100 Upton Rd, Mount Shasta (96067-9169)
P.O. Box 157 (96067-0157)
PHONE...................530 926-4485
Gregory Juell, *Mng Member*
EMP: 17 **EST:** 1976
SQ FT: 1,200
SALES (est): 4.9MM **Privately Held**
WEB: www.sousareadymix.com
SIC: 3273 Ready-mixed concrete

(P-4509)
SOUTH VALLEY MATERIALS INC (DH)
114 E Shaw Ave Ste 100, Fresno (93710-7621)
P.O. Box 26240 (93729-6240)
PHONE...................559 277-7060
James G Brown, *President*
EMP: 60 **EST:** 1996
SQ FT: 6,000
SALES (est): 11.9MM
SALES (corp-wide): 20.8B **Privately Held**
WEB: www.lehighhanson.com
SIC: 3273 Ready-mixed concrete

(P-4510)
TEICHERT INC (PA)
5200 Franklin Dr Ste 115, Pleasanton (94588-3363)
P.O. Box 15002, Sacramento (95851-0002)
PHONE...................916 484-3011
Judson T Riggs, *President*
Louis V Riggs, *Ch of Bd*
Ron Gatto, *CFO*
Narendra M Pathipati, *CFO*
Sonja Herne, *Exec VP*
▲ **EMP:** 853 **EST:** 1887
SALES (est): 842MM **Privately Held**
WEB: www.teichert.com
SIC: 3273 5032 1611 1442 Ready-mixed concrete; brick, stone & related material; highway & street construction; construction sand & gravel; single-family housing construction; air ducts, sheet metal

3274 Lime

(P-4511)
LIME LIGHT CRM INC
89 De Boom St, San Francisco (94107-1425)
PHONE...................800 455-9645
Brian A Bogosian, *President*
Joanny Spina, *Opers Mgr*
Matthew Abdalah, *Accounts Exec*
EMP: 23 **EST:** 2015
SALES (est): 4.5MM **Privately Held**
WEB: www.sticky.io
SIC: 3274 Lime

3275 Gypsum Prdts

(P-4512)
PABCO BUILDING PRODUCTS LLC
Also Called: Pabco Gypsum
37851 Cherry St, Newark (94560-4348)
P.O. Box 405 (94560-0405)
PHONE...................510 792-9555
Charlie Coleman, *Manager*
EMP: 53
SALES (corp-wide): 1.1B **Privately Held**
WEB: www.pabcogypsum.com
SIC: 3275 Gypsum products
HQ: Pabco Building Products, Llc
10600 White Rock Rd Ste 1
Rancho Cordova CA 95670
510 792-1577

(P-4513)
PABCO BUILDING PRODUCTS LLC
37849 Cherry St, Newark (94560-4348)
PHONE...................510 792-1577
Ryan Lucchetti, *President*
EMP: 53
SALES (corp-wide): 1.1B **Privately Held**
WEB: www.pabcogypsum.com
SIC: 3275 3251 3259 Gypsum products; brick clay: common face, glazed, vitrified or hollow; architectural terra cotta
HQ: Pabco Building Products, Llc
10600 White Rock Rd Ste 1
Rancho Cordova CA 95670
510 792-1577

(P-4514)
PABCO BUILDING PRODUCTS LLC (HQ)
Also Called: Quietrock
10600 White Rock Rd Ste 1, Rancho Cordova (95670-6293)
P.O. Box 419074 (95741-9074)
PHONE...................510 792-1577
Phil Bonnell, *President*
Brian Hobdy, *CFO*
Jack Haarlander, *Bd of Directors*
Alfred Mueller, *Bd of Directors*
Larry Solari, *Bd of Directors*
▲ **EMP:** 20 **EST:** 1976
SALES (est): 171.4MM
SALES (corp-wide): 1.1B **Privately Held**
WEB: www.pabcogypsum.com
SIC: 3275 3251 3259 Gypsum products; brick clay: common face, glazed, vitrified or hollow; architectural terra cotta
PA: Pacific Coast Building Products, Inc.
10600 White Rock Rd # 100
Rancho Cordova CA 95670
916 631-6500

3281 Cut Stone Prdts

(P-4515)
ART CRAFT STATUARY INC
10441 Edes Ave, Oakland (94603-3015)
PHONE...................510 633-1411
Alipio Fabbri, *President*
Ivana Fabbri, *Vice Pres*
EMP: 22 **EST:** 1961
SQ FT: 43,000
SALES (est): 1.1MM **Privately Held**
WEB: www.artcraftstatuary.com
SIC: 3281 3272 Cut stone & stone products; concrete products

(P-4516)
BARRYS CULTURED MARBLE INC
866 Teal Dr, Benicia (94510-1249)
PHONE...................707 745-3444
Barry Martin, *President*
Carole Martin, *Vice Pres*
EMP: 19 **EST:** 1989
SALES (est): 1.2MM **Privately Held**
SIC: 3281 5211 1799 Cut stone & stone products; bathroom fixtures, equipment & supplies; counter top installation

(P-4517)
GGF MARBLE & SUPPLY INC
1375 Franquette Ave Ste F, Concord (94520-7932)
PHONE...................925 676-8385
Gaspare Giorgio Fundaro, *President*
Gregory Markeil,
Vince Rizzuto,
◆ **EMP:** 24 **EST:** 1986
SQ FT: 2,500
SALES (est): 315.5K **Privately Held**
WEB: www.gmmarbleandgranite.net
SIC: 3281 Furniture, cut stone

(P-4518)
HALABI INC (PA)
Also Called: Duracite
4447 Green Valley Rd, Fairfield (94534-1365)
PHONE...................707 402-1600
Fadi M Halabi, *CEO*
George Marino, *CFO*
Lenna Geist, *Human Res Dir*
EMP: 137 **EST:** 1995
SALES (est): 26.5MM **Privately Held**
SIC: 3281 1799 Cut stone & stone products; counter top installation

(P-4519)
PARAGON INDUSTRIES INC (PA)
Also Called: Bedrosian's Tiles & Stone
4285 N Golden State Blvd, Fresno (93722-6316)
PHONE...................559 275-5000
Larry Bedrosian, *CEO*
Gardnar O 'brien, *CFO*
Linda Bedrosian, *Treasurer*
Gary Bedrosian, *Vice Pres*
Janice Bedrosian, *Admin Sec*
◆ **EMP:** 78 **EST:** 1974

3281 - Cut Stone Prdts County (P-4520)

SQ FT: 35,000
SALES (est): 251.5MM **Privately Held**
SIC: **5211** 3281 3251 Tile, ceramic; curbing, granite or stone; granite, cut & shaped; brick & structural clay tile

(P-4520)
PARAGON INDUSTRIES II INC
4285 N Golden State Blvd, Fresno (93722-6316)
PHONE...................................559 275-5000
Larry E Bedrosian, *President*
EMP: 128 EST: 2012
SALES (est): 8.4MM
SALES (corp-wide): 251.5MM **Privately Held**
SIC: **5211** 3281 3251 Tile, ceramic; curbing, granite or stone; granite, cut & shaped; brick & structural clay tile
PA: Paragon Industries, Inc.
4285 N Golden State Blvd
Fresno CA 93722
559 275-5000

(P-4521)
PAVESTONE LLC
27600 County Road 90, Winters (95694-9003)
PHONE...................................530 795-4400
Wes May, *Manager*
Brad Hayes, *Plant Mgr*
Jeannie Del Toro, *Transptn Dir*
EMP: 17 **Privately Held**
WEB: www.pavestone.com
SIC: **3281** Paving blocks, cut stone
HQ: Pavestone, Llc
5 Concourse Pkwy Ste 1900
Atlanta GA 30328
404 926-3167

(P-4522)
SHARCAR ENTERPRISES INC
Also Called: Custom Marble & Onyx
201 Winmoore Way, Modesto (95358-5743)
P.O. Box 581710 (95358-0030)
PHONE...................................209 531-2200
Daryl Schenewark, *President*
Sharon Schenewark, *Admin Sec*
EMP: 20 EST: 1988
SQ FT: 10,000
SALES (est): 2.9MM **Privately Held**
WEB: www.custommarbleandonyx.com
SIC: **3281** 1799 Bathroom fixtures, cut stone; counter top installation

(P-4523)
SINOSOURCE INTL CO INC
230 Adrian Rd, Millbrae (94030-3103)
PHONE...................................650 697-6668
Ken Jiang, *President*
Lindsay Petterson, *Cust Mgr*
◆ EMP: 15 EST: 1999
SALES (est): 2MM **Privately Held**
WEB: www.shopping.na3.netsuite.com
SIC: **3281** Urns, cut stone

(P-4524)
SOUTH BAY MARBLE INC (PA)
1770 Old Bayshore Hwy, San Jose (95112-4306)
PHONE...................................650 594-4251
Bob Sutton, *President*
▲ EMP: 29 EST: 1978
SALES (est): 2.4MM **Privately Held**
WEB: www.southbaymarble.com
SIC: **3281** Marble, building: cut & shaped; building stone products; granite, cut & shaped

3291 Abrasive Prdts

(P-4525)
MIPOX INTERNATIONAL CORP
1065 E Hillsdale Blvd # 401, Foster City (94404-1689)
PHONE...................................650 638-9830
Tetsujiro Tada, *President*
◆ EMP: 24 EST: 1989
SQ FT: 14,000
SALES (est): 1.3MM **Privately Held**
WEB: www.mipox.co.jp
SIC: **3291** Abrasive products

PA: Mipox Corporation
6-11-3, Nishishinjuku
Shinjuku-Ku TKY 160-0
-

3292 Asbestos products

(P-4526)
LAMART CORPORATION
Also Called: Orcon Aerospace
2600 Central Ave Ste E, Union City (94587-3187)
P.O. Box 487, Kentfield (94914-0487)
PHONE...................................510 489-8100
EMP: 110
SALES (corp-wide): 93.6MM **Privately Held**
WEB: www.lamartcorp.com
SIC: **3292** 3559 Blankets, insulating for aircraft asbestos; bag seaming & closing machines (sewing machinery)
PA: Lamart Corporation
16 Richmond St
Clifton NJ 07011
973 772-6262

3295 Minerals & Earths: Ground Or Treated

(P-4527)
A&M PRODUCTS MANUFACTURING CO (HQ)
1221 Broadway Ste 51, Oakland (94612-1837)
PHONE...................................510 271-7000
Lawrence Peiros, *Principal*
▲ EMP: 100 EST: 1999
SALES (est): 16MM
SALES (corp-wide): 7.3B **Publicly Held**
WEB: www.thecloroxcompany.com
SIC: **3295** Minerals, ground or treated
PA: The Clorox Company
1221 Broadway Ste 1300
Oakland CA 94612
510 271-7000

(P-4528)
DICALITE MINERALS CORP (HQ)
36994 Summit Lake Rd, Burney (96013-9636)
PHONE...................................530 335-5451
Raymond Perlman, *President*
Derek J Cusack, *Vice Pres*
Ben Lazar, *Controller*
Rocky Torgrimson, *Opers Mgr*
Doug Witherspoon, *Director*
◆ EMP: 40 EST: 1995
SQ FT: 3,000
SALES (est): 28.3MM
SALES (corp-wide): 81.9MM **Privately Held**
WEB: www.dicalite.com
SIC: **3295** Minerals, ground or treated
PA: Dicalite Management Group, Llc
1001 Cnshohckn State Rd
Conshohocken PA 19428
610 660-8808

(P-4529)
IMERYS FILTRATION MINERALS INC (DH)
1732 N 1st St Ste 450, San Jose (95112-4579)
PHONE...................................805 562-0200
Douglas A Smith, *CEO*
John Oskan, *President*
Rick Heer, *Treasurer*
Fred Weber, *Treasurer*
Daniel Moncino, *Vice Pres*
◆ EMP: 50 EST: 1992
SQ FT: 11,600
SALES (est): 570.7MM
SALES (corp-wide): 3.2MM **Privately Held**
WEB: www.imerys-performance-minerals.com
SIC: **3295** Minerals, ground or treated
HQ: Imerys Usa, Inc.
100 Mansell Ct E Ste 300
Roswell GA 30076
770 576-3999

(P-4530)
ISP GRANULE PRODUCTS INC
1900 Hwy 104, Ione (95640)
PHONE...................................209 274-2930
Sunil Kumar, *President*
EMP: 195 EST: 2002
SALES (est): 4.1MM
SALES (corp-wide): 106.6MM **Privately Held**
SIC: **3295** Roofing granules
HQ: Isp Minerals Llc
34 Charles St
Hagerstown MD 21740

(P-4531)
PABCO CLAY PRODUCTS LLC
1500 Shridan Lincoln Blvd, Lincoln (95648-9102)
PHONE...................................916 645-8937
EMP: 23
SALES (corp-wide): 1.1B **Privately Held**
SIC: **3295** Minerals, ground or treated
HQ: Pabco Clay Products, Llc
605 Industrial Way
Dixon CA 95620

(P-4532)
SPECIALTY GRANULES LLC
1900 State Hwy 104, Ione (95640)
P.O. Box 400 (95640-0400)
PHONE...................................209 274-5323
George Dias, *Plant Mgr*
EMP: 50
SALES (corp-wide): 106.6MM **Privately Held**
WEB: www.specialtygranules.com
SIC: **3295** Roofing granules
PA: Specialty Granules Llc
13424 Pa Ave Ste 303
Hagerstown MD 21742
301 733-4000

3296 Mineral Wool

(P-4533)
KNAUF INSULATION INC
3100 Ashby Rd, Shasta Lake (96019-9136)
PHONE...................................530 275-9665
Bill Taylor, *Branch Mgr*
Jennifer Pirro,
Dwain Chabolla, *Manager*
Iain James, *Manager*
EMP: 103
SALES (corp-wide): 10.7B **Privately Held**
WEB: www.knaufnorthamerica.com
SIC: **3296** Fiberglass insulation
HQ: Knauf Insulation, Inc.
1 Knauf Dr
Shelbyville IN 46176
317 398-4434

3297 Nonclay Refractories

(P-4534)
TERRA MILLENNIUM CORP
1060 Hensley St, Richmond (94801-2117)
PHONE...................................510 233-2500
Michael Elam, *CFO*
Rich Giaramita, *Regional Mgr*
Josh Bibbs, *Project Mgr*
Madison Allred, *Marketing Mgr*
EMP: 27 EST: 2002
SALES (est): 379.3K **Privately Held**
WEB: www.tmcorp.us
SIC: **3297** Nonclay refractories

3299 Nonmetallic Mineral Prdts, NEC

(P-4535)
BRANDELLI ARTS INC
1250 Shaws Flat Rd, Sonora (95370-5433)
PHONE...................................714 537-0969
Robert Brandelli, *President*
Aurora Brandelli, *Vice Pres*
EMP: 46 EST: 1969

SALES (est): 2MM **Privately Held**
SIC: **3299** 3272 Statuary: gypsum, clay, papier mache, metal, etc.; concrete products

(P-4536)
LOMELIS STATUARY INC (PA)
Also Called: Lomeli's Gardens
11921 E Brandt Rd, Lockeford (95237-9708)
P.O. Box 1356 (95237-1356)
PHONE...................................209 367-1131
Doris Lomeli, *President*
Adriana Lomeli, *Treasurer*
Carlos Lomeli, *Admin Sec*
Elsa Lomeli, *Admin Sec*
EMP: 25 EST: 1971
SQ FT: 28,000
SALES (est): 2.3MM **Privately Held**
SIC: **3299** 5021 5261 Statuary: gypsum, clay, papier mache, metal, etc.; outdoor & lawn furniture; nurseries & garden centers

(P-4537)
MORGAN TECHNICAL CERAMICS INC
2425 Whipple Rd, Hayward (94544-7807)
PHONE...................................510 491-1100
Mark Robertshaw, *CEO*
Andrew Hosty, *COO*
Kevin Dangerfield, *CFO*
Andrew Shilston, *Chairman*
Ron Delevan, *Technical Mgr*
EMP: 29 EST: 1991
SALES (est): 5.1MM **Privately Held**
SIC: **3299** Ceramic fiber

(P-4538)
OMEGA PRODUCTS CORP (HQ)
Also Called: Omega Products International
8111 Fruitridge Rd, Sacramento (95826-4759)
P.O. Box 77220, Corona (92877-0107)
PHONE...................................916 635-3335
Kenneth R Thompson, *President*
Lutz Lamparter, *COO*
Todd Martin, *Vice Pres*
Alejandra Becerra, *Credit Mgr*
Sam Shen, *Purch Mgr*
▲ EMP: 60 EST: 1973
SQ FT: 11,000
SALES (est): 34MM
SALES (corp-wide): 90.1MM **Privately Held**
WEB: www.omega-products.com
SIC: **3299** 2899 Stucco; chemical preparations
PA: Opal Service, Inc.
282 S Anita Dr
Orange CA 92868
714 935-0900

3312 Blast Furnaces, Coke Ovens, Steel & Rolling Mills

(P-4539)
BAMBACIGNO STEEL COMPANY
4930 Mchenry Ave, Modesto (95356-9669)
PHONE...................................209 524-9681
Mary Bambacigno, *CEO*
Bill Boughton, *Vice Pres*
Sheila Arnold, *Admin Sec*
Rich Custer, *Project Mgr*
Nicole Kochman, *Accountant*
EMP: 48
SQ FT: 51,440
SALES (est): 10.3MM **Privately Held**
WEB: www.bambacigno.com
SIC: **3312** Structural shapes & pilings, steel

(P-4540)
CALIFORNIA STL STAIR RAIL MFR
587 Carnegie St, Manteca (95337-6102)
PHONE...................................209 824-1785
Richard G Lee, *President*
Dave Geserick, *CFO*
EMP: 28 EST: 1997
SQ FT: 30,000
SALES (est): 1.4MM **Privately Held**
SIC: **3312** Rails, steel or iron; structural shapes & pilings, steel

PRODUCTS & SERVICES SECTION

3353 - Aluminum Sheet, Plate & Foil County (P-4560)

(P-4541)
DIETRICH INDUSTRIES INC
2525 S Airport Way, Stockton (95206-3521)
PHONE.................................209 547-9066
Randy Rose, *Manager*
EMP: 84
SALES (corp-wide): 3.1B **Publicly Held**
SIC: 3312 Blast furnaces & steel mills
HQ: Dietrich Industries, Inc.
200 W Wlson Bridge Rd
Worthington OH 43085
800 873-2604

(P-4542)
HOLT TOOL & MACHINE INC
2909 Middlefield Rd, Redwood City (94063-3328)
PHONE.................................650 364-2547
Leo Hoenighausen, *President*
Ulrich Hoenighausen, *CFO*
Karen Garcia, *Technology*
Remus Regnelala, *Mfg Mgr*
EMP: 21 **EST:** 1933
SQ FT: 12,000
SALES (est): 3.6MM **Privately Held**
WEB: www.holttool.com
SIC: 3312 3469 7692 3544 Tool & die steel & alloys; metal stampings; welding repair; special dies, tools, jigs & fixtures

(P-4543)
LAMAR TOOL & DIE CASTING INC
4230 Technology Dr, Modesto (95356-9484)
PHONE.................................209 545-5525
Larry Snoreen, *President*
Margie Snoreen, *Treasurer*
Brian Kolsters, *Vice Pres*
Carol Lemmons, *Executive*
Kelli Jones, *Office Mgr*
▲ **EMP:** 41 **EST:** 1982
SQ FT: 20,000
SALES (est): 7.4MM **Privately Held**
WEB: www.lamartoolanddie.com
SIC: 3322 3463 3364 Tool & die steel & alloys; nonferrous forgings; nonferrous die-castings except aluminum

3315 Steel Wire Drawing & Nails & Spikes

(P-4544)
NEW PRDUCT INTGRTION SLTONS IN (PA)
Also Called: Npi Solutions
685 Jarvis Dr Ste A, Morgan Hill (95037-2813)
PHONE.................................408 944-9178
Kevin R Andersen, *President*
Dawn Casterson, *CFO*
Glenda Hernandez, *Top Exec*
Scott Ngo, *Project Engr*
Cindy E Chambers, *Controller*
▲ **EMP:** 64 **EST:** 2000
SQ FT: 15,000
SALES (est): 31.9MM **Privately Held**
WEB: www.npisolutions.com
SIC: 3315 Cable, steel: insulated or armored

(P-4545)
SILICON VALLEY MFG INC
6520 Central Ave, Newark (94560-3933)
PHONE.................................510 791-9450
Mark Serpa, *Principal*
EMP: 18 **EST:** 2007
SALES (est): 9.7MM **Privately Held**
WEB: www.svmfg.com
SIC: 3315 Steel wire & related products

(P-4546)
SUN POWER SECURITY GATES INC
438 Tyler Rd, Merced (95341-8807)
P.O. Box 2044 (95344-0044)
PHONE.................................209 722-3990
Robert Osborn, *President*
Gene Felling, *Vice Pres*
Dusty Major, *General Mgr*
EMP: 17 **EST:** 1990
SQ FT: 3,500
SALES (est): 2MM **Privately Held**
WEB: www.sun-power.com
SIC: 3315 3677 Fence gates posts & fittings: steel; transformers power supply, electronic type

3316 Cold Rolled Steel Sheet, Strip & Bars

(P-4547)
NEXCOIL STEEL LLC
1265 Shaw Rd, Stockton (95215-4020)
PHONE.................................209 900-1919
Gary Stein, *Principal*
Robert Elkington, *Principal*
Fred Morrison, *Principal*
EMP: 17 **EST:** 2012
SALES (est): 2MM **Privately Held**
SIC: 3316 Bars, steel, cold finished, from purchased hot-rolled

3321 Gray Iron Foundries

(P-4548)
LODI IRON WORKS INC (PA)
Also Called: Galt Steel Foundry
820 S Sacramento St, Lodi (95240-4710)
P.O. Box 1150 (95241-1150)
PHONE.................................209 368-5395
Kevin Van Steenberge, *President*
Michael Van Steenberge, *Vice Pres*
Michael Vansteenberg, *Purch Mgr*
Mike Van Steenberge, *VP Mfg*
Steve Horvath, *Manager*
EMP: 37 **EST:** 1943
SQ FT: 11,000
SALES (est): 10.4MM **Privately Held**
WEB: www.lodiiron.com
SIC: 3321 3312 Gray iron castings; stainless steel

(P-4549)
MCWANE INC
AB & I Foundry
7825 San Leandro St, Oakland (94621-2515)
PHONE.................................510 632-3467
Allan Boscacci, *President*
Michael Lowe, *Vice Pres*
Jenny Landon, *Personnel Assit*
Richard Watson, *Plant Mgr*
Matthew Maziarz, *Regl Sales Mgr*
▲ **EMP:** 215
SALES (corp-wide): 970.3MM **Privately Held**
WEB: www.abifoundry.com
SIC: 3321 3494 Gray & ductile iron foundries; valves & pipe fittings
PA: Mcwane, Inc.
2900 Highway 280 S # 300
Birmingham AL 35223
205 414-3100

(P-4550)
MCWANE INC
Also Called: A B & I
2581 S Golden State Blvd, Fowler (93625-2681)
PHONE.................................559 834-4630
Kirt Winter, *Branch Mgr*
EMP: 15
SALES (corp-wide): 970.3MM **Privately Held**
WEB: www.abifoundry.com
SIC: 3321 Soil pipe & fittings: cast iron
PA: Mcwane, Inc.
2900 Highway 280 S # 300
Birmingham AL 35223
205 414-3100

(P-4551)
RIDGE FOUNDRY
Also Called: Ridge Cast Metals
1554 Doolittle Dr, San Leandro (94577-2271)
PHONE.................................510 352-0551
Norman Stamm, *President*
EMP: 33 **EST:** 1956
SQ FT: 25,000
SALES (est): 1.1MM **Privately Held**
SIC: 3321 3325 3369 3365 Gray iron castings; ductile iron castings; steel foundries; nonferrous foundries; aluminum foundries; malleable iron foundries

3324 Steel Investment Foundries

(P-4552)
REED MANUFACTURING INC
Also Called: American Casting Co
205 Apollo Way Ste A, Hollister (95023-2507)
PHONE.................................831 637-5641
John Reed, *President*
Simeon Bauer, *Vice Pres*
Chris St John, *Vice Pres*
Jeff Ferrara, *Engineer*
Oliver Hayes, *Engineer*
EMP: 35 **EST:** 1977
SQ FT: 7,200
SALES (est): 5.7MM **Privately Held**
WEB: www.americancastingco.com
SIC: 3324 Commercial investment castings, ferrous

3325 Steel Foundries, NEC

(P-4553)
TUSCO CASTING CORPORATION
934 E Victor Rd, Lodi (95240-0722)
P.O. Box 537 (95241-0537)
PHONE.................................209 368-5137
Kevin Steiger, *President*
Tanen Steiger, *Vice Pres*
EMP: 28 **EST:** 1965
SQ FT: 20,000
SALES (est): 1.1MM **Privately Held**
WEB: www.tuscocasting.com
SIC: 3325 3365 3322 Alloy steel castings, except investment; aluminum foundries; malleable iron foundries

3334 Primary Production Of Aluminum

(P-4554)
KAISER ALUMINUM INTL CORP
6177 Sunal Blvd, Pleasanton (94566)
PHONE.................................949 614-1740
Jack A Hockema, *President*
EMP: 103 **EST:** 1957
SALES (est): 42.2MM
SALES (corp-wide): 1.1B **Publicly Held**
WEB: www.kaiseraluminum.com
SIC: 3334 3353 3354 3355 Primary aluminum; aluminum sheet, plate & foil; aluminum extruded products; aluminum rolling & drawing
PA: Kaiser Aluminum Corporation
27422 Portola Pkwy # 350
Foothill Ranch CA 92610
949 614-1740

3339 Primary Nonferrous Metals, NEC

(P-4555)
SUPERIOR QUARTZ INC
Also Called: Silica Engineering Group
3370 Edward Ave, Santa Clara (95054-2309)
PHONE.................................408 844-9663
Nermin Aganbegovic, *President*
Mirela Aganbegovic, *Director*
EMP: 15 **EST:** 1999
SQ FT: 13,000 **Privately Held**
WEB: www.superiorqtz.com
SIC: 3339 3679 3264 Silicon, pure; quartz crystals, for electronic application; magnets, permanent: ceramic or ferrite

3341 Secondary Smelting & Refining Of Nonferrous Metals

(P-4556)
ALL METALS INC (PA)
Also Called: Ecs Refining
705 Reed St, Santa Clara (95050-3942)
PHONE.................................408 200-7000
James L Taggart, *President*
Kenneth Taggart, *Vice Pres*
Ken Taggart, *Program Mgr*
Jim Nelson, *General Mgr*
Kent Taggart, *General Mgr*
▲ **EMP:** 20 **EST:** 1980
SQ FT: 24,000
SALES (est): 10.4MM **Privately Held**
SIC: 3341 4953 3339 Secondary precious metals; tin smelting & refining (secondary); lead smelting & refining (secondary); silver recovery from used photographic film; refuse systems; primary nonferrous metals

(P-4557)
AQUA METALS INC
1010 Atlantic Ave, Alameda (94501-1199)
PHONE.................................510 479-7635
Judd Merrill, *CFO*
EMP: 38
SALES (corp-wide): 108K **Publicly Held**
WEB: www.aquametals.com
SIC: 3341 Secondary nonferrous metals
PA: Aqua Metals, Inc.
2500 Peru Dr
Sparks NV 89437
510 479-7635

3353 Aluminum Sheet, Plate & Foil

(P-4558)
GOLDEN STATE ASSEMBLY INC
18220 Butterfield Blvd, Morgan Hill (95037-2824)
PHONE.................................408 438-0314
Jose Mardueno, *Site Mgr*
EMP: 19 **Privately Held**
WEB: www.gsassembly.com
SIC: 3353 3569 Aluminum sheet & strip; assembly machines, non-metalworking
PA: Golden State Assembly, Inc.
47823 Westinghouse Dr
Fremont CA 94539

(P-4559)
GOLDEN STATE ASSEMBLY INC (PA)
47823 Westinghouse Dr, Fremont (94539-7437)
P.O. Box 611913, San Jose (95161-1913)
PHONE.................................510 226-8155
Yesenia Castillo, *CEO*
Cesar E Madrueno, *President*
Maria Arellano, *Engineer*
Nancy Martinez, *Accounting Mgr*
Laura Santana, *Clerk*
EMP: 181 **EST:** 2009
SALES (est): 58MM **Privately Held**
WEB: www.gsassembly.com
SIC: 3353 3357 3679 Aluminum sheet & strip; aluminum wire & cable; assembly machines, non-metalworking; harness assemblies for electronic use: wire or cable; wire products, steel or iron

(P-4560)
ITW SEMISYSTEMS INC
625 Wool Creek Dr Ste G, San Jose (95112-2622)
PHONE.................................408 350-0244
EMP: 30
SALES (est): 3.7MM
SALES (corp-wide): 41MM **Privately Held**
WEB: www.mdc-vacuum.com
SIC: 3353 Tube Bending Weldment

3353 - Aluminum Sheet, Plate & Foil County (P-4561)

PA: Mdc Vacuum Products, Llc
30962 Santana St
Hayward CA 94544
510 265-3500

(P-4561)
MAVERICK ENTERPRISES INC
751 E Gobbi St, Ukiah (95482-6205)
PHONE..................707 463-5591
Steve Otterbeck, *President*
Cai N Berg, *President*
Trish Estep, *President*
Mike Benett, *Officer*
Jon Henderson, *Exec VP*
▲ EMP: 105 EST: 1992
SQ FT: 30,000
SALES (est): 30.1MM **Privately Held**
WEB: www.maverickcaps.com
SIC: 3353 Foil, aluminum
PA: Pcm Companies, Llc
2150 Dodd Rd
Mendota Heights MN 55120

3355 Aluminum Rolling & Drawing, NEC

(P-4562)
ARCADIA INC
2324 Del Monte St, West Sacramento (95691-3807)
PHONE..................916 375-1478
Eddy Sala, *Branch Mgr*
EMP: 29
SALES (corp-wide): 116.8MM **Privately Held**
WEB: www.arcadiainc.com
SIC: 3355 Extrusion ingot, aluminum: made in rolling mills
PA: Arcadia Inc.
2301 E Vernon Ave
Vernon CA 90058
323 269-7200

(P-4563)
METALS USA BUILDING PDTS LP
11340 White Rock Rd Ste B, Rancho Cordova (95742-6606)
PHONE..................916 635-2245
EMP: 25
SALES (corp-wide): 9.2B **Publicly Held**
SIC: 3355 Mfg & Whol Exterior Aluminum Building Products
HQ: Metals Usa Building Products Lp
2440 Albright Dr
Houston TX 92821
713 946-9000

(P-4564)
SOUTHERN ALUM FINSHG CO INC
Also Called: Saf West
4356 Caterpillar Rd, Redding (96003-1422)
PHONE..................530 244-7518
Sam Heier, *Branch Mgr*
Scott Thayer, *Project Mgr*
EMP: 90
SALES (corp-wide): 42.5MM **Privately Held**
WEB: www.saf.com
SIC: 3355 Structural shapes, rolled, aluminum
PA: Southern Aluminum Finishing Company, Inc.
1581 Huber St Nw
Atlanta GA 30318
404 355-1560

3356 Rolling, Drawing-Extruding Of Nonferrous Metals

(P-4565)
ENERVENUE INC
47621 Westinghouse Dr, Fremont (94539-7474)
PHONE..................408 664-0355
Jorg Heinemann, *CEO*
Frank Blohm, *COO*
Yi Cui, *Chairman*
Vikash Venkataramana, *Surgery Dir*
Majid Keshavarz, *CTO*
EMP: 30 EST: 2020
SALES (est): 10.3MM **Privately Held**
SIC: 3356 Battery metal

(P-4566)
FLASHCO MANUFACTURING INC (PA)
150 Todd Rd Ste 400, Santa Rosa (95407-8412)
PHONE..................707 824-4448
Gregory J Morrow, *CEO*
Marielle Blais, *Controller*
Brian Edison, *Sales Staff*
Phil Gatti, *Sales Staff*
▲ EMP: 26 EST: 1999
SQ FT: 7,500
SALES (est): 11.3MM **Privately Held**
WEB: www.flashco.com
SIC: 3356 Lead & lead alloy bars, pipe, plates, shapes, etc.

3357 Nonferrous Wire Drawing

(P-4567)
ARIA TECHNOLOGIES INC
102 Wright Brothers Ave, Livermore (94551-9240)
PHONE..................925 292-1616
Paula McGuinness, *CEO*
Joe McGuinness, *President*
Dave Dickens, *Vice Pres*
Ryan Gilbert, *Engineer*
Justin Tidd, *Mfg Staff*
▲ EMP: 20 EST: 1991
SQ FT: 15,000
SALES (est): 5.6MM **Privately Held**
WEB: www.ariatech.com
SIC: 3357 Communication wire

(P-4568)
CFKBA INC (PA)
150 Jefferson Dr, Menlo Park (94025-1115)
PHONE..................650 847-3900
Richard Johns, *Ch of Bd*
Laurent Mayer, *Vice Pres*
Wendell Jesseman, *Admin Sec*
◆ EMP: 49 EST: 1962
SQ FT: 43,000
SALES (est): 5.8MM **Privately Held**
SIC: 3357 5063 Nonferrous wiredrawing & insulating; wire & cable

(P-4569)
CFKBA INC
508 2nd Ave, Redwood City (94063-3848)
PHONE..................650 302-6331
EMP: 15
SALES (corp-wide): 5.8MM **Privately Held**
SIC: 3357 Nonferrous wiredrawing & insulating
PA: Cfkba Inc.
150 Jefferson Dr
Menlo Park CA 94025
650 847-3900

(P-4570)
DICAR INC
1285 Alma Ct, San Jose (95112-5943)
P.O. Box 1653, Morgan Hill (95038-1653)
PHONE..................408 295-1106
Edward Garcia, *CEO*
Ed Garcia, *President*
Diana M Garcia, *CFO*
Carol Garcia, *Vice Pres*
EMP: 26
SQ FT: 9,900
SALES (est): 6.4MM **Privately Held**
WEB: www.dicarinc.com
SIC: 3357 3599 3089 3679 Coaxial cable, nonferrous; communication wire; machine & other job shop work; blow molded finished plastic products; harness assemblies for electronic use: wire or cable

(P-4571)
NEPTEC OS INC
Also Called: Neptec Optical Solutions
48603 Warm Springs Blvd, Fremont (94539-7782)
PHONE..................510 687-1101
David Cheng, *President*
Chaoyu Yue, *Vice Pres*
EMP: 25 EST: 2008
SALES (est): 3.7MM **Privately Held**
WEB: www.neptecos.com
SIC: 3357 Fiber optic cable (insulated)

(P-4572)
PHAMTEC INC (PA)
1526 Centre Pointe Dr, Milpitas (95035-8230)
PHONE..................408 210-4606
Steven Pham, *Administration*
EMP: 30 EST: 2012
SALES (est): 2.3MM **Privately Held**
WEB: www.phamtecinc.com
SIC: 3357 Nonferrous wiredrawing & insulating

(P-4573)
WINTRONICS INTERNATIONAL INC
Also Called: Winstronics
3817 Spinnaker Ct, Fremont (94538-6537)
PHONE..................510 226-7588
Ben Yueh, *President*
Bobby Zhang, *Engineer*
Eileen Hsu, *Accounts Mgr*
▲ EMP: 25 EST: 1992
SQ FT: 12,000
SALES (est): 9.5MM **Privately Held**
WEB: www.winstronics.com
SIC: 3357 Communication wire

3363 Aluminum Die Castings

(P-4574)
A & B DIE CASTING CO INC
900 Alfred Nobel Dr, Hercules (94547-1814)
PHONE..................877 708-0009
Bernard E Dathe, *President*
Stephen Dathe, *COO*
Robert Dathe, *Corp Secy*
Alex Hantke, *Vice Pres*
George Donatello, *Info Tech Mgr*
EMP: 47 EST: 1951
SQ FT: 19,000
SALES (est): 2.7MM **Privately Held**
WEB: www.abdiecasting.com
SIC: 3363 3364 Aluminum die-castings; zinc & zinc-base alloy die-castings

(P-4575)
COOLING SOURCE INC
2021 Las Positas Ct # 101, Livermore (94551-7311)
PHONE..................925 292-1293
Michel Gelinas, *President*
Ray Arcena, *Engineer*
Jason Shrider, *Sales Staff*
Wayne Finger, *Manager*
Brian Rubner, *Manager*
▲ EMP: 118 EST: 2009
SQ FT: 4,000
SALES (est): 11.3MM **Privately Held**
WEB: www.coolingsource.com
SIC: 3363 3354 3325 3469 Aluminum die-castings; shapes, extruded aluminum; alloy steel castings, except investment; metal stampings

(P-4576)
EAST BAY BRASS FOUNDRY INC
1200 Chesley Ave, Richmond (94801-2144)
PHONE..................510 233-7171
Milton G Stewart, *President*
Teresa K Stewart, *Admin Sec*
EMP: 25 EST: 1947
SQ FT: 16,700
SALES (est): 2.5MM **Privately Held**
WEB: www.eastbaybrass.com
SIC: 3363 3364 3366 3369 Aluminum die-castings; brass & bronze die-castings; bronze foundry; nonferrous foundries; aluminum foundries

(P-4577)
HYATT DIE CAST ENGRG CORP - S
Also Called: Hyatt Die Casting
1250 Kifer Rd, Sunnyvale (94086-5304)
PHONE..................408 523-7000
Kul Dhanota, *Branch Mgr*
EMP: 39
SALES (corp-wide): 26.8MM **Privately Held**
WEB: www.hyattdiecast.com
SIC: 3363 Aluminum die-castings
PA: Hyatt Die Cast And Engineering Corporation - South
4656 Lincoln Ave
Cypress CA 90630
714 826-7550

(P-4578)
KEARNEYS ALUMINUM FOUNDRY INC (PA)
2660 S Dearing Ave, Fresno (93725-2104)
P.O. Box 2926 (93745-2926)
PHONE..................559 233-2591
Victor T Kearney Sr, *CEO*
Gary A Kearney, *President*
Michael Kearney, *President*
William Kearney, *President*
Robert Kearney Jr, *Vice Pres*
▲ EMP: 20 EST: 1944
SQ FT: 80,000
SALES (est): 3.5MM **Privately Held**
WEB: www.kearneysaluminumfoundry.com
SIC: 3363 Aluminum die-castings

(P-4579)
SAN JOSE DIE CASTING CORP
600 Business Park Dr # 100, Lincoln (95648-9364)
PHONE..................408 262-6500
Everett Callaghan, *President*
Leonid Kirshon, *Vice Pres*
Mark Callaghan, *Engineer*
▲ EMP: 27 EST: 1955
SALES (est): 3.7MM **Privately Held**
WEB: www.sjdiecasting.com
SIC: 3363 3364 3599 3441 Aluminum die-castings; zinc & zinc-base alloy die-castings; machine shop, jobbing & repair; fabricated structural metal; nonferrous foundries

(P-4580)
SKS DIE CAST & MACHINING INC (PA)
1849 Oak St, Alameda (94501-1412)
PHONE..................510 523-2541
Sean Keating, *CEO*
Jerome W Keating, *President*
Menelos J Moore, *Treasurer*
Leonore Keating, *Admin Sec*
Jesusa Fusade, *Asst Treas*
▲ EMP: 64 EST: 1947
SQ FT: 50,000
SALES (est): 5.4MM **Privately Held**
WEB: www.sksdiecasting.com
SIC: 3363 3845 Aluminum die-castings; electromedical equipment

3364 Nonferrous Die Castings, Exc Aluminum

(P-4581)
PRESSURE CAST PRODUCTS CORP
4210 E 12th St, Oakland (94601-4411)
PHONE..................510 532-7310
Willis Mc Neil, *President*
Vikki Cantwell, *General Mgr*
Jean Mc Neil, *Admin Sec*
▲ EMP: 32 EST: 1958
SQ FT: 30,000
SALES (est): 5.1MM **Privately Held**
WEB: www.pressurecastproducts.com
SIC: 3364 3363 Zinc & zinc-base alloy die-castings; aluminum die-castings

(P-4582)
PROTECH MATERIALS INC
20919 Cabot Blvd, Hayward (94545-1155)
PHONE..................510 887-5870
MEI Zhang, *President*
Larry Liu, *Vice Pres*

▲ = Import ▼ = Export
◆ = Import/Export

PRODUCTS & SERVICES SECTION

3421 - Cutlery County (P-4603)

Jacques Matteau, *VP Bus Dvlpt*
▲ **EMP:** 16 **EST:** 2006
SQ FT: 7,100
SALES (est): 2.5MM **Privately Held**
WEB: www.protechmaterials.com
SIC: 3364 3443 Nonferrous die-castings except aluminum; high vacuum coaters, metal plate

3365 Aluminum Foundries

(P-4583)
CHOICE FOODSERVICES INC
Also Called: Children's Choice
569 San Ramon Valley Blvd, Danville (94526-4024)
PHONE.................925 837-0104
Justin Gagnon, *President*
Ryan Mariopti, *CFO*
Mario Gonzalez, *Production*
Sam Totah, *Sales Staff*
Keith Cosbey, *Director*
▲ **EMP:** 80 **EST:** 2003
SALES (est): 22.9MM **Privately Held**
WEB: www.choicelunch.com
SIC: 3365 5049 Cooking/kitchen utensils, cast aluminum; school supplies

(P-4584)
GENERAL FOUNDRY SERVICE CORP
1390 Business Center Pl, San Leandro (94577-2212)
PHONE.................510 297-5040
Edward J Ritelli Jr, *CEO*
Edward J Ritelli Sr, *President*
Steve Bybee, *COO*
John Ritelli, *Technical Staff*
John Fehringer, *QC Mgr*
EMP: 70 **EST:** 1946
SQ FT: 15,200
SALES (est): 10.4MM **Privately Held**
WEB: www.genfoundry.com
SIC: 3365 3543 3369 3324 Aluminum & aluminum-based alloy castings; machinery castings, aluminum; industrial patterns; nonferrous foundries; steel investment foundries

(P-4585)
K B W INC
2660 S Dearing Ave, Fresno (93725-2104)
P.O. Box 2926 (93745-2926)
PHONE.................559 233-2591
William P Kearney, *President*
EMP: 20 **EST:** 1969
SALES (est): 1.1MM **Privately Held**
SIC: 3365 Aluminum foundries

3369 Nonferrous Foundries: Castings, NEC

(P-4586)
PCC STRUCTURALS INC
Also Called: PCC Structurals-San Leandro
414 Hester St, San Leandro (94577-1024)
PHONE.................510 568-6400
Craig Milton, *Branch Mgr*
Justin Meek, *Analyst*
Laura Norberg, *Accountant*
Brian Keegan, *VP Human Res*
Taylor Schaack, *Facilities Mgr*
EMP: 180
SALES (corp-wide): 245.5B **Publicly Held**
WEB: www.pccstructurals.com
SIC: 3369 Nonferrous foundries
HQ: Pcc Structurals, Inc.
 4600 Se Harney Dr
 Portland OR 97206
 503 777-3881

(P-4587)
RADIAN THERMAL PRODUCTS INC
Also Called: Radian Heat Sinks
2160 Walsh Ave, Santa Clara (95050-2512)
PHONE.................408 988-6200
Gerald L McIntyre, *Chairman*
Mong Hu, *CEO*
Nancy Cortez, *CIO*
Andrew Masto, *Engineer*
Kevin Pinheiro, *Engineer*
▲ **EMP:** 54 **EST:** 1984
SQ FT: 26,500
SALES (est): 8MM **Privately Held**
WEB: www.radianheatsinks.com
SIC: 3369 Castings, except die-castings, precision

3398 Metal Heat Treating

(P-4588)
METAL IMPROVEMENT COMPANY LLC
7655 Longard Rd Bldg A, Livermore (94551-8208)
PHONE.................925 960-1090
Jim McManus, *Manager*
Marissa Skog, *Manager*
EMP: 40
SALES (est): 2.3B **Publicly Held**
WEB: www.cwst.com
SIC: 3398 Shot peening (treating steel to reduce fatigue)
HQ: Metal Improvement Company, Llc
 80 E Rte 4 Ste 310
 Paramus NJ 07652
 201 843-7800

3399 Primary Metal Prdts, NEC

(P-4589)
CELLMOBILITY INC
808 Gilman St, Berkeley (94710-1422)
PHONE.................510 549-3300
Heeman Choe, *CEO*
EMP: 30
SALES (est): 1.2MM **Privately Held**
WEB: www.cellmoinc.com
SIC: 3399 Metal powders, pastes & flakes

(P-4590)
PARMATECH CORPORATION
2221 Pine View Way, Petaluma (94954-5688)
PHONE.................707 778-2266
Peter Frost, *CEO*
Caryn E Mitchell, *Treasurer*
Tracy Macneal, *Officer*
Bryan Mc Bride, *General Mgr*
▲ **EMP:** 75 **EST:** 1973
SQ FT: 22,000
SALES (est): 22.6MM
SALES (corp-wide): 87.5MM **Privately Held**
WEB: www.atwcompanies.com
SIC: 3399 Powder, metal
PA: Atw Companies, Inc.
 125 Metro Center Blvd # 300
 Warwick RI 02886
 401 244-1002

(P-4591)
PERRY TOOL & RESEARCH INC
3415 Enterprise Ave, Hayward (94545-3284)
PHONE.................510 782-9226
Kenneth Fasselman, *CEO*
EMP: 35 **EST:** 1962
SQ FT: 13,000
SALES (est): 4MM **Privately Held**
WEB: www.perrytool.com
SIC: 3399 Powder, metal

(P-4592)
SCAFCO CORPORATION
2443 Foundry Park Ave, Fresno (93706-4531)
PHONE.................559 256-9911
Larry Stone, *President*
EMP: 29
SALES (corp-wide): 75.8MM **Privately Held**
WEB: www.scafco.com
SIC: 3399 Iron ore recovery from open hearth slag
PA: Scafco Corporation
 2800 E Main Ave
 Spokane WA 99202
 509 343-9000

(P-4593)
SENJU COMTEK CORP
1171 N 4th St Ste 80, San Jose (95112-4968)
PHONE.................408 792-3830
Ryoichi Suzuki, *Branch Mgr*
Hiro Ota, *Info Tech Mgr*
Mari Kuhn, *Manager*
EMP: 16 **Privately Held**
WEB: www.senju.com
SIC: 3399 Paste, metal
HQ: Senju Comtek Corp.
 2989 San Ysidro Way
 Santa Clara CA 95051

(P-4594)
SIMPSON MANUFACTURING CO INC (PA)
5956 W Las Positas Blvd, Pleasanton (94588-8540)
PHONE.................925 560-9000
Karen Colonias, *CEO*
Peter N Louras Jr, *Ch of Bd*
Michael Olosky, *COO*
Brian J Magstadt, *CFO*
Celeste Ford, *Bd of Directors*
EMP: 150 **EST:** 1956
SALES (est): 1.2B **Publicly Held**
WEB: www.simpsonmfg.com
SIC: 3399 3441 Metal fasteners; building components, structural steel

(P-4595)
VALIMET INC (PA)
431 Sperry Rd, Stockton (95206-3907)
P.O. Box 31690 (95213-1690)
PHONE.................209 444-1600
Kurt F Leopold, *CEO*
George Campbell, *President*
Chris Adam, *Exec VP*
Michaela Leopold, *Admin Sec*
Sifan Zhu, *Engineer*
EMP: 57 **EST:** 1957
SQ FT: 200,000
SALES (est): 13.4MM **Privately Held**
WEB: www.valimet.com
SIC: 3399 Powder, metal

3411 Metal Cans

(P-4596)
AMERICAN PRODUCTION CO INC
Also Called: Super Chef
2734 Spring St, Redwood City (94063-3524)
P.O. Box 5766 (94063-0766)
PHONE.................650 368-5334
Owen Conley, *President*
EMP: 27 **EST:** 1945
SQ FT: 35,000
SALES (est): 1.8MM
SALES (corp-wide): 4.9MM **Privately Held**
WEB: www.americanproduction.com
SIC: 3411 2656 3412 Food & beverage containers; sanitary food containers; metal barrels, drums & pails
PA: Tilley Manufacturing Co., Inc.
 2734 Spring St
 Redwood City CA 94063
 650 365-3598

(P-4597)
BALL CORPORATION
Also Called: Metal Fd Hhld Pdts Pckging Div
300 Greger St, Oakdale (95361-8613)
PHONE.................209 848-6500
Michael Wright, *Branch Mgr*
Dave Miller, *President*
Joe Simcik, *Engineer*
Fred Orieny, *Analyst*
Candyce Knisely, *Buyer*
EMP: 260
SALES (corp-wide): 11.7B **Publicly Held**
WEB: www.ball.com
SIC: 3411 Metal cans
PA: Ball Corporation
 9200 W 108th Cir
 Westminster CO 80021
 303 469-3131

(P-4598)
KLEAN KANTEEN INC
3960 Morrow Ln, Chico (95928-8912)
PHONE.................530 592-4552
James Osgood, *CEO*
Darrell Cresswell, *President*
Jeff Cresswell, *COO*
Erika Bruhn, *CIO*
Kevin Welch, *Info Tech Mgr*
▲ **EMP:** 79 **EST:** 1976
SQ FT: 5,000
SALES (est): 11.4MM **Privately Held**
WEB: www.kleankanteen.com
SIC: 3411 Food containers, metal

(P-4599)
SILGAN CONTAINERS MFG CORP
4000 Yosemite Blvd, Modesto (95357-1580)
PHONE.................209 521-6469
EMP: 24 **Publicly Held**
WEB: www.silgancontainers.com
SIC: 3411 Metal cans
HQ: Silgan Containers Manufacturing Corporation
 21600 Oxnard St Ste 1600
 Woodland Hills CA 91367

(P-4600)
SILGAN CONTAINERS MFG CORP
2200 Wilbur Ave, Antioch (94509-8506)
PHONE.................925 778-8000
Arnold Naimark, *Branch Mgr*
EMP: 24 **Publicly Held**
WEB: www.silgancontainers.com
SIC: 3411 Metal cans
HQ: Silgan Containers Manufacturing Corporation
 21600 Oxnard St Ste 1600
 Woodland Hills CA 91367

(P-4601)
SILGAN CONTAINERS MFG CORP
6180 Roselle Ave, Riverbank (95367-2837)
PHONE.................209 869-3637
Steven Wolfgram, *Branch Mgr*
EMP: 24 **Publicly Held**
WEB: www.silgancontainers.com
SIC: 3411 Metal cans
HQ: Silgan Containers Manufacturing Corporation
 21600 Oxnard St Ste 1600
 Woodland Hills CA 91367

(P-4602)
SILGAN CONTAINERS MFG CORP
3250 Patterson Rd, Riverbank (95367-2938)
PHONE.................209 869-3601
Gary Miller, *Branch Mgr*
EMP: 24
SQ FT: 200,000 **Publicly Held**
WEB: www.silgancontainers.com
SIC: 3411 Metal cans
HQ: Silgan Containers Manufacturing Corporation
 21600 Oxnard St Ste 1600
 Woodland Hills CA 91367

3421 Cutlery

(P-4603)
ARCH FOODS INC (PA)
25817 Clawiter Rd, Hayward (94545-3217)
P.O. Box 2355, Clovis (93613-2355)
PHONE.................510 331-8352
Jeff Lim, *CEO*
▼ **EMP:** 45 **EST:** 2009
SQ FT: 2,000
SALES (est): 5.7MM **Privately Held**
WEB: www.archfoods.com
SIC: 3421 5149 Cutlery; dried or canned foods

3423 - Hand & Edge Tools

3423 Hand & Edge Tools

(P-4604)
ASSEMBLY SYSTEMS (PA)
16595 Englewood Ave, Los Gatos (95032-5622)
PHONE.................................408 395-5313
Malcolm Macdonald, *President*
EMP: 20 **EST:** 1977
SQ FT: 10,000
SALES (est): 1.9MM **Privately Held**
WEB: www.assemblysystems.net
SIC: 3423 Hand & edge tools

(P-4605)
DIRECT STONE TOOL SUPPLY INC (PA)
2400 Teagarden St, San Leandro (94577-4336)
PHONE.................................510 747-9720
Keith Mitchell, *CEO*
Monica Cass, *CFO*
Joanna Fernandez, *Branch Mgr*
▲ **EMP:** 19 **EST:** 2008
SALES (est): 5MM **Privately Held**
WEB: www.directstonetoolsupply.com
SIC: 3423 Masons' hand tools; stonecutters' hand tools

(P-4606)
LEVINE ARTHUR LANSKY & ASSOC (PA)
Also Called: Lansky Sharpeners
3914 Delmont Ave, Oakland (94605-2233)
PHONE.................................415 234-6020
Arthur Lansky Levine, *President*
EMP: 16 **EST:** 1974
SQ FT: 68,000
SALES (est): 1.7MM **Privately Held**
WEB: www.waterfordlexington.com
SIC: 3423 Hand & edge tools

(P-4607)
MORGAN MANUFACTURING INC
521 2nd St, Petaluma (94952-5121)
P.O. Box 737 (94953-0737)
PHONE.................................707 763-6848
Carl T Palmgren, *President*
Lillian Raposo, *Vice Pres*
Mary Kinney, *Marketing Mgr*
EMP: 15 **EST:** 1954
SALES (est): 1.7MM **Privately Held**
WEB: www.morganmfg.com
SIC: 3423 3499 Hand & edge tools; stabilizing bars (cargo), metal

(P-4608)
STANLEY ACCESS TECH LLC
1312 Dupont Ct, Manteca (95336-6004)
PHONE.................................209 221-4066
Brian Sheppard, *Manager*
EMP: 20
SALES (corp-wide): 14.5B **Publicly Held**
WEB: www.stanleyaccess.com
SIC: 3423 Hand & edge tools
HQ: Stanley Access Technologies Llc
65 Scott Swamp Rd
Farmington CT 06032

(P-4609)
SUPERCLOSET
Also Called: Kind Led Grow Lights
3555 Airway Dr, Santa Rosa (95403-1605)
P.O. Box 6105 (95406-0105)
PHONE.................................831 588-7829
Kip Lewis Andersen, *CEO*
Nicholas Schweitzer, *COO*
Nick Schweitzer, *COO*
Rory Kagan, *Officer*
Jeff James, *Purchasing*
▲ **EMP:** 20 **EST:** 2002
SQ FT: 18,000
SALES (est): 2.7MM **Privately Held**
WEB: www.supercloset.com
SIC: 3423 5261 Garden & farm tools, including shovels; lawn & garden equipment

(P-4610)
TRONEX TECHNOLOGY INCORPORATED
2860 Cordelia Rd Ste 230, Fairfield (94534-1808)
PHONE.................................707 426-2550
Arne Salvesen, *President*
Karin Salvesen, *Vice Pres*
EMP: 20 **EST:** 1982
SQ FT: 4,000
SALES (est): 1.5MM **Privately Held**
WEB: www.tronex.descoindustries.com
SIC: 3423 5049 Screw drivers, pliers, chisels, etc. (hand tools); precision tools

3425 Hand Saws & Saw Blades

(P-4611)
NORDIC SAW & TOOL MFRS INC
2114 Divanian Dr, Turlock (95382-9680)
P.O. Box 1128 (95381-1128)
PHONE.................................209 634-9015
Dewey Larson, *President*
EMP: 27 **EST:** 1962
SQ FT: 11,000
SALES (est): 694.5K **Privately Held**
WEB: www.nordicsaw.com
SIC: 3425 3421 3545 Saw blades & handsaws; knives: butchers', hunting, pocket, etc.; bits for use on lathes, planers, shapers, etc.

(P-4612)
SAWBIRDS INC (PA)
Also Called: Cal Saw
721 Brannan St, San Francisco (94103-4927)
P.O. Box 165, Winchester OR (97495-0165)
PHONE.................................415 861-0644
Warren M Bird, *President*
Benson L Joseph, *Vice Pres*
Hazel E Bird, *Admin Sec*
▲ **EMP:** 20 **EST:** 1886
SQ FT: 17,500
SALES (est): 1.9MM **Privately Held**
SIC: 3425 7699 3423 Saw blades for hand or power saws; knife, saw & tool sharpening & repair; knives, agricultural or industrial

3429 Hardware, NEC

(P-4613)
AMERICAN EMPEROR INC
888 Doolittle Dr, San Leandro (94577-1020)
PHONE.................................713 478-5973
Wai Ming Ng, *CEO*
EMP: 41 **EST:** 1983
SALES (est): 6MM **Privately Held**
WEB: www.emperorelectrical.com
SIC: 3429 Furniture builders' & other household hardware

(P-4614)
AUGUST HOME INC
657 Bryant St, San Francisco (94107-1612)
PHONE.................................415 891-0866
Jason Johnson, *CEO*
Peter Fornell, *President*
Kathy Sanders, *Chief Mktg Ofcr*
Yves Behar, *Officer*
Nate Williams, *Officer*
▲ **EMP:** 42 **EST:** 2012
SQ FT: 7,000
SALES (est): 11MM
SALES (corp-wide): 10.1B **Privately Held**
WEB: www.assaabloy.com
SIC: 5251 3429 Door locks & lock sets; security cable locking system
PA: Assa Abloy Ab
Klarabergsviadukten 90
Stockholm 111 6
850 648-500

(P-4615)
CRAIN CUTTER COMPANY INC
1155 Wrigley Way, Milpitas (95035-5426)
PHONE.................................408 946-6100
Millard Crain Jr, *CEO*
Jennifer Crain, *Shareholder*
Lance Crain, *Shareholder*
Eric Brungardt, *Representative*
▲ **EMP:** 87 **EST:** 1956
SQ FT: 110,000
SALES (est): 17.4MM **Privately Held**
WEB: www.craintools.com
SIC: 3429 3545 Manufactured hardware (general); machine tool accessories

(P-4616)
GARDNER FAMILY LTD PARTNERSHIP
Also Called: HMC Display
300 Commerce Dr, Madera (93637-5215)
PHONE.................................559 675-8149
Curtis K Gardner, *President*
Christine G Gardner, *Manager*
▲ **EMP:** 25 **EST:** 1967
SQ FT: 45,000
SALES (est): 6.6MM **Privately Held**
WEB: www.hmcdisplay.com
SIC: 3429 Manufactured hardware (general)

(P-4617)
HEARTHCO INC
5781 Pleasant Valley Rd, El Dorado (95623-4200)
PHONE.................................530 622-3877
Dan Zacher, *President*
Laurene Zacher, *CFO*
Paul Amador, *Sales Mgr*
EMP: 20 **EST:** 2001
SALES (est): 3.3MM **Privately Held**
WEB: www.hearthco.com
SIC: 3429 Fireplace equipment, hardware: andirons, grates, screens

(P-4618)
INTELLIGENT ENERGY INC
1731 Tech Dr Ste 755, San Jose (95110)
PHONE.................................562 997-3600
Henri Winand, *President*
Larry Frost, *Corp Secy*
Hazen Burford, *Vice Pres*
Iain Fraser, *Engineer*
EMP: 39 **EST:** 2002
SQ FT: 9,600
SALES (est): 5.2MM
SALES (corp-wide): 3MM **Privately Held**
WEB: www.intelligent-energy.com
SIC: 3429 3694 Bicycle racks, automotive; alternators, automotive
PA: Intelligent Energy Limited
Charnwood Building
Loughborough LEICS LE11
150 927-1271

(P-4619)
MCDANIEL MANUFACTURING INC
6180 Enterprise Dr Ste D, Diamond Springs (95619-9471)
PHONE.................................530 626-6336
John McDaniel, *President*
Nora McDaniel, *Corp Secy*
EMP: 15 **EST:** 1992
SALES (est): 2.3MM **Privately Held**
WEB: www.mcdanielmfg.com
SIC: 3429 3443 3089 Manufactured hardware (general); stills, pressure: metal plate; hardware, plastic

(P-4620)
SEARS ROEBUCK AND CO
Also Called: Sears 1468
5540 Winfield Blvd, San Jose (95123-1216)
PHONE.................................408 864-6600
EMP: 250
SALES (corp-wide): 16.7B **Publicly Held**
SIC: 5311 3429 Department Store Mfg Hardware
HQ: Sears, Roebuck And Co.
3333 Beverly Rd
Hoffman Estates IL 60179
847 286-2500

(P-4621)
T G SCHMEISER CO INC
Also Called: Schmeiser Farm Equipment
3160 E California Ave, Fresno (93702-4108)
P.O. Box 1047 (93714-1047)
PHONE.................................559 486-4569
Andrew W Cummings, *CEO*
Andrew Wcummings, *CEO*
Shirley Cummings, *Corp Secy*
Mitchell Jacoby, *Engineer*
Olga Pirogova, *Engineer*
▼ **EMP:** 35 **EST:** 1929
SQ FT: 36,000
SALES (est): 6MM **Privately Held**
WEB: www.tgschmeiser.com
SIC: 3429 3523 Manufactured hardware (general); soil preparation machinery, except turf & grounds

3431 Enameled Iron & Metal Sanitary Ware

(P-4622)
OZIG LLC ◆
490 43rd St Ste 206, Oakland (94609-2138)
PHONE.................................510 588-7952
Guanglin Duan, *Mng Member*
EMP: 50 **EST:** 2021
SALES (est): 10MM **Privately Held**
SIC: 3431 5084 Sinks: enameled iron, cast iron or pressed metal; countersinks

3432 Plumbing Fixture Fittings & Trim, Brass

(P-4623)
CENTRAL VLY ASSEMBLY PACKG INC
5515 E Lamona Ave 103, Fresno (93727-2226)
PHONE.................................559 486-4260
Nate Perry, *CEO*
John Perry, *COO*
David Fuentes, *Opers Mgr*
EMP: 24 **EST:** 2003
SALES (est): 2.1MM **Privately Held**
WEB: www.centralvalleyassembly.com
SIC: 3432 3565 3089 3824 Plastic plumbing fixture fittings, assembly; bag opening, filling & closing machines; vacuum packaging machinery; blister or bubble formed packaging, plastic; linear counters

3433 Heating Eqpt

(P-4624)
ACR SOLAR INTERNATIONAL CORP
Also Called: Solarroofs.com
5840 Gibbons Dr Ste H, Carmichael (95608-6903)
PHONE.................................916 481-7200
Al Rich, *President*
Albert C Rich, *President*
Ashley Rich, *Vice Pres*
Chris McKay, *Parts Mgr*
EMP: 20 **EST:** 1997
SQ FT: 7,500
SALES (est): 2.4MM **Privately Held**
WEB: www.acrsolar.com
SIC: 5211 3433 1711 Solar heating equipment; solar heaters & collectors; solar energy contractor

(P-4625)
BENCHMARK THERMAL CORPORATION
13185 Nevada City Ave, Grass Valley (95945-9568)
PHONE.................................530 477-5011
Vincent Palmieri, *CEO*
Gil Mathew, *President*
Laralee Hannah, *Admin Sec*
EMP: 52 **EST:** 1984
SQ FT: 20,000

PRODUCTS & SERVICES SECTION

3441 - Fabricated Structural Steel County (P-4649)

SALES (est): 6.5MM **Privately Held**
WEB: www.benchmarkthermal.com
SIC: 3433 Heating equipment, except electric

(P-4626)
BIOTHERM HYDRONIC INC
Also Called: True Leaf Technologies
476 Primero Ct, Cotati (94931-3014)
P.O. Box 750967, Petaluma (94975-0967)
PHONE.................................707 794-9660
Jim K Rearden, *CEO*
Michael G Muchow, *CFO*
Suzy Arnette, *Office Mgr*
Joel Rechin, *Information Mgr*
Thad Humphrey, *Engineer*
▲ EMP: 15 EST: 1989
SQ FT: 10,000
SALES (est): 5.5MM **Privately Held**
WEB: www.biothermsolutions.com
SIC: 3433 Heating equipment, except electric

(P-4627)
COEN COMPANY INC (DH)
951 Mariners Island Blvd, San Mateo (94404-1558)
PHONE.................................650 522-2100
Earl W Schnell, *President*
Steve Londerville, *Executive*
Tony Santiago, *Executive*
Samantha Jones, *Administration*
Mey Saephan, *Administration*
◆ EMP: 40 EST: 1912
SALES (est): 57.6MM
SALES (corp-wide): 36.9B **Privately Held**
WEB: www.johnzinkhamworthy.com
SIC: 3433 3823 Burners, furnaces, boilers & stokers; combustion control instruments
HQ: Koch Engineered Solutions, Llc
4111 E 37th St N
Wichita KS 67220
316 828-8515

(P-4628)
FAFCO INC (PA)
435 Otterson Dr, Chico (95928-8207)
PHONE.................................530 332-2100
Freeman A Ford, *Ch of Bd*
Robert C Leckinger, *CEO*
Bob Leckinger, *COO*
Nancy I Garvin, *CFO*
Phil Delnegro, *Vice Pres*
◆ EMP: 46 EST: 1969
SQ FT: 57,500
SALES (est): 12.4MM **Privately Held**
WEB: www.fafco.com
SIC: 3433 Heaters, swimming pool: oil or gas

(P-4629)
GEMTECH SALES CORP
Also Called: Free Hot Water
2146 Bering Dr, San Jose (95131-2013)
P.O. Box 112045, Campbell (95011-2045)
PHONE.................................408 432-9900
Gal Moyal, *President*
Brian Dombrowski, *Sales Staff*
Brian Harrison, *Sales Staff*
EMP: 20 EST: 1999
SQ FT: 9,000
SALES (est): 2.3MM **Privately Held**
SIC: 3433 Solar heaters & collectors

(P-4630)
INNOVATIVE COMBUSTION TECH (PA)
Also Called: S.T. Johnson Company
5160 Fulton Dr, Fairfield (94534-1639)
PHONE.................................510 652-6000
Antonio De La O, *President*
Todd Cole, *Executive*
Barbara Florio, *Admin Sec*
Scott Krahn, *Engineer*
Bob Nickeson, *Engineer*
▼ EMP: 16 EST: 1903
SALES (est): 8.5MM **Privately Held**
WEB: www.stjohnson.com
SIC: 3433 Gas-oil burners, combination

(P-4631)
MANUFACTURERS COML FIN LLC
Also Called: Benchmark Thermal
13185 Nevada City Ave, Grass Valley (95945-9568)
PHONE.................................530 477-5011
Michael Kayman,
Roger Ruttenberg, *Vice Pres*
Eric Doan, *Accountant*
EMP: 40
SQ FT: 8,000
SALES (est): 3.1MM **Privately Held**
WEB: www.benchmarkthermal.com
SIC: 3433 Room & wall heaters, including radiators

(P-4632)
PEGASUS SOLAR INC
506 W Ohio Ave, Richmond (94804-2040)
PHONE.................................510 210-3797
Kai Stephan, *CEO*
Olav Junttila, *CFO*
Anne Wright, *VP Sales*
Brady Miramontes, *Manager*
EMP: 25 EST: 2012
SALES (est): 3.2MM **Privately Held**
WEB: www.pegassusolar.com
SIC: 5211 3433 Solar heating equipment; solar heaters & collectors

(P-4633)
RE TRANQUILLITY 8 LLC
300 California St Fl 7, San Francisco (94104-1415)
PHONE.................................415 675-1500
Yumin Liu, *President*
Helen Kang Shin, *Vice Pres*
EMP: 32 EST: 2013
SALES (est): 8.1MM
SALES (corp-wide): 3.4B **Privately Held**
SIC: 3433 Solar heaters & collectors
HQ: Recurrent Energy Development Holdings, Llc
3000 Oak Rd Ste 300
Walnut Creek CA 94597
415 675-1501

(P-4634)
SKYLINE SOLAR INC
185 E Dana St, Mountain View (94041-1507)
PHONE.................................650 864-9770
Thomas M Rohrs, *CEO*
John Backer, *Vice Pres*
Danny C Cheung, *Vice Pres*
Robert L Macdonald, *CTO*
▲ EMP: 21 EST: 2007
SQ FT: 14,000
SALES (est): 1.6MM **Privately Held**
WEB: www.skyline-solar.com
SIC: 3433 5211 Solar heaters & collectors; solar heating equipment

(P-4635)
SMA AMERICA PRODUCTION LLC
6020 West Oaks Blvd # 300, Rocklin (95765-5472)
PHONE.................................720 347-6000
Pierre Pascal Urbon,
Sarah Svaerd, *Project Mgr*
Ravi Dodballapur, *Technical Staff*
Kerry Kvenlog, *Technical Staff*
Jesus Martinez, *Engineer*
◆ EMP: 200 EST: 2009
SQ FT: 150,000
SALES (est): 43.3MM
SALES (corp-wide): 1.2B **Privately Held**
WEB: www.sma-america.com
SIC: 3433 Solar heaters & collectors
HQ: Sma Solar Technology America Llc
6020 West Oaks Blvd
Rocklin CA 95765
916 625-0870

(P-4636)
SOLAR INDUSTRIES INC
731 N Market Blvd Ste J, Sacramento (95834-1211)
PHONE.................................916 567-9650
Kerry Bradford, *Manager*
EMP: 22
SALES (est): 6.5MM **Privately Held**
WEB: www.solarindustriesinc.com
SIC: 3433 Solar heaters & collectors
PA: Solar Industries, Inc.
4940 S Alvernon Way
Tucson AZ 85706
520 790-8989

(P-4637)
SOLARROOFSCOM INC
5840 Gibbons Dr Ste H, Carmichael (95608-6903)
PHONE.................................916 481-7200
Albert C Rich, *President*
Susan Rich, *CEO*
EMP: 17 EST: 1997
SQ FT: 8,000
SALES (est): 1.5MM **Privately Held**
WEB: www.solarroofs.com
SIC: 3433 Solar heaters & collectors

(P-4638)
SPI SOLAR INC
4677 Old Ironsides Dr # 1, Santa Clara (95054-1809)
PHONE.................................408 919-8000
Xiaofeng Peng, *CEO*
EMP: 566 EST: 2006
SALES (est): 62MM **Privately Held**
SIC: 3433 Solar heaters & collectors

(P-4639)
ST JOHNSON COMPANY LLC
5160 Fulton Dr, Fairfield (94534-1639)
PHONE.................................510 652-6000
Antonio De La O, *President*
Barbara Florio, *CFO*
Shirley Redditt, *Admin Asst*
EMP: 40 EST: 2013
SALES (est): 7.3MM
SALES (corp-wide): 8.5MM **Privately Held**
WEB: www.johnsonburners.com
SIC: 3433 Heating equipment, except electric
PA: Innovative Combustion Technologies Inc
5160 Fulton Dr
Fairfield CA 94534
510 652-6000

(P-4640)
SUNTECH AMERICA INC (PA)
Also Called: Suntech Power
2721 Shattuck Ave, Berkeley (94705-1008)
PHONE.................................415 882-9922
Zhengrong Shi, *CEO*
John Lefebvre, *President*
David King, *CFO*
▲ EMP: 15 EST: 2006
SALES (est): 2.8MM **Privately Held**
WEB: www.suntech-power.com
SIC: 3433 Solar heaters & collectors

3441 Fabricated Structural Steel

(P-4641)
ADTEK INC
1460 Ellerd Dr, Turlock (95380-5749)
PHONE.................................209 634-0300
Bob Zinzenoul, *Principal*
Mike Spence, *Prgrmr*
Tom Ady, *Opers Mgr*
EMP: 30 EST: 2003
SALES (est): 2.9MM **Privately Held**
SIC: 3441 Building components, structural steel

(P-4642)
AHLBORN STRUCTURAL STEEL INC
1230 Century Ct, Santa Rosa (95403-1042)
PHONE.................................707 573-0742
Thomas Ahlborn, *CEO*
Lance Ballenger, *Vice Pres*
Cathy Ahlborn, *Admin Sec*
Ian Burns, *Project Mgr*
Chris Johannesen, *Project Mgr*
EMP: 34 EST: 2004

SALES (est): 5.2MM **Privately Held**
WEB: www.ahlbornstructural.com
SIC: 3441 Fabricated structural metal

(P-4643)
ALL WEST FABRICATORS INC
44875 Fremont Blvd, Fremont (94538-6318)
PHONE.................................510 623-1200
Gary J Lee, *President*
Keith Lee, *Vice Pres*
EMP: 16 EST: 1996
SALES (est): 544.3K **Privately Held**
SIC: 3441 Fabricated structural metal for bridges

(P-4644)
AMT METAL FABRICATORS INC
211 Parr Blvd, Richmond (94801-1119)
PHONE.................................510 236-1414
Michael R Turpen, *President*
Cheryl Turpen, *CFO*
Chuck McKinney, *General Mgr*
Will Fowler, *Manager*
EMP: 20 EST: 1950
SQ FT: 12,000
SALES (est): 4.9MM **Privately Held**
WEB: www.amtmetals.com
SIC: 3441 Building components, structural steel

(P-4645)
B METAL FABRICATION INC
318 S Maple Ave, South San Francisco (94080-6306)
PHONE.................................650 615-7705
Robert Steinebel, *CEO*
Berthold Steinebel, *President*
Brigitte Steinebel, *CFO*
Barbara Blundell, *Vice Pres*
EMP: 30 EST: 1987
SQ FT: 14,000
SALES (est): 6MM **Privately Held**
WEB: www.bmetalfabrication.com
SIC: 3441 Fabricated structural metal

(P-4646)
BERGER STEEL CORPORATION
4728 Kilzer Ave 692, McClellan (95652-2300)
PHONE.................................916 640-8778
Jason Michael Berger, *President*
Cody Berger, *Vice Pres*
Mellisa Dockins, *Office Mgr*
Phil Berger, *Controller*
Dave Back, *Director*
EMP: 27 EST: 2012
SALES (est): 6.2MM **Privately Held**
WEB: www.bergersteel.com
SIC: 3441 5051 Fabricated structural metal; structural shapes, iron or steel

(P-4647)
BIG VALLEY METALS LP
620 Houston St Ste 1, West Sacramento (95691-2255)
P.O. Box 934 (95691-0934)
PHONE.................................916 372-2383
J Robert Vela, *Owner*
EMP: 15 EST: 2004
SALES (est): 3.2MM **Privately Held**
SIC: 3441 Fabricated structural metal

(P-4648)
BOBS IRON INC
629 Whitney St, San Leandro (94577-1115)
PHONE.................................510 567-8983
Robert Smith, *President*
EMP: 25 EST: 1989
SALES (est): 2.5MM **Privately Held**
SIC: 3441 Fabricated structural metal

(P-4649)
CALIFORNIA STL FABRICATORS INC
1120 Reno Ave, Modesto (95351-1128)
PHONE.................................209 566-0629
Paul R Osborne, *CEO*
EMP: 31 EST: 2013
SALES (est): 5MM **Privately Held**
WEB: www.calsteelfab.com
SIC: 3441 Fabricated structural metal

3441 - Fabricated Structural Steel County (P-4650)

PRODUCTS & SERVICES SECTION

(P-4650)
CAPITOL IRON WORKS INC
7009 Power Inn Rd, Sacramento (95828-2498)
PHONE..................916 381-1554
Daniel D Howard, *President*
Steve Hartzell, *President*
Diana Howard, *Treasurer*
Michael Collier, *Vice Pres*
Bee Hillen, *Project Mgr*
EMP: 20
SQ FT: 3,000
SALES (est): 2.2MM **Privately Held**
WEB: www.capitolironworks.com
SIC: 3441 Fabricated structural metal

(P-4651)
CARTER GROUP (PA)
Also Called: Alling Iron Works
3709 Seaport Blvd, West Sacramento (95691-3558)
PHONE..................916 373-0148
Joe Neal Carter, *President*
Renee Mason, *Corp Secy*
EMP: 20 **EST:** 1920
SALES (est): 3.1MM **Privately Held**
WEB: www.farallonboats.com
SIC: 3441 5551 Fabricated structural metal; boat dealers

(P-4652)
CENTRAL VALLEY MACHINING INC
5820 E Harvard Ave, Fresno (93727-1373)
PHONE..................559 291-7749
Long MAI, *President*
Peter MAI, *Vice Pres*
EMP: 22 **EST:** 2003
SQ FT: 5,000
SALES (est): 3.1MM **Privately Held**
SIC: 3441 Fabricated structural metal

(P-4653)
CH INDUSTRIAL TECHNOLOGY INC
3160 E California Ave, Fresno (93702-4108)
PHONE..................559 485-8011
Cameron Williams, *President*
Jeremiah Burleson, *Admin Sec*
▲ **EMP:** 17 **EST:** 2008
SQ FT: 17,000
SALES (est): 1.6MM **Privately Held**
WEB: www.chindustrialtech.com
SIC: 3441 3479 Fabricated structural metal; painting of metal products

(P-4654)
CONCORD IRON WORKS INC
Also Called: C I W
1 Leslie Dr, Pittsburg (94565-2654)
PHONE..................925 432-0136
Jill Lee, *President*
Rita Gonsalves, *Corp Secy*
Jill M Lee, *Vice Pres*
David Maggi, *Vice Pres*
Rosa Cendejas, *Office Mgr*
EMP: 50 **EST:** 1975
SALES (est): 10.3MM **Privately Held**
WEB: www.concordiron.com
SIC: 3441 Fabricated structural metal

(P-4655)
CONXTECH INC
6600 Koll Center Pkwy # 210, Pleasanton (94566-3167)
PHONE..................510 264-9111
Robert J Simmons, *President*
Alan Thomas, *Exec VP*
Raymond G Kitasoe, *Vice Pres*
Kelly Luttrell, *VP Bus Dvlpt*
Scott Fortune, *Info Tech Mgr*
◆ **EMP:** 150 **EST:** 2004
SQ FT: 100,000
SALES (est): 47.6MM **Privately Held**
WEB: www.conxtech.com
SIC: 3441 Building components, structural steel

(P-4656)
DAVISON IRON WORKS INC
8845 Elder Creek Rd Ste A, Sacramento (95826-1835)
PHONE..................916 381-2121
Andrew Peszynski, *President*
Candy Holland, *Vice Pres*
Jeff Kellar, *Project Mgr*
Marsha Longacre, *Finance*
Cathy Defazio, *Purch Agent*
EMP: 50 **EST:** 1959
SQ FT: 3,500
SALES (est): 12.2MM **Privately Held**
WEB: www.davisoniron.com
SIC: 3441 Fabricated structural metal

(P-4657)
ELIGIUS MANUFACTURING INC
1177 N 15th St, San Jose (95112-1422)
PHONE..................408 437-0337
Leon Schaper, *President*
EMP: 30 **EST:** 2017
SALES (est): 3.1MM **Privately Held**
WEB: www.eligiusmfg.com
SIC: 3441 Fabricated structural metal

(P-4658)
EXCELSIOR INC
2681 N Business Park Ave, Fresno (93727-8639)
PHONE..................559 346-0932
Raymond R Roush III, *President*
Lester Rogers, *Manager*
EMP: 27 **EST:** 1996
SQ FT: 10,000
SALES (est): 5MM **Privately Held**
WEB: www.excelsiormetals.com
SIC: 3441 Fabricated structural metal

(P-4659)
FERROSAUR INC
Also Called: Industrial Welding
4821 Mountain Lakes Blvd, Redding (96003-1454)
PHONE..................530 246-7843
Thomas Largent, *Vice Pres*
Thomas R Largent, *CEO*
EMP: 31 **EST:** 1993
SQ FT: 33,000
SALES (est): 6.7MM **Privately Held**
SIC: 3441 7692 2298 5932 Fabricated structural metal; welding repair; rope, except asbestos & wire; building materials, secondhand

(P-4660)
FIFE METAL FABRICATING INC
2305 Radio Ln, Redding (96001-3884)
PHONE..................530 243-4696
Doyle Fife Jr, *President*
Joanne Fife, *Corp Secy*
EMP: 37 **EST:** 1965
SALES (est): 1.3MM **Privately Held**
SIC: 3441 3446 Building components, structural steel; architectural metalwork

(P-4661)
FLORIAN INDUSTRIES INC
151 Industrial Way, Brisbane (94005-1003)
PHONE..................415 330-9000
Chuck Lutz, *President*
Allan Baquilar, *Project Mgr*
EMP: 15 **EST:** 2007
SQ FT: 2,000
SALES (est): 3.9MM **Privately Held**
WEB: www.florianindustries.com
SIC: 3441 Fabricated structural metal

(P-4662)
FRESNO FAB-TECH INC
1035 K St, Sanger (93657-3383)
PHONE..................559 875-9800
Chris Kisling, *President*
EMP: 40 **EST:** 1988
SQ FT: 35,000
SALES (est): 8.2MM **Privately Held**
WEB: www.fresnofabtech.com
SIC: 3441 Fabricated structural metal

(P-4663)
G2 METAL FAB
4205 S B St Ste A, Stockton (95206-3941)
PHONE..................925 443-7903
Orlando Gutierrez, *President*
Nohora Gutierrez, *Vice Pres*
Erik Jorgenson, *General Mgr*
Jeremy Silva, *General Mgr*
Rob Goncalves, *Office Mgr*
EMP: 31 **EST:** 2007
SALES (est): 7.8MM **Privately Held**
WEB: www.g2metalfab.com
SIC: 3441 Fabricated structural metal

(P-4664)
GERLINGER FNDRY MCH WORKS INC (PA)
1527 Sacramento St, Redding (96001-1914)
P.O. Box 992195 (96099-2195)
PHONE..................530 243-1053
Fred Gerlinger, *CEO*
Jo Gerlinger, *CFO*
Tim Gerlinger, *Vice Pres*
EMP: 37
SQ FT: 45,000
SALES (est): 12MM **Privately Held**
WEB: www.gerlinger.com
SIC: 3441 3494 7692 5051 Fabricated structural metal; valves & pipe fittings; welding repair; steel

(P-4665)
GLAZIER STEEL INC
650 Sandoval Way, Hayward (94544-7129)
PHONE..................510 471-5300
Craig Glazier, *CEO*
Harold Glazier, *President*
Terry Caldwell, *Project Mgr*
Austin Nunez, *Project Mgr*
Rene Macias, *Manager*
EMP: 75 **EST:** 1982
SQ FT: 26,897
SALES (est): 31.1MM **Privately Held**
WEB: www.glaziersteel.com
SIC: 3441 Fabricated structural metal

(P-4666)
HERRICK CORPORATION (PA)
Also Called: San Bernandina Steel
3003 E Hammer Ln, Stockton (95212-2801)
P.O. Box 8429 (95208-0429)
PHONE..................209 956-4751
David H Dornsife, *CEO*
Doug Griffin, *President*
Peter Abila, *CFO*
Adan Preciado, *Vice Pres*
John Reitmeier, *Vice Pres*
▲ **EMP:** 50 **EST:** 1921
SALES (est): 221.8MM **Privately Held**
WEB: www.herricksteel.com
SIC: 3441 Fabricated structural metal

(P-4667)
IRON DOG FABRICATION INC
3450 Regional Pkwy Ste E, Santa Rosa (95403-8247)
PHONE..................707 579-7831
Duncan Woods, *President*
Cynthia Woods, *Corp Secy*
EMP: 17 **EST:** 1994
SQ FT: 18,000
SALES (est): 2.3MM **Privately Held**
WEB: www.irondogfab.com
SIC: 3441 7692 1791 Building components, structural steel; welding repair; structural steel erection

(P-4668)
JC METAL SPECIALISTS INC (PA)
220 Michelle Ct, San Francisco (94124)
PHONE..................415 822-3878
Judy Chan, *President*
Jeffrey Chan, *CFO*
EMP: 19 **EST:** 1979
SQ FT: 7,500
SALES (est): 8.5MM **Privately Held**
WEB: www.tomsmetal.com
SIC: 3441 Building components, structural steel

(P-4669)
KASCO FAB INC
4529 S Chestnut Ave Lowr, Fresno (93725-9244)
PHONE..................559 442-1018
Hidemi Kimura, *CEO*
Ken Kimura, *Vice Pres*
Eva Padilla, *Bookkeeper*
Richard Stewart, *Manager*
EMP: 75 **EST:** 1980
SQ FT: 200,000
SALES (est): 6.4MM **Privately Held**
WEB: www.kascofab.com
SIC: 3441 3449 Building components, structural steel; miscellaneous metalwork

(P-4670)
KC METAL PRODUCTS INC (PA)
Also Called: Kc Metals
1960 Hartog Dr, San Jose (95131-2212)
PHONE..................408 436-8754
Robert J Daugherty, *President*
Sandra Daugherty, *Admin Sec*
EMP: 72 **EST:** 1971
SQ FT: 60,000
SALES (est): 8.9MM **Privately Held**
WEB: www.kcmetals.com
SIC: 3441 3429 Fabricated structural metal; manufactured hardware (general)

(P-4671)
L & H IRON INC
Also Called: Lartech
1049 Felipe Ave, San Jose (95122-2602)
PHONE..................408 287-8797
Kirk Larson, *President*
EMP: 23 **EST:** 1986
SALES (est): 4.1MM **Privately Held**
SIC: 3441 3446 Fabricated structural metal; stairs, staircases, stair treads: prefabricated metal

(P-4672)
LEES IMPERIAL WELDING INC
3300 Edison Way, Fremont (94538-6150)
PHONE..................510 657-4900
Gary Lee, *CEO*
Keith Lee, *Vice Pres*
Sam Cromwell, *Project Mgr*
David Beers, *Purch Agent*
Colton Beebe, *Manager*
EMP: 150 **EST:** 1958
SQ FT: 59,000
SALES (est): 25.6MM **Privately Held**
WEB: www.leeiw.com
SIC: 3441 Fabricated structural metal

(P-4673)
LEHMANS MANUFACTURING CO INC
4960 E Jensen Ave, Fresno (93725-1897)
PHONE..................559 486-1700
Adam Lehman, *Ch of Bd*
Kenneth Lehman, *President*
Joyce Lehman, *Corp Secy*
EMP: 15 **EST:** 1946
SQ FT: 36,000
SALES (est): 2.5MM **Privately Held**
WEB: www.lehmansmfg.com
SIC: 3441 Fabricated structural metal

(P-4674)
MADRUGA IRON WORKS INC
305 Gandy Dancer Dr, Tracy (95377-9083)
PHONE..................209 832-7003
Joseph Raymond Madruga, *CEO*
Elizabeth Betsy Madruga, *President*
Raymond M Madruga, *President*
Darlene Taylor, *Purchasing*
Mary E Weber, *Agent*
EMP: 45 **EST:** 1914
SQ FT: 50,000
SALES (est): 9.7MM **Privately Held**
WEB: www.madrugaironworks.com
SIC: 3441 3599 Fabricated structural metal; machine shop, jobbing & repair

(P-4675)
MARIN MANUFACTURING INC
195 Mill St, San Rafael (94901-4020)
PHONE..................415 453-1825
Daniel G Seright, *President*
Richard A Simanek, *Corp Secy*
EMP: 26 **EST:** 1970
SQ FT: 12,000
SALES (est): 1.5MM **Privately Held**
SIC: 3441 3599 7692 Building components, structural steel; machine shop, jobbing & repair; welding repair

(P-4676)
METALSET INC
1200 Hensley St, Richmond (94801-1900)
PHONE..................510 233-9998
Wesley Sillineri, *President*
Jaime Alvarez, *Plant Supt*
Chris Peacock, *Director*
Lee Bizicki, *Superintendent*
EMP: 22 **EST:** 1995
SALES (est): 5.2MM **Privately Held**
WEB: www.metalsetinc.com
SIC: 3441 Fabricated structural metal

▲ = Import ▼ = Export
◆ = Import/Export

3442 - Metal Doors, Sash, Frames, Molding & Trim County (P-4701)

(P-4677)
MONTEREY STRUCTURAL STEEL INC
404 W Beach St, Watsonville (95076-4533)
PHONE..................................831 768-1277
Kenneth J Bachini, *President*
EMP: 15 **EST:** 2000
SALES (est): 2.2MM **Privately Held**
WEB: www.montereystructuralsteel.the-bluebook.com
SIC: 3441 Fabricated structural metal

(P-4678)
NATIONAL METAL FABRICATORS
28435 Century St, Hayward (94545-4862)
P.O. Box 56478 (94545-6478)
PHONE..................................510 887-6231
Steven L Kint, *CEO*
Gayle Kint, *Corp Secy*
Mark Nickles, *Vice Pres*
Mike Wieber, *Vice Pres*
EMP: 37 **EST:** 1975
SQ FT: 26,000
SALES (est): 2.4MM **Privately Held**
WEB: www.nationalmetalfab.com
SIC: 3441 Fabricated structural metal

(P-4679)
OLSON AND CO STEEL
3488 W Ashlan Ave, Fresno (93722-4443)
PHONE..................................559 224-7811
Del Stephens, *Branch Mgr*
Lan Lu, *Controller*
Steve Rivera, *Safety Mgr*
Christopher Reid, *Production*
Jose De Leon, *Manager*
EMP: 125
SALES (corp-wide): 57.4MM **Privately Held**
WEB: www.olsonsteel.com
SIC: 3441 3446 Building components, structural steel; architectural metalwork
PA: Olson And Co. Steel
1941 Davis St
San Leandro CA 94577
510 489-4680

(P-4680)
PLACER WATERWORKS INC
1325 Furneaux Rd, Plumas Lake (95961-7485)
PHONE..................................530 742-9675
Karl Kern, *President*
Sheila Kern, *Vice Pres*
EMP: 20 **EST:** 1993
SQ FT: 10,500
SALES (est): 3.8MM **Privately Held**
WEB: www.placerwaterworks.com
SIC: 3441 Fabricated structural metal

(P-4681)
ROBECKS WLDG & FABRICATION INC
1150 Mabury Rd Ste 1, San Jose (95133-1031)
PHONE..................................408 287-0202
Armon Robeck, *President*
Laurie Morado, *Corp Secy*
Ronald Robeck, *Vice Pres*
EMP: 22 **EST:** 1993
SQ FT: 6,000
SALES (est): 4.7MM **Privately Held**
WEB: www.robecks.com
SIC: 3441 7692 Fabricated structural metal; welding repair

(P-4682)
ROBERT J ALANDT & SONS
Also Called: Central Cal Metals
4692 N Brawley Ave, Fresno (93722-3921)
PHONE..................................559 275-1391
Frank Alandt, *President*
Joseph Alandt, *Corp Secy*
Robert Alandt, *Vice Pres*
EMP: 45 **EST:** 1950
SQ FT: 50,000
SALES (est): 7MM **Privately Held**
WEB: www.cencalmetals.com
SIC: 3441 Fabricated structural metal

(P-4683)
SIERRA METAL FABRICATORS INC
Also Called: Sierra Metalk Fabricators
529 Searls Ave, Nevada City (95959-3003)
P.O. Box 1359 (95959-1359)
PHONE..................................530 265-4591
Jason White, *President*
Steve Sears, *Supervisor*
EMP: 30 **EST:** 1974
SQ FT: 30,000
SALES (est): 3.8MM **Privately Held**
WEB: www.sierrametal.com
SIC: 3441 Fabricated structural metal

(P-4684)
SMB INDUSTRIES INC (PA)
Also Called: Metal Works Supply
550 Georgia Pacific Way, Oroville (95965-9638)
PHONE..................................530 534-6266
Sean Pierce, *President*
Mike Phulps, *Treasurer*
Travis Quinonez, *Project Mgr*
Jesse Bessmer, *Manager*
EMP: 69 **EST:** 1988
SQ FT: 45,000
SALES (est): 216K **Privately Held**
WEB: www.mtlwks.com
SIC: 3441 Expansion joints (structural shapes), iron or steel

(P-4685)
SUBURBAN STEEL INC (PA)
706 W California Ave, Fresno (93706-3599)
PHONE..................................559 268-6281
Stan J Cavalla, *President*
Ron Cavalla, *Vice Pres*
Jerry Wood, *Office Mgr*
EMP: 28 **EST:** 1945
SQ FT: 12,000
SALES (est): 5.2MM **Privately Held**
SIC: 3441 3446 Building components, structural steel; railings, bannisters, guards, etc.: made from metal pipe

(P-4686)
SUMMIT STEEL WORKS CORPORATION
850 Faulstich Ct, San Jose (95112-1361)
PHONE..................................408 510-5880
Peter Kockelman, *President*
Nicola Kockelman, *CFO*
Ian Gravina, *Vice Pres*
Jeremiah Randa, *Project Engr*
Jeryn Sampson, *Project Engr*
EMP: 30 **EST:** 1988
SQ FT: 4,500
SALES (est): 6.7MM **Privately Held**
WEB: www.summitsteelworks.com
SIC: 3441 Fabricated structural metal

(P-4687)
SVM MACHINING INC
6520 Central Ave, Newark (94560-3933)
PHONE..................................510 791-9450
Mark Serpa, *President*
EMP: 39 **EST:** 1997
SQ FT: 21,000
SALES (est): 2.5MM **Privately Held**
WEB: www.svmfg.com
SIC: 3441 Building components, structural steel

(P-4688)
T&S MANUFACTURING TECH LLC
Also Called: Atech Manufacturing
1530 Oakland Rd Ste 120, San Jose (95112-1241)
PHONE..................................408 441-0285
Tony Tolani,
Peter Nguyen, *VP Opers*
Shalini Tolani,
EMP: 18 **EST:** 2008
SQ FT: 6,000
SALES (est): 2.9MM **Privately Held**
WEB: www.atechmanufacturing.com
SIC: 3441 3999 Fabricated structural metal; atomizers, toiletry

(P-4689)
TERMINAL MANUFACTURING CO LLC
Also Called: T M C
707 Gilman St, Berkeley (94710-1312)
PHONE..................................510 526-3071
Steve Millinger, *Mng Member*
Isaac Viscarra, *Engineer*
Robert Magtibay, *Purchasing*
Resty Fernandez, *Buyer*
Richard Robison,
EMP: 30 **EST:** 1918
SQ FT: 30,000
SALES (est): 6.6MM **Privately Held**
WEB: www.terminalmanufacturing.com
SIC: 3441 Fabricated structural metal

(P-4690)
TRANS BAY STEEL CORPORATION (PA)
2801 Giant Rd Ste H, San Pablo (94806-2275)
PHONE..................................510 277-3756
William Kavicky, *President*
William H Kroplin, *Vice Pres*
EMP: 35 **EST:** 1987
SALES (est): 4.8MM **Privately Held**
WEB: www.transbaysteel.com
SIC: 3441 Fabricated structural metal

(P-4691)
UNITED MISC & ORNA STL INC
Also Called: Umo Steel
4700 Horner St, Union City (94587-2531)
PHONE..................................510 429-8755
Juan M Romero, *President*
Jose Barrera, *Vice Pres*
Jose G Romero, *Principal*
Victoria Barrera, *Admin Mgr*
EMP: 48 **EST:** 2004
SALES (est): 2.7MM **Privately Held**
SIC: 3441 Fabricated structural metal

(P-4692)
WADE METAL PRODUCTS INC
1818 Los Angeles St, Fresno (93721-3113)
P.O. Box 1945, Clovis (93613-1945)
PHONE..................................559 237-9233
Marian Esquibel, *CEO*
Curtis Esquibel, *CFO*
John Spier, *Manager*
EMP: 15 **EST:** 2003
SQ FT: 12,000
SALES (est): 1.6MM **Privately Held**
WEB: www.wademetalproducts.com
SIC: 3441 Fabricated structural metal

(P-4693)
WELDWAY INC
521 Hi Tech Pkwy, Oakdale (95361-9395)
PHONE..................................209 847-8083
Mike Sala, *President*
Steve Brooks, *Corp Secy*
Lee Murrison, *Manager*
EMP: 35 **EST:** 1983
SQ FT: 4,500
SALES (est): 7.1MM **Privately Held**
WEB: www.weldwayinc.com
SIC: 3441 Fabricated structural metal

(P-4694)
WESTCO IRON WORKS INC (PA)
1080 Concannon Blvd # 110, Livermore (94550-6576)
PHONE..................................925 961-9152
Mark Shoermsser, *President*
Scott Hofstede, *CFO*
Brad Thompson, *Vice Pres*
John Winger, *Vice Pres*
Nick Hieber, *Manager*
EMP: 70 **EST:** 2005
SALES (est): 18.4MM **Privately Held**
WEB: www.westcoironworks.com
SIC: 3441 Fabricated structural metal

(P-4695)
YUBA CITY STEEL PRODUCTS CO
532 Crestmont Ave, Yuba City (95991-6209)
PHONE..................................530 673-4554
Clinton L West, *Ch of Bd*
Robert Zellner, *President*
▼ **EMP:** 34 **EST:** 1944
SQ FT: 81,000
SALES (est): 3.5MM **Privately Held**
WEB: www.yubacitysteelproductsco.city-fos.com
SIC: 3441 Fabricated structural metal

3442 Metal Doors, Sash, Frames, Molding & Trim

(P-4696)
ANLIN WINDOWS & DOORS ✪
1665 Tollhouse Rd, Clovis (93611-0523)
PHONE..................................800 287-7996
EMP: 120 **EST:** 2021
SALES (est): 330.8K
SALES (corp-wide): 882.6MM **Publicly Held**
WEB: www.pgtwindows.com
SIC: 3442 Metal doors, sash & trim
PA: Pgt Innovations, Inc.
1070 Technology Dr
North Venice FL 34275
941 480-1600

(P-4697)
ARCHITECTURAL BLOMBERG LLC
Also Called: Blomberg Window Systems
1453 Blair Ave, Sacramento (95822-3410)
P.O. Box 22485 (95822-0485)
PHONE..................................916 428-8060
Jeremy Drucker, *Mng Member*
EMP: 32 **EST:** 2014 **Privately Held**
WEB: www.blombergwindows.com
SIC: 3442 Window & door frames

(P-4698)
BAYFAB METALS INC
870 Doolittle Dr, San Leandro (94577-1079)
PHONE..................................510 568-8950
Susan Miranda, *President*
EMP: 20 **EST:** 1969
SQ FT: 21,000
SALES (est): 4MM **Privately Held**
WEB: www.bayfabmetals.com
SIC: 3442 3444 3446 3499 Metal doors, sash & trim; metal housings, enclosures, casings & other containers; louvers, ventilating; shims, metal; name plates: except engraved, etched, etc.: metal

(P-4699)
BELCO CABINETS INC
1109 Black Diamond Way, Lodi (95240-0746)
PHONE..................................209 334-5437
Roy Belanger, *President*
EMP: 15 **EST:** 1978
SQ FT: 21,000
SALES (est): 2.3MM **Privately Held**
WEB: www.belcocabinetsinc.com
SIC: 3442 2434 Metal doors; wood kitchen cabinets

(P-4700)
BLOMBERG BUILDING MATERIALS (PA)
Also Called: Blomberg Window Systems
1453 Blair Ave, Sacramento (95822-3410)
PHONE..................................916 428-8060
Philip Collier, *CEO*
Bud Warren, *Executive*
Mikal Dinsdale, *Sales Staff*
Jan Miller, *Sales Staff*
EMP: 99 **EST:** 1956
SALES (est): 9.5MM **Privately Held**
WEB: www.blombergwindows.com
SIC: 3442 Metal doors, sash & trim

(P-4701)
BLUM CONSTRUCTION CO INC
Also Called: European Rolling Shutters
404a Umbarger Rd A, San Jose (95111-2087)
PHONE..................................408 629-3740
Helmut Blum, *President*
Renate Blum, *Vice Pres*
▲ **EMP:** 15 **EST:** 1984
SQ FT: 10,500

3442 - Metal Doors, Sash, Frames, Molding & Trim County

(P-4702)
SALES (est): 2.3MM Privately Held
SIC: 3442 3444 1751 1799 Shutters, door or window: metal; awnings & canopies; window & door installation & erection; awning installation

(P-4702)
CLEAR VIEW LLC
1650 Las Plumas Ave Ste A, San Jose (95133-1657)
PHONE 408 271-2734
Daniel Lezotte,
Brittanny Nakamoto, *Vice Pres*
Andrew Lezotte, *Mng Member*
EMP: 15 EST: 2015
SALES (est): 1.8MM Privately Held
WEB: www.clearviewdoor.com
SIC: 3442 5084 Screen doors, metal; industrial machinery & equipment

(P-4703)
DIABLO MOLDING & TRIM COMPANY
5600 Sunol Blvd Ste C, Pleasanton (94566-8802)
P.O. Box 2190, Dublin (94568-0218)
PHONE 925 417-0663
Alex Blumin, *President*
EMP: 15 EST: 1992
SALES (est): 473.7K Privately Held
WEB: www.diablomolding.com
SIC: 3442 Molding, trim & stripping

(P-4704)
GILWIN COMPANY
2354 Lapham Dr, Modesto (95354-3912)
PHONE 209 522-9775
Donald P Miller, *President*
Wanda SAI, *Office Mgr*
EMP: 23 EST: 1990
SQ FT: 27,000
SALES (est): 2.8MM Privately Held
WEB: www.gilwin.com
SIC: 3442 Window & door frames; casements, aluminum

(P-4705)
METAL MANUFACTURING CO INC
2240 Evergreen St, Sacramento (95815-3281)
PHONE 916 922-3484
Jerry Guest, *President*
Troy Smith, *Treasurer*
Henry Baum, *Admin Sec*
EMP: 20 EST: 1972
SQ FT: 19,000
SALES (est): 2MM Privately Held
WEB: www.metalmfgco.com
SIC: 3442 Metal doors

(P-4706)
NOR-CAL OVERHEAD INC
Also Called: Garage Doors
2145 Elkins Way Ste E, Brentwood (94513-7363)
PHONE 925 240-5141
William McElmurry, *President*
William A McElmurry, *CEO*
Stephenie Massoth, *General Mgr*
Melissa McElmurry, *Opers Staff*
EMP: 15 EST: 2003
SALES (est): 2.5MM Privately Held
WEB: www.norcaloverheaddoor.com
SIC: 5211 3442 Garage doors, sale & installation; garage doors, overhead: metal; rolling doors for industrial buildings or warehouses, metal

(P-4707)
QUANEX SCREENS LLC
5901 88th St, Sacramento (95828-1121)
PHONE 916 386-8728
EMP: 17 Publicly Held
WEB: www.quanex.com
SIC: 3442 Screen doors, metal
HQ: Quanex Screens Llc
1800 West Loop S Ste 1500
Houston TX 77027
713 961-4200

(P-4708)
R & S MANUFACTURING INC (HQ)
Also Called: R & S Rolling Door Products
33955 7th St, Union City (94587-3521)
P.O. Box 2737 (94587-7737)
PHONE 510 429-1788
Gordon J Ong, *President*
James Greaves, *Treasurer*
Ray Zarodney, *Admin Sec*
Robert R Smith, *Director*
▲ EMP: 25 EST: 1979
SQ FT: 36,136
SALES (est): 12.9MM Privately Held
WEB: www.rsdoorproducts.com
SIC: 3442 3231 Rolling doors for industrial buildings or warehouses, metal; louvers, shutters, jalousies & similar items; products of purchased glass
PA: R & S Erection, Incorporated
2057 W Avenue 140th
San Leandro CA 94577
510 483-3710

(P-4709)
STILES CUSTOM METAL INC
1885 Kinser Rd, Ceres (95307-4606)
PHONE 209 538-3667
David Stiles, *President*
Jim Ludlow, *CFO*
Steve Stiles, *Vice Pres*
Adam Hale, *Project Mgr*
Juan Rios, *Project Mgr*
EMP: 87 EST: 1973
SQ FT: 56,000
SALES (est): 17.4MM Privately Held
WEB: www.stilesdoors.com
SIC: 3442 Metal doors; window & door frames

(P-4710)
TMP LLC
Also Called: Titan Metal Products
3011 Academy Way, Sacramento (95815-1540)
PHONE 916 920-2555
Glen Harélson, *President*
Flora Harelson, *Treasurer*
EMP: 24 EST: 1977
SQ FT: 18,000
SALES (est): 246.6K Privately Held
SIC: 3442 Metal doors; window & door frames; sash, door or window: metal; moldings & trim, except automobile: metal

3443 Fabricated Plate Work

(P-4711)
AM AND S MFG INC
Also Called: AM&s Mnufactruing Design Group
1394 Tully Rd Ste 203, San Jose (95122-3057)
PHONE 408 396-3027
Andrew Le, *CEO*
Vincent Rondas, *CFO*
EMP: 15 EST: 2013
SALES (est): 1.3MM Privately Held
WEB: www.amnsmfg.com
SIC: 3443 3599 3541 3728 Metal parts; machine shop, jobbing & repair; electrical discharge machining (EDM); lathes; aircraft body & wing assemblies & parts; welding wire, bare & coated

(P-4712)
BENICIA FABRICATION & MCH INC
101 E Channel Rd, Benicia (94510-1155)
PHONE 707 745-8111
Thomas D Cepernich, *CEO*
Dennis Michael Rose, *President*
Steven Rose, *Exec VP*
Mike McKay, *Design Engr*
Robert Mattsson, *Engineer*
EMP: 150 EST: 1983
SQ FT: 80,000
SALES (est): 26.5MM Privately Held
WEB: www.beniciafab.com
SIC: 3443 3599 Fabricated plate work (boiler shop); machine shop, jobbing & repair

(P-4713)
CENTRAL VALLEY TANK OF CAL
4752 E Carmen Ave, Fresno (93703-4501)
PHONE 559 456-3500
Kathy Tackett, *President*
EMP: 16 EST: 2008
SALES (est): 4.9MM Privately Held
WEB: www.centralvalleytank.com
SIC: 3443 Boiler shop products: boilers, smokestacks, steel tanks

(P-4714)
CERTIFIED STAINLESS SVC INC
Also Called: Westmark
441 Business Park Way, Atwater (95301-9499)
PHONE 209 356-3300
Chris Portmann, *Branch Mgr*
Barinder Singh, *Engineer*
John Davis, *Purch Mgr*
EMP: 82
SALES (corp-wide): 35.6MM Privately Held
WEB: www.west-mark.com
SIC: 3443 3569 Tanks for tank trucks, metal plate; firefighting apparatus & related equipment
PA: Certified Stainless Service Inc.
2704 Railroad Ave
Ceres CA 95307
209 537-4747

(P-4715)
CERTIFIED STAINLESS SVC INC (PA)
Also Called: West-Mark
2704 Railroad Ave, Ceres (95307-4600)
P.O. Box 100 (95307-0100)
PHONE 209 537-4747
Scott Vincent, *CEO*
Tara Hogan, *Partner*
Teo Serrano, *Partner*
Dale Steeley, *Partner*
Jack Smith, *Shareholder*
▲ EMP: 40
SQ FT: 64,000
SALES (est): 35.6MM Privately Held
WEB: www.west-mark.com
SIC: 3443 3715 7538 Tanks for tank trucks, metal plate; truck trailers; general truck repair

(P-4716)
CERTIFIED STAINLESS SVC INC
Also Called: West-Mark
581 Industry Way, Atwater (95301-9457)
P.O. Box 100, Ceres (95307-0100)
PHONE 209 537-4747
Grant Smith, *Branch Mgr*
Jason Higgins, *Prdtn Mgr*
Wayne Kindred, *Marketing Staff*
Heather Silveira, *Manager*
EMP: 82
SALES (corp-wide): 35.6MM Privately Held
WEB: www.west-mark.com
SIC: 3443 3569 Tanks for tank trucks, metal plate; firefighting apparatus & related equipment
PA: Certified Stainless Service Inc.
2704 Railroad Ave
Ceres CA 95307
209 537-4747

(P-4717)
CHART INC
46441 Landing Pkwy, Fremont (94538-6496)
PHONE 408 371-3303
Daniel Sullivan, *Branch Mgr*
EMP: 23 Publicly Held
WEB: www.chartindustries.com
SIC: 3443 Fabricated plate work (boiler shop)
HQ: Chart Inc.
407 7th St Nw
New Prague MN 56071
952 758-4484

(P-4718)
CONTAINMENT CONSULTANTS INC
Also Called: Ideal Envmtl Pdts & Svcs
110 Old Gilroy St, Gilroy (95020-6948)
P.O. Box 307 (95021-0307)
PHONE 408 848-6998
Anne Anderson, *President*
EMP: 16 EST: 1992
SQ FT: 14,000
SALES (est): 1.9MM Privately Held
WEB: www.chem-stor.com
SIC: 3443 8748 Tanks, standard or custom fabricated: metal plate; environmental consultant

(P-4719)
CRYOWEST INC
25 Hangar Way, Watsonville (95076-2403)
PHONE 831 786-9721
John Wolfe, *President*
◆ EMP: 30 EST: 2011
SALES (est): 3.4MM Privately Held
WEB: www.cryowest.com
SIC: 3443 Cryogenic tanks, for liquids & gases

(P-4720)
EDGE ELECTRONICS CORPORATION
Also Called: Mc Intyre Coil
164 21st Ave, San Francisco (94121-1206)
PHONE 510 614-7988
Dennis T Wong, *President*
William Schwartz, *Vice Pres*
EMP: 20 EST: 1982
SALES (est): 2.5MM Privately Held
WEB: www.edgeelectronics.com
SIC: 3443 Heat exchangers, plate type

(P-4721)
GTM TECHNOLOGIES LLC (PA)
Also Called: Luxfer-GTM
1619 Shattuck Ave, Berkeley (94709-1611)
PHONE 415 856-0570
Michael Koonce, *President*
EMP: 16 EST: 2012
SQ FT: 1,700
SALES (est): 3.6MM Privately Held
WEB: www.luxfergtm.com
SIC: 3443 Tanks for tank trucks, metal plate

(P-4722)
ITW BLDING CMPONENTS GROUP INC
Also Called: ITW Alpine
8801 Folsom Blvd Ste 107, Sacramento (95826-3249)
PHONE 916 387-0116
Sally Thomas, *Sales/Mktg Mgr*
Russell Tangren, *Engineer*
Chao Yang, *Engineer*
EMP: 37
SALES (corp-wide): 12.5B Publicly Held
WEB: www.alpineacademyitw.com
SIC: 3443 3469 Truss plates, metal; stamping metal for the trade
HQ: Itw Building Components Group, Inc.
13389 Lakefront Dr
Earth City MO 63045
314 344-9121

(P-4723)
JONNA CORP INC
348 Phelan Ave, San Jose (95112-4103)
PHONE 408 297-7910
Robert W Hill, *President*
EMP: 21 EST: 2001
SALES (est): 1.4MM Privately Held
SIC: 3443 Fabricated plate work (boiler shop)

(P-4724)
KSM VACUUM PRODUCTS INC
102 Persian Dr Ste 203, Sunnyvale (94089-1561)
PHONE 408 514-2400
Yun Ho Kim, *CEO*
▲ EMP: 15 EST: 2002
SALES (est): 1.2MM Privately Held
WEB: www.ksm.co.kr
SIC: 3443 High vacuum coaters, metal plate

PRODUCTS & SERVICES SECTION

3444 - Sheet Metal Work County (P-4748)

(P-4725)
MODERN CUSTOM FABRICATION INC
4922 E Jensen Ave, Fresno (93725-1806)
P.O. Box 11925 (93775-1925)
PHONE..................559 264-4741
James E Jones, *CEO*
James W Gray, *Vice Pres*
John W Jones, *Principal*
Barbara Nix, *Human Res Mgr*
Carl Pearson, *Sales Staff*
EMP: 35 **EST:** 2001
SALES (est): 14.4MM
SALES (corp-wide): 159.6MM **Privately Held**
WEB: www.modweldco.com
SIC: 3443 Fabricated plate work (boiler shop)
PA: Modern Welding Company, Inc.
2880 New Hartford Rd
Owensboro KY 42303
270 685-4400

(P-4726)
NATIONWIDE BOILER INCORPORATED (PA)
42400 Christy St, Fremont (94538-3141)
PHONE..................510 490-7100
Larry Day, *President*
James Hermerding, *Vice Pres*
Michele Tomas, *Vice Pres*
Philip Blake, *Project Mgr*
Luke Honnen, *Engineer*
◆ **EMP:** 47 **EST:** 1967
SQ FT: 35,000
SALES: 29.2MM **Privately Held**
WEB: www.nationwideboiler.com
SIC: 3443 Fabricated plate work (boiler shop)

(P-4727)
NWPC LLC
Also Called: Nothwest Pipe Company
10100 W Linne Rd, Tracy (95377-9128)
PHONE..................209 836-5050
Scott Montross, *CEO*
EMP: 75 **EST:** 2019
SALES (est): 39MM
SALES (corp-wide): 285.9MM **Publicly Held**
WEB: www.nwpipe.com
SIC: 3443 3317 Fabricated plate work (boiler shop); steel pipe & tubes
PA: Northwest Pipe Company
201 Ne Park Plaza Dr # 100
Vancouver WA 98684
360 397-6250

(P-4728)
PREMIERE RECYCLE CO
348 Phelan Ave, San Jose (95112-4103)
PHONE..................408 297-7910
Robert Hill, *President*
Adit Shrestha, *Project Mgr*
Jene Garcia, *Manager*
EMP: 50 **EST:** 1998
SALES (est): 5.2MM **Privately Held**
WEB: www.premierrecycle.com
SIC: 3443 4953 4212 Dumpsters, garbage; garbage: collecting, destroying & processing; local trucking, without storage

(P-4729)
S & H WELDING INC
8604 Elder Creek Rd, Sacramento (95828-1803)
PHONE..................916 386-8921
John Jones, *President*
EMP: 15 **EST:** 1990
SQ FT: 10,000
SALES (est): 2.1MM **Privately Held**
SIC: 3443 Fabricated plate work (boiler shop)

(P-4730)
SAN-I-PAK PACIFIC INC
23535 S Bird Rd, Tracy (95304-9339)
P.O. Box 1183 (95378-1183)
PHONE..................209 836-2310
John L Hall, *CEO*
Wilburn Hall, *Vice Pres*
EMP: 50 **EST:** 1982
SQ FT: 25,000
SALES (est): 11.1MM **Privately Held**
WEB: www.sanipak.com
SIC: 3443 Sterilizing chambers, metal plate

(P-4731)
SONOMA STAINLESS
170 Todd Rd Ste 100, Santa Rosa (95407-8155)
PHONE..................707 546-3945
EMP: 15 **EST:** 2015
SALES (est): 3MM **Privately Held**
WEB: www.sonomastainless.com
SIC: 3443 Fabricated plate work (boiler shop)

(P-4732)
STEEL STRUCTURES INC
28777 Avenue 15 1/2, Madera (93638-2316)
PHONE..................559 673-8021
Daniel Riley, *President*
Tracy Riley, *Vice Pres*
EMP: 22 **EST:** 1953
SQ FT: 44,000 **Privately Held**
WEB: www.steelstructuresinc.com
SIC: 3443 Tanks, standard or custom fabricated: metal plate; process vessels, industrial: metal plate

(P-4733)
WANTZ EQUIPMENT COMPANY INC
3300 W Capitol Ave, West Sacramento (95691-2111)
PHONE..................916 372-1792
Donna Vaughn, *President*
Donna Vaughan, *Treasurer*
EMP: 20 **EST:** 1988
SQ FT: 18,000
SALES (est): 3MM **Privately Held**
WEB: www.wantzinc.com
SIC: 3443 Fabricated plate work (boiler shop)

(P-4734)
XCHANGER MANUFACTURING CORP
Also Called: Wiegmann & Rose
263 S Vasco Rd, Livermore (94551-9203)
P.O. Box 4187, Oakland (94614-4187)
PHONE..................510 632-8828
Scott E Logan, *President*
Suzette I Logan, *Admin Asst*
Sam Flores, *Purchasing*
Jon E Hammons, *Plant Supt*
K Gardner, *Mktg Dir*
EMP: 21 **EST:** 1950
SQ FT: 80,000
SALES (est): 5.3MM **Privately Held**
WEB: www.wiegmannandrose.com
SIC: 3443 Heat exchangers: coolers (after, inter), condensers, etc.

3444 Sheet Metal Work

(P-4735)
A & J PRECISION SHEETMETAL INC
2233 Paragon Dr Ste A, San Jose (95131-1339)
PHONE..................408 885-9134
Amrik Atwal, *CEO*
Jagtar Atwal, *President*
Suki Atwal, *Vice Pres*
▲ **EMP:** 52 **EST:** 1994
SALES (est): 11.7MM **Privately Held**
WEB: www.ajsheetmetal.com
SIC: 3444 Sheet metalwork

(P-4736)
A H K ELECTRONIC SHTMTL INC
875 Jarvis Dr Ste 120, Morgan Hill (95037-2887)
PHONE..................408 778-3901
Vinai Kumar, *President*
Farid Ghantous, *COO*
EMP: 20 **EST:** 1983
SQ FT: 30,000
SALES (est): 2.4MM **Privately Held**
WEB: www.ahksheetmetal.com
SIC: 3444 Sheet metal specialties, not stamped

(P-4737)
ACCURATE HEATING & COOLING INC
Also Called: Tru-Fit Manufacturing
3515 Yosemite Ave, Lathrop (95330-9748)
PHONE..................209 858-4125
Joan Kauffman, *President*
Melvin Kauffman, *Shareholder*
Jill Brandenburg, *Corp Secy*
Janet Murray, *Manager*
EMP: 23 **EST:** 1954
SQ FT: 30,000
SALES (est): 3.1MM **Privately Held**
SIC: 3444 Ducts, sheet metal

(P-4738)
ADVANCED MFG & DEV INC
Also Called: Metalfx
200 N Lenore Ave, Willits (95490-3209)
PHONE..................707 459-9451
Henry Moss, *President*
Ed Shoulders, *Production*
Kristy Moss, *Supervisor*
▲ **EMP:** 165 **EST:** 1976
SQ FT: 65,000
SALES: 28.7MM
SALES (corp-wide): 1.3B **Publicly Held**
WEB: www.metalfx.com
SIC: 3444 2541 3469 3567 Housings for business machines, sheet metal; cabinets, except refrigerated: show, display, etc.: wood; metal stampings; industrial furnaces & ovens; coin-operated amusement machines; boxes, wood
PA: Avista Corporation
1411 E Mission Ave
Spokane WA 99202
509 489-0500

(P-4739)
AIRTRONICS METAL PRODUCTS INC (PA)
140 San Pedro Ave, Morgan Hill (95037-5123)
PHONE..................408 977-7800
Jeff Burke, *CEO*
John Richardson, *Ch of Bd*
James Ellis, *Vice Pres*
Fermin Rodriguez, *Vice Pres*
Kyle O'Leary, *CIO*
▲ **EMP:** 213 **EST:** 1962
SQ FT: 55,000
SALES (est): 27.6MM **Privately Held**
WEB: www.airtronics.com
SIC: 3444 3479 Sheet metalwork; painting, coating & hot dipping

(P-4740)
AKAS MANUFACTURING CORPORATION
Also Called: Labtronix
3200 Investment Blvd, Hayward (94545-3807)
PHONE..................510 786-3200
Santosh Sud, *President*
Artie Sud, *Vice Pres*
EMP: 21 **EST:** 1999
SQ FT: 60,000
SALES (est): 702.9K **Privately Held**
SIC: 3444 3441 Sheet metalwork; fabricated structural metal

(P-4741)
ANDRUS SHEET METAL INC
Also Called: Seaport Stainless
5021 Seaport Ave, Richmond (94804-4638)
PHONE..................510 232-8687
Ray Doving, *President*
Linda Doving, *Vice Pres*
Ryan Doving, *Vice Pres*
EMP: 30 **EST:** 1977
SQ FT: 14,000
SALES (est): 4.6MM **Privately Held**
SIC: 3444 Restaurant sheet metalwork

(P-4742)
ASCENT TECHNOLOGY INC
838 Jury Ct, San Jose (95112-2815)
PHONE..................408 213-1080
Mark S Fanelli, *President*
▲ **EMP:** 17 **EST:** 1996
SALES (est): 2.9MM **Privately Held**
WEB: www.ascenttech.com
SIC: 3444 3364 Sheet metalwork; nonferrous die-castings except aluminum

(P-4743)
ASM PRECISION INC
613 Martin Ave Ste 106, Rohnert Park (94928-2000)
PHONE..................707 584-7950
Mario R Felciano, *President*
Jay Sandoval, *Vice Pres*
Jeff Murray, *Project Mgr*
EMP: 15 **EST:** 2007
SQ FT: 9,000
SALES (est): 3.8MM **Privately Held**
WEB: www.asmprecision.com
SIC: 3444 Sheet metal specialties, not stamped

(P-4744)
BMB METAL PRODUCTS CORPORATION
Also Called: B M B
11460 Elks Cir, Rancho Cordova (95742-7332)
PHONE..................916 631-9120
Jerry Mc Donald, *President*
Jolene Harlos,
EMP: 24 **EST:** 1966
SQ FT: 23,000
SALES (est): 4.9MM **Privately Held**
WEB: www.bmbmetalproductsc.openfos.com
SIC: 3444 Sheet metalwork

(P-4745)
BURLINGAME HTG VENTILATION INC
821 Malcolm Rd, Burlingame (94010-1406)
PHONE..................650 697-9142
Douglass Ulrich, *CEO*
Fred Ulrich, *President*
Patricia Ann Ulrich, *Corp Secy*
EMP: 24 **EST:** 1976
SQ FT: 3,000
SALES (est): 2.6MM **Privately Held**
WEB: www.burlingameheating.com
SIC: 3444 1711 Sheet metalwork; heating & air conditioning contractors

(P-4746)
CAPTIVE-AIRE SYSTEMS INC
6856 Lockheed Dr, Redding (96002-9769)
PHONE..................530 351-7150
Csaba Sikur, *Branch Mgr*
Bill Griffin, *Vice Pres*
Bart Chandler, *Regional Mgr*
Mike Little, *Regional Mgr*
Beyene Asmare, *Sr Software Eng*
EMP: 140
SALES (corp-wide): 401.1MM **Privately Held**
WEB: www.captiveaire.com
SIC: 3444 Metal ventilating equipment
PA: Captive-Aire Systems, Inc.
4641 Paragon Park Rd # 104
Raleigh NC 27616
919 882-2410

(P-4747)
COMCO SHEET METAL COMPANY
237 Southbrook Pl, Clayton (94517-1035)
PHONE..................510 832-6433
Armand Butticci III, *President*
Maria Butticci, *Corp Secy*
EMP: 16 **EST:** 1945
SQ FT: 13,000
SALES (est): 1MM **Privately Held**
SIC: 3444 Restaurant sheet metalwork

(P-4748)
COMPACTOR MANAGEMENT CO LLC
32420 Central Ave, Union City (94587-2007)
PHONE..................510 623-2323
David Lucio, *CEO*
Sandra Garcia,
Emilio Lucio,
Eric Duran, *Manager*
EMP: 26 **EST:** 2006

3444 - Sheet Metal Work County (P-4749)

SALES (est): 7.5MM Privately Held
SIC: 3444 4953 Bins, prefabricated sheet metal; recycling, waste materials

(P-4749)
CONTRACT METAL PRODUCTS INC
6451 W Schulte Rd Ste 110, Tracy (95377-8131)
PHONE..................510 979-0000
John Young, *President*
EMP: 30 EST: 1974
SALES (est): 5MM Privately Held
WEB: www.contractmetalproducts.com
SIC: 3444 3599 7692 Sheet metal specialties, not stamped; machine shop, jobbing & repair; welding repair

(P-4750)
CORTEC PRECISION SHTMTL INC (PA)
2231 Will Wool Dr, San Jose (95112-2628)
PHONE..................408 278-8540
Mike Corrales, *Vice Pres*
John Corrales, *President*
Richard Corrales, *Vice Pres*
Melanie Wilcox, *Executive*
Manuel Teschera, *General Mgr*
EMP: 153 EST: 1989
SQ FT: 78,000
SALES (est): 78.7MM Privately Held
WEB: www.cortecprecision.com
SIC: 3444 Sheet metal specialties, not stamped

(P-4751)
CREATIVE MFG SOLUTIONS INC
18400 Sutter Blvd, Morgan Hill (95037-2819)
PHONE..................408 327-0600
Tim Patrick Herlihy, *President*
Tammy Herlihy, *CFO*
Jorge Magana, *Prgrmr*
Israel Ruiz, *Buyer*
Gilbert Ruiz, *QC Mgr*
EMP: 22 EST: 2006
SQ FT: 12,000
SALES (est): 5.7MM Privately Held
WEB: www.creativemanufacturingsolutions.com
SIC: 3444 Sheet metal specialties, not stamped

(P-4752)
DALE BRISCO INC
2132 S Temperance Ave, Fowler (93625-9760)
PHONE..................559 834-5926
Jamie Brisco, *President*
Cheryl Brisco, *Office Mgr*
Pat Phelan, *Sales Staff*
EMP: 17 EST: 1967
SQ FT: 50,000
SALES (est): 3.5MM Privately Held
WEB: www.dalebriscoinc.com
SIC: 3444 Pipe, sheet metal; ducts, sheet metal; flues & pipes, stove or furnace: sheet metal; pile shells, sheet metal

(P-4753)
DECK WEST INC
1900 Sanguinetti Ln, Stockton (95205-3403)
PHONE..................209 939-9700
Patty Shipman, *CEO*
Cliff Heard, *Project Mgr*
EMP: 23 EST: 1995
SQ FT: 26,000
SALES (est): 2.3MM Privately Held
WEB: www.deckwest.com
SIC: 3444 Metal roofing & roof drainage equipment; metal flooring & siding

(P-4754)
DEPENDABLE PRECISION MFG INC
1111 S Stockton St Ste A, Lodi (95240-5933)
PHONE..................209 369-1055
Clifford L McBride, *President*
EMP: 17 EST: 1978
SQ FT: 30,000
SALES (est): 3.4MM Privately Held
WEB: www.dependableprecision.com
SIC: 3444 Sheet metal specialties, not stamped

(P-4755)
DEVINCENZI METAL PRODUCTS INC
1809 Castenada Dr, Burlingame (94010-5716)
PHONE..................650 692-5800
Robert C Devincenzi, *CEO*
Janice Samuelson, *Corp Secy*
Steven Devincenzi, *Vice Pres*
Jan Samuelson, *Controller*
▲ EMP: 75 EST: 1978
SQ FT: 90,000
SALES (est): 8.7MM Privately Held
WEB: www.celestica.com
SIC: 3444 Sheet metal specialties, not stamped

(P-4756)
DURAVENT INC (DH)
877 Cotting Ct, Vacaville (95688-9354)
PHONE..................800 835-4429
Simon Davis, *CEO*
◆ EMP: 350 EST: 1982
SALES (est): 122MM
SALES (corp-wide): 148MM Privately Held
WEB: www.duravent.com
SIC: 3444 Metal ventilating equipment
HQ: M & G Group Europe B.V.
  Dr. A.F. Philipsweg 39
  Assen 9403
  503 139-944

(P-4757)
E-M MANUFACTURING INC
1290 Dupont Ct, Manteca (95336-6003)
P.O. Box 397, Half Moon Bay (94019-0397)
PHONE..................209 825-1800
Jody Elliot, *President*
Mike Elliot, *Corp Secy*
EMP: 19 EST: 2009
SQ FT: 15,500
SALES (est): 2.8MM Privately Held
WEB: www.emmanufacturing.com
SIC: 3444 Sheet metal specialties, not stamped; metal housings, enclosures, casings & other containers

(P-4758)
ECB CORP
Also Called: Omni Duct Systems
1650 Parkway Blvd, West Sacramento (95691-5020)
PHONE..................916 492-8900
Lou Yuhas, *Branch Mgr*
Adam Barstad, *General Mgr*
Scott Barstad, *General Mgr*
Veronica Negrete, *Credit Staff*
Eddie Carbajal, *Purchasing*
EMP: 25
SALES (corp-wide): 39.4MM Privately Held
WEB: www.omniduct.com
SIC: 3444 Ducts, sheet metal
PA: Ecb Corp.
  6400 Artesia Blvd
  Buena Park CA 90620
  714 385-8900

(P-4759)
ECLIPSE METAL FABRICATION INC
17700 Shideler Pkwy, Lathrop (95330-9356)
PHONE..................650 298-8731
Joe Anaya, *President*
Eduardo Molina, *CFO*
Eduardo Melina, *Treasurer*
Al Cuevas, *Executive*
EMP: 50 EST: 1999
SALES (est): 6.6MM Privately Held
WEB: www.eclipsemf.com
SIC: 3444 Sheet metalwork

(P-4760)
ELITE E/M INC
340 Martin Ave, Santa Clara (95050-3112)
PHONE..................408 988-3505
Igor Brovarny, *President*
Tim Parsley, *General Mgr*
Benny Guira, *Manager*
EMP: 32 EST: 1988
SQ FT: 12,300
SALES (est): 5.8MM Privately Held
WEB: www.eliteem.com
SIC: 3444 3559 3593 3542 Forming machine work, sheet metal; semiconductor manufacturing machinery; machine & other job shop work; presses: forming, stamping, punching, sizing (machine tools); design, commercial & industrial; mechanical engineering

(P-4761)
EMTEC ENGINEERING
16840 Joleen Way Ste F1, Morgan Hill (95037-4606)
PHONE..................408 779-5800
Edward R Ruminski, *President*
EMP: 32 EST: 1986
SQ FT: 16,000
SALES (est): 5.1MM Privately Held
WEB: www.emtec.cc
SIC: 3444 3599 3469 Sheet metalwork; machine shop, jobbing & repair; metal stampings

(P-4762)
ENCORE INDUSTRIES
597 Brennan St, San Jose (95131-1202)
PHONE..................408 416-0501
Gary Vogel, *CEO*
Tom Fitzgerald, *Treasurer*
Gordon Tigue, *Vice Pres*
▲ EMP: 50 EST: 1997
SALES (est): 10.9MM Privately Held
WEB: www.encoreindustries.com
SIC: 3444 3441 Sheet metalwork; fabricated structural metal

(P-4763)
FABRITEC PRECISION INC
1060 Reno Ave, Modesto (95351-1233)
P.O. Box 32370, San Jose (95152-2370)
PHONE..................209 529-8504
Jack Taek Bong Kim, *President*
Hester Lou-Kim, *Corp Secy*
EMP: 37 EST: 1997
SQ FT: 16,800
SALES (est): 2.5MM Privately Held
SIC: 3444 Sheet metalwork

(P-4764)
GCM MEDICAL & OEM INC (PA)
Also Called: Global Contract Manufacturing
1350 Atlantic St, Union City (94587-2004)
PHONE..................510 475-0404
Seanus Meaghr, *President*
Brandon Miller, *Technician*
John Pasillas, *Technician*
Rafael Ojeda, *Mfg Mgr*
Andre Finney, *Opers Staff*
◆ EMP: 77 EST: 1983
SQ FT: 80,000
SALES (est): 25.5MM Privately Held
WEB: www.gogcm.com
SIC: 3444 3541 Sheet metalwork; machine tools, metal cutting type

(P-4765)
GRAYSIX COMPANY
2427 4th St, Berkeley (94710-2488)
PHONE..................510 845-5936
Robert Gray, *President*
Matthew D Gray, *Marketing Staff*
EMP: 24 EST: 1946
SQ FT: 16,000
SALES (est): 2.5MM Privately Held
SIC: 3444 3469 Housings for business machines, sheet metal; metal stampings

(P-4766)
GROUP MANUFACTURING SVCS INC (PA)
1928 Hartog Dr, San Jose (95131-2212)
PHONE..................408 436-1040
Curtis Molyneaux, *President*
Patti Thatcher, *CFO*
Patty Thtcher, *CFO*
David Guerra, *VP Business*
Antonio Matos, *General Mgr*
EMP: 80
SQ FT: 30,000
SALES (est): 14.7MM Privately Held
WEB: www.groupmanufacturing.com
SIC: 3444 Ducts, sheet metal

(P-4767)
GROUP MANUFACTURING SVCS INC
2751 Merc Dr Ste 900, Rancho Cordova (95742)
PHONE..................916 858-3270
Jerry Myrick, *Manager*
EMP: 18
SALES (corp-wide): 14.7MM Privately Held
WEB: www.groupmanufacturing.com
SIC: 3444 Sheet metal specialties, not stamped
PA: Group Manufacturing Services, Inc.
  1928 Hartog Dr
  San Jose CA 95131
  408 436-1040

(P-4768)
HARDCRAFT INDUSTRIES INC
Also Called: Peninsula Metal Fabrication
2221 Ringwood Ave, San Jose (95131-1736)
PHONE..................408 432-8340
Andrew Brandt Kwiram, *President*
Melissa Eakin, *Human Res Mgr*
Jim Scocca, *Prdtn Mgr*
EMP: 52 EST: 2016
SALES (est): 7.9MM Privately Held
WEB: www.hardcraft.com
SIC: 3444 Forming machine work, sheet metal

(P-4769)
HILL MANUFACTURING COMPANY LLC
3363 Edward Ave, Santa Clara (95054-2334)
PHONE..................408 988-4744
J Douglas Wickham, *President*
Barbara A Wickham, *CFO*
Barbara Wickham, *CFO*
Anthony Knezevich, *General Mgr*
Dave Crabb, *Prgrmr*
EMP: 46 EST: 1971
SQ FT: 24,500
SALES (est): 9.3MM Privately Held
WEB: www.hill-mfg.com
SIC: 3444 Sheet metal specialties, not stamped

(P-4770)
HSI MECHANICAL INC
1013 N Emerald Ave, Modesto (95351-2851)
PHONE..................209 408-0183
Tim Scott, *Principal*
Preston Stephens, *President*
Brent Holloway, *Vice Pres*
EMP: 21 EST: 2015
SQ FT: 4,000
SALES (est): 2.7MM Privately Held
WEB: www.hsimechanicalinc.com
SIC: 3444 Sheet metalwork

(P-4771)
I & A INC
Also Called: Peninsula Metal Fabrication
2221 Ringwood Ave, San Jose (95131-1736)
PHONE..................408 432-8340
Anthony Davis, *President*
Heather Jevens, *CFO*
Ishbel Davis, *Vice Pres*
Ian Davis, *Principal*
EMP: 41 EST: 2002
SQ FT: 48,000
SALES (est): 6.8MM Privately Held
WEB: www.pmf.com
SIC: 3444 Sheet metal specialties, not stamped

(P-4772)
IMPAKT HOLDINGS LLC
490 Gianni St, Santa Clara (95054-2413)
PHONE..................408 727-0880
Dan Rubin, *CEO*
Daniel Yang, *COO*
Kirk Johnson, *CFO*
EMP: 50 EST: 2016
SALES (est): 5.5MM Privately Held
WEB: www.celestica.com
SIC: 3444 Sheet metalwork

▲ = Import ▼ = Export
◆ = Import/Export

PRODUCTS & SERVICES SECTION

3444 - Sheet Metal Work County (P-4797)

(P-4773)
INLAND MARINE INDUSTRIES INC
Also Called: Inland Metal Technologies
3245 Depot Rd, Hayward (94545-2709)
PHONE.....................510 785-8555
Jennifer Sutton, *President*
Kieran Brady, *Engineer*
Mike Berg, *Purchasing*
George Bielert, *Opers Staff*
Jessica Dickinson, *Manager*
◆ **EMP:** 180
SALES (est): 41MM **Privately Held**
WEB: www.inlandmetal.wpengine.com
SIC: 3444 Sheet metalwork

(P-4774)
JRI INC
Also Called: John Russo Industrial Metal
38021 Cherry St, Newark (94560-4524)
PHONE.....................510 494-5300
Ralph Colet, *President*
Carmen Colet, *Vice Pres*
EMP: 46 **EST:** 1905
SQ FT: 170,000
SALES (est): 2.9MM **Privately Held**
SIC: 3444 Sheet metalwork

(P-4775)
KARGO MASTER INC
11261 Trade Center Dr, Rancho Cordova (95742-6223)
PHONE.....................916 638-8370
John Hancock, *President*
David Lewis, *Vice Pres*
Terri Aquino, *Accounting Mgr*
David Schnur, *Sales Staff*
Jay Graves, *Manager*
EMP: 40 **EST:** 1983
SALES (est): 4.1MM **Privately Held**
WEB: www.kargomaster.com
SIC: 3444 Sheet metalwork

(P-4776)
LAPTALO ENTERPRISES INC
Also Called: J L Precision Sheet Metal
2360 Zanker Rd, San Jose (95131-1115)
PHONE.....................408 727-6633
Jakov Laptalo, *CEO*
Michael Laptalo, *President*
Tony Grizelj, *Vice Pres*
Todd Morey, *Vice Pres*
Slavko Laptalo, *Admin Sec*
EMP: 100
SQ FT: 60,000
SALES (est): 31.1MM **Privately Held**
WEB: www.jlprecision.com
SIC: 3444 Sheet metal specialties, not stamped

(P-4777)
LEVMAR INC
Also Called: Concord Sheet Metal
1666 Willow Pass Rd, Pittsburg (94565-1702)
PHONE.....................925 680-8723
Mark Riley, *President*
EMP: 15 **EST:** 2011
SALES (est): 1.8MM **Privately Held**
WEB: www.concordsheetmetal.com
SIC: 3444 Sheet metalwork

(P-4778)
LOR-VAN MANUFACTURING LLC
3307 Edward Ave, Santa Clara (95054-2341)
PHONE.....................408 980-1045
Christopher Girardot,
Ismelda Lopez, *Engineer*
Lorena Lopez,
EMP: 26 **EST:** 2005
SQ FT: 6,400
SALES (est): 4.3MM **Privately Held**
WEB: www.lor-vanmfg.com
SIC: 3444 3699 Sheet metal specialties, not stamped; laser welding, drilling & cutting equipment

(P-4779)
LUNAS SHEET METAL INC
3125 Molinaro St Ste 102, Santa Clara (95054-2433)
PHONE.....................408 492-1260
Antonio Luna, *President*
Maria Luna, *CFO*
EMP: 15 **EST:** 1989
SQ FT: 10,000
SALES (est): 2.2MM **Privately Held**
WEB: www.lunasheetmetal.com
SIC: 3444 Sheet metalwork

(P-4780)
LYNX ENTERPRISES INC
724 E Grant Line Rd Ste B, Tracy (95304-2800)
PHONE.....................209 833-3400
Vance R Anderson, *President*
Keith J Anderson, *CFO*
Keith Anderson, *CFO*
Carlos Aldona, *Admin Sec*
Rosalinda Orta, *Purchasing*
▲ **EMP:** 60 **EST:** 1993
SQ FT: 52,000
SALES (est): 13.5MM **Privately Held**
SIC: 3444 3446 3443 3441 Sheet metalwork; architectural metalwork; fabricated plate work (boiler shop); fabricated structural metal

(P-4781)
M C I MANUFACTURING INC (PA)
1020 Rock Ave, San Jose (95131-1610)
PHONE.....................408 456-2700
Henry LI, *President*
EMP: 45 **EST:** 1992
SQ FT: 22,000
SALES (est): 5MM **Privately Held**
WEB: www.mcimfg.com
SIC: 3444 Metal housings, enclosures, casings & other containers

(P-4782)
M-T METAL FABRICATIONS INC
536 Lewelling Blvd Ste A, San Leandro (94579-1845)
PHONE.....................510 357-5262
Ross Bigler, *President*
Justin Bigler, *Vice Pres*
Manny Ferreira, *Manager*
EMP: 37 **EST:** 1962
SQ FT: 12,900
SALES (est): 4MM **Privately Held**
WEB: www.mtmetalfab.com
SIC: 3444 Sheet metal specialties, not stamped

(P-4783)
MAC CAL COMPANY
Also Called: Mac Cal Manufacturing
2520 Zanker Rd, San Jose (95131-1127)
PHONE.....................408 441-1435
Michael Hall, *President*
Renee Hall, *CEO*
Cathy McDonald, *CFO*
Marlene Kamiya, *Executive*
Dave Whitaker, *General Mgr*
EMP: 80
SALES (est): 17.1MM **Privately Held**
WEB: www.maccal.com
SIC: 3444 3479 7336 Sheet metal specialties, not stamped; housings for business machines, sheet metal; name plates: engraved, etched, etc.; silk screen design

(P-4784)
MASS PRECISION INC
46555 Landing Pkwy, Fremont (94538-6421)
PHONE.....................408 954-0200
Greg Kraus, *Manager*
EMP: 125
SALES (corp-wide): 88.6MM **Privately Held**
WEB: www.massprecision.com
SIC: 3444 3599 Sheet metalwork; machine shop, jobbing & repair
PA: Mass Precision, Inc.
2110 Oakland Rd
San Jose CA 95131
408 954-0200

(P-4785)
MASS PRECISION INC (PA)
Also Called: Machining and Frame Division
2110 Oakland Rd, San Jose (95131-1565)
PHONE.....................408 954-0200
Al Stucky Jr, *President*
W Ray Allen, *CFO*
Jake Garrett, *Administration*
Mike Subocz, *Technology*
Jeremy Stucky, *Engineer*
▲ **EMP:** 200
SQ FT: 200,000
SALES (est): 88.6MM **Privately Held**
WEB: www.massprecision.com
SIC: 3444 3599 Sheet metal specialties, not stamped; machine shop, jobbing & repair

(P-4786)
MELROSE METAL PRODUCTS INC
44533 S Grimmer Blvd, Fremont (94538-6309)
P.O. Box 1780, Pleasanton (94566-0177)
PHONE.....................510 657-8771
Mitchell A Hoppe, *CEO*
Harry Hoppe, *Shareholder*
Shirley Hoppe, *Vice Pres*
EMP: 20 **EST:** 1925
SQ FT: 40,000
SALES (est): 3.6MM **Privately Held**
WEB: www.gomelrose.com
SIC: 3444 Sheet metal specialties, not stamped

(P-4787)
METAL SALES MANUFACTURING CORP
1326 Paddock Pl, Woodland (95776-5919)
PHONE.....................707 826-2653
Ray Kirchner, *Manager*
Dwight Isaac, *Manager*
EMP: 32
SALES (corp-wide): 347.3MM **Privately Held**
WEB: www.metalsales.us.com
SIC: 3444 3448 Roof deck, sheet metal; siding, sheet metal; prefabricated metal buildings
HQ: Metal Sales Manufacturing Corporation
545 S 3rd St Ste 200
Louisville KY 40202
502 855-4300

(P-4788)
METALS DIRECT INC
6771 Eastside Rd, Redding (96001-5059)
PHONE.....................530 605-1931
Dale Williams, *President*
Terry Williams, *Vice Pres*
EMP: 29 **EST:** 2009
SALES (est): 3.1MM **Privately Held**
WEB: www.metalsdirect.com
SIC: 3444 5082 1761 5039 Siding, sheet metal; contractors' materials; roofing, siding & sheet metal work; metal buildings; agricultural building contractors

(P-4789)
MEYERS SHEET METAL BOX INC
138 W Harris Ave, South San Francisco (94080-6009)
PHONE.....................650 873-8889
James H C Liang, *President*
Chung Lai Liang, *Corp Secy*
EMP: 31 **EST:** 1987
SQ FT: 7,500
SALES (est): 2.9MM **Privately Held**
SIC: 3444 Sheet metalwork

(P-4790)
MICROFORM PRECISION LLC
4244 S Market Ct Ste A, Sacramento (95834-1243)
PHONE.....................916 419-0580
Timothy E Rice, *Mng Member*
Tim Rice, *Data Proc Staff*
Brian Cook, *Engineer*
Bryan Wallace, *Buyer*
Adam Rice, *Director*
▲ **EMP:** 55 **EST:** 1981
SQ FT: 42,000
SALES (est): 9.6MM **Privately Held**
WEB: www.mform.com
SIC: 3444 Sheet metal specialties, not stamped

(P-4791)
MIKES SHEET METAL PDTS INC
Also Called: Uniproducts
3315 Elkhorn Blvd, North Highlands (95660-3112)
PHONE.....................916 348-3800
Michael R Meredith, *President*
Ginny Meredith, *Vice Pres*
EMP: 25 **EST:** 1978
SQ FT: 10,000
SALES (est): 3.3MM **Privately Held**
SIC: 3444 Ducts, sheet metal

(P-4792)
MILLENNIUM METALCRAFT INC
3201 Osgood Cmn, Fremont (94539-5029)
PHONE.....................510 657-4700
Kenneth Watson, *President*
Gwendolyn Watson, *CFO*
EMP: 36 **EST:** 1994
SQ FT: 8,100
SALES (est): 3.1MM **Privately Held**
WEB: www.mmcraft.com
SIC: 3444 Sheet metal specialties, not stamped

(P-4793)
NEW CAL METALS INC
Also Called: Artesian Home Products
3495 Swetzer Rd, Granite Bay (95746)
P.O. Box 1126, Loomis (95650-1126)
PHONE.....................916 652-7424
Larry Dumm, *President*
Slate Bryer, *Shareholder*
Chris Tataschiore, *Vice Pres*
▲ **EMP:** 15 **EST:** 2008
SQ FT: 15,000
SALES (est): 2.7MM **Privately Held**
WEB: www.newcalmetals.com
SIC: 3444 Metal ventilating equipment

(P-4794)
NOLL/NORWESCO LLC
1320 Performance Dr, Stockton (95206-4925)
PHONE.....................209 234-1600
Gary Henry, *Mng Member*
EMP: 130 **EST:** 2007
SALES (est): 66.3MM
SALES (corp-wide): 1B **Publicly Held**
WEB: www.gibraltar1.com
SIC: 3444 Sheet metalwork
PA: Gibraltar Industries, Inc.
3556 Lake Shore Rd # 100
Buffalo NY 14219
716 826-6500

(P-4795)
NOR-CAL METAL FABRICATORS
1121 3rd St, Oakland (94607-2509)
PHONE.....................510 350-0121
Robert C Hall, *Ch of Bd*
Michael Tran, *President*
Lac Nguyen, *Prgrmr*
Troy Nickles, *Mfg Staff*
▲ **EMP:** 51 **EST:** 1960
SQ FT: 100,000
SALES (est): 11.2MM **Privately Held**
WEB: www.nc-mf.com
SIC: 3444 3661 Sheet metal specialties, not stamped; telephone & telegraph apparatus

(P-4796)
NORTH VALLEY RAIN GUTTERS
27 Freight Ln Ste C, Chico (95973-8962)
PHONE.....................530 894-3347
Michael Gaston, *Owner*
EMP: 16 **EST:** 1983
SQ FT: 3,000
SALES (est): 893.2K **Privately Held**
WEB: www.northvalleyraingutter.com
SIC: 3444 1761 Gutters, sheet metal; downspouts, sheet metal; gutter & downspout contractor

(P-4797)
OKEEFFES INC
Also Called: Safti
220 S R St, Merced (95341-6833)
PHONE.....................209 388-9072
William Keeffe, *Branch Mgr*
William O 'keeffe Jr, *Vice Pres*
John Gordon, *Comp Tech*
Paolo Mercado, *Project Mgr*
Peter Cheung, *Finance*

3444 - Sheet Metal Work County (P-4798)

PRODUCTS & SERVICES SECTION

EMP: 134
SALES (corp-wide): 29.6MM **Privately Held**
WEB: www.okeeffes.com
SIC: 5211 3444 3354 Lumber & other building materials; sheet metalwork; aluminum extruded products
PA: O'keeffe's, Inc.
100 N Hill Dr Ste 12
Brisbane CA 94005
415 822-4222

(P-4798)
ONETO MANUFACTURING CO INC
146 S Maple Ave, South San Francisco (94080-6302)
PHONE.................650 875-1710
Jack Liberatore, *President*
Barbara L Liberatore, *Vice Pres*
Robert Liberatore, *Admin Sec*
EMP: 23 EST: 1959
SQ FT: 20,000
SALES (est): 2.4MM **Privately Held**
SIC: 3444 Sheet metal specialties, not stamped

(P-4799)
PACIFIC MODERN HOMES INC
9723 Railroad St, Elk Grove (95624-2456)
P.O. Box 670 (95759-0670)
PHONE.................916 685-9514
Anthony Colbert, *President*
Anthony B Colbert, *President*
Chris J Fellersen, *Senior VP*
Kenneth S Rader, *Vice Pres*
Thomas Dyer, *CTO*
▼ EMP: 20 EST: 1968
SQ FT: 3,800
SALES (est): 3.1MM **Privately Held**
WEB: www.pmhi.com
SIC: 3444 5031 Metal roofing & roof drainage equipment; building materials, exterior; building materials, interior

(P-4800)
PALEX METALS INC
3601 Thomas Rd, Santa Clara (95054-2040)
PHONE.................408 496-6111
Donald J Russo, *President*
John Jameson, *CFO*
Mary Magda Russo, *Vice Pres*
Rudy Valenzuela, *VP Bus Dvlpt*
EMP: 34 EST: 1973
SALES (est): 2.9MM **Privately Held**
WEB: www.palex-metals.com
SIC: 3444 Sheet metal specialties, not stamped

(P-4801)
PEGA PRECISION INC
18800 Adams Ct, Morgan Hill (95037-2816)
PHONE.................408 776-3700
Lewis H Fast, *President*
Aaron Fast, *Vice Pres*
EMP: 20
SQ FT: 30,000
SALES (est): 3.4MM **Privately Held**
WEB: www.pegaprecision.com
SIC: 3444 3599 Housings for business machines, sheet metal; machine shop, jobbing & repair

(P-4802)
PENFIELD PRODUCTS INC
Also Called: Custom Home Accessories
11300 Trade Center Dr A, Rancho Cordova (95742-6329)
PHONE.................916 635-0231
Jeffrey Feldman, *CEO*
EMP: 22 EST: 2013
SQ FT: 18,000
SALES (est): 5MM **Privately Held**
WEB: www.store.mailboxes.info
SIC: 3444 5999 Mail (post office) collection or storage boxes, sheet metal; trophies & plaques

(P-4803)
PETERSON SHEET METAL INC
Also Called: Peterson Sheetmetal
12925 Alcosta Blvd Ste 2, San Ramon (94583-1341)
PHONE.................925 830-1766
Carl Peterson, *President*
Darlene Peterson, *Vice Pres*
EMP: 37 EST: 1997
SQ FT: 3,200
SALES (est): 6.6MM **Privately Held**
WEB: www.petersonsheetmetal.com
SIC: 3444 Sheet metalwork

(P-4804)
PINNACLE MANUFACTURING CORP
17680 Bttrfield Blvd Ste 1, Morgan Hill (95037)
PHONE.................408 778-6100
Philip Stolzman, *President*
Byron Scarlett, *Purchasing*
Emil Strehlow, *QC Mgr*
Kristin Mullen, *Manager*
▲ EMP: 35 EST: 2002
SALES (est): 8.1MM **Privately Held**
WEB: www.team-pinnacle.com
SIC: 3444 Sheet metalwork

(P-4805)
PITTSBURG GENERAL INC
Also Called: Merit Ends Inc.
620 Clark Ave, Pittsburg (94565-5000)
PHONE.................800 445-6374
Peter Ryner, *CEO*
David Berry, *CFO*
EMP: 25 EST: 1967
SQ FT: 200,000
SALES (est): 16.7MM **Privately Held**
WEB: www.meritsteel.com
SIC: 3444 5051 Sheet metalwork; sheets, metal
PA: Viking Processing Corporation
620 Clark Ave
Pittsburg CA 94565

(P-4806)
PRO-TEK MANUFACTURING INC
4849 Southfront Rd, Livermore (94551-9482)
PHONE.................925 454-8100
Steven M Krider, *President*
Sargon Alkurge, *Vice Pres*
Daniel McKenzie, *Vice Pres*
Ron Biela, *Sales Staff*
Eddie Mendez, *Supervisor*
▲ EMP: 49 EST: 1980
SQ FT: 35,240
SALES (est): 10.9MM **Privately Held**
WEB: www.protekmfg.com
SIC: 3444 3449 Sheet metalwork; miscellaneous metalwork

(P-4807)
PROMPT PRECISION METALS INC
1649 E Whitmore Ave, Ceres (95307-7203)
PHONE.................209 531-1210
Don Widdifield, *President*
Joan Widdifield, *Admin Sec*
Larry McNertney, *Opers Staff*
EMP: 33 EST: 1988
SQ FT: 70,000
SALES (est): 7.6MM **Privately Held**
WEB: www.promptprecision.com
SIC: 3444 Sheet metal specialties, not stamped

(P-4808)
QUALITY METAL FABRICATION LLC
2350 Wilbur Way, Auburn (95602-9500)
PHONE.................530 887-7388
Thomas Neithercutt, *Mng Member*
Hailey Graspointner, *Office Mgr*
Greg Quayle, *Office Mgr*
EMP: 27 EST: 1996
SQ FT: 12,000
SALES (est): 5.2MM **Privately Held**
WEB: www.qualitymetalfabrication.com
SIC: 3444 1799 Sheet metalwork; welding on site

(P-4809)
RECOATING-WEST INC (PA)
Also Called: Rwi
4170 Douglas Blvd Ste 120, Granite Bay (95746-9703)
PHONE.................916 652-8290
Brian Hope, *President*
Ian Cameron, *CFO*
Jamie McCartney, *Office Mgr*
Cheryl Poderzay, *Office Mgr*
Glenn Shafto, *Analyst*
▲ EMP: 35 EST: 1982
SQ FT: 41,000
SALES (est): 5.9MM **Privately Held**
WEB: www.recoatingwest.com
SIC: 3444 Sheet metalwork

(P-4810)
REDDING METAL CRAFTERS INC
3871 Rancho Rd, Redding (96002-9328)
PHONE.................530 222-4400
Robert Robinson III, *President*
Barbara Robinson, *Corp Secy*
Gregory Robinson, *Vice Pres*
EMP: 21 EST: 1982
SQ FT: 10,000
SALES (est): 2.3MM **Privately Held**
SIC: 3444 Restaurant sheet metalwork

(P-4811)
RESPONSIBLE METAL FAB INC
1256 Lawrence Station Rd, Sunnyvale (94089-2218)
PHONE.................408 734-0713
Peter Goglia, *President*
Syed Ahmed, *Finance*
EMP: 45 EST: 1979
SALES (est): 4.2MM **Privately Held**
WEB: www.responsiblemetal.com
SIC: 3444 Sheet metalwork

(P-4812)
RON NUNES ENTERPRISES LLC
7703 Las Positas Rd, Livermore (94551-8205)
PHONE.................925 371-0220
Ron Nunes, *President*
Hiliary Cruse, *Bookkeeper*
Mark Timm, *Mktg Dir*
EMP: 20 EST: 1972
SQ FT: 28,000
SALES (est): 5.1MM **Privately Held**
WEB: www.ronnunes.com
SIC: 3444 7692 3443 3441 Sheet metal specialties, not stamped; welding repair; fabricated plate work (boiler shop); fabricated structural metal

(P-4813)
RONALD F OGLETREE INC
Also Called: Ogletree's
935 Vintage Ave, Saint Helena (94574-1400)
PHONE.................707 963-3537
Ronald Ogletree, *President*
Matthew CIA, *Vice Pres*
EMP: 34 EST: 1946
SQ FT: 22,500
SALES (est): 4.8MM **Privately Held**
SIC: 3444 3441 1791 Sheet metal specialties, not stamped; fabricated structural metal; structural steel erection

(P-4814)
SAL J ACSTA SHEETMETAL MFG INC
Also Called: Acosta Sheet Metal Mfg Co
930 Remillard Ct, San Jose (95122-2625)
PHONE.................408 275-6370
Sal J Acosta, *CEO*
Anthony Morales, *CFO*
Randy Acosta, *Treasurer*
Sandi Acosta, *Vice Pres*
Michelle Acosta, *Admin Sec*
▲ EMP: 65 EST: 1974
SQ FT: 118,000
SALES (est): 8.8MM **Privately Held**
SIC: 3444 Sheet metal specialties, not stamped

(P-4815)
SCREEN TECH INC
4754 Bennett Dr, Livermore (94551-4800)
P.O. Box 23484, San Jose (95153-3484)
PHONE.................408 885-9750
Stevan S Robertson, *Principal*
Marsha Robertson, *Vice Pres*
Steve Robertson, *CIO*
Matt Larson, *Engineer*
Tony Phan, *Senior Engr*
▲ EMP: 60 EST: 1964
SQ FT: 52,000
SALES (est): 11.1MM **Privately Held**
WEB: www.screentechinc.com
SIC: 3444 Sheet metal specialties, not stamped

(P-4816)
SEGUNDO METAL PRODUCTS INC
Also Called: Advantage Metal Products
7855 Southfront Rd, Livermore (94551-8230)
PHONE.................925 667-2009
Mike Segundo, *President*
Ramsey Ackad, *CFO*
Janis Deroche, *Vice Pres*
Phil Segundo, *Vice Pres*
Mike Subocz, *Program Mgr*
▲ EMP: 80 EST: 1988
SQ FT: 60,000
SALES (est): 19.6MM **Privately Held**
WEB: www.advantagemetal.com
SIC: 3444 Sheet metalwork

(P-4817)
SHEET MTAL FABRICATION SUP INC
2020 Railroad Dr, Sacramento (95815-3515)
PHONE.................916 641-6884
Cipriano Espinor, *President*
Mark Johnston, *President*
John Espinor, *Vice Pres*
EMP: 52 EST: 1983
SQ FT: 14,000
SALES (est): 1.2MM **Privately Held**
SIC: 3444 Ducts, sheet metal

(P-4818)
SONOMA METAL PRODUCTS INC
601 Aviation Blvd, Santa Rosa (95403-1025)
PHONE.................707 484-9876
Brian K Herndon, *President*
Wanda Dunbar, *Shareholder*
Sharon Herndon, *Treasurer*
Don Dunbar, *Admin Sec*
EMP: 20 EST: 1982
SQ FT: 54,000
SALES (est): 683.6K **Privately Held**
WEB: www.fab2spec.info
SIC: 3444 3496 2522 Housings for business machines, sheet metal; miscellaneous fabricated wire products; office furniture, except wood

(P-4819)
SOUTH BAY DIVERSFD SYSTEMS INC
Also Called: U S Fabrications
1841 National Ave, Hayward (94545-1707)
PHONE.................510 784-3094
Thomas S Waller, *President*
Horatio Finley, *Purchasing*
▲ EMP: 15 EST: 1981
SALES (est): 4.5MM **Privately Held**
SIC: 3444 Sheet metalwork

(P-4820)
SPACESONICS INCORPORATED
Also Called: Paysonic
30300 Union City Blvd, Union City (94587-1514)
PHONE.................650 610-0999
Ignacio C Palomarez, *President*
Elizabeth Palomarez, *Treasurer*
Hortencia Villanuedo, *Admin Sec*
Carlos Palomarez, *Info Tech Dir*
Diane Palomarez, *Info Tech Mgr*
▲ EMP: 90 EST: 1967
SQ FT: 55,000
SALES (est): 22.5MM **Privately Held**
WEB: www.spacesonic.com
SIC: 3444 Metal housings, enclosures, casings & other containers

(P-4821)
SUN SHEETMETAL SOLUTIONS INC
3565 Charter Park Dr, San Jose (95136-1346)
P.O. Box 731244 (95173-1244)
PHONE.................408 445-8047
Chau Nguyen, *President*

▲ = Import ▼ = Export
◆ = Import/Export

PRODUCTS & SERVICES SECTION

3448 - Prefabricated Metal Buildings & Cmpnts County (P-4844)

Rebecca Trinhle, *CFO*
Tom Nguyen, *Vice Pres*
Kevin Trinhle, *Accounts Mgr*
EMP: 20 **EST:** 2000
SQ FT: 10,000
SALES (est): 4.1MM Privately Held
WEB: www.sunmfgsolutions.com
SIC: 3444 3552 Sheet metal specialties, not stamped; fabric forming machinery & equipment

(P-4822)
SUPERIOR METALS INC
838 Jury Ct Ste B, San Jose (95112-2815)
PHONE...................408 938-3488
Hugo Navarez, *President*
EMP: 15 **EST:** 1999
SQ FT: 7,000
SALES (est): 3.5MM Privately Held
WEB: www.smiprecision.com
SIC: 3444 Sheet metalwork

(P-4823)
TAYLOR WINGS INC
8392 Carbide Ct, Sacramento (95828-5638)
PHONE...................916 851-9464
Brad Durga, *President*
EMP: 25 **EST:** 1979
SALES (est): 3MM Privately Held
WEB: www.taylorwings.com
SIC: 3444 Sheet metalwork

(P-4824)
TEOHC CALIFORNIA INC
1320 Performance Dr, Stockton (95206-4925)
PHONE...................209 234-1600
Nicholas L Saakvitne, *CEO*
Gary Henry, *President*
Jim Willis, *CFO*
Mark J Comfort, *Vice Pres*
Bruce Couturier, *Vice Pres*
EMP: 264 **EST:** 1943
SQ FT: 350,000
SALES (est): 134.8MM
SALES (corp-wide): 1B Publicly Held
WEB: www.gibraltar1.com
SIC: 3444 3479 Furnace casings, sheet metal; gutters, sheet metal; galvanizing of iron, steel or end-formed products
PA: Gibraltar Industries, Inc.
  3556 Lake Shore Rd # 100
  Buffalo NY 14219
  716 826-6500

(P-4825)
THERMA LLC
1601 Las Plumas Ave, San Jose (95133-1613)
PHONE...................408 347-3400
Joseph Parisi, *CEO*
Nicki Parisi, *CFO*
Scott Carstairs, *Exec VP*
Francis Wong, *Exec VP*
Pete Portesi, *Executive*
▲ **EMP:** 1200 **EST:** 1967
SALES (est): 228.8MM
SALES (corp-wide): 402.3MM Privately Held
WEB: www.therma.com
SIC: 3444 3448 Sheet metalwork; prefabricated metal components
PA: Therma Holdings Llc
  1601 Las Plumas Ave
  San Jose CA 95133
  408 347-3100

(P-4826)
TRI FAB ASSOCIATES INC
48351 Lakeview Blvd, Fremont (94538-6533)
PHONE...................510 651-7628
Ronald A Brochu, *President*
Joseph R Santosuosso, *CEO*
James McDonald, *Prgrmr*
Jennifer De La Fuente, *Controller*
Larry Rohrbacher, *Plant Mgr*
EMP: 90 **EST:** 1989
SQ FT: 35,000
SALES (est): 18.3MM Privately Held
WEB: www.trifab.com
SIC: 3444 Sheet metal specialties, not stamped

(P-4827)
UNITED MECH MET FBRICATORS INC
Also Called: Umec
33353 Lewis St, Union City (94587-2205)
PHONE...................510 537-4744
Gina Wang, *CEO*
Barry Brescia, *Vice Chairman*
Garrett Lewis, *Prgrmr*
Isabel Mato, *Buyer*
Camille Alcayde, *Manager*
EMP: 50 **EST:** 1982
SALES (est): 12.8MM Privately Held
WEB: www.umec.net
SIC: 3444 3443 3841 Sheet metalwork; fabricated plate work (boiler shop); surgical & medical instruments

(P-4828)
USK MANUFACTURING INC
720 Zwissig Way, Union City (94587-3602)
PHONE...................510 471-7555
Moon Do Kim, *CEO*
Jina Kim, *Vice Pres*
Cindy Fong, *Principal*
▲ **EMP:** 45 **EST:** 1987
SQ FT: 85,000
SALES (est): 5MM Privately Held
WEB: www.uskmfg.com
SIC: 3444 Sheet metalwork

(P-4829)
W A CALL MANUFACTURING CO INC
1710 Rogers Ave, San Jose (95112-1189)
PHONE...................408 436-1450
W A Pat Call Jr, *President*
Justin Pourroy, *Vice Pres*
EMP: 23 **EST:** 1950
SQ FT: 36,250
SALES (est): 4.6MM Privately Held
WEB: www.wacallmfg.com
SIC: 3444 5075 Metal ventilating equipment; warm air heating & air conditioning

(P-4830)
WEST COAST FAB INC
700 S 32nd St, Richmond (94804-4106)
PHONE...................510 529-0177
Thomas Nelson, *President*
Scott Shelby, *Manager*
EMP: 15 **EST:** 1973
SQ FT: 18,000
SALES (est): 2.6MM Privately Held
WEB: www.westcoastfab.com
SIC: 3444 Sheet metal specialties, not stamped

(P-4831)
WESTFAB MANUFACTURING INC
3370 Keller St, Santa Clara (95054-2612)
PHONE...................408 727-0550
Akbar Soleimanieh, *President*
Homeira Lotfi, *CFO*
EMP: 45
SQ FT: 22,000
SALES (est): 5MM Privately Held
WEB: www.westfab.com
SIC: 3444 Sheet metalwork

3446 Architectural & Ornamental Metal Work

(P-4832)
ACTIANCE INC
1400 Seaport Blvd, Redwood City (94063-5594)
PHONE...................650 631-6300
EMP: 42
SALES (est): 10.3MM Privately Held
SIC: 3446 Mfg Architectural Metalwork

(P-4833)
AMERICAN STEEL & STAIRWAYS INC
8525 Forest St Ste A, Gilroy (95020-3797)
PHONE...................408 848-2992
Martin Vollrath, *President*
Margit Vollrath, *Corp Secy*
Thomas Vollrath, *Vice Pres*
Lilia Lara, *Admin Asst*
Nancy Vollrath, *Purchasing*
EMP: 33 **EST:** 1975
SQ FT: 18,000
SALES (est): 7.8MM Privately Held
WEB: www.americansteelandstairways.com
SIC: 3446 3441 Ornamental metalwork; fabricated structural metal

(P-4834)
ARBOR FENCE INC
22660 Broadway, Sonoma (95476-8217)
PHONE...................707 938-3133
Ronald Wooden, *President*
EMP: 22 **EST:** 1990
SALES (est): 2.6MM Privately Held
WEB: www.arborfenceinc.com
SIC: 3446 3315 2499 5211 Fences, gates, posts & flagpoles; chain link fencing; fencing, wood; fencing; security devices

(P-4835)
BORGA STL BLDNGS CMPONENTS INC
300 W Peach St, Fowler (93625-2530)
P.O. Box 35 (93625-0035)
PHONE...................559 834-5375
Ronald Heskett, *CEO*
Scott Boatwright, *Controller*
Marissa Heskett, *Controller*
Arthur Tanner, *Controller*
Amila Roberts, *Human Resources*
EMP: 51
SQ FT: 90,000
SALES (est): 10.4MM Privately Held
WEB: www.borgasteel.com
SIC: 3446 3448 Railings, prefabricated metal; buildings, portable: prefabricated metal

(P-4836)
MC METAL INC
1347 Donner Ave, San Francisco (94124-3612)
PHONE...................415 822-2288
Jeffrey Mark, *President*
EMP: 17 **EST:** 1997
SALES (est): 3.8MM Privately Held
WEB: www.mcmetalinc.com
SIC: 3446 Architectural metalwork

(P-4837)
NGO METALS INC
Also Called: Moz Designs
711 Kevin Ct, Oakland (94621-4039)
PHONE...................510 632-0853
Murry Sandford, *CEO*
Herbert M Sandford III, *Vice Pres*
Tripp Sandford, *Vice Pres*
Juan Alatorre, *Project Mgr*
Deandre Montgomery, *Project Mgr*
◆ **EMP:** 25 **EST:** 1990
SQ FT: 10,000
SALES (est): 8.6MM
SALES (corp-wide): 936.9MM Publicly Held
WEB: www.mozdesigns.com
SIC: 3446 Architectural metalwork
PA: Armstrong World Industries, Inc.
  2500 Columbia Ave
  Lancaster PA 17603
  717 397-0611

(P-4838)
OLSON AND CO STEEL (PA)
1941 Davis St, San Leandro (94577-1262)
PHONE...................510 489-4680
David Olson, *CEO*
Dylan Olson, *President*
Kevin Cullen, *CFO*
Del Stephens, *District Mgr*
Jacob Perrin, *CIO*
▲ **EMP:** 225 **EST:** 1960
SQ FT: 130,000
SALES (est): 57.4MM Privately Held
WEB: www.olsonsteel.com
SIC: 3446 3441 Architectural metalwork; fabricated structural metal

(P-4839)
SONOMA ACCESS CTRL SYSTEMS INC
21600 8th St E, Sonoma (95476-2821)
PHONE...................707 935-3458
David Nisenson, *President*
Paula Nisenson, *Vice Pres*
EMP: 21 **EST:** 1988
SQ FT: 8,000
SALES (est): 1.6MM Privately Held
WEB: www.accesscontrolsonoma.com
SIC: 3446 1799 Gates, ornamental metal; fence construction

(P-4840)
TAURUS FABRICATION INC
22818 Industrial Pl, Grass Valley (95949-6326)
PHONE...................530 268-2650
Beau Huiskens, *CEO*
Beau Huisaens, *President*
Andrew Whiting, *General Mgr*
EMP: 25 **EST:** 2015
SQ FT: 1,200
SALES (est): 4.7MM Privately Held
WEB: www.taurusfab.com
SIC: 3446 3599 3499 3999 Gratings, tread: fabricated metal; machine shop, jobbing & repair; fire- or burglary-resistive products; barber & beauty shop equipment

(P-4841)
TECHNIBUILDERS IRON INC
1049 Felipe Ave, San Jose (95122-2602)
PHONE...................408 287-8797
Roy S Larson, *President*
EMP: 18 **EST:** 1966
SQ FT: 7,200
SALES (est): 1.4MM Privately Held
SIC: 3446 Ornamental metalwork

(P-4842)
VALLEY STAIRWAY INC
5684 E Shields Ave, Fresno (93727-7818)
P.O. Box 245, Clovis (93613-0245)
PHONE...................559 299-0151
Jerry De George, *President*
Anthony De George Jr, *Corp Secy*
EMP: 16 **EST:** 1957
SQ FT: 29,464
SALES (est): 1.7MM Privately Held
WEB: www.valleystairwayinc.com
SIC: 3446 Stairs, staircases, stair treads: prefabricated metal

(P-4843)
WESTERN SQUARE INDUSTRIES INC
1621 N Brdwy, Stockton (95205)
PHONE...................209 944-0921
David Bowyer, *CEO*
Trygue Mikkelsen, *Chairman*
Serisha S Ana, *Office Mgr*
Larry Bartko, *Chief Engr*
Ben Rebuldela, *Prdtn Mgr*
◆ **EMP:** 40 **EST:** 1978
SQ FT: 44,000
SALES (est): 9.5MM Privately Held
WEB: www.westernsquare.com
SIC: 3446 2542 2514 3441 Fences or posts, ornamental iron or steel; gates, ornamental metal; racks, merchandise display or storage: except wood; tables, household: metal; fabricated structural metal

---

3448 Prefabricated Metal Buildings & Cmpnts

(P-4844)
ALLIED CONTAINER SYSTEMS INC
Also Called: ACS
511 Wilbur Ave Ste B4, Antioch (94509-7563)
PHONE...................925 944-7600
Brian Horsfall, *Ch of Bd*
Robbin Kilgore, *Officer*
Matthew Horsfall, *Vice Pres*
Susan Horsfall, *Vice Pres*
Lester Sanui, *Vice Pres*
◆ **EMP:** 140 **EST:** 1992
SQ FT: 20,000
SALES (est): 19.6MM Privately Held
SIC: 3448 8748 3559 Prefabricated metal buildings; environmental consultant; chemical machinery & equipment

3448 - Prefabricated Metal Buildings & Cmpnts County (P-4845)

(P-4845)
ALUMAWALL INC
1701 S 7th St Ste 9, San Jose (95112-6000)
PHONE.................................408 275-7165
David M Warda, *President*
Lori Warda, *Vice Pres*
Maureen Sullivan, *Project Mgr*
Steven Aguilar, *Technology*
Dagmar Van Fleet, *Controller*
EMP: 65
SQ FT: 50,000
SALES (est): 16.4MM **Privately Held**
WEB: www.alumawall.com
SIC: 3448 Prefabricated metal components

(P-4846)
AMERICAN CARPORTS INC (PA)
1415 Clay St, Colusa (95932-2064)
PHONE.................................866 730-9865
Primo Castillo, *President*
Milton Castillo, *President*
Venani Torres, *Corp Secy*
EMP: 43 **EST:** 2001
SQ FT: 500,000
SALES (est): 1MM **Privately Held**
WEB: www.americancarportsinc.com
SIC: 3448 Garages, portable: prefabricated metal; carports: prefabricated metal

(P-4847)
AMERICORE INC
19705 August Ave, Hilmar (95324-9302)
P.O. Box 1353 (95324-1353)
PHONE.................................209 632-5679
Ryan Marques Cunha, *President*
EMP: 47 **EST:** 2007
SALES (est): 5.9MM **Privately Held**
WEB: www.americoremechanical.com
SIC: 3448 3699 3841 Prefabricated metal buildings; electrical welding equipment; diagnostic apparatus, medical

(P-4848)
CALIFORNIA EXPANDED MET PDTS
Also Called: Cemco
1001a Pttsburg Antoch Hwy, Pittsburg (94565-4199)
PHONE.................................925 473-9340
Ned Martin, *Manager*
Bob Ladd, *General Mgr*
Barry Anstett, *Engineer*
Monique Acosta, *Human Resources*
Todd McCrite, *Opers Staff*
EMP: 15
SALES (corp-wide): 78.1MM **Privately Held**
WEB: www.cemcosteel.com
SIC: 3448 3449 3444 3441 Prefabricated metal buildings; miscellaneous metalwork; sheet metalwork; fabricated structural metal
PA: California Expanded Metal Products Company
13191 Crssrads Pkwy N Ste
City Of Industry CA 91746
626 369-3564

(P-4849)
CBC STEEL BUILDINGS LLC
1700 E Louise Ave, Lathrop (95330-9795)
P.O. Box 1009 (95330-1009)
PHONE.................................209 858-2425
Steve Campbell, *President*
EMP: 120 **EST:** 2007
SQ FT: 105,000
SALES (est): 36.7MM
SALES (corp-wide): 20.1B **Publicly Held**
WEB: www.cbcsteelbuildings.com
SIC: 3448 Prefabricated metal buildings
PA: Nucor Corporation
1915 Rexford Rd Ste 400
Charlotte NC 28211
704 366-7000

(P-4850)
EMERALD KINGDOM GREENHOUSE LLC (PA)
104 Masonic Ln, Weaverville (96093-1127)
PHONE.................................530 215-5670
Kate Brown, *Project Mgr*
▲ **EMP:** 41 **EST:** 2014
SALES (est): 2.5MM **Privately Held**
WEB: www.emeraldkingdomgreenhouse.com
SIC: 3448 5191 Greenhouses: prefabricated metal; greenhouse equipment & supplies

(P-4851)
ENVIROPLEX INC
4777 Carpenter Rd, Stockton (95215-8106)
PHONE.................................209 466-8000
Glenn Owens, *President*
Sharon Castello, *Administration*
Casey Koester, *Project Mgr*
John Kozler, *Project Mgr*
Ola Abell, *Purchasing*
EMP: 60 **EST:** 1991
SQ FT: 102,000
SALES (est): 15.7MM
SALES (corp-wide): 572.5MM **Publicly Held**
WEB: www.enviroplex.com
SIC: 3448 Buildings, portable: prefabricated metal
PA: Mcgrath Rentcorp
5700 Las Positas Rd
Livermore CA 94551
925 606-9200

(P-4852)
KINGSPAN INSULATED PANELS INC
Kingspan API
2000 Morgan Rd, Modesto (95358-9407)
PHONE.................................209 531-9091
Russell Shiels, *President*
Donal Curtin, *General Mgr*
Steve Mauro, *Regl Sales Mgr*
David Lohsen, *Supervisor*
EMP: 72 **Privately Held**
WEB: www.kingspan.com
SIC: 3448 Prefabricated metal buildings
HQ: Kingspan Insulated Panels Inc.
726 Summerhill Dr
Deland FL 32724
386 626-6789

(P-4853)
KRAEMER & CO MFG INC
3778 County Road 99w, Orland (95963-9785)
PHONE.................................530 865-7982
Ben Kraemer, *President*
Nancy Kraemer, *Treasurer*
Gerald Kraemer, *Admin Sec*
Don Sheets, *Opers Staff*
EMP: 29 **EST:** 1984
SQ FT: 6,500
SALES (est): 5.5MM **Privately Held**
WEB: www.kraemermanufacturing.com
SIC: 3448 3523 3441 3412 Farm & utility buildings; farm machinery & equipment; elevators, farm; fabricated structural metal; metal barrels, drums & pails

(P-4854)
PACIFIC METAL BUILDINGS INC
270 Old Highway 99, Maxwell (95955-8076)
P.O. Box 485 (95955-0485)
PHONE.................................530 438-2777
EMP: 19
SALES (est): 2.9MM **Privately Held**
WEB: www.pacificbuildingsinc.com
SIC: 3448 Prefabricated Metal Buildings, Nsk

(P-4855)
PRE-INSULATED METAL TECH INC (HQ)
Also Called: All Weather Insulated Panels
929 Aldridge Rd, Vacaville (95688-9282)
PHONE.................................707 359-2280
William H Lowery, *President*
Kim Harrell, *Vice Pres*
Michael T Lowery, *Vice Pres*
Anne Sison, *Administration*
Troy Speers, *Technician*
▲ **EMP:** 48 **EST:** 2010
SQ FT: 96,000
SALES (est): 24.6MM **Privately Held**
WEB: www.kingspan.com
SIC: 3448 Panels for prefabricated metal buildings

(P-4856)
SARAMARK INC
15660 Mckinley Ave, Lathrop (95330-8525)
P.O. Box 1369 (95330-1369)
PHONE.................................408 971-3881
Mark A Collishaw, *CEO*
Markus Deleeuw, *Sales Mgr*
EMP: 50 **EST:** 1900
SALES (est): 5.1MM **Privately Held**
WEB: www.saramark.com
SIC: 3448 Prefabricated metal buildings

3449 Misc Structural Metal Work

(P-4857)
JR DANIELS COMMERCIAL BLDRS
Also Called: Innovative Steel Structures
907 Maze Blvd, Modesto (95351-1851)
PHONE.................................209 545-6040
James R Daniels, *President*
EMP: 21 **EST:** 1991
SQ FT: 1,900
SALES (est): 1.2MM **Privately Held**
SIC: 3449 Bars, concrete reinforcing: fabricated steel

(P-4858)
PACIFIC STEEL GROUP
2301 Napa Vallejo Hwy, NAPA (94558-6242)
PHONE.................................707 669-3136
Alfredo Gonzalez, *Branch Mgr*
EMP: 21
SALES (corp-wide): 95.3MM **Privately Held**
WEB: www.pacificsteelgroup.com
SIC: 3449 Bars, concrete reinforcing: fabricated steel
PA: Pacific Steel Group Corporation
4805 Murphy Canyon Rd
San Diego CA 92123
858 251-1100

(P-4859)
PACIFIC STEEL GROUP
355 S Vasco Rd, Livermore (94550-5300)
PHONE.................................858 251-1100
EMP: 53
SALES (corp-wide): 180.7MM **Privately Held**
WEB: www.pacificsteelgroup.com
SIC: 3449 Miscellaneous Metalwork
PA: Pacific Steel Group Corporation
4805 Murphy Canyon Rd
San Diego CA 92123
858 251-1100

(P-4860)
PACIFIC WEST FOREST PRODUCTS
13434 Browns Valley Dr, Chico (95973-9322)
P.O. Box 2082 (95927-2082)
PHONE.................................530 899-7313
Keith Lindquist, *President*
Kevin Linquist, *Vice Pres*
▲ **EMP:** 16 **EST:** 1997
SQ FT: 37,000
SALES (est): 2.2MM **Privately Held**
WEB: www.pacificwestforest.com
SIC: 3449 5031 Custom roll formed products; lumber: rough, dressed & finished

(P-4861)
SIMPSON STRONG-TIE COMPANY INC (HQ)
5956 W Las Positas Blvd, Pleasanton (94588-8540)
P.O. Box 10789 (94588-0789)
PHONE.................................925 560-9000
Karen Colonias, *CEO*
Phillip Kingsfather, *President*
Terry Kingsfather, *President*
Bryan Magstaet, *CFO*
Jacinta Pister, *Senior VP*
♦ **EMP:** 150 **EST:** 1914
SQ FT: 89,000
SALES (est): 847.7MM
SALES (corp-wide): 1.2B **Publicly Held**
WEB: www.strongtie.com
SIC: 3449 2891 Joists, fabricated bar; adhesives
PA: Simpson Manufacturing Co., Inc.
5956 W Las Positas Blvd
Pleasanton CA 94588
925 560-9000

(P-4862)
SIMPSON STRONG-TIE COMPANY INC
5151 S Airport Way, Stockton (95206-3991)
PHONE.................................209 234-7775
Bruce Lewis, *Branch Mgr*
Ricardo Arevalo, *Vice Pres*
Brian Todd, *Program Mgr*
Allison Edenzon, *Office Mgr*
Brandy Reyes, *Office Mgr*
EMP: 100
SALES (corp-wide): 1.2B **Publicly Held**
WEB: www.strongtie.com
SIC: 3449 3444 3441 Joists, fabricated bar; sheet metalwork; fabricated structural metal
HQ: Simpson Strong-Tie Company Inc.
5956 W Las Positas Blvd
Pleasanton CA 94588
925 560-9000

(P-4863)
SIMPSON STRONG-TIE INTL INC (DH)
5956 W Las Positas Blvd, Pleasanton (94588-8540)
P.O. Box 10789 (94588-0789)
PHONE.................................925 560-9000
Karen Colonias, *CEO*
▲ **EMP:** 100 **EST:** 1993
SQ FT: 89,000
SALES (est): 51.1MM
SALES (corp-wide): 1.2B **Publicly Held**
WEB: www.strongtie.com
SIC: 3449 Joists, fabricated bar
HQ: Simpson Strong-Tie Company Inc.
5956 W Las Positas Blvd
Pleasanton CA 94588
925 560-9000

(P-4864)
SRSS LLC
1400 Airport Blvd, Santa Rosa (95403-1023)
PHONE.................................707 544-7777
Mark Ferronato, *Manager*
Nathan Williams, *Prdtn Mgr*
Rodney Ferronato, *Manager*
EMP: 17 **EST:** 2001
SALES (est): 3.6MM **Privately Held**
WEB: www.srss.com
SIC: 3449 Bars, concrete reinforcing: fabricated steel

3451 Screw Machine Prdts

(P-4865)
ACCU-SWISS INC (PA)
544 Armstrong Way, Oakdale (95361-9367)
PHONE.................................209 847-1016
Sohel Sareshwala, *President*
Asfiya Sareshwala, *Treasurer*
Ali Gabajiwala, *Engineer*
EMP: 17 **EST:** 1977
SQ FT: 10,000
SALES (est): 2.8MM **Privately Held**
WEB: www.accuswissinc.com
SIC: 3451 8711 Screw machine products; engineering services

(P-4866)
H&M PRECISION MACHINING
Also Called: H & M Precision Machining
504 Robert Ave, Santa Clara (95050-2955)
PHONE.................................408 982-9184
Jane Harvey, *President*
EMP: 18 **EST:** 1960
SQ FT: 8,000
SALES (est): 1.1MM **Privately Held**
WEB: www.h-mprecisionmachining.com
SIC: 3451 3469 Screw machine products; machine parts, stamped or pressed metal

▲ = Import ▼ = Export
♦ = Import/Export

PRODUCTS & SERVICES SECTION

3469 - Metal Stampings, NEC County (P-4889)

(P-4867)
MERCED SCREW PRODUCTS INC
1861 Grogan Ave, Merced (95341-6432)
PHONE.............................209 723-7706
Steve Centivich, *President*
Pamela McGlynn, *Office Mgr*
EMP: 40 **EST:** 1980
SQ FT: 17,000
SALES (est): 3.5MM **Privately Held**
WEB: www.mercedscrewproducts.com
SIC: 3451 Screw machine products

(P-4868)
PENCOM/ACCURACY INC
Also Called: Accuracy Screw Machine Pdts
1300 Industrial Rd Ste 21, San Carlos (94070-4141)
PHONE.............................510 785-5022
Bill Gardiner, *President*
Deborah Gardiner, *Treasurer*
Brian Wilkenson, *Vice Pres*
EMP: 91 **EST:** 1978
SQ FT: 8,000
SALES (est): 2.1MM **Privately Held**
WEB: www.pencomsf.com
SIC: 3451 Screw machine products
PA: Peninsula Components, Inc.
   1300 Industrial Rd Ste 21
   San Carlos CA 94070

(P-4869)
SANMINA CORPORATION
8455 Cabot Ct, Newark (94560-3336)
PHONE.............................510 494-2421
Lyn Morris, *Branch Mgr*
Tadd Thomas, *General Mgr*
Cathy Brake, *Info Tech Mgr*
Nick Gorshen, *Maintence Staff*
EMP: 200 **Publicly Held**
WEB: www.sanmina.com
SIC: 3451 Screw machine products
PA: Sanmina Corporation
   2700 N 1st St
   San Jose CA 95134

(P-4870)
SWISS-TECH MACHINING LLC
Also Called: Manufacturer
10564 Industrial Ave, Roseville (95678-6223)
PHONE.............................916 797-6010
Pete Kummli,
Ben Schlichting, *General Mgr*
Cheryl Kummli, *Controller*
EMP: 25
SQ FT: 20,000
SALES (est): 4.1MM **Privately Held**
WEB: www.stmachining.com
SIC: 3451 Screw machine products

3452 Bolts, Nuts, Screws, Rivets & Washers

(P-4871)
BAY STANDARD MANUFACTURING INC (PA)
Also Called: Bsmi
24485 Marsh Creek Rd, Brentwood (94513-4319)
P.O. Box 801 (94513-0801)
PHONE.............................925 634-1181
Gary W Landgraf, *CEO*
Gregory Iverson, *President*
Karen Landgraf, *Vice Pres*
Jeri Hoffman, *Sales Staff*
Alison Watts, *Property Mgr*
◆ **EMP:** 50 **EST:** 1959
SQ FT: 25,000
SALES (est): 11MM **Privately Held**
WEB: www.baystandard.com
SIC: 3452 5072 Bolts, metal; bolts

(P-4872)
CONKLIN & CONKLIN INCORPORATED
34201 7th St, Union City (94587-3655)
PHONE.............................510 489-5500
James Edward Conklin, *President*
Barbara Conklin, *Vice Pres*
▲ **EMP:** 30 **EST:** 1969
SQ FT: 23,000
SALES (est): 4.6MM **Privately Held**
SIC: 3452 Bolts, nuts, rivets & washers

(P-4873)
U-C COMPONENTS INC (PA)
18700 Adams Ct, Morgan Hill (95037-2804)
P.O. Box 430 (95038-0430)
PHONE.............................408 782-1929
Nancy Anderson, *President*
Gary Broeder, *QC Dir*
Aileen Bui, *Sales Staff*
Tim Renggli, *Manager*
EMP: 23 **EST:** 1974
SQ FT: 16,000
SALES (est): 5MM **Privately Held**
WEB: www.uccomponents.com
SIC: 3452 Screws, metal

3462 Iron & Steel Forgings

(P-4874)
BAY EQUIPMENT CO INC
44221 S Grimmer Blvd, Fremont (94538-6309)
PHONE.............................510 226-8800
Pat Pecoraro, *President*
Gerry Pecoraro, *Vice Pres*
EMP: 31 **EST:** 1972
SQ FT: 18,000
SALES (est): 2.4MM **Privately Held**
WEB: www.bayequipmentsales.com
SIC: 3462 5082 Construction or mining equipment forgings, ferrous; scaffolding

(P-4875)
BIERWITH FORGE & TOOL INC
Also Called: Berkeley Forge & Tool
1331 Eastshore Hwy, Berkeley (94710-1320)
PHONE.............................510 526-5034
Peter Bierwith, *President*
Paul Bierwith, *Shareholder*
Tony Latini, *COO*
Robert Bierwith, *Corp Secy*
Ed Hinckley, *Vice Pres*
▲ **EMP:** 88
SQ FT: 50,000
SALES (est): 21.9MM **Privately Held**
WEB: www.berkforge.com
SIC: 3462 Construction or mining equipment forgings, ferrous

(P-4876)
COULTER FORGE TECHNOLOGY INC
Also Called: Coulter Steel and Forge
1494 67th St, Emeryville (94608-1016)
P.O. Box 8008 (94662-0901)
PHONE.............................510 420-3500
Peter Bierwith, *President*
Robert Bierwith, *Vice Pres*
John Martin, *Executive*
Cola Chan, *Asst Controller*
Joseph Holmes, *VP Mktg*
▲ **EMP:** 18 **EST:** 2002
SQ FT: 20,000
SALES (est): 4.1MM **Privately Held**
WEB: www.coulter-forge.com
SIC: 3462 Iron & steel forgings

3465 Automotive Stampings

(P-4877)
ROOTLIEB INC
815 S Soderquist Rd, Turlock (95380-5723)
P.O. Box 1810 (95381-1810)
PHONE.............................209 632-2203
Thomas H Rootlieb, *President*
EMP: 22 **EST:** 1957
SQ FT: 25,000
SALES (est): 967.5K **Privately Held**
WEB: www.rootlieb.com
SIC: 3465 Fenders, automobile: stamped or pressed metal; body parts, automobile: stamped metal

3466 Crowns & Closures

(P-4878)
RIEKE CORPORATION
1200 Valley House Dr # 100, Rohnert Park (94928-4934)
PHONE.............................707 238-9250
Rohnert Park, *Branch Mgr*
Kathleen Gogola, *Vice Pres*
Kate Gandy, *Accountant*
Jacob Noack, *Accountant*
Collins Teri, *Human Resources*
EMP: 180
SALES (corp-wide): 769.9MM **Publicly Held**
WEB: www.riekepackaging.com
SIC: 3466 Closures, stamped metal
HQ: Rieke Llc
   500 W 7th St
   Auburn IN 46706
   260 925-3700

3469 Metal Stampings, NEC

(P-4879)
CARSONS COATINGS INC
550 Industrial Dr Ste 200, Galt (95632-1647)
PHONE.............................209 745-2387
Duane Carson, *President*
Terry Carson, *Vice Pres*
▲ **EMP:** 20 **EST:** 1991
SQ FT: 53,000
SALES (est): 2.5MM **Privately Held**
WEB: www.carsonscoatings.com
SIC: 3469 Architectural panels or parts, porcelain enameled

(P-4880)
CONTEXT ENGINEERING CO
Also Called: Sidco Labelling Systems
1043 Di Giulio Ave, Santa Clara (95050-2805)
PHONE.............................408 748-9112
David Clemson, *President*
Martin Clemson, *Vice Pres*
Lucy Del Real, *General Mgr*
Maral Panossian, *General Mgr*
Mary Clemson, *Admin Sec*
▲ **EMP:** 25 **EST:** 1983
SQ FT: 4,500
SALES (est): 3.8MM **Privately Held**
WEB: www.contextengineering.com
SIC: 3469 5131 5084 Electronic enclosures, stamped or pressed metal; labels; industrial machinery & equipment

(P-4881)
DIE AND TOOL PRODUCTS INC
1842 Sabre St, Hayward (94545-1024)
PHONE.............................415 822-2888
Victor Tschirky, *President*
Mariette Tschirky, *Corp Secy*
EMP: 16 **EST:** 1948
SALES (est): 2MM **Privately Held**
SIC: 3469 Stamping metal for the trade

(P-4882)
E2E MFG LLC
3500 Yale Way, Fremont (94538-6180)
PHONE.............................925 862-2057
Igonni Fajardo,
Humera Nawaz, *Program Mgr*
Raja Maruthu, *Engineer*
Jeffery Vinyard, *Sales Staff*
Christine Luna,
▲ **EMP:** 46 **EST:** 2000
SALES (est): 9.2MM **Privately Held**
WEB: www.e2emfg.com
SIC: 3469 Metal stampings

(P-4883)
FORM & FUSION MFG INC (PA)
Also Called: Urgent Upfits
11261 Trade Center Dr, Rancho Cordova (95742-6223)
PHONE.............................916 638-8576
John Hancock, *President*
Dave Lewis, *Shareholder*
EMP: 27 **EST:** 1971
SQ FT: 40,000 **Privately Held**
WEB: www.form-fusion.com

SIC: 3469 3465 Metal stampings; automotive stampings

(P-4884)
HUGIN COMPONENTS INC
Also Called: H C I
4231 Pacific St Ste 23, Rocklin (95677-2135)
PHONE.............................916 652-1070
Steve Katonis, *President*
Sharon Katonis, *Vice Pres*
Wayne Paul,
EMP: 22 **EST:** 1990
SQ FT: 18,000
SALES (est): 1.9MM **Privately Held**
WEB: www.hugincomponents.com
SIC: 3469 Stamping metal for the trade

(P-4885)
LEMTECH USA INC
185 Estancia Dr Unit 117, San Jose (95134-2211)
PHONE.............................408 824-5352
CHI-Feng Hsu, *President*
Maurice K Chan, *Treasurer*
Muralidharan N Das, *Admin Sec*
EMP: 16 **EST:** 2013
SALES (est): 1.2MM **Privately Held**
WEB: www.lemtech.com
SIC: 3469 Metal stampings
HQ: Lemtech Technology Limited
   Rm 2702-03 27/F Cc Wu Bldg
   Wan Chai HK

(P-4886)
MEYER CORPORATION US (HQ)
Also Called: Meyer Wines
1 Meyer Plz, Vallejo (94590-5925)
PHONE.............................707 551-2800
Stanley Kin Sui Cheng, *CEO*
Ed Blackman, *COO*
Christopher Banning, *Director*
◆ **EMP:** 80 **EST:** 1980
SQ FT: 180,000
SALES (est): 128.8MM **Privately Held**
WEB: www.meyerus.com
SIC: 3469 3631 5023 Cooking ware, except porcelain enamelled; household cooking equipment; kitchenware

(P-4887)
PERIDOT CORPORATION
1072 Serpentine Ln, Pleasanton (94566-4731)
PHONE.............................925 461-8830
Patrick Pickerell, *President*
Debra Vansickle, *Vice Pres*
John Lindsay, *Engineer*
Ken Buell, *Manager*
Debra Pickerell, *Manager*
EMP: 60 **EST:** 1996
SQ FT: 30,000
SALES (est): 15.3MM **Privately Held**
WEB: www.peridotcorp.com
SIC: 3469 Metal stampings
PA: Seisa Medical, Inc.
   9005 Montana Ave
   El Paso TX 79925

(P-4888)
QUALITY METAL SPINNING AND
4047 Transport St, Palo Alto (94303-4914)
PHONE.............................650 858-2491
Joseph Czisch Jr, *President*
Xenia Czisch, *Vice Pres*
EMP: 30 **EST:** 1967
SQ FT: 34,000
SALES (est): 5.6MM **Privately Held**
WEB: www.qualitymetalspinning.us
SIC: 3469 3599 Stamping metal for the trade; machine shop, jobbing & repair

(P-4889)
RAGO & SON INC
1029 51st Ave, Oakland (94601-5653)
P.O. Box 7309 (94601-0309)
PHONE.............................510 536-5700
Dominic Anthony Rago, *CEO*
Dominic Rago, *President*
Deborah Rago, *Corp Secy*
Gerald Accardo Jr, *Vice Pres*
Gerald Accardo Sr, *Vice Pres*
EMP: 80 **EST:** 1969
SQ FT: 38,000

3471 - Electroplating, Plating, Polishing, Anodizing & Coloring County (P-4890)

PRODUCTS & SERVICES SECTION

SALES (est): 21.8MM **Privately Held**
WEB: www.ragoandson.com
SIC: 3469 Stamping metal for the trade

3471 Electroplating, Plating, Polishing, Anodizing & Coloring

(P-4890)
A & E ANODIZING INC
652 Charles St Ste A, San Jose (95112-1433)
PHONE................408 297-5910
Edwardo Ibanez, *President*
Angelica Ibanez, *CFO*
EMP: 15 **EST:** 1988
SALES (est): 2.2MM **Privately Held**
WEB: www.aeanodizing.com
SIC: 3471 Electroplating of metals or formed products

(P-4891)
A&A METAL FINISHING ENTPS LLC
8290 Alpine Ave, Sacramento (95826-4748)
PHONE................916 442-1063
Anthony R Nole, *Vice Pres*
Nancy M Casale, *Admin Sec*
EMP: 20 **EST:** 2008
SALES (est): 1.9MM **Privately Held**
WEB: www.mfg-5.com
SIC: 3471 Electroplating of metals or formed products; finishing, metals or formed products

(P-4892)
ABLE METAL PLATING INC
932 86th Ave, Oakland (94621-1642)
P.O. Box 43480 (94624-0480)
PHONE................510 569-6539
Jose Vasquez, *President*
Rafael De La Paz, *Vice Pres*
Elizabeth Vasquez, *Vice Pres*
Joann Kern, *Office Mgr*
EMP: 25 **EST:** 1998
SQ FT: 7,500
SALES (est): 2.8MM **Privately Held**
SIC: 3471 Electroplating of metals or formed products

(P-4893)
ADVANCED METAL FINISHING LLC
Also Called: AMF
2130 March Rd, Roseville (95747-9308)
PHONE................530 888-7772
Mischelle Von Rembov,
EMP: 20 **EST:** 2000
SQ FT: 4,500
SALES (est): 2.5MM **Privately Held**
WEB: www.amfservices.net
SIC: 3471 Electroplating of metals or formed products

(P-4894)
AI INDUSTRIES LLC (PA)
1725 E Byshore Rd Ste 101, Redwood City (94063)
PHONE................650 366-4099
Shannon Lew,
Mackenzie Martin, *Assistant*
EMP: 87 **EST:** 1977
SQ FT: 27,000
SALES (est): 20.1MM **Privately Held**
WEB: www.aiindustries.com
SIC: 3471 3479 Anodizing (plating) of metals or formed products; coating of metals & formed products

(P-4895)
ALUMINUM COATING TECH INC
Also Called: A.C.T.
8290 Alpine Ave, Sacramento (95826-4748)
PHONE................916 442-1063
Steven G Hickey, *CEO*
EMP: 20 **EST:** 1991
SALES (est): 2.1MM **Privately Held**
WEB: www.mfg-5.com
SIC: 3471 Electroplating of metals or formed products

(P-4896)
AMEX PLATING INCORPORATED
3333 Woodward Ave, Santa Clara (95054-2628)
PHONE................408 986-8222
Jose Rodriguez, *President*
Sylvia D Rodriguez, *CEO*
Rebeca Rodriguez, *Vice Pres*
Nhan Lu, *General Mgr*
EMP: 30 **EST:** 1983
SQ FT: 10,850
SALES (est): 4.1MM **Privately Held**
WEB: www.amexplating.com
SIC: 3471 Finishing, metals or formed products; anodizing (plating) of metals or formed products

(P-4897)
APPLIED ANODIZE INC
622 Charcot Ave Ste D, San Jose (95131-2205)
PHONE................408 435-9191
Jose Muguerza, *President*
Charlie Richmond, *Manager*
EMP: 27 **EST:** 1978
SQ FT: 14,000
SALES (est): 1.5MM **Privately Held**
WEB: www.appliedanodize.com
SIC: 3471 Coloring & finishing of aluminum or formed products; finishing, metals or formed products; plating of metals or formed products

(P-4898)
ARA TECHNOLOGY
1286 Anvilwood Ave, Sunnyvale (94089-2203)
PHONE................408 734-8131
Mardig Chakalian, *President*
Haig Chakalian, *Vice Pres*
EMP: 20 **EST:** 1977
SQ FT: 10,000
SALES (est): 1.9MM **Privately Held**
SIC: 3471 Plating of metals or formed products

(P-4899)
ATMF INC
Also Called: Ano-Tech Metal Finishing
807 Lincoln Ave, Clovis (93612-2245)
PHONE................559 299-6836
Carol Downs, *CEO*
Kelly S Downs, *President*
Gregory Ott, *Vice Pres*
Rich Tuman, *Purch Mgr*
Brett Hunter, *Plant Mgr*
EMP: 30 **EST:** 1981
SQ FT: 8,000
SALES (est): 6.1MM **Privately Held**
WEB: www.ano-tech.com
SIC: 3471 Anodizing (plating) of metals or formed products; coloring & finishing of aluminum or formed products

(P-4900)
BONNER PROCESSING INC
6052 Industrial Way Ste A, Livermore (94551-9711)
PHONE................925 455-3833
Robert Bonner, *President*
EMP: 21 **EST:** 2004
SQ FT: 19,500
SALES (est): 1MM **Privately Held**
SIC: 3471 Tumbling (cleaning & polishing) of machine parts

(P-4901)
CHROME DEPOSIT CORP
Also Called: Roll Technology West
900 Loveridge Rd, Pittsburg (94565-2808)
P.O. Box 472 (94565-0047)
PHONE................925 432-4507
Jim Goehring, *General Mgr*
EMP: 25 **EST:** 1994
SALES (est): 2.5MM **Privately Held**
WEB: www.chromedeposit.com
SIC: 3471 Chromium plating of metals or formed products

(P-4902)
DU-ALL ANODIZING INC
730 Chestnut St, San Jose (95110-1803)
PHONE................408 275-6694
Gregrey Marchand, *President*
Tony Athens, *Vice Pres*
EMP: 21 **EST:** 1961
SQ FT: 10,000
SALES (est): 508.2K **Privately Held**
WEB: www.duallanodizing.com
SIC: 3471 6531 Anodizing (plating) of metals or formed products; finishing, metals or formed products; real estate agents & managers

(P-4903)
ELECTRO-PLATING SPC INC
2436 American Ave, Hayward (94545-1810)
PHONE................510 786-1881
Mary L Hall, *President*
Debbie McPeek, *Executive*
Mary Ha, *General Mgr*
EMP: 32 **EST:** 1973
SQ FT: 10,000
SALES (est): 3.3MM **Privately Held**
WEB: www.eps-plating.com
SIC: 3471 Electroplating of metals or formed products

(P-4904)
ELECTROCHEM SOLUTIONS INC
32500 Central Ave, Union City (94587-2032)
PHONE................510 476-1840
David Rossiter, *CEO*
Janet Nielsen, *Sales Mgr*
EMP: 256 **EST:** 2012
SALES (est): 2.6MM
SALES (corp-wide): 93MM **Privately Held**
WEB: www.electro-chem.com
SIC: 3471 Electroplating of metals or formed products
PA: Pioneer Metal Finishing, Llc
480 Pilgrim Way Ste 1400
Green Bay WI 54304
877 721-1100

(P-4905)
ELECTROCHEM SOLUTIONS LLC
32500 Central Ave, Union City (94587-2032)
PHONE................510 476-1840
David Rossiter, *President*
Scott Sammons, *Cust Mgr*
EMP: 27 **EST:** 2003
SQ FT: 21,315
SALES (est): 2.8MM **Privately Held**
WEB: www.electro-chem.com
SIC: 3471 Electroplating of metals or formed products

(P-4906)
FOUR D METAL FINISHING
1065 Memorex Dr, Santa Clara (95050-2809)
PHONE................408 730-5722
Peter Deguara, *President*
EMP: 30 **EST:** 1973
SQ FT: 11,000
SALES (est): 3.8MM **Privately Held**
WEB: www.fourdmetal.com
SIC: 3471 Electroplating of metals or formed products

(P-4907)
GENERAL GRINDING INC
Also Called: Stailess Polishing Co.
801 51st Ave, Oakland (94601-5694)
PHONE................510 261-5557
Michael Bardon, *President*
Daniel Bardon, *Corp Secy*
Jonathan Bardon, *Manager*
EMP: 34 **EST:** 1944
SQ FT: 22,500
SALES (est): 3.5MM **Privately Held**
WEB: www.generalgrindinginc.com
SIC: 3471 Finishing, metals or formed products

(P-4908)
GLOBAL PLATING INC
44620 S Grimmer Blvd, Fremont (94538-6386)
PHONE................510 659-8764
Douglas Brothers, *President*
Doug Brothers, *Executive*
Charles Liggett, *Opers Staff*
EMP: 35 **EST:** 1985
SQ FT: 23,000 **Privately Held**
WEB: www.globalplating.com
SIC: 3471 Plating of metals or formed products; finishing, metals or formed products; electroplating of metals or formed products

(P-4909)
HAMMON PLATING CORPORATION
890 Commercial St, Palo Alto (94303-4905)
PHONE................650 494-2691
Tom Wooten, *President*
Glen Phinney, *Corp Secy*
Michelle Hammel, *Accounting Mgr*
Phillip Kelman, *Opers Staff*
John Montoya, *Director*
EMP: 35 **EST:** 1960
SQ FT: 5,000
SALES (est): 6.1MM **Privately Held**
WEB: www.hammonplating.com
SIC: 3471 Electroplating of metals or formed products; plating of metals or formed products

(P-4910)
HANE AND HANE INC
Also Called: University Plating Co
303 Piercy Rd, San Jose (95138-1403)
PHONE................408 292-2140
Carter Hane, *President*
EMP: 20 **EST:** 1958
SALES (est): 2.1MM **Privately Held**
SIC: 3471 Electroplating of metals or formed products

(P-4911)
HY-TECH PLATING INC
1011 American St, San Carlos (94070-5303)
PHONE................650 593-4566
Wendell Wessbecher, *President*
EMP: 15 **EST:** 1988
SALES (est): 652.6K **Privately Held**
WEB: www.hy-techplating.com
SIC: 3471 Electroplating of metals or formed products; plating of metals or formed products

(P-4912)
MENCARINI & JARWIN INC
Also Called: Chrome Craft
5950 88th St, Sacramento (95828-1109)
PHONE................916 383-1660
Philip B Jarwin, *Ch of Bd*
Lillian J Jarwin, *President*
Judith Marrs, *Admin Sec*
EMP: 23 **EST:** 1963
SQ FT: 46,000
SALES (est): 2MM **Privately Held**
WEB: www.chromecraftreman.com
SIC: 3471 Chromium plating of metals or formed products

(P-4913)
MILNERS ANODIZING
3330 Mcmaude Pl, Santa Rosa (95407-8120)
PHONE................707 584-1188
Terry Burson, *Owner*
Claire Burson, *Co-Owner*
EMP: 25 **EST:** 1983
SQ FT: 7,200
SALES (est): 2.2MM **Privately Held**
WEB: www.milnersanodizing.com
SIC: 3471 Electroplating of metals or formed products

(P-4914)
MONTOYA & JARAMILLO INC
Also Called: Swift Metal Finishing
1161 Richard Ave, Santa Clara (95050-2843)
PHONE................408 727-5776
Robert Montoya Jr, *President*
Dyanne Castro, *Treasurer*
EMP: 18 **EST:** 1963
SQ FT: 6,000
SALES (est): 3.4MM **Privately Held**
SIC: 3471 Electroplating of metals or formed products

▲ = Import ▼=Export
◆ =Import/Export

3479 - Coating & Engraving, NEC County (P-4938)

(P-4915)
NEW AGE METAL FINISHING LLC
2169 N Pleasant Ave, Fresno (93705-4730)
PHONE..................559 498-8585
Michael Zelinski,
EMP: 28 EST: 1995
SQ FT: 5,000
SALES (est): 3.5MM Privately Held
WEB: www.newagemetalfinishing.com
SIC: 3471 Electroplating of metals or formed products

(P-4916)
NXEDGE CSL LLC
529 Aldo Ave, Santa Clara (95054-2205)
PHONE..................408 727-0893
Mahesh Naik, President
Kavita Patel, Human Res Mgr
Tim Mickael, Manager
▲ EMP: 55 EST: 2011
SQ FT: 16,000
SALES (est): 6.9MM Privately Held
WEB: www.nxedge.com
SIC: 3471 Anodizing (plating) of metals or formed products; cleaning & descaling metal products; electroplating of metals or formed products; cleaning, polishing & finishing

(P-4917)
PROCESS STAINLESS LAB INC (PA)
Also Called: Advance Elctro Polishing
1280 Memorex Dr, Santa Clara (95050-2812)
PHONE..................408 980-0535
Clay Hudson, Owner
David Hays, Co-Owner
EMP: 27 EST: 1993
SQ FT: 8,000
SALES (est): 5MM Privately Held
WEB: www.pslinc.com
SIC: 3471 Polishing, metals or formed products

(P-4918)
PRODIGY SURFACE TECH INC
Also Called: Arrhenius
807 Aldo Ave Ste 103, Santa Clara (95054-2254)
PHONE..................408 492-9390
John Shaw, President
Mark Danitschek, COO
James Kikoshima, Vice Pres
Randy Souza, Marketing Mgr
Sheila Tosado, Cust Mgr
EMP: 38 EST: 2002
SQ FT: 14,500
SALES (est): 5.9MM Privately Held
WEB: www.prodigysurfacetech.com
SIC: 3471 Electroplating of metals or formed products; plating of metals or formed products

(P-4919)
SANTA CLARA PLATING CO INC
1773 Grant St, Santa Clara (95050-3974)
PHONE..................408 727-9315
Thomas L Coss, President
Wendy Coss, Shareholder
EMP: 85 EST: 1974
SQ FT: 13,000
SALES (est): 6.9MM Privately Held
WEB: www.santaclaraplating.com
SIC: 3471 Electroplating of metals or formed products

(P-4920)
SEMANO INC
31757 Knapp St, Hayward (94544-7827)
PHONE..................510 489-2360
Frank Largusa, President
Terry Dillon, Corp Secy
Devin Kerns, Project Mgr
Shanti Raikar, Safety Mgr
Jose Dacorro, Prdtn Mgr
▲ EMP: 35 EST: 1993
SQ FT: 13,000
SALES (est): 4.5MM Privately Held
WEB: www.semanoinc.com
SIC: 3471 Electroplating of metals or formed products

(P-4921)
SJ VALLEY PLATING INC
491 Perry Ct, Santa Clara (95054-2624)
PHONE..................408 988-5502
Jeff Adams, President
Michele Adams, Admin Sec
EMP: 22 EST: 1980
SQ FT: 10,000
SALES (est): 1.4MM Privately Held
SIC: 3471 Chromium plating of metals or formed products; plating of metals or formed products

(P-4922)
THERMIONICS LABORATORY INC
Thermionics Metal Proc Inc
3118 Depot Rd, Hayward (94545-2708)
PHONE..................510 786-0680
Al Nielsen, Manager
EMP: 75
SQ FT: 1,300
SALES (corp-wide): 36.5MM Privately Held
WEB: www.thermionics.com
SIC: 3471 8711 7342 Cleaning & descaling metal products; engineering services; disinfecting & pest control services
HQ: Thermionics Laboratory, Inc.
3118 Depot Rd
Hayward CA 94545
510 538-3304

(P-4923)
VALLEY CHROME PLATING INC
Also Called: Wing Master
1028 Hoblitt Ave, Clovis (93612-2805)
P.O. Box 189 (93613-0189)
PHONE..................559 298-8094
Thomas A Lucas, CEO
Ray Lucas, President
Catherine L Booey, Corp Secy
Greg Lucas, Vice Pres
Matthew Lucas, Vice Pres
▲ EMP: 70 EST: 1961
SQ FT: 30,000
SALES (est): 16MM Privately Held
WEB: www.valleychrome.com
SIC: 3471 3714 Plating of metals or formed products; bumpers & bumperettes, motor vehicle

---

3479 Coating & Engraving, NEC

(P-4924)
ACI ALLOYS INC
1458 Seareel Pl, San Jose (95131-1572)
PHONE..................408 259-7337
Paul Albert, President
Charles Albert, Vice Pres
Larry Albert, Vice Pres
EMP: 15 EST: 1982
SQ FT: 4,800
SALES (est): 1.5MM Privately Held
WEB: www.acialloys.com
SIC: 3479 Coating of metals & formed products

(P-4925)
ADVANCED GRINDING INCORPORATED
812 49th Ave, Oakland (94601-5136)
PHONE..................510 536-3465
Ronald L Wegstein, President
Ronald Wegstein, President
Karen Wegstein, Vice Pres
EMP: 30 EST: 1980
SQ FT: 13,000
SALES (est): 2.6MM Privately Held
WEB: www.advancedgrindinginc.com
SIC: 3479 Coating of metals & formed products

(P-4926)
ADVANCED INDUS COATINGS INC
950 Industrial Dr, Stockton (95206-3927)
PHONE..................209 234-2700
Toll Free:..................877 -
Ronald Cymanski, President
David Arney, COO
Marianne Arney, Corp Secy
Steve Hockett, Vice Pres
Joann Cymanski, Marketing Mgr
EMP: 53 EST: 1984
SQ FT: 48,000
SALES (est): 9.9MM Privately Held
WEB: www.aic-coatings.com
SIC: 3479 Coating of metals & formed products

(P-4927)
B & C PAINTING SOLUTIONS INC
107 Val Dervin Pkwy, Stockton (95206-4001)
PHONE..................209 982-0422
Gary Maggard, CEO
Gloria Parker, Manager
EMP: 28 EST: 2002
SQ FT: 40,000
SALES (est): 3.8MM Privately Held
WEB: www.bcpaintingsolutions.com
SIC: 3479 Coating of metals & formed products

(P-4928)
B R & F SPRAY INC
3380 De La Cruz Blvd, Santa Clara (95054-2608)
PHONE..................408 988-7582
Ronald Grainger, President
Florence Grainger, Corp Secy
EMP: 20 EST: 1972
SQ FT: 14,000
SALES (est): 1.6MM Privately Held
WEB: www.brf-spray.com
SIC: 3479 3471 Painting of metal products; plating & polishing

(P-4929)
CAL-SPRAY INC
1905 Bay Rd, East Palo Alto (94303-1314)
P.O. Box 50203, Palo Alto (94303-0203)
PHONE..................650 325-0096
John Garcia, President
EMP: 16 EST: 1966
SQ FT: 10,000
SALES (est): 1.2MM Privately Held
SIC: 3479 Painting of metal products

(P-4930)
CLASS A POWDERCOAT INC
7506 Henrietta Dr, Sacramento (95822-5145)
PHONE..................916 681-7474
Klay Stubbs, President
Kirk Stubbs, Vice Pres
EMP: 25 EST: 1991
SQ FT: 5,000
SALES (est): 2.4MM Privately Held
WEB: www.classapc.com
SIC: 3479 3471 Painting of metal products; sand blasting of metal parts

(P-4931)
E-FAB INC
1075 Richard Ave, Santa Clara (95050-2815)
P.O. Box 239 (95052-0239)
PHONE..................408 727-5218
James W Scales, President
Carol Spicker, CFO
Jerry Banks, Vice Pres
Aubrey Lopez, Accounts Mgr
EMP: 22 EST: 1981
SQ FT: 4,000
SALES (est): 3.4MM Privately Held
WEB: www.e-fab.com
SIC: 3479 Etching & engraving

(P-4932)
ELECTRO STAR INDUS COATING INC
Also Called: Electro Star Powder Coatings
1945 Airport Blvd, Red Bluff (96080-4518)
PHONE..................530 527-5400
Baron E Pierce, President
Susan Pierce, CFO
EMP: 15
SQ FT: 4,000
SALES (est): 1.4MM Privately Held
WEB: www.electrostar.net
SIC: 3479 Coating of metals & formed products

(P-4933)
FUSION COATINGS INC
6589 Las Positas Rd, Livermore (94551-5157)
PHONE..................925 443-8083
Paul Fleury, President
Julie Fleury, Co-Owner
EMP: 15 EST: 1984
SQ FT: 7,000
SALES (est): 1.7MM Privately Held
WEB: www.fusioncoatingsonline.com
SIC: 3479 Coating of metals & formed products

(P-4934)
GILBERT SPRAY COAT INC
300 Laurelwood Rd, Santa Clara (95054-2311)
PHONE..................408 988-0747
Todd McLean, President
Lisa McLean, Vice Pres
EMP: 40 EST: 1939
SQ FT: 5,000
SALES (est): 1.2MM Privately Held
WEB: www.gilbertspray.com
SIC: 3479 Painting of metal products; painting, coating & hot dipping

(P-4935)
ITALIX COMPANY INC
120 Mast St Ste A, Morgan Hill (95037-5154)
PHONE..................408 988-2487
Robert L Armanasco, President
Frank Fantino, CEO
Jeff Zweers, Engineer
EMP: 19 EST: 1977
SQ FT: 8,000
SALES (est): 2.9MM Privately Held
WEB: www.italix.com
SIC: 3479 3471 Etching, photochemical; finishing, metals or formed products

(P-4936)
KION TECHNOLOGY INC
2190 Oakland Rd, San Jose (95131-1571)
PHONE..................408 435-3008
Moto Hayashi, President
Shirley Chau, Admin Sec
EMP: 22 EST: 1992
SQ FT: 8,000
SALES (est): 1MM Privately Held
WEB: www.kiontech.com
SIC: 3479 Coating of metals & formed products

(P-4937)
MAAS BROTHERS INC
Also Called: Maas Brothers Powder Coating
285 S Vasco Rd, Livermore (94551-9203)
PHONE..................925 294-8200
Kevin Maas, President
Kraig Maas, Vice Pres
EMP: 75 EST: 1998
SQ FT: 80,000
SALES (est): 6.7MM Privately Held
WEB: www.maasbrothersinc.com
SIC: 3479 Coating of metals & formed products

(P-4938)
MELROSE NAMEPLATE LABEL CO INC (PA)
26575 Corporate Ave, Hayward (94545-3920)
PHONE..................510 732-3100
Chris Somers, President
Cindy Choy, CFO
Kathy Brenner, Admin Sec
▼ EMP: 29 EST: 1939
SQ FT: 33,000
SALES (est): 4MM Privately Held
WEB: www.melrose-nl.com
SIC: 3479 3993 3643 3355 Name plates: engraved, etched, etc.; signs & advertising specialties; current-carrying wiring devices; aluminum plating & drawing; laminated plastics plate & sheet; coated & laminated paper

3479 - Coating & Engraving, NEC County (P-4939)

(P-4939)
MOORE QUALITY GALVANIZING INC
3001 Falcon Dr, Madera (93637-8601)
P.O. Box 420 (93639-0420)
PHONE.................................559 673-2822
Thomas E Moore, *President*
Kellie Moore, *Corp Secy*
Marie Moore, *Vice Pres*
EMP: 26 **EST:** 1984
SQ FT: 11,000
SALES (est): 4.6MM **Privately Held**
WEB: www.mooregalvanizing.com
SIC: 3479 Coating of metals & formed products

(P-4940)
MOORE QUALITY GALVANIZING LP
3001 Falcon Dr, Madera (93637-8601)
P.O. Box 420 (93639-0420)
PHONE.................................559 673-2822
Marie Moore, *General Ptnr*
Kellie Moore, *Partner*
Alex Oestriecher, *Accountant*
Shelly Zirbel, *Personnel*
Shawn Deiter, *Agent*
EMP: 20 **EST:** 1984
SQ FT: 18,000
SALES (est): 2.2MM **Privately Held**
WEB: www.mooregalvanizing.com
SIC: 3479 Coating of metals & formed products

(P-4941)
OPTICAL COATING LABORATORY LLC (HQ)
Also Called: Ocli
2789 Northpoint Pkwy, Santa Rosa (95407-7397)
PHONE.................................707 545-6440
Fred Van Milligen, *President*
Pat Higgins, *Vice Pres*
Shawn Cullen, *General Mgr*
Marina Nedeltcheva, *Admin Asst*
Morgan Huber, *Buyer*
EMP: 400 **EST:** 1963
SQ FT: 490,000
SALES (est): 131MM
SALES (corp-wide): 1.2B **Publicly Held**
WEB: www.viavisolutions.com
SIC: 3479 3577 3827 Coating of metals & formed products; computer peripheral equipment; optical instruments & lenses
PA: Viavi Solutions Inc.
7047 E Greenway Pkwy # 25
Scottsdale AZ 85254
408 404-3600

(P-4942)
PACIFIC GALVANIZING INC
715 46th Ave, Oakland (94601-5096)
PHONE.................................510 261-7331
William Branagh, *President*
EMP: 25 **EST:** 1969
SQ FT: 16,000
SALES: 5.1MM
SALES (corp-wide): 18.4MM **Privately Held**
WEB: www.pacificgalvanizing.com
SIC: 3479 Coating of metals & formed products
PA: Branagh Inc.
750 Kevin Ct
Oakland CA 94621
510 638-6455

(P-4943)
PACIFIC POWDER COATING INC
8637 23rd Ave, Sacramento (95826-4903)
PHONE.................................916 381-1154
Jeffrey M Rochester, *President*
Danielle Gugin, *Admin Asst*
Gabriel Ayala, *Production*
Jolene Mark, *Manager*
▲ **EMP:** 30
SQ FT: 40,000
SALES: 6.3MM **Privately Held**
WEB: www.pacpowder.com
SIC: 3479 3449 Coating of metals & formed products; miscellaneous metalwork

(P-4944)
PACIFIC SHORING PRODUCTS LLC (PA)
265 Roberts Ave, Santa Rosa (95407-5836)
PHONE.................................707 575-9014
Bruce Russell, *CEO*
Bruce Russel,
Robert Pitts, *Mng Member*
EMP: 55 **EST:** 2006
SALES (est): 14.3MM **Privately Held**
WEB: www.pacificshoring.com
SIC: 3479 3334 Aluminum coating of metal products; primary aluminum

(P-4945)
PLASMA RGGEDIZED SOLUTIONS INC (PA)
2284 Ringwood Ave Ste A, San Jose (95131-1722)
PHONE.................................408 954-8405
Jim Stameson, *CEO*
Evan Persky, *CFO*
Roger Adams, *Technical Staff*
EMP: 68 **EST:** 2008
SALES (est): 16.7MM **Privately Held**
WEB: www.plasmarugged.com
SIC: 3479 Coating of metals & formed products

(P-4946)
PREMIER COATINGS INC
Also Called: Premier Finishing
7910 Longe St, Stockton (95206-3933)
PHONE.................................209 982-5585
Craig M Walters, *President*
Thom Foulks, *Vice Pres*
Wendy Foulks, *Admin Sec*
Gustavo Vega, *Controller*
Kim Brown, *Manager*
EMP: 75 **EST:** 1996
SQ FT: 30,000
SALES (est): 10.7MM **Privately Held**
WEB: www.premierfinishing.com
SIC: 3479 Coating of metals & formed products

(P-4947)
PROFESSIONAL FINISHING INC
770 Market Ave, Richmond (94801-1303)
PHONE.................................510 233-7629
Ricardo E Gomez, *President*
EMP: 60 **EST:** 1979
SQ FT: 18,000
SALES (est): 7.2MM **Privately Held**
WEB: www.professionalfinishing.com
SIC: 3479 Coating of metals & formed products

(P-4948)
SCIENTIFIC METAL FINISHING INC
3180 Molinaro St, Santa Clara (95054-2425)
PHONE.................................408 970-9011
Theodore G Otto III, *President*
Kathleen Otto, *CFO*
Carolyn Silberman, *Manager*
Carolyn W Silberman, *Manager*
EMP: 40 **EST:** 1987
SQ FT: 18,000
SALES (est): 5MM **Privately Held**
WEB: www.scientificmetal.com
SIC: 3479 2851 Coating of metals & formed products; paints & allied products

(P-4949)
SPECIALIZED COATING SERVICES
42680 Christy St, Fremont (94538-3135)
PHONE.................................510 226-8700
Richard Ramirez, *President*
Kim Atkins, *Vice Pres*
Roger Hartshorn, *Opers Staff*
Priscilla Reyes, *Accounts Mgr*
EMP: 62 **EST:** 1998
SALES (est): 5MM **Privately Held**
WEB: www.speccoat.com
SIC: 3479 Coating of metals & formed products

(P-4950)
SPRAYTRONICS INC
6001 Butler Ln Ste 204, Scotts Valley (95066-3548)
PHONE.................................408 988-3636
EMP: 20
SQ FT: 30,000
SALES (est): 1.9MM **Privately Held**
SIC: 3479 Painting Electronic Components & Panels

(P-4951)
STAR FINISHES INC
40429 Brickyard Dr, Madera (93636-9515)
PHONE.................................559 261-1076
Doug Hagen, *President*
EMP: 25 **EST:** 2000
SQ FT: 7,760
SALES (est): 1MM **Privately Held**
WEB: www.starfinishes.com
SIC: 3479 Coating of metals & formed products

3489 Ordnance & Access, NEC

(P-4952)
CONCEALED CARRIER LLC
Also Called: Tacgicon Armament
11315 Sunrise Gold Cir F, Rancho Cordova (95742-6534)
PHONE.................................916 530-6205
Jacob Dines, *Mng Member*
EMP: 21 **EST:** 2015
SALES (est): 15.4MM **Privately Held**
SIC: 3489 Ordnance & accessories

3491 Industrial Valves

(P-4953)
AUTOMATION & ENTERTAINMENT INC
25870 Soquel San Jose Rd, Los Gatos (95033-9235)
PHONE.................................408 353-4223
Paul Wilkinson, *CEO*
Richard Barnes, *CIO*
Jeri Tjon, *Manager*
EMP: 20 **EST:** 2011
SALES (est): 2.6MM **Privately Held**
WEB: www.automationandentertainment.com
SIC: 3491 Automatic regulating & control valves

(P-4954)
BAILEY VALVE INC
264 W Fallbrook Ave # 105, Fresno (93711-5807)
PHONE.................................559 434-2838
Eric Brewer, *President*
John Edward, *Vice Pres*
▲ **EMP:** 35 **EST:** 2004
SQ FT: 3,500
SALES (est): 3.6MM **Privately Held**
WEB: www.baileyvalve.com
SIC: 3491 Industrial valves

(P-4955)
MDC VACUUM PRODUCTS LLC
23874b Cabot Blvd, Hayward (94545-1661)
PHONE.................................510 265-3500
EMP: 117
SALES (corp-wide): 104.1MM **Privately Held**
WEB: www.mdcprecision.com
SIC: 3491 Industrial valves
PA: Mdc Vacuum Products, Llc
30962 Santana St
Hayward CA 94544
510 265-3500

3493 Steel Springs, Except Wire

(P-4956)
BETTS COMPANY
3025 E Palm Ave Ste 104, Manteca (95337-9516)
PHONE.................................209 599-1824
EMP: 78
SALES (corp-wide): 65.3MM **Privately Held**
WEB: www.betts1868.com
SIC: 3493 Mfg Steel Springs-Nonwire
PA: Betts Company
2843 S Maple Ave
Fresno CA 93725
559 498-3304

(P-4957)
OHARA METAL PRODUCTS
4949 Fulton Dr Ste E, Fairfield (94534-1648)
PHONE.................................707 863-9090
Tim Ives, *President*
Irene O'Hara, *CEO*
Robin Ives, *CFO*
Kathleen O'Hara,
EMP: 30 **EST:** 1964
SQ FT: 20,000
SALES (est): 3.5MM **Privately Held**
WEB: www.oharamfg.com
SIC: 3493 3721 5051 5085 Steel springs, except wire; helicopters; metals service centers & offices; industrial supplies

3494 Valves & Pipe Fittings, NEC

(P-4958)
AMERICAN AVK CO
5286 E Home Ave, Fresno (93727-2103)
PHONE.................................559 452-4305
Michael Enos, *Principal*
John Martin, *Vice Pres*
Terrie Martin, *Admin Asst*
Bento Owens, *Info Tech Mgr*
John Wilber, *Engrg Dir*
◆ **EMP:** 15 **EST:** 2011
SALES (est): 1.9MM **Privately Held**
WEB: www.americanavk.com
SIC: 3494 Pipe fittings

(P-4959)
BERMAD INC (PA)
Also Called: Bermad Control Valves
3816 S Willow Ave Ste 101, Fresno (93725-9241)
PHONE.................................877 577-4283
Nadav Yakir, *President*
Tannice Skinner, *Controller*
Giora Cameron, *Marketing Staff*
Yiftah Enav, *Marketing Staff*
Barbara Demarchi,
▲ **EMP:** 34 **EST:** 1977
SQ FT: 10,000
SALES (est): 6.6MM **Privately Held**
WEB: www.bermadinc.com
SIC: 3494 Sprinkler systems, field

(P-4960)
EVALVE INC
4045 Campbell Ave, Menlo Park (94025-1006)
PHONE.................................650 330-8100
Ferolyn T Powell, *President*
Doug Hughes, *CFO*
Sean Cleary, *Senior VP*
Bunty Banerjee, *Vice Pres*
Jonathan D Feuchtwang, *Vice Pres*
EMP: 91 **EST:** 1999
SQ FT: 38,000
SALES (est): 12.1MM
SALES (corp-wide): 34.6B **Publicly Held**
WEB: www.abbott.com
SIC: 3494 Valves & pipe fittings
PA: Abbott Laboratories
100 Abbott Park Rd
Abbott Park IL 60064
224 667-6100

PRODUCTS & SERVICES SECTION
3499 - Fabricated Metal Prdts, NEC County (P-4984)

(P-4961)
MORRILL INDUSTRIES INC
24754 E River Rd, Escalon (95320-8601)
PHONE...................................209 838-2550
Ken Morrill, *President*
Wayne Morrill, *CFO*
Diane Cordray, *Admin Sec*
Ed Morrill, *Analyst*
Bob Morrill, *Prdtn Mgr*
▲ **EMP:** 55 **EST:** 1954
SALES (est): 6.9MM **Privately Held**
WEB: www.morrillinc.com
SIC: 3494 Sprinkler systems, field

(P-4962)
NOR-CAL PRODUCTS INC (DH)
1967 S Oregon St, Yreka (96097-3462)
P.O. Box 518 (96097-0518)
PHONE...................................530 842-4457
Tom Deany, *President*
David Stone, *CFO*
Julie White, *Engineer*
Anna Baker, *Finance*
Jack Coupens, *Purchasing*
▲ **EMP:** 140 **EST:** 1946
SQ FT: 57,000
SALES (est): 53.7MM
SALES (corp-wide): 1.3B **Privately Held**
WEB: www.n-c.com
SIC: 3494 Valves & pipe fittings

3495 Wire Springs

(P-4963)
AMERICAN PRECISION SPRING CORP
1513 Arbuckle Ct, Santa Clara (95054-3401)
PHONE...................................408 986-1020
Kathleen Chu, *President*
Mike Remily, *Vice Pres*
Tuan Nguyen, *Opers Mgr*
Gladys Calvillo, *Accounts Exec*
EMP: 23 **EST:** 1979
SQ FT: 1,500
SALES (est): 4MM **Privately Held**
WEB: www.americanprecspring.com
SIC: 3495 Mechanical springs, precision

(P-4964)
BETTS COMPANY (PA)
Also Called: Betts Spring Manufacturing
2843 S Maple Ave, Fresno (93725-2217)
PHONE...................................559 498-3304
William Betts IV, *Ch of Bd*
Bill Betts, *President*
Don Devany, *Senior VP*
Donald Devany, *Vice Pres*
David Peterson, *Administration*
▲ **EMP:** 75 **EST:** 1873
SQ FT: 7,500
SALES (est): 58.7MM **Privately Held**
WEB: www.betts1868.com
SIC: 3495 3493 Wire springs; instrument springs, precision; mechanical springs, precision; automobile springs

(P-4965)
PENINSULA SPRING CORPORATION
6750 Silacci Way, Gilroy (95020-7035)
P.O. Box 1782 (95021-1782)
PHONE...................................408 848-3361
Joe Kilmer, *President*
Laura Hampel, *CFO*
Muriel Kilmer, *Vice Pres*
EMP: 18 **EST:** 1977
SQ FT: 10,000 **Privately Held**
WEB: www.peninsulaspring.com
SIC: 3495 3444 3498 3496 Precision springs; forming machine work, sheet metal; fabricated pipe & fittings; miscellaneous fabricated wire products

3496 Misc Fabricated Wire Prdts

(P-4966)
BLACKTALON INDUSTRIES INC
481 Technology Way, NAPA (94558-7571)
P.O. Box 300 (94559-0300)
PHONE...................................707 256-1812
Brent Morgan, *President*
EMP: 15 **EST:** 2006
SALES (est): 243.1K **Privately Held**
SIC: 3496 7382 Fencing, made from purchased wire; burglar alarm maintenance & monitoring

(P-4967)
CABLE MOORE INC (PA)
4700 Coliseum Way, Oakland (94601-5008)
P.O. Box 4067 (94614-4067)
PHONE...................................510 436-8000
Sandra Moore, *CEO*
Gregory Moore, *Corp Secy*
Lis Adams, *Education*
Tere T Oconnor, *Program Dir*
▲ **EMP:** 30 **EST:** 1986
SQ FT: 12,500
SALES (est): 8.3MM **Privately Held**
WEB: www.cablemoore.com
SIC: 3496 Wire chain

(P-4968)
DAHLHAUSER MFG CO INC
1855 Russell Ave, Santa Clara (95054-2035)
PHONE...................................408 988-3717
Dan Dahlhauser, *President*
EMP: 23 **EST:** 1966
SQ FT: 22,000
SALES (est): 2MM **Privately Held**
WEB: www.dmchooks.com
SIC: 3496 Wire fasteners

(P-4969)
FEENEY INC
2603 Union St, Oakland (94607-2423)
PHONE...................................510 893-9473
Grissell Ralston, *CEO*
Katrina Ralston, *President*
Steven Imbrenda, *CFO*
Richard Ralston, *Principal*
Jennifer Trejo, *Administration*
▼ **EMP:** 48 **EST:** 1948
SQ FT: 29,000
SALES (est): 10.5MM **Privately Held**
WEB: www.feeneyinc.com
SIC: 3496 Miscellaneous fabricated wire products

(P-4970)
GROSSI FABRICATION INC
3200 Tully Rd, Hughson (95326-9816)
P.O. Box 937 (95326-0937)
PHONE...................................209 883-2817
Larry Grossi, *President*
Shanon Grossi, *Vice Pres*
EMP: 19 **EST:** 1998
SALES (est): 5.3MM **Privately Held**
WEB: www.grossifabrication.com
SIC: 3496 Netting, woven wire: made from purchased wire

(P-4971)
INTAKE SCREENS INC
8417 River Rd, Sacramento (95832-9710)
PHONE...................................916 665-2727
Russell Berry IV, *President*
Russ Berry, *Founder*
Russell M Berry III, *Vice Pres*
Judy McAvoy, *Office Mgr*
Ronaele Berry, *Admin Sec*
EMP: 15 **EST:** 1996
SQ FT: 3,300
SALES (est): 3.5MM **Privately Held**
WEB: www.intakescreensinc.com
SIC: 3496 Screening, woven wire: made from purchased wire

(P-4972)
VOLK ENTERPRISES INC
618 S Kilroy Rd, Turlock (95380-9531)
PHONE...................................209 632-3826
Anthony Volks, *Manager*
EMP: 60 **Privately Held**
WEB: www.volkenterprises.com
SIC: 3496 3089 Miscellaneous fabricated wire products; plastic processing
PA: Volk Enterprises, Inc.
1335 Ridgeland Pkwy # 120
Alpharetta GA 30004

3498 Fabricated Pipe & Pipe Fittings

(P-4973)
ACCURATE TUBE BENDING INC
37770 Timber St, Newark (94560-4443)
P.O. Box 990, Fremont (94537-0990)
PHONE...................................510 790-6500
Jon Morrow, *President*
EMP: 33 **EST:** 1994
SQ FT: 28,000
SALES (est): 6.9MM **Privately Held**
WEB: www.atbending.com
SIC: 3498 Tube fabricating (contract bending & shaping)

(P-4974)
JIFCO INC (PA)
Also Called: Jifco Fabricated Piping
571 Exchange Ct, Livermore (94550-2400)
P.O. Box 589 (94551-0589)
PHONE...................................925 449-4665
Jay Forni Jr, *President*
Kerry Thach, *Project Mgr*
Monica Spina Forni, *Director*
Jeffrey Hill, *Director*
Kevin N Krausgill, *Director*
EMP: 58 **EST:** 1983
SALES (est): 16.5MM **Privately Held**
WEB: www.jifco.com
SIC: 3498 Tube fabricating (contract bending & shaping)

(P-4975)
KAISER ENTERPRISES INC
Also Called: Insight Mfg Services
798 Murphys Creek Rd, Murphys (95247-9562)
P.O. Box 2609 (95247-2609)
PHONE...................................209 728-2091
Loretta Dietz Kaiser, *President*
Herman Kaiser, *COO*
Adela Alfonso, *Assistant*
EMP: 75 **EST:** 2007
SQ FT: 6,900
SALES (est): 11.8MM **Privately Held**
SIC: 3498 Coils, pipe: fabricated from purchased pipe

(P-4976)
MARINE & INDUSTRIAL SVCS INC
2391 W 10th St, Antioch (94509-1366)
PHONE...................................925 757-8791
Thomas M Hannaford, *President*
Stanley Pipes, *Treasurer*
EMP: 16 **EST:** 1988
SQ FT: 21,000
SALES (est): 2MM **Privately Held**
WEB: www.marineandindustrialservices.com
SIC: 3498 Pipe fittings, fabricated from purchased pipe

(P-4977)
SF TUBE INC
23099 Connecticut St, Hayward (94545-1605)
PHONE...................................510 785-9148
Michelle Valdez, *Manager*
EMP: 46
SALES (corp-wide): 119.3MM **Privately Held**
SIC: 3498 Tube fabricating (contract bending & shaping)
HQ: Sf Tube, Inc.
640 N Lasalle Dr Ste 670
Chicago IL 60654
312 374-4829

(P-4978)
SHAPCO INC
5220 S Peach Ave, Fresno (93725-9708)
PHONE...................................559 834-1342
Garette Scott, *Branch Mgr*
Donna Vogt, *Accountant*
Erline Cardenas, *Human Res Mgr*
Linda Bender, *Sales Mgr*
Jesse Stagg, *Sales Staff*
EMP: 95
SALES (corp-wide): 98.4MM **Privately Held**
WEB: www.custompipe.com
SIC: 3498 Fabricated pipe & fittings
PA: Shapco Inc.
1666 20th St Ste 100
Santa Monica CA 90404
310 264-1666

(P-4979)
SUPERIOR TUBE PIPE BNDING FBCO
Also Called: Superior Tbepe Bnding Fbrctn
2407 Industrial Pkwy W, Hayward (94545-5007)
PHONE...................................510 782-9311
Jon T Morrow Jr, *President*
EMP: 26 **EST:** 1965
SQ FT: 22,000
SALES (est): 502.1K **Privately Held**
SIC: 3498 Tube fabricating (contract bending & shaping); pipe sections fabricated from purchased pipe

3499 Fabricated Metal Prdts, NEC

(P-4980)
ARVI MANUFACTURING INC
1256 Birchwood Dr Ste B, Sunnyvale (94089-2205)
PHONE...................................408 734-4776
Harold Kirksey, *CEO*
Rita Kirksey, *CFO*
▲ **EMP:** 28 **EST:** 1977
SQ FT: 5,000
SALES (est): 2.7MM **Privately Held**
WEB: www.arvi.net
SIC: 3499 Machine bases, metal

(P-4981)
BARRICADE CO & TRAFFIC SUP INC (PA)
Also Called: T B C
3963 Santa Rosa Ave, Santa Rosa (95407-8274)
PHONE...................................707 523-2350
Jennifer R Pitts, *President*
Robert F Pitts, *Admin Sec*
EMP: 17 **EST:** 2000
SQ FT: 21,000
SALES (est): 2.5MM **Privately Held**
WEB: www.unitedrentals.com
SIC: 3499 Barricades, metal

(P-4982)
BISHOP-WISECARVER CORPORATION (PA)
2104 Martin Way, Pittsburg (94565-5027)
PHONE...................................925 439-8272
Pamela Kan, *CEO*
Ali Jabbari, *President*
Shelley Galvin, *Treasurer*
Timothy Silsbee, *Exec Dir*
Judith S Wiscarver, *Admin Sec*
▲ **EMP:** 53 **EST:** 1950
SQ FT: 80,000
SALES (est): 13.1MM **Privately Held**
WEB: www.bwc.com
SIC: 3499 5085 3823 Machine bases, metal; bearings; industrial instrmnts msrmnt display/control process variable

(P-4983)
BMF - BAKTEK METAL FABRICATION
290 Lindbergh Ave, Livermore (94551-9512)
PHONE...................................925 245-0200
Eric Lunsford, *Owner*
EMP: 15 **EST:** 2010
SALES (est): 129.6K **Privately Held**
WEB: www.bmfabrication.com
SIC: 3499 Fabricated metal products

(P-4984)
CAL-WELD INC
4308 Solar Way, Fremont (94538-6335)
PHONE...................................510 226-0100
Maurice Carson, *President*
EMP: 116 **EST:** 1978
SALES (est): 20.2MM
SALES (corp-wide): 124.8MM **Publicly Held**
WEB: www.ichorsystems.com
SIC: 3499 Aerosol valves, metal

3499 - Fabricated Metal Prdts, NEC County (P-4985)

PRODUCTS & SERVICES SECTION

HQ: Ichor Holdings, Llc
9660 Sw Herman Rd
Tualatin OR 97062
503 625-2251

(P-4985)
MOHIN INC
5040 Commercial Cir Ste A, Concord (94520-1250)
P.O. Box 1798, Pittsburg (94565-0179)
PHONE..................................925 798-5572
Kirana Banga, *President*
EMP: 24 **EST:** 2019
SALES (est): 1.1MM **Privately Held**
SIC: 3499 Machine bases, metal

(P-4986)
R & K INDUSTRIAL PRODUCTS CO
Also Called: R&K Industrial Wheels
1945 7th St, Richmond (94801-1639)
PHONE..................................510 234-7212
Jorge Ramirez, *President*
June Woodruff, *Manager*
EMP: 30 **EST:** 1945
SQ FT: 48,000
SALES (est): 4.2MM **Privately Held**
SIC: 3499 Wheels: wheelbarrow, stroller, etc.: disc, stamped metal

(P-4987)
STRYKER ENTERPRISES INC
Also Called: Recognition Products Mfg
1358 E San Fernando St, San Jose (95116-2329)
PHONE..................................408 295-6300
William J Stryker Jr, *President*
Elizabeth Rich, *Cust Mgr*
Becky Ryalls, *Accounts Exec*
▲ **EMP:** 19 **EST:** 1948
SQ FT: 12,000
SALES (est): 3.4MM **Privately Held**
WEB: www.plaque.com
SIC: 3499 Trophies, metal, except silver

(P-4988)
STURDY GUN SAFE INC
Also Called: Sturdy Safe
2030 S Sarah St, Fresno (93721-3316)
PHONE..................................559 485-8361
Terry Pratt, *CEO*
▲ **EMP:** 29 **EST:** 1981
SQ FT: 15,000
SALES (est): 400K **Privately Held**
WEB: www.sturdysafe.com
SIC: 3499 Safes & vaults, metal

(P-4989)
WOODSIDE INVESTMENT INC
Also Called: Michael and Company
12405 E Brandt Rd, Lockeford (95237-9571)
P.O. Box 1100 (95237-1100)
PHONE..................................209 787-8040
Dennis E Wood, *CEO*
Dennis Wood, *President*
James Mettler, *Project Mgr*
Erica I Zuiga, *Accounting Mgr*
Heath Pettygrove, *Opers Mgr*
EMP: 70 **EST:** 1991
SQ FT: 50,000
SALES (est): 14.9MM **Privately Held**
SIC: 3499 Aerosol valves, metal

3511 Steam, Gas & Hydraulic Turbines & Engines

(P-4990)
AERO TURBINE INC
6800 Lindbergh St, Stockton (95206-3934)
PHONE..................................209 983-1112
Douglas R Clayton, *President*
C W Dinsley, *Treasurer*
David Mattson, *Exec VP*
▲ **EMP:** 60
SQ FT: 51,000
SALES (est): 11.6MM **Privately Held**
WEB: www.aeroturbine.aero
SIC: 3511 Turbines & turbine generator sets

3519 Internal Combustion Engines, NEC

(P-4991)
CUMMINS PACIFIC LLC
875 Riverside Pkwy, West Sacramento (95605-1502)
PHONE..................................916 371-0630
Mike Goodwin, *Branch Mgr*
Robert Dickie, *Manager*
EMP: 15
SALES (corp-wide): 19.8B **Publicly Held**
WEB: www.cummins.com
SIC: 3519 5063 7629 Diesel engine rebuilding; generators; generator repair
HQ: Cummins Pacific, Llc
1939 Deere Ave
Irvine CA 92606

(P-4992)
ROLLS-ROYCE CORPORATION
7200 Earhart Rd, Oakland (94621-4511)
PHONE..................................510 635-1500
Marion C Blakey, *President*
Jeff Craig, *IT/INT Sup*
Rajesh Sharma, *Technology*
Kevin Campbell, *Engineer*
Gary Lewis, *Engineer*
EMP: 500
SALES (corp-wide): 15.7B **Privately Held**
WEB: www.rolls-roycemotorcars.com
SIC: 5511 3519 New & used car dealers; jet propulsion engines; marine engines
HQ: Rolls-Royce Corporation
450 S Meridian St
Indianapolis IN 46225

(P-4993)
SOUTHWEST PRODUCTS CORPORATION
85 Enterprise Ct Ste B, Galt (95632-8162)
PHONE..................................209 745-6000
Patrick Cofild, *Branch Mgr*
EMP: 35
SALES (corp-wide): 18.1MM **Privately Held**
WEB: www.southwestproducts.com
SIC: 3519 Diesel engine rebuilding
HQ: Southwest Products Corporation
11690 N 132nd Ave
Surprise AZ 85379
306 887-7400

3523 Farm Machinery & Eqpt

(P-4994)
AGRIFIM IRRIGATION PDTS INC
Also Called: Nds
2855 S East Ave, Fresno (93725-1908)
PHONE..................................559 443-6680
Rael Sacks, *President*
▲ **EMP:** 15 **EST:** 1985
SQ FT: 15,200
SALES (est): 3.9MM
SALES (corp-wide): 1.1B **Privately Held**
SIC: 3523 Farm machinery & equipment
HQ: National Diversified Sales, Inc.
21300 Victory Blvd # 215
Woodland Hills CA 91367
559 562-9888

(P-4995)
AMERICAN INTERNATIONAL MFG CO
Also Called: Aim Mail Centers
1230 Fortna Ave, Woodland (95776-5905)
PHONE..................................530 666-2446
John Bridges, *CEO*
David Neilson, *President*
Chistophre Neilson, *Principal*
Michael Webster, *Engineer*
Leslie Besseghini, *Manager*
EMP: 29 **EST:** 1973
SQ FT: 23,000
SALES (est): 5.2MM **Privately Held**
WEB: www.aimfab.com
SIC: 3523 3556 Farm machinery & equipment; food products machinery

(P-4996)
AWETA-AUTOLINE INC (DH)
4516 E Citron, Fresno (93725-9861)
PHONE..................................559 244-8340
Otto Vink, *CEO*
Art Lopez, *President*
David Olson, *Finance*
Pete Biers, *Regl Sales Mgr*
▲ **EMP:** 45 **EST:** 1995
SQ FT: 20,000
SALES (est): 10.3MM
SALES (corp-wide): 62.8MM **Privately Held**
WEB: www.aweta.com
SIC: 3523 Grading, cleaning, sorting machines, fruit, grain, vegetable
HQ: Aweta Holding B.V.
Kwakelweg 2
Pijnacker 2641
886 688-000

(P-4997)
CAL-COAST DAIRY SYSTEMS INC
424 S Tegner Rd, Turlock (95380-9406)
P.O. Box 737 (95381-0737)
PHONE..................................209 634-9026
Lon Baptista, *President*
Lori Baptista, *Vice Pres*
Stacy Souza, *Office Mgr*
EMP: 28 **EST:** 1990
SQ FT: 16,000
SALES (est): 2.1MM **Privately Held**
WEB: www.calcoastinc.com
SIC: 3523 1542 8711 5083 Dairy equipment (farm); agricultural building contractors; structural engineering; dairy machinery & equipment; residential construction; fabricated plate work (boiler shop)

(P-4998)
CENTRAL IRRIGATION INC
2941 N Highway 59, Merced (95348-4350)
PHONE..................................209 262-3723
Keith R Yamamoto, *CEO*
EMP: 23 **EST:** 2014
SALES (est): 7MM **Privately Held**
WEB: www.centralirrigation.com
SIC: 3523 Planting, haying, harvesting & processing machinery

(P-4999)
COE ORCHARD EQUIPMENT INC
3453 Riviera Rd, Live Oak (95953-9713)
PHONE..................................530 695-5121
Lyman Coe, *CEO*
Lois A Coe, *CFO*
Chris Alexander, *Vice Pres*
Martin Vargas, *Prdtn Mgr*
Stacie Mackay, *Marketing Staff*
▲ **EMP:** 100
SQ FT: 45,000
SALES (est): 9.4MM **Privately Held**
WEB: www.coeshakers.com
SIC: 3523 Harvesters, fruit, vegetable, tobacco, etc.

(P-5000)
D&M MANUFACTURING CO LLC
5400 S Villa Ave, Fresno (93725-9798)
PHONE..................................559 834-4668
Judy Tolentino, *Owner*
EMP: 18 **EST:** 1987
SQ FT: 10,000
SALES (est): 2.6MM **Privately Held**
WEB: www.dnmmfgco.com
SIC: 3523 Fertilizing, spraying, dusting & irrigation machinery

(P-5001)
D-K-P INC
275 N Marks Ave, Fresno (93706-1102)
PHONE..................................559 266-2695
Douglas R King, *President*
EMP: 15 **EST:** 1969
SQ FT: 12,000
SALES (est): 1.3MM
SALES (corp-wide): 5.6MM **Privately Held**
WEB: www.rmking.com
SIC: 3523 Cotton pickers & strippers

PA: R. M. King Company Exports
315 N Marks Ave
Fresno CA
559 266-0258

(P-5002)
DAVIS MACHINE SHOP INC
Also Called: Meridian Supply
15805 Central St, Meridian (95957-9517)
PHONE..................................530 696-2577
Clifton Davis, *CEO*
Thomas Davis, *Vice Pres*
EMP: 34 **EST:** 1913
SQ FT: 5,000
SALES (est): 5.5MM **Privately Held**
WEB: www.davismachineshop.net
SIC: 3523 3599 5251 Farm machinery & equipment; machine shop, jobbing & repair; hardware

(P-5003)
DOMRIES ENTERPRISES INC
12281 Road 29, Madera (93638-8332)
PHONE..................................559 485-4306
Candyce L Domries, *CEO*
Lorraine Domries, *Treasurer*
▲ **EMP:** 35 **EST:** 1924
SQ FT: 65,000
SALES (est): 8.4MM **Privately Held**
WEB: www.domries.com
SIC: 3523 5084 Soil preparation machinery, except turf & grounds; fertilizing, spraying, dusting & irrigation machinery; industrial machinery & equipment

(P-5004)
FLORY INDUSTRIES
4737 Toomes Rd, Salida (95368)
P.O. Box 908 (95368-0908)
PHONE..................................209 545-1167
Howard Flory, *CEO*
Mike Eger, *CFO*
Rodney Flory, *Treasurer*
Marlin Flory, *Vice Pres*
Ben Eller, *Store Mgr*
EMP: 75 **EST:** 1904
SQ FT: 12,000
SALES (est): 35.9MM **Privately Held**
WEB: www.goflory.com
SIC: 3523 5083 3441 0173 Harvesters, fruit, vegetable, tobacco, etc.; farm equipment parts & supplies; fabricated structural metal; tree nuts

(P-5005)
GUSS AUTOMATION LLC
2545 Simpson St, Kingsburg (93631-9501)
PHONE..................................559 897-0245
Dave Crinklaw, *Mng Member*
EMP: 15 **EST:** 2019
SALES (est): 2.5MM **Privately Held**
WEB: www.gussag.com
SIC: 3523 Sprayers & spraying machines, agricultural

(P-5006)
HYDROPOINT DATA SYSTEMS INC
1720 Corporate Cir, Petaluma (94954-6924)
PHONE..................................707 769-9696
Chris Spain, *CEO*
Paul Ciandrini, *President*
Mardi Diamond, *Vice Pres*
Chris Manchuck, *Vice Pres*
Amir Omar, *Vice Pres*
▲ **EMP:** 50 **EST:** 2002
SQ FT: 18,000
SALES (est): 15.5MM **Privately Held**
WEB: www.hydropoint.com
SIC: 3523 Irrigation equipment, self-propelled

(P-5007)
INTERNATIONAL HORT TECH LLC
Also Called: Interntional Horticulture Tech
150 Acquistapace Rd, Hollister (95023-9350)
P.O. Box 1035 (95024-1035)
PHONE..................................831 637-1800
Gary R Hartman, *Mng Member*
Cammile Hartman,
David Pruitt, *Manager*
▲ **EMP:** 25 **EST:** 1998
SQ FT: 60,000

▲ = Import ▼ = Export
◆ = Import/Export

PRODUCTS & SERVICES SECTION
3531 - Construction Machinery & Eqpt County (P-5031)

SALES (est): 3.1MM **Privately Held**
WEB: www.ihort.com
SIC: 3523 Farm machinery & equipment

(P-5008)
IRRITEC USA INC
1420 N Irritec Way, Fresno (93703-4432)
PHONE..................................559 275-8825
Mitchell Martin, *CEO*
Kevin Dieker, *Natl Sales Mgr*
Mitchell Blum, *Marketing Staff*
Greg Gostanian, *Sales Staff*
Fernando Mejorada, *Sales Staff*
◆ **EMP:** 56 **EST:** 2009
SALES (est): 13.8MM **Privately Held**
WEB: www.irritec.com
SIC: 3523 Irrigation equipment, self-propelled

(P-5009)
JACKRABBIT (PA)
Also Called: Dakota AG Welding
471 Industrial Ave, Ripon (95366-2768)
PHONE..................................209 599-6118
Bill Kirkendall, *CEO*
▲ **EMP:** 60
SQ FT: 15,000
SALES (est): 13.8MM **Privately Held**
WEB: www.jackrabbitequipment.com
SIC: 3523 Harvesters, fruit, vegetable, tobacco, etc.

(P-5010)
JACKRABBIT
Also Called: Dakota AG Welding
1318 Dakota Ave, Modesto (95358-9505)
PHONE..................................209 521-9325
Earl Anderson, *Branch Mgr*
EMP: 15
SALES (corp-wide): 13.8MM **Privately Held**
WEB: www.jackrabbitequipment.com
SIC: 3523 7692 Farm machinery & equipment; welding repair
PA: Jackrabbit
   471 Industrial Ave
   Ripon CA 95366
   209 599-6118

(P-5011)
KAMPER FABRICATION INC
20107 N Ripon Rd, Ripon (95366-9758)
P.O. Box 177 (95366-0177)
PHONE..................................209 599-7137
Richard Kamper, *President*
Brenda Kamper, *Corp Secy*
Greg Kamper, *Sales Staff*
EMP: 23 **EST:** 1983
SQ FT: 24,800
SALES: 7MM **Privately Held**
WEB: www.kamperfab.com
SIC: 3523 Farm machinery & equipment

(P-5012)
KINGSBURG CULTIVATOR INC
40190 Road 36, Kingsburg (93631-9621)
PHONE..................................559 897-3662
Clint Erling, *President*
Allen Scheidt, *Vice Pres*
EMP: 37 **EST:** 1954
SQ FT: 1,400
SALES (est): 5.6MM **Privately Held**
WEB: www.kcimfg.com
SIC: 3523 Harvesters, fruit, vegetable, tobacco, etc.

(P-5013)
KIRBY MANUFACTURING INC (PA)
484 S St 59, Merced (95341-6541)
P.O. Box 989 (95341-0989)
PHONE..................................209 723-0778
Richard M Kirby, *President*
William T Kirby, *Treasurer*
Madeleine Kirby Davenport, *Vice Pres*
Kelly Sellers, *Admin Sec*
Jonthan Garcia, *Purch Mgr*
◆ **EMP:** 68 **EST:** 1970
SQ FT: 45,000
SALES (est): 12.8MM **Privately Held**
WEB: www.kirbymanufacturing.com
SIC: 3523 Cattle feeding, handling & watering equipment; haying machines: mowers, rakes, stackers, etc.

(P-5014)
LAIRD MFG LLC (PA)
Also Called: Laird Manufacturing
531 S State Highway 59, Merced (95341-6925)
P.O. Box 1053 (95341-1053)
PHONE..................................209 722-4145
Lee Cansler,
David Landry, *Administration*
Steve Lemos, *Sales Staff*
Manuel Rosa, *Sales Staff*
Issac Isako,
◆ **EMP:** 40 **EST:** 1937
SQ FT: 15,000
SALES (est): 9.9MM **Privately Held**
WEB: www.lairdmanufacturing.com
SIC: 3523 7692 Cattle feeding, handling & watering equipment; welding repair

(P-5015)
ORCHARD MACHINERY CORP DISC (PA)
Also Called: Orchard Harvest
2700 Colusa Hwy, Yuba City (95993-8927)
PHONE..................................530 673-2822
Don Mayo, *CEO*
Brian Andersen, *Vice Pres*
Brian Anderson, *Vice Pres*
Greg Kriss, *Vice Pres*
Joe Martinez, *Vice Pres*
▲ **EMP:** 60 **EST:** 1961
SQ FT: 70,000
SALES (est): 25.7MM **Privately Held**
WEB: www.shakermaker.com
SIC: 3523 Shakers, tree: nuts, fruits, etc.

(P-5016)
PELLENC AMERICA INC (DH)
3171 Guerneville Rd, Santa Rosa (95401-4028)
PHONE..................................707 568-7286
Marc Paisnel, *President*
J L Guigues, *Director*
Roger Pellenc, *Director*
J P Pettavino, *Director*
Alex Dragos, *Manager*
▲ **EMP:** 24 **EST:** 1996
SQ FT: 50,000
SALES (corp-wide): 2.6MM **Privately Held**
WEB: www.pellencus.com
SIC: 3523 Farm machinery & equipment
HQ: Pellenc
   Quartier Notre Dames Des Anges
   Pertuis 84120
   490 088-086

(P-5017)
PERRYS CUSTOM CHOPPING LLC
21365 Williams Ave, Hilmar (95324-9602)
PHONE..................................209 667-8777
Jeff Perry, *Principal*
EMP: 15 **EST:** 2003
SALES (est): 2.2MM **Privately Held**
SIC: 3523 Harvesters, fruit, vegetable, tobacco, etc.

(P-5018)
SIMPLY COUNTRY INC
10110 Harvest Ln, Rough and Ready (95975-9783)
PHONE..................................530 615-0565
EMP: 15 **EST:** 2011
SQ FT: 6,800
SALES (est): 1.2MM **Privately Held**
SIC: 3523 Mfg Farm Machinery/Equipment

(P-5019)
TG SCHMEISER CO INC
8135 E Dinuba Ave, Selma (93662-9411)
PHONE..................................559 268-8128
Andrew W Cummings, *Administration*
EMP: 15 **EST:** 2016
SALES (est): 5.3MM **Privately Held**
WEB: www.tgschmeiser.com
SIC: 3523 Farm machinery & equipment

(P-5020)
WASCO HARDFACING CO
4585 E Citron, Fresno (93725-9861)
P.O. Box 2395 (93745-2395)
PHONE..................................559 485-5860
Robin R Messick, *CEO*
▲ **EMP:** 60 **EST:** 1952
SQ FT: 20,000
SALES (est): 9.6MM **Privately Held**
WEB: www.wascohardfacing.com
SIC: 3523 Farm machinery & equipment

(P-5021)
WEISS-MCNAIR LLC (DH)
100 Loren Ave, Chico (95928-7450)
PHONE..................................530 891-6214
Larry Demmer, *President*
Glenn Stanley, *President*
Sinath Chiem, *Engineer*
Josh Gertsch, *Engineer*
Patti Patheal, *Human Res Mgr*
▲ **EMP:** 80 **EST:** 1974
SQ FT: 32,000
SALES (est): 21.7MM **Privately Held**
WEB: www.weissmcnair.com
SIC: 3523 Farm machinery & equipment
HQ: Gould Paper Corporation
   99 Park Ave Fl 10
   New York NY 10016
   212 301-0000

(P-5022)
WILCOX BROTHERS INC
Also Called: Wilcox AG Products
14180 State Highway 160, Walnut Grove (95690-9741)
P.O. Box 70 (95690-0070)
PHONE..................................916 776-1784
Alan Wilcox, *President*
Bruce Wilcox, *Vice Pres*
▲ **EMP:** 57
SQ FT: 10,800
SALES (est): 13.5MM **Privately Held**
WEB: www.wilcoxap.com
SIC: 3523 Farm machinery & equipment

3524 Garden, Lawn Tractors & Eqpt

(P-5023)
FRESNO FORD TRACTOR INC
Also Called: Kuckenbecker Tractor Co
3040 S Parkway Dr, Fresno (93725-2323)
P.O. Box 11786 (93775-1786)
PHONE..................................559 485-9090
Richard Kuckenbecker, *President*
EMP: 26 **EST:** 1968
SQ FT: 33,808
SALES (est): 2.9MM
SALES (corp-wide): 13.6MM **Privately Held**
WEB: www.kuckenbeckertractor.com
SIC: 5999 3524 Farm tractors; farm machinery; lawn & garden tractors & equipment
PA: Kuckenbecker Incorporated
   800 S Madera Ave
   Madera CA 93637
   559 233-0519

3531 Construction Machinery & Eqpt

(P-5024)
ARCBYT INC (PA)
548 Market St Pmb 39975, San Francisco (94104-5401)
PHONE..................................415 449-4852
Kimberly Abrams, *CEO*
EMP: 26 **EST:** 2018
SALES (est): 2.7MM **Privately Held**
SIC: 3531 Construction machinery

(P-5025)
BRODERICK GENERAL ENGINEERING
21750 8th St E Ste B, Sonoma (95476-9803)
PHONE..................................707 996-7809
Jeffrey Carlson, *Principal*
Jesus Fernandez, *Principal*
Sean Martin, *Principal*
Nik Patridis, *Principal*
Ryan Poore, *Principal*
EMP: 68 **EST:** 1998
SALES (est): 2.6MM **Privately Held**
SIC: 3531 Construction machinery

(P-5026)
CAL VSTA EROSION CTRL PDTS LLC
459 Country Rd 99w 99 W, Arbuckle (95912)
PHONE..................................530 476-0706
Renee Shadinger, *CEO*
Bryan Shadinger, *President*
John Shadinger, *CFO*
Maggie Shadinger, *Controller*
EMP: 35 **EST:** 2006
SALES (est): 2.9MM **Privately Held**
WEB: www.calvistaerosion.com
SIC: 3531 Construction machinery

(P-5027)
CALIFORNIA MFG & ENGRG CO LLC
1401 S Madera Ave, Kerman (93630-9139)
PHONE..................................559 842-1500
Frank Shanahan,
Douglas Kemp, *QC Mgr*
Karen Emery,
Richard Spencer,
▲ **EMP:** 130 **EST:** 2004
SALES (est): 19MM **Privately Held**
WEB: www.mecawp.com
SIC: 3531 Construction machinery

(P-5028)
CARON COMPACTOR CO
1204 Ullrey Ave, Escalon (95320-8618)
PHONE..................................800 448-8236
James O Caron, *CEO*
Judith S Caron, *Vice Pres*
David Williams, *Production*
▲ **EMP:** 25 **EST:** 1969
SQ FT: 18,000
SALES (est): 3.7MM **Privately Held**
WEB: www.caroncompactor.com
SIC: 3531 3441 Construction machinery attachments; fabricated structural metal

(P-5029)
CLEASBY MANUFACTURING CO INC (PA)
1414 Bancroft Ave, San Francisco (94124-3603)
P.O. Box 24132 (94124-0132)
PHONE..................................415 822-6565
Leslie John Cleasby, *President*
John Cleasby, *President*
Thomas Zickgraf, *Controller*
EMP: 20 **EST:** 1949
SQ FT: 21,000
SALES (est): 5.8MM **Privately Held**
WEB: www.cleasby.com
SIC: 3531 5033 Roofing equipment; roofing & siding materials

(P-5030)
CUSTOM BUILDING PRODUCTS INC
3525 Zephyr Ct, Stockton (95206-4210)
PHONE..................................209 983-8322
EMP: 40 **Privately Held**
WEB: www.custombuildingproducts.com
SIC: 3531 Concrete grouting equipment
HQ: Custom Building Products Llc
   7711 Center Ave Ste 500
   Huntington Beach CA 92647
   800 272-8786

(P-5031)
EAGLE ROCK INCORPORATED
40029 La Grange Rd, Junction City (96048)
P.O. Box 1498, Weaverville (96093-1498)
PHONE..................................530 623-4444
Larry E Yingling, *President*
David W Yingling, *Vice Pres*
EMP: 15 **EST:** 1980
SQ FT: 720
SALES (est): 2.6MM **Privately Held**
WEB: www.eagle-rock-incorporated.sbcontract.com
SIC: 3531 2951 1423 Rock crushing machinery, portable; capstans, ship; asphalt & asphaltic paving mixtures (not from refineries); crushed & broken granite

---
(PA)=Parent Co (HQ)=Headquarters (DH)=Div Headquarters
✪ = New Business established in last 2 years

3531 - Construction Machinery & Eqpt County

(P-5032)
ENDEAVOR HOMES INC
655 Cal Oak Rd, Oroville (95965-9621)
P.O. Box 1947 (95965-1947)
PHONE..................530 534-0300
Del Fleener, *President*
Shonie Schufeldt, *Treasurer*
William Wicklas, *Vice Pres*
EMP: 20 **EST:** 1996
SALES (est): 2.7MM Privately Held
WEB: www.endeavorhomes.com
SIC: 3531 2439 Construction machinery; trusses, wooden roof

(P-5033)
GUNTERT ZMMERMAN CONST DIV INC
222 E 4th St, Ripon (95366-2761)
PHONE..................209 599-0066
Ronald M Guntert Jr, *CEO*
Jan Scholl, *COO*
Denise Guntert, *Vice Pres*
Jeremy Henley, *Technician*
Iovtcho Delev, *Engineer*
◆ **EMP:** 50 **EST:** 1942
SQ FT: 10,000
SALES (est): 13.4MM Privately Held
WEB: www.guntert.com
SIC: 3531 3599 Pavers; machine & other job shop work

(P-5034)
JAMIE G WATT
833 Curlew Rd, Livermore (94551-6103)
PHONE..................925 580-2805
Jamie Watt, *Principal*
EMP: 15 **EST:** 2006
SALES (est): 2.9MM Privately Held
SIC: 3531 Backhoes

(P-5035)
KDF ENTERPRISES LLC
3941 Park Dr, El Dorado Hills (95762-4549)
PHONE..................803 928-7073
James Dearing, *Director*
EMP: 250
SALES (corp-wide): 33.4MM Privately Held
WEB: www.kdfllc.com
SIC: 3531 Construction machinery
PA: Kdf Enterprises Llc
  370 Mountain View Rd
  Springville AL 35146
  205 687-1875

(P-5036)
KENCO ENGINEERING INC
2155 Pfe Rd, Roseville (95747-9765)
P.O. Box 1467 (95678-8467)
PHONE..................916 782-8494
David Lutz, *President*
Brian Handshoe, *Vice Pres*
Donald Lutz, *Vice Pres*
Ron Geimer, *Sales Mgr*
EMP: 30 **EST:** 1957
SQ FT: 25,000
SALES (est): 4.7MM Privately Held
WEB: www.kencoengineering.com
SIC: 3531 5082 Construction machinery attachments; general construction machinery & equipment

(P-5037)
SILICON VALLEY CRANE INC
10700 Bigge St, San Leandro (94577-1032)
PHONE..................408 452-1537
Kenneth R Hensley, *Principal*
EMP: 16 **EST:** 2008
SALES (est): 334.1K Privately Held
SIC: 3531 Construction machinery

(P-5038)
SOLARJUICE AMERICAN INC
Also Called: Solar 4 America
6950 Preston Ave, Livermore (94551-9545)
PHONE..................925 474-8821
Denton Teng, *President*
EMP: 322 **EST:** 2019
SALES (est): 23.6MM Privately Held
SIC: 3531 5211 Roofing equipment; solar heating equipment

(P-5039)
SUPERWINCH HOLDING LLC
3945 Freedom Cir Ste 560, Santa Clara (95054-1269)
PHONE..................860 412-1476
Edward Cunningham,
EMP: 70 **EST:** 2009
SALES (est): 6.4MM Privately Held
SIC: 3531 Winches

(P-5040)
TANFIELD ENGRG SYSTEMS US INC
Also Called: Upright
2686 S Maple Ave, Fresno (93725-2108)
PHONE..................559 443-6602
Roy Stanley, *President*
Charles Brooks, *CFO*
David Sternweis, *Controller*
Darren Kell, *Director*
EMP: 15 **EST:** 2006
SQ FT: 67,727
SALES (est): 11.5MM
SALES (corp-wide): 3MM Privately Held
WEB: www.tanfieldgroup.com
SIC: 3531 Aerial work platforms: hydraulic/elec. truck/carrier mounted
PA: Tanfield Group Plc
  Sandgate House
  Newcastle-Upon-Tyne

(P-5041)
TINK INC
2361 Durham Dayton Hwy, Durham (95938-9604)
PHONE..................530 895-0897
Robert J Du Bose, *CEO*
Dan Bose, *Vice Pres*
Dan M Du Bose, *Vice Pres*
Dan D Bose, *VP Finance*
Rosie Birmingham, *Controller*
EMP: 40
SQ FT: 53,000
SALES (est): 13.7MM Privately Held
WEB: www.tinkinc.com
SIC: 3531 3444 Construction machinery; sheet metalwork

(P-5042)
TNT INDUSTRIAL CONTRACTORS INC (PA)
3800 Happy Ln, Sacramento (95827-9721)
PHONE..................916 395-8400
Josh Twist, *CEO*
John Morrill, *Project Mgr*
Dave Richter, *Sr Project Mgr*
Mike Richardson, *Superintendent*
EMP: 35 **EST:** 1991
SQ FT: 4,000
SALES (est): 16.1MM Privately Held
WEB: www.tntindustrial.com
SIC: 3531 Construction machinery

3532 Mining Machinery & Eqpt

(P-5043)
REED INTERNATIONAL (HQ)
Also Called: Saunco Air Technologies
13024 Lake Rd, Hickman (95323-9667)
P.O. Box 178 (95323-0178)
PHONE..................209 874-2357
Wendell Reed, *President*
Kevin Clark, *Project Engr*
Sandy Salas, *Supervisor*
▼ **EMP:** 19 **EST:** 1973
SALES (est): 5.3MM
SALES (corp-wide): 163.9MM Privately Held
WEB: www.macropaver.com
SIC: 3532 5531 3564 3444 Mining machinery; automotive & home supply stores; blowers & fans; sheet metalwork
PA: Basic Resources, Inc.
  928 12th St Ste 700
  Modesto CA 95354
  209 521-9771

3533 Oil Field Machinery & Eqpt

(P-5044)
AERA ENERGY SERVICES COMPANY
29010 Shell Rd, Coalinga (93210-9235)
PHONE..................559 935-7418
Kevin Peck, *Branch Mgr*
Ed Patterson, *Opers Staff*
EMP: 30
SALES (corp-wide): 180.5B Privately Held
WEB: www.aeraenergy.com
SIC: 3533 1311 Oil & gas drilling rigs & equipment; crude petroleum & natural gas production
HQ: Aera Energy Services Company
  10000 Ming Ave
  Bakersfield CA 93311
  661 665-5000

(P-5045)
CAMERON INTERNATIONAL CORP
Also Called: Cooper Cameron Valves
562 River Park Dr, Redding (96003-5381)
PHONE..................530 242-6965
EMP: 56
SALES (corp-wide): 10.3B Publicly Held
SIC: 3533 Mfg Oil/Gas Field Machinery
PA: Cameron International Corporation
  1333 West Loop S Ste 1700
  Houston TX 77041
  713 513-3300

3534 Elevators & Moving Stairways

(P-5046)
ELEVATOR INDUSTRIES INC
110 Main Ave, Sacramento (95838-2015)
PHONE..................916 921-1495
Guy Buckman, *President*
Jason Buckman, *Vice Pres*
Denise Rasberry, *Sales Mgr*
▲ **EMP:** 16 **EST:** 2013
SALES (est): 2.8MM Privately Held
WEB: www.elevator-industries.com
SIC: 3534 7699 Elevators & equipment; elevators: inspection, service & repair

(P-5047)
NIDEC MOTOR CORPORATION
Also Called: McE
11380 White Rock Rd, Rancho Cordova (95742-6522)
PHONE..................916 463-9200
Mohamed Ezzeddine, *Business Dir*
Jim Kitz, *Admin Sec*
Jessica Robert, *Admin Asst*
David Adcock, *Administration*
Marsha Eubank, *Administration*
EMP: 400 Privately Held
WEB: www.acim.nidec.com
SIC: 3534 3613 Elevators & equipment; switchgear & switchboard apparatus
HQ: Nidec Motor Corporation
  8050 West Florissant Ave
  Saint Louis MO 63136

(P-5048)
POWERLIFT DUMBWAITERS INC
2444 Georgia Slide Rd, Georgetown (95634-2201)
P.O. Box 4390 (95634-4390)
PHONE..................800 409-5438
John B Reite, *President*
Brian Schmit, *Sales Staff*
▲ **EMP:** 17 **EST:** 2000
SQ FT: 7,500
SALES (est): 3MM Privately Held
WEB: www.dumbwaiters.com
SIC: 3534 Dumbwaiters

(P-5049)
SCHINDLER ELEVATOR CORPORATION
555 Mccormick St, San Leandro (94577-1107)
PHONE..................510 382-2075
Dennis Devos, *Manager*
William Fletcher, *Manager*
EMP: 30
SALES (corp-wide): 753.4MM Privately Held
WEB: www.schindler.com
SIC: 3534 1796 7699 Elevators & equipment; elevator installation & conversion; elevators: inspection, service & repair
HQ: Schindler Elevator Corporation
  20 Whippany Rd
  Morristown NJ 07960
  973 397-6500

3535 Conveyors & Eqpt

(P-5050)
COMPASS EQUIPMENT INC (PA)
4688 Pacific Heights Rd, Oroville (95965-9239)
P.O. Box 1048 (95965-1048)
PHONE..................530 533-7284
Stephen Appleby, *President*
Ron Moras, *Corp Secy*
Victor Abreo, *Vice Pres*
Matthew Hunt, *Foreman/Supr*
Steve Appleby, *Sales Mgr*
EMP: 22 **EST:** 1976
SQ FT: 22,400
SALES (est): 12.8MM Privately Held
WEB: www.compassequip.com
SIC: 3535 Belt conveyor systems, general industrial use

(P-5051)
FLO STOR ENGINEERING INC (PA)
Also Called: Flostor
21371 Cabot Blvd, Hayward (94545-1650)
PHONE..................510 887-7179
Robert Weeks, *Owner*
Keith Bawa, *Controller*
John Fisher, *Sales Engr*
John Jackson, *Sales Engr*
Alicia Capps,
▼ **EMP:** 21 **EST:** 1983
SALES (est): 5.4MM Privately Held
WEB: www.flostor.com
SIC: 3535 Conveyors & conveying equipment

(P-5052)
HECO-PACIFIC MANUFACTURING INC
1510 Pacific St, Union City (94587-2099)
PHONE..................510 487-1155
Malik A Alarab, *President*
Allan M Alarab, *Admin Sec*
Dwight Chew, *Project Engr*
Teli Capino, *Associate*
▼ **EMP:** 25 **EST:** 1961
SQ FT: 34,000
SALES (est): 4.9MM Privately Held
WEB: www.hecopacific.com
SIC: 3535 3536 3531 Conveyors & conveying equipment; cranes, overhead traveling; construction machinery

(P-5053)
OMRON ROBOTICS SAFETY TECH INC (HQ)
Also Called: Adept Technology
4550 Norris Canyon Rd # 150, San Ramon (94583-1369)
PHONE..................925 245-3400
Rob Cain, *President*
Joachim Melis, *President*
Seth Halio, *CFO*
Deron Jackson, *CTO*
Neil Wilber, *Technician*
▲ **EMP:** 156 **EST:** 2005
SQ FT: 57,000
SALES (est): 90MM Privately Held
WEB: www.robotics.omron.com
SIC: 3535 7372 Robotic conveyors; prepackaged software; operating systems computer software

▲ = Import ▼ = Export
◆ = Import/Export

PRODUCTS & SERVICES SECTION

3541 - Machine Tools: Cutting County (P-5077)

(P-5054)
PRIDE CONVEYANCE SYSTEMS INC
Also Called: P C S
1700 Shelton Dr, Hollister (95023-9404)
PHONE 831 637-1787
Shannon Pride, *President*
Pat Jordon, *Vice Pres*
Ruben Padilla, *Vice Pres*
Bill Stewart, *Vice Pres*
Mike Zgragen, *Vice Pres*
◆ EMP: 75 EST: 1990
SQ FT: 36,000
SALES (est): 16.3MM **Privately Held**
WEB: www.roeslein.com
SIC: **3535** Conveyors & conveying equipment

(P-5055)
RALPHS-PUGH CO INC
3931 Oregon St, Benicia (94510-1301)
PHONE 707 745-6222
William G Pugh, *CEO*
Deborah Pugh, *Treasurer*
Tom Anderson, *Vice Pres*
Scott Fukayama, *Engineer*
Derrick Shelton, *Natl Sales Mgr*
EMP: 65
SQ FT: 36,000
SALES (est): 20.2MM **Privately Held**
WEB: www.ralphs-pugh.com
SIC: **3535** Conveyors & conveying equipment

(P-5056)
SARDEE CORPORATION CALIFORNIA
2731 E Myrtle St, Stockton (95205-4793)
PHONE 209 466-1526
Steve Sarovich, *President*
Dolores Sarovich, *Corp Secy*
Alan Bassett, *Vice Pres*
Alex Graham, *Vice Pres*
EMP: 16 EST: 1965
SQ FT: 20,000
SALES (est): 807.4K **Privately Held**
WEB: www.sardee.com
SIC: **3535** Conveyors & conveying equipment

(P-5057)
SMART MACHINES INC
46702 Bayside Pkwy, Fremont (94538-6582)
PHONE 510 661-5000
K C Janac, *President*
Sharon Andres, *Controller*
EMP: 34 EST: 1994
SQ FT: 15,258
SALES (est): 4.6MM **Publicly Held**
WEB: www.brooks.com
SIC: **3535** Robotic conveyors
PA: Brooks Automation, Inc.
   15 Elizabeth Dr
   Chelmsford MA 01824

(P-5058)
STOCKTON TRI-INDUSTRIES LLC
2141 E Anderson St, Stockton (95205-7010)
P.O. Box 6097 (95206-0097)
PHONE 209 948-9701
Courtney Rogers, *Mng Member*
Harrison Freddie Wells, *CEO*
Ray Smith, *Corp Secy*
Luis Leon, *Project Engr*
Jeff Yon, *Accounts Mgr*
EMP: 39 EST: 1976
SQ FT: 32,000
SALES (est): 6.7MM **Privately Held**
WEB: www.stocktontri.com
SIC: **3535** 3599 Conveyors & conveying equipment; machine shop, jobbing & repair

3536 Hoists, Cranes & Monorails

(P-5059)
CARPENTER GROUP (PA)
Also Called: Cable-Cisco
222 Napoleon St, San Francisco (94124-1017)
PHONE 415 285-1954
Bernard L Martin, *CEO*
Bruce Yoder, *President*
Frank Joost, *Vice Pres*
Patty Oliverio, *Admin Sec*
Jeff Scott, *Info Tech Mgr*
▲ EMP: 33 EST: 1950
SQ FT: 26,000
SALES (est): 20.1MM **Privately Held**
WEB: www.carpenterrigging.com
SIC: **3536** 2394 5085 3496 Hoists; liners & covers, fabric: made from purchased materials; industrial supplies; cable, uninsulated wire: made from purchased wire

3537 Indl Trucks, Tractors, Trailers & Stackers

(P-5060)
ALL-AMERICAN LUMPING LLC
5665 N Pershing Ave A1, Stockton (95207-4948)
PHONE 209 715-0309
Crystal Garcia, *CEO*
EMP: 76 EST: 2019
SALES (est): 3.2MM **Privately Held**
WEB: www.allamericanlumping.com
SIC: **3537** Pallet loaders & unloaders

(P-5061)
FREMONT PACKAGE EXPRESS
734 Still Breeze Way, Sacramento (95831-5544)
PHONE 916 541-1812
Terrence Wong, *Owner*
EMP: 15 EST: 2015
SALES (est): 800K **Privately Held**
SIC: **3537** Trucks: freight, baggage, etc.: industrial, except mining

(P-5062)
GOLDEN GATE FREIGHTLINER INC
Also Called: Golden Gate Truck Center
2727 E Central Ave, Fresno (93725-2425)
P.O. Box 12346 (93777-2346)
PHONE 559 486-4310
Gurpreet Bhangoo, *Finance*
EMP: 300
SALES (corp-wide): 100.3MM **Privately Held**
WEB: www.freightliner.com
SIC: **3537** 5511 Trucks: freight, baggage, etc.: industrial, except mining; new & used car dealers
HQ: Golden Gate Freightliner Inc.
   8200 Baldwin St
   Oakland CA 94621
   559 486-4310

(P-5063)
GOLDEN VALLEY & ASSOCIATES INC
Also Called: Cal Central Catering Trailers
3511 Finch Rd A, Modesto (95357-4143)
PHONE 209 549-1549
Estafani Ochoa, *CEO*
Carlos Osorio, *Recruiter*
EMP: 22 EST: 2004
SQ FT: 30,000
SALES (est): 3.6MM **Privately Held**
SIC: **3537** Aircraft engine cradles

(P-5064)
JS TRUCKING INC
2930 Geer Rd, Turlock (95382-1142)
PHONE 209 252-0007
Balbir Dhaliwal, *President*
EMP: 40 EST: 2010
SALES (est): 3MM **Privately Held**
SIC: **3537** Trucks: freight, baggage, etc.: industrial, except mining

(P-5065)
NOR CAL TRUCK SALES & MFG
Also Called: Nor Car Truck Sales
200 Industrial Way, Benicia (94510-1191)
PHONE 925 787-9735
David Jenkins, *Owner*
EMP: 18 EST: 1980
SALES (est): 1MM **Privately Held**
WEB: www.norcaltrucksales.com
SIC: **3537** 5511 Trucks, tractors, loaders, carriers & similar equipment; trucks, tractors & trailers: new & used

(P-5066)
PRODUCTBOARD INC (PA)
612 Howard St Fl 4, San Francisco (94105-3944)
PHONE 844 472-6273
Hubert Palan, *CEO*
Emily Brown, *CEO*
Noah Barr, *Vice Pres*
Karly Knipp, *Sales Staff*
Jack Langenback, *Accounts Exec*
EMP: 249 EST: 2014
SALES (est): 33.2MM **Privately Held**
WEB: www.productboard.com
SIC: **3537** Platforms, cargo

(P-5067)
PROFESSIONAL LUMPER SVC INC
1943 Alex Way, Turlock (95382-9207)
P.O. Box 729, Ceres (95307-0729)
PHONE 209 613-5397
Tony Kauffman, *President*
Connie Kauffman, *Co-Owner*
EMP: 35 EST: 2004
SALES (est): 2.6MM **Privately Held**
SIC: **3537** Trucks, tractors, loaders, carriers & similar equipment

(P-5068)
STROPPINI ENTERPRISES
2546 Mercantile Dr Ste A, Rancho Cordova (95742-8203)
PHONE 916 635-8181
Gilbert Stroppini, *Owner*
Dave Yungling, *General Mgr*
▲ EMP: 23 EST: 1970
SQ FT: 12,000
SALES (est): 1.2MM **Privately Held**
WEB: www.stroppini.com
SIC: **3537** Platforms, stands, tables, pallets & similar equipment; tables, lift: hydraulic

(P-5069)
VALLEY FORKLIFT
3834 Commerce Dr, West Sacramento (95691-2179)
PHONE 916 371-6165
Gerry Hudson, *Principal*
Shawn Lyons, *Sales Mgr*
Gabe Elmore, *Accounts Mgr*
EMP: 15 EST: 2014
SALES (est): 1.4MM **Privately Held**
WEB: www.forkliftssacramento.net
SIC: **3537** 7699 Forklift trucks; industrial truck repair

3541 Machine Tools: Cutting

(P-5070)
ACCEL MANUFACTURING INC
1709 Grant St, Santa Clara (95050-3939)
PHONE 408 727-5883
Loc Pham, *President*
EMP: 15 EST: 2010
SALES (est): 4.5MM **Privately Held**
WEB: www.accelmfg.com
SIC: **3541** Machine tool replacement & repair parts, metal cutting types

(P-5071)
AKIRA SEIKI USA INC
255 Capitol St, Livermore (94551-5210)
PHONE 925 443-1200
Alan Kludjian, *President*
▲ EMP: 23 EST: 1995
SALES (est): 1.5MM **Privately Held**
WEB: www.akira-seiki.com
SIC: **3541** Machine tools, metal cutting type

(P-5072)
CAL-WEST PRECISION SOLUTIONS
3485 Edward Ave, Santa Clara (95054-2131)
PHONE 408 988-8069
EMP: 15 EST: 2010
SALES (est): 2.2MM **Privately Held**
WEB: www.calwestprecision.com
SIC: **3541** Lathes, metal cutting & polishing

(P-5073)
DMG MORI MANUFACTURING USA INC (HQ)
Also Called: DTL Research & Technical Ctr
3601 Faraday Ave, Davis (95618-7776)
PHONE 530 746-7400
Adam Hansel, *President*
Hiroshi Takami, *Treasurer*
Zach Piner, *Vice Pres*
Natsuo Okada, *Admin Sec*
▲ EMP: 115 EST: 2011
SALES (est): 30.8MM **Privately Held**
WEB: www.dmgmori.co.jp
SIC: **3541** Machine tools, metal cutting type

(P-5074)
GNB CORPORATION
Also Called: GNB Vacuum Excellence Defined
3200 Dwight Rd Ste 100, Elk Grove (95758-6461)
PHONE 916 233-3543
Kenneth W Harrison, *President*
Donald A Bendix, *Corp Secy*
Klaus Rindt, *Vice Pres*
Amy Long, *Human Resources*
▲ EMP: 60
SQ FT: 62,500
SALES (est): 14.5MM **Privately Held**
WEB: www.gnbvac.com
SIC: **3541** 3491 Machine tools, metal cutting type; industrial valves
HQ: Ellison Technologies, Inc.
   9828 Arlee Ave
   Santa Fe Springs CA 90670
   562 949-8311

(P-5075)
J&N ENGINEERING INC
1310 N 4th St, San Jose (95112-4713)
PHONE 408 680-1810
John Pham, *CEO*
Tu Pham, *Director*
EMP: 20 EST: 2017
SALES (est): 2.5MM **Privately Held**
WEB: www.jnstructural.com
SIC: **3541** Machine tools, metal cutting type

(P-5076)
METLSAW SYSTEMS INC
2950 Bay Vista Ct, Benicia (94510-1123)
PHONE 707 746-6200
Lisa Kvech, *CEO*
Bruce Rowland, *Officer*
Tom Kvech, *Engineer*
Kenneth Forman, *Controller*
Robert Sanchez, *Plant Mgr*
◆ EMP: 21 EST: 1984
SQ FT: 30,000
SALES (est): 7.3MM **Privately Held**
WEB: www.metlsaw.com
SIC: **3541** Saws & sawing machines

(P-5077)
ROBB-JACK CORPORATION (PA)
3300 Nicolaus Rd Ste 1, Lincoln (95648-9574)
PHONE 916 645-6045
David Baker, *President*
Steve Handrop, *Exec VP*
Khadidja Norris, *Vice Pres*
Kenji Castro, *Telecom Exec*
Patrick Barroga, *Engineer*
EMP: 74 EST: 1959
SQ FT: 42,000
SALES (est): 14.9MM **Privately Held**
WEB: www.robbjack.com
SIC: **3541** Machine tools, metal cutting type

3542 Machine Tools: Forming

(P-5078)
CARANDO TECHNOLOGIES INC
345 N Harrison St, Stockton (95203-2801)
P.O. Box 1167 (95201-1167)
PHONE.................................209 948-6500
Sidney A Scheutz, *CEO*
Laura Keir, *CFO*
Shannon Crawford, *Office Mgr*
Elise Woods, *Purch Mgr*
▼ **EMP:** 25 **EST:** 2003
SQ FT: 35,000
SALES (est): 7.3MM **Privately Held**
WEB: www.carando.net
SIC: 3542 3548 3599 Machine tools; metal forming type; welding apparatus; custom machinery; machine shop, jobbing & repair

(P-5079)
HORN MACHINE TOOLS INC (PA)
Also Called: H M T
40455 Brickyard Dr # 101, Madera (93636-9516)
PHONE.................................559 431-4131
Kent Horn, *President*
Bradley Carter, *Design Engr*
Paul Kuehlwein, *Regl Sales Mgr*
Will Winn, *Sales Staff*
William Winn, *Sales Staff*
▲ **EMP:** 31 **EST:** 1996
SALES (est): 7.7MM **Privately Held**
WEB: www.hornmachinetools.com
SIC: 3542 5084 Bending machines; industrial machinery & equipment

(P-5080)
POLAR SERVICE CENTER
4432 Winters Ave, McClellan (95652-2315)
PHONE.................................916 643-4689
EMP: 31 **EST:** 2014
SALES (est): 2.4MM **Privately Held**
WEB: www.polarservicecenters.com
SIC: 5531 3542 5961 Truck equipment & parts; mechanical (pneumatic or hydraulic) metal forming machines; automotive supplies & equipment, mail order

3544 Dies, Tools, Jigs, Fixtures & Indl Molds

(P-5081)
BENDA TOOL & MODEL WORKS INC
Also Called: A & B Diecasting
900 Alfred Nobel Dr, Hercules (94547-1814)
PHONE.................................510 741-3170
Robert Dathe, *President*
Stephen Dathe, *CEO*
Judy Newsome, *COO*
Stephen Daintith, *Exec VP*
Ben Dathe, *Vice Pres*
▲ **EMP:** 35
SQ FT: 60,000
SALES (est): 8MM **Privately Held**
WEB: www.abdiecasting.com
SIC: 3544 Dies, steel rule; industrial molds

(P-5082)
COMPUTER PLASTICS
1914 National Ave, Hayward (94545-1784)
PHONE.................................510 785-3600
Wayne L Harshbarger, *President*
EMP: 21 **EST:** 1969
SQ FT: 12,700
SALES (est): 4.6MM **Privately Held**
WEB: www.computerplastics.com
SIC: 3544 3089 Special dies & tools; molding primary plastic

(P-5083)
DECREVEL INCORPORATED
1836 Soscol Ave, NAPA (94559-1349)
PHONE.................................707 258-8065
P James Decrevel Sr, *President*
Sara Decrevel, *CFO*
EMP: 26 **EST:** 1979
SQ FT: 4,500
SALES (est): 1.5MM **Privately Held**
WEB: www.decrevel.com
SIC: 3544 2752 Special dies & tools; die sets for metal stamping (presses); commercial printing, lithographic

(P-5084)
PROTOTEK CALIFORNIA LLC
215 Devcon Dr, San Jose (95112-4211)
PHONE.................................408 730-5035
Matthew Hayes, *President*
James Fletcher, *Prgrmr*
Doloris V Longoria, *Manager*
EMP: 27 **EST:** 1991
SALES (est): 7.9MM
SALES (corp-wide): 52.8MM **Privately Held**
WEB: www.prototek.com
SIC: 3544 3089 Industrial molds; plastic processing
PA: Core Industrial Partners, Llc
    200 N La Salle St # 2360
    Chicago IL 60601
    312 566-4880

(P-5085)
TMK MANUFACTURING
2110 Oakland Rd, San Jose (95131-1565)
PHONE.................................408 732-3200
EMP: 60
SQ FT: 15,700
SALES (est): 3.3MM **Privately Held**
SIC: 3544 3599 3469 Mfg Dies/Tools/Jigs/Fixtures Mfg Industrial Machinery Mfg Metal Stampings

(P-5086)
TOOL MAKERS INTERNATIONAL INC
Also Called: T M I
3390 Woodward Ave, Santa Clara (95054-2629)
P.O. Box 4840 (95056-4840)
PHONE.................................408 980-8888
Patrick Chronis, *President*
EMP: 32 **EST:** 1961
SQ FT: 22,000
SALES (est): 1.1MM **Privately Held**
SIC: 3544 Special dies, tools, jigs & fixtures

(P-5087)
US DIES INC (PA)
1992 Rockefeller Dr # 300, Ceres (95307-7274)
PHONE.................................209 664-1402
Thomas Mason, *President*
Diana L Mason, *Corp Secy*
Ken Thomas, *Vice Pres*
EMP: 23 **EST:** 1971
SQ FT: 21,000
SALES (est): 7MM **Privately Held**
SIC: 3544 Dies, steel rule

(P-5088)
WRIGHT ENGINEERED PLASTICS INC
3681 N Laughlin Rd, Santa Rosa (95403-1027)
PHONE.................................707 575-1218
Barbara F Roberts, *President*
Mike Nellis, *COO*
Matt Calahan, *QC Mgr*
▲ **EMP:** 47 **EST:** 1970
SQ FT: 25,000
SALES (est): 10.2MM
SALES (corp-wide): 103.5MM **Privately Held**
WEB: www.wepmolding.com
SIC: 3544 3089 Special dies, tools, jigs & fixtures; plastic hardware & building products
HQ: Seaway Plastics Engineering Llc
    6006 Siesta Ln
    Port Richey FL 34668

3545 Machine Tool Access

(P-5089)
BEAM DYNAMICS INC
5100 Patrick Henry Dr, Santa Clara (95054-1112)
PHONE.................................408 764-4805
Mathew Bye, *President*
Jon Maroney, *Vice Pres*
Blaine Boloich, *Director*
EMP: 39 **EST:** 1997
SQ FT: 4,200
SALES (est): 4.7MM
SALES (corp-wide): 1.2B **Publicly Held**
WEB: www.coherent.com
SIC: 3545 Machine tool accessories
PA: Coherent, Inc.
    5100 Patrick Henry Dr
    Santa Clara CA 95054
    408 764-4000

(P-5090)
BROACH MASTERS INC
2160 Precision Pl, Auburn (95603-9096)
PHONE.................................530 885-1939
Mark Vian, *President*
Elizabeth Vian, *Vice Pres*
Scott Vian, *Vice Pres*
Aaron Hill, *Prgrmr*
EMP: 27 **EST:** 1978
SALES (est): 3.3MM **Privately Held**
WEB: www.broachmasters.com
SIC: 3545 3599 Precision tools, machinists'; machine shop, jobbing & repair

(P-5091)
CONCEPT PART SOLUTIONS INC
2047 Zanker Rd, San Jose (95131-2107)
PHONE.................................408 748-1244
Richard L Diehl, *CEO*
Bruce Dickson, *Managing Dir*
MO Yi, *General Mgr*
Ikuko Kato, *Sales Dir*
Saori Ishii, *Sales Staff*
EMP: 39 **EST:** 2007
SALES (est): 4.3MM **Privately Held**
WEB: www.conceptpartsolutions.com
SIC: 3545 Machine tool accessories

(P-5092)
DEWEYL TOOL CO INC
959 Transport Way, Petaluma (94954-1474)
PHONE.................................707 765-5779
William Cline, *President*
Susan Blow, *Vice Pres*
Linda Cline, *Vice Pres*
Terrie Cline, *Manager*
EMP: 35 **EST:** 1969
SQ FT: 20,000
SALES (est): 3.8MM **Privately Held**
WEB: www.deweyl.com
SIC: 3545 Machine tool attachments & accessories

(P-5093)
DMG MORI DIGITAL TECH LAB CORP
Also Called: DTL Mori Seiki
3601 Faraday Ave, Davis (95618-7776)
PHONE.................................530 746-7400
Zach Piner, *President*
Hiroshi Takami, *Treasurer*
Adam Hansel, *Vice Pres*
Natsuo Okada, *Admin Sec*
▲ **EMP:** 49 **EST:** 2002
SALES (est): 8.5MM **Privately Held**
WEB: www.us.dmgmori.com
SIC: 3545 Machine tool accessories
HQ: Dmg Mori Usa, Inc.
    2400 Huntington Blvd
    Hoffman Estates IL 60192
    847 593-5400

(P-5094)
DRILLING & TRENCHING SUP INC (PA)
Also Called: Drilling World
1458 Mariani Ct, Tracy (95376-2825)
PHONE.................................510 895-1650
David Wellington Moran, *CEO*
Karen Arnett, *Admin Sec*
Erin B Moran, *Admin Sec*
Vince Averett, *Opers Mgr*
Sandy Clark,
▲ **EMP:** 17 **EST:** 1987
SQ FT: 52,000
SALES (est): 9.3MM **Privately Held**
WEB: www.drillingworld.com
SIC: 3545 Drilling machine attachments & accessories

(P-5095)
DYNATEX INTERNATIONAL
5577 Skylane Blvd, Santa Rosa (95403-1048)
PHONE.................................707 542-4227
Kate Henry, *CEO*
John Tyler, *President*
Leanne Sarcy, *CFO*
Leanne Sarasy, *Vice Pres*
Richard Gaona, *Engineer*
EMP: 21 **EST:** 1958
SQ FT: 15,000
SALES (est): 4MM **Privately Held**
WEB: www.dynatex.com
SIC: 3545 Cutting tools for machine tools

(P-5096)
ELCON PRECISION LLC
1009 Timothy Dr, San Jose (95133-1043)
PHONE.................................408 292-7800
Dan Brumlik, *Chairman*
Pater Smith, *President*
Evonne Yang, *Admin Asst*
Dan Schick, *Engineer*
Trinh Tran, *Accountant*
EMP: 35 **EST:** 2011
SALES (est): 5.9MM **Privately Held**
WEB: www.elconprecision.com
SIC: 3545 Precision tools, machinists'

(P-5097)
FRT OF AMERICA LLC
1101 S Winchester Blvd, San Jose (95128-3901)
PHONE.................................408 261-2632
Thomas Fries,
EMP: 18 **EST:** 2004
SALES (est): 2.5MM
SALES (corp-wide): 7.4MM **Privately Held**
WEB: www.frtmetrology.com
SIC: 3545 Measuring tools & machines, machinists' metalworking type
PA: Fries Research & Technology Gmbh
    Friedrich-Ebert-Str. 75
    Bergisch Gladbach NW 51429
    220 484-2430

(P-5098)
PELAGIC PRESSURE SYSTEMS CORP
480 Mccormick St, San Leandro (94577-1106)
PHONE.................................510 569-3100
Michael Hollis, *CEO*
Paul Elsinga, *Principal*
Robert Hollis, *Principal*
▲ **EMP:** 75 **EST:** 1979
SALES (est): 23.5MM
SALES (corp-wide): 11.9MM **Privately Held**
WEB: www.pelagicnet.com
SIC: 3545 Gauges (machine tool accessories)
HQ: Aqua-Lung America, Inc.
    2340 Cousteau Ct
    Vista CA 92081
    760 597-5000

(P-5099)
STEP TOOLS UNLIMITED INC
Also Called: Destiny Tool
18434 Technology Dr, Morgan Hill (95037-2844)
PHONE.................................408 988-8898
Guy Calamia, *President*
Nettie Calamia, *Corp Secy*
EMP: 63 **EST:** 1980
SALES (est): 12.1MM **Privately Held**
WEB: www.destinytool.com
SIC: 3545 Cutting tools for machine tools

(P-5100)
STEWART TOOL COMPANY
3647 Omec Cir, Rancho Cordova (95742-7302)
PHONE.................................916 635-8321
Mark Richard Stewart, *CEO*
Craig Harrington, *Corp Secy*
Dave Hassemeyer, *Admin Sec*
Jeff Boyett, *Engineer*
Brady Yount, *Controller*
EMP: 55 **EST:** 1968
SQ FT: 22,000

PRODUCTS & SERVICES SECTION

3555 - Printing Trades Machinery & Eqpt County (P-5122)

SALES (est): 9.7MM **Privately Held**
WEB: www.stewarttool.com
SIC: **3545** 3544 7692 Precision tools, machinists'; jigs & fixtures; welding repair

(P-5101)
TLC MACHINING INCORPORATED
Also Called: US Machining
2571 Chant Ct, San Jose (95122-1004)
PHONE..................................408 321-9002
EMP: 35
SQ FT: 5,000
SALES (est): 4.5MM **Privately Held**
SIC: **3545** Mfg Machine Tool Accessories

3546 Power Hand Tools

(P-5102)
GRANBERG PUMP AND METER LTD
Also Called: Granberg International
1051 Los Medanos St, Pittsburg (94565-2561)
PHONE..................................707 562-2099
Erik Granberg, *President*
John Mahley, *General Mgr*
Brian Mohr, *Project Mgr*
Lindsey Granberg, *Marketing Mgr*
Ben Hawkins, *Sales Mgr*
◆ EMP: 19 EST: 1956
SQ FT: 9,000 **Privately Held**
WEB: www.granberg.com
SIC: **3546** Power-driven handtools

(P-5103)
ZIRCON CORPORATION (PA)
1580 Dell Ave, Campbell (95008-6918)
PHONE..................................408 866-8600
John Stauss, *President*
Charles J Stauss, *Ch of Bd*
John R Stauss, *President*
Ron Bourque, *CFO*
Robert Wyler, *Admin Sec*
◆ EMP: 45 EST: 1977
SQ FT: 6,000
SALES (est): 28MM **Privately Held**
WEB: www.zircon.com
SIC: **3546** Power-driven handtools

3548 Welding Apparatus

(P-5104)
LONGEVITY GLOBAL INC
23591 Foley St, Hayward (94545-1676)
PHONE..................................877 566-4462
Simon Katz, *CEO*
Daniel Aviles, *Manager*
▲ EMP: 17 EST: 2007
SQ FT: 7,000
SALES (est): 1.3MM **Privately Held**
WEB: www.longevity-inc.com
SIC: **3548** 3545 3541 3699 Welding apparatus; machine tool accessories; machine tools, metal cutting type; welding machines & equipment, ultrasonic; metalworking machinery

(P-5105)
SENSBEY INC (PA)
833 Mahler Rd Ste 3, Burlingame (94010-1609)
PHONE..................................650 697-2032
Katsuhiro Enokawa, *President*
Hiro Ito, *Vice Pres*
EMP: 15
SQ FT: 22,000
SALES (est): 1.5MM **Privately Held**
WEB: www.sensbey.com
SIC: **3548** 3634 3822 Soldering equipment, except hand soldering irons; heating units, for electric appliances; built-in thermostats, filled system & bimetal types

3549 Metalworking Machinery, NEC

(P-5106)
5-STARS ENGINEERING ASSOCIATES
3393 De La Cruz Blvd, Santa Clara (95054-2633)
PHONE..................................408 380-4849
EMP: 26
SQ FT: 46,000
SALES (est): 4.1MM **Privately Held**
SIC: **3549** Metalworking Machinery, Nec

(P-5107)
BRIGHT MACHINES INC (PA)
132 Hawthorne St, San Francisco (94107-1308)
PHONE..................................415 867-4402
Amar Hanspal, *CEO*
Tzahi Rodrig, *COO*
Tzani Rodrig, *COO*
Craig Foster, *CFO*
Pat O'Malley, *CFO*
EMP: 378 EST: 2018
SALES (est): 76MM **Privately Held**
WEB: www.brightmachines.com
SIC: **3549** Assembly machines, including robotic

(P-5108)
HAEGER INCORPORATED (DH)
811 Wakefield Dr, Oakdale (95361-7792)
PHONE..................................209 848-4000
Alan Phillips, *CEO*
Wouter Kleizen, *President*
Angela Asbroek, *Office Mgr*
Jeannet N Trott, *Controller*
Gena Beck, *Human Res Mgr*
▲ EMP: 23 EST: 1979
SQ FT: 36,000
SALES (est): 7.6MM **Privately Held**
WEB: www.haeger.com
SIC: **3549** Metalworking machinery
HQ: Phillips Corporation
    7390 Coca Cola Dr Ste 200
    Hanover MD 21076
    410 564-2900

(P-5109)
LTI BOYD
600 S Mcclure Rd, Modesto (95357-0520)
PHONE..................................800 554-0200
Mitch Aiello, *President*
Kurt Wetzel, *CFO*
▲ EMP: 2746 EST: 2011
SALES (est): 2.7MM **Privately Held**
WEB: www.boydcorp.com
SIC: **3549** 3053 8711 Metalworking machinery; gaskets, packing & sealing devices; industrial engineers
PA: Sentinel Capital Partners Llc
    330 Madison Ave Fl 27
    New York NY 10017

(P-5110)
NEATO ROBOTICS INC (HQ)
50 Rio Robles, San Jose (95134-1806)
PHONE..................................510 795-1351
Giacomo Marini, *CEO*
Thomas Nedder, *CEO*
Holly Anderson, *CFO*
Bruce McAllister, *CFO*
Frank Meyer, *Vice Pres*
◆ EMP: 92 EST: 2005
SALES (est): 34.6MM
SALES (corp-wide): 3.2B **Privately Held**
WEB: www.neatorobotics.com
SIC: **3549** 3524 Assembly machines, including robotic; blowers & vacuums, lawn
PA: Vorwerk Se & Co. Kg
    Muhlenweg 17-37
    Wuppertal NW 42275
    202 564-0

(P-5111)
OHMNILABS INC
2367 Bering Dr, San Jose (95131-1125)
PHONE..................................408 675-9565
Thuc Vu, *CEO*
EMP: 23 EST: 2016

SALES (est): 4.1MM **Privately Held**
WEB: www.ohmnilabs.com
SIC: **3549** Assembly machines, including robotic

(P-5112)
POSITRONICS INCORPORATED
173 Spring St Ste 120, Pleasanton (94566-9401)
PHONE..................................925 931-0211
Howard Miles, *President*
Vincent Leung, *Vice Pres*
Richard Barnes, *CIO*
Dan Bryant, *CTO*
John Thoits, *Software Engr*
EMP: 15 EST: 2001
SQ FT: 2,200
SALES (est): 2.2MM **Privately Held**
WEB: www.posincorp.com
SIC: **3549** Assembly machines, including robotic

(P-5113)
SAILDRONE INC
1050 W Tower Ave, Alameda (94501-5003)
PHONE..................................415 670-9700
Richard Jenkins, *CEO*
Kimberly Sparling, *Vice Pres*
Yuriy Smolyakov, *Software Engr*
Daama Sheepo, *VP Engrg*
Casey Brown, *Engineer*
EMP: 15 EST: 2012
SQ FT: 32,500
SALES (est): 3MM **Privately Held**
WEB: www.saildrone.com
SIC: **3549** Assembly machines, including robotic

3552 Textile Machinery

(P-5114)
SURFACE ENGINEERING SPC
919 Hamlin Ct, Sunnyvale (94089-1402)
PHONE..................................408 734-8810
Richard Peattie, *President*
Jane Peattie, *Vice Pres*
David Rich, *Engineer*
EMP: 20 EST: 1976
SQ FT: 18,000
SALES (est): 4.8MM **Privately Held**
WEB: www.surfeng.com
SIC: **3552** 7389 Spindles, textile; grinding, precision: commercial or industrial

3553 Woodworking Machinery

(P-5115)
KVAL INC
Also Called: Kval Machinery Co
825 Petaluma Blvd S, Petaluma (94952-5134)
PHONE..................................707 762-4363
Gerald Kvalheim, *CEO*
Andrew M Kvalheim, *Treasurer*
Dave Kvalheim, *Vice Pres*
Mark Kvalheim, *Vice Pres*
John Miller, *CTO*
▲ EMP: 125 EST: 1950
SALES (est): 25.1MM **Privately Held**
WEB: www.kvalinc.com
SIC: **3553** 5084 Woodworking machinery; industrial machinery & equipment

(P-5116)
VOORWOOD COMPANY
Also Called: Turbosand
2350 Barney Rd, Anderson (96007-4306)
PHONE..................................530 365-3311
Adam Britton, *CEO*
Larry Ackernecht, *Vice Pres*
Steve Shifflet, *Admin Sec*
Brian Evans, *Technician*
Jason Morasch, *Electrical Engi*
▼ EMP: 30 EST: 1961
SQ FT: 60,000
SALES (est): 7.5MM **Privately Held**
WEB: www.voorwood.com
SIC: **3553** Woodworking machinery

(P-5117)
WANESHEAR TECHNOLOGIES LLC
3471 N State St, Ukiah (95482-3080)
PHONE..................................707 462-4761
▼ EMP: 35
SALES: 2.5MM **Privately Held**
SIC: **3553** Mfg Woodworking Machinery

3554 Paper Inds Machinery

(P-5118)
GEO M MARTIN COMPANY (PA)
1250 67th St, Emeryville (94608-1121)
PHONE..................................510 652-2200
Merrill D Martin, *CEO*
Robert A Morgan, *President*
Lillian Martin, *CFO*
George R Martin, *Exec VP*
Daniel J D'Angelo, *Vice Pres*
▲ EMP: 99 EST: 1957
SQ FT: 50,000
SALES (est): 22.2MM **Privately Held**
WEB: www.geomartin.com
SIC: **3554** Corrugating machines, paper

3555 Printing Trades Machinery & Eqpt

(P-5119)
FISHER GRAPHIC INDS A CAL CORP
1137 Graphics Dr, Modesto (95351-1501)
PHONE..................................209 577-0181
Phillip Saunders, *President*
EMP: 33 EST: 1978
SQ FT: 36,000
SALES (est): 2MM
SALES (corp-wide): 55.9MM **Privately Held**
WEB: www.containergraphics.com
SIC: **3555** 2796 Printing plates; platemaking services
PA: Container Graphics Corp.
    114 Ednbrgh S Dr Ste 104
    Cary NC 27511
    919 481-4200

(P-5120)
GRAPHICS MICROSYSTEMS INC (HQ)
484 Oakmead Pkwy, Sunnyvale (94085-4708)
PHONE..................................408 731-2000
Shlomo Amir, *CEO*
Steven Runyan, *President*
Tim Reed, *VP Finance*
EMP: 70 EST: 1983
SQ FT: 20,000
SALES (est): 11.5MM **Privately Held**
WEB: www.avt-inc.com
SIC: **3555** Printing trades machinery

(P-5121)
HARRIS & BRUNO MACHINE CO INC (PA)
Also Called: Harris & Bruno International
8555 Washington Blvd, Roseville (95678-5901)
PHONE..................................916 781-7676
Nick Bruno, *CEO*
Scott Alvarado, *Vice Pres*
Jessica Mitchell, *Admin Asst*
Shaun Densley, *Administration*
Joe Braun, *Project Mgr*
▲ EMP: 64
SQ FT: 45,000
SALES (est): 23.6MM **Privately Held**
WEB: www.harris-bruno.com
SIC: **3555** Printing trades machinery

(P-5122)
OCE DSPLAY GRPHICS SYSTEMS INC
2811 Orchard Pkwy, San Jose (95134-2013)
PHONE..................................773 714-8500
▼ EMP: 100

3555 - Printing Trades Machinery & Eqpt County

SALES (est): 34.5K
SALES (corp-wide): 30.7B Privately Held
SIC: 3555 3577 Mfg Printing Trades Machinery Mfg Computer Peripheral Equipment
HQ: Oce Holding B.V.
Sint Urbanusweg 43
Venlo 5914
773 592-222

(P-5123)
QUINTEL CORPORATION
685 Jarvis Dr Ste A, Morgan Hill (95037-2813)
PHONE 408 776-5190
Jeffrey C Lane, *President*
Howard Green, *Chief Mktg Ofcr*
Robert Borawski, *Admin Sec*
Keith Radousky, *CTO*
EMP: 20 **EST:** 1978
SQ FT: 12,500
SALES (est): 1.7MM Privately Held
WEB: www.neutronixinc.com
SIC: 3555 Printing trades machinery

(P-5124)
XEROX INTERNATIONAL PARTNERS (DH)
Also Called: Fuji Xerox
2100 Geng Rd Ste 210, Palo Alto (94303-3307)
PHONE 408 953-2700
Sunil Gupta, *Partner*
Daniel Avrahami, *Research*
▲ **EMP:** 74 **EST:** 1991
SALES (est): 24.7MM
SALES (corp-wide): 7B Publicly Held
WEB: www.xerox.com
SIC: 3555 Leads, printers'
HQ: Xerox Corporation
201 Merritt 7
Norwalk CT 06851
800 835-6100

3556 Food Prdts Machinery

(P-5125)
BILLINGTON WELDING & MFG INC
Also Called: Bwm
1442 N Emerald Ave, Modesto (95351-1115)
P.O. Box 4460 (95352-4460)
PHONE 209 526-0846
Timothy Ryan Billington, *CEO*
Francis Billington, *President*
EMP: 60 **EST:** 1969
SQ FT: 26,000
SALES (est): 7.4MM Privately Held
WEB: www.billington-mfg.com
SIC: 3556 3535 Food products machinery; conveyors & conveying equipment

(P-5126)
BLENTECH CORPORATION
2899 Dowd Dr, Santa Rosa (95407-7897)
PHONE 707 523-5949
Darrell Horn, *President*
Gina Muelrath, *President*
Daniel Voit, *COO*
Joseph Yarnall, *Exec VP*
Vanessa Wallace, *Admin Asst*
▲ **EMP:** 60 **EST:** 1986
SQ FT: 27,000
SALES (est): 15.1MM Privately Held
WEB: www.blentech.com
SIC: 3556 Mixers, commercial, food; meat processing machinery; poultry processing machinery; pasta machinery

(P-5127)
COMMERCIAL MANUFACTURING
2432 S East Ave, Fresno (93706-5119)
P.O. Box 947 (93714-0947)
PHONE 559 237-1855
Larry Hagopian, *President*
Michael Tarver, *Engineer*
Tom Harrison, *Marketing Staff*
Nick Loewen, *Manager*
EMP: 45 **EST:** 1938
SQ FT: 45,000
SALES (est): 7.7MM Privately Held
WEB: www.commercialmfg.com
SIC: 3556 Food products machinery

(P-5128)
CRIVELLER CALIFORNIA CORP
185 Grant Ave, Healdsburg (95448-9539)
PHONE 707 431-2211
Bruno Criveller, *President*
Mario Creveller, *Vice Pres*
Mario Criveller, *Vice Pres*
Shane Curtis, *Executive*
Jennifer Johnson, *Opers Staff*
▲ **EMP:** 15 **EST:** 2000
SALES (est): 5MM Privately Held
WEB: www.criveller.com
SIC: 3556 Brewers' & maltsters' machinery

(P-5129)
DALE GROVE CORPORATION
Also Called: Gdc
1501 Stone Creek Dr, San Jose (95132-1933)
PHONE 408 251-7220
Stephanie Mattos, *CEO*
John R Mattos, *Vice Pres*
Ruth Howell, *Bookkeeper*
EMP: 19 **EST:** 1965
SQ FT: 28,000
SALES (est): 3MM Privately Held
WEB: www.grovedale.com
SIC: 3556 3535 3429 Food products machinery; conveyors & conveying equipment; manufactured hardware (general)

(P-5130)
FOOD EQUIPMENT MFG CO
Also Called: Femco
175 Mitchell Rd, Hollister (95023-9603)
P.O. Box 257 (95024-0257)
PHONE 831 637-1624
Sal Felice, *President*
Elizabeth Felice, *Treasurer*
EMP: 26 **EST:** 1982
SQ FT: 2,800
SALES (est): 2.5MM Privately Held
SIC: 3556 Food products machinery

(P-5131)
HACKETT INDUSTRIES INC
Also Called: West Star Industries
4445 E Fremont St, Stockton (95215-4007)
PHONE 209 955-8220
Michelle E Focke, *CEO*
Richard Hackett, *President*
Mark Lathrop, *CFO*
Carolyn Hackett, *Admin Sec*
EMP: 43 **EST:** 1973
SQ FT: 90,000
SALES (est): 8.8MM Privately Held
SIC: 3556 3444 3431 Food products machinery; sheet metalwork; metal sanitary ware

(P-5132)
JOHN BEAN TECHNOLOGIES CORP
Also Called: Jbt Food Tech Madera
2300 W Industrial Ave, Madera (93637-5210)
PHONE 559 661-3200
Eric Madsen, *Branch Mgr*
Clara Rovedo, *Engineer*
Alex Sandoval, *Engineer*
Christina Joachim, *Mfg Staff*
EMP: 165 Publicly Held
WEB: www.jbtc.com
SIC: 3556 Food products machinery
PA: John Bean Technologies Corporation
70 W Madison St Ste 4400
Chicago IL 60602

(P-5133)
O H I COMPANY
820 S Pershing Ave, Stockton (95206-1176)
P.O. Box 622 (95201-0622)
PHONE 209 466-8921
Thomas W Hubbard, *CEO*
Ben Wallace, *Vice Pres*
▲ **EMP:** 26 **EST:** 1970
SQ FT: 40,000
SALES (est): 8.1MM Privately Held
SIC: 3556 3443 Food products machinery; fabricated plate work (boiler shop)

(P-5134)
RIPON MFG CO
Also Called: RMC
652 S Stockton Ave, Ripon (95366-2798)
PHONE 209 599-2148
Glenn Navarro, *President*
Ursula Navarro, *Corp Secy*
Alana Navarro, *Admin Asst*
Kenny Hoogendoorn, *Superintendent*
EMP: 20 **EST:** 1964
SQ FT: 45,000
SALES (est): 4.9MM Privately Held
WEB: www.riponmfgco.com
SIC: 3556 3535 Food products machinery; conveyors & conveying equipment

(P-5135)
STALFAB
131 Algen Ln, Watsonville (95076-8624)
P.O. Box 780 (95077-0780)
PHONE 831 786-1600
Eric Buksa, *Owner*
EMP: 21 **EST:** 1994
SQ FT: 5,000
SALES (est): 976.3K Privately Held
SIC: 3556 Food products machinery

(P-5136)
VALLEY PACKLINE SOLUTIONS
5259 Avenue 408, Reedley (93654-9131)
PHONE 559 638-7821
Jim Parra, *President*
Jerry Patterson, *Engineer*
EMP: 30 **EST:** 2008
SALES (est): 3.2MM Privately Held
WEB: www.packlinesolutions.com
SIC: 3556 Dehydrating equipment, food processing

(P-5137)
VERSACO MANUFACTURING INC
550 E Luchessa Ave, Gilroy (95020-7068)
PHONE 408 848-2880
Alan R Owens, *President*
John K Ishizuka, *Vice Pres*
EMP: 16 **EST:** 1983
SQ FT: 30,000
SALES (est): 2.4MM Privately Held
WEB: www.versacomfg.com
SIC: 3556 3661 3312 3537 Food products machinery; telephone & telegraph apparatus; structural & rail mill products; industrial trucks & tractors

3559 Special Ind Machinery, NEC

(P-5138)
AC PHOTONICS INC
2701 Northwestern Pkwy, Santa Clara (95051-0947)
PHONE 408 986-9838
Yongjian Wang, *President*
Steve Walton, *COO*
Zuhong Qu, *Vice Pres*
Tony Cortez, *Business Mgr*
Marcella Jiang, *Sales Staff*
▲ **EMP:** 24 **EST:** 1997
SQ FT: 10,000
SALES (est): 3.2MM Privately Held
WEB: www.acphotonics.com
SIC: 3559 Fiber optics strand coating machinery

(P-5139)
ADVANCED INDUSTRIAL CERAMICS
2449 Zanker Rd, San Jose (95131-1116)
PHONE 408 955-9990
Chau Nguyen, *Owner*
EMP: 25 **EST:** 2002
SQ FT: 7,500
SALES (est): 6.3MM Privately Held
WEB: www.aiceramics.com
SIC: 3559 3674 Semiconductor manufacturing machinery; stud bases or mounts for semiconductor devices

(P-5140)
APERIA TECHNOLOGIES INC
1616 Rollins Rd, Burlingame (94010-2302)
PHONE 415 494-9624
Joshua Carter, *CEO*
Josue Rojas, *Software Dev*
Brian Finones, *Technician*
Lucas Cooter, *Engineer*
Brandon Haws, *Engineer*
▲ **EMP:** 33 **EST:** 2010
SALES (est): 7.6MM Privately Held
WEB: www.aperiatech.com
SIC: 3559 Automotive maintenance equipment

(P-5141)
APPLIED MATERIALS INC (PA)
3050 Bowers Ave Bldg 1, Santa Clara (95054-3298)
P.O. Box 58039 (95052-8039)
PHONE 408 727-5555
Gary E Dickerson, *President*
Thomas J Iannotti, *Ch of Bd*
Daniel J Durn, *CFO*
Teri Little,
Thomas F Larkins, *Senior VP*
▲ **EMP:** 800 **EST:** 1967
SALES (est): 17.2B Publicly Held
WEB: www.appliedmaterials.com
SIC: 3559 3674 Semiconductor manufacturing machinery; semiconductors & related devices

(P-5142)
AUTOMETRIX INC
12098 Charles Dr, Grass Valley (95945-8418)
PHONE 530 477-5065
John Palmer, *President*
John Yates, *Vice Pres*
Rob Lewis, *Technician*
Tyler Green, *Engineer*
Aaron McMahan, *Sales Staff*
EMP: 18 **EST:** 1980
SQ FT: 11,000
SALES (est): 5.4MM Privately Held
WEB: www.autometrix.com
SIC: 3559 5084 Ammunition & explosives, loading machinery; industrial machinery & equipment

(P-5143)
CHA INDUSTRIES INC
Also Called: Cha Vacuum Technology
250 S Vasco Rd, Livermore (94551-9060)
PHONE 510 683-8554
Stephen Kaplan, *President*
Sharon Krawiecki, *Treasurer*
Paul Metzler, *Vice Pres*
Stephen Dipietro, *Admin Sec*
Charles Hester, *Technician*
▼ **EMP:** 25 **EST:** 1953
SALES (est): 5.8MM Privately Held
WEB: www.chaindustries.com
SIC: 3559 Semiconductor manufacturing machinery

(P-5144)
CLEANPARTSET INC
3530 Bassett St, Santa Clara (95054-2704)
PHONE 408 886-3300
Patrick Bogart, *CEO*
Joreg Hohnloser, *President*
Lisa Peddy, *CFO*
Ken Pelan, *CFO*
Bernard Adams, *Principal*
▲ **EMP:** 161 **EST:** 1979
SQ FT: 35,000
SALES (est): 9.8MM
SALES (corp-wide): 14.1MM Privately Held
WEB: www.cleanpart.com
SIC: 3559 Semiconductor manufacturing machinery
HQ: Cleanpart Usa, Inc.
631 Interntl Pkwy Ste 20
Richardson TX 75081

(P-5145)
CRIST GROUP INC
1324 E Beamer St, Woodland (95776-6003)
PHONE 530 661-0700
Paul Crist, *President*
Michelle Schnepp, *Admin Asst*

PRODUCTS & SERVICES SECTION
3559 - Special Ind Machinery, NEC County (P-5169)

EMP: 20 EST: 2000
SALES (est): 2.5MM **Privately Held**
WEB: www.cristgroup.com
SIC: **3559** 3821 2821 Semiconductor manufacturing machinery; laboratory apparatus & furniture; polytetrafluoroethylene resins (teflon)

(P-5146)
EKSO BIONICS INC (PA)
1414 Hrbour Way S Ste 120, Richmond (94804)
PHONE 510 984-1761
Eythor Bender, *CEO*
Nathan Harding, *COO*
Max Scheder-Biesehin, *CFO*
Thomas A Schreck, *Bd of Directors*
Russ Delonzor, *Vice Pres*
EMP: 73 EST: 2005
SALES (est): 14.5MM **Privately Held**
WEB: www.eksobionics.com
SIC: **3559** Cryogenic machinery, industrial

(P-5147)
ELITE SERVICE EXPERTS INC (PA)
725 Del Paso Rd, Sacramento (95834-1106)
PHONE 916 568-1400
Roy Hill, *President*
Ryan Petree, *Vice Pres*
Keith Holtz, *Maintence Staff*
EMP: 59 EST: 2017
SALES (est): 5MM **Privately Held**
WEB: www.elite.gs
SIC: **3559** 1711 0782 1731 Parking facility equipment & supplies; plumbing contractors; landscape contractors; electrical work

(P-5148)
ENERGY RECOVERY INC (PA)
1717 Doolittle Dr, San Leandro (94577-2231)
PHONE 510 483-7370
Robert Yu Lang Mao, *President*
Hans Peter Michelet, *Ch of Bd*
Josh Ballard, *CFO*
Joshua Ballard, *CFO*
David Barnes, *Officer*
▲ EMP: 214 EST: 1992
SQ FT: 171,000
SALES (est): 118.9MM **Publicly Held**
WEB: www.energyrecovery.com
SIC: **3559** Desalination equipment

(P-5149)
EPOCH INTERNATIONAL ENTPS INC (PA)
46583 Fremont Blvd, Fremont (94538-6409)
PHONE 510 556-1225
Foad Ghalili, *President*
Monireh Meshgin, *CFO*
Ladon Ghalili, *General Mgr*
Betty Su, *Engineer*
Neda Meshkin, *Controller*
▲ EMP: 178 EST: 1993
SQ FT: 5,550
SALES: 38.7MM **Privately Held**
WEB: www.epoch-int.com
SIC: **3559** Electronic component making machinery

(P-5150)
EXPERT SEMICONDUCTOR TECH INC
Also Called: Expertech
10 Victor Sq Ste 100, Scotts Valley (95066-3562)
P.O. Box 66508 (95067-6508)
PHONE 831 439-9300
Jonathan George, *CEO*
Mark Cooper, *Vice Pres*
Ralph Mason, *Sales Staff*
Colin Wilson, *Manager*
EMP: 25 EST: 1992
SQ FT: 40,000
SALES (est): 5.2MM **Privately Held**
WEB: www.exper-tech.com
SIC: **3559** Semiconductor manufacturing machinery

(P-5151)
HANTRONIX INC
10080 Bubb Rd, Cupertino (95014-4132)
PHONE 408 252-1100
Wayne Choi, *CEO*
Latha Ravi, *Purchasing*
Richard Kim, *Sales Staff*
Richard Choi, *Manager*
Max Mun, *Manager*
▲ EMP: 22 EST: 1975
SQ FT: 10,000
SALES (est): 26.3MM **Privately Held**
WEB: www.hantronix.com
SIC: **3559** 5065 3577 Electronic component making machinery; electronic parts & equipment; computer peripheral equipment

(P-5152)
IMG ALTAIR LLC
41970 Christy St, Fremont (94538-3160)
PHONE 650 508-8700
Chris Ferrari, *CEO*
EMP: 56 EST: 2019
SALES (est): 15.5MM **Privately Held**
WEB: www.imgprecision.com
SIC: **3559** 7692 Electronic component making machinery; brazing
PA: Img Companies, Llc
225 Mountain Vista Pkwy
Livermore CA 94551

(P-5153)
IMTEC ACCULINE LLC
Also Called: Intelligent Quartz Solutions
49036 Milmont Dr, Fremont (94538-7301)
PHONE 510 770-1800
Paul V Mendes, *Mng Member*
Emily Xiang, *Senior Buyer*
Lynn Culver, *Manager*
▲ EMP: 24 EST: 1977
SQ FT: 27,000
SALES (est): 5.9MM **Privately Held**
WEB: www.wkfluidhandling.com
SIC: **3559** Semiconductor manufacturing machinery

(P-5154)
INTEVAC INC (PA)
3560 Bassett St, Santa Clara (95054-2704)
PHONE 408 986-9888
Wendell T Blonigan, *President*
David S Dury, *Ch of Bd*
James Moniz, *CFO*
Jay Cho, *Exec VP*
Timothy Justyn, *Exec VP*
▲ EMP: 238 EST: 1990
SQ FT: 169,583
SALES: 97.8MM **Publicly Held**
WEB: www.intevac.com
SIC: **3559** Semiconductor manufacturing machinery

(P-5155)
JASPER DISPLAY CORP
3235 Kifer Rd Ste 150, Santa Clara (95051-0815)
PHONE 408 831-5788
Kenneth Tai, *CEO*
Kaushik Sheth, *General Mgr*
Ed Hudson, *CTO*
Robert Lo, *Software Engr*
Robert Savage, *Software Engr*
EMP: 20 EST: 2009
SALES (est): 3.2MM **Privately Held**
WEB: www.jasperdisplay.com
SIC: **3559** Electronic component making machinery
PA: Investar Holdings Inc.
7f-16, 81, Shui Li Rd.,
Hsinchu City 30059

(P-5156)
KANTHAL THERMAL PROCESS INC
19500 Nugget Blvd, Sonora (95370-9248)
PHONE 209 533-1990
James T Johnson, *CEO*
Eric Anderson, *Design Engr*
Bradley Blackmore, *Design Engr*
Darwin Tadena, *Project Engr*
Jay Husher, *Engineer*
▲ EMP: 75 EST: 1981
SQ FT: 100,000
SALES (est): 17.8MM
SALES (corp-wide): 9.9B **Privately Held**
WEB: www.home.sandvik
SIC: **3559** Semiconductor manufacturing machinery
HQ: Sandvik, Inc.
1483 Dogwood Way
Mebane NC 27302
201 794-5000

(P-5157)
MEEDER EQUIPMENT COMPANY (PA)
Also Called: Ransome Manufacturing
3495 S Maple Ave, Fresno (93725-2494)
P.O. Box 12446 (93777-2446)
PHONE 559 485-0979
Jeffrey D Vertz, *President*
Jeffrey Vertz, *President*
James Moe, *Corp Secy*
Angrest Harris, *Vice Pres*
Shawn Huffman, *Vice Pres*
▲ EMP: 45 EST: 1954
SQ FT: 13,000
SALES (est): 16.9MM **Privately Held**
WEB: www.meeder.com
SIC: **3559** 5084 3714 8711 Refinery, chemical processing & similar machinery; industrial machinery & equipment; propane conversion equipment; propane conversion equipment, motor vehicle; building construction consultant

(P-5158)
MICROBAR INC
45473 Warm Springs Blvd, Fremont (94539-6104)
PHONE 510 659-9770
EMP: 295
SQ FT: 50,000
SALES (est): 29.8MM **Privately Held**
SIC: **3559** Mfg Misc Industry Machinery

(P-5159)
MT SYSTEMS INC
Also Called: Micro Tech Systems
49040 Milmont Dr, Fremont (94538-7301)
PHONE 510 651-5277
Thomas Mike Vukosav, *President*
Kelly Vukosav, *Manager*
▼ EMP: 17 EST: 2000
SQ FT: 16,000
SALES (est): 3MM **Privately Held**
WEB: www.microtechprocess.com
SIC: **3559** Semiconductor manufacturing machinery

(P-5160)
MULTIBEAM CORPORATION
3951 Burton Dr, Santa Clara (95054-1583)
PHONE 408 980-1800
Dr David K Lam, *Ch of Bd*
Lynn Barringer, *President*
Ted Prescop, *Principal*
EMP: 35 EST: 2011
SALES (est): 3.3MM **Privately Held**
WEB: www.multibeamcorp.com
SIC: **3559** Semiconductor manufacturing machinery

(P-5161)
NURO INC
1300 Terra Bella Ave # 100, Mountain View (94043-1850)
PHONE 650 476-2687
David Ferguson, *CEO*
Jiajun Zhu, *Principal*
Thomas Langevin, *Program Mgr*
Chris Beall, *Software Engr*
Nicholas Jiang, *Software Engr*
EMP: 170 EST: 2017
SALES (est): 23MM **Privately Held**
WEB: www.nuro.ai
SIC: **3559** Robots, molding & forming plastics

(P-5162)
P & L SPECIALTIES
1650 Almar Pkwy, Santa Rosa (95403-8253)
PHONE 707 573-3141
Edwin Barr, *President*
Lisa Hyde, *Vice Pres*
Jeff Allen, *Finance*
Joe Pelleriti, *Sales Associate*
Halley Osborne, *Marketing Staff*
◆ EMP: 15 EST: 1984
SQ FT: 15,000
SALES (est): 4.1MM **Privately Held**
WEB: www.pnlspecialties.com
SIC: **3559** 3556 Recycling machinery; beverage machinery

(P-5163)
PACIFIC COAST OPTICS LLC
10604 Industrial Ave # 100, Roseville (95678-6227)
PHONE 916 789-0111
Hai Vu,
EMP: 15 EST: 2016
SALES (est): 646.5K **Privately Held**
SIC: **3559** Optical lens machinery

(P-5164)
PERCEPTIMED INC
365 San Antonio Rd, Mountain View (94040-1213)
P.O. Box 731338, San Jose (95173-1338)
PHONE 650 941-7000
Frank Starn, *CEO*
Alan Jacobs, *President*
Hamutal Anavi Russo, *CFO*
Terry Cater, *VP Bus Dvlpt*
Sheila Wallace, *Admin Sec*
EMP: 27 EST: 2011
SALES (est): 1.9MM **Privately Held**
WEB: www.interlinkai.com
SIC: **3559** Pharmaceutical machinery

(P-5165)
QUALITY MACHINING & DESIGN INC
2857 Aiello Dr, San Jose (95111-2155)
PHONE 408 224-7976
Ryszard Ott, *President*
EMP: 30 EST: 1998
SQ FT: 23,000
SALES (est): 6.3MM **Privately Held**
WEB: www.qualitymd.com
SIC: **3559** 3365 Semiconductor manufacturing machinery; aerospace castings, aluminum

(P-5166)
RCH ASSOCIATES INC
6111 Southfront Rd Ste C, Livermore (94551-5136)
PHONE 510 657-7846
Robert C Hoelsch, *President*
Matthew Furlo, *Engineer*
Isidro Trujillo, *Prdtn Mgr*
EMP: 21 EST: 1989
SALES (est): 2.5MM **Privately Held**
WEB: www.rchassociates.com
SIC: **3559** Semiconductor manufacturing machinery

(P-5167)
RITE TRACK EQUIPMENT SVCS INC
2151 Otoole Ave Ste 40, San Jose (95131-1330)
PHONE 408 432-0131
EMP: 15 **Privately Held**
SIC: **3559** Mfg Misc Industry Machinery
PA: Rite Track Equipment Services, Inc.
8655 Rite Track Way
West Chester OH 45069

(P-5168)
RIVOS INC ✪
2811 Mission College Blvd F, Santa Clara (95054-1884)
PHONE 408 663-6746
Puneet Kumar, *CEO*
EMP: 27 EST: 2021
SALES (est): 1MM **Privately Held**
SIC: **3559** Semiconductor manufacturing machinery

(P-5169)
RUCKER & KOLLS INC (PA)
1064 Yosemite Dr, Milpitas (95035-5410)
PHONE 408 934-9875
Arlen Chou, *President*
Juventino Montez, *Technician*
Hsun Chou, *Director*
EMP: 26 EST: 1976
SQ FT: 6,000

3559 - Special Ind Machinery, NEC County

(P-5170)
SALES (est): 4.6MM Privately Held
WEB: www.ruckerkolls.com
SIC: 3559 3825 Semiconductor manufacturing machinery; instruments to measure electricity

(P-5170)
SANTUR CORPORATION (HQ)
40931 Encyclopedia Cir, Fremont (94538-2436)
PHONE 510 933-4100
Paul Meissner, *President*
George W Laplante, *CFO*
Bardia Pezeshki, *CTO*
Sabeur Siala, *VP Engrg*
Richard Wilmer, *VP Opers*
EMP: 188 EST: 2000
SQ FT: 20,000
SALES (est): 1.1MM Publicly Held
WEB: www.neophotonics.com
SIC: 3559 Electronic component making machinery

(P-5171)
SPT MICROTECHNOLOGIES USA INC (PA)
5750 Hellyer Ave Ste 10, San Jose (95138-1000)
PHONE 408 571-1400
Vivek RAO, *COO*
Seiichi Ogino, *President*
Takayoshi Kikuchi, *Treasurer*
Masayoshi Tanaka, *Admin Sec*
Cody Ray, *Electrical Engi*
EMP: 42 EST: 2015
SQ FT: 28,000
SALES (est): 9.8MM Privately Held
WEB: www.sptmicro.com
SIC: 3559 Semiconductor manufacturing machinery

(P-5172)
TRI-C MANUFACTURING INC
517 Houston St, West Sacramento (95691-2213)
PHONE 916 371-1700
Lilburn Clyde Lamar, *President*
EMP: 20 EST: 1969
SALES (est): 4.1MM
SALES (corp-wide): 5.4MM Privately Held
WEB: www.tri-cshredders.com
SIC: 3559 Rubber working machinery, including tires
PA: Tri-C Machine Corporation
    520 Harbor Blvd
    West Sacramento CA 95691
    916 371-8090

(P-5173)
ULTRATECH INC (HQ)
3050 Zanker Rd, San Jose (95134-2126)
PHONE 408 321-8835
EMP: 115
SQ FT: 100,000
SALES: 194MM Publicly Held
WEB: www.veeco.com
SIC: 3559 Special Industry Machinery, Nec, Nsk

(P-5174)
WEST COAST CRYOGENICS INC
Also Called: West Coast Cryogenics Services
503 W Larch Rd Ste K, Tracy (95304-1670)
PHONE 800 657-0545
Danny Silveira, *President*
Krystal Silveria, *Vice Pres*
Ron Hensley, *Manager*
Anita Hollingsworth, *Manager*
EMP: 21 EST: 2013
SALES (est): 3.6MM Privately Held
WEB: www.westcoastcryo.com
SIC: 3559 Cryogenic machinery, industrial

(P-5175)
WESTCOAST PRECISION INC
2091 Fortune Dr, San Jose (95131-1824)
PHONE 408 943-9998
Sang A Nhin, *CEO*
Helen Nhin, *Principal*
EMP: 55 EST: 2004
SALES (est): 7.6MM Privately Held
WEB: www.westcoastprecision.com
SIC: 3559 Semiconductor manufacturing machinery

3561 Pumps & Pumping Eqpt

(P-5176)
HP WATER SYSTEMS INC
9338 W Whites Bridge Ave, Fresno (93706-9515)
PHONE 559 268-4751
Hollis Priest Jr, *President*
Joyce Priest, *Admin Sec*
EMP: 30 EST: 1995
SQ FT: 3,000
SALES (est): 4.5MM Privately Held
WEB: www.hepelectricinc.com
SIC: 3561 1781 Pumps & pumping equipment; water well drilling

(P-5177)
MESSER LLC
Boc Edwards Systems Chemistry
2041 Mission College Blvd, Santa Clara (95054-1517)
PHONE 408 496-1177
Tom Haren, *Manager*
EMP: 24
SQ FT: 30,000
SALES (corp-wide): 1.3B Privately Held
WEB: www.messeramericas.com
SIC: 3561 Pumps & pumping equipment
HQ: Messer Llc
    200 Smrst Corp Blvd # 7000
    Bridgewater NJ 08807
    800 755-9277

(P-5178)
PROVAC SALES INC
3131 Soquel Dr Ste A, Soquel (95073-2098)
PHONE 831 462-8900
Paul Flood, *CEO*
Leah Smith, *Marketing Staff*
EMP: 23 EST: 1990
SALES (est): 2.6MM Privately Held
WEB: www.provac.com
SIC: 3561 5084 Pumps & pumping equipment; pumps & pumping equipment

(P-5179)
SULZER PUMP SOLUTIONS US INC
1650 Bell Ave Ste 140, Sacramento (95838-2869)
PHONE 916 925-8508
Dale Gretzinger, *Manager*
EMP: 21
SALES (corp-wide): 11MM Privately Held
SIC: 3561 Pumps & pumping equipment
PA: Sulzer Pump Solutions (Us) Inc.
    110 Hoxie Rd
    Lebanon CT 06249
    203 238-2700

(P-5180)
TRILLIUM PUMPS USA INC (DH)
Also Called: Trillium Pump USA
2495 S Golden State Blvd, Fresno (93706-4533)
P.O. Box 164 (93707-0164)
PHONE 559 442-4000
John Kavalam, *President*
Vera Haitayan, *President*
Jim Doxey, *Bd of Directors*
Ken Black, *Officer*
Tom Howard, *Area Mgr*
◆ EMP: 130 EST: 1934
SQ FT: 128,000
SALES (est): 123.4MM Privately Held
WEB: www.firstreserve.com
SIC: 3561 Industrial pumps & parts
HQ: First Reserve Corporation, L.L.C.
    290 Harbor Dr Fl 1
    Stamford CT 06902
    203 661-6601

(P-5181)
WILLOW INNOVATIONS INC
1975 W El Cmino Real Ste, Mountain View (94040)
PHONE 650 472-0300
Laura Chambers, *CEO*
EMP: 175 EST: 2014
SALES (est): 10.9MM Privately Held
SIC: 3561 Pumps & pumping equipment

3563 Air & Gas Compressors

(P-5182)
COMPRESSED A BENZ SYSTEMS INC (DH)
Also Called: Benz Engineering
48434 Milmont Dr, Fremont (94538-7326)
PHONE 510 413-5200
Scott Smith, *President*
EMP: 75 EST: 2001
SALES (est): 14.6MM
SALES (corp-wide): 11.5B Privately Held
WEB: www.ceobenzcas.com
SIC: 3563 Air & gas compressors

(P-5183)
EBARA TECHNOLOGIES INC (DH)
51 Main Ave, Sacramento (95838-2014)
PHONE 916 920-5451
Nasao Asami, *Ch of Bd*
Mitsuhiko Shirakashi, *President*
Tadashi Urata, *President*
Naoki Ando, *CEO*
Masumi Shionuma, *Corp Secy*
▲ EMP: 100
SQ FT: 160,000
SALES (est): 86.7MM Privately Held
WEB: www.ebaratech.com
SIC: 3563 Vacuum pumps, except laboratory

(P-5184)
EDWARDS VACUUM LLC (PA)
2041 Mission College Blvd, Santa Clara (95054-1517)
PHONE 978 658-5410
Geert Follens, *President*
Mike Allison, *Vice Pres*
Steve Goldspring, *Vice Pres*
Gary Harte, *Vice Pres*
Neil Lavender-Jones, *Vice Pres*
EMP: 29 EST: 2015
SALES (est): 1.9MM Privately Held
WEB: www.edwardsvacuum.com
SIC: 3563 Air & gas compressors

(P-5185)
HUNTINGTON MECHANICAL LABS INC
Also Called: Huntington Mechanical Labs
13355 Nevada City Ave, Grass Valley (95945-9091)
PHONE 530 273-9533
Ronald Scott Hooper, *CEO*
Ron Hooper, *President*
Kyle Lind, *Engineer*
Tami Isaacson, *Accounting Mgr*
EMP: 36 EST: 1969
SQ FT: 45,000
SALES (est): 9.8MM Privately Held
WEB: www.huntvac.com
SIC: 3563 Vacuum pumps, except laboratory; vacuum (air extraction) systems, industrial

(P-5186)
MDC VACUUM PRODUCTS LLC (PA)
Also Called: Mdc Precision
30962 Santana St, Hayward (94544-7058)
P.O. Box 398436, San Francisco (94139-8436)
PHONE 510 265-3500
David Dutton, *CEO*
Paul Downey, *CFO*
Timothy Lima, *CFO*
Erick Forbes, *Vice Pres*
Rob Holoboff, *General Mgr*
▲ EMP: 100 EST: 1975
SQ FT: 45,000
SALES (est): 104.1MM Privately Held
WEB: www.mdcprecision.com
SIC: 3563 Vacuum pumps, except laboratory

(P-5187)
NORDSON MARCH INC (HQ)
Also Called: March Plasma Systems
2470 Bates Ave Ste A, Concord (94520-1294)
PHONE 925 827-1240
James Getty, *CEO*
Raymond L Cushing, *CFO*
Denise Getty, *General Mgr*
Jack Newlin, *Software Engr*
Jack Crutchfield, *Technician*
▲ EMP: 24 EST: 1984
SQ FT: 6,000
SALES (est): 16.1MM
SALES (corp-wide): 2.1B Publicly Held
WEB: www.nordson.com
SIC: 3563 Air & gas compressors
PA: Nordson Corporation
    28601 Clemens Rd
    Westlake OH 44145
    440 892-1580

(P-5188)
TAYLOR INVESTMENTS LLC
Also Called: Global Precision Manufacturing
13355 Nevada City Ave, Grass Valley (95945-9091)
PHONE 530 273-4135
Edwin Taylor, *President*
Ronald Hooper, *Vice Pres*
EMP: 34 EST: 2007
SALES (est): 2.9MM Privately Held
SIC: 3563 Air & gas compressors

3564 Blowers & Fans

(P-5189)
AIR FACTORS INC
4771 Arroyo Vis Ste D, Livermore (94551-4847)
PHONE 925 579-0040
Robert Browning, *President*
Melvin Killinen, *Executive*
EMP: 18 EST: 2004
SALES (est): 2.3MM Privately Held
WEB: www.airfactors.com
SIC: 3564 Blowers & fans

(P-5190)
AIRGARD INC (PA)
1755 Mccarthy Blvd, Milpitas (95035-7416)
PHONE 408 573-0701
Dan White, *President*
Dyana Chargin, *CFO*
Martin Johnson, *CFO*
Mark Johnsgard, *Vice Pres*
Kevin McGinnis, *Vice Pres*
▲ EMP: 22 EST: 1988
SALES (est): 6MM Privately Held
WEB: www.airgard.net
SIC: 3564 Air purification equipment

(P-5191)
ENVIROCARE INTERNATIONAL INC
507 Green Island Rd, American Canyon (94503-9649)
PHONE 707 638-6800
John Tate III, *President*
Russell Helfond, *COO*
Lisa Helfond, *Vice Pres*
Brian Higgins, *CTO*
John Fosgate, *Project Engr*
EMP: 22 EST: 1991
SQ FT: 10,000
SALES (est): 7.7MM Privately Held
WEB: www.envirocare.com
SIC: 3564 Air cleaning systems; air purification equipment; dust or fume collecting equipment, industrial; precipitators, electrostatic

(P-5192)
TEMPEST TECHNOLOGY CORPORATION
4708 N Blythe Ave, Fresno (93722-3930)
PHONE 559 277-7577
Leroy B Coffman III, *President*
Joseph Schanda, *COO*
Danette Dunn, *Officer*
Melinda Vines, *General Mgr*
Dannette Dunn, *Controller*
▲ EMP: 25 EST: 1982
SQ FT: 22,000

▲ = Import ▼ = Export
◆ = Import/Export

PRODUCTS & SERVICES SECTION

3566 - Speed Changers, Drives & Gears County (P-5214)

SALES (est): 5.2MM **Privately Held**
WEB: www.tempest.us.com
SIC: **3564** Ventilating fans: industrial or commercial

(P-5193)
WHIPPLE INDUSTRIES INC
3292 N Weber Ave, Fresno (93722-4942)
PHONE..................................559 442-1261
Arthur Whipple, *CEO*
Sherry Anderson, *Admin Sec*
▲ EMP: 15 EST: 1989
SQ FT: 5,258
SALES (est): 3.3MM **Privately Held**
WEB: www.whipplesuperchargers.com
SIC: **3564** 3732 3724 3714 Turbo-blowers, industrial; boat building & repairing; aircraft engines & engine parts; motor vehicle parts & accessories

3565 Packaging Machinery

(P-5194)
ADCO MANUFACTURING
2170 Academy Ave, Sanger (93657-3795)
PHONE..................................559 875-5563
Kate King, *President*
Glen Long, *COO*
Frank Hoffman, *Vice Pres*
◆ EMP: 150 EST: 1957
SQ FT: 75,000
SALES (est): 33.3MM **Privately Held**
WEB: www.adcomfg.com
SIC: **3565** Carton packing machines

(P-5195)
AVP TECHNOLOGY LLC
4140 Business Center Dr, Fremont (94538-6354)
PHONE..................................510 683-0157
Hugh Chau, *CEO*
Son Tran, *Opers Staff*
Lynn Chau,
▲ EMP: 45 EST: 2005
SQ FT: 4,000
SALES (est): 9MM **Privately Held**
WEB: www.avptechnologyllc.com
SIC: **3565** Vacuum packaging machinery

(P-5196)
B & H MANUFACTURING CO INC (PA)
Also Called: B & H Labeling Systems
3461 Roeding Rd, Ceres (95307-9442)
P.O. Box 247 (95307-0247)
PHONE..................................209 537-5785
Roman M Eckols, *CEO*
Calvin E Bright, *Ch of Bd*
Lyn E Bright, *President*
Marjorie Bright, *Corp Secy*
Bob Adamson, *Vice Pres*
◆ EMP: 149 EST: 1969
SQ FT: 65,000
SALES (est): 27.4MM **Privately Held**
WEB: www.bhlabeling.com
SIC: **3565** Labeling machines, industrial

(P-5197)
BLC WC INC
Also Called: Imperial System
2900 Faber St, Union City (94587-1228)
PHONE..................................510 489-5400
John Kramer, *Branch Mgr*
Janet Rozier, *Manager*
Marisol Yarrish, *Accounts Mgr*
EMP: 35
SALES (corp-wide): 21.2MM **Privately Held**
WEB: www.resourcelabel.com
SIC: **3565** 2679 3953 2672 Labeling machines, industrial; labels, paper: made from purchased material; marking devices; coated & laminated paper
PA: Blc Wc, Inc.
13260 Moore St
Cerritos CA 90703
562 926-1452

(P-5198)
BW INTEGRATED SYSTEMS
1949 E Manning Ave, Reedley (93654-9462)
PHONE..................................559 638-8484
EMP: 19 EST: 2018
SALES (est): 4.8MM **Privately Held**
WEB: www.bwflexiblesystems.com
SIC: **3565** Packaging machinery

(P-5199)
KLIPPENSTEIN CORPORATION
2246 E Date Ave, Fresno (93706-5425)
PHONE..................................559 834-4258
Kenneth Ray Klippenstein, *CEO*
Wendy Klippenstein, *Corp Secy*
Alec Weins, *Project Engr*
Jason Reimer, *Master*
▲ EMP: 25 EST: 1979
SALES (est): 9.5MM **Privately Held**
WEB: www.klippenstein.com
SIC: **3565** Packaging machinery

(P-5200)
KODIAK CARTONERS INC
Also Called: Ywd Cartoners
2550 S East Ave Ste 101, Fresno (93706-5121)
PHONE..................................559 266-4844
Casandra Tanney, *President*
EMP: 24 EST: 1997
SALES (est): 8.1MM **Privately Held**
WEB: www.kodiakcartoners.com
SIC: **3565** Packing & wrapping machinery

(P-5201)
PACKAGING AIDS CORPORATION (PA)
Also Called: P A C
25 Tiburon St, San Rafael (94901-4721)
P.O. Box 9144 (94912-9144)
PHONE..................................415 454-4868
Serge Berguig, *President*
Mark Goldman, *COO*
Greg Berguig, *Vice Pres*
Adam Greenlief, *General Mgr*
Greg Quinn, *General Mgr*
▲ EMP: 30 EST: 1963
SQ FT: 27,000
SALES (est): 9MM **Privately Held**
WEB: www.pacmachinery.com
SIC: **3565** 5084 Bag opening, filling & closing machines; industrial machinery & equipment

(P-5202)
SABEL ENGINEERING CORPORATION
1579 N Castle Rd, Sonoma (95476-4864)
P.O. Box 1223 (95476-1223)
PHONE..................................707 938-4771
Herbert Sabel, *President*
June Sabel, *Corp Secy*
Vikki Braldi, *Admin Mgr*
Brad Hanky, *Sales Mgr*
EMP: 27 EST: 1971
SQ FT: 11,400
SALES (est): 1.1MM **Privately Held**
WEB: www.massmanllc.com
SIC: **3565** 5084 Carton packing machines; industrial machinery & equipment

(P-5203)
SARDEE INDUSTRIES INC
2731 E Myrtle St, Stockton (95205-4718)
PHONE..................................209 466-1526
Alan Basset, *Branch Mgr*
EMP: 20
SALES (corp-wide): 13.5MM **Privately Held**
WEB: www.sardee.com
SIC: **3565** 3536 Packaging machinery; hoists, cranes & monorails
PA: Sardee Industries, Inc.
5100 Academy Dr Ste 400
Lisle IL 60532
630 824-4200

(P-5204)
SIMPLEX FILLER INC
Also Called: Simplex Filler Co
640 Airpark Rd Ste A, NAPA (94558-7569)
PHONE..................................707 265-6801
G Donald Murray III, *President*
Edna Murray, *CFO*
Jonathan Fuller, *Plant Mgr*
EMP: 15 EST: 1966
SQ FT: 15,500
SALES (est): 2MM **Privately Held**
WEB: www.simplexfiller.com
SIC: **3565** Packaging machinery

(P-5205)
SPT MICROTECHNOLOGIES USA INC
5750 Hellyer Ave, San Jose (95138-1000)
PHONE..................................408 571-1400
MEI Yin Lin, *President*
▲ EMP: 15 EST: 2008
SALES (est): 340.5K **Privately Held**
WEB: www.sptmicro.com
SIC: **3565** Vacuum packaging machinery

(P-5206)
THIELE TECHNOLOGIES INC
1949 E Manning Ave, Reedley (93654-9462)
PHONE..................................559 638-8484
Ed Suarez, *Manager*
Doug Pool, *Engineer*
Mark Reimer, *Engineer*
Louie Braun, *Sales Staff*
John Deprospero, *Manager*
EMP: 24 **Privately Held**
WEB: www.bwflexiblesystems.com
SIC: **3565** Packaging machinery
HQ: Thiele Technologies, Inc.
315 27th Ave Ne
Minneapolis MN 55418
612 782-1200

(P-5207)
VERICOOL INC
7066 Las Positas Rd Ste C, Livermore (94551-5134)
PHONE..................................925 337-0808
Darrell Jobe, *CEO*
Danny Dubuk, *CFO*
Leslie Errington, *Vice Pres*
Michael Mathias, *VP Bus Dvlpt*
EMP: 41 EST: 2016
SALES (est): 8.7MM **Privately Held**
WEB: www.vericoolpackaging.com
SIC: **3565** Packaging machinery

(P-5208)
VISTECH MFG SOLUTIONS LLC (HQ)
Also Called: Vis Tech
1156 Scenic Dr Ste 120, Modesto (95350-6100)
PHONE..................................209 544-9333
John Jacinto, *Mng Member*
Tim Martin, *Engineer*
Alex Ramirez, *Plant Mgr*
Lane Simpson,
▲ EMP: 75 EST: 2003
SQ FT: 32,500
SALES (est): 92.5MM
SALES (corp-wide): 15.6MM **Privately Held**
WEB: www.vistechmfg.com
SIC: **3565** Packaging machinery
PA: National Minority Supplier Development Council Business Consortium Fund, Inc.
90 Park Ave Fl 37
New York NY 10016
212 944-2430

(P-5209)
W E PLEMONS MCHY SVCS INC
13479 E Industrial Dr, Parlier (93648-9678)
P.O. Box 787 (93648-0787)
PHONE..................................559 646-6630
William Plemons, *President*
John Robinson, *Shareholder*
Edward Baskette, *CFO*
Olivia Kozera, *Vice Pres*
Jeff Winters, *Vice Pres*
▲ EMP: 25 EST: 1986
SQ FT: 30,000
SALES (est): 4.8MM **Privately Held**
WEB: www.weplemons.com
SIC: **3565** 7699 Packaging machinery; industrial machinery & equipment repair

3566 Speed Changers, Drives & Gears

(P-5210)
AMERICAN PRECISION GEAR CO
365 Foster City Blvd, Foster City (94404-1104)
PHONE..................................650 627-8060
Steve W Lefczik, *President*
EMP: 20 EST: 1956
SQ FT: 22,000
SALES (est): 4.6MM **Privately Held**
WEB: www.amgear.com
SIC: **3566** Gears, power transmission, except automotive

(P-5211)
CELESTICA PRCSION MCHINING LTD (PA)
49235 Milmont Dr, Fremont (94538-7349)
PHONE..................................510 742-0500
Darren Myers, *CEO*
Angelo Grestoni, *President*
John S Winter, *Vice Pres*
Marie Delage, *Administration*
Judy Tseng, *Finance*
EMP: 32 EST: 1954
SQ FT: 40,000
SALES (est): 7.9MM **Privately Held**
WEB: www.celestica.com
SIC: **3566** 3599 3469 3544 Gears, power transmission, except automotive; machine shop, jobbing & repair; stamping metal for the trade; special dies & tools

(P-5212)
HARMONIC DRIVE LLC
333 W San Carlos St # 10, San Jose (95110-2726)
PHONE..................................800 921-3332
EMP: 17 **Privately Held**
WEB: www.harmonicdrive.net
SIC: **3566** Speed changers, drives & gears
HQ: Harmonic Drive L.L.C.
42 Dunham Rd
Beverly MA 01915

(P-5213)
HECO INC
Also Called: Pascal Systems
2350 Del Monte St, West Sacramento (95691-3807)
P.O. Box 1388 (95691-1388)
PHONE..................................916 372-5411
Michael H Jacobs, *President*
Allen Rasmussen, *Vice Pres*
Mike Jacobs, *Marketing Staff*
◆ EMP: 30 EST: 1975
SQ FT: 10,000
SALES (est): 4.8MM **Privately Held**
WEB: www.hecogear.com
SIC: **3566** Speed changers (power transmission equipment), except auto

(P-5214)
SEW-EURODRIVE INC
30599 San Antonio St, Hayward (94544-7101)
PHONE..................................510 487-3560
Marvin Leeper, *Branch Mgr*
Tom Ellis, *Regional Mgr*
Katy Helman, *Admin Mgr*
Bernadette Jones, *Admin Mgr*
David Ebert, *Administration*
EMP: 44
SALES (corp-wide): 3.5B **Privately Held**
WEB: www.seweurodrive.com
SIC: **3566** Speed changers, drives & gears
HQ: Sew-Eurodrive, Inc.
1295 Old Spartanburg Hwy
Lyman SC 29365
864 439-7537

3567 Indl Process Furnaces & Ovens

(P-5215)
FLUIDIX INC (PA)
1422 Mammoth Tav Rd C6, Mammoth Lakes (93546)
P.O. Box 1807 (93546-1807)
PHONE..................................760 935-2016
Kent A Rianda, *President*
EMP: 22 **EST:** 1982
SALES (est): 1MM **Privately Held**
WEB: www.fluidixinc.com
SIC: 3567 Heating units & devices, industrial: electric

(P-5216)
MILLER CAT CORPORATION
384 Laurelwood Rd, Santa Clara (95054-2311)
PHONE..................................408 510-5224
Chung Lee, *CEO*
EMP: 24 **EST:** 2011
SALES (est): 6.8MM **Privately Held**
WEB: www.millercat.com
SIC: 3567

(P-5217)
SCHMID THERMAL SYSTEMS INC
200 Westridge Dr, Watsonville (95076-4172)
PHONE..................................831 763-0113
Thomas Stewart, *CEO*
William Daley, *Admin Sec*
Chuck Attema, *Engineer*
Scott Pervorse, *Engineer*
Evelyn Esparza, *Purchasing*
◆ **EMP:** 110 **EST:** 1992
SQ FT: 34,000
SALES (est): 25.7MM
SALES (corp-wide): 355.8K **Privately Held**
WEB: www.sierratherm.com
SIC: 3567 3559 3674 Electrical furnaces, ovens & heating devices, exc. induction; broom making machinery; semiconductors & related devices
HQ: Gebr. Schmid Gmbh
Robert-Bosch-Str. 32-36
Freudenstadt BW 72250
744 153-80

(P-5218)
SMARTTHINGS INC (PA)
665 Clyde Ave, Mountain View (94043-2235)
PHONE..................................757 633-2308
Alex Hawkinson, *CEO*
Andrew Brooks, *COO*
Simon Seungmin Kim, *CFO*
Robert Parker, *Senior VP*
James Stolp, *Senior VP*
EMP: 103 **EST:** 2015
SALES (est): 42.4MM **Privately Held**
WEB: www.smartthings.com
SIC: 5251 3567 3663 Door locks & lock sets; electrical furnaces, ovens & heating devices, exc. induction; cameras, television

(P-5219)
WARMBOARD INC
100 Enterprise Way G300, Scotts Valley (95066-3245)
PHONE..................................831 685-9276
Terry Alberg, *President*
Casey Kunselman, *Project Mgr*
Mark Florez, *Manager*
EMP: 20 **EST:** 2001
SQ FT: 1,250
SALES (est): 7.2MM **Privately Held**
WEB: www.warmboard.com
SIC: 3567 Radiant heating systems, industrial process

3568 Mechanical Power Transmission Eqpt, NEC

(P-5220)
BALL SCREWS & ACTUATORS CO INC (HQ)
Also Called: B S A
48767 Kato Rd, Fremont (94538-7313)
PHONE..................................510 770-5932
Steve Randazzo, *President*
Yuly Jeng, *Controller*
▲ **EMP:** 73 **EST:** 1971
SQ FT: 30,000
SALES (est): 10.4MM
SALES (corp-wide): 22.2B **Publicly Held**
WEB: www.danaher.com
SIC: 3568 3625 3593 3562 Power transmission equipment; actuators, industrial; fluid power cylinders & actuators; ball & roller bearings; bolts, nuts, rivets & washers
PA: Danaher Corporation
2200 Penn Ave Nw Ste 800w
Washington DC 20037
202 828-0850

(P-5221)
FERROTEC (USA) CORPORATION (HQ)
3945 Freedom Cir Ste 450, Santa Clara (95054-1207)
PHONE..................................408 964-7700
Eiji Miyamaga, *CEO*
Nigel Hunton, *President*
Robert Otey, *President*
Richard R Cesati, *CFO*
Akira Yamamura, *Chairman*
◆ **EMP:** 90 **EST:** 1968
SQ FT: 55,000
SALES (est): 121MM **Privately Held**
WEB: www.ferrotec.com
SIC: 3568 3053 Bearings, bushings & blocks; gaskets & sealing devices

(P-5222)
KLA TENCOR
Also Called: Air Bearing Technology
2260 American Ave Ste 1, Hayward (94545-1815)
PHONE..................................510 887-2647
Art Cormier, *Principal*
Roger Peters, *Principal*
Jeff Rhoton, *Principal*
Jing Zhou, *Design Engr*
Deanne Hein, *Technical Staff*
EMP: 27 **EST:** 1989
SALES (est): 4.1MM **Privately Held**
WEB: www.airbearingtechnology.com
SIC: 3568 3545 Bearings, bushings & blocks; machine tool accessories

3569 Indl Machinery & Eqpt, NEC

(P-5223)
ABUNDANT ROBOTICS
3521 Investment Blvd, Hayward (94545-3704)
PHONE..................................510 274-5846
Jordan Caress, *Opers Staff*
EMP: 15 **EST:** 2016
SALES (est): 2.7MM **Privately Held**
SIC: 3569 Robots, assembly line: industrial & commercial

(P-5224)
ARUNDO ANALYTICS INC (PA)
470 Ramona St, Palo Alto (94301-1707)
PHONE..................................713 256-7584
Tor Jacob Ramsoy, *CEO*
Wayne Purboo, *Senior VP*
Cody Falcon, *Vice Pres*
Piers Wells, *Vice Pres*
Martin Lundqvist, *General Mgr*
EMP: 32 **EST:** 2015
SALES (est): 1.1MM **Privately Held**
WEB: www.arundo.com
SIC: 3569 Filters

(P-5225)
BAY AREA INDUS FILTRATION INC
6355 Coliseum Way, Oakland (94621-3719)
P.O. Box 2071, San Leandro (94577-0207)
PHONE..................................510 562-6373
Thomas S Schneider, *President*
Diana E Schneider, *Vice Pres*
EMP: 24 **EST:** 1972
SALES (est): 2.6MM **Privately Held**
WEB: www.bayareafiltration.com
SIC: 3569 5085 3564 2674 Filters, general line: industrial; filters, industrial; blowers & fans; bags: uncoated paper & multiwall

(P-5226)
BEAM ON TECHNOLOGY CORPORATION
317 Brokaw Rd, Santa Clara (95050-4335)
PHONE..................................408 982-0161
Rajoo Venkat, *President*
Herbert Martinez, *CFO*
EMP: 27 **EST:** 1992
SALES (est): 4.6MM **Privately Held**
WEB: www.beamon.com
SIC: 3569 3544 3543 Assembly machines, non-metalworking; special dies, tools, jigs & fixtures; industrial patterns

(P-5227)
COUNTY OF SAN BENITO
25820 Airline Hwy, Paicines (95043-9738)
PHONE..................................831 389-4591
EMP: 54
SALES (corp-wide): 110.2MM **Privately Held**
WEB: www.cosb.us
SIC: 9224 3569 Fire protection; firefighting apparatus
PA: County Of San Benito
481 4th St Fl 2
Hollister CA 95023
831 636-4000

(P-5228)
FJA INDUSTRIES INC
1230 Coleman Ave, Santa Clara (95050-4338)
P.O. Box 242 (95052-0242)
PHONE..................................408 727-0100
Frank J Ardezzone, *CEO*
▲ **EMP:** 17 **EST:** 1991
SQ FT: 10,000
SALES (est): 600K **Privately Held**
WEB: www.fjaind.com
SIC: 3569 Robots, assembly line: industrial & commercial

(P-5229)
GUSMER ENTERPRISES INC
Also Called: Cellulo Co Division
81 M St, Fresno (93721-3215)
PHONE..................................908 301-1811
Fred Mazanec, *Manager*
Roger Pachelbel, *General Mgr*
Orlando Gomez, *Info Tech Dir*
Peter Stenfort, *Marketing Staff*
EMP: 56
SQ FT: 18,644
SALES (corp-wide): 43MM **Privately Held**
WEB: www.gusmerenterprises.com
SIC: 3569 Filters, general line: industrial
PA: Gusmer Enterprises, Inc.
1165 Globe Ave
Mountainside NJ 07092
908 301-1811

(P-5230)
PARKER-HANNIFIN CORPORATION
Racor Division
1640 Cummins Dr, Modesto (95358-6400)
PHONE..................................209 521-7860
Brian Hook, *Branch Mgr*
Leeanne McInerny, *Executive Asst*
Sharon Bobowski, *Purch Mgr*
Dan Walter, *Sales Staff*
EMP: 700
SALES (corp-wide): 13.7B **Publicly Held**
WEB: www.parker.com
SIC: 3569 3561 3714 3564 Filters, general line: industrial; pumps & pumping equipment; motor vehicle parts & accessories; blowers & fans
PA: Parker-Hannifin Corporation
6035 Parkland Blvd
Cleveland OH 44124
216 896-3000

(P-5231)
PUROLATOR LIQUID PROCESS INC
8314 Tiogawoods Dr, Sacramento (95828-5048)
PHONE..................................916 689-2328
Norm Johnson, *President*
EMP: 41 **EST:** 1967
SQ FT: 40,000
SALES (est): 898.2K **Privately Held**
WEB: www.purolator-lp.com
SIC: 3569 Filters

(P-5232)
RESCUE 42 INC
370 Ryan Ave Ste 120, Chico (95973-9530)
P.O. Box 1242 (95927-1242)
PHONE..................................530 891-3473
Tim Oconnell, *President*
Keith Fegley, *Opers Mgr*
Marteen Busby, *Sales Mgr*
EMP: 15 **EST:** 1995
SALES (est): 3.6MM **Privately Held**
WEB: www.rescue42.com
SIC: 3569 Firefighting apparatus & related equipment

(P-5233)
SOUTH SKYLINE FIREFIGHTERS
Also Called: South Skyline Vlntr Fire Rscue
12900 Skyline Blvd, Los Gatos (95033-9401)
PHONE..................................408 354-0025
Greg Redden, *Exec Dir*
EMP: 18 **EST:** 1983
SALES (est): 1.1MM **Privately Held**
WEB: www.southskyline.org
SIC: 3569 Firefighting apparatus & related equipment

(P-5234)
SP3 DIAMOND TECHNOLOGIES INC
1605 Wyatt Dr, Santa Clara (95054-1587)
PHONE..................................877 773-9940
EMP: 15
SALES (est): 2.4MM
SALES (corp-wide): 7.8MM **Privately Held**
SIC: 3569 Mfg General Industrial Machinery
PA: Sp3, Inc.
1605 Wyatt Dr
Santa Clara CA 95054
408 492-0630

(P-5235)
WOMACK INTERNATIONAL INC
3855 Cypress Dr Ste H, Petaluma (94954-5690)
PHONE..................................707 763-1800
Thomas Womack, *President*
Michael Oakes, *COO*
▼ **EMP:** 16 **EST:** 1980
SQ FT: 130,000
SALES (est): 1.4MM **Privately Held**
WEB: www.womack.com
SIC: 3569 Filter elements, fluid, hydraulic line

3571 Electronic Computers

(P-5236)
3PAR INC (HQ)
4209 Technology Dr, Fremont (94538-6339)
PHONE..................................510 445-1046
David C Scott, *President*
Adriel G Lares, *CFO*
Alastair A Short, *Vice Pres*
Ashok Singhal PHD, *CTO*
Kevin Minh Lam, *Technology*

PRODUCTS & SERVICES SECTION

3571 - Electronic Computers County (P-5259)

EMP: 188 **EST:** 1999
SQ FT: 263,000
SALES (est): 108.1MM
SALES (corp-wide): 26.9B **Publicly Held**
WEB: www.hpe.com
SIC: 3571 2542 Electronic computers; partitions & fixtures, except wood
PA: Hewlett Packard Enterprise Company
  11445 Compaq Center W Dr
  Houston TX 77070
  650 687-5817

(P-5237)
ACCURATE ALWAYS INC
127 Ocean Ave, Half Moon Bay (94019-4042)
PHONE 650 728-9428
Yousef Shemisa, *CEO*
Kate Shemisa, *President*
Kate Haley, *Chief Mktg Ofcr*
EMP: 25 **EST:** 2004
SQ FT: 3,500
SALES (est): 1.8MM **Privately Held**
WEB: www.accuratealways.com
SIC: 3571 Electronic computers

(P-5238)
AECHELON TECHNOLOGY INC (PA)
888 Brannan St Ste 210, San Francisco (94103-4930)
PHONE 415 255-0120
Nacho Sanz-Pastor, *CEO*
Chris Blumenthal, *COO*
Bruce Johnson, *COO*
Luis Barcena, *Exec VP*
Jon Boettcher, *CIO*
▲ **EMP:** 106 **EST:** 1998
SQ FT: 40,000
SALES (est): 26.8MM **Privately Held**
WEB: www.aechelon.com
SIC: 3571 Electronic computers

(P-5239)
ALPHA RESEARCH & TECH INC
Also Called: Art
5175 Hillsdale Cir # 100, El Dorado Hills (95762-5776)
PHONE 916 431-9340
Deann Kerr, *President*
Donne W Smith, *Vice Pres*
Donne Smith, *Vice Pres*
Mark Eggers, *Info Tech Mgr*
John Pleines, *Technology*
EMP: 73 **EST:** 1993
SQ FT: 22,000
SALES (est): 16.9MM **Privately Held**
WEB: www.artruggedsystems.com
SIC: 3571 Electronic computers

(P-5240)
AMPRO ADLINK TECHNOLOGY INC
6450 Via Del Oro, San Jose (95119-1208)
PHONE 408 360-0200
Elizabeth Campbell, *CEO*
Mark Peterson, *Ch of Bd*
Joanne M Williams, *President*
George Feng, *COO*
Charles M Frank, *CFO*
▲ **EMP:** 65 **EST:** 1995
SQ FT: 25,000
SALES (est): 29.6MM **Privately Held**
WEB: www.adlinktech.com
SIC: 3571 Electronic computers
PA: Adlink Technology Inc.
  9f, No. 166, Jian 1st Rd,
  New Taipei City TAP 23511

(P-5241)
AMTEK ELECTRONIC INC
Also Called: Manufacturers Import & Export
1150 N 5th St, San Jose (95112-4415)
PHONE 408 971-8787
Kathryn Yuen, *President*
John Yuen, *Vice Pres*
T C Yuen, *Vice Pres*
EMP: 17 **EST:** 1978
SQ FT: 22,000
SALES (est): 1.3MM **Privately Held**
SIC: 3571 3679 3577 Electronic computers; power supplies, all types: static; computer peripheral equipment

(P-5242)
AYAR LABS INC (PA)
3351 Olcott St, Santa Clara (95054-3029)
PHONE 650 963-7200
Charlie Wuischpard, *CEO*
Mark Wade, *President*
Lisa Cummins Dulchinos, *COO*
Roy Meade, *Vice Pres*
Hugo Saleh, *Vice Pres*
EMP: 46 **EST:** 2015
SALES (est): 17.2MM **Privately Held**
WEB: www.ayarlabs.com
SIC: 3571 Electronic computers

(P-5243)
BOLD DATA TECHNOLOGY INC
Also Called: Crown Micro
47540 Seabridge Dr, Fremont (94538-6547)
PHONE 510 490-8296
Eugene Kiang, *President*
Marco Yee, *CFO*
Winston Xia, *Exec VP*
Bonnie Silva, *Administration*
Kevin Chang, *Technology*
▲ **EMP:** 45 **EST:** 1991
SQ FT: 50,000
SALES (est): 13.7MM **Privately Held**
WEB: www.boldata.com
SIC: 3571 3577 3674 Personal computers (microcomputers); computer peripheral equipment; computer logic modules

(P-5244)
COASTAL PVA OPCO LLC
2929 Grandview St, Placerville (95667-4635)
PHONE 530 406-3303
Joseph P Binkley,
Jeff Miller, *CFO*
EMP: 15 **EST:** 2016
SALES (est): 1.4MM **Privately Held**
SIC: 3571 Electronic computers

(P-5245)
COBALT ROBOTICS INC
4019 Transport St Ste De, Palo Alto (94303-4914)
PHONE 650 781-3626
Travis Deyle, *CEO*
Nick Olson, *Sales Executive*
Kriselle Laran, *Marketing Staff*
EMP: 60 **EST:** 2016
SALES (est): 9.2MM **Privately Held**
WEB: www.cobaltrobotics.com
SIC: 3571 Electronic computers

(P-5246)
COLFAX INTERNATIONAL
2805 Bowers Ave Ste 230, Santa Clara (95051-0971)
PHONE 408 730-2275
Gautam Shah, *CEO*
Barbara Karvonen, *COO*
Andrey Vladimirov, *Research*
William Edward, *Engineer*
Achim Wengeler, *Director*
▼ **EMP:** 31 **EST:** 1987
SALES (est): 10.1MM **Privately Held**
WEB: www.colfax-intl.com
SIC: 3571 Electronic computers

(P-5247)
COMPUTER ACCESS TECH CORP
3385 Scott Blvd, Santa Clara (95054-3115)
PHONE 408 727-6600
Fax: 408 727-6622
EMP: 67
SQ FT: 14,000
SALES (est): 6.1MM
SALES (corp-wide): 2.1B **Publicly Held**
SIC: 3571 7371 3577 Mfg Electronic Computers Custom Computer Programing Mfg Computer Peripheral Equipment
HQ: Teledyne Lecroy, Inc.
  700 Chestnut Ridge Rd
  Chestnut Ridge NY 10977
  845 425-2000

(P-5248)
ELECTRONIC COOLING SOLUTIONS
2344 Walsh Ave Ste B, Santa Clara (95051-1327)
PHONE 408 738-8331
EMP: 15
SALES (est): 2.2MM **Privately Held**
WEB: www.ecooling.com
SIC: 3571 Mfg Electronic Computers

(P-5249)
ELMA ELECTRONIC INC (HQ)
44350 S Grimmer Blvd, Fremont (94538-6385)
PHONE 510 656-3400
Fred Ruegg, *CEO*
Shan Morgan, *President*
Peter Brunner, *Exec VP*
Ram Rajan, *Senior VP*
Badri Rajan, *Vice Pres*
▲ **EMP:** 150 **EST:** 1985
SQ FT: 100,000
SALES: 70.5K
SALES (corp-wide): 161MM **Privately Held**
WEB: www.elma.com
SIC: 3571 3575 3577 Electronic computers; computer terminals; computer peripheral equipment
PA: Elma Electronic Ag
  Hofstrasse 93
  Wetzikon ZH 8620
  449 334-111

(P-5250)
HP INC
303 2nd St Ste S500, San Francisco (94107-1373)
PHONE 415 979-3700
Ben Nelson, *General Mgr*
Justin Du, *Software Dev*
Jennifer Kwan, *Marketing Staff*
Srujana Mutyala, *Marketing Staff*
Peter Lanzinni, *Sales Staff*
EMP: 70
SALES (corp-wide): 56.6B **Publicly Held**
WEB: www.hp.com
SIC: 3571 Personal computers (microcomputers)
PA: Hp Inc.
  1501 Page Mill Rd
  Palo Alto CA 94304
  650 857-1501

(P-5251)
HP INC (PA)
1501 Page Mill Rd, Palo Alto (94304-1126)
P.O. Box 10301 (94303-0890)
PHONE 650 857-1501
Enrique Lores, *President*
Charles V Bergh, *Ch of Bd*
Alex Cho, *President*
Didier Deltort, *President*
Tuan Tran, *President*
EMP: 2500 **EST:** 1939
SALES (est): 56.6B **Publicly Held**
WEB: www.hp.com
SIC: 3571 7372 3861 3577 Personal computers (microcomputers); minicomputers; prepackaged software; cameras, still & motion picture (all types); diazotype (whiteprint) reproduction machines & equipment; printers, computer; optical scanning devices; computer storage devices; computer terminals

(P-5252)
HP R&D HOLDING LLC (HQ)
1501 Page Mill Rd, Palo Alto (94304-1126)
PHONE 650 857-1501
EMP: 75 **EST:** 2015
SALES (est): 3.3MM
SALES (corp-wide): 56.6B **Publicly Held**
WEB: www.hp.com
SIC: 3571 Personal computers (microcomputers)
PA: Hp Inc.
  1501 Page Mill Rd
  Palo Alto CA 94304
  650 857-1501

(P-5253)
HPI FEDERAL LLC (HQ)
1501 Page Mill Rd, Palo Alto (94304-1126)
PHONE 650 857-1501
Mark T Prather, *President*
Todd Wallace, *Mfg Staff*
Jordan Traynor, *Sales Staff*
Dave Block, *Senior Mgr*
EMP: 123 **EST:** 2015
SALES (est): 77.4MM
SALES (corp-wide): 56.6B **Publicly Held**
WEB: www.hp.com
SIC: 3571 Personal computers (microcomputers)
PA: Hp Inc.
  1501 Page Mill Rd
  Palo Alto CA 94304
  650 857-1501

(P-5254)
INDIGO AMERICA INC
1501 Page Mill Rd, Palo Alto (94304-1126)
PHONE 650 857-1501
Catherine A Lesjak, *Branch Mgr*
Kevin Schwab, *District Mgr*
Larry Dale, *Technical Staff*
Julie Saurage, *Marketing Staff*
Dan Desrosiers, *Sales Staff*
EMP: 171
SALES (corp-wide): 56.6B **Publicly Held**
SIC: 3571 7372 Personal computers (microcomputers); prepackaged software
HQ: Indigo America Inc
  165 Dascomb Rd Ste 1
  Andover MA 01810

(P-5255)
INNOWI INC
3240 Scott Blvd, Santa Clara (95054-3011)
PHONE 408 609-9404
Zia Hasnain, *CEO*
Asis REO, *President*
Saisel Seed, *CFO*
Saad Ahmed, *Engineer*
Jaykishan Choksi, *Engineer*
◆ **EMP:** 40 **EST:** 2014
SALES (est): 3.3MM **Privately Held**
WEB: www.innowi.com
SIC: 3571 Electronic computers

(P-5256)
INSPUR SYSTEMS INC (HQ)
1501 Mccarthy Blvd, Milpitas (95035-7420)
PHONE 800 697-5893
Ziliang Leon Zheng, *President*
Meng Zhu, *CFO*
Dolly Wu, *General Mgr*
Nat Dai, *Marketing Staff*
Ali Irani, *Manager*
▲ **EMP:** 50 **EST:** 2015
SALES: 617.8MM **Privately Held**
WEB: www.inspursystems.com
SIC: 3571 Electronic computers

(P-5257)
INSPUR SYSTEMS INC
Also Called: Inspur US R&D Technology Ctr
3347 Gateway Blvd, Fremont (94538-6526)
PHONE 510 400-7599
EMP: 26 **Privately Held**
WEB: www.inspursystems.com
SIC: 3571 Electronic computers
HQ: Inspur Systems, Inc.
  1501 Mccarthy Blvd
  Milpitas CA 95035
  800 697-5893

(P-5258)
LENOVO (UNITED STATES) INC
602 Charcot Ave, San Jose (95131-2204)
PHONE 510 813-3331
EMP: 89 **Privately Held**
WEB: www.lenovo.com
SIC: 3571 Electronic computers
HQ: Lenovo (United States) Inc.
  8001 Development Dr
  Morrisville NC 27560
  855 253-6686

(P-5259)
MEDIATEK USA INC (PA)
2840 Junction Ave, San Jose (95134-1922)
PHONE 408 526-1899
Ming-Kai Tsai, *Ch of Bd*
Jyh-Jer Cho, *Vice Chairman*
Ching-Jiang Hsieh, *President*
David Ku, *CFO*
Cheng-Te Chuang, *Senior VP*

3571 - Electronic Computers County (P-5260)

▲ EMP: 199 EST: 1997
SALES (est): 13MM **Privately Held**
WEB: www.mediatek.com
SIC: **3571** 3674 Electronic computers; semiconductors & related devices

(P-5260)
MERCURY SYSTEMS INC
47200 Bayside Pkwy, Fremont (94538-6567)
PHONE...........................510 252-0870
Mark Aslett, *President*
EMP: 65
SALES (corp-wide): 924MM **Publicly Held**
WEB: www.mrcy.com
SIC: **3571** Electronic computers
PA: Mercury Systems, Inc.
50 Minuteman Rd
Andover MA 01810
978 256-1300

(P-5261)
MITAC INFORMATION SYSTEMS CORP
Also Called: Blue Coat
44131 Nobel Dr, Fremont (94538-3173)
PHONE...........................510 668-3507
Karen Soong, *CFO*
EMP: 24 **Privately Held**
WEB: www.mitac.com
SIC: **3571** Electronic computers
HQ: Mitac Information Systems Corp.
39889 Eureka Dr
Newark CA 94560

(P-5262)
MOCKINGBIRD NETWORKS
10040 Bubb Rd, Cupertino (95014-4132)
PHONE...........................408 342-5300
Pong Lim, *CEO*
Ken Murray, *President*
John Chun, *COO*
Steve Y Kim, *Principal*
Alex Finch, *Finance*
EMP: 17 EST: 1983
SQ FT: 8,000
SALES (est): 432.9K **Privately Held**
SIC: **3571** 3672 3577 Electronic computers; printed circuit boards; computer peripheral equipment

(P-5263)
OMNICELL INC (PA)
590 E Middlefield Rd, Mountain View (94043-4008)
PHONE...........................650 251-6100
Randall A Lipps, *Ch of Bd*
Peter J Kuipers, *CFO*
Scott P Seidelmann, *Ch Credit Ofcr*
Gary Petersmeyer, *Bd of Directors*
Dan S Johnston, *Exec VP*
▲ EMP: 273 EST: 1992
SQ FT: 99,900
SALES (est): 892.2MM **Publicly Held**
WEB: www.omnicell.com
SIC: **3571** Electronic computers

(P-5264)
OMNICELL INC
1201 Charleston Rd, Mountain View (94043-1337)
PHONE...........................650 251-6100
Randall Lipps, *President*
Haiko Horn, *Chief Mktg Ofcr*
Raja Kara, *Sr Software Eng*
Ashwini Sharma, *Sr Software Eng*
Ram Kovuru, *Software Engr*
EMP: 23 EST: 2018
SALES (est): 4.9MM **Privately Held**
WEB: www.omnicell.com
SIC: **3571** Electronic computers

(P-5265)
OMNICELL INTERNATIONAL INC (HQ)
590 E Middlefield Rd, Mountain View (94043-4008)
PHONE...........................650 251-6100
Randall A Lipps, *Ch of Bd*
Dan S Johnston, *Exec VP*
Nhat H Ngo, *Exec VP*
Robin G Seim, *Exec VP*
Saranya Sanampudi, *Software Dev*
EMP: 41 EST: 2010

SALES (est): 1.8MM **Publicly Held**
WEB: www.omnicell.com
SIC: **3571** Electronic computers

(P-5266)
ORACLE AMERICA INC (HQ)
Also Called: Sun Microsystems
500 Oracle Pkwy, Redwood City (94065-1677)
PHONE...........................650 506-7000
Jeffrey O Henley, *Chairman*
Colleen Voltz, *Partner*
Jeffrey Henley, *Vice Chairman*
Safra A Catz, *President*
Kevin Melia, *CFO*
▲ EMP: 3500 EST: 1986
SALES (est): 2.7B
SALES (corp-wide): 40.4B **Publicly Held**
WEB: www.oracle.com
SIC: **3571** 7379 7373 7372 Minicomputers; computer related consulting services; systems integration services; operating systems computer software; microprocessors
PA: Oracle Corporation
2300 Oracle Way
Austin TX 78741
737 867-1000

(P-5267)
PALM LATIN AMERICA INC
1501 Page Mill Rd, Palo Alto (94304-1126)
PHONE...........................650 857-1501
Charles V Bergh, *Ch of Bd*
EMP: 43 EST: 2000
SALES (est): 3.9MM
SALES (corp-wide): 56.6B **Publicly Held**
WEB: www.hp.com
SIC: **3571** Personal computers (microputers)
PA: Hp Inc.
1501 Page Mill Rd
Palo Alto CA 94304
650 857-1501

(P-5268)
PARALLAX INCORPORATED
Also Called: Parallax Research
599 Menlo Dr Ste 100, Rocklin (95765-3725)
PHONE...........................916 624-8333
Charles Gracey III, *President*
Charles Gracey II, *Treasurer*
Heller Carolyn, *Info Tech Mgr*
Mary Beth Gracey, *Controller*
Carolyn Montzingo, *Manager*
▲ EMP: 33
SQ FT: 11,000
SALES (est): 8.1MM **Privately Held**
WEB: www.parallax.com
SIC: **3571** 5045 3577 Minicomputers; computers, peripherals & software; computer peripheral equipment

(P-5269)
PIRANHA EMS INC
2681 Zanker Rd, San Jose (95134-2107)
PHONE...........................408 520-3963
Richard Walkup, *CEO*
Roger Malmrose, *CEO*
Kiu Chong, *Materials Dir*
EMP: 45 EST: 2013
SALES (est): 7.2MM **Privately Held**
WEB: www.piranhaems.com
SIC: **3571** Electronic computers

(P-5270)
QANTEL TECHNOLOGIES INC
9812 Vasquez Cir, Loomis (95650-8535)
PHONE...........................510 731-2080
Michael Galvin, *President*
Jerry Devries, *Vice Pres*
Shirley Fernandez, *Prgrmr*
Barrie Moore, *Prgrmr*
Joan Morgan, *Programmer Anys*
EMP: 19 EST: 1996
SALES (est): 2.9MM **Privately Held**
WEB: www.qantel.com
SIC: **3571** 7371 Electronic computers; computer software development

(P-5271)
SHASTA ELECTRONIC MFG SVCS INC
Also Called: Shasta Ems
525 E Brokaw Rd, San Jose (95112-1004)
PHONE...........................408 436-1267
Vinh Nguyen, *President*
Rang Nguyen, *Vice Pres*
EMP: 18 EST: 2006
SQ FT: 11,000
SALES (est): 2.5MM **Privately Held**
WEB: www.shastaems.com
SIC: **3571** Electronic computers

(P-5272)
SIGMA MFG & LOGISTICS LLC
10050 Fthlls Blvd Ste 100, Roseville (95747)
PHONE...........................916 781-3052
Ushadevi Chenna,
Tanuja Chenna,
Venkatasubbanna Chenna,
EMP: 20 EST: 2002
SQ FT: 35,000
SALES (est): 4.3MM **Privately Held**
WEB: www.sigmamfg.com
SIC: **3571** Computers, digital, analog or hybrid

(P-5273)
SUPER MICRO COMPUTER INC (PA)
Also Called: Supermicro
980 Rock Ave, San Jose (95131-1615)
PHONE...........................408 503-8000
Charles Liang, *Ch of Bd*
David Weigand, *CFO*
Don Clegg, *Senior VP*
George KAO, *Senior VP*
Sara Liu, *Senior VP*
▲ EMP: 2367 EST: 1993
SQ FT: 1,097,000
SALES: 3.5B **Publicly Held**
WEB: www.supermicro.com.tw
SIC: **3571** 3572 7372 Electronic computers; computer storage devices; prepackaged software

(P-5274)
TALL TREE INSURANCE COMPANY
1501 Page Mill Rd, Palo Alto (94304-1126)
PHONE...........................650 857-1501
William Hewlet, *CEO*
EMP: 24 EST: 1939
SALES (est): 3.2MM
SALES (corp-wide): 56.6B **Publicly Held**
WEB: www.talltreehealth.com
SIC: **3571** Electronic computers
PA: Hp Inc.
1501 Page Mill Rd
Palo Alto CA 94304
650 857-1501

(P-5275)
TANGENT COMPUTER INC (PA)
Also Called: Tanget Fastnet
191 Airport Blvd, Burlingame (94010-2006)
PHONE...........................888 683-2881
Douglas James Monsour, *CEO*
Ron Perkes, *Chief Mktg Ofcr*
Maher Zabaneh, *Vice Pres*
Chris Lee, *Engineer*
Lannie Tran, *Accounting Mgr*
EMP: 97 EST: 1989
SQ FT: 80,000
SALES (est): 13.5MM **Privately Held**
WEB: www.tangent.com
SIC: **5734** 3571 Computer & software stores; personal computers (microcomputers)

(P-5276)
TARACOM CORPORATION
1220 Memorex Dr, Santa Clara (95050-2845)
PHONE...........................408 691-6655
Farhad Haghighi, *CEO*
EMP: 15 EST: 2006
SALES (est): 2.5MM **Privately Held**
WEB: www.taracom.net
SIC: **3571** Electronic computers

(P-5277)
THOUSANDSHORES INC
37707 Cherry St, Newark (94560-4347)
PHONE...........................510 477-0249
Ding He, *CEO*
Zhi Liu, *President*
Sam Liu, *Vice Pres*
◆ EMP: 15 EST: 2010
SALES (est): 4.3MM **Privately Held**
WEB: www.thousandshores.com
SIC: **3571** 5999 Electronic computers; mobile telephones & equipment

(P-5278)
TRANSLATTICE INC (PA)
3398 Londonderry Dr, Santa Clara (95050-6619)
PHONE...........................408 749-8478
Frank Huerta, *CEO*
Michael Lyle, *President*
EMP: 20 EST: 2007
SQ FT: 4,197
SALES (est): 2.4MM **Privately Held**
WEB: www.translattice.com
SIC: **3571** Electronic computers

(P-5279)
VECTOR DATA LLC
801 Addison St, Berkeley (94710-2053)
PHONE...........................408 933-3266
Timothy Naple, *Mng Member*
Greg Orciuch, *Info Tech Mgr*
Bryan Foster, *Manager*
EMP: 76 EST: 2006
SALES (est): 10.1MM **Privately Held**
WEB: www.vectordata.com
SIC: **3571** Electronic computers

3572 Computer Storage Devices

(P-5280)
2CRSI CORPORATION
894 Faulstich Ct Ste B, San Jose (95112-1361)
PHONE...........................408 598-3176
Alain Wilmouth, *CEO*
Wally Liaw, *President*
EMP: 19 EST: 2018
SALES (est): 9.8MM
SALES (corp-wide): 205.8K **Privately Held**
WEB: www.2crsi.com
SIC: **3572** Computer storage devices
HQ: 2crsi
32 Rue Jacobi Netter
Strasbourg 67200
390 204-310

(P-5281)
AMPEX DATA SYSTEMS CORPORATION (HQ)
26460 Corporate Ave, Hayward (94545-3914)
PHONE...........................650 367-2011
Gary Thom, *President*
Krystl Donaldson, *Administration*
Hudson Kevin, *Engineer*
Richard Stone, *Engineer*
David Trytko, *Engineer*
▲ EMP: 58 EST: 1990
SQ FT: 15,661
SALES (est): 29.9MM
SALES (corp-wide): 35.8MM **Privately Held**
WEB: www.ampex.com
SIC: **3572** Computer storage devices
PA: Delta Information Systems, Inc.
747 Dresher Rd Ste 100
Horsham PA 19044
215 657-5270

(P-5282)
APPRO INTERNATIONAL INC (DH)
Also Called: Cray Cluster Solutions
220 Devcon Dr, San Jose (95112-4210)
PHONE...........................408 941-8100
Daniel Kim, *President*
James Yi, *CFO*
Steve Lyness, *Vice Pres*
Giri Chukkapalli, *CTO*
John Lee, *Engineer*

PRODUCTS & SERVICES SECTION

3572 - Computer Storage Devices County (P-5305)

▲ EMP: 75 EST: 1991
SQ FT: 40,000
SALES (est): 19.5MM
SALES (corp-wide): 26.9B Publicly Held
SIC: 3572 3577 3571 Computer storage devices; computer peripheral equipment; electronic computers
HQ: Cray Inc.
901 5th Ave Ste 1000
Seattle WA 98164
206 701-2000

(P-5283)
BITMICRO NETWORKS INC (PA)
47929 Fremont Blvd, Fremont (94538-6508)
PHONE.....................510 743-3124
EMP: 16
SQ FT: 14,000
SALES (est): 10MM Privately Held
WEB: www.bitmicro.com
SIC: 3572 Mfg Computer Storage Devices

(P-5284)
CORAID INC (PA)
255 Shoreline Dr Ste 650, Redwood City (94065-1431)
PHONE.....................650 517-9300
EMP: 91
SALES (est): 21.6MM Privately Held
WEB: www.coraid.com
SIC: 3572 Mfg Computer Storage Devices

(P-5285)
FORTASA MEMORY SYSTEMS INC
1670 S Amphlett Blvd, San Mateo (94402-2510)
PHONE.....................888 367-8588
Tatyana Nakhimovsky, *President*
Robert Noyes, *CFO*
Samuel Nakhimovsky, *General Mgr*
Toni Briski, *Accounting Mgr*
▼ EMP: 21 EST: 2009
SQ FT: 1,500
SALES (est): 9.6MM Privately Held
WEB: www.fortasa.com
SIC: 3572 Computer storage devices

(P-5286)
HEADWAY TECHNOLOGIES INC
463 S Milpitas Blvd, Milpitas (95035-5438)
PHONE.....................408 935-1020
Nabil Arnaout, *Branch Mgr*
David Wagner, *Vice Pres*
Linda Silva, *Administration*
Kowang Liu, *Technical Staff*
Jeff Hagen, *Engineer*
EMP: 588 Privately Held
WEB: www.headway.com
SIC: 3572 Computer disk & drum drives & components
HQ: Headway Technologies, Inc.
682 S Hillview Dr
Milpitas CA 95035
408 934-5300

(P-5287)
HEADWAY TECHNOLOGIES INC (HQ)
682 S Hillview Dr, Milpitas (95035-5457)
PHONE.....................408 934-5300
Mao-Min Chen, *President*
Thomas Surran, *CFO*
Gary Pester, *Vice Pres*
Brenda Baltazar, *Administration*
Lanette Sarte, *Administration*
▲ EMP: 200 EST: 1994
SALES (est): 596.7MM Privately Held
WEB: www.headway.com
SIC: 3572 Magnetic storage devices, computer

(P-5288)
HEADWAY TECHNOLOGIES INC
497 S Hillview Dr, Milpitas (95035-7702)
PHONE.....................408 934-5300
Yoshiro Nakagawa, *VP Opers*
Po-Kang Wang, *Senior VP*
Robert Yang, *Technical Staff*
Mike Couch, *Engineer*
John Revelez, *Supervisor*
EMP: 588 Privately Held
WEB: www.headway.com
SIC: 3572 Computer storage devices

HQ: Headway Technologies, Inc.
682 S Hillview Dr
Milpitas CA 95035
408 934-5300

(P-5289)
HEADWAY TECHNOLOGIES INC
550 S Hillview Dr, Milpitas (95035-5445)
PHONE.....................408 934-3262
John Racz, *Regional Mgr*
Sue Rowatt, *Human Res Mgr*
EMP: 588 Privately Held
WEB: www.headway.com
SIC: 3572 Magnetic storage devices, computer
HQ: Headway Technologies, Inc.
682 S Hillview Dr
Milpitas CA 95035
408 934-5300

(P-5290)
HGST INC
Also Called: Skyera
5601 Great Oaks Pkwy, San Jose (95119-1003)
PHONE.....................408 954-8100
Dominic Bayani, *Technician*
Sergio Singh, *Project Mgr*
Donald Pence, *Technology*
Gautam Chawra, *Technical Staff*
Kenny Melendrez, *Technical Staff*
EMP: 50
SALES (corp-wide): 16.9B Publicly Held
WEB: www.westerndigital.com
SIC: 3572 Computer storage devices
HQ: Hgst, Inc.
5601 Great Oaks Pkwy
San Jose CA 95119
408 717-6000

(P-5291)
HGST INC (DH)
5601 Great Oaks Pkwy, San Jose (95119-1003)
PHONE.....................408 717-6000
John Coyne, *CEO*
Florian Risso, *Partner*
Stephen Milligan, *President*
Douglas A Gross, *COO*
Michael A Murray, *CFO*
▲ EMP: 1942 EST: 2002
SALES (est): 596.7MM
SALES (corp-wide): 16.9B Publicly Held
WEB: www.westerndigital.com
SIC: 3572 Computer storage devices

(P-5292)
HIGHPOINT TECHNOLOGIES INC
41650 Christy St, Fremont (94538-3114)
PHONE.....................408 942-5800
Michael Whang, *President*
Yuan-Lang Chang, *CFO*
From Yu, *Engineer*
May Hwang, *Sales Dir*
Corey Baker, *Marketing Mgr*
◆ EMP: 22 EST: 1995
SQ FT: 14,500
SALES (est): 3MM Privately Held
WEB: www.highpoint-tech.com
SIC: 3572 8731 Computer disk & drum drives & components; computer (hardware) development

(P-5293)
HITACHI VANTARA CORPORATION (DH)
2535 Augustine Dr, Santa Clara (95054-3003)
PHONE.....................408 970-1000
Jack Domme, *President*
Minoru Kosuge, *Ch of Bd*
Brian Householder, *President*
Catriona Fallon, *CFO*
Rick Martig, *CFO*
▲ EMP: 450 EST: 1979
SQ FT: 250,000
SALES (est): 1.7B Privately Held
WEB: www.hitachivantara.com
SIC: 3572 Computer storage devices
HQ: Hitachi Vantara Corporation
2535 Augustine Dr
Santa Clara CA 95054
408 970-1000

(P-5294)
INEDA SYSTEMS INC (PA)
5201 Great America Pkwy # 532, Santa Clara (95054-1122)
PHONE.....................408 400-7375
Gude Dasaradha, *CEO*
Balaji Kanigicherla, *Vice Pres*
Ramkumar Subramanian, *Vice Pres*
EMP: 37 EST: 2011
SALES (est): 1.1MM Privately Held
SIC: 5734 3572 Computer peripheral equipment; computer disk & drum drives & components

(P-5295)
INTELLIGENT STORAGE SOLUTION
2073 Otoole Ave, San Jose (95131-1303)
PHONE.....................408 428-0105
Dat Do, *President*
Ian Wallace, *Engineer*
Lan Vuong, *Sales Staff*
Mark Wallace, *Rector*
▲ EMP: 33 EST: 2004
SALES (est): 1MM Privately Held
WEB: www.iss-phil.com
SIC: 3572 Computer disk & drum drives & components

(P-5296)
IOSAFE INC
10600 Industrial Ave # 120, Roseville (95678-6210)
PHONE.....................888 984-6723
Robb Moore, *CEO*
Christine Davis, *CFO*
Andrea Moore, *Treasurer*
John Boston, *Technical Staff*
Matt Eargis, *VP Sales*
▲ EMP: 18 EST: 2005
SQ FT: 20,000
SALES (est): 4.3MM Privately Held
WEB: www.iosafe.com
SIC: 3572 Computer storage devices

(P-5297)
JTS CORPORATION
Also Called: Atari Corporation
166 Baypointe Pkwy, San Jose (95134-1621)
PHONE.....................408 468-1800
David T Mitchell, *President*
Sirjang Lal Tandon, *Ch of Bd*
Kenneth D Wing, *COO*
Joseph A Prezioso, *CFO*
Steven L Kaczeus, *Officer*
EMP: 6000 EST: 1994
SQ FT: 52,000
SALES (est): 67.8MM Privately Held
SIC: 3572 Disk drives, computer

(P-5298)
MASS MICROSYSTEMS INC
810 W Maude Ave, Sunnyvale (94085-2910)
PHONE.....................408 522-1200
Bill R Finley, *President*
▼ EMP: 15 EST: 1987
SQ FT: 36,662
SALES (est): 227K Privately Held
SIC: 3572 Computer auxiliary storage units

(P-5299)
MAXTOR CORPORATION (DH)
4575 Scotts Valley Dr, Scotts Valley (95066-4517)
PHONE.....................831 438-6550
▲ EMP: 100
SALES (est): 418.7MM Privately Held
WEB: www.maxtor.com
SIC: 3572 Mfg Computer Storage Devices
HQ: Seagate Technology (Us) Holdings, Inc
920 Disc Dr
Scotts Valley CA 95014
831 438-6550

(P-5300)
MICRON CONSUMER PDTS GROUP INC (HQ)
540 Alder Dr, Fremont (94538)
PHONE.....................669 226-3000
Gerald Pittman, *President*
Vincent Nguyen, *Vice Pres*
Fred Jensen, *Sr Software Eng*
Luong Phu, *Technical Staff*

Gang Zhao, *Engineer*
▲ EMP: 75 EST: 2000
SALES (est): 2.4MM
SALES (corp-wide): 27.7B Publicly Held
WEB: www.micron.com
SIC: 3572 Computer storage devices
PA: Micron Technology, Inc.
8000 S Federal Way
Boise ID 83716
208 368-4000

(P-5301)
MITAC INFORMATION SYSTEMS CORP (DH)
39889 Eureka Dr, Newark (94560-4811)
PHONE.....................510 284-3000
Charlotte Chou, *President*
Billy Ho, *President*
Karen Soong, *CFO*
Matthew Miau, *Chairman*
◆ EMP: 103 EST: 2010
SQ FT: 240,000
SALES (est): 111.7MM Publicly Held
WEB: www.mitac.com
SIC: 3572 Computer storage devices

(P-5302)
NETAPP INC (PA)
3060 Olsen Dr, San Jose (95128-2155)
PHONE.....................408 822-6000
George Kurian, *CEO*
T Michael Nevens, *Ch of Bd*
Cesar Cernuda, *President*
Michael J Berry, *CFO*
Brad Anderson, *Exec VP*
▲ EMP: 1600 EST: 1992
SQ FT: 300,000
SALES: 5.7B Publicly Held
WEB: www.netapp.com
SIC: 3572 7373 7372 Computer storage devices; computer integrated systems design; systems software development services; computer system selling services; prepackaged software

(P-5303)
NEXSAN TECHNOLOGIES INC (DH)
1289 Anvilwood Ave, Sunnyvale (94089-2204)
PHONE.....................408 724-9809
Philip Black, *CEO*
Gene Spies, *Officer*
George Symons, *Officer*
James R Molenda, *Admin Sec*
Keith Desilvey, *Sales Staff*
▲ EMP: 40 EST: 2001
SALES (est): 26.1MM
SALES (corp-wide): 41MM Privately Held
WEB: www.nexsan.com
SIC: 3572 Computer storage devices
HQ: Nexsan Corporation
325 E Hillcrest Dr # 150
Thousand Oaks CA 91360
408 724-9809

(P-5304)
NFLASH INC (PA)
3080 Kenneth St, Santa Clara (95054-3415)
PHONE.....................408 350-0341
Nathan Litinski, *CEO*
EMP: 34 EST: 2016
SALES (est): 879.6K Privately Held
SIC: 3572 Magnetic storage devices, computer

(P-5305)
NIMBLE STORAGE INC (HQ)
900 N Mccarthy Blvd, Milpitas (95035-5128)
PHONE.....................408 432-9600
Suresh Vasudevan, *CEO*
Anup Singh, *CFO*
Janet Matsuda, *Chief Mktg Ofcr*
Lloyd Santy, *Vice Pres*
Nate Bloomer, *Executive*
▲ EMP: 1299 EST: 2007
SALES: 402.6MM
SALES (corp-wide): 26.9B Publicly Held
WEB: www.hpe.com
SIC: 3572 Computer storage devices

3572 - Computer Storage Devices County (P-5306)

PA: Hewlett Packard Enterprise Company
11445 Compaq Center W Dr
Houston TX 77070
650 687-5817

(P-5306)
NWE TECHNOLOGY INC
1688 Richard Ave, Santa Clara (95050-2844)
PHONE.................................408 919-6100
S C Huang, *President*
▲ **EMP:** 150 **EST:** 1998
SQ FT: 63,000
SALES (est): 10.7MM **Privately Held**
WEB: www.nwetechnology.com
SIC: 3572 Computer disk & drum drives & components

(P-5307)
ORYX ADVANCED MATERIALS INC (PA)
46458 Fremont Blvd, Fremont (94538-6469)
PHONE.................................510 249-1158
Victor Tan, *CEO*
Kwei-San Teng, *Vice Pres*
Diana Lai, *Office Admin*
Michelle Phan, *Accountant*
Tan Geok San, *Director*
▲ **EMP:** 33 **EST:** 1976
SQ FT: 7,000
SALES (est): 5.4MM **Privately Held**
WEB: www.oryxadv.com
SIC: 3572 Disk drives, computer

(P-5308)
OVERLAND STORAGE INC (HQ)
Also Called: Overland-Tandberg
2633 Camino Ramon Ste 325, San Ramon (94583-9149)
PHONE.................................408 283-4700
Eric L Kelly, *CEO*
Kurt L Kalbfleisch, *CFO*
Carol Dixon, *Vice Pres*
Larry Hansen, *Vice Pres*
David Ochser, *Vice Pres*
◆ **EMP:** 458 **EST:** 1980
SALES (est): 108.5MM
SALES (corp-wide): 1.1MM **Privately Held**
WEB: www.overlandtandberg.com
SIC: 3572 7372 Computer storage devices; prepackaged software
PA: Sphere 3d Inc
240 Matheson Blvd E
Mississauga ON L4Z 1
416 749-5999

(P-5309)
PHILIPS LT-ON DGTAL SLTONS USA (DH)
Also Called: P L D S
720 S Hillview Dr, Milpitas (95035-5455)
PHONE.................................510 687-1800
Charlie Pseng, *President*
Armando Abella, *CFO*
Walker Su, *Admin Sec*
June Ly, *Administration*
▼ **EMP:** 50 **EST:** 2006
SQ FT: 17,088
SALES (est): 16.3MM
SALES (corp-wide): 133.6MM **Privately Held**
WEB: www.pldsnet.com
SIC: 3572 Disk drives, computer

(P-5310)
QUANTUM CORPORATION (PA)
224 Airport Pkwy Ste 550, San Jose (95110-1097)
PHONE.................................408 944-4000
James J Lerner, *Ch of Bd*
J Michael Dodson, *CFO*
Brian Cabrera, *Ch Credit Ofcr*
Rick Valentine, *Ch Credit Ofcr*
Regan Macpherson,
▲ **EMP:** 314 **EST:** 1980
SALES (est): 402.9MM **Publicly Held**
WEB: www.quantum.com
SIC: 3572 Tape storage units, computer

(P-5311)
QUANTUM GOVERNMENT INC
224 Airport Pkwy Ste 550, San Jose (95110-1097)
PHONE.................................408 944-4000
Don Maruca, *President*
Lewis Moorehead, *Principal*
EMP: 21 **EST:** 2020
SALES (est): 1.3MM **Privately Held**
WEB: www.quantum.com
SIC: 3572 Computer storage devices

(P-5312)
RANK TECHNOLOGY CORP
1190 Miraloma Way Ste Q, Sunnyvale (94085-4607)
PHONE.................................408 737-1488
Fred Barez, *President*
Henry Barez, *Vice Pres*
EMP: 22 **EST:** 1987
SQ FT: 6,000
SALES (est): 1.3MM **Privately Held**
SIC: 3572 Computer storage devices

(P-5313)
RASILIENT SYSTEMS INC (PA)
3281 Kifer Rd, Santa Clara (95051-0826)
PHONE.................................408 730-2568
Sean Chang, *CEO*
Mohammad Rydhan, *Technical Staff*
Tracy Nguyen, *Controller*
Brian Mahamongkol, *Opers Staff*
Brian Johnpaoli, *Sales Staff*
◆ **EMP:** 49 **EST:** 2001
SALES (est): 10.5MM **Privately Held**
WEB: www.rasilient.com
SIC: 3572 5045 Computer storage devices; disk drives

(P-5314)
SALE 121 CORP (PA)
1467 68th Ave, Sacramento (95822-4728)
P.O. Box 190969, Brooklyn NY (11219-0969)
PHONE.................................888 233-7667
Mohammad Naz, *Principal*
EMP: 61 **EST:** 2014
SQ FT: 3,500
SALES (est): 3.5MM **Privately Held**
SIC: 3572 8748 7373 Disk drives, computer; systems engineering consultant, ex. computer or professional; systems software development services

(P-5315)
SANDISK LLC (DH)
Also Called: Western Digital
951 Sandisk Dr, Milpitas (95035-7933)
PHONE.................................408 801-1000
Sanjay Mehrotra, *President*
Michael Marks, *Ch of Bd*
Judy Bruner, *CFO*
John Joy, *Treasurer*
Sumit Sadana, *Exec VP*
▲ **EMP:** 141 **EST:** 1988
SQ FT: 589,000
SALES (est): 1.7B
SALES (corp-wide): 16.9B **Publicly Held**
WEB: www.shop.westerndigital.com
SIC: 3572 Computer storage devices

(P-5316)
SAP AG
3410 Hillview Ave, Palo Alto (94304-1395)
PHONE.................................650 849-4000
EMP: 167
SALES (est): 17.1MM **Privately Held**
WEB: www.sap.com
SIC: 3572 Computer Storage Devices

(P-5317)
SCALITY INC
149 New Montgomery St # 4, San Francisco (94105-3740)
PHONE.................................650 356-8500
Jerome Lecat, *CEO*
Erwan Menard, *COO*
Philippe Mechanick, *CFO*
Paul Turner, *Chief Mktg Ofcr*
David Harvey, *Vice Pres*
EMP: 45 **EST:** 2010
SALES (est): 11.1MM
SALES (corp-wide): 21.9MM **Privately Held**
WEB: www.scality.com
SIC: 3572 Computer storage devices
PA: Scality
11 Rue Tronchet
Paris 75008
142 948-470

(P-5318)
SEAGATE SYSTEMS (US) INC (DH)
Also Called: Xyratex
46831 Lakeview Blvd, Fremont (94538-6552)
PHONE.................................510 687-5200
Steve J Luczo, *Principal*
Ernest Sampias, *CEO*
Richard Pearce, *CFO*
Ken Claffey, *Senior VP*
Todd Gresham, *Senior VP*
▲ **EMP:** 70 **EST:** 1986
SALES (est): 46.6MM **Privately Held**
WEB: www.seagate.com
SIC: 3572 Disk drives, computer
HQ: Seagate Technology Llc
47488 Kato Rd
Fremont CA 94538
800 732-4283

(P-5319)
SEAGATE TECHNOLOGY LLC (DH)
47488 Kato Rd, Fremont (94538-7319)
P.O. Box 4030, Cupertino (95015-4030)
PHONE.................................800 732-4283
Stephen J Luczo, *President*
Terry Cunningham, *President*
Robert Whitmore, *COO*
Patrick O Malley, *CFO*
Patrick J O'Malley, *CFO*
▲ **EMP:** 3000 **EST:** 2000
SQ FT: 383,000
SALES (est): 1.4B **Privately Held**
WEB: www.seagate.com
SIC: 3572 Computer storage devices
HQ: Seagate Technology (Us) Holdings, Inc
10200 S De Anza Blvd
Cupertino CA 95014
831 438-6550

(P-5320)
SEAGATE US LLC
10200 S De Anza Blvd, Cupertino (95014-3029)
PHONE.................................408 658-1000
Stephen J Luczo, *CEO*
EMP: 45 **EST:** 2000
SALES (est): 6.3MM **Privately Held**
WEB: www.seagate.com
SIC: 3572 Magnetic storage devices, computer
PA: Seagate Technology Unlimited Company
38/39 Fitzwilliam Square West
Dublin D02 N

(P-5321)
SMART STORAGE SYSTEMS INC (DH)
39672 Eureka Dr, Newark (94560-4805)
PHONE.................................510 623-1231
Iain Mackenzie, *CEO*
Alan Marten, *President*
Ann T Nguyen, *CFO*
▲ **EMP:** 29 **EST:** 1985
SALES (est): 4.6MM
SALES (corp-wide): 16.9B **Publicly Held**
WEB: www.shop.westerndigital.com
SIC: 3572 5045 Computer storage devices; computers, peripherals & software
HQ: Sandisk Llc
951 Sandisk Dr
Milpitas CA 95035
408 801-1000

(P-5322)
SOLID DATA SYSTEMS INC
3542 Bassett St, Santa Clara (95054-2704)
P.O. Box 320095, Los Gatos (95032-0101)
PHONE.................................408 845-5700
EMP: 15
SQ FT: 3,500
SALES (est): 2.4MM **Privately Held**
WEB: www.soliddata.com
SIC: 3572 Mfg Computer Storage Devices

(P-5323)
SYNAPSENSE CORPORATION
340 Palladio Pkwy Ste 530, Folsom (95630-8833)
PHONE.................................916 294-0110
Bart Tichelman, *President*
Dr Raju Pandey, *CTO*
Anthony Brandshaw, *Warehouse Mgr*
EMP: 35 **EST:** 2006
SALES (est): 7.3MM
SALES (corp-wide): 932MM **Privately Held**
WEB: www.panduit.com
SIC: 3572 Computer storage devices
PA: Panduit Corp.
18900 Panduit Dr
Tinley Park IL 60487
708 532-1800

(P-5324)
VICOM SYSTEMS INC
2336 Walsh Ave Ste H, Santa Clara (95051-1313)
P.O. Box 6375 (95056-6375)
PHONE.................................408 588-1286
Samuel Tam, *President*
Daryl Adams, *Office Mgr*
EMP: 31 **EST:** 1981
SQ FT: 13,000
SALES (est): 3.3MM **Privately Held**
WEB: www.vicom.com
SIC: 3572 7371 Computer storage devices; custom computer programming services

(P-5325)
WD MEDIA LLC
1710 Automation Pkwy, San Jose (95131-1873)
PHONE.................................408 576-2000
Timothy D Harris, *CEO*
Kathleen A Bayless, *CFO*
Mr Jan Schwartz, *Treasurer*
Richard A Kashnow, *Bd of Directors*
Peter S Norris, *Exec VP*
▲ **EMP:** 426 **EST:** 1983
SQ FT: 188,000
SALES (est): 66MM
SALES (corp-wide): 16.9B **Publicly Held**
WEB: www.westerndigital.com
SIC: 3572 Computer storage devices
PA: Western Digital Corporation
5601 Great Oaks Pkwy
San Jose CA 95119
408 717-6000

(P-5326)
WESTERN DIGITAL CORPORATION (PA)
5601 Great Oaks Pkwy, San Jose (95119-1003)
PHONE.................................408 717-6000
David V Goeckeler, *CEO*
Matthew E Massengill, *Ch of Bd*
Srinivasan Sivaram, *President*
Robert K Eulau, *CFO*
Michael C Ray,
▲ **EMP:** 1158 **EST:** 1970
SQ FT: 2,275,000
SALES: 16.9B **Publicly Held**
WEB: www.westerndigital.com
SIC: 3572 Computer storage devices; disk drives, computer

(P-5327)
WESTERN DIGITAL TECH INC (HQ)
Also Called: WD
5601 Great Oaks Pkwy, San Jose (95119-1003)
PHONE.................................408 717-6000
David Goeckeler, *CEO*
John F Coyne, *President*
John Sawyer, *President*
Michael D Cordano, *COO*
Olivier C Leonetti, *CFO*
▲ **EMP:** 4300 **EST:** 1986
SQ FT: 257,000
SALES (est): 2.3B
SALES (corp-wide): 16.9B **Publicly Held**
WEB: www.westerndigital.com
SIC: 3572 Disk drives, computer
PA: Western Digital Corporation
5601 Great Oaks Pkwy
San Jose CA 95119
408 717-6000

▲ = Import ▼ = Export
◆ = Import/Export

PRODUCTS & SERVICES SECTION
3577 - Computer Peripheral Eqpt, NEC County (P-5348)

3575 Computer Terminals

(P-5328)
ACCO BRANDS USA LLC
Kensington Computer Pdts Group
1500 Fashion Island Blvd # 300, San Mateo (94404-1597)
PHONE 650 572-2700
Patty Coffee, *Branch Mgr*
Fawn Wane, *Partner*
Ben Thacker, *Vice Pres*
Mirian Choi, *Executive Asst*
Jeff Smith, *Planning*
EMP: 100
SALES (corp-wide): 1.6B **Publicly Held**
WEB: www.accobrands.com
SIC: 3575 Keyboards, computer, office machine
HQ: Acco Brands Usa Llc
  4 Corporate Dr
  Lake Zurich IL 60047
  800 222-6462

(P-5329)
AG NEOVO TECHNOLOGY CORP
48501 Warm Springs Blvd # 114, Fremont (94539-7750)
PHONE 408 321-8210
Phillip Chang, *President*
David LI, *Sales Staff*
Daniel Tsao, *Manager*
▲ **EMP:** 18 **EST:** 1999
SALES (est): 8.5MM **Privately Held**
WEB: www.agneovo.com
SIC: 3575 Computer terminals, monitors & components
PA: Associated Industries China, Inc.
  5f-1, No. 3-1, Park St.
  Taipei City TAP 11503

(P-5330)
CYBERNETIC MICRO SYSTEMS INC
3000 La Honda Rd, San Gregorio (94074-9839)
P.O. Box 3000 (94074-3000)
PHONE 650 726-3000
Edwin E Klingman, *President*
Karen Moty, *Treasurer*
EMP: 20 **EST:** 1974
SQ FT: 6,960
SALES (est): 1.5MM **Privately Held**
WEB: www.controlchips.com
SIC: 3575 7371 Computer terminals, monitors & components; computer software development

(P-5331)
DIAMANTI INC (PA)
111 N Market St Ste 800, San Jose (95113-1102)
PHONE 408 645-5111
Tom Barton, *CEO*
Karthik Govindhasamy, *COO*
Jony Hartono, *CFO*
Mark Balch, *Vice Pres*
Jenny Fong, *Vice Pres*
EMP: 40 **EST:** 2014
SALES (est): 9.6MM **Privately Held**
WEB: www.diamanti.com
SIC: 3575 Keyboards, computer, office machine

(P-5332)
HPE GOVERNMENT LLC
46600 Landing Pkwy, Fremont (94538-6420)
PHONE 916 435-9200
EMP: 100
SALES (corp-wide): 26.9B **Publicly Held**
WEB: www.hpe.com
SIC: 3575 3572 7371 7378 Mfg Computer Terminals Mfg Computer Storage Dvc Computer Programming Svc Computer Maint/Repair Mfg Electronic Computers
HQ: Hpe Government, Llc.
  420 Natl Bus Pkwy Ste 18
  Annapolis Junction MD 20701
  301 572-1980

(P-5333)
JUPITER SYSTEMS INC
Also Called: Infocus Jupiter
31015 Huntwood Ave, Hayward (94544-7007)
PHONE 510 675-1000
Sidney Rittenberg, *President*
Jack Klingelhofer, *Ch of Bd*
Bob Worthington, *CFO*
Robert Worthington, *CFO*
Daniel Lecour, *Vice Pres*
◆ **EMP:** 42 **EST:** 1981
SQ FT: 33,000
SALES (est): 10.9MM **Privately Held**
WEB: www.jupiter.com
SIC: 3575 Computer terminals
HQ: Infocus Corporation
  13190 Sw 68th Pkwy Ste 12
  Portland OR 97223
  503 207-4700

(P-5334)
MASHGIN INC
849 E Charleston Rd, Palo Alto (94303-4612)
PHONE 650 847-8050
Abhinai Srivastava, *CEO*
Mukul Dhankhar, *Principal*
Max Olson, *Opers Staff*
EMP: 17 **EST:** 2013
SALES (est): 5.1MM **Privately Held**
WEB: www.mashgin.com
SIC: 3575 Computer terminals, monitors & components

(P-5335)
MOTOROLA SOLUTIONS INC
6001 Shellmound St Fl 4th, Emeryville (94608-1968)
PHONE 510 420-7400
EMP: 26
SALES (corp-wide): 5.7B **Publicly Held**
SIC: 3575 Mfg Computer Terminals
PA: Motorola Solutions, Inc.
  1303 E Algonquin Rd
  Schaumburg IL 60661
  847 576-5000

(P-5336)
RGB DISPLAY CORPORATION
22525 Kingston Ln, Grass Valley (95949-7706)
PHONE 530 268-2222
Lori Mc Laughlin, *President*
Michelle Hilger, *CFO*
Joan Mc Laughlin, *Corp Secy*
Mike Newman, *Engineer*
EMP: 19 **EST:** 1978
SQ FT: 14,000
SALES (est): 2.8MM **Privately Held**
WEB: www.rgbdisplay.com
SIC: 3575 Computer terminals, monitors & components

(P-5337)
UNI-PIXEL DISPLAYS INC
4699 Old Ironsides Dr # 3, Santa Clara (95054-1824)
PHONE 281 825-4500
Jeff Hawthorne, *CEO*
Frank Delape, *Ch of Bd*
Reed Killion, *President*
Donna Grumgles, *COO*
Jim Tassone, *CFO*
◆ **EMP:** 89 **EST:** 1998
SQ FT: 30,000
SALES (est): 3.4MM **Privately Held**
WEB: www.method.ventures
SIC: 3575 Computer terminals, monitors & components
PA: Uni-Pixel, Inc.
  4699 Old Ironsides Dr # 3
  Santa Clara CA 95054

3577 Computer Peripheral Eqpt, NEC

(P-5338)
3DCONNEXION INC
6505 Kaiser Dr, Fremont (94555-3614)
PHONE 510 713-6000
Rory Dooley, *President*
James V McCanna, *CFO*
Lew Epstein, *Vice Pres*
Niraj Swarup, *Vice Pres*
EMP: 75 **EST:** 2001
SALES (est): 24.8MM
SALES (corp-wide): 2.9B **Privately Held**
WEB: www.3dconnexion.com
SIC: 3577 5045 Computer peripheral equipment; computers & accessories, personal & home entertainment
HQ: Logitech Inc.
  7700 Gateway Blvd
  Newark CA 94560
  510 795-8500

(P-5339)
ACER AMERICAN HOLDINGS CORP (DH)
1730 N 1st St Ste 400, San Jose (95112-4642)
PHONE 408 533-7700
Emmanuel Fromont, *CEO*
J T Wang, *CEO*
Abhishek Singh, *Executive*
Suzanne Musselman, *Administration*
Jon Chandler, *Telecomm Mgr*
EMP: 1494 **EST:** 2007
SALES (est): 1.7B **Privately Held**
SIC: 3577 3571 Computer peripheral equipment; electronic computers

(P-5340)
ACTIVEWIRE INC (PA)
895 Commercial St Ste 700, Palo Alto (94303-4906)
P.O. Box 60280 (94306-0280)
PHONE 650 969-4000
Mato Hatori, *President*
Eric Berwer, *COO*
EMP: 69 **EST:** 1997
SALES (est): 143.3K **Privately Held**
WEB: www.activewireinc.com
SIC: 3577 5045 Computer peripheral equipment; computers, peripherals & software

(P-5341)
ADVANCE MODULAR TECHNOLOGY INC
Also Called: A M T
2075 Bering Dr Ste C, San Jose (95131-2011)
PHONE 408 453-9880
Crispian SOO, *President*
Pauline SOO, *Vice Pres*
▲ **EMP:** 26 **EST:** 1995
SALES (est): 3.6MM **Privately Held**
WEB: www.amchip.com
SIC: 3577 Computer peripheral equipment

(P-5342)
ALLIED TELESIS INC
3041 Orchard Pkwy, San Jose (95134-2017)
PHONE 408 519-8700
Taki Oshima, *Manager*
Lisa Rosetta, *COO*
Sultan Cochinwala, *Vice Pres*
Jim Holland, *Vice Pres*
Diem Doan, *CTO*
EMP: 20 **Privately Held**
WEB: www.alliedtelesis.com
SIC: 3577 Computer peripheral equipment
HQ: Allied Telesis, Inc.
  19800 North Creek Pkwy # 100
  Bothell WA 98011
  408 519-8700

(P-5343)
ARIES RESEARCH INC
Also Called: Aries Solutions
46750 Fremont Blvd # 107, Fremont (94538-6573)
P.O. Box 1112, Alamo (94507-7112)
PHONE 925 818-1078
Lawrence T Kou, *CEO*
Ilain Kou, *President*
J Bar Houston, *Engineer*
EMP: 38 **EST:** 1989
SQ FT: 8,600
SALES (est): 1.5MM **Privately Held**
WEB: www.ari.com
SIC: 3577 3571 Computer peripheral equipment; electronic computers

(P-5344)
ARUBA NETWORKS INC
1322 Crossman Ave, Sunnyvale (94089-1113)
PHONE 408 227-4500
Amol Kelkar, *Branch Mgr*
Glenn Ferreira, *Vice Pres*
David Miller, *Vice Pres*
John W Turner, *General Mgr*
Steve Carlock, *Admin Sec*
EMP: 602
SALES (corp-wide): 26.9B **Publicly Held**
WEB: www.arubanetworks.com
SIC: 3577 Computer peripheral equipment
HQ: Aruba Networks, Inc.
  3333 Scott Blvd
  Santa Clara CA 95054
  408 227-4500

(P-5345)
ARUBA NETWORKS INC (HQ)
Also Called: Aruba Networks Cafe
3333 Scott Blvd, Santa Clara (95054-3103)
PHONE 408 227-4500
Keerti Melkote, *President*
Vishal Lall, *COO*
Jon Faust, *CFO*
Carl Mower, *Vice Pres*
Michael Wais, *Vice Pres*
EMP: 270 **EST:** 2002
SALES (est): 669MM
SALES (corp-wide): 26.9B **Publicly Held**
WEB: www.arubanetworks.com
SIC: 3577 3663 7371 Computer peripheral equipment; mobile communication equipment; computer software development
PA: Hewlett Packard Enterprise Company
  11445 Compaq Center W Dr
  Houston TX 77070
  650 687-5817

(P-5346)
ARUBA NETWORKS INC
634 E Caribbean Dr, Sunnyvale (94089-1108)
PHONE 408 227-4500
Carly Hunt, *Partner*
Murali Duvvury, *Vice Pres*
Ryan Rhea, *Administration*
Anil Kamath, *Network Enginr*
Abdul Sameem, *Network Enginr*
EMP: 602
SALES (corp-wide): 26.9B **Publicly Held**
WEB: www.arubanetworks.com
SIC: 3577 Computer peripheral equipment
HQ: Aruba Networks, Inc.
  3333 Scott Blvd
  Santa Clara CA 95054
  408 227-4500

(P-5347)
ASANTE TECHNOLOGIES INC (PA)
2223 Oakland Rd, San Jose (95131-1402)
PHONE 408 435-8388
Jeff Yuan-Kai Lin, *President*
David Kichar, *COO*
Y C Wang, *Exec VP*
Sun WEI, *Human Res Dir*
Phil Berkowitz, *VP Sales*
EMP: 29 **EST:** 1988
SQ FT: 7,000
SALES (est): 5.5MM **Privately Held**
WEB: www.asante.com
SIC: 3577 Computer peripheral equipment

(P-5348)
AVERMEDIA TECHNOLOGIES INC
4038 Clipper Ct, Fremont (94538-6540)
PHONE 510 403-0006
Michael Cooke, *President*
David KAO, *Sales Dir*
▲ **EMP:** 21 **EST:** 2013
SALES (est): 9.8MM **Privately Held**
WEB: www.avermedia.com
SIC: 3577 Computer peripheral equipment
PA: Avermedia Technologies, Inc.
  No. 135, Jan 1st Rd.
  New Taipei City TAP 23585

(PA)=Parent Co (HQ)=Headquarters (DH)=Div Headquarters
✪ = New Business established in last 2 years

3577 - Computer Peripheral Eqpt, NEC County (P-5349)

(P-5349)
AVISTAR COMMUNICATIONS CORP (PA)
1875 S Grant St Fl 10, San Mateo (94402-2666)
PHONE..................650 525-3300
Robert F Kirk, *CEO*
Elias A Murraymetzger, *CFO*
Stephen M Epstein, *Chief Mktg Ofcr*
Michael J Dignen, *Senior VP*
R Jan Afridi, *Vice Pres*
EMP: 29 **EST:** 1993
SQ FT: 29,600
SALES (est): 9.4MM **Privately Held**
WEB: www.avistar.com
SIC: 3577 Computer peripheral equipment

(P-5350)
BESTEK MANUFACTURING INC
675 Sycamore Dr Ste 170, Milpitas (95035-7469)
PHONE..................408 321-8834
Frank Dang, *President*
Tyler Dang, *Director*
EMP: 40 **EST:** 1994
SQ FT: 8,000
SALES (est): 7.2MM **Privately Held**
WEB: www.bestekmfg.com
SIC: 3577 3679 3672 Computer peripheral equipment; harness assemblies for electronic use: wire or cable; printed circuit boards

(P-5351)
BLACK DIAMOND VIDEO INC
503 Canal Blvd, Richmond (94804-3517)
PHONE..................510 439-4500
Peter Metcalf, *CEO*
Donald Martell, *Project Mgr*
David Martell, *Controller*
▲ **EMP:** 90
SQ FT: 30,000
SALES (est): 25MM **Privately Held**
WEB: www.steris.com
SIC: 3577 3679 Computer peripheral equipment; electronic switches
HQ: Steris Corporation
5960 Heisley Rd
Mentor OH 44060
440 354-2600

(P-5352)
BLUE CEDAR NETWORKS INC
325 Pacific Ave Fl 1, San Francisco (94111-1711)
PHONE..................415 329-0401
John Aisien, *CEO*
Jeanne Angelo-Pardo, *CFO*
Chris Ford, *Officer*
Alan Robertson, *Vice Pres*
EMP: 36 **EST:** 2016
SQ FT: 8,000
SALES (est): 4.4MM **Privately Held**
WEB: www.bluecedar.com
SIC: 3577 Computer peripheral equipment

(P-5353)
BRIDGECREW INC
1 Market St, San Francisco (94105-1420)
PHONE..................510 304-4622
Idan Tendler, *CEO*
EMP: 20 **EST:** 2019
SALES (est): 11MM
SALES (corp-wide): 4.2B **Publicly Held**
WEB: www.paloaltonetworks.com
SIC: 3577 7371 Computer peripheral equipment; custom computer programming services
PA: Palo Alto Networks Inc.
3000 Tannery Way
Santa Clara CA 95054
408 753-2200

(P-5354)
BROCADE CMMNCTIONS SYSTEMS LLC (DH)
1320 Ridder Park Dr, San Jose (95131-2313)
PHONE..................408 333-8000
Hock E Tan, *President*
Lissa Walline, *Partner*
Thomas H Krause Jr, *CFO*
Jean Samuel Furter, *Treasurer*
Alexis Bjrlin, *Vice Pres*
EMP: 800 **EST:** 1995
SQ FT: 562,000
SALES (est): 1.5B
SALES (corp-wide): 23.8B **Publicly Held**
WEB: www.broadcom.com
SIC: 3577 4813 Computer peripheral equipment;
HQ: Lsi Corporation
1320 Ridder Park Dr
San Jose CA 95131
408 433-8000

(P-5355)
CARBON INC
1089 Mills Way, Redwood City (94063-3119)
PHONE..................650 285-6307
Ellen J Kullman, *President*
Dana McCallum, *Partner*
Elisa De Martel, *CFO*
Joseph M Desimone, *Chairman*
Erika Berg, *Program Mgr*
EMP: 210 **EST:** 2013
SQ FT: 87,000
SALES (est): 65.6MM **Privately Held**
WEB: www.carbon3d.com
SIC: 3577 3841 Computer peripheral equipment; surgical & medical instruments

(P-5356)
CASPIAN NETWORKS INC
101 University Ave # 100, Palo Alto (94301-1638)
PHONE..................408 382-5200
L William Krause, *President*
Thomas Carlson, *CFO*
Penny St Clairre, *Mktg Dir*
David Robison, *Sales Staff*
EMP: 22 **EST:** 1998
SALES (est): 1.2MM **Privately Held**
SIC: 3577 Computer peripheral equipment

(P-5357)
CISCO SYSTEMS INC (PA)
170 W Tasman Dr, San Jose (95134-1706)
PHONE..................408 526-4000
Charles H Robbins, *Ch of Bd*
Gerri Elliott, *Partner*
Maria Martinez, *COO*
R Scott Herren, *CFO*
Deborah L Stahlkopf,
EMP: 700 **EST:** 1984
SALES (est): 49.8B **Publicly Held**
WEB: www.cisco.com
SIC: 3577 7379 Data conversion equipment, media-to-media: computer;

(P-5358)
CISCO TECHNOLOGY INC (HQ)
170 W Tasman Dr, San Jose (95134-1706)
PHONE..................408 526-4000
Evan Sloves, *CEO*
Marc Briceno, *Vice Pres*
Tony Cox, *Business Dir*
John Mann, *Program Mgr*
Kavitha Kodali, *Software Engr*
EMP: 75 **EST:** 1997
SALES (est): 15MM
SALES (corp-wide): 49.8B **Publicly Held**
WEB: www.cisco.com
SIC: 3577 7379 Data conversion equipment, media-to-media: computer;
PA: Cisco Systems, Inc.
170 W Tasman Dr
San Jose CA 95134
408 526-4000

(P-5359)
CONVERGENT MANUFACTURING TECH
966 Shulman Ave, Santa Clara (95050-2822)
PHONE..................408 987-2770
Kevin C Lettire, *President*
Steve Alexander, *Opers Staff*
EMP: 20 **EST:** 1997
SQ FT: 5,000
SALES (est): 1.3MM **Privately Held**
WEB: www.cmt-mtc.com
SIC: 3577 Computer peripheral equipment

(P-5360)
CORSAIR GAMING INC (PA)
47100 Bayside Pkwy, Fremont (94538-6563)
PHONE..................510 657-8747
Andrew J Paul, *CEO*
George L Majoros Jr, *Ch of Bd*
Thi L La, *President*
Michael G Potter, *CFO*
Bertrand Chevalier, *Exec VP*
EMP: 414 **EST:** 1994
SQ FT: 60,000
SALES (est): 1.7B **Publicly Held**
WEB: www.corsair.com
SIC: 3577 5045 5734 Computer peripheral equipment; computer peripheral equipment; computers & accessories, personal & home entertainment; computer peripheral equipment; software, computer games

(P-5361)
CPACKET NETWORKS INC
Also Called: Cwr Labs
2130 Gold St 200, San Jose (95002-3700)
P.O. Box 430, Alviso (95002-0430)
PHONE..................650 969-9500
Rony Kay, *CEO*
Ron Nevo, *Vice Pres*
Brendan O'Flaherty, *Vice Pres*
Jasmine Wang, *General Mgr*
Juneed Ahamed, *Sr Software Eng*
EMP: 22
SALES (est): 6.9MM **Privately Held**
WEB: www.cpacket.com
SIC: 3577 Computer peripheral equipment

(P-5362)
DTEN INC (PA)
97 E Brokaw Rd Ste 180, San Jose (95112-1031)
PHONE..................866 936-3836
WEI Liu, *President*
Karthik Chandran, *CFO*
Peter Yaskowitz, *Chief Mktg Ofcr*
Kash Khetia, *Sales Staff*
EMP: 31 **EST:** 2017
SALES (est): 2.6MM **Privately Held**
WEB: www.dten.com
SIC: 3577 Input/output equipment, computer

(P-5363)
ELECTRONIC RESOURCES NETWORK
Also Called: Tern
1950 5th St, Davis (95616-4018)
PHONE..................530 758-0180
Tom Tang, *President*
Ning Lu, *CFO*
Ziqiang Tang, *Vice Pres*
Chon Tang, *Manager*
EMP: 26 **EST:** 1993
SQ FT: 6,000
SALES (est): 4.2MM **Privately Held**
WEB: www.tern.com
SIC: 3577 5045 3679 Computer peripheral equipment; computer peripheral equipment; electronic circuits

(P-5364)
ELISITY INC
100 Century Center Ct # 710, San Jose (95112-4537)
PHONE..................408 839-3971
James Winebrenner, *CEO*
Matthew Krieg, *VP Sales*
EMP: 15 **EST:** 2019
SALES (est): 1.1MM **Privately Held**
WEB: www.elisity.com
SIC: 3577 Computer output to microfilm units

(P-5365)
ELITEGROUP CMPT SYSTEMS INC
6851 Mowry Ave, Newark (94560-4925)
PHONE..................510 226-7333
Ray Lin, *CEO*
Lena Ruan, *Corp Secy*
See See Lo, *Principal*
Shirley Peng, *Purch Mgr*
◆ **EMP:** 200 **EST:** 1990
SQ FT: 60,000
SALES (est): 42.2MM **Privately Held**
WEB: www.ecsusa.com
SIC: 3577 Computer peripheral equipment
HQ: Ecs Holding (America) Co.
6600 Sands Point Dr # 288
Houston TX

(P-5366)
EVEREST NETWORKS INC
205 Ravendale Dr, Mountain View (94043-5216)
P.O. Box 391602 (94039-1602)
PHONE..................408 300-9236
Simon Wright, *CEO*
Scott Jeffcoat, *Vice Pres*
Christopher Twiggs, *Manager*
EMP: 15 **EST:** 2014
SALES (est): 2.8MM **Privately Held**
WEB: www.everestnetworks.com
SIC: 3577 Computer peripheral equipment

(P-5367)
FIRETIDE INC (DH)
2105 S Bascom Ave Ste 220, Campbell (95008-3292)
PHONE..................408 399-7771
Corry S Hong, *President*
Gordon Lowe, *Partner*
Angela Zhou, *Manager*
▲ **EMP:** 99 **EST:** 2001
SQ FT: 30,000
SALES (est): 31.1MM
SALES (corp-wide): 579.1MM **Privately Held**
WEB: www.unicomsi.com
SIC: 3577 3825 4899 Computer peripheral equipment; network analyzers; communication signal enhancement network system
HQ: Unicom Systems Inc.
15535 San Fernando Missio
Mission Hills CA 91345
818 838-0606

(P-5368)
FORTINET INC (PA)
899 Kifer Rd, Sunnyvale (94086-5205)
PHONE..................408 235-7700
Ken Xie, *Ch of Bd*
Sarah Bigley Barnett, *Partner*
Vincent Delbar, *Partner*
Michael Xie, *President*
Keith Jensen, *CFO*
▲ **EMP:** 5213 **EST:** 2000
SQ FT: 160,000
SALES (est): 2.5B **Publicly Held**
WEB: www.fortinet.com
SIC: 3577 Computer peripheral equipment

(P-5369)
FUJIFILM DIMATIX INC (DH)
2250 Martin Ave, Santa Clara (95050-2704)
PHONE..................408 565-9150
Kenji Sukeno, *Ch of Bd*
Teiichi Goto, *President*
Wendy Arienzo, *Vice Pres*
Karen Hebert, *Vice Pres*
Cassidy Jarrell, *Software Engr*
◆ **EMP:** 569 **EST:** 1996
SQ FT: 125,000
SALES (est): 105.4MM **Privately Held**
WEB: www.dimatix.com
SIC: 3577 Printers, computer

(P-5370)
GDCA INC
1799 Portola Ave Ste 1, Livermore (94551-7947)
PHONE..................925 456-9900
Ethan Plotkin, *CEO*
Sue Plotkin, *Executive*
Lynn McFarland, *Marketing Staff*
Anne Bennedsen, *Director*
Kip Kingsland, *Director*
EMP: 38 **EST:** 1993
SQ FT: 6,000
SALES (est): 7.4MM **Privately Held**
WEB: www.gdca.com
SIC: 3577 3571 Computer peripheral equipment; electronic computers

(P-5371)
GIGAMON INC (HQ)
3300 Olcott St, Santa Clara (95054-3005)
PHONE..................408 831-4000
Paul Hooper, *CEO*
Michelle Hodges, *Partner*
Shane Buckley, *President*
Karl Van Den Bergh, *Chief Mktg Ofcr*
Christel Ventura,
▲ **EMP:** 635 **EST:** 2009
SQ FT: 105,600

▲ = Import ▼=Export
◆ =Import/Export

PRODUCTS & SERVICES SECTION
3577 - Computer Peripheral Eqpt, NEC County (P-5394)

SALES (est): 310.8MM **Privately Held**
WEB: www.gigamon.com
SIC: **3577** 7372 Computer peripheral equipment; prepackaged software

(P-5372)
HANAPS ENTERPRISES
Also Called: Digital Storm
8100 Camino Arroyo, Gilroy (95020-7304)
PHONE..................................669 235-3810
Paramjit Chana, *CEO*
Surnderjit Chana, *Vice Pres*
Thanh Phan, *General Mgr*
Stephen Dalton, *Technical Staff*
▲ EMP: 70 EST: 2003
SALES (est): 27MM **Privately Held**
WEB: www.digitalstorm.com
SIC: **3577** 7379 Computer peripheral equipment; computer related maintenance services

(P-5373)
IDENTIV INC (PA)
2201 Walnut Ave Ste 100, Fremont (94538-2334)
PHONE..................................949 250-8888
Steven Humphreys, *CEO*
James E Ousley, *Ch of Bd*
John Guerrero, *Vice Pres*
Louis Modell, *Vice Pres*
Scott Sieracki, *Vice Pres*
EMP: 172 EST: 1990
SQ FT: 3,082
SALES (est): 86.9MM **Publicly Held**
WEB: www.identiv.com
SIC: **3577** 7372 Computer peripheral equipment; prepackaged software

(P-5374)
IMMERSION CORPORATION (PA)
330 Townsend St Ste 234, San Francisco (94107-1659)
PHONE..................................408 467-1900
Jared Smith, *CEO*
Eric Singer, *Ch of Bd*
Aaron Akerman, *CFO*
Manuel Cruz, *Research*
Stephen Ferrari, *Finance Dir*
EMP: 48 EST: 1993
SQ FT: 5,000
SALES (est): 30.4MM **Publicly Held**
WEB: www.immersion.com
SIC: **3577** 7371 Computer peripheral equipment; computer software development & applications

(P-5375)
INCAL TECHNOLOGY INC
46420 Fremont Blvd, Fremont (94538-6469)
PHONE..................................510 657-8405
Cary Caywood, *CEO*
Bruce Simikowski, *Vice Pres*
Naveed Syed, *Design Engr*
Lopez Grace, *Purchasing*
Grace Lopez, *Purchasing*
EMP: 25 EST: 1988
SQ FT: 7,500
SALES (est): 4.4MM **Privately Held**
WEB: www.incal.com
SIC: **3577** Computer peripheral equipment

(P-5376)
INFOBLOX INTERNATIONAL INC (DH)
2390 Mission College Blvd, Santa Clara (95054-1530)
PHONE..................................408 986-4000
Robert Thomas, *Principal*
Scott Fulton, *Exec VP*
Lester Igo, *Engineer*
Irene Duldulao, *Opers Staff*
▲ EMP: 279 EST: 2004
SALES (est): 2.2MM
SALES (corp-wide): 27.1MM **Privately Held**
WEB: www.infoblox.com
SIC: **3577** Computer peripheral equipment
HQ: Infoblox Inc.
2390 Mission College Blvd # 501
Santa Clara CA 95054
408 986-4000

(P-5377)
INTEL AMERICAS INC (HQ)
2200 Mission College Blvd, Santa Clara (95054-1549)
PHONE..................................408 765-8080
Craig R Barrett, *CEO*
Gary Dunkin, *Engineer*
Thomas Pieser, *Business Mgr*
Balaji Srinivasan, *Manager*
▲ EMP: 232 EST: 1999
SALES (est): 43MM
SALES (corp-wide): 77.8B **Publicly Held**
WEB: www.intel.com
SIC: **3577** Computer peripheral equipment
PA: Intel Corporation
2200 Mission College Blvd
Santa Clara CA 95054
408 765-8080

(P-5378)
INTEL CORPORATION
3065 Bowers Ave, Santa Clara (95054-3293)
PHONE..................................408 765-2508
Andrew S Grove, *CEO*
Jennifer Luo, *Technical Staff*
Emily Dowey, *Engineer*
Manoj Selvatharasu, *Engineer*
Sundar Subramaniam, *Director*
EMP: 17
SQ FT: 78,336
SALES (corp-wide): 77.8B **Publicly Held**
WEB: www.intel.com
SIC: **3577** Computer peripheral equipment
PA: Intel Corporation
2200 Mission College Blvd
Santa Clara CA 95054
408 765-8080

(P-5379)
INTEL CORPORATION
2300 Mission College Blvd, Santa Clara (95054-1531)
PHONE..................................408 425-8398
Ziya MA, *Manager*
Chad Barrington, *Technician*
EMP: 200
SALES (corp-wide): 77.8B **Publicly Held**
WEB: www.intel.com
SIC: **3577** Computer peripheral equipment
PA: Intel Corporation
2200 Mission College Blvd
Santa Clara CA 95054
408 765-8080

(P-5380)
INTEL CORPORATION
101 Innovation Dr Bldg 1, San Jose (95134-1941)
PHONE..................................408 544-7000
Dan McNamara, *Branch Mgr*
Vincent Hu, *Vice Pres*
Kevin Lyman, *Vice Pres*
David Moore, *Vice Pres*
Dermot Hargaden, *General Mgr*
EMP: 3000
SALES (corp-wide): 77.8B **Publicly Held**
WEB: www.intel.com
SIC: **3577** Computer peripheral equipment
PA: Intel Corporation
2200 Mission College Blvd
Santa Clara CA 95054
408 765-8080

(P-5381)
INTEL INTERNATIONAL INC
2200 Mission College Blvd, Santa Clara (95054-1549)
PHONE..................................408 765-8080
Sharon Lynn Heck, *CEO*
EMP: 43 EST: 1971
SALES (est): 2.9MM
SALES (corp-wide): 77.8B **Publicly Held**
WEB: www.intel.com
SIC: **3577** Computer peripheral equipment
PA: Intel Corporation
2200 Mission College Blvd
Santa Clara CA 95054
408 765-8080

(P-5382)
INTEL MICROELECTRONICS ASIA LTD (HQ)
2200 Mission College Blvd, Santa Clara (95054-1549)
PHONE..................................408 765-8080
Henry A Orphys, *Principal*
Alvin Lim, *Program Mgr*
EMP: 53 EST: 2008
SALES (est): 7.9MM
SALES (corp-wide): 77.8B **Publicly Held**
WEB: www.intel.com
SIC: **3577** Computer peripheral equipment
PA: Intel Corporation
2200 Mission College Blvd
Santa Clara CA 95054
408 765-8080

(P-5383)
INTEL OVERSEAS CORPORATION
2200 Mission College Blvd, Santa Clara (95054-1549)
PHONE..................................408 765-8080
Raju Nallapa, *Principal*
EMP: 16 EST: 2007
SALES (est): 211.1K **Privately Held**
WEB: www.intel.com
SIC: **3577** Computer peripheral equipment

(P-5384)
INTEL PHILS HOLDING LLC (HQ)
2200 Mission Blvd, Santa Clara (95054)
PHONE..................................408 765-8080
EMP: 319 EST: 2008
SALES (est): 1.3MM
SALES (corp-wide): 77.8B **Publicly Held**
WEB: www.intel.com
SIC: **3577** Computer peripheral equipment
PA: Intel Corporation
2200 Mission College Blvd
Santa Clara CA 95054
408 765-8080

(P-5385)
INTEL RESALE CORPORATION
2200 Mission College Blvd, Santa Clara (95054-1549)
PHONE..................................408 765-8080
Nanci S Palmintere, *President*
▼ EMP: 41 EST: 1986
SALES (est): 10.1MM
SALES (corp-wide): 77.8B **Publicly Held**
WEB: www.intel.com
SIC: **3577** Computer peripheral equipment
PA: Intel Corporation
2200 Mission College Blvd
Santa Clara CA 95054
408 765-8080

(P-5386)
INTEL SERVICES LLC (HQ)
2200 Mission College Blvd, Santa Clara (95054-1549)
PHONE..................................408 765-8080
EMP: 934 EST: 1968
SALES (est): 31MM
SALES (corp-wide): 77.8B **Publicly Held**
WEB: www.intel.com
SIC: **3577** Computer peripheral equipment
PA: Intel Corporation
2200 Mission College Blvd
Santa Clara CA 95054
408 765-8080

(P-5387)
INTEL TECHNOLOGIES INC (HQ)
2200 Mission College Blvd, Santa Clara (95054-1549)
PHONE..................................408 765-8080
Roger Whittier, *Principal*
Stacy Smith, *CFO*
EMP: 485 EST: 1991
SALES (est): 38.3MM
SALES (corp-wide): 77.8B **Publicly Held**
WEB: www.intel.com
SIC: **3577** Computer peripheral equipment
PA: Intel Corporation
2200 Mission College Blvd
Santa Clara CA 95054
408 765-8080

(P-5388)
INTERFACE MASTERS INC
150 E Brokaw Rd, San Jose (95112-4203)
P.O. Box 612228 (95161-2228)
PHONE..................................408 441-9341
EMP: 17 EST: 2013
SALES (est): 3.3MM **Privately Held**
WEB: www.interfacemasters.com
SIC: **3577** Computer peripheral equipment

(P-5389)
ITUNER NETWORKS CORPORATION
44244 Fremont Blvd, Fremont (94538-6000)
PHONE..................................510 573-0783
Andrei Bulucea, *President*
Raluca Neacsu, *Vice Pres*
Adina Pricop, *Technology*
▲ EMP: 15 EST: 1999
SALES (est): 1.2MM **Privately Held**
WEB: www.mini-box.com
SIC: **3577** 5961 5045 Computer peripheral equipment; computers & peripheral equipment, mail order; computer peripheral equipment

(P-5390)
JUNIPER NETWORKS INC (PA)
1133 Innovation Way, Sunnyvale (94089-1228)
PHONE..................................408 745-2000
Rami Rahim, *CEO*
Scott Kriens, *Ch of Bd*
Manoj Leelanivas, *COO*
Kenneth B Miller, *CFO*
Anand Athreya, *Exec VP*
EMP: 300 EST: 1996
SALES (est): 4.4B **Publicly Held**
WEB: www.juniper.net
SIC: **3577** 7372 Computer peripheral equipment; prepackaged software

(P-5391)
KELLY COMPUTER SYSTEMS INC
1060 La Avenida St, Mountain View (94043-1422)
PHONE..................................650 960-1010
Larry Kelly, *President*
Tim Kelly, *Vice Pres*
Lawrence Kelly, *Sales Executive*
EMP: 22 EST: 1984
SQ FT: 20,000
SALES (est): 1.2MM **Privately Held**
SIC: **3577** 7371 7373 Computer peripheral equipment; computer software development; systems integration services

(P-5392)
LITE-ON TECHNOLOGY INTL INC (HQ)
720 S Hillview Dr, Milpitas (95035-5455)
PHONE..................................408 945-0222
Kung Soong, *Principal*
Paul Lin, *Vice Chairman*
Joseph Chen, *Vice Pres*
Daisy Young, *Principal*
Harry Guo, *CIO*
▲ EMP: 75 EST: 1994
SALES (est): 5MM **Privately Held**
WEB: www.liteon.com
SIC: **3577** 3572 Computer peripheral equipment; computer storage devices

(P-5393)
LOGITECH INC (HQ)
7700 Gateway Blvd, Newark (94560-1046)
PHONE..................................510 795-8500
Bracken P Darrell, *President*
Guerrino De Luca, *Ch of Bd*
Josh Duncan, *Vice Pres*
Michele Hermann, *Vice Pres*
Joe Sullivan, *Vice Pres*
◆ EMP: 276 EST: 1982
SQ FT: 295,560
SALES (est): 1.8B
SALES (corp-wide): 2.9B **Privately Held**
WEB: www.logitech.com
SIC: **3577** Input/output equipment, computer
PA: Logitech International S.A.
Les Chatagnis
Apples VD
218 635-511

(P-5394)
LOGITECH LATIN AMERICA INC
7700 Gateway Blvd, Newark (94560-1046)
PHONE..................................510 795-8500
Bracken Darrell, *CEO*
EMP: 19 EST: 2011

3577 - Computer Peripheral Eqpt, NEC County (P-5395)

SALES (est): 1.2MM
SALES (corp-wide): 2.9B **Privately Held**
WEB: www.logitech.com
SIC: 3577 Input/output equipment, computer
PA: Logitech International S.A.
Les Chatagnis
Apples VD
218 635-511

(P-5395)
LOGITECH STREAMING MEDIA INC
7600 Gateway Blvd, Newark (94560-1159)
PHONE..................................510 795-8500
Bracken Darrell, *CEO*
Travis Tanimura, *Managing Dir*
Cissy Zhang, *Executive Asst*
Jeff Eisenman, *Sr Ntwrk Engine*
Dean Blackketter, *CTO*
▲ **EMP:** 63 **EST:** 1999
SQ FT: 18,000
SALES (est): 7.3MM
SALES (corp-wide): 2.9B **Privately Held**
WEB: www.logitech.com
SIC: 3577 Computer peripheral equipment
PA: Logitech International S.A.
Les Chatagnis
Apples VD
218 635-511

(P-5396)
MANDIANT INC (PA)
601 Mccarthy Blvd, Milpitas (95035-7932)
PHONE..................................408 321-6300
Kevin R Mandia, *CEO*
Enrique Salem, *Ch of Bd*
John P Watters, *President*
Frank E Verdecanna, *CFO*
Vikram Ramesh, *Chief Mktg Ofcr*
EMP: 2630 **EST:** 2004
SQ FT: 190,000
SALES (corp-wide): 940.5MM **Publicly Held**
WEB: www.fireeye.com
SIC: 3577 7372 Computer peripheral equipment; prepackaged software

(P-5397)
MARBURG TECHNOLOGY INC
Also Called: Glide-Write
304 Turquoise St, Milpitas (95035-5431)
PHONE..................................408 262-8400
Francis Burga, *CEO*
Mohammed Ebrahimi, *CFO*
Francis Guevara, *Vice Pres*
▲ **EMP:** 54 **EST:** 1988
SALES (est): 3.7MM **Privately Held**
WEB: www.glidewrite.com
SIC: 3577 Disk & diskette equipment, except drives

(P-5398)
MEGA FORCE CORPORATION
Also Called: Megaforce
2035 Otoole Ave, San Jose (95131-1301)
PHONE..................................408 956-9989
Stanley Trenh, *President*
Joann Nguyen, *Program Mgr*
Manuel Villalobos, *Area Mgr*
Matt Robledo, *Technician*
Hieu Tran, *Purchasing*
EMP: 45 **EST:** 1994
SQ FT: 15,000
SALES (est): 13.2MM **Privately Held**
WEB: www.megaforcecorp.com
SIC: 3577 Computer peripheral equipment

(P-5399)
MICRO CONNECTORS INC
2700 Mccone Ave, Hayward (94545-1615)
PHONE..................................510 266-0299
Charlie Lin, *President*
▲ **EMP:** 29 **EST:** 1986
SALES (est): 2.5MM **Privately Held**
WEB: www.microconnectors.com
SIC: 3577 Computer peripheral equipment

(P-5400)
MICROTECH INTERNATIONAL INC (DH)
466 Kato Ter, Fremont (94539-8332)
PHONE..................................510 360-0210
Robert Schneider, *CEO*
Brian Campbell, *President*
Motoyuki Matsubara, *Exec VP*
N H Menon, *Vice Pres*
EMP: 147 **EST:** 1985
SALES (est): 5.7MM **Publicly Held**
WEB: www.identiv.com
SIC: 3577 3695 3674 Computer peripheral equipment; magnetic & optical recording media; semiconductors & related devices
HQ: Identiv Gmbh
Oskar-Messter-Str. 12
Ismaning BY 85737
899 595-5441

(P-5401)
MITAC INFORMATION SYSTEMS
39889 Eureka Dr, Newark (94560-4811)
PHONE..................................510 668-3679
EMP: 50 **Privately Held**
SIC: 3577 Mfg Computer Peripheral Equipment
HQ: Mitac Information Systems Corp.
44131 Nobel Dr
Fremont CA 94560
510 668-3679

(P-5402)
OPTIBASE INC (HQ)
931 Benecia Ave, Sunnyvale (94085-2805)
P.O. Box 448, Mountain View (94042-0448)
PHONE..................................800 451-5101
Shlomo Wyler, *CEO*
Michael Chorpash, *President*
Yakir Ben-Naim, *CFO*
EMP: 27 **EST:** 1991
SQ FT: 15,000
SALES (est): 37.2MM **Privately Held**
WEB: www.optibase-holdings.com
SIC: 3577 Computer peripheral equipment

(P-5403)
PALO ALTO NETWORKS INC (PA)
3000 Tannery Way, Santa Clara (95054-2832)
PHONE..................................408 753-4000
Nikesh Arora, *Ch of Bd*
William Jenkins, *President*
Jean Compeau, *CFO*
Dipak Golechha, *CFO*
Mark D McLaughlin, *Vice Ch Bd*
EMP: 500 **EST:** 2005
SQ FT: 941,000
SALES (est): 4.2B **Publicly Held**
WEB: www.paloaltonetworks.com
SIC: 3577 7371 Computer peripheral equipment; computer software development & applications

(P-5404)
PANO LOGIC INC
1100 La Avenida St Ste A, Mountain View (94043-1453)
PHONE..................................650 743-1773
John Kish, *President*
Parmeet S Chaddha, *Exec VP*
Aly Orady, *CTO*
Nils Bunger, *VP Engrg*
▲ **EMP:** 47 **EST:** 2006
SQ FT: 11,800
SALES (est): 3.5MM **Privately Held**
SIC: 3577 Computer peripheral equipment

(P-5405)
PRINTWORX INC
195 Aviation Way Ste 201, Watsonville (95076-2059)
PHONE..................................831 722-7147
James B Riches, *Ch of Bd*
David Willmon, *President*
EMP: 17 **EST:** 1987
SQ FT: 15,000
SALES (est): 1.5MM **Privately Held**
SIC: 3577 5112 7378 3861 Printers, computer; computer & photocopying supplies; computer & data processing equipment repair/maintenance; photographic equipment & supplies; commercial printing

(P-5406)
REVERA INCORPORATED
3090 Oakmead Village Dr, Santa Clara (95051-0862)
PHONE..................................408 510-7400
Glyn Davies, *President*
Timothy Welch, *CFO*
Jim Pouquette, *Vice Pres*
Dave Reed, *CTO*
Aniruddha Deshpande, *Engineer*
▲ **EMP:** 40 **EST:** 2003
SQ FT: 20,000
SALES (est): 9.3MM **Privately Held**
WEB: www.novami.com
SIC: 3577 Optical scanning devices
PA: Nova Ltd
Rehovot
Rehovot

(P-5407)
RGB SPECTRUM
1101 Marina Village Pkwy # 101, Alameda (94501-3579)
PHONE..................................510 814-7000
Robert Marcus, *CEO*
Scott Norder, *Senior VP*
Jed Deame, *Vice Pres*
Tony Spica, *Vice Pres*
Jason Tirado, *Vice Pres*
▲ **EMP:** 81 **EST:** 1987
SALES (est): 18.3MM **Privately Held**
WEB: www.rgb.com
SIC: 3577 5731 3679 Graphic displays, except graphic terminals; video cameras, recorders & accessories; recording & playback apparatus, including phonograph

(P-5408)
ROBOTLAB INC
Also Called: Robotslab US
1981 N Broadway Ste 322, Walnut Creek (94596-3841)
PHONE..................................415 702-3033
Elad Inbar, *CEO*
Michael Rogero, *CFO*
Priscilla Eklund, *Administration*
Paul Knaack, *Manager*
Charles Nimrad, *Consultant*
EMP: 25 **EST:** 2011
SQ FT: 1,500
SALES (est): 4.7MM **Privately Held**
WEB: www.robotlab.com
SIC: 3577 7373 8732 8742 Computer peripheral equipment; turnkey vendors, computer systems; commercial sociological & educational research; educational research; automation & robotics consultant
PA: E.I.C.S Ltd
/14
Metar 85025

(P-5409)
SECUGEN CORPORATION
2065 Martin Ave Ste 102, Santa Clara (95050-2707)
PHONE..................................408 834-7712
Won Lee, *President*
Winnie Ahn, *Marketing Staff*
James Wedel, *Director*
◆ **EMP:** 30 **EST:** 2006
SALES (est): 5.1MM **Privately Held**
WEB: www.secugen.com
SIC: 3577 Computer peripheral equipment
PA: Pivotec Corperation
Rm 502
Seongnam
-

(P-5410)
SEGMENTIO INC
101 Spear St Fl 1, San Francisco (94105-1580)
PHONE..................................844 611-0621
Peter Kristian Reinhardt, *President*
Sandra Smith, *CFO*
Joe Morrissey, *Officer*
Tido Carriero, *Vice Pres*
Prakash Durgani, *Vice Pres*
EMP: 313 **EST:** 2011
SALES (est): 68MM
SALES (corp-wide): 1.7B **Publicly Held**
WEB: www.segment.com
SIC: 3577 Data conversion equipment, media-to-media: computer
PA: Twilio Inc.
101 Spear St Fl 1
San Francisco CA 94105
415 390-2337

(P-5411)
SILICON GRAPHICS INTL CORP (HQ)
940 N Mccarthy Blvd, Milpitas (95035-5128)
PHONE..................................669 900-8000
Jorge L Titinger, *CEO*
Cassio Conceicao, *COO*
Mack Asrat, *CFO*
Eng Lim Goh, *Senior VP*
Peter E Hilliard, *Senior VP*
▲ **EMP:** 673 **EST:** 2002
SALES (est): 268.5MM
SALES (corp-wide): 26.9B **Publicly Held**
WEB: www.sgi.com
SIC: 3577 7371 Computer peripheral equipment; computer software development & applications
PA: Hewlett Packard Enterprise Company
11445 Compaq Center W Dr
Houston TX 77070
650 687-5817

(P-5412)
SOLFLOWER COMPUTER INC
3337 Kifer Rd, Santa Clara (95051-0719)
PHONE..................................408 733-8100
Kim Vu, *President*
Janet Doan, *Vice Pres*
Paul Nguyen, *Manager*
EMP: 20 **EST:** 1988
SQ FT: 8,000
SALES (est): 4.1MM **Privately Held**
WEB: www.solflower.com
SIC: 3577 Computer peripheral equipment

(P-5413)
SP CONTROLS INC
930 Linden Ave, South San Francisco (94080-1754)
PHONE..................................650 392-7880
Paul Anson Brown, *CEO*
Gary Arcudi, *Exec VP*
Bob Toleno, *Technical Staff*
▲ **EMP:** 15 **EST:** 1997
SQ FT: 5,000
SALES (est): 3.1MM **Privately Held**
WEB: www.spcontrols.com
SIC: 3577 Computer peripheral equipment

(P-5414)
SPYRUS INC (PA)
103 Bonaventura Dr, San Jose (95134-2106)
PHONE..................................408 392-9131
Sue Pontius, *CEO*
Tom Dickens, *COO*
Ed Almojuela, *Treasurer*
Steve Kadash, *Vice Pres*
Sheelah Gott, *Clerk*
EMP: 20 **EST:** 1992
SQ FT: 15,000
SALES (est): 5.5MM **Privately Held**
WEB: www.spyrus.com
SIC: 3577 7371 7372 Computer peripheral equipment; computer software development; prepackaged software

(P-5415)
SYNAPTICS INCORPORATED
1109 Mckay Dr, San Jose (95131-1706)
PHONE..................................408 904-1100
EMP: 81
SALES (corp-wide): 1.3B **Publicly Held**
WEB: www.synaptics.com
SIC: 3577 7372 Computer peripheral equipment; prepackaged software
PA: Synaptics Incorporated
1251 Mckay Dr
San Jose CA 95131
408 904-1100

(P-5416)
SYNAPTICS INCORPORATED (PA)
1251 Mckay Dr, San Jose (95131-1709)
PHONE..................................408 904-1100
Michael Hurlston, *President*
Nelson C Chan, *Ch of Bd*
Dean Butler, *CFO*
John McFarland, *Senior VP*
Kermit Nolan, *Vice Pres*
EMP: 1059 **EST:** 1986
SQ FT: 210,000

PRODUCTS & SERVICES SECTION

3589 - Service Ind Machines, NEC County (P-5439)

SALES: 1.3B **Publicly Held**
WEB: www.synaptics.com
SIC: 3577 7372 Computer peripheral equipment; application computer software

(P-5417)
SYNAPTICS INTERNATIONAL INC
1251 Mckay Dr, San Jose (95131-1709)
PHONE 408 955-0783
Kermit Nolan, *CFO*
John McFarland, *Admin Sec*
EMP: 30 **EST:** 2016
SALES (est): 592K **Privately Held**
WEB: www.synaptics.com
SIC: 3577 Computer peripheral equipment

(P-5418)
TELEPATHY INC
1202 Kifer Rd, Sunnyvale (94086-5304)
PHONE 408 306-8421
EMP: 25 **EST:** 2013
SQ FT: 600
SALES (est): 2.5MM **Privately Held**
SIC: 3577 Mfg Computer Peripheral Equipment

(P-5419)
TERARECON INC
93141 Civic Ct Dr, Fremont (94538)
PHONE 650 372-1100
Jeff Sorenson, *Branch Mgr*
EMP: 35
SALES (corp-wide): 53.1MM **Privately Held**
WEB: www.terarecon.com
SIC: 3577 5734 Computer peripheral equipment; computer & software stores
PA: Terarecon Inc.
  4309 Emperor Blvd Ste 310
  Durham NC 27703
  650 372-1100

(P-5420)
USI MANUFACTURING SERVICES INC
1255 E Arques Ave, Sunnyvale (94085-4701)
PHONE 408 636-9600
Frank Halvorson, *Producer*
EMP: 31 **EST:** 2000
SALES (est): 1.1MM **Privately Held**
SIC: 3577 Computer peripheral equipment

(P-5421)
VISIONEER INC (HQ)
5696 Stewart Ave, Fremont (94538-3174)
PHONE 925 251-6300
J Larry Smart, *Ch of Bd*
Walt Thinsen, *President*
Greg Elder, *CFO*
John C Dexter, *Vice Pres*
Jennifer Willems, *Business Dir*
▲ **EMP:** 49 **EST:** 1994
SALES (est): 38.8MM **Privately Held**
WEB: www.visioneer.com
SIC: 3577 Computer peripheral equipment

3578 Calculating & Accounting Eqpt

(P-5422)
EDWARDS & ANDERSON INC
2845 Day Rd, Gilroy (95020-8827)
PHONE 408 847-6770
Jerry Anderson, *Branch Mgr*
EMP: 24
SALES (corp-wide): 1.1MM **Privately Held**
SIC: 3578 Automatic teller machines (ATM)
PA: Edwards & Anderson, Inc.
  3649 Jamison Way
  Castro Valley CA 94546
  510 581-0230

(P-5423)
POS PORTAL INC (HQ)
180 Promenade Cir Ste 215, Sacramento (95834-2940)
PHONE 530 695-3005
Mike Baur, *CEO*
Scott Agatep, *COO*
Evamarie K Ghiggeri, *Vice Pres*
Sarah Klose, *Vice Pres*
Joe Villamil, *Vice Pres*
▲ **EMP:** 27 **EST:** 2000
SQ FT: 12,500
SALES (est): 14.1MM **Publicly Held**
WEB: www.posportal.com
SIC: 3578 3699 Point-of-sale devices; security control equipment & systems

(P-5424)
VERIFONE INTRMDATE HLDINGS INC
2099 Gateway Pl, San Jose (95110-1093)
PHONE 408 232-7800
German Romero, *Technical Staff*
James Edwards, *Engineer*
Joel Sampson, *Engineer*
Ian Smith, *Engineer*
Carl Brandis, *Director*
EMP: 99 **EST:** 2002
SALES (est): 10.3MM
SALES (corp-wide): 695.1MM **Privately Held**
WEB: www.verifone.com
SIC: 3578 Point-of-sale devices
HQ: Verifone, Inc.
  2744 N University Dr
  Coral Springs FL 33065
  800 837-4366

3579 Office Machines, NEC

(P-5425)
PARKER POWIS INC
2929 5th St, Berkeley (94710-2736)
PHONE 510 848-2463
Kevin Parker, *President*
Charles Marino, *COO*
Tony Cheng, *CFO*
Sacramento Gonzalez, *Technical Staff*
Angela Knutzon, *Purch Agent*
▲ **EMP:** 75 **EST:** 1982
SQ FT: 54,000
SALES (est): 12.9MM **Privately Held**
WEB: www.mypowis.com
SIC: 3579 Binding machines, plastic & adhesive

3581 Automatic Vending Machines

(P-5426)
CARACAL ENTERPRISES LLC
Also Called: Ventek International
1260 Holm Rd Ste A, Petaluma (94954-7152)
PHONE 707 773-3373
Gary Catt, *President*
Philip Wilkinson, *COO*
Bill Paulin, *CFO*
Joan Barrie, *Executive Asst*
Carol Kresse, *Controller*
▲ **EMP:** 30 **EST:** 2003
SALES (est): 5.3MM **Privately Held**
WEB: www.ventek-intl.com
SIC: 3581 Automatic vending machines

3582 Commercial Laundry, Dry Clean & Pressing Mchs

(P-5427)
WESTERN STATE DESIGN INC
2331 Tripaldi Way, Hayward (94545-5022)
PHONE 510 786-9271
Michael Ambrose, *Sales Staff*
EMP: 80 **EST:** 2016
SALES (est): 19.6MM **Publicly Held**
WEB: www.westernstatedesign.com
SIC: 3582 Commercial laundry equipment; dryers, laundry: commercial, including coin-operated; extractors, commercial laundry; washing machines, laundry: commercial, incl. coin-operated
PA: Evi Industries, Inc.
  4500 Biscayne Blvd # 340
  Miami FL 33137

3585 Air Conditioning & Heating Eqpt

(P-5428)
AVIATE ENTERPRISES INC
5844 Price Ave, McClellan (95652-2407)
PHONE 916 993-4000
Timothy Devine, *CEO*
Michael A Bush, *VP Business*
Carolyn Wells, *VP Business*
Sayed Mahboobi, *IT/INT Sup*
Diane Devine, *Finance*
EMP: 27 **EST:** 2014
SQ FT: 3,700
SALES (est): 10.2MM **Privately Held**
WEB: www.aviateinc.com
SIC: 3585 3843 5599 3629 Refrigeration & heating equipment; dental equipment & supplies; golf cart, powered; electronic generation equipment; medical & hospital equipment

(P-5429)
BALTIMORE AIRCOIL COMPANY INC
B A C
15341 Road 28 1/2, Madera (93638-2395)
P.O. Box 960 (93639-0960)
PHONE 559 673-9231
Han Yen, *Branch Mgr*
Candice Nager, *Comms Mgr*
Chad Shaffer, *General Mgr*
Adam Garcia, *Info Tech Dir*
Michael Raabe, *Info Tech Mgr*
EMP: 150
SQ FT: 45,000
SALES (corp-wide): 2.4B **Privately Held**
WEB: www.baltimoreaircoil.com
SIC: 3585 Condensers, refrigeration; refrigeration equipment, complete
HQ: Baltimore Aircoil Company, Inc.
  7600 Dorsey Run Rd
  Jessup MD 20794
  410 799-6200

(P-5430)
FLUID INDUSTRIAL MFG INC
340 S Milpitas Blvd, Milpitas (95035-5421)
PHONE 408 782-9900
Kerry Kirchenbauer, *President*
Nichole Karavlan, *Project Mgr*
EMP: 19 **EST:** 2004
SALES (est): 3MM **Privately Held**
WEB: www.chillermen.com
SIC: 3585 Refrigeration equipment, complete

(P-5431)
GOODMAN MANUFACTURING CO LP
3018 Alvarado St Ste C, San Leandro (94577-5726)
PHONE 510 265-1212
Toni Boglin, *Branch Mgr*
EMP: 292 **Privately Held**
WEB: www.goodmanmfg.com
SIC: 3585 Refrigeration & heating equipment
HQ: Goodman Manufacturing Company, Lp
  19001 Kermier Rd
  Waller TX 77484
  713 861-2500

(P-5432)
J P LAMBORN CO (PA)
Also Called: J P L
3663 E Wawona Ave, Fresno (93725-9236)
PHONE 559 650-2120
John P Lamborn Jr, *CEO*
Katlyn Garcia, *Executive*
Pam Lamborn, *Admin Sec*
Jonathon Lamborn, *Technology*
Jason Shelton, *Engineer*
▲ **EMP:** 375 **EST:** 1961
SQ FT: 125,000
SALES (est): 33.1MM **Privately Held**
WEB: www.jplflex.com
SIC: 3585 Heating & air conditioning combination units

(P-5433)
MACINTYRE CORP
27403 Industrial Blvd, Hayward (94545-3348)
PHONE 800 229-3560
John-Paul Farsight, *CEO*
EMP: 25 **EST:** 2020
SALES (est): 1.2MM **Privately Held**
SIC: 3585 Refrigeration & heating equipment

(P-5434)
MYDAX INC
12260 Shale Ridge Ln # 4, Auburn (95602-8400)
PHONE 530 888-6662
Richard S Frankel, *CEO*
Gary Kramer, *President*
Thomas Spesick, *Vice Pres*
Justin Clark, *QC Mgr*
Buck Brogdon, *Mfg Staff*
EMP: 19 **EST:** 1986
SQ FT: 15,000
SALES (est): 2.5MM **Privately Held**
WEB: www.mydax.com
SIC: 3585 Refrigeration & heating equipment

(P-5435)
TREAU INC
375 Alabama St Ste 220, San Francisco (94110-1361)
PHONE 866 945-3514
Vincent Romanin, *President*
EMP: 22 **EST:** 2017
SALES: 2.7MM **Privately Held**
WEB: www.gradientcomfort.com
SIC: 3585 8731 Air conditioning condensers & condensing units; energy research

(P-5436)
VINOTHEQUE WINE CELLARS
1738 E Alpine Ave, Stockton (95205-2505)
PHONE 209 466-9463
Thomas R Schneider, *CEO*
Franklin Pfaller-Martin, *Prdtn Mgr*
Samantha Matlock, *Marketing Staff*
Rocky Zuniga, *Sales Staff*
Joaquin Jasso, *Facilities Mgr*
▼ **EMP:** 16 **EST:** 1999
SQ FT: 30,000
SALES (est): 3.9MM **Privately Held**
WEB: www.vinotheque.com
SIC: 3585 Refrigeration equipment, complete

3589 Service Ind Machines, NEC

(P-5437)
ACM RESEARCH INC (PA)
42307 Osgood Rd Ste I, Fremont (94539-5062)
PHONE 510 445-3700
David H Wang, *President*
Mark McKechnie, *CFO*
Sally Henry, *Marketing Staff*
EMP: 540 **EST:** 1998
SALES (est): 156.6MM **Publicly Held**
WEB: www.acmrcsh.com
SIC: 3589 Commercial cleaning equipment

(P-5438)
AUTO-CHLOR SYSTEM NY CY INC (PA)
450 Ferguson Dr, Mountain View (94043-5214)
PHONE 650 967-3085
Jerry Ivy, *President*
Debbie Ivy, *Corp Secy*
EMP: 179 **EST:** 1988
SALES (est): 950.6K **Privately Held**
WEB: www.autochlor.com
SIC: 3589 Dishwashing machines, commercial

(P-5439)
B M D ENTERPRISES INC
Also Called: Pure Water Pool Service
4959 E Dakota Ave Ste A, Fresno (93727-7402)
PHONE 559 291-7708

3589 - Service Ind Machines, NEC County (P-5440)

Todd Yingling, *President*
Charles Ben Dunn, *CEO*
Suzanne Yingling, *Corp Secy*
Marilyn Dunn, *Vice Pres*
EMP: 18 **EST:** 1961
SQ FT: 5,000
SALES (est): 1.7MM **Privately Held**
WEB: www.purewaterpoolsfresno.com
SIC: 5999 **3589** Swimming pool chemicals, equipment & supplies; swimming pools, hot tubs & sauna equipment & supplies; swimming pool filter & water conditioning systems

(P-5440)
CHEMICAL TECHNOLOGIES INTL INC
Also Called: CTI
2747 Merc Dr Ste 200, Rancho Cordova (95742)
P.O. Box 968 (95741-0968)
PHONE.....................916 638-1315
Clint Townsend, *CEO*
Risa Townsend, *Treasurer*
Todd Hinde, *Technical Staff*
Diane Corey, *Human Resources*
Chad Townsend, *Plant Mgr*
▲ **EMP:** 18 **EST:** 1998
SQ FT: 50,000
SALES (est): 4.8MM **Privately Held**
WEB: www.proschoice.com
SIC: 3589 2842 Commercial cleaning equipment; cleaning or polishing preparations

(P-5441)
MAR COR PURIFICATION INC
2606 Barrington Ct, Hayward (94545-1100)
PHONE.....................510 397-0025
EMP: 29 **Privately Held**
WEB: www.mcpur.com
SIC: 3589 Water treatment equipment, industrial
HQ: Mar Cor Purification, Inc.
  4450 Township Line Rd
  Skippack PA 19474
  800 633-3080

(P-5442)
MCC CONTROLS LLC
Also Called: Primex
859 Cotting Ct Ste G, Vacaville (95688-9354)
P.O. Box 1708, Detroit Lakes MN (56502-1708)
PHONE.....................218 847-1317
David Thomas, *President*
Taunia Suckert, *Corp Secy*
Joseph Martell, *Prgrmr*
Pete Santos, *Purch Agent*
Sead Filipovic, *Production*
EMP: 27 **EST:** 2016
SALES (est): 3.7MM **Privately Held**
SIC: 3589 Sewage & water treatment equipment

(P-5443)
MONTAGUE COMPANY
1830 Stearman Ave, Hayward (94545-1018)
P.O. Box 4954 (94540-4954)
PHONE.....................510 785-8822
Thomas M Whalen, *President*
Robert M Whalen, *Chairman*
George A Malloch, *Admin Sec*
◆ **EMP:** 105 **EST:** 1857
SQ FT: 100,000
SALES (est): 25.5MM **Privately Held**
WEB: www.montaguecompany.com
SIC: 3589 Cooking equipment, commercial

(P-5444)
NEW WAVE INDUSTRIES LTD (PA)
Also Called: Pur-Clean Pressure Car Wash
3315 Orange Grove Ave, North Highlands (95660-5807)
PHONE.....................800 882-8854
Gary Hirsh, *CEO*
Dave Sharma, *Vice Pres*
Nicolle Hearne, *Project Mgr*
Teresa Borchard, *Technical Staff*
Greg Oliver, *Engineer*
EMP: 17 **EST:** 1985
SQ FT: 24,000

SALES (est): 5.2MM **Privately Held**
WEB: www.purclean.com
SIC: 3589 Car washing machinery

(P-5445)
NIECO CORPORATION
7950 Cameron Dr, Windsor (95492-8594)
PHONE.....................707 838-3226
Edward D Baker Sr, *President*
Jamie Nau, *President*
Edward Baker Jr, *Vice Pres*
Matthew Baker, *Vice Pres*
Patrick Baker, *Vice Pres*
◆ **EMP:** 70 **EST:** 1972
SQ FT: 80,000
SALES (est): 18.4MM
SALES (corp-wide): 2.5B **Publicly Held**
WEB: www.nieco.com
SIC: 3589 Commercial cooking & food-warming equipment
PA: The Middleby Corporation
  1400 Toastmaster Dr
  Elgin IL 60120
  847 741-3300

(P-5446)
OZOTECH INC (PA)
1015 S Main St, Yreka (96097-3324)
PHONE.....................530 842-4189
Stephen Christiansen, *President*
Steve Christiansen, *Opers Staff*
Lance Vogel, *Opers Staff*
▲ **EMP:** 18 **EST:** 1986
SALES (est): 2.9MM **Privately Held**
WEB: www.ozotech.com
SIC: 3589 Water purification equipment, household type; water treatment equipment, industrial

(P-5447)
PURONICS INCORPORATED (HQ)
5775 Las Positas Rd, Livermore (94551-7819)
PHONE.....................925 456-7000
Gregg C Sengstack, *CEO*
EMP: 66 **EST:** 2005
SALES (est): 12.7MM
SALES (corp-wide): 1.2B **Publicly Held**
WEB: www.puronics.com
SIC: 3589 Swimming pool filter & water conditioning systems
PA: Franklin Electric Co., Inc.
  9255 Coverdale Rd
  Fort Wayne IN 46809
  260 824-2900

(P-5448)
RYKO SOLUTIONS INC
3939 W Capitol Ave Ste D, West Sacramento (95691-2105)
PHONE.....................916 372-8815
EMP: 21
SALES (corp-wide): 2.3B **Privately Held**
SIC: 3589 5087 Mfg Service Industry Machinery Whol Service Establishment Equipment
HQ: Ryko Solutions, Inc.
  1500 Se 37th St
  Grimes IA 50111
  515 986-3700

(P-5449)
THERMIONICS LABORATORY INC
10230 Twin Pines Pl, Grass Valley (95949-9530)
PHONE.....................530 272-3436
Steve Rolland, *Principal*
EMP: 48
SALES (corp-wide): 36.5MM **Privately Held**
WEB: www.thermionics.com
SIC: 3589 Asbestos removal equipment
HQ: Thermionics Laboratory, Inc.
  3118 Depot Rd
  Hayward CA 94545
  510 538-3304

(P-5450)
VANDER LANS & SONS INC (PA)
Also Called: Lansas Products
1320 S Sacramento St, Lodi (95240-5705)
P.O. Box 758 (95241-0758)
PHONE.....................209 334-4115
Gerald Vanderlans, *President*

Nick Bettencourt, *Corp Secy*
Victor Schuh, *Corp Secy*
Nora Linley, *Admin Asst*
April Hayles, *Bookkeeper*
▲ **EMP:** 41 **EST:** 1958
SQ FT: 30,000
SALES (est): 8.7MM **Privately Held**
WEB: www.lansas.com
SIC: 3589 5084 Commercial cleaning equipment; industrial machinery & equipment

(P-5451)
WATER ONE INDUSTRIES INC (PA)
5410 Gateway Plaza Dr, Benicia (94510-2122)
PHONE.....................707 747-4300
Hans-Erik Fuchs, *CEO*
Erin Steiger, *Corp Secy*
Tim Russell, *Vice Pres*
Brian Robinson, *Regional Mgr*
Matt Steiger, *Regional Mgr*
EMP: 25 **EST:** 2006
SQ FT: 3,500
SALES (est): 4MM **Privately Held**
WEB: www.wateroneonline.com
SIC: 3589 Water treatment equipment, industrial

(P-5452)
YUBA CY WSTE WTR TRTMNT FCILTY
302 Burns Dr, Yuba City (95991-7205)
PHONE.....................530 822-7698
John Buckland, *Mayor*
Pat Posthumus, *Executive*
EMP: 24 **EST:** 2003
SALES (est): 2.3MM **Privately Held**
WEB: www.yubacity.net
SIC: 3589 Water treatment equipment, industrial

3593 Fluid Power Cylinders & Actuators

(P-5453)
TURLOCK MACHINE WORKS
Also Called: Hypower Hydraulics
1240 S 1st St, Turlock (95380-6023)
P.O. Box 3788 (95381-3788)
PHONE.....................209 632-2275
Vivian Manha, *CEO*
Konrad Hack, *Treasurer*
Judy Hunt, *Vice Pres*
EMP: 30 **EST:** 1937
SQ FT: 35,000
SALES (est): 3.4MM **Privately Held**
WEB: www.hypowerhydraulics.com
SIC: 3593 8611 Fluid power cylinders & actuators; manufacturers' institute

3596 Scales & Balances, Exc Laboratory

(P-5454)
BIOMICROLAB INC
2500 Dean Lesher Dr Ste A, Concord (94520-1273)
PHONE.....................925 689-1200
David B Miller, *President*
William Hess, *Vice Pres*
David Miller, *Info Tech Mgr*
Brian Lechman, *Electrical Engi*
Alex Drynkin, *Engineer*
EMP: 20 **EST:** 2004
SALES (est): 7MM
SALES (corp-wide): 50.2MM **Privately Held**
WEB: www.sptlabtech.com
SIC: 3596 Weighing machines & apparatus
HQ: Spt Labtech Limited
  Melbourn Science Park
  Royston HERTS SG8 6
  122 362-7555

3599 Machinery & Eqpt, Indl & Commercial, NEC

(P-5455)
478826 LIMITED
Also Called: Zi Machine Manufacturing
5050 Hillsdale Cir, El Dorado Hills (95762-5706)
PHONE.....................916 933-5280
Steve Zeldag, *CEO*
Stephen Zeldag, *Sales Mgr*
EMP: 21 **EST:** 1983
SQ FT: 26,000
SALES (est): 3.1MM **Privately Held**
WEB: www.zimachine.com
SIC: 3599 Machine shop, jobbing & repair

(P-5456)
A & D PRECISION MACHINING INC
4155 Business Center Dr, Fremont (94538-6355)
PHONE.....................510 657-6781
David A Dreifort, *CEO*
Anson Nguyen, *Engineer*
Marcus Rosevear, *Engineer*
Nick Le, *Mfg Staff*
Caprice Dreifort, *Marketing Mgr*
EMP: 45 **EST:** 1977
SQ FT: 28,000
SALES (est): 12.7MM **Privately Held**
WEB: www.adprecision.com
SIC: 3599 Machine shop, jobbing & repair

(P-5457)
A&T PRECISION MACHINING
330 Piercy Rd, San Jose (95138-1401)
PHONE.....................408 363-1198
James Le, *Partner*
An Le, *Partner*
Hieu Le, *Partner*
Michael Vo, *Sales Staff*
EMP: 34 **EST:** 1993
SALES (est): 3.3MM **Privately Held**
SIC: 3599 Machine shop, jobbing & repair; machine & other job shop work

(P-5458)
A-1 JAYS MACHINING INC (PA)
2228 Oakland Rd, San Jose (95131-1414)
PHONE.....................408 262-1845
James K Machathil, *CEO*
Thomas Abraham, *General Mgr*
EMP: 80 **EST:** 1990
SQ FT: 10,000
SALES (est): 19.3MM **Privately Held**
WEB: www.a1jays.com
SIC: 3599 Machine shop, jobbing & repair

(P-5459)
A-1 MACHINE MANUFACTURING INC (PA)
490 Gianni St, Santa Clara (95054-2413)
PHONE.....................408 727-0880
Yong Kil, *President*
Yong Su Pak, *Vice Pres*
▲ **EMP:** 175 **EST:** 1986
SQ FT: 250,000
SALES (est): 28.2MM **Privately Held**
SIC: 3599 Machine shop, jobbing & repair

(P-5460)
ABSOLUTE MACHINE INC
5020 Mountain Lakes Blvd, Redding (96003-1457)
PHONE.....................530 242-6840
Alfred Madena, *President*
EMP: 16 **EST:** 2004
SALES (est): 1.4MM **Privately Held**
WEB: www.absolutem.com
SIC: 3599 Machine shop, jobbing & repair

(P-5461)
ACCURATE TECHNOLOGY MFG INC
930 Thompson Pl, Sunnyvale (94085-4517)
PHONE.....................408 733-4344
Ivo Dukanovic, *CEO*
John Dukanovic, *Owner*
EMP: 60 **EST:** 1994
SQ FT: 40,000

PRODUCTS & SERVICES SECTION
3599 - Machinery & Eqpt, Indl & Commercial, NEC County (P-5487)

SALES (est): 10.1MM **Privately Held**
WEB: www.accuratetm.com
SIC: **3599** Machine shop, jobbing & repair

(P-5462)
ACM MACHINING INC
Also Called: Alfred's Machining
240 State Highway 16 # 18, Plymouth (95669-9701)
PHONE..................916 804-9489
Carlos Balbacas, *Owner*
Phil Garcia, *QC Mgr*
EMP: 35
SALES (corp-wide): 16.2MM **Privately Held**
WEB: www.acmmachining.com
SIC: **3599** 3494 Machine shop, jobbing & repair; valves & pipe fittings
PA: Acm Machining, Inc.
  11390 Gold Dredge Way
  Rancho Cordova CA 95742
  916 852-8600

(P-5463)
ACM MACHINING INC (PA)
11390 Gold Dredge Way, Rancho Cordova (95742-6867)
PHONE..................916 852-8600
Alfred Balbach, *President*
Carlos Balbachas, *Vice Pres*
Pete Reynen, *General Mgr*
Mariano Ispas, *Engineer*
Alexander Shamota, *Engineer*
▲ EMP: 41 EST: 1974
SQ FT: 29,000
SALES (est): 16.2MM **Privately Held**
WEB: www.acmmachining.com
SIC: **3599** Machine shop, jobbing & repair

(P-5464)
ADEM LLC
Also Called: Advanced Design Engrg & Mfg
1040 Di Giulio Ave # 160, Santa Clara (95050-2847)
PHONE..................408 727-8955
Boris Kesil,
Jacob Obolsky,
Valery Sokolsky,
EMP: 30 EST: 1997
SQ FT: 11,000
SALES (est): 6.9MM **Privately Held**
WEB: www.ademllc.com
SIC: **3599** 8711 Machine shop, jobbing & repair; engineering services

(P-5465)
ADVANCED COMPONENTS MFG
Also Called: A C M
1415 N Carolan Ave, Burlingame (94010-2403)
PHONE..................650 344-6272
Craig Corey, *President*
Jack Corey, *Treasurer*
Gloria Corey, *Admin Sec*
EMP: 26 EST: 1984
SQ FT: 6,500
SALES (est): 1.2MM **Privately Held**
SIC: **3599** 3444 Machine shop, jobbing & repair; sheet metalwork

(P-5466)
ADVANCED MCHNING TCHNIQUES INC
16205 Vineyard Blvd, Morgan Hill (95037-7124)
PHONE..................408 778-4500
Frank C Dutra, *President*
Susan Dutra, *Vice Pres*
Marla Abeyta, *Admin Sec*
Dj Bain, *Purchasing*
Sharyn Gibbs, *Sales Staff*
EMP: 49 EST: 1985
SQ FT: 24,000 **Privately Held**
WEB: www.advancedmachining.com
SIC: **3599** Machine shop, jobbing & repair

(P-5467)
ALL-IN MACHINING LLC
157 Sloan Ct Ste B, Tracy (95304-1649)
PHONE..................209 839-8672
Jake Flanigan,
EMP: 21 EST: 2017
SALES (est): 2.5MM **Privately Held**
WEB: www.allinmach.com
SIC: **3599** Machine shop, jobbing & repair

(P-5468)
ALL-TECH MACHINE & ENGRG INC
2700 Prune Ave, Fremont (94539-6780)
PHONE..................510 353-2000
Richard M Gale, *CEO*
Boydine Michaels, *Vice Pres*
Janice Moan, *Admin Sec*
EMP: 49 EST: 1987
SALES (est): 5.6MM **Privately Held**
WEB: www.alltechinc.com
SIC: **3599** Machine shop, jobbing & repair

(P-5469)
ALPHA MACHINE COMPANY INC
933 Chittenden Ln Ste A, Capitola (95010-3600)
PHONE..................831 462-7400
Pemo Saraliev, *President*
Chris Jenschke, *Partner*
Jonathan Saraliev, *Engineer*
Marlene Saraliev, *Agent*
EMP: 18 EST: 1978
SQ FT: 12,000
SALES (est): 3MM **Privately Held**
WEB: www.alphamco.com
SIC: **3599** Machine shop, jobbing & repair

(P-5470)
ALTAMONT MANUFACTURING INC
241 Rickenbacker Cir, Livermore (94551-7216)
PHONE..................925 371-5401
Robert Stivers, *President*
Richard Stivers, *Vice Pres*
EMP: 18 EST: 2003
SALES (est): 3.1MM **Privately Held**
WEB: www.altamontmfg.com
SIC: **3599** Machine shop, jobbing & repair

(P-5471)
ALTEST CORPORATION
898 Faulstich Ct, San Jose (95112-1361)
PHONE..................408 436-9900
Savann Seng, *CEO*
Brian Sen, *President*
Amy Tung, *Vice Pres*
Sanjay Agarwal, *Engineer*
Chad Chhoun, *Production*
EMP: 29 EST: 1998
SQ FT: 30,000
SALES (est): 7.9MM **Privately Held**
WEB: www.altestcorp.com
SIC: **3599** 3672 Machine shop, jobbing & repair; printed circuit boards

(P-5472)
ALVELLAN INC
Also Called: East Bay Machine and Shtmtl
1030 Shary Ct, Concord (94518-2409)
P.O. Box 1206 (94522-1206)
PHONE..................925 689-2421
Sean M McLellan, *CEO*
Tim Alvey, *CFO*
EMP: 28 EST: 2006
SQ FT: 30,000
SALES (est): 3.9MM **Privately Held**
SIC: **3599** 5083 Machine shop, jobbing & repair; lawn & garden machinery & equipment

(P-5473)
ANGULAR MACHINING INC
2040 Hartog Dr, San Jose (95131-2214)
PHONE..................408 954-8326
Kiet Nguyen, *President*
Tina Tran, *Office Mgr*
EMP: 46 EST: 2001
SALES (est): 3.7MM **Privately Held**
WEB: www.angularmachining.com
SIC: **3599** Machine shop, jobbing & repair

(P-5474)
APEX MACHINING INC
1997 Hartog Dr, San Jose (95131-2222)
PHONE..................408 441-1335
Carl Kennedy, *General Mgr*
Gilbert Gutierrez, *Purch Mgr*
EMP: 23 EST: 1993
SQ FT: 1,200
SALES (est): 1.5MM **Privately Held**
WEB: www.apex-machining.com
SIC: **3599** Machine shop, jobbing & repair

(P-5475)
APPLIED PROCESS EQUIPMENT
2620 Bay Rd, Redwood City (94063-3501)
PHONE..................650 365-6895
Michael T Hertert, *Partner*
Chris Dale, *Partner*
EMP: 21 EST: 1984
SQ FT: 5,000
SALES (est): 1MM **Privately Held**
SIC: **3599** Machine shop, jobbing & repair

(P-5476)
ARMSTRONG TECHNOLOGY SV INC
1271 Anvilwood Ave, Sunnyvale (94089-2204)
PHONE..................408 734-4434
Julie Armstrong, *Vice Pres*
Tim Fast, *Manager*
Rito Velarde, *Manager*
EMP: 19
SALES (corp-wide): 9.1MM **Privately Held**
WEB: www.armstrong-tech.com
SIC: **3599** Machine shop, jobbing & repair
PA: Armstrong Technology S.V., Inc.
  1121 Elko Dr
  Sunnyvale CA 94089
  408 734-4434

(P-5477)
ARMSTRONG TECHNOLOGY SV INC
12780 Earhart Ave, Auburn (95602-9027)
PHONE..................530 888-6262
Arthur Armstrong, *Branch Mgr*
Julie Armstrong, *Vice Pres*
Brandy Haring, *Office Mgr*
Jim Burkhart, *Plant Mgr*
EMP: 19
SALES (corp-wide): 9.1MM **Privately Held**
WEB: www.armstrong-tech.com
SIC: **3599** Machine shop, jobbing & repair
PA: Armstrong Technology S.V., Inc.
  1121 Elko Dr
  Sunnyvale CA 94089
  408 734-4434

(P-5478)
AZTEC MACHINE CO INC
3156 Fitzgerald Rd Ste A, Rancho Cordova (95742-6889)
PHONE..................916 638-4894
Alfredo Alvarez, *President*
EMP: 19 EST: 1994
SQ FT: 7,200
SALES (est): 1MM **Privately Held**
WEB: www.aztecmachine.com
SIC: **3599** Machine shop, jobbing & repair

(P-5479)
B & G PRECISION INC
45450 Industrial Pl Ste 9, Fremont (94538-6474)
PHONE..................510 438-9785
Daniel Datta, *CEO*
EMP: 19 EST: 1986
SQ FT: 3,600
SALES (est): 3.1MM **Privately Held**
WEB: www.bgprecisioninc.com
SIC: **3599** Machine shop, jobbing & repair; machine & other job shop work

(P-5480)
B&Z MANUFACTURING COMPANY INC
1478 Seareel Ln, San Jose (95131-1567)
PHONE..................408 943-1117
Dennis Kimball, *President*
Thomas Simpson, *Corp Secy*
Linda Franks, *Accounting Mgr*
Karen House, *Manager*
EMP: 42 EST: 1960
SQ FT: 18,000
SALES (est): 5.6MM **Privately Held**
WEB: www.bzmfg.com
SIC: **3599** Machine shop, jobbing & repair

(P-5481)
BABBITT BEARING CO INC
Also Called: B B C
1170 N 5th St, San Jose (95112-4483)
PHONE..................408 298-1101
Stanley Sinn, *President*
Jerry Mann, *Vice Pres*
Steve Oliveira, *General Mgr*
EMP: 25 EST: 1946
SQ FT: 16,000
SALES (est): 5.3MM **Privately Held**
WEB: www.bbcmachine.com
SIC: **3599** Machine shop, jobbing & repair

(P-5482)
BAY PRECISION MACHINING INC
Also Called: Emkay Mfg.
815 Sweeney Ave Ste D, Redwood City (94063-3029)
PHONE..................650 365-3010
Anne Feher, *President*
George Koncz, *Vice Pres*
EMP: 33 EST: 1978
SQ FT: 7,500
SALES (est): 1.9MM **Privately Held**
SIC: **3599** Machine shop, jobbing & repair

(P-5483)
BEGOVIC INDUSTRIES INC
Also Called: B & H Engineering Company
1725 Old County Rd, San Carlos (94070-5206)
PHONE..................650 594-2861
Bakir Begovic, *CEO*
Kenan Begovic, *President*
Hamida Begovic, *Vice Pres*
Majid Suljic, *Mfg Staff*
EMP: 20 EST: 1972
SALES (est): 5.6MM **Privately Held**
WEB: www.bhengineering.com
SIC: **3599** 3444 Machine shop, jobbing & repair; sheet metalwork

(P-5484)
BRUDER INDUSTRY
3920 Sandstone Dr, El Dorado Hills (95762-9652)
PHONE..................916 939-6888
Rex Kamphfner, *General Mgr*
Mike Kerbow, *Project Engr*
EMP: 76 EST: 1969
SQ FT: 35,000
SALES (est): 1.4MM
SALES (corp-wide): 44.2MM **Privately Held**
WEB: www.aerometals.aero
SIC: **3599** Machine shop, jobbing & repair
PA: Aerometals, Inc.
  3920 Sandstone Dr
  El Dorado Hills CA 95762
  916 939-6888

(P-5485)
C L HANN INDUSTRIES INC
1020 Timothy Dr, San Jose (95133-1042)
PHONE..................408 293-4800
Pete Hann, *President*
Erich Von Shofstall, *COO*
Cheyne Hann, *CFO*
Art Korp, *Vice Pres*
Georgette Hann, *Office Mgr*
EMP: 15 EST: 1971
SQ FT: 30,000
SALES (est): 4.3MM **Privately Held**
WEB: www.clhann.com
SIC: **3599** Machine shop, jobbing & repair; machine & other job shop work

(P-5486)
CALMAX TECHNOLOGY INC
3491 Lafayette St, Santa Clara (95054-2707)
PHONE..................408 748-8600
Manny Adame, *Sls & Mktg Exec*
Gary Hintz, *Exec VP*
Linda M Walters, *Finance*
Michael Irany, *Purchasing*
Israel Leal, *Manager*
EMP: 20 **Privately Held**
WEB: www.calmaxtechnology.com
SIC: **3599** Machine shop, jobbing & repair
PA: Calmax Technology, Inc.
  526 Laurelwood Rd
  Santa Clara CA 95054

(P-5487)
CALMAX TECHNOLOGY INC
558 Laurelwood Rd, Santa Clara (95054-2418)
PHONE..................408 506-2035

3599 - Machinery & Eqpt, Indl & Commercial, NEC County (P-5488)

PRODUCTS & SERVICES SECTION

Boguslaw J Marcinkowski, *Branch Mgr*
EMP: 15 **Privately Held**
WEB: www.calmaxtechnology.com
SIC: 3599 Machine shop, jobbing & repair
PA: Calmax Technology, Inc.
526 Laurelwood Rd
Santa Clara CA 95054

(P-5488)
CALMAX TECHNOLOGY INC (PA)
526 Laurelwood Rd, Santa Clara (95054-2418)
PHONE.................................408 748-8660
Boguslaw J Marcinkowski, *CEO*
Katherine Marcinkowski, *Office Admin*
Linda Walters, *Administration*
Matt Hintz, *Project Mgr*
Haili Liu, *Engineer*
EMP: 50 **EST:** 1987
SQ FT: 78,822
SALES (est): 25.2MM **Privately Held**
WEB: www.calmaxtechnology.com
SIC: 3599 Machine shop, jobbing & repair

(P-5489)
CAMPBELL GRINDING INC
1003 E Vine St, Lodi (95240-3127)
PHONE.................................209 339-8838
Dan Fritz, *President*
EMP: 21 **EST:** 1980
SQ FT: 17,000
SALES (est): 805.6K **Privately Held**
SIC: 3599 Machine shop, jobbing & repair

(P-5490)
CASON ENGINEERING INC
4952 Windplay Dr Ste D, El Dorado Hills (95762-9338)
PHONE.................................916 939-9311
Bradford Cason, *President*
Michelle Cason, *Executive*
EMP: 35 **EST:** 1969
SQ FT: 27,500
SALES (est): 653.4K **Privately Held**
WEB: www.casoneng.com
SIC: 3599 Machine shop, jobbing & repair

(P-5491)
CELESTICA PRCSION MCHINING LTD
40725 Encyclopedia Cir, Fremont (94538-2451)
PHONE.................................510 252-2100
EMP: 16
SALES (corp-wide): 7.9MM **Privately Held**
WEB: www.celestica.com
SIC: 3599 Machine shop, jobbing & repair
PA: Celestica Precision Machining Ltd.
49235 Milmont Dr
Fremont CA 94538
510 742-0500

(P-5492)
CENCAL CNC INC
2491 Simpson St, Kingsburg (93631-9501)
PHONE.................................559 897-8706
Abe Wiebe, *President*
Ann Wiebe, *Vice Pres*
Nick Wiebe, *Vice Pres*
Viktor Reimer, *Production*
Shelby Vincent, *Sales Staff*
EMP: 25 **EST:** 2006
SQ FT: 5,000
SALES (est): 4.8MM **Privately Held**
WEB: www.cencalcnc.com
SIC: 3599 Electrical discharge machining (EDM)

(P-5493)
CERAMIC TECH INC
46211 Research Ave, Fremont (94539-6113)
PHONE.................................510 252-8500
Kanu Gandhi, *President*
Vivek Gandhi, *Treasurer*
EMP: 30 **EST:** 1989
SQ FT: 30,000
SALES (est): 7MM
SALES (corp-wide): 70.2MM **Privately Held**
WEB: www.fralock.com
SIC: 3599 3264 Machine & other job shop work; porcelain electrical supplies

PA: Fralock Holdings Llc
28525 Industry Dr
Valencia CA 91355
661 702-6999

(P-5494)
COLLEEN & HERB ENTERPRISES INC
Also Called: C & H Enterprises
46939 Bayside Pkwy, Fremont (94538-6527)
PHONE.................................510 226-6083
Herbert Schmidt, *CEO*
Colleen Schmidt, *President*
Jake Schmidt, *COO*
Linda Daly, *Human Res Mgr*
Janet Soto, *Human Res Mgr*
EMP: 115 **EST:** 1984
SQ FT: 50,000
SALES (est): 16.7MM **Privately Held**
WEB: www.candhenterprises.com
SIC: 3599 7692 Machine shop, jobbing & repair; welding repair

(P-5495)
CONSOLDTED HNGE MNFCTURED PDTS
Also Called: Champ Co
1150b Dell Ave, Campbell (95008-6640)
PHONE.................................408 379-6550
Karl L Herbst, *President*
Ursula Gueldner, *Treasurer*
Alfred Riesenhuber, *Vice Pres*
Leanne Crockett, *Opers Mgr*
Laurie Guerra, *Production*
EMP: 17 **EST:** 1969
SQ FT: 23,000
SALES (est): 2.8MM **Privately Held**
WEB: www.champcompany.com
SIC: 3599 Machine shop, jobbing & repair

(P-5496)
COUGHRAN MECHANICAL SVCS INC
3053 Liberty Island Rd, Rio Vista (94571-1018)
P.O. Box 158 (94571-0158)
PHONE.................................707 374-2100
Kirk Coughran, *President*
Karla Graham, *CFO*
EMP: 32 **EST:** 1990
SQ FT: 2,400
SALES (est): 1.8MM **Privately Held**
WEB: www.coughranmechanicalservices.com
SIC: 3599 Machine shop, jobbing & repair

(P-5497)
CPK MANUFACTURING INC
2188 Del Franco St Ste 70, San Jose (95131-1583)
PHONE.................................408 971-4019
Khamsy Syluangkhot, *President*
Paul Wendall, *Vice Pres*
EMP: 16 **EST:** 1995
SALES (est): 4.2MM **Privately Held**
WEB: www.cpkmfg.net
SIC: 3599 Machine shop, jobbing & repair; machine & other job shop work

(P-5498)
CREATIVE METAL PRODUCTS CORP
6284 San Ignacio Ave D, San Jose (95119-1366)
PHONE.................................408 281-0797
Kenneth Hutchinson, *President*
Shirley Hutchinson, *Corp Secy*
▲ **EMP:** 26 **EST:** 1984
SQ FT: 4,606
SALES (est): 1.7MM **Privately Held**
WEB: www.creativemetalproducts.com
SIC: 3599 3544 Machine shop, jobbing & repair; special dies, tools, jigs & fixtures

(P-5499)
CUSTOM MICRO MACHINING INC
707 Brown Rd, Fremont (94539-7014)
PHONE.................................510 651-9434
Tao Chou, *President*
Victor Nguyen, *Vice Pres*
Christina Le, *General Mgr*
Kim Nguyen, *Planning Mgr*
EMP: 26 **EST:** 1990

SQ FT: 8,000
SALES (est): 3.5MM **Privately Held**
WEB: www.cmmusa.com
SIC: 3599 Machine shop, jobbing & repair

(P-5500)
CUTTING EDGE MACHINING INC (PA)
1331 Old County Rd, Belmont (94002-3967)
PHONE.................................408 738-8677
Jack Corey, *CEO*
Gloria L Corey, *Corp Secy*
EMP: 25 **EST:** 1973
SALES (est): 5.5MM **Privately Held**
WEB: www.cemachining.com
SIC: 3599 Machine shop, jobbing & repair

(P-5501)
D & F STANDLER INC
195 Lewis Rd Ste 39, San Jose (95111-2192)
PHONE.................................408 226-8188
Dennis Styczynski, *President*
Alain Styczynski, *Vice Pres*
EMP: 23 **EST:** 1980
SQ FT: 11,000
SALES (est): 1.2MM **Privately Held**
WEB: www.dfstandler.com
SIC: 3599 Machine shop, jobbing & repair

(P-5502)
D & T MACHINING INC
3360 Victor Ct, Santa Clara (95054-2316)
PHONE.................................408 486-6035
Tom Nguyen, *President*
EMP: 18 **EST:** 1994
SQ FT: 1,800
SALES (est): 677.4K **Privately Held**
WEB: www.dtmachining.com
SIC: 3599 Machine shop, jobbing & repair

(P-5503)
DARKO PRECISION INC
470 Gianni St, Santa Clara (95054-2413)
PHONE.................................408 988-6133
Dardo Simunic, *President*
Vesna Simunic, *Vice Pres*
EMP: 78 **EST:** 1987
SQ FT: 35,000
SALES (est): 20.7MM **Privately Held**
WEB: www.darkoprecision.com
SIC: 3599 Machine shop, jobbing & repair

(P-5504)
DCPM INC
Also Called: DC Valve Mfg & Precision Mchs
885 Jarvis Dr, Morgan Hill (95037-2858)
PHONE.................................408 928-2510
Cuu Banh, *CEO*
James Swartzbaugh, *Manager*
EMP: 43 **EST:** 1998
SQ FT: 3,200
SALES (est): 6.7MM **Privately Held**
SIC: 3599 Machine shop, jobbing & repair

(P-5505)
DELONG MANUFACTURING CO INC
967 Parker Ct, Santa Clara (95050-2808)
PHONE.................................408 727-3348
David De Long, *CEO*
William A De Long Jr, *CFO*
EMP: 16 **EST:** 1966
SQ FT: 8,400 **Privately Held**
WEB: www.delongmfg.com
SIC: 3599 Machine shop, jobbing & repair

(P-5506)
DELTA MATRIX INC
Also Called: Delta Machine
2180 Oakland Rd, San Jose (95131-1571)
PHONE.................................408 955-9140
Tad Slowikowski, *President*
Edgar Gayon, *Vice Pres*
Yolanda Slowikowski, *Admin Sec*
Brianna Perez, *Administration*
Alex Slowikowski, *Project Engr*
EMP: 38 **EST:** 2001
SQ FT: 9,000
SALES (est): 9.1MM **Privately Held**
SIC: 3599 Machine shop, jobbing & repair

(P-5507)
DETENTION DEVICE SYSTEMS
Also Called: DDS
25545 Seaboard Ln, Hayward (94545-3209)
PHONE.................................510 783-0771
Steven R Allington, *President*
Tom Heath, *Vice Pres*
Ron Blair, *Plant Supt*
EMP: 45 **EST:** 1985
SQ FT: 20,000
SALES (est): 5.7MM **Privately Held**
WEB: www.detentiondevicesystems.com
SIC: 3599 3429 Machine shop, jobbing & repair; locks or lock sets

(P-5508)
DIAMOND TOOL AND DIE INC
Also Called: Lab Clear
508 29th Ave, Oakland (94601-2198)
PHONE.................................510 534-7050
Darrell G Holt, *President*
Dan Welter, *Vice Pres*
Daniel Walter, *Admin Sec*
Larry Regas, *Prdtn Mgr*
Eric Jorgenson, *QC Mgr*
▲ **EMP:** 32 **EST:** 1967
SQ FT: 22,000
SALES (est): 5.1MM **Privately Held**
WEB: www.dtdjobshop.com
SIC: 3599 Machine shop, jobbing & repair

(P-5509)
DKW PRECISION MACHINING INC
17731 Ideal Pkwy, Manteca (95336-8991)
PHONE.................................209 824-7899
Kurt Franklin, *President*
Brian Kott, *General Mgr*
EMP: 20 **EST:** 1984
SQ FT: 10,000
SALES (est): 1.4MM **Privately Held**
WEB: www.dkwmachine.com
SIC: 3599 Machine shop, jobbing & repair

(P-5510)
DONAL MACHINE INC
591 N Mcdowell Blvd, Petaluma (94954-2340)
P.O. Box 750637 (94975-0637)
PHONE.................................707 763-6625
John Chris Bergstedt, *President*
Donna Bergstedt, *CFO*
Bob Bergstedt, *Vice Pres*
Robert Bergstedt, *Vice Pres*
Thomas Dollard, *General Mgr*
EMP: 31 **EST:** 1969
SQ FT: 30,000
SALES (est): 6.4MM **Privately Held**
WEB: www.donalmachine.com
SIC: 3599 3444 3548 Machine shop, jobbing & repair; sheet metalwork; welding & cutting apparatus & accessories

(P-5511)
DYLERN INCORPORATED
14444 Greenwood Cir, Nevada City (95959-9690)
PHONE.................................530 470-8785
EMP: 20
SQ FT: 9,000
SALES (est): 1.7MM **Privately Held**
SIC: 3599 Mfg Industrial Machinery

(P-5512)
E & S PRECISION MACHINE INC
4631 Enterprise Way, Modesto (95356-8715)
PHONE.................................209 545-6161
Jim Elzner, *President*
Donita Elzner, *CFO*
Alice Green, *Office Mgr*
Cas Casados, *Prdtn Mgr*
Steve Hegedus, *Manager*
EMP: 18 **EST:** 1989
SQ FT: 5,000
SALES (est): 3MM **Privately Held**
WEB: www.esprecision.comcastbiz.net
SIC: 3599 Machine shop, jobbing & repair

(P-5513)
E D M SACRAMENTO INC
Also Called: Sac EDM & Waterjet
11341 Sunrise Park Dr, Rancho Cordova (95742-6532)
PHONE.................................916 851-9285

▲ = Import ▼ = Export
♦ = Import/Export

PRODUCTS & SERVICES SECTION
3599 - Machinery & Eqpt, Indl & Commercial, NEC County (P-5540)

Daniel Folk, *CEO*
Jeff Foster, *Bookkeeper*
Jeffrey Foster,
EMP: 24 **EST:** 1983
SQ FT: 20,000
SALES (est): 6.4MM **Privately Held**
WEB: www.sacedm.com
SIC: 3599 Machine shop, jobbing & repair

(P-5514)
E R T INC
Also Called: T E R
306 Mathew St, Santa Clara (95050-3104)
PHONE 408 986-9920
Edward Cech III, *President*
Daryl Gillum, *COO*
Tom Cech, *Vice Pres*
EMP: 21 **EST:** 1984
SQ FT: 12,000
SALES (est): 2.6MM **Privately Held**
SIC: 3599 3444 Machine shop, jobbing & repair; sheet metalwork

(P-5515)
EH SUDA INC (PA)
Also Called: Fabtron
611 Industrial Rd Ste 3, San Carlos (94070-3337)
PHONE 650 622-9700
Edwin H Suda, *CEO*
EMP: 15 **EST:** 1979
SALES (est): 4.5MM **Privately Held**
SIC: 3599 Machine shop, jobbing & repair

(P-5516)
EH SUDA INC
Also Called: Fabtron
210 Texas Ave, Lewiston (96052)
P.O. Box 171 (96052-0171)
PHONE 530 778-9830
Mark Suda, *Branch Mgr*
Luis Munoz, *Supervisor*
EMP: 20
SALES (corp-wide): 4.5MM **Privately Held**
SIC: 3599 Machine shop, jobbing & repair
PA: E.H. Suda, Inc.
611 Industrial Rd Ste 3
San Carlos CA 94070
650 622-9700

(P-5517)
ELITE METAL FABRICATION INC
2299 Ringwood Ave Ste C1, San Jose (95131-1732)
PHONE 408 433-9926
Mario Flores, *Manager*
EMP: 15 **EST:** 2000
SALES (est): 638.9K **Privately Held**
WEB: www.eelitemetal.com
SIC: 3599 Machine & other job shop work

(P-5518)
ELLIOTT MANUFACTURING CO INC
2664 S Cherry Ave, Fresno (93706-5494)
P.O. Box 11277 (93772-1277)
PHONE 559 233-6235
Terry Aluisi, *CEO*
Thomas E Cole, *Ch of Bd*
Luellen Newman, *COO*
Sarah Cole, *Bd of Directors*
Richard E Cole, *Vice Pres*
▲ **EMP:** 15 **EST:** 1929
SALES (est): 3.6MM **Privately Held**
WEB: www.elliott-mfg.com
SIC: 3599 3556 3565 7692 Machine shop, jobbing & repair; food products machinery; packaging machinery; welding repair; sheet metalwork

(P-5519)
EME TECHNOLOGIES INC
3485 Victor St, Santa Clara (95054-2319)
PHONE 408 720-8817
Walter Nguyen, *President*
Rosario Bonilla, *Finance Mgr*
Lien Nguyen, *Manager*
▲ **EMP:** 27 **EST:** 1986
SQ FT: 20,000
SALES (est): 1.8MM **Privately Held**
WEB: www.emetec.com
SIC: 3599 Machine shop, jobbing & repair

(P-5520)
ENGINEERED AUTOMATION LLC
Also Called: Cope Manufacturing Co
20400 N Kennefick Rd, Acampo (95220-9708)
P.O. Box 2660, Lodi (95241-2660)
PHONE 209 368-6363
Daniel Mills,
Assaad Elkhouri, *Founder*
Howard Burns, *Sales Mgr*
EMP: 15 **EST:** 1964
SQ FT: 12,000
SALES (est): 1MM **Privately Held**
SIC: 3599 Machine shop, jobbing & repair

(P-5521)
ERC CONCEPTS CO INC
1255 Birchwood Dr, Sunnyvale (94089-2206)
P.O. Box 62019 (94088-2019)
PHONE 408 734-5345
Felix Oramas, *President*
Reina Oramas, *Vice Pres*
EMP: 46 **EST:** 1993
SQ FT: 17,000
SALES (est): 2.1MM **Privately Held**
WEB: www.erc-concepts.com
SIC: 3599 Machine shop, jobbing & repair

(P-5522)
EXCEL CNC MACHINING INC
Also Called: Excel Machining
3185 De La Cruz Blvd, Santa Clara (95054-2405)
PHONE 408 970-9460
Krzysztof Wisinski, *President*
EMP: 48 **EST:** 1996
SALES (est): 8.9MM **Privately Held**
WEB: www.excel-cnc.com
SIC: 3599 Machine shop, jobbing & repair

(P-5523)
EXPEDITE PRECISION WORKS INC
931 Berryessa Rd, San Jose (95133-1002)
PHONE 408 437-1893
Orlando Teixeira, *President*
Yousuff Habibullahkhan, *General Mgr*
Fatima Teixeira, *CTO*
Chet Gaede, *Manager*
EMP: 45 **EST:** 1994
SQ FT: 5,500
SALES (est): 5.1MM **Privately Held**
WEB: www.expediteprecision.com
SIC: 3599 3089 Machine shop, jobbing & repair; plastic hardware & building products

(P-5524)
EXTREME PRECISION INC
1717 Little Orchard St B, San Jose (95125-1049)
PHONE 408 275-8365
Matthew Ellis, *President*
Rosa Pace, *General Mgr*
EMP: 15 **EST:** 1993
SQ FT: 7,500
SALES (est): 2.2MM **Privately Held**
SIC: 3599 Machine shop, jobbing & repair; machine & other job shop work

(P-5525)
FERAL PRODUCTIONS LLC
1935 N Macarthur Dr, Tracy (95376-2833)
PHONE 510 791-5392
Robert Potts,
Lynn Potts,
EMP: 28 **EST:** 1997
SQ FT: 10,400
SALES (est): 4MM **Privately Held**
WEB: www.feralprodinc.com
SIC: 3599 Machine shop, jobbing & repair

(P-5526)
FM INDUSTRIES INC (DH)
221 E Warren Ave, Fremont (94539-7916)
PHONE 510 668-1900
Hidenori Nanto, *Chairman*
David S Miller, *CEO*
Kevin Balsan, *General Mgr*
Ariel Gubatina, *Prgrmr*
Raymond Kolstad, *Prgrmr*
EMP: 110 **EST:** 1989
SQ FT: 56,000
SALES (est): 78.5MM **Privately Held**
WEB: www.fmindustries.com
SIC: 3599 3544 3999 Machine shop, jobbing & repair; special dies, tools, jigs & fixtures; atomizers, toiletry
HQ: Ngk North America, Inc.
1105 N Market St Ste 1300
Wilmington DE 19801
302 654-1344

(P-5527)
FMW MACHINE SHOP
519 Claire St, Hayward (94541-6411)
PHONE 650 363-1313
Humberto Fabris, *General Ptnr*
Annette Fabris, *Partner*
Maria Fabris, *Partner*
EMP: 39 **EST:** 1978
SALES (est): 2MM **Privately Held**
SIC: 3599 Machine shop, jobbing & repair

(P-5528)
FRED MATTER INC
Also Called: Alloy Metal Products
7801 Las Positas Rd, Livermore (94551-8206)
PHONE 925 371-1234
Fred Matter, *President*
EMP: 21 **EST:** 1977
SQ FT: 30,000
SALES (est): 3.4MM **Privately Held**
SIC: 3599 Machine shop, jobbing & repair

(P-5529)
GARABEDIAN BROS INC (PA)
Also Called: Valley Welding & Machine Works
2543 S Orange Ave, Fresno (93725-1329)
P.O. Box 2455 (93745-2455)
PHONE 559 268-5014
Michael J Garabedian, *CEO*
Joanne Garabedian, *Corp Secy*
▼ **EMP:** 30 **EST:** 1946
SQ FT: 45,000
SALES (est): 7.7MM **Privately Held**
SIC: 3599 3523 Machine shop, jobbing & repair; driers (farm): grain, hay & seed

(P-5530)
GATEWAY PRECISION INC
480 Vista Way, Milpitas (95035-5406)
PHONE 408 855-8849
EMP: 15
SALES (est): 2.9MM **Privately Held**
WEB: www.gatewayprecision.com
SIC: 3599 Mfg Industrial Machinery

(P-5531)
GEIGER MANUFACTURING INC
1110 E Scotts Ave, Stockton (95205-6148)
P.O. Box 1449 (95201-1449)
PHONE 209 464-7746
Roger Haack, *President*
Dennis D Geiger, *Treasurer*
EMP: 16 **EST:** 1904
SQ FT: 27,250
SALES (est): 1.8MM **Privately Held**
WEB: www.geigermfg.com
SIC: 3599 Machine shop, jobbing & repair

(P-5532)
GENTEC MANUFACTURING INC
2241 Ringwood Ave, San Jose (95131-1737)
PHONE 408 432-6220
Mark Diaz, *President*
Delia Garcia, *Office Mgr*
Michael Elder, *Production*
Carlos Ramos, *Manager*
EMP: 15 **EST:** 1976
SQ FT: 5,700
SALES (est): 3.1MM **Privately Held**
WEB: www.gentecmfg.com
SIC: 3599 Machine shop, jobbing & repair

(P-5533)
HAIG PRECISION MFG CORP
3616 Snell Ave, San Jose (95136-1305)
PHONE 408 378-4920
Daniel S Sarkisian, *CEO*
Paul Sarkisian, *Vice Pres*
Aaron Valenta, *Executive*
Naida Katz, *Office Mgr*
John Tower, *Design Engr*
▲ **EMP:** 60 **EST:** 1960
SQ FT: 26,000
SALES (est): 11.4MM **Privately Held**
WEB: www.haigprecision.com
SIC: 3599 7692 Machine shop, jobbing & repair; welding repair

(P-5534)
HAMMOND ENTERPRISES INC
549 Garcia Ave Ste C, Pittsburg (94565-7402)
PHONE 925 432-3537
Alan B Hammond, *CEO*
▲ **EMP:** 20 **EST:** 1990
SQ FT: 12,500
SALES (est): 2.3MM **Privately Held**
WEB: www.hammondenterprises.com
SIC: 3599 Machine shop, jobbing & repair

(P-5535)
HEIGHTEN AMERICA INC
Also Called: Heighten Manfacturing
1144 Post Rd, Oakdale (95361-9384)
PHONE 209 845-0455
Linda Smeck, *President*
Jerrold W Smeck, *Treasurer*
Debbie Lasiter,
EMP: 21 **EST:** 1984
SQ FT: 8,000
SALES (est): 3.5MM **Privately Held**
WEB: www.hi10usa.com
SIC: 3599 Machine shop, jobbing & repair

(P-5536)
HIEP NGUYEN CORPORATION
Also Called: Silicon Valley Precision Mch
1641 Rogers Ave, San Jose (95112-1126)
PHONE 408 451-9042
Hen Tran, *President*
Hua Tran, *Vice Pres*
Buu Thai, *Admin Sec*
EMP: 20 **EST:** 1988
SQ FT: 6,400
SALES (est): 1MM **Privately Held**
SIC: 3599 Machine shop, jobbing & repair

(P-5537)
HIRSCH MACHINE INC
1030 Autumn Ln, Los Altos (94024-6035)
PHONE 408 738-8844
Robert Hirsch, *President*
Paula Hirsch, *CFO*
EMP: 23 **EST:** 1981
SQ FT: 10,000
SALES (est): 1.3MM **Privately Held**
WEB: www.hirschmachine.com
SIC: 3599 7692 7629 Machine shop, jobbing & repair; welding repair; electrical repair shops

(P-5538)
IMG COMPANIES LLC (PA)
225 Mountain Vista Pkwy, Livermore (94551-8210)
PHONE 925 273-1100
Kam Pasha, *CEO*
Kiran Mukkamala, *CFO*
Mahesh Kumar, *Vice Pres*
Brian Magann, *Managing Dir*
Suleiman Aboutaam, *CIO*
▲ **EMP:** 70 **EST:** 2004
SALES (est): 20MM **Privately Held**
WEB: www.imgprecision.com
SIC: 3599 Machine shop, jobbing & repair

(P-5539)
IMT PRECISION INC
31902 Hayman St, Hayward (94544-7925)
PHONE 510 324-8926
Timoteo Ilario, *President*
Zack Lemley, *Planning*
Peter Kunze, *QC Mgr*
EMP: 50 **EST:** 1993
SQ FT: 50,000
SALES (est): 9.6MM **Privately Held**
WEB: www.imtp.com
SIC: 3599 Machine shop, jobbing & repair

(P-5540)
INNOVATIVE MACHINING INC
845 Yosemite Way, Milpitas (95035-6329)
PHONE 408 262-2270
Thang Vo, *President*
Bich Nguyen, *Vice Pres*
Lauren Vo, *Project Mgr*
EMP: 64 **EST:** 1997
SQ FT: 3,000

3599 - Machinery & Eqpt, Indl & Commercial, NEC County (P-5541)

SALES (est): 6.6MM **Privately Held**
WEB: www.innomachcorp.com
SIC: 3599 Machine shop, jobbing & repair

(P-5541)
INTEGRATED MFG TECH INC
Also Called: IMT
1477 N Milpitas Blvd, Milpitas (95035-3160)
PHONE 510 366-8793
Andy Luong, *President*
Whyemun Chan, *Treasurer*
Sally Luong, *Vice Pres*
EMP: 17 **EST:** 2005
SALES (est): 311.9K **Privately Held**
WEB: www.imt-intl.com
SIC: 3599 3471 3498 7692 Machine shop, jobbing & repair; polishing, metals or formed products; fabricated pipe & fittings; welding repair

(P-5542)
INVERSE SOLUTIONS INC
3922 Valley Ave Ste A, Pleasanton (94566-4873)
PHONE 925 931-9500
David Jordan, *Principal*
Josh Jordon, *Vice Pres*
Ronda Jordan, *Admin Sec*
EMP: 24 **EST:** 1999
SQ FT: 12,500
SALES (est): 4.8MM **Privately Held**
WEB: www.inversesolutionsinc.com
SIC: 3599 Machine shop, jobbing & repair

(P-5543)
ITSJ GROUP INC
490 Parrott St, San Jose (95112-4118)
PHONE 408 609-6392
Chau Tran, *CEO*
EMP: 20 **EST:** 2020
SALES (est): 1.8MM **Privately Held**
WEB: www.itsj-group.com
SIC: 3599 Machine & other job shop work

(P-5544)
J A-CO MACHINE WORKS LLC
Also Called: Jaco Machine Works
4 Carbonero Way, Scotts Valley (95066-4200)
PHONE 877 429-8175
Andy Smith, *Mng Member*
Jeffrey A Smith, *Managing Prtnr*
Gabby Tracey, *Office Mgr*
EMP: 20 **EST:** 1979
SQ FT: 9,000
SALES (est): 3.9MM **Privately Held**
WEB: www.jacoworks.com
SIC: 3599 Machine shop, jobbing & repair

(P-5545)
JARVIS MANUFACTURING INC
210 Hillsdale Ave, San Jose (95136-1392)
PHONE 408 226-2600
Tony Grewal, *CEO*
EMP: 17 **EST:** 1957
SALES (est): 2MM **Privately Held**
WEB: www.jarvismfg.com
SIC: 3599 Machine shop, jobbing & repair

(P-5546)
JENSON MECHANICAL INC
Also Called: J M I
32420 Central Ave, Union City (94587-2007)
P.O. Box 1006, Tracy (95378-1006)
PHONE 510 429-8078
Greg Jenson, *President*
Matt Jenson, *Business Mgr*
EMP: 20 **EST:** 1976
SQ FT: 30,000
SALES (est): 4.1MM **Privately Held**
WEB: www.jensonmechanical.com
SIC: 3599 7699 Custom machinery; industrial machinery & equipment repair

(P-5547)
JESSEE BROTHERS MACHINE SP INC
Also Called: J B Precision
1640 Dell Ave, Campbell (95008-6951)
PHONE 408 866-1755
Chett Jessee, *President*
Marcia Balfour, *Sales Mgr*
EMP: 16 **EST:** 1975
SQ FT: 12,500

SALES (est): 2.5MM **Privately Held**
WEB: www.jesseebrothersinc.com
SIC: 3599 Machine shop, jobbing & repair

(P-5548)
JL HALEY ENTERPRISES INC
3510 Luyung Dr, Rancho Cordova (95742-6872)
PHONE 916 631-6375
James L Haley, *CEO*
◆ **EMP:** 140 **EST:** 1971
SQ FT: 67,000
SALES (est): 21.3MM
SALES (corp-wide): 138.5MM **Privately Held**
WEB: www.vander-bend.com
SIC: 3599 3471 3312 7692 Machine shop, jobbing & repair; blast furnaces & steel mills; welding repair
PA: Vander-Bend Manufacturing, Inc.
2701 Orchard Pkwy
San Jose CA 95134
408 245-5150

(P-5549)
JWP MANUFACTURING LLC
3500 De La Cruz Blvd, Santa Clara (95054-2111)
PHONE 408 970-0641
Jerzy W Prokop, *Mng Member*
Peter Prokop, *Engineer*
Andy Eden, *Sales Staff*
Suzanna Prokop,
Zuzanna Prokop, *Mng Member*
EMP: 25 **EST:** 1986
SQ FT: 12,000
SALES (est): 5MM **Privately Held**
WEB: www.jwpmfg.com
SIC: 3599 Machine shop, jobbing & repair

(P-5550)
KAL MACHINING INC
18450 Sutter Blvd, Morgan Hill (95037-2819)
PHONE 408 782-8989
Qing Ye, *President*
David Long, *Vice Pres*
▲ **EMP:** 20 **EST:** 2000
SQ FT: 10,000
SALES (est): 1.5MM **Privately Held**
WEB: www.kalmachining.com
SIC: 3599 Machine shop, jobbing & repair

(P-5551)
KALMAN MANUFACTURING INC
780 Jarvis Dr Ste 150, Morgan Hill (95037-2886)
PHONE 408 776-7664
Alan D Kalman, *President*
Freia Kalman, *Vice Pres*
EMP: 43 **EST:** 1983
SQ FT: 35,000
SALES (est): 6.3MM **Privately Held**
WEB: www.kalman.com
SIC: 3599 Machine shop, jobbing & repair

(P-5552)
KDF INC
Also Called: Pro-Cision Machining
15875 Concord Cir, Morgan Hill (95037-5448)
PHONE 408 779-3731
Ken Fredenburg, *President*
EMP: 30 **EST:** 1984
SQ FT: 20,000
SALES (est): 3.9MM **Privately Held**
SIC: 3599 Machine shop, jobbing & repair; electrical discharge machining (EDM)

(P-5553)
KHUUS INC
Also Called: Kamet
1778 Mccarthy Blvd, Milpitas (95035-7421)
PHONE 408 522-8000
Peter Khuu, *President*
Donald Cheng, *General Mgr*
John Gitonga, *Sales Executive*
▲ **EMP:** 60 **EST:** 1986
SQ FT: 25,000
SALES (est): 10.9MM **Privately Held**
WEB: www.kamet.com
SIC: 3599 Machine shop, jobbing & repair

(P-5554)
KIMZEY WELDING WORKS
164 Kentucky Ave, Woodland (95695-2743)
PHONE 530 662-9331
John W Kimzey, *President*
Edith Kimzey, *Corp Secy*
EMP: 18 **EST:** 1953
SQ FT: 14,400
SALES (est): 2.4MM **Privately Held**
WEB: www.kimzeyweldingworks.com
SIC: 3599 7692 5251 3842 Custom machinery; welding repair; hardware; surgical appliances & supplies; surgical & medical instruments

(P-5555)
KNT INC
Also Called: Knt Manufacturing
39760 Eureka Dr, Newark (94560-4808)
PHONE 510 651-7163
Keith Ngo, *CEO*
EMP: 150 **EST:** 2001
SQ FT: 50,000
SALES (est): 34MM **Privately Held**
WEB: www.kntmfg.com
SIC: 3599 Machine shop, jobbing & repair

(P-5556)
KODIAK PRECISION INC (PA)
444 S 1st St, Richmond (94804-2107)
PHONE 510 234-4165
Paul Bacchi, *President*
Neil Divers, *Vice Pres*
Dave Harris, *Vice Pres*
EMP: 17 **EST:** 1976
SQ FT: 10,000
SALES (est): 3MM **Privately Held**
WEB: www.kodiakprecisioninc.com
SIC: 3599 Machine shop, jobbing & repair

(P-5557)
KRISALIS PRECISION MACHINING
3366 Golden Gate Ct, San Andreas (95249-9625)
PHONE 209 296-6866
Charles R Tinney, *President*
EMP: 17 **EST:** 2017
SALES (est): 1.4MM **Privately Held**
SIC: 3599 Machine shop, jobbing & repair

(P-5558)
L & T PRECISION ENGRG INC
2395 Qume Dr, San Jose (95131-1813)
PHONE 408 441-1890
Luc Tran, *President*
My Truong, *General Mgr*
Thang Dinh, *Technical Staff*
Thai Le, *Manager*
EMP: 40 **EST:** 1988
SALES (est): 6.2MM **Privately Held**
WEB: www.lt-engineering.com
SIC: 3599 8711 Machine shop, jobbing & repair; consulting engineer

(P-5559)
LANGILLS GENERAL MACHINE INC
7850 14th Ave, Sacramento (95826-4302)
PHONE 916 452-0167
James Langill Sr, *President*
EMP: 35 **EST:** 1969
SQ FT: 10,000
SALES (est): 5.5MM **Privately Held**
WEB: www.langills.com
SIC: 3599 Machine shop, jobbing & repair

(P-5560)
LENZ PRECISION TECHNOLOGY INC
Also Called: Lenz Technology
355 Pioneer Way Ste A, Mountain View (94041-1542)
PHONE 650 966-1784
Eric Lenz, *President*
Shannon Lenz, *CFO*
Valerie Lenz, *Corp Secy*
Paul Lera, *Manager*
EMP: 23 **EST:** 1972
SQ FT: 18,000
SALES (est): 1.6MM **Privately Held**
WEB: www.lenztech.com
SIC: 3599 Machine shop, jobbing & repair

(P-5561)
LOCK-N-STITCH INC
1015 S Soderquist Rd, Turlock (95380-5726)
PHONE 209 632-2345
Gary J Reed, *CEO*
Louise Reed, *President*
Brandi Rollins, *Treasurer*
Arthur Reyes, *Human Res Mgr*
Derrik Holmes, *Foreman/Supr*
▲ **EMP:** 42
SQ FT: 33,000
SALES: 4.9MM
SALES (corp-wide): 5.4B **Privately Held**
WEB: www.locknstitch.com
SIC: 3599 Machine shop, jobbing & repair
PA: Wartsila Oyj Abp
Hiililaiturinkuja 2
Helsinki 00180
107 090-000

(P-5562)
LYRU ENGINEERING INC
965 San Leandro Blvd, San Leandro (94577-1532)
PHONE 510 357-5951
Jeff Snyder, *President*
Greg A Snyder, *Admin Sec*
EMP: 22 **EST:** 1965
SQ FT: 12,500
SALES (est): 1MM **Privately Held**
WEB: www.lyruengineering.com
SIC: 3599 Machine shop, jobbing & repair

(P-5563)
M & L PRECISION MACHINING INC (PA)
18665 Madrone Pkwy, Morgan Hill (95037-2868)
PHONE 408 436-3955
Mark Laisure, *President*
Harold Laisure, *Vice Pres*
Karen Laisure, *Vice Pres*
Ross Laisure, *Vice Pres*
Garine Ricco, *Office Mgr*
▲ **EMP:** 20 **EST:** 1971
SQ FT: 10,000
SALES (est): 6MM **Privately Held**
WEB: www.mlprecision.com
SIC: 3599 3451 3444 Machine shop, jobbing & repair; screw machine products; sheet metalwork

(P-5564)
M & W ENGINEERING INC
3880 Dividend Dr Ste 100, Shingle Springs (95682-7229)
PHONE 530 676-7185
Frank E Marsh, *President*
Kim Waters, *Treasurer*
EMP: 20 **EST:** 1979
SQ FT: 10,800
SALES (est): 4MM **Privately Held**
WEB: www.mandwengineering.biz
SIC: 3599 Machine shop, jobbing & repair

(P-5565)
MARS ENGINEERING COMPANY INC
Also Called: Vin-Max
699 Montague St, San Leandro (94577-4323)
PHONE 510 483-0541
Manny Ambrosio, *President*
Christy Ambrosio, *Corp Secy*
EMP: 35 **EST:** 1964
SQ FT: 15,000
SALES (est): 6.4MM **Privately Held**
WEB: www.marseng.com
SIC: 3599 Machine shop, jobbing & repair

(P-5566)
MARX DIGITAL MFG INC (PA)
Also Called: Marx Digital Cnc Machine Shop
3551 Victor St, Santa Clara (95054-2321)
PHONE 408 748-1783
Marek Smiech, *President*
Krzysztof Juszczynski, *Treasurer*
Shane Johnson, *General Mgr*
EMP: 83 **EST:** 2008

▲ = Import ▼ = Export
◆ = Import/Export

PRODUCTS & SERVICES SECTION

3599 - Machinery & Eqpt, Indl & Commercial, NEC County (P-5593)

SALES (est): 2.3MM Privately Held
WEB: www.marxdigital.com
SIC: 3599 3639 3829 Machine shop, jobbing & repair; sewing machines & attachments, domestic; drafting instruments & machines: t-square, template, etc.

(P-5567)
MASTER PRECISION MACHINING
2199 Ronald St, Santa Clara (95050-2883)
PHONE..................................408 727-0185
Richard Rossi, *President*
Rich Parchman, *COO*
Robert Paolinetti, *Corp Secy*
Eric Parchman, *Officer*
William Regnani, *Vice Pres*
EMP: 30 EST: 1969
SQ FT: 10,000
SALES (est): 3.1MM Privately Held
WEB: www.master-precision.com
SIC: 3599 Machine shop, jobbing & repair

(P-5568)
MCKENZIE MACHINING INC
481 Perry Ct, Santa Clara (95054-2624)
PHONE..................................408 748-8885
Scott McKenzie, *Owner*
EMP: 18 EST: 1996
SQ FT: 10,400
SALES (est): 1.6MM Privately Held
WEB: www.mckenziemachining.com
SIC: 3599 Machine shop, jobbing & repair

(P-5569)
MECOPTRON INC
3115 Osgood Ct, Fremont (94539-5652)
PHONE..................................510 226-9966
Andy Law, *Founder*
Christine Law, *Human Res Mgr*
EMP: 17 EST: 1986
SQ FT: 12,000
SALES (est): 638.1K Privately Held
WEB: www.mecoptron.com
SIC: 3599 3444 Machine shop, jobbing & repair; sheet metalwork

(P-5570)
MECPRO INC
980 George St, Santa Clara (95054-2705)
PHONE..................................408 727-9757
Son Ho, *President*
Kelly Ho, *Vice Pres*
Colin Wintrup, *Vice Pres*
Ty Ho, *Mfg Staff*
EMP: 64 EST: 1979
SQ FT: 15,000
SALES (est): 5.4MM Privately Held
WEB: www.mecproinc.com
SIC: 3599 Machine shop, jobbing & repair

(P-5571)
MID VALLEY MFG INC
2039 W Superior Ave, Caruthers (93609-9531)
P.O. Box 295 (93609-0295)
PHONE..................................559 864-9441
Robert Smith, *President*
Rex Tyler, *Vice Pres*
EMP: 22 EST: 1977
SQ FT: 7,200
SALES (est): 1.2MM Privately Held
SIC: 3599 Machine shop, jobbing & repair

(P-5572)
MILITARY AIRCRAFT PARTS (PA)
116 Oxburough Dr, Folsom (95630-3293)
PHONE..................................916 635-8010
Robert E Marin, *President*
EMP: 45 EST: 2000
SALES (est): 5MM Privately Held
WEB: www.mail.ex2.secureserver.net
SIC: 3599 Machine shop, jobbing & repair

(P-5573)
MINIATURE PRECISION INC
4488 Mountain Lakes Blvd, Redding (96003-1445)
PHONE..................................530 244-4181
Don Anderson, *President*
Diana Anderson, *Vice Pres*
Mike Twoney, *QC Mgr*
EMP: 23 EST: 1971
SQ FT: 8,000
SALES (est): 3.1MM Privately Held
WEB: www.miniature-precision.com
SIC: 3599 Machine shop, jobbing & repair

(P-5574)
MISSION TOOL AND MFG CO INC
3440 Arden Rd, Hayward (94545-3906)
PHONE..................................510 782-8383
Gary W Smith, *President*
Carol Smith, *Vice Pres*
Greg Hernandez, *Prgrmr*
Thomas Zaw, *QC Mgr*
▲ EMP: 40 EST: 1968
SQ FT: 28,000
SALES (est): 8MM Privately Held
WEB: www.mtmprecision.com
SIC: 3599 3465 3469 3544 Machine & other job shop work; automotive stampings; metal stampings; special dies, tools, jigs & fixtures

(P-5575)
MOTIV DESIGN GROUP INC
430 Perrymont Ave, San Jose (95125-1444)
PHONE..................................408 441-0611
Lino R Covarrubias, *CEO*
Carlos Barrientos, *Vice Pres*
EMP: 16 EST: 2006
SQ FT: 2,400
SALES (est): 4.2MM Privately Held
WEB: www.motiv-dgi.com
SIC: 3599 Custom machinery; machine & other job shop work

(P-5576)
MR GEARS INC
428 Stanford Ave, Redwood City (94063-3423)
PHONE..................................650 364-7793
Jack Hybl, *President*
EMP: 15 EST: 1972
SQ FT: 4,100
SALES (est): 280.6K Privately Held
SIC: 3599 3751 3462 3714 Machine shop, jobbing & repair; gears, motorcycle & bicycle; gears, forged steel; gears, motor vehicle

(P-5577)
NANEZ MFG INC
164 Commercial St, Sunnyvale (94086-5201)
PHONE..................................408 830-9903
Francisco Nanez, *President*
EMP: 20 EST: 2012
SQ FT: 500
SALES (est): 3.5MM Privately Held
WEB: www.nanezmfg.com
SIC: 3599 Machine shop, jobbing & repair

(P-5578)
NEW WORLD MACHINING INC
2799 Aiello Dr, San Jose (95111-2156)
PHONE..................................408 227-3810
Marvin Elsten, *President*
Dianne Elsten, *Vice Pres*
Richard Barnes, *VP Opers*
Quang Le, *Prdtn Mgr*
Janice Flores, *Cust Mgr*
EMP: 25 EST: 1973
SQ FT: 30,000
SALES (est): 2.8MM Privately Held
WEB: www.newworldmachining.com
SIC: 3599 5084 Machine shop, jobbing & repair; industrial machinery & equipment

(P-5579)
NEW YORK MACHINE SHOP INC
2875 Feather River Blvd, Oroville (95965-9630)
PHONE..................................530 534-7965
Albert M King Jr, *Principal*
EMP: 15 EST: 2001
SALES (est): 166.6K Privately Held
SIC: 3599 Machine shop, jobbing & repair

(P-5580)
NM MACHINING INC
175 Lewis Rd Ste 25, San Jose (95111-2175)
PHONE..................................408 972-8978
Mike Tran, *President*
Jerzy Glinka, *Vice Pres*
Sylvia MAI, *Manager*
EMP: 38 EST: 1995
SQ FT: 8,272
SALES (est): 2MM Privately Held
WEB: www.nmmachining.com
SIC: 3599 Machine shop, jobbing & repair

(P-5581)
NORTH STATE MANUFACURING
8794 Airport Rd, Redding (96002-9212)
PHONE..................................530 378-5750
Norman Dreyer, *Administration*
EMP: 15 EST: 2015
SALES (est): 680.2K Privately Held
SIC: 3599 Machine shop, jobbing & repair

(P-5582)
NTL PRECISION MACHINING INC
1355 Vander Way, San Jose (95112-2809)
PHONE..................................408 298-6650
Henry Ngo, *CEO*
Hai Ngo, *Vice Pres*
Thao Ngo, *Admin Sec*
EMP: 15 EST: 1996
SQ FT: 7,500
SALES (est): 2.7MM Privately Held
WEB: www.ntlprecision.com
SIC: 3599 Machine shop, jobbing & repair

(P-5583)
OT PRECISION MACHINING INC
1450 Seareel Ln, San Jose (95131-1580)
PHONE..................................408 435-8818
Tam Dang, *President*
Minh Ly, *Manager*
EMP: 25 EST: 1995
SQ FT: 2,000
SALES (est): 3.1MM Privately Held
WEB: www.otprecision.com
SIC: 3599 Machine shop, jobbing & repair

(P-5584)
OWENS DESIGN INCORPORATED
47427 Fremont Blvd, Fremont (94538-6504)
PHONE..................................510 659-1800
John Apgar, *President*
Paul Shufflebotham, *Vice Pres*
Maria Luna, *Admin Sec*
Carl Josey, *Engineer*
Eugene Petrushansky, *Engineer*
EMP: 45 EST: 1983
SQ FT: 30,000
SALES (est): 12.4MM Privately Held
WEB: www.owensdesign.com
SIC: 3599 Custom machinery

(P-5585)
P M S D INC (PA)
Also Called: Danco Machine
3411 Leonard Ct, Santa Clara (95054-2053)
PHONE..................................408 988-5235
Timothy Rohr, *CEO*
Ron Simonetti, *Vice Pres*
Jodie Lim, *Program Mgr*
Marcel Micael, *Info Tech Mgr*
Rich Olesen, *Info Tech Mgr*
EMP: 102 EST: 1978
SALES (est): 16.9MM Privately Held
WEB: www.dancomachine.com
SIC: 3599 Machine shop, jobbing & repair

(P-5586)
P M S D INC
Also Called: K-Fab
3411 Leonard Ct, Santa Clara (95054-2053)
PHONE..................................408 727-5322
Denise Bachur, *Admin Mgr*
Hudson Wheldon, *Materials Mgr*
Tam Hoang, *Prdtn Mgr*
Neil Starr, *QC Mgr*
EMP: 40
SALES (corp-wide): 16.9MM Privately Held
WEB: www.dancomachine.com
SIC: 3599 Machine shop, jobbing & repair
PA: P M S D Inc
  3411 Leonard Ct
  Santa Clara CA 95054
  408 988-5235

(P-5587)
PACIFIC ROLLER DIE CO INC
Also Called: Prd Company
1321 W Winton Ave, Hayward (94545-1407)
PHONE..................................510 244-7286
Robert F Miller, *CEO*
Michael Kraut, *Sales Mgr*
◆ EMP: 16 EST: 1961
SQ FT: 25,000
SALES (est): 4.2MM Privately Held
WEB: www.prdcompany.com
SIC: 3599 3547 3542 Machine shop, jobbing & repair; rolling mill machinery; machine tools, metal forming type

(P-5588)
PACIFIC SCREW PRODUCTS INC
Also Called: Rollin J. Lobaugh
1331 Old County Rd Ste C, Belmont (94002-3968)
PHONE..................................650 583-9682
Jack Corey, *President*
Gloria Corey, *Corp Secy*
EMP: 52 EST: 1922
SQ FT: 24,000
SALES (est): 5.3MM Privately Held
SIC: 3599 Machine shop, jobbing & repair

(P-5589)
PACON MFG INC
4777 Bennett Dr Ste H, Livermore (94551-4860)
PHONE..................................925 961-0445
Steven McClure, *CEO*
EMP: 20 EST: 2013
SALES (est): 3.6MM Privately Held
WEB: www.paconquality.com
SIC: 3599 Machine shop, jobbing & repair

(P-5590)
PARAGON MACHINE WORKS INC
253 S 25th St, Richmond (94804-2856)
PHONE..................................510 232-3223
Mark Norstad, *Owner*
Donna Norstad, *Office Mgr*
EMP: 60 EST: 1983
SQ FT: 55,000
SALES (est): 7.2MM Privately Held
WEB: www.paragonmachineworks.com
SIC: 3599 Machine shop, jobbing & repair

(P-5591)
PARAGON SWISS
545 Aldo Ave Ste 1, Santa Clara (95054-2206)
PHONE..................................408 748-1617
Kevin Beatty, *President*
David R Beatty, *Vice Pres*
Joanne Beatty, *Admin Sec*
Craig Kay, *Technology*
Christopher Kay, *Prdtn Mgr*
EMP: 30 EST: 1984
SQ FT: 10,200
SALES (est): 3.1MM Privately Held
WEB: www.paragonswiss.com
SIC: 3599 3451 Machine shop, jobbing & repair; screw machine products

(P-5592)
PARAMETRIC MANUFACTURING INC
3465 Edward Ave, Santa Clara (95054-2131)
PHONE..................................408 654-9845
Jon Drury, *President*
EMP: 16 EST: 2005
SQ FT: 7,500
SALES (est): 2MM Privately Held
WEB: www.parametric-usa.com
SIC: 3599 Machine shop, jobbing & repair

(P-5593)
PAULI SYSTEMS INC
1820 Walters Ct, Fairfield (94533-2759)
PHONE..................................707 429-2434
Robert Pauli, *CEO*
Craig Corson, *Engineer*
Josef Spridgen, *Sales Staff*
Jerry Montgomery, *Manager*
EMP: 22 EST: 1996
SQ FT: 13,500

3599 - Machinery & Eqpt, Indl & Commercial, NEC County (P-5594)

SALES (est): 5.4MM Privately Held
WEB: www.paulisystems.com
SIC: 3599 Custom machinery

(P-5594)
PERFORMEX MACHINING INC
963 Terminal Way, San Carlos (94070-3224)
PHONE..................650 595-2228
Joseph Iffla, Owner
EMP: 20 EST: 1977
SQ FT: 5,600
SALES (est): 2.4MM Privately Held
WEB: www.performexmachining.com
SIC: 3599 Machine shop, jobbing & repair

(P-5595)
PETERSEN PRECISION ENGRG LLC
611 Broadway St, Redwood City (94063-3102)
PHONE..................650 365-4373
Fred Petersen, CEO
Sunil Chandar, Department Mgr
Mike Kunis, Maintence Staff
Milton Philip Olson,
Brian Malenfant, Supervisor
EMP: 120 EST: 1999
SQ FT: 55,000
SALES (est): 16.5MM Privately Held
WEB: www.petersenprecision.com
SIC: 3599 Machine shop, jobbing & repair

(P-5596)
PISOR INDUSTRIES INC
7201 32nd St, North Highlands (95660-2500)
PHONE..................916 944-2851
Tony Free, President
Joy Pisor, Corp Secy
EMP: 31 EST: 1978
SQ FT: 4,500
SALES (est): 1.1MM Privately Held
SIC: 3599 3498 3446 Machine shop, jobbing & repair; fabricated pipe & fittings; architectural metalwork

(P-5597)
PLEASANTON TOOL & MFG INC
1181 Quarry Ln Ste 450, Pleasanton (94566-8460)
PHONE..................925 426-0500
Chester Thomas, President
Rich Thomas, President
Shirley Thomas, CFO
Steve Hallock, Vice Pres
Ray Forbes, General Mgr
EMP: 25 EST: 1989
SQ FT: 18,000
SALES (est): 3.6MM Privately Held
WEB: www.pleasantontool.com
SIC: 3599 Machine shop, jobbing & repair

(P-5598)
PNM COMPANY
2547 N Business Park Ave, Fresno (93727-8637)
PHONE..................559 291-1986
Dave Counts, Partner
Precision Numeric Machine, Partner
Mark Winters, Partner
Bev Caldwell, Bookkeeper
Mario Persicone, Director
▲ EMP: 48 EST: 1987
SQ FT: 5,500
SALES (est): 8.4MM Privately Held
WEB: www.pnmcnc.com
SIC: 3599 Machine shop, jobbing & repair

(P-5599)
POLYTEC PRODUCTS CORPORATION
3390 Valley Square Ln, San Jose (95117-3068)
PHONE..................650 322-7555
John Parissenti, President
Tony Hertado, Principal
Peggy Blevins, Director
EMP: 45 EST: 1968
SALES (est): 7.2MM Privately Held
WEB: www.polytecproducts.com
SIC: 3599 Machine shop, jobbing & repair

(P-5600)
PPM PRODUCTS INC
1538 Gladding Ct, Milpitas (95035-6814)
PHONE..................408 946-4710
Yasuhiro Hayashi, President
Kathy Sato, Executive Asst
Clifford Hayashi, Info Tech Dir
Nina Hayashi, Accounting Mgr
EMP: 20 EST: 1984
SQ FT: 3,000
SALES (est): 1.6MM Privately Held
WEB: www.ppmproducts.com
SIC: 3599 Machine shop, jobbing & repair

(P-5601)
PRECISION CNC LLC
16818 Sycamore Ave, Patterson (95363-9724)
PHONE..................209 277-2082
Kyle Ferry, Branch Mgr
EMP: 22
SALES (corp-wide): 728.8K Privately Held
SIC: 3599 Machine shop, jobbing & repair
PA: Precision Cnc, Llc
    2818 Olive Ave
    Patterson CA

(P-5602)
PRECISION IDENTITY CORPORATION
804 Camden Ave, Campbell (95008-4119)
PHONE..................408 374-2346
Karl Kamber, President
Pierre Kamber, Vice Pres
Roland Kamber, Vice Pres
Jennifer Birch, Bookkeeper
Glenn Clark, Human Res Mgr
EMP: 16 EST: 1970
SQ FT: 12,000
SALES (est): 1MM Privately Held
WEB: www.precisionidentity.com
SIC: 3599 3451 Machine shop, jobbing & repair; screw machine products

(P-5603)
PREFERRED MFG SVCS INC (PA)
Also Called: Snowline Engineering
4261 Business Dr, Cameron Park (95682-7217)
PHONE..................530 677-2675
Calvin Reynolds, President
Lee Block, Exec VP
John Caparella, Engineer
Danette Hart, Inv Control Mgr
Tim Bartosh, Foreman/Supr
EMP: 65
SQ FT: 34,000
SALES (est): 3.4MM Privately Held
WEB: www.snowlineengineering.com
SIC: 3599 Machine shop, jobbing & repair

(P-5604)
PTEC SOLUTIONS INC (PA)
48633 Warm Springs Blvd, Fremont (94539-7782)
PHONE..................510 358-3578
Peter Pham, President
Phuong Lam, Accounting Mgr
Tram Nguyen, Accounts Mgr
▲ EMP: 66 EST: 2010
SQ FT: 25,000
SALES (est): 12MM Privately Held
WEB: www.ptecsolutions.com
SIC: 3599 8711 3357 Machine shop, jobbing & repair; engineering services; fiber optic cable (insulated)

(P-5605)
PTR MANUFACTURING INC
Also Called: Ptr Sheet Metal & Fabrication
33390 Transit Ave, Union City (94587-2014)
PHONE..................510 477-9654
SAI La, President
Phong La, Vice Pres
Eric Tran, Opers Mgr
Todd W Phillips, QC Mgr
EMP: 40 EST: 1994
SQ FT: 45,000
SALES (est): 6.1MM Privately Held
WEB: www.ptrmanufacturing.com
SIC: 3599 3444 Machine shop, jobbing & repair; sheet metalwork

(P-5606)
QUALITY MACHINE ENGRG INC
2559 Grosse Ave, Santa Rosa (95404-2608)
PHONE..................707 528-1900
Rudy Hirschnitz, President
Shawn Barnett, Vice Pres
John F Wright, Vice Pres
EMP: 36 EST: 1991
SQ FT: 13,500
SALES (est): 1.2MM Privately Held
WEB: www.qmeinc.com
SIC: 3599 Machine shop, jobbing & repair

(P-5607)
R & L ENTERPRISES INC
Also Called: Rand Machine Works
1955 S Mary St, Fresno (93721-3309)
PHONE..................559 233-1608
Robert Rand, President
Linda Rand, Vice Pres
Kristin Henson, Executive
Leon Malding, Plant Mgr
EMP: 26
SQ FT: 27,000
SALES (est): 3MM Privately Held
WEB: www.randmachineworks.com
SIC: 3599 7692 Machine shop, jobbing & repair; welding repair

(P-5608)
R STEPHENSON & D CRAM MFG INC
Also Called: R & D Mfg Services
800 Faulstich Ct, San Jose (95112-1361)
PHONE..................408 452-0882
Rick Stephenson, President
EMP: 20 EST: 1976
SQ FT: 14,000
SALES (est): 1.1MM Privately Held
WEB: www.rdmfg.net
SIC: 3599 3369 3324 Machine shop, jobbing & repair; nonferrous foundries; steel investment foundries

(P-5609)
RAPID PRECISION MFG INC
1516 Montague Expy, San Jose (95131-1408)
PHONE..................408 617-0771
Paul Yi, CEO
EMP: 35 EST: 2006
SQ FT: 11,000
SALES (est): 4.8MM Privately Held
WEB: www.rapidprecision.net
SIC: 3599 Machine shop, jobbing & repair

(P-5610)
RDC MACHINE INC
2011 Stone Ave, San Jose (95125-1447)
PHONE..................408 970-0721
Randolph D Cuilla, President
Janene Cuilla, Treasurer
Mark Cuilla, Vice Pres
Dana Depew Sr, VP Opers
EMP: 41 EST: 1991
SALES (est): 5.8MM Privately Held
WEB: www.rdcmachine.com
SIC: 3599 Machine shop, jobbing & repair

(P-5611)
RELIANCE MACHINE PRODUCTS INC
4265 Solar Way, Fremont (94538-6389)
PHONE..................510 438-6760
Kelly L Hill, President
EMP: 45 EST: 1981
SQ FT: 12,000
SALES (est): 6MM Privately Held
WEB: www.rmp-inc.com
SIC: 3599 Machine shop, jobbing & repair

(P-5612)
RICHARDS MACHINING CO INC
382 Martin Ave, Santa Clara (95050-3112)
PHONE..................408 526-9219
Gustavo Chavez, President
Odin Chavez, Vice Pres
Yovannah Chavez, Executive
Yamir Chavez, Admin Sec
EMP: 16 EST: 1988 Privately Held
WEB: www.rmco-inc.com
SIC: 3599 Machine shop, jobbing & repair

(P-5613)
RMC ENGINEERING CO INC (PA)
255 Mayock Rd, Gilroy (95020-7032)
P.O. Box 575 (95021-0575)
PHONE..................408 842-2525
Betty Mc Kenzie, President
Shawna Kenzie, Treasurer
Shawna Mc Kenzie, Corp Secy
Kevin Mc Kenzie, Vice Pres
Scott Mc Kenzie, Vice Pres
▲ EMP: 30 EST: 1978
SQ FT: 14,000
SALES (est): 5.2MM Privately Held
WEB: www.rmcengineering.com
SIC: 3599 7692 7538 3715 Machine shop, jobbing & repair; automotive welding; general automotive repair shops; truck trailers

(P-5614)
ROBSON TECHNOLOGIES INC
Also Called: R T I
135 E Main Ave Ste 130, Morgan Hill (95037-7522)
PHONE..................408 779-8008
William W Robson, President
Ryan Block, Vice Pres
Lori Robson, Vice Pres
Chris O 'connor, Director
EMP: 27 EST: 1989
SQ FT: 3,000
SALES (est): 9.5MM Privately Held
WEB: www.testfixtures.com
SIC: 3599 3823 Machine shop, jobbing & repair; computer interface equipment for industrial process control

(P-5615)
S F ENTERPRISES INCORPORATED
707 Warrington Ave, Redwood City (94063-3525)
PHONE..................650 455-3223
Ben Schloss, President
EMP: 17 EST: 2012
SQ FT: 4,000
SALES (est): 3.2MM Privately Held
SIC: 3599 Air intake filters, internal combustion engine, except auto

(P-5616)
SAMAX PRECISION INC
926 W Evelyn Ave, Sunnyvale (94086-5957)
PHONE..................408 245-9555
Vicki Murray, President
Jodi McCash, Admin Sec
Scott McClung, QC Dir
EMP: 36 EST: 1963
SQ FT: 10,000
SALES (est): 6.3MM Privately Held
WEB: www.samaxinc.com
SIC: 3599 Custom machinery

(P-5617)
SHARP DIMENSION INC
4240 Business Center Dr, Fremont (94538-6356)
PHONE..................510 656-8938
Scott Vo, President
EMP: 21 EST: 1991
SQ FT: 12,000
SALES (est): 5.3MM Privately Held
WEB: www.sharpdimension.com
SIC: 3599 Machine shop, jobbing & repair

(P-5618)
SIERRA PACIFIC MACHINING INC
530 Parrott St, San Jose (95112-4120)
PHONE..................408 924-0281
Richard Wagner, President
Steven Young, Vice Pres
EMP: 26 EST: 1974
SALES (est): 1.3MM Privately Held
WEB: www.sierrapacificmachining.com
SIC: 3599 Machine shop, jobbing & repair

PRODUCTS & SERVICES SECTION
3599 - Machinery & Eqpt, Indl & Commercial, NEC County (P-5644)

(P-5619)
SILICON VALLEY ELITE MFG
460 Aldo Ave, Santa Clara (95054-2301)
PHONE....................408 654-9534
Kim Oanh Ngo, *CEO*
EMP: 19 **EST:** 2012
SALES (est): 1.1MM Privately Held
WEB: www.svemfg.com
SIC: 3599 Machine shop, jobbing & repair

(P-5620)
SKYLIGHT TOOLS INC
2797 Bryant St, San Francisco (94110-4225)
PHONE....................800 961-2580
Jasper Malcolmson, *Principal*
EMP: 22 **EST:** 2016
SALES (est): 3MM Privately Held
SIC: 3599 Industrial machinery

(P-5621)
SOUTH BAY SOLUTIONS INC (PA)
Also Called: SBS
37399 Centralmont Pl, Fremont (94536-6549)
PHONE....................650 843-1800
Adam Drewniany, *CEO*
Valerie Guseva, *Vice Pres*
Lyka Gonzales, *Program Mgr*
Michael Drewniany, *Marketing Staff*
EMP: 30 **EST:** 1992
SQ FT: 20,000
SALES (est): 31.5MM Privately Held
WEB: www.southbaysolutions.com
SIC: 3599 Machine shop, jobbing & repair

(P-5622)
SQUAGLIA MANUFACTURING COMPANY (PA)
275 Polaris Ave, Mountain View (94043-4588)
PHONE....................650 965-9644
Pat Pellizzari, *President*
Ken Pellizzari, *Vice Pres*
EMP: 35 **EST:** 1962
SQ FT: 10,000
SALES (est): 2.5MM Privately Held
WEB: www.squaglia.com
SIC: 3599 Machine shop, jobbing & repair

(P-5623)
SURFACE MANUFACTURING INC
2025 Airpark Ct Ste 10, Auburn (95602-9069)
PHONE....................530 885-0700
Lee Baker, *President*
Richard Peattie, *CFO*
Jane Peattie, *Corp Secy*
EMP: 24 **EST:** 1986
SQ FT: 10,000
SALES (est): 1.1MM Privately Held
WEB: www.surfacemfg.com
SIC: 3599 3577 Machine shop, jobbing & repair; computer peripheral equipment

(P-5624)
SUTTER P DAHLGLEN ENTPS INC
Also Called: Metalfab
1650 Grant St, Santa Clara (95050-3981)
PHONE....................408 727-4640
Linda Terestra, *President*
Jack Paravagna, *President*
EMP: 18 **EST:** 1966
SQ FT: 16,000
SALES (est): 425.5K Privately Held
SIC: 3599 1611 Machine & other job shop work; grading

(P-5625)
SWISS SCREW PRODUCTS INC
339 Mathew St, Santa Clara (95050-3113)
PHONE....................408 748-8400
Sung H Hwang, *President*
Mike Hwang, *Vice Pres*
Young S Hwang, *Vice Pres*
Young Hwang, *Technical Staff*
EMP: 25 **EST:** 1969
SQ FT: 12,750
SALES (est): 2.7MM Privately Held
WEB: www.swissscrew.com
SIC: 3599 3541 3451 Machine shop, jobbing & repair; machine tools, metal cutting type; screw machine products

(P-5626)
TAPEMATION MACHINING INC (PA)
13 Janis Way, Scotts Valley (95066-3537)
PHONE....................831 438-3069
Ericka Stevens, *President*
Josolyn Bradshaw, *Vice Pres*
EMP: 25 **EST:** 1961
SALES (est): 5.6MM Privately Held
WEB: www.tapemation.com
SIC: 3599 Machine shop, jobbing & repair

(P-5627)
TEDON SPECIALTIES A CAL CORP
Also Called: Rock Systems
1255 Vista Way, Red Bluff (96080-4506)
P.O. Box 1236 (96080-1236)
PHONE....................530 527-6600
Donald E Hake, *President*
John Kate, *Manager*
EMP: 15 **EST:** 1980
SQ FT: 14,000
SALES (est): 2.3MM Privately Held
WEB: www.tedon-specialties.hub.biz
SIC: 3599 Machine shop, jobbing & repair

(P-5628)
TRIDECS CORPORATION
3513 Arden Rd, Hayward (94545-3907)
PHONE....................510 785-2620
Frank Schenkhuizen Sr, *Ch of Bd*
Frank Schenkhuizen Jr, *President*
Emma J Schenkhuizen, *Admin Sec*
Joe La, *Prgrmr*
EMP: 25 **EST:** 1970
SQ FT: 15,000
SALES (est): 3MM Privately Held
WEB: www.tridecs.com
SIC: 3599 Machine shop, jobbing & repair

(P-5629)
TRONSON MANUFACTURING INC
3421 Yale Way, Fremont (94538-6171)
PHONE....................408 533-0369
Michael Lieu, *President*
▲ **EMP:** 20 **EST:** 1998
SQ FT: 11,040
SALES (est): 4.5MM Privately Held
WEB: www.tronsonmfg.com
SIC: 3599 Machine shop, jobbing & repair

(P-5630)
TRU MACHINING
45979 Warm Springs Blvd, Fremont (94539-6765)
PHONE....................510 573-3408
Quocthuy Truong, *President*
Diep Nguyen, *Vice Pres*
EMP: 15 **EST:** 2013
SALES (est): 1.6MM Privately Held
WEB: www.trumachining.com
SIC: 3599 3569 Machine shop, jobbing & repair; liquid automation machinery & equipment

(P-5631)
UNITECH TOOL & MACHINE INC
3025 Stender Way, Santa Clara (95054-3216)
PHONE....................408 566-0333
Ramin Lak, *CEO*
▲ **EMP:** 17 **EST:** 1995
SALES (est): 2.5MM Privately Held
WEB: www.unitechtool.com
SIC: 3599 Machine shop, jobbing & repair

(P-5632)
UNITED WESTERN INDUSTRIES INC
3515 N Hazel Ave, Fresno (93722-4913)
P.O. Box 13099 (93794-3099)
PHONE....................559 226-7236
L G Simmons, *President*
Gale Pirtle, *Managing Prtnr*
Bruce Ketch, *Vice Pres*
Camilo Salas, *Opers Mgr*
EMP: 49 **EST:** 1971
SQ FT: 15,000
SALES (est): 8.7MM Privately Held
WEB: www.uwi.us
SIC: 3599 3469 3544 Custom machinery; machine shop, jobbing & repair; metal stampings; die sets for metal stamping (presses)

(P-5633)
V-TECH MANUFACTURING INC
Also Called: V Tech
1140 W Evelyn Ave, Sunnyvale (94086-5742)
PHONE....................408 730-9200
Robert Gluchowski, *President*
Jamie Sandidge, *Office Mgr*
EMP: 15 **EST:** 1990
SQ FT: 2,000
SALES (est): 2.3MM Privately Held
WEB: www.vtechmanufacturing.com
SIC: 3599 Machine shop, jobbing & repair

(P-5634)
VALLEY TOOL & MFG CO INC
2507 Tully Rd, Hughson (95326-9824)
P.O. Box 220 (95326-0220)
PHONE....................209 883-4093
Fred G Brenda, *CEO*
Carol Finn, *Corp Secy*
Daniel C Finn, *Vice Pres*
Paul Swanson, *Engineer*
Luann Klann, *Controller*
▲ **EMP:** 40
SQ FT: 50,000
SALES (est): 9.2MM Privately Held
WEB: www.valleytoolmfg.com
SIC: 3599 Machine shop, jobbing & repair

(P-5635)
VANDER-BEND MANUFACTURING INC
Also Called: J.L. Haley
3510 Luyung Dr, Rancho Cordova (95742-6872)
PHONE....................916 631-6375
Steve Butts, *Branch Mgr*
Lori Murdock, *Manager*
EMP: 140
SALES (corp-wide): 138.5MM Privately Held
WEB: www.vander-bend.com
SIC: 3599 3312 7692 Machine shop, jobbing & repair; blast furnaces & steel mills; welding repair
PA: Vander-Bend Manufacturing, Inc.
2701 Orchard Pkwy
San Jose CA 95134
408 245-5150

(P-5636)
VANDERHULST ASSOCIATES INC
3300 Victor Ct, Santa Clara (95054-2316)
PHONE....................408 727-1313
Hank Vanderhulst, *CEO*
Sandy Thompson, *Vice Pres*
Corrie Vanderhulst, *Admin Sec*
Chad Weaver, *Prgrmr*
EMP: 30 **EST:** 1975
SQ FT: 11,000 Privately Held
WEB: www.vanderhulst.com
SIC: 3599 Machine shop, jobbing & repair

(P-5637)
VIAN ENTERPRISES INC
2120 Precision Pl, Auburn (95603-9096)
PHONE....................530 885-1997
Christopher Vian, *CEO*
Liz Popsicle, *President*
William Kirby, *CFO*
Carol Ann Vian, *Vice Pres*
Elizabeth Vian, *Executive*
EMP: 87 **EST:** 1968
SALES (est): 12.6MM Privately Held
WEB: www.vianenterprises.com
SIC: 3599 Machine shop, jobbing & repair

(P-5638)
VISGER PRECISION INC
1815 Russell Ave, Santa Clara (95054-2035)
PHONE....................408 988-0184
Terrance M Visger, *President*
Terry Visger, *Manager*
EMP: 18 **EST:** 1975
SQ FT: 10,000
SALES (est): 2.5MM Privately Held
WEB: www.visger.com
SIC: 3599 Machine shop, jobbing & repair

(P-5639)
WATTS MACHINING INC
3370 Victor Ct, Santa Clara (95054-2316)
PHONE....................408 654-9300
Doug Watts, *President*
Bob Hazle, *General Mgr*
Karen Watts, *Supervisor*
EMP: 30 **EST:** 1982
SALES (est): 3.4MM Privately Held
WEB: www.wattsmachining.com
SIC: 3599 Machine shop, jobbing & repair

(P-5640)
WB MACHINING & MECH DESIGN
1670 Zanker Rd, San Jose (95112-1134)
PHONE....................408 453-5005
Max Ho, *CEO*
EMP: 22 **EST:** 1992
SQ FT: 20,000
SALES (est): 5MM Privately Held
WEB: www.wb-precision.com
SIC: 3599 3569 3699 Machine shop, jobbing & repair; assembly machines, non-metalworking; electrical equipment & supplies

(P-5641)
WES MANUFACTURING INC
431 Greenwood Dr, Santa Clara (95054-2134)
PHONE....................408 727-0750
Garn Nelson, *CEO*
Carl Michaels, *Vice Pres*
Dennis Whightman, *Vice Pres*
Susan Nelson, *Accounts Mgr*
EMP: 20 **EST:** 1995
SALES (est): 3.2MM Privately Held
WEB: www.accuratetm.com
SIC: 3599 8711 Machine shop, jobbing & repair; consulting engineer

(P-5642)
WESTERN GRINDING SERVICE INC
2375 De La Cruz Blvd, Santa Clara (95050-2920)
PHONE....................650 591-2635
David P Wilson, *Ch of Bd*
Ethan C Wilson, *President*
Rob Brindle, *VP Mfg*
Cathy Day, *Director*
EMP: 30 **EST:** 1953
SQ FT: 28,000
SALES (est): 4.7MM Privately Held
WEB: www.westerngrinding.com
SIC: 3599 Machine shop, jobbing & repair

(P-5643)
WOLFS PRECISION WORKS INC
3549 Haven Ave Ste F, Menlo Park (94025-1070)
PHONE....................650 364-1341
Wolfgang Pohl, *President*
Karen Pohl, *Corp Secy*
EMP: 27 **EST:** 1979
SQ FT: 5,000
SALES (est): 1.9MM Privately Held
WEB: www.wpw-inc.com
SIC: 3599 Machine shop, jobbing & repair

(P-5644)
YUHAS TOOLING & MACHINING INC
Also Called: Slawomira Sobczyk
1031 Pecten Ct, Milpitas (95035-6804)
PHONE....................408 934-9196
Slava Sobczyk, *CEO*
EMP: 28 **EST:** 1993
SQ FT: 6,000
SALES (est): 750.1K Privately Held
WEB: www.yuhasmachining.com
SIC: 3599 Machine shop, jobbing & repair

3612 Power, Distribution & Specialty Transformers

(P-5645)
ABB INC
1321 Harbor Bay Pkwy # 101, Alameda (94502-6582)
PHONE.................................510 987-7111
Beth Reid, *Branch Mgr*
EMP: 63
SALES (corp-wide): 26.1B **Privately Held**
WEB: www.global.abb
SIC: 3612 Transformers, except electric
HQ: Abb Inc.
 305 Gregson Dr
 Cary NC 27511

(P-5646)
ALGONQUIN POWER SANGER LLC
1125 Muscat Ave, Sanger (93657-4000)
P.O. Box 397 (93657-0397)
PHONE.................................559 875-0800
Ian Robertson, *Mng Member*
Travis Clendenen, *Plant Mgr*
EMP: 22 EST: 1988
SQ FT: 16,225
SALES (est): 7.7MM
SALES (corp-wide): 1.6B **Privately Held**
WEB: www.sanger.org
SIC: 3612 Power transformers, electric
PA: Algonquin Power & Utilities Corp
 354 Davis Rd
 Oakville ON L6J 2
 905 465-4500

(P-5647)
QUALITY TRANSFORMER & ELEC
Also Called: Quality Transformer & Elec Co
963 Ames Ave, Milpitas (95035-6326)
PHONE.................................408 935-0231
Carl Clift, *CEO*
Frank W Hendershot, *President*
Adam Clouse, *General Mgr*
Yogesh Dua, *Engineer*
Preston Hullen, *Engineer*
EMP: 40 EST: 1964
SQ FT: 32,500
SALES (est): 9.8MM **Privately Held**
WEB: www.qte.com
SIC: 3612 Transformers, except electric

(P-5648)
SIWIBI WHOLESALE
625 Ellis St, Mountain View (94043-2226)
PHONE.................................650 448-1041
EMP: 30 EST: 2020
SALES (est): 1.3MM **Privately Held**
WEB: www.siwibi.com
SIC: 3612 Distribution transformers, electric

3613 Switchgear & Switchboard Apparatus

(P-5649)
BRILLIANT HOME TECHNOLOGY INC
155 Bovet Rd Ste 500, San Mateo (94402-3157)
PHONE.................................650 539-5320
Aaron Emigh, *CEO*
Brian Cardanha, *Vice Pres*
Michael Williams, *Vice Pres*
Anoop Mehta, *CIO*
Steven Stanek, *CTO*
EMP: 46 EST: 2016
SALES (est): 500K **Privately Held**
WEB: www.brilliant.tech
SIC: 3613 Switchgear & switchboard apparatus

(P-5650)
BUFFALO DISTRIBUTION INC
30750 San Clemente St, Hayward (94544-7131)
PHONE.................................510 324-3800
Earl I Ramer Jr, *CEO*
▲ EMP: 17 EST: 2002
SALES (est): 1.4MM **Privately Held**
WEB: www.buffalodistribution.com
SIC: 3613 Distribution cutouts

(P-5651)
DIGITAL LOGGERS INC
2695 Walsh Ave, Santa Clara (95051-0920)
PHONE.................................408 330-5599
▲ EMP: 34 EST: 2009
SQ FT: 21,000
SALES (est): 2.8MM **Privately Held**
SIC: 3613 3679 Mfg Switchgear/Switchboards Mfg Electronic Components

(P-5652)
NEW IEM LLC
Also Called: Industrial Electric Mfg
48205 Warm Springs Blvd, Fremont (94539-7654)
PHONE.................................510 656-1600
Edward Herman, *CEO*
Clayton Such, *COO*
John Hulme, *CFO*
Tim Ferguson, *Vice Pres*
Daniel O'Callaghan, *Vice Pres*
▲ EMP: 240 EST: 2003
SQ FT: 131,000
SALES (est): 90MM
SALES (corp-wide): 250MM **Privately Held**
WEB: www.iemfg.com
SIC: 3613 Switchboards & parts, power; switchboard apparatus, except instruments; control panels, electric; switchgear & switchgear accessories
HQ: Abd El & Larson Holdings, Llc
 48205 Warm Springs Blvd
 Fremont CA 94539
 510 656-1600

(P-5653)
RELECTRIC INC
2390 Zanker Rd, San Jose (95131-1115)
PHONE.................................408 467-2222
Anthony Robinson, *President*
Michael Richardson, *Vice Pres*
Jessica Clifford, *Executive*
Kelly Pihera, *Purch Agent*
Michael Lisle, *Sales Dir*
▲ EMP: 30 EST: 2003
SQ FT: 35,000
SALES (est): 9.9MM **Privately Held**
WEB: www.relectric.com
SIC: 3613 3625 5063 8734 Switchgear & switchboard apparatus; relays & industrial controls; electrical apparatus & equipment; testing laboratories

(P-5654)
SILICON VLY WORLD TRADE CORP
Also Called: American Skynet Electronics
1474 Gladding Ct, Milpitas (95035-6831)
PHONE.................................408 945-6355
Ching-Hung Liang, *President*
▲ EMP: 25 EST: 1985
SQ FT: 10,000
SALES (est): 3.4MM **Privately Held**
WEB: www.skynetpower.com.tw
SIC: 3613 7379 Power switching equipment; computer related maintenance services
PA: Skynet Electronic Co., Ltd.
 4f, No. 76,78,80, Chenggong Rd., Sec. 1
 Taipei City TAP 11570

(P-5655)
SOLARBOS (HQ)
2019 Elkins Way Ste A, Brentwood (94513-7372)
PHONE.................................925 456-7744
William L Vietas, *CEO*
Timothy F Murphy, *CFO*
Bryanna Monelo, *Opers-Prdtn-Mfg*
Joseph Bieri, *Production*
EMP: 51 EST: 2006
SALES (est): 27MM
SALES (corp-wide): 1B **Publicly Held**
WEB: www.solarbos.com
SIC: 3613 Switchgear & switchboard apparatus

PA: Gibraltar Industries, Inc.
 3556 Lake Shore Rd # 100
 Buffalo NY 14219
 716 826-6500

(P-5656)
TRAYER ENGINEERING CORPORATION
1569 Alvarado St, San Leandro (94577-2640)
PHONE.................................415 285-7770
John Trayer, *President*
Neil Morris, *COO*
Kirit Patel, *COO*
Ben Wong, *CFO*
Andrew Bond, *Officer*
▼ EMP: 84 EST: 1962
SQ FT: 21,000
SALES (est): 20.4MM **Privately Held**
WEB: www.trayer.com
SIC: 3613 Switchgear & switchgear accessories

3621 Motors & Generators

(P-5657)
AKRIBIS SYSTEMS INCORPORATED
780 Montague Expy Ste 508, San Jose (95131-1319)
PHONE.................................408 913-1300
Howe Yuen Lim, *CEO*
Thomas Barrett, *Engineer*
EMP: 15 EST: 2012
SALES (est): 6.5MM **Privately Held**
WEB: www.akribis-sys.com
SIC: 3621 5084 Servomotors, electric; industrial machinery & equipment
PA: Akribis Systems Pte. Ltd.
 5012 Ang Mo Kio Avenue 5
 Singapore 56987

(P-5658)
CHARGEPOINT HOLDINGS INC (PA)
240 E Hacienda Ave, Campbell (95008-6617)
PHONE.................................408 841-4500
Pasquale Romano, *President*
Rex Jackson, *CFO*
Michael Hughes, *Ch Credit Ofcr*
Colleen Jansen, *Chief Mktg Ofcr*
Lawrence Lee, *Senior VP*
EMP: 798 EST: 2007
SQ FT: 72,000 **Publicly Held**
WEB: www.chargepoint.com
SIC: 3621 Generators for gas-electric or oil-electric vehicles

(P-5659)
CHI WEST LLC (DH)
660 4th St, San Francisco (94107-1618)
PHONE.................................415 608-8757
Kevin J Louie, *Principal*
▲ EMP: 72 EST: 2012
SALES (est): 7.9MM
SALES (corp-wide): 137.3MM **Privately Held**
WEB: www.enelx.com
SIC: 3621 Windmills, electric generating
HQ: Enel North America, Inc.
 100 Brickstone Sq Ste 300
 Andover MA 01810
 978 681-1900

(P-5660)
ES WEST COAST LLC
Also Called: Energy Systems
7100 Longe St Ste 300, Stockton (95206-3962)
PHONE.................................209 870-1900
Don Richter, *President*
Robert Gabriel, *Department Mgr*
Allen Ridgway, *Technician*
Rocky Bear, *Project Engr*
Heather Gum, *Sales Staff*
EMP: 45 EST: 2012
SALES (est): 10.6MM
SALES (corp-wide): 95MM **Privately Held**
SIC: 3621 Electric motor & generator auxilary parts

HQ: The Shane Group Llc
 215 W Mechanic St
 Hillsdale MI 49242
 517 439-4316

(P-5661)
FARASIS ENERGY USA INC
21363 Cabot Blvd, Hayward (94545-1650)
PHONE.................................510 732-6600
Yu Wang, *CEO*
EMP: 67 EST: 2019
SALES (est): 5.6MM **Privately Held**
SIC: 3621 Generators for storage battery chargers

(P-5662)
FREEWIRE TECHNOLOGIES INC
1933 Davis St Ste 301a, San Leandro (94577-1259)
PHONE.................................415 779-5515
Arcady Sosinov, *CEO*
Martin Lynch, *COO*
Michael Beer, *CFO*
Rob Anderson, *Vice Pres*
Jawann Swislow, *CTO*
EMP: 50 EST: 2014
SALES (est): 1.5MM **Privately Held**
WEB: www.freewiretech.com
SIC: 3621 3714 7389 Storage battery chargers, motor & engine generator type; motor vehicle electrical equipment;

(P-5663)
LIN ENGINEERING INC
16245 Vineyard Blvd, Morgan Hill (95037-7123)
PHONE.................................408 919-0200
Ted T Lin, *President*
Rouyu Loughry, *CFO*
Cynthia Lin, *Corp Secy*
Ryan Lin, *Vice Pres*
Viviana Ramalho, *Administration*
▲ EMP: 125 EST: 1987
SQ FT: 16,000
SALES (est): 33.8MM
SALES (corp-wide): 259.6MM **Privately Held**
WEB: www.linengineering.com
SIC: 3621 Motors, electric
HQ: Moons' International Trading (Shanghai) Co., Ltd.
 Caohejing Hi-Tech Zone
 Shanghai 20023

(P-5664)
NATURENER USA LLC (HQ)
435 Pacific Ave Fl 4, San Francisco (94133-4611)
PHONE.................................415 217-5500
Jose M S Seara,
Greg Copeland, *Vice Pres*
Gregory Copeland, *Vice Pres*
Marc Denarie, *CIO*
Andy Whelchel, *Technician*
EMP: 30 EST: 2007
SALES (est): 17.9MM
SALES (corp-wide): 834.2K **Privately Held**
WEB: www.naturener.us
SIC: 3621 Windmills, electric generating
PA: Grupo Naturener, Sa
 Calle Nulez De Balboa, 120 - 7
 Madrid 28006
 915 625-410

(P-5665)
NOVATORQUE INC
281 Greenoaks Dr, Atherton (94027-2114)
PHONE.................................510 933-2700
Emily Liggett, *CEO*
Tim McNally, *CFO*
Kim Baker, *Engineer*
Scott Johnson, *Vice Pres*
Joe Weber, *Vice Pres*
▲ EMP: 29 EST: 2008
SQ FT: 27,000
SALES (est): 4.9MM **Privately Held**
WEB: www.regalbeloit.com
SIC: 3621 Motors & generators

(P-5666)
POWERFLEX SYSTEMS LLC
392 1st St, Los Altos (94022-3601)
P.O. Box 3155 (94024-0155)
PHONE.................................650 469-3392

PRODUCTS & SERVICES SECTION

3625 - Relays & Indl Controls County (P-5688)

George Lee, *CEO*
Steven Low, *Ch of Bd*
Wyatt Kozelka, *Project Mgr*
Daniel Carrillo, *Project Engr*
Max Wilcox, *Director*
EMP: 24 **EST:** 2016
SALES (est): 2.9MM **Privately Held**
WEB: www.powerflex.com
SIC: 3621 Generators for gas-electric or oil-electric vehicles

(P-5667)
R K LARRABEE COMPANY INC
Also Called: Construction Electrical Pdts
7800 Las Positas Rd, Livermore (94551-8240)
PHONE.................................925 828-9420
Robert Larrabee, *President*
Nancy Larrabee, *Vice Pres*
Scott Larrabee, *Vice Pres*
Rob Larrabee, *VP Sales*
◆ **EMP:** 65
SALES (est): 18.6MM
SALES (corp-wide): 1.6B **Privately Held**
WEB: www.cepnow.com
SIC: 3621 3699 3648 3646 Power generators; electrical equipment & supplies; lighting equipment; commercial indusl & institutional electric lighting fixtures; non-current-carrying wiring services; nonferrous wiredrawing & insulating
PA: Southwire Company, Llc
1 Southwire Dr
Carrollton GA 30119
770 832-4242

(P-5668)
STEM INC (PA)
100 Rollins Rd, Millbrae (94030-3115)
PHONE.................................415 937-7816
John Carrington, *CEO*
Mark Triplett, *COO*
Bill Bush, *CFO*
Alan Russo, *Risk Mgmt Dir*
Prakesh Patel, *Security Dir*
EMP: 90 **EST:** 2018 **Publicly Held**
WEB: www.stem.com
SIC: 3621 7372 Storage battery chargers, motor & engine generator type; prepackaged software

3624 Carbon & Graphite Prdts

(P-5669)
ADVANCE CARBON PRODUCTS INC
2036 National Ave, Hayward (94545-1712)
PHONE.................................510 293-5930
Ronald D Crader, *President*
James Michael Crader, *Vice Pres*
Gary Kloss, *Vice Pres*
Janice Guerrero, *Admin Asst*
Geoff Carbon, *Engineer*
EMP: 40 **EST:** 1955
SQ FT: 20,000
SALES (est): 3.6MM **Privately Held**
WEB: www.store.advancecarbon.com
SIC: 3624 3678 3643 3568 Brush blocks, carbon or molded graphite; electronic connectors; current-carrying wiring devices; power transmission equipment; gaskets, packing & sealing devices; industrial inorganic chemicals

(P-5670)
CARBON DESIGN INNOVATIONS INC (PA)
1745 Adrian Rd Ste 20, Burlingame (94010-2100)
PHONE.................................650 697-7070
Vance J Nau, *CEO*
EMP: 32 **EST:** 2009
SALES (est): 340.7K **Privately Held**
WEB: www.carbondesigninnovations.com
SIC: 3624 Carbon & graphite products

(P-5671)
CDG TECHNOLOGY LLC
779 Twin View Blvd, Redding (96003-2008)
PHONE.................................530 243-4451
Manny Ornellas,
EMP: 21 **EST:** 2003

SALES (est): 3.5MM **Privately Held**
WEB: www.cdgtech.com
SIC: 3624 Fibers, carbon & graphite

(P-5672)
MITSUBSHI CHEM CRBN FIBR CMPST (DH)
5900 88th St, Sacramento (95828-1109)
PHONE.................................916 386-1733
Susumu Sasaki, *CEO*
Donald Carter, *CFO*
Masayoshi Ozeki, *Vice Pres*
Takeshi Sasaki, *Vice Pres*
Denise Di Fabbio, *Admin Asst*
▲ **EMP:** 125 **EST:** 1991
SQ FT: 60,000
SALES (est): 60.7MM **Privately Held**
WEB: www.mccfc.com
SIC: 3624 Fibers, carbon & graphite

(P-5673)
SANGRAF INTERNATIONAL INC
3171 Independence Dr, Livermore (94551-7595)
PHONE.................................216 800-9999
Jamie Hansen, *CEO*
Helen Hou, *CFO*
EMP: 23 **EST:** 2012
SALES (est): 2.6MM **Privately Held**
WEB: www.sangrafintl.com
SIC: 3624 Carbon & graphite products

3625 Relays & Indl Controls

(P-5674)
AIRSPACE SYSTEMS INC
1933 Davis St Ste 229, San Leandro (94571-1257)
PHONE.................................415 226-7779
Jasminder Banga, *CEO*
Dan Dalton, *Partner*
Guy Bar-Nahum, *Vice Pres*
Navneet Mosey, *Managing Dir*
Trevor Owens, *Engineer*
EMP: 30 **EST:** 2015
SALES (est): 3.2MM **Privately Held**
WEB: www.airspace.co
SIC: 3625 Control equipment, electric

(P-5675)
AMES FIRE WATERWORKS
1485 Tanforan Ave, Woodland (95776-6108)
PHONE.................................530 666-2493
Nancy West, *CEO*
Steve Loya, *Prdtn Mgr*
▲ **EMP:** 88 **EST:** 1910
SQ FT: 10,000
SALES (est): 11.3MM
SALES (corp-wide): 1.5B **Publicly Held**
WEB: www.watts.com
SIC: 3625 3494 Relays & industrial controls; valves & pipe fittings
PA: Watts Water Technologies, Inc.
815 Chestnut St
North Andover MA 01845
978 688-1811

(P-5676)
APPLIED CONTROL ELECTRONICS
5480 Merchant Cir, Placerville (95667-8250)
PHONE.................................530 626-5181
Terry Burke, *President*
Natalie Burke, *CFO*
Edd Todd, *Prdtn Mgr*
EMP: 15 **EST:** 1988
SQ FT: 10,000
SALES (est): 5.3MM **Privately Held**
WEB: www.appconx.com
SIC: 3625 8711 Motor controls & accessories; electrical or electronic engineering; consulting engineer

(P-5677)
ASCOR INC (HQ)
4650 Norris Canyon Rd, San Ramon (94583-1320)
PHONE.................................925 328-4650
Jeffrey Lum, *President*
John Regazzi, *CEO*
EMP: 100 **EST:** 1987
SQ FT: 19,000

SALES (est): 5.8MM
SALES (corp-wide): 13MM **Publicly Held**
WEB: www.go-asg.gigatronics.com
SIC: 3625 Switches, electronic applications
PA: Giga-Tronics Incorporated
5990 Gleason Dr
Dublin CA 94568
925 328-4650

(P-5678)
CTI-CONTROLTECH INC
22 Beta Ct, San Ramon (94583-1202)
PHONE.................................925 208-4250
George P Constas, *President*
Adam Pennell, *Sales Associate*
EMP: 15 **EST:** 1976
SQ FT: 5,000
SALES (est): 4.3MM **Privately Held**
WEB: www.cti-ct.com
SIC: 3625 5084 Relays & industrial controls; controlling instruments & accessories

(P-5679)
GNA INDUSTRIES INC
Also Called: Alex Tronix
4761 W Jacquelyn Ave, Fresno (93722-6438)
PHONE.................................559 276-0953
EMP: 29
SQ FT: 5,000
SALES (est): 4.8MM **Privately Held**
WEB: www.alextronix.com
SIC: 3625 Mfg Relays/Industrial Controls

(P-5680)
ITT LLC
ITT BIW Connector Systems
500 Tesconi Cir, Santa Rosa (95401-4665)
PHONE.................................707 523-2300
Robert Roeser, *Branch Mgr*
Shari Eshem, *CFO*
Carlo Ghirardo, *Senior VP*
Mary Gerstner, *Vice Pres*
Eckhard Konkel, *Vice Pres*
EMP: 109
SQ FT: 35,000
SALES (corp-wide): 2.4B **Publicly Held**
WEB: www.itt.com
SIC: 3625 Control equipment, electric
HQ: Itt Llc
1133 Westchester Ave N-100
White Plains NY 10604
914 641-2000

(P-5681)
KAPSCH TRAFFICCOM USA INC
4256 Hacienda Dr Ste 100, Pleasanton (94588-8595)
PHONE.................................925 225-1600
David Dimlich, *President*
Thien Nguyen, *Sr Software Eng*
Paul Camarena, *Senior Engr*
Timothy McGuire, *Supervisor*
EMP: 109
SALES (corp-wide): 1.1B **Privately Held**
WEB: www.kapsch.net
SIC: 3625 Industrial electrical relays & switches
HQ: Kapsch Trafficcom Usa, Inc.
8201 Greensboro Dr # 1002
Mc Lean VA 22102
703 885-1976

(P-5682)
KENSINGTON LABORATORIES LLC (PA)
6200 Village Pkwy, Dublin (94568-3004)
PHONE.................................510 324-0126
Raj Kaul, *Mng Member*
EMP: 17 **EST:** 1972
SQ FT: 72,000
SALES (est): 10MM **Privately Held**
WEB: www.kensingtonlabs.com
SIC: 3625 3825 3674 Positioning controls, electric; measuring instruments & meters, electric; semiconductors & related devices

(P-5683)
LAIRD TECHNOLOGIES INC
2755 Great America Way, Santa Clara (95054-1166)
PHONE.................................408 726-5329
EMP: 19 **EST:** 2015

SALES (est): 1.8MM **Privately Held**
WEB: www.lairdtech.com
SIC: 3625 Relays & industrial controls

(P-5684)
MICROSEMI FREQUENCY TIME CORP (DH)
3870 N 1st St, San Jose (95134-1702)
PHONE.................................480 792-7200
Ganesh Moorthy, *President*
J Eric Bjornholt, *CFO*
Steve Sanghi, *Chairman*
Robert Clarkson, *Director*
▲ **EMP:** 170 **EST:** 2001
SALES (est): 152MM
SALES (corp-wide): 5.4B **Publicly Held**
WEB: www.microsemi.com
SIC: 3625 7372 Timing devices, electronic; business oriented computer software
HQ: Microsemi Corporation
11861 Western Ave
Garden Grove CA 92841
949 380-6100

(P-5685)
NEXTINPUT INC (HQ)
980 Linda Vista Ave, Mountain View (94043-1903)
PHONE.................................408 770-9293
Ali Foughi, *CEO*
Sameer Bidichandani, *Vice Pres*
Philip Thach, *Vice Pres*
Mehrnaz Youssefi, *Engineer*
William Bowman, *Opers Staff*
EMP: 43 **EST:** 2012
SALES (est): 6.9MM
SALES (corp-wide): 4B **Publicly Held**
WEB: www.nextinput.com
SIC: 3625 Switches, electronic applications
PA: Qorvo, Inc.
7628 Thorndike Rd
Greensboro NC 27409
336 664-1233

(P-5686)
PECO INSPX
1616 Culpepper Ave Ste A, Modesto (95351-1220)
PHONE.................................209 576-3345
Jeff Souza, *Vice Pres*
Rae Holloway, *Accountant*
EMP: 17
SALES (corp-wide): 4.4MM **Privately Held**
WEB: www.peco-inspx.com
SIC: 3625 Relays & industrial controls
PA: Peco Inspx
1835 Rollins Rd
Burlingame CA 94010
209 576-3345

(P-5687)
PIVOTAL SYSTEMS CORPORATION
48389 Fremont Blvd # 100, Fremont (94538-6513)
PHONE.................................510 770-9125
John Hoffman, *CEO*
EMP: 20 **EST:** 2003
SQ FT: 1,000
SALES (est): 8.8MM **Privately Held**
WEB: www.pivotalsys.com
SIC: 3625 Control equipment, electric

(P-5688)
RCD ENGINEERING INC
17100 Salmon Mine Rd, Nevada City (95959-9350)
P.O. Box 119, North San Juan (95960-0119)
PHONE.................................530 292-3133
Steve Leach, *CEO*
Pat Leach, *Admin Sec*
Roger Fogarty, *Foreman/Supr*
Paco Garcia, *Marketing Staff*
Barry Bryne, *Sales Staff*
EMP: 53 **EST:** 1967
SQ FT: 12,000
SALES (est): 3.6MM **Privately Held**
WEB: www.rcdengineering.com
SIC: 3625 3714 Motor controls & accessories; motor starters & controllers, electric; motor vehicle parts & accessories

3625 - Relays & Indl Controls County (P-5689)

(P-5689)
ROCKWELL AUTOMATION INC
111 N Market St Ste 200, San Jose (95113-1116)
PHONE....................408 443-5425
EMP: 67 Publicly Held
SIC: 3625 Mfg Relays/Industrial Controls
PA: Rockwell Automation, Inc.
　　1201 S 2nd St
　　Milwaukee WI 53204

(P-5690)
SILICON MICROSTRUCTURES INC
1701 Mccarthy Blvd, Milpitas (95035-7416)
PHONE....................408 473-9700
Frank D Guidone, *President*
Tommy Truong, *Technician*
Tobias Ilchmann, *Technology*
Jeremy Gao, *Sales Staff*
▲ EMP: 76 EST: 1991
SQ FT: 34,000
SALES (est): 28.2MM
SALES (corp-wide): 12.1B Privately Held
WEB: www.si-micro.com
SIC: 3625 3823 Relays & industrial controls; industrial instrmnts msrmnt display/control process variable
HQ: Measurement Specialties, Inc.
　　1000 Lucas Way
　　Hampton VA 23666
　　757 766-1500

(P-5691)
VARIOUS TECHNOLOGIES INC
2720 Aiello Dr Ste C, San Jose (95111-2186)
PHONE....................408 972-4460
Kurt Sebben, *President*
Eric Chan, *Sales Staff*
EMP: 22 EST: 1986
SQ FT: 8,200
SALES (est): 1.3MM Privately Held
WEB: www.vari-tech.com
SIC: 3625 Solenoid switches (industrial controls); electric controls & control accessories, industrial

3629 Electrical Indl Apparatus, NEC

(P-5692)
ALTERGY SYSTEMS
140 Blue Ravine Rd, Folsom (95630-4703)
PHONE....................916 458-8590
Eric S Mettler, *President*
Audrey Cook, *President*
Michael Benoff, *CFO*
Nate Cammack, *CFO*
Jeremy Wolfe, *CFO*
▲ EMP: 29 EST: 2001
SQ FT: 37,000
SALES (est): 8.6MM Privately Held
WEB: www.altergy.com
SIC: 3629 Electrochemical generators (fuel cells)

(P-5693)
CHARGEPOINT INC (PA)
254 E Hacienda Ave, Campbell (95008-6617)
PHONE....................408 841-4500
Pasquale Romano, *President*
Rex Jackson, *CFO*
Colleen Jansen, *Chief Mktg Ofcr*
Bill Loewenthal, *Senior VP*
Eric Sidle, *Senior VP*
◆ EMP: 566 EST: 2007
SQ FT: 120,000
SALES: 146.4MM Privately Held
WEB: www.chargepoint.com
SIC: 3629 Battery chargers, rectifying or nonrotating

(P-5694)
CLEAR SHAPE TECHNOLOGIES INC
2655 Seely Ave Bldg 5, San Jose (95134-1931)
PHONE....................408 943-1234
Lip-Bu Tan, *Principal*
EMP: 15 EST: 2008
SALES (est): 1.3MM
SALES (corp-wide): 2.6B Publicly Held
WEB: www.cadence.com
SIC: 3629 Electrical industrial apparatus
PA: Cadence Design Systems, Inc.
　　2655 Seely Ave Bldg 5
　　San Jose CA 95134
　　408 943-1234

(P-5695)
MOJO MOBILITY INC
3707 Heron Way, Palo Alto (94303-4254)
PHONE....................650 446-0004
Afshin Partovi, *CEO*
Zack Deiri, *Vice Pres*
Bob Lang, *Vice Pres*
EMP: 21 EST: 2005
SALES (est): 537.1K Privately Held
WEB: www.mojomobility.com
SIC: 3629 Battery chargers, rectifying or nonrotating

(P-5696)
SOLAREDGE TECHNOLOGIES INC (PA)
700 Tasman Dr, Milpitas (95035-7456)
PHONE....................510 498-3200
Zvi Lando, *CEO*
Sehwoong Jeong, *CEO*
Uri Bechor, *COO*
Ronen Faier, *CFO*
Nadav Zafrir, *Co-COB*
◆ EMP: 431 EST: 2006
SALES (est): 121.9MM Privately Held
WEB: www.solaredge.com
SIC: 3629 Power conversion units, a.c. to d.c.: static-electric

(P-5697)
SOUTH BAY SOLUTIONS TEXAS LLC
37399 Centralmont Pl, Fremont (94536-6549)
PHONE....................936 494-0180
Theresa Brooks, *Vice Pres*
Parveen Johal, *QC Mgr*
▲ EMP: 15 EST: 2012
SALES (est): 489.5K Privately Held
WEB: www.southbaysolutions.com
SIC: 3629 Electronic generation equipment

(P-5698)
SPARQTRON CORPORATION
5079 Brandin Ct, Fremont (94538-3140)
PHONE....................510 657-7198
Shu Hung Kung, *CEO*
Mitchell Kung, *President*
Stephanie Nelson, *CFO*
May Tsao, *Program Mgr*
Ella MA, *Prgrmr*
▲ EMP: 100 EST: 1998
SQ FT: 70,000
SALES (est): 32.5MM Privately Held
WEB: www.sparqtron.com
SIC: 3629 3672 Static elimination equipment, industrial; printed circuit boards

(P-5699)
ULTRACELL CORPORATION (PA)
399 Lindbergh Ave, Livermore (94551-9291)
PHONE....................925 292-4226
Keith Scott, *CEO*
Gerry Tucker, *Engineer*
Miguel Rio Tinto, *Director*
EMP: 16 EST: 2002
SALES (est): 2.1MM Privately Held
WEB: www.ultracell-llc.com
SIC: 3629 Electrochemical generators (fuel cells)

3631 Household Cooking Eqpt

(P-5700)
BULL OUTDOOR PRODUCTS INC
1011 E Pine St Ste A, Lodi (95240-3158)
PHONE....................909 770-8626
Mark Nureddine, *President*
Jeremy Seats, *Opers Staff*
◆ EMP: 50 EST: 1989
SQ FT: 25,000
SALES (est): 16.5MM Privately Held
WEB: www.bullbbq.com
SIC: 5712 3631 Outdoor & garden furniture: barbecues, grills & braziers (outdoor cooking)

(P-5701)
TELEDYNE WIRELESS INC
Also Called: Teledyne Microwave
3236 Scott Blvd, Santa Clara (95054-3011)
PHONE....................408 986-5060
EMP: 110
SALES (corp-wide): 2.3B Publicly Held
SIC: 3631 Mfg Microwave
HQ: Teledyne Wireless, Llc
　　1274 Terra Bella Ave
　　Mountain View CA 94043
　　650 691-9800

3632 Household Refrigerators & Freezers

(P-5702)
LARRY SCHLUSSLER
Also Called: Sun Frost
824 L St Ste 7, Arcata (95521-5766)
P.O. Box 1101 (95518-1101)
PHONE....................707 822-9095
Larry Schussler, *Owner*
▼ EMP: 15 EST: 1982
SQ FT: 6,000
SALES (est): 1.2MM Privately Held
WEB: www.sunfrost.com
SIC: 3632 Household refrigerators & freezers

3634 Electric Household Appliances

(P-5703)
BRAVA HOME INC
312 Chestnut St, Redwood City (94063-2222)
PHONE....................408 675-2569
John Pleasants, *CEO*
Shih Yu Cheng, *COO*
Dan Yue,
Mark Janoff, *Admin Sec*
EMP: 26 EST: 2015
SALES (est): 6.8MM
SALES (corp-wide): 2.5B Publicly Held
WEB: www.middleby.com
SIC: 3634 Ovens, portable: household
PA: The Middleby Corporation
　　1400 Toastmaster Dr
　　Elgin IL 60120
　　847 741-3300

(P-5704)
KATADYN DESALINATION LLC
Also Called: Spectra Watermakers
2220 S Mcdowell Blvd Ext, Petaluma (94954-5659)
PHONE....................415 526-2780
Shawn Hostetter, *Mng Member*
Chris Voxland,
EMP: 20 EST: 2014
SQ FT: 8,400
SALES (est): 4MM Privately Held
SIC: 3634 3732 Water pulsating devices, electric; yachts, building & repairing

(P-5705)
MILA USA INC
11 Laurel Ave, Belvedere Tiburon (94920-2305)
PHONE....................415 734-8540
Grant Prigge, *CEO*
EMP: 20 EST: 2018
SALES (est): 1.2MM Privately Held
SIC: 3634 7389 Air purifiers, portable;

(P-5706)
OLISO INC
1200 Harbour Way S 215, Richmond (94804-3636)
PHONE....................415 864-7600
Ehsan Alipour, *CEO*
John Melot, *CFO*
Susan Wayland, *CFO*
Thomas J Beatty, *Administration*
Janice Wong, *Administration*
▲ EMP: 16 EST: 2004
SQ FT: 7,000
SALES (est): 2.7MM Privately Held
WEB: www.oliso.com
SIC: 3634 Personal electrical appliances

3635 Household Vacuum Cleaners

(P-5707)
BETTER CLEANING SYSTEMS INC
Also Called: Kleenrite
1122 Maple St, Madera (93637-5368)
P.O. Box 359 (93639-0359)
PHONE....................559 673-5700
William Hachtmann, *CEO*
Bill Hachtmann, *President*
Mason Wheeler, *CIO*
Pat Hibben, *Controller*
Jeremy Wheeler, *Opers Staff*
◆ EMP: 37 EST: 1975
SQ FT: 27,620
SALES (est): 6.4MM Privately Held
WEB: www.kleenritemfg.com
SIC: 3635 Carpet shampooer

3641 Electric Lamps

(P-5708)
APPLIED PHOTON TECHNOLOGY INC
3346 Arden Rd, Hayward (94545-3923)
PHONE....................510 780-9500
Leonard Goldfine, *President*
Rafael Olano, *Vice Pres*
Rodney Romero, *Vice Pres*
Tian Liu, *Director*
▲ EMP: 29 EST: 2002
SQ FT: 12,850
SALES (est): 4.2MM Privately Held
WEB: www.appliedphoton.com
SIC: 3641 Ultraviolet lamps

3643 Current-Carrying Wiring Devices

(P-5709)
AMPHENOL DC ELECTRONICS INC
1870 Little Orchard St, San Jose (95125-1041)
P.O. Box 28463 (95159-8463)
PHONE....................408 947-4500
Ruben Matias, *General Mgr*
David Cianciulli Jr, *President*
Adrienne Bugayong, *Program Mgr*
Loc Huynh, *Program Mgr*
Ruben Macias, *General Mgr*
EMP: 300 EST: 1979
SQ FT: 33,000
SALES (est): 73.9MM
SALES (corp-wide): 8.6B Publicly Held
WEB: www.dcelectronics.com
SIC: 3643 Current-carrying wiring devices
PA: Amphenol Corporation
　　358 Hall Ave
　　Wallingford CT 06492
　　203 265-8900

(P-5710)
BIZLINK TECHNOLOGY INC (HQ)
47211 Bayside Pkwy, Fremont (94538-6517)
PHONE....................510 252-0786
Annie Kuo, *President*
David McKee, *CEO*
Ted Hsiao, *Vice Pres*
Roger Liang, *Vice Pres*
Anders Peterson, *Vice Pres*
◆ EMP: 80 EST: 1996
SQ FT: 62,000
SALES (est): 68.1MM Privately Held
WEB: www.bizlinktech.com
SIC: 3643 Current-carrying wiring devices

PRODUCTS & SERVICES SECTION

3646 - Commercial, Indl & Institutional Lighting Fixtures County (P-5732)

(P-5711)
CABLE CONNECTION INC
Also Called: Lorom West
1035 Mission Ct, Fremont (94539-8203)
PHONE..................................510 249-9000
Greg Gaches, *President*
Nikki Del Campo, *Administration*
Pat Matthews, *Data Proc Exec*
Diane Sowerbrower, *Human Res Mgr*
Harry Hildebrand, *Sales Staff*
▲ **EMP:** 100 **EST:** 1992
SQ FT: 55,000
SALES (est): 27MM Privately Held
WEB: www.cable-connection.com
SIC: 3643 Current-carrying wiring devices

(P-5712)
CALPICO INC
1387 San Mateo Ave, South San Francisco (94080-6511)
PHONE..................................650 588-2241
Carey Wilson, *President*
Edna Wilson, *Treasurer*
Fran Crosby, *Sales Staff*
▲ **EMP:** 23 **EST:** 1963
SQ FT: 20,000
SALES (est): 3.5MM Privately Held
WEB: www.calpicoinc.com
SIC: 3643 3317 3089 3498 Current-carrying wiring devices; steel pipe & tubes; plastic hardware & building products; fabricated pipe & fittings; gaskets, packing & sealing devices

(P-5713)
CMOR MANUFACTURING INC
3625 Cincinnati Ave, Rocklin (95765-1234)
PHONE..................................916 626-3100
Chris L Moore, *President*
Gerald Moore, *Vice Pres*
EMP: 80
SQ FT: 62,600
SALES (est): 8.6MM Privately Held
SIC: 3643 3661 Current-carrying wiring devices; telephone & telegraph apparatus

(P-5714)
DC ELECTRONICS INC
1870 Little Orchard St, San Jose (95125-1041)
P.O. Box 67126, Scotts Valley (95067-7126)
PHONE..................................408 947-4531
Dave Cianciulli, *President*
Ruben Macias Jr, *COO*
Eric Hynes, *CFO*
Steve Gulesserian, *Vice Pres*
Alex Friedrich, *Info Tech Mgr*
EMP: 69 **EST:** 1983
SALES (est): 17.4MM Privately Held
WEB: www.dcelectronics.com
SIC: 3643 Current-carrying wiring devices

(P-5715)
G D M ELECTRONIC ASSEMBLY INC
Also Called: Gdm Electronic & Medical
2070 Ringwood Ave, San Jose (95131-1745)
PHONE..................................408 945-4100
Michael Sobolewski, *CEO*
Grant Murphy, *Partner*
Susie Perches, *Partner*
Tamee Pires, *Executive*
Diego Martinez, *Controller*
EMP: 77 **EST:** 1983
SQ FT: 24,000
SALES (est): 12.1MM Privately Held
WEB: www.gdm1.com
SIC: 3643 3565 Current-carrying wiring devices; packaging machinery

(P-5716)
GOLD TECHNOLOGIES INC
Also Called: Goldtec USA
1648 Mabury Rd Ste A, San Jose (95133-1097)
PHONE..................................408 321-9568
Patricia Tran, *President*
EMP: 25 **EST:** 1998
SQ FT: 12,000
SALES (est): 2.1MM Privately Held
WEB: www.goldtec.com
SIC: 3643 Electric connectors

(P-5717)
JOY SIGNAL TECHNOLOGY LLC
1020 Marauder St Ste A, Chico (95973-9028)
PHONE..................................530 891-3551
Steve Jones, *President*
EMP: 50 **EST:** 1987
SQ FT: 21,000
SALES (est): 10.8MM
SALES (corp-wide): 77.3MM Privately Held
WEB: www.joysignal.com
SIC: 3643 Power line cable
PA: Ohio Associated Enterprises Llc
97 Corwin Dr
Painesville OH 44077
440 354-2106

(P-5718)
SPIRE MANUFACTURING INC
49016 Milmont Dr, Fremont (94538-7301)
PHONE..................................510 226-1070
Christine Bui, *CEO*
Achilleas Vezirir, *President*
Hai Dau, *Vice Pres*
▲ **EMP:** 20 **EST:** 2008
SALES (est): 3MM Privately Held
WEB: www.spiremfg.com
SIC: 3643 3674 Power outlets & sockets; lamp sockets & receptacles (electric wiring devices); integrated circuits, semiconductor networks, etc.

(P-5719)
TOBAR INDUSTRIES INC
912 Olinder Ct, San Jose (95122-2619)
PHONE..................................408 494-3530
Elias Antoun, *CEO*
Farid Ghantous, *COO*
William Delaney, *CFO*
Jeffrey Reitman, *Office Mgr*
Ron Santos, *Manager*
EMP: 95 **EST:** 1976
SQ FT: 58,516
SALES (est): 12.8MM Privately Held
WEB: www.tobarind.com
SIC: 3643 3444 Current-carrying wiring devices; sheet metalwork

(P-5720)
WATT STOPPER INC (DH)
Also Called: Watt Stopper Le Grand
2700 Zanker Rd Ste 168, San Jose (95134-2140)
PHONE..................................408 988-5331
Tom Lowery, *CEO*
Aaron Lee, *Admin Sec*
Trudy Whong, *Planning*
Ting Chu, *Technician*
Britton Dickey, *Project Mgr*
▲ **EMP:** 30 **EST:** 1980
SQ FT: 16,000
SALES (est): 96.9MM
SALES (corp-wide): 25.9MM Privately Held
WEB: www.legrand.us
SIC: 3643 3646 3645 Current-carrying wiring devices; commercial indusl & institutional electric lighting fixtures; residential lighting fixtures
HQ: Legrand Holding, Inc.
60 Woodlawn St
West Hartford CT 06110
860 233-6251

3644 Noncurrent-Carrying Wiring Devices

(P-5721)
FRASE ENTERPRISES
Also Called: Kortick Manufacturer Co
2261 Carion Ct, Pittsburg (94565-4029)
PHONE..................................510 856-3600
Robert C Frase, *CEO*
Robert Spigel, *President*
Jim Szymanski, *Vice Pres*
George Gammell, *Engineer*
Lily Frey, *Controller*
▲ **EMP:** 26 **EST:** 1891
SQ FT: 90,000
SALES (est): 7.6MM Privately Held
WEB: www.kortick.com
SIC: 3644 3462 Insulators & insulation materials, electrical; pole line hardware forgings, ferrous

3645 Residential Lighting Fixtures

(P-5722)
AMERICAN LEISURE COMPANY (PA)
Also Called: American Leisure Patio
135 Ingalls St, Santa Cruz (95060-5813)
PHONE..................................831 427-4270
Brett Freiberg, *President*
Kathleen Freiberg, *Vice Pres*
Hugh Fike, *Project Mgr*
EMP: 18 **EST:** 2016
SALES (est): 501.9K Privately Held
WEB: www.americanleisurepatio.com
SIC: 3645 2511 5021 5712 Garden, patio, walkway & yard lighting fixtures: electric; garden furniture: wood; outdoor & lawn furniture; outdoor & garden furniture

(P-5723)
B-K LIGHTING INC
40429 Brickyard Dr, Madera (93636-9515)
PHONE..................................559 438-5800
Douglas W Hagen, *President*
Nathan Sloan, *President*
Mark Hansston, *Design Engr*
Carlos Padilla, *Engineer*
Leilani Talty, *Controller*
▲ **EMP:** 90 **EST:** 1985
SQ FT: 70,000
SALES (est): 18.6MM Privately Held
WEB: www.bklighting.com
SIC: 3645 3646 5063 Residential lighting fixtures; commercial indusl & institutional electric lighting fixtures; electrical apparatus & equipment

(P-5724)
PHOENIX DAY INC
3431 Regatta Blvd, Richmond (94804-4594)
PHONE..................................415 822-4414
Tony Brenta, *President*
▲ **EMP:** 15 **EST:** 1850
SQ FT: 8,000
SALES (est): 2.5MM Privately Held
WEB: www.phoenixday.com
SIC: 3645 3646 3446 Residential lighting fixtures; commercial indusl & institutional electric lighting fixtures; ornamental metalwork

(P-5725)
SEASCAPE LAMPS INC
125a Lee Rd, Watsonville (95076-9422)
PHONE..................................831 728-5699
Michael Shenk, *President*
◆ **EMP:** 15 **EST:** 1983
SQ FT: 16,000
SALES (est): 1.1MM Privately Held
WEB: www.seascapelamps.com
SIC: 3645 Boudoir lamps; lamp & light shades

(P-5726)
SPECTRUM SYSTEMS SF
1585 Folsom St, San Francisco (94103-3728)
PHONE..................................415 361-2429
Timothy Brian Smith, *Principal*
John Dannenberg, *Vice Pres*
Louise Galindo, *Office Mgr*
EMP: 15 **EST:** 2016
SALES (est): 2.5MM Privately Held
WEB: www.spectrumsystemssf.net
SIC: 3645 Residential lighting fixtures

(P-5727)
TECHTRON PRODUCTS INC
2694 W Winton Ave, Hayward (94545-1108)
PHONE..................................510 293-3500
William Swen, *President*
Shiow Shya Swen, *Vice Pres*
EMP: 43 **EST:** 1977
SQ FT: 50,500
SALES (est): 8.3MM Privately Held
WEB: www.techtronproducts.com
SIC: 3645 5063 Residential lighting fixtures; lighting fixtures, residential

(P-5728)
VODE LIGHTING LLC
21684 8th St E Ste 700, Sonoma (95476-2818)
PHONE..................................707 996-9898
Thomas Warton, *President*
Tom Warton, *President*
Scott Yu, *Officer*
George Santan, *Managing Dir*
Devon Bacon, *Web Dvlpr*
▲ **EMP:** 19 **EST:** 2005
SALES (est): 10.9MM Privately Held
WEB: www.vode.com
SIC: 3645 3646 Residential lighting fixtures; commercial indusl & institutional electric lighting fixtures

(P-5729)
WASHOE EQUIPMENT INC
Also Called: Sunoptics Prismatic Skylights
6201 27th St, Sacramento (95822-3712)
PHONE..................................916 395-4700
Jim Blomberg, *President*
Jerry Blomberg, *Treasurer*
Thomas Blomberg, *Vice Pres*
Grant Grabble, *VP Sales*
▼ **EMP:** 97 **EST:** 1978
SQ FT: 16,000
SALES (est): 11.9MM
SALES (corp-wide): 3.4B Publicly Held
WEB: www.sunoptics.acuitybrands.com
SIC: 3645 5031 Residential lighting fixtures; commercial indusl & institutional electric lighting fixtures; skylights, all materials
PA: Acuity Brands, Inc.
1170 Peachtree St Ne # 23
Atlanta GA 30309
404 853-1400

(P-5730)
XICATO INC (PA)
102 Cooper Ct, Los Gatos (95032-7604)
PHONE..................................866 223-8395
Menko Deroos, *CEO*
Mark Pugh, *President*
John Yriberri, *President*
Steve Workman, *CFO*
Joanna Brace, *Exec VP*
▲ **EMP:** 36 **EST:** 2007
SALES (est): 10.1MM Privately Held
WEB: www.xicato.com
SIC: 3645 Garden, patio, walkway & yard lighting fixtures: electric

(P-5731)
ZUO MODERN CONTEMPORARY INC (PA)
80 Swan Way Ste 150, Oakland (94621-1451)
PHONE..................................510 877-4087
Luis Ruesga, *CEO*
Steven Poon, *COO*
Terrence Tam, *CFO*
Roberto Chavez, *Branch Mgr*
Cristy Maxwell, *Sales Staff*
◆ **EMP:** 26 **EST:** 2004
SQ FT: 64,000
SALES (est): 22.9MM Privately Held
WEB: www.zuomod.com
SIC: 3645 5021 Residential lighting fixtures; office furniture

3646 Commercial, Indl & Institutional Lighting Fixtures

(P-5732)
BORDEN LIGHTING
2355 Verna Ct, San Leandro (94577-4205)
P.O. Box 2817, Alameda (94501-0817)
PHONE..................................510 357-0171
Randy Borden, *Principal*
James Borden, *Principal*
Barry Gould, *Site Mgr*
EMP: 24 **EST:** 1962

3646 - Commercial, Indl & Institutional Lighting Fixtures County (P-5733)

SALES (est): 5.1MM **Privately Held**
WEB: www.bordenlighting.com
SIC: **3646** 3645 Fluorescent lighting fixtures, commercial; ornamental lighting fixtures, commercial; fluorescent lighting fixtures, residential

(P-5733)
BOYD LIGHTING FIXTURE COMPANY (PA)
200a Harbor Dr, Sausalito (94965-1427)
PHONE..................................415 778-4300
John S Sweet Jr, *President*
Udell Blackham, *CFO*
Isma Khan, *Office Mgr*
Linda Kiner, *CIO*
Schuyler Sweet, *CIO*
◆ **EMP:** 20 **EST:** 1921
SQ FT: 13,000
SALES (est): 10.5MM **Privately Held**
WEB: www.boydlighting.com
SIC: **3646** 3645 Commercial indusl & institutional electric lighting fixtures; residential lighting fixtures

(P-5734)
ENLIGHTED INC
3979 Freedom Cir Ste 210, Santa Clara (95054-1248)
PHONE..................................650 964-1094
Joe Costello, *Ch of Bd*
Amy Stacy, *Partner*
Mike Martini, *CFO*
Eamonn Hughes, *Exec VP*
Colm Nee, *Senior VP*
▲ **EMP:** 91 **EST:** 2009
SALES (est): 24.9MM **Privately Held**
WEB: www.enlightedinc.com
SIC: **3646** Commercial indusl & institutional electric lighting fixtures

(P-5735)
FINELITE INC (PA)
30500 Whipple Rd, Union City (94587-1530)
PHONE..................................510 441-1100
Jerome Mix, *CEO*
Jane White, *President*
Mark Benguerel, *COO*
Margaret Fenton, *CFO*
Walter B Clark, *Chairman*
◆ **EMP:** 137 **EST:** 1991
SQ FT: 140,132
SALES (est): 133.5MM **Privately Held**
WEB: www.finelite.com
SIC: **3646** Commercial indusl & institutional electric lighting fixtures

(P-5736)
HOLOPHANE CORPORATION
2231 4th St, Berkeley (94710-2214)
PHONE..................................510 540-0156
Denise Bernard, *Principal*
Renee Sekanovich, *Sales Staff*
EMP: 239
SALES (corp-wide): 3.4B **Publicly Held**
WEB: www.holophane.acuitybrands.com
SIC: **3646** Commercial indusl & institutional electric lighting fixtures
HQ: Holophane Corporation
3825 Columbus Rd Bldg A
Granville OH 43023

(P-5737)
LUMIGROW INC
6550 Vallejo St Ste 200, Emeryville (94608-2166)
PHONE..................................800 514-0487
Jay Albere II, *CEO*
Kevin Wells, *President*
Dan Lee, *CFO*
Brandon Newkirk, *Chief Mktg Ofcr*
Jessica Vaughan, *Opers Staff*
EMP: 28 **EST:** 2008
SALES (est): 5MM **Privately Held**
WEB: www.lumigrow.com
SIC: **3646** Ornamental lighting fixtures, commercial

(P-5738)
SCOTT LAMP COMPANY INC
Also Called: Scott Architectural
355 Watt Dr, Fairfield (94534-4207)
PHONE..................................707 864-2066
Dennis J Scott, *CEO*

Dennis Scott, *CEO*
Paul R Scott, *Vice Pres*
Eileen K Scott-Emerson, *Admin Sec*
Ann Seffens, *Controller*
▲ **EMP:** 90 **EST:** 1957
SQ FT: 71,000
SALES (est): 19.8MM **Privately Held**
WEB: www.scottlamp.com
SIC: **3646** 3645 Ceiling systems, luminous; chandeliers, commercial; desk lamps, commercial; ornamental lighting fixtures, commercial; residential lighting fixtures

(P-5739)
TANKO STREETLIGHTING INC
Also Called: Tanko Streetlighting Services
220 Bay Shore Blvd, San Francisco (94124-1323)
PHONE..................................415 254-7579
Jason Tanko, *President*
Clare Bressani, *Vice Pres*
Julie Juarez, *CIO*
Joe Bollinger, *Engineer*
Chris Pettengill, *Opers Mgr*
▲ **EMP:** 31 **EST:** 2004
SQ FT: 5,000
SALES (est): 4.4MM **Privately Held**
WEB: www.tankolighting.com
SIC: **3646** Commercial indusl & institutional electric lighting fixtures

3647 Vehicular Lighting Eqpt

(P-5740)
SIERRA DESIGN MFG INC (PA)
Also Called: Dry Launch Light Co
2602 Superior Dr, Livermore (94550-6614)
PHONE..................................925 443-3140
Dennis Moore, *President*
Cindy Moore, *Vice Pres*
◆ **EMP:** 20 **EST:** 1969
SALES (est): 3.4MM **Privately Held**
SIC: **3647** Taillights, motor vehicle

3648 Lighting Eqpt, NEC

(P-5741)
AL KRAMP SPECIALTIES
Also Called: J K Lighting Systems
1707 El Pinal Dr, Stockton (95205-2553)
P.O. Box 8867 (95208-0867)
PHONE..................................209 464-7539
Al Kramp, *Owner*
Sharon Lundquist, *Controller*
EMP: 18 **EST:** 1977
SQ FT: 67,000
SALES (est): 1.9MM **Privately Held**
SIC: **3648** 5063 3699 Lighting equipment; lighting fixtures; electrical equipment & supplies

(P-5742)
COMCAST SPOTLIGHT
4733 Chabot Dr Ste 101, Pleasanton (94588-3970)
PHONE..................................415 264-6267
EMP: 25
SALES (corp-wide): 103.5B **Publicly Held**
WEB: www.effectv.com
SIC: **3648** Spotlights
HQ: Comcast Spotlight, Lp
55 W 46th St Fl 33
New York NY 10036
212 907-8641

(P-5743)
HYDROFARM LLC (HQ)
2249 S Mcdowell Blvd Ext, Petaluma (94954-5661)
PHONE..................................707 765-9990
Peter Wardenburg, *Mng Member*
Gerard Cantwell, *Senior VP*
Derrick Hughes, *IT/INT Sup*
Ole Kern, *Analyst*
Greg Thiel, *Natl Sales Mgr*
◆ **EMP:** 29 **EST:** 1977

SALES (est): 32.9MM
SALES (corp-wide): 342.2MM **Publicly Held**
WEB: www.hydrofarm.com
SIC: **3648** 3999 Lighting equipment; hydroponic equipment
PA: Hydrofarm Holdings Group, Inc.
290 Canal Rd
Fairless Hills PA 19030
707 765-9990

(P-5744)
INNOVALIGHT INC
965 W Maude Ave, Sunnyvale (94085-2802)
PHONE..................................408 419-4400
Thomas Linn, *CEO*
Michael Johnson, *CFO*
Conrad Burke, *Principal*
▲ **EMP:** 40 **EST:** 2001
SALES (est): 5.9MM
SALES (corp-wide): 14.2B **Publicly Held**
WEB: www.dupont.com
SIC: **3648** Lighting equipment
HQ: E. I. Du Pont De Nemours And Company
974 Centre Rd Bldg 735
Wilmington DE 19805
302 485-3000

(P-5745)
LUMINUS INC (HQ)
Also Called: Lightera
1145 Sonora Ct, Sunnyvale (94086-5384)
PHONE..................................408 708-7000
Decai Sun, *CEO*
Mark Pugh, *Exec VP*
Mike Kennedy, *Vice Pres*
Ting LI, *Vice Pres*
Tao T Tong, *Vice Pres*
EMP: 120 **EST:** 2012
SALES (est): 50.7MM **Privately Held**
WEB: www.luminus.com
SIC: **3648** Lighting equipment

(P-5746)
LUMINUS DEVICES INC
1145 Sonora Ct, Sunnyvale (94086-5384)
PHONE..................................978 528-8000
Decai Sun, *CEO*
Kevin Shih, *CFO*
Mark Pugh, *Exec VP*
Ting LI, *Vice Pres*
Shaohua Huang, *CTO*
▲ **EMP:** 156 **EST:** 2002
SALES (est): 37.8MM **Privately Held**
WEB: www.luminus.com
SIC: **3648** Lighting equipment
HQ: Luminus, Inc.
1145 Sonora Ct
Sunnyvale CA 94086
408 708-7000

(P-5747)
MW MCWONG INTERNATIONAL INC (PA)
Also Called: Pacific Lighting & Electrical
1921 Arena Blvd, Sacramento (95834-3770)
PHONE..................................916 371-8080
Margaret Y Wong, *CEO*
Emily MEI, *CFO*
Blane Goettle, *Vice Pres*
Stephen Zhou, *Vice Pres*
Christina Dyson, *Administration*
▲ **EMP:** 31 **EST:** 1984
SQ FT: 47,430
SALES (est): 8.5MM **Privately Held**
WEB: www.mcwonginc.com
SIC: **3648** Lighting fixtures, except electric; residential

(P-5748)
PACIFIC COAST STAGE LIGHTING
10774 Melody Rd, Smartsville (95977-9538)
PHONE..................................916 765-4396
Mark Mehlman, *President*
EMP: 16
SALES (corp-wide): 613.7K **Privately Held**
WEB:
www.pacificcoastlightingandvideo.com
SIC: **3648** Arc lighting fixtures

PA: Pacific Coast Stage Lighting
23529 Connecticut St
Hayward CA 94545
530 913-7541

(P-5749)
Q TECHNOLOGY INC
336 Lindbergh Ave, Livermore (94551-9511)
PHONE..................................925 373-3456
Samuel S Lee, *President*
◆ **EMP:** 30 **EST:** 1992
SQ FT: 10,000
SALES (est): 10MM **Privately Held**
WEB: www.q-techinc.com
SIC: **3648** Lighting equipment

(P-5750)
TEKA ILLUMINATION INC
40429 Brickyard Dr, Madera (93636-9515)
PHONE..................................559 438-5800
Douglas W Hagen, *President*
EMP: 15 **EST:** 1993
SQ FT: 3,000
SALES (est): 1.1MM **Privately Held**
WEB: www.tekaillumination.com
SIC: **3648** Lighting equipment

3651 Household Audio & Video Eqpt

(P-5751)
AUDIO VISUAL MGT SOLUTIONS
3425 Solano Ave, NAPA (94558-2709)
PHONE..................................707 254-3395
Jason Woods, *Branch Mgr*
EMP: 38 **Privately Held**
WEB: www.avms.com
SIC: **3651** Electronic kits for home assembly: radio, TV, phonograph
PA: Audio Visual Management Solutions, Inc
814 6th Ave S
Seattle WA 98134

(P-5752)
AV NOW INC
225 Technology Cir, Scotts Valley (95066-3525)
PHONE..................................831 425-2500
Robert Dehart, *President*
Dulce Sixtos, *General Mgr*
Ken Lyon, *Opers Mgr*
▲ **EMP:** 20 **EST:** 1987
SQ FT: 2,000
SALES (est): 3.4MM **Privately Held**
WEB: www.avnow.com
SIC: **3651** 7929 Audio electronic systems; disc jockey service

(P-5753)
COUNTRYMAN ASSOCIATES INC
195 Constitution Dr, Menlo Park (94025-1106)
PHONE..................................650 364-9988
Carl Countryman, *President*
Carolyn Countryman, *Treasurer*
Rosa Pimentel, *General Mgr*
Andy Davies, *Engineer*
Nathan Hatch, *Engineer*
▲ **EMP:** 17 **EST:** 1967
SQ FT: 4,000
SALES (est): 3.3MM **Privately Held**
WEB: www.countryman.com
SIC: **3651** 5065 Audio electronic systems; electronic parts & equipment

(P-5754)
DOLBY LABORATORIES INC (PA)
1275 Market St Fl 15, San Francisco (94103-1426)
PHONE..................................415 558-0200
Kevin Yeaman, *President*
Peter Gotcher, *Ch of Bd*
Lewis Chew, *CFO*
Robert Park, *CFO*
Avadis Tevanian, *Bd of Directors*
▲ **EMP:** 1118 **EST:** 1965

PRODUCTS & SERVICES SECTION
3652 - Phonograph Records & Magnetic Tape County (P-5777)

SALES: 1.2B **Publicly Held**
WEB: www.dolby.com
SIC: 3651 7819 6794 Audio electronic systems; laboratory service, motion picture; music licensing & royalties; music licensing to radio stations

(P-5755)
DOLBY LABS LICENSING CORP
100 Potrero Ave, San Francisco (94103-4886)
PHONE..............................415 558-0200
Ray Dolby, *Chairman*
Aya Itokawa, *Partner*
N William Jasper Jr, *President*
Jeffrey Eid, *Vice Pres*
Brian Link, *Vice Pres*
▲ **EMP:** 125 **EST:** 1965
SQ FT: 50,000
SALES (est): 26.2MM
SALES (corp-wide): 1.2B **Publicly Held**
WEB: www.dolby.com
SIC: 3651 Audio electronic systems
PA: Dolby Laboratories, Inc.
  1275 Market St Fl 15
  San Francisco CA 94103
  415 558-0200

(P-5756)
EI CORP
13355 Grass Valley Ave A, Grass Valley (95945-9521)
PHONE..............................530 274-1240
Michael Castorino, *Principal*
Syed Zaidi, *CFO*
Michael Ahmadi, *Exec VP*
Ram Narayanan, *Vice Pres*
EMP: 26 **EST:** 1975
SQ FT: 27,000
SALES (est): 4.2MM **Privately Held**
SIC: 3651 3845 3841 Recording machines, except dictation & telephone answering; electromedical equipment; surgical & medical instruments

(P-5757)
FRESNO DISTRIBUTING CO
Also Called: Fresno D"
2055 E Mckinley Ave, Fresno (93703-2997)
P.O. Box 6078 (93703-6078)
PHONE..............................559 442-8800
Stephen Ronald Cloud, *CEO*
Mary Iness, *Corp Secy*
Ryan Cloud, *Vice Pres*
Steve Cloud Jr, *Vice Pres*
EMP: 33 **EST:** 1946
SALES (est): 8.1MM **Privately Held**
WEB: www.fresnod.com
SIC: 3651 3494 Home entertainment equipment, electronic; plumbing & heating valves

(P-5758)
GALLIEN TECHNOLOGY INC (PA)
Also Called: Galliien Krueger
2234 Industrial Dr, Stockton (95206-4937)
PHONE..............................209 234-7300
Robert Gallien, *President*
Christine Simpson, *Sales Staff*
◆ **EMP:** 59 **EST:** 1970
SQ FT: 21,000
SALES (est): 8MM **Privately Held**
WEB: www.gallien-krueger.com
SIC: 3651 Amplifiers: radio, public address or musical instrument

(P-5759)
ISOLATION NETWORK INC (PA)
Also Called: Ingrooves
55 Francisco St Ste 350, San Francisco (94133-2112)
PHONE..............................415 489-7000
Jay Boberg, *Ch of Bd*
Adam Hiles, *President*
Bob Roback, *CEO*
Vincent Freda, *COO*
Clifton Wong, *CFO*
EMP: 26 **EST:** 2003
SQ FT: 5,000
SALES (est): 6.9MM **Privately Held**
WEB: www.ingrooves.com
SIC: 3651 7829 Music distribution apparatus; musical entertainers

(P-5760)
JEFF BURGESS & ASSOCIATES INC (DH)
Also Called: JB&a Distribution
1050 Northgate Dr Ste 200, San Rafael (94903-2562)
PHONE..............................415 256-2800
Jeff Burgess, *CEO*
Gregory Burgess, *President*
Joseph Taylor, *Technical Staff*
Laura Genoway, *Marketing Mgr*
Jeff Briggs, *Regl Sales Mgr*
EMP: 37 **EST:** 1996
SQ FT: 10,000
SALES (est): 12.7MM **Privately Held**
WEB: www.jbanda.com
SIC: 3651 Household audio equipment

(P-5761)
M F A INCORPORATED (PA)
5530 Moraga Pl, Piedmont (94611-3165)
PHONE..............................510 547-8444
Peter L Evans, *President*
EMP: 53 **EST:** 1984
SALES (est): 131K **Privately Held**
SIC: 3651 Audio electronic systems

(P-5762)
MAGICO LLC
3170 Corporate Pl, Hayward (94545-3916)
PHONE..............................510 649-9700
Alon Wolf, *CEO*
Pete Maher, *CFO*
Peter Maher, *CFO*
Tuan Trinh, *CFO*
David Shackleton, *Opers Staff*
▲ **EMP:** 26 **EST:** 1996
SQ FT: 12,000
SALES (est): 6.2MM **Privately Held**
WEB: www.magicoaudio.com
SIC: 3651 Speaker systems

(P-5763)
MESA/BOOGIE LIMITED (HQ)
1317 Ross St, Petaluma (94954-1124)
PHONE..............................707 765-1805
James Curleigh, *CEO*
James Aschow, *Vice Pres*
Tom Waugh, *Engineer*
Jo Leach, *Controller*
Shawn Farbman, *Sales Mgr*
▲ **EMP:** 100 **EST:** 1975
SQ FT: 47,000
SALES (est): 12.4MM
SALES (corp-wide): 295.4MM **Privately Held**
WEB: www.mesaboogie.com
SIC: 3651 5736 Amplifiers: radio, public address or musical instrument; musical instrument stores
PA: Gibson Brands, Inc.
  209 10th Ave S Ste 460
  Nashville TN 37203
  615 871-4500

(P-5764)
MEYER SOUND LABORATORIES INC (PA)
Also Called: Meyer Sound Labs
2832 San Pablo Ave, Berkeley (94702-2258)
PHONE..............................510 486-1166
John D Meyer, *President*
Brad Friedman, *CFO*
John McMahon, *Senior VP*
Marc Chutczer, *Vice Pres*
Pablo Espinosa, *Vice Pres*
◆ **EMP:** 140 **EST:** 1979
SQ FT: 15,800
SALES (est): 28.4MM **Privately Held**
WEB: www.meyersound.com
SIC: 3651 Loudspeakers, electrodynamic or magnetic

(P-5765)
NADY SYSTEMS INC
3341 Vincent Rd, Pleasant Hill (94523-4354)
PHONE..............................510 652-2411
John Nady, *President*
Crystal Vasquez, *Executive*
Marc Schneider, *Sales Staff*
Charlie Beutter, *Manager*
Joy Ferrer, *Manager*
▲ **EMP:** 27 **EST:** 1976

SALES (est): 4.9MM **Privately Held**
WEB: www.nady.com
SIC: 3651 3669 Audio electronic systems; intercommunication systems, electric

(P-5766)
NCA LABORATORIES INC
Also Called: The Clearwater Company
11305 Sunrise Gold Cir, Rancho Cordova (95742-7213)
P.O. Box 428, Folsom (95763-0428)
PHONE..............................916 852-7029
Glenn A Stasky, *President*
◆ **EMP:** 18 **EST:** 2001
SALES (est): 1.1MM
SALES (corp-wide): 174.3MM **Privately Held**
WEB: www.clearwateraudio.com
SIC: 3651 Audio electronic systems
HQ: Simpson Performance Products, Inc.
  328 Fm 306
  New Braunfels TX 78130
  830 625-1774

(P-5767)
PASS LABORATORIES INC
13395 New Arprt Rd Ste G, Auburn (95602)
P.O. Box 219, Foresthill (95631-0219)
PHONE..............................530 878-5350
Desmond Harrinton, *President*
Desmond Harrington, *President*
▲ **EMP:** 15 **EST:** 1991
SQ FT: 4,000
SALES (est): 2.3MM **Privately Held**
WEB: www.passlabs.com
SIC: 3651 Amplifiers: radio, public address or musical instrument

(P-5768)
PETCUBE INC (PA)
555 De Haro St Ste 280a, San Francisco (94107-2363)
PHONE..............................424 302-6107
Iaroslav Azhniuk, *CEO*
Alexander Neskin, *CFO*
Alex Davidenko, *Vice Pres*
Andrii Kulbaba, *Admin Sec*
EMP: 27 **EST:** 2013
SALES (est): 8.1MM **Privately Held**
WEB: www.petcube.com
SIC: 3651 Video camera-audio recorders, household use

(P-5769)
SOUNDSTREAM TECHNOLOGIES MFG
11365 Sunrise Park Dr, Rancho Cordova (95742-6556)
PHONE..............................916 635-3011
Donna Haas, *President*
Melissa Chapman, *Administration*
EMP: 50 **EST:** 1997
SALES (est): 3.1MM **Privately Held**
SIC: 3651 Amplifiers: radio, public address or musical instrument

(P-5770)
ULTIMATUM RECORDS LLC ✪
4695 Chabot Dr Ste 200, Pleasanton (94588-2756)
PHONE..............................925 353-5202
John Perenchio,
EMP: 16 **EST:** 2021
SALES (est): 1.2MM **Privately Held**
SIC: 3651 Music distribution apparatus

(P-5771)
VELODYNE ACOUSTICS INC
850 Tanglewood Dr, Lafayette (94549-4929)
PHONE..............................408 465-2800
David Hall, *CEO*
Joseph B Culkin, *Shareholder*
Vincent C Hall, *Shareholder*
Bruce Hall, *President*
Michael Jellen, *President*
▲ **EMP:** 70 **EST:** 1983
SALES (est): 11.4MM **Privately Held**
WEB: www.velodyneacoustics.com
SIC: 3651 5731 Speaker systems; radio, television & electronic stores

(P-5772)
VUDU INC
600 W California Ave, Sunnyvale (94086-2486)
PHONE..............................408 492-1010
Neil Madden Ashe, *CEO*
Edward Lichty, *COO*
Chris Watts, *CFO*
Scott Blanksteen, *Vice Pres*
Tony Miranz, *Vice Pres*
EMP: 86 **EST:** 2005
SALES (est): 10.8MM
SALES (corp-wide): 559.1B **Publicly Held**
WEB: www.vudu.com
SIC: 5731 3651 Television sets; electronic kits for home assembly: radio, TV, phonograph
PA: Walmart Inc.
  702 Sw 8th St
  Bentonville AR 72716
  479 273-4000

(P-5773)
WINNOV INC
3945 Freedom Cir Ste 560, Santa Clara (95054-1269)
PHONE..............................888 315-9460
Olivier Garbe, *CEO*
EMP: 22 **EST:** 1992
SALES (est): 3.2MM **Privately Held**
SIC: 3651 Household audio & video equipment

(P-5774)
XIAOMI USA INC
97 E Brokaw Rd Ste 310, San Jose (95112-1031)
PHONE..............................833 942-6648
Lin Bin, *President*
Chew Shouzi, *CFO*
Lei Jun, *Chairman*
Wang Chuan, *Senior VP*
Liu De, *Senior VP*
EMP: 25 **EST:** 2017
SALES (est): 2.7MM
SALES (corp-wide): 1B **Privately Held**
WEB: www.mi.com
SIC: 5731 3651 5999 Radio, television & electronic stores; household audio & video equipment; mobile telephones & equipment
HQ: Xiaomi Corporation
  C/O: Maples Corporate Services Limited
  George Town GR CAYMAN

3652 Phonograph Records & Magnetic Tape

(P-5775)
ACCRUALIFY INC
14 N San Mateo Dr, San Mateo (94401-2824)
PHONE..............................650 437-7225
Brent Jackson, *Executive*
EMP: 16 **EST:** 2016
SALES (est): 455.4K **Privately Held**
WEB: www.accrualify.com
SIC: 3652 Pre-recorded records & tapes

(P-5776)
DEMAND KNOWN INC
943 Addison Ave, Palo Alto (94301-3002)
PHONE..............................310 929-5930
Eric A Fong, *Principal*
EMP: 18 **EST:** 2015
SALES (est): 82.8K **Privately Held**
WEB: www.demandknown.com
SIC: 3652 Pre-recorded records & tapes

(P-5777)
FANTASY INC
Also Called: Contemporary Records
2600 10th St Ste 100, Berkeley (94710-2512)
PHONE..............................510 486-2038
EMP: 100
SQ FT: 40,000
SALES (est): 10.7MM **Privately Held**
WEB: www.berkeleyfilmscreening.com
SIC: 3652 2741 7389 Prerecorded Records And Tapes, Nsk

3652 - Phonograph Records & Magnetic Tape County (P-5778)

PRODUCTS & SERVICES SECTION

(P-5778)
ISOMEDIA LLC
43297 Osgood Rd, Fremont (94539-5657)
PHONE..................510 668-1656
Howard Xu,
Greg Evans, *Accounts Exec*
▲ EMP: 25 EST: 2004
SALES (est): 3.5MM **Privately Held**
WEB: www.isomediainc.com
SIC: 3652 Compact laser discs, prerecorded

(P-5779)
MOTIVEMETRICS
425 Sherman Ave Ste 300, Palo Alto (94306-1851)
PHONE..................800 216-5207
Frank Slaughter, *CTO*
Kyle Thomas, *Research*
EMP: 19 EST: 2019
SALES (est): 656.9K **Privately Held**
WEB: www.motivemetrics.com
SIC: 3652 Pre-recorded records & tapes

(P-5780)
OPSWARE INC
599 N Mathilda Ave, Sunnyvale (94085-3505)
PHONE..................408 744-7517
EMP: 22 EST: 2016
SALES (est): 423.3K **Privately Held**
SIC: 3652 Pre-recorded records & tapes

(P-5781)
STREAMLIO INC
801 Middlefield Rd Apt 9, Palo Alto (94301-2924)
PHONE..................949 701-9729
Lewis Kaneshiro, *Principal*
EMP: 17 EST: 2016
SALES (est): 501.3K
SALES (corp-wide): 2.2B **Publicly Held**
WEB: www.splunk.com
SIC: 3652 Pre-recorded records & tapes
PA: Splunk Inc.
    270 Brannan St
    San Francisco CA 94107
    415 848-8400

(P-5782)
THROUGHPUT INC
2100 Geng Rd, Palo Alto (94303-3343)
PHONE..................215 606-8552
Ali Raza, *CEO*
Seth Page, *COO*
Khizer Hayat, *Principal*
Cameronna Nazeri, *Opers Staff*
EMP: 15 EST: 2016
SALES (est): 1.3MM **Privately Held**
WEB: www.throughput.world
SIC: 3652 Pre-recorded records & tapes

3661 Telephone & Telegraph Apparatus

(P-5783)
3JAM INC
2108 Sand Hill Rd, Menlo Park (94025-6903)
PHONE..................415 867-1339
Marc Lefkowitz, *Principal*
Brad Kellett, *Engineer*
EMP: 16 EST: 2006
SALES (est): 270.2K **Privately Held**
WEB: www.3jam.com
SIC: 3661 Message concentrators

(P-5784)
ADAPS PHOTONICS INC (PA)
252 Corral Ave, Sunnyvale (94086-7007)
PHONE..................650 521-3925
Jieyang Jia, *CEO*
EMP: 55 EST: 2018
SALES (est): 1.1MM **Privately Held**
SIC: 3661 Fiber optics communications equipment

(P-5785)
ALCATEL-LUCENT USA INC
777 E Middlefield Rd, Mountain View (94043-4023)
PHONE..................650 623-3300
Sudhanshu Jain, *Principal*
EMP: 58
SALES (corp-wide): 25.8B **Privately Held**
WEB: www.alcatel-lucent.com
SIC: 3661 Telephone & telegraph apparatus
HQ: Nokia Of America Corporation
    600 Mountain Ave Ste 700
    New Providence NJ 07974

(P-5786)
ALCATEL-LUCENT USA INC
30971a San Benito St, Hayward (94544-7936)
PHONE..................510 475-5000
EMP: 25
SALES (corp-wide): 27.3B **Privately Held**
SIC: 3661 Mfg Telephone/Telegraph Apparatus
HQ: Nokia Of America Corporation
    600 Mountain Ave Ste 700
    New Providence NJ 07974

(P-5787)
ALTIGEN COMMUNICATIONS INC
670 N Mccarthy Blvd # 20, Milpitas (95035-5119)
PHONE..................408 597-9000
Jeremiah J Fleming, *President*
Philip M McDermott, *CFO*
David Tang, *Officer*
Simon Chouldjian, *Vice Pres*
Joe Hamblin, *Vice Pres*
▲ EMP: 115
SQ FT: 27,576
SALES (est): 16.9MM **Privately Held**
WEB: www.altigen.com
SIC: 3661 1731 Telephone & telegraph apparatus; communications specialization

(P-5788)
AYANTRA INC
47873 Fremont Blvd, Fremont (94538-6506)
PHONE..................510 623-7526
Ashok Teckchandani, *President*
Harbans Rattia, *Vice Pres*
Albert Calpito, *Project Engr*
Mauro Ortega, *Engineer*
Ravi Koppula,
▲ EMP: 15 EST: 1995
SQ FT: 2,300
SALES (est): 2.6MM **Privately Held**
WEB: www.ayantra.com
SIC: 3661 Telephone & telegraph apparatus

(P-5789)
BLACK POINT PRODUCTS INC
2700 Rydin Rd Ste G, Richmond (94804-5800)
P.O. Box 70074 (94807-0074)
PHONE..................510 232-7723
Thomas Tognetti, *President*
Karin M Ashford, *Vice Pres*
▲ EMP: 30 EST: 1985
SALES (est): 3.2MM **Privately Held**
WEB: www.blkpoint.com
SIC: 3661 3651 Telephones & telephone apparatus; video cassette recorders/players & accessories

(P-5790)
CALMAR OPTCOM INC
Also Called: Calmar Laser
951 Commercial St, Palo Alto (94303-4908)
PHONE..................408 733-7800
Anthony Lin, *President*
Sha Tong, *Director*
EMP: 20 EST: 1996
SQ FT: 7,000
SALES (est): 4MM **Privately Held**
WEB: www.calmarlaser.com
SIC: 3661 3699 Fiber optics communications equipment; pulse amplifiers; laser systems & equipment

(P-5791)
COADNA PHOTONICS INC (HQ)
1012 Stewart Dr, Sunnyvale (94085-3914)
PHONE..................408 736-1100
Jim Yuan, *CEO*
Fang Wang, *COO*
Irene Yum, *CFO*
Jack Kelly, *Vice Pres*
▲ EMP: 60 EST: 2000
SQ FT: 12,000
SALES (est): 18.9MM
SALES (corp-wide): 3.1B **Publicly Held**
WEB: www.ii-vi.com
SIC: 3661 Fiber optics communications equipment
PA: Ii-Vi Incorporated
    375 Saxonburg Blvd
    Saxonburg PA 16056
    724 352-4455

(P-5792)
DANTEL INC
4210 N Brawley Ave 108, Fresno (93722-3979)
PHONE..................559 292-1111
Alan J Brown, *Chairman*
Alan G Hutcheson, *CEO*
Robin Weir, *COO*
Joel Siering, *CFO*
Frank Martinez, *Vice Pres*
EMP: 23 EST: 1971
SALES (est): 5.2MM **Privately Held**
WEB: www.dantel.com
SIC: 3661 Telephones & telephone apparatus

(P-5793)
DITECH NETWORKS INC (HQ)
3099 N 1st St, San Jose (95134-2006)
PHONE..................408 883-3636
Thomas L Beaudoin, *President*
Paul A Ricci, *CEO*
William Tamblyn, *Vice Pres*
EMP: 54 EST: 1983
SQ FT: 20,100
SALES (est): 11MM **Publicly Held**
WEB: www.nuance.com
SIC: 3661 Telephones & telephone apparatus

(P-5794)
ENABLENCE USA COMPONENTS INC
2933 Bayview Dr, Fremont (94538-6520)
PHONE..................510 226-8900
Evan Chen, *CEO*
Andy Spector, *Surgery Dir*
Jacob Sun, *Principal*
Peter Sung, *Finance Dir*
Fang Wang, *Sales Staff*
EMP: 98 EST: 2003
SQ FT: 26,000
SALES (est): 33.1MM
SALES (corp-wide): 1.4MM **Privately Held**
WEB: www.enablence.com
SIC: 3661 Fiber optics communications equipment
PA: Enablence Technologies Inc
    390 March Rd Suite 119
    Kanata ON K2K 0
    613 656-2850

(P-5795)
EXTREME NETWORKS INC (PA)
6480 Via Del Oro, San Jose (95119-1208)
PHONE..................408 579-2800
Edward B Meyercord, *President*
Sam Flansbaum, *Partner*
Christopher Walden, *Partner*
John C Shoemaker, *Ch of Bd*
Remi Thomas, *CFO*
◆ EMP: 400 EST: 1996
SQ FT: 185,000
SALES: 1B **Publicly Held**
WEB: www.extremenetworks.com
SIC: 3661 7373 7372 Telephone & telegraph apparatus; computer integrated systems design; systems integration services; prepackaged software

(P-5796)
FIBER SYSTEMS INC
101 Soquel Ave Apt 418, Santa Cruz (95060-4564)
PHONE..................831 430-0700
▲ EMP: 21
SALES (est): 3.2MM **Privately Held**
WEB: www.fibersys.com
SIC: 3661 Telephone And Telegraph Apparatus

(P-5797)
FINISAR CORPORATION (HQ)
1389 Moffett Park Dr, Sunnyvale (94089-1134)
PHONE..................408 548-1000
Mary Jane Raymond, *CFO*
Roger Ferguson, *Bd of Directors*
Helene Simonet, *Bd of Directors*
Eric Bentley, *Vice Pres*
John Wachsman, *Vice Pres*
▲ EMP: 24 EST: 1987
SQ FT: 92,000
SALES (est): 1.2B
SALES (corp-wide): 3.1B **Publicly Held**
WEB: www.ii-vi.com
SIC: 3661 3663 Fiber optics communications equipment; antennas, transmitting & communications
PA: Ii-Vi Incorporated
    375 Saxonburg Blvd
    Saxonburg PA 16056
    724 352-4455

(P-5798)
GRASS VALLEY USA LLC (PA)
125 Crown Point Ct, Grass Valley (95945-9515)
P.O. Box 599000, Nevada City (95959-7900)
PHONE..................800 547-8949
Timothy Shoulders, *President*
Christian Bernard, *Vice Pres*
Neil Maycock, *Vice Pres*
Tim Ordaz, *Vice Pres*
Jared Timmins, *Vice Pres*
▲ EMP: 300 EST: 2010
SALES (est): 163.8MM **Privately Held**
WEB: www.grassvalley.com
SIC: 3661 3999 3663 3651 Telephone sets, all types except cellular radio; ; radio & TV communications equipment; television receiving sets

(P-5799)
INFINERA CORPORATION (PA)
6373 San Ignacio Ave, San Jose (95119-1200)
PHONE..................408 572-5200
Thomas J Fallon, *CEO*
Kambiz Y Hooshmand, *Ch of Bd*
David W Heard, *COO*
Nancy Erba, *CFO*
Marcel Gani, *Bd of Directors*
▼ EMP: 450 EST: 2000
SQ FT: 321,000
SALES (est): 1.3B **Publicly Held**
WEB: www.infinera.com
SIC: 3661 7372 Fiber optics communications equipment; prepackaged software

(P-5800)
INSIEME NETWORKS LLC
210 W Tasman Dr Bldg F, San Jose (95134-1714)
PHONE..................408 424-1227
Luca Cafiero, *Principal*
EMP: 31 EST: 2012
SALES (est): 1.7MM
SALES (corp-wide): 49.8B **Publicly Held**
WEB: www.cisco.com
SIC: 3661 Telephone & telegraph apparatus
PA: Cisco Systems, Inc.
    170 W Tasman Dr
    San Jose CA 95134
    408 526-4000

(P-5801)
NETGEAR INC (PA)
350 E Plumeria Dr, San Jose (95134-1911)
PHONE..................408 907-8000
Patrick C S Lo, *Ch of Bd*
Michael F Falcon, *COO*
Bryan D Murray, *CFO*
Heidi B Cormack, *Senior VP*
David J Henry, *Senior VP*
◆ EMP: 130 EST: 1996
SQ FT: 142,700
SALES (est): 1.2B **Publicly Held**
WEB: www.netgear.com
SIC: 3661 4813 Fiber optics communications equipment; modems; carrier equipment, telephone or telegraph; telephone communication, except radio;

▲ = Import ▼=Export
◆ =Import/Export

PRODUCTS & SERVICES SECTION
3663 - Radio & T V Communications, Systs & Eqpt, Broadcast/Studio County (P-5822)

(P-5802)
OCLARO (NORTH AMERICA) INC
252 Charcot Ave, San Jose (95131)
PHONE..................408 383-1400
Jerry Turin, *CEO*
Pete Mangan, *CEO*
Paul Jiang, *Senior VP*
Kate Rundle, *Admin Sec*
EMP: 576 **EST:** 2000
SQ FT: 54,000
SALES (est): 95.1MM
SALES (corp-wide): 1.7B **Publicly Held**
WEB: www.oclaro.com
SIC: 3661 Fiber optics communications equipment
HQ: Oclaro, Inc.
  400 N Mccarthy Blvd
  Milpitas CA 95035

(P-5803)
OCLARO SUBSYSTEMS INC
400 N Mccarthy Blvd, Milpitas (95035-9100)
PHONE..................408 383-1400
Jerry Turin, *CEO*
Bob Barron, *Partner*
Shri Dodani, *President*
Bruce D Horn, *CFO*
John Ralston, *Vice Pres*
▲ **EMP:** 200 **EST:** 2008
SALES (est): 87.9MM
SALES (corp-wide): 1.7B **Publicly Held**
SIC: 3661 Fiber optics communications equipment
HQ: Oclaro Fiber Optics, Inc.
  400 N Mccarthy Blvd
  Milpitas CA 95035
  408 383-1400

(P-5804)
OPTOPLEX CORPORATION
48500 Kato Rd, Fremont (94538-7338)
PHONE..................510 490-9930
James C Sha, *President*
Dar-Yuan Song, *Exec VP*
Emily Wang, *Office Mgr*
Yung-Chieh Hsieh, *CTO*
Yue Chen, *Electrical Engi*
EMP: 300 **EST:** 2000
SQ FT: 16,000
SALES (est): 54.9MM **Privately Held**
WEB: www.optoplex.com
SIC: 3661 7361 3827 Fiber optics communications equipment; employment agencies; optical instruments & lenses

(P-5805)
PLANTRONICS INC (PA)
345 Encinal St, Santa Cruz (95060-2146)
PHONE..................831 420-3002
David M Shull, *President*
Robert Hagerty, *Ch of Bd*
Charles D Boynton, *CFO*
Marv Tseu, *Vice Ch Bd*
Lisa Bodensteiner, *Exec VP*
▲ **EMP:** 1643 **EST:** 1961
SQ FT: 123,047
SALES: 3.7MM **Publicly Held**
WEB: www.poly.com
SIC: 3661 3679 Telephones & telephone apparatus; headsets, telephone; telephone sets, all types except cellular radio; headphones, radio

(P-5806)
POLYCOM INC (HQ)
6001 America Center Dr, San Jose (95002-2562)
PHONE..................831 426-5858
Robert C Hagerty, *CEO*
Julie Azzarello, *Partner*
Marco Landi, *President*
Jennifer Sanchez-Valenci, *President*
Dave Schull, *CEO*
▲ **EMP:** 2631 **EST:** 1990
SALES (est): 29.8MM
SALES (corp-wide): 3.7MM **Publicly Held**
WEB: www.poly.com
SIC: 3661 3679 Telephones & telephone apparatus; headphones, radio
PA: Plantronics, Inc.
  345 Encinal St
  Santa Cruz CA 95060
  831 420-3002

(P-5807)
RAYMAR INFORMATION TECH INC (PA)
Also Called: Computer Exchange, The
7325 Roseville Rd, Sacramento (95842-1600)
PHONE..................916 783-1951
Donald L Breidenbach, *CEO*
David Figueroa, *CFO*
Gary Portellas, *Managing Dir*
Carole Murnane, *Admin Asst*
Corinna Gross, *Technology*
EMP: 37 **EST:** 1982
SALES (est): 5.9MM **Privately Held**
WEB: www.raymarinc.com
SIC: 3661 5045 Telephone & telegraph apparatus; computers

(P-5808)
SKYLOOM GLOBAL CORP
1901 Poplar St, Oakland (94607-2310)
PHONE..................415 696-4894
Marcos Dario Franceschini, *President*
Flavio Guidotti, *Director*
Santiago Tempone, *Director*
Patricia Wexler, *Director*
EMP: 20 **EST:** 2019
SALES (est): 2.5MM **Privately Held**
WEB: www.skyloom.co
SIC: 3661 Telephone & telegraph apparatus

(P-5809)
SORRENTO NETWORKS CORPORATION (HQ)
7195 Oakport St, Oakland (94621-1947)
PHONE..................510 577-1400
Phillip W Arneson, *President*
Joe R Armstrong, *CFO*
Richard L Jacobson, *Senior VP*
EMP: 18 **EST:** 1981
SQ FT: 36,000
SALES (est): 10.2MM
SALES (corp-wide): 300.6MM **Publicly Held**
WEB: www.sorrentonet.com
SIC: 3661 Telephones & telephone apparatus; switching equipment, telephone; multiplex equipment, telephone & telegraph; fiber optics communications equipment
PA: Dzs Inc.
  5700 Tennyson Pkwy # 400
  Plano TX 75024
  469 327-1531

(P-5810)
SYSTEM STUDIES INCORPORATED (PA)
21340 E Cliff Dr, Santa Cruz (95062-4862)
PHONE..................831 475-5777
Robert A Simpkins, *President*
Diane Bordoni, *Corp Secy*
William D Simpkins, *Vice Pres*
Sheryll Hiatt, *Sales Mgr*
EMP: 42 **EST:** 1980
SQ FT: 11,000
SALES (est): 9MM **Privately Held**
WEB: www.airtalk.com
SIC: 3661 Telephone & telegraph apparatus

(P-5811)
SYSTEM STUDIES INCORPORATED
2900 Research Park Dr, Soquel (95073-2253)
PHONE..................831 475-5777
Gary Cramer, *Branch Mgr*
David Serry, *Engineer*
Tim Taylor, *Director*
EMP: 38
SALES (corp-wide): 9MM **Privately Held**
WEB: www.airtalk.com
SIC: 3661 Telephone & telegraph apparatus
PA: System Studies Incorporated
  21340 E Cliff Dr
  Santa Cruz CA 95062
  831 475-5777

(P-5812)
TATUNG TELECOM CORPORATION
2660 Marine Way, Mountain View (94043-1124)
P.O. Box 2012, Menlo Park (94026-2012)
PHONE..................650 961-2288
Douglas Lau, *President*
T S Lin, *Ch of Bd*
Grace Lau, *CFO*
Sue J Lau, *Admin Sec*
EMP: 61 **EST:** 1985
SQ FT: 10,000
SALES (est): 3.3MM **Privately Held**
WEB: www.tatung.com.tw
SIC: 3661 Telephone & telegraph apparatus
PA: Tatung Co.
  22, Zhongshan N. Rd., Sec. 3,
  Taipei City TAP 10435

(P-5813)
TITAN PHOTONICS INC
1241 Quarry Ln Ste 140, Pleasanton (94566-8462)
PHONE..................510 687-0488
Eric Liu, *President*
Charlie Chen, *Treasurer*
▲ **EMP:** 20 **EST:** 2005
SQ FT: 2,000
SALES (est): 2.5MM **Privately Held**
WEB: www.titanphotonics.com
SIC: 3661 Telephone & telegraph apparatus

(P-5814)
UTSTARCOM INC (HQ)
2635 N 1st St Ste 148, San Jose (95134-2062)
PHONE..................408 791-6168
▲ **EMP:** 102
SALES (est): 86.9MM **Privately Held**
WEB: www.utstarcom.com
SIC: 3661 3663 Mfg Telephone/Telegraph Apparatus Mfg Radio/Tv Communication Equipment

(P-5815)
VOX NETWORK SOLUTIONS INC
130 Produce Ave Ste C, South San Francisco (94080-6523)
PHONE..................650 989-1000
Scott Landis, *CEO*
Chanley Geveshausen, *Vice Pres*
Aaron Wilson, *Vice Pres*
Kevin Bryant, *Executive*
Todd Harcarik, *Executive*
EMP: 150 **EST:** 2006
SALES (est): 67.4MM **Privately Held**
WEB: www.voxns.com
SIC: 3661 8748 4813 Switching equipment, telephone; telephone central office equipment, dial or manual; telephone sets, all types except cellular radio; telecommunications consultant;

(P-5816)
WEST COAST VENTURE CAPITAL LLC (PA)
10050 Bandley Dr, Cupertino (95014-2102)
PHONE..................408 725-0700
Carl Berg, *President*
EMP: 478 **EST:** 1981
SALES (est): 46.4MM **Privately Held**
SIC: 3661 Telephone & telegraph apparatus

3663 Radio & T V Communications, Systs & Eqpt, Broadcast/Studio

(P-5817)
AJA VIDEO SYSTEMS INC (PA)
180 Litton Dr, Grass Valley (95945-5076)
P.O. Box 1033 (95945-1033)
PHONE..................530 274-2048
John O ABT, *Principal*
Darlene ABT, *CFO*
Eric Gysen, *Vice Pres*
Beryl Beckwith, *Administration*
Sean Long, *Software Engr*
▲ **EMP:** 29 **EST:** 1993
SQ FT: 9,800
SALES (est): 11MM **Privately Held**
WEB: www.aja.com
SIC: 3663 Television broadcasting & communications equipment

(P-5818)
ALDETEC INC
3560 Business Dr Ste 100, Sacramento (95820-2161)
PHONE..................916 453-3382
Jeff Russ, *Exec VP*
Jenny Tham, *General Mgr*
Richard Silvers, *Engineer*
John McCarthy, *Director*
EMP: 46 **EST:** 1999
SQ FT: 16,038
SALES (est): 7.1MM **Privately Held**
WEB: www.aldetec.com
SIC: 3663 Amplifiers, RF power & IF

(P-5819)
ALIEN TECHNOLOGY LLC (PA)
845 Embedded Way Ste 100, San Jose (95138-1091)
PHONE..................408 782-3900
Weijie Yun, *CEO*
Duane E Zitzner, *Ch of Bd*
Patrick Ervin, *President*
Glenn Gengel, *President*
John Payne, *COO*
▲ **EMP:** 50 **EST:** 1994
SQ FT: 81,000
SALES (est): 40MM **Privately Held**
WEB: www.alientechnology.com
SIC: 3663 Radio broadcasting & communications equipment; transmitting apparatus, radio or television

(P-5820)
AMINO TECHNOLOGIES (US) LLC (HQ)
20823 Stevens Creek Blvd, Cupertino (95014-2108)
PHONE..................408 861-1400
Steve D McKay, *Bd of Directors*
Brian Garrett, *Partner*
Dennis Chong, *Manager*
◆ **EMP:** 30 **EST:** 2006
SALES (est): 22MM **Privately Held**
WEB: www.amino.tv
SIC: 3663 5064 Television broadcasting & communications equipment; electrical appliances, television & radio; television sets

(P-5821)
ANACOM INC
11682 Vineyard Spring Ct, Cupertino (95014-5135)
PHONE..................408 519-2062
James Tom, *CEO*
May Tom, *President*
Ram Chandran, *Vice Pres*
Adam Weinstein, *Executive*
Long Tran, *Engineer*
▲ **EMP:** 40 **EST:** 1991
SALES (est): 6.5MM **Privately Held**
WEB: www.anacominc.com
SIC: 3663 Receiver-transmitter units (transceiver)

(P-5822)
ANRITSU COMPANY (DH)
490 Jarvis Dr, Morgan Hill (95037-2834)
P.O. Box 39000, San Francisco (94139-0001)
PHONE..................800 267-4878
Hirokazu Hashimoto, *CEO*
Lisa Aragon, *President*
Donn Mulder, *President*
Andrea Culler, *Sr Corp Ofcr*
Toshihiko Takahashi, *Senior VP*
▲ **EMP:** 485 **EST:** 1960
SQ FT: 242,000
SALES: 96.5MM **Privately Held**
WEB: www.anritsu.com
SIC: 3663 3825 Radio & TV communications equipment; instruments to measure electricity; test equipment for electronic & electric measurement

3663 - Radio & TV Communications, Systs & Eqpt, Broadcast/Studio County (P-5823)

PRODUCTS & SERVICES SECTION

HQ: Anritsu U.S. Holding, Inc.
490 Jarvis Dr
Morgan Hill CA 95037
408 778-2000

(P-5823)
APPLE INC (PA)
1 Apple Park Way, Cupertino (95014-0642)
PHONE.....................408 996-1010
Timothy D Cook, *CEO*
Maggie Berkhouse, *Partner*
Ethan Brauel, *Partner*
Arthur D Levinson, *Ch of Bd*
Jeff Williams, *COO*
◆ EMP: 2000 EST: 1977
SALES: 365.8B **Publicly Held**
WEB: www.apple.com
SIC: 3663 3571 3575 3577 Mobile communication equipment; personal computers (microcomputers); computer terminals, monitors & components; printers, computer; sound reproducing equipment; operating systems computer software; application computer software

(P-5824)
ARUBA NETWORKS INC
392 Acoma Way, Fremont (94539-7508)
PHONE.....................408 227-4500
EMP: 29
SALES (corp-wide): 50.1B **Publicly Held**
SIC: 3663 Mfg Radio/Tv Communication Equipment
HQ: Aruba Networks, Inc.
3333 Scott Blvd
Santa Clara CA 95054
408 227-4500

(P-5825)
ARUBA NETWORKS INC
390 W Caribbean Dr, Sunnyvale (94089-1010)
PHONE.....................408 227-4500
Alain Carpentier, *Vice Pres*
Partha Narasimhan, *CTO*
Kathy Winters, *Human Resources*
Pradeep Iyer, *Chief*
EMP: 722
SALES (corp-wide): 26.9B **Publicly Held**
WEB: www.arubanetworks.com
SIC: 3663 3577 7371 Mobile communication equipment; data conversion equipment, media-to-media: computer; computer software development
HQ: Aruba Networks, Inc.
3333 Scott Blvd
Santa Clara CA 95054
408 227-4500

(P-5826)
ASTRANIS SPACE TECH CORP
420 Bryant St, San Francisco (94107-1303)
PHONE.....................415 854-0586
John Gedmark, *CEO*
Ryan McLinko, *Founder*
Miki Heller, *Vice Pres*
Kevin Dluzen, *Electrical Engi*
Anjali Majumdar, *Electrical Engi*
EMP: 105 EST: 2015
SQ FT: 13,000
SALES (est): 21MM **Privately Held**
WEB: www.astranis.com
SIC: 3663 Satellites, communications

(P-5827)
AVID SYSTEMS INC (HQ)
280 Bernardo Ave, Mountain View (94043-5238)
PHONE.....................650 526-1600
Ken A Sexton, *CEO*
Patti S Hart, *Ch of Bd*
Georg Blinn, *President*
Ajay Chopra, *President*
Arthur D Chadwick, *CFO*
▲ EMP: 225 EST: 1986
SQ FT: 106,000
SALES (est): 195.8MM
SALES (corp-wide): 360.4MM **Publicly Held**
WEB: www.avid.com
SIC: 3663 3577 Radio & TV communications equipment; computer peripheral equipment

PA: Avid Technology, Inc.
75 Network Dr
Burlington MA 01803
978 640-6789

(P-5828)
CANARY COMMUNICATIONS INC
6040 Hellyer Ave Ste 150, San Jose (95138-1041)
PHONE.....................408 365-0609
Vinh Tran, *President*
Roland Yamaguchi, *Vice Pres*
Charles McKee, *Executive*
▲ EMP: 15 EST: 1987
SALES (est): 1.3MM **Privately Held**
WEB: www.canarycom.com
SIC: 3663 Receiver-transmitter units (transceiver)

(P-5829)
CARLSON WIRELESS TECH INC
3134 Jacobs Ave Ste C, Eureka (95501-0960)
PHONE.....................707 443-0100
James R Carlson, *CEO*
Shamus Jennings, *Technical Staff*
Mindy Hiley, *Opers Staff*
EMP: 15 EST: 1998
SQ FT: 6,000
SALES (est): 2.8MM **Privately Held**
WEB: www.carlsonwireless.com
SIC: 3663 Airborne radio communications equipment; receivers, radio communications; transmitter-receivers, radio

(P-5830)
CELLPHONE-MATE INC
Also Called: Surecall
48346 Milmont Dr, Fremont (94538-7324)
PHONE.....................510 770-0469
Hongtao Zhan, *President*
Laine Matthews, *Vice Pres*
Frankie Smith, *Vice Pres*
Scott Terry, *Vice Pres*
Beverley Tate, *Office Mgr*
▲ EMP: 52 EST: 2001
SQ FT: 22,800
SALES (est): 13.7MM **Privately Held**
WEB: www.surecall.com
SIC: 3663 Amplifiers, RF power & IF; antennas, transmitting & communications; cable television equipment

(P-5831)
CLEAR-COM LLC (HQ)
Also Called: Clear-Com Communications
1301 Marina Village Pkwy # 105, Alameda (94501-1058)
PHONE.....................510 337-6600
Mitzi Dominguez, *CEO*
Bob Boster, *President*
Harry Miyahira, *Chairman*
Helen Miyahira, *Admin Sec*
Yves PSM, *Sr Software Eng*
▲ EMP: 792 EST: 1968
SQ FT: 23,700
SALES (est): 176.9MM
SALES (corp-wide): 495.2MM **Privately Held**
WEB: www.clearcom.com
SIC: 3663 Radio & TV communications equipment
PA: H.M. Electronics, Inc.
2848 Whiptail Loop
Carlsbad CA 92010
858 535-6000

(P-5832)
COMMUNICATIONS & PWR INDS LLC
Also Called: CPI
811 Hansen Way, Palo Alto (94304-1031)
PHONE.....................650 846-3729
Robert Sickett, *Manager*
Andy Tafler, *President*
Alan Maffei, *Vice Pres*
Carl Schoeneberger, *Vice Pres*
Jennifer Trainor, *Vice Pres*
EMP: 1500
SQ FT: 25,000 **Privately Held**
WEB: www.cpii.com
SIC: 3663 Radio & TV communications equipment

HQ: Communications & Power Industries Llc
811 Hansen Way
Palo Alto CA 94304

(P-5833)
COMTECH STLLITE NTWRK TECH INC
3550 Bassett St, Santa Clara (95054-2704)
PHONE.....................408 213-3000
Kevin Kirkpatrick, *Manager*
EMP: 160
SALES (corp-wide): 581.7MM **Publicly Held**
WEB: www.comtechefdata.com
SIC: 3663 3679 Amplifiers, RF power & IF; power supplies, all types: static
HQ: Comtech Satellite Network Technologies, Inc.
2114 W 7th St
Tempe AZ 85281

(P-5834)
CPI SATCOM & ANTENNA TECH INC
2205 Fortune Dr, San Jose (95131-1806)
PHONE.....................408 955-1900
Steve Michaud, *Branch Mgr*
Christopher Marzilli, *President*
Eric Estrada, *Program Mgr*
Michael Amireh, *Administration*
Tom Faure-Goda, *Engineer*
EMP: 70 **Privately Held**
WEB: www.cpii.com
SIC: 3663 Radio & TV communications equipment
HQ: Cpi Satcom & Antenna Technologies Inc.
1700 Cable Dr Ne
Conover NC 28613
704 462-7330

(P-5835)
CREDENCE ID LLC
2335 Broadway Ste 100, Oakland (94612-2495)
PHONE.....................888 243-5452
Bruce Hanson, *CEO*
Donald Shimer, *CFO*
Robert Garrigan, *Senior VP*
Yash Shah, *Senior VP*
Machiel Vander Harst, *VP Sales*
EMP: 32 EST: 2012
SALES (est): 2.9MM **Privately Held**
WEB: www.credenceid.com
SIC: 3663 Mobile communication equipment

(P-5836)
CRL SYSTEMS INC
Also Called: Orban
14798 Wicks Blvd, San Leandro (94577-6718)
PHONE.....................510 351-3500
Derek Pilkington, *President*
C J Brentlinger, *President*
Robert McMartin, *CFO*
EMP: 123 EST: 1969
SQ FT: 75,000
SALES (est): 8.6MM
SALES (corp-wide): 15.5MM **Publicly Held**
WEB: www.orban.com
SIC: 3663 Radio & TV communications equipment
PA: Circuit Research Labs, Inc.
7970 S Kyrene Rd
Tempe AZ 85284
480 403-8300

(P-5837)
CTT INC (PA)
5870 Hellyer Ave Ste 70, San Jose (95138-1004)
PHONE.....................408 541-0596
David Tai, *CEO*
Thanh Thai, *Vice Pres*
John Campbell, *Admin Sec*
Ken Pickard, *Technical Staff*
Darre Brokeshoulder, *Engineer*
▼ EMP: 80 EST: 1981
SQ FT: 45,000

SALES: 7.3MM **Privately Held**
WEB: www.cttinc.com
SIC: 3663 Microwave communication equipment; amplifiers, RF power & IF

(P-5838)
DIGITAL PROTOTYPE SYSTEMS INC
Also Called: Dps Telecom
4955 E Yale Ave, Fresno (93727-1523)
PHONE.....................559 454-1600
Robert A Berry, *CEO*
Marshall Denhartog, *President*
Ron Stover, *Vice Pres*
Samantha Johnson, *Executive Asst*
Richard Howell, *Software Engr*
EMP: 46 EST: 1986
SQ FT: 50,000
SALES (est): 10.8MM **Privately Held**
WEB: www.dpstele.com
SIC: 3663 Telemetering equipment, electronic

(P-5839)
ENDWAVE CORPORATION (DH)
6024 Silver Creek Vly Rd, San Jose (95138-1011)
PHONE.....................408 522-3100
AVI Katz PHD, *President*
James R Croen, *President*
Curt P Sacks, *CFO*
Steven F Layton, *Senior VP*
Daniel P Teuthorn, *Senior VP*
EMP: 374 EST: 1995
SQ FT: 33,000
SALES (est): 65.4MM **Privately Held**
WEB: www.idt.com
SIC: 3663 Radio broadcasting & communications equipment; radio receiver networks; receiver-transmitter units (transceiver)
HQ: Gigpeak, Inc.
6024 Silver Creek Vly Rd
San Jose CA 95138
408 546-3316

(P-5840)
ENERGOUS CORPORATION
3590 N 1st St Ste 210, San Jose (95134-1812)
PHONE.....................408 963-0200
Stephen R Rizzone, *President*
Dan Fairfax, *Ch of Bd*
Cesar Johnston, *COO*
Brian Sereda, *CFO*
Neeraj Sahejpal, *Senior VP*
EMP: 68 EST: 2012
SALES (est): 327.3K **Privately Held**
WEB: www.energous.com
SIC: 3663 3674 Radio broadcasting & communications equipment; antennas, transmitting & communications; semiconductors & related devices

(P-5841)
ERICSSON INC
250 Holger Way, San Jose (95134-1300)
PHONE.....................408 970-2000
EMP: 24
SALES (corp-wide): 30.8B **Publicly Held**
SIC: 3663 Mfg Radio/Tv Communication Equipment
HQ: Ericsson Inc.
6300 Legacy Dr
Plano TX 75024
972 583-0000

(P-5842)
ETM—ELECTROMATIC INC (PA)
35451 Dumbarton Ct, Newark (94560-1100)
PHONE.....................510 797-1100
Thomas M Hayse, *CEO*
Jesse Iverson, *Vice Pres*
Kayte Mariani, *Vice Pres*
Richard Marquez, *Vice Pres*
Bill Nighan, *Vice Pres*
◆ EMP: 97 EST: 1973
SQ FT: 56,000
SALES (est): 24.6MM **Privately Held**
WEB: www.etm-inc.com
SIC: 3663 3825 Microwave communication equipment; amplifiers, RF power & IF; test equipment for electronic & electric measurement

▲ = Import ▼=Export
◆ =Import/Export

PRODUCTS & SERVICES SECTION
3663 - Radio & T V Communications, Systs & Eqpt, Broadcast/Studio County (P-5863)

(P-5843)
EUPHONIX INC (HQ)
280 Bernardo Ave, Mountain View (94043-5238)
PHONE 650 526-1600
Jeffrey A Chew, *CEO*
Paul L Hammel, *Senior VP*
▲ **EMP:** 95 **EST:** 1988
SQ FT: 40,000
SALES (est): 36.9MM
SALES (corp-wide): 360.4MM **Publicly Held**
WEB: www.avid.com
SIC: 3663 Studio equipment, radio & television broadcasting
PA: Avid Technology, Inc.
75 Network Dr
Burlington MA 01803
978 640-6789

(P-5844)
GRASS VALLEY INC
125 Crown Point Ct, Grass Valley (95945-9515)
P.O. Box 599000, Nevada City (95959-7900)
PHONE 530 478-3000
Marc Valentine, *President*
Rick Stannard, *Administration*
Stephen Baures, *Engineer*
Donald Childers, *Engineer*
Katy Hanna, *Opers Mgr*
▲ **EMP:** 114 **EST:** 1999
SALES (est): 17.7MM
SALES (corp-wide): 3.5MM **Privately Held**
WEB: www.grassvalley.com
SIC: 3663 Radio & TV communications equipment
HQ: Grass Valley Canada
3499 Rue Douglas-B.-Floreani
Saint-Laurent QC H4S 2
514 333-1772

(P-5845)
GRASS VALLEY INC (DH)
Also Called: Miranda
125 Crown Point Ct, Grass Valley (95945-9515)
P.O. Box 1658, Nevada City (95959-1658)
PHONE 530 265-1000
Strath Goodship, *CEO*
Marco Lopez, *President*
Charles Meyer, *President*
Luc St-Georges, *COO*
Kevin Joyce, *Chief Mktg Ofcr*
EMP: 100 **EST:** 1989
SQ FT: 42,000
SALES (est): 49.4MM
SALES (corp-wide): 3.5MM **Privately Held**
WEB: www.grassvalley.com
SIC: 3663 Radio & TV communications equipment
HQ: Grass Valley Canada
3499 Rue Douglas-B.-Floreani
Saint-Laurent QC H4S 2
514 333-1772

(P-5846)
GROUND CONTROL INC
1485 Bay Shore Blvd Ste 4, San Francisco (94124-3002)
PHONE 415 508-8589
Jae Shin, *President*
EMP: 20 **EST:** 2018
SALES (est): 2.7MM **Privately Held**
WEB: www.groundci.com
SIC: 3663 Satellites, communications

(P-5847)
HARMONIC INC (PA)
2590 Orchard Pkwy, San Jose (95131-1033)
PHONE 408 542-2500
Patrick J Harshman, *President*
Patrick Gallagher, *Ch of Bd*
Sanjay Kalra, *CFO*
Nimrod Ben-Natan, *Senior VP*
Ian Graham, *Senior VP*
◆ **EMP:** 1007 **EST:** 1988
SALES (est): 378.8MM **Publicly Held**
WEB: www.harmonicinc.com
SIC: 3663 3823 Television broadcasting & communications equipment; industrial instrmnts msrmnt display/control process variable

(P-5848)
HEROTEK INC
155 Baytech Dr, San Jose (95134-2303)
PHONE 408 941-8399
Cheng W Lai, *President*
James Wong, *Design Engr*
Cheng Lai, *Finance Other*
Donna Morgan, *Human Res Dir*
Michael Lai, *Purch Mgr*
EMP: 46 **EST:** 1982
SQ FT: 9,600
SALES (est): 5.2MM **Privately Held**
WEB: www.herotek.com
SIC: 3663 3812 Microwave communication equipment; search & navigation equipment

(P-5849)
JAMPRO ANTENNAS INC
6340 Sky Creek Dr, Sacramento (95828-1025)
PHONE 916 383-1177
Alex Perchevitch, *President*
Doug McCabe, *COO*
Ken Mueller, *CFO*
Cyndi Sanderson, *Vice Pres*
Aaron Callahan, *Engineer*
◆ **EMP:** 60 **EST:** 1986
SQ FT: 12,000
SALES (est): 12.7MM **Privately Held**
WEB: www.jampro.com
SIC: 3663 Antennas, transmitting & communications; television antennas (transmitting) & ground equipment

(P-5850)
KATEEVA INC
7015 Gateway Blvd, Newark (94560-1011)
PHONE 800 385-7802
May Su, *CEO*
Conor Madigan, *President*
Eli Vronsky,
Tom Wu, *Exec VP*
Lonnie Ellingson, *Senior VP*
▲ **EMP:** 200 **EST:** 2007
SQ FT: 11,000
SALES (est): 52.4MM **Privately Held**
WEB: www.kateeva.com
SIC: 3663 Cable television equipment

(P-5851)
KMIC TECHNOLOGY INC
2095 Ringwood Ave Ste 10, San Jose (95131-1786)
PHONE 408 240-3600
David Kim, *President*
Paul Truong, *Design Engr*
Jinho Park, *Opers Mgr*
Arthur Ignacio, *Sales Mgr*
EMP: 25 **EST:** 2002
SQ FT: 15,800
SALES (est): 3.6MM **Privately Held**
WEB: www.kmictech.com
SIC: 3663 Receivers, radio communications

(P-5852)
L3 TECHNOLOGIES INC
Also Called: Randtron Antenna Systems
130 Constitution Dr, Menlo Park (94025-1141)
PHONE 650 326-9500
Robert Friedman, *Branch Mgr*
Kevin McCullough, *President*
David Butler, *Vice Pres*
Winston Tai, *Engineer*
Paul Castro, *Director*
EMP: 160
SALES (corp-wide): 18.1B **Publicly Held**
WEB: www.l3harris.com
SIC: 3663 Telemetering equipment, electronic; antennas, transmitting & communications
HQ: L3 Technologies, Inc.
600 3rd Ave Fl 34
New York NY 10016
321 727-9100

(P-5853)
LEGEND SILICON CORP
440 Mission Ct, Fremont (94539)
PHONE 510 656-9888
Zhengyu Zhang, *President*
Hong Dong, *Vice Chairman*
Lin Yang, *Chairman*
EMP: 21 **EST:** 1996
SQ FT: 8,000
SALES (est): 1.6MM **Privately Held**
WEB: www.legendsilicon.com
SIC: 3663 8733 Antennas, transmitting & communications; research institute

(P-5854)
MAXAR SPACE LLC
5130 Rbert J Mathews Pkwy, El Dorado Hills (95762-5703)
PHONE 916 605-5448
Bob White, *Plant Mgr*
Bruce Stephenson, *Senior VP*
Bryan Fitzgerald, *Vice Pres*
Joe Foust, *Vice Pres*
Joseph Foust, *Vice Pres*
EMP: 776
SALES (corp-wide): 1.7B **Publicly Held**
WEB: www.maxar.com
SIC: 3663 Space satellite communications equipment
HQ: Maxar Space Llc
3825 Fabian Way
Palo Alto CA 94303
650 852-4000

(P-5855)
MDA CMMUNICATIONS HOLDINGS LLC
3825 Fabian Way, Palo Alto (94303-4604)
PHONE 650 852-4000
Anil Wirasekara,
William McCombe,
EMP: 39 **EST:** 2014
SALES (est): 3.6MM
SALES (corp-wide): 1.7B **Publicly Held**
WEB: www.maxar.com
SIC: 3663 Satellites, communications
PA: Maxar Technologies Inc.
1300 W 120th Ave
Westminster CO 80234
303 684-2207

(P-5856)
MOTOROLA SOLUTIONS INC
1101 Marina Village Pkwy # 200, Alameda (94501-6472)
PHONE 510 217-7400
EMP: 142
SALES (corp-wide): 6.3B **Publicly Held**
SIC: 3663 5046 3674 3571 Mfg Radio/Tv Comm Equip
PA: Motorola Solutions, Inc.
500 W Monroe St Ste 4400
Chicago IL 60661
847 576-5000

(P-5857)
NORDEN MILLIMETER INC
5441 Merchant Cir Ste C, Placerville (95667-8643)
PHONE 530 642-9123
JC Rosenberg, *Chairman*
Duncan Smith, *President*
Kary Robertson, *Treasurer*
Lorrie Hartsough, *Admin Sec*
Jessica Paden, *Administration*
EMP: 22 **EST:** 2001
SQ FT: 10,000
SALES (est): 4.8MM **Privately Held**
WEB: www.nordengroup.com
SIC: 3663 Amplifiers, RF power & IF

(P-5858)
NVIDIA US INVESTMENT COMPANY
2701 San Tomas Expy, Santa Clara (95050-2519)
PHONE 408 615-2500
Jen-Hsun Huang, *President*
EMP: 73 **EST:** 2000
SALES (est): 10.3MM **Publicly Held**
WEB: www.nvidia.com
SIC: 3663 Radio & TV communications equipment
PA: Nvidia Corporation
2788 San Tomas Expy
Santa Clara CA 95051

(P-5859)
OTI ENGINEERING CONS INC
24926 State Highway 108, MI Wuk Village (95346-9714)
PHONE 209 586-1022
Thomas A Olson, *CEO*
Janice Sue Olson, *Vice Pres*
EMP: 30 **EST:** 1985
SQ FT: 2,600
SALES (est): 6.2MM
SALES (corp-wide): 61.8MM **Privately Held**
WEB: www.olsontech.com
SIC: 3663 Cable television equipment
HQ: Antronix Of California, Inc.
24926 State Highway 108
Mi Wuk Village CA 95346
800 545-1022

(P-5860)
PALM INC (HQ)
950 W Maude Ave, Sunnyvale (94085-2801)
PHONE 408 617-7000
Jonathan J Rubinstein, *President*
▲ **EMP:** 400
SQ FT: 347,144
SALES (est): 122.1MM **Privately Held**
WEB: www.palm.com
SIC: 3663 Mobile communication equipment

(P-5861)
PRECISION CONTACTS INC
990 Suncast Ln, El Dorado Hills (95762-9626)
PHONE 916 939-4147
Mat Wroblewski, *President*
Mathew Wroblewski, *President*
Nancy Wroblewski, *Corp Secy*
Dean Wroblewski, *Vice Pres*
Steven Wroblewski, *Vice Pres*
EMP: 37 **EST:** 1976
SQ FT: 24,000
SALES (est): 4.8MM **Privately Held**
WEB: www.precisioncontacts.com
SIC: 3663 3829 Radio & TV communications equipment; measuring & controlling devices

(P-5862)
RADITEK INC (PA)
1702 Meridian Ave Ste L, San Jose (95125-5586)
PHONE 408 266-7404
Malcolm R Lee, *President*
Peter Corbett, *COO*
Hima Thakkar, *Sales Staff*
▲ **EMP:** 69 **EST:** 1993
SALES (est): 5.5MM **Privately Held**
WEB: www.raditek.com
SIC: 3663 Microwave communication equipment

(P-5863)
RAYTHEON APPLIED SGNAL TECH IN (DH)
460 W California Ave, Sunnyvale (94086-5148)
PHONE 408 749-1888
John R Treichler, *CEO*
William B Van Vleet III, *CEO*
Mark M Andersson, *COO*
James E Doyle, *CFO*
R Fred Roscher, *Exec VP*
EMP: 294 **EST:** 1984
SQ FT: 266,077
SALES (est): 1.8MM
SALES (corp-wide): 56.5B **Publicly Held**
WEB: www.raytheon.com
SIC: 3663 Radio & TV communications equipment
HQ: Raytheon Company
870 Winter St
Waltham MA 02451
781 522-3000

3663 - Radio & TV Communications, Systs & Eqpt, Broadcast/Studio County (P-5864)

PRODUCTS & SERVICES SECTION

(P-5864)
REVIVERMX INC
4170 Douglas Blvd Ste 200, Granite Bay (95746-9704)
PHONE.................................916 580-3495
Robert Wood, *CEO*
Neville Boston, *Principal*
Mark Luhdorff, *Principal*
Siva Saravanan, *CIO*
EMP: 21 **EST:** 2017
SALES (est): 3.1MM **Privately Held**
WEB: www.reviver.com
SIC: 3663 3469 5531 Mobile communication equipment; automobile license tags, stamped metal; automotive parts

(P-5865)
RUCKUS WIRELESS INC (DH)
Also Called: Ruckus Networks
350 W Java Dr, Sunnyvale (94089-1026)
PHONE.................................650 265-4200
Ken Cheng, *CEO*
Andrew Barkoff, *Partner*
Jean Furter, *CFO*
Ian Whiting, *Officer*
Pramod Badjate, *Senior VP*
▲ **EMP:** 712 **EST:** 2004
SQ FT: 95,000
SALES (est): 1.4B **Publicly Held**
WEB: www.commscope.com
SIC: 3663 Radio & TV communications equipment
HQ: Arris International Limited
Salts Mill
Shipley
127 453-2000

(P-5866)
SATELLITE AV LLC
Also Called: Glorystar Satellite Systems
4021 Alvis Ct Ste 5, Rocklin (95677-4031)
PHONE.................................916 677-0720
Bred Kelly, *Mng Member*
Tony Ochoa, *Info Tech Mgr*
Donald Fenton, *Engineer*
Rocio De, *Finance*
Hope Lothrop, *Accountant*
◆ **EMP:** 20 **EST:** 2004
SQ FT: 15,000
SALES (est): 1.7MM **Privately Held**
WEB: www.satelliteav.com
SIC: 5731 3663 Antennas, satellite dish; radio & TV communications equipment

(P-5867)
SIERRA NEVADA CORPORATION
39465 Paseo Padre Pkwy # 2900, Fremont (94538-5350)
PHONE.................................510 446-8400
Fatih Ozmen, *CEO*
Eren Ozmen, *President*
Jerry Harvey, *Administration*
Jasen Murphy, *Electrical Engi*
Collin Smith, *Engineer*
EMP: 34
SALES (corp-wide): 2.3B **Privately Held**
WEB: www.sncorp.com
SIC: 3663 4812 Radio & TV communications equipment; radio telephone communication
PA: Sierra Nevada Corporation
444 Salomon Cir
Sparks NV 89434
775 331-0222

(P-5868)
SITUNE CORPORATION
2216 Ringwood Ave, San Jose (95131-1714)
PHONE.................................408 712-3350
Vahid Toosi, *CEO*
Sam Heidari, *Chairman*
Marzieh Veyseh, *CTO*
EMP: 35 **EST:** 2006
SQ FT: 3,200
SALES (est): 4.6MM **Privately Held**
WEB: www.situne-ic.com
SIC: 3663 Television closed circuit equipment

(P-5869)
SOCKET MOBILE INC
39700 Eureka Dr, Newark (94560-4808)
PHONE.................................510 933-3000
Kevin J Mills, *President*
Charlie Bass, *Ch of Bd*
Lynn Zhao, *CFO*
Leonard L Ott, *Exec VP*
▲ **EMP:** 48 **EST:** 1992
SQ FT: 37,100
SALES (est): 15.7MM **Privately Held**
WEB: www.socketmobile.com
SIC: 3663 7372 Mobile communication equipment; prepackaged software

(P-5870)
SONY MBL CMMUNICATIONS USA INC
2207 Bridgepoint Pkwy, San Mateo (94404)
PHONE.................................866 766-9374
▲ **EMP:** 170
SQ FT: 10,000
SALES (est): 87.1MM **Privately Held**
SIC: 3663 5999 Mfg Radio/Tv Communication Equipment Ret Misc Merchandise

(P-5871)
STELLANT SYSTEMS INC
Also Called: Narda Microwave West
107 Woodmere Rd, Folsom (95630-4706)
PHONE.................................916 351-4500
Michael Claggett, *Manager*
Eddie Rodgers, *Engineer*
Phyllis Townsend, *Manager*
EMP: 165 **Privately Held**
WEB: www.l3harris.com
SIC: 3663 Telemetering equipment, electronic
HQ: Stellant Systems, Inc.
3100 Lomita Blvd
Torrance CA 90505

(P-5872)
STONECROP TECHNOLOGIES LLC
103 H St Ste B, Petaluma (94952-5125)
P.O. Box 550 (94953-0550)
PHONE.................................781 659-0007
Jeff Baum, *VP Bus Dvlpt*
Page Williams, *General Mgr*
Elizabeth Prince, *Planning*
Damion Soto, *IT/INT Sup*
Phil Bailey, *Engineer*
EMP: 18 **Privately Held**
WEB: www.stonecroptech.com
SIC: 3663 Microwave communication equipment
PA: Stonecrop Technologies, Llc
80 Washington St Ste M50
Norwell MA 02061

(P-5873)
SWIFT NAVIGATION INC (PA)
201 Mission St Ste 2400, San Francisco (94105-1853)
PHONE.................................415 484-9026
Timothy Harris, *CEO*
Anthony Cole, *Exec VP*
Leith Bade, *Sr Software Eng*
Darren Luisi, *Technician*
Guillaume Decerprit, *Engineer*
EMP: 52 **EST:** 2014
SALES (est): 7.4MM **Privately Held**
WEB: www.swiftnav.com
SIC: 3663 Radio & TV communications equipment

(P-5874)
TAIWAN APPLE LLC (HQ)
1 Apple Park Way, Cupertino (95014-0642)
PHONE.................................408 996-1010
Timothy Cook, *CEO*
EMP: 47 **EST:** 2020
SALES (est): 1.4MM
SALES (corp-wide): 365.8B **Publicly Held**
WEB: www.headquartersoffice.com
SIC: 3663 Mobile communication equipment
PA: Apple Inc.
1 Apple Park Way
Cupertino CA 95014
408 996-1010

(P-5875)
TARANA WIRELESS INC (PA)
590 Alder Dr, Milpitas (95035-7443)
PHONE.................................408 365-8483
Sergiu Nedeski, *President*
Kranti Kilaru, *President*
Harry May, *Vice Pres*
Rabin K Patra, *Vice Pres*
Rj Honicky, *Sr Software Eng*
EMP: 15 **EST:** 2009
SALES (est): 2MM **Privately Held**
WEB: www.taranawireless.com
SIC: 3663 Radio & TV communications equipment

(P-5876)
TCI INTERNATIONAL INC (HQ)
3541 Gateway Blvd, Fremont (94538-6585)
PHONE.................................510 687-6100
Slobodan Tkalcevic, *Vice Pres*
Stephen Stein, *Vice Pres*
Roy Woolsey, *Vice Pres*
▲ **EMP:** 103 **EST:** 1986
SQ FT: 60,000
SALES (est): 35.7MM
SALES (corp-wide): 1.5B **Publicly Held**
WEB: www.tcibr.com
SIC: 3663 3812 3661 Radio broadcasting & communications equipment; antennas, transmitting & communications; antennas, radar or communications; modems
PA: Spx Corporation
6325 Ardrey Kell Rd # 400
Charlotte NC 28277
980 474-3700

(P-5877)
TECHNICOLOR USA INC
400 Providence Mine Rd, Nevada City (95959-2953)
PHONE.................................530 478-3000
Jeff Rosica, *Senior VP*
EMP: 628
SALES (corp-wide): 57.9MM **Privately Held**
SIC: 3663 Radio & TV communications equipment
HQ: Technicolor Usa, Inc.
6040 W Sunset Blvd
Hollywood CA 90028
317 587-4287

(P-5878)
TELECOMMUNICATIONS ENGRG ASSOC
1160 Industrial Rd Ste 15, San Carlos (94070-4128)
PHONE.................................650 590-1801
Daryl Jones, *President*
EMP: 24 **EST:** 1974
SQ FT: 5,500
SALES (est): 519.5K **Privately Held**
SIC: 3663 7622 Radio & TV communications equipment; communication equipment repair

(P-5879)
TELEWAVE INC
48421 Milmont Dr, Fremont (94538-7327)
PHONE.................................408 929-4400
Roberta Boward, *President*
Allen Collins, *COO*
Jeff Cornehl, *Engineer*
Frank Peek, *Engineer*
Caroline Tooma, *Director*
◆ **EMP:** 46 **EST:** 1972
SALES (est): 12.1MM **Privately Held**
WEB: www.telewave.com
SIC: 3663 Radio broadcasting & communications equipment

(P-5880)
TERRASAT COMMUNICATIONS INC
315 Digital Dr, Morgan Hill (95037-2878)
PHONE.................................408 782-5911
Jit Patel, *President*
Carl Hurst, *COO*
Rod Benson, *Vice Pres*
Mike Gold, *Vice Pres*
Jos Hecht, *Vice Pres*
▲ **EMP:** 47 **EST:** 1994
SALES (est): 15.2MM **Privately Held**
WEB: www.terrasatinc.com
SIC: 3663 Satellites, communications

(P-5881)
THAWTE INC
Also Called: Thawte Consulting USA
405 Clyde Ave, Mountain View (94043-2209)
PHONE.................................650 426-7400
Mark Shuttleworth, *President*
EMP: 49 **EST:** 1995
SALES (est): 21.6MM
SALES (corp-wide): 2.5B **Publicly Held**
WEB: www.thawte.com
SIC: 3663 7371 Digital encoders; custom computer programming services
PA: Nortonlifelock Inc.
60 E Rio Salado Pkwy # 1
Tempe AZ 85281
650 527-8000

(P-5882)
TRIQUINT WJ INC
3099 Orchard Dr, San Jose (95134-2005)
PHONE.................................408 577-6200
W Dexter Paine III, *Ch of Bd*
Bruce W Diamond, *President*
Ralph G Quinsey, *CEO*
R Gregory Miller, *CFO*
Haresh P Patel, *Senior VP*
EMP: 92 **EST:** 2000
SQ FT: 124,000
SALES (est): 12.3MM
SALES (corp-wide): 4B **Publicly Held**
WEB: www.qorvo.com
SIC: 3663 3674 Radio broadcasting & communications equipment; semiconductors & related devices
HQ: Qorvo Us, Inc.
2300 Ne Brookwood Pkwy
Hillsboro OR 97124
336 664-1233

(P-5883)
WEST-COM NRSE CALL SYSTEMS INC (PA)
Also Called: Wc
2200 Cordelia Rd, Fairfield (94534-1912)
PHONE.................................707 428-5900
C Larry Peters, *CEO*
Dania Atanassova-Een, *CFO*
Paul Langstroth, *Vice Pres*
Colleen Ryan, *Managing Dir*
David Daum, *Regional Mgr*
EMP: 40 **EST:** 1988
SQ FT: 15,000
SALES (est): 10.3MM **Privately Held**
WEB: www.westcomncs.com
SIC: 3663 Radio broadcasting & communications equipment

(P-5884)
WI2WI INC (PA)
1879 Lundy Ave Ste 218, San Jose (95131-1881)
PHONE.................................408 416-4200
Zachariah J Mathews, *President*
EMP: 50 **EST:** 2005
SALES (est): 8.3MM **Privately Held**
WEB: www.wi2wi.com
SIC: 3663 Radio & TV communications equipment

(P-5885)
WOHLER TECHNOLOGIES INC
1280 San Luis Obispo St, Hayward (94544-7916)
PHONE.................................510 870-0810
Michael Kelly, *President*
John Palmer, *Chairman*
Aaron Aiken, *Admin Sec*
Ian Caldwell, *Sales Mgr*
▲ **EMP:** 25 **EST:** 1991
SALES (est): 7.4MM **Privately Held**
WEB: www.wohler.com
SIC: 3663 Radio & TV communications equipment

3669 Communications Eqpt, NEC

(P-5886)
CITY OF FOLSOM
50 Natoma St, Folsom (95630-2614)
PHONE.................................916 355-7272
Fax: 916 351-0525

PRODUCTS & SERVICES SECTION

3672 - Printed Circuit Boards County (P-5907)

EMP: 100 **Privately Held**
SIC: 9511 3669 Air/Water/Waste Management Mfg Communications Equipment
PA: City Of Folsom
  50 Natoma St
  Folsom CA 95630
  916 355-7200

(P-5887)
GENERAL DYNAMICS MISSION
2688 Orchard Pkwy, San Jose (95134-2020)
PHONE.............................408 908-7300
Christopher Brady, *President*
Christopher Marzilli, *President*
Terry McLachlan, *Info Tech Dir*
Marek Kozina, *Software Engr*
Charlie Fray, *Technology*
EMP: 449
SALES (corp-wide): 37.9B **Publicly Held**
WEB: www.gdmissionsystems.com
SIC: 3669 3812 Transportation signaling devices; search & navigation equipment
HQ: General Dynamics Mission Systems, Inc.
  12450 Fair Lakes Cir
  Fairfax VA 22033
  877 449-0600

(P-5888)
LUMENTUM HOLDINGS INC (PA)
1001 Ridder Park Dr, San Jose (95131-2314)
PHONE.............................408 546-5483
Alan S Lowe, *President*
Vincent Retort, *COO*
Wajid Ali, *CFO*
Jason Reinhardt, *Exec VP*
Christopher Coldren, *Senior VP*
EMP: 1072 **EST:** 1979
SALES: 1.7B **Publicly Held**
WEB: www.lumentum.com
SIC: 3669 3674 Intercommunication systems, electric; semiconductors & related devices; optical isolators

(P-5889)
LUMENTUM INC
400 N Mccarthy Blvd, Milpitas (95035-9100)
PHONE.............................408 546-5483
Alan Lowe, *CEO*
Rama Kambhapati, *Engineer*
Yunsong Zhao, *Engineer*
Vincent Issier, *Director*
Shay O 'reilly, *Manager*
EMP: 22 **EST:** 2015
SALES (est): 1.3MM
SALES (corp-wide): 1.7B **Publicly Held**
WEB: www.lumentum.com
SIC: 3669 Emergency alarms
PA: Lumentum Holdings Inc.
  1001 Ridder Park Dr
  San Jose CA 95131
  408 546-5483

(P-5890)
MERU NETWORKS INC (HQ)
894 Ross Dr, Sunnyvale (94089-1403)
PHONE.............................408 215-5300
Ken Xie, *CEO*
Michael Xie, *President*
Andrew Del Matto, *CFO*
Kishore Reddy, *Vice Pres*
Don Trimble, *Vice Pres*
▲ **EMP:** 415 **EST:** 2002
SQ FT: 44,000
SALES (est): 70.4MM
SALES (corp-wide): 2.5B **Publicly Held**
WEB: www.meruwlantest.com
SIC: 3669 Intercommunication systems, electric
PA: Fortinet, Inc.
  899 Kifer Rd
  Sunnyvale CA 94086
  408 235-7700

(P-5891)
MYERS & SONS HI-WAY SAFETY INC
9510 Jackson Rd, Sacramento (95827-9724)
PHONE.............................909 591-1781
EMP: 15

SALES (corp-wide): 24.6MM **Privately Held**
WEB: www.hiwaysafety.com
SIC: 3669 Pedestrian traffic control equipment
PA: Myers & Son's Hi-Way Safety Inc.
  13310 5th St
  Chino CA 91710
  909 591-1781

(P-5892)
NIGHT OPTICS USA INC
605 Oro Dam Blvd E, Oroville (95965-5718)
PHONE.............................714 899-4475
Ilya Reyngold, *CEO*
Rimma Epelbaum, *CFO*
Israel Reyngold, *Vice Pres*
◆ **EMP:** 48 **EST:** 2003
SQ FT: 4,600
SALES (est): 5.8MM
SALES (corp-wide): 2.2B **Publicly Held**
WEB: www.nightoptics.com
SIC: 3669 3827 Visual communication systems; optical instruments & apparatus
PA: Vista Outdoor Inc.
  1 Vista Way
  Anoka MN 55303
  763 433-1000

(P-5893)
PRESENTERTEK INC
3710 N Lakeshore Blvd, Loomis (95650-9789)
PHONE.............................916 251-7190
Thomas J Tanner, *CEO*
Steven McNerney, *President*
Debbi Sutton, *General Mgr*
EMP: 22 **EST:** 2017
SQ FT: 2,500
SALES (est): 525K **Privately Held**
WEB: www.presentertek.com
SIC: 3669 Visual communication systems

(P-5894)
PROXIM WIRELESS CORPORATION (PA)
2114 Ringwood Ave, San Jose (95131-1715)
PHONE.............................408 383-7600
Greg Marzullo, *President*
Steve Button, *CFO*
David Porte, *Senior VP*
David L Renauld, *Vice Pres*
David Sumi, *Vice Pres*
▲ **EMP:** 55 **EST:** 2003
SQ FT: 42,500
SALES (est): 63.1MM **Publicly Held**
WEB: www.proxim.com
SIC: 3669 Signaling apparatus, electric

(P-5895)
SAFETY NTWRK TRAFFIC SIGNS INC
1345 N Rabe Ave, Fresno (93727-2249)
PHONE.............................559 291-8000
Russ Johnson, *President*
Leonard Contreras, *Manager*
Alys Day, *Manager*
EMP: 20 **EST:** 2014
SALES (est): 2.6MM **Privately Held**
WEB: www.safetynetworkinc.com
SIC: 3669 Traffic signals, electric

(P-5896)
SENSYS NETWORKS INC (HQ)
Also Called: Senetrics International
1608 4th St Ste 110, Berkeley (94710-1749)
PHONE.............................510 548-4620
Amine Haoui, *President*
Robert Kavaler, *Senior VP*
Hamed Benouar, *Vice Pres*
Brian Fuller, *Vice Pres*
Luca Fusina, *Vice Pres*
▲ **EMP:** 79 **EST:** 2003
SALES (est): 10.8MM
SALES (corp-wide): 33.1MM **Privately Held**
WEB: www.sensysnetworks.com
SIC: 3669 Transportation signaling devices
PA: Tagmaster Ab
  Kronborgsgrand 11
  Kista 164 4
  863 219-50

(P-5897)
VOCERA COMMUNICATIONS INC (PA)
525 Race St Ste 150, San Jose (95126-3497)
PHONE.............................408 882-5100
Brent D Lang, *Ch of Bd*
Justin Bezilla, *President*
Justin R Spencer, *CFO*
M Bridget Duffy, *Chief Mktg Ofcr*
Sue Dooley, *Officer*
▲ **EMP:** 644 **EST:** 2000
SQ FT: 70,000
SALES (est): 198.4MM **Publicly Held**
WEB: www.vocera.com
SIC: 3669 Intercommunication systems, electric

(P-5898)
WATT STOPPER INC
2800 De La Cruz Blvd, Santa Clara (95050-2619)
PHONE.............................408 988-5331
Joan Williams, *Vice Pres*
David Fox, *Technical Staff*
Mike Ballard, *Engineer*
Kendall Johnston, *Engineer*
Jeff Davis, *Manager*
EMP: 19 **EST:** 2020
SALES (est): 2.8MM **Privately Held**
SIC: 3669 Communications equipment

(P-5899)
WESTERN PACIFIC SIGNAL LLC
15890 Foothill Blvd, San Leandro (94578-2101)
PHONE.............................510 276-6400
Heidi Shupp, *President*
Donald R Shupp, *Vice Pres*
Pedro Lopez, *Technical Staff*
Aron McEvoy, *Manager*
EMP: 15 **EST:** 1997
SQ FT: 6,500
SALES (est): 3.3MM **Privately Held**
WEB: www.wpsignal.com
SIC: 3669 Traffic signals, electric

3671 Radio & T V Receiving Electron Tubes

(P-5900)
COMMUNICATIONS & PWR INDS LLC (HQ)
Also Called: CPI
811 Hansen Way, Palo Alto (94304-1031)
PHONE.............................650 846-2900
Robert A Fickett, *President*
Joel A Littman, *CFO*
John Beighley, *Vice Pres*
Don C Coleman, *Vice Pres*
Sean Villa-Lovoz, *Vice Pres*
◆ **EMP:** 720 **EST:** 1950
SQ FT: 429,000
SALES (est): 587.8MM **Privately Held**
WEB: www.cpii.com
SIC: 3671 3679 3699 3663 Vacuum tubes; microwave components; power supplies, all types: static; electrical equipment & supplies; radio & TV communications equipment

(P-5901)
GLOBALFOUNDRIES US INC (DH)
Also Called: Global Foundries
2600 Great America Way, Santa Clara (95054-1169)
PHONE.............................408 462-3900
Thomas Caulfield, *CEO*
Stephen Beebe, *COO*
Dr John Goldsberry, *CFO*
Louis Lupin, *Officer*
Daniel Durn, *Exec VP*
▲ **EMP:** 4859 **EST:** 2008
SALES (est): 1.5B **Publicly Held**
WEB: www.gf.com
SIC: 3671 3592 Electron tubes; valves

(P-5902)
HEATWAVE LABS INC
195 Aviation Way Ste 100, Watsonville (95076-2059)
PHONE.............................831 722-9081

Kim Gunther, *President*
David Sailer, *Manager*
EMP: 18 **EST:** 1994
SQ FT: 10,000
SALES (est): 3MM **Privately Held**
WEB: www.cathode.com
SIC: 3671 Electron tubes

(P-5903)
LEEMAH CORPORATION (PA)
155 S Hill Dr, Brisbane (94005-1203)
PHONE.............................415 394-1288
Efrem Mah, *CEO*
Bing Hong Mah, *President*
Warren Gee, *CFO*
Dick Wong, *Vice Pres*
John Sim, *Branch Mgr*
▲ **EMP:** 150 **EST:** 1971
SQ FT: 60,000
SALES (est): 63.9MM **Privately Held**
WEB: www.leemah.com
SIC: 3671 3672 3669 3663 Electron tubes; printed circuit boards; intercommunication systems, electric; radio & TV communications equipment; computer peripheral equipment

(P-5904)
THERMO KEVEX X-RAY INC
320 El Pueblo Rd, Scotts Valley (95066-4219)
PHONE.............................831 438-5940
Marijn Dekkers, *President*
Mark Chatfield, *Director*
EMP: 92 **EST:** 1996
SQ FT: 16,800
SALES (est): 8.7MM
SALES (corp-wide): 32.2B **Publicly Held**
WEB: www.thermofisher.com
SIC: 3671 3679 3844 Transmittal, industrial & special purpose electron tubes; power supplies, all types: static; X-ray apparatus & tubes
PA: Thermo Fisher Scientific Inc.
  168 3rd Ave
  Waltham MA 02451
  781 622-1000

3672 Printed Circuit Boards

(P-5905)
ABSOLUTE TURNKEY SERVICES INC
555 Aldo Ave, Santa Clara (95054-2205)
PHONE.............................408 850-7530
Jeffrey Bullis, *CEO*
Michelle Gaynor, *Vice Pres*
EMP: 40 **EST:** 1996
SQ FT: 17,000
SALES (est): 10.6MM **Privately Held**
WEB: www.absolute-ems.com
SIC: 3672 Printed circuit boards

(P-5906)
ADDISON TECHNOLOGY INC
Also Called: Addison Engineering
150 Nortech Pkwy, San Jose (95134-2305)
PHONE.............................408 749-1000
Gibson Cobb, *President*
Jim Landis, *Vice Pres*
Mark Ridgeway, *Vice Pres*
Jeff Besterman, *Accounts Mgr*
▲ **EMP:** 45 **EST:** 1983
SQ FT: 40,000
SALES (est): 5.4MM **Privately Held**
WEB: www.addisonengineering.com
SIC: 3672 5065 Printed circuit boards; semiconductor devices

(P-5907)
ADVANCED CIRCUITS INC
Also Called: Coastal Circuit
1602 Tacoma Way, Redwood City (94063-1109)
PHONE.............................415 602-6834
Ralph Richart Jr, *President*
EMP: 16 **Publicly Held**
WEB: www.4pcb.com
SIC: 3672 Circuit boards, television & radio printed
HQ: Advanced Circuits, Inc.
  21101 E 32nd Pkwy
  Aurora CO 80011

3672 - Printed Circuit Boards County (P-5908) — PRODUCTS & SERVICES SECTION

(P-5908)
ALL QUALITY & SERVICES INC
Also Called: Aqs
47817 Fremont Blvd, Fremont (94538-6506)
PHONE...................510 249-5800
So Jin Lee, *President*
Jack Walton, *COO*
John Park, *Chief Mktg Ofcr*
Paul Kang, *Officer*
Kang Samuel, *Vice Pres*
▲ **EMP:** 120 **EST:** 1991
SALES (est): 28.2MM **Privately Held**
WEB: www.aqs-inc.com
SIC: 3672 3651 Printed circuit boards; electronic kits for home assembly: radio, TV, phonograph

(P-5909)
ALPHA EMS CORPORATION
44193 S Grimmer Blvd, Fremont (94538-6350)
PHONE...................510 498-8788
Eric Chang, *CEO*
Chingping Chang, *CEO*
Jim Creel, *Vice Pres*
Dave Kichar, *Vice Pres*
Anthony Ureta, *Program Mgr*
EMP: 150
SQ FT: 50,000
SALES: 18.6MM **Privately Held**
WEB: www.alphaemscorp.com
SIC: 3672 Printed circuit boards

(P-5910)
ALTA MANUFACTURING INC
47650 Westinghouse Dr, Fremont (94539-7473)
PHONE...................510 668-1870
Anne Lee, *CEO*
EMP: 30 **EST:** 1998
SQ FT: 24,000
SALES (est): 7.9MM **Privately Held**
WEB: www.altamfg.com
SIC: 3672 Printed circuit boards

(P-5911)
ALTAFLEX
336 Martin Ave, Santa Clara (95050-3112)
PHONE...................408 727-6614
Paul Morben, *President*
Robert Jung, *General Mgr*
EMP: 70 **EST:** 2000
SQ FT: 20,200
SALES: 13MM
SALES (corp-wide): 1.1B **Publicly Held**
WEB: www.altaflex.com
SIC: 3672 Printed circuit boards
HQ: Osi Electronics, Inc.
  12533 Chadron Ave
  Hawthorne CA 90250
  310 978-0516

(P-5912)
AMPRO SYSTEMS INC
1000 Page Ave, Fremont (94538-7340)
PHONE...................510 624-9000
Elliot Wang, *President*
▲ **EMP:** 42 **EST:** 1997
SQ FT: 21,000
SALES (est): 4.8MM **Privately Held**
WEB: www.amprosystems.com
SIC: 3672 Printed circuit boards

(P-5913)
AMTECH MICROELECTRONICS INC
485 Cochrane Cir, Morgan Hill (95037-2831)
PHONE...................408 612-8888
Walter Chavez, *President*
Chris Wright, *Engineer*
Dave Bringuel, *Sales Staff*
EMP: 42 **EST:** 1993
SQ FT: 14,500
SALES (est): 7.8MM **Privately Held**
WEB: www.amtechmicro.com
SIC: 3672 Printed circuit boards

(P-5914)
APCT INC (HQ)
Also Called: (FORMER: ADVANCED PRINTED CIRCUIT TECHNOLOGY)
3495 De La Cruz Blvd, Santa Clara (95054-2110)
PHONE...................408 727-6442
Steve Robinson, *CEO*
Greg Elder, *CFO*
Joe Gisch, *CFO*
Jeff De Serrano, *Exec VP*
Kimberly Johnson, *Exec VP*
▲ **EMP:** 137 **EST:** 1977
SQ FT: 30,000
SALES (est): 12.6MM
SALES (corp-wide): 7MM **Privately Held**
WEB: www.apct.com
SIC: 3672 Circuit boards, television & radio printed
PA: Apct Holdings, Llc
  3495 De La Cruz Blvd
  Santa Clara CA 95054
  408 727-6442

(P-5915)
APCT HOLDINGS LLC (PA)
3495 De La Cruz Blvd, Santa Clara (95054-2110)
PHONE...................408 727-6442
Steve Robinson, *CEO*
Greg Elder, *CFO*
Tony Torres, *Marketing Staff*
Amy Paulino, *Sales Staff*
EMP: 26 **EST:** 2013
SQ FT: 30,000
SALES (est): 7MM **Privately Held**
WEB: www.apct.com
SIC: 3672 Printed circuit boards

(P-5916)
ARDENT SYSTEMS INC
2040 Ringwood Ave, San Jose (95131-1728)
PHONE...................408 526-0100
Thomas Han, *President*
Young C Kang, *Admin Sec*
EMP: 35 **EST:** 1989
SQ FT: 8,000
SALES (est): 3MM **Privately Held**
WEB: www.ardentsi.com
SIC: 3672 Printed circuit boards

(P-5917)
ASTEEL FLASH USA CORP (DH)
Also Called: Asteelflash
4211 Starboard Dr, Fremont (94538-6427)
PHONE...................510 440-2840
Gilles Benhamou, *President*
Craig Young, *President*
Claude Savard, *CFO*
Pierre Laboisse, *Exec VP*
Vince Pradia, *Exec VP*
▲ **EMP:** 146 **EST:** 2011
SALES (est): 95.2MM **Privately Held**
WEB: www.asteelflash.com
SIC: 3672 3679 Printed circuit boards; electronic circuits
HQ: Asteelflash Group
  6 Rue Vincent Van Gogh
  Neuilly Plaisance 93360
  149 445-300

(P-5918)
BAY AREA CIRCUITS INC
44358 Old Warm Sprng Blvd, Fremont (94538-6148)
PHONE...................510 933-9000
Barbara Nobriga, *President*
Brian Paper, *COO*
Cassandra Mubayed, *Office Mgr*
James Vansant, *Info Tech Mgr*
Wayne Dieck, *Manager*
▲ **EMP:** 48 **EST:** 1975
SQ FT: 7,500
SALES (est): 12.4MM **Privately Held**
WEB: www.bayareacircuits.com
SIC: 3672 Circuit boards, television & radio printed

(P-5919)
BAY ELCTRNIC SPPORT TRNICS INC
Also Called: Bestronics
2090 Fortune Dr, San Jose (95131-1823)
PHONE...................408 432-3222
Nat Mani, *CEO*
Ron Menigoz, *Vice Pres*
Steve Yetso, *Vice Pres*
Connie Andrade, *Program Mgr*
Sohee Jung, *Program Mgr*
▲ **EMP:** 155 **EST:** 1990
SQ FT: 150,000
SALES (est): 101.1MM **Privately Held**
SIC: 3672 Circuit boards, television & radio printed
PA: Bestronics Holdings, Inc.
  2090 Fortune Dr
  San Jose CA 95131
  408 385-7777

(P-5920)
BEMA ELECTRONIC MFG INC
4545 Cushing Pkwy, Fremont (94538-6466)
PHONE...................510 490-7770
Helen Kwong, *President*
Suju Kwong, *CFO*
Charles Evans, *Program Mgr*
Tiffany Vu, *Division Mgr*
Song Kang, *Info Tech Mgr*
▲ **EMP:** 100 **EST:** 1999
SQ FT: 26,205
SALES (est): 22.5MM **Privately Held**
WEB: www.bemaelectronics.com
SIC: 3672 Printed circuit boards

(P-5921)
BENCHMARK ELEC MFG SLTIONS INC (HQ)
5550 Hellyer Ave, San Jose (95138-1005)
PHONE...................805 222-1303
Jayne Desorcie, *Administration*
Bruce McCreary, *Bd of Directors*
Mike Buseman, *Exec VP*
Miles Sattelmeier, *Software Engr*
Bonny Barsabal, *Prgrmr*
▲ **EMP:** 100 **EST:** 1986
SQ FT: 80,000
SALES (est): 116.7MM
SALES (corp-wide): 2B **Publicly Held**
WEB: www.bench.com
SIC: 3672 Printed circuit boards
PA: Benchmark Electronics, Inc.
  56 S Rockford Dr
  Tempe AZ 85281
  623 300-7000

(P-5922)
CIREXX CORPORATION
791 Nuttman St, Santa Clara (95054-2623)
PHONE...................408 988-3980
Phillip Menges, *President*
Kurt Menges, *CFO*
Harendra Sheth, *Planning Mgr*
Tamala Steele, *Accounting Mgr*
Al Wasserzug, *Business Mgr*
▲ **EMP:** 49 **EST:** 1980
SQ FT: 22,000
SALES (est): 6.2MM **Privately Held**
WEB: www.cirexx.com
SIC: 3672 8711 Printed circuit boards; engineering services

(P-5923)
CIREXX INTERNATIONAL INC (PA)
791 Nuttman St, Santa Clara (95054-2623)
PHONE...................408 988-3980
Philip Menges, *President*
Kurt H Menges, *Vice Pres*
Ken Brown, *Executive*
Carlo Dominguez, *CTO*
Duy Le, *Software Dev*
EMP: 115 **EST:** 2005
SALES (est): 21.4MM **Privately Held**
WEB: www.cirexx.com
SIC: 3672 Circuit boards, television & radio printed

(P-5924)
CORDOVA PRINTED CIRCUITS INC
1648 Watson Ct, Milpitas (95035-6822)
PHONE...................408 942-1100
Josel Buada, *President*
EMP: 15 **EST:** 1978
SQ FT: 8,176
SALES (est): 4.8MM **Privately Held**
WEB: www.cordovaprintedcircuits.com
SIC: 3672 Printed circuit boards

(P-5925)
CREATION TECH SANTA CLARA INC
2801 Northwestern Pkwy, Santa Clara (95051-0903)
PHONE...................408 235-7500
Arthur Tymos, *CEO*
Dennis Kottke, *Ch of Bd*
Kurt Pagnini, *Vice Pres*
▲ **EMP:** 93 **EST:** 2001
SQ FT: 32,000
SALES (est): 7.3MM
SALES (corp-wide): 212.6MM **Privately Held**
WEB: www.creationtech.com
SIC: 3672 Printed circuit boards
PA: Creation Technologies Ltd.
  8999 Fraserton Crt
  Burnaby BC V5J 5

(P-5926)
DIGICOM ELECTRONICS INC
7799 Pardee Ln, Oakland (94621-1425)
PHONE...................510 639-7003
Mohammed R Ohady, *CEO*
Arthur Fung, *Technology*
Norma Criglar, *Controller*
Jonathan Chuong, *Manager*
EMP: 32
SALES (est): 6.1MM **Privately Held**
WEB: www.digicom.org
SIC: 3672 Printed circuit boards

(P-5927)
ELECTROMAX INC
1960 Concourse Dr, San Jose (95131-1719)
PHONE...................408 428-9474
Aaron Wong, *President*
Ken Wong, *Vice Pres*
Fung Leung, *Administration*
▲ **EMP:** 50 **EST:** 1991
SQ FT: 30,000
SALES (est): 9.6MM **Privately Held**
WEB: www.electromaxinc.com
SIC: 3672 Printed circuit boards

(P-5928)
EMBER INDUSTRIES
812 Barstow Ave, Clovis (93612-2274)
PHONE...................310 490-8926
Robert Vieira, *Principal*
EMP: 16 **EST:** 2018
SALES (est): 778K **Privately Held**
WEB: www.emberindustries.com
SIC: 3672 Printed circuit boards

(P-5929)
FABRINET WEST INC
4900 Patrick Henry Dr, Santa Clara (95054-1822)
PHONE...................408 748-0900
Tom Mitchell, *CEO*
▲ **EMP:** 101 **EST:** 2015
SALES (est): 42MM **Privately Held**
WEB: www.fabrinetwest.com
SIC: 3672 3999 Printed circuit boards; atomizers, toiletry
PA: Fabrinet
  C/O Intertrust Corporate Services (Cayman) Limited
  George Town GR CAYMAN

(P-5930)
FLEX INTERCONNECT TECH INC
1603 Watson Ct, Milpitas (95035-6806)
PHONE...................408 956-8204
Chetan Shah, *CEO*
Dean Matsuo, *Corp Secy*
Nitin Desai, *Engineer*
EMP: 41 **EST:** 1998
SQ FT: 15,000
SALES (est): 5.4MM **Privately Held**
WEB: www.fit4flex.com
SIC: 3672 Printed circuit boards

(P-5931)
FLEXTRONICS AMERICA LLC (DH)
6201 America Center Dr, San Jose (95002-2563)
PHONE...................408 576-7000
David Bennett, *Mng Member*
Regina Tay, *Legal Staff*
Chris Collier,
▲ **EMP:** 230
SALES (est): 830.1MM **Privately Held**
WEB: www.flex.com
SIC: 3672 Printed circuit boards

PRODUCTS & SERVICES SECTION

3672 - Printed Circuit Boards County (P-5956)

(P-5932)
FLEXTRONICS INTL USA INC
6201 America Center Dr, San Jose (95002-2563)
PHONE................................408 576-7000
Henry Bzeih, *Officer*
Mark Holman, *Vice Pres*
Marty Nicodemus, *Vice Pres*
Melissa Zujkowski, *Vice Pres*
Nancy Rodriguez, *Executive*
EMP: 2000 **Privately Held**
WEB: www.flex.com
SIC: 3672 Printed circuit boards
HQ: Flextronics International Usa, Inc.
6201 America Center Dr
San Jose CA 95002

(P-5933)
FLEXTRONICS INTL USA INC (HQ)
6201 America Center Dr, San Jose (95002-2563)
PHONE................................408 576-7000
Jason Spicer, *CEO*
David Bennett, *CFO*
Kelly Hampton, *Vice Pres*
Brigette Hendrix, *Vice Pres*
Sol Hutson, *Vice Pres*
▲ **EMP:** 892 **EST:** 1987
SQ FT: 100,000
SALES (est): 2.1B **Privately Held**
WEB: www.flex.com
SIC: 3672 Printed circuit boards

(P-5934)
FLEXTRONICS LOGISTICS USA INC (DH)
6201 America Center Dr # 6, San Jose (95002-2563)
PHONE................................408 576-7000
Michael McNamara, *President*
Steven Proctor, *Vice Pres*
Jack Chang, *Buyer*
Sarveswara Basa, *Senior Mgr*
▲ **EMP:** 292 **EST:** 2001
SALES (est): 135MM **Privately Held**
WEB: www.flex.com
SIC: 3672 Printed circuit boards

(P-5935)
GENERAL ELEC ASSEMBLY INC
1525 Atteberry Ln, San Jose (95131-1412)
PHONE................................408 980-8819
Eric Chang, *President*
Matthew McClendon, *Program Mgr*
Grace Ling, *Human Res Mgr*
Donna Field, *QC Mgr*
Ben Bobo, *VP Mktg*
EMP: 45 **EST:** 1992
SQ FT: 16,000
SALES (est): 8.5MM **Privately Held**
WEB: www.geamfg.com
SIC: 3672 Wiring boards

(P-5936)
GORILLA CIRCUITS (PA)
1445 Oakland Rd, San Jose (95112-1203)
PHONE................................408 294-9897
Hershel Petty, *CEO*
Jaime Gutierrez, *Vice Pres*
Cody Vandenburgh, *Business Mgr*
Mario Borjon, *Finance*
Jennifer Petty, *Buyer*
▲ **EMP:** 166 **EST:** 1967
SQ FT: 60,000
SALES (est): 54MM **Privately Held**
WEB: www.gorillacircuits.com
SIC: 3672 Circuit boards, television & radio printed

(P-5937)
GREEN CIRCUITS INC
1130 Ringwood Ct, San Jose (95131-1726)
PHONE................................408 526-1700
Joseph O'Neil, *CEO*
Ted Park, *COO*
Michael Nguyen, *Vice Pres*
Henry Luu, *Program Mgr*
John Suh, *Program Mgr*
▲ **EMP:** 187 **EST:** 2006
SQ FT: 15,000
SALES (est): 56.8MM **Privately Held**
WEB: www.greencircuits.com
SIC: 3672 Printed circuit boards

(P-5938)
HARBOR ELECTRONICS INC (PA)
3021 Kenneth St, Santa Clara (95054-3416)
PHONE................................408 988-6544
Christopher Cuda, *President*
Qing Lin, *CFO*
Thomas Bleakley, *Vice Pres*
Sean Yi, *Technician*
Tom Bleakley, *Engineer*
EMP: 190 **EST:** 2016
SQ FT: 50,000
SALES (est): 56.7MM **Privately Held**
WEB: www.harbor-electronics.com
SIC: 3672 Printed circuit boards

(P-5939)
HYTEK R&D INC (PA)
Also Called: R & D Tech
2044 Corporate Ct, Milpitas (95035)
PHONE................................408 761-5266
Dave Linedaugh, *President*
EMP: 22 **EST:** 2008
SALES (est): 1.7MM **Privately Held**
SIC: 3672 5063 Printed circuit boards; electrical supplies

(P-5940)
INFINITI SOLUTIONS USA INC (PA)
Also Called: Adaptive Electronics
3910 N 1st St, San Jose (95134-1501)
PHONE................................408 923-7300
Inderjit Singh, *President*
Kumar Patel, *President*
Pin Patel, *Vice Pres*
Dhaval Patel, *Executive*
William Pham, *Technician*
EMP: 113 **EST:** 1975
SQ FT: 70,000
SALES (est): 20.4MM **Privately Held**
WEB: www.infinitisolutions.com
SIC: 3672 3825 8711 Printed circuit boards; test equipment for electronic & electrical circuits; engineering services

(P-5941)
JABIL INC
Also Called: Jabil Circuit
30 Great Oaks Blvd, San Jose (95119-1309)
PHONE................................408 361-3200
Courtney J Ryan, *Exec VP*
Andrew Priestley, *Vice Pres*
Mike Warner, *Vice Pres*
Matt Behringer, *Executive*
Tariq Mir, *CIO*
EMP: 500
SALES (corp-wide): 29.2B **Publicly Held**
WEB: www.jabil.com
SIC: 3672 Printed circuit boards
PA: Jabil Inc.
10560 Dr Mrtn Lther King
Saint Petersburg FL 33716
727 577-9749

(P-5942)
JATON CORPORATION
47677 Lakeview Blvd, Fremont (94538-6544)
PHONE................................510 933-8888
Vicky Hong, *President*
J S Chiang, *CEO*
Aurora Wao, *Human Res Mgr*
▲ **EMP:** 59 **EST:** 1982
SQ FT: 85,000
SALES (est): 2.1MM **Privately Held**
WEB: www.jaton.com
SIC: 3672 3674 3661 3577 Printed circuit boards; modules, solid state; modems; computer peripheral equipment

(P-5943)
KALKAI ADVANCE MFG INC
630 Martin Ave, Rohnert Park (94928-2099)
PHONE................................707 588-9906
Robert Weed, *CEO*
Suzanne Landeros, *CFO*
Roberto Monteros, *CFO*
Eduardo Lopez, *Engineer*
Antonio Corona, *Production*
EMP: 28 **EST:** 2015
SQ FT: 28,000
SALES (est): 6.6MM **Privately Held**
SIC: 3672 Printed circuit boards

(P-5944)
KIMBALL ELECTRONICS IND INC
Also Called: Global Equipment Services
5215 Hellyer Ave Ste 130, San Jose (95138-1090)
PHONE................................669 234-1110
Christopher Thyen, *Vice Pres*
EMP: 40 **EST:** 2018
SQ FT: 154
SALES: 1.2B
SALES (corp-wide): 1.2B **Publicly Held**
WEB: www.kimballelectronics.com
SIC: 3672 8711 7371 Printed circuit boards; engineering services; computer software development
PA: Kimball Electronics, Inc.
1205 Kimball Blvd
Jasper IN 47546
812 634-4000

(P-5945)
MC ELECTRONICS LLC
1891 Airway Dr, Hollister (95023-9099)
PHONE................................831 637-1651
Jan Kreminski,
Crystal Herrera, *Accounting Mgr*
Bishop McElvaney, *Mfg Mgr*
Doug Hooton, *Director*
EMP: 399 **EST:** 1981
SQ FT: 6,000
SALES (est): 83.5MM
SALES (corp-wide): 443.3MM **Privately Held**
WEB: www.mcelectronics.com
SIC: 3672 Printed circuit boards
PA: Volex Plc
Unit C1
Basingstoke HANTS RG24
203 370-8830

(P-5946)
MERITRONICS INC (PA)
500 Yosemite Dr Ste 108, Milpitas (95035-5467)
PHONE................................408 969-0888
Cherng Dior Wu, *President*
Kiet Pham, *Vice Pres*
▲ **EMP:** 34 **EST:** 1995
SQ FT: 34,000
SALES (est): 13.3MM **Privately Held**
WEB: www.meritronics.com
SIC: 3672 Printed circuit boards

(P-5947)
MERITRONICS MATERIALS INC
42660 Christy St, Fremont (94538-3135)
PHONE................................408 390-5642
Richard Maldonado, *President*
EMP: 18 **EST:** 2017
SALES (est): 3.1MM **Privately Held**
WEB: www.meritronics.com
SIC: 3672 3679 Printed circuit boards; electronic circuits

(P-5948)
MULTIMEK INC
357 Reed St, Santa Clara (95050-3107)
PHONE................................408 653-1300
Doug McCown, *President*
Doug Mc Cown, *VP Human Res*
Kevin McCown, *Materials Mgr*
EMP: 20 **EST:** 1980
SQ FT: 8,000
SALES (est): 3.9MM **Privately Held**
WEB: www.multimekinc.com
SIC: 3672 Printed circuit boards

(P-5949)
MVINIX CORPORATION
1759 Mccarthy Blvd, Milpitas (95035-7416)
PHONE................................408 321-9109
Daniel Tran, *CEO*
Huynh P Tan, *President*
Bien Vo, *Vice Pres*
Gene Nguyen, *Business Mgr*
Yamille Platero, *Sales Associate*
EMP: 38 **EST:** 2008
SALES (est): 9.5MM **Privately Held**
WEB: www.mvinix.com
SIC: 5731 3672 Consumer electronic equipment; printed circuit boards

(P-5950)
N D E INC
Also Called: New Dimension Electronics
3301 Keller St, Santa Clara (95054-2601)
PHONE................................408 727-3955
Richard Le, *CEO*
EMP: 30 **EST:** 1991
SQ FT: 6,000
SALES (est): 4.3MM **Privately Held**
SIC: 3672 3679 Printed circuit boards; harness assemblies for electronic use: wire or cable

(P-5951)
NEXLOGIC TECHNOLOGIES INC
2085 Zanker Rd, San Jose (95131-2107)
PHONE................................408 436-8150
Zulki Khan, *President*
Minh Ly, *Program Mgr*
Tariq Nisar, *Program Mgr*
Sanam Shaikh, *Sr Software Eng*
Yaseen Haroon, *Controller*
▲ **EMP:** 76 **EST:** 1995
SALES (est): 15.2MM **Privately Held**
WEB: www.nexlogic.com
SIC: 3672 Printed circuit boards

(P-5952)
NOVA DRILLING SERVICES INC
1500 Buckeye Dr, Milpitas (95035-7418)
PHONE................................408 732-6682
Mike McKibbin, *President*
Michael Doherty, *Vice Pres*
Stephanie Bell, *Admin Sec*
Kathleen McKibbin, *Admin Sec*
EMP: 33 **EST:** 1978
SQ FT: 15,000
SALES (est): 4.4MM **Privately Held**
WEB: www.novadrilling.com
SIC: 3672 3083 Printed circuit boards; laminated plastics plate & sheet

(P-5953)
ONCORE MANUFACTURING LLC
6600 Stevenson Blvd, Fremont (94538-2471)
PHONE................................510 516-5488
James Liow, *Branch Mgr*
EMP: 99
SALES (corp-wide): 1.1B **Privately Held**
WEB: www.neotech.com
SIC: 3672 8711 Printed circuit boards; electrical or electronic engineering
HQ: Oncore Manufacturing Llc
9340 Owensmouth Ave
Chatsworth CA 91311

(P-5954)
ORION MANUFACTURING INC
5550 Hellyer Ave, San Jose (95138-1005)
PHONE................................408 955-9001
Matthew L Davis, *President*
EMP: 19 **EST:** 2002
SALES (est): 899.8K **Privately Held**
SIC: 3672 Printed circuit boards

(P-5955)
PACTRON
3000 Patrick Henry Dr, Santa Clara (95054-1814)
PHONE................................408 329-5500
Sriram Iyer, *CEO*
K Prakash, *COO*
Lokesh Verma, *COO*
Sanjay Singh, *Vice Pres*
Danny Danyali, *Technical Staff*
EMP: 99 **EST:** 1995
SQ FT: 35,000
SALES (est): 22.4MM **Privately Held**
WEB: www.pactroninc.com
SIC: 3672 Printed circuit boards

(P-5956)
PALPILOT INTERNATIONAL CORP (PA)
500 Yosemite Dr, Milpitas (95035-5467)
PHONE................................408 855-8866
Eddy Niu, *President*
Jerry Barnes, *Vice Pres*
Yichien Hwang, *Vice Pres*
Bruce Lee, *Vice Pres*
Meilee Cheng, *Administration*
▲ **EMP:** 40 **EST:** 1992
SQ FT: 7,000

(PA)=Parent Co (HQ)=Headquarters (DH)=Div Headquarters
✪ = New Business established in last 2 years

3672 - Printed Circuit Boards County (P-5957)

SALES (est): 17.7MM **Privately Held**
WEB: www.palpilot.com
SIC: 3672 Wiring boards

(P-5957)
PARAMIT CORPORATION (PA)
Also Called: Lathrop Engineering
18735 Madrone Pkwy, Morgan Hill (95037-2876)
PHONE..................408 782-5600
Balbir Rataul, *President*
Bruce Richardson, *President*
Tom La Rose, *CFO*
Donna Wheatley, *Program Mgr*
Harpreet Pannu, *Software Engr*
▲ EMP: 198 EST: 1990
SQ FT: 150,000
SALES (est): 107.3MM **Privately Held**
WEB: www.paramit.com
SIC: 3672 Printed circuit boards

(P-5958)
PLEXUS CORP
431 Kato Ter, Fremont (94539-8333)
P.O. Box 156, Neenah WI (54957-0156)
PHONE..................510 668-9000
Fax: 510 668-9090
EMP: 120
SALES (corp-wide): 2.6B **Publicly Held**
SIC: 3672 Mfg Printed Circuit Boards
PA: Plexus Corp.
   1 Plexus Way
   Neenah WI 54956
   920 969-6000

(P-5959)
PRECISION DESIGN INC
Also Called: Pdi
1160 Industrial Rd Ste 16, San Carlos (94070-4128)
PHONE..................650 508-8041
Alexandra Sgolombis, *President*
EMP: 20 EST: 1983
SQ FT: 5,030
SALES (est): 502.3K **Privately Held**
SIC: 3672 7373 Printed circuit boards; computer integrated systems design

(P-5960)
QOSTRONICS INC
2044 Corporate Ct, San Jose (95131-1753)
PHONE..................408 719-1286
Shawn Do, *Principal*
MAI Tran, *Admin Sec*
Dai Le, *Engineer*
EMP: 33 EST: 2002
SQ FT: 5,500
SALES (est): 5.9MM **Privately Held**
WEB: www.qostronics.com
SIC: 3672 3845 Circuit boards, television & radio printed; electromedical equipment

(P-5961)
QUALITEK INC (HQ)
1116 Elko Dr, Sunnyvale (94089-2207)
PHONE..................408 734-8686
Louise Crisham, *CEO*
Jose N Martinez, *Info Tech Mgr*
▲ EMP: 75 EST: 1972
SQ FT: 20,000
SALES (est): 22.1MM
SALES (corp-wide): 80.7MM **Privately Held**
WEB: www.westak.com
SIC: 3672 Printed circuit boards
PA: Westak, Inc.
   1116 Elko Dr
   Sunnyvale CA 94089
   408 734-8686

(P-5962)
QUALITEK INC
Also Called: Westak
1272 Forgewood Ave, Sunnyvale (94089-2215)
PHONE..................408 752-8422
Ray Giancola, *Manager*
EMP: 75
SALES (corp-wide): 80.7MM **Privately Held**
WEB: www.westak.com
SIC: 3672 Printed circuit boards

HQ: Qualitek, Inc.
   1116 Elko Dr
   Sunnyvale CA 94089

(P-5963)
QUALITY CIRCUIT ASSEMBLY INC
Also Called: Q C A
1709 Junction Ct Ste 380, San Jose (95112-1044)
PHONE..................408 441-1001
Jeff Moss, *President*
Dwight Hargrave, *Vice Pres*
Nancy Moss, *Sales Dir*
Steve Giron, *Manager*
EMP: 65 EST: 1988
SQ FT: 30,000
SALES (est): 22.3MM **Privately Held**
WEB: www.qcamfg.com
SIC: 3672 Circuit boards, television & radio printed

(P-5964)
R&D ALTANOVA INC
6389 San Ignacio Ave, San Jose (95119-1206)
PHONE..................408 225-7011
James Russell, *CEO*
Ken Pawloski, *CFO*
Mark Yaeger, *Vice Pres*
Anh Ngo, *Engineer*
Don Thompson, *Director*
EMP: 48 EST: 2000
SQ FT: 15,000
SALES (est): 15.1MM
SALES (corp-wide): 54.5MM **Privately Held**
WEB: www.rdaltanova.com
SIC: 3672 7389 Printed circuit boards; design services
PA: R & D Circuits Inc
   3601 S Clinton Ave
   South Plainfield NJ 07080
   732 549-4554

(P-5965)
RASTERGRAF INC (PA)
7145 Marlborough Ter, Berkeley (94705-1736)
PHONE..................510 849-4801
Victor R Gold Jr, *President*
EMP: 25 EST: 1979
SALES (est): 423.3K **Privately Held**
WEB: www.rastergraf.com
SIC: 3672 Printed circuit boards

(P-5966)
ROCKET EMS INC
2950 Patrick Henry Dr, Santa Clara (95054-1813)
PHONE..................408 727-3700
Craig Arcuri, *CEO*
Michael Kottke, *President*
Katherine Danh, *Program Mgr*
Curtis Nguy, *Engineer*
Vipul Chapla, *QC Mgr*
EMP: 140 EST: 2010
SQ FT: 40,000
SALES (est): 64MM **Privately Held**
WEB: www.rocketems.com
SIC: 3672 Printed circuit boards

(P-5967)
ROYAL CIRCUIT SOLUTIONS INC (PA)
21 Hamilton Ct, Hollister (95023-2535)
PHONE..................831 636-7789
Milan Shah, *President*
Mary Nydegger, *Accountant*
Rahim Nosrati, *Production*
Amber Marini, *Regl Sales Mgr*
Johnny Dearmas, *Sales Staff*
▲ EMP: 30 EST: 2008
SQ FT: 15,000
SALES (est): 11.4MM **Privately Held**
WEB: www.royalcircuits.com
SIC: 3672 Circuit boards, television & radio printed

(P-5968)
SANMINA CORPORATION
San Jose Plant 1337
2700 N 1st St, San Jose (95134-2015)
PHONE..................408 964-3500
Thomas Mosier, *President*
Jacquelyn Ward, *Bd of Directors*
Dennis Young, *Exec VP*
Mohammed Israr, *Vice Pres*
Daniel Liddle, *Vice Pres*
EMP: 20 **Publicly Held**
WEB: www.sanmina.com
SIC: 3672 Printed circuit boards
PA: Sanmina Corporation
   2700 N 1st St
   San Jose CA 95134

(P-5969)
SANMINA CORPORATION
2050 Bering Dr, San Jose (95131-2009)
PHONE..................408 964-6400
Eileen Card, *Branch Mgr*
Jure Sola, *CEO*
Barry Hegarty, *Vice Pres*
Daniel Liddle, *Vice Pres*
Jose Martinez, *Vice Pres*
EMP: 375 **Publicly Held**
WEB: www.sanmina.com
SIC: 3672 Printed circuit boards
PA: Sanmina Corporation
   2700 N 1st St
   San Jose CA 95134

(P-5970)
SANMINA CORPORATION
42735 Christy St, Fremont (94538-3146)
PHONE..................510 897-2000
Tony Princiotta, *Branch Mgr*
Mohammed Israr, *Vice Pres*
Eduardo Davalos, *IT/INT Sup*
Daniel Messah, *Analyst*
Pk Chan, *Controller*
EMP: 500
SQ FT: 155,000 **Publicly Held**
WEB: www.sanmina.com
SIC: 3672 Printed circuit boards
PA: Sanmina Corporation
   2700 N 1st St
   San Jose CA 95134

(P-5971)
SANMINA CORPORATION (PA)
2700 N 1st St, San Jose (95134-2015)
P.O. Box 7, Huntsville AL (35804-0007)
PHONE..................408 964-3500
Jure Sola, *Ch of Bd*
Mike Landy, *COO*
Kurt Adzema, *CFO*
Eugene A Delaney, *Bd of Directors*
Alan Reid, *Exec VP*
▲ EMP: 318 EST: 1980
SALES: 6.7B **Publicly Held**
WEB: www.sanmina.com
SIC: 3672 3674 Printed circuit boards; semiconductors & related devices; light emitting diodes

(P-5972)
SANMINA-SCI USA INC
30 E Plumeria Dr, San Jose (95134-2102)
PHONE..................408 964-3500
Jure Sola, *CEO*
Bob Eulau, *Exec VP*
Charles Kostalnick, *Exec VP*
Alan Reid, *Exec VP*
Dennis Young, *Exec VP*
EMP: 22 EST: 2005
SALES (est): 929.1K **Privately Held**
WEB: www.sanmina.com
SIC: 3672 Printed circuit boards

(P-5973)
SIERRA CIRCUITS INC
Also Called: Sierra Proto Express
1108 W Evelyn Ave, Sunnyvale (94086-5745)
PHONE..................408 735-7137
Kenneth Bahl, *CEO*
Steve Arobio, *Vice Pres*
S Bala Bahl, *Vice Pres*
Satpreet Kaur, *Office Admin*
Quyen Nguyen, *Admin Asst*
▲ EMP: 105 EST: 1978
SQ FT: 22,000
SALES (est): 73.4MM **Privately Held**
WEB: www.protoexpress.com
SIC: 3672 Printed circuit boards

(P-5974)
SMTC CORPORATION (HQ)
431 Kato Ter, Fremont (94539-8333)
PHONE..................510 737-0700
John Caldwell, *CEO*
Joe Bustos, *Vice Pres*
Andy Cai, *Vice Pres*
Josh Chien, *Vice Pres*
Bob Miller, *Vice Pres*
▲ EMP: 96 EST: 1994
SALES (est): 43MM
SALES (corp-wide): 386.4MM **Privately Held**
WEB: www.smtc.com
SIC: 3672 Printed circuit boards
PA: Smtc Corporation
   7050 Woodbine Ave
   Markham ON L3R 4
   905 479-1810

(P-5975)
SMTC MANUFACTURING CORP CAL
431 Kato Ter, Fremont (94539-8333)
PHONE..................408 934-7100
Larry Silber, *CEO*
John Caldwell, *President*
Claude Germain, *President*
Alex Walker, *President*
Jane Todd, *CFO*
▲ EMP: 1875 EST: 1994
SALES (est): 145.1MM
SALES (corp-wide): 386.4MM **Privately Held**
WEB: www.smtc.com
SIC: 3672 Printed circuit boards
HQ: Smtc Manufacturing Corporation Of Canada
   7050 Woodbine Ave
   Markham ON L3R 4
   905 479-1810

(P-5976)
SNA ELECTRONICS INC
3249 Laurelview Ct, Fremont (94538-6535)
PHONE..................510 656-3903
Sung W Shin, *CEO*
CHI Shin, *CFO*
Steve Hahn, *Vice Pres*
Philip Hwang, *Program Mgr*
Andrew Shin, *Program Mgr*
EMP: 44 EST: 2002
SQ FT: 40,800
SALES (est): 11MM **Privately Held**
WEB: www.sna-electronic.com
SIC: 3672 Printed circuit boards

(P-5977)
SONIC MANUFACTURING TECH INC
47931 Westinghouse Dr, Fremont (94539-7483)
PHONE..................510 580-8551
Kenneth B Raab, *President*
Chris Hanson, *Engineer*
Mike Mayes, *Purch Mgr*
EMP: 20 EST: 2015
SALES (est): 5.1MM **Privately Held**
WEB: www.sonicmfg.com
SIC: 3672 Printed circuit boards

(P-5978)
SONIC MANUFACTURING TECH INC
47951 Westinghouse Dr, Fremont (94539-7483)
PHONE..................510 580-8500
Kenneth Raab, *President*
Robert Pereyda, *Vice Pres*
Henry Woo, *Vice Pres*
▲ EMP: 300 EST: 1996
SQ FT: 80,000
SALES (est): 102.3MM **Privately Held**
WEB: www.sonicmfg.com
SIC: 3672 Printed circuit boards

(P-5979)
SPARTRONICS MILPITAS INC (DH)
1940 Milmont Dr, Milpitas (95035-2578)
PHONE..................408 957-1300
Paul Fraipont, *President*
Greg Kelble, *Admin Sec*
▲ EMP: 101 EST: 1987
SQ FT: 62,500

PRODUCTS & SERVICES SECTION
3672 - Printed Circuit Boards County (P-6004)

SALES (est): 22.1MM
SALES (corp-wide): 810.8MM **Privately Held**
WEB: www.sparton.com
SIC: 3672 Printed circuit boards
HQ: Spartronics, Llc
2333 Reach Rd
Williamsport PA 17701
763 703-4321

(P-5980)
STREAMLINE CIRCUITS LLC
Also Called: Summit Intrconnect Santa Clara
1410 Martin Ave, Santa Clara (95050-2621)
PHONE.....................415 279-8650
Shane Whiteside, *CEO*
Thomas P Caldwell, *CFO*
Clay Swain, *VP Sls/Mktg*
◆ **EMP:** 300 **EST:** 2003
SALES (est): 50.4MM
SALES (corp-wide): 1.7B **Privately Held**
WEB: www.summit-pcb.com
SIC: 3672 Printed circuit boards
HQ: Summit Interconnect, Inc.
223 N Crescent Way
Anaheim CA 92801
714 239-2433

(P-5981)
STREAMLINE ELECTRONICS MFG INC
Also Called: S E M
4285 Technology Dr, Fremont (94538-6339)
PHONE.....................408 263-3600
Shahab Jafri, *President*
Ash Bokhari, *Administration*
Michelle Nava, *Purchasing*
EMP: 50 **EST:** 1975
SQ FT: 26,000
SALES (est): 6.1MM **Privately Held**
WEB: www.sem-inc.com
SIC: 3672 8711 2542 Printed circuit boards; engineering services; partitions & fixtures, except wood

(P-5982)
SUBA TECHNOLOGY INC
46501 Landing Pkwy, Fremont (94538-6421)
PHONE.....................408 434-6500
Rolando M Suba, *CEO*
Alex Obice, *COO*
Winston Punzalan, *Executive*
EMP: 69 **EST:** 2001
SQ FT: 35,000
SALES (est): 11.6MM **Privately Held**
WEB: www.subatech.com
SIC: 3672 Printed circuit boards

(P-5983)
SUMMIT INTERCONNECT INC
Also Called: Santa Clara Facility
1401 Martin Ave, Santa Clara (95050-2614)
PHONE.....................408 727-1418
Shane Whiteside, *Branch Mgr*
EMP: 240
SALES (corp-wide): 1.7B **Privately Held**
WEB: www.summit-pcb.com
SIC: 3672 Printed circuit boards
HQ: Summit Interconnect, Inc.
223 N Crescent Way
Anaheim CA 92801
714 239-2433

(P-5984)
SUNNYTECH
2243 Ringwood Ave, San Jose (95131-1737)
PHONE.....................408 943-8100
Siu Fong Chow, *President*
Virgil Chen, *Vice Pres*
Vigil Chen, *Executive*
Winny Chow, *Finance*
▲ **EMP:** 18 **EST:** 1986
SQ FT: 5,500
SALES (est): 3.3MM **Privately Held**
WEB: www.sunnytech.biz
SIC: 3672 Printed circuit boards

(P-5985)
SYMPROTEK CO
950 Yosemite Dr, Milpitas (95035-5452)
PHONE.....................408 956-0700
Eric Chon, *President*
Sangkyoo Jang, *Buyer*
Winona Medroso, *QC Mgr*
Harry La, *Director*
Maria Masdriga, *Manager*
▲ **EMP:** 35 **EST:** 1994
SQ FT: 36,000
SALES (est): 7MM **Privately Held**
WEB: www.symprotek.com
SIC: 3672 Printed circuit boards

(P-5986)
TELIRITE TECHNICAL SVCS INC
2857 Lakeview Ct, Fremont (94538-6534)
PHONE.....................510 440-3888
Patrick Chan, *CEO*
Kue Chau Loh, *CFO*
Kue Loh, *CFO*
Henry Gong, *Vice Pres*
▲ **EMP:** 22 **EST:** 1995
SQ FT: 12,000
SALES (est): 4.4MM **Privately Held**
WEB: www.telirite.com
SIC: 3672 Printed circuit boards

(P-5987)
TEMPO AUTOMATION INC
2460 Alameda St, San Francisco (94103-4806)
PHONE.....................415 320-1261
Jeffrey McAlvay, *CEO*
Jesse Koenig, *COO*
Robert Papa, *Officer*
Hugh Coffee, *Technician*
Jessica Grijalva, *Technician*
EMP: 35 **EST:** 2014
SQ FT: 2,000
SALES (est): 6.4MM **Privately Held**
WEB: www.tempoautomation.com
SIC: 3672 Printed circuit boards

(P-5988)
TRI-PHASE INC
Also Called: Valley Services Electronics
6190 San Ignacio Ave, San Jose (95119-1378)
PHONE.....................408 284-7700
Andy Pecota, *CEO*
Beth Kendrick, *President*
Tammy Tran, *Technology*
Jason Fisher, *Engineer*
John Grilli, *Engineer*
EMP: 160 **EST:** 1978
SQ FT: 52,000
SALES (est): 48.3MM **Privately Held**
WEB: www.vse.com
SIC: 3672 Printed circuit boards

(P-5989)
TTM PRINTED CIRCUIT GROUP INC
407 Mathew St, Santa Clara (95050-3105)
PHONE.....................408 486-3100
Jeff Gonsman, *Manager*
EMP: 32
SALES (corp-wide): 2.1B **Publicly Held**
WEB: www.ttm.com
SIC: 3672 Printed circuit boards
HQ: Ttm Printed Circuit Group, Inc.
2630 S Harbor Blvd
Santa Ana CA 92704

(P-5990)
TTM TECHNOLOGIES INC
407 Mathew St, Santa Clara (95050-3105)
PHONE.....................408 486-3100
Kathy Davis, *Human Res Dir*
Sue Adams, *Director*
EMP: 260
SALES (corp-wide): 2.1B **Publicly Held**
WEB: www.ttm.com
SIC: 3672 Printed circuit boards
PA: Ttm Technologies, Inc.
200 Sandpointe Ave # 400
Santa Ana CA 92707
714 327-3000

(P-5991)
TTM TECHNOLOGIES INC
355 Turtle Creek Ct, San Jose (95125-1316)
PHONE.....................408 280-0422
Arnold Amaral, *Branch Mgr*
Joanna Zhao, *Program Mgr*
EMP: 118

SALES (corp-wide): 2.1B **Publicly Held**
WEB: www.ttm.com
SIC: 3672 Printed circuit boards
PA: Ttm Technologies, Inc.
200 Sandpointe Ave # 400
Santa Ana CA 92707
714 327-3000

(P-5992)
TWIN INDUSTRIES INC
2303 Camino Ramon Ste 106, San Ramon (94583-1389)
PHONE.....................925 866-8946
Joe O'Neil, *General Mgr*
Adom Moutafian, *President*
▲ **EMP:** 15 **EST:** 1972
SQ FT: 26,000
SALES (est): 1MM **Privately Held**
WEB: www.twinind.com
SIC: 3672 Printed circuit boards

(P-5993)
UNITED SUPERTEK INC
Also Called: U S I
14930 Vintner Ct, Saratoga (95070-9712)
PHONE.....................408 922-0730
Samson Zarnegar, *President*
EMP: 17 **EST:** 1983
SQ FT: 25,000
SALES (est): 2.4MM **Privately Held**
SIC: 3672 Printed circuit boards

(P-5994)
URI TECH INC
1670 Santa Lucia Dr, San Jose (95125-5229)
PHONE.....................408 456-0115
Sea Heon Kim, *President*
EMP: 15 **EST:** 1996
SALES (est): 1.2MM **Privately Held**
SIC: 3672 Printed circuit boards

(P-5995)
VECTOR FABRICATION INC (PA)
1629 Watson Ct, Milpitas (95035-6806)
PHONE.....................408 942-9800
Quang Luong, *President*
Issac Stringer, *Vice Pres*
Vinh Luong, *General Mgr*
▲ **EMP:** 19 **EST:** 1995
SQ FT: 18,000
SALES (est): 2.8MM **Privately Held**
WEB: www.vectorfab.com
SIC: 3672 Printed circuit boards

(P-5996)
VENTURE ELECTRONICS INTL INC
6701 Mowry Ave, Newark (94560-4927)
PHONE.....................510 744-3720
C T Wong, *President*
EMP: 46 **EST:** 2002
SALES (est): 2.8MM **Privately Held**
WEB: www.venture.com.sg
SIC: 3672 Printed circuit boards
PA: Venture Corporation Limited
5006 Ang Mo Kio Avenue 5
Singapore 56987

(P-5997)
VITRON ELECTRONIC SERVICES INC
Also Called: Vitron Electronics Mfg & Svcs
5400 Hellyer Ave, San Jose (95138-1019)
PHONE.....................408 251-1600
Huan Cong Tran, *CEO*
Huan Tran, *COO*
Hien Duong, *Purchasing*
▲ **EMP:** 60 **EST:** 1988
SQ FT: 3,500
SALES (est): 15MM **Privately Held**
WEB: www.vitronmfg.com
SIC: 3672 Printed circuit boards

(P-5998)
WESTAK INC (PA)
Also Called: A2
1116 Elko Dr, Sunnyvale (94089-2207)
PHONE.....................408 734-8686
Louise Crisham, *CEO*
Lou George, *COO*
Dicie Hinaga, *CFO*
Lisa Kennedy, *Office Mgr*
Ted Chee, *Administration*
EMP: 100 **EST:** 1972

SQ FT: 20,000
SALES (est): 80.7MM **Privately Held**
WEB: www.westak.com
SIC: 3672 Circuit boards, television & radio printed

(P-5999)
WESTAK INTERNATIONAL SALES INC (HQ)
1116 Elko Dr, Sunnyvale (94089-2207)
PHONE.....................408 734-8686
Louise Crisham, *President*
▲ **EMP:** 130 **EST:** 1982
SQ FT: 20,000
SALES (est): 24.7MM
SALES (corp-wide): 80.7MM **Privately Held**
WEB: www.westak.com
SIC: 3672 Printed circuit boards
PA: Westak, Inc.
1116 Elko Dr
Sunnyvale CA 94089
408 734-8686

(P-6000)
WHIZZ SYSTEMS INC
3240 Scott Blvd, Santa Clara (95054-3011)
PHONE.....................408 207-0400
Munawar Karimjee, *CEO*
Muhammad Irfan, *President*
Yome Salinas, *Administration*
Will Ziakas, *Project Mgr*
Jared Davis, *Facilities Mgr*
▲ **EMP:** 50
SQ FT: 35,000
SALES (est): 23.3MM **Privately Held**
WEB: www.whizzsystems.com
SIC: 3672 Printed circuit boards

(P-6001)
WILLIAM HO
Also Called: MBA Electronics
40760 Encyclopedia Cir, Fremont (94538-2473)
PHONE.....................510 226-9089
William Ho, *Owner*
EMP: 18 **EST:** 1991
SQ FT: 21,000
SALES (est): 7.2MM **Privately Held**
WEB: www.mbaelectronics.com
SIC: 3672 Printed circuit boards

(P-6002)
XILINX INC (PA)
2100 All Programable, San Jose (95124-4355)
PHONE.....................408 559-7778
Victor Peng, *President*
Andrea Nieto, *Partner*
Dennis Segers, *Ch of Bd*
Brice Hill, *CFO*
William Christopher Madden, *Exec VP*
EMP: 3824 **EST:** 1984
SQ FT: 588,000
SALES: 3.1B **Publicly Held**
WEB: www.xilinx.com
SIC: 3672 3674 7372 Printed circuit boards; microcircuits, integrated (semiconductor); application computer software

(P-6003)
ZOLLNER ELECTRONICS INC
575 Cottonwood Dr, Milpitas (95035-7402)
PHONE.....................408 434-5400
Markus Aschenbrenner,
Stephan Weiss, *COO*
Sean Dang, *Program Mgr*
Michael Diep, *Program Mgr*
Nessa Hunt, *Admin Sec*
▲ **EMP:** 29 **EST:** 1965
SALES (est): 16.9MM
SALES (corp-wide): 1.8B **Privately Held**
WEB: www.zollner-electronics.com
SIC: 3672 Printed circuit boards
PA: Zollner Elektronik Ag
Manfred-Zollner-Str. 1
Zandt BY 93499
994 420-10

(P-6004)
ZYTEK CORP (PA)
Also Called: Zytek Ems
1755 Mccarthy Blvd, Milpitas (95035-7416)
PHONE.....................408 520-4287
Rabia Khan, *President*
EMP: 39 **EST:** 2011

3674 - Semiconductors County (P-6005)

SQ FT: 21,000
SALES (est): 5.2MM **Privately Held**
SIC: 3672 Printed circuit boards

3674 Semiconductors

(P-6005)
3PLUS1 TECHNOLOGY INC
18809 Cox Ave Ste 250, Saratoga (95070-6617)
PHONE..........................408 374-1111
Robert Dunnett, *Principal*
EMP: 23 **EST:** 2006
SALES (est): 1.3MM **Privately Held**
SIC: 3674 Semiconductors & related devices

(P-6006)
ABOUND LOGIC INC
19200 Stevens Creek Blvd # 200, Cupertino (95014-2530)
PHONE..........................408 873-3400
Frederick Reblewski, *CEO*
Karen Wong, *Finance Dir*
EMP: 22 **EST:** 2006
SALES (est): 2.3MM **Privately Held**
SIC: 3674 Semiconductor circuit networks

(P-6007)
ACACIA COMMUNICATIONS INC
2700 Zanker Rd Ste 160, San Jose (95134-2139)
PHONE..........................212 331-8417
EMP: 71
SALES (corp-wide): 49.8B **Publicly Held**
WEB: www.acacia-inc.com
SIC: 3674 Semiconductors & related devices
HQ: Acacia Communications, Inc.
3 Mill And Main Pl # 400
Maynard MA 01754
978 938-4896

(P-6008)
ACHRONIX SEMICONDUCTOR CORP
2903 Bunker Hill Ln # 200, Santa Clara (95054-1148)
PHONE..........................408 889-4100
Robert Blake, *President*
John Holt, *Ch of Bd*
Ravi Aripirala, *COO*
Howard Brodsky, *CFO*
Mark Voll, *CFO*
EMP: 75 **EST:** 2006
SQ FT: 25,000
SALES (est): 17.3MM **Privately Held**
WEB: www.achronix.com
SIC: 3674 Integrated circuits, semiconductor networks, etc.

(P-6009)
ACTSOLAR INC
2900 Semiconductor Dr, Santa Clara (95051-0606)
PHONE..........................408 721-5000
Andrew Foss, *President*
Brian Dupin, *Vice Pres*
EMP: 45 **EST:** 2006
SQ FT: 3,000
SALES (est): 10.7MM
SALES (corp-wide): 14.4B **Publicly Held**
SIC: 3674 Semiconductors & related devices
HQ: National Semiconductor Corporation
2900 Semiconductor Dr
Santa Clara CA 95051
408 721-5000

(P-6010)
ADESTO TECHNOLOGIES CORP (HQ)
3600 Peterson Way, Santa Clara (95054-2808)
PHONE..........................408 400-0578
Narbeh Derhacobian, *President*
Nelson Chan, *Ch of Bd*
Ron Shelton, *CFO*
David Aaron, *Vice Pres*
Seyed Attaran, *Vice Pres*
◆ **EMP:** 121 **EST:** 2006
SQ FT: 34,000

SALES (est): 118.1MM
SALES (corp-wide): 1.3B **Privately Held**
WEB: www.dialog-semiconductor.com
SIC: 3674 Semiconductors & related devices
PA: Dialog Semiconductor Limited
100 Longwater Avenue Green Park
Reading BERKS
179 375-7700

(P-6011)
ADVANCED ANALOGIC TECH INC
2740 Zanker Rd, San Jose (95134-2128)
PHONE..........................408 330-1400
Richard K Williams, *President*
David J Aldrich, *CEO*
Parviz Ghaffaripour, *COO*
Ashok Chandran, *CFO*
Bijan Mohandes, *Exec VP*
EMP: 105 **EST:** 1962
SQ FT: 42,174
SALES (est): 25.6MM
SALES (corp-wide): 3.3B **Publicly Held**
WEB: www.analogictech.com
SIC: 3674 Integrated circuits, semiconductor networks, etc.
PA: Skyworks Solutions, Inc.
5260 California Ave
Irvine CA 92617
949 231-3000

(P-6012)
ADVANCED COMPONENT LABS INC
Also Called: A C L
990 Richard Ave Ste 118, Santa Clara (95050-2828)
PHONE..........................408 327-0200
Michael J Oswald, *CEO*
Winston Labucay, *CFO*
Deborah Herting, *Vice Pres*
Nerissa De Ramos, *Sales Mgr*
EMP: 20 **EST:** 1994
SQ FT: 20,000
SALES (est): 2.2MM **Privately Held**
WEB: www.aclusa.com
SIC: 3674 Semiconductor circuit networks

(P-6013)
ADVANCED LINEAR DVCS RES INC
415 Tasman Dr, Sunnyvale (94089-1706)
PHONE..........................408 747-1155
Robert L Chao, *President*
EMP: 21 **EST:** 1985
SQ FT: 12,000
SALES (est): 3.2MM **Privately Held**
WEB: www.aldinc.com
SIC: 3674 8711 Integrated circuits, semiconductor networks, etc.; engineering services

(P-6014)
ADVANCED MICRO DEVICES INC (PA)
Also Called: AMD
2485 Augustine Dr, Santa Clara (95054-3002)
PHONE..........................408 749-4000
Lisa T Su, *President*
John E Caldwell, *Ch of Bd*
Poh-Choo Chuah, *President*
Devinder Kumar, *CFO*
Ahmed Al Idrissi, *Bd of Directors*
EMP: 6631 **EST:** 1969
SQ FT: 251,000
SALES (est): 9.7B **Publicly Held**
WEB: www.amd.com
SIC: 3674 Integrated circuits, semiconductor networks, etc.; microprocessors; memories, solid state; microcircuits, integrated (semiconductor)

(P-6015)
ADVANTEST AMERICA INC (HQ)
3061 Zanker Rd, San Jose (95134-2127)
PHONE..........................408 456-3600
Douglas Lefever, *CEO*
Keith Hardwick, *CFO*
Myron Lee, *Treasurer*
Gerald Chan, *Vice Pres*
Judy Davies, *Vice Pres*
▲ **EMP:** 90 **EST:** 1982

SALES (est): 219MM **Privately Held**
WEB: www.advantest.com
SIC: 3674 Semiconductors & related devices

(P-6016)
AIXTRON INC
1700 Wyatt Dr Ste 15, Santa Clara (95054-1526)
PHONE..........................669 228-3759
Martin Goetzeler, *CEO*
Randy Singh, *CFO*
Martin Fischer, *Vice Pres*
Michael Heuken, *Vice Pres*
Ken Teo, *Managing Dir*
▲ **EMP:** 156 **EST:** 1981
SQ FT: 100,500
SALES (est): 196.4K
SALES (corp-wide): 318.4MM **Privately Held**
WEB: www.aixtron.com
SIC: 3674 Semiconductors & related devices
PA: Aixtron Se
Dornkaulstr. 2
Herzogenrath NW 52134
240 790-300

(P-6017)
AKM SEMICONDUCTOR INC
Also Called: A K M
1731 Tech Dr Ste 500, San Jose (95110)
PHONE..........................408 436-8580
S Kido, *President*
Makoto Konosu, *CEO*
Lyle Knudsen, *Vice Pres*
Paul Werner, *VP Business*
Chris Baltar, *Engineer*
▲ **EMP:** 33 **EST:** 1995
SQ FT: 5,402
SALES (est): 20.4MM **Privately Held**
WEB: www.akm.com
SIC: 3674 Semiconductors & related devices
HQ: Asahi Kasei Microdevices Corporation
1-1-2, Yurakucho
Chiyoda-Ku TKY 100-0

(P-6018)
AKT AMERICA INC (HQ)
3101 Scott Blvd Bldg 91, Santa Clara (95054-3318)
PHONE..........................408 563-5455
In Doo Kang, *Vice Pres*
Chang Olivia, *Admin Asst*
Zhongchuan Eddy, *Software Engr*
Daksha Nagpal, *Project Mgr*
Gautam Hemani, *Engineer*
▲ **EMP:** 400 **EST:** 1994
SQ FT: 200,000
SALES (est): 121.2MM
SALES (corp-wide): 17.2B **Publicly Held**
WEB: www.appliedmaterials.com
SIC: 3674 Semiconductors & related devices
PA: Applied Materials, Inc.
3050 Bowers Ave Bldg 1
Santa Clara CA 95054
408 727-5555

(P-6019)
AKT AMERICA INC
1245 Walsh Ave, Santa Clara (95050-2662)
PHONE..........................408 563-5455
EMP: 400
SALES (corp-wide): 17.2B **Publicly Held**
WEB: www.appliedmaterials.com
SIC: 3674 Semiconductors & related devices
HQ: Akt America, Inc.
3101 Scott Blvd Bldg 91
Santa Clara CA 95054
408 563-5455

(P-6020)
ALACRITECH INC
1995 N 1st St Ste 200, San Jose (95112-4220)
P.O. Box 20307 (95160-0307)
PHONE..........................408 867-3809
Larry Boucher, *President*
Theresa Begiebing, *CEO*
Esther Lee, *CFO*
Richard Blackborow, *Vice Pres*

Russ Lait, *Vice Pres*
EMP: 39 **EST:** 1997
SQ FT: 10,600
SALES (est): 5.5MM **Privately Held**
WEB: www.alacritech.com
SIC: 3674 Semiconductors & related devices

(P-6021)
ALION ENERGY INC
2200 Central St D, Richmond (94801-1213)
PHONE..........................510 965-0868
Mark Kingsley, *President*
Jesse Atkinson, *Vice Pres*
Linda Ramos, *Office Mgr*
Luigi Petrigh-Dove, *Engineer*
Craig Wildman, *Engineer*
▲ **EMP:** 51 **EST:** 2008
SALES (est): 7.7MM **Privately Held**
WEB: www.alionenergy.com
SIC: 3674 Solar cells

(P-6022)
ALL SENSORS CORPORATION
16035 Vineyard Blvd, Morgan Hill (95037-5480)
PHONE..........................408 776-9434
Dennis Dauenhauer, *President*
Gary Arnold, *Vice Pres*
Delly Paiva, *Admin Asst*
Tim Shotter, *Planning*
Usman Bhatti, *Engineer*
◆ **EMP:** 38 **EST:** 1999
SQ FT: 20,000
SALES (est): 9MM
SALES (corp-wide): 8.6B **Publicly Held**
WEB: www.allsensors.com
SIC: 3674 Infrared sensors, solid state
PA: Amphenol Corporation
358 Hall Ave
Wallingford CT 06492
203 265-8900

(P-6023)
ALLTEQ INDUSTRIES INC
215 Rustic Pl, San Ramon (94582-5618)
PHONE..........................925 833-7666
Phil Davies, *President*
Tony Draga, *Vice Pres*
William Miller, *Vice Pres*
EMP: 19 **EST:** 1983
SQ FT: 11,000
SALES (est): 534.1K **Privately Held**
WEB: www.allteq.com
SIC: 3674 3825 Semiconductors & related devices; integrated circuit testers

(P-6024)
ALLVIA INC
445 Fairway Dr, Half Moon Bay (94019-2200)
PHONE..........................408 234-8778
Sergey Savastiouk, *CEO*
EMP: 20 **EST:** 1996
SALES (est): 2.8MM **Privately Held**
WEB: www.allvia.com
SIC: 3674 Integrated circuits, semiconductor networks, etc.

(P-6025)
ALPHA AND OMEGA SEMICDTR INC (HQ)
475 Oakmead Pkwy, Sunnyvale (94085-4709)
PHONE..........................408 789-0008
Mike F Chang, *CEO*
Ephraim Kwok, *President*
Yueh-SE N Ho, *COO*
Mary Dotz, *CFO*
Lucas Chang, *Bd of Directors*
▲ **EMP:** 107 **EST:** 2000
SQ FT: 50,000
SALES (est): 54.3MM **Privately Held**
WEB: www.aosmd.com
SIC: 3674 Semiconductors & related devices

(P-6026)
ALTA DEVICES INC
545 Oakmead Pkwy, Sunnyvale (94085-4023)
PHONE..........................408 988-8600
Jian Ding, *CEO*
Mallorie Burak, *CFO*
Harry Atwater, *Bd of Directors*

▲ = Import ▼ = Export
◆ = Import/Export

PRODUCTS & SERVICES SECTION

3674 - Semiconductors County (P-6048)

Eli Yablonovitch, *Bd of Directors*
Stephen Fisher, *Vice Pres*
EMP: 250 **EST:** 2013
SQ FT: 115,000
SALES (est): 57.9MM **Privately Held**
WEB: www.altadevices.com
SIC: 3674 Semiconductors & related devices
PA: Jinjiang Hydroelectric Power Group Co., Ltd.
No.0-A, Anli Road, Chaoyang Dist.
Beijing 10010
-

(P-6027)
ALTERA CORPORATION (HQ)
101 Innovation Dr, San Jose (95134-1941)
PHONE.................................408 544-7000
John P Daane, *Ch of Bd*
Ronald J Pasek, *CFO*
John Sotir, *Officer*
Supreet Manchanda, *Exec VP*
Danny Biran, *Senior VP*
▲ **EMP:** 2740 **EST:** 1983
SQ FT: 505,000
SALES (est): 440.4MM
SALES (corp-wide): 77.8B **Publicly Held**
WEB: www.altera.com
SIC: 3674 7371 Semiconductors & related devices; computer software development & applications
PA: Intel Corporation
2200 Mission College Blvd
Santa Clara CA 95054
408 765-8080

(P-6028)
ALTIERRE CORPORATION
1980 Concourse Dr, San Jose (95131-1719)
P.O. Box 640527 (95164-0527)
PHONE.................................408 435-7343
Tony Alvarez, *CEO*
Anurag Goel, *COO*
Shan Kumar, *CFO*
Ravi Bhatnagar, *Vice Pres*
Ken Cioffi, *Vice Pres*
▲ **EMP:** 50
SQ FT: 85,367
SALES (est): 14.8MM **Privately Held**
WEB: www.altierre.com
SIC: 3674 Integrated circuits, semiconductor networks, etc.

(P-6029)
AMAT
3101 Scott Blvd, Santa Clara (95054-3318)
PHONE.................................408 563-5385
Dennis Chang, *Program Mgr*
Aron Rosenfeld, *Info Tech Dir*
Aniruddha Pal, *Project Engr*
Jian Chen, *Electrical Engi*
Duc Buckius, *Engineer*
EMP: 16 **EST:** 2018
SALES (est): 4.1MM **Privately Held**
WEB: www.appliedmaterials.com
SIC: 3674 Semiconductors & related devices

(P-6030)
AMBARELLA INC (PA)
3101 Jay St, Santa Clara (95054-3329)
PHONE.................................408 734-8888
Feng-Ming Wang, *Ch of Bd*
Chan W Lee, *COO*
Kevin C Eichler, *CFO*
John Young, *CFO*
CHI-Hong Ju, *Senior VP*
EMP: 739 **EST:** 2004
SQ FT: 58,700
SALES: 222.9MM **Publicly Held**
WEB: www.ambarella.com
SIC: 3674 Semiconductors & related devices

(P-6031)
AMBARELLA CORPORATION
3101 Jay St, Santa Clara (95054-3329)
PHONE.................................408 734-8888
EMP: 47 **EST:** 2004
SALES (est): 2MM
SALES (corp-wide): 222.9MM **Publicly Held**
WEB: www.ambarella.com
SIC: 3674 Semiconductors & related devices

PA: Ambarella, Inc.
3101 Jay St
Santa Clara CA 95054
408 734-8888

(P-6032)
AMBIOS TECHNOLOGY INC (PA)
1 Technology Dr, Milpitas (95035-7916)
PHONE.................................831 427-1160
Patrick O'Hara, *President*
▲ **EMP:** 22 **EST:** 1996
SQ FT: 5,800
SALES (est): 6.2MM **Privately Held**
WEB: www.kla-tencor.com
SIC: 3674 Semiconductors & related devices

(P-6033)
AMD FAR EAST LTD (HQ)
1 Amd Pl, Sunnyvale (94085-3905)
PHONE.................................408 749-4000
EMP: 361 **EST:** 1987
SALES (est): 4.1MM
SALES (corp-wide): 9.7B **Publicly Held**
WEB: www.amd.com
SIC: 3674 Integrated circuits, semiconductor networks, etc.
PA: Advanced Micro Devices, Inc.
2485 Augustine Dr
Santa Clara CA 95054
408 749-4000

(P-6034)
AMLOGIC INC
2518 Mission College Blvd, Santa Clara (95054-1239)
PHONE.................................408 850-9688
John Zhong, *President*
Xie James, *Vice Pres*
Yeeping Zhong, *Vice Pres*
Kedar Roy, *Technology*
Tim Yao, *Architect*
EMP: 20 **EST:** 1995
SALES (est): 4.2MM **Privately Held**
SIC: 3674 Integrated circuits, semiconductor networks, etc.

(P-6035)
AMPAC TECHNOLOGY CORPORATION
425 Market St Fl 22, San Francisco (94105-2532)
PHONE.................................415 912-2838
Allen Yue, *President*
EMP: 15 **EST:** 2002
SALES (est): 327.9K **Privately Held**
SIC: 3674 Computer logic modules

(P-6036)
ANALOG BITS
945 Stewart Dr, Sunnyvale (94085-3861)
PHONE.................................650 279-9323
Alan Rogers, *Owner*
Mahesh Tirupattur, *Exec VP*
Aarthi Ramadhas, *Engineer*
EMP: 30 **EST:** 1996
SALES (est): 4.5MM **Privately Held**
WEB: www.analogbits.com
SIC: 3674 Semiconductors & related devices

(P-6037)
ANALOGIX SEMICONDUCTOR INC
Also Called: PACIFIC ANALOGIX SEMICONDUCTOR
3211 Scott Blvd Ste 100, Santa Clara (95054-3009)
PHONE.................................408 988-8848
Kewei Yang, *Ch of Bd*
Bill Eichen, *President*
Patrick LI, *President*
Mike Seifert, *CFO*
Hing Chu, *Vice Pres*
▲ **EMP:** 24 **EST:** 2002
SALES (est): 93.7MM **Privately Held**
SIC: 3674 Integrated circuits, semiconductor networks, etc.

(P-6038)
APPLIED CERAMICS INC (PA)
48630 Milmont Dr, Fremont (94538-7253)
PHONE.................................510 249-9700
Matt Darko Sertic, *CEO*
David Kolaric, *CFO*
Roman Mischenko, *Exec VP*

Brandon Talaich, *CTO*
Hrnji Erves, *Prdtn Mgr*
▲ **EMP:** 134 **EST:** 1994
SQ FT: 57,000
SALES (est): 15.7MM **Privately Held**
WEB: www.appliedceramics.net
SIC: 3674 3264 Semiconductors & related devices; porcelain electrical supplies

(P-6039)
APPLIED FILMS CORPORATION
3050 Bowers Ave, Santa Clara (95054-3201)
PHONE.................................408 727-5555
Thomas T Edman, *President*
Richard P Beck, *Ch of Bd*
Lawrence D Firestone, *CFO*
Joachim Nell, *Exec VP*
James P Scholhamer, *Senior VP*
▲ **EMP:** 192 **EST:** 1994
SQ FT: 87,000
SALES (est): 7.2MM
SALES (corp-wide): 17.2B **Publicly Held**
WEB: www.appliedmaterials.com
SIC: 3674 Semiconductors & related devices
PA: Applied Materials, Inc.
3050 Bowers Ave Bldg 1
Santa Clara CA 95054
408 727-5555

(P-6040)
APPLIED MATERIALS INC
3340 Scott Blvd, Santa Clara (95054-3101)
PHONE.................................408 727-5555
Gary E Dickerson, *Branch Mgr*
Kyle Van Dusen, *QC Mgr*
Lance Mace, *Director*
Nathan Hanrahan, *Manager*
Daniel Herkalo, *Manager*
EMP: 56
SALES (corp-wide): 17.2B **Publicly Held**
WEB: www.appliedmaterials.com
SIC: 3674 Semiconductors & related devices
PA: Applied Materials, Inc.
3050 Bowers Ave Bldg 1
Santa Clara CA 95054
408 727-5555

(P-6041)
APPLIED MATERIALS INC
1700 E Pescadero Ave, Tracy (95304-8532)
PHONE.................................408 679-2925
EMP: 27
SALES (corp-wide): 17.2B **Publicly Held**
WEB: www.appliedmaterials.com
SIC: 3674 Semiconductors & related devices
PA: Applied Materials, Inc.
3050 Bowers Ave Bldg 1
Santa Clara CA 95054
408 727-5555

(P-6042)
APPLIED MATERIALS INC
974 E Arques Ave, Sunnyvale (94085-4520)
PHONE.................................408 727-5555
James Morgan, *Branch Mgr*
Pravin Narwankar, *Vice Pres*
Wayne Tu, *Info Tech Dir*
Walters Shen, *Info Tech Mgr*
Dave Dunne, *Software Engr*
EMP: 48
SALES (corp-wide): 17.2B **Publicly Held**
WEB: www.appliedmaterials.com
SIC: 3674 Semiconductors & related devices
PA: Applied Materials, Inc.
3050 Bowers Ave Bldg 1
Santa Clara CA 95054
408 727-5555

(P-6043)
APPLIED MATERIALS (HOLDINGS) (HQ)
3050 Bowers Ave, Santa Clara (95054-3298)
P.O. Box 58039 (95052-8039)
PHONE.................................408 727-5555
Michael R Splinter, *CEO*
Gary E Dickerson, *President*
George S Davise, *Exec VP*
Randhir Thakur, *Exec VP*

Joseph Flanagan, *Senior VP*
EMP: 223 **EST:** 1982
SALES: 9.7MM
SALES (corp-wide): 17.2B **Publicly Held**
WEB: www.appliedmaterials.com
SIC: 3674 Semiconductors & related devices
PA: Applied Materials, Inc.
3050 Bowers Ave Bldg 1
Santa Clara CA 95054
408 727-5555

(P-6044)
APPLIED MFR GROUP INC
941 George St, Santa Clara (95054-2706)
PHONE.................................408 855-8857
Ewa Gregorczuk, *President*
Jackie Ng, *COO*
EMP: 20 **EST:** 2003
SALES (est): 3.4MM **Privately Held**
WEB: www.appliedmaterials.com
SIC: 3674 3999 Semiconductors & related devices; barber & beauty shop equipment

(P-6045)
APPLIED MICRO CIRCUITS CORP (HQ)
4555 Great America Pkwy # 6, Santa Clara (95054-1243)
PHONE.................................408 542-8600
Paramesh Gopi, *President*
Martin S McDermut, *CFO*
L William Caraccio,
▲ **EMP:** 394 **EST:** 1979
SQ FT: 55,000
SALES (est): 159.2MM **Publicly Held**
WEB: www.macom.com
SIC: 3674 Microcircuits, integrated (semiconductor)

(P-6046)
APPLIED MTLS ASIA-PACIFIC LLC (HQ)
3050 Bowers Ave, Santa Clara (95054-3201)
PHONE.................................408 727-5555
Franz Janker, *President*
Kevin Odonnell, *Prgrmr*
EMP: 1059 **EST:** 1989
SQ FT: 3,000
SALES (est): 23.1MM
SALES (corp-wide): 17.2B **Publicly Held**
WEB: www.appliedmaterials.com
SIC: 3674 Semiconductors & related devices
PA: Applied Materials, Inc.
3050 Bowers Ave Bldg 1
Santa Clara CA 95054
408 727-5555

(P-6047)
AQUANTIA CORP (DH)
5488 Marvell Ln, Santa Clara (95054-3606)
PHONE.................................408 228-8300
Matt Murphy, *President*
Pirooz Parvarandeh, *COO*
Dmitry Akhanov, *Bd of Directors*
Anders Swahn, *Bd of Directors*
Lip-Bu Tan, *Bd of Directors*
EMP: 290 **EST:** 2004
SALES: 120.7MM
SALES (corp-wide): 682.9MM **Privately Held**
WEB: www.marvell.com
SIC: 3674 Semiconductors & related devices

(P-6048)
ARM INC (HQ)
150 Rose Orchard Way, San Jose (95134-1358)
PHONE.................................408 576-1500
Simon Segars, *CEO*
Pavan Bathla, *Partner*
Victoria Ingrey, *Partner*
David Seider, *Partner*
Graham Budd, *COO*
EMP: 270 **EST:** 1991
SQ FT: 54,489
SALES (est): 1B **Privately Held**
WEB: www.arminc.us
SIC: 3674 Integrated circuits, semiconductor networks, etc.

(PA)=Parent Co (HQ)=Headquarters (DH)=Div Headquarters
✪ = New Business established in last 2 years

3674 - Semiconductors County (P-6049)

(P-6049)
ARRIVE TECHNOLOGIES INC
3693 Westchester Dr, Roseville (95747-6353)
PHONE..................916 715-9775
Peter W Keeler, *Ch of Bd*
Murat Uraz, *President*
EMP: 15 **EST:** 2001
SALES (est): 11K **Privately Held**
WEB: www.arrivetechnologies.com
SIC: 3674 Integrated circuits, semiconductor networks, etc.

(P-6050)
ARTERIS INC (PA)
595 Millich Dr Ste 200, Campbell (95008-0550)
PHONE..................408 470-7300
Charles K Janac, *President*
Stephane Mehat, *CFO*
Joe Butler, *Vice Pres*
Bhavin Vaidya, *IT/INT Sup*
Farnaz Alim, *Technical Staff*
EMP: 38 **EST:** 2004
SQ FT: 6,287
SALES (est): 10.4MM **Publicly Held**
WEB: www.arteris.com
SIC: 3674 Semiconductors & related devices

(P-6051)
ARTERIS HOLDINGS INC
591 W Hamilton Ave # 250, Campbell (95008-0559)
PHONE..................408 470-7300
Charles K Janac, *President*
Nick Hawkins, *CFO*
Stephane Mehat, *CFO*
Khaled Labib, *Vice Pres*
Ty Garibay, *CTO*
EMP: 45 **EST:** 2007
SQ FT: 4,500
SALES (est): 5.1MM **Privately Held**
WEB: www.arteris.com
SIC: 3674 Semiconductors & related devices

(P-6052)
ASIC ADVANTAGE INC
3850 N 1st St, San Jose (95134-1702)
PHONE..................408 541-8686
EMP: 52
SQ FT: 20,077
SALES (est): 6.7MM **Privately Held**
WEB: www.asicadvantage.com
SIC: 3674 Mfg Semiconductors/Related Devices

(P-6053)
ATP ELECTRONICS INC
2590 N 1st St Ste 150, San Jose (95131-1049)
PHONE..................408 732-5000
Jeffray Hsieh, *CEO*
Dean Chang, *Ch of Bd*
Danny Lin, *Vice Pres*
Winnie Chan, *Human Res Dir*
Larry Farnam, *Sales Staff*
▲ **EMP:** 23
SQ FT: 10,000
SALES (est): 6.3MM **Privately Held**
WEB: www.atpinc.com
SIC: 3674 Semiconductors & related devices
PA: Atp Electronics Taiwan Inc.
10f, No. 185, Tiding Blvd., Sec. 2,
Taipei City TAP 11493

(P-6054)
AUXIN SOLAR INC
6835 Via Del Oro, San Jose (95119-1315)
PHONE..................408 225-4380
Sherry Tai, *CEO*
Mamum Rashid, *Vice Pres*
▲ **EMP:** 45 **EST:** 2008
SQ FT: 100,000
SALES (est): 9.6MM **Privately Held**
WEB: www.auxinsolar.com
SIC: 3674 Solar cells; modules, solid state

(P-6055)
AVAGO TECH WRELESS USA MFG LLC
1320 Ridder Park Dr, San Jose (95131-2313)
PHONE..................800 433-8778
Benjamin Yohe, *Engineer*
EMP: 49 **EST:** 2017
SALES (est): 17.3MM
SALES (corp-wide): 23.8B **Publicly Held**
WEB: www.broadcom.com
SIC: 3674 Semiconductors & related devices
HQ: Broadcom Corporation
1320 Ridder Park Dr
San Jose CA 95131

(P-6056)
AVAGO TECHNOLOGIES US INC
1730 Fox Dr, San Jose (95131-2311)
PHONE..................408 433-4068
Hock E Tan, *Branch Mgr*
EMP: 1218
SALES (corp-wide): 23.8B **Publicly Held**
SIC: 3674 Semiconductors & related devices
HQ: Avago Technologies U.S. Inc.
1320 Ridder Park Dr
San Jose CA 95131

(P-6057)
AVAGO TECHNOLOGIES US INC
350 W Trimble Rd, San Jose (95131-1008)
PHONE..................408 435-7400
EMP: 17
SALES (corp-wide): 23.8B **Publicly Held**
WEB: www.broadcom.com
SIC: 3674 Mfg Semiconductors/Related Devices
HQ: Avago Technologies U.S. Inc.
1320 Ridder Park Dr
San Jose CA 95131

(P-6058)
AVAGO TECHNOLOGIES US INC (HQ)
1320 Ridder Park Dr, San Jose (95131-2313)
P.O. Box 3643, Santa Clara (95055-3643)
PHONE..................800 433-8778
Hock Tan, *President*
Dick Chang, *Ch of Bd*
Douglas Bettinger, *CFO*
Kristen Spears, *CFO*
Jeff Henderson, *Senior VP*
▲ **EMP:** 400 **EST:** 2005
SALES (est): 1.3B
SALES (corp-wide): 23.8B **Publicly Held**
WEB: www.broadcom.com
SIC: 3674 5065 Semiconductor diodes & rectifiers; semiconductor devices
PA: Broadcom Inc.
1320 Ridder Park Dr
San Jose CA 95131
408 433-8000

(P-6059)
AVALANCHE TECHNOLOGY INC
3450 W Warren Ave, Fremont (94538-6425)
PHONE..................510 438-0148
Petro Estakhri, *President*
Bob Netter, *CFO*
Ebrahim Abedifard, *Vice Pres*
Haidari Hamid, *Vice Pres*
Yiming Huai, *Vice Pres*
EMP: 25 **EST:** 2006
SALES (est): 5.1MM **Privately Held**
WEB: www.avalanche-technology.com
SIC: 3674 Magnetic bubble memory device

(P-6060)
AXIS GROUP INC
1220 Whipple Rd, Union City (94587-2026)
P.O. Box 1192 (94587-1192)
PHONE..................510 487-7393
Kofi A Tawiah, *President*
EMP: 31 **EST:** 1989
SQ FT: 15,000
SALES (est): 1MM **Privately Held**
WEB: www.e3systems.com
SIC: 3674 Semiconductors & related devices

(P-6061)
AXT INC
Also Called: American Etal Technology
4311 Solar Way, Fremont (94538-6389)
PHONE..................510 683-5900
Maureen Wang, *Manager*
Leonard Leblanc, *Bd of Directors*
Raymond Low, *Vice Pres*
Bob Ochrym, *VP Bus Dvlpt*
EMP: 764
SALES (corp-wide): 95.3MM **Publicly Held**
WEB: www.axt.com
SIC: 3674 Integrated circuits, semiconductor networks, etc.
PA: Axt, Inc.
4281 Technology Dr
Fremont CA 94538
510 438-4700

(P-6062)
AXT INC (PA)
4281 Technology Dr, Fremont (94538-6339)
PHONE..................510 438-4700
Morris S Young, *CEO*
Jesse Chen, *Ch of Bd*
Gary L Fischer, *CFO*
▲ **EMP:** 27 **EST:** 1986
SQ FT: 19,467
SALES (est): 95.3MM **Publicly Held**
WEB: www.axt.com
SIC: 3674 Semiconductors & related devices; integrated circuits, semiconductor networks, etc.; diodes, solid state (germanium, silicon, etc.)

(P-6063)
AXT-TONGMEI INC
4281 Technology Dr, Fremont (94538-6339)
PHONE..................510 438-4700
Dr Morris Young, *CEO*
Alan Chan, *Controller*
EMP: 26 **EST:** 2020
SALES (est): 53MM
SALES (corp-wide): 95.3MM **Publicly Held**
WEB: www.axt.com
SIC: 3674 Semiconductor diodes & rectifiers
PA: Axt, Inc.
4281 Technology Dr
Fremont CA 94538
510 438-4700

(P-6064)
AZIMUTH INDUSTRIAL CO INC
Also Called: Azimuth Semiconductor Assembly
30593 Un Cy Blvd Ste 110, Union City (94587)
PHONE..................510 441-6000
David Lee, *President*
Sandra Lee, *Officer*
Sunny Tseng, *Accountant*
Panny Hsu, *Manager*
▲ **EMP:** 20 **EST:** 1988
SQ FT: 16,000
SALES (est): 3.1MM **Privately Held**
WEB: www.azimuthsemi.com
SIC: 3674 Semiconductors & related devices

(P-6065)
BAE SYSTEMS IMGING SLTIONS INC
1841 Zanker Rd Ste 50, San Jose (95112-4223)
PHONE..................408 433-2500
Kwang Bo Cho, *President*
Steve Onishi, *VP Engrg*
Victoria Madamba, *Project Mgr*
Alberto Magnani, *Technical Staff*
George Wang, *Engineer*
EMP: 99 **EST:** 2001
SQ FT: 60,000
SALES (est): 22.8MM
SALES (corp-wide): 25.6B **Privately Held**
WEB: www.fairchildimaging.com
SIC: 3674 3577 Semiconductors & related devices; computer peripheral equipment
HQ: Bae Systems Information And Electronic Systems Integration Inc.
65 Spit Brook Rd
Nashua NH 03060
603 885-4321

(P-6066)
BERKELEY DESIGN AUTOMATION INC
46871 Bayside Pkwy, Fremont (94538-6572)
PHONE..................408 496-6600
EMP: 25
SQ FT: 25,000
SALES (est): 2.6MM **Privately Held**
WEB: www.new.siemens.com
SIC: 3674 Integrated Circuits

(P-6067)
BIPOLARICS INC
45920 Sentinel Pl, Fremont (94539-6942)
PHONE..................408 372-7574
Dr Charles Leung, *President*
Colin Levy, *Treasurer*
Jessica Leung, *Controller*
EMP: 16 **EST:** 1988
SALES (est): 1.1MM **Privately Held**
WEB: www.bipolaricsinc.business.site
SIC: 3674 3677 Integrated circuits, semiconductor networks, etc.; electronic coils, transformers & other inductors

(P-6068)
BLAIZE INC (PA)
4370 Town Center Blvd # 24, El Dorado Hills (95762-7140)
PHONE..................916 347-0050
Dinakar C Munagala, *CEO*
Dado Banatao, *Bd of Directors*
Tony Cannestra, *Bd of Directors*
Santiago Fernandez, *Vice Pres*
Santiago Fernandez-Gomez, *Vice Pres*
EMP: 297 **EST:** 2011
SALES (est): 28.1MM **Privately Held**
WEB: www.blaize.com
SIC: 3674 Semiconductors & related devices

(P-6069)
BLOOM ENERGY CORPORATION (PA)
4353 N 1st St, San Jose (95134-1259)
PHONE..................408 543-1500
K R Sridhar, *Ch of Bd*
Susan Brennan, *COO*
Gregory Cameron, *CFO*
Mary Bush, *Bd of Directors*
Matt Ross, *Chief Mktg Ofcr*
▲ **EMP:** 300 **EST:** 2001
SQ FT: 181,000
SALES (est): 794.2MM **Publicly Held**
WEB: www.bloomenergy.com
SIC: 3674 Fuel cells, solid state

(P-6070)
BOLB INC
52 Wright Brothers Ave, Livermore (94551-9496)
PHONE..................925 453-6293
Ling Zhou, *CEO*
EMP: 15 **EST:** 2014
SALES (est): 3.3MM **Privately Held**
WEB: www.bolb.co
SIC: 3674 3641 Light emitting diodes; health lamps, infrared or ultraviolet

(P-6071)
BRIDGELUX INC
46410 Fremont Blvd, Fremont (94538-6469)
PHONE..................925 583-8400
Tim Lester, *CEO*
Bradley J Bullington, *COO*
Mark Van Den Berg, *Vice Pres*
Fs Chang, *Vice Pres*
Brian Cumpston, *Vice Pres*
▲ **EMP:** 90 **EST:** 2008
SALES (est): 18.4MM **Privately Held**
WEB: www.bridgelux.com
SIC: 3674 Light emitting diodes

PRODUCTS & SERVICES SECTION
3674 - Semiconductors County (P-6092)

(P-6072)
BROADCOM CORPORATION
250 Innovation Dr, San Jose (95134-3390)
PHONE.................................408 922-7000
Carol Barrett, *Branch Mgr*
Don Bird, *Sr Ntwrk Engine*
Albert Chin, *Info Tech Dir*
Raphy Alamparambil, *Software Engr*
Alberto Campos, *Design Engr*
EMP: 39
SALES (corp-wide): 23.8B **Publicly Held**
WEB: www.broadcom.com
SIC: 3674 Integrated circuits, semiconductor networks, etc.
HQ: Broadcom Corporation
1320 Ridder Park Dr
San Jose CA 95131

(P-6073)
BROADCOM CORPORATION (HQ)
1320 Ridder Park Dr, San Jose (95131-2313)
P.O. Box 57013, Irvine (92619-7013)
PHONE.................................408 433-8000
Hock Tan, *CEO*
Anthony Maslowski, *CFO*
Vijay Janapaty, *Vice Pres*
Asad Khamisy, *Vice Pres*
Leo Kaplan, *Associate Dir*
▲ **EMP:** 1259 **EST:** 1991
SALES (est): 2.4B
SALES (corp-wide): 23.8B **Publicly Held**
WEB: www.broadcom.com
SIC: 3674 Integrated circuits, semiconductor networks, etc.
PA: Broadcom Inc.
1320 Ridder Park Dr
San Jose CA 95131
408 433-8000

(P-6074)
BROADCOM INC (PA)
1320 Ridder Park Dr, San Jose (95131-2313)
PHONE.................................408 433-8000
Hock E Tan, *President*
Henry Samueli, *Ch of Bd*
Thomas H Krause Jr, *President*
Ch:arlie B Kawwas, *COO*
Kirsten M Spears, *CFO*
EMP: 262 **EST:** 2005
SALES (est): 23.8B **Publicly Held**
WEB: www.broadcom.com
SIC: 3674 Semiconductor diodes & rectifiers

(P-6075)
BROADCOM TECHNOLOGIES INC (HQ)
1320 Ridder Park Dr, San Jose (95131-2313)
PHONE.................................408 433-8000
David Brown, *Exec VP*
Dave Patel, *Principal*
Chau Huynh, *Design Engr*
Mark Wang, *Technology*
Saket Bhide, *Engineer*
EMP: 773 **EST:** 2018
SALES (est): 4.1MM
SALES (corp-wide): 23.8B **Publicly Held**
WEB: www.broadcom.com
SIC: 3674 Semiconductors & related devices
PA: Broadcom Inc.
1320 Ridder Park Dr
San Jose CA 95131
408 433-8000

(P-6076)
BROADLIGHT INC
2901 Tasman Dr Ste 218, Santa Clara (95054-1138)
PHONE.................................408 982-4210
Raanan Gewirtzman, *CEO*
Dror Heldenberg, *CFO*
Didi Ivancovsky, *Vice Pres*
Eli Weitz, *CTO*
EMP: 68 **EST:** 2003
SALES (est): 8.5MM
SALES (corp-wide): 23.8B **Publicly Held**
WEB: www.broadcom.com
SIC: 3674 Semiconductors & related devices

HQ: Broadcom Corporation
1320 Ridder Park Dr
San Jose CA 95131

(P-6077)
C & D SEMICONDUCTOR SVCS INC (PA)
Also Called: C&D Precision Machining
2031 Concourse Dr, San Jose (95131-1727)
PHONE.................................408 383-1888
Dong Van Nguyen, *CEO*
Dong Nguyen, *Vice Pres*
Tien Nguyen, *Vice Pres*
Thanh Truong, *Design Engr*
Thuy Truong, *Design Engr*
◆ **EMP:** 45 **EST:** 1990
SQ FT: 3,600
SALES (est): 10.8MM **Privately Held**
WEB: www.cdsemi.com
SIC: 3674 Semiconductors & related devices

(P-6078)
CA INC
1320 Ridder Park Dr, San Jose (95131-2313)
PHONE.................................408 433-8000
EMP: 100
SALES (corp-wide): 23.8B **Publicly Held**
WEB: www.broadcom.com
SIC: 3674 Semiconductors & related devices
HQ: Ca, Inc.
520 Madison Ave
New York NY 10022
800 225-5224

(P-6079)
CAMTEK USA INC
48389 Fremont Blvd # 112, Fremont (94538-6558)
PHONE.................................510 624-9905
Cathy Hamilton, *Principal*
Amy Zhong, *Treasurer*
Tommy Weiss, *Vice Pres*
EMP: 28 **EST:** 1997
SQ FT: 10,000
SALES (est): 6MM **Privately Held**
WEB: www.camtek.com
SIC: 3674 Integrated circuits, semiconductor networks, etc.
PA: Camtek Ltd
7 Haarig
Migdal Haemek 23094

(P-6080)
CAVIUM LLC (DH)
5488 Marvell Ln, Santa Clara (95054-3606)
P.O. Box 67151, Scotts Valley (95067-7151)
PHONE.................................408 222-2500
Jean Hu, *President*
Bradley Buss, *Bd of Directors*
Raj Singh, *Vice Pres*
Edward Wee, *General Mgr*
Diane Donnell, *Office Mgr*
EMP: 281 **EST:** 2000
SALES: 984MM
SALES (corp-wide): 682.9MM **Privately Held**
WEB: www.cavium.com
SIC: 3674 Semiconductors & related devices

(P-6081)
CAVIUM NETWORKS INTL INC (DH)
2315 N 1st St, San Jose (95131-1010)
PHONE.................................650 625-7000
Syed Ali, *CEO*
Rakesh Bindlish, *General Mgr*
Raj Singh, *General Mgr*
Amit Madupu, *Engrg Dir*
Iqbal Rana, *Technology*
EMP: 78 **EST:** 2005
SALES (est): 22.5MM
SALES (corp-wide): 682.9MM **Privately Held**
WEB: www.cavium.com
SIC: 3674 Semiconductor diodes & rectifiers

(P-6082)
CHRONTEL INC (PA)
2210 Otoole Ave Ste 100, San Jose (95131-1300)
PHONE.................................408 383-9328
Bruce Wooley, *Ch of Bd*
David C SOO, *President*
John Milner, *COO*
James Lin, *CFO*
Demonder Chan, *Officer*
EMP: 70 **EST:** 1986
SQ FT: 40,000
SALES (est): 10.9MM **Privately Held**
WEB: www.chrontel.com
SIC: 3674 8711 Integrated circuits, semiconductor networks, etc.; engineering services

(P-6083)
CNEX LABS INC (PA)
2880 Stevens Creek Blvd # 300, San Jose (95128-4608)
PHONE.................................408 695-1045
Alan Armstrong, *CEO*
Kenny Coker, *Vice Pres*
Joe Defranco, *Vice Pres*
Ronnie Huang, *Vice Pres*
Kyoungryun Bae, *Technical Staff*
EMP: 50 **EST:** 2013
SALES (est): 10MM **Privately Held**
WEB: www.cnexlabs.com
SIC: 3674 Semiconductors & related devices

(P-6084)
COMPUGRAPHICS USA INC (HQ)
43455 Osgood Rd, Fremont (94539-5609)
PHONE.................................510 249-2600
Lawrence Amon, *President*
Mark Crownover, *Administration*
Mark Nehrenz, *Info Tech Mgr*
Joe Lister, *Database Admin*
EMP: 56 **EST:** 1983
SQ FT: 25,000
SALES (est): 11.2MM
SALES (corp-wide): 1.8B **Publicly Held**
WEB: www.compsus.com
SIC: 3674 Integrated circuits, semiconductor networks, etc.
PA: Element Solutions Inc
500 E Broward Blvd # 1860
Fort Lauderdale FL 33394
561 207-9600

(P-6085)
CONCEPT SYSTEMS MFG INC
2047 Zanker Rd, San Jose (95131-2107)
PHONE.................................408 855-8595
Richard Diehl, *President*
Christie Shannon, *CFO*
Perry Hough, *Engrg Dir*
▲ **EMP:** 21 **EST:** 2006
SALES (est): 3MM **Privately Held**
WEB: www.csmanufacturing.net
SIC: 3674 Semiconductors & related devices

(P-6086)
CONDOR RELIABILITY SVCS INC
2175 De La Cruz Blvd, Santa Clara (95050-3036)
PHONE.................................408 486-9600
Punam Patel, *President*
Tushar Patel, *Executive*
EMP: 21 **EST:** 1980
SQ FT: 5,000
SALES (est): 1.8MM **Privately Held**
WEB: www.crsigroup.com
SIC: 3674 8999 8734 8731 Semiconductors & related devices; weather related services; testing laboratories; commercial physical research

(P-6087)
CONTECH SOLUTIONS INCORPORATED
631 Montague St, San Leandro (94577-4323)
PHONE.................................510 357-7900
Afshin Nouri, *President*
Mehran Jafarcadeh, *Vice Pres*
Nicole Scott, *Office Mgr*
Mehran Jafarzaden, *Info Tech Mgr*
Jafarzaden Mehran, *Director*

EMP: 21 **EST:** 1995
SQ FT: 4,000
SALES (est): 2.6MM **Privately Held**
WEB: www.contechsolutions.com
SIC: 3674 Semiconductors & related devices

(P-6088)
CORE SYSTEMS INCORPORATED
47757 Warm Springs Blvd, Fremont (94539-7470)
PHONE.................................510 933-2300
Donald W Lindsey, *CEO*
Walter J Wriggins, *President*
Steve Lindsey, *Treasurer*
Lynda Jones, *Mktg Dir*
▲ **EMP:** 25 **EST:** 1990
SQ FT: 14,095
SALES (est): 6.7MM **Privately Held**
WEB: www.ii-vi.com
SIC: 3674 Semiconductors & related devices

(P-6089)
CORPORATECOUCH
Also Called: Corp Couch
260 Vicente St, San Francisco (94127-1331)
PHONE.................................415 312-6078
EMP: 25
SALES (est): 2MM **Privately Held**
SIC: 3674 Mfg Semiconductors/Related Devices

(P-6090)
CORSAIR MEMORY INC
47100 Bayside Pkwy, Fremont (94538-6563)
PHONE.................................510 657-8747
Andrew J Paul, *President*
Liz Wallsom, *Sales Mgr*
Kevin Gao, *Manager*
EMP: 150
SALES (corp-wide): 1.7B **Publicly Held**
WEB: www.corsair.com
SIC: 3674 7373 8731 Memories, solid state; computer integrated systems design; computer (hardware) development
HQ: Corsair Memory, Inc.
47100 Bayside Pkwy
Fremont CA 94538

(P-6091)
CORSAIR MEMORY INC (HQ)
47100 Bayside Pkwy, Fremont (94538-6563)
PHONE.................................510 657-8747
Andrew J Paul, *President*
Ronald Van Veen, *Vice Pres*
Don Lieberman, *CTO*
Adam Steinberg, *Technical Staff*
Caren Bautista, *Analyst*
◆ **EMP:** 149 **EST:** 2007
SQ FT: 44,000
SALES (est): 132.1MM
SALES (corp-wide): 1.7B **Publicly Held**
WEB: www.corsair.com
SIC: 3674 7373 8731 Memories, solid state; computer integrated systems design; computer (hardware) development
PA: Corsair Gaming, Inc.
47100 Bayside Pkwy
Fremont CA 94538
510 657-8747

(P-6092)
CORTINA SYSTEMS INC (DH)
2953 Bunker Hill Ln # 300, Santa Clara (95054-1131)
PHONE.................................408 481-2300
Amir Nayyerhabibi, *President*
Bruce Margtson, *CFO*
EMP: 120 **EST:** 2001
SQ FT: 41,645
SALES (est): 104.5MM
SALES (corp-wide): 682.9MM **Privately Held**
WEB: www.marvell.com
SIC: 3674 Integrated circuits, semiconductor networks, etc.
HQ: Inphi Corporation
110 Rio Robles
San Jose CA 95134
408 217-7300

(PA)=Parent Co (HQ)=Headquarters (DH)=Div Headquarters
✪ = New Business established in last 2 years

3674 - Semiconductors County (P-6093)

(P-6093)
CROSSBAR INC
3200 Patrick Henry Dr # 110, Santa Clara (95054-1865)
PHONE.................................408 884-0281
George Minassian, *CEO*
Sundar Narayanan, *Vice Pres*
Hagop Nazarian, *Vice Pres*
Sylvain Dubois, *VP Bus Dvlpt*
Zorina Mercado, *Executive Asst*
EMP: 20 **EST:** 2008
SALES (est): 4.6MM **Privately Held**
WEB: www.crossbar-inc.com
SIC: 3674 Semiconductors & related devices

(P-6094)
CYOPTICS INC
1320 Ridder Park Dr, San Jose (95131-2313)
PHONE.................................408 433-7343
EMP: 19 **EST:** 2018
SALES (est): 11.4MM
SALES (corp-wide): 23.8B **Publicly Held**
WEB: www.broadcom.com
SIC: 3674 Semiconductors & related devices
HQ: Broadcom Corporation
1320 Ridder Park Dr
San Jose CA 95131

(P-6095)
CYPRESS SEMICONDUCTOR CORP (HQ)
198 Champion Ct, San Jose (95134-1709)
PHONE.................................408 943-2600
Hassane El-Khoury, *President*
Robert Lefort, *President*
Jack Artman, *CFO*
Sabbas Daniel, *Exec VP*
James Nulty, *Vice Pres*
◆ **EMP:** 650 **EST:** 2019
SQ FT: 171,370
SALES: 2.2B
SALES (corp-wide): 10.1B **Privately Held**
WEB: www.cypress.com
SIC: 3674 Semiconductors & related devices
PA: Infineon Technologies Ag
Am Campeon 1-15
Neubiberg BY 85579
892 340-

(P-6096)
CYPRESS SEMICONDUCTOR INTL INC (DH)
4001 N 1st St, San Jose (95134-1503)
PHONE.................................408 943-2600
Neil Weiss, *Vice Pres*
Vijay Kadam, *IT/INT Sup*
Rochelle Arreola, *Engineer*
Tomasz Cewe, *Engineer*
Toan Ong, *Engineer*
EMP: 234 **EST:** 1982
SALES (est): 10.7MM
SALES (corp-wide): 10.1B **Privately Held**
WEB: www.cypress.com
SIC: 3674 Semiconductors & related devices
HQ: Cypress Semiconductor Corporation
198 Champion Ct
San Jose CA 95134
408 943-2600

(P-6097)
D-TEK MANUFACTURING
3245 Woodward Ave, Santa Clara (95054-2626)
PHONE.................................408 588-1574
Dung Nguyen, *President*
Thanh L Dang, *Vice Pres*
EMP: 20 **EST:** 2010
SQ FT: 5,000
SALES (est): 4.2MM **Privately Held**
WEB: www.d-tekmfg.com
SIC: 3674 Semiconductors & related devices

(P-6098)
DAYSTAR TECHNOLOGIES INC
1010 S Milpitas Blvd, Milpitas (95035-6307)
PHONE.................................408 582-7100
Tina Carrillo, *Branch Mgr*
EMP: 60
SALES (corp-wide): 10.4MM **Privately Held**
WEB: www.daystartech.com
SIC: 3674 Solar cells
PA: Daystar Technologies Inc.
3556 Alvarado Niles Rd S
Union City CA 94587
408 582-7100

(P-6099)
DIALOG SEMICONDUCTOR INC (DH)
2560 Mission College Blvd # 110, Santa Clara (95054-1217)
P.O. Box 2369, Clifton NJ (07015-2369)
PHONE.................................408 845-8500
Jalal Bagherli, *CEO*
Karim Arabi, *Vice Pres*
Andrew Austin, *Vice Pres*
Jim Caravella, *Vice Pres*
Christophe Chene, *Vice Pres*
EMP: 224 **EST:** 1998
SALES (est): 52.2MM
SALES (corp-wide): 1.3B **Privately Held**
WEB: www.dialog-semiconductor.com
SIC: 3674 Semiconductors & related devices
HQ: Dialog Semiconductor Gmbh
Neue Str. 95
Kirchheim Unter Teck BW 73230
702 180-50

(P-6100)
DOLPHIN TECHNOLOGY INC
333 W Santa Clara St # 9, San Jose (95113-1713)
PHONE.................................408 392-0012
Mohammad Tamjidi, *President*
John Atkinson, *CFO*
Sushil Panda, *Engineer*
Yongchao Xu, *Engineer*
Joe Giordano, *Analyst*
EMP: 31 **EST:** 1996
SALES (est): 3.5MM **Privately Held**
WEB: www.dolphin-ic.com
SIC: 3674 Semiconductors & related devices

(P-6101)
DREAMBIG SEMICONDUCTOR INC
2860 Zanker Rd Ste 210, San Jose (95134-2120)
PHONE.................................408 839-1232
Sohail A Syed, *CEO*
EMP: 75 **EST:** 2019
SALES (est): 3.9MM **Privately Held**
WEB: www.dreambigsemi.com
SIC: 3674 Semiconductor circuit networks

(P-6102)
DSP GROUP INC (PA)
2055 Gateway Pl Ste 480, San Jose (95110-1019)
PHONE.................................408 986-4300
Ofer Elyakim, *CEO*
Kenneth H Traub, *Ch of Bd*
Dror Levy, *CFO*
EMP: 67 **EST:** 1987
SQ FT: 1,723
SALES (est): 114.4MM **Publicly Held**
WEB: www.dspg.com
SIC: 3674 7371 Integrated circuits, semiconductor networks, etc.; computer software development

(P-6103)
DUST NETWORKS INC
32990 Alvarado Niles Rd, Union City (94587-8106)
PHONE.................................510 400-2900
Joy Weiss, *President*
Eva Chen, *Vice Pres*
Brenda Glaze, *Vice Pres*
Dave Lynch, *Vice Pres*
EMP: 67 **EST:** 2002
SQ FT: 15,000
SALES (est): 16.1MM
SALES (corp-wide): 5.6B **Publicly Held**
WEB: www.analog.com
SIC: 3674 Semiconductors & related devices
HQ: Linear Technology Llc
1630 Mccarthy Blvd
Milpitas CA 95035
408 432-1900

(P-6104)
DYNAMIC INTGRTED SOLUTIONS LLC
1710 Fortune Dr, San Jose (95131-1744)
PHONE.................................408 727-3400
Eric Hummel, *Director*
EMP: 17 **Privately Held**
WEB: www.dynamicsolutionsusa.com
SIC: 3674 Semiconductors & related devices
PA: Dynamic Integrated Solutions Llc
3964 Rivermark Plz # 104
Santa Clara CA 95054

(P-6105)
DYNAMIC INTGRTED SOLUTIONS LLC (PA)
3964 Rivermark Plz # 104, Santa Clara (95054-4155)
PHONE.................................408 727-3400
David Diep,
Pratity Jani, *HR Admin*
EMP: 29 **EST:** 2006
SALES (est): 7.5MM **Privately Held**
WEB: www.dynamicsolutionsusa.com
SIC: 3674 Semiconductors & related devices

(P-6106)
EDGEQ INC
2550 Great America Way # 3, Santa Clara (95054-1159)
PHONE.................................408 209-0368
Vinay Ravuri, *CEO*
EMP: 20 **EST:** 2018
SALES (est): 3.1MM **Privately Held**
WEB: www.edgecompute.io
SIC: 3674 Semiconductors & related devices

(P-6107)
EG SYSTEMS LLC (PA)
Also Called: Electroglas
6200 Village Pkwy, Dublin (94568-3004)
PHONE.................................510 324-0126
Raj Kaul, *Mng Member*
▲ **EMP:** 59 **EST:** 2009
SALES (est): 1.2MM **Privately Held**
SIC: 3674 Semiconductors & related devices

(P-6108)
ELEMENTCXI
25 E Trimble Rd, San Jose (95131-1108)
PHONE.................................408 935-8090
EMP: 20
SALES (est): 2.4MM **Privately Held**
WEB: www.elementcxi.com
SIC: 3674 Mfg Semiconductors/Related Devices

(P-6109)
ENDWAVE DEFENSE SYSTEMS INC (DH)
130 Baytech Dr, San Jose (95134-2302)
PHONE.................................408 522-3180
Ed Keible, *CEO*
David M Hall, *Senior VP*
EMP: 100 **EST:** 1986
SQ FT: 15,000
SALES (est): 4.8MM **Privately Held**
SIC: 3674 Semiconductors & related devices

(P-6110)
ENERPARC CA3 LLC
1999 Harrison St Ste 830, Oakland (94612-4707)
PHONE.................................844 367-7272
Florent Abadie,
EMP: 15 **EST:** 2014
SQ FT: 2,000
SALES (est): 100K **Privately Held**
SIC: 3674 Solar cells

(P-6111)
ENFABRICA CORPORATION
295 Bernardo Ave Ste 200, Mountain View (94043-5205)
PHONE.................................650 206-8533
Rochan Sankar, *President*
EMP: 30 **EST:** 2020
SALES (est): 2MM **Privately Held**
SIC: 3674 Semiconductors & related devices

(P-6112)
ENPHASE ENERGY INC (PA)
47281 Bayside Pkwy, Fremont (94538-6517)
PHONE.................................707 774-7000
Jennifer Sayre, *Partner*
Badrinarayanan Kothandaraman, *President*
Jeffrey McNeil, *COO*
Eric Branderiz, *CFO*
David Ranhoff, *Ch Credit Ofcr*
▲ **EMP:** 825 **EST:** 2006
SQ FT: 40,446
SALES (est): 774.4MM **Publicly Held**
WEB: www.enphase.com
SIC: 3674 Semiconductors & related devices

(P-6113)
ENVIRON-CLEAN TECHNOLOGY INC
Also Called: Environ Clean Technology
1710 Ringwood Ave, San Jose (95131-1711)
PHONE.................................408 487-1770
EMP: 16
SALES (corp-wide): 332.4MM **Privately Held**
SIC: 3674 Mfg Semiconductors/Related Devices
HQ: Environ-Clean Technology Inc
3844 E University Dr # 2
Phoenix AZ 85034
602 438-9131

(P-6114)
ESILICON CORPORATION (DH)
2953 Bunker Hill Ln # 300, Santa Clara (95054-1131)
PHONE.................................408 217-7300
Seth Neiman, *Ch of Bd*
Jens Andersen, *President*
Jack Harding, *President*
Hugh Durdan, *COO*
Dennis Hollenbeck, *COO*
EMP: 187 **EST:** 1999
SALES (est): 53.6MM
SALES (corp-wide): 682.9MM **Privately Held**
WEB: www.marvell.com
SIC: 3674 Integrated circuits, semiconductor networks, etc.; hybrid integrated circuits
HQ: Inphi Corporation
110 Rio Robles
San Jose CA 95134
408 217-7300

(P-6115)
ESPERANTO TECHNOLOGIES INC (PA)
800 W El Cmino Real Ste 4, Mountain View (94040)
PHONE.................................650 319-7357
Art Swift, *CEO*
Nick Aretakis, *Vice Pres*
David Glasco, *Vice Pres*
EMP: 99 **EST:** 2014
SALES (est): 6.3MM **Privately Held**
WEB: www.esperanto.ai
SIC: 3674 7371 Integrated circuits, semiconductor networks, etc.; computer software development

(P-6116)
ESS TECHNOLOGY HOLDINGS INC (HQ)
109 Bonaventura Dr, San Jose (95134-2106)
PHONE.................................408 643-8818
Robert L Blair, *President*
Robert Plachno, *President*
John A Marsh, *CFO*
Dan Christman, *Chief Mktg Ofcr*
Peter Frith, *Officer*

PRODUCTS & SERVICES SECTION

3674 - Semiconductors County (P-6138)

▲ **EMP:** 45 **EST:** 1984
SALES (est): 28.5MM **Privately Held**
WEB: www.esstech.com
SIC: 3674 Microcircuits, integrated (semiconductor); semiconductor circuit networks

(P-6117)
EXAR CORPORATION (HQ)
1060 Rincon Cir, San Jose (95131-1325)
PHONE..................669 265-6100
Ryan A Benton, *CEO*
Keith Tainsky, *CFO*
Diane Hill, *Vice Pres*
Edward Yang, *Vice Pres*
Sherry Lin,
EMP: 184 **EST:** 1971
SQ FT: 151,000
SALES (est): 51.8MM
SALES (corp-wide): 478.6MM **Publicly Held**
WEB: www.maxlinear.com
SIC: 3674 Integrated circuits, semiconductor networks, etc.; metal oxide silicon (MOS) devices; microcircuits, integrated (semiconductor)
PA: Maxlinear, Inc.
  5966 La Place Ct Ste 100
  Carlsbad CA 92008
  760 692-0711

(P-6118)
EXCLARA INC
4701 Patrick Henry Dr, Santa Clara (95054-1819)
PHONE..................408 329-9319
Shrichand Dodani, *President*
Stephanie Leung, *CFO*
Anwar Aslam, *Engineer*
▲ **EMP:** 16 **EST:** 2006
SALES (est): 833.7K **Privately Held**
WEB: www.exclara.com
SIC: 3674 3677 Semiconductors & related devices; transformers power supply, electronic type

(P-6119)
FAIRCHILD SEMICDTR INTL INC (HQ)
Also Called: On Semiconductor
1272 Borregas Ave, Sunnyvale (94089-1310)
PHONE..................408 822-2000
Keith D Jackson, *President*
Sik-Han Soh, *Vice Chairman*
William A Schromm, *COO*
Bernard Gutmann, *CFO*
George H Cave, *Exec VP*
EMP: 1654 **EST:** 1959
SALES (est): 1B
SALES (corp-wide): 5.2B **Publicly Held**
WEB: www.onsemi.com
SIC: 3674 Semiconductors & related devices
PA: On Semiconductor Corporation
  5005 E Mcdowell Rd
  Phoenix AZ 85008
  602 244-6200

(P-6120)
FLEXTRONICS SEMICONDUCTOR (DH)
2241 Lundy Ave Bldg 2, San Jose (95131-1822)
PHONE..................408 576-7000
Ash Bhardwaj, *President*
Duncan Robertson, *Vice Pres*
Dean Kennedy, *Program Mgr*
Melvin Agustin, *Network Tech*
Dawn Collier, *Director*
EMP: 40 **EST:** 1976
SQ FT: 54,000
SALES (est): 39.4MM **Privately Held**
SIC: 3674 8711 Semiconductors & related devices; engineering services

(P-6121)
FOCUS ENHANCEMENTS INC (DH)
Also Called: Focus Enhncments Systems Group
931 Benecia Ave, Sunnyvale (94085-2805)
PHONE..................650 230-2400
Brett A Moyer, *President*
Gary Williams, *CFO*

▲ **EMP:** 100 **EST:** 1992
SQ FT: 27,500
SALES (est): 13.4MM **Privately Held**
WEB: www.vitec.com
SIC: 3674 3861 Semiconductors & related devices; editing equipment, motion picture: viewers, splicers, etc.
HQ: Vitec Multimedia, Inc.
  2200 Century Pkwy Ne # 900
  Atlanta GA 30345
  404 320-0110

(P-6122)
FORMFACTOR INC (PA)
7005 Southfront Rd, Livermore (94551-8201)
PHONE..................925 290-4000
Michael D Slessor, *CEO*
Thomas St Dennis, *Ch of Bd*
Shai Shahar, *CFO*
Tom Begley, *Vice Pres*
Tony Cellucci, *Vice Pres*
▲ **EMP:** 200 **EST:** 1993
SQ FT: 168,636
SALES (est): 693.6MM **Publicly Held**
WEB: www.formfactor.com
SIC: 3674 3825 Semiconductors & related devices; thermoelectric devices, solid state; instruments to measure electricity

(P-6123)
FORTEMEDIA INC (PA)
4051 Burton Dr, Santa Clara (95054-1585)
PHONE..................408 716-8028
Paul Huang, *CEO*
Scott Yang, *Vice Pres*
Xiaoyan Lu, *Senior Mgr*
Harry Liu, *Regional*
▼ **EMP:** 25 **EST:** 1996
SQ FT: 9,000
SALES (est): 13MM **Privately Held**
WEB: www.fortemedia.com
SIC: 3674 Semiconductors & related devices

(P-6124)
FRONTIER SEMICONDUCTOR (PA)
Also Called: Fsm
165 Topaz St, Milpitas (95035-5430)
PHONE..................408 432-8338
Yuen F Lim, *CEO*
Wojtek Walecki, *CTO*
Jason Yeung, *Technology*
Nikos Jger, *Technical Staff*
Mihail Mihaylov, *Electrical Engi*
EMP: 34 **EST:** 1988
SQ FT: 40,000
SALES (est): 5.7MM **Privately Held**
WEB: www.frontiersemi.com
SIC: 3674 Integrated circuits, semiconductor networks, etc.

(P-6125)
GCT SEMICONDUCTOR INC (PA)
2121 Ringwood Ave Ste A, San Jose (95131-1741)
PHONE..................408 434-6040
John Schlaefer, *CEO*
Kyeong Ho Lee, *Ch of Bd*
Gene Kulzer, *CFO*
David Yoon, *Vice Pres*
Alex Sum, *VP Mktg*
EMP: 30 **EST:** 2001
SQ FT: 15,000
SALES (est): 24.1MM **Privately Held**
WEB: www.gctsemi.com
SIC: 3674 Semiconductors & related devices

(P-6126)
GENESYS LOGIC AMERICA INC
2880 Zanker Rd Ste 105, San Jose (95134-2121)
PHONE..................408 435-8899
Nancy Chien, *General Mgr*
Vincent Chang, *Sales Staff*
EMP: 49 **EST:** 2003
SALES (est): 5.2MM **Privately Held**
WEB: www.genesyslogic.com
SIC: 3674 Semiconductors & related devices
PA: Genesys Logic, Inc.
  12f,14f, No. 205, Beixin Rd., Sec. 3
  New Taipei City TAP 23143

(P-6127)
GEO SEMICONDUCTOR INC (PA)
101 Metro Dr Ste 620, San Jose (95110-1342)
PHONE..................408 638-0400
Paul Russo, *CEO*
Simon Westbrook, *CFO*
Ronald Allard, *Vice Pres*
Herv Brelay, *Vice Pres*
John Casey, *Vice Pres*
EMP: 70 **EST:** 2009
SALES (est): 11.3MM **Privately Held**
WEB: www.geosemi.com
SIC: 3674 Semiconductors & related devices

(P-6128)
GIGAMAT TECHNOLOGIES INC
47269 Fremont Blvd, Fremont (94538-6502)
PHONE..................510 770-8008
Edmond Abrahamians, *CEO*
▲ **EMP:** 17 **EST:** 2002
SQ FT: 7,000
SALES (est): 1.5MM **Privately Held**
WEB: www.gigamat.com
SIC: 3674 Semiconductors & related devices

(P-6129)
GIGPEAK INC (DH)
6024 Silver Creek Vly Rd, San Jose (95138-1011)
PHONE..................408 546-3316
Gregory L Waters, *President*
Brian C White, *CFO*
Matthew D Brandalise, *Admin Sec*
EMP: 132 **EST:** 2008
SQ FT: 32,805
SALES (est): 58.7MM **Privately Held**
WEB: www.idt.com
SIC: 3674 Integrated circuits, semiconductor networks, etc.; hybrid integrated circuits
HQ: Renesas Electronics America Inc.
  6024 Silver Creek Vly Rd
  San Jose CA 95138
  408 432-8888

(P-6130)
GLOBAL TESTING CORPORATION
225 Pamela Dr Apt 205, Mountain View (94040-3236)
PHONE..................408 745-0718
Jon Hwu, *CEO*
EMP: 22 **EST:** 1998
SQ FT: 12,000
SALES (est): 457.4K **Privately Held**
WEB: www.gttw.com.tw
SIC: 3674 Semiconductors & related devices
HQ: Global Testing Corporation
  75 & 77, Guangfu Rd.,
  Hukou Hsiang HSI 30351

(P-6131)
GLOBALFOUNDRIES DRESDEN
1050 E Arques Ave, Sunnyvale (94085-4601)
PHONE..................408 462-3900
Faina Medzonsky,
Hans Deppe,
James E Doran,
Thomas M McCoy,
Bruce McDougall,
EMP: 951 **EST:** 2004
SALES (est): 14MM **Publicly Held**
WEB: www.gf.com
SIC: 3674 3369 Integrated circuits, semiconductor networks, etc.; nonferrous foundries
HQ: Globalfoundries U.S. Inc.
  2600 Great America Way
  Santa Clara CA 95054

(P-6132)
GLOBALFOUNDRIES US INC
1278 Reamwood Ave, Sunnyvale (94089-2233)
PHONE..................408 462-3900
EMP: 89 **Publicly Held**
WEB: www.gf.com

SIC: 3674 Semiconductors & related devices
HQ: Globalfoundries U.S. Inc.
  2600 Great America Way
  Santa Clara CA 95054

(P-6133)
GREENLIANT SYSTEMS INC
3970 Freedom Cir Ste 100, Santa Clara (95054-1298)
PHONE..................408 217-7400
Bing Yeh, *CEO*
Arthur Hsu, *President*
Yoshinobu Higuchi, *Vice Pres*
Danny MA, *Surgery Dir*
Tan Ho, *Software Dev*
EMP: 105
SALES (est): 14.4MM **Privately Held**
WEB: www.greenliant.com
SIC: 3674 5065 Semiconductors & related devices; electronic parts & equipment

(P-6134)
GRINDING & DICING SERVICES INC
Also Called: Gdsi
925 Berryessa Rd, San Jose (95133-1002)
PHONE..................408 451-2000
Joe D Collins, *CEO*
Laila H Collins, *Vice Pres*
Saira Haq, *Vice Pres*
Rey Sana, *Engineer*
Beatrice Duarte, *QC Mgr*
▲ **EMP:** 24 **EST:** 1992
SQ FT: 14,500
SALES (est): 7.8MM **Privately Held**
WEB: www.stealthdicing.com
SIC: 3674 2672 Semiconductors & related devices; adhesive papers, labels or tapes: from purchased material

(P-6135)
GSI TECHNOLOGY INC
2360 Owen St, Santa Clara (95054-3210)
PHONE..................408 980-8388
Shu Lee-Lean, *Branch Mgr*
Daniel Hsiao, *Info Tech Mgr*
EMP: 95 **Publicly Held**
WEB: www.gsitechnology.com
SIC: 3674 Semiconductors & related devices
PA: Gsi Technology, Inc.
  1213 Elko Dr
  Sunnyvale CA 94089

(P-6136)
GSI TECHNOLOGY INC (PA)
1213 Elko Dr, Sunnyvale (94089-2211)
PHONE..................408 331-8800
Lee-Lean Shu, *Ch of Bd*
Douglas Schirle, *CFO*
Avidan Akerib, *Vice Pres*
Patrick Chuang, *Vice Pres*
Didier Lasserre, *Vice Pres*
EMP: 62 **EST:** 1995
SQ FT: 44,277
SALES (est): 27.7MM **Publicly Held**
WEB: www.gsitechnology.com
SIC: 3674 3572 Integrated circuits, semiconductor networks, etc.; computer storage devices

(P-6137)
GULSHAN INTERNATIONAL CORP
Also Called: Invax Technologies
1355 Geneva Dr, Sunnyvale (94089-1121)
PHONE..................408 745-6090
Abid Khan, *President*
Susy Khan, *Office Mgr*
Brandon Shalin, *Engineer*
EMP: 31 **EST:** 1980
SALES (est): 7MM **Privately Held**
SIC: 3674 Modules, solid state

(P-6138)
GYRFALCON TECHNOLOGY INC (PA)
1900 Mccarthy Blvd # 412, Milpitas (95035-7457)
PHONE..................408 944-9219
Frank Lyn, *President*
Marc Naddell, *Vice Pres*

3674 - Semiconductors County (P-6139)

Frank Lin, *Executive*
Daniel Liu, *Program Mgr*
Rihua WEI, *Engineer*
EMP: 49 **EST:** 2017
SALES (est): 5.2MM **Privately Held**
WEB: www.gyrfalcontech.ai
SIC: 3674 Semiconductors & related devices

(P-6139)
H-SQUARE CORPORATION
Also Called: H2 Co
3100 Patrick Henry Dr, Santa Clara (95054-1850)
PHONE 408 732-1240
Bud Barclay, *President*
Larry Dean, *Shareholder*
▲ **EMP:** 42 **EST:** 1975
SQ FT: 20,000
SALES (est): 9.8MM **Privately Held**
WEB: www.h-square.com
SIC: 3674 Semiconductor circuit networks; solid state electronic devices; stud bases or mounts for semiconductor devices

(P-6140)
HANERGY HOLDING (AMERICA) LLC (HQ)
1350 Bayshore Hwy, Burlingame (94010-1823)
PHONE 650 288-3722
Yi Wu, *CEO*
EMP: 107 **EST:** 2010
SALES (est): 51.7MM **Privately Held**
WEB: www.hanergymobileenergy.com
SIC: 3674 6719 Solar cells; investment holding companies, except banks

(P-6141)
HAYWARD QUARTZ TECHNOLOGY INC
Also Called: Hayward Quartz Machining Co
1700 Corporate Way, Fremont (94539-6107)
PHONE 510 657-9605
Nhe Thi Le, *CEO*
Ha Vinh Ly, *President*
Duong Nguyen, *CIO*
Rafik Ayvazyan, *Software Dev*
Ken Jacoby, *Project Mgr*
▲ **EMP:** 250 **EST:** 1984
SQ FT: 250,000
SALES (est): 61.1MM **Privately Held**
WEB: www.haywardquartz.com
SIC: 3674 Semiconductor circuit networks

(P-6142)
HELITEK COMPANY LTD
4033 Clipper Ct, Fremont (94538-6540)
PHONE 510 933-7688
Ping-Hai Chiao, *President*
Hd Chiou, *CTO*
Nancy Lin, *Purchasing*
▲ **EMP:** 82 **EST:** 1994
SQ FT: 30,000
SALES (est): 5.2MM **Privately Held**
WEB: www.helitek.com
SIC: 3674 Semiconductors & related devices
PA: Wafer Works Corporation
100, Longyuan 1st Rd.,
Taoyuan City TAY 32542

(P-6143)
HERMES-MICROVISION INC
1762 Automation Pkwy, San Jose (95131-1873)
PHONE 408 597-8600
Jack Jau, *CEO*
Chung Shih Pan, *President*
Charles Yang, *Electrical Engi*
Bill Chiang, *Engineer*
Jie Fang, *Engineer*
▲ **EMP:** 25 **EST:** 1998
SQ FT: 80,000
SALES (est): 12.6MM
SALES (corp-wide): 16.5B **Privately Held**
WEB: www.asml.com
SIC: 3674 Integrated circuits, semiconductor networks, etc.
HQ: Hermes Microvision Incorporated B.V.
De Run 6501
Veldhoven

(P-6144)
HI RELBLITY MCRELECTRONICS INC
1804 Mccarthy Blvd, Milpitas (95035-7410)
PHONE 408 764-5500
Zafar Malik, *President*
Alex Barrios, *Vice Pres*
Larry Jorstad, *CTO*
Fatemeh Kiaei, *Finance Mgr*
Catherine Tijo, *Finance Mgr*
EMP: 56 **EST:** 2008
SALES (est): 21.7MM
SALES (corp-wide): 191.4MM **Privately Held**
WEB: www.hirelmicro.com
SIC: 3674 7389 Semiconductors & related devices; inspection & testing services
HQ: Silicon Turnkey Solutions, Inc.
1804 Mccarthy Blvd
Milpitas CA 95035
408 904-0200

(P-6145)
HITECH GLOBAL DISTRIBUTION LLC
2059 Camden Ave Ste 160, San Jose (95124-2024)
PHONE 408 781-8043
Samantha Alimardani, *President*
Cyrus Mousavi, *General Mgr*
Fred Cohen, *Technical Staff*
◆ **EMP:** 29 **EST:** 2004
SALES (est): 2.8MM **Privately Held**
WEB: www.hitechglobal.com
SIC: 3674 Semiconductors & related devices

(P-6146)
IC SENSORS INC
45738 Northport Loop W, Fremont (94538-6476)
PHONE 510 498-1570
Frank Guibone, *President*
Victor Chatigny, *General Mgr*
EMP: 78 **EST:** 1982
SQ FT: 34,000
SALES (est): 4.2MM
SALES (corp-wide): 12.1B **Privately Held**
SIC: 3674 8711 3625 Semiconductors & related devices; engineering services; switches, electronic applications
HQ: Measurement Specialties, Inc.
1000 Lucas Way
Hampton VA 23666
757 766-1500

(P-6147)
ICHOR SYSTEMS INC (HQ)
3185 Laurelview Ct, Fremont (94538-6535)
PHONE 510 897-5200
Thomas M Rohrs, *CEO*
Peter English, *President*
Jeffrey Anderson, *CFO*
John Spence, *Managing Dir*
Trevor Harmon, *IT/INT Sup*
▲ **EMP:** 20 **EST:** 2009
SALES (est): 49.8MM
SALES (corp-wide): 124.8MM **Publicly Held**
WEB: www.ichorsystems.com
SIC: 3674 Semiconductors & related devices
PA: Ichor Holdings, Ltd.
3185 Laurelview Ct
Fremont CA 94538
510 897-5200

(P-6148)
ILLINOIS TOOL WORKS INC
ITW Rippey
5000 Hillsdale Cir, El Dorado Hills (95762-5706)
PHONE 916 939-4332
Brent Best, *Manager*
EMP: 69
SALES (corp-wide): 12.5B **Publicly Held**
WEB: www.itw.com
SIC: 3674 Semiconductors & related devices
PA: Illinois Tool Works Inc.
155 Harlem Ave
Glenview IL 60025
847 724-7500

(P-6149)
INFINEON TECH AMERICAS CORP
640 N Mccarthy Blvd, Milpitas (95035-5113)
PHONE 866 951-9519
Robert Lefort, *President*
Sandra Garcia, *Technician*
Odile Ronat, *Technical Staff*
Christian Rosengarten, *Purch Mgr*
Spencer Allan, *Regl Sales Mgr*
EMP: 1200
SALES (corp-wide): 10.1B **Privately Held**
WEB: www.infineon.com
SIC: 3674 Semiconductors & related devices
HQ: Infineon Technologies Americas Corp.
101 N Pacific Coast Hwy
El Segundo CA 90245
310 726-8200

(P-6150)
INFINEON TECH N AMER CORP (DH)
640 N Mccarthy Blvd, Milpitas (95035-5113)
PHONE 408 503-2642
Robert Lefort, *President*
Andrew Prillwitz, *CFO*
Machaiah Thammaiah, *Executive*
Cherry Tseng, *Executive*
Paul Johnson, *Exec Dir*
▲ **EMP:** 500 **EST:** 1982
SQ FT: 400,000
SALES (est): 300.8MM
SALES (corp-wide): 10.1B **Privately Held**
SIC: 3674 Semiconductors & related devices
HQ: Infineon Technologies Us Holdco Inc.
640 N Mccarthy Blvd
Milpitas CA 95035
866 951-9519

(P-6151)
INFINEON TECH N AMER CORP
30805 Santana St, Hayward (94544-7030)
P.O. Box 60000 File 0670, San Francisco (94102)
PHONE 919 768-0315
Robert Lefort, *President*
Scott Delgiudice, *Regional*
EMP: 162
SALES (corp-wide): 10.1B **Privately Held**
SIC: 3674 Semiconductors & related devices
HQ: Infineon Technologies North America Corporation
640 N Mccarthy Blvd
Milpitas CA 95035
408 503-2642

(P-6152)
INFINEON TECH US HOLDCO INC (HQ)
Also Called: Infineon Technologies AG
640 N Mccarthy Blvd, Milpitas (95035-5113)
PHONE 866 951-9519
David Lewis, *CEO*
Andrew Prillwitz, *CFO*
Gernot Langguth, *Sr Corp Ofcr*
Helmut Gassel, *Chief Mktg Ofcr*
Dominik Asam, *Vice Pres*
EMP: 100 **EST:** 2014
SQ FT: 62,874
SALES (est): 309.6MM
SALES (corp-wide): 10.1B **Privately Held**
WEB: www.infineon.com
SIC: 3674 Integrated circuits, semiconductor networks, etc.
PA: Infineon Technologies Ag
Am Campeon 1-15
Neubiberg BY 85579
892 340-

(P-6153)
INNODISK USA CORPORATION
42996 Osgood Rd, Fremont (94539-5627)
PHONE 510 770-9421
Victor Le, *President*
▲ **EMP:** 30 **EST:** 2011
SALES (est): 10MM **Privately Held**
WEB: www.innodisk.tumblr.com
SIC: 3674 Random access memory (RAM)

PA: Innodisk Corporation
5f, No. 237, Datong Rd., Sec. 1,
New Taipei City TAP 22161

(P-6154)
INNOGRIT CORPORATION
1735 Technology Dr, San Jose (95110-1313)
PHONE 408 785-3678
Zining Wu, *CEO*
EMP: 34 **EST:** 2016
SALES (est): 3.1MM **Privately Held**
WEB: www.innogritcorp.com
SIC: 3674 Semiconductors & related devices

(P-6155)
INOLUX CORPORATION
619 Bainbridge St, Foster City (94404-3601)
PHONE 650 483-6227
Holton Lee, *Branch Mgr*
EMP: 18
SALES (corp-wide): 1.6MM **Privately Held**
WEB: www.inolux-corp.com
SIC: 3674 Semiconductors & related devices
PA: Inolux Corporation
3350 Scott Blvd Ste 4102
Santa Clara CA 95054
408 844-8734

(P-6156)
INPHENIX INC
250 N Mines Rd, Livermore (94551-2238)
PHONE 925 606-8809
David Eu, *President*
Tong MO, *Administration*
Meena Kaur, *Software Dev*
Simon Cohen, *Engineer*
Tao Huang, *Engineer*
EMP: 25 **EST:** 2003
SALES (est): 6.1MM **Privately Held**
WEB: www.inphenix.com
SIC: 3674 Semiconductors & related devices

(P-6157)
INPHI CORPORATION (HQ)
110 Rio Robles, San Jose (95134-1813)
PHONE 408 217-7300
Jean Hu, *President*
Mitchell Gaynor,
Timothy Heenan, *Vice Pres*
Nariman Yousefi, *Vice Pres*
Gabrielle Kleyh, *Executive*
EMP: 229 **EST:** 2000
SQ FT: 110,611
SALES: 682.9MM **Privately Held**
WEB: www.marvell.com
SIC: 3674 Integrated circuits, semiconductor networks, etc.
PA: Marvell Technology, Inc.
1000 N West St Ste 1200
Wilmington DE 19801
302 295-4840

(P-6158)
INTEGRA TECH SILICON VLY LLC (DH)
1635 Mccarthy Blvd, Milpitas (95035-7415)
PHONE 408 618-8700
Matt Bergeron, *CEO*
Joe Foerstel, *Vice Pres*
Joseph Foerstel, *Vice Pres*
Janice Pinson, *Program Mgr*
Angie Smead, *Senior Buyer*
EMP: 109 **EST:** 1990
SQ FT: 48,000
SALES (est): 22.5MM **Privately Held**
WEB: www.integra-tech.com
SIC: 3674 3825 Semiconductors & related devices; semiconductor test equipment
HQ: Integra Technologies Llc
3450 N Rock Rd Ste 100
Wichita KS 67226
316 630-6800

(P-6159)
INTEGRTED SILICON SOLUTION INC (PA)
1623 Buckeye Dr, Milpitas (95035-7423)
PHONE 408 969-6600
Jimmy Lee, *CEO*

PRODUCTS & SERVICES SECTION
3674 - Semiconductors County (P-6179)

KY Han, *Vice Chairman*
Scott Howarth, *President*
Jianyue Pan, *Bd of Directors*
Allen Chang, *Vice Pres*
▲ **EMP:** 581 **EST:** 1988
SQ FT: 55,612
SALES (est): 85.4MM **Privately Held**
WEB: www.issi.com
SIC: 3674 Semiconductors & related devices

(P-6160)
INTEL CORPORATION (PA)
2200 Mission College Blvd, Santa Clara (95054-1549)
P.O. Box 58119 (95052-8119)
PHONE...................408 765-8080
Patrick Gelsinger, *CEO*
Omar Ishrak, *Ch of Bd*
George S Davis, *CFO*
Gregory M Bryant, *Exec VP*
Steven R Rodgers, *Exec VP*
◆ **EMP:** 54360 **EST:** 1968
SALES (est): 77.8B **Publicly Held**
WEB: www.intel.com
SIC: 3674 3577 7372 Microprocessors; computer peripheral equipment; prepackaged software; application computer software

(P-6161)
INTEL CORPORATION
1900 Prairie City Rd, Folsom (95630-9599)
PHONE...................916 356-8080
Conrad Wiederhold, *Manager*
Dave Aubin, *Vice Pres*
Rolando Saldana, *Vice Pres*
Alan Bumgarner, *Program Mgr*
Laura Vujovich, *Program Mgr*
EMP: 57
SALES (corp-wide): 77.8B **Publicly Held**
WEB: www.intel.com
SIC: 3674 3572 3577 Microprocessors; computer storage devices; computer peripheral equipment
PA: Intel Corporation
2200 Mission College Blvd
Santa Clara CA 95054
408 765-8080

(P-6162)
INTEL INTERNATIONAL LIMITED (HQ)
2200 Mission College Blvd, Santa Clara (95054-1549)
PHONE...................408 765-8080
Lee Johnny, *Principal*
EMP: 15 **EST:** 1971
SALES (est): 27MM
SALES (corp-wide): 77.8B **Publicly Held**
WEB: www.intel.com
SIC: 3674 3571 Memories, solid state; microprocessors; computers, digital, analog or hybrid
PA: Intel Corporation
2200 Mission College Blvd
Santa Clara CA 95054
408 765-8080

(P-6163)
INTEL PUERTO RICO INC
2200 Mission College Blvd, Santa Clara (95054-1549)
PHONE...................408 765-8080
Craig Barrett, *President*
Shashi Jain, *Senior VP*
John Mitchell, *IT/INT Sup*
Shirley Isip, *Technician*
Louis Luong, *Technician*
EMP: 95 **EST:** 1981
SALES (est): 6.4MM
SALES (corp-wide): 77.8B **Publicly Held**
WEB: www.intel.com
SIC: 3674 3571 Memories, solid state; microprocessors; computers, digital, analog or hybrid
PA: Intel Corporation
2200 Mission College Blvd
Santa Clara CA 95054
408 765-8080

(P-6164)
INTEL SEMICONDUCTOR (US) LLC (HQ)
2200 Mission College Blvd, Santa Clara (95054-1549)
PHONE...................408 765-8080
Robert H Swan, *CEO*
▲ **EMP:** 55 **EST:** 1996
SALES (est): 54.6MM
SALES (corp-wide): 77.8B **Publicly Held**
WEB: www.intel.com
SIC: 3674 7372 Semiconductors & related devices; prepackaged software
PA: Intel Corporation
2200 Mission College Blvd
Santa Clara CA 95054
408 765-8080

(P-6165)
INTERMOLECULAR INC (HQ)
3011 N 1st St, San Jose (95134-2004)
PHONE...................408 582-5700
Chris Kramer, *President*
Bruce M McWilliams, *Ch of Bd*
C Richard Neely, *CFO*
Bill Roeschlein, *CFO*
Scot A Griffin, *Exec VP*
EMP: 174 **EST:** 2004
SQ FT: 146,000
SALES (est): 33.6MM
SALES (corp-wide): 20.7B **Privately Held**
WEB: www.intermolecular.com
SIC: 3674 Integrated circuits, semiconductor networks, etc.
PA: Merck Kg Auf Aktien
Frankfurter Str. 250
Darmstadt HE 64293
615 172-0

(P-6166)
INVECAS INC (PA)
2350 Mission College Blvd # 777, Santa Clara (95054-1561)
PHONE...................408 758-5636
Dasaradha Gude, *CEO*
Khanh Le, *President*
Prasad Chalasani, *Vice Pres*
Srinivasa Gutta, *Vice Pres*
Bhaskar Kolla, *Vice Pres*
EMP: 23 **EST:** 2014
SALES (est): 68MM **Privately Held**
WEB: www.invecas.com
SIC: 3674 Semiconductors & related devices

(P-6167)
IWATT INC (DH)
Also Called: Dialog Semiconductor
675 Campbell Tech Pkwy # 150, Campbell (95008-5053)
PHONE...................408 374-4200
Ronald P Edgerton, *CEO*
James V McCanna, *CFO*
Andrew Bray, *Vice Pres*
Scott Brown, *Vice Pres*
Gary Happ, *Vice Pres*
▲ **EMP:** 45 **EST:** 1999
SQ FT: 26,000
SALES (est): 52.9MM
SALES (corp-wide): 1.3B **Privately Held**
WEB: www.dialog-semiconductor.de
SIC: 3674 Semiconductors & related devices
HQ: Dialog Semiconductor Gmbh
Neue Str. 95
Kirchheim Unter Teck BW 73230
702 180-50

(P-6168)
IXYS LLC (HQ)
1590 Buckeye Dr, Milpitas (95035-7418)
PHONE...................408 457-9000
Meenal Sethna,
Vladimir Tsukanov, *Vice Pres*
Nathan Zommer, *Principal*
Timothy Richardson, *Director*
EMP: 493 **EST:** 1983
SQ FT: 51,000
SALES: 322.1MM
SALES (corp-wide): 1.4B **Publicly Held**
WEB: www.ixys.com
SIC: 3674 Integrated circuits, semiconductor networks, etc.
PA: Littelfuse, Inc.
8755 W Higgins Rd Ste 500
Chicago IL 60631
773 628-1000

(P-6169)
JDJ SEMICONDUCTOR LLC
1249 Reamwood Ave, Sunnyvale (94089-2226)
PHONE...................408 542-9430
Joe Rothstein,
Douglas Beaubien,
EMP: 21 **EST:** 2003
SQ FT: 8,400
SALES (est): 4MM **Privately Held**
WEB: www.pyramidsemiconductor.com
SIC: 3674 Integrated circuits, semiconductor networks, etc.

(P-6170)
JINKOSOLAR (US) INC
595 Market St Ste 2200, San Francisco (94105-2834)
PHONE...................415 402-0502
Xiande LI, *CEO*
Jeff Szczepanski, *Treasurer*
Nigel Cockroft, *General Mgr*
LI Hui, *Controller*
Glenn Tomasyan, *Regl Sales Mgr*
▲ **EMP:** 58 **EST:** 2010
SALES (est): 9.4MM
SALES (corp-wide): 20.1MM **Privately Held**
SIC: 3674 Semiconductors & related devices
PA: Jinkosolar (U.S.) Holding Inc.
595 Market St Ste 2200
San Francisco CA 94105
415 402-0502

(P-6171)
KEYSSA INC (PA)
3945 Freedom Cir Ste 560, Santa Clara (95054-1269)
PHONE...................408 637-2300
Tony Fadell, *CEO*
Gordon Almquist, *Vice Pres*
Nick Antonopoulos, *Vice Pres*
Srikanth Gondi, *Vice Pres*
Roger Isaac, *Vice Pres*
EMP: 37 **EST:** 2009
SALES (est): 9.5MM **Privately Held**
WEB: www.keyssa.com
SIC: 3674 3577 Semiconductors & related devices; computer peripheral equipment

(P-6172)
KLA CORPORATION
Also Called: Promesys Division
5451 Patrick Henry Dr, Santa Clara (95054-1167)
PHONE...................408 986-5600
EMP: 16
SALES (corp-wide): 6.9B **Publicly Held**
WEB: www.kla-tencor.com
SIC: 3674 Semiconductors & related devices
PA: Kla Corporation
1 Technology Dr
Milpitas CA 95035
408 875-3000

(P-6173)
KLA-TENCOR ASIA-PAC DIST CORP
1 Technology Dr, Milpitas (95035-7916)
PHONE...................408 875-4144
Mark Nordstrom, *Principal*
Theodore Castro, *Treasurer*
Dan Wack, *Surgery Dir*
Prasookumar Bharathkumar, *Sr Ntwrk Engine*
Ruil Yang, *Design Engr*
▲ **EMP:** 51 **EST:** 2002
SALES (est): 15.5MM
SALES (corp-wide): 6.9B **Publicly Held**
WEB: www.kla-tencor.com
SIC: 3674 Semiconductors & related devices
PA: Kla Corporation
1 Technology Dr
Milpitas CA 95035
408 875-3000

(P-6174)
KSM CORP
1959 Concourse Dr, San Jose (95131-1708)
PHONE...................408 514-2400
Jooswan Kim, *CEO*
Harvinder P Singh, *President*
EMP: 87 **EST:** 2003
SQ FT: 18,000
SALES (est): 1.8MM **Privately Held**
WEB: www.ksm.co.kr
SIC: 3674 Semiconductors & related devices
PA: Ksm Component Co., Ltd.
90 Wolha-Ro 589beon-Gil, Haseong-Myeon
Gimpo 10011

(P-6175)
LAM RESEARCH CORPORATION (PA)
4650 Cushing Pkwy, Fremont (94538-6401)
PHONE...................510 572-0200
Timothy M Archer, *President*
Abhijit Y Talwalkar, *Ch of Bd*
Samantha Tan, *COO*
Douglas R Bettinger, *CFO*
Ava M Hahn,
EMP: 100 **EST:** 1980
SALES: 14.6B **Publicly Held**
WEB: www.lamresearch.com
SIC: 3674 Wafers (semiconductor devices)

(P-6176)
LAM RESEARCH CORPORATION
1 Portola Ave, Livermore (94551-7647)
PHONE...................510 572-8400
Kay Maruhashi, *Program Mgr*
Prit Samra, *Program Mgr*
Terry Bloom, *Business Mgr*
Rich Witherspoon, *Business Mgr*
Brian Boyd, *Finance*
EMP: 25
SALES (corp-wide): 14.6B **Publicly Held**
WEB: www.lamresearch.com
SIC: 3674 Semiconductors & related devices
PA: Lam Research Corporation
4650 Cushing Pkwy
Fremont CA 94538
510 572-0200

(P-6177)
LAM RESEARCH CORPORATION
1201 Voyager St, Livermore (94550-2568)
PHONE...................209 597-2194
EMP: 30 **EST:** 2011
SALES (est): 4.8MM **Privately Held**
WEB: www.lamresearch.com
SIC: 3674 Semiconductors & related devices

(P-6178)
LATTICE SEMICONDUCTOR CORP
2115 Onel Dr, San Jose (95131-2032)
PHONE...................408 826-6000
Al Chan, *Manager*
Mark Nelson, *Vice Pres*
Eric Wong, *Software Engr*
James Khong, *Engineer*
Hank Kwon, *Engineer*
EMP: 300
SALES (corp-wide): 408.1MM **Publicly Held**
WEB: www.latticesemi.com
SIC: 3674 Integrated circuits, semiconductor networks, etc.
PA: Lattice Semiconductor Corp
5555 Ne Moore Ct
Hillsboro OR 97124
503 268-8000

(P-6179)
LINEAR INTEGRATED SYSTEMS INC
4042 Clipper Ct, Fremont (94538-6540)
PHONE...................510 490-9160
Cindy Cook Johnson, *CEO*
Tim McCune, *President*
Timothy McCune, *President*
Michael Ansberry, *Vice Pres*
Vicky Tang, *Technology*

3674 - Semiconductors County (P-6180)

EMP: 25 EST: 1987
SQ FT: 5,000
SALES (est): 2.7MM Privately Held
WEB: www.linearsystems.com
SIC: 3674 Integrated circuits, semiconductor networks, etc.

(P-6180)
LINEAR TECHNOLOGY LLC (HQ)
1630 Mccarthy Blvd, Milpitas (95035-7417)
PHONE 408 432-1900
Lothar Maier, *CEO*
Alexander R McCann, *COO*
Donald P Zerio, *CFO*
Cuyler Latorraca, *Vice Pres*
Steve Pietkiewicz, *Vice Pres*
▲ EMP: 900 EST: 1981
SQ FT: 430,000
SALES (est): 1.4B
SALES (corp-wide): 5.6B Publicly Held
WEB: www.analog.com
SIC: 3674 Integrated circuits, semiconductor networks, etc.
PA: Analog Devices, Inc.
1 Analog Way
Wilmington MA 01887
781 329-4700

(P-6181)
LRE SILICON SERVICES
Also Called: L R Enterprises
1235 Torres Ave, Milpitas (95035-4015)
P.O. Box 360869 (95036-0869)
PHONE 408 262-8725
Linda Robinson, *Owner*
EMP: 18 EST: 1999
SALES (est): 1MM Privately Held
SIC: 3674 Silicon wafers, chemically doped

(P-6182)
LSI CORPORATION (DH)
Also Called: Broadcom
1320 Ridder Park Dr, San Jose (95131-2313)
PHONE 408 433-8000
Hock E Tan, *CEO*
Jean F Rankin, *Exec VP*
Janet Jerin, *Executive Asst*
Mark Brazeal, *Admin Sec*
Joab Kong, *Administration*
▲ EMP: 2400 EST: 1980
SQ FT: 240,000
SALES (est): 1.7B
SALES (corp-wide): 23.8B Publicly Held
SIC: 3674 Microcircuits, integrated (semiconductor)

(P-6183)
M-PULSE MICROWAVE INC
576 Charcot Ave, San Jose (95131-2201)
PHONE 408 432-1480
Billy Long, *President*
Wendell Sanders, *Shareholder*
Hector Flores, *Admin Sec*
John Richards, *Sales Executive*
Walt Medeiros, *Facilities Mgr*
EMP: 25 EST: 1987
SQ FT: 24,000
SALES (est): 3.3MM Privately Held
WEB: www.mpulsemw.com
SIC: 3674 Integrated circuits, semiconductor networks, etc.

(P-6184)
MACOM CNNCTIVITY SOLUTIONS LLC
4555 Great America Pkwy, Santa Clara (95054-1243)
PHONE 408 542-8686
EMP: 22 EST: 2017
SALES (est): 933.3K Privately Held
WEB: www.macom.com
SIC: 3674 7699 Light emitting diodes; metal reshaping & replating services
PA: Macom Technology Solutions (India) Private Limited
601, 6th Floor,
Pune MH 41100

(P-6185)
MACQUARIE ELECTRONICS INC
2153 Otoole Ave Ste 20, San Jose (95131-1331)
PHONE 408 965-3860
Matt Hayes, *Vice Pres*
Jana Daley, *Sales Staff*
▲ EMP: 21 EST: 2005
SALES (est): 1.1MM Privately Held
WEB: www.macquarie.com
SIC: 3674 Semiconductors & related devices

(P-6186)
MAGNUM SEMICONDUCTOR INC
6024 Silver Creek Vly Rd, San Jose (95138-1011)
PHONE 408 934-3700
Gopal Solanki, *President*
Terry Griffin, *CFO*
Fure-Ching Jeng, *Vice Pres*
Torrie Su, *Engineer*
Srinivas Ambati, *Director*
▲ EMP: 233 EST: 2005
SALES (est): 30.4MM Privately Held
WEB: www.magnumsemi.com
SIC: 3674 Integrated circuits, semiconductor networks, etc.
HQ: Gigpeak, Inc.
6024 Silver Creek Vly Rd
San Jose CA 95138
408 546-3316

(P-6187)
MARSEILLE INC
3211 Scott Blvd Ste 205, Santa Clara (95054-3009)
PHONE 408 855-9003
EMP: 45 EST: 2002
SALES (est): 244.1K Privately Held
WEB: www.marseilleinc.com
SIC: 3674 Semiconductors & related devices

(P-6188)
MARVELL SEMICONDUCTOR
700 First Ave, Sunnyvale (94089-1020)
PHONE 408 222-2500
Allan Lim, *Manager*
EMP: 23 EST: 2020
SALES (est): 661K Privately Held
SIC: 3674 Semiconductors & related devices

(P-6189)
MARVELL SEMICONDUCTOR INC
890 Glenn Dr, Folsom (95630-3185)
PHONE 916 605-3700
EMP: 217
SALES (corp-wide): 682.9MM Privately Held
WEB: www.marvell.com
SIC: 3674 Semiconductors & related devices
HQ: Marvell Semiconductor, Inc.
5488 Marvell Ln
Santa Clara CA 95054

(P-6190)
MARVELL SEMICONDUCTOR INC (DH)
5488 Marvell Ln, Santa Clara (95054-3606)
PHONE 408 222-2500
Matthew Murphy, *CEO*
Jean Hu, *CFO*
Juergen Gromer, *Bd of Directors*
Henry Tan, *Bd of Directors*
Neil Kim, *Exec VP*
◆ EMP: 900 EST: 1995
SALES (est): 678.9MM
SALES (corp-wide): 682.9MM Privately Held
WEB: www.marvell.com
SIC: 3674 Semiconductors & related devices

(P-6191)
MARVELL TECHNOLOGY GROUP LTD
5488 Marvell Ln, Santa Clara (95054-3606)
PHONE 408 222-2500
Kevin O 'buckley, *Vice Pres*
Mike Dudek, *Engineer*
Jae Choi, *Sales Staff*
Todd Manley, *Director*
Ajay Prasad, *Director*
EMP: 52 EST: 1991
SALES (est): 2.4MM Privately Held
SIC: 3674 Semiconductors & related devices

(P-6192)
MATTSON TECHNOLOGY INC (DH)
47131 Bayside Pkwy, Fremont (94538-6517)
PHONE 510 657-5900
Allen Lu, *President*
Frank Moreman, *COO*
Subhash Deshmukh, *Officer*
Michael Z Shi, *Officer*
Shannon Hart, *Senior VP*
▲ EMP: 293 EST: 1988
SQ FT: 101,000
SALES (est): 251.4MM Privately Held
WEB: www.mattson.com
SIC: 3674 Semiconductors & related devices
HQ: Beijing E-Town International Investment & Development Co., Ltd.
2501, Floor 25, Building 1, No.22 Courtyard, Ronghua M. Road, Be Beijing 10000
108 105-7999

(P-6193)
MAXIM INTEGRATED PRODUCTS INC (HQ)
160 Rio Robles, San Jose (95134-1813)
PHONE 408 601-1000
Tunc Doluca, *President*
William P Sullivan, *Ch of Bd*
Brian C White, *CFO*
Edwin B Medlin,
Jon Imperato, *Senior VP*
EMP: 956 EST: 1983
SQ FT: 435,000
SALES: 2.6B
SALES (corp-wide): 5.6B Publicly Held
WEB: www.maximintegrated.com
SIC: 3674 Semiconductors & related devices; microcircuits, integrated (semiconductor)
PA: Analog Devices, Inc.
1 Analog Way
Wilmington MA 01887
781 329-4700

(P-6194)
MCUBE INC (PA)
2570 N 1st St Ste 300, San Jose (95131-1018)
PHONE 408 637-5503
Ben Lee, *CEO*
Sanjay Bhandari, *Vice Pres*
Crystal Kwong, *Accountant*
Robert Sun, *Opers Staff*
Mehdi Behnami, *Marketing Staff*
EMP: 91 EST: 2011
SALES (est): 10.6MM Privately Held
WEB: www.movella.com
SIC: 3674 Semiconductors & related devices

(P-6195)
MEGACHIPS LSI USA CORPORATION
910 E Hamilton Ave # 120, Campbell (95008-0612)
PHONE 408 570-0555
Ikuo Iwama, *CEO*
Akihide Maeda, *CFO*
EMP: 75 EST: 2018
SALES (est): 9.7MM Privately Held
WEB: www.megachips.com
SIC: 3674 5065 Semiconductors & related devices; semiconductor devices
PA: Megachips Corporation
1-1-1, Miyahara, Yodogawa-Ku Osaka OSK 532-0

(P-6196)
MEIVAC INCORPORATED
5830 Hellyer Ave, San Jose (95138-1004)
PHONE 408 362-1000
Richard Meidinger, *CEO*
David Meidinger, *President*
Marcela Gonzalez, *Administration*
Alfonso Gonzalez, *Technology*
Brian Meidinger, *Manager*
EMP: 30 EST: 1993
SQ FT: 27,000
SALES (est): 7.8MM Privately Held
WEB: www.meivac.ferrotec.com
SIC: 3674 Semiconductors & related devices

(P-6197)
MELLANOX TECHNOLOGIES INC
Also Called: Accounts Payable
2530 Zanker Rd, San Jose (95131-1127)
P.O. Box 67143, Scotts Valley (95067-7143)
PHONE 408 970-3400
Eyal Waldman, *CEO*
Pegah Seddighian, *Senior Engr*
Naama Avriel, *Opers Staff*
John Kim, *Marketing Staff*
EMP: 18 Publicly Held
WEB: www.nvidia.com
SIC: 3674 Semiconductors & related devices
HQ: Mellanox Technologies, Inc.
2530 Zanker Rd
San Jose CA 95131
408 970-3400

(P-6198)
MELLANOX TECHNOLOGIES INC (DH)
2530 Zanker Rd, San Jose (95131-1127)
PHONE 408 970-3400
Eyal Waldman, *Ch of Bd*
Chris Shea, *President*
Alon Webman, *President*
Shai Cohen, *COO*
Michael Gray, *CFO*
EMP: 651 EST: 1999
SALES: 1.3B Publicly Held
WEB: www.nvidia.com
SIC: 3674 Integrated circuits, semiconductor networks, etc.

(P-6199)
MERLIN SOLAR TECHNOLOGIES INC (HQ)
5891 Rue Ferrari, San Jose (95138-1857)
PHONE 650 740-1160
Arthur Tan, *CEO*
Olaf Gresens, *President*
Dinna Bayangas, *CFO*
Venkatesan Murali, *Founder*
Kira Vargas, *Program Mgr*
EMP: 39 EST: 2016
SQ FT: 26,773
SALES (est): 1.1MM
SALES (corp-wide): 2MM Privately Held
WEB: www.merlinsolar.com
SIC: 3674 Solar cells
PA: Aci Solar Holdings Na, Inc.
303 Twin Dolphin Dr Ste 6
Redwood City CA 94065
650 227-3271

(P-6200)
MIASOLE
2590 Walsh Ave, Santa Clara (95051-1315)
PHONE 408 919-5700
Jeff Zhou, *CEO*
Merle McClendon, *CFO*
Elyrose Zavagno, *Executive Asst*
Atiye Bayman, *CTO*
Seila Chim, *Technician*
▲ EMP: 315 EST: 2001
SALES (est): 49.6MM Privately Held
WEB: www.miasole.com
SIC: 3674 Solar cells

(P-6201)
MIASOLE HI-TECH CORP (DH)
3211 Scott Blvd Ste 201, Santa Clara (95054-3009)
PHONE 408 919-5700
Jie Zhang, *CEO*
Lyndsey Zhang, *CFO*
Stephen Barry, *Vice Pres*
Atiye Bayman, *Vice Pres*
Jason Corneille, *Vice Pres*
EMP: 250
SALES (est): 51.7MM Privately Held
WEB: www.miasole.com
SIC: 3674 5074 Solar cells; heating equipment & panels, solar

▲ = Import ▼ =Export
◆ =Import/Export

PRODUCTS & SERVICES SECTION

3674 - Semiconductors County (P-6223)

HQ: Hanergy Holding (America) Llc
1350 Bayshore Hwy
Burlingame CA 94010
650 288-3722

(P-6202)
MICREL LLC
2180 Fortune Dr, San Jose (95131-1815)
PHONE..........................408 944-0800
Raymond Zinn, *CEO*
Lisa Jones, *Administration*
Peter Stavish, *Info Tech Mgr*
Betty Sausele, *Business Anlyst*
Jenny Sun, *Design Engr*
EMP: 728
SALES (corp-wide): 5.4B **Publicly Held**
WEB: www.microchip.com
SIC: 3674 Integrated circuits, semiconductor networks, etc.
HQ: Micrel Llc
2355 W Chandler Blvd
Chandler AZ 85224
480 792-7200

(P-6203)
MICROCHIP TECHNOLOGY
1931 Fortune Dr, San Jose (95131-1724)
PHONE..........................408 474-3640
Thomas Mendoza, *Manager*
Swetha Pakala, *Sr Software Eng*
Bo Chai, *Software Engr*
Phuc Tang, *Technician*
Jeffrey Chou, *Design Engr*
EMP: 20 **EST:** 2015
SALES (est): 5.9MM **Privately Held**
WEB: www.microchip.com
SIC: 3674 Semiconductors & related devices

(P-6204)
MICRON TECHNOLOGY INC
570 Alder Dr Bldg 2, Milpitas (95035-7443)
PHONE..........................408 855-4000
EMP: 48
SALES (corp-wide): 21.4B **Publicly Held**
WEB: www.micron.com
SIC: 3674 Mfg Semiconductors/Related Devices
PA: Micron Technology, Inc.
8000 S Federal Way
Boise ID 83716
208 368-4000

(P-6205)
MICROSEMI CORP - ANLOG MXED SG
3850 N 1st St, San Jose (95134-1702)
PHONE..........................408 643-6000
Shafy Eltoukhy, *General Mgr*
EMP: 50
SALES (corp-wide): 5.4B **Publicly Held**
WEB: www.microsemi.com
SIC: 3674 Semiconductors & related devices
HQ: Microsemi Corp. - Analog Mixed Signal Group
11861 Western Ave
Garden Grove CA 92841

(P-6206)
MICROSEMI CORPORATION
3295 Scott Blvd 150, Santa Clara (95054-3014)
PHONE..........................408 240-4560
Elan Atian, *Manager*
Radjendirane Codandaramane, *Engineer*
EMP: 100
SALES (corp-wide): 5.4B **Publicly Held**
WEB: www.microsemi.com
SIC: 3674 Semiconductors & related devices
HQ: Microsemi Corporation
11861 Western Ave
Garden Grove CA 92841
949 380-6100

(P-6207)
MICROSEMI CRP- RF INTGRTED SLT (DH)
Also Called: Microsemi Rfis
105 Lake Forest Way, Folsom (95630-4708)
PHONE..........................916 850-8640
James J Peterson, *President*
Ralph Brandi, *COO*
John W Hohener, *CFO*
David H Hall, *Vice Pres*
Mar Caballero, *Engineer*
▲ **EMP:** 115 **EST:** 2009
SALES (est): 48.8MM
SALES (corp-wide): 5.4B **Publicly Held**
WEB: www.microsemi.com
SIC: 3674 Semiconductors & related devices
HQ: Microsemi Corporation
11861 Western Ave
Garden Grove CA 92841
949 380-6100

(P-6208)
MICROSEMI FREQUENCY TIME CORP
3870 N 1st St, San Jose (95134-1702)
PHONE..........................408 433-0910
Justin Spencer, *President*
Robert Amos, *Administration*
James Auker, *Design Engr*
Chris Myrick, *Technical Staff*
Tony Bartyczak, *Engineer*
EMP: 23
SALES (corp-wide): 5.4B **Publicly Held**
WEB: www.microsemi.com
SIC: 3674 Semiconductors & related devices
HQ: Microsemi Frequency And Time Corporation
3870 N 1st St
San Jose CA 95134
480 792-7200

(P-6209)
MICROSEMI SEMICONDUCTOR US INC
3843 Brickway Blvd # 100, Santa Rosa (95403-9059)
PHONE..........................707 568-5900
Julio Perdomo, *CEO*
Hiroshi Kondoh, *COO*
Jerome C Nathan, *CFO*
Jerome Nathan, *Executive*
Jeff Meyer, *CTO*
▼ **EMP:** 41 **EST:** 2001
SQ FT: 26,000
SALES (est): 10.5MM
SALES (corp-wide): 5.4B **Publicly Held**
WEB: www.centellax.com
SIC: 3674 Semiconductors & related devices
HQ: Cnt Acquisition Corp.
1 Enterprise
Aliso Viejo CA 92656
949 380-6100

(P-6210)
MICROSEMI SOC CORP (DH)
3870 N 1st St, San Jose (95134-1702)
PHONE..........................408 643-6000
James J Peterson, *CEO*
John W Hohener, *CFO*
Esmat Z Hamdy, *Senior VP*
Fares N Mubarak, *Senior VP*
David L Van De Hey, *Vice Pres*
▲ **EMP:** 385 **EST:** 1985
SQ FT: 158,000
SALES (est): 147.5MM
SALES (corp-wide): 5.4B **Publicly Held**
WEB: www.microsemi.com
SIC: 3674 7371 Microcircuits, integrated (semiconductor); computer software development
HQ: Microsemi Corporation
11861 Western Ave
Garden Grove CA 92841
949 380-6100

(P-6211)
MICROSEMI SOC CORP
2051 Stierlin Ct, Mountain View (94043-4655)
PHONE..........................650 318-4200
Mary Segura, *Manager*
Esmat Z Hamdy, *Vice Pres*
Esmat Hamdy, *Vice Pres*
Barbara McArthur, *Vice Pres*
Louis Sisniegas, *Info Tech Dir*
EMP: 48
SALES (corp-wide): 5.4B **Publicly Held**
WEB: www.microsemi.com
SIC: 3674 Microcircuits, integrated (semiconductor)
HQ: Microsemi Soc Corp.
3870 N 1st St
San Jose CA 95134
408 643-6000

(P-6212)
MICROSEMI STOR SOLUTIONS INC (DH)
1380 Bordeaux Dr, Sunnyvale (94089-1005)
PHONE..........................408 239-8000
Paul Pickle, *President*
Adhir Mattu, *President*
John W Hohener, *CFO*
Bob Hall, *Program Mgr*
Dennis Allyn, *Opers Staff*
EMP: 1069 **EST:** 1983
SQ FT: 85,000
SALES (est): 112.6MM
SALES (corp-wide): 5.4B **Publicly Held**
WEB: www.microsemi.com
SIC: 3674 Modules, solid state
HQ: Microsemi Corporation
11861 Western Ave
Garden Grove CA 92841
949 380-6100

(P-6213)
MIPS TECH INC (HQ)
300 Orchard Cy Dr Ste 170, Campbell (95008)
PHONE..........................408 530-5000
Sandeep Vij, *President*
Krishna Raghavan, *COO*
William Slater, *CFO*
Mark Butler, *Vice Pres*
Brad Holtzinger, *Vice Pres*
▲ **EMP:** 157 **EST:** 1992
SALES (est): 49.3MM
SALES (corp-wide): 53.2MM **Privately Held**
WEB: www.mips.com
SIC: 3674 Microprocessors
PA: Wave Computing, Inc.
780 Montague Expy Ste 308
San Jose CA 95131
408 412-8645

(P-6214)
MOBILYGEN CORPORATION
160 Rio Robles, San Jose (95134-1813)
PHONE..........................408 601-1000
Joseph Perl, *Ch of Bd*
Chris Day, *President*
EMP: 93 **EST:** 1998
SQ FT: 13,000
SALES (est): 56MM
SALES (corp-wide): 5.6B **Publicly Held**
WEB: www.maximintegrated.com
SIC: 3674 Semiconductors & related devices
HQ: Maxim Integrated Products, Inc.
160 Rio Robles
San Jose CA 95134
408 601-1000

(P-6215)
MOBIVEIL INC
890 Hillview Ct Ste 250, Milpitas (95035-4574)
PHONE..........................408 791-2977
Ravikumar R Thummarukudy, *CEO*
Dale Olstinske, *Vice Pres*
Amit Saxena, *Vice Pres*
D Srinivasan, *Principal*
Gopa Periyadan, *Council Mbr*
EMP: 18 **EST:** 2011
SALES (est): 3.4MM **Privately Held**
WEB: www.mobiveil.com
SIC: 3674 Semiconductors & related devices

(P-6216)
MONOLITHIC POWER SYSTEMS INC
79 Great Oaks Blvd, San Jose (95119-1311)
PHONE..........................408 826-0600
Paul Ueunten, *Principal*
Victor Lee, *Bd of Directors*
Jeff Zhou, *Bd of Directors*
Maurice Sciammas, *Vice Pres*
Saria Tseng, *Vice Pres*
EMP: 81 **EST:** 2004
SALES (est): 6.6MM **Privately Held**
WEB: www.monolithicpower.cn
SIC: 3674 Read-only memory (ROM)

(P-6217)
MONTAGE TECHNOLOGY INC
101 Metro Dr Ste 500, San Jose (95110-1342)
PHONE..........................408 982-2788
Howard Yang, *Principal*
Lee Khem, *Sales Staff*
Robert Jin, *Manager*
EMP: 17 **EST:** 2005
SALES (est): 3.6MM **Privately Held**
WEB: www.montage-tech.com
SIC: 3674 Semiconductors & related devices

(P-6218)
MOSYS INC
2309 Bering Dr, San Jose (95131-1125)
PHONE..........................408 418-7500
Daniel Lewis, *President*
James W Sullivan, *CFO*
EMP: 24 **EST:** 1991
SQ FT: 10,000
SALES (est): 6.8MM **Privately Held**
WEB: www.mosys.com
SIC: 3674 Semiconductors & related devices; integrated circuits, semiconductor networks, etc.

(P-6219)
MPI AMERICA INC
2360 Qume Dr Ste C, San Jose (95131-1838)
PHONE..........................408 770-3650
Richard William Dock, *President*
Janet Chiang, *General Mgr*
Wayne Lee, *General Mgr*
Carrie Huang, *Engineer*
Devon Vongdeng, *Sales Staff*
EMP: 17
SALES: 16.8MM **Privately Held**
SIC: 3674 Semiconductors & related devices

(P-6220)
MPS INTERNATIONAL LTD
79 Great Oaks Blvd, San Jose (95119-1311)
PHONE..........................408 826-0600
Michael R Hsing, *CEO*
▼ **EMP:** 1891 **EST:** 1997
SQ FT: 100,000
SALES (est): 1.3MM **Publicly Held**
WEB: www.monolithicpower.cn
SIC: 3674 Semiconductors & related devices
PA: Monolithic Power Systems, Inc.
5808 Lake Washington Blvd
Kirkland WA 98033

(P-6221)
MULTIPHY INC
125 University Ave # 200, Palo Alto (94301-1622)
PHONE..........................650 600-9194
AVI Shabtai, *Principal*
EMP: 18 **EST:** 2013
SALES (est): 591.4K **Privately Held**
SIC: 3674 Integrated circuits, semiconductor networks, etc.

(P-6222)
NANOSILICON INC
2461 Autumnvale Dr, San Jose (95131-1802)
PHONE..........................408 263-7341
Lincoln Bejan, *President*
Jackie Bejan, *CFO*
John Ayala, *Vice Pres*
EMP: 22 **EST:** 2009
SQ FT: 30,000
SALES (est): 3.5MM **Privately Held**
WEB: www.nanosiliconinc.com
SIC: 3674 Semiconductors & related devices

(P-6223)
NANOSYS INC (PA)
233 S Hillview Dr, Milpitas (95035-5417)
PHONE..........................408 240-6700
Jason Hartlove, *CEO*
Noland Granberry, *Exec VP*

(PA)=Parent Co (HQ)=Headquarters (DH)=Div Headquarters
✪ = New Business established in last 2 years

3674 - Semiconductors County (P-6224)

John Hanlow, *Senior VP*
Charlie Hotz, *Vice Pres*
Seila Chim, *Technician*
EMP: 275 **EST:** 2001
SQ FT: 32,000
SALES (est): 48.2MM **Privately Held**
WEB: www.nanosys.com
SIC: 3674 Semiconductors & related devices

(P-6224)
NATIONAL SEMICONDUCTOR CORP (HQ)
2900 Semiconductor Dr, Santa Clara (95051-0695)
PHONE..................408 721-5000
Ellen L Barker, *CEO*
Lewis Chew, *CFO*
Todd M Duchene, *Senior VP*
Edward J Sweeney, *Senior VP*
Jamie E Samath, *Vice Pres*
▲ **EMP:** 1700 **EST:** 1959
SALES (est): 388.2MM
SALES (corp-wide): 14.4B **Publicly Held**
WEB: www.ti.com
SIC: 3674 Microprocessors
PA: Texas Instruments Incorporated
12500 Ti Blvd
Dallas TX 75243
214 479-3773

(P-6225)
NDK AMERICA INC
1551 Mccarthy Blvd, Milpitas (95035-7387)
PHONE..................408 428-0800
EMP: 16 **EST:** 2005
SALES (est): 283.2K **Privately Held**
WEB: www.ndk.com
SIC: 3674 Semiconductors & related devices

(P-6226)
NDSP DELAWARE INC
Also Called: Ndsp Crp
224 Airport Pkwy Ste 400, San Jose (95110-1095)
PHONE..................408 626-1640
Ven L Lee, *President*
Leonard Liu, *Chairman*
Hongmin Zhang, *CTO*
EMP: 41 **EST:** 1997
SQ FT: 9,285
SALES (est): 1.8MM
SALES (corp-wide): 40.8MM **Publicly Held**
WEB: www.pixelworks.com
SIC: 3674 Integrated circuits, semiconductor networks, etc.
PA: Pixelworks, Inc.
226 Airport Pkwy Ste 595
San Jose CA 95110
408 200-9200

(P-6227)
NEOCONIX INC
4020 Moorpark Ave Ste 108, San Jose (95117-1845)
PHONE..................408 530-9393
Asuri Raghavan, *President*
Jim Witham, *CEO*
Dirk Brown, *Exec VP*
Phil Damberg, *Vice Pres*
Dinesh Kalakkad, *Vice Pres*
EMP: 40 **EST:** 2002
SQ FT: 5,000
SALES (est): 4.5MM **Privately Held**
WEB: www.neoconix.com
SIC: 3674 Semiconductors & related devices

(P-6228)
NEOPHOTONICS CORPORATION (PA)
3081 Zanker Rd, San Jose (95134-2127)
PHONE..................408 232-9200
Timothy S Jenks, *President*
Raymond Cheung, *COO*
Elizabeth EBY, *CFO*
Wupen Yuen,
Bradford W Wright, *Senior VP*
EMP: 993 **EST:** 1996
SQ FT: 103,314
SALES (est): 371.1MM **Publicly Held**
WEB: www.neophotonics.com
SIC: 3674 Semiconductors & related devices

(P-6229)
NETHRA IMAGING INC (PA)
2855 Bowers Ave, Santa Clara (95051-0917)
PHONE..................408 257-5880
Ramesh Singh, *President*
EMP: 40 **EST:** 2003
SALES (est): 9.4MM **Privately Held**
WEB: www.nethra-imaging.com
SIC: 3674 Semiconductors & related devices

(P-6230)
NETXEN INC (DH)
205 Ravendale Dr, Mountain View (94043-5216)
PHONE..................949 389-6000
Govind Kizhepat, *President*
Jag Setlur, *Controller*
EMP: 408 **EST:** 2001
SQ FT: 20,950
SALES (est): 6.6MM
SALES (corp-wide): 682.9MM **Privately Held**
WEB: www.marvell.com
SIC: 3674 Microcircuits, integrated (semiconductor)

(P-6231)
NEXGEN POWER SYSTEMS INC
3151 Jay St Ste 201, Santa Clara (95054-3338)
PHONE..................408 230-7698
Dinesh Ramanathan, *President*
Narayanan Karu, *CFO*
EMP: 30 **EST:** 2017
SALES (est): 5.1MM **Privately Held**
WEB: www.nexgenpowersystems.com
SIC: 3674 Semiconductor circuit networks

(P-6232)
NGCODEC INC
440 N Wolfe Rd Ste 2187, Sunnyvale (94085-3869)
PHONE..................408 766-4382
Oliver Gunasekara, *CEO*
Alberto Duenas, *Chairman*
EMP: 20 **EST:** 2012
SALES (est): 2.7MM
SALES (corp-wide): 3.1B **Publicly Held**
WEB: www.xilinx.com
SIC: 3674 Semiconductors & related devices
PA: Xilinx, Inc.
2100 All Programmable
San Jose CA 95124
408 559-7778

(P-6233)
NIMSOFT INC (DH)
3965 Freedom Cir Fl 6, Santa Clara (95054-1286)
PHONE..................408 796-3400
Chris O'Malley, *CEO*
Dave Dwyer, *General Ptnr*
Mark Harris, *CFO*
Lokesh Jindal, *Senior VP*
Ron Doyle, *Vice Pres*
EMP: 387 **EST:** 2002
SQ FT: 6,000
SALES (est): 81.2MM
SALES (corp-wide): 23.8B **Publicly Held**
WEB: www.broadcom.com
SIC: 3674 Semiconductors & related devices
HQ: Ca, Inc.
520 Madison Ave
New York NY 10022
800 225-5224

(P-6234)
NUVIA INC
2811 Mission College Blvd F, Santa Clara (95054-1884)
PHONE..................408 654-9696
Gerard Williams, *CEO*
Jon Masters, *Vice Pres*
Jon Carvill, *VP Mktg*
EMP: 20 **EST:** 2019
SALES (est): 9.9MM
SALES (corp-wide): 23.5B **Publicly Held**
WEB: www.qualcomm.com
SIC: 3674 8731 Metal oxide silicon (MOS) devices; computer (hardware) development

HQ: Qualcomm Technologies, Inc.
5775 Morehouse Dr
San Diego CA 92121
858 587-1121

(P-6235)
NVIDIA CORPORATION (PA)
2788 San Tomas Expy, Santa Clara (95051-0952)
PHONE..................408 486-2000
Jen-Hsun Huang, *President*
Shae Fogg, *Partner*
Vanita Sodha, *Partner*
Colette M Kress, *CFO*
Mark Perry, *Bd of Directors*
◆ **EMP:** 458 **EST:** 1993
SALES (est): 16.6B **Publicly Held**
WEB: www.nvidia.com
SIC: 3674 Semiconductors & related devices

(P-6236)
NVIDIA INTL HOLDINGS INC (HQ)
2788 San Tomas Expy, Santa Clara (95051-0952)
PHONE..................408 486-2000
Jen-Hsun Huang, *President*
EMP: 100 **EST:** 2015
SALES (est): 19.3MM **Publicly Held**
WEB: www.nvidia.com
SIC: 3674 Semiconductors & related devices

(P-6237)
NXEDGE SAN CARLOS LLC
1000 Commercial St, San Carlos (94070-4024)
PHONE..................650 422-2269
EMP: 24 **EST:** 2015
SALES (est): 3.9MM **Privately Held**
WEB: www.nxedge.com
SIC: 3674 Semiconductors & related devices

(P-6238)
NXP USA INC
411 E Plumeria Dr, San Jose (95134-1924)
PHONE..................408 518-5500
Fari Assaderaghi, *Senior VP*
Tracy Fisher, *Software Engr*
George Arce, *Engineer*
Barbara Casas, *Engineer*
Bala Muccala, *Engineer*
EMP: 500
SALES (corp-wide): 8.6B **Privately Held**
WEB: www.nxp.com
SIC: 3674 Integrated circuits, semiconductor networks, etc.
HQ: Nxp Usa, Inc.
6501 W William Cannon Dr
Austin TX 78735
512 933-8214

(P-6239)
OCLARO INC (HQ)
400 N Mccarthy Blvd, Milpitas (95035-9100)
PHONE..................408 383-1400
Greg Dougherty, *CEO*
Craig Cocchi, *COO*
Pete Mangan, *CFO*
Adam Carter, *Ch Credit Ofcr*
Lisa Paul, *Exec VP*
EMP: 331 **EST:** 1988
SALES (est): 543.1MM
SALES (corp-wide): 1.7B **Publicly Held**
WEB: www.oclaro.com
SIC: 3674 3826 3827 Light emitting diodes; laser scientific & engineering instruments; optical instruments & apparatus
PA: Lumentum Holdings Inc.
1001 Ridder Park Dr
San Jose CA 95131
408 546-5483

(P-6240)
OCLARO FIBER OPTICS INC (DH)
400 N Mccarthy Blvd, Milpitas (95035-9100)
PHONE..................408 383-1400
Harry L Bosco, *President*
Robert J Nobile, *CFO*
Atsushi Horiuchi, *Senior VP*
Justin J O'Neill, *Senior VP*

Pinaki Mohapatra, *Controller*
EMP: 245 **EST:** 2000
SALES (est): 160.6MM
SALES (corp-wide): 1.7B **Publicly Held**
WEB: www.oclaro.com
SIC: 3674 Photoconductive cells

(P-6241)
OEPIC SEMICONDUCTORS INC
1231 Bordeaux Dr, Sunnyvale (94089-1203)
PHONE..................408 747-0388
Yi-Ching Pao, *President*
EMP: 35 **EST:** 2000
SQ FT: 18,000
SALES (est): 6.2MM **Privately Held**
WEB: www.oepic.com
SIC: 3674 Semiconductors & related devices

(P-6242)
OMNIVISION TECHNOLOGIES INC (PA)
4275 Burton Dr, Santa Clara (95054-1512)
PHONE..................408 567-3000
Shaw Hong, *CEO*
Raymond Wu, *President*
Henry Yang, *COO*
Anson Chan, *CFO*
Michelle Milunovic, *Vice Pres*
▲ **EMP:** 1943 **EST:** 1995
SQ FT: 207,000
SALES (est): 238.1MM **Privately Held**
WEB: www.ovt.com
SIC: 3674 Semiconductors & related devices

(P-6243)
ON SEMCNDCTOR CNNCTVITY SLTONS (HQ)
1704 Automation Pkwy, San Jose (95131-1873)
PHONE..................669 209-5500
Keith D Jackson, *President*
Lionel Bonnot, *Senior VP*
David Carroll, *Senior VP*
Marge Blair, *Admin Asst*
Hongping Liu, *Design Engr*
EMP: 323 **EST:** 2005
SQ FT: 84,000
SALES: 220.4MM
SALES (corp-wide): 5.2B **Publicly Held**
WEB: www.onsemi.com
SIC: 3674 Semiconductors & related devices
PA: On Semiconductor Corporation
5005 E Mcdowell Rd
Phoenix AZ 85008
602 244-6600

(P-6244)
ONSPEC TECHNOLOGY PARTNERS INC
Also Called: Bi Cmos Foundry
975 Comstock St, Santa Clara (95054-3407)
PHONE..................408 654-7627
Peter Liljegren, *Vice Pres*
Sona Joe, *Vice Pres*
EMP: 45 **EST:** 2004
SALES (est): 2.9MM **Privately Held**
SIC: 3674 Wafers (semiconductor devices)

(P-6245)
ONTERA INC
2161 Delaware Ave Ste B, Santa Cruz (95060-5790)
PHONE..................831 222-2193
Murielle Thinard McLane, *CEO*
Paul Marr, *Officer*
Raparti Swayambhu, *Senior VP*
Andrea Chow, *Vice Pres*
Mark Rose, *Vice Pres*
EMP: 107
SQ FT: 12,000
SALES (est): 20.5MM **Privately Held**
WEB: www.ontera.bio
SIC: 3674 3826 Semiconductors & related devices; analytical instruments

(P-6246)
OORJA CORPORATION
45473 Warm Springs Blvd, Fremont (94539-6104)
PHONE..................510 659-1899

▲ = Import ▼ = Export
◆ = Import/Export

PRODUCTS & SERVICES SECTION

3674 - Semiconductors County (P-6269)

EMP: 50 EST: 2018
SALES (est): 3.4MM Privately Held
WEB: www.oorjafuelcells.com
SIC: 3674 Semiconductors & related devices

(P-6247)
OPEN-SILICON INC (DH)
Also Called: Openfive
490 N Mccarthy Blvd # 220, Milpitas (95035-5118)
PHONE...................................408 240-5700
Taher Madraswala, *President*
Jay Vyas, *Senior VP*
Anand Bariya, *Vice Pres*
Gerry Benson, *Vice Pres*
Hans Bouwmeester, *Vice Pres*
EMP: 33 EST: 2003
SQ FT: 10,000
SALES (est): 13.6MM Privately Held
WEB: www.openfive.com
SIC: 3674 Integrated circuits, semiconductor networks, etc.

(P-6248)
ORBOTECH LT SOLAR LLC
Also Called: Olt Solar
5970 Optical Ct, San Jose (95138-1400)
PHONE...................................408 414-3777
Georg Bremer, *Mng Member*
Kam Law,
Matt Toshima,
EMP: 20 EST: 2009
SALES (est): 3.8MM
SALES (corp-wide): 6.9B Publicly Held
WEB: www.kla-tencor.com
SIC: 3674 Integrated circuits, semiconductor networks, etc.
PA: Kla Corporation
   1 Technology Dr
   Milpitas CA 95035
   408 875-3000

(P-6249)
PANTRONIX CORPORATION
2710 Lakeview St, Fremont (94538-6534)
P.O. Box 1460, Los Altos (94023-1460)
PHONE...................................510 656-5898
▲ EMP: 250
SQ FT: 82,000
SALES (est): 34MM Privately Held
WEB: www.pantronix.com
SIC: 3674 8734 Mfg Semiconductors/Related Devices Testing Laboratory

(P-6250)
PATRIOT MEMORY INC (PA)
47027 Benicia St, Fremont (94538-7331)
PHONE...................................510 979-1021
Paul Jones, *Mng Member*
Hung Pham, *Info Tech Mgr*
Sarah Lien, *Marketing Staff*
Doug Diggs,
Jim Jones, *Director*
▲ EMP: 125 EST: 1985
SALES (est): 35.1MM Privately Held
WEB: www.patriotmemory.com
SIC: 3674 5045 Semiconductors & related devices; computers

(P-6251)
PIXELWORKS INC (PA)
226 Airport Pkwy Ste 595, San Jose (95110-3704)
PHONE...................................408 200-9200
Todd A Debonis, *President*
Daniel J Heneghan, *Ch of Bd*
Elias N Nader, *CFO*
Anthony Gioeli, *Exec VP*
Peter Carson, *Vice Pres*
EMP: 147 EST: 1997
SQ FT: 10,000
SALES (est): 40.8MM Publicly Held
WEB: www.pixelworks.com
SIC: 3674 7372 Semiconductors & related devices; prepackaged software; utility computer software

(P-6252)
POLISHING CORPORATION AMERICA
Also Called: PCA
442 Martin Ave, Santa Clara (95050-2911)
PHONE...................................888 892-3377
Stuart Becker, *CEO*
▲ EMP: 40 EST: 1970

SQ FT: 10,000
SALES (est): 5.5MM Privately Held
WEB: www.pcasilicon.com
SIC: 3674 Silicon wafers, chemically doped

(P-6253)
POWER INTEGRATIONS INC (PA)
5245 Hellyer Ave, San Jose (95138-1002)
PHONE...................................408 414-9200
Balu Balakrishnan, *President*
William George, *Ch of Bd*
Sandeep Nayyar, *CFO*
Wendy A Arienzo, *Bd of Directors*
Sunil Gupta, *Vice Pres*
EMP: 706 EST: 1988
SALES (est): 488.3MM Publicly Held
WEB: www.power.com
SIC: 3674 Integrated circuits, semiconductor networks, etc.

(P-6254)
POWER INTGRTONS INTL HLDNGS IN
5245 Hellyer Ave, San Jose (95138-1002)
PHONE...................................408 414-8528
Balu Balakrishnan, *President*
Wolfgang Ademmer, *Vice Pres*
Joe Schiffer, *Director*
EMP: 60 EST: 1997
SALES (est): 2.6MM
SALES (corp-wide): 488.3MM Publicly Held
WEB: www.power.com
SIC: 3674 Integrated circuits, semiconductor networks, etc.
PA: Power Integrations, Inc.
   5245 Hellyer Ave
   San Jose CA 95138
   408 414-9200

(P-6255)
PRIME SOLUTIONS INC (PA)
4261 Business Center Dr, Fremont (94538-6357)
PHONE...................................510 490-2255
Harry H Moroyan, *President*
Vera Moroyan, *Admin Sec*
EMP: 72 EST: 1988
SQ FT: 1,200
SALES (est): 3.2MM Privately Held
WEB: www.primesolutions.com
SIC: 3674 Integrated circuits, semiconductor networks, etc.

(P-6256)
PRIMENANO INC
4701 Patrick Henry Dr # 8, Santa Clara (95054-1819)
PHONE...................................650 300-5115
Eduard Weichselbaum, *CEO*
EMP: 15 EST: 2010
SALES (est): 1.2MM Privately Held
WEB: www.primenanoinc.com
SIC: 3674 Semiconductors & related devices

(P-6257)
PROBE-LOGIC INC
1885 Lundy Ave Ste 101, San Jose (95131-1887)
PHONE...................................408 416-0777
Hon Cheng, *CEO*
Tai Nguyen, *Engineer*
Luis Morales, *Sales Mgr*
Ken Chen, *Manager*
EMP: 42 EST: 2002
SQ FT: 15,000
SALES (est): 5.4MM Privately Held
WEB: www.probelogic.com
SIC: 3674 Semiconductors & related devices

(P-6258)
PROCESS SPECIALTIES INC
1660 W Linne Rd Ste A, Tracy (95377-8025)
PHONE...................................209 832-1344
Edward Morris, *President*
Mark Hinkle, *Vice Pres*
Manny D Arroz, *Admin Sec*
Steve Hayashi, *Engineer*
Garry Jenkins, *Engineer*
EMP: 27 EST: 1988
SQ FT: 35,910

SALES: 10.3MM Privately Held
WEB: www.processspecialties.com
SIC: 3674 Wafers (semiconductor devices)

(P-6259)
PROMEX INDUSTRIES INCORPORATED (PA)
3075 Oakmead Village Dr, Santa Clara (95051-0811)
PHONE...................................408 496-0222
Richard F Otte, *CEO*
Chris Pugh, *Vice Pres*
Dr Edward Binkley, *Principal*
▲ EMP: 65 EST: 1999
SQ FT: 30,000
SALES (est): 23.5MM Privately Held
WEB: www.promex-ind.com
SIC: 3674 Modules, solid state; hybrid integrated circuits; integrated circuits, semiconductor networks, etc.

(P-6260)
PROTONEX LLC
Also Called: Pni Sensor
2331 Circadian Way, Santa Rosa (95407-5437)
PHONE...................................707 566-2260
Eric Walters,
Becky OH,
EMP: 18 EST: 2017
SALES (est): 1.8MM Privately Held
SIC: 3674 Radiation sensors

(P-6261)
QMAT INC
Also Called: Quenta Material
2424 Walsh Ave, Santa Clara (95051-1303)
P.O. Box 110644, Campbell (95011-0644)
PHONE...................................408 228-5880
Francois Henley, *Principal*
Kristine Ryan, *Admin Sec*
EMP: 15 EST: 2012
SALES (est): 1.2MM Privately Held
WEB: www.qmatinc.com
SIC: 3674 Wafers (semiconductor devices)

(P-6262)
QUALCOMM ATHEROS INC (HQ)
1700 Technology Dr, San Jose (95110-1383)
PHONE...................................408 773-5200
Lilia Munoz, *Executive*
Gary Szilagyi, *General Mgr*
Nathaniel Houghton, *Sr Software Eng*
Susan Schwarz, *Info Tech Dir*
MAI Hoang, *Technician*
▲ EMP: 600 EST: 1998
SALES (est): 221.5MM
SALES (corp-wide): 23.5B Publicly Held
WEB: www.qualcomm.com
SIC: 3674 4899 Integrated circuits, semiconductor networks, etc.; communication signal enhancement network system
PA: Qualcomm Incorporated
   5775 Morehouse Dr
   San Diego CA 92121
   858 587-1121

(P-6263)
QUANTUMSCAPE BATTERY INC
1730 Technology Dr, San Jose (95110-1331)
PHONE...................................408 452-2000
Jagdeep Singh, *President*
Howard Lukens, *Officer*
PH D Joseph Han, *Technical Staff*
Marie Mayer, *Technical Staff*
Ann Truong, *Controller*
EMP: 121 EST: 2010
SALES (est): 24.1MM
SALES (corp-wide): 35.9MM Publicly Held
WEB: www.quantumscape.com
SIC: 3674 Semiconductors & related devices
PA: Quantumscape Corporation
   1730 Technology Dr
   San Jose CA 95110
   408 452-2000

(P-6264)
QUANTUMSCAPE CORPORATION (PA)
1730 Technology Dr, San Jose (95110-1331)
PHONE...................................408 452-2000
Jagdeep Singh, *CEO*
Kevin Hettrich, *CFO*
Celina Mikolajczak, *Vice Pres*
Timothy Holme, *CTO*
EMP: 100 EST: 2020
SALES (est): 35.9MM Publicly Held
WEB: www.quantumscape.com
SIC: 3674 Semiconductors & related devices

(P-6265)
QUELLAN INC
Also Called: Intersil Quellan
1001 Murphy Ranch Rd, Milpitas (95035-7912)
PHONE...................................408 546-3487
Tony Stelliga, *CEO*
Donalc Macleod, *Ch of Bd*
James Diller, *CEO*
Guy Anthony, *CFO*
Joy Laskar, *CTO*
EMP: 26 EST: 2001
SALES (est): 1.5MM Privately Held
SIC: 3674 Semiconductors & related devices

(P-6266)
QUICKLOGIC CORPORATION (PA)
2220 Lundy Ave, San Jose (95131-1816)
PHONE...................................408 990-4000
Brian C Faith, *President*
Michael R Farese, *Ch of Bd*
Anthony Contos, *CFO*
Timothy Saxe, *Senior VP*
Rajiv Jain, *Vice Pres*
EMP: 46 EST: 1988
SQ FT: 24,164
SALES: 8.6MM Publicly Held
WEB: www.quicklogic.com
SIC: 3674 3823 Integrated circuits, semiconductor networks, etc.; programmers, process type

(P-6267)
R2 SEMICONDUCTOR INC
3600 W Byshore Rd Ste 205, Palo Alto (94303)
PHONE...................................408 745-7400
David Fisher, *President*
Frank Sasselli, *Vice Pres*
Larry Burns, *Principal*
Andrew Hartland, *Principal*
Ravi Ramachandran, *Principal*
EMP: 19 EST: 2008
SALES (est): 2.3MM Privately Held
WEB: www.r2semi.com
SIC: 3674 Integrated circuits, semiconductor networks, etc.

(P-6268)
RAMBUS INC (PA)
4453 N 1st St Ste 100, San Jose (95134-1260)
PHONE...................................408 462-8000
Luc Seraphin, *President*
Charles Kissner, *Ch of Bd*
Sean Fan, *COO*
Rahul Mathur, *CFO*
John Shinn, *Ch Credit Ofcr*
◆ EMP: 398 EST: 1990
SALES (est): 246.3MM Publicly Held
WEB: www.rambus.com
SIC: 3674 6794 Integrated circuits, semiconductor networks, etc.; patent owners & lessors

(P-6269)
REACTION TECHNOLOGY INC (HQ)
3400 Bassett St, Santa Clara (95054-2703)
PHONE...................................408 970-9601
Uzi Sasson, *CEO*
James Jacobson, *President*
David Sallous, *Vice Pres*
Janice Baker, *Manager*
EMP: 20 EST: 1991
SQ FT: 10,800

(PA)=Parent Co (HQ)=Headquarters (DH)=Div Headquarters
✪ = New Business established in last 2 years

3674 - Semiconductors County (P-6270)

SALES (est): 7.9MM
SALES (corp-wide): 1.4B **Publicly Held**
WEB: www.reactiontechnology.com
SIC: 3674 Integrated circuits, semiconductor networks, etc.
PA: Littelfuse, Inc.
 8755 W Higgins Rd Ste 500
 Chicago IL 60631
 773 628-1000

(P-6270)
REFLEX PHOTONICS INC
1250 Oakmead Pkwy, Sunnyvale (94085-4027)
PHONE..............408 501-8886
EMP: 30
SALES (est): 1.8MM **Privately Held**
WEB: www.reflexphotonics.com
SIC: 3674 Mfg Semiconductors/Related Devices

(P-6271)
RELIANCE COMPUTER CORP
2451 Mission College Blvd, Santa Clara (95054-1214)
PHONE..............408 492-1915
▲ EMP: 115
SALES (est): 6MM
SALES (corp-wide): 4.2B **Publicly Held**
SIC: 3674 3672 Mfg Semiconductors/Related Devices Mfg Printed Circuit Boards
HQ: Broadcom Corporation
 5300 California Ave
 Irvine CA 95131
 949 926-5000

(P-6272)
RENESAS ELECTRONICS AMER INC (HQ)
6024 Silver Creek Vly Rd, San Jose (95138-1011)
P.O. Box 67071, Scotts Valley (95067-7071)
PHONE..............408 432-8888
Sailesh Chittipeddi, *President*
Tiffani Costa, *President*
James Shih, *COO*
Aris Bolisay, *CFO*
James Vu, *Treasurer*
▲ EMP: 880 EST: 1980
SQ FT: 263,000
SALES (est): 758.4MM **Privately Held**
WEB: www.renesas.com
SIC: 3674 Integrated circuits, semiconductor networks, etc.

(P-6273)
RENESAS ELECTRONICS AMER INC
Also Called: Intersil Techwell
240a Lawrence Ave, South San Francisco (94080-6817)
PHONE..............408 588-6750
Tom Thompson, *Engineer*
Martin Baker, *Marketing Staff*
Willie Chan, *Sales Staff*
Vince Villajoaquin, *Manager*
EMP: 600 **Privately Held**
WEB: www.renesas.com
SIC: 3674 Semiconductors & related devices
HQ: Renesas Electronics America Inc.
 6024 Silver Creek Vly Rd
 San Jose CA 95138
 408 432-8888

(P-6274)
ROBERTSON PRECISION INC
2971 Spring St, Redwood City (94063-3935)
PHONE..............408 230-3044
Bernadette Robertson, *CEO*
William B Robertson, *President*
Eric Paulsen, *General Mgr*
EMP: 24 EST: 1984
SALES (est): 1.2MM **Privately Held**
WEB: www.robertsonprecision.com
SIC: 3674 3842 3829 Wafers (semiconductor devices); implants, surgical; measuring & controlling devices

(P-6275)
ROCKLEY PHOTONICS INC
333 W San Carlos St # 850, San Jose (95110-2711)
PHONE..............408 579-9210
Andrew George Rickman, *Branch Mgr*
EMP: 15
SALES (corp-wide): 20.1MM **Privately Held**
WEB: www.rockleyphotonics.com
SIC: 3674 Semiconductors & related devices
HQ: Rockley Photonics, Inc.
 234 E Colo Blvd Ste 600
 Pasadena CA 91101
 626 304-9960

(P-6276)
S3 GRAPHICS INC
940 Mission Ct, Fremont (94539-8202)
PHONE..............510 687-4900
Wenchih Chen, *President*
Iming Pai, *Vice Pres*
EMP: 108 EST: 2000
SALES (est): 6.8MM **Privately Held**
SIC: 3674 Semiconductors & related devices
PA: S3 Graphics Co., Ltd
 C/O: Card Corporate Services Ltd
 George Town GR CAYMAN

(P-6277)
SAMIL POWER US LTD
3478 Buskirk Ave Ste 1000, Pleasant Hill (94524-4378)
PHONE..............925 930-3924
Peter Peiju Cui, *CEO*
▲ EMP: 43 EST: 2012
SQ FT: 2,000
SALES (est): 5MM
SALES (corp-wide): 81.6K **Privately Held**
WEB: www.samilpower.com
SIC: 3674 Solar cells
PA: Wuxi Samil Power Co., Ltd.
 No.52, Huigu Venture Park, Zhenghe Boulevard, Huishan District
 Wuxi 21417
 510 835-9313

(P-6278)
SANKALP USA INC
Also Called: Sankalp Semiconductor
2225 E Bayshore Rd 200, Palo Alto (94303-3220)
PHONE..............408 372-6090
Vivek Pawar, *Chairman*
Samir Patel, *CEO*
Atul Arora, *Vice Pres*
Mrinal Das, *Vice Pres*
Madhav RAO, *Vice Pres*
EMP: 35 EST: 2009
SALES (est): 9.9MM **Privately Held**
WEB: www.sankalpsemi.com
SIC: 3674 Integrated circuits, semiconductor networks, etc.
HQ: Sankalp Semiconductor Private Limited
 Plot No:9, Survey No 89
 Hubballi KA 58002

(P-6279)
SCINTERA NETWORKS INC
160 Rio Robles, San Jose (95134-1813)
PHONE..............408 636-2600
Davin Lee, *CEO*
Scott M Gibson, *CFO*
Steffen Hahn, *Vice Pres*
Bob Koupal, *Vice Pres*
Rajeev Krishnamoorthy, *Vice Pres*
EMP: 47 EST: 2001
SQ FT: 20,000
SALES (est): 5.1MM **Privately Held**
SIC: 3674 Semiconductors & related devices

(P-6280)
SEMI AUTOMATION & TECH INC
Also Called: Noel Technologies
1510 Dell Ave Ste C, Campbell (95008-6917)
PHONE..............408 374-9549
Kristin Boyce, *President*
Brenda Hill, *Vice Pres*
▲ EMP: 42 EST: 1996
SQ FT: 7,500
SALES (est): 7MM **Privately Held**
WEB: www.noeltech.com
SIC: 3674 Semiconductors & related devices

(P-6281)
SEMICAT INC (PA)
47900 Fremont Blvd, Fremont (94538-6507)
PHONE..............408 514-6900
Jae Yeol Park, *CEO*
Mike Nam, *COO*
Joon Suh Juhn, *CFO*
Young Seok You, *CFO*
Tam Tran, *Engineer*
◆ EMP: 23 EST: 2003
SQ FT: 46,000
SALES (est): 4MM **Privately Held**
WEB: www.semicat.com
SIC: 3674 Semiconductors & related devices

(P-6282)
SEMICNDCTOR CMPONENTS INDS LLC
Also Called: On Semiconductor
3001 Stender Way, Santa Clara (95054-3216)
PHONE..............408 660-2699
Bernie Colpitts, *Officer*
Bernie R Colpitts, *Officer*
Rajeev Govil, *Design Engr*
Mollie Olarte, *Design Engr*
Michael Jensen, *Engineer*
EMP: 30
SALES (corp-wide): 5.2B **Publicly Held**
WEB: www.onsemi.com
SIC: 3674 3825 3651 Semiconductors & related devices; diode & transistor testers; amplifiers: radio, public address or musical instrument
HQ: Semiconductor Components Industries, Llc
 5005 E Mcdowell Rd
 Phoenix AZ 85008
 602 244-6600

(P-6283)
SEMINET INC
150 Great Oaks Blvd, San Jose (95119-1347)
PHONE..............408 754-8537
Humayun Kabir, *Principal*
Greg Krikorian, *Principal*
EMP: 20 EST: 1988
SALES (est): 2.2MM **Privately Held**
WEB: www.seminet.com
SIC: 3674 Semiconductors & related devices

(P-6284)
SENTONS USA INC
627 River Oaks Pkwy, San Jose (95134-1907)
PHONE..............408 732-9000
Jess Lee, *President*
Dawn Cao, *Engineer*
EMP: 24 EST: 2011
SALES (est): 3.1MM **Privately Held**
WEB: www.sentons.com
SIC: 3674 Semiconductors & related devices

(P-6285)
SILICON GENESIS CORPORATION
46816 Lakeview Blvd, Fremont (94538-6543)
PHONE..............408 228-5885
Theodore E Fong, *Branch Mgr*
EMP: 20 **Privately Held**
WEB: www.sigen.net
SIC: 3674 Semiconductors & related devices
PA: Silicon Genesis Corporation
 145 Baytech Dr
 San Jose CA 95134

(P-6286)
SILICON IMAGE INC (HQ)
2115 Onel Dr, San Jose (95131-2032)
PHONE..............408 616-4000
Joe Bedewi, *CFO*
Kurt Thielen, *President*
Byron Milstead, *Vice Pres*
David L Rutledge, *CTO*
Victor Da Costa, *Engng Exec*
▲ EMP: 571 EST: 1995
SQ FT: 128,154
SALES (est): 119.8MM
SALES (corp-wide): 408.1MM **Publicly Held**
WEB: www.latticesemi.com
SIC: 3674 7371 Semiconductors & related devices; computer software development & applications
PA: Lattice Semiconductor Corp
 5555 Ne Moore Ct
 Hillsboro OR 97124
 503 268-8000

(P-6287)
SILICON LABS INTEGRATION INC (HQ)
Also Called: Silicon Laboratories
2708 Orchard Pkwy 30, San Jose (95134-1968)
PHONE..............408 702-1400
Jean Luc Nauleau, *President*
Pierre Lamond, *Chairman*
Britta Young, *Office Mgr*
Vladimir Mesarovic, *Engineer*
Kyle Beckmeyer, *Marketing Mgr*
EMP: 48 EST: 1989
SALES (est): 11.3MM **Publicly Held**
WEB: www.silabs.com
SIC: 3674 Semiconductors & related devices

(P-6288)
SILICON LIGHT MACHINES CORP (DH)
820 Kifer Rd Ste B, Sunnyvale (94086-5200)
PHONE..............408 240-4700
Lars Eng, *CEO*
Ken Fukui, *Senior VP*
EMP: 19 EST: 1994
SQ FT: 18,000
SALES (est): 7.9MM **Privately Held**
WEB: www.siliconlight.com
SIC: 3674 Semiconductors & related devices
HQ: Screen North America Holdings, Inc.
 150 Innovation Dr Ste A
 Elk Grove Village IL 60007
 847 870-7400

(P-6289)
SILICON MOTION INC
690 N Mccarthy Blvd # 200, Milpitas (95035-5134)
PHONE..............408 501-5300
Wallace Kou, *President*
Richard Chang, *Vice Pres*
Lien-Chun Liu, *Exec Dir*
Bernadette Aguilon, *Admin Asst*
Amanda Huang, *Administration*
EMP: 60 EST: 1995
SQ FT: 12,000
SALES (est): 13.6MM **Privately Held**
WEB: www.siliconmotion.com
SIC: 3674 Integrated circuits, semiconductor networks, etc.
PA: Silicon Motion Technology Corporation
 C/O: Conyers Trust Company (Cayman) Limited
 George Town GR CAYMAN

(P-6290)
SILICON STANDARD CORP
Also Called: SSC
4701 Patrick Henry Dr # 16, Santa Clara (95054-1863)
PHONE..............408 234-6964
EMP: 20
SALES (est): 2.2MM **Privately Held**
WEB: www.siliconstandard.com
SIC: 3674 Mfg Semiconductors/Related Devices

(P-6291)
SILICON STORAGE TECHNOLOGY INC (HQ)
1020 Kifer Rd, Sunnyvale (94086-5301)
PHONE..............408 735-9110
Steve Sanghi, *President*
James B Boyd, *CFO*
Wade F Meyercord, *Bd of Directors*
Chen Tsai, *Senior VP*
Bomy Chen, *Vice Pres*
EMP: 451 EST: 1989
SQ FT: 132,000

▲ = Import ▼ = Export
◆ = Import/Export

PRODUCTS & SERVICES SECTION
3674 - Semiconductors County (P-6310)

SALES (est): 128.1MM
SALES (corp-wide): 5.4B Publicly Held
WEB: www.sst.com
SIC: 3674 5065 Memories, solid state; semiconductor devices
PA: Microchip Technology Inc
2355 W Chandler Blvd
Chandler AZ 85224
480 792-7200

(P-6292)
SILICON TURNKEY SOLUTIONS INC (HQ)
1804 Mccarthy Blvd, Milpitas (95035-7410)
PHONE 408 904-0200
Richard Kingdon, *President*
Virginia Benguerel, *COO*
Michael Rooney, *CFO*
Steve Lew, *Program Mgr*
Jerry W Chang, *General Mgr*
EMP: 17 **EST:** 2000
SQ FT: 35,000
SALES (est): 21.7MM
SALES (corp-wide): 191.4MM Privately Held
WEB: www.sts-usa.com
SIC: 3674 5065 Microcircuits, integrated (semiconductor); semiconductor devices
PA: Micross Components, Inc.
7725 N Orange Blossom Trl
Orlando FL 32810
407 298-7100

(P-6293)
SILICON VLY MCRELECTRONICS INC
2985 Kifer Rd, Santa Clara (95051-0802)
PHONE 408 844-7100
Van Pham, *Accounting Mgr*
Vance Callinan, *Business Mgr*
Roger Neef, *Sales Mgr*
Svm Wong, *Sales Staff*
David Alcantar, *Manager*
◆ **EMP:** 30 **EST:** 1990
SQ FT: 30,000
SALES (est): 9.7MM Privately Held
WEB: www.svmi.com
SIC: 3674 Silicon wafers, chemically doped

(P-6294)
SILICONCORE TECHNOLOGY INC
890 Hillview Ct Ste 120, Milpitas (95035-4573)
PHONE 408 946-8185
Eric LI, *President*
Heng Liu, *Officer*
Nicos Syrimis, *Senior VP*
Glenn Bailey, *Vice Pres*
Maggie Huang, *Vice Pres*
▲ **EMP:** 23
SQ FT: 6,000
SALES (est): 25.2MM Privately Held
WEB: www.silicon-core.com
SIC: 3674 Integrated circuits, semiconductor networks, etc.; light emitting diodes; television monitors

(P-6295)
SILICONIX INCORPORATED (HQ)
2585 Junction Ave, San Jose (95134-1923)
PHONE 408 988-8000
Serge Jaunay, *CEO*
King Owyang, *President*
Nick Bacile, *COO*
▲ **EMP:** 610 **EST:** 1962
SQ FT: 220,100
SALES (est): 322.9MM
SALES (corp-wide): 2.5B Publicly Held
WEB: www.vishay.com
SIC: 3674 Transistors
PA: Vishay Intertechnology, Inc.
63 Lancaster Ave
Malvem PA 19355
610 644-1300

(P-6296)
SILICONIX SEMICONDUCTOR INC
2201 Laurelwood Rd, Santa Clara (95054-1593)
PHONE 408 988-8000
EMP: 54 **EST:** 1999

SALES (est): 5.8MM
SALES (corp-wide): 2.5B Publicly Held
SIC: 3674 Semiconductors & related devices
HQ: Siliconix Incorporated
2585 Junction Ave
San Jose CA 95134
408 988-8000

(P-6297)
SILVER PEAK SYSTEMS INC (HQ)
2860 De La Cruz Blvd, Santa Clara (95050-2635)
PHONE 408 935-1800
David Hughes, *CEO*
Ian Whiting, *President*
Eric Yeaman, *CFO*
Rick Valentine, *Ch Credit Ofcr*
John Vincenzo, *Chief Mktg Ofcr*
EMP: 116 **EST:** 2004
SQ FT: 29,000
SALES (est): 72.8MM
SALES (corp-wide): 26.9B Publicly Held
WEB: www.silver-peak.com
SIC: 3674 Integrated circuits, semiconductor networks, etc.
PA: Hewlett Packard Enterprise Company
11445 Compaq Center W Dr
Houston TX 77070
650 687-5817

(P-6298)
SIPEX CORPORATION (DH)
48720 Kato Rd, Fremont (94538-7312)
PHONE 669 265-6100
Ralph Schmitt, *CEO*
Clyde R Wallin, *CFO*
Lee Cleveland, *Senior VP*
John Phan, *Info Tech Dir*
Guy Adams, *Director*
EMP: 115 **EST:** 1965
SQ FT: 95,700
SALES (est): 10.7MM
SALES (corp-wide): 478.6MM Publicly Held
WEB: www.maxlinear.com
SIC: 3674 Integrated circuits, semiconductor networks, etc.
HQ: Exar Corporation
1060 Rincon Cir
San Jose CA 95131
669 265-6100

(P-6299)
SIRF TECHNOLOGY HOLDINGS INC
1060 Rincon Cir, San Jose (95131-1325)
PHONE 408 523-6500
Diosdado B Banatao, *Ch of Bd*
Diosdado P Banatao, *Ch of Bd*
Dennis Bencala, *CFO*
Geoffrey Ribar, *CFO*
Kanwar Chadha, *Vice Pres*
EMP: 753 **EST:** 2001
SQ FT: 48,000
SALES (est): 176.4MM
SALES (corp-wide): 23.5B Publicly Held
WEB: www.qualcomm.com
SIC: 3674 3663 Semiconductors & related devices;
HQ: Csr Limited
Churchill House
Cambridge CAMBS CB4 0
122 369-2000

(P-6300)
SITEK PROCESS SOLUTIONS
233 Technology Way Ste 3, Rocklin (95765-1208)
PHONE 916 797-9000
James Mullany, *CEO*
Terri Mullany, *Vice Pres*
Blake Mullany, *Technician*
Daniel Mullany, *Sales Staff*
Tyler Israel, *Manager*
▲ **EMP:** 18 **EST:** 1998
SQ FT: 8,000
SALES (est): 5.1MM Privately Held
WEB: www.sitekprocess.com
SIC: 3674 Semiconductors & related devices

(P-6301)
SITIME CORPORATION
5451 Patrick Henry Dr, Santa Clara (95054-1167)
PHONE 408 328-4400
Rajesh Vashist, *Ch of Bd*
Arthur D Chadwick, *CFO*
Vincent P Pangrazio,
Fariborz Assaderaghi, *Exec VP*
Lionel Bonnot, *Exec VP*
EMP: 187 **EST:** 2003
SQ FT: 50,400
SALES (est): 116.1MM Privately Held
WEB: www.sitime.com
SIC: 3674 Semiconductors & related devices

(P-6302)
SK HYNIX MEMORY SOLUTIONS INC
3103 N 1st St, San Jose (95134-1934)
PHONE 408 514-3500
Tony Yoon, *CEO*
Sang SOO Son, *CFO*
Chee Hoe Chu, *Vice Pres*
Khaled Labib, *Vice Pres*
Albert Hu, *Sr Software Eng*
EMP: 270 **EST:** 2004
SALES (est): 41MM Privately Held
WEB: www.skhms.com
SIC: 3674 Semiconductors & related devices
PA: Sk Hynix Inc.
2091 Gyeongchung-Daero, Bubal-Eup
Icheon 17336

(P-6303)
SMALL PRECISION TOOLS INC
Also Called: Wire Bonding Tools
1330 Clegg St, Petaluma (94954-1127)
PHONE 707 765-4545
Peter Glutz, *President*
Joe Gracia, *CFO*
Mary Ong, *Vice Pres*
Megumi Kuroda, *General Mgr*
Susan Poti, *Administration*
▲ **EMP:** 94 **EST:** 1969
SQ FT: 25,000
SALES (est): 16.5MM
SALES (corp-wide): 216.2MM Privately Held
WEB: www.smallprecisiontools.com
SIC: 3674 Semiconductors & related devices
PA: Spt Roth Ag
Werkstrasse 28
Lyss BE 3250
323 878-080

(P-6304)
SMART GLOBAL HOLDINGS INC (PA)
39870 Eureka Dr, Newark (94560-4809)
PHONE 510 623-1231
Mark Adams, *President*
Ajay Shah, *Ch of Bd*
Thierry Pellegrino, *President*
Jack Pacheco, *COO*
Bruce Goldberg,
EMP: 475 **EST:** 1988
SQ FT: 79,480
SALES (est): 1.5B Publicly Held
WEB: www.smartm.com
SIC: 3674 Semiconductors & related devices

(P-6305)
SMART MODULAR TECH DE INC (HQ)
45800 Northport Loop W, Fremont (94538-6413)
PHONE 510 623-1231
Jack Pacheco, *CEO*
Frank Perezalonso, *VP Bus Dvlpt*
Paolo Pugno, *Business Mgr*
Lee C CBA, *Credit Staff*
Rick Hazell, *Director*
EMP: 100 **EST:** 2004
SALES (est): 166.5MM
SALES (corp-wide): 1.5B Publicly Held
WEB: www.smartm.com
SIC: 3674 Semiconductors & related devices

PA: Smart Global Holdings, Inc.
39870 Eureka Dr
Newark CA 94560
510 623-1231

(P-6306)
SMART MODULAR TECHNOLOGIES INC (HQ)
39870 Eureka Dr, Newark (94560-4809)
PHONE 510 623-1231
Jack Pacheco, *CEO*
Kiwan Kim, *Vice Pres*
Mike Rubino, *Vice Pres*
Kimberley McKinney, *Executive*
Vivian Thai, *Program Mgr*
▲ **EMP:** 1148 **EST:** 1988
SALES (est): 312.7MM
SALES (corp-wide): 1.5B Publicly Held
WEB: www.smartm.com
SIC: 3674 Semiconductors & related devices
PA: Smart Global Holdings, Inc.
39870 Eureka Dr
Newark CA 94560
510 623-1231

(P-6307)
SONIC TECHNOLOGY PRODUCTS INC
108 Boulder St, Nevada City (95959-2610)
P.O. Box 539, Grass Valley (95945-0539)
PHONE 530 272-4607
Melanie Sullivan, *CEO*
Justin Reinholz, *President*
Craig Ashcraft, *Vice Pres*
Marianne Boyer, *Executive*
Susan Walsh, *Sales Staff*
▲ **EMP:** 22 **EST:** 1986
SQ FT: 2,000
SALES (est): 1.1MM Privately Held
WEB: www.sonictechnologyproducts.com
SIC: 3674 3651 Semiconductors & related devices; household audio & video equipment

(P-6308)
SORAA INC (HQ)
6500 Kaiser Dr Ste 110, Fremont (94555-3662)
PHONE 510 456-2200
Jeffery Parker, *Ch of Bd*
Charles Giancarlo, *Bd of Directors*
Ann REO, *Senior VP*
Neal Woods, *Senior VP*
Nahid Afshar, *Vice Pres*
▲ **EMP:** 90 **EST:** 2007
SQ FT: 50,000
SALES (est): 27.6MM
SALES (corp-wide): 101.4MM Privately Held
WEB: www.soraa.com
SIC: 3674 3641 Semiconductors & related devices; electric lamps; electric lamp (bulb) parts
PA: Ecosense Lighting Inc.
837 N Spring St Ste 103
Los Angeles CA 90012
855 632-6736

(P-6309)
SPANSION LLC (DH)
198 Champion Ct, San Jose (95134-1709)
P.O. Box 3453, Sunnyvale (94088-3453)
PHONE 512 691-8500
Thad Trent, *President*
Eugene Spevakov, *Treasurer*
Randy Blair, *Vice Pres*
John Wang, *Vice Pres*
Joseph Dean, *Planning*
▲ **EMP:** 378 **EST:** 2003
SALES (est): 107.1MM
SALES (corp-wide): 10.1B Privately Held
WEB: www.cypress.com
SIC: 3674 Semiconductors & related devices
HQ: Cypress Semiconductor Corporation
198 Champion Ct
San Jose CA 95134
408 943-2600

(P-6310)
SPECTRUM SEMICONDUCTOR MTLS
155 Nicholson Ln, San Jose (95134-1359)
PHONE 408 435-5555
Steve Ochoa, *President*

3674 - Semiconductors County (P-6311)

Laura Bisceglia, *Purchasing*
Emily Muth, *Materials Mgr*
EMP: 16 EST: 1990
SQ FT: 7,100
SALES (est): 2.7MM Privately Held
WEB: www.spectrum-semi.com
SIC: 3674 Semiconductors & related devices

(P-6311)
SPIN MEMORY INC
45500 Northport Loop W, Fremont (94538-6498)
PHONE.................510 933-8200
Tom Sparkman, *President*
John Kispert, *Ch of Bd*
Antoine Bruyns, *CFO*
Mustafa Pinarbasi, *Senior VP*
Thomas Boone, *Vice Pres*
▲ EMP: 50 EST: 2007
SALES (est): 9.5MM Privately Held
WEB: www.spinmemory.com
SIC: 3674 Random access memory (RAM)

(P-6312)
STATS CHIPPAC INC (DH)
880 N Mccarthy Blvd # 250, Milpitas (95035-5121)
PHONE.................510 979-8000
Tan Lay Koon, *President*
Wan Choong Hoe, *Exec VP*
Han Byung Joon, *Exec VP*
John Lau Tai Chong, *Senior VP*
Janet Taylor, *Senior VP*
▲ EMP: 50 EST: 2000
SALES (est): 24.3MM Privately Held
WEB: www.jcetglobal.com
SIC: 3674 Integrated circuits, semiconductor networks, etc.

(P-6313)
STATS CHIPPAC TEST SVCS INC (DH)
Also Called: Fastramp
46429 Landing Pkwy, Fremont (94538-6496)
PHONE.................510 979-8000
Tan Lay Koon, *President*
David Goldberg, *Admin Sec*
Manuel Landavazo, *Sales Mgr*
EMP: 15 EST: 2001
SALES (est): 13.6MM Privately Held
WEB: www.jcetglobal.com
SIC: 3674 Semiconductors & related devices

(P-6314)
SUMMIT WIRELESS TECH INC (PA)
6840 Via Del Oro Ste 280, San Jose (95119-1380)
PHONE.................408 627-4716
Brett Moyer, *Ch of Bd*
Gary Williams, *CFO*
Yung Han, *Manager*
EMP: 30 EST: 2010
SQ FT: 1,500
SALES (est): 2.4MM Publicly Held
WEB: www.summitwireless.com
SIC: 3674 Semiconductors & related devices

(P-6315)
SUNPOWER CORPORATION (DH)
51 Rio Robles, San Jose (95134-1858)
PHONE.................408 240-5500
Peter Faricy, *President*
Dominic Kubelka, *Partner*
Thomas Werner, *Ch of Bd*
Manavendra Sial, *CFO*
Regan J Macpherson
▲ EMP: 600 EST: 1985
SQ FT: 61,000
SALES: 1.1B
SALES (corp-wide): 4.6B Publicly Held
WEB: www.us.sunpower.com
SIC: 3674 3679 Solar cells; photoelectric cells, solid state (electronic eye); power supplies, all types: static
HQ: Totalenergies Solar Intl
 La Defense
 Courbevoie 92400
 147 444-546

(P-6316)
SUNPREME INC
4701 Patrick Henry Dr # 25, Santa Clara (95054-1863)
PHONE.................408 419-9281
Ashok K Sinha, *CEO*
Mike Wanebo, *President*
Ratson Morad, *COO*
Surinder S Bedi, *Exec VP*
Homi Fateni, *Senior VP*
▲ EMP: 30 EST: 2009
SALES (est): 9.3MM Privately Held
WEB: www.sunpreme.com
SIC: 3674 Solar cells

(P-6317)
SUNSIL INC (PA)
3174 Danville Blvd Ste 1, Alamo (94507-1919)
P.O. Box 220 (94507-0220)
PHONE.................925 648-7779
Seth Alavi, *President*
Vivek Dutta, *Adv Board Mem*
Terry Snowden, *Sales Staff*
▲ EMP: 37 EST: 1999
SALES (est): 3.1MM Privately Held
WEB: www.sunsil.com
SIC: 3674 Semiconductors & related devices

(P-6318)
SUNSYSTEM TECHNOLOGY LLC
Also Called: Next Phase Solar
2802 10th St, Berkeley (94710-2711)
PHONE.................510 984-2027
Adam Burstein, *Branch Mgr*
David Hughes, *CIO*
Garrett Holtzen, *Technician*
EMP: 118
SALES (corp-wide): 28.3MM Privately Held
WEB: www.sstsolar.com
SIC: 3674 Photovoltaic devices, solid state
PA: Sunsystem Technology, Llc
 2731 Citrus Rd Ste D
 Rancho Cordova CA 95742
 916 671-3351

(P-6319)
SUNWORKS INC (PA)
2270 Douglas Blvd Ste 216, Roseville (95661-4239)
PHONE.................916 409-6900
Gaylon Morris, *CEO*
Judith Hall, *Ch of Bd*
Jason Bonfigt, *CFO*
Paul McDonnel, *CFO*
Stanley Speer, *Bd of Directors*
EMP: 55 EST: 2002
SALES (est): 37.9MM Publicly Held
WEB: www.sunworksusa.com
SIC: 3674 Integrated circuits, semiconductor networks, etc.

(P-6320)
SUPERTEX INC (HQ)
1235 Bordeaux Dr, Sunnyvale (94089-1203)
PHONE.................408 222-8888
Henry C Pao PH D, *President*
Benedict C K Choy, *Senior VP*
Phillip Kagel, *General Mgr*
Dean Converse, *Engineer*
Howard Lee, *Engineer*
▲ EMP: 316 EST: 1975
SQ FT: 42,000
SALES (est): 37.4MM
SALES (corp-wide): 5.4B Publicly Held
WEB: www.microchip.com
SIC: 3674 Integrated circuits, semiconductor networks, etc.
PA: Microchip Technology Inc
 2355 W Chandler Blvd
 Chandler AZ 85224
 480 792-7200

(P-6321)
SURFACE ART ENGINEERING INC
81 Bonaventura Dr, San Jose (95134-2105)
PHONE.................408 433-4700
Jennifer Lee, *CEO*
Richard Kundert, *President*

Esther Lee, *Program Mgr*
Grace Nam, *Program Mgr*
Sandy Chun, *General Mgr*
▲ EMP: 50 EST: 1993
SQ FT: 24,000
SALES (est): 11.7MM Privately Held
SIC: 3674 Computer logic modules

(P-6322)
SYMANTEC SEC HOLDINGS I INC
350 Ellis St, Mountain View (94043-2202)
PHONE.................650 527-8000
David Mahoney, *Bd of Directors*
William Wentz, *Bd of Directors*
Adam Bromwich, *Vice Pres*
Sheila Jordan, *Vice Pres*
Ken Schneider, *Vice Pres*
EMP: 18 EST: 2019
SALES (est): 6.4MM
SALES (corp-wide): 2.5B Publicly Held
WEB: www.nortonlifelock.com
SIC: 3674 Semiconductors & related devices
PA: Nortonlifelock Inc.
 60 E Rio Salado Pkwy # 1
 Tempe AZ 85281
 650 527-8000

(P-6323)
T-RAM SEMICONDUCTOR INC
2109 Landings Dr, Mountain View (94043-0839)
PHONE.................408 597-3670
Dado Banatao, *Ch of Bd*
Sam R Nakib, *President*
Scott Robins, *Vice Pres*
EMP: 18 EST: 2000
SQ FT: 28,000
SALES (est): 888.2K Privately Held
WEB: www.t-ram.com
SIC: 3674 Semiconductors & related devices

(P-6324)
TAHOE RF SEMICONDUCTOR INC
12834 Earhart Ave, Auburn (95602-9027)
PHONE.................530 823-9786
Irshad A Rasheed, *CEO*
Brian Kabaker, *CFO*
Christopher Saint, *Vice Pres*
EMP: 22 EST: 2002
SQ FT: 6,000
SALES (est): 1.1MM Privately Held
WEB: www.business.nasdaq.com
SIC: 3674 8711 Semiconductors & related devices; engineering services

(P-6325)
TAKEX AMERICA INC
1810 Oakland Rd Ste F, San Jose (95131-2316)
PHONE.................877 371-2727
Yuji Egawa, *President*
▲ EMP: 26 EST: 1997
SALES (est): 2.5MM Privately Held
WEB: www.takexinc.com
SIC: 3674 Infrared sensors, solid state

(P-6326)
TECHNOPROBE AMERICA INC
2526 Qume Dr Ste 27, San Jose (95131-1870)
PHONE.................408 573-9911
Stefano Felici, *President*
Jody Johnston, *Engineer*
Michael Palumbo, *Marketing Staff*
Steven Radford, *Sales Staff*
EMP: 25 EST: 2007
SQ FT: 800
SALES (est): 4.1MM Privately Held
WEB: www.technoprobe.com
SIC: 3674 Semiconductors & related devices

(P-6327)
TELA INNOVATIONS INC
475 Alberto Way Ste 120, Los Gatos (95032-5480)
P.O. Box 320162 (95032-0102)
PHONE.................408 558-6300
Scott Becker, *CEO*
Carney Becker, *President*
Peter Calverley, *CFO*
Liz Stewart, *Vice Pres*

Roxane Ng, *Office Mgr*
EMP: 27 EST: 2006
SALES (est): 761.3K Privately Held
WEB: www.tela-inc.com
SIC: 3674 Integrated circuits, semiconductor networks, etc.

(P-6328)
TELEDYNE DEFENSE ELEC LLC
Also Called: Teledyne E2v Hirel Electronics
765 Sycamore Dr, Milpitas (95035-7465)
PHONE.................408 737-0992
Amy Saylors, *Manager*
EMP: 105
SALES (corp-wide): 3B Publicly Held
WEB: www.teledynedefenseelectronics.com
SIC: 3674 Semiconductors & related devices
HQ: Teledyne Defense Electronics, Llc
 1274 Terra Bella Ave
 Mountain View CA 94043
 650 691-9800

(P-6329)
TELEDYNE E2V, INC.
Also Called: Teledyne Hirel Electronics
765 Sycamore Dr, Milpitas (95035-7465)
PHONE.................408 737-0992
EMP: 44
SALES (corp-wide): 3B Publicly Held
WEB: www.teledyne-e2v.com
SIC: 3674 Semiconductors & related devices
HQ: E2v Holdings Inc.
 660 White Plains Rd # 525
 Tarrytown NY 10591
 415 987-2211

(P-6330)
TESSERA INC (DH)
3025 Orchard Pkwy, San Jose (95134-2017)
PHONE.................408 321-6000
Richard Chernicoff, *President*
Simon McElrea, *President*
Donald Stout, *Bd of Directors*
Christopher Pickett, *Vice Pres*
C Richard Neely Jr, *Principal*
EMP: 71 EST: 1992
SQ FT: 51,000
SALES (est): 34.3MM
SALES (corp-wide): 892MM Publicly Held
WEB: www.tessera.com
SIC: 3674 8999 Integrated circuits, semiconductor networks, etc.; inventor
HQ: Tessera Technologies, Inc.
 3025 Orchard Pkwy
 San Jose CA 95134
 408 321-6000

(P-6331)
TESSERA TECHNOLOGIES INC (DH)
3025 Orchard Pkwy, San Jose (95134-2017)
PHONE.................408 321-6000
Tom Lacey, *CEO*
Jon E Kirchner, *President*
Robert Andersen, *CFO*
Peter Van Deventer, *Chief Mktg Ofcr*
Kevin Doohan, *Officer*
▲ EMP: 131 EST: 1990
SALES (est): 87.4MM
SALES (corp-wide): 892MM Publicly Held
WEB: www.tessera.com
SIC: 3674 6794 Integrated circuits, semiconductor networks, etc.; memories, solid state; patent buying, licensing, leasing
HQ: Xperi Corporation
 3025 Orchard Pkwy
 San Jose CA 95134
 408 321-6000

(P-6332)
TEST-UM INC
430 N Mccarthy Blvd, Milpitas (95035-5112)
PHONE.................818 464-5021
David Vellequette, *CEO*
▲ EMP: 39 EST: 1993
SQ FT: 8,000

PRODUCTS & SERVICES SECTION
3674 - Semiconductors County (P-6353)

SALES (est): 4.7MM
SALES (corp-wide): 1.2B **Publicly Held**
WEB: www.viavisolutions.com
SIC: 3674 Semiconductors & related devices
PA: Viavi Solutions Inc.
7047 E Greenway Pkwy # 25
Scottsdale AZ 85254
408 404-3600

(P-6333)
THERMAL CONDUCTIVE BONDING INC (PA)
Also Called: T C B
19 Great Oaks Blvd Ste 20, San Jose (95119-1364)
PHONE..................408 920-0255
Wayne Simpson, *President*
Ryan Scatena, *Vice Pres*
Brandon Quintana, *Principal*
Angus McFadden, *Technology*
Robbin Dier, *Production*
EMP: 21 **EST:** 2012
SALES (est): 5.7MM **Privately Held**
WEB: www.tcbonding.com
SIC: 3674 Semiconductors & related devices

(P-6334)
TOWER SEMICONDUCTOR USA INC
2570 N 1st St Ste 480, San Jose (95131-1018)
PHONE..................408 770-1320
Doron Simon, *President*
Marco Racanelli, *Vice Pres*
Michael Song, *Vice Pres*
Gene Monnin, *Engineer*
Julie Akina, *Human Resources*
EMP: 15 **EST:** 1996
SQ FT: 4,100
SALES (est): 2.6MM **Privately Held**
WEB: www.towersemi.com
SIC: 3674 Semiconductors & related devices
PA: Tower Semiconductor Ltd
20 Shaul Amor Blvd
Migdal Haemek 23530

(P-6335)
TROPIAN INC
20813 Stevens Creek Blvd, Cupertino (95014-2185)
PHONE..................408 865-1300
Tim Unger, *President*
Earl Mc Cune, *CTO*
▲ **EMP:** 27 **EST:** 1996
SQ FT: 26,000
SALES (est): 404.1K **Privately Held**
WEB: www.tropian.com
SIC: 3674 Semiconductors & related devices

(P-6336)
TSI SEMICONDUCTORS AMERICA LLC (PA)
Also Called: Telefunken Semiconductors Amer
7501 Foothills Blvd, Roseville (95747-6504)
PHONE..................916 786-3900
Bruce Gray, *CEO*
Michael Gontar, *Ch of Bd*
John Doricko, *President*
Roger Lee, *COO*
Randy Ruegg, *CFO*
▲ **EMP:** 125 **EST:** 2011
SALES (est): 37.6MM **Privately Held**
WEB: www.tsisemi.com
SIC: 3674 Semiconductors & related devices

(P-6337)
TSMC TECHNOLOGY INC
2851 Junction Ave, San Jose (95134-1910)
PHONE..................408 382-8052
Lora Ho, *President*
Dick Thurston, *President*
Wendell Huang, *Treasurer*
Kc Chou, *Program Mgr*
Richard L Thurston, *Admin Sec*
EMP: 69 **EST:** 1996
SALES (est): 15.6MM **Privately Held**
WEB: www.tsmc.com
SIC: 3674 Semiconductor circuit networks
HQ: Tsmc Partners Ltd.
C/O: Portcullis Trusnet (Bvi) Limited
Road Town
-

(P-6338)
TVIA INC (PA)
4800 Great America Pkwy, Santa Clara (95054-1213)
PHONE..................408 982-8591
Eli Porat, *Ch of Bd*
Keith Yee, *CFO*
David Medin, *Vice Pres*
EMP: 27 **EST:** 1993
SQ FT: 16,500
SALES (est): 17.2MM **Privately Held**
WEB: www.tvia.com
SIC: 3674 Semiconductors & related devices

(P-6339)
UBICOM INC
195 Baypointe Pkwy, San Jose (95134-1697)
PHONE..................408 433-3330
EMP: 75
SQ FT: 15,000
SALES (est): 7.2MM **Privately Held**
WEB: www.ubicom.com
SIC: 3674 Mfg Semiconductors/Related Devices

(P-6340)
UBICOM INC (PA)
635 Clyde Ave, Mountain View (94043-2213)
PHONE..................408 523-7800
Doug Spreng, *Principal*
EMP: 48 **EST:** 2016
SALES (est): 181.2K **Privately Held**
SIC: 3674 3559 Integrated circuits, semiconductor networks, etc.; special industry machinery

(P-6341)
UHV SPUTTERING INC
275 Digital Dr, Morgan Hill (95037-2878)
PHONE..................408 779-2826
Rick Wooden, *President*
Mila Clement, *Marketing Staff*
EMP: 28 **EST:** 1989
SQ FT: 10,000
SALES (est): 7.6MM **Privately Held**
WEB: www.uhvsputtering.com
SIC: 3674 3471 Thin film circuits; electroplating & plating

(P-6342)
ULTRA CLEAN TECH SYSTEMS SVC I (HQ)
Also Called: Uct
26462 Corporate Ave, Hayward (94545-3914)
PHONE..................510 576-4400
Jim Skullhammer, *CEO*
Leonard Mezhvinsky, *President*
Casey Eichler, *CFO*
Ernest Maddock, *Bd of Directors*
Deborah Hayward, *Senior VP*
▲ **EMP:** 120 **EST:** 1991
SQ FT: 12,000
SALES (est): 191.7MM
SALES (corp-wide): 1.4B **Publicly Held**
WEB: www.uct.com
SIC: 3674 Semiconductors & related devices
PA: Ultra Clean Holdings, Inc.
26462 Corporate Ave
Hayward CA 94545
510 576-4400

(P-6343)
ULTRASIL LLC
3527 Breakwater Ave, Hayward (94545-3610)
PHONE..................510 266-3700
Nghia Nguyen, *CEO*
Len Anderson, *Vice Pres*
Tim Kivlin, *Sales Staff*
EMP: 20 **EST:** 2019
SALES (est): 2MM **Privately Held**
WEB: www.ultrasil.com
SIC: 3674 Silicon wafers, chemically doped

(P-6344)
UMC GROUP (USA)
488 De Guigne Dr, Sunnyvale (94085-3903)
PHONE..................408 523-7800
Robert Tsao, *Chairman*
Peter Chang, *Vice Chairman*
Ing-Dar Liu, *Vice Chairman*
Fu Tai Liou, *President*
Jason S Wang, *CEO*
▲ **EMP:** 75 **EST:** 1997
SQ FT: 40,000
SALES (est): 22.5MM **Privately Held**
WEB: www.umc.com
SIC: 3674 5065 Wafers (semiconductor devices); electronic parts & equipment
PA: United Microelectronics Corporation
3, Lixing 2nd Rd., Hsinchu Science Park,
Hsinchu City 30078

(P-6345)
VEECO INSTRUMENTS INC
Also Called: Veeco C V C
3100 Laurelview Ct, Santa Clara (95054)
PHONE..................510 657-8523
EMP: 28
SALES (corp-wide): 392.8MM **Publicly Held**
SIC: 3674 5065 Mfg Semiconductors/Related Devices Whol Electronic Parts/Equipment
PA: Veeco Instruments Inc.
Terminal Dr
Plainview NY 11803
516 677-0200

(P-6346)
VERISILICON INC (HQ)
2150 Gold St Ste 200, San Jose (95002-3702)
P.O. Box 1090 (95108-1090)
PHONE..................408 844-8560
Wayne WEI Ming Dai, *President*
Robert Brown, *CFO*
David Jarmon, *Vice Pres*
Wenqian Shi, *Vice Pres*
Yang Wang, *Vice Pres*
▲ **EMP:** 17 **EST:** 2003
SQ FT: 55,000
SALES (est): 13.1MM **Privately Held**
WEB: www.verisilicon.com
SIC: 3674 Semiconductors & related devices

(P-6347)
VIA TECHNOLOGIES INC
Also Called: Via Embedded Store
940 Mission Ct, Fremont (94539-8202)
PHONE..................510 683-3300
Wenchi Chen, *President*
Cher Wang, *CFO*
Tzumu Lin, *Vice Pres*
Fan Lu, *Project Mgr*
Andy Hwang, *Technical Staff*
▲ **EMP:** 130 **EST:** 1993
SQ FT: 55,000
SALES (est): 30.5MM **Privately Held**
WEB: www.viatech.com
SIC: 3674 Semiconductors & related devices
PA: Via Usa Inc
940 Mission Ct
Fremont CA 94539
510 683-3300

(P-6348)
VIRAGE LOGIC CORPORATION (HQ)
700 E Middlefield Rd, Mountain View (94043-4024)
PHONE..................650 584-5000
Alexander Shubat, *President*
Brian Sereda, *CFO*
Jian Y Pan, *Vice Pres*
Andreas Kuehlmann, *General Mgr*
Paul Furnanz, *Engineer*
EMP: 354 **EST:** 1995
SQ FT: 61,500
SALES (est): 102MM
SALES (corp-wide): 3.6B **Publicly Held**
WEB: www.synopsys.com
SIC: 3674 Integrated circuits, semiconductor networks, etc.
PA: Synopsys, Inc.
690 E Middlefield Rd
Mountain View CA 94043
650 584-5000

(P-6349)
VISHAY SILICONIX LLC
2585 Junction Ave, San Jose (95134-1923)
PHONE..................408 988-8000
Felix Zandman, *Ch of Bd*
Peter G Henrici, *Senior VP*
Darin Yost, *General Mgr*
Denise Walsh, *Administration*
Carl Haner, *CIO*
▲ **EMP:** 700 **EST:** 1999
SALES (est): 140.5MM
SALES (corp-wide): 2.5B **Publicly Held**
WEB: www.vishay.com
SIC: 3674 Semiconductors & related devices
HQ: Siliconix Incorporated
2585 Junction Ave
San Jose CA 95134
408 988-8000

(P-6350)
VISIONARY ELECTRONICS INC
141 Parker Ave, San Francisco (94118-2607)
PHONE..................415 751-8811
Brad Mc Millan, *President*
Roger Peterson, *Shareholder*
Jeff Fearn, *Treasurer*
Robin McMullen, *Marketing Staff*
EMP: 18 **EST:** 1974
SALES (est): 2.1MM **Privately Held**
WEB: www.viselect.com
SIC: 3674 3679 Microprocessors; recording & playback heads, magnetic

(P-6351)
VOLTERRA SEMICONDUCTOR LLC (DH)
160 Rio Robles, San Jose (95134-1813)
PHONE..................408 601-1000
Mark Casper, *President*
Christopher Paisley, *Ch of Bd*
Craig Teuscher, *COO*
Mike Burns, *CFO*
William Numann, *Senior VP*
EMP: 100 **EST:** 1996
SQ FT: 73,000
SALES (est): 82.7MM
SALES (corp-wide): 5.6B **Publicly Held**
WEB: www.maximintegrated.com
SIC: 3674 3612 Semiconductors & related devices; voltage regulators, transmission & distribution
HQ: Maxim Integrated Products, Inc.
160 Rio Robles
San Jose CA 95134
408 601-1000

(P-6352)
VOLTERRA SEMICONDUCTOR LLC
3839 Spinnaker Ct, Fremont (94538-6537)
PHONE..................510 743-1200
Jeff Staszak, *CEO*
EMP: 164
SALES (corp-wide): 5.6B **Publicly Held**
SIC: 3674 3612 Semiconductors & related devices; voltage regulators, transmission & distribution
HQ: Volterra Semiconductor Llc
160 Rio Robles
San Jose CA 95134
408 601-1000

(P-6353)
W2 OPTRONICS INC (PA)
5500 Stewart Ave, Fremont (94538-3100)
PHONE..................510 207-8320
Xinshi Xu, *CEO*
Yuezhong Feng, *Vice Pres*
Xuehua Wu, *Vice Pres*
Guoqiang Xu, *Vice Pres*
EMP: 19 **EST:** 2009
SQ FT: 10,000
SALES (est): 1.6MM **Privately Held**
WEB: www.w2opt.com
SIC: 3674 3661 3827 Microprocessors; fiber optics communications equipment; lenses, optical: all types except ophthalmic; prisms, optical

---

(PA)=Parent Co (HQ)=Headquarters (DH)=Div Headquarters
✪ = New Business established in last 2 years

3674 - Semiconductors County (P-6354)

PRODUCTS & SERVICES SECTION

(P-6354)
WAFER PROCESS SYSTEMS INC
3641 Charter Park Dr, San Jose (95136-1312)
PHONE................408 445-3010
Douglas H Caldwell, *CEO*
Christopher J Schmitz, *Vice Pres*
EMP: 15 **EST:** 1983
SALES (est): 3.1MM **Privately Held**
WEB: www.waferprocess.com
SIC: 3674 Semiconductors & related devices

(P-6355)
WAFERNET INC
2142 Paragon Dr, San Jose (95131-1305)
PHONE................408 437-9747
Lori L Vann, *President*
Jon Mewes, *CFO*
Frank Chang, *Officer*
Dave Mewes, *Vice Pres*
Lisa Zhang, *Engineer*
▲ **EMP:** 17 **EST:** 1988
SALES (est): 3.9MM **Privately Held**
WEB: www.wafernet.com
SIC: 3674 Semiconductors & related devices

(P-6356)
WINSLOW AUTOMATION INC
Also Called: Six Sigma
905 Montague Expy, Milpitas (95035-6817)
PHONE................408 262-9004
Russell Winslow, *CEO*
Daryl Sawtelle, *CFO*
Amy Phan, *Controller*
Edna Daos, *Human Res Mgr*
Tisha Wolf, *Opers Mgr*
EMP: 58
SQ FT: 24,784
SALES (est): 12.4MM **Privately Held**
WEB: www.winslowautomation.com
SIC: 3674 Semiconductors & related devices

(P-6357)
WINTEC INDUSTRIES INC (PA)
8674 Thornton Ave, Newark (94560-3330)
PHONE................510 953-7440
David Jeng, *CEO*
Sue Jeng, *COO*
Bob Neher, *Bd of Directors*
Frank Patchel, *Officer*
Jennifer Chen, *Vice Pres*
▲ **EMP:** 96 **EST:** 1988
SQ FT: 85,000
SALES (est): 53.5MM **Privately Held**
WEB: www.wintecind
SIC: 3674 3571 8742 7389 Semiconductors & related devices; electronic computers; computers, digital, analog or hybrid; mainframe computers; materials mgmt. (purchasing, handling, inventory) consultant; site location consultant; inventory computing service

(P-6358)
WINWAY USA INC
1800 Wyatt Dr Ste 2, Santa Clara (95054-1527)
PHONE................203 775-9311
Mark Wang, *CEO*
Stephen A Evans, *President*
Robert Bollo, *CFO*
Rob Lanoce, *Sales Staff*
EMP: 16 **EST:** 2014
SQ FT: 5,000
SALES (est): 1.1MM **Privately Held**
WEB: www.winwayglobal.com
SIC: 3674 Semiconductors & related devices
PA: Winway Technology Co., Ltd.
68, Chuangyi S. Rd.,
Kaohsiung City 81156

(P-6359)
WORLDWIDE ENERGY AND MFG USA (PA)
1675 Rollins Rd Ste F, Burlingame (94010-2320)
PHONE................650 692-7788
John Ballard, *Ch of Bd*
Tiffany Margaret Shum, *Director*
▲ **EMP:** 511 **EST:** 2000
SQ FT: 9,680
SALES (est): 33.8MM **Privately Held**
WEB: www.wwmusa.com
SIC: 3674 Semiconductors & related devices

(P-6360)
XILINX DEVELOPMENT CORPORATION (HQ)
2100 All Programable, San Jose (95124-4355)
P.O. Box 240010 (95154-2410)
PHONE................408 559-7778
Jon A Olson, *CEO*
John Hieb, *Sales Staff*
EMP: 100 **EST:** 1993
SALES (est): 18.1MM
SALES (corp-wide): 3.1B **Publicly Held**
WEB: www.xilinx.com
SIC: 3674 Semiconductors & related devices
PA: Xilinx, Inc.
2100 All Programable
San Jose CA 95124
408 559-7778

(P-6361)
XPERI CORPORATION (HQ)
3025 Orchard Pkwy, San Jose (95134-2017)
PHONE................408 321-6000
Jon Kirchner, *CEO*
Richard S Hill, *Ch of Bd*
Robert Andersen, *CFO*
Geir Skaaden, *Officer*
Paul Davis, *Admin Sec*
EMP: 104 **EST:** 2002
SALES (est): 280MM
SALES (corp-wide): 892MM **Publicly Held**
WEB: www.xperi.com
SIC: 3674 7379 7819 8742 Semiconductors & related devices; data processing consultant; ; consultants, motion picture; management information systems consultant
PA: Xperi Holding Corporation
3025 Orchard Pkwy
San Jose CA 95134
408 321-6000

(P-6362)
YADAV TECHNOLOGY INC
48371 Fremont Blvd # 101, Fremont (94538-6554)
PHONE................510 438-0148
Petro Estakhri, *CEO*
Bob Netter, *CFO*
Rani Ranjan, *Principal*
EMP: 16 **EST:** 2007
SALES (est): 194.8K **Privately Held**
WEB: www.avalanche-technology.com
SIC: 3674 Semiconductors & related devices

(P-6363)
YIELD ENGINEERING SYSTEMS INC
3178 Laurelview Ct, Fremont (94538-6535)
PHONE................510 954-6889
Ramakanth Alapati, *CEO*
Alex Chow, *President*
Rezwan Lateef, *President*
Ken Macwilliams, *CFO*
Fred Garcy, *CFO*
EMP: 70 **EST:** 1980
SQ FT: 20,000
SALES (est): 25.8MM **Privately Held**
WEB: www.yieldengineering.com
SIC: 3674 Semiconductors & related devices

(P-6364)
ZEP SOLAR LLC (DH)
161 Mitchell Blvd Ste 104, San Rafael (94903-2085)
PHONE................415 479-6900
Michael John Miskovsky, *CEO*
Peter David, *CFO*
Christina Manansala, *Vice Pres*
Jack West, *CTO*
▲ **EMP:** 28 **EST:** 2009
SQ FT: 8,200
SALES (est): 12.9MM
SALES (corp-wide): 31.5B **Publicly Held**
WEB: www.solarcity.com
SIC: 3674 Photovoltaic devices, solid state

(P-6365)
ZEST LABS INC (HQ)
2349 Bering Dr, San Jose (95131-1125)
P.O. Box 641810 (95164-1810)
PHONE................408 200-6500
Peter Mehring, *CEO*
Tocd Clayton, *Senior VP*
Scott Durgin, *CTO*
Dean Kawaguchi, *Technology*
EMP: 41 **EST:** 2004
SQ FT: 8,000
SALES (est): 28.5MM **Publicly Held**
WEB: www.zestlabs.com
SIC: 3674 Semiconductors & related devices

(P-6366)
ZILOG INC (DH)
1590 Buckeye Dr, Milpitas (95035-7418)
PHONE................408 513-1500
Darin G Billerbeck, *President*
Mike Speckman, *President*
Perry J Grace, *CFO*
Steve Darrough, *Vice Pres*
Dan Eaton, *Vice Pres*
EMP: 100 **EST:** 1997
SQ FT: 42,000
SALES (est): 32.8MM
SALES (corp-wide): 1.4B **Publicly Held**
WEB: www.zilog.com
SIC: 3674 Microcircuits, integrated (semiconductor)
HQ: Ixys, Llc
1590 Buckeye Dr
Milpitas CA 95035
408 457-9000

(P-6367)
ZNSHINE PV-TECH INC
400 Oyster Point Blvd # 326, South San Francisco (94080-1994)
PHONE................415 810-0861
Wangsheng Kong, *CEO*
▲ **EMP:** 25 **EST:** 2011
SALES (est): 910K **Privately Held**
WEB: www.znshinesolar.com
SIC: 3674 Solar cells
PA: Znshine Pv Tech Co., Ltd.
No.1, Zhenxing S. Road, Zhixi Industrial Cluster Zone, Jintan Di
Changzhou 21325

(P-6368)
ZOLA ELECTRIC LABS INC
555 De Haro St Ste 220, San Francisco (94107-2399)
PHONE................650 542-6939
William Lenihan, *CEO*
Guido Frantzen, *CFO*
Ranjan Prasad, *Vice Pres*
EMP: 25 **EST:** 2015
SQ FT: 2,500
SALES (est): 5MM **Privately Held**
WEB: www.zolaelectric.com
SIC: 3674 Solar cells
PA: Off Grid Electric Ltd
C/O: Estera Trust (Cayman) Limited
Grand Cayman GR CAYMAN

(P-6369)
ZORAN CORPORATION (DH)
1060 Rincon Cir, San Jose (95131-1325)
PHONE................972 673-1600
Daniel Willard Gardiner, *CEO*
Mustafa Ozgen, *President*
Karl Schneider, *CFO*
Isaac Shenberg PHD, *Senior VP*
Robert Krk, *Vice Pres*
◆ **EMP:** 1024 **EST:** 1981
SQ FT: 89,000
SALES (est): 101.6MM
SALES (corp-wide): 23.5B **Publicly Held**
WEB: www.qualcomm.com
SIC: 3674 Integrated circuits, semiconductor networks, etc.
HQ: Csr Limited
Churchill House
Cambridge CAMBS CB4 0
122 369-2000

3675 Electronic Capacitors

(P-6370)
BESTRONICS HOLDINGS INC (PA)
2090 Fortune Dr, San Jose (95131-1823)
PHONE................408 385-7777
Nat Mani, *CEO*
Ron Menigoz, *Exec VP*
Steve Yetso, *Vice Pres*
Ben Calub, *VP Mfg*
EMP: 62 **EST:** 2011
SQ FT: 73,000
SALES (est): 101.1MM **Privately Held**
SIC: 3675 Electronic capacitors

(P-6371)
JENNINGS TECHNOLOGY CO LLC (DH)
970 Mclaughlin Ave, San Jose (95122-2611)
PHONE................408 292-4025
W David Smith, *CEO*
Kurt Gallo, *Vice Pres*
Jamie Horton, *Vice Pres*
Roderick Mosely, *Director*
▲ **EMP:** 70 **EST:** 1942
SALES (est): 12MM
SALES (corp-wide): 26.1B **Privately Held**
WEB: www.tnb.com
SIC: 3675 3679 3625 Electronic capacitors; electronic circuits; relays, for electronic use
HQ: Abb Installation Products Inc.
860 Ridge Lake Blvd
Memphis TN 38120
901 252-5000

(P-6372)
ZF ARRAY TECHNOLOGY INC
2302 Trade Zone Blvd, San Jose (95131-1819)
PHONE................408 433-9920
Robert Zinn, *CEO*
Richard Freiberger, *COO*
Jim Viviani, *Vice Pres*
▲ **EMP:** 31 **EST:** 2003
SQ FT: 33,000
SALES (est): 1.4MM
SALES (corp-wide): 386.4MM **Privately Held**
WEB: www.smtc.com
SIC: 3675 Electronic capacitors
PA: Smtc Corporation
7050 Woodbine Ave
Markham ON L3R 4
905 479-1810

3676 Electronic Resistors

(P-6373)
SEMICNDCTOR CMPONENTS INDS LLC
3001 Stender Way, Santa Clara (95054-3216)
PHONE................408 542-1051
EMP: 103
SALES (corp-wide): 5.2B **Publicly Held**
WEB: www.onsemi.com
SIC: 3676 3675 3672 3674 Electronic resistors; electronic capacitors; printed circuit boards; microcircuits, integrated (semiconductor)
HQ: Semiconductor Components Industries, Llc
5005 E Mcdowell Rd
Phoenix AZ 85008
602 244-6600

(P-6374)
YAGEO AMERICA CORPORATION
2550 N 1st St Ste 480, San Jose (95131-1038)
PHONE................408 240-6200
CHI Wen Chang, *President*
John Blackerby, *Regl Sales Mgr*
Dean Rambo, *Regl Sales Mgr*
Richard TSE, *Sales Staff*
▲ **EMP:** 20 **EST:** 2006
SALES (est): 3.5MM **Privately Held**
WEB: www.yageo.com
SIC: 3676 Electronic resistors

PRODUCTS & SERVICES SECTION
3679 - Electronic Components, NEC County (P-6396)

PA: Yageo Corporation
3f, 233-1, 233-2, Baoqiao Rd.,
New Taipei City TAP 23145

3677 Electronic Coils & Transformers

(P-6375)
AHN ENTERPRISES LLC
Also Called: Santronics
1240 Birchwood Dr Ste 2, Sunnyvale (94089-2205)
PHONE..................408 734-1878
Raymond Ahn,
Joanna Abes,
Garrick Ahn,
Grant Ahn,
Jeewon Ahn,
◆ EMP: 17 EST: 1980
SQ FT: 5,000
SALES (est): 3MM Privately Held
WEB: www.santronics-usa.com
SIC: 3677 Electronic transformers

(P-6376)
ARAS POWER TECHNOLOGIES (PA)
371 Fairview Way, Milpitas (95035-3024)
PHONE..................408 935-8877
Fariborz RAD, President
▲ EMP: 30 EST: 2002
SQ FT: 5,000
SALES (est): 4MM Privately Held
WEB: www.araspower.com
SIC: 3677 3679 Transformers power supply, electronic type; static power supply converters for electronic applications

(P-6377)
BEL POWER SOLUTIONS INC
Also Called: Power One
2390 Walsh Ave, Santa Clara (95051-1301)
PHONE..................866 513-2839
Dennis Ackerman, President
Colin Dunn, Vice Pres
Steve Dawson, Director
▲ EMP: 2000 EST: 1949
SALES (est): 124.3MM
SALES (corp-wide): 465.7MM Publicly Held
WEB: www.belfuse.com
SIC: 3677 Electronic coils, transformers & other inductors
PA: Bel Fuse Inc.
206 Van Vorst St
Jersey City NJ 07302
201 432-0463

(P-6378)
CHILISIN AMERICA LTD
2880 Zanker Rd Ste 203, San Jose (95134-2122)
PHONE..................408 954-7389
Yao-Ching Kuo, CEO
Melanie Chen, Marketing Staff
EMP: 20 EST: 2011
SALES (est): 1.6MM Privately Held
WEB: www.chilisin.com
SIC: 3677 Electronic coils, transformers & other inductors
PA: Chilisin Electronics Corp.
No. 29, Lane 301, Dexing Rd.
Hukou Hsiang HSI 30346

(P-6379)
CUSTOM COILS INC
4000 Industrial Way, Benicia (94510-1242)
PHONE..................707 752-8633
Tom Quinn, President
John Quinn, CEO
Brian Quinn, Vice Pres
EMP: 15 EST: 1978
SQ FT: 7,200
SALES (est): 2.7MM Privately Held
WEB: www.ccoils.com
SIC: 3677 Electronic coils, transformers & other inductors

(P-6380)
FILTRATION DEVELOPMENT CO LLC
Also Called: Fdc Aerofilter
3920 Sandstone Dr, El Dorado Hills (95762-9652)
PHONE..................415 884-0555
Andrew Rowen,
Lorie Symon, Info Tech Mgr
John Holland, Sales Staff
Sharon Stark, Sales Staff
EMP: 22 EST: 1998
SQ FT: 3,000
SALES (est): 4.3MM Privately Held
WEB: www.fdcaerofilter.com
SIC: 3677 Filtration devices, electronic

(P-6381)
JAMES L HALL CO INCORPORATED
Also Called: Jetronics Company
218 Roberts Ave, Santa Rosa (95401-6146)
P.O. Box U (95402-0280)
PHONE..................707 544-2436
Stephen Vallarino, Mng Member
EMP: 55 EST: 1961
SALES (est): 14.9MM Privately Held
WEB: www.jetronics.com
SIC: 3677 3679 Electronic coils, transformers & other inductors; electronic circuits
PA: James L. Hall Co., Incorporated
360 Tesconi Cir Ste B
Santa Rosa CA 95401
707 547-0775

(P-6382)
MAGNETIC COILS INC
150 San Hedrin Cir, Willits (95490-8753)
PHONE..................707 459-5994
Don Setzco, Manager
EMP: 61
SALES (corp-wide): 5.2MM Privately Held
WEB: www.mcitransformer.com
SIC: 3677 Electronic coils, transformers & other inductors
PA: Magnetic Coils Inc.
411 Manhattan Ave
West Babylon NY
631 587-0510

(P-6383)
SCOTTS VALLEY MAGNETICS INC
300 El Pueblo Rd Ste 107, Scotts Valley (95066-4238)
P.O. Box 66575 (95067-6575)
PHONE..................831 438-3600
Norma Humphries, President
Karina Humphries, Treasurer
Jerry Humphries, Vice Pres
Karina Linn, Executive
John F Humphries, Admin Sec
▲ EMP: 24 EST: 1976
SQ FT: 15,000
SALES (est): 4.3MM Privately Held
WEB: www.svmagnetics.com
SIC: 3677 3679 3829 Filtration devices, electronic; electronic transformers; inductors, electronic; transformers power supply, electronic type; power supplies, all types: static; measuring & controlling devices

(P-6384)
SMART WIRES INC (PA)
Also Called: S W G
3292 Whipple Rd, Union City (94587-1217)
PHONE..................415 800-5555
Peter Wells, President
Scott Homes, Officer
Michael Walsh, Officer
Karamjit Singh, Vice Pres
Eduardo Aguilar, Admin Asst
EMP: 85 EST: 2010
SALES (est): 15.4MM Privately Held
WEB: www.smartwires.com
SIC: 3677 Electronic coils, transformers & other inductors

(P-6385)
SONOMA PHOTONICS INC
1750 Northpoint Pkwy C, Santa Rosa (95407-7597)
PHONE..................707 568-1202
Mark A Caylor, President
Wesley G Bush, President
Karen Wallen, General Mgr
EMP: 50 EST: 2000
SQ FT: 30,000
SALES (est): 14.2MM Publicly Held
WEB: www.sonomaphotonics.com
SIC: 3677 3827 Filtration devices, electronic; optical instruments & lenses
HQ: Northrop Grumman Systems Corporation
2980 Fairview Park Dr
Falls Church VA 22042
703 280-2900

(P-6386)
STANGENES INDUSTRIES INC (PA)
1052 E Meadow Cir, Palo Alto (94303-4271)
PHONE..................650 855-9926
Magne Stangenes, CEO
Kari Stangenes, CFO
Paul Holen, Administration
Chris Yeckel, Electrical Engi
Kelli Noel, Engineer
▲ EMP: 77 EST: 1974
SQ FT: 15,500
SALES (est): 26.9MM Privately Held
WEB: www.stangenes.com
SIC: 3677 Electronic transformers

(P-6387)
SYNDER INC (PA)
Also Called: Synder Filtration
4941 Allison Pkwy, Vacaville (95688-8795)
PHONE..................707 451-6060
Edward Yeh, CEO
Joseph Y Wang, President
Y C Jao PHD, Vice Pres
Kevin Carlson, General Mgr
Kimberly D 'costa, Sales Staff
▲ EMP: 29 EST: 1989
SQ FT: 26,000
SALES (est): 7.9MM Privately Held
WEB: www.synderfiltration.com
SIC: 3677 8748 8742 Filtration devices, electronic; systems analysis or design; industry specialist consultants

(P-6388)
WJLP COMPANY INC
Also Called: West Coast Magnetics
4848 Frontier Way Ste 100, Stockton (95215-9649)
P.O. Box 31330 (95213-1330)
PHONE..................800 628-1123
Weyman Lundquist, President
Luz Jimenez, Admin Sec
Shuang Feng, Electrical Engi
Maria Larios, Human Res Mgr
Toni Jimenez, Purch Mgr
▲ EMP: 100 EST: 1974
SQ FT: 8,000
SALES (est): 23.4MM Privately Held
WEB: www.wcmagnetics.com
SIC: 3677 3357 Electronic transformers; coaxial cable, nonferrous

3678 Electronic Connectors

(P-6389)
BRANTNER HOLDING LLC (DH)
501 Oakside Ave, Redwood City (94063-3800)
PHONE..................650 361-5292
Harold Barksdale, President
EMP: 100 EST: 2014
SALES (est): 47.4MM
SALES (corp-wide): 12.1B Privately Held
SIC: 3678 Electronic connectors
HQ: Te Connectivity Mog Inc.
501 Oakside Ave
Redwood City CA 94063
650 361-5292

(P-6390)
CALCULEX
131 Stony Cir Ste 500a, Santa Rosa (95401-9520)
PHONE..................707 578-2307
Martin Small, President
EMP: 50 EST: 1985
SALES (est): 7MM Privately Held
SIC: 3678 Electronic connectors

(P-6391)
DUEL SYSTEMS INC
2025 Galeway Pl Ste 235, San Jose (95110)
PHONE..................408 453-9500
Don Duda, President
▲ EMP: 62 EST: 1988
SQ FT: 34,000
SALES (est): 5.3MM
SALES (corp-wide): 1B Publicly Held
WEB: www.methode.com
SIC: 3678 Electronic connectors
PA: Methode Electronics, Inc
8750 W Bryn Mawr Ave # 1000
Chicago IL 60631
708 867-6777

(P-6392)
HIGH CONNECTION DENSITY INC
820 Kifer Rd Ste A, Sunnyvale (94086-5200)
PHONE..................408 743-9700
Tsuyoshi Taira, President
Charlie Stevenson, COO
Richard Barnes, CIO
EMP: 25 EST: 2000
SALES (est): 3MM Privately Held
WEB: www.hcdcorp.com
SIC: 3678 8734 Electronic connectors; testing laboratories

(P-6393)
LACO INC
6767 Preston Ave, Livermore (94551-8529)
P.O. Box 3069, Danville (94526-8069)
PHONE..................775 461-2960
EMP: 20 Privately Held
WEB: www.lacoinc.com
SIC: 3678 Electronic connectors
PA: Laco, Inc.
1150 Trademark Dr Ste 111
Reno NV 89521

(P-6394)
ONANON INC
720 S Milpitas Blvd, Milpitas (95035-5449)
PHONE..................408 262-8990
Dennis Joel Johnson, CEO
Thomas R Sahakian, CFO
Misael Miranda, Managing Dir
Brian Fang, Engineer
Keyon Keshtgar, Engineer
EMP: 49 EST: 1979
SQ FT: 25,000
SALES (est): 12MM Privately Held
WEB: www.onanon.com
SIC: 3678 3089 Electronic connectors; laminating of plastic

3679 Electronic Components, NEC

(P-6395)
AEI ELECTECH CORP
Also Called: Sunpower USA
33485 Western Ave, Union City (94587-3201)
PHONE..................510 489-5088
David Shu, President
Tristan Wang, Manager
◆ EMP: 15 EST: 1986
SALES (est): 532.1K Privately Held
WEB: www.sunpower-usa.com
SIC: 3679 Power supplies, all types: static

(P-6396)
AHEAD MAGNETICS INC
Also Called: Aheadtek
6410 Via Del Oro, San Jose (95119-1208)
PHONE..................408 226-9800
Tim Higgins, Principal

3679 - Electronic Components, NEC County (P-6397)

Ed Soldani, *CFO*
Patrick Johnston, *Exec VP*
Yolanda Verdugo, *Executive*
Sam Guerriero, *Engineer*
▲ **EMP:** 78
SQ FT: 32,000
SALES (est): 13.4MM **Privately Held**
WEB: www.aheadtek.com
SIC: 3679 Recording & playback heads, magnetic
PA: Huritga International Holding (S) Pte. Ltd.
   10 Anson Road
   Singapore 07990

(P-6397)
AKASH SYSTEMS INC (PA)
600 California St Fl 11, San Francisco (94108-2727)
PHONE.....................................408 887-6682
Felix Ejeckam, *CEO*
Tyrone Mitchell, *COO*
Fabrizio Montauti, *Vice Pres*
EMP: 15 **EST:** 2015
SQ FT: 120
SALES (est): 3.9MM **Privately Held**
WEB: www.akashsystems.com
SIC: 3679 Antennas, satellite; household use

(P-6398)
APPLIED THIN-FILM PRODUCTS (HQ)
Also Called: Atp
3620 Yale Way, Fremont (94538-6182)
PHONE.....................................510 661-4287
David J Adams, *CEO*
Ryan Nguyen, *COO*
Franco Pietroforte, *Vice Pres*
Todd Dillman, *Executive*
David Adams, *Branch Mgr*
EMP: 112 **EST:** 1995
SQ FT: 18,000
SALES (est): 25MM
SALES (corp-wide): 2.5B **Publicly Held**
WEB: www.thinfilm.com
SIC: 3679 Microwave components
PA: Vishay Intertechnology, Inc.
   63 Lancaster Ave
   Malvern PA 19355
   610 644-1300

(P-6399)
APPLIED THIN-FILM PRODUCTS
3439 Edison Way, Fremont (94538-6179)
PHONE.....................................510 661-4287
David Adams, *Branch Mgr*
EMP: 16
SALES (corp-wide): 2.5B **Publicly Held**
WEB: www.thinfilm.com
SIC: 3679 Microwave components
HQ: Applied Thin-Film Products
   3620 Yale Way
   Fremont CA 94538

(P-6400)
BANH AN BINH
1965 Stonewood Ln, San Jose (95132-1354)
PHONE.....................................408 935-8950
EMP: 20
SALES (est): 1.9MM **Privately Held**
SIC: 3679 Mfg Electronic Components

(P-6401)
BENTEK CORPORATION
Also Called: Bentek Solar
1991 Senter Rd, San Jose (95112-2631)
PHONE.....................................408 954-9600
Mitchell Schoch, *President*
Lou Marzano, *President*
Mel Pagdanganan, *Info Tech Mgr*
Jamie Aimonetti, *Human Res Dir*
Tuan Tran, *Mfg Spvr*
▲ **EMP:** 100 **EST:** 2005
SALES (est): 30.9MM **Privately Held**
WEB: www.bentek.com
SIC: 3679 Electronic circuits

(P-6402)
BRANDT ELECTRONICS INC
1971 Tarob Ct, Milpitas (95035-6825)
P.O. Box 3255, Santa Clara (95055-3255)
PHONE.....................................408 240-0004
Phillip D Duvall, *CEO*
Denice Deaville, *CFO*
Steve Hall, *Vice Pres*
Rogelio Jose, *Engineer*
EMP: 40 **EST:** 1979
SQ FT: 12,000
SALES (est): 5MM **Privately Held**
WEB: www.brandtelectronics.com
SIC: 3679 Power supplies, all types: static

(P-6403)
C D INTERNATIONAL TECH INC
695 Pinnacle Pl, Livermore (94550-9705)
PHONE.....................................408 986-0725
Zhong Cao, *President*
▲ **EMP:** 19 **EST:** 1993
SQ FT: 10,000
SALES (est): 1.2MM **Privately Held**
WEB: www.cdint.com
SIC: 3679 3357 Transducers, electrical; coaxial cable, nonferrous

(P-6404)
CELESTICA LLC
Also Called: D&H Manufacturing
49235 Milmont Dr, Fremont (94538-7349)
PHONE.....................................510 770-5100
Mark Morris, *Branch Mgr*
Jack Jacobs, *Vice Pres*
Craig Oberg, *Vice Pres*
Monica Bragado, *Business Dir*
Josh Kanne, *Business Dir*
EMP: 200
SALES (corp-wide): 1.1B **Privately Held**
WEB: www.celestica.com
SIC: 3679 Electronic circuits
HQ: Celestica Llc
   645 Harvey Rd Ste 1
   Manchester NH 03103

(P-6405)
CELLINK CORPORATION
610 Quarry Rd, San Carlos (94070-6224)
PHONE.....................................650 799-3018
Kevin Coakley, *CEO*
EMP: 38 **EST:** 2012
SALES (est): 11.5MM
SALES (corp-wide): 17B **Publicly Held**
WEB: www.cellinkcircuits.com
SIC: 3679 Electronic circuits
PA: Lear Corporation
   21557 Telegraph Rd
   Southfield MI 48033
   248 447-1500

(P-6406)
CERNEX INC
1710 Zanker Rd Ste 103, San Jose (95112-4219)
PHONE.....................................408 541-9226
Chanh Huynh, *President*
▲ **EMP:** 21 **EST:** 1988
SQ FT: 5,200
SALES (est): 8.1MM **Privately Held**
WEB: www.cernex.com
SIC: 3679 Microwave components

(P-6407)
COHERENT ASIA INC
5100 Patrick Henry Dr, Santa Clara (95054-1112)
PHONE.....................................408 764-4000
Helene Simonet, *Exec VP*
EMP: 51 **EST:** 2006
SALES (est): 38.1MM
SALES (corp-wide): 1.2B **Publicly Held**
WEB: www.coherent.com
SIC: 3679 3827 Electronic crystals; optical instruments & lenses
PA: Coherent, Inc.
   5100 Patrick Henry Dr
   Santa Clara CA 95054
   408 764-4000

(P-6408)
COLLARIS LLC
Also Called: Collaris Defense
685 Jarvis Dr Ste C, Morgan Hill (95037-2813)
PHONE.....................................510 825-9995
Yasser Khan, *Principal*
Ajmal Khan, *Principal*
EMP: 56 **EST:** 2010
SALES (est): 2.2MM **Privately Held**
WEB: www.collaris.biz
SIC: 3679 3812 Rheostats, for electronic end products; search & navigation equipment

(P-6409)
COMPASS COMPONENTS INC (PA)
Also Called: Compass Manufacturing Service
48133 Warm Springs Blvd, Fremont (94539-7498)
PHONE.....................................510 656-4700
Jack Maxwell, *CEO*
Bob Duplantier, *President*
Joe Werner, *Bd of Directors*
Joseph Ayala, *Vice Pres*
Irene Domingo, *Associate Dir*
EMP: 110 **EST:** 1979
SC FT: 36,000
SALES (est): 63.1MM **Privately Held**
WEB: www.compassmade.com
SIC: 3679 5065 Harness assemblies for electronic use: wire or cable; electronic parts

(P-6410)
COMPSERV INC
42 Golf Rd, Pleasanton (94566-9752)
PHONE.....................................415 331-4571
Michael J Maslana, *President*
Christopher Alessio, *Vice Pres*
Robert Boguski, *Vice Pres*
Brian Hill, *Sr Ntwrk Engine*
Goretti Correia, *Buyer*
▲ **EMP:** 15 **EST:** 1988
SQ FT: 9,000
SALES (est): 521.4K **Privately Held**
SIC: 3679 Electronic circuits

(P-6411)
CPI INTERNATIONAL HOLDING CORP
811 Hansen Way, Palo Alto (94304-1031)
PHONE.....................................650 846-2900
O Joe Caldarelli, *CEO*
Robert A Fickett, *President*
John R Beighley, *Vice Pres*
John Overstreet, *Vice Pres*
Andrew E Tafler, *Vice Pres*
EMP: 104 **EST:** 2011
SALES (est): 3MM **Privately Held**
WEB: www.cpii.com
SIC: 3679 Electronic circuits

(P-6412)
CPI INTERNATIONAL HOLDING LLC
811 Hansen Way, Palo Alto (94304-1031)
P.O. Box 51110 (94303-0687)
PHONE.....................................650 846-2900
Joe O Caldarelli, *CEO*
Andrew Ivers, *COO*
Peter Kolda, *COO*
Sear Villa-Lovoz, *Vice Pres*
Karl Schmitt, *Info Tech Dir*
EMP: 65 **EST:** 2011
SALES (est): 2.4MM **Privately Held**
WEB: www.cpii.com
SIC: 3679 Electronic circuits

(P-6413)
CPI SUBSIDIARY HOLDINGS LLC (DH)
811 Hansen Way, Palo Alto (94304-1031)
PHONE.....................................650 846-2900
Robert A Fickett, *CEO*
Laura Brown, *Officer*
Jojo Wade, *Sales Executive*
Alan McClelland, *Manager*
Chris Hainsworth, *Supervisor*
EMP: 162 **EST:** 1995
SALES (est): 10.7MM **Privately Held**
WEB: www.cpii.com
SIC: 3679 Electronic circuits

(P-6414)
CSR TECHNOLOGY INC (DH)
1060 Rincon Cir, San Jose (95131-1325)
PHONE.....................................408 523-6500
Brett Gladden, *CEO*
Ron Mackintosh, *Chairman*
Chris Ladas, *Exec VP*
Lesta Brady, *Vice Pres*
Igor Chirashnya, *Vice Pres*

▲ **EMP:** 452 **EST:** 1995
SALES (est): 106.7MM
SALES (corp-wide): 23.5B **Publicly Held**
WEB: www.qualcomm.com
SIC: 3679 3812 3674 Electronic circuits; search & navigation equipment; semiconductors & related devices
HQ: Qualcomm Technologies International, Ltd.
   Churchill House
   Cambridge CAMBS CB4 0
   289 046-3140

(P-6415)
DAWN VME PRODUCTS
47915 Westinghouse Dr, Fremont (94539-7483)
PHONE.....................................510 657-4444
Barry W Burnsides, *CEO*
Cheryl A Burnsides, *Vice Pres*
Tim Collins, *IT/INT Sup*
Jorge Hernandez, *Engineer*
Sharnjit Sekhon, *QC Mgr*
▲ **EMP:** 45
SQ FT: 20,000
SALES (est): 9.6MM **Privately Held**
WEB: www.dawnvme.com
SIC: 3679 Electronic parts & equipment

(P-6416)
DE ANZA MANUFACTURING SVCS INC
1271 Reamwood Ave, Sunnyvale (94089-2275)
PHONE.....................................408 734-2020
Art Takahara, *President*
Michael Takahara, *Vice Pres*
Mike Takahara, *Vice Pres*
Linda Walker, *Admin Mgr*
Kristine Walker, *Admin Asst*
▼ **EMP:** 60 **EST:** 1978
SQ FT: 24,000
SALES (est): 11.4MM **Privately Held**
WEB: www.deanzamfg.com
SIC: 3679 3643 Harness assemblies for electronic use: wire or cable; current-carrying wiring devices

(P-6417)
DENRON INC
2135 Ringwood Ave, San Jose (95131-1725)
P.O. Box 612797 (95161-2797)
PHONE.....................................408 435-8588
Don Mills, *VP Opers*
EMP: 400 **EST:** 1980
SQ FT: 40,000
SALES (est): 18.5MM **Privately Held**
SIC: 3679 Harness assemblies for electronic use: wire or cable

(P-6418)
DICON FIBEROPTICS INC (PA)
Also Called: Kessil
1689 Regatta Blvd, Richmond (94804-7438)
PHONE.....................................510 620-5000
Ho-Shang Lee, *President*
Dr Gilles Corcos, *Ch of Bd*
Robert Schleicher, *Vice Pres*
Wuucheng Huang, *Info Tech Mgr*
Miguel Garcia, *Purch Mgr*
▲ **EMP:** 364 **EST:** 1986
SQ FT: 202,000
SALES (est): 70.8MM **Privately Held**
WEB: www.godicon.com
SIC: 3679 3827 Electronic switches; optical instruments & lenses

(P-6419)
DJ GREY COMPANY INC
455 Allan Ct, Healdsburg (95448-4802)
PHONE.....................................707 431-2779
Marla J Grey, *President*
Michele Perry, *Vice Pres*
EMP: 15 **EST:** 1978
SQ FT: 4,500
SALES (est): 2.1MM **Privately Held**
WEB: www.djgreycable.com
SIC: 3679 Electronic circuits

(P-6420)
DREAMCTCHERS EMPWERMENT NETWRK
2201 Tuolumne St, Vallejo (94589-2524)
PHONE.....................................707 558-1775

▲ = Import ▼ = Export
♦ = Import/Export

PRODUCTS & SERVICES SECTION
3679 - Electronic Components, NEC County (P-6444)

George Lytal, *Ch of Bd*
Regina Kaiser, *Prgrmr*
EMP: 25 **EST:** 2012
SALES (est): 1.1MM Privately Held
SIC: 3679 Voice controls

(P-6421)
ECLIPSE MICROWAVE INC
Also Called: Eclipse Mdi
4425 Fortran Dr Ste 40, San Jose (95134-2300)
PHONE..............................408 806-8938
Jeffrey Rapadas, *President*
John Choe, *CFO*
Hazel Rapaas, *Treasurer*
▼ **EMP:** 18 **EST:** 2001
SQ FT: 5,000
SALES (est): 1.4MM Privately Held
WEB: www.eclipsemdi.com
SIC: 3679 3674 Microwave components; semiconductors & related devices

(P-6422)
ELCON INC
1009 Timothy Dr, San Jose (95133-1043)
PHONE..............................408 292-7800
Anthony J Barraco, *CEO*
Steve Loveless, *Principal*
Nutan Bhiwandker, *Manager*
EMP: 50 **EST:** 1967
SQ FT: 31,000
SALES (est): 10MM Privately Held
WEB: www.elconprecision.com
SIC: 3679 Commutators, electronic

(P-6423)
ELMECH INC
195 San Pedro Ave Ste E15, Morgan Hill (95037-5140)
P.O. Box 2606 (95038-2606)
PHONE..............................408 782-2990
Paul Balog, *President*
Mathew Schreyer, *Supervisor*
EMP: 15 **EST:** 1980
SQ FT: 4,400
SALES (est): 3.3MM Privately Held
WEB: www.elmechinc.com
SIC: 3679 Harness assemblies for electronic use: wire or cable

(P-6424)
EMVCO LLC
900 Metro Center Blvd, Foster City (94404-2172)
PHONE..............................650 432-3149
Robert Burns,
Karen Shunk, *Opers Staff*
EMP: 22 **EST:** 1999
SALES (est): 1.7MM Privately Held
WEB: www.emvco.com
SIC: 3679 Electronic circuits

(P-6425)
ENSURGE MICROPOWER INC
Also Called: NFC Innovation Center
2581 Junction Ave, San Jose (95134-1923)
PHONE..............................408 503-7300
Kevin Dale Barber, *CEO*
Richard Van Der Linde, *Engineer*
Matthew Bright, *Marketing Staff*
EMP: 70 **EST:** 2011
SQ FT: 61,000
SALES (est): 18.6MM Privately Held
WEB: www.ensurge.com
SIC: 3679 Electronic circuits
PA: Ensurge Micropower Asa
    House Of Business Fridtjof Nansens
    Plass 4
    Oslo 0160
    -

(P-6426)
FABRI-TECH COMPONENTS INC
49038 Milmont Dr, Fremont (94538-7301)
PHONE..............................510 249-2000
Terry Anest, *President*
Teo Seow Phong, *CEO*
Gerald Lim, *Manager*
EMP: 15 **EST:** 1998
SQ FT: 7,000
SALES (est): 8.3MM Privately Held
WEB: www.fabritech.net
SIC: 3679 Electronic circuits

PA: Fabri-Tech Components (S) Pte Ltd
    3 Tuas Basin Link
    Singapore 63875

(P-6427)
FASTRAK MANUFACTURING SVCS INC
1275 Alma Ct, San Jose (95112-5943)
PHONE..............................408 298-6414
Phillip Guzman, *CEO*
Michelle Hilty, *President*
EMP: 20 **EST:** 1985
SALES (est): 3.5MM Privately Held
WEB: www.fastrakmfg.com
SIC: 3679 8711 Harness assemblies for electronic use: wire or cable; electronic circuits; electrical or electronic engineering

(P-6428)
FLEXTRONICS CORPORATION (DH)
6201 America Center Dr, Alviso (95002-2563)
PHONE..............................803 936-5200
Marc A Onetto, *President*
Adeline Tan, *Bd of Directors*
Andy Powell, *Senior VP*
Christian Bauwens, *Vice Pres*
Marcin FIC, *Vice Pres*
▲ **EMP:** 224 **EST:** 1998
SQ FT: 350,000
SALES (est): 811.9MM Privately Held
WEB: www.flex.com
SIC: 3679 3577 3571 Electronic circuits; computer peripheral equipment; electronic computers

(P-6429)
FOTONATION CORPORATION (PA)
3025 Orchard Pkwy, San Jose (95134-2017)
PHONE..............................650 843-9025
Sumat Mehra, *VP Bus Dvlpt*
Ilariu Raducan, *Sr Project Mgr*
Pradeep Bardia, *Manager*
EMP: 52 **EST:** 2016
SALES (est): 1.8MM Privately Held
WEB: www.dts.com
SIC: 3679 Electronic circuits

(P-6430)
GM ASSOCIATES INC
Also Called: G M Quartz
9824 Kitty Ln, Oakland (94603-1070)
PHONE..............................510 430-0806
Melvyn Nutter, *President*
Deborah Camp, *Vice Pres*
Karen Beato, *Business Mgr*
▲ **EMP:** 58 **EST:** 1973
SQ FT: 8,000
SALES (est): 10.8MM Privately Held
WEB: www.gm-quartz.com
SIC: 3679 3229 Quartz crystals, for electronic application; scientific glassware

(P-6431)
GOOCH & HOUSEGO PALO ALTO LLC (HQ)
Also Called: Crystal Technology
44247 Nobel Dr, Fremont (94538-3178)
PHONE..............................650 856-7911
Jon Fowler, *President*
Mark Batzdorf, *CFO*
Iwan Dodd, *Vice Pres*
Michael Chapman, *Controller*
Michael Bailey, *Manager*
▲ **EMP:** 64 **EST:** 1967
SQ FT: 25,000
SALES (est): 18.4MM
SALES (corp-wide): 159.5MM Privately Held
WEB: www.gandh.com
SIC: 3679 Electronic crystals
PA: Gooch & Housego Plc
    Dowlish Ford
    Ilminster TA19
    146 025-6440

(P-6432)
HELIOVOLT CORPORATION
3945 Freedom Cir Ste 560, Santa Clara (95054-1269)
PHONE..............................512 767-6079
Dong S Kim, *President*
Billy J Stanbery, *President*
John Prater, *Vice Pres*
Steve Darnell, *Principal*
Louay Eldada, *CTO*
▲ **EMP:** 36 **EST:** 2001
SALES (est): 2MM Privately Held
SIC: 3679 Power supplies, all types: static

(P-6433)
HTI TURNKEY MANUFACTURING SVCS
2200 Zanker Rd Ste A, San Jose (95131-1111)
PHONE..............................408 955-0807
MAI Linh Tran, *CEO*
Nhan Nguyen, *General Mgr*
Thanah MAI Tran, *Admin Sec*
Vic Tinio, *Consultant*
EMP: 25
SQ FT: 10,000
SALES (est): 2MM Privately Held
WEB: www.hti9001.com
SIC: 3679 Harness assemblies for electronic use: wire or cable

(P-6434)
INTEGRITY TECHNOLOGY CORP
2505 Technology Dr, Hayward (94545-4869)
PHONE..............................270 812-8867
J P Young, *President*
Susan Whichard, *VP Sales*
J Garcia, *Manager*
J Jefferson, *Manager*
EMP: 17 **EST:** 1986
SQ FT: 4,000
SALES (est): 1MM Privately Held
SIC: 3679 3677 Electronic circuits; electronic coils, transformers & other inductors

(P-6435)
INTERFACE MASTERS TECH INC
150 E Brokaw Rd, San Jose (95112-4203)
PHONE..............................408 441-9341
Benjamin Askarinam, *CEO*
Sima Askarinam, *President*
Brian Shannon, *Vice Pres*
Jennifer Hang, *Program Mgr*
June Nguyen-Dell, *Program Mgr*
EMP: 50 **EST:** 1997
SQ FT: 3,000
SALES (est): 13.4MM Privately Held
WEB: www.interfacemasters.com
SIC: 3679 Electronic switches

(P-6436)
ISOLINK INC
880 Yosemite Way, Milpitas (95035-6360)
PHONE..............................408 946-1968
David Aldrich, *CEO*
Jorge Rosario, *Treasurer*
Bill Cantarini, *Engrg Dir*
▲ **EMP:** 32 **EST:** 1987
SQ FT: 16,600
SALES (est): 8MM
SALES (corp-wide): 3.3B Publicly Held
WEB: www.skyworksinc.com
SIC: 3679 3827 Electronic circuits; optical instruments & lenses
PA: Skyworks Solutions, Inc.
    5260 California Ave
    Irvine CA 92617
    949 231-3000

(P-6437)
J & L DIGITAL PRECISION INC
551 Taylor Way Ste 15, San Carlos (94070-6252)
PHONE..............................650 592-0170
John L Obertelli, *President*
Loretta Obertelli, *Corp Secy*
Gail Firpo, *Vice Pres*
Louis Firpo, *Vice Pres*
Jeff Obertelli, *Vice Pres*
EMP: 16 **EST:** 1966
SALES (est): 4MM Privately Held
WEB: www.jldigital.net
SIC: 3679 Electronic circuits

(P-6438)
J&M MANUFACTURING INC
430 Aaron St, Cotati (94931-3016)
P.O. Box 2435, Rohnert Park (94927-2435)
PHONE..............................707 795-8223
James O Judd Jr, *Owner*
Paul L Matthias, *CFO*
▲ **EMP:** 34 **EST:** 1984
SQ FT: 25,000
SALES (est): 2.9MM Privately Held
WEB: www.jmmfg.com
SIC: 3679 3444 Electronic circuits; metal housings, enclosures, casings & other containers

(P-6439)
JAVAD EMS INC
900 Rock Ave, San Jose (95131-1615)
PHONE..............................408 770-1700
Javad Ashjaee, *President*
Gary Walker, *Vice Pres*
Linda Bezoni, *Principal*
Pam Walke, *Vice Pres*
Jamie Jazmin, *Program Mgr*
▲ **EMP:** 95 **EST:** 2009
SALES (est): 23MM Privately Held
WEB: www.javadgnss.com
SIC: 3679 Electronic circuits

(P-6440)
JDI DISPLAY AMERICA INC (PA)
1740 Tech Dr Ste 460, San Jose (95110)
PHONE..............................408 501-3720
Atsuhiko Tokinosu, *President*
Shuichi Odsuka, *CEO*
Koichiro Taniyama, *CFO*
Michael Du, *Vice Pres*
Robert Bogdanoff, *Administration*
EMP: 23 **EST:** 2012
SALES (est): 3.2MM Privately Held
WEB: www.j-display.com
SIC: 3679 7374 Liquid crystal displays (LCD); computer processing services

(P-6441)
JIC INDUSTRIAL CO INC
978 Hanson Ct, Milpitas (95035-3165)
PHONE..............................408 935-9880
Frank Yen, *President*
▲ **EMP:** 28 **EST:** 1988
SALES (est): 1.7MM Privately Held
WEB: www.jicusa.com
SIC: 3679 3678 3357 Electronic circuits; electronic connectors; nonferrous wire-drawing & insulating

(P-6442)
KELYTECH CORPORATION
1482 Gladding Ct, Milpitas (95035-6831)
PHONE..............................408 935-0888
K C Wong, *President*
Stanley Chiu, *Vice Pres*
Katie Wong, *Executive*
Kevin Wong, *Office Mgr*
Irene Wong, *Admin Sec*
EMP: 40 **EST:** 1990
SQ FT: 8,500
SALES (est): 5.9MM Privately Held
WEB: www.kelytech.com
SIC: 3679 Electronic circuits

(P-6443)
KG TECHNOLOGIES INC
6028 State Farm Dr, Rohnert Park (94928-2133)
PHONE..............................888 513-1874
Erik Zhang, *President*
Massimo Perucchini, *Vice Pres*
Jing LI, *Electrical Engi*
Jacqueline Gesner, *Engineer*
Karli Haws, *Opers Staff*
▲ **EMP:** 18 **EST:** 2009
SQ FT: 5,600
SALES (est): 2.7MM Privately Held
WEB: www.kgtechnologies.net
SIC: 3679 Electronic circuits

(P-6444)
KRYTAR INC
1288 Anvilwood Ave, Sunnyvale (94089-2203)
PHONE..............................408 734-5999
Nancy Russell, *Ch of Bd*
Douglas Hagan, *President*
Robyn Brallier, *Controller*
Hilda Clayton, *Purchasing*

3679 - Electronic Components, NEC County (P-6445)

EMP: 20 **EST:** 1975
SALES (est): 3.8MM Privately Held
WEB: www.krytar.com
SIC: 3679 Microwave components; electronic circuits

(P-6445)
L P GLASSBLOWING INC
2322 Calle Del Mundo, Santa Clara (95054-1007)
PHONE..................408 988-7561
Leopold Pivk, *President*
Hilda Pivk, *Vice Pres*
EMP: 29 **EST:** 1975
SQ FT: 6,700
SALES (est): 5.9MM Privately Held
WEB: www.lpglassblowing.com
SIC: 3679 3229 Quartz crystals, for electronic application; pressed & blown glass

(P-6446)
LANDMARK TECHNOLOGY INC
1660 Mckee Rd, San Jose (95116-1263)
PHONE..................408 435-8890
Sun Lu, *President*
Jean Lu, *CFO*
Fanny Yip, *Admin Asst*
▲ **EMP:** 32 **EST:** 1985
SQ FT: 13,000
SALES (est): 2.5MM Privately Held
WEB: www.landmarktek.com
SIC: 3679 3674 Liquid crystal displays (LCD); semiconductors & related devices

(P-6447)
LG INNOTEK USA INC (HQ)
2540 N 1st St Ste 400, San Jose (95131-1016)
PHONE..................408 955-0364
Sung IL Yang, *President*
Harry Kang, *Marketing Mgr*
Eugene Kang, *Marketing Staff*
Patrick Kang, *Marketing Staff*
Lawrence Madanda, *Director*
▲ **EMP:** 153 **EST:** 1994
SQ FT: 71,168
SALES (est): 26.5MM Privately Held
WEB: www.lginnotek.com
SIC: 3679 Antennas, receiving

(P-6448)
LIGHTECH FIBEROPTIC INC
1987 Adams Ave, San Leandro (94577-1005)
PHONE..................510 567-8700
Tracy Scott, *COO*
Jimmy Ko, *President*
▲ **EMP:** 15 **EST:** 1995
SQ FT: 11,000
SALES (est): 4.5MM Privately Held
WEB: www.lightech.net
SIC: 3679 3229 Electronic switches; pressed & blown glass

(P-6449)
LUCERO CABLES INC
193 Stauffer Blvd, San Jose (95125-1042)
PHONE..................408 536-0340
Madeline Eliasnia, *CEO*
Surendra Gupta, *President*
Art Eliasnia, *Chairman*
Iraj Pessian, *Treasurer*
Serjik Avanes, *Vice Pres*
▲ **EMP:** 110 **EST:** 1978
SQ FT: 50,000
SALES (est): 8.8MM Privately Held
WEB: www.luceromfg.com
SIC: 3679 3571 Harness assemblies for electronic use: wire or cable; electronic computers

(P-6450)
M2 ANTENNA SYSTEMS INC
Also Called: Msquared
4402 N Selland Ave, Fresno (93722-4191)
PHONE..................559 221-2271
Myrna Staal, *President*
Mike Staal, *Vice Pres*
Mathew Staal, *General Mgr*
Matt Staal, *General Mgr*
Carrie Patton, *Manager*
EMP: 15 **EST:** 1985
SQ FT: 10,000
SALES (est): 2.9MM Privately Held
WEB: www.m2inc.com
SIC: 3679 5999 3625 Antennas, receiving; mobile telephones & equipment; positioning controls, electric

(P-6451)
MAGNITUDE ELECTRONICS LLC
926 Bransten Rd, San Carlos (94070-4029)
PHONE..................650 551-1850
Hal White, *Mng Member*
Gilles Grosgurin,
▲ **EMP:** 19 **EST:** 1995
SQ FT: 2,500
SALES (est): 1.7MM Privately Held
WEB: www.magnitude-electronics.com
SIC: 3679 Electronic circuits

(P-6452)
MANUTRONICS INC
736 S Hillview Dr, Milpitas (95035-5455)
PHONE..................408 262-6579
Cuong Tran, *CEO*
EMP: 15 **EST:** 2013
SALES (est): 4.5MM Privately Held
WEB: www.manutronics.net
SIC: 3679 Electronic circuits

(P-6453)
MENLO INDUSTRIES INC
44060 Old Warm Sprng Blvd, Fremont (94538-6145)
PHONE..................510 770-2350
EMP: 55
SQ FT: 24,899
SALES (est): 10MM Privately Held
WEB: www.menloindustries.com
SIC: 3679 Electronic Components, Nec, Nsk
PA: Kauthar Sdn Bhd
  15th Flr Menara Tr
  Kuala Lumpur KLP 50450

(P-6454)
MICRO LAMBDA WIRELESS INC
46515 Landing Pkwy, Fremont (94538-6421)
PHONE..................510 770-9221
John Nguyen, *President*
David Suddarth, *Vice Pres*
Susan Sun, *Vice Pres*
Myra Verret, *Administration*
MAI Lam, *Accountant*
EMP: 39 **EST:** 1990
SQ FT: 19,000
SALES (est): 6.6MM Privately Held
WEB: www.microlambdawireless.com
SIC: 3679 5065 3663 Microwave components; electronic parts & equipment; radio & TV communications equipment

(P-6455)
MICROWAVE TECHNOLOGY INC (DH)
4268 Solar Way, Fremont (94538-6335)
PHONE..................510 651-6700
Nathan Zommer, *CEO*
Zong Cai, *Engineer*
Gary Glaze, *Engineer*
Shawn Smith, *Engineer*
Ted Tu, *Engineer*
EMP: 61 **EST:** 1982
SQ FT: 30,800
SALES (est): 17.4MM
SALES (corp-wide): 1.4B Publicly Held
WEB: www.mwtinc.com
SIC: 3679 3663 Commutators, electronic; amplifiers, RF power & IF
HQ: Ixys, Llc
  1590 Buckeye Dr
  Milpitas CA 95035
  408 457-9000

(P-6456)
MORROW SNOWBOARDS INC
Also Called: Granite Bay Technologies
599 Menlo Dr Ste 200, Rocklin (95765-3725)
PHONE..................916 415-0645
▼ **EMP:** 1500
SQ FT: 9,300
SALES (est): 24.1MM Privately Held
WEB: www.morrowsnowboards.com
SIC: 3679 3728 3674 Mfg Liquid Crystal Display Products Turnkey Assemblies Front Panel Display & Subassemlies With Integrated Circuits

(P-6457)
MTI CORPORATION
Also Called: Material Technology Intl
860 S 19th St, Richmond (94804-3809)
PHONE..................510 525-3070
Xiao P Jiang, *President*
Zhao Liu, *Corp Secy*
Andy Huang, *Sales Engr*
◆ **EMP:** 43 **EST:** 1995
SQ FT: 5,000
SALES (est): 7.5MM Privately Held
WEB: www.mtixtl.com
SIC: 3679 Electronic crystals

(P-6458)
MURDOC TECHNOLOGY LLC
5683 E Fountain Way, Fresno (93727-7813)
PHONE..................559 497-1580
Larry R Harris,
Greg Miller, *Administration*
Karie Shaw, *Sales Executive*
Xeng Vang, *Assistant*
▲ **EMP:** 40 **EST:** 1999
SQ FT: 12,000
SALES (est): 7.7MM Privately Held
WEB: www.murdoc.com
SIC: 3679 Electronic circuits

(P-6459)
MYNTAHL CORPORATION
Also Called: East Electronics
48273 Lakeview Blvd, Fremont (94538-6519)
PHONE..................510 413-0002
Tingyi Xu, *CEO*
Ben Lawrence, *Software Dev*
▲ **EMP:** 30 **EST:** 1996
SQ FT: 7,000
SALES (est): 3.3MM Privately Held
WEB: www.east-elec.com
SIC: 3679 Electronic circuits

(P-6460)
NEONODE INC (PA)
2880 Zanker Rd, San Jose (95134-2117)
PHONE..................408 496-6722
Urban Forssell, *President*
Ulf Rosberg, *Ch of Bd*
Maria Ek, *CFO*
Alexander Jubner, *Vice Pres*
Bruce Banter, *Engineer*
EMP: 45 **EST:** 1997
SALES (est): 5.9MM Privately Held
WEB: www.neonode.com
SIC: 3679 3826 Cryogenic cooling devices for infrared detectors, masers; infrared analytical instruments

(P-6461)
NEW VISION DISPLAY INC (DH)
1430 Blue Oaks Blvd # 100, Roseville (95747-5156)
PHONE..................916 786-8111
Jeff Olyniec, *CEO*
Owen Chen, *Ch of Bd*
Alan M Lefko, *CFO*
Alan Lefko, *CFO*
Jack Powers, *Engineer*
◆ **EMP:** 28
SQ FT: 2,000
SALES (est): 300MM Privately Held
WEB: www.newvisiondisplay.com
SIC: 3679 Liquid crystal displays (LCD)

(P-6462)
NORTRA CABLES INC
570 Gibraltar Dr, Milpitas (95035-6315)
PHONE..................408 942-1106
Jim Love, *President*
Lyn Hickey, *Shareholder*
Andy O 'brien, *IT/INT Sup*
Gabriel Venegas, *Facilities Mgr*
Michelle Lateur, *Manager*
EMP: 60 **EST:** 1985
SQ FT: 14,000
SALES (est): 15.3MM Privately Held
WEB: www.nortra-cables.com
SIC: 3679 Harness assemblies for electronic use: wire or cable

(P-6463)
NRC MANUFACTURING INC
500 Yosemite Dr Ste 108, Milpitas (95035-5467)
PHONE..................510 438-9400
Rata Chea, *President*
David Hang, *CFO*
David Godinez, *Engineer*
Pete Soto, *Manager*
EMP: 18 **EST:** 2008
SALES (est): 3MM Privately Held
WEB: www.nrcmfg.com
SIC: 3679 Electronic circuits

(P-6464)
OBERON CO
7216 Via Colina, San Jose (95139-1130)
PHONE..................408 227-3730
Inez Termerson, *President*
Ian Temerson, *Manager*
▲ **EMP:** 17 **EST:** 1997
SALES (est): 320.2K Privately Held
WEB: www.oberoninc.com
SIC: 3679 Electronic circuits

(P-6465)
OMNIYIG INC
3350 Scott Blvd Bldg 66, Santa Clara (95054-3174)
PHONE..................408 988-0843
William Capogeannis, *Ch of Bd*
Cathleen Capogeannis, *Treasurer*
Maria Rosales, *Office Mgr*
Michaela Nieblas, *Manager*
▲ **EMP:** 26 **EST:** 1973
SQ FT: 12,000
SALES (est): 4.4MM Privately Held
WEB: www.omniyig.com
SIC: 3679 Microwave components

(P-6466)
OXFORD INSTRS X-RAY TECH INC
Also Called: X-Ray Technology Group
360 El Pueblo Rd, Scotts Valley (95066-4228)
PHONE..................831 439-9729
Bernard Scanlan, *CEO*
Bryant Grigsby, *Engrg Dir*
Viveka Barnes, *Controller*
▲ **EMP:** 69 **EST:** 1979
SQ FT: 6,600
SALES (est): 23.4MM
SALES (corp-wide): 448.8MM Privately Held
WEB: www.oxinst.com
SIC: 3679 3844 Power supplies, all types: static; X-ray apparatus & tubes
HQ: Oxford Instruments Holdings, Inc.
  600 Milik St
  Carteret NJ 07008
  732 541-1300

(P-6467)
REGAL ELECTRONICS INC (PA)
820 Charcot Ave, San Jose (95131-2226)
P.O. Box 60008, Sunnyvale (94088-0008)
PHONE..................408 988-2288
Tony Lee, *President*
Madeleine Lee, *CEO*
Dr William Kunz, *Exec VP*
▲ **EMP:** 24 **EST:** 1976
SALES (est): 2.4MM Privately Held
WEB: www.regalusa.net
SIC: 3679 3678 3612 Electronic circuits; electronic connectors; transformers, except electric

(P-6468)
SECURITY PEOPLE INC
Also Called: Digilock
9 Willowbrook Ct, Petaluma (94954-6507)
PHONE..................707 766-6000
Asil Gokcebay, *CEO*
Russell Petersen, *Owner*
Bill Gordon, *President*
Julie Advocate, *Vice Pres*
Anthony Dinh, *Software Dev*
▲ **EMP:** 30 **EST:** 1981

▲ = Import ▼=Export
◆ =Import/Export

PRODUCTS & SERVICES SECTION

3691 - Storage Batteries County (P-6491)

SALES (est): 9.3MM Privately Held
WEB: www.digilock.com
SIC: 3679 Electronic circuits

(P-6469)
SILITRONICS INC
1957 Concourse Dr, San Jose (95131-1708)
PHONE..................408 605-1148
Dhiraj Bora, CEO
EMP: 30 EST: 2011
SQ FT: 15,000
SALES (est): 6MM Privately Held
WEB: www.silitronics.com
SIC: 3679 3672 Electronic circuits; printed circuit boards

(P-6470)
SOUTH BAY CIRCUITS INC
210 Hillsdale Ave, San Jose (95136-1392)
PHONE..................408 978-8992
EMP: 164
SALES (corp-wide): 70.7MM Privately Held
SIC: 3679 Mfg Electronic Components
PA: South Bay Circuits, Inc.
 99 N Mckemy Ave
 Chandler AZ 85226
 480 940-3125

(P-6471)
STORE INTELLIGENCE INC
6700 Koll Center Pkwy # 10, Pleasanton (94566-7060)
PHONE..................925 400-8499
Cristina Sava, Vice Pres
EMP: 30 EST: 2020
SALES (est): 34MM Privately Held
WEB: www.store-intelligence.com
SIC: 3679 Electronic circuits

(P-6472)
SUPPORT SYSTEMS INTL CORP
Also Called: Fiber Optic Cable Shop
136 S 2nd St Dept B, Richmond (94804-2110)
PHONE..................510 234-9090
Ben G Parsons, President
Richard St John, Vice Pres
Ben Parsons, Manager
▼ EMP: 65 EST: 1976
SQ FT: 15,000
SALES (est): 7.3MM Privately Held
SIC: 3679 Harness assemblies for electronic use: wire or cable

(P-6473)
SYSTRON DONNER INERTIAL INC
2700 Systron Dr, Concord (94518-1399)
PHONE..................925 979-4400
Dave Peace, CEO
Nasrullah Nas Ebrahimi, Technician
Arturo Escobedo, Technician
Kathleen Herrington, Technician
Troy Seehawer, Network Analyst
EMP: 117 EST: 2015
SALES (est): 25.8MM
SALES (corp-wide): 110.1MM Publicly Held
WEB: www.emcore.com
SIC: 3679 3829 Electronic circuits; accelerometers
PA: Emcore Corporation
 2015 Chestnut St
 Alhambra CA 91803
 626 293-3400

(P-6474)
T R MANUFACTURING
41938 Christy St, Fremont (94538-3159)
PHONE..................510 657-3850
Long Tran, Principal
Joanne Harris, Purch Agent
Socorro Ignacio, Accounts Mgr
EMP: 17 EST: 1998
SALES (est): 678.4K Privately Held
SIC: 3679 Electronic components

(P-6475)
TE CONNECTIVITY LTD
Also Called: Te Circuit Protection
6900 Paseo Padre Pkwy, Fremont (94555-3641)
PHONE..................650 361-4923
Thomas J Lynch, CEO

Terrence Curtin, President
Joe Donahue, COO
Mario Calastri, CFO
John Jenkins, Exec VP
EMP: 26 EST: 2014
SALES (est): 10.5MM
SALES (corp-wide): 1.4B Publicly Held
WEB: www.littelfuse.com
SIC: 3679 Electronic circuits
PA: Littelfuse, Inc.
 8755 W Higgins Rd Ste 500
 Chicago IL 60631
 773 628-1000

(P-6476)
TELEDYNE DEFENSE ELEC LLC
Also Called: Teledyne Microwave Solutions
11361 Sunrise Park Dr, Rancho Cordova (95742-6587)
PHONE..................916 638-3344
Bob Dipple, Branch Mgr
David A Zavadil, Vice Pres
Jerry Stevens, Program Mgr
John Tennant, Program Mgr
Cindy Clark, General Mgr
EMP: 200
SALES (corp-wide): 3B Publicly Held
WEB: www.teledynedefenseelectronics.com
SIC: 3679 3672 3663 3651 Microwave components; printed circuit boards; radio & TV communications equipment; household audio & video equipment; traveling wave tubes
HQ: Teledyne Defense Electronics, Llc
 1274 Terra Bella Ave
 Mountain View CA 94043
 650 691-9800

(P-6477)
TELEDYNE DEFENSE ELEC LLC (HQ)
Also Called: Teledyne Microwave Solutions
1274 Terra Bella Ave, Mountain View (94043-1820)
PHONE..................650 691-9800
Richard Palilonis, CEO
Ralph Fullerton, Engineer
Kiet Pham, Engineer
Ron Korber, Senior Engr
Sal Hanhan, Controller
▲ EMP: 25 EST: 2003
SALES (est): 55.2MM
SALES (corp-wide): 3B Publicly Held
WEB: www.teledynedefenseelectronics.com
SIC: 3679 Microwave components
PA: Teledyne Technologies Inc
 1049 Camino Dos Rios
 Thousand Oaks CA 91360
 805 373-4545

(P-6478)
TELEDYNE WIRELESS LLC
11361 Sunrise Park Dr, Rancho Cordova (95742-6587)
PHONE..................916 638-3344
EMP: 111
SALES (corp-wide): 2.3B Publicly Held
SIC: 3679 Mfg Electronic Components
HQ: Teledyne Wireless, Llc
 1274 Terra Bella Ave
 Mountain View CA 94043
 650 691-9800

(P-6479)
TR MANUFACTURING LLC (HQ)
33210 Central Ave, Union City (94587-2010)
PHONE..................510 657-3850
Dom Tran, CEO
Jack Cho, COO
Armando Manlutac, Engineer
▲ EMP: 250 EST: 1998
SQ FT: 52,000
SALES (est): 42.4MM
SALES (corp-wide): 11.3B Publicly Held
WEB: www.corning.com
SIC: 3679 Electronic circuits
PA: Corning Incorporated
 1 Riverfront Plz
 Corning NY 14831
 607 974-9000

(P-6480)
UNIQUIFY INC
2030 Fortune Dr Ste 200, San Jose (95131-1835)
PHONE..................408 235-8810
Josh Lee, CEO
Jung Ho Lee, President
Sam Kim, COO
Robert Sheffield, CFO
Robert Smith, Senior VP
EMP: 50 EST: 2005
SALES (est): 10.7MM Privately Held
WEB: www.uniquify.com
SIC: 3679 Electronic circuits

(P-6481)
VANDER-BEND MANUFACTURING INC (PA)
2701 Orchard Pkwy, San Jose (95134-2008)
PHONE..................408 245-5150
Greg Biggs, President
Boris Gorelik, CFO
Jason Bortoli, Program Mgr
Steve Wolf, General Mgr
Jill De Dios, Admin Sec
▲ EMP: 323 EST: 1999
SQ FT: 207,000
SALES (est): 138.5MM Privately Held
WEB: www.vander-bend.com
SIC: 3679 3444 3549 3599 Harness assemblies for electronic use: wire or cable; sheet metalwork; metalworking machinery; machine & other job shop work

(P-6482)
WELLEX CORPORATION (PA)
551 Brown Rd, Fremont (94539-7003)
PHONE..................510 743-1818
Tzu Tai Tsai, CEO
Richard Fitzgerald, President
Edward Lin, COO
Jackson Wang, Chairman
Gina Cheng, Executive
▲ EMP: 146 EST: 1983
SQ FT: 88,516
SALES (est): 42.3MM Privately Held
WEB: www.wellex.com
SIC: 3679 3672 Harness assemblies for electronic use: wire or cable; printed circuit boards

(P-6483)
WINCHESTER INTERCONNECT RF CORP
5590 Skylane Blvd, Santa Rosa (95403-1030)
PHONE..................707 573-1900
Robert Wallick, Engineer
Dan Hirschnitz, General Mgr
EMP: 1109
SALES (corp-wide): 14.3B Publicly Held
SIC: 3679 3357 Harness assemblies for electronic use: wire or cable; microwave components; coaxial cable, nonferrous
HQ: Winchester Interconnect Rf Corporation
 245 Lynnfield St
 Peabody MA 01960
 978 532-0775

3691 Storage Batteries

(P-6484)
AA PORTABLE POWER CORPORATION
825 S 19th St, Richmond (94804-3808)
PHONE..................510 525-2328
Xiao Ping Jiang, President
Reiko Aso, Admin Sec
▲ EMP: 35 EST: 1995
SQ FT: 15,000
SALES (est): 4.1MM Privately Held
WEB: www.aaportablepower.com
SIC: 3691 Storage batteries

(P-6485)
ADARA POWER INC
15466 Los Gatos Blvd 10, Los Gatos (95032-2542)
PHONE..................844 223-2969
Neil Maguire, CEO
Greg Maguire, Vice Pres
◆ EMP: 17 EST: 2014

SQ FT: 5,000
SALES (est): 470.2K Privately Held
SIC: 3691 Storage batteries

(P-6486)
CABAN SYSTEMS INC
858 Stanton Rd, Burlingame (94010-1404)
PHONE..................831 245-1608
Alexandra Rasch, CEO
Christian Handley, Engineer
EMP: 25 EST: 2018
SALES (est): 3.1MM Privately Held
WEB: www.cabansystems.com
SIC: 3691 Storage batteries

(P-6487)
INEVIT INC
541 Jefferson Ave Ste 100, Redwood City (94063-1700)
PHONE..................650 298-6001
Michael Miskovsky, CEO
Mark White, Admin Sec
EMP: 104 EST: 2016
SALES (est): 3.8MM Privately Held
WEB: www.driveseres.com
SIC: 3691 Storage batteries
HQ: Sf Motors, Inc.
 3303 Scott Blvd
 Santa Clara CA 95054
 408 617-7878

(P-6488)
NANOTECH ENERGY INC
311 Otterson Dr Ste 60, Chico (95928-8236)
PHONE..................310 806-9202
Jack Kavanaugh, CEO
Maher Kady, CTO
Scott Jacobson, Director
Edie Gray, Manager
EMP: 28 EST: 2014
SALES (est): 3MM Privately Held
WEB: www.nanotechenergy.com
SIC: 3691 Storage batteries

(P-6489)
NATRON ENERGY INC
3542 Bassett St, Santa Clara (95054-2704)
PHONE..................408 498-5828
Colin Wessells, CEO
Rob Rogan, Officer
Ali Fircuzi, Vice Pres
Jack Pouchet, Vice Pres
Patrick Geng, Engineer
EMP: 60 EST: 2012
SQ FT: 2,500
SALES (est): 12.6MM Privately Held
WEB: www.natron.energy
SIC: 3691 7389 Batteries, rechargeable;

(P-6490)
SILA NANOTECHNOLOGIES INC
2450 Mariner Square Loop, Alameda (94501-1010)
PHONE..................707 901-7452
Gene Berdichevsky, CEO
Byron Deeter, Partner
Bill Mulligan, COO
Desouza Warren, CFO
Kurt Kelty, Vice Pres
EMP: 160 EST: 2011
SQ FT: 87,531
SALES (est): 49.3MM Privately Held
WEB: www.silanano.com
SIC: 3691 Storage batteries

(P-6491)
TENERGY CORPORATION
Also Called: All-Battery.com
436 Kato Ter, Fremont (94539-8332)
PHONE..................510 687-0388
Xiangbing LI, CEO
Katherine Zhuang, Vice Pres
Ling Ch Liang, Admin Sec
Alberto Lam, Graphic Designe
Lisa Wu, Engineer
▲ EMP: 90 EST: 2004
SALES (est): 18.5MM Privately Held
WEB: www.tenergy.com
SIC: 3691 5063 Alkaline cell storage batteries; batteries

3691 - Storage Batteries County (P-6492)

PRODUCTS & SERVICES SECTION

(P-6492)
ZEROBASE ENERGY LLC
Also Called: Zero Base
46609 Fremont Blvd, Fremont
(94538-6410)
PHONE..................................888 530-9376
Steve Hogge, *President*
Roger Rose, *Vice Pres*
Wayne Labrie, *Production*
Mark Lucas, *Sales Staff*
EMP: 22 **EST:** 2009
SALES (est): 5.5MM **Privately Held**
WEB: www.zerobaseenergy.com
SIC: 3691 3699 4911 Storage batteries; generators, ultrasonic; generation, electric power

---

3692 Primary Batteries: Dry & Wet

(P-6493)
ENOVIX CORPORATION
3501 W Warren Ave, Fremont
(94538-6400)
PHONE..................................510 695-2350
Harrold J Rust, *President*
Thurman J Rodgers, *Ch of Bd*
Steffen Pietzke, *CFO*
Cameron Dales, *Ch Credit Ofcr*
Ashok Lahiri, *CTO*
EMP: 173 **EST:** 2006
SQ FT: 68,658
SALES (est): 14.7MM **Privately Held**
SIC: 3692 Primary batteries, dry & wet

(P-6494)
ENOVIX CORPORATION
3501 W Warren Ave, Fremont
(94538-6400)
PHONE..................................510 695-2399
Harrold Rust, *CEO*
Jim Gilbreath, *President*
Cameron Dales, *COO*
Steffen Pietzke, *CFO*
Ashok Lahiri, *Officer*
EMP: 115 **EST:** 2006
SALES (est): 51.9MM **Privately Held**
WEB: www.enovix.com
SIC: 3692 Primary batteries, dry & wet

(P-6495)
IMPRINT ENERGY INC
1320 Harbor Bay Pkwy # 110, Alameda
(94502-6578)
PHONE..................................510 847-7027
Christine Ho, *CEO*
Eliodoro Batingana Jr, *CFO*
Mark Laich, *Vice Pres*
Ying Lin, *Research*
Albert Aumentado, *Engineer*
EMP: 17 **EST:** 2010
SALES (est): 1.2MM **Privately Held**
WEB: www.imprintenergy.com
SIC: 3692 Primary batteries, dry & wet

(P-6496)
PRIMUS POWER CORPORATION
3967 Trust Way, Hayward (94545-3723)
P.O. Box 4557 (94540-4557)
PHONE..................................510 342-7600
Thomas Stepien, *CEO*
Jorg Heinemann, *Officer*
Paul Kreiner, *Vice Pres*
Tracy Omagbemi, *Office Mgr*
Richard Winter, *CTO*
EMP: 50
SALES (est): 15.1MM **Privately Held**
WEB: www.primuspower.com
SIC: 3692 Primary batteries, dry & wet

3694 Electrical Eqpt For Internal Combustion Engines

(P-6497)
JAPAN ENGINE INC
2131 Williams St, San Leandro
(94577-3224)
PHONE..................................510 532-7878
Yu Feng Lin, *CEO*
Michael Yi, *Principal*
▲ **EMP:** 16 **EST:** 1997
SALES (est): 4.9MM **Privately Held**
WEB: www.japanengine.com
SIC: 3694 Engine electrical equipment

(P-6498)
SERES INC
3303 Scott Blvd, Santa Clara (95054-3102)
PHONE..................................214 585-3356
Mingxu Yao, *CEO*
EMP: 200 **EST:** 2019
SALES (est): 21.5MM **Privately Held**
WEB: www.driveseres.com
SIC: 3694 Motors, starting: automotive & aircraft

3695 Recording Media

(P-6499)
BORQS INTERNATIONAL HOLDG CORP
5201 Great America Pkwy, Santa Clara
(95054-1122)
PHONE..................................619 363-3168
Pat Chan, *President*
Anthony Chan, *CFO*
Bob LI, *Exec VP*
Hareesh Ramanna, *Exec VP*
Simon Sun, *Exec VP*
EMP: 42 **EST:** 2017
SALES (est): 8.5MM **Privately Held**
SIC: 3695 Computer software tape & disks: blank, rigid & floppy
PA: Borqs Technologies Inc.
C/O:intertrust Fiduciary Services (Bvi) Limited
Road Town

(P-6500)
CAPELLA PHOTONICS INC
1100 La Avenida St Ste A, Mountain View
(94043-1453)
PHONE..................................408 360-4240
Larry Schwerin, *President*
Rafael Torres, *CFO*
William O'Hollaren, *Vice Pres*
Byron Trop, *Vice Pres*
Long Yang, *Vice Pres*
EMP: 50 **EST:** 2000
SQ FT: 6,600
SALES (est): 30.2MM
SALES (corp-wide): 25.8B **Privately Held**
WEB: www.capellainc.com
SIC: 3695 Optical disks & tape, blank
HQ: Nokia Of America Corporation
600 Mountain Ave Ste 700
New Providence NJ 07974

(P-6501)
ELECTRONIC ARTS REDWOOD INC (HQ)
Also Called: Ea Sports
209 Redwood Shores Pkwy, Redwood City
(94065-1175)
PHONE..................................650 628-1500
Larry Probst, *CEO*
Daryl Holt, *Vice Pres*
Stuart Lang, *Vice Pres*
William Payne, *Director*
Larre Sterling, *Director*
EMP: 716 **EST:** 2001
SALES (est): 2.9MM
SALES (corp-wide): 5.5B **Publicly Held**
WEB: www.ea.com
SIC: 3695 Video recording tape, blank
PA: Electronic Arts Inc.
209 Redwood Shores Pkwy
Redwood City CA 94065
650 628-1500

(P-6502)
JULY SYSTEMS INC (PA)
533 Airport Blvd Ste 395, Burlingame
(94010-2012)
PHONE..................................650 685-2460
BJ Arun, *CEO*
Rajash Reddy, *President*
Ashook Narasimhan, *Principal*
Deann Swanson, *Consultant*
EMP: 88 **EST:** 2001

SALES (est): 12.4MM **Privately Held**
WEB: www.dnaspaces.cisco.com
SIC: 3695 Computer software tape & disks: blank, rigid & floppy

(P-6503)
MICROTECH SYSTEMS INC
1334 Brommer St Ste B6, Santa Cruz
(95062-2955)
PHONE..................................650 596-1900
Corwin Nichols, *CEO*
Van Cluck, *CFO*
Helen Carter, *Treasurer*
Michael Fallavollita, *Vice Pres*
Lance Danbe, *Executive*
EMP: 15 **EST:** 1977
SALES (est): 2.6MM **Privately Held**
WEB: www.mtsystemsinc.com
SIC: 3695 Optical disks & tape, blank

(P-6504)
MONTEREY DESIGN SYSTEMS INC
2171 Landings Dr, Mountain View
(94043-0837)
PHONE..................................408 747-7370
Jacques Benkoski, *President*
Aidan Cullen, *CFO*
James Koford, *Chairman*
▲ **EMP:** 17 **EST:** 1996
SALES (est): 354.7K **Privately Held**
SIC: 3695 5045 3675 Computer software tape & disks: blank, rigid & floppy; computer software; electronic capacitors

(P-6505)
MOTA GROUP INC (PA)
Also Called: Unorth
60 S Market St Ste 1100, San Jose
(95113-2366)
PHONE..................................408 370-1248
Michael Faro, *CEO*
Jeffrey L Garon, *CFO*
Lily Q Ju, *Admin Sec*
◆ **EMP:** 24 **EST:** 2003
SALES (est): 3.8MM **Privately Held**
WEB: www.mota.com
SIC: 3695 Computer software tape & disks: blank, rigid & floppy

(P-6506)
RECOMMIND INC (HQ)
550 Kearny St Ste 700, San Francisco
(94108-2589)
PHONE..................................415 394-7899
Steve King, *CEO*
Bernard Huger, *CFO*
Eric S Cissp, *Regional Mgr*
Jan Puzicha, *CTO*
Connie Janise, *Project Mgr*
EMP: 100
SQ FT: 15,000
SALES (est): 50.1MM
SALES (corp-wide): 3.1B **Privately Held**
WEB: www.recommind.com
SIC: 3695 Computer software tape & disks: blank, rigid & floppy
PA: Open Text Corporation
275 Frank Tompa Dr
Waterloo ON N2L 0
519 888-7111

(P-6507)
THINKWAVE INC
103 Morris St Ste F, Sebastopol
(95472-3863)
P.O. Box 2418 (95473-2418)
PHONE..................................707 824-6200
John Poluektov, *CEO*
EMP: 15 **EST:** 1997
SALES (est): 193.5K **Privately Held**
WEB: www.thinkwave.com
SIC: 3695 7371 Computer software tape & disks: blank, rigid & floppy; custom computer programming services

---

3699 Electrical Machinery, Eqpt & Splys, NEC

(P-6508)
3D ROBOTICS INC (PA)
Also Called: Diy Drones
1165 Miller Ave, Berkeley (94708-1754)
PHONE..................................415 599-1404

Chris Anderson, *CEO*
Jordi Munoz, *President*
Andy Jensen, *COO*
John Cherbini, *Vice Pres*
Merlin Love, *Vice Pres*
▲ **EMP:** 70 **EST:** 2009
SALES (est): 28.7MM **Privately Held**
WEB: www.3dr.com
SIC: 3699 Electrical equipment & supplies

(P-6509)
BRIX GROUP INC
Also Called: Panapacific Shipping
80 Van Ness Ave, Fresno (93721-3223)
PHONE..................................559 457-4750
Harrison Brix, *CEO*
Sylvia Molina, *Office Admin*
Carmen Lopez, *Human Resources*
Nathaniel Birdsong, *Marketing Staff*
Tina Ellis, *Marketing Staff*
EMP: 47
SALES (corp-wide): 156.6MM **Privately Held**
WEB: www.panapacific.com
SIC: 3699 Electrical equipment & supplies
PA: The Brix Group Inc
838 N Laverne Ave
Fresno CA 93727
559 457-4700

(P-6510)
CENTRAL TECH INC
2271 Ringwood Ave, San Jose
(95131-1717)
PHONE..................................408 955-0919
EMP: 23 **EST:** 2016
SALES (est): 5.9MM **Privately Held**
WEB: www.centraltechinc.com
SIC: 3699 Electronic training devices

(P-6511)
CONSTRUCTION INNOVATIONS LLC
Also Called: Ci
10630 Mather Blvd Ste 200, Mather
(95655-4125)
PHONE..................................855 725-9555
Larry A Devore, *President*
James B Littlejohn, *CFO*
Levi Sirbu, *Buyer*
Jes Vargas, *Education*
Martha Ledesma, *Manager*
EMP: 150 **EST:** 2012
SQ FT: 17,000
SALES (est): 160MM **Privately Held**
WEB: www.constructioninnovations.com
SIC: 3699 8711 Electrical equipment & supplies; consulting engineer
PA: Bdg Innovations, Llc
6001 Outfall Cir
Sacramento CA 95828
855 725-9555

(P-6512)
DIY CO
3360 20th St, San Francisco (94110-2655)
PHONE..................................844 564-6349
Zach Klein, *CEO*
EMP: 16 **EST:** 2011
SALES (est): 1.6MM **Privately Held**
WEB: www.diy.org
SIC: 3699 Teaching machines & aids, electronic
HQ: Littlebits Electronics Inc.
601 W 26th St Rm M274
New York NY 10001

(P-6513)
DPSS LASERS INC
2525 Walsh Ave, Santa Clara
(95051-1316)
PHONE..................................408 988-4300
Alex Laymon, *President*
Thomas Hogan, *CEO*
Timothy Houtz, *Technician*
Paul Crothers, *Engineer*
Malinna Tian, *Accounting Mgr*
EMP: 30 **EST:** 1998
SQ FT: 25,000
SALES (est): 5.1MM **Privately Held**
WEB: www.dpss-lasers.com
SIC: 3699 Laser systems & equipment

▲ = Import ▼ = Export
◆ = Import/Export

PRODUCTS & SERVICES SECTION
3699 - Electrical Machinery, Eqpt & Splys, NEC County (P-6539)

(P-6514)
DUNAN SENSING LLC
1953 Concourse Dr, San Jose (95131-1708)
PHONE 408 613-1015
Tom Nguyen, *Principal*
Annie Tran, *Finance*
◆ **EMP:** 36 **EST:** 2014
SQ FT: 15,000
SALES (est): 1.8MM **Privately Held**
WEB: www.dunansensing.com
SIC: 3699 Laser welding, drilling & cutting equipment

(P-6515)
E-FUEL CORPORATION
15466 Los Gatos Blvd 37, Los Gatos (95032-2542)
PHONE 408 267-2667
EMP: 32
SALES (est): 3MM **Privately Held**
SIC: 3699 Mfg Energy Equipment

(P-6516)
ELECTRONIC INTERFACE CO INC
Also Called: Applied Engineering
6341 San Ignacio Ave # 10, San Jose (95119-1202)
PHONE 408 286-2134
Jack Yao, *President*
Jesus Vasquez, *Technician*
Greg Flick, *Engineer*
Sean Galligan, *Engineer*
Katherine Nguyen, *Controller*
EMP: 75 **EST:** 1979
SALES (est): 18.9MM **Privately Held**
SIC: 3699 7694 Electrical equipment & supplies; armature rewinding shops

(P-6517)
ENVIA SYSTEMS INC
7979 Gateway Blvd Ste 101, Newark (94560-1157)
P.O. Box 14142, Fremont (94539-1342)
PHONE 510 509-1367
Sujeet Kumar, *President*
▲ **EMP:** 50 **EST:** 2007
SALES (est): 8.1MM **Privately Held**
SIC: 3699 Electrical equipment & supplies

(P-6518)
EOPLEX INC
1321 Ridder Park Dr 10, San Jose (95131-2306)
PHONE 408 638-5100
Arthur L Chait, *CEO*
EMP: 20 **EST:** 1995
SALES (est): 1.1MM **Privately Held**
WEB: www.eoplex.com
SIC: 3699 Electrical equipment & supplies

(P-6519)
EOPLEX TECHNOLOGIES INC
2940 N 1st St, San Jose (95134-2021)
PHONE 408 638-5100
Arthur Chait, *President*
Charles Taylor, *Founder*
Philip E Rogren, *VP Mktg*
Sean Foote, *Director*
Michio Fujimura, *Director*
▲ **EMP:** 20 **EST:** 2001
SALES (est): 1.4MM **Privately Held**
WEB: www.eoplex.com
SIC: 3699 Electrical equipment & supplies

(P-6520)
ETON CORPORATION
1015 Corporation Way, Palo Alto (94303-4305)
PHONE 650 903-3866
Esmail Amid-Hozour, *President*
Meiling Liao, *CFO*
John Smith, *Senior VP*
Winston Wang, *Engineer*
Elena Hui, *Business Mgr*
▲ **EMP:** 45 **EST:** 1986
SQ FT: 10,400
SALES (est): 10.5MM **Privately Held**
WEB: www.etoncorp.com
SIC: 3699 Electrical equipment & supplies

(P-6521)
FORMAX TECHNOLOGIES INC
Also Called: Fti
305 S Soderquist Rd, Turlock (95380-5130)
PHONE 209 668-1001
Ryan Lindsay, *President*
T Ryan Lindsay, *President*
Timothy D Lindsay, *CEO*
Melody Wright, *Cust Svc Dir*
▲ **EMP:** 16 **EST:** 2002
SQ FT: 66,000
SALES (est): 1.3MM **Privately Held**
SIC: 3699 Electrical equipment & supplies

(P-6522)
FULLER MANUFACTURING INC
130 Ridge Rd, Sutter Creek (95685-9690)
P.O. Box 999 (95685-0999)
PHONE 209 267-5071
Christopher Fuller, *President*
Shirley Fuller, *Corp Secy*
EMP: 16 **EST:** 1979
SQ FT: 5,000
SALES (est): 1.4MM **Privately Held**
WEB: www.fullermfg.com
SIC: 3699 3694 3679 Electrical equipment & supplies; automotive electrical equipment; electronic circuits

(P-6523)
GEFEN LLC
1800 S Mcdowell Blvd Ext, Petaluma (94954-6962)
PHONE 818 772-9100
Hagai Gefen, *CEO*
Tony Dowzall, *President*
Jill Gefen, *Vice Pres*
Aaron Hernandez, *Director*
Robert Lemer, *Director*
▲ **EMP:** 42 **EST:** 1987
SQ FT: 8,000
SALES (est): 17.4MM **Privately Held**
WEB: www.gefen.com
SIC: 3699 High-energy particle physics equipment
HQ: Nortek Security & Control Llc
5919 Sea Otter Pl Ste 100
Carlsbad CA 92010
760 438-7000

(P-6524)
GHANGOR CLOUD INC
2001 Gateway Pl Ste 710w, San Jose (95110-1077)
PHONE 408 713-3303
Tarique Mustafa, *CEO*
Bhanu Panda, *COO*
Ellen Brigham, *Vice Pres*
John Racioppi, *Vice Pres*
John Metzler, *Chief*
EMP: 65 **EST:** 2014
SALES (est): 3.1MM **Privately Held**
WEB: www.ghangorcloud.com
SIC: 3699 7371 Security devices; software programming applications

(P-6525)
IJK & CO INC
Also Called: Bayshore Lights
225 Industrial St, San Francisco (94124-1928)
PHONE 415 826-8899
Michael Tseng, *CEO*
EMP: 50 **EST:** 1991
SALES (est): 9.1MM **Privately Held**
WEB: www.bayshoresupply.com
SIC: 3699 5063 1711 7349 Electrical equipment & supplies; electrical supplies; plumbing, heating, air-conditioning contractors; lighting maintenance service

(P-6526)
INO-TECH LASER PROCESSING INC
2228 Oakland Rd, San Jose (95131-1414)
PHONE 408 262-1845
James K Machathil, *CEO*
Socorro Salado, *Administration*
EMP: 23 **EST:** 2011
SALES (est): 1.5MM **Privately Held**
WEB: www.a1jays.com
SIC: 3699 3826 Laser systems & equipment; laser welding, drilling & cutting equipment; laser scientific & engineering instruments

(P-6527)
INTERGEN INC
1145 Tasman Dr, Sunnyvale (94089-2228)
PHONE 408 245-2737
Kris Madeyski, *President*
John Horn, *Admin Sec*
EMP: 15 **EST:** 1992
SQ FT: 7,000
SALES (est): 688.4K **Privately Held**
SIC: 3699 7371 Laser systems & equipment; computer software development & applications

(P-6528)
IONETIX CORPORATION (PA)
101 The Embarcadero # 210, San Francisco (94105-1222)
PHONE 415 944-1440
Kevin Cameron, *CEO*
David Eve, *Vice Pres*
Mark Leuschner, *Vice Pres*
Joshua McCurry, *Technician*
Jay Paquette, *Engineer*
EMP: 17 **EST:** 2009
SALES (est): 5.8MM **Privately Held**
WEB: www.ionetix.com
SIC: 3699 Cyclotrons

(P-6529)
KERI SYSTEMS INC (PA)
302 Enzo Dr Ste 190, San Jose (95138-1801)
PHONE 408 435-8400
Ted Geiszler, *President*
Ken Geiszler, *President*
Dave Miller, *Software Engr*
Phillip Smith, *Technology*
Gary Colman, *Technical Staff*
◆ **EMP:** 53 **EST:** 1990
SQ FT: 20,000
SALES (est): 10MM **Privately Held**
WEB: www.kerisys.com
SIC: 3699 3829 Security control equipment & systems; measuring & controlling devices

(P-6530)
KNIGHTSCOPE INC
1070 Terra Bella Ave, Mountain View (94043-1830)
PHONE 650 924-1025
William Santana LI, *CEO*
Jack Schenk, *President*
Mallorie Burak, *CFO*
Marina Hardof, *CFO*
Aaron Lehnhardt, *Exec VP*
EMP: 65 **EST:** 2013
SALES (est): 10.1MM **Privately Held**
WEB: www.knightscope.com
SIC: 3699 Security devices

(P-6531)
KYOCERA SLD LASER INC
6500 Kaiser Dr, Fremont (94555-3661)
PHONE 805 696-6999
Steven Denbaars, *CEO*
Kay Ozaki Ms, *VP Human Res*
EMP: 23 **Privately Held**
WEB: www.kyocera-sldlaser.com
SIC: 3699 Laser systems & equipment
HQ: Kyocera Sld Laser, Inc.
485 Pine Ave
Goleta CA 93117
805 696-6999

(P-6532)
LIFELINE SEC & AUTOMTN INC
2081 Arena Blvd Ste 260, Sacramento (95834-2309)
PHONE 916 285-9078
Gordon Johnson, *President*
EMP: 61 **EST:** 2005
SALES (est): 2.5MM **Privately Held**
WEB: www.viosecurity.com
SIC: 3699 Security devices
PA: Vio Security, Llc
3100 Premier Dr Unit 206
Irving TX 75063

(P-6533)
NANOTRONICS IMAGING INC
Also Called: Nanotronics Automation
777 Flynn Rd, Hollister (95023-9558)
PHONE 831 630-0700
Randy Griffith, *Branch Mgr*
Oleg Alferov, *Software Engr*
Julio Coppo, *Sales Dir*
Jennifer Sanandres, *Marketing Mgr*
EMP: 24
SALES (corp-wide): 10.7MM **Privately Held**
WEB: www.nanotronics.co
SIC: 3699 Electronic training devices
PA: Nanotronics Imaging, Inc.
2251 Front St Ste 110
Cuyahoga Falls OH 44221
330 926-9809

(P-6534)
NETWORKED ENERGY SERVICES CORP (HQ)
Also Called: Grid Modernization Division
5215 Hellyer Ave Ste 150, San Jose (95138-1089)
PHONE 408 622-9900
Michael Anderson, *CEO*
Jonathan Main, *COO*
Will Mathieson, *CFO*
Damian Inglin, *VP Bus Dvlpt*
David Demoney, *Sr Software Eng*
▲ **EMP:** 55 **EST:** 2014
SALES (est): 12.6MM **Privately Held**
WEB: www.networkedenergy.com
SIC: 3699 Grids, electric

(P-6535)
PATRICK RYNEARSON RULIN
Also Called: Pearl Electric Co
5320 Section Ave, Stockton (95215-9602)
PHONE 209 943-2705
Patrick R Rynearson, *Mng Member*
Patrick Rynearson, *Owner*
Juan Perez, *Vice Pres*
EMP: 17 **EST:** 2004
SALES (est): 2.8MM **Privately Held**
WEB: www.pearlelectricinc.com
SIC: 3699 1731 Electrical equipment & supplies; electrical work

(P-6536)
PENDULUM INSTRUMENTS INC
1123 Madison Ave, Redwood City (94061-1544)
PHONE 866 644-1230
Harald Kruger, *President*
Marcin Sawicki, *General Mgr*
Eva Chapa, *Sales Staff*
EMP: 22 **EST:** 2018
SALES (est): 250K **Privately Held**
WEB: www.pendulum-instruments.com
SIC: 3699 3825 Electrical equipment & supplies; instruments to measure electricity

(P-6537)
PINE GROVE GROUP INC
25500 State Highway 88, Pioneer (95666-9647)
PHONE 209 295-7733
Dan Nolting, *CEO*
EMP: 30 **EST:** 1997
SQ FT: 8,000
SALES (est): 3.2MM **Privately Held**
WEB: www.pinegrovegroup.com
SIC: 3699 Electrical equipment & supplies

(P-6538)
R J R TECHNOLOGIES INC (PA)
7875 Edgewater Dr, Oakland (94621-2001)
PHONE 480 800-2300
Wil Salhuana, *President*
Tony Bregante, *CFO*
Richard J Ross, *Principal*
John Ni, *CTO*
George Penney, *Engineer*
EMP: 69 **EST:** 1987
SQ FT: 50,000
SALES (est): 25.6MM **Privately Held**
WEB: www.rjrtechnologies.com
SIC: 3699 Cleaning equipment, ultrasonic, except medical & dental

(P-6539)
RACO MANUFACTURING & ENGRG CO
1400 62nd St, Emeryville (94608-2099)
PHONE 510 658-6713
Constance Brown, *President*
James Brown, *Vice Pres*
EMP: 39 **EST:** 1947
SQ FT: 5,500

3699 - Electrical Machinery, Eqpt & Splys, NEC County (P-6540)

PRODUCTS & SERVICES SECTION

SALES (est): 6.3MM **Privately Held**
WEB: www.racoman.com
SIC: **3699** 3823 Electrical equipment & supplies; temperature instruments: industrial process type

(P-6540)
SCHNEDER ELC BLDNGS AMRCAS INC
Also Called: TAC Yamas
5735 W Las Psts Blvd, Pleasanton (94588-4002)
PHONE..........................925 463-7100
Daroowe Torkelson, *Manager*
Allan Beckman, *Software Engr*
Oscar Esquer, *Technician*
Lisa Brewer, *Project Mgr*
Ivan Bui, *Technical Staff*
EMP: 45
SALES (corp-wide): 177.9K **Privately Held**
SIC: **3699** Electrical equipment & supplies
HQ: Schneider Electric Buildings Americas, Inc.
1650 W Crosby Rd
Carrollton TX 75006
972 323-1111

(P-6541)
SCHNEIDER ELECTRIC
200 W Pontiac Way, Clovis (93612-5612)
PHONE..........................615 691-2586
Sudhir Gonugunta, *General Mgr*
Brian Fagan, *Manager*
EMP: 17 EST: 2018
SALES (est): 6.6MM **Privately Held**
WEB: www.se.com
SIC: **3699** Electrical equipment & supplies

(P-6542)
SIENNA CORPORATION INC
41350 Christy St, Fremont (94538-3115)
PHONE..........................510 440-0200
EMP: 21 EST: 1995
SALES (est): 3.2MM **Privately Held**
SIC: **3699** Mfg Electrical Equipment/Supplies

(P-6543)
SPECTRA-PHYSICS INC (DH)
Also Called: Laser Division
1565 Barber Ln, Milpitas (95035-7409)
P.O. Box 19607, Irvine (92623-9607)
PHONE..........................877 835-9620
Robert J Phillippy, *CEO*
Pete Williams, *Vice Pres*
Anne Eichhorn, *Planning*
Jack Brookshaw, *Technician*
Thuan Dinh, *Technician*
▼ EMP: 795 EST: 1961
SQ FT: 129,500
SALES (est): 103.6MM
SALES (corp-wide): 2.3B **Publicly Held**
WEB: www.spectra-physics.com
SIC: **3699** 8731 Laser systems & equipment; commercial physical research
HQ: Newport Corporation
1791 Deere Ave
Irvine CA 92606
949 863-3144

(P-6544)
TASCENT INC
475 Alberto Way Ste 200, Los Gatos (95032-5480)
PHONE..........................650 799-4611
Dean Senner, *CEO*
Peter Dabrowski, *CFO*
Scott Clark, *Vice Pres*
Alastair Partington, *Vice Pres*
Joey Pritikin, *Vice Pres*
EMP: 16 EST: 2015
SALES (est): 3.3MM **Privately Held**
WEB: www.tascent.com
SIC: **3699** Security control equipment & systems

(P-6545)
TURNER DSGNS HYDRCRBON INSTRS
2023 N Gateway Blvd # 101, Fresno (93727-1623)
PHONE..........................559 253-1414
Gary Bartman, *President*
Mark Fletcher, *Corp Secy*
Susan Bartman, *Manager*

EMP: 43 EST: 2002
SALES (est): 6.2MM **Privately Held**
WEB: www.oilinwatermonitors.com
SIC: **3699** Electrical equipment & supplies

(P-6546)
VIAVI SOLUTIONS INC
Also Called: Jsdu
2789 Northpoint Pkwy, Santa Rosa (95407-7350)
PHONE..........................707 545-6440
Toni McWilliamns, *Principal*
Leland Black, *Design Engr*
Tj Mills, *Engineer*
Wilhelm Hebenstreit, *Manager*
EMP: 200
SALES (corp-wide): 1.2B **Publicly Held**
WEB: www.viavisolutions.com
SIC: **3699** Laser systems & equipment
PA: Viavi Solutions Inc.
7047 E Greenway Pkwy # 25
Scottsdale AZ 85254
408 404-3600

(P-6547)
WG SECURITY PRODUCTS INC (PA)
591 W Hamilton Ave # 260, Campbell (95008-0568)
PHONE..........................408 241-8000
Xiao Hui Yang, *CEO*
Graham Handyside, *Vice Pres*
Stephen Johnson, *Accounts Mgr*
▲ EMP: 39 EST: 1998
SALES (est): 5.5MM **Privately Held**
WEB: www.wgspi.com
SIC: **3699** 5065 Security devices; security control equipment & systems

3711 Motor Vehicles & Car Bodies

(P-6548)
AMERICAN CARRIER SYSTEMS
2285 E Date Ave, Fresno (93706-5426)
PHONE..........................559 442-1500
Philip Sweet, *President*
David Sweet, *Admin Sec*
▲ EMP: 24 EST: 1974
SQ FT: 36,552
SALES (est): 1.2MM **Privately Held**
WEB: www.americancarrierequipment.com
SIC: **3711** Motor vehicles & car bodies

(P-6549)
BYTON NORTH AMERICA CORP
4201 Burton Dr, Santa Clara (95054-1512)
PHONE..........................408 966-5078
Carsten Breitfield, *CEO*
Albert LI, *CFO*
Scott Bang, *Engineer*
Claire Wang, *Commissioner*
Andrew Hussey, *Director*
EMP: 225 EST: 2016
SALES (est): 22.8MM **Privately Held**
WEB: www.byton.com
SIC: **3711** Cars, electric, assembly of

(P-6550)
CRUISE LLC
333 Brannan St, San Francisco (94107-1810)
PHONE..........................415 787-2346
Dan Ammann, *CEO*
Logan Perreault, *Software Engr*
Carl Jenkins, *VP Engrg*
Ayan Chakrabarty, *Research*
Aaron Asbill, *Technology*
EMP: 82 EST: 2013
SALES (est): 43.9MM **Publicly Held**
WEB: www.getcruise.com
SIC: **3711** Cars, electric, assembly of
PA: General Motors Company
300 Renaissance Ctr L1
Detroit MI 48243

(P-6551)
GOLDEN STATE FIRE APPRATUS INC
7400 Reese Rd, Sacramento (95828-3706)
PHONE..........................916 330-1638
Ryan Wright, *President*

Marie Wright, *Admin Sec*
Dave Klockzien, *Sales Mgr*
EMP: 16 EST: 1989
SQ FT: 5,000
SALES (est): 25MM **Privately Held**
WEB: www.goldenstatefire.com
SIC: **3711** 3713 Truck & tractor truck assembly; truck & bus bodies

(P-6552)
LUCID GROUP INC (PA) ◆
7373 Gateway Blvd, Newark (94560-1149)
PHONE..........................510 648-3553
Peter Rawlinson, *CEO*
Andrew Liveris, *Ch of Bd*
Sherry House, *CFO*
Eric Bach, *Senior VP*
Michael Bell, *Senior VP*
EMP: 27 EST: 2021
SALES (est): 514.5MM **Publicly Held**
SIC: **3711** Cars, electric, assembly of

(P-6553)
LUCID USA INC (HQ)
Also Called: Lucid Motors
7373 Gateway Blvd, Newark (94560-1149)
PHONE..........................510 648-3553
Peter Rawlinson, *CEO*
Sherry House, *CFO*
Derek Jenkins, *Senior VP*
Jonathan Butler, *Vice Pres*
Khaled Abdo, *Engineer*
▲ EMP: 233 EST: 2007
SQ FT: 65,000
SALES (est): 216.9MM
SALES (corp-wide): 514.5MM **Publicly Held**
WEB: www.lucidmotors.com
SIC: **3711** 8711 Motor vehicles & car bodies; engineering services
PA: Lucid Group, Inc.
7373 Gateway Blvd
Newark CA 94560
510 648-3553

(P-6554)
PREVOST CAR (US) INC
28702 Hall Rd, Hayward (94545-5012)
PHONE..........................951 202-2064
EMP: 32
SALES (corp-wide): 39.1B **Privately Held**
WEB: www.prevostcar.com
SIC: **3711** Motor vehicles & car bodies
HQ: Prevost Car (Us) Inc.
7817 National Service Rd
Greensboro NC 27409
908 222-7211

(P-6555)
PROTERRA INC (PA)
1815 Rollins Rd, Burlingame (94010-2204)
PHONE..........................864 438-0000
John J Allen, *Ch of Bd*
Chris Bailey, *President*
Gareth T Joyce, *President*
Joshua P Ensign, *COO*
Amy E Ard, *CFO*
EMP: 199 EST: 2004
SQ FT: 34,400
SALES (est): 181.2MM **Publicly Held**
WEB: www.arclightclean.com
SIC: **3711** Motor vehicles & car bodies

(P-6556)
PROTERRA OPERATING COMPANY INC (HQ)
1815 Rollins Rd, Burlingame (94010-2204)
PHONE..........................864 438-0000
Jack Allen, *CEO*
Josh Ensign, *COO*
Amy Ard, *CFO*
Joann Covington,
Rick Huibregtse, *Senior VP*
▲ EMP: 183 EST: 2004
SQ FT: 14,000
SALES (est): 181.2MM **Publicly Held**
WEB: www.proterra.com
SIC: **3711** Bus & other large specialty vehicle assembly
PA: Proterra Inc
1815 Rollins Rd
Burlingame CA 94010
864 438-0000

(P-6557)
ROBOMART INC
555 California St # 4925, San Francisco (94104-1503)
PHONE..........................669 350-4463
Ali Ahmed, *Principal*
EMP: 18 EST: 2017
SALES (est): 639K **Privately Held**
WEB: www.robomart.co
SIC: **3711** 5599 Automobile assembly, including specialty automobiles; automotive dealers

(P-6558)
SF MOTORS INC (DH)
3303 Scott Blvd, Santa Clara (95054-3102)
PHONE..........................408 617-7878
Michael Deng, *CEO*
Martin Eberhard, *Officer*
Mike Miskovsky, *Officer*
Thomas Fritz, *General Mgr*
David Baker, *Engineer*
EMP: 250 EST: 2016
SQ FT: 18,000
SALES (est): 56.9MM **Privately Held**
WEB: www.driveseres.com
SIC: **3711** Cars, electric, assembly of

(P-6559)
SHYFT GROUP INC
4242 Forcum Ave B-640, McClellan (95652-2110)
PHONE..........................916 921-2639
EMP: 26
SALES (corp-wide): 146.2MM **Publicly Held**
WEB: www.spartanmotors.com
SIC: **3711** 3714 7519 Chassis, motor vehicle; motor vehicle parts & accessories; utility trailer rental
PA: The Shyft Group Inc
41280 Bridge St
Novi MI 48375
517 543-6400

(P-6560)
SIEMENS MOBILITY INC
7464 French Rd, Sacramento (95828-4600)
PHONE..........................916 681-3000
Dariusz Chrominski, *Administration*
Sean Tabrizi, *Engineer*
Dario Fabrizi, *Analyst*
Lisette Castillo, *Recruiter*
Mary Guzman, *Buyer*
EMP: 957
SALES (corp-wide): 67.4B **Privately Held**
SIC: **3711** 3743 Motor vehicles & car bodies; railway motor cars
HQ: Siemens Mobility, Inc.
1 Penn Plz Ste 1100
New York NY 10119
212 672-4000

(P-6561)
TESLA INC (PA)
3500 Deer Creek Rd, Palo Alto (94304-1317)
PHONE..........................650 681-5000
Elon Musk, *CEO*
Robyn Denholm, *Ch of Bd*
Zachary Kirkhorn, *CFO*
Andrew Baglino, *Senior VP*
Vaibhav Taneja,
▲ EMP: 225 EST: 2003
SALES (est): 31.5B **Publicly Held**
WEB: www.tesla.com
SIC: **3711** 3714 3674 Automobile assembly, including specialty automobiles; cars, electric, assembly of; motor vehicle parts & accessories; solar cells

(P-6562)
ZOOX INC (HQ)
Also Called: Zoox Labs
1149 Chess Dr, Foster City (94404-1102)
PHONE..........................650 539-9669
Carl Bass, *Chairman*
Aicha Evans, *CEO*
Ilan Hart, *CFO*
Jesse Levinson, *Principal*
Audie Jr Concordia, *Program Mgr*
EMP: 50 EST: 2014

▲ = Import ▼ =Export
◆ =Import/Export

PRODUCTS & SERVICES SECTION
3728 - Aircraft Parts & Eqpt, NEC County (P-6631)

(P-6609)
DFC INC
Also Called: Advanced Helicopter Svs
17986 County Road 94b, Woodland (95695-9238)
PHONE...................530 669-7115
Sparrow Tang, *President*
Patricia Laustalot, *Treasurer*
Carol Aronson, *Vice Pres*
Adam Burriss, *Director*
David Chaplin, *Director*
EMP: 80 **EST:** 2001
SQ FT: 55,000
SALES (est): 12.1MM **Privately Held**
WEB: www.advancedhelicopterservices.com
SIC: 3721 Aircraft

(P-6610)
GDAS-LINCOLN INC
Also Called: Gulfstream California
1501 Aviation Blvd, Lincoln (95648-9388)
PHONE...................916 645-8961
David Pearman, *General Mgr*
Luis E Leal, *Regl Sales Mgr*
James Kratz, *Sales Mgr*
Bob Rice, *Associate*
EMP: 47 **EST:** 2012
SALES (est): 7.9MM **Privately Held**
SIC: 3721 Aircraft

(P-6611)
IMPOSSIBLE AEROSPACE CORP
1709 Junction Ct, San Jose (95112-1044)
P.O. Box 7468, Menlo Park (94026-7468)
PHONE...................707 293-9367
Albert Spencer Gore, *CEO*
Eric Davidson, *COO*
Kingsley Chen, *Engineer*
Sahil Bhojwani, *Regl Sales Mgr*
Travis Quimby, *Sales Staff*
EMP: 15 **EST:** 2017
SALES (est): 2.8MM **Privately Held**
WEB: www.vayuaerospace.com
SIC: 3721 Aircraft

(P-6612)
JOBY AVIATION INC
2155 Delaware Ave Ste 225, Santa Cruz (95060-5735)
PHONE...................831 426-3733
Joeben Bevirt, *CEO*
Paul Sciarra, *Ch of Bd*
Matthew Field, *CFO*
Kate Dehoff, *Admin Sec*
Didier Papadopoulos, *Engineer*
EMP: 956 **EST:** 2020
SALES (est): 105.2MM **Privately Held**
SIC: 3721 Aircraft

(P-6613)
LOCKHEED MARTIN (HQ)
1111 Lockheed Martin Way, Sunnyvale (94089-1212)
PHONE...................408 834-9741
Dave Turkington, *Principal*
EMP: 100 **EST:** 1987
SALES (est): 39.8MM **Publicly Held**
WEB: www.lockheedmartinjobs.com
SIC: 3721 Aircraft

(P-6614)
LOCKHEED MARTIN CORPORATION
2655 S Macarthur Dr, Tracy (95376-8188)
PHONE...................408 756-3008
EMP: 430
SALES (corp-wide): 45.3B **Publicly Held**
SIC: 3721 Mfg Aircraft
PA: Lockheed Martin Corporation
  6801 Rockledge Dr
  Bethesda MD 20817
  301 897-6000

(P-6615)
LOCKHEED MARTIN CORPORATION
1374 Holland Ct, San Jose (95118-3423)
PHONE...................408 742-5219
EMP: 430
SALES (corp-wide): 47.1B **Publicly Held**
SIC: 3721 Mfg Global Security Systems
PA: Lockheed Martin Corporation
  6801 Rockledge Dr
  Bethesda MD 20817
  301 897-6000

(P-6616)
NORTHROP GRUMMAN SYSTEMS CORP
Also Called: Electronic Systems Co Esco
401 E Hendy Ave, Sunnyvale (94086-5100)
P.O. Box 3499 (94088-3499)
PHONE...................408 735-2241
William Pitts, *Branch Mgr*
Dave Maxwell, *Administration*
Tyron Nguyen, *Administration*
Hanif Subedar, *Engrg Dir*
William Ho, *Technical Staff*
EMP: 305 **Publicly Held**
WEB: www.northropgrumman.com
SIC: 3721 Motorized aircraft; research & development on aircraft by the manufacturer
HQ: Northrop Grumman Systems Corporation
  2980 Fairview Park Dr
  Falls Church VA 22042
  703 280-2900

(P-6617)
NORTHROP GRUMMAN SYSTEMS CORP
Also Called: Northrop Grumman Mar Systems
401 E Hendy Ave Ms33-3, Sunnyvale (94086-5100)
P.O. Box 3499 (94088-3499)
PHONE...................408 735-3011
J Hupton, *Branch Mgr*
Nandor Horvath, *Engineer*
John Hultin, *Engineer*
EMP: 200 **Publicly Held**
WEB: www.northropgrumman.com
SIC: 3721 3519 3511 Aircraft; internal combustion engines; turbines & turbine generator sets
HQ: Northrop Grumman Systems Corporation
  2980 Fairview Park Dr
  Falls Church VA 22042
  703 280-2900

(P-6618)
SKYDIO INC (PA)
114 Hazel Ave, Redwood City (94061-3112)
PHONE...................855 463-5902
Adam P Bry, *CEO*
Alberto Farronato, *Chief Mktg Ofcr*
Abraham Bachrach, *Engineer*
Justine Pimentel-Czerwi, *Office Mgr*
Hayk Martirosyan, *Software Dev*
EMP: 79 **EST:** 2014
SQ FT: 15,000
SALES (est): 17.9MM **Privately Held**
WEB: www.skydio.com
SIC: 3721 Non-motorized & lighter-than-air aircraft

(P-6619)
TDL AERO ENTERPRISES INC
44 Macready Dr, Merced (95341-6405)
P.O. Box 249, Hilmar (95324-0249)
PHONE...................209 722-7300
Tom Lopez, *President*
EMP: 18 **EST:** 1994
SALES (est): 1.6MM **Privately Held**
WEB: www.gatewayaircenter.com
SIC: 3721 5088 7389 Airplanes, fixed or rotary wing; transportation equipment & supplies;

(P-6620)
WEATHERLY AIRCRAFT COMPANY
5000 Bailey Loop Bldg 360, McClellan (95652-2501)
PHONE...................916 640-0120
Gary Beck, *President*
Gloria Burns, *Office Mgr*
EMP: 32 **EST:** 2000
SALES (est): 2.9MM **Privately Held**
SIC: 3721 3728 Aircraft; aircraft parts & equipment

3724 Aircraft Engines & Engine Parts

(P-6621)
PRATT & WHITNEY
800 S Airport Blvd, San Francisco (94128-3115)
PHONE...................650 634-3122
Regina Ganbrell, *Manager*
Adrienna Yan, *Project Engr*
EMP: 17 **EST:** 2014
SALES (est): 2.8MM **Privately Held**
WEB: www.rtx.com
SIC: 3724 Aircraft engines & engine parts

(P-6622)
TURBINE ENG CMPNENTS TECH CORP
Also Called: Tect Aerospace
1211 Old Albany Rd, San Francisco (94103)
PHONE...................415 626-2000
EMP: 322
SALES (corp-wide): 232.9MM **Privately Held**
SIC: 3724 Turbines, aircraft type
PA: Turbine Engine Components Technologies Corporation
  1211 Old Albany Rd
  Thomasville GA 31792
  229 228-2600

(P-6623)
VIP MANUFACTURING & ENGRG CORP
Also Called: VIP Mfg & Engr
1084 Martin Ave, Santa Clara (95050-2609)
P.O. Box 2314, Los Gatos (95031-2314)
PHONE...................408 727-6545
L A Vargo Jr, *President*
Emma Vargo, *CFO*
EMP: 76 **EST:** 1963
SQ FT: 10,500
SALES (est): 2MM **Privately Held**
SIC: 3724 3451 3599 Aircraft engines & engine parts; screw machine products; machine shop, jobbing & repair

(P-6624)
WKF (FRIEDMAN ENTERPRISES INC (PA)
Also Called: Eff Aero
2334 Stagecoach Rd Ste B, Stockton (95215-7939)
PHONE...................925 673-9100
Wayne Friedman, *President*
EMP: 19 **EST:** 2011
SALES (est): 1.5MM **Privately Held**
SIC: 3724 Aircraft engines & engine parts

3728 Aircraft Parts & Eqpt, NEC

(P-6625)
AEG INDUSTRIES INC
1219 Briggs Ave, Santa Rosa (95401-4761)
PHONE...................707 575-0697
Peggy McIlnay Moe, *President*
Aaron McIlnay-Moe, *Partner*
Peg McIlnay-Moe, *President*
William Pottorff, *President*
Dennis McIlnay Moe, *Vice Pres*
EMP: 30 **EST:** 1991
SQ FT: 6,500
SALES (est): 6.7MM **Privately Held**
WEB: www.aegindustries.com
SIC: 3728 Aircraft parts & equipment

(P-6626)
AERO PRECISION HOLDINGS LP
2525 Collier Canyon Rd, Livermore (94551-7545)
PHONE...................925 455-9900
Frank Cowle, *Partner*
Gregory Friedman, *Buyer*
EMP: 200 **EST:** 2016
SALES (est): 12.9MM **Privately Held**
WEB: www.goallclear.com
SIC: 3728 Aircraft parts & equipment

(P-6627)
AEROJET ROCKETDYNE INC
Also Called: Rocket Shop
1180 Iron Point Rd # 350, Folsom (95630-8321)
PHONE...................916 355-4000
Craig Halterman, *Vice Pres*
Warren Yasuhara, *Vice Pres*
Gene Goldman, *Exec Dir*
Brian Robbers, *Program Mgr*
Zenu Sarcadi, *Telecomm Mgr*
EMP: 22
SALES (corp-wide): 2B **Publicly Held**
WEB: www.rocket.com
SIC: 3728 Aircraft body & wing assemblies & parts
HQ: Aerojet Rocketdyne, Inc.
  2001 Aerojet Rd
  Rancho Cordova CA 95742
  916 355-4000

(P-6628)
AEROJET ROCKETDYNE INC
160 Blue Ravine Rd Ste C, Folsom (95630-4718)
PHONE...................916 355-4000
John Barker, *Engineer*
Michael Lynch, *Engineer*
EMP: 22
SALES (corp-wide): 2B **Publicly Held**
WEB: www.rocket.com
SIC: 3728 Aircraft body & wing assemblies & parts
HQ: Aerojet Rocketdyne, Inc.
  2001 Aerojet Rd
  Rancho Cordova CA 95742
  916 355-4000

(P-6629)
AEROMETALS INC (PA)
3920 Sandstone Dr, El Dorado Hills (95762-9652)
PHONE...................916 939-6888
Lorie Symon, *President*
Lori Symon, *Chief Mktg Ofcr*
Anthony Bohm, *Program Mgr*
Tony Bohm, *Program Mgr*
Rex Kamphfner, *General Mgr*
◆ **EMP:** 76 **EST:** 1982
SQ FT: 150,000
SALES (est): 44.2MM **Privately Held**
WEB: www.aerometals.aero
SIC: 3728 Aircraft parts & equipment

(P-6630)
AEROSPACE COMPOSITE PRODUCTS (PA)
Also Called: Acp Composites
78 Lindbergh Ave, Livermore (94551-9503)
PHONE...................925 443-5900
George William Sparr, *President*
Greg Caulder, *Vice Pres*
Barbara Sparr, *Admin Sec*
Michele Flores, *Data Proc Staff*
Connie Austin, *Human Res Mgr*
EMP: 19 **EST:** 2003
SALES (est): 8.9MM **Privately Held**
WEB: www.acpcomposites.com
SIC: 3728 5961 3624 Aircraft assemblies, subassemblies & parts; mail order house; carbon & graphite products

(P-6631)
APPLIED AROSPC STRUCTURES CORP (PA)
Also Called: Aasc
3437 S Airport Way, Stockton (95206-3853)
P.O. Box 6189 (95206-0189)
PHONE...................209 982-0160
John E Rule, *President*
Rhonda Ward, *Corp Secy*
Burton Weil, *Admin Sec*
Allen Stephens, *Design Engr*
Mike Noyes, *Engineer*
▲ **EMP:** 229 **EST:** 1995
SQ FT: 100,000
SALES (est): 129.6MM **Privately Held**
WEB: www.aascworld.com
SIC: 3728 Aircraft parts & equipment

3728 - Aircraft Parts & Eqpt, NEC County (P-6632)

(P-6632)
GENERAL DYNMICS OTS NCVLLE INC (DH)
511 Grove St, Healdsburg (95448-4747)
PHONE............707 473-9200
Phebe N Novakovic, *CEO*
Richard Schroeder, *Vice Pres*
Laura Ortega, *Executive*
Timothy Finks, *Engineer*
Jennifer Fuchs, *Materials Mgr*
EMP: 65 EST: 1999
SQ FT: 28,000
SALES (est): 29.1MM
SALES (corp-wide): 37.9B **Publicly Held**
WEB: www.gd-ots.com
SIC: 3728 Aircraft parts & equipment
HQ: General Dynamics Ordnance And Tactical Systems, Inc.
11399 16th Ct N Ste 200
Saint Petersburg FL 33716
727 578-8100

(P-6633)
HILLER AIRCRAFT CORPORATION
925 M St, Firebaugh (93622-2234)
P.O. Box 246 (93622-0246)
PHONE............559 659-5959
Steven Palm, *General Mgr*
EMP: 27 EST: 1994
SQ FT: 100,000
SALES (est): 2.9MM **Privately Held**
WEB: www.hilleraircraftcorporation.com
SIC: 3728 Aircraft parts & equipment

(P-6634)
ICON AIRCRAFT INC (PA)
2141 Icon Way, Vacaville (95688-8766)
PHONE............707 564-4000
Kirk Hawkins, *CEO*
Thomas Wieners, *COO*
Rich Bridge, *Vice Pres*
Simi Gupta, *Controller*
Jerry Meyer, *Marketing Staff*
EMP: 198 EST: 2006
SALES (est): 53.9MM **Privately Held**
WEB: www.iconaircraft.com
SIC: 3728 Aircraft parts & equipment

(P-6635)
MATTERNET INC (PA)
185 E Dana St, Mountain View (94041-1507)
PHONE............650 260-2727
Andreas Ratopoulos, *CEO*
Matthew Dawes, *Tech Recruiter*
Akshay Bajaj, *Engineer*
Brandon Landry, *Engineer*
EMP: 27 EST: 2014
SALES (est): 4.4MM **Privately Held**
WEB: www.mttr.net
SIC: 3728 Target drones

(P-6636)
ORCON AEROSPACE
2600 Central Ave Ste E, Union City (94587-3187)
P.O. Box 487, Kentfield (94914-0487)
PHONE............510 489-8100
Hollis Bascom, *President*
Dennis Murray, *Vice Pres*
Tom Macedo, *Opers Staff*
EMP: 67 EST: 2006
SQ FT: 200,000
SALES (est): 2.4MM **Privately Held**
WEB: www.orcon.com
SIC: 3728 Aircraft parts & equipment

(P-6637)
WEST VALLEY AVIATION INC
1011 12th St, Firebaugh (93622-2600)
PHONE............559 659-7378
Charlie Witrado, *President*
Sylvester Ochoa, *Manager*
Joel Witrado, *Manager*
EMP: 15 EST: 2005
SALES (est): 1.5MM **Privately Held**
SIC: 3728 Dusting & spraying equipment, aircraft

3731 Shipbuilding & Repairing

(P-6638)
BAY SHIP & YACHT CO (PA)
2900 Main St Ste 2100, Alameda (94501-7739)
PHONE............510 337-9122
William Elliott, *CEO*
Bill Elliott, *President*
Maggie Collins, *COO*
Shirley Smith, *COO*
Vicki Elliott, *Treasurer*
▲ EMP: 175 EST: 1990
SQ FT: 20,000
SALES (est): 75.4MM **Privately Held**
WEB: www.bay-ship.com
SIC: 3731 3732 Commercial cargo ships, building & repairing; combat vessels, building & repairing; barges, building & repairing; yachts, building & repairing

(P-6639)
MARE ISLAND DRY DOCK LLC
1180 Nimitz Ave, Vallejo (94592-1053)
PHONE............707 652-7356
Stephen Dileo, *Mng Member*
William Dunbar, *Vice Pres*
Christina Snyder, *Administration*
Dan Schaab, *Project Mgr*
Chris Snyder, *Contract Mgr*
EMP: 60
SALES (est): 32.4MM **Privately Held**
WEB: www.midllc.com
SIC: 3731 Shipbuilding & repairing

(P-6640)
WALASHEK INDUSTRIAL & MAR INC
2826 8th St, Berkeley (94710-2707)
PHONE............206 624-2880
Frank Walashek, *Manager*
EMP: 31
SALES (corp-wide): 27.4MM **Privately Held**
WEB: www.walashek.com
SIC: 3731 Shipbuilding & repairing
HQ: Walashek Industrial & Marine, Inc.
3411 Amherst St
Norfolk VA 23513

3732 Boat Building & Repairing

(P-6641)
DEEP OCEAN ENGINEERING INC
2403 Qume Dr, San Jose (95131-1821)
PHONE............408 436-1102
Fang LI, *CEO*
EMP: 15 EST: 2010
SALES (est): 1.7MM **Privately Held**
WEB: www.deepocean.com
SIC: 3732 Boat building & repairing

(P-6642)
FINELINE INDUSTRIES INC (PA)
Also Called: Centurion
2047 Grogan Ave, Merced (95341-6440)
PHONE............209 384-0255
Richard D Lee, *President*
Clark Bird, *CFO*
Pamela Lee, *Corp Secy*
Jeffrey Polan, *Vice Pres*
▼ EMP: 75 EST: 1983
SQ FT: 38,000
SALES (est): 27.6MM **Privately Held**
WEB: www.centurionboats.com
SIC: 3732 Boats, fiberglass: building & repairing

(P-6643)
KAYE SANDY ENTERPRISES INC
Also Called: Porta-Bote International
1074 Independence Ave, Mountain View (94043-1602)
PHONE............650 961-5334
Alex R Kaye, *President*
Frances Kaye, *Corp Secy*
▼ EMP: 35 EST: 1973
SQ FT: 4,000
SALES (est): 2.6MM **Privately Held**
WEB: www.porta-bote.com
SIC: 3732 5551 Boat building & repairing; boat dealers

(P-6644)
MB SPORTS INC
280 Airpark Rd, Atwater (95301-9535)
PHONE............209 357-4153
Myung Bo Hong, *CEO*
Dustin Brendel, *Purchasing*
▲ EMP: 40 EST: 1993
SQ FT: 16,000
SALES (est): 4.6MM **Privately Held**
WEB: www.mbsportsusa.com
SIC: 3732 5551 5091 Motorboats, inboard or outboard: building & repairing; boat dealers; boats, canoes, watercrafts & equipment

(P-6645)
MOOSE BOATS INC
1175 Nimitz Ave Ste 150, Vallejo (94592-1003)
PHONE............707 778-9828
Christian Lind, *CEO*
Aaron Lind, *Treasurer*
Roger N Fleck, *Exec VP*
Mark Stott, *Vice Pres*
Stephen Dirkes, *General Mgr*
EMP: 16 EST: 2016
SQ FT: 20,000
SALES (est): 3.1MM **Privately Held**
SIC: 3732 Boat building & repairing

3751 Motorcycles, Bicycles & Parts

(P-6646)
4INTO1 INC
280 Wattis Way B, South San Francisco (94080-6714)
PHONE............650 741-6175
Rufus Ashford, *Principal*
EMP: 15 EST: 2014
SALES (est): 219.4K **Privately Held**
WEB: www.4into1.com
SIC: 3751 Motorcycles & related parts

(P-6647)
AMERICAN HARD BAG LLC
1467 Stoney Cross Ln, Lincoln (95648-3247)
PHONE............707 484-1283
Robert Gomez,
Colleen Finn,
EMP: 17 EST: 2014
SALES (est): 1MM **Privately Held**
WEB: www.americanhardbag.com
SIC: 3751 Motorcycles & related parts

(P-6648)
CYCLE SHACK
816 Murchison Dr, Millbrae (94030-3026)
PHONE............650 583-7014
Homer H Dyer, *President*
Buzz Dyer, *President*
Grove Hoover II, *Vice Pres*
Steve Reedy, *Admin Sec*
EMP: 18 EST: 1966
SQ FT: 35,000
SALES (est): 629.6K **Privately Held**
SIC: 3751 Motorcycles & related parts; motorcycle accessories

(P-6649)
GILROY MOTORCYCLE CENTER INC
7661 Monterey St, Gilroy (95020-5215)
PHONE............408 842-9955
Stephen J Schaub, *CEO*
EMP: 21 EST: 1985
SALES (est): 2.6MM **Privately Held**
WEB: www.gilroymotorcyclecenter.com
SIC: 3751 5571 Motorcycles, bicycles & parts; motorcycle dealers

(P-6650)
GLOBAL MOTORSPORT PARTS INC
15750 Vineyard Blvd # 100, Morgan Hill (95037-7119)
PHONE............408 778-0500
Joseph F Keenan, *Ch of Bd*
Seth Murdock, *CFO*
◆ EMP: 106 EST: 1998
SALES (est): 2.6MM **Privately Held**
WEB: www.customchrome.com
SIC: 3751 5013 Motorcycle accessories; motorcycle parts
HQ: Dae-Il Usa, Inc.
112 Robert Young Blvd
Murray KY 42071

(P-6651)
KIBBLWHITE PRCSION MCHNING INC
580 Crespi Dr Ste H, Pacifica (94044-3426)
PHONE............650 359-4704
Will Kibblewhite, *President*
Maria Kibblewhite, *Purchasing*
▲ EMP: 23 EST: 1961
SQ FT: 3,000
SALES (est): 3.1MM **Privately Held**
WEB: www.kpmi.us
SIC: 3751 3599 Motorcycles & related parts; machine shop, jobbing & repair

(P-6652)
MAIER MANUFACTURING INC
416 Crown Point Cir Ste 1, Grass Valley (95945-9558)
PHONE............530 272-9036
Charles A Maier, *President*
George Maier, *Vice Pres*
Mark Maier, *Vice Pres*
▲ EMP: 45 EST: 1971
SQ FT: 79,000
SALES (est): 4.4MM **Privately Held**
WEB: www.maierusa.com
SIC: 3751 3082 Motorcycle accessories; unsupported plastics profile shapes

(P-6653)
MEGACYCLE ENGINEERING INC
Also Called: Megacycle Cams
90 Mitchell Blvd, San Rafael (94903-2039)
PHONE............415 472-3195
James H Dour, *President*
Barbara Dour, *Treasurer*
Lisa Dour, *Office Mgr*
EMP: 23 EST: 1963
SQ FT: 7,500
SALES (est): 706.4K **Privately Held**
WEB: www.megacyclecams.com
SIC: 3751 3714 5013 Motorcycles & related parts; camshafts, motor vehicle; automotive supplies & parts; motorcycle parts

(P-6654)
SANTA CRUZ BICYCLES LLC
Also Called: Santa Cruz Bikes
2841 Mission St, Santa Cruz (95060-5705)
PHONE............831 459-7560
Rob Roskopp,
Willie Bullian, *Department Mgr*
Adam Guske, *Planning*
Niki Woodward, *Planning*
Faith Zack, *Business Anlyst*
◆ EMP: 70 EST: 2015
SQ FT: 70,000
SALES (est): 16.4MM
SALES (corp-wide): 2B **Privately Held**
WEB: www.santacruzbicycles.com
SIC: 3751 5941 Motorcycles, bicycles & parts; bicycle & bicycle parts
HQ: Pon Holdings B.V.
Stadionplein 28
Amsterdam
202 460-900

3764 Guided Missile/Space Vehicle Propulsion Units & parts

(P-6655)
AEROJET ROCKETDYNE INC (HQ)
2001 Aerojet Rd, Rancho Cordova (95742-6418)
P.O. Box 13222, Sacramento (95813-3222)
PHONE..................................916 355-4000
Eileen Drake, *CEO*
Amy Gowder, *COO*
Huseyin Gulcu, *CFO*
Paul Landstrom, *CFO*
John Joy, *Treasurer*
▲ **EMP:** 1400 **EST:** 1944
SALES (est): 763.9MM
SALES (corp-wide): 2B **Publicly Held**
WEB: www.rocket.com
SIC: 3764 3728 3769 3761 Propulsion units for guided missiles & space vehicles; aircraft body & wing assemblies & parts; guided missile & space vehicle parts & auxiliary equipment; guided missiles & space vehicles
PA: Aerojet Rocketdyne Holdings, Inc.
222 N Pcf Cast Hwy Ste 50
El Segundo CA 90245
310 252-8100

3792 Travel Trailers & Campers

(P-6656)
FOUR WHEEL CAMPERS INC
1400 Churchill Downs Ave A, Woodland (95776-6147)
PHONE..................................530 666-1442
Tom Hanagan, *President*
Dan Welty, *Vice Pres*
Sonam Chand, *Admin Asst*
Jay Roper, *Manager*
▲ **EMP:** 25 **EST:** 1973
SALES (est): 5.1MM **Privately Held**
WEB: www.fourwheelcampers.com
SIC: 3792 5561 Travel trailers & campers; recreational vehicle dealers

3795 Tanks & Tank Components

(P-6657)
SANTA ROSA STAIN
1400 Airport Blvd, Santa Rosa (95403-1023)
P.O. Box 518 (95402-0518)
PHONE..................................707 544-7777
Mark Ferronato, *President*
Michele Cotta, *Corp Secy*
Rod Ferronato, *Vice Pres*
Danny Cotta, *Prdtn Mgr*
EMP: 45 **EST:** 1969
SQ FT: 12,000
SALES (est): 7.5MM **Privately Held**
WEB: www.srss.com
SIC: 3795 Tanks & tank components

3799 Transportation Eqpt, NEC

(P-6658)
DHM ENTERPRISES INC
7609 Wilbur Way, Sacramento (95828-4927)
PHONE..................................916 688-7767
George Backovich, *President*
John Pennell, *Treasurer*
Bruce Pennell, *Vice Pres*
EMP: 16 **EST:** 1985
SALES (est): 1.4MM **Privately Held**
SIC: 3799 5551 Boat trailers; boat dealers

(P-6659)
SPORT BOAT TRAILERS INC
430 C St, Patterson (95363-2724)
P.O. Box 1686 (95363-1686)
PHONE..................................209 892-5388
Robert J Kehl, *President*
EMP: 17 **EST:** 1974
SQ FT: 3,700
SALES (est): 2.2MM **Privately Held**
WEB: www.sbtrailers.com
SIC: 3799 7539 Boat trailers; trailer repair

3812 Search, Detection, Navigation & Guidance Systs & Instrs

(P-6660)
ALLIANT TCHSYSTEMS OPRTONS LLC
151 Martinvale Ln Ste 150, San Jose (95119-1455)
PHONE..................................408 513-3271
EMP: 33 **Publicly Held**
WEB: www.northropgrumman.com
SIC: 3812 Search & navigation equipment
HQ: Alliant Techsystems Operations Llc
2980 Fairview Park Dr
Falls Church VA 22042

(P-6661)
AO SKY CORPORATION
4989 Pedro Hill Rd, Pilot Hill (95664-9610)
PHONE..................................415 717-9901
Craig Miller, *President*
EMP: 15 **EST:** 2011
SALES (est): 786.2K **Privately Held**
WEB: www.ao-sky.com
SIC: 3812 Aircraft/aerospace flight instruments & guidance systems

(P-6662)
ASRC AEROSPACE CORP
Nasa Ames Research Ctr, Mountain View (94035)
PHONE..................................650 604-5946
Ted Price, *Manager*
Davin Chan, *Technical Mgr*
EMP: 232
SALES (corp-wide): 2.7B **Privately Held**
WEB: www.asrcfederal.com
SIC: 3812 7371 7373 5088 Search & navigation equipment; custom computer programming services; computer integrated systems design; transportation equipment & supplies
HQ: Asrc Aerospace Corp
7000 Muirkirk Meadows Dr # 100
Beltsville MD 20705
301 837-5500

(P-6663)
ASTRO DIGITAL US INC
3171 Jay St, Santa Clara (95054-3308)
PHONE..................................650 804-3210
Chris Biddy, *CEO*
Melinda Horberg, *Administration*
Alex Kudriashova, *Sr Software Eng*
EMP: 32 **EST:** 2018
SALES (est): 4.1MM **Privately Held**
WEB: www.astrodigital.com
SIC: 3812 Aircraft/aerospace flight instruments & guidance systems

(P-6664)
BAE SYSTEMS LAND ARMAMENTS LP
6331 San Ignacio Ave, San Jose (95119-1202)
P.O. Box 5300958 (95153-5398)
PHONE..................................408 289-0111
John Spiller, *Officer*
Robert Sankovich, *Vice Pres*
Paul Kim, *Program Mgr*
Ted Kimes, *Program Mgr*
Loren Van Huystee, *Program Mgr*
EMP: 407
SALES (corp-wide): 25.6B **Privately Held**
WEB: www.baesystems.com
SIC: 3812 Search & navigation equipment
HQ: Bae Systems Land & Armaments L.P.
2941 Frview Pk Dr Ste 100
Falls Church VA 22042
571 461-6000

(P-6665)
COBHAM ADV ELEC SOL INC
5300 Hellyer Ave, San Jose (95138-1003)
PHONE..................................408 624-3000
Charles Stuff, *President*
Marc Holloway, *Program Mgr*
Scott Sacks, *Program Mgr*
Kathleen Thomas, *Program Mgr*
Alan Takahashi, *General Mgr*
EMP: 316
SALES (corp-wide): 177.9K **Privately Held**
WEB: www.cobham.com
SIC: 3812 3679 Search & navigation equipment; microwave components
HQ: Cobham Advanced Electronic Solutions Inc.
305 Richardson Rd
Lansdale PA 19446

(P-6666)
DAVIS INSTRUMENTS CORPORATION
3465 Diablo Ave, Hayward (94545-2778)
PHONE..................................510 732-9229
James S Acquistapace, *Ch of Bd*
Robert W Selig Jr, *President*
Kevin McCarthy, *COO*
Diane Padilla, *CFO*
Susan Tatum, *CFO*
◆ **EMP:** 100 **EST:** 1964
SQ FT: 77,000
SALES (est): 22MM **Privately Held**
WEB: www.davisinstruments.com
SIC: 3812 3429 3829 3823 Navigational systems & instruments; marine hardware; measuring & controlling devices; industrial instrmnts msrmnt display/control process variable; farm machinery & equipment

(P-6667)
EVICTION DEF CLLBRTIVE INC A C
1338 Mission St Fl 4, San Francisco (94103-2643)
PHONE..................................415 947-0797
Martina I Cucullu Lim, *Exec Dir*
Sarah F Hinks, *Litigation*
EMP: 70 **EST:** 2017
SALES (est): 3.8MM **Privately Held**
WEB: www.evictiondefense.org
SIC: 3812 Defense systems & equipment

(P-6668)
GARNER PRODUCTS INC
10620 Industrial Ave # 100, Roseville (95678-6241)
PHONE..................................916 784-0200
Ronald Stofan, *CEO*
Michelle M Stofan, *Admin Sec*
Jason McMillen, *Mfg Dir*
Justin Stofan, *Accounts Mgr*
Chris Trevino, *Accounts Mgr*
EMP: 15
SQ FT: 24,000
SALES (est): 3.1MM **Privately Held**
WEB: www.garnerproducts.com
SIC: 3812 3663 7389 Degaussing equipment; radio broadcasting & communications equipment; document & office record destruction

(P-6669)
GENERAL DYNMICS OTS VRSTRON IN
950 Iron Point Rd Ste 110, Folsom (95630-8303)
PHONE..................................916 355-7700
Marshall Cousineau, *Director*
EMP: 60
SALES (corp-wide): 37.9B **Publicly Held**
WEB: www.gd-ots.com
SIC: 3812 3769 Search & navigation equipment; guided missile & space vehicle parts & auxiliary equipment
HQ: General Dynamics Ots (Niceville), Inc.
511 Grove St
Healdsburg CA 95448
707 473-9200

(P-6670)
GENERAL RADAR CORP
616 Mountain View Ave, Belmont (94002-2533)
PHONE..................................626 319-5827
Nolan Browne, *CEO*
Dmitry Turbiner, *Admin Sec*
EMP: 20 **EST:** 2015
SALES (est): 2.2MM **Privately Held**
WEB: www.genrad.io
SIC: 3812 Antennas, radar or communications; aircraft/aerospace flight instruments & guidance systems

(P-6671)
GMW ASSOCIATES
955 Industrial Rd, San Carlos (94070-4117)
PHONE..................................650 802-8292
Ian Walker, *Vice Pres*
Jocelyn Walker, *Admin Sec*
Lou Law, *Engineer*
Ludovic Letourneur, *Engineer*
Michael Duffy, *Senior Engr*
EMP: 43 **EST:** 2018
SALES (est): 5.1MM **Privately Held**
WEB: www.gmw.com
SIC: 3812 Search & navigation equipment

(P-6672)
INVENSENSE INC (HQ)
1745 Tech Dr Ste 200, San Jose (95110)
PHONE..................................408 501-2200
Amit Shah, *Ch of Bd*
Behrooz Abdi, *President*
Mark Dentinger, *CFO*
Daniel Goehl, *Vice Pres*
Al Heshmati, *Vice Pres*
EMP: 631 **EST:** 2004
SQ FT: 159,000
SALES (est): 86MM **Privately Held**
WEB: www.invensense.tdk.com
SIC: 3812 Gyroscopes

(P-6673)
L-3 COMMUNICATIONS WESCAM
428 Aviation Blvd Ste 3l, Santa Rosa (95403-1069)
PHONE..................................707 568-3000
Dan Heibel, *President*
EMP: 57 **EST:** 1986
SALES (est): 11.5MM
SALES (corp-wide): 18.1B **Publicly Held**
WEB: www.l3harris.com
SIC: 3812 3861 Search & navigation equipment; photographic equipment & supplies
HQ: L3 Technologies, Inc.
600 3rd Ave Fl 34
New York NY 10016
321 727-9100

(P-6674)
LG INNOTEK USA INC
Also Called: San Jose Office
2540 N 1st St Ste 400, San Jose (95131-1016)
PHONE..................................408 234-6356
Won Kim, *Engineer*
Luke Han, *Business Mgr*
Hwaseub Lee, *QC Mgr*
Jeesun Lim, *Opers Staff*
Eugene Kang, *Marketing Staff*
EMP: 24 **Privately Held**
SIC: 3812 Defense systems & equipment
HQ: Lg Innotek Usa, Inc.
2540 N 1st St Ste 400
San Jose CA 95131
408 955-0364

(P-6675)
METROTECH CORPORATION (PA)
Also Called: Vivax-Metrotech
3251 Olcott St, Santa Clara (95054-3006)
PHONE..................................408 734-3880
Christian Stolz, *CEO*
Andrew Hoare, *President*
Mark Drew, *Vice Pres*
Mark Royle, *Vice Pres*
Kristin Lee, *IT/INT Sup*
▲ **EMP:** 78 **EST:** 1976
SQ FT: 65,000

3812 - Search, Detection, Navigation & Guidance Systs & Instrs County (P-6676)

SALES (est): 17.3MM Privately Held
SIC: 3812 3599 3829 Detection apparatus: electronic/magnetic field, light/heat; water leak detectors; measuring & controlling devices

(P-6676)
MORPHO DETECTION LLC
7151 Gateway Blvd, Newark (94560-1012)
PHONE 510 739-2400
Mike McGowan, *Telecomm Mgr*
Dave Petry, *Technology*
Sue Sauvageau, *Technology*
Robert Hilliard, *Mfg Staff*
EMP: 77
SALES (corp-wide): 13.1MM Privately Held
WEB: www.smithsdetection.com
SIC: 3812 Detection apparatus: electronic/magnetic field, light/heat
PA: Morpho Detection Llc
  2202 Lakeside Blvd
  Edgewood MD 21040
  714 476-3570

(P-6677)
NORTHROP GRUMMAN SYSTEMS CORP
6379 San Ignacio Ave, San Jose (95119-1200)
PHONE 703 968-1239
Stacy Moffett, *Branch Mgr*
Alice Reed, *Principal*
EMP: 200 Publicly Held
WEB: www.northropgrumman.com
SIC: 3812 Search & navigation equipment
HQ: Northrop Grumman Systems Corporation
  2980 Fairview Park Dr
  Falls Church VA 22042
  703 280-2900

(P-6678)
NORTHROP GRUMMAN SYSTEMS CORP
Northrop Grumman Info Systems
5441 Luce Ave, McClellan (95652-2417)
PHONE 916 570-4454
John Dydiw, *Manager*
Ron Garrison, *Design Engr*
Kelley Ristau, *Engineer*
EMP: 200 Publicly Held
WEB: www.northropgrumman.com
SIC: 3812 Search & navigation equipment
HQ: Northrop Grumman Systems Corporation
  2980 Fairview Park Dr
  Falls Church VA 22042
  703 280-2900

(P-6679)
PRENAV INC
1909 Lyon Ave, Belmont (94002-1728)
PHONE 650 264-7279
Nathan Schuett, *CEO*
Nick Rossi, *President*
Marc Ausman, *COO*
Mark Bercow, *VP Bus Dvlpt*
Reza Anvari, *Engineer*
EMP: 25 **EST:** 2013
SALES (est): 3.1MM Privately Held
WEB: www.prenav.com
SIC: 3812 Aircraft/aerospace flight instruments & guidance systems

(P-6680)
QUANERGY SYSTEMS INC (PA)
433 Lakeside Dr, Sunnyvale (94085-4704)
PHONE 408 245-9500
Kevin J Kennedy, *CEO*
Louay Eldada, *President*
Axel Fuchs, *President*
Mike Healy, *CFO*
Enzo Signore, *Chief Mktg Ofcr*
EMP: 199 **EST:** 2012
SALES (est): 47.3MM Privately Held
WEB: www.quanergy.com
SIC: 3812 Infrared object detection equipment

(P-6681)
QUANTUM3D INC (PA)
920 Hillview Ct Ste 145, Milpitas (95035-4558)
PHONE 408 600-2500
Clayton Conrad, *President*
Murat Kose, *CFO*
Timothy Stewart, *Vice Pres*
Burak Aksoy, *Managing Dir*
Jeff Belote, *Engineer*
◆ **EMP:** 19 **EST:** 1994
SQ FT: 20,000
SALES (est): 7.1MM Privately Held
WEB: www.quantum3d.com
SIC: 3812 Aircraft control instruments

(P-6682)
SIERRA NEVADA CORP
3034 Gold Canal Dr, Rancho Cordova (95670-6464)
PHONE 775 331-0222
Tim Black, *Principal*
EMP: 17 **EST:** 2016
SALES (est): 2.1MM Privately Held
WEB: www.sncorp.com
SIC: 3812 Search & navigation equipment

(P-6683)
SIERRA NEVADA CORPORATION
985 University Ave Ste 4, Los Gatos (95032-7639)
PHONE 408 395-2004
Michael Weiland, *Branch Mgr*
Eren Ozmen, *President*
Fatih Ozmen, *CEO*
Luciano Saccani, *Business Dir*
EMP: 34
SALES (corp-wide): 2.3B Privately Held
WEB: www.sncorp.com
SIC: 3812 Search & navigation equipment
PA: Sierra Nevada Corporation
  444 Salomon Cir
  Sparks NV 89434
  775 331-0222

(P-6684)
SIERRA NEVADA CORPORATION
145 Parkshore Dr, Folsom (95630-4734)
PHONE 916 985-8799
Carolyn Cain, *Branch Mgr*
Aaron Bennetts, *Program Mgr*
Brian Dunlop, *Software Engr*
George Figueroa, *Engineer*
Lisa Weisman, *Business Mgr*
EMP: 34
SALES (corp-wide): 2.3B Privately Held
WEB: www.sncorp.com
SIC: 3812 Search & navigation equipment
PA: Sierra Nevada Corporation
  444 Salomon Cir
  Sparks NV 89434
  775 331-0222

(P-6685)
SMITHS DETECTION INC
7151 Gateway Blvd, Newark (94560-1012)
PHONE 410 612-2625
Shan Hood, *President*
EMP: 1009
SALES (corp-wide): 3.3B Privately Held
WEB: www.smithsdetection.com
SIC: 3812 Detection apparatus: electronic/magnetic field, light/heat
HQ: Smiths Detection Inc.
  2202 Lakeside Blvd
  Edgewood MD 21040
  410 612-2625

(P-6686)
TELENAV INC (PA)
4655 Great America Pkwy, Santa Clara (95054-1236)
PHONE 408 245-3800
HP Jin, *Ch of Bd*
Salman Dhanani, *President*
Hassan Wahla, *President*
Adeel Manzoor, *CFO*
Karen Francis, *Bd of Directors*
EMP: 685 **EST:** 1999
SQ FT: 55,000
SALES: 240.3MM Privately Held
WEB: www.telenav.com
SIC: 3812 Navigational systems & instruments

(P-6687)
TINI AEROSPACE INC
2505 Kerner Blvd, San Rafael (94901-5571)
PHONE 415 524-2124
Michael Bokaie, *President*
Vicki Lasky, *Treasurer*

David Bokaie, *Vice Pres*
Trudy Sachs, *Vice Pres*
▼ **EMP:** 30 **EST:** 1996
SQ FT: 5,400
SALES (est): 7.3MM Privately Held
WEB: www.ebad.com
SIC: 3812 Search & navigation equipment

(P-6688)
TRIMBLE MILITARY & ADVNCED SYS
510 De Guigne Dr, Sunnyvale (94085-3920)
P.O. Box 3642 (94088-3642)
PHONE 408 481-8000
Ron Smith, *President*
Allan Riccetti, *Senior Buyer*
▼ **EMP:** 55 **EST:** 2007
SQ FT: 22,000
SALES (est): 15.8MM
SALES (corp-wide): 3.2B Publicly Held
WEB: www.trimble.com
SIC: 3812 3829 Search & navigation equipment; measuring & controlling devices
PA: Trimble Inc.
  935 Stewart Dr
  Sunnyvale CA 94085
  408 481-8000

(P-6689)
VELODYNE LIDAR USA INC (HQ)
5521 Hellyer Ave, San Jose (95138-1017)
PHONE 408 465-2800
Anand Gopalan, *CEO*
David Hall, *Ch of Bd*
Rick Tewell, *COO*
Andrew Hamer, *CFO*
Mircea Gradu, *Vice Pres*
EMP: 233 **EST:** 1983
SALES (est): 74.4MM
SALES (corp-wide): 95.3MM Publicly Held
WEB: www.velodynelidar.com
SIC: 5731 3812 Video cameras & accessories; altimeters, standard & sensitive
PA: Velodyne Lidar, Inc.
  5521 Hellyer Ave
  San Jose CA 95138
  669 275-2251

3821 Laboratory Apparatus & Furniture

(P-6690)
APPLIED CELLS INC
3350 Scott Blvd Bldg 6, Santa Clara (95054-3108)
PHONE 800 960-3004
Yuchen Zhou, *CEO*
Yu Liping, *President*
EMP: 20 **EST:** 2017
SALES (est): 1.7MM Privately Held
SIC: 3821 Sample preparation apparatus

(P-6691)
BERLIN FOOD & LAB EQUIPMENT CO
43 S Linden Ave, South San Francisco (94080-6407)
PHONE 650 589-4231
Michael F Ulrich, *President*
Mark Cottonaro, *COO*
Jackie McClymond, *CFO*
Bron Cottonaro, *Vice Pres*
Kimberly Rojas, *Admin Asst*
EMP: 23 **EST:** 1947
SQ FT: 50,000
SALES (est): 4.2MM Privately Held
WEB: www.berlinusa.com
SIC: 3821 1799 Laboratory apparatus & furniture; home/office interiors finishing, furnishing & remodeling; food service equipment installation

(P-6692)
ENDRUN TECHNOLOGIES LLC
2270 Northpoint Pkwy, Santa Rosa (95407-7398)
PHONE 707 573-8633
Georgia Johnson, *CFO*
Susan Coryell,

David Lobsinger,
EMP: 15 **EST:** 1998
SQ FT: 7,400
SALES (est): 4.7MM Privately Held
WEB: www.endruntechnologies.com
SIC: 3821 3825 Time interval measuring equipment, electric (lab type); frequency meters: electrical, mechanical & electronic

(P-6693)
IDEX HEALTH & SCIENCE LLC (HQ)
600 Park Ct, Rohnert Park (94928-7906)
PHONE 707 588-2000
Jeff Cannon, *President*
Abhi Khandelwal, *Vice Pres*
Christal Morris, *Vice Pres*
Abigail Roche, *Vice Pres*
Dan Salliotte, *Vice Pres*
▲ **EMP:** 87 **EST:** 2002
SQ FT: 70,000
SALES (est): 219.7MM
SALES (corp-wide): 2.3B Publicly Held
WEB: www.idex-hs.com
SIC: 3821 3829 3826 3823 Laboratory apparatus & furniture; measuring & controlling devices; analytical instruments; industrial instrmnts msrmnt display/control process variable; valves & pipe fittings
PA: Idex Corporation
  3100 Sanders Rd Ste 301
  Northbrook IL 60062
  847 498-7070

(P-6694)
LASER REFERENCE INC
151 Martinvale Ln, San Jose (95119-1454)
PHONE 408 361-0220
Lee Robson, *President*
Christopher Middleton, *Treasurer*
Mike Middleton, *Admin Sec*
David Kawano, *Sales Mgr*
Tracy Davis, *Manager*
▲ **EMP:** 22 **EST:** 1991
SQ FT: 9,500
SALES (est): 1.1MM Privately Held
WEB: www.proshotlaser.com
SIC: 3821 3829 3699 Laser beam alignment devices; measuring & controlling devices; electrical equipment & supplies

(P-6695)
MARVAC SCIENTIFIC MFG CO
3231 Monument Way Ste I, Concord (94518-2444)
PHONE 925 825-4636
George Marin, *President*
Steve Marin, *Treasurer*
Douglas Marin, *Vice Pres*
Lisa Miller, *Buyer*
EMP: 18 **EST:** 1959
SQ FT: 20,000
SALES (est): 4.1MM Privately Held
WEB: www.marvacscientific.com
SIC: 3821 Vacuum pumps, laboratory

(P-6696)
MINARIS MEDICAL AMERICA INC
630 Clyde Ct, Mountain View (94043-2239)
PHONE 800 233-6278
Takashi Miyamoto, *CEO*
Kazuyoshi Tsunoda, *President*
Keiichi Takeda, *CFO*
Cinda Curley, *Administration*
Steve Schwalen, *Administration*
EMP: 190 **EST:** 1982
SQ FT: 31,000
SALES (est): 35.5MM Privately Held
WEB: www.minarismedical.com
SIC: 3821 2835 8071 Laboratory measuring apparatus; in vitro diagnostics; medical laboratories
HQ: Showa Denko Materials Co., Ltd.
  1-9-2, Marunouchi
  Chiyoda-Ku TKY 100-0

(P-6697)
TECAN SYSTEMS INC
2450 Zanker Rd, San Jose (95131-1126)
PHONE 408 953-3100
David Martyr, *CEO*
Rudolf Eugster, *CFO*
Martin Brusdeilins, *Exec VP*

▲ = Import ▼ =Export
◆ =Import/Export

PRODUCTS & SERVICES SECTION
3823 - Indl Instruments For Meas, Display & Control County (P-6718)

Christian Herr, *General Mgr*
Joe Pham, *IT/INT Sup*
▲ **EMP:** 100 **EST:** 1972
SQ FT: 23,400
SALES (est): 28.1MM
SALES (corp-wide): 641.7MM Privately Held
WEB: www.tecan.com
SIC: 3821 3829 5561 3494 Laboratory apparatus, except heating & measuring; measuring & controlling devices; pumps & pumping equipment; valves & pipe fittings; unsupported plastics profile shapes; commercial physical research
HQ: Tecan U.S. Group, Inc.
9401 Globe Center Dr # 140
Morrisville NC 27560
919 361-5200

(P-6698)
TLI ENTERPRISES INC (PA)
3118 Depot Rd, Hayward (94545-2708)
P.O. Box 3711 (94540-3711)
PHONE...................510 538-3304
John Trujillo, *CEO*
Shawn Trujillo, *President*
EMP: 30 **EST:** 1937
SQ FT: 18,000
SALES (est): 36.5MM Privately Held
WEB: www.thermionics.com
SIC: 3821 3471 Vacuum pumps, laboratory; cleaning, polishing & finishing

3822 Automatic Temperature Controls

(P-6699)
AUTOMATED SOLUTIONS GROUP INC
Also Called: ASG
2150 Bering Dr, San Jose (95131-2013)
PHONE...................408 432-0300
Tony Skibinski, *President*
Joe Olivier, *Project Mgr*
Joseph Olivier, *Project Engr*
Michael Anderson, *Engineer*
Bruce Peddy, *Opers Mgr*
EMP: 43 **EST:** 2012
SQ FT: 2,500
SALES (est): 6.5MM Privately Held
WEB: www.asgbms.com
SIC: 3822 Building services monitoring controls, automatic

(P-6700)
C3-ILEX LLC (PA)
46609 Fremont Blvd, Fremont (94538-6410)
P.O. Box 3224, Los Altos (94024-0224)
PHONE...................510 659-8300
EMP: 21
SQ FT: 15,000
SALES (est): 4.9MM Privately Held
SIC: 3822 Environmental Controls, Nsk

(P-6701)
COMPAC ENGINEERING INC
1111 Noffsinger Ln, Paradise (95969-6323)
P.O. Box 9 (95967-0009)
PHONE...................530 872-2042
James W Jones, *President*
EMP: 36 **EST:** 1964
SQ FT: 5,000
SALES (est): 5.7MM Privately Held
WEB: www.compac.com
SIC: 3822 Liquid level controls, residential or commercial heating

(P-6702)
NVENT THERMAL LLC (DH)
899 Broadway St, Redwood City (94063-3104)
PHONE...................650 474-7414
Brad Faulconer, *President*
Adam Sherman, *Senior Engr*
Rita Duncan, *Human Resources*
Eugene Ho, *Marketing Staff*
Chad Banzhaf, *Director*
◆ **EMP:** 300 **EST:** 2000
SQ FT: 65,000
SALES (est): 750MM Privately Held
WEB: www.raychem.nvent.com
SIC: 3822 1711 Auto controls regulating residntl & coml environmt & applncs; heating & air conditioning contractors
HQ: Nvent Management Company
1665 Utica Ave S Ste 700
Saint Louis Park MN 55416
763 204-7700

(P-6703)
PARAGON CONTROLS INCORPORATED
Also Called: PCI
2371 Circadian Way, Santa Rosa (95407-5439)
P.O. Box 99, Forestville (95436-0099)
PHONE...................707 579-1424
Richard Thomas Reis, *President*
Cheryl Reis, *Treasurer*
Larry E Winterbourne, *Vice Pres*
Dennis Reis, *Admin Sec*
Justin Caswell, *Engineer*
▲ **EMP:** 15 **EST:** 1984
SQ FT: 8,200
SALES (est): 3.5MM Privately Held
WEB: www.paragoncontrols.com
SIC: 3822 3823 Air flow controllers, air conditioning & refrigeration; fan control, temperature responsive; pressure controllers, air-conditioning system type; primary elements for process flow measurement

(P-6704)
RESIDENTIAL CTRL SYSTEMS INC
Also Called: R C S
11481 Sunrise Gold Cir # 1, Rancho Cordova (95742-6545)
PHONE...................916 635-6784
Michael Kuhlmann, *President*
Michael Hoffman, *Officer*
Mike Hoffman, *Vice Pres*
EMP: 27 **EST:** 1992
SALES (est): 3.1MM Privately Held
SIC: 3822 Damper operators: pneumatic, thermostatic, electric; pneumatic relays, air-conditioning type; energy cutoff controls, residential or commercial types

(P-6705)
SIEMENS INDUSTRY INC
7464 French Rd, Sacramento (95828-4600)
PHONE...................916 681-3000
Oliver Hauck, *Branch Mgr*
Nicola Terry, *Executive Asst*
Vasiliy Karamalak, *Electrical Engi*
Lennart Bergstrom, *Engineer*
David Mendenhall, *Accounts Mgr*
EMP: 200
SALES (corp-wide): 67.4B Privately Held
WEB: www.siemens.com
SIC: 3822 5063 3669 1731 Air conditioning & refrigeration controls; thermostats & other environmental sensors; electric alarms & signaling equipment; emergency alarms; safety & security specialization; security systems services; relays & industrial controls
HQ: Siemens Industry, Inc.
1000 Deerfield Pkwy
Buffalo Grove IL 60089
847 215-1000

(P-6706)
SUPERIOR SENSOR TECHNOLOGY INC
103 Cooper Ct, Los Gatos (95032-7604)
PHONE...................408 703-2950
James Finch, *CEO*
EMP: 25 **EST:** 2016
SALES (est): 2.4MM Privately Held
WEB: www.superiorsensors.com
SIC: 3822 Pressure controllers, air-conditioning system type

(P-6707)
VIGILENT CORPORATION (PA)
1111 Broadway Fl 3, Oakland (94607-4139)
PHONE...................888 305-4451
David Hudson, *CEO*
Andrew Gordon, *Vice Pres*
Bob Thronson, *Vice Pres*
John Taylor, *Managing Dir*
Cedric Clotilde, *Sr Software Eng*
EMP: 47 **EST:** 2008
SALES (est): 13MM Privately Held
WEB: www.vigilent.com
SIC: 3822 Auto controls regulating residntl & coml environmt & applncs

(P-6708)
VOLTUS INC
542b Presidio Blvd, San Francisco (94129-1403)
PHONE...................415 617-9602
Gregg Dixon, *CEO*
Matthew Plante, *President*
Doug Perrygo, *CFO*
Stephanie Hendricks, *Vice Pres*
Neil Lakin, *VP Engrg*
EMP: 38 **EST:** 2016
SALES (est): 3.5MM Privately Held
WEB: www.voltus.co
SIC: 3822 3829 Auto controls regulating residntl & coml environmt & applncs; measuring & controlling devices

(P-6709)
X THERM
3325 Investment Blvd, Hayward (94545-3808)
PHONE...................510 441-7566
H Johnson, *Principal*
Parnell Ellison, *Partner*
Raymund Cruz, *Engineer*
Kunal Gharat, *Engineer*
Erik Olivar, *Engineer*
EMP: 18 **EST:** 2018
SALES (est): 5.7MM Privately Held
WEB: www.therm-x.com
SIC: 3822 Auto controls regulating residntl & coml environmt & applncs

3823 Indl Instruments For Meas, Display & Control

(P-6710)
ACS INSTRUMENTATION VALVES INC
3065 Richmond Pkwy # 106, Richmond (94806-5719)
PHONE...................510 262-1880
Elizabeth Niemczyk, *CEO*
EMP: 99 **EST:** 2017
SALES (est): 7.3MM Privately Held
SIC: 3823 Industrial instrmnts msrmnt display/control process variable

(P-6711)
ADVANCED PRESSURE TECHNOLOGY
Also Called: AP Tech
687 Technology Way, NAPA (94558-7512)
PHONE...................707 259-0102
Rene Zakhour, *President*
Kathy Wright, *CFO*
Joseph Briski, *Vice Pres*
Kambiz Farnaam, *Vice Pres*
Karena Zakhour, *Business Anlyst*
▲ **EMP:** 95
SALES (est): 32.8MM Privately Held
WEB: www.aptech-online.com
SIC: 3823 Pressure gauges, dial & digital

(P-6712)
AIR MONITOR CORPORATION (PA)
1050 Hopper Ave, Santa Rosa (95403-1695)
P.O. Box 6358 (95406-0358)
PHONE...................707 544-2706
Dean De Baun, *CEO*
Sharon Hughes, *CFO*
Rob Neumann, *Vice Pres*
Chris De Baun, *Admin Sec*
Eddie Serrano, *Technician*
EMP: 70 **EST:** 1967
SQ FT: 50,000
SALES (est): 10.6MM Privately Held
WEB: www.airmonitor.com
SIC: 3823 Industrial instrmnts msrmnt display/control process variable

(P-6713)
ANDROS INCORPORATED
3301 Leonard Ct, Santa Clara (95054-2054)
PHONE...................510 837-3525
Richard Paterson, *President*
Cindee Beechwood, *CFO*
Heidi Hughes, *Sales Staff*
EMP: 18 **EST:** 2006
SALES (est): 373.9K Privately Held
WEB: www.advancedenergy.com
SIC: 3823 Industrial instrmnts msrmnt display/control process variable

(P-6714)
COLTER & PETERSON MICROSYSTEMS
Also Called: C & P Microsystems
1260 Holm Rd Ste C, Petaluma (94954-7152)
PHONE...................707 776-4500
Bruce Peterson, *President*
Wayne Smith, *VP Sales*
Tom L Luciani, *Manager*
▲ **EMP:** 20 **EST:** 1979
SQ FT: 7,500
SALES (est): 3.1MM
SALES (corp-wide): 29MM Privately Held
WEB: www.papercutters.com
SIC: 3823 5084 3554 Computer interface equipment for industrial process control; printing trades machinery, equipment & supplies; paper mill machinery: plating, slitting, waxing, etc.
PA: Colter & Peterson, Inc.
19 Fairfield Pl
West Caldwell NJ 07006
973 684-0901

(P-6715)
DIGITAL DYNAMICS INC
5 Victor Sq, Scotts Valley (95066-3531)
PHONE...................831 438-4444
William P Ledeen, *Ch of Bd*
Bill Murvihill, *VP Bus Dvlpt*
Carolyn Jerde, *Admin Sec*
William Waggoner, *Info Tech Mgr*
Woody Craig, *Technician*
EMP: 45 **EST:** 1974
SQ FT: 18,000
SALES (est): 11.4MM Privately Held
WEB: www.digitaldynamics.com
SIC: 3823 Industrial instrmnts msrmnt display/control process variable

(P-6716)
DUSOUTH INDUSTRIES
Also Called: Dst Controls
651 Stone Rd, Benicia (94510-1141)
PHONE...................707 745-5117
William Southard, *President*
Read Hayward, *Vice Pres*
EMP: 30 **EST:** 1975
SQ FT: 14,000
SALES (est): 8.3MM Privately Held
WEB: www.dusouthindustries.openfos.com
SIC: 3823 Industrial instrmnts msrmnt display/control process variable

(P-6717)
EAGLE TECH MANUFACTURING INC
841 Walker St, Watsonville (95076-4116)
PHONE...................831 768-7467
Alfredo Madrigal, *President*
Hector Madrigal, *Vice Pres*
Bertha Guerrero, *Bookkeeper*
▲ **EMP:** 38 **EST:** 1996
SQ FT: 5,000
SALES (est): 4.7MM Privately Held
WEB: www.eagletechman.com
SIC: 3823 Electrolytic conductivity instruments, industrial process

(P-6718)
EDC-BIOSYSTEMS INC (PA)
170 Rose Orchard Way # 200, San Jose (95134-1374)
PHONE...................510 257-1500
◆ **EMP:** 25
SALES (est): 2.7MM Privately Held
WEB: www.edcbiosystems.com
SIC: 3823 Mfg Process Control Instruments

3823 - Indl Instruments For Meas, Display & Control County (P-6719)

(P-6719)
FORTREND ENGINEERING CORP
2220 Otoole Ave, San Jose (95131-1326)
PHONE................................408 734-9311
Chris Wu PHD, *CEO*
Joseph MA PHD, *Chairman*
Richard Morgan, *Vice Pres*
Donna Cheng, *Controller*
EMP: 41 EST: 1979
SQ FT: 20,000
SALES (est): 6.6MM Privately Held
WEB: www.fortrend.com
SIC: 3823 Industrial instrmnts msrmnt display/control process variable

(P-6720)
FRONTLINE ENVMTL TECH GROUP IN
Also Called: Frontline Technologies
3195 Park Rd Ste C, Benicia (94510-1185)
P.O. Box 426 (94510-0426)
PHONE................................707 745-1116
Randall L Sherwood, *President*
Gary Whitehead, *Opers Staff*
Lynne Trammell, *Manager*
EMP: 30 EST: 1992
SQ FT: 5,000
SALES (est): 4.2MM Privately Held
WEB: www.frontlineworldwide.net
SIC: 3823 1731 Industrial instrmnts msrmnt display/control process variable; environmental system control installation

(P-6721)
GALIL MOTION CONTROL INC
270 Technology Way, Rocklin (95765-1228)
PHONE................................800 377-6329
Jacob Tal, *Principal*
Wayne Baron, *President*
Brian Kambe, *Vice Pres*
Kaushal Shah, *Vice Pres*
John Thompson, *Vice Pres*
EMP: 36 EST: 1983
SQ FT: 30,000
SALES (est): 9.2MM Privately Held
WEB: www.galil.com
SIC: 3823 Industrial instrmnts msrmnt display/control process variable

(P-6722)
INTEGRATED FLOW SYSTEMS LLC (HQ)
Also Called: Advanced Integration Tech
26462 Corporate Ave, Hayward (94545-3914)
PHONE................................510 659-4900
Michael Mallinen, *Mng Member*
◆ EMP: 80 EST: 1983
SQ FT: 3,000
SALES (est): 31.4MM
SALES (corp-wide): 1.4B Publicly Held
WEB: www.uct.com
SIC: 3823 Industrial instrmnts msrmnt display/control process variable
PA: Ultra Clean Holdings, Inc.
26462 Corporate Ave
Hayward CA 94545
510 576-4400

(P-6723)
JOHN ZINK COMPANY LLC
2151 River Plaza Dr # 200, Sacramento (95833-4133)
PHONE................................918 234-1884
EMP: 22
SALES (corp-wide): 36.9B Privately Held
WEB: www.johnzinkhamworthy.com
SIC: 3823 Industrial instrmnts msrmnt display/control process variable
HQ: John Zink Company, Llc
11920 E Apache St
Tulsa OK 74116
918 234-1800

(P-6724)
KEYSIGHT TECHNOLOGIES INC (PA)
1400 Fountaingrove Pkwy, Santa Rosa (95403-1738)
P.O. Box 4026 (95402-4026)
PHONE................................800 829-4444
Ron Nersesian, *President*
Huei Sin EE, *President*
John Page, *President*
Satish Dhanasekaran, *COO*
Neil Dougherty, *CFO*
EMP: 5182 EST: 1939
SALES (est): 4.2B Publicly Held
WEB: www.keysight.com
SIC: 3823 3829 7629 Industrial instrmnts msrmnt display/control process variable; measuring & controlling devices; electronic equipment repair

(P-6725)
MAX MACHINERY INC
33 Healdsburg Ave Ste A, Healdsburg (95448-4043)
PHONE................................707 433-2662
Oliver Max, *President*
Sonia Max, *Vice Pres*
Dan Turek, *General Mgr*
Daniel Turek, *General Mgr*
Tejpal Sekhon, *Engineer*
EMP: 21 EST: 1967
SQ FT: 10,000
SALES (est): 5MM Privately Held
WEB: www.maxmachinery.com
SIC: 3823 Industrial instrmnts msrmnt display/control process variable

(P-6726)
MICRO LITHOGRAPHY INC
1247 Elko Dr, Sunnyvale (94089-2211)
PHONE................................408 747-1769
Yung-Tsai Yen, *CEO*
Chris Yen, *President*
Sandy Yen, *Exec VP*
David Wang, *Administration*
Buu Le, *Software Dev*
▲ EMP: 225 EST: 1981
SQ FT: 100,000
SALES (est): 35MM Privately Held
WEB: www.mliusa.com
SIC: 3823 3674 Industrial instrmnts msrmnt display/control process variable; semiconductors & related devices

(P-6727)
MODUTEK CORP
6387 San Ignacio Ave, San Jose (95119-1206)
PHONE................................408 362-2000
Douglas G Wagner, *President*
Robert Brody, *Vice Pres*
Anthony Rutland, *Technician*
Mitch Tojima, *Engineer*
Joanne Turley, *Human Res Dir*
EMP: 21 EST: 1980
SQ FT: 21,000
SALES (est): 5.6MM Privately Held
WEB: www.modutek.com
SIC: 3823 7373 Temperature instruments: industrial process type; systems integration services

(P-6728)
MOUNTZ INC (PA)
Also Called: Dg Mountz Associates
1080 N 11th St, San Jose (95112-2927)
PHONE................................408 292-2214
Brad Mountz, *President*
David Aviles, *CFO*
Lorna U Mountz, *Treasurer*
Alex Gregorios, *Admin Asst*
John Brackmann, *Technical Staff*
▲ EMP: 43 EST: 1964
SQ FT: 30,000
SALES (est): 15MM Privately Held
WEB: www.mountztorque.com
SIC: 3823 5085 Industrial instrmnts msrmnt display/control process variable; fasteners & fastening equipment

(P-6729)
PENSANDO SYSTEMS INC
570 Alder Dr, Milpitas (95035-7443)
PHONE................................408 451-9012
Prem Chand Jain, *CEO*
John Chambers, *Chairman*
EMP: 55 EST: 2017
SALES (est): 10.6MM Privately Held
SIC: 3823 Computer interface equipment for industrial process control

(P-6730)
PHOTON INC
1671 Dell Ave Ste 208, Campbell (95008-6900)
PHONE................................408 226-1000
John Fleisher, *President*
Teena Guenther, *CFO*
Judith Fleisher, *Corp Secy*
Mary Russell, *Marketing Staff*
EMP: 18 EST: 1980
SQ FT: 10,000
SALES (est): 1.7MM Privately Held
SIC: 3823 8711 Industrial instrmnts msrmnt display/control process variable; consulting engineer

(P-6731)
PROTEUS INDUSTRIES INC
340 Pioneer Way, Mountain View (94041-1577)
PHONE................................650 964-4163
Jon Heiner, *CEO*
Mark Nicewonger, *Vice Pres*
Jane Rendon, *Info Tech Mgr*
Angelo Palacios, *IT/INT Sup*
Mark Malfatti, *Technical Staff*
▲ EMP: 50 EST: 1978
SQ FT: 40,000
SALES (est): 11.3MM Privately Held
SIC: 3823 3829 3826 3824 Industrial instrmnts msrmnt display/control process variable; measuring & controlling devices; analytical instruments; fluid meters & counting devices; relays & industrial controls

(P-6732)
PSI WATER TECHNOLOGIES INC
550 Sycamore Dr, Milpitas (95035-7412)
PHONE................................408 819-3043
Brent Simmons, *CEO*
Rick Riddle, *Vice Pres*
Gunnar Thortarson, *Vice Pres*
Gunnar Thordarson, *Human Res Mgr*
Gary Turner, *Director*
▲ EMP: 32 EST: 2003
SALES (est): 9.5MM Privately Held
WEB: www.4psi.net
SIC: 3823 Water quality monitoring & control systems

(P-6733)
SEMIFAB INC
2027 Otoole Ave, San Jose (95131-1301)
PHONE................................408 414-5928
Hauynium Kabir, *President*
Greg Krikorian, *CFO*
Gerry Reynolds, *Program Mgr*
◆ EMP: 60 EST: 1978
SALES (est): 8.1MM Privately Held
WEB: www.semifab.com
SIC: 3823 3822 Industrial instrmnts msrmnt display/control process variable; temperature instruments: industrial process type; temperature controls, automatic

(P-6734)
TEST ENTERPRISES INC (PA)
Also Called: Thermonics
1288 Reamwood Ave, Sunnyvale (94089-2233)
PHONE................................408 542-5900
James C Kufis, *CEO*
Joachim Kunkel, *General Mgr*
▲ EMP: 20 EST: 1976
SQ FT: 22,000
SALES (est): 2.6MM Privately Held
WEB: www.testenterprises.com
SIC: 3823 3825 Temperature measurement instruments, industrial; semiconductor test equipment

(P-6735)
UNITED STTES THRMLCTRIC CNSRTI
Also Called: Ustc
13267 Contrs Dr Ste D, Chico (95973)
PHONE................................530 345-8000
James M Kerner, *President*
▲ EMP: 20 EST: 1995
SALES (est): 9MM Privately Held
WEB: www.ustechcon.com
SIC: 3823 3999 Industrial instrmnts msrmnt display/control process variable; barber & beauty shop equipment

(P-6736)
VALLEY CONTROLS INC
583 E Dinuba Ave, Reedley (93654-3531)
P.O. Box 1205 (93654-1205)
PHONE................................559 638-5115
Verl A Tyler, *President*
Robin Tyler, *Corp Secy*
Doyle Anderson, *Vice Pres*
EMP: 15 EST: 1978
SQ FT: 14,500
SALES (est): 1.1MM Privately Held
SIC: 3823 1731 Industrial instrmnts msrmnt display/control process variable; electrical work

(P-6737)
VEEX INC
2827 Lakeview Ct, Fremont (94538-6534)
PHONE................................510 651-0500
Cyrille Morelle, *President*
Keith Cole, *Vice Pres*
Mike Venter, *Vice Pres*
Lucie Cartaya, *Office Mgr*
Kyler Collins, *Software Engr*
EMP: 19 EST: 2006
SQ FT: 8,000
SALES (est): 4.9MM Privately Held
WEB: www.veexinc.com
SIC: 3823 Programmers, process type

(P-6738)
WATER RESOURCES CAL DEPT
901 P St Lbby, Sacramento (95814-6424)
PHONE................................916 651-9203
Mark Cowin, *Branch Mgr*
Raphael Torres, *Deputy Dir*
EMP: 20 Privately Held
WEB: www.ca.gov
SIC: 3823 Water quality monitoring & control systems
HQ: California Department Of Water Resources
1416 9th St
Sacramento CA 95814
916 653-9394

3824 Fluid Meters & Counters

(P-6739)
BRITELAB INC
6341 San Ignacio Ave, San Jose (95119-1202)
PHONE................................650 961-0671
Robert De Neve, *CEO*
Paul Rogan, *CFO*
Jae Jung, *Officer*
Kip Smith, *Officer*
Suki Hong, *Exec VP*
▲ EMP: 65 EST: 2007
SQ FT: 52,000
SALES (est): 14.4MM Privately Held
WEB: www.britelab.com
SIC: 3824 8741 8742 Mechanical & electromechanical counters & devices; management services; management consulting services

(P-6740)
EXELIXIS INC
Division 1
1851 Harbor Bay Pkwy, Alameda (94502-3010)
PHONE................................650 837-7000
Michael M Morrissey, *President*
EMP: 371 Publicly Held
WEB: www.exelixis.com
SIC: 3824 8731 Fluid meters & counting devices; commercial physical research; biological research
PA: Exelixis, Inc.
1851 Harbor Bay Pkwy
Alameda CA 94502

3825 - Instrs For Measuring & Testing Electricity County (P-6763)

(P-6741)
TRI-CONTINENT SCIENTIFIC INC
12740 Earhart Ave, Auburn (95602-9027)
PHONE.....................530 273-8888
Lee Carter, *CEO*
Brenton Hanlon, *President*
Sandra Zoch, *Treasurer*
▲ **EMP:** 85 **EST:** 1975
SQ FT: 34,000
SALES (est): 11.6MM
SALES (corp-wide): 4.9B **Publicly Held**
WEB: www.gardnerdenver.com
SIC: 3824 3829 3821 3561 Integrating & totalizing meters for gas & liquids; totalizing meters, consumption registering; measuring & controlling devices; laboratory apparatus & furniture; pumps & pumping equipment
HQ: Gardner Denver, Inc.
 800 Beaty St
 Davidson NC 28036

3825 Instrs For Measuring & Testing Electricity

(P-6742)
ADVANCED MICROTECHNOLOGY
3511 Thomas Rd Ste 8, Santa Clara (95054-2039)
PHONE.....................408 945-9191
Eugene R Wertz, *President*
EMP: 16 **EST:** 1977
SALES (est): 2.8MM **Privately Held**
WEB: www.advancedmicrotech.com
SIC: 3825 8711 Test equipment for electronic & electrical circuits; engineering services

(P-6743)
AEHR TEST SYSTEMS (PA)
400 Kato Ter, Fremont (94539-8332)
PHONE.....................510 623-9400
Gayn Erickson, *President*
Rhea J Posedel, *Ch of Bd*
Kunio Sano, *President*
Kenneth B Spink, *CFO*
Howard Slayen, *Bd of Directors*
▲ **EMP:** 85 **EST:** 1977
SQ FT: 51,289
SALES: 16.6MM **Publicly Held**
WEB: www.aehr.com
SIC: 3825 Test equipment for electronic & electrical circuits

(P-6744)
AGILENT TECH FOUNDATION
5301 Stevens Creek Blvd, Santa Clara (95051-7201)
PHONE.....................408 345-8886
William P Sullivan, *CEO*
EMP: 33 **EST:** 1999
SALES (est): 4.3K **Privately Held**
WEB: www.agilent.com
SIC: 3825 Instruments to measure electricity

(P-6745)
AGILENT TECH WORLD TRADE INC (HQ)
5301 Stevens Creek Blvd, Santa Clara (95051-7201)
PHONE.....................408 345-8886
Adrian Dillon, *CEO*
D Craig Norlund, *Treasurer*
Marie O Huber, *Asst Sec*
EMP: 762 **EST:** 1999
SALES (est): 17.5MM
SALES (corp-wide): 5.3B **Publicly Held**
WEB: www.agilent.com
SIC: 3825 Instruments to measure electricity
PA: Agilent Technologies, Inc.
 5301 Stevens Creek Blvd
 Santa Clara CA 95051
 800 227-9770

(P-6746)
ANRITSU US HOLDING INC (HQ)
Also Called: Anritsu Company
490 Jarvis Dr, Morgan Hill (95037-2834)
PHONE.....................408 778-2000
Wade Hulon, *President*
Jon Martens, *Vice Chairman*
Toby Echelberry, *Planning*
Rod Boles, *CIO*
Dendi Kurniawan, *Engineer*
▲ **EMP:** 500 **EST:** 1990
SQ FT: 244,000
SALES (est): 317MM **Privately Held**
WEB: www.anritsu.com
SIC: 3825 3663 5065 Test equipment for electronic & electric measurement; radio & TV communications equipment; electronic parts & equipment

(P-6747)
CALOGIC (PA)
237 Whitney Pl, Fremont (94539-7664)
PHONE.....................510 656-2900
Jonathan Kaye, *President*
Kathryn Kaye, *Vice Pres*
Eric Prinz, *General Mgr*
EMP: 21 **EST:** 2001
SQ FT: 10,314
SALES (est): 3.7MM **Privately Held**
WEB: www.calogic.net
SIC: 3825 Instruments to measure electricity

(P-6748)
ECHELON CORPORATION (DH)
3600 Peterson Way, Santa Clara (95054-2808)
PHONE.....................408 938-5200
Ronald Sege, *President*
Alicia Jayne Moore, *Officer*
Ian Phan, *General Mgr*
Glen Riley, *Software Engr*
Mike Wytyshyn, *Engineer*
▲ **EMP:** 55 **EST:** 1988
SQ FT: 32,000
SALES: 31.6MM
SALES (corp-wide): 1.3B **Privately Held**
WEB: www.dialog-semiconductor.com
SIC: 3825 7371 Network analyzers; computer software systems analysis & design, custom; computer software development

(P-6749)
ELECRAFT INCORPORATED
125 Westridge Dr, Watsonville (95076-4167)
P.O. Box 69, Aptos (95001-0069)
PHONE.....................831 763-4211
Eric Swartz, *President*
Wayne Burdick, *Principal*
Giannini Paul, *Materials Mgr*
Burdick Wayne, *Opers Staff*
Anderson Brent, *Production*
EMP: 35 **EST:** 1997
SALES (est): 7.3MM **Privately Held**
WEB: www.elecraft.com
SIC: 3825 Oscillators, audio & radio frequency (instrument types)

(P-6750)
ELECTRIQ POWER INC
1937 Davis St Unit A1, San Leandro (94577-1262)
PHONE.....................833 462-2883
Frank Magnotti, *CEO*
Jim Lovewell, *President*
Jeffrey Besen, *Vice Pres*
Jamie James, *Vice Pres*
Neha Palmer, *Vice Pres*
EMP: 17 **EST:** 2014
SALES (est): 1.8MM **Privately Held**
WEB: www.electriqpower.com
SIC: 3825 7371 Electrical energy measuring equipment; computer software development & applications

(P-6751)
ESSAI INC (DH)
48580 Kato Rd, Fremont (94538-7338)
PHONE.....................510 580-1700
Nasser Barabi, *CEO*
Iraj Barabi, *CFO*
Keith Hardwick, *CFO*
Derek Curry, *Info Tech Mgr*
Kenneth Cartwright, *Technician*
EMP: 202 **EST:** 2003

SALES (est): 60MM **Privately Held**
WEB: www.advantest.com
SIC: 3825 Semiconductor test equipment

(P-6752)
EUGENUS INC (HQ)
677 River Oaks Pkwy, San Jose (95134-1907)
PHONE.....................669 235-8244
Pyung Yong Um, *CEO*
Satish Dasam, *CIO*
Justin Baltazar, *Engineer*
Leslie Luu, *Senior Buyer*
Sherry Chapman, *Director*
EMP: 78 **EST:** 2009
SQ FT: 2,700
SALES (est): 26.9MM **Privately Held**
WEB: www.eugenustech.com
SIC: 3825 Semiconductor test equipment

(P-6753)
EVERACTIVE INC
2986 Oakmead Village Ct, Santa Clara (95051-0807)
PHONE.....................517 256-0679
Bob Nunn, *CEO*
Nathan Roberts, *Vice Pres*
John Greenfield, *Business Dir*
Benton Calhoun MD, *CTO*
David Wentzloff MD, *CTO*
EMP: 86 **EST:** 2012
SALES (est): 15.7MM **Privately Held**
WEB: www.everactive.com
SIC: 3825 3674 Analog-digital converters, electronic instrumentation type; semiconductors & related devices

(P-6754)
EXATRON INC
2842 Aiello Dr, San Jose (95111-2154)
PHONE.....................408 629-7600
Robert Howell, *CEO*
Eric Hagquist, *Treasurer*
Vincent Vu, *Electrical Engi*
Adam Nomura, *Engineer*
Gloria Matson, *Sales Staff*
EMP: 25 **EST:** 1974
SQ FT: 15,500
SALES (est): 4.8MM **Privately Held**
WEB: www.exatron.com
SIC: 3825 Integrated circuit testers

(P-6755)
EXCEL PRECISION CORP USA
3350 Scott Blvd Bldg 62, Santa Clara (95054-3125)
PHONE.....................408 727-4260
John Tsai, *CEO*
Lon Allen, *Admin Sec*
EMP: 25 **EST:** 1984
SQ FT: 5,500
SALES (est): 4.8MM **Privately Held**
WEB: www.excelprecision.com
SIC: 3825 3829 3827 3826 Measuring instruments & meters, electric; measuring & controlling devices; optical instruments & lenses; analytical instruments

(P-6756)
FOUR DIMENSIONS INC
3140 Diablo Ave, Hayward (94545-2702)
PHONE.....................510 782-1843
James T Chen, *President*
Constance Chen, *Corp Secy*
▲ **EMP:** 15 **EST:** 1978
SQ FT: 8,800
SALES (est): 2.4MM **Privately Held**
WEB: www.4dimensions.com
SIC: 3825 Semiconductor test equipment

(P-6757)
GIGA-TRONICS INCORPORATED (PA)
5990 Gleason Dr, Dublin (94568-7644)
PHONE.....................925 328-4650
John R Regazzi, *CEO*
William J Thompson, *Ch of Bd*
Lutz P Henckels, *COO*
Gordon Almquist, *Bd of Directors*
Daniel S Kirby, *Vice Pres*
EMP: 15 **EST:** 1980
SQ FT: 23,873

SALES: 13MM **Publicly Held**
WEB: www.go-asg.gigatronics.com
SIC: 3825 3674 3823 Microwave test equipment; pulse (signal) generators; signal generators & averagers; sweep generators; microcircuits, integrated (semiconductor); modules, solid state; computer interface equipment for industrial process control

(P-6758)
GOLDEN ALTOS CORPORATION
402 S Hillview Dr, Milpitas (95035-5464)
PHONE.....................408 956-1010
Alexander H C Chang, *CEO*
Hsun K Chou, *Ch of Bd*
Winston Kuok, *Marketing Staff*
▲ **EMP:** 50 **EST:** 1991
SQ FT: 10,000
SALES (est): 13.4MM **Privately Held**
WEB: www.goldenaltos.com
SIC: 3825 3674 3672 Integrated circuit testers; semiconductors & related devices; printed circuit boards

(P-6759)
GREGORY ASSOCIATES INC
1233 Belknap Ct, Cupertino (95014-4904)
PHONE.....................408 446-5725
EMP: 24
SQ FT: 21,000
SALES (est): 3.3MM **Privately Held**
SIC: 3825 8711 3674 Mfg Electronic Test Equipment & Semiconductors

(P-6760)
GUIDETECH INC
774 Charcot Ave, San Jose (95131-2224)
PHONE.....................408 733-6555
Frank McKiney, *President*
Hans Betz, *Ch of Bd*
▲ **EMP:** 25 **EST:** 1988
SALES (est): 3.1MM **Privately Held**
WEB: www.guidetech.com
SIC: 3825 Test equipment for electronic & electric measurement

(P-6761)
GUZIK TECHNICAL ENTERPRISES (PA)
2443 Wyandotte St, Mountain View (94043-2350)
PHONE.....................650 625-8000
Nahum Guzik, *President*
Vladislav Klimov, *Director*
▲ **EMP:** 50 **EST:** 1982
SQ FT: 60,000
SALES (est): 18.1MM **Privately Held**
WEB: www.guzik.com
SIC: 3825 3829 3577 Test equipment for electronic & electrical circuits; measuring & controlling devices; computer peripheral equipment

(P-6762)
HOLO INC
39684 Eureka Dr, Newark (94560-4805)
PHONE.....................510 221-4177
Arian Aghababaie, *CEO*
Hal Zarem, *COO*
Hany Eitouni, *Vice Pres*
Anthony Lee, *Research*
Michael Smith, *VP Opers*
EMP: 30 **EST:** 2017
SALES (est): 3.1MM **Privately Held**
WEB: www.holoam.com
SIC: 3825 Digital test equipment, electronic & electrical circuits

(P-6763)
INFORMATION SCAN TECH INC
Also Called: I S T
487 Gianni St, Santa Clara (95054-2414)
PHONE.....................408 988-1908
Richard Chang, *President*
Peter Chou, *Vice Pres*
Tony Lee, *Vice Pres*
▲ **EMP:** 18 **EST:** 1978
SQ FT: 12,000
SALES (est): 734.3K **Privately Held**
WEB: www.infoscantech.com
SIC: 3825 Test equipment for electronic & electrical circuits

3825 - Instrs For Measuring & Testing Electricity County (P-6764)

(P-6764)
INGRASYS TECHNOLOGY USA INC
2025 Gateway Pl Ste 190, San Jose (95110-1052)
PHONE................863 271-8266
Jang-Ping Chen, *CEO*
EMP: 15 **EST:** 2009
SALES (est): 12.6MM **Privately Held**
WEB: www.ingrasys.com
SIC: 3825 4899 Network analyzers; communication signal enhancement network system
HQ: Ingrasys Technology Inc.
No. 1188, Nanqing Rd.,
Taoyuan City TAY 33849

(P-6765)
LIBERTY LABORATORIES INC
10869 Sycamore Ct, Cupertino (95014-6559)
PHONE................408 262-6633
Gary W Caywood, *President*
Ahmad Ammouri, *General Mgr*
Cynthia Ly, *Office Mgr*
Edmund Arucan, *Engineer*
Bosco Nguyen, *Engineer*
EMP: 39 **EST:** 1978
SALES (est): 1.7MM **Privately Held**
WEB: www.iselabs.com
SIC: 3825 Instruments to measure electricity

(P-6766)
LUCAS/SIGNATONE CORPORATION (PA)
Also Called: Lucas Labs
393 Tomkins Ct Ste J, Gilroy (95020-3632)
PHONE................408 848-2851
Richard Dickson, *President*
Dennis Dickson, *CFO*
James Dickson, *Technology*
Marc Pinard, *Sales Mgr*
Mark Pinard, *Sales Staff*
EMP: 28 **EST:** 1990
SALES (est): 5.2MM **Privately Held**
WEB: www.signatone.com
SIC: 3825 3559 Semiconductor test equipment; semiconductor manufacturing machinery

(P-6767)
LUMILEDS LLC (HQ)
370 W Trimble Rd, San Jose (95131-1008)
PHONE................408 964-2900
Matt Roney, *CEO*
Jan Paaul Teuwen, *CFO*
Cheree McAlpine, *Senior VP*
Steve Barlow, *General Mgr*
Jy Bhardwaj, *CTO*
◆ **EMP:** 40 **EST:** 1999
SALES (est): 174.7MM
SALES (corp-wide): 133.6MM **Privately Held**
WEB: www.lumileds.com
SIC: 3825 3674 Instruments to measure electricity; light emitting diodes
PA: Koninklijke Philips N.V.
High Tech Campus 52
Eindhoven 5656
402 791-111

(P-6768)
MAGNETIC RCRDING SOLUTIONS INC
3080 Oakmead Village Dr, Santa Clara (95051-0808)
PHONE................408 970-8266
Vladimir Pogrebinsky, *President*
Wayne Erickson, *Exec VP*
EMP: 17 **EST:** 1997
SQ FT: 6,000
SALES (est): 566.3K **Privately Held**
SIC: 3825 Test equipment for electronic & electrical circuits

(P-6769)
MARVELL SEMICONDUCTOR INC
5450 Bayfront Plz, Santa Clara (95054-3600)
PHONE................408 855-8839
EMP: 31 **Privately Held**
SIC: 3825 Mfg Electrical Measuring Instruments
HQ: Marvell Semiconductor, Inc.
5488 Marvell Ln
Santa Clara CA 95054

(P-6770)
MEASUREMENT SPECIALTIES INC
Also Called: Te Connectivity
424 Crown Point Cir, Grass Valley (95945-9089)
PHONE................530 273-4608
Frank Guidone, *CEO*
EMP: 60
SALES (corp-wide): 12.1B **Privately Held**
SIC: 3825 3676 Instruments to measure electricity; electronic resistors
HQ: Measurement Specialties, Inc.
1000 Lucas Way
Hampton VA 23666
757 766-1500

(P-6771)
MULTITEST ELCTRNIC SYSTEMS INC (DH)
3021 Kenneth St, Santa Clara (95054-3416)
PHONE................408 988-6544
Dave Tacelli, *President*
Paul Diehl, *Engineer*
Stefan Binder, *Manager*
▲ **EMP:** 280 **EST:** 1986
SQ FT: 40,000
SALES (est): 54.4MM
SALES (corp-wide): 636MM **Publicly Held**
WEB: www.cohu.com
SIC: 3825 3674 3624 Semiconductor test equipment; semiconductors & related devices; brushes & brush stock contacts, electric
HQ: Xcerra Corporation
825 University Ave
Norwood MA 02062
781 461-1000

(P-6772)
NAPTECH TEST EQUIPMENT INC
9781 Pt Lkeview Rd Unit 3, Kelseyville (95451)
PHONE................707 995-7145
Roger Briggs, *President*
Indigo Perry, *Train & Dev Mgr*
Jim Davis, *Sales Associate*
Ray Reynolds, *Sales Staff*
◆ **EMP:** 15 **EST:** 1991
SQ FT: 12,000
SALES (est): 2.9MM **Privately Held**
WEB: www.naptech.com
SIC: 3825 7629 Instruments to measure electricity; electrical repair shops

(P-6773)
NEOSEM TECHNOLOGY INC (DH)
1965 Concourse Dr, San Jose (95131-1708)
PHONE................408 643-7000
DH Yeom, *President*
Michael Bellon, *President*
Mike Rogowski, *COO*
Jin Choi, *Vice Pres*
Roger Leisy, *VP Sales*
▲ **EMP:** 20 **EST:** 1981
SQ FT: 18,000
SALES (est): 7.6MM **Privately Held**
WEB: www.neosem.com
SIC: 3825 Test equipment for electronic & electrical circuits

(P-6774)
NEXTEST SYSTEMS CORPORATION
Also Called: Nextest Systems Teradyne Co
875 Embedded Way, San Jose (95138-1030)
PHONE................408 960-2400
Mark Jadiela, *CEO*
Tim F Moriarty, *President*
James P Moniz, *CFO*
Robin Adler, *Bd of Directors*
Paul Barics, *Vice Pres*
▲ **EMP:** 125 **EST:** 1997
SQ FT: 33,200
SALES (est): 39.9MM
SALES (corp-wide): 3.1B **Publicly Held**
WEB: www.teradyne.com
SIC: 3825 Instruments to measure electricity
PA: Teradyne, Inc.
600 Riverpark Dr
North Reading MA 01864
978 370-2700

(P-6775)
NIKON RESEARCH CORP AMERICA
1399 Shoreway Rd, Belmont (94002-4107)
PHONE................800 446-4566
W Thomas Novak, *CEO*
Donis Flagello, *President*
Hamid Zarringhalam, *Exec VP*
Mitsuaki Yonekawa, *Senior VP*
Mohamad Zarringhalam, *Senior VP*
EMP: 40 **EST:** 1996
SQ FT: 15,000
SALES (est): 11MM **Privately Held**
WEB: www.nikonprecision.com
SIC: 3825 Semiconductor test equipment
HQ: Nikon Americas Inc.
1300 Walt Whitman Rd Fl 2
Melville NY 11747

(P-6776)
NOVA MEASURING INSTRUMENTS INC
3342 Gateway Blvd, Fremont (94538-6525)
PHONE................408 510-7400
May Su, *President*
Dror David, *Officer*
Daniel Kandel, *Technology*
Nicholas Antoniou, *Manager*
Dmitry Yoffe, *Manager*
EMP: 45 **EST:** 1996
SALES (est): 15.1MM **Privately Held**
WEB: www.novami.com
SIC: 3825 Semiconductor test equipment
PA: Nova Ltd
Rehovot
Rehovot

(P-6777)
PACIFIC WESTERN SYSTEMS INC (PA)
505 E Evelyn Ave, Mountain View (94041-1613)
PHONE................650 961-8855
Daniel A Worsham, *Ch of Bd*
Becky Worsham, *Corp Secy*
EMP: 20 **EST:** 1967
SQ FT: 40,000
SALES (est): 2.5MM **Privately Held**
SIC: 3825 3567 Semiconductor test equipment; industrial furnaces & ovens

(P-6778)
PERICOM SEMICONDUCTOR CORP (HQ)
1545 Barber Ln, Milpitas (95035-7409)
PHONE................408 232-9100
Alex C Hui, *President*
Kevin S Bauer, *CFO*
Angela Chen, *Senior VP*
CHI-Hung Hui, *Senior VP*
Michael Chen, *Vice Pres*
◆ **EMP:** 909 **EST:** 1990
SQ FT: 85,040
SALES (est): 264.8MM
SALES (corp-wide): 1.2B **Publicly Held**
WEB: www.diodes.com
SIC: 3825 3674 Instruments to measure electricity; integrated circuits, semiconductor networks, etc.
PA: Diodes Incorporated
4949 Hedgcoxe Rd Ste 200
Plano TX 75024
972 987-3900

(P-6779)
PHOTON DYNAMICS INC
Flat Panel Display Division
5970 Optical Ct, San Jose (95138-1400)
PHONE................408 723-7118
Jeffrey Hawthorne, *President*
Steve Ku, *Administration*
Bob Berens, *Sr Software Eng*
Karla Gutierrez, *Research*
Todd Hultsman, *Director*
EMP: 128
SALES (corp-wide): 6.9B **Publicly Held**
WEB: www.orbotech.com
SIC: 3825 Test equipment for electronic & electric measurement
HQ: Photon Dynamics, Inc.
5970 Optical Ct
San Jose CA 95138
408 226-9900

(P-6780)
PHOTON DYNAMICS INC (HQ)
5970 Optical Ct, San Jose (95138-1400)
PHONE................408 226-9900
Malcolm J Thompson PHD, *Ch of Bd*
Amichai Steimberg, *President*
Errol Moore, *CEO*
James P Moniz, *CFO*
Dr Abraham Gross, *Exec VP*
▲ **EMP:** 112 **EST:** 1986
SQ FT: 128,520
SALES (est): 91.9MM
SALES (corp-wide): 6.9B **Publicly Held**
WEB: www.orbotech.com
SIC: 3825 3829 Test equipment for electronic & electrical circuits; measuring & controlling devices
PA: Kla Corporation
1 Technology Dr
Milpitas CA 95035
408 875-3000

(P-6781)
PHOTON DYNAMICS INC
17 Great Oaks Blvd, San Jose (95119-1359)
PHONE................408 226-9900
Malcolm J Thompson, *Manager*
EMP: 128
SALES (corp-wide): 6.9B **Publicly Held**
WEB: www.orbotech.com
SIC: 3825 Test equipment for electronic & electric measurement
HQ: Photon Dynamics, Inc.
5970 Optical Ct
San Jose CA 95138
408 226-9900

(P-6782)
POWER STANDARDS LAB INC
Also Called: Powerside
980 Atlantic Ave Ste 100, Alameda (94501-1098)
PHONE................510 522-4400
Alex McEachern, *President*
Barry Tangney, *COO*
Mike Burns, *Vice Pres*
Marco Mancilla, *Vice Pres*
Carlos Mendes, *Engineer*
EMP: 32 **EST:** 2000
SQ FT: 12,000
SALES (est): 8.7MM
SALES (corp-wide): 505.9K **Privately Held**
WEB: www.powerside.com
SIC: 3825 8734 Power measuring equipment, electrical; testing laboratories
PA: Les Equipements Power Survey Ltee
7850 Rte Transcanadienne
Saint-Laurent QC H4T 1
514 333-8392

(P-6783)
QUALITAU INCORPORATED (PA)
5303 Betsy Ross Dr, Santa Clara (95054-1102)
PHONE................408 675-3034
Gadi Krieger, *CEO*
Jacob Herschmann, *President*
Nava Ben-Yehuda, *Vice Pres*
Tony Chavez, *Principal*
Peter Y Cuevas, *Principal*
EMP: 59 **EST:** 1990
SQ FT: 16,000
SALES (est): 10.8MM **Privately Held**
WEB: www.qualitau.com
SIC: 3825 Semiconductor test equipment

PRODUCTS & SERVICES SECTION
3826 - Analytical Instruments County (P-6806)

(P-6784)
QXQ INC
44113 S Grimmer Blvd, Fremont (94538-6350)
PHONE....................510 252-1522
Roger Quan, *President*
Kelly Nguyen, *CFO*
Weili Aguilar, *Officer*
Jack Jenkins, *Admin Sec*
George Quan, *Opers Mgr*
▲ **EMP:** 33 **EST:** 1992
SQ FT: 2,600
SALES (est): 7.5MM **Privately Held**
WEB: www.qxq.com
SIC: 3825 Instruments to measure electricity

(P-6785)
ROHDE & SCHWARZ USA INC
409 Dixon Landing Rd, Milpitas (95035-2579)
PHONE....................818 846-3600
EMP: 17
SALES (corp-wide): 2.8B **Privately Held**
WEB: www.rohde-schwarz.com
SIC: 3825 Instruments to measure electricity
HQ: Rohde & Schwarz Usa, Inc.
6821 Benjamin Franklin Dr
Columbia MD 21046
410 910-7800

(P-6786)
ROLLINS ROAD ACQUISITION CO (HQ)
100 Rollins Rd, Millbrae (94030-3115)
PHONE....................415 937-7836
John Carrington, *CEO*
Mary Adam, *Partner*
William Bush, *CFO*
Karen Butterfield, *Officer*
Alan Russo, *Officer*
◆ **EMP:** 80 **EST:** 2009
SQ FT: 20,000
SALES (est): 38.7MM **Publicly Held**
WEB: www.stem.com
SIC: 3825 Electrical power measuring equipment
PA: Stem, Inc.
100 Rollins Rd
Millbrae CA 94030
415 937-7816

(P-6787)
ROOS INSTRUMENTS INC
Also Called: RI
2285 Martin Ave, Santa Clara (95050-2715)
PHONE....................408 748-8589
Mark Roos, *CEO*
Mark D Roos, *President*
Catherine Roos, *Officer*
Esther Chen, *Sr Software Eng*
Sian-Tek Chen, *Sr Software Eng*
EMP: 21 **EST:** 1989
SQ FT: 22,000
SALES (est): 6MM **Privately Held**
WEB: www.roos.com
SIC: 3825 Semiconductor test equipment

(P-6788)
SAGE INSTRUMENTS INC
240 Airport Blvd, Freedom (95019-2636)
PHONE....................831 761-1000
Dave McIntosh, *CEO*
Brett M Mackinnon, *President*
Ray Levasseur, *CFO*
Renshou Dai, *Officer*
Al Key, *Technical Staff*
EMP: 90 **EST:** 1984
SQ FT: 20,000
SALES (est): 8.4MM **Privately Held**
WEB: www.sageinst.com
SIC: 3825 Test equipment for electronic & electric measurement

(P-6789)
SATELLITE TELEWORK CENTERS INC (PA)
6265 Highway 9, Felton (95018-9710)
PHONE....................831 222-2100
Barbara Sprenger, *President*
Daryn Dezengotita, *Marketing Staff*
Aaron Caponigro, *Manager*
EMP: 60 **EST:** 2008

SALES (est): 5.1MM **Privately Held**
WEB: www.satellitecenters.com
SIC: 3825 7389 Network analyzers; office facilities & secretarial service rental

(P-6790)
SEAGULL SOLUTIONS INC
15105 Concord Cir Ste 100, Morgan Hill (95037-5487)
PHONE....................408 778-1127
Carol Lawless, *CFO*
Donald L Ekhoff, *CTO*
EMP: 15 **EST:** 1999
SQ FT: 8,717
SALES (est): 2.4MM **Privately Held**
WEB: www.seagullsolutions.net
SIC: 3825 Instruments to measure electricity

(P-6791)
SEMPREX CORPORATION
782 Camden Ave, Campbell (95008-4102)
PHONE....................408 379-3230
Karl Volk, *President*
Lou Volk, *COO*
EMP: 20 **EST:** 1966
SQ FT: 12,500
SALES (est): 2.2MM **Privately Held**
WEB: www.semprex.com
SIC: 3825 Instruments to measure electricity

(P-6792)
SOTCHER MEASUREMENT INC
115 Phelan Ave Ste 10, San Jose (95112-6122)
PHONE....................408 574-0112
Marc Sotcher, *President*
Don Vuong, *Finance Mgr*
EMP: 22 **EST:** 1970
SQ FT: 9,000
SALES (est): 2.7MM **Privately Held**
WEB: www.sotcher.com
SIC: 3825 Test equipment for electronic & electrical circuits

(P-6793)
SPIRENT COMMUNICATIONS INC
2708 Orchard Pkwy Ste 20, San Jose (95134-1968)
PHONE....................408 752-7100
Laura Chavez, *Manager*
Chrisanne Milko, *Admin Asst*
James Williams, *Technician*
Tim Dellinger, *Engineer*
Patrick Magee, *Engineer*
EMP: 111
SALES (corp-wide): 522.4MM **Privately Held**
WEB: www.spirent.com
SIC: 3825 3829 3663 Instruments to measure electricity; measuring & controlling devices; radio & TV communications equipment
HQ: Spirent Communications Inc.
27349 Agoura Rd
Calabasas CA 91301

(P-6794)
SV PROBE INC
6680 Via Del Oro, San Jose (95119-1392)
PHONE....................480 635-4700
Kevin Kurtz, *Principal*
EMP: 318 **Privately Held**
WEB: www.svprobe.com
SIC: 3825 Test equipment for electronic & electrical circuits
HQ: Sv Probe, Inc.
7810 S Hardy Dr Ste 113
Tempe AZ 85284

(P-6795)
TESTMETRIX INC
1141 Ringwood Ct Ste 90, San Jose (95131-1757)
PHONE....................408 730-5511
Christian Cojocneanu, *President*
Stephanie Haag, *CFO*
Mike Bulat, *Director*
EMP: 28 **EST:** 1983

SALES (est): 2.7MM **Privately Held**
WEB: www.testmetrix.com
SIC: 3825 3674 Test equipment for electronic & electric measurement; semiconductors & related devices

(P-6796)
TRANSLARITY INC
46575 Fremont Blvd, Fremont (94538-6409)
PHONE....................510 371-7900
Laura Oliphant, *CEO*
Mark Gardiner, *COO*
Mike Chrastecky, *VP Bus Dvlpt*
Chuck Wiley,
J Kelly Truman, *Principal*
EMP: 19 **EST:** 2002
SQ FT: 20,000
SALES (est): 4MM **Privately Held**
WEB: www.translarity.com
SIC: 3825 Semiconductor test equipment

(P-6797)
TTT-CUBED INC
1120 Auburn St, Fremont (94538-7328)
PHONE....................510 656-2325
Jeff Tindall, *President*
EMP: 90 **EST:** 2011
SALES (est): 16.4MM **Publicly Held**
WEB: www.dbcontrol.com
SIC: 3825 Test equipment for electronic & electric measurement
HQ: Db Control Corp.
1120 Auburn St
Fremont CA 94538

(P-6798)
TURNONGREEN INC
Also Called: Coolisys
1635 S Main St, Milpitas (95035-6262)
PHONE....................510 657-2635
Amos Kohn, *CEO*
Seth Murdoch, *CFO*
Russ Woodmansee, *Vice Pres*
EMP: 25 **EST:** 2020
SALES (est): 25.4MM
SALES (corp-wide): 23.8MM **Publicly Held**
WEB: www.coolisys.com
SIC: 3825 3812 3613 3679 Electrical energy measuring equipment; defense systems & equipment; power switching equipment; power supplies, all types: static; battery chargers, rectifying or non-rotating
HQ: Digital Power Corporation
1635 S Main St
Milpitas CA 95035
510 657-2635

(P-6799)
VALDOR FIBER OPTICS INC (PA)
1838 D St, Hayward (94541-4435)
PHONE....................510 293-1212
Las Yabut, *President*
EMP: 15 **EST:** 1993
SQ FT: 12,000
SALES (est): 2.5MM **Privately Held**
SIC: 3825 Measuring instruments & meters, electric

(P-6800)
VLSI STANDARDS INC
5 Technology Dr, Milpitas (95035-7916)
PHONE....................408 428-1800
Ian Smith, *President*
EMP: 36 **EST:** 1984
SQ FT: 17,500
SALES (est): 11.1MM
SALES (corp-wide): 6.9B **Publicly Held**
WEB: www.vlsistandards.com
SIC: 3825 Standards & calibration equipment for electrical measuring
PA: Kla Corporation
1 Technology Dr
Milpitas CA 95035
408 875-3000

(P-6801)
XANDEX INC
1360 Redwood Way Ste A, Petaluma (94954-1104)
PHONE....................707 763-7799
Kamran Shamsavari, *President*

Nariman Manoochehri, *CEO*
Annena Herndon, *Asst Controller*
Sherri Hanson, *Human Resources*
▲ **EMP:** 42 **EST:** 1980
SQ FT: 20,000
SALES (est): 10.1MM **Privately Held**
WEB: www.xandex.com
SIC: 3825 3674 Instruments to measure electricity; wafers (semiconductor devices)

3826 Analytical Instruments

(P-6802)
AB SCIEX LLC (HQ)
1201 Radio Rd, Redwood City (94065-1217)
PHONE....................877 740-2129
Rainer Blair, *Mng Member*
Veronique A Berger, *Vice Pres*
Tamara Bond, *Vice Pres*
Tara Illiano, *Vice Pres*
Brent Ladd, *Vice Pres*
EMP: 92 **EST:** 2009
SALES (est): 67.4MM
SALES (corp-wide): 22.2B **Publicly Held**
WEB: www.sciex.com
SIC: 3826 Analytical instruments
PA: Danaher Corporation
2200 Penn Ave Nw Ste 800w
Washington DC 20037
202 828-0850

(P-6803)
ACCESS SYSTEMS INC
4947 Hillsdale Cir, El Dorado Hills (95762-5707)
PHONE....................916 941-8099
Michael Herd, *President*
Greg Johnston, *Opers Mgr*
Mike Herd, *Sales Staff*
EMP: 26 **EST:** 2002
SQ FT: 3,000
SALES (est): 2.8MM **Privately Held**
WEB: www.accesssystems.us
SIC: 3826 3699 Integrators (mathematical instruments); security control equipment & systems

(P-6804)
AFFYMETRIX INC (HQ)
3380 Central Expy, Santa Clara (95051-0704)
PHONE....................408 731-5000
Seth H Hoogasian, *President*
Gary McMaster, *Officer*
John Batty, *Exec VP*
Siang Chin, *Vice Pres*
John Dangelo, *Vice Pres*
EMP: 962 **EST:** 2015
SALES (est): 192MM
SALES (corp-wide): 32.2B **Publicly Held**
WEB: www.thermofisher.com
SIC: 3826 Analytical instruments
PA: Thermo Fisher Scientific Inc.
168 3rd Ave
Waltham MA 02451
781 622-1000

(P-6805)
AGILENT TECHNOLOGIES INC (PA)
5301 Stevens Creek Blvd, Santa Clara (95051-7201)
P.O. Box 58059 (95052-8059)
PHONE....................800 227-9770
Michael McMullen, *President*
Robert McMahon, *CFO*
Allison Ballmer, *Senior VP*
Padraig McDonnell, *Senior VP*
Rick Burdsall, *Vice Pres*
▲ **EMP:** 9233 **EST:** 1999
SALES (est): 5.3B **Publicly Held**
WEB: www.agilent.com
SIC: 3826 7372 Analytical instruments; gas testing apparatus; instruments measuring magnetic & electrical properties; prepackaged software

(P-6806)
ALZA CORPORATION
1010 Joaquin Rd, Mountain View (94043-1242)
PHONE....................650 564-5000
Duane Frise, *Branch Mgr*

3826 - Analytical Instruments County (P-6807)

EMP: 725
SALES (corp-wide): 82.5B **Publicly Held**
WEB: www.alza.com
SIC: 3826 Analytical instruments
HQ: Alza Corporation
  700 Eubanks Dr
  Vacaville CA 95688
  707 453-6400

(P-6807)
ALZA CORPORATION
700 Eubanks Dr, Vacaville (95688-9470)
PHONE 707 453-6400
David Danks, *Vice Pres*
EMP: 650
SQ FT: 23,040
SALES (corp-wide): 82.5B **Publicly Held**
WEB: www.alza.com
SIC: 3826 Analytical instruments
HQ: Alza Corporation
  700 Eubanks Dr
  Vacaville CA 95688
  707 453-6400

(P-6808)
ANALYTCAL SCENTIFIC INSTRS INC
Also Called: A S I
3023 Research Dr, San Pablo (94806-5206)
PHONE 510 669-2250
Stephen H Graham, *President*
Yasu Graham, *Vice Pres*
Yasu Kagayama, *Vice Pres*
Michael Pinkerton, *Technical Staff*
Rishpal Brar, *Controller*
EMP: 30 **EST:** 1989
SQ FT: 12,000
SALES (est): 4.3MM **Privately Held**
WEB: www.hplc-asi.com
SIC: 3826 3494 Analytical instruments; valves & pipe fittings

(P-6809)
ART ROBBINS INSTRUMENTS LLC
1293 Mountain View Alviso, Sunnyvale (94089-2241)
PHONE 408 734-8400
Matt Robbins, *General Mgr*
Erik Norgren, *Design Engr*
Paul May, *Marketing Staff*
Arthur Robbins,
Heather Robbins,
EMP: 31 **EST:** 2003
SQ FT: 6,000
SALES (est): 8.7MM **Privately Held**
WEB: www.artrobbins.com
SIC: 3826 Analytical instruments

(P-6810)
ASA CORPORATION
3111 Sunset Blvd Ste V, Rocklin (95677-3090)
PHONE 530 305-3720
EMP: 15
SALES (est): 5MM **Privately Held**
SIC: 3826 Analytical Instruments, Nsk

(P-6811)
ATONARP US INC
Also Called: Smart Spectrometer
46653 Fremont Blvd, Fremont (94538-6410)
PHONE 650 714-6290
David King, *CEO*
Kirk Johnson, *CFO*
Prakash Murthy, *Principal*
Karthik Madathil, *Director*
EMP: 43 **EST:** 2015
SALES (est): 10.3MM **Privately Held**
WEB: www.atonarp.com
SIC: 3826 Spectrometers

(P-6812)
AXYGEN INC (HQ)
Also Called: Axygen Scientific
33210 Central Ave, Union City (94587-2010)
PHONE 510 494-8900
Hemant Gupta, *President*
Amit Bansal, *CFO*
◆ **EMP:** 194 **EST:** 1993
SQ FT: 33,000
SALES (est): 32.5MM
SALES (corp-wide): 11.3B **Publicly Held**
WEB: www.corning.com
SIC: 3826 Analytical instruments
PA: Corning Incorporated
  1 Riverfront Plz
  Corning NY 14831
  607 974-9000

(P-6813)
BAB ACQUISITION CORP
Also Called: Phynexus
3670 Charter Park Dr A, San Jose (95136-1396)
PHONE 408 267-7214
Torben Jorgensen, *CEO*
Tiffany Thao Nguyen, *Vice Pres*
Jonathan Grambow, *Research*
Lee Hoang, *Research*
Devin Clunn, *Engineer*
EMP: 17 **EST:** 2018
SALES (est): 5.9MM **Privately Held**
WEB: www.phynexus.com
SIC: 3826 Analytical instruments
PA: Biotage Ab

  Uppsala 751 0

(P-6814)
BAYSPEC INC
1101 Mckay Dr, San Jose (95131-1706)
PHONE 408 512-5928
William Yang, *President*
Eric Bergles, *Vice Pres*
Chase Wang, *Engineer*
Mike Chai, *Production*
Brad Sohnlein, *Sales Staff*
EMP: 35 **EST:** 1999
SQ FT: 48,000
SALES (est): 9.9MM **Privately Held**
WEB: www.bayspec.com
SIC: 3826 Analytical instruments

(P-6815)
BERKELEY LIGHTS INC (PA)
5858 Horton St Ste 320, Emeryville (94608-2183)
PHONE 510 858-2855
Eric D Hobbs, *CEO*
Gregory T Lucier, *Ch of Bd*
Shaun M Holt, *CFO*
Matthew W Rosinack, *Senior VP*
Eric Esser, *Vice Pres*
EMP: 214 **EST:** 2011
SQ FT: 54,063
SALES (est): 64.3MM **Publicly Held**
WEB: www.berkeleylights.com
SIC: 3826 8733 Analytical instruments; research institute

(P-6816)
BIO-RAD LABORATORIES INC (PA)
1000 Alfred Nobel Dr, Hercules (94547-1898)
PHONE 510 724-7000
Norman Schwartz, *Ch of Bd*
Andrew J Last, *COO*
Ilan Daskal, *CFO*
Ronald W Hutton, *Treasurer*
Michael Crowley, *Exec VP*
◆ **EMP:** 3554 **EST:** 1952
SALES (est): 2.5B **Publicly Held**
WEB: www.bio-rad.com
SIC: 3826 3845 2835 Electrophoresis equipment; electromedical equipment; in vitro & in vivo diagnostic substances

(P-6817)
BIO-RAD LABORATORIES INC
Also Called: Finance Department
225 Linus Pauling Dr, Hercules (94547-1816)
PHONE 510 741-6916
Lanette Ewing, *Branch Mgr*
Robert Cooper, *Vice Pres*
Claudia Yatsko, *Executive*
Alfredo Ornelas, *Program Mgr*
Jessie Jeyapalan, *Admin Sec*
EMP: 1500
SALES (corp-wide): 2.5B **Publicly Held**
WEB: www.bio-rad.com
SIC: 3826 Electrophoresis equipment
PA: Bio-Rad Laboratories, Inc.
  1000 Alfred Nobel Dr
  Hercules CA 94547
  510 724-7000

(P-6818)
BIOLOG INC
21124 Cabot Blvd, Hayward (94545-1130)
PHONE 510 785-2564
Barry R Bochner, *President*
Edwin Fineman, *Vice Pres*
Karen Freeman, *Vice Pres*
Doug Rife, *Vice Pres*
Andrew Wung, *Marketing Staff*
EMP: 40 **EST:** 1981
SQ FT: 25,000
SALES (est): 9.7MM **Privately Held**
WEB: www.biolog.com
SIC: 3826 Analytical instruments

(P-6819)
BRIDGER TECHNOLOGIES INC
Also Called: Bti
1000 Alfred Nobel Dr, Hercules (94547-1811)
PHONE 406 556-0300
Fred Albert, *President*
Brad Wright, *Vice Pres*
EMP: 26 **EST:** 2003
SQ FT: 5,400
SALES (est): 1.1MM
SALES (corp-wide): 2.5B **Publicly Held**
WEB: www.bio-rad.com
SIC: 3826 Analytical instruments
PA: Bio-Rad Laboratories, Inc.
  1000 Alfred Nobel Dr
  Hercules CA 94547
  510 724-7000

(P-6820)
CEPHEID (HQ)
904 E Caribbean Dr, Sunnyvale (94089-1189)
PHONE 408 541-4191
Warren Kocmond, *President*
Daniel E Madden, *CFO*
William E Murray,
Jacobin Zorin, *Officer*
Michael Fitzgerald, *Exec VP*
◆ **EMP:** 1653 **EST:** 1996
SALES (est): 538.5MM
SALES (corp-wide): 22.2B **Publicly Held**
WEB: www.cepheid.com
SIC: 3826 3841 Analytical instruments; surgical & medical instruments
PA: Danaher Corporation
  2200 Penn Ave Nw Ste 800w
  Washington DC 20037
  202 828-0850

(P-6821)
COHERENT INC (PA)
5100 Patrick Henry Dr, Santa Clara (95054-1112)
PHONE 408 764-4000
Andreas W Mattes, *President*
Garry W Rogerson, *Ch of Bd*
Mark Sobey, *COO*
Kevin Palatnik, *CFO*
Susan M James, *Bd of Directors*
▲ **EMP:** 1082 **EST:** 1966
SQ FT: 200,000
SALES (est): 1.2B **Publicly Held**
WEB: www.coherent.com
SIC: 3826 3845 3699 Laser scientific & engineering instruments; laser systems & equipment, medical; laser systems & equipment

(P-6822)
CONTINUUM ELECTRO-OPTICS INC
532 Gibraltar Dr, Milpitas (95035-6315)
PHONE 408 727-3240
Robert Buckley, *CEO*
Larry Cramer, *President*
Frank Romero, *Treasurer*
Curt Fredrickson, *Vice Pres*
◆ **EMP:** 75 **EST:** 1976
SQ FT: 44,000
SALES (est): 22.1MM **Privately Held**
WEB: www.amplitude-laser.com
SIC: 3826 Laser scientific & engineering instruments

(P-6823)
CYTEK BIOSCIENCES INC (PA)
46107 Landing Pkwy, Fremont (94538-6407)
PHONE 877 922-9835
Wenbin Jiang, *President*
Patrik Jeanmonod, *CFO*
Allen Poirson, *Senior VP*
Ray Lannigan, *Vice Pres*
Steve Ziganti, *Vice Pres*
EMP: 390 EST: 2014
SQ FT: 12,000
SALES (est): 92.8MM **Publicly Held**
WEB: www.cytekbio.com
SIC: 3826 Analytical instruments

(P-6824)
DIONEX CORPORATION (HQ)
1228 Titan Way Ste 1002, Sunnyvale (94085-4074)
P.O. Box 3603 (94088-3603)
PHONE 408 737-0700
Mark Casper, *President*
Craig A McCollam, *CFO*
Bruce Barton, *Exec VP*
Jasmine Gruia Gray PHD, *Vice Pres*
Bill Baker, *Regional Mgr*
EMP: 400 **EST:** 1986
SQ FT: 252,000
SALES (est): 627.1MM
SALES (corp-wide): 32.2B **Publicly Held**
WEB: www.thermofisher.com
SIC: 3826 2819 3087 3841 Chromatographic equipment, laboratory type; chemicals, reagent grade: refined from technical grade; custom compound purchased resins; surgical & medical instruments
PA: Thermo Fisher Scientific Inc.
  168 3rd Ave
  Waltham MA 02451
  781 622-1000

(P-6825)
DRY VAC ENVIRONMENTAL INC (PA)
864 Saint Francis Way, Rio Vista (94571-1250)
PHONE 707 374-7500
Dan Simpson, *President*
Greg Crocco, *Shareholder*
EMP: 25 **EST:** 1996
SQ FT: 50,000
SALES (est): 5.1MM **Privately Held**
WEB: www.desllc.biz
SIC: 3826 3531 Liquid testing apparatus; construction machinery

(P-6826)
DUKE SCIENTIFIC CORPORATION
46360 Fremont Blvd, Fremont (94538-6406)
P.O. Box 50005, Palo Alto (94303-0005)
PHONE 650 424-1177
Stanley D Duke, *CEO*
Philip Warren, *President*
Ellen Layendecker, *Treasurer*
Heather Vail, *Admin Sec*
EMP: 66 **EST:** 1970
SQ FT: 14,000
SALES (est): 5MM
SALES (corp-wide): 32.2B **Publicly Held**
WEB: www.thermofisher.com
SIC: 3826 Analytical instruments
PA: Thermo Fisher Scientific Inc.
  168 3rd Ave
  Waltham MA 02451
  781 622-1000

(P-6827)
EUV TECH INC
2830 Howe Rd A, Martinez (94553-4000)
PHONE 925 229-4388
Rupert Perera, *President*
Chami Perera, *Vice Pres*
Matt Hettermann, *Engineer*
Omar Mussa, *Engineer*
Michelle Lawson, *Purchasing*
EMP: 15 **EST:** 1996
SALES (est): 4.6MM **Privately Held**
WEB: www.euvtech.com
SIC: 3826 Laser scientific & engineering instruments

PRODUCTS & SERVICES SECTION
3826 - Analytical Instruments County (P-6850)

(P-6828)
FEI EFA INC (DH)
Also Called: Dcg Systems
3400 W Warren Ave, Fremont
(94538-6425)
PHONE..................510 897-6800
Israel Niv, *CEO*
Ronen Benzion, *President*
Bob Conners, *CFO*
Tameyasu Anayama, *Vice Pres*
Aaron Nestor, *Engineer*
EMP: 95 **EST:** 2008
SQ FT: 45,000
SALES (est): 51.4MM
SALES (corp-wide): 32.2B **Publicly Held**
WEB: www.fei.com
SIC: 3826 Analytical instruments
HQ: Fei Company
5350 Ne Dawson Creek Dr
Hillsboro OR 97124
503 726-7500

(P-6829)
FIBERLITE CENTRIFUGE LLC
Also Called: Thermo Fisher Scientific
422 Aldo Ave, Santa Clara (95054-2301)
PHONE..................408 492-1109
Al Piramoon, *Mng Member*
Dennis Crane, *Facilities Mgr*
Markus Affolter, *Manager*
▲ **EMP:** 70 **EST:** 1994
SQ FT: 18,000
SALES (est): 31MM
SALES (corp-wide): 32.2B **Publicly Held**
WEB: www.thermofisher.com
SIC: 3826 Analytical instruments
PA: Thermo Fisher Scientific Inc.
168 3rd Ave
Waltham MA 02451
781 622-1000

(P-6830)
FLUIDIGM CORPORATION (PA)
2 Tower Pl Ste 2000, South San Francisco
(94080-1844)
PHONE..................650 266-6000
Carlos Paya, *Ch of Bd*
Vikram Jog, *CFO*
Colin McCracken, *Officer*
Nicholas Khadder, *Senior VP*
Bradley Kreger, *Senior VP*
EMP: 608 **EST:** 1999
SQ FT: 78,000
SALES (est): 138.1MM **Publicly Held**
WEB: www.fluidigm.com
SIC: 3826 8731 Analytical instruments; biotechnical research, commercial

(P-6831)
FLUIDIGM SCIENCES INC
2 Tower Pl Fl 20, South San Francisco
(94080-1826)
PHONE..................408 900-7205
Joseph J Victor, *President*
Mark Tebneoer, *CFO*
Scott Tanner, *Officer*
Heather Meeks, *Admin Asst*
EMP: 20 **EST:** 2011
SALES (est): 2.1MM
SALES (corp-wide): 138.1MM **Publicly Held**
WEB: www.fluidigm.com
SIC: 3826 2819 Analytical instruments; chemicals, reagent grade: refined from technical grade
PA: Fluidigm Corporation
2 Tower Pl Ste 2000
South San Francisco CA 94080
650 266-6000

(P-6832)
GATAN INTERNATIONAL INC
5794a W Las Positas Blvd, Pleasanton
(94588-4083)
PHONE..................925 463-0200
William E Offenberg, *President*
EMP: 50 **EST:** 1992
SALES (est): 7.9MM
SALES (corp-wide): 5.5B **Publicly Held**
WEB: www.gatan.com
SIC: 3826 Analytical optical instruments
PA: Roper Technologies, Inc.
6901 Prof Pkwy E Ste 200
Sarasota FL 34240
941 556-2601

(P-6833)
INFRASTRUCTUREWORLD LLC
377 Margarita Dr, San Rafael
(94901-2376)
PHONE..................415 699-1543
Barbara L Treat, *Mng Member*
Chris Sherman, *Managing Dir*
Cordell Hull,
EMP: 20 **EST:** 2010
SALES (est): 954.4K **Privately Held**
WEB: www.infrastructureworld.com
SIC: 3826 Infrared analytical instruments

(P-6834)
INTEGENX INC (HQ)
5720 Stoneridge Dr # 300, Pleasanton
(94588-2739)
PHONE..................925 701-3400
Robert A Schueren, *CEO*
David V Smith, *COO*
David King, *Exec VP*
▲ **EMP:** 69 **EST:** 2003
SQ FT: 10,000
SALES (est): 34.6MM
SALES (corp-wide): 32.2B **Publicly Held**
WEB: www.thermofisher.com
SIC: 3826 Analytical instruments
PA: Thermo Fisher Scientific Inc.
168 3rd Ave
Waltham MA 02451
781 622-1000

(P-6835)
MARINE SPILL RESPONSE CORP
990 W Waterfront Dr, Eureka (95501-0173)
PHONE..................707 442-6087
EMP: 21 **Privately Held**
WEB: www.msrc.org
SIC: 3826 Environmental testing equipment
PA: Marine Spill Response Corporation
220 Spring St Ste 500
Herndon VA 20170

(P-6836)
MARKES INTERNATIONAL INC
Also Called: Alms Company
2355 Gold Meadow Way # 120, Gold River
(95670-6325)
PHONE..................513 745-0241
Elizabeth Woolfenden, *Director*
Kaylen Prior, *Sales Staff*
Alun Cole, *Director*
EMP: 17 **EST:** 2010
SALES (est): 15.5MM
SALES (corp-wide): 240.4MM **Privately Held**
WEB: www.markes.com
SIC: 3826 Analytical instruments
HQ: Markes International Limited
Unit 3-4 Gwaun Elai
Pontyclun M GLAM CF72

(P-6837)
MEDICAL ANALYSIS SYSTEMS INC (DH)
46360 Fremont Blvd, Fremont
(94538-6406)
PHONE..................510 979-5000
Steve Kondor, *President*
Eric Scheinerman, *CFO*
Darwin Richardson, *Vice Pres*
EMP: 150 **EST:** 1974
SQ FT: 180,000
SALES (est): 46.7MM
SALES (corp-wide): 32.2B **Publicly Held**
WEB: www.thermofisher.com
SIC: 3826 Analytical instruments

(P-6838)
MICROGENICS CORPORATION (HQ)
46500 Kato Rd, Fremont (94538-7310)
PHONE..................510 979-9147
Seth H Hoogasian, *CEO*
David Rubinfien, *President*
Lakshmi Anne, *Manager*
▲ **EMP:** 230 **EST:** 1998
SQ FT: 108,000
SALES (est): 498.3MM
SALES (corp-wide): 32.2B **Publicly Held**
SIC: 3826 Analytical instruments
PA: Thermo Fisher Scientific Inc.
168 3rd Ave
Waltham MA 02451
781 622-1000

(P-6839)
MICROGENICS CORPORATION
44660 Osgood Rd, Fremont (94539-6410)
PHONE..................510 979-5000
EMP: 5846
SALES (corp-wide): 32.2B **Publicly Held**
SIC: 3826 Analytical instruments
HQ: Microgenics Corporation
46500 Kato Rd
Fremont CA 94538
510 979-9147

(P-6840)
MOLECULAR DEVICES LLC
47661 Fremont Blvd, Fremont
(94538-6577)
PHONE..................408 747-3546
Susan Murphy, *President*
Marlene Ogawa, *Director*
Remco De Vries, *Accounts Mgr*
EMP: 17 **EST:** 2016
SALES (est): 2.2MM **Privately Held**
WEB: www.moleculardevices.com
SIC: 3826 Analytical instruments

(P-6841)
MOLECULAR DEVICES LLC (HQ)
3860 N 1st St, San Jose (95134-1702)
PHONE..................408 747-1700
Kevin Chance, *Mng Member*
Steven Qian, *Officer*
Laurent Claisse, *Vice Pres*
Dean Ding, *Vice Pres*
Susan Murphy, *Vice Pres*
▲ **EMP:** 125 **EST:** 2011
SALES (est): 154.1MM
SALES (corp-wide): 22.2B **Publicly Held**
WEB: www.moleculardevices.com
SIC: 3826 3841 Analytical instruments; surgical & medical instruments
PA: Danaher Corporation
2200 Penn Ave Nw Ste 800w
Washington DC 20037
202 828-0850

(P-6842)
NUTCRACKER THERAPEUTICS INC
5858 Horton St Ste 540, Emeryville
(94608-2170)
PHONE..................:510 473-8478
Igor Khandros, *CEO*
EMP: 37 **EST:** 2018
SALES (est): 5.6MM **Privately Held**
WEB: www.nutcrackerx.com
SIC: 3826 Analytical instruments

(P-6843)
PACIFIC BIOSCIENCES CAL INC (PA)
1305 Obrien Dr, Menlo Park (94025-1445)
PHONE..................650 521-8000
Michael Hunkapiller, *CEO*
Mark Van Oene, *COO*
Ben Gong, *CFO*
Kathy Ordonez, *Ch Credit Ofcr*
John Milligan, *Bd of Directors*
EMP: 389 **EST:** 2000
SQ FT: 180,000
SALES (est): 78.8MM **Publicly Held**
WEB: www.pacb.com
SIC: 3826 Analytical instruments

(P-6844)
PICARRO INC (PA)
3105 Patrick Henry Dr, Santa Clara
(95054-1815)
PHONE..................408 962-3900
Alex Balkanski, *President*
Betsy Kais, *CFO*
Yonggang He, *Vice Pres*
Renato Winkler, *Business Dir*
Kathy Johnson, *Executive Asst*
EMP: 182 **EST:** 2001
SQ FT: 15,250
SALES (est): 48.1MM **Privately Held**
WEB: www.picarro.com
SIC: 3826 Analytical instruments

(P-6845)
RAINDANCE TECHNOLOGIES INC
5731 W Las Positas Blvd, Pleasanton
(94588-4084)
PHONE..................978 495-3300
Kathy Ordonez, *CEO*
Jonathan Rothberg, *Ch of Bd*
Roch Kelly, *COO*
Alfred G Merriweather, *CFO*
Andy Watson, *Chief Mktg Ofcr*
EMP: 45 **EST:** 2004
SALES (est): 14MM
SALES (corp-wide): 2.5B **Publicly Held**
WEB: www.bio-rad.com
SIC: 3826 Analytical instruments
PA: Bio-Rad Laboratories, Inc.
1000 Alfred Nobel Dr
Hercules CA 94547
510 724-7000

(P-6846)
REMEL INC
46500 Kato Rd, Fremont (94538-7310)
PHONE..................916 425-2651
EMP: 1091
SALES (corp-wide): 32.2B **Publicly Held**
WEB: www.thermofisher.com
SIC: 3826 Analytical instruments
HQ: Remel Inc.
12076 Santa Fe Trail Dr
Lenexa KS 66215
800 255-6730

(P-6847)
RS TECHNICAL SERVICES INC (PA)
1327 Clegg St, Petaluma (94954-1126)
P.O. Box 66, Perry OK (73077-0066)
PHONE..................707 778-1974
Michael Sutliff, *Principal*
Michael W Sutliff, *CEO*
Kathey Sutliff, *Admin Sec*
EMP: 88 **EST:** 1983
SQ FT: 15,000
SALES (est): 9.4MM **Privately Held**
WEB: www.subsite.com
SIC: 3826 3823 Sewage testing apparatus; industrial instrmnts msrmnt display/control process variable

(P-6848)
RTEC-INSTRUMENTS INC
1810 Oakland Rd Ste B, San Jose
(95131-2316)
PHONE..................408 456-0801
Vishal Khosla, *CEO*
Jun Xiao, *Vice Pres*
Ming Chan, *Engineer*
Liz Chen, *Sales Mgr*
EMP: 25
SQ FT: 3,000
SALES (est): 6.5MM **Privately Held**
WEB: www.rtec-instruments.com
SIC: 3826 Analytical instruments

(P-6849)
SEER INC
3800 Bridge Pkwy Ste 102, Redwood City
(94065-1171)
PHONE..................650 453-0000
Omid Farokhzad, *Ch of Bd*
Omead Ostadan, *President*
David R Horn, *CFO*
Elona Kogan, *Admin Sec*
EMP: 60 **EST:** 2017
SQ FT: 25,600
SALES (est): 656K **Privately Held**
WEB: www.seer.bio
SIC: 3826 8733 Analytical instruments; medical research

(P-6850)
SEPRAGEN CORPORATION
33470 Western Ave, Union City
(94587-3202)
PHONE..................510 475-0650
Vinit Saxena, *Ch of Bd*
Henry N Edmunds, *CFO*
Ron Genise, *Software Engr*
EMP: 28 **EST:** 1985
SQ FT: 23,000

3826 - Analytical Instruments County (P-6851) — PRODUCTS & SERVICES SECTION

SALES (est): 5.7MM Privately Held
WEB: www.sepragen.com
SIC: 3826 Liquid chromatographic instruments

(P-6851)
SERADYN INC
46360 Fremont Blvd, Fremont (94538-6406)
PHONE..................317 610-3800
Mark Roberts, President
EMP: 56 EST: 1984
SQ FT: 40,000
SALES (est): 13.2MM
SALES (corp-wide): 32.2B Publicly Held
WEB: www.thermofisher.com
SIC: 3826 Analytical instruments
HQ: Fisher Scientific International Llc
 81 Wyman St
 Waltham MA 02451

(P-6852)
SIGRAY INC
5750 Imhoff Dr Ste I, Concord (94520-5348)
PHONE..................925 207-0925
Wenbing Yun, Ch of Bd
Sylvia Yun, Vice Pres
Sylvia Lewis, General Mgr
Vladimir Semenov, Engineer
Vikram Singh, Engineer
EMP: 24 EST: 2013
SALES (est): 5.2MM Privately Held
WEB: www.sigray.com
SIC: 3826 Analytical instruments

(P-6853)
SLOUBER ENTERPRISES INC (PA)
Also Called: High Sierra Electronics
11885 Sunrise Ln, Grass Valley (95945-8898)
PHONE..................530 273-2080
Katherine L Slouber, CEO
James E Slouber, Vice Pres
Eric Gibbons, General Mgr
Carrie Lery, Engineer
Troy Nofziger, Engineer
EMP: 22 EST: 1992
SQ FT: 13,500
SALES (est): 8MM Privately Held
SIC: 3826 8748 8731 Environmental testing equipment; communications consulting; electronic research

(P-6854)
STANFORD RESEARCH SYSTEMS INC
Also Called: SRS
1290 Reamwood Ave Ste D, Sunnyvale (94089-2279)
PHONE..................408 744-9040
William R Green, President
John Willison, Vice Pres
Dave Ames, Executive
Judi Cushing, Info Tech Mgr
Steven Tran, Software Engr
EMP: 212 EST: 1980
SQ FT: 20,000
SALES (est): 20.4MM Privately Held
WEB: www.thinksrs.com
SIC: 3826 Analytical instruments

(P-6855)
TALIS BIOMEDICAL CORPORATION (PA)
230 Constitution Dr, Menlo Park (94025-1109)
PHONE..................650 433-3000
Kimberly J Popovits, CEO
Robert Kelley, COO
J Roger Moody Jr, CFO
Karen E Flick, Senior VP
Douglas Liu, Senior VP
EMP: 67 EST: 2010
SQ FT: 24,000
SALES (est): 10.9MM Publicly Held
WEB: www.talisbio.com
SIC: 3826 Spectroscopic & other optical properties measuring equipment

(P-6856)
TESSOLVE SERVICES INC (DH)
Also Called: Tessolve Dts
14567 Big Basin Way A3, Saratoga (95070-6039)
PHONE..................408 865-0873
Pakkirisamy Rajamanickam, CEO
EMP: 70 EST: 2006
SALES (est): 6.4MM Privately Held
WEB: www.tessolve.com
SIC: 3826 Laser scientific & engineering instruments

(P-6857)
THERMO FINNIGAN LLC (HQ)
355 River Oaks Pkwy, San Jose (95134-1908)
PHONE..................408 965-6000
Anthony H Smith, Mng Member
Jonathan C Wilk,
▲ EMP: 500 EST: 2001
SALES (est): 496.2MM
SALES (corp-wide): 32.2B Publicly Held
WEB: www.thermofisher.com
SIC: 3826 Analytical instruments
PA: Thermo Fisher Scientific Inc.
 168 3rd Ave
 Waltham MA 02451
 781 622-1000

(P-6858)
THERMO FISHER SCIENTIFIC
Also Called: Thermofinnegan
355 River Oaks Pkwy, San Jose (95134-1908)
P.O. Box 49031 (95161-9031)
PHONE..................408 894-9835
Ian Jardin, Branch Mgr
King Poon, President
Vlad Eberman, Senior Engr
Ed Goncalves, Finance
Terry Zhang, Analyst
EMP: 400
SALES (corp-wide): 32.2B Publicly Held
SIC: 3826 Analytical instruments
HQ: Thermo Fisher Scientific (Asheville) Llc
 275 Aiken Rd
 Asheville NC 28804
 828 658-2711

(P-6859)
THERMO FISHER SCIENTIFIC INC
3380 Central Expy, Santa Clara (95051-0704)
PHONE..................408 731-5056
Gene Tanimoto, Branch Mgr
Ron Fitzgerald, Mfg Staff
Candia Brown, Director
EMP: 29
SALES (corp-wide): 32.2B Publicly Held
WEB: www.thermofisher.com
SIC: 3826 Analytical instruments
PA: Thermo Fisher Scientific Inc.
 168 3rd Ave
 Waltham MA 02451
 781 622-1000

(P-6860)
THERMOQUEST CORPORATION
355 River Oaks Pkwy, San Jose (95134-1908)
P.O. Box 49031 (95161-9031)
PHONE..................408 965-6000
EMP: 1215
SALES: 431.8MM
SALES (corp-wide): 16.9B Publicly Held
SIC: 3826 3823 Mfg Mass Spectrometers & Liquid & Gas Chromatographs
PA: Thermo Fisher Scientific Inc.
 168 3rd Ave
 Waltham MA 02451
 781 622-1000

(P-6861)
TURNER DESIGNS INC
1995 N 1st St, San Jose (95112-4220)
PHONE..................408 749-0994
Jim Crawford, President
Lisette Montes, Human Res Mgr
Jen Sluga, Marketing Staff
Albert Aceves, Manager
EMP: 45 EST: 1972
SQ FT: 20,000
SALES (est): 10.9MM Privately Held
WEB: www.turnerdesigns.com
SIC: 3826 Analytical instruments

(P-6862)
VIAVI SOLUTIONS INC
430 N Mccarthy Blvd, Milpitas (95035-5112)
PHONE..................408 546-5000
Barry Johnson, Vice Pres
John Kavanagh, Vice Pres
Luiz-Cesar Oliveira, Vice Pres
Sinclair Vass, Vice Pres
Brad Duffy, Program Mgr
EMP: 191
SALES (corp-wide): 1.2B Publicly Held
WEB: www.viavisolutions.com
SIC: 3826 3674 Analytical instruments; optical isolators
PA: Viavi Solutions Inc.
 7047 E Greenway Pkwy # 25
 Scottsdale AZ 85254
 408 404-3600

(P-6863)
VIBRANT SCIENCES LLC
1021 Howard Ave Ste B, San Carlos (94070-4034)
PHONE..................408 203-9383
John Rajasekaran, Mng Member
EMP: 111 EST: 2011
SALES (est): 6.6MM Privately Held
WEB: www.vibrantsci.com
SIC: 3826 Electrolytic conductivity instruments

(P-6864)
XIA LLC
2744 E 11th St Ste H2, Oakland (94601-1443)
PHONE..................510 401-5760
William K Warburton,
Michael Sears, Vice Pres
Nicole Thomas, Admin Asst
Shawn Hoover, Engineer
Brendan McNally, Engineer
EMP: 31 EST: 2004
SQ FT: 8,000
SALES (est): 6.3MM Privately Held
WEB: www.xia.com
SIC: 3826 Analytical instruments

3827 Optical Instruments

(P-6865)
AMERICAN TECH NETWRK CORP (PA)
Also Called: American Technologies Network
1341 San Mateo Ave, South San Francisco (94080-6511)
PHONE..................800 910-2862
Marc Vayn, CEO
James Munn, COO
Gennady Shpiler, Engrg Dir
Sunny Lum, Engineer
Krassimir Gentchev, Production
▲ EMP: 48 EST: 1995
SQ FT: 25,000
SALES (est): 12.7MM Privately Held
WEB: www.atncorp.com
SIC: 3827 Optical instruments & lenses; aiming circles (fire control equipment)

(P-6866)
BLUE SKY RESEARCH INCORPORATED (PA)
510 Alder Dr, Milpitas (95035-7443)
PHONE..................408 941-6068
Christopher Gladding, President
Sandip Basu, CFO
Joe Kulakofsky, Vice Pres
EMP: 48 EST: 1986
SQ FT: 21,000
SALES (est): 8.5MM Privately Held
WEB: www.blueskyresearch.com
SIC: 3827 3674 Lenses, optical: all types except ophthalmic; semiconductors & related devices

(P-6867)
CARL ZEISS MEDITEC INC (DH)
5300 Central Pkwy, Dublin (94568-4999)
P.O. Box 100372, Pasadena (91189-0003)
PHONE..................925 557-4100
James V Mazzo, President
Roberto Deger, CFO
Thomas Simmerer, Officer
Craig Altschuler, Vice Pres
Jeff Rospert, Vice Pres
▲ EMP: 445 EST: 2000
SALES (est): 177.5MM Privately Held
WEB: www.zeiss.com
SIC: 3827 Optical instruments & apparatus
HQ: Carl Zeiss Meditec Ag
 Goschwitzer Str. 51-52
 Jena TH 07745
 364 122-00

(P-6868)
COLLIMATED HOLES INC
460 Division St, Campbell (95008-6923)
PHONE..................408 374-5080
Richard Mead, President
Dan Dickerson, Vice Pres
Lori Driggs, Opers Staff
EMP: 42 EST: 1975
SQ FT: 11,600
SALES (est): 1.6MM Privately Held
WEB: www.collimatedholes.com
SIC: 3827 Optical instruments & apparatus; optical elements & assemblies, except ophthalmic

(P-6869)
COMCORE TECHNOLOGIES INC
Also Called: Comcore Opcital Communication
48834 Kato Rd Ste 108a, Fremont (94538-7368)
PHONE..................408 623-9704
EMP: 20
SQ FT: 22,000
SALES (est): 3.6MM Privately Held
WEB: www.comcore.com
SIC: 3827 Mfg Optical Instruments/Lenses
PA: Manfredini Gennaro
 Via Sant' Anna 109/B
 Nocera Inferiore SA

(P-6870)
DIGILENS INC
1288 Hammerwood Ave, Sunnyvale (94089-2232)
PHONE..................408 734-0219
Christopher Pickett, CEO
Ratson Morad, COO
Michael Angel, CFO
Jonathan David Waldern, Chairman
Alastair Grant, Senior VP
EMP: 40 EST: 2003
SQ FT: 15,000
SALES (est): 8.9MM Privately Held
WEB: www.digilens.com
SIC: 3827 Optical instruments & lenses

(P-6871)
DIMAXX TECHNOLOGIES LLC
11838 Kemper Rd, Auburn (95603-9531)
P.O. Box 21810, Eugene OR (97402-0412)
PHONE..................530 888-1942
Leonard Mott,
Glenell Myers, Office Mgr
Norm Blankenship, Sales Staff
Gary Debell,
Tony Louderback,
EMP: 16 EST: 2000
SALES (est): 2.3MM Privately Held
WEB: www.dimaxxtech.com
SIC: 3827 Optical instruments & lenses

(P-6872)
FLEX PRODUCTS INC
1402 Mariner Way, Santa Rosa (95407-7370)
PHONE..................707 525-9200
Michael B Sullivan, President
Joseph Zils, CFO
Mary Ellen King, IT/INT Sup
Larry Mathis, Engineer
Paul Cavallo, Supervisor
EMP: 225 EST: 1988
SQ FT: 70,000
SALES (est): 48.7MM
SALES (corp-wide): 1.2B Publicly Held
SIC: 3827 3081 Lens coating equipment; unsupported plastics film & sheet
HQ: Optical Coating Laboratory, Llc
 2789 Northpoint Pkwy
 Santa Rosa CA 95407
 707 545-6440

▲ = Import ▼=Export
♦ =Import/Export

PRODUCTS & SERVICES SECTION
3829 - Measuring & Controlling Devices, NEC County (P-6895)

(P-6873)
FOREAL SPECTRUM INC
2370 Qume Dr Ste A, San Jose (95131-1842)
PHONE..................408 923-1675
Anmin Zheng, *CEO*
Liang Zhou, *President*
Baorui Gao, *Vice Pres*
Ronggui Shen, *Vice Pres*
Claire Nippress, *Office Mgr*
▲ EMP: 25 EST: 2003
SALES (est): 4.6MM **Privately Held**
WEB: www.forealspectrum.com
SIC: 3827 Optical instruments & lenses

(P-6874)
GUIDED WAVE INC
3033 Gold Canal Dr, Rancho Cordova (95670-6129)
PHONE..................916 638-4944
Susan Foulk, *CEO*
Don Goldman, *Vice Pres*
William Grooms, *Vice Pres*
James Low, *Info Tech Mgr*
Janell Leysath, *Marketing Staff*
EMP: 32 EST: 2001
SQ FT: 15,000
SALES (est): 6.9MM **Privately Held**
WEB: www.guided-wave.com
SIC: 3827 Optical instruments & apparatus

(P-6875)
INNEOS LLC
5700 Stoneridge Dr # 200, Pleasanton (94588-2897)
PHONE..................925 226-0138
Brian C Peters, *CEO*
Eric Grann, *Vice Pres*
Scott Oleary, *Vice Pres*
Todd Whitaker, *Vice Pres*
Martin Smith, *Business Dir*
EMP: 27 EST: 2005
SALES (est): 6.2MM **Privately Held**
WEB: www.inneos.com
SIC: 3827 Optical elements & assemblies, except ophthalmic

(P-6876)
INSCOPIX INC
2462 Embarcadero Way, Palo Alto (94303-3313)
PHONE..................650 600-3886
Kunal Ghosh, *President*
Martin Verhoef, *Ch Credit Ofcr*
David Gray, *Officer*
Vikram Brar, *Vice Pres*
Glenn Powell, *Vice Pres*
EMP: 15 EST: 2010
SQ FT: 6,041
SALES (est): 5.1MM **Privately Held**
WEB: www.inscopix.com
SIC: 3827 Microscopes, except electron, proton & corneal

(P-6877)
INTEVAC PHOTONICS INC (HQ)
3560 Bassett St, Santa Clara (95054-2704)
PHONE..................408 986-9888
Joseph Pietras III, *President*
Timothy Justyn, *Exec VP*
Kevin Barber, *Director*
EMP: 79 EST: 2008
SALES (est): 10.5MM **Publicly Held**
WEB: www.intevac.com
SIC: 3827 Optical instruments & lenses

(P-6878)
KLA CORPORATION (PA)
1 Technology Dr, Milpitas (95035-7916)
PHONE..................408 875-3000
Richard P Wallace, *President*
Edward W Barnholt, *Ch of Bd*
Bren D Higgins, *CFO*
Oreste Donzella, *Exec VP*
Brian Lorig, *Exec VP*
◆ EMP: 300 EST: 1975
SALES: 6.9B **Publicly Held**
WEB: www.kla-tencor.com
SIC: 3827 3825 7699 7629 Optical instruments & lenses; optical test & inspection equipment; semiconductor test equipment; optical instrument repair; electronic equipment repair

(P-6879)
LIGHT LABS INC
725 Shasta St, Redwood City (94063-2124)
PHONE..................650 257-8100
Dave Grannan, *CEO*
Tom Barone, *CFO*
Bradley Lautenbach, *Senior VP*
Sumit Chawla, *Vice Pres*
Harish Sarma, *Vice Pres*
EMP: 78
SALES (est): 21.8MM **Privately Held**
WEB: www.light.co
SIC: 3827 Optical instruments & lenses

(P-6880)
MICRO-VU CORP CALIFORNIA (PA)
7909 Conde Ln, Windsor (95492-9779)
PHONE..................707 838-6272
Edward P Amormino, *President*
Virginia Amormino, *Corp Secy*
Rebecca Pozzi, *Administration*
Jordan Reese, *Administration*
Kevin Johnson, *Project Engr*
◆ EMP: 79 EST: 1958
SQ FT: 60,000
SALES (est): 29MM **Privately Held**
WEB: www.microvu.com
SIC: 3827 Optical comparators

(P-6881)
OCLARO TECHNOLOGY INC
400 N Mccarthy Blvd, Milpitas (95035-9100)
PHONE..................408 383-1400
Greg Dougherty, *CEO*
Jim Haynes, *President*
Terry Unter, *COO*
Pete Mangan, *CFO*
Mike Fernicola, *Officer*
EMP: 800 EST: 1997
SALES (est): 255.4MM
SALES (corp-wide): 1.7B **Publicly Held**
WEB: www.oclaro.com
SIC: 3827 Optical instruments & lenses
HQ: Oclaro, Inc.
    400 N Mccarthy Blvd
    Milpitas CA 95035

(P-6882)
ONYX OPTICS INC
6551 Sierra Ln, Dublin (94568-2798)
PHONE..................925 833-1969
Helmuthe Meissner, *Ch of Bd*
David Meissner, *President*
Stephanie Meissner, *CEO*
Karen Meissner, *CFO*
Roberto Rodriguez, *Plant Mgr*
EMP: 15 EST: 1992
SQ FT: 8,500
SALES (est): 2.5MM **Privately Held**
WEB: www.onyxoptics.com
SIC: 3827 Optical instruments & lenses

(P-6883)
ORAYA THERAPEUTICS INC
3 Twin Dolphin Dr Ste 175, Redwood City (94065-5160)
P.O. Box 5122, Belmont (94002-5122)
PHONE..................510 456-3700
Jim Taylor, *President*
Michael Gertner, *Shareholder*
▲ EMP: 26 EST: 2007
SALES (est): 3.9MM **Privately Held**
WEB: www.zeiss.com
SIC: 3827 Optical instruments & lenses

(P-6884)
REDFERN INTEGRATED OPTICS INC
3350 Scott Blvd Bldg 1, Santa Clara (95054-3107)
PHONE..................408 970-3500
Larry Marshall, *CEO*
EMP: 20 EST: 2001
SALES (est): 3.4MM **Privately Held**
WEB: www.rio-lasers.com
SIC: 3827 Optical elements & assemblies, except ophthalmic
HQ: Optasense Holdings Limited
    Cody Technology Park
    Farnborough HANTS
    125 239-2000

(P-6885)
RVISION INC
2365 Paragon Dr Ste D, San Jose (95131-1335)
PHONE..................408 437-5777
Brian M Kelly, *President*
Ryan Wald, *President*
Robb Warwick, *Treasurer*
Daniel Spradling, *Admin Sec*
Lance Rosenzweig, *Director*
EMP: 20 EST: 1997
SQ FT: 11,000
SALES: 3.6MM
SALES (corp-wide): 4MM **Privately Held**
WEB: www.rvisionusa.com
SIC: 3827 3861 1731 5063 Optical instruments & lenses; cameras & related equipment; electrical work; electrical apparatus & equipment
PA: Industrial Security Alliance Partners, Inc.
    10350 Science Center Dr # 100
    San Diego CA 92121
    619 232-7041

(P-6886)
SIERRA PRECISION OPTICS INC
12830 Earhart Ave, Auburn (95602-9027)
PHONE..................530 885-6979
Michael Dorich, *CEO*
Eloise Dorich, *Admin Sec*
Shery Burr, *Purchasing*
Russ Lowe, *Marketing Staff*
EMP: 25 EST: 2001
SQ FT: 15,000
SALES (est): 4MM **Privately Held**
WEB: www.sierraoptics.com
SIC: 3827 Optical instruments & apparatus

(P-6887)
VSP LABS INC (PA)
Also Called: Vspone
3333 Quality Dr, Rancho Cordova (95670-7985)
PHONE..................866 569-8800
Donald E Oakley, *President*
Don Ball, *CFO*
EMP: 439 EST: 2009
SALES (est): 151MM **Privately Held**
WEB: www.vspglobal.com
SIC: 3827 5049 Optical instruments & lenses; optical goods

(P-6888)
ZYGO EPO
3900 Lakeside Dr, Richmond (94806-1963)
PHONE..................510 243-7592
EMP: 16 EST: 2011
SALES (est): 2.8MM **Privately Held**
SIC: 3827 Optical instruments & lenses

3829 Measuring & Controlling Devices, NEC

(P-6889)
ABAXIS INC (HQ)
3240 Whipple Rd, Union City (94587-1217)
PHONE..................510 675-6500
Clinton H Severson, *CEO*
Donald P Wood, *President*
Ross Taylor, *CFO*
Ilya Frumkin, *Vice Pres*
Gene Hart, *Vice Pres*
◆ EMP: 180 EST: 1989
SQ FT: 158,378
SALES: 244.7MM
SALES (corp-wide): 6.6B **Publicly Held**
WEB: www.abaxis.com
SIC: 3829 2835 Medical diagnostic systems, nuclear; in vitro & in vivo diagnostic substances
PA: Zoetis Inc.
    10 Sylvan Way
    Parsippany NJ 07054
    973 822-7000

(P-6890)
ACLARA BIOSCIENCES INC
Also Called: A Company In Development Stage
345 Oyster Point Blvd, South San Francisco (94080-1913)
PHONE..................800 297-2728
Thomas G Klopack, *CEO*
Thomas J Baruch, *Ch of Bd*
Jerry Rahon, *Director*
EMP: 24 EST: 1995
SQ FT: 44,000
SALES (est): 703.4K **Privately Held**
SIC: 3829 8731 3826 3821 Measuring & controlling devices; commercial physical research; analytical instruments; laboratory apparatus & furniture; chemical preparations

(P-6891)
ALL WEATHER INC
Also Called: AWI
1065 National Dr Ste 1, Sacramento (95834-1927)
PHONE..................916 928-1000
Jason Hall, *President*
Bob Perrin, *Exec VP*
Bartlomiej Klusek, *Software Engr*
Rajesh Kommu, *Software Engr*
Brian Porter, *Technician*
◆ EMP: 65 EST: 2000
SQ FT: 50,000
SALES (est): 20.1MM **Privately Held**
WEB: www.allweatherinc.com
SIC: 3829 8999 3674 Weather tracking equipment; weather related services; radiation sensors

(P-6892)
APPLIED PHYSICS SYSTEMS (PA)
Also Called: 2-G Enterprises
425 Clyde Ave, Mountain View (94043-2209)
PHONE..................650 965-0500
William Goodman, *President*
Maxwell Goodman, *Vice Pres*
Robert Goodman, *Vice Pres*
Dwayne Bakaas, *General Mgr*
Christine Goodman, *Admin Sec*
EMP: 111 EST: 1978
SALES (est): 22.9MM **Privately Held**
WEB: www.appliedphysics.com
SIC: 3829 8711 Magnetometers; consulting engineer

(P-6893)
ATMOS ENGINEERING INC
443 Dearborn Park Rd, Pescadero (94060-9706)
P.O. Box 807 (94060-0807)
PHONE..................650 879-1674
Rodger Reinhart, *President*
EMP: 16 EST: 1989
SALES (est): 226.6K **Privately Held**
WEB: www.atmos.com
SIC: 3829 Temperature sensors, except industrial process & aircraft

(P-6894)
AUTOMATIC CONTROL ENGRG CORP
Also Called: Johnson Contrls Authorized Dlr
20788 Corsair Blvd, Hayward (94545-1010)
P.O. Box 20788 (94546-8788)
PHONE..................510 293-6040
Robert Crowder, *CEO*
Stephen Crowder, *Vice Pres*
Wilson Lee, *Project Mgr*
Marc Davilla, *Technical Staff*
Alfred Espudo, *Project Engr*
EMP: 46 EST: 1975
SQ FT: 15,000
SALES (est): 7.4MM **Privately Held**
WEB: www.johnsoncontrols.com
SIC: 3829 5084 5075 Measuring & controlling devices; instruments & control equipment; warm air heating & air conditioning

(P-6895)
C&C BUILDING AUTOMATION CO INC
26062 Eden Landing Rd # 8, Hayward (94545-3712)
PHONE..................650 292-7450
Chuck Chavez, *Principal*
Sheran Jones, *Admin Asst*
Francisco Jauregui, *Design Engr*
Steve Roth, *Technology*
Cliff McIntire, *Engineer*
EMP: 25 EST: 2001

3829 - Measuring & Controlling Devices, NEC County (P-6896)

PRODUCTS & SERVICES SECTION

SALES (est): 5.3MM **Privately Held**
WEB: www.ccbac.com
SIC: 3829 Measuring & controlling devices

(P-6896)
CARROS SENSORS SYSTEMS CO LLC
Also Called: Systron Donner Inertial
355 Lennon Ln, Walnut Creek (94598-2475)
PHONE.....................925 979-4400
Victor Dragotti, *Design Engr*
David Hoyh, *Sales Dir*
Harry Angus, *Manager*
EMP: 438
SALES (corp-wide): 3B **Privately Held**
WEB: www.sensata.com
SIC: 3829 Measuring & controlling devices
HQ: Carros Sensors & Systems Company, Llc
1461 Lawrence Dr
Thousand Oaks CA 91320

(P-6897)
COMET TECHNOLOGIES USA INC
2360 Bering Dr, San Jose (95131-1121)
PHONE.....................408 325-8770
Paul Smith, *Manager*
Jose Cervantes, *Representative*
EMP: 205
SALES (corp-wide): 433.4MM **Privately Held**
WEB: www.comet-pct.com
SIC: 3829 Measuring & controlling devices
HQ: Comet Technologies Usa Inc.
100 Trap Falls Road Ext
Shelton CT 06484
203 447-3200

(P-6898)
DELTATRAK INC
1236 Doker Dr, Modesto (95351-1587)
PHONE.....................209 579-5343
Allen Hui, *Manager*
Brian Edwards, *Vice Pres*
Jeanne Solis, *Administration*
Jamil Ali, *Technician*
Charles Craig, *Engineer*
EMP: 50
SQ FT: 25,468 **Privately Held**
WEB: www.deltatrak.com
SIC: 3829 Temperature sensors, except industrial process & aircraft
PA: Deltatrak, Inc.
6801 Koll Center Pkwy # 120
Pleasanton CA 94566

(P-6899)
DELTATRAK INC (PA)
6801 Koll Center Pkwy # 120, Pleasanton (94566-7076)
P.O. Box 398 (94566-0039)
PHONE.....................925 249-2250
Frederick L Wu, *CEO*
Stephen Hibbs, *Vice Pres*
Cecilia Sun, *Vice Pres*
Charles Langbehn, *Engineer*
Michelle Alvino, *Business Mgr*
▲ **EMP:** 25 **EST:** 1989
SALES (est): 16.6MM **Privately Held**
WEB: www.deltatrak.com
SIC: 3829 3823 3822 Temperature sensors, except industrial process & aircraft; industrial instrmnts msrmnt display/control process variable; auto controls regulating residntl & coml environmt & applncs

(P-6900)
ET WATER SYSTEMS LLC
384 Bel Marin Keys Blvd, Novato (94949-5361)
PHONE.....................415 945-9383
Bruce J Cardinal,
Tyler Schien, *Opers Mgr*
Daniel Martinez, *Sales Staff*
David Curtis,
▲ **EMP:** 28 **EST:** 2002
SALES (est): 3.1MM **Privately Held**
WEB: www.jainsusa.com
SIC: 3829 Measuring & controlling devices

(P-6901)
FITBIT LLC (DH)
199 Fremont St Fl 14, San Francisco (94105-2253)
PHONE.....................415 513-1000
James Park, *Ch of Bd*
Stephen Shaw, *Owner*
Lori Huss, *Partner*
Ronald W Kisling, *CFO*
Steven Murray, *Bd of Directors*
EMP: 1611 **EST:** 2007
SQ FT: 260,000
SALES: 1.4B
SALES (corp-wide): 182.5B **Publicly Held**
WEB: www.fitbit.com
SIC: 3829 Measuring & controlling devices
HQ: Google Llc
1600 Amphitheatre Pkwy
Mountain View CA 94043
650 253-0000

(P-6902)
FOUR D IMAGING
808 Gilman St, Berkeley (94710-1422)
PHONE.....................510 290-3533
Glen Stevick, *President*
EMP: 15 **EST:** 2004
SALES (est): 293.8K **Privately Held**
WEB: www.4dimaging.com
SIC: 3829 Measuring & controlling devices

(P-6903)
GEOMETRICS INC
2190 Fortune Dr, San Jose (95131-1815)
PHONE.....................408 428-4244
Mark Prouty, *President*
Rod Bravo, *CFO*
Bart Hoekstra, *Vice Pres*
Craig Lippus, *Vice Pres*
Ron Royal, *Vice Pres*
EMP: 80 **EST:** 1969
SALES (est): 22.1MM **Privately Held**
WEB: www.geometrics.com
SIC: 3829 Geophysical or meteorological electronic equipment
HQ: Oyo Corporation U.S.A.
245 N Carmelo Ave Ste 101
Pasadena CA 91107

(P-6904)
GUNNEBO ENTRANCE CONTROL INC (HQ)
Also Called: Omega Turnstiles
535 Getty Ct Ste F, Benicia (94510-1179)
PHONE.....................707 748-0885
John Haining, *CEO*
Susanne Larsson, *CFO*
Janet Button, *Executive*
Laurie Mugride, *General Mgr*
Jenifer Babbitt, *Admin Sec*
▲ **EMP:** 17 **EST:** 2001
SQ FT: 20,000
SALES (est): 4.7MM
SALES (corp-wide): 492.5MM **Privately Held**
WEB: www.gunnebo.com.us
SIC: 3829 Automatic turnstiles & related apparatus
PA: Gunnebo Ab
Johan Pa Gardas Gata 7
Goteborg 412 5
102 095-000

(P-6905)
HIGHLAND TECHNOLOGY
650 Potrero Ave, San Francisco (94110-2117)
PHONE.....................415 551-1700
John Larkin, *President*
Denise Thiry, *Shareholder*
Hugh Callahan, *Vice Pres*
Elizabeth Larkin, *Vice Pres*
Rebecca McKee, *Admin Sec*
EMP: 20 **EST:** 1984
SQ FT: 6,000
SALES (est): 3.1MM **Privately Held**
WEB: www.highlandtechnology.com
SIC: 3829 Measuring & controlling devices

(P-6906)
KALILA MEDICAL INC
1400 Dell Ave Ste C, Campbell (95008-6620)
PHONE.....................408 819-5175
Joshua Hagerman, *Surgery Dir*
EMP: 25 **EST:** 2011
SQ FT: 12,536
SALES (est): 900K **Privately Held**
WEB: www.terumomedical.com
SIC: 3829 Thermometers, including digital; clinical
HQ: Terumo Americas Holding, Inc.
265 Davidson Ave Ste 320
Somerset NJ 08873
732 302-4900

(P-6907)
KWJ ENGINEERING INC (PA)
Also Called: Eco Sensors
8430 Central Ave Ste C, Newark (94560-3457)
PHONE.....................510 794-4296
Joseph R Stetter, *President*
Edward F Stetter, *CFO*
Tasneem Ali, *Admin Asst*
Mel Findlay, *Senior Engr*
Bennett Meulendyk, *Senior Engr*
EMP: 20 **EST:** 1993
SQ FT: 10,000
SALES (est): 5.7MM **Privately Held**
WEB: www.kwjengineering.com
SIC: 3829 5084 Gas detectors; instruments & control equipment

(P-6908)
LEICA GEOSYSTEMS HDS LLC
5000 Executive Pkwy # 500, San Ramon (94583-4210)
PHONE.....................925 790-2300
Kem Mooyman,
EMP: 61 **EST:** 2000
SQ FT: 25,000
SALES (est): 12.6MM
SALES (corp-wide): 4.5B **Privately Held**
WEB: www.leica-geosystems.com
SIC: 3829 Measuring & controlling devices
HQ: Leica Geosystems Ag
Heinrich-Wild-Strasse 201
Heerbrugg SG 9435
717 273-131

(P-6909)
MARATHON PRODUCTS INCORPORATED
14500 Doolittle Dr, San Leandro (94577-6615)
P.O. Box 21579, Piedmont (94620-1579)
PHONE.....................510 562-6450
Jon Nakagawa, *President*
Kevin Flynn, *Vice Pres*
▲ **EMP:** 26 **EST:** 1991
SALES (est): 3.2MM **Privately Held**
WEB: www.marathonproducts.com
SIC: 3829 Temperature sensors, except industrial process & aircraft

(P-6910)
METTLER-TOLEDO RAININ LLC (HQ)
7500 Edgewater Dr, Oakland (94621-3027)
PHONE.....................510 564-1600
Gerhard Keller, *General Mgr*
Olivier Filliol, *CEO*
Henri Chahine, *COO*
Shawn Vadala, *CFO*
David Greenwood, *IT/INT Sup*
▲ **EMP:** 120 **EST:** 1963
SQ FT: 55,000
SALES (est): 95.2MM
SALES (corp-wide): 3B **Publicly Held**
WEB: www.mt.com
SIC: 3829 3821 Measuring & controlling devices; pipettes, hemocytometer
PA: Mettler-Toledo International Inc.
1900 Polaris Pkwy Fl 6
Columbus OH 43240
614 438-4511

(P-6911)
MICRO-METRIC INC
1050 Commercial St, San Jose (95112-1419)
PHONE.....................408 452-8505
Fax: 408 452-8412
EMP: 15
SQ FT: 6,500

SALES (est): 3.2MM **Privately Held**
WEB: www.micro-metric.com
SIC: 3829 7699 8734 Mfg Measuring/Controlling Devices Repair Services Testing Laboratory

(P-6912)
MIRION TECHNOLOGIES INC (PA)
3000 Executive Pkwy # 518, San Ramon (94583-4355)
PHONE.....................925 543-0800
John Viscovic, *CEO*
Michael Flynn, *CFO*
Mike Brumbaugh, *Exec VP*
Seth Rosen, *Exec VP*
Mike Edelman, *Vice Pres*
EMP: 158 **EST:** 2005
SQ FT: 10,300
SALES (est): 558.1MM **Privately Held**
WEB: www.mirion.com
SIC: 3829 Measuring & controlling devices

(P-6913)
NOAH MEDICAL CORPORATION
1501 Industrial Rd, San Carlos (94070-4111)
PHONE.....................718 564-3717
Jian Zhang, *CEO*
Emma Yang, *Finance*
EMP: 75 **EST:** 2018
SALES (est): 6MM **Privately Held**
WEB: www.noahmed.com
SIC: 3829 Medical diagnostic systems, nuclear

(P-6914)
OUSTER INC (PA)
350 Treat Ave Ste 1, San Francisco (94110-1948)
PHONE.....................415 949-0108
Charles Pacala, *CEO*
Susan Heystee, *Ch of Bd*
Mark Frichtl, *COO*
Oliver Hutaff, *CFO*
Wil Selby, *Project Mgr*
EMP: 84 **EST:** 2015
SALES (est): 10.7MM **Privately Held**
WEB: www.ouster.com
SIC: 3829 Surveying instruments & accessories

(P-6915)
PACIFIC INSTRUMENTS INC
4080 Pike Ln, Concord (94520-1227)
PHONE.....................925 827-9010
John Hueckel, *President*
Norm Hueckel, *Vice Pres*
Timothy Pellegrini, *Engineer*
Patrick Rule, *Manager*
▲ **EMP:** 21 **EST:** 1966
SQ FT: 18,000
SALES (est): 5.7MM
SALES (corp-wide): 269.8MM **Publicly Held**
WEB: www.pacificinstruments.com
SIC: 3829 Measuring & controlling devices
HQ: Vishay Precision Israel Ltd
26 Harokmim, Entrance
Holon 58858

(P-6916)
PETASENSE INC
860 Hillview Ct Ste 150, Milpitas (95035-4570)
PHONE.....................650 336-0480
Arun Santhebennur, *COO*
Abhinav Khushraj, *CEO*
Zach Shelby, *Vice Pres*
Ken Madsen, *Executive*
Kuldeep Amarnath, *CTO*
EMP: 20 **EST:** 2015
SALES (est): 2.9MM **Privately Held**
WEB: www.petasense.com
SIC: 3829 Accelerometers

(P-6917)
PROMEGA BSYSTEMS SUNNYVALE INC
3945 Freedom Cir Ste 200, Santa Clara (95054-1264)
PHONE.....................408 636-2400
William A Linton, *Principal*
Ivan Ivanov, *Manager*
Sean Woods, *Manager*

▲ = Import ▼ = Export
◆ = Import/Export

PRODUCTS & SERVICES SECTION

3841 - Surgical & Medical Instrs & Apparatus County (P-6936)

EMP: 27 EST: 2002
SQ FT: 20,000
SALES (est): 1.6MM
SALES (corp-wide): 487.9MM Privately Held
WEB: www.promega.com
SIC: 3829 Measuring & controlling devices
PA: Promega Corporation
    2800 Woods Hollow Rd
    Fitchburg WI 53711
    608 274-4330

(P-6918)
RAE SYSTEMS INC (DH)
1349 Moffett Park Dr, Sunnyvale (94089-1134)
PHONE.................................408 952-8200
Robert Chen, *President*
Christopher Toney, *COOO*
Michael Hansen, *CFO*
Ming Ting Tang PHD, *Exec VP*
Thomas N Gre, *Vice Pres*
▲ EMP: 700 EST: 1991
SQ FT: 67,000
SALES (est): 104.3MM
SALES (corp-wide): 32.6B Publicly Held
WEB: www.honeywell.com
SIC: 3829 3812 3699 Gas detectors; search & detection systems & instruments; security control equipment & systems
HQ: Honeywell Analytics Inc.
    405 Barclay Blvd
    Lincolnshire IL 60069
    847 955-8200

(P-6919)
SACRAMENTO COOLING SYSTEMS INC
5466 E Lamona Ave # 1022, Fresno (93727-2359)
PHONE.................................559 253-9660
Kevin Castle, *President*
EMP: 17
SALES (corp-wide): 11.9MM Privately Held
WEB: www.lhairco.com
SIC: 3829 Measuring & controlling devices
PA: Sacramento Cooling Systems, Inc.
    2530 Warren Dr
    Rocklin CA 95677
    916 677-1000

(P-6920)
SECO MANUFACTURING COMPANY INC
4155 Oasis Rd, Redding (96003-0859)
PHONE.................................530 225-8155
Steven W Berglund, *CEO*
Mike Dahl, *General Mgr*
Mike Copeland, *Manager*
▲ EMP: 120
SQ FT: 73,400
SALES (est): 31.8MM
SALES (corp-wide): 3.2B Publicly Held
WEB: www.surveying.com
SIC: 3829 Surveying instruments & accessories
PA: Trimble Inc.
    935 Stewart Dr
    Sunnyvale CA 94085
    408 481-8000

(P-6921)
SIERRA MONITOR CORPORATION (HQ)
1991 Tarob Ct, Milpitas (95035-6840)
PHONE.................................408 262-6611
Nishan J Vartanian, *President*
Steve Shaw, *Vice Pres*
▲ EMP: 56 EST: 1967
SQ FT: 28,000
SALES: 22MM
SALES (corp-wide): 1.3B Publicly Held
WEB: www.us.msasafety.com
SIC: 3829 3822 Measuring & controlling devices; auto controls regulating residntl & coml environmt & applncs
PA: Msa Safety Incorporated
    1000 Cranberry Woods Dr
    Cranberry Township PA 16066
    724 776-8600

(P-6922)
SOLANO DIAGNOSTICS IMAGING
1101 B Gale Wilson Blvd # 100, Fairfield (94533-3771)
PHONE.................................707 646-4646
Adrian Ritts, *Manager*
Laverna Hubbard, *Administration*
EMP: 44 EST: 1990
SQ FT: 4,000
SALES (est): 5.3MM Privately Held
WEB: www.northbay.org
SIC: 3829 8071 8011 Medical diagnostic systems, nuclear; medical laboratories; radiologist

(P-6923)
SOLMETRIC CORPORATION
Also Called: Suneye
117 Morris St Ste 100, Sebastopol (95472-3846)
PHONE.................................707 823-4600
Macdonald Willand, *President*
Robert Macdonald, *VP Finance*
▲ EMP: 94 EST: 2006
SALES (est): 15.2MM Publicly Held
WEB: www.solmetric.com
SIC: 3829 Solarimeters
HQ: Vivint Solar, Inc.
    1800 W Ashton Blvd
    Lehi UT 84043
    877 404-4129

(P-6924)
SPECTRAL DYNAMICS INC (PA)
2199 Zanker Rd, San Jose (95131-2109)
PHONE.................................760 761-0440
Stewart J Slykhous, *CEO*
James D Tucker, *CFO*
Rick Ellis, *Engineer*
Tony Keller, *Sales Mgr*
▲ EMP: 20 EST: 1988
SQ FT: 12,000
SALES (est): 7.9MM Privately Held
WEB: www.spectraldynamics.com
SIC: 3829 Measuring & controlling devices

(P-6925)
TELEDYNE DGITAL IMAGING US INC
Also Called: Teledyne RAD-Iccn Imaging
765 Sycamore Dr, Milpitas (95035-7465)
PHONE.................................408 736-6000
EMP: 15
SALES (corp-wide): 3B Publicly Held
WEB: www.photometrics.com
SIC: 3829 3674 Measuring & controlling devices; semiconductors & related devices
HQ: Teledyne Digital Imaging Us, Inc.
    700 Technology Park Dr # 2
    Billerica MA 01821
    978 670-2000

(P-6926)
THERM-X OF CALIFORNIA INC (HQ)
3200 Investment Blvd, Hayward (94545-3807)
P.O. Box 768, Alamo (94507-0768)
PHONE.................................510 441-7566
Dan Trujillo, *CEO*
Skip Johnson, *President*
Linda Trujillo, *Corp Secy*
Chris Moe, *Technician*
Hazeleen Carpio, *Engineer*
EMP: 229 EST: 1976
SQ FT: 74,300
SALES (est): 72.2MM
SALES (corp-wide): 3.1B Privately Held
WEB: www.therm-x.com
SIC: 3829 Measuring & controlling devices
PA: Nibe Industrier Ab
    Jarnvagsgatan 40
    Markaryd 285 3
    433 730-00

(P-6927)
TOPCON POSITIONING SYSTEMS INC (DH)
7400 National Dr, Livermore (94550-7340)
PHONE.................................925 245-8300
Raymond O'Connor, *President*
Mick Yamazaki, *COO*
David Mudrick, *CFO*
Philip Thach, *CFO*
Cindy Hudson, *Exec VP*
◆ EMP: 122
SQ FT: 80,000
SALES (est): 125.2MM Privately Held
WEB: www.topconpositioning.com
SIC: 3829 3625 3823 3699 Surveying instruments & accessories; relays & industrial controls; industrial instrmnts msrmnt display/control process variable; electrical equipment & supplies; surveying services; excavation work
HQ: Topcon America Corporation
    111 Bauer Dr
    Oakland NJ 07436
    201 599-5100

(P-6928)
TRIMBLE INC (PA)
935 Stewart Dr, Sunnyvale (94085-3913)
PHONE.................................408 481-8000
Robert G Painter, *President*
Ulf J Johansson, *Ch of Bd*
Nickolas V Steeg, *Vice Chairman*
Annamarie Curry, *Officer*
Jaime Nielsen, *Officer*
◆ EMP: 750 EST: 1978
SQ FT: 139,000
SALES (est): 3.2B Publicly Held
WEB: www.trimble.com
SIC: 3829 3812 Measuring & controlling devices; navigational systems & instruments

(P-6929)
VISBY MEDICAL INC
3010 N 1st St, San Jose (95134-2023)
PHONE.................................408 650-8878
Adam De La Zerda, *CEO*
Thomas Prescott, *Ch of Bd*
Teresa Abraham, *General Mgr*
Jonathan Hong, *Opers Staff*
EMP: 100 EST: 2012
SALES (est): 22.4MM Privately Held
WEB: www.visbymedical.com
SIC: 3829 Medical diagnostic systems, nuclear

3841 Surgical & Medical Instrs & Apparatus

(P-6930)
ABBOTT LABORATORIES
Also Called: Abbott Diagnostics Division
4551 Great America Pkwy, Santa Clara (95054-1208)
PHONE.................................408 330-0057
Jim Janik, *Branch Mgr*
Savuth Vann, *Technician*
Joe Melnick, *Research*
Paul Nguyen, *Technical Staff*
Scott Shoffner, *Engineer*
EMP: 450
SQ FT: 117,500
SALES (corp-wide): 34.6B Publicly Held
WEB: www.abbott.com
SIC: 3841 Medical instruments & equipment, blood & bone work
PA: Abbott Laboratories
    100 Abbott Park Rd
    Abbott Park IL 60064
    224 667-6100

(P-6931)
ABBOTT LABORATORIES
Also Called: Abbott Vascular
3200 Lakeside Dr, Santa Clara (95054-2807)
P.O. Box 58167 (95052-8167)
PHONE.................................408 845-3000
Jean Reyda, *Branch Mgr*
Elizabeth Cushman, *President*
Alexey Nepogodiev, *Division VP*
Neil Moat, *Vice Pres*
Jeff Buchmann, *Executive*
EMP: 750
SALES (corp-wide): 34.6B Publicly Held
WEB: www.abbott.com
SIC: 3841 8731 Surgical & medical instruments; commercial physical research
PA: Abbott Laboratories
    100 Abbott Park Rd
    Abbott Park IL 60064
    224 667-6100

(P-6932)
ABBOTT VASCULAR INC (HQ)
3200 Lakeside Dr, Santa Clara (95054-2807)
PHONE.................................408 845-3000
John M Capek, *President*
Charles D Foltz, *CEO*
Mark Murray, *CFO*
Nikhil Tundwal, *Area Mgr*
Chris Kinsey, *Admin Asst*
▲ EMP: 1429 EST: 1995
SQ FT: 370,000
SALES (est): 701.6MM
SALES (corp-wide): 34.6B Publicly Held
WEB: www.cardiovascular.abbott
SIC: 3841 Surgical & medical instruments
PA: Abbott Laboratories
    100 Abbott Park Rd
    Abbott Park IL 60064
    224 667-6100

(P-6933)
ACCESS CLOSURE INC
5452 Betsy Ross Dr, Santa Clara (95054-1101)
PHONE.................................408 610-6500
Gregory D Casciaro, *President*
John J Buckley, *CFO*
Susan Aloyan, *Exec VP*
Stephen Mackinnon, *Vice Pres*
Ariel Sutton, *Vice Pres*
EMP: 344 EST: 2002
SQ FT: 40,000
SALES (est): 54.1MM
SALES (corp-wide): 152.9B Publicly Held
WEB: www.cardinalhealth.com
SIC: 3841 Surgical & medical instruments
PA: Cardinal Health, Inc.
    7000 Cardinal Pl
    Dublin OH 43017
    614 757-5000

(P-6934)
ACCURAY INCORPORATED (PA)
1310 Chesapeake Ter, Sunnyvale (94089-1100)
PHONE.................................408 716-4600
Joshua H Levine, *President*
Louis J Lavigne Jr, *Ch of Bd*
Elizabeth Davila, *Vice Chairman*
Andy Kirkpatrick, *COO*
Shigeyuki Hamamatsu, *CFO*
▲ EMP: 117 EST: 1992
SQ FT: 124,000
SALES: 396.2MM Publicly Held
WEB: www.accuray.com
SIC: 3841 Surgical instruments & apparatus

(P-6935)
ADVANCEDCATH TECHNOLOGIES LLC (HQ)
176 Component Dr, San Jose (95131-1119)
PHONE.................................408 433-9505
Randall Sword, *CEO*
Lucian Bejinariu, *Vice Pres*
Nitin Mathur, *Vice Pres*
Chris Mikkelson, *Engineer*
Amy Tran, *Accountant*
EMP: 32 EST: 2013
SALES (est): 35MM
SALES (corp-wide): 12.1B Privately Held
WEB: www.te.com
SIC: 3841 Catheters
PA: Te Connectivity Ltd.
    Muhlenstrasse 26
    Schaffhausen SH 8200
    526 336-677

(P-6936)
AEGEA MEDICAL INC
4055 Campbell Ave, Menlo Park (94025-1006)
PHONE.................................650 701-1125
Maria Sainz, *CEO*
Connie Rey, *Vice Pres*
Don Gurskis, *CTO*
Micah Harris, *Director*
EMP: 21 EST: 2007
SALES (est): 6.2MM
SALES (corp-wide): 2.4B Publicly Held
WEB: www.maratreatment.com
SIC: 3841 Surgical & medical instruments

3841 - Surgical & Medical Instrs & Apparatus County (P-6937)

HQ: Coopersurgical, Inc.
95 Corporate Dr
Trumbull CT 06611

(P-6937)
ALEYEGN INC (PA)
23600 Big Basin Way, Saratoga
(95070-9755)
PHONE............................301 758-2949
Michael Ballard, *President*
Satish Herekar, *Principal*
EMP: 72 **EST:** 2015
SALES (est): 202.2K **Privately Held**
WEB: www.aleyegn.com
SIC: 3841 3845 Surgical lasers; laser systems & equipment, medical

(P-6938)
ALLAY THERAPEUTICS INC
4040 Campbell Ave Ste 110, Menlo Park
(94025-1053)
PHONE............................650 514-6284
Adam Gridley, *CEO*
EMP: 28 **EST:** 2016
SALES (est): 2.5MM **Privately Held**
SIC: 3841 8733 Surgical & medical instruments; noncommercial research organizations

(P-6939)
ALPINE BIOMED CORP
1501 Industrial Rd, San Carlos
(94070-4111)
PHONE............................650 802-0400
James B Hawkins, *President*
EMP: 86 **EST:** 1994
SQ FT: 1,460
SALES (est): 9.8MM
SALES (corp-wide): 415.6MM **Publicly Held**
WEB: www.natus.com
SIC: 3841 Catheters
PA: Natus Medical Incorporated
6701 Koll Center Pkwy # 12
Pleasanton CA 94566
925 223-6700

(P-6940)
AMEDICA BIOTECH INC
28301 Industrial Blvd K, Hayward
(94545-4429)
PHONE............................510 785-5980
▲ **EMP:** 17
SALES (est): 1.7MM
SALES (corp-wide): 27.3B **Publicly Held**
WEB: www.amedicabiotech.com
SIC: 3841 8731 Mfg Surgical/Medical Instruments Commercial Physical Research
HQ: Alere Inc.
51 Sawyer Rd Ste 200
Waltham MA 02453
781 647-3900

(P-6941)
AMERICAN MSTR TECH SCNTFIC INC
Also Called: American Histology Reagent Co
1330 Thurman St, Lodi (95240-3145)
P.O. Box 2539 (95241-2539)
PHONE............................209 368-4031
Dan Eckert, *CEO*
Brandon B Jones, *President*
Kameron Teyes, *COO*
Jeff Kupp, *CFO*
Judy Masciasini, *Mktg Dir*
▲ **EMP:** 126 **EST:** 1979
SQ FT: 25,000
SALES (est): 17.1MM
SALES (corp-wide): 84.6MM **Privately Held**
WEB: www.statlab.com
SIC: 3841 2835 Medical instruments & equipment, blood & bone work; cytology & histology diagnostic agents
PA: Slmp, Llc
2090 Commerce Dr
Mckinney TX 75069
972 436-1010

(P-6942)
ANCORA HEART INC
4001 Burton Dr, Santa Clara (95054-1585)
PHONE............................408 727-1105
Jeffrey M Closs, *President*
Russel Sampson, *Officer*
Russ Sampson, *Vice Pres*
Linda Lu, *Finance*
Joni Cronin, *Manager*
EMP: 50 **EST:** 2002
SALES (est): 7.5MM **Privately Held**
WEB: www.gdsmed.com
SIC: 3841 Diagnostic apparatus, medical

(P-6943)
APPLIED SCIENCE INC (PA)
983 Golden Gate Ter, Grass Valley
(95945-5938)
PHONE............................530 273-8299
Jonathan G Morgan, *Director*
Thomas Vick, *Purchasing*
Tom Vick, *Purchasing*
Dale Richardson, *VP Sales*
◆ **EMP:** 15 **EST:** 1991
SQ FT: 6,200
SALES (est): 3.8MM **Privately Held**
WEB: www.applied-science.com
SIC: 3841 Surgical & medical instruments

(P-6944)
ARSTASIS INC
6500 Kaiser Dr Ste 120, Fremont
(94555-3662)
PHONE............................650 508-1549
David I Bruce, *CEO*
Alex Arrow, *CFO*
Richard G Castro, *Senior VP*
Michael McNulty, *Vice Pres*
D Bruce Modesitt, *CTO*
EMP: 15 **EST:** 2004
SQ FT: 61,000
SALES (est): 825.6K **Privately Held**
WEB: www.arstasis.com
SIC: 3841 5047 Surgical & medical instruments; medical equipment & supplies; medical laboratory equipment

(P-6945)
ASTERO BIO CORPORATION
3475 Edison Way Ste A, Menlo Park
(94025-1821)
PHONE............................800 749-0898
EMP: 42
SALES (est): 113.7K **Publicly Held**
WEB: www.biolifesolutions.com
SIC: 3841 Manufactures Surgical/Medical Instruments
PA: Biolife Solutions, Inc.
3303 Mnte Vlla Pkwy Ste 3
Bothell WA 98021

(P-6946)
ATHELAS INC
10209 Danube Dr, Cupertino (95014-2141)
PHONE............................408 603-1954
Tanay Tandon, *CEO*
EMP: 23 **EST:** 2016
SALES (est): 5.2MM **Privately Held**
WEB: www.athelas.com
SIC: 3841 Diagnostic apparatus, medical

(P-6947)
AURIS HEALTH INC (DH)
150 Shoreline Dr, Redwood City
(94065-1400)
PHONE............................650 610-0750
Frederic Moll, *CEO*
David M Styka, *CFO*
Josh Defonzo, *Officer*
Dan Bradford, *VP Opers*
EMP: 100 **EST:** 2007
SALES (est): 59MM
SALES (corp-wide): 82.5B **Publicly Held**
WEB: www.aurishealth.com
SIC: 3841 Surgical & medical instruments
HQ: Ethicon Inc.
1000 Route 202
Raritan NJ 08869
732 524-0400

(P-6948)
AVAIL MEDSYSTEMS INC
2953 Bunker Hill Ln # 101, Santa Clara
(95054-1131)
PHONE............................650 772-1529
Daniel Hawkins, *CEO*
EMP: 20 **EST:** 2012
SALES (est): 2.8MM **Privately Held**
WEB: www.avail.io
SIC: 3841 Surgical & medical instruments

(P-6949)
AVANTEC VASCULAR CORPORATION
870 Hermosa Ave, Sunnyvale
(94085-4104)
PHONE............................408 329-5400
Kiminori Toda, *CEO*
Motasim Sirhan, *President*
Jim Shy, *Vice Pres*
Nat Bowditch, *Principal*
Marsha Tran, *Human Res Mgr*
▲ **EMP:** 35 **EST:** 1999 **Privately Held**
WEB: www.avantecvascular.com
SIC: 3841 Medical instruments & equipment, blood & bone work

(P-6950)
AVINGER INC
400 Chesapeake Dr, Redwood City
(94063-4739)
PHONE............................650 241-7900
James G Cullen, *Ch of Bd*
Jeffrey M Soinski, *President*
Mark Weinswig, *CFO*
Philip Preuss, *Vice Pres*
Jeff Miller, *Planning*
EMP: 65 **EST:** 2007
SQ FT: 44,200
SALES (est): 8.7MM **Privately Held**
WEB: www.avinger.com
SIC: 3841 Catheters

(P-6951)
BARRX MEDICAL INC
Also Called: Covidien
540 Oakmead Pkwy, Sunnyvale
(94085-4022)
PHONE............................408 328-7300
Vafa Jamali, *Vice Pres*
Richard Short, *President*
Kevin Cordell, *Vice Pres*
William Dippel, *Vice Pres*
Robert Haggerty, *Vice Pres*
EMP: 94 **EST:** 2003
SQ FT: 19,000
SALES (est): 13.9MM **Privately Held**
WEB: www.barrx.com
SIC: 3841 Surgical & medical instruments
HQ: Covidien Limited
1st Floor
Dublin

(P-6952)
BECTON DICKINSON AND COMPANY
Bd Biosciences
2350 Qume Dr, San Jose (95131-1812)
PHONE............................408 432-9475
William Rhodes, *Principal*
Donna Boles, *Vice Pres*
Karthik Ranganathan, *Vice Pres*
Mark Yale, *Surgery Dir*
Rasheedia Aigoro, *Associate Dir*
EMP: 332
SALES (corp-wide): 17.1B **Publicly Held**
WEB: www.bd.com
SIC: 3841 3826 2899 2835 Surgical & medical instruments; analytical instruments; chemical preparations; in vitro & in vivo diagnostic substances
PA: Becton, Dickinson And Company
1 Becton Dr
Franklin Lakes NJ 07417
201 847-6800

(P-6953)
BENTEC MEDICAL OPCO LLC
1380 E Beamer St, Woodland
(95776-6003)
PHONE............................530 406-3333
JG Singh, *CEO*
Ralph Germscheid, *Vice Pres*
Chris Mazelin, *Business Dir*
Jerry Bravo, *Engineer*
Cheryl Shimek, *Marketing Staff*
EMP: 50 **EST:** 2016
SALES (est): 7.1MM **Privately Held**
WEB: www.bentecmed.com
SIC: 3841 Surgical & medical instruments

(P-6954)
BIOCARE MEDICAL LLC
60 Berry Dr, Pacheco (94553-5601)
PHONE............................925 603-8000
Luis De Luzuriaga, *CEO*
Jamie Conroy, *CFO*
Nicolas Barthelemy, *Chairman*
Eric Stewart, *VP Bus Dvlpt*
Thomas Barnaba, *Executive*
▼ **EMP:** 154 **EST:** 1997
SQ FT: 51,000
SALES (est): 61.2MM **Privately Held**
WEB: www.biocare.net
SIC: 3841 2835 5047 Diagnostic apparatus, medical; in vitro & in vivo diagnostic substances; diagnostic equipment, medical

(P-6955)
BIOCHECK INC (HQ)
425 Eccles Ave, South San Francisco
(94080-1902)
PHONE............................650 573-1968
Roy Paxton Yih, *CEO*
EMP: 100 **EST:** 1996
SQ FT: 7,000
SALES (est): 56.4MM **Privately Held**
WEB: www.biocheckinc.com
SIC: 3841 5047 Diagnostic apparatus, medical; diagnostic equipment, medical

(P-6956)
BIOGENEX LABORATORIES (PA)
48810 Kato Rd Ste 200, Fremont
(94538-7311)
PHONE............................510 824-1400
Krishan Lal Kalra, *CEO*
Sunil Aggarwal, *Research*
Ajay Kumar, *Financial Analy*
Ajay Kumar Valluri, *Finance*
Jason Nguyen, *Prdtn Mgr*
◆ **EMP:** 24 **EST:** 1981
SALES (est): 8.5MM **Privately Held**
WEB: www.biogenex.com
SIC: 3841 2835 8731 2819 Diagnostic apparatus, medical; cytology & histology diagnostic agents; commercial physical research; chemicals, reagent grade: refined from technical grade

(P-6957)
BIOTRICITY INC
275 Shoreline Dr Ste 150, Redwood City
(94065-1494)
PHONE............................650 832-1626
Waqaas Al-Siddiq, *CEO*
Alice Gaber, *CEO*
Spencer Ladow, *Vice Pres*
Chad Isbell, *Business Dir*
EMP: 25 **EST:** 2016
SALES (est): 3.3MM **Privately Held**
WEB: www.biotricity.com
SIC: 3841 Surgical & medical instruments

(P-6958)
BLOOMLIFE INC
181 2nd St, San Francisco (94105-3808)
PHONE............................415 215-4251
Eric Dy, *CEO*
Julian Penders, *COO*
EMP: 20 **EST:** 2014
SALES (est): 1.8MM **Privately Held**
WEB: www.bloomlife.com
SIC: 3841 7389 Surgical & medical instruments;

(P-6959)
CARDIVA MEDICAL INC
1615 Wyatt Dr, Santa Clara (95054-1587)
PHONE............................408 470-7100
John Russell, *President*
Rick Anderson, *Ch of Bd*
Glenn Foy, *President*
Malcolm Farnsworth, *CFO*
Randy Hubbell, *Officer*
EMP: 135 **EST:** 2002
SALES (est): 31.2MM
SALES (corp-wide): 988.4MM **Publicly Held**
WEB: www.cardivamedical.com
SIC: 3841 Surgical & medical instruments
PA: Haemonetics Corporation
125 Summer St
Boston MA 02110
781 848-7100

▲ = Import ▼ = Export
◆ = Import/Export

PRODUCTS & SERVICES SECTION

3841 - Surgical & Medical Instrs & Apparatus County (P-6983)

(P-6960)
CARL ZEISS OPHTHALMIC SYSTEMS
5300 Central Pkwy, Dublin (94568-4999)
PHONE.................................925 557-4100
Lothar Coob, *President*
EMP: 27 **EST:** 2000
SALES (est): 438.9K **Privately Held**
SIC: 3841 Medical instruments & equipment, blood & bone work

(P-6961)
CETERIX ORTHOPAEDICS INC
6500 Kaiser Dr Ste 120, Fremont (94555-3662)
PHONE.................................650 241-1748
John McCutcheon, *President*
Michael Hendricksen, *COO*
Justin Saliman, *Chief Mktg Ofcr*
Patty Perla, *Human Resources*
Mark Saxton, *VP Sls/Mktg*
EMP: 28 **EST:** 2010
SALES (est): 7.7MM
SALES (corp-wide): 4.5B **Privately Held**
WEB: www.smith-nephew.com
SIC: 3841 Surgical instruments & apparatus
PA: Smith & Nephew Plc
  Building 5, Croxley Park
  Watford HERTS WD18
  800 015-7573

(P-6962)
CIRTEC MEDICAL CORP
101b Cooper Ct, Los Gatos (95032-7604)
PHONE.................................408 395-0443
Michael Forman, *Branch Mgr*
Asheesh Divetia, *General Mgr*
Richard Nicolas, *General Mgr*
Jeffrey Gariepy, *Technician*
Carl Bauer, *Engineer*
EMP: 60
SALES (corp-wide): 200MM **Privately Held**
WEB: www.cirtecmed.com
SIC: 3841 Surgical & medical instruments
PA: Cirtec Medical Corp.
  9200 Xylon Ave N
  Brooklyn Park MN 55445
  763 493-8556

(P-6963)
COOPER MEDICAL INC (HQ)
6140 Stnrdge Mall Rd Ste, Pleasanton (94588)
PHONE.................................925 460-3600
Robert S Weiss, *CEO*
EMP: 100 **EST:** 2012
SALES (est): 184.1MM
SALES (corp-wide): 2.4B **Publicly Held**
WEB: www.coopercos.com
SIC: 3841 Medical instruments & equipment, blood & bone work
PA: The Cooper Companies Inc
  6101 Bollinger Canyon Rd # 5
  San Ramon CA 94583
  925 460-3600

(P-6964)
CORDIS CORPORATION
5452 Betsy Ross Dr, Santa Clara (95054-1101)
PHONE.................................408 273-3700
Thomas Gonchar, *Engineer*
Linda Husseini, *Marketing Mgr*
David Cepek, *Director*
EMP: 47
SALES (corp-wide): 728.4MM **Privately Held**
SIC: 3841 3842 Surgical & medical instruments; catheters; surgical appliances & supplies; implants, surgical
PA: Cordis Corporation
  7000 Cardinal Pl
  Dublin OH 43017
  408 273-3700

(P-6965)
COVIDIEN HOLDING INC
540 Oakmead Pkwy, Sunnyvale (94085-4022)
PHONE.................................408 585-7700
Jose E Almeida, *Chairman*
EMP: 125 **Privately Held**
SIC: 3841 Surgical & medical instruments
HQ: Covidien Holding Inc.
  710 Medtronic Pkwy
  Minneapolis MN 55432

(P-6966)
COVIDIEN HOLDING INC
6531 Dumbarton Cir, Fremont (94555-3619)
PHONE.................................510 456-1500
Duke Rohlen, *Branch Mgr*
EMP: 125 **Privately Held**
SIC: 3841 Surgical & medical instruments
HQ: Covidien Holding Inc.
  710 Medtronic Pkwy
  Minneapolis MN 55432

(P-6967)
CREDENCE MEDSYSTEMS INC
1430 Obrien Dr Ste D, Menlo Park (94025-1446)
PHONE.................................844 263-3797
Dr Frank Litvack, *Ch of Bd*
Jeff F Shanley, *President*
Jeff Tillack, *COO*
Mark Hassett, *Vice Pres*
Mina Leung, *Research*
EMP: 18 **EST:** 2013
SALES (est): 4.2MM **Privately Held**
WEB: www.credencemed.com
SIC: 3841 Surgical & medical instruments; hypodermic needles & syringes

(P-6968)
CREGANNA MEDICAL DEVICES INC (DH)
Also Called: Creganna-Tactx Medical
1353 Dell Ave, Campbell (95008-6609)
PHONE.................................408 364-7100
Robert Bell Hance, *CEO*
Helen Ryan, *President*
Padraic Clarke, *CFO*
Richard Leyden, *Admin Sec*
Brian Bechtold, *Technician*
EMP: 40 **EST:** 2007
SALES (est): 65.4MM
SALES (corp-wide): 12.1B **Privately Held**
WEB: www.creganna.com
SIC: 3841 Surgical & medical instruments

(P-6969)
DEPUY SYNTHES PRODUCTS INC
130 Knowles Dr Ste E, Los Gatos (95032-1832)
PHONE.................................408 246-4300
EMP: 15
SALES (corp-wide): 82.5B **Publicly Held**
SIC: 3841 Diagnostic apparatus, medical
HQ: Depuy Synthes Products, Inc.
  325 Paramount Dr
  Raynham MA 02767
  508 880-8100

(P-6970)
DFINE INC (HQ)
3047 Orchard Pkwy, San Jose (95134-2129)
PHONE.................................408 321-9999
Greg Barrett, *President*
Rick Short, *CFO*
Bob Poser, *Vice Pres*
Cindee Van Vleck, *Vice Pres*
Rahul Gupta, *Engineer*
▲ **EMP:** 161 **EST:** 2004
SQ FT: 18,000
SALES (est): 9.4MM
SALES (corp-wide): 963.8MM **Publicly Held**
WEB: www.merit.com
SIC: 3841 Surgical & medical instruments
PA: Merit Medical Systems, Inc.
  1600 W Merit Pkwy
  South Jordan UT 84095
  801 253-1600

(P-6971)
DUKE EMPIRICAL INC
2829 Mission St, Santa Cruz (95060-5755)
PHONE.................................831 420-1104
Robert C Laduca, *CEO*
Beatriz Collazo, *Project Mgr*
Ryan Drake, *Purchasing*
EMP: 60 **EST:** 2000
SQ FT: 9,000
SALES (est): 9.9MM **Privately Held**
WEB: www.dukeempirical.com
SIC: 3841 Diagnostic apparatus, medical

(P-6972)
EVOLVE MANUFACTURING TECH INC
47300 Bayside Pkwy, Fremont (94538-6516)
PHONE.................................650 968-9292
Noreen King, *President*
Dave Devine, *President*
Sarvar Samia, *Human Resources*
Barbara Espinoza, *Purch Mgr*
Michelle Perez, *Buyer*
▲ **EMP:** 65 **EST:** 1999
SQ FT: 45,000
SALES (est): 14.1MM **Privately Held**
WEB: www.evolvemfg.com
SIC: 3841 3674 8731 Ultrasonic medical cleaning equipment; semiconductors & related devices; biotechnical research, commercial

(P-6973)
FLUXION BIOSCIENCES INC
1600 Harbor Bay Pkwy # 150, Alameda (94502-3011)
PHONE.................................650 241-4777
Jeff Jenson, *CEO*
Jody Beecher, *Vice Pres*
Niall Murphy, *Vice Pres*
Cristian Ionescuzanetti, *CTO*
Cristian Ionescu Zanetti, *CTO*
▲ **EMP:** 30 **EST:** 2005
SQ FT: 10,000
SALES (est): 6.5MM **Privately Held**
WEB: www.fluxionbio.com
SIC: 3841 Diagnostic apparatus, medical

(P-6974)
GALA THERAPEUTICS INC (PA)
1531 Industrial Rd, San Carlos (94070-4111)
PHONE.................................628 800-1154
Jonathan Reuben, *CEO*
Brett Bannan, *Surgery Dir*
Kevin Taylor, *Research*
Genevieve Foster, *Manager*
EMP: 149 **EST:** 2016
SALES (est): 12.6MM **Privately Held**
WEB: www.galatherapeutics.com
SIC: 3841 Surgical & medical instruments

(P-6975)
GALAXY MEDICAL INC
1531 Industrial Rd, San Carlos (94070-4111)
PHONE.................................510 847-5189
Jonathan Waldstreicher, *CEO*
EMP: 49 **EST:** 2020
SALES (est): 5MM **Privately Held**
SIC: 3841 Stethoscopes & stethographs

(P-6976)
GAUSS SURGICAL INC
4085 Campbell Ave, Menlo Park (94025-1939)
PHONE.................................650 949-4153
Siddarth Satish, *CEO*
EMP: 42 **EST:** 2019
SALES (est): 6MM
SALES (corp-wide): 14.3B **Publicly Held**
WEB: www.gausssurgical.com
SIC: 3841 Surgical & medical instruments
PA: Stryker Corporation
  2825 Airview Blvd
  Portage MI 49002
  269 385-2600

(P-6977)
GE VENTURES INC
3000 Sand Hill Rd 2-160, Menlo Park (94025-7145)
PHONE.................................650 233-3900
Sue Siegal, *CEO*
EMP: 16 **EST:** 2015
SALES (est): 1MM **Privately Held**
WEB: www.ge.com
SIC: 3841 Surgical & medical instruments

(P-6978)
GENMARK DIAGNOSTICS INC (DH)
1 Dna Way, South San Francisco (94080-4918)
PHONE.................................650 225-1000
Scott Mendel, *President*
Johnny Ek, *CFO*
Michael Gleeson, *Senior VP*
Michael Harkins, *Senior VP*
Tyler Jensen, *Senior VP*
EMP: 598 **EST:** 2020
SALES (est): 171.5MM
SALES (corp-wide): 69.8B **Privately Held**
WEB: www.genmarkdx.com
SIC: 3841 Surgical & medical instruments
HQ: Roche Holdings, Inc.
  1 Dna Way
  South San Francisco CA 94080
  650 225-1000

(P-6979)
GUIDANT SALES LLC
825 E Middlefield Rd, Mountain View (94043-4025)
PHONE.................................650 965-2634
EMP: 324
SALES (corp-wide): 9.9B **Publicly Held**
WEB: www.bostonscientific.com
SIC: 3841 Surgical & medical instruments
HQ: Guidant Sales Llc
  4100 Hamline Ave N
  Saint Paul MN 55112

(P-6980)
HANSEN MEDICAL INC
Also Called: Braid Logistics
800 E Middlefield Rd, Mountain View (94043-4030)
PHONE.................................650 404-5800
Cary Vance, *President*
Michael L Eagle, *Ch of Bd*
Cary G Vance, *President*
Christopher P Lowe, *CFO*
Robert Cathcart, *Senior VP*
EMP: 130 **EST:** 2002
SQ FT: 63,000
SALES (est): 43.6MM
SALES (corp-wide): 82.5B **Publicly Held**
WEB: www.aurishealth.com
SIC: 3841 Catheters
HQ: Auris Health, Inc.
  150 Shoreline Dr
  Redwood City CA 94065
  650 610-0750

(P-6981)
HANTEL TECHNOLOGIES INC
3496 Breakwater Ct, Hayward (94545-3613)
PHONE.................................510 400-1164
Mary M Pascual Gallup, *CEO*
David Gallup, *President*
Dennis Mello, *Manager*
▲ **EMP:** 40 **EST:** 1998
SQ FT: 18,000
SALES (est): 5.3MM **Privately Held**
WEB: www.hanteltech.com
SIC: 3841 Surgical & medical instruments

(P-6982)
HAROLD REICHS PHARMACY
Also Called: Reichs Pharmacy and Med Sup
39 W 10th St, Tracy (95376-3901)
PHONE.................................209 835-1832
Harold Reich, *Owner*
EMP: 15 **EST:** 1968
SQ FT: 1,000
SALES (est): 1.5MM **Privately Held**
WEB: www.reichsrx.com
SIC: 5912 3841 Drug stores; medical instruments & equipment, blood & bone work

(P-6983)
ICU MEDICAL INC
5729 Fontanoso Way, San Jose (95138-1015)
PHONE.................................408 284-7064
Joe Belloah, *Manager*
Julio Javier Duclos, *Director*
EMP: 100
SALES (corp-wide): 1.2B **Publicly Held**
WEB: www.icumed.com
SIC: 3841 Surgical & medical instruments

3841 - Surgical & Medical Instrs & Apparatus County (P-6984)

PA: Icu Medical, Inc.
951 Calle Amanecer
San Clemente CA 92673
949 366-2183

(P-6984)
INTELLA INTERVENTIONAL SYSTEMS
Also Called: Iwi
605 W California Ave, Sunnyvale (94086-4831)
PHONE.................650 269-1375
EMP: 62
SQ FT: 14,500
SALES (est): 7.3MM **Privately Held**
WEB: www.i-i-s-i.com
SIC: 3841 Designs And Mfg Catheters

(P-6985)
INTERSECT ENT INC (PA)
1555 Adams Dr, Menlo Park (94025-1439)
PHONE.................650 641-2100
Thomas A West, *President*
Kieran T Gallahue, *Ch of Bd*
Richard A Meier, *CFO*
Patrick A Broderick, *Exec VP*
Cher Mitchell, *Research*
▲ **EMP:** 404 **EST:** 2003
SQ FT: 10,200
SALES (est): 80.5MM **Publicly Held**
WEB: www.intersectent.com
SIC: 3841 Surgical & medical instruments

(P-6986)
INTUITIVE SRGCAL OPRATIONS INC (HQ)
1020 Kifer Rd, Sunnyvale (94086-5301)
PHONE.................408 523-2100
Gary S Guthart, *CEO*
EMP: 654 **EST:** 2009
SALES (est): 5.5MM **Publicly Held**
WEB: www.intuitive.com
SIC: 3841 Surgical & medical instruments

(P-6987)
INTUITIVE SRGICAL HOLDINGS LLC (HQ)
1020 Kifer Rd, Sunnyvale (94086-5301)
PHONE.................408 523-2100
Gary S Guthart PHD, *CEO*
Gokul Ramaswamy, *Info Tech Dir*
▼ **EMP:** 100 **EST:** 2007
SALES (est): 998.3K **Publicly Held**
WEB: www.intuitive.com
SIC: 3841 Surgical & medical instruments

(P-6988)
INTUITY MEDICAL INC
Also Called: Rosedale Medical
3500 W Warren Ave, Fremont (94538-6499)
PHONE.................408 530-1700
Emory Anderson, *President*
Emory V Anderson III, *President*
Robb Hesley, *Vice Pres*
Kelley Lipman, *Vice Pres*
Christopher Woeste, *Vice Pres*
EMP: 64 **EST:** 2002
SQ FT: 18,000
SALES (est): 20.5MM **Privately Held**
WEB: www.presspogo.com
SIC: 3841 Surgical & medical instruments

(P-6989)
INVUITY INC
Also Called: Intelligent Photonics
444 De Haro St Ste 110, San Francisco (94107-2350)
PHONE.................415 665-2100
Kevin A Lobo, *Ch of Bd*
James H Mackaness, *CFO*
Paul Davison, *Vice Pres*
Joseph Guido, *Vice Pres*
Valerie Dawydiak, *Area Mgr*
▲ **EMP:** 172 **EST:** 2004
SQ FT: 38,135
SALES: 39.6MM
SALES (corp-wide): 14.3B **Publicly Held**
WEB: www.stryker.com
SIC: 3841 5047 Surgical instruments & apparatus; surgical equipment & supplies
PA: Stryker Corporation
2825 Airview Blvd
Portage MI 49002
269 385-2600

(P-6990)
IOGYN INC
150 Baytech Dr, San Jose (95134-2302)
PHONE.................408 996-2517
Csaba Truckai, *Exec Dir*
John Shadduck, *Exec Dir*
David Clapper, *Director*
Rodney Perkins, *Director*
Bruno Strul, *Director*
EMP: 34 **EST:** 2010
SALES (est): 2.5MM
SALES (corp-wide): 9.9B **Publicly Held**
WEB: www.bostonscientific.com
SIC: 3841 Surgical & medical instruments
PA: Boston Scientific Corporation
300 Boston Scientific Way
Marlborough MA 01752
508 683-4000

(P-6991)
IRHYTHM TECHNOLOGIES INC (PA)
699 8th St Ste 600, San Francisco (94103-4901)
PHONE.................415 632-5700
Douglas J Devine, *CEO*
Abhijit Y Talwalkar, *Ch of Bd*
Mark J Day, *Exec VP*
Dietra N Jones, *Exec VP*
Derrick Sung, *Exec VP*
EMP: 30 **EST:** 2006
SQ FT: 117,560
SALES (est): 265.1MM **Publicly Held**
WEB: www.irhythmtech.com
SIC: 3841 3845 Surgical & medical instruments; diagnostic apparatus, medical; electrocardiographs

(P-6992)
ISCIENCE INTERVENTIONAL CORP
41316 Christy St, Fremont (94538-3115)
PHONE.................650 421-2700
Michael Nash, *President*
Matt Franklin, *CFO*
Stan Conston, *Vice Pres*
Ernie Edwards, *Vice Pres*
Mark Hayward, *Vice Pres*
EMP: 23 **EST:** 2000
SALES (est): 1.5MM **Privately Held**
WEB: www.iscienceinterventional.com
SIC: 3841 Instruments, microsurgical: except electromedical

(P-6993)
JOHNSON MATTHEY INC
Also Called: Shape Memory Applications
1070 Coml St Ste 110, San Jose (95112)
PHONE.................408 727-2221
Brian Woodward, *Branch Mgr*
Paramjit Sheena, *Technician*
Rebecca Delgado, *Master*
EMP: 34
SALES (corp-wide): 22B **Privately Held**
WEB: www.matthey.com
SIC: 3841 3496 3356 3357 Surgical & medical instruments; miscellaneous fabricated wire products; nonferrous rolling & drawing; nonferrous wiredrawing & insulating; steel wire & related products
HQ: Johnson Matthey Inc.
435 Devon Park Dr Ste 600
Wayne PA 19087
610 971-3000

(P-6994)
KAINOS DENTAL TECHNOLOGIES LLC (PA)
2975 Treat Blvd Ste A3, Concord (94518-3690)
PHONE.................800 331-4834
William Gianni, *CEO*
Andrew Nam, *COO*
Michael Finke, *CTO*
EMP: 24 **EST:** 2011
SQ FT: 3,000
SALES (est): 3MM **Privately Held**
WEB: www.kainosdental.com
SIC: 3841 3843 8072 Surgical & medical instruments; dental equipment & supplies; artificial teeth production

(P-6995)
KINEMATIC AUTOMATION INC
21085 Longeway Rd, Sonora (95370-8968)
P.O. Box 69, Twain Harte (95383-0069)
PHONE.................209 532-3200
David Carlberg, *President*
Ted Meigs, *Vice Pres*
Patricia Webster, *Analyst*
Jane Hebel, *Sales Staff*
EMP: 55 **EST:** 1980
SQ FT: 19,000
SALES (est): 14.4MM **Privately Held**
WEB: www.kinematic.com
SIC: 3841 7389 Diagnostic apparatus, medical; design, commercial & industrial

(P-6996)
LIFESCAN PRODUCTS LLC (HQ)
1000 Gibraltar Dr, Milpitas (95035-6312)
PHONE.................408 719-8443
Eric Milledge, *Ch of Bd*
Louis Caro, *CFO*
James Martin, *Business Mgr*
Sonia Rodriguez, *Buyer*
EMP: 413 **EST:** 2006
SALES (est): 107.5MM
SALES (corp-wide): 82.5B **Publicly Held**
WEB: www.lifescan.com
SIC: 3841 3845 Surgical & medical instruments; ultrasonic scanning devices, medical
PA: Johnson & Johnson
1 Johnson And Johnson Plz
New Brunswick NJ 08933
732 524-0400

(P-6997)
LOMA VISTA MEDICAL INC
863a Mitten Rd Ste 100a, Burlingame (94010-1303)
PHONE.................650 490-4747
Alex Tilson, *CEO*
Mark Scheeff, *Vice Pres*
EMP: 30 **EST:** 2007
SQ FT: 4,500
SALES (est): 2.1MM
SALES (corp-wide): 17.1B **Publicly Held**
WEB: www.bd.com
SIC: 3841 Surgical & medical instruments
PA: Becton, Dickinson And Company
1 Becton Dr
Franklin Lakes NJ 07417
201 847-6800

(P-6998)
LUMENIS BE INC ◆
2077 Gateway Pl Ste 300, San Jose (95110-1149)
PHONE.................408 764-3000
Zipora Ozer-Armon, *CEO*
Brad Oliver, *President*
Shalom Cohen, *CFO*
Oded Paz, *Admin Sec*
Jason Stinger, *VP Finance*
EMP: 230 **EST:** 2021
SQ FT: 13,500
SALES (est): 37.6MM **Privately Held**
WEB: www.lumenis.com
SIC: 3841 Surgical & medical instruments
HQ: Lumenis Ltd.
6 Hakidma
Yokneam Illit 20692

(P-6999)
LUMENIS INC (DH)
2077 Gateway Pl Ste 300, San Jose (95110-1149)
PHONE.................408 764-3000
Tzipi Ozer Armon, *CEO*
Brad Oliver, *President*
Shlomi Cohen, *CFO*
David Cavanaugh, *Vice Pres*
Audrey Szutu, *Vice Pres*
▲ **EMP:** 150 **EST:** 1992
SQ FT: 13,500
SALES (est): 160MM **Privately Held**
WEB: www.lumenis.com
SIC: 3841 Surgical & medical instruments

(P-7000)
LUMINOSTICS INC
446 S Hillview Dr, Milpitas (95035-5464)
PHONE.................760 709-2230
Balakrishnan Raja, *Director*

Bharat Jain, *Research*
Gavin Garvey, *Director*
James Hodges, *Director*
Andrew Paterson, *Director*
EMP: 20 **EST:** 2014
SALES (est): 3.4MM **Privately Held**
WEB: www.cliphealth.com
SIC: 3841 Surgical & medical instruments

(P-7001)
MCKESSON CORPORATION
3775 Seaport Blvd, West Sacramento (95691-3558)
PHONE.................916 372-4600
EMP: 19 **EST:** 1994
SALES (est): 276.2K **Privately Held**
WEB: www.mckesson.com
SIC: 3841 5122 8062 Diagnostic apparatus, medical; proprietary (patent) medicines; general medical & surgical hospitals

(P-7002)
MEDEONBIO INC
452 Oakmead Pkwy, Sunnyvale (94085-4708)
PHONE.................650 397-5100
Yue-Teh Jang, *CEO*
EMP: 22 **EST:** 2012
SALES (est): 5.3MM **Privately Held**
WEB: www.medeonbio.com
SIC: 3841 Surgical & medical instruments
PA: Medeon Biodesign, Inc.
7f, 116, Hougang St.,
Taipei City TAP 11170

(P-7003)
MEDICAL INSTR DEV LABS INC
Also Called: Mid Labs
557 Mccormick St, San Leandro (94577-1107)
PHONE.................510 357-3952
Dr Rob Peabody Sr, *CEO*
Carl Wang, *President*
Rong Wang, *Vice Pres*
Jim Gaab, *Engineer*
David Riley, *Engineer*
EMP: 35 **EST:** 1991
SQ FT: 17,000
SALES (est): 6.8MM **Privately Held**
WEB: www.midlabs.com
SIC: 3841 Ophthalmic instruments & apparatus

(P-7004)
MEDTRONIC INC
5345 Skyllane Blvd, Santa Rosa (95403)
PHONE.................707 541-3144
Eric Kunz, *Branch Mgr*
EMP: 30 **Privately Held**
WEB: www.medtronic.com
SIC: 3841 5047 5999 Surgical & medical instruments; medical equipment & supplies; medical apparatus & supplies
HQ: Medtronic, Inc.
710 Medtronic Pkwy
Minneapolis MN 55432
763 514-4000

(P-7005)
MEDTRONIC SPINE LLC
1221 Crossman Ave, Sunnyvale (94089-1103)
PHONE.................408 548-6500
Bill Hawkins, *President*
Karen D Talmadge, *Vice Pres*
EMP: 1090 **EST:** 2008
SQ FT: 151,000
SALES (est): 224.1MM **Privately Held**
WEB: www.medtronic.com
SIC: 3841 Surgical & medical instruments
HQ: Medtronic, Inc.
710 Medtronic Pkwy
Minneapolis MN 55432
763 514-4000

(P-7006)
MERAQI MEDICAL INC
47225 Fremont Blvd, Fremont (94538-6502)
PHONE.................669 222-7710
Alan Hershey, *CEO*
EMP: 407 **EST:** 2017

▲ = Import ▼ = Export
◆ = Import/Export

PRODUCTS & SERVICES SECTION

3841 - Surgical & Medical Instrs & Apparatus County (P-7030)

SALES (est): 5MM
SALES (corp-wide): 1.1B **Privately Held**
WEB: www.viantmedical.com
SIC: **3841** Surgical & medical instruments
HQ: Viant Medical, Llc
2 Hampshire St
Foxborough MA 02035

(P-7007)
MICRUS ENDOVASCULAR LLC (HQ)
821 Fox Ln, San Jose (95131-1601)
PHONE..................408 433-1400
P Laxminarain, *President*
Robert A Stern, *President*
John T Kilcoyne, *CEO*
Gordon T Sangster, *CFO*
Edward F Ruppel Jr, *Ch Credit Ofcr*
EMP: 139 EST: 1997
SQ FT: 42,000
SALES (est): 94.3MM
SALES (corp-wide): 82.5B **Publicly Held**
WEB: www.jnj.com
SIC: **3841** Surgical instruments & apparatus
PA: Johnson & Johnson
1 Johnson And Johnson Plz
New Brunswick NJ 08933
732 524-0400

(P-7008)
MINERVA SURGICAL INC
4255 Burton Dr, Santa Clara (95054-1512)
PHONE..................855 646-7874
David M Clapper, *President*
Ross A Jaffe, *Ch of Bd*
Dominique J Filloux, *COO*
Joel R Jung, *CFO*
Evgueni V Skalnyi, *Vice Pres*
▲ EMP: 139 EST: 2008
SQ FT: 32,719
SALES (est): 37.7MM **Privately Held**
WEB: www.minervasurgical.com
SIC: **3841** Surgical & medical instruments

(P-7009)
MIZUHO ORTHOPEDIC SYSTEMS INC (HQ)
Also Called: Mizuho OSI
30031 Ahern Ave, Union City (94587-1234)
P.O. Box 1468 (94587-6468)
PHONE..................510 429-1500
Takashi Nemoto, *CEO*
Steve Lamb, *President*
Yosup Kim, *Treasurer*
Patrick Rimroth, *General Mgr*
Shamili Koduru, *Business Anlyst*
◆ EMP: 299 EST: 1977
SQ FT: 111,100
SALES (est): 83.9MM **Privately Held**
WEB: www.mizuhosi.com
SIC: **3841** Operating tables

(P-7010)
NEUROPACE INC
455 Bernardo Ave, Mountain View (94043-5237)
PHONE..................650 237-2700
Michael Favet, *President*
Frank Fischer, *Ch of Bd*
Rebecca Kuhn, *CFO*
Martha Morrell, *Chief Mktg Ofcr*
Isabella Abati, *Vice Pres*
EMP: 152 EST: 1997
SQ FT: 53,000
SALES (est): 41.1MM **Privately Held**
WEB: www.neuropace.com
SIC: **3841** Surgical & medical instruments

(P-7011)
NEVRO CORP (PA)
1800 Bridge Pkwy, Redwood City (94065-1164)
PHONE..................650 251-0005
D Keith Grossman, *Ch of Bd*
Roderick H Macleod, *CEO*
Niamh Pellegrini, *Ch Credit Ofcr*
David Caraway, *Officer*
Lori Ciano, *Officer*
EMP: 835 EST: 2006
SQ FT: 50,740
SALES (est): 362MM **Publicly Held**
WEB: www.nevro.com
SIC: **3841** Surgical & medical instruments

(P-7012)
NOVA EYE INC
41316 Christy St, Fremont (94538-3115)
PHONE..................510 291-1300
Victor Previn, *CEO*
John Craig, *Vice Pres*
Patrick Tucker, *Regional Mgr*
Jennifer Hagan, *Admin Sec*
Mario Del Rosario, *Engineer*
EMP: 26 EST: 2013
SALES (est): 5.3MM **Privately Held**
SIC: **3841** Surgical & medical instruments

(P-7013)
OPTIMEDICA CORPORATION
510 Cottonwood Dr, Milpitas (95035-7403)
PHONE..................408 850-8600
Miles White, *CEO*
Mark J Forchette, *President*
Mark A Murray, *CFO*
EMP: 116 EST: 2004
SALES (est): 6.8MM
SALES (corp-wide): 82.5B **Publicly Held**
WEB: www.jnj.com
SIC: **3841** Eye examining instruments & apparatus
PA: Johnson & Johnson
1 Johnson And Johnson Plz
New Brunswick NJ 08933
732 524-0400

(P-7014)
OPTOVUE INC (PA)
2800 Bayview Dr, Fremont (94538-6518)
PHONE..................510 623-8868
Jay WEI, *CEO*
David Voris, *President*
Paul Kealey, *Senior VP*
Joe Garibaldi, *Vice Pres*
Gordon Wong, *Vice Pres*
▲ EMP: 85 EST: 2003
SQ FT: 12,400
SALES (est): 37.1MM **Privately Held**
WEB: www.optovue.com
SIC: **3841** 5048 Surgical & medical instruments; ophthalmic goods

(P-7015)
ORBIS WHEELS INC
Also Called: Orbis Bioaid
3200 Dutton Ave, Santa Rosa (95407-5703)
PHONE..................415 548-4160
Marcus Hays, *CEO*
EMP: 19 EST: 2014
SALES (est): 2.4MM **Privately Held**
WEB: www.orbisdriven.com
SIC: **3841** Surgical & medical instruments

(P-7016)
ORTHOFIX MEDICAL INC
501 Mercury Dr, Sunnyvale (94085-4019)
PHONE..................214 937-2000
EMP: 974
SALES (corp-wide): 459.9MM **Privately Held**
WEB: www.orthofix.com
SIC: **3841** Surgical & medical instruments
PA: Orthofix Medical Inc.
3451 Plano Pkwy
Lewisville TX 75056
214 937-2000

(P-7017)
ORTHOGROUP INC
11280 Sanders Dr Ste A, Rancho Cordova (95742-6888)
PHONE..................916 859-0881
Henry Fletcher, *President*
EMP: 15 EST: 2005
SALES (est): 2MM **Privately Held**
WEB: www.orthogroup.com
SIC: **3841** Medical instruments & equipment, blood & bone work

(P-7018)
OSSEON LLC
2301 Circadian Way # 300, Santa Rosa (95407-5461)
PHONE..................707 636-5940
Ronald Clough, *CEO*
Spencer Hill,
EMP: 22 EST: 2014
SQ FT: 10,000

SALES (est): 407.1K **Privately Held**
WEB: www.merit.com
SIC: **3841** Surgical & medical instruments

(P-7019)
PENUMBRA INC (PA)
1 Penumbra, Alameda (94502-7676)
PHONE..................510 748-3200
Adam Elsesser, *Ch of Bd*
James Pray, *President*
Maggie Yuen, *CFO*
Johanna Roberts, *Exec VP*
Lynn Rothman, *Exec VP*
EMP: 3067 EST: 2004
SQ FT: 305,000
SALES (est): 560.4MM **Publicly Held**
WEB: www.penumbrainc.com
SIC: **3841** Surgical & medical instruments

(P-7020)
PHOENIX DEVENTURES INC
18655 Madrone Pkwy # 180, Morgan Hill (95037-8101)
PHONE..................408 782-6240
Jeffrey Christian, *President*
Chris Watson, *Prgrmr*
Marty Bloem, *Project Engr*
Valerie Hickey, *Controller*
Dacy Coleman, *Opers Staff*
EMP: 47 EST: 2000
SQ FT: 30,000
SALES (est): 9.2MM **Privately Held**
WEB: www.phoenixdeventures.com
SIC: **3841** Surgical & medical instruments

(P-7021)
POTRERO MEDICAL
26142 Eden Landing Rd, Hayward (94545-3710)
PHONE..................888 635-7280
Joe Urban, *CEO*
Andrew Offer, *CFO*
Vanessa Moll, *Chief Mktg Ofcr*
Kenna Sylliaasen, *Office Mgr*
Saheel Sutaria, *CTO*
EMP: 52 EST: 2014
SQ FT: 15,000
SALES (est): 1.1MM **Privately Held**
WEB: www.potreromed.com
SIC: **3841** Diagnostic apparatus, medical

(P-7022)
PRINTERPREZZ INC
47929 Fremont Blvd, Fremont (94538-6508)
PHONE..................510 225-8412
Shrinivas Shetty, *CEO*
Shri Shetty, *CEO*
Teresa Thuruthiyil, *Officer*
EMP: 18 EST: 2018
SALES (est): 2.3MM **Privately Held**
WEB: www.printerprezz.com
SIC: **3841** Surgical & medical instruments; medical instruments & equipment, blood & bone work

(P-7023)
PROCEPT BIOROBOTICS CORP (PA)
900 Island Dr Ste 170, Redwood City (94065-5176)
PHONE..................650 232-7200
Reza Zadno, *President*
Frederic Moll, *Ch of Bd*
Kevin Waters, *CFO*
Alaleh Nouri, *Senior VP*
Hisham Shiblaq, *Senior VP*
EMP: 203 EST: 2007
SQ FT: 43,485
SALES (est): 7.7MM **Publicly Held**
WEB: www.procept-biorobotics.com
SIC: **3841** Surgical & medical instruments

(P-7024)
PROSURG INC
Also Called: Ximed Medical Systems
2195 Trade Zone Blvd, San Jose (95131-1743)
PHONE..................408 945-4040
Ashvin H Desai, *President*
EMP: 40 EST: 1987
SQ FT: 14,800 **Privately Held**
WEB: www.prosurg.com
SIC: **3841** 3823 Surgical & medical instruments; industrial instrmnts msrmnt display/control process variable

(P-7025)
PULSAR VASCULAR INC
47709 Fremont Blvd, Fremont (94538-6512)
PHONE..................408 246-4300
Robert M Abrams, *President*
Chas Roue, *Vice Pres*
EMP: 15 EST: 2007
SALES (est): 4.8MM
SALES (corp-wide): 82.5B **Publicly Held**
SIC: **3841** Diagnostic apparatus, medical
HQ: Depuy Synthes Products, Inc.
325 Paramount Dr
Raynham MA 02767
508 880-8100

(P-7026)
RENOVORX INC
4546 El Cmino Real Ste B1, Los Altos (94022)
PHONE..................650 284-4433
Shaun Bagai, *Principal*
Imtiaz Qureshi, *Director*
EMP: 16 EST: 2015
SALES (est): 1.4MM **Privately Held**
WEB: www.renovorx.com
SIC: **3841** Catheters

(P-7027)
RH USA INC
Also Called: Lumenis
455 N Canyons Pkwy Ste B, Livermore (94551-7682)
PHONE..................925 245-7900
Jeannette Trujillo, *Vice Pres*
Bob Schultz, *Engineer*
Miranda Yee, *Controller*
Gladys Copeland, *Director*
▲ EMP: 42 EST: 2004
SQ FT: 40,000
SALES (est): 12.2MM **Privately Held**
WEB: www.rh-global.com
SIC: **3841** Surgical & medical instruments
PA: R.H. Technologies Ltd
5 Hatzoref
Nof Hagalil 17880

(P-7028)
SADRA MEDICAL INC
160 Knowles Dr, Los Gatos (95032-1828)
PHONE..................408 370-1550
Michael F Mahoney, *President*
Ken Martin, *President*
Jon Bohane, *CFO*
Robert Chang, *Exec VP*
Dave Paul, *Vice Pres*
EMP: 73 EST: 2003
SALES (est): 4.8MM
SALES (corp-wide): 9.9B **Publicly Held**
WEB: www.bostonscientific.com
SIC: **3841** Surgical & medical instruments
PA: Boston Scientific Corporation
300 Boston Scientific Way
Marlborough MA 01752
508 683-4000

(P-7029)
SANOVAS INC
2597 Kerner Blvd, San Rafael (94901-5571)
P.O. Box 2129 (94912-2129)
PHONE..................415 729-9391
Lawrence Gerrans, *President*
Jerry Katzman, *CEO*
Robert Farrell, *CFO*
Steve Budill, *Vice Pres*
Mike Humason, *Vice Pres*
EMP: 36 EST: 2010
SALES (est): 5MM **Privately Held**
WEB: www.sanovas.com
SIC: **3841** Surgical & medical instruments

(P-7030)
SCHOLTEN SURGICAL INSTRS INC
170 Commerce St Ste 101, Lodi (95240-0871)
PHONE..................209 365-1393
Arie Scholten, *President*
Jim Van Andel, *COO*
EMP: 17 EST: 1978
SALES (est): 628.1K **Privately Held**
WEB: www.novatome.com
SIC: **3841** Surgical & medical instruments

3841 - Surgical & Medical Instrs & Apparatus County (P-7031)

(P-7031)
SCITON INC
925 Commercial St, Palo Alto (94303-4908)
PHONE..................650 493-9155
James Hobart, *CEO*
Tina Bock, *Partner*
Shannyn Harrison, *Partner*
Ariel Weaver, *Partner*
Dan Negus, *President*
▼ **EMP:** 74 **EST:** 1997
SQ FT: 15,000
SALES (est): 25.1MM **Privately Held**
WEB: www.sciton.com
SIC: 3841 Surgical lasers

(P-7032)
SEMLER SCIENTIFIC INC (PA)
2340-2348 Wlsh Ave Ste 23, Santa Clara (95051)
PHONE..................877 774-4211
Douglas Murphy-Chutorian, *CEO*
Andrew B Weinstein, *Senior VP*
Sandra Caughlan, *Technical Staff*
Mike Demarco, *Technical Staff*
Daniel E Conger, *VP Finance*
EMP: 54 **EST:** 2007
SALES (est): 38.6MM **Publicly Held**
WEB: www.semlerscientific.com
SIC: 3841 Surgical & medical instruments

(P-7033)
SHEATHING TECHNOLOGIES INC
675 Jarvis Dr Ste A, Morgan Hill (95037-2815)
PHONE..................408 782-2720
Larry Polayes, *President*
Kathy Scroggins, *Officer*
Kipp Herman, *Personnel Assit*
Jazmin Velazquez, *Sales Associate*
Shannan Matthews, *Sales Staff*
▲ **EMP:** 39 **EST:** 1992
SQ FT: 10,000
SALES (est): 9MM **Privately Held**
WEB: www.sheathes.com
SIC: 3841 Diagnostic apparatus, medical

(P-7034)
SHOCKWAVE MEDICAL INC (PA)
5403 Betsy Ross Dr, Santa Clara (95054-1162)
PHONE..................510 279-4262
Douglas Godshall, *President*
C Raymond Larkin Jr, *Ch of Bd*
Dan Puckett, *CFO*
Isaac Zacharias, *Ch Credit Ofcr*
Keith D Dawkins, *Chief Mktg Ofcr*
EMP: 158 **EST:** 2009
SQ FT: 35,000
SALES (est): 67.7MM **Publicly Held**
WEB: www.shockwavemedical.com
SIC: 3841 Diagnostic apparatus, medical

(P-7035)
SIGHT SCIENCES INC (PA)
4040 Campbell Ave Ste 100, Menlo Park (94025-1053)
PHONE..................650 352-4400
Paul Badawi, *President*
Staffan Encrantz, *Ch of Bd*
Sam Park, *COO*
Jesse Selnick, *CFO*
Shawn O'Neil, *Ch Credit Ofcr*
EMP: 183 **EST:** 2010
SQ FT: 10,823
SALES (est): 27.6MM **Publicly Held**
WEB: www.sightsciences.com
SIC: 3841 Surgical & medical instruments

(P-7036)
SILARA MEDTECH (PA)
451 Aviation Blvd 107a, Santa Rosa (95403-9099)
PHONE..................707 757-5750
Becky Thomas, *Office Mgr*
EMP: 35 **EST:** 2019
SALES (est): 768.4K **Privately Held**
SIC: 3841 Surgical & medical instruments

(P-7037)
SILK ROAD MEDICAL INC
1213 Innsbruck Dr, Sunnyvale (94089-1317)
PHONE..................408 720-9002
Erica J Rogers, *President*
Lucas W Buchanan, *COO*
Lucas Buchanan, *CFO*
Andrew Davis, *Ch Credit Ofcr*
Randall Sullivan, *Exec VP*
EMP: 176 **EST:** 2007
SQ FT: 31,000
SALES (est): 75.2MM **Privately Held**
WEB: www.silkroadmed.com
SIC: 3841 Surgical & medical instruments

(P-7038)
SIMPLIFY MEDICAL INC
685 N Pastoria Ave, Sunnyvale (94085-2917)
P.O. Box 60879 (94088-0879)
PHONE..................650 946-2025
J Christopher Barry, *CEO*
Nicole Czaplewski, *Consultant*
EMP: 17 **EST:** 2014
SALES (est): 5.3MM
SALES (corp-wide): 1.1B **Publicly Held**
WEB: www.simplifymedical.com
SIC: 3841 Surgical & medical instruments
PA: Nuvasive, Inc.
7475 Lusk Blvd
San Diego CA 92121
858 909-1800

(P-7039)
SOLTA MEDICAL INC (DH)
7031 Koll Center Pkwy # 260, Pleasanton (94566-3134)
PHONE..................510 786-6946
J Michael Pearson, *President*
Howard B Schiller, *Treasurer*
Robert Chai-Onn, *Admin Sec*
▲ **EMP:** 100 **EST:** 1996
SQ FT: 88,000
SALES (est): 61.4MM
SALES (corp-wide): 8.6B **Privately Held**
WEB: www.solta.com
SIC: 3841 Surgical & medical instruments
HQ: Bausch Health Americas, Inc.
400 Somerset Corp Blvd
Bridgewater NJ 08807
908 927-1400

(P-7040)
SONOMA ORTHOPEDIC PRODUCTS INC
50 W San Fernando St Fl 5, San Jose (95113-2433)
PHONE..................847 807-4378
Charles Nelson, *CEO*
Matt Jerome, *President*
Rick Epstein, *CEO*
Kyle Lappin, *Vice Pres*
Alex Winber, *Vice Pres*
EMP: 15 **EST:** 2008
SALES (est): 745.5K **Privately Held**
SIC: 3841 Surgical & medical instruments

(P-7041)
SPECIFIC DIAGNOSTICS INC
855 Maude Ave, Mountain View (94043-4021)
PHONE..................650 938-2030
Paul Rhodes, *CEO*
Anthony Bazarko, *Ch Credit Ofcr*
EMP: 20 **EST:** 2011
SALES (est): 4.3MM **Privately Held**
WEB: www.specificdx.com
SIC: 3841 Surgical & medical instruments

(P-7042)
SPECTRANETICS CORPORATION
5055 Brandin Ct, Fremont (94538-3140)
PHONE..................510 933-7964
Gil Paet, *Principal*
EMP: 80 **EST:** 2017
SALES (est): 3.6MM **Privately Held**
SIC: 3841 5047 5999 Surgical & medical instruments; medical equipment & supplies; medical apparatus & supplies

(P-7043)
SPINE VIEW INC
110 Pioneer Way Ste A, Mountain View (94041-1519)
PHONE..................510 490-1753
Roy Chin, *CEO*
Sam Park, *COO*
EMP: 56 **EST:** 2004
SALES (est): 5MM **Privately Held**
WEB: www.spineview.com
SIC: 3841 Surgical & medical instruments

(P-7044)
STRYKER SALES LLC
Also Called: Stryker Neurovascular
47900 Bayside Pkwy, Fremont (94538-6515)
PHONE..................510 413-2500
Mark O'Brien, *Vice Pres*
Dwight Fowler, *Principal*
Scott Courts, *Program Mgr*
David Hess, *Program Mgr*
Andrea Scicli, *Program Mgr*
EMP: 38
SALES (corp-wide): 14.3B **Publicly Held**
WEB: www.stryker.com
SIC: 3841 Surgical & medical instruments
HQ: Stryker Sales, Llc
2825 Airview Blvd
Portage MI 49002

(P-7045)
SUPIRA MEDICAL INC
590 Division St, Campbell (95008-6906)
PHONE..................408 560-2500
AMR Salahieh, *CEO*
Janine Robinson, *Vice Pres*
EMP: 36 **EST:** 2019
SALES (est): 4.2MM **Privately Held**
WEB: www.supiramedical.com
SIC: 3841 Surgical & medical instruments

(P-7046)
SYNVASIVE TECHNOLOGY INC
4925 Robert J Mathews Pkw, El Dorado Hills (95762-5700)
PHONE..................916 939-3913
Kelly Fisher, *Principal*
EMP: 112
SALES (corp-wide): 7B **Publicly Held**
WEB: www.synvasive.com
SIC: 3841 Surgical knife blades & handles
HQ: Synvasive Technology, Inc.
8690 Technology Way
Reno NV 89521

(P-7047)
TACTX MEDICAL INC (DH)
Also Called: Creganna - Tactx Medical
1353 Dell Ave, Campbell (95008-6609)
PHONE..................408 364-7100
Robert Bell Hance, *CEO*
Nitin Matani, *President*
Helen Ryan, *President*
Jeff Kraus, *Vice Pres*
Doug Wilkins, *Vice Pres*
▼ **EMP:** 115 **EST:** 2002
SQ FT: 12,000
SALES: 34.3MM
SALES (corp-wide): 12.1B **Privately Held**
WEB: www.tactxmed.com
SIC: 3841 Surgical stapling devices

(P-7048)
THERANOS INC (PA)
7373 Gateway Blvd, Newark (94560-1149)
PHONE..................650 838-9292
David Taylor, *CEO*
Daniel Guggenheim, *Ch Credit Ofcr*
Patrick O'Neill, *Ch Credit Ofcr*
Antti Korhonen, *Administration*
So Han Spivey, *Controller*
EMP: 100 **EST:** 2004
SALES (est): 32MM **Privately Held**
WEB: www.theranos.com
SIC: 3841 8748 Diagnostic apparatus, medical; testing services

(P-7049)
THERASENSE INC
1360 S Loop Rd, Alameda (94502-7000)
PHONE..................510 749-5400
W Mark Lortz, *CEO*
EMP: 20 **EST:** 2007
SALES (est): 1.5MM
SALES (corp-wide): 34.6B **Publicly Held**
WEB: www.abbott.com
SIC: 3841 Surgical & medical instruments
PA: Abbott Laboratories
100 Abbott Park Rd
Abbott Park IL 60064
224 667-6100

(P-7050)
THERMOGENESIS HOLDINGS INC (PA)
Also Called: CESCA THERAPEUTICS
2711 Citrus Rd, Rancho Cordova (95742-6228)
PHONE..................916 858-5100
Xiaochun Xu, *Ch of Bd*
Jeff Cauble, *CFO*
Jeffery Cauble, *CFO*
Eric Hellebust, *Program Mgr*
Jillian Miller, *Research*
▲ **EMP:** 22 **EST:** 1986
SQ FT: 28,000
SALES (est): 9.7MM **Publicly Held**
WEB: www.thermogenesis.com
SIC: 3841 Surgical & medical instruments

(P-7051)
TOP SHELF MANUFACTURING LLC
1851 Paradise Rd Ste A, Tracy (95304-8524)
PHONE..................209 834-8185
Mark Hirsch,
Jeff Leonard,
▲ **EMP:** 15 **EST:** 2002
SALES (est): 6MM **Privately Held**
WEB: www.topshelforthopedics.com
SIC: 3841 Diagnostic apparatus, medical
PA: Pacific Medical, Inc.
1700 N Chrisman Rd
Tracy CA 95304

(P-7052)
TRIREME MEDICAL LLC
7060 Koll Center Pkwy # 30, Pleasanton (94566-3106)
PHONE..................925 931-1300
Eitan Konstantino, *President*
Khang Nguyen, *Research*
▲ **EMP:** 70 **EST:** 2005
SQ FT: 15,000
SALES (est): 7.1MM **Privately Held**
WEB: www.qtvascular.com
SIC: 3841 Suction therapy apparatus

(P-7053)
TYCHE MEDTECH INC
3022 Scott Blvd, Santa Clara (95054-3315)
PHONE..................408 919-0098
Anatoly Ryzhikh, *CEO*
▲ **EMP:** 17 **EST:** 2012
SALES (est): 1.3MM **Privately Held**
WEB: www.tychemedtech.com
SIC: 3841 Surgical & medical instruments

(P-7054)
VARIAN ASSOCIATES LIMITED
3100 Hansen Way, Palo Alto (94304-1038)
PHONE..................650 493-4000
EMP: 32
SALES (est): 5MM
SALES (corp-wide): 3.1B **Privately Held**
WEB: www.varian.com
SIC: 3841 3829 Mfg Surgical/Medical Instruments Mfg Measuring/Controlling Devices
PA: Varian Medical Systems, Inc.
3100 Hansen Way
Palo Alto CA 94304
650 493-4000

(P-7055)
VARIAN MEDICAL SYSTEMS INC
3120 Hansen Way, Palo Alto (94304-1030)
PHONE..................650 213-8000
George Zdasiuk, *Vice Pres*
EMP: 45
SALES (corp-wide): 67.4B **Privately Held**
WEB: www.varian.com
SIC: 3841 Surgical & medical instruments
HQ: Varian Medical Systems, Inc.
3100 Hansen Way
Palo Alto CA 94304
650 493-4000

(P-7056)
VARIAN MEDICAL SYSTEMS INC
660 N Mccarthy Blvd, Milpitas (95035-5113)
PHONE..................408 321-9400

▲ = Import ▼=Export
◆ =Import/Export

PRODUCTS & SERVICES SECTION
3842 - Orthopedic, Prosthetic & Surgical Appliances/Splys County (P-7078)

Viki Sparks, *Branch Mgr*
Keith Askoff, *Vice Pres*
Corinn Whann, *Executive Asst*
Patricia Hotz, *Sales Staff*
LI Xu, *Senior Mgr*
EMP: 200
SALES (corp-wide): 67.4B **Privately Held**
WEB: www.varian.com
SIC: 3841 Surgical & medical instruments
HQ: Varian Medical Systems, Inc.
   3100 Hansen Way
   Palo Alto CA 94304
   650 493-4000

(P-7057)
VENUS CONCEPT INC
128 Baytech Dr, San Jose (95134-2302)
PHONE 855 882-7827
EMP: 87 **Privately Held**
WEB: www.venustreatments.com
SIC: 3841 5047 Mfg Surgical/Medical Instruments Whol Medical/Hospital Equipment
HQ: Venus Concept Canada Corp
   235 Yorkland Blvd Suite 900
   Toronto ON M2J 4
   877 848-8430

(P-7058)
VERB SURGICAL INC
5490 Great America Pkwy, Santa Clara (95054-3644)
PHONE 408 438-3363
Kurt Azarbarzin, *President*
Michael Deghuee, *Assoc VP*
Maria Chung, *Vice Pres*
Dave Herrmann, *Vice Pres*
Pablo E Garcia Kilroy, *Vice Pres*
EMP: 60 **EST:** 2015
SALES (est): 13.9MM
SALES (corp-wide): 82.5B **Publicly Held**
WEB: www.jnj.com
SIC: 3841 Surgical & medical instruments
PA: Johnson & Johnson
   1 Johnson And Johnson Plz
   New Brunswick NJ 08933
   732 524-0400

(P-7059)
VERSATILE POWER INC
743 Camden Ave Ste B, Campbell (95008-4101)
PHONE 408 341-4600
Jerry Price, *CEO*
Dave Hoffman, *President*
Mark Brown, *Sales Staff*
▲ **EMP:** 24 **EST:** 2002
SALES (est): 3.9MM
SALES (corp-wide): 1.4B **Publicly Held**
WEB: www.versatilepower.com
SIC: 3841 3825 Medical instruments & equipment, blood & bone work; semiconductor test equipment
PA: Advanced Energy Industries, Inc.
   1595 Wynkoop St Ste 800
   Denver CO 80202
   970 407-6626

(P-7060)
VNUS MEDICAL TECHNOLOGIES INC
5799 Fontanoso Way, San Jose (95138-1015)
PHONE 408 360-7200
Brian E Farley, *President*
Peter Osborne, *CFO*
Kirti Kamdar, *Senior VP*
John W Kapples, *Vice Pres*
Mark S Saxton, *Vice Pres*
EMP: 119 **EST:** 1995
SQ FT: 93,650
SALES (est): 8.7MM **Privately Held**
WEB: www.vnus.fr
SIC: 3841 Catheters
HQ: Covidien Lp
   15 Hampshire St
   Mansfield MA 02048
   763 514-4000

(P-7061)
W L GORE & ASSOCIATES INC
2890 De La Cruz Blvd, Santa Clara (95050-2619)
PHONE 928 864-2705
Mohan Sancheti, *Branch Mgr*
EMP: 184

SALES (corp-wide): 3.8B **Privately Held**
WEB: www.gore.com
SIC: 3841 Surgical & medical instruments
PA: W. L. Gore & Associates, Inc.
   555 Paper Mill Rd
   Newark DE 19711
   302 738-4880

(P-7062)
WANG NMR INC
550 N Canyons Pkwy, Livermore (94551-9472)
PHONE 925 443-0212
Sou-Tien Wang, *CEO*
Bert Wang, *President*
Henry Chen, *Vice Pres*
Clyde Taylor, *Vice Pres*
▲ **EMP:** 28 **EST:** 1983
SQ FT: 36,000
SALES (est): 3.1MM **Privately Held**
WEB: www.wangnmr.openfos.com
SIC: 3841 Diagnostic apparatus, medical

(P-7063)
XOFT INC
101 Nicholson Ln, San Jose (95134-1359)
PHONE 408 493-1500
Ken Ferry, *CEO*
Kevin Burns, *Exec VP*
Dan Arnoff, *Vice Pres*
John A Delucia, *Vice Pres*
Robert Kirby, *Vice Pres*
EMP: 29 **EST:** 2012
SALES (est): 4.9MM
SALES (corp-wide): 29.7MM **Publicly Held**
WEB: www.xoftinc.com
SIC: 3841 Surgical & medical instruments
PA: Icad, Inc.
   98 Spit Brook Rd Ste 100
   Nashua NH 03062
   603 882-5200

(P-7064)
ZELTIQ AESTHETICS INC (DH)
Also Called: Coolsculpting
4410 Rosewood Dr, Pleasanton (94588-3050)
PHONE 925 474-2500
Mark J Foley, *President*
Todd E Zavodnick, *President*
Taylor Harris, *CFO*
Sergio Garcia, *Senior VP*
Joe Piazza, *Vice Pres*
▲ **EMP:** 653 **EST:** 2005
SQ FT: 71,670
SALES (est): 354.2MM **Privately Held**
WEB: www.coolsculpting.com
SIC: 3841 Surgical & medical instruments
HQ: Allergan Holdco Us, Inc.
   400 Interpace Pkwy Ste D
   Parsippany NJ 07054
   862 261-7000

(P-7065)
ZIPLINE MEDICAL INC
747 Camden Ave Ste A, Campbell (95008-4147)
PHONE 408 412-7228
John R Tighe, *President*
Amir Belson, *Founder*
Bauback Safa, *Officer*
Eric Storne, *Vice Pres*
Petrina Picariello, *Office Admin*
EMP: 19 **EST:** 2007
SALES (est): 3.8MM
SALES (corp-wide): 14.3B **Publicly Held**
WEB: www.stryker.com
SIC: 3841 7389 Surgical & medical instruments;
PA: Stryker Corporation
   2825 Airview Blvd
   Portage MI 49002
   269 385-2600

3842 Orthopedic, Prosthetic & Surgical Appliances/Splys

(P-7066)
AXIOM INDUSTRIES INC
Also Called: Prime Engineering
4202 W Sierra Madre Ave, Fresno (93722-3932)
PHONE 559 276-1310

Mary Wilson Boegel, *President*
Bruce Boegel, *CFO*
Mark Allen, *Vice Pres*
Rick Michael, *Natl Sales Mgr*
◆ **EMP:** 26 **EST:** 1987
SALES (est): 4.7MM **Privately Held**
WEB: www.primeengineering.com
SIC: 3842 Technical aids for the handicapped

(P-7067)
BOSTON SCIENTIFIC CORPORATION
150 Baytech Dr, San Jose (95134-2302)
PHONE 408 935-3400
Tom Flemming, *Manager*
Warren Wang, *Vice Pres*
Danielle Saunders, *Info Tech Mgr*
Noah Gruber, *Engineer*
Stephanie Nguyen, *Engineer*
EMP: 125
SALES (corp-wide): 9.9B **Publicly Held**
WEB: www.bostonscientific.com
SIC: 3842 3841 Surgical appliances & supplies; grafts, artificial: for surgery; diagnostic apparatus, medical
PA: Boston Scientific Corporation
   300 Boston Scientific Way
   Marlborough MA 01752
   508 683-4000

(P-7068)
EARGO INC (PA)
1600 Technology Dr Fl 6, San Jose (95110-1382)
PHONE 650 351-7700
Christian Gormsen, *President*
Josh Makower, *Ch of Bd*
William Brownie, *COO*
Adam Laponis, *CFO*
EMP: 80 **EST:** 2010
SQ FT: 30,434
SALES: 69.1MM **Publicly Held**
WEB: www.eargo.com
SIC: 3842 Hearing aids

(P-7069)
EKSO BIONICS HOLDINGS INC
1414 Hrbour Way S Ste 120, Richmond (94804)
PHONE 510 984-1761
Jack Peurach, *President*
Steven Sherman, *Ch of Bd*
John Glenn, *CFO*
Bill Shaw, *Ch Credit Ofcr*
Michael Pratt, *Vice Pres*
EMP: 82 **EST:** 2012
SQ FT: 45,000
SALES (est): 8.8MM **Privately Held**
WEB: www.ir.eksobionics.com
SIC: 3842 5999 Crutches & walkers; walkers; canes, orthopedic; medical apparatus & supplies

(P-7070)
ELITE BIOMECHANICAL DESIGN (PA)
9 Governors Ln, Chico (95926-1991)
PHONE 530 894-6913
Michael Patrick Casey, *Principal*
Matthew Daniels, *Co-Owner*
EMP: 20 **EST:** 2010
SALES (est): 467.9K **Privately Held**
WEB: www.elitebiomechanicaldesign.com
SIC: 5999 3842 Orthopedic & prosthesis applications; braces, orthopedic

(P-7071)
HAND BIOMECHANICS LAB INC
77 Scripps Dr Ste 104, Sacramento (95825-6209)
PHONE 916 923-5073
John Agee MD, *President*
Ivan Davila, *Orthopedist*
EMP: 16 **EST:** 1982
SQ FT: 2,600
SALES (est): 2.3MM **Privately Held**
WEB: www.handbiolab.com
SIC: 3842 Orthopedic appliances

(P-7072)
IMPERATIVE CARE INC (PA)
1359 Dell Ave, Campbell (95008-6609)
PHONE 669 228-3814
Daniel Davis, *President*
Matthew Garrett, *CFO*

Ariel Sutton, *Exec VP*
Brian Armijo, *Vice Pres*
Chad Roue, *Vice Pres*
EMP: 24 **EST:** 2016
SQ FT: 20,000
SALES (est): 5.9MM **Privately Held**
WEB: www.imperativecare.com
SIC: 3842 Surgical appliances & supplies

(P-7073)
INNERSCOPE HEARING TECH INC
2151 Professional Dr Fl 2, Roseville (95661-3761)
PHONE 916 218-4100
Matthew Moore, *CEO*
Mark Moore, *Ch of Bd*
Kim Moore, *Treasurer*
Adnan Shennib, *CTO*
Patrick Muchiri, *Cust Svc Dir*
EMP: 19 **EST:** 2012
SQ FT: 6,944
SALES (est): 324.8K **Privately Held**
WEB: www.innd.com
SIC: 5999 3842 7629 Hearing aids; hearing aids; hearing aid repair

(P-7074)
INTUITIVE SURGICAL INC (PA)
1020 Kifer Rd, Sunnyvale (94086-5301)
PHONE 408 523-2100
Gary S Guthart, *President*
Craig H Barratt, *Ch of Bd*
Marshall L Mohr, *CFO*
Kara Andersen Reiter, *Ch Credit Ofcr*
Myriam J Curet, *Chief Mktg Ofcr*
▲ **EMP:** 183 **EST:** 1995
SQ FT: 1,200,000
SALES (est): 4.3B **Publicly Held**
WEB: www.intuitive.com
SIC: 3842 3841 Surgical appliances & supplies; surgical & medical instruments

(P-7075)
KAISE PERMA SAN FRANC MEDIC CE
2425 Geary Blvd, San Francisco (94115-3358)
PHONE 415 833-2000
Michael Alexander, *Senior VP*
Karen Bass, *Vice Pres*
Vikas Thakur, *Vice Pres*
Minh Lam, *Engineer*
Wendy Retzloff, *Purchasing*
EMP: 32 **EST:** 2013
SALES (est): 4.4MM **Privately Held**
SIC: 3842 Autoclaves, hospital & surgical

(P-7076)
NUPRODX INC
161 S Vasco Rd Ste G, Livermore (94551-5131)
PHONE 925 292-0866
David Gaskell, *President*
Debbie Carbone, *Human Resources*
Jared Federico, *Accounts Mgr*
EMP: 15
SALES (corp-wide): 2.4MM **Privately Held**
WEB: www.nuprodx.com
SIC: 3842 3999 Wheelchairs; wheelchair lifts
PA: Nuprodx, Inc.
   889 Hayes St
   Sonoma CA 95476
   415 472-1699

(P-7077)
PACIFIC COAST LABORATORIES
Also Called: PCL Communications
2100 Orchard Ave, San Leandro (94577-3415)
PHONE 510 351-2770
Monte Martinez, *President*
EMP: 39 **EST:** 1949
SALES (est): 1.6MM **Privately Held**
WEB: www.pcl-cfa.com
SIC: 3842 Hearing aids; ear plugs; noise protectors, personal

(P-7078)
PULSE SYSTEMS LLC
4090 Nelson Ave, Concord (94520-8513)
PHONE 925 798-4080

3842 - Orthopedic, Prosthetic & Surgical Appliances/Splys County (P-7079)

Herb Bellucci,
Jeremy Wallace, *Prgrmr*
Wen Ho, *Engineer*
Justin Koos, *Engineer*
Neda Nasr, *Sales Engr*
EMP: 80 **EST:** 1997
SQ FT: 12,600
SALES (est): 13.5MM
SALES (corp-wide): 355.8K **Privately Held**
WEB: www.heraeus.com
SIC: 3842 3841 Surgical appliances & supplies; surgical & medical instruments
HQ: Heraeus Holding Gesellschaft Mit Beschrankter Haftung
Heraeusstr. 12-14
Hanau HE 63450
618 135-0

(P-7079)
SAN JQUIN ORTHTICS PRSTHTICS C
2211 N California St, Stockton (95204-5503)
PHONE..................209 932-0170
Matthew Shane Evans, *CEO*
Mike Beck, *Principal*
EMP: 15 **EST:** 2006
SALES (est): 1.5MM **Privately Held**
SIC: 3842 Orthopedic appliances

(P-7080)
SPECTRUM PRSTHTCS/RTHTICS RDDI
1844 South St, Redding (96001-1809)
PHONE..................530 243-4500
Forest Sexton, *President*
Jeff Zeller, *Admin Sec*
Tina Zeller, *Manager*
EMP: 47 **EST:** 2005
SALES (est): 2.4MM **Privately Held**
WEB: www.spectrumoandp.com
SIC: 3842 Limbs, artificial

(P-7081)
STRYKER SALES LLC
Also Called: Stryker Endoscopy
5900 Optical Ct, San Jose (95138-1400)
PHONE..................800 624-4422
Kim Gonia, *Director*
Aileen Maderich, *Officer*
Bill Piwnica, *Exec Dir*
David Hess, *Program Mgr*
John Murray, *General Mgr*
EMP: 38
SQ FT: 20,000
SALES (corp-wide): 14.3B **Publicly Held**
WEB: www.stryker.com
SIC: 3842 Personal safety equipment
HQ: Stryker Sales, Llc
2825 Airview Blvd
Portage MI 49002

(P-7082)
THINK SURGICAL INC
47201 Lakeview Blvd, Fremont (94538-6530)
PHONE..................510 249-2300
Stuart F Simpson, *CEO*
David C Dvorak, *Ch of Bd*
Paul Weiner, *Officer*
Steve Whiseant, *Vice Pres*
Cynthia Kalb, *VP Bus Dvlpt*
EMP: 160 **EST:** 2007
SQ FT: 70,000
SALES (est): 50MM **Privately Held**
WEB: www.thinksurgical.com
SIC: 3842 Surgical appliances & supplies

3843 Dental Eqpt & Splys

(P-7083)
DENTISTS SUPPLY COMPANY
1201 K St Ste 740, Sacramento (95814-4039)
PHONE..................888 253-1223
James Wiggett, *CEO*
Jamie Gabe, *Marketing Staff*
EMP: 25 **EST:** 2014
SALES (est): 3MM **Privately Held**
WEB: www.tdsc.com
SIC: 3843 Dental equipment & supplies

(P-7084)
DEXTA CORPORATION
957 Enterprise Way, NAPA (94558-6209)
PHONE..................707 255-2454
Mark M Rusin, *President*
Paul Rusin, *Vice Pres*
Justin Magnelli, *Manager*
EMP: 52 **EST:** 1966
SQ FT: 19,000
SALES (est): 10MM **Privately Held**
WEB: www.dexta.com
SIC: 3843 Dental chairs

(P-7085)
LARES RESEARCH
295 Lockheed Ave, Chico (95973-9026)
PHONE..................530 345-1767
Craig Lares, *President*
Christian Godoy, *Sr Exec VP*
David Mosey, *Technician*
Bruce Holderbein, *Electrical Engi*
Larry McCulloch, *Engineer*
EMP: 39 **EST:** 1956
SQ FT: 30,000
SALES (est): 7MM **Privately Held**
WEB: www.laresdental.com
SIC: 3843 5047 Dental equipment & supplies; dental equipment & supplies

(P-7086)
MICRODENTAL LABORATORIES INC
7475 Southfront Rd, Livermore (94551-8224)
PHONE..................800 229-0936
Dazia Bosworth, *Branch Mgr*
Ivan Siu, *CFO*
Eric Hill, *Division Mgr*
Mike Milne, *General Mgr*
Trisha Hoofard, *Office Mgr*
EMP: 45
SALES (corp-wide): 6.7MM **Privately Held**
WEB: www.microdental.com
SIC: 3843 Dental equipment & supplies
PA: Microdental Laboratories, Inc.
500 Stephenson Hwy
Troy MI 48083
877 711-8778

(P-7087)
PATTERSON DENTAL SUPPLY INC
5087 Commercial Cir, Concord (94520-1268)
PHONE..................925 603-6350
Mark Webb, *Branch Mgr*
EMP: 19
SALES (corp-wide): 5.9B **Publicly Held**
WEB: www.pattersoncompanies.com
SIC: 3843 Dental equipment & supplies
HQ: Patterson Dental Supply, Inc.
1031 Mendota Heights Rd
Saint Paul MN 55120
651 686-1600

(P-7088)
PURELINE ORALCARE INC
804 Estates Dr Ste 104, Aptos (95003-3571)
P.O. Box 1070, Capitola (95010-1070)
PHONE..................831 662-9500
Jack Conrey, *President*
EMP: 19 **EST:** 1996
SQ FT: 8,500
SALES (est): 321.9K **Privately Held**
WEB: www.purelineoralcare.com
SIC: 3843 5047 Dental equipment; dental equipment & supplies

(P-7089)
TECH WEST VACUUM INC
2625 N Argyle Ave, Fresno (93727-1304)
PHONE..................559 291-1650
John Napier, *President*
▲ **EMP:** 52 **EST:** 1983
SQ FT: 30,000
SALES (est): 9.2MM **Privately Held**
WEB: www.tech-west.com
SIC: 3843 Dental equipment

(P-7090)
WELLS DENTAL INC
Also Called: Wells Precision Machining
5860 Flynn Creek Rd, Comptche (95427-9500)
P.O. Box 106 (95427-0106)
PHONE..................707 937-0521
Richard B Wells, *President*
Marvin Wells, *Corp Secy*
Ginger Wells, *Exec VP*
EMP: 15 **EST:** 1929
SQ FT: 15,000
SALES (est): 2.3MM **Privately Held**
WEB: www.wellsdental.com
SIC: 3843 Dental laboratory equipment

3844 X-ray Apparatus & Tubes

(P-7091)
CARL ZISS X-RAY MICROSCOPY INC
5300 Central Pkwy, Dublin (94568-4999)
PHONE..................925 701-3600
Bobby Blair, *CEO*
Peter Jackson, *President*
Timothy Hart, *Corp Secy*
Jin Yoon, *Principal*
Vladimir Solovyev, *Program Mgr*
EMP: 66 **EST:** 2000
SALES (est): 17.7MM **Privately Held**
WEB: www.zeiss.com
SIC: 3844 5047 X-ray apparatus & tubes; X-ray machines & tubes
HQ: Carl Zeiss Microscopy Gmbh
Carl-Zeiss-Promenade 10
Jena TH 07745

(P-7092)
LYNCEAN TECHNOLOGIES INC
47633 Westinghouse Dr, Fremont (94539-7474)
PHONE..................650 320-8300
Ronald Ruth, *CEO*
Rod Loewen, *Shareholder*
Carol Ruth, *CFO*
Jeff Rifkin, *Vice Pres*
Kasahara Jack, *VP Bus Dvlpt*
▲ **EMP:** 17 **EST:** 2001
SALES (est): 4.7MM **Privately Held**
WEB: www.lynceantech.com
SIC: 3844 X-ray generators

(P-7093)
RAPISCAN LABORATORIES INC (HQ)
46718 Fremont Blvd, Fremont (94538-6538)
PHONE..................408 961-9700
Shiva Kumar, *President*
Deborah Cegielski, *Vice Pres*
▲ **EMP:** 60 **EST:** 1997
SALES (est): 33.6MM
SALES (corp-wide): 1.1B **Publicly Held**
WEB: www.rapiscansystems.com
SIC: 3844 X-ray apparatus & tubes
PA: Osi Systems, Inc.
12525 Chadron Ave
Hawthorne CA 90250
310 978-0516

(P-7094)
TRUFOCUS CORPORATION
468 Westridge Dr, Watsonville (95076-4159)
PHONE..................831 761-9981
George G Howard, *President*
Kevin Bedolla, *Admin Sec*
Dianne Moody, *Exec Sec*
EMP: 16 **EST:** 1987
SQ FT: 12,500
SALES (est): 2MM **Privately Held**
WEB: www.trufocus.com
SIC: 3844 X-ray apparatus & tubes

(P-7095)
VAREX IMAGING WEST LLC (HQ)
2175 Mission College Blvd, Santa Clara (95054-1520)
PHONE..................408 565-0850
Brian Giambattista, *Mng Member*
Darryl Hoeffner, *Engineer*
Rania Khalife, *Manager*
◆ **EMP:** 169 **EST:** 2015
SQ FT: 74,000
SALES (est): 90MM
SALES (corp-wide): 738.3MM **Publicly Held**
WEB: www.vareximaging.com
SIC: 3844 X-ray apparatus & tubes
PA: Varex Imaging Corporation
1678 S Pioneer Rd
Salt Lake City UT 84104
801 972-5000

3845 Electromedical & Electrotherapeutic Apparatus

(P-7096)
AVANTIS MEDICAL SYSTEMS INC
2367 Bering Dr, San Jose (95131-1125)
P.O. Box 70845, Sunnyvale (94086-0845)
PHONE..................408 733-1901
Matt Frushell, *President*
Anthony Ditonno, *Ch of Bd*
Scott Dodson, *President*
Larry Tannenbaum, *CFO*
Salmaan Hameed, *CTO*
EMP: 38 **EST:** 2004
SQ FT: 4,700
SALES (est): 3.3MM **Privately Held**
WEB: www.avantismedicalsystems.com
SIC: 3845 Endoscopic equipment, electromedical

(P-7097)
BIOINTELLISENSE INC
570 El Cmino Real Ste 200, Redwood City (94063)
PHONE..................650 481-8140
James Mault, *CEO*
David Wang, *CTO*
EMP: 26 **EST:** 2018
SALES (est): 8.9MM **Privately Held**
WEB: www.biointellisense.com
SIC: 3845 Electromedical apparatus

(P-7098)
CALA HEALTH INC
875 Mahler Rd Ste 168, Burlingame (94010-1606)
PHONE..................415 890-3961
Renee Ryan, *CEO*
John Colombo, *Vice Pres*
Chris Daniel, *Vice Pres*
Manish Gupta, *Vice Pres*
Denise Wright, *Surgery Dir*
EMP: 75 **EST:** 2013
SALES (est): 11.1MM **Privately Held**
WEB: www.calahealth.com
SIC: 3845 7389 Transcutaneous electrical nerve stimulators (TENS); business services

(P-7099)
CARE INNOVATIONS LLC
950 Iron Point Rd Ste 160, Folsom (95630-9304)
PHONE..................800 450-0970
Randy Swanson, *CEO*
Marcus Grindstaff, *COO*
Bruce Pruden, *CFO*
Kevon Kothari, *Vice Pres*
Alan O 'kelly, *Sr Software Eng*
EMP: 50 **EST:** 2011
SALES (est): 10MM **Privately Held**
WEB: www.careinnovations.com
SIC: 3845 3641 Electromedical apparatus; electrotherapeutic lamp units

(P-7100)
CHALGREN ENTERPRISES
Also Called: Jari Electro Supply
380 Tomkins Ct, Gilroy (95020-3631)
PHONE..................408 847-3994
Richard Kaiser, *President*
Michael Kaiser, *Treasurer*
Diana Kaiser, *Vice Pres*
EMP: 15 **EST:** 1965
SQ FT: 4,200
SALES (est): 2.1MM **Privately Held**
WEB: www.rhythmlink.com
SIC: 3845 Electromedical equipment

▲ = Import ▼ = Export
◆ = Import/Export

PRODUCTS & SERVICES SECTION
3845 - Electromedical & Electrotherapeutic Apparatus County (P-7124)

(P-7101)
CLI LIQUIDATING CORPORATION
47266 Benicia St, Fremont (94538-7330)
PHONE.................................510 354-0300
Fax: 510 657-4476
EMP: 81
SQ FT: 29,000
SALES (est): 11MM Privately Held
WEB: www.cardima.com
SIC: 3845 Mfg Electromedical Equipment

(P-7102)
CUTERA INC (PA)
3240 Bayshore Blvd, Brisbane (94005-1021)
PHONE.................................415 657-5500
David H Mowry, *CEO*
J Daniel Plants, *Ch of Bd*
Fuad Ahmad, *CFO*
Sandra A Gardiner, *CFO*
Rohan Seth, *CFO*
EMP: 358 EST: 1998
SQ FT: 66,000
SALES (est): 147.6MM Publicly Held
WEB: www.cutera.com
SIC: 3845 Laser systems & equipment, medical

(P-7103)
EBR SYSTEMS INC (PA)
480 Oakmead Pkwy, Sunnyvale (94085-4708)
PHONE.................................408 720-1906
John McCutcheon, *President*
Allan Will, *Ch of Bd*
Stephen Oconnor, *President*
Mark Schwartz, *President*
Rick Riley, *COO*
EMP: 22 EST: 2003
SQ FT: 8,500
SALES (est): 5.1MM Privately Held
WEB: www.ebrsystemsinc.com
SIC: 3845 Cardiographs

(P-7104)
EKO DEVICES INC
1212 Broadway Ste 100, Oakland (94612-1835)
PHONE.................................844 356-3384
Connor Landgraf, *CEO*
Adam Saltman, *Officer*
Phu Trinh, *Vice Pres*
Subbu Venkatraman, *CTO*
Steven Avila, *Opers Staff*
EMP: 100 EST: 2013
SALES (est): 10.7MM Privately Held
WEB: www.ekohealth.com
SIC: 3845 5047 3841 Electromedical equipment; medical & hospital equipment; diagnostic equipment, medical; diagnostic apparatus, medical

(P-7105)
EXPLORAMED NC7 INC
Also Called: Willow
1975 W El Cmino Real Ste, Mountain View (94040)
PHONE................................ 650 559-5805
Naomi Kelman, *President*
EMP: 58 EST: 2014
SQ FT: 5,175
SALES (est): 6.3MM Privately Held
WEB: www.exploramed.com
SIC: 3845 Electromedical apparatus

(P-7106)
HALO NEURO INC
Also Called: Halo Neuroscience
735 Market St Fl 4, San Francisco (94103-2034)
PHONE.................................415 851-3338
Daniel Chao, *CEO*
Daniel S Chao, *Bd of Directors*
Mark Mastalir, *Chief Mktg Ofcr*
Mark Mastlier, *Chief Mktg Ofcr*
Brett Wingeier, *CTO*
EMP: 17 EST: 2013
SQ FT: 8,000
SALES (est): 1.8MM Privately Held
WEB: www.haloneuro.com
SIC: 3845 Electrotherapeutic apparatus

(P-7107)
HOSPITAL SYSTEMS INC
750 Garcia Ave, Pittsburg (94565-5012)
PHONE.................................925 427-7800
Jennifer M Miller, *Ch of Bd*
David H Miller, *President*
Rebecca Miller, *President*
Kathie Campbell, *Vice Pres*
Becca Miller, *Vice Pres*
EMP: 72 EST: 1970
SQ FT: 20,000
SALES (est): 8.5MM Privately Held
WEB: www.hsiheadwalls.com
SIC: 3845 Electromedical equipment

(P-7108)
IRIDEX CORPORATION (PA)
1212 Terra Bella Ave, Mountain View (94043-1824)
PHONE.................................650 940-4700
David I Bruce, *President*
Patrick Mercer, *COO*
Fuad Ahmad, *CFO*
EMP: 83 EST: 1989
SQ FT: 37,166
SALES (est): 36.3MM Publicly Held
WEB: www.iridex.com
SIC: 3845 Electromedical equipment

(P-7109)
IRIS MEDICAL INSTRUMENTS INC
Also Called: Iridex
1212 Terra Bella Ave, Mountain View (94043-1824)
PHONE.................................650 940-4700
Ted Boutacoff, *CEO*
EMP: 43 EST: 1989
SALES (est): 1.1MM Publicly Held
WEB: www.iridex.com
SIC: 3845 Laser systems & equipment, medical
PA: Iridex Corporation
    1212 Terra Bella Ave
    Mountain View CA 94043

(P-7110)
KYMA MEDICAL TECHNOLOGIES INC
2000 Ringwood Ave, San Jose (95131-1728)
PHONE.................................650 386-5089
Assaf Bernstein, *CEO*
Uriel Weinstein, *CTO*
Melissa Atienza, *Manager*
EMP: 17 EST: 2014
SALES (est): 758K Privately Held
SIC: 3845 Automated blood & body fluid analyzers, except laboratory
PA: Zoll Medical Israel Ltd
    14 Atirei Yeda
    Kfar Saba

(P-7111)
LUMASENSE TECHNOLOGIES INC (HQ)
888 Tasman Dr 100, Milpitas (95035-7439)
PHONE.................................408 727-1600
Steve Abely, *CEO*
Vivek Joshi, *President*
Steve Uhlir, *President*
Tina M Donikowski, *Bd of Directors*
John A Roush, *Bd of Directors*
▲ EMP: 80 EST: 2005
SALES (est): 97.6MM
SALES (corp-wide): 1.4B Publicly Held
WEB: www.advancedenergy.com
SIC: 3845 3829 3825 3823 Electromedical equipment; measuring & controlling devices; instruments to measure electricity; temperature instruments: industrial process type
PA: Advanced Energy Industries, Inc.
    1595 Wynkoop St Ste 800
    Denver CO 80202
    970 407-6526

(P-7112)
MC LIQUIDATION INC
Also Called: Intraop Medical Services
570 Del Rey Ave, Sunnyvale (94085-3528)
PHONE.................................408 636-1020
John Powers, *President*
J K Hullett, *CFO*
Richard A Belford, *Vice Pres*
Winfield Jones, *VP Sales*
EMP: 56 EST: 1999
SQ FT: 14,419
SALES (est): 1.4MM Privately Held
WEB: www.intraop.com
SIC: 3845 Electromedical equipment

(P-7113)
MENTZER ELECTRONICS
858 Stanton Rd, Burlingame (94010-1404)
P.O. Box 610, Barrington IL (60011-0610)
PHONE.................................650 697-2642
Fax: 650 697-2405
EMP: 24
SQ FT: 14,000
SALES (est): 2.1MM Privately Held
WEB: www.mentzerelectronics.com
SIC: 3845 3672 Mfg Electromedical Equipment Mfg Printed Circuit Boards

(P-7114)
MOVANO INC
1652 Chestnut St, San Francisco (94123-2903)
PHONE.................................415 651-3172
Michael Leabman, *President*
Emily Wang Fairbairn, *Ch of Bd*
Jeremy J Cogan, *CFO*
Phil Kelly, *Vice Pres*
EMP: 15 EST: 2018 Privately Held
WEB: www.movano.com
SIC: 3845 Electromedical equipment

(P-7115)
NATUS MEDICAL INCORPORATED (PA)
6701 Koll Center Pkwy # 12, Pleasanton (94566-8061)
PHONE.................................925 223-6700
Jonathan Kennedy, *President*
Robert A Gunst, *Ch of Bd*
Drew Davies, *CFO*
Austin F Noll III, *Ch Credit Ofcr*
Doris Engibous, *Bd of Directors*
▲ EMP: 392 EST: 1987
SQ FT: 8,200
SALES (est): 415.6MM Publicly Held
WEB: www.natus.com
SIC: 3845 Electromedical equipment

(P-7116)
NEW SOURCE TECHNOLOGY LLC
6678 Owens Dr Ste 105, Pleasanton (94588-3324)
PHONE.................................925 462-6888
Gregory A Pon, *President*
Jocelyn Long, *Vice Pres*
Jenny Jiang, *Business Mgr*
Hannah Smith, *Director*
EMP: 15 EST: 1996
SALES (est): 1.6MM Privately Held
WEB: www.newsourcetechnology.com
SIC: 3845 Laser systems & equipment, medical

(P-7117)
NEW STAR LASERS INC
Also Called: Cooltouch
8331 Sierra College Blvd # 204, Roseville (95661-9412)
PHONE.................................916 677-1900
Ilan Ben-David, *CEO*
Nina Davis, *President*
David R Hennings, *President*
Peter Giove, *Buyer*
EMP: 41 EST: 1994
SQ FT: 20,000
SALES (est): 8.2MM Privately Held
SIC: 3845 Laser systems & equipment, medical

(P-7118)
ORATEC INTERVENTIONS INC (DH)
3696 Haven Ave, Redwood City (94063-4604)
PHONE.................................901 396-2121
Ron Sparks, *CEO*
Mark Frost, *Treasurer*
Jerry Goodman, *Vice Pres*
Reuben Rosales, *Vice Pres*
James Ralston, *Admin Sec*
EMP: 100 EST: 1993
SQ FT: 37,000
SALES (est): 2.9MM
SALES (corp-wide): 4.5B Privately Held
WEB: www.ceosmith-nephew.com
SIC: 3845 8011 3841 Electromedical equipment; offices & clinics of medical doctors; surgical & medical instruments
HQ: Smith & Nephew, Inc.
    1450 E Brooks Rd
    Memphis TN 38116
    901 396-2121

(P-7119)
OUTSET MEDICAL INC
3052 Orchard Dr, San Jose (95134-2011)
PHONE.................................669 231-8200
Leslie Trigg, *President*
D Keith Grossman, *Ch of Bd*
Martin Vazquez, *COO*
Nabeel Ahmed, *CFO*
Steve Williamson, *Ch Credit Ofcr*
EMP: 313 EST: 2003
SALES (est): 49.9MM Privately Held
WEB: www.outsetmedical.com
SIC: 3845 Electromedical equipment

(P-7120)
PACESETTER INC
6035 Stoneridge Dr, Pleasanton (94588-3270)
PHONE.................................925 730-4171
David Villarreal, *Branch Mgr*
Darrell Ebuen, *Engineer*
Alicia Baumberger, *Senior Mgr*
EMP: 212
SALES (corp-wide): 34.6B Publicly Held
SIC: 3845 Defibrillator
HQ: Pacesetter, Inc.
    15900 Valley View Ct
    Sylmar CA 91342

(P-7121)
PARACOR MEDICAL INC
19200 Stevns Crk Blvd, Cupertino (95014-2530)
PHONE.................................408 207-1050
William Mavity, *President*
Pooja Joshipura, *Supervisor*
EMP: 19 EST: 1999
SQ FT: 12,000
SALES (est): 1.5MM Privately Held
WEB: www.paracormedical.com
SIC: 3845 Ultrasonic scanning devices, medical

(P-7122)
REFLEXION MEDICAL INC
25841 Industrial Blvd # 275, Hayward (94545-2991)
PHONE.................................650 239-9070
Samuel R Mazin, *President*
Todd Powell, *President*
Martyn Webster, *CFO*
Leonard Lyons, *Vice Pres*
Kathy Oshaughnessy, *Vice Pres*
EMP: 120 EST: 2009
SALES (est): 32.8MM Privately Held
WEB: www.reflexion.com
SIC: 3845 Electromedical equipment

(P-7123)
SALUTRON INCORPORATED (PA)
8371 Central Ave Ste A, Newark (94560-3473)
PHONE.................................510 795-2876
Mike Tsai, *CEO*
Michael Tsai, *CFO*
Gerstenberger Bob, *Vice Pres*
Bob Gerstenberger, *Vice Pres*
Yong Jin Lee, *CTO*
◆ EMP: 29 EST: 1995
SQ FT: 11,000
SALES (est): 5.6MM Privately Held
WEB: www.salutron.com
SIC: 3845 Patient monitoring apparatus

(P-7124)
SOLTA MEDICAL INC
25901 Industrial Blvd, Hayward (94545-2995)
PHONE.................................510 782-2286
Doug Heigo, *Branch Mgr*
Jack Ham, *Engineer*

3845 - Electromedical & Electrotherapeutic Apparatus County (P-7125)

Patrick Babcock, *Opers Staff*
Ana Cardenas, *Opers Staff*
Lay Kee, *Marketing Staff*
EMP: 150
SALES (corp-wide): 8.6B **Privately Held**
WEB: www.solta.com
SIC: 3845 Electromedical equipment
HQ: Solta Medical, Inc.
7031 Koll Center Pkwy # 260
Pleasanton CA 94566
510 786-6946

(P-7125)
THORATEC LLC (HQ)
6035 Stoneridge Dr, Pleasanton (94588-3270)
PHONE..................925 847-8600
Donald J Zurbay,
Taylor C Harris, *CFO*
Taylor Harris, *CFO*
Rich Bonito, *Officer*
Lauren Hernandez, *Vice Pres*
▲ **EMP:** 193 **EST:** 1976
SQ FT: 66,000
SALES (est): 386.8MM
SALES (corp-wide): 34.6B **Publicly Held**
WEB: www.abbott.com
SIC: 3845 3841 Electromedical equipment; surgical & medical instruments; diagnostic apparatus, medical
PA: Abbott Laboratories
100 Abbott Park Rd
Abbott Park IL 60064
224 667-6100

(P-7126)
TOPCON MED LASER SYSTEMS INC
606 Enterprise Ct, Livermore (94550-5200)
PHONE..................888 760-8657
Dean Scotch, *Vice Pres*
Rob Orsino, *President*
Hidehary Suzuki, *President*
Dan Van Buskirk, *Program Mgr*
▲ **EMP:** 45 **EST:** 2010
SALES (est): 12.6MM **Privately Held**
WEB: www.pascalvision.com
SIC: 3845 Laser systems & equipment, medical
HQ: Topcon America Corporation
111 Bauer Dr
Oakland NJ 07436
201 599-5100

(P-7127)
TOSHIBA AMERICA INC
280 Utah Ave, South San Francisco (94080-6812)
PHONE..................212 596-0600
Umesh Arora, *Director*
EMP: 150 **Privately Held**
SIC: 3845 Electromedical equipment
HQ: Toshiba America Inc
1251 Ave Of Amrcas Ste 41
New York NY 10020
212 596-0600

(P-7128)
TURNCARE INC
2225 E Byshore Rd Ste 200, Palo Alto (94303)
PHONE..................203 437-6768
Carol Juhl, *Opers Staff*
Rafael Squitieri, *Senior Mgr*
EMP: 16 **EST:** 2011
SALES (est): 4.2MM **Privately Held**
WEB: www.turncare.com
SIC: 3845 Electromedical equipment

(P-7129)
TUSKER MEDICAL INC
155 Jefferson Dr, Menlo Park (94025-1114)
PHONE..................650 223-6900
Amir Abolfathi, *President*
EMP: 31 **EST:** 2016
SALES (est): 5.7MM
SALES (corp-wide): 4.5B **Privately Held**
WEB: www.smith-nephew.com
SIC: 3845 Audiological equipment, electromedical
PA: Smith & Nephew Plc
Building 5, Croxley Park
Watford HERTS WD18
800 015-7573

(P-7130)
TWENTY TWENTY THERAPEUTICS LLC
259 E Grand Ave, South San Francisco (94080-4804)
PHONE..................208 696-2020
Dimitri Azar, *Mng Member*
EMP: 25 **EST:** 2020
SALES (est): 900K **Privately Held**
WEB: www.twentytwenty.com
SIC: 3845 Electromedical equipment

(P-7131)
VARIAN MEDICAL SYSTEMS INC (DH)
3100 Hansen Way, Palo Alto (94304-1030)
PHONE..................650 493-4000
Christopher Toth, *CEO*
Francis R Facchini, *President*
Kevin O'Reilly, *President*
Tim Fox, *Assoc VP*
Matthias Platsch, *Exec VP*
EMP: 1710 **EST:** 1948
SQ FT: 481,000
SALES (est): 3.1B
SALES (corp-wide): 67.4B **Privately Held**
WEB: www.varian.com
SIC: 3845 7372 Electromedical equipment; electromedical apparatus; prepackaged software
HQ: Siemens Healthineers Ag
Henkestr. 127
Erlangen BY 91052
800 188-1885

(P-7132)
VAVE HEALTH INC
2350 Mission College Blvd # 1200, Santa Clara (95054-1565)
PHONE..................650 387-7059
Amin Nikoozadeh, *CEO*
Lynn Bender, *Vice Pres*
Joe Ko, *Vice Pres*
Caroline Zeisbrich, *Med Doctor*
EMP: 15 **EST:** 2014
SALES (est): 2MM **Privately Held**
WEB: www.vavehealth.com
SIC: 3845 Ultrasonic medical equipment, except cleaning

(P-7133)
VIBRYNT INC
2570 W El Camino Real # 310, Mountain View (94040-1306)
PHONE..................650 362-6100
EMP: 30
SQ FT: 4,121
SALES (est): 3.1MM **Privately Held**
SIC: 3845 Mfg Electromedical Equipment

(P-7134)
VITAL CONNECT INC
224 Airport Pkwy Ste 300, San Jose (95110-1022)
PHONE..................408 963-4600
Nersi Nazari, *President*
Michael Dillhyon, *President*
Martin Webster, *CFO*
Bill Brodie, *Officer*
Johanna Beckmen, *Vice Pres*
EMP: 50 **EST:** 2012
SALES (est): 12MM **Privately Held**
WEB: www.vitalconnect.com
SIC: 3845 Ultrasonic scanning devices, medical

(P-7135)
XINTEC CORPORATION (PA)
Also Called: Convergent Laser Technologies
1660 S Loop Rd, Alameda (94502-7091)
PHONE..................510 832-2130
Mark H K Chim, *President*
Marilyn M Chou, *Exec VP*
Michael Haskin, *Engineer*
Dang Nguyen, *Engineer*
Jenny Ha, *Purchasing*
▲ **EMP:** 20 **EST:** 1984
SQ FT: 20,000
SALES (est): 7.3MM **Privately Held**
SIC: 3845 Laser systems & equipment, medical

(P-7136)
ZOLL CIRCULATION INC
2000 Ringwood Ave, San Jose (95131-1728)
PHONE..................408 541-2140
Richard A Packer, *CEO*
James Palabzolo, *President*
Hal Harmon, *Vice Pres*
Rick Helkowski, *Vice Pres*
Kenneth E Ludlum, *Principal*
▲ **EMP:** 130
SALES (est): 35.9MM **Privately Held**
WEB: www.zoll.com
SIC: 3845 3841 Electromedical equipment; surgical & medical instruments
HQ: Zoll Medical Corporation
269 Mill Rd
Chelmsford MA 01824
978 421-9655

3851 Ophthalmic Goods

(P-7137)
BESPOKE INC
Also Called: Topology Eyewear
3260 19th St, San Francisco (94110-1917)
PHONE..................612 201-6800
Eric Varady, *President*
Rob Varady, *COO*
Robert Varady, *COO*
Alexis Gallagher, *Officer*
EMP: 20 **EST:** 2014
SALES (est): 2.3MM **Privately Held**
WEB: www.topologyeyewear.com
SIC: 3851 Frames & parts, eyeglass & spectacle

(P-7138)
COOPER COMPANIES INC (PA)
6101 Bollinger Canyon Rd # 5, San Ramon (94583-5108)
PHONE..................925 460-3600
Albert G White III, *President*
Daniel G McBride, *COO*
Brian G Andrews, *CFO*
Agostino Ricupati, *Senior VP*
Mark J Drury, *Vice Pres*
EMP: 1829 **EST:** 1980
SQ FT: 103,990
SALES (est): 2.4B **Publicly Held**
WEB: www.coopercos.com
SIC: 3851 3842 Contact lenses; surgical appliances & supplies; gynecological supplies & appliances

(P-7139)
EYEFLUENCE INC
1600 Amphitheatre Pkwy, Mountain View (94043-1351)
PHONE..................408 586-8632
EMP: 29
SALES (est): 3.7MM **Privately Held**
SIC: 3851 Mfg Ophthalmic Goods

(P-7140)
GRIFFIN & REED A MEDICAL CORP
651 Fulton Ave, Sacramento (95825-4813)
PHONE..................916 483-2525
D Brent Reed, *President*
EMP: 16 **EST:** 1977
SALES (est): 482.5K **Privately Held**
WEB: www.lasikworld.com
SIC: 3851 Protective eyeware

(P-7141)
HOYA OPTICAL INC (PA)
1400 Carpenter Ln, Modesto (95351-1102)
P.O. Box 580870 (95358-0016)
PHONE..................209 579-7739
Fred Fink, *CEO*
EMP: 90 **EST:** 1954
SQ FT: 17,700
SALES (est): 7.6MM **Privately Held**
WEB: www.hoyavision.com
SIC: 3851 8011 5995 5048 Ophthalmic goods; offices & clinics of medical doctors; optical goods stores; ophthalmic goods

(P-7142)
IRD ACQUISITIONS LLC
Also Called: Trijicon Electro Optics
12810 Earhart Ave, Auburn (95602-9027)
PHONE..................530 210-2966
Stephen Bindon, *CEO*
EMP: 17 **EST:** 2013
SQ FT: 7,500
SALES (est): 2.1MM
SALES (corp-wide): 69.7MM **Privately Held**
WEB: www.trijicon.com
SIC: 3851 3949 3827 Goggles: sun, safety, industrial, underwater, etc.; target shooting equipment; telescopes: elbow, panoramic, sighting, fire control, etc.
PA: Trijicon, Inc.
49385 Shafer Ct
Wixom MI 48393
248 960-7700

(P-7143)
LENS C-C INC (PA)
Also Called: Con-Cise Contact Lens Co
1750 N Loop Rd Ste 150, Alameda (94502-8013)
PHONE..................800 772-3911
Carl Moore, *President*
Lynda Baker, *Vice Pres*
Dan Davis, *Vice Pres*
EMP: 100 **EST:** 1949
SQ FT: 34,000
SALES (est): 24.7MM **Privately Held**
WEB: www.abboptical.com
SIC: 3851 Contact lenses

(P-7144)
LENSVECTOR INC
6203 San Ignacio Ave, San Jose (95119-1371)
PHONE..................408 542-0300
Howard Earhart, *CEO*
Mark Gemello, *CFO*
Thomas Killick, *VP Bus Dvlpt*
Lifan Zhang, *Executive*
EMP: 70 **EST:** 2006
SALES (est): 8MM **Privately Held**
WEB: www.lensvector.com
SIC: 3851 Ophthalmic goods

(P-7145)
NITINOL DEVELOPMENT CORP
Also Called: Nitinol Devices & Components
47533 Westinghouse Dr, Fremont (94539-7463)
PHONE..................510 683-2000
Tom Duerig, *President*
Chun Tam, *CFO*
Brian Adcock, *Officer*
Craig Bonsignore, *Vice Pres*
John Dicello, *Vice Pres*
EMP: 600 **EST:** 1991
SQ FT: 30,000
SALES (est): 49.5MM **Privately Held**
WEB: www.nitinol.com
SIC: 3851 3496 Frames & parts, eyeglass & spectacle; miscellaneous fabricated wire products

(P-7146)
VSP RETAIL INC
3333 Quality Dr, Rancho Cordova (95670-7985)
PHONE..................800 852-7600
Nicola Zotta, *President*
EMP: 15 **EST:** 2016
SALES (est): 854.5K **Privately Held**
WEB: www.vspglobal.com
SIC: 3851 Frames, lenses & parts, eyeglass & spectacle

(P-7147)
WILEY X INC (PA)
Also Called: Wiley X Eyewear
7800 Patterson Pass Rd, Livermore (94550-9544)
PHONE..................925 243-9810
Myles J Freeman Jr, *President*
Myles R Freeman Sr, *CEO*
Mike Bilby, *CFO*
Karen Stevens, *Info Tech Dir*
Christian G Gerlovich, *Info Tech Mgr*
◆ **EMP:** 120 **EST:** 1987
SQ FT: 35,000

▲ = Import ▼ = Export
◆ = Import/Export

PRODUCTS & SERVICES SECTION

3914 - Silverware, Plated & Stainless Steel Ware County (P-7168)

SALES (est): 28.5MM **Privately Held**
WEB: www.wileyx.com
SIC: **3851** 5048 2381 2339 Frames, lenses & parts, eyeglass & spectacle; ophthalmic goods; gloves, work: woven or knit, made from purchased materials; women's & misses' athletic clothing & sportswear

3861 Photographic Eqpt & Splys

(P-7148)
ALTIA SYSTEMS INC
20400 Stevns Crk Blvd # 750, Cupertino (95014-2291)
PHONE......................................408 996-9710
Aurangzeb Khan, *CEO*
Ram Natarajan, *Officer*
Brian Bodmer, *Vice Pres*
Eric Smith, *Vice Pres*
Alex Hausman, *Executive*
▲ **EMP:** 25 **EST:** 2011
SALES (est): 4.8MM
SALES (corp-wide): 2.1B **Privately Held**
WEB: www.gn.com
SIC: **3861** Cameras & related equipment
PA: Gn Store Nord A/S
    Lautrupbjerg 7
    Ballerup 2750
    457 500-00

(P-7149)
GLOBAL INFORMATION DIST INC
2635 Zanker Rd, San Jose (95134-2107)
PHONE......................................408 232-5500
Ernstfried Driesen, *President*
Leon Hefner, *Engineer*
Guenter Heissler, *Manager*
EMP: 19 **EST:** 1989
SQ FT: 11,000
SALES (est): 3.4MM
SALES (corp-wide): 3.4MM **Privately Held**
WEB: www.gid-it.de
SIC: **3861** 5112 7379 Microfiche readers & reader printers; computer & photocopying supplies; computer related maintenance services
PA: Global Information Distribution GmbH
    Brugelmannstr. 5
    Koln NW 50679
    221 837-9020

(P-7150)
GOPRO INC (PA)
3000 Clearview Way, San Mateo (94402-3710)
PHONE......................................650 332-7600
Nicholas Woodman, *Ch of Bd*
Brian McGee, *COO*
Dean Jahnke, *Vice Pres*
Eve Saltman, *Vice Pres*
Chris Clark, *Comms Dir*
◆ **EMP:** 495 **EST:** 2004
SQ FT: 201,000
SALES (est): 891.9MM **Publicly Held**
WEB: www.gopro.com
SIC: **3861** 7372 Cameras & related equipment; prepackaged software

(P-7151)
HOYA HOLDINGS INC (HQ)
680 N Mccarthy Blvd # 120, Milpitas (95035-5120)
PHONE......................................408 654-2300
Hiroshi Suzuki, *CEO*
Eiichiro Ikeda, *COO*
Ryo Hirooka, *CFO*
▲ **EMP:** 180 **EST:** 1973
SALES (est): 58.4MM **Privately Held**
WEB: www.hoyaoptics.com
SIC: **3861** 3825 3827 Photographic sensitized goods; test equipment for electronic & electric measurement; optical instruments & lenses

(P-7152)
L-3 CMMNICATIONS SONOMA EO INC
Also Called: Wescam Sonoma Operations
428 Aviation Blvd, Santa Rosa (95403-1069)
PHONE......................................707 568-3000
Andy Fordham, *General Mgr*
Felice Marrone, *Info Tech Mgr*
Tyler Bushman, *Network Enginr*
Ken Landaiche, *Electrical Engi*
Scott Sellner, *Finance Mgr*
EMP: 200 **EST:** 1997
SQ FT: 20,000
SALES (est): 41.2MM
SALES (corp-wide): 18.1B **Publicly Held**
WEB: www.l3harris.com
SIC: **3861** 3812 Photographic equipment & supplies; heads-up display systems (HUD), aeronautical
HQ: L3 Technologies, Inc.
    600 3rd Ave Fl 34
    New York NY 10016
    321 727-9100

(P-7153)
LEOPARD IMAGING INC (PA)
48820 Kato Rd Ste 100b, Fremont (94538-7323)
PHONE......................................408 263-0988
Xiaowu Pu, *CEO*
EMP: 95 **EST:** 2008
SALES (est): 9.8MM **Privately Held**
WEB: www.leopardimaging.com
SIC: **3861** 5946 8071 3663 Cameras & related equipment; camera & photographic supply stores; X-ray laboratory, including dental; cameras, television

(P-7154)
LUMENS INTEGRATION INC
4116 Clipper Ct, Fremont (94538-6514)
PHONE......................................510 657-8367
Andy Chang, *President*
Helen Perlegos, *Marketing Mgr*
Haiho Tran, *Sales Staff*
Paul Munoz, *Mktg Coord*
Christopher Skaggs, *Manager*
◆ **EMP:** 36 **EST:** 2001
SQ FT: 5,200
SALES (est): 5.1MM **Privately Held**
WEB: www.mylumens.com
SIC: **3861** 5043 Projectors, still or motion picture, silent or sound; projection apparatus, motion picture & slide
HQ: Lumens Digital Optics Inc.
    5f-1, 20, Taiyuan St.,
    Chupei City HSI 30288

(P-7155)
NEFELI NETWORKS INC
2150 Shattuck Ave # 1300, Berkeley (94704-1345)
PHONE......................................510 859-4665
Kevin Fall, *Administration*
EMP: 23 **EST:** 2017
SALES (est): 644.9K **Privately Held**
WEB: www.nefeli.io
SIC: **3861** Photographic equipment & supplies

(P-7156)
NEUVECTOR INC
2880 Zanker Rd Ste 100, San Jose (95134-2121)
PHONE......................................408 455-4034
Fei Huang, *President*
Glen Kosaka, *Vice Pres*
Selvam Thangaraj, *Engineer*
Anssi Harjunpaa, *Sales Staff*
EMP: 21 **EST:** 2016
SALES (est): 2.7MM **Privately Held**
WEB: www.neuvector.com
SIC: **3861** Photographic equipment & supplies

(P-7157)
OPTOMA TECHNOLOGY INC
47697 Westinghouse Dr, Fremont (94539-7474)
PHONE......................................510 897-8600
Robert Sterzing, *Principal*
Hans Wang, *Exec VP*
Gen Page, *Admin Asst*
Nick Quinn, *Web Dvlpr*
Szyleatmaw Bravo, *Software Engr*
▲ **EMP:** 120 **EST:** 1995
SQ FT: 34,000
SALES (est): 35.5MM **Privately Held**
WEB: www.optoma.com
SIC: **3861** Projectors, still or motion picture, silent or sound
HQ: Optoma Corporation
    12f, No. 213, Beixin Rd., Sec. 3
    New Taipei City TAP 23143

(P-7158)
SUSS MCRTEC PRCSION PHTMASK IN
Also Called: Image Technology
821 San Antonio Rd, Palo Alto (94303-4618)
PHONE......................................415 494-3113
Frank Averdung, *CEO*
Alex Naderi, *President*
Patricia Christiansen, *CFO*
EMP: 17 **EST:** 1963
SQ FT: 10,000
SALES (est): 11MM
SALES (corp-wide): 298.1MM **Privately Held**
WEB: www.suss.com
SIC: **3861** Photographic equipment & supplies
HQ: Suss Microtec Inc.
    2520 Palisades Dr
    Corona CA 92882
    408 940-0300

(P-7159)
SWENSON GROUP
Also Called: Swenson Group Inc Xerox
1620 S Amphlett Blvd, San Mateo (94402-2521)
PHONE......................................650 655-4990
Dean Swenson, *President*
Carrie Rosada, *Sales Staff*
EMP: 36 **Privately Held**
WEB: www.theswensongroup.com
SIC: **3861** Photographic equipment & supplies
PA: The Swenson Group
    1410 Stealth St
    Livermore CA 94551

3873 Watch & Clock Devices & Parts

(P-7160)
ACCUSPLIT (PA)
1262 Quarry Ln Ste B, Pleasanton (94566-4733)
PHONE......................................925 290-1900
W Ron Sutton, *President*
Byron Dana Lindstrom, *Exec VP*
Joey Sutton, *Sales Staff*
▲ **EMP:** 17 **EST:** 1980
SALES (est): 2.6MM **Privately Held**
WEB: www.accusplit.com
SIC: **3873** 3824 Watches & parts, except crystals & jewels; controls, revolution & timing instruments; pedometers

(P-7161)
CLUB DONATELLO OWNERS ASSN
501 Post St, San Francisco (94102-1228)
PHONE......................................415 474-7333
Daryl Clark, *President*
Marie Vergara, *Administration*
Sherwin David, *Manager*
Mandy Vergara, *Manager*
▲ **EMP:** 21 **EST:** 1984
SALES (est): 3.4MM **Privately Held**
WEB: www.clubdonatello.org
SIC: **3873** Timers for industrial use, clockwork mechanism only

(P-7162)
PEBBLE TECHNOLOGY CORP
900 Middlefield Rd Ste 5, Redwood City (94063-1681)
PHONE......................................888 224-5820
EMP: 44
SALES (est): 18.9MM **Privately Held**
SIC: **3873** Mfg Watches/Clocks/Parts

3911 Jewelry: Precious Metal

(P-7163)
ALUMA USA INC
435 Tesconi Cir, Santa Rosa (95401-4619)
PHONE......................................707 545-9344
▲ **EMP:** 22
SQ FT: 8,867
SALES: 15MM **Privately Held**
WEB: www.alumausa.net
SIC: **3911** Jewelry, Precious Metal

(P-7164)
ANATOMETAL INC
165 Dubois St, Santa Cruz (95060-2108)
PHONE......................................831 454-9880
Barry Blanchard, *President*
Cheng Tan, *Bookkeeper*
Mary Todryk, *Sales Staff*
Traci Furtado, *Manager*
EMP: 40 **EST:** 1990
SALES (est): 6.7MM **Privately Held**
WEB: www.anatometal.com
SIC: **3911** Jewelry, precious metal

(P-7165)
CONNERS ORO-CAL MFG CO
1720 Bird St, Oroville (95965-4806)
PHONE......................................530 533-5065
David J Conner, *President*
Susan Y Conner, *Admin Sec*
EMP: 18 **EST:** 1941
SQ FT: 2,850
SALES (est): 9.2MM **Privately Held**
WEB: www.orocal.com
SIC: **3911** 3873 5094 Jewelry, precious metal; watches, clocks, watchcases & parts; jewelry & precious stones

(P-7166)
HOLLY YASHI INC
1300 9th St, Arcata (95521-5703)
PHONE......................................707 822-0389
Paul S Lubitz, *President*
Holly A Hosterman, *Vice Pres*
Trevor Shirk, *Research*
Danielle Demartini, *Graphic Designe*
Robin Weburg, *Accountant*
▲ **EMP:** 54 **EST:** 1981
SQ FT: 4,800
SALES (est): 7.1MM **Privately Held**
WEB: www.hollyyashi.com
SIC: **3911** Earrings, precious metal; necklaces, precious metal

(P-7167)
JOSTENS INC
P.O. Box 1747 (95677-7747)
PHONE......................................916 408-2295
EMP: 44
SALES (corp-wide): 307.6MM **Privately Held**
SIC: **3911** Mfg Precious Mtl Jewelry Commercial Printing Misc Publishing
HQ: Jostens, Inc.
    3601 Minnesota Dr Ste 400
    Minneapolis MN 55435
    952 830-3300

3914 Silverware, Plated & Stainless Steel Ware

(P-7168)
STREIVOR INC
Also Called: Streivor Air Systems
2150 Kitty Hawk Rd, Livermore (94551-9522)
PHONE......................................925 960-9090
Jeffrey S Lambertson, *CEO*
Jose Lopez, *Sales Staff*
EMP: 18 **EST:** 1989
SQ FT: 35,250
SALES (est): 5.4MM **Privately Held**
WEB: www.streivor.com
SIC: **3914** Stainless steel ware

3931 - Musical Instruments County (P-7169)   PRODUCTS & SERVICES SECTION

3931 Musical Instruments

(P-7169)
ALEMBIC INC
240 Classic Ct, Rohnert Park (94928-1619)
PHONE................707 523-2611
Susan L Wickersham, *President*
Ron Wickersham, *Treasurer*
EMP: 15 EST: 1969
SALES (est): 2.1MM **Privately Held**
WEB: www.alembic.com
SIC: 3931 5736 Guitars & parts, electric & nonelectric; musical instrument stores

(P-7170)
AXL MUSICAL INSTRUMENTS CO LTD (PA)
401 Forbes Blvd, South San Francisco (94080-2016)
PHONE................415 508-1398
Alan X Liu, *CEO*
EMP: 50 EST: 1998
SALES (est): 331K **Privately Held**
WEB: www.axlmusic.com
SIC: 3931 Musical instruments

(P-7171)
DUNLOP MANUFACTURING INC (PA)
150 Industrial Way, Benicia (94510-1112)
P.O. Box 846 (94510-0846)
PHONE................707 745-2722
James Andrew Dunlop, *CEO*
Julie Forristall, *CFO*
Jasmin Powell, *Vice Pres*
Sally Balmaceda, *Info Tech Mgr*
Michael Hole, *Info Tech Mgr*
◆ EMP: 87 EST: 1977
SQ FT: 40,000
SALES (est): 23.5MM **Privately Held**
WEB: www.jimdunlop.com
SIC: 3931 Guitars & parts, electric & non-electric

(P-7172)
EMG INC
675 Aviation Blvd Ste B, Santa Rosa (95403-1025)
P.O. Box 4394 (95402-4394)
PHONE................707 525-9941
Robert A Turner, *President*
Andy Gravelle, *COO*
Margot Schrank, *Vice Pres*
Gary Rush, *General Mgr*
Derek Bartlett, *Sales Staff*
EMP: 81 EST: 1977
SQ FT: 10,000
SALES (est): 13.1MM **Privately Held**
WEB: www.emgpickups.com
SIC: 3931 5736 Guitars & parts, electric & nonelectric; musical instrument stores

(P-7173)
SANTA CRUZ GUITAR CORPORATION
151 Harvey West Blvd C, Santa Cruz (95060-2167)
PHONE................831 425-0999
Richard Hoover, *President*
John Anderson, *CFO*
Nathan Arrison, *Engineer*
▲ EMP: 22 EST: 1976
SQ FT: 6,800
SALES (est): 3.3MM **Privately Held**
WEB: www.santacruzguitar.com
SIC: 3931 5736 Guitars & parts, electric & nonelectric; musical instrument stores

(P-7174)
SCHOENSTEIN & CO
4001 Industrial Way, Benicia (94510-1241)
PHONE................707 747-5858
Jack M Bethards, *President*
Louis Patterson, *Vice Pres*
Diane Delu, *Admin Sec*
EMP: 25 EST: 1877
SQ FT: 10,000
SALES (est): 1.2MM **Privately Held**
WEB: www.schoenstein.com
SIC: 3931 7699 Pipes, organ; organ tuning & repair

3944 Games, Toys & Children's Vehicles

(P-7175)
CRYPTIC STUDIOS INC
980 University Ave, Los Gatos (95032-7620)
PHONE................408 399-1969
Jack Emmert, *CEO*
Michael C Lewis, *President*
Edward Dibbs, *Software Engr*
Macoy Madson, *Software Engr*
Max Krembs, *Technical Staff*
EMP: 100 EST: 2000
SALES (est): 26.5MM **Privately Held**
WEB: www.crypticstudios.com
SIC: 3944 Video game machines, except coin-operated
HQ: Perfect World Co., Ltd.
701-14, Floor 7, Building 5, No.1 Courtyard, Shangdi E. Road, Ha Beijing 10010

(P-7176)
EXTRON CONTRACT MFG INC
Also Called: Extron Contract Packaging
496 S Abbott Ave, Milpitas (95035-5258)
PHONE................510 353-0177
Andy Nguyen, *President*
EMP: 28 EST: 1979
SQ FT: 200,000
SALES (est): 337.3K **Privately Held**
WEB: www.extroninc.com
SIC: 3944 3672 Electronic games & toys; printed circuit boards

(P-7177)
LEAPFROG ENTERPRISES INC (HQ)
2200 Powell St Ste 500, Emeryville (94608-1818)
PHONE................510 420-5000
Nick Delany, *CEO*
William To, *President*
Alec Anderson, *CFO*
Paul Bennett, *Vice Pres*
Scott A Steinberg, *Vice Pres*
▲ EMP: 357 EST: 1995
SALES (est): 88.1MM **Privately Held**
WEB: www.leapfrog.com
SIC: 3944 Games, toys & children's vehicles

(P-7178)
LEARNING SQUARED INC (PA)
935 Benecia Ave, Sunnyvale (94085-2805)
PHONE................650 567-9995
Andrew Butler, *CEO*
Thomas Boeckle, *Ch of Bd*
Wendy Hsu, *CFO*
Dhruv Bhargava, *Vice Pres*
Ashish Jhalani, *CTO*
EMP: 198 EST: 2014
SQ FT: 12,000
SALES (est): 21.3MM **Privately Held**
WEB: www.squarepanda.com
SIC: 3944 Electronic toys

(P-7179)
LITTLE PASSPORTS INC
27 Maiden Ln Fl 4, San Francisco (94108-5444)
PHONE................415 874-9577
Stella MA, *CEO*
Amy Norman, *Principal*
Jennifer Rey, *Controller*
Michelle Shen, *Opers Staff*
Nicole Gerona, *Merchandising*
▲ EMP: 34 EST: 2012
SALES (est): 11.9MM **Privately Held**
WEB: www.littlepassports.com
SIC: 5945 3944 Hobby & craft supplies; craft & hobby kits & sets

(P-7180)
LIVE2KITE LLC (PA)
44 Industrial Way, Greenbrae (94904-2406)
PHONE................415 924-9463
▲ EMP: 21 EST: 2006
SALES (est): 614.9K **Privately Held**
WEB: www.live2kite.com
SIC: 3944 Kites

(P-7181)
POCKET GEMS INC
220 Montgomery St Ste 750, San Francisco (94104-3479)
PHONE................415 371-1333
Ben Liu, *CEO*
Jon Selin, *Vice Pres*
Lu Su, *Software Engr*
Bowen Zhu, *Software Engr*
Jesse Lam, *Technician*
EMP: 196 EST: 2009
SALES (est): 55.2MM **Privately Held**
WEB: www.pocketgems.com
SIC: 3944 Electronic games & toys

(P-7182)
POOLMASTER INC
770 Del Paso Rd, Sacramento (95834-1117)
P.O. Box 340308 (95834-0308)
PHONE................916 567-9800
Leon H Tager, *President*
Carol Tager, *Corp Secy*
Nora Davis, *Vice Pres*
Will Heizer, *Safety Mgr*
Lisa Goshgarian, *Marketing Mgr*
◆ EMP: 55 EST: 1959
SQ FT: 100,000
SALES (est): 11.3MM **Privately Held**
WEB: www.poolmaster.com
SIC: 3944 5091 Games, toys & children's vehicles; sporting & recreation goods

(P-7183)
RUMBLE ENTERTAINMENT INC
Also Called: Rumble Games
2121 S El Cmino Real Ste, San Mateo (94403)
PHONE................650 316-8819
Greg Richardson, *CEO*
EMP: 24 EST: 2011
SALES (est): 1.7MM **Privately Held**
WEB: www.rumblegames.com
SIC: 3944 Electronic games & toys

(P-7184)
TANGLE INC DBA TANGLE CREAT
310 Littlefield Ave, South San Francisco (94080-6103)
PHONE................703 478-0500
Nicholas Zawitz, *CEO*
Richard Zawitz, *President*
Nick Zawitz, *CFO*
Geoff McKee, *Vice Pres*
Joclynn Alioto, *Opers Staff*
▲ EMP: 26 EST: 1982
SQ FT: 5,000
SALES (est): 3.9MM **Privately Held**
WEB: www.tanglecreations.com
SIC: 3944 Games, toys & children's vehicles

3949 Sporting & Athletic Goods, NEC

(P-7185)
ALTERG INC
48368 Milmont Dr, Fremont (94538-7324)
PHONE................510 270-5900
Sanjay Gupta, *CEO*
Kevin Davidge, *CFO*
Dev Mishra, *Chief Mktg Ofcr*
Gabriel Griego, *Vice Pres*
Clement Leung, *Vice Pres*
▲ EMP: 60 EST: 2004
SQ FT: 15,247
SALES (est): 12.9MM **Privately Held**
WEB: www.alterg.com
SIC: 3949 Lacrosse equipment & supplies, general

(P-7186)
AMERICAN UNDERWATER PRODUCTS (HQ)
Also Called: Oceanic
2002 Davis St, San Leandro (94577-1211)
PHONE................800 435-3483
Robert R Hollis, *CEO*
Paul Elsinga, *COO*
◆ EMP: 93 EST: 1973
SQ FT: 74,000
SALES (est): 25.6MM **Privately Held**
WEB: www.oceanicworldwide.com
SIC: 3949 5941 Sporting & athletic goods; skin diving, scuba equipment & supplies

(P-7187)
ARROW SURF PRODUCTS (PA)
1115 Thompson Ave Ste 7, Santa Cruz (95062-3253)
PHONE................831 462-2791
Bob Pearson, *Owner*
EMP: 15 EST: 1975
SQ FT: 1,200
SALES (est): 1.3MM **Privately Held**
WEB: www.arrowsurfshop.com
SIC: 3949 Surfboards

(P-7188)
BELL SPORTS INC (HQ)
Also Called: Easton Bell Sports
5550 Scotts Valley Dr, Scotts Valley (95066-3438)
PHONE................469 417-6600
Dan Arment, *President*
◆ EMP: 75 EST: 1952
SQ FT: 27,197
SALES (est): 74.1MM
SALES (corp-wide): 2.2B **Publicly Held**
WEB: www.bellhelmets.com
SIC: 3949 3751 Helmets, athletic; bicycles & related parts
PA: Vista Outdoor Inc.
1 Vista Way
Anoka MN 55303
763 433-1000

(P-7189)
BOOSTED INC (PA)
Also Called: Boosted Boards
400 Oyster Point Blvd # 229, South San Francisco (94080-1952)
PHONE................650 933-5151
Sanjay Dastoor, *CEO*
Richard Bridge, *CFO*
Ashley Wilburne, *Office Mgr*
Alberto Cayabyab, *Technician*
Oliver Riihiluoma, *Engineer*
EMP: 25 EST: 2012
SALES (est): 8.6MM **Privately Held**
WEB: www.boostedusa.com
SIC: 3949 Skateboards

(P-7190)
CALIFORNIA TRACK & ENGINEERING
4668 N Sonora Ave Ste 101, Fresno (93722-3970)
PHONE................559 237-2590
Karol Fair, *President*
Ken Brown, *Controller*
Julie Werfelmann, *Manager*
▲ EMP: 33 EST: 1981
SQ FT: 2,500
SALES (est): 10MM **Privately Held**
SIC: 3949 1629 Track & field athletic equipment; athletic field construction

(P-7191)
CAMELBAK ACQUISITION CORP
2000 S Mcdwell Blvd Ste 2, Petaluma (94954-6901)
PHONE................707 792-9700
EMP: 37 EST: 2011
SALES (est): 698.3K
SALES (corp-wide): 2.2B **Publicly Held**
WEB: www.vistaoutdoor.com
SIC: 3949 Camping equipment & supplies
PA: Vista Outdoor Inc.
1 Vista Way
Anoka MN 55303
763 433-1000

(P-7192)
CAMELBAK PRODUCTS LLC (HQ)
2000 S Mcdwell Blvd Ste 2, Petaluma (94954-6901)
PHONE................707 792-9700
Scott D Chaplin, *Mng Member*
Jody Brunner,
Glenn Gross,
Stephen M Nolan,
J Marty O'Donohue,
▲ EMP: 98 EST: 1989
SQ FT: 50,000

▲ = Import ▼ = Export
◆ = Import/Export

PRODUCTS & SERVICES SECTION

3993 - Signs & Advertising Displays County (P-7213)

SALES (est): 33.7MM
SALES (corp-wide): 2.2B **Publicly Held**
WEB: www.camelbak.com
SIC: 3949 Camping equipment & supplies
PA: Vista Outdoor Inc.
1 Vista Way
Anoka MN 55303
763 433-1000

(P-7193)
CLEANWORLD
2330 Gold Meadow Way, Gold River (95670-4471)
PHONE.................................916 635-7300
Michele Wong, *CEO*
Terry Carlone, *Officer*
Joshua Rapport, *Vice Pres*
Josh Rapport, *Research*
Jennifer Claiborne, *Manager*
EMP: 17 **EST:** 2009
SALES (est): 512.9K **Privately Held**
WEB: www.cleanworld.com
SIC: 3949 Exercise equipment

(P-7194)
ERMICO ENTERPRISES INC
1111 17th St Ste B, San Francisco (94107-2406)
P.O. Box 885403 (94188-5403)
PHONE.................................415 822-6776
Rebekah Engel, *President*
Linda Decay, *Corp Secy*
Gwynned Vitello, *Vice Pres*
▲ **EMP:** 100 **EST:** 1976
SQ FT: 19,000
SALES (est): 9.2MM **Privately Held**
SIC: 3949 3599 3365 3366 Skateboards; machine shop, jobbing & repair; aluminum foundries; brass foundry

(P-7195)
EXACTACATOR INC (PA)
2237 Stagecoach Rd, Stockton (95215-7915)
P.O. Box 8501 (95208-0501)
PHONE.................................209 464-8979
James G Nesbitt, *President*
Shelley Holcomb, *Treasurer*
John Nakashima, *Vice Pres*
Barbara Nesbitt, *Admin Sec*
Melissa Ping, *Admin Sec*
▲ **EMP:** 22 **EST:** 1983
SQ FT: 21,000
SALES (est): 3MM **Privately Held**
WEB: www.viseinserts.com
SIC: 3949 Bowling equipment & supplies; bows, archery

(P-7196)
FINIS INC (PA)
Also Called: Finis USA
5849 W Schulte Rd Ste 104, Tracy (95377-8135)
PHONE.................................925 454-0111
John Mix, *CEO*
Byron Lindstrom, *Exec VP*
Plamen Nikolov, *General Mgr*
Clarke Dolliver, *Graphic Designe*
Clarence De Ramos, *Controller*
▲ **EMP:** 24 **EST:** 1993
SALES (est): 5.1MM **Privately Held**
WEB: www.apps.finisswim.com
SIC: 3949 Surfboards

(P-7197)
HYDRAPAK INC
6605 San Leandro St, Oakland (94621-3317)
PHONE.................................510 632-8318
Matthew Lyon, *CEO*
Jacqueline Takeshita, *Admin Mgr*
Graham Mendell, *Natl Sales Mgr*
Sam Lopez, *Director*
Michael Massucco, *Director*
▲ **EMP:** 25 **EST:** 2001
SALES (est): 2.5MM **Privately Held**
WEB: www.hydrapak.com
SIC: 3949 Sporting & athletic goods

(P-7198)
KEISER CORPORATION (PA)
Also Called: Keiser Sports Health Equipment
2470 S Cherry Ave, Fresno (93706-5004)
PHONE.................................559 256-8000
Dennis L Keiser, *CEO*
Portlinn Pangburn, *CFO*
Kathy Keiser, *Treasurer*
Randy Keiser, *Vice Pres*
Gyl Keiser, *Admin Sec*
◆ **EMP:** 97 **EST:** 1977
SQ FT: 100,000
SALES (est): 20.6MM **Privately Held**
WEB: www.keiser.com
SIC: 3949 Exercise equipment

(P-7199)
NHS INC
Also Called: Santa Cruz Skateboards
104 Bronson St Ste 9, Santa Cruz (95062-3487)
P.O. Box 2718 (95063-2718)
PHONE.................................831 459-7800
Robert A Denike, *CEO*
Caylin Tardif, *CFO*
Richard H Novak, *Chairman*
Jeff Kendall, *Chief Mktg Ofcr*
Jaime Medrano, *Department Mgr*
▲ **EMP:** 92 **EST:** 1972
SQ FT: 50,000
SALES (est): 31.9MM **Privately Held**
WEB: www.p2skateboards.com
SIC: 3949 2329 Skateboards; winter sports equipment; athletic (warmup, sweat & jogging) suits: men's & boys'

(P-7200)
RAINBOW FIN COMPANY INC
677 Beach Dr, Watsonville (95076-1904)
PHONE.................................831 728-2998
Glen Dewitt, *Principal*
Kathleen Dewitt, *Principal*
Shawd Dewitt, *Principal*
▲ **EMP:** 16 **EST:** 1968
SQ FT: 4,000
SALES (est): 514.7K **Privately Held**
WEB: www.rainbowfins.com
SIC: 3949 Windsurfing boards (sailboards) & equipment; surfboards

(P-7201)
STX INC
Also Called: Alta Industries
412 Aviation Blvd Ste K, Santa Rosa (95403-1089)
P.O. Box 4407, Petaluma (94955-4407)
PHONE.................................707 284-3549
William S Anderson, *President*
Mark Lee, *Materials Mgr*
▲ **EMP:** 50 **EST:** 1978
SALES (est): 4.2MM **Privately Held**
WEB: www.altaindustries.com
SIC: 3949 Protective sporting equipment

(P-7202)
USA PRODUCTS GROUP (PA)
Also Called: Progrip Cargo Control
1300 E Vine St, Lodi (95240-3148)
P.O. Box 1750 (95241-1750)
PHONE.................................209 334-1460
Stephen D Jackson, *President*
Yolanda Bernasconi, *Executive*
Raymond S Brown, *Director*
Mike Wilcox, *Manager*
▲ **EMP:** 30 **EST:** 1995
SALES (est): 10.6MM **Privately Held**
WEB: www.usaprogrip.com
SIC: 3949 2399 Bags, golf; golf equipment; seat covers, automobile

3952 Lead Pencils, Crayons & Artist's Mtrls

(P-7203)
DOSTAL STUDIO
17 Woodland Ave, San Rafael (94901-5301)
PHONE.................................415 721-7080
Frank Dostal, *Owner*
EMP: 15 **EST:** 1990
SALES (est): 600K **Privately Held**
WEB: www.dostalstudio.com
SIC: 3952 Frames for artists' canvases

3953 Marking Devices

(P-7204)
BLUE RING STENCILS LLC
675 Trade Zone Blvd, Milpitas (95035-6803)
PHONE.................................866 763-3873
Ahmad Abualrub, *Principal*
EMP: 16
SALES (corp-wide): 10MM **Privately Held**
WEB: www.blueringstencils.com
SIC: 3953 Stencils, painting & marking
PA: Blue Ring Stencils Llc
140 Mount Holly By Pass # 10
Lumberton NJ 08048
866 763-3873

(P-7205)
GREEN LAKE INVESTORS LLC
Also Called: Laser Excel
3310 Coffey Ln, Santa Rosa (95403-1917)
PHONE.................................707 577-1301
Ron Macken, *Manager*
Dan Marschall, *Director*
Tyler Keenlance, *Associate*
EMP: 20
SALES (corp-wide): 5.1MM **Privately Held**
WEB: www.visitgreenlake.com
SIC: 3953 2759 3699 Stencils, painting & marking; screen printing; electrical equipment & supplies
PA: Green Lake Investors Llc
620 Cardinal Ln
Hartland WI 53029
262 369-5000

(P-7206)
HERO ARTS RUBBER STAMPS INC
1200 Hrbour Way S Ste 201, Richmond (94804)
PHONE.................................510 232-4200
Aaron Leventhal, *CEO*
Jacqueline Leventhal, *President*
Tim Urrizola, *CFO*
Cornell Gray, *Prdtn Mgr*
Tami Hartley, *Legal Staff*
▲ **EMP:** 59
SQ FT: 70,000
SALES (est): 7.1MM **Privately Held**
WEB: www.heroarts.com
SIC: 3953 Marking devices; arts & crafts supplies

3955 Carbon Paper & Inked Ribbons

(P-7207)
LASER RECHARGE INC (PA)
Also Called: Encompass
8250 Belvedere Ave Ste C, Sacramento (95826-4754)
PHONE.................................916 813-2717
Michael Mooney, *CEO*
Dave Michon, *President*
Shannon Mooney, *CFO*
Brendan Phillips, *Technician*
Vickie Morgan, *Manager*
EMP: 21 **EST:** 1990
SQ FT: 10,000
SALES (est): 3.8MM **Privately Held**
SIC: 3955 7699 5943 Print cartridges for laser & other computer printers; office equipment & accessory customizing; office forms & supplies

3961 Costume Jewelry & Novelties

(P-7208)
BELLABEAT INC
16 Merced Ave, San Francisco (94127-1026)
PHONE.................................415 317-6153
Jelena Jozovic, *President*
Urska Srsen, *Officer*
EMP: 21 **EST:** 2016
SALES (est): 148.8K **Privately Held**
WEB: www.bellabeat.com
SIC: 3961 Pins (jewelry), except precious metal

(P-7209)
LINDEBURG & CO
Also Called: Lindeburg Jewelers
758 Industrial Rd, San Carlos (94070-3300)
PHONE.................................650 592-6275
Vera Lindeburg, *President*
Ruth Lindeburg, *Corp Secy*
EMP: 22 **EST:** 1917
SQ FT: 13,000
SALES (est): 801.2K **Privately Held**
WEB: www.lindeburg.com
SIC: 5944 3961 5094 Watches; jewelry, precious stones & precious metals; costume jewelry; watches & parts; diamonds (gems); jewelry

(P-7210)
LIZ PALACIOS DESIGNS LTD
1 Stanton Way, Mill Valley (94941-1421)
PHONE.................................628 444-3339
Liz Palacios, *President*
Mingyu Fang, *Office Mgr*
Rosa Garcia, *Office Mgr*
EMP: 16 **EST:** 1991
SQ FT: 7,500
SALES (est): 1.9MM **Privately Held**
WEB: www.lizpalacios.com
SIC: 3961 Costume jewelry

3965 Fasteners, Buttons, Needles & Pins

(P-7211)
GIST INC
Also Called: Gist Silversmiths
4385 Pleasant Valley Rd, Placerville (95667-8430)
PHONE.................................530 644-8000
Gary Gist, *President*
Jennifer Folsom, *Vice Pres*
Jason Migliore, *Graphic Designe*
Branden Gist, *Engineer*
Wende Heinen, *Sales Staff*
▲ **EMP:** 85 **EST:** 1977
SQ FT: 15,000
SALES (est): 11.6MM **Privately Held**
WEB: www.gistsilversmiths.com
SIC: 3965 3911 Buckles & buckle parts; jewelry apparel

(P-7212)
TOTAL CONCEPT ENTERPRISES INC
3745 E Jensen Ave, Fresno (93725-1334)
PHONE.................................559 485-8413
Liz Limoune, *President*
Carol Jacobs, *Vice Pres*
Gina McGowen, *Sales Mgr*
EMP: 17 **EST:** 2004
SQ FT: 18,000
SALES (est): 4MM **Privately Held**
WEB: www.totalconceptent.com
SIC: 3965 5085 3842 Fasteners; fasteners & fastening equipment; abdominal supporters, braces & trusses

3993 Signs & Advertising Displays

(P-7213)
A PLUS SIGNS INC
4270 N Brawley Ave, Fresno (93722-3979)
PHONE.................................559 275-0700
Chris Pacheco, *President*
Jeff Ashlock, *Vice Pres*
Lauren Gibson, *Project Mgr*
Bo Ross, *Prdtn Mgr*
Don Underdown, *Accounts Mgr*
EMP: 47 **EST:** 1986
SQ FT: 12,000
SALES (est): 5.3MM **Privately Held**
WEB: www.a-plussigns.com
SIC: 3993 7389 2399 Electric signs; signs, not made in custom sign painting shops; sign painting & lettering shop; banners, pennants & flags

3993 - Signs & Advertising Displays County (P-7214)

(P-7214)
AD ART INC (PA)
Also Called: Ad Art Sign Company
150 Executive Park Blvd # 2100, San Francisco (94134-3364)
PHONE..................................415 869-6460
Terry J Long, *CEO*
Robert Kiereczyk, *President*
Doug Head, *Exec VP*
Duane Contento, *Senior VP*
David Esajian, *Vice Pres*
▲ **EMP:** 70
SQ FT: 4,000
SALES (est): 27MM **Privately Held**
WEB: www.adart.com
SIC: 3993 Electric signs

(P-7215)
AINOR SIGNS INC
5443 Stationers Way, Sacramento (95842-1900)
PHONE..................................916 348-4370
Joseph Ainor, *President*
Catherine Bettencourt, *Admin Sec*
Sarah Bergh, *Project Mgr*
Carrie Patterson, *Project Mgr*
Theresa Bergh, *Controller*
EMP: 27 **EST:** 2006
SQ FT: 1,500
SALES (est): 3.3MM **Privately Held**
WEB: www.ainorsigns.com
SIC: 3993 Signs, not made in custom sign painting shops

(P-7216)
ARROW SIGN CO (PA)
Also Called: Arrow Sign Company
1051 46th Ave, Oakland (94601-4436)
PHONE..................................209 931-5522
Charles Sterne, *President*
James L Golden, *Vice Pres*
Jeremy Blackburn, *Project Mgr*
Lauren McSorley, *Controller*
Lauren Taylor, *Human Res Mgr*
EMP: 48 **EST:** 1958
SQ FT: 119,375
SALES (est): 11MM **Privately Held**
WEB: www.arrowsigncompany.com
SIC: 3993 Electric signs

(P-7217)
ARROW SIGN CO
3133 N Ad Art Rd, Stockton (95215-2217)
PHONE..................................209 931-7852
Chuck Sterne, *Branch Mgr*
EMP: 27
SALES (corp-wide): 11MM **Privately Held**
WEB: www.arrowsigncompany.com
SIC: 3993 Electric signs
PA: Arrow Sign Co.
 1051 46th Ave
 Oakland CA 94601
 209 931-5522

(P-7218)
ATHLETIC SPORTS LLC
11327 Trade Center Dr # 33, Rancho Cordova (95742-6238)
PHONE..................................310 709-3944
Ronnie Moers, *Mng Member*
EMP: 42 **EST:** 2020
SALES (est): 1MM **Privately Held**
SIC: 3993 Signs & advertising specialties

(P-7219)
BEELINE GROUP LLC
30941 San Clemente St, Hayward (94544-7128)
P.O. Box 757, Carthage MO (64836-0757)
PHONE..................................510 477-5400
Susan Terry, *President*
Josh Roberts, *CEO*
Wayne Kimball, *CFO*
Phil Green, *Vice Pres*
Julie Stier, *Exec Dir*
EMP: 70 **EST:** 2014
SALES (est): 13.7MM **Privately Held**
WEB: www.beelinegroup.com
SIC: 3993 2542 Signs & advertising specialties; fixtures: display, office or store: except wood

(P-7220)
BLAZER EXHIBITS & GRAPHICS INC
4227 Technology Dr, Fremont (94538-6339)
PHONE..................................408 263-7000
David Graham, *CEO*
Loren Ellis, *President*
Susan Graham, *Treasurer*
Vanessa Ellis, *Vice Pres*
EMP: 15 **EST:** 1983
SQ FT: 20,000
SALES (est): 2.5MM **Privately Held**
WEB: www.blazerexhibits.com
SIC: 3993 Signs & advertising specialties

(P-7221)
BRIGHTSIGN LLC
983 University Ave Bldg A, Los Gatos (95032-7637)
P.O. Box 320250 (95032-0104)
PHONE..................................408 852-9263
Anthony Wood,
Bryan Kennedy, *President*
Phil Blundell, *Vice Pres*
Keith Byres, *Vice Pres*
Robert Gardner, *Vice Pres*
▲ **EMP:** 88 **EST:** 2010
SQ FT: 19,362
SALES (est): 6.7MM **Privately Held**
WEB: www.brightsign.biz
SIC: 3993 Signs & advertising specialties

(P-7222)
CAL-SIGN WHOLESALE INC
5260 Jerusalem Ct, Modesto (95356-9219)
PHONE..................................209 523-7446
Greg Johnson, *President*
Roger Johnson, *Corp Secy*
Mark Johnson, *Vice Pres*
Rhonda Shafer, *Admin Asst*
EMP: 17 **EST:** 1974
SQ FT: 4,050
SALES (est): 2.1MM **Privately Held**
WEB: www.calsignwholesale.com
SIC: 3993 Electric signs

(P-7223)
CELLOTAPE INC (HQ)
39611 Eureka Dr, Newark (94560-4806)
PHONE..................................510 651-5551
Toll Free:...............................888 -
Pete Offermann, *Ch of Bd*
Renee Rhodes, *Executive*
Eric Lomas, *Admin Sec*
Nick Testanero, *Director*
Robert Devincenzi, *Accounts Mgr*
EMP: 102 **EST:** 1949
SQ FT: 55,000
SALES (est): 26.7MM **Privately Held**
WEB: www.cellotape.com
SIC: 3993 2675 2672 2759 Signs & advertising specialties; die-cut paper & board; coated & laminated paper; labels & seals: printing

(P-7224)
CLEARIST INC
2105 Lundy Ave, San Jose (95131-1849)
PHONE..................................408 835-8620
Paul Nguyen, *President*
EMP: 18 **EST:** 2012
SALES (est): 2.2MM **Privately Held**
SIC: 3993 Advertising artwork

(P-7225)
CORPORATE SIGN SYSTEMS INC
2464 De La Cruz Blvd, Santa Clara (95050-2923)
PHONE..................................408 292-1600
Danny Moran, *CEO*
Phil Wyatt, *Vice Pres*
Heather Bjorklund, *Project Mgr*
Dichoso Joe, *Project Mgr*
Jeff Lang, *Technology*
EMP: 20 **EST:** 1961
SQ FT: 7,000
SALES (est): 4.6MM **Privately Held**
WEB: www.corporatesigns.com
SIC: 3993 7389 Signs & advertising specialties; sign painting & lettering shop

(P-7226)
CRAIGO INVESTMENTS INC
Also Called: Fastsigns
2745 W Shaw Ave Ste 120, Fresno (93711-3315)
PHONE..................................559 222-9293
Robert Glenn Craigo, *CEO*
EMP: 24 **EST:** 2010
SALES (est): 1.4MM **Privately Held**
WEB: www.fastsigns.com
SIC: 3993 Signs & advertising specialties

(P-7227)
D N G CUMMINGS INC
Also Called: Action Sign Systems
3580 Haven Ave Ste 1, Redwood City (94063-4639)
PHONE..................................650 593-8974
Dorothy Cummings, *President*
Greg Cummings, *Vice Pres*
Richard Cummings, *Vice Pres*
Gregory Patrick, *General Mgr*
EMP: 18 **EST:** 1983
SQ FT: 9,600
SALES (est): 1MM **Privately Held**
SIC: 3993 Signs, not made in custom sign painting shops

(P-7228)
D3 LED LLC (PA)
Also Called: Dynamic Digital Displays
11370 Sunrise Park Dr, Rancho Cordova (95742-6542)
PHONE..................................916 669-7408
George Pappas, *Mng Member*
Jason Barak, *Managing Prtnr*
Eric Bland, *Vice Pres*
Bob Magnus, *Vice Pres*
Anil Reddy, *Vice Pres*
◆ **EMP:** 20 **EST:** 2005
SQ FT: 60,000
SALES (est): 18.6MM **Privately Held**
WEB: www.d3led.com
SIC: 3993 Signs & advertising specialties

(P-7229)
FASTSIGNS
650 Harrison St, San Francisco (94107-1311)
PHONE..................................415 537-6900
Jason Moline, *Owner*
Bruce Vaughn, *Vice Pres*
Richard Jongordon, *Admin Sec*
EMP: 39 **EST:** 2000
SQ FT: 7,000
SALES (est): 1MM **Privately Held**
WEB: www.fastsigns.com
SIC: 3993 Signs & advertising specialties

(P-7230)
GARNETT SIGNS LLC
Also Called: Garnett Sign Studio
48531 Warm Springs Blvd # 412, Fremont (94539-7793)
PHONE..................................650 871-9518
Stephen Savoy, *President*
Masaki Kitamori, *Graphic Designe*
Clifford Kane, *Manager*
EMP: 15 **EST:** 1946 **Privately Held**
SIC: 3993 3479 Signs, not made in custom sign painting shops; name plates: engraved, etched, etc.

(P-7231)
GMPC LLC
Also Called: Big Accessories
2180 S Mcdwell Blvd Ext S, Petaluma (94954-6974)
PHONE..................................707 766-1702
Steve Wegner, *Principal*
Bridget Mc Coy, *CFO*
Patti Kinzer, *Analyst*
Kathryn Meehan, *Prdtn Mgr*
Kriya Stevens, *Sales Staff*
EMP: 18
SALES (corp-wide): 15.7MM **Privately Held**
WEB: www.gmpc.com
SIC: 3993 7336 Advertising novelties; commercial art & graphic design
PA: Gmpc, Llc
 11390 W Olympic Blvd
 Los Angeles CA 90064
 310 392-4070

(P-7232)
HUPP SIGNS & LIGHTING INC
70 Loren Ave, Chico (95928-7433)
P.O. Box 7730 (95927-7730)
PHONE..................................530 345-7078
Joe Hupp,
Britanie Hupp, *Human Resources*
Sandra Valerio, *Supervisor*
EMP: 19 **EST:** 1993
SQ FT: 18,000
SALES (est): 1.4MM **Privately Held**
WEB: www.huppsigns.com
SIC: 3993 Neon signs

(P-7233)
ILLUMINATED CREATIONS INC
Also Called: Ellis and Ellis Sign
1111 Joellis Way, Sacramento (95815-3914)
PHONE..................................916 924-1936
Bret E Ellis, *CEO*
Sydney Ellis, *President*
Sarah Summers, *CFO*
Sharon Ellis, *Corp Secy*
Brad Edward Ellis, *Vice Pres*
EMP: 40 **EST:** 1975
SQ FT: 60,000
SALES (est): 7.4MM **Privately Held**
WEB: www.ellissigns.com
SIC: 3993 Signs, not made in custom sign painting shops

(P-7234)
IMPACT MARKETING DISPLAYS LLC
Also Called: Impact Displays
1725 De La Cruz Blvd, Santa Clara (95050-3011)
PHONE..................................408 217-6850
Theodore Ridgway, *Mng Member*
▲ **EMP:** 15 **EST:** 2008
SALES (est): 475.2K **Privately Held**
WEB: www.impact-displays.com
SIC: 3993 Signs & advertising specialties

(P-7235)
J S HCKLEY ARCHTCTRAL SGNAGE
1999 Alpine Way, Hayward (94545-1701)
PHONE..................................510 940-2608
John Hackley, *President*
EMP: 20 **EST:** 1981
SQ FT: 20,000
SALES (est): 1.2MM **Privately Held**
SIC: 3993 Signs & advertising specialties

(P-7236)
JAR VENTURES INC
Also Called: Sign-A-Rama
4351 Caterpillar Rd, Redding (96003-1423)
PHONE..................................530 224-9655
John Robbins, *President*
EMP: 17 **EST:** 2005
SALES (est): 1.5MM **Privately Held**
WEB: www.signarama.com
SIC: 3993 Signs & advertising specialties

(P-7237)
JEFF FRANK
Also Called: Northwest Signs
120 Encinal St, Santa Cruz (95060-2111)
PHONE..................................831 469-8208
Jeff Frank, *Owner*
Chris Merrell, *Office Mgr*
Jon Mata, *Project Mgr*
EMP: 15 **EST:** 1987
SQ FT: 5,000
SALES (est): 1.2MM **Privately Held**
WEB: www.northwestsigns.com
SIC: 3993 7349 Signs & advertising specialties; lighting maintenance service

(P-7238)
JOHNSON UNITED INC (PA)
Also Called: United Sign Systems
5201 Pentecost Dr, Modesto (95356-9271)
PHONE..................................209 543-1320
Darryl Johnson, *CEO*
Andy Soares, *Principal*
Mike Noordewier, *Admin Sec*
Diane Lenzora, *Project Mgr*
Marco A Ospina, *Project Mgr*
▼ **EMP:** 31 **EST:** 1967
SQ FT: 23,000

PRODUCTS & SERVICES SECTION
3993 - Signs & Advertising Displays County (P-7263)

SALES (est): 5.3MM **Privately Held**
WEB: www.unitedsign.net
SIC: 3993 Signs & advertising specialties

(P-7239)
JSJ ELECTRICAL DISPLAY CORP
340 Via Palo Linda, Fairfield (94534-1528)
PHONE.................................707 747-5595
Brian Schneider, *President*
Jeff Jensen, *Managing Prtnr*
Clayton Jensen, *Vice Pres*
Larry Koyle, *Director*
EMP: 18 EST: 1994 **Privately Held**
WEB: www.jsjdisplay.com
SIC: 3993 Neon signs

(P-7240)
JUSTIPHER INC
Also Called: Fastsigns
1248 W Winton Ave, Hayward (94545-1406)
PHONE.................................510 918-6800
Linda Fong, *Branch Mgr*
EMP: 15 **Privately Held**
WEB: www.fastsigns.com
SIC: 3993 Signs & advertising specialties
PA: Justipher, Inc.
325 5th St
Oakland CA 94607

(P-7241)
LEOTEK ELECTRONICS USA LLC
1955 Lundy Ave, San Jose (95131-1848)
PHONE.................................408 380-1788
James C Hwang, *CEO*
Chen-Ho Wu, *President*
Chris Berumen, *Regional Mgr*
Eric Dun, *Engineer*
Pushun Sheth, *Engineer*
▲ EMP: 23 EST: 1996
SQ FT: 10,000
SALES (est): 12.1MM **Privately Held**
WEB: www.leotek.com
SIC: 3993 5046 Electric signs; signs, electrical
PA: Lite-On Technology Corporation
22f, 392, Ruey Kuang Rd.,
Taipei City TAP 11492

(P-7242)
MARKETSHARE INC (PA)
2001 Tarob Ct, Milpitas (95035-6825)
PHONE.................................408 262-0677
Frederick Wilhelm, *CEO*
Alexis Bybel, *CFO*
John Lovell, *Vice Pres*
James Gochnauer, *Opers Staff*
Shawn Oliver, *Marketing Staff*
EMP: 65
SQ FT: 16,000
SALES (est): 11.8MM **Privately Held**
WEB: www.marketshareonline.com
SIC: 3993 7312 Electric signs; billboard advertising

(P-7243)
MARTINELLI ENVMTL GRAPHICS
Also Called: Martinelli Envmtl Graphics
1829 Egbert Ave, San Francisco (94124-2519)
PHONE.................................415 468-4000
Jack Martinelli, *President*
Patty Martinelli, *Treasurer*
Jeff Osicka, *Vice Pres*
Candace Savoie, *Executive*
Jason Joe, *Project Mgr*
EMP: 15 EST: 1988
SQ FT: 8,000
SALES (est): 1.9MM **Privately Held**
WEB: www.martinelli-graphics.com
SIC: 3993 Electric signs

(P-7244)
MINA-TREE SIGNS INCORPORATED (PA)
1233 E Ronald St, Stockton (95205-3331)
P.O. Box 8406 (95208-0406)
PHONE.................................209 941-2921
Harold Leroy Minatre, *President*
EMP: 36 EST: 1967
SALES (est): 4.2MM **Privately Held**
WEB: www.mina-treesigns.com
SIC: 3993 Electric signs; advertising novelties

(P-7245)
OKI DOKI SIGNS
Also Called: Od Signs
3490 Depot Rd, Hayward (94545-2714)
PHONE.................................510 940-7446
Kin So, *Owner*
▲ EMP: 18 EST: 1994
SALES (est): 831.5K **Privately Held**
WEB: www.odsigns.com
SIC: 3993 Signs & advertising specialties

(P-7246)
PACIFIC COAST SIGNS INC (PA)
1754 Hempstead Pl, Redwood City (94061-3251)
PHONE.................................650 520-0724
Paul Maynes, *Principal*
EMP: 32 EST: 2008
SALES (est): 543.9K **Privately Held**
WEB: www.fastsigns.com
SIC: 3993 Signs & advertising specialties

(P-7247)
PACIFIC NEON
2939 Academy Way, Sacramento (95815-1802)
P.O. Box 15100 (95851-0100)
PHONE.................................916 927-0527
Oleta Lambert, *Ch of Bd*
John Drury, *President*
Brian Rath, *Sr Corp Ofcr*
Bill Dickson, *Design Engr*
Candace Groomes, *Project Mgr*
EMP: 40 EST: 1946
SQ FT: 65,000
SALES (est): 6.9MM **Privately Held**
WEB: www.pacificneon.com
SIC: 3993 1799 7359 Electric signs; sign installation & maintenance; sign rental

(P-7248)
PELICAN SIGN SERVICE INC
391 Bundy Ave, San Jose (95117-3978)
PHONE.................................408 246-3833
Frank Pleican, *CEO*
Frank E Pelican Jr, *President*
EMP: 20 EST: 1975
SALES (est): 1.3MM **Privately Held**
SIC: 3993 Signs & advertising specialties

(P-7249)
RAGO NEON INC
235 Laurel Ave, Hayward (94541-3822)
PHONE.................................510 537-1903
Antone F Rago II, *President*
EMP: 18 EST: 1977
SQ FT: 9,600
SALES (est): 1.6MM **Privately Held**
WEB: www.ragoneon.com
SIC: 3993 Neon signs

(P-7250)
RAPID DISPLAYS INC
33195 Lewis St, Union City (94587-2201)
PHONE.................................510 471-6955
EMP: 17
SALES (corp-wide): 472MM **Privately Held**
WEB: www.rapiddisplays.com
SIC: 3993 Mfg Signs/Advertising Specialties
HQ: Rapid Displays, Inc.
4300 W 47th St
Chicago IL 60632
773 927-5000

(P-7251)
SCOTT AG LLC
1275 N Dutton Ave, Santa Rosa (95401-4663)
PHONE.................................707 545-4519
Jimmy D Burch, *Principal*
Susan Burch, *Office Mgr*
Katie Popov, *Project Mgr*
Jim Popov, *Supervisor*
EMP: 16 EST: 2011
SALES (est): 2.5MM **Privately Held**
WEB: www.scottag.com
SIC: 3993 Signs & advertising specialties

(P-7252)
SIGN DESIGNS INC
Also Called: Macdonald Screen Print
204 Campus Way, Modesto (95350-5845)
P.O. Box 4590 (95352-4590)
PHONE.................................209 524-4484
David Johnston, *President*
Pete Michelini, *CFO*
Doug Smith, *Vice Pres*
Douglas Smith, *Vice Pres*
Jeff Stockton, *Project Mgr*
EMP: 44 EST: 1971
SQ FT: 35,000
SALES (est): 4.6MM **Privately Held**
WEB: www.signdesigns.com
SIC: 3993 Electric signs

(P-7253)
SIGN TECHNOLOGY INC
1700 Entp Blvd Ste F, West Sacramento (95691)
PHONE.................................916 372-1200
Michael Wilmer, *CEO*
Dan Worsley, *Vice Pres*
Dallas Dorn, *Sales Staff*
EMP: 30 EST: 1979
SQ FT: 11,660
SALES (est): 5.1MM **Privately Held**
WEB: www.signtechnology.com
SIC: 3993 Signs, not made in custom sign painting shops

(P-7254)
SIMPLY SMASHING INC
Also Called: Fruehe Design
4790 W Jacquelyn Ave, Fresno (93722-6406)
PHONE.................................559 658-2367
Tim Fruehe, *President*
EMP: 16 EST: 1994
SALES (est): 598.7K **Privately Held**
WEB: www.simplysmashing.com
SIC: 3993 7336 Advertising novelties; graphic arts & related design

(P-7255)
STREET GRAPHICS INC
Also Called: Delta Signs
1834 W Euclid Ave, Stockton (95204-2911)
PHONE.................................209 948-1713
EMP: 20
SQ FT: 12,000
SALES (est): 2.5MM **Privately Held**
WEB: www.deltasigns.net
SIC: 3993 Mfg Signs/Advertising Specialties

(P-7256)
SUPERSONIC ADS INC
Also Called: Ironsource
17 Bluxome St, San Francisco (94107-1605)
PHONE.................................650 825-6010
Gil Shoham, *CEO*
Rujul Patel, *Vice Pres*
Daphne Saragosti, *Vice Pres*
Damon B Marshall, *VP Bus Dvlpt*
Giles Davis, *Business Dir*
EMP: 43 EST: 2011
SALES (est): 4.3MM **Privately Held**
SIC: 3993 Advertising artwork

(P-7257)
THOMAS-SWAN SIGN COMPANY INC
2717 Goodrick Ave, Richmond (94801-1109)
PHONE.................................415 621-1511
Allen E Thomas, *CEO*
Michael Roberts, *President*
John Soares, *CFO*
Donna Thomas, *Treasurer*
Stacy Roberts, *Vice Pres*
EMP: 35 EST: 1877
SQ FT: 40,000
SALES (est): 8.1MM **Privately Held**
WEB: www.thomasswan.com
SIC: 3993 Electric signs

(P-7258)
UNIVERSAL CUSTOM DISPLAY
Also Called: Universal Custom Design
9104 Elkmont Dr Ste 100, Elk Grove (95624-9724)
PHONE.................................916 714-2505
Daniel Hayes, *CEO*
Daniel Lopez, *COO*
Don Almeda, *Vice Pres*
Charles Dickenson, *Vice Pres*
Jeanne Hayes, *Admin Sec*
▲ EMP: 175 EST: 1999
SQ FT: 120,000
SALES (est): 35.9MM **Privately Held**
WEB: www.unicusdis.com
SIC: 3993 2541 Signs & advertising specialties; display fixtures, wood

(P-7259)
VOMELA SPECIALTY COMPANY
Corporate Identity Systems
1342 San Mateo Ave, South San Francisco (94080-6501)
PHONE.................................650 877-8000
Robert Pietila, *Branch Mgr*
Homer Capistrano, *Supervisor*
EMP: 28
SALES (corp-wide): 258MM **Privately Held**
WEB: www.vomela.com
SIC: 3993 2759 Signs & advertising specialties; screen printing
PA: Vomela Specialty Company
845 Minnehaha Ave E
Saint Paul MN 55106
651 228-2200

(P-7260)
WEIDNER ARCHTCTRAL SGNG/HUSE S
Also Called: WEIDNERCA
5001 24th St, Sacramento (95822-2201)
PHONE.................................800 561-7446
Mark Douglas Copeland, *Ch of Bd*
Edwin F Weidner III, *President*
Arie Korver, *COO*
Kathy Weidner, *Treasurer*
Randy Wagner, *Vice Pres*
EMP: 58
SQ FT: 20,450
SALES: 11.6MM **Privately Held**
WEB: www.weidnerca.com
SIC: 3993 2759 7389 Signs & advertising specialties; screen printing; sign painting & lettering shop

(P-7261)
WESTERN SIGN COMPANY INC
6221a Enterprise Dr Ste A, Diamond Springs (95619-9398)
PHONE.................................916 933-3765
David Brazelton, *President*
Todd Johnston, *Vice Pres*
Keith Wills, *Vice Pres*
Cindy Brazelton, *Admin Sec*
Wendie Denham, *Opers Mgr*
EMP: 20 EST: 1959
SQ FT: 12,000
SALES (est): 3.9MM **Privately Held**
WEB: www.westernsign.com
SIC: 3993 1799 Electric signs; neon signs; sign installation & maintenance

(P-7262)
YOUNG ELECTRIC SIGN COMPANY
Also Called: Yesco
875 National Dr Ste 107, Sacramento (95834-1162)
PHONE.................................916 419-8101
Rachel Williamson, *Branch Mgr*
EMP: 35
SALES (corp-wide): 498.1MM **Privately Held**
WEB: www.yesco.com
SIC: 3993 5999 1799 Electric signs; awnings; sign installation & maintenance
PA: Young Electric Sign Company Inc
2401 S Foothill Dr
Salt Lake City UT 84109
801 464-4600

(P-7263)
YOUNG ELECTRIC SIGN COMPANY
Also Called: Yesco
46750 Fremont Blvd # 101, Fremont (94538-6573)
PHONE.................................510 877-7815
Kip Kitto, *Branch Mgr*
EMP: 35

3995 - Burial Caskets County (P-7264)

SALES (corp-wide): 498.1MM **Privately Held**
WEB: www.yesco.com
SIC: 3993 Signs & advertising specialties
PA: Young Electric Sign Company Inc
2401 S Foothill Dr
Salt Lake City UT 84109
801 464-4200

3995 Burial Caskets

(P-7264)
UNIVERSAL MEDITECH INC
1320 E Fortune Ave # 102, Fresno (93725-1958)
PHONE 559 366-7798
Zhaoyan Wang, *President*
EMP: 45 EST: 2015
SALES (est): 3.4MM **Privately Held**
WEB: www.universal-meditech.com
SIC: 3995 2835 Casket linings; pregnancy test kits

3996 Linoleum & Hard Surface Floor Coverings, NEC

(P-7265)
PARMA FLOORS INC
2079 Hartog Ave S, San Jose (95131)
PHONE 408 638-0247
Kaaveh Letafat, *CEO*
Chad Lopez, *Principal*
▲ EMP: 18 EST: 2013
SALES (est): 10MM **Privately Held**
WEB: www.parmaflooring.com
SIC: 3996 Tile, floor: supported plastic

(P-7266)
RENOS FLOOR COVERING INC
1515 Solano Ave, Vallejo (94590-5736)
P.O. Box 503, NAPA (94559-0503)
PHONE 415 459-1403
Carolyn Reno, *President*
John Norman, *Vice Pres*
EMP: 20 EST: 2006
SALES (est): 2.1MM **Privately Held**
SIC: 3996 Asphalted-felt-base floor coverings: linoleum, carpet

3999 Manufacturing Industries, NEC

(P-7267)
AKON INCORPORATED
2135 Ringwood Ave, San Jose (95131-1725)
PHONE 408 432-8039
Surya Sareen, *President*
Dan Brassfield, *Officer*
Louis Seieroe, *Business Dir*
Ajay Dalal, *Engineer*
Avinash Ratra, *Engineer*
EMP: 60
SQ FT: 35,000
SALES (est): 10.6MM **Privately Held**
WEB: www.akoninc.com
SIC: 3999 Slot machines

(P-7268)
ALOHA BAY
Also Called: Bright Lights Candle Company
16275 A Main St, Lower Lake (95457)
P.O. Box 539 (95457-0539)
PHONE 707 994-3267
Bernard S Burger, *CEO*
Roy Dixon, *Principal*
▲ EMP: 35 EST: 1992
SQ FT: 1,500
SALES (est): 4.1MM **Privately Held**
WEB: www.alohabay.com
SIC: 3999 5199 Candles; candles

(P-7269)
BALSAM BRANDS INC (PA)
Also Called: Balsam Hill
50 Woodside Plz Ste 111, Redwood City (94061-2500)
PHONE 877 442-2572
Thomas Harman, *CEO*
Caroline Tuan, *COO*
Kristen Gasior, *Chief Mktg Ofcr*
Mike Rockwood, *Exec VP*
Erin Chow, *Vice Pres*
EMP: 70 EST: 2006
SALES (est): 31.7MM **Privately Held**
WEB: www.balsambrands.com
SIC: 3999 Christmas trees, artificial

(P-7270)
BART MANUFACTURING INC (PA)
3787 Spinnaker Ct, Fremont (94538-6537)
PHONE 408 320-4373
Dave Weissbart, *CEO*
Vishal Kyatham, *Project Mgr*
Prathamesh Ghankutkar, *Engineer*
EMP: 74 EST: 2010
SALES (est): 6.8MM **Privately Held**
WEB: www.bartmanufacturing.com
SIC: 3999 Chairs, hydraulic, barber & beauty shop

(P-7271)
BRICHETTO BROS
8700 Crane Rd, Oakdale (95361-8108)
P.O. Box 11600 (95361-0595)
PHONE 209 847-2775
John Brichetto, *Partner*
John M Brichetto, *Partner*
Joseph P Brichetto, *Partner*
EMP: 23 EST: 1971
SALES (est): 876.4K **Privately Held**
SIC: 3999 Nut shells, grinding, from purchased nuts

(P-7272)
BRITE INDUSTRIES INC
Also Called: Brite Labs
1746 13th St, Oakland (94607-1510)
PHONE 510 250-9330
Brian Brown, *CEO*
EMP: 96 EST: 2017
SALES (est): 5.2MM **Privately Held**
SIC: 3999 5159 ;

(P-7273)
CALIFORNIA INDUSTIRAL MFG LLC (PA)
1221 Independence Pl, Gridley (95948-9341)
P.O. Box 830, Durham (95938-0830)
PHONE 530 846-9960
EMP: 18 EST: 2014
SALES (est): 261.5K **Privately Held**
SIC: 3999 Manufacturing industries

(P-7274)
CENTURIONI INDUSTRIES INC
580 Crespi Dr, Pacifica (94044-3487)
PHONE 858 213-7433
Deanna Aleese, *Principal*
EMP: 16 EST: 2010
SALES (est): 122.1K **Privately Held**
WEB: www.centurionind.com
SIC: 3999 Manufacturing industries

(P-7275)
CITY OF WOODLAND
Also Called: Woodland Fire Department
1000 Lincoln Ave, Woodland (95695-4100)
PHONE 530 661-5860
Dan Belline, *Chief*
EMP: 101
SALES (corp-wide): 98.4MM **Privately Held**
WEB: www.cityofwoodland.org
SIC: 9224 3999 Fire department, not including volunteer; badges, metal: policemen, firemen, etc.
PA: City Of Woodland
300 1st St
Woodland CA 95695
530 661-5830

(P-7276)
CLAMP SWING PRICING CO INC
8386 Capwell Dr, Oakland (94621-2114)
PHONE 510 567-1600
Benjamin Garfinkle, *President*
Wilma Garfinkle, *Ch of Bd*
Richard Barnes, *CIO*
Kamran Faizi, *Sales Mgr*
◆ EMP: 30 EST: 1924
SQ FT: 47,000
SALES (est): 4.5MM **Privately Held**
WEB: www.clampswing.com
SIC: 3999 Identification plates

(P-7277)
CONNECTED CANNABIS
2831 Fruitridge Rd, Sacramento (95820-6339)
PHONE 916 308-4175
Jordan Aguilar, *General Mgr*
Makenzie Smith, *Human Res Mgr*
Alicia Busse, *Marketing Staff*
Alex Clatterbuck, *Sales Staff*
Nate Richardson, *Manager*
EMP: 22 EST: 2019
SALES (est): 6MM **Privately Held**
WEB: www.connectedcannabisco.com
SIC: 3999

(P-7278)
CONSOLIDATED TRAINING LLC
144 Holm Rd Spc 47, Watsonville (95076-2428)
PHONE 831 768-8888
EMP: 22
SALES (est): 15MM **Privately Held**
SIC: 3999 Mfg Misc Products

(P-7279)
D&H MANUFACTURING COMPANY
Also Called: D&H / R&D
49235 Milmont Dr, Fremont (94538-7349)
PHONE 510 770-5100
Marie Dunaway, *Human Res Mgr*
EMP: 22 EST: 2015
SALES (est): 4.5MM **Privately Held**
SIC: 3999 Manufacturing industries

(P-7280)
ECO-SHELL INC
5230 Grange Rd, Corning (96021-9239)
PHONE 530 824-8794
Charles R Crain Jr, *CEO*
◆ EMP: 22 EST: 1996
SQ FT: 60,000
SALES (est): 7MM **Privately Held**
WEB: www.ecoshell.com
SIC: 3999 Nut shells, grinding, from purchased nuts

(P-7281)
EDS MANUFACTURING
1494 Gladding Ct, Milpitas (95035-6831)
PHONE 408 982-3688
EMP: 28 EST: 2019
SALES (est): 2.2MM **Privately Held**
WEB: www.edsmanufacturing.com
SIC: 3999 Manufacturing industries

(P-7282)
EDS MFG INC
1725 De La Cruz Blvd # 5, Santa Clara (95050-3011)
PHONE 408 900-8941
EMP: 15 EST: 2016
SALES (est): 384.2K **Privately Held**
SIC: 3999 Manufacturing industries

(P-7283)
EMERALD TRIANGLE MGT GROUP INC
5550 West End Rd Ste 11, Arcata (95521-9298)
PHONE 707 630-5040
Per A Jacobsen, *CEO*
EMP: 15 EST: 2016
SALES (est): 315.1K **Privately Held**
SIC: 3999 5159 5993 8741 ; ; ; management services

(P-7284)
END TIMEY INDUSTRIES LLC (PA)
250 Fell St, San Francisco (94102-5150)
PHONE 202 550-7570
EMP: 15 EST: 2017
SALES (est): 65.7K **Privately Held**
SIC: 3999 Manufacturing industries

(P-7285)
FOLKMANIS INC
1219 Park Ave, Emeryville (94608-3607)
PHONE 510 658-7677
Atis Folkmanis, *President*
Dan Folkmanis, *Vice Pres*
Judy Folkmanis, *Vice Pres*
Jack Tallman, *Human Res Mgr*
Elaine Kollias, *Mktg Dir*
▲ EMP: 40 EST: 1972
SALES (est): 4.4MM **Privately Held**
WEB: www.folkmanis.com
SIC: 3999 3942 Puppets & marionettes; dolls & stuffed toys

(P-7286)
HOGAN MFG INC (PA)
1638 Main St, Escalon (95320-1722)
P.O. Box 398 (95320-0398)
PHONE 209 838-7323
Mark Hogan, *CEO*
Joe Debiasio, *CFO*
John Fusco, *Vice Pres*
Jeff Hogan, *Vice Pres*
Zach Hogan, *Vice Pres*
▲ EMP: 150
SQ FT: 43,000
SALES (est): 38.5MM **Privately Held**
WEB: www.hoganmfg.com
SIC: 3999 3441 3443 1791 Wheelchair lifts; fabricated structural metal; fabricated plate work (boiler shop); structural steel erection

(P-7287)
HOGAN MFG INC
Lift-U
1520 1st St, Escalon (95320-1703)
P.O. Box 398 (95320-0398)
PHONE 209 838-2400
Paul Riechmuth, *Admin Mgr*
David Johnson, *Engineer*
John Woods, *Plant Supt*
John Fusco, *Mktg Dir*
Zach Hogan, *Manager*
EMP: 125
SALES (corp-wide): 38.5MM **Privately Held**
WEB: www.hoganmfg.com
SIC: 3999 3842 3714 3534 Wheelchair lifts; surgical appliances & supplies; motor vehicle parts & accessories; elevators & moving stairways
PA: Hogan Mfg., Inc.
1638 Main St
Escalon CA 95320
209 838-7323

(P-7288)
IAB BRANDS INC
Also Called: Iab Mfg
4060 Clarewood Way, Sacramento (95835-2015)
PHONE 844 426-2634
Thomas Patterson, *CEO*
EMP: 16 EST: 1996
SALES (est): 724.6K **Privately Held**
WEB: www.iabmfg.zendesk.com
SIC: 3999 Manufacturing industries

(P-7289)
J & A JEFFERY INC
Also Called: Western Stabilization
395 Industrial Way Ste B, Dixon (95620-9787)
P.O. Box 1022 (95620-1022)
PHONE 707 678-0369
John Jordan, *CEO*
Judy Jeffery, *President*
Ashley Jeffery, *Vice Pres*
Justine Jeffery, *Controller*
Tim Robben, *Superintendent*
EMP: 50 EST: 1988
SQ FT: 16,000
SALES (est): 9.8MM **Privately Held**
WEB: www.wstabilization.com
SIC: 3999 0711 Custom pulverizing & grinding of plastic materials; soil preparation services

(P-7290)
JUUL LABS INC (PA)
560 20th St, San Francisco (94107-4344)
PHONE 415 829-2336
Kc Crosthwaite, *CEO*
Elaine Paik, *CFO*
Matt David, *Officer*
Saurabh Sinha, *Senior VP*
Rajeev Bhalla, *Vice Pres*
EMP: 312 EST: 2007

PRODUCTS & SERVICES SECTION
3999 - Manufacturing Industries, NEC County (P-7317)

SALES (est): 151.4MM **Privately Held**
WEB: www.juullabs.com
SIC: **3999** Cigarette & cigar products & accessories

(P-7291)
KDS NAIL PRODUCTS
Also Called: Texchem Chemical
8580 Younger Creek Dr, Sacramento (95828-1000)
PHONE.................................916 381-9358
Dat Vinh MA, *Principal*
▲ EMP: 34 EST: 1995
SALES (est): 1.5MM **Privately Held**
WEB: www.kdsproducts.com
SIC: **3999** 2899 Fingernails, artificial; chemical preparations

(P-7292)
KITANICA LLC
867 Isabella St, Oakland (94607-3429)
PHONE.................................707 272-7286
Spencer Tien, *Partner*
Chris Cronin, *Partner*
Leonard Riccio, *Principal*
EMP: 18 EST: 2015
SALES (est): 1.1MM **Privately Held**
WEB: www.kitanica.com
SIC: **3999** Manufacturing industries

(P-7293)
KIVA MANUFACTURING INC
Also Called: Kiva Confections
445 Lesser St, Oakland (94601-4901)
PHONE.................................510 780-0777
Scott Palmer, *CEO*
Monica Trujillo, *Purchasing*
EMP: 26 EST: 2019
SALES (est): 6.6MM **Privately Held**
WEB: www.kivaconfections.com
SIC: **3999**

(P-7294)
KNT MANUFACTURING INC
39760 Eureka Dr, Newark (94560-4808)
PHONE.................................510 896-1699
Keith Ngo, *CEO*
Felipe Rodriguez, *Manager*
Raul Samson, *Manager*
EMP: 67 EST: 2013
SALES (est): 7.8MM **Privately Held**
WEB: www.kntmfg.com
SIC: **3999** Barber & beauty shop equipment

(P-7295)
L & B LABORATORIES INC
1660 Mabury Rd, San Jose (95133-1032)
PHONE.................................408 251-7888
Viet Le, *Principal*
EMP: 21 EST: 2004
SALES (est): 1.2MM **Privately Held**
WEB: www.landblabs.com
SIC: **3999** Barber & beauty shop equipment

(P-7296)
LIXIT CORPORATION (PA)
Also Called: Equitex
100 Coombs St, NAPA (94559-3941)
P.O. Box 2580 (94558-0525)
PHONE.................................800 358-8254
Linda Parks, *President*
Elizabeth Dennis, *COO*
Chris Parks, *CFO*
Laurie Corona, *Vice Pres*
Howard Pickens, *Vice Pres*
▲ EMP: 101 EST: 1968
SQ FT: 50,000
SALES (est): 13.6MM **Privately Held**
WEB: www.lixit.com
SIC: **3999** Pet supplies

(P-7297)
LUXSHARE-ICT INC
890 Hillview Ct Ste 200, Milpitas (95035-4573)
PHONE.................................408 957-0535
Jerry Tsai, *CEO*
EMP: 41 EST: 2011
SALES (est): 9.3MM **Privately Held**
WEB: www.en.luxshare-ict.com
SIC: **3999** Manufacturing industries
HQ: Luxshare-Ict Co., Ltd.
2f, No. 252, Neihu Rd., Sec. 1
Taipei City TAP 11493

(P-7298)
LYSTEK INTERNATIONAL INC
1014 Chadbourne Rd, Fairfield (94534-9700)
PHONE.................................707 419-0084
James Dunbar, *Principal*
Alex West, *Senior Engr*
Samantha Halloran, *Manager*
EMP: 16 EST: 2016
SALES (est): 11.7MM
SALES (corp-wide): 206.5MM **Privately Held**
WEB: www.lystek.com
SIC: **3999** Manufacturing industries
PA: R. W. Tomlinson Limited
100 Citigate Dr
Ottawa ON K2J 6
613 822-1867

(P-7299)
MIDWAY GAMES WEST INC
675 Sycamore Dr, Milpitas (95035-7458)
PHONE.................................408 434-3700
Dan Van Elderen, *President*
Mickey Lynch, *CFO*
Mark Pierce, *Senior VP*
Steve Calsee, *Vice Pres*
Masao Chata, *Vice Pres*
EMP: 130 EST: 1972
SALES (est): 5.3MM **Privately Held**
SIC: **3999** 3944 Coin-operated amusement machines; video game machines, except coin-operated

(P-7300)
MOSAIC BRANDS INC
Also Called: Hair ACC By Mia Minnelli
3266 Buskirk Ave, Pleasant Hill (94523-4315)
P.O. Box 585, Alamo (94507-0585)
PHONE.................................925 322-8700
Mia Minnelli, *President*
▲ EMP: 25 EST: 2000
SQ FT: 20,000
SALES (est): 2.7MM **Privately Held**
SIC: **3999** 3069 Hair & hair-based products; rubber hair accessories

(P-7301)
POWERHOUSE ENGINEERING INC
101 Industrial Way Ste 13, Belmont (94002-8207)
PHONE.................................650 226-3560
Carlo Bertocchini, *President*
EMP: 16 EST: 2007
SALES (est): 718.4K **Privately Held**
SIC: **3999** Manufacturing industries

(P-7302)
PRIDE INDUSTRIES ONE INC
10030 Foothills Blvd, Roseville (95747-7102)
P.O. Box 1200, Rocklin (95677-7200)
PHONE.................................916 788-2100
Jeff Dern, *CFO*
Pete Berghuis, *COO*
Chris Bunch, *Vice Pres*
Dan Robin, *Vice Pres*
David Wickersham, *Vice Pres*
EMP: 4300 EST: 1997
SALES (est): 102.7MM
SALES (corp-wide): 232.7MM **Privately Held**
WEB: www.prideindustries.com
SIC: **3999** Barber & beauty shop equipment
PA: Pride Industries
10030 Foothills Blvd
Roseville CA 95747
916 788-2100

(P-7303)
PRYSM INC (PA)
513 Fairview Way, Milpitas (95035-3059)
PHONE.................................408 586-1727
Amit Jain, *President*
Don Williams, *President*
Jasbir Singh, *CFO*
Tushar Kothari, *Exec VP*
Dana Corey, *Vice Pres*
▲ EMP: 70
SQ FT: 25,000
SALES (est): 33.6MM **Privately Held**
WEB: www.prysm.com
SIC: **3999** Advertising display products

(P-7304)
R&D EDUCATIONAL SYSTEMS INC
Also Called: Sombrero Time
9719 Village Center Dr # 125, Granite Bay (95746-6499)
PHONE.................................916 934-6223
Ruth Finsthwait, *President*
David Finsthwait, *COO*
Angie Martinez, *Teacher*
EMP: 15 EST: 2007
SQ FT: 2,000
SALES (est): 1.8MM **Privately Held**
WEB: www.myspanishjourney.com
SIC: **8299** 3999 Educational services; education aids, devices & supplies

(P-7305)
RESQ MANUFACTURING
11430 White Rock Rd, Rancho Cordova (95742-6600)
PHONE.................................916 638-6786
Martin Szegedy, *CEO*
EMP: 45
SALES (est): 4.7MM **Privately Held**
WEB: www.resqmfg.com
SIC: **3999** Airplane models, except toy

(P-7306)
SAVAGE INDUSTRIES
48 Linda St, San Francisco (94110-1616)
PHONE.................................415 845-6264
Adam Savage, *Principal*
EMP: 22 EST: 2010
SALES (est): 375.3K **Privately Held**
WEB: www.savageservices.com
SIC: **3999** Manufacturing industries

(P-7307)
SHELLPRO INC
18378 Atkins Rd, Lodi (95240-9649)
P.O. Box 2680 (95241-2680)
PHONE.................................209 334-2081
Calvin Suess, *President*
Virgil Suess, *Vice Pres*
Rocky Suess, *VP Prdtn*
EMP: 22 EST: 2000
SQ FT: 225,000
SALES (est): 1.6MM **Privately Held**
WEB: www.shellproinc.com
SIC: **3999** Nut shells, grinding, from purchased nuts

(P-7308)
SOCIAL BRANDS LLC
6575 Simson St, Oakland (94605-2271)
PHONE.................................415 728-1761
Benjamin Seabury, *Mng Member*
EMP: 20 EST: 2017
SALES (est): 544.3K **Privately Held**
SIC: **3999** Manufacturing industries

(P-7309)
SUBLIMATION INC
Also Called: Sublime
2537 Willow St Unit 6, Oakland (94607-1723)
PHONE.................................888 994-2726
Matthew Hawkins, *CEO*
Ahmer Iqbal, *COO*
EMP: 25 EST: 2016
SALES (est): 2.2MM
SALES (corp-wide): 3.9MM **Privately Held**
WEB: www.shopharborside.com
SIC: **3999** 5159 ;
PA: Harborside Inc.
66205 Paul Rd
Desert Hot Springs CA 92240
888 994-2726

(P-7310)
SUBLIME MACHINING INC
2537 Willow St, Oakland (94607-1723)
PHONE.................................858 349-2445
Alexander Fang, *Principal*
EMP: 17 EST: 2016
SALES (est): 1MM **Privately Held**
SIC: **3999** 5159 7699 ; ; industrial machinery & equipment repair

(P-7311)
SUN VALLEY FLORAL GROUP LLC
3160 Upper Bay Rd, Arcata (95521-9690)
PHONE.................................707 826-8700
Lane Devries, *CEO*
Conor Maguire, *Sales Staff*
Jack Merrill, *Sales Staff*
Cisco Haggerty, *Manager*
▲ EMP: 750
SALES (est): 72.9MM **Privately Held**
WEB: www.thesunvalleygroup.com
SIC: **3999** Flowers, artificial & preserved

(P-7312)
T4 MANUFACTURING INC (PA)
51 Poppy House Rd, Rio Vista (94571-1201)
P.O. Box 691 (94571-0691)
PHONE.................................707 689-3849
EMP: 16 EST: 2018
SALES (est): 267.4K **Privately Held**
WEB: www.t4manufacturing.com
SIC: **3999** Manufacturing industries

(P-7313)
TAKT MANUFACTURING INC
1300 E Victor Rd, Lodi (95240-0800)
PHONE.................................408 250-4975
Trevor Weissbart, *Principal*
EMP: 15 EST: 2018
SALES (est): 723.3K **Privately Held**
SIC: **3999** Manufacturing industries

(P-7314)
TRICK OR TREAT STDIOS HLDNGS L
1005 17th Ave, Santa Cruz (95062-3033)
PHONE.................................831 713-9665
Christopher M Zephro, *CEO*
Julie Stockwell, *Manager*
▲ EMP: 20 EST: 2013
SQ FT: 3,000
SALES (est): 1.1MM **Privately Held**
WEB: www.trickortreatstudios.com
SIC: **3999** 7922 2389 Magic equipment, supplies & props; costume design, theatrical; lodge costumes

(P-7315)
VIRTUAL TECHNOLOGIES INC
Also Called: Global V R
1380 Piper Dr, Milpitas (95035-6820)
PHONE.................................408 597-3400
Ken Bayr, *President*
Gregory J Lima, *Exec VP*
Frank Ballouz, *Senior VP*
Caryn Mical, *Vice Pres*
Debbie Minardi, *Vice Pres*
◆ EMP: 50 EST: 1998
SQ FT: 60,000
SALES (est): 10.5MM **Privately Held**
SIC: **3999** Coin-operated amusement machines

(P-7316)
VOLTA INDUSTRIES INC (HQ)
155 De Haro St, San Francisco (94103-5121)
PHONE.................................415 583-3805
Scott Mercer, *Ch of Bd*
Christopher Wendel, *President*
Francois P Chadwick, *CFO*
James S Degraw, *Officer*
Praveen Mandal, *CTO*
EMP: 100 EST: 2010
SALES (est): 19.4MM
SALES (corp-wide): 25.7MM **Publicly Held**
WEB: www.voltacharging.com
SIC: **3999** Barber & beauty shop equipment
PA: Volta Inc.
155 De Haro St
San Francisco CA 94103
415 583-3805

(P-7317)
XODUS MANUFACTURING INC
45999 Warm Springs Blvd, Fremont (94539-6766)
PHONE.................................510 413-7925
Hector Carballo, *CEO*
EMP: 15 EST: 2015

4011 Railroads, Line-Hauling Operations

(P-7318)
CALIFRNIA HIGH SPEED RAIL AUTH
770 L St Ste 620, Sacramento (95814-3385)
PHONE 916 324-1541
Dan Richard, *Ch of Bd*
EMP: 100 EST: 2010
SALES (est): 16.6MM **Privately Held**
WEB: www.hsr.ca.gov
SIC: 4011 Railroads, line-haul operating
PA: State Of California
State Capital
Sacramento CA 95814
916 445-2864

(P-7319)
SIERRA ENTERTAINMENT
341 Industrial Way, Woodland (95776-6012)
PHONE 530 666-9646
David Magew, *President*
Alan H Lambert, *Vice Pres*
Robert Pinoli, *Vice Pres*
Torgny Nilsson, *Admin Sec*
EMP: 36 EST: 1999
SALES (est): 60.3K **Privately Held**
WEB: www.sierrarailroad.com
SIC: 4011 Railroads, line-haul operating
PA: Sierra Railroad Company
341 Industrial Way
Woodland CA 95776

4111 Local & Suburban Transit

(P-7320)
A-PARA TRANSIT CORP
Also Called: Yefllow Shttle Vtrans Sdan Svc
1400 Doolittle Dr, San Leandro (94577-2226)
PHONE 510 562-5500
Shiv D Kumar, *President*
Mark Weinstein, *Senior VP*
Alicia Paschal, *Human Resources*
Gana Kumar, *Director*
Leslie Thornton, *Manager*
EMP: 110 EST: 1992
SQ FT: 2,200
SALES (est): 24.6MM **Privately Held**
WEB: www.aparatransit.com
SIC: 4111 Local & suburban transit

(P-7321)
AERO TECHNOLOGIES INC (PA)
555 Mission St, San Francisco (94105-0920)
PHONE 415 314-7479
Garrett Camp, *CEO*
EMP: 47 EST: 2013
SALES (est): 2.1MM **Privately Held**
SIC: 4111 Airport transportation

(P-7322)
AIRLINE COACH SERVICE INC
San Francisco Intl Arprt, San Francisco (94125)
P.O. Box 250147 (94125-0147)
PHONE 650 697-7733
Alex Morrison, *Vice Pres*
EMP: 45
SALES (corp-wide): 9.1MM **Privately Held**
WEB: www.airlinecoach.com
SIC: 4111 Airport transportation services, regular route
PA: Airline Coach Service, Inc.
863 Malcolm Rd
Burlingame CA 94010
650 697-7733

(P-7323)
AIRLINE COACH SERVICE INC (PA)
863 Malcolm Rd, Burlingame (94010-1406)
P.O. Box 282998, San Francisco (94128-2998)
PHONE 650 697-7733
Alex Morrison, *CEO*
Gregory Choo, *Ch of Bd*
Kyung C Lee, *President*
EMP: 45 EST: 1982
SQ FT: 7,000
SALES (est): 9.1MM **Privately Held**
WEB: www.airlinecoach.com
SIC: 4111 4581 Airport transportation services, regular route; airport terminal services

(P-7324)
ALAMEDA-CONTRA COSTA TRNST DST (PA)
Also Called: AC TRANSIT
1600 Franklin St, Oakland (94612-2806)
P.O. Box 28507 (94604-8507)
PHONE 510 891-4777
Michael Hursh, *General Mgr*
Claudia Allen, *CFO*
Lewis Clinton, *CFO*
Jeff Davis, *Bd of Directors*
Kathleen Kelly, *Officer*
▲ EMP: 250 EST: 1956
SQ FT: 100,000
SALES: 62MM **Privately Held**
WEB: www.actransit.org
SIC: 4111 Bus line operations

(P-7325)
BLACK CAR NETWORK LLC (PA)
Also Called: Urbanbcn Worldwide
1184 San Mateo Ave, South San Francisco (94080-6602)
PHONE 877 277-0208
Nadia Abdelfattah,
EMP: 37 EST: 2011
SALES (est): 2.1MM **Privately Held**
WEB: www.urbanbcn.com
SIC: 4111 Airport transportation

(P-7326)
CITY OF FOLSOM
1300 Leidesdorff St, Folsom (95630-2449)
PHONE 916 355-8395
EMP: 122
SALES (corp-wide): 116.1MM **Privately Held**
WEB: www.folsom.ca.us
SIC: 4111 Local & suburban transit
PA: City Of Folsom
50 Natoma St
Folsom CA 95630
916 355-7200

(P-7327)
CITY OF FRESNO
Fresno Area Express
2223 G St, Fresno (93706-1631)
PHONE 559 621-7433
Bruce Red, *General Mgr*
Clifford Traugh, *Analyst*
Karen Hillius, *Accountant*
Randy Clays, *Supervisor*
Bruce Robinson, *Supervisor*
EMP: 460
SALES (corp-wide): 462.5MM **Privately Held**
WEB: www.fresno.gov
SIC: 4111 Bus transportation
PA: City Of Fresno
2600 Fresno St
Fresno CA 93721
559 621-7001

(P-7328)
CITY OF RIO VISTA
Also Called: RIO VISTA DELTA BREEZE
1 Main St, Rio Vista (94571-1842)
PHONE 707 374-5337
Norm Richardson, *Mayor*
Rob Hickey, *City Mgr*
Constance Boulware, *Council Mbr*
Rick Dolk, *Council Mbr*
Tim Kubli, *Council Mbr*
EMP: 35 EST: 2012
SQ FT: 9,000
SALES (est): 10.2MM **Privately Held**
WEB: www.riovistacity.com
SIC: 4111 Local & suburban transit

(P-7329)
EASTERN CNTRA COSTA TRNST AUTH
Also Called: Tri Delta Transit
801 Wilbur Ave, Antioch (94509-7500)
PHONE 925 754-6622
Jennie Krieg, *CEO*
Steve Ponte, *COO*
Thomas J Harais, *CFO*
Kevin Romick, *Bd of Directors*
Mike Furnary, *Buyer*
EMP: 35 EST: 1976
SQ FT: 38,000
SALES (est): 7.6MM **Privately Held**
WEB: www.trideltatransit.com
SIC: 4111 Bus line operations

(P-7330)
FIRST TRANSIT INC
2047 Grogan Ave, Merced (95341-6440)
PHONE 209 385-1226
Caryn Borba, *Branch Mgr*
Miles Turpin, *Director*
EMP: 127
SALES (corp-wide): 903.8MM **Privately Held**
WEB: www.firsttransit.com
SIC: 4111 Bus transportation
PA: First Transit, Inc.
600 Vine St Ste 1400
Cincinnati OH 45202
513 241-2200

(P-7331)
FIRST TRANSIT INC
Also Called: Laidlaw Transit Services
117 Fern St Ste 100, Santa Cruz (95060-2155)
PHONE 831 460-9911
Camilla Shaffer, *Manager*
EMP: 127
SALES (corp-wide): 903.8MM **Privately Held**
WEB: www.firsttransit.com
SIC: 4111 Local & suburban transit
PA: First Transit, Inc.
600 Vine St Ste 1400
Cincinnati OH 45202
513 241-2200

(P-7332)
FIRST TRANSIT INC
500 W Hospital Rd, French Camp (95231-9693)
PHONE 866 244-6383
EMP: 127
SALES (corp-wide): 903.8MM **Privately Held**
WEB: www.firsttransit.com
SIC: 4111 Local & suburban transit
PA: First Transit, Inc.
600 Vine St Ste 1400
Cincinnati OH 45202
513 241-2200

(P-7333)
FIRST TRANSIT INC
Also Called: Dispatch Office
407 High St, Oakland (94601-3903)
PHONE 510 437-8990
EMP: 127
SALES (corp-wide): 903.8MM **Privately Held**
WEB: www.firsttransit.com
SIC: 4111 Bus transportation
PA: First Transit, Inc.
600 Vine St Ste 1400
Cincinnati OH 45202
513 241-2200

(P-7334)
GLOCOL INC
980 9th St Fl 16, Sacramento (95814-2736)
PHONE 650 224-2108
Ranju Verma, *Exec Dir*
Harsh Verma, *Principal*
EMP: 20 EST: 2003
SALES (est): 1.3MM **Privately Held**
WEB: www.glocol.net
SIC: 4111 7375 7371 7372 Local & suburban transit; information retrieval services; computer software systems analysis & design, custom; computer software development & applications; computer software development; business oriented computer software

(P-7335)
GMJ AIR SHUTTLE LLC
5411 Luce Ave 201, McClellan (95652-2447)
PHONE 916 884-2001
Jerome Joondeph, *Mng Member*
Aimee Robello, *Business Mgr*
Roland Vargas, *Manager*
EMP: 100 EST: 2012
SALES (est): 4.5MM **Privately Held**
WEB: www.xojetaviation.com
SIC: 4111 Airport transportation

(P-7336)
GREYHOUND LINES INC
Also Called: Boltbus
5275 W Shaw Ave, Fresno (93722-5031)
PHONE 559 268-1829
David Hall, *General Mgr*
EMP: 69
SALES (corp-wide): 6.5B **Privately Held**
WEB: www.greyhound.com
SIC: 4111 Commuter bus operation
HQ: Greyhound Lines, Inc.
350 N Saint Paul St # 300
Dallas TX 75201
214 849-8000

(P-7337)
JEREMIAH PHILLIPS LLC
Also Called: Airline Coach Service
863 Malcolm Rd, Burlingame (94010-1406)
P.O. Box 4427 (94011-4427)
PHONE 650 697-7733
Alex Morrison, *Mng Member*
Charles Morrison,
EMP: 99 EST: 2016
SQ FT: 10,000
SALES (est): 5.3MM **Privately Held**
SIC: 4111 Airport transportation

(P-7338)
KOTOBUKI-YA INC
Also Called: CPS
720 Woodside Way, San Mateo (94401-1610)
PHONE 650 344-7955
Koichi Suyama, *President*
EMP: 70 EST: 1983
SALES (est): 2MM **Privately Held**
WEB: www.kotobukiyausa.com
SIC: 4111 Airport transportation

(P-7339)
LIVERMORE AMDOR VLY TRNST AUTH
Also Called: Wheels
1362 Rutan Dr Ste 100, Livermore (94551-7318)
PHONE 925 455-7555
Paul Matsuoka, *Exec Dir*
Christy Wegener, *Plan/Corp Dev D*
Kadri Kulm, *Planning*
Tamara Edwards, *Finance*
Tony McCaulay, *Marketing Staff*
EMP: 44 EST: 1985
SALES (est): 14.5MM **Privately Held**
WEB: www.wheelsbus.com
SIC: 4111 8611 Bus transportation; business associations

(P-7340)
MARIN AIRPORTER INC
1455 N Hamilton Pkwy, Novato (94949-8205)
PHONE 415 884-2878
Guy Murta, *Branch Mgr*
Lawrence Forrest, *Project Mgr*
Margie Franklin, *Bookkeeper*
EMP: 59
SALES (corp-wide): 9.5MM **Privately Held**
WEB: www.marinairporter.com
SIC: 4111 Local & suburban transit

PRODUCTS & SERVICES SECTION
4111 - Local & Suburban Transit County (P-7360)

PA: Marin Airporter
8 Lovell Ave
San Rafael CA 94901
415 256-8833

(P-7341) MENDOCINO TRANSIT AUTHORITY (PA)
241 Plant Rd, Ukiah (95482-6944)
PHONE 707 462-3881
Bruce Richard, *Owner*
Jacob King, *Exec Dir*
Bob Butler, *Maintence Staff*
EMP: 45 **EST:** 1975
SALES (est): 6.9MM **Privately Held**
WEB: www.mendocinotransit.org
SIC: 4111 7538 Bus line operations; general automotive repair shops

(P-7342) METROPOLITAN TRNSP COMM (PA)
Also Called: M T C
375 Beale St Ste 800, San Francisco (94105-2179)
PHONE 415 778-6700
Steve Hieminger, *Exec Dir*
Brian Mayhew, *CFO*
Jake Mackenzie, *Vice Ch Bd*
Julie Teglovic, *Officer*
Therese McMillan, *Exec Dir*
EMP: 93 **EST:** 1970
SQ FT: 21,000
SALES: 161.9MM **Privately Held**
WEB: www.mtc.ca.gov
SIC: 4111 Bus line operations

(P-7343) MV TRANSPORTATION INC
1944 Williams St, San Leandro (94577-2304)
PHONE 510 351-1603
Jay Jeter, *Branch Mgr*
Miriam Cifuentes, *General Mgr*
Mark Centeno, *Manager*
EMP: 171
SALES (corp-wide): 378.4MM **Privately Held**
WEB: www.mvtransit.com
SIC: 4111 Local & suburban transit
PA: Mv Transportation, Inc.
2711 N Haskell Ave # 1500
Dallas TX 75204
972 391-4600

(P-7344) PENINSULA CRRDOR JINT PWERS BD
Also Called: Caltrain
1250 San Carlos Ave, San Carlos (94070-2468)
P.O. Box 3006 (94070-1306)
PHONE 650 508-6200
Michael J Scanlon, *Exec Dir*
Virginia Harrington, *CEO*
Chuck Harvey, *CEO*
Michelle Bouchard, *COO*
Jeremy Lipps, *Officer*
EMP: 105
SALES: 84.4MM **Privately Held**
WEB: www.caltrain.com
SIC: 4111 Local railway passenger operation

(P-7345) REDDING AERO ENTERPRISES INC
Also Called: Redding Jet Center
3775 Flight Ave Ste 100, Redding (96002-9376)
PHONE 530 224-2300
Jack Kilpatrick, *President*
Steve Hoppes, *Corp Secy*
Victor Clarke, *Vice Pres*
Douglas Coble, *General Mgr*
EMP: 60 **EST:** 1972
SQ FT: 31,000
SALES (est): 6MM **Privately Held**
WEB: www.reddingjet.com
SIC: 4111 4581 Airport transportation services, regular route; aircraft servicing & repairing

(P-7346) SACRAMENTO REGIONAL TRNST DIST (PA)
1400 29th St, Sacramento (95816-6406)
P.O. Box 2110 (95812-2110)
PHONE 916 726-2877
Mike Wiley, *CEO*
Lisa Hinz, *Vice Pres*
Neil Nance, *Vice Pres*
Angela Roy, *Admin Asst*
Jose Gonzalez, *Business Anlyst*
▲ **EMP:** 700 **EST:** 1955
SQ FT: 10,000
SALES: 21MM **Privately Held**
WEB: www.sacrt.com
SIC: 4111 Bus line operations; commuter rail passenger operation

(P-7347) SACRAMENTO REGIONAL TRNST DIST
Transit System Development
1400 29th St, Sacramento (95816-6406)
P.O. Box 2110 (95812-2110)
PHONE 916 362-9490
Beverly Scott, *Manager*
Laura Ham, *Vice Pres*
Sandra Buck, *Technician*
Robin Haswell, *Technology*
Craig Norman, *Engineer*
EMP: 40
SALES (corp-wide): 21MM **Privately Held**
WEB: www.sacrt.com
SIC: 4111 Bus line operations
PA: Sacramento Regional Transit Dist.
1400 29th St
Sacramento CA 95816
916 726-2877

(P-7348) SAN FRANCISCO BAY AREA RAPID
Also Called: Oakland Shops/Annex
601 E 8th St, Oakland (94606-3606)
PHONE 510 286-2893
Tom Delaney, *Superintendent*
Deborah Avaro, *COO*
John Goodwin, *General Mgr*
Christina Hohorst, *Planning*
Joni McCarty, *Technician*
EMP: 2000
SALES (corp-wide): 394.9MM **Privately Held**
WEB: www.bart.gov
SIC: 4111 Local railway passenger operation
PA: San Francisco Bay Area Rapid Transit District
2150 Webster St
Oakland CA 94612
510 464-6000

(P-7349) SAN FRNCSCO BAY AREA RPID TRNS (PA)
Also Called: Bart
2150 Webster St, Oakland (94612-3012)
P.O. Box 12688 (94604-2688)
PHONE 510 464-6000
Robert Powers, *General Mgr*
Dominic Cisneros, *Officer*
Paul Fadelli, *Officer*
Taylor Huckaby, *Officer*
William Longstaff, *Vice Pres*
▲ **EMP:** 400 **EST:** 1957
SQ FT: 150,000
SALES: 394.9MM **Privately Held**
WEB: www.bart.gov
SIC: 4111 Local railway passenger operation

(P-7350) SAN JOAQUIN REGIONAL TRNST DST
Also Called: Sjrtd
421 E Weber Ave, Stockton (95202-3024)
P.O. Box 201010 (95201-9010)
PHONE 209 948-5566
Gloria G Salazar, *CEO*
Gloria Salazar, *CFO*
Cameron Isaacson, *Officer*
Donna Kelsay, *General Mgr*
Judith Spiro, *Admin Asst*
EMP: 201 **EST:** 1964
SQ FT: 29,100
SALES (est): 45.4MM **Privately Held**
WEB: www.sanjoaquinrtd.com
SIC: 4111 Bus line operations

(P-7351) SAN MATEO COUNTY TRANSIT DST (PA)
Also Called: SAMTRANS
1250 San Carlos Ave, San Carlos (94070-2468)
P.O. Box 3006 (94070-1306)
PHONE 650 508-6200
Jim Hartnett, *CEO*
Bill Likens, *President*
Ch Harvey, *COO*
Virginia Harrington, *CFO*
Rita Haskin, *Ch Credit Ofcr*
EMP: 250 **EST:** 1976
SQ FT: 20,000
SALES: 11.6MM **Privately Held**
WEB: www.smctd.com
SIC: 4111 Bus line operations

(P-7352) SAN MATEO COUNTY TRANSIT DST
Also Called: Sam Trans
301 N Access Rd, South San Francisco (94080-6901)
PHONE 650 588-4860
John Gerbo, *Branch Mgr*
Elliot Rivas, *Maint Spvr*
EMP: 349
SQ FT: 2,000
SALES (corp-wide): 11.6MM **Privately Held**
WEB: www.smctd.com
SIC: 4111 Bus line operations
PA: San Mateo County Transit District
1250 San Carlos Ave
San Carlos CA 94070
650 508-6200

(P-7353) SANTA CLARA VALLEY TRNSP AUTH (PA)
3331 N 1st St, San Jose (95134-1906)
PHONE 408 321-2300
Nuria Fernandez, *CEO*
Benito Torrecillas, *Comms Mgr*
Carroll W Huff, *Principal*
Armida Alvarez, *Admin Sec*
Valerie Tucker, *Admin Sec*
▲ **EMP:** 1053 **EST:** 1972
SQ FT: 217,000
SALES: 1.2B **Privately Held**
WEB: www.vta.org
SIC: 4111 Local & suburban transit

(P-7354) SANTA CLARA VALLEY TRNSP AUTH
Document Control-Central File
3331 N 1st St Bldg B, San Jose (95134-1906)
PHONE 408 321-5559
Michael Burns, *Manager*
EMP: 82
SALES (corp-wide): 1.2B **Privately Held**
WEB: www.vta.org
SIC: 4111 9621 Local & suburban transit; subway operation;
PA: Santa Clara Valley Transportation Authority
3331 N 1st St
San Jose CA 95134
408 321-2300

(P-7355) SANTA CRUZ METRO TRNST DST
Also Called: Maintenance Dept
138 Golf Club Dr, Santa Cruz (95060-2121)
PHONE 831 429-5455
Tom Stickle, *Manager*
EMP: 93
SALES (corp-wide): 7.7MM **Privately Held**
WEB: www.scmtd.com
SIC: 4111 Local & suburban transit
PA: Santa Cruz Metropolitan Transit District
110 Vernon St
Santa Cruz CA 95060
831 426-6143

(P-7356) SANTA CRUZ METRO TRNST DST
Also Called: Fleet Maintenance Dept
110 Vernon St Ste B, Santa Cruz (95060-2130)
PHONE 831 469-1954
Tom Stickel, *Manager*
EMP: 93
SALES (corp-wide): 7.7MM **Privately Held**
WEB: www.scmtd.com
SIC: 4111 Local & suburban transit
PA: Santa Cruz Metropolitan Transit District
110 Vernon St
Santa Cruz CA 95060
831 426-6143

(P-7357) SANTA CRUZ METRO TRNST DST
135 Aviation Way Ste 2, Watsonville (95076-2046)
PHONE 831 426-6080
Lesley White, *Branch Mgr*
Angel Aken, *Finance Mgr*
Kevin Walter, *Human Res Mgr*
Debbie Kinslow, *Manager*
EMP: 93
SALES (corp-wide): 7.7MM **Privately Held**
WEB: www.scmtd.com
SIC: 4111 Local & suburban transit
PA: Santa Cruz Metropolitan Transit District
110 Vernon St
Santa Cruz CA 95060
831 426-6143

(P-7358) SFO AIRPORTER INC (PA)
Also Called: Compass Transportation Charter
1535 S 10th St, San Jose (95112-2516)
PHONE 650 246-2734
Nicholas C Leonoudakis, *Ch of Bd*
Jeffrey G Leonoudakis, *President*
Stephan C Leonoudakis, *Exec VP*
Timothy K Leonoudakis, *Vice Pres*
▼ **EMP:** 100 **EST:** 1976
SALES (est): 19.2MM **Privately Held**
WEB: www.sfoairporter.com
SIC: 4111 4141 4131 Airport transportation; local bus charter service; intercity bus line

(P-7359) SFO AIRPORTER INC
325 5th St, San Francisco (94107-1040)
PHONE 415 495-3909
Gordis Esposto, *Branch Mgr*
EMP: 100
SALES (corp-wide): 19.2MM **Privately Held**
WEB: www.sfoairporter.com
SIC: 4111 4141 4131 Airport transportation; local bus charter service; intercity bus line
PA: Sfo Airporter, Inc.
1535 S 10th St
San Jose CA 95112
650 246-2734

(P-7360) SONOMA COUNTY AIRPORT EX INC
5807 Old Redwood Hwy, Santa Rosa (95403-1167)
PHONE 707 837-8700
Howard Emigh, *President*
Tony Geraldi, *Corp Secy*
Janet Emigh, *Vice Pres*
Anthony Geraldi, *Vice Pres*
Amy Neese, *Human Res Dir*
EMP: 409 **EST:** 1981
SQ FT: 5,500
SALES (est): 6.5MM
SALES (corp-wide): 69.6MM **Privately Held**
WEB: www.airportexpressinc.com
SIC: 4111 4141 Airport transportation services, regular route; local bus charter service

4111 - Local & Suburban Transit County (P-7361)
PRODUCTS & SERVICES SECTION

(P-7361)
SUPERSHUTTLE INTERNATIONAL INC
323 S Canal St, South San Francisco (94080-4605)
PHONE..................650 246-2786
Eric Butler, *Principal*
EMP: 85
SALES (corp-wide): 1.3B **Privately Held**
SIC: 4111 Local & suburban transit
HQ: Supershuttle International, Inc.
14500 N Northsight Blvd # 329
Scottsdale AZ 85260
480 609-3000
PA: Groome Transportation, Incorporated
2289 Dabney Rd
Richmond VA 23230
804 222-7226

(P-7362)
SUPERSHUTTLE INTERNATIONAL INC
160 S Linden Ave, South San Francisco (94080-6419)
PHONE..................650 246-2704
EMP: 85
SALES (corp-wide): 1.3B **Privately Held**
SIC: 4111 Airport transportation
HQ: Supershuttle International, Inc.
14500 N Northsight Blvd # 329
Scottsdale AZ 85260
480 609-3000

(P-7363)
SUPERSHUTTLE INTERNATIONAL INC
700 16th St, San Francisco (94158-2531)
PHONE..................415 558-8500
Ruth T West, *Branch Mgr*
EMP: 85
SALES (corp-wide): 1.3B **Privately Held**
SIC: 4111 Airport transportation services, regular route
HQ: Supershuttle International, Inc.
14500 N Northsight Blvd # 329
Scottsdale AZ 85260
480 609-3000

(P-7364)
TRANSITAMERICA SERVICES INC
93 Cahill St, San Jose (95110-2501)
PHONE..................408 961-4350
Robert J Smith, *CEO*
EMP: 47 **EST:** 2005
SALES (est): 20.5MM **Privately Held**
WEB: www.herzog.com
SIC: 4111 Local & suburban transit

(P-7365)
WEST COUNTY TRNSP AGCY
367 W Robles Ave, Santa Rosa (95407-8126)
PHONE..................707 206-9988
Chad Barksdale, *Exec Dir*
Michael REA, *Principal*
Emily Keeran, *Instructor*
Janice Siebert, *Manager*
Carey Cox, *Supervisor*
EMP: 177
SQ FT: 125,017
SALES (est): 18.2MM **Privately Held**
WEB: www.schoolbusing.org
SIC: 4111 Local & suburban transit

(P-7366)
WISK AERO LLC (PA)
2700 Broderick Way, Mountain View (94043-1108)
PHONE..................650 641-0920
Gary Gysin, *CEO*
Dan Dalton, *Vice Pres*
Yuichi Sakashita, *Controller*
EMP: 269 **EST:** 2019
SALES (est): 35.6MM **Privately Held**
WEB: www.wisk.aero
SIC: 4111 Airport transportation

4119 Local Passenger Transportation: NEC

(P-7367)
AMATO INDUSTRIES INCORPORATED
Also Called: Gateway Limousine
1550 Gilbreth Rd, Burlingame (94010-1605)
PHONE..................650 697-5548
Sam Amato, *CEO*
Joel Amato, *Vice Pres*
Karen Amato, *Vice Pres*
Tom Amato, *Finance*
Gerri Jacinto, *Human Res Mgr*
EMP: 48 **EST:** 1979
SQ FT: 9,500
SALES (est): 6.2MM **Privately Held**
WEB: www.gatewayglobalsf.com
SIC: 4119 Limousine rental, with driver

(P-7368)
AMERICAN MED RSPNSE INLAND EMP
1041 Fee Dr, Sacramento (95815-3908)
PHONE..................916 563-0600
Doug Petric, *Director*
Karl Pedroni, *Director*
EMP: 253 **Privately Held**
SIC: 4119 Ambulance service
HQ: American Medical Response Of Inland Empire
879 Marlborough Ave
Riverside CA 92507

(P-7369)
AMERICAN MED RSPNSE INLAND EMP
4451 Caterpillar Rd Ste 1, Redding (96003-1493)
PHONE..................530 246-9111
John Lord, *Director*
EMP: 253 **Privately Held**
SIC: 4119 Ambulance service
HQ: American Medical Response Of Inland Empire
879 Marlborough Ave
Riverside CA 92507

(P-7370)
AMERICAN MED RSPNSE INLAND EMP
1300 Illinois St, San Francisco (94107-3107)
PHONE..................415 922-9400
James Salvante, *Manager*
EMP: 253 **Privately Held**
SIC: 4119 Ambulance service
HQ: American Medical Response Of Inland Empire
879 Marlborough Ave
Riverside CA 92507

(P-7371)
AMERICAN MED RSPNSE INLAND EMP
116 Hubbard St, Santa Cruz (95060-2938)
PHONE..................831 423-7030
David Zenker, *Manager*
EMP: 253 **Privately Held**
SIC: 4119 Ambulance service
HQ: American Medical Response Of Inland Empire
879 Marlborough Ave
Riverside CA 92507

(P-7372)
AMERICAN MEDICAL RESPONSE INC
13992 Catalina St, San Leandro (94577-5506)
PHONE..................415 794-9204
Thomas Wagner, *CEO*
EMP: 250 **EST:** 1992
SALES (est): 15.6MM **Publicly Held**
WEB: www.evhc.net
SIC: 4119 7372 Ambulance service; application computer software
HQ: Envision Healthcare Corporation
1a Burton Hills Blvd
Nashville TN 37215
615 665-1283

(P-7373)
BAUERS INTELLIGENT TRNSP INC (PA)
50 Pier, San Francisco (94158-2193)
PHONE..................415 263-4020
Gary Bauer, *CEO*
Dennis Jackson, *COO*
Gary Schwartz, *CFO*
Mike Harshfield MBA, *Senior VP*
Carlee Loya, *Executive*
EMP: 250 **EST:** 1989
SQ FT: 125,000
SALES: 38.5MM **Privately Held**
WEB: www.bauersit.com
SIC: 4119 Limousine rental, with driver

(P-7374)
BAY MEDIC TRANSPORTATION INC
959 Detroit Ave, Concord (94518-2501)
PHONE..................800 689-9511
Nesar Abdiani, *CEO*
Ali Abdani, *President*
EMP: 56 **EST:** 1995
SQ FT: 1,600
SALES (est): 5.3MM **Privately Held**
WEB: www.baymedic.com
SIC: 4119 Ambulance service

(P-7375)
BAYSHORE AMBULANCE INC (PA)
370 Hatch Dr, Foster City (94404-1106)
P.O. Box 4622 (94404-0622)
PHONE..................650 525-9700
William Bockholt, *President*
David Bockholt, *Treasurer*
EMP: 51 **EST:** 1990
SQ FT: 5,000
SALES (est): 6.1MM **Privately Held**
WEB: www.bayshoreambulance.com
SIC: 4119 Ambulance service

(P-7376)
BELLS HALDSBURG AMBULANCE SVC
438 Powell Ave, Healdsburg (95448-3430)
P.O. Box 726 (95448-0726)
PHONE..................707 433-1114
Wayne Bell, *President*
EMP: 41 **EST:** 1956
SALES (est): 507.7K **Privately Held**
WEB: www.bellsambulance.com
SIC: 4119 Ambulance service

(P-7377)
BI-COUNTY AMBULANCE SVC INC
1700 Poole Blvd, Yuba City (95993-2610)
P.O. Box 3130 (95992-3130)
PHONE..................530 674-2780
Kelly W Bumpus, *President*
Alex Bumpus, *Vice Pres*
EMP: 50 **EST:** 1976
SQ FT: 1,600
SALES (est): 5MM **Privately Held**
WEB: www.bicountyambulance.com
SIC: 4119 Ambulance service

(P-7378)
BLACK TIE TRANSPORTATION LLC
7080 Commerce Dr, Pleasanton (94588-8021)
PHONE..................925 847-0747
Bill Wheeler, *Mng Member*
Debbie Moore,
Jennifer Wheeler,
EMP: 130 **EST:** 1997
SQ FT: 18,000
SALES (est): 11.7MM **Privately Held**
WEB: www.blacktietrans.com
SIC: 4119 4724 Limousine rental, with driver; travel agencies

(P-7379)
CALIFRNIA SHOCK TRUMA A RESCUE (PA)
Also Called: Calstar
4933 Bailey Loop, McClellan (95652-2516)
PHONE..................916 921-4000
Lynn Malmstrom, *President*
Sonja Vargas, *Admin Asst*
EMP: 63 **EST:** 1983
SQ FT: 44,000
SALES (est): 35.9K **Privately Held**
WEB: www.calstar.org
SIC: 4119 Ambulance service

(P-7380)
CRUISE LLC (HQ)
1201 Bryant St, San Francisco (94103-4306)
PHONE..................415 335-4097
Daniel Ammann, *CEO*
Gil West, *COO*
Sheldon Quan, *Vice Pres*
John Taylor, *Vice Pres*
Louise Zhang, *Vice Pres*
EMP: 75 **EST:** 2016
SALES (est): 170.1MM **Publicly Held**
WEB: www.getcruise.com
SIC: 4119 Automobile rental, with driver

(P-7381)
DAV-EL RESERVATIONS SYSTEM INC
Also Called: Dav El Chuffeured Trnsp Networ
2025 Mckinnon Ave, San Francisco (94124-1608)
PHONE..................415 206-7950
Irwin Rosnel, *Manager*
EMP: 91
SALES (corp-wide): 10.8MM **Privately Held**
SIC: 4119 Limousine rental, with driver
PA: Dav-El Reservations System, Inc.
200 2nd St
Chelsea MA
617 887-0900

(P-7382)
ENLOE MEDICAL CENTER
Also Called: Tty-Deaf Hndcppd-Cmmnction Ctr
W 5th Av & Esplanade, Chico (95926)
PHONE..................530 891-7347
Bob Quitu, *Manager*
EMP: 118
SALES (corp-wide): 675.2MM **Privately Held**
WEB: www.enloe.org
SIC: 4119 Ambulance service
PA: Enloe Medical Center
1531 Esplanade
Chico CA 95926
530 332-7300

(P-7383)
FIRST RESPONDER EMS INC
Also Called: Paradise Ambulance Service
333 Huss Dr Ste 100, Chico (95928-8242)
PHONE..................530 897-6345
Byron Parsons, *President*
Meghan Woods, *Human Resources*
Joe Madrigal,
Scott Raper,
Bob Hall, *Manager*
EMP: 80 **EST:** 1988
SALES (est): 3.7MM **Privately Held**
WEB: www.firstresponder.com
SIC: 4119 Ambulance service

(P-7384)
KMA EMERGENCY SERVICES INC
Also Called: West Medions
14275 Wicks Blvd, San Leandro (94577-5613)
PHONE..................510 614-1420
Erik Mandler, *President*
EMP: 68 **EST:** 1995
SALES (est): 5MM **Privately Held**
WEB: www.westmedambulance.com
SIC: 4119 Ambulance service

PRODUCTS & SERVICES SECTION
4119 - Local Passenger Transportation: NEC County (P-7409)

(P-7385)
KWPH ENTERPRISES
Also Called: American Ambulance
2911 E Tulare St, Fresno (93721-1502)
PHONE.................................559 443-5900
Todd Valeri, *President*
Todd R Valeri, *President*
James Wampler, *CFO*
Hal Fielding, *Supervisor*
EMP: 700 **EST:** 1975
SQ FT: 22,000
SALES (est): 275MM **Privately Held**
WEB: www.americanambulance.com
SIC: 4119 Ambulance service

(P-7386)
LYFT INC (PA)
185 Berry St Ste 5000, San Francisco (94107-2503)
PHONE.................................844 250-2773
Logan Green, *CEO*
Prashant Aggarwal, *Ch of Bd*
John Zimmer, *President*
Brian Roberts, *CFO*
Sean Aggarwal, *Bd of Directors*
EMP: 4628 **EST:** 2007
SQ FT: 430,000
SALES (est): 2.3B **Publicly Held**
WEB: www.lyft.com
SIC: 4119 Local rental transportation; automobile rental, with driver

(P-7387)
MEDIC AMBULANCE SERVICE INC (PA)
506 Couch St, Vallejo (94590-2408)
P.O. Box 4467 (94590-0459)
PHONE.................................707 644-1761
Rodolfo Manfredi, *President*
Helen Pierson, *CFO*
Marissa Luchini, *Vice Pres*
Sandy Whaley, *Vice Pres*
Kristi Kendall, *VP Finance*
EMP: 130
SQ FT: 7,000
SALES (est): 13.7MM **Privately Held**
WEB: www.medicambulance.net
SIC: 4119 Ambulance service

(P-7388)
MEDIC AMBULANCE SERVICE INC
1001 Texas St Ste C, Fairfield (94533-5723)
PHONE.................................916 564-9011
Helen Pierson, *Manager*
Tucson Lee, *Technician*
Elisa Martinez, *Opers Spvr*
Kim Jeffery, *Opers Mgr*
Michael Fenwick,
EMP: 45
SALES (corp-wide): 13.7MM **Privately Held**
WEB: www.medicambulance.net
SIC: 4119 Ambulance service
PA: Medic Ambulance Service, Inc.
506 Couch St
Vallejo CA 94590
707 644-1761

(P-7389)
MEDSTAR LLC
20 Business Park Way # 100, Sacramento (95828-0965)
PHONE.................................916 669-0550
Adam C Ruggles, *President*
Adam Ruggles, *CFO*
Girma Tadesse, *Vice Pres*
Shawn Tweedt, *Surgeon*
Wilbur Roese, *Internal Med*
EMP: 65
SALES (est): 2.9MM **Privately Held**
WEB: www.medstarllc.com
SIC: 4119 Ambulance service

(P-7390)
MEDSTAR AMBLNCE MNDCINO CNTY I
130 Ford St, Ukiah (95482-4012)
P.O. Box 277 (95482-0277)
PHONE.................................707 462-3808
Leonard Winter, *CEO*
Brian Hajik, *Director*
EMP: 41 **EST:** 2012
SALES (est): 1.9MM **Privately Held**
WEB: www.medstarmendocino.org
SIC: 4119 Ambulance service

(P-7391)
NATIONAL EXPRESS LLC
880 Thornton Rd, Merced (95341-8003)
PHONE.................................209 201-9345
EMP: 64 **Privately Held**
WEB: www.nellc.com
SIC: 4119 Vanpool operation
HQ: National Express Llc
2601 Navistar Dr Bldg 4
Lisle IL 60532

(P-7392)
NORCAL AMBULANCE LLC
6761 Sierra Ct Ste G, Dublin (94568-2692)
PHONE.................................925 452-8300
Karla Nazareno, *Mng Member*
Jason Raddatz, *VP Bus Dvlpt*
Jacqueline Mitchell, *Human Resources*
Josh Islas, *Supervisor*
Melissa Popnoe, *Supervisor*
EMP: 38
SALES (corp-wide): 6.1MM **Privately Held**
WEB: www.norcalambulance.com
SIC: 4119 Ambulance service
PA: Norcal Ambulance Llc
3025 Independence Dr H
Livermore CA 94551
925 452-8301

(P-7393)
NORTH STAR EMERGENCY SVCS INC
Also Called: Norcal Ambulance Services
2537 Willow St, Oakland (94607-1723)
P.O. Box 12347, Pleasanton (94588-2347)
PHONE.................................510 452-3400
David Plaza, *COO*
Barry Sutherland, *CEO*
Makenzie Kelly, *CFO*
Karla Nazareno, *Administration*
William Vance, *Manager*
EMP: 52 **EST:** 2005
SALES (est): 7.3MM **Privately Held**
SIC: 4119 Ambulance service

(P-7394)
PARATRANSIT INCORPORATED (PA)
2501 Florin Rd, Sacramento (95822-4467)
P.O. Box 231100 (95823-0401)
PHONE.................................916 429-2009
Linda Jean Deavens, *CEO*
Ninh Dao-Dickinson, *COO*
Steve Robinson-Burmester, *CFO*
Patricia Williams, *Rector*
Jamila Lee, *Asst Mgr*
EMP: 210 **EST:** 1978
SQ FT: 250,000
SALES (est): 23.6MM **Privately Held**
WEB: www.paratransit.org
SIC: 4119 7539 Ambulance service; automotive repair shops

(P-7395)
PISTORESI AMBLNCE SVC OF MDERA
113 N R St, Madera (93637-4465)
PHONE.................................559 673-8004
Monte Pistoresi, *President*
Leona Pistoresi, *Vice Pres*
EMP: 63 **EST:** 1963
SQ FT: 1,000
SALES (est): 3.1MM **Privately Held**
WEB: www.pistoresiambulance.com
SIC: 4119 Ambulance service

(P-7396)
PROTRANSPORT-1 LLC (HQ)
720 Portal St, Cotati (94931-3060)
PHONE.................................707 975-2386
Michael Sechrist,
Matt Condie, *Business Anlyst*
Marc Dorsett, *IT/INT Sup*
Travis Spencer, *Accounting Mgr*
Kelley Sechrist,
EMP: 541 **EST:** 2000
SQ FT: 2,600
SALES (est): 102.3MM
SALES (corp-wide): 249MM **Privately Held**
WEB: www.protransport-1.com
SIC: 4119 Ambulance service
PA: Pt-1 Holdings, Llc
720 Portal St
Cotati CA 94931
707 665-4295

(P-7397)
PURE LUXURY LIMOUSINE SERVICE
Also Called: Pure Luxury Worldwide Trnsp
4246 Petaluma Blvd N, Petaluma (94952-1240)
P.O. Box 910, Penngrove (94951-0910)
PHONE.................................800 626-5466
Gary L Buffo Jr, *CEO*
Antoinette Allison, *Business Mgr*
Linda Reinecke, *Business Mgr*
Debbie Hawkins, *Human Resources*
John Byers, *Opers Staff*
EMP: 111 **EST:** 1991
SQ FT: 35,000
SALES (est): 14.5MM **Privately Held**
WEB: www.pureluxury.com
SIC: 4119 Limousine rental, with driver

(P-7398)
QUICKSILVER DELIVERY INC
Also Called: Quicksilver Delivery Service
129 Kissling St, San Francisco (94103-3726)
PHONE.................................415 431-1600
Phil Mc Cafee, *President*
EMP: 57 **EST:** 1981
SQ FT: 5,000
SALES (est): 395.4K **Privately Held**
SIC: 4119 Limousine rental, with driver

(P-7399)
REACH AIR MEDICAL SERVICES LLC (HQ)
8880 Cal Center Dr 125, Sacramento (95826-3222)
PHONE.................................707 324-2400
Brian Fladhammer, *General Mgr*
Patrick J McDonald, *President*
James E Adams, *CEO*
Ken A Lillo, *CFO*
Robert H Fish, *Chairman*
EMP: 40 **EST:** 1990
SALES (est): 53.5MM **Privately Held**
WEB: www.reachair.com
SIC: 4119 Ambulance service

(P-7400)
RM EXECUTIVE TRANSPORTATION
Also Called: Mosaic Global Transportation
525 Sunol St, San Jose (95126-3752)
PHONE.................................650 260-1240
Maurice Brewster, *President*
Lloyd J Vassell, *President*
Rhonda Brewster, *COO*
Lloyd Vassell, *VP Bus Dvlpt*
Jenny Duong, *Controller*
EMP: 35 **EST:** 2006
SALES (est): 5.2MM **Privately Held**
WEB: www.mosaicglobaltransportation.com
SIC: 4119 Limousine rental, with driver

(P-7401)
ROYAL AMBULANCE INC
14472 Wicks Blvd, San Leandro (94577-6712)
PHONE.................................877 995-6161
Steve Grau, *President*
Leon Botoshansky, *CFO*
Amri Pascual, *Technician*
Sean Young, *Opers Mgr*
Arkady Kaminski, *Director*
EMP: 120 **EST:** 2005
SQ FT: 5,000
SALES (est): 10.8MM **Privately Held**
WEB: www.royalambulance.com
SIC: 4119 Ambulance service

(P-7402)
RURAL/METRO CORPORATION
2364 W Winton Ave, Hayward (94545-1102)
PHONE.................................510 266-0885
EMP: 111
SALES (corp-wide): 3.7B **Publicly Held**
SIC: 4119 Local Passenger Transportation
HQ: Rural/Metro Corporation
8465 N Pima Rd
Scottsdale AZ 85258
480 606-3886

(P-7403)
SANTA CRUZ CNTY RGNAL TRNSP CO
1523 Pacific Ave, Santa Cruz (95060-3911)
PHONE.................................831 460-3200
George Dondero, *Exec Dir*
Guy Preston, *Exec Dir*
EMP: 35 **EST:** 1967
SALES (est): 3.5MM **Privately Held**
WEB: www.sccrtc.org
SIC: 4119 Local passenger transportation

(P-7404)
SEQUOIA SAFETY COUNCIL INC
500 E 11th St, Reedley (93654-2526)
PHONE.................................559 638-9995
Mark Watkins, *Administration*
Scott Brockett, *Manager*
EMP: 45 **EST:** 1953
SQ FT: 5,062
SALES (est): 2.7MM **Privately Held**
WEB: www.sequoiasafetycouncil.com
SIC: 4119 Ambulance service

(P-7405)
SILICON VALLEY AMBULANCE INC
181 Martinvale Ln, San Jose (95119-1319)
PHONE.................................408 225-2262
Randy Hooks, *President*
Lisa Hooks, *Vice Pres*
Angela Seitz,
EMP: 58 **EST:** 2002
SALES (est): 6.2MM **Privately Held**
WEB: www.sva-ems.com
SIC: 4119 Ambulance service

(P-7406)
STORER TRANSIT SYSTEMS (PA)
Also Called: Modesto Dial-Ride
3519 Mcdonald Ave, Modesto (95358-9770)
PHONE.................................209 527-4900
Donald Storer, *President*
Alexis Tamayo, *Representative*
EMP: 37 **EST:** 1981
SALES (est): 3.9MM **Privately Held**
WEB: www.storerbus.com
SIC: 4119 4725 Limousine rental, with driver; sightseeing tour companies

(P-7407)
TRANSDEV SERVICES INC
2361 Airport Blvd, San Jose (95110-1207)
PHONE.................................408 282-4706
Dwayne Brown, *Planning*
Christopher Bates, *Manager*
EMP: 441
SALES (corp-wide): 1.3B **Privately Held**
WEB: www.transdevna.com
SIC: 4119 4121 Local passenger transportation; taxicabs
HQ: Transdev Services, Inc.
720 E Bttrfield Rd Ste 300
Lombard IL 60148
630 571-7070

(P-7408)
UCS LIMO LLC
Also Called: Ucs Worldwide
1710 S Amphlett Blvd, San Mateo (94402-2703)
PHONE.................................866 345-5640
Lohan Caetano, *Mng Member*
EMP: 45 **EST:** 2012
SALES (est): 5MM **Privately Held**
WEB: www.ucslimo.com
SIC: 4119 Limousine rental, with driver

(P-7409)
UNIVERSAL LIMOUSINE & TRNSP CO
9944 Mills Station Rd C, Sacramento (95827-2202)
PHONE.................................916 361-5466
Marc Sievers, *CEO*
EMP: 70 **EST:** 1994

4119 - Local Passenger Transportation: NEC County (P-7410)

SQ FT: 10,000
SALES (est): 4.4MM **Privately Held**
WEB: www.universallimo.com
SIC: **4119** Limousine rental, with driver

(P-7410)
URBANBCN WORLDWIDE
1184 San Mateo Ave, South San Francisco (94080-6602)
PHONE.................................415 494-8122
Dave Uziel, *President*
EMP: 50 EST: 2015
SALES (est): 2.2MM **Privately Held**
WEB: www.urbanbcn.com
SIC: **4119** Limousine rental, with driver

(P-7411)
WEST SIDE COMMUNITY AMBULANCE
151 State Highway 33, Newman (95360-9603)
PHONE.................................209 862-2951
Chuck Coelho, *Director*
EMP: 49 EST: 2010
SALES (est): 821.6K **Privately Held**
WEB: www.westsideambulance.com
SIC: **4119** Ambulance service

(P-7412)
WESTMED AMBULANCE
14275 Wicks Blvd, San Leandro (94577-5613)
PHONE.................................510 401-5420
Alan Cress, *Director*
Joe Chiedley, *Director*
EMP: 58 EST: 1995
SALES (est): 7.9MM **Privately Held**
WEB: www.westmedambulance.com
SIC: **4119** Ambulance service

4121 Taxi Cabs

(P-7413)
LUXOR CABS INC
531 Bay Shore Blvd, San Francisco (94124-1511)
PHONE.................................415 282-4141
John Lazar, *CEO*
William Falcon, *Corp Secy*
Dolores Parlomenko, *Vice Pres*
Rick Larsen, *Manager*
EMP: 49 EST: 1946
SALES (est): 4.8MM **Privately Held**
WEB: www.luxorcab.com
SIC: **4121** 7521 Taxicabs; parking lots

(P-7414)
SERRA YELLOW CAB DALY CITY INC
195 87th St Ste D, Daly City (94015-1692)
PHONE.................................650 333-9598
Talib Saliman, *President*
Nidal Zaro, *Vice Pres*
EMP: 40 EST: 1986
SQ FT: 3,200
SALES (est): 1.7MM **Privately Held**
SIC: **4121** 4111 Taxicabs; airport transportation

(P-7415)
YELLOW CHECKER CAB COMPANY INC
Also Called: Yellow Cab Company
646 N King Rd Ste A, San Jose (95133-1755)
PHONE.................................408 286-3400
Lawrence A Silva, *President*
Harout Karanfilian, *Shareholder*
Donald A Silva, *Vice Pres*
Elect Mayor, *Manager*
Megan Lynch, *Contractor*
EMP: 49 EST: 1974
SALES: 4.7MM **Privately Held**
WEB: www.yellowcheckercab.com
SIC: **4121** Taxicabs

4131 Intercity & Rural Bus Transportation

(P-7416)
SANTA ROSA BUS LINES
Also Called: Santa Rosa City of
45 Stony Point Rd, Santa Rosa (95401-4446)
PHONE.................................707 543-3333
David Wachter, *Principal*
Matt Crosbie, *Officer*
Rachael Gilligan, *Marketing Staff*
Kevin King, *Marketing Staff*
Gina Giomi, *Corp Comm Staff*
EMP: 67 EST: 1997
SQ FT: 11,432
SALES (est): 5.9MM **Privately Held**
WEB: www.srcity.org
SIC: **4131** Intercity bus line

4141 Local Bus Charter Svc

(P-7417)
MICHAELS TRNSP SVC INC
140 Yolano Dr, Vallejo (94589-2251)
PHONE.................................707 674-6013
Michael Brown, *President*
Lam Phimmachack, *Director*
Geneva Thornton, *Director*
Adriana Catledge, *Manager*
EMP: 95 EST: 1983
SQ FT: 26,000
SALES (est): 19.9MM **Privately Held**
WEB: www.bustransportation.com
SIC: **4141** 7363 8331 4111 Local bus charter service; employee leasing service; job training services; bus transportation; school buses

(P-7418)
MINITRANS CORPORATION (PA)
Also Called: SF Mini Bus
2260 Palou Ave, San Francisco (94124-1505)
P.O. Box 882374 (94188-2374)
PHONE.................................415 970-8091
Miguel Guerrero, *Managing Dir*
Teresa Guerrero, *CFO*
EMP: 44 EST: 1976
SQ FT: 20,000
SALES (est): 5.9MM **Privately Held**
WEB: www.sfminibus.com
SIC: **4141** 4142 Local bus charter service; bus charter service, except local

(P-7419)
STORER TRANSPORTATION SERVICE (PA)
Also Called: Storer Travel Service
3519 Mcdonald Ave, Modesto (95358-9771)
PHONE.................................209 521-8250
Donald Storer, *CEO*
Warren Storer, *CEO*
Erica Gonzales, *Executive*
Kimberlie Orosco, *General Mgr*
Alberta Deanda, *Business Mgr*
EMP: 275
SQ FT: 6,000
SALES (est): 33.8MM **Privately Held**
WEB: www.storercoachways.com
SIC: **4141** 4725 4724 4151 Local bus charter service; tours, conducted; travel agencies; school buses; bus charter service, except local

4142 Bus Charter Service, Except Local

(P-7420)
AMADOR STAGE LINES INC
Also Called: Allen Transportation Co
1331 C St, Sacramento (95814-0913)
P.O. Box 15707 (95852-0707)
PHONE.................................916 444-7880
W R Allen, *CEO*
Alex B Allen, *President*
William R Allen, *Treasurer*
R E Allen, *Vice Pres*
Sherri Peters, *Admin Asst*
EMP: 80 EST: 1947
SQ FT: 2,000
SALES (est): 11.5MM **Privately Held**
WEB: www.amadorstagelines.com
SIC: **4142** Bus charter service, except local

(P-7421)
DELTA CHARTER SERVICE INC
4900 E Mariposa Rd, Stockton (95215-8150)
P.O. Box 5547 (95205-0547)
PHONE.................................209 465-1053
Jim Foust, *CEO*
John Martin, *CFO*
Ryan Lackmann, *Opers Mgr*
EMP: 40 EST: 1969
SQ FT: 8,000
SALES (est): 2.2MM **Privately Held**
WEB: www.deltacharterbus.com
SIC: **4142** Bus charter service, except local

(P-7422)
ROYAL COACH TOURS (PA)
630 Stockton Ave, San Jose (95126-2433)
PHONE.................................408 279-4801
Sandra Allen, *CEO*
Joanne Smith Christian, *Shareholder*
Daniel Smith, *Vice Pres*
Rene Fernandez, *Sales Staff*
Tawny Hicks, *Sales Staff*
EMP: 108 EST: 1960
SQ FT: 2,500
SALES (est): 24MM **Privately Held**
WEB: www.royal-coach.com
SIC: **4142** Bus charter service, except local

(P-7423)
VIA ADVENTURES INC (PA)
Also Called: Via Charter Lines
300 Grogan Ave, Merced (95341-6446)
PHONE.................................209 384-1315
Curtis A Riggs, *President*
Gaye Riggs, *Corp Secy*
Denise Demery, *Opers Mgr*
EMP: 50 EST: 1989
SALES (est): 9.6MM **Privately Held**
WEB: www.viatrailways.com
SIC: **4142** 4724 4725 Bus charter service, except local; travel agencies; sightseeing tour companies

4151 School Buses

(P-7424)
CATHOLIC CHRTIES CYO OF THE AR
699 Serramonte Blvd 210, Daly City (94015-4132)
PHONE.................................650 757-2110
Bill Avalos, *Manager*
EMP: 63
SALES (corp-wide): 63.3MM **Privately Held**
WEB: www.catholiccharitiessf.org
SIC: **4151** 8322 School buses; individual & family services
PA: Catholic Charities Cyo Of The Archdiocese Of San Francisco
1 Saint Vincents Dr
San Rafael CA 94903
415 972-1200

(P-7425)
DURHAM SCHOOL SERVICES L P
379 Earhart Way, Livermore (94551-9509)
PHONE.................................925 606-0871
Phillys Decia, *Manager*
EMP: 157 **Privately Held**
WEB: www.durhamschoolservices.com
SIC: **4151** School buses
HQ: Durham School Services, L. P.
2601 Navistar Dr
Lisle IL 60532
630 836-0292

(P-7426)
DURHAM SCHOOL SERVICES L P
27577 Industrial Blvd A, Hayward (94545-4044)
PHONE.................................510 887-6005
EMP: 190
SQ FT: 1,200 **Privately Held**
SIC: **4151** School Bus Transportation Service
HQ: Durham School Services, L. P.
2601 Navistar Dr
Lisle IL 60532
630 836-0292

(P-7427)
DURHAM SCHOOL SERVICES L P
10701 E Bennett Rd, Grass Valley (95945-9361)
P.O. Box 1393 (95945-1393)
PHONE.................................530 273-7282
Paula Davidson, *General Mgr*
Shawn Powers, *Opers Mgr*
EMP: 157 **Privately Held**
WEB: www.durhamschoolservices.com
SIC: **4151** 4119 4111 School buses; local passenger transportation; local & suburban transit
HQ: Durham School Services, L. P.
2601 Navistar Dr
Lisle IL 60532
630 836-0292

(P-7428)
DURHAM SCHOOL SERVICES L P
2121 Piedmont Way, Pittsburg (94565-5017)
PHONE.................................925 686-3391
Joe Cobillas, *Branch Mgr*
EMP: 157 **Privately Held**
WEB: www.durhamschoolservices.com
SIC: **4151** School buses
HQ: Durham School Services, L. P.
2601 Navistar Dr
Lisle IL 60532
630 836-0292

(P-7429)
ELK GROVE UNIFIED SCHOOL DST
Also Called: Transportation Department
8421 Gerber Rd, Sacramento (95828-3711)
PHONE.................................916 686-7733
Jill Gayaldo, *Branch Mgr*
EMP: 44
SALES (corp-wide): 741.9MM **Privately Held**
WEB: www.egusd.net
SIC: **4151** School buses
PA: Grove Elk Unified School District
9510 Elk Grove Florin Rd
Elk Grove CA 95624
916 686-5085

(P-7430)
FIRST STUDENT INC
436 Parr Blvd, Richmond (94801-1123)
PHONE.................................510 237-6677
Brian Rutford, *Principal*
EMP: 120 **Privately Held**
WEB: www.firststudentinc.com
SIC: **4151** School buses
PA: First Student, Inc.
600 Vine St Ste 1400
Cincinnati OH 45202

(P-7431)
FIRST STUDENT INC
59 Jordan St, San Rafael (94901-3918)
PHONE.................................415 455-9098
Cindy Srering, *Branch Mgr*
EMP: 120 **Privately Held**
WEB: www.firststudentinc.com
SIC: **4151** School buses
PA: First Student, Inc.
600 Vine St Ste 1400
Cincinnati OH 45202

(P-7432)
FIRST STUDENT INC
2368 Bates Ave, Concord (94520-1244)
PHONE.................................510 628-0014
EMP: 120 **Privately Held**
WEB: www.firststudentinc.com
SIC: **4151** School buses

PRODUCTS & SERVICES SECTION

4212 - Local Trucking Without Storage County (P-7456)

PA: First Student, Inc.
600 Vine St Ste 1400
Cincinnati OH 45202

(P-7433)
FIRST STUDENT INC
520 Bragato Rd, San Carlos (94070-6227)
PHONE..................................650 685-8245
EMP: 120 Privately Held
WEB: www.firststudentinc.com
SIC: 4151 School buses
PA: First Student, Inc.
600 Vine St Ste 1400
Cincinnati OH 45202

(P-7434)
FIRST STUDENT INC
2005 Navy Dr, Stockton (95206-1142)
PHONE..................................209 466-7737
Drigden Summers, Manager
EMP: 120 Privately Held
WEB: www.firststudentinc.com
SIC: 4151 School buses
PA: First Student, Inc.
600 Vine St Ste 1400
Cincinnati OH 45202

(P-7435)
FIRST STUDENT INC
2805 S East Ave, Fresno (93725-1942)
PHONE..................................559 268-4077
EMP: 120 Privately Held
WEB: www.firststudentinc.com
SIC: 4151 School buses
PA: First Student, Inc.
600 Vine St Ste 1400
Cincinnati OH 45202

(P-7436)
FIRST STUDENT INC
2270 Jerrold Ave, San Francisco (94124-1012)
PHONE..................................415 647-9012
Bob Gonzales, Manager
EMP: 120 Privately Held
WEB: www.firststudentinc.com
SIC: 4151 School buses
PA: First Student, Inc.
600 Vine St Ste 1400
Cincinnati OH 45202

(P-7437)
FIRST STUDENT INC
931 Remillard Ct, San Jose (95122-2625)
PHONE..................................408 971-3466
Susan Moorehaed, Manager
EMP: 120 Privately Held
WEB: www.firststudentinc.com
SIC: 4151 School buses
PA: First Student, Inc.
600 Vine St Ste 1400
Cincinnati OH 45202

(P-7438)
FIRST STUDENT INC
801 Wilbur Ave, Antioch (94509-7500)
PHONE..................................925 754-4878
Susan Hinson, Branch Mgr
EMP: 120 Privately Held
WEB: www.firststudentinc.com
SIC: 4151 School buses
PA: First Student, Inc.
600 Vine St Ste 1400
Cincinnati OH 45202

(P-7439)
FIRST STUDENT INC
Also Called: Laidlaw Transit Services
123 N E St Ste 102, Madera (93638-3286)
PHONE..................................559 661-7433
Roberta Collins, Branch Mgr
EMP: 120 Privately Held
WEB: www.firststudentinc.com
SIC: 4151 School buses
PA: First Student, Inc.
600 Vine St Ste 1400
Cincinnati OH 45202

(P-7440)
LODI UNIFIED SCHOOL DISTRICT
Also Called: Transportation
820 S Cuff Ave, Lodi (95240)
PHONE..................................209 331-7169
Carlos Garcia, Director
EMP: 35
SALES (corp-wide): 428.1MM Privately Held
WEB: www.lodiusd.net
SIC: 4151 School buses
PA: Lodi Unified School District
1305 E Vine St
Lodi CA 95240
209 331-7000

(P-7441)
MERCED TRANSPORTATION COMPANY
300 Grogan Ave, Merced (95341-6446)
PHONE..................................209 384-2575
Curtis Riggs, President
Gaye Riggs, CFO
EMP: 71 EST: 1980
SQ FT: 8,000
SALES (est): 6.5MM Privately Held
WEB: www.mercedfleetservice.com
SIC: 4151 School buses

(P-7442)
MID-PLACER PUBLIC SCHOOLS
13121 Bill Francis Dr, Auburn (95603-9022)
PHONE..................................530 823-4820
Martin Ward, CEO
EMP: 36 EST: 2018
SALES (est): 2.1MM Privately Held
WEB: www.midplacer.com
SIC: 4151 School buses

(P-7443)
UNIVERSITY CALIFORNIA DAVIS
Also Called: Transportation Services
1 Shields Ave, Davis (95616-8500)
PHONE..................................530 752-8277
Cliff Contreras, Director
EMP: 92 Privately Held
WEB: www.ucdavis.edu
SIC: 4151 7521 School buses; automobile parking
HQ: University Of California, Davis
1 Shields Ave
Davis CA 95616

4173 Bus Terminal & Svc Facilities

(P-7444)
ALAMEDA-CONTRA COSTA TRNST DST
A C Transit
10626 International Blvd, Oakland (94603-3806)
PHONE..................................510 577-8816
Glen Andrade, Manager
Jose Vega, Business Anlyst
Renan Manzanero, Technical Staff
Christy McCree, Analyst
Julia Kocs, Corp Comm Staff
EMP: 1307
SALES (corp-wide): 62MM Privately Held
WEB: www.actransit.org
SIC: 4173 Maintenance facilities for motor vehicle passenger transport
PA: Alameda-Contra Costa Transit District
1600 Franklin St
Oakland CA 94612
510 891-4777

(P-7445)
SAN MATEO COUNTY TRANSIT DST
Also Called: Sam Trans
501 Pico Blvd, San Carlos (94070-2706)
PHONE..................................650 508-6412
Ed Proctor, Manager
John Roberts, Maintence Staff
EMP: 146
SALES (corp-wide): 11.6MM Privately Held
WEB: www.smctd.com
SIC: 4173 4111 Maintenance facilities, buses; local & suburban transit
PA: San Mateo County Transit District
1250 San Carlos Ave
San Carlos CA 94070
650 508-6200

4212 Local Trucking Without Storage

(P-7446)
AGRI-COMM EXPRESS INC
3915 S Hunt Rd, Gustine (95322-9771)
PHONE..................................209 854-2474
John Mello, CEO
Antone Mello III, Vice Pres
EMP: 37 EST: 1981
SQ FT: 3,000
SALES (est): 8.5MM Privately Held
SIC: 4212 4213 Local trucking, without storage; trucking, except local

(P-7447)
ALL WEST COAST SHIPPING INC (PA)
1200 Wright Ave, Richmond (94804-3646)
PHONE..................................510 236-3008
Andrey Naumov, President
Felix Cater, Business Mgr
Al Bogatov, Opers Staff
Ilia Chasov, Opers Staff
Melinda Gjertsen, Manager
EMP: 57 EST: 2007
SALES (est): 5MM Privately Held
WEB: www.wcshipping.com
SIC: 4212 4213 Delivery service, vehicular; trucking, except local

(P-7448)
AMS RELOCATION INCORPORATED
Also Called: AMS Bekins Van Lines
1873 Rollins Rd, Burlingame (94010-2209)
PHONE..................................650 697-3530
Mike Foster, General Mgr
Gary P Wolfe, President
Bill Evans, Sales Staff
EMP: 55 EST: 1954
SQ FT: 45,000
SALES (est): 8.1MM Privately Held
WEB: www.bekinsmovingservices.com
SIC: 4212 Moving services

(P-7449)
ANDERSNCTTONWOOD DISPOSAL SVCS (PA)
8592 Commercial Way, Redding (96002-3901)
PHONE..................................530 221-6510
Rick King, Administration
Maury Myers, President
EMP: 49 EST: 1986
SQ FT: 6,000
SALES (est): 8.3MM Privately Held
SIC: 4212 Garbage collection & transport, no disposal

(P-7450)
ANDERSNCTTONWOOD DISPOSAL SVCS
Also Called: Waste Managment
3281 State Highway 99w S, Corning (96021-9736)
P.O. Box 496 (96021-0496)
PHONE..................................530 824-4700
Bill Manneo, Manager
EMP: 51
SALES (corp-wide): 8.3MM Privately Held
SIC: 4212 Garbage collection & transport, no disposal
PA: Andersoncottonwood Disposal Services Inc
8592 Commercial Way
Redding CA 96002
530 221-6510

(P-7451)
B & C CHANDLER TRUCKING INC
Also Called: B & C Trucking
16930 Road 26 Ste C, Madera (93638-0691)
PHONE..................................559 674-7181
Shiela Chandler, President
Curtis Chandler, Admin Sec
Sheila Chandler, Admin Sec
EMP: 43 EST: 1998
SQ FT: 200
SALES (est): 2.5MM Privately Held
WEB: www.fivestarfreight.net
SIC: 4212 Local trucking, without storage

(P-7452)
BFI WASTE SYSTEMS N AMER INC
Also Called: Site 915
1601 Dixon Landing Rd, Milpitas (95035-8100)
PHONE..................................408 432-1234
Desi Reno, General Mgr
EMP: 40
SALES (corp-wide): 10.1B Publicly Held
SIC: 4212 4959 4953 Garbage collection & transport, no disposal; sanitary services; refuse systems
HQ: Bfi Waste Systems Of North America, Inc.
2394 E Camelback Rd
Phoenix AZ 85016

(P-7453)
BLUE EAGLE CONTRACTING INC
113 Presley Way Ste 8, Grass Valley (95945-5847)
PHONE..................................530 272-0287
Daniel L Rackley, President
Marvin L Rackley, Ch of Bd
Dan Rackley, Vice Pres
Ray Rackley, Vice Pres
EMP: 59 EST: 1973
SALES (est): 5.2MM Privately Held
WEB: www.blueeaglecontracting.net
SIC: 4212 Mail carriers, contract

(P-7454)
CALIFORNIA MATERIALS INC
Also Called: Cmat
3736 S Highway 99, Stockton (95215-8028)
P.O. Box 32314 (95213-2314)
PHONE..................................209 472-7422
Earl Rogers, President
Renee Limon, Traffic Dir
EMP: 50 EST: 2008
SALES (est): 7.9MM Privately Held
WEB: www.californiamaterials.com
SIC: 4212 Dump truck haulage

(P-7455)
CARTEL TRANSPORT LLC (PA)
1487 13th St, Firebaugh (93622-2305)
P.O. Box 96 (93622-0096)
PHONE..................................559 659-3981
Dominic S Carlucci, Mng Member
Ruben Magallanes, General Mgr
Santiago Pimentel, Safety Mgr
Tommy Weaver, Opers Staff
EMP: 135 EST: 1989
SQ FT: 3,000 Privately Held
WEB: www.carluccitransport.com
SIC: 4212 4213 Local trucking, without storage; trucking, except local

(P-7456)
CARTEL TRANSPORT LLC
154 Poppy Ave, Patterson (95363-9717)
PHONE..................................209 892-3880
Dominic Carlucci, Mng Member
EMP: 35 Privately Held
WEB: www.carluccitransport.com
SIC: 4212 Local trucking, without storage
PA: Cartel Transport, Llc
1487 13th St
Firebaugh CA 93622
559 659-3981

4212 - Local Trucking Without Storage County (P-7457)   PRODUCTS & SERVICES SECTION

(P-7457)
CENTRAL VALLEY CONCRETE INC (PA)
Also Called: Central Valley Trucking
3823 N State Highway 59, Merced (95348-9370)
PHONE..................209 723-8846
Scott Neal, *CEO*
Brandon Williams, *General Mgr*
EMP: 150 EST: 1975
SQ FT: 2,000
SALES (est): 34.4MM **Privately Held**
WEB: www.centralvalleyconcrete.com
SIC: 4212 3273 Local trucking, without storage; ready-mixed concrete

(P-7458)
CERUTTI & SONS TRNSP CO
750 N Valentine Ave, Fresno (93706-1040)
PHONE..................559 275-6608
Alvin Cerutti, *President*
Henry L Cerutti, *Vice Pres*
EMP: 45 EST: 1945
SQ FT: 1,000
SALES (est): 6.7MM **Privately Held**
SIC: 4212 Dump truck haulage

(P-7459)
CLAY MIRANDA TRUCKING INC
3220 W Belmont Ave, Fresno (93722-5905)
P.O. Box 11983 (93776-1983)
PHONE..................559 275-6250
Debbie Cooper, *Vice Pres*
Mike Miranda, *President*
EMP: 40 EST: 1967
SQ FT: 9,600
SALES (est): 2.8MM **Privately Held**
SIC: 4212 5032 Dump truck haulage; asphalt mixture; gravel; sand, construction; stone, crushed or broken

(P-7460)
DEPENDABLE HIGHWAY EXPRESS INC
830 E St, West Sacramento (95605-2309)
PHONE..................916 374-0782
Tim Wallmark, *Branch Mgr*
Mike La Porte, *Manager*
EMP: 50
SALES (corp-wide): 206.3MM **Privately Held**
WEB: www.godependable.com
SIC: 4212 4213 Local trucking, without storage; trucking, except local
PA: Dependable Highway Express, Inc.
2555 E Olympic Blvd
Los Angeles CA 90023
323 526-2200

(P-7461)
DHILLON BROS TRUCKING INC
6251 E American Ave, Fresno (93725-9376)
PHONE..................559 834-5600
Jagjiwan S Dhillon, *CEO*
EMP: 50 EST: 2001
SALES (est): 6.1MM **Privately Held**
SIC: 4212 Local trucking, without storage

(P-7462)
EMBARK TRUCKS INC
424 Townsend St, San Francisco (94107-1510)
PHONE..................765 409-4499
Alexander Rodrigues, *CEO*
EMP: 35 EST: 2016
SALES (est): 3.3MM **Privately Held**
WEB: www.embarktrucks.com
SIC: 4212 Local trucking, without storage

(P-7463)
FEATHER RIVER DISPOSAL INC
1166 Industrial Way, Quincy (95971-9724)
PHONE..................530 283-2065
Mike Clemetf, *Principal*
EMP: 832 EST: 1964
SALES (est): 1.7MM
SALES (corp-wide): 15.2B **Publicly Held**
SIC: 4212 Garbage collection & transport, no disposal
HQ: Waste Management Of Texas, Inc.
1001 Fannin St Ste 4000
Houston TX 77002

(P-7464)
FIRST CLASS SVC TRCKG CO INC
400 Gandy Dancer Dr, Tracy (95377-8917)
PHONE..................209 832-4669
James A Alves, *CEO*
Tom Green, *General Mgr*
Gale Green, *Office Mgr*
Joe Monkhouse, *Manager*
EMP: 43 EST: 1990
SQ FT: 320,760
SALES (est): 5.8MM **Privately Held**
WEB: www.fcstrucking.com
SIC: 4212 Truck rental with drivers

(P-7465)
FIVE RIVER TRUCKING INC
1020 Oswald Rd, Yuba City (95991-9719)
PHONE..................530 212-4477
Gurbinder Singh, *President*
Amneet Singh, *Vice Pres*
EMP: 35 EST: 2015
SQ FT: 1,000
SALES (est): 4.1MM **Privately Held**
SIC: 4212 Local trucking, without storage

(P-7466)
FRANK GHIGLIONE INC (PA)
Also Called: Rodgers Trucking Co
1622 Moreland Dr, Alameda (94501-3018)
PHONE..................510 483-7000
Frank Ghiglione, *President*
Winifred Ghiglione, *Admin Sec*
Steve Strom, *Personnel*
John Ghiglione, *Opers Staff*
EMP: 80 EST: 1972
SALES (est): 10.1MM **Privately Held**
WEB: www.rodgerstrucking.com
SIC: 4212 Delivery service, vehicular

(P-7467)
FRANK GHIGLIONE INC
Also Called: Rogers Trucking
2972 Alvarado St Ste H, San Leandro (94577-5732)
PHONE..................510 483-2063
Frank Ghiglione, *Manager*
EMP: 80
SALES (corp-wide): 10.1MM **Privately Held**
WEB: www.rodgerstrucking.com
SIC: 4212 4214 Delivery service, vehicular; local trucking with storage
PA: Frank Ghiglione, Inc.
1622 Moreland Dr
Alameda CA 94501
510 483-7000

(P-7468)
GARY BEEBE INDUSTRIES INC
500 Wise Rd, Lincoln (95648-8518)
P.O. Box 665 (95648-0665)
PHONE..................916 645-6073
Gary Beebe, *President*
EMP: 26 EST: 1989
SQ FT: 4,200
SALES (est): 1.4MM **Privately Held**
SIC: 4212 2875 5032 Local trucking, without storage; fertilizers, mixing only; sand, construction

(P-7469)
GEORGE KISHIDA INC
Also Called: Kishida Geo Trucking
1725 Ackerman Dr, Lodi (95240-6330)
PHONE..................209 368-0603
George Kishida Jr, *President*
Shizuko Kishida, *Corp Secy*
EMP: 51 EST: 1946
SQ FT: 16,000
SALES (est): 2.6MM **Privately Held**
WEB: www.georgekishida.com
SIC: 4212 Local trucking, without storage

(P-7470)
GILLIES TRUCKING INC
3931 Newton Rd, Stockton (95205-2488)
P.O. Box 8303 (95208-0303)
PHONE..................209 948-6268
Randy Gilles, *President*
James T Gillies, *Treasurer*
Ken Gillies, *Vice Pres*
Brenda Hill, *Bookkeeper*
EMP: 47
SQ FT: 5,000
SALES (est): 6.7MM **Privately Held**
WEB: www.gilliestrucking.com
SIC: 4212 Local trucking, without storage

(P-7471)
GO EXPRESS LLC
4067 W Shaw Ave, Fresno (93722-6214)
PHONE..................559 274-0168
Richard Malcolm, *Mng Member*
Jose Garcia, *Warehouse Mgr*
Richard Malcom,
Manuel Gomez, *Manager*
Erika Vilhauer, *Assistant*
EMP: 36 EST: 2013
SALES (est): 2.5MM **Privately Held**
WEB: www.goexpress1.com
SIC: 4212 Delivery service, vehicular

(P-7472)
GREWAL BROS TRUCKING INC
515 E Greenway Ave, Turlock (95380-8720)
PHONE..................209 678-2557
Jasvir Grewal, *CEO*
Gurjit Grewal, *President*
Jafvir Grewal, *Vice Pres*
EMP: 36 EST: 2011
SALES (est): 3MM **Privately Held**
WEB: www.grewaltrucking.com
SIC: 4212 Local trucking, without storage

(P-7473)
HILDEBRAND & SONS TRUCKING INC (PA)
6 Lewis Rd, Royal Oaks (95076-5395)
PHONE..................831 722-3006
Dorothea Hildebrand, *President*
Theron Hildebrand, *Vice Pres*
EMP: 54 EST: 1956
SQ FT: 5,000
SALES (est): 6.7MM **Privately Held**
SIC: 4212 Local trucking, without storage

(P-7474)
HUMBOLDT SANITATION CO
Also Called: Humboldt Sanitatation & Recycl
2585 Central Ave, McKinleyville (95519-3617)
P.O. Box 2812 (95519-2812)
PHONE..................707 839-3285
Greg Cain, *President*
Christine Cain, *Admin Sec*
EMP: 66 EST: 1968
SQ FT: 4,000
SALES (est): 1.4MM **Privately Held**
WEB: www.humboldtsanitation.com
SIC: 4212 4953 Garbage collection & transport, no disposal; recycling, waste materials

(P-7475)
INDUSTRIAL WSTE DBRIS BOX RNTA
Also Called: Industrial Carting
3911 Santa Rosa Ave, Santa Rosa (95407-8274)
PHONE..................707 585-0511
Curtis Michelini Sr, *CEO*
Charles R Hardin, *Corp Secy*
EMP: 32 EST: 1971
SQ FT: 2,000
SALES (est): 1.2MM **Privately Held**
WEB: www.industrial-carting.com
SIC: 4212 4953 2631 2621 Garbage collection & transport, no disposal; recycling, waste materials; cardboard; paper mills

(P-7476)
JOHN AGUILAR & COMPANY INC
Also Called: Vernon Transportation Company
1505 Navy Dr, Stockton (95206-4104)
P.O. Box 31450 (95213-1450)
PHONE..................209 546-0171
Gregg Wilson, *President*
Joe Lacey, *CFO*
Dennis Carey, *Vice Pres*
Dave Wilson, *Admin Sec*
Nicole Rose, *Controller*
EMP: 85 EST: 1986
SQ FT: 5,600
SALES (est): 14.8MM **Privately Held**
WEB: www.vernontransportation.com
SIC: 4212 Liquid haulage, local

(P-7477)
JS HOMEN TRUCKING INC
4224 Turlock Rd, Snelling (95369-9729)
P.O. Box 382 (95369-0382)
PHONE..................209 723-9559
Joe Homen, *President*
Margaret Homen, *Corp Secy*
EMP: 65 EST: 1989
SQ FT: 2,484
SALES (est): 5.2MM **Privately Held**
SIC: 4212 Local trucking, without storage

(P-7478)
JUNK KING LLC (PA)
389 Oyster Point Blvd # 6, South San Francisco (94080-1951)
PHONE..................888 888-5865
Brian Reardon,
Allen Wasson, *Vice Pres*
Dallas Ferguson, *General Mgr*
Thys Kuitert, *General Mgr*
James Van Buren, *General Mgr*
EMP: 111 EST: 2005
SALES (est): 10.7MM **Privately Held**
WEB: www.junk-king.com
SIC: 4212 6794 Garbage collection & transport, no disposal; franchises, selling or licensing

(P-7479)
KENNIE C KNOWLES TRUCKING
3411 S Market St, Redding (96001-3823)
P.O. Box 994732 (96099-4732)
PHONE..................530 243-1366
Kennie Knowles, *President*
Wilma Knowles, *Treasurer*
Michael Knowles, *Principal*
EMP: 49 EST: 1970
SQ FT: 3,000
SALES (est): 2.8MM **Privately Held**
SIC: 4212 Lumber & timber trucking; timber trucking, local

(P-7480)
MAD DOG EXPRESS INC (PA)
299 Lawrence Ave, South San Francisco (94080-6818)
P.O. Box 281585, San Francisco (94128-1585)
PHONE..................650 588-1900
Steve Harth, *President*
John Coleman, *Vice Pres*
EMP: 70 EST: 1989
SQ FT: 18,500
SALES (est): 6.2MM **Privately Held**
SIC: 4212 Local trucking, without storage

(P-7481)
MAGNATRANS LLC
8620 Antelope North Rd A, Antelope (95843-3973)
PHONE..................916 969-6300
EMP: 45
SALES (corp-wide): 8.8MM **Privately Held**
SIC: 4212 Local Trucking, Without Storage, Nsk
PA: Magnatrans, Llc
10700 Jersey Blvd Ste 400
Rancho Cucamonga CA 91730
909 736-0800

(P-7482)
MAPLEBEAR INC (PA)
Also Called: Instacart
50 Beale St Ste 600, San Francisco (94105-1871)
PHONE..................888 246-7822
Fidji Simo, *CEO*
Robert Adams, *Partner*
Jennifer Meyer, *Partner*
Eric Sadkin, *Partner*
Eunice Tsui, *Partner*
EMP: 7154 EST: 2012
SALES (est): 950.5MM **Privately Held**
WEB: www.instacart.com
SIC: 4212 4215 Delivery service, vehicular; package delivery, vehicular

PRODUCTS & SERVICES SECTION

4213 - Trucking, Except Local County (P-7507)

(P-7483)
MARATHON BUSINESS GROUP INC
Also Called: Marathon Express
3210 Coffey Ln Ste A, Santa Rosa (95403-1924)
P.O. Box 463 (95402-0463)
PHONE..................707 575-8252
Morris M Anwarzai, *CEO*
EMP: 56 **EST:** 1980
SQ FT: 2,500
SALES (est): 2.8MM **Privately Held**
WEB: www.marathonexpress.com
SIC: 4212 Delivery service, vehicular

(P-7484)
MISSION TRAIL WSTE SYSTEMS INC
Also Called: Recycle Waste
1060 Richard Ave, Santa Clara (95050-2816)
PHONE..................408 727-5365
Louie Pellegrini, *President*
William Dobert, *CFO*
Robert Molinaro, *Vice Pres*
Douglas Button, *Admin Sec*
EMP: 75 **EST:** 1960
SALES (est): 14.3MM **Privately Held**
WEB: www.missiontrail.com
SIC: 4212 4953 Garbage collection & transport, no disposal; recycling, waste materials

(P-7485)
MT DBLO RESOURCE RECOVERY LLC
4080 Mallard Dr, Concord (94520-1245)
PHONE..................925 682-9113
Gregory Brumfield, *President*
Patrick Dolim, *CFO*
Kish Rajan, *Officer*
Bob Hammons, *Manager*
EMP: 300 **EST:** 2017
SALES (est): 46.4MM **Privately Held**
WEB: www.mdrr.com
SIC: 4212 4953 Garbage collection & transport, no disposal; liquid waste, collection & disposal; recycling, waste materials

(P-7486)
RDM EXPRESS INC (PA)
750 La Playa St, San Francisco (94121-3262)
PHONE..................415 642-4916
Lev Reykhel, *Principal*
EMP: 71 **EST:** 1998
SALES (est): 1.3MM **Privately Held**
WEB: www.russianbooksmusic.com
SIC: 4212 5149 Local trucking, without storage; groceries & related products

(P-7487)
RUAN
830 W Glenwood Ave, Turlock (95380-5751)
PHONE..................209 634-4928
Bill Hagney, *Manager*
EMP: 126
SALES (corp-wide): 4.5MM **Privately Held**
SIC: 4212 Local trucking, without storage
PA: Ruan
1354 S Blackstone St
Tulare CA 93274
559 688-0591

(P-7488)
SAIA MOTOR FREIGHT LINE LLC
1705 Rogers Ave, San Jose (95112-1108)
PHONE..................408 487-1740
Nick Candea, *Branch Mgr*
EMP: 49
SALES (corp-wide): 1.8B **Publicly Held**
SIC: 4212 4213 Animal & farm product transportation services; trucking, except local
HQ: Saia Motor Freight Line, Llc
11465 Johns Creek Pkwy # 400
Duluth GA 30097
770 232-5067

(P-7489)
SILVA TRUCKING
36 W Mathews Rd, French Camp (95231-9684)
P.O. Box 1449 (95231-1449)
PHONE..................209 982-1114
David Silva, *President*
EMP: 50
SQ FT: 4,000
SALES (est): 8MM **Privately Held**
WEB: www.silvatrucking.com
SIC: 4212 Dump truck haulage

(P-7490)
SPECIALIZED TRANSPORT INC
Also Called: Taylor Heavy Hauling
9325 Viking Pl, Roseville (95747-9753)
PHONE..................916 969-6300
Richard Taylor, *President*
Sheila Taylor, *Corp Secy*
EMP: 47 **EST:** 2002
SQ FT: 1,000
SALES (est): 5.3MM **Privately Held**
SIC: 4212 Light haulage & cartage, local

(P-7491)
STAT DELIVERY SERVICE INC
14755 Catalina St, San Leandro (94577-6609)
P.O. Box 56358, Hayward (94545-6358)
PHONE..................510 681-6125
Ray Elizondo, *President*
EMP: 60 **EST:** 1998
SALES (est): 2.6MM **Privately Held**
WEB: www.statdel.org
SIC: 4212 Delivery service, vehicular

(P-7492)
SUNSET DISPOSAL SERVICE INC
Also Called: Allied Waste
1145 W Charter Way, Stockton (95206-1106)
PHONE..................209 466-5192
Bobbi Furst, *Controller*
EMP: 40 **EST:** 1998
SQ FT: 1,000
SALES (est): 1.5MM
SALES (corp-wide): 10.1B **Publicly Held**
WEB: www.republicservices.com
SIC: 4212 Garbage collection & transport, no disposal
PA: Republic Services, Inc.
18500 N Allied Way # 100
Phoenix AZ 85054
480 627-2700

(P-7493)
TALLEY TRANSPORTATION
12325 Road 29, Madera (93638-8401)
P.O. Box 568 (93639-0568)
PHONE..................559 673-9013
Martin Talley, *CEO*
Kenneth Talley, *Vice Pres*
EMP: 57
SQ FT: 5,500
SALES (est): 6.4MM **Privately Held**
SIC: 4212 Local trucking, without storage

(P-7494)
TERESI TRUCKING LLC (PA)
900 1/2 E Victor Rd, Lodi (95240-0722)
P.O. Box 1270 (95241-1270)
PHONE..................209 368-2472
John M Teresi, *Mng Member*
John Teresi, *Opers Mgr*
Anthony T Teresi,
Varene Teresi,
Phil Zazzarino, *Representative*
EMP: 45 **EST:** 1954
SQ FT: 20,000
SALES (est): 7.9MM **Privately Held**
WEB: www.teresitrucking.com
SIC: 4212 Local trucking, without storage

(P-7495)
UNITED PARCEL SERVICE INC
Also Called: UPS
1601 W Mckinley Ave, Fresno (93728-1220)
PHONE..................559 442-2950
Michael Eskew, *Branch Mgr*
EMP: 137
SALES (corp-wide): 84.6B **Publicly Held**
WEB: www.ups.com
SIC: 4212 Delivery service, vehicular
HQ: United Parcel Service, Inc.
55 Glenlake Pkwy
Atlanta GA 30328
404 828-6000

(P-7496)
VALLEY TRANSPORTATION INC (PA)
2837 S East Ave, Fresno (93725-1943)
P.O. Box 12663 (93778-2663)
PHONE..................559 266-6674
Deborah B Simpson, *President*
Rodney D Heintz, *COO*
Myra Gales, *VP Finance*
Robert Styles, *Maintence Staff*
Tara Simpson,
EMP: 55 **EST:** 1988
SQ FT: 6,000
SALES (est): 12.6MM **Privately Held**
WEB: www.valleytransportation.com
SIC: 4212 Delivery service, vehicular

(P-7497)
WASTE MGT COLLECTN RECYCL INC
2658 N Main St, Walnut Creek (94597-2729)
PHONE..................925 935-8900
Ronald J Proto, *Manager*
EMP: 132
SALES (corp-wide): 15.2B **Publicly Held**
SIC: 4212 4953 Garbage collection & transport, no disposal; refuse systems
HQ: Waste Management Collection And Recycling, Inc.
1001 Fannin St Ste 4000
Houston TX 77002

(P-7498)
WATERS MOVING & STORAGE INC
37 Bridgehead Rd, Martinez (94553-1300)
P.O. Box 1029 (94553-0102)
PHONE..................925 372-0914
Ken Waters, *CEO*
Paulette Waters, *CFO*
Linda Gilmore, *General Mgr*
EMP: 75 **EST:** 1975
SQ FT: 50,000
SALES (est): 8MM **Privately Held**
WEB: www.watersmoving.com
SIC: 4212 Moving services

(P-7499)
WESTERN MESSENGER SERVICE INC
75 Columbia Sq, San Francisco (94103-4099)
PHONE..................415 487-4229
Dennis Golladay, *President*
Joe McManus, *President*
Patty Sokolecki, *Admin Sec*
Evan Magayanes, *Admin Asst*
Raymond Crosetti, *Assistant VP*
EMP: 115 **EST:** 1979
SQ FT: 11,000
SALES (est): 11.4MM **Privately Held**
WEB: www.westernmessenger.com
SIC: 4212 Delivery service, vehicular

4213 Trucking, Except Local

(P-7500)
A & I TRUCKING INC (PA)
Also Called: A & I Transportation
123 Lee Rd Ste E, Watsonville (95076-9422)
P.O. Box 1270 (95077-1270)
PHONE..................831 763-7805
Albert Tadevosyan, *CEO*
EMP: 46 **EST:** 2013
SQ FT: 1,000
SALES (est): 11.1MM **Privately Held**
WEB: www.aiexpressinc.com
SIC: 4213 Trucking, except local

(P-7501)
A C TRUCKING INC
1974 E Yosemite Ave, Manteca (95336-9562)
P.O. Box 987 (95336-1139)
PHONE..................209 823-3224
Albert Nunes, *President*
Carol Nunes, *Vice Pres*
Susan Reinke, *Controller*
EMP: 46 **EST:** 1971
SQ FT: 1,000
SALES (est): 6.7MM **Privately Held**
WEB: www.acttrucking.com
SIC: 4213 Trucking, except local

(P-7502)
AM & S TRANSPORTATION CO
1700 24th St, Oakland (94607-1733)
P.O. Box 23822 (94623-0822)
PHONE..................510 208-0271
Mateus Morais, *President*
Paula Gouveia, *Shareholder*
William Morais, *Shareholder*
Maria Morais, *Vice Pres*
EMP: 61 **EST:** 1981
SQ FT: 2,000
SALES (est): 6.9MM **Privately Held**
WEB: www.amstrans.com
SIC: 4213 4225 Contract haulers; general warehousing

(P-7503)
AMAR TRANSPORTATION INC (PA)
Also Called: Paul Trucking
144 W Lake Ave Ste C, Watsonville (95076-4554)
P.O. Box 39 (95077-0039)
PHONE..................831 728-8209
Amarjit S Tut, *President*
Surjit S Tut, *Treasurer*
Paritan S Tut, *Vice Pres*
Ranjit S Tut, *Vice Pres*
EMP: 130 **EST:** 1976
SQ FT: 4,872
SALES (est): 8.9MM **Privately Held**
SIC: 4213 4212 Trucking, except local; local trucking, without storage

(P-7504)
ASSOCIATED TRUCKING INC
1065 San Mateo Ave, San Bruno (94066-1525)
PHONE..................650 652-3960
Saul Gonzales, *President*
Eduardo Gonzalez, *President*
Chely Guzman, *Office Mgr*
Corinna Vega, *Executive Asst*
EMP: 49 **EST:** 2005 **Privately Held**
WEB: www.associatedtruckinginc.com
SIC: 4213 1795 Contract haulers; demolition, buildings & other structures

(P-7505)
ATECH WAREHOUSING & DIST INC (PA)
7 College Ave, Santa Rosa (95401-4702)
P.O. Box 6836 (95406-0836)
PHONE..................707 526-1910
Jesse E Amaral, *President*
Geri Amaral, *Vice Pres*
Travis Amaral, *Manager*
EMP: 60 **EST:** 1993
SQ FT: 35,000
SALES (est): 12.9MM **Privately Held**
WEB: www.atechlogistics.com
SIC: 4213 Less-than-truckload (LTL) transport

(P-7506)
BAGGIE FARMS EXPRESS INC
6385 E North Ave, Fresno (93725-9309)
PHONE..................559 486-7330
Mitchel Bagdasarian, *President*
EMP: 48 **EST:** 1976
SQ FT: 15,000
SALES (est): 4.5MM **Privately Held**
WEB: www.baggiefarms.com
SIC: 4213 Contract haulers

(P-7507)
BERT E JESSUP TRANSPORTATION
641 Old Gilroy St, Gilroy (95020-6233)
PHONE..................408 848-3390
Leonard Milanowski, *CEO*
Len Milanowski, *CFO*
Robin Jessup, *Admin Sec*
EMP: 85 **EST:** 1967
SQ FT: 10,000

4213 - Trucking, Except Local County (P-7508)

PRODUCTS & SERVICES SECTION

SALES (est): 9.8MM **Privately Held**
WEB: www.jessup.net
SIC: 4213 Trucking, except local

(P-7508)
BERTETTA TANKLINES INC
1486 Huntington Ave # 300, South San Francisco (94080-5970)
PHONE.................................650 872-2900
Mark Silva, *President*
Rocky Bertetta, *President*
EMP: 35 EST: 2003
SALES (est): 2.6MM **Privately Held**
WEB: www.bertetta.com
SIC: 4213 Contract haulers

(P-7509)
BETTENDORF ENTERPRISES INC (PA)
Also Called: Bettendorf Trucking
4545 West End Rd, Arcata (95521-9205)
P.O. Box 4689 (95518-4689)
PHONE.................................707 822-0173
Monty Bettendorf, *CEO*
Rick Roberts, *CFO*
Karen Cavers, *Executive*
Ron Borges, *Admin Sec*
Mike Tully, *Human Res Dir*
EMP: 40 EST: 1960
SQ FT: 6,000
SALES (est): 28.1MM **Privately Held**
WEB: www.bettendorftrucking.com
SIC: 4213 Contract haulers

(P-7510)
BHANDAL BROS INC
2490 San Juan Rd, Hollister (95023-9107)
P.O. Box 190 (95024-0190)
PHONE.................................831 728-2691
Maninder Singh, *President*
EMP: 50 EST: 2012
SALES (est): 8.8MM **Privately Held**
SIC: 4213 Trucking, except local

(P-7511)
BHANDAL BROS TRUCKING INC
2490 San Juan Rd, Hollister (95023-9107)
P.O. Box 1900 (95024-1900)
PHONE.................................831 728-2691
Mangal S Bhandal, *President*
EMP: 55 EST: 1987
SQ FT: 4,000
SALES (est): 10.4MM **Privately Held**
SIC: 4213 Refrigerated products transport

(P-7512)
BILLET TRANSPORTATION INC (PA)
255 Lombard Rd Ste B, American Canyon (94503-9717)
PHONE.................................707 649-9200
Gerald A Francis, *President*
George Francis, *Treasurer*
◆ EMP: 43 EST: 1997
SQ FT: 40,000
SALES (est): 5MM **Privately Held**
WEB: www.billet-transportation-inc.hub.biz
SIC: 4213 Trucking, except local

(P-7513)
BJJ COMPANY LLC (PA)
Also Called: Westland Trailer Mfg
1040 W Kettleman Ln, Lodi (95240-6056)
PHONE.................................209 941-8361
Fax: 209 941-0476
EMP: 70
SQ FT: 4,000
SALES (est): 12.1MM **Privately Held**
SIC: 4213 Trucking Operator-Nonlocal

(P-7514)
BRENT REDMOND TRNSP INC
1800 Lana Way, Hollister (95023-2566)
P.O. Box 1359 (95024-1359)
PHONE.................................831 637-5382
Brent R Redmond, *President*
Susan Redmond, *CFO*
Larry Brem, *Exec VP*
George Voorhis, *Opers Mgr*
Patrick Kenny, *Manager*
EMP: 38 EST: 1987
SQ FT: 10,000

SALES (est): 8.7MM **Privately Held**
WEB: www.brentredmond.com
SIC: 4213 Trucking, except local

(P-7515)
BUTTON TRANSPORTATION INC
7000 Button Ln, Dixon (95620-9116)
PHONE.................................707 678-7434
Robert Button, *President*
Anthony Iten, *President*
Dalton Reardon, *Maintence Staff*
Kris Bowen, *Manager*
Bob Button, *Manager*
EMP: 175 EST: 1975
SQ FT: 5,000
SALES (est): 39.9MM **Privately Held**
WEB: www.buttontransportation.com
SIC: 4213 Contract haulers

(P-7516)
C LINE EXPRESS
75 Mezzetta Ct, American Canyon (94503-9625)
P.O. Box 540, NAPA (94559-0540)
PHONE.................................707 553-6041
Maurice P Clay III, *President*
Todd Walker, *Vice Pres*
▲ EMP: 38 EST: 1947
SQ FT: 20,000
SALES (est): 4.9MM **Privately Held**
WEB: www.c-linexp.com
SIC: 4213 Trucking, except local

(P-7517)
CAL NOR TRUCKING INC (PA)
2670 Apricot St, Live Oak (95953-2200)
P.O. Box 174 (95953-0174)
PHONE.................................530 695-9219
Harjinder Singh Bains, *President*
EMP: 66 EST: 2004
SALES (est): 862.6K **Privately Held**
SIC: 4213 Trucking, except local

(P-7518)
CALIFORNIA BULK INC
Also Called: Alegre Trucking
3939 Producers Dr, Stockton (95206-4204)
PHONE.................................209 983-1069
Robert Fowler, *Manager*
EMP: 197 **Privately Held**
WEB: www.alegretrucking.com
SIC: 4213 Trucking, except local
PA: California Bulk, Inc.
5100 W Highway 12
Lodi CA 95242

(P-7519)
CHIPMAN CORPORATION (PA)
Also Called: Caton Moving & Storage
1040 Marina Village Pkwy # 100, Alameda (94501-6478)
PHONE.................................510 748-8700
Tom Chipman, *CEO*
Justin Chipman, *President*
John H Chipman Sr, *Chairman*
Rick Carreon, *Vice Pres*
Ron Grant, *Vice Pres*
▲ EMP: 50 EST: 1939
SQ FT: 400,000
SALES (est): 43.5MM **Privately Held**
WEB: www.chipmanrelo.com
SIC: 4213 4731 Household goods transport; foreign freight forwarding

(P-7520)
COLONIAL VAN & STORAGE INC (PA)
6001 88th St Ste A, Sacramento (95828-1134)
PHONE.................................916 546-3600
Douglas B Welton, *President*
David Cabral, *General Mgr*
Dawn Porter, *Admin Sec*
Kerri Walker, *Manager*
EMP: 42 EST: 1946
SQ FT: 60,000
SALES: 7.3MM **Privately Held**
WEB: www.colonialvan.com
SIC: 4213 4214 Trucking, except local; household goods moving & storage, local

(P-7521)
CROWN WORLDWIDE MVG & STOR LLC (PA)
Also Called: Crown Worldwide Moving & Stor
14826 Wicks Blvd, San Leandro (94577-6606)
PHONE.................................510 895-8050
Robert S Bowen, *CEO*
Salvator Ferrante, *President*
Joyce Burrows, *CFO*
Terry Weber, *Exec VP*
Janet Bowen, *Senior VP*
◆ EMP: 35 EST: 1972
SQ FT: 150,000
SALES (est): 29.4MM **Privately Held**
WEB: www.crownwms.com
SIC: 4213 4731 4214 Trucking, except local; household goods transport; foreign freight forwarding; local trucking with storage

(P-7522)
CUNHA DRAYING INC
1500 Madruga Rd, Lathrop (95330-9779)
PHONE.................................209 858-1400
Paul Buttini, *President*
Peggy Deforest, *Vice Pres*
EMP: 65 EST: 1977
SQ FT: 10,000
SALES (est): 8.4MM **Privately Held**
WEB: www.cunhatruck.com
SIC: 4213 Contract haulers

(P-7523)
DEPENDABLE HIGHWAY EXPRESS INC
1343 Lone Palm Ave, Modesto (95351-1536)
PHONE.................................209 342-0184
Don Hillman, *President*
EMP: 79
SALES (corp-wide): 206.3MM **Privately Held**
WEB: www.godependable.com
SIC: 4213 Trucking, except local
PA: Dependable Highway Express, Inc.
2555 E Olympic Blvd
Los Angeles CA 90023
323 526-2200

(P-7524)
DEPENDABLE HIGHWAY EXPRESS INC
3012 Alvarado St, San Leandro (94577-5735)
PHONE.................................510 357-2223
Trevor Schirmer, *Manager*
EMP: 79
SALES (corp-wide): 206.3MM **Privately Held**
WEB: www.godependable.com
SIC: 4213 Trucking, except local
PA: Dependable Highway Express, Inc.
2555 E Olympic Blvd
Los Angeles CA 90023
323 526-2200

(P-7525)
DEPENDABLE HIGHWAY EXPRESS INC
Also Called: Dhe
3199 Alvarado St, San Leandro (94577-5709)
PHONE.................................510 357-2223
Georgia Briggs, *Branch Mgr*
EMP: 79
SALES (corp-wide): 206.3MM **Privately Held**
WEB: www.godependable.com
SIC: 4213 4225 Trucking, except local; general warehousing & storage
PA: Dependable Highway Express, Inc.
2555 E Olympic Blvd
Los Angeles CA 90023
323 526-2200

(P-7526)
DK EXPRESS CARGO INC
Also Called: D K Express
2000 W Charter Way, Stockton (95206-1117)
PHONE.................................209 954-9354
Daljit Singh, *CEO*
EMP: 41 EST: 1997

SALES (est): 4.9MM **Privately Held**
WEB: www.dkexpressinc.net
SIC: 4213 Trucking, except local

(P-7527)
DOUDELL TRUCKING COMPANY (PA)
1505 N 4th St, San Jose (95112-4607)
P.O. Box 5879 (95150-5879)
PHONE.................................408 263-7300
Armand Kunde, *President*
John Kunde, *CFO*
EMP: 80 EST: 1944
SQ FT: 20,000
SALES (est): 17.8MM **Privately Held**
WEB: www.doudell.com
SIC: 4213 4214 4212 Contract haulers; local trucking with storage; local trucking, without storage

(P-7528)
EAGLE TRANSPORTATION CO INC
4325 Santa Rosa Ave, Santa Rosa (95407-8278)
PHONE.................................707 586-9766
Mark Burris, *President*
Lori Galeazzi-Hafner, *Treasurer*
Tony Nagora, *Broker*
EMP: 35 EST: 1977
SQ FT: 24,000
SALES (est): 5.4MM **Privately Held**
WEB: www.eagle-redwood.com
SIC: 4213 4212 Trucking, except local; local trucking, without storage

(P-7529)
ED ROCHA LIVESTOCK TRNSP INC
Also Called: Rocha Transportation
2400 Nickerson Dr, Modesto (95358-9409)
P.O. Box 40, Ceres (95307-0040)
PHONE.................................209 538-1302
Henry Dirksen, *President*
Zachary Dirksen, *Treasurer*
Corrie M Toste, *Admin Sec*
Grant Hannink, *Opers Mgr*
Carl Gisler, *Opers Staff*
EMP: 70 EST: 1963
SQ FT: 5,500
SALES (est): 12.4MM **Privately Held**
WEB: www.rochatrans.com
SIC: 4213 Contract haulers

(P-7530)
ESTES EXPRESS LINES
2100 Fair St, Chico (95928-6746)
PHONE.................................530 895-5123
Kevin Treff, *Manager*
EMP: 51
SALES (corp-wide): 3.5B **Privately Held**
WEB: www.estes-express.com
SIC: 4213 4212 Less-than-truckload (LTL) transport; local trucking, without storage
PA: Estes Express Lines
3901 W Broad St
Richmond VA 23230
804 353-1900

(P-7531)
ESTES EXPRESS LINES
4355 S Chestnut Ave, Fresno (93725-9372)
PHONE.................................559 441-0915
Michael Haynes, *Manager*
EMP: 51
SALES (corp-wide): 3.5B **Privately Held**
WEB: www.estes-express.com
SIC: 4213 4212 Less-than-truckload (LTL) transport; local trucking, without storage
PA: Estes Express Lines
3901 W Broad St
Richmond VA 23230
804 353-1900

(P-7532)
ESTES EXPRESS LINES
650 Carlson Ct, Rohnert Park (94928-2037)
PHONE.................................707 585-7961
Mike Gamel, *Manager*
John Eastland, *Vice Pres*
Brian Kurowsky, *Vice Pres*
John Rodgers, *Vice Pres*
Paul Dugent, *Executive*

▲ = Import ▼ = Export
◆ = Import/Export

PRODUCTS & SERVICES SECTION
4213 - Trucking, Except Local County (P-7557)

EMP: 51
SALES (corp-wide): 3.5B **Privately Held**
WEB: www.estes-express.com
SIC: 4213 Contract haulers
PA: Estes Express Lines
3901 W Broad St
Richmond VA 23230
804 353-1900

(P-7533)
ESTES EXPRESS LINES
1634 S 7th St, San Jose (95112-5931)
PHONE 408 286-3894
John Martin, *Branch Mgr*
Elaine Gonzales, *Accounts Mgr*
EMP: 51
SALES (corp-wide): 3.5B **Privately Held**
WEB: www.estes-express.com
SIC: 4213 Contract haulers
PA: Estes Express Lines
3901 W Broad St
Richmond VA 23230
804 353-1900

(P-7534)
ESTES EXPRESS LINES
1750 Adams Ave, San Leandro (94577-1002)
PHONE 510 635-0165
Bill Wardell, *Manager*
EMP: 51
SALES (corp-wide): 3.5B **Privately Held**
WEB: www.estes-express.com
SIC: 4213 Contract haulers
PA: Estes Express Lines
3901 W Broad St
Richmond VA 23230
804 353-1900

(P-7535)
ESTES EXPRESS LINES
7611 S Airport Way, Stockton (95206-3918)
PHONE 209 982-1841
Mark Hancock, *Branch Mgr*
Natascha Baker, *Accounts Mgr*
EMP: 51
SALES (corp-wide): 3.5B **Privately Held**
WEB: www.estes-express.com
SIC: 4213 Contract haulers
PA: Estes Express Lines
3901 W Broad St
Richmond VA 23230
804 353-1900

(P-7536)
FEDEX FREIGHT WEST INC
3050 Teagarden St, San Leandro (94577-5721)
PHONE 650 244-9522
EMP: 89
SALES (corp-wide): 47.4B **Publicly Held**
SIC: 4213 Trucking Operator-Nonlocal
HQ: Fedex Freight West, Inc.
6411 Guadalupe Mines Rd
San Jose CA 95120
775 356-7600

(P-7537)
FEDEX FREIGHT WEST INC
4570 S Maple Ave, Fresno (93725-9358)
PHONE 559 266-0732
EMP: 125
SALES (corp-wide): 47.4B **Publicly Held**
SIC: 4213 4231 4214 Trucking Operator-Nonlocal Truck Terminal Facility Local Trucking-With Storage
HQ: Fedex Freight West, Inc.
6411 Guadalupe Mines Rd
San Jose CA 95120
775 356-7600

(P-7538)
FEDEX FREIGHT WEST INC
1230 N Mcdowell Blvd, Petaluma (94954-1113)
PHONE 707 778-3191
EMP: 50
SQ FT: 13,920
SALES (corp-wide): 47.4B **Publicly Held**
SIC: 4213 Long Distance Trucking Company
HQ: Fedex Freight West, Inc.
6411 Guadalupe Mines Rd
San Jose CA 95120
775 356-7600

(P-7539)
FOODLINER INC
2431 E Mariposa Rd, Stockton (95205)
PHONE 209 941-8361
Steve Hronek, *Manager*
EMP: 59
SALES (corp-wide): 92.2MM **Privately Held**
WEB: www.foodliner.com
SIC: 4213 Contract haulers
PA: Foodliner, Inc.
2099 Southpark Ct Ste 1
Dubuque IA 52003
563 584-2670

(P-7540)
FRANK C ALEGRE TRUCKING INC (PA)
5100 W Highway 12, Lodi (95242-9529)
P.O. Box 1508 (95241-1508)
PHONE 209 334-2112
Anthony J Alegre, *President*
Michelle Schultz, *General Mgr*
EMP: 185 **EST:** 1963
SQ FT: 34,200
SALES (est): 26.4MM **Privately Held**
WEB: www.alegretrucking.com
SIC: 4213 4212 Contract haulers; dump truck haulage

(P-7541)
FREDERICKSEN TANK LINES INC (PA)
Also Called: Nevada Truck & Trailer Repair
840 Delta Ln, West Sacramento (95691-2801)
PHONE 916 371-4960
Leonard D Robinson, *CEO*
Jeanne Haskell, *President*
Larry Kenobbie, *Vice Pres*
EMP: 45 **EST:** 1940
SQ FT: 8,000
SALES (est): 4.5MM **Privately Held**
SIC: 4213 4212 Liquid petroleum transport, non-local; petroleum haulage, local

(P-7542)
FTG CONSTRUCTION MTLS INC
5100 W Highway 12, Lodi (95242-9529)
P.O. Box 1508 (95241-1508)
PHONE 209 334-4038
Anthony J Alegre, *CEO*
Frank C Alegre Jr, *Shareholder*
Gary D Alegre, *Shareholder*
Michelle Shultz, *Admin Sec*
EMP: 102 **EST:** 1973
SQ FT: 1,200
SALES (est): 4.9MM **Privately Held**
WEB: www.alegretrucking.com
SIC: 4213 Trucking, except local; less-than-truckload (LTL) transport; heavy machinery transport

(P-7543)
FUEL DELIVERY SERVICES INC
4895 S Airport Way, Stockton (95206-3915)
P.O. Box 1369 (95201-1369)
PHONE 209 751-2185
Ronald M Vandepol, *CEO*
David Atwater, *Shareholder*
Mike Boswart, *Shareholder*
Tom V Depol, *Shareholder*
Jennifer Clark, *Vice Pres*
EMP: 94 **EST:** 1998
SQ FT: 2,000
SALES (est): 15.9MM **Privately Held**
WEB: www.fueldeliveryservices.net
SIC: 4213 Liquid petroleum transport, non-local

(P-7544)
GCU TRUCKING INC
7819 Crane Rd, Oakdale (95361-8114)
P.O. Box 1423 (95361-1423)
PHONE 209 845-2117
Leo Arcos, *CEO*
EMP: 52 **EST:** 1995
SQ FT: 7,000
SALES (est): 7.3MM **Privately Held**
WEB: www.gcutrucking.com
SIC: 4213 5032 Contract haulers; brick, stone & related material

(P-7545)
GILLSON TRUCKING INC
1801 E Dr Mrtn Lther King, Stockton (95205-7013)
PHONE 925 400-9094
Harsimran Singh, *CEO*
Bikramjit Singh, *CEO*
EMP: 250 **EST:** 2013
SALES (est): 29.3MM **Privately Held**
SIC: 4213 Trucking, except local

(P-7546)
GK TRANSPORT INC
2175 N Brawley Ave, Fresno (93722-5408)
PHONE 559 275-3628
Gurwinder Singh, *President*
EMP: 45 **EST:** 2009
SALES (est): 3.8MM **Privately Held**
SIC: 4213 Heavy hauling

(P-7547)
GLS US FREIGHT INC (PA)
6750 Longe St Ste 100, Stockton (95206-4938)
P.O. Box 2569, Manteca (95336-1167)
PHONE 209 823-2168
James Scott Blevins, *President*
Phil Rankin, *Vice Pres*
Penny Regelman, *Office Mgr*
Ryan V Veen, *Info Tech Mgr*
Ryan Veen, *Info Tech Mgr*
EMP: 100 **EST:** 1976
SALES (est): 78.1MM **Privately Held**
WEB: www.mtnvly.com
SIC: 4213 Contract haulers

(P-7548)
GREEN VALLEY TRNSP CORP
30131 Highway 33, Tracy (95304-9319)
PHONE 209 836-5192
Mike Taylor, *CEO*
Nancy J Houghton, *President*
Kevin West, *COO*
Cathy Gilbert, *Executive*
Linda Larson, *Safety Mgr*
EMP: 50 **EST:** 1987
SALES (est): 9.7MM **Privately Held**
WEB: www.greenvalleytransportation.com
SIC: 4213 4212 Contract haulers; local trucking, without storage

(P-7549)
HANSEN ADKINS AUTO TRNSPT INC
650 Hammond Way, Milpitas (95035-5328)
PHONE 408 514-2345
Steve West, *Branch Mgr*
Mark Friedman, *Engineer*
EMP: 38 **Privately Held**
WEB: www.hansenadkins.com
SIC: 4213 Automobiles, transport & delivery
PA: Hansen & Adkins Auto Transport, Inc.
3552 Green Ave
Los Alamitos CA 90720

(P-7550)
HENDRICKSON TRUCK LINES INC
7080 Florin Perkins Rd, Sacramento (95828-2609)
P.O. Box 277806 (95827-7806)
PHONE 916 387-9614
William Hendrickson, *Chairman*
Ward Hendrickson, *CEO*
Alban Lang, *CFO*
EMP: 148 **EST:** 2013
SALES (est): 23MM **Privately Held**
WEB: www.htlines.com
SIC: 4213 Trucking, except local

(P-7551)
HENDRICKSON TRUCKING INC
7080 Florin Perkins Rd, Sacramento (95828-2609)
P.O. Box 292219 (95829-2219)
PHONE 916 387-9614
William Hendrickson, *CEO*
Ward Hendrickson, *President*
EMP: 280 **EST:** 1976
SQ FT: 5,480
SALES (est): 25.8MM **Privately Held**
WEB: www.htlines.com
SIC: 4213 Trucking, except local

(P-7552)
INLAND STAR DIST CTRS INC (PA)
3146 S Chestnut Ave, Fresno (93725-2606)
P.O. Box 2396 (93745-2396)
PHONE 559 237-2052
Michael K Kelton, *CEO*
Kimberly Shirkey, *Vice Pres*
John Neale, *Comms Dir*
Daniel Alvarado, *General Mgr*
Dave Donathan, *Technology*
◆ **EMP:** 60 **EST:** 1985
SQ FT: 550,000
SALES (est): 52.7MM **Privately Held**
WEB: www.inlandstar.com
SIC: 4213 4225 Trucking, except local; general warehousing

(P-7553)
J B HUNT TRANSPORT INC
2660 Loomis Rd, Stockton (95205-8008)
PHONE 209 235-1371
Shane O'Connor, *Manager*
Dominique Knowles, *Analyst*
Deshawn Phillips, *Maintence Staff*
Mike Davis, *Manager*
John Walker, *Accounts Mgr*
EMP: 165
SALES (corp-wide): 9.6B **Publicly Held**
WEB: www.jbhunt.com
SIC: 4213 Trucking, except local
HQ: J. B. Hunt Transport, Inc.
615 J B Hunt Corp Dr
Lowell AR 72745
479 820-0000

(P-7554)
J B HUNT TRANSPORT INC
3170 Crow Canyon Pl # 180, San Ramon (94583-1155)
PHONE 866 759-1127
Arifa Tuzin, *Manager*
EMP: 165
SALES (corp-wide): 9.6B **Publicly Held**
WEB: www.jbhunt.com
SIC: 4213 Trucking, except local
HQ: J. B. Hunt Transport, Inc.
615 J B Hunt Corp Dr
Lowell AR 72745
479 820-0000

(P-7555)
J B HUNT TRANSPORT SVCS INC
Also Called: J.B. Hunt Transport Services
3124 E Manning Ave, Fowler (93625-9785)
PHONE 559 834-3852
EMP: 687
SALES (corp-wide): 9.6B **Publicly Held**
WEB: www.jbhunt.com
SIC: 4213 Trucking, except local
PA: J. B. Hunt Transport Services, Inc.
615 J B Hunt Corporate Dr
Lowell AR 72745
479 820-0000

(P-7556)
JJ BARN TRANSPORT INC
3030 Morrow Bay St, West Sacramento (95691-5895)
PHONE 916 371-5800
Amandeep Singh, *CEO*
EMP: 35 **EST:** 2013
SALES (est): 2.5MM **Privately Held**
SIC: 4213 4731 Trucking, except local; freight forwarding

(P-7557)
JOHNSON & DALY MOVING & STRG
Also Called: Atlas Van Lines Agent
110 Belvedere St Ste 200, San Rafael (94901-4763)
PHONE 415 435-1192
James Daly, *President*
Tim Johnson, *Vice Pres*
Mario Batz, *General Mgr*
EMP: 35 **EST:** 1979
SQ FT: 10,000
SALES (est): 2.9MM **Privately Held**
WEB: www.johnsondalymoving.com
SIC: 4213 4225 Household goods transport; general warehousing

4213 - Trucking, Except Local County (P-7558)

(P-7558)
KHALSA TRANSPORTATION INC
13371 S Fowler Ave, Selma (93662-9501)
PHONE..................559 697-6557
Bhupinder Singh, *President*
Sandokh K Singh, *Vice Pres*
EMP: 40 EST: 2004
SALES (est): 6.1MM **Privately Held**
WEB: www.khalsatransportation.com
SIC: 4213 7389 Trucking, except local;

(P-7559)
KS TRANS SERVICE CO
3190 S Elm Ave, Fresno (93706-5619)
P.O. Box 12005 (93776-2005)
PHONE..................559 264-5650
Rajinder K Nijjar, *CEO*
Kevin Nijjar, *President*
EMP: 60 EST: 2007
SALES (est): 7MM **Privately Held**
SIC: 4213 Trucking, except local

(P-7560)
L A S TRANSPORTATION INC
Also Called: Produces Dairy
250 E Belmont Ave, Fresno (93701-1405)
P.O. Box 1231 (93715-1231)
PHONE..................559 264-6583
Richard Shehady, *President*
Lawrence Shehady, *Chairman*
Jeremy Crow, *Asst Controller*
Paul Garoogian, *Controller*
Dewayne Scott, *Buyer*
EMP: 36 EST: 1954
SQ FT: 30,000
SALES (est): 2.6MM **Privately Held**
WEB: www.producersdairy.com
SIC: 4213 Refrigerated products transport

(P-7561)
LEMORE TRANSPORTATION INC (PA)
Also Called: Royal Trucking
1420 Royal Industrial Way, Concord (94520-4914)
P.O. Box 6085 (94524-1085)
PHONE..................925 689-6444
Barbara Querio, *CEO*
Roy Querio, *President*
Heidi Becker, *Vice Pres*
Jeremy Hunt, *Administration*
Dan Sander, *Controller*
EMP: 73 EST: 1965
SQ FT: 6,000
SALES (est): 11.9MM **Privately Held**
WEB: www.royaltrucking.com
SIC: 4213 Contract haulers

(P-7562)
LR LEASING INC
5411 Raley Blvd, Sacramento (95838-1726)
PHONE..................916 438-0888
Andrew Romanov, *President*
Sergey Romanov, *Vice Pres*
Evelina R Popovich, *Admin Sec*
Evelina Popovich, *Admin Sec*
Slava Chmel, *Opers Mgr*
EMP: 45 EST: 2000
SQ FT: 21,000
SALES (est): 8.2MM **Privately Held**
WEB: www.dctransport.biz
SIC: 4213 Trucking, except local

(P-7563)
LYONS TRANSPORTATION INC (PA)
3198 Willow Ave Ste 104, Clovis (93612-4716)
PHONE..................559 299-0123
Albert Peterson, *CEO*
Earl Smittcamp, *Ch of Bd*
Robert E Smittcamp, *Vice Pres*
William Smittcamp, *Admin Sec*
EMP: 42 EST: 1972
SALES (est): 9MM **Privately Held**
WEB: www.lyonstransportation.com
SIC: 4213 Refrigerated products transport; contract haulers

(P-7564)
MAJOR TRANSPORTATION SVCS INC
3342 N Weber Ave, Fresno (93722-4909)
PHONE..................559 485-5949
Gill Baljinder, *President*
Bhupinde Gill, *Vice Pres*
Joe Garcia, *Principal*
EMP: 50 EST: 2005
SALES (est): 7.3MM **Privately Held**
SIC: 4213 Trucking, except local

(P-7565)
MATHESON FAST FREIGHT INC
9785 Goethe Rd, Sacramento (95827-3559)
PHONE..................209 342-0184
Mark Matheson, *Branch Mgr*
Paul Viers, *General Mgr*
Travis King, *Human Resources*
Daniel Shandy, *Maintence Staff*
Muguet Cochran, *Manager*
EMP: 265
SALES (corp-wide): 390MM **Privately Held**
WEB: www.mathesoninc.com
SIC: 4213 Less-than-truckload (LTL) transport
HQ: Matheson Fast Freight, Inc.
     9780 Dino Dr
     Elk Grove CA 95624
     916 686-4600

(P-7566)
MATHESON FAST FREIGHT INC (HQ)
9780 Dino Dr, Elk Grove (95624-9477)
PHONE..................916 686-4600
Robert B Matheson, *Ch of Bd*
Mark B Matheson, *President*
Laurie Johnson, *Corp Secy*
Carole L Matheson, *Exec VP*
Donald G Brocca, *Vice Pres*
EMP: 70 EST: 1984
SQ FT: 7,200
SALES (est): 43.5MM
SALES (corp-wide): 390MM **Privately Held**
WEB: www.mathesoninc.com
SIC: 4213 Less-than-truckload (LTL) transport
PA: Matheson Trucking, Inc.
    9785 Goethe Rd
    Sacramento CA 95827
    916 685-2330

(P-7567)
MATHESON TRUCKING INC (PA)
9785 Goethe Rd, Sacramento (95827-3559)
PHONE..................916 685-2330
Mark Matheson, *President*
Patricia Kepner, *CEO*
Tamrya Ford, *CFO*
Charles J Mellor, *Officer*
Carole L Matheson, *Exec VP*
EMP: 50 EST: 1964
SQ FT: 3,000
SALES (est): 390MM **Privately Held**
WEB: www.mathesoninc.com
SIC: 4213 4731 Contract haulers; less-than-truckload (LTL) transport; freight transportation arrangement

(P-7568)
METROPOLITAN VAN AND STOR INC (PA)
5400 Industrial Way, Benicia (94510-1037)
P.O. Box 829, Martinez (94553-0082)
PHONE..................707 745-1150
Dennis Paulley, *President*
Keith Estes, *Vice Pres*
Alex Finley, *Office Mgr*
Trisha Simon, *Office Mgr*
Julia Paulley-Shafer, *Project Mgr*
EMP: 40 EST: 1969
SQ FT: 121,400
SALES (est): 13.5MM **Privately Held**
WEB: www.metrovan.com
SIC: 4213 4214 Household goods transport; household goods moving & storage, local

(P-7569)
MI GROUP INC
Also Called: Movers Intl World Scope
25821 Industrial Blvd # 400, Hayward (94545-2919)
PHONE..................510 887-8200
Vince Hererra, *Vice Pres*
EMP: 73
SALES (corp-wide): 134MM **Privately Held**
SIC: 4213 Trucking, except local
HQ: The Mi Group Inc
    5 Woodhollow Rd Ste 7
    Parsippany NJ 07054
    973 463-0712

(P-7570)
NEW LEGEND INC
Also Called: Legend Transpotation
1235 Oswald Rd, Yuba City (95991-9719)
PHONE..................530 674-3100
Baveljit Singh Samara, *Branch Mgr*
John Hammond, *CFO*
Sherry Ayuyu, *Payroll Mgr*
Travis Moore, *Recruiter*
Stephen Cope-Jenner, *Accounts Mgr*
EMP: 316 **Privately Held**
SIC: 4213 4212 Trucking, except local; local trucking, without storage
PA: New Legend, Inc.
    811 S 59th Ave
    Phoenix AZ 85043

(P-7571)
NOBLE MOVERS INC
101 Creekside Ridge Ct # 2, Roseville (95678-3595)
PHONE..................415 260-1000
Frank Didonato, *CEO*
EMP: 57 EST: 2020
SQ FT: 17,000
SALES (est): 5MM **Privately Held**
SIC: 4213 Trucking, except local

(P-7572)
NORTHERN RFRIGERATED TRNSP INC (PA)
2700 W Main St, Turlock (95380-9537)
PHONE..................209 664-3800
Richard Mello, *CEO*
Judi Mello, *Treasurer*
John Doidge, *Vice Pres*
EMP: 120
SQ FT: 25,000
SALES (est): 32.4MM **Privately Held**
WEB: www.northernrefrigerated.com
SIC: 4213 Refrigerated products transport

(P-7573)
POPPY STATE EXPRESS INC
2700 W Main St, Turlock (95380-9537)
PHONE..................209 664-3950
Richard D Mello, *President*
Daniel N Watson, *CFO*
Judy Mello, *Treasurer*
John Doidge, *Vice Pres*
Claudia Doidge, *Admin Sec*
EMP: 80 EST: 1980
SQ FT: 30,000
SALES (est): 7.4MM **Privately Held**
WEB: www.northernrefrigerated.com
SIC: 4213 Refrigerated products transport

(P-7574)
R&L CARRIERS SHARED SVCS LLC
15651 Worthley Dr, San Lorenzo (94580-1800)
PHONE..................510 258-0547
Frank Gill, *Branch Mgr*
EMP: 45 **Privately Held**
WEB: www.rlcarriers.com
SIC: 4213 Trucking, except local
PA: R&L Carriers Shared Services, L.L.C.
    600 Gilliam Rd
    Wilmington OH 45177

(P-7575)
RAPID COURIER & FREIGHT INC
Also Called: RFI Logistics Warehouse
8760 Younger Creek Dr, Sacramento (95828-1022)
P.O. Box 97, Rancho Cordova (95741-0097)
PHONE..................916 387-5505
Albert Heath, *President*
Cynthia Heath, *Admin Sec*
Dale Selee, *Sales Executive*
EMP: 35 EST: 1990
SQ FT: 75,000 **Privately Held**
WEB: www.rfilogistics.com
SIC: 4213 Contract haulers

(P-7576)
RCG LOGISTICS LLC
Also Called: Rcg Auto Logistics
9300 Tech Center Dr # 190, Sacramento (95826-2575)
PHONE..................916 999-1234
Vitaliy Kezmenko, *CEO*
Aleksandr Marinov, *President*
Vitaliy Kuzmenko, *CEO*
Donald Neverov, *COO*
Sean Cabin, *Ch Credit Ofcr*
EMP: 95 EST: 2010
SALES (est): 15.3MM **Privately Held**
WEB: www.rcgauto.com
SIC: 4213 4731 Automobiles, transport & delivery; freight transportation arrangement

(P-7577)
REEVE TRUCKING COMPANY INC (PA)
5050 Carpenter Rd, Stockton (95215-8105)
P.O. Box 5126 (95205-0126)
PHONE..................209 948-4061
Lori J Reeve, *President*
Don Reeve, *Vice Pres*
Donald E Reeve, *Vice Pres*
Donald J Reeve Aka Spike, *Vice Pres*
Scott Moyers, *Purchasing*
▲ EMP: 70 EST: 1972
SQ FT: 100,000
SALES (est): 26.1MM **Privately Held**
WEB: www.reevetrucking.com
SIC: 4213 Contract haulers

(P-7578)
RELIANCE INTERMODAL INC
1919 Mrtin Lther King Ste, Stockton (95210)
P.O. Box 31238 (95213-1238)
PHONE..................209 946-0200
Lakhbir S Deol, *CEO*
EMP: 65 EST: 2011 **Privately Held**
WEB: www.relianceintermodal.com
SIC: 4213 Trucking, except local

(P-7579)
RENN TRANSPORTATION INC
8845 Forest St, Gilroy (95020-3651)
PHONE..................408 842-3545
Brad E Renn, *President*
Robert Renn, *Vice Pres*
Patricia Renn, *Admin Sec*
Jill Steinmetz, *Human Res Mgr*
Jeremiah Beale, *Maintence Staff*
EMP: 100
SQ FT: 9,609
SALES (est): 17.2MM **Privately Held**
WEB: www.renntransportation.com
SIC: 4213 Trucking, except local

(P-7580)
ROADSTAR TRUCKING INC
30527 San Antonio St, Hayward (94544-7101)
PHONE..................510 487-2404
Charles Ramorino, *Chairman*
Robert Ramorino, *President*
EMP: 55 EST: 1959
SQ FT: 43,000
SALES (est): 8.9MM **Privately Held**
WEB: www.roadstartruckinginc.com
SIC: 4213 Trucking, except local

PRODUCTS & SERVICES SECTION
4213 - Trucking, Except Local County (P-7604)

(P-7581)
RUAN TRANSPORT CORPORATION
830 W Glenwood Ave, Turlock (95380-5751)
PHONE...............................209 599-5000
Mike Elliott, *Branch Mgr*
EMP: 44
SALES (corp-wide): 1.6B Privately Held
WEB: www.ruan.com
SIC: 4213 Contract haulers
HQ: Ruan Transport Corporation
666 Grand Ave Ste 3100
Des Moines IA 50309
515 245-2500

(P-7582)
RUAN TRANSPORT CORPORATION
475 S Tegner Rd, Turlock (95380-9406)
PHONE...............................209 634-2768
Ken Becker, *Branch Mgr*
EMP: 44
SALES (corp-wide): 1.6B Privately Held
WEB: www.ruan.com
SIC: 4213 Contract haulers
HQ: Ruan Transport Corporation
666 Grand Ave Ste 3100
Des Moines IA 50309
515 245-2500

(P-7583)
RUAN TRANSPORT CORPORATION
6035 Giant Rd, Richmond (94806-2388)
PHONE...............................510 758-7383
Erik Rose, *Branch Mgr*
EMP: 44
SALES (corp-wide): 1.6B Privately Held
WEB: www.ruan.com
SIC: 4213 Contract haulers
HQ: Ruan Transport Corporation
666 Grand Ave Ste 3100
Des Moines IA 50309
515 245-2500

(P-7584)
RUAN TRANSPORT CORPORATION
2000 Loveridge Rd, Pittsburg (94565-4114)
PHONE...............................925 427-3983
EMP: 44
SALES (corp-wide): 1.6B Privately Held
WEB: www.ruan.com
SIC: 4213 Contract haulers
HQ: Ruan Transport Corporation
666 Grand Ave Ste 3100
Des Moines IA 50309
515 245-2500

(P-7585)
S & M MOVING SYSTEMS
Also Called: SM International
48551 Warm Springs Blvd, Fremont (94539-7765)
PHONE...............................510 497-2300
Gerald P Stadler, *Principal*
John Stadler, *Vice Pres*
Judy Clark, *Cust Mgr*
Rose Tristao, *Manager*
▲ EMP: 60 EST: 1985
SQ FT: 38,000
SALES (est): 12.9MM
SALES (corp-wide): 99.8MM Privately Held
WEB: www.smmoving.com
SIC: 4213 4214 Trucking, except local; local trucking with storage
PA: Torrance Van & Storage Company
12128 Burke St
Santa Fe Springs CA 90670

(P-7586)
SAIA INC
Also Called: Saia S Reno Barbara K
1508 Wyant Way, Sacramento (95864-2642)
PHONE...............................916 483-8331
EMP: 74
SALES (corp-wide): 1.8B Publicly Held
WEB: www.saia.com
SIC: 4213 Contract haulers
PA: Saia, Inc.
11465 Johns Creek Pkwy # 400
Johns Creek GA 30097
770 232-5067

(P-7587)
SAIA MOTOR FREIGHT LINE LLC
9119 Elkmont Dr, Elk Grove (95624-9706)
PHONE...............................916 690-8417
Joe Meyer, *Branch Mgr*
EMP: 55
SALES (corp-wide): 1.8B Publicly Held
SIC: 4213 Contract haulers
HQ: Saia Motor Freight Line, Llc
11465 Johns Creek Pkwy # 400
Duluth GA 30097
770 232-5067

(P-7588)
SAIA MOTOR FREIGHT LINE LLC
1095 N Court St, Redding (96001-0439)
P.O. Box 991210 (96099-1210)
PHONE...............................530 243-5540
Joe Myers, *Manager*
EMP: 55
SALES (corp-wide): 1.8B Publicly Held
SIC: 4213 Contract haulers
HQ: Saia Motor Freight Line, Llc
11465 Johns Creek Pkwy # 400
Duluth GA 30097
770 232-5067

(P-7589)
SAIA MOTOR FREIGHT LINE LLC
1755 Aurora Dr, San Leandro (94577-3103)
PHONE...............................510 347-6890
John Dentony, *Manager*
EMP: 55
SALES (corp-wide): 1.8B Publicly Held
SIC: 4213 4212 Contract haulers; local trucking, without storage
HQ: Saia Motor Freight Line, Llc
11465 Johns Creek Pkwy # 400
Duluth GA 30097
770 232-5067

(P-7590)
SAIA MOTOR FREIGHT LINE LLC
2575 S Sunland Ave, Fresno (93725-1330)
PHONE...............................559 499-6970
Adolph Lopez, *Branch Mgr*
EMP: 55
SALES (corp-wide): 1.8B Publicly Held
SIC: 4213 Contract haulers
HQ: Saia Motor Freight Line, Llc
11465 Johns Creek Pkwy # 400
Duluth GA 30097
770 232-5067

(P-7591)
SCAN-VINO LLC (PA)
Also Called: Cherokee Freight Lines
5463 Cherokee Rd, Stockton (95215-1128)
P.O. Box 5509 (95205-0509)
PHONE...............................209 931-3570
Leanne Scannavino, *Principal*
Barbara Lance, *Admin Sec*
Patrick Finch, *CIO*
James Fisher, *Controller*
John Ott, *Safety Mgr*
EMP: 69 EST: 1965
SQ FT: 1,000
SALES (est): 23.4MM Privately Held
SIC: 4213 Contract haulers

(P-7592)
SEA-LOGIX LLC
1425 Maritime St, Oakland (94607-1022)
PHONE...............................510 271-1400
Mary Brown, *Superintendent*
EMP: 60
SALES (corp-wide): 632.2MM Privately Held
WEB: www.sealogix.com
SIC: 4213 Trucking, except local
HQ: Sea-Logix, Llc
4040 Civic Center Dr # 350
San Rafael CA 94903
415 927-6400

(P-7593)
SEA-LOGIX LLC (HQ)
4040 Civic Center Dr # 350, San Rafael (94903-4150)
PHONE...............................415 927-6400
Peter McLoughlin,
George Pasha IV, *Ch of Bd*
James Britton, *CFO*
Amy Sherburne Manning,
▲ EMP: 37 EST: 1989
SALES (est): 24.6MM
SALES (corp-wide): 632.2MM Privately Held
WEB: www.sealogix.com
SIC: 4213 Trucking, except local
PA: The Pasha Group
4040 Civic Center Dr # 350
San Rafael CA 94903
415 927-6400

(P-7594)
SEASIDE RFRIGERATED TRNSPT INC (PA)
7041 Las Positas Rd Ste H, Livermore (94551-5124)
PHONE...............................510 732-0472
Lynn Johnson, *President*
Beverly Johnson, *Treasurer*
Dianna Johnson, *Human Res Dir*
EMP: 46 EST: 1972
SQ FT: 9,000
SALES (est): 9.7MM Privately Held
WEB: www.seasidetransport.com
SIC: 4213 Trucking, except local

(P-7595)
SNOOZIE SHAVINGS INC (PA)
525 Elk Valley Rd, Crescent City (95531-9460)
P.O. Box 14 (95531-0014)
PHONE...............................707 464-6186
Dwayne C Reichlin, *President*
Robert Matthess, *Treasurer*
Jay M Freeman, *Vice Pres*
Charlie F Compton, *Admin Sec*
EMP: 51 EST: 1967
SQ FT: 18,000
SALES (est): 2.5MM Privately Held
SIC: 4213 5099 Trucking, except local; shavings, wood; wood & wood by-products

(P-7596)
SOUTHWEST TRUCK SERVICE
Also Called: Southwest Logistics Services
50 Pine St, Watsonville (95076)
P.O. Box 1810 (95077-1810)
PHONE...............................831 724-1041
Robert Spear, *President*
Patricia Buckley, *Shareholder*
Denise Spear, *Shareholder*
Noe Legaspi, *General Mgr*
Inder Singh, *Manager*
EMP: 50 EST: 1964
SQ FT: 3,000
SALES (est): 3MM Privately Held
WEB: www.swtrucking.com
SIC: 4213 4212 Refrigerated products transport; local trucking, without storage

(P-7597)
SUDDATH RLCTION SYSTEMS NTHRN
2020 S 10th St, San Jose (95112-4112)
PHONE...............................904 858-1273
Jacob Moreno, *President*
EMP: 50 EST: 2017
SALES (est): 2.9MM Privately Held
SIC: 4213 Household goods transport

(P-7598)
SUDDATH RLCTION SYSTEMS NTHRN
2055 S 7th St, San Jose (95112-6141)
PHONE...............................408 288-3030
Gene Kopecky, *President*
EMP: 51 EST: 2001
SALES (est): 9.9MM
SALES (corp-wide): 820.8MM Privately Held
WEB: www.acerelocation.com
SIC: 4213 4731 4214 Household goods transport; freight forwarding; household goods moving & storage, local
HQ: Suddath Van Lines Inc
815 S Main St Ste 400
Jacksonville FL 32207
904 390-7100

(P-7599)
SUPERIOR TRUCK LINES INC (PA)
1457 Main St Ste A, Newman (95360-1342)
P.O. Box 307, Gustine (95322-0307)
PHONE...............................209 862-9430
Frank R Amaral III, *President*
Deanie Azevedo, *Corp Secy*
Frank R Amaral Jr, *Vice Pres*
EMP: 40 EST: 1988
SQ FT: 1,238
SALES (est): 16.3MM Privately Held
WEB: www.superiortruckline.com
SIC: 4213 Contract haulers

(P-7600)
T & T TRUCKING INC (PA)
11396 N Hwy 99, Lodi (95240-6899)
PHONE...............................800 692-3457
Terry M Tarditi, *President*
John King, *Treasurer*
Mary Lou Tarditi, *Admin Sec*
EMP: 107
SQ FT: 25,000
SALES (est): 18.6MM Privately Held
WEB: www.tttrucking.com
SIC: 4213 Contract haulers

(P-7601)
TIGER LINES LLC (HQ)
927 Black Diamond Way, Lodi (95240-0738)
P.O. Box 1120 (95241-1120)
PHONE...............................209 334-4100
Dennis Altnow, *CEO*
David Hembree, *Vice Pres*
Emil Canlas, *Human Resources*
Don Stone, *Terminal Mgr*
Donald Altnow, *Mng Member*
EMP: 75 EST: 1935
SQ FT: 20,000
SALES (est): 27.4MM Privately Held
WEB: www.tigerlines.com
SIC: 4213 4214 4212 Contract haulers; local trucking with storage; local trucking, without storage
PA: Lts Rentals, Llc
927 Black Diamond Way
Lodi CA 95240
209 334-4100

(P-7602)
TIMMERMAN STARLITE TRCKG INC
3955 Starlite Dr, Ceres (95307-9733)
P.O. Box 2710 (95307-7710)
PHONE...............................209 538-1706
Colby Bell, *CEO*
Agnes Timmerman, *Corp Secy*
Geneveve Timmerman, *Vice Pres*
EMP: 65 EST: 1976
SALES (est): 9.7MM Privately Held
WEB: www.starlitetrucking.com
SIC: 4213 4212 Trucking, except local; farm to market haulage, local

(P-7603)
TMT ENTERPRISES INC
1996 Oakland Rd, San Jose (95131-1606)
PHONE...............................408 432-9040
Ted H Moore, *President*
Colleen Moore, *Vice Pres*
Lynette Bernardi, *Executive Asst*
Matt Moore, *Opers Mgr*
EMP: 35 EST: 1971
SQ FT: 1,000
SALES (est): 5MM Privately Held
WEB: www.tmtenterprises.net
SIC: 4213 Trucking, except local

(P-7604)
TONYS EXPRESS INC
4727 Fite Ct Ste C, Stockton (95215-8338)
PHONE...............................209 234-1000
Dave Mendes, *Manager*
EMP: 63
SALES (corp-wide): 17.2MM Privately Held
WEB: www.tonysexpress.com
SIC: 4213 Trucking, except local

4213 - Trucking, Except Local County (P-7605)

PA: Tony's Express Inc.
10613 Jasmine St
Fontana CA 92337
909 427-8700

(P-7605)
TRANS VALLEY TRANSPORT
450 E 9th St, Gilroy (95020-6686)
P.O. Box 485 (95021-0485)
PHONE..................................408 842-2188
Kerry Winfield Burnham, *CEO*
Donald J Triolo, *Shareholder*
Eric J Triolo, *President*
John P Triolo, *Vice Pres*
EMP: 35 **EST:** 1967
SQ FT: 7,200
SALES (est): 9.5MM **Privately Held**
WEB: www.tvtli.com
SIC: 4213 Trucking, except local

(P-7606)
TRIMAC TRNSP SVCS WSTN INC
331 E Channel Rd, Benicia (94510-1127)
PHONE..................................707 745-5414
Tom Munseny, *Manager*
EMP: 35
SALES (corp-wide): 626.9MM **Privately Held**
WEB: www.trimac.com
SIC: 4213 Trucking, except local
HQ: Trimac Transportation Services (Western), Inc.
15333 John F Kennedy Blvd
Houston TX 77032
281 985-0000

(P-7607)
TRIUS TRUCKING INC
4692 E Lincoln Ave, Fowler (93625-9685)
P.O. Box 2700, Fresno (93745-2700)
PHONE..................................559 834-4000
Tehal Singh Thandi, *CEO*
Michelle Eaves, *Controller*
EMP: 87
SQ FT: 3,900
SALES (est): 27.4MM **Privately Held**
WEB: www.triustrucking.com
SIC: 4213 Trucking, except local

(P-7608)
UPS GROUND FREIGHT INC
925 Morse Ave, Sunnyvale (94089-1601)
PHONE..................................408 400-0595
EMP: 95
SALES (corp-wide): 58.2B **Publicly Held**
SIC: 4213 Less-Than-Truckload Carrier
HQ: Ups Ground Freight, Inc.
1000 Semmes Ave
Richmond VA 23224
804 231-8000

(P-7609)
UPS GROUND FREIGHT INC
900 E St, West Sacramento (95605-2310)
PHONE..................................916 371-9101
EMP: 60
SALES (corp-wide): 58.2B **Publicly Held**
SIC: 4213 Class One Motor Carrier
HQ: Ups Ground Freight, Inc.
1000 Semmes Ave
Richmond VA 23224
804 231-8000

(P-7610)
VITO TRUCKING LLC
1415 Sandpoint Dr, Ceres (95307-7463)
PHONE..................................209 342-5104
Vito Ranuio, *Mng Member*
EMP: 60 **EST:** 2005
SALES (est): 5.6MM **Privately Held**
WEB: www.vitotrucking.com
SIC: 4213 Trucking, except local

(P-7611)
WILDWOOD EXPRESS
12416 Swanson Ave, Kingsburg (93631-9516)
P.O. Box 397 (93631-0397)
PHONE..................................559 805-3237
Mark Anthony Woods, *President*
Matthew Woods, *Treasurer*
Sue Woods, *Vice Pres*
EMP: 50 **EST:** 1980
SQ FT: 3,500

SALES (est): 7.9MM **Privately Held**
WEB: www.wildwoodex.com
SIC: 4213 Contract haulers

(P-7612)
WILLIAMS TANK LINES (PA)
1477 Tillie Lewis Dr, Stockton (95206-1130)
PHONE..................................209 944-5613
Michael I Williams, *CEO*
Marlys A Williams, *Admin Sec*
Ricky Green, *Manager*
Scott Murdock, *Manager*
Lee Sizemore, *Manager*
EMP: 90 **EST:** 1978
SQ FT: 15,000
SALES (est): 42.8MM **Privately Held**
WEB: www.williamstanklines.com
SIC: 4213 Liquid petroleum transport, nonlocal

(P-7613)
XPO ENTERPRISE SERVICES INC
Also Called: Con-Way
3810 Hill Rd, Lakeport (95453-7015)
PHONE..................................916 399-8291
EMP: 120
SALES (corp-wide): 7.6B **Publicly Held**
SIC: 4213 Trucking Operator-Nonlocal
HQ: Xpo Enterprise Services, Inc.
2211 Old Earhart Rd # 100
Ann Arbor MI 48105
734 998-4200

(P-7614)
XPO LOGISTICS FREIGHT INC
5475 S Airport Way, Stockton (95206-3918)
PHONE..................................209 983-8285
Rudy Romo, *Manager*
EMP: 70
SQ FT: 1,000
SALES (corp-wide): 16.2B **Publicly Held**
WEB: www.xpo.com
SIC: 4213 Contract haulers
HQ: Xpo Logistics Freight, Inc.
2211 Old Earhart Rd # 10
Ann Arbor MI 48105
800 755-2728

(P-7615)
XPO LOGISTICS FREIGHT INC
3516 Kiessig Ave, Sacramento (95823-1036)
PHONE..................................916 399-8291
John Sullivan, *Branch Mgr*
Tim Myles, *Human Res Dir*
EMP: 70
SALES (corp-wide): 16.2B **Publicly Held**
WEB: www.xpo.com
SIC: 4213 Contract haulers
HQ: Xpo Logistics Freight, Inc.
2211 Old Earhart Rd # 10
Ann Arbor MI 48105
800 755-2728

(P-7616)
XPO LOGISTICS FREIGHT INC
Also Called: Con-Way
4095 S Moorland Ave, Santa Rosa (95407-8110)
PHONE..................................707 584-0211
Rich Gonzales, *Manager*
EMP: 70
SALES (corp-wide): 16.2B **Publicly Held**
WEB: www.xpo.com
SIC: 4213 Contract haulers
HQ: Xpo Logistics Freight, Inc.
2211 Old Earhart Rd # 10
Ann Arbor MI 48105
800 755-2728

(P-7617)
XPO LOGISTICS FREIGHT INC
2200 Claremont Ct, Hayward (94545-5002)
PHONE..................................510 785-6920
Terry Smith, *Manager*
EMP: 70
SQ FT: 28,704
SALES (corp-wide): 16.2B **Publicly Held**
WEB: www.xpo.com
SIC: 4213 4212 4731 Contract haulers; local trucking, without storage; freight transportation arrangement

HQ: Xpo Logistics Freight, Inc.
2211 Old Earhart Rd # 10
Ann Arbor MI 48105
800 755-2728

4214 Local Trucking With Storage

(P-7618)
CUSTOM FREIGHT SYSTEMS INC (PA)
2484 Baumann Ave, San Lorenzo (94580-1802)
PHONE..................................510 728-7515
David Williams, *CEO*
Harvey Selnik, *Corp Secy*
Edmond Epps, *Vice Pres*
Mishell Macias, *Office Mgr*
Marke Tyrrell, *Sales Staff*
EMP: 45 **EST:** 1985
SQ FT: 175,000
SALES (est): 12.8MM **Privately Held**
SIC: 4214 Local trucking with storage

(P-7619)
DGA SERVICES INC (PA)
Also Called: J I T Transportation
1075 Montague Expy, Milpitas (95035-6828)
P.O. Box 41372, San Jose (95160-1372)
PHONE..................................408 232-4800
Gene Ashley, *President*
Deborah S Ashley, *CEO*
David Butcher, *Executive*
Dave Butcher, *General Mgr*
Ross Williams, *Info Tech Mgr*
EMP: 54 **EST:** 1993
SQ FT: 125,000
SALES (est): 20.5MM **Privately Held**
SIC: 4214 4213 Local trucking with storage; trucking, except local

(P-7620)
DURKEE DRAYAGE COMPANY
539 Stone Rd, Benicia (94510-1113)
PHONE..................................510 970-7550
Jeffrey J Fenton, *President*
Cathy Lashin, *Vice Pres*
▲ **EMP:** 80 **EST:** 1933
SQ FT: 80,000
SALES (est): 9MM **Privately Held**
WEB: www.durkeedrayage.com
SIC: 4214 Local trucking with storage

(P-7621)
FRONTIER TRANSPORTATION INC
425 W Larch Rd, Tracy (95304-1614)
PHONE..................................209 836-0251
Tom Moffitt, *Manager*
Joe Arellano, *Training Spec*
Susan Badgett, *Clerk*
EMP: 47
SALES (corp-wide): 18.5MM **Privately Held**
WEB: www.osterkampgrp.com
SIC: 4214 4231 Local trucking with storage; trucking terminal facilities
PA: Frontier Transportation Inc.
3577 Philadelphia St
Chino CA 91710
909 590-8245

(P-7622)
GSC LOGISTICS INC (PA)
530 Water St Fl 5, Oakland (94607-3532)
PHONE..................................510 844-3700
Scott E Taylor, *CEO*
Garcia Andres, *Vice Pres*
Dennis Lee, *Vice Pres*
Ingrid McFarland, *Analyst*
Jerome Musni, *Analyst*
▲ **EMP:** 106 **EST:** 1988
SQ FT: 8,000
SALES (est): 62MM **Privately Held**
WEB: www.gsclogistics.com
SIC: 4214 4225 4213 Local trucking with storage; general warehousing; trucking, except local

(P-7623)
JAVELIN LOGISTICS CORPORATION (PA)
7025 Central Ave, Newark (94560-4201)
PHONE..................................510 795-7287
Malcolm George Winspear, *CEO*
Jeff Hoover, *Vice Pres*
Mary White, *Admin Mgr*
Mike Sacrey, *General Mgr*
Gail Endrina, *Administration*
EMP: 50 **EST:** 1995
SALES (est): 28.9MM **Privately Held**
WEB: www.javelinlogistics.com
SIC: 4214 4731 4225 Local trucking with storage; freight transportation arrangement; general warehousing & storage

(P-7624)
LEGACY TRANSPORTATION SVCS INC (PA)
Also Called: Legacy Global Logistics Svcs
935 Mclaughlin Ave, San Jose (95122-2612)
PHONE..................................408 294-9800
John Migliozzi, *President*
Kerry Carlson, *President*
Shelly Gipson, *Exec VP*
Michael Quinn, *Exec VP*
Shelly J McAllister, *Vice Pres*
▲ **EMP:** 140 **EST:** 1991
SQ FT: 200,000
SALES (est): 57.1MM **Privately Held**
WEB: www.legacytsi.com
SIC: 4214 4213 Local trucking with storage; trucking, except local

(P-7625)
MARIN STORAGE & TRUCKING INC (PA)
Also Called: Reliable Crane & Rigging
801 Lindberg Ln, Petaluma (94952-3358)
P.O. Box 126, Kentfield (94914-0126)
PHONE..................................707 778-8313
Michael Geister, *President*
William Magee, *Corp Secy*
Mark Sotak, *Superintendent*
EMP: 35 **EST:** 1964
SQ FT: 20,000
SALES (est): 6.2MM **Privately Held**
SIC: 4214 Local trucking with storage

(P-7626)
MEES MOVING & STORAGE INC (PA)
2561 Grennan Ct, Rancho Cordova (95742-6296)
P.O. Box 189 (95741-0189)
PHONE..................................916 635-8262
William E Mee, *Ch of Bd*
Jerry Ryan, *Vice Pres*
Mark Filer, *Manager*
Julie Filer, *Representative*
EMP: 39 **EST:** 1969
SQ FT: 24,000
SALES (est): 5.5MM **Privately Held**
WEB: www.meemoving.com
SIC: 4214 4213 4783 Household goods moving & storage, local; contract haulers; packing & crating

(P-7627)
MOVING SOLUTIONS INC
Also Called: North American Van Lines
7093 Central Ave, Newark (94560-4201)
PHONE..................................408 920-0110
Rick S Philpott, *CEO*
Janet Philpott, *Vice Pres*
EMP: 150 **EST:** 1984
SQ FT: 200,000
SALES (est): 20.2MM **Privately Held**
WEB: www.northamerican.com
SIC: 4214 8742 7376 1799 Local trucking with storage; construction project management consultant; computer facilities management; office furniture installation

(P-7628)
NATIONAL TRANSFER AND STOR INC
Also Called: Olsen & Fielding Moving Svcs
6350 Sky Creek Dr Ste 600, Sacramento (95828-1057)
PHONE..................................916 383-8800
Toll Free:..................................866

PRODUCTS & SERVICES SECTION

4215 - Courier Svcs, Except Air County (P-7653)

C Reid Olsen, *CEO*
Curtis R Olsen Jr, *President*
Suzanne Fielding, *Corp Secy*
Curt Olsen, *Vice Pres*
EMP: 43 **EST:** 1953
SQ FT: 42,000
SALES (est): 1.6MM **Privately Held**
SIC: 4214 4213 Household goods moving & storage, local; household goods transport

(P-7629)
NEW WORLD VAN LINES INC
Also Called: New Wrld Van Lnes San Frncisco
33373 Lewis St, Union City (94587-2205)
PHONE..................................510 487-1091
Shirley Marx, *Branch Mgr*
EMP: 58
SALES (corp-wide): 96.9MM **Privately Held**
WEB: www.nwvl.com
SIC: 4214 Local trucking with storage
PA: New World Van Lines, Inc.
5875 N Rogers Ave
Chicago IL 60646
773 685-3399

(P-7630)
NOR-CAL MOVING SERVICES (PA)
Also Called: Allied Intl San Franisco
3129 Corporate Pl, Hayward (94545-3915)
PHONE..................................510 371-4942
Peter Mazzetti Jr, *CEO*
Dennis D Goza, *President*
John Mizera, *CFO*
Dave Konecny, *Exec VP*
James Thomas, *Vice Pres*
▲ **EMP:** 125 **EST:** 1982
SQ FT: 200,000
SALES (est): 24.8MM **Privately Held**
WEB: www.nor-calmoving.com
SIC: 4214 4213 Household goods moving & storage, local; household goods transport

(P-7631)
PODS OF SAN FRANCISCO LLC (HQ)
21001 Cabot Blvd, Hayward (94545-1109)
PHONE..................................510 780-1654
Tom Ryan, *Mng Member*
EMP: 51 **EST:** 2004
SALES (est): 1.4MM **Privately Held**
WEB: www.pods.com
SIC: 4214 4225 Local trucking with storage; general warehousing & storage

(P-7632)
REDDING LUMBER TRANSPORT INC
Also Called: R L T
4301 Eastside Rd, Redding (96001-3801)
P.O. Box 492110 (96049-2110)
PHONE..................................530 241-8193
Albert Shufelberger, *President*
William Weber, *Vice Pres*
Matthew Lord, *Manager*
EMP: 93 **EST:** 1972
SQ FT: 4,000
SALES (est): 10.2MM **Privately Held**
WEB: www.rlttrucking.com
SIC: 4214 4213 Local trucking with storage; refrigerated products transport

(P-7633)
ROYAL EXPRESS INC (PA)
3545 E Date Ave, Fresno (93725-1933)
PHONE..................................559 272-3500
Kirpal S Shiota, *CEO*
EMP: 111 **EST:** 1975
SQ FT: 435,600
SALES (est): 15.1MM **Privately Held**
WEB: www.royalexp.com
SIC: 4214 Local trucking with storage

(P-7634)
SS SKIKOS INCORPORATED
1289 Sebastopol Rd, Santa Rosa (95407-6834)
PHONE..................................707 575-3000
Shad Skikos, *CEO*
Pete Skikos, *President*
EMP: 80 **EST:** 2002

SALES (est): 14.6MM **Privately Held**
WEB: www.skikostrucking.com
SIC: 4214 Local trucking with storage

(P-7635)
STARVING STUDENTS INC
2150 Bell Ave Ste 110, Sacramento (95838-3008)
PHONE..................................916 927-7071
EMP: 48
SALES (corp-wide): 140.3MM **Privately Held**
SIC: 4214 Local Trucking-With Storage
PA: Starving Students, Inc.
6220 Kimberly Ave Ste 2
Las Vegas NV 89122

(P-7636)
TEOCAL TRANSPORT INC
2101 Carden St, San Leandro (94577-2245)
PHONE..................................510 569-3485
Rafael Aguirre, *CEO*
EMP: 35 **EST:** 1990
SALES (est): 424.1MM **Privately Held**
WEB: www.teocaltransport.com
SIC: 4214 Local trucking with storage

(P-7637)
TREVIS BERRY TRANSPORTATION
655 E Luchessa Ave, Gilroy (95020-7009)
P.O. Box 1802 (95021-1802)
PHONE..................................408 842-8238
David Reynolds, *President*
Paula Reynolds, *Corp Secy*
Missy Lopez, *Bookkeeper*
Trevis R Berry, *Transportation*
EMP: 57 **EST:** 1940
SQ FT: 57,000
SALES (est): 5.1MM **Privately Held**
WEB: www.trevisberry.com
SIC: 4214 4213 7699 Local trucking with storage; trucking, except local; contract haulers; pallet repair

(P-7638)
VALLEY RLCTION STOR NTHRN CAL (PA)
Also Called: Valley Northamerican
5000 Marsh Dr, Concord (94520-5322)
PHONE..................................925 230-2025
James Robson, *President*
John A Burks, *CEO*
EMP: 50 **EST:** 1985
SQ FT: 58,000
SALES (est): 20.6MM **Privately Held**
WEB: www.valleyrelocation.com
SIC: 4214 Local trucking with storage

(P-7639)
VALLEY RLCTION STOR NTHRN CAL
Also Called: Valley Northamerican
3230 Reed Ave, West Sacramento (95605-1622)
PHONE..................................916 375-0001
Mark Palatier, *Branch Mgr*
EMP: 74
SALES (corp-wide): 20.6MM **Privately Held**
WEB: www.valleyrelocation.com
SIC: 4214 Local trucking with storage
PA: Valley Relocation And Storage Of Northern California, Inc.
5000 Marsh Dr
Concord CA 94520
925 230-2025

(P-7640)
VALLEY RLCTION STOR NTHRN CAL
Also Called: Valley Northamerican
835 Sinclair Frontage Rd, Milpitas (95035-6308)
PHONE..................................408 938-3672
Ralph Rojas, *Branch Mgr*
EMP: 74
SALES (corp-wide): 20.6MM **Privately Held**
WEB: www.valleyrelocation.com
SIC: 4214 Local trucking with storage

PA: Valley Relocation And Storage Of Northern California, Inc.
5000 Marsh Dr
Concord CA 94520
925 230-2025

(P-7641)
VIN LUX LLC
1200 Green Island Rd, American Canyon (94503-9639)
PHONE..................................707 265-4100
Thomas Tunt, *Mng Member*
Mandy Rocio, *Manager*
EMP: 50 **EST:** 2007
SALES (est): 9.9MM **Privately Held**
WEB: www.vinluxtransport.com
SIC: 4214 Local trucking with storage

4215 Courier Svcs, Except Air

(P-7642)
DYNAMEX INC
4790 Frontier Way Ste A, Stockton (95215-9424)
PHONE..................................209 464-7008
EMP: 60
SALES (corp-wide): 3.2B **Privately Held**
SIC: 4215 Courier Service
HQ: Dynamex Inc.
5429 L B Johnson Fwy 90 Ste 900
Dallas TX 75254
214 560-9000

(P-7643)
EXPRESS MESSENGER SYSTEMS INC
3830 Cypress Dr, Petaluma (94954-5613)
PHONE..................................707 773-1564
Steve Brenner, *General Mgr*
Jane Arge, *Admin Asst*
Elicia Cano, *Manager*
EMP: 50 **Privately Held**
WEB: www.ontrac.com
SIC: 5941 4215 Sporting goods & bicycle shops; courier services, except by air
PA: Express Messenger Systems, Inc.
2501 S Price Rd Ste 201
Chandler AZ 85286

(P-7644)
EXPRESS MESSENGER SYSTEMS INC
Also Called: California Overnight
1635 Main Ave Ste 3, Sacramento (95838-2452)
PHONE..................................916 921-6016
Ian Burton, *Manager*
EMP: 71 **Privately Held**
WEB: www.ontrac.com
SIC: 4215 Package delivery, vehicular
PA: Express Messenger Systems, Inc.
2501 S Price Rd Ste 201
Chandler AZ 85286

(P-7645)
EXPRESS MESSENGER SYSTEMS INC
Also Called: Ontrac
4603 N Brawley Ave # 103, Fresno (93722-3960)
PHONE..................................559 277-4910
EMP: 56 **Privately Held**
SIC: 4215 Courier Service
PA: Express Messenger Systems, Inc.
2501 S Price Rd Ste 201
Chandler AZ 85286

(P-7646)
EXPRESS MESSENGER SYSTEMS INC
Also Called: California Overnight
101 Spear St Ste A1, San Francisco (94105-1557)
PHONE..................................415 495-7300
Fax: 415 495-7420
EMP: 63 **Privately Held**
SIC: 4215 Courier Service
PA: Express Messenger Systems, Inc.
2501 S Price Rd Ste 201
Chandler AZ 85286

(P-7647)
FEDERAL EXPRESS CORPORATION
Also Called: Fedex
9190 Edes Ave, Oakland (94603-1116)
PHONE..................................510 382-2344
EMP: 300
SALES (corp-wide): 47.4B **Publicly Held**
SIC: 4215 4513 Air & Ground Cargo Service
HQ: Federal Express Corporation
3610 Hacks Cross Rd
Memphis TN 38125
901 369-3600

(P-7648)
GENERAL LGSTICS SYSTEMS US INC
4601 Malat St, Oakland (94601-4903)
PHONE..................................800 322-5555
Patrick Stoops, *Principal*
EMP: 143
SALES (corp-wide): 17.8B **Privately Held**
WEB: www.gls-us.com
SIC: 4215 Package delivery, vehicular
HQ: General Logistics Systems Us, Inc.
4000 Executive Pkwy # 295
San Ramon CA 94583

(P-7649)
GENERAL LGSTICS SYSTEMS US INC
760 Cabin Dr, Mill Valley (94941-3915)
PHONE..................................415 492-1112
Steve Koller, *Manager*
EMP: 143
SALES (corp-wide): 17.8B **Privately Held**
WEB: www.gls-us.com
SIC: 4215 4212 Package delivery, vehicular; delivery service, vehicular
HQ: General Logistics Systems Us, Inc.
4000 Executive Pkwy # 295
San Ramon CA 94583

(P-7650)
KARSSLI CORPORATION
901 Corcoran Ave, Santa Cruz (95062-4266)
PHONE..................................831 420-8900
Mustafa M Karssli, *Principal*
EMP: 36 **EST:** 2008
SALES (est): 1.4MM **Privately Held**
SIC: 4215 Parcel delivery, vehicular

(P-7651)
NEWGISTICS INC
27 Maiden Ln Fl 4, San Francisco (94108-5444)
PHONE..................................415 465-0564
EMP: 62
SALES (corp-wide): 3.5B **Publicly Held**
WEB: www.pitneybowes.com
SIC: 4215 Courier services, except by air
HQ: Newgistics, Inc.
7171 Sw Pkwy
Austin TX 78735

(P-7652)
ROAD RUNNER DELIVERY LLC
530 Chestnut St Apt 17, San Carlos (94070-2101)
PHONE..................................312 468-6940
James McKinney,
EMP: 50 **EST:** 2020
SALES (est): 2.2MM **Privately Held**
SIC: 4215 Courier services, except by air

(P-7653)
SERVE ROBOTICS INC ✪
1050 Noriega St, San Francisco (94122-4514)
PHONE..................................415 590-0160
Ali Kashani, *CEO*
Touraj Parang, *COO*
EMP: 58 **EST:** 2021
SALES (est): 3MM **Privately Held**
SIC: 4215 Package delivery, vehicular

4215 - Courier Svcs, Except Air

(P-7654)
SYNC LOGISTICS LLC (PA)
44308 Pcf Commons Blvd, Fremont (94538-3815)
PHONE...................510 353-3749
Theseus Scott, *Mng Member*
Michael White,
EMP: 44 **EST:** 2018
SALES (est): 400K **Privately Held**
SIC: 4215 Package delivery, vehicular

(P-7655)
SYNCTRUCK LLC (PA)
510 Eccles Ave, South San Francisco (94080-1905)
PHONE...................650 239-6231
Luis Antonio Toledo, *Mng Member*
EMP: 120 **EST:** 2015
SQ FT: 500
SALES (est): 8.7MM **Privately Held**
WEB: www.synctruck.com
SIC: 4215 Package delivery, vehicular

(P-7656)
TENTER ENTERPRISES INC
180 Redbud Dr, Paradise (95969-3719)
PHONE...................530 680-9917
Elliot Tenter, *President*
EMP: 35 **EST:** 2011
SALES (est): 1.5MM **Privately Held**
SIC: 4215 Parcel delivery, vehicular

(P-7657)
TRIPLE H SOLUTIONS INC
Also Called: Ths
9575 Stablegate Rd, Wilton (95693-9214)
PHONE...................916 475-8367
Jason Hall, *President*
EMP: 35 **EST:** 2020
SALES (est): 1.4MM **Privately Held**
SIC: 4215 Package delivery, vehicular

(P-7658)
UNITED PARCEL SERVICE INC
Also Called: UPS
1601 Atlas Rd, Richmond (94806-1101)
PHONE...................510 262-2338
Jim Kelly, *President*
EMP: 152
SALES (corp-wide): 84.6B **Publicly Held**
WEB: www.ups.com
SIC: 4215 4513 Parcel delivery, vehicular; air courier services
HQ: United Parcel Service, Inc.
  55 Glenlake Pkwy
  Atlanta GA 30328
  404 828-6000

(P-7659)
UNITED PARCEL SERVICE INC
Also Called: UPS
6845 Eastside Rd, Anderson (96007-9406)
PHONE...................530 365-7850
Lauren Lnd, *Manager*
EMP: 152
SALES (corp-wide): 84.6B **Publicly Held**
WEB: www.ups.com
SIC: 4215 4213 Parcel delivery, vehicular; trucking, except local
HQ: United Parcel Service, Inc.
  55 Glenlake Pkwy
  Atlanta GA 30328
  404 828-6000

(P-7660)
UNITED PARCEL SERVICE INC
Also Called: UPS
5000 W Cordelia Rd, Fairfield (94534-1628)
PHONE...................707 864-8200
EMP: 152
SALES (corp-wide): 84.6B **Publicly Held**
WEB: www.ups.com
SIC: 4215 Parcel delivery, vehicular
HQ: United Parcel Service, Inc.
  55 Glenlake Pkwy
  Atlanta GA 30328
  404 828-6000

(P-7661)
UNITED PARCEL SERVICE INC
Also Called: UPS
1400 Hil Mor Dr, Ceres (95307-9292)
PHONE...................800 742-5877
Dave Walker, *Principal*
EMP: 152
SALES (corp-wide): 84.6B **Publicly Held**
WEB: www.ups.com
SIC: 4215 Parcel delivery, vehicular
HQ: United Parcel Service, Inc.
  55 Glenlake Pkwy
  Atlanta GA 30328
  404 828-6000

(P-7662)
UNITED PARCEL SERVICE INC
Also Called: UPS
1380 Shore St, West Sacramento (95691-3522)
PHONE...................916 373-4076
Tom Karls, *Manager*
EMP: 152
SALES (corp-wide): 84.6B **Publicly Held**
WEB: www.ups.com
SIC: 4215 Parcel delivery, vehicular
HQ: United Parcel Service, Inc.
  55 Glenlake Pkwy
  Atlanta GA 30328
  404 828-6000

(P-7663)
UNITED PARCEL SERVICE INC
Also Called: UPS
2531 Napa Valley Corp Dr, NAPA (94558)
PHONE...................707 224-1205
Josh Young, *Principal*
EMP: 152
SALES (corp-wide): 84.6B **Publicly Held**
WEB: www.ups.com
SIC: 4215 Package delivery, vehicular
HQ: United Parcel Service, Inc.
  55 Glenlake Pkwy
  Atlanta GA 30328
  404 828-6000

(P-7664)
UNITED PARCEL SERVICE INC
Also Called: UPS
128 Shore St, Sacramento (95829)
PHONE...................916 373-4089
Chris Wagner, *Manager*
EMP: 152
SALES (corp-wide): 84.6B **Publicly Held**
WEB: www.ups.com
SIC: 4215 Parcel delivery, vehicular
HQ: United Parcel Service, Inc.
  55 Glenlake Pkwy
  Atlanta GA 30328
  404 828-6000

(P-7665)
UNITED PARCEL SERVICE INC
Also Called: UPS
1999 S 7th St, San Jose (95112-6009)
PHONE...................408 291-2942
Frank Cademarti, *Manager*
EMP: 152
SALES (corp-wide): 84.6B **Publicly Held**
WEB: www.ups.com
SIC: 4215 Parcel delivery, vehicular
HQ: United Parcel Service, Inc.
  55 Glenlake Pkwy
  Atlanta GA 30328
  404 828-6000

(P-7666)
UNITED PARCEL SERVICE INC
UPS
2222 17th St, San Francisco (94103-5015)
PHONE...................415 252-4564
Tom Dalto, *Manager*
EMP: 152
SALES (corp-wide): 84.6B **Publicly Held**
WEB: www.ups.com
SIC: 4215 4513 Parcel delivery, vehicular; air courier services
HQ: United Parcel Service, Inc.
  55 Glenlake Pkwy
  Atlanta GA 30328
  404 828-6000

(P-7667)
UNITED PARCEL SERVICE INC
Also Called: UPS
1012 Sterling St, Vallejo (94591-8686)
PHONE...................707 252-4560
EMP: 152
SALES (corp-wide): 84.6B **Publicly Held**
WEB: www.ups.com
SIC: 4215 Parcel delivery, vehicular

(P-7668)
UNITED PARCEL SERVICE INC
Also Called: UPS
8400 Pardee Dr, Oakland (94621-1456)
PHONE...................510 813-5662
Shurn Rick, *Technician*
EMP: 152
SALES (corp-wide): 84.6B **Publicly Held**
WEB: www.ups.com
SIC: 4215 Parcel delivery, vehicular
HQ: United Parcel Service, Inc.
  55 Glenlake Pkwy
  Atlanta GA 30328
  404 828-6000

(P-7669)
UNITED PARCEL SERVICE INC
Also Called: UPS
259 Cherry St, Ukiah (95482-5804)
PHONE...................707 468-5481
EMP: 152
SALES (corp-wide): 84.6B **Publicly Held**
WEB: www.ups.com
SIC: 4215 Parcel delivery, vehicular
HQ: United Parcel Service, Inc.
  55 Glenlake Pkwy
  Atlanta GA 30328
  404 828-6000

(P-7670)
UNITED PARCEL SERVICE INC
Also Called: UPS
2342 Gun Club Rd, Angels Camp (95222-9248)
PHONE...................209 736-0878
EMP: 152
SALES (corp-wide): 84.6B **Publicly Held**
WEB: www.ups.com
SIC: 4215 Parcel delivery, vehicular
HQ: United Parcel Service, Inc.
  55 Glenlake Pkwy
  Atlanta GA 30328
  404 828-6000

(P-7671)
UNITED PARCEL SERVICE INC
Also Called: UPS
2275 Sierra Meadows Dr, Rocklin (95677-2111)
PHONE...................916 632-4826
Kathy Scott, *President*
EMP: 152
SALES (corp-wide): 84.6B **Publicly Held**
WEB: www.ups.com
SIC: 4215 Parcel delivery, vehicular
HQ: United Parcel Service, Inc.
  55 Glenlake Pkwy
  Atlanta GA 30328
  404 828-6000

(P-7672)
UNITED PARCEL SERVICE INC
Also Called: UPS
251 Sylvania Ave, Santa Cruz (95060-2161)
PHONE...................831 425-1054
EMP: 152
SALES (corp-wide): 84.6B **Publicly Held**
WEB: www.ups.com
SIC: 4215 Parcel delivery, vehicular
HQ: United Parcel Service, Inc.
  55 Glenlake Pkwy
  Atlanta GA 30328
  404 828-6000

(P-7673)
UNITED PARCEL SERVICE INC
Also Called: UPS
4500 Norris Canyon Rd, San Ramon (94583-1369)
PHONE...................800 833-9943
EMP: 152
SALES (corp-wide): 84.6B **Publicly Held**
WEB: www.ups.com
SIC: 4215 Parcel delivery, vehicular
HQ: United Parcel Service, Inc.
  55 Glenlake Pkwy
  Atlanta GA 30328
  404 828-6000

(P-7674)
UNITED PARCEL SERVICE INC
Also Called: UPS
3930 Kristi Ct, Sacramento (95827-9716)
PHONE...................916 857-0311
EMP: 152
SALES (corp-wide): 84.6B **Publicly Held**
WEB: www.ups.com
SIC: 4215 Parcel delivery, vehicular
HQ: United Parcel Service, Inc.
  55 Glenlake Pkwy
  Atlanta GA 30328
  404 828-6000

(P-7675)
UNITY COURIER SERVICE INC
1132 Beecher St, San Leandro (94577-1252)
PHONE...................510 568-8890
Michael Wynant, *Branch Mgr*
EMP: 356
SALES (corp-wide): 44.9MM **Privately Held**
WEB: www.unitycourier.com
SIC: 4215 Package delivery, vehicular
PA: Unity Courier Service, Inc.
  3231 Fletcher Dr
  Los Angeles CA 90065
  323 255-9800

4221 Farm Product Warehousing & Storage

(P-7676)
RIVERSIDE LTD
Also Called: Riverside Elevators
14400 Andrus Island Rd, Isleton (95641-9804)
PHONE...................916 777-6076
Daniel Wilson, *Managing Prtnr*
Dixie Wilson, *Partner*
George C Wilson, *Partner*
EMP: 47 **EST:** 1983
SALES (est): 5.6MM **Privately Held**
WEB: www.ucr.edu
SIC: 4221 Grain elevator, storage only

4222 Refrigerated Warehousing & Storage

(P-7677)
CAL PACKING & STORAGE LP
Also Called: Bravante Produce
1356 S Buttonwillow Ave, Reedley (93654-9333)
PHONE...................559 638-2929
George Bravante, *Managing Prtnr*
Eric Coy, *Sales Staff*
Mike Keelin, *Sales Staff*
Mike Keeline, *Sales Staff*
Adriana Plascenci, *Sales Staff*
EMP: 70 **EST:** 2005
SQ FT: 100,000
SALES (est): 12.7MM **Privately Held**
WEB: www.bravanteproduce.com
SIC: 4222 7389 5148 Warehousing, cold storage or refrigerated; packaging & labeling services; fresh fruits & vegetables

(P-7678)
ECKERT COLD STORAGE COMPANY
757 Moffat Blvd, Manteca (95336-5819)
PHONE...................209 823-3181
Steve West, *Manager*
EMP: 200
SALES (corp-wide): 141.5MM **Privately Held**
WEB: www.eckertcs.com
SIC: 4222 2037 Storage, frozen or refrigerated goods; frozen fruits & vegetables
PA: Eckert Cold Storage Company
  905 Clough Rd
  Escalon CA 95320
  209 838-4040

PRODUCTS & SERVICES SECTION

4225 - General Warehousing & Storage County (P-7701)

(P-7679)
LINEAGE LOGISTICS HOLDINGS LLC
Also Called: M&L Refrigerated Terminal
2323 Port Road A, Stockton (95203-2918)
PHONE...................................209 942-2323
John Weihrouch, *Branch Mgr*
EMP: 70 Privately Held
WEB: www.lineagelogistics.com
SIC: 4222 Warehousing, cold storage or refrigerated
HQ: Lineage Logistics Holdings, Llc
46500 Humboldt Dr
Novi MI 48377
800 678-7271

(P-7680)
USKO EXPRESS INC
11290 Point East Dr # 200, Rancho Cordova (95742-6243)
PHONE...................................916 515-8065
Vladimir Skots, *President*
Maksim Andrianov, *Opers Staff*
Max Andrianov, *Opers Staff*
Ivan Kushnir, *Opers Staff*
Yaro Naumchuk, *Manager*
EMP: 90 EST: 2010
SALES (est): 21.5MM Privately Held
WEB: www.uskoinc.com
SIC: 4222 4221 Refrigerated warehouse & storage; farm product warehousing & storage

4225 General Warehousing & Storage

(P-7681)
BACO REALTY CORPORATION
2071 Camino Ramon, San Ramon (94583-1378)
PHONE...................................925 275-0100
George Bamburg, *Principal*
EMP: 85
SQ FT: 48,000
SALES (corp-wide): 43MM Privately Held
WEB: www.bacorealty.com
SIC: 4225 Warehousing, self-storage
PA: Baco Realty Corporation
51 Federal St Ste 202
San Francisco CA 94107
415 281-3700

(P-7682)
C&S WHOLESALE GROCERS INC
8301 Fruitridge Rd, Sacramento (95826-4806)
PHONE...................................916 383-5275
Ric Clark, *General Mgr*
Kristi Peredo, *Buyer*
Verseman Roger, *Merchandising*
Jeremy Cullifer, *Manager*
Kelly Weaver, *Manager*
EMP: 51
SALES (corp-wide): 5.9MM Privately Held
WEB: www.cswg.com
SIC: 4225 General warehousing
PA: C&S Wholesale Grocers, Inc.
7 Corporate Dr
Keene NH 03431
603 354-7000

(P-7683)
CASTLE DISTRIBUTION SVCS INC
16505 Avenue 24 1/2, Chowchilla (93610-9564)
P.O. Box 995 (93610-0995)
PHONE...................................559 665-3716
Toll Free:......................................888 -
Brenda Zubeck, *President*
H Ronald Child, *President*
Diane Child, *Vice Pres*
▲ **EMP:** 37 EST: 1983
SQ FT: 155,000
SALES (est): 1.2MM Privately Held
WEB: www.castledistribution.com
SIC: 4225 General warehousing

(P-7684)
CFR RINKENS LLC
Also Called: Cfr San Francisco
2875 Prune Ave, Fremont (94539-6731)
PHONE...................................310 297-8488
EMP: 36
SALES (corp-wide): 49.6MM Privately Held
WEB: www.cfrrinkens.com
SIC: 4225 Miniwarehouse, warehousing
PA: Cfr Rinkens, Llc
15501 Texaco Ave
Paramount CA 90723
310 639-7725

(P-7685)
CHARLES MATOIAN ENTPS INC (PA)
Also Called: OK Produce
1888 S East Ave, Fresno (93721-3231)
P.O. Box 12838 (93779-2838)
PHONE...................................559 445-8600
Matty Matoian, *President*
Angel Burnett, *Partner*
Chris Castro, *General Mgr*
Chad Matoian, *Purchasing*
Tim Monteath, *Buyer*
EMP: 196 EST: 1941
SQ FT: 70,000
SALES (est): 64.8MM Privately Held
WEB: www.okproduce.com
SIC: 4225 General warehousing; miniwarehouse, warehousing

(P-7686)
CJ LOGISTICS AMERICA LLC
1565 N Macarthur Dr, Tracy (95376-2846)
PHONE...................................209 362-2232
Bob Justice, *Manager*
Kent Sparks, *Opers Mgr*
Eloisa Rodriguez, *Clerk*
EMP: 90 Privately Held
WEB: www.america.cjlogistics.com
SIC: 4225 General warehousing & storage
HQ: Cj Logistics America, Llc
1750 S Wolf Rd
Des Plaines IL 60018

(P-7687)
CONTINENTAL TERMINALS INC ✪
300 Mitchell Ave, Alameda (94501-7885)
PHONE...................................510 746-1100
Dustin Weber, *Vice Pres*
EMP: 50 EST: 2021
SALES (est): 2.2MM Privately Held
WEB: www.annextryco.net
SIC: 4225 General warehousing

(P-7688)
COSTCO WHOLESALE CORPORATION
Also Called: Costco Depot 179
25501 S Gateway Blvd, Tracy (95377-8631)
PHONE...................................209 835-5222
EMP: 300
SALES (corp-wide): 166.7B Publicly Held
SIC: 4225 Distribution Center
PA: Costco Wholesale Corporation
999 Lake Dr Ste 200
Issaquah WA 98027
425 313-8100

(P-7689)
G3 ENTERPRISES INC (PA)
502 E Whitmore Ave, Modesto (95358-9411)
P.O. Box 624 (95353-0624)
PHONE...................................209 341-7515
Robert Lubeck, *President*
Michael Ellis, *CFO*
Thomas Gallo, *Vice Pres*
Taran Hay, *Vice Pres*
John Cunningham, *Executive*
▲ **EMP:** 160 EST: 1961
SQ FT: 10,000
SALES (est): 116.5MM Privately Held
WEB: www.g3enterprises.com
SIC: 4225 General warehousing & storage

(P-7690)
G3 ENTERPRISES INC
Also Called: Delaware G3 Enterprises
4995 Hillsdale Cir, El Dorado Hills (95762-5707)
PHONE...................................209 341-8670
EMP: 35
SALES (corp-wide): 116.5MM Privately Held
WEB: www.g3enterprises.com
SIC: 4225 General warehousing & storage
PA: G3 Enterprises, Inc.
502 E Whitmore Ave
Modesto CA 95358
209 341-7515

(P-7691)
GENESIS LOGISTICS INC
4013 Whipple Rd, Union City (94587-1521)
PHONE...................................510 476-0790
Scott Mullins, *General Mgr*
Aran Kahn, *Executive*
EMP: 39 EST: 2001
SQ FT: 37,000
SALES (est): 3.4MM
SALES (corp-wide): 79B Privately Held
WEB: www.onestoporderform.com
SIC: 4225 General warehousing & storage
HQ: Exel Inc.
360 Westar Blvd
Westerville OH 43082
614 865-8500

(P-7692)
KANDY INVESTMENTS LLC
Also Called: Storage Masters Self Storage
3205 Dutton Ave, Santa Rosa (95407-7891)
PHONE...................................707 584-8363
Jeffrey Sommers,
Robert Oates, *General Ptnr*
Cynthia Oates, *Ltd Ptnr*
Karen Sommers, *Principal*
EMP: 37 EST: 1999
SALES (est): 1.6MM Privately Held
WEB: www.storagemastersr.com
SIC: 4225 General warehousing; warehousing, self-storage

(P-7693)
LONGS DRUG STORES CAL LLC
2400 Keystone Pcf Pkwy, Patterson (95363-8866)
PHONE...................................209 895-7839
Stephen McCormick, *Manager*
EMP: 139
SALES (corp-wide): 268.7B Publicly Held
WEB: www.cvs.com
SIC: 4225 General warehousing & storage
HQ: Longs Drug Stores California L.L.C.
1 Cvs Dr
Woonsocket RI 02895

(P-7694)
MAXAR SPACE LLC
1140 Hamilton Ct, Menlo Park (94025-1425)
PHONE...................................650 852-4000
Pat Downey, *Branch Mgr*
EMP: 518
SALES (corp-wide): 1.7B Publicly Held
WEB: www.maxar.com
SIC: 4225 General warehousing
HQ: Maxar Space Llc
3825 Fabian Way
Palo Alto CA 94303
650 852-4000

(P-7695)
NATIONAL DISTRIBUTION AGCY INC (HQ)
Also Called: Pacific Coast Warehouse Co
7025 Central Ave, Newark (94560-4201)
PHONE...................................510 487-6226
Sheryl Sadler, *President*
▲ **EMP:** 62 EST: 1982
SQ FT: 305,000
SALES (est): 5.1MM
SALES (corp-wide): 15.8MM Privately Held
SIC: 4225 General warehousing

PA: Public Investment Corporation
1207 W Magnolia Blvd C
Burbank CA 91506
310 451-5227

(P-7696)
NORTH BAY DISTRIBUTION INC (PA)
2050 Cessna Dr, Vacaville (95688-8712)
PHONE...................................707 452-9984
Lee Perry, *President*
Riza Suma, *Vice Pres*
Ethel Arhin, *Admin Asst*
Ray George, *Administration*
Elena Salinas, *Human Resources*
EMP: 100 EST: 1997
SQ FT: 220,000
SALES (est): 40MM Privately Held
WEB: www.nbd3pl.com
SIC: 4225 General warehousing

(P-7697)
ONFULFILLMENT INC
8678 Thornton Ave, Newark (94560-3330)
PHONE...................................510 793-3009
Steve Friar, *President*
Claude Poirier, *Senior VP*
Daniel Barnett, *Vice Pres*
Charlie Pugh, *Planning*
Steve Elliott, *Technology*
▲ **EMP:** 38 EST: 1999
SQ FT: 100,000 Privately Held
WEB: www.onfulfillment.com
SIC: 4225 General warehousing

(P-7698)
PACIFIC SOUTHWEST CONT LLC
568 S Riverside Dr, Modesto (95354-4009)
PHONE...................................209 526-0444
EMP: 35
SALES (corp-wide): 143.5MM Privately Held
WEB: www.teampsc.com
SIC: 4225 General warehousing
PA: Pacific Southwest Container, Llc
4530 Leckron Rd
Modesto CA 95357
209 526-0444

(P-7699)
PDC LOGISTICS INC (PA)
6383 Las Positas Rd, Livermore (94551-5103)
PHONE...................................925 583-0200
Joseph Palestro, *President*
Catherine Palestro, *VP Admin*
Zech Van Puffelen, *CTO*
▲ **EMP:** 45 EST: 1981
SQ FT: 206,000
SALES (est): 6.9MM Privately Held
WEB: www.pdc-logistics.com
SIC: 4225 4214 General warehousing; local trucking with storage

(P-7700)
RAS MANAGEMENT INC (PA)
Also Called: Aaaaa Rent-A-Space
4545 Crow Canyon Pl, Castro Valley (94552-4803)
P.O. Box 20385 (94546-8385)
PHONE...................................510 727-1800
H James Knuppe, *President*
Barbara Knuppe, *Corp Secy*
David O' Brien, *Manager*
EMP: 50 EST: 1989
SQ FT: 6,000
SALES (est): 14.5MM Privately Held
SIC: 4225 Warehousing, self-storage

(P-7701)
REVANCE THERAPEUTICS INC
Rm 144 Mffett Blvd Bldg 2, Moffett Field (94035)
PHONE...................................510 742-3400
Mark Foley, *CEO*
EMP: 65
SALES (corp-wide): 15.3MM Publicly Held
WEB: www.revance.com
SIC: 4225 General warehousing & storage
PA: Revance Therapeutics, Inc.
1222 Demonbreun St # 1001
Nashville TN 37203
615 724-7755

4225 - General Warehousing & Storage County (P-7702)

PRODUCTS & SERVICES SECTION

(P-7702)
RUSH ORDER INC (PA)
6600 Silacci Way, Gilroy (95020-7019)
PHONE..............................408 848-3525
James Chapman, *President*
Doris Kanemura, *Vice Pres*
Jennifer Casey, *Project Mgr*
Jj Alcantar, *Business Mgr*
Tim Gallardo, *Sr Project Mgr*
▲ **EMP:** 40 **EST:** 1991
SQ FT: 50,000
SALES (est): 15.7MM **Privately Held**
WEB: www.rushorder.com
SIC: 4225 General warehousing & storage

(P-7703)
UNITED NATURAL FOODS WEST INC (HQ)
Also Called: Unfi
1101 Sunset Blvd, Rocklin (95765-3786)
PHONE..............................916 625-4100
Kurt M Luttecke, *CEO*
Michael S Funk, *Ch of Bd*
Steven L Spinner, *President*
Eric A Dorne, *Senior VP*
Sean F Griffin, *Vice Pres*
▲ **EMP:** 385 **EST:** 1976
SQ FT: 150,000
SALES (est): 207.8MM **Publicly Held**
WEB: www.west.unfi.com
SIC: 4225 5141 General warehousing & storage; groceries, general line

(P-7704)
UNIVERSITY CAL SAN FRANCISCO
Materiel Management
616 Forbes Blvd, South San Francisco (94080-2009)
PHONE..............................510 987-0700
Diana Hopper, *Principal*
EMP: 51 **Privately Held**
WEB: www.ucsf.edu
SIC: 4225 8221 9411 General warehousing & storage; university; administration of educational programs
HQ: University Cal San Francisco
513 Parnassus Ave 115f
San Francisco CA 94143

(P-7705)
WESTERN WINE SERVICES INC (PA)
880 Hanna Dr, American Canyon (94503-9605)
PHONE..............................800 999-8463
Michael W Hodes, *President*
Bruce Cohen, *Senior VP*
Marc Cohen, *Vice Pres*
Tad Franzman, *Vice Pres*
▲ **EMP:** 99 **EST:** 1988
SALES (est): 28.2MM **Privately Held**
WEB: www.westerncarriers.com
SIC: 4225 General warehousing & storage

(P-7706)
WORLD CLASS DISTRIBUTION INC
2121 Boeing Way, Stockton (95206-4934)
PHONE..............................909 574-4140
Michael Campbell, *Principal*
EMP: 68
SALES (corp-wide): 355.8K **Privately Held**
SIC: 4225 General warehousing & storage
HQ: World Class Distribution Inc.
10288 Calabash Ave
Fontana CA 92335

4226 Special Warehousing & Storage, NEC

(P-7707)
DATASAFE INC (PA)
2237 Palou Ave, San Francisco (94124-1504)
P.O. Box 7794 (94120-7794)
PHONE..............................650 875-3800
Robert S Reis, *Ch of Bd*
Thomas S Reis, *CEO*
Rob Reis, *COO*
Ronald P Reis, *Vice Pres*
Arnold Cabrera, *Administration*
EMP: 50 **EST:** 1898
SALES (est): 10.8MM **Privately Held**
WEB: www.datasafe.com
SIC: 4226 Document & office records storage

(P-7708)
GRM INFORMATION MGT SVCS INC (PA)
Also Called: Guarantee Records Management
41099 Boyce Rd, Fremont (94538-2434)
PHONE..............................201 798-7100
Jerry Glatt, *President*
Moishe Mana, *CEO*
Amyn Maskati, *CFO*
Mario Amato, *Vice Pres*
Tod Olsen, *Vice Pres*
EMP: 300 **EST:** 1988
SQ FT: 1,000,000
SALES (est): 102MM **Privately Held**
WEB: www.grmdocumentmanagement.com
SIC: 4226 7389 Document & office records storage; document storage service

(P-7709)
PRIDE INDUSTRIES (PA)
10030 Foothills Blvd, Roseville (95747-7102)
P.O. Box 1200, Rocklin (95677-7200)
PHONE..............................916 788-2100
Jeffery Dern, *President*
Bob Olsen, *Ch of Bd*
Peter Berghuis, *COO*
Casey Blake, *COO*
Leslie King, *COO*
▲ **EMP:** 250 **EST:** 1966
SQ FT: 177,000
SALES (est): 232.7MM **Privately Held**
WEB: www.prideindustries.com
SIC: 4226 7349 3679 Special warehousing & storage; building maintenance services; electronic circuits

4231 Terminal & Joint Terminal Maint Facilities

(P-7710)
PS BAJWA INC
5400 W Highway 12, Lodi (95242-9170)
PHONE..............................209 334-2011
EMP: 40
SALES: 3.5MM **Privately Held**
SIC: 4231 Truck Terminal Facility

4412 Deep Sea Foreign Transportation Of Freight

(P-7711)
PATRIOT CONTRACT SERVICES LLC
Also Called: P C S
1320 Willow Pass Rd # 485, Concord (94520-7940)
PHONE..............................925 296-2000
Jordan Truchan, *CEO*
Judy Collins, *CFO*
Frank Angelacci, *Vice Pres*
Timothy M Gill,
EMP: 400 **EST:** 1997
SQ FT: 7,500
SALES (est): 23.6MM **Privately Held**
WEB: www.patriotships.com
SIC: 4412 4424 4449 4481 Deep sea foreign transportation of freight; deep sea domestic transportation of freight; canal & intracoastal freight transportation; deep sea passenger transportation, except ferry; marine surveyors

4424 Deep Sea Domestic Transportation Of Freight

(P-7712)
MATSON NAVIGATION COMPANY
1710 Springwood Dr, Modesto (95350-3875)
PHONE..............................209 577-1081
EMP: 49
SALES (corp-wide): 1.8B **Publicly Held**
SIC: 4424 Domestic Sea Freight Transportation
HQ: Matson Navigation Company, Inc.
555 12th St
Oakland CA 94607
510 628-4000

(P-7713)
MATSON NAVIGATION COMPANY INC (HQ)
555 12th St Fl 7, Oakland (94607-4046)
PHONE..............................510 628-4000
Matthew J Cox, *Ch of Bd*
Ronald J Forest, *President*
Joel M Wine, *CFO*
Ben Bowler, *Treasurer*
John P Lauer, *Ch Credit Ofcr*
◆ **EMP:** 200 **EST:** 1882
SQ FT: 105,000
SALES (est): 1.6B
SALES (corp-wide): 2.3B **Publicly Held**
WEB: www.matson.com
SIC: 4424 4491 4492 Deep sea domestic transportation of freight; marine cargo handling; tugboat service
PA: Matson, Inc.
1411 Sand Island Pkwy
Honolulu HI 96819
808 848-1211

(P-7714)
PASHA HAWAII TRNSPT LINES LLC
1425 Maritime St, Oakland (94607-1022)
PHONE..............................510 271-1400
Mary Brown, *Office Mgr*
EMP: 100
SALES (corp-wide): 30.3MM **Privately Held**
WEB: www.pashagroup.com
SIC: 4424 4783 Deep sea domestic transportation of freight; containerization of goods for shipping
PA: Pasha Hawaii Transport Lines Llc
4040 Civic Center Dr # 350
San Rafael CA 94903
415 927-6400

4449 Water Transportation Of Freight, NEC

(P-7715)
CHEEMA LOGISTICS
968 Sierra St Ste 130, Kingsburg (93631-1554)
PHONE..............................559 702-1444
Parminder Singh, *President*
EMP: 65 **EST:** 2014
SALES (est): 1.9MM **Privately Held**
SIC: 4449 Intracoastal (freight) transportation

(P-7716)
DEVINE & SON TRUCKING CO INC (PA)
Also Called: Devine Intermodal
3870 Channel Dr, West Sacramento (95691-3466)
P.O. Box 980160 (95798-0160)
PHONE..............................559 486-7440
John Frederick Drewes, *CEO*
Richard Coyle, *President*
Amanda Nichols, *Vice Pres*
EMP: 200
SQ FT: 6,000
SALES (est): 28.3MM **Privately Held**
WEB: www.devineintermodal.com
SIC: 4449 4213 Canal & intracoastal freight transportation; trucking, except local

4482 Ferries

(P-7717)
BAY MARITIME CORP (PA)
Also Called: Bay Ship & Yacht
2900 Main St Ste 2100, Alameda (94501-7739)
PHONE..............................510 337-9122
Joel Welter, *CIO*
Richard Neuman, *Sr Project Mgr*
David Ashton, *Manager*
EMP: 21 **EST:** 2011
SALES (est): 23.4MM **Privately Held**
WEB: www.bay-ship.com
SIC: 4482 8711 7699 7539 Ferries; engineering services; hydraulic equipment repair; machine shop, automotive; welding repair; paint shop, automotive

4489 Water Transport Of Passengers, NEC

(P-7718)
BLUE AND GOLD FLEET
Also Called: Pier Restaurant
Marine Terminal Pier 41 St Pier, San Francisco (94133)
PHONE..............................415 705-8200
Ron Duckhorn, *Owner*
Patrick Murphy, *President*
Molly South, *Treasurer*
Kent McGrath, *Vice Pres*
Robert Moore, *Admin Sec*
▲ **EMP:** 70 **EST:** 1979
SALES (est): 14MM
SALES (corp-wide): 40MM **Privately Held**
WEB: www.blueandgoldfleet.com
SIC: 4489 4724 Excursion boat operators; travel agencies
PA: Pier 39 Limited Partnership
Beach Embarcadero Level 3
San Francisco CA 94133
415 705-5500

(P-7719)
COMMODORE DINING CRUISES INC
Mainers Sq, Alameda (94501)
PHONE..............................510 337-9000
Jewell Chung, *Sales Staff*
Victoria Sablan, *Sales Staff*
EMP: 95
SALES (corp-wide): 5.9MM **Privately Held**
WEB: www.commodoreevents.com
SIC: 4489 Excursion boat operators
PA: Commodore Dining Cruises Inc
2394 Mariner Square Dr A
Alameda CA 94501
510 337-9000

(P-7720)
GOLDEN GATE SCNIC STMSHIP CORP
Also Called: Red and White Fleet
Shed C Pier 45 St Pier, San Francisco (94133)
PHONE..............................415 901-5249
Thomas E Escher, *President*
Jeffrey Unverferth, *Human Res Mgr*
EMP: 50 **EST:** 1997
SALES (est): 10MM **Privately Held**
SIC: 4489 4482 Sightseeing boats; ferries

(P-7721)
HORNBLOWER YACHTS LLC
200 Marina Blvd, Berkeley (94710-1608)
PHONE..............................916 446-1185
Daniel Montoya, *Manager*
Linda Beimfohr, *Vice Pres*
Rob Dallisson, *Engineer*
Chris Gallup, *Opers Staff*
Shay Rosner, *Marketing Staff*
EMP: 55
SALES (corp-wide): 536MM **Privately Held**
WEB: www.hornblower.com
SIC: 4489 Excursion boat operators

▲ = Import ▼ = Export
◆ = Import/Export

PRODUCTS & SERVICES SECTION

4512 - Air Transportation, Scheduled County (P-7744)

PA: Hornblower Yachts, Llc
On The Embarcadero Pier 3 St Pier
San Francisco CA 94111
415 788-8866

4491 Marine Cargo Handling

(P-7722)
LEVIN-RICHMOND TERMINAL CORP
402 Wright Ave, Richmond (94804-3532)
PHONE.................................510 232-4422
Gary Levin, *President*
Sylvia San Andres, *Admin Asst*
Nenita Magpayo, *Accountant*
Pat O'Driscoll, *Opers Mgr*
Joe Rotter, *Opers Mgr*
EMP: 47 **EST:** 1981
SALES (est): 14.6MM
SALES (corp-wide): 16.4MM **Privately Held**
SIC: 4491 Marine cargo handling
PA: Levin Enterprises Inc
112 Wshington Ave Ste 250
Richmond CA 94801
510 215-1515

(P-7723)
MTC HOLDINGS (DH)
3 Embarcadero Ctr Ste 550, San Francisco (94111-4048)
PHONE.................................912 651-4000
Michael Hassing, *President*
Gail Parris, *CFO*
Christopher Redlich Jr, *Chairman*
EMP: 50 **EST:** 2000
SALES (est): 88.1MM **Privately Held**
WEB: www.portsamerica.com
SIC: 4491 Stevedoring; marine terminals; loading vessels; unloading vessels
HQ: Ports America, Inc.
525 Wshngton Blvd Ste 166
Jersey City NJ 07310
732 635-3899

(P-7724)
PORT DEPT CITY OF OAKLAND (PA)
Also Called: Port of Oakland
530 Water St Fl 3, Oakland (94607-3525)
P.O. Box 2064 (94604-2064)
PHONE.................................510 627-1100
Veteran Chris Lytle, *Exec Dir*
Laurice Henry-Ross, *President*
Julie Lam, *CFO*
Sara Lee, *CFO*
Donna Cason, *Officer*
EMP: 350 **EST:** 1927
SQ FT: 285,600
SALES (est): 196.2MM **Privately Held**
WEB: www.portofoakland.com
SIC: 4491 4581 Marine cargo handling; airport leasing, if operating airport

(P-7725)
SACRAMNT-YOLO PORT DST FING CO
Also Called: Port of Sacramento
1110 W Capitol Ave, West Sacramento (95691-2717)
PHONE.................................916 371-8000
Mike Luken, *Principal*
Polly Harris, *Admin Sec*
EMP: 53 **EST:** 1963
SALES (est): 1MM **Privately Held**
WEB: www.cityofwestsacramento.org
SIC: 4491 Marine terminals

(P-7726)
STOCKTON PORT DISTRICT
Also Called: PORT OF STOCKTON
2201 W Washington St # 13, Stockton (95203-2991)
P.O. Box 2089 (95201-2089)
PHONE.................................209 946-0246
Richard Aschieris, *Director*
Juan Villanueva, *Admin Asst*
Jim Cooper, *Info Tech Mgr*
Davin Garcia, *Technology*
Tricia Rosenow, *Technology*
EMP: 100
SQ FT: 18,000

SALES: 55MM **Privately Held**
WEB: www.portofstockton.com
SIC: 4491 4225 Waterfront terminal operation; warehousing, self-storage

4492 Towing & Tugboat Svcs

(P-7727)
CROSS LINK INC
Also Called: Westar Marine Services
50 Pier Bldg C, San Francisco (94158-2193)
P.O. Box 78100 (94107-8100)
PHONE.................................415 495-3191
Mary C McMillan, *CEO*
Wendy Heffron-Morrow, *Vice Pres*
▲ **EMP:** 65 **EST:** 1975
SQ FT: 16,000
SALES (est): 11.6MM **Privately Held**
WEB: www.westarmarineservices.com
SIC: 4492 Marine towing services

4493 Marinas

(P-7728)
DELTA MARINA YACHT HARBOR
100 Marina Dr, Rio Vista (94571-2098)
PHONE.................................707 374-2315
Richard H Baumann, *President*
James Baumann, *Vice Pres*
EMP: 35 **EST:** 1959
SQ FT: 2,500
SALES (est): 1.4MM **Privately Held**
WEB: www.deltamarina.com
SIC: 4493 5551 7033 Boat yards, storage & incidental repair; marine supplies; recreational vehicle parks

(P-7729)
HOLIDAY HARBOR INC (PA)
20061 Shasta Caverns Rd, Lakehead (96051-9642)
PHONE.................................530 238-2383
Stephen C Barry, *President*
EMP: 49 **EST:** 1965
SQ FT: 10,000
SALES (est): 5.9MM **Privately Held**
WEB: www.lakeshasta.com
SIC: 4493 Marinas

(P-7730)
HUMBOLDT BAY HBR RCRTION CNSRV
Also Called: Humboldt Bay Harbor, The
601 Startare Dr, Eureka (95501-0765)
P.O. Box 1030 (95502-1030)
PHONE.................................707 443-0801
David Hull, *CEO*
Larry Oetker, *Exec Dir*
Roy Curless, *Commissioner*
Larry Doss, *Commissioner*
Ronald Fritzsche, *Commissioner*
EMP: 62 **EST:** 1973
SALES (est): 6.4MM **Privately Held**
WEB: www.humboldtbay.org
SIC: 4493 Boat yards, storage & incidental repair

(P-7731)
KEN & LAURA SCHEIDEGGER
Also Called: Delta Boatworks
106 W Brannan Island Rd, Isleton (95641-9760)
PHONE.................................916 777-6462
Kenneth Scheidegger, *Owner*
Elvera Scheidegger, *Co-Owner*
EMP: 24 **EST:** 1966
SQ FT: 3,750
SALES (est): 1.1MM **Privately Held**
WEB: www.deltaboatworks.com
SIC: 4493 3732 5812 Boat yards, storage & incidental repair; boat building & repairing; eating places

(P-7732)
SAN MATEO COUNTY HARBOR DST
504 Avenue Alhambra Fl 2, El Granada (94018-8133)
P.O. Box 1449 (94018-1449)
PHONE.................................650 583-4400
Steve McGrath, *General Mgr*
EMP: 35 **EST:** 2010

SALES (est): 2.8MM **Privately Held**
WEB: www.smharbor.com
SIC: 4493 Marinas

(P-7733)
ST FRANCIS MARINE CENTER INC
Also Called: Ramp Restaurant, The
835 Terry A Francois Blvd, San Francisco (94158-2209)
PHONE.................................415 621-2876
Michael R Denman, *CEO*
Arvind Patel, *Vice Pres*
Joan Robins, *General Mgr*
Richard Chang, *Controller*
Arlene Deguzman, *Controller*
EMP: 47 **EST:** 1984
SQ FT: 7,000
SALES (est): 6.3MM **Privately Held**
WEB: www.sfboatworks.com
SIC: 5812 4493 3732 7699 American restaurant; boat yards, storage & incidental repair; boat building & repairing; boat repair; outboard motors; marine crafts & supplies

4499 Water Transportation Svcs, NEC

(P-7734)
ANGEL ISLAND-TIBURON FERRY INC
21 Main St, Belvedere Tiburon (94920-2533)
P.O. Box 1231 (94920-4231)
PHONE.................................415 435-2131
Margaret McDonogh, *President*
Ashley Kristensen, *Director*
EMP: 44 **EST:** 1998
SALES (est): 6.1MM **Privately Held**
WEB: www.angelislandferry.com
SIC: 4499 4482 Chartering of commercial boats; ferries

(P-7735)
MATSON ALASKA INC
555 12th St Ste 700, Oakland (94607-3652)
PHONE.................................704 973-7000
EMP: 40 **EST:** 2019
SALES (est): 961.5K
SALES (corp-wide): 2.3B **Publicly Held**
WEB: www.matson.com
SIC: 4499 Water transportation cleaning services
PA: Matson, Inc.
1411 Sand Island Pkwy
Honolulu HI 96819
808 848-1211

(P-7736)
MATSON NAVIGATION CO ALSK LLC
555 12th St Ste 700, Oakland (94607-3652)
P.O. Box 30170, College Station TX (77842-3170)
PHONE.................................510 628-4000
EMP: 85 **EST:** 2001
SALES (est): 1.7MM
SALES (corp-wide): 2.3B **Publicly Held**
WEB: www.matson.com
SIC: 4499 4491 5551 Water transportation services; marine terminals; marine supplies
PA: Matson, Inc.
1411 Sand Island Pkwy
Honolulu HI 96819
808 848-1211

4512 Air Transportation, Scheduled

(P-7737)
AMERIFLIGHT LLC
21889 Skywest Dr, Hayward (94541-7021)
PHONE.................................510 569-6000
EMP: 57
SALES (corp-wide): 183.1MM **Privately Held**
SIC: 4512 Scheduled Air Transportation

PA: Ameriflight, Llc
4700 W Empire Ave
Burbank CA 75261
818 847-0000

(P-7738)
CALIFORNIA SIERRA EXPRESS INC
1842 G St, Fresno (93725)
PHONE.................................559 441-1300
Jeff Phillips, *Vice Pres*
Isaias Martinez, *Opers Mgr*
EMP: 39 **Privately Held**
WEB: www.calsierraexpress.info
SIC: 4512 Air cargo carrier, scheduled
PA: California Sierra Express, Inc.
4965 Joule St
Reno NV 89502

(P-7739)
PIEDMONT AIRLINES INC
Also Called: American Airlines/Eagle
5175 E Clinton Way, Fresno (93727-2086)
PHONE.................................559 269-5694
Pete Ellgrande, *Manager*
EMP: 170
SALES (corp-wide): 17.3B **Publicly Held**
WEB: www.piedmont-airlines.com
SIC: 4512 Air passenger carrier, scheduled
HQ: Piedmont Airlines, Inc.
5443 Airport Terminal Rd
Salisbury MD 21804
410 572-5100

(P-7740)
SKYWEST AIRLINES INC
Also Called: Baggage & Air Freight Service
Fresno Air Terminal, Fresno (93727)
PHONE.................................559 252-3400
Renae Kramer, *Branch Mgr*
EMP: 351
SALES (corp-wide): 2.1B **Publicly Held**
WEB: www.skywest.com
SIC: 4512 Air passenger carrier, scheduled
HQ: Skywest Airlines, Inc.
444 S River Rd
St George UT 84790
435 634-3000

(P-7741)
UNITED PARCEL SERVICE INC
Also Called: UPS
26557 Danti Ct Fl 1, Hayward (94545-3917)
PHONE.................................510 264-8880
Mel Valencia, *Admin Sec*
EMP: 76
SALES (corp-wide): 84.6B **Publicly Held**
WEB: www.ups.com
SIC: 4512 Air cargo carrier, scheduled
HQ: United Parcel Service, Inc.
55 Glenlake Pkwy
Atlanta GA 30328
404 828-6000

(P-7742)
UNITED PARCEL SERVICE INC
Also Called: UPS
10295 Truemper Way, Mather (95655-4003)
PHONE.................................916 231-0814
EMP: 76
SALES (corp-wide): 84.6B **Publicly Held**
WEB: www.ups.com
SIC: 4512 Air cargo carrier, scheduled
HQ: United Parcel Service, Inc.
55 Glenlake Pkwy
Atlanta GA 30328
404 828-6000

(P-7743)
VIRGIN AMERICA CRISIS FUND (PA)
555 Airport Blvd, Burlingame (94010-2000)
PHONE.................................650 762-7000
Matthew Larson, *Principal*
EMP: 48 **EST:** 2011
SALES (est): 87.5K **Privately Held**
SIC: 4512 Air transportation, scheduled

(P-7744)
VIRGIN AMERICA INC (HQ)
555 Airport Blvd, Burlingame (94010-2000)
PHONE.................................877 359-8474
Benito Minicucci, *CEO*

4513 - Air Courier Svcs County (P-7745)

Donald J Carty, *Ch of Bd*
Michele O'Connor, *CEO*
Stephen A Forte, *COO*
Peter D Hunt, *CFO*
EMP: 2964 **EST:** 2004
SQ FT: 85,674
SALES (est): 249.6MM
SALES (corp-wide): 3.5B **Publicly Held**
WEB: www.alaskaair.com
SIC: 4512 Air passenger carrier, scheduled
PA: Alaska Air Group, Inc
19300 International Blvd
Seatac WA 98188
206 392-5040

4513 Air Courier Svcs

(P-7745)
DHL EXPRESS (USA) INC
401 23rd St, San Francisco (94107-3102)
PHONE..................................415 826-7338
Jeffrey Funk, *Manager*
Troy Kozie, *Executive*
Cynthia Clark, *Sales Staff*
Barry Lopiccolo, *Manager*
James Sun, *Representative*
EMP: 70
SALES (corp-wide): 79B **Privately Held**
WEB: www.dhl-usa.com
SIC: 4513 Air courier services
HQ: Dhl Express (Usa), Inc.
16592 Collections Ctr Dr
Chicago IL 60693
954 888-7000

(P-7746)
FEDERAL EXPRESS CORPORATION
Also Called: Fedex
3541 Regional Pkwy, Petaluma (94954)
PHONE..................................800 463-3339
EMP: 80
SALES (corp-wide): 47.4B **Publicly Held**
SIC: 4513 Air Courier Services
HQ: Federal Express Corporation
3610 Hacks Cross Rd
Memphis TN 38125
901 369-3600

(P-7747)
FEDERAL EXPRESS CORPORATION
Also Called: Fedex
1601 Aurora Dr, San Leandro (94577-3101)
PHONE..................................510 347-2430
EMP: 130
SALES (corp-wide): 47.4B **Publicly Held**
SIC: 4513 4215 Air Courier Services
Courier Service
HQ: Federal Express Corporation
3610 Hacks Cross Rd
Memphis TN 38125
901 369-3600

(P-7748)
FEDERAL EXPRESS CORPORATION
Also Called: Fedex
500 10th St Ste 139, Oakland (94607-4010)
PHONE..................................510 465-5209
EMP: 107
SALES (corp-wide): 47.4B **Publicly Held**
SIC: 4513 Air Courier Services
HQ: Federal Express Corporation
3610 Hacks Cross Rd
Memphis TN 38125
901 369-3600

(P-7749)
FEDERAL EXPRESS CORPORATION
Also Called: Fedex
8950 Cal Center Dr # 370, Sacramento (95826-3262)
PHONE..................................916 361-5500
EMP: 100
SALES (corp-wide): 47.4B **Publicly Held**
SIC: 4513 4512 4212 4213 Air & Surface Courier Services

HQ: Federal Express Corporation
3610 Hacks Cross Rd
Memphis TN 38125
901 369-3600

(P-7750)
LBC MUNDIAL CORPORATION (DH)
Also Called: LBC North America
3563 Inv Blvd Ste 3, Hayward (94545)
PHONE..................................650 873-0750
Miguel Angel Camahort, *President*
Fely Ruiz, *Treasurer*
Patricia Garcia, *Advt Staff*
James Taylor, *Warehouse Mgr*
EMP: 60 **EST:** 1985
SQ FT: 25,000
SALES (est): 49.4MM **Privately Held**
WEB: www.lbcexpressholdings.com
SIC: 4513 4215 6099 6221 Air courier services; courier services, except by air; foreign currency exchange; commodity contracts brokers, dealers

(P-7751)
ULTRAEX INC
2633 Barrington Ct, Hayward (94545-1100)
PHONE..................................800 882-1000
Ernest Holbrook, *President*
Shirley Sun, *Technology*
Alejandra Flores-Campos, *Supervisor*
EMP: 35 **EST:** 1983
SQ FT: 10,000
SALES (est): 1.1MM **Privately Held**
WEB: www.ultraex.com
SIC: 4513 4214 4215 Air courier services; local trucking with storage; package delivery, vehicular

(P-7752)
WEST AIR INC
5005 E Andersen Ave, Fresno (93727-1502)
PHONE..................................559 454-7843
Lawrence W Olson, *Ch of Bd*
Timothy Flynn, *Shareholder*
Maurice Gallagher, *Shareholder*
Beth Wood, *President*
David Agbisit, *Manager*
EMP: 70 **EST:** 1940
SQ FT: 10,000
SALES (est): 7.5MM **Privately Held**
WEB: www.westair.net
SIC: 4513 Package delivery, private air

(P-7753)
WING AVIATION LLC
1600 Amphitheatre Pkwy, Mountain View (94043-1351)
PHONE..................................650 224-1198
James Burgess, *CEO*
EMP: 120
SALES (est): 8.3MM **Privately Held**
SIC: 4513 Package delivery, private air

(P-7754)
WING AVIATION LLC
100 Mayfield Ave, Mountain View (94043-4122)
PHONE..................................650 260-8170
James Burgess, *CEO*
Adam Woodworth, *CTO*
Divya Chandra, *Controller*
EMP: 100 **EST:** 2017
SALES (est): 19.7MM
SALES (corp-wide): 182.5B **Publicly Held**
WEB: www.abc.xyz
SIC: 4513 Package delivery, private air
PA: Alphabet Inc.
1600 Amphitheatre Pkwy
Mountain View CA 94043
650 253-0000

4522 Air Transportation, Nonscheduled

(P-7755)
BOUTIQUE AIR INC (PA)
5 3rd St Ste 925, San Francisco (94103-3220)
PHONE..................................415 449-0505
Shawn Simpson, *President*
Brian Murphy, *COO*
Brian Kondrad, *Vice Pres*
Anastasiya Levchenko, *Project Mgr*
Matt Butcher, *Opers Staff*
EMP: 435 **EST:** 2007
SALES (est): 55.7MM **Privately Held**
WEB: www.boutiqueair.com
SIC: 4522 4512 Flying charter service; air passenger carrier, scheduled

(P-7756)
ELDORADO AIR LLC
Also Called: Axis Jet
6133 Freport Blvd Ste 300, Sacramento (95822)
PHONE..................................916 391-5000
Daniel Kimmel, *Principal*
Matthew Bosco, *Principal*
EMP: 52 **EST:** 2003
SALES (est): 1MM **Privately Held**
SIC: 4522 Air transportation, nonscheduled

(P-7757)
KAISERAIR INC (PA)
8735 Earhart Rd, Oakland (94621-4547)
P.O. Box 2626 (94614-0626)
PHONE..................................510 569-9622
Ronald J Guerra, *President*
Rob Guerra, *Senior VP*
Glenn Barrett, *Vice Pres*
David A Mancebo, *Vice Pres*
Gregg Rorabaugh, *Vice Pres*
EMP: 148 **EST:** 1979
SQ FT: 970,000
SALES (est): 16.8MM **Privately Held**
WEB: www.kaiserair.com
SIC: 4522 Flying charter service

(P-7758)
MODESTO EXECUTIVE A CHRTR INC
Also Called: Sky Trek Aviation
825 Airport Way, Modesto (95354-3929)
PHONE..................................209 577-4654
Walter J Van Heukelem, *President*
Barry Meuse, *CFO*
Pennie Weber, *Corp Secy*
John Rogers, *Vice Pres*
John Freitas, *Technician*
EMP: 73 **EST:** 1982
SQ FT: 100,000
SALES (est): 9.2MM **Privately Held**
WEB: www.skytrekaviation.com
SIC: 4522 4581 Air passenger carriers, nonscheduled; flying charter service; aircraft servicing & repairing

(P-7759)
REACH MEDICAL HOLDINGS LLC (PA)
2360 Becker Blvd, Santa Rosa (95403-8270)
PHONE..................................707 324-2400
Ken A Dilillo, *Officer*
Casey Ping, *Director*
EMP: 40 **EST:** 2007
SALES (est): 53.8MM **Privately Held**
WEB: www.reachair.com
SIC: 4522 Ambulance services, air

(P-7760)
ROGERS HELICOPTERS INC
5508 E Aircorp Way, Fresno (93727-1201)
PHONE..................................559 299-4903
Sandy Kilby, *General Mgr*
Brian Guenthart, *Opers Staff*
EMP: 88
SALES (corp-wide): 21.2MM **Privately Held**
WEB: www.rogershelicopters.com
SIC: 4522 Flying charter service
PA: Rogers Helicopters, Inc.
5484 E Perimeter Rd
Fresno CA 93727
559 299-4903

(P-7761)
SILLER HELICOPTERS INC
1250 Smith Rd, Yuba City (95991-6948)
PHONE..................................530 674-9460
Tom Siller, *President*
Jack Parnell, *Ch of Bd*
Andy Jansen, *Corp Secy*
Jim Anderson, *Opers Staff*
Hunt Norriss, *Director*
EMP: 40 **EST:** 2009
SALES (est): 3.2MM **Privately Held**
WEB: www.sillerhelicopters.com
SIC: 4522 7389 Helicopter carriers, nonscheduled; fire protection service other than forestry or public

4581 Airports, Flying Fields & Terminal Svcs

(P-7762)
ABM AVIATION INC
601 Gateway Blvd Ste 1145, South San Francisco (94080-7413)
PHONE..................................650 872-5400
Doug Kreuckamp, *Vice Pres*
EMP: 96
SALES (corp-wide): 5.9B **Publicly Held**
WEB: www.abm.com
SIC: 4581 Airport
HQ: Abm Aviation, Inc.
3399 Peachtree Rd Ne # 15
Atlanta GA 30326
404 926-4200

(P-7763)
AEROGROUND INC (DH)
Also Called: Air Cargo Handling Service
270 Lawrence Ave, South San Francisco (94080-6817)
PHONE..................................650 266-6965
Anthony Bonino, *CEO*
Dave Beekman, *Vice Pres*
Raymond Lo, *Managing Dir*
Sean McCool, *Regional Mgr*
AB El Akmadi, *General Mgr*
▲ **EMP:** 800 **EST:** 1989
SQ FT: 175,000
SALES (est): 67.2MM
SALES (corp-wide): 1.1B **Privately Held**
WEB: www.aeroground.com
SIC: 4581 4213 Air freight handling at airports; trucking, except local

(P-7764)
ALLIANCE GROUND INTL LLC
648 Rest Field Rd, San Francisco (94128)
PHONE..................................650 821-0855
Peter Ferrantelli, *General Mgr*
Jermaine Sanders, *General Mgr*
Juan Silva, *General Mgr*
Isaac Donkor, *Opers Mgr*
EMP: 167
SALES (corp-wide): 213.1MM **Privately Held**
WEB: www.allianceground.com
SIC: 4581 Airfreight loading & unloading services
PA: Alliance Ground International, Llc
9130 S Ddland Blvd Ste 18
Miami FL 33156
305 740-3252

(P-7765)
ALLIED AVIATION FUELING CO INC
7330 Earhart Dr, Sacramento (95837-1134)
PHONE..................................916 924-1002
Robert Rose, *President*
EMP: 53 **EST:** 1994
SALES (est): 1.4MM **Privately Held**
WEB: www.alliedaviation.com
SIC: 4581 Aircraft servicing & repairing

(P-7766)
ATLANTIC AVIATION SVC
1250 Aviation Ave Ste 235, San Jose (95110-1119)
PHONE..................................408 297-7552
Dan Ryan, *President*
Harold Deguzman, *CFO*
Jim Blair, *Treasurer*
Jim Rutherford, *Exec VP*
Barry Fernald, *Admin Sec*
EMP: 52 **EST:** 1984
SQ FT: 196,000
SALES (est): 1.5MM **Privately Held**
WEB: www.atlanticaviation.com
SIC: 4581 Aircraft maintenance & repair services; hangars & other aircraft storage facilities

PRODUCTS & SERVICES SECTION

4581 - Airports, Flying Fields & Terminal Svcs County (P-7788)

(P-7767)
CITY OF CHICO
Also Called: Chico Municipal Airport
150 Airpark Blvd Ste 20, Chico (95973-9095)
P.O. Box 3420 (95927-3420)
PHONE..................................530 896-7699
Robert Grierson, *Branch Mgr*
EMP: 77
SALES (corp-wide): 89.1MM **Privately Held**
WEB: www.chico.ca.us
SIC: **4581** Airport
PA: City Of Chico
    411 Main St Fl 1
    Chico CA 95928
    530 896-7200

(P-7768)
CITY OF HAYWARD
Also Called: Hayward Air Terminal
20301 Skywest Dr, Hayward (94541-4639)
PHONE..................................510 293-8678
Ross Dubarry, *Mng Member*
Douglas McNeeley, *Manager*
EMP: 46
SALES (corp-wide): 229.5MM **Privately Held**
WEB: www.hayward-ca.gov
SIC: **4581** 9111 Airport; mayors' offices
PA: City Of Hayward
    777 B St
    Hayward CA 94541
    510 583-4000

(P-7769)
CITY OF SAN JOSE
Also Called: Airport
801 N 1st St, San Jose (95110-1704)
PHONE..................................650 965-4156
Nina Grayson, *Principal*
Amy Jasinski, *Partner*
Martina Davis, *Officer*
Daniel Hall, *Officer*
Andrea Maestre, *Officer*
EMP: 80 EST: 2009
SALES (est): 3.7MM
SALES (corp-wide): 1.8B **Privately Held**
WEB: www.sanjoseca.gov
SIC: **4581** Airport
PA: City Of San Jose
    200 E Santa Clara St 13th
    San Jose CA 95113
    408 535-3500

(P-7770)
COUNTY OF HUMBOLDT
Humboldt County Aviation
3561 Boeing Ave, Eureka (95501)
PHONE..................................707 839-5402
Jacquelyn Hulsey, *Branch Mgr*
EMP: 49 **Privately Held**
WEB: www.humboldtgov.org
SIC: **4581** Airport
PA: County Of Humboldt
    825 5th St
    Eureka CA 95501
    707 268-2543

(P-7771)
COUNTY OF MENDOCINO
Also Called: Department of Transportation
340 Lake Mendocino Dr, Ukiah (95482-9432)
PHONE..................................707 463-4363
Howard Dashiell, *Branch Mgr*
Chamise Cubbison, *Info Tech Mgr*
Matt Kendall, *Sheriff*
Shannon Barney, *Director*
EMP: 42
SALES (corp-wide): 289.1MM **Privately Held**
WEB: www.mendocinocounty.org
SIC: **4581** Airport
PA: County Of Mendocino
    501 Low Gap Rd Rm 1010
    Ukiah CA 95482
    707 463-4441

(P-7772)
COUNTY OF SACRAMENTO
Also Called: Airports Dept
6900 Airport Blvd, Sacramento (95837-1109)
PHONE..................................916 874-0912
Hardy Acree, *Director*
Joe Luna, *Technology*
EMP: 98
SALES (corp-wide): 3.1B **Privately Held**
WEB: www.saccounty.net
SIC: **4581** 9621 Airport; aircraft regulating agencies;
PA: County Of Sacramento
    700 H St Ste 7650
    Sacramento CA 95814
    916 874-8515

(P-7773)
GAT - ARLN GROUND SUPPORT INC
6701 Lindbergh Dr, Sacramento (95837-1138)
PHONE..................................916 923-2349
Tina Stupa, *Admin Asst*
Brian Laliberte, *Manager*
EMP: 357 **Privately Held**
WEB: www.gatags.com
SIC: **4581** Aircraft maintenance & repair services; airfreight loading & unloading services
PA: Gat - Airline Ground Support, Inc.
    246 City Cir Ste 2000
    Peachtree City GA 30269

(P-7774)
KAISERAIR INC
Also Called: Santa Rosa Jet Center
2240 Airport Blvd, Santa Rosa (95403-1003)
PHONE..................................707 528-7400
Glenn Barrett, *Vice Pres*
Pamela Whitty, *President*
Davida Mancebo, *Vice Pres*
Jim Bolar, *Human Res Mgr*
Diane Hinds, *Human Resources*
EMP: 37
SALES (corp-wide): 16.8MM **Privately Held**
WEB: www.kaiserair.com
PA: Kaiserair, Inc.
    8735 Earhart Rd
    Oakland CA 94621
    510 569-9622

(P-7775)
MATHER AVIATION LLC (PA)
10360 Macready Ave, Mather (95655-4109)
PHONE..................................916 364-4711
Victor Cushing, *President*
Anita Cushing, *Vice Pres*
Candice Cushing, *Vice Pres*
Eric Negendank, *Info Tech Dir*
Quinten House, *Maintence Staff*
EMP: 45 EST: 1991
SQ FT: 95,000
SALES (est): 12.7MM **Privately Held**
WEB: www.matheraviation.com
SIC: **4581** 7699 Airport hangar rental; aircraft maintenance & repair services; aircraft & heavy equipment repair services

(P-7776)
MCCLELLAND AVIATION INC
Also Called: Aperture Aviation
2500 Robert Fowler Way, San Jose (95148-1004)
PHONE..................................408 258-4075
Michael McClelland, *Branch Mgr*
Evan Antolin, *Opers Mgr*
Jason Utpadel, *Prdtn Mgr*
EMP: 45
SALES (corp-wide): 561.2K **Privately Held**
SIC: **4581** Aircraft maintenance & repair services
PA: Mcclelland Aviation, Inc.
    2513 Cherry Ave
    San Jose CA 95125
    408 440-2378

(P-7777)
NAPA JET CENTER INC
Also Called: Bridgeford Flying Services
2030 Airport Rd, NAPA (94558-6208)
PHONE..................................707 224-0887
Andrew L Hoxsey, *Ch of Bd*
Harold Morrison, *President*
Larry Christensen, *CFO*
EMP: 54 EST: 1947
SQ FT: 15,000
SALES (est): 6.4MM **Privately Held**
WEB: www.napajetcenter.com
SIC: **4581** 4522 5172 Aircraft servicing & repairing; air passenger carriers, non-scheduled; aircraft fueling services

(P-7778)
PACIFIC AVIATION CORPORATION
P.O. Box 250758 (94125-0758)
PHONE..................................650 821-1190
Addie E Castillo, *Branch Mgr*
EMP: 193 **Privately Held**
WEB: www.pacificaviation.com
SIC: **4581** Airport
PA: Pacific Aviation Corporation
    201 Continental Blvd # 220
    El Segundo CA 90245

(P-7779)
PAUL LOEWEN
Also Called: Lasar
900f Sky Park Rd, Lakeport (95453-8748)
PHONE..................................707 263-0452
Paul Loewen, *Owner*
David Henneman, *Officer*
Robert Brown, *General Mgr*
EMP: 16 EST: 1976
SQ FT: 102,700
SALES (est): 2.2MM **Privately Held**
WEB: www.lasar.com
SIC: **4581** 3728 5599 Aircraft servicing & repairing; aircraft assemblies, subassemblies & parts; aircraft instruments, equipment or parts

(P-7780)
PORT DEPT CITY OF OAKLAND
9532 Earhart Rd Ste 205, Oakland (94621-4551)
PHONE..................................510 563-3697
Mike Mantino, *Manager*
EMP: 91
SALES (corp-wide): 196.2MM **Privately Held**
WEB: www.portofoakland.com
SIC: **4581** Airport terminal services
PA: Port Department Of The City Of Oakland
    530 Water St Fl 3
    Oakland CA 94607
    510 627-1100

(P-7781)
PORT DEPT OF THE CY OAKLAND
Also Called: Metropliatan Oakland Intl Arprt
1 Airport Dr Ste 45, Oakland (94621-1476)
PHONE..................................510 563-3300
Bill Wade, *Manager*
Gina Carradine, *Officer*
Mike Zampa, *Comms Dir*
Cheryl Ho, *Admin Sec*
Kor Yan, *Electrical Engi*
EMP: 91
SALES (corp-wide): 196.2MM **Privately Held**
WEB: www.portofoakland.com
SIC: **4581** Airport
PA: Port Department Of The City Of Oakland
    530 Water St Fl 3
    Oakland CA 94607
    510 627-1100

(P-7782)
PRIMEFLIGHT AVIATION SVCS INC
612 Mcdonald Rd Ste 100, San Francisco (94128)
PHONE..................................650 877-1560
Robert Prescott, *Manager*
Anne Bauzon, *Train & Dev Mgr*
EMP: 202
SALES (corp-wide): 240.1MM **Privately Held**
WEB: www.primeflight.com
SIC: **4581** Airports, flying fields & services
HQ: Primeflight Aviation Services, Inc.
    7135 Charlotte Pike # 100
    Nashville TN 37209
    615 312-7856

(P-7783)
SAN FRANCISCO INTL ARPRT
Also Called: Sfo
670 W Field Rd, San Francisco (94128)
P.O. Box 8097 (94128-8097)
PHONE..................................650 821-6700
EMP: 35
SALES (est): 4.8MM **Privately Held**
WEB: www.flysfo.com
SIC: **4581** Airport/Airport Services

(P-7784)
SAN FRANCISCO INTL ARPRT CORP
Also Called: San Francisco Intl Arprt
780 S Airport Blvd, San Francisco (94128)
PHONE..................................650 616-2400
Ivar C Satero, *Director*
Jeff Littlefield, *COO*
Amanda Ashton, *Officer*
Flynn Bradley, *Program Mgr*
Tina Ko, *General Mgr*
▲ EMP: 35 EST: 1927
SQ FT: 1,200
SALES: 193.7K
SALES (est): 7.1B **Privately Held**
WEB: www.flysfo.com
SIC: **4581** Airport
PA: City & County Of San Francisco
    1 Dr Carlton B Goodlett P
    San Francisco CA 94102
    415 554-7500

(P-7785)
SUNSET AVIATION LLC (PA)
Also Called: Solairus Aviation
201 1st St Ste 307, Petaluma (94952-4290)
PHONE..................................707 775-2786
Daniel Drohan, *CEO*
John King, *President*
Greg Petersen, *COO*
Mark Dennen, *CFO*
Bob Marinace, *Exec VP*
EMP: 50 EST: 2008
SALES (est): 88.3MM **Privately Held**
WEB: www.solairus.aero
SIC: **4581** Airports, flying fields & services

(P-7786)
SWISSPORT USA INC
San Francisco Intl Arprt, San Francisco (94128)
PHONE..................................650 821-6220
Cecilia Guillen, *Station Mgr*
EMP: 73
SALES (corp-wide): 355.8K **Privately Held**
WEB: www.swissport.com
SIC: **4581** Airport terminal services
HQ: Swissport Usa, Inc.
    227 Fayetteville St # 900
    Raleigh NC 27601

(P-7787)
SWISSPORT USA INC
Delta Crgo Bldg 612 Rm 21, San Francisco (94128)
PHONE..................................571 214-7068
Joe Phelan, *Exec VP*
EMP: 73
SALES (corp-wide): 355.8K **Privately Held**
WEB: www.swissport.com
SIC: **4581** Airport terminal services
HQ: Swissport Usa, Inc.
    227 Fayetteville St # 900
    Raleigh NC 27601

(P-7788)
TOTAL AIRPORT SERVICES LLC
900 N Access Rd, San Francisco (94128-3169)
P.O. Box 280955 (94128-0955)
PHONE..................................650 589-8560
Jack Evans, *CEO*
EMP: 69
SALES (corp-wide): 155.3MM **Privately Held**
WEB: www.totalairportservices.com
SIC: **4581** Airport

4581 - Airports, Flying Fields & Terminal Svcs County (P-7789)

HQ: Total Airport Services, Llc
28420 Hardy Toll Rd # 220
Spring TX 77373
832 592-0048

(P-7789)
TOTAL AIRPORT SERVICES LLC
3537 Branson Dr, San Mateo (94403-2901)
PHONE 650 358-0144
Faith Lopez, *Hum Res Coord*
Justin Karanikolas, *Manager*
Michael Plachy, *Manager*
Albert Ware, *Manager*
EMP: 69
SALES (corp-wide): 155.3MM **Privately Held**
WEB: www.totalairportservices.com
SIC: 4581 Aircraft maintenance & repair services
HQ: Total Airport Services, Llc
28420 Hardy Toll Rd # 220
Spring TX 77373
832 592-0048

(P-7790)
TRAVIS FLIGHT SERVICE INC
2112 Adams Ave, San Leandro (94577-1010)
P.O. Box Hh, Fairfield (94533-0657)
PHONE 707 437-4900
August John Loustau, *President*
Lillian Loustau, *Corp Secy*
EMP: 60 **EST:** 1964
SQ FT: 5,000
SALES (est): 3.5MM **Privately Held**
SIC: 4581 Aircraft servicing & repairing

(P-7791)
TRUX TRANSPORT
237 Harbor Way, South San Francisco (94080-6811)
P.O. Box 2505 (94083-2505)
PHONE 650 244-0200
Robert Simms, *President*
Edna Simms, *Admin Sec*
▲ **EMP:** 100 **EST:** 1968
SQ FT: 50,000
SALES (est): 11.4MM **Privately Held**
WEB: www.truxairlinecargo.com
SIC: 4581 Air freight handling at airports

(P-7792)
UNIVERSITY CALIFORNIA DAVIS
Also Called: Transportation Service Dept
1 Shields Ave, Davis (95616-8500)
PHONE 530 752-5435
EMP: 166 **Privately Held**
WEB: www.ucdavis.edu
SIC: 4581 8221 9411 Airports, flying fields & services; university; administration of educational programs
HQ: University Of California, Davis
1 Shields Ave
Davis CA 95616

4619 Pipelines, NEC

(P-7793)
BRASS ENGINEERING INTL
2551 San Ramon Valley Blv, San Ramon (94583-1662)
PHONE 925 867-1000
Brad Ricks, *President*
Guohua Shou, *Admin Sec*
Roy G Betinol, *
EMP: 200 **EST:** 2002
SALES (est): 39.9MM **Privately Held**
WEB: www.brassengineering.com
SIC: 4619 1731 Slurry pipeline operation; energy management controls

4724 Travel Agencies

(P-7794)
CALIFORNIA TRVL & TOURISM COMM
Also Called: Visit California
555 Capitol Mall Ste 1100, Sacramento (95814-4601)
P.O. Box 1499 (95812-1499)
PHONE 916 444-4429
Caroline Beteta, *President*
Matthew T Sabbatini, *CFO*
Ryan Becker, *Vice Pres*
Leona Reed, *Vice Pres*
Troy Cantrell, *Info Tech Dir*
EMP: 40 **EST:** 1997
SALES (est): 21MM **Privately Held**
WEB: www.visitcalifornia.com
SIC: 4724 Travel agencies; tourist agency arranging transport, lodging & car rental

(P-7795)
CLASSIC CUSTOM VACATIONS INC
5893 Rue Ferrari, San Jose (95138-1857)
PHONE 800 221-3949
Timothy Scott Macdonald, *CEO*
Gregge Brockway, *President*
Anil Prasad, *Accounting Mgr*
Linda Ladeck, *Business Mgr*
David Ryan, *Business Mgr*
EMP: 74 **EST:** 2002
SQ FT: 31,000
SALES (est): 13.1MM
SALES (corp-wide): 5.2B **Publicly Held**
WEB: www.classicvacations.com
SIC: 4724 Tourist agency arranging transport, lodging & car rental
PA: Expedia Group, Inc.
1111 Expedia Group Way W
Seattle WA 98119
206 481-7200

(P-7796)
FLYTBASE INC
1900 Camden Ave, San Jose (95124-2942)
PHONE 805 470-8985
Nitin Gupta, *Director*
Kaushik Gala, *Officer*
EMP: 44 **EST:** 2016
SALES (est): 4.5MM **Privately Held**
WEB: www.flytbase.com
SIC: 4724 Travel agencies

(P-7797)
GEOGRAPHIC EXPEDITIONS INC
Also Called: Innerasia Travel Group
1016 Lincoln Blvd Ste 316, San Francisco (94129-1609)
P.O. Box 29902 (94129-0902)
PHONE 415 922-0448
George Doubleday, *Ch of Bd*
Alysa Pakkidis, *Creative Dir*
Jennine Cohen, *Managing Dir*
Wen Minkoff, *Managing Dir*
Lisa Parker, *Admin Sec*
EMP: 54 **EST:** 1982
SALES (est): 10.6MM **Privately Held**
WEB: www.geoex.com
SIC: 4724 Travel agencies

(P-7798)
HIPCAMP INC
965 Market St Ste 480, San Francisco (94103-1701)
PHONE 242 377-8982
Alyssa Ravasio, *CEO*
Zach Conn, *Sr Software Eng*
Jon Eckstein, *Sr Software Eng*
Myles Tan, *Sr Software Eng*
Richard Barnes, *CIO*
EMP: 115 **EST:** 2013
SALES (est): 14.5MM **Privately Held**
WEB: www.hipcamp.com
SIC: 4724 Travel agencies; tourist agency arranging transport, lodging & car rental

(P-7799)
HORNBLOWER GROUP INC (PA)
The Embarcadero Pier 3 St Pier, San Francisco (94111)
PHONE 415 635-2210
Terry Macrae, *Chairman*
Kevin Rabbitt, *CEO*
EMP: 270 **EST:** 2008
SALES (est): 63.6MM **Privately Held**
WEB: www.hornblower.com
SIC: 4724 Travel agencies

(P-7800)
HORNBLOWER YACHTS LLC (PA)
Also Called: Hornblower Cruises & Event
On The Embarcadero Pier 3 St Pier, San Francisco (94111)
PHONE 415 788-8866
Terry Macrae, *CEO*
Gordon Loebl, *Vice Pres*
Annabella Stagner, *Vice Pres*
Justin Thulien, *Vice Pres*
Kim Wright, *Vice Pres*
EMP: 250 **EST:** 1980
SALES (est): 536MM **Privately Held**
WEB: www.hornblower.com
SIC: 4724 Travel agencies

(P-7801)
IDEA TRAVEL COMPANY
13145 Byrd Ln Ste 101, Los Altos Hills (94022-3211)
PHONE 650 948-0207
Michael Schoendorf, *CEO*
Ram Bodapati, *CTO*
Beverly Hoh, *Software Dev*
Sharen Schoendorf, *Agent*
EMP: 1100 **EST:** 1973
SALES (est): 453.4MM **Privately Held**
WEB: www.ideatravel.com
SIC: 4724 Tourist agency arranging transport, lodging & car rental

(P-7802)
L B C HOLDINGS U S A CORP (PA)
362 E Grand Ave, South San Francisco (94080-6210)
PHONE 650 873-0750
Carlos Araneta, *Ch of Bd*
EMP: 164 **EST:** 1986
SQ FT: 25,000
SALES (est): 21MM **Privately Held**
SIC: 4724 4513 4412 Travel agencies; air courier services; deep sea foreign transportation of freight

(P-7803)
MOZIO INC (PA)
44 Tehama St Fl 4, San Francisco (94105-3110)
PHONE 916 719-9213
David Litwak, *CEO*
Jj Metzinger, *CTO*
EMP: 55 **EST:** 2012
SALES (est): 4.9MM **Privately Held**
WEB: www.mozio.com
SIC: 4724 4111 Travel agencies; airport transportation

(P-7804)
PATTERSON TRAVEL AGENCY
1750 Howe Ave Ste 320, Sacramento (95825-3986)
PHONE 916 929-5555
James Whillock, *President*
Bruce Douglass, *Shareholder*
Laurel Whillock, *Chairman*
Marijo Douglass, *Admin Sec*
EMP: 43 **EST:** 1948
SQ FT: 8,100
SALES (est): 8.7MM **Privately Held**
WEB: www.travelstore.com
SIC: 4724 Travel agencies

(P-7805)
PEAK TRAVEL GROUP
Also Called: Rt Peak Travel Group
1723 Hamilton Ave Ste A, San Jose (95125-5428)
PHONE 408 286-2633
Tyler Peak, *President*
Kim Peak, *Corp Secy*
Helen Leon, *Exec VP*
Will Dawes, *Software Dev*
Beth Ebner, *Sales Staff*
EMP: 43 **EST:** 1963
SQ FT: 4,000
SALES (est): 9.1MM
SALES (corp-wide): 189MM **Privately Held**
WEB: www.dt.com
SIC: 4724 Tourist agency arranging transport, lodging & car rental
PA: Direct Travel Inc.
7430 E Caley Ave Ste 220
Centennial CO 80111
952 746-3575

(P-7806)
PERFORMANCE GRP OF NRTHN CA
Also Called: T P G
4701 Doyle St Ste 510, Emeryville (94608-2939)
PHONE 510 923-9123
Janet Traphagen, *President*
Arlene Motter, *VP Finance*
Cynthia Tsuchimoto, *Controller*
Lilia Romero, *Buyer*
Kim Demus, *Opers Staff*
EMP: 46 **EST:** 1998
SQ FT: 6,000
SALES (est): 14.5MM
SALES (corp-wide): 189MM **Privately Held**
WEB: www.tpgnc.com
SIC: 4724 Travel agencies
HQ: Creative Group, Inc.
1500 N Casaloma Dr # 201
Appleton WI 54913
920 739-8850

(P-7807)
SNAPCOMMERCE INC
Also Called: Snap Travel
18 Bartol St, San Francisco (94133-4501)
PHONE 917 704-4588
Hussein Fazal, *CEO*
Henry Shi, *COO*
Daniel Weisenfeld, *CFO*
Yan Lau, *Finance*
EMP: 115 **EST:** 2016
SALES (est): 39.9MM **Privately Held**
WEB: www.snaptravel.com
SIC: 4724 Travel agencies

(P-7808)
TRAVELMASTERS INC
Also Called: Goldrush Getaways
8350 Auburn Blvd Ste 200, Citrus Heights (95610-0396)
PHONE 916 722-1648
Brian A Carr, *President*
Beatriz De La Torre, *Director*
Tracy Stevens, *Advisor*
Elizabeth Connors, *Agent*
EMP: 50 **EST:** 2000
SALES (est): 10MM **Privately Held**
SIC: 4724 Tourist agency arranging transport, lodging & car rental

(P-7809)
TRIPACTIONS INC (PA)
1501 Page Mill Rd, Palo Alto (94304-1126)
PHONE 888 505-8747
Ariel Cohen, *CEO*
Thomas Tuchscherer, *CFO*
Carlos Delatorre, *Officer*
Ilan Twig, *Officer*
Bob Brindley, *Vice Pres*
EMP: 891 **EST:** 2015
SALES (est): 228MM **Privately Held**
WEB: www.tripactions.com
SIC: 4724 Travel agencies

(P-7810)
UBER
101 Jefferson Dr, Menlo Park (94025-1114)
PHONE 866 440-6700
Brent Ritz, *Ch of Bd*
EMP: 100 **EST:** 2006
SALES (est): 6.8MM **Privately Held**
WEB: www.uberrealestate.com
SIC: 4724 7299 6531 Travel agencies; information services, consumer; real estate brokers & agents

(P-7811)
WORLD PROJECTS CORPORATION
110 E D St Ste K, Benicia (94510-3252)
PHONE 707 556-5885
Deborah Gibbs, *CEO*
Keith Bishop, *Vice Pres*
Chris Robinson, *Executive Asst*
Richard Barnes, *CIO*
Lacey Kahley, *Prdtn Mgr*
EMP: 30 **EST:** 1984

PRODUCTS & SERVICES SECTION

4731 - Freight Forwarding & Arrangement County (P-7834)

SALES (est): 3.5MM **Privately Held**
WEB: www.world-projects.net
SIC: **4724** 4725 2741 Travel agencies; tour operators; music book & sheet music publishing

---

4725 Tour Operators

(P-7812)
ACCENT HOSPITALITY GROUP LLC
Also Called: Nature Expeditions Africa
2830 I St Ste 104, Sacramento (95816-4311)
PHONE.................................415 286-2867
Kimani Adam,
EMP: 149 **EST:** 2016
SALES (est): 4MM **Privately Held**
SIC: **4725** Tour operators; arrangement of travel tour packages, wholesale; sightseeing tour companies

(P-7813)
ALCATRAZ CRUISES LLC
Hrnblwer Alctraz Pier 33 St Pier, San Francisco (94111)
PHONE.................................415 981-7625
Terry A Macrae,
Denise McKevitt-Rasmus, *General Mgr*
Michael Badolato, *Administration*
Atwood Gaines, *Engineer*
Ivonne Guido, *Human Res Mgr*
EMP: 66 **EST:** 2005
SALES (est): 21.4MM **Privately Held**
WEB: www.alcatrazcruises.com
SIC: **4725** Tours, conducted

(P-7814)
APPELLATION TOURS INC
Also Called: Beau Wine Tours
21707 8th St E, Sonoma (95476-9781)
PHONE.................................707 938-8001
Thomas Buck, *President*
EMP: 50 **EST:** 2001
SQ FT: 21,000
SALES (est): 8.7MM **Privately Held**
WEB: www.appellationtours.com
SIC: **4725** 4111 4141 Tours, conducted; airport limousine, scheduled service; local bus charter service

(P-7815)
BACKROADS (PA)
801 Cedar St, Berkeley (94710-1800)
PHONE.................................510 527-1555
Tom Hale, *CEO*
Robert Greeneisen, *Principal*
Mark Selcon, *Regional Mgr*
Stacy Loucks, *General Mgr*
Oscar Hernandez, *Administration*
EMP: 100 **EST:** 1979
SQ FT: 10,000
SALES (est): 119.6MM **Privately Held**
WEB: www.backroads.com
SIC: **4725** 4724 Sightseeing tour companies; travel agencies

(P-7816)
BLUE BUS TOURS LLC
Also Called: Grayline of San Francisco
216 Ryan Way, South San Francisco (94080-6308)
PHONE.................................415 353-5310
Xavier Valls Pinilla, *CEO*
EMP: 120 **EST:** 2011
SALES (est): 350K **Privately Held**
WEB: www.graylineofsanfrancisco.com
SIC: **4725** Tours, conducted

(P-7817)
CLASSIC VACATIONS LLC
Also Called: Classic Custom Vacations
5893 Rue Ferrari, San Jose (95138-1857)
PHONE.................................408 287-4550
David Hu, *President*
Jonna Jackson, *Partner*
Eddie Sanchez, *Vice Pres*
Denis Fastert, *Surgery Dir*
Dajana Levy, *Info Tech Dir*
EMP: 149 **EST:** 2005
SALES (est): 44.7MM **Privately Held**
WEB: www.classicvacations.com
SIC: **4725** Arrangement of travel tour packages, wholesale

PA: Najafi Companies, Llc
2525 E Camelback Rd Ste 8
Phoenix AZ 85016

(P-7818)
JOGURU INC
2600 El Camino Real Ste 4, Palo Alto (94306-1705)
PHONE.................................855 526-4332
Praveen Kumar, *CEO*
Saket Newaskar, *Director*
EMP: 75
SQ FT: 2,500
SALES (est): 500K **Privately Held**
SIC: **4725** Arrangement of travel tour packages, wholesale

(P-7819)
NAPA VALLEY BALLOONS INC
4086 Byway E, NAPA (94558-2289)
PHONE.................................707 253-2224
Don Surplus, *President*
Kim Kleist, *Vice Pres*
EMP: 39 **EST:** 1979
SQ FT: 660
SALES (est): 8.2MM **Privately Held**
WEB: www.napavalleyballoons.com
SIC: **4725** Tours, conducted

(P-7820)
OKABE INTERNATIONAL INC (PA)
Also Called: Pacific Leisure Management
1739 Buchanan St Ste B, San Francisco (94115-3208)
PHONE.................................415 921-0808
Mitsufumi Okabe, *President*
Rumi Okabe, *Corp Secy*
EMP: 50 **EST:** 1973
SQ FT: 3,600
SALES (est): 7.5MM **Privately Held**
SIC: **4725** 4833 5941 Tours, conducted; television broadcasting stations; sporting goods & bicycle shops; tennis goods & equipment; golf goods & equipment

(P-7821)
OLIVIA COMPANIES LLC
Also Called: Olivia Cruises & Resorts
434 Brannan St, San Francisco (94107-1714)
PHONE.................................415 962-5700
EMP: 31
SQ FT: 9,000
SALES (est): 5.6MM **Privately Held**
WEB: www.olivia.com
SIC: **4725** 5961 3652 Tour Operators

4729 Passenger Transportation Arrangement, NEC

(P-7822)
ZIRO RIDE LLC
201 Spear St Ste 1100, San Francisco (94105-6164)
PHONE.................................951 801-4981
Jai Randwani,
Maria Macario, *Exec Dir*
Santosh Vishnubhotla,
EMP: 40 **EST:** 2019
SALES (est): 1.7MM **Privately Held**
SIC: **4729** Carpool/vanpool arrangement

4731 Freight Forwarding & Arrangement

(P-7823)
APM TERMINALS PACIFIC LTD
5801 Christie Ave, Emeryville (94608-1964)
PHONE.................................510 992-6430
EMP: 350
SALES (corp-wide): 38.6B **Privately Held**
SIC: **4731** Freight Services
HQ: Apm Terminals Pacific Ltd.
9300 Arrowpoint Blvd
Charlotte NC 90731
704 571-2768

(P-7824)
ATECH LOGISTICS INC
7 College Ave, Santa Rosa (95401-4702)
P.O. Box 6836 (95406-0836)
PHONE.................................707 526-1910
Jesse E Amaral, *President*
Geri Amaral, *Vice Pres*
Michelle Feeney, *Human Resources*
Santos Isaias, *Opers Staff*
EMP: 130 **EST:** 2002
SQ FT: 35,000
SALES (est): 31.8MM **Privately Held**
WEB: www.atechlogistics.com
SIC: **4731** Freight forwarding

(P-7825)
BLACKROCK LOGISTICS INC (PA)
7031 Koll Center Pkwy # 250, Pleasanton (94566-3134)
PHONE.................................925 523-3878
Larry T James, *President*
Jeff R Mitchell, *CFO*
Jeff Mitchell, *CFO*
Mark J Polland, *Vice Pres*
Mark Polland, *Vice Pres*
EMP: 143 **EST:** 2013
SALES (est): 211.9MM **Privately Held**
WEB: www.blackrock-logistics.net
SIC: **4731** Freight forwarding

(P-7826)
BROCK LLC (PA)
Also Called: Brock Transportation
3025 Independence Dr C, Livermore (94551-7683)
PHONE.................................925 371-2184
Christopher R Obrien, *Mng Member*
William T Obrien, *Mng Member*
Renee Obrien, *Manager*
EMP: 64 **EST:** 1997
SQ FT: 3,000
SALES (est): 37MM **Privately Held**
WEB: www.brockweb.com
SIC: **4731** 4789 Brokers, shipping; pipeline terminal facilities, independently operated

(P-7827)
CALIFORNIA SIERRA EXPRESS INC
2975 Oates St Ste 30, West Sacramento (95691-6401)
PHONE.................................916 375-7070
Jeff Phillips, *Manager*
Christina Cordova, *Technology*
Kelli Scurti, *Asst Controller*
Matt Gaines, *Opers Mgr*
Kris McGlown, *Opers Staff*
EMP: 39 **Privately Held**
WEB: www.calsierraexpress.info
SIC: **4731** 4212 Agents, shipping; delivery service, vehicular
PA: California Sierra Express, Inc.
4965 Joule St
Reno NV 89502

(P-7828)
CALIFORNIA SIERRA EXPRESS INC
2720 W Winton Ave, Hayward (94545-1120)
PHONE.................................510 786-9974
EMP: 39 **Privately Held**
WEB: www.calsierraexpress.info
SIC: **4731** Agents, shipping
PA: California Sierra Express, Inc.
4965 Joule St
Reno NV 89502

(P-7829)
CHEVRON SHIPPING COMPANY LLC
6001 Bollinger Canyon Rd, San Ramon (94583-5737)
PHONE.................................925 842-1000
John S Watson, *CEO*
James W Johnson, *Exec VP*
George L Kirkland, *Exec VP*
Gabriel Grimaldi, *Vice Pres*
Hendro Santoso, *Vice Pres*
▲ **EMP:** 96 **EST:** 1997

SALES (est): 111.5MM
SALES (corp-wide): 94.6B **Publicly Held**
WEB: www.chevron.com
SIC: **5541** 4731 Filling stations, gasoline; brokers, shipping
PA: Chevron Corporation
6001 Bollinger Canyon Rd
San Ramon CA 94583
925 842-1000

(P-7830)
CONNER LOGISTICS INC
4069 W Shaw Ave Ste 103, Fresno (93722-6215)
PHONE.................................888 939-4637
Dave Conner, *President*
Megan Conner, *General Mgr*
Beatriz Rios, *Admin Asst*
Donna Puett, *Accounting Mgr*
Sean Conner, *Opers Mgr*
EMP: 90 **EST:** 2002
SALES (est): 11.6MM **Privately Held**
WEB: www.connerlogistics.com
SIC: **4731** Freight forwarding

(P-7831)
DHX-DEPENDABLE HAWAIIAN EX INC
3623 Munster St, Hayward (94545-1646)
PHONE.................................510 686-2600
Wilfred Robello, *General Mgr*
Georgia Briggs, *Office Mgr*
EMP: 61
SALES (corp-wide): 108.7MM **Privately Held**
WEB: www.dhx.com
SIC: **4731** Freight forwarding
PA: Dhx-Dependable Hawaiian Express, Inc.
19201 S Susana Rd
Compton CA 90221
310 537-2000

(P-7832)
DISCOPYLABS (PA)
Also Called: Dcl
48641 Milmont Dr, Fremont (94538-7354)
PHONE.................................510 651-5100
Norman Tu, *CEO*
David Tu, *President*
Antonia Tu, *Corp Secy*
Victoria Maddux, *Vice Pres*
Vikhar Baquer, *Human Resources*
▲ **EMP:** 50 **EST:** 1982
SQ FT: 300,000
SALES (est): 75.4MM **Privately Held**
WEB: www.dclcorp.com
SIC: **5961** 4731 7389 ; freight forwarding

(P-7833)
EXPEDITORS INTL WASH INC
Also Called: Sfo-3 - San Francisco Full Svc
425 Valley Dr, Brisbane (94005-1209)
PHONE.................................415 657-3600
Kevin Niduaza, *General Mgr*
Soparah Keo, *Opers Staff*
Katrina Elicagaray Mela, *Manager*
Lance Ohira, *Accounts Mgr*
EMP: 50
SALES (corp-wide): 10.1B **Publicly Held**
WEB: www.expeditors.com
SIC: **4731** Freight forwarding
PA: Expeditors International Of Washington, Inc.
1015 3rd Ave
Seattle WA 98104
206 674-3400

(P-7834)
EXPRESS SYSTEM INTERMODAL INC
2633 Camino Ramon Ste 400, San Ramon (94583-2176)
PHONE.................................801 302-6625
Peter Leng, *President*
EMP: 37 **EST:** 1985
SALES (est): 9.5MM **Privately Held**
WEB: www.oocl.com
SIC: **4731** Freight forwarding
HQ: Oocl (Usa) Inc.
10913 S Rver Front Pkwy S
South Jordan UT 84095
801 302-6625

4731 - Freight Forwarding & Arrangement County (P-7835)

PRODUCTS & SERVICES SECTION

(P-7835)
FORWARD AIR INC
30108 Eigenbrodt Way # 100, Union City (94587-1225)
PHONE..................................415 570-6040
Fax: 650 794-9923
EMP: 50
SALES (corp-wide): 1.1B Publicly Held
SIC: 4731 Freight Transportation Arrangement Freight Transportation Arrangement
HQ: Forward Air, Inc.
    430 Airport Rd
    Greeneville TN 37745
    423 639-7196

(P-7836)
G3 ENTERPRISES INC
G3 Enterprises Mineral Div
1300 Camino Diablo Rd, Byron (94514)
P.O. Box 216 (94514-0216)
PHONE..................................209 341-3441
EMP: 44
SALES (corp-wide): 116.5MM Privately Held
WEB: www.g3enterprises.com
SIC: 4731 Truck transportation brokers
PA: G3 Enterprises, Inc.
    502 E Whitmore Ave
    Modesto CA 95358
    209 341-7515

(P-7837)
G3 ENTERPRISES INC
G3 Enterprises Closure Div
500 S Santa Rosa Ave, Modesto (95354-3717)
PHONE..................................209 341-4045
EMP: 44
SALES (corp-wide): 116.5MM Privately Held
WEB: www.g3enterprises.com
SIC: 4731 Truck transportation brokers
PA: G3 Enterprises, Inc.
    502 E Whitmore Ave
    Modesto CA 95358
    209 341-7515

(P-7838)
HES TRANSPORTATION SVCS INC
3623 Munster St, Hayward (94545-1646)
P.O. Box 57136 (94545-7136)
PHONE..................................510 783-6100
Jeff Graham, President
Joyce C Schaul, Vice Pres
EMP: 50 EST: 1986
SQ FT: 38,000
SALES (est): 9.9MM Privately Held
SIC: 4731 Freight forwarding

(P-7839)
INNOVEL SOLUTIONS INC
Also Called: Sears
521 Stone Rd, Benicia (94510-1113)
PHONE..................................707 748-1940
Dixie Shaw, Manager
EMP: 592
SALES (corp-wide): 4.1B Privately Held
WEB: www.sears.com
SIC: 4731 Agents, shipping
HQ: Innovel Solutions, Inc.
    3333 Beverly Rd
    Hoffman Estates IL 60179
    847 286-2500

(P-7840)
J F HILLEBRAND USA INC
5325 Industrial Way, Benicia (94510-1026)
PHONE..................................707 996-5686
EMP: 38
SALES (corp-wide): 2.6MM Privately Held
WEB: www.hillebrand.com
SIC: 4731 Agents, shipping; brokers, shipping; foreign freight forwarding
HQ: J. F. Hillebrand Usa, Inc.
    2147 Route 27 Ste 401
    Edison NJ 08817
    732 388-0101

(P-7841)
JAVELIN LOGISTICS COMPANY INC
7025 Central Ave, Newark (94560-4201)
PHONE..................................800 577-1060
Malcolm Winspear, President
Michael Sacrey, General Mgr
EMP: 225 EST: 2018
SALES (est): 13.3MM Privately Held
WEB: www.javelinlogistics.com
SIC: 4731 Freight forwarding

(P-7842)
JOHANSON TRANSPORTATION SVC (PA)
5583 E Olive Ave, Fresno (93727-2559)
P.O. Box 55003 (93747-5003)
PHONE..................................559 458-2200
Larry Johanson, President
Richard Johanson, Ch of Bd
Janice Spicer, CFO
Randy Gabardi, Vice Pres
Craig Johannson, Vice Pres
EMP: 40 EST: 1971
SQ FT: 11,000
SALES (est): 20.9MM Privately Held
WEB: www.johansontrans.com
SIC: 4731 Brokers, shipping

(P-7843)
JUMBO LOGISTICS LLC
801 E Roth Rd, French Camp (95231-9777)
PHONE..................................216 662-5420
Ramanpreet Bhinder, CEO
Ray Bhinder,
Jabarjeet S Bhinder, Mng Member
EMP: 40 EST: 2005
SALES (est): 8.1MM Privately Held
WEB: www.femsinc.com
SIC: 4731 Freight forwarding

(P-7844)
KSI CORP (PA)
839 Mitten Rd, San Bruno (94066)
P.O. Box 2182, South San Francisco (94083-2182)
PHONE..................................650 952-0815
Carl Bellante, CEO
Dennis Siu, CFO
Michael Ford, Senior VP
Chris Ramos, Vice Pres
Albert Foong, Manager
EMP: 64 EST: 1989
SQ FT: 13,000
SALES (est): 10.2MM Privately Held
WEB: www.ksicorp.com
SIC: 4731 8741 Customhouse brokers; management services

(P-7845)
LEE JENNINGS TARGET EX INC
Also Called: L J E Enterprises
815 Moffat Blvd, Manteca (95336-5820)
PHONE..................................209 823-0071
Lee Jennings Jr, Manager
EMP: 66
SALES (corp-wide): 12MM Privately Held
WEB: www.ljetarget.com
SIC: 4731 4213 Domestic freight forwarding; trucking, except local
PA: Lee Jennings Target Express, Inc.
    1465 E Franklin Ave
    Pomona CA 91766
    909 868-1040

(P-7846)
MATSON LOGISTICS INC
1855 Gateway Blvd Ste 550, Concord (94520-8461)
PHONE..................................925 887-6207
Rusty K Rolfe, Exec VP
Lori Geraty, President
Randall Reynolds, Administration
Chad Dawson, Manager
EMP: 40
SALES (corp-wide): 2.3B Publicly Held
WEB: www.matson.com
SIC: 4731 Agents, shipping
HQ: Matson Logistics, Inc.
    1815 S Meyers Rd Ste 700
    Oakbrook Terrace IL 60181
    630 203-3500

(P-7847)
MENDOCINO RAILWAY
Also Called: Skunk Train, The
100 W Laurel St, Fort Bragg (95437-3410)
PHONE..................................707 964-6371
David Magaw, President
Ed Ring, Treasurer
Chris Hart, Vice Pres
Torgny Nilsson, Admin Sec
EMP: 63 EST: 2004
SALES (est): 105.5K Privately Held
WEB: www.skunktrain.com
SIC: 4731 4011 Railroad freight agency; railroads, line-haul operating
PA: Sierra Railroad Company
    341 Industrial Way
    Woodland CA 95776

(P-7848)
PANALPINA INC
400 Oyster Point Blvd # 300, South San Francisco (94080-1919)
P.O. Box 1850 (94083-1850)
PHONE..................................650 825-3036
Tommy Lau, Branch Mgr
Yuko Nakano, Export Mgr
EMP: 40
SALES (corp-wide): 18.4B Privately Held
WEB: www.ssc-solutions.com
SIC: 4731 Freight forwarding
HQ: Panalpina, Inc.
    12430 Nw 25th St 100
    Miami FL 33182
    305 894-1300

(P-7849)
PASHA GROUP (PA)
Also Called: Pasha Freight
4040 Civic Center Dr # 350, San Rafael (94903-4187)
PHONE..................................415 927-6400
George W Pasha III, Ch of Bd
James Britton, CFO
Steve Hunter, Treasurer
Jeff Burgin, Senior VP
Amy Sherburne, Vice Pres
◆ EMP: 400 EST: 1973
SQ FT: 18,000
SALES (est): 632.2MM Privately Held
WEB: www.pashagroup.com
SIC: 4731 Freight forwarding

(P-7850)
PREMIER GLOBAL LOGISTICS LLC
1656 Germano Way, Pleasanton (94566-2259)
PHONE..................................877 671-0254
Robert Buell, Mng Member
Derek Pridgeon, VP Opers
Jacqueline Paiso, Opers Mgr
Thomas A Storey Jr,
Ashley Bush, Director
EMP: 38 EST: 2010
SALES (est): 13.6MM Privately Held
WEB: www.premiergl.com
SIC: 4731 Freight forwarding

(P-7851)
PROGISTICS DISTRIBUTION INC
480 Roland Way Ste 103, Oakland (94621-2052)
PHONE..................................415 369-8845
Joel G Ritch, CEO
Julian Ludlow, President
James Liguori, CFO
Jamie Myers, Vice Pres
Rick Schad, Vice Pres
EMP: 576 EST: 2012
SQ FT: 7,500
SALES (est): 91.1MM Privately Held
WEB: www.progisticsdistribution.com
SIC: 4731 Freight transportation arrangement

(P-7852)
RK LOGISTICS GROUP INC
44951 Industrial Dr, Fremont (94538-6486)
P.O. Box 610670, San Jose (95161-0670)
PHONE..................................510 298-5128
EMP: 40
SALES (corp-wide): 29MM Privately Held
WEB: www.rklogisticsgroup.com
SIC: 4731 Freight transportation arrangement
PA: The Rk Logistics Group Inc
    41707 Christy St
    Fremont CA 94538
    408 942-8107

(P-7853)
SHINE LOGISTICS LLC
9012 Pebble Field Way, Sacramento (95829-9267)
PHONE..................................916 518-9393
Navjot Madahar, CEO
Katie Diaz, Manager
EMP: 120 EST: 2018
SALES (est): 15MM Privately Held
WEB: www.shinelogisticsllc.com
SIC: 4731 Freight forwarding

(P-7854)
THREE WAY LOGISTICS INC (PA)
42505 Christy St, Fremont (94538-3993)
P.O. Box 1806 (94538-0032)
PHONE..................................408 748-3929
Anthony J Bonino, CEO
Kevin Scherer, President
Philipp Scherer, CFO
Stan Aikman, Vice Pres
Michael Bonino, Vice Pres
▲ EMP: 60 EST: 2003
SQ FT: 135,000
SALES (est): 55.3MM Privately Held
WEB: www.threeway.com
SIC: 4731 Freight forwarding

(P-7855)
UNITED STTES INTRMDAL SVCS LLC
Also Called: G3 Enterprises
502 E Whitmore Ave, Modesto (95358-9411)
PHONE..................................209 341-4045
John R Gallo,
Gregory J Coleman, President
EMP: 88 EST: 1983
SQ FT: 10,000
SALES (est): 24.5MM Privately Held
SIC: 4731 5182 Truck transportation brokers; bottling wines & liquors

(P-7856)
UNITRANS INTERNATIONAL CORP (HQ)
351 Swift Ave, South San Francisco (94080-6206)
P.O. Box 17044, Inglewood (90308-7044)
PHONE..................................650 588-1233
Andrew Schadegg, President
Paige Weiss, CFO
Chris Amberg, Exec VP
Mark Bichsel, Vice Pres
Rene M Schaub, Regional Mgr
◆ EMP: 45 EST: 1977
SQ FT: 22,500
SALES (est): 49.7MM
SALES (corp-wide): 760.4MM Privately Held
WEB: www.unitrans-us.com
SIC: 4731 Foreign freight forwarding
PA: Ait Worldwide Logistics, Inc.
    701 N Rohlwing Rd
    Itasca IL 60143
    630 766-8300

(P-7857)
UPS SUPPLY CHAIN SOLUTIONS INC
1150 E Arbor Ave Ste 101, Tracy (95304-8440)
PHONE..................................209 319-4116
Jesse Anguiano, Branch Mgr
EMP: 55
SALES (corp-wide): 84.6B Publicly Held
WEB: www.theupsstore.com
SIC: 4731 Freight forwarding
HQ: Ups Supply Chain Solutions, Inc.
    12380 Morris Rd
    Alpharetta GA 30005
    678 258-2000

(P-7858)
USKO EXPEDITE INC (PA)
11290 Point East Dr # 110, Rancho Cordova (95742-6243)
PHONE..................................916 233-4455
Vlad Skots, CEO
Artur Liulkovich, Manager
EMP: 49 EST: 2017
SALES (est): 6.7MM Privately Held
WEB: www.uskoinc.com
SIC: 4731 Transportation agents & brokers

▲ = Import ▼ = Export
◆ = Import/Export

4789 - Transportation Svcs, NEC County (P-7882)

(P-7859)
WATCHPOINT LOGISTICS INC
50 Tanforan Ave, South San Francisco (94080-6608)
PHONE.....................650 871-4747
Jay Bellin, *President*
Alec Binnie, *Director*
Julie Busch, *Director*
Michael Schweinberg, *Director*
◆ **EMP:** 110 **EST:** 1988
SQ FT: 35,000
SALES (est): 27.3MM **Privately Held**
WEB: www.watchpointlogistics.com
SIC: 4731 Freight forwarding

(P-7860)
WEDRIVEU INC
700 Airport Blvd Ste 250, Burlingame (94010-1937)
PHONE.....................650 645-6800
Dennis Carlson, *CEO*
Erick Vanwagenen, *President*
Tim Wayland, *Ch Credit Ofcr*
Matthew Streem, *Vice Pres*
Pat McConn, *VP Finance*
EMP: 40 **EST:** 1988
SALES (est): 13.2MM **Privately Held**
WEB: www.wedriveu.com
SIC: 4731 Freight transportation arrangement
HQ: Wedriveu Holdings, Inc.
700 Airport Blvd Ste 250
Burlingame CA 94010

(P-7861)
XPO LOGISTICS FREIGHT INC
2171 Otoole Ave, San Jose (95131-1314)
PHONE.....................408 435-3876
Jon Sullivan, *Branch Mgr*
EMP: 35
SQ FT: 8,834
SALES (corp-wide): 16.2B **Publicly Held**
WEB: www.xpo.com
SIC: 4731 Freight transportation arrangement
HQ: Xpo Logistics Freight, Inc.
2211 Old Earhart Rd # 10
Ann Arbor MI 48105
800 755-2728

(P-7862)
XPO LOGISTICS FREIGHT INC
4195 E Central Ave, Fresno (93725-9026)
PHONE.....................559 485-1164
Bud Whitney, *Principal*
EMP: 35
SQ FT: 39,620
SALES (corp-wide): 16.2B **Publicly Held**
WEB: www.xpo.com
SIC: 4731 Freight transportation arrangement
HQ: Xpo Logistics Freight, Inc.
2211 Old Earhart Rd # 10
Ann Arbor MI 48105
800 755-2728

(P-7863)
XPO LOGISTICS FREIGHT INC
Also Called: Con-Way Freight
2201 Branstetter Ln, Redding (96001-4458)
PHONE.....................530 243-6175
Todd Kellerstiass, *Manager*
EMP: 35
SALES (corp-wide): 16.2B **Publicly Held**
WEB: www.xpo.com
SIC: 4731 Freight transportation arrangement
HQ: Xpo Logistics Freight, Inc.
2211 Old Earhart Rd # 10
Ann Arbor MI 48105
800 755-2728

4741 Railroad Car Rental

(P-7864)
CENTRAL VALLEY AG TRNSPT INC
Also Called: Central Valley AG Transload
330 Codoni Ave, Modesto (95357-0506)
PHONE.....................209 544-9246
Michael Barry, *President*
Ryan Hogan, *CFO*

Paul Konzen, *Vice Pres*
EMP: 45 **EST:** 2003
SQ FT: 286,000
SALES (est): 4.8MM **Privately Held**
WEB: www.cv-ag.com
SIC: 4741 4214 2041 Grain leveling in railroad cars; local trucking with storage; flour & other grain mill products

4783 Packing & Crating Svcs

(P-7865)
CENTRA FREIGHT SERVICES INC (PA)
279 Lawrence Ave, South San Francisco (94080-6818)
PHONE.....................650 873-8147
Jonathan Wang, *CEO*
Stanley Wang, *President*
Goldine Wang, *Vice Pres*
Julie Wang, *Admin Sec*
Dale Lowe, *Controller*
◆ **EMP:** 53 **EST:** 1980
SQ FT: 11,500
SALES (est): 10.4MM **Privately Held**
WEB: www.centrafreight.com
SIC: 4783 4731 Containerization of goods for shipping; domestic freight forwarding

(P-7866)
INNOVATED PACKAGING CO INC
38505 Cherry St Ste C, Newark (94560-4700)
PHONE.....................510 745-8180
Ben F Polando, *President*
Adele Daszko, *Exec VP*
Donna Fernandez, *Senior VP*
Santina Polando, *Exec Sec*
EMP: 75 **EST:** 1988
SQ FT: 110,000
SALES (est): 20.2MM **Privately Held**
WEB: www.innovpak.com
SIC: 4783 Packing & crating

(P-7867)
INTEGRATED PKG & CRATING SVCS
Also Called: Inovative Packaging
38505 Cherry St, Newark (94560-4700)
PHONE.....................510 745-8180
EMP: 50
SQ FT: 90,000
SALES (est): 7.2MM **Privately Held**
SIC: 4783 Packing And Crating, Nsk

(P-7868)
MOONLIGHT PACKING CORPORATION
Also Called: Plant 04
17770 E Huntsman Ave, Reedley (93654-9205)
PHONE.....................559 638-7799
EMP: 635 **Privately Held**
WEB: www.moonlightcompanies.com
SIC: 4783 5148 Packing & crating; fruits, fresh
PA: Moonlight Packing Corporation
17719 E Huntsman Ave
Reedley CA 93654

4785 Fixed Facilities, Inspection, Weighing Svcs Transptn

(P-7869)
CALIFORNIA GOVERNMENT TRNSP
Also Called: Cal Trans
600 Lewelling Blvd, San Leandro (94579-1805)
PHONE.....................510 614-5942
Bill Kimball, *General Mgr*
Tanya Mejia, *IT/INT Sup*
Jaime Velasquez, *IT/INT Sup*
Deandre Forks, *Traffic Dir*
Shelley Caldwell, *Agent*
EMP: 38 **EST:** 1930
SALES (est): 2.9MM **Privately Held**
SIC: 4785 Transportation inspection services

(P-7870)
GOLDEN GATE BRDGE HWY TRNSP DS (PA)
Toll Plz, San Francisco (94129)
PHONE.....................415 921-5858
James C Eddie, *President*
Tino Molossi, *Officer*
D'ann Moore, *Officer*
Denis J Mulligan, *General Mgr*
Dennis Mulligan, *General Mgr*
▲ **EMP:** 250 **EST:** 1928
SQ FT: 20,000
SALES (est): 145.6MM **Privately Held**
WEB: www.goldengate.org
SIC: 4785 4131 4482 4111 Toll bridge operation; interstate bus line; ferries operating across rivers or within harbors; bus transportation

(P-7871)
GOLDEN GATE BRDGE HWY TRNSP DS
Also Called: Golden Gate Ferry
101 E Sir Frncis Drake Bl, Larkspur (94939-1803)
PHONE.....................415 455-2000
David Clark, *Manager*
Peter Pomies, *Technician*
Paolo Cosulich-Schwar, *Manager*
EMP: 69
SALES (corp-wide): 145.6MM **Privately Held**
WEB: www.goldengate.org
SIC: 4785 4482 Toll bridge operation; ferries operating across rivers or within harbors
PA: Golden Gate Bridge Highway & Transportation District
Toll Plz
San Francisco CA 94129
415 921-5858

(P-7872)
GOLDEN GATE BRIDGE HIGH
Also Called: Golden Gate Transit
1011 Andersen Dr, San Rafael (94901-5318)
PHONE.....................415 457-3110
Susan Chiaroni, *Manager*
Kathy Amoroso, *Bd of Directors*
Amorette Ko, *Executive Asst*
Marcus Lo, *Admin Sec*
Mary Lucas, *Admin Asst*
EMP: 535
SQ FT: 50,000
SALES (corp-wide): 145.6MM **Privately Held**
WEB: www.goldengate.org
SIC: 4785 4111 Toll bridge operation; airport transportation services, regular route
PA: Golden Gate Bridge Highway & Transportation District
Toll Plz
San Francisco CA 94129
415 921-5858

4789 Transportation Svcs, NEC

(P-7873)
ACERTUS
3044 Elkhorn Blvd Ste J, North Highlands (95660-3025)
PHONE.....................916 331-2355
Shirley Tyler, *Principal*
EMP: 39
SALES (corp-wide): 92.6MM **Privately Held**
WEB: www.amerifleet.com
SIC: 4789 Car loading
HQ: Amerifleet Transportation, Inc.
1111 Alderman Dr Ste 350
Alpharetta GA 30005
770 442-0222

(P-7874)
ARLEEN LOGISTICS INC (PA)
5556 Honor Pkwy, Sacramento (95835-1700)
PHONE.....................916 514-9746
Balvinder Singh, *CEO*
EMP: 55 **EST:** 2015

SALES (est): 1.1MM **Privately Held**
SIC: 4789 Transportation services

(P-7875)
B & F LOGISTICS LLC (PA) ✪
175 Santa Barbara Way, Fairfield (94533-2262)
PHONE.....................707 720-6101
Brian Jones,
EMP: 40 **EST:** 2021
SALES (est): 78.4K **Privately Held**
SIC: 4789 Transportation services

(P-7876)
CAPSTONE LOGISTICS LLC
16888 Mckinley Ave, Lathrop (95330-9705)
PHONE.....................209 858-1401
EMP: 525
SALES (corp-wide): 1.1B **Privately Held**
WEB: www.capstonelogistics.com
SIC: 4789 Cargo loading & unloading services
PA: Capstone Logistics, Llc
30 Technology Pkwy S # 200
Peachtree Corners GA 30092
770 414-1929

(P-7877)
CHEEMA TRANSPORT INC
1483 Avenue 396, Kingsburg (93631-9132)
P.O. Box 737 (93631-0737)
PHONE.....................559 634-9109
Bahadur Singh, *President*
EMP: 45 **EST:** 2010
SALES (est): 6MM **Privately Held**
WEB: www.cheematransports.com
SIC: 4789 Cargo loading & unloading services

(P-7878)
DELIVERIMATES LLC
5311 Escover Ln, San Jose (95118-3025)
PHONE.....................857 445-7736
EMP: 60 **EST:** 2020
SALES (est): 4MM **Privately Held**
WEB: www.deliverimates.com
SIC: 4789 Transportation services

(P-7879)
DRAKAINA LOGISTICS
958 Ryan Ave, Clovis (93611-3423)
PHONE.....................559 765-1347
EMP: 70 **EST:** 2020
SALES (est): 3.1MM **Privately Held**
SIC: 4789 Transportation services

(P-7880)
DW MORGAN LLC
4185 Blackhawk Plaza Cir # 260, Danville (94506-4906)
PHONE.....................925 460-2700
David W Morgan, *CEO*
EMP: 63 **EST:** 2013
SALES (est): 10.7MM **Privately Held**
WEB: www.dwmorgan.com
SIC: 4789 4731 4212 Cargo loading & unloading services; domestic freight forwarding; local trucking, without storage

(P-7881)
FAST AG SVCS TRNSPT INC (PA)
1303 S Cornelia Ave, Fresno (93706-9414)
PHONE.....................559 233-0970
Chris Cubre, *CEO*
EMP: 45 **EST:** 2017
SALES (est): 374.4K **Privately Held**
SIC: 4789 Stockyards, not primarily for fattening or selling livestock

(P-7882)
FULFILLMENT WHSNG SLUTIONS INC
31137 Wiegman Rd, Hayward (94544-7854)
PHONE.....................760 685-5388
Tony Nguyen, *CEO*
EMP: 50 **EST:** 2019
SALES (est): 3.3MM **Privately Held**
WEB: www.fulfillmentsolutionsinc.com
SIC: 4789 4225 Freight car loading & unloading; general warehousing & storage

4789 - Transportation Svcs, NEC County (P-7883)

(P-7883)
INDUSTRIAL RELATIONS CAL DEPT
1515 Clay St Ste 1201, Oakland (94612-1474)
PHONE..................510 286-7000
Robert Jones, *Director*
EMP: 97 **Privately Held**
SIC: 4789 Pipeline terminal facilities, independently operated
HQ: California Department Of Industrial Relations
455 Golden Gate Ave Fl 10
San Francisco CA 94102

(P-7884)
JAC LOGISTICS LLC
1750 Pririe Cy Rd Ste 130, Folsom (95630)
PHONE..................954 881-2231
Cornell Campbell, *CEO*
EMP: 39 **EST:** 2020
SALES (est): 1.3MM **Privately Held**
SIC: 4789 Transportation services

(P-7885)
JIT TRANSPORTATION INC
1075 Montague Expy, Milpitas (95035-6828)
PHONE..................408 232-4800
Gene Ashley, *President*
Travis Wells, *Manager*
Edward Knudsen, *Supervisor*
EMP: 350 **EST:** 2007
SALES (est): 31.7MM **Privately Held**
WEB: www.jittransportation.com
SIC: 4789 Space flight operations, except government

(P-7886)
JJ EXPRESS FREIGHT INC
4196 Valtara Rd, Cameron Park (95682-8986)
PHONE..................916 914-3231
Zeljko Mijovic, *President*
EMP: 35 **EST:** 2016
SALES (est): 2.1MM **Privately Held**
SIC: 4789 Transportation services

(P-7887)
LOCATION SERVICES LLC (PA)
Also Called: Pathfinder Services
2365 Iron Point Rd # 160, Folsom (95630-8711)
PHONE..................800 588-0097
Lee McCarty, *CEO*
Karen Gordon, *CFO*
Jim Cousino, *Vice Pres*
Emory White, *Vice Pres*
Richard Barnes, *CIO*
EMP: 90 **EST:** 2014
SQ FT: 15,000
SALES (est): 27.1MM **Privately Held**
WEB: www.location-services.com
SIC: 4789 Car loading

(P-7888)
NEWLINE TRANSPORT INC
4460 W Shaw Ave Ste 234, Fresno (93722-6210)
PHONE..................559 515-5000
Gurjant Singh, *President*
EMP: 38 **EST:** 2017
SALES (est): 2.5MM **Privately Held**
SIC: 4789 Transportation services

(P-7889)
PACIFIC COAST CONTAINER INC (PA)
Also Called: PCC Northwest
432 Estudillo Ave Ste 1, San Leandro (94577-4908)
PHONE..................510 346-6100
Michael Mc Donnell, *CEO*
Abdel Zaharan, *CFO*
◆ **EMP:** 139 **EST:** 1988
SQ FT: 12,000
SALES (est): 65.9MM **Privately Held**
WEB: www.pcclogistics.com
SIC: 4789 4225 4222 Cargo loading & unloading services; general warehousing; warehousing, cold storage or refrigerated

(P-7890)
PATTAR TRANS INC
4325 W Taylor Rd, Turlock (95380-9558)
PHONE..................209 634-3849
Harwinder Singh Pattar, *CEO*
Ranjit Pattar, *Vice Pres*
EMP: 40 **EST:** 2000
SALES (est): 4.9MM **Privately Held**
SIC: 4789 Cargo loading & unloading services

(P-7891)
POSTMATES INC (HQ)
950 23rd St, San Francisco (94107-3401)
PHONE..................800 882-6106
Bastian Lehmann, *CEO*
Vivek Patel, *COO*
Kristen Schaefer, *CFO*
Justin Esch, *Vice Pres*
Wilson Korte, *Executive*
EMP: 333 **EST:** 2011
SALES (est): 307.8MM
SALES (corp-wide): 11.1B **Publicly Held**
WEB: www.postmates.com
SIC: 4789 Cargo loading & unloading services
PA: Uber Technologies, Inc.
1515 3rd St
San Francisco CA 94158
415 612-8582

(P-7892)
R MILLENNIUM TRANSPORT INC
Also Called: R Millennium Transport
1670 Fulkerth Rd, Turlock (95380-6885)
PHONE..................209 668-9700
Surjit Malhi, *President*
Rajwant Kaur Malhi, *Principal*
EMP: 35 **EST:** 2010
SALES (est): 4MM **Privately Held**
SIC: 4789 Cargo loading & unloading services

(P-7893)
RUSSO BROTHERS TRANSPORT INC
6108 Hedge Ave, Sacramento (95829-9340)
PHONE..................916 519-1334
Oleg Khomich, *CEO*
EMP: 51 **EST:** 2010
SALES (est): 3.6MM **Privately Held**
WEB: www.russotransport.com
SIC: 4789 Passenger train services

(P-7894)
SCUSD
3101 Redding Ave, Sacramento (95820-2124)
PHONE..................916 277-6705
Scusd Mnt, *Principal*
Christe Farnum, *Teacher*
Rosa Hernandez, *Teacher*
Suzan Lee, *Teacher*
Kim Loquaci, *Teacher*
EMP: 47 **EST:** 2008
SALES (est): 11MM **Privately Held**
WEB: www.scusd.edu
SIC: 4789 Transportation services

(P-7895)
STAR TRANSPORT LLC
9500 S De Wolf Ave, Selma (93662-9534)
P.O. Box 1350 (93662-1350)
PHONE..................559 834-3021
Jeff Lion, *Mng Member*
Brittany Westbrook, *Admin Asst*
Steve Serpa, *Opers Staff*
Bruce Lion,
Dan Lion,
EMP: 45 **EST:** 2007
SALES (est): 4.1MM **Privately Held**
WEB: www.startransport.net
SIC: 4789 Pipeline terminal facilities, independently operated

---

4812 Radiotelephone Communications

(P-7896)
AT&T CORP
330 R, San Ramon (94583)
PHONE..................925 823-6949
EMP: 416
SALES (corp-wide): 171.7B **Publicly Held**
WEB: www.att.com
SIC: 4812 Cellular telephone services
HQ: At&T Corp.
1 At&T Way
Bedminster NJ 07921
800 403-3302

(P-7897)
BLACKWATER CELLULAR CORP
Also Called: Cellular One
125 E Sir Frncis Drake Bl, Larkspur (94939-1860)
PHONE..................415 526-2200
Kevin Douglas, *Ch of Bd*
Tim Mc Gaw, *President*
EMP: 150 **EST:** 1991
SALES (est): 6.5MM **Privately Held**
WEB: www.cellularone.com
SIC: 4812 Cellular telephone services

(P-7898)
BRIX GROUP INC
4762 W Jennifer Ave # 103, Fresno (93722-6423)
PHONE..................800 726-2333
Kristina Reed, *Branch Mgr*
Harrison Brix, *COO*
EMP: 40
SALES (corp-wide): 156.6MM **Privately Held**
WEB: www.panapacific.com
SIC: 4812 Cellular telephone services
PA: The Brix Group Inc
838 N Laverne Ave
Fresno CA 93727
559 457-4700

(P-7899)
CELLCO PARTNERSHIP
Also Called: Verizon Wireless
682 Freeman Ln, Grass Valley (95949-9616)
PHONE..................530 477-8042
EMP: 71
SALES (corp-wide): 128.2B **Publicly Held**
WEB: www.verizonwireless.com
SIC: 4812 Cellular telephone services
HQ: Cellco Partnership
1 Verizon Way
Basking Ridge NJ 07920

(P-7900)
CELLCO PARTNERSHIP
Also Called: Verizon Wireless
5815 Stockton Blvd Ste D, Sacramento (95824-3051)
PHONE..................916 838-9525
EMP: 71
SALES (corp-wide): 128.2B **Publicly Held**
WEB: www.verizonwireless.com
SIC: 4812 Cellular telephone services
HQ: Cellco Partnership
1 Verizon Way
Basking Ridge NJ 07920

(P-7901)
CELLCO PARTNERSHIP
Also Called: Verizon Wireless
300 W Shaw Ave, Clovis (93612-3680)
PHONE..................559 321-8116
EMP: 71
SALES (corp-wide): 128.2B **Publicly Held**
WEB: www.verizonwireless.com
SIC: 4812 Cellular telephone services
HQ: Cellco Partnership
1 Verizon Way
Basking Ridge NJ 07920

(P-7902)
CELLCO PARTNERSHIP
18012 Bollinger Canyon Rd, San Ramon (94583-1502)
PHONE..................925 743-9327
EMP: 74
SALES (corp-wide): 127B **Publicly Held**
SIC: 4812 Radiotelephone Communication
HQ: Cellco Partnership
1 Verizon Way
Basking Ridge NJ 07920

(P-7903)
CELLCO PARTNERSHIP
Also Called: Verizon Wireless
10952 Trinity Pkwy, Stockton (95219-7235)
PHONE..................209 474-9071
EMP: 71
SALES (corp-wide): 128.2B **Publicly Held**
WEB: www.verizonwireless.com
SIC: 4812 Cellular telephone services
HQ: Cellco Partnership
1 Verizon Way
Basking Ridge NJ 07920

(P-7904)
CLFRN/CLRD/FLRD/RGON I COMCAST
3011 Comcast Pl, Livermore (94551-7594)
PHONE..................925 424-0273
Stephen B Burke, *President*
Kristeen Cominiello, *Vice Pres*
Markos Moussa, *Planning*
Tonya Kelly, *Finance*
Angela Mead, *Human Res Mgr*
EMP: 222 **EST:** 1996
SALES (est): 29.1MM
SALES (corp-wide): 103.5B **Publicly Held**
WEB: www.comcast.com
SIC: 4812 4841 Radio telephone communication; cable television services
PA: Comcast Corporation
1701 John F Kennedy Blvd
Philadelphia PA 19103
215 286-1700

(P-7905)
CONTRA COSTA COUNTY
30 Douglas Dr, Martinez (94553-4068)
PHONE..................925 313-1323
Tim Rocco, *Treasurer*
Scott Alonso, *Officer*
Teresa Gerringer, *Comms Dir*
Ed Woo, *CIO*
Jeff Cameron, *Network Mgr*
EMP: 125 **EST:** 2016
SALES (est): 23.7MM **Privately Held**
WEB: www.cchealth.org
SIC: 4812 Radio telephone communication

(P-7906)
CREDO MOBILE INC
Also Called: Working Assets Long Distance
101 Market St Ste 700, San Francisco (94105-1533)
P.O. Box 88878, Carol Stream IL (60188-0878)
PHONE..................415 369-2000
Michael Hall Kieschnick, *CEO*
Douglas Moore, *CFO*
Stephen Gunn, *Vice Pres*
Cecilia Parisi, *Vice Pres*
Mary Wu, *Vice Pres*
EMP: 100 **EST:** 1985
SQ FT: 21,000
SALES (est): 26.2MM **Privately Held**
WEB: www.credomobile.com
SIC: 4812 Cellular telephone services

(P-7907)
INDIAN ROCK UNIVERSAL INC
4132 Manzanita Ave # 400, Carmichael (95608-8200)
PHONE..................916 696-6973
Adrianna Blea, *Principal*
EMP: 39
SALES (corp-wide): 116.5K **Privately Held**
SIC: 4812 Cellular telephone services

PRODUCTS & SERVICES SECTION

4813 - Telephone Communications, Except Radio County (P-7930)

PA: Indian Rock Universal Inc.
8939 S Sepulveda Blvd
Los Angeles CA

(P-7908) NSA WIRELESS INC (PA)
12893 Alcosta Blvd Ste G, San Ramon (94583-1450)
P.O. Box 1073 (94583-1073)
PHONE...............925 867-2817
James Irish, *President*
EMP: 44 **EST:** 2005
SALES (est): 8.8MM **Privately Held**
WEB: www.nsawireless.com
SIC: 4812 Cellular telephone services

(P-7909) PACIFIC BELL TELEPHONE COMPANY
262 19th Ave, San Mateo (94403-1419)
PHONE...............650 572-6807
Carl Edwards, *Principal*
EMP: 4444
SALES (corp-wide): 171.7B **Publicly Held**
WEB: www.att.com
SIC: 4812 Cellular telephone services
HQ: Pacific Bell Telephone Company
430 Bush St Fl 3
San Francisco CA 94108
415 542-9000

(P-7910) PACIFIC BELL TELEPHONE COMPANY
2040 Polk St 267, San Francisco (94109-2520)
PHONE...............415 978-0881
EMP: 4444
SALES (corp-wide): 171.7B **Publicly Held**
WEB: www.att.com
SIC: 4812 Cellular telephone services
HQ: Pacific Bell Telephone Company
430 Bush St Fl 3
San Francisco CA 94108
415 542-9000

(P-7911) SBC LONG DISTANCE LLC
Also Called: AT&T Long Distance
5850 W Las Positas Blvd, Pleasanton (94588-8522)
PHONE...............314 505-0582
Marla Cruse, *Manager*
EMP: 39 **EST:** 2006
SALES (est): 1.4MM
SALES (corp-wide): 171.7B **Publicly Held**
WEB: www.att.com
SIC: 4812 Cellular telephone services
PA: At&T Inc.
208 S Akard St
Dallas TX 75202
210 821-4105

(P-7912) SLING MEDIA LLC
1051 E Hillsdale Blvd # 500, Foster City (94404-1640)
PHONE...............650 293-8000
Charles W Ergen, *CEO*
Linda Ng, *Executive Asst*
Chris Ferro, *Software Dev*
Peter Haase, *Technical Staff*
Harshal Zele, *Technical Staff*
▲ **EMP:** 180 **EST:** 2004
SALES (est): 36.1MM **Publicly Held**
WEB: www.sling.com
SIC: 4812 Radio telephone communication
PA: Dish Network Corporation
9601 S Meridian Blvd
Englewood CO 80112

(P-7913) SPIDERCLOUD WIRELESS INC (HQ)
475 Sycamore Dr, Milpitas (95035-7428)
PHONE...............408 567-9165
Michael Gallagher, *CEO*
Thomas Scott, *CFO*
Theresa McCarthy, *Vice Pres*
Ron Pelley, *Vice Pres*
Kumarakrishna Ramkumar, *QA Dir*
▲ **EMP:** 50 **EST:** 2007
SALES (est): 23MM
SALES (corp-wide): 11.3B **Publicly Held**
WEB: www.corning.com
SIC: 4812 Cellular telephone services
PA: Corning Incorporated
1 Riverfront Plz
Corning NY 14831
607 974-9000

(P-7914) T-MOBILE USA INC
Also Called: Metropcs-Modesto
2225 Plaza Pkwy Ste I1b, Modesto (95350-6220)
PHONE...............209 529-0539
EMP: 170
SALES (corp-wide): 88.3B **Publicly Held**
SIC: 4812 4813 Radiotelephone Communication Telephone Communications Ret Misc Merchandise
HQ: T-Mobile Usa, Inc.
12920 Se 38th St
Bellevue WA 98006
425 378-4000

(P-7915) TAGGLE SYSTEMS LLC
2804 Gateway Oaks Dr 10, Sacramento (95833-4345)
PHONE...............800 619-2919
George Zisis, *Manager*
EMP: 50 **EST:** 2018
SALES (est): 1.7MM **Privately Held**
SIC: 4812 1522 Cellular telephone services; multi-family dwellings, new construction

(P-7916) TKS WIRELESS INC
Also Called: Cricket Wireless
3320 Foothill Blvd, Oakland (94601-3115)
P.O. Box 2225, Union City (94587-7225)
PHONE...............510 227-6440
Sami D Aldajani, *President*
Khalid Aldajani, *Admin Sec*
EMP: 200 **EST:** 2013
SALES (est): 20.7MM **Privately Held**
SIC: 4812 Cellular telephone services

(P-7917) UNLIMITED R US INC (PA)
Also Called: Metro Unlimited Wireless
10535 E Stockton Blvd F, Elk Grove (95624-9758)
PHONE...............916 509-4496
Fathi Abboushi, *President*
EMP: 41 **EST:** 2013 **Privately Held**
SIC: 4812 Cellular telephone services

4813 Telephone Communications, Except Radio

(P-7918) 11 MAIN INC
527 Flume St, Chico (95928-5608)
PHONE...............530 892-9191
Jeff Schlicht, *CEO*
Mike Effle, *President*
Ray Kaminski, *Vice Pres*
Christina Liu, *Vice Pres*
Amber Minson, *Vice Pres*
EMP: 105 **EST:** 2013
SALES (est): 15.2MM **Privately Held**
SIC: 4813
HQ: Alibaba.Com Us Llc
525 Almanor Ave Ste 400
Sunnyvale CA 94085
408 785-5580

(P-7919) 1HEALTHIO INC
388 Market St, San Francisco (94111-5311)
PHONE...............208 681-4058
Mehdi Maghsoodnia, *CEO*
Nikhil Arun, *Vice Pres*
Haley Goldlist, *Principal*
EMP: 44 **EST:** 2014
SALES (est): 7.6MM **Privately Held**
WEB: www.vitagene.com
SIC: 4813

(P-7920) 2WIRE INC (DH)
2450 Walsh Ave, Santa Clara (95051-1303)
PHONE...............408 235-5500
Tim O'Loughlin, *CEO*
Pasquale Romano, *President*
Mary S Chan, *Bd of Directors*
Tom McLaughlin, *Vice Pres*
Kim Hanson, *Office Mgr*
▲ **EMP:** 138
SQ FT: 82,000
SALES (est): 72.6MM **Publicly Held**
WEB: www.commscope.com
SIC: 4813

(P-7921) 8X8 INC (PA)
675 Creekside Way, Campbell (95008-0636)
PHONE...............408 727-1885
Dave Sipes, *CEO*
Bryan R Martin, *Ch of Bd*
Samuel Wilson, *CFO*
Walt Weisner, *Ch Credit Ofcr*
Amritesh Chaudhuri, *Chief Mktg Cfcr*
EMP: 1095 **EST:** 1987
SQ FT: 140,831
SALES: 532.3MM **Publicly Held**
WEB: www.8x8.com
SIC: 4813 7372 ; ; prepackaged software

(P-7922) ADAPTIVE SPCTRUM SGNAL ALGNMT (PA)
Also Called: Adaptive Spctrum Signal Algnmt
203 Rdwood Shres Pkwy Ste, Redwood City (94065)
PHONE...............650 654-3400
John M Cioffi, *CEO*
James Lindstrom, *CFO*
Philip Bednarz, *Exec VP*
Assia Cioffi, *Exec VP*
Barry Gray, *Vice Pres*
EMP: 72 **EST:** 2010
SALES (est): 10.6MM **Privately Held**
WEB: www.assia-inc.com
SIC: 4813

(P-7923) AERIS COMMUNICATIONS INC (PA)
2099 Gateway Pl Ste 600, San Jose (95110-1048)
PHONE...............408 557-1900
Marc Jones, *CEO*
John Molise, *CFO*
Raj Kanaya, *Chief Mktg Ofcr*
Mark Cratsenburg, *Vice Pres*
Michael Doran, *Vice Pres*
EMP: 180 **EST:** 2013
SQ FT: 30,000
SALES (est): 56.4MM **Privately Held**
WEB: www.aeris.com
SIC: 4813 4812 Local & long distance telephone communications: cellular telephone services

(P-7924) ALTEP CALIFORNIA LLC (DH)
Also Called: Elitigation Solutions
2479 E Bayshore Rd # 215, Palo Alto (94303-3230)
PHONE...............650 691-4500
Roger Miller,
EMP: 80 **EST:** 2013
SALES (est): 1MM
SALES (corp-wide): 50.7MM **Privately Held**
WEB: www.elitinc.com
SIC: 4813
HQ: Altep, Inc.
1828 L St Nw Ste 1070
Washington DC 20036
915 533-8722

(P-7925) ANOTHER CORPORATE ISP LLC
Also Called: Monkeybrains
286 12th St, San Francisco (94103-3718)
PHONE...............415 974-1313
Rudy Rucker, *Mng Member*
Lewis Morales, *Administration*
Matt Luzius, *Technical Staff*
Laurie Hall, *Counsel*
EMP: 50 **EST:** 2011
SALES (est): 8.3MM **Privately Held**
WEB: www.monkeybrains.net
SIC: 4813

(P-7926) ARROW SYSTEMS INTEGRATION INC
46425 Landing Pkwy, Fremont (94538-6496)
PHONE...............510 897-2900
Fax: 510 897-2901
EMP: 19
SALES (corp-wide): 23.8B **Publicly Held**
SIC: 4813 3661 1731 Telephone Communications Mfg Telephone/Telegraph Apparatus Electrical Contractor
HQ: Arrow Systems Integration, Inc.
1820 Preston Park Blvd # 2800
Plano TX 55121
972 462-5800

(P-7927) ASIAINFO-LINKAGE INC
5201 Great America Pkwy # 356, Santa Clara (95054-1122)
PHONE...............408 970-9788
Steve Zhang, *CEO*
Ying Han, *CFO*
Yadong Jin, *Exec VP*
Jie LI, *Vice Pres*
Lihua Yan, *Vice Pres*
EMP: 1500 **EST:** 1994 **Privately Held**
WEB: www.asiainfo-linkage.com
SIC: 4813
HQ: Asiainfo Technologies (China), Inc.
101, 1st Floor, Building 19, East District, No. 10, Northwest Wa
Beijing 10019

(P-7928) AT&T SERVICES INC
610 Brannan St, San Francisco (94107-1512)
PHONE...............415 545-9051
EMP: 187
SALES (corp-wide): 146.8B **Publicly Held**
SIC: 4813 Telephone Communications
HQ: At&T Services, Inc.
208 S Akard St Ste 110
Dallas TX 75202
210 821-4105

(P-7929) AT&T SERVICES INC
666 Folsom St Rm 1132, San Francisco (94107-1397)
PHONE...............415 545-9058
EMP: 90
SALES (corp-wide): 160.5B **Publicly Held**
SIC: 4813 4812 Telephone Communications Radiotelephone Communication
HQ: At&T Services, Inc.
208 S Akard St Ste 110
Dallas TX 75202
210 821-4105

(P-7930) AT&T SERVICES INC
Also Called: SBC
485 S Monroe St 13a, San Jose (95128)
PHONE...............408 554-3335
EMP: 168
SALES (corp-wide): 160.5B **Publicly Held**
SIC: 4813 Telephone Communications
HQ: At&T Services, Inc.
208 S Akard St Ste 110
Dallas TX 75202
210 821-4105

4813 - Telephone Communications, Except Radio County (P-7931)

(P-7931)
AUTOMATTIC INC (PA)
Also Called: Woocommerce
2601 Mission St Ste 900, San Francisco (94110-3143)
PHONE..................................877 273-3049
Mattew Mullenweg, *CEO*
Stuart West, *CFO*
Michelle Weber, *Bd of Directors*
Toni Schneider, *Admin Sec*
Josh Betz, *Sr Software Eng*
EMP: 60 EST: 2005
SALES (est): 48.2MM **Privately Held**
WEB: www.automattic.com
SIC: **4813** 7375 7371 ; information retrieval services; data base information retrieval; on-line data base information retrieval; computer software development & applications

(P-7932)
AUTOMTED MDIA PROC SLTIONS INC
Also Called: Equilibrium Solutions Group
500 Tamal Plz Ste 520, Corte Madera (94925-1184)
PHONE..................................415 332-4343
Sean Barger, *Bd of Directors*
Damien Wigley, *General Mgr*
EMP: 30 EST: 2004
SQ FT: 4,800
SALES (est): 5.6MM **Privately Held**
WEB: www.equilibrium.com
SIC: **4813** 7371 7373 7372 ; computer software systems analysis & design, custom; systems software development services; business oriented computer software

(P-7933)
AVAYA INC
1030 Commercial St, San Jose (95112-1436)
PHONE..................................408 437-2504
EMP: 36 **Publicly Held**
WEB: www.avaya.com
SIC: **4813** Telephone communication, except radio
HQ: Avaya Inc.
2605 Meridian Pkwy # 200
Durham NC 27713
908 953-6000

(P-7934)
BIGSTEPCOM
2601 Mission St Ste 500, San Francisco (94110-3142)
PHONE..................................415 229-8500
Lucy Reid, *CEO*
Andrew Beebe, *President*
Tim Roberts, *Sales Mgr*
EMP: 202 EST: 1998
SALES (est): 1.2MM **Privately Held**
WEB: www.hosand.com
SIC: **4813** 8742 ; management consulting services
HQ: Affinity Internet, Inc.
3250 W Coml Blvd Ste 200
Fort Lauderdale FL 33309
954 334-8181

(P-7935)
BLOOMREACH INC (PA)
82 Pioneer Way, Mountain View (94041-1525)
PHONE..................................650 964-1541
Raj De Datta, *CEO*
Dave Pomeroy, *CFO*
David Hurwitz, *Chief Mktg Ofcr*
Rob Rosenthal, *Officer*
Tjeerd Brenninkmeijer, *Exec VP*
EMP: 130 EST: 2009
SALES (est): 30.5MM **Privately Held**
WEB: www.bloomreach.com
SIC: **4813**

(P-7936)
CAL CONSOLDATED COMMUNICATIONS
211 Lincoln St, Roseville (95678-2614)
P.O. Box 619969 (95661-0969)
PHONE..................................916 786-6141
Bob Udell, *CEO*
David Herrick, *Vice Pres*
Kathleen Glenn, *Analyst*
Joe Glenn, *Director*
Mike Johnson, *Manager*
EMP: 385 EST: 1914
SQ FT: 21,500
SALES (est): 15.9MM
SALES (corp-wide): 1.3B **Publicly Held**
WEB: www.consolidated.com
SIC: **4813** Local telephone communications; long distance telephone communications
HQ: Surewest Communications
211 Lincoln St
Roseville CA 95678
916 786-6141

(P-7937)
CALNET INC
4101 Wild Chaparral Dr, Shingle Springs (95682-8739)
P.O. Box 1041 (95682-1041)
PHONE..................................530 672-1078
John Lane, *CEO*
Ken Garnett, *COO*
Rob Graf, *Officer*
Helena Scott, *Senior VP*
Mary Bryan, *Vice Pres*
EMP: 78 EST: 1996
SALES (est): 34.7MM **Privately Held**
WEB: www.cal.net
SIC: **4813**

(P-7938)
CBS MAXPREPS INC
4364 Town Center Blvd # 320, El Dorado Hills (95762-7127)
PHONE..................................530 676-6440
Andy Beal, *President*
Matt Locke, *Info Tech Dir*
John Stockett, *Merchandising*
Todd Shurtleff, *Director*
Christina Martin, *Assistant*
EMP: 42 EST: 1993
SQ FT: 9,000
SALES (est): 1.5MM
SALES (corp-wide): 25.3B **Publicly Held**
WEB: www.viacomcbs.com
SIC: **4813**
HQ: Viacomcbs Inc.
1515 Broadway
New York NY 10036
212 258-6000

(P-7939)
CITIZENS TELECOM CO CAL INC (HQ)
Also Called: Frontier
9260 E Stockton Blvd, Elk Grove (95624-1456)
PHONE..................................317 208-3567
Mary Agnes Wilderotter, *Ch of Bd*
Livingston E Ross, *Vice Pres*
John Casey, *Admin Sec*
Mark Devoll, *Technician*
EMP: 318 EST: 1927
SQ FT: 1,000
SALES (est): 47.8MM
SALES (corp-wide): 7.1B **Privately Held**
WEB: www.frontier.com
SIC: **4813** Local telephone communications; long distance telephone communications
PA: Frontier Communications Corporation
401 Merritt 7 Ste 7
Norwalk CT 06851
203 614-5600

(P-7940)
CLEARCAPTIONS LLC
3001 Lava Ridge Ct # 100, Roseville (95661-2837)
PHONE..................................866 868-8695
Robert Rae, *President*
Corrine Perritano, *COO*
Raghu Dhulipala, *Officer*
Rita Beier Braman, *Vice Pres*
Gordon L Ellis, *Vice Pres*
EMP: 50 EST: 2015
SALES (est): 25.2MM
SALES (corp-wide): 103.6MM **Privately Held**
WEB: www.clearcaptions.com
SIC: **4813**
PA: Purple Communications, Inc.
13620 Ranch Road 620 N C100
Austin TX 78717
888 900-4780

(P-7941)
CLOVER NETWORK INC
415 N Mathilda Ave, Sunnyvale (94085-4222)
PHONE..................................650 210-7888
Leonard Speiser, *CEO*
Zan Aronowitz, *COO*
John Beatty, *Vice Pres*
Michael Lazzaro, *Vice Pres*
Mark Schulze, *VP Business*
EMP: 65 EST: 2010
SQ FT: 8,200
SALES (est): 25.4MM
SALES (corp-wide): 14.8B **Publicly Held**
WEB: www.clover.com
SIC: **4813**
HQ: First Data Corporation
255 Fiserv Dr
Brookfield WI 53045

(P-7942)
CONSOLE (PA)
Also Called: Iix Peering
3131 Jay St Ste 210, Santa Clara (95054-3336)
PHONE..................................855 858-5497
Bill Norton, *Principal*
Stephen Wilcox, *President*
Paul Gampe, *CTO*
Blake Gillman, *Director*
EMP: 35 EST: 2013
SALES (est): 996.1K **Privately Held**
WEB: www.console.to
SIC: **4813**

(P-7943)
CORE+DATA CORPORATION
37 Roble Rd, Berkeley (94705-2826)
PHONE..................................510 540-0168
Russ Watson Jr, *President*
Terry Walker, *Treasurer*
Jay Wolford, *Vice Pres*
EMP: 50 EST: 1994
SALES (est): 2.2MM **Privately Held**
SIC: **4813**

(P-7944)
COVAD COMMUNICATIONS GROUP INC (DH)
Also Called: Megapath
6800 Koll Center Pkwy # 20, Pleasanton (94566-7045)
PHONE..................................408 952-6400
D Craig Young, *CEO*
Brett Flinchum, *COO*
Jeffrey Bailey, *CFO*
Douglas A Carlen, *Senior VP*
Chris Tsichlis, *VP Human Res*
▲ EMP: 131 EST: 1996
SQ FT: 133,310
SALES (est): 279.3MM
SALES (corp-wide): 844.2MM **Privately Held**
WEB: www.gtt.net
SIC: **4813** Voice telephone communications; data telephone communications;
HQ: Fusion Mphc Holding Corporation
6800 Koll Center Pkwy
Pleasanton CA 94566
925 201-2500

(P-7945)
DECENTRAL TV CORPORATION
Also Called: Kyte
442 Post St Fl 10, San Francisco (94102-1524)
PHONE..................................415 480-6800
Daniel Graf, *CEO*
Gannon Hall, *COO*
Anne Dorman, *CFO*
Dan Fitzsimons, *Risk Mgmt Dir*
Erik Abair, *CTO*
EMP: 86 EST: 2006
SQ FT: 2,000
SALES (est): 6.9MM
SALES (corp-wide): 22.7MM **Privately Held**
WEB: www.piksel.com
SIC: **4813**
PA: Piksel, Inc.
2100 Powers Ferry Rd Se # 400
Atlanta GA 30339
877 664-6137

(P-7946)
DIGITAL PATH INC
1065 Marauder St, Chico (95973-9039)
PHONE..................................800 676-7284
James A Higgins, *President*
Erica Higgins, *CFO*
Michelle Wright, *Vice Pres*
Jeanne Burroughs, *Info Tech Mgr*
Cathy Houghtby, *Teacher*
▲ EMP: 50 EST: 2005
SALES (est): 27MM **Privately Held**
WEB: www.digitalpath.net
SIC: **4813** 5045 ; ; computers, peripherals & software

(P-7947)
ENVIVIO INC
2795 Augustine Dr, Santa Clara (95054-2957)
PHONE..................................650 243-2700
Julien Signes, *President*
Terry D Kramer, *Ch of Bd*
Erik E Miller, *CFO*
Jean-Pierre Henot, *CTO*
EMP: 163 EST: 2000
SALES (est): 46.1MM
SALES (corp-wide): 26.8B **Privately Held**
WEB: www.mediakind.com
SIC: **4813** Telephone/video communications
HQ: Ericsson Inc.
6300 Legacy Dr
Plano TX 75024
972 583-0000

(P-7948)
EQUINIX PACIFIC LLC (HQ)
Also Called: Equinix Pacific, Inc.
1 Lagoon Dr Ste 400, Redwood City (94065-1564)
PHONE..................................650 598-6000
Samuel Lee, *President*
Keith D Taylor, *CFO*
▲ EMP: 254 EST: 2012
SALES (est): 5.9MM
SALES (corp-wide): 6B **Publicly Held**
WEB: www.equinix.com
SIC: **4813**
PA: Equinix, Inc.
1 Lagoon Dr Ste 400
Redwood City CA 94065
650 598-6000

(P-7949)
EQUINIX PROFESSIONAL SVCS INC
1 Lagoon Dr, Redwood City (94065-1562)
PHONE..................................800 322-9280
Andrew Peitsch, *Analyst*
EMP: 39 EST: 2016
SALES (est): 2.5MM
SALES (corp-wide): 6B **Publicly Held**
WEB: www.equinix.com
SIC: **4813**
PA: Equinix, Inc.
1 Lagoon Dr Ste 400
Redwood City CA 94065
650 598-6000

(P-7950)
ERICSSON INC
2755 Augustine Dr, Santa Clara (95054-2919)
PHONE..................................408 750-5000
Kevin A Denuccio, *Manager*
Sheleila Valderama, *Project Mgr*
Mirko Prizmic, *Engineer*
Shah Rahman, *Director*
Sergio Czernichow, *Manager*
EMP: 1100
SALES (corp-wide): 26.8B **Privately Held**
SIC: **4813** Telephone communication, except radio
HQ: Ericsson Inc.
6300 Legacy Dr
Plano TX 75024
972 583-0000

(P-7951)
FRONTIER CALIFORNIA INC
Also Called: Verizon
525 E Yosemite Ave, Manteca (95336-5806)
P.O. Box 992 (95336-1139)
PHONE..................................209 239-4128
Luanne Weldon, *Branch Mgr*

PRODUCTS & SERVICES SECTION
4813 - Telephone Communications, Except Radio County (P-7973)

EMP: 305
SALES (corp-wide): 7.1B **Privately Held**
WEB: www.frontier.sale
SIC: 4813 4812 Local telephone communications; radio telephone communication
HQ: Frontier California Inc.
401 Merritt 7
Norwalk CT 06851

(P-7952)
FRONTIER CALIFORNIA INC
Also Called: Verizon
295 Parkshore Dr, Folsom (95630-4716)
PHONE 212 395-1000
Victor Andersen, *Branch Mgr*
EMP: 305
SALES (corp-wide): 7.1B **Privately Held**
WEB: www.frontier.sale
SIC: 4813 Telephone communication, except radio
HQ: Frontier California Inc.
401 Merritt 7
Norwalk CT 06851

(P-7953)
FUSION CLOUD COMPANY LLC (DH)
6800 Koll Center Pkwy # 20, Pleasanton (94566-7045)
PHONE 925 201-2500
Donald C Young, *Mng Member*
Brian George, *CTO*
Derek Heins,
Paul Milley,
EMP: 80 **EST:** 2015
SALES (est): 127.6MM
SALES (corp-wide): 844.2MM **Privately Held**
WEB: www.gtt.net
SIC: 4813 Data telephone communications
HQ: Covad Communications Group, Inc.
6800 Koll Center Pkwy # 20
Pleasanton CA 94566
408 952-6400

(P-7954)
FUTUREWEI TECHNOLOGIES INC
2330 Central Expy, Santa Clara (95050-2516)
PHONE 469 277-5700
EMP: 119
SALES (corp-wide): 37.3B **Privately Held**
SIC: 4813 Telephone communication, except radio
HQ: Futurewei Technologies, Inc.
5700 Tennyson Pkwy # 600
Plano TX 75024
469 277-5700

(P-7955)
GLOBAL VALLEY NETWORKS INC
Also Called: Gvn
515 Keystone Blvd, Patterson (95363-8861)
PHONE 209 892-4100
Carla Reichelderfer, *President*
Ed Tisdale, *CFO*
Angel Covarrubias, *Real Est Agnt*
EMP: 48 **EST:** 1913
SQ FT: 15,000
SALES (est): 282.4K **Privately Held**
WEB: www.frontier.sale
SIC: 4813 Long distance telephone communications

(P-7956)
GOGRID LLC
Also Called: Coloserve
150 S 1st St Ste 101, San Jose (95113-2605)
PHONE 415 869-7444
John Keagy, *Mng Member*
Brett Newsome, *CFO*
Jeff Samuels, *Chief Mktg Ofcr*
Mark Worsey, *CTO*
Jerry Mun, *Network Enginr*
EMP: 112 **EST:** 2001
SQ FT: 20,000
SALES (est): 16.4MM **Privately Held**
SIC: 4813 7374 7375 7371 ; ; data processing & preparation; computer graphics service; data base information retrieval; computer software development & applications

(P-7957)
GTT COMMUNICATIONS (MP) INC (DH)
Also Called: Megapath
6700 Koll Center Pkwy # 33, Pleasanton (94566-7060)
PHONE 415 687-3870
Craig Young, *CEO*
Paul Milley, *CFO*
Kurt Hoffman, *Co-President*
Steve Chisholm, *Senior VP*
David Williams, *Senior VP*
EMP: 150 **EST:** 1997
SQ FT: 12,000
SALES (est): 87.4MM **Privately Held**
SIC: 4813 7375 ; information retrieval services
HQ: Gtt Americas, Llc
7900 Tysons One Pl Fl 14
Mc Lean VA 22102
703 783-3124

(P-7958)
HOTWIRE INC
114 Sansome St Ste 400, San Francisco (94104-3810)
PHONE 415 343-8400
Dara Khosrowshahi, *CEO*
Clem Bason, *President*
Melissa Postier, *Social Dir*
Gabriela Contreras, *Executive Asst*
ARI Gunawan, *Sr Software Eng*
EMP: 175 **EST:** 1999
SALES (est): 58.5MM
SALES (corp-wide): 5.2B **Publicly Held**
WEB: www.hotwire.com
SIC: 4813
PA: Expedia Group, Inc.
1111 Expedia Group Way W
Seattle WA 98119
206 481-7200

(P-7959)
HUAWEI ENTERPRISE USA INC
20400 Stevens Creek Blvd, Cupertino (95014-2217)
PHONE 408 394-4295
EMP: 80
SALES (est): 6.4MM **Privately Held**
SIC: 4813 Telephone Communications
PA: Huawei Investment & Holding Co., Ltd.
Bantian Huawei Base, Longgang District
Shenzhen 51812

(P-7960)
IAC PUBLISHING LLC
555 12th St Ste 300, Oakland (94607-3698)
PHONE 510 985-7400
Adam Roston, *CEO*
Jeffrey Spitzer, *Vice Pres*
Stephanie Williams, *Executive Asst*
Daniel Wiener, *Marketing Mgr*
EMP: 100 **EST:** 2017
SQ FT: 47,679
SALES (est): 7.9MM **Privately Held**
WEB: www.iacpublishing.com
SIC: 4813

(P-7961)
INDIEGOGO INC
965 Mission St Fl 7, San Francisco (94103-2955)
PHONE 866 641-4646
Andy Bailey, *CEO*
Kerry Barker, *Trust Officer*
Deana Burke, *Vice Pres*
Genevieve Conaty, *Vice Pres*
Tim French, *Vice Pres*
EMP: 138 **EST:** 2007
SALES (est): 45.2MM **Privately Held**
WEB: www.filmgogo.com
SIC: 4813 7371 ; computer code authors; software programming applications

(P-7962)
INGENIO INC
182 Howard St 826, San Francisco (94105-1611)
PHONE 415 248-4000
Warren Heffelfinger, *CEO*
Mark Britto, *CEO*
EMP: 120 **EST:** 1999
SQ FT: 25,000
SALES (est): 23.7MM
SALES (corp-wide): 171.7B **Publicly Held**
WEB: www.ingenio.com
SIC: 4813
PA: At&T Inc.
208 S Akard St
Dallas TX 75202
210 821-4105

(P-7963)
INREACH INTERNET LLC (HQ)
4635 Georgetown Pl, Stockton (95207-6203)
P.O. Box 312, West Enfield ME (04493-0312)
PHONE 888 467-3224
EMP: 57
SQ FT: 5,075
SALES (est): 7.5MM
SALES (corp-wide): 16.4MM **Privately Held**
SIC: 4813 Telephone Communications
PA: Mobilepro Corp.
6100 Oak Tree Blvd # 200
Independence OH 44131
216 986-2745

(P-7964)
INTER STAR INC
Also Called: Shasta.com
833 Mistletoe Ln Ste A1, Redding (96002-0247)
PHONE 530 224-6866
Andrew Main, *President*
Darren White, *Corp Secy*
Becky Hemp, *Exec VP*
Frank J Bramante, *Controller*
Mark Caulfield, *Sales Associate*
EMP: 65 **EST:** 1995
SQ FT: 3,000
SALES (est): 9MM **Privately Held**
SIC: 4813

(P-7965)
INTERMEDIA COMMUNICATIONS INC (DH)
100 Mathilda Pl Ste 600, Sunnyvale (94086-6081)
PHONE 800 940-0011
David C Ruberg, *President*
James M Walters, *President*
Jeanne M Walters, *President*
Robert M Manning, *CFO*
EMP: 225 **EST:** 1986
SALES (est): 805.6MM
SALES (corp-wide): 128.2B **Publicly Held**
WEB: www.verizon.com
SIC: 4813 Local & long distance telephone communications; voice telephone communications; data telephone communications;

(P-7966)
IPASS INC (HQ)
3800 Bridge Pkwy, Redwood City (94065-1171)
PHONE 650 232-4100
Darin R Vickery, *CFO*
Christine Braelow, *Vice Pres*
Christopher Calhoun, *Vice Pres*
Gilbert Rios, *Info Tech Mgr*
Monish Bhorali, *Software Engr*
EMP: 181 **EST:** 1996
SQ FT: 25,000
SALES: 54.4MM
SALES (corp-wide): 69.6MM **Publicly Held**
WEB: www.ipass.com
SIC: 4813 7374 ; ; data processing & preparation
PA: Pareteum Corporation
1185 Ave Of The Amrcas Fl
New York NY 10036
646 975-0400

(P-7967)
JIGSAW OPERATIONS LLC (PA)
1600 Amphitheatre Pkwy, Mountain View (94043-1351)
PHONE 212 565-8046
John Sarapata, *Exec Dir*
EMP: 30 **EST:** 2017
SALES (est): 2.1MM **Privately Held**
WEB: www.jigsaw.google.com
SIC: 4813 7372 ; application computer software

(P-7968)
JUSTANSWER LLC
38 Keyes Ave Ste 150, San Francisco (94129-1761)
PHONE 800 785-2305
Andrew Kurtzig,
Jeremy Liegl,
Jason Kellerman, *Exec VP*
Jeff Cavellini, *Vice Pres*
Robert Ellison, *CTO*
EMP: 38 **EST:** 2011
SALES (est): 3.4MM **Privately Held**
WEB: www.justanswer.com
SIC: 4813

(P-7969)
LIVEWORLD INC (PA)
2105 S Bascom Ave Ste 159, Campbell (95008-3276)
PHONE 800 301-9507
Peter H Friedman, *CEO*
David Houston, *CFO*
Chris N Christensen, *Exec VP*
Jenna Woodul, *Exec VP*
Martin Bishop, *Vice Pres*
EMP: 68 **EST:** 1996
SALES (est): 20MM **Publicly Held**
WEB: www.liveworld.com
SIC: 4813

(P-7970)
LUMEN TECH GVRNMENT SLTONS INC
2240 Douglas Blvd Ste 250, Roseville (95661-3874)
PHONE 916 781-7772
Peter Kusendahl, *Branch Mgr*
EMP: 5004
SALES (corp-wide): 20.7B **Publicly Held**
SIC: 4813 Local telephone communications
HQ: Lumen Technologies Government Solutions, Inc.
931 14th St Ste 1000b
Denver CO 80202
303 992-1400

(P-7971)
LUMEN TECHNOLOGIES INC
1085 Marguerite Ct, Lafayette (94549-2847)
PHONE 925 974-0200
EMP: 45
SALES (corp-wide): 20.7B **Publicly Held**
WEB: www.centurylink.com
SIC: 4813 Telecommunications & Cellular Services
PA: Lumen Technologies, Inc.
100 Centurylink Dr
Monroe LA 71203
318 388-9000

(P-7972)
MAILCENTRO INC
715 Sutter St Ste B, Folsom (95630-2569)
PHONE 916 985-4445
David Saykally, *President*
EMP: 120 **EST:** 2001
SALES (est): 477.3K **Privately Held**
WEB: www.cpsoftwaregroup.com
SIC: 4813
PA: Computer Power Software Group Inc.
716 Figueroa St
Folsom CA 95630

(P-7973)
MOBITV INC (PA)
1900 Powell St Ste 900, Emeryville (94608-1885)
PHONE 510 981-1303
Charlie Nooney, *Ch of Bd*
Stephen Coney, *President*
Paul Scanlan, *President*

4813 - Telephone Communications, Except Radio County (P-7974)

Anders Norstr M, *COO*
Anders Norstrom, *COO*
EMP: 99 **EST:** 2000
SQ FT: 3,200
SALES (est): 43.9MM **Privately Held**
WEB: www.mobitv.com
SIC: 4813 4899 ; data communication services

(P-7974)
NEO ADVISORY INC
Also Called: Neoit
2880 Zanker Rd Ste 203, San Jose (95134-2122)
PHONE................................415 462-0569
EMP: 40
SQ FT: 2,500
SALES (est): 1.2MM **Privately Held**
WEB: www.neogroup.com
SIC: 4813 Telephone Communications

(P-7975)
NING INC
2000 Sierra Point Pkwy # 10, Brisbane (94005-1845)
PHONE................................650 244-4000
EMP: 40
SALES (est): 7.7MM
SALES (corp-wide): 57.4MM **Privately Held**
SIC: 4813 Telephone Communications
PA: Mode Media Corporation
1100 La Avenida St
Mountain View CA 94043
650 244-4000

(P-7976)
O1 COMMUNICATIONS INC
4359 Town Center Blvd # 21, El Dorado Hills (95762-7113)
PHONE................................888 444-1111
Bradley Jenkins, *CEO*
Jim Beausoleil, *CFO*
Max Seely, *Senior VP*
EMP: 89 **EST:** 1998
SQ FT: 20,000
SALES (est): 19.3MM **Privately Held**
WEB: www.o1phone.com
SIC: 4813 Data telephone communications

(P-7977)
ONLINE GAME SERVICES INC
100 W San Fernando St # 365, San Jose (95113-2219)
PHONE................................408 333-9663
EMP: 36
SALES (est): 1.1MM
SALES (corp-wide): 8.9MM **Privately Held**
SIC: 4813 Telephone Communications
PA: Global Netoptex, Inc.
75 E Santa Clara St # 800
San Jose CA
408 289-9395

(P-7978)
OPENGOV INC (PA)
6525 Crown Blvd # 41340, San Jose (95160-4099)
P.O. Box 41340 (95160-1340)
PHONE................................650 336-7167
Zac Bookman, *CEO*
David Reeves, *President*
Paul Denton, *CFO*
Ainslie Mayberry, *CFO*
Joe Lonsdale, *Chairman*
EMP: 22 **EST:** 2011
SALES (est): 10.7MM **Privately Held**
WEB: www.opengov.com
SIC: 4813 7372 ; publishers' computer software

(P-7979)
OUTSPARK INC
434 Brannan St 1, San Francisco (94107-1714)
PHONE................................415 495-1905
EMP: 45
SQ FT: 4,600
SALES (est): 2.9MM **Privately Held**
WEB: www.outspark.com
SIC: 4813 7999 Telephone Communications Amusement/Recreation Services

(P-7980)
PACIFIC BELL TELEPHONE COMPANY (HQ)
Also Called: Pacbell
430 Bush St Fl 3, San Francisco (94108-3735)
PHONE................................415 542-9000
Kenneth P McNeely, *CEO*
Ray Wilkins Jr, *President*
Leslie Thomas, *Technician*
Howard Duff, *Engineer*
Sameer Maheshwari, *Human Resources*
▲ **EMP:** 2000 **EST:** 1906
SQ FT: 500,000
SALES (est): 1B
SALES (corp-wide): 171.7B **Publicly Held**
WEB: www.att.com
SIC: 4813 2741 4822 Local & long distance telephone communications; local telephone communications; voice telephone communications; data telephone communications; directories, telephone; publishing only, not printed on site; telegraph & other communications; electronic mail
PA: At&T Inc.
208 S Akard St
Dallas TX 75202
210 821-4105

(P-7981)
PARETO NETWORKS INC
1183 Bordeaux Dr Ste 22, Sunnyvale (94089-1201)
PHONE................................877 727-8020
Daniel Ryan, *CEO*
EMP: 78 **EST:** 2008
SALES (est): 3.3MM **Publicly Held**
WEB: www.extremenetworks.com
SIC: 4813
HQ: Aerohive Networks, Inc.
1011 Mccarthy Blvd
Milpitas CA 95035

(P-7982)
PAYCYCLE INC
210 Portage Ave, Palo Alto (94306-2242)
P.O. Box 397850, Mountain View (94039-7850)
PHONE................................650 852-9650
EMP: 75
SQ FT: 15,000
SALES (est): 4.2MM
SALES (corp-wide): 7.6B **Publicly Held**
SIC: 4813 8721 Telephone Communications Accounting/Auditing/Bookkeeping
PA: Intuit Inc.
2700 Coast Ave
Mountain View CA 94043
650 944-6000

(P-7983)
PLANETOUT INC (HQ)
795 Folsom St Fl 1, San Francisco (94107-4226)
PHONE................................415 834-6500
Daniel E Steimle, *CEO*
Karen Magee, *CEO*
EMP: 80 **EST:** 2000
SQ FT: 56,000
SALES (est): 17.5MM **Privately Held**
WEB: www.planetoutinc.com
SIC: 4813

(P-7984)
PONDEROSA TELEPHONE CO (PA)
47034 Rd 201, O Neals (93645)
PHONE................................559 868-6000
E L Silkwood, *CEO*
Franklin E Bigelow, *Vice Pres*
Kristann Silkwood-Mattes, *Vice Pres*
J F Wagner, *Admin Sec*
Doug Patterson, *Technician*
EMP: 43 **EST:** 1944
SQ FT: 5,000
SALES (est): 23.4MM **Privately Held**
WEB: www.goponderosa.com
SIC: 4813 Local telephone communications

(P-7985)
RACE TELECOMMUNICATIONS INC (PA)
601 Gateway Blvd Ste 280, South San Francisco (94080-7074)
PHONE................................650 246-8900
Raul Alcaraz, *CEO*
EMP: 60 **EST:** 2006
SALES (est): 5.1MM **Privately Held**
SIC: 4813 7374 ; data processing & preparation

(P-7986)
RAKUTEN USA INC (HQ)
800 Concar Dr Ste 175, San Mateo (94402-7044)
PHONE................................617 491-5252
Amit Patel, *CEO*
Mario Pinho, *CFO*
Wai Yan Sun, *Treasurer*
Travis Abbott, *Vice Pres*
Ben Harris, *Vice Pres*
EMP: 80 **EST:** 2006
SALES (est): 82.5MM **Privately Held**
WEB: www.global.rakuten.com
SIC: 4813

(P-7987)
RELAY2 INC (PA)
1525 Mccrthy Bllvard Ste, Milpitas (95035)
PHONE................................408 380-0031
Greg Daily, *CEO*
Eric Chen, *President*
Scott Gorton, *CFO*
WEI Lu, *Vice Pres*
Andreas Steinmetzler, *Vice Pres*
EMP: 70 **EST:** 2011
SALES (est): 1.6MM **Privately Held**
WEB: www.relay2.com
SIC: 4813

(P-7988)
SENDMAIL INC
892 Ross Dr, Sunnyvale (94089-1443)
PHONE................................510 594-5400
Gary Steele, *CEO*
Sandy Abbott, *CFO*
Paul Auvil, *CFO*
Kimberly Getgem Bargero, *Vice Pres*
Stephanie Nevin, *Vice Pres*
EMP: 110 **EST:** 2013
SQ FT: 30,000
SALES (est): 29.2MM
SALES (corp-wide): 1B **Privately Held**
WEB: www.proofpoint.com
SIC: 4813 7371 7372 7373 ; computer software development; prepackaged software; computer integrated systems design
PA: Proofpoint, Inc.
925 W Maude Ave
Sunnyvale CA 94085
408 517-4710

(P-7989)
SIERRA TEL CMMUNICATIONS GROUP (PA)
Also Called: Seirra Telephone
49150 Road 426, Oakhurst (93644-8702)
P.O. Box 219 (93644-0219)
PHONE................................559 683-4611
John H Baker, *CEO*
Harry H Baker, *Ch of Bd*
Linda Oldfield, *Administration*
Cindy Huber, *Controller*
Lee Lambert, *Purchasing*
EMP: 46 **EST:** 1997
SQ FT: 12,000
SALES (est): 97.8MM **Privately Held**
WEB: www.sierratel.com
SIC: 4813 Local telephone communications

(P-7990)
SIERRA TELEPHONE COMPANY INC
49150 Road 426, Oakhurst (93644-8702)
P.O. Box 219 (93644-0219)
PHONE................................559 683-4611
Harry H Baker, *President*
John H Baker, *Vice Pres*
Heidi D Baker, *Admin Sec*
Judi Thomas, *Info Tech Mgr*
Kevin Meeker, *Supervisor*
EMP: 190 **EST:** 1908

SALES (est): 58.6MM
SALES (corp-wide): 97.8MM **Privately Held**
WEB: www.sierratel.com
SIC: 4813 Local telephone communications; long distance telephone communications
PA: Sierra Tel Communications Group
49150 Road 426
Oakhurst CA 93644
559 683-4611

(P-7991)
SKYPE INC
1 Microsoft Way Redmond, Palo Alto (94304)
PHONE................................650 493-7900
Donald Albert, *President*
Tony Bates, *CEO*
Laura Shesgreen, *Vice Pres*
Shauna Kline, *Controller*
▲ **EMP:** 70 **EST:** 2005
SQ FT: 90,698
SALES (est): 10.6MM
SALES (corp-wide): 168B **Publicly Held**
WEB: www.skype.com
SIC: 4813 ;
PA: Microsoft Corporation
1 Microsoft Way
Redmond WA 98052
425 882-8080

(P-7992)
SLASHSUPPORT INC (HQ)
Also Called: CSS
75 E Santa Clara St # 900, San Jose (95113-1842)
P.O. Box 361226, Milpitas (95036-1226)
PHONE................................408 985-4377
Manish Tandon, *CEO*
Sunil Mittal, *President*
Raghavendran Krishnamurthy, *Program Mgr*
Randy Parker, *CTO*
Sandra Azpilcueta, *Project Mgr*
EMP: 206 **EST:** 1999
SQ FT: 11,000
SALES: 140.9MM **Privately Held**
SIC: 4813

(P-7993)
STRAVA INC (PA)
208 Utah St Fl 2, San Francisco (94103-4871)
PHONE................................415 374-7298
Michael Horvath, *CEO*
James Quarles, *CEO*
Christine Park, *CFO*
Yandong Liu, *CTO*
Alexandre Aybes, *Software Engr*
EMP: 194 **EST:** 2009
SALES (est): 38.6MM **Privately Held**
WEB: www.strava.com
SIC: 4813

(P-7994)
SUREWEST BROADBAND
5411 Lucey Ave, Roseville (95661)
PHONE................................916 772-5000
William R Lawver, *President*
Carin Hendelberg-Lawver, *Admin Sec*
EMP: 212 **EST:** 1994
SALES (est): 1.2MM
SALES (corp-wide): 1.3B **Publicly Held**
WEB: www.consolidated.com
SIC: 4813
HQ: Surewest Communications
211 Lincoln St
Roseville CA 95678
916 786-6141

(P-7995)
SYNAPTICS INCORPORATED
3120 Scott Blvd, Santa Clara (95054-3326)
PHONE................................408 454-5100
EMP: 65
SALES (corp-wide): 1.3B **Publicly Held**
WEB: www.synaptics.com
SIC: 4813 4899 Data telephone communications; data communication services
PA: Synaptics Incorporated
1251 Mckay Dr
San Jose CA 95131
408 904-1100

PRODUCTS & SERVICES SECTION
4832 - Radio Broadcasting Stations County (P-8017)

(P-7996)
TACTIVOS INC (PA)
Also Called: Mural
650 Clfrnia St Fl 7 Ste 1 Flr 7, San Francisco (94108)
PHONE..............................415 687-2501
Mariano Suarez Battan, CEO
Pato Jutard, CTO
Justin Kazwell, Marketing Staff
Gino Valencia, Manager
EMP: 51 EST: 2011
SALES (est): 10.4MM **Privately Held**
WEB: www.mural.co
SIC: 4813

(P-7997)
TALKPLUS INC
1825 S Grant St Ste 400, San Mateo (94402-7039)
PHONE..............................650 403-5800
Michael Toepel, President
Jeffery Black, Ch of Bd
Steven Denebeim, CFO
EMP: 48 EST: 2006
SQ FT: 8,370
SALES (est): 1MM **Privately Held**
WEB: www.talkplus.com
SIC: 4813 Data telephone communications

(P-7998)
TELMATE LLC (DH)
20 California St Ste 600, San Francisco (94111-4834)
P.O. Box 1137, Fruitland ID (83619-1137)
PHONE..............................866 516-0115
Kevin O' Neil, President
Christian McCarrick, President
Morgan Collins, Technology
Reuben Garcia, Technology
Pablo Nichols, General Counsel
EMP: 88 EST: 2009
SALES (est): 49MM **Privately Held**
WEB: www.telmate.com
SIC: 4813 Local & long distance telephone communications
HQ: Global Tel-Link Corporation
3120 Frview Pk Dr Ste 300
Falls Church VA 22042
703 955-3910

(P-7999)
TEXTNOW INC
Also Called: Enflick
1 Sutter St Ste 800, San Francisco (94104-4917)
PHONE..............................226 476-1578
Derek Ting, CEO
Maria Santamaria, Technical Staff
Denny Lee, Manager
EMP: 15 EST: 2017
SALES (est): 4.9MM **Privately Held**
WEB: www.careers.textnow.com
SIC: 4813 7372 ; application computer software

(P-8000)
TIZETI INC
1437 Chilco St, Menlo Park (94025-1329)
PHONE..............................281 377-6715
Kendall Ananyi, CEO
EMP: 40 EST: 2016
SALES (est): 1.8MM **Privately Held**
SIC: 4813

(P-8001)
TOGETHER LABS INC
1001 Marshall St, Redwood City (94063-2052)
P.O. Box 2772 (94064-2772)
PHONE..............................650 231-4688
Daren Tsui, CEO
Cary Rosenzweig, CEO
Lauren Bigelow,
Pamela Kelly, Senior VP
Victor Zaud, Senior VP
EMP: 103 EST: 2005
SALES (est): 38.8MM **Privately Held**
WEB: www.secure.imvu.com
SIC: 4813

(P-8002)
USTREAM INC
410 Townsend St Fl 4, San Francisco (94107-1581)
PHONE..............................415 489-9400
John Ham, CEO
Brad Hunstable, President
EMP: 65 EST: 2007
SALES (est): 10.3MM
SALES (corp-wide): 73.6B **Publicly Held**
WEB: www.video.ibm.com
SIC: 4813
PA: International Business Machines Corporation
1 New Orchard Rd Ste 1 # 1
Armonk NY 10504
914 499-1900

(P-8003)
VERIZON BUSINESS GLOBAL LLC
6023 Jqn Murieta Ave, Newark (94560-8513)
PHONE..............................415 328-1020
Siva Velusamy, Principal
Mike Stephen, Partner
Amir Hojjatnia, Executive
EMP: 49
SALES (corp-wide): 128.2B **Publicly Held**
WEB: www.verizon.com
SIC: 4813 Telephone communication, except radio
HQ: Verizon Business Global Llc
22001 Loudoun County Pkwy
Ashburn VA 20147

(P-8004)
VOLCANO COMMUNICATIONS COMPANY (PA)
Also Called: Volcano Telephone Company
20000 State Highway 88, Pine Grove (95665-9512)
P.O. Box 1070 (95665-1070)
PHONE..............................209 296-7502
Sharon J Lundgren, President
Elizabeth Lundgren, Treasurer
William Harder, Vice Pres
John M Lundgren, Vice Pres
Robert Bob Passeri, Vice Pres
EMP: 100 EST: 1903
SQ FT: 19,600
SALES (est): 29.2MM **Privately Held**
WEB: www.volcanocommunications.com
SIC: 4813 4841 Local telephone communications; cable television services

(P-8005)
VSS MONITORING INC (HQ)
178 E Tasman Dr, San Jose (95134-1619)
PHONE..............................408 585-6800
Terrence M Breslin, President
James McNicholas, CFO
Andrew R Harding, Vice Pres
EMP: 156 EST: 2003
SQ FT: 10,000
SALES (est): 23.4MM
SALES (corp-wide): 831.2MM **Publicly Held**
WEB: www.vssmonitoring.com
SIC: 4813
PA: Netscout Systems, Inc.
310 Littleton Rd
Westford MA 01886
978 614-4000

(P-8006)
VTA TELEPHONE INFORMATION
3331 N 1st St, San Jose (95134-1927)
PHONE..............................408 321-7127
Ash Kalra, Ch of Bd
Lapreasha Gentry, Executive Asst
Ehab Azab, Administration
Robert Valenzuela, Administration
Ronak Naik, Project Leader
EMP: 67 EST: 2011
SALES (est): 10.1MM **Privately Held**
WEB: www.vta.org
SIC: 4813 Local & long distance telephone communications

(P-8007)
VUCLIP INC
Also Called: Xinlab
1551 Mccarthy Blvd # 214, Milpitas (95035-7437)
PHONE..............................408 649-2240
Nickhil Jakatdar, CEO
Xinhui Niu, President
Apurva Desai, CFO
Salman Hussain, Officer
Arun Prakash, Exec VP
EMP: 46 EST: 2002
SALES (est): 7.7MM **Privately Held**
WEB: www.vuclip.com
SIC: 4813 Telephone/video communications
PA: Pccw Limited
41/F Taikoo Place Pccw Twr
Quarry Bay HK

(P-8008)
WEBPASS INC
267 8th St, San Francisco (94103-3910)
PHONE..............................415 233-4100
Dinni Jain, CEO
Ed Florence, General Mgr
Brenton Hale, Info Tech Mgr
Eli Brown, IT/INT Sup
Brian Gomez, Technician
EMP: 75 EST: 2006
SQ FT: 8,000
SALES (est): 12.2MM
SALES (corp-wide): 182.5B **Publicly Held**
WEB: www.webpass.net
SIC: 4813
HQ: Google Fiber Inc.
35018 Avenue D
Yucaipa CA 92399
650 253-0000

(P-8009)
WORLD TRADE NETWORK INC (PA)
Also Called: Wt.net
4635 Georgetown Pl, Stockton (95207-6203)
P.O. Box 460293, Houston TX (77056-8293)
PHONE..............................713 358-5603
Toll Free:..............................888 -
◆ EMP: 40 EST: 1995
SQ FT: 10,000
SALES (est): 3.5MM **Privately Held**
SIC: 4813 7371 Telephone Communications Custom Computer Programing

(P-8010)
XOBEE NETWORKS INC
7910 N Ingram Ave Ste 101, Fresno (93711-5828)
PHONE..............................559 579-1300
Eric Raw, President
Edie Roach, Executive Asst
Trino Correa, Administration
Marciano Rodriguez, Administration
Matt Sotomayor, Administration
EMP: 53 EST: 2013
SQ FT: 5,500
SALES (est): 5MM **Privately Held**
WEB: www.xobee.com
SIC: 4813 7379 8741 8748 ; computer related consulting services; management services; telecommunications consultant

(P-8011)
ZADAONET
685 Scofield Ave Apt 22, East Palo Alto (94303-2350)
PHONE..............................650 556-6377
Wenda Zhao, President
EMP: 60 EST: 2017
SALES (est): 1.6MM **Privately Held**
SIC: 4813

(P-8012)
ZOOSK INC (HQ)
989 Market St Fl 5, San Francisco (94103-1741)
PHONE..............................415 728-9543
Jeronimo Folgueira, CEO
Kelsey Walker, Executive
Veera Arrabolu, Software Engr
Larry Chen, Software Engr
Ketul Shah, Software Engr
EMP: 50 EST: 2007
SALES (est): 25.1MM
SALES (corp-wide): 559.6K **Privately Held**
WEB: www.zoosk.com
SIC: 4813 7299 ; dating service
PA: Spark Networks Se
Kohlfurter Str. 41/
Berlin BE 10999
309 919-4951

4822 Telegraph & Other Message Communications

(P-8013)
INTRADO INTERACTIVE SVCS CORP
100 Enterprise Way A-3, Scotts Valley (95066-3248)
PHONE..............................888 527-5225
EMP: 89
SALES (corp-wide): 2.2B **Privately Held**
WEB: www.intrado.com
SIC: 4822 Nonvocal message communications
HQ: Intrado Interactive Services Corporation
11808 Miracle Hills Dr
Omaha NE 68154

(P-8014)
LEENA AI INC
3260 Hillview Ave, Palo Alto (94304-1220)
PHONE..............................332 232-9740
Adit Jain, CEO
EMP: 150 EST: 2018
SALES (est): 4.6MM **Privately Held**
SIC: 4822 Nonvocal message communications

4832 Radio Broadcasting Stations

(P-8015)
AMAZING FACTS INTERNATIONAL
Also Called: Amazing Facts Ministries
6615 Sierra College Blvd, Roseville (95746-7366)
P.O. Box 1058 (95678-8058)
PHONE..............................916 434-3880
Allen Hrenyk, Principal
Todd Parrish, Partner
Doug Batchelor, President
Dan Andries, IT/INT Sup
Wanda Davis, Asst Treas
EMP: 85 EST: 2017
SALES (est): 24MM **Privately Held**
WEB: www.amazingfacts.org
SIC: 4832 Radio broadcasting stations, except music format

(P-8016)
CAPITAL PUBLIC RADIO INC
7055 Folsom Blvd, Sacramento (95826-2625)
PHONE..............................916 278-8900
Rick Eytcheson, President
Joe Barr, Officer
Frank Maranzino, CTO
Hazel Oriel, Controller
Jen Picard, Producer
EMP: 50 EST: 1979
SQ FT: 19,838
SALES: 14.9MM **Privately Held**
WEB: www.capradio.org
SIC: 4832 Radio broadcasting stations

(P-8017)
DEER CREEK BROADCASTING LLC
Also Called: Ktay Kmxi Khsl Kwe Khhz Krer
2654 Cramer Ln, Chico (95928-8838)
PHONE..............................530 345-0021
Dino Corbin,
Richard Barnes, CIO
Mark Chase, Prdtn Dir
Jaime Perry, Natl Sales Mgr
Larry Scott, Program Dir
EMP: 40 EST: 2004
SQ FT: 2,500
SALES (est): 2MM **Privately Held**
WEB: www.1035theblaze.com
SIC: 4832 Radio broadcasting stations

4832 - Radio Broadcasting Stations County (P-8018)

(P-8018)
EDUCATIONAL MEDIA FOUNDATION (PA)
Also Called: K-Love Radio Network
5700 West Oaks Blvd, Rocklin (95765-3719)
PHONE.................916 251-1600
Darrell Chambliss, *Ch of Bd*
Dean Stordahl, *Vice Chairman*
Richard Jenkins, *President*
Mike Novak, *CEO*
Jon Taylor, *CFO*
EMP: 200 EST: 1981
SQ FT: 55,000
SALES (est): 201.2MM **Privately Held**
WEB: www.klove.com
SIC: 4832 Radio broadcasting stations

(P-8019)
EMF BROADCASTING
5700 West Oaks Blvd, Rocklin (95765-3719)
PHONE.................601 992-6988
Novak Upped, *Principal*
Michelle Riddell, *Vice Pres*
Felipe Aguilar, *Regional Mgr*
Lisa Williams, *Administration*
John Ovalle, *Engineer*
EMP: 53 EST: 2016
SALES (est): 6.2MM **Privately Held**
SIC: 4832 Radio broadcasting stations

(P-8020)
ENTERCOM COMMUNICATIONS CORP
Also Called: Kseg-FM
5345 Madison Ave, Sacramento (95841-3141)
PHONE.................916 766-5000
John Geary, *Manager*
Lance Richard, *Vice Pres*
Amy Feldman, *Executive*
Derrick Dodson, *Info Tech Mgr*
Brooke Holbus, *Project Mgr*
EMP: 120
SALES (corp-wide): 1B **Publicly Held**
WEB: www.entercom.com
SIC: 4832 7929 Radio broadcasting stations, music format; entertainers & entertainment groups
PA: Audacy, Inc.
2400 Market St Fl 4
Philadelphia PA 19103
610 660-5610

(P-8021)
ENTERCOM MEDIA CORP
Also Called: CBS
1071 W Shaw Ave, Fresno (93711-3702)
PHONE.................559 490-0106
El Smith, *Manager*
EMP: 82
SQ FT: 5,938
SALES (corp-wide): 1B **Publicly Held**
SIC: 4832 Radio broadcasting stations, music format
HQ: Entercom Media Corp.
345 Hudson St
New York NY 10014
212 314-9200

(P-8022)
ENTERCOM MEDIA CORP
Also Called: CBS
865 Battery St Fl 3, San Francisco (94111-1503)
PHONE.................415 765-4097
Michael Martin, *Vice Pres*
Marisha Roberts, *Marketing Staff*
Suzie Martellaro, *Manager*
Howard Silver, *Manager*
EMP: 82
SALES (corp-wide): 1B **Publicly Held**
SIC: 4832 Radio broadcasting stations, music format
HQ: Entercom Media Corp.
345 Hudson St
New York NY 10014
212 314-9200

(P-8023)
ENTERCOM MEDIA CORP
Also Called: CBS
280 Commerce Cir, Sacramento (95815-4212)
PHONE.................916 923-6800
Micheal Hornetto, *Manager*
Katy Brown Jones, *Natl Sales Mgr*
EMP: 82
SALES (corp-wide): 1B **Publicly Held**
SIC: 4832 Radio broadcasting stations, music format
HQ: Entercom Media Corp.
345 Hudson St
New York NY 10014
212 314-9200

(P-8024)
FAMILY STATIONS INC (PA)
Also Called: Family Radio
1350 S Loop Rd, Alameda (94502-7095)
PHONE.................510 568-6200
Harold Camping, *President*
Gary Cook, *CFO*
Bill Thornton, *Treasurer*
Jeff Zimmer, *Engineer*
Tom Evans, *Maint Spvr*
EMP: 130 EST: 1958
SQ FT: 3,000
SALES (est): 7.2MM **Privately Held**
WEB: www.familyradio.org
SIC: 4832 Radio broadcasting stations

(P-8025)
FOOTHLL-DE ANZA CMNTY CLLEGE D
Also Called: Kfjc FM
12345 S El Monte Rd # 6202, Los Altos Hills (94022-4504)
PHONE.................650 949-7260
Eric Johnson, *General Mgr*
John Fox, *Instructor*
Mallory Newell, *Director*
Mandy Thai, *Assistant*
EMP: 285
SALES (corp-wide): 108.9MM **Privately Held**
WEB: www.fhda.edu
SIC: 4832 Radio broadcasting stations, music format
PA: Foothill-De Anza Community College District Financing Corporation
12345 S El Monte Rd
Los Altos Hills CA 94022
650 949-6100

(P-8026)
HENRY BROADCASTING CO
2277 Jerrold Ave, San Francisco (94124-1011)
PHONE.................415 285-1133
C H Buckley, *President*
EMP: 35 EST: 1996
SALES (est): 2.4MM
SALES (corp-wide): 1B **Publicly Held**
WEB: www.wzlx.iheart.com
SIC: 4832 Radio broadcasting stations
HQ: Cbs Radio Inc.
83 Leo M Birmingham Pkwy
Boston MA

(P-8027)
IHEARTCOMMUNICATIONS INC
Also Called: Krzr 103 7 FM
83 E Shaw Ave Ste 150, Fresno (93710-7622)
PHONE.................559 230-4300
Jeff Negrete, *Branch Mgr*
EMP: 75 **Publicly Held**
WEB: www.iheartmedia.com
SIC: 4832 Radio broadcasting stations
HQ: Iheartcommunications, Inc.
20880 Stone Oak Pkwy
San Antonio TX 78258
210 822-2828

(P-8028)
K G O T V NEWS BUREAU
520 3rd St Ste 200, Oakland (94607-3505)
PHONE.................510 451-4772
Ed Kosowski, *Principal*
EMP: 100 EST: 2002
SALES (est): 618K **Privately Held**
SIC: 4832 Radio broadcasting stations

HQ: San Francisco Radio Assets Llc
750 Battery St Fl 2
San Francisco CA 94111

(P-8029)
KUIC INC
Also Called: Kuic-FM
555 Mason St Ste 245, Vacaville (95688-4640)
PHONE.................707 446-0200
James Levitt, *Ch of Bd*
John F Levitt, *President*
Robin Mitchell, *Executive*
Joe Scholtes, *Executive*
Jim Hampton, *Program Dir*
EMP: 60 EST: 1969
SQ FT: 4,200
SALES (est): 668.6K
SALES (corp-wide): 7MM **Privately Held**
WEB: www.kuic.com
SIC: 4832 2711 Radio broadcasting stations; newspapers
PA: Coast Radio Company, Inc.
555 Mason St Ste 245
Vacaville CA 95688
707 446-0200

(P-8030)
PANDORA MEDIA LLC (DH)
2100 Franklin St Ste 700, Oakland (94612-3145)
PHONE.................510 451-4100
Roger Lynch, *President*
Peter Ruzicka, *Ch of Bd*
David Gerbitz, *COO*
Etienne Handman, *COO*
Naveen Chopra, *CFO*
EMP: 1622 EST: 2000
SQ FT: 250,000
SALES: 1.4MM
SALES (corp-wide): 9.3B **Publicly Held**
WEB: www.pandora.com
SIC: 4832 Radio broadcasting stations

(P-8031)
REDWOOD EMPIRE STEREOCASTERS
Also Called: Kzst Radio
3392 Mendocino Ave Fl 2, Santa Rosa (95403-2213)
P.O. Box 100 (95402-0100)
PHONE.................707 528-4434
Gordon D Zlot, *President*
Tom Skinner, *Vice Pres*
Denise Stevensen, *Marketing Staff*
Leanna Wetmore, *Marketing Staff*
EMP: 35 EST: 1971
SQ FT: 10,000
SALES (est): 4.9MM **Privately Held**
WEB: www.kzst.com
SIC: 4832 Radio broadcasting stations, music format

(P-8032)
RESULTS RADIO LLC (PA)
Also Called: Results Radio Licensee
1355 N Dutton Ave Ste 225, Santa Rosa (95401-7107)
PHONE.................707 546-9185
Jack W Fritz II,
Misty Jackson, *Executive Asst*
Ron Castro, *CTO*
Kathleen Ackerman, *Controller*
Eric White, *Opers Mgr*
EMP: 68 EST: 1999
SALES (est): 13.7MM **Privately Held**
WEB: www.resultsradio.com
SIC: 4832 Radio broadcasting stations

(P-8033)
RURAL CAL BRDCSTG CORP KRCB KP
Also Called: Northern California Pub Media
5850 Labath Ave, Rohnert Park (94928-2041)
PHONE.................707 584-2062
Nancy Dobbs, *President*
Steve Mencher, *Director*
Karen Bell, *Manager*
EMP: 38
SQ FT: 5,500
SALES: 2.3MM **Privately Held**
WEB: www.norcalpublicmedia.org
SIC: 4832 4833 Radio broadcasting stations; television broadcasting stations

(P-8034)
SAN FRANCISCO RADIO ASSETS LLC (DH)
Also Called: Kgo 810am
750 Battery St Fl 2, San Francisco (94111-1523)
PHONE.................415 216-1300
Deidrea Lieberman,
Jack Swanson, *Administration*
Loren Award, *Advisor*
EMP: 150 EST: 1946
SQ FT: 51,000
SALES (est): 20.5MM **Privately Held**
SIC: 4832 Radio broadcasting stations

(P-8035)
TUNEIN INC
Also Called: Radio Time
210 King St Fl 3, San Francisco (94107-1702)
PHONE.................650 319-7100
Richard Stern, *CEO*
Jason Hable, *President*
Holly Lim, *CFO*
George Kristin, *Vice Pres*
Ren Perez, *Administration*
EMP: 200 EST: 2010
SALES (est): 73.7MM **Privately Held**
WEB: www.tunein.com
SIC: 4832 Radio broadcasting stations

(P-8036)
WALT DISNEY COMPANY
Also Called: Kiid
8265 Sierra College Blvd # 21, Roseville (95661-9403)
PHONE.................916 780-1470
EMP: 53 **Publicly Held**
SIC: 4832 Radio Broadcast Station
PA: The Walt Disney Company
500 S Buena Vista St
Burbank CA 91521

(P-8037)
WHITE ASH BROADCASTING INC
Also Called: Valley Public Radio
2589 Alluvial Ave, Clovis (93611-9505)
PHONE.................559 862-2480
Joseph Moore, *President*
Alice Daniel, *Director*
EMP: 58 EST: 1975
SQ FT: 10,000
SALES (est): 2.3MM **Privately Held**
WEB: www.kvpr.org
SIC: 4832 Radio broadcasting stations

4833 Television Broadcasting Stations

(P-8038)
ABC CABLE NETWORKS GROUP
900 Front St, San Francisco (94111-1427)
PHONE.................415 954-7911
Lynn Dooley, *Branch Mgr*
Rosendo Pena, *Info Tech Mgr*
EMP: 200
SALES (corp-wide): 65.3B **Publicly Held**
WEB: www.abc.com
SIC: 4833 Television broadcasting stations
HQ: Abc Cable Networks Group
500 S Buena Vista St
Burbank CA 91521
818 460-7477

(P-8039)
CALIFORNIA OREGON BROADCASTING (HQ)
Also Called: Krcr TV
755 Auditorium Dr, Redding (96001-0920)
PHONE.................530 243-7777
Sarah Smith, *General Mgr*
Natasa Bansagi, *Producer*
EMP: 60 EST: 1963
SQ FT: 14,000
SALES (est): 15.5MM
SALES (corp-wide): 24.7MM **Privately Held**
SIC: 4833 Television broadcasting stations

PRODUCTS & SERVICES SECTION

4841 - Cable & Other Pay TV Svcs County (P-8061)

PA: Appalachian Broadcasting Corp
101 Lee St
Bristol VA
276 645-1555

(P-8040)
CATAMUNT BRDCSTG CHC-RDDING IN (PA)
Also Called: Khsl TV
3460 Silverbell Rd, Chico (95973-0388)
PHONE..................................530 893-2424
Raymond Johns, *President*
EMP: 104 **EST:** 1950
SQ FT: 18,000
SALES (est): 8MM **Privately Held**
WEB: www.actionnewsnow.com
SIC: 4833 Television broadcasting stations

(P-8041)
CHANNEL 40 INC
Also Called: Ktxl-Fox 40
4655 Fruitridge Rd, Sacramento (95820-5201)
PHONE..................................916 454-4422
Jerry Del Core, *Vice Pres*
Leigh White, *Vice Pres*
Allison Gregory, *Graphic Designe*
Jocelyn Tham, *Production*
Monika Diaz, *Director*
EMP: 105 **EST:** 1989
SQ FT: 25,000
SALES (est): 17MM
SALES (corp-wide): 4.5B **Publicly Held**
WEB: www.fox40.com
SIC: 4833 Television translator station
HQ: Tribune Media Company
515 N State St Ste 2400
Chicago IL 60654
312 222-3394

(P-8042)
CHRONICLE BROADCASTING CO
Also Called: Kron-TV
900 Front St, San Francisco (94111-1427)
PHONE..................................415 561-8000
Francis A Martin III, *President*
Glen E Pickell, *Treasurer*
Ronald Ingram, *Vice Pres*
Robert M Raymer, *Admin Sec*
Christina Bennett, *Producer*
EMP: 400 **EST:** 1966
SQ FT: 90,000
SALES (est): 83.8MM
SALES (corp-wide): 4.2B **Privately Held**
WEB: www.kron4.com
SIC: 4833 Television broadcasting stations
HQ: Hearst Communications, Inc.
300 W 57th St
New York NY 10019
212 649-2000

(P-8043)
COMCAST SPRTSNET BAY AREA HLDN
360 3rd St Fl 2, San Francisco (94107-2154)
PHONE..................................415 896-2557
Richard Cotton, *Mng Member*
National Broadcasting, *General Ptnr*
Jared Grayson, *Executive*
Ye Hu, *Software Dev*
David Ferrell, *Sales Staff*
EMP: 47 **EST:** 1989
SALES (est): 9.4MM
SALES (corp-wide): 103.5B **Publicly Held**
WEB: www.nbcsports.com
SIC: 4833 Television broadcasting stations
HQ: Nbcuniversal Media, Llc
30 Rockefeller Plz Fl 2
New York NY 10112

(P-8044)
HEARST STATIONS INC
Also Called: Kcra
3 Television Cir, Sacramento (95814-0750)
PHONE..................................916 446-3333
E Proshinsky, *General Mgr*
Steve Mellish, *Producer*
EMP: 102
SALES (corp-wide): 4.2B **Privately Held**
WEB: www.kcra.com
SIC: 4833 Television broadcasting stations
HQ: Hearst Stations Inc.
3 Television Cir
Sacramento CA 95814
916 446-3333

(P-8045)
HEARST STATIONS INC
Also Called: Kqca
3 Television Cir, Sacramento (95814-0750)
PHONE..................................916 447-5858
Dave York, *Technology*
EMP: 102
SALES (corp-wide): 4.2B **Privately Held**
WEB: www.kcra.com
SIC: 4833 Television broadcasting stations
HQ: Hearst Stations Inc.
3 Television Cir
Sacramento CA 95814
916 446-3333

(P-8046)
HEARST STATIONS INC (DH)
Also Called: Kmbc/Kcwe
3 Television Cir, Sacramento (95814-0750)
PHONE..................................916 446-3333
Jordan Wertlieb, *President*
Catharine Blakemore, *Director*
EMP: 80 **EST:** 1994
SALES (est): 117MM
SALES (corp-wide): 4.2B **Privately Held**
WEB: www.kcra.com
SIC: 4833 Television broadcasting stations

(P-8047)
KFSN TELEVISION LLC
Also Called: ABC 30
1777 G St, Fresno (93706-1688)
PHONE..................................559 442-1170
Dan Adams, *President*
Patrice Coulter, *Accounts Exec*
EMP: 117 **EST:** 2005
SQ FT: 26,962
SALES (est): 10.1MM
SALES (corp-wide): 65.3B **Publicly Held**
WEB: www.abc30.com
SIC: 4833 Television broadcasting stations
HQ: Disney Enterprises, Inc.
500 S Buena Vista St
Burbank CA 91521
818 560-1000

(P-8048)
KMPH FOX 26
Also Called: Pappas Telecasting Company
5111 E Mckinley Ave, Fresno (93727-2033)
PHONE..................................559 255-2600
Harry Pappas, *Principal*
EMP: 203 **EST:** 1971
SALES (est): 3.6MM
SALES (corp-wide): 5.9B **Publicly Held**
WEB: www.kmph.com
SIC: 4833 Television broadcasting stations
PA: Sinclair Broadcast Group, Inc.
10706 Beaver Dam Rd
Hunt Valley MD 21030
410 568-1500

(P-8049)
KQED INC (PA)
Also Called: Kqed Public Media
2601 Mariposa St, San Francisco (94110-1426)
P.O. Box 410865 (94141-0865)
PHONE..................................415 864-2000
John Boland, *President*
Donald W Derheim, *COO*
Mitzie Kelley, *CFO*
Craig Martin, *Officer*
Jo Anne Wallace, *Vice Pres*
EMP: 258 **EST:** 1952
SQ FT: 75,000
SALES: 121.4MM **Privately Held**
WEB: www.kqed.org
SIC: 4833 4832 Television broadcasting stations; radio broadcasting stations

(P-8050)
KTVU PARTNERSHIP INC
Also Called: Ktvu Television Fox 2
2 Jack London Sq, Oakland (94607-3727)
PHONE..................................510 834-1212
Murdock Lachlan, *CEO*
Kathie Smith, *Vice Pres*
Mark Richardson, *Engineer*
Stacey Rikard, *Natl Sales Mgr*
Mike Sklut, *Sales Staff*
◆ **EMP:** 230 **EST:** 1963
SALES (est): 47.7MM
SALES (corp-wide): 12.9B **Publicly Held**
WEB: www.ktvu.com
SIC: 4833 Television broadcasting stations
HQ: Fox Television Stations, Inc.
1999 S Bundy Dr
Los Angeles CA 90025
310 584-2000

(P-8051)
KVIE INC (PA)
Also Called: KVIE CHANNEL 6
2030 W El Cmino Ave Ste 1, Sacramento (95833)
P.O. Box 6 (95812-0006)
PHONE..................................916 929-5843
David Lowe, *CEO*
David Hosley, *President*
Julie Saqueton, *CFO*
Janet Coshow, *Officer*
Khalid Muslih, *Administration*
EMP: 60 **EST:** 1955
SQ FT: 69,000
SALES: 15MM **Privately Held**
WEB: www.kvie.org
SIC: 4833 Television broadcasting stations

(P-8052)
KXTV INC
Also Called: K X T V Channel 10
400 Broadway, Sacramento (95818-2041)
PHONE..................................916 441-2345
Risa Omega, *President*
Evangelista Hinojos, *Opers Staff*
Mellisa Paul, *Marketing Staff*
John Bartell, *Author*
Zach Fuentes, *Author*
EMP: 160 **EST:** 1940
SQ FT: 29,000
SALES (est): 10.3MM
SALES (corp-wide): 2.9B **Publicly Held**
WEB: www.abc10.com
SIC: 4833 Television broadcasting stations
PA: Tegna Inc.
8350 Broad St Ste 2000
Tysons VA 22102
703 873-6600

(P-8053)
LINCOLN BRDCSTG A CAL LTD PRTN (PA)
Also Called: Station Ktsf-TV
100 Valley Dr, Brisbane (94005-1318)
PHONE..................................415 508-1056
Lincoln Howell, *Partner*
Lillian Lincoln Howell, *Partner*
EMP: 82 **EST:** 1976
SQ FT: 20,800
SALES (est): 12.6MM **Privately Held**
SIC: 4833 Television broadcasting stations

(P-8054)
SACRAMENTO TELEVISION STNS INC (DH)
Also Called: Kmax TV
2713 Kovr Dr, West Sacramento (95605-1600)
PHONE..................................916 374-1452
Peter Dunn, *CEO*
EMP: 152 **EST:** 1954
SQ FT: 40,000
SALES (est): 47.2MM
SALES (corp-wide): 25.3B **Publicly Held**
WEB: www.sacramentomediamarket.com
SIC: 4833 Television broadcasting stations
HQ: Viacomcbs Inc.
1515 Broadway
New York NY 10036
212 258-6000

(P-8055)
TELEMUNDO OF FRESNO LLC
500 Media Pl, Sacramento (95815-3733)
PHONE..................................559 252-5101
Alberto Martinez, *Mng Member*
EMP: 39 **EST:** 2002
SALES (est): 3.5MM
SALES (corp-wide): 103.5B **Publicly Held**
WEB: www.nbcuniversal.com
SIC: 4833 Television broadcasting stations
HQ: Nbcuniversal Media, Llc
30 Rockefeller Plz Fl 2
New York NY 10112

(P-8056)
VALLEY PUBLIC TELEVISION INC
Also Called: VALLEYPBS
1544 Van Ness Ave, Fresno (93721-1213)
PHONE..................................559 266-1800
Paula Castadio, *President*
Phyllis Brotherton, *CFO*
Douglas Enoll, *Chairman*
Andy Vu, *Chief Engr*
Vicki Lund, *Accounting Mgr*
EMP: 56 **EST:** 1984
SQ FT: 22,000
SALES (est): 4.5MM **Privately Held**
WEB: www.valleypbs.org
SIC: 4833 Television broadcasting stations

(P-8057)
YOUNG BRDCSTG OF SAN FRANCISCO
Also Called: Kron-TV
900 Front St, San Francisco (94111-1427)
PHONE..................................415 441-4444
Deb McDermot, *President*
Chris McDonnell, *Vice Pres*
Kron News, *Director*
EMP: 92 **EST:** 2000
SALES (est): 22.3MM
SALES (corp-wide): 4.5B **Publicly Held**
WEB: www.kron4.com
SIC: 4833 Television broadcasting stations
HQ: Young Broadcasting, Llc
599 Lexington Ave
New York NY 10022
517 372-8282

4841 Cable & Other Pay TV Svcs

(P-8058)
ABS-CBN INTERNATIONAL (DH)
432 N Canal St Ste 21, South San Francisco (94080-4666)
PHONE..................................800 527-2820
Eugenio Lopez III, *CEO*
Raffy Lopez, *COO*
Juan Manahan, *Vice Pres*
Ronnie Supelana, *Administration*
Genemar Simpao, *CIO*
▲ **EMP:** 140
SALES: 605.1K **Privately Held**
WEB: www.abscbnfoundation.org
SIC: 4841 7822 Cable & other pay television services; television & video tape distribution

(P-8059)
COMCAST CALIFORNIA IX INC
1111 Andersen Dr, San Rafael (94901-5394)
PHONE..................................215 286-3345
Paul Gibson, *Vice Pres*
EMP: 41 **EST:** 2009
SALES (est): 11.6MM
SALES (corp-wide): 103.5B **Publicly Held**
WEB: www.nbcuniversal.com
SIC: 4841 Cable television services
HQ: Nbcuniversal Media, Llc
30 Rockefeller Plz Fl 2
New York NY 10112

(P-8060)
COX ENTERPRISES INC
1549 W Menlo Ave, Fresno (93711-1308)
PHONE..................................559 432-3947
EMP: 38
SALES (corp-wide): 22.3B **Publicly Held**
SIC: 4841 Cable/Pay Television Service
PA: Cox Enterprises, Inc.
6205 Pachtree Dunwoody Rd
Atlanta GA 30328
678 645-0000

(P-8061)
DIRECTV GROUP INC
340 Commerce Ave, Fairfield (94533)
PHONE..................................707 452-7409
EMP: 128
SALES (corp-wide): 31.7B **Publicly Held**
SIC: 4841 Cable/Pay Television Service

(PA)=Parent Co (HQ)=Headquarters (DH)=Div Headquarters
✪ = New Business established in last 2 years

4841 - Cable & Other Pay TV Svcs County (P-8062) — PRODUCTS & SERVICES SECTION

HQ: The Directv Group Inc
2260 E Imperial Hwy
El Segundo CA 90245
310 964-5000

(P-8062)
DIRECTV GROUP INC
1129 B St, San Lorenzo (94580)
PHONE.....................510 481-1324
EMP: 128
SALES (corp-wide): 31.7B Publicly Held
SIC: 4841 Cable/Pay Television Service
HQ: The Directv Group Inc
2260 E Imperial Hwy
El Segundo CA 90245
310 964-5000

(P-8063)
INTEL MEDIA INC
2200 Mission College Blvd, Santa Clara (95054-1549)
PHONE.....................408 765-0063
Erik Huggers, President
EMP: 350 EST: 1999
SALES (est): 89.9MM
SALES (corp-wide): 77.8B Publicly Held
WEB: www.intel.com
SIC: 4841 Subscription television services
PA: Intel Corporation
2200 Mission College Blvd
Santa Clara CA 95054
408 765-8080

(P-8064)
PLAXO INC
Also Called: Comcast Slcon Vly Innvtion Ctr
1050 Enterprise Way # 200, Sunnyvale (94089-1415)
PHONE.....................408 900-8701
Justin Miller, President
Michael Yurochko, Vice Pres
Jai Saxena, Exec Dir
Preston Smalley, Exec Dir
Steven Hsu, Administration
EMP: 80 EST: 2002
SALES (est): 23.7MM
SALES (corp-wide): 103.5B Publicly Held
WEB: www.comcast.com
SIC: 4841 Cable & other pay television services
PA: Comcast Corporation
1701 John F Kennedy Blvd
Philadelphia PA 19103
215 286-1700

(P-8065)
ROKU INC (PA)
1155 Coleman Ave, San Jose (95110-1104)
PHONE.....................408 556-9040
Anthony Wood, Ch of Bd
Bridgette BEK, Partner
Jason Weber, Partner
Steve Louden, CFO
Stephen H Kay, Senior VP
▲ EMP: 250 EST: 2002
SALES (est): 1.7B Publicly Held
WEB: www.roku.com
SIC: 4841 7822 Cable & other pay television services; motion picture & tape distribution

(P-8066)
SACO ENTERPRISES INC
Also Called: Pactech
2260 Trade Zone Blvd, San Jose (95131-1845)
PHONE.....................408 526-9363
Aaron Chui, President
Sandy Cheng, CFO
◆ EMP: 18 EST: 2007
SQ FT: 8,000
SALES (est): 7.5MM Privately Held
WEB: www.pactech-inc.com
SIC: 4841 5051 3678 Cable television services; cable, wire; electronic connectors

(P-8067)
TIME WARNER CABLE ENTPS LLC
360 W Caribbean Dr, Sunnyvale (94089-1010)
PHONE.....................408 747-7330
Alex Quilici, Branch Mgr
Jennifer Watral, Partner
EMP: 48
SALES (corp-wide): 48.1B Publicly Held
SIC: 4841 Cable television services
HQ: Time Warner Cable Enterprises Llc
400 Atlantic St Ste 6
Stamford CT 06901

(P-8068)
VOLCANO VISION INC
Also Called: Volcano Telephone Co.
20000 State Highway 88, Pine Grove (95665-9512)
P.O. Box 1070 (95665-1070)
PHONE.....................209 296-2288
Toll Free:...................888 -
Sharon J Lundgren, President
John M Lundgren, Vice Pres
Deilia P Harder, Human Resources
EMP: 46 EST: 1984
SQ FT: 1,000
SALES (est): 676K Privately Held
WEB: www.volcanocommunications.com
SIC: 4841 Cable television services

4899 Communication Svcs, NEC

(P-8069)
AT&T MOBILITY LLC
Also Called: Cingular Wireless
3 Bay View Dr, San Carlos (94070-1665)
PHONE.....................650 638-1188
EMP: 107
SALES (corp-wide): 171.7B Publicly Held
WEB: www.att.com
SIC: 4899 4812 Communication Services Radiotelephone Communication
HQ: At&T Mobility Llc
1025 Lenox Park Blvd Ne A
Brookhaven GA 30319
800 331-0500

(P-8070)
BELLA TERRA TECHNOLOGIES INC
1600 Amphitheatre Pkwy, Mountain View (94043-1351)
PHONE.....................650 316-6660
Tom Ingersoll, CEO
Dan Berkenstock,
EMP: 54 EST: 2009
SALES (est): 29.2MM
SALES (corp-wide): 182.5B Publicly Held
WEB: www.knightscope.com
SIC: 4899 Satellite earth stations
HQ: Google Llc
1600 Amphitheatre Pkwy
Mountain View CA 94043
650 253-0000

(P-8071)
BLUE JEANS NETWORK INC (HQ)
Also Called: Verizon Sourcing
3098 Olsen Dr, San Jose (95128-2048)
PHONE.....................408 550-2828
Tami Erwin, CEO
Chrissy Goyhenetche, Partner
James Aviani, Vice Pres
Adam Hyder, Vice Pres
Tim Miller, Vice Pres
EMP: 145 EST: 2009
SALES (est): 198.3MM
SALES (corp-wide): 128.2B Publicly Held
WEB: www.bluejeans.com
SIC: 4899 Data communication services
PA: Verizon Communications Inc.
1095 Ave Of The Americas
New York NY 10036
212 395-1000

(P-8072)
BYTEMOBILE INC (DH)
Also Called: Byte Mobile
2860 De La Cruz Blvd # 200, Santa Clara (95050-2635)
PHONE.....................408 327-7788
Hatim Tyabji, CEO
Adrian Hall, COO
Thomas Hubbs, CFO
JD Howard, Vice Pres
Andy Missan, Vice Pres
▲ EMP: 258 EST: 2000
SQ FT: 30,000
SALES (est): 78.8MM Publicly Held
WEB: www.citrix.com
SIC: 4899 7361 Communication signal enhancement network system; employment agencies
HQ: Citrix Systems International Gmbh
Rheinweg 7
Schaffhausen SH 8200
526 357-700

(P-8073)
CALIX INC (PA)
2777 Orchard Pkwy, San Jose (95134-2008)
PHONE.....................408 514-3000
Carl Russo, Ch of Bd
Michael Weening, President
Cory Sindelar, CFO
Martha Galley, Vice Pres
Gordon Magee, Admin Sec
◆ EMP: 647 EST: 1999
SALES (est): 541.2MM Publicly Held
WEB: www.calix.com
SIC: 4899 7372 4813 Data communication services; prepackaged software;

(P-8074)
CHAYACHITRA MEDIA LLC (PA)
38713 Chimaera Cir, Fremont (94536-3247)
PHONE.....................510 397-8344
Sudhir Kolli, Principal
EMP: 37 EST: 2016
SALES (est): 302.8K Privately Held
SIC: 4899 Communication services

(P-8075)
EDTUIT INC (PA)
3527 Hamlin Rd, Lafayette (94549-5005)
PHONE.....................415 269-4471
Marten Nelson, CEO
Christopher Haupt, CTO
EMP: 39 EST: 2008
SALES (est): 506.6K Privately Held
WEB: www.edtuit.com
SIC: 4899 Communication services

(P-8076)
EQUINIX (US) ENTERPRISES INC (HQ)
1 Lagoon Dr, Redwood City (94065-1562)
PHONE.....................650 598-6363
Donald Campbell, CFO
EMP: 80 EST: 2005
SALES (est): 59.1MM
SALES (corp-wide): 6B Publicly Held
WEB: www.equinix.com
SIC: 4899 Communication signal enhancement network system
PA: Equinix, Inc.
1 Lagoon Dr Ste 400
Redwood City CA 94065
650 598-6000

(P-8077)
GAMUT SMART MEDIA FROM COX LLC
611 Gateway Blvd, South San Francisco (94080-7017)
PHONE.....................650 392-6238
Larry Braitman, Principal
EMP: 50
SALES (corp-wide): 1.6MM Privately Held
WEB: www.gamut.media
SIC: 4899 7313 Data communication services; electronic media advertising representatives
HQ: Gamut Smart Media From Cox, Llc.
1 Dag Hammarskjold Plz
New York NY 10017
212 588-2800

(P-8078)
INTELPEER CLOUD CMMNCTIONS LLC
155 Bovet Rd Ste 405, San Mateo (94402-3137)
PHONE.....................650 525-9200
Frank Fawzi, President
Andre Simone, CFO
Rob Clarke, Ch Credit Ofcr
Robert Galop, Chief Mktg Ofcr
Michael Jerich, Officer
EMP: 106 EST: 2002
SQ FT: 6,000
SALES (est): 52.1MM Privately Held
WEB: www.intelepeer.com
SIC: 4899 Data communication services

(P-8079)
ITRON NETWORKED SOLUTIONS INC (HQ)
230 W Tasman Dr, San Jose (95134-1714)
PHONE.....................669 770-4000
Thomas L Deitrich, President
Robert Farrow, Treasurer
Catriona M Fallon, Senior VP
Don Reeves, Vice Pres
Terry Pashoian, Admin Mgr
▲ EMP: 400 EST: 2002
SQ FT: 191,800
SALES: 311MM
SALES (corp-wide): 2.1B Publicly Held
WEB: www.itron.com
SIC: 4899 7372 Communication signal enhancement network system; prepackaged software
PA: Itron, Inc.
2111 N Molter Rd
Liberty Lake WA 99019
509 924-9900

(P-8080)
MAXAR SPACE LLC (HQ)
3825 Fabian Way, Palo Alto (94303-4604)
PHONE.....................650 852-4000
John Celli, President
Barbara Ellis, President
Ed McFarlane, President
Ron Haley, CFO
Paul Estey, Exec VP
◆ EMP: 75 EST: 1892
SALES (est): 785.7MM
SALES (corp-wide): 1.7B Publicly Held
WEB: www.maxar.com
SIC: 4899 3663 Satellite earth stations; satellites, communications
PA: Maxar Technologies Inc.
1300 W 120th Ave
Westminster CO 80234
303 684-2207

(P-8081)
MOBILEUM INC (PA)
20813 Stevns Crk Blvd, Cupertino (95014-2185)
PHONE.....................408 844-6600
Bobby Srinivasan, CEO
CP Murali, President
Andrew Warner, CFO
James Doyle, Chief Mktg Ofcr
Bernardo Lucas, Chief Mktg Ofcr
EMP: 180 EST: 2000
SQ FT: 4,000
SALES (est): 68.3MM Privately Held
WEB: www.mobileum.com
SIC: 4899 7373 Data communication services; computer systems analysis & design

(P-8082)
OPLINK COMMUNICATIONS LLC (DH)
46360 Fremont Blvd, Fremont (94538-6406)
PHONE.....................510 933-7200
Joseph Y Liu, CEO
Peter Lee, President
Shirley Yin, CFO
River Gong, Exec VP
Jim LI, Senior VP
▲ EMP: 3674 EST: 1995
SQ FT: 51,000
SALES (est): 579MM
SALES (corp-wide): 36.9B Privately Held
WEB: www.oplink.com
SIC: 4899 3661 Communication signal enhancement network system; data communication services; fiber optics communications equipment
HQ: Molex, Llc
2222 Wellington Ct
Lisle IL 60532
630 969-4550

▲ = Import ▼ = Export
◆ = Import/Export

PRODUCTS & SERVICES SECTION

4911 - Electric Svcs County (P-8110)

(P-8083)
PLURIBUS NETWORKS INC (PA)
5201 Great America Pkwy # 422, Santa Clara (95054-1143)
PHONE.................650 289-4717
Kumar Srikantan, *CEO*
George De Urioste, *CFO*
Ken Yang, *Bd of Directors*
David Ginsburg, *Officer*
Sunay Tripathi, *Officer*
EMP: 57 **EST:** 2011
SALES (est): 12.9MM **Privately Held**
WEB: www.pluribusnetworks.com
SIC: 4899 Communication signal enhancement network system

(P-8084)
RING2 COMMUNICATIONS LLC
Also Called: Loopup
282 2nd St Ste 200, San Francisco (94105-3122)
PHONE.................415 829-2952
Michael Hughes, *CEO*
Simon Healey, *CEO*
Marcus Greensit, *COO*
Robert Baugh, *Exec VP*
Alex Breen, *Exec VP*
EMP: 47 **EST:** 2003
SALES (est): 8.2MM **Privately Held**
WEB: www.loopup.com
SIC: 4899 Data communication services

(P-8085)
SS8 NETWORKS INC (PA)
Also Called: S S 8
750 Tasman Dr, Milpitas (95035-7456)
PHONE.................408 894-8400
Dennis Haar, *CEO*
Keith Bhatia, *COO*
Kam Wong, *CFO*
Cemal Dikmen, *Principal*
EMP: 120 **EST:** 1999
SQ FT: 83,000
SALES (est): 43.6MM **Privately Held**
WEB: www.ss8.com
SIC: 4899 7381 Communication signal enhancement network system; detective services

(P-8086)
TIBIT COMMUNICATIONS INC
1465 N Mcdowell Blvd # 150, Petaluma (94954-6571)
PHONE.................707 664-5906
Richard Stanfield, *President*
Edward Boyd, *Vice Pres*
Jerry Wojtowicz, *Vice Pres*
Paul Runcy, *Managing Dir*
Kevin Noll, *Director*
EMP: 35 **EST:** 2014
SALES (est): 2.8MM **Privately Held**
WEB: www.tibitcom.com
SIC: 4899 Data communication services

(P-8087)
VERTICAL COMMUNICATION (HQ)
3979 Freedom Cir Ste 400, Santa Clara (95054-1257)
PHONE.................408 969-9600
William Tauscher, *CEO*
David Krietzberg, *CFO*
Clinton Childress, *Officer*
Fran Blackburn, *Vice Pres*
David House, *Vice Pres*
▲ **EMP:** 65 **EST:** 1996
SALES (est): 24.7MM
SALES (corp-wide): 40MM **Privately Held**
WEB: www.vertical.com
SIC: 4899 Data communication services
PA: Vertical Communications, Inc.
1000 Holcomb Woods Pkwy # 415
Roswell GA 30076
877 837-8422

(P-8088)
WHATSAPP LLC (HQ)
1601 Willow Rd, Menlo Park (94025-1452)
PHONE.................650 336-3079
Jan Koum, *CEO*
Derek Konigsberg, *Software Engr*
Ehren Kret, *Software Engr*
Thuy Ho, *Tech Recruiter*
EMP: 68 **EST:** 2013
SALES (est): 31.4MM
SALES (corp-wide): 85.9B **Publicly Held**
WEB: www.whatsapp.com
SIC: 4899 5999 Data communication services; mobile telephones & equipment
PA: Meta Platforms, Inc.
1601 Willow Rd
Menlo Park CA 94025
650 543-4800

4911 Electric Svcs

(P-8089)
ALAMEDA BUREAU ELEC IMPRV CORP (HQ)
Also Called: Alameda Municipal Power
2000 Grand St, Alameda (94501-1228)
P.O. Box H (94501-0263)
PHONE.................510 748-3902
Edwin Dankworth, *CEO*
Gregory Hamm, *President*
Dean Batchelor, *COO*
Laura Giuntini, *Vice Pres*
Peter Holmes, *Vice Pres*
▲ **EMP:** 85 **EST:** 1882
SALES (est): 79.1MM
SALES (corp-wide): 162MM **Privately Held**
WEB: www.alamedamp.com
SIC: 4911 Distribution, electric power; transmission, electric power
PA: City Of Alameda
2263 Santa Clara Ave
Alameda CA 94501
510 747-7400

(P-8090)
CALIFRNIA IND SYS OPRATOR CORP (PA)
Also Called: California ISO
250 Outcropping Way, Folsom (95630-8773)
P.O. Box 639014 (95763-9014)
PHONE.................916 351-4400
Bob Foster, *Ch of Bd*
William J Regan, *CFO*
Andrew Ulmer, *Bd of Directors*
Anne Gonzales, *Officer*
Roger Collanton, *Vice Pres*
EMP: 450 **EST:** 1997
SQ FT: 79,000
SALES (est): 222.6MM **Privately Held**
WEB: www.caiso.com
SIC: 4911 Distribution, electric power; transmission, electric power

(P-8091)
CALPINE CORPORATION
5029 S Township Rd, Yuba City (95993-9748)
PHONE.................530 821-2075
Scott Reynolds, *Branch Mgr*
Allison Bryan, *Opers Staff*
Bill Burnett, *Manager*
Jamie Wright, *Manager*
EMP: 50
SALES (corp-wide): 10B **Privately Held**
WEB: www.calpine.com
SIC: 4911 Generation, electric power;
HQ: Calpine Corporation
717 Texas St Ste 1000
Houston TX 77002
713 830-2000

(P-8092)
CLEARWAY ENERGY GROUP LLC (PA)
100 California St Ste 400, San Francisco (94111-4509)
PHONE.................415 627-1600
Craig Cornelius, *CEO*
Jonathan Bram, *Ch of Bd*
Randy Hickok, *COO*
Ray Long, *Senior VP*
Daniel Abbott, *Finance*
EMP: 377 **EST:** 2016
SQ FT: 3,000
SALES (est): 330.4MM **Privately Held**
WEB: www.clearwayenergygroup.com
SIC: 4911 Distribution, electric power

(P-8093)
CLEARWAY RENEW LLC (HQ)
Also Called: NRG Energy
100 California St Ste 400, San Francisco (94111-4509)
PHONE.................415 627-1600
Craig Cornelius, *President*
Randall Hickok, *Vice Pres*
Steven Ryder, *Vice Pres*
EMP: 41 **EST:** 2009
SALES (est): 147.7MM **Privately Held**
WEB: www.global-infra.com
SIC: 4911

(P-8094)
CYPRESS CREEK RENEWABLES LLC
445 Bush St Fl 7, San Francisco (94108-3728)
PHONE.................415 306-5300
Matthew McGovern, *Branch Mgr*
Chris Norqual, *Vice Pres*
EMP: 60
SALES (corp-wide): 419MM **Privately Held**
WEB: www.ccrenew.com
SIC: 4911
PA: Cypress Creek Renewables, Llc
3250 Ocean Park Blvd # 355
Santa Monica CA 90405
310 581-6299

(P-8095)
EDWARD W SCOTT ELECTRIC CO INC
1555 Burke Ave Ste L, San Francisco (94124-1442)
PHONE.................415 206-7120
Eileen B Lynch, *Principal*
EMP: 40
SALES (corp-wide): 56.3MM **Privately Held**
WEB: www.edwardwscottelectric.com
SIC: 4911 Electric services
PA: Edward W. Scott Electric Co., Inc.
500 W Ohio Ave
Richmond CA 94804
415 206-7120

(P-8096)
ENPOWER MANAGEMENT CORP
2603 Camino Ramon Ste 263, San Ramon (94583-9143)
PHONE.................925 244-1100
Edward Tomeo, *President*
Alex Sugaoka, *Vice Pres*
EMP: 79 **EST:** 1994
SALES (est): 3.2MM
SALES (corp-wide): 33.5MM **Privately Held**
WEB: www.enpowercorp.com
SIC: 4911 Generation, electric power; distribution, electric power
PA: Enpower Corp.
2603 Camino Ramon Ste 263
San Ramon CA 94583
925 244-1100

(P-8097)
GASNA 10P LLC
50 California St Ste 820, San Francisco (94111-4617)
PHONE.................775 562-4104
EMP: 35
SALES (est): 4.2MM **Privately Held**
SIC: 4911 Electric Services

(P-8098)
GASNA 36P LLC
50 California St Ste 820, San Francisco (94111-4617)
PHONE.................775 562-4104
EMP: 35
SALES (est): 3MM **Privately Held**
SIC: 4911 Electric Services

(P-8099)
GASNA 38P LLC
50 California St Ste 820, San Francisco (94111-4617)
PHONE.................775 562-4104
EMP: 35 **EST:** 2010
SALES (est): 3.1MM **Privately Held**
SIC: 4911 Electric Services

(P-8100)
GASNA 39P LLC
50 California St Ste 820, San Francisco (94111-4617)
PHONE.................415 230-5601
EMP: 35 **EST:** 2010
SALES (est): 3.1MM **Privately Held**
SIC: 4911 Electric Services

(P-8101)
GASNA 44P LLC
50 California St Ste 820, San Francisco (94111-4617)
PHONE.................415 230-5601
EMP: 35
SALES (est): 3MM **Privately Held**
SIC: 4911 Electric Services

(P-8102)
GASNA 45P LLC
50 California St Ste 820, San Francisco (94111-4617)
PHONE.................415 230-5601
EMP: 35 **EST:** 2011
SALES (est): 3MM **Privately Held**
SIC: 4911 Electric Services

(P-8103)
GASNA 57P LLC
50 California St Ste 820, San Francisco (94111-4617)
PHONE.................415 230-5601
EMP: 35 **EST:** 2011
SALES (est): 4.7MM **Privately Held**
SIC: 4911 Electric Services

(P-8104)
GASNA 60P LLC
50 California St Ste 820, San Francisco (94111-4617)
PHONE.................415 230-5601
EMP: 35
SALES (est): 4.1MM **Privately Held**
SIC: 4911 Electric Services

(P-8105)
GASNA 61P LLC
50 California St Ste 820, San Francisco (94111-4617)
PHONE.................415 230-5601
EMP: 35 **EST:** 2011
SALES (est): 4.7MM **Privately Held**
SIC: 4911 Electric Services

(P-8106)
GASNA 65P LLC
50 California St Ste 820, San Francisco (94111-4617)
PHONE.................775 562-4104
EMP: 35 **EST:** 2011
SALES (est): 3.1MM **Privately Held**
SIC: 4911 Electric Services

(P-8107)
GASNA 69P LLC
50 California St Ste 820, San Francisco (94111-4617)
PHONE.................415 230-5601
EMP: 35
SALES (est): 4.7MM **Privately Held**
SIC: 4911 Electric Services

(P-8108)
GASNA 75P LLC
50 California St Ste 820, San Francisco (94111-4617)
PHONE.................775 562-4104
EMP: 35
SALES (est): 4.7MM **Privately Held**
SIC: 4911 Electric Services

(P-8109)
GASNA 76P LLC
50 California St Ste 820, San Francisco (94111-4617)
PHONE.................775 562-4104
EMP: 35
SALES (est): 4.7MM **Privately Held**
SIC: 4911 Electric Services

(P-8110)
GASNA 78P LLC
50 California St Ste 820, San Francisco (94111-4617)
PHONE.................415 230-5601

4911 - Electric Svcs County (P-8111)

PRODUCTS & SERVICES SECTION

EMP: 35
SALES (est): 4.7MM **Privately Held**
SIC: 4911 Electric Services

(P-8111)
GASNA 79P LLC
50 California St Ste 820, San Francisco (94111-4617)
PHONE 415 230-5601
EMP: 35
SALES (est): 3.1MM **Privately Held**
SIC: 4911 Electric Services

(P-8112)
GASNA 81P LLC
50 California St Ste 820, San Francisco (94111-4617)
PHONE 775 562-4104
EMP: 35
SALES (est): 4.7MM **Privately Held**
SIC: 4911 Electric Services

(P-8113)
GEYSERS POWER COMPANY LLC
10350 Socrates Mine Rd, Middletown (95461-9732)
PHONE 707 431-6000
Jim Horn, *Director*
EMP: 35 **EST:** 1999
SALES (est): 14.5MM
SALES (corp-wide): 10B **Privately Held**
WEB: www.calpine.com
SIC: 4911 Generation, electric power
HQ: Calpine Corporation
717 Texas St Ste 1000
Houston TX 77002
713 830-2000

(P-8114)
GREENLEAF POWER LLC (PA)
2600 Capitol Ave, Sacramento (95816-5927)
PHONE 916 596-2500
Hugh Smith, *CEO*
James Huffman, *Vice Pres*
Michael Dwyer, *Business Anlyst*
Mitchell Martin, *Project Engr*
Kevin Lawrence, *Opers Mgr*
EMP: 47 **EST:** 2012
SALES (est): 38.3MM **Privately Held**
WEB: www.greenleaf-power.com
SIC: 4911 Generation, electric power

(P-8115)
HANERGY HOLDING AMERICA INC
1350 Bayshore Hwy Ste 825, Burlingame (94010-1848)
PHONE 650 288-3722
Yi Wu, *Ch of Bd*
Jeff Zhou, *President*
Richard Gaertner, *COO*
Anny Hu, *Executive*
Abraham Liu, *Technology*
EMP: 360 **EST:** 2011
SQ FT: 7,000
SALES (est): 227.3MM **Privately Held**
WEB: www.hanergymobileenergy.com
SIC: 4911 6719 Generation, electric power; investment holding companies, except banks
PA: Jinjiang Hydroelectric Power Group Co., Ltd.
No.0-A, Anli Road, Chaoyang Dist.
Beijing 10010

(P-8116)
HL POWER COMPANY
732-025 Wendel Rd, Wendel (96136-9705)
PHONE 530 254-6161
Ralph Sanders, *Principal*
EMP: 38 **EST:** 1988
SQ FT: 3,200
SALES (est): 43.3MM **Privately Held**
WEB: www.hlpower.com
SIC: 4911 Generation, electric power

(P-8117)
IP PORTFOLIO I LLC
548 Market St 68743, San Francisco (94104-5401)
PHONE 510 260-2192
Luke Dunnington, *COO*
EMP: 45 **EST:** 2017

SALES (est): 17.1MM
SALES (corp-wide): 847MM **Publicly Held**
WEB: www.macquarie.com
SIC: 4911 Electric services
PA: Macquarie Infrastructure Corporation
125 W 55th St Fl 15
New York NY 10019
212 231-1000

(P-8118)
LASSEN MUNICIPAL UTILITY DST
65 S Roop St, Susanville (96130-4335)
PHONE 530 257-4174
Mary Anderson, *Accounts Mgr*
Doug Smith, *General Mgr*
William Stewart, *General Mgr*
Nick Dominguez, *Info Tech Mgr*
Catherine Schroeder, *Technician*
EMP: 38
SQ FT: 6,000
SALES (est): 18.3MM **Privately Held**
WEB: www.lmud.org
SIC: 4911 Distribution, electric power

(P-8119)
LEEMAH ELECTRONICS INC
Also Called: (415 LOCATION)
1080 Sansome St, San Francisco (94111-1308)
PHONE 415 394-1288
Jack Wang, *Manager*
EMP: 21
SALES (corp-wide): 63.9MM **Privately Held**
WEB: www.leemah.com
SIC: 4911 3672 3669 3571 Electric services; printed circuit boards; intercommunication systems, electric; electronic computers
HQ: Leemah Electronics, Inc.
155 S Hill Dr
Brisbane CA 94005

(P-8120)
LIBERTY UTLTIES CLPECO ELC LLC
Also Called: LIBERTY ENERGY
933 Eloise Ave, South Lake Tahoe (96150-6470)
PHONE 800 782-2506
Ian Robertson, *Mng Member*
Mike Smart, *President*
Brent Baker, *Vice Pres*
Chico Dafonte, *Vice Pres*
Tony Penna, *Vice Pres*
EMP: 60 **EST:** 2009
SQ FT: 10,000
SALES (est): 92.9MM **Privately Held**
SIC: 4911 Distribution, electric power

(P-8121)
MARIN CLEAN ENERGY
Also Called: McE
1125 Tamalpais Ave, San Rafael (94901-3221)
PHONE 415 464-6028
Dawn Weisz, *CEO*
Troy Nordquist, *Admin Asst*
Jay Marshall, *Technology*
Karamvir Singh, *Technology*
David Potovsky, *Contract Mgr*
EMP: 75 **EST:** 2008
SQ FT: 10,000
SALES (est): 26.3MM **Privately Held**
WEB: www.mcecleanenergy.org
SIC: 4911 Distribution, electric power

(P-8122)
MARTINEZ COGEN LTD PARTNERSHIP
550 Solano Way, Pacheco (94553-1446)
PHONE 925 313-0800
John Trider, *CEO*
EMP: 55 **EST:** 1989
SALES (est): 3.4MM
SALES (corp-wide): 7.5B **Privately Held**
WEB: www.woodplc.com
SIC: 4911 Generation, electric power
HQ: Amec Foster Wheeler Limited
23rd Floor
London E14 5
203 215-1700

(P-8123)
MERCED IRRIGATION DISTRICT (PA)
744 W 20th St, Merced (95340-3601)
P.O. Box 2288 (95344-0288)
PHONE 209 722-5761
Tim Pellissier, *President*
Andre Urquidez, *Treasurer*
Dave Long, *Vice Pres*
Hicham Eltal, *General Mgr*
Bryan Kelly, *General Mgr*
EMP: 50 **EST:** 1919
SQ FT: 20,000
SALES: 101.7MM **Privately Held**
WEB: www.mercedid.com
SIC: 4911 4971 Generation, electric power; water distribution or supply systems for irrigation

(P-8124)
MERCED IRRIGATION DISTRICT
Also Called: Hydro Division
9188 Village Dr, Snelling (95369-9605)
PHONE 209 378-2421
Dan Pope, *Manager*
EMP: 52
SALES (corp-wide): 101.7MM **Privately Held**
WEB: www.mercedid.com
SIC: 4911 Electric services
PA: Merced Irrigation District
744 W 20th St
Merced CA 95340
209 722-5761

(P-8125)
MODESTO IRRIGATION DISTRICT
1231 11th St, Modesto (95354-0701)
P.O. Box 4060 (95352-4060)
PHONE 209 526-7563
Don Durman, *Treasurer*
Stu Gilman, *Director*
EMP: 83
SALES (corp-wide): 430.9MM **Privately Held**
WEB: www.mid.org
SIC: 4911 4941 ; water supply
PA: Modesto Irrigation District (Inc)
1231 11th St
Modesto CA 95354
209 526-7337

(P-8126)
MODESTO IRRIGATION DISTRICT (PA)
1231 11th St, Modesto (95354-0701)
P.O. Box 4060 (95352-4060)
PHONE 209 526-7337
Allen Short, *President*
Scott Furgerson, *General Mgr*
Joy Warren, *Administration*
Heliane Burns, *CIO*
Chris Dow, *Prgrmr*
EMP: 175 **EST:** 1887
SQ FT: 90,000
SALES: 430.9MM **Privately Held**
WEB: www.mid.org
SIC: 4911 4971 ; water distribution or supply systems for irrigation

(P-8127)
MODESTO IRRIGATION DISTRICT
929 Woodland Ave, Modesto (95351-1553)
P.O. Box 4060 (95352-4060)
PHONE 209 526-7373
Ellen Short, *General Mgr*
Martin Stokman, *Vice Pres*
Karen Mullins, *General Mgr*
Richard Barnes, *CIO*
Tracy Holt, *Info Tech Dir*
EMP: 83
SALES (corp-wide): 430.9MM **Privately Held**
WEB: www.mid.org
SIC: 4911 4971 Distribution, electric power; irrigation systems
PA: Modesto Irrigation District (Inc)
1231 11th St
Modesto CA 95354
209 526-7337

(P-8128)
NORTHERN CALIFORNIA POWER AGCY (PA)
Also Called: Ncpa
651 Commerce Dr, Roseville (95678-6411)
PHONE 916 781-3636
Sondra Ainsworth, *Treasurer*
Vicki Cichocki, *General Mgr*
Randy Howard, *General Mgr*
Cary A Padgett, *Executive Asst*
Michelle Schellentrager, *Admin Asst*
EMP: 65 **EST:** 1968
SQ FT: 17,400
SALES (est): 104.2MM **Privately Held**
WEB: www.ncpa.com
SIC: 4911 Transmission, electric power

(P-8129)
NRG CALIFORNIA NORTH LLC (HQ)
1350 Treat Blvd Ste 500, Walnut Creek (94597-8853)
P.O. Box 192, Pittsburg (94565-0019)
PHONE 925 287-3133
Mike Lyons,
David Frandsen, *Senior Engr*
EMP: 141 **EST:** 1999
SALES (est): 471.9MM **Publicly Held**
WEB: www.nrg.com
SIC: 4911 Generation, electric power

(P-8130)
PACIFIC GAS AND ELECTRIC CO
Also Called: PG&e
425 Beck Ave, Fairfield (94533-6808)
PHONE 415 973-7000
Dana McKiddin, *Principal*
EMP: 120 **Publicly Held**
WEB: www.pge.com
SIC: 4911 Transmission, electric power
HQ: Pacific Gas And Electric Company
77 Beale St
San Francisco CA 94105
415 973-7000

(P-8131)
PACIFIC GAS AND ELECTRIC CO (HQ)
Also Called: PG&E
77 Beale St, San Francisco (94105-1814)
P.O. Box 770000 (94177-0001)
PHONE 415 973-7000
Michael Lewis, *President*
Dean Seavers, *Ch of Bd*
Adam Wright, *COO*
David Thomason, *CFO*
Margaret K Becker, *Treasurer*
▲ **EMP:** 3000 **EST:** 1905
SALES (est): 18.4B **Publicly Held**
WEB: www.pge.com
SIC: 4911 4924 Generation, electric power; transmission, electric power; distribution, electric power; natural gas distribution

(P-8132)
PACIFIC GAS AND ELECTRIC CO
Also Called: PG&e
885 Embarcadero Dr, West Sacramento (95605-1503)
PHONE 916 375-5005
Richard Yamacuchi, *Branch Mgr*
EMP: 120 **Publicly Held**
WEB: www.pge.com
SIC: 4911 Transmission, electric power
HQ: Pacific Gas And Electric Company
77 Beale St
San Francisco CA 94105
415 973-7000

(P-8133)
PACIFIC GAS AND ELECTRIC CO
Also Called: PG&e
P.O. Box 930 (95201-3093)
PHONE 209 932-6550
EMP: 120 **Publicly Held**
WEB: www.pge.com
SIC: 4911 Transmission, electric power
HQ: Pacific Gas And Electric Company
77 Beale St
San Francisco CA 94105
415 973-7000

▲ = Import ▼ = Export
◆ = Import/Export

PRODUCTS & SERVICES SECTION

4911 - Electric Svcs County (P-8159)

(P-8134)
PACIFIC GAS AND ELECTRIC CO
Also Called: PG&e
8 E River Park Pl W, Fresno (93720-1551)
PHONE..................209 726-7650
Sharla Jennings, *Treasurer*
Dustin Chappel, *Opers Spvr*
EMP: 120 **Publicly Held**
WEB: www.pge.com
SIC: 4911 Transmission, electric power
HQ: Pacific Gas And Electric Company
  77 Beale St
  San Francisco CA 94105
  415 973-7000

(P-8135)
PACIFIC GAS AND ELECTRIC CO
Also Called: PG&e
2730 Gateway Oaks Dr # 220, Sacramento
(95833-3503)
PHONE..................916 923-7007
Russ Jackson, *Manager*
Bridget Engbretson, *Administration*
EMP: 120 **Publicly Held**
WEB: www.pge.com
SIC: 4911 Transmission, electric power
HQ: Pacific Gas And Electric Company
  77 Beale St
  San Francisco CA 94105
  415 973-7000

(P-8136)
PACIFIC GAS AND ELECTRIC CO
Also Called: PG&e
350 Salem St, Chico (95928-5331)
P.O. Box 49 (95927-0049)
PHONE..................530 258-6215
Rodney J Strub, *Branch Mgr*
EMP: 120 **Publicly Held**
WEB: www.pge.com
SIC: 4911 4932 Transmission, electric power; gas & other services combined
HQ: Pacific Gas And Electric Company
  77 Beale St
  San Francisco CA 94105
  415 973-7000

(P-8137)
PACIFIC GAS AND ELECTRIC CO
PG&e
4525 Hollis St, Oakland (94608-2911)
PHONE..................510 450-5744
Shawnmarie Gonzalez, *Program Mgr*
James Hale, *Project Mgr*
EMP: 120 **Publicly Held**
WEB: www.pge.com
SIC: 4911 Transmission, electric power
HQ: Pacific Gas And Electric Company
  77 Beale St
  San Francisco CA 94105
  415 973-7000

(P-8138)
PACIFIC GAS AND ELECTRIC CO
Also Called: PG&e
4940 Allison Pkwy, Vacaville (95688-9346)
PHONE..................707 446-7381
EMP: 120 **Publicly Held**
WEB: www.pge.com
SIC: 4911 Transmission, electric power
HQ: Pacific Gas And Electric Company
  77 Beale St
  San Francisco CA 94105
  415 973-7000

(P-8139)
PACIFIC GAS AND ELECTRIC CO
PG&e
1970 Industrial Way, Belmont (94002)
PHONE..................650 592-9411
Michele A Silva, *Branch Mgr*
Wendy Bossier, *Supervisor*
EMP: 120 **Publicly Held**
WEB: www.pge.com
SIC: 4911 4923 Transmission, electric power; gas transmission & distribution
HQ: Pacific Gas And Electric Company
  77 Beale St
  San Francisco CA 94105

(P-8140)
PACIFIC GAS AND ELECTRIC CO
Also Called: PG&e
12626 Jackson Gate Rd, Jackson
(95642-9543)
PHONE..................209 223-5259
Mark Johnson, *Branch Mgr*
EMP: 120 **Publicly Held**
WEB: www.pge.com
SIC: 4911 Transmission, electric power
HQ: Pacific Gas And Electric Company
  77 Beale St
  San Francisco CA 94105
  415 973-7000

(P-8141)
PACIFIC GAS AND ELECTRIC CO
Also Called: PG&e
3965 Occidental Rd, Santa Rosa
(95401-5898)
PHONE..................707 579-6337
Leo Conner, *Principal*
Bryan Hennessy, *Engineer*
EMP: 120 **Publicly Held**
WEB: www.pge.com
SIC: 4911 Transmission, electric power
HQ: Pacific Gas And Electric Company
  77 Beale St
  San Francisco CA 94105
  415 973-7000

(P-8142)
PACIFIC GAS AND ELECTRIC CO
Also Called: PG&e
6537 Foothill Blvd, Oakland (94605-2016)
PHONE..................510 437-2222
Audey Ford, *Manager*
Vincent Rego, *Officer*
EMP: 120 **Publicly Held**
WEB: www.pge.com
SIC: 4911 4924 Generation, electric power; natural gas distribution
HQ: Pacific Gas And Electric Company
  77 Beale St
  San Francisco CA 94105
  415 973-7000

(P-8143)
PACIFIC GAS AND ELECTRIC CO
Also Called: PG&e
3400 Crow Canyon Rd, San Ramon
(94583-1308)
PHONE..................650 513-0700
Robert Kohne, *Engr R&D*
Michael Herz, *Manager*
EMP: 200
SQ FT: 3,000 **Publicly Held**
WEB: www.pge.com
SIC: 4911 Transmission, electric power
HQ: Pacific Gas And Electric Company
  77 Beale St
  San Francisco CA 94105
  415 973-7000

(P-8144)
PACIFIC GAS AND ELECTRIC CO
Also Called: PG&e
777 Railroad Ave, Pittsburg (94565-2651)
P.O. Box 590 (94565-0590)
PHONE..................925 757-2000
Barbara Corsi, *Branch Mgr*
EMP: 120 **Publicly Held**
WEB: www.pge.com
SIC: 4911 Transmission, electric power
HQ: Pacific Gas And Electric Company
  77 Beale St
  San Francisco CA 94105
  415 973-7000

(P-8145)
PACIFIC GAS AND ELECTRIC CO
Also Called: PG&e
1220 Andersen Dr, San Rafael
(94901-5332)
PHONE..................800 743-5000
Jeffrey Bleich, *Branch Mgr*
EMP: 120 **Publicly Held**
WEB: www.pge.com
SIC: 4911 Transmission, electric power
HQ: Pacific Gas And Electric Company
  77 Beale St
  San Francisco CA 94105
  415 973-7000

(P-8146)
PACIFIC GAS AND ELECTRIC CO
Also Called: PG&e
650 O St, Fresno (93721-2708)
PHONE..................559 263-7361
C R Martin, *Branch Mgr*
Clarence Blythe, *Engineer*
EMP: 120 **Publicly Held**
WEB: www.pge.com
SIC: 4911 4922 Generation, electric power; natural gas transmission
HQ: Pacific Gas And Electric Company
  77 Beale St
  San Francisco CA 94105
  415 973-7000

(P-8147)
PACIFIC GAS AND ELECTRIC CO
Also Called: PG&e
3955 Arch Rd Ste 100, Stockton
(95215-8328)
PHONE..................209 942-5142
Richard Kolodzie, *Principal*
EMP: 120 **Publicly Held**
WEB: www.pge.com
SIC: 4911 Transmission, electric power
HQ: Pacific Gas And Electric Company
  77 Beale St
  San Francisco CA 94105
  415 973-7000

(P-8148)
PACIFIC GAS AND ELECTRIC CO
Also Called: PG&e
210 Corona Rd, Petaluma (94954-1319)
PHONE..................707 765-5118
Tom Reimer, *Manager*
EMP: 120
SQ FT: 168,577 **Publicly Held**
WEB: www.pge.com
SIC: 4911 Transmission, electric power
HQ: Pacific Gas And Electric Company
  77 Beale St
  San Francisco CA 94105
  415 973-7000

(P-8149)
PACIFIC GAS AND ELECTRIC CO
Also Called: PG&e
631 N Colusa St, Willows (95988-2209)
PHONE..................530 229-4164
Sam Burton, *Manager*
EMP: 120 **Publicly Held**
WEB: www.pge.com
SIC: 4911 4922 Transmission, electric power; natural gas transmission
HQ: Pacific Gas And Electric Company
  77 Beale St
  San Francisco CA 94105
  415 973-7000

(P-8150)
PACIFIC GAS AND ELECTRIC CO
PG&e
111 Stony Cir, Santa Rosa (95401-9599)
PHONE..................800 756-7243
Gary F Heitz, *Principal*
EMP: 120
SQ FT: 100,000 **Publicly Held**
WEB: www.pge.com
SIC: 4911 Transmission, electric power
HQ: Pacific Gas And Electric Company
  77 Beale St
  San Francisco CA 94105
  415 973-7000

(P-8151)
PACIFIC GAS AND ELECTRIC CO
Also Called: PG&e
14550 Tuolumne Rd, Sonora (95370-9769)
PHONE..................916 904-9035
EMP: 120 **Publicly Held**
WEB: www.pge.com
SIC: 4911 Transmission, electric power
HQ: Pacific Gas And Electric Company
  77 Beale St
  San Francisco CA 94105
  415 973-7000

(P-8152)
PACIFIC GAS AND ELECTRIC CO
Also Called: PG&e
4690 Evora Rd, Concord (94520-1004)
PHONE..................925 676-0948
John Glenn, *Branch Mgr*
EMP: 120 **Publicly Held**

(P-8153)
PACIFIC GAS AND ELECTRIC CO
Also Called: PG&e
160 Peabody Rd 166, Vacaville
(95687-4729)
PHONE..................800 684-4648
EMP: 120 **Publicly Held**
WEB: www.pge.com
SIC: 4911 Transmission, electric power
HQ: Pacific Gas And Electric Company
  77 Beale St
  San Francisco CA 94105
  415 973-7000

(P-8154)
PACIFIC GAS AND ELECTRIC CO
Also Called: PG&e
2-98 7th St, Marysville (95901)
PHONE..................800 743-5000
EMP: 120 **Publicly Held**
WEB: www.pge.com
SIC: 4911 Transmission, electric power
HQ: Pacific Gas And Electric Company
  77 Beale St
  San Francisco CA 94105
  415 973-7000

(P-8155)
PACIFIC GAS AND ELECTRIC CO
Also Called: PG&e
235 Industrial Rd, San Carlos
(94070-6211)
PHONE..................800 684-4648
EMP: 120 **Publicly Held**
WEB: www.pge.com
SIC: 4911 Transmission, electric power
HQ: Pacific Gas And Electric Company
  77 Beale St
  San Francisco CA 94105
  415 973-7000

(P-8156)
PACIFIC GAS AND ELECTRIC CO
Also Called: PG&e
3050 Geneva Ave, Daly City (94014-1640)
PHONE..................800 684-4648
EMP: 120 **Publicly Held**
WEB: www.pge.com
SIC: 4911 Transmission, electric power
HQ: Pacific Gas And Electric Company
  77 Beale St
  San Francisco CA 94105
  415 973-7000

(P-8157)
PACIFIC GAS AND ELECTRIC CO
Also Called: PG&e
624 W 15th St, Merced (95340-5914)
PHONE..................800 684-4648
EMP: 120 **Publicly Held**
WEB: www.pge.com
SIC: 4911 Transmission, electric power
HQ: Pacific Gas And Electric Company
  77 Beale St
  San Francisco CA 94105
  415 973-7000

(P-8158)
PACIFIC GAS AND ELECTRIC CO
Also Called: PG&e
1745 2nd St, Selma (93662-3625)
P.O. Box 180 (93662-0180)
PHONE..................559 891-2143
Gary Truitt, *Manager*
EMP: 120 **Publicly Held**
WEB: www.pge.com
SIC: 4911 Transmission, electric power
HQ: Pacific Gas And Electric Company
  77 Beale St
  San Francisco CA 94105
  415 973-7000

(P-8159)
PACIFIC GAS AND ELECTRIC CO
Also Called: PG&e
4636 Missouri Flat Rd, Placerville
(95667-6823)
PHONE..................530 621-7237
Gordon Smith, *Branch Mgr*

4911 - Electric Svcs County (P-8160)

PRODUCTS & SERVICES SECTION

EMP: 120 **Publicly Held**
WEB: www.pge.com
SIC: **4911** Transmission, electric power
HQ: Pacific Gas And Electric Company
    77 Beale St
    San Francisco CA 94105
    415 973-7000

(P-8160)
PACIFIC GAS AND ELECTRIC CO
Also Called: PG&e
  1567 Huntoon St, Oroville (95965-4921)
  PHONE.................................530 532-4093
  Gene Murray, *Branch Mgr*
  EMP: 120 **Publicly Held**
  WEB: www.pge.com
  SIC: **4911** Transmission, electric power
  HQ: Pacific Gas And Electric Company
    77 Beale St
    San Francisco CA 94105
    415 973-7000

(P-8161)
PACIFIC GAS AND ELECTRIC CO
Also Called: PG&e
  33995 Alta Bonny Nook Rd, Alta (95701)
  P.O. Box 688 (95701-0688)
  PHONE.................................530 389-2202
  Dave Barret, *Foreman/Supr*
  EMP: 120 **Publicly Held**
  WEB: www.pge.com
  SIC: **4911** Transmission, electric power
  HQ: Pacific Gas And Electric Company
    77 Beale St
    San Francisco CA 94105
    415 973-7000

(P-8162)
PACIFIC GAS AND ELECTRIC CO
Also Called: PG&e
  3600 Meadow View Dr, Redding (96002-9701)
  PHONE.................................530 365-7672
  John Duncan, *Manager*
  Anandi De La Fuente, *Engineer*
  EMP: 120 **Publicly Held**
  WEB: www.pge.com
  SIC: **4911** Transmission, electric power
  HQ: Pacific Gas And Electric Company
    77 Beale St
    San Francisco CA 94105
    415 973-7000

(P-8163)
PACIFIC GAS AND ELECTRIC CO
Also Called: PG&e
  31295 Manton Viola Rd, Manton (96059)
  PHONE.................................530 474-3333
  Chip Stalica, *Manager*
  EMP: 120 **Publicly Held**
  WEB: www.pge.com
  SIC: **4911** Transmission, electric power
  HQ: Pacific Gas And Electric Company
    77 Beale St
    San Francisco CA 94105
    415 973-7000

(P-8164)
PACIFIC GAS AND ELECTRIC CO
Also Called: PG&e
  3395 Mcmaude Pl, Santa Rosa (95407-8120)
  PHONE.................................707 577-7283
  Rolando Trevino, *VP Engrg*
  EMP: 120 **Publicly Held**
  WEB: www.pge.com
  SIC: **4911** Transmission, electric power
  HQ: Pacific Gas And Electric Company
    77 Beale St
    San Francisco CA 94105
    415 973-7000

(P-8165)
PACIFIC GAS AND ELECTRIC CO
Also Called: PG&e
  12840 Bill Clark Way, Auburn (95602-9527)
  PHONE.................................530 889-3102
  Steve Pennett, *Manager*
  EMP: 120 **Publicly Held**
  WEB: www.pge.com
  SIC: **4911** Transmission, electric power
  HQ: Pacific Gas And Electric Company
    77 Beale St
    San Francisco CA 94105
    415 973-7000

(P-8166)
PACIFIC GAS AND ELECTRIC CO
Also Called: PG&e
  1850 Gateway Blvd Ste 800, Concord (94520-8473)
  PHONE.................................925 674-6305
  EMP: 65 **Publicly Held**
  SIC: **4911** Electric Services
  HQ: Pacific Gas And Electric Company
    77 Beale St
    San Francisco CA 94105
    415 973-7000

(P-8167)
PACIFIC GAS AND ELECTRIC CO
Also Called: PG&e
  202 Pearson Rd, Paradise (95969-5046)
  PHONE.................................530 327-7633
  Molly Williams, *Branch Mgr*
  EMP: 120 **Publicly Held**
  WEB: www.pge.com
  SIC: **4911** Transmission, electric power
  HQ: Pacific Gas And Electric Company
    77 Beale St
    San Francisco CA 94105
    415 973-7000

(P-8168)
PACIFIC GAS AND ELECTRIC CO
Also Called: PG&e
  4040 West Ln, Stockton (95204-2436)
  PHONE.................................209 942-1523
  Ken Wells, *Manager*
  EMP: 120 **Publicly Held**
  WEB: www.pge.com
  SIC: **4911** Transmission, electric power
  HQ: Pacific Gas And Electric Company
    77 Beale St
    San Francisco CA 94105
    415 973-7000

(P-8169)
PACIFIC GAS AND ELECTRIC CO
Also Called: PG&e
  Hwy 299, Willow Creek (95573)
  P.O. Box 238 (95573-0238)
  PHONE.................................530 629-2128
  Randall L Dieterie, *Branch Mgr*
  EMP: 120 **Publicly Held**
  WEB: www.pge.com
  SIC: **4911** Transmission, electric power
  HQ: Pacific Gas And Electric Company
    77 Beale St
    San Francisco CA 94105
    415 973-7000

(P-8170)
PACIFIC GAS AND ELECTRIC CO
Also Called: PG&e
  42105 Boyce Rd, Fremont (94538-3110)
  PHONE.................................510 770-2025
  Gary Commick, *Principal*
  EMP: 120 **Publicly Held**
  WEB: www.pge.com
  SIC: **4911** Transmission, electric power
  HQ: Pacific Gas And Electric Company
    77 Beale St
    San Francisco CA 94105
    415 973-7000

(P-8171)
PACIFIC GAS AND ELECTRIC CO
Also Called: PG&e
  1000 King Salmon Ave, Eureka (95503-6859)
  PHONE.................................707 444-0700
  Roy Willis, *Manager*
  EMP: 120 **Publicly Held**
  WEB: www.pge.com
  SIC: **4911** Transmission, electric power
  HQ: Pacific Gas And Electric Company
    77 Beale St
    San Francisco CA 94105
    415 973-7000

(P-8172)
PACIFIC GAS AND ELECTRIC CO
Also Called: PG&e
  33755 Old Mill Rd, Auberry (93602-9655)
  P.O. Box 425 (93602-0425)
  PHONE.................................559 855-6112
  John Moore, *General Mgr*
  EMP: 120 **Publicly Held**
  WEB: www.pge.com
  SIC: **4911** Transmission, electric power; generation, electric power

(P-8173)
PACIFIC GAS AND ELECTRIC CO
Also Called: PG&e
  1028 6th St, Los Banos (93635-4218)
  PHONE.................................209 826-5131
  Stephen Rath, *Branch Mgr*
  EMP: 120 **Publicly Held**
  WEB: www.pge.com
  SIC: **4911** Transmission, electric power
  HQ: Pacific Gas And Electric Company
    77 Beale St
    San Francisco CA 94105
    415 973-7000

(P-8174)
PACIFIC GAS AND ELECTRIC CO
Also Called: PG&e
  450 Eastmoor Ave, Daly City (94015-2041)
  PHONE.................................650 755-1236
  EMP: 150 **Publicly Held**
  WEB: www.pge.com
  SIC: **4911** Electric And Other Services Combined
  HQ: Pacific Gas And Electric Company
    77 Beale St
    San Francisco CA 94105
    415 973-7000

(P-8175)
PACIFIC GAS AND ELECTRIC CO
Also Called: PG&e
  1524 N Carpenter Rd, Modesto (95351-1110)
  PHONE.................................209 576-6636
  Sheila Radford, *Branch Mgr*
  Kevin Chacon, *Manager*
  EMP: 120 **Publicly Held**
  WEB: www.pge.com
  SIC: **4911** **4923** **4932** Transmission, electric power; gas transmission & distribution; gas & other services combined
  HQ: Pacific Gas And Electric Company
    77 Beale St
    San Francisco CA 94105
    415 973-7000

(P-8176)
PACIFIC GAS AND ELECTRIC CO
Also Called: PG&e
  811 W J St, Oakdale (95361-3669)
  PHONE.................................800 743-5000
  Ross Leveretg, *Manager*
  EMP: 120 **Publicly Held**
  WEB: www.pge.com
  SIC: **4911** **4923** **4939** Transmission, electric power; gas transmission & distribution; combination utilities
  HQ: Pacific Gas And Electric Company
    77 Beale St
    San Francisco CA 94105
    415 973-7000

(P-8177)
PACIFIC GAS AND ELECTRIC CO
Also Called: PG&e
  3136 Boeing Way Fl 2, Stockton (95206-4989)
  PHONE.................................209 942-1787
  Robert Eggert, *Branch Mgr*
  EMP: 120
  SQ FT: 138,000 **Publicly Held**
  WEB: www.pge.com
  SIC: **4911** **4922** Generation, electric power; natural gas transmission
  HQ: Pacific Gas And Electric Company
    77 Beale St
    San Francisco CA 94105
    415 973-7000

(P-8178)
PACIFIC GAS AND ELECTRIC CO
Also Called: PG&e
  2221 S Orange Ave, Fresno (93725-1011)
  PHONE.................................559 263-7152
  Robert Martin, *Manager*
  EMP: 120 **Publicly Held**
  WEB: www.pge.com
  SIC: **4911** Transmission, electric power
  HQ: Pacific Gas And Electric Company
    77 Beale St
    San Francisco CA 94105
    415 973-7000

(P-8179)
PACIFIC GAS AND ELECTRIC CO
Also Called: PG&e
  5221 Quinn Rd, Vacaville (95688-9453)
  PHONE.................................707 452-1983
  Dagoberto Fierros, *Analyst*
  EMP: 120 **Publicly Held**
  WEB: www.pge.com
  SIC: **4911** Transmission, electric power
  HQ: Pacific Gas And Electric Company
    77 Beale St
    San Francisco CA 94105
    415 973-7000

(P-8180)
PACIFIC GAS AND ELECTRIC CO
Also Called: PG&e
  5555 Florin Perkins Rd, Sacramento (95826-4815)
  P.O. Box 997300 (95899-7300)
  PHONE.................................916 275-2763
  Maria Jordan, *Manager*
  Bobby Daley, *Technology*
  Amelia Harter, *Manager*
  David Liang, *Manager*
  Kenneth Meyer, *Supervisor*
  EMP: 200 **Publicly Held**
  WEB: www.pge.com
  SIC: **4911** **4923** Distribution, electric power; generation, electric power; transmission, electric power; gas transmission & distribution
  HQ: Pacific Gas And Electric Company
    77 Beale St
    San Francisco CA 94105
    415 973-7000

(P-8181)
PACIFIC GAS AND ELECTRIC CO
Also Called: PG&e
  11239 Midway, Chico (95928-8219)
  PHONE.................................530 896-4318
  Russ Bates, *Branch Mgr*
  EMP: 120 **Publicly Held**
  WEB: www.pge.com
  SIC: **4911** Transmission, electric power
  HQ: Pacific Gas And Electric Company
    77 Beale St
    San Francisco CA 94105
    415 973-7000

(P-8182)
PACIFIC GAS AND ELECTRIC CO
Also Called: PG&e
  502 E Grant Line Rd, Tracy (95376-2800)
  P.O. Box 356 (95378-0356)
  PHONE.................................559 263-5438
  Matt Storment, *Branch Mgr*
  EMP: 120 **Publicly Held**
  WEB: www.pge.com
  SIC: **4911** Transmission, electric power
  HQ: Pacific Gas And Electric Company
    77 Beale St
    San Francisco CA 94105
    415 973-7000

(P-8183)
PACIFIC GAS AND ELECTRIC CO
Also Called: PG&e
  3797 1st St, Livermore (94551-4905)
  PHONE.................................925 373-2623
  Kermit Pol, *Branch Mgr*
  EMP: 120 **Publicly Held**
  WEB: www.pge.com
  SIC: **4911** Transmission, electric power
  HQ: Pacific Gas And Electric Company
    77 Beale St
    San Francisco CA 94105
    415 973-7000

(P-8184)
PACIFIC GAS AND ELECTRIC CO
Also Called: PG&e
  316 L St, Davis (95616-4231)
  PHONE.................................530 757-5803
  Gail Sanchez, *Manager*
  EMP: 120 **Publicly Held**
  WEB: www.pge.com
  SIC: **4911** Transmission, electric power

PRODUCTS & SERVICES SECTION
4911 - Electric Svcs County (P-8205)

HQ: Pacific Gas And Electric Company
  77 Beale St
  San Francisco CA 94105
  415 973-7000

(P-8185)
PACIFIC GAS AND ELECTRIC CO
Also Called: PG&e
2111 Hillcrest Ave, Antioch (94509-2862)
PHONE.................................925 779-7745
Mike Diaz, *Manager*
EMP: 120 **Publicly Held**
WEB: www.pge.com
SIC: 4911 4922 4924 1311 Distribution, electric power; generation, electric power; transmission, electric power; pipelines, natural gas; natural gas distribution; crude petroleum production; natural gas production; land subdividers & developers, commercial; land subdividers & developers, residential; power plant construction
HQ: Pacific Gas And Electric Company
  77 Beale St
  San Francisco CA 94105
  415 973-7000

(P-8186)
PACIFIC GAS AND ELECTRIC CO
Also Called: PG&e
2180 Harrison St, San Francisco (94110-1300)
PHONE.................................415 695-3513
Dave Bradley, *Branch Mgr*
Jessica Vandyke, *Analyst*
EMP: 120 **Publicly Held**
WEB: www.pge.com
SIC: 4911 4922 4924 1311 Generation, electric power; transmission, electric power; distribution, electric power; pipelines, natural gas; natural gas distribution; natural gas production; crude petroleum production; land subdividers & developers, residential; land subdividers & developers, commercial; power plant construction
HQ: Pacific Gas And Electric Company
  77 Beale St
  San Francisco CA 94105
  415 973-7000

(P-8187)
PACIFIC GAS AND ELECTRIC CO
Also Called: PG&e
66 Ranch Dr, Milpitas (95035-5103)
PHONE.................................408 945-6215
Jeff Klotz, *Branch Mgr*
EMP: 120 **Publicly Held**
WEB: www.pge.com
SIC: 4911 Transmission, electric power
HQ: Pacific Gas And Electric Company
  77 Beale St
  San Francisco CA 94105
  415 973-7000

(P-8188)
PACIFIC GAS AND ELECTRIC CO
Also Called: PG&e
28570 Tiger Creek Rd, Pioneer (95666-9646)
PHONE.................................209 295-2651
EMP: 120 **Publicly Held**
WEB: www.pge.com
SIC: 4911 Transmission, electric power
HQ: Pacific Gas And Electric Company
  77 Beale St
  San Francisco CA 94105
  415 973-7000

(P-8189)
PATTERN ENERGY GROUP ONE LP (PA)
1088 Sansome St, San Francisco (94111-1308)
PHONE.................................415 283-4000
Michael Garland, *CEO*
Alan Batkin, *Partner*
Brandon Inabinet, *IT/INT Sup*
Kim Liou, *General Counsel*
Gareth Walker, *Director*
EMP: 58 EST: 2009
SALES (est): 59.4MM **Privately Held**
WEB: www.patternenergy.com
SIC: 4911 Transmission, electric power

(P-8190)
PATTERN PANHANDLE WIND LLC
1088 Sansome St, San Francisco (94111-1308)
PHONE.................................415 283-4000
Michael Garland, *President*
EMP: 38 EST: 2007
SQ FT: 27,000
SALES (est): 14MM
SALES (corp-wide): 220.9K **Privately Held**
WEB: www.patternenergy.com
SIC: 4911 Generation, electric power
HQ: Pattern Energy Group Inc.
  1088 Sansome St
  San Francisco CA 94111
  415 283-4000

(P-8191)
PATTERN US FINANCE COMPANY LLC
1088 Sansome St, San Francisco (94111-1308)
PHONE.................................415 283-4000
Michael M Garland, *President*
Cary Kottler, *Vice Pres*
Brenda MEI, *Administration*
Chello French, *Accountant*
Nathan Durfey, *Manager*
EMP: 35 EST: 2017
SALES (est): 16.2MM
SALES (corp-wide): 220.9K **Privately Held**
WEB: www.patternenergy.com
SIC: 4911 Electric services
HQ: Pattern Energy Group Inc.
  1088 Sansome St
  San Francisco CA 94111
  415 283-4000

(P-8192)
PG&E CORPORATION
705 P St, Fresno (93721-2709)
PHONE.................................559 263-5303
EMP: 71 **Publicly Held**
WEB: www.pgecorp.com
SIC: 4911 Electric services
PA: Pg&e Corporation
  77 Beale St
  San Francisco CA 94105

(P-8193)
PLACER COUNTY WATER AGENCY
Also Called: Power Systems Division
24625 Harrison St, Foresthill (95631-9328)
P.O. Box 667 (95631-0667)
PHONE.................................530 367-6701
Stephen Jones, *Manager*
Joseph H Parker, *CFO*
Angela Pratt, *Admin Mgr*
Richard Vorous, *CIO*
Ross Branch, *Info Tech Mgr*
EMP: 83
SALES (corp-wide): 70.7MM **Privately Held**
WEB: www.pcwa.net
SIC: 4911 Electric services
PA: Placer County Water Agency
  144 Ferguson Rd
  Auburn CA 95603
  530 823-4850

(P-8194)
PLACER COUNTY WATER AGENCY (PA)
144 Ferguson Rd, Auburn (95603-3231)
P.O. Box 6570 (95604-6570)
PHONE.................................530 823-4850
Andy Fecko, *General Mgr*
Joseph Parker, *CFO*
David Breninger, *General Mgr*
Nichol Snyder, *Admin Asst*
Stephan Raper, *Technician*
EMP: 90 EST: 1957
SQ FT: 22,750
SALES (est): 70.7MM **Privately Held**
WEB: www.pcwa.net
SIC: 4911 4941 4971 Distribution, electric power; water supply; irrigation systems

(P-8195)
PLUMAS-SIERRA RURAL ELC COOP (PA)
73233 State Route 70, Portola (96122-7069)
PHONE.................................530 832-4261
Robert Marshall, *CEO*
Bill Hubert, *CFO*
Suzie Henson, *Admin Asst*
Judy May, *Sales Mgr*
Emily Compton, *Manager*
EMP: 37 EST: 1937
SQ FT: 6,000
SALES (est): 26.3MM **Privately Held**
WEB: www.psrec.coop
SIC: 4911 Generation, electric power

(P-8196)
SACRAMENTO MUNICPL UTILITY DST (PA)
Also Called: S M U D
6201 S St, Sacramento (95817-1818)
P.O. Box 15830 (95852-0830)
PHONE.................................916 452-3211
Arlen Orchard, *CEO*
Jim Tracy, *CFO*
Paul Lau, *Officer*
Laura Lewis, *Officer*
Michael Deangelis, *Program Mgr*
▲ EMP: 710 EST: 1923
SQ FT: 118,000
SALES: 1.5B **Privately Held**
WEB: www.smud.org
SIC: 4911 Distribution, electric power

(P-8197)
SACRAMENTO MUNICPL UTILITY DST
6201 S St, Sacramento (95817-1818)
PHONE.................................916 452-3211
Carlos Diaz, *Branch Mgr*
EMP: 377
SALES (corp-wide): 1.5B **Privately Held**
WEB: www.smud.org
SIC: 4911 Generation, electric power
PA: Sacramento Municipal Utility District
  6201 S St
  Sacramento CA 95817
  916 452-3211

(P-8198)
SACRAMENTO MUNICPL UTILITY DST
Also Called: Smud Energy Services
6301 S St, Sacramento (95817)
P.O. Box 15830 (95852-0830)
PHONE.................................916 732-5155
Jan Schori, *Manager*
Suzanne Dizon, *Partner*
Phyllis Figlioli, *COO*
Patricia Parent, *Officer*
Gregory Hensley, *CIO*
EMP: 88
SALES (corp-wide): 1.5B **Privately Held**
WEB: www.smud.org
SIC: 4911 Generation, electric power
PA: Sacramento Municipal Utility District
  6201 S St
  Sacramento CA 95817
  916 452-3211

(P-8199)
SACRAMENTO MUNICPL UTILITY DST
Also Called: Supply Change Services
6201 S St, Sacramento (95817-1818)
P.O. Box 15830 (95852-0830)
PHONE.................................916 732-5616
Frankie McDermott, *Manager*
Jerry Clark, *Agent*
EMP: 377
SALES (corp-wide): 1.5B **Privately Held**
WEB: www.smud.org
SIC: 4911
PA: Sacramento Municipal Utility District
  6201 S St
  Sacramento CA 95817
  916 452-3211

(P-8200)
SIEMENS ENERGY INC
3215 47th Ave, Sacramento (95824-2400)
PHONE.................................916 391-2993
Frank Miller, *Plant Mgr*
Nalin Bhatt, *Manager*
EMP: 95
SALES (corp-wide): 32.3B **Privately Held**
WEB: www.siemens.com
SIC: 4911 Generation, electric power
HQ: Siemens Energy, Inc.
  4400 N Alafaya Trl
  Orlando FL 32826
  407 736-2000

(P-8201)
SOUTHERN CALIFORNIA EDISON CO
Also Called: Northern Hydro
54205 Mt Poplar Ave, Big Creek (93605)
PHONE.................................559 893-3611
David Dormire, *Manager*
John Hamilton, *Project Mgr*
Bryan Troll, *Human Res Mgr*
EMP: 151
SALES (corp-wide): 13.5B **Publicly Held**
WEB: www.sce.com
SIC: 4911 Electric services
HQ: Southern California Edison Company
  2244 Walnut Grove Ave
  Rosemead CA 91770
  626 302-1212

(P-8202)
SOUTHERN CALIFORNIA EDISON CO
55481 Mt Poplar, Big Creek (93605)
P.O. Box 130 (93605-0130)
PHONE.................................559 893-2037
Southern Edison, *Branch Mgr*
EMP: 151
SALES (corp-wide): 13.5B **Publicly Held**
WEB: www.sce.com
SIC: 4911 Distribution, electric power; transmission, electric power
HQ: Southern California Edison Company
  2244 Walnut Grove Ave
  Rosemead CA 91770
  626 302-1212

(P-8203)
SURPRISE VLY ELCTRFCATION CORP
800 W 12th St, Alturas (96101-3132)
PHONE.................................530 233-3511
Wesley Cook,
Ray Cloud,
Joseph Johnson,
EMP: 48 EST: 1937
SQ FT: 5,000
SALES (est): 46.8MM **Privately Held**
WEB: www.surprisevalleyelectric.org
SIC: 4911 Distribution, electric power

(P-8204)
TRUCKEE DNNER PUB UTLITY DST F
Also Called: Truckee Donner Pud
11570 Donner Pass Rd, Truckee (96161-4992)
PHONE.................................530 587-3896
Michael D Holley, *General Mgr*
Trey Griffin, *IT/INT Sup*
Shanna Kuhlemier, *Finance*
Melissa Kleffman, *Buyer*
Grant Sacks, *Cust Mgr*
EMP: 68 EST: 1927
SQ FT: 48,000
SALES: 41.7MM **Privately Held**
WEB: www.tdpud.org
SIC: 4911 4941 Distribution, electric power; water supply

(P-8205)
TURLOCK IRRGTION DST EMPLYEES (PA)
333 E Canal Dr, Turlock (95380-3946)
P.O. Box 949 (95381-0949)
PHONE.................................209 883-8222
Joe Alamo, *President*
Constance Anderson, *Division Mgr*
Jim McCoy, *Division Mgr*
Benjamin Plaa, *Division Mgr*
Michael Frantz, *Admin Sec*
EMP: 204 EST: 1887
SQ FT: 20,000
SALES (est): 342.9MM **Privately Held**
WEB: www.tid.org
SIC: 4911 Distribution, electric power

4911 - Electric Svcs County

(P-8206)
V3 ELECTRIC INC
4925 Robert J Mathews Pkw, El Dorado Hills (95762-5700)
PHONE................916 597-2627
Joshua D Collette, *CEO*
Rachel Ravel, *Admin Asst*
Jason Baggett, *Analyst*
Margaret Carroll, *Opers Mgr*
Peder McOmber, *Sales Mgr*
EMP: 184 **EST:** 2015
SQ FT: 15,000
SALES (est): 23.8MM **Privately Held**
WEB: www.v3electric.com
SIC: 4911 1731 ; electric power systems contractors

(P-8207)
WELLHEAD ELECTRIC COMPANY INC
650 Bercut Dr Ste C, Sacramento (95811-0100)
PHONE................916 447-5171
Harold Dittner, *President*
Paul Cummins, *Vice Pres*
Sharon Stureman, *Administration*
Mike Gonzalez, *Info Tech Mgr*
Josh Curtis, *Technician*
EMP: 50 **EST:** 2011
SALES (est): 27.4MM **Privately Held**
WEB: www.wellhead.com
SIC: 4911 Generation, electric power

(P-8208)
WOODLAND BIOMASS POWER LTD
1786 E Kentucky Ave, Woodland (95776)
P.O. Box 1560 (95776-1560)
PHONE................530 661-6095
Larry Oneal, *Manager*
EMP: 45 **EST:** 1988
SALES (est): 4.7MM **Privately Held**
WEB: www.woodlandchamber.org
SIC: 4911

4922 Natural Gas Transmission

(P-8209)
WILD GOOSE STORAGE INC
2780 W Liberty Rd, Gridley (95948-9335)
P.O. Box 8 (95948-0008)
PHONE................530 846-7350
David Pope, *President*
EMP: 70 **EST:** 1996
SALES (est): 23.7MM **Privately Held**
WEB: www.rockpointgs.com
SIC: 4922 Storage, natural gas

4924 Natural Gas Distribution

(P-8210)
PACIFIC ENERGY FUELS COMPANY
Also Called: PG&e
77 Beale St Ste 100, San Francisco (94105-1814)
PHONE................415 973-8200
Gordon Smith, *President*
Justin Tomljanovic, *Vice Pres*
John Villalobos, *Comp Spec*
Glenda Scarbrough, *Human Res Dir*
Sean Mackay, *Senior Mgr*
EMP: 3131 **EST:** 1988
SALES (est): 16.2MM **Publicly Held**
WEB: www.pge.com
SIC: 4924 Natural gas distribution
HQ: Pacific Gas And Electric Company
77 Beale St
San Francisco CA 94105
415 973-7000

(P-8211)
PACIFIC GAS AND ELECTRIC CO
Also Called: PG&e
24300 Clawiter Rd, Hayward (94545-2218)
PHONE................510 784-3253
Tom Webb, *Branch Mgr*
Adam Soto, *Project Mgr*
WEI Chen, *Credit Staff*
EMP: 120 **Publicly Held**
WEB: www.pge.com
SIC: 4924 4911 Natural gas distribution; distribution, electric power
HQ: Pacific Gas And Electric Company
77 Beale St
San Francisco CA 94105
415 973-7000

(P-8212)
PACIFIC GAS AND ELECTRIC CO
Also Called: PG&e
460 Rio Lindo Ave, Chico (95926-1815)
PHONE................530 894-4739
Todd Stewart, *Manager*
EMP: 120 **Publicly Held**
WEB: www.pge.com
SIC: 4924 4911 4923 Natural gas distribution; electric services; gas transmission & distribution
HQ: Pacific Gas And Electric Company
77 Beale St
San Francisco CA 94105
415 973-7000

(P-8213)
STEELRVER INFRSTRCTURE FUND N (HQ)
Also Called: Steelrver Infrstrcture Prtners
1 Letterman Dr Bldg D, San Francisco (94129-1494)
PHONE................415 291-2200
Chris Kinney, *Partner*
John Anderson, *Partner*
Dennis Mahoney, *Partner*
John Fenton, *Consultant*
EMP: 200
SALES (est): 143.2MM **Privately Held**
WEB: www.steelriverpartners.com
SIC: 4924 Natural gas distribution

4931 Electric & Other Svcs Combined

(P-8214)
LOGANS GAP B MEMBER LLC (DH)
1088 Sansome St, San Francisco (94111-1308)
PHONE................415 283-4000
Michael Garland, *President*
Alexander Bennet,
EMP: 80 **EST:** 2014
SQ FT: 27,000
SALES (est): 30.8MM
SALES (corp-wide): 220.9K **Privately Held**
WEB: www.patternenergy.com
SIC: 4931 Electric & other services combined
HQ: Pattern Energy Group Inc.
1088 Sansome St
San Francisco CA 94111
415 283-4000

(P-8215)
PG&E RECOVERY FUNDING LLC ◆
77 Beale St, San Francisco (94105-1814)
P.O. Box 770000 (94177-0001)
PHONE................415 973-1000
EMP: 128 **EST:** 2021
SALES (est): 44K **Publicly Held**
SIC: 4931 Electric & other services combined
PA: Pg&E Corporation
77 Beale St
San Francisco CA 94105

(P-8216)
UNDERGROUND CNSTR CO INC
5145 Industrial Way, Benicia (94510-1042)
PHONE................707 746-8800
Christopher Ronco, *President*
Jeff Tinsley, *CFO*
George R Bradshaw, *Exec VP*
George Bradshaw, *Exec VP*
Loren Hudson, *Vice Pres*
EMP: 250 **EST:** 1936
SQ FT: 32,946
SALES (est): 172.7MM
SALES (corp-wide): 11.2B **Publicly Held**
WEB: www.undergroundconstruction.com
SIC: 4931 5172 4923 Electric & other services combined; aircraft fueling services; gas transmission & distribution
PA: Quanta Services, Inc.
2800 Post Oak Blvd # 2600
Houston TX 77056
713 629-7600

4939 Combination Utilities, NEC

(P-8217)
NOR-CAL CONTROLS ES INC
4790 Golden Foothill Pkwy # 110, El Dorado Hills (95762-9332)
PHONE................916 836-0800
Rob O Lopez, *CEO*
Ian Lopez, *COO*
Nu Chareunrath, *CFO*
Sean Keven, *Technical Staff*
Troy Morlan, *Engineer*
EMP: 92 **EST:** 2006
SALES (est): 31MM **Privately Held**
WEB: www.norcalcontrols.net
SIC: 4939 7373 8711 Combination utilities; computer integrated systems design; engineering services

4941 Water Sply

(P-8218)
ALAMEDA COUNTY WATER DISTRICT (PA)
Also Called: Acwd
43885 S Grimmer Blvd, Fremont (94538-6375)
P.O. Box 5110 (94537-5110)
PHONE................510 668-4200
Walt Wadlow, *General Mgr*
Roslyn Fuller, *Officer*
Steve Peterson, *Department Mgr*
Paul Piraino, *General Mgr*
Robert Shaver, *General Mgr*
EMP: 182 **EST:** 1914
SQ FT: 60,000
SALES: 130.9MM **Privately Held**
WEB: www.acwd.org
SIC: 4941 Water supply

(P-8219)
ALAMEDA COUNTY WATER DISTRICT
42436 Mission Blvd, Fremont (94539-4791)
PHONE................510 668-6631
Milan Viau, *Principal*
Cynthia Coutee, *Office Admin*
Kathy Barnes-Jones, *Administration*
Thomas Niesar, *Planning*
Erick Villalobos, *Technician*
EMP: 35
SALES (corp-wide): 130.9MM **Privately Held**
WEB: www.acwd.org
SIC: 4941 Water supply
PA: Alameda County Water District Inc
43885 S Grimmer Blvd
Fremont CA 94538
510 668-4200

(P-8220)
AMADOR WATER AGENCY
12800 Ridge Rd, Sutter Creek (95685-9630)
PHONE................209 223-3018
Jim Abercrombie, *District Mgr*
Terance W Moore, *President*
David N McGee, *CFO*
Paul Molinelli, *Bd of Directors*
John P Swift, *Vice Pres*
EMP: 52 **EST:** 1959
SQ FT: 2,000
SALES: 11.1MM **Privately Held**
WEB: www.amadorwater.org
SIC: 4941 4952 Water supply; sewerage systems

(P-8221)
ANDERSON PUMP COMPANY
Also Called: Dragon Engineering
24719 Robertson Blvd, Chowchilla (93610-9090)
P.O. Box 906 (93610-0906)
PHONE................559 665-4477
Daniel Skeen, *President*
Imogene Anderson, *Corp Secy*
Leon Anderson, *Vice Pres*
Jim Smith, *Vice Pres*
Jolene Skeen, *Office Mgr*
EMP: 55 **EST:** 1948
SQ FT: 10,000
SALES (est): 20.1MM **Privately Held**
WEB: www.andersonpumpcompany.com
SIC: 4941 4971 Water supply; irrigation systems

(P-8222)
AZULWORKS INC
1400 Egbert Ave, San Francisco (94124-3222)
PHONE................415 558-1507
Sandra R Hernandez, *President*
Christopher Kahney, *COO*
Audrey Kailly, *Office Admin*
Eoin Sullivan, *Project Mgr*
Hina Patel, *Controller*
EMP: 103 **EST:** 2001
SALES (est): 36.8MM **Privately Held**
WEB: www.azulworks.com
SIC: 4941 1623 1389 1622 Water supply; water, sewer & utility lines; communication line & transmission tower construction; construction, repair & dismantling services; tunnel construction; concrete work; stucco, gunite & grouting contractors; structural steel erection; concrete reinforcement, placing of

(P-8223)
BYRON BETHANY IRRIGATION DST
7995 Bruns Rd, Byron (94514-1625)
PHONE................209 835-0375
Rick Gilmore, *General Mgr*
Jeff Brown, *Director*
EMP: 51 **EST:** 1914
SQ FT: 800
SALES (est): 18.1MM **Privately Held**
WEB: www.bbid.org
SIC: 4941 Water supply

(P-8224)
CALAVERAS COUNTY WATER DST
120 Toma Ct, San Andreas (95249-9335)
P.O. Box 608 (95249-0608)
PHONE................209 754-3543
Scott Ratterman, *President*
Jeff Davidson, *Vice Pres*
Michael Minkler, *General Mgr*
Ben Stopper, *Opers Staff*
Joel Metzger, *Manager*
EMP: 66 **EST:** 1946
SQ FT: 5,000
SALES: 12.6MM **Privately Held**
WEB: www.ccwd.org
SIC: 4941 Water supply

(P-8225)
CALIFORNIA WATER SERVICE CO (HQ)
1720 N 1st St, San Jose (95112-4598)
PHONE................408 367-8200
Martin A Kropelnicki, *CEO*
Nishaik Tillman, *Partner*
Michael P Ireland, *President*
Oscar Ramos,
Helen Del Grosso, *Vice Pres*
EMP: 160 **EST:** 1926
SQ FT: 43,000
SALES (est): 391.4MM
SALES (corp-wide): 794.3MM **Publicly Held**
WEB: www.calwater.com
SIC: 4941 Water supply
PA: California Water Service Group
1720 N 1st St
San Jose CA 95112
408 367-8200

PRODUCTS & SERVICES SECTION

4941 - Water Sply County (P-8246)

(P-8226)
CALIFORNIA WATER SERVICE GROUP (PA)
1720 N 1st St, San Jose (95112-4598)
PHONE..................................408 367-8200
Martin A Kropelnicki, *President*
Peter C Nelson, *Ch of Bd*
Thomas F Smegal III, *CFO*
Todd K Peters, *Officer*
Shannon C Dean, *Vice Pres*
EMP: 142 **EST:** 1999
SALES (est): 794.3MM **Publicly Held**
WEB: www.calwatergroup.com
SIC: 4941 Water supply

(P-8227)
CALIFORNIA-AMERICAN WATER CO
4701 Beloit Dr, Sacramento (95838-2434)
PHONE..................................916 568-4216
Robert Bloor, *CFO*
Walter Sadler, *Engineer*
EMP: 50
SALES (corp-wide): 3.7B **Publicly Held**
WEB: www.amwater.com
SIC: 4941 4953 Water supply; refuse systems
HQ: California-American Water Company
655 W Broadway Ste 1410
San Diego CA 92101
619 446-4760

(P-8228)
CITY OF FAIRFIELD
Also Called: North Bay Regional Water
5110 Peabody Rd, Fairfield (94533-8908)
PHONE..................................707 428-7680
Ken Britz, *Manager*
EMP: 50
SALES (corp-wide): 146.2MM **Privately Held**
WEB: www.fairfield.ca.gov
SIC: 4941 Water supply
PA: City Of Fairfield
1000 Webster St
Fairfield CA 94533
707 428-7569

(P-8229)
CITY OF FRESNO
Also Called: Water Division
1910 E University Ave, Fresno (93703-2927)
PHONE..................................559 621-5300
Lon Martin, *Manager*
Ben Barnes, *Officer*
Art Estrada, *Officer*
Julie Skamel, *Officer*
Patty Laygo, *Executive Asst*
EMP: 165
SALES (corp-wide): 462.5MM **Privately Held**
WEB: www.fresno.gov
SIC: 4941 Water supply
PA: City Of Fresno
2600 Fresno St
Fresno CA 93721
559 621-7001

(P-8230)
CONTRA COSTA WATER DISTRICT (PA)
Also Called: Ccwd
1331 Concord Ave, Concord (94520-4907)
PHONE..................................925 688-8000
Lisa Borba, *President*
Chris Dundon, *Vice Pres*
Wendy Chriss, *Admin Sec*
Christine Helton, *Admin Sec*
Kathy Hildenbrand, *Admin Sec*
▲ **EMP:** 225 **EST:** 1936
SQ FT: 22,000
SALES: 3.8MM **Privately Held**
WEB: www.ccwater.com
SIC: 4941 Water supply

(P-8231)
CONTRA COSTA WATER DISTRICT
Also Called: Bollman Treatment Plant
2015 Bates Ave, Concord (94520-1254)
PHONE..................................925 688-8090
Carl Voight, *Branch Mgr*
Lauren Curiel, *Admin Sec*
Donnella Smigiel-Amdahl, *Analyst*
Jeff Tschudi, *Accountant*
Lisa Borba, *Director*
EMP: 36
SALES (corp-wide): 3.8MM **Privately Held**
WEB: www.ccwater.com
SIC: 4941 Water supply
PA: Contra Costa Water District Inc
1331 Concord Ave
Concord CA 94520
925 688-8000

(P-8232)
CONTRA COSTA WATER DISTRICT
Also Called: Randall-Bold Wtr Trtmnt Plant
3760 Neroly Rd, Oakley (94561-2084)
PHONE..................................925 383-2576
Walter Bishop, *General Mgr*
EMP: 36
SALES (corp-wide): 3.8MM **Privately Held**
WEB: www.ccwater.com
SIC: 4941 Water supply
PA: Contra Costa Water District Inc
1331 Concord Ave
Concord CA 94520
925 688-8000

(P-8233)
DUBLIN SAN RAMON SERVICES DST (PA)
7051 Dublin Blvd, Dublin (94568-3018)
PHONE..................................925 875-2276
Bert Michalczyk, *CEO*
Lori Rose, *Treasurer*
Irene Suroso, *Engineer*
▲ **EMP:** 109
SQ FT: 19,400
SALES: 71.4MM **Privately Held**
WEB: www.dsrsd.com
SIC: 4941 Water supply

(P-8234)
EAST BAY MNCPL UTLITY DST WSTW
Also Called: Ebmud
15083 Camanche Pkwy S, Valley Springs (95252-8330)
PHONE..................................209 772-8204
Kent Lambert, *Branch Mgr*
Jill Gaskins, *Analyst*
Anthony Ukena, *Auditor*
EMP: 187
SALES (corp-wide): 625MM **Privately Held**
WEB: www.ebmud.com
SIC: 4941 Water supply
HQ: East Bay Municipal Utility District, Wastewater System
375 11th St
Oakland CA 94607

(P-8235)
EAST BAY MNCPL UTLITY DST WTR
Also Called: Ebmud
3999 Lakeside Dr, Richmond (94806-1964)
PHONE..................................866 403-2683
Karl Gillson, *Branch Mgr*
EMP: 43
SALES (corp-wide): 625MM **Privately Held**
WEB: www.ebmud.com
SIC: 4941 Water supply
PA: East Bay Municipal Utility District, Water System
375 11th St
Oakland CA 94607
866 403-2683

(P-8236)
EAST BAY MNCPL UTLITY DST WTR (PA)
Also Called: EBMUD
375 11th St, Oakland (94607-4246)
P.O. Box 24055 (94623-1055)
PHONE..................................866 403-2683
Alexander Coate, *General Mgr*
John Coleman, *Bd of Directors*
Andy Katz, *Bd of Directors*
Serge Terentieff, *Division Mgr*
Gina Bellingham, *Admin Sec*
EMP: 629 **EST:** 1923
SQ FT: 264,427
SALES: 625MM **Privately Held**
WEB: www.ebmud.com
SIC: 4941 Water supply

(P-8237)
EAST BAY MNCPL UTLITY DST WTR
Also Called: Ebmud
6921 Chabot Rd, Oakland (94618-1921)
PHONE..................................866 403-2683
David White, *Branch Mgr*
EMP: 43
SALES (corp-wide): 625MM **Privately Held**
WEB: www.ebmud.com
SIC: 4941 Water supply
PA: East Bay Municipal Utility District, Water System
375 11th St
Oakland CA 94607
866 403-2683

(P-8238)
EAST BAY MNCPL UTLITY DST WTR
Also Called: Ebmud
1 Winemaster Way Ste K, Lodi (95240-0860)
PHONE..................................209 333-2095
Alexander Coate, *General Mgr*
EMP: 43
SALES (corp-wide): 625MM **Privately Held**
WEB: www.ebmud.com
SIC: 4941 Water supply
PA: East Bay Municipal Utility District, Water System
375 11th St
Oakland CA 94607
866 403-2683

(P-8239)
EAST BAY MNCPL UTLITY DST WTR
Also Called: East Bay Water
500 San Pablo Dam Rd, Orinda (94563-1604)
P.O. Box 24055, Oakland (94623-1055)
PHONE..................................925 254-3778
Steve Abbors, *Branch Mgr*
Jason Mitchell, *Supervisor*
EMP: 43
SQ FT: 1,000
SALES (corp-wide): 625MM **Privately Held**
WEB: www.ebmud.com
SIC: 4941 Water supply
PA: East Bay Municipal Utility District, Water System
375 11th St
Oakland CA 94607
866 403-2683

(P-8240)
EAST BAY MNCPL UTLITY DST WTR
Also Called: Ebmud
Pardee Ctr, Valley Springs (95252)
PHONE..................................209 772-8200
Pat Lydon, *Superintendent*
Lisa Stuart, *Clerk*
EMP: 43
SALES (corp-wide): 625MM **Privately Held**
WEB: www.ebmud.com
SIC: 4941 Water supply
PA: East Bay Municipal Utility District, Water System
375 11th St
Oakland CA 94607
866 403-2683

(P-8241)
EAST BAY MNCPL UTLITY DST WTR
Also Called: Water Supply Division
1804 W Main St, Stockton (95203-2902)
P.O. Box 228 (95201-0228)
PHONE..................................209 946-8000
Andrew Enos, *Branch Mgr*
EMP: 43
SALES (corp-wide): 625MM **Privately Held**
WEB: www.ebmud.com
SIC: 4941 Water supply
PA: East Bay Municipal Utility District, Water System
375 11th St
Oakland CA 94607
866 403-2683

(P-8242)
EAST BAY MNCPL UTLITY DST WTR
Also Called: Oakland Business Office
375 11th St, Oakland (94607-4246)
P.O. Box 2060 (94604-2060)
PHONE..................................510 287-0600
EMP: 43
SALES (corp-wide): 625MM **Privately Held**
WEB: www.ebmud.com
SIC: 4941 Water supply
PA: East Bay Municipal Utility District, Water System
375 11th St
Oakland CA 94607
866 403-2683

(P-8243)
EAST BAY MUNICIPL UTILTY DISTR
Also Called: Ebmud
3849 Mount Diablo Blvd, Lafayette (94549)
PHONE..................................866 403-2683
Alexander Coate, *General Mgr*
David Klein, *Controller*
EMP: 43
SALES (corp-wide): 625MM **Privately Held**
WEB: www.ebmud.com
SIC: 4941 Water supply
PA: East Bay Municipal Utility District, Water System
375 11th St
Oakland CA 94607
866 403-2683

(P-8244)
EAST BAY MUNICIPL UTILTY DISTR
Also Called: Ebmud
1100 21st St, Oakland (94607-2887)
PHONE..................................866 403-2683
Dennis Dimer, *Branch Mgr*
Susan Lord, *Opers Staff*
EMP: 43
SALES (corp-wide): 625MM **Privately Held**
WEB: www.ebmud.com
SIC: 4941 Water supply
PA: East Bay Municipal Utility District, Water System
375 11th St
Oakland CA 94607
866 403-2683

(P-8245)
EAST BAY MUNICIPL UTILTY DISTR
Also Called: East Area Office
2551 N Main St, Walnut Creek (94597-3122)
P.O. Box 1000, Oakland (94649-0001)
PHONE..................................866 403-2683
Alexander Coate, *Manager*
EMP: 43
SALES (corp-wide): 625MM **Privately Held**
WEB: www.ebmud.com
SIC: 4941 Water supply
PA: East Bay Municipal Utility District, Water System
375 11th St
Oakland CA 94607

(P-8246)
EAST BAY MUNICIPL UTILTY DISTR
Also Called: Ebmud - Construction and Maint
2149 Union St, Oakland (94607)
PHONE..................................866 403-2683
Alexander Coate, *Branch Mgr*
EMP: 54

4941 - Water Sply County (P-8247)

SALES (corp-wide): 625MM **Privately Held**
WEB: www.ebmud.com
SIC: 4941 Water supply
PA: East Bay Municipal Utility District, Water System
375 11th St
Oakland CA 94607
866 403-2683

(P-8247)
EL DORADO HILLS COUNTY WTR DST
Also Called: El Dorado Hills Fire Dept
1050 Wilson Blvd, El Dorado Hills (95762-7263)
PHONE.................................916 933-6623
John Hidahl, *President*
James O'Camb, *COO*
Christina Burroughs, *Admin Asst*
Christopher Landry, *Engineer*
Jessica Braddock, *Finance*
EMP: 51 EST: 1963
SALES (est): 19.7MM **Privately Held**
WEB: www.edhfire.com
SIC: 4941 Water supply

(P-8248)
EL DORADO IRRIGATION DISTRICT
2890 Mosquito Rd, Placerville (95667-4700)
PHONE.................................530 622-4513
George Osborne, *President*
Darcy Millward, *Vice Pres*
Ane Deister, *General Mgr*
Pat Johnson, *Executive Asst*
Linda King, *Admin Asst*
EMP: 300 EST: 1925
SQ FT: 27,000
SALES: 71.9MM **Privately Held**
WEB: www.eid.org
SIC: 4941 4952 8741 4971 Water supply; sewerage systems; management services; irrigation systems

(P-8249)
FAIR OAKS WATER DISTRICT
10326 Fair Oaks Blvd, Fair Oaks (95628-7114)
PHONE.................................916 967-5723
Tom Gray, *Manager*
EMP: 42 EST: 1917
SQ FT: 10,000
SALES (est): 10.3MM **Privately Held**
WEB: www.fowd.com
SIC: 4941 Water supply

(P-8250)
HIGHLANDS WATER COMPANY
14580 Lakeshore Dr, Clearlake (95422-8100)
PHONE.................................707 994-2393
John Eckhardt, *President*
Ermen Ghiorzi, *Admin Sec*
Richard Sisco, *Controller*
Magen Estep,
EMP: 37 EST: 1923
SQ FT: 500
SALES (est): 5.7MM **Privately Held**
WEB: www.highlandswater.com
SIC: 4941 Water supply

(P-8251)
HUMBOLDT COMMUNITY SERVICE DST
5055 Walnut Dr, Eureka (95503-6595)
P.O. Box 158, Cutten (95534-0158)
PHONE.................................707 443-4558
Mark Bryant, *General Mgr*
David Walkley, *Finance Mgr*
Brenda Franklin, *Manager*
EMP: 42 EST: 1952
SQ FT: 4,500
SALES: 10.4MM **Privately Held**
WEB: www.humboldtcsd.org
SIC: 4941 4952 Water supply; sewerage systems

(P-8252)
MADERA IRRIGATION DISTRICT
12152 Road 28 1/4, Madera (93637-9199)
PHONE.................................559 673-3514
Carl Jansen, *President*
Cynthia Rascoe, *Admin Sec*
James Rosel, *Technician*
Dina Nolan, *Manager*
Manuel Guillen, *Supervisor*
EMP: 40 EST: 1920
SQ FT: 8,600
SALES (est): 26.2MM **Privately Held**
WEB: www.madera-id.org
SIC: 4941 Water supply

(P-8253)
MAMMOTH COMMUNITY WATER DST
1315 Meridian Blvd, Mammoth Lakes (93546-2074)
P.O. Box 597 (93546-0597)
PHONE.................................760 934-2596
Sandra Hageman, *Finance Mgr*
Patrick Hayes, *General Mgr*
Mark Busby, *Technician*
Clay Murray, *Opers Staff*
Jeff Beatty, *Manager*
EMP: 42 EST: 1957
SQ FT: 9,000
SALES (est): 15.6MM **Privately Held**
WEB: www.mcwd.dst.ca.us
SIC: 4941 4952 Water supply; sewerage systems

(P-8254)
NORTH MARIN WATER DISTRICT (PA)
Also Called: Nmwd
999 Rush Creek Pl, Novato (94945-7716)
P.O. Box 146 (94948-0146)
PHONE.................................415 897-4133
Chris Degabriele, *Principal*
Carmela Chandrasekera, *Engineer*
Rocky Vogler, *Chief Engr*
Nancy Holton, *Accountant*
Robert Clark, *Opers Staff*
EMP: 50 EST: 1948
SQ FT: 7,200
SALES (est): 21.7MM **Privately Held**
WEB: www.nmwd.com
SIC: 4941 Water supply

(P-8255)
NORTHSTAR COMMUNITY SVCS DST
900 Northstar Dr, Truckee (96161-4204)
PHONE.................................530 562-0747
Michael Staudenmayer, *Manager*
Jeann Green, *Vice Pres*
Steve Goates, *Technology*
Joshua Detwiler, *Technical Staff*
Matt Ryan, *Opers Staff*
EMP: 41 EST: 1990
SQ FT: 6,150
SALES (est): 6.2MM **Privately Held**
WEB: www.northstarcsd.org
SIC: 4941 Water supply

(P-8256)
OAKDALE IRRGTION DST FING CORP
1205 E F St, Oakdale (95361-4112)
PHONE.................................209 847-0341
Alfred Bairos, *President*
Kathy Cook, *CFO*
Steve Knell, *Exec Dir*
▲ EMP: 51 EST: 1909
SQ FT: 5,000
SALES (est): 15MM **Privately Held**
WEB: www.oakdaleirrigation.com
SIC: 4941 Water supply

(P-8257)
OPERATIONS MANAGEMENT INTL INC
1500 Southside Dr, Gilroy (95020-7042)
PHONE.................................408 848-0480
Paul Roy, *Opers-Prdtn-Mfg*
EMP: 35
SALES (corp-wide): 13.5B **Publicly Held**
SIC: 4941 4952 Water supply; sewerage systems
HQ: Operations Management International, Inc.
9193 S Jamaica St Ste 400
Englewood CO 80112
303 740-0019

(P-8258)
PANOCHE WATER DISTRICT
52027 W Althea Ave, Firebaugh (93622-9401)
PHONE.................................209 364-6136
ARA Azhderian, *General Mgr*
John Bennet, *President*
Sue Redfern, *Vice Pres*
Michael Linneman, *Director*
Mike Sterns, *Director*
EMP: 50 EST: 1989
SQ FT: 1,200
SALES (est): 13.9MM **Privately Held**
SIC: 4941 Water supply

(P-8259)
RANCHO MURIETA CMNTY SVCS DST
15160 Jackson Rd, Sloughhouse (95683)
P.O. Box 1050 (95683-1050)
PHONE.................................916 354-3700
Edward R Crouse, *Manager*
Les Clark, *Director*
▲ EMP: 35 EST: 1982
SQ FT: 5,000
SALES (est): 5.8MM **Privately Held**
WEB: www.ranchomurietacsd.com
SIC: 4941 7381 4952 Water supply; protective services, guard; sewerage systems

(P-8260)
RECLAMATION DISTRICT 108
975 Wilson Bend Rd, Grimes (95950)
P.O. Box 50 (95950-0050)
PHONE.................................530 437-2221
Fred Durst, *President*
Lewis Bair, *General Mgr*
Cathy Busch, *General Mgr*
Cathy Miller, *Admin Sec*
EMP: 47 EST: 1893
SALES (est): 18.5MM **Privately Held**
WEB: www.rd108.org
SIC: 4941 Water supply

(P-8261)
SAC RIVER WATER TREATMENT PLAN
301 Water St, Sacramento (95811-0241)
PHONE.................................916 808-3101
David Herrmann, *Superintendent*
EMP: 40 EST: 2008
SALES (est): 1.7MM **Privately Held**
SIC: 4941 Water supply

(P-8262)
SACRAMENTO SUBURBAN WATER DST
3701 Marconi Ave Ste 100, Sacramento (95821-5346)
PHONE.................................916 972-7171
Daniel York, *General Mgr*
Ben Harris, *Officer*
Craig Locke, *Vice Pres*
Matthew Winans, *CIO*
Kyle Jividen, *Technician*
EMP: 60 EST: 1958
SQ FT: 13,500
SALES: 49.2MM **Privately Held**
WEB: www.sswd.org
SIC: 4941 Water supply

(P-8263)
SACRAMENTO SUBURBAN WATER DST
3701 Marconi Ave Ste 100, Sacramento (95821-5346)
PHONE.................................916 972-7171
Robert Rosco, *General Mgr*
Greg Bundesen, *Supervisor*
EMP: 52 EST: 2002
SALES (est): 10.6MM **Privately Held**
WEB: www.sswd.org
SIC: 4941 Water supply

(P-8264)
SAN JOSE WATER COMPANY (HQ)
Also Called: S J W
110 W Taylor St, San Jose (95110-2131)
PHONE.................................408 288-5314
W Richard Roth, *CEO*
Charles Toeniskoetter, *Ch of Bd*
Angela Yip, *CFO*
Richard Balocco, *Vice Pres*
Geaorge Belhumeur, *Vice Pres*
EMP: 140 EST: 1866
SQ FT: 5,000
SALES: 411.4MM
SALES (corp-wide): 564.5MM **Publicly Held**
WEB: www.sjwgroup.com
SIC: 4941 Water supply
PA: Sjw Group
110 W Taylor St
San Jose CA 95110
408 279-7800

(P-8265)
SAN JOSE WATER COMPANY
1221 S Bascom Ave, San Jose (95128-3514)
PHONE.................................408 298-0364
Paul Schreiber, *Manager*
EMP: 180
SALES (corp-wide): 564.5MM **Publicly Held**
WEB: www.sjwgroup.com
SIC: 4941 Water supply
HQ: San Jose Water Company
110 W Taylor St
San Jose CA 95110
408 288-5314

(P-8266)
SAN JUAN WATER DISTRICT
9935 Auburn Folsom Rd, Granite Bay (95746-9690)
P.O. Box 2157 (95746-2157)
PHONE.................................916 791-0115
Shauna Lorance, *Exec Dir*
Mary A Morris, *CFO*
Paul Helliker, *General Mgr*
Robert Nush, *Administration*
Kurt Corothers, *Technician*
EMP: 44 EST: 1954
SQ FT: 3,800
SALES: 24.4MM **Privately Held**
WEB: www.sjwd.org
SIC: 4941 Water supply

(P-8267)
SANTA CLARA VALLEY WATER (PA)
5750 Almaden Expy, San Jose (95118-3614)
P.O. Box 20670 (95160-0670)
PHONE.................................408 265-2600
Beau Goldie, *CEO*
Gary Kremen, *Bd of Directors*
Rachael Gibson, *Officer*
Olga Steele, *Officer*
Hernan Rivero, *Risk Mgmt Dir*
▲ EMP: 250 EST: 1951
SQ FT: 40,780
SALES: 144.6MM **Privately Held**
WEB: www.valleywater.org
SIC: 4941 Water supply

(P-8268)
SANTA CLARA VLY WTR DST PUB FC
Also Called: Penitencia Water Trtmnt Plant
3959 Whitman Way, San Jose (95132-3168)
PHONE.................................408 630-2560
EMP: 164
SALES (corp-wide): 144.6MM **Privately Held**
WEB: www.valleywater.org
SIC: 4941 Water supply
PA: Santa Clara Valley Water District Public Facilities Financing Corporation
5750 Almaden Expy
San Jose CA 95118
408 265-2600

(P-8269)
SANTA CLARA VLY WTR DST PUB FC
400 More Ave, Los Gatos (95032-1111)
PHONE.................................408 395-8121
Greg Gibson, *Branch Mgr*
Heather Williams, *Admin Asst*
Lale Eristurk, *Engineer*
EMP: 164
SALES (corp-wide): 144.6MM **Privately Held**
WEB: www.valleywater.org
SIC: 4941 Water supply

▲ = Import ▼ = Export
◆ = Import/Export

PRODUCTS & SERVICES SECTION
4952 - Sewerage Systems County (P-8290)

PA: Santa Clara Valley Water District Public Facilities Financing Corporation
5750 Almaden Expy
San Jose CA 95118
408 265-2600

(P-8270)
SANTA CRUZ CITY OF
Also Called: City Snta Cruz Mncpl Utilities
212 Locust St Ste D, Santa Cruz (95060-3812)
PHONE 831 420-5200
Bill Kocher, *Director*
EMP: 36
SALES (corp-wide): 116.6MM **Privately Held**
WEB: www.cityofsantacruz.com
SIC: **9111** 4941 Mayors' offices; water supply
PA: City Of Santa Cruz
809 Center St Rm 8
Santa Cruz CA 95060
831 420-5055

(P-8271)
SJW GROUP (PA)
110 W Taylor St, San Jose (95110-2131)
PHONE 408 279-7800
Eric W Thornburg, *Ch of Bd*
James P Lynch, *CFO*
Suzy Papazian, *Admin Sec*
Wendy Avila-Walker, *Controller*
EMP: 357 EST: 1866
SALES (est): 564.5MM **Publicly Held**
WEB: www.sjwgroup.com
SIC: **4941** 6531 Water supply; real estate agent, commercial

(P-8272)
SONOMA COUNTY WATER AGENCY
404 Aviation Blvd Ste 0, Santa Rosa (95403-9019)
PHONE 707 526-5370
Grant Davis, *General Mgr*
Lori Soto, *Exec Dir*
Kevin Booker, *General Mgr*
Wendy Gjestland, *General Mgr*
Carrie Pollard, *CIO*
EMP: 200 EST: 1950
SQ FT: 57,000
SALES: 52.7MM **Privately Held**
WEB: www.sonomawater.org
SIC: **4941** Water supply

(P-8273)
SOQUEL CREEK WATER DISTRICT
5180 Soquel Dr, Soquel (95073-2549)
P.O. Box 1550, Capitola (95010-1550)
PHONE 831 475-0195
Laura D Brown, *Manager*
Bruce Jaffe, *Bd of Directors*
Jayne Wallner, *Bd of Directors*
Tom Lahue, *Vice Pres*
Ron Duncan, *General Mgr*
EMP: 40
SQ FT: 4,200
SALES: 23.2MM **Privately Held**
WEB: www.soquelcreekwater.org
SIC: **4941** Water supply

(P-8274)
SOUTH FEATHER WATER & PWR AGCY (PA)
2310 Oro Quincy Hwy, Oroville (95966-5226)
PHONE 530 533-4578
James Edward, *Director*
Lou Lodigiani, *President*
Patricia A Sands, *Treasurer*
Matt Colwell, *Division Mgr*
Daniel Leon, *Division Mgr*
EMP: 45 EST: 1919
SQ FT: 5,000
SALES (est): 22.2MM **Privately Held**
WEB: www.southfeather.com
SIC: **4941** Water supply

(P-8275)
SOUTH SAN JQUIN CNTY FIRE AUTH
Also Called: South County Fire
835 N Central Ave, Tracy (95376-4105)
PHONE 209 831-6702
David Bramell, *Principal*
Jackie Heefner, *Principal*
Robert Rickman, *Principal*
EMP: 95 EST: 2018
SALES (est): 8.5MM **Privately Held**
WEB: www.sjcfire.org
SIC: **4941** Water supply

(P-8276)
SOUTH SAN JQUIN IRRIGATION DST
Also Called: Ssjid
11011 E Highway 120, Manteca (95336-9751)
P.O. Box 747, Ripon (95366-0747)
PHONE 209 249-4600
Betty Garcia, *Exec Sec*
Mike Weststeyn, *Vice Pres*
Tim Hagins, *Division Mgr*
Joe Hasten, *Division Mgr*
Collin Hodge, *Division Mgr*
EMP: 93
SQ FT: 8,500
SALES: 9.6MM **Privately Held**
WEB: www.ssjid.com
SIC: **4941** Water supply

(P-8277)
TUOLUMNE UTILITIES DISTRICT
Also Called: T U D
18885 Nugget Blvd, Sonora (95370-9284)
PHONE 209 532-5536
Pet Kampa, *General Mgr*
John Maciel, *Bd of Directors*
Edwinr Pattison, *General Mgr*
Corey Adams, *Administration*
Jennifer Batt, *Engineer*
EMP: 80 EST: 1947
SQ FT: 6,000
SALES (est): 38.2MM **Privately Held**
WEB: www.tudwater.com
SIC: **4941** 4952 Water supply; sewerage systems

4952 Sewerage Systems

(P-8278)
ARIES INDUSTRIES INC
Also Called: Ccv Engineering & Mfg
5748 E Shields Ave # 101, Fresno (93727-7854)
PHONE 559 291-0383
Kevin Blackhurse, *Manager*
Dustin Harp, *Technician*
Joe Zweep, *Technician*
Kenneth Ebenhoch, *Engineer*
Jeff Patin, *Engineer*
EMP: 101
SALES (corp-wide): 27.9MM **Privately Held**
WEB: www.ariesindustries.com
SIC: **4952** Sewerage systems
PA: Aries Industries, Inc.
550 Elizabeth St
Waukesha WI 53186
800 234-7205

(P-8279)
CENTRAL CONTRA COSTA SANI DST
5019 Imhoff Pl, Martinez (94553-4316)
PHONE 925 228-9500
Roger Bailey, *CEO*
Katie Young, *Admin Sec*
Todd Smithey, *Administration*
Anne Gemmell, *Planning*
Donna Anderson, *Technician*
EMP: 275
SQ FT: 40,000
SALES: 87.2MM **Privately Held**
WEB: www.centralsan.org
SIC: **4952** Sewerage systems

(P-8280)
COVELLO GROUP INC
1660 Olympic Blvd Ste 300, Walnut Creek (94596-5190)
PHONE 925 933-2300
Bruce Presser, *CEO*
Gary Skrel, *President*
Joseph Covello, *Chairman*
Ed Obrien, *Vice Pres*
Steven Wrightson, *Vice Pres*
EMP: 50 EST: 1994
SQ FT: 5,780
SALES (est): 5MM **Privately Held**
WEB: www.covellogroup.com
SIC: **4952** Sewerage systems

(P-8281)
EAST BAY MNCPL UTLTY DST WSTW (HQ)
Also Called: EBMUD - SPECIAL DISTRICT NO. 1
375 11th St, Oakland (94607-4246)
PHONE 866 403-2683
Alexander Coate, *General Mgr*
Karl Yakich, *Engineer*
Linda Gillock, *Purchasing*
Carlton Chan, *Manager*
EMP: 39 EST: 1944
SQ FT: 264,427
SALES: 122.3MM
SALES (corp-wide): 625MM **Privately Held**
WEB: www.ebmud.com
SIC: **4952** 4953 Sewerage systems;
PA: East Bay Municipal Utility District, Water System
375 11th St
Oakland CA 94607
866 403-2683

(P-8282)
FAIRFIELD-SUISUN SEWER DST
1010 Chadbourne Rd, Fairfield (94534-9700)
PHONE 707 429-8930
Richard F Luthy Jr, *General Mgr*
Steve Ray, *Technology*
Benjamin Carver, *Engineer*
Olivia Ruiz, *Accountant*
Brian Hawley, *Opers Mgr*
EMP: 65 EST: 1951
SQ FT: 15,000
SALES (est): 23MM **Privately Held**
WEB: www.fssd.com
SIC: **4952** Sewerage systems

(P-8283)
HIDDEN VLY LK CMNTY SVCS DST
19400 Hartmann Rd, Hidden Valley Lake (95467-8371)
PHONE 707 987-9201
Roland Sanford, *General Mgr*
Carolyn Graham, *Bd of Directors*
Kirk Cloyd, *General Mgr*
Tami Ipsen, *Admin Sec*
Brandon Bell, *Technician*
EMP: 37 EST: 1968
SALES: 661.3K **Privately Held**
WEB: www.hvlcsd.org
SIC: **4952** Sewerage systems

(P-8284)
MALAGA COUNTY WATER DISTRICT
3580 S Frank Ave, Fresno (93725-2511)
PHONE 559 485-7353
Charles Garabedian Jr, *President*
John Leyva, *Vice Pres*
Laurie Cortez, *Admin Asst*
Irma Casteneda, *Director*
Sal Cerrillo, *Director*
EMP: 40 EST: 1958
SQ FT: 2,500
SALES (est): 971.8K **Privately Held**
WEB: www.malagacwd.org
SIC: **4952** 7999 Sewerage systems; recreation center

(P-8285)
MCKINLEYVILLE CMNTY SVCS DST
1656 Sutter Rd, McKinleyville (95519-4217)
P.O. Box 2037 (95519-2037)
PHONE 707 839-3251
Helen Edwards, *President*
Norman Shopay, *Bd of Directors*
Thomas Marking, *General Mgr*
Gregory Orsini, *General Mgr*
April Sousa, *Admin Sec*
EMP: 49 EST: 1970
SQ FT: 26,400
SALES (est): 13.9MM **Privately Held**
WEB: www.mckinleyvillecsd.com
SIC: **4952** 4941 Sewerage systems; water supply

(P-8286)
NAPA SANITATION DISTRICT
1515 Soscol Ferry Rd, NAPA (94558-6247)
P.O. Box 2480 (94558-0522)
PHONE 707 254-9231
Tim Healy, *General Mgr*
John Cuevas, *CFO*
Andrew Damron, *Engineer*
Daniel Fritz, *Opers Spvr*
Jim Keller, *Plant Mgr*
EMP: 50
SQ FT: 3,600
SALES: 35.6MM **Privately Held**
WEB: www.napasan.com
SIC: **4952** Sewerage systems

(P-8287)
NORTH TAHOE PUBLIC UTILITY DST (PA)
Also Called: North Tahoe P U D
875 National Ave, Tahoe Vista (96148-9867)
P.O. Box 139 (96148-0139)
PHONE 530 546-4212
Leon Schegg, *General Mgr*
Vanetta Van Cleave, *CFO*
Amy Fontana, *Technician*
David Bowker, *Opers Staff*
Jason Dicey, *Opers Staff*
EMP: 45 EST: 1948
SALES (est): 14.5MM **Privately Held**
WEB: www.ntpud.org
SIC: **4952** 4941 7999 Sewerage systems; water supply; recreation services

(P-8288)
SACRAMENTO REG CO SANIT DIST
Sacramento Regional Waste
8521 Laguna Station Rd, Elk Grove (95758-9550)
PHONE 916 875-9000
Ruben Robles, *Manager*
Christina Brown, *Project Mgr*
Chris Heikkila, *Technology*
Dean Wyley, *Engineer*
Chris Blackburn, *Analyst*
EMP: 500
SALES (corp-wide): 101.6MM **Privately Held**
WEB: www.regionalsan.com
SIC: **4952** Sewerage systems
PA: Sacramento Regional County Sanitation District
10060 Goethe Rd
Sacramento CA 95827
916 876-6000

(P-8289)
SELMA-KNGSBURG-FOWLER CNTY STN
Also Called: S-K-F County Sanitation Dist
11301 E Conejo Ave, Kingsburg (93631-9511)
P.O. Box 158 (93631-0158)
PHONE 559 897-6500
Judy Case, *Chairman*
Veronica Cazares, *Engineer*
Ralph Gonzales, *Director*
EMP: 43 EST: 1971
SQ FT: 12,000
SALES (est): 17.5MM **Privately Held**
WEB: www.skfcsd.org
SIC: **4952** Sewerage systems

(P-8290)
SILICON VALLEY CLEAN WATER
Also Called: SBSA
1400 Radio Rd, Redwood City (94065-1220)
PHONE 650 591-7121
Ronald W Shepherd, *Principal*
Daniel T Child, *Manager*
EMP: 79 EST: 1975
SQ FT: 180,000
SALES: 54.1MM **Privately Held**
WEB: www.svcw.org
SIC: **4952** Sewerage systems

4952 - Sewerage Systems County (P-8291)

PRODUCTS & SERVICES SECTION

(P-8291)
SOUTH TAHOE PUBLIC UTILITY DST
1275 Meadow Crest Dr, South Lake Tahoe (96150-7401)
PHONE..................................530 544-6474
Richard Solbrig, *General Mgr*
Paul Hughes, *CFO*
Paul Sciuto, *Principal*
Debbie Henderson, *General Mgr*
John Thiel, *General Mgr*
EMP: 113 EST: 1950
SALES (est): 53.7MM **Privately Held**
WEB: www.stpud.us
SIC: 4952 4941 Sewerage systems; water supply

(P-8292)
TAHOE CITY PUBLIC UTILITY DIST
221 Fairway Dr, Tahoe City (96145-1746)
P.O. Box 5249 (96145-5249)
PHONE..................................530 583-3796
Lucinda M Gustafson, *CEO*
James Dykstra, *Treasurer*
Cindy Gustafson, *Exec Dir*
Brandi Stirton, *Admin Sec*
Carol Hackbarth, *Admin Asst*
EMP: 40 EST: 1993
SQ FT: 9,500
SALES (est): 6MM **Privately Held**
WEB: www.tcpud.org
SIC: 4952 4941 7999 Sewerage systems; water supply; recreation services

(P-8293)
TAHOE-TRUCKEE SANITATION AGCY
Also Called: Ttsa
13720 Butterfield Dr, Truckee (96161-3316)
PHONE..................................530 587-2525
Marcia Beals, *General Mgr*
Laura Mader, *Lab Dir*
Michael Peak, *Department Mgr*
Roshelle Chavez, *Executive Asst*
Kristin Schrandt, *Technician*
▲ EMP: 59 EST: 1972
SQ FT: 500,083
SALES (est): 12.7MM **Privately Held**
WEB: www.ttsa.net
SIC: 4952 Sewerage systems

(P-8294)
TRUCKEE SANITARY DISTRICT
12304 Joerger Dr, Truckee (96161-3386)
PHONE..................................530 587-3804
Thomas S Elfridge, *General Mgr*
Dennis Anderson, *Bd of Directors*
Brian K Smart, *Vice Pres*
Rene Lopez, *CIO*
Liz Carstens, *Technician*
EMP: 36 EST: 1906
SALES (est): 10.8MM **Privately Held**
WEB: www.truckeesan.org
SIC: 4952 Sewerage systems

(P-8295)
UNION SANITARY DISTRICT
Also Called: USD
5072 Benson Rd, Union City (94587-2508)
PHONE..................................510 477-7500
Paul Eldredge, *Principal*
Michael Gill, *Technology*
Richard Scobee, *Technology*
Sami Ghossain, *Technical Staff*
Roslyn Fuller, *Purch Agent*
▲ EMP: 130 EST: 1918
SALES (est): 61.6MM **Privately Held**
WEB: www.unionsanitary.ca.gov
SIC: 4952 Sewerage systems

(P-8296)
WEST COUNTY WASTEWATER DST
2377 Garden Tract Rd, Richmond (94801-1001)
PHONE..................................510 237-6603
Brian Hill, *Superintendent*
Claudia Anderson, *Admin Sec*
Michael Savannah, *Sr Project Mgr*
Sherry A Stanley, *Director*
Geraldine Gonzales, *Supervisor*
EMP: 41
SALES (corp-wide): 28.9MM **Privately Held**
WEB: www.wcwd.org
SIC: 4952 Sewerage systems
PA: West County Wastewater District
2910 Hilltop Dr
Richmond CA 94806
510 222-6700

4953 Refuse Systems

(P-8297)
ACES WASTE SERVICES INC
6500 Buena Vista Rd, Ione (95640-9443)
PHONE..................................209 274-2237
Colleen Ianni, *President*
Kari Ianni, *Treasurer*
Peggy Assereto, *Vice Pres*
Paul Molinelli, *Vice Pres*
Susan Evans-Moreira, *Office Mgr*
EMP: 35 EST: 1995
SALES (est): 13.2MM **Privately Held**
WEB: www.aceswaste.com
SIC: 4953 Garbage: collecting, destroying & processing

(P-8298)
AER ELECTRONICS INC (PA)
Also Called: Aerelectronics
42744 Boscell Rd, Fremont (94538-5132)
PHONE..................................510 300-0500
Andre Weiglein, *President*
William Schoening, *CFO*
John Dickenson, *Vice Pres*
Janet Rianda, *Vice Pres*
James Quintal, *Admin Sec*
▲ EMP: 55 EST: 1996
SQ FT: 75,000
SALES (est): 18.4MM **Privately Held**
WEB: www.aerworldwide.com
SIC: 4953 5093 Recycling, waste materials; scrap & waste materials

(P-8299)
ALAMEDA COUNTY INDUSTRIES INC
610 Aladdin Ave, San Leandro (94577-4302)
PHONE..................................510 357-7282
Louis Pellegrini, *Exec VP*
Robert Molinaro, *CEO*
Kent Kenney, *CFO*
Jason Dobert, *Sales Staff*
Carrie Dobert, *Manager*
EMP: 50 EST: 2000
SQ FT: 39,648
SALES (est): 17.8MM **Privately Held**
WEB: www.alamedacountyindustries.com
SIC: 4953 Rubbish collection & disposal

(P-8300)
ALCO IRON & METAL CO
1091 Doolittle Dr C, San Leandro (94577-1022)
PHONE..................................510 562-1107
Kim Kantor, *President*
Kevin Kantor, *Exec VP*
Walter Chang, *General Mgr*
Emilio Zamora, *General Mgr*
Brian Harvey, *Plant Engr Mgr*
EMP: 48
SALES (corp-wide): 50.5MM **Privately Held**
WEB: www.alcometals.com
SIC: 4953 Recycling, waste materials
PA: Alco Iron & Metal Co.
2140 Davis St
San Leandro CA 94577
510 562-1107

(P-8301)
ALEMEDA COUNTY INDUSTRIES LLC
610 Aladdin Ave, San Leandro (94577-4302)
PHONE..................................510 357-7282
Robert Molinaro,
Gricelda Sanchez, *Asst Controller*
Kent Kenney, *Controller*
Vigil Mary, *Human Resources*
Jason Dobert, *Supervisor*
EMP: 70 EST: 1999
SQ FT: 5,400
SALES (est): 8.7MM **Privately Held**
WEB: www.alamedacountyindustries.com
SIC: 4953 Recycling, waste materials

(P-8302)
AMADOR DISPOSAL SERVICE INC
Also Called: Amador County Landfill
6500 Buena Vista Rd, Ione (95640-9443)
PHONE..................................209 274-4095
John Jordan, *General Mgr*
Jason Craft, *Manager*
EMP: 58 EST: 1965
SQ FT: 1,500
SALES (est): 5.8MM
SALES (corp-wide): 5.4B **Privately Held**
WEB: www.aceswaste.com
SIC: 4953 Rubbish collection & disposal
HQ: Waste Connections Us, Inc.
3 Waterway Square Pl # 110
The Woodlands TX 77380

(P-8303)
ARCATA GARBAGE CO
30 S G St, Arcata (95521-6692)
PHONE..................................707 822-0304
Riccardo Fusi, *President*
EMP: 39 EST: 1961
SQ FT: 125
SALES (est): 646.5K **Privately Held**
WEB: www.recology.com
SIC: 4953 Recycling, waste materials

(P-8304)
ATLAS DISPOSAL INDUSTRIES LLC
3035 Prospect Park Dr # 40, Rancho Cordova (95670-6070)
PHONE..................................916 455-2800
Dave Sikich, *CEO*
Nick Sikich, *COO*
Steven Bruce, *Vice Pres*
Sean Moen, *General Mgr*
Natalie Peebles, *Sales Staff*
EMP: 70 EST: 1998
SALES (est): 18.9MM **Privately Held**
WEB: www.atlasdisposal.com
SIC: 4953 Garbage: collecting, destroying & processing; refuse collection & disposal services

(P-8305)
BAY AREA CONCRETE LLC
1580 Chabot Ct, Hayward (94545-2423)
PHONE..................................510 294-0220
Preet Johal,
EMP: 100 EST: 2012
SALES (est): 10.4MM **Privately Held**
WEB: www.bayareaconcreterecycling.com
SIC: 4953 1771 Recycling, waste materials; concrete work

(P-8306)
BAY CITIES REFUSE SERVICE INC
Also Called: Bay View Refuse & Recycling
2525 Garden Tract Rd, Richmond (94801-1005)
PHONE..................................510 237-4614
Lewis Figone, *President*
Ray Walter Morrison, *Shareholder*
Gregory Harman, *Officer*
Kimberly Christie, *General Mgr*
Greg Christie, *Technology*
EMP: 52 EST: 1959
SQ FT: 3,750
SALES (est): 4.6MM **Privately Held**
WEB: www.baycitiesrefuse.com
SIC: 4953 Refuse collection & disposal services

(P-8307)
BAY COUNTIES WASTE SVCS INC
Also Called: Specialty Solid Waste & Recycl
3355 Thomas Rd, Santa Clara (95054-2060)
PHONE..................................408 565-9900
Robert J Molinaro, *CEO*
William Dobert, *CFO*
Douglas Button, *Treasurer*
Jerry Nabhan, *General Mgr*
Nick Nabhan, *General Mgr*
▲ EMP: 80 EST: 1930
SQ FT: 2,000
SALES (est): 18.5MM **Privately Held**
WEB: www.sswr.com
SIC: 4953 Recycling, waste materials

(P-8308)
BAY POLYMERS CORP
Also Called: BP
44530 S Grimmer Blvd, Fremont (94538-6386)
PHONE..................................510 490-1791
John La Fontain, *President*
▲ EMP: 40 EST: 1978
SQ FT: 16,000
SALES (est): 14.5MM **Privately Held**
WEB: www.baypolymer.com
SIC: 4953 Recycling, waste materials

(P-8309)
BERTOLOTTI DISPOSAL INC
231 Flamingo Dr, Modesto (95358-6128)
P.O. Box 127, Ceres (95307-0127)
PHONE..................................209 537-1500
Bert Bertolotti, *President*
Steve Holloway, *Treasurer*
Delouries Bertolotti, *Vice Pres*
Melissa Acosta, *Manager*
EMP: 40
SQ FT: 10,000
SALES (est): 9.1MM **Privately Held**
WEB: www.bertolottidisposal.com
SIC: 4953 Garbage: collecting, destroying & processing

(P-8310)
BLUE LINE TRANSFER INC
500 E Jamie Ct, South San Francisco (94080-6222)
P.O. Box 348 (94083-0348)
PHONE..................................650 589-5511
Doug Button, *President*
Paul Formosa, *Treasurer*
Michael Achiro, *Vice Pres*
Ron Fornesi, *Vice Pres*
Vince Fornesi, *Vice Pres*
EMP: 49 EST: 1970
SQ FT: 22,500
SALES (est): 5.5MM **Privately Held**
WEB: www.ssfscavenger.com
SIC: 4953 Recycling, waste materials

(P-8311)
BROWNING-FERRIS INDS CAL INC
Also Called: Site L71
12310 San Mateo Rd, Half Moon Bay (94019-7112)
PHONE..................................650 726-1819
Jim Gunderson, *Manager*
EMP: 35
SALES (corp-wide): 10.1B **Publicly Held**
SIC: 4953 Sanitary landfill operation
HQ: Browning-Ferris Industries Of California, Inc.
9200 Glenoaks Blvd
Sun Valley CA 91352
818 790-5410

(P-8312)
BROWNING-FERRIS INDS CAL INC
Also Called: Site 211
951 Waterbird Way, Martinez (94553-1469)
PHONE..................................925 313-8901
Oscar Vase, *Manager*
EMP: 35
SQ FT: 60,000
SALES (corp-wide): 10.1B **Publicly Held**
SIC: 4953 Refuse systems
HQ: Browning-Ferris Industries Of California, Inc.
9200 Glenoaks Blvd
Sun Valley CA 91352
818 790-5410

(P-8313)
BRUNOS IRON & METAL LP
3211 S Golden State Blvd, Fresno (93725-2404)
PHONE..................................559 233-6543
Freda Tosi, *Partner*
Nick Tosi, *Cust Mgr*
Gloria M Richardson, *Manager*
Rick White, *Manager*
▼ EMP: 45 EST: 1947
SQ FT: 3,528

PRODUCTS & SERVICES SECTION
4953 - Refuse Systems County (P-8336)

SALES (est): 5MM Privately Held
WEB: www.brunosrecycling.com
SIC: 4953 Recycling, waste materials

(P-8314)
CALIFORNIA WASTE SOLUTIONS INC (PA)
1005 Timothy Dr, San Jose (95133-1043)
PHONE 510 832-8111
David Duong, *CEO*
Kristina Duong, *CFO*
Joel Corona, *Officer*
Victor Duong, *Vice Pres*
Linda Duong, *Admin Sec*
◆ EMP: 75 EST: 1992
SQ FT: 120,000
SALES (est): 34.9MM Privately Held
WEB: www.calwaste.com
SIC: 4953 Recycling, waste materials

(P-8315)
CALIFRNIA ELCTRNIC ASSET RCVER
3678 Lemay St, Mather (95655-4117)
PHONE 916 388-1777
Paul Y Gao, *CEO*
Chee Vang, *Data Proc Staff*
George Garofalo, *Opers Staff*
◆ EMP: 35 EST: 2000
SQ FT: 80,000
SALES (est): 13.1MM Privately Held
WEB: www.cearinc.com
SIC: 4953 Recycling, waste materials

(P-8316)
CALIFRNIA WSTE RCVERY SYSTEMS
175 Enterprise Ct Ste A, Galt (95632-9047)
P.O. Box 670, Woodbridge (95258-0670)
PHONE 209 369-6887
Dave Vaccarezza,
Cindy Kline, *CFO*
Jack Fiori, *Vice Pres*
Todd Snider, *Business Dir*
Michael Sinclair, *Controller*
EMP: 42 EST: 1972
SQ FT: 2,012
SALES (est): 24.1MM Privately Held
WEB: www.cal-waste.com
SIC: 4953 8641 Garbage: collecting, destroying & processing; civic social & fraternal associations

(P-8317)
CIRCOSTA IRON AND METAL CO INC
1801 Evans Ave, San Francisco (94124-1103)
P.O. Box 24494 (94124-0494)
PHONE 415 282-8568
Steven Circosta, *President*
Nick Circosta Jr, *President*
Lee Woodall, *Vice Pres*
▼ EMP: 39 EST: 1933
SQ FT: 4,000
SALES (est): 7MM Privately Held
WEB: www.circostametals.com
SIC: 4953 Recycling, waste materials; refuse collection & disposal services

(P-8318)
CITY OF SACRAMENTO
Also Called: Department of Public Works
2812 Meadowview Rd, Sacramento (95832-1441)
PHONE 916 808-4949
Terrance Davis, *Manager*
Daniel G Bowers, *Director*
EMP: 35
SALES (corp-wide): 838.2MM Privately Held
WEB: www.cityofsacramento.org
SIC: 4953 4212 9511 Rubbish collection & disposal; garbage collection & transport, no disposal;
PA: City Of Sacramento
    915 I St Fl 5
    Sacramento CA 95814
    916 808-5300

(P-8319)
CIVICORPS
6315 San Leandro St, Oakland (94621-3727)
PHONE 510 992-7800
Bill Zenoni, *Branch Mgr*
Rachel Eisner, *Director*
EMP: 48 Privately Held
WEB: www.cvcorps.org
SIC: 4953 Recycling, waste materials
PA: Civicorps
    101 Myrtle St
    Oakland CA 94607

(P-8320)
COUNTY QUARRY PRODUCTS
5501 Imhoff Pl, Martinez (94553-4391)
PHONE 925 682-0707
Doug Foskett, *Partner*
Sonny Mc Dowell, *Partner*
Randy Grim, *Office Mgr*
Austin Snyder, *Purchasing*
EMP: 20 EST: 1986
SQ FT: 1,000
SALES (est): 5.2MM Privately Held
WEB: www.countyquarryproducts.com
SIC: 4953 5032 3272 2951 Recycling, waste materials; brick, stone & related material; concrete products; asphalt paving mixtures & blocks

(P-8321)
COVANTA STANISLAUS INC
4040 Fink Rd, Crows Landing (95313-9686)
P.O. Box 278 (95313-0278)
PHONE 209 837-4423
Karen Henry, *Financial Exec*
Karen L Wilhelm, *Business Mgr*
Jeffrey Ruoss, *Plant Mgr*
EMP: 47 EST: 1989
SALES (est): 19.2MM
SALES (corp-wide): 1.9B Publicly Held
SIC: 4953 Recycling, waste materials
HQ: Covanta Projects, Llc
    445 South St
    Morristown NJ 07960

(P-8322)
EAST BAY MUNICIPL UTILTY DISTR
Also Called: Ebmud
2020 Wake Ave, Oakland (94607-5100)
PHONE 866 403-2683
Alexander Coate, *General Mgr*
EMP: 43
SALES (corp-wide): 625MM Privately Held
WEB: www.ebmud.com
SIC: 4953 9511
PA: East Bay Municipal Utility District, Water System
    375 11th St
    Oakland CA 94607
    866 403-2683

(P-8323)
ECULLET INC
1 Vintage Ct, Woodside (94062-2560)
PHONE 650 493-7300
Craig J London, *CEO*
Mark D Muenchow, *CFO*
Farook Afsari, *Chairman*
Dr Yue Min Wong, *Director*
EMP: 100 EST: 1999
SALES (est): 11.1MM Privately Held
WEB: www.support.website-creator.org
SIC: 4953 Recycling, waste materials

(P-8324)
ELECTRNIC RCYCLERS INTL - IND
7815 N Palm Ave Ste 140, Fresno (93711-5531)
PHONE 317 522-1414
John S Shegerian, *President*
Tammy L Shegerian, *Treasurer*
Linda L Ramos, *Admin Sec*
Shyann Caudel, *CIO*
Justin Ledoux, *Opers Staff*
▼ EMP: 99
SALES (est): 13MM Privately Held
WEB: www.eridirect.com
SIC: 4953 Recycling, waste materials
PA: Electronic Recyclers International Inc.
    7815 N Palm Ave Ste 140
    Fresno CA 93711

(P-8325)
ELECTRNIC RCYCLERS INTL - WASH
7815 N Palm Ave Ste 140, Fresno (93711-5531)
PHONE 253 736-2627
John Shegerian, *President*
Tammy Shegerian, *Treasurer*
Linda Ramos, *Admin Sec*
EMP: 45 EST: 2008
SALES (est): 2.2MM Privately Held
WEB: www.eridirect.com
SIC: 4953 Non-hazardous waste disposal sites
PA: Electronic Recyclers International Inc.
    7815 N Palm Ave Ste 140
    Fresno CA 93711

(P-8326)
ELECTRONIC RECYCLERS INTL INC (PA)
Also Called: Electronic Recyclers America
7815 N Palm Ave Ste 140, Fresno (93711-5531)
PHONE 800 374-3473
John S Shegerian, *CEO*
Dann V Angeloff, *President*
Kelly Thomas, *COO*
James Kim, *CFO*
Brendan Egan, *Bd of Directors*
▲ EMP: 540 EST: 2006
SQ FT: 75,000
SALES (est): 499.9MM Privately Held
WEB: www.eridirect.com
SIC: 4953 Recycling, waste materials

(P-8327)
EMPIRE WASTE MANAGEMENT
450 Orr Springs Rd, Ukiah (95482-3131)
PHONE 707 462-2063
Robert Thornsberry, *Owner*
EMP: 72 EST: 1982
SALES (est): 20.3MM
SALES (corp-wide): 15.2B Publicly Held
WEB: www.wm.com
SIC: 4953 Garbage: collecting, destroying & processing
PA: Waste Management, Inc.
    800 Capitol St Ste 3000
    Houston TX 77002
    713 512-6200

(P-8328)
EVERGREEN ENVMTL SVCS INC
6880 Smith Ave, Newark (94560-4224)
PHONE 510 795-4400
Gary Colbert, *President*
EMP: 179 EST: 1977
SQ FT: 10,000
SALES (est): 1.2MM
SALES (corp-wide): 20.6MM Privately Held
SIC: 4953 Liquid waste, collection & disposal
PA: Evergreen Holdings Inc.
    18952 Macarthur Blvd # 410
    Irvine CA 92612
    949 757-7770

(P-8329)
FIBRES INTERNATIONAL INC
Also Called: Fibres International Recycling
88 Rowland Way Ste 300, Novato (94945-5049)
PHONE 425 455-9811
Tony Rounds, *General Mgr*
EMP: 38 Privately Held
SIC: 4953 4212 3341 3231 Refuse collection & disposal services; local trucking, without storage; secondary nonferrous metals; products of purchased glass; pulp mills
PA: Fibres International, Inc.
    88 Rowland Way Ste 300
    Novato CA 94945

(P-8330)
FIBRES INTERNATIONAL INC
88 Rowland Way Ste 300, Novato (94945-5049)
PHONE 425 455-9811
Rich Yost, *Manager*
EMP: 38 Privately Held
SIC: 4953 3231 Recycling, waste materials; products of purchased glass
PA: Fibres International, Inc.
    88 Rowland Way Ste 300
    Novato CA 94945

(P-8331)
FORWARD INC (DH)
1145 W Charter Way, Stockton (95206-1106)
PHONE 209 466-4482
Kevin Basso, *General Mgr*
EMP: 40 EST: 1961
SQ FT: 7,000
SALES (est): 44MM
SALES (corp-wide): 10.1B Publicly Held
WEB: www.republicservices.com
SIC: 4953 Sanitary landfill operation
HQ: Allied Waste Industries, Llc
    18500 N Allied Way # 100
    Phoenix AZ 85054
    480 627-2700

(P-8332)
FORWARD INC
Also Called: Site 204
9999 S Austin Rd, Manteca (95336-8924)
PHONE 209 982-4298
Ruben Ramirez, *Manager*
EMP: 110
SALES (corp-wide): 10.1B Publicly Held
SIC: 4953 Sanitary landfill operation
HQ: Forward, Inc.
    1145 W Charter Way
    Stockton CA 95206
    209 466-4482

(P-8333)
GILTON RSRCE RCVERY TRNSF FCLT (PA)
755 S Yosemite Ave, Oakdale (95361-4039)
PHONE 209 527-3781
Richard Gilton, *President*
Tedford Gilton, *Vice Pres*
Karen Gilton Hardister, *Vice Pres*
Donna Love, *Vice Pres*
EMP: 54 EST: 1990
SALES (est): 12.3MM Privately Held
WEB: www.gilton.com
SIC: 4953 Recycling, waste materials

(P-8334)
GILTON SOLID WASTE MGT INC
755 S Yosemite Ave, Oakdale (95361-4991)
PHONE 209 527-3781
Richard Gilton, *President*
Tedford Gilton, *Vice Pres*
Karen Gilton Hardister, *Vice Pres*
Karen Hardister, *Vice Pres*
Donna Gilton Love, *Vice Pres*
EMP: 136 EST: 1961
SQ FT: 3,000
SALES (est): 33.3MM Privately Held
WEB: www.gilton.com
SIC: 4953 Recycling, waste materials

(P-8335)
GREENWASTE RECOVERY INC (PA)
1500 Berger Dr, Watsonville (95077)
P.O. Box 2347 (95077-2347)
PHONE 408 283-4800
Richard Christina, *President*
Frank Weigel, *COO*
Don Dean, *CFO*
Dave Tilton, *CFO*
Jesse Weigel, *Corp Secy*
EMP: 95 EST: 1991
SQ FT: 115,000
SALES (est): 51.7MM Privately Held
WEB: www.greenwaste.com
SIC: 4953 Rubbish collection & disposal; waste materials, disposal at sea

(P-8336)
GREY BEARS
2710 Chanticleer Ave, Santa Cruz (95065-1812)
PHONE 831 479-1055
Tim Brattan, *CEO*
Danielle Wong, *Program Mgr*
Sharon Gross, *Office Mgr*
Mary Buck, *Opers Mgr*

(PA)=Parent Co (HQ)=Headquarters (DH)=Div Headquarters
✪ = New Business established in last 2 years

4953 - Refuse Systems County (P-8337)

Howard Feldstein, *Asst Director*
EMP: 40 **EST:** 1973
SQ FT: 1,200
SALES (est): 2.7MM **Privately Held**
WEB: www.greybears.org
SIC: 4953 8399 8611 Recycling, waste materials; community action agency; community affairs & services

(P-8337)
INDUSTRIAL METAL RECYCLING INC
260 Phelan Ave, San Jose (95112-6109)
PHONE................408 294-2334
Jeff Brown, *President*
EMP: 47 **EST:** 1999
SALES (est): 3.9MM **Privately Held**
WEB: www.industrialmetalservice.com
SIC: 4953 Recycling, waste materials

(P-8338)
KELLER CANYON LANDFILL COMPANY
Also Called: Site 212
901 Bailey Rd, Bay Point (94565-4309)
PHONE................925 458-9800
Jeff D Andrews, *CEO*
Norm Christiansen, *Manager*
EMP: 526 **EST:** 1992
SQ FT: 50,000
SALES (est): 5.7MM
SALES (corp-wide): 10.1B **Publicly Held**
SIC: 4953 Sanitary landfill operation
HQ: Browning-Ferris Industries Of California, Inc.
    9200 Glenoaks Blvd
    Sun Valley CA 91352
    818 790-5410

(P-8339)
M & M SERVICES INC (PA)
Also Called: Pacific Sanitation
590 Caletti Ave, Windsor (95492-8768)
PHONE................707 838-2597
Doug Moreda, *President*
Dustin Abbott, *CFO*
EMP: 41 **EST:** 2002
SALES (est): 11.1MM **Privately Held**
WEB: www.pacificsanitation.com
SIC: 4953 Refuse collection & disposal services

(P-8340)
MADERA DISPOSAL SYSTEMS INC (DH)
Also Called: M D S I
21739 Road 19, Chowchilla (93610-8218)
P.O. Box 12227, Fresno (93777-2227)
PHONE................559 665-3099
Ron Mittelstaedt, *President*
EMP: 85 **EST:** 1965
SQ FT: 1,200
SALES (est): 20.7MM
SALES (corp-wide): 5.4B **Privately Held**
WEB: www.wasteconnections.com
SIC: 4953 4212 Street refuse systems; local trucking, without storage

(P-8341)
MAMMOTH DISPOSAL COMPANY
59 Commerce Dr, Mammoth Lakes (93546-6206)
P.O. Box 237 (93546-0237)
PHONE................760 934-2201
Ronald Mittelstaedt, *CEO*
Darrell Chambliss, *Vice Pres*
Brian Bigham, *Manager*
EMP: 81 **EST:** 1962
SALES (est): 3.1MM
SALES (corp-wide): 5.4B **Privately Held**
WEB: www.mammothdisposal.com
SIC: 4953 Garbage: collecting, destroying & processing; refuse collection & disposal services
HQ: Waste Connections Us, Inc.
    3 Waterway Square Pl # 110
    The Woodlands TX 77380

(P-8342)
MARIN SANITARY SERVICE (PA)
Also Called: Marin Resource Recovery Center
1050 Andersen Dr, San Rafael (94901-5316)
P.O. Box 10067 (94912-0067)
PHONE................415 456-2601
Patricia Garbarino, *CEO*
Jason Raleigh, *CFO*
Dave Garbarino, *Vice Pres*
Ron Piombo, *Vice Pres*
Mardell Sarkela
EMP: 85
SALES (est): 78.5MM **Privately Held**
WEB: www.marinsanitaryservice.com
SIC: 4953 5099 4212 Garbage: collecting, destroying & processing; recycling, waste materials; wood chips; local trucking, without storage

(P-8343)
MARIN SANITARY SERVICE
565 Jacoby St, San Rafael (94901-5305)
PHONE................415 485-5646
Ruben Valtierra, *Branch Mgr*
Steve Rosa, *Vice Pres*
Mardell Sarkela,
Mardell Sarkela, *Technician*
Rudy Tescallo, *Foreman/Supr*
EMP: 60
SALES (corp-wide): 78.5MM **Privately Held**
WEB: www.marinsanitaryservice.com
SIC: 4953 Recycling, waste materials
PA: Marin Sanitary Service
    1050 Andersen Dr
    San Rafael CA 94901
    415 456-2601

(P-8344)
MCCOURTNEY ROAD TRANSFER STN
Also Called: Wm
14741 Wolf Mountain Rd, Grass Valley (95949-8734)
PHONE................530 274-2215
Bob Elder, *Principal*
EMP: 42 **EST:** 2006
SALES (est): 11.8MM
SALES (corp-wide): 15.2B **Publicly Held**
WEB: www.wm.com
SIC: 5541 4953 Gasoline service stations; recycling, waste materials
PA: Waste Management, Inc.
    800 Capitol St Ste 3000
    Houston TX 77002
    713 512-6200

(P-8345)
MILL VALLEY REFUSE SERVICE INC
112 Front St, San Rafael (94901-4011)
P.O. Box 3557 (94912-3557)
PHONE................415 457-2287
Dave Biggio, *President*
James Iavarone, *Treasurer*
Dave Dellazoppa, *Vice Pres*
Jennifer Dami, *VP Admin*
Lynda Mendoza, *Sales Mgr*
EMP: 57 **EST:** 1906
SQ FT: 52,000
SALES (est): 11.7MM **Privately Held**
WEB: www.millvalleyrefuse.com
SIC: 4953 Rubbish collection & disposal; recycling, waste materials

(P-8346)
NORTECH WASTE LLC
3033 Fiddyment Rd, Roseville (95747-9705)
PHONE................916 645-5230
Paul Szura, *Mng Member*
Tina Steiner, *Administration*
Keith Schmidt, *Engineer*
Arthur A Daniels,
Donald M Moriel,
EMP: 120 **EST:** 1992
SQ FT: 9,000
SALES (est): 25.3MM **Privately Held**
WEB: www.nortechwaste.com
SIC: 4953 3341 3312 3231 Sanitary landfill operation; secondary nonferrous metals; blast furnaces & steel mills; products of purchased glass; pulp mills

(P-8347)
NOVATO DISPOSAL SERVICE INC (PA)
Also Called: Total Waste Systems
3417 Standish Ave, Santa Rosa (95407-8135)
P.O. Box 1916 (95402-1916)
PHONE................707 765-9995
James Ratto, *President*
Diana Ratto, *Corp Secy*
Markj Arsenault, *Exec VP*
Julie Bertani-Kiser, *Vice Pres*
Catherine Langridge, *Vice Pres*
EMP: 40 **EST:** 1947
SQ FT: 3,000
SALES (est): 13.2MM **Privately Held**
SIC: 4953 Recycling, waste materials

(P-8348)
PENINSULA SANITARY SERVICE INC
339 Bonair Siding Rd, Stanford (94305-7201)
PHONE................650 321-4236
Louis Pellegrini Sr, *President*
Louis Pellegrini Jr, *Vice Pres*
Deanna Halleck Ventura, *Manager*
EMP: 35 **EST:** 1933
SQ FT: 1,840
SALES (est): 6.6MM **Privately Held**
WEB: www.lbre.stanford.edu
SIC: 4953 Garbage: collecting, destroying & processing; recycling, waste materials

(P-8349)
POTRERO HILLS LANDFILL INC
3675 Potrero Hills Ln, Suisun City (94585)
P.O. Box 68, Fairfield (94533-0628)
PHONE................707 429-9600
Richard Granzella, *President*
EMP: 39 **EST:** 1984
SALES (est): 18.5MM
SALES (corp-wide): 5.4B **Privately Held**
WEB: www.wasteconnections.com
SIC: 4953 Sanitary landfill operation
HQ: Waste Connections Us, Inc.
    3 Waterway Square Pl # 110
    The Woodlands TX 77380

(P-8350)
PSC LLC
189 Stauffer Blvd, San Jose (95125-1042)
PHONE................408 295-0607
Bruce Boman, *Branch Mgr*
EMP: 273 **Privately Held**
WEB: www.hydrochempsc.com
SIC: 4953 Refuse systems
HQ: Psc, Llc
    5151 San Felipe St Ste 11
    Houston TX 77056

(P-8351)
RECOLOGY INC (PA)
50 California St Ste 2400, San Francisco (94111-4796)
PHONE................415 875-1000
Sal Coniglio, *CEO*
George P McGrath, *COO*
Mark R Lomele, *CFO*
Dennis Wu, *Chairman*
Cary Chen, *Vice Pres*
EMP: 60 **EST:** 1988
SQ FT: 25,000
SALES (est): 1.4B **Privately Held**
WEB: www.recology.com
SIC: 4953 Garbage: collecting, destroying & processing; recycling, waste materials

(P-8352)
RECOLOGY INC
245 N 1st St, Dixon (95620-3027)
PHONE................916 379-3300
Jim Sullivan, *Administration*
Marc Castelli, *Safety Mgr*
EMP: 63
SALES (corp-wide): 1.4B **Privately Held**
WEB: www.recology.com
SIC: 4953 Recycling, waste materials
PA: Recology Inc.
    50 California St Ste 2400
    San Francisco CA 94111
    415 875-1000

(P-8353)
RECOLOGY SONOMA MARIN
3400 Standish Ave, Santa Rosa (95407-8112)
PHONE................707 586-8261
Fred Stemmler, *General Mgr*
EMP: 450 **EST:** 2017
SALES (est): 86MM
SALES (corp-wide): 1.4B **Privately Held**
WEB: www.recology.com
SIC: 4953 Recycling, waste materials
PA: Recology Inc.
    50 California St Ste 2400
    San Francisco CA 94111
    415 875-1000

(P-8354)
RECOLOGY SOUTH VALLEY (HQ)
1351 Pacheco Pass Hwy, Gilroy (95020-9579)
PHONE................408 842-3358
Robert Coyle, *President*
Mike Sanjiacomo, *Vice Pres*
Monica Estrada, *General Mgr*
EMP: 65 **EST:** 1949
SQ FT: 6,000
SALES (est): 22.5MM
SALES (corp-wide): 1.4B **Privately Held**
WEB: www.recology.com
SIC: 4953 Sanitary landfill operation; recycling, waste materials
PA: Recology Inc.
    50 California St Ste 2400
    San Francisco CA 94111
    415 875-1000

(P-8355)
RECOLOGY VALLEJO (HQ)
Also Called: Vallejo Garbage & Recycling
2021 Broadway St, Vallejo (94589-1701)
PHONE................707 552-3110
Ed Farewell, *General Mgr*
EMP: 108 **EST:** 1926
SQ FT: 40,000
SALES (est): 30.5MM
SALES (corp-wide): 1.4B **Privately Held**
WEB: www.recology.com
SIC: 4953 Recycling, waste materials
PA: Recology Inc.
    50 California St Ste 2400
    San Francisco CA 94111
    415 875-1000

(P-8356)
RECOLOGY YUBA-SUTTER
3001 N Levee Rd, Marysville (95901-3600)
P.O. Box G (95901-0062)
PHONE................530 743-6933
Robert Coyle, *COO*
EMP: 90 **EST:** 1974
SQ FT: 7,000
SALES (est): 10.2MM
SALES (corp-wide): 1.4B **Privately Held**
WEB: www.recology.com
SIC: 4953 4212 Garbage: collecting, destroying & processing; recycling, waste materials; hazardous waste collection & disposal; hazardous waste transport
PA: Recology Inc.
    50 California St Ste 2400
    San Francisco CA 94111
    415 875-1000

(P-8357)
RECYCLING INDUSTRIES INC
4741 Watt Ave, North Highlands (95660-5526)
PHONE................916 452-3961
Scott Kuhnen, *President*
David Kuhnen, *CFO*
Adam Gese, *Plant Mgr*
Michael Rexroad, *Manager*
EMP: 75 **EST:** 1981
SQ FT: 155,000
SALES (est): 17.9MM **Privately Held**
WEB: www.recyclingindustries.com
SIC: 4953 Recycling, waste materials

(P-8358)
REDWOOD LANDFILL INC
8950 Redwood Hwy, Novato (94945-1435)
P.O. Box 793 (94948-0793)
PHONE................415 892-2851
Ramin Khany, *Site Mgr*
Barry Skolnick, *Vice Pres*

PRODUCTS & SERVICES SECTION

4953 - Refuse Systems County (P-8379)

Jessica K Jones, *Manager*
EMP: 114 **EST:** 1958
SALES (est): 32.2MM
SALES (corp-wide): 15.2B **Publicly Held**
WEB: www.redwoodlandfill.wm.com
SIC: 4953 Sanitary landfill operation; recycling, waste materials
PA: Waste Management, Inc.
800 Capitol St Ste 3000
Houston TX 77002
713 512-6200

(P-8359)
REDWOOD SERVICES INC
350 Lang Rd, Burlingame (94010-2003)
PHONE..............................650 872-2310
Steve Willett, *President*
Gary Button, *Vice Pres*
EMP: 38 **EST:** 1996
SALES (est): 1.8MM **Privately Held**
WEB: www.rdsredwood.com
SIC: 4953 Recycling, waste materials

(P-8360)
REPUBLIC SVCS VSCO RD LANDFILL
4001 N Vasco Rd, Livermore (94551-9766)
PHONE..............................925 447-0491
Kevin Finn, *President*
Eric Horton, *General Mgr*
H Wayne Huizenga,
▲ **EMP:** 50 **EST:** 1958
SQ FT: 600
SALES (est): 10.3MM
SALES (corp-wide): 10.1B **Publicly Held**
WEB: www.republicservices.com
SIC: 4953 Recycling, waste materials
PA: Republic Services, Inc.
18500 N Allied Way # 100
Phoenix AZ 85054
480 627-2700

(P-8361)
REUSE PEOPLE OF AMERICA INC
Also Called: Reuse People, The
9235 San Leandro St, Oakland (94603-1237)
PHONE..............................510 383-1983
Ted Reiff, *President*
Tim Jackson, *Exec Dir*
EMP: 49 **EST:** 1999
SALES (est): 6.5MM **Privately Held**
WEB: www.thereusepeople.org
SIC: 4953 Recycling, waste materials

(P-8362)
SACRAMENTO AREA SEWER DISTRICT (PA)
10060 Goethe Rd, Sacramento (95827-3553)
PHONE..............................916 876-6000
Joseph Maestretti, *CFO*
Claudia Goss, *COO*
Joe Maestretti, *CFO*
Prabhaker Somavarapu, *Principal*
Elizabeth Allan, *Exec Dir*
EMP: 300 **EST:** 2008
SALES (est): 98.5MM **Privately Held**
WEB: www.sacsewer.com
SIC: 4953 Rubbish collection & disposal

(P-8363)
SOUTH SAN FRNCSCO SCVENGER INC
500 E Jamie Ct, South San Francisco (94080-6222)
P.O. Box 348 (94083-0348)
PHONE..............................650 589-4020
Doug Button, *President*
Paul Formosa, *CFO*
Michael Achiro, *Vice Pres*
Daniel Bertoldi Jr, *Vice Pres*
Ron Fornesi, *Vice Pres*
EMP: 65 **EST:** 1907
SQ FT: 10,000
SALES (est): 17.8MM **Privately Held**
WEB: www.ssfscavenger.com
SIC: 4953 Garbage: collecting, destroying & processing

(P-8364)
SOUTH TAHOE REFUSE CO
Also Called: Sierra Disposal Service
2140 Ruth Ave, South Lake Tahoe (96150-4357)
PHONE..............................530 541-5105
Jeffrey Tillman, *President*
Gloria Lehman, *Treasurer*
John Tillman, *Vice Pres*
John De Marchini, *Admin Sec*
EMP: 100
SQ FT: 5,000
SALES (est): 17.2MM **Privately Held**
WEB: www.southtahoerefuse.com
SIC: 4953 Garbage: collecting, destroying & processing

(P-8365)
SUNSET SCAVENGER COMPANY
Also Called: Recology Sunset Scavenger
250 Executive Park Blvd # 2100, San Francisco (94134-3306)
PHONE..............................415 330-1300
Archie Humphrey, *COO*
Gary Kirk, *Administration*
Joe Goldstein, *Opers Staff*
John Ratto, *Opers Staff*
John Legnitto, *Manager*
EMP: 420 **EST:** 1920
SQ FT: 3,800
SALES (est): 54MM
SALES (corp-wide): 1.4B **Privately Held**
WEB: www.recology.com
SIC: 4953 Recycling, waste materials
PA: Recology Inc.
50 California St Ste 2400
San Francisco CA 94111
415 875-1000

(P-8366)
TAMALPAIS COMMUNITY SVCS DST
305 Bell Ln, Mill Valley (94941-4037)
PHONE..............................415 388-6393
Jon Elam, *General Mgr*
Mike Quecke, *Director*
EMP: 40 **EST:** 1967
SQ FT: 2,047
SALES (est): 1.3MM **Privately Held**
WEB: www.tamcsd.org
SIC: 4953 Recycling, waste materials

(P-8367)
TITUS MINT INSTLLTION SVCS INC
Also Called: Titus Industrial Supply
1430 Willow Pass Rd # 25, Concord (94520-7928)
PHONE..............................909 357-3156
Mike Centers, *President*
Eddy Olmos, *Controller*
EMP: 35 **EST:** 2002
SQ FT: 16,500
SALES (est): 8.1MM **Privately Held**
WEB: www.titusservices.net
SIC: 4953 Recycling, waste materials

(P-8368)
TOMRA SORTING INC (DH)
Also Called: Best USA
875 Embarcadero Dr, West Sacramento (95605-1503)
PHONE..............................720 870-2240
Bert Van Der Auwera, *CEO*
Paul Berghmans, *President*
Valeria Kompen, *Officer*
Eddy De Reyes, *Vice Pres*
Lorraine Dundon, *Vice Pres*
▲ **EMP:** 109 **EST:** 2000
SQ FT: 6,000
SALES (est): 51.1MM
SALES (corp-wide): 1.1B **Privately Held**
WEB: www.tomra.com
SIC: 4953 Recycling, waste materials
HQ: Tomra Sorting Nv
Romeinse Straat 20
Leuven 3001
164 085-80

(P-8369)
TRACY DLTA SOLID WASTE MGT INC
Also Called: Delta Disposal Service Co
30703 S Macarthur Dr, Tracy (95377-9170)
P.O. Box 274 (95378-0274)
PHONE..............................209 835-0601
Michael Repetto, *President*
Carl Repetto, *Vice Pres*
Anna Lovecchio, *General Mgr*
Gina Baker, *Controller*
Susan Hudson, *Controller*
EMP: 61 **EST:** 1951
SQ FT: 1,000
SALES (est): 12MM **Privately Held**
WEB: www.tdswm.com
SIC: 4953 Garbage: collecting, destroying & processing; recycling, waste materials

(P-8370)
TRACY MTL RCVERY SLID WSTE TRN
30703 S Macarthur Dr, Tracy (95377-9170)
P.O. Box 93 (95378-0093)
PHONE..............................209 832-2355
Mike Repetto, *President*
Kurt Repetto, *Admin Sec*
EMP: 43 **EST:** 1993
SALES (est): 3MM **Privately Held**
WEB: www.tracymaterialrecovery.com
SIC: 4953 Recycling, waste materials; liquid waste, collection & disposal

(P-8371)
TRI-CITY ECONOMIC DEV CORP
Also Called: Tri Ced Community Recycling
33377 Western Ave, Union City (94587-2210)
PHONE..............................510 429-8030
Richard Valle, *Principal*
Mangee Austria, *Opers Staff*
Wilson Lee, *Manager*
EMP: 59 **EST:** 1980
SQ FT: 74,055
SALES (est): 11MM **Privately Held**
WEB: www.tri-ced.org
SIC: 4953 Recycling, waste materials

(P-8372)
TRIPLE S METAL INC
567 Exchange Ct, Livermore (94550-2400)
PHONE..............................925 449-3262
Tom Chiang, *CEO*
◆ **EMP:** 50 **EST:** 2012
SALES (est): 10.8MM **Privately Held**
WEB: www.triplesmetal.com
SIC: 4953 Recycling, waste materials

(P-8373)
TURLOCK SCAVENGER COMPANY
1200 S Walnut Rd, Turlock (95380-9221)
P.O. Box 1865 (95381-1865)
PHONE..............................209 668-7274
Allan Marchant, *CEO*
Lee Marchant, *Treasurer*
Greg Marchant, *Vice Pres*
Jerilyn Yerby, *Controller*
Art Machado, *Opers Mgr*
EMP: 40 **EST:** 1935
SQ FT: 3,000
SALES (est): 9.8MM **Privately Held**
WEB: www.turlockscavengercompany.com
SIC: 4953 Garbage: collecting, destroying & processing

(P-8374)
UNIVERSAL SERVICE RECYCL INC (PA)
Also Called: U S R
3200 S El Dorado St, Stockton (95206-3459)
PHONE..............................209 944-9555
Guilherme Mendonca, *Chairman*
William Mendonca, *President*
Dennis Decosta, *CEO*
Anna Olsen, *CFO*
Anthony Bonilla, *General Mgr*
▼ **EMP:** 45 **EST:** 1996
SQ FT: 100,000
SALES (est): 14.3MM **Privately Held**
WEB: www.usrscrap.com
SIC: 4953 Recycling, waste materials

(P-8375)
UNIVERSAL SVC RCYCL MERCED INC (PA)
3200 S El Dorado St, Stockton (95206-3459)
PHONE..............................209 944-9555
William Mendonca, *CEO*
Alexis Williams, *CFO*
Jason Antypas, *Senior Buyer*
Thomas Hightower, *Opers Mgr*
Kent Rieger, *Accounts Mgr*
EMP: 64 **EST:** 2002
SALES (est): 6.7MM **Privately Held**
WEB: www.usrscrap.com
SIC: 4953 Recycling, waste materials

(P-8376)
UPPER VALLEY DISPOSAL SERVICE (PA)
1285 Whitehall Ln, Saint Helena (94574-9682)
P.O. Box 382 (94574-0382)
PHONE..............................707 963-7988
Robert Pestoni, *President*
Linda Sereni, *Admin Sec*
Michael Karl, *Controller*
Mike Karl, *Controller*
EMP: 45 **EST:** 1963
SQ FT: 30,000
SALES (est): 19.7MM **Privately Held**
WEB: www.uvds.com
SIC: 4953 Refuse collection & disposal services; garbage: collecting, destroying & processing; recycling, waste materials

(P-8377)
USA WASTE OF CALIFORNIA INC (HQ)
Also Called: Waste Management
11931 Foundation Pl # 200, Gold River (95670-4540)
PHONE..............................916 387-1400
Barry S Skolnick, *CEO*
Mike Witt, *CEO*
Earl E Defrates, *Treasurer*
Ed Aurand, *Ch Credit Ofcr*
Alex Oseguera, *Vice Pres*
EMP: 35 **EST:** 1978
SQ FT: 3,200
SALES (est): 42.4MM
SALES (corp-wide): 15.2B **Publicly Held**
WEB: www.wm.com
SIC: 4953 Garbage: collecting, destroying & processing
PA: Waste Management, Inc.
800 Capitol St Ste 3000
Houston TX 77002
713 512-6200

(P-8378)
VEHICLE RECYCLING SERVICES LLC
Also Called: Ipull U Pull Auto Parts
2274 E Muscat Ave, Fresno (93725-2420)
PHONE..............................916 870-4383
Kendig Kneen, *Manager*
EMP: 35
SALES (corp-wide): 20MM **Privately Held**
WEB: www.ipullupull.com
SIC: 4953 5015 Recycling, waste materials; automotive parts & supplies, used; engines, used
PA: Vehicle Recycling Services Llc
3151 S Highway 99
Stockton CA 95215
916 870-4383

(P-8379)
VISIONS RECYCLING INC
Also Called: Visions Paint Recycling
4105 S Market Ct Ste A, Sacramento (95834-1215)
PHONE..............................916 564-9121
Jerry Noel, *CEO*
Marie Noel, *Treasurer*
Gina Balsz, *Sales Staff*
Jess Elshere, *Accounts Mgr*
▲ **EMP:** 42 **EST:** 2001
SQ FT: 47,000
SALES (est): 11.7MM **Privately Held**
WEB: www.visionsqualitycoatings.com
SIC: 4953 2851 Recycling, waste materials; paints & paint additives

4953 - Refuse Systems County (P-8380)

(P-8380)
WASTE CONNECTIONS CAL INC (DH)
Also Called: Greenteam of San Jose
1333 Oakland Rd, San Jose (95112-1364)
PHONE..................408 282-4400
Paul Nelson, *Vice Pres*
Ron Mittelstaedt, *CEO*
Michael Harlan, *Bd of Directors*
Pual Nelson, *Vice Pres*
Glen Long, *District Mgr*
EMP: 150 **EST:** 1976
SQ FT: 6,000
SALES (est): 38.6MM
SALES (corp-wide): 5.4B **Privately Held**
WEB: www.greenteam.com
SIC: 4953 Garbage: collecting, destroying & processing

(P-8381)
WASTE MANAGEMENT CAL INC
910 Coyote Creek Golf Dr, Morgan Hill (95037)
P.O. Box 1870 (95038-1870)
PHONE..................408 779-2206
Joe Morse, *Sales/Mktg Mgr*
Christian Sook, *Accounts Mgr*
EMP: 117
SALES (corp-wide): 15.2B **Publicly Held**
SIC: 4953 Recycling, waste materials
HQ: Waste Management Of California, Inc.
9081 Tujunga Ave
Sun Valley CA 91352
877 836-6526

(P-8382)
WASTE MANAGEMENT WISCONSIN INC
1166 Industrial Way, Quincy (95971-9724)
PHONE..................530 283-2065
Mike Clements, *Branch Mgr*
EMP: 47
SALES (corp-wide): 15.2B **Publicly Held**
SIC: 4953 Garbage: collecting, destroying & processing
HQ: Waste Management Of Wisconsin, Inc.
1021 Main St Ste 2123b
Houston TX 77002
262 251-4000

(P-8383)
WASTE MGT ALAMEDA CNTY INC (HQ)
172 98th Ave, Oakland (94603-1004)
PHONE..................510 613-8710
Barry S Skolnick, *CEO*
James C Fish Jr, *Exec VP*
James E Trevathan, *Exec VP*
Regina Beale,
Dino Fontana, *Manager*
EMP: 550 **EST:** 1920
SALES (est): 240.6MM
SALES (corp-wide): 15.2B **Publicly Held**
WEB: www.wm.com
SIC: 4953 Garbage: collecting, destroying & processing
PA: Waste Management, Inc.
800 Capitol St Ste 3000
Houston TX 77002
713 512-6200

(P-8384)
WASTE MGT COLLECTN RECYCL INC
219 Pudding Creek Rd, Fort Bragg (95437-8136)
PHONE..................707 964-9172
Robert Thornsberry, *Manager*
EMP: 88
SALES (corp-wide): 15.2B **Publicly Held**
SIC: 4953 Garbage: collecting, destroying & processing
HQ: Waste Management Collection And Recycling, Inc.
1001 Fannin St Ste 4000
Houston TX 77002

(P-8385)
WASTE MGT COLLECTN RECYCL INC
1324 Paddock Pl, Woodland (95776-5919)
PHONE..................530 662-8748
John Duncan, *Manager*
Larry Picard, *Human Resources*
EMP: 88
SALES (corp-wide): 15.2B **Publicly Held**
SIC: 4953 Garbage: collecting, destroying & processing
HQ: Waste Management Collection And Recycling, Inc.
1001 Fannin St Ste 4000
Houston TX 77002

(P-8386)
WASTE MGT COLLECTN RECYCL INC
1340 W Beach St, Watsonville (95076-5122)
P.O. Box 2347 (95077-2347)
PHONE..................831 768-9505
James Moresco, *Branch Mgr*
Rini Van Every, *Info Tech Dir*
EMP: 88
SALES (corp-wide): 15.2B **Publicly Held**
SIC: 4953 Garbage: collecting, destroying & processing
HQ: Waste Management Collection And Recycling, Inc.
1001 Fannin St Ste 4000
Houston TX 77002

(P-8387)
WASTE MGT COLLECTN RECYCL INC
219 Pudding Creek Rd, Fort Bragg (95437-8136)
PHONE..................707 462-0210
Kaladas Ginger, *Branch Mgr*
EMP: 88
SALES (corp-wide): 15.2B **Publicly Held**
SIC: 4953 Recycling, waste materials
HQ: Waste Management Collection And Recycling, Inc.
1001 Fannin St Ste 4000
Houston TX 77002

(P-8388)
WASTE MGT COLLECTN RECYCL INC
450 Orr Springs Rd, Ukiah (95482-3131)
PHONE..................707 462-0210
Lee Hicks, *Branch Mgr*
EMP: 88
SALES (corp-wide): 15.2B **Publicly Held**
SIC: 4953 Garbage: collecting, destroying & processing
HQ: Waste Management Collection And Recycling, Inc.
1001 Fannin St Ste 4000
Houston TX 77002

(P-8389)
WEST COUNTY RESOURCE RECOVERY
101 Pittsburg Ave, Richmond (94801-1201)
PHONE..................510 231-4200
Richard Granzella, *President*
EMP: 45 **EST:** 1989
SALES (est): 12.8MM
SALES (corp-wide): 10.1B **Publicly Held**
WEB: www.recyclemore.com
SIC: 4953 Recycling, waste materials
HQ: Richmond Sanitary Service, Inc.
3260 Blume Dr Ste 100
Richmond CA 94806
510 262-7100

(P-8390)
WHEELABRATOR LASSEN INC (DH)
20811 Industry Rd, Anderson (96007-8703)
PHONE..................530 365-9173
John Kehoe, *President*
▲ **EMP:** 66 **EST:** 1996
SQ FT: 4,000
SALES (est): 10.1MM **Privately Held**
WEB: www.wtienergy.com
SIC: 4953 Refuse systems
HQ: Wheelabrator Technologies Holdings Inc.
100 Aboretum Dr Ste 310
Portsmouth NH 03801
603 929-3000

(P-8391)
ZANKER RD RSRCE MGT LTD A CAL
Also Called: Zanker Road Landfill
980 State Highway 25, Gilroy (95020-8080)
PHONE..................408 846-1575
Greg Ryan, *Manager*
EMP: 37
SALES (corp-wide): 35.5MM **Privately Held**
WEB: www.zankerrecycling.com
SIC: 4953 Sanitary landfill operation
PA: Zanker Road Resource Management, Ltd., A California Limited Partnership
705 Los Esteros Rd
San Jose CA 95134
408 263-2385

(P-8392)
ZANKER ROAD RESOURCE MGT LTD
4201 Florin Perkins Rd, Sacramento (95826-4829)
PHONE..................916 738-9279
Cliff Busekist, *Branch Mgr*
Rosario Serna, *Office Mgr*
Ying Rong, *Accountant*
Spencer Morgan, *Opers Staff*
EMP: 37
SALES (corp-wide): 35.5MM **Privately Held**
WEB: www.zankerrecycling.com
SIC: 4953 Recycling, waste materials
PA: Zanker Road Resource Management, Ltd., A California Limited Partnership
705 Los Esteros Rd
San Jose CA 95134
408 263-2385

4959 Sanitary Svcs, NEC

(P-8393)
CENTRAL MARIN SANITATION AGCY
1301 Andersen Dr, San Rafael (94901-5339)
PHONE..................415 459-1455
Jason Dow, *General Mgr*
Joyce Cheung, *Engineer*
Michael Silva, *Opers Staff*
Kenneth Spray, *Manager*
EMP: 47 **EST:** 1985
SQ FT: 871,000
SALES: 18.8MM **Privately Held**
WEB: www.cmsa.us
SIC: 4959 Sanitary services

(P-8394)
CONTRA CSTA MSQITO VCTOR CTRL
155 Mason Cir, Concord (94520-1213)
PHONE..................925 685-9301
Craig Downs, *General Mgr*
Paula Macedo, *General Mgr*
Chris Doll, *Technician*
Shaun Redman, *Technician*
Natalie Martini, *Analyst*
EMP: 46 **EST:** 1926
SQ FT: 4,800
SALES (est): 4.1MM **Privately Held**
WEB: www.contracostamosquito.com
SIC: 4959 Mosquito eradication

(P-8395)
CONTRACT SWEEPING SERVICES LLC
760 E Capitol Ave, Milpitas (95035-6812)
PHONE..................408 828-5280
Jason Browne, *Branch Mgr*
EMP: 46
SALES (corp-wide): 10.2MM **Privately Held**
WEB: www.contractsweeping.com
SIC: 4959 Sweeping service: road, airport, parking lot, etc.
PA: Contract Sweeping Services, Llc
760 E Capitol Ave
Milpitas CA 95035
888 837-9337

(P-8396)
CONTRACT SWEEPING SERVICES LLC
1113 Shaw Rd, Stockton (95215-4044)
PHONE..................408 828-5280
Dan Baca, *Manager*
EMP: 46
SALES (corp-wide): 10.2MM **Privately Held**
WEB: www.contractsweeping.com
SIC: 4959 Sweeping service: road, airport, parking lot, etc.
PA: Contract Sweeping Services, Llc
760 E Capitol Ave
Milpitas CA 95035
888 837-9337

(P-8397)
COUNTY OF STANISLAUS
Also Called: East Side Msqito Abatement Dst
2000 Santa Fe Ave, Modesto (95357-0650)
PHONE..................209 522-4098
J Wakoli Wekesa, *Branch Mgr*
EMP: 49
SALES (corp-wide): 1.2B **Privately Held**
WEB: www.stancounty.com
SIC: 4959 Mosquito eradication
PA: County Of Stanislaus
1010 10th St Ste 5100
Modesto CA 95354
209 525-6398

(P-8398)
ENGINRNG/RMDTION RSRCES GROUP (PA)
Also Called: Errg
4585 Pacheco Blvd Ste 200, Martinez (94553-2228)
PHONE..................925 839-2200
Cynthia Liu, *CEO*
Cynthia A Liu, *CEO*
Todd Katz, *CFO*
Caitlin Gorman, *Regional Mgr*
Melanie Enman, *Division Mgr*
EMP: 70 **EST:** 1997
SQ FT: 31,000
SALES: 58.9MM **Privately Held**
WEB: www.errg.com
SIC: 4959 8744 Environmental cleanup services;

(P-8399)
FLAGSHIP SWEEPING SERVICES INC (HQ)
1050 N 5th St, San Jose (95112-4400)
PHONE..................408 977-0155
David Pasek, *CEO*
EMP: 35 **EST:** 1994
SQ FT: 4,200
SALES (est): 7.4MM **Privately Held**
WEB: www.flagshipinc.com
SIC: 4959 7349 Sweeping service: road, airport, parking lot, etc.; janitorial service, contract basis

(P-8400)
NRC ENVIRONMENTAL SERVICES INC (DH)
1605 Ferry Pt, Alameda (94501-5021)
PHONE..................510 749-1390
Steven Candito, *President*
Neil Challis, *Senior VP*
Mike Reese, *Senior VP*
Todd Roloff, *Senior VP*
Sal Sacco, *Senior VP*
▲ **EMP:** 80 **EST:** 1988
SQ FT: 18,000
SALES (est): 193.3MM
SALES (corp-wide): 933.8MM **Publicly Held**
WEB: www.nrcc.com
SIC: 4959 Toxic or hazardous waste cleanup; oil spill cleanup; environmental cleanup services

(P-8401)
NRC ENVIRONMENTAL SERVICES INC
2450 Rice Ave, West Sacramento (95691-2319)
PHONE..................916 371-7202
Frank Garrett, *Branch Mgr*
EMP: 35

PRODUCTS & SERVICES SECTION
5012 - Automobiles & Other Motor Vehicles Wholesale County (P-8422)

SALES (corp-wide): 933.8MM **Publicly Held**
WEB: www.nrcc.com
SIC: **4959** Environmental cleanup services
HQ: Nrc Environmental Services, Inc.
1605 Ferry Pt
Alameda CA 94501

(P-8402)
ORO LOMA SANITARY DISTRICT
2655 Grant Ave, San Lorenzo (94580-1839)
PHONE..................................510 276-4700
Jason Warner, *Treasurer*
Bob Glaze, *Admin Sec*
Shelia Young, *Admin Sec*
Lacey Aldridge, *Admin Asst*
Anna Wilewski Turon, *Finance*
EMP: 49
SQ FT: 7,300
SALES: 25.9MM **Privately Held**
WEB: www.oroloma.org
SIC: **4959** Sanitary services

(P-8403)
SACRAMENTO REG CO SANIT DIST (PA)
Also Called: Srcsd
10060 Goethe Rd, Sacramento (95827-3553)
PHONE..................................916 876-6000
Prabhakar Somavarapu, *Director*
Peter Castles, *Bd of Directors*
Phil Serna, *Principal*
Glen Iwamura, *Info Tech Mgr*
Shabab Shams, *Project Mgr*
EMP: 200 EST: 1973
SQ FT: 136,000
SALES (est): 101.6MM **Privately Held**
WEB: www.regionalsan.com
SIC: **4959** Sanitary services

(P-8404)
SACRAMENTO YOLO CNTY MOSQUITO
8631 Bond Rd, Elk Grove (95624-1477)
PHONE..................................916 685-1022
Raul Deanda, *President*
Vern Bruhn, *Vice Pres*
Raj Badhan, *Technology*
Gary Goodman, *Manager*
Marty Scholl, *Manager*
EMP: 51 EST: 1946
SALES (est): 8.5MM **Privately Held**
WEB: www.fightthebite.net
SIC: **4959** Mosquito eradication

(P-8405)
SAN MTEO CNTY MSQITO VCTOR CTR
Also Called: Smcmad
1351 Rollins Rd, Burlingame (94010-2409)
PHONE..................................650 344-8592
Dennis Prager, *Superintendent*
EMP: 44 EST: 1916
SALES (est): 5.4MM **Privately Held**
WEB: www.smcmvcd.org
SIC: **4959** Mosquito eradication

(P-8406)
SANITARY DST 1 MARIN CNTY
Also Called: Ross Valley Sanitary District
2960 Kerner Blvd, San Rafael (94901-5517)
PHONE..................................415 259-2949
Greg Norby, *Principal*
Celia Peterson, *Principal*
EMP: 42 EST: 1899
SQ FT: 7,400
SALES: 22.7MM **Privately Held**
SIC: **4959** Sanitary services

(P-8407)
SANTA CLARA COUNTY OF
101 Skyport Dr, San Jose (95110-1302)
PHONE..................................408 573-2400
Michael Murdter, *Director*
Ron McCurry, *Technician*
Roy Cabaltera, *Project Engr*
Herbert Naraval, *Engineer*
Thien Pham, *Engineer*
EMP: 41
SQ FT: 25,600 **Privately Held**
WEB: www.sccgov.org

SIC: **4959** 9621 Road, airport & parking lot maintenance services; regulation, administration of transportation
PA: County Of Santa Clara
70 W Hedding St 2wing
San Jose CA 95110
408 299-5200

(P-8408)
STATEWIDE CNSTR SWEEPING LLC
45945 Warm Springs Blvd, Fremont (94539-6746)
PHONE..................................510 683-9584
Manny Saxena, *CEO*
Dennis Pierce, *Manager*
EMP: 50 EST: 2007
SQ FT: 8,000
SALES (est): 9.1MM **Privately Held**
WEB: www.statewidesweeping.com
SIC: **4959** Sweeping service: road, airport, parking lot, etc.

(P-8409)
SUPERIOR EQUIPMENT COMPANY INC
2301 Napa Vallejo Hwy, NAPA (94558-6242)
P.O. Box 10369 (94581-2369)
PHONE..................................707 256-3600
Jack Pagendarm, *President*
Kathleen Pagendarm, *Corp Secy*
Nicolas Pagendarm, *Vice Pres*
EMP: 28 EST: 1995
SQ FT: 4,300 **Privately Held**
WEB: www.superiorequipco.com
SIC: **4959** 5084 5093 7692 Sanitary services; compaction equipment; metal scrap & waste materials; welding repair

4971 Irrigation Systems

(P-8410)
FRESNO IRRIGATION DISTRICT
2907 S Maple Ave, Fresno (93725-2218)
PHONE..................................559 233-7161
Gary R Serrato, *General Mgr*
Deann Hailey, *CFO*
Hugo Egle, *Opers Staff*
Laurence Kimura, *Manager*
Mike Prestridge, *Superintendent*
EMP: 83 EST: 1920
SQ FT: 18,000
SALES: 27.6MM **Privately Held**
WEB: www.fresnoirrigation.com
SIC: **4971** Water distribution or supply systems for irrigation

(P-8411)
FRESNO VALVES & CASTINGS INC (PA)
7736 E Springfield Ave, Selma (93662-9408)
P.O. Box 40 (93662-0040)
PHONE..................................559 834-2511
Jeffery Showalter, *CEO*
Kevin Follansbee, *CFO*
Rich Bonzo, *Engineer*
Joni Roam, *Controller*
Denise Cano, *Human Res Mgr*
◆ EMP: 165 EST: 1952
SALES (est): 104.5MM **Privately Held**
WEB: www.fresnovalves.com
SIC: **4971** 3491 3498 3441 Water distribution or supply systems for irrigation; industrial valves; fabricated pipe & fittings; fabricated structural metal; nonferrous foundries; commercial indusl & institutional electric lighting fixtures

(P-8412)
GLENN-COLUSA IRRIGATION DST (PA)
344 E Laurel St, Willows (95988-3114)
P.O. Box 150 (95988-0150)
PHONE..................................530 934-8881
Donald Bransford, *President*
Dennis Michum, *Treasurer*
EMP: 72 EST: 1920
SQ FT: 5,000
SALES: 14MM **Privately Held**
WEB: www.gcid.net
SIC: **4971** Water distribution or supply systems for irrigation

(P-8413)
MARIN MUNICIPAL WATER DISTRICT (PA)
220 Nellen Ave, Corte Madera (94925-1169)
P.O. Box 994 (94976-0994)
PHONE..................................415 945-1455
Krishna Kumar, *President*
Jack Gibson, *Vice Chairman*
Terry Stigall, *CFO*
Frank Fung, *Officer*
Mike Strom, *Vice Pres*
EMP: 220 EST: 1912
SQ FT: 32,000
SALES: 97.2MM **Privately Held**
WEB: www.marinwater.org
SIC: **4971** 4941 Irrigation systems; water supply

(P-8414)
MERCED IRRIGATION DISTRICT
3321 Franklin Rd, Merced (95348-9345)
PHONE..................................209 722-2719
Jarith Krause, *Manager*
Joseph Chance, *Network Enginr*
Marco Orozco, *Engineer*
EMP: 62
SALES (corp-wide): 101.7MM **Privately Held**
WEB: www.mercedid.com
SIC: **4971** Water distribution or supply systems for irrigation
PA: Merced Irrigation District
744 W 20th St
Merced CA 95340
209 722-5761

(P-8415)
NEVADA IRRIGATION DISTRICT (PA)
Also Called: N I D
1036 W Main St, Grass Valley (95945-5424)
PHONE..................................530 273-6185
Remleh Scherzinger, *General Mgr*
John H Drew, *President*
Keane Sommers, *CEO*
Marie Owens, *Treasurer*
Monica Reyes, *Vice Pres*
▲ EMP: 160 EST: 1921
SQ FT: 11,050
SALES (est): 55.3MM **Privately Held**
WEB: www.nidwater.com
SIC: **4971** 4911 Water distribution or supply systems for irrigation; generation, electric power

(P-8416)
SAN LUIS DLTA-MENDOTA WTR AUTH
15990 Kelso Rd, Byron (94514-1916)
PHONE..................................209 835-2593
Frances Mizuno, *Principal*
Joyce Machado, *Treasurer*
Charles Reyes, *Technician*
Andrew Garcia, *Engineer*
Jaime McNeil, *Engineer*
EMP: 42
SALES (corp-wide): 2.1MM **Privately Held**
WEB: www.sldmwa.org
SIC: **4971** 8611 Water distribution or supply systems for irrigation; public utility association
PA: San Luis & Delta-Mendota Water Authority
842 6th St
Los Banos CA 93635
209 826-9696

(P-8417)
SAN LUIS DLTA-MENDOTA WTR AUTH (PA)
Also Called: San Joaquinn Vly Draing Auth
842 6th St, Los Banos (93635-4214)
P.O. Box 2157 (93635-2157)
PHONE..................................209 826-9696
Daniel G Nelson, *Exec Dir*
Jacob Oxenrider, *Comms Dir*
Stephanie Harris, *Hum Res Coord*
Nicho Ontiveros, *Purchasing*
Paul Stearns, *Opers Staff*
EMP: 45 EST: 1992

SALES: 2.1MM **Privately Held**
WEB: www.sldmwa.org
SIC: **4971** 8611 Water distribution or supply systems for irrigation; public utility association

(P-8418)
SOLANO IRRIGATION DISTRICT
810 Vaca Valley Pkwy # 201, Vacaville (95688-8834)
PHONE..................................707 448-6847
Robert Hansen, *President*
Victor Fortenberry, *Officer*
Guido E Colla, *Vice Pres*
Jeff Sullivan, *Technician*
Paul Fuchslin, *Engineer*
EMP: 99 EST: 1948
SQ FT: 8,500
SALES (est): 12.9MM **Privately Held**
WEB: www.sidwater.org
SIC: **4971** Irrigation systems

(P-8419)
STREAMLINE IRRIGATION INC
3630 Avenue 384, Kingsburg (93631-9672)
PHONE..................................559 897-1516
Phillip Benjamin Bartel, *CEO*
Steven Moreno, *Manager*
EMP: 40 EST: 2011
SALES (est): 7.4MM **Privately Held**
WEB: www.streamlineirrigation.net
SIC: **4971** Water distribution or supply systems for irrigation

5012 Automobiles & Other Motor Vehicles Wholesale

(P-8420)
ABC BUS INC
3508 Haven Ave, Redwood City (94063-4603)
PHONE..................................650 368-3364
Mike Lawrence, *Manager*
EMP: 85
SALES (corp-wide): 182.4MM **Privately Held**
WEB: www.abc-companies.com
SIC: **5012** 4173 Buses; bus terminal & service facilities
HQ: Abc Bus, Inc.
1506 30th St Nw
Faribault MN 55021
507 334-1871

(P-8421)
FRESNO AUTO DEALERS AUCTION
278 N Marks Ave, Fresno (93706-1136)
PHONE..................................559 268-8051
Darryl Ceccolli, *President*
▼ EMP: 1381 EST: 1975
SQ FT: 15,000
SALES (est): 8.7MM
SALES (corp-wide): 1.6MM **Privately Held**
WEB: www.manheim.com
SIC: **5012** Automobile auction
HQ: Manheim Investments, Inc.
6205 Pachtree Dunwoody Rd
Atlanta GA 30328
866 626-4346

(P-8422)
FRESNO TRUCK CENTER
2727 E Central Ave, Fresno (93725-2425)
P.O. Box 12346 (93777-2346)
PHONE..................................559 486-4310
Randy Moore, *Manager*
Michael Belles, *Principal*
EMP: 80
SQ FT: 40,000
SALES (corp-wide): 100.3MM **Privately Held**
WEB: www.affinitytruck.com
SIC: **5012** 5511 7538 5531 Truck tractors; trucks, tractors & trailers: new & used; general truck repair; truck equipment & parts; truck tires & tubes
PA: Fresno Truck Center
2727 E Central Ave
Fresno CA 93725
559 486-4310

5012 - Automobiles & Other Motor Vehicles Wholesale County (P-8423)

(P-8423)
FRESNO TRUCK CENTER
Also Called: Delta Truck Center
10182 S Harlan Rd, French Camp (95231-9647)
P.O. Box 20 (95231-0020)
PHONE..................................209 983-2400
John Gannon, *Manager*
Glenn Richardson, *Sales Mgr*
Jim Jones, *Sales Associate*
Brandon Botelho, *Sales Staff*
David Jones, *Manager*
EMP: 125
SALES (corp-wide): 100.3MM **Privately Held**
WEB: www.affinitytruck.com
SIC: **5012** 5013 7538 5531 Trucks, commercial; automotive supplies & parts; general automotive repair shops; truck equipment & parts; pickups, new & used; engines & parts, diesel
PA: Fresno Truck Center
2727 E Central Ave
Fresno CA 93725
559 486-4310

(P-8424)
FRONTIER FORD (PA)
Also Called: Frontier Rent-A-Car
3701 Stevens Creek Blvd, Santa Clara (95051-7396)
PHONE..................................408 241-1800
James F Landes, *CEO*
Andrew L Breech, *Treasurer*
E Robert Breech Jr, *Vice Pres*
Hal Arnon, *General Mgr*
Harold D Arnon, *Admin Sec*
▲ EMP: 140 EST: 1960
SQ FT: 10,000
SALES (est): 52.3MM **Privately Held**
WEB: www.frontierford.com
SIC: **5511** 5521 5012 Automobiles, new & used; used car dealers; automobiles & other motor vehicles

(P-8425)
HENDRICK AUTOMOTIVE GROUP
Also Called: Acura Pleasanton
4355 Rosewood Dr, Pleasanton (94588-3003)
P.O. Box 9050 (94566-9050)
PHONE..................................925 463-4700
Bob Slapp, *General Mgr*
Robert Slap, *General Mgr*
Steve Heise, *Controller*
Stephen Lao, *Sales Staff*
Alfred Revelli, *Sales Staff*
EMP: 82
SQ FT: 16,967
SALES (corp-wide): 2B **Privately Held**
WEB: www.hendrickcars.com
SIC: **5511** 5012 Automobiles, new & used; automobiles & other motor vehicles
PA: Hendrick Automotive Group
6000 Monroe Rd Ste 100
Charlotte NC 28212
704 568-5550

(P-8426)
INTERSTATE TRUCK CENTER LLC (PA)
Also Called: Valley Peterbilt
2110 S Sinclair Ave, Stockton (95215-7556)
PHONE..................................209 944-5821
David T Morganson, *Mng Member*
Radawna Hanson, *Asst Controller*
Bill Dugo, *Sales Staff*
Ryan Sabean, *Sales Staff*
Rick Coslett,
EMP: 100 EST: 1974
SQ FT: 22,000
SALES (est): 47.3MM **Privately Held**
WEB: www.itctrucks.com
SIC: **5012** 7513 Trucks, commercial; truck rental, without drivers

(P-8427)
REDDING FREIGHTLINER INC
Also Called: Eureka Freightliner Parts
4991 Caterpillar Rd, Redding (96003-1404)
P.O. Box 992070 (96099-2070)
PHONE..................................530 241-4412
Alan Shufelberger, *President*
Shawn Gamble, *Vice Pres*
Jon Morgan, *Manager*
EMP: 41 EST: 1995
SQ FT: 60,000
SALES (est): 16.1MM **Privately Held**
WEB: www.freightliner.com
SIC: **5012** 7538 Trucks, commercial; general truck repair

(P-8428)
SR SHROEDER INC
1150 N 1st St, Dixon (95620-3164)
P.O. Box 65 (95620-0065)
PHONE..................................707 693-8166
Diane Schroeder, *President*
Michelle Schroeder, *Treasurer*
EMP: 18 EST: 1971
SALES (est): 3.2MM **Privately Held**
SIC: **5571** 5012 3949 Motorcycle dealers; automobiles & other motor vehicles; water skiing equipment & supplies, except skis

(P-8429)
SSMB PACIFIC HOLDING CO INC (HQ)
Also Called: Bay Area Kenworth
1755 Adams Ave, San Leandro (94577-1001)
PHONE..................................510 836-6100
Harry Mamizuka, *President*
Tom Bertolino, *Vice Pres*
▼ EMP: 55 EST: 1942
SQ FT: 35,000
SALES (est): 47.6MM
SALES (corp-wide): 17.3B **Publicly Held**
WEB: www.norcalkw.com
SIC: **5012** 7699 Trucks, commercial; industrial truck repair
PA: Paccar Inc
777 106th Ave Ne
Bellevue WA 98004
425 468-7400

(P-8430)
SSMB PACIFIC HOLDING CO INC
20769 Industry Rd, Anderson (96007-8703)
PHONE..................................530 222-1212
Glenn Reed, *Branch Mgr*
EMP: 36
SALES (corp-wide): 17.3B **Publicly Held**
WEB: www.norcalkw.com
SIC: **5012** Trucks, commercial
HQ: Ssmb Pacific Holding Co Inc
1755 Adams Ave
San Leandro CA 94577
510 836-6100

(P-8431)
SSMB PACIFIC HOLDING CO INC
16715 Condit Rd, Morgan Hill (95037-9552)
PHONE..................................408 500-3400
Mandeep Johal, *Branch Mgr*
EMP: 36
SALES (corp-wide): 17.3B **Publicly Held**
WEB: www.norcalkw.com
SIC: **5012** 7699 Trucks, commercial; industrial truck repair
HQ: Ssmb Pacific Holding Co Inc
1755 Adams Ave
San Leandro CA 94577
510 836-6100

(P-8432)
TRUECAR INC
2 Embarcadero Ctr Fl 8, San Francisco (94111-3833)
PHONE..................................415 821-8270
Greg Stacknick, *Senior VP*
Joe Broccoli, *Vice Pres*
Paul Edmonds, *Vice Pres*
Andrew Gordon, *Vice Pres*
Nick Sarnoff, *Vice Pres*
EMP: 36 **Publicly Held**
WEB: www.truecar.com
SIC: **5012** 7299 Automotive brokers; information services, consumer
PA: Truecar, Inc.
120 Broadway Ste 200
Santa Monica CA 90401

(P-8433)
TSC MOTORS INC
Also Called: Morgan Hl Chrysler Ddge Jeep R
17085 Condit Rd, Morgan Hill (95037-3301)
PHONE..................................408 580-0410
Salvatore Cardinale, *President*
Christian Pullara, *Vice Pres*
EMP: 35 EST: 2020
SALES (est): 2.9MM **Privately Held**
WEB: www.chrysler.com
SIC: **5012** Automobiles

(P-8434)
WIND RIVER ENTERPRISES INC
Also Called: North Bay Auto Auction
250 Dittmer Rd, Fairfield (94534-1621)
PHONE..................................707 864-1040
Don Morrow, *President*
Maureen Green, *Corp Secy*
David Aahl, *Vice Pres*
Audra Kelly, *Marketing Staff*
EMP: 95
SQ FT: 20,000
SALES: 14.3MM **Privately Held**
WEB: www.nbauto.com
SIC: **5012** Automobile auction

5013 Motor Vehicle Splys & New Parts Wholesale

(P-8435)
1-800 RADIATOR & A/C (DH)
Also Called: 1-800-Radiator
4401 Park Rd, Benicia (94510-1124)
PHONE..................................707 747-7400
Mike Rippey, *Ch of Bd*
Joe Rippey, *President*
Ted Rippey, *Exec VP*
Al Francis, *Vice Pres*
Kurtis Keala, *Vice Pres*
◆ EMP: 100 EST: 1985
SALES (est): 79.9MM
SALES (corp-wide): 904.2MM **Publicly Held**
WEB: www.radiator.com
SIC: **5013** Radiators

(P-8436)
AIRPORT AUTO PARTS INC
Also Called: NAPA Auto Parts
520 San Mateo Ave, San Bruno (94066-4325)
PHONE..................................650 952-1135
Raj Singh, *President*
EMP: 17 EST: 1976
SQ FT: 4,500
SALES (est): 1.3MM **Privately Held**
WEB: www.napaonline.com
SIC: **5531** 5013 3714 Automotive parts; automotive supplies & parts; motor vehicle parts & accessories

(P-8437)
ALL KLIN CORPORATION (PA)
Also Called: Intex Auto Parts
1432 Old Bayshore Hwy, San Jose (95112-2813)
PHONE..................................408 327-1000
Fred Feng-Sung Ho, *CEO*
Wendy Ho, *Vice Pres*
▲ EMP: 35 EST: 1979
SQ FT: 27,000
SALES (est): 10.5MM **Privately Held**
WEB: www.autopartsbayarea.com
SIC: **5013** Automotive supplies & parts; automobile & truck equipment & parts

(P-8438)
ALLIED EXHAUST SYSTEMS INC (PA)
Also Called: Team Allied Distribution
3928 Oregon St, Benicia (94510-1102)
P.O. Box 2004 (94510-0818)
PHONE..................................707 745-0506
Darrel Kurth, *CEO*
Patrick Kelly, *CFO*
Lawrence Contreras, *Vice Pres*
Jeff Jorgensen, *Admin Sec*
Harold William Maneth, *Accountant*
▲ EMP: 35 EST: 1986
SQ FT: 34,000
SALES (est): 54.9MM **Privately Held**
WEB: www.team-allied.com
SIC: **5013** Exhaust systems (mufflers, tail pipes, etc.); automotive supplies & parts

(P-8439)
ASSOCIATED R V ENT INC
Also Called: All-Rite
1500 Shelton Dr Frnt, Hollister (95023-2573)
PHONE..................................831 636-9566
Michael Zevar, *President*
Nancy Lopez, *Vice Pres*
Jeannie Cezar, *General Mgr*
EMP: 45 EST: 1975
SQ FT: 20,000
SALES (est): 9MM **Privately Held**
SIC: **5013** 3442 Automotive supplies & parts; metal doors

(P-8440)
AUTOHAUS AUTOMOTIVE INC (PA)
21650 Mission Blvd, Hayward (94541-2693)
PHONE..................................510 881-1915
Rebecca Moncada, *President*
Manuel F Moncada, *Corp Secy*
EMP: 38 EST: 1957
SQ FT: 10,000
SALES (est): 5.6MM **Privately Held**
WEB: www.autohausautomotive.net
SIC: **5013** 5531 Automotive supplies & parts; automotive accessories

(P-8441)
AUTOMOBILE ACCESSORIES COMPANY
Also Called: Enterprise Auto Parts
2304 Churn Creek Rd, Redding (96002-0736)
PHONE..................................530 223-1561
Jerry D Ross, *President*
EMP: 45
SALES (corp-wide): 10.3MM **Privately Held**
WEB: www.napaonline.com
SIC: **5531** 5013 Automobile & truck equipment & parts; automotive supplies & parts
PA: Automobile Accessories Company
1264 California St
Redding CA 96001
530 243-1142

(P-8442)
BERT WILLIAMS AND SONS INC
525 Northbay Dr, NAPA (94559-1425)
PHONE..................................707 255-7003
Herbert L Williams, *President*
Keith Abernethy, *Sales Staff*
EMP: 36 EST: 1946
SQ FT: 8,400
SALES (est): 5.9MM **Privately Held**
WEB: www.bertwilliamsandsons.com
SIC: **5531** 5013 3714 Automotive parts; truck parts & accessories; motor vehicle parts & accessories

(P-8443)
BI WAREHOUSING INC (PA)
Also Called: Anheuser-Busch
5404 Pacific St, Rocklin (95677-2714)
PHONE..................................916 624-0654
Bart W Riebes, *CEO*
Mel Todd, *Vice Pres*
EMP: 83 EST: 1992
SQ FT: 30,000
SALES (est): 44.1MM **Privately Held**
WEB: www.napaonline.com
SIC: **5531** 5013 7539 Automotive parts; automotive supplies & parts; machine shop, automotive

(P-8444)
BI WAREHOUSING INC
Also Called: Riebe's Auto Parts
3865 Taylor Rd Ste A, Loomis (95650-9276)
PHONE..................................916 652-4433
David Mc Claren, *Manager*
EMP: 94

▲ = Import ▼=Export
◆ =Import/Export

PRODUCTS & SERVICES SECTION

5013 - Motor Vehicle Splys & New Parts Wholesale County (P-8466)

SALES (corp-wide): 44.1MM **Privately Held**
WEB: www.napaonline.com
SIC: **5531** 5013 7539 Automotive parts; automotive supplies & parts; machine shop, automotive
PA: Bi Warehousing, Inc.
5404 Pacific St
Rocklin CA 95677
916 624-0654

(P-8445)
BI WAREHOUSING INC
Also Called: Riebe's Auto Parts
5404 Pacific St Ste B, Rocklin (95677-2714)
PHONE..................916 624-0654
Mel Todd, *General Mgr*
EMP: 94
SALES (corp-wide): 44.1MM **Privately Held**
WEB: www.napaonline.com
SIC: **5531** 5013 Automotive parts; automotive supplies & parts
PA: Bi Warehousing, Inc.
5404 Pacific St
Rocklin CA 95677
916 624-0654

(P-8446)
BI WAREHOUSING INC
Also Called: Riebes Auto Parts
1490 Bridge St, Yuba City (95993-3506)
PHONE..................530 671-8787
Doug Duncan, *Branch Mgr*
EMP: 50
SALES (corp-wide): 44.1MM **Privately Held**
WEB: www.napaonline.com
SIC: **5013** 5531 Automotive supplies & parts; automotive parts
PA: Bi Warehousing, Inc.
5404 Pacific St
Rocklin CA 95677
916 624-0654

(P-8447)
CAPITOL CLUTCH & BRAKE INC
3100 Duluth St, West Sacramento (95691-2208)
PHONE..................916 371-5970
Charles Vincent Mathews, *CEO*
EMP: 37
SQ FT: 50,000
SALES (est): 9MM **Privately Held**
WEB: www.capitolclutch.com
SIC: **5531** 5013 Truck equipment & parts; automotive brakes

(P-8448)
CUSTOM CHROME MANUFACTURING
15750 Vineyard Blvd # 100, Morgan Hill (95037-7119)
PHONE..................408 825-5000
Dan Cook, *Principal*
Bill Prescott, *VP Admin*
Jolene Ramirez, *Finance Mgr*
Sharon Dela Cruz, *Marketing Staff*
◆ EMP: 299 EST: 1990
SALES (est): 18MM **Privately Held**
WEB: www.customchrome.com
SIC: **5013** Motorcycle parts
HQ: Dae-Il Usa, Inc.
112 Robert Young Blvd
Murray KY 42071

(P-8449)
DANA MOTORS INC (PA)
Also Called: Motor Warehouse
901 Arden Way, Sacramento (95815-3289)
P.O. Box 15152 (95851-0152)
PHONE..................916 920-0150
David A Kenmonth, *President*
Steven Bowler, *Sales Mgr*
EMP: 19 EST: 1959
SQ FT: 31,000
SALES (est): 4.8MM **Privately Held**
WEB: www.npwcompanies.com
SIC: **5013** 3714 Automotive supplies & parts; motor vehicle parts & accessories

(P-8450)
FAST PRO INC
Also Called: Fast Undercar
2555 Lafayette St Ste 103, Santa Clara (95050-2644)
PHONE..................408 566-0200
Brian Smits, *President*
Miles Muelder, *Inv Control Mgr*
EMP: 60 EST: 1996
SQ FT: 13,000
SALES (est): 8.8MM **Privately Held**
WEB: www.fastundercar.com
SIC: **5013** Automotive supplies; automotive supplies & parts

(P-8451)
FLEETPRIDE INC
1164 Old Bayshore Hwy, San Jose (95112-2807)
PHONE..................408 286-9200
EMP: 28 **Privately Held**
WEB: www.fleetpride.com
SIC: **5013** 3714 Automotive brakes; clutches; motor vehicle parts & accessories
HQ: Fleetpride, Inc.
600 Las Colinas Blvd E # 400
Irving TX 75039
469 249-7500

(P-8452)
GENERAL AUTO REPAIR INC
Also Called: NAPA Auto Parts
4425 International Blvd, Oakland (94601-4510)
PHONE..................510 533-3333
Timothy Gerrity, *Principal*
Rhea Gerrity, *Vice Pres*
EMP: 35 EST: 1957
SQ FT: 45,000
SALES (est): 2.1MM **Privately Held**
WEB: www.generalauto.com
SIC: **5531** 5013 Automotive parts; automotive supplies & parts

(P-8453)
HANSEL - PRESTIGE INC
Also Called: Hansel BMW of Santa Rosa
2925 Corby Ave, Santa Rosa (95407-7846)
PHONE..................707 578-4717
Cooper Marinak, *Technician*
Pedro Perez, *Technician*
Rob Young, *Technician*
David Berbiglia, *Finance Mgr*
Shawn Hartnett, *Opers Staff*
EMP: 42 **Privately Held**
WEB: www.bmwgroup.com
SIC: **5511** 5013 7539 Automobiles, new & used; motor vehicle supplies & new parts; automotive repair shops
HQ: Hansel - Prestige, Inc.
3075 Corby Ave
Santa Rosa CA
707 545-6602

(P-8454)
KROEGER EQP SUP CO A CAL CORP
2645 S Chestnut Ave, Fresno (93725-2113)
P.O. Box 2427 (93745-2427)
PHONE..................559 485-9900
Bruce Greer, *CEO*
EMP: 27 EST: 1970
SQ FT: 53,000
SALES (est): 10.8MM **Privately Held**
WEB: www.emtharp.com
SIC: **5013** 5531 3714 Truck parts & accessories; automotive parts; truck equipment & parts; motor vehicle parts & accessories; motor vehicle brake systems & parts
PA: Tharp Truck Rental, Inc.
15243 Road 192
Porterville CA 93257
559 782-5800

(P-8455)
LEVAN IMPORT-EXPORT INC
Also Called: Levan Auto Body Parts
6935 Stockton Blvd, Sacramento (95823-2425)
PHONE..................916 381-5712
Harry Levan, *President*
▲ EMP: 35 EST: 1988
SQ FT: 25,000
SALES (est): 5.3MM **Privately Held**
SIC: **5013** Automotive supplies & parts

(P-8456)
MOTION PRO INC
3171 Swetzer Rd, Loomis (95650-9579)
PHONE..................650 594-9600
Christopher Carter, *President*
Kevin Veltfort, *Admin Sec*
◆ EMP: 38
SQ FT: 64,000
SALES (est): 11MM **Privately Held**
WEB: www.motionpro.com
SIC: **5013** Motorcycle parts

(P-8457)
MYGRANT GLASS COMPANY INC (PA)
3271 Arden Rd, Hayward (94545-3901)
PHONE..................510 785-4360
Michael Mygrant, *CEO*
Kathy Mygrant, *Corp Secy*
Vince Burger, *Regional Mgr*
Steve Johnson, *Regional Mgr*
Scott Hughan, *Branch Mgr*
◆ EMP: 50
SQ FT: 128,222
SALES (est): 153.6MM **Privately Held**
WEB: www.mygrantglassonline.com
SIC: **5013** Automobile glass

(P-8458)
NAPA NISSAN INC
510 Soscol Ave, NAPA (94559-3406)
PHONE..................707 253-1551
Vince Compagno, *President*
Vincent Compagno, *President*
Gregory Compagno, *Vice Pres*
Michael Williams, *Purchasing*
Pat Madrazo, *Sales Mgr*
EMP: 44 EST: 1975
SQ FT: 14,000
SALES (est): 12.6MM **Privately Held**
WEB: www.napanissan.com
SIC: **5511** 5013 Automobiles, new & used; automotive engines & engine parts

(P-8459)
NATIONAL AUTO PRTS WHSE - CA I (HQ)
Also Called: Speed Warehouse
901 Arden Way, Sacramento (95815-3201)
PHONE..................510 786-3555
Laurence M Pacey, *CEO*
Sandra Daniels, *Principal*
Mike Montgomery, *General Mgr*
Al Liggins, *Buyer*
Robert Bigham, *Warehouse Mgr*
EMP: 40 EST: 2011
SALES (est): 12.2MM
SALES (corp-wide): 142.5MM **Privately Held**
WEB: www.npwcompanies.com
SIC: **5013** Automotive supplies & parts
PA: National Auto Parts Warehouse, Llc
11150 Nw 32nd Ave
Miami FL 33167
305 953-7270

(P-8460)
PIERCEY NORTH INC
Also Called: Piercey Toyota
950 Thompson St, Milpitas (95035-6296)
PHONE..................408 240-1400
William R Piercey, *CEO*
Artus V Whicker, *President*
Tom A Chadwell, *Corp Secy*
Ricardo Aguilar, *Finance Mgr*
Kathi Martarano, *Controller*
EMP: 110 EST: 1969
SQ FT: 20,800
SALES (est): 29.9MM
SALES (corp-wide): 114.1MM **Privately Held**
WEB: www.pierceytoyota.com
SIC: **5511** 5531 5521 5013 Automobiles, new & used; automotive & home supply stores; used car dealers; motor vehicle supplies & new parts
PA: Piercey Management Services, Inc.
16901 Millikan Ave
Irvine CA 92606
949 379-3701

(P-8461)
R V KARLS INC
Also Called: Wholesale Trailer Supply
1470 Vinci Ave, Sacramento (95838-1716)
PHONE..................916 992-9703
Karl Potter, *President*
Susan Potter, *Admin Sec*
Curtis Myers, *IT/INT Sup*
Patti Plymesser, *Purchasing*
Lou Stanton, *Safety Mgr*
▲ EMP: 46 EST: 1979
SQ FT: 30,000
SALES (est): 16.8MM **Privately Held**
SIC: **5013** Automotive supplies & parts

(P-8462)
S F AUTO PARTS WHSE INC
Also Called: Mac Kenzie Warehouse
6000 3rd St, San Francisco (94124-3106)
PHONE..................415 255-0115
M Mackenzie Menendez, *President*
Michelle Mackenzie Menendez, *President*
Anna-Maria Mac Kenzie, *Treasurer*
Eduardo Menendez, *Exec VP*
EMP: 56 EST: 1951
SQ FT: 53,000
SALES (est): 17.5MM **Privately Held**
SIC: **5013** Automotive supplies

(P-8463)
SAIC INNOVATION CENTER LLC
2680 Zanker Rd Ste 100, San Jose (95134-2143)
PHONE..................408 614-9391
Yi Lu,
EMP: 88 EST: 2015
SALES (est): 8.1MM **Privately Held**
WEB: www.saicusa.com
SIC: **5013** Automotive supplies & parts
HQ: Saic Usa, Inc.
322 N Old Woodward Ave # 3
Birmingham MI 48009
248 267-9117

(P-8464)
SANTOS FORD INC
617 W Pacheco Blvd, Los Banos (93635-3936)
PHONE..................209 826-4921
Marion G Santos III, *President*
EMP: 41 EST: 1996
SQ FT: 12,000
SALES (est): 14.3MM **Privately Held**
WEB: www.santosford.net
SIC: **5511** 5013 7538 Automobiles, new & used; automotive engines & engine parts; automotive supplies & parts; truck parts & accessories; general automotive repair shops

(P-8465)
SCOGGAN CO INC (PA)
Also Called: Drive Line Service Sacramento
704 Houston St, West Sacramento (95691-2217)
PHONE..................916 371-3984
James Scoggan, *President*
Elaine Scoggan, *Principal*
▲ EMP: 25 EST: 1971
SQ FT: 8,000
SALES (est): 8.1MM **Privately Held**
SIC: **5013** 3714 7539 Automotive supplies & parts; drive shafts, motor vehicle automotive repair shops

(P-8466)
SERRATO-MCDERMOTT INC
Also Called: Allied Auto Store
43815 S Grimmer Blvd, Fremont (94538-6348)
PHONE..................510 656-6233
Bill Bailey, *CEO*
Tom Croker, *Sales Mgr*
Anthony Barnes, *Sales Staff*
Manuel Pereira, *Sales Staff*
EMP: 55 EST: 1970
SQ FT: 17,000
SALES (est): 19.5MM **Privately Held**
WEB: www.alliedautostores.com
SIC: **5013** 5531 Automotive supplies & parts; automotive parts

5013 - Motor Vehicle Splys & New Parts Wholesale County (P-8467)

(P-8467)
SOUTHERN CAL DISC TIRE CO INC
11127 Folsom Blvd, Rancho Cordova (95670-6132)
PHONE 916 638-2388
Dave Tagliaferi, *Manager*
EMP: 106
SALES (corp-wide): 3.6B **Privately Held**
WEB: www.discounttire.com
SIC: 5531 5013 Automotive tires; wheels, motor vehicle
HQ: Southern California Discount Tire Co., Inc.
16100 N Grnway Hyden Loop
Scottsdale AZ 85260
602 996-0201

(P-8468)
SOUTHERN CAL DISC TIRE CO INC
6434 Florin Rd, Sacramento (95823-2327)
PHONE 916 427-1961
Amos Bennett, *Manager*
Paul Slobodnjak, *Manager*
EMP: 106
SALES (corp-wide): 3.6B **Privately Held**
WEB: www.discounttire.com
SIC: 5531 5013 Automotive tires; wheels, motor vehicle
HQ: Southern California Discount Tire Co., Inc.
16100 N Grnway Hyden Loop
Scottsdale AZ 85260
602 996-0201

(P-8469)
SPECIALTY TRUCK PARTS INC (PA)
7700 Arroyo Cir, Gilroy (95020-7312)
P.O. Box 871, San Jose (95106-0871)
PHONE 408 998-7272
Roger L Stanton, *President*
Alvin B Davidson, *Ch of Bd*
Danny Green, *Vice Pres*
Ron Lutz, *Vice Pres*
Brian Stanton, *Vice Pres*
EMP: 36 **EST:** 1923
SALES (est): 10.4MM **Privately Held**
WEB: www.specialtytruck.com
SIC: 5531 5511 5013 3713 Truck equipment & parts; trucks, tractors & trailers: new & used; automotive supplies & parts; truck & bus bodies

(P-8470)
SSF IMPORTED AUTO PARTS LLC (DH)
Also Called: S S F
466 Forbes Blvd, South San Francisco (94080-2015)
PHONE 800 203-9287
Thomas Beer, *Mng Member*
Nancy Sanguinetti, *Info Tech Dir*
Dante Jerlich, *IT/INT Sup*
Mark Gunson, *Graphic Designe*
Russ Jones, *Asst Controller*
▲ **EMP:** 100 **EST:** 1976
SALES (est): 118.9MM
SALES (corp-wide): 64.2K **Privately Held**
WEB: www.ssfautoparts.com
SIC: 5013 Automotive supplies & parts
HQ: Wm Se
Pagenstecherstr. 121
Osnabruck NI 49090
541 998-90

(P-8471)
SUPERWINCH LLC
3945 Freedom Cir Ste 560, Santa Clara (95054-1269)
PHONE 800 323-2031
Edward Cunningham,
Brent Nasset, *President*
◆ **EMP:** 40 **EST:** 1970
SALES (est): 8MM **Privately Held**
WEB: www.superwinch.com
SIC: 5013 3531 Automotive supplies; winches

(P-8472)
VALLEJO NISSAN INC
3287 Sonoma Blvd, Vallejo (94590-2989)
PHONE 707 643-8291
Gregory Compagno, *President*
Vincent Compagno, *Corp Secy*
Yvette Correa, *Administration*
Carlos Ramirez, *Sales Mgr*
Ryan Macoy, *Sales Staff*
EMP: 48 **EST:** 1968
SQ FT: 15,000
SALES (est): 31.4MM **Privately Held**
WEB: www.vallejonissan.com
SIC: 5511 5531 5013 7538 Automobiles, new & used; automotive parts; automotive supplies & parts; general automotive repair shops

(P-8473)
WABASH NATIONAL TRLR CTRS INC
3600 W Capitol Ave, West Sacramento (95691-2114)
PHONE 916 371-6921
Jack Scarff, *Manager*
EMP: 43
SALES (corp-wide): 1.4B **Publicly Held**
WEB: www.wabashnational.com
SIC: 5013 5012 7539 Motor vehicle supplies & new parts; automobiles & other motor vehicles; automotive repair shops
HQ: Wabash National Trailer Centers, Inc.
1000 Sagamore Pkwy S
Lafayette IN 47905
765 771-5300

(P-8474)
WAGAN CORPORATION
31088 San Clemente St, Hayward (94544-7811)
PHONE 510 471-9221
Alex Hsu, *CEO*
John Hsu, *Ch of Bd*
Po-Jung Hsu, *CEO*
Christina Vanderbeek, *COO*
Mamie Hsu, *CFO*
▲ **EMP:** 50
SQ FT: 30,000
SALES (est): 11.3MM **Privately Held**
WEB: www.wagan.com
SIC: 5013 Automotive supplies & parts

5014 Tires & Tubes Wholesale

(P-8475)
AMCS INC
Also Called: Aquamatic Cover Systems
200 Mayock Rd, Gilroy (95020-7029)
PHONE 408 846-9274
Harry Last, *CEO*
Barbara E Last, *Corp Secy*
Debra Dankel, *Vice Pres*
Tom Dankel, *Vice Pres*
Juliana Hardin, *Vice Pres*
◆ **EMP:** 40 **EST:** 1980
SQ FT: 17,600
SALES (est): 14.7MM **Privately Held**
SIC: 5014 3069 Tire & tube repair materials; sheeting, rubber or rubberized fabric

(P-8476)
BRIDGSTONE AMRCAS TIRE OPRTONS
GCR Tires & Service 859
1401 Richards Blvd, Sacramento (95811-0423)
PHONE 916 447-4220
Christopher Chadwick, *Manager*
EMP: 72 **Privately Held**
WEB: www.bridgestoneamericas.com
SIC: 5531 5014 Automotive tires; truck tires & tubes
HQ: Bridgestone Americas Tire Operations, Llc
200 4th Ave S Ste 100
Nashville TN 37201
615 937-1000

(P-8477)
MC LEAS TIRE SERVICE INC (PA)
Also Called: Mc Leas Tire & Automotive Svc
800 Piner Rd, Santa Rosa (95403-2021)
PHONE 707 542-0363
Larry L McLea, *CEO*
Lester V McLea, *President*
Richard W McLea, *Vice Pres*
Ozzie Flores, *Manager*
EMP: 38 **EST:** 1966
SQ FT: 10,000
SALES (est): 17.7MM **Privately Held**
WEB: www.mcleastire.com
SIC: 5531 5014 7539 Automotive tires; automobile tires & tubes; truck tires & tubes; brake repair, automotive; tune-up service, automotive; front end repair, automotive; wheel alignment, automotive

(P-8478)
SOUTHERN CAL DISC TIRE CO INC
34734 Alvarado Niles Rd, Union City (94587-4502)
PHONE 510 429-1977
Mike Balestreri, *Branch Mgr*
EMP: 106
SALES (corp-wide): 3.6B **Privately Held**
WEB: www.discounttire.com
SIC: 5531 5014 5013 Automotive tires; automobile tires & tubes; wheels, motor vehicle
HQ: Southern California Discount Tire Co., Inc.
16100 N Grnway Hyden Loop
Scottsdale AZ 85260
602 996-0201

(P-8479)
SOUTHERN CAL DISC TIRE CO INC
1610 Broadway St, Redwood City (94063-2402)
PHONE 650 366-4003
Dan Richards, *Branch Mgr*
EMP: 106
SALES (corp-wide): 3.6B **Privately Held**
WEB: www.discounttire.com
SIC: 5531 5014 5013 Automotive tires; automobile tires & tubes; wheels, motor vehicle
HQ: Southern California Discount Tire Co., Inc.
16100 N Grnway Hyden Loop
Scottsdale AZ 85260
602 996-0201

(P-8480)
SOUTHERN CAL DISC TIRE CO INC
32 W El Camino Real, Mountain View (94040-2602)
PHONE 650 988-9611
Dan Appleman, *Branch Mgr*
EMP: 106
SALES (corp-wide): 3.6B **Privately Held**
WEB: www.discounttire.com
SIC: 5531 5014 5013 Automotive tires; automobile tires & tubes; wheels, motor vehicle
HQ: Southern California Discount Tire Co., Inc.
16100 N Grnway Hyden Loop
Scottsdale AZ 85260
602 996-0201

(P-8481)
SOUTHERN CAL DISC TIRE CO INC
980 E Hamilton Ave, Campbell (95008-0615)
PHONE 408 377-5010
Marlon Arevall, *Manager*
EMP: 106
SALES (corp-wide): 3.6B **Privately Held**
WEB: www.discounttire.com
SIC: 5531 5014 Automotive tires; automobile tires & tubes
HQ: Southern California Discount Tire Co., Inc.
16100 N Grnway Hyden Loop
Scottsdale AZ 85260
602 996-0201

(P-8482)
SOUTHERN CAL DISC TIRE CO INC
536 E Brokaw Rd, San Jose (95112-1003)
PHONE 408 436-8274
Tracy Stevens, *Principal*
EMP: 106
SALES (corp-wide): 3.6B **Privately Held**
WEB: www.discounttire.com
SIC: 5531 5014 5013 Automotive tires; automobile tires & tubes; wheels, motor vehicle
HQ: Southern California Discount Tire Co., Inc.
16100 N Grnway Hyden Loop
Scottsdale AZ 85260
602 996-0201

5015 Motor Vehicle Parts, Used Wholesale

(P-8483)
PICK PULL AUTO DISMANTLING INC
19919 Viking Way, Redding (96003-8229)
PHONE 530 221-6184
Mike Craska, *Branch Mgr*
EMP: 37
SALES (corp-wide): 2.7B **Publicly Held**
SIC: 5015 Automotive parts & supplies, used
HQ: Pick And Pull Auto Dismantling, Inc.
10850 Gold Center Dr # 325
Rancho Cordova CA 95670
916 689-2000

(P-8484)
PICK PULL AUTO DISMANTLING INC
3230 E Jensen Ave, Fresno (93706-5114)
PHONE 559 233-3881
EMP: 37
SALES (corp-wide): 2.7B **Publicly Held**
SIC: 5015 Automotive parts & supplies, used
HQ: Pick And Pull Auto Dismantling, Inc.
10850 Gold Center Dr # 325
Rancho Cordova CA 95670
916 689-2000

(P-8485)
PICK PULL AUTO DISMANTLING INC
10475 Old Redwood Hwy, Windsor (95492-9256)
PHONE 707 838-4691
Roberto Mendoza, *Manager*
EMP: 37
SALES (corp-wide): 2.7B **Publicly Held**
SIC: 5015 Automotive parts & supplies, used
HQ: Pick And Pull Auto Dismantling, Inc.
10850 Gold Center Dr # 325
Rancho Cordova CA 95670
916 689-2000

(P-8486)
PICK PULL AUTO DISMANTLING INC
4659 Air Base Pkwy, Fairfield (94533-7108)
PHONE 707 425-1044
Kevin Bosche, *Manager*
EMP: 37
SALES (corp-wide): 2.7B **Publicly Held**
SIC: 5015 Automotive parts & supplies, used
HQ: Pick And Pull Auto Dismantling, Inc.
10850 Gold Center Dr # 325
Rancho Cordova CA 95670
916 689-2000

(P-8487)
PICK PULL AUTO DISMANTLING INC (HQ)
Also Called: Auto Parts Group
10850 Gold Center Dr # 325, Rancho Cordova (95670-6045)
PHONE 916 689-2000
Thomas Klauer, *President*
Byron Breshears, *District Mgr*
Mike Craig, *General Mgr*
Katherine Dunn, *Store Mgr*
Sandra Harrison, *Executive Asst*
EMP: 50 **EST:** 1987
SQ FT: 9,000
SALES (est): 290.6MM
SALES (corp-wide): 2.7B **Publicly Held**
WEB: www.schnitzersteel.com
SIC: 5015 Automotive parts & supplies, used

▲ = Import ▼ = Export
◆ = Import/Export

PRODUCTS & SERVICES SECTION

5023 - Home Furnishings Wholesale County (P-8509)

PA: Schnitzer Steel Industries, Inc.
299 Sw Clay St Ste 350
Portland OR 97201
503 224-9900

(P-8488)
PICK PULL AUTO DISMANTLING INC
6355 Pacific St, Rocklin (95677-3424)
PHONE...............................916 784-6350
Sylvia Lyser, *Manager*
EMP: 37
SALES (corp-wide): 2.7B **Publicly Held**
SIC: 5015 Automotive parts & supplies, used
HQ: Pick And Pull Auto Dismantling, Inc.
10850 Gold Center Dr # 325
Rancho Cordova CA 95670
916 689-2000

(P-8489)
PICK PULL AUTO DISMANTLING INC
7400 Mowry Ave, Newark (94560-4932)
PHONE...............................510 742-2277
Undtermine BR, *Manager*
EMP: 37
SALES (corp-wide): 2.7B **Publicly Held**
SIC: 5015 7549 Automotive parts & supplies, used; towing services
HQ: Pick And Pull Auto Dismantling, Inc.
10850 Gold Center Dr # 325
Rancho Cordova CA 95670
916 689-2000

5021 Furniture Wholesale

(P-8490)
COG GROUP LLC (PA)
Also Called: Contract Office Group
1731 Tech Dr Ste 100, San Jose (95110)
PHONE...............................408 213-1790
Davyd Funk,
Lindsey Frimming, *Officer*
Justin Loeber, *CIO*
Robert Caywood, *Project Mgr*
Helen Hall, *Human Resources*
EMP: 54 **EST:** 2015
SALES (est): 22.7MM **Privately Held**
WEB: www.cog.com
SIC: 5021 Office furniture; office & public building furniture; public building furniture

(P-8491)
COMMERCIAL STING SPCALISTS INC
481 Laurelwood Rd, Santa Clara (95054-2416)
PHONE...............................408 453-8983
James E Day, *President*
Richard Buchner, *Vice Pres*
Daniel Bae, *Manager*
Manuel Gonzalez, *Manager*
EMP: 39 **EST:** 1998
SQ FT: 24,000
SALES (est): 3.7MM **Privately Held**
WEB: www.comseat.com
SIC: 5021 Restaurant furniture

(P-8492)
CONTRACT INTERIORS SAN DIEGO
4450 N Brawley Ave # 125, Fresno (93722-3952)
PHONE...............................559 276-0561
Douglas Davidian, *CEO*
Robyn Davidian, *President*
Douglas B Davidian, *CEO*
Robin Hankins, *Vice Pres*
Dusre Grove, *Admin Sec*
EMP: 80 **EST:** 1985
SQ FT: 18,480
SALES (est): 12.9MM **Privately Held**
SIC: 5021 Office & public building furniture

(P-8493)
COORDNTED RSRCES INC SAN FRNCS
Also Called: C R I
130 Sutter St Fl 3, San Francisco (94104-4012)
PHONE...............................415 989-0773
Gerald E Slagter, *Ch of Bd*
William J Watson, *CEO*
Jaimee Arent, *Vice Pres*
Aaron Gruver, *Executive*
Danielle Sablan, *Project Mgr*
▲ **EMP:** 45 **EST:** 1986
SQ FT: 6,400
SALES (est): 22.1MM **Privately Held**
WEB: www.cri-sf.com
SIC: 5021 5712 Office furniture; office furniture

(P-8494)
HOMELEGANCE INC (PA)
Also Called: A G A
48200 Fremont Blvd, Fremont (94538-6509)
PHONE...............................510 933-6888
Puhsien C Chao, *CEO*
Rosa Chao, *President*
Hutch Chao, *Vice Pres*
Chrissy Chang, *General Mgr*
◆ **EMP:** 88 **EST:** 1984
SQ FT: 800,000
SALES (est): 25.6MM **Privately Held**
WEB: www.homelegance.com
SIC: 5021 Household furniture

(P-8495)
IBEX ENTERPRISES
Also Called: Resource Design Interiors
350 Brannan St Fl 1, San Francisco (94107-3803)
PHONE...............................415 777-0202
Ann Pantera, *President*
Alex Cvetkov, *Exec VP*
Maryann McCarthy, *Vice Pres*
Kalee Woo, *Vice Pres*
Dan McCarthy, *Office Admin*
EMP: 35 **EST:** 1989
SQ FT: 9,192
SALES: 40.2MM **Privately Held**
WEB: www.ibexent.com
SIC: 5021 5023 7389 Office & public building furniture; window furnishings; floor coverings; interior design services

(P-8496)
INTERFORM COMMERCIAL INTERIORS
3000 Executive Pkwy # 175, San Ramon (94583-4255)
PHONE...............................925 867-1001
Richard Watts, *President*
Alex Gilmete, *Senior VP*
Linda Newton, *Vice Pres*
EMP: 42 **EST:** 1982
SQ FT: 6,600
SALES (est): 3.7MM **Privately Held**
WEB: www.interform.com
SIC: 5021 7389 5713 Office furniture; interior design services; floor covering stores

(P-8497)
K B M OFFICE EQUIPMENT INC (PA)
Also Called: Kbm-Hogue
225 W Santa Clara St, San Jose (95113-1723)
PHONE...............................408 351-7100
Stan Vuckovich, *CEO*
Anthony De Maio, *CFO*
Mark Dailey, *Vice Pres*
Kristi Rolak, *Vice Pres*
Richard Barnes, *CIO*
◆ **EMP:** 57 **EST:** 1946
SQ FT: 10,400
SALES (est): 32.5MM **Privately Held**
WEB: www.kbmofficeeque.openfos.com
SIC: 5021 7389 Office furniture; interior design services

(P-8498)
K&I INTERNATIONAL TRADE INC
1267 Willis St Ste 200, Redding (96001-0400)
PHONE...............................320 228-2788
Jinhong Lin, *CEO*
EMP: 50 **EST:** 2013
SALES (est): 3.1MM **Privately Held**
SIC: 5021 Furniture

(P-8499)
LARRY FISHER & SONS LTD PARTNR
5242 E Home Ave, Fresno (93727-2103)
PHONE...............................559 252-2575
Larry Fisher, *Partner*
Jennifer Fisher, *Partner*
Sophia Fisher, *Partner*
▲ **EMP:** 19 **EST:** 1987
SQ FT: 10,000
SALES (est): 8MM **Privately Held**
WEB: www.larryfisherandsons.com
SIC: 5021 2542 3535 Racks; racks, merchandise display or storage: except wood; conveyors & conveying equipment

(P-8500)
LFTM INC
Also Called: Top Dawg Modular Service
49035 Milmont Dr, Fremont (94538-7317)
PHONE...............................510 249-0900
EMP: 15
SQ FT: 10,000
SALES (est): 3.2MM **Privately Held**
WEB: www.californiausedofficefurniture.com
SIC: 5021 2522 Whol Furniture Mfg Office Furniture-Nonwood

(P-8501)
ONE WORKPLACE L FERRARI LLC
Also Called: One Workplace L Ferrari
475 Brannan St, San Francisco (94107-5418)
PHONE...............................415 357-2200
Brian Wilson, *Mng Member*
Aaron Uyehara, *Info Tech Mgr*
Deborah Maddock, *Credit Staff*
Maria Preciado, *Credit Staff*
Nancy Silvey, *Opers Staff*
EMP: 50 **EST:** 2011
SALES (est): 16.7MM
SALES (corp-wide): 329.1MM **Privately Held**
WEB: www.oneworkplace.com
SIC: 5021 Filing units; office furniture
PA: One Workplace L. Ferrari, Llc
2500 De La Cruz Blvd
Santa Clara CA 95050
669 800-2500

(P-8502)
PALECEK IMPORTS INC (PA)
601 Parr Blvd, Richmond (94801-1316)
PHONE...............................510 236-7730
Allan Palecek, *President*
Andrew T Palecek, *Vice Pres*
Chuck Riesbol, *MIS Staff*
Leona Burkes, *Credit Staff*
Rose CHI, *Accountant*
◆ **EMP:** 77 **EST:** 1972
SQ FT: 250,000
SALES (est): 36.9MM **Privately Held**
WEB: www.palecek.com
SIC: 5021 5023 Household furniture; home furnishings

(P-8503)
RANDALL HORTON ASSOCIATES INC (PA)
Also Called: Sidemark Corporate Furniture
4353 N 1st St Ste 100, San Jose (95134-1259)
PHONE...............................408 490-3300
EMP: 40
SQ FT: 10,000
SALES (est): 19.9MM **Privately Held**
WEB: www.sidemark.com
SIC: 5021 7389 Whol Furniture Business Services

(P-8504)
ZOCALO
1551 Bancroft Ave 1508, San Francisco (94124-3216)
PHONE...............................415 293-1600
Jeremy Sommer, *President*
Steve Fox, *CFO*
Ronaldo Zalaya, *Opers Staff*
◆ **EMP:** 62 **EST:** 1995
SQ FT: 150,000
SALES (est): 8.9MM **Privately Held**
WEB: www.zocalo.org
SIC: 5021 Furniture

5023 Home Furnishings Wholesale

(P-8505)
ARMIN MAIER AND ASSOCIATES INC (PA)
2149 Powell St, San Francisco (94133-1948)
PHONE...............................415 332-6467
Armin Maier, *CEO*
Jon Hart, *Vice Pres*
John Callahan, *Sales Staff*
EMP: 37 **EST:** 2001
SALES (est): 2.9MM **Privately Held**
WEB: www.maierandassoc.com
SIC: 5023 Floor coverings

(P-8506)
B R FUNSTEN & CO
Also Called: BR Funsten
105 Lndustrial Park, Manteca (95337)
PHONE...............................209 825-5375
Rod Tilson, *Branch Mgr*
Kevin Schock, *Technician*
Steve Johnson, *Purchasing*
EMP: 60
SALES (corp-wide): 384.1MM **Privately Held**
WEB: www.brfunsten.com
SIC: 5023 5713 Resilient floor coverings: tile or sheet; floor covering stores
PA: B. R. Funsten & Co.
5200 Watt Ct Ste B
Fairfield CA 94534
209 825-5375

(P-8507)
B T MANCINI CO INC
8571 23rd Ave, Sacramento (95826-4993)
P.O. Box 276128 (95827-6128)
PHONE...............................916 381-3660
Mike Quirk, *Sales/Mktg Mgr*
Joe Camilleri, *Vice Pres*
Peggy Briggs, *Admin Sec*
Ryan Breakstone, *Project Mgr*
Megan Stockdale, *Project Mgr*
EMP: 106
SQ FT: 13,000
SALES (corp-wide): 58.2MM **Privately Held**
WEB: www.btmancini.com
SIC: 5023 Floor coverings
PA: B. T. Mancini Co., Inc.
876 S Milpitas Blvd
Milpitas CA 95035
408 942-7900

(P-8508)
CALIFORNIA BACKYARD INC (PA)
Also Called: Nevada Backyard Stores
130 Cyber Ct, Rocklin (95765-1214)
PHONE...............................916 543-1900
Wilma Homsy, *President*
Denise Homsy-Tapken, *Vice Pres*
Jerry Petkovich, *Branch Mgr*
Thomas J Tapken, *Admin Sec*
Thomas Tapken, *Admin Sec*
▲ **EMP:** 50 **EST:** 1994
SQ FT: 44,000
SALES (est): 20MM **Privately Held**
WEB: www.californiabackyard.com
SIC: 5999 5719 5023 Christmas lights & decorations; wicker, rattan or reed home furnishings; housewares; grills, barbecue

(P-8509)
CONKLIN BROS SAN JOSE INC (PA)
Also Called: Abbey Carpet
2250 Almaden Expy, San Jose (95125-2050)
PHONE...............................408 266-2250
Richard Oderio Jr, *CEO*
Barbara Zibell, *CFO*
Richard Barnes, *Vice Pres*
Craig Nourie, *Vice Pres*
John Shiels, *Vice Pres*
EMP: 37 **EST:** 1963
SQ FT: 23,000
SALES (est): 13.9MM **Privately Held**
WEB: www.conklinbros.com
SIC: 5713 5023 Carpets; carpets

5023 - Home Furnishings Wholesale County (P-8510)

(P-8510)
DSB INC
Also Called: DSB Commercial Floor Finishes
2157 Otoole Ave Ste 20, San Jose (95131-1332)
PHONE..............................408 228-3000
Jim Hardush, *President*
Steve Wells, *Superintendent*
EMP: 40 EST: 1995
SALES (est): 5.3MM Privately Held
WEB: www.dsb-plus.com
SIC: 5023 Floor coverings

(P-8511)
E & E CO LTD (PA)
Also Called: Jla Home
45875 Northport Loop E, Fremont (94538-6414)
PHONE..............................510 490-9788
Edmund Jin, *CEO*
Michael Mullen, *Exec VP*
Hellen Xu, *Exec VP*
Winnie Cheung, *Vice Pres*
Adriana Divizich, *Vice Pres*
◆ EMP: 180 EST: 1994
SQ FT: 60,000
SALES (est): 249.4MM Privately Held
WEB: www.ee1994.com
SIC: 5023 Sheets, textile

(P-8512)
GATE FIVE GROUP LLC
Also Called: Roost
200 Gate 5 Rd Ste 116, Sausalito (94965-1456)
P.O. Box 399 (94966-0399)
PHONE..............................415 339-9500
Scott Donnellan,
Diane Panelo, *Controller*
Kim Lee, *Merchandising*
Tommy Sisco, *Sales Staff*
Michael Kohlmann, *Director*
◆ EMP: 50 EST: 2001
SQ FT: 1,500
SALES (est): 19.3MM Privately Held
SIC: 5023 Decorative home furnishings & supplies

(P-8513)
HOMESITE SVCS INC A CAL CORP (PA)
6611 Preston Ave Ste E, Livermore (94551-5108)
PHONE..............................925 237-3050
Tina Tomei, *CEO*
Darryl Phelps, *COO*
Tami Dowell, *Project Mgr*
Crysta Estimo, *Project Mgr*
Haleigh Ray, *Project Mgr*
▲ EMP: 61 EST: 2004
SALES (est): 81.4MM Privately Held
WEB: www.homesiteservices.net
SIC: 5713 5211 5023 Floor covering stores; counter tops; window covering parts & accessories

(P-8514)
KOEHLER LEFFORGE INC
Also Called: Wyman-Empires Fabric
2647 Mercantile Dr Ste B, Rancho Cordova (95742-6608)
P.O. Box 276221, Sacramento (95827-6221)
PHONE..............................916 381-9333
James M Lefforge, *President*
Katheryn Lefforge, *Corp Secy*
EMP: 35 EST: 1945
SQ FT: 35,000
SALES (est): 4.4MM Privately Held
SIC: 5023 Window covering parts & accessories

(P-8515)
LION TRADING COMPANY LLC (PA)
1838 N Milpitas Blvd, Milpitas (95035-2714)
PHONE..............................408 946-0888
EMP: 78 EST: 2011
SALES (est): 170.8K Privately Held
SIC: 5023 Sheets, textile

(P-8516)
MAJESTIC FLOORS INC
5111 Port Chicago Hwy, Concord (94520-1216)
PHONE..............................925 825-0771
Vince Steel, *CEO*
Kristy Steel, *Corp Secy*
EMP: 35 EST: 1984
SQ FT: 17,000
SALES (est): 21.1MM Privately Held
WEB: www.majesticfloors.com
SIC: 5023 Wood flooring

(P-8517)
OBERON DESIGN AND MFG LLC
1076 Illinois St, San Francisco (94107-3120)
PHONE..............................415 865-5440
Michael Ogura,
Marshall J Lane,
▲ EMP: 23 EST: 1997
SALES (est): 5.3MM Privately Held
WEB: www.oberondesign.net
SIC: 5023 5063 2519 Frames & framing, picture & mirror; mirrors & pictures, framed & unframed; lighting fixtures; household furniture, except wood or metal; upholstered

(P-8518)
PEKING HANDICRAFT INC (PA)
Also Called: P H I
1388 San Mateo Ave, South San Francisco (94080-6501)
PHONE..............................650 871-3788
Derrick Lo, *CEO*
Clinton Chien, *COO*
Wendy So, *Technology*
Elizabeth Almeda, *Sales Executive*
Ann Nensel, *Sales Mgr*
◆ EMP: 120 EST: 1977
SQ FT: 150,000
SALES (est): 43.1MM Privately Held
WEB: www.pkhc.com
SIC: 5023 Linens & towels; bedspreads; sheets, textile; decorative home furnishings & supplies

(P-8519)
POTTERY WORLD LLC
1006 White Rock Rd, El Dorado Hills (95762-5684)
PHONE..............................916 358-8788
James W Rodda, *Branch Mgr*
EMP: 56
SALES (corp-wide): 14.9MM Privately Held
WEB: www.potteryworld.com
SIC: 5023 Pottery
PA: Pottery World Inc.
4419 Granite Dr
Rocklin CA 95677
916 624-8080

(P-8520)
PSI3G INC (PA)
Also Called: Partition Specialties
505 San Marin Dr Ste A120, Novato (94945-1355)
PHONE..............................415 493-3854
Randall E Squires, *CEO*
Ryan Iwasa, *Vice Pres*
Shawn Still, *Vice Pres*
Karen Dohemann, *Controller*
Robert Kaminski, *Sales Mgr*
EMP: 67 EST: 2009
SALES (est): 17.8MM Privately Held
WEB: www.psi3g.com
SIC: 5713 5023 1752 Floor covering stores; floor coverings; access flooring system installation

(P-8521)
TOM DUFFY CO
Also Called: Wholesale Flooring Products
5200 Watt Ct Ste B, Fairfield (94534-4209)
PHONE..............................800 479-5671
Jim Funsten, *CEO*
Anne Funsten, *President*
Judy Bruce, *CFO*
Dave Bolton, *Vice Pres*
Tom Duffy, *Vice Pres*
EMP: 51 EST: 2014
SALES (est): 22.7MM
SALES (corp-wide): 384.1MM Privately Held
WEB: www.tomduffy.com
SIC: 5023 Carpets
PA: B. R. Funsten & Co.
5200 Watt Ct Ste B
Fairfield CA 94534
209 825-5375

(P-8522)
TRUCKEE-TAHOE LUMBER COMPANY (PA)
10242 Church St, Truckee (96161-0350)
P.O. Box 369 (96160-0369)
PHONE..............................530 587-9211
Andrew M Cross, *President*
Ira Cross, *Vice Pres*
Fred H Salzinger, *Vice Pres*
Steve Stevenson, *Executive*
Pat Jones, *Store Mgr*
▲ EMP: 36 EST: 1931
SQ FT: 5,400
SALES (est): 25.3MM Privately Held
WEB: www.ttlco.com
SIC: 5211 5023 Millwork & lumber; resilient floor coverings: tile or sheet

(P-8523)
VALYRIA LLC (HQ)
Also Called: Transpac
1050 Aviator Dr, Vacaville (95688-8900)
PHONE..............................707 452-0600
Laurie Gilner, *President*
Tara Dikos, *Exec VP*
Karen Garcia, *Executive*
Courtney Guerino, *Executive*
Jose Gomez, *Technology*
▲ EMP: 80 EST: 2016
SQ FT: 175,000
SALES (est): 26.1MM
SALES (corp-wide): 61.3MM Privately Held
WEB: www.shoptii.com
SIC: 5023 Decorative home furnishings & supplies
PA: C & F Enterprises, Inc.
819 Bluecrab Rd
Newport News VA 23606
757 873-5688

5031 Lumber, Plywood & Millwork Wholesale

(P-8524)
AMERICAN BUILDING SUPPLY INC (HQ)
Also Called: Abs-American Building Supply
8360 Elder Creek Rd, Sacramento (95828-1705)
P.O. Box 293030 (95829-3030)
PHONE..............................916 503-4100
Mark Ballantyne, *CEO*
Dave Baker, *President*
Jan Leonard, *Vice Pres*
Greg Leffers, *General Mgr*
Son Nguyen, *CTO*
▲ EMP: 250 EST: 1965
SQ FT: 230,000
SALES (est): 368.3MM Publicly Held
WEB: www.abs-abs.com
SIC: 5031 3231 Doors; doors, glass: made from purchased glass

(P-8525)
AMERICAN BUILDING SUPPLY INC
Also Called: ABS- American Building Supply
8920 43rd Ave, Sacramento (95828-1123)
PHONE..............................916 387-4101
Liz Robertson, *Branch Mgr*
EMP: 99 Publicly Held
WEB: www.abs-abs.com
SIC: 5031 3231 Doors; door frames, all materials; doors, glass: made from purchased glass
HQ: American Building Supply, Inc.
8360 Elder Creek Rd
Sacramento CA 95828
916 503-4100

(P-8526)
AMERICAN BUILDING SUPPLY INC
1488 Tillie Lewis Dr, Stockton (95206-1131)
PHONE..............................209 941-8852
Randy Neto, *Branch Mgr*
Jake Pronio, *Vice Pres*
Adam Jacuinde, *Production*
David Dennie, *Sales Mgr*
James Fleming, *Sales Staff*
EMP: 99 Publicly Held
WEB: www.abs-abs.com
SIC: 5031 Doors
HQ: American Building Supply, Inc.
8360 Elder Creek Rd
Sacramento CA 95828
916 503-4100

(P-8527)
AMERICAN BUILDING SUPPLY INC
Also Called: Abs-American Building Supply
1 Wayne Ct, Sacramento (95825-1300)
PHONE..............................916 503-4100
Ray Fletcher, *Principal*
Cory Lainhart, *Project Mgr*
EMP: 99 Publicly Held
WEB: www.abs-abs.com
SIC: 5031 Doors
HQ: American Building Supply, Inc.
8360 Elder Creek Rd
Sacramento CA 95828
916 503-4100

(P-8528)
ARGONAUT WINDOW & DOOR INC
1901 S Bascom Ave Ste 800, Campbell (95008-2240)
PHONE..............................408 376-4018
Martin C Ettema, *President*
Chris Ettema, *Owner*
Kirstin Joyce, *Project Mgr*
Brent Anderson, *Sales Staff*
Glenn Anisman, *Sales Staff*
EMP: 55 EST: 2002
SALES (est): 13.6MM Privately Held
WEB: www.argowin.com
SIC: 5211 5031 1751 7299 Door & window products; windows; door frames, all materials; cabinet & finish carpentry; window & door (prefabricated) installation; home improvement & renovation contractor agency

(P-8529)
BERKE DOOR & HARDWARE INC
8255 Belvedere Ave, Sacramento (95826-4713)
PHONE..............................916 452-7331
Erwin M Berke, *President*
Merna Berke, *Corp Secy*
Erik Berke, *Vice Pres*
Erik Bjerke, *General Mgr*
EMP: 18 EST: 1950
SQ FT: 24,000
SALES (est): 3.1MM Privately Held
WEB: www.berkedoorandhardware.com
SIC: 5031 5072 2431 Doors; builders' hardware; door frames, wood

(P-8530)
BINBIN WINDOWS INC (PA)
272 Bay Shore Blvd, San Francisco (94124-1323)
PHONE..............................415 282-1688
Yubin Chen, *President*
EMP: 53 EST: 2017
SALES (est): 203.1K Privately Held
SIC: 5031 Windows

(P-8531)
BMC STOCK HOLDINGS INC
Also Called: Heritage One Door & Carpentry
4300 Jetway Ct, North Highlands (95660-5702)
PHONE..............................916 481-5030
Madeleine Beezer, *Finance*
Dayna Buttacavoli, *Manager*
Jared Hooker, *Manager*
EMP: 350

PRODUCTS & SERVICES SECTION
5031 - Lumber, Plywood & Millwork Wholesale County (P-8551)

SALES (corp-wide): 8.5B **Publicly Held**
SIC: **5031** 2431 Doors & windows; windows & window parts & trim, wood
HQ: Bmc Stock Holdings, Inc.
4800 Falls Of Neuse Rd # 400
Raleigh NC 27609

(P-8532)
BUILDING MATERIAL DISTRS INC (PA)
Also Called: B M D
225 Elm Ave, Galt (95632-1558)
P.O. Box 606 (95632-0606)
PHONE..................................209 745-3001
Mike Garrison, *Chairman*
Jeff Gore, *President*
Cynthia Thompson, *CFO*
Steven Ellinwood, *Chairman*
Joe Burdge, *Business Mgr*
◆ **EMP:** 170
SQ FT: 100,000
SALES (est): 145.1MM **Privately Held**
WEB: www.bmdusa.com
SIC: **5031** Building materials, exterior; building materials, interior; window frames, all materials; door frames, all materials

(P-8533)
CAPITAL LUMBER
160 Commerce Cir, Sacramento (95815-4208)
PHONE..................................916 922-8861
Sam Sanregret, *President*
EMP: 15 **EST:** 2017
SALES (est): 601.7K **Privately Held**
WEB: www.capital-lumber.com
SIC: **5211 5031** 2421 Lumber products; lumber: rough, dressed & finished; lumber: rough, sawed or planed

(P-8534)
CAPITAL LUMBER COMPANY
13480 Old Redwood Hwy, Healdsburg (95448)
P.O. Box 1396 (95448-1396)
PHONE..................................707 433-7070
Jeff Howard, *Principal*
Bethany Doss, *Business Mgr*
EMP: 26
SALES (corp-wide): 375MM **Privately Held**
WEB: www.capital-lumber.com
SIC: **5031** 2493 Lumber: rough, dressed & finished; reconstituted wood products
PA: Capital Lumber Company
5110 N 40th St Ste 242
Phoenix AZ 85018
602 381-0709

(P-8535)
CHA-DOR REALTY LLC
Also Called: Meek's
2763 Lake Tahoe Blvd, South Lake Tahoe (96150-7724)
P.O. Box 7647 (96158-0647)
PHONE..................................530 544-2237
Mike Willford, *Branch Mgr*
EMP: 102
SQ FT: 28,515
SALES (corp-wide): 45.5MM **Privately Held**
WEB: www.doitbest.com
SIC: **5251 5031** Hardware; lumber: rough, dressed & finished
PA: Cha-Dor Realty Llc
1651 Response Rd Ste 200
Sacramento CA 95815
916 565-1586

(P-8536)
COLLIER WAREHOUSE INC
Also Called: Cwi
90 Dorman Ave, San Francisco (94124-1807)
PHONE..................................415 920-9720
Paul C Akin, *CEO*
David C Freer, *President*
Christy Akin, *Admin Sec*
Clark Akin, *Project Mgr*
Ryan Macphee, *Human Resources*
◆ **EMP:** 50 **EST:** 1977
SQ FT: 8,000
SALES (est): 26.5MM **Privately Held**
WEB: www.colliergroup.com
SIC: **5031** 1751 Windows; window & door (prefabricated) installation

(P-8537)
COMPLETE MILLWORK SERVICES INC
405 Aldo Ave, Santa Clara (95054-2302)
PHONE..................................408 567-9664
Andrew Hoxsey, *Project Mgr*
Jamal Farhoud, *Opers Mgr*
EMP: 50
SALES (corp-wide): 29.8MM **Privately Held**
WEB: www.cmsrno.com
SIC: **5031** Millwork
PA: Complete Millwork Services, Inc.
4909 Goni Rd Ste A
Carson City NV 89706
775 246-0485

(P-8538)
CONSOLIDATED PALLET COMPANY
4400 Florin Perkins Rd, Sacramento (95826-4814)
P.O. Box 292141 (95829-2141)
PHONE..................................916 381-8123
Dan Lund, *President*
Cheryl Lund, *Vice Pres*
EMP: 15 **EST:** 1994
SQ FT: 60,000
SALES (est): 9.6MM **Privately Held**
SIC: **5031** 2448 5211 Pallets, wood; pallets, wood; lumber & other building materials

(P-8539)
COUNTY BUILDING MATERIALS INC
Also Called: Ace Hardware
2927 S King Rd, San Jose (95122-1597)
PHONE..................................408 274-4920
Jay Robert Williams Jr, *CEO*
Jay R William Sr, *President*
Harry Glaze, *Vice Pres*
▲ **EMP:** 60 **EST:** 1974
SQ FT: 26,000
SALES (est): 11.4MM **Privately Held**
WEB: www.paylesshardwareandrockery.com
SIC: **5031** 5032 5261 5193 Building materials, exterior; building materials, interior; brick, stone & related material; nursery stock, seeds & bulbs; nursery stock; masonry materials & supplies

(P-8540)
D & J LUMBER CO INC (PA)
Also Called: Ace Hardware
600 Tennant Ave, Morgan Hill (95037-5519)
P.O. Box 7 (95038-0007)
PHONE..................................408 778-1550
Michael Johnson, *President*
Michael Seda, *CFO*
Joe Mc Avoy, *Sales Executive*
EMP: 70 **EST:** 1980
SQ FT: 20,000
SALES (est): 21.7MM **Privately Held**
WEB: www.benjaminmoore.com
SIC: **5251 5031 5231** Hardware; lumber: rough, dressed & finished; paint, glass & wallpaper

(P-8541)
DISCOUNT BUILDERS SUPPLY
1695 Mission St, San Francisco (94103-2432)
PHONE..................................415 285-2800
Charles Goodman, *President*
Mike Heffernan, *Manager*
▲ **EMP:** 69
SQ FT: 40,000
SALES (est): 29.9MM **Privately Held**
WEB: www.discountbuilderssupplysf.com
SIC: **5031** 5211 Building materials, exterior; lumber & other building materials

(P-8542)
DOLANS PINOLE LBR BLDG MTLS CO
2750 Camino Diablo, Lafayette (94597-3906)
PHONE..................................925 927-4662
Jane Dolan, *Branch Mgr*
EMP: 44
SALES (corp-wide): 26.9MM **Privately Held**
WEB: www.dolanlumber.com
SIC: **5211 5031** 1761 Door & window products; doors & windows; skylight installation
PA: Dolans Of Pinole Lumber And Building Materials Co.
3355 Vincent Rd
Pleasant Hill CA 94523
925 926-1030

(P-8543)
DOORS UNLIMITED
1685 Sutter Rd, McKinleyville (95519-4216)
PHONE..................................707 822-5959
EMP: 40
SALES (est): 3.1MM **Privately Held**
SIC: **5031** Whol Wooden Doors

(P-8544)
EL & EL WOOD PRODUCTS CORP
10149 Iron Rock Way, Elk Grove (95624-2700)
PHONE..................................916 685-1855
Cathy Vidas, *President*
Michelle Levotch, *Controller*
Al Bhakta, *Sales Staff*
Dan Moroni, *Representative*
EMP: 47
SQ FT: 100,000
SALES (corp-wide): 27.7MM **Privately Held**
WEB: www.elandelwoodproducts.com
SIC: **5031** Molding, all materials; millwork
PA: El & El Wood Products Corp.
6011 Schaefer Ave
Chino CA 91710
909 591-0339

(P-8545)
EXPERT DRY WALL SYSTEMS INC
1141 Old Byshore Hwy Ste, San Jose (95112)
PHONE..................................408 271-5044
Laura Grabar, *Principal*
EMP: 70 **EST:** 2013
SALES (est): 5MM **Privately Held**
SIC: **5031** 1742 Wallboard; drywall

(P-8546)
GLESBY BUILDING MTLS CO INC
Also Called: Glesby Wholesale
2015 W Avenue 140th, San Leandro (94577-5623)
P.O. Box 1955 (94577-0294)
PHONE..................................510 639-9350
Dennis Scharssenberg, *Manager*
EMP: 43
SALES (corp-wide): 28.6MM **Privately Held**
WEB: www.glesby.com
SIC: **5031** Building materials, exterior; building materials, interior
PA: Glesby Building Materials Co., Inc.
15119 Oxnard St
Van Nuys CA 91411
818 785-2166

(P-8547)
HARDWOODS SPECIALTY PDTS US LP
620 Quinn Ave, San Jose (95112-2604)
PHONE..................................408 275-1990
Lance Blanco, *Manager*
EMP: 70
SALES (corp-wide): 950.6MM **Privately Held**
WEB: www.hardwoods-inc.com
SIC: **5031** 5211 Lumber: rough, dressed & finished; lumber products
HQ: Hardwoods Specialty Products Us Lp
2700 Lind Ave Sw Ste 100
Renton WA 98057
425 251-1213

(P-8548)
HERITAGE 1 WINDOW AND BUILDING
4300 Jetway Ct, North Highlands (95660-5702)
P.O. Box 214609, Sacramento (95821-0609)
PHONE..................................916 481-5030
Charles Gardemeyer, *CEO*
Stephen Beckham, *COO*
Geoff Hughes, *CFO*
John Ballou, *Sales Mgr*
Tyler Randolth, *Manager*
EMP: 171 **EST:** 2012
SQ FT: 80,000
SALES (est): 24MM
SALES (corp-wide): 51.2MM **Privately Held**
WEB: www.heritageonewindow.com
SIC: **5031** Doors & windows
PA: Heritage Interests, Llc
4300 Jetway Ct
North Highlands CA 95660
916 481-5030

(P-8549)
HERITAGE ONE DOOR CRPENTRY LLC
4300 Jetway Ct, North Highlands (95660-5702)
P.O. Box 214609, Sacramento (95821-0609)
PHONE..................................916 481-5030
Charles Gardemeyer, *Mng Member*
John Dutter, *COO*
Geoff Hughes, *CFO*
John Ballou, *Sales Mgr*
Candice Kenney, *Manager*
EMP: 86 **EST:** 2011
SQ FT: 80,000
SALES (est): 19.5MM
SALES (corp-wide): 51.2MM **Privately Held**
WEB: www.buildwithbmc.com
SIC: **5031** 2431 Doors & windows; windows & window parts & trim, wood
PA: Heritage Interests, Llc
4300 Jetway Ct
North Highlands CA 95660
916 481-5030

(P-8550)
HILLS FLAT LUMBER CO (PA)
380 Railroad Ave, Grass Valley (95945-5909)
P.O. Box 1630, Colfax (95713-1630)
PHONE..................................530 273-6171
Edward J Pardini Jr, *CEO*
Jason Pardini, *Vice Pres*
Kennan Pardini, *Vice Pres*
Sandra Pardini, *Vice Pres*
Shannon Banks, *Purch Agent*
EMP: 80
SQ FT: 12,000
SALES (est): 26.8MM **Privately Held**
WEB: www.hillsflatlumber.com
SIC: **5251 5031** 5193 5999 Hardware; doors & windows; nursery stock; plumbing & heating supplies; general merchandise, non-durable; equipment rental & leasing

(P-8551)
HILMAR LUMBER INC
Also Called: Ace Hardware
8150 Lander Ave, Hilmar (95324-8325)
P.O. Box 310 (95324-0310)
PHONE..................................209 668-8123
Keith Waterson, *CEO*
Arlon Waterson, *CFO*
Jerry Durjava, *Purchasing*
Mary Mendex, *Purchasing*
Janelle Mendes, *Advt Staff*
EMP: 35 **EST:** 1971
SQ FT: 11,600
SALES (est): 13MM **Privately Held**
WEB: www.hilmarlumber.com
SIC: **5031** 5211 5251 Lumber: rough, dressed & finished; lumber & other building materials; builders' hardware

5031 - Lumber, Plywood & Millwork Wholesale County (P-8552)

(P-8552)
HOSKIN & MUIR INC
Also Called: Hmi Cardinal
6611 Preston Ave Ste C, Livermore (94551-5108)
PHONE.................................925 373-1135
Joe Eglin, *Opers Mgr*
Mitchell Goodman, *Sales Staff*
Jonathan Herbst, *Sales Staff*
Stephanie Stratford, *Director*
Mark Schulte, *Manager*
EMP: 35
SALES (corp-wide): 126.7MM **Privately Held**
WEB: www.hmiglass.com
SIC: 5031 Molding, all materials
PA: Hoskin & Muir, Inc.
4795 Shepherdsville Rd
Louisville KY 40218
502 969-4059

(P-8553)
HUMBOLDT REDWOOD COMPANY LLC (HQ)
125 Main St, Scotia (95565)
P.O. Box 712 (95565-0712)
PHONE.................................707 764-4472
Bob Mertz,
Mike Jani,
Marty Olhiser,
EMP: 221 EST: 2008
SALES (est): 382.8MM **Privately Held**
WEB: www.hrcllc.com
SIC: 5031 Lumber: rough, dressed & finished
PA: Mendocino Redwood Company, Llc
850 Kunzler Ranch Rd
Ukiah CA 95482
707 463-5110

(P-8554)
KELLEHER CORPORATION
201 Opportunity St, Sacramento (95838-3258)
PHONE.................................916 561-2860
John Ahlers, *Vice Pres*
Steve Hoffelt, *Sales Staff*
Bill Mattorano, *Sales Staff*
EMP: 46
SALES (corp-wide): 50.1MM **Privately Held**
WEB: www.kelleher.com
SIC: 5031 Lumber: rough, dressed & finished
PA: The Kelleher Corporation
1543 5th Ave
San Rafael CA 94901
415 454-8861

(P-8555)
KELLEHER CORPORATION
10 Grandview Ave, Novato (94945)
PHONE.................................415 898-8440
Kevin Mason, *Manager*
EMP: 46
SALES (corp-wide): 50.1MM **Privately Held**
WEB: www.kelleher.com
SIC: 5031 Lumber: rough, dressed & finished
PA: The Kelleher Corporation
1543 5th Ave
San Rafael CA 94901
415 454-8861

(P-8556)
LOWES HOME CENTERS LLC
7651 N Blackstone Ave, Fresno (93720-4306)
PHONE.................................559 436-6266
Dale Delmanowski, *Manager*
EMP: 119
SQ FT: 136,597
SALES (corp-wide): 89.6B **Publicly Held**
WEB: www.lowes.com
SIC: 5211 5031 5722 5064 Home centers; building materials, exterior; building materials, interior; household appliance stores; electrical appliances, television & radio
HQ: Lowe's Home Centers, Llc
1000 Lowes Blvd
Mooresville NC 28117
336 658-4000

(P-8557)
LOWES HOME CENTERS LLC
3801 Plndale Ave Side Frn Side Frnt, Modesto (95356)
PHONE.................................209 545-7676
Rick Christman, *Branch Mgr*
Luis Nogami, *Merchandising*
EMP: 119
SALES (corp-wide): 89.6B **Publicly Held**
WEB: www.lowes.com
SIC: 5211 5031 5722 5064 Home centers; building materials, exterior; building materials, interior; household appliance stores; electrical appliances, television & radio
HQ: Lowe's Home Centers, Llc
1000 Lowes Blvd
Wilkesboro NC 28117
336 658-4000

(P-8558)
LOWES HOME CENTERS LLC
491 Bay Shore Blvd, San Francisco (94124-1508)
PHONE.................................415 486-8611
Jonathon Schultz, *Store Mgr*
Genevieve Wynsen, *Human Res Mgr*
Henry Chavez, *Sales Staff*
Danny Devore, *Sales Staff*
Brian Piscanio, *Sales Staff*
EMP: 119
SALES (corp-wide): 89.6B **Publicly Held**
WEB: www.lowes.com
SIC: 5211 5031 5722 5064 Home centers; building materials, exterior; building materials, interior; household appliance stores; electrical appliances, television & radio
HQ: Lowe's Home Centers, Llc
1000 Lowes Blvd
Mooresville NC 28117
336 658-4000

(P-8559)
LOWES HOME CENTERS LLC
800 E Bidwell St, Folsom (95630-3350)
PHONE.................................916 984-7979
Dave Ward, *Executive*
Felicia Madrid, *Opers Staff*
Jerry Victoriano, *Sales Staff*
EMP: 119
SALES (corp-wide): 89.6B **Publicly Held**
WEB: www.lowes.com
SIC: 5211 5031 5722 5064 Home centers; building materials, exterior; building materials, interior; household appliance stores; electrical appliances, television & radio
HQ: Lowe's Home Centers, Llc
1000 Lowes Blvd
Mooresville NC 28117
336 658-4000

(P-8560)
LOWES HOME CENTERS LLC
775 Ridder Park Dr, San Jose (95131-2489)
PHONE.................................408 518-4165
EMP: 119
SALES (corp-wide): 89.6B **Publicly Held**
WEB: www.lowes.com
SIC: 5211 5031 5722 5064 Home centers; building materials, exterior; building materials, interior; household appliance stores; electrical appliances, television & radio
HQ: Lowe's Home Centers, Llc
1000 Lowes Blvd
Wilkesboro NC 28117
336 658-4000

(P-8561)
LOWES HOME CENTERS LLC
1751 E Monte Vista Ave, Vacaville (95688-3103)
PHONE.................................707 455-4400
EMP: 119
SALES (corp-wide): 89.6B **Publicly Held**
WEB: www.lowes.com
SIC: 5211 5031 5722 5064 Home centers; building materials, exterior; building materials, interior; household appliance stores; electrical appliances, television & radio
HQ: Lowe's Home Centers, Llc
1000 Lowes Blvd
Mooresville NC 28117
336 658-4000

(P-8562)
LOWES HOME CENTERS LLC
1951 Auto Center Dr, Antioch (94509-3100)
PHONE.................................925 756-0370
Chris Cool, *Manager*
EMP: 119
SALES (corp-wide): 89.6B **Publicly Held**
WEB: www.lowes.com
SIC: 5211 5031 5722 5064 Home centers; building materials, exterior; building materials, interior; household appliance stores; electrical appliances, television & radio
HQ: Lowe's Home Centers, Llc
1000 Lowes Blvd
Wilkesboro NC 28117
336 658-4000

(P-8563)
LOWES HOME CENTERS LLC
32040 Union Lndg, Union City (94587-1769)
PHONE.................................510 476-0600
Nick Perry, *Manager*
EMP: 119
SALES (corp-wide): 89.6B **Publicly Held**
WEB: www.lowes.com
SIC: 5211 5031 7389 Home centers; building materials, exterior; building materials, interior; interior designer
HQ: Lowe's Home Centers, Llc
1000 Lowes Blvd
Mooresville NC 28117
336 658-4000

(P-8564)
LOWES HOME CENTERS LLC
1340 El Camino Real, San Bruno (94066-1304)
PHONE.................................650 616-7800
Chris Marino, *Manager*
EMP: 119
SALES (corp-wide): 89.6B **Publicly Held**
WEB: www.lowes.com
SIC: 5211 5031 5722 5064 Home centers; building materials, exterior; building materials, interior; household appliance stores; electrical appliances, television & radio
HQ: Lowe's Home Centers, Llc
1000 Lowes Blvd
Mooresville NC 28117
336 658-4000

(P-8565)
LOWES HOME CENTERS LLC
10201 Fairway Dr, Roseville (95678-1969)
PHONE.................................916 771-7111
Chris Ralls, *Branch Mgr*
EMP: 119
SALES (corp-wide): 89.6B **Publicly Held**
WEB: www.lowes.com
SIC: 5211 5031 5722 5064 Home centers; building materials, exterior; building materials, interior; household appliance stores; electrical appliances, television & radio
HQ: Lowe's Home Centers, Llc
1000 Lowes Blvd
Mooresville NC 28117
336 658-4000

(P-8566)
LOWES HOME CENTERS LLC
4255 First St, Livermore (94551-4967)
PHONE.................................925 245-2440
Steve Harada, *Manager*
EMP: 119
SALES (corp-wide): 89.6B **Publicly Held**
WEB: www.lowes.com
SIC: 5211 5031 5722 5064 Home centers; building materials, exterior; building materials, interior; household appliance stores; electrical appliances, television & radio
HQ: Lowe's Home Centers, Llc
1000 Lowes Blvd
Mooresville NC 28117
336 658-4000

(P-8567)
LOWES HOME CENTERS LLC
8369 Power Inn Rd, Elk Grove (95624-3464)
PHONE.................................916 688-1922
Barry Wood, *Branch Mgr*
EMP: 119
SALES (corp-wide): 89.6B **Publicly Held**
WEB: www.lowes.com
SIC: 5211 5031 5722 5064 Home centers; building materials, exterior; building materials, interior; household appliance stores; electrical appliances, television & radio
HQ: Lowe's Home Centers, Llc
1000 Lowes Blvd
Mooresville NC 28117
336 658-4000

(P-8568)
LOWES HOME CENTERS LLC
2350 Forest Ave, Chico (95928-7600)
PHONE.................................530 895-5130
Mike Marrs, *Branch Mgr*
EMP: 119
SALES (corp-wide): 89.6B **Publicly Held**
WEB: www.lowes.com
SIC: 5211 5031 5722 5064 Home centers; building materials, exterior; building materials, interior; household appliance stores; electrical appliances, television & radio
HQ: Lowe's Home Centers, Llc
1000 Lowes Blvd
Mooresville NC 28117
336 658-4000

(P-8569)
LOWES HOME CENTERS LLC
3645 E Hammer Ln, Stockton (95212-2823)
PHONE.................................209 956-7200
Rose Rozich, *Branch Mgr*
EMP: 119
SALES (corp-wide): 89.6B **Publicly Held**
WEB: www.lowes.com
SIC: 5211 5031 5722 5064 Home centers; building materials, exterior; building materials, interior; household appliance stores; electrical appliances, television & radio
HQ: Lowe's Home Centers, Llc
1000 Lowes Blvd
Wilkesboro NC 28117
336 658-4000

(P-8570)
LOWES HOME CENTERS LLC
7151 Camino Arroyo, Gilroy (95020-7308)
PHONE.................................408 413-6000
Joe Solis, *Manager*
EMP: 119
SQ FT: 146,682
SALES (corp-wide): 89.6B **Publicly Held**
WEB: www.lowes.com
SIC: 5211 5031 5722 5064 Home centers; building materials, exterior; building materials, interior; household appliance stores; electrical appliances, television & radio
HQ: Lowe's Home Centers, Llc
1000 Lowes Blvd
Mooresville NC 28117
336 658-4000

(P-8571)
LOWES HOME CENTERS LLC
7840 Greenback Ln, Citrus Heights (95610-5910)
PHONE.................................916 728-7800
Ron Latta, *Manager*
Hazel Mapa, *Sales Staff*
EMP: 119
SALES (corp-wide): 89.6B **Publicly Held**
WEB: www.lowes.com
SIC: 5211 5031 5722 5064 Home centers; building materials, exterior; building materials, interior; household appliance stores; electrical appliances, television & radio
HQ: Lowe's Home Centers, Llc
1000 Lowes Blvd
Mooresville NC 28117
336 658-4000

5031 - Lumber, Plywood & Millwork Wholesale County (P-8592)

(P-8572)
LOWES HOME CENTERS LLC
1750 W Olive Ave, Merced (95348-1201)
PHONE 209 385-5000
Terry Stewart, *Manager*
EMP: 119
SALES (corp-wide): 89.6B **Publicly Held**
WEB: www.lowes.com
SIC: 5211 5031 5722 5064 Home centers; building materials, exterior; building materials, interior; household appliance stores; electrical appliances, television & radio
HQ: Lowe's Home Centers, Llc
   1000 Lowes Blvd
   Wilkesboro NC 28117
   336 658-4000

(P-8573)
LOWES HOME CENTERS LLC
875 Shaw Ave, Clovis (93612-3911)
PHONE 559 322-3000
John Metcalf, *Branch Mgr*
EMP: 119
SALES (corp-wide): 89.6B **Publicly Held**
WEB: www.lowes.com
SIC: 5211 5031 5722 5064 Home centers; building materials, exterior; building materials, interior; household appliance stores; electrical appliances, television & radio
HQ: Lowe's Home Centers, Llc
   1000 Lowes Blvd
   Mooresville NC 28117
   336 658-4000

(P-8574)
LOWES HOME CENTERS LLC
1389 S Lwer Sacramento Rd, Lodi (95242)
PHONE 209 339-2600
Erik Hajek, *Manager*
EMP: 119
SALES (corp-wide): 89.6B **Publicly Held**
WEB: www.lowes.com
SIC: 5211 5031 5722 5064 Home centers; building materials, exterior; building materials, interior; household appliance stores; electrical appliances, television & radio
HQ: Lowe's Home Centers, Llc
   1000 Lowes Blvd
   Mooresville NC 28117
   336 658-4000

(P-8575)
LOWES HOME CENTERS LLC
43612 Pcf Commons Blvd, Fremont (94538-3808)
PHONE 510 344-4920
Jason McNutt, *Manager*
EMP: 119
SALES (corp-wide): 89.6B **Publicly Held**
WEB: www.lowes.com
SIC: 5211 5031 5722 5064 Home centers; building materials, exterior; building materials, interior; household appliance stores; electrical appliances, television & radio
HQ: Lowe's Home Centers, Llc
   1000 Lowes Blvd
   Wilkesboro NC 28117
   336 658-4000

(P-8576)
LOWES HOME CENTERS LLC
5503 Lone Tree Way, Antioch (94531-8444)
PHONE 925 779-4560
Kevin Harrison, *Branch Mgr*
Julie Schrader, *Sales Mgr*
EMP: 119
SALES (corp-wide): 89.6B **Publicly Held**
WEB: www.lowes.com
SIC: 5211 5031 5722 5064 Home centers; building materials, exterior; building materials, interior; household appliance stores; electrical appliances, television & radio
HQ: Lowe's Home Centers, Llc
   1000 Lowes Blvd
   Mooresville NC 28117
   336 658-4000

(P-8577)
LOWES HOME CENTERS LLC
10342 Trinity Pkwy, Stockton (95219-7243)
PHONE 209 513-9843
Robert Tedford, *Sales Executive*
EMP: 119
SALES (corp-wide): 89.6B **Publicly Held**
WEB: www.lowes.com
SIC: 5211 5031 5722 5064 Home centers; building materials, exterior; building materials, interior; household appliance stores; electrical appliances, television & radio
HQ: Lowe's Home Centers, Llc
   1000 Lowes Blvd
   Wilkesboro NC 28117
   336 658-4000

(P-8578)
LOWES HOME CENTERS LLC
7921 Redwood Dr, Cotati (94931-3032)
PHONE 707 242-5000
Dave Berlin, *Manager*
EMP: 119
SALES (corp-wide): 89.6B **Publicly Held**
WEB: www.lowes.com
SIC: 5211 5031 5722 5064 Home centers; building materials, exterior; building materials, interior; household appliance stores; electrical appliances, television & radio
HQ: Lowe's Home Centers, Llc
   1000 Lowes Blvd
   Mooresville NC 28117
   336 658-4000

(P-8579)
LOWES HOME CENTERS LLC
12071 Industry Blvd, Jackson (95642-9310)
PHONE 209 223-6140
EMP: 119
SALES (corp-wide): 89.6B **Publicly Held**
WEB: www.lowes.com
SIC: 5211 5031 5722 5064 Home centers; building materials, exterior; building materials, interior; household appliance stores; electrical appliances, television & radio
HQ: Lowe's Home Centers, Llc
   1000 Lowes Blvd
   Mooresville NC 28117
   336 658-4000

(P-8580)
LOWES HOME CENTERS LLC
811 E Arques Ave, Sunnyvale (94085-4523)
PHONE 408 470-1680
Sandy Guerra, *Sales Staff*
EMP: 119
SALES (corp-wide): 89.6B **Publicly Held**
WEB: www.lowes.com
SIC: 5211 5031 5722 5064 Home centers; building materials, exterior; building materials, interior; household appliance stores; electrical appliances, television & radio
HQ: Lowe's Home Centers, Llc
   1000 Lowes Blvd
   Mooresville NC 28117
   336 658-4000

(P-8581)
LOWES HOME CENTERS LLC
1200 E Cypress Ave, Redding (96002-1162)
PHONE 530 351-0181
Kevin Lowe, *Executive*
EMP: 119
SALES (corp-wide): 89.6B **Publicly Held**
WEB: www.lowes.com
SIC: 5211 5031 5722 5064 Home centers; building materials, exterior; building materials, interior; household appliance stores; electrical appliances, television & radio
HQ: Lowe's Home Centers, Llc
   1000 Lowes Blvd
   Mooresville NC 28117
   336 658-4000

(P-8582)
LOWES HOME CENTERS LLC
935 Tharp Rd, Yuba City (95993-8998)
PHONE 530 844-5000
Matt Heichlinger, *Manager*
Jillian Staib, *Department Mgr*
EMP: 119
SALES (corp-wide): 89.6B **Publicly Held**
WEB: www.lowes.com
SIC: 5211 5031 5722 5064 Home centers; building materials, exterior; building materials, interior; household appliance stores; electrical appliances, television & radio
HQ: Lowe's Home Centers, Llc
   1000 Lowes Blvd
   Mooresville NC 28117
   336 658-4000

(P-8583)
LOWES HOME CENTERS LLC
3303 Entertainment Way, Turlock (95380-8437)
PHONE 209 656-3020
Rick Christman, *Manager*
Scott Miller, *Office Mgr*
EMP: 119
SALES (corp-wide): 89.6B **Publicly Held**
WEB: www.lowes.com
SIC: 5211 5031 5722 5064 Home centers; building materials, exterior; building materials, interior; household appliance stores; electrical appliances, television & radio
HQ: Lowe's Home Centers, Llc
   1000 Lowes Blvd
   Wilkesboro NC 28117
   336 658-4000

(P-8584)
LOWES HOME CENTERS LLC
3251 Zinfandel Dr, Rancho Cordova (95670-6378)
PHONE 916 267-2850
Randy Sergeant, *Branch Mgr*
EMP: 119
SALES (corp-wide): 89.6B **Publicly Held**
WEB: www.lowes.com
SIC: 5211 5031 5722 5064 Home centers; building materials, exterior; building materials, interior; household appliance stores; electrical appliances, television & radio
HQ: Lowe's Home Centers, Llc
   1000 Lowes Blvd
   Wilkesboro NC 28117
   336 658-4000

(P-8585)
LOWES HOME CENTERS LLC
3750 Dublin Blvd, Dublin (94568-7352)
PHONE 925 241-3082
Sly Renard, *General Mgr*
EMP: 119
SALES (corp-wide): 89.6B **Publicly Held**
WEB: www.lowes.com
SIC: 5211 5031 5722 5064 Home centers; building materials, exterior; building materials, interior; household appliance stores; electrical appliances, television & radio
HQ: Lowe's Home Centers, Llc
   1000 Lowes Blvd
   Wilkesboro NC 28117
   336 658-4000

(P-8586)
LOWES HOME CENTERS LLC
2100 W Cleveland Ave, Madera (93637-8756)
PHONE 559 416-4000
Jay Mahabir, *Branch Mgr*
EMP: 119
SALES (corp-wide): 89.6B **Publicly Held**
WEB: www.lowes.com
SIC: 5211 5031 5722 5064 Home centers; building materials, exterior; building materials, interior; household appliance stores; electrical appliances, television & radio
HQ: Lowe's Home Centers, Llc
   1000 Lowes Blvd
   Wilkesboro NC 28117
   336 658-4000

(P-8587)
LOWES HOME CENTERS LLC
1935 Arnold Indus Way, Concord (94520-5312)
PHONE 925 566-9000
EMP: 119
SALES (corp-wide): 89.6B **Publicly Held**
WEB: www.lowes.com
SIC: 5211 5031 5722 5064 Home centers; building materials, exterior; building materials, interior; household appliance stores; electrical appliances, television & radio
HQ: Lowe's Home Centers, Llc
   1000 Lowes Blvd
   Wilkesboro NC 28117
   336 658-4000

(P-8588)
M J&C HOLDING INC
Also Called: Wayside Lumber
11277 Trade Center Dr, Rancho Cordova (95742-6223)
PHONE 916 635-9090
James McVey, *CEO*
Robin Infausto, *Office Mgr*
Cheryl McVey, *Admin Sec*
EMP: 46 EST: 1999
SQ FT: 22,000
SALES (est): 12.2MM **Privately Held**
WEB: www.waysidelumber.com
SIC: 5211 5031 Lumber products; lumber: rough, dressed & finished

(P-8589)
MEDALLION INDUSTRIES INC
4771 Arroyo Vis Ste F, Livermore (94551-4847)
PHONE 925 449-9040
Jay Deyo, *Branch Mgr*
EMP: 15
SALES (corp-wide): 12.4MM **Privately Held**
WEB: www.medallionindustries.com
SIC: 5031 2421 2421 Windows; window frames, all materials; millwork; sawmills & planing mills, general
PA: Medallion Industries, Inc.
   3221 Nw Yeon Ave
   Portland OR 97210
   503 221-0170

(P-8590)
MENDOCINO FOREST PDTS CO LLC
Also Called: Sawmill
850 Kunzler Ranch Rd, Ukiah (95482-7294)
P.O. Box 996 (95482-0996)
PHONE 707 468-1431
Dean Kerstetter, *Exec VP*
EMP: 200
SALES (corp-wide): 134.9MM **Privately Held**
WEB: www.mfp.com
SIC: 5031 2421 2499 Lumber: rough, dressed & finished; fencing, wood; sawmills & planing mills, general; fencing, docks & other outdoor wood structural products
PA: Mendocino Forest Products Company Llc
   3700 Old Redwood Hwy # 200
   Santa Rosa CA 95403
   707 620-2961

(P-8591)
MENDOCINO FOREST PDTS CO LLC (PA)
3700 Old Redwood Hwy # 200, Santa Rosa (95403-5739)
P.O. Box 390, Calpella (95418-0390)
PHONE 707 620-2961
Sandy Dean, *CEO*
John Russell, *President*
Bob Mertz, *CEO*
Jim Pelkey, *CFO*
EMP: 400
SQ FT: 5,000
SALES (est): 134.9MM **Privately Held**
WEB: www.mfp.com
SIC: 5031 2421 Lumber: rough, dressed & finished; sawmills & planing mills, general

(P-8592)
MENDOCINO FOREST PDTS CO LLC
Also Called: Calpella Distribution Center
6375 N State St, Calpella (95418)
P.O. Box 336 (95418-0336)
PHONE 707 485-6800

5031 - Lumber, Plywood & Millwork Wholesale County (P-8593)

Mike Benetti, *Branch Mgr*
EMP: 39
SALES (corp-wide): 134.9MM **Privately Held**
WEB: www.mfp.com
SIC: 5031 2421 Lumber: rough, dressed & finished; sawmills & planing mills, general
PA: Mendocino Forest Products Company Llc
3700 Old Redwood Hwy # 200
Santa Rosa CA 95403
707 620-2961

(P-8593)
MENDOCINO FOREST PDTS CO LLC
1360 19th Hole Dr Ste 200, Windsor (95492-7717)
PHONE 707 620-2961
EMP: 39
SALES (corp-wide): 134.9MM **Privately Held**
WEB: www.mfp.com
SIC: 5031 2421 Lumber: rough, dressed & finished; sawmills & planing mills, general
PA: Mendocino Forest Products Company Llc
3700 Old Redwood Hwy # 200
Santa Rosa CA 95403
707 620-2961

(P-8594)
MENDOCINO REDWOOD COMPANY LLC (PA)
850 Kunzler Ranch Rd, Ukiah (95482-7294)
P.O. Box 996 (95482-0996)
PHONE 707 463-5110
Richard Higgenbottom, *Mng Member*
Michael Jani,
Jim Pelkey,
EMP: 40 **EST:** 1998
SALES (est): 382.8MM **Privately Held**
WEB: www.hrcllc.com
SIC: 5031 Lumber: rough, dressed & finished; kitchen cabinets

(P-8595)
MILGARD MANUFACTURING LLC
Also Called: Milgard Windows
6050 88th St, Sacramento (95828-1119)
PHONE 916 387-0700
Bert Dimauro, *Branch Mgr*
Stanley Chiu, *Sales Staff*
Tom Munoz, *Sales Staff*
Erika Bonnett, *Manager*
David Glenn, *Manager*
EMP: 179
SALES (corp-wide): 822.1MM **Privately Held**
WEB: www.milgard.com
SIC: 5031 Windows
HQ: Milgard Manufacturing Llc
1010 54th Ave E
Tacoma WA 98424
253 922-4343

(P-8596)
MINTON DOOR COMPANY (PA)
1150 Elko Dr, Sunnyvale (94089-2207)
PHONE 650 961-9800
Allen Minton, *President*
Richard Minton, *CEO*
Tony Lew, *COO*
Joe Turner, *COO*
Nancy Minton, *CFO*
EMP: 23 **EST:** 1992
SQ FT: 100,000
SALES (est): 10.9MM **Privately Held**
WEB: www.mintondoor.com
SIC: 5031 5072 3429 2431 Doors; door frames, all materials; hardware; manufactured hardware (general); millwork

(P-8597)
NANA WALL SYSTEMS INC
100 Madowcreek Dr Ste 250, Corte Madera (94925)
PHONE 415 383-3148
Ebrahim M Nana, *President*
Ilyas Nana, *Treasurer*
Ahmad M Nana, *Vice Pres*
Taha Nana, *Vice Pres*
Ozair Nana, *Admin Sec*
◆ **EMP:** 47 **EST:** 1989

SQ FT: 10,000
SALES (est): 20.7MM **Privately Held**
WEB: www.nanawall.com
SIC: 5031 Windows

(P-8598)
NU FOREST PRODUCTS INC
280 Asti Rd, Cloverdale (95425)
P.O. Box 189 (95425-0189)
PHONE 707 433-3313
Douglas Hart, *CEO*
Bruce Brogden, *CFO*
Thomas Alexander, *Mill Mgr*
Liane Mills, *Sales Staff*
Roz Pierce, *Sales Staff*
▲ **EMP:** 73 **EST:** 1971
SALES (est): 23.5MM **Privately Held**
WEB: www.iwpllc.com
SIC: 5031 Lumber: rough, dressed & finished
PA: International Building Materials Llc
14421 Se 98th Ct
Clackamas OR 97015

(P-8599)
OAKLAND PALLET COMPANY INC (PA)
2500 Grant Ave, San Lorenzo (94580-1810)
PHONE 510 278-1291
Jose G Padilla, *President*
Javier Padilla, *Treasurer*
Carlos Padilla, *Vice Pres*
Graciela Padilla, *Sales Staff*
Manuel Padilla, *Sales Staff*
EMP: 130
SALES (est): 45.1MM **Privately Held**
WEB: www.oaklandpallet.com
SIC: 5031 7699 Pallets, wood; pallet repair

(P-8600)
OREGON PCF BLDG PDTS CALIF INC
Also Called: Orepac Building Products
8185 Signal Ct Ste A, Sacramento (95824-2354)
PHONE 916 381-8051
John Dutter, *Manager*
Cesar Moreno, *Manager*
EMP: 88
SALES (corp-wide): 322.9MM **Privately Held**
SIC: 5031 Building materials, exterior; building materials, interior; lumber: rough, dressed & finished; millwork
HQ: Oregon Pacific Building Products (Calif.), Inc.
30170 Sw Ore Pac Ave
Wilsonville OR 97070
503 685-5499

(P-8601)
PACIFIC COAST CONTG SPC INC
946 N Market Blvd, Sacramento (95834-1268)
PHONE 916 929-3100
Heather Lim, *President*
Sonny Kooner, *Admin Sec*
David McNellis,
Darren Morris,
Robert Rivinius,
EMP: 51 **EST:** 2008
SALES (est): 10.2MM
SALES (corp-wide): 1.1B **Privately Held**
WEB: www.paccoast.com
SIC: 5031 1761 1742 1799 Lumber, plywood & millwork; roofing contractor; plastering, drywall & insulation; coating, caulking & weather, water & fireproofing; garage door, installation or erection
HQ: Pacific Coast Building Services, Inc.
946 N Market Blvd
Sacramento CA 95834

(P-8602)
PACIFIC COAST SUPPLY LLC (HQ)
4290 Roseville Rd, North Highlands (95660-5710)
PHONE 916 971-2301
Curt Gomes, *President*

Lisa Goeppner, *CFO*
Walter Payne, *Bd of Directors*
Joe Gower, *Vice Pres*
Nina Tran, *Accounting Mgr*
EMP: 454 **EST:** 2001
SALES (est): 575.2MM
SALES (corp-wide): 1.1B **Privately Held**
WEB: www.paccoastsupply.com
SIC: 5031 Lumber, plywood & millwork
PA: Pacific Coast Building Products, Inc.
10600 White Rock Rd # 100
Rancho Cordova CA 95670
916 631-6500

(P-8603)
PJS LUMBER INC
Also Called: P J'S Construction Supplies
45055 Fremont Blvd, Fremont (94538-6318)
PHONE 510 743-5300
Shane McMillan, *CEO*
Carlton J McMillan, *President*
Terry W Protto, *CEO*
Jeff Veilleux, *COO*
Roberto De Lara, *Project Mgr*
EMP: 145
SQ FT: 2,000
SALES (est): 82.1MM **Privately Held**
WEB: www.pjsrebar.com
SIC: 5031 5051 Lumber: rough, dressed & finished; steel

(P-8604)
RONBOW CORPORATION
7150 Patterson Pass Rd F, Livermore (94550-9507)
PHONE 510 713-1188
Jason Chen, *President*
Theresa Chen, *CFO*
Stuart Stanton, *Exec VP*
Rene Derose, *Vice Pres*
Peiru Guo, *Business Anlyst*
◆ **EMP:** 38 **EST:** 2002
SALES (est): 20.1MM **Privately Held**
WEB: www.ronbow.com
SIC: 5031 Kitchen cabinets

(P-8605)
ROYAL PLYWOOD COMPANY LLC
6003 88th St Ste 100, Sacramento (95828-1143)
P.O. Box 728, La Mirada (90637-0728)
PHONE 916 426-3292
Gabriel N Marshi, *Mng Member*
Sally Hicks, *Manager*
EMP: 78
SALES (corp-wide): 62.2MM **Privately Held**
WEB: www.royalplywood.com
SIC: 5031 Lumber: rough, dressed & finished
PA: Royal Plywood Company, Llc
14171 Park Pl
Cerritos CA 90703
562 404-2989

(P-8606)
SCARBOROUGH LBR & BLDG SUP INC (PA)
Also Called: Ace Hardware
20 El Pueblo Rd, Scotts Valley (95066-3505)
P.O. Box 66599 (95067-6599)
PHONE 831 438-0331
Alvin L Scarborough, *CEO*
Linda Gilbert, *Vice Pres*
Mike Scarborough, *Vice Pres*
EMP: 40 **EST:** 1968
SQ FT: 12,500
SALES (est): 12.7MM **Privately Held**
WEB: www.scarboroughlumber.com
SIC: 5251 5031 Hardware; lumber, plywood & millwork

(P-8607)
SIERRA PT LBR & PLYWD CO INC (PA)
601 Tunnel Ave, Brisbane (94005-1106)
PHONE 415 468-1000
Lee P Nobmann, *President*
EMP: 67 **EST:** 1980
SQ FT: 16,000

SALES (est): 8.2MM **Privately Held**
WEB: www.goldenstatelumber.com
SIC: 5211 5031 Lumber products; lumber: rough, dressed & finished

(P-8608)
SILVERADO BUILDING MTLS INC (PA)
Also Called: Thompson Bldg Mtls Sacramento
9297 Jackson Rd, Sacramento (95826-9710)
PHONE 916 361-7374
Kenneth R Thompson, *CEO*
Leonard Crabtree, *President*
Joe Barkley, *General Mgr*
Jamie Hildebrand, *Office Mgr*
Israel Villarreal, *Purch Agent*
EMP: 37 **EST:** 1992
SQ FT: 18,000
SALES (est): 23MM **Privately Held**
WEB: www.silveradobldg.com
SIC: 5031 5032 Wallboard; plastering materials

(P-8609)
SUPER PALLET RECYCLING CORP (PA)
Also Called: Super Pallet Recycling Center
10401 Grant Line Rd, Elk Grove (95624-9404)
P.O. Box 1832 (95759-1832)
PHONE 916 686-1700
Gyan Kalwani, *President*
Kenneth D Holer, *Vice Pres*
EMP: 78 **EST:** 1994
SALES (est): 10.3MM **Privately Held**
SIC: 5031 Pallets, wood

(P-8610)
TRINITY RIVER LUMBER COMPANY (PA)
1375 Main St, Weaverville (96093)
P.O. Box 249 (96093-0249)
PHONE 530 623-5561
Frank A Schmidbauer, *CEO*
Dee Sanders, *Vice Pres*
Alex Cousins, *District Mgr*
Mike Shorten, *Sales Staff*
▲ **EMP:** 145 **EST:** 1983
SQ FT: 10,000
SALES (est): 26.9MM **Privately Held**
WEB: www.trinityriverlumbercompany.com
SIC: 5031 Lumber: rough, dressed & finished

(P-8611)
USG INTERIORS LLC
2575 Loomis Rd, Stockton (95205-8045)
PHONE 209 466-4636
Sandy Hirzel, *Manager*
EMP: 342
SALES (corp-wide): 10.7B **Privately Held**
WEB: www.usg.com
SIC: 5031 Building materials, exterior
HQ: Usg Interiors, Llc
125 S Franklin St
Chicago IL 60606
800 874-4968

(P-8612)
WESTERN BUYERS LLC (PA)
Also Called: Meek's Lumber & Hardware
1030 Winding Creek Rd, Roseville (95678-7045)
PHONE 916 576-3042
Carrie O'Brien Meek, *President*
William C Meek, *President*
Lois Parson, *Treasurer*
Jill Reynolds, *Corp Secy*
Terry O Meek, *Vice Pres*
EMP: 40 **EST:** 1964
SALES (est): 29MM **Privately Held**
SIC: 5031 Lumber: rough, dressed & finished

(P-8613)
WESTERN WOODS INC (PA)
275 Sikorsky Ave, Chico (95973-9049)
P.O. Box 4402 (95927-4402)
PHONE 530 343-5821
Gerald K Richter, *President*
Linda Yale, *Info Tech Mgr*
Bill Weaver, *IT/INT Sup*
Scott Brewer, *Sales Staff*
Kevin Richter, *Sales Staff*

▲ = Import ▼ = Export
◆ = Import/Export

PRODUCTS & SERVICES SECTION
5032 - Brick, Stone & Related Construction Mtrls Wholesale County (P-8635)

◆ **EMP:** 44 **EST:** 1971
SQ FT: 25,000
SALES (est): 32.1MM **Privately Held**
WEB: www.westernwoodsinc.com
SIC: 5031 Lumber: rough, dressed & finished

5032 Brick, Stone & Related Construction Mtrls Wholesale

(P-8614)
A TEICHERT & SON INC (HQ)
Also Called: Teichert Construction
5200 Franklin Dr Ste 115, Pleasanton (94588-3363)
P.O. Box 15002, Sacramento (95851-0002)
PHONE.................................916 484-3011
Judson T Riggs, *President*
Dana M Davis, *President*
Kenneth A Kayser, *President*
Narendra M Pathipati, *CFO*
Terri A Bakken, *Vice Pres*
▼ **EMP:** 1016 **EST:** 1887
SALES (est): 798.7MM
SALES (corp-wide): 842MM **Privately Held**
WEB: www.teichert.com
SIC: 5032 3273 1611 1442 Brick, stone & related material; ready-mixed concrete; highway & street construction; construction sand & gravel; single-family housing construction
PA: Teichert, Inc.
5200 Franklin Dr Ste 115
Pleasanton CA 94588
916 484-3011

(P-8615)
ADVANCED COMPANIES INC
Also Called: Advanced Asphalt
40165 Trk Arpt Rd 30, Truckee (96161-4113)
P.O. Box 2602 (96160-2602)
PHONE.................................530 582-0800
Jerry T Bellon, *President*
Jerome D Krug Jr, *Vice Pres*
EMP: 40 **EST:** 1992
SQ FT: 1,800
SALES (est): 8.5MM **Privately Held**
SIC: 5032 Paving mixtures

(P-8616)
ALPHA GRANITE & MARBLE INC
2303 Merced St, San Leandro (94577-4208)
PHONE.................................303 373-4911
Kevin Murphy, *President*
Brian Geasa, *CFO*
Suzanne Morosoli, *Admin Sec*
EMP: 39 **EST:** 1990
SQ FT: 43,000
SALES (est): 576.6K **Privately Held**
WEB: www.alphagranite.com
SIC: 5032 5211 Building stone; masonry materials & supplies

(P-8617)
ANTIOCH BUILDING MATERIALS CO (PA)
Also Called: A B M
1375 California Ave, Pittsburg (94565-4119)
P.O. Box 870, Antioch (94509-0086)
PHONE.................................925 432-0171
Niels Larsen, *CEO*
Susan Larsen, *President*
EMP: 24 **EST:** 1920
SQ FT: 4,000
SALES (est): 10MM **Privately Held**
WEB: www.antiochbuilding.com
SIC: 5032 3273 Asphalt mixture; ready-mixed concrete

(P-8618)
ARIZONA TILE LLC
11115 Folsom Blvd, Rancho Cordova (95670-6463)
PHONE.................................916 853-0100
Jon Hulshoff, *Branch Mgr*
Chris Anda, *Manager*
EMP: 35

SALES (corp-wide): 263MM **Privately Held**
WEB: www.arizonatile.com
SIC: 5211 5032 Tile, ceramic; tile, clay or other ceramic, excluding refractory
PA: Arizona Tile, L.L.C.
8829 S Priest Dr
Tempe AZ 85284
480 893-9393

(P-8619)
ARIZONA TILE LLC
10576 Industrial Ave, Roseville (95678-6212)
PHONE.................................916 782-3200
John Williams, *Manager*
Joshua McCord,
EMP: 35
SALES (corp-wide): 263MM **Privately Held**
WEB: www.arizonatile.com
SIC: 5211 5032 3253 Tile, ceramic; ceramic wall & floor tile; ceramic wall & floor tile
PA: Arizona Tile, L.L.C.
8829 S Priest Dr
Tempe AZ 85284
480 893-9393

(P-8620)
CALAVERAS MATERIALS INC
2095 E Central Ave, Fresno (93725-2708)
PHONE.................................559 233-2311
Jeff Rash, *Office Mgr*
EMP: 37
SALES (corp-wide): 20.8B **Privately Held**
SIC: 5211 5032 Sand & gravel; paving materials
HQ: Calaveras Materials Inc.
1100 Lowe Rd
Hughson CA 95326
209 883-0448

(P-8621)
CEMEX CNSTR MTLS PCF LLC
Also Called: Aggregate Clayton Quarry
515 Mitchell Canyon Rd, Clayton (94517-1529)
PHONE.................................925 672-4900
George J Allen, *Branch Mgr*
EMP: 42 **Privately Held**
SIC: 5032 3271 Cement; concrete block & brick
HQ: Cemex Construction Materials Pacific, Llc
1501 Belvedere Rd
West Palm Beach FL 33406
561 833-5555

(P-8622)
CEMEX CORP
22101 W Sunset Ave, Los Banos (93635-9683)
PHONE.................................800 992-3639
EMP: 129 **Privately Held**
WEB: www.cemex.com
SIC: 5032 3273 Cement; ready-mixed concrete
HQ: Cemex Corp.
4646 E Van Buren St # 25
Phoenix AZ 85008
602 416-2600

(P-8623)
CEMEX CORP
808 Gilman St, Berkeley (94710-1422)
PHONE.................................800 992-3639
EMP: 129 **Privately Held**
WEB: www.cemex.com
SIC: 5032 3273 Cement; ready-mixed concrete
HQ: Cemex Corp.
4646 E Van Buren St # 25
Phoenix AZ 85008
602 416-2600

(P-8624)
CLARK - PACIFIC CORPORATION (PA)
Also Called: Clark Pacific
710 Riverpoint Ct Ste 100, West Sacramento (95605-1690)
PHONE.................................916 371-0305
Robert Clark, *President*
Don Clark, *President*
Aaron Alhady, *General Mgr*

Tom Anderson, *General Mgr*
Terry Street, *General Mgr*
▲ **EMP:** 300 **EST:** 1966
SALES (est): 243.7MM **Privately Held**
WEB: www.clarkpacific.com
SIC: 5032 3272 Brick, stone & related material; concrete products, precast

(P-8625)
ELEGANT SURFACES
3640 Amrcn Rver Dr Ste 15, Sacramento (95864)
P.O. Box 705, Byron (94514-0705)
PHONE.................................209 823-9388
John Polimeno, *CEO*
Dan Thompson, *President*
Kristie Polimeno, *Vice Pres*
▲ **EMP:** 26 **EST:** 1967
SQ FT: 48,000
SALES (est): 2.7MM **Privately Held**
WEB: www.elegantsurfaces.com
SIC: 5032 3281 Marble building stone; marble, building: cut & shaped

(P-8626)
GRANITE ROCK CO
303 Coral St, Santa Cruz (95060-2106)
PHONE.................................831 471-3440
Jim Holnquist, *General Mgr*
EMP: 42
SALES (corp-wide): 390.3MM **Privately Held**
WEB: www.graniterock.com
SIC: 5032 Brick, stone & related material
PA: Granite Rock Co.
350 Technology Dr
Watsonville CA 95076
831 768-2000

(P-8627)
GRANITE ROCK CO
540 W Beach St, Watsonville (95076-5125)
P.O. Box 50001 (95077-5001)
PHONE.................................831 724-3847
Mark Trainer, *Manager*
Jalyssa Rodriguez, *Office Admin*
EMP: 42
SALES (corp-wide): 390.3MM **Privately Held**
WEB: www.graniterock.com
SIC: 5032 Brick, stone & related material
PA: Granite Rock Co.
350 Technology Dr
Watsonville CA 95076
831 768-2000

(P-8628)
HEATH CERAMICS LTD
101 The Embarcadero, San Francisco (94105-1216)
PHONE.................................415 399-9284
Michael Annth, *Branch Mgr*
EMP: 40
SALES (corp-wide): 22.7MM **Privately Held**
WEB: www.heathceramics.com
SIC: 5719 5032 Bath accessories; tile & clay products
PA: Heath Ceramics, Ltd.
400 Gate 5 Rd
Sausalito CA 94965
415 332-3732

(P-8629)
LYNGSO GARDEN MATERIALS INC
345 Shoreway Rd, San Carlos (94070-2708)
PHONE.................................650 364-1730
Theresa Lyngso, *President*
Theresa N Lyngso, *CFO*
James Kolter, *Vice Pres*
Linda K Lyngso, *Vice Pres*
Pamela Parkinson, *Admin Sec*
▲ **EMP:** 50 **EST:** 1950
SALES (est): 24.6MM **Privately Held**
WEB: www.lyngsogarden.com
SIC: 5032 5261 5211 5191 Brick, stone & related material; nurseries & garden centers; lumber & other building materials; greenhouse equipment & supplies

(P-8630)
MILPITAS MATERIALS COMPANY
1125 N Milpitas Blvd, Milpitas (95035-3152)
P.O. Box 360003 (95036-0003)
PHONE.................................650 969-4401
Jon B Minnis, *President*
Val Fisher, *Vice Pres*
Gretchen Hill, *Manager*
Rita Minnis, *Manager*
EMP: 20 **EST:** 1954
SQ FT: 1,000
SALES (est): 8.2MM **Privately Held**
WEB: www.milpitasmaterials.com
SIC: 5032 5211 3273 Concrete mixtures; concrete & cinder block; ready-mixed concrete

(P-8631)
PAREX USA INC
Alta Building Materials
111290 S Vallejo Ct, French Camp (95231)
P.O. Box 2399, Oakland (94614-0399)
PHONE.................................510 444-2497
Steve Horn, *Opers-Prdtn-Mfg*
EMP: 15
SQ FT: 66,000
SALES (corp-wide): 8.6B **Privately Held**
WEB: www.parexusa.com
SIC: 5032 3299 Brick, stone & related material; stucco
HQ: Parex Usa, Inc.
2150 Eastridge Ave
Riverside CA 92507
714 778-2266

(P-8632)
RAILWAY DISTRIBUTING INC
Also Called: Foundation Building Material
675 Emory St, San Jose (95110-1824)
PHONE.................................408 280-7625
Joe Salvador, *President*
Narda Salvador, *Vice Pres*
Gary Mazzurco, *Sales Executive*
Eric Lorenzo, *Sales Staff*
Kai Markee, *Sales Staff*
EMP: 50 **EST:** 1978
SQ FT: 2,000
SALES (est): 8.9MM **Privately Held**
WEB: www.fbmsales.com
SIC: 5032 5033 Drywall materials; insulation, thermal

(P-8633)
SACRAMENTO STUCCO CO
Also Called: Western Blended Products
1550 Parkway Blvd, West Sacramento (95691-5009)
P.O. Box 981088 (95798-1088)
PHONE.................................916 372-7442
Lewis Winchell, *CEO*
Walter Rozewski, *Corp Secy*
Pat Marshall, *Office Mgr*
Manuel Herrera, *Accountant*
Matt Boker, *Manager*
◆ **EMP:** 28
SQ FT: 55,000
SALES (est): 13.1MM **Privately Held**
WEB: www.sacramentostucco.com
SIC: 5032 2851 Stucco; paints & allied products

(P-8634)
SEQUOIA STEEL AND SUPPLY CO
Also Called: Eagle Building Materials
1407 N Clark St, Fresno (93703-3615)
PHONE.................................559 485-4100
Tom Graves, *President*
Carol Summers, *Vice Pres*
Sal Lopez, *Manager*
EMP: 15 **EST:** 1958
SQ FT: 12,000
SALES (est): 1.4MM **Privately Held**
SIC: 5211 5032 3299 Masonry materials & supplies; cement; sand & gravel; lime & plaster; stucco; cement; sand, construction; lime, except agricultural; mica products

(P-8635)
SOUTHERNCARLSON INC
801 Striker Ave, Sacramento (95834-1115)
PHONE.................................916 375-8322

5032 - Brick, Stone & Related Construction Mtrls Wholesale

Vinnie Villano, *President*
EMP: 16 **Privately Held**
WEB: www.southerncarlson.com
SIC: 5032 3429 Brick, stone & related material; builders' hardware
HQ: Southerncarlson, Inc.
10840 Harney St
Omaha NE 68154

(P-8636)
TRIANGLE ROCK PRODUCT INC
Also Called: Triangle Rock Products
22101 W Sunset Ave, Los Banos (93635-9683)
P.O. Box 1111 (93635-1111)
PHONE 209 826-5066
Don James, *Principal*
EMP: 231 **EST:** 1945
SALES (est): 13MM **Publicly Held**
SIC: 5032 3273 5211 Brick, stone & related material; ready-mixed concrete; lumber & other building materials
HQ: Calmat Co.
500 N Brand Blvd Ste 500 # 500
Glendale CA 91203
818 553-8821

(P-8637)
U S TECHNICAL CERAMICS INC
15400 Concord Cir, Morgan Hill (95037-5428)
PHONE 408 779-0303
Walt Carbonell, *CEO*
Joe Escobedo, *Vice Pres*
▲ **EMP:** 40 **EST:** 1987
SQ FT: 30,000
SALES (est): 8.1MM **Privately Held**
WEB: www.ustc.net
SIC: 5032 3677 3264 Ceramic construction materials, excluding refractory; electronic coils, transformers & other inductors; porcelain electrical supplies

(P-8638)
UNITED STATES GYPSUM COMPANY
2049 Senter Rd, San Jose (95112-2600)
PHONE 408 279-3001
Paul Clark, *Branch Mgr*
EMP: 105
SALES (corp-wide): 10.7B **Privately Held**
WEB: www.usg.com
SIC: 5032 Drywall materials
HQ: United States Gypsum Company
550 W Adams St Ste 1300
Chicago IL 60661
312 606-4000

5033 Roofing, Siding & Insulation Mtrls Wholesale

(P-8639)
BURLINGAME INDUSTRIES INC
Also Called: Eagle Roofing Products
4555 Mckinley Ave, Stockton (95206-4008)
PHONE 209 464-9001
Hersch Beahm, *Manager*
Mark Lowrey, *Representative*
EMP: 192
SALES (corp-wide): 120.4MM **Privately Held**
WEB: www.eagleroofing.com
SIC: 5033 Roofing, siding & insulation
PA: Burlingame Industries, Incorporated
3546 N Riverside Ave
Rialto CA 92377
909 355-7000

(P-8640)
OWENS CORNING SALES LLC
960 Central Expy, Santa Clara (95050-2665)
PHONE 408 235-1351
Chris Rukman, *Branch Mgr*
Alan Renner, *QC Mgr*
Kevin Hatten, *Sales Staff*
EMP: 400 **Publicly Held**
WEB: www.owenscorning.com
SIC: 5033 3296 Fiberglass building materials; mineral wool
HQ: Owens Corning Sales, Llc
1 Owens Corning Pkwy
Toledo OH 43659
419 248-8000

(P-8641)
TRI-VALLEY SUPPLY INC (HQ)
Also Called: Tri Valley Wholesale
39300 Civic Center Dr # 300, Fremont (94538-2338)
PHONE 510 494-9982
James P Petersen, *President*
Joe Dean, *Vice Pres*
David Van Beek, *Vice Pres*
▲ **EMP:** 85 **EST:** 1993
SQ FT: 15,000
SALES (est): 20MM **Privately Held**
WEB: www.trivalleysupply.com
SIC: 5033 Roofing & siding materials

5039 Construction Materials, NEC Wholesale

(P-8642)
COASTAL CONSTRUCTION SVCS LLC
1633 Industrial Pkwy W, Hayward (94544-7046)
PHONE 510 785-9220
Bruce E Green, *Mng Member*
EMP: 35 **EST:** 2014
SALES (est): 2.8MM **Privately Held**
SIC: 5039 1521 1799 Construction materials; single-family housing construction; kitchen cabinet installation

(P-8643)
DONS MOBILE GLASS INC (PA)
Also Called: Wardrobe and Bath Specialties
3800 Finch Rd, Modesto (95357-4100)
PHONE 209 548-7000
Stephen W Mort, *President*
Robert Serpa, *CFO*
Bill Manuel, *Vice Pres*
Clinton Mort, *Admin Sec*
Jacques Navant, *Technical Staff*
▲ **EMP:** 60 **EST:** 1960
SQ FT: 60,000
SALES (est): 33.8MM **Privately Held**
WEB: www.donsmobileglass.com
SIC: 5231 5039 Glass; glass construction materials; exterior flat glass: plate or window; interior flat glass: plate or window

(P-8644)
GLASS & SASH INC (PA)
425 Irwin St, San Rafael (94901-5112)
PHONE 415 456-2240
Fariborz Arfaian, *President*
Tom Hess, *Vice Pres*
Arlene Phillips, *Admin Sec*
▲ **EMP:** 23 **EST:** 1958
SQ FT: 100,000
SALES (est): 4.9MM **Privately Held**
WEB: www.glassandsash.com
SIC: 5039 3231 5231 1793 Glass construction materials; products of purchased glass; doors, glass: made from purchased glass; glass; glass & glazing work

(P-8645)
JENSEN ENTERPRISES INC
Also Called: Jensen Precast
5400 Raley Blvd, Sacramento (95838-1700)
PHONE 916 992-8301
Mark Voiselle, *General Mgr*
Miles Bennett, *President*
Digna Barton, *Sales Staff*
Brian Burton, *Sales Staff*
Jay Devries, *Sales Staff*
EMP: 70
SALES (corp-wide): 237.2MM **Privately Held**
WEB: www.jensenprecast.com
SIC: 5039 5211 Septic tanks; masonry materials & supplies
PA: Jensen Enterprises, Inc.
9895 Double R Blvd
Reno NV 89521
775 352-2700

(P-8646)
SECURITY CONTRACTOR SVCS INC (PA)
Also Called: S C S
5339 Jackson St, North Highlands (95660-5004)
PHONE 916 338-4200
Barry J Marrs, *CEO*
John Goodman, *Branch Mgr*
Steve Mann, *Branch Mgr*
Ron Meyer, *Branch Mgr*
Barry Figel, *General Mgr*
EMP: 60 **EST:** 1961
SQ FT: 50,000
SALES (est): 50MM **Privately Held**
WEB: www.scsfence.com
SIC: 5039 7359 3315 Wire fence, gates & accessories; equipment rental & leasing; steel wire & related products

(P-8647)
SOUTHGATE GLASS & SCREEN INC (PA)
6852 Franklin Blvd, Sacramento (95823-1810)
PHONE 916 476-8396
Scott Davis, *President*
Tim Wolhart, *Division Mgr*
Dave Megarry, *General Mgr*
Stacy Kramer, *Marketing Staff*
Brian Moen, *Manager*
EMP: 50
SQ FT: 5,000
SALES (est): 10MM **Privately Held**
WEB: www.southgateglass.com
SIC: 5039 5231 Glass construction materials; glass

(P-8648)
SOUTHGATE GLASS & SCREEN INC
6199 Warehouse Way, Sacramento (95826-4907)
PHONE 916 476-8396
Dave Megeary, *Branch Mgr*
Jim Boller, *Project Mgr*
EMP: 50
SALES (corp-wide): 10MM **Privately Held**
WEB: www.southgateglass.com
SIC: 5039 5231 Glass construction materials; glass
PA: Southgate Glass & Screen, Inc.
6852 Franklin Blvd
Sacramento CA 95823
916 476-8396

(P-8649)
VAN DUERR INDUSTRIES INC
Also Called: Safe Path Products
21 Valley Ct, Chico (95973-0171)
PHONE 530 893-1596
Timothy Vanderheiden, *President*
Timothy Vander Heiden, *Executive*
Marcos Silva, *Sales Mgr*
▲ **EMP:** 20 **EST:** 2002
SQ FT: 2,600
SALES (est): 5.2MM **Privately Held**
WEB: www.safepathproducts.com
SIC: 5039 5031 2822 Prefabricated structures; lumber, plywood & millwork; acrylic rubbers, polyacrylate

(P-8650)
WILLIAMS SCOTSMAN INC
Also Called: Williams Scotsman - Fresno
2829 S Chestnut Ave, Fresno (93725-2224)
PHONE 559 441-8181
Rob Gebhard, *Manager*
EMP: 41
SALES (corp-wide): 1.3B **Publicly Held**
WEB: www.willscot.com
SIC: 5039
HQ: Williams Scotsman, Inc.
901 S Bond St Ste 600
Baltimore MD 21231
410 931-6000

5044 Office Eqpt Wholesale

(P-8651)
ALLMODULAR SYSTEMS INC
21005 Cabot Blvd, Hayward (94545-1109)
PHONE 510 887-9000
Donald Marquez, *President*
Lou Bettino, *Vice Pres*
Vince Contreras, *Vice Pres*
Rosa Pelayo, *Principal*
Juan P Valera, *Principal*
▲ **EMP:** 46 **EST:** 2008
SALES (est): 10MM **Privately Held**
WEB: www.allmodularsystems.com
SIC: 5044 Office equipment

(P-8652)
INTERNATIONAL BUS MCHS CORP
Also Called: IBM
425 Market St, San Francisco (94105-2532)
PHONE 415 545-4747
Wirt Cook, *CEO*
Karmen Leung, *Executive*
Gevin Diep, *Administration*
Alan Chin, *Software Engr*
Chin Huang, *Software Engr*
EMP: 208
SALES (corp-wide): 73.6B **Publicly Held**
WEB: www.ibm.com
SIC: 5044 5045 3571 Office equipment; computers, peripherals & software; electronic computers
PA: International Business Machines Corporation
1 New Orchard Rd Ste 1 # 1
Armonk NY 10504
914 499-1900

(P-8653)
OFFICE DEPOT INC
5405 E Home Ave Ste 109, Fresno (93727-2120)
PHONE 559 255-1711
Fax: 559 255-6647
EMP: 40
SALES (corp-wide): 10.2B **Publicly Held**
SIC: 5943 5044 5045 Ret Stationery Whol Office Equipment Whol Computer/Peripheral
PA: Office Depot, Inc.
6600 N Military Trl
Boca Raton FL 33496
561 438-4800

(P-8654)
OFFICEMAX NORTH AMERICA INC
2800 Power Inn Rd, Sacramento (95826-2601)
PHONE 916 388-0120
Stacy Blackhursc, *Branch Mgr*
EMP: 35
SALES (corp-wide): 9.7B **Publicly Held**
SIC: 5712 5044 5943 Office furniture; copying equipment; stationery stores
HQ: Officemax North America, Inc.
263 Shuman Blvd Ste 145
Naperville IL 60563
630 717-0791

(P-8655)
SAITECH INC
42640 Christy St, Fremont (94538-3135)
PHONE 510 440-0256
Vikram Mahajan, *CEO*
Sachin Sharma, *CFO*
Sunny Bhatia, *Manager*
Sally ACC, *Clerk*
▲ **EMP:** 18 **EST:** 2002
SQ FT: 9,000
SALES (est): 18.6MM **Privately Held**
WEB: www.saitechincorporated.com
SIC: 5044 5734 7373 3572 Office equipment; computer peripheral equipment; modems, monitors, terminals & disk drives: computers; value-added resellers, computer systems; computer storage devices; computers; peripherals & software

PRODUCTS & SERVICES SECTION

5045 - Computers & Peripheral Eqpt & Software Wholesale County (P-8676)

(P-8656)
SOURCECORP BPS NTHRN CAL INC
900 Fortress St, Chico (95973-9514)
PHONE.................530 893-7900
Steve Grieco, *CEO*
Katy Murray, *CFO*
Russel Birk, *Treasurer*
Charles Gilbert, *General Counsel*
EMP: 91 **EST:** 2013
SALES (est): 2.7MM
SALES (corp-wide): 1.2B **Publicly Held**
WEB: www.exelatech.com
SIC: 5044 7389 Microfilm equipment; microfilm recording & developing service
HQ: Sourcecorp Bps Inc.
2701 E Grauwyler Rd
Irving TX 75061
866 321-5854

(P-8657)
YUBICO INC
530 Lytton Ave Ste 301, Palo Alto (94301-1541)
PHONE.................408 774-4064
Stina Ehrensvard, *CEO*
John Salter, *COO*
Mattias Danielsson, *Officer*
Jeff Kukowski, *Officer*
Rick O'Rourke, *Officer*
EMP: 150 **EST:** 2007
SALES (est): 28.7MM **Privately Held**
WEB: www.yubico.com
SIC: 5044 7379 Office equipment;

5045 Computers & Peripheral Eqpt & Software Wholesale

(P-8658)
ACCESS INTERNATIONAL COMPANY (DH)
45630 Northport Loop E, Fremont (94538-6477)
PHONE.................510 226-1000
▲ **EMP:** 50 **EST:** 1998
SALES (est): 45.6MM **Privately Held**
SIC: 5045 Computers, peripherals & software

(P-8659)
ACMA COMPUTERS INC
1565 Reliance Way, Fremont (94539-6103)
PHONE.................510 497-8626
CHI Lei Ni, *President*
Jerry Shih, *Shareholder*
Jean Shih, *CEO*
EMP: 36 **EST:** 1979
SQ FT: 23,000
SALES (est): 1.9MM **Privately Held**
WEB: www.amax.com
SIC: 5045 Computers, peripherals & software

(P-8660)
ADVANCED DGITAL SOLUTIONS INTL
7026 Koll Center Pkwy #21, Pleasanton (94566-3105)
PHONE.................510 490-6667
Shahid H Sheikh, *CEO*
Roya Sheikh, *Treasurer*
EMP: 35 **EST:** 1991
SALES (est): 9.1MM **Privately Held**
WEB: www.adsii.com
SIC: 5734 5045 5112 Computer peripheral equipment; computers, peripherals & software; stationery & office supplies

(P-8661)
ADVANCED TECHNOLOGY DISTRS INC
Also Called: Adtech Computers
1571 E Whitmore Ave, Ceres (95307-9215)
PHONE.................209 541-1111
James Lawson, *President*
Kevin Qualle, *Exec VP*
Richard Perez, *Engineer*
EMP: 40 **EST:** 1986
SQ FT: 20,000
SALES (est): 9.1MM **Privately Held**
WEB: www.adtech-it.com
SIC: 5045 5734 5961 7373 Computers, peripherals & software; computer & software stores; computers & peripheral equipment, mail order; computer integrated systems design; computer software systems analysis & design, custom; computer installation

(P-8662)
AGENT IQ INC
95 3rd St, San Francisco (94103-3103)
PHONE.................844 243-6847
Slaven Bilac, *CEO*
Eugene Soriano, *Treasurer*
Weidan Du, *Engineer*
Daniel Coever, *Human Resources*
Sally Dang, *Manager*
EMP: 40 **EST:** 2016
SALES (est): 6.5MM **Privately Held**
WEB: www.agentiq.com
SIC: 5045 Computer software

(P-8663)
AIRMAGNET INC
178 E Tasman Dr, San Jose (95134-1619)
PHONE.................408 571-5000
Robert S Lutz, *CEO*
Dean Au, *President*
Miles Wu, *Treasurer*
Greg Yates, *Exec VP*
▲ **EMP:** 45 **EST:** 2001
SQ FT: 26,000
SALES (est): 7.3MM
SALES (corp-wide): 831.2MM **Publicly Held**
WEB: www.netscout.com
SIC: 5045 Computers, peripherals & software
PA: Netscout Systems, Inc.
310 Littleton Rd
Westford MA 01886
978 614-4000

(P-8664)
ALLOY TECHNOLOGIES INC (PA)
528 Folsom St, San Francisco (94105-3102)
PHONE.................415 990-5140
Joel Beal, *CEO*
EMP: 73 **EST:** 2015
SALES (est): 7.3MM **Privately Held**
WEB: www.alloy.ai
SIC: 5045 Computer software

(P-8665)
AMAX ENGINEERING CORPORATION (PA)
Also Called: Amax Computer
1565 Reliance Way, Fremont (94539-6103)
PHONE.................510 651-8886
Jerry Kc Shih, *CEO*
CHI-Lei Ni, *Vice Pres*
Jean Shih, *Vice Pres*
▲ **EMP:** 150
SQ FT: 110,000
SALES (est): 174.4MM **Privately Held**
WEB: www.amax.com
SIC: 5045 Computer peripheral equipment; computer software

(P-8666)
AMERICAN PORTWELL TECH INC (PA)
Also Called: AP Tech
44200 Christy St, Fremont (94538-3179)
PHONE.................510 403-3399
Allen Lee, *CEO*
Susan WEI, *Executive*
Joyce Wang, *Admin Sec*
Jason Chen, *Project Mgr*
Jackson Liu, *Technology*
▲ **EMP:** 60 **EST:** 1999
SQ FT: 42,515
SALES (est): 82.3MM **Privately Held**
WEB: www.portwell.com
SIC: 5045 Computer peripheral equipment

(P-8667)
AMETEK INC
Also Called: Cognex
1288 San Luis Obispo St, Hayward (94544-7916)
PHONE.................510 431-6718
Markku Jaaskelainen, *Branch Mgr*
Darryl Troxel, *Software Engr*
EMP: 45
SALES (corp-wide): 4.5B **Publicly Held**
WEB: www.ametek.com
SIC: 5045 3829 3826 Computers, peripherals & software; measuring & controlling devices; analytical instruments
PA: Ametek, Inc.
1100 Cassatt Rd
Berwyn PA 19312
610 647-2121

(P-8668)
AOPEN AMERICA INCORPORATED
2150 N 1st St Ste 400, San Jose (95131-2043)
PHONE.................408 586-1200
Dale Tsai, *President*
Stephen Borg, *Officer*
James Huang, *Vice Pres*
Chris Liu, *Vice Pres*
Julie Ruffin, *CIO*
▲ **EMP:** 70 **EST:** 1997
SALES (est): 13MM **Privately Held**
WEB: www.aopen.com
SIC: 5045 Computer software
PA: Aopen Incorporated
21f, No. 92, Sec. 1, Xintai 5th Rd.,
New Taipei City TAP 22102

(P-8669)
APPSROI INC
1765 Landess Ave 121, Milpitas (95035-7019)
PHONE.................510 470-0095
Yogendra Chordia, *President*
EMP: 53 **EST:** 2008
SALES (est): 389.4K
SALES (corp-wide): 21.4MM **Privately Held**
WEB: www.appsroi.com
SIC: 5045 7379 Computer software; computer related consulting services
PA: Soaprojects, Inc.
495 N Whisman Rd Ste 100
Mountain View CA 94043
650 960-9900

(P-8670)
ASI COMPUTER TECHNOLOGIES INC (PA)
Also Called: A S I
48289 Fremont Blvd, Fremont (94538-6510)
PHONE.................510 226-8000
Christine Liang, *CEO*
Brian Clark, *Exec VP*
Marcel Liang, *Principal*
Dinah De La Vega, *Administration*
Kelvin Smith, *Administration*
◆ **EMP:** 52 **EST:** 1987
SQ FT: 155,000
SALES (est): 145.6MM **Privately Held**
WEB: www.asipartner.com
SIC: 5045 3577 Disk drives; keying equipment; printers, computer; terminals, computer; computer output to microfilm units

(P-8671)
ASUS COMPUTER INTERNATIONAL
48720 Kato Rd, Fremont (94538-7312)
PHONE.................510 739-3777
Steve Chang, *CEO*
Ivan Hoe, *President*
Raymond Chen, *Vice Pres*
Alan Hsieh, *Vice Pres*
Leslie Shen, *Executive*
▲ **EMP:** 130 **EST:** 1994
SQ FT: 13,000
SALES (est): 116MM **Privately Held**
WEB: www.asus.com.tw
SIC: 5045 3577 Computer peripheral equipment; computer peripheral equipment
PA: Asustek Computer Incorporation
15, Lide Rd.,
Taipei City TAP 11259

(P-8672)
ATTIVO NETWORKS INC (PA)
46601 Fremont Blvd, Fremont (94538-6410)
PHONE.................510 623-1000
Tushar Kothari, *CEO*
Jilbert Washten, *CFO*
Sarah Ashburn, *Vice Pres*
Matthew Parker, *Vice Pres*
Ashok Shah, *Vice Pres*
EMP: 69 **EST:** 2011
SQ FT: 5,200
SALES (est): 10.1MM **Privately Held**
WEB: www.attivonetworks.com
SIC: 5045 7371 7372 7373 Computers, peripherals & software; software programming applications; prepackaged software; systems software development services; computer related maintenance services

(P-8673)
AVER INFORMATION INC
668 Mission Ct, Fremont (94539-8206)
PHONE.................408 263-3828
Arthur S Pait, *President*
Sinar Pait, *CEO*
Jeff McNall, *Business Mgr*
Jay Lyons, *Manager*
▲ **EMP:** 50 **EST:** 2008
SQ FT: 15,000
SALES (est): 28MM **Privately Held**
WEB: www.averusa.com
SIC: 5045 7382 5099 Computer software; computers & accessories, personal & home entertainment; security systems services; confinement surveillance systems maintenance & monitoring; video & audio equipment
PA: Aver Information Inc.
8f, No. 157, Daan Rd,
New Taipei City TAP 23673

(P-8674)
BAYNETWORK INC (PA)
961 Hamilton Ave, Menlo Park (94025-1431)
PHONE.................650 561-8120
Yuriy Petushaov, *President*
EMP: 65 **EST:** 2009
SALES (est): 1MM **Privately Held**
WEB: www.baynetworks.com
SIC: 5045 5065 Computer software; computer peripheral equipment; modems, computer

(P-8675)
BIG HAIRY DOG INFO SYSTEMS
Also Called: Bhd Information Systems
3205 Ramos Cir, Sacramento (95827-2501)
PHONE.................916 368-3939
Sandy Strom Malaney, *CEO*
Michael Malaney, *President*
Cynthia Paez-Dichoso, *CFO*
Cynthia Paez, *Executive*
Buddy Gobbell, *IT/INT Sup*
EMP: 40 **EST:** 1993
SQ FT: 6,400
SALES (est): 14.7MM **Privately Held**
WEB: www.bighairydog.com
SIC: 5045 Computer software

(P-8676)
BIZCOM ELECTRONICS INC (HQ)
1361 El Camino Real, Santa Clara (95050-4280)
PHONE.................408 262-7877
Ray Chen, *CEO*
Duan Wang, *President*
Gary Lu, *CFO*
Tony Bonadero, *Vice Pres*
Eric Peng, *Vice Pres*
▲ **EMP:** 140 **EST:** 1992
SALES (est): 51.4MM **Privately Held**
WEB: www.bizcom-us.com
SIC: 5045 7629 7378 Computers; telecommunication equipment repair (except telephones); computer maintenance & repair

5045 - Computers & Peripheral Eqpt & Software Wholesale County (P-8677)

(P-8677)
BOOLE INC
2979 Basil Cmn, Livermore (94551-6370)
PHONE..............................408 368-2515
Sunil Coushik, *President*
EMP: 50 **EST:** 2015
SALES (est): 950.1K **Privately Held**
SIC: 5961 5045 Computers & peripheral equipment, mail order; computers, peripherals & software

(P-8678)
BRAMASOL INC
3979 Freedom Cir Ste 620, Santa Clara (95054-1262)
PHONE..............................408 831-0046
Dave Fellers, *CEO*
Jonathan Bell, *CFO*
Dave Leong, *Executive*
Anna Guibao, *IT/INT Sup*
Robert Liszew, *Project Mgr*
EMP: 80 **EST:** 1996
SQ FT: 2,000
SALES (est): 20MM **Privately Held**
WEB: www.bramasol.com
SIC: 5045 Computer software

(P-8679)
CABLE WHOLESALECOM INC (PA)
1200 Voyager St, Livermore (94551-9498)
P.O. Box 11775, Pleasanton (94588-1775)
PHONE..............................925 455-0800
Shenrong Jiang, *President*
Michael Capone, *COO*
Monique De Mar, *Sales Mgr*
Diana Goodman, *Sales Mgr*
Kyle Ludwig, *Sales Mgr*
◆ **EMP:** 22 **EST:** 2000
SQ FT: 30,500
SALES (est): 10.5MM **Privately Held**
WEB: www.cablewholesale.com
SIC: 5045 2298 Computer peripheral equipment; cable, fiber

(P-8680)
CANON FINANCIAL SERVICES INC
Also Called: Oce USA
3265 Ramos Cir Ste 200, Sacramento (95827-2500)
PHONE..............................916 368-7610
Dave Olfon, *Manager*
EMP: 37 **Privately Held**
SIC: 5045 Printers, computer
HQ: Canon Financial Services, Inc.
5600 Broken Sound Blvd Nw
Boca Raton FL 33487

(P-8681)
CHRONICLED INC
116 Natoma St Fl 2, San Francisco (94105-3745)
PHONE..............................415 355-4681
Susanne Somerville, *CEO*
Cecily Welch, *CIO*
Maurizio Greco, *CTO*
Grant Harris, *Software Engr*
James McNamara, *Engineer*
EMP: 31 **EST:** 2014
SQ FT: 3,200
SALES (est): 4.8MM **Privately Held**
WEB: www.chronicled.com
SIC: 5045 7372 5734 Computer software; application computer software; software, business & non-game

(P-8682)
COMPUTER PERFORMANCE INC
Also Called: Digital Loggers
2695 Walsh Ave, Santa Clara (95051-0920)
PHONE..............................408 330-5599
Martin Bodo, *Ch of Bd*
Jamal Keikha, *COO*
Valerie Bodo, *Corp Secy*
Kathryn Tyson, *Department Mgr*
Thai Kim, *Sales Staff*
▲ **EMP:** 35 **EST:** 1987
SQ FT: 42,000

SALES (est): 5.3MM **Privately Held**
WEB: www.dlidirect.com
SIC: 5734 5045 3572 Computer peripheral equipment; computer peripheral equipment; disk drives; computer disk & drum drives & components

(P-8683)
CONVERSICA INC (PA)
950 Tower Ln Ste 1200, Foster City (94404-4245)
PHONE..............................650 290-7674
Alex Terry, *CEO*
Jared Keller, *President*
Jason Lund, *CFO*
Rashmi Vittal, *Chief Mktg Ofcr*
Brian Kaminski, *Officer*
EMP: 16 **EST:** 2016
SQ FT: 8,000
SALES (est): 8.8MM **Privately Held**
WEB: www.conversica.com
SIC: 5734 5045 7372 Software, business & non-game; computer software; business oriented computer software

(P-8684)
CONVRGD DATA TECH INC
999 Commercial St Ste 202, Palo Alto (94303-4909)
PHONE..............................650 461-4483
Akash Rajkumar Saraf, *CEO*
EMP: 110 **EST:** 2017
SALES (est): 16.3MM **Privately Held**
WEB: www.convrgd.com
SIC: 5045 Computers, peripherals & software

(P-8685)
CREATIVE LABS INC (DH)
1901 Mccarthy Blvd, Milpitas (95035-7427)
PHONE..............................408 428-6600
Keh Long Ng, *CEO*
Craig McHugh, *President*
Danielle Dunlap, *Executive Asst*
MAI Cheng, *Info Tech Mgr*
Arlene Hodges, *Accounting Mgr*
▲ **EMP:** 200 **EST:** 1988
SQ FT: 57,000
SALES (est): 214MM **Privately Held**
WEB: www.us.creative.com
SIC: 5045 5734 3577 Computer peripheral equipment; computer & software stores; computer peripheral equipment

(P-8686)
CYARA SOLUTIONS CORP
805 Veterans Blvd Ste 105, Redwood City (94063-1750)
PHONE..............................650 549-8522
Alok Kulkarni, *CEO*
James Isaacs, *President*
Mark Verbeck, *CFO*
Geoff Willshire, *Officer*
George Skaryak, *Exec VP*
EMP: 174 **EST:** 2010
SALES (est): 23.2MM **Privately Held**
WEB: www.cyara.com
SIC: 5045 Computer software

(P-8687)
CYBERCSI INC
3511 Thomas Rd Ste 5, Santa Clara (95054-2039)
PHONE..............................408 727-2900
Dave Sanders, *CEO*
David Wurfer, *Vice Pres*
Amanda Walters, *Administration*
Eduardo Saldana, *Technician*
Dave Yu, *Technician*
EMP: 95 **EST:** 1993
SQ FT: 11,000
SALES (est): 17.3MM **Privately Held**
WEB: www.cybercsi.com
SIC: 5045 7378 Computers, peripherals & software; computer maintenance & repair

(P-8688)
CYBERGUYS INC
11321 White Rock Rd, Rancho Cordova (95742-6505)
PHONE..............................800 892-1010
Wesley K Sumida, *President*
EMP: 48 **EST:** 2001
SQ FT: 51,000

SALES (est): 5.7MM **Privately Held**
WEB: www.cyberguys.com
SIC: 5734 5045 Modems, monitors, terminals & disk drives: computers; printers & plotters: computers; computer software

(P-8689)
DATA PHYSICS CORPORATION (PA)
Also Called: Dp
3100 De La Cruz Blvd # 101, Santa Clara (95054-2438)
PHONE..............................408 437-0100
SRI R Welaratna, *CEO*
David C Snyder, *Chairman*
Kevin McIntosh, *Vice Pres*
John Ho, *Regional Mgr*
Jim Prange, *Regional Mgr*
▲ **EMP:** 15 **EST:** 1984
SALES (est): 17MM **Privately Held**
WEB: www.dataphysics.com
SIC: 5045 3672 7371 3577 Computer software; wiring boards; custom computer programming services; computer peripheral equipment

(P-8690)
DATAENDURE
Also Called: Computer Media Technology
1960 Zanker Rd 10, San Jose (95112-4216)
PHONE..............................408 734-3339
Kurt M Klein, *President*
Patrick Chris, *Officer*
Dennis Ferrara, *Vice Pres*
Gary Klausner, *Executive*
Joe Lockhart, *Executive*
EMP: 35 **EST:** 1984
SQ FT: 110,000
SALES (est): 24.1MM
SALES (corp-wide): 38.1MM **Privately Held**
WEB: www.dataendure.com
SIC: 5045 Computer software
PA: Cmt Holdings, Inc.
590 Laurelwood Rd
Santa Clara CA 95054
408 734-3339

(P-8691)
DATRIUM INC
385 Moffett Park Dr # 205, Sunnyvale (94089-1217)
PHONE..............................650 485-2165
Tim Page, *CEO*
Michael Mullany, *Bd of Directors*
Brian Biles, *Officer*
George LI, *Senior VP*
Brett Foy, *Vice Pres*
EMP: 57 **EST:** 2013
SALES (est): 16.9MM
SALES (corp-wide): 11.7B **Publicly Held**
WEB: www.datrium.com
SIC: 5045 Computer software
PA: Vmware, Inc.
3401 Hillview Ave
Palo Alto CA 94304
650 427-5000

(P-8692)
DFI TECHNOLOGIES LLC
5501 Monte Claire Ln, Loomis (95650-7947)
PHONE..............................916 378-4166
David Lu, *President*
Alan Paro, *Treasurer*
Dave Stickles, *Vice Pres*
Charlie Yang, *General Mgr*
Gavin Chan, *Executive Asst*
▲ **EMP:** 58 **EST:** 1985
SALES (est): 10.5MM **Privately Held**
WEB: www.dfi.com.tw
SIC: 5045 Computer peripheral equipment
PA: Dfi Inc.
10f, 97, Xintai 5th Rd., Sec. 1,
New Taipei City TAP 22175

(P-8693)
DIALPAD INC
Also Called: Voiceai
1 Letterman Dr Bldg C, San Francisco (94129-2402)
PHONE..............................760 648-3282
EMP: 280 **Privately Held**
WEB: www.dialpad.com

SIC: 5045 Computer software
PA: Dialpad, Inc.
100 California St Ste 500
San Francisco CA 94111

(P-8694)
DOME9 SECURITY INC
Also Called: Checkpoint Cloudguard Dome9
800 W El Cmino Real Ste 1, Mountain View (94040)
PHONE..............................831 212-2353
Zohar Alon, *CEO*
Susan Cloud, *Business Mgr*
Tim Duffy, *Sales Staff*
Arthur Rutherford, *Sales Staff*
Shiran Aviram, *Manager*
EMP: 25 **EST:** 2011
SALES (est): 6.3MM **Privately Held**
WEB: www.checkpoint.com
SIC: 5734 5045 7372 7382 Software, business & non-game; computer software; business oriented computer software; security systems services
HQ: Check Point Public Cloud Security Ltd
5 Shlomo Kaplan, Entrance D
Tel Aviv-Jaffa

(P-8695)
DROBO INC (HQ)
1289 Anvilwood Ave, Sunnyvale (94089-2204)
PHONE..............................408 454-4200
Mihir H Shah, *CEO*
Stefan Drege, *Partner*
Tom Buiocchi, *President*
Mark Herbert, *President*
James Gardner, *COO*
▲ **EMP:** 79 **EST:** 2005
SQ FT: 15,000
SALES (est): 19.3MM
SALES (corp-wide): 41MM **Privately Held**
WEB: www.drobo.com
SIC: 5045 Computer software
PA: Storcentric, Inc.
1289 Anvilwood Ave
Sunnyvale CA 94089
408 454-4200

(P-8696)
E-FILLIATE INC
Also Called: West Coast Office & Dist Ctr
11321 White Rock Rd, Rancho Cordova (95742-6505)
PHONE..............................916 858-1000
Wesley Sumida, *CEO*
Mark Luhdorff, *CFO*
Greg Lutz, *CFO*
Aurelia Martian, *Admin Asst*
Kyle Gong, *CIO*
◆ **EMP:** 48 **EST:** 1987
SQ FT: 62,000
SALES (est): 14.5MM **Privately Held**
WEB: www.efilliate.com
SIC: 5961 5045 Computers & peripheral equipment, mail order; computer peripheral equipment; computers & accessories, personal & home entertainment

(P-8697)
ELECTRIC CLOUD INC (HQ)
125 S Market St Ste 400, San Jose (95113-2241)
PHONE..............................408 419-4300
Sacha Labourey, *CEO*
Matt Parson, *CFO*
Jim Ensell, *Chief Mktg Ofcr*
Prathap Dendi, *Vice Pres*
John Giannitsis, *Risk Mgmt Dir*
EMP: 102 **EST:** 2002
SQ FT: 10,000
SALES (est): 22.4MM **Privately Held**
WEB: www.cloudbees.com
SIC: 5045 7371 Computer software; computer software development & applications; software programming applications

(P-8698)
ELITEGROUP COMPUTER SYSTEMS HO
Also Called: E C S-Elitegroup Cmpt Systems
6851 Mowry Ave, Newark (94560-4925)
PHONE..............................510 794-2952
Sam Tsai, *President*

▲ = Import ▼ = Export
◆ = Import/Export

PRODUCTS & SERVICES SECTION **5045 - Computers & Peripheral Eqpt & Software Wholesale County (P-8720)**

Joseph Chang, *CFO*
Jon R Parsons, *Asst Sec*
▼ **EMP:** 240 **EST:** 1999
SQ FT: 108,000
SALES (est): 74.8MM **Privately Held**
WEB: www.hiyes-group.com.tw
SIC: 5045 3577 Computer peripheral equipment; computer peripheral equipment
PA: Hiyes International Co., Ltd.
7f., No.260, Dunhua N. Rd.,
Taipei City TAP 10548

(P-8699)
ELO TOUCH SOLUTIONS INC (HQ)
670 N Mccarthy Blvd # 100, Milpitas (95035-5119)
PHONE...........................408 597-8000
Craig Witsoe, *CEO*
Michael Duong, *Partner*
Dan Ludwick, *President*
Roxi Wen, *CFO*
John Lamb, *Chief Mktg Ofcr*
◆ **EMP:** 333 **EST:** 2012
SQ FT: 75,000
SALES (est): 150.4MM
SALES (corp-wide): 1.8B **Privately Held**
WEB: www.elotouch.com
SIC: 5045 Computers, peripherals & software
PA: The Gores Group Llc
9800 Wilshire Blvd
Beverly Hills CA 90212
310 209-3010

(P-8700)
ENDORSE CORP
60 E 3rd Ave, San Mateo (94401-4030)
PHONE...........................617 470-8332
Steven Carpenter, *CEO*
EMP: 53 **EST:** 2010
SALES (est): 1.1MM **Publicly Held**
WEB: www.dropbox.com
SIC: 5045 Computer software
PA: Dropbox, Inc.
1800 Owens St Ste 200
San Francisco CA 94158

(P-8701)
ENVISION PERIPHERALS INC (PA)
Also Called: E P I
490 N Mccarthy Blvd # 12, Milpitas (95035-5118)
PHONE...........................510 770-9988
David MO, *CEO*
Tom Kang, *Vice Pres*
Dale Feyereisen, *Regl Sales Mgr*
Shelly Herring, *Sales Staff*
Timothy Lawler, *Sales Staff*
◆ **EMP:** 39 **EST:** 1998
SALES (est): 15.6MM **Privately Held**
WEB: www.envisiondisplay.com
SIC: 5045 3577 Computers & accessories, personal & home entertainment; computer peripheral equipment

(P-8702)
EPMWARE INC
333 W San Carlos St # 60, San Jose (95110-2726)
PHONE...........................408 614-0442
Tony Kiratsous, *Mng Member*
Abhi Nerurkar, *Co-Owner*
Deven Shah, *Co-Owner*
EMP: 20 **EST:** 2013
SALES (est): 1.7MM **Privately Held**
WEB: www.epmware.com
SIC: 5045 7372 Computer software; business oriented computer software

(P-8703)
EXCLUSIVE NETWORKS USA INC
2075 Zanker Rd, San Jose (95131-2107)
PHONE...........................408 943-9193
Olivier Breittmayer, *CEO*
James Zhi Fang Shen, *Vice Pres*
Lucy Shen, *Admin Sec*
Vinicius Moehlecke, *Sales Staff*
Ta Kontakt, *Manager*
◆ **EMP:** 29 **EST:** 1992
SQ FT: 20,000

SALES (est): 58.3MM **Privately Held**
WEB: www.exclusive-networks.com
SIC: 5045 3571 Computer peripheral equipment; electronic computers

(P-8704)
EXXACT CORPORATION
46221 Landing Pkwy, Fremont (94538-6407)
PHONE...........................510 226-7366
Peter Chen, *CEO*
Jason Chen, *COO*
Andrew Nelson, *Vice Pres*
Kevin Wong, *Senior Engr*
Guy Purser, *Sales Mgr*
▼ **EMP:** 53 **EST:** 1992
SQ FT: 8,000
SALES (est): 53.9MM **Privately Held**
WEB: www.exxactcorp.com
SIC: 5045 Computer peripheral equipment

(P-8705)
F-SECURE INC (HQ)
470 Ramona St, Palo Alto (94301-1707)
PHONE...........................888 432-8233
Risto Siilasmaa, *Ch of Bd*
Mikko Peltola, *President*
Eriikka Soderstrom, *CFO*
Ilkka Starck, *Exec VP*
Sean Obrey, *Vice Pres*
EMP: 35 **EST:** 1995
SALES (est): 30.2MM
SALES (corp-wide): 260.4MM **Privately Held**
WEB: www.f-secure.com
SIC: 5045 Computer software
PA: F-Secure Oyj
Tammasaarenkatu 7
Helsinki 00180
925 200-700

(P-8706)
FORGEROCK INC (PA)
201 Mission St Ste 2900, San Francisco (94105-1858)
PHONE...........................415 599-1100
Francis Rosch, *President*
Bruce Golden, *Ch of Bd*
John Fernandez, *CFO*
Atri Chatterjee, *Chief Mktg Ofcr*
Sam Fleischmann,
EMP: 699 **EST:** 2009
SALES (est): 127.6MM **Publicly Held**
WEB: www.forgerock.com
SIC: 5045 5734 7371 Computer software; software, business & non-game; computer software systems analysis & design, custom; computer software development & applications; computer software development; software programming applications

(P-8707)
FUJIFILM BI INTRNTNAL OPRTONS
3174 Porter Dr, Palo Alto (94304-1212)
PHONE...........................650 240-3740
Takashi Nawata, *President*
EMP: 39 **EST:** 1991
SALES (est): 3.1MM **Privately Held**
SIC: 5045 Printers, computer

(P-8708)
G C MICRO CORPORATION
3910 Cypress Dr, Petaluma (94954-5694)
PHONE...........................707 789-0600
Belinda Guadarrama, *President*
Lonnie Landers, *Program Mgr*
Wilfred Leung, *Technology*
Erin Newton, *Sales Associate*
Stacey Pemberton, *Sales Associate*
EMP: 40 **EST:** 1986
SQ FT: 9,000
SALES (est): 49MM **Privately Held**
WEB: www.gcmicro.com
SIC: 5045 Computer software

(P-8709)
GUPTA TECHNOLOGIES LLC
2101 Arena Blvd Ste 100, Sacramento (95834-2307)
PHONE...........................916 928-6400
Todd Wille,
Steven Bonham,
EMP: 61 **EST:** 2001

SALES (est): 2.6MM
SALES (corp-wide): 3.1B **Privately Held**
WEB: www.opentext.com
SIC: 5045 Computer software
HQ: Daegis Inc.
600 Las Colinas Blvd E # 1500
Irving TX 75039
214 584-6400

(P-8710)
HPM INCORPORATED
Also Called: Cancom USA
850 Auburn Ct, Fremont (94538-7306)
PHONE...........................510 353-0770
Charles Miano, *CEO*
Alex Lindsay, *COO*
Prabhjot K Randhawa, *Treasurer*
Shawn Scanlon, *Vice Pres*
John Todd, *Vice Pres*
◆ **EMP:** 67 **EST:** 1994
SQ FT: 11,000
SALES (est): 75MM
SALES (corp-wide): 1.9B **Privately Held**
WEB: www.hpmnetworks.com
SIC: 5045 7378 Computer software; computer peripheral equipment repair & maintenance
PA: Cancom Se
Erika-Mann-Str. 69
Munchen BY 80636
895 405-40

(P-8711)
HULA NETWORKS INC (PA)
929 Berryessa Rd Ste 10, San Jose (95133-1084)
PHONE...........................866 485-2638
Joe Commendatore, *CEO*
Scott Hobin, *CFO*
Stephen Robinson, *Principal*
▲ **EMP:** 16 **EST:** 2002
SALES (est): 11.7MM **Privately Held**
WEB: www.hulanetworks.com
SIC: 5045 5065 3572 3577 Computers & accessories, personal & home entertainment; electronic parts & equipment; computer storage devices; computer peripheral equipment

(P-8712)
I2C INC
100 Redwood Shores Pkwy # 100, Redwood City (94065-1253)
PHONE...........................650 593-5400
Amir Wain, *CEO*
Charlie Noreen, *CFO*
Heather Clifton, *Chief Mktg Ofcr*
Marc Winitz, *Chief Mktg Ofcr*
Joseph Derosa, *Exec VP*
EMP: 400 **EST:** 2000
SALES (est): 120.9MM **Privately Held**
WEB: www.i2cinc.com
SIC: 5045 Computer software

(P-8713)
INSIDEVIEW TECHNOLOGIES INC
444 De Haro St Ste 210, San Francisco (94107-2398)
PHONE...........................415 728-9309
Gabe Rogol, *CEO*
Kevin Matsushita, *Partner*
Jim Lightsey, *CFO*
Gordon Anderson, *Vice Pres*
Loree Farrar, *Vice Pres*
EMP: 150 **EST:** 2005
SALES (est): 47.1MM **Privately Held**
WEB: www.insideview.com
SIC: 5045 Computer software
PA: Demandbase, Inc.
680 Folsom St Ste 400
San Francisco CA 94107

(P-8714)
IRON SYSTEMS INC
980 Mission Ct, Fremont (94539-8202)
PHONE...........................408 943-8000
Billy Bath, *President*
Harvey Bath, *Vice Pres*
Ben Davidson, *Vice Pres*
Bob Sidhu, *Vice Pres*
Bobby B Sidhu, *Vice Pres*
▲ **EMP:** 75 **EST:** 2002
SQ FT: 43,000

SALES (est): 117.8MM **Privately Held**
WEB: www.ironsystems.com
SIC: 5045 Computers, peripherals & software

(P-8715)
JANE TECHNOLOGIES INC
1347 Pacific Ave Ste 201, Santa Cruz (95060-3940)
PHONE...........................617 285-2466
Socrates Rosenfeld, *President*
EMP: 93 **EST:** 2017
SALES (est): 10.3MM **Privately Held**
SIC: 5045 Computers, peripherals & software

(P-8716)
JIVOX CORPORATION (HQ)
1810 Gateway Dr Ste 280, San Mateo (94404-4062)
PHONE...........................650 412-1125
Diaz Nesamoney, *CEO*
EMP: 91 **EST:** 2007
SALES (est): 30.6MM **Privately Held**
WEB: www.jivox.com
SIC: 5045 Computer software

(P-8717)
JUNIPER SQUARE INC
343 Sansome St Ste 600, San Francisco (94104-5603)
PHONE...........................415 841-2722
Alex Robinson, *CEO*
Wilson Chan, *Vice Pres*
Esther Park, *Sr Software Eng*
Chris Saden, *Sr Software Eng*
Allen Tsai, *CIO*
EMP: 355 **EST:** 2014
SALES (est): 62.4MM **Privately Held**
WEB: www.junipersquare.com
SIC: 5045 Computer software

(P-8718)
KEMEERA LLC (PA)
Also Called: Fathom
620 3rd St, Oakland (94607-3551)
PHONE...........................510 281-9000
Michelle Malia Mihevc, *CEO*
Richard Stumo, *CFO*
Rich Spott, *Vice Pres*
Randall Oglesby, *CIO*
Ashik Hossain, *IT Specialist*
EMP: 40 **EST:** 2008
SALES (est): 23.1MM **Privately Held**
WEB: www.studiofathom.com
SIC: 5045 Printers, computer

(P-8719)
LANNER ELECTRONICS USA INC
Also Called: Lanner USA
47790 Westinghouse Dr, Fremont (94539-7475)
PHONE...........................510 979-0688
Emily Chou, *CEO*
Jackie Wang, *General Mgr*
Jason Wang, *Project Mgr*
Aung Han, *Engineer*
Jie Lin, *Engineer*
▲ **EMP:** 45 **EST:** 1996
SQ FT: 10,099
SALES (est): 23.1MM **Privately Held**
WEB: www.lannerusa.com
SIC: 5045 Computers, peripherals & software
PA: Lanner Electronics Inc.
7f, No. 173, Datong Rd., Sec. 2
New Taipei City TAP 22183

(P-8720)
LEANDATA INC
2901 Patrick Henry Dr, Santa Clara (95054-1831)
PHONE...........................669 600-5676
Taifu Liang, *CEO*
Maeve Naughton, *Partner*
Karen Steele, *Chief Mktg Ofcr*
Brian Birkett, *Vice Pres*
Larry Cheng, *Vice Pres*
EMP: 59 **EST:** 2012
SALES (est): 10MM **Privately Held**
WEB: www.leandata.com
SIC: 5045 Computer software

5045 - Computers & Peripheral Eqpt & Software Wholesale County (P-8721)

(P-8721)
LITE-ON TRADING USA INC (PA)
720 S Hillview Dr, Milpitas (95035-5455)
PHONE..............................408 946-4873
Sonny Chao, *President*
Steven Shou Yen Liao, *CEO*
Vivian Kwan, *Accountant*
Charlotte Kwok, *Accountant*
Yuen Yue Yeung, *Controller*
◆ **EMP:** 41 **EST:** 2003
SALES (est): 7.6MM **Privately Held**
WEB: www.us.liteon.com
SIC: 5045 Computer peripheral equipment

(P-8722)
LITMUS AUTOMATION INC
2107 N 1st St Ste 440, San Jose (95131-2028)
PHONE..............................765 418-7405
Vatsal Shah, *CEO*
John Younes, *COO*
Sacha Sawaya, *CFO*
Parth Desai, *Technical Staff*
William Wong, *Engineer*
EMP: 50 **EST:** 2016
SQ FT: 3,500
SALES (est): 9.6MM **Privately Held**
WEB: www.litmus.io
SIC: 5045 7372 Computer software; prepackaged software

(P-8723)
MAGMA DESIGN AUTOMATION INC
2880 Zanker Rd Ste 203, San Jose (95134-2122)
PHONE..............................408 432-7288
Andy Huang, *Principal*
EMP: 48
SALES (corp-wide): 3.6B **Publicly Held**
WEB: www.synopsys.com
SIC: 5045 7371 7361 Computer software; computer software development; employment agencies
HQ: Magma Design Automation, Inc.
1650 Tech Dr Ste 100
San Jose CA 95110
408 565-7500

(P-8724)
MARIADB USA INC
350 Bay St Ste 100-319, San Francisco (94133-1966)
PHONE..............................847 562-9000
Michael Howard, *Branch Mgr*
Sameer Tiwari, *CIO*
Hyrum Hilario, *Sales Staff*
EMP: 42
SALES (corp-wide): 7.8MM **Privately Held**
WEB: www.mariadb.com
SIC: 5045 Computer software
PA: Mariadb Usa, Inc.
68 Willow Rd
Menlo Park CA 94025
855 562-7423

(P-8725)
MATTERPORT OPERATING LLC (HQ)
352 E Java Dr, Sunnyvale (94089-1328)
PHONE..............................650 641-2241
Raymond J Pittman, *Ch of Bd*
James D Fay, *CFO*
Jean Barbagelata, *Officer*
Jay Remley, *Officer*
Nicholas Wiley, *Executive*
EMP: 217 **EST:** 2011
SQ FT: 28,322
SALES (est): 61.2MM **Publicly Held**
WEB: www.matterport.com
SIC: 5045 Computer software
PA: Matterport, Inc.
352 E Java Dr
Sunnyvale CA 94089
650 641-2241

(P-8726)
MICROLAND ELECTRONICS CORP (PA)
1883 Ringwood Ave, San Jose (95131-1721)
PHONE..............................408 441-1688
Abraham Chen, *President*
V M Kumar, *Chief Mktg Ofcr*
Randy Yuan, *Vice Pres*
Sam Cho, *Exec Sec*
▲ **EMP:** 40 **EST:** 1986
SQ FT: 40,000
SALES (est): 34.6MM **Privately Held**
WEB: www.microlandusa.com
SIC: 5045 3577 3572 3571 Computer peripheral equipment; computer peripheral equipment; computer storage devices; electronic computers

(P-8727)
MICROMENDERS INC (PA)
1388 Sutter St Ste 650, San Francisco (94109-5452)
PHONE..............................415 344-0917
Toll Free:...............................888 -
Dave Sperry, *CEO*
Scott Estrella, *Partner*
Corey Choi, *Vice Pres*
Joshua Roybal, *Administration*
Tony Dodson, *Technician*
EMP: 38 **EST:** 1985
SQ FT: 5,375
SALES (est): 13.8MM **Privately Held**
WEB: www.micromenders.com
SIC: 5045 7373 7371 4813 Computers, peripherals & software; local area network (LAN) systems integrator; computer software systems analysis & design, custom

(P-8728)
MIRAPATH INC (PA)
Also Called: Data Center Gear
10950 N Blaney Ave, Cupertino (95014-0555)
PHONE..............................408 873-7883
Doris Yeh, *CEO*
Diana LI, *Chief Mktg Ofcr*
Dave Bercovich, *Executive*
MAI Tran, *Administration*
Steve Singleton, *Info Tech Mgr*
▲ **EMP:** 42 **EST:** 2003
SALES (est): 21.6MM **Privately Held**
WEB: www.mirapath.com
SIC: 5045 Computer peripheral equipment

(P-8729)
NEW TECH SOLUTIONS INC
Also Called: NTS
4179 Business Center Dr, Fremont (94538-6355)
PHONE..............................510 353-4070
Vijay Kumar, *CEO*
Rajesh Patel, *President*
Maulik Gandhi, *Engineer*
Rosanna Belda, *Sales Staff*
Jacob Hirshberg, *Sales Staff*
EMP: 45 **EST:** 1997
SQ FT: 10,000
SALES (est): 150MM **Privately Held**
WEB: www.newtechsolutions.com
SIC: 5734 5045 7373 3571 Computer & software stores; computers, peripherals & software; computer integrated systems design; electronic computers; custom computer programming services

(P-8730)
ORACLE AMERICA INC
500 Oracle Pkwy, Redwood City (94065-1677)
PHONE..............................800 633-0584
EMP: 58
SALES (corp-wide): 40.4B **Publicly Held**
WEB: www.oracle.com
SIC: 5045 8731 Computer software; computer (hardware) development
HQ: Oracle America, Inc.
500 Oracle Pkwy
Redwood City CA 94065
650 506-7000

(P-8731)
PALAMIDA INC
215 2nd St Lbby 2, San Francisco (94105-3140)
PHONE..............................415 777-9400
Mark E Tolliver, *CEO*
Eric Free, *Officer*
Jeff Luszcz, *CTO*
Marshall Stevenson, *Regl Sales Mgr*
EMP: 40 **EST:** 2005
SALES (est): 12MM
SALES (corp-wide): 15.9MM **Privately Held**
WEB: www.revenera.com
SIC: 5045 Computer software; application computer software
HQ: Flexera Software Llc
300 Park Blvd Ste 500
Itasca IL 60143

(P-8732)
PENGUIN COMPUTING INC (DH)
45800 Northport Loop W, Fremont (94538-6413)
PHONE..............................415 954-2800
Tom Coull, *President*
Lisa Cummins, *CFO*
Daniel Dowling, *Vice Pres*
Bryan Hanson, *Vice Pres*
Garth Thompson, *Vice Pres*
▲ **EMP:** 85 **EST:** 1999
SQ FT: 86,000
SALES: 166.5MM
SALES (corp-wide): 1.5B **Publicly Held**
WEB: www.penguincomputing.com
SIC: 5045 7371 7379 Computer software; custom computer programming services; computer related maintenance services

(P-8733)
PHIHONG USA CORP (HQ)
47800 Fremont Blvd, Fremont (94538-6551)
PHONE..............................510 445-0100
Fei Hung Alex Lin, *President*
Michael Tena, *CFO*
Russ Hu, *Info Tech Mgr*
Kevin Hsu, *Project Mgr*
Dominick Lamaida, *Project Engr*
▲ **EMP:** 58 **EST:** 1990
SQ FT: 33,000
SALES (est): 35.3MM **Privately Held**
WEB: www.phihong.com
SIC: 5045 3572 Computer peripheral equipment; computer disk & drum drives & components

(P-8734)
PHOENIX SYSTEMS EXCHANGE INC
2401 Kerner Blvd, San Rafael (94901-5569)
PHONE..............................415 485-4500
Gus Constantin, *President*
Paritosh K Choksi, *Senior VP*
Kerby Fegal, *Senior VP*
Bryant Tong, *Senior VP*
Andrew Constantin, *Vice Pres*
EMP: 50 **EST:** 1988
SQ FT: 60,000
SALES (est): 12.8MM
SALES (corp-wide): 40MM **Privately Held**
WEB: www.phxa.com
SIC: 5045 Computers, peripherals & software
PA: Phoenix American Incorporated
2401 Kerner Blvd
San Rafael CA 94901
415 485-4500

(P-8735)
POSIFLEX BUSINESS MACHINES INC
30689 Huntwood Ave, Hayward (94544-7021)
PHONE..............................510 429-7097
Steven Young, *CEO*
Owen Cheng, *President*
Dora Heepow, *Corp Secy*
M Z Chen, *Vice Pres*
David Hoang, *Info Tech Dir*
▲ **EMP:** 37 **EST:** 1992
SQ FT: 30,021
SALES (est): 22.1MM **Privately Held**
WEB: www.posiflexusa.com
SIC: 5045 Computer peripheral equipment
PA: Posiflex Technology, Inc.
23, Datong St.,
New Taipei City TAP 23679

(P-8736)
POWER FACTORS LLC (PA)
135 Main St Ste 1750, San Francisco (94105-4801)
PHONE..............................415 299-7448
Gary Meyers, *CEO*
Richard Barnes, *Vice Pres*
Jeremy Baxter, *Vice Pres*
Robert Johnson, *Vice Pres*
Dave Roberts, *Vice Pres*
EMP: 49 **EST:** 2012
SALES (est): 13.5MM **Privately Held**
WEB: www.pfdrive.com
SIC: 5045 Computer software

(P-8737)
PROMISE TECHNOLOGY INC
3241 Keller St, Santa Clara (95054-2646)
PHONE..............................408 228-1400
Tung-Hsu Lin, *CEO*
James Lee, *President*
Michael Lin, *Officer*
Sherri Anderson, *Admin Sec*
David Bautista, *Info Tech Mgr*
▲ **EMP:** 80 **EST:** 1988
SALES (est): 47.3MM **Privately Held**
WEB: www.promise.com
SIC: 5045 7379 Computers, peripherals & software; data processing consultant
PA: Promise Technology Inc.
2f, No. 30, Gongye E. 9th Rd.,
Xinzhukexuegongyexueyuan District
Paoshan Hsiang HSI 30075

(P-8738)
QCT LLC
1010 Rincon Cir, San Jose (95131-1325)
PHONE..............................510 270-6111
Alan Lam, *Mng Member*
Gary TSE, *Software Engr*
Keunsung Lee, *Engineer*
Vanessa Lu, *Accountant*
Anita Liu, *Opers Staff*
▲ **EMP:** 1000 **EST:** 2011
SALES (est): 91MM **Privately Held**
WEB: www.qct.io
SIC: 5045 Computers, peripherals & software
PA: Quanta Computer Inc.
No. 188, Wenhua 2nd Rd.
Taoyuan City TAY 33383

(P-8739)
QUANTA COMPUTER USA INC (HQ)
45630 Northport Loop E, Fremont (94538-6477)
PHONE..............................510 226-1000
Barry Lam, *Chairman*
Alan Lam, *President*
CC Leung, *President*
Pak Lee Lam, *CEO*
Winnie Lee, *Vice Pres*
▲ **EMP:** 307 **EST:** 1991
SQ FT: 93,000
SALES (est): 99.7MM **Privately Held**
WEB: www.quantatw.com
SIC: 5045 Computers, peripherals & software

(P-8740)
QUANTA SERVICE INCORPORATION (DH)
45630 Northport Loop E, Fremont (94538-6477)
PHONE..............................510 226-1000
Alan Pak Lin Lam, *Principal*
▲ **EMP:** 74 **EST:** 1998
SALES (est): 10.5MM **Privately Held**
SIC: 5045 Computers, peripherals & software

(P-8741)
QUORUMLABS INC
2870 Zanker Rd Ste 130, San Jose (95134-2133)
PHONE..............................408 708-4500
Doug Garn, *CEO*
Andrew Swart, *Ch of Bd*
Edward Sharp, *CEO*
Marty Bradford, *CFO*
Chris Moore, *Senior VP*
EMP: 42 **EST:** 2007

▲ = Import ▼ = Export ◆ = Import/Export

PRODUCTS & SERVICES SECTION
5046 - Commercial Eqpt, NEC Wholesale County (P-8764)

SALES (est): 10.1MM **Privately Held**
WEB: www.quorum.com
SIC: **5045** Computer software

(P-8742)
RAVIG INC
Also Called: Salient Global Technologies
510 Garcia Ave Ste E, Pittsburg (94565-7405)
PHONE 925 526-1234
Ravikanth Ganapavarapu, *CEO*
EMP: 60 **EST:** 1999
SQ FT: 34,000
SALES: 2.7MM
SALES (corp-wide): 6.3MM **Privately Held**
WEB: www.salientglobaltech.com
SIC: **5045** 7373 3571 Computers, peripherals & software; systems software development services; electronic computers
PA: Salient Global Technologies
 11252 Leo Ln
 Dallas TX 75229
 925 526-1234

(P-8743)
REAL INTENT
932 Hamlin Ct, Sunnyvale (94089-1401)
PHONE 408 830-0700
Prakash Narain, *President*
Rajiv Kumar, *COO*
Ramesh Dewangan, *Vice Pres*
Hamed Emami, *Vice Pres*
Insoo Park, *Vice Pres*
EMP: 40 **EST:** 1997
SQ FT: 15,000
SALES (est): 7MM **Privately Held**
WEB: www.realintent.com
SIC: **5045** Computer software

(P-8744)
RETRONYMS INC (PA)
595 Pacific Ave Fl 4, San Francisco (94133-4685)
PHONE 614 589-3121
EMP: 124 **EST:** 2011
SALES (est): 715.7K **Privately Held**
WEB: www.retronymslabs.com
SIC: **5045** Computer software

(P-8745)
RFXCEL CORPORATION (PA)
12667 Alcosta Blvd # 375, San Ramon (94583-5272)
PHONE 925 824-0300
Glenn Abood, *CEO*
Lincoln Manning, *Officer*
Atul Mohidekar, *Officer*
Brian Bilyeu, *Vice Pres*
Rose Campasano, *Vice Pres*
EMP: 54 **EST:** 2004
SQ FT: 10,000
SALES (est): 16.8MM **Privately Held**
WEB: www.rfxcel.com
SIC: **5045** 7371 Computer software; custom computer programming services

(P-8746)
RIVERBED TECHNOLOGY INC (HQ)
680 Folsom St Ste 600, San Francisco (94107-2155)
PHONE 415 247-8800
Dan Smoot, *CEO*
John Tyler, *CFO*
Subbu Iyer, *Chief Mktg Ofcr*
Paul Mountford, *Officer*
Lori Spence, *Officer*
▲ **EMP:** 70 **EST:** 2002
SQ FT: 167,000
SALES (est): 864.9MM
SALES (corp-wide): 1.7B **Privately Held**
WEB: www.riverbed.com
SIC: **5045** 3577 Computer software; computer peripheral equipment
PA: Riverbed Holdings, Inc.
 300 N La Salle Dr # 4350
 Chicago IL 60654
 312 254-2100

(P-8747)
SIBLINGS INVESTMENT INC
Also Called: Vantec Thermal Technologies
43951 Boscell Rd, Fremont (94538-5139)
PHONE 510 668-0368
Chin-Che Huang, *President*

Sheena L Chang, *Vice Pres*
▲ **EMP:** 25 **EST:** 1992
SQ FT: 12,000
SALES (est): 4.3MM **Privately Held**
WEB: www.vantecusa.com
SIC: **5045** 3577 Computer peripheral equipment; computer peripheral equipment

(P-8748)
SK HYNIX AMERICA INC (HQ)
3101 N 1st St, San Jose (95134-1934)
PHONE 408 232-8000
Kun Chul Suh, *CEO*
Song Ho-Keun, *Ch of Bd*
Jae H Park, *President*
C Charles Cho, *Info Tech Mgr*
Sergio De La Torre, *Technology*
▲ **EMP:** 80 **EST:** 1983
SQ FT: 190,000
SALES (est): 244.5MM **Privately Held**
WEB: www.skhynix.com
SIC: **5045** 5065 Computer peripheral equipment; semiconductor devices

(P-8749)
SOLID STATE STOR TECH USA CORP
726 S Hillview Dr, Milpitas (95035-5455)
PHONE 510 687-1800
Ren-Wu Gong, *President*
Chin-Sou Tsai Hong, *CFO*
June Ly, *Administration*
Zahir Aziz, *Senior Engr*
Yung-Huei Chen, *Director*
▲ **EMP:** 100 **EST:** 2003
SQ FT: 8,100
SALES (est): 16.5MM **Privately Held**
WEB: www.ssstc.com
SIC: **5045** Computer peripheral equipment
HQ: Solid State Storage Technology Corporation
 12f-14f, No. 392, Ruiguang Rd.
 Taipei City TAP 11492

(P-8750)
ST CYBERLINK CORPORATION
44063 Fremont Blvd, Fremont (94538-6045)
PHONE 510 623-9888
Yinpeng Huang, *CEO*
Jian Chen, *CFO*
Lu Huang, *Director*
▲ **EMP:** 38 **EST:** 2001
SQ FT: 33,000
SALES (est): 12.5MM **Privately Held**
WEB: www.globalpcdirect.com
SIC: **5045** Computers

(P-8751)
SUNVALLEYTEK INTERNATIONAL INC
160 E Tasman Dr, San Jose (95134-1619)
PHONE 510 255-6101
Caijin Sun, *CEO*
▲ **EMP:** 60 **EST:** 2007
SALES (est): 12.1MM **Privately Held**
WEB: www.sunvalley-group.com
SIC: **5045** 5961 Computer software; computer equipment & electronics, mail order

(P-8752)
SUPER TALENT TECHNOLOGY CORP
2077 N Capitol Ave, San Jose (95132-1009)
PHONE 408 957-8133
Abraham MA, *President*
◆ **EMP:** 670 **EST:** 1991
SALES (est): 46.8MM **Privately Held**
WEB: www.supertalent.com
SIC: **5045** Computer peripheral equipment

(P-8753)
T B B INC
Also Called: Data Consultants
3586 N Hazel Ave, Fresno (93722-4912)
PHONE 559 222-4100
William Pardini, *President*
Greg Hutchings, *Executive*
Jean Smiley, *CTO*
Gregory Hutchings, *Info Tech Mgr*
Jason Ramsey, *Software Dev*
EMP: 37 **EST:** 1976

SQ FT: 16,000
SALES (est): 3.9MM **Privately Held**
WEB: www.dataconsultants.com
SIC: **5045** 7372 Computers; terminals, computer; computer peripheral equipment; business oriented computer software

(P-8754)
TEAMSABLE INC
1911 Hartog Dr, San Jose (95131-2213)
PHONE 408 452-8788
Tzuchiang Hsieh, *CEO*
Simon Wang, *VP Sales*
Kathy Wu, *Sales Staff*
EMP: 22 **EST:** 2018
SQ FT: 10,000
SALES (est): 3.1MM **Privately Held**
WEB: www.teamsable.com
SIC: **5045** 3861 5043 Computer peripheral equipment; cameras & related equipment; motion picture cameras, equipment & supplies

(P-8755)
TRANQUILMONEY INC
5823 Ruddy Duck Ct, Stockton (95207-4518)
PHONE 800 979-6739
EMP: 75
SALES (corp-wide): 12MM **Privately Held**
WEB: www.tranquilmoney.com
SIC: **5045** Whol Computers/Peripherals
PA: Tranquilmoney Inc.
 461 Vose Ave
 South Orange NJ 07079
 212 494-0383

(P-8756)
TRIVAD INC
1350 Bayshore Hwy Ste 799, Burlingame (94010-1838)
PHONE 650 286-1086
Jenna Lim, *CEO*
William Allen, *Vice Pres*
Dave Thompson, *Vice Pres*
Gayle Godkin, *Executive*
Mike Ross, *Executive*
EMP: 230 **EST:** 2002
SALES (est): 117.3MM **Privately Held**
WEB: www.trivad.com
SIC: **5045** 7373 5734 3721 Computers, peripherals & software; computer integrated systems design; computer & software stores; airplanes, fixed or rotary wing; airborne radio communications equipment; search & navigation equipment; aircraft control systems, electronic; navigational systems & instruments

(P-8757)
TWIN BRIDGES TECHNOLOGIES LLC
Also Called: Crushvirus
30286 Oakbrook Rd, Hayward (94544-6670)
PHONE 707 591-4500
Seema Dhingra, *Mng Member*
EMP: 16 **EST:** 2016
SALES (est): 1MM **Privately Held**
WEB: www.twinbridgestech.com
SIC: **5045** 7372 Computer software; utility computer software

(P-8758)
UNIXSURPLUS INC
3060 Raymond St, Santa Clara (95054-3430)
PHONE 408 844-0082
John Edward Bodo, *CEO*
Hector Ramirez, *Vice Pres*
Teresa Bodo, *Admin Sec*
Kara Ligda, *Assistant*
EMP: 42 **EST:** 2006
SALES (est): 9.2MM **Privately Held**
WEB: www.unixsurplus.com
SIC: **5045** Computers, peripherals & software

(P-8759)
VALGENESIS INC (PA)
395 Oyster Point Blvd # 228, South San Francisco (94080-1930)
PHONE 510 445-0505
Siva Samy, *President*

Kevin O'Donnell, *CFO*
Steve Reynolds, *Risk Mgmt Dir*
Shanti Mulyadi, *Office Mgr*
Shaun Leblanc, *Admin Sec*
▼ **EMP:** 54 **EST:** 2005
SQ FT: 1,000
SALES (est): 9.9MM **Privately Held**
WEB: www.valgenesis.com
SIC: **5045** 7371 Computer software; computer software development & applications

(P-8760)
VICARIOUS FPC INC
1320 Decoto Rd Ste 200, Union City (94587-3599)
PHONE 415 604-3278
David Scott Phoenix, *CEO*
Trevor Bauchou, *Office Mgr*
Bianca Hudetz, *Executive Asst*
Ken Kansky, *Software Engr*
Simon Lapeyry, *Director*
EMP: 40 **EST:** 2010
SALES (est): 12.1MM **Privately Held**
WEB: www.vicarious.com
SIC: **5045** 3549 Computer software; assembly machines, including robotic

(P-8761)
VISCIRA LLC
360 3rd St Ste 500, San Francisco (94107-2165)
PHONE 415 848-8010
Dave Gulezian, *President*
Rick Barker, *COO*
Hagop Kane Kaneboughazian, *Vice Pres*
EMP: 100 **EST:** 2018
SALES (est): 36.6MM
SALES (corp-wide): 15.9B **Privately Held**
WEB:
SIC: **5045** 7371 Computer software; computer software development & applications
HQ: Sudler & Hennessey, Llc
 3 Columbus Cir Fl 7
 New York NY 10019
 212 614-4100

(P-8762)
WRANGLER TOPCO LLC (HQ)
555 California St # 2900, San Francisco (94104-1503)
PHONE 415 439-1400
Andrey Filev, *CEO*
Ryan Atlas, *Vice Pres*
Patrick Severson, *Vice Pres*
EMP: 87 **EST:** 2018
SALES (est): 348.6MM **Publicly Held**
WEB: www.citrix.com
SIC: **5045** Computer peripheral equipment

(P-8763)
XTRAPLUS CORPORATION
Also Called: Zipzoomfly
39889 Eureka Dr, Newark (94560-4811)
PHONE 510 897-1890
MEI F Chan, *President*
◆ **EMP:** 28 **EST:** 1998
SALES (est): 4.9MM **Privately Held**
SIC: **5045** 3577 Computer peripheral equipment; computer peripheral equipment

5046 Commercial Eqpt, NEC Wholesale

(P-8764)
B & N INDUSTRIES INC (PA)
1409 Chapin Ave Fl 2nd, Burlingame (94010-4082)
PHONE 650 593-4127
Brad Somberg, *President*
Cherie Azzopardi, *Administration*
Talene Kapeghian, *Administration*
Lexi Dingman, *Project Mgr*
David Largusa, *Project Mgr*
◆ **EMP:** 77 **EST:** 1975
SQ FT: 30,000
SALES (est): 29.1MM **Privately Held**
WEB: www.bnind.com
SIC: **5046** 3089 2541 2542 Store fixtures & display equipment; injection molded finished plastic products; wood partitions & fixtures; office & store showcases & display fixtures

5046 - Commercial Eqpt, NEC Wholesale County

(P-8765)
HARMAN MANAGEMENT CORPORATION (PA)
Also Called: A&W Restaurant
595 Millich Dr Ste 106, Campbell (95008-0550)
PHONE..................650 941-5681
James Jackson, *President*
Vern Wardle, *COO*
Joe Pullin, *Vice Pres*
Tammie Meikle, *Prgrmr*
David Coombs, *Business Mgr*
EMP: 406 **EST:** 1966
SQ FT: 10,000
SALES (corp-wide): 333.7MM **Privately Held**
WEB: www.harmans.biz
SIC: 5812 5046 8741 Fast-food restaurant, chain; restaurant equipment & supplies; management services

(P-8766)
MAX PROCESS EQUIPMENT LLC
1420 Healdsburg Ave, Healdsburg (95448-3207)
PHONE..................707 433-7281
David Whitney, *CEO*
Tim March, *COO*
EMP: 44
SALES (est): 17.8MM **Privately Held**
WEB: www.maxprocessequipment.com
SIC: 5046 Commercial equipment

(P-8767)
MYERS RESTAURANT SUPPLY LLC
1599 Cleveland Ave, Santa Rosa (95401-4280)
PHONE..................707 570-1200
Charlie Fusari, *CEO*
Rob Myers, *President*
Bruce Balla, *Administration*
Pj Patton, *Project Mgr*
Kim Cochran, *Manager*
EMP: 114 **EST:** 2011
SALES (est): 30.4MM
SALES (corp-wide): 707.3MM **Privately Held**
WEB: www.myersrestaurantsupply.com
SIC: 5046 Restaurant equipment & supplies
PA: Edward Don & Company, Llc
9801 Adam Don Pkwy
Woodridge IL 60517
708 442-9400

(P-8768)
NOVA EQUIPMENT LEASING LLC
185 Devlin Rd, NAPA (94558-6255)
P.O. Box 4050 (94558-0450)
PHONE..................707 265-1116
Carole L Bionda, *General Counsel*
EMP: 39 **EST:** 2014
SALES (est): 1.9MM
SALES (corp-wide): 11.2B **Publicly Held**
WEB: www.quantaservices.com
SIC: 5046 Commercial equipment
PA: Quanta Services, Inc.
2800 Post Oak Blvd # 2600
Houston TX 77056
713 629-7600

(P-8769)
PSI MANAGEMENT TEAM INC
Also Called: Partition Specialties
20996 Cabot Blvd, Hayward (94545-1129)
PHONE..................510 266-0076
Lei Ghann, *Manager*
Beth Osmidoff, *Administration*
Brad Johnson, *Project Mgr*
Barbara Parkman, *Contract Mgr*
Tiffany McDonald, *Purchasing*
EMP: 54
SALES (corp-wide): 19.2MM **Privately Held**
WEB: www.psi3g.com
SIC: 5046 Partitions
PA: Psi Management Team, Inc.
7428 Redwood Blvd Ste 101
Novato CA 94945
415 193-3859

(P-8770)
TRIMARK ERF INC
415 Richards Blvd, Sacramento (95811-0219)
PHONE..................916 447-6600
William Braca, *Branch Mgr*
Ella Montes, *Project Mgr*
Richard Flatto, *Buyer*
Lucinda Tromblay, *Opers Spvr*
Jason Husby, *Marketing Mgr*
EMP: 45
SALES (corp-wide): 42.5MM **Privately Held**
WEB: www.bigtray.com
SIC: 5046 7699 Restaurant equipment & supplies; restaurant equipment repair
PA: Trimark Erf, Inc.
1200 7th St
San Francisco CA 94107
415 626-5611

5047 Medical, Dental & Hospital Eqpt & Splys Wholesale

(P-8771)
ADMEDES INC (DH)
2800 Collier Canyon Rd, Livermore (94551-9201)
PHONE..................925 417-0778
Andreas Schuessler, *President*
Michael Ehrlinspiel, *General Mgr*
Kim Williams, *Admin Asst*
Susan Moua, *Technician*
Satya Gollapudi, *Engineer*
▲ **EMP:** 38 **EST:** 2006
SALES (est): 11.9MM
SALES (corp-wide): 231.2MM **Privately Held**
WEB: www.admedes.com
SIC: 5047 Medical equipment & supplies
HQ: Admedes Gmbh
Rastatter Str. 15
Pforzheim BW 75179
723 192-2310

(P-8772)
ALPHA INNOTECH CORP (DH)
Also Called: Cell Biosciences
81 Daggett Dr, San Jose (95134-2109)
PHONE..................510 483-9620
Ronald H Bissinger, *CEO*
Michael P Henighan, *CFO*
Jeff Whitmore, *Vice Pres*
Siavash Ghazvini, *VP Mktg*
▲ **EMP:** 162 **EST:** 1987
SQ FT: 35,000
SALES (est): 9.7MM
SALES (corp-wide): 931MM **Publicly Held**
WEB: www.proteinsimple.com
SIC: 5047 7372 Diagnostic equipment, medical; electro-medical equipment; prepackaged software
HQ: Proteinsimple
3001 Orchard Pkwy
San Jose CA 95134
408 510-5500

(P-8773)
ARTERYS INC
2021 Fillmore St 100, San Francisco (94115-2708)
PHONE..................650 319-7230
Fabien Beckers, *CEO*
John Axerio-Cilies, *Founder*
CIA McCaffrey, *Vice Pres*
Adrianne Martinez, *Executive Asst*
Gio De Francesco, *Technical Staff*
EMP: 57 **EST:** 2011
SALES (est): 5.1MM **Privately Held**
WEB: www.arterys.com
SIC: 5047 Medical equipment & supplies

(P-8774)
BASIS SCIENCE INC
150 Chestnut St, San Francisco (94111-1004)
PHONE..................415 367-7477
Jeffrey Holove, *CEO*
Bharat Vasan, *COO*
John Marshall, *Vice Pres*
Marco Della Torre, *Vice Pres*
Chris Verplaetse, *Vice Pres*
EMP: 35 **EST:** 2010
SALES (est): 5MM
SALES (corp-wide): 77.8B **Publicly Held**
WEB: www.mybasis.com
SIC: 5047 Medical equipment & supplies
PA: Intel Corporation
2200 Mission College Blvd
Santa Clara CA 95054
408 765-8080

(P-8775)
BONGMI INC
68 Harriet St Unit 3, San Francisco (94103-4094)
PHONE..................415 823-8595
Snow LI, *Director*
EMP: 50 **EST:** 2015
SALES (est): 20K **Privately Held**
SIC: 5047 7389 Medical equipment & supplies; business services

(P-8776)
BRADEN PRTNERS LP A CAL LTD PR (HQ)
Also Called: Pacific Pulmonary Services Co
1304 Sthpint Blvd Ste 130, Petaluma (94954)
PHONE..................415 893-1518
Jane Thomas, *CEO*
Tsutomu Igawa, *Ch of Bd*
Edwin Deleon, *Purchasing*
Nancy V Natta, *VP Mktg*
Kristin Allman, *Sales Staff*
▲ **EMP:** 65 **EST:** 1990
SALES (est): 194MM
SALES (corp-wide): 257.9MM **Privately Held**
SIC: 5047 Medical equipment & supplies

(P-8777)
COLOR HEALTH INC (PA)
Also Called: Color Genomic Danny
831 Mitten Rd Ste 100, Burlingame (94010-1300)
PHONE..................650 651-7116
Othman Laraki, *President*
Ziga Mahkovec, *Software Engr*
Desloover Daniel, *Research*
Justin Lock, *Research*
Jeff Dejelo, *VP Finance*
EMP: 482 **EST:** 2013
SQ FT: 2,000
SALES (est): 85.8MM **Privately Held**
WEB: www.color.com
SIC: 5047 Medical & hospital equipment

(P-8778)
CONRAD CORPORATION
Also Called: Conquest Imaging
1815 Industrial Dr # 100, Stockton (95206-4975)
P.O. Box 31796 (95213-1796)
PHONE..................209 942-2654
Jean Conrad, *CEO*
Mark Conrad, *President*
Effie Fryer, *Vice Pres*
Matt Tomory, *Vice Pres*
Jacqueline Guerra, *Executive*
EMP: 44 **EST:** 2000
SQ FT: 34,000
SALES (est): 18.1MM **Privately Held**
WEB: www.conquestimaging.com
SIC: 5047 Medical equipment & supplies

(P-8779)
DIGITAL DOC LLC
4789 Golden Foothill Pkwy, El Dorado Hills (95762-9641)
PHONE..................916 941-8010
Don Berg, *Mng Member*
Jim Schmied, *Design Engr*
Brian Brennan, *Sales Staff*
Ben Moore, *Manager*
Brit Sexton, *Manager*
▲ **EMP:** 44 **EST:** 1998
SALES (est): 10.7MM **Privately Held**
WEB: www.digi-doc.com
SIC: 5047 3069 Medical equipment & supplies; medical & laboratory rubber sundries & related products

(P-8780)
GOLD STANDARD DIAGNOSTICS CORP (PA)
2795 2nd St Ste 300, Davis (95618-6505)
PHONE..................530 759-8000
John M Griffiths, *President*
James Thompson, *CFO*
Jennifer Roth, *Vice Pres*
Amanda Cormier-Adams, *Technical Staff*
Christina Brusca, *Opers Staff*
▲ **EMP:** 65 **EST:** 2006
SQ FT: 2,750
SALES (est): 38.8MM **Privately Held**
WEB: www.gsdx.us
SIC: 5047 Diagnostic equipment, medical

(P-8781)
H AND H DRUG STORES INC
Also Called: Western Drug Medical Supply
4692 E Waterloo Rd, Stockton (95215-2309)
PHONE..................209 931-5200
Haig J Youredjian, *Principal*
EMP: 77
SALES (corp-wide): 52.8MM **Privately Held**
WEB: www.westerndrug.com
SIC: 5047 Medical equipment & supplies
PA: H And H Drug Stores, Inc.
3604 San Fernando Rd
Glendale CA 91204
818 956-6691

(P-8782)
HELIX MEDICAL COMM LLC (DH)
1400 Fashion Island Blvd, San Francisco (94104)
PHONE..................650 357-0958
Neil Matheson, *President*
Jeff Mullican, *CFO*
Lynn Nye, *Manager*
Bianca Ruzicka, *Manager*
EMP: 45 **EST:** 2001
SQ FT: 11,389
SALES (est): 25.9MM
SALES (corp-wide): 5.8MM **Privately Held**
WEB: www.hhealth.com
SIC: 5047 Medical equipment & supplies
HQ: Huntsworth Health North America Llc
800 Town Line Rd Ste 100
Yardley PA 19067
215 550-8300

(P-8783)
ITA-MED CO
25377 Huntwood Ave, Hayward (94544-2212)
PHONE..................510 200-9249
Lev Tripolsky, *President*
Alex Bond, *Marketing Staff*
◆ **EMP:** 49
SQ FT: 35,000
SALES (est): 8MM **Privately Held**
WEB: www.itamed.com
SIC: 5047 Medical equipment & supplies

(P-8784)
JAMESTOWN HLTH MED SUP CO LLC (PA)
879 F St Ste 120, West Sacramento (95605-2384)
PHONE..................916 431-8046
Deepal S Wannakuwatte,
Deepal Wannakuwatte, *Principal*
EMP: 35 **EST:** 2005
SALES (est): 8MM **Privately Held**
SIC: 5047 Medical equipment & supplies

(P-8785)
KAISER FOUNDATION HOSPITALS
275 W Macarthur Blvd, Oakland (94611-5641)
PHONE..................510 752-6808
Anne Burnett, *Director*
Shelley Lee, *Web Dvlpr*
Morali Sharma, *Endocrinology*
Ivy Yu, *Med Doctor*
Carol Starks, *Asst Director*
EMP: 104
SALES (corp-wide): 30.5B **Privately Held**
WEB: www.kaisercenter.com
SIC: 5047 Medical equipment & supplies

▲ = Import ▼ = Export
◆ = Import/Export

PRODUCTS & SERVICES SECTION

5051 - Metals Service Centers County (P-8807)

HQ: Kaiser Foundation Hospitals Inc
1 Kaiser Plz
Oakland CA 94612
510 271-6611

(P-8786)
LIFE-ASSIST INCORPORATED (PA)
11277 Sunrise Park Dr, Rancho Cordova (95742-6528)
PHONE..................................916 635-3822
Ramona M Davis, *CEO*
Linda Bergaus, *CFO*
Linda M Bergaus, *Treasurer*
Brett Archer, *Regional Mgr*
Judith Sproul Davis, *Admin Sec*
EMP: 35 **EST:** 1977
SQ FT: 50,000
SALES (est): 19.5MM **Privately Held**
WEB: www.life-assist.com
SIC: 5047 Medical equipment & supplies

(P-8787)
LIN-ZHI INTERNATIONAL INC
2945 Oakmead Village Ct, Santa Clara (95051-0812)
PHONE..................................408 970-8811
Marie Lin, *CEO*
Sushmita Choudhury, *Human Resources*
Kenneth Yeung, *Purchasing*
Allen Wang, *Associate*
EMP: 48 **EST:** 1998
SALES (est): 18.1MM **Privately Held**
WEB: www.lin-zhi.com
SIC: 5047 Diagnostic equipment, medical

(P-8788)
MY TRUE IMAGE MFG INC
Also Called: Design Veronique
999 Marina Way S, Richmond (94804-3738)
PHONE..................................510 970-7990
Veronica C Smith, *President*
Michael Qi, *Accounting Mgr*
Macarthur Alfaro, *Prdtn Mgr*
Asali Saterfield, *Sales Staff*
Cheli Espinoza, *Cust Mgr*
▲ **EMP:** 80 **EST:** 1987
SQ FT: 30,000
SALES (est): 23.4MM **Privately Held**
SIC: 5047 Medical equipment & supplies

(P-8789)
PRACTICE WARES INC
Also Called: Practicewares Dental Supply
2377 Gold Meadow Way, Gold River (95670-4405)
PHONE..................................916 526-2674
EMP: 50
SALES (corp-wide): 12.5MM **Privately Held**
SIC: 5047 Whol Medical/Hospital Equipment
PA: Practice Wares, Inc
3400 E Mcdowell Rd
Phoenix AZ
602 225-9090

(P-8790)
PRECISION MEDICAL PRODUCTS INC
2217 Plaza Dr, Rocklin (95765-4421)
PHONE..................................888 963-6265
Marc Reynolds, *CEO*
Bruce Capagli, *COO*
Austin Phillips, *Chief Mktg Ofcr*
Mark Bernardini, *Officer*
Chris Barton, *Vice Pres*
EMP: 35 **EST:** 2010
SQ FT: 1,200
SALES (est): 8.1MM **Privately Held**
WEB: www.pmpmed.com
SIC: 5047 Medical equipment & supplies

(P-8791)
SAN JOSE SURGICAL SUPPLY INC (PA)
902 S Bascom Ave, San Jose (95128-3599)
PHONE..................................408 293-9033
Dennis J Collins, *President*
Emile Fatha, *Director*
▲ **EMP:** 44 **EST:** 1964
SQ FT: 15,000
SALES (est): 13.4MM **Privately Held**
WEB: www.sjsurgical.com
SIC: 5047 5122 Surgical equipment & supplies; pharmaceuticals

(P-8792)
SUNRISE MEDICAL (US) LLC
2842 N Business Park Ave, Fresno (93727-1328)
PHONE..................................559 292-2171
Thomas Rossnagel, *CEO*
Larry Jackson, *President*
▲ **EMP:** 28 **EST:** 2010
SALES (est): 11.4MM **Privately Held**
WEB: www.sunrisemedical.com
SIC: 5047 3842 Medical equipment & supplies; wheelchairs

(P-8793)
TRACPATCH HEALTH INC
1115 Windfield Way # 100, El Dorado Hills (95762-9835)
PHONE..................................916 355-7123
Collen Gray, *President*
Curt Wiedenhoefer, *President*
Gail V Dalen, *Exec VP*
Carolyn Hayes, *Vice Pres*
Dan Richards, *Vice Pres*
EMP: 82 **EST:** 1992
SQ FT: 25,000
SALES (est): 24.5MM **Privately Held**
WEB: www.consensusortho.com
SIC: 5047 3841 Medical equipment & supplies; surgical & medical instruments

(P-8794)
VETERINARY SERVICE INC
4048 Strolling Ct, Merced (95340-8104)
PHONE..................................209 722-7600
Michelle Garcia, *Branch Mgr*
EMP: 50
SALES (corp-wide): 70.6MM **Privately Held**
WEB: www.vsi.cc
SIC: 5047 5199 5083 Veterinarians' equipment & supplies; pet supplies; poultry equipment
PA: Veterinary Service, Inc.
4100 Bangs Ave
Modesto CA 95356
209 545-5100

(P-8795)
VIEWRAY TECHNOLOGIES INC
815 E Middlefield Rd, Mountain View (94043-4025)
PHONE..................................650 252-0920
Caley Castelein, *Bd of Directors*
Theodore Wang, *Bd of Directors*
Rob Fuchs, *Officer*
Christopher Walz, *Engineer*
Eddie Martinez, *Director*
EMP: 75
SALES (corp-wide): 87.7MM **Publicly Held**
WEB: www.viewray.com
SIC: 5047 Medical & hospital equipment
HQ: Viewray Technologies, Inc.
2 Thermo Fisher Way
Oakwood Village OH 44146
440 703-3210

(P-8796)
VISIONCARE DEVICES INC
Also Called: Biotronics
6100 Bellevue Ln, Anderson (96007-4950)
PHONE..................................530 364-2271
Wayne Cook, *President*
Rick Morgan, *Project Engr*
Tom Ackernecht, *Manager*
EMP: 20 **EST:** 1990
SQ FT: 8,000
SALES (est): 3.3MM **Privately Held**
WEB: www.visioncaredevices.com
SIC: 5047 5048 3841 3851 Medical equipment & supplies; ophthalmic goods; surgical & medical instruments; ophthalmic goods; electromedical equipment

5048 Ophthalmic Goods Wholesale

(P-8797)
ABB/CON-CISE OPTICAL GROUP LLC
Also Called: Primary Eyecare Network
1750 N Loop Rd Ste 150, Alameda (94502-8013)
PHONE..................................800 852-8089
EMP: 80
SALES (corp-wide): 1.3B **Privately Held**
SIC: 5048 5044 Wholesales Ophthalmic Goods And Professional Equipment Specializing In Optical Goods
HQ: Abb/Con-Cise Optical Group Llc
12301 Nw 39th St
Coral Springs FL 33065
800 852-8089

(P-8798)
ABB/CON-CISE OPTICAL GROUP LLC
Also Called: ABB Optical Group
1750 N Loop Rd Ste 150, Alameda (94502-8013)
PHONE..................................510 483-9400
Angel Alvarez, *CEO*
Tom Penot, *Analyst*
Melissa Bernath, *Manager*
Schwartz Eric, *Manager*
Jesse Fuentes, *Manager*
EMP: 147 **Privately Held**
WEB: www.abboptical.com
SIC: 5048 5049 Ophthalmic goods; optical goods
HQ: Abb/Con-Cise Optical Group Llc
12301 Nw 39th St
Coral Springs FL 33065

(P-8799)
MARCOLIN USA INC
Also Called: Viva International
6 Janet Way Apt 116, Belvedere Tiburon (94920-2164)
PHONE..................................415 383-6348
EMP: 66 **Privately Held**
SIC: 5048 5099 Whol Ophthalmic Goods Whol Durable Goods
HQ: Marcolin U.S.A., Inc.
3140 Us Highway 22
Branchburg NJ 08876
800 345-8482

5049 Professional Eqpt & Splys, NEC Wholesale

(P-8800)
ABB ENTERPRISE SOFTWARE INC
Also Called: ABB - Los Gatos Research
3055 Orchard Dr, San Jose (95134-2005)
P.O. Box 80065, Raleigh NC (27623-0065)
PHONE..................................408 770-8968
Doug Baer, *General Mgr*
Michaela Tatro, *Executive Asst*
Abd Al Kareem Qaram, *Accounts Mgr*
EMP: 63
SALES (corp-wide): 26.1B **Privately Held**
WEB: www.global.abb
SIC: 5049 3826 Analytical instruments; analytical instruments
HQ: Abb Inc.
305 Gregson Dr
Cary NC 27511

(P-8801)
CPI INTERNATIONAL
5580 Skylane Blvd, Santa Rosa (95403-1030)
PHONE..................................707 521-6327
Ryan Vice, *CEO*
Joseph Phillips, *CFO*
Tommy Mitchell, *Vice Pres*
Brenda Sims, *Office Mgr*
▲ **EMP:** 70 **EST:** 1996
SQ FT: 20,000
SALES (est): 18.7MM **Privately Held**
WEB: www.cpiinternational.com
SIC: 5049 3826 Analytical instruments; analytical instruments

(P-8802)
QUARTZY INC
28321 Industrial Blvd, Hayward (94545-4428)
PHONE..................................855 782-7899
Jayant Kulkarni, *CEO*
Adam Regelmann, *COO*
Virginia Lindgren, *Office Mgr*
Tristan Pemble, *Sr Software Eng*
Kha-Ai Nguyen, *Analyst*
EMP: 55 **EST:** 2007
SALES (est): 26.4MM **Privately Held**
WEB: www.quartzy.com
SIC: 5049 Laboratory equipment, except medical or dental

(P-8803)
SILICON VALLEY OPTICS TECH
44141 S Grimmer Blvd, Fremont (94538-6350)
PHONE..................................510 623-1161
John Jao, *President*
▲ **EMP:** 40 **EST:** 2002
SALES (est): 3.4MM **Privately Held**
WEB: www.svotek.com
SIC: 5995 5049 Optical goods stores; optical goods

(P-8804)
TECHNICAL INSTR SAN FRANCISCO (PA)
Also Called: Technical Instrument SF
1826 Rollins Rd Ste 100, Burlingame (94010-2215)
P.O. Box 2340, Mill Valley (94942-2340)
PHONE..................................650 651-3000
Brian F Lundy, *CEO*
Silvia Foppiano, *Manager*
EMP: 29 **EST:** 1996
SQ FT: 11,000
SALES (est): 9.4MM **Privately Held**
SIC: 5049 3827 Optical goods; optical instruments & lenses

5051 Metals Service Centers

(P-8805)
AOC TECHNOLOGIES INC
5960 Inglewood Dr, Pleasanton (94588-8610)
PHONE..................................925 875-0808
Gordon Gu, *President*
▲ **EMP:** 315 **EST:** 1999
SALES (est): 57.6MM **Privately Held**
WEB: www.aocchina.net
SIC: 5051 3357 Metal wires, ties, cables & screening; fiber optic cable (insulated)

(P-8806)
ARCHITECTURAL GL & ALUM CO INC (PA)
6400 Brisa St, Livermore (94550-2550)
PHONE..................................925 583-2460
Joseph Brescia, *CEO*
John Buckley, *President*
William Coll Jr, *Vice Pres*
William Coll Sr, *Admin Sec*
Julie Montes, *Admin Asst*
▲ **EMP:** 155 **EST:** 1970
SQ FT: 33,000
SALES (est): 73.5MM **Privately Held**
WEB: www.aga-ca.com
SIC: 5051 1793 1791 3442 Aluminum bars, rods, ingots, sheets, pipes, plates, etc.; glass & glazing work; exterior wall system installation; sash, door or window: metal

(P-8807)
ASC PROFILES LLC (DH)
Also Called: ASC Building Products
2110 Enterprise Blvd, West Sacramento (95691-3428)
PHONE..................................916 376-2800
Sarah Deukmejian, *CEO*
Paul Warme, *CFO*
Marie Ortega, *Info Tech Dir*
Shane Smith, *Info Tech Mgr*
Scott Sonneborn, *Project Mgr*

5051 - Metals Service Centers County (P-8808)

EMP: 85 EST: 1972
SQ FT: 87,120
SALES (est): 108.2MM **Privately Held**
WEB: www.ascprofiles.com
SIC: **5051** Steel

(P-8808)
BAYSHORE METALS
4240 San Andres Way, El Dorado Hills (95762-5066)
PHONE.................................415 647-7981
Ron Marchand, *President*
Staci Marchand, *Corp Secy*
▲ EMP: 40 EST: 1917
SALES (est): 5.7MM **Privately Held**
WEB: www.bayshoremetals.com
SIC: **5051** Ferrous metals; nonferrous metal sheets, bars, rods, etc.

(P-8809)
BEL AIRE ENGINEERING INC
22740 Alice St, Hayward (94541-6499)
PHONE.................................510 538-6950
Joseph T Kessler Jr, *President*
C Eleanor Kessler, *Corp Secy*
C Kessler, *Admin Sec*
EMP: 16 EST: 1971
SQ FT: 18,000
SALES (est): 4.7MM **Privately Held**
WEB: www.belairee.com
SIC: **5051** 5211 3444 2394 Aluminum bars, rods, ingots, sheets, pipes, plates, etc.; lumber & other building materials; sheet metalwork; canvas & related products

(P-8810)
CAPITOL STEEL COMPANY
1932 Auburn Blvd, Sacramento (95815-1910)
P.O. Box 215239 (95821-1239)
PHONE.................................916 924-3195
Craig M Elowson, *President*
EMP: 25 EST: 1968
SALES (est): 17.6MM **Privately Held**
WEB: www.capitolsteelcompany.com
SIC: **5051** 5032 3444 Steel; brick, stone & related material; concrete forms, sheet metal

(P-8811)
CMC REBAR WEST
5160 Fulton Dr, Fairfield (94534-1639)
PHONE.................................707 759-1400
Howard Bennion, *Branch Mgr*
EMP: 56 **Privately Held**
SIC: **5051** Steel
HQ: Cmc Rebar West
3880 Murphy Canyon Rd # 100
San Diego CA 92123

(P-8812)
CONCRETEWORKS STUDIO INC
1998 Republic Ave, San Leandro (94577-4224)
PHONE.................................510 534-7141
Mark Rogero, *CEO*
EMP: 84 EST: 2015
SALES (est): 7.6MM **Privately Held**
WEB: www.concreteworks.com
SIC: **5712** 5051 Custom made furniture, except cabinets; forms, concrete construction (steel)

(P-8813)
CONSOLDTED METAL FBRCTNG CO INC
2780 S Cherry Ave, Fresno (93706-5424)
P.O. Box 12064 (93776-2064)
PHONE.................................559 268-7887
Philip Alcorn, *President*
Brent Alcorn, *Vice Pres*
Deanna Alcorn, *Vice Pres*
Scott Alcorn, *Admin Sec*
Richard McBride, *Opers Staff*
EMP: 30 EST: 1975
SQ FT: 40,080
SALES (est): 10.1MM **Privately Held**
SIC: **5051** 3444 3441 Aluminum bars, rods, ingots, sheets, pipes, plates, etc.; steel; sheet metalwork; fabricated structural metal

(P-8814)
D P NICOLI INC
266 Harbor Way, South San Francisco (94080-6816)
PHONE.................................650 873-2999
Mike Welton, *Branch Mgr*
Michael Casas, *Sales Staff*
EMP: 15
SALES (corp-wide): 10.6MM **Privately Held**
WEB: www.dpnicoli.com
SIC: **5051** 7359 3325 Steel; equipment rental & leasing; steel foundries
PA: D. P. Nicoli, Inc.
17888 Sw Mcewan Rd
Lake Oswego OR 97035
503 692-6080

(P-8815)
DIVERSE STEEL SALES INC (PA)
1666 Willow Pass Rd, Pittsburg (94565-1702)
PHONE.................................925 756-0555
Mark Riley, *President*
Barbara Riley, *Corp Secy*
▲ EMP: 18 EST: 1989
SQ FT: 65,000
SALES (est): 10.9MM **Privately Held**
WEB: www.diversesteelsales.com
SIC: **5051** 3444 Steel; sheet metalwork

(P-8816)
GERLINGER FNDRY MCH WORKS INC
Also Called: Gerlinger Steel & Supply Co
1510 Tanforan Ave, Woodland (95776-6109)
P.O. Box 992195, Redding (96099-2195)
PHONE.................................530 243-1053
Fred Gerlinger, *Branch Mgr*
Jo Gerlinger, *CFO*
Don Vanderpool, *Buyer*
Rick Eagle, *Sales Staff*
Justin Lindell, *Sales Staff*
EMP: 17
SALES (corp-wide): 12MM **Privately Held**
WEB: www.gerlinger.com
SIC: **5051** 5015 3441 Steel; motor vehicle parts, used; fabricated structural metal
PA: Gerlinger Foundry And Machine Works, Inc.
1527 Sacramento St
Redding CA 96001
530 243-1053

(P-8817)
GUNTERT SALES DIV INC
Also Called: Guntert Steel
222 E 4th St, Ripon (95366-2761)
PHONE.................................209 599-6131
Ronald M Guntert Jr, *CEO*
Christine Stanbrough, *CFO*
Ronald Ruffoni, *Vice Pres*
Timothy Arends,
Rod Hudson, *Design Engr*
EMP: 45 EST: 1945
SQ FT: 10,000
SALES (est): 22MM **Privately Held**
WEB: www.guntertsteel.com
SIC: **5051** Plates, metal

(P-8818)
HANSFORD INDUSTRIES INC (PA)
Also Called: Ciking Steel
8610 Elder Creek Rd, Sacramento (95828-1803)
PHONE.................................916 379-0210
Danny L Hansford, *CEO*
EMP: 39 EST: 1991
SQ FT: 1,800
SALES (est): 10.8MM **Privately Held**
WEB: www.vikingsteel.net
SIC: **5051** Viking

(P-8819)
HITACHI METALS AMERICA LTD
880 N Mccarthy Blvd # 200, Milpitas (95035-5126)
PHONE.................................408 467-8900
Rick Shigashara, *Branch Mgr*
Megan Kiernan, *Technology*
Ryan Johnson, *Engineer*
Kenneth Cheung, *Sales Staff*
Joedel Dizon, *Sales Staff*
EMP: 70 **Privately Held**
WEB: www.hitachimetals.com
SIC: **5051** Steel; castings, rough: iron or steel
HQ: Hitachi Metals America, Ltd.
2 Manhattanville Rd # 301
Purchase NY 10577
914 694-9200

(P-8820)
KEARNEYS METALS INC
4731 E Vine Ave, Fresno (93725-2112)
P.O. Box 2926 (93745-2926)
PHONE.................................559 233-2591
Michael Kearney, *Principal*
Gary Kearney, *Corp Secy*
Sylvia Perez, *Executive*
▲ EMP: 41 EST: 1965
SQ FT: 80,000
SALES (est): 11.8MM **Privately Held**
WEB: www.kearneysaluminumfoundry.com
SIC: **5051** Steel

(P-8821)
MAXX METALS INC
355 Quarry Rd, San Carlos (94070-6217)
P.O. Box 10963, Pleasanton (94588-0963)
PHONE.................................650 654-1500
Paul A Wallace, *President*
Debra L Wallace, *CFO*
EMP: 68 EST: 2007
SQ FT: 13,000
SALES (est): 9.5MM **Privately Held**
WEB: www.maxxmetals.com
SIC: **5051** Steel

(P-8822)
ORION GROUP WORLD LLC
143 Seminary Dr Apt Q, Mill Valley (94941-6212)
PHONE.................................415 602-5233
Ace Stojanovski, *President*
Monika Szczuka,
EMP: 120 EST: 2017
SALES (est): 8.5MM **Privately Held**
SIC: **5051** 7389 3812 3482 Iron & steel (ferrous) products; ; defense systems & equipment; cartridges, 30 mm. & below; rocket launchers; rockets (ammunition)

(P-8823)
PDM STEEL SERVICE CENTERS INC
3500 Bassett St, Santa Clara (95054-2704)
P.O. Box 329 (95052-0329)
PHONE.................................408 988-3000
John Norman, *General Mgr*
Casey Haldeman, *Vice Pres*
Adam Ivankovic, *Vice Pres*
Andrew Sanchez, *Executive*
Jesse Farrer, *General Mgr*
EMP: 17
SQ FT: 46,080
SALES (corp-wide): 8.8B **Publicly Held**
WEB: www.pdmsteel.com
SIC: **5051** 3444 3272 Steel; sheet metalwork; concrete products
HQ: Pdm Steel Service Centers, Inc.
3535 E Myrtle St
Stockton CA 95205
209 943-0555

(P-8824)
PDM STEEL SERVICE CENTERS INC (HQ)
Also Called: Specialty Steel Service
3535 E Myrtle St, Stockton (95205-4721)
PHONE.................................209 943-0555
Derick Halecky, *President*
Jennifer Gardner, *CFO*
Joseph Anderson, *Vice Pres*
Randy H Kearns, *Vice Pres*
William Nixon, *Vice Pres*
▲ EMP: 100 EST: 1954
SALES (est): 214.5MM
SALES (corp-wide): 8.8B **Publicly Held**
WEB: www.pdmsteel.com
SIC: **5051** Steel
PA: Reliance Steel & Aluminum Co.
350 S Grand Ave Ste 5100
Los Angeles CA 90071
213 687-7700

(P-8825)
PDM STEEL SERVICE CENTERS INC
9245 Laguna Springs Dr # 350, Elk Grove (95758-7987)
PHONE.................................916 513-4548
Randy Kearns, *President*
Luann Berndt, *Purchasing*
EMP: 200
SALES (corp-wide): 8.8B **Publicly Held**
WEB: www.pdmsteel.com
SIC: **5051** Steel
HQ: Pdm Steel Service Centers, Inc.
3535 E Myrtle St
Stockton CA 95205
209 943-0555

(P-8826)
PJS REBAR INC
45055 Fremont Blvd, Fremont (94538-6318)
PHONE.................................510 490-0321
Stuart Lowe, *CEO*
Elva Salmeron, *Dept Chairman*
Rick Lopez, *Project Mgr*
Shane McMillan, *VP Opers*
Bill Bryan, *Maint Spvr*
EMP: 70 EST: 2015
SALES (est): 14MM **Privately Held**
WEB: www.pjsrebar.com
SIC: **5051** Steel

(P-8827)
RELIANCE STEEL & ALUMINUM CO
Reliance Metal Center
33201 Western Ave, Union City (94587-2208)
PHONE.................................510 476-4400
Dave Buchanan, *Manager*
Kristen Hernandez, *Credit Mgr*
Mike Waller, *Opers Staff*
EMP: 90
SQ FT: 137,757
SALES (corp-wide): 8.8B **Publicly Held**
WEB: www.rsac.com
SIC: **5051** Steel; aluminum bars, rods, ingots, sheets, pipes, plates, etc.; bars, metal; copper
PA: Reliance Steel & Aluminum Co.
350 S Grand Ave Ste 5100
Los Angeles CA 90071
213 687-7700

(P-8828)
SPECIALTY STEEL SERVICE CO INC
1224 Coloma Way Ste 150, Roseville (95661-4673)
PHONE.................................800 777-4258
EMP: 39
SALES (corp-wide): 10.4B **Publicly Held**
SIC: **5051** Metals Service Center
HQ: Specialty Steel Service Co., Inc.
3300 Douglas Blvd Ste 128
Roseville CA 95661
916 771-4737

(P-8829)
SPECIALTY STEEL SERVICE CO INC (HQ)
3300 Douglas Blvd Ste 128, Roseville (95661-3897)
PHONE.................................916 771-4737
Fax: 916 771-8658
▲ EMP: 70
SQ FT: 3,000
SALES (est): 24.4MM
SALES (corp-wide): 10.4B **Publicly Held**
WEB: www.specialtysteel.net
SIC: **5051** Metals Service Center
PA: Reliance Steel & Aluminum Co.
350 S Grand Ave Ste 5100
Los Angeles CA 90071
213 687-7700

(P-8830)
TCI ALUMINUM/NORTH INC
2353 Davis Ave, Hayward (94545-1111)
PHONE.................................510 786-3750
Jeff Bordalampe, *President*
Jim Clifton, *Vice Pres*
George Lambros, *Opers Mgr*
Mark Oatley, *Sales Engr*
Hugh Odonnell, *Sales Engr*

PRODUCTS & SERVICES SECTION

5063 - Electrl Apparatus, Eqpt, Wiring Splys Wholesale County (P-8853)

EMP: 60 **EST:** 1972
SQ FT: 60,000
SALES (est): 25.3MM **Privately Held**
WEB: www.tcialuminum.com
SIC: 5051 Steel

(P-8831)
THYSSENKRUPP INDUS SVCS NA INC
201 Discovery Dr, Livermore (94551-9532)
PHONE 209 395-9111
EMP: 94
SALES (corp-wide): 34B **Privately Held**
WEB: www.thyssenkrupp-materials-na.com
SIC: 5051 Steel
HQ: Thyssenkrupp Industrial Services Na, Inc.
22355 W 11 Mile Rd
Southfield MI 48033
248 233-5600

(P-8832)
VIKING PROCESSING CORPORATION (PA)
620 Clark Ave, Pittsburg (94565-5000)
PHONE 925 427-2518
Spencer M Brog, *CEO*
David Berry, *Finance*
◆ **EMP:** 40 **EST:** 1986
SQ FT: 50,000
SALES (est): 46.4MM **Privately Held**
SIC: 5051 Steel

(P-8833)
WHOLESALE OUTLET INC (PA)
4920 Raley Blvd, Sacramento (95838-1719)
PHONE 916 338-2444
Joe Schmidt, *President*
EMP: 46 **EST:** 1986
SQ FT: 10,000
SALES (est): 24.1MM **Privately Held**
WEB: www.wohvac.com
SIC: 5051 5075 Sheets, metal; warm air heating & air conditioning; air conditioning & ventilation equipment & supplies

(P-8834)
WILLIS REBAR INC
2333 Courage Dr Ste H9, Fairfield (94533-6748)
PHONE 707 419-5949
Raymond Willis III, *CEO*
EMP: 42 **EST:** 2012
SALES (est): 3.7MM **Privately Held**
WEB: www.willisrebarinc.com
SIC: 5051 Steel

5063 Electrl Apparatus, Eqpt, Wiring Splys Wholesale

(P-8835)
16500 SIXTEEN FIVE HUNDRED
2001 Broadway Fl 4th, Oakland (94612-2302)
PHONE 510 208-5005
Paul McDowell, *President*
Jonathan Snyder, *Engineer*
Angela Loceo, *Controller*
Rojae Lake, *Opers-Prdtn-Mfg*
Tyler Elliott, *Sales Staff*
EMP: 48 **EST:** 1998
SQ FT: 14,000
SALES (est): 8MM **Privately Held**
WEB: www.16500.com
SIC: 5063 Electrical supplies

(P-8836)
ABB INC
6650 Goodyear Rd, Benicia (94510-1250)
PHONE 808 497-7240
EMP: 79
SALES (corp-wide): 26.1B **Privately Held**
WEB: www.global.abb
SIC: 5063 Switchgear
HQ: Abb Inc.
305 Gregson Dr
Cary NC 27511

(P-8837)
AEE SOLAR INC
Also Called: Alternative Energy Engineering
1227 Striker Ave Ste 200, Sacramento (95834-1179)
PHONE 800 777-6609
Jude Ekwedike, *Principal*
Aaron Liggett, *Engineer*
Cassandra Bernstein, *Credit Staff*
Patrick Lewis, *Buyer*
Rick Silva, *Prdtn Mgr*
EMP: 57 **Publicly Held**
WEB: www.aeesolar.com
SIC: 5063 Generators
HQ: Aee Solar, Inc.
775 Fiero Ln Ste 200
San Luis Obispo CA 93401
800 777-6609

(P-8838)
ALAMEDA ELECTRIC SUPPLY (HQ)
Also Called: Alameda Electrical Distrs
3875 Bay Center Pl, Hayward (94545-3619)
PHONE 510 786-1400
Robert E Larue, *CEO*
Greg Berkowitz, *Vice Pres*
Criag Larue, *Executive*
Paul Kline, *Buyer*
Jeanette Ward, *Marketing Staff*
▲ **EMP:** 49 **EST:** 1976
SQ FT: 28,000
SALES (est): 152.6MM
SALES (corp-wide): 175.9MM **Privately Held**
WEB: www.alamedaelectric.com
SIC: 5063 Electrical supplies
PA: Alcal Industries, Inc.
25823 Clawiter Rd
Hayward CA 94545
510 786-1400

(P-8839)
ALCAL INDUSTRIES INC (PA)
25823 Clawiter Rd, Hayward (94545-3217)
P.O. Box 4138 (94540-4138)
PHONE 510 786-1400
Bob La Rue, *President*
Courtney Paulsen, *Marketing Mgr*
Misahel Aldaco, *Sales Staff*
Jack Zunich, *Manager*
EMP: 40 **EST:** 2003
SALES (est): 175.9MM **Privately Held**
SIC: 5063 Electrical fittings & construction materials

(P-8840)
ALLIED ELECTRIC MOTOR SVC INC (PA)
4690 E Jensen Ave, Fresno (93725-1698)
PHONE 559 486-4222
Salvatore Rome, *Ch of Bd*
Gail Mandal, *President*
Joyce Barnes, *Corp Secy*
Henry Mandal, *Senior VP*
Richard Johnson, *Vice Pres*
EMP: 55 **EST:** 1955
SQ FT: 100,000
SALES (est): 25.1MM **Privately Held**
SIC: 5063 7694 Electrical supplies; electric motor repair

(P-8841)
AMERICAN WHOLESALE LTG INC
Also Called: Brilliant Lighting Products
1725 Rutan Dr, Livermore (94551-7638)
PHONE 510 252-1088
Jeffrey David Jensen, *President*
Jeremy Adamson, *CFO*
Julie Hannon, *Office Mgr*
Kelly Houston, *Executive Asst*
Alysia Clark, *Admin Asst*
▲ **EMP:** 60 **EST:** 1985
SQ FT: 12,000
SALES (est): 25MM **Privately Held**
WEB: www.awlighting.com
SIC: 5063 Lighting fixtures

(P-8842)
AMPRIUS TECHNOLOGIES INC
1180 Page Ave, Fremont (94538-7342)
PHONE 800 425-8803
Kang Sun, *CEO*

Sandra Wallach, *CFO*
EMP: 50 **EST:** 2020
SALES (est): 2.9MM **Privately Held**
WEB: www.amprius.com
SIC: 5063 Batteries

(P-8843)
ANIXTER INC
5000 Franklin Dr 200, Pleasanton (94588-3354)
PHONE 925 469-8500
Sabrina Vasquez, *Manager*
Lmeshelle Davis, *Credit Staff*
Brent McClintock, *Manager*
Navid Aflatooni, *Accounts Mgr*
EMP: 50 **Publicly Held**
WEB: www.anixterlabstesting.com
SIC: 5063 Wire & cable
HQ: Anixter Inc.
2301 Patriot Blvd
Glenview IL 60026
224 521-8000

(P-8844)
ASSOCIATED LIGHTING REP INC (PA)
7777 Pardee Ln, Oakland (94621-1425)
P.O. Box 2265 (94621-0165)
PHONE 510 638-3800
Darrell Packard Sr, *President*
Sean Darcy, *Vice Pres*
Bruce Laing, *Vice Pres*
Neva Benavides, *Administration*
Gwen Smallwood, *Administration*
EMP: 41 **EST:** 1962
SQ FT: 10,000
SALES (est): 16.5MM **Privately Held**
WEB: www.alrinc.com
SIC: 5063 Lighting fixtures, commercial & industrial

(P-8845)
BELL ELECTRICAL SUPPLY INC (PA)
Also Called: Industrial Control Components
316 Mathew St, Santa Clara (95050-3104)
PHONE 408 727-2355
David Wallen, *President*
Marisol Iriondo, *Project Mgr*
Vanessa Arrington, *VP Opers*
Rosalie Adragna, *Sales Staff*
David Guevara, *Sales Staff*
EMP: 44 **EST:** 1966
SQ FT: 24,000
SALES (est): 37MM **Privately Held**
WEB: www.bell-electrical.com
SIC: 5063 Electrical supplies

(P-8846)
BUY 4 LESS
Also Called: G & R Wholesale Distribution
401 W Lockeford St, Lodi (95240-2035)
PHONE 209 368-3614
Steve Fetzer, *President*
EMP: 55 **EST:** 1991
SQ FT: 8,000
SALES (est): 3MM **Privately Held**
WEB: www.buy4lesslodi.com
SIC: 5411 5063 5149 Convenience stores; electrical apparatus & equipment; groceries & related products

(P-8847)
CALIFRNIA ARCHTECTURAL LTG INC (PA)
Also Called: Cal Lighting
4000 Executive Pkwy # 350, San Ramon (94583-4257)
PHONE 925 242-0111
Kenneth A Selvidge Sr, *President*
Suzanne Carroll, *Corp Secy*
David Bacher, *Vice Pres*
Anthony Dowling, *Sales Staff*
Ron Scott, *Sales Staff*
EMP: 35 **EST:** 1984
SALES (est): 8.2MM **Privately Held**
WEB: www.cal.lighting
SIC: 5063 Lighting fixtures, commercial & industrial; lighting fixtures

(P-8848)
CANDLE3 LLC
101 California St # 2710, San Francisco (94111-5802)
PHONE 415 365-9679

EMP: 47
SALES (corp-wide): 12.5MM **Privately Held**
SIC: 5063 Whol Electrical Equipment
PA: Candle3, Llc
555 Middle Creek Pkwy # 200
Colorado Springs CO 80921
719 602-6000

(P-8849)
CAPELLA SPACE CORP
438 Shotwell St, San Francisco (94110-1914)
PHONE 650 334-7734
Payam Banazadeh, *CEO*
Kevin Chen, *Vice Pres*
Christian Lenz, *Vice Pres*
Matt Wood, *Vice Pres*
Cheryl He, *Software Engr*
EMP: 75 **EST:** 2016
SALES (est): 12.2MM **Privately Held**
WEB: www.capellaspace.com
SIC: 5063 Antennas, receiving, satellite dishes

(P-8850)
CENTURY COMMERCIAL SERVICE
12820 Earhart Ave, Auburn (95602-9027)
P.O. Box 6793 (95604-6793)
PHONE 530 823-1004
Keith Estes, *President*
Brent Estes, *Vice Pres*
Traci Estes, *Vice Pres*
Brian Kolitsch, *Department Mgr*
Lorin Estes, *Technician*
EMP: 50 **EST:** 1984
SQ FT: 6,500
SALES (est): 20.2MM **Privately Held**
WEB: www.centuryservice.com
SIC: 5063 1731 8748 Light bulbs & related supplies; lighting contractor; energy conservation consultant

(P-8851)
CHESTER C LEHMANN CO INC (PA)
Also Called: Electrical Distributors Co
1135 Auzerais Ave, San Jose (95126-3402)
P.O. Box 26830 (95159-6830)
PHONE 408 293-5818
Chester C Lehmann III, *CEO*
Scott Lehmann, *President*
Melissa Lankford, *Project Mgr*
Jackie Murdaugh, *Project Mgr*
Teresa T Nielsen, *Project Mgr*
▼ **EMP:** 65 **EST:** 1948
SQ FT: 80,000
SALES (est): 181MM **Privately Held**
SIC: 5063 Electrical supplies

(P-8852)
CITY ELECTRIC SUPPLY
360 Tesconi Cir, Santa Rosa (95401-4677)
PHONE 707 523-4600
Steve Acuri, *Manager*
Bobbyjean Payne, *Project Mgr*
Martin Sass, *Sales Associate*
EMP: 25 **EST:** 2009
SALES (est): 10.8MM **Privately Held**
WEB: www.ces-santarosa.shopced.com
SIC: 5063 3699 3634 Electrical supplies; electrical equipment & supplies; electric housewares & fans

(P-8853)
CITY LIGHTS LIGHTING SHOWROOM
1585 Folsom St, San Francisco (94103-3728)
PHONE 415 863-2020
Nina Klotz, *President*
Javier Garcia, *Sales Staff*
Michael Moody, *Sales Staff*
Joy Perez, *Sales Staff*
Raymond Yee, *Sales Staff*
EMP: 40 **EST:** 1978
SALES (est): 23.7MM **Privately Held**
WEB: www.citylightssf.com
SIC: 5063 Lighting fixtures

5063 - Electrl Apparatus, Eqpt, Wiring Splys Wholesale County (P-8854)

(P-8854)
CJS LIGHTING INC
300 Derek Pl, Roseville (95678-7011)
P.O. Box 1269 (95678-8269)
PHONE..................................916 774-6888
Robert Oflaherty, *President*
Robert O'Flaherty, *President*
Robert O'flaherty, *Branch Mgr*
Christina Szeremi, *Project Mgr*
Jeff McCrary, *Sales Associate*
EMP: 40 **EST:** 1974
SQ FT: 4,330
SALES (est): 6.2MM **Privately Held**
WEB: www.cjslighting.com
SIC: 5063 Lighting fixtures

(P-8855)
CONTINENTAL SALES & MKTG INC (PA)
2360 Alvarado St, San Leandro (94577-4314)
PHONE..................................510 895-1881
Steven Scheiner, *President*
Feroun Khan, *Vice Pres*
Lewis Ted, *Vice Pres*
Patrick Jenkinson, *VP Bus Dvlpt*
CJ Tocco, *Regional Mgr*
◆ **EMP:** 40 **EST:** 1978
SQ FT: 40,000
SALES (est): 10.3MM **Privately Held**
WEB: www.csmlink.com
SIC: 5063 Electrical apparatus & equipment

(P-8856)
DAHL-BECK ELECTRIC CO
2775 Goodrick Ave, Richmond (94801-1109)
PHONE..................................510 237-2325
Roger Beck, *CEO*
William R Beck, *President*
James Ross, *Corp Secy*
Gerald Vaio, *Vice Pres*
▲ **EMP:** 65 **EST:** 1932
SQ FT: 75,000
SALES (est): 21.8MM **Privately Held**
WEB: www.dahlbeckelectric.com
SIC: 5063 1731 Electrical supplies; general electrical contractor

(P-8857)
E & S WESTCOAST LLC (PA)
Also Called: John Deere Authorized Dealer
7100 Longe St Ste 300, Stockton (95206-3962)
P.O. Box 31420 (95213-1420)
PHONE..................................209 870-1900
Donald Richter, *President*
Gail Cressley, *Vice Pres*
Bob Denning, *General Mgr*
Adam Collins, *Technician*
Heather Gum, *Project Mgr*
EMP: 35 **EST:** 1992
SQ FT: 19,000
SALES (est): 13.6MM **Privately Held**
WEB: www.espowergen.com
SIC: 5063 7629 5082 Generators; generator repair; construction & mining machinery

(P-8858)
EDGES ELECTRICAL GROUP LLC (HQ)
1135 Auzerais Ave, San Jose (95126-3402)
P.O. Box 26830 (95159-6830)
PHONE..................................408 293-5818
Mark Arndt, *CFO*
Randy Phares, *Branch Mgr*
Linsey Doneilo, *Project Mgr*
Nadine White, *Project Mgr*
Nancy Cooper, *Human Res Mgr*
EMP: 84 **EST:** 2014
SALES (est): 65.8MM
SALES (corp-wide): 181MM **Privately Held**
WEB: www.edgesgroup.com
SIC: 5063 Electrical supplies
PA: Chester C. Lehmann Co., Inc.
   1135 Auzerais Ave
   San Jose CA 95126
   408 293-5818

(P-8859)
ELECTRIC MOTOR SHOP (PA)
Also Called: Electric Motor & Supply
253 Fulton St, Fresno (93721-3164)
P.O. Box 446 (93709-0446)
PHONE..................................559 233-1153
Richard M Caglia, *President*
Sally Caglia, *Treasurer*
Sally M Caglia, *Corp Secy*
Theresa Azevedo, *Officer*
Steven Ray,
EMP: 24 **EST:** 1913
SQ FT: 7,500
SALES (est): 51.9MM **Privately Held**
WEB: www.electricmotorshop.com
SIC: 5063 1731 7694 7922 Motor controls, starters & relays: electric; motors, electric; electrical work; electric motor repair; theatrical producers & services

(P-8860)
ELECTRIC MOTOR SHOP
Also Called: Electric Motor & Supply Co.
250 Broadway St, Fresno (93721-3103)
P.O. Box 446 (93709-0446)
PHONE..................................559 233-1153
Dicks Caglia, *President*
Wilson Rodney, *Branch Mgr*
Theresa Azevedo, *Office Mgr*
Glenda Ritter, *Office Mgr*
Jon Wiseman, *Sales Staff*
EMP: 148
SQ FT: 1,296
SALES (corp-wide): 51.9MM **Privately Held**
WEB: www.electricmotorshop.com
SIC: 5063 Electrical supplies
PA: Electric Motor Shop
   253 Fulton St
   Fresno CA 93721
   559 233-1153

(P-8861)
GREATLINK INTERNATIONAL INC
44168 S Grimmer Blvd, Fremont (94538-6310)
PHONE..................................510 657-1667
Anjee Huang, *CEO*
David Lai, *Project Engr*
Boris Shklyarevsky, *Sales Staff*
▲ **EMP:** 659 **EST:** 1997
SQ FT: 10,000
SALES (est): 64MM **Privately Held**
WEB: www.greatlinkus.com
SIC: 5063 Cable conduit
PA: Greatlink Electronics Taiwan Ltd.
   5f, 7, Ln. 45, Baoxing Rd.,
   New Taipei City TAP 23145

(P-8862)
INDEPENDENT ELECTRIC SUP INC (DH)
2001 Marina Blvd, San Leandro (94577-3204)
PHONE..................................510 877-9850
David Jones, *President*
Rick Crew, *Branch Mgr*
Brett Massip, *Branch Mgr*
Pete Schneider, *Branch Mgr*
Lorraine Hidalgo, *Admin Asst*
EMP: 166 **EST:** 1973
SALES (est): 631.3MM
SALES (corp-wide): 13.2MM **Privately Held**
WEB: www.soneparusa.com
SIC: 5063 Electrical supplies
HQ: Sonepar Management Us, Inc.
   510 Walnut St Ste 400
   Philadelphia PA 19106
   215 399-5900

(P-8863)
INSULATION SOURCES INC (PA)
Also Called: ICO Rally
2575 E Bayshore Rd, Palo Alto (94303-3210)
PHONE..................................650 856-8378
Edwina M Cioffi, *CEO*
Brian Cioffi, *Vice Pres*
Janet Ashley, *Technology*
Greg Ghiozzi, *Manager*
▲ **EMP:** 45 **EST:** 1997
SQ FT: 15,000

SALES (est): 39.2MM **Privately Held**
SIC: 5063 5065 3671 Wire & cable; electronic parts; cathode ray tubes, including rebuilt

(P-8864)
KOFFLER ELEC MECH APPRTUS REPR
527 Whitney St, San Leandro (94577-1113)
PHONE..................................510 567-0630
Lari Koffler, *President*
Michael Bucedi, *Treasurer*
Wayne Kelder, *Vice Pres*
Charles H Koffler, *Vice Pres*
Kevin Koffler, *General Mgr*
▲ **EMP:** 80 **EST:** 1994
SQ FT: 77,548
SALES (est): 27MM **Privately Held**
WEB: www.koffler.com
SIC: 5063 7694 Motors, electric; electric motor repair

(P-8865)
LGE ELECTRICAL SALES INC
755 E Evelyn Ave, Sunnyvale (94086-6527)
P.O. Box 1263, San Carlos (94070-1263)
PHONE..................................408 992-4145
Ray Landgraf, *Manager*
EMP: 102
SALES (corp-wide): 13.2MM **Privately Held**
WEB: www.lgesales.com
SIC: 5063 Electrical supplies
HQ: Lge Electrical Sales, Inc.
   650 University Ave # 218
   Sacramento CA 95825
   916 563-2737

(P-8866)
LUMENS LLC (DH)
2020 L St Ste LI10, Sacramento (95811-4260)
PHONE..................................916 444-5585
Ken Plumlee, *President*
Peter Weight, *Admin Sec*
Brian Del Vecchio, *Sr Software Eng*
Melanie Robledo, *Opers Staff*
Richard Tawney, *Marketing Staff*
◆ **EMP:** 50 **EST:** 2003
SQ FT: 5,700
SALES (est): 31.7MM
SALES (corp-wide): 177.9K **Privately Held**
WEB: www.lumens.com
SIC: 5063 5712 Lighting fixtures; furniture stores

(P-8867)
MALTBY ELECTRIC SUPPLY CO INC (PA)
336 7th St, San Francisco (94103-4092)
PHONE..................................415 863-5000
John A Maltby, *President*
Broadney Jason, *Vice Pres*
Justin Phelan, *Branch Mgr*
Lily Maltby, *Admin Sec*
Armand Pantaleon, *Business Mgr*
EMP: 35 **EST:** 1955
SQ FT: 31,378
SALES (est): 32.2MM **Privately Held**
WEB: www.maltbyelecsf.com
SIC: 5063 Electrical supplies

(P-8868)
MCS OPCO LLC
Also Called: US Power
905 Cottinlane Dr, Vacaville (95688)
PHONE..................................203 740-4236
Dan Pfahlert, *Manager*
EMP: 35
SALES (corp-wide): 8.7MM **Privately Held**
SIC: 5063 Power transmission equipment, electric
PA: Mcs Opco, Llc
   9 Park Lawn Dr
   Bethel CT 06801
   203 740-4236

(P-8869)
MPOWER ELECTRONICS INC
3046 Scott Blvd, Santa Clara (95054-3301)
PHONE..................................408 320-1266
Hong Tao Sun, *President*
Weimin Cai, *Chairman*

Peter Hsi, *Bd of Directors*
Yongbiao Qian, *General Mgr*
Werner Haag, *Engineer*
◆ **EMP:** 60 **EST:** 2018
SALES (est): 2.7MM **Privately Held**
WEB: www.mpowerinc.com
SIC: 5063 3829 3624 Fire alarm systems; signaling equipment, electrical; gas detectors; carbon & graphite products

(P-8870)
OPTIMAS OE SOLUTIONS LLC
5940 E Shields Ave # 102, Fresno (93727-8066)
PHONE..................................559 492-4441
Andrew Marlow, *Manager*
EMP: 41
SALES (corp-wide): 714.8MM **Privately Held**
WEB: www.optimas.com
SIC: 5063 Electrical apparatus & equipment
HQ: Optimas Oe Solutions, Llc
   1441 N Wood Dale Rd
   Wood Dale IL 60191
   224 999-1000

(P-8871)
OPTIMAS OE SOLUTIONS LLC
1931 Lundy Ave, San Jose (95131-1847)
PHONE..................................408 934-1001
Barry Torno, *Principal*
EMP: 41
SALES (corp-wide): 714.8MM **Privately Held**
WEB: www.optimas.com
SIC: 5063 Wire & cable; control & signal wire & cable, including coaxial
HQ: Optimas Oe Solutions, Llc
   1441 N Wood Dale Rd
   Wood Dale IL 60191
   224 999-1000

(P-8872)
OSRAM SYLVANIA INC
651 River Oaks Pkwy, San Jose (95134-1907)
PHONE..................................408 922-7200
EMP: 35
SALES (corp-wide): 4.1B **Privately Held**
WEB: www.osram.us
SIC: 5063 Lighting fixtures
HQ: Osram Sylvania Inc
   200 Ballardvale St # 305
   Wilmington MA 01887
   978 570-3000

(P-8873)
QUANTUM PRECISION INC
1307 66th St, Emeryville (94608-1116)
PHONE..................................908 928-1115
EMP: 28 **EST:** 1976
SQ FT: 845
SALES: 1.4MM **Privately Held**
SIC: 5063 3825 Wholesaler & Export Agent Of Electrical Equipment And Through Subsidiary Manufactures Electrical Testing Equipment

(P-8874)
REXEL USA INC
Also Called: Gexpro
2301 Armstrong St Ste 205, Livermore (94551-9349)
PHONE..................................510 476-3400
David Mahoney, *Branch Mgr*
Tina Terry, *Office Admin*
Jeffrey Fisk, *Project Mgr*
Karen Lee, *Project Mgr*
Blair Martin, *Project Mgr*
EMP: 45
SALES (corp-wide): 533.7K **Privately Held**
WEB: www.rexelusainc.com
SIC: 5063 Electrical supplies
HQ: Rexel Usa, Inc.
   14951 Dallas Pkwy
   Dallas TX 75254

(P-8875)
SATCO PRODUCTS OF CALIFORNIA
31288 San Benito St, Hayward (94544-7914)
PHONE..................................510 487-4822

PRODUCTS & SERVICES SECTION
5065 - Electronic Parts & Eqpt Wholesale County (P-8897)

Allen Ginsburg, *Manager*
EMP: 54
SALES (corp-wide): 124.4MM **Privately Held**
WEB: www.satco.com
SIC: 5063 Lighting fixtures; light bulbs & related supplies
HQ: Satco Products Of California, Inc
110 Heartland Blvd
Edgewood NY 11717
631 243-2022

(P-8876)
SHOWA DENKO MATERIALS AMER INC (DH)
2150 N 1st St Ste 350, San Jose (95131-2061)
PHONE..................408 873-2200
Dennis Parker, *President*
Tomoe Kalnay, *CFO*
Terry Fischer, *Vice Pres*
Naoyuki Koyama, *General Mgr*
Nelson Kuo, *Engineer*
◆ **EMP:** 45
SQ FT: 14,000
SALES (est): 150.1MM **Privately Held**
WEB: www.ma.showadenko.com
SIC: 5063 5065 Wiring devices; circuit breakers; semiconductor devices; capacitors, electronic

(P-8877)
SIEMENS
1001 Marina Village Pkwy, Alameda (94501-1091)
PHONE..................510 263-0367
EMP: 46 **Privately Held**
SIC: 9611 5211 5063 3699 Admn General Economy Pgm Ret Lumber/Building Mtrl Whol Electrical Equip Mfg Elec Mach/Equip/Supp

(P-8878)
STEVEN ENGINEERING INC (PA)
230 Ryan Way, South San Francisco (94080-6370)
PHONE..................650 588-9200
Bonnie A Walter, *CEO*
Kenneth D Walter, *President*
Bryan J Woifgram, *Exec VP*
Bryan Wolfgram, *Exec VP*
Paul E Burk III, *Vice Pres*
◆ **EMP:** 93 **EST:** 1975
SQ FT: 66,000
SALES (est): 72.4MM **Privately Held**
WEB: www.stevenengineering.com
SIC: 5063 Electrical apparatus & equipment

(P-8879)
WINDY CY WIRE CBLE TECH PDTS L
8024 Central Ave, Newark (94560-3450)
PHONE..................510 284-3956
Sonia Daquioag, *Manager*
EMP: 217
SALES (corp-wide): 703.5MM **Privately Held**
WEB: www.smartwire.com
SIC: 5063 Wire & cable
HQ: Windy City Wire Cable And Technology Products, Llc
386 Internationale Dr H
Bolingbrook IL 60440

(P-8880)
YDESIGN GROUP LLC (DH)
Also Called: Yliving
2020 L St Ste Ll10, Sacramento (95811-4260)
PHONE..................866 842-6209
Graham C Weaver,
Suzan Davis, *Vice Pres*
Jennifer Neto, *Office Mgr*
Branden Tillman, *CIO*
Henry Cai, *Controller*
◆ **EMP:** 50 **EST:** 2008
SALES (est): 106.9MM
SALES (corp-wide): 177.9K **Privately Held**
WEB: www.ydesigngroup.com
SIC: 5063 5031 Lighting fixtures; lighting fittings & accessories; lighting fixtures, commercial & industrial; lighting fixtures, residential; building materials, interior

(P-8881)
ZSPACE INC (PA)
55 Nicholson Ln Ste 2, San Jose (95134-1366)
PHONE..................408 498-4050
Paul Kellenberger, *CEO*
Joseph Powers, *CFO*
EMP: 68 **EST:** 2006
SALES (est): 17.5MM **Privately Held**
WEB: www.zspace.com
SIC: 5063 Transformers, electric

5064 Electrical Appliances, TV & Radios Wholesale

(P-8882)
AAC TECHNOLOGIES HOLDINGS INC (HQ)
20380 Town Center Ln, Cupertino (95014-3210)
PHONE..................408 490-4263
Charles Slutzky, *Surgery Dir*
Desiree Sanchez, *Office Mgr*
Timo Gerasimow, *Sr Software Eng*
Jon Eccleston, *Engineer*
Silviu Tanase, *Engineer*
EMP: 25 **EST:** 2017
SALES (est): 2.6MM **Privately Held**
WEB: www.aactechnologies.com
SIC: 5064 3651 Tape players & recorders; audio electronic systems

(P-8883)
BRIX GROUP INC
HG BRIX CO
80 Van Ness Ave, Fresno (93721-3223)
PHONE..................559 457-4794
EMP: 49
SALES (corp-wide): 151.7MM **Privately Held**
SIC: 5064 Whol Appliances/Tv/Radio
PA: The Brix Group Inc
838 N Laverne Ave
Fresno CA 93727
559 457-4700

(P-8884)
LOWES HOME CENTERS LLC
3400 N Texas St, Fairfield (94533-7242)
PHONE..................707 207-2070
Susan Moores, *Branch Mgr*
EMP: 119
SALES (corp-wide): 89.6B **Publicly Held**
WEB: www.lowes.com
SIC: 5211 5064 5722 Home centers; electrical appliances, television & radio; household appliance stores
HQ: Lowe's Home Centers, Llc
1000 Lowes Blvd
Mooresville NC 28117
336 658-4000

(P-8885)
NOVO MASTERS WHOLESALE INC ✪
Also Called: Masters Whosales
2504 Mercantile Dr, Rancho Cordova (95742-8201)
PHONE..................916 665-0390
Angela Liu, *CEO*
EMP: 45 **EST:** 2021
SALES (est): 24MM **Privately Held**
SIC: 5064 Appliance parts, household

(P-8886)
RIGGS DISTRIBUTING INC (PA)
Also Called: Sub Zero
1755 Rollins Rd, Burlingame (94010-2207)
PHONE..................650 240-3000
Robert P Riggs, *President*
Larry Short, *Vice Pres*
Molly Dagnelie, *Technology*
Bryan Nies, *Marketing Mgr*
Jammy Charan, *Sales Staff*
▲ **EMP:** 40 **EST:** 2007
SQ FT: 25,000
SALES (est): 13.2MM **Privately Held**
WEB: www.riggsdistributing.com
SIC: 5064 Refrigerators & freezers

(P-8887)
SIERRA SELECT DISTRIBUTORS INC
4320 Roseville Rd, North Highlands (95660-5711)
PHONE..................916 483-9295
Patrick Russell Tatro, *CEO*
John Tatro, *Vice Pres*
Arnie Vierra, *Division Mgr*
Michael W Tatro, *General Mgr*
Lita Martinez, *Admin Sec*
▲ **EMP:** 65 **EST:** 1982
SQ FT: 54,000
SALES (est): 27.3MM **Privately Held**
WEB: www.sierraselect.com
SIC: 5064 Radios; television sets; video cassette recorders & accessories; microwave ovens, non-commercial

---

5065 Electronic Parts & Eqpt Wholesale

(P-8888)
ABX ENGINEERING INC
875 Stanton Rd, Burlingame (94010-1403)
PHONE..................650 552-2300
Paul Leininger, *CEO*
Brian Helm, *Vice Pres*
Rigo Alonso, *Project Mgr*
Silvia De Leon, *Purch Mgr*
Silvia De Leon-Lind, *Purch Mgr*
EMP: 100
SQ FT: 16,000
SALES (est): 51.8MM **Privately Held**
WEB: www.abxengineering.com
SIC: 5065 7373 3672 Electronic parts; turnkey vendors, computer systems; printed circuit boards

(P-8889)
AMERICAN TELESOURCE INC
Also Called: ATI
1311 63rd St Ste B, Emeryville (94608-2156)
PHONE..................510 428-1111
Stephen Viets, *President*
Steve Karthan, *CFO*
Joseph Ball, *Prgrmr*
H Emamifar, *Engineer*
Craig Wada, *Engineer*
EMP: 38 **EST:** 1987
SALES (est): 9.6MM **Privately Held**
WEB: www.ati-connect.com
SIC: 5065 7629 7371 Telephone equipment; telecommunication equipment repair (except telephones); computer software systems analysis & design, custom

(P-8890)
APACER MEMORY AMERICA INC
46732 Lakeview Blvd, Fremont (94538-6529)
PHONE..................408 518-8699
Austin Chen, *President*
Jane Koo, *CFO*
Lawrence Lo, *Vice Pres*
Deborah Guo, *Opers Staff*
Jack Luo, *Sales Staff*
▲ **EMP:** 47 **EST:** 1997
SQ FT: 3,500
SALES (est): 10.3MM **Privately Held**
WEB: www.apacer.com
SIC: 5065 Electronic parts & equipment
PA: Apacer Technology Inc.
1f, No. 32, Zhongcheng Rd.
New Taipei City TAP 23674

(P-8891)
APPLIED WIRELESS IDENTIFIC (PA)
Also Called: Awid
18300 Sutter Blvd, Morgan Hill (95037-2841)
PHONE..................408 779-1929
Dr Edward Liao, *CEO*
Sara Stein, *Regl Sales Mgr*
Hakima Abbas, *Director*
▲ **EMP:** 30 **EST:** 1997
SQ FT: 20,000

SALES (est): 13.8MM **Privately Held**
WEB: www.awid.com
SIC: 5065 3699 Security control equipment & systems; security control equipment & systems

(P-8892)
ASE (US)INC (DH)
Also Called: Advance Semiconductor Engrg
1255 E Arques Ave, Sunnyvale (94085-4701)
PHONE..................408 636-9500
Pien Wu, *President*
Ingu Chang, *Vice Pres*
Richard Barnes, *CIO*
Terry Hsiang, *Sales Staff*
Jon Howard, *Manager*
EMP: 54 **EST:** 1983
SQ FT: 21,000
SALES (est): 48.5MM **Privately Held**
WEB: www.asetechforum.com
SIC: 5065 Electronic parts & equipment

(P-8893)
ATMOSIC TECHNOLOGIES INC
2105 S Bascom Ave Ste 220, Campbell (95008-3292)
PHONE..................650 678-7864
David Su, *CEO*
Thomas Chen, *Vice Pres*
EMP: 35 **EST:** 2017
SALES (est): 7.2MM **Privately Held**
WEB: www.atmosic.com
SIC: 5065 Semiconductor devices

(P-8894)
AVI SYSTEMS INC
44150 S Grimmer Blvd, Fremont (94538-6310)
PHONE..................415 915-2070
EMP: 55
SALES (corp-wide): 250.2MM **Privately Held**
WEB: www.avisystems.com
SIC: 5065 Sound equipment, electronic
PA: Avi Systems, Inc.
9675 W 76th St Ste 200
Eden Prairie MN 55344
952 949-3700

(P-8895)
AXIAD IDS INC (HQ)
900 Lafayette St Ste 600, Santa Clara (95050-4931)
PHONE..................408 841-4670
Bassam Al-Khalidi, *CEO*
Yves Audebert, *President*
Thomas Jahn, *CFO*
Gurpreet Manes, *Vice Pres*
Brian Culhane, *VP Bus Dvlpt*
EMP: 39 **EST:** 2010
SALES (est): 16.2MM **Privately Held**
WEB: www.axiad.com
SIC: 5065 7382 7373 Security control equipment & systems; security systems services; computer integrated systems design

(P-8896)
BEYOND SECURITY INC
2267 Lava Ridge Ct # 100, Roseville (95661-3062)
PHONE..................279 201-7150
Aviram Jenik, *President*
Benjamin Moyer, *Administration*
Noam Rathaus, *CTO*
Cameron O'connor, *Sales Staff*
EMP: 70 **EST:** 2005
SALES (est): 12.5MM **Privately Held**
WEB: www.beyondsecurity.com
SIC: 5065 Security control equipment & systems

(P-8897)
BRAEMAC (CA) LLC
43134 Osgood Rd, Fremont (94539-5608)
PHONE..................510 687-1000
Ben Kingsley, *Mng Member*
Sid Batra, *General Mgr*
Dan Cao, *Sales Staff*
Rey Lingad, *Warehouse Mgr*
Raymond Ford,
◆ **EMP:** 80 **EST:** 1997
SQ FT: 16,000

5065 - Electronic Parts & Eqpt Wholesale County (P-8898)

PRODUCTS & SERVICES SECTION

SALES (est): 24.2MM Privately Held
WEB: www.braemac.com
SIC: 5065 Semiconductor devices

(P-8898)
BRIX GROUP INC (PA)
Also Called: Pana-Pacific
838 N Laverne Ave, Fresno (93727-6868)
PHONE.....................559 457-4700
Harrison Brix, CEO
Kristina Reed, President
John Trenberth, CEO
Dennis Pastirik, CFO
John Tingleff, CFO
▲ EMP: 80
SQ FT: 35,000
SALES (est): 156.6MM Privately Held
WEB: www.panapacific.com
SIC: 5065 5013 Mobile telephone equipment; paging & signaling equipment; motor vehicle supplies & new parts

(P-8899)
CALEX MFG CO INC
2401 Stanwell Dr Frnt, Concord (94520-4872)
PHONE.....................925 687-4411
Paul S Cuff, CEO
Milivoje Brkovic, CTO
Ed Wong, Senior Engr
Robert Zorovic, Buyer
Goble Loren, Mfg Mgr
▲ EMP: 45 EST: 1962
SALES (est): 19.5MM Privately Held
WEB: www.calex.com
SIC: 5065 Electronic parts & equipment; coils, electronic

(P-8900)
CALIFORNIA EASTERN LABS INC (PA)
5201 Great America Pkwy, Santa Clara (95054-1122)
PHONE.....................408 919-2500
Paul Minton, CEO
Jerry A Arden, Ch of Bd
Paul A S Minton, President
Mark A Sargent, CFO
Kevin Beber, Vice Pres
▲ EMP: 80 EST: 1959
SQ FT: 42,000
SALES (est): 37.1MM Privately Held
WEB: www.cel.com
SIC: 5065 Semiconductor devices

(P-8901)
CAVENDISH KINETICS INC
2960 N 1st St, San Jose (95134-2021)
PHONE.....................408 627-4504
Paul Dal Santo, President
Patrick Murray, CFO
Atul P Shingal, Vice Pres
EMP: 50 EST: 2006
SALES (est): 18.4MM
SALES (corp-wide): 4B Publicly Held
WEB: www.cavendish-kinetics.com
SIC: 5065 Semiconductor devices
PA: Qorvo, Inc.
 7628 Thorndike Rd
 Greensboro NC 27409
 336 664-1233

(P-8902)
CENZIC INC
655 Campbell Tech Pkwy # 100, Campbell (95008-5088)
PHONE.....................408 200-0700
John Weinschenk, President
Dave Ferguson, CFO
Bala Venkat, Chief Mktg Ofcr
Glenn Gramling, Vice Pres
Tyler Rorabaugh, Vice Pres
EMP: 68 EST: 2000
SQ FT: 7,600
SALES (est): 14MM Privately Held
WEB: www.trustwave.com
SIC: 5065 Security control equipment & systems
HQ: Trustwave Holdings, Inc.
 70 W Madison St Ste 600
 Chicago IL 60602
 312 750-0950

(P-8903)
CNET TECHNOLOGY CORPORATION (HQ)
26291 Prod Ave Ste 205, Hayward (94545)
PHONE.....................408 392-9966
Simon J Chang, President
▲ EMP: 179 EST: 1987
SQ FT: 50,000
SALES (est): 30MM Privately Held
WEB: www.cnetusa.com
SIC: 5065 3661 3577 Communication equipment; modems, computer; telephone & telegraph apparatus; computer peripheral equipment

(P-8904)
COMBA TELECOM INC
568 Gibraltar Dr, Milpitas (95035-6315)
PHONE.....................408 526-0130
Tung Ling Fok, President
Luo Rui Bo, Vice Pres
Bu Bin Long, Vice Pres
Chen Sui Yang, Vice Pres
Zhang Jin Yu, Vice Pres
EMP: 18 EST: 2005
SALES (est): 23MM Privately Held
WEB: www.comba-telecom.com
SIC: 5065 3661 Telephone & telegraphic equipment; telephones & telephone apparatus
PA: Comba Telecom Systems Limited
 Rm 611 6/F East Wing Hong Kong Science Park
 Tai Po NT

(P-8905)
CREATEPROS LLC
4353 N 1st St, San Jose (95134-1259)
PHONE.....................844 752-7328
EMP: 105
SALES (est): 22K Privately Held
WEB: www.createpros.net
SIC: 5065 8748 Electronic Parts And Equipment, Nec, Nsk

(P-8906)
DELTA AMERICA LTD (HQ)
Also Called: Delta Products
46101 Fremont Blvd, Fremont (94538-6468)
PHONE.....................510 668-5100
Ming H Huang, President
Armin Paya, Vice Pres
Wayne Brown, Office Mgr
Yao Chou, Admin Sec
Bin Su, Info Tech Dir
◆ EMP: 130 EST: 1988
SALES (est): 261.5MM Privately Held
WEB: www.delta-america.com
SIC: 5065 3679 8731 Electronic parts & equipment; switches, stepping; power supplies, all types: static; electronic research

(P-8907)
DIALOG SEMICONDUCTOR INC
1515 Wyatt Dr, Santa Clara (95054-1586)
PHONE.....................408 327-8800
EMP: 235
SALES (corp-wide): 1.3B Privately Held
WEB: www.dialog-semiconductor.com
SIC: 5065 Semiconductor devices
HQ: Dialog Semiconductor, Inc.
 2560 Mission College Blvd # 110
 Santa Clara CA 95054
 408 845-8500

(P-8908)
DYNAMIC SECURITY TECH INC
28301 Industrial Blvd B, Hayward (94545-4429)
PHONE.....................510 786-1121
Bryan Buenaventura, CEO
Nora Juarez-Faddis, General Mgr
EMP: 24
SALES (est): 2.4MM Privately Held
WEB: www.dystinc.com
SIC: 5065 7382 3699 Security control equipment & systems; security systems services; security devices

(P-8909)
ERIC ELECTRONICS INC
2220 Lundy Ave, San Jose (95131-1816)
P.O. Box 610010 (95161-0010)
PHONE.....................408 432-1111
Donald Turnquist, CEO
Curt Gordon, President
EMP: 26 EST: 1969
SQ FT: 21,000
SALES (est): 3.2MM Privately Held
WEB: www.ericnet.com
SIC: 5065 3679 Electronic parts; electronic circuits

(P-8910)
EWING-FOLEY INC (PA)
10061 Bubb Rd Ste 100, Cupertino (95014-4162)
PHONE.....................408 342-1201
Richard Foley, Ch of Bd
Todd Henry, Partner
Gary Lessing, President
Robert Lessing, Corp Secy
Jessica Jagger, Executive
EMP: 50 EST: 1964
SQ FT: 13,000
SALES (est): 22.7MM Privately Held
WEB: www.ewingfoley.com
SIC: 5065 Electronic parts

(P-8911)
EXIS INC
1590 The Alameda Ste 110, San Jose (95126-2314)
PHONE.....................408 944-4600
Jim Bailey, President
Lisa Carter, Executive Asst
Tanya Gonzales, Administration
Tanya Gromova, Administration
Suzie Ferreira, Sales Staff
EMP: 50 EST: 1984
SALES (est): 6.7MM Privately Held
WEB: www.exisqci.com
SIC: 5065 Electronic parts

(P-8912)
FAI ELECTRONICS CORP
Also Called: Future Active Industrial Elec
690 N Mccarthy Blvd Ste 2, Milpitas (95035-5134)
PHONE.....................408 434-0369
Debbie Miller, Manager
EMP: 49
SALES (corp-wide): 3.1B Privately Held
SIC: 5065 Electronic parts
HQ: Fai Electronics Corp
 41 Main St
 Bolton MA 01740

(P-8913)
FAI ELECTRONICS CORP
2220 Otoole Ave, San Jose (95131-1326)
PHONE.....................408 829-7581
McCormick Don, Branch Mgr
EMP: 49
SALES (corp-wide): 3.1B Privately Held
SIC: 5065 Electronic parts
HQ: Fai Electronics Corp
 41 Main St
 Bolton MA 01740

(P-8914)
FUJITSU COMPONENTS AMERICA INC (DH)
1230 E Arques Ave Ms160, Sunnyvale (94085-5401)
PHONE.....................408 745-4900
Robert L Thornton, President
Don Cramb, President
Donald J Dealtry, President
Yasuhiro Ogura, CFO
Yasuhito Hara, Chairman
◆ EMP: 35 EST: 1993
SQ FT: 24,000
SALES (est): 24.4MM Privately Held
WEB: www.scanners.us.fujitsu.com
SIC: 5065 Electronic parts & equipment

(P-8915)
HANA MICROELECTRONICS INC
3100 De La Cruz Blvd, Santa Clara (95054-2438)
PHONE.....................408 452-7474
Sanjay Mitra, President
Thang Bui, Business Mgr
Leana Bui, Accounts Mgr
EMP: 36 EST: 1987
SQ FT: 2,500
SALES (est): 5.5MM Privately Held
WEB: www.hanagroup.com
SIC: 5065 Electronic parts
HQ: Hana Semiconductor (Bkk) Company Limited
 65/98 Soi Vibhavadi Rangsit 64 Yeak 2 Lak Si

(P-8916)
HDX INTERNATIONAL INC (PA)
2036 Avanti Ave, Dublin (94568-3252)
PHONE.....................925 922-1448
Xiao-Yang Huang, President
Ning Yu, Project Engr
▲ EMP: 48 EST: 2003
SALES (est): 744.6K Privately Held
WEB: www.hdx-international.com
SIC: 5065 Electronic parts

(P-8917)
HITACHI HIGH-TECH AMERICA INC
5960 Inglewood Dr Ste 200, Pleasanton (94588-8611)
PHONE.....................925 218-2800
Bob Gordon, Manager
Robert Gordon, Vice Pres
Gene Procopio, Vice Pres
John Giudicessi, Executive
Donna Armanino, Managing Dir
EMP: 70 Privately Held
WEB: www.hitachi-hightech.com
SIC: 5065 Electronic parts
HQ: Hitachi High-Tech America, Inc.
 10 N Martingale Rd # 500
 Schaumburg IL 60173
 847 273-4141

(P-8918)
HOTAN CORP
630 Hardcastle Ct, San Ramon (94583-6015)
PHONE.....................925 290-1000
Tom Hsieh, CEO
Andrea Wong, President
Li-Jung Yang, CFO
Jenny Yang, Admin Sec
◆ EMP: 35 EST: 1996
SALES (est): 10.1MM Privately Held
WEB: www.philips.hotan.com
SIC: 5065 Diskettes, computer
PA: Cmc Magnetics Corporation
 15f, 53, Min Chuan W. Rd.,
 Taipei City TAP 10452

(P-8919)
IDEC CORPORATION (HQ)
1175 Elko Dr, Sunnyvale (94089-2209)
PHONE.....................408 747-0550
Toshiyuki Funaki, CEO
Mikio Funaki, President
Roger Proffer, COO
Donald L Scrivner, CFO
Donald Scrivner, CFO
▲ EMP: 89 EST: 1975
SQ FT: 84,000
SALES (est): 49MM Privately Held
WEB: www.us.idec.com
SIC: 5065 Electronic parts

(P-8920)
INTERNTNAL ELCTRNIC CMPNNTS US (HQ)
809 Aldo Ave Ste 104, Santa Clara (95054-2255)
PHONE.....................408 477-2755
Shawn Stone, President
Chuck Williams, General Mgr
Ludmila Soltes, Accountant
Michael Runowski, Controller
Scott Anderson, Sales Staff
▲ EMP: 16 EST: 1999

▲ = Import ▼=Export
◆ =Import/Export

PRODUCTS & SERVICES SECTION

5065 - Electronic Parts & Eqpt Wholesale County (P-8941)

SQ FT: 13,500
SALES (est): 11.1MM
SALES (corp-wide): 8.7MM **Privately Held**
WEB: www.ieccan.com
SIC: **5065** 3679 Electronic parts; electronic circuits
PA: International Electronic Components Inc
352 Signet Dr
North York ON M9L 1
416 293-2961

(P-8921)
JAI INC
6800 Santa Teresa Blvd # 175, San Jose (95119-1238)
PHONE.................................408 383-0300
Jorgen Andersen, *President*
Jimi Meshulam, *CFO*
Tomas Baek, *Vice Pres*
Usman Syed, *CIO*
Cindy Phan, *CTO*
▲ EMP: 29 EST: 1982
SQ FT: 35,000
SALES (est): 14MM
SALES (corp-wide): 37MM **Privately Held**
WEB: www.jai.com
SIC: **5065** 3663 Security control equipment & systems; electronic parts; television broadcasting & communications equipment
HQ: Jai A/S
Valby Torvegade 17, Sal 1
Valby 2500
445 788-88

(P-8922)
JAMES ELECTRONICS LIMITED
Also Called: Jameco Electronics
1355 Shoreway Rd, Belmont (94002-4105)
PHONE.................................650 592-6718
Dennis D Farrey, *Ch of Bd*
James Farrey, *CEO*
Gloria Leong, *CFO*
Phil Greeves, *Vice Pres*
Eric Wood, *Principal*
▲ EMP: 70 EST: 1973
SQ FT: 50,000
SALES (est): 24.9MM **Privately Held**
WEB: www.jameco.com
SIC: **5961 5065 5063** Electronic kits & parts, mail order; electronic parts & equipment; electrical apparatus & equipment

(P-8923)
JEI
Also Called: Jei
3087 Alhambra Dr, Cameron Park (95682-8849)
PHONE.................................530 677-3210
Jack Mahoney, *President*
Steve Vodoklys, *CFO*
Novikoff Roxanne, *Office Mgr*
▲ EMP: 18 EST: 1959
SQ FT: 4,400
SALES (est): 4.7MM **Privately Held**
WEB: www.jei-inc.com
SIC: **5065** 3651 Electronic parts & equipment; recording machines, except dictation & telephone answering

(P-8924)
JEM AMERICA CORP
3000 Laurelview Ct, Fremont (94538-6575)
PHONE.................................510 683-9234
Kazumasa Okubo, *Owner*
Eddie Kazama, *President*
Karen Wong, *General Mgr*
Trisha Quach, *Technician*
Hirotaka Inoue, *Technology*
EMP: 50 EST: 1987
SQ FT: 17,000
SALES (est): 12.7MM **Privately Held**
WEB: www.jemam.com
SIC: **5065** Electronic parts
PA: Japan Electronic Materials Corporation
2-5-13, Nishinagasucho
Amagasaki HYO 660-0

(P-8925)
KIOXIA AMERICA INC (PA)
2610 Orchard Pkwy, San Jose (95134-2020)
PHONE.................................408 526-2400
Toshiaki Fujikawa, *CEO*
Takanori Nakazawa, *CFO*
Julius Christensen, *Vice Pres*
Sean Collins, *Vice Pres*
Joel Dedrick, *Vice Pres*
EMP: 200 EST: 2017
SQ FT: 60,000
SALES (est): 100.6MM **Privately Held**
SIC: **5065** Electronic parts & equipment

(P-8926)
KYCON INC
305 Digital Dr, Morgan Hill (95037-2878)
PHONE.................................408 494-0330
Kaya Erk, *President*
Carl Furumasu, *President*
Helen Burr, *Technology*
William Cook, *Engineer*
Anh Lam, *Human Res Mgr*
▲ EMP: 35 EST: 1988
SQ FT: 25,000
SALES (est): 10.7MM **Privately Held**
WEB: www.kycon.com
SIC: **5065** 3678 Connectors, electronic; electronic connectors

(P-8927)
LEMO USA INC
635 Park Ct, Rohnert Park (94928-7940)
P.O. Box 2408 (94927-2408)
PHONE.................................707 206-3700
Dinshaw Pohwala, *CEO*
Marian Brown, *CFO*
Greg Mielke, *Executive*
Tim Hassett, *General Mgr*
Wendy Christiansen, *Executive Asst*
EMP: 100 EST: 1972
SQ FT: 55,000
SALES (est): 52.3MM
SALES (corp-wide): 355.8K **Privately Held**
WEB: www.lemo.com
SIC: **5065** 3678 Connectors, electronic; electronic connectors
HQ: Interlemo U.S.A. Inc.
635 Park Ct
Rohnert Park CA 94928

(P-8928)
LG DISPLAY AMERICA INC (HQ)
2540 N 1st St Ste 400, San Jose (95131-1016)
PHONE.................................408 350-0190
Chris Min, *President*
Davis Lee, *President*
James Jeong, *CFO*
Yong Kee Huang, *Senior VP*
Domingo Park, *Vice Pres*
▲ EMP: 70 EST: 1999
SQ FT: 1,000
SALES (est): 42.6MM **Privately Held**
WEB: www.lgcorp.com
SIC: **5065** Modems, computer

(P-8929)
LITE-ON INC (HQ)
Also Called: Lite-On U S A
720 S Hillview Dr, Milpitas (95035-5455)
PHONE.................................408 946-4873
Sonny Hsuen-Ching Chao, *President*
Anson Chiu, *General Mgr*
Sophie Lin, *Project Mgr*
Scott Davis, *Business Mgr*
Paxion Chen, *Human Resources*
◆ EMP: 50 EST: 1987
SQ FT: 25,000
SALES (est): 31.6MM **Privately Held**
WEB: www.liteon.com
SIC: **5065** Semiconductor devices

(P-8930)
MACRONIX AMERICA INC (HQ)
Also Called: Mxic
680 N Mccarthy Blvd # 200, Milpitas (95035-5120)
PHONE.................................408 262-8887
Arthur Yang, *CEO*
John J Wong, *President*
Yen-Hie Chao, *Vice Pres*
Jui-Kun Chen, *Vice Pres*
Jon-Ten Chung, *Vice Pres*
EMP: 53 EST: 1994
SQ FT: 20,000
SALES (est): 38.2MM **Privately Held**
WEB: www.macronix.com
SIC: **5065** 3674 Semiconductor devices; semiconductors & related devices

(P-8931)
MARKI MICROWAVE INC
345 Digital Dr, Morgan Hill (95037-2878)
PHONE.................................408 778-4200
Christopher Marki, *CEO*
David Shepard, *COO*
Ralf Liebermann, *CFO*
Terrance Stebbins, *Officer*
Christine Marki, *Vice Pres*
EMP: 45 EST: 1991
SQ FT: 9,800
SALES (est): 23.8MM **Privately Held**
WEB: www.markimicrowave.com
SIC: **5065** Electronic parts & equipment

(P-8932)
METRIC EQUIPMENT SALES INC
Also Called: Microlease
25841 Industrial Blvd # 200, Hayward (94545-2991)
PHONE.................................510 264-0887
Nigel Brown, *CEO*
Mike Clark, *CEO*
Nathan Hurst, *CFO*
David Sherve, *Senior VP*
Gordon Curwen, *Vice Pres*
EMP: 70 EST: 1992
SQ FT: 25,000
SALES (est): 21.4MM
SALES (corp-wide): 254.4MM **Privately Held**
SIC: **5065** 5084 7359 3825 Electronic parts; measuring & testing equipment, electrical; electronic equipment rental, except computers; instruments to measure electricity
HQ: Microlease Inc.
6060 Sepulveda Blvd
Van Nuys CA 91411
866 520-0200

(P-8933)
MICRO-MECHANICS INC
465 Woodview Ave, Morgan Hill (95037-2800)
PHONE.................................408 779-2927
Christopher R Borch, *President*
Shirley Bautista, *Sales Engr*
Carol Bean, *Manager*
Thomas Nunez, *Manager*
Swan Rai, *Manager*
EMP: 50 EST: 1997
SQ FT: 42,000
SALES (est): 20.3MM **Privately Held**
WEB: www.micro-mechanics.com
SIC: **5065** 3674 Semiconductor devices; semiconductors & related devices
PA: Micro-Mechanics (Holdings) Ltd.
31 Kaki Bukit Place
Singapore 41620

(P-8934)
MINIMATICS INC (PA)
3445 De La Cruz Blvd, Santa Clara (95054-2110)
PHONE.................................650 969-5630
Walter Chew, *President*
Charles R Fowler, *Shareholder*
Marjorie Chew, *Admin Sec*
EMP: 39 EST: 1973
SALES (est): 10.8MM **Privately Held**
WEB: www.minimatics.com
SIC: **5065** 3599 Semiconductor devices; machine shop, jobbing & repair

(P-8935)
MIO TECHNOLOGY USA LTD
47988 Fremont Blvd, Fremont (94538-6507)
PHONE.................................510 252-6900
▲ EMP: 35
SALES (est): 4.6MM
SALES (corp-wide): 1.3B **Privately Held**
SIC: **5065** 3663 Whol Electronic Parts/Equipment
HQ: Booming Enterprises Inc
C/O: Offshore Incorporation Limited
Road Town
284 494-8184

(P-8936)
NAN YA TECHNOLOGY CORP USA
Also Called: Nanya Technologies U S A
1735 Tech Dr Ste 400, San Jose (95110)
PHONE.................................408 961-4000
Jih Lien, *CEO*
Brian Donahue, *President*
Steve Hsu, *CFO*
Pamela Chen, *Office Mgr*
Joe Makley, *Sales Staff*
▲ EMP: 38 EST: 1997
SALES (est): 16.2MM **Privately Held**
WEB: www.nanya.com
SIC: **5065** Semiconductor devices
PA: Nanya Technology Corporation
98, Nanlin Rd.,
New Taipei City TAP 24352

(P-8937)
NEST LABS INC
3400 Hillview Ave, Palo Alto (94304-1346)
PHONE.................................855 469-6378
Tony Fadell, *CEO*
Bryan James, *Vice Pres*
Matthew Rogers, *Principal*
Kathy Vick, *Executive Asst*
Toshiro Yamada, *Sr Software Eng*
◆ EMP: 70 EST: 2010
SALES (est): 37.1MM
SALES (corp-wide): 182.5B **Publicly Held**
WEB: www.google.com
SIC: **5065** 5999 Electronic parts & equipment; electronic parts & equipment
HQ: Google Llc
1600 Amphitheatre Pkwy
Mountain View CA 94043
650 253-0000

(P-8938)
NGK ELECTRONICS USA INC
2520 Mission College Blvd # 104, Santa Clara (95054-1238)
PHONE.................................408 330-6900
Koji Hasegawa, *Treasurer*
▲ EMP: 36 EST: 2002
SALES (est): 9.5MM **Privately Held**
SIC: **5065** Semiconductor devices
HQ: Ngk North America, Inc.
1105 N Market St Ste 1300
Wilmington DE 19801
302 654-1344

(P-8939)
NORDSON CORPORATION
2470 Bates Ave Ste A, Concord (94520-1294)
PHONE.................................925 827-1240
Michael F Hilton, *CEO*
James Getty, *President*
Scott Sleeman, *Area Mgr*
Floriana Suriawidjaja, *Engineer*
Eric Rabjohns, *Analyst*
EMP: 23 EST: 1966
SALES (est): 537.7K **Privately Held**
WEB: www.nordson.com
SIC: **5065** 3559 Semiconductor devices; semiconductor manufacturing machinery

(P-8940)
NU HORIZONS ELECTRONICS CORP
890 N Mccarthy Blvd, San Jose (95131)
PHONE.................................408 946-4154
EMP: 50
SALES (corp-wide): 23.2B **Publicly Held**
SIC: **5065** Whol Electronic Parts/Equipment
HQ: Nu Horizons Electronics Corp.
70 Maxess Rd
Melville NY 11747
631 396-5000

(P-8941)
NUVOTON TECHNOLOGY CORP AMER
2727 N 1st St, San Jose (95134-2029)
PHONE.................................408 544-1718

5065 - Electronic Parts & Eqpt Wholesale County (P-8942)

PRODUCTS & SERVICES SECTION

Arthur Yu-Cheng Chiao, *Chairman*
Robert Hsu, *President*
Wen Cho, *CFO*
Mark Hemming, *Chief Mktg Ofcr*
Stephen Rei-Min Huang, *Vice Pres*
EMP: 60 **EST:** 2008
SALES (est): 22.9MM **Privately Held**
WEB: www.nuvoton.com
SIC: 5065 Semiconductor devices
HQ: Nuvoton Technology Corporation
No. 4, Yanxin 3rd Rd.,
Hsinchu City 30077

(P-8942)
NXEDGE INC
925 Lightpost Way, Morgan Hill (95037-2869)
PHONE.............................208 362-7200
Jackson Chao, *CEO*
Tina Robinson, *Administration*
Allyson Rollins-Carr, *Manager*
EMP: 37 **EST:** 2001
SALES (est): 4.7MM **Privately Held**
WEB: www.nxedge.com
SIC: 5065 Electronic parts & equipment

(P-8943)
OMEGA EMS (PA)
Also Called: Omega Electronic Mfg Svcs
5400 Hellyer Ave, San Jose (95138-1019)
PHONE.............................408 206-4260
Chris Alessio, *President*
Phil Aguiar, *Vice Pres*
Ian Grover, *Vice Pres*
Larry Zhiou, *Program Mgr*
Hong Cox, *Buyer*
EMP: 99 **EST:** 2015
SQ FT: 700
SALES: 21.2MM **Privately Held**
WEB: www.omega-ems.com
SIC: 5065 Electronic parts & equipment

(P-8944)
OSRAM OPTO SEMICONDUCTORS INC (DH)
1150 Kifer Rd Ste 100, Sunnyvale (94086-5302)
PHONE.............................408 962-3736
Olaf Berlien, *CEO*
Markus Arzberger, *General Mgr*
Matt Eaton, *Planning*
Dennis Vanzilen, *Technology*
Zheng Dai, *Engineer*
▲ **EMP:** 50 **EST:** 2000
SALES (est): 54.7MM
SALES (corp-wide): 4.1B **Privately Held**
WEB: www.osram.de
SIC: 5065 Semiconductor devices
HQ: Osram Licht Ag
Marcel-Breuer-Str. 6
Munchen BY 80807
896 213-0

(P-8945)
PARADE TECHNOLOGIES INC
2720 Orchard Pkwy, San Jose (95134-2012)
PHONE.............................408 329-5540
Ji Zhao, *CEO*
Joe Montalbo, *Senior VP*
Randy Baker, *Vice Pres*
Jowie Chung, *Engineer*
Jeffery Dahlin, *Engineer*
EMP: 80 **EST:** 2005
SQ FT: 5,500
SALES (est): 19.2MM **Privately Held**
WEB: www.paradetech.com
SIC: 5065 Semiconductor devices
PA: Parade Technologies, Ltd
C/O: Maples Corporate Services Limited
George Town GR CAYMAN

(P-8946)
PHASE MATRIX INC
Also Called: Ni Microwave Components
4600 Patrick Henry Dr, Santa Clara (95054-1817)
PHONE.............................954 490-9429
Pete Pragastis, *President*
Charanbir Mahal, *Vice Pres*
George Clark, *Administration*
Mark Espinosa, *QC Mgr*
EMP: 50 **EST:** 1999

SQ FT: 24,000
SALES (est): 25.2MM
SALES (corp-wide): 1.2B **Publicly Held**
WEB: www.phasematrix.net
SIC: 5065 Electronic parts & equipment
PA: National Instruments Corporation
11500 N Mopac Expy
Austin TX 78759
512 683-0100

(P-8947)
PRISM ELECTRONICS CORP (PA)
900 Lightpost Way 100, Morgan Hill (95037-2869)
PHONE.............................408 778-7050
John Jules Mauro, *CEO*
Sofia Fedotova, *Admin Sec*
Kevin Pabst, *Business Mgr*
Linda Kim, *Opers Mgr*
◆ **EMP:** 47 **EST:** 2002
SQ FT: 21,373
SALES (est): 18.8MM **Privately Held**
WEB: www.prismelectronics.net
SIC: 5065 Electronic parts

(P-8948)
R&M USA INC
Also Called: Realm
840 Yosemite Way, Milpitas (95035-6360)
PHONE.............................408 945-6625
Christopher Stratas, *President*
Kimberly Horowitz, *Treasurer*
Lidan Gu, *Purchasing*
Bryce Alvarez, *Mfg Mgr*
Michel Riva, *Director*
▲ **EMP:** 80 **EST:** 1999
SQ FT: 34,865
SALES: 20.2MM
SALES (corp-wide): 106.7MM **Privately Held**
WEB: www.rdm.com
SIC: 5065 Communication equipment
HQ: Reichle & De-Massari Ag
Binzstrasse 32
Wetzikon ZH 8620
449 319-777

(P-8949)
ROSE ELECTRONICS DISTRG CO LLC
2030 Ringwood Ave, San Jose (95131-1728)
PHONE.............................408 943-0200
Itamar Frankenthal, *CEO*
Katherine Mack, *Vice Pres*
Mike Schrader, *Department Mgr*
JM Bourdon, *VP Sls/Mktg*
Annette Campos, *Services*
▲ **EMP:** 34 **EST:** 1963
SALES (est): 9.9MM **Privately Held**
WEB: www.rosebatteries.com
SIC: 5065 3691 Electronic parts; capacitors, electronic; resistors, electronic; storage batteries

(P-8950)
SAMSUNG ELECTRONICS AMER INC
665 Clyde Ave, Mountain View (94043-2235)
PHONE.............................650 210-1000
Evan Maxei, *Director*
Adriana Park, *Bd of Directors*
Hyun Park, *Bd of Directors*
Jungsun Lee, *Officer*
Seungmin Kim, *Vice Pres*
EMP: 1000
SQ FT: 395 **Privately Held**
WEB: www.samsung.com
SIC: 5065 Electronic parts & equipment
HQ: Samsung Electronics America, Inc.
85 Challenger Rd
Ridgefield Park NJ 07660
201 229-4000

(P-8951)
SAMSUNG SEMICONDUCTOR INC (DH)
3655 N 1st St, San Jose (95134-1707)
PHONE.............................408 544-4000
Young Chang Bae, *President*
Damian Huh, *CFO*
Hong Hao, *Senior VP*
Tom Quinn, *Senior VP*

Shankar Chandran, *Vice Pres*
◆ **EMP:** 216 **EST:** 1979
SQ FT: 206,816
SALES (est): 715.3MM **Privately Held**
WEB: www.samsungsemi.com
SIC: 5065 5045 Semiconductor devices; computers, peripherals & software
HQ: Samsung Electronics America, Inc.
85 Challenger Rd
Ridgefield Park NJ 07660
201 229-4000

(P-8952)
SHINKO ELECTRIC AMERICA INC (DH)
1280 E Arques Ave, Sunnyvale (94085-5401)
PHONE.............................408 232-0499
Greg Bettencourt, *President*
Hietoshi Arai, *Vice Pres*
John Cotugno, *Regional Mgr*
Yuka Luyen, *Admin Asst*
Greg Bettencoast, *CIO*
EMP: 20 **EST:** 1977
SALES (est): 27.9MM **Privately Held**
WEB: www.shinko.co.jp
SIC: 5065 3674 Electronic parts & equipment; semiconductors & related devices

(P-8953)
SILICONWARE USA INC (DH)
1735 Tech Dr Ste 300 Fl 3, San Jose (95110)
PHONE.............................408 573-5500
Bough Lin, *Ch of Bd*
Randy Hsiao Yu Lo, *President*
Yi Hsin Lin, *CFO*
Alex Chenok, *Vice Pres*
EMP: 50 **EST:** 1996
SQ FT: 8,000
SALES (est): 24.4MM **Privately Held**
WEB: www.spil.com.tw
SIC: 5065 Semiconductor devices

(P-8954)
SIMCO-ION TECHNOLOGY GROUP (PA)
1601 Harbor Bay Pkwy # 150, Alameda (94502-3028)
PHONE.............................510 217-0600
Craig Hindman, *CEO*
Ronald Weigner, *President*
Michael Sheperia, *Managing Dir*
Berry Brown, *General Mgr*
Lyle Nelsen, *Engineer*
▲ **EMP:** 110 **EST:** 1936
SQ FT: 55,000
SALES (est): 17.2MM **Privately Held**
WEB: www.simco-ion.com
SIC: 5065 Electronic parts

(P-8955)
SMA SOLAR TECHNOLOGY AMER LLC (HQ)
Also Called: SMA America
6020 West Oaks Blvd, Rocklin (95765-5472)
PHONE.............................916 625-0870
Jurgen Krehnke,
Charles Morrill, *Vice Pres*
Juan Bojorquez, *CIO*
Casey Wright, *Project Mgr*
Timothy Chapin, *Technical Staff*
◆ **EMP:** 130 **EST:** 2000
SQ FT: 25,000
SALES: 247.2MM
SALES (corp-wide): 1.2B **Privately Held**
WEB: www.sma-america.com
SIC: 5065 Electronic parts
PA: Sma Solar Technology Ag
Sonnenallee 1
Niestetal HE 34266
561 952-20

(P-8956)
SMTC MEX HOLDINGS INC (HQ)
431 Kato Ter, Fremont (94539-8333)
PHONE.............................915 849-6752
Ed Smith, *President*
Kenny Lai, *Vice Pres*
Terry Wegman, *Vice Pres*
Mandy York, *Program Mgr*
Chris Pierce, *Engineer*
EMP: 99 **EST:** 1999

SALES (est): 34.3MM
SALES (corp-wide): 386.4MM **Privately Held**
WEB: www.smtc.com
SIC: 5065 8711 Electronic parts & equipment; electrical or electronic engineering
PA: Smtc Corporation
7050 Woodbine Ave
Markham ON L3R 4
905 479-1810

(P-8957)
SMTC MEX HOLDINGS INC
431 Kato Ter, Fremont (94539-8333)
PHONE.............................510 737-0729
EMP: 158
SALES (corp-wide): 386.4MM **Privately Held**
WEB: www.smtc.com
SIC: 5065 Electronic parts & equipment
HQ: Smtc Mex Holdings, Inc.
431 Kato Ter
Fremont CA 94539
915 849-6752

(P-8958)
SOLIGENT DISTRIBUTION LLC (HQ)
1400 N Mcdowell Blvd # 201, Petaluma (94954-6553)
P.O. Box 751539 (94975-1539)
PHONE.............................707 992-3100
Jonathan Doochin, *CEO*
Thomas Enzendorfer, *President*
Mark Laabs, *COO*
Austin Blackmon, *Vice Pres*
Justin Davidson, *Vice Pres*
▼ **EMP:** 128 **EST:** 2013
SALES (est): 95.7MM
SALES (corp-wide): 139.1MM **Privately Held**
WEB: www.soligent.net
SIC: 5065 8711 Electronic parts & equipment; engineering services
PA: Soligent Holdings Inc.
1500 Valley House Dr # 210
Rohnert Park CA 94928
707 992-3100

(P-8959)
STANFORD EQUIPMENT COMPANY
1500 Wyatt Dr Ste 2, Santa Clara (95054-1522)
PHONE.............................408 855-8040
Alex Rapoport, *Director*
Chuck Nolan, *Engineer*
EMP: 45
SQ FT: 2,500
SALES: 4.6MM **Privately Held**
SIC: 5065 5047 Electronic parts & equipment; medical & hospital equipment

(P-8960)
STMICROELECTRONICS INC
2755 Great America Way, Santa Clara (95054-1166)
PHONE.............................408 452-8585
EMP: 140
SALES (corp-wide): 8.3B **Privately Held**
SIC: 5065 Whol Electronic Parts/Equipment
HQ: Stmicroelectronics, Inc
750 Canyon Dr Ste 300
Coppell TX 75019
972 466-6000

(P-8961)
SUMITOMO ELC DVC INNVTONS USA
2355 Zanker Rd, San Jose (95131-1109)
PHONE.............................408 232-9500
Mike Nishiguchi, *CEO*
John Wyatt, *CFO*
Eddie Tsumura, *Vice Pres*
Chris Wiggins, *Vice Pres*
Norma Simeon, *Accountant*
▲ **EMP:** 80 **EST:** 2000
SQ FT: 52,600
SALES (est): 26.1MM **Privately Held**
WEB: www.sei-device.com
SIC: 5065 Electronic parts
PA: Sumitomo Electric Industries, Ltd.
4-5-33, Kitahama, Chuo-Ku
Osaka OSK 541-0

PRODUCTS & SERVICES SECTION
5072 - Hardware Wholesale County (P-8983)

(P-8962)
SURVELLNCE SYSTEMS INTGRTION I
Also Called: Ssi
4465 Granite Dr Ste 700, Rocklin (95677-2143)
PHONE 800 508-6981
Michael T Flowers, *CEO*
Jon Ward, *President*
Mark Haney, *Chairman*
Meichel Garrett, *Project Mgr*
Olga Suarez, *Accounting Mgr*
EMP: 50 EST: 2002
SQ FT: 15,000
SALES (est): 37.1MM **Privately Held**
WEB: www.ssicctv.com
SIC: 5065 Video equipment, electronic; security control equipment & systems

(P-8963)
TABULA INC
1100 La Avenida St, Mountain View (94043-1452)
PHONE 408 986-9140
Dennis Segers, *CEO*
Steven Teig, *President*
Adam Hartman, *Research*
EMP: 100 EST: 2003
SALES (est): 22.1MM **Privately Held**
WEB: www.tabula.com
SIC: 5065 Semiconductor devices

(P-8964)
TILE INC
1900 S Norfolk St Ste 310, San Mateo (94403-1171)
PHONE 650 274-0676
Charles Prober, *CEO*
Michael Farley, *COO*
Robert O'Hare, *CFO*
Kirsten Daru, *Vice Pres*
Kristin Markworth, *Vice Pres*
▲ EMP: 168 EST: 2012
SQ FT: 4,000
SALES (est): 64.9MM **Privately Held**
WEB: www.thetileapp.com
SIC: 5065 Security control equipment & systems

(P-8965)
TPS AVIATION INC (PA)
1515 Crocker Ave, Hayward (94544-7038)
PHONE 510 475-1010
George Sozaburo Kujiraoka, *CEO*
George Kujiraoka, *COO*
Jane Milanes, *Controller*
Kevin Suyeyasu, *Purch Mgr*
Maia Corpuz, *Purchasing*
◆ EMP: 100 EST: 1963
SQ FT: 58,700
SALES (est): 67.2MM **Privately Held**
WEB: www.tpsaviation.com
SIC: 5065 3728 3429 5088 Electronic parts; aircraft parts & equipment; manufactured hardware (general); aircraft & parts; aircraft engines & engine parts; guided missiles & space vehicles; hardware

(P-8966)
TRINET COMMUNICATIONS INC (PA)
6567 Brisa St, Livermore (94550-2519)
PHONE 925 294-1720
Jon J Fernandez, *President*
Jason Skeoch, *Vice Pres*
▲ EMP: 15 EST: 1990
SQ FT: 30,000
SALES (est): 8.2MM **Privately Held**
SIC: 5065 3661 Communication equipment; telephone & telegraph apparatus

(P-8967)
TTI INC
Also Called: Rfmw
188 Martinvale Ln, San Jose (95119-1356)
PHONE 408 414-1450
Joel Levine, *Branch Mgr*
Liz Pruhsmeier, *Director*
EMP: 80
SALES (corp-wide): 245.5B **Publicly Held**
WEB: www.tti.com
SIC: 5065 Electronic parts

HQ: Tti, Inc.
2441 Northeast Pkwy
Fort Worth TX 76106
817 740-9000

(P-8968)
U-2 HOME ENTERTAINMENT INC
Also Called: Tai Seng Entertainment
170 S Spruce Ave Ste 200, South San Francisco (94080-4557)
P.O. Box 818, San Bruno (94066-0818)
PHONE 650 871-8118
▲ EMP: 50
SALES (est): 10.2MM **Privately Held**
SIC: 5065 Motion Picture/Tape Distribution

(P-8969)
VIVOTEK USA INC
2050 Ringwood Ave, San Jose (95131-1782)
PHONE 408 773-8686
Wen Chang Chen, *CEO*
Harry Hu, *President*
Stanley Chih, *Regional Mgr*
Michael Tao, *Office Admin*
Kelly Lee, *Admin Asst*
◆ EMP: 36 EST: 2008
SQ FT: 13,000
SALES (est): 34.9MM **Privately Held**
WEB: www.vivotek.com
SIC: 5065 Security control equipment & systems
HQ: Vivotek Inc.
6f, 192, Lien Cheng Rd.,
New Taipei City TAP 23553

(P-8970)
W-NEWEB CORPORATION
1525 Mccarthy Blvd # 206, Milpitas (95035-7451)
PHONE 408 457-6800
Richard Juang, *CFO*
▲ EMP: 35 EST: 1999
SQ FT: 4,100
SALES (est): 6.7MM **Privately Held**
WEB: www.wnc.com.tw
SIC: 5065 Communication equipment
PA: Wistron Neweb Corporation
20 Park Aveue Ii, Hsinchu Science Park,
Paoshan Hsiang HSI 30844

(P-8971)
WARD/DAVIS ASSOCIATES INC
1155 N 1st St Ste 205, San Jose (95112-4925)
PHONE 408 213-1090
Eva Bernier, *Manager*
Kirk Reger, *Partner*
William Breyer, *President*
Carole Gavalyas, *CFO*
Michael Pluchar, *Vice Pres*
EMP: 35
SQ FT: 6,000
SALES (corp-wide): 18.7MM **Privately Held**
WEB: www.warddavis.com
SIC: 5065 Electronic parts
PA: Ward/Davis Associates, Inc.
2623 Manhattan Beach Blvd
Redondo Beach CA 90278
310 297-5990

(P-8972)
WESTEK ELECTRONICS INC
165 Westridge Dr, Watsonville (95076-4167)
PHONE 831 740-6300
Kevin Larkin, *CEO*
Amy Eades, *Principal*
Susie Freitas, *Principal*
Javier Ramirez, *Principal*
Michael Hushaw, *Administration*
▲ EMP: 40 EST: 1986
SALES (est): 11.6MM **Privately Held**
WEB: www.westek.com
SIC: 5065 Electronic parts & equipment

(P-8973)
WINBOND ELECTRONICS CORP AMER
2727 N 1st St, San Jose (95134-2029)
PHONE 408 943-6666
Yuan Mou Shu, *Principal*
JW Park, *Vice Pres*
Ming-Huei Shieh, *Executive*
Eries Tseng, *Planning*
Johnny Chan, *Design Engr Mgr*
▲ EMP: 60 EST: 1990
SQ FT: 50,000
SALES (est): 25.6MM **Privately Held**
WEB: www.winbond.com
SIC: 5065 8731 3674 Electronic parts; commercial physical research; semiconductors & related devices
PA: Winbond Electronics Corporation
8, Keya 1st Rd.,
Taichung City 42881

(P-8974)
XCERRA CORPORATION
Also Called: Western Region
880 N Mccarthy Blvd # 100, Milpitas (95035-5126)
PHONE 408 635-4300
Ken Daub, *Branch Mgr*
Michael Goldbach, *Vice Pres*
Tim Hallock, *Vice Pres*
Sandy Salinas, *Planning*
Steve Blanchette, *Info Tech Mgr*
EMP: 200
SALES (corp-wide): 636MM **Publicly Held**
WEB: www.cohu.com
SIC: 5065 Semiconductor devices
HQ: Xcerra Corporation
825 University Ave
Norwood MA 02062
781 461-1000

(P-8975)
XP POWER LLC
Also Called: Emco High Voltage
11383 Prospect Dr, Jackson (95642-9311)
PHONE 209 267-1630
Michael Doherty, *Vice Pres*
EMP: 56 **Privately Held**
WEB: www.xppower.com
SIC: 5065 Electronic parts & equipment
HQ: Xp Power Llc
990 Benecia Ave
Sunnyvale CA 94085

(P-8976)
XP POWER LLC (HQ)
990 Benecia Ave, Sunnyvale (94085-2804)
PHONE 408 732-7777
Mike Laver, *Mng Member*
Barbara Roberts, *Executive Asst*
Camilla Godleman, *IT/INT Sup*
Douglas Beuerman, *Engrg Dir*
Ryan Barnes, *Technology*
▲ EMP: 60 EST: 2008
SQ FT: 58,000
SALES (est): 332.2MM **Privately Held**
WEB: www.xppower.com
SIC: 5065 Electronic parts & equipment

(P-8977)
YAMAICHI ELECTRONICS USA INC (HQ)
475 Holger Way, San Jose (95134-1369)
PHONE 408 435-9800
Alfred Muranaga, *President*
Joel Gentleman, *General Mgr*
Ernesto Rosa, *Comp Lab Dir*
Brian Ferreira, *Technology*
Ichiro Fujishiro, *Engineer*
▲ EMP: 48 EST: 1983
SALES (est): 36.5MM **Privately Held**
WEB: www.yeu.com
SIC: 5065 Electronic parts

5072 Hardware Wholesale

(P-8978)
ACF COMPONENTS & FASTENERS INC (PA)
Also Called: Acf Industrial Solutions
2512 Tripaldi Way, Hayward (94545-5033)
PHONE 510 487-2100
John Y Mizutani, *Ch of Bd*
Robert Mandler, *COO*
Tanya Moore, *Credit Staff*
Christina Thompson, *Purchasing*
Dan Seanez, *QC Mgr*
▲ EMP: 38 EST: 1976
SALES (est): 20.5MM **Privately Held**
WEB: www.acfcom.com
SIC: 5072 5065 Miscellaneous fasteners; electronic parts & equipment

(P-8979)
BAY BOLT INC
4610 Malat St, Oakland (94601-4904)
PHONE 510 532-1188
Richard R Anderson, *President*
EMP: 15 EST: 1981
SQ FT: 30,000
SALES (est): 3.3MM **Privately Held**
WEB: www.baybolt.com
SIC: 5072 5051 3452 Bolts; nuts (hardware); screws; steel; nonferrous metal sheets, bars, rods, etc.; bolts, nuts, rivets & washers

(P-8980)
CHARLES MCMURRAY CO (PA)
2520 N Argyle Ave, Fresno (93727-1399)
P.O. Box 569 (93709-0569)
PHONE 559 292-5751
Charles McMurray, *CEO*
Louis Mc Murray, *President*
Cassie Mc Murray, *Admin Sec*
Starla Schletewitz, *Administration*
Kathy Earnhart, *Credit Mgr*
▲ EMP: 62
SQ FT: 58,000
SALES (est): 38.3MM **Privately Held**
WEB: www.charlesmcmurray.com
SIC: 5072 Builders' hardware

(P-8981)
CHARLES MCMURRAY CO
2601 Land Ave, Sacramento (95815-2383)
P.O. Box 569, Fresno (93709-0569)
PHONE 916 929-9560
Bill Whitaker, *Manager*
Curt Daily, *Officer*
Stu Kidd, *Admin Sec*
Danny Graham, *Purchasing*
Matt Sullivan, *Opers Staff*
EMP: 46
SALES (corp-wide): 38.3MM **Privately Held**
WEB: www.charlesmcmurray.com
SIC: 5072 Builders' hardware
PA: Charles Mcmurray Co.
2520 N Argyle Ave
Fresno CA 93727
559 292-5751

(P-8982)
FASTENING SYSTEMS INTL
Also Called: F S I
1206 E Macarthur St Ste 1, Sonoma (95476-3800)
PHONE 707 935-1170
Roger Nikkel, *President*
Kathryn Nikkel, *CFO*
Diane Nikkel, *Corp Secy*
Mark Herrand, *Vice Pres*
Lucia Picard, *Office Mgr*
▲ EMP: 20 EST: 1983
SALES (est): 14.2MM **Privately Held**
WEB: www.fsirivet.com
SIC: 5072 3429 Miscellaneous fasteners; aircraft hardware

(P-8983)
FRIEDMANS HOME IMPROVEMENT
Also Called: Friedman Bros Home Imprv Ctr
4055 Santa Rosa Ave, Santa Rosa (95407-8222)
PHONE 707 584-7811
Steve Chapman, *Manager*
EMP: 58
SQ FT: 100,000
SALES (corp-wide): 70.9MM **Privately Held**
WEB: www.friedmanshome.com
SIC: 5251 5261 5072 5031 Hardware; nurseries & garden centers; hardware; building materials, exterior; building materials, interior; lumber & other building materials
PA: Friedman's Home Improvement
4055 Santa Rosa Ave
Santa Rosa CA 95407
707 584-7811

5072 Hardware Wholesale County

(P-8984)
J MILANO CO INC
910 W Charter Way, Stockton (95206-1104)
P.O. Box 688 (95201-0688)
PHONE.................................209 944-0902
Gary L Milano, *President*
Don Milano, *Vice Pres*
▲ EMP: 18
SQ FT: 9,000
SALES: 5.2MM **Privately Held**
SIC: 5072 3599 Hardware; machine shop, jobbing & repair

(P-8985)
JACKSONS HARDWARE INC
Also Called: Marin Industrial Distributors
435 Du Bois St, San Rafael (94901-3910)
P.O. Box 10247 (94912-0247)
PHONE.................................415 870-4083
Matthew R Olson, *President*
Anna Buss, *Treasurer*
Steve Hossfeld, *General Mgr*
Karen Adolphson, *Office Mgr*
Bill Dudley, *Sales Mgr*
EMP: 61 EST: 1964
SQ FT: 50,000
SALES (est): 16MM **Privately Held**
WEB: www.jacksonshardware.com
SIC: 5072 5251 Hardware; hardware

(P-8986)
JAMCOR CORPORATION
Also Called: S J S Products
6261 Angelo Ct, Loomis (95650-9565)
P.O. Box 90 (95650-0090)
PHONE.................................916 652-7713
William Mc Gillivray, *Ch of Bd*
▲ EMP: 38 EST: 1931
SQ FT: 15,696
SALES (est): 8.8MM **Privately Held**
WEB: www.sjsproducts.com
SIC: 5072 Miscellaneous fasteners

(P-8987)
MCKENZIE HARDWARE INC
Also Called: Ace Hardware
627 Merchant St, Vacaville (95688-6907)
PHONE.................................707 448-2978
David McKenzie, *President*
Scott McKenzie, *Treasurer*
James McKenzie, *Vice Pres*
Darcy McKenzie, *Admin Sec*
Ian McKenzie, *Sales Associate*
▲ EMP: 45 EST: 1952
SQ FT: 17,000
SALES (est): 6.6MM **Privately Held**
WEB: www.acehardware.com
SIC: 5251 5072 5231 Hardware; hardware; paint, glass & wallpaper

(P-8988)
MID-VALLEY DISTRIBUTORS INC
3886 E Jensen Ave, Fresno (93725-1343)
PHONE.................................559 485-2660
Richard Porter, *President*
David Porter, *Vice Pres*
Richard A Porter Jr, *Vice Pres*
Raul Rosario, *Buyer*
Al McKnight, *Sales Staff*
EMP: 38 EST: 1946
SQ FT: 80,000
SALES (est): 14.5MM **Privately Held**
WEB: www.mvdinc.com
SIC: 5072 5251 Nuts (hardware); bolts; screws; hardware

(P-8989)
SANTA ROSA HARDWARE CO INC
489 Portal St, Cotati (94931-3072)
P.O. Box 1428, Rohnert Park (94927-1428)
PHONE.................................707 795-2500
Randall Roe, *President*
Zenna Roe, *Vice Pres*
EMP: 17 EST: 1970
SQ FT: 23,000
SALES (est): 2.3MM **Privately Held**
SIC: 5072 5031 3442 2431 Builders' hardware; doors; door frames, all materials; metal doors, sash & trim; millwork

(P-8990)
SUNKIST ENTERPRISES
1308 Rollins Rd, Burlingame (94010-2410)
PHONE.................................650 347-3900
Ali Husain, *Owner*
EMP: 75 EST: 1983
SQ FT: 6,000
SALES (est): 6.9MM **Privately Held**
WEB: www.se.supply
SIC: 5072 5031 Hardware; lumber, plywood & millwork

(P-8991)
WILDENRADT-MCMURRAY INC
Also Called: Macmurray Pacific
568 7th St, San Francisco (94103-4710)
PHONE.................................510 835-5500
Eric Wildenradt, *CEO*
Theodore Wildenradt, *President*
Vernelle Wildenradt, *Corp Secy*
William Wong, *Sales Staff*
▲ EMP: 70 EST: 1951
SQ FT: 25,000
SALES (est): 15MM **Privately Held**
SIC: 5072 Builders' hardware

5074 Plumbing & Heating Splys Wholesale

(P-8992)
BRITA PRODUCTS COMPANY
1221 Broadway Ste 290, Oakland (94612-1838)
P.O. Box 24305 (94623-1305)
PHONE.................................510 271-7000
Greg Frank, *President*
EMP: 85 EST: 1988
SALES (est): 49.9MM
SALES (corp-wide): 7.3B **Publicly Held**
WEB: www.brita.com
SIC: 5074 Water purification equipment
PA: The Clorox Company
1221 Broadway Ste 1300
Oakland CA 94612
510 271-7000

(P-8993)
BUILDCOM INC
Also Called: Faucetdirect.com
402 Otterson Dr Ste 100, Chico (95928-8247)
PHONE.................................800 375-3403
Christian B Friedland, *President*
Erik Lukasek, *President*
Danielle Porto Mohn, *Chief Mktg Ofcr*
Lindsay Fee, *Vice Pres*
David Luebke, *Vice Pres*
▼ EMP: 380 EST: 2000
SQ FT: 22,100
SALES (est): 221.8MM
SALES (corp-wide): 21.8B **Privately Held**
WEB: www.ferguson.com
SIC: 5074 5999 Plumbing fittings & supplies; plumbing & heating supplies
HQ: Ferguson Enterprises, Llc
12500 Jefferson Ave
Newport News VA 23602
757 874-7795

(P-8994)
CENTER STATE PIPE AND SUP CO
2750 Cherokee Rd, Stockton (95205-2476)
P.O. Box 939 (95201-0939)
PHONE.................................209 466-0871
Jeff Timbo, *Manager*
Jeff Turndeaguh, *Manager*
EMP: 16
SALES (corp-wide): 4.9MM **Privately Held**
WEB: www.buttespipe.com
SIC: 5074 5085 5963 5064 Plumbing & heating valves; industrial fittings; bottled water delivery; water heaters, electric; pipe & tubing, steel; pipe fittings, fabricated from purchased pipe
PA: Center State Pipe And Supply Co.
1348 Mcwilliams Way
Modesto CA 95351
209 521-1151

(P-8995)
CIVICSOLAR INC (PA)
304 12th St Ste 3b, Oakland (94607-4532)
P.O. Box 398730, San Francisco (94139-8730)
PHONE.................................800 409-2257
Stewart Rentz, *CEO*
Kerim Baran, *Vice Pres*
Michael Jeffrey Goldberg, *Vice Pres*
Michael Palar, *Vice Pres*
Mike Leone, *CIO*
▼ EMP: 40 EST: 2009
SALES (est): 19.8MM **Privately Held**
WEB: www.cedgreentech.com
SIC: 5074 5211 Heating equipment & panels, solar; solar heating equipment

(P-8996)
FRESNO PIPE & SUPPLY INC (PA)
Also Called: Stockton Pipe & Supply
4696 E Commerce Ave, Fresno (93725-2299)
P.O. Box 2760 (93745-2760)
PHONE.................................559 233-0500
Steve Allen, *CEO*
Gary Kearney, *Corp Secy*
Robert Musso, *Executive*
▲ EMP: 35 EST: 1984
SALES (est): 22.6MM **Privately Held**
WEB: www.fresnopipe.net
SIC: 5074 Pipes & fittings, plastic; plumbers' brass goods & fittings; plumbing & heating valves

(P-8997)
GCO INC (PA)
27750 Industrial Blvd, Hayward (94545-4043)
PHONE.................................510 786-3333
Michael H Groeniger, *Ch of Bd*
Beverly J Groeniger, *Treasurer*
Richard Alexander, *Exec VP*
Richard Old, *Vice Pres*
James Wunsche, *Vice Pres*
EMP: 50 EST: 1949
SQ FT: 15,000
SALES (est): 34MM **Privately Held**
SIC: 5074 5087 Pipe & boiler covering; pipes & fittings, plastic; plumbing & heating valves; firefighting equipment; sprinkler systems

(P-8998)
GENERAL PLUMBING SUPPLY CO INC (PA)
1530 San Luis Rd, Walnut Creek (94597-3114)
P.O. Box 4666 (94596-0666)
PHONE.................................925 939-4622
Richard P Amaro Jr, *CEO*
Evelyn Amaro, *Treasurer*
Richard R Amaro, *Vice Pres*
Richard Amaro Jr, *Vice Pres*
Patricia Garcia, *Office Mgr*
▲ EMP: 36 EST: 1965
SQ FT: 14,000
SALES (est): 94.8MM **Privately Held**
WEB: www.generalplumbingsupply.com
SIC: 5074 5063 Plumbing fittings & supplies; electrical apparatus & equipment

(P-8999)
IRONRIDGE INC (DH)
28357 Industrial Blvd, Hayward (94545-4428)
PHONE.................................800 227-9523
William Kim, *Ch of Bd*
Rich Tiu, *CEO*
Corey Geiger, *COO*
Jim Clark, *Pres*
Jon Ash, *Vice Pres*
▲ EMP: 50 EST: 1998
SQ FT: 10,000
SALES: 78.8MM
SALES (corp-wide): 288.5MM **Privately Held**
WEB: www.ironridge.com
SIC: 5074 3433 Heating equipment & panels, solar; solar heaters & collectors
HQ: Esdec, Inc.
976 Brady Ave Nw Ste 100
Atlanta GA 30318
404 512-0716

(P-9000)
J W WOOD CO INC (PA)
3676 Old Hwy 44 Dr, Redding (96003)
P.O. Box 991600 (96099-1600)
PHONE.................................530 894-1325
John Alan Wood, *President*
Kellie Wood, *Corp Secy*
Dave Forsman, *Manager*
Lucie Murphy, *Manager*
EMP: 35 EST: 1954
SQ FT: 33,000
SALES (est): 32.5MM **Privately Held**
WEB: www.jwwoodco.com
SIC: 5074 5051 Plumbing fittings & supplies; metals service centers & offices

(P-9001)
NEXTRACKER INC (DH)
6200 Paseo Padre Pkwy, Fremont (94555-3601)
PHONE.................................510 270-2500
Daniel Shugar, *CEO*
Bruce Ledesma, *President*
Tyroan Hardy, *COO*
Marco Garcia, *Ch Credit Ofcr*
Mike Mehawich, *Chief Mktg Ofcr*
◆ EMP: 250 EST: 2013
SQ FT: 30,000
SALES (est): 101.3MM **Privately Held**
WEB: www.nextracker.com
SIC: 5074 Heating equipment & panels, solar

(P-9002)
ONE BLOCK OFF GRID INC
164 S Park St, San Francisco (94107-1809)
PHONE.................................530 304-3969
Dave Llorens, *Principal*
Nicole Lal, *Recruiter*
EMP: 60 EST: 2010
SALES (est): 5.8MM
SALES (corp-wide): 2.8MM **Privately Held**
SIC: 5074 Heating equipment & panels, solar
PA: Solar Pure Energies Inc
5700-100 King St W
Toronto ON M5X 2
416 913-0787

(P-9003)
PACE SUPPLY CORP (PA)
6000 State Farm Dr # 200, Rohnert Park (94928-2226)
P.O. Box 6407 (94927-6407)
PHONE.................................707 755-2499
Keith Hubbard, *President*
Ted M Green, *Ch of Bd*
Ben Campanile, *Bd of Directors*
Steve Coleman, *Executive*
Mike Barton, *Branch Mgr*
▲ EMP: 80 EST: 1994
SQ FT: 10,000
SALES (est): 161.1MM **Privately Held**
WEB: www.pacesupply.com
SIC: 5074 Plumbing fittings & supplies

(P-9004)
PURCELL-MURRAY COMPANY INC (PA)
235 Kansas St Fl 1, San Francisco (94103-5170)
PHONE.................................415 468-6620
Timothy J Murray, *President*
Larissa Taboryski, *COO*
Stanley Kisver, *CFO*
Larry Purcell, *Vice Pres*
Laurence D Purcell, *Vice Pres*
▲ EMP: 67 EST: 1981
SALES (est): 70.5MM **Privately Held**
WEB: www.purcellmurray.com
SIC: 5074 5064 Plumbing fittings & supplies; electrical appliances, major

(P-9005)
R V CLOUD CO
3000 Winchester Blvd, Campbell (95008-6599)
PHONE.................................408 378-7943
Steven Cloud, *CEO*
Kay Cloud, *Vice Pres*
EMP: 50 EST: 1963
SQ FT: 79,651

▲ = Import ▼ = Export
◆ = Import/Export

PRODUCTS & SERVICES SECTION
5082 - Construction & Mining Mach & Eqpt Wholesale County (P-9024)

SALES (est): 6.5MM **Privately Held**
WEB: www.rvcloud.com
SIC: 5074 5083 Plumbing fittings & supplies; irrigation equipment

(P-9006)
WESTERN NEVADA SUPPLY CO
10990 Industrial Way A, Truckee (96161-0257)
PHONE...................................530 582-5009
Theodore Reviglio, *Vice Pres*
Chris Bush, *Purchasing*
Weezie Cox, *Sales Staff*
John Reilly, *Sales Staff*
EMP: 129
SALES (corp-wide): 267.5MM **Privately Held**
WEB: www.goblueteam.com
SIC: 5074 Plumbing fittings & supplies
PA: Western Nevada Supply Co.
950 S Rock Blvd
Sparks NV 89431
775 359-5800

5075 Heating & Air Conditioning Eqpt & Splys Wholesale

(P-9007)
CALIFORNIA HYDRONICS CORP (PA)
Also Called: Columbia Hydronics Co.
2293 Tripaldi Way, Hayward (94545-5024)
P.O. Box 5049 (94540-5049)
PHONE...................................510 293-1993
David Attard, *President*
Jim Frueh,
John Arthur, *CFO*
Kevin McCloud, *Treasurer*
James A Attard, *Vice Pres*
EMP: 50 EST: 1957
SQ FT: 50,000
SALES (est): 47.2MM **Privately Held**
WEB: www.chchydro.com
SIC: 5075 3585 Warm air heating equipment & supplies; refrigeration & heating equipment

(P-9008)
CFM EQUIPMENT DISTRIBUTORS INC (PA)
1644 Main Ave Ste 1, Sacramento (95838-2409)
PHONE...................................916 447-7022
Andrew Barton, *CEO*
Chester Flint, *President*
Joe Souza, *Admin Sec*
Dolores Desousa, *Admin Asst*
Dawn Kehrwald, *Human Res Mgr*
▲ EMP: 31 EST: 1984
SQ FT: 10,000
SALES (est): 35.3MM **Privately Held**
WEB: www.cfmequipment.com
SIC: 5075 3678 3999 Air conditioning equipment, except room units; furnaces, warm air; electronic connectors; atomizers, toiletry

(P-9009)
EDWARD B WARD & COMPANY INC (DH)
Also Called: Ward, E B
99 S Hill Dr Ste B, Brisbane (94005-1282)
PHONE...................................415 330-6600
James Lazor, *President*
John Ward, *Ch of Bd*
Robert McDonough, *CEO*
Edward B Ward, *COO*
Paul Caputi, *Vice Pres*
▲ EMP: 50 EST: 1957
SQ FT: 45,000
SALES (est): 35.9MM
SALES (corp-wide): 17.4B **Publicly Held**
WEB: www.rtx.com
SIC: 5075 Air conditioning equipment, except room units
HQ: Carrier Corporation
13995 Pasteur Blvd
Palm Beach Gardens FL 33418
800 379-6484

(P-9010)
EDWARD B WARD & COMPANY INC
Valair Division
2345 Los Angeles St, Fresno (93721-3115)
PHONE...................................559 487-1860
Paul Caputi, *Manager*
EMP: 85
SALES (corp-wide): 17.4B **Publicly Held**
SIC: 5075 Air conditioning equipment, except room units
HQ: Edward B. Ward & Company, Inc.
99 S Hill Dr Ste B
Brisbane CA 94005
415 330-6600

(P-9011)
NORMAN S WRGHT MECH EQP CRPRTN (PA)
99 S Hill Dr Ste A, Brisbane (94005-1282)
PHONE...................................415 467-7600
Richard F Leao, *President*
Robert L Beyer, *Exec VP*
Salvatore M Giglio, *Exec VP*
Pete McLaughlin, *General Mgr*
Carlos Gil, *Engineer*
EMP: 80 EST: 1906
SQ FT: 50,000
SALES (est): 127.8MM **Privately Held**
SIC: 5075 1711 Warm air heating equipment & supplies; air conditioning & ventilation equipment & supplies; heating & air conditioning contractors

(P-9012)
PACIFIC COAST SALES & SVC INC
Also Called: Fix Air
890 Service St Ste A, San Jose (95112-1374)
PHONE...................................408 437-0390
Richard Muetze, *Manager*
EMP: 44
SALES (corp-wide): 15.4MM **Privately Held**
WEB: www.pacificcoasttrane.com
SIC: 5075 Air conditioning & ventilation equipment & supplies; warm air heating equipment & supplies
PA: Pacific Coast Sales & Service, Inc.
310 Soquel Way
Sunnyvale CA 94085
408 481-3600

(P-9013)
RUSSELL SIGLER INC
8615 23rd Ave, Sacramento (95826-4903)
PHONE...................................916 387-3000
Sydney Rustemeyer, *President*
Spencer Reider, *Project Mgr*
Stuart Satterfield, *Engineer*
Colby Fischer, *Opers Staff*
Mary Gerhardt, *Sales Staff*
EMP: 55
SALES (corp-wide): 174.2MM **Privately Held**
WEB: www.siglers.com
SIC: 5075 Warm air heating & air conditioning
PA: Russell Sigler, Inc.
9702 W Tonto St
Tolleson AZ 85353
623 388-5100

(P-9014)
RUSSELL SIGLER INC
1920 Mark Ct, Concord (94520-8536)
PHONE...................................925 726-0141
Russell Sigler, *Branch Mgr*
Mohit Verma, *Sales Engr*
Fernando Cerbantes, *Sales Staff*
Steve Moorhead, *Manager*
EMP: 55
SALES (corp-wide): 174.2MM **Privately Held**
WEB: www.siglers.com
SIC: 5075 Warm air heating & air conditioning
PA: Russell Sigler, Inc.
9702 W Tonto St
Tolleson AZ 85353
623 388-5100

(P-9015)
SIERRA PCF HM & COMFORT INC
Also Called: Sierra Pacific Htg & Air-Solar
2550 Mercantile Dr Ste D, Rancho Cordova (95742-8202)
PHONE...................................916 638-0543
Jason Hanson, *President*
Mike Loer, *Vice Pres*
Lynne Bertolino, *Accounting Mgr*
Lynne Lockwood, *Accounting Mgr*
Kathleen Webster, *Finance Mgr*
EMP: 75 EST: 1984
SALES (est): 30.2MM **Privately Held**
WEB: www.sierrapacifichome.com
SIC: 5075 5074 Warm air heating & air conditioning; heating equipment & panels, solar

5078 Refrigeration Eqpt & Splys Wholesale

(P-9016)
NOR-CAL BEVERAGE CO INC
1347 Shore St, West Sacramento (95691-3511)
PHONE...................................916 371-8219
Al Barbagelata, *Branch Mgr*
EMP: 49
SALES (corp-wide): 231.7MM **Privately Held**
WEB: www.ncbev.com
SIC: 5078 Refrigeration equipment & supplies
PA: Nor-Cal Beverage Co., Inc.
2150 Stone Blvd
West Sacramento CA 95691
916 372-0600

(P-9017)
THERMO KING FRESNO INC (PA)
3247 E Annadale Ave, Fresno (93725-1902)
P.O. Box 2367 (93745-2367)
PHONE...................................559 496-3500
Norman Nelson, *President*
Cornelius Van Beek, *Vice Pres*
Ron Dawson, *Manager*
▲ EMP: 43 EST: 1984
SQ FT: 7,000
SALES (est): 19.1MM **Privately Held**
WEB: www.thermokingca.com
SIC: 5531 5078 Truck equipment & parts; refrigeration units, motor vehicles

5082 Construction & Mining Mach & Eqpt Wholesale

(P-9018)
ASOMEO ENVMTL RSTRTION INDUST
2151 River Plaza Dr # 105, Sacramento (95833-3881)
PHONE...................................530 434-6869
Akan Ismaili, *President*
L Kahn, *Officer*
EMP: 90 EST: 2018
SALES (est): 24.4MM **Privately Held**
SIC: 5082 5083 Logging & forestry machinery & equipment; landscaping equipment

(P-9019)
BOUTON CONSTRUCTION INC
420 E Mcglincy Ln, Campbell (95008-4905)
PHONE...................................408 375-0829
Chad Bouton, *CEO*
Albert Munoz, *Manager*
EMP: 89 EST: 2010
SALES (est): 11.1MM **Privately Held**
SIC: 5082 1799 1741 1611 Road construction equipment; waterproofing; retaining wall construction; surfacing & paving

(P-9020)
CASE DEALER HOLDING CO LLC (DH)
1751 Bell Ave, Sacramento (95838-2862)
PHONE...................................916 649-0096
Trevor Ward, *Mng Member*
EMP: 57 EST: 2008
SALES (est): 8.8MM
SALES (corp-wide): 25.9B **Privately Held**
SIC: 5082 General construction machinery & equipment
HQ: Cnh Industrial America Llc
700 State St
Racine WI 53404
262 636-6011

(P-9021)
HOC HOLDINGS INC (PA)
7310 Pacific Ave, Pleasant Grove (95668-9708)
PHONE...................................916 921-8950
Kenneth Monroe, *President*
EMP: 222 EST: 2008
SALES (est): 292.8MM **Privately Held**
WEB: www.holtca.com
SIC: 5082 5084 5083 7359 General construction machinery & equipment; materials handling machinery; agricultural machinery; equipment rental & leasing

(P-9022)
HOLT OF CALIFORNIA (HQ)
Also Called: Holt CA
7310 Pacific Ave, Pleasant Grove (95668-9708)
PHONE...................................916 991-8200
Victor Wykoff Jr, *Ch of Bd*
Gordon Beatie, *Vice Chairman*
Kenneth Monroe, *President*
Daniel Johns, *CFO*
Ronald Monroe, *Exec VP*
◆ EMP: 155 EST: 1998
SQ FT: 160,000
SALES (est): 292.8MM **Privately Held**
WEB: www.holtca.com
SIC: 5082 5084 5083 7359 General construction machinery & equipment; tractors, construction; materials handling machinery; agricultural machinery; equipment rental & leasing
PA: Hoc Holdings, Inc.
7310 Pacific Ave
Pleasant Grove CA 95668
916 921-8950

(P-9023)
HOLT OF CALIFORNIA
Also Called: Caterpillar Authorized Dealer
3850 Channel Dr, West Sacramento (95691-3466)
PHONE...................................916 373-4100
Toll Free:.................................888 -
Carry Roulet, *Manager*
EMP: 150
SALES (corp-wide): 292.8MM **Privately Held**
WEB: www.holtca.com
SIC: 5082 5083 5084 General construction machinery & equipment; agricultural machinery & equipment; materials handling machinery
HQ: Holt Of California
7310 Pacific Ave
Pleasant Grove CA 95668
916 991-8200

(P-9024)
HOLT RENTAL SERVICES
7310 Pacific Ave, Pleasant Grove (95668-9708)
PHONE...................................916 921-8800
Harry Rife, *CIO*
Kevin Freeman, *Sales Staff*
Megan Humlick, *Sales Staff*
EMP: 64 EST: 2017
SALES (est): 5.4MM
SALES (corp-wide): 292.8MM **Privately Held**
WEB: www.holtca.com
SIC: 5082 General construction machinery & equipment
HQ: Holt Of California
7310 Pacific Ave
Pleasant Grove CA 95668
916 991-8200

5082 - Construction & Mining Mach & Eqpt Wholesale County (P-9025)

(P-9025)
PETERSON MACHINERY CO (PA)
Also Called: Peterson Cat
955 Marina Blvd, San Leandro (94577-3440)
P.O. Box 5258 (94577-0610)
PHONE.....................541 302-9199
Duane D Doyle, *CEO*
Mark Ehni, *President*
Ernie Fierro, *Vice Pres*
Jack Hancock, *Principal*
Bill Bean, *General Mgr*
EMP: 1055 **EST:** 2006
SALES (est): 320.5MM **Privately Held**
WEB: www.petersoncat.com
SIC: 5082 General construction machinery & equipment

(P-9026)
QUINN LIFT INC (HQ)
10273 S Golden State Blvd, Selma (93662-9410)
P.O. Box 12625, Fresno (93778-2625)
PHONE.....................559 896-4040
Blake Quinn, *CEO*
Michelle Locke, *CFO*
Paul Lucini, *Vice Pres*
Eric Greene, *Regional Mgr*
Parker Quinn, *Admin Sec*
◆ **EMP:** 40 **EST:** 1996
SALES (est): 34.7MM
SALES (corp-wide): 378.6MM **Privately Held**
WEB: www.quinncompany.com
SIC: 5082 General construction machinery & equipment
PA: Quinn Group, Inc.
10006 Rose Hills Rd
City Of Industry CA 90601
562 463-4000

(P-9027)
RGW EQUIPMENT SALES LLC
550 Greenville Rd, Livermore (94550-9297)
PHONE.....................925 606-2456
Dane Lowry, *Vice Pres*
Warren Hanson, *Sales Staff*
Todd Provines, *Sales Staff*
Rick Albert,
EMP: 45 **EST:** 2003
SALES (est): 33MM **Privately Held**
WEB: www.rgwequipment.com
SIC: 5082 General construction machinery & equipment

(P-9028)
SAFWAY SERVICES LP
1660 Gilbreth Rd, Burlingame (94010-1408)
PHONE.....................650 652-9255
Fax: 650 652-9255
EMP: 50
SALES (corp-wide): 1.7B **Privately Held**
SIC: 5082 Whol Construction/Mining Equipment
HQ: Safway Services, L.P.
N19w24200 Riverwood Dr # 200
Waukesha WI 53188
262 523-6500

5083 Farm & Garden Mach & Eqpt Wholesale

(P-9029)
ALSCO - GEYER IRRIGATION INC
700 5th St, Arbuckle (95912-9550)
P.O. Box 111 (95912-0111)
PHONE.....................530 476-2253
Charles Geyer, *President*
Andrew Geyer, *CFO*
Andy Geyer, *Treasurer*
Marjoria Martinez, *Admin Sec*
EMP: 90 **EST:** 1996
SQ FT: 3,000
SALES (est): 25.1MM **Privately Held**
WEB: www.alscogeyerirrigation.com
SIC: 5083 Irrigation equipment

(P-9030)
AMERICAN GRAPE HARVESTERS INC
Also Called: Agh
5778 W Barstow Ave, Fresno (93722-5024)
PHONE.....................559 277-7380
Tom M Thompson, *CEO*
Rick Garcia, *Purchasing*
Jason Thompson, *Sales Mgr*
▲ **EMP:** 22 **EST:** 1990
SQ FT: 30,000
SALES (est): 6.7MM **Privately Held**
WEB: www.aghinc.com
SIC: 5083 0722 3523 7699 Farm equipment parts & supplies; grapes, machine harvesting services; harvesters, fruit, vegetable, tobacco, etc.; shakers, tree: nuts, fruits, etc.; agricultural equipment repair services

(P-9031)
ATI MACHINERY INC
Also Called: NAPA West
21436 S Lassen Ave, Five Points (93624)
P.O. Box 445 (93624-0445)
PHONE.....................559 884-2471
Toll Free:.....................888
Leo A Marihart, *Ch of Bd*
Mark Moorhead, *President*
Richard Demler, *Admin Sec*
EMP: 50 **EST:** 1985
SQ FT: 22,000
SALES (est): 13.2MM **Privately Held**
WEB: www.atimachinery.com
SIC: 5083 7699 7359 5531 Farm equipment parts & supplies; farm machinery repair; equipment rental & leasing; automotive parts

(P-9032)
BIANCHI AG SERVICES INC (PA)
1210 Richvale Hwy, Richvale (95974-8008)
P.O. Box 1216, Durham (95938-1216)
PHONE.....................530 882-4575
Jim Bianchi, *CEO*
Moe Dean, *CFO*
EMP: 118 **EST:** 2007
SALES (est): 17.4MM **Privately Held**
WEB: www.bianchiagservices.com
SIC: 5083 Agricultural machinery & equipment

(P-9033)
CENTRAL VALLEY BUILDERS SUPPLY
Also Called: Do It Best
1100 Vintage Ave, Saint Helena (94574-1440)
PHONE.....................707 963-3622
Jack Nelson, *General Mgr*
EMP: 49
SALES (corp-wide): 52MM **Privately Held**
WEB: www.central-valley.com
SIC: 5211 5083 5251 5031 Lumber & other building materials; irrigation equipment; hardware; lumber, plywood & millwork
PA: Central Valley Builders Supply
1790 Soscol Ave
Napa CA 94559
707 252-2889

(P-9034)
DRIPWORKS INC
Also Called: Everliner
190 San Hedrin Cir, Willits (95490-8753)
PHONE.....................707 459-6323
Leon Springer, *CEO*
Jerry Jordan, *Admin Sec*
Amanda Roth, *Business Mgr*
◆ **EMP:** 35 **EST:** 1992
SQ FT: 1,000
SALES (est): 8.7MM **Privately Held**
WEB: www.dripworks.com
SIC: 5083 5961 Irrigation equipment; catalog & mail-order houses

(P-9035)
EURODRIP USA INC
1850 W Almond Ave, Madera (93637-5214)
PHONE.....................559 674-2670
Rowland Wilkinson, *CEO*
◆ **EMP:** 80 **EST:** 1996
SQ FT: 33,180
SALES (est): 25.7MM **Privately Held**
WEB: www.eurodripusa.com
SIC: 5083 3084 Irrigation equipment; plastics pipe
HQ: Eurodrip S.A.
Athinon - Lamias National Rd (55th Km), P.O. Box 34
Oinofyta 32011

(P-9036)
EXACT CORP
5143 Blue Gum Ave, Modesto (95356-9516)
PHONE.....................209 544-8600
Jonathan J Flora, *CEO*
Sharon Eddleman, *Purchasing*
Heath Flora, *Sales Mgr*
Jason Bayer, *Marketing Staff*
▼ **EMP:** 41 **EST:** 1977
SALES (est): 19.8MM **Privately Held**
WEB: www.exactcorp.com
SIC: 5083 Agricultural machinery & equipment

(P-9037)
FORTIER & FORTIER INC
Also Called: Reedley Irrigation & Supply
1260 S Buttonwillow Ave, Reedley (93654-9359)
P.O. Box 592 (93654-0592)
PHONE.....................559 638-5774
Paul Fortier, *CEO*
Mary E Fortier, *President*
Shelly Fortier, *Admin Sec*
David Stuart, *Finance*
Chris Gueder, *Sales Associate*
EMP: 34 **EST:** 1961
SQ FT: 6,500
SALES (est): 10.8MM **Privately Held**
WEB: www.reedleyirrigation.com
SIC: 5083 5261 5999 3272 Irrigation equipment; nurseries & garden centers; farm equipment & supplies; pipe, concrete or lined with concrete

(P-9038)
GARTON TRACTOR INC (PA)
Also Called: Kubota Authorized Dealer
2400 N Golden State Blvd, Turlock (95382-9408)
P.O. Box 1849 (95381-1849)
PHONE.....................209 632-3931
William L Garton, *President*
Thomas Garton, *Treasurer*
Tom Garton, *Vice Pres*
Kevin Ballard, *General Mgr*
Denis Evans, *General Mgr*
▲ **EMP:** 63 **EST:** 1953
SQ FT: 20,000
SALES (est): 54.2MM **Privately Held**
WEB: www.gartontractor.com
SIC: 5999 5083 Farm machinery; farm & garden machinery

(P-9039)
GREEN ACRES NURSERY & SUP LLC
604 Sutter St Ste 350, Folsom (95630-2698)
PHONE.....................916 673-9720
Mark Gill,
Erik Snare, *Project Mgr*
Andrew Emmert, *Buyer*
James Jessup, *Buyer*
Kevin Gill, *Opers Staff*
▲ **EMP:** 90 **EST:** 2002
SALES (est): 26.6MM **Privately Held**
WEB: www.idiggreenacres.com
SIC: 5083 5261 Irrigation equipment; nursery stock, seeds & bulbs

(P-9040)
JENSEN & PILEGARD (PA)
1739 E Terrace Ave, Fresno (93703-1737)
PHONE.....................559 268-9221
Don J Pilegard, *President*
Chris Pilegard, *Corp Secy*
EMP: 25 **EST:** 1952
SQ FT: 15,500
SALES (est): 13.9MM **Privately Held**
WEB: www.jensenandpilegard.com
SIC: 5083 2048 5261 Farm equipment parts & supplies; garden machinery & equipment; livestock feeds; poultry feeds; lawn & garden supplies

(P-9041)
NETAFIM IRRIGATION INC (HQ)
5470 E Home Ave, Fresno (93727-2107)
PHONE.....................559 453-6800
Igal Aisenberg, *President*
Lauri Hanover, *CFO*
Iris Ron, *Officer*
Rami Miron, *Vice Pres*
Guy Sagie, *Vice Pres*
▲ **EMP:** 110 **EST:** 1965
SQ FT: 100,000
SALES (est): 91.1MM
SALES (corp-wide): 699.4MM **Privately Held**
WEB: www.netafimusa.com
SIC: 5083 3523 Irrigation equipment; irrigation equipment, self-propelled
PA: Netafim Ltd
10 Hashalom Rd.
Tel Aviv-Jaffa 67892
864 747-47

(P-9042)
NORTHCAST HORTICULTURE SUP INC (PA)
Also Called: Northcoast Hydroponics
513 K St, Arcata (95521-6173)
PHONE.....................707 839-0245
Stephen Gieder, *Ch of Bd*
Daniel Brumbaugh, *General Mgr*
Garry Nelson, *Controller*
EMP: 35 **EST:** 2005
SALES (est): 5.9MM **Privately Held**
WEB: www.nhs-hydroponics.com
SIC: 5083 Hydroponic equipment & supplies

(P-9043)
RDO CONSTRUCTION EQUIPMENT CO
7650 Hawthorne Ave Ste 1, Livermore (94550-7126)
PHONE.....................925 454-3100
Ken Hugen, *Manager*
Stephanie Lipich, *Officer*
EMP: 38
SALES (corp-wide): 2.5B **Privately Held**
WEB: www.rdoequipment.com
SIC: 5083 Agricultural machinery & equipment
HQ: Rdo Construction Equipment Co.
2000 Industrial Dr
Bismarck ND 58501
701 223-5798

(P-9044)
THOMASON TRACTOR CO CALIFORNIA
Also Called: John Deere Authorized Dealer
985 12th St, Firebaugh (93622)
P.O. Box 97 (93622-0097)
PHONE.....................559 659-2039
Audrey Thomason, *President*
Rodney Thomason, *Vice Pres*
Jessica Diaz, *Office Admin*
Angelica Fuentes, *Administration*
Francisco Nunez, *Technician*
EMP: 50 **EST:** 1967
SQ FT: 33,000
SALES (est): 17.4MM **Privately Held**
WEB: www.thomasontractor.com
SIC: 5083 Agricultural machinery & equipment

(P-9045)
TURLOCK DAIRY & RFRGN INC
Also Called: T D R
1819 S Walnut Rd, Turlock (95380-9219)
P.O. Box 1530 (95381-1530)
PHONE.....................209 667-6455
Mathew Anthony Bruno, *CEO*
Tony Bruno, *President*
Jonathan Risley, *Analyst*
EMP: 100 **EST:** 1972
SQ FT: 10,000
SALES (est): 27.4MM **Privately Held**
WEB: www.tdr-inc.com
SIC: 5083 7699 1542 Dairy machinery & equipment; industrial equipment services; nonresidential construction

▲ = Import ▼ =Export
◆ =Import/Export

PRODUCTS & SERVICES SECTION
5084 - Industrial Mach & Eqpt Wholesale County (P-9067)

(P-9046)
UNITED GREEN MARK INC
Also Called: Sprinkler Irrgtion Specialists
1145 N 13th St, San Jose (95112-2903)
PHONE.................408 295-3376
Dave Usher, *Manager*
EMP: 98
SALES (corp-wide): 2.7B **Publicly Held**
SIC: 5083 Lawn & garden machinery & equipment; landscaping equipment
HQ: United Green Mark Inc
650 Stephenson Hwy
Troy MI 48083
248 588-2100

(P-9047)
URBAN FARMER STORE INC (PA)
2833 Vicente St, San Francisco (94116-2721)
PHONE.................415 661-2204
Thomas Bressan, *CEO*
Adrian Smith, *President*
Colleen Omeara, *Controller*
Brian Murphy, *Sales Staff*
▲ **EMP:** 20 **EST:** 1983
SQ FT: 6,000
SALES (est): 9.6MM **Privately Held**
WEB: www.urbanfarmerstore.com
SIC: 5083 3645 Irrigation equipment; garden, patio, walkway & yard lighting fixtures; electric

(P-9048)
VALLEY TRUCK AND TRACTOR INC
Also Called: John Deere Authorized Dealer
Hwy 113, Robbins (95676)
P.O. Box 256 (95676-0256)
PHONE.................530 738-4421
Mike Cardoza, *Sales/Mktg Mgr*
Margie Reynoso, *Admin Asst*
Marc Boomgaarden, *Opers Mgr*
Mick Dinsdale, *Sales Staff*
Mark Harris, *Sales Staff*
EMP: 63
SALES (corp-wide): 90MM **Privately Held**
WEB: www.valleytruckandtractor.com
SIC: 5083 5261 Agricultural machinery & equipment; farm equipment parts & supplies; lawnmowers & tractors
PA: Valley Truck And Tractor Inc.
1003 Stabler Ln
Yuba City CA 95993
530 673-4615

(P-9049)
VUCOVICH INC (PA)
Also Called: John Deere Authorized Dealer
4288 S Bagley Ave, Fresno (93725-9014)
P.O. Box 2513 (93745-2513)
PHONE.................559 486-8020
Marsha Vucovich, *President*
Reid Pinion, *Controller*
Juan Gonzalez, *Sales Associate*
Carlos Maldonado, *Sales Associate*
Greg Ruiz, *Sales Associate*
EMP: 60 **EST:** 1961
SQ FT: 42,800
SALES (est): 24MM **Privately Held**
WEB: www.deere.com
SIC: 5083 Farm equipment parts & supplies

5084 Industrial Mach & Eqpt Wholesale

(P-9050)
ADVANCED GASES AND EQP INC
4639 Missouri Flat Rd, Placerville (95667-6816)
PHONE.................530 344-0771
Clif Brewer, *Branch Mgr*
EMP: 72
SALES (corp-wide): 14.1MM **Privately Held**
WEB: www.advancedgases.com
SIC: 5999 5084 Welding supplies; industrial machinery & equipment
PA: Advanced Gases And Equipment Inc.
520 Houston St
West Sacramento CA 95691
916 374-0771

(P-9051)
ANRITSU AMERICAS SALES COMPANY
490 Jarvis Dr, Morgan Hill (95037-2834)
PHONE.................408 778-2000
Hirokazu Hamada, *CEO*
EMP: 540 **EST:** 2018
SQ FT: 250,000
SALES (est): 218.3MM **Privately Held**
SIC: 5084 Measuring & testing equipment, electrical
HQ: Anritsu U.S. Holding, Inc.
490 Jarvis Dr
Morgan Hill CA 95037
408 778-2000

(P-9052)
BAY ADVANCED TECHNOLOGIES LLC
Also Called: Bay Advanced Tech 0045
8100 Central Ave, Newark (94560-3449)
PHONE.................510 857-0900
Mike Stimson, *Branch Mgr*
Yvette Kindred, *Technician*
EMP: 37
SALES (corp-wide): 3.2B **Publicly Held**
WEB: www.bayat.com
SIC: 5084 Pneumatic tools & equipment
HQ: Bay Advanced Technologies, Llc
8100 Central Ave
Newark CA 94560
510 857-0900

(P-9053)
BHOGART LLC
1919 Monterey Hwy Ste 80, San Jose (95112-6147)
PHONE.................855 553-3887
Kimberly Schaefer, *Partner*
Kevin Dolan, *Partner*
Thomas Lynch, *CEO*
David Schaefer, *CTO*
EMP: 38 **EST:** 2013
SALES (est): 9.5MM **Privately Held**
WEB: www.bhogart.com
SIC: 5084 Industrial machinery & equipment

(P-9054)
BIG JOE CALIFORNIA NORTH INC (PA)
Also Called: Big Joe Handling Systems
25932 Eden Landing Rd, Hayward (94545-3816)
PHONE.................510 785-6900
Boyd J Kiefus, *CEO*
Rod D Kiefus, *CFO*
Rod Kiefus, *CFO*
Steve Cox, *General Mgr*
Juan Garcia, *Technician*
EMP: 110 **EST:** 2003
SQ FT: 52,000
SALES (est): 43.2MM **Privately Held**
WEB: www.bigjoelift.com
SIC: 5084 5999 7359 8331 Lift trucks & parts; business machines & equipment; equipment rental & leasing; job training services

(P-9055)
BUCKEYE FIRE EQUIPMENT COMPANY
2416 Teagarden St, San Leandro (94577-4336)
PHONE.................510 483-1815
Mark Libardos, *Principal*
EMP: 291
SALES (corp-wide): 73.3MM **Privately Held**
WEB: www.buckeyefire.com
SIC: 5084 Industrial machinery & equipment
PA: Buckeye Fire Equipment Company
110 Kings Rd
Kings Mountain NC 28086
704 739-7415

(P-9056)
BUCKLES-SMITH ELECTRIC COMPANY (PA)
540 Martin Ave, Santa Clara (95050-2954)
PHONE.................408 280-7777
Art Cook, *CEO*
Pat Berry, *Vice Pres*
Roger Stanger, *Vice Pres*
Ron Zimmerman, *Admin Sec*
EMP: 55 **EST:** 1939
SALES (est): 60.6MM **Privately Held**
WEB: www.buckles-smith.com
SIC: 5084 5063 Industrial machinery & equipment; electrical supplies

(P-9057)
BUILDING ROBOTICS INC
Also Called: Comfy
1504 Franklin St Ste 200, Oakland (94612-2819)
PHONE.................510 972-9709
Erica Eaton, *CEO*
EMP: 57 **EST:** 2012
SALES (est): 17.3MM
WEB: www.comfyapp.com
SIC: 5084 Robots, industrial
HQ: Siemens Industry, Inc.
1000 Deerfield Pkwy
Buffalo Grove IL 60089
847 215-1000

(P-9058)
C N C SOLUTIONS (PA)
945 Ames Ave, Milpitas (95035-6326)
PHONE.................408 586-8236
EMP: 39 **EST:** 2002
SALES (est): 660.4K **Privately Held**
WEB: www.cncsolutions.biz
SIC: 5084 Industrial machinery & equipment

(P-9059)
CAPITAL ASSET EXCH & TRDG LLC (PA)
Also Called: Cae Online
870 E Charleston Rd # 210, Palo Alto (94303-4611)
PHONE.................650 326-3313
Ryan Jacob, *Mng Member*
Jeff Robbins, *President*
Andrei Fiadkovich, *Vice Pres*
Erin Hoang, *VP Finance*
▲ **EMP:** 45 **EST:** 1983
SQ FT: 10,000
SALES (est): 75MM **Privately Held**
SIC: 5084 Industrial machinery & equipment

(P-9060)
CAPITOL BARRICADE INC (PA)
6001 Elvas Ave, Sacramento (95819-4357)
PHONE.................916 451-5176
Joseph Reihl, *President*
Suzanne Reihl, *Treasurer*
Dave Sherman, *Opers Staff*
Ed Pal, *Sales Executive*
Todd Woolford, *Sales Mgr*
◆ **EMP:** 62 **EST:** 1966
SQ FT: 3,200
SALES: 73.7K **Privately Held**
WEB: www.capitolbarricade.com
SIC: 5084 7359 Safety equipment; equipment rental & leasing

(P-9061)
CROSSING AUTOMATION INC (HQ)
46702 Bayside Pkwy, Fremont (94538-6582)
PHONE.................510 661-5000
Robert B Macknight Kkk, *President*
Mark D Morelli, *President*
Stephen S Schwartz, *CEO*
Lindon G Robertson, *Exec VP*
David C Gray, *Senior VP*
▲ **EMP:** 1036 **EST:** 2004
SQ FT: 5,500
SALES (est): 113.3MM **Publicly Held**
WEB: www.crossinginc.com
SIC: 5084 Industrial machinery & equipment

(P-9062)
DENNIS DESIGN & MFG INC
Also Called: Designs Metals
4202 Jessup Rd, Ceres (95307-9604)
P.O. Box 576372, Modesto (95357-6372)
PHONE.................209 632-9956
EMP: 20 **EST:** 1980
SQ FT: 10,000
SALES (est): 3.4MM **Privately Held**
WEB: www.designmetals.com
SIC: 5084 1796 3441 3556 Whol Industrial Equip Bldg Equip Installation Structural Metal Fabrctn Mfg Food Prdts Mach

(P-9063)
DIRECTED LIGHT INC
Also Called: Unitek Miyachi International
74 Bonaventura Dr, San Jose (95134-2123)
PHONE.................408 321-8500
Mike McCourt, *CEO*
Neil Bell, *President*
▲ **EMP:** 25 **EST:** 1983
SQ FT: 13,000
SALES (est): 8.3MM **Privately Held**
WEB: www.directedlight.com
SIC: 5084 2759 7699 5072 Industrial machinery & equipment; laser printing; industrial machinery & equipment repair; hardware

(P-9064)
E & M ELECTRIC AND MCHY INC (PA)
Also Called: E&M
126 Mill St, Healdsburg (95448-4438)
PHONE.................707 433-5578
Steven Edgar Deas, *CEO*
Paul Deas, *Principal*
Dan Mossberg, *Office Admin*
Marc Johnson, *Technical Staff*
Joe Schlitzer, *Engineer*
◆ **EMP:** 50
SQ FT: 25,000
SALES (est): 91MM **Privately Held**
WEB: www.eandm.com
SIC: 5084 5999 5063 7694 Instruments & control equipment; motors, electric; motors, electric; electric motor repair

(P-9065)
EAST BAY CLARKLIFT INC (PA)
Also Called: Cromer Clarklift
4701 Oakport St, Oakland (94601-4906)
P.O. Box 14338 (94614-2338)
PHONE.................510 534-6566
Marshall Cromer, *President*
Holly Cromer, *Admin Sec*
▲ **EMP:** 49 **EST:** 1989
SQ FT: 20,000
SALES (est): 48.7MM **Privately Held**
WEB: www.cromer.com
SIC: 5084 7359 7699 Materials handling machinery; equipment rental & leasing; industrial equipment services

(P-9066)
EAST BAY PUMP & EQUIPMENT CO
4900 E 12th St, Oakland (94601-5110)
PHONE.................510 532-1800
Mark Ratto, *President*
EMP: 19 **EST:** 1970
SQ FT: 8,900
SALES (est): 5MM **Privately Held**
WEB: www.pumpsalesandservice.com
SIC: 5084 7699 3561 Pumps & pumping equipment; pumps & pumping equipment repair; pumps, domestic; water or sump

(P-9067)
FRESNO OXGN WLDG SUPPLIERS INC (PA)
Also Called: Barnes Welding Supply
2825 S Elm Ave Ste 101, Fresno (93706-5460)
P.O. Box 1666 (93717-1666)
PHONE.................559 233-6684
Michael L Barnes, *CEO*
David Barnes, *COO*
Jami Bradshaw, *Store Mgr*
James Michael Mc Cann, *Admin Sec*
Keith Swertfager, *Purchasing*
▲ **EMP:** 30 **EST:** 1949
SQ FT: 5,000

5084 - Industrial Mach & Eqpt Wholesale County (P-9068)

(P-9068)
SALES (est): 56.4MM **Privately Held**
WEB: www.barnesspecialtygases.com
SIC: **5084** 5169 3548 2813 Welding machinery & equipment; industrial gases; welding apparatus; industrial gases

(P-9068)
GENMARK AUTOMATION (DH)
46723 Lakeview Blvd, Fremont (94538-6528)
PHONE.....................510 897-3400
Yuji Shioga, *CEO*
Danny Hinckley, *QC Mgr*
Marlowe Markov, *Marketing Staff*
▼ **EMP: 98 EST:** 1985
SQ FT: 86,000
SALES (est): 57.1MM **Privately Held**
WEB: www.genmarkautomation.com
SIC: **5084** 3674 Industrial machinery & equipment; wafers (semiconductor devices)

(P-9069)
GMW ASSOCIATES
951 Industrial Rd Ste D, San Carlos (94070-4154)
PHONE.....................650 802-8292
Brian J Richter, *President*
Lalo Guitron, *Vice Pres*
Ben Hertzell, *Vice Pres*
Ian J Walker, *Vice Pres*
Sandro Renteria, *Lab Dir*
▲ **EMP: 18 EST:** 1983
SQ FT: 13,000
SALES (est): 8.7MM **Privately Held**
WEB: www.gmw.com
SIC: **5084** 3823 Instruments & control equipment; industrial process control instruments

(P-9070)
GOLDEN EAGLE DISTRIBUTING CORP
1251 Tinker Rd, Rocklin (95765-1311)
P.O. Box 1560 (95677-7560)
PHONE.....................916 645-6600
Gary Bussell, *CEO*
Steven L Clark, *Vice Pres*
Jason Herron, *Opers Mgr*
Paul Balint, *Sales Staff*
Dan Sumner, *Sales Staff*
◆ **EMP: 165 EST:** 1946
SQ FT: 90,000
SALES (est): 12.1MM **Privately Held**
WEB: www.goldeneagledist.com
SIC: **5084** Chainsaws; pumps & pumping equipment
HQ: Echo, Incorporated
400 Oakwood Rd
Lake Zurich IL 60047
847 540-8400

(P-9071)
HOUSTON MFG & INSTALLATION INC
520 E Service Rd, Modesto (95358-9306)
P.O. Box 2258, Ceres (95307-8758)
PHONE.....................209 556-0163
Ramon Villarreal, *President*
Mirna Torres, *Administration*
Ray Villarreal, *Mfg Staff*
EMP: 36 EST: 2006
SALES (est): 9.1MM **Privately Held**
WEB: www.hmi2006.com
SIC: **5084** Industrial machinery & equipment

(P-9072)
INOXPA USA INC
3721 Santa Rosa Ave B4, Santa Rosa (95407-8240)
PHONE.....................707 585-3900
Candi Granes Campasol, *President*
▲ **EMP: 300 EST:** 2004
SQ FT: 1,600
SALES (est): 26.7MM **Privately Held**
WEB: www.inoxpausa.com
SIC: **5084** Pumps & pumping equipment

(P-9073)
JOHNSTON INDUSTRIAL SUPPLY INC (PA)
Also Called: Jisco
2433 S Cherry Ave, Fresno (93706-5090)
P.O. Box 209 (93708-0209)
PHONE.....................559 233-1322
Leo S Johnston III, *President*
Charlotte Cassano, *Accountant*
John Tejes, *Director*
▲ **EMP: 35 EST:** 1963
SQ FT: 38,500
SALES (est): 11.6MM **Privately Held**
WEB: www.jiscodirect.com
SIC: **5084** 5211 Machine tools & accessories; metalworking tools (such as drills, taps, dies, files); lumber & other building materials

(P-9074)
KBA DOCUSYS INC (PA)
32900 Alvarado Niles Rd # 1, Union City (94587-3106)
PHONE.....................510 214-4040
James E Graf, *President*
Todd Moody, *Treasurer*
Michelle Graf, *Bd of Directors*
Brian Carias, *Branch Mgr*
James A Hennefer, *Admin Sec*
EMP: 43 EST: 2007
SALES (est): 21MM **Privately Held**
WEB: www.kbadocusys.com
SIC: **5084** 5044 7371 Printing trades machinery, equipment & supplies; photocopy machines; computer software systems analysis & design, custom; computer software writers, freelance

(P-9075)
LAKOS CORPORATION
1365 N Clovis Ave, Fresno (93727-2282)
P.O. Box 398936, San Francisco (94139-8936)
PHONE.....................559 255-1601
Scott Marion, *CEO*
Brian Ketcham, *CFO*
Kathy Colby, *Exec VP*
Randy Delenikos, *Vice Pres*
Craig Malsam, *Vice Pres*
◆ **EMP: 90 EST:** 1972
SQ FT: 100,000
SALES (est): 27.7MM **Privately Held**
WEB: www.lakos.com
SIC: **5084** 3491 Industrial machinery & equipment; pressure valves & regulators, industrial
PA: Lakos Acquisition Holdco, Llc
1365 N Clovis Ave
Fresno CA 93727
559 255-1601

(P-9076)
LMC WEST INC
5300 Claus Rd, Riverbank (95367)
P.O. Box 325 (95367-0325)
PHONE.....................209 869-0144
Fax: 209 869-0258
EMP: 50
SQ FT: 50,000
SALES (est): 10.3MM
SALES (corp-wide): 2.3B **Publicly Held**
SIC: **5084** Whol Industrial Equipment Mfg Blowers/Fans
PA: Donaldson Company, Inc.
1400 W 94th St
Minneapolis MN 55431
952 887-3131

(P-9077)
LORING SMART ROAST INC
3200 Dutton Ave Ste 413, Santa Rosa (95407-5736)
PHONE.....................707 526-7215
Mark Ludwig, *Founder*
Greg Schiller, *Sr Software Eng*
Scott Robinson, *Mfg Dir*
Sylvia Alvarez, *Materials Mgr*
Dennis Vogel, *Marketing Staff*
EMP: 54 EST: 2007
SQ FT: 19,000
SALES (est): 12MM **Privately Held**
WEB: www.loring.com
SIC: **5084** Food industry machinery

(P-9078)
MCGRATH RENTCORP
Also Called: Mobile Modular
5700 Las Positas Rd, Livermore (94551-7806)
PHONE.....................877 221-2813
Philip Hawkins, *Vice Pres*
Kristina Vantrease, *Vice Pres*
Chris Snyder, *Surgery Dir*
Gary Carleton, *Branch Mgr*
Greg Hurley, *Branch Mgr*
EMP: 102
SALES (corp-wide): 572.5MM **Publicly Held**
WEB: www.mgrc.com
SIC: **5084** 7359 Measuring & testing equipment, electrical; electronic equipment rental, except computers
PA: Mcgrath Rentcorp
5700 Las Positas Rd
Livermore CA 94551
925 606-9200

(P-9079)
MCGRATH RENTCORP (PA)
5700 Las Positas Rd, Livermore (94551-7806)
PHONE.....................925 606-9200
Joseph F Hanna, *President*
Ronald H Zech, *Ch of Bd*
Keith E Pratt, *CFO*
John P Skenesky, *Treasurer*
Kim A Box, *Bd of Directors*
EMP: 312 EST: 1979
SQ FT: 26,000
SALES (est): 572.5MM **Publicly Held**
WEB: www.mgrc.com
SIC: **5084** 7359 Measuring & testing equipment, electrical; electronic equipment rental, except computers

(P-9080)
MCLAUGHLIN WASTE EQUIPMENT INC (PA)
11900 Locke Rd, Lockeford (95237-9701)
P.O. Box 637, Galt (95632-0637)
PHONE.....................209 367-8810
Danny McLaughlin, *CEO*
Danny Michael McLaughlin, *CEO*
Alice Rabara, *Controller*
EMP: 51 EST: 2013
SALES (est): 10.4MM **Privately Held**
WEB: www.mwecans.com
SIC: **5084** Industrial machinery & equipment

(P-9081)
MOREFLAVOR INC (PA)
Also Called: Beer Beer & More Beer
701 Willow Pass Rd, Pittsburg (94565-1803)
PHONE.....................800 600-0033
Olin Schultz, *CEO*
Darrin Schelth, *Shareholder*
Casey Cobb, *COO*
Dan Lipscomb, *COO*
Chris Graham, *CFO*
◆ **EMP: 21 EST:** 1995
SQ FT: 10,000
SALES (est): 25.5MM **Privately Held**
WEB: www.moreflavor.com
SIC: **5084** 3556 Brewery products manufacturing machinery, commercial; brewers' & maltsters' machinery

(P-9082)
NAN FANG DIST GROUP INC
2100 Williams St, San Leandro (94577-3225)
PHONE.....................510 297-5382
Ze Pan, *CEO*
Zhen Poon, *Vice Pres*
▲ **EMP: 100 EST:** 1994
SALES (est): 12.7MM **Privately Held**
SIC: **5084** Engines & parts, diesel

(P-9083)
NIKON PRECISION INC (DH)
1399 Shoreway Rd, Belmont (94002-4107)
PHONE.....................650 508-4674
Toyohiro Takamine, *CEO*
Takao Naito, *President*
Shintaro Nishimura, *Executive*
Steven Barnett, *Associate Dir*
Mahmoud Moukalled, *Software Engr*
▲ **EMP: 250 EST:** 1982
SQ FT: 30,000
SALES (est): 161.2MM **Privately Held**
WEB: www.nikonprecision.com
SIC: **5084** 5065 Industrial machinery & equipment; electronic parts & equipment

(P-9084)
PACIFIC MTL HDLG SOLUTIONS INC
2242 Hoover Ave, Modesto (95354-3906)
PHONE.....................209 524-5194
Thys Schurer, *Manager*
EMP: 43 Privately Held
WEB: www.pmhsi.com
SIC: **5511 5084** Trucks, tractors & trailers: new & used; lift trucks & parts
PA: Pacific Material Handling Solutions, Inc.
30361 Whipple Rd
Union City CA 94587

(P-9085)
PAPE MATERIAL HANDLING INC
47132 Kato Rd, Fremont (94538-7333)
PHONE.....................510 659-4100
Ken Mader, *Branch Mgr*
Chris Wetle, *President*
Jordan Pape, *CEO*
Jason Vincent, *Manager*
EMP: 80
SQ FT: 37,536 **Privately Held**
WEB: www.papemh.com
SIC: **5084** 8743 7359 5082 Materials handling machinery; sales promotion; stores & yards equipment rental; contractors' materials
HQ: Pape' Material Handling, Inc.
355 Goodpasture Island Rd
Eugene OR 97401

(P-9086)
PARAGON PRODUCTS LIMITED LLC (PA)
4475 Golden Foothill Pkwy, El Dorado Hills (95762-9638)
PHONE.....................916 941-9717
Ted Keefer, *President*
Renee Lajou, *CFO*
Jo Boxell, *Office Mgr*
Paul Davies,
◆ **EMP: 40 EST:** 1997
SQ FT: 12,000
SALES (est): 32MM **Privately Held**
WEB: www.paragonproducts.net
SIC: **5084** Pumps & pumping equipment

(P-9087)
R F MACDONALD CO (PA)
25920 Eden Landing Rd, Hayward (94545-3816)
PHONE.....................510 784-0110
Michael D Macdonald, *Co-President*
James T Macdonald, *President*
Joel Lesser, *CFO*
James Macdonald, *Treasurer*
Chris Sentner, *Vice Pres*
EMP: 124 EST: 1956
SQ FT: 25,000
SALES (est): 97.1MM **Privately Held**
WEB: www.rfmacdonald.com
SIC: **5084** 7699 5074 Pumps & pumping equipment; industrial machinery & equipment repair; boilers, power (industrial)

(P-9088)
RELIABLE ROBOTICS CORPORATION
950 N Rengstorff Ave E, Mountain View (94043-1746)
PHONE.....................650 336-0608
Richard Barnes, *CIO*
Amy Beacham, *Opers Mgr*
EMP: 37 EST: 2017
SALES (est): 6.8MM **Privately Held**
WEB: www.reliable.co
SIC: **5084** Robots, industrial

(P-9089)
RITTER MANUFACTURING INC
321 Eastgate Ln, Martinez (94553-6543)
PHONE.....................925 757-7296
Ase J Stornetta, *President*
Jean Stornetta, *Vice Pres*
EMP: 15 EST: 1976

▲ = Import ▼ = Export
◆ = Import/Export

PRODUCTS & SERVICES SECTION
5085 - Industrial Splys Wholesale County (P-9110)

SALES (est): 2.7MM **Privately Held**
WEB: www.rittermachinery.com
SIC: **5084** 3553 Industrial machinery & equipment; woodworking machinery

(P-9090)
RKI INSTRUMENTS INC (PA)
Also Called: R K I
33248 Central Ave, Union City (94587-2010)
PHONE..................510 441-5656
Robert Pellissier, *President*
Sandra Gallagher, *Vice Pres*
Teresa Carlino, *Administration*
John Villalovos, *Administration*
Ramey Packer, *CIO*
▲ **EMP:** 54 **EST:** 1994
SQ FT: 10,000
SALES (est): 21.2MM **Privately Held**
WEB: www.rkiinstruments.com
SIC: **5084** 3823 Industrial machinery & equipment; on-stream gas/liquid analysis instruments, industrial

(P-9091)
ROSE JOAQUIN INC
Also Called: B & B Mfg Co
410 S Golden State Blvd, Turlock (95380-4959)
PHONE..................209 632-0616
Joaquin A Rose, *President*
David A Rose, *CFO*
Michael A Rose, *Vice Pres*
EMP: 31 **EST:** 1936
SQ FT: 20,000
SALES (est): 11.2MM **Privately Held**
WEB: www.bbmfgpower.com
SIC: **5084** 7692 3599 Hydraulic systems equipment & supplies; welding repair; machine shop, jobbing & repair

(P-9092)
S4 LLC
601 California St Ste 100, San Francisco (94108-2828)
P.O. Box 77385 (94107-0385)
PHONE..................415 979-9640
EMP: 15
SALES (est): 1.9MM **Privately Held**
SIC: **5084** 3823 Whol And Ret Industrial And Commercial Machinery And Computer Equipment

(P-9093)
SAN FRANCISCO ELEV SVCS INC
6517 Sierra Ln, Dublin (94568-2798)
PHONE..................925 829-5400
Donovan McKeever, *President*
Tarek Elgendi, *Project Mgr*
Brian McLemore, *Sales Mgr*
EMP: 50 **EST:** 2015
SALES (est): 8.1MM **Privately Held**
WEB: www.ascentelevator.com
SIC: **5084** Elevators

(P-9094)
SELWAY MACHINE TOOL CO INC (PA)
29250 Union City Blvd, Union City (94587-1279)
PHONE..................510 487-9291
William R Selway, *President*
Pat Hayes, *President*
Dan Selway, *Corp Secy*
Joe Madden, *Executive*
Kate Gray, *Admin Sec*
▲ **EMP:** 37 **EST:** 1963
SQ FT: 48,000
SALES (est): 46.4MM **Privately Held**
WEB: www.selwaytool.com
SIC: **5084** Metalworking machinery; machine tools & accessories

(P-9095)
SHANNON PUMP CO
275 S State Highway 59, Merced (95341-6919)
PHONE..................209 723-3904
Delbert Shannon, *CEO*
Claudia Shannon, *Corp Secy*
Christopher Shannon, *Vice Pres*
EMP: 40 **EST:** 1944
SQ FT: 12,000
SALES (est): 15.4MM **Privately Held**
WEB: www.shannonpump.com
SIC: **5084** 7699 Pumps & pumping equipment; pumps & pumping equipment repair

(P-9096)
SMIC AMERICAS
1732 N 1st St Ste 200, San Jose (95112-4518)
PHONE..................408 550-8888
David N K Wang, *CEO*
Michael J Rekuc, *President*
Simon Yang, *COO*
Yonggang Gao, *CFO*
Gary Tseng, *CFO*
▲ **EMP:** 39 **EST:** 2001
SALES (est): 5.8MM **Privately Held**
WEB: www.smics.com
SIC: **5084** Industrial machinery & equipment
PA: Semiconductor Manufacturing International Corporation
C/O: Conyers Trust Company (Cayman) Limited
George Town GR CAYMAN

(P-9097)
TK ELEVATOR CORPORATION
14400 Catalina St, San Leandro (94577-5516)
PHONE..................510 476-1900
Ed Persico, *Manager*
Mike Dugan, *Senior Engr*
Daniel Giaramita, *Director*
EMP: 53
SALES (corp-wide): 1B **Privately Held**
WEB: www.tkelevator.com
SIC: **5084** 1796 3534 Elevators; elevator installation & conversion; elevators & moving stairways
HQ: Tk Elevator Corporation
11605 Haynes Bridge Rd
Alpharetta GA 30009
678 319-3240

(P-9098)
TK ELEVATOR CORPORATION
520 Townsend St Fl 1, San Francisco (94103-6242)
PHONE..................415 544-8150
David Stanley, *Manager*
Kyle Bushon, *Branch Mgr*
Alireza Mohammadi, *Sr Project Mgr*
EMP: 53
SALES (corp-wide): 1B **Privately Held**
WEB: www.tkelevator.com
SIC: **5084** Elevators
HQ: Tk Elevator Corporation
11605 Haynes Bridge Rd
Alpharetta GA 30009
678 319-3240

(P-9099)
TK ELEVATOR CORPORATION
3711 W Swift Ave, Fresno (93722-6350)
PHONE..................559 271-1238
Brian Hodges, *Manager*
EMP: 53
SALES (corp-wide): 1B **Privately Held**
WEB: www.tkelevator.com
SIC: **5084** Elevators
HQ: Tk Elevator Corporation
11605 Haynes Bridge Rd
Alpharetta GA 30009
678 319-3240

(P-9100)
TRI TOOL INC (HQ)
3041 Sunrise Blvd, Rancho Cordova (95742-6502)
PHONE..................916 288-6100
Christopher M Belle, *CEO*
George J Wernette III, *President*
Chris Soriano, *CFO*
Jerri Wernette, *Treasurer*
Scott Stanton, *Vice Pres*
▲ **EMP:** 224 **EST:** 1972
SQ FT: 125,000
SALES (est): 74.9MM **Privately Held**
WEB: www.tritool.com
SIC: **5084** 3548 3541 Industrial machinery & equipment; welding apparatus; pipe cutting & threading machines
PA: The Wernette Family Limited Partnership Of 1995
3041 Sunrise Blvd
Rancho Cordova CA 95742
916 288-6100

(P-9101)
UNICO MECHANICAL CORP
1209 Polk St, Benicia (94510-2906)
P.O. Box 847 (94510-0847)
PHONE..................707 745-4540
Michael Potter, *President*
Randy Potter, *President*
Michael Guthrie, *COO*
Karen Begley, *Admin Asst*
Tom Clougher, *Info Tech Mgr*
▲ **EMP:** 80 **EST:** 2006
SQ FT: 80,000
SALES (est): 18.6MM **Privately Held**
WEB: www.unicomechanical.com
SIC: **5084** 7699 Industrial machinery & equipment; industrial machinery & equipment repair

(P-9102)
VALIN CORPORATION (PA)
5225 Hellyer Ave Ste 250, San Jose (95138-1023)
PHONE..................408 730-9850
Joseph C Nettemeyer, *President*
John Pregenzer, *COO*
David Hefler, *CFO*
Anne Vranicic, *Vice Pres*
Timothy Tritch, *VP Bus Dvlpt*
◆ **EMP:** 96 **EST:** 1974
SALES (est): 132.1MM **Privately Held**
WEB: www.valin.com
SIC: **5084** Materials handling machinery; processing & packaging equipment

(P-9103)
VALLEY POWER SYSTEMS INC
Also Called: John Deere Authorized Dealer
2070 Farallon Dr, San Leandro (94577-6602)
PHONE..................510 635-8991
Mickey Smith, *Branch Mgr*
EMP: 17
SALES (corp-wide): 178.7MM **Privately Held**
WEB: www.valleypowersystems.com
SIC: **5084** 3531 5063 Engines & parts, diesel; road construction & maintenance machinery; generators
PA: Valley Power Systems, Inc.
425 S Hacienda Blvd
City Of Industry CA 91745
626 333-1243

(P-9104)
WATTS EQUIPMENT COMPANY
17547 Comconex Rd, Manteca (95336-8105)
P.O. Box 2570 (95336-1167)
PHONE..................209 825-1700
Shirley Perreira, *Vice Pres*
Virgil Watts, *Ch of Bd*
Brock Watts, *President*
Destiny Jauregui, *Executive Asst*
Marolyn Watts, *Admin Asst*
EMP: 40 **EST:** 1967
SQ FT: 18,000
SALES (est): 12MM **Privately Held**
WEB: www.wattsequipment.com
SIC: **5084** 7699 7359 Lift trucks & parts; industrial equipment services; equipment rental & leasing

(P-9105)
WH ACQUISITIONS INC (HQ)
800 Concar Dr Ste 100, San Mateo (94402-7045)
PHONE..................650 358-5000
Jeff Drazan, *CEO*
Ingrid Swanson, *Principal*
Kevin Yamashita, *Principal*
EMP: 242 **EST:** 2012
SALES (est): 406.8MM
SALES (corp-wide): 1.8B **Privately Held**
WEB: www.berwind.com
SIC: **5084** 6719 Industrial machinery & equipment; investment holding companies, except banks
PA: Berwind Corporation
2929 Walnut St Ste 900
Philadelphia PA 19104
215 563-2800

5085 Industrial Splys Wholesale

(P-9106)
ACTION GYPSUM SUPPLY WEST LP (PA)
21040 Forbes Ave, Hayward (94545-1116)
PHONE..................510 259-1965
EMP: 45 **EST:** 2015
SALES (est): 5.3MM **Privately Held**
WEB: www.actiongypsum.com
SIC: **5085** Industrial supplies

(P-9107)
ADVANTEK TAPING SYSTEMS INC (DH)
6839 Mowry Ave, Newark (94560-4925)
PHONE..................510 623-1877
Andy Byron, *President*
▲ **EMP:** 89 **EST:** 1991
SQ FT: 24,600
SALES (est): 19.8MM **Privately Held**
WEB: www.advantek.com
SIC: **5085** 3674 Abrasives; integrated circuits, semiconductor networks, etc.
HQ: Advantek, Llc
20969 Cabot Blvd
Hayward CA 94545
510 623-1877

(P-9108)
ALCAN PACKG CAPSULES CAL LLC
5425 Broadway St, American Canyon (94503-9678)
PHONE..................707 257-6481
Richard Evans, *President*
Michael Schmitt, *Exec VP*
Federick Catteau, *Vice Pres*
▲ **EMP:** 21 **EST:** 1982
SQ FT: 20,618
SALES (est): 13.7MM
SALES (corp-wide): 12.4B **Privately Held**
WEB: www.amcor.com
SIC: **5085** 3466 Bottler supplies; crowns & closures
HQ: Amcor European Holdings Pty Ltd
L 11 60 City Rd
Southbank VIC 3006

(P-9109)
ALFRED CONHAGEN INC CALIFORNIA
Also Called: Rotating Equipment Specialist
3900 Oregon St Ste 1, Benicia (94510-1148)
PHONE..................707 746-4848
Len Cucciare, *Manager*
EMP: 50
SALES (corp-wide): 11.5MM **Privately Held**
SIC: **5085** 7699 Industrial supplies; pumps & pumping equipment repair
PA: Conhagen, Alfred, Inc Of California
2555 Severn Ave Ste 110
Metairie LA 70002
908 753-9800

(P-9110)
BAY STANDARD INC
24485 Marsh Creek Rd, Brentwood (94513-4319)
P.O. Box 801 (94513-0801)
PHONE..................925 634-1181
Gary W Landgraf, *President*
Karen Landgraf, *Corp Secy*
Tom Landgraf, *Vice Pres*
Paige Shamblin, *Purch Mgr*
▲ **EMP:** 100 **EST:** 1966
SALES (est): 13MM **Privately Held**
WEB: www.baystandard.com
SIC: **5085** 3965 Fasteners & fastening equipment; fasteners

5085 - Industrial Splys Wholesale County (P-9111)

(P-9111)
CALIFORNIA INDUSTRIAL RBR CO (PA)
2539 S Cherry Ave, Fresno (93706-5007)
PHONE.................................559 268-7321
Larry T Cain Sr, *President*
Jeff T Brust, *CEO*
Carol Ann Cain, *Treasurer*
Russell Lemburg, *Branch Mgr*
Vivian Tur, *Administration*
▲ EMP: 25 EST: 1958
SQ FT: 45,000
SALES (est): 74.8MM **Privately Held**
WEB: www.californiaindustrialrubber.net
SIC: **5085** 5999 3052 Hose, belting & packing; seals, industrial; rubber goods, mechanical; rubber stamps; rubber & plastics hose & beltings

(P-9112)
CARBONIC SERVICE
1920 De La Cruz Blvd, Santa Clara (95050-3004)
PHONE.................................408 727-8835
Geordel C Allison, *CEO*
Geordel Allison, *Admin Sec*
EMP: 43 EST: 1948
SQ FT: 1,200
SALES (est): 10MM **Privately Held**
WEB: www.carbonicservice.com
SIC: **5085** 5149 Gas equipment, parts & supplies; beverage concentrates

(P-9113)
COFAN USA INC
48664 Milmont Dr, Fremont (94538-7353)
PHONE.................................510 490-7533
Chang S Han, *President*
Steven Cooper, *Sales Staff*
Ben Finn, *Sales Staff*
▲ EMP: 40 EST: 1994
SQ FT: 66,000
SALES (est): 23.9MM **Privately Held**
WEB: www.cofangroup.com
SIC: **5085** 3444 3089 3672 Industrial supplies; sheet metalwork; injection molded finished plastic products; printed circuit boards

(P-9114)
COMPASS CONTAINER GROUP INC (PA)
6345 Coliseum Way, Oakland (94621-3719)
P.O. Box 340771, Sacramento (95834-0771)
PHONE.................................510 839-7500
Toll Free:...............................888 -
Ricardo Lacayo, *CEO*
Brian Crosby, *Vice Pres*
Paul Crosby, *Vice Pres*
Orlando Fernandes, *General Mgr*
◆ EMP: 36 EST: 2000
SQ FT: 6,000
SALES (est): 9.9MM **Privately Held**
WEB: www.compasscontainer.com
SIC: **5085** Commercial containers

(P-9115)
CONTINENTAL WESTERN CORP (PA)
Also Called: C W C
2950 Merced St Ste 200, San Leandro (94577-5641)
P.O. Box 2418 (94577-0241)
PHONE.................................510 352-3133
Frederick J Oshay, *President*
George Garcia, *Vice Pres*
Frank Larson, *Vice Pres*
Donn Mouw, *Branch Mgr*
Craig Steinke, *Controller*
◆ EMP: 50 EST: 1957
SQ FT: 25,000
SALES (est): 60MM **Privately Held**
WEB: www.cwcglobal.com
SIC: **5085** 3069 Twine; rapping, rubber

(P-9116)
DARCOID COMPANY OF CALIFORNIA
Also Called: Darcoid Nor-Cal Seal
950 3rd St, Oakland (94607-2502)
PHONE.................................510 836-2449
Robert M Loback, *CEO*
Steve Barton, *Engineer*
Jason Hainer, *Engineer*
Chuanyu Zhang, *QC Mgr*
Alexandra Loback, *Opers Staff*
▲ EMP: 48 EST: 1945
SQ FT: 27,000
SALES (est): 25MM **Privately Held**
WEB: www.darcoid.com
SIC: **5085** 3053 Rubber goods, mechanical; gaskets, all materials

(P-9117)
ERIKS NORTH AMERICA INC
Also Called: Valley Rubber & Gasket
10182 Croydon Way, Sacramento (95827-2102)
PHONE.................................916 366-9340
Les A Shively, *CEO*
Debbie Herbers, *Technology*
Keith Hoelscher, *Manager*
EMP: 98 **Privately Held**
WEB: www.eriksna.com
SIC: **5085** 3053 3052 Hose, belting & packing; gaskets & seals; gaskets, packing & sealing devices; rubber & plastics hose & beltings
HQ: Eriks North America, Inc.
  650 Washington Rd Ste 500
  Pittsburgh PA 15228
  800 937-9070

(P-9118)
GCO INC
4130 S Moorland Ave, Santa Rosa (95407-8154)
PHONE.................................707 584-3333
Bob Barstar, *Manager*
EMP: 35
SALES (corp-wide): 34MM **Privately Held**
SIC: **5085** Valves & fittings
PA: Gco, Inc.
  27750 Industrial Blvd
  Hayward CA 94545
  510 786-3333

(P-9119)
IMACC CORPORATION
Also Called: Myers Container
2200 Central St, Richmond (94801-1213)
PHONE.................................510 233-4865
EMP: 45
SQ FT: 5,000
SALES (corp-wide): 43.2MM **Privately Held**
SIC: **5085** 3443 3412 Whol Industrial Supplies Mfg Fabricated Plate Wrk Mfg Metal Barrels/Pails
PA: Imacc Corporation
  2303 Dalton Industrial Ct
  Dalton GA 30721
  706 270-8635

(P-9120)
INDUSTRIAL CONT SVCS - CA N LL
Also Called: Ics-CA North
749 Galleria Blvd, Roseville (95678-1331)
PHONE.................................916 781-2775
Charles Veniez, *CEO*
Gerald Butler,
Alain G Magnan,
Kay Rykowski,
Calvin G Lee, *Mng Member*
EMP: 52 EST: 1986
SQ FT: 10,000
SALES (est): 24.2MM
SALES (corp-wide): 1.1B **Privately Held**
WEB: www.mauserpackaging.com
SIC: **5085** 2655 Commercial containers; fiber cans, drums & similar products
HQ: Industrial Container Services Llc
  375 Northridge Rd Ste 600
  Atlanta GA 30350
  407 930-4182

(P-9121)
LENACO CORPORATION
Also Called: Blue Ribbon Supply Company Brs
451 E Jamie Ct, South San Francisco (94080-6204)
P.O. Box 2867 (94083-2867)
PHONE.................................650 873-3500
Daisy Dilena, *CEO*
Frank Dilena, *Shareholder*
Carolyn Dilena, *Treasurer*
John Dilena, *Vice Pres*
Randy Dilena, *Vice Pres*
▲ EMP: 45 EST: 1958
SQ FT: 40,000
SALES (est): 23.4MM **Privately Held**
WEB: www.lenaco.com
SIC: **5085** 5087 Industrial supplies; laundry equipment & supplies

(P-9122)
MACPHERSON WSTN TL SUP CO LLC (PA)
203 Lawrence Dr Ste D, Livermore (94551-5152)
P.O. Box 420, Tracy (95378-0420)
PHONE.................................925 443-8665
Jerry L Gerardot, *President*
Judy Gerardot, *Corp Secy*
Kevin Young, *Vice Pres*
Eric Bernal, *Branch Mgr*
Connie Cottrell, *Branch Mgr*
EMP: 40 EST: 1946
SQ FT: 28,000
SALES (est): 50.4MM **Privately Held**
WEB: www.westtool.com
SIC: 5251 **5085** Tools; tools

(P-9123)
MELO MACHINE & MFG INC
1707 Magnolia Ave, Patterson (95363-9630)
P.O. Box 517 (95363-0517)
PHONE.................................209 892-2661
Jim Melo, *Owner*
EMP: 17 EST: 1987
SQ FT: 7,000
SALES (est): 2.7MM **Privately Held**
SIC: **5085** 3599 Industrial supplies; machine shop, jobbing & repair

(P-9124)
OLANDER COMPANY INC
144 Commercial St, Sunnyvale (94086-5298)
PHONE.................................408 735-1850
Ronald Olander, *CEO*
Melissa Warren, *Admin Asst*
Anna Olander, *Technology*
Rey Del Fierro, *Buyer*
Paul Lloyd, *Marketing Staff*
EMP: 48 EST: 1962
SQ FT: 26,000
SALES (est): 24.1MM **Privately Held**
WEB: www.olander.com
SIC: **5085** Fasteners, industrial: nuts, bolts, screws, etc.

(P-9125)
PACIFIC RUBBER & PACKING INC (PA)
1160 Industrial Rd Ste 3, San Carlos (94070-4128)
PHONE.................................650 595-5888
Peter Burfield, *Ch of Bd*
Ashley Burfield, *President*
Joyce Burfield, *Vice Pres*
John Farcich, *Vice Pres*
Judy Lara, *Human Res Mgr*
EMP: 27 EST: 1973
SQ FT: 12,000
SALES (est): 27.2MM **Privately Held**
WEB: www.pacificrubber.com
SIC: **5085** 3061 Rubber goods, mechanical; seals, industrial; mechanical rubber goods

(P-9126)
PBM SUPPLY & MFG
Also Called: P B M
324 Meyers St, Chico (95928-7175)
P.O. Box 3129 (95927-3129)
PHONE.................................530 345-1334
Barry S Jones, *CEO*
Tim Williams, *General Mgr*
Zack Stephens, *Technology*
Craig Vonseggern, *Manager*
▲ EMP: 24 EST: 1969
SQ FT: 10,100
SALES (est): 15MM **Privately Held**
WEB: www.pbmsprayers.com
SIC: **5085** 5191 3715 Industrial supplies; farm supplies; bus trailers, tractor type

(P-9127)
PRECISION FLUID CONTROLS INC
3860 Cincinnati Ave, Rocklin (95765-1312)
PHONE.................................916 626-3029
Peggy Stevens, *President*
John Roth, *Technician*
EMP: 70
SALES (est): 1.4MM **Privately Held**
WEB: www.precisionfluidcontrols.com
SIC: **5085** 3728 Valves & fittings; accumulators, aircraft propeller

(P-9128)
RJMS CORPORATION (PA)
Also Called: Toyota Material Hdlg Nthrn Cal
6999 Southfront Rd, Livermore (94551-8221)
PHONE.................................510 675-0500
Richard Andres, *CEO*
Mark Andres, *Vice Pres*
Stephen Andres, *Vice Pres*
Gregg Robinson, *Branch Mgr*
Timo Soeganda, *Administration*
▲ EMP: 100 EST: 1921
SQ FT: 45,000
SALES (est): 115.1MM **Privately Held**
WEB: www.tmhnc.com
SIC: 5511 **5085** 7699 Automobiles, new & used; industrial supplies; industrial machinery & equipment repair

(P-9129)
ROPE PARTNER INC
125 Mcpherson St Ste B, Santa Cruz (95060-5883)
PHONE.................................831 460-9448
Eric Stanfield, *President*
Chris Bley, *Founder*
Kalil Allon, *Technician*
Linda Benko, *Technician*
Jaime Castagnetto, *Technician*
EMP: 65 EST: 2001
SQ FT: 1,900 **Privately Held**
WEB: www.ropepartner.com
SIC: **5085** Rope, cord & thread

(P-9130)
RS HUGHES COMPANY INC (PA)
Also Called: Saunders
1162 Sonora Ct, Sunnyvale (94086-5378)
PHONE.................................408 739-3211
William Matthews, *CEO*
Robert McCollum, *Ch of Bd*
Peter Biocini, *President*
Thomas Smith, *CFO*
George Mallinckrodt, *Vice Pres*
EMP: 45 EST: 1954
SQ FT: 20,000
SALES: 429.8MM **Privately Held**
WEB: www.rshughes.com
SIC: **5085** Abrasives & adhesives

(P-9131)
S & S TOOL & SUPPLY INC (HQ)
Also Called: S & S Supplies and Solutions
2700 Maxwell Way, Fairfield (94534-9708)
P.O. Box 1111, Martinez (94553-0111)
PHONE.................................800 430-8665
Tracy Tomkovicz, *CEO*
Tanya Powell, *CFO*
Aaron Hershman, *Branch Mgr*
Robert Peers, *CIO*
Phil Jones, *Info Tech Mgr*
▲ EMP: 100 EST: 1983
SQ FT: 90,000
SALES (est): 153.2MM
SALES (corp-wide): 950.5MM **Privately Held**
WEB: www.igate2.suppliesandsolutions.com
SIC: **5085** 7699 5072 7359 Industrial tools; industrial equipment services; hand tools; equipment rental & leasing
PA: Total Safety U.S., Inc.
  3151 Briarpark Dr Ste 500
  Houston TX 77042
  713 353-7100

(P-9132)
SAN JOAQUIN HYDRAULIC INC (PA)
Also Called: Central Supply Co
530 Van Ness Ave, Fresno (93721-2924)
PHONE.................................559 264-7325

Robert F Egan, *Ch of Bd*
Lowell D Smith, *Shareholder*
Timothy Cornelius, *Sales Mgr*
▲ **EMP:** 15 **EST:** 1950
SQ FT: 40,000
SALES (est): 6.3MM **Privately Held**
WEB: www.centralsupply.com
SIC: 5085 3053 5251 Industrial fittings; seals, industrial; packing, industrial; gaskets, packing & sealing devices; hardware

(P-9133)
SEGUIN MREAU NAPA COPERAGE INC
Also Called: Fine Northern Oak
151 Camino Dorado, NAPA (94558-6213)
PHONE....................707 252-3408
Nicolas Mahler-Besse, *Principal*
◆ **EMP:** 57
SQ FT: 40,000
SALES (est): 15.5MM **Privately Held**
WEB: www.seguinmoreaunapa.com
SIC: 5085 2449 Barrels, new or reconditioned; barrels, wood: coopered
PA: Seguin Moreau Holdings Inc
  151 Camino Dorado
  Napa CA 94558

(P-9134)
STEWART SUPERIOR
14487 Griffith St, San Leandro (94577-6701)
PHONE....................510 346-9811
Jack Donnelly Jr, *President*
John Kuhr, *Vice Pres*
▲ **EMP:** 17 **EST:** 1885
SQ FT: 22,000
SALES (est): 4.9MM **Privately Held**
WEB: www.stewartsuperior.com
SIC: 5085 3953 Industrial supplies; marking devices

(P-9135)
SUNBELT SUPPLY LP
Also Called: Sunbelt Supply 9256
4754 Bennett Dr Ste C, Livermore (94551-4800)
PHONE....................925 449-5900
Scott Jackson, *Branch Mgr*
EMP: 39
SALES (corp-wide): 573.9MM **Privately Held**
WEB: www.sunbeltsupply.com
SIC: 5085 Valves & fittings
HQ: Sunbelt Supply L.P.
  3750 Hwy 225
  Pasadena TX 77503

(P-9136)
SUNNYVALE FLUID SYS TECH INC (PA)
Also Called: Swagelok Northern California
3393 W Warren Ave, Fremont (94538-6424)
PHONE....................510 933-2500
Rod Fallow, *CEO*
Rachel Mittler, *Technology*
Victor Jung, *Cust Mgr*
Jeff Hopkins, *Manager*
Eric Morrison, *Representative*
EMP: 49 **EST:** 1956
SQ FT: 14,000
SALES (est): 29.2MM **Privately Held**
WEB: www.northerncal.swagelok.com
SIC: 5085 3492 Valves & fittings; fluid power valves & hose fittings

(P-9137)
TE TECH LLC
44380 Osgood Rd, Fremont (94539-6404)
PHONE....................510 770-8610
E Hiedi Monaco,
Anthony Monaco,
◆ **EMP:** 15 **EST:** 1981
SALES (est): 2MM **Privately Held**
WEB: www.mallorytechrangers.com
SIC: 5085 2679 Clean room supplies; paper products, converted

(P-9138)
TITAN NEWMAN INC
Also Called: Newman Flange & Fitting Co
1649 L St, Newman (95360-1048)
P.O. Box 905 (95360-0905)
PHONE....................209 862-2977
Samuel Liebelt, *President*
Penny Mello, *Chairman*
Helmut Liebelt, *Treasurer*
Annette Poel, *Office Mgr*
Julio Nogueda, *Plant Mgr*
◆ **EMP:** 70 **EST:** 1974
SQ FT: 1,800
SALES (est): 15.7MM **Privately Held**
WEB: www.newmanflange.com
SIC: 5085 Valves & fittings

(P-9139)
VAT INCORPORATED (DH)
655 River Oaks Pkwy, San Jose (95134-1907)
PHONE....................800 935-1446
Andrew Witken, *President*
Robert Campbell, *President*
Simon Mansbridge, *President*
Brian J Darcy, *Treasurer*
Rafma Torre, *Controller*
▲ **EMP:** 49 **EST:** 1984
SALES (est): 46.5MM
SALES (corp-wide): 574.8MM **Privately Held**
WEB: www.vatvalve.com
SIC: 5085 7699 3491 Valves & fittings; valve repair, industrial; industrial valves
HQ: Vat Holding Ag
  Seelistrasse 1
  Haag (Rheintal) SG 9469
  817 716-161

5087 Service Establishment Eqpt & Splys Wholesale

(P-9140)
A-A LOCK & ALARM INC (PA)
1251 El Camino Real, Menlo Park (94025-4208)
PHONE....................650 326-9020
James B Maclachlan, *President*
Jean Maclachlan, *Corp Secy*
EMP: 45 **EST:** 1957
SQ FT: 6,000
SALES (est): 13.4MM **Privately Held**
WEB: www.aalock.com
SIC: 5087 7382 7699 Locksmith equipment & supplies; security systems services; locksmith shop

(P-9141)
CENTRAL SANITARY SUPPLY LLC (DH)
416 N 9th St Ste A, Modesto (95350-5868)
PHONE....................209 523-3002
Kenneth Sweder, *CEO*
Elsa Espinoza, *Office Mgr*
Veronica Baker, *Executive Asst*
Sargon Kheedo, *Controller*
Karen Foust, *Purchasing*
▲ **EMP:** 40 **EST:** 1956
SQ FT: 60,000
SALES (est): 34.6MM
SALES (corp-wide): 870.7MM **Privately Held**
WEB: www.centralsanitary.com
SIC: 5087 Janitors' supplies
HQ: Perrin Bernard Supowitz, Llc
  5496 Lindbergh Ln
  Bell CA 90201
  323 981-2800

(P-9142)
ETTORE PRODUCTS CO
2100 N Loop Rd, Alameda (94502-8010)
P.O. Box 2164, Oakland (94621-0064)
PHONE....................510 748-4130
Michael A Smahlik, *Principal*
Rufus Bunch, *COO*
Diane S Smahli, *Treasurer*
Diane Smahlik, *Corp Secy*
Wayne Schultz, *Vice Pres*
▲ **EMP:** 85 **EST:** 1958
SQ FT: 30,000
SALES (est): 23.9MM **Privately Held**
WEB: www.ettore.com
SIC: 5087 Janitors' supplies

(P-9143)
FLIP HOSPITALITY & ENTRMT LLC (PA)
101 Golf Course Dr A220, Rohnert Park (94928-1737)
PHONE....................707 584-1405
Nino Rabbaa, *Mng Member*
EMP: 73 **EST:** 2014
SALES (est): 9.4MM **Privately Held**
SIC: 5087 Restaurant supplies

(P-9144)
JN RESTAURANTS INC (PA)
Also Called: Denny's
933 6th St Ste B, Los Banos (93635-4215)
PHONE....................209 710-8385
James Chaeyu RHO, *CEO*
EMP: 342 **EST:** 2009
SALES (est): 518K **Privately Held**
WEB: www.dennys.com
SIC: 5812 5087 Restaurant, family: chain; restaurant supplies

(P-9145)
LN CURTIS AND SONS (PA)
185 Lennon Ln 110, Walnut Creek (94598-2549)
P.O. Box 60000, San Francisco (94160-0001)
PHONE....................510 839-5111
John Viboch, *CFO*
Jeff Curtis, *Vice Pres*
Roger Curtis, *Vice Pres*
Tim Henderson, *Vice Pres*
Steve Price, *Division Mgr*
▲ **EMP:** 65 **EST:** 1929
SQ FT: 25,000
SALES (est): 102.7MM **Privately Held**
WEB: www.lncurtis.com
SIC: 5087 5099 Firefighting equipment; safety equipment & supplies

(P-9146)
SANTA ROSA FIRE EQP SVC INC
595a Portal St, Cotati (94931-3023)
P.O. Box 7070, Santa Rosa (95407-0070)
PHONE....................707 546-0797
Michael Reeser, *President*
EMP: 42 **EST:** 1954
SQ FT: 3,200
SALES (est): 1.9MM **Privately Held**
WEB: www.santarosafireequip.com
SIC: 5999 5087 Fire extinguishers; alarm signal systems; safety supplies & equipment; firefighting equipment

(P-9147)
TRADER VICS
9 Anchor Dr, Emeryville (94608-1510)
PHONE....................510 653-3400
Lynn Bergeron, *Ch of Bd*
Erik Heggen, *Executive Asst*
Eve Caumont, *Marketing Staff*
Tradervics Bahrain, *Director*
Justin Becker, *Director*
▲ **EMP:** 62 **EST:** 1950
SALES (est): 5.4MM **Privately Held**
WEB: www.tradervicsemeryville.com
SIC: 5812 5087 6794 Eating places; restaurant supplies; franchises, selling or licensing

(P-9148)
WAXIES ENTERPRISES LLC
901 N Canyon Pkwy, Livermore (94551)
PHONE....................925 454-2900
John Bielenberg, *General Mgr*
Ivan Lopez, *Executive*
Matthew Lacivita, *Opers Mgr*
Tiffany McLaughlin, *Sales Mgr*
Diane Leider, *Sales Staff*
EMP: 44
SALES (corp-wide): 1.2B **Privately Held**
WEB: www.info.waxie.com
SIC: 5087 Janitors' supplies
HQ: Waxie's Enterprises, Llc
  9353 Waxie Way
  San Diego CA 92123
  800 995-4466

5088 Transportation Eqpt & Splys, Except Motor Vehicles Wholesale

(P-9149)
AERO PRECISION INDUSTRIES LLC (PA)
2525 Collier Canyon Rd, Livermore (94551-7545)
PHONE....................424 252-8294
Greg Beason, *CEO*
Brad Morton, *Bd of Directors*
Rich Archer, *Vice Pres*
Anthony Grant, *Vice Pres*
Brian Hladek, *Vice Pres*
▼ **EMP:** 128 **EST:** 1993
SALES (est): 278MM **Privately Held**
WEB: www.goallclear.com
SIC: 5088 Aircraft engines & engine parts; aircraft equipment & supplies

(P-9150)
E & B MARINE INC (HQ)
500 Westridge Dr, Watsonville (95076-6710)
PHONE....................831 728-2700
Randolph K Repass, *Ch of Bd*
Peter Harris, *President*
▲ **EMP:** 100 **EST:** 1956
SQ FT: 200,000
SALES (est): 48.3MM
SALES (corp-wide): 1B **Privately Held**
WEB: www.westmarine.com
SIC: 5551 5961 5088 Marine supplies; mail order house; marine supplies
PA: West Marine, Inc.
  500 Westridge Dr
  Watsonville CA 95076
  831 728-2700

(P-9151)
LJ WALCH CO INC
6600 Preston Ave, Livermore (94551-5132)
P.O. Box 2798 (94551-2798)
PHONE....................925 449-9252
Ron Luty, *CEO*
Tony Ippolito, *President*
Mark Nelson, *Senior VP*
Bill Luty, *Vice Pres*
Tom Walch, *Vice Pres*
▲ **EMP:** 60
SQ FT: 38,500
SALES (est): 24.9MM **Privately Held**
WEB: www.ljwalch.com
SIC: 5088 7629 Aircraft & parts; aircraft electrical equipment repair

(P-9152)
SVENDSEN ENTERPRISES LLC
2900 Main St, Alameda (94501-7522)
PHONE....................510 522-2886
Bill Elliott, *CEO*
EMP: 45 **EST:** 2016
SALES (est): 3.5MM **Privately Held**
WEB: www.svendsens.com
SIC: 5088 Boats, non-recreational

(P-9153)
WEST MARINE INC (PA)
500 Westridge Dr, Watsonville (95076-6710)
PHONE....................831 728-2700
Matthew L Hyde, *President*
Jeffrey L Lasher, *CFO*
Patrick Rayray, *Treasurer*
Aaron Carpenter, *Chief Mktg Ofcr*
Andy Cross, *Chief Mktg Ofcr*
◆ **EMP:** 484 **EST:** 1968
SQ FT: 98,000
SALES (est): 1B **Privately Held**
WEB: www.westmarine.com
SIC: 5551 5961 5088 5611 Marine supplies; mail order house; marine supplies; clothing, sportswear, men's & boys'; clothing accessories: men's & boys'; hats, men's & boys'; children's shoes; women's shoes; men's boots; ready-to-wear apparel, women's

5091 - Sporting & Recreational Goods & Splys Wholesale County (P-9154)

PRODUCTS & SERVICES SECTION

5091 Sporting & Recreational Goods & Splys Wholesale

(P-9154)
CHEM QUIP INC
Also Called: White House Sales
2551 Land Ave, Sacramento (95815-2363)
PHONE..................800 821-1678
Don Aston, *CEO*
Greg Durkee, *President*
Steve Hubbard, *CFO*
Brain Long, *Admin Sec*
EMP: 62 **EST:** 1961
SQ FT: 20,000
SALES (est): 11.5MM Privately Held
WEB: www.chemquip.com
SIC: 5091 5169 Swimming pools, equipment & supplies; chlorine

(P-9155)
CREATIVE RECRTL SYSTEMS INC
2377 Gold Meadow Way # 10, Gold River (95670-4405)
PHONE..................916 638-5375
Paul Stanfel, *CEO*
Cole St-Pierre, *Software Dev*
Austin Stanfel, *Author*
EMP: 67 **EST:** 1972
SALES (est): 8.7MM Privately Held
WEB: www.creativesystems.com
SIC: 5091 Sporting & recreation goods

(P-9156)
GENERAL POOL & SPA SUPPLY INC (PA)
11285 Sunco Dr, Rancho Cordova (95742-6517)
PHONE..................916 853-2401
Philip Gelhaus, *President*
Patty Gelhaus, *Corp Secy*
Mark Yomogida, *Vice Pres*
Kathy Schulte, *Purchasing*
▼ **EMP:** 55 **EST:** 1966
SQ FT: 25,000
SALES (est): 13.8MM Privately Held
SIC: 5091 Swimming pools, equipment & supplies; spa equipment & supplies

(P-9157)
KAL-KUSTOM ENTERPRISES (PA)
43289 Osgood Rd, Fremont (94539-5657)
P.O. Box 1155, Discovery Bay (94505-7155)
PHONE..................510 651-8400
Karl Koster, *President*
Jane Kiffel, *Corp Secy*
EMP: 15 **EST:** 1964
SQ FT: 14,000
SALES (est): 12.6MM Privately Held
SIC: 5091 3732 5012 Motorboats, inboard or outboard: building & repairing; trailers for passenger vehicles

(P-9158)
MARIN MOUNTAIN BIKES (PA)
1450 Tech Ln Ste 100, Petaluma (94954)
PHONE..................415 382-6000
Robert F Buckley, *Ch of Bd*
Lisa Jaggard, *Vice Pres*
Cathy Licht, *Credit Mgr*
Caitlin Lutz, *Mktg Coord*
Chris Holmes, *Director*
▲ **EMP:** 19 **EST:** 1986
SQ FT: 18,000
SALES (est): 8.2MM Privately Held
WEB: www.marinbikes.com
SIC: 5091 3751 Bicycles; bicycles & related parts

(P-9159)
POOL COVERS INC
4925 Fulton Dr, Fairfield (94534-1640)
PHONE..................707 864-6674
William Pickens, *CEO*
Claire King, *President*
EMP: 40 **EST:** 1977
SQ FT: 14,000
SALES (est): 4.2MM Privately Held
WEB: www.poolcoversinc.com
SIC: 5999 5091 Swimming pool chemicals, equipment & supplies; swimming pools, equipment & supplies

(P-9160)
POOL WATER PRODUCTS
1940 Arnold Industrial Pl, Concord (94520-5318)
PHONE..................925 827-4300
Joe Roberts, *Manager*
EMP: 18
SALES (corp-wide): 89.8MM Privately Held
WEB: www.poolwaterproducts.com
SIC: 5091 2899 7389 Swimming pools, equipment & supplies; chemical preparations; swimming pool & hot tub service & maintenance
PA: Pool Water Products
  17872 Mitchell N Ste 250
  Irvine CA 92614
  949 756-1666

(P-9161)
PORTCO INC
Also Called: Bay Company, The
496 Jefferson St, San Francisco (94109-1315)
PHONE..................415 771-5200
Arthur N Hoppe, *President*
David Berbey, *Vice Pres*
Rhoda Berbey, *Admin Sec*
Juliet Navarro, *Info Tech Mgr*
Rich Conway, *Manager*
EMP: 60 **EST:** 2003
SQ FT: 6,000
SALES (est): 5.4MM Privately Held
SIC: 5812 5651 5091 Eating places; unisex clothing stores; boat accessories & parts

(P-9162)
SCP DISTRIBUTORS LLC
Also Called: Lincoln Aquatics
2051 Commerce Ave, Concord (94520-4901)
PHONE..................925 687-9500
Roque Santos, *Vice Pres*
Andrea Lopez, *Office Mgr*
Myron Clifton, *Opers Staff*
Dwight Thurman, *Sales Mgr*
EMP: 35 Publicly Held
WEB: www.scppool.com
SIC: 5091 Swimming pools, equipment & supplies
HQ: Scp Distributors Llc
  109 Northpark Blvd
  Covington LA 70433
  985 892-5521

(P-9163)
TITAN MFG & DISTRG INC
480 E North Ave Ste 101, Fresno (93706-5466)
PHONE..................559 475-0882
EMP: 65
SALES (corp-wide): 32.5MM Privately Held
WEB: www.titan.fitness
SIC: 5091 5961 Fitness equipment & supplies;
PA: Titan Manufacturing And Distributing, Inc.
  3839 Frest Hl Irene Rd St
  Memphis TN 38125
  800 605-8241

5092 Toys & Hobby Goods & Splys Wholesale

(P-9164)
BANDAI NAMCO ENTRMT AMER INC
Also Called: Ndga
2051 Mission College Blvd, Santa Clara (95054-1519)
PHONE..................408 235-2000
Naoki Katashima, *CEO*
Nick O 'leary, *President*
Masaaki Tsuji, *President*
Hide Irie, *COO*
Arnaud Muller, *COO*
▲ **EMP:** 200 **EST:** 1990
SQ FT: 51,118
SALES (est): 52.2MM Privately Held
WEB: www.bandainamcoent.com
SIC: 5092 Video games
HQ: Bandai Namco Holdings Usa Inc.
  2120 Park Pl Ste 120
  El Segundo CA 90245

(P-9165)
BIOWARE SACRAMENTO (HQ)
1015 20th St, Sacramento (95811-4202)
PHONE..................916 403-3500
Mark Otero, *CEO*
Kenneth Walton, *COO*
EMP: 45 **EST:** 2008
SQ FT: 11,000
SALES (est): 24.4MM
SALES (corp-wide): 5.5B Publicly Held
WEB: www.bioware.com
SIC: 5092 Video games
PA: Electronic Arts Inc.
  209 Redwood Shores Pkwy
  Redwood City CA 94065
  650 628-1500

(P-9166)
BLACKSTONE GAMING LLC
1887 Matrix Blvd, San Jose (95110-2309)
P.O. Box 3753, Alhambra (91803-0753)
PHONE..................424 488-0505
EMP: 53
SALES (corp-wide): 5MM Privately Held
SIC: 5092 Video games
PA: Blackstone Gaming, Llc
  100 W Broadway Ste 255
  Long Beach CA 90802
  562 800-0905

(P-9167)
CAPCOM ENTERTAINMENT INC
Also Called: Capcom U.S.a
185 Berry St Ste 1200, San Francisco (94107-1794)
PHONE..................650 350-6500
Kazuhiro Abe, *CEO*
Hiroshi Tobisawa, *President*
Mark Beaumont, *COO*
Ted Tsung, *Project Mgr*
Peggy Sincerbox, *Credit Staff*
▲ **EMP:** 80 **EST:** 1995
SALES (est): 29.2MM Privately Held
WEB: www.capcom-unity.com
SIC: 5092 Video games
HQ: Capcom U.S.A. Inc
  185 Berry St Ste 1200
  San Francisco CA 94107
  650 350-6500

(P-9168)
CAPCOM U S A INC (HQ)
185 Berry St Ste 1200, San Francisco (94107-1794)
PHONE..................650 350-6500
Koko Ishikawa, *President*
Rob Dyer, *COO*
Hiro Tachibana, *Vice Pres*
William Yagibacon, *Vice Pres*
Tom James, *Info Tech Dir*
▲ **EMP:** 180
SALES (est): 51.9MM Privately Held
WEB: www.capcomusa.com
SIC: 5092 7993 7372 Video games; arcades; prepackaged software

(P-9169)
MELISSA & DOUG LLC
4718 Newcastle Rd, Stockton (95215-9454)
PHONE..................209 830-7900
Melissa Douglas, *Principal*
EMP: 54
SALES (corp-wide): 91.6MM Privately Held
WEB: www.melissaanddoug.com
SIC: 5092 Toys & hobby goods & supplies
PA: Melissa & Doug, Llc
  10 Westport Rd
  Wilton CT 06897
  203 762-4500

(P-9170)
SALTERS DISTRIBUTING INC
711 S 3rd St, Chowchilla (93610-3502)
PHONE..................559 825-3220
David Salter, *President*
Cheryl Salter, *Manager*
EMP: 54 **EST:** 1990
SQ FT: 50,000
SALES (est): 11.4MM Privately Held
WEB: www.saltersdistributing.com
SIC: 5092 5199 Toys; general merchandise, non-durable

(P-9171)
WILD PLANET ENTERTAINMENT INC (DH)
Also Called: Wild Planet Toys
225 Bush St Fl 13, San Francisco (94104-4256)
P.O. Box 420 (94104-0420)
PHONE..................415 705-8300
Daniel Louis Grossman, *President*
Arman Miamidian, *CFO*
Leonard Kingsley, *Director*
▲ **EMP:** 49 **EST:** 1993
SQ FT: 18,000
SALES (est): 10MM
SALES (corp-wide): 1.5B Privately Held
WEB: www.wildplanetfoods.com
SIC: 5092 Toys
HQ: Spin Master Ltd
  225 King St W Suite 200
  Toronto ON M5V 1
  416 364-6002

5093 Scrap & Waste Materials Wholesale

(P-9172)
ALCO IRON & METAL CO (PA)
2140 Davis St, San Leandro (94577-1062)
PHONE..................510 562-1107
Kem Kantor, *President*
Sung Park, *CFO*
Kari Fletcher, *Vice Pres*
Keith Kantor, *Vice Pres*
Kevin Kantor, *Vice Pres*
◆ **EMP:** 100 **EST:** 1955
SQ FT: 35,000
SALES (est): 50.5MM Privately Held
WEB: www.alcometals.com
SIC: 5093 5051 Metal scrap & waste materials; steel

(P-9173)
B T AUTOMOTIVE INC
Also Called: All Frign Dmestics Auto Bdy Sp
1917 Navy Dr, Stockton (95206-1141)
P.O. Box 908 (95201-0908)
PHONE..................209 462-4444
Toll Free:..................888 -
Behzad Akhavan Tavakoli, *President*
Ben Tavakoli, *Finance*
Aj Tavakoli, *Master*
EMP: 40 **EST:** 1986
SQ FT: 27,000 Privately Held
WEB: www.afdbodyshop.com
SIC: 5093 7532 7549 5015 Automotive wrecking for scrap; body shop, automotive; towing services; automotive parts & supplies, used

(P-9174)
CASS INC (PA)
2730 Peralta St, Oakland (94607-1707)
P.O. Box 24222 (94623-1222)
PHONE..................510 893-6476
Edward B Kangeter IV, *CEO*
Richard Scharfen, *Vice Chairman*
Chal Sulprizio, *President*
Carmen Zeng, *CFO*
Eric Whitenight, *Sales Staff*
◆ **EMP:** 60 **EST:** 1973
SQ FT: 20,000
SALES (est): 50.8MM Privately Held
WEB: www.customalloy.com
SIC: 5093 Nonferrous metals scrap

(P-9175)
CUSTOM ALLOY SCRAP SALES INC (HQ)
2730 Peralta St, Oakland (94607-1707)
P.O. Box 24222 (94623-1222)
PHONE..................510 893-6476
Chal Sulprizio, *President*
Dan Gellepes, *Auditor*
Martha Bisso, *Buyer*
Sarah Tideman, *QC Mgr*

PRODUCTS & SERVICES SECTION

5099 - Durable Goods: NEC Wholesale County (P-9196)

Mitchell Donovan, *Maintence Staff*
EMP: 43 **EST:** 1980
SQ FT: 1,000
SALES (est): 10.8MM
SALES (corp-wide): 50.8MM **Privately Held**
WEB: www.customalloy.com
SIC: 5093 Metal scrap & waste materials; nonferrous metals scrap
PA: Cass, Inc.
 2730 Peralta St
 Oakland CA 94607
 510 893-6476

(P-9176)
SCHNITZER FRESNO INC
2727 S Chestnut Ave, Fresno (93725-2114)
P.O. Box 12085 (93776-2085)
PHONE...................559 233-3211
Leonard Schnitzer, *CEO*
Gilbert Schnitzer, *Ch of Bd*
Barry Rosen, *Treasurer*
Gary Schnitzer, *Vice Pres*
Cody Lacy, *General Mgr*
EMP: 119 **EST:** 1917
SQ FT: 2,400
SALES (est): 11.3MM
SALES (corp-wide): 2.7B **Publicly Held**
WEB: www.schnitzersteel.com
SIC: 5093 Junk & scrap; ferrous metal scrap & waste
PA: Schnitzer Steel Industries, Inc.
 299 Sw Clay St Ste 350
 Portland OR 97201
 503 224-9900

(P-9177)
SIMS GROUP USA CORPORATION (DH)
Also Called: Simsmetal America
600 S 4th St, Richmond (94804-3504)
PHONE...................510 412-5300
Alistair Field, *CEO*
Bob Kelman, *President*
Myles Partridge, *CFO*
Jimmie Buckland, *Exec VP*
John Crabb, *Principal*
◆ **EMP:** 100 **EST:** 1987
SQ FT: 4,000
SALES (est): 142.1MM **Privately Held**
WEB: www.simsmm.com
SIC: 5093 4953 Ferrous metal scrap & waste; nonferrous metals scrap; recycling, waste materials
HQ: Sims Group Usa Holdings Corp
 16 W 22nd St Fl 10
 New York NY 10010
 212 604-0710

(P-9178)
STANDARD IRON & METALS CO
4525 San Leandro St, Oakland (94601-4449)
PHONE...................510 535-0222
Jason Allen, *Principal*
Lloyd Weinstein, *Corp Secy*
Carolina Garcia, *Traffic Mgr*
▼ **EMP:** 50 **EST:** 1978
SQ FT: 20,000
SALES (est): 14.8MM **Privately Held**
WEB: www.standardiron.net
SIC: 5093 Ferrous metal scrap & waste; nonferrous metals scrap

---

5094 Jewelry, Watches, Precious Stones Wholesale

(P-9179)
BJS RESTAURANTS INC
3401 Dale Rd Ste 840, Modesto (95356-0549)
PHONE...................209 526-8850
Brandon Mynear, *Principal*
EMP: 39
SALES (corp-wide): 1.1B **Publicly Held**
WEB: www.bjsrestaurants.com
SIC: 5094 Jewelry
PA: Bj's Restaurants, Inc.
 7755 Center Ave Ste 300
 Huntington Beach CA 92647
 714 500-2400

(P-9180)
BLISS WORLD LLC
39 Pier, San Francisco (94133-1006)
PHONE...................415 217-7047
Ori Kedem, *Branch Mgr*
EMP: 70 **Privately Held**
WEB: www.blissworld.com
SIC: 5094 Jewelry
HQ: Bliss World Llc
 145 S Fairfax Ave Ste 400
 Los Angeles CA 90036
 212 931-6383

(P-9181)
DERCO INC
Also Called: Derco Jewelers
888 Brannan St Ste 137, San Francisco (94103-5601)
PHONE...................415 626-7442
Ohan Derabrahamian, *President*
Jack Derabrahamian, *Co-President*
Aberi Mashid, *Consultant*
EMP: 35 **EST:** 1979
SQ FT: 2,700
SALES (est): 15MM **Privately Held**
WEB: www.m.mainstreethub.com
SIC: 5094 5999 Jewelry; gems & precious stones

(P-9182)
GOLDEN STATE IMPORTS INTL INC (PA)
Also Called: G S I
2417 Mariner Square Loop # 25, Alameda (94501-1027)
P.O. Box 31088, Oakland (94604-7088)
PHONE...................510 995-1320
Jane Lai, *Ch of Bd*
Jimmy Lai, *President*
Iling Chiang, *Admin Sec*
▲ **EMP:** 19 **EST:** 1974
SQ FT: 12,000
SALES (est): 5.5MM **Privately Held**
SIC: 5094 2034 Clocks, watches & parts; dehydrated fruits, vegetables, soups

(P-9183)
JEWELRY SUPPLY INC
Also Called: Jewelrysupply.com
301 Derek Pl, Roseville (95678-7026)
PHONE...................916 780-9610
Ken Roberts, *President*
Tony Roberts, *Vice Pres*
Jeanette Roberts, *Admin Sec*
◆ **EMP:** 35 **EST:** 2002
SQ FT: 20,000
SALES (est): 8.9MM **Privately Held**
WEB: www.jewelrysupply.com
SIC: 5094 Jewelry

(P-9184)
OTTO FREI-JULES BOREL INC (PA)
126 2nd St, Oakland (94607-4514)
P.O. Box 796 (94604-0796)
PHONE...................800 772-3456
Steven A Frei, *CEO*
Jim Frei, *Treasurer*
John Frei Jr, *Vice Pres*
Rhett Frei, *Marketing Staff*
Wyatt Frei, *Manager*
▲ **EMP:** 35 **EST:** 1930
SQ FT: 15,000
SALES (est): 10.1MM **Privately Held**
WEB: www.ofrei.com
SIC: 5094 Jewelers' findings

(P-9185)
TOUCAN INC (PA)
Also Called: Tomas Jewelry
824 L St Ste 6, Arcata (95521-5766)
P.O. Box 4899 (95518-4899)
PHONE...................707 822-6662
Thomas S Perrett, *President*
Karen Lu, *Manager*
▲ **EMP:** 80 **EST:** 1980
SQ FT: 25,000
SALES (est): 18.5MM **Privately Held**
WEB: www.toucanjewelry.com
SIC: 5094 Jewelry; precious metals

(P-9186)
WILSON TROPHY CO CALIFORNIA
Also Called: Awards By Wilson
1724 Frienza Ave, Sacramento (95815-2710)
PHONE...................916 927-9733
Gerald Loomis, *President*
Michelle Loomis, *Vice Pres*
▲ **EMP:** 17 **EST:** 1971
SQ FT: 12,500
SALES (est): 3.1MM **Privately Held**
WEB: www.wilsontrophy.com
SIC: 5999 5094 3993 2396 Trophies & plaques; trophies; signs & advertising specialties; automotive & apparel trimmings; pleating & stitching

---

5099 Durable Goods: NEC Wholesale

(P-9187)
AIRFIELD SUPPLY CO
1190 Coleman Ave, San Jose (95110-1190)
PHONE...................408 320-0230
Marc Matulich, *Principal*
Ryan Petulla, *Treasurer*
Dustin McDonald, *Vice Pres*
Hudson Moore, *Train & Dev Mgr*
Lesley Nickus, *Manager*
EMP: 100 **EST:** 2017
SALES (est): 8.8MM **Privately Held**
WEB: www.airfieldsupplyco.com
SIC: 5099 Durable goods

(P-9188)
BAY MARINE & INDUS SUP LLC
2900 Main St, Alameda (94501-7522)
PHONE...................510 337-9122
Bill Elliott, *Principal*
James Whitman, *Principal*
EMP: 50 **EST:** 2017
SALES (est): 5.1MM **Privately Held**
SIC: 5099 Durable goods

(P-9189)
BOSSA NOVA ROBOTICS INC (HQ)
610 22nd St Ste 250, San Francisco (94107-3576)
P.O. Box 590979 (94159-0979)
PHONE...................415 234-5136
Bruce McWilliams, *CEO*
Amy Han, *Vice Pres*
Dorothea Rueger, *Office Mgr*
Kyle Stanhouse, *Software Engr*
Mostafa Fahmy, *Engineer*
▼ **EMP:** 70 **EST:** 2011
SQ FT: 5,000
SALES (est): 67.4MM **Privately Held**
WEB: www.bossanova.com
SIC: 5099 Robots, service or novelty

(P-9190)
BOSSA NOVA ROBOTICS INC
709 N Shoreline Blvd, Mountain View (94043-3208)
P.O. Box 590979, San Francisco (94159-0979)
PHONE...................415 234-5136
EMP: 101 **Privately Held**
WEB: www.bossanova.com
SIC: 5099 Robots, service or novelty
HQ: Bossa Nova Robotics, Inc.
 610 22nd St Ste 250
 San Francisco CA 94107
 415 234-5136

(P-9191)
BRUNI GLASS PACKAGING INC
2750 Maxwell Way, Fairfield (94534-9708)
PHONE...................707 752-6200
Gino Del Bon, *CEO*
Roberto Del Bon, *President*
Ray Kor, *CFO*
Jessica Baldwin, *Sales Staff*
Richard Richmond, *Sales Staff*
◆ **EMP:** 39 **EST:** 2004

SALES (est): 5.7MM
SALES (corp-wide): 542.2MM **Privately Held**
WEB: www.bruniglass.com
SIC: 5231 5099 Glass; containers: glass, metal or plastic
PA: Berlin Packaging L.L.C.
 525 W Monroe St Ste 1400
 Chicago IL 60661
 312 876-9292

(P-9192)
BURGETT INCORPORATED (PA)
Also Called: Piano Disc
4111a N Freeway Blvd, Sacramento (95834-1209)
PHONE...................916 567-9999
Gary Burgett, *CEO*
Stephanie Johnston, *President*
Edward Ringgold, *CFO*
Kirk Burgett, *Vice Pres*
Brad Thompson, *Technician*
▲ **EMP:** 69 **EST:** 1977
SQ FT: 48,000
SALES (est): 17.8MM **Privately Held**
WEB: www.theburgettgroup.com
SIC: 5099 3429 3931 3651 Pianos; piano hardware; musical instruments; household audio & video equipment

(P-9193)
CELLMARK INC (DH)
Also Called: United International
88 Rowland Way Ste 300, Novato (94945-5049)
PHONE...................415 927-1700
Jimmy Derrico, *Division Pres*
Mike Franquiz, *Exec VP*
Shaun Day, *Vice Pres*
Robes Nelson, *Vice Pres*
Gregory Saba, *Vice Pres*
◆ **EMP:** 65 **EST:** 1984
SQ FT: 13,000
SALES (est): 604.1MM **Privately Held**
WEB: www.cellmark.com
SIC: 5099 5093 5111 Pulpwood; waste paper; fine paper
HQ: Cellmark Ab
 Lilla Bommen 3c
 Goteborg 411 0
 311 900-07

(P-9194)
ELSA L INC
800 A St, San Rafael (94901-3011)
PHONE...................415 472-8388
Elsa Leung, *CEO*
Jacqueline Hamm, *Vice Pres*
Frank Leung, *Admin Sec*
Rich Walter, *VP Finance*
Norman Chan, *Accountant*
▲ **EMP:** 35 **EST:** 1992
SALES (est): 10.2MM **Privately Held**
WEB: www.elsal.com
SIC: 5099 Wood & wood by-products

(P-9195)
FRESH PICK PRODUCE
195 San Pedro Ave Ste D, Morgan Hill (95037-5142)
PHONE...................408 315-4612
Stephanie Tsigaris,
EMP: 50 **EST:** 2017
SALES (est): 2.5MM **Privately Held**
SIC: 5099 Durable goods

(P-9196)
INGRAM ENTERTAINMENT INC
1130 Iron Point Rd, Folsom (95630-8308)
PHONE...................916 235-5400
Matt Lam, *Purchasing*
EMP: 17
SALES (corp-wide): 400MM **Privately Held**
WEB: www.ingramentertainment.com
SIC: 5099 3695 Pulpwood; drums, magnetic
HQ: Ingram Entertainment Inc.
 2 Ingram Blvd
 La Vergne TN 37089

5099 - Durable Goods: NEC Wholesale County (P-9197)

(P-9197)
IRON OX INC
955 Terminal Way, San Carlos (94070-3224)
PHONE..................281 381-0409
Brandon Alexander, *Mng Member*
Sarah Osentoski, *Vice Pres*
Hamzah Shakeel, *Principal*
Brianna Viviani, *Office Mgr*
Preethi Kumar, *Technical Staff*
EMP: 37 **EST:** 2016
SALES (est): 7.3MM **Privately Held**
WEB: www.ironox.com
SIC: 5099 Robots, service or novelty

(P-9198)
JORGENSEN & SONS INC (PA)
Also Called: Jorgensen & Co
2467 Foundry Park Ave, Fresno (93706-4531)
PHONE..................559 268-6241
Darrell Hefley, *CEO*
Donald Jorgensen, *Ch of Bd*
Leon Young, *President*
Jim Rushing, *Treasurer*
Al V Jorgensen, *Vice Ch Bd*
EMP: 55
SQ FT: 28,000
SALES (est): 30.7MM **Privately Held**
WEB: www.jorgensenco.com
SIC: 5099 1731 Safety equipment & supplies; fire detection & burglar alarm systems specialization

(P-9199)
MONSTER INC (PA)
Also Called: Monster Products
601 Gateway Blvd Ste 900, South San Francisco (94080-7070)
P.O. Box 435, Brisbane (94005-0435)
PHONE..................415 840-2000
Noel Lee, *President*
Irene Baron, *Vice Pres*
Einstein Galang, *Administration*
Cris Alqueza, *IT/INT Sup*
Tony Dichiro, *Director*
◆ **EMP:** 330 **EST:** 1978
SQ FT: 50,000
SALES (est): 150.7MM **Privately Held**
WEB: www.monsterstore.com
SIC: 5099 4841 3679 Video & audio equipment; cable & other pay television services; headphones, radio

(P-9200)
PEL WHOLESALE INC
6818 Patterson Pass Rd H, Livermore (94550-4230)
PHONE..................925 373-3628
Cindy Trinh, *Mng Member*
EMP: 20 **EST:** 2003
SALES (est): 1.3MM **Privately Held**
SIC: 5099 3999 Durable goods; pet supplies

(P-9201)
SAFETYMAX CORPORATION
Also Called: Cityaid First Aid Direct
2256 Palou Ave, San Francisco (94124-1505)
PHONE..................415 626-4650
Tony Lembo, *President*
Carol Gutierrez-Manne, *Opers Mgr*
EMP: 35 **EST:** 1991
SQ FT: 4,000
SALES (est): 6.4MM **Privately Held**
WEB: www.safetymax.com
SIC: 5099 5199 Safety equipment & supplies; first aid supplies

(P-9202)
SOUVENIR COFFEE CORPORATION (PA)
2849 Garber St, Berkeley (94705-1314)
PHONE..................510 919-2777
EMP: 36 **EST:** 2018
SALES (est): 1.8MM **Privately Held**
WEB: www.souvenir-coffee.com
SIC: 5099 Souvenirs

(P-9203)
WEST COAST NOVELTY CORPORATION (PA)
2401 Monarch St, Alameda (94501-7513)
PHONE..................510 748-4248
Brian T McCroden, *CEO*
John Allenberg, *CEO*
Lance Littlejohn, *COO*
Dave Barckholtz, *Vice Pres*
John Bragg, *Vice Pres*
▲ **EMP:** 35 **EST:** 1915
SQ FT: 64,000
SALES (est): 12.7MM **Privately Held**
WEB: www.thewcngroup.com
SIC: 5099 Souvenirs

(P-9204)
YALEY ENTERPRISES INC
7664 Avianca Dr, Redding (96002-9703)
P.O. Box 1426, Anderson (96007-1426)
PHONE..................530 365-5252
Patricia J Yaley, *CEO*
Thomas O'Rourke, *Corp Secy*
Thomas J Yaley, *Vice Pres*
▲ **EMP:** 16 **EST:** 1976
SQ FT: 30,000
SALES (est): 1.7MM **Privately Held**
WEB: www.vinewickcandle.com
SIC: 5099 3544 Brass goods; special dies, tools, jigs & fixtures

5112 Stationery & Office Splys Wholesale

(P-9205)
CANON SOLUTIONS AMERICA INC
1651 Myrtle Ave Ste C, Eureka (95501-1495)
PHONE..................707 442-9397
EMP: 39 **Privately Held**
WEB: www.csa.canon.com
SIC: 5112 Computer & photocopying supplies
HQ: Canon Solutions America, Inc.
1 Canon Park
Melville NY 11747
631 330-5000

(P-9206)
DIETRICH POST CO INC
945 Bryant St, San Francisco (94103-4523)
PHONE..................510 596-0080
EMP: 50
SALES (est): 4.1MM **Privately Held**
SIC: 5112 Whol Stationery/Office Supplies

(P-9207)
EMPIRE PAPER CORPORATION
Also Called: Baron
4930 Waterstone Dr, Roseville (95747-6385)
P.O. Box 24073, Oakland (94623-1073)
PHONE..................510 534-2700
Henry F Scarpelli, *President*
Olga Kazakova, *COO*
Matthew Meixell, *Vice Pres*
EMP: 20 **EST:** 1963
SQ FT: 40,000
SALES (est): 3.8MM **Privately Held**
SIC: 5112 2752 7389 2759 Office supplies; commercial printing, offset; engraving service; commercial printing

(P-9208)
MINTED LLC (PA)
747 Front St Ste 200, San Francisco (94111-1945)
PHONE..................415 399-1100
Mariam Naficy, *CEO*
John Foster, *Officer*
Wendy Bergh, *Vice Pres*
Vlad Kuznetsov, *Vice Pres*
Namrata Patel, *Vice Pres*
▲ **EMP:** 1974 **EST:** 2007
SALES (est): 1.2MM **Privately Held**
WEB: www.minted.com
SIC: 5112 Social stationery & greeting cards

(P-9209)
OFFICEMAX NORTH AMERICA INC
1800 Oakdale Rd Ste B, Modesto (95355-2988)
PHONE..................209 551-9700
Lee Blankenship, *Branch Mgr*
EMP: 58
SALES (corp-wide): 9.7B **Publicly Held**
SIC: 5112 5943 Stationery & office supplies; office forms & supplies
HQ: Officemax North America, Inc.
263 Shuman Blvd Ste 145
Naperville IL 60563
630 717-0791

(P-9210)
PAPER CULTURE LLC
475 El Cmino Real Ste 202, Millbrae (94030)
PHONE..................650 249-0800
Christopher Wu, *CEO*
Spencer Ballo, *IT/INT Sup*
Deb D Hochheiser, *Marketing Staff*
Jamie Michael, *Marketing Staff*
Anurag Mendhekar,
EMP: 50 **EST:** 2008
SALES (est): 7MM **Privately Held**
WEB: www.paperculture.com
SIC: 5112 5999 7336 Social stationery & greeting cards; alarm & safety equipment stores; art design services

(P-9211)
TROWBRIDGE ENTERPRISES (PA)
Also Called: Palace Business Solutions
2606 Chanticleer Ave, Santa Cruz (95065-1810)
PHONE..................831 476-3815
Toll Free..................888
Roy M Trowbridge, *CEO*
Frank H Trowbridge III, *CFO*
Margaret Trowbridge, *Corp Secy*
Daniel Bechtold, *Vice Pres*
Neal Heckman, *Vice Pres*
EMP: 45 **EST:** 1949
SQ FT: 11,000
SALES (est): 41.7MM **Privately Held**
WEB: www.gopalace.com
SIC: 5112 5943 5999 Office supplies; stationery stores; artists' supplies & materials

5113 Indl & Personal Svc Paper Wholesale

(P-9212)
CALPINE CONTAINERS INC (PA)
380 W Spruce Ave, Clovis (93611-8705)
PHONE..................559 519-7199
Walter D Tindell, *CEO*
Kenneth A Sommers, *CFO*
Kenneth Sommers, *CFO*
Scott R Hickman, *Vice Pres*
E C Rathbun, *Principal*
▲ **EMP:** 15 **EST:** 1895
SALES (est): 51.2MM **Privately Held**
SIC: 5113 5085 2441 2448 Corrugated & solid fiber boxes; box shooks; boxes, wood; pallets, wood

(P-9213)
GAHVEJIAN ENTERPRISES INC
Also Called: Mid Valley Packaging & Sup Co
2004 S Temperance Ave, Fowler (93625-9759)
P.O. Box 96 (93625-0096)
PHONE..................559 834-5956
Carrie L Gahvejian, *President*
John Gahvejian, *President*
Lorrie Gahvejian, *Corp Secy*
Erik Creede, *Principal*
Carrie Gahvejian-Hudso, *General Mgr*
◆ **EMP:** 50 **EST:** 1980
SQ FT: 150,000
SALES (est): 51.3MM **Privately Held**
WEB: www.mvpsupply.com
SIC: 5113 Bags, paper & disposable plastic

(P-9214)
GOLDEN GATE DEBRIS BOX SERVICE (HQ)
515 Tunnel Ave, San Francisco (94134)
PHONE..................415 626-4000
Mark Malatesta, *Principal*
EMP: 45 **EST:** 1984
SALES (est): 5.4MM
SALES (est): 1.4B **Privately Held**
WEB: www.recology.com
SIC: 5113 Boxes & containers; patterns, paper
PA: Recology Inc.
50 California St Ste 2400
San Francisco CA 94111
415 875-1000

(P-9215)
MAXCO SUPPLY INC (PA)
605 S Zediker Ave, Parlier (93648-2033)
P.O. Box 814 (93648-0814)
PHONE..................559 646-8449
Max Flaming, *President*
David Bryant, *COO*
Joe Sepe, *Research*
Robert Grote, *VP Mfg*
Mario Morales, *Production*
▲ **EMP:** 45 **EST:** 1972
SQ FT: 8,500
SALES (est): 72.1MM **Privately Held**
WEB: www.maxcopackaging.com
SIC: 5113 2436 3554 Shipping supplies; softwood veneer & plywood; box making machines, paper

(P-9216)
P&P INTERNATIONAL INC
2014 2nd St, Selma (93662-3722)
PHONE..................559 891-9888
William A Spencer, *President*
James Tienken, *Sales Mgr*
Ryan Mejia, *Marketing Staff*
▲ **EMP:** 15 **EST:** 2003
SALES (est): 8.8MM **Privately Held**
WEB: www.usa-ppi.com
SIC: 5113 3221 5085 Cups, disposable plastic & paper; water bottles, glass; glass bottles

(P-9217)
PACKAGING INNOVATORS LLC
6850 Brisa St, Livermore (94550-2521)
P.O. Box 1110 (94551-1110)
PHONE..................925 371-2000
William E Mazzocco, *President*
Beverly J Flynt, *Corp Secy*
Mark Andrew Mazzocco, *Vice Pres*
Mark Mazzocco, *Vice Pres*
Mike Mazzocco, *Vice Pres*
▲ **EMP:** 90 **EST:** 1975
SALES (est): 48.1MM
SALES (corp-wide): 317.1MM **Privately Held**
WEB: www.packaginginnovators.com
SIC: 5113 2653 3993 Shipping supplies; corrugated & solid fiber boxes; display items, solid fiber: made from purchased materials; signs & advertising specialties
PA: Golden West Packaging Group Llc
15400 Don Julian Rd
City Of Industry CA 91745
888 501-5893

(P-9218)
SAMBRAILO PACKAGING (PA)
800 Walker St, Watsonville (95076-4117)
P.O. Box 50090 (95077-5090)
PHONE..................831 724-7581
Mark Sambrailo, *Ch of Bd*
Rachel Montoya, *CFO*
Michael Sambrailo, *Pres*
Michael Keegan, *Business Dir*
Scott Gray, *Technology*
▲ **EMP:** 35 **EST:** 1923
SQ FT: 45,000
SALES (est): 69.8MM **Privately Held**
WEB: www.sambrailo.com
SIC: 5113 5162 Bags, paper & disposable plastic; plastics materials & basic shapes

(P-9219)
STASHER INC
Also Called: Modern-Twist
1310 63rd St, Emeryville (94608-2104)
PHONE..................510 531-2100
Kat Nouri, *CEO*
Katousha Nouri, *CEO*
Tom Johnson, *Vice Pres*
Staci Gilmore, *Graphic Designe*
Ashley Gonias, *Pub Rel Dir*
EMP: 15 **EST:** 2015

PRODUCTS & SERVICES SECTION

5131 - Piece Goods, Notions & Dry Goods Wholesale County (P-9240)

SALES (est): 4.8MM **Privately Held**
WEB: www.stasherbag.com
SIC: 5113 2656 Sanitary food containers; frozen food containers; made from purchased material

(P-9220)
UNISOURCE PACKAGING INC
4225 Hacienda Dr Ste A, Pleasanton (94588-2720)
P.O. Box 8803 (94588)
PHONE......................925 227-6000
Allan Dragone, *CEO*
▲ **EMP:** 112 **EST:** 1993
SALES (est): 42.4MM
SALES (corp-wide): 6.3B **Publicly Held**
WEB: www.veritivcorp.com
SIC: 5113 Shipping supplies
HQ: Veritiv Operating Company
1000 Abernathy Rd Bldg 4
Atlanta GA 30328
770 391-8200

(P-9221)
VERITIV OPERATING COMPANY
Northern California Mkt Area
4395 S Minnewawa Ave # 101, Fresno (93725-9479)
P.O. Box 11368 (93773-1368)
PHONE......................559 268-0467
Fax: 559 233-9136
EMP: 90
SALES (corp-wide): 8.3B **Publicly Held**
SIC: 5113 Whol Industrial/Service Paper
HQ: Veritiv Operating Company
1000 Abernathy Rd
Atlanta GA 30328
770 391-8200

5122 Drugs, Drug Proprietaries & Sundries Wholesale

(P-9222)
AMERISOURCEBERGEN DRUG CORP
Also Called: ABC Sacramento Striker
1325 Striker Ave, Sacramento (95834-1164)
PHONE......................916 830-4500
Bruce Bennett, *Branch Mgr*
Nancy Pointer, *Executive*
Randy Howery, *Research*
Bob Laubacher, *Director*
Scott Ashe, *Manager*
EMP: 102
SALES (corp-wide): 189.8B **Publicly Held**
WEB: www.amerisourcebergen.com
SIC: 5122 Pharmaceuticals
HQ: Amerisourcebergen Drug Corporation
1 W 1st Ave
Conshohocken PA 19428
610 727-7000

(P-9223)
BADASS BRAND INC
Also Called: Badass Beard Care
8400 Moss Ct, Granite Bay (95746-7367)
PHONE......................916 990-3873
Charles Moyer, *CEO*
Ashley Moyer, *Vice Pres*
Ashley Aka, *Human Res Dir*
Chad A 'pickles, *Marketing Staff*
EMP: 20 **EST:** 2014
SALES: 3.1MM **Privately Held**
WEB: www.badassbeardcare.com
SIC: 5122 2844 Cosmetics, perfumes & hair products; hair preparations, including shampoos; shaving preparations; deodorants, personal

(P-9224)
BENEFIT COSMETICS LLC (DH)
Also Called: Lvmh Moet Hnnssy Louis Vuitton
225 Bush St Fl 20, San Francisco (94104-4279)
PHONE......................415 781-8153
Christie Fleischer, *CEO*
Sara Botwood-Guest, *Vice Pres*
Emmanuel D'Halluin, *Vice Pres*
Hannah Malott, *Creative Dir*
Nora Lee, *Planning*

▲ **EMP:** 100 **EST:** 1976
SQ FT: 800
SALES (est): 193MM
SALES (corp-wide): 419.1MM **Privately Held**
WEB: www.benefitcosmetics.com
SIC: 5122 5999 Cosmetics; cosmetics
HQ: Lvmh Moet Hennessy Louis Vuitton Inc.
19 E 57th St
New York NY 10022
212 931-2700

(P-9225)
BRONDELL INC
1830 Harrison St, San Francisco (94103-4228)
P.O. Box 470085 (94147-0085)
PHONE......................415 315-9000
David Samuel, *Chairman*
Steven Scheer, *President*
Sara Adams, *CFO*
Alison Patella, *Marketing Staff*
Parker Benthin, *Sales Staff*
◆ **EMP:** 25 **EST:** 2003
SQ FT: 3,300
SALES (est): 13.9MM **Privately Held**
WEB: www.brondell.com
SIC: 5122 2499 Toiletries; seats, toilet

(P-9226)
EO PRODUCTS LLC
90 Windward Way, San Rafael (94901-7200)
PHONE......................415 945-1900
Susan Griffin Black, *CEO*
EMP: 185 **EST:** 2020
SALES (est): 21.7MM **Privately Held**
WEB: www.eoproducts.com
SIC: 5122 Cosmetics

(P-9227)
GOLDEN N-LIFE DIAMITE INTL INC (PA)
3500 Gateway Blvd, Fremont (94538-6584)
PHONE......................510 651-0405
Roget Uys, *CEO*
Daniel L Lewis, *COO*
Rico Brown, *Vice Pres*
Renato Dicarlo, *Vice Pres*
Robert Galano, *Vice Pres*
▲ **EMP:** 80 **EST:** 1958
SQ FT: 66,000
SALES (est): 77.2MM **Privately Held**
WEB: www.gnld.com.ph
SIC: 5122 Cosmetics

(P-9228)
KENDO HOLDINGS INC (HQ)
Also Called: Marc Jacobs Beauty
425 Market St Fl 19, San Francisco (94105-2425)
PHONE......................415 284-6000
David Suliteanu, *President*
Karen Tate, *CFO*
Catie Neel, *Chief Mktg Ofcr*
Kirsten Walcott, *Senior VP*
Michael Lee, *Vice Pres*
▲ **EMP:** 325 **EST:** 2010
SALES (est): 112.2MM
SALES (corp-wide): 419.1MM **Privately Held**
WEB: www.kendobrands.com
SIC: 5122 5961 Cosmetics, perfumes & hair products; cosmetics & perfumes, mail order
PA: Lvmh Moet Hennessy Louis Vuitton
22 Avenue Montaigne
Paris 75008
962 177-144

(P-9229)
LUCKY STORES II LLC
Also Called: Save Mart
875 S Tracy Blvd, Tracy (95376-4744)
PHONE......................209 830-1977
Vince McFarland, *Managing Prtnr*
Ken Gaines, *Manager*
EMP: 80 **EST:** 2011
SALES (est): 2.1MM **Privately Held**
SIC: 5411 5122 Grocery stores, chain; pharmaceuticals

(P-9230)
MCKESSON CORPORATION
3000 Colby St, Berkeley (94705-2083)
PHONE......................510 666-0854
Micah Wakamatsu, *Branch Mgr*
EMP: 66
SALES (corp-wide): 238.2B **Publicly Held**
WEB: www.mckesson.com
SIC: 5122 Pharmaceuticals
PA: Mckesson Corporation
6555 State Highway 161
Irving TX 75039
972 446-4800

(P-9231)
MCKESSON MEDICAL-SURGICAL INC
Also Called: McKesson Medical Surgical
1 Post St Fl 18, San Francisco (94104-5284)
PHONE......................415 983-8300
John H Hammergren, *President*
Jorge L Figueredo, *Exec VP*
Paul C Julian, *Exec VP*
James Beer, *Vice Pres*
Patrick J Blake, *Vice Pres*
EMP: 54 **EST:** 1980
SALES (est): 38.6MM
SALES (corp-wide): 238.2B **Publicly Held**
WEB: www.mckgenmed.com
SIC: 5122 Pharmaceuticals
PA: Mckesson Corporation
6555 State Highway 161
Irving TX 75039
972 446-4800

(P-9232)
MCKESSON SPCLTY HLTH TECH PDTS (HQ)
1 Post St Fl 18, San Francisco (94104-5284)
PHONE......................415 983-8300
John H Hammergren, *CEO*
EMP: 50 **EST:** 2009
SALES (est): 199MM
SALES (corp-wide): 238.2B **Publicly Held**
WEB: www.mckesson.com
SIC: 5122 Pharmaceuticals
PA: Mckesson Corporation
6555 State Highway 161
Irving TX 75039
972 446-4800

(P-9233)
MYOVANT SCIENCES INC
2000 Sierra Point Pkwy # 9, Brisbane (94005-1845)
PHONE......................650 392-0222
Dave Marek, *CEO*
Uneek Mehra, *CFO*
Angie Lewis-White, *Vice Pres*
Gary Palmer, *Vice Pres*
Minli Xie, *Vice Pres*
EMP: 132 **EST:** 2016
SALES (est): 63.5MM **Privately Held**
WEB: www.myovant.com
SIC: 5122 Pharmaceuticals
HQ: Myovant Holdings Limited
Suite 1, 3rd Floor
London
207 400-3347

(P-9234)
NATURES PRODUCTS INC (DH)
1221 Broadway, Oakland (94612-1837)
PHONE......................954 233-3300
Jose Minski, *President*
Meyer Minski, *Vice Pres*
Ruben Minski, *Vice Pres*
Mario Murillo, *Planning Mgr*
Magaly Flores, *Purch Mgr*
◆ **EMP:** 156 **EST:** 1986
SALES (est): 132.1MM
SALES (corp-wide): 7.3B **Publicly Held**
SIC: 5122 5499 Vitamins & minerals; health & dietetic food stores

(P-9235)
QUESTCOR PHARMACEUTICALS
26118 Research Pl, Hayward (94545-3732)
PHONE......................510 400-0700

EMP: 44 **EST:** 2007
SALES (est): 11.4MM **Privately Held**
SIC: 5122 2833 Whol Drugs/Sundries Mfg Medicinal/Botanical Products

(P-9236)
SAFEWAY CORPORATE INC
5918 Stoneridge Mall Rd, Pleasanton (94588-3229)
PHONE......................925 467-3000
EMP: 5011
SALES (est): 1.1MM
SALES (corp-wide): 59.9B **Privately Held**
SIC: 5411 5122 Ret Groceries Whol Drugs/Sundries
HQ: Safeway Inc.
11555 Dublin Canyon Rd
Pleasanton CA 94588
925 226-5000

(P-9237)
SMALL WORLD TRADING CO
Also Called: Eo Products
90 Windward Way, San Rafael (94901-7200)
PHONE......................415 945-1900
Susan Griffin-Black, *Ch of Bd*
Sam Borri, *Partner*
Fran Strachan, *VP Bus Dvlpt*
Michael Cronin, *CTO*
Stephanie Quevedo, *Software Dev*
EMP: 185 **EST:** 1991
SQ FT: 40,000
SALES (est): 50.5MM **Privately Held**
WEB: www.eoproducts.com
SIC: 5122 Cosmetics

(P-9238)
SMITH & VANDIVER CORPORATION
Also Called: Sinclair & Valentine
480 Airport Blvd, Watsonville (95076-2002)
PHONE......................831 722-9526
Graham Orriss, *CEO*
Jeffrey K Slaboden, *President*
Charles Chestnutt, *CFO*
Irvaz Husic, *Vice Pres*
Stephen Rosich, *Planning*
▲ **EMP:** 75 **EST:** 1979
SQ FT: 55,000
SALES (est): 50.3MM **Privately Held**
WEB: www.svnaturally.com
SIC: 5122 2844 Cosmetics; toilet preparations

(P-9239)
VALLEY WHOLESALE DRUG CO LLC
1401 W Fremont St, Stockton (95203-2627)
P.O. Box 247, Thorofare NJ (08086-0247)
PHONE......................209 466-0131
Henry Dale Smith, *CEO*
Dan Matteoli, *Vice Pres*
Angelo Grande, *Principal*
Joseph Caswell, *Technology*
EMP: 75 **EST:** 1948
SQ FT: 10,000
SALES (est): 47.3MM
SALES (corp-wide): 189.8B **Publicly Held**
WEB: www.smartsourcerx.com
SIC: 5122 Pharmaceuticals
HQ: H. D. Smith, Llc
1 W 1st Ave Ste 100
Conshohocken PA 19428
866 232-1222

5131 Piece Goods, Notions & Dry Goods Wholesale

(P-9240)
AP UNLIMITED CORPORATION
Also Called: American Plastic
1225 N Macarthur Dr # 200, Tracy (95376-2843)
PHONE......................209 834-0287
Gary Grewal, *President*
◆ **EMP:** 15 **EST:** 1999
SQ FT: 18,000

5131 - Piece Goods, Notions & Dry Goods Wholesale

SALES (est): 5.6MM **Privately Held**
WEB: www.americanplastics.com
SIC: 5131 3965 Plastic piece goods, woven; zippers; buckles & buckle parts; zipper

(P-9241)
CHARMING TRIM & PACKAGING LLC
28 Brookside Ct, Novato (94947-3847)
PHONE....................................415 302-7021
Richard Ringeisen, *President*
Barry Chan, *Exec Dir*
EMP: 1000 **EST:** 2011
SALES (est): 29.1MM **Privately Held**
WEB: www.charmingtrim.com
SIC: 5131 3111 Trimmings, apparel; garment leather

(P-9242)
TEIJIN PHARMA USA LLC
1 Harbor Dr Ste 200, Sausalito (94965-1434)
PHONE....................................415 893-1518
Kavuo Imose,
EMP: 566 **EST:** 2008
SALES (est): 16.7MM **Privately Held**
WEB: www.mail.teijinny.com
SIC: 5131 Piece goods & notions
HQ: Teijin Holdings Usa Inc.
600 Lexington Ave Fl 27
New York NY 10022
212 308-8744

5136 Men's & Boys' Clothing & Furnishings Wholesale

(P-9243)
DORFMAN-PACIFIC CO (HQ)
Also Called: Dorfman Pacific
2615 Boeing Way, Stockton (95206-3984)
P.O. Box 213005 (95213-9005)
PHONE....................................209 982-1400
Douglas Edward Highsmith, *CEO*
Bakul Patel, *Vice Pres*
Carla Hoffman, *Executive*
Debra Highsmith, *Admin Sec*
Stephanie Gohman, *Purchasing*
◆ **EMP:** 140 **EST:** 1921
SQ FT: 275,000
SALES (est): 90.9MM **Privately Held**
WEB: www.dorfmanmilano.com
SIC: 5136 5137 Caps, men's & boys'; hats, men's & boys'; men's & boys' outerwear; caps & gowns; hats: women's, children's & infants'; women's & children's outerwear

(P-9244)
GONZALES PARK LLC
Also Called: Fifth Sun
495 Ryan Ave, Chico (95973-8846)
PHONE....................................530 343-8725
Daniel Gonzales, *Mng Member*
Erik Johnson, *CFO*
Dawn Gonzales, *Treasurer*
▲ **EMP:** 192 **EST:** 1995
SQ FT: 26,000
SALES (est): 134.8MM
SALES (corp-wide): 195.4MM **Privately Held**
WEB: www.5sun.com
SIC: 5136 2326 5699 Shirts, men's & boys'; men's & boys' work clothing; T-shirts, custom printed
PA: Mad Engine, Llc
6740 Cobra Way Ste 100
San Diego CA 92121
858 558-5270

(P-9245)
JA APPAREL CORP (HQ)
6100 Stevenson Blvd, Fremont (94538-2490)
PHONE....................................877 986-9669
Anthony Sapienza, *President*
Kenton Selvey, *President*
Jose Bahena, *Sr Exec VP*
Jamie Bragg, *Exec VP*
Salvator Mellace, *Exec VP*
◆ **EMP:** 50 **EST:** 1988
SQ FT: 9,500

County (P-9241)

SALES (est): 97.1MM
SALES (corp-wide): 2.8B **Privately Held**
WEB: www.tailoredbrands.com
SIC: 5136 Men's & boys' clothing
PA: Tailored Brands, Inc.
6380 Rogerdale Rd
Houston TX 77072
281 776-7000

(P-9246)
KILAM INC
39678 Mission Blvd, Fremont (94539-3000)
PHONE....................................510 943-4040
Sunil Kilam, *Administration*
▼ **EMP:** 160 **EST:** 2006
SQ FT: 1,600
SALES (est): 20.9MM **Privately Held**
WEB: www.eastessence.com
SIC: 5136 5137 3842 5047 Apparel belts, men's & boys'; apparel belts, women's & children's; gloves, safety; medical equipment & supplies; industrial safety devices; first aid kits & masks; shoe accessories

(P-9247)
LLC NOBLE RIDER (PA)
Also Called: Noble Outfitters
4300 Spyres Way, Modesto (95356-9259)
PHONE....................................209 566-7800
Dan J Costa, *Mng Member*
Elizabeth Ureste, *Purchasing*
Jeremy Pevehouse, *VP Sls/Mktg*
Victoria Philipp, *Sales Staff*
Abigail Murphy, *Mktg Coord*
▲ **EMP:** 95 **EST:** 2012
SALES (est): 15.4MM **Privately Held**
WEB: www.nobleoutfitters.com
SIC: 5136 5137 7389 Sportswear, men's & boys'; sportswear, women's & children's; apparel designers, commercial

(P-9248)
MJC INTERNATIONAL GROUP LLC (HQ)
25 Park Pl, Brisbane (94005-1306)
PHONE....................................415 467-9500
Michael Shina, *Mng Member*
Stephen Goldhorn, *Software Dev*
Jing Chen, *Production*
Ang Phan, *Manager*
Keith Prymak, *Accounts Mgr*
▲ **EMP:** 39 **EST:** 2008
SQ FT: 40,000
SALES (est): 25.6MM **Privately Held**
WEB: www.gomjc.com
SIC: 5136 5137 Neckwear, men's & boys'; women's & children's dresses, suits, skirts & blouses

(P-9249)
MURPHY HARTELIUS/M&H UNIFORMS (PA)
Also Called: M & H Uniforms
845 Stanton Rd, Burlingame (94010-1403)
P.O. Box 4365 (94011-4365)
PHONE....................................650 344-2997
Damian Murphy, *CEO*
Declan Murphy, *President*
Aidan Del, *Manager*
Aidan Del Canizo, *Manager*
Marie Selvaggio, *Manager*
EMP: 30 **EST:** 1960
SALES (est): 10.9MM **Privately Held**
WEB: www.mandhuniforms.com
SIC: 5136 5137 2339 2326 Uniforms, men's & boys'; uniforms, women's & children's; women's & misses' outerwear; men's & boys' work clothing

5137 Women's, Children's & Infants Clothing Wholesale

(P-9250)
AMOUR VERT INC
1278 Minnesota St Ste A, San Francisco (94107-3408)
PHONE....................................650 388-4284
Aaron Hoey, *CEO*
Ashley Witt, *Store Mgr*
Dmitri Litin, *Controller*
Amanda Halper, *Marketing Staff*
Cooper Lauren, *Manager*
EMP: 64 **EST:** 2011

SALES (est): 13MM **Privately Held**
WEB: www.amourvert.com
SIC: 5137 Women's & children's clothing

(P-9251)
BYER CALIFORNIA
811 Factory Stores Dr, NAPA (94558-5660)
PHONE....................................707 259-1225
EMP: 134
SALES (corp-wide): 395MM **Privately Held**
SIC: 5621 5137 2389 Ret Women's Clothing Whol Women's/Child's Clothing Mfg Apparel/Accessories
PA: Byer California
66 Potrero Ave
San Francisco CA 94103
415 626-7844

(P-9252)
JD FINE & COMPANY INC
Also Called: Tart Collections
2304 Willow Pass Rd, Concord (94520-2115)
PHONE....................................925 521-3300
Jamie Finegold, *President*
Dana Finegold, *CFO*
Berthiaume Denise, *Prdtn Mgr*
Brown Wendy-Lynn, *VP Mktg*
Katherine Delpit, *Sales Staff*
▲ **EMP:** 35 **EST:** 1996
SALES (est): 16.6MM **Privately Held**
WEB: www.jdfine.com
SIC: 5137 Nightwear: women's, children's & infants'

(P-9253)
MICHAEL KORS (USA) INC
1071 Santa Rosa Plz, Santa Rosa (95401-6397)
PHONE....................................707 535-0301
EMP: 45 **Privately Held**
SIC: 5651 5621 5137 2389 Jeans stores; women's specialty clothing stores; women's & children's outerwear; men's miscellaneous accessories
HQ: Michael Kors (Usa), Inc.
11 W 42nd St Fl 28
New York NY 10036
212 201-8100

(P-9254)
MICHAEL KORS (USA) INC
925 Blossom Hill Rd, San Jose (95123-1230)
PHONE....................................408 362-9537
Josef Lizotte, *Store Dir*
EMP: 45 **Privately Held**
SIC: 5651 5621 5137 2389 Family clothing stores; women's clothing stores; women's & children's clothing; apparel for handicapped
HQ: Michael Kors (Usa), Inc.
11 W 42nd St Fl 28
New York NY 10036
212 201-8100

(P-9255)
RUBY RIBBON
856 Mitten Rd Ste 101, Burlingame (94010-1333)
PHONE....................................650 525-4141
Loly Hlade, *Chief Mktg Ofcr*
Peter Fichtel, *Vice Pres*
Fichtel Peter, *Vice Pres*
Elaine Johnson, *Sales Staff*
Dane Nakamura, *Sales Staff*
EMP: 37 **EST:** 2018
SALES (est): 11.4MM **Privately Held**
WEB: www.rubyribbon.com
SIC: 5137 Women's & children's lingerie & undergarments

(P-9256)
SAK BRAND GROUP
400 Alabama St, San Francisco (94110-1315)
PHONE....................................415 486-1200
Matt Speight, *Manager*
Andrea Coppola, *Relations*
EMP: 19 **Privately Held**
WEB: www.thesak.com
SIC: 5137 5632 3171 Women's & children's clothing; women's accessory & specialty stores; women's handbags & purses

PA: The Sak Brand Group
339 5th Ave Fl 2
New York NY 10016

(P-9257)
TECHSTYLES SPORTSWEAR LLC
2051 Alpine Way, Hayward (94545-1703)
PHONE....................................800 733-3629
Jonathan W Bruml,
Paul Hellwig, *Production*
James Trevallion, *Production*
Melissa Fuquay, *Sales Mgr*
Michele Miller, *Manager*
EMP: 50 **EST:** 1986
SQ FT: 20,000
SALES (est): 13.2MM **Privately Held**
WEB: www.techstyles.com
SIC: 5137 5136 Women's & children's clothing; men's & boys' clothing

5139 Footwear Wholesale

(P-9258)
BIRKENSTOCK USA LP (DH)
8171 Redwood Blvd, Novato (94945-1403)
PHONE....................................415 884-3200
Stephan Birkenstock, *Partner*
Bernd Hillen, *Partner*
Christa Skov, *Partner*
Karen Anathan, *Vice Pres*
Scott Raddcliffe, *Vice Pres*
▲ **EMP:** 50 **EST:** 1971
SQ FT: 15,000
SALES (est): 55.3MM
SALES (corp-wide): 861.8MM **Privately Held**
WEB: www.birkenstock.com
SIC: 5139 Footwear
HQ: Ockenfels Services Gmbh
Burg Ockenfels
Linz
264 594-20

(P-9259)
L & L LOGIC AND LOGISTICS LP
6 Hamilton Landing # 250, Novato (94949-8264)
PHONE....................................707 795-2475
▲ **EMP:** 50
SALES (est): 3.9MM **Privately Held**
WEB: www.ll-logistics.com
SIC: 5139 Whol Footwear

(P-9260)
MILLENNIAL BRANDS LLC (PA)
Also Called: Rocket Dog Brands
2002 Diablo Rd, Danville (94506-2021)
PHONE....................................866 938-4806
Scott Briskie, *Mng Member*
Doug Younce, *Treasurer*
Mia Goodman, *Vice Pres*
Carly Marie, *Vice Pres*
Joe Shaheen, *Vice Pres*
▲ **EMP:** 85 **EST:** 2007
SALES (est): 23.8MM **Privately Held**
SIC: 5139 Footwear

5141 Groceries, General Line Wholesale

(P-9261)
ADVANTAGE SALES & MARKETING
5064 Franklin Dr, Pleasanton (94588-3354)
PHONE....................................925 463-5600
Clyde Le Baron, *President*
Steve Derking, *Exec VP*
Larissa Baker, *Manager*
EMP: 46 **EST:** 1945
SQ FT: 27,000
SALES (est): 2.2MM **Privately Held**
WEB: www.advantagesolutions.net
SIC: 5141 5142 5122 Food brokers; packaged frozen goods; druggists' sundries

▲ = Import ▼ = Export
◆ = Import/Export

PRODUCTS & SERVICES SECTION

5141 - Groceries, General Line Wholesale County (P-9283)

(P-9262)
BI-RITE RESTAURANT SUP CO INC
Also Called: Bi-Rite Foodservice Distrs
123 S Hill Dr, Brisbane (94005-1203)
PHONE................................415 656-0187
William Barulich, *CEO*
Steve Barulich, *President*
Zachary Barulich, *CFO*
Zack Barulich, *CFO*
Tom Whiteside, *Exec VP*
◆ **EMP:** 300
SQ FT: 220,000
SALES: 324MM **Privately Held**
WEB: www.birite.com
SIC: 5141 5147 5148 5023 Groceries, general line; meats & meat products; fresh fruits & vegetables; kitchenware; linens, table; towels; commercial equipment; direct selling establishments

(P-9263)
BOX LUNCH COMPANY INC
319 S Maple Ave Ste 206, South San Francisco (94080-5864)
P.O. Box 131 (94083-0131)
PHONE................................650 589-1886
Julie De Masi, *President*
John Jacob, *General Mgr*
Cristina Acevedo, *Sales Staff*
EMP: 36 **EST:** 1987
SQ FT: 12,500
SALES (est): 1.5MM **Privately Held**
SIC: 5812 5141 Caterers; food brokers

(P-9264)
C W BROWER INC (PA)
Also Called: Stop 'n' Save Liquors
413 S Riverside Dr Ste A, Modesto (95354-4079)
PHONE................................209 523-1828
Libby Pomeroy, *President*
EMP: 65 **EST:** 1962
SQ FT: 100,000
SALES (est): 75.1MM **Privately Held**
SIC: 5541 5921 5141 5411 Filling stations, gasoline; hard liquor; groceries, general line; convenience stores, independent

(P-9265)
C&S WHOLESALE GROCERS INC
2797 S Orange Ave, Fresno (93725-1919)
P.O. Box 11097 (93771-1097)
PHONE................................559 442-4700
Randy Wood, *Branch Mgr*
Asad Husain, *Exec VP*
Alan Kintisch, *Senior VP*
Raymond Schrumpf, *Vice Pres*
Terrell Jones, *General Mgr*
EMP: 164
SALES (corp-wide): 5.9MM **Privately Held**
WEB: www.cswg.com
SIC: 5141 Food brokers
PA: C&S Wholesale Grocers, Inc.
7 Corporate Dr
Keene NH 03431
603 354-7000

(P-9266)
COASTAL PACIFIC FD DISTRS INC (PA)
1015 Performance Dr, Stockton (95206-4925)
P.O. Box 30910 (95213-0910)
PHONE................................909 947-2066
Terrence Wood, *CEO*
Jeff King, *COO*
Matthew Payne, *CFO*
John Payne, *Treasurer*
Brian Murdoch, *Exec VP*
◆ **EMP:** 220 **EST:** 1986
SQ FT: 500,000
SALES (est): 312MM **Privately Held**
WEB: www.cpfd.com
SIC: 5141 5149 Groceries, general line; bakery products

(P-9267)
COASTAL PACIFIC FD DISTRS INC
California Pacific
1801 Murchison Dr Ste 300, Burlingame (94010-4517)
PHONE................................650 692-8211
Frank Pecoraro, *President*
Michelle Alberto, *Manager*
EMP: 52
SALES (corp-wide): 312MM **Privately Held**
WEB: www.cpfd.com
SIC: 5141 Groceries, general line
PA: Coastal Pacific Food Distributors, Inc.
1015 Performance Dr
Stockton CA 95206
909 947-2066

(P-9268)
CORE-MARK HOLDING COMPANY INC
2959 Thomas Pl Ste 150, West Sacramento (95691-5751)
PHONE................................866 791-4210
Thomas Perkins, *Branch Mgr*
EMP: 50
SQ FT: 79,000
SALES (corp-wide): 30.4B **Publicly Held**
WEB: www.core-mark.com
SIC: 5141 Groceries, general line
HQ: Core-Mark Holding Company, Inc.
1500 Solana Blvd Ste 3400
Westlake TX 76262
940 293-8600

(P-9269)
DEL MONTE CAPITOL MEAT CO LLC (HQ)
4051 Seaport Blvd, West Sacramento (95691-3416)
PHONE................................916 927-0595
Christopher Pappas, *President*
John Debenedetti, *Exec VP*
Brian Hansen, *Vice Pres*
James Romeo, *Vice Pres*
Jeff Root, *Sales Executive*
EMP: 81 **EST:** 2015
SALES (est): 54.8MM **Publicly Held**
WEB: www.chefswarehouse.com
SIC: 5141 Food brokers

(P-9270)
DOT FOODS INC
2200 Nickerson Dr, Modesto (95358-9489)
PHONE................................209 581-9090
Fax: 209 581-9082
EMP: 134
SALES (corp-wide): 5.4B **Privately Held**
SIC: 5141 Whol General Groceries
PA: Dot Foods, Inc.
1 Dot Way
Mount Sterling IL 62353
217 773-4411

(P-9271)
E G AYERS DISTRIBUTING INC
5819 S Broadway St, Eureka (95503-6906)
PHONE................................707 445-2077
Paul A Ayers, *CEO*
Phillip Ayers, *Treasurer*
EMP: 50 **EST:** 1947
SQ FT: 15,000
SALES (est): 23.7MM **Privately Held**
WEB: www.ayersdistributing.com
SIC: 5141 5149 Food brokers; beverages, except coffee & tea

(P-9272)
GROCERY OUTLET HOLDING CORP (PA)
5650 Hollis St, Emeryville (94608-2597)
PHONE................................510 845-1999
Eric J Lindberg Jr, *CEO*
Erik D Ragatz, *Ch of Bd*
Robert Joseph Sheedy Jr, *President*
Charles C Bracher, *CFO*
S Macgregor Read Jr, *Vice Ch Bd*
EMP: 311 **EST:** 1946
SALES: 3.1B **Publicly Held**
WEB: www.groceryoutlet.com
SIC: 5411 5141 Grocery stores, independent; groceries, general line

(P-9273)
HIGHLAND WHOLESALE FOODS INC
1604 Tillie Lewis Dr, Stockton (95206-1159)
PHONE................................209 933-0580
T Gregory Stagnitto, *President*
Tommy Sodaro, *Senior VP*
Cliff Coler, *Controller*
Josh Lang, *Sales Staff*
▼ **EMP:** 80 **EST:** 1999
SQ FT: 240,000
SALES (est): 54.1MM **Privately Held**
WEB: www.highlandwholesalefoods.com
SIC: 5141 Food brokers

(P-9274)
ITALFOODS INC
205 Shaw Rd, South San Francisco (94080-6605)
P.O. Box 2563 (94083-2563)
PHONE................................650 877-0724
Georgette Guerra, *CEO*
Donald Raphael, *General Mgr*
Dan Ginn, *Human Res Mgr*
Richard Degaetano, *Purchasing*
Lorenzo Chiostri, *Sales Staff*
▲ **EMP:** 80 **EST:** 1978
SQ FT: 114,000
SALES (est): 31.2MM **Privately Held**
WEB: www.italfoodsinc.com
SIC: 5141 Food brokers

(P-9275)
LASSEN CANYON NURSERY INC (PA)
10364 Salmon Creek Rd, Redding (96003-8267)
P.O. Box 992400 (96099-2400)
PHONE................................530 223-1075
Elizabeth Elwood Ponce, *CEO*
Kenneth Elwood Jr, *President*
Liz Ponce, *Vice Pres*
Garrett Wallis, *CIO*
Crystal Amen, *Sales Mgr*
▼ **EMP:** 125 **EST:** 1964
SQ FT: 3,000
SALES (est): 93.1MM **Privately Held**
WEB: www.lassencanyonnursery.com
SIC: 5141 5191 0171 Groceries, general line; hay; raspberry farm

(P-9276)
LEE BROS FOODSERVICES INC (PA)
Also Called: Lee Industrial Catering
660 E Gish Rd, San Jose (95112-2707)
PHONE................................408 275-0700
Chieu Van Le, *CEO*
Tu Lee, *COO*
Huong Le, *Vice Pres*
Jimmy Lee, *Vice Pres*
Nick Nguyen, *Manager*
▲ **EMP:** 100 **EST:** 1985
SQ FT: 15,000
SALES (est): 61.9MM **Privately Held**
SIC: 5141 5142 Food brokers; packaged frozen goods

(P-9277)
MARQUEZ BROTHERS INTL INC (PA)
Also Called: M B
5801 Rue Ferrari, San Jose (95138-1857)
PHONE................................408 960-2700
Gustavo Marquez, *CEO*
Jaime Marquez, *Exec VP*
Angel Garza, *General Mgr*
Toby Murray, *Executive Asst*
Jerry Santamaria, *Admin Sec*
◆ **EMP:** 150 **EST:** 1981
SQ FT: 160,000
SALES (est): 104.1MM **Privately Held**
WEB: www.marquezbrothers.com
SIC: 5141 Food brokers

(P-9278)
MCLANE FOODSERVICE DIST INC
800 Mellon Ave, Manteca (95337-6135)
PHONE................................209 823-7157
EMP: 114
SALES (corp-wide): 245.5B **Publicly Held**
WEB: www.mbmcorp.com
SIC: 5141 Groceries, general line
HQ: Mclane Foodservice Distribution, Inc.
2641 Meadowbrook Rd
Rocky Mount NC 27801
252 985-7200

(P-9279)
MCLANE/PACIFIC INC
3876 E Childs Ave, Merced (95341-9520)
P.O. Box 2107 (95344-0107)
PHONE................................209 725-2500
William G Rosier, *CEO*
Mike Youngblood, *President*
Kevin Koch, *Treasurer*
Jim Kent, *Exec VP*
Michelle Chesnutt, *VP Sales*
▲ **EMP:** 498 **EST:** 1983
SQ FT: 220,000
SALES (est): 92.5MM
SALES (corp-wide): 245.5B **Publicly Held**
WEB: www.mclaneco.com
SIC: 5141 Food brokers
HQ: Mclane Company, Inc.
4747 Mclane Pkwy
Temple TX 76504
254 771-7500

(P-9280)
MERCADO LATINO INC
33430 Western Ave, Union City (94587-3202)
PHONE................................510 475-5500
Robert Rodriguez, *Principal*
EMP: 113
SALES (corp-wide): 87MM **Privately Held**
WEB: www.mercadolatinoinc.com
SIC: 5141 Food brokers
PA: Mercado Latino, Inc.
245 Baldwin Park Blvd
City Of Industry CA 91746
626 333-6862

(P-9281)
OAKHURST INDUSTRIES INC
Also Called: Freund Baking Co
3265 Investment Blvd, Hayward (94545-3806)
PHONE................................510 265-2400
Jim Freund, *Principal*
Larry Lumley, *Plant Mgr*
Terry Vincej, *Plant Mgr*
Steven A Freund, *Litigation*
EMP: 178
SQ FT: 67,896 **Privately Held**
SIC: 5141 2051 Groceries, general line; bread, cake & related products
PA: Oakhurst Industries, Inc.
2050 S Tubeway Ave
Commerce CA 90040

(P-9282)
PALO ALTO EGG AND FOOD SVC CO
Also Called: Palo Alto Food Company
6691 Clark Ave, Newark (94560-3925)
P.O. Box 327 (94560-0327)
PHONE................................510 456-2420
Eric Jensen, *CEO*
Paul Jensen, *Vice Pres*
Natalie Timboe, *Sales Staff*
EMP: 50 **EST:** 1967
SQ FT: 15,000
SALES (est): 10MM **Privately Held**
SIC: 5141 Food brokers

(P-9283)
PERFORMANCE FOOD GROUP INC
Also Called: Performnce Foodservice-Ledyard
1047 17th Ave, Santa Cruz (95062-3033)
PHONE................................831 462-4400
Steve Rebottaro, *Branch Mgr*
Cody Walz, *General Mgr*
Remy Connor, *Human Res Dir*
Rob Beres, *Manager*
Jesse Jacobs, *Manager*
EMP: 101

5141 - Groceries, General Line Wholesale County (P-9284)

SALES (corp-wide): 30.4B **Publicly Held**
WEB: www.pfgc.com
SIC: 5141 5046 5087 Food brokers; restaurant equipment & supplies; janitors' supplies
HQ: Performance Food Group, Inc.
  12500 West Creek Pkwy
  Richmond VA 23238
  804 484-7700

(P-9284)
PITTSBURG WHOLESALE GROC INC
Also Called: Pitco
385 Valley Dr, Brisbane (94005-1207)
PHONE.................................415 865-0404
Mike Ashtiani, *Branch Mgr*
Marilou Labuguen,
Reza Neghabat, *Sr Consultant*
Maria Green, *Manager*
Mark Perez, *Manager*
EMP: 46 **Privately Held**
WEB: www.pitcofoods.com
SIC: 5141 Food brokers
PA: Pittsburg Wholesale Grocers, Inc.
  567 Cinnabar St
  San Jose CA 95110

(P-9285)
PITTSBURG WHOLESALE GROC INC
1800 Merced St, San Leandro
(94577-3228)
PHONE.................................408 701-7326
EMP: 46 **Privately Held**
WEB: www.pitcofoods.com
SIC: 5141 Food brokers
PA: Pittsburg Wholesale Grocers, Inc.
  567 Cinnabar St
  San Jose CA 95110

(P-9286)
PITTSBURG WHOLESALE GROC INC
Also Called: Pitco Foods
3575 Ramos Dr, West Sacramento
(95691-5753)
PHONE.................................916 372-7772
Farzam Hariri, *Manager*
Adeline Baugh, *Technology*
Mary Mehr, *Human Res Dir*
Ryan Anhari, *Opers Staff*
Eliza Tartt, *Marketing Staff*
EMP: 46 **Privately Held**
WEB: www.pitcofoods.com
SIC: 5141 Food brokers
PA: Pittsburg Wholesale Grocers, Inc.
  567 Cinnabar St
  San Jose CA 95110

(P-9287)
PITTSBURG WHOLESALE GROC INC
Also Called: Pitco Foods
1800 Merced St, San Leandro
(94577-3228)
PHONE.................................510 533-3444
Steve Perez, *Director*
Fernando Neyra, *Supervisor*
EMP: 46 **Privately Held**
WEB: www.pitcofoods.com
SIC: 5141 5194 5145 Food brokers; tobacco & tobacco products; candy
PA: Pittsburg Wholesale Grocers, Inc.
  567 Cinnabar St
  San Jose CA 95110

(P-9288)
PK KINDER CO INC
Also Called: Kinder's
245 Ygnacio Valley Rd # 200, Walnut Creek
(94596-7029)
PHONE.................................925 939-7242
Joseph Rainero, *CEO*
Rebecca Hollingsworth, *CFO*
Jim Hart, *Chairman*
EMP: 50 **EST:** 1996
SALES (est): 42.2MM **Privately Held**
WEB: www.kinders.com
SIC: 5141 5421 Groceries, general line; meat & fish markets

(P-9289)
RESERS FINE FOODS INC
1540 Giuntoli Ln, Arcata (95521-4419)
PHONE.................................503 643-6431
EMP: 56
SALES (corp-wide): 1.5B **Privately Held**
WEB: www.resers.com
SIC: 5141 Groceries, general line
PA: Reser's Fine Foods, Inc.
  15570 Sw Jenkins Rd
  Beaverton OR 97006
  503 643-6431

(P-9290)
RESERS FINE FOODS INC
5800 Airport Rd, Redding (96002-9359)
PHONE.................................503 643-6431
EMP: 56
SALES (corp-wide): 1.5B **Privately Held**
WEB: www.resers.com
SIC: 5141 Groceries, general line
PA: Reser's Fine Foods, Inc.
  15570 Sw Jenkins Rd
  Beaverton OR 97006
  503 643-6431

(P-9291)
RETAIL REALM DISTRIBUTION INC (PA)
454 W Napa St B, Sonoma (95476-6519)
PHONE.................................707 996-5400
Afshin Amir Alikhani, *President*
Rachel Smith, *Vice Pres*
EMP: 88 **EST:** 2009
SALES (est): 8.3MM **Privately Held**
WEB: www.retailrealm.com
SIC: 5141 Food brokers

(P-9292)
S AND L MEAT SALES COMPANY
Also Called: S and L Food Sales
2 Bellarmine Ct, Chico (95928-7149)
P.O. Box 1189 (95927-1189)
PHONE.................................530 343-7953
Larry J Stephenson, *CEO*
Chris Leitner, *General Mgr*
Bob Brown, *Sales Staff*
Angie Castro, *Sales Staff*
Anton Dwyer, *Manager*
EMP: 40 **EST:** 1972
SQ FT: 25,000
SALES (est): 13.9MM **Privately Held**
WEB: www.slfoodsales.com
SIC: 5141 5147 5144 Food brokers; meats & meat products; poultry & poultry products

(P-9293)
SALADINOS INC
3045 Mulvany Pl, West Sacramento
(95691-5745)
PHONE.................................559 271-3700
Craig Saladino, *President*
EMP: 54
SALES (corp-wide): 288.6MM **Privately Held**
WEB: www.saladinos.com
SIC: 5141 Food brokers
PA: Saladino's, Inc.
  3325 W Figarden Dr
  Fresno CA 93711
  559 271-3700

(P-9294)
SALADINOS INC (PA)
3325 W Figarden Dr, Fresno (93711-3909)
P.O. Box 12266 (93777-2266)
PHONE.................................559 271-3700
Craig A Saladino, *CEO*
Patrick Peters, *COO*
Don Saladino, *Chairman*
Matthew Jost, *Administration*
Craig Urrizola, *CIO*
EMP: 113 **EST:** 1944
SQ FT: 40,000
SALES (est): 288.6MM **Privately Held**
WEB: www.saladinos.com
SIC: 5141 2099 Food brokers; food preparations

(P-9295)
SAVE MART SUPERMARKETS
8839 Greenback Ln, Orangevale
(95662-4061)
PHONE.................................916 989-3915
EMP: 75
SALES (corp-wide): 4.1B **Privately Held**
SIC: 5411 5141 Ret Groceries Whol General Groceries
PA: Save Mart Supermarkets
  1800 Standiford Ave
  Modesto CA 95350
  209 577-1600

(P-9296)
SAVE MART SUPERMARKETS DISC (PA)
Also Called: S-Mart
1800 Standiford Ave, Modesto
(95350-0180)
P.O. Box 4278 (95352-4278)
PHONE.................................209 577-1600
Robert M Piccinini, *CEO*
James Orr, *COO*
Ronald Riesenbeck, *CFO*
James Sims, *Officer*
Steve Junqueiro, *Vice Pres*
EMP: 250 **EST:** 1952
SQ FT: 34,000
SALES (est): 414.7K **Privately Held**
WEB: www.savemart.com
SIC: 5411 5141 4213 4212 Supermarkets, chain; groceries, general line; refrigerated products transport; local trucking, without storage

(P-9297)
SAVE MART SUPERMARKETS DISC
5671 E Kings Canyon Rd, Fresno
(93727-4641)
PHONE.................................559 253-1220
Michele D Snider, *Manager*
EMP: 85
SALES (corp-wide): 414.7K **Privately Held**
WEB: www.thesavemartcompanies.com
SIC: 5411 5141 Supermarkets, chain; groceries, general line
PA: Save Mart Supermarkets Disc
  1800 Standiford Ave
  Modesto CA 95350
  209 577-1600

(P-9298)
SAVE MART SUPERMARKETS DISC
2237 Claribel Rd, Riverbank (95367-9473)
PHONE.................................209 863-1480
Tony Angoletta, *Manager*
Pranish Lal, *Marketing Staff*
EMP: 85
SALES (corp-wide): 414.7K **Privately Held**
WEB: www.thesavemartcompanies.com
SIC: 5411 5141 Supermarkets, chain; groceries, general line
PA: Save Mart Supermarkets Disc
  1800 Standiford Ave
  Modesto CA 95350
  209 577-1600

(P-9299)
SAVE MART SUPERMARKETS DISC
100 River Rd, Tahoe City (96145-1716)
PHONE.................................530 583-5231
Donna Finn, *Manager*
EMP: 85
SALES (corp-wide): 414.7K **Privately Held**
WEB: www.savemart.com
SIC: 5411 5141 Supermarkets, chain; groceries, general line
PA: Save Mart Supermarkets Disc
  1800 Standiford Ave
  Modesto CA 95350
  209 577-1600

(P-9300)
SAVE MART SUPERMARKETS DISC
11399 Deerfield Dr, Truckee (96161-0505)
PHONE.................................530 587-5522
Donna Sinn, *Manager*
EMP: 85
SALES (corp-wide): 414.7K **Privately Held**
WEB: www.savemart.com
SIC: 5411 5141 Supermarkets, chain; groceries, general line
PA: Save Mart Supermarkets Disc
  1800 Standiford Ave
  Modesto CA 95350
  209 577-1600

(P-9301)
SAVE MART SUPERMARKETS DISC
Also Called: Foodmaxx
6982 Sunrise Blvd, Citrus Heights
(95610-3144)
PHONE.................................916 723-2446
Richard Fay, *Branch Mgr*
EMP: 85
SALES (corp-wide): 414.7K **Privately Held**
WEB: www.savemart.com
SIC: 5411 5141 Supermarkets, chain; groceries, general line
PA: Save Mart Supermarkets Disc
  1800 Standiford Ave
  Modesto CA 95350
  209 577-1600

(P-9302)
SHOEI FOODS (USA) INC
1900 Feather River Blvd, Olivehurst
(95961-9709)
PHONE.................................530 742-7866
Don Soetaert, *CEO*
Sumio Kawanabe, *President*
Tall Matsushima, *President*
Dwight Davis, *Opers Staff*
John Gaffney, *Sales Staff*
◆ **EMP:** 100
SQ FT: 68,000
SALES (est): 83.2MM **Privately Held**
WEB: www.shoeifoodsusa.com
SIC: 5141 Food brokers
PA: Shoei Foods Corporation
  5-7, Akihabara
  Taito-Ku TKY 110-0

(P-9303)
SIMCO FOODS INC
Also Called: Wipeout Bar & Grill
39 Pier Ste A202, San Francisco
(94133-1067)
PHONE.................................415 982-5872
Sandra Fletcher, *Vice Pres*
Caroline Simmons,
Nancy Simmons,
Warren Simmons,
EMP: 60 **EST:** 1986
SALES (est): 2.1MM **Privately Held**
WEB: www.simco.us
SIC: 5141 Groceries, general line

(P-9304)
SL ONE GLOBAL INC (PA)
4211 Norwood Ave, Sacramento
(95838-4945)
PHONE.................................916 993-4100
Sean Loloee, *President*
EMP: 59 **EST:** 2008
SALES (est): 1.7MM **Privately Held**
SIC: 5141 Groceries, general line

(P-9305)
SMART & FINAL STORES INC
7223 Fair Oaks Blvd, Carmichael
(95608-6410)
PHONE.................................916 486-6315
EMP: 243
SALES (corp-wide): 4.7B **Privately Held**
SIC: 5141 Groceries, general line
HQ: Smart & Final Stores Llc
  600 Citadel Dr
  Commerce CA 90040
  323 869-7500

(P-9306)
SMART & FINAL STORES INC
1180 S King Rd, San Jose (95122-2143)
PHONE.................................408 251-0109
EMP: 243
SALES (corp-wide): 4.7B **Privately Held**
SIC: 5141 Groceries, general line

PRODUCTS & SERVICES SECTION
5142 - Packaged Frozen Foods Wholesale County (P-9328)

HQ: Smart & Final Stores Llc
600 Citadel Dr
Commerce CA 90040
323 869-7500

(P-9307)
SMART & FINAL STORES INC
2825 Grass Valley Hwy, Auburn (95603-2542)
PHONE......................530 823-1205
EMP: 243
SALES (corp-wide): 4.7B **Privately Held**
SIC: 5141 Groceries, general line
HQ: Smart & Final Stores Llc
600 Citadel Dr
Commerce CA 90040
323 869-7500

(P-9308)
SMART & FINAL STORES INC
2425 N Blackstone Ave, Fresno (93703-1748)
PHONE......................559 229-2944
EMP: 243
SALES (corp-wide): 4.7B **Privately Held**
SIC: 5141 Groceries, general line
HQ: Smart & Final Stores Llc
600 Citadel Dr
Commerce CA 90040
323 869-7500

(P-9309)
SMART & FINAL STORES INC
401 Jacklin Rd, Milpitas (95035-3226)
PHONE......................408 941-9642
EMP: 243
SALES (corp-wide): 4.7B **Privately Held**
SIC: 5141 Groceries, general line
HQ: Smart & Final Stores Llc
600 Citadel Dr
Commerce CA 90040
323 869-7500

(P-9310)
SMART & FINAL STORES INC
790 W Shaw Ave, Clovis (93612-3216)
PHONE......................559 297-9376
EMP: 243
SALES (corp-wide): 4.7B **Privately Held**
SIC: 5141 Groceries, general line
HQ: Smart & Final Stores Llc
600 Citadel Dr
Commerce CA 90040
323 869-7500

(P-9311)
SOUTHWEST TRADERS INCORPORATED
4747 Frontier Way, Stockton (95215-9671)
PHONE......................209 462-1607
Jerry Alestra, *Branch Mgr*
Mike Bredemeier, *CFO*
Erin Arrivillaga, *Vice Pres*
David Shaw, *General Mgr*
Tina Sterling, *Administration*
EMP: 102
SALES (corp-wide): 398.7MM **Privately Held**
WEB: www.southwesttraders.com
SIC: 5141 Food brokers
PA: Southwest Traders Incorporated
27565 Diaz Rd
Temecula CA 92590
951 699-7800

(P-9312)
SPROUTS FARMERS MARKET INC
1700 Mchenry Ave, Modesto (95350-4373)
PHONE......................209 527-7575
Andrew Jhawar, *Branch Mgr*
EMP: 65
SALES (corp-wide): 6.4B **Publicly Held**
WEB: www.sprouts.com
SIC: 5141 Groceries, general line
PA: Sprouts Farmers Market, Inc.
5455 E High St Ste 111
Phoenix AZ 85054
480 814-8016

(P-9313)
SUNFOODS LLC (HQ)
Also Called: Hinode
1620 E Kentucky Ave, Woodland (95776-6110)
P.O. Box 8729 (95776-8729)
PHONE......................530 661-1923
Matt Alonso, *CEO*
Jacqueline Hartshorn,
John Koury,
Clyde Uchida,
◆ EMP: 70 EST: 2008
SQ FT: 1,600
SALES (est): 22MM **Privately Held**
WEB: www.hinoderice.com
SIC: 5141 Food brokers

(P-9314)
SUPERIOR FOODS INC
Also Called: Superior Foods Companies, The
275 Westgate Dr, Watsonville (95076-2470)
PHONE......................831 728-3691
David E Moore, *Ch of Bd*
Mateo Lettunich, *President*
R Neil Happee, *CEO*
Neil Happee, *COO*
H Monroe Howser III, *CFO*
◆ EMP: 100 EST: 1980
SQ FT: 10,782
SALES (est): 53.7MM **Privately Held**
WEB: www.superiorfoods.com
SIC: 5141 Food brokers

(P-9315)
SYGMA NETWORK INC
3741 Gold River Ln, Stockton (95215-9669)
PHONE......................209 932-5300
John Rivers, *Manager*
Don Thornburg, *Executive*
EMP: 185
SALES (corp-wide): 52.8B **Publicly Held**
WEB: www.sygmanetwork.com
SIC: 5141 Food brokers
HQ: The Sygma Network Inc
5550 Blazer Pkwy Ste 300
Dublin OH 43017

(P-9316)
SYSCO CENTRAL CALIFORNIA INC
136 Mariposa Rd, Modesto (95354-4122)
P.O. Box 729 (95353-0729)
PHONE......................209 527-7700
Elizabeth Aspray, *President*
Robin Kawashima, *CFO*
Patrick Kissee, *Vice Pres*
Simon To, *Vice Pres*
Tisha Escoto, *Buyer*
▲ EMP: 312 EST: 1938
SQ FT: 177,000
SALES (est): 112.6MM
SALES (corp-wide): 52.8B **Publicly Held**
WEB: www.syscocentralca.com
SIC: 5141 5142 5046 5148 Food brokers; meat, frozen; packaged; vegetables, frozen; restaurant equipment & supplies; fruits, fresh; vegetables, fresh
PA: Sysco Corporation
1390 Enclave Pkwy
Houston TX 77077
281 584-1390

(P-9317)
SYSCO SACRAMENTO INC
7062 Pacific Ave, Pleasant Grove (95668-9731)
P.O. Box 138007, Sacramento (95813-8007)
PHONE......................916 275-2714
Jackie L Ward, *Ch of Bd*
Bill Delaney, *President*
Delmer Schnuelle, *President*
Tom Bene, *Exec VP*
Brian Beach, *Senior VP*
▼ EMP: 393 EST: 2000
SQ FT: 350,000
SALES (est): 221.8MM
SALES (corp-wide): 52.8B **Publicly Held**
WEB: www.sysco.com
SIC: 5141 5142 Food brokers; packaged frozen goods

PA: Sysco Corporation
1390 Enclave Pkwy
Houston TX 77077
281 584-1390

(P-9318)
SYSCO SAN FRANCISCO INC
5900 Stewart Ave, Fremont (94538-3147)
P.O. Box 5019 (94537-5019)
PHONE......................510 226-3000
James Ehlers, *President*
Glory Law, *Officer*
Bruce Luong, *Vice Pres*
Patrick Bily, *Principal*
Jane Brett, *Principal*
▼ EMP: 650 EST: 1939
SQ FT: 470,000
SALES (est): 221.8MM
SALES (corp-wide): 52.8B **Publicly Held**
WEB: www.syscosf.com
SIC: 5141 5147 5142 Food brokers; meats, fresh; packaged frozen goods
PA: Sysco Corporation
1390 Enclave Pkwy
Houston TX 77077
281 584-1390

(P-9319)
TALAMO FOOD SERVICE INC
Also Called: Talamo Foods
18675 Madrone Pkwy 100, Morgan Hill (95037-2868)
PHONE......................408 612-8751
Mario Talamo, *President*
Joseph Talamo, *COO*
Fred Gotto, *Purchasing*
Rebecca Cabrera, *Sales Staff*
EMP: 49 EST: 1989
SQ FT: 10,000
SALES (est): 23MM **Privately Held**
WEB: www.talamofoods.net
SIC: 5141 Food brokers

(P-9320)
TAPIA ENTERPRISES INC
Also Called: Tapia Bros Company
2324 S Barton Ave, Fresno (93725-1101)
PHONE......................559 486-8347
Grazila Tapia, *Manager*
EMP: 37
SALES (corp-wide): 95.1MM **Privately Held**
WEB: www.tapiabrothers.com
SIC: 5141 Food brokers
PA: Tapia Enterprises, Inc.
6067 District Blvd
Maywood CA 90270
323 560-7415

(P-9321)
US FOODS INC
300 Lawrence Dr Frnt, Livermore (94551-5139)
PHONE......................925 606-3525
Phil Collins, *Branch Mgr*
Rob West, *Warehouse Mgr*
John Amore, *Manager*
Scott Hart, *Manager*
Cat Lindquist, *Accounts Exec*
EMP: 500 **Publicly Held**
WEB: www.usfoods.com
SIC: 5141 Food brokers
HQ: Us Foods, Inc.
9399 W Higgins Rd # 100
Rosemont IL 60018

(P-9322)
USTOV INC
Also Called: U.S. Trading Company
21118 Cabot Blvd, Hayward (94545-1130)
PHONE......................510 781-1818
Paul M Tov, *CEO*
Joseph Cho, *General Mgr*
◆ EMP: 50 EST: 1985
SQ FT: 132,000
SALES (est): 23.3MM **Privately Held**
SIC: 5141 Food brokers

(P-9323)
WIN WOO TRADING LLC
Also Called: New Berry Trading
31056 Genstar Rd, Hayward (94544-7830)
PHONE......................510 259-1888
Jia Jing Zheng, *Mng Member*
Hua Gui Liang,

▲ EMP: 49 EST: 2004
SQ FT: 100,000
SALES (est): 43.2MM
SALES (corp-wide): 566.8MM **Publicly Held**
WEB: www.rnjfood.com
SIC: 5141 Food brokers
PA: Hf Foods Group Inc.
19319 Arenth Ave
City Of Industry CA 91748
626 338-1090

5142 Packaged Frozen Foods Wholesale

(P-9324)
CALBEE NORTH AMERICA LLC
2600 Maxwell Way, Fairfield (94534-1915)
PHONE......................707 427-2500
Gene Jensen, *Branch Mgr*
CJ Bischoff, *Vice Pres*
Frank Rogers, *Regional Mgr*
John Moran, *General Mgr*
Lisa Jernigan, *Administration*
EMP: 50 **Privately Held**
WEB: www.calbeena.com
SIC: 5142 5145 2038 Packaged frozen goods; snack foods; snacks, including onion rings, cheese sticks, etc.
HQ: Calbee North America, Llc
72600 Lewis & Clark Dr
Boardman OR 97818

(P-9325)
D AND T FOODS INC
Also Called: D & T Foods Company
1261 Martin Ave, Santa Clara (95050-2652)
PHONE......................408 727-8331
Daniel Yet, *CEO*
◆ EMP: 48 EST: 1991
SQ FT: 80,000
SALES (est): 33.8MM **Privately Held**
WEB: www.dtfoods.com
SIC: 5142 5146 Packaged frozen goods; fish & seafoods

(P-9326)
MCLANE FOODSERVICE DIST INC
Also Called: M B M
5675 Sunol Blvd, Pleasanton (94566-7765)
PHONE......................252 985-7200
Al Monceaux, *Manager*
EMP: 70
SALES (corp-wide): 245.5B **Publicly Held**
WEB: www.mbmcorp.com
SIC: 5142 Packaged frozen goods
HQ: Mclane Foodservice Distribution, Inc.
2641 Meadowbrook Rd
Rocky Mount NC 27801
252 985-7200

(P-9327)
MOONLIGHT PACKING CORPORATION
1300 I St, Reedley (93654-3301)
PHONE......................559 638-7799
David Gonzalez, *Opers Staff*
Luis Licea, *Manager*
EMP: 726 **Privately Held**
WEB: www.moonlightcompanies.com
SIC: 5142 Frozen vegetables & fruit products
PA: Moonlight Packing Corporation
17719 E Huntsman Ave
Reedley CA 93654

(P-9328)
NEWPORT MEAT NORTHERN CAL INC (HQ)
Also Called: Newport Meat Company
48811 Warm Springs Blvd, Fremont (94539-7712)
PHONE......................800 535-6328
Denise L Van Voorhis, *CEO*
Robert Facciola, *President*
Marilyn Terantino, *Admin Sec*
▲ EMP: 35 EST: 1954
SQ FT: 84,000

5142 - Packaged Frozen Foods Wholesale County (P-9329)

SALES (est): 56.1MM
SALES (corp-wide): 52.8B **Publicly Held**
WEB: www.newportmeat.com
SIC: 5142 5147 Packaged frozen goods; meats, fresh
PA: Sysco Corporation
1390 Enclave Pkwy
Houston TX 77077
281 584-1390

(P-9329)
PACIFIC SFOOD - SACRAMENTO LLC
Also Called: Pacific Fresh Seafood
1420 National Dr, Sacramento (95834-1967)
PHONE..................................916 419-5500
Frank Dominic Dulcich, *President*
Tim Horgan, *COO*
Kara Aakre, *Controller*
Anna Hoyt, *Sales Staff*
Miranda Ries, *Director*
◆ EMP: 180 EST: 1989
SQ FT: 50,000
SALES (est): 52MM
SALES (corp-wide): 617.5MM **Privately Held**
WEB: www.pacificseafood.com
SIC: 5142 5146 Fish, frozen: packaged; fish, fresh
HQ: Pacific Seafood Distribution, Llc
16797 Se 130th Ave
Clackamas OR 97015
503 905-4500

(P-9330)
PRODUCERS DAIRY FOODS INC (PA)
250 E Belmont Ave, Fresno (93701-1405)
PHONE..................................559 264-6583
Lawrence A Shehadey, *Ch of Bd*
Richard Shehadey, *CEO*
Nick Kelble, *COO*
Brandi Williams, *Officer*
Scott Shehadey, *Vice Pres*
▲ EMP: 200 EST: 1932
SALES (est): 199.8MM **Privately Held**
WEB: www.producersdairy.com
SIC: 5142 5143 Fruit juices, frozen; dairy products, except dried or canned

(P-9331)
VAN WOLFS LLC
Also Called: Fatcat Scones
8130 Berry Ave Ste 100, Sacramento (95828-1696)
PHONE..................................916 372-6464
Erik Finnerty, *Owner*
Tony Vanrees,
Angie Westberg, *Manager*
EMP: 44 EST: 2002
SALES (est): 5.6MM **Privately Held**
SIC: 5142 Bakery products, frozen

(P-9332)
VPS COMPANIES INC (PA)
310 Walker St, Watsonville (95076-4525)
P.O. Box 118 (95077-0118)
PHONE..................................831 724-7551
Jack Randle, *Ch of Bd*
Byron Johnson, *President*
Ronald Marker, *CFO*
Fred Haas, *Treasurer*
Fred J Haas, *Corp Secy*
▲ EMP: 50 EST: 1966
SQ FT: 10,000
SALES (est): 327.5MM **Privately Held**
WEB: www.vpsco.com
SIC: 5142 0723 4731 Fruits, frozen; vegetables, frozen; crop preparation services for market; freight transportation arrangement

5143 Dairy Prdts, Except Dried Or Canned Wholesale

(P-9333)
ARCTIC EXPRESS NORCAL LLC
3130 Crow Canyon Pl # 210, San Ramon (94583-1346)
PHONE..................................925 553-3681
Michael Zumbo, *Principal*
EMP: 45 EST: 2017
SALES (est): 8.6MM **Privately Held**
WEB: www.arcticexpress.net
SIC: 5143 Ice cream & ices

(P-9334)
CENTRAL VALLEY CHEESE INC
115 S Kilroy Rd, Turlock (95380-9531)
PHONE..................................209 664-1080
Antranik Baghdassarian, *CEO*
EMP: 70 EST: 1999
SALES (est): 53.5MM **Privately Held**
WEB: www.centralvalleycheese.com
SIC: 5143 Cheese
PA: Karoun Dairies, Inc.
13023 Arroyo St
San Fernando CA 91340

(P-9335)
CHALLENGE DAIRY PRODUCTS INC (HQ)
6701 Donlon Way, Dublin (94568-2850)
P.O. Box 2369 (94568-0706)
PHONE..................................925 828-6160
Michael Burdeny, *President*
Jonathon Aclin, *President*
Tod Ditto, *President*
John Hvizda, *President*
Stanford Alan Maag, *CFO*
▼ EMP: 57
SQ FT: 8,500
SALES: 335.3MM
SALES (corp-wide): 3.3B **Privately Held**
WEB: www.challengedairy.com
SIC: 5143 5149 Butter; milk, canned or dried
PA: California Dairies, Inc.
2000 N Plaza Dr
Visalia CA 93291
559 625-2200

(P-9336)
CIRCUS ICE CREAM
345 N Montgomery St, San Jose (95110-2326)
PHONE..................................408 977-1134
Jose Alvardo, *Principal*
EMP: 15 EST: 2007
SALES (est): 135.5K **Privately Held**
SIC: 5812 5143 2024 Ice cream stands or dairy bars; frozen dairy desserts; ice cream & frozen desserts

(P-9337)
DREYERS GRND ICE CREAM HLDNGS (DH)
5929 College Ave, Oakland (94618-1325)
PHONE..................................510 652-8187
Michael T Mitchell, *CEO*
Steve Barbour, *CFO*
Sherri Bjelka, *Officer*
Darin Perry, *Vice Pres*
Suzanne Saltzman, *Principal*
◆ EMP: 230 EST: 2002
SQ FT: 64,000
SALES (est): 1.3B
SALES (corp-wide): 177.9K **Privately Held**
WEB: www.nestleusa.com
SIC: 5143 5451 2024 Frozen dairy desserts; ice cream (packaged); ice cream & frozen desserts
HQ: Froneri International Limited
Leeming Lane Industrial Estate Leeming Bar
Northallerton
167 742-3397

(P-9338)
FOSTER DAIRY FARMS (PA)
Also Called: Crystal Creamery
529 Kansas Ave, Modesto (95351-1515)
PHONE..................................209 576-3400
Dennis Roberts, *President*
Mark Shaw, *CFO*
Steve Brownfield, *Foreman/Supr*
Manuel Machado, *Foreman/Supr*
Elijah Walker, *Manager*
▼ EMP: 800 EST: 1958
SALES (est): 374.1MM **Privately Held**
WEB: www.crystalcreamery.com
SIC: 5143 2026 Dairy products, except dried or canned; fluid milk

(P-9339)
FOSTER DAIRY PRODUCTS DISTRG (PA)
529 Kansas Ave, Modesto (95351-1515)
PHONE..................................209 576-3400
Jeff Foster, *President*
EMP: 25 EST: 1951
SALES (est): 35.3MM **Privately Held**
SIC: 5143 2026 Dairy products, except dried or canned; fluid milk

(P-9340)
HDP ENTERPRISES INC
Also Called: Mike Hudson Distributing
2237 S Mcdowell Blvd Ext, Petaluma (94954-5661)
P.O. Box 6010 (94955-6010)
PHONE..................................707 763-7388
George R Parisi, *CEO*
Frank Haynes, *Exec VP*
James Davis, *Project Mgr*
Chuck Barbee, *Regional Mgr*
Jim Beels, *Regional Mgr*
◆ EMP: 48 EST: 2000
SQ FT: 55,000
SALES (est): 26.9MM **Privately Held**
WEB: www.mikehudsondist.com
SIC: 5143 5147 5113 Cheese; meats, cured or smoked; disposable plates, cups, napkins & eating utensils
PA: Mike Hudson Distributing, Inc.
1297 Dynamic St
Petaluma CA 94954
707 763-7388

(P-9341)
PACIFIC CHEESE CO INC (PA)
21090 Cabot Blvd, Hayward (94545-1110)
P.O. Box 56598 (94545-6598)
PHONE..................................510 784-8800
Stephen B Gaddis, *President*
Dale Tate, *CFO*
June M Gaddis, *Corp Secy*
Brian Santos, *MIS Mgr*
Diana Rivera, *Analyst*
◆ EMP: 229 EST: 1966
SQ FT: 107,000
SALES (est): 1B **Privately Held**
WEB: www.pacificcheese.com
SIC: 5143 Cheese

(P-9342)
TONYS FINE FOODS (HQ)
3575 Reed Ave, West Sacramento (95605-1628)
P.O. Box 1501, Broderick (95605-0698)
PHONE..................................916 374-4000
Karl Berger, *President*
Steve Dietz, *Vice Pres*
Tom McMurtrey, *Vice Pres*
Tom Baiocchi, *Project Mgr*
David Nasater, *Technology*
▲ EMP: 390 EST: 1934
SQ FT: 143,000
SALES (est): 414.4MM **Publicly Held**
WEB: www.unfifresh.com
SIC: 5143 5149 Cheese; groceries & related products

(P-9343)
YOLO ICE & CREAMERY INC
1462 Churchill Downs Ave, Woodland (95776-6113)
PHONE..................................530 662-7337
David J Molinaro, *CEO*
EMP: 17 EST: 1960
SQ FT: 2,500
SALES (est): 6.1MM **Privately Held**
WEB: www.yoloiceandcreamery.com
SIC: 5143 2097 Dairy products, except dried or canned; manufactured ice

5144 Poultry & Poultry Prdts Wholesale

(P-9344)
3STONEDEGGS INC
Also Called: California Sandwich Company
840 Embarcadero Dr Ste 40, West Sacramento (95605-1509)
PHONE..................................541 225-7491
Michael Rose, *President*
Jesse Rice, *Managing Prtnr*

EMP: 40 EST: 2018
SALES (est): 4.3MM **Privately Held**
SIC: 5144 Eggs

(P-9345)
CHEVRON STATIONS INC
755 S Tracy Blvd, Tracy (95376-4753)
PHONE..................................209 830-0370
Kathy Carter, *Manager*
EMP: 133
SALES (corp-wide): 94.6B **Publicly Held**
WEB: www.chevron.com
SIC: 5541 5144 Filling stations, gasoline; poultry & poultry products
HQ: Chevron Stations, Inc.
6001 Bollinger Canyon Rd
San Ramon CA 94583
925 842-1000

(P-9346)
CHEVRON STATIONS INC
18060 San Ramon Vly Blvd, San Ramon (94583-4405)
PHONE..................................925 328-0292
Mark Howard, *Manager*
EMP: 133
SQ FT: 4,250
SALES (corp-wide): 94.6B **Publicly Held**
WEB: www.chevron.com
SIC: 5541 5144 Filling stations, gasoline; poultry & poultry products
HQ: Chevron Stations, Inc.
6001 Bollinger Canyon Rd
San Ramon CA 94583
925 842-1000

(P-9347)
LEHAR SALES CO
477 Forbes Blvd, South San Francisco (94080-2017)
PHONE..................................510 465-3255
Harold J De Luca, *CEO*
Rick Charles, *President*
Hariette Young, *Treasurer*
Tarry Winfrey, *Vice Pres*
Claire Venturini, *Admin Sec*
EMP: 65 EST: 1949
SALES (est): 3.4MM
SALES (corp-wide): 43.1MM **Privately Held**
WEB: www.pacagri.com
SIC: 5144 Poultry: live, dressed or frozen (unpackaged); poultry products
PA: Pacific Agri-Products, Inc.
477 Forbes Blvd
South San Francisco CA 94080
650 873-0440

(P-9348)
MODESTO FOOD DISTRIBUTORS INC
7601 El Camino Real, Colma (94014-3107)
PHONE..................................650 756-3603
John Granahan, *President*
Gray Kael, *Vice Pres*
David Granahan, *Admin Sec*
EMP: 35 EST: 1972
SQ FT: 7,000
SALES (est): 8.3MM **Privately Held**
WEB: www.modestofood.com
SIC: 5144 5149 Poultry products; specialty food items

(P-9349)
NULAID FOODS INC (PA)
200 W 5th St, Ripon (95366-2793)
PHONE..................................209 599-2121
David K Crockett, *President*
Scott Hennecke, *CFO*
Kari Bohannan, *Cust Mgr*
Sonja Murray, *Director*
Jim Vangorkom, *Manager*
EMP: 79 EST: 1963
SQ FT: 5,000
SALES (est): 26.1MM **Privately Held**
WEB: www.nulaid.com
SIC: 5144 2047 2015 2023 Eggs; eggs: cleaning, oil treating, packing & grading; dog food; egg processing; cream substitutes

(P-9350)
RACE STREET PARTNERS INC (PA)
967 W Hedding St, San Jose (95126-1257)
PHONE..................................408 294-6161

▲ = Import ▼=Export
◆ =Import/Export

PRODUCTS & SERVICES SECTION

5146 - Fish & Seafood Wholesale County (P-9374)

Gino Barsanti, *Chairman*
Michael Barsanti, *Corp Secy*
Dan Barsanti, *Vice Pres*
David Riparbelli, *Vice Pres*
James Riparbelli, *Vice Pres*
EMP: 80 **EST:** 1946
SQ FT: 63,000
SALES (est): 20.5MM Privately Held
WEB: www.racestreetpartners.com
SIC: 5144 5146 5147 5142 Poultry & poultry products; fish & seafoods; meats & meat products; packaged frozen goods; frozen fish, meat & poultry

(P-9351)
ROCKY MOUNTAIN EGGS INC
720 S Stockton Ave, Ripon (95366-2790)
PHONE 209 254-2200
Charles Elste, *President*
Joseph Le Bel, *Warehouse Mgr*
EMP: 35 **EST:** 2001
SQ FT: 1,500
SALES (est): 8.2MM Privately Held
WEB: www.rockymountaineggs.com
SIC: 5144 Eggs

(P-9352)
SQUAB PRODUCERS CALIF INC
409 Primo Way, Modesto (95358-5721)
PHONE 209 537-4744
Robert Shipley, *President*
EMP: 55 **EST:** 1943
SQ FT: 11,000
SALES (est): 14MM Privately Held
WEB: www.squab.com
SIC: 5144 2015 Poultry: live, dressed or frozen (unpackaged); poultry slaughtering & processing

(P-9353)
SUNRISE FARMS LLC
395 Liberty Rd, Petaluma (94952-8104)
PHONE 707 778-6450
James Carlson, *Manager*
Larry Johnson,
Al Nissen,
Arnold Rieb li,
Richard Weber,
▲ **EMP:** 65 **EST:** 1966
SQ FT: 10,000
SALES (est): 14MM Privately Held
SIC: 5144 2015 Eggs: cleaning, oil treating, packing & grading; poultry slaughtering & processing

5145 Confectionery Wholesale

(P-9354)
GOURMET PLUS INC
Also Called: Thatcher's Gourmet Popcorn
1201 Minnesota St, San Francisco (94107-3407)
PHONE 415 643-9945
Abrahim Aboukhalil, *President*
◆ **EMP:** 42 **EST:** 1983
SQ FT: 20,000
SALES: 5.1MM Privately Held
WEB: www.tgsp.com
SIC: 5145 5441 2064 Popcorn & supplies; popcorn, including caramel corn; breakfast bars

(P-9355)
INSIGNIA CAPITAL PARTNERS LP (PA)
1333 N Calif Blvd Ste 520, Walnut Creek (94596-4543)
PHONE 925 399-8900
Dave Lowe, *Managing Prtnr*
Saaheb Sidana, *Associate*
EMP: 70 **EST:** 2013
SALES (est): 177.6MM Privately Held
WEB: www.insigniacap.com
SIC: 5145 2064 Nuts, salted or roasted; nuts, candy covered

(P-9356)
R W GARCIA CO INC (PA)
100 Enterprise Way C230, Scotts Valley (95066-3274)
P.O. Box 8290, San Jose (95155-8290)
PHONE 408 287-4616
Robert W Garcia, *President*

Margaret Garcia, *Vice Pres*
Janette Rosales, *Office Mgr*
Allan Perkins, *Plant Mgr*
Cody Howell, *QC Mgr*
◆ **EMP:** 50 **EST:** 1981
SQ FT: 30,000
SALES (est): 61.2MM Privately Held
WEB: www.rwgarcia.com
SIC: 5145 2096 2099 Snack foods; tortilla chips; food preparations

(P-9357)
TREE NUTS LLC
451 W F St, Turlock (95380-6079)
P.O. Box 1009 (95381-1009)
PHONE 209 669-6400
Steve Warda,
◆ **EMP:** 40 **EST:** 2008
SQ FT: 50,000 Privately Held
SIC: 5145 2068 Nuts, salted or roasted; salted & roasted nuts & seeds

5146 Fish & Seafood Wholesale

(P-9358)
ALOHA SEAFOOD INC
Shed D6 Pier 45, San Francisco (94133)
PHONE 415 441-4484
Michael Willing, *CEO*
Mitch Gronner, *Vice Pres*
EMP: 43
SQ FT: 3,500
SALES (est): 15MM Privately Held
WEB: www.alohaseafood.net
SIC: 5146 Seafoods

(P-9359)
BAY AREA SEAFOOD INC (PA)
30248 Santucci Ct, Hayward (94544-7100)
PHONE 510 475-7100
Marisela Lisa Duran, *CEO*
EMP: 44 **EST:** 2009
SALES (est): 22.2MM Privately Held
WEB: www.bayarea-seafood.com
SIC: 5146 Seafoods

(P-9360)
BLUE RIVER SEAFOOD INC
Also Called: Joe Pucci & Sons Seafoods
25447 Industrial Blvd, Hayward (94545-2931)
PHONE 510 300-6800
Chris Lam, *CEO*
Sean Nguyen, *General Mgr*
Chuck Scharmann, *General Mgr*
Colleen Laa, *Buyer*
Ana Santiago, *Supervisor*
▲ **EMP:** 53 **EST:** 1918
SQ FT: 53,000
SALES (est): 27.7MM Privately Held
WEB: www.puccifoods.com
SIC: 5146 2092 Fish, fresh; fish, frozen, unpackaged; fresh or frozen packaged fish

(P-9361)
CAITO FISHERIES INC (PA)
19400 Harbor Ave, Fort Bragg (95437-5615)
P.O. Box 1370 (95437-1370)
PHONE 707 964-6368
Joseph A Caito, *CEO*
James G Caito, *Vice Pres*
EMP: 73 **EST:** 1975
SQ FT: 10,000
SALES (est): 23.4MM Privately Held
WEB: www.caitofisheries.com
SIC: 5146 Seafoods

(P-9362)
CAL SOUTHERN SEAFOOD INC (PA)
125 Salinas Rd Ste 5b, Royal Oaks (95076-6706)
P.O. Box 939, Los Olivos (93441-0939)
PHONE 805 698-8262
Pete J Guglielmo, *President*
Mike Salcedo, *Principal*
EMP: 82 **EST:** 2012
SALES (est): 9.3MM Privately Held
SIC: 5146 2092 Seafoods; seafoods, frozen: prepared

(P-9363)
CALIFORNIA SHELLFISH CO INC
Point St George Fisheries
1280 Columbus Ave 300r, San Francisco (94133-1302)
P.O. Box 1386, Santa Rosa (95402-1386)
PHONE 707 542-9490
Tony Delima, *Branch Mgr*
EMP: 175
SALES (corp-wide): 58MM Privately Held
SIC: 5146 Fish, fresh; fish, frozen, unpackaged
PA: California Shellfish Company, Inc.
 818 E Broadway C
 San Gabriel CA 91776
 415 923-7400

(P-9364)
CENTRAL FISH INC
1535 Kern St, Fresno (93706-3382)
PHONE 559 237-2049
Ernest Doizaki, *CEO*
EMP: 55 **EST:** 2020
SALES (est): 6.4MM Privately Held
WEB: www.centralfish.com
SIC: 5146 Seafoods

(P-9365)
EXCLUSIVE FRESH INC
165 Airport St, El Granada (94018-8044)
P.O. Box 308 (94018-0308)
PHONE 650 728-7321
Philip Bruno, *CEO*
Margie Macdougall, *Corp Secy*
Greg Hampton, *Vice Pres*
EMP: 26 **EST:** 1993
SQ FT: 12,000
SALES (est): 11MM Privately Held
WEB: www.exclusivefresh.com
SIC: 5146 2092 Seafoods; fresh or frozen packaged fish

(P-9366)
FISH MKT RSTRANTS- SAN JOSE LP
Also Called: San Mateo Fish Market
1855 S Norfolk St, San Mateo (94403-1155)
PHONE 650 349-3474
Simon Johnson, *Manager*
Aire Hjelle, *Human Resources*
EMP: 75
SALES (corp-wide): 8.9MM Privately Held
WEB: www.thefishmarket.com
SIC: 5812 5146 5813 5421 Seafood restaurants; fish & seafoods; drinking places; meat & fish markets
PA: Fish Market Restaurants- San Jose, L.P.
 1 Tuna Ln Ste 3
 San Diego CA 92101
 619 232-8862

(P-9367)
LUSAMERICA FOODS INC (PA)
16480 Railroad Ave, Morgan Hill (95037-5210)
PHONE 408 778-7200
Fernando Luis Frederico, *CEO*
Ana Frederico, *Vice Pres*
Anna Frederico, *Vice Pres*
Jose Hernandez, *General Mgr*
Jacob Salas, *IT/INT Sup*
▲ **EMP:** 128 **EST:** 1976
SQ FT: 40,000
SALES (est): 84.3MM Privately Held
WEB: www.lusamerica.com
SIC: 5146 5142 Fish, fresh; packaged frozen goods

(P-9368)
PACIFIC HARVEST SEAFOODS INC
Also Called: Pacific Harvest Trading
800 Salinas Rd, San Juan Bautista (95045-9788)
P.O. Box 788 (95045-0788)
PHONE 408 295-2455
Michael Litchko, *President*
Rhonda Simon, *Treasurer*
David Dewitt, *Opers Staff*
Robert Bragg, *Production*
EMP: 40 **EST:** 1974

SQ FT: 22,000
SALES (est): 11.4MM Privately Held
WEB: www.pacificharvestseafoods.com
SIC: 5146 Seafoods

(P-9369)
SJ DISTRIBUTORS INC (PA)
625 Vista Way, Milpitas (95035-5433)
PHONE 888 988-2328
Scott Chun Ho Suen, *CEO*
Jerry Yeung, *CFO*
Jenny Lin, *Admin Sec*
EMP: 71
SQ FT: 60,000
SALES (est): 266.9MM Privately Held
WEB: www.sjfood.com
SIC: 5146 5149 5148 5142 Seafoods; canned goods: fruit, vegetables, seafood, meats, etc.; fresh fruits & vegetables; meat, frozen: packaged

(P-9370)
SSC INC (HQ)
Also Called: Sunnyvale Seafood
2910 Faber St, Union City (94587-1214)
PHONE 510 477-0008
Jeff Sedacca, *CEO*
James Dimino, *Vice Pres*
Tracy Ha, *Accounting Mgr*
Wendy Jin, *Controller*
Steven Zhou, *Opers Mgr*
▲ **EMP:** 66 **EST:** 1983
SQ FT: 74,000
SALES (est): 52.5MM Privately Held
WEB: www.sunnyvaleseafood.com
SIC: 5146 5147 Seafoods; meats, fresh

(P-9371)
STAGNARO BROTHERS SEAFOOD INC
320 Washington St, Santa Cruz (95060-4929)
PHONE 831 423-1188
Giovanni Stagnaro, *Ch of Bd*
Robert Tara, *President*
Virginia Stagnaro, *Treasurer*
Ernest M Stagnaro, *Vice Ch Bd*
Robert Mc Pherson, *Vice Pres*
EMP: 73 **EST:** 1937
SQ FT: 12,000
SALES (est): 19.6MM Privately Held
WEB: www.stagnarobrothers.com
SIC: 5146 5812 5421 Seafoods; seafood restaurants; seafood markets

(P-9372)
TRUE WRLD FODS SAN FRNCSCO LLC
1815 Williams St, San Leandro (94577-2301)
PHONE 510 352-8140
Shinryo Shimada, *Mng Member*
Makoto Kikuchi,
David Miller,
◆ **EMP:** 62 **EST:** 1978
SQ FT: 27,000
SALES (est): 33.8MM
SALES (corp-wide): 1.2B Privately Held
WEB: www.trueworldfoods.com
SIC: 5146 Seafoods
HQ: True World Holdings Llc
 24 Link Dr Unit D
 Rockleigh NJ 07647
 201 750-0024

(P-9373)
VINCES SHELLFISH CO INC
1063 Montgomery Ave, San Bruno (94066-1517)
P.O. Box 326 (94066-0326)
PHONE 650 589-5385
Christopher Svedise, *CEO*
Vincent Svedise, *President*
Vince Svedise, *Sales Staff*
Tim Wieland, *Manager*
▲ **EMP:** 35 **EST:** 1973
SQ FT: 5,500
SALES (est): 8.6MM Privately Held
WEB: www.vincesshellfish.com
SIC: 5146 Fish, fresh; seafoods

(P-9374)
WILD PLANET FOODS INC (DH)
1585 Heartwood Dr Ste F, McKinleyville (95519-3993)
PHONE 707 840-9116

5147 - Meats & Meat Prdts Wholesale County (P-9375) — PRODUCTS & SERVICES SECTION

Terry Hunt, *CEO*
William Carvalho, *President*
William D Walters, *CFO*
Bill McCarthy, *Vice Pres*
Karen McDonald, *Vice Pres*
◆ **EMP:** 54 **EST:** 2004
SALES (est): 36.8MM
SALES (corp-wide): 177.4K **Privately Held**
WEB: www.wildplanetfoods.com
SIC: 5146 Seafoods
HQ: Bolton Group Srl
   Via Giovanni Battista Pirelli 0019
   Milano MI 20124
   026 775-04

5147 Meats & Meat Prdts Wholesale

(P-9375) BASSIAN FARMS INC
4051 Seaport Blvd, West Sacramento (95691-3416)
P.O. Box 21160, San Jose (95151-1160)
PHONE 408 286-6262
Daniel Bassian, *President*
Lee Bassian, *Vice Pres*
EMP: 35 **EST:** 1990
SALES (est): 14.7MM **Publicly Held**
WEB: www.bassianfarms.com
SIC: 5147 5142 Meats, fresh; meat, frozen: packaged
PA: The Chefs' Warehouse Inc
   100 E Ridge Rd
   Ridgefield CT 06877

(P-9376) CALVADA SALES COMPANY (PA)
450 Richards Blvd, Sacramento (95811-0220)
P.O. Box 13159 (95813-3159)
PHONE 916 441-6290
Thomas B Mackey, *President*
Laura Bent, *Office Mgr*
Thomas W Mackey, *Admin Sec*
Dan Johnson, *CIO*
Gustavo Aguiar, *Sales Staff*
EMP: 45
SQ FT: 20,000
SALES (est): 29.8MM **Privately Held**
WEB: www.calvadafoods.com
SIC: 5147 5144 5142 Meats, fresh; poultry products; meat, frozen: packaged

(P-9377) DUPONT MARKET INC (PA)
Also Called: Grimaud Farms
8612 Younger Creek Dr, Sacramento (95828-1022)
PHONE 510 562-3593
Fukming Chan, *CEO*
Howard Chan, *President*
EMP: 60 **EST:** 1977
SQ FT: 4,000
SALES (est): 12.8MM **Privately Held**
SIC: 5421 5147 5146 Fish markets; meat markets, including freezer provisioners; meats & meat products; fish & seafoods

(P-9378) GOLDEN GATE MEAT COMPANY INC (PA)
803 Wright Ave, Richmond (94804-3639)
PHONE 415 861-3800
Jim Offenbach, *Principal*
James Offenbach, *President*
Patricia Offenbach, *Vice Pres*
Justin Offenbach, *Human Res Mgr*
Jamie Lloyd, *Buyer*
EMP: 36 **EST:** 1990
SQ FT: 15,000
SALES (est): 25.2MM **Privately Held**
WEB: www.goldengatemeatcompany.com
SIC: 5147 5144 Meats, fresh; poultry & poultry products

(P-9379) RICHMOND WHOLESALE MEAT LLC (PA)
Also Called: Pro Foods Solutions
2920 Regatta Blvd, Richmond (94804-4528)
PHONE 510 233-5111
Richard Doellstedt, *President*
Alan Bell, *CFO*
Laura Steinebach, *CFO*
Carl Doellstedt, *Vice Pres*
John Doellstedt, *Principal*
◆ **EMP:** 55 **EST:** 1961
SQ FT: 100,000
SALES (est): 56.3MM **Privately Held**
WEB: www.richmondwholesale.com
SIC: 5147 Meats, fresh

(P-9380) SPECIALTY BRANDED PRODUCTS INC
Also Called: Ol' Smokey
523 N Brawley Ave, Fresno (93706-1015)
P.O. Box 11987 (93776-1987)
PHONE 559 222-8895
Rafael Russian, *CEO*
Sonya Stelfox, *Shareholder*
Shane Stelfox, *Treasurer*
Shelley Stelfox, *Admin Sec*
EMP: 45 **EST:** 1988
SQ FT: 18,000
SALES (est): 8MM **Privately Held**
WEB: www.flavorsotw.com
SIC: 5147 Meats, fresh; meats, cured or smoked

(P-9381) VOLUME SNACKS
Also Called: Derosa Sales
1948 Hays Ln, Woodland (95776-6216)
PHONE 530 662-3500
Denise O'Brien, *President*
Miguel Bran, *Vice Pres*
Chuck Harper, *Vice Pres*
Tracy Freeman, *Admin Sec*
Joseph Dibartolo, *Opers Mgr*
EMP: 40 **EST:** 1981
SQ FT: 70,000
SALES (est): 20.5MM **Privately Held**
SIC: 5147 5145 Meats, cured or smoked; nuts, salted or roasted

(P-9382) WEBERS QUALITY MEATS INC
Also Called: Butcher's Brand
990 Carden St, San Leandro (94577-1164)
PHONE 510 635-9892
Stefan Weber, *President*
Linda Weber, *Corp Secy*
EMP: 60 **EST:** 1979
SQ FT: 10,000
SALES (est): 26.9MM **Privately Held**
SIC: 5147 5142 Meats, fresh; meat, frozen: packaged

(P-9383) YOSEMITE FOODS INC
4221 E Mariposa Rd, Stockton (95215-8139)
PHONE 209 990-5400
Michael Lau, *Exec Dir*
EMP: 120 **EST:** 2016
SALES (est): 20.8MM **Privately Held**
SIC: 5147 Meats & meat products

(P-9384) YOSEMITE MEAT COMPANY INC
601 Zeff Rd, Modesto (95351-3942)
P.O. Box 31480, Stockton (95213-1480)
PHONE 209 524-5117
Johnnie F Lau, *President*
Gay Lau, *Vice Pres*
Yolanda White, *Human Res Dir*
Chance Reeder, *Plant Supt*
▲ **EMP:** 100 **EST:** 1974
SQ FT: 3,600
SALES (est): 25.4MM **Privately Held**
WEB: www.yosemitemeat.com
SIC: 5147 2013 Meats, fresh; bacon, side & sliced: from purchased meat

5148 Fresh Fruits & Vegetables Wholesale

(P-9385) 1ST QUALITY PRODUCE INC
2445 S Gearhart Ave, Fresno (93725-1300)
P.O. Box 2307 (93745-2307)
PHONE 559 442-1932
Michael Kahaian, *President*
Rita Kahaian, *Vice Pres*
Zack Anderson, *Controller*
Victor Wilcox, *Sales Staff*
James Valenzuela, *Manager*
EMP: 45 **EST:** 2004
SQ FT: 28,000
SALES (est): 23.9MM **Privately Held**
WEB: www.firstqualityproduce.com
SIC: 5148 Fruits, fresh

(P-9386) ANDRIGHETTO PRODUCE INC (PA)
Also Called: Shasta Produce Co
155 Terminal Ct 15-33, South San Francisco (94080-6532)
P.O. Box 2328 (94083-2328)
PHONE 650 588-0930
David Andrighetto, *CEO*
Peter Carcione, *President*
Steven Andrighetto, *CEO*
Steven Hurwitz, *Treasurer*
Domenic Andrighetto, *Vice Pres*
EMP: 104 **EST:** 1986
SQ FT: 10,000
SALES (est): 49.3MM **Privately Held**
WEB: www.shastaproduce.com
SIC: 5148 Fruits, fresh

(P-9387) ANDYS PRODUCE MARKET INC
1691 Gravenstein Hwy N, Sebastopol (95472-2610)
P.O. Box 870 (95473-0870)
PHONE 707 823-8661
Kathrin Skikos, *President*
EMP: 40 **EST:** 1962
SQ FT: 10,000
SALES (est): 12MM **Privately Held**
WEB: www.andysproduce.com
SIC: 5148 5431 6531 Fruits, fresh; fruit stands or markets; vegetable stands or markets; real estate agent, residential

(P-9388) BAY AREA HERBS & SPC LLC
Also Called: American Herbs & Specialties
155 Terminal Ct Ste G, South San Francisco (94080-6525)
P.O. Box 1968 (94083-1968)
PHONE 650 583-0857
Steve Hurwitz,
Tom Maag,
EMP: 41 **EST:** 1989
SALES (est): 16.1MM **Privately Held**
WEB: www.bayareaherbs.com
SIC: 5148 Fruits, fresh

(P-9389) CALIFORNIA FRUIT EXCHANGE LLC (PA)
Also Called: Farmstead Gourmet
6011 E Pine St, Lodi (95240-0815)
P.O. Box 1264 (95241-1264)
PHONE 209 334-2988
Paul Marchand,
Suzanne Hernandez, *Mktg Dir*
Chiles Wilson Jr,
▲ **EMP:** 150 **EST:** 2008
SQ FT: 47,200
SALES (est): 57.2MM **Privately Held**
SIC: 5148 5499 Fruits; food gift baskets

(P-9390) CALIFORNIA VEGETABLE SPC INC
Also Called: California Endive Farm
15 Poppy House Rd, Rio Vista (94571-1201)
P.O. Box 638 (94571-0638)
PHONE 707 374-2111
Alexandre Pierron-Darbonne, *CEO*
Richard Collins, *President*
Luc Darbonne, *CEO*
Jose Arias, *Vice Pres*
David Moen, *Sales Staff*
▲ **EMP:** 70 **EST:** 1987
SQ FT: 11,000
SALES (est): 22.2MM **Privately Held**
WEB: www.endive.com
SIC: 5148 Fresh fruits & vegetables

(P-9391) CAPAY INCORPORATED (PA)
Also Called: Capay Fruits and Vegetables
3880 Seaport Blvd, West Sacramento (95691-3449)
PHONE 530 796-0730
Thaddeus Barsotti, *CEO*
Noah Barnes, *President*
Moyra Barsotti, *Admin Sec*
Greg Novak, *Sales Staff*
Kianna Small, *Accounts Mgr*
EMP: 98 **EST:** 1979
SALES (est): 41.8MM **Privately Held**
WEB: www.capayorganic.com
SIC: 5148 Fresh fruits & vegetables

(P-9392) CECELIA PACKING CORPORATION
24780 E South Ave, Orange Cove (93646-9426)
PHONE 559 626-5000
James J Cotter, *CEO*
David G Roth, *President*
Karen Vargas, *Controller*
Randy Jacobson, *Sales Staff*
◆ **EMP:** 130 **EST:** 1937
SQ FT: 55,000
SALES (est): 29.5MM **Privately Held**
WEB: www.ceceliapack.com
SIC: 5148 Fresh fruits & vegetables

(P-9393) CHICO PRODUCE INC (PA)
Also Called: Pro Pacific Fresh
70 Pepsi Way, Durham (95938-9798)
P.O. Box 1069 (95938-1069)
PHONE 530 893-0596
Terry Richardson, *CEO*
Bruce Parks, *Ch of Bd*
Tony Fierro, *Database Admin*
Ron Ulrici, *Human Res Dir*
Jamar Carter, *Buyer*
▼ **EMP:** 141 **EST:** 1983
SQ FT: 70,000
SALES (est): 72.6MM **Privately Held**
WEB: www.ppf-foods.com
SIC: 5148 5149 Fruits, fresh; dried or canned foods

(P-9394) CHICO PRODUCE INC
Also Called: Redding Produce
70 Pepsi Way, Durham (95938-9798)
PHONE 530 241-1124
Bill Patchen, *Manager*
Larry Maligie, *Info Tech Dir*
Tony Knight, *VP Sales*
Melinda Bowers, *Manager*
EMP: 36
SALES (corp-wide): 72.6MM **Privately Held**
WEB: www.ppf-foods.com
SIC: 5148 Fruits, fresh; vegetables
PA: Chico Produce, Inc.
   70 Pepsi Way
   Durham CA 95938
   530 893-0596

(P-9395) COAST CITRUS DISTRIBUTORS
Also Called: Coast Tropical
2885 Volpey Way, Union City (94587-1244)
PHONE 213 955-3448
Jim Alvarez, *President*
EMP: 40
SQ FT: 10,000
SALES (corp-wide): 335.5MM **Privately Held**
WEB: www.coasttropical.com
SIC: 5148 Fruits, fresh
PA: Coast Citrus Distributors
   7597 Bristow Ct
   San Diego CA 92154
   619 661-7950

PRODUCTS & SERVICES SECTION
5148 - Fresh Fruits & Vegetables Wholesale County (P-9418)

(P-9396)
CUSTOM PRODUCE SALES (PA)
13475 E Progress Dr, Parlier (93648-9674)
P.O. Box 977, Kingsburg (93631-0977)
PHONE..............................559 254-5800
Marvin Farris, *CEO*
Vanessa Biggs, *Sales Staff*
Lorena Luna, *Sales Staff*
▲ **EMP:** 180 **EST:** 1995
SALES (est): 33.8MM **Privately Held**
SIC: 5148 Fruits, fresh

(P-9397)
DAYLIGHT FOODS INC
30200 Whipple Rd, Union City (94587-1524)
PHONE..............................510 931-4207
Chris Vlahopouliotis, *President*
Robert Tantillo, *Exec VP*
Paul Jennings, *Vice Pres*
Bob Kaspereen, *Vice Pres*
Sheila Chandy, *Analyst*
▲ **EMP:** 120 **EST:** 2003
SALES (est): 50MM **Privately Held**
WEB: www.daylightfoods.com
SIC: 5148 Fruits, fresh; vegetables, fresh

(P-9398)
DRISCOLLS INC (PA)
345 Westridge Dr, Watsonville (95076-4169)
P.O. Box 50045 (95077-5045)
PHONE..............................831 424-0506
Miles Reiter, *CEO*
Joseph Miles Reiter, *Ch of Bd*
Sean Martin, *CFO*
Elly Hoever, *Treasurer*
Jerry D'Amore, *Vice Pres*
◆ **EMP:** 60 **EST:** 1953
SQ FT: 19,932
SALES (est): 454.8MM **Privately Held**
WEB: www.driscolls.com
SIC: 5148 5431 Fruits, fresh; fruit & vegetable markets

(P-9399)
DRISCOLLS INC
150 Westridge Dr, Watsonville (95076-6709)
PHONE..............................800 871-3333
Ivyenna Davis, *Internal Med*
Shannon Corbin, *Director*
Dan McClure, *Manager*
EMP: 75
SALES (corp-wide): 454.8MM **Privately Held**
WEB: www.driscolls.com
SIC: 5148 Fruits, fresh
PA: Driscoll's, Inc.
345 Westridge Dr
Watsonville CA 95076
831 424-0506

(P-9400)
EARLS ORGANIC
Also Called: Earl's Organic Produce
2101 Jerrold Ave Ste 100, San Francisco (94124-1009)
PHONE..............................415 824-7419
Earl Herrick, *Principal*
Juan Gamino, *Officer*
Jose Cruz, *Administration*
Michele Smith-Jefferies, *Administration*
Kat Vining, *Human Res Dir*
▲ **EMP:** 78
SALES (est): 50MM **Privately Held**
WEB: www.earlsorganic.com
SIC: 5148 Fresh fruits & vegetables

(P-9401)
FAMILY TREE FARMS MKTG LLC
41646 Road 62, Reedley (93654-9124)
P.O. Box 396, Dinuba (93618-0396)
PHONE..............................559 591-6280
David Jackson, *Mng Member*
Andrew Muxlow,
EMP: 50 **EST:** 2002
SALES (est): 1.2MM **Privately Held**
WEB: www.familytreefarms.com
SIC: 5148 Fruits, fresh

(P-9402)
FIELD FRESH FARMS LLC
320 Industrial Rd, Watsonville (95076-5116)
P.O. Box 2731 (95077-2731)
PHONE..............................831 722-1422
Mike Dobler,
Paul Betancourt, *Controller*
Cary Lee, *Opers Staff*
Manny Diaz, *Sales Staff*
Craig Dobler,
EMP: 80
SQ FT: 66,000
SALES (est): 49MM **Privately Held**
WEB: www.fieldfreshproduce.com
SIC: 5148 Fruits, fresh

(P-9403)
FRESH INNOVATIONS CAL LLC
7735 S Highway 99, Stockton (95215-9623)
PHONE..............................209 983-9700
Timothy Stejskal, *CEO*
Richard Turner, *CFO*
Todd Nelson, *Branch Mgr*
EMP: 135 **EST:** 2006
SALES (est): 25.4MM **Privately Held**
WEB: www.fresh-innovations.com
SIC: 5148 Fruits

(P-9404)
FRESHKO PRODUCE SERVICES INC
2155 E Muscat Ave, Fresno (93725-2326)
P.O. Box 11097 (93771-1097)
PHONE..............................559 497-7000
Manny Robles, *Principal*
Randall Shepherd, *Principal*
EMP: 142 **EST:** 2002
SQ FT: 47,000
SALES (est): 49.7K
SALES (corp-wide): 5.9MM **Privately Held**
WEB: www.freshkoproduce.com
SIC: 5148 5499 Fruits, fresh; juices, fruit or vegetable
PA: C&S Wholesale Grocers, Inc.
7 Corporate Dr
Keene NH 03431
603 354-7000

(P-9405)
FRESHPOINT CENTRAL CALIFORNIA
5900 N Golden State Blvd, Turlock (95382-9671)
PHONE..............................209 216-0200
Brian M Sturgeon, *President*
Jeffrey A Sacchini, *CEO*
EMP: 150 **EST:** 2000
SQ FT: 54,000
SALES (est): 55.8MM
SALES (corp-wide): 52.8B **Publicly Held**
WEB: www.freshpoint.com
SIC: 5148 Fresh fruits & vegetables
HQ: Freshpoint, Inc.
1390 Enclave Pkwy
Houston TX 77077

(P-9406)
FRESNO PRODUCE INC
1415 B St, Fresno (93706-1917)
P.O. Box 12204 (93776-2204)
PHONE..............................559 495-0143
Sean Leer, *CEO*
Laura Miller, *Vice Pres*
Jason Davis, *General Mgr*
Gabe Martinez, *Sales Associate*
Carol Benke, *Manager*
EMP: 40 **EST:** 1990
SQ FT: 18,000
SALES (est): 15MM
SALES (corp-wide): 86MM **Privately Held**
WEB: www.fresnoproduce.com
SIC: 5148 Fruits, fresh
PA: Gs Foods Group
11755 Wilshire Blvd # 14
Los Angeles CA
310 806-9780

(P-9407)
GALLI PRODUCE COMPANY
1650 Old Bayshore Hwy, San Jose (95112-4304)
PHONE..............................408 436-6100
Gerald Pieracci, *President*
Kristin Killin, *Corp Secy*
Jeff Pieracci, *Vice Pres*
Dennis Tinucci, *Vice Pres*
Joseph Vanni, *Vice Pres*
EMP: 60 **EST:** 1950
SQ FT: 10,000
SALES (est): 19.7MM **Privately Held**
WEB: www.galliproduce.com
SIC: 5148 5142 Fruits, fresh; vegetables, fresh; fruits, frozen; vegetables, frozen

(P-9408)
GAZZALIS SUPERMARKET INC
7000 Bancroft Ave, Oakland (94605-2404)
PHONE..............................510 569-8159
Abdo S Algazzali, *President*
Amani Algazzali, *Admin Sec*
EMP: 50 **EST:** 2003
SALES (est): 6.7MM **Privately Held**
WEB: www.gazzalis.com
SIC: 5411 5148 5147 Grocery stores, independent; fresh fruits & vegetables; meats, fresh

(P-9409)
GENERAL PROD A CAL LTD PARTNR (PA)
1330 N B St, Sacramento (95811-0605)
P.O. Box 308 (95812-0308)
PHONE..............................916 441-6431
Jeff Sacchini, *CEO*
Dan Chan, *President*
Tony Calleja, *CFO*
Don Weersing, *Vice Pres*
Sheryl Weichert, *Vice Pres*
◆ **EMP:** 200 **EST:** 1933
SQ FT: 110,000
SALES (est): 80.1MM **Privately Held**
WEB: www.generalproduce.com
SIC: 5148 Fruits, fresh; vegetables, fresh

(P-9410)
HERMAN PRODUCE SALES LLC
2370 W Cleveland Ave # 108, Madera (93637-8742)
PHONE..............................559 661-8253
EMP: 75
SALES (corp-wide): 500K **Privately Held**
SIC: 5431 5148 Fruit & vegetable markets; fresh fruits & vegetables
PA: Herman Produce Sales Llc
2985 Airport Dr
Madera CA 93637
559 871-3161

(P-9411)
HERMAN PRODUCE SALES LLC (PA)
2985 Airport Dr, Madera (93637-9288)
PHONE..............................559 871-3161
Erik L Herman,
EMP: 35 **EST:** 2017
SALES (est): 500K **Privately Held**
SIC: 5431 5148 Fruit & vegetable markets; fresh fruits & vegetables

(P-9412)
KINGSBURG APPLE PACKERS INC
Also Called: Kingsburg Orchards
10363 Davis Ave, Kingsburg (93631-9539)
P.O. Box 38 (93631-0038)
PHONE..............................559 897-5132
George H Jackson, *President*
Colleen Jackson, *Corp Secy*
Becky Stark, *Controller*
Brian Keavy, *Export Mgr*
Ken Okajima, *Marketing Staff*
◆ **EMP:** 450 **EST:** 1984
SQ FT: 10,000
SALES (est): 44MM **Privately Held**
WEB: www.kingsburgorchards.com
SIC: 5148 Fruits, fresh

(P-9413)
KINGSBURG ORCHARDS
10363 Davis Ave, Kingsburg (93631-9539)
P.O. Box 38 (93631-0038)
PHONE..............................559 897-2986
Michael Jackson, *President*
Chad Allred, *President*
Rachel Flores, *Finance Mgr*
Michael Elwinger, *Marketing Mgr*
Charlie Airoza, *Marketing Staff*
◆ **EMP:** 58 **EST:** 2011
SALES (est): 23.8MM **Privately Held**
WEB: www.kingsburgorchards.com
SIC: 5148 Fruits, fresh

(P-9414)
LIBERTY PACKING COMPANY LLC (PA)
Also Called: Morning Star Company The
724 Main St, Woodland (95695-3491)
PHONE..............................209 826-7100
Chris Rufer,
Ernesto De Loza, *Opers Staff*
▲ **EMP:** 22 **EST:** 2001
SALES (est): 102.8MM **Privately Held**
SIC: 5148 2033 Vegetables; tomato products: packaged in cans, jars, etc.

(P-9415)
LIVINGSTON FARMERS ASSOCIATION
11019 Eucalyptus Ave, Livingston (95334-9705)
PHONE..............................209 394-7941
Ted Kurooski, *Principal*
EMP: 41
SALES (corp-wide): 5.8MM **Privately Held**
SIC: 5148 Fresh fruits & vegetables
PA: Livingston Farmers Association
641 6th St
Livingston CA 95334
209 394-7941

(P-9416)
MARIPOSA NATURAL FOODS
Also Called: Mariposa Market
500 S Main St, Willits (95490-3910)
PHONE..............................707 459-9630
Mary Anne Roth Trevey, *President*
EMP: 35 **EST:** 1979
SQ FT: 300
SALES (est): 5.5MM **Privately Held**
WEB: www.mariposamarket.com
SIC: 5431 5148 Fruit stands or markets; vegetable stands or markets; fruits, fresh; vegetables, fresh

(P-9417)
MERCADO LATINO INC
2006 Jerrold Ave, San Francisco (94124-1605)
P.O. Box 6168, El Monte (91734-6168)
PHONE..............................415 282-5563
Roberto Rodriquez, *Manager*
EMP: 35
SALES (corp-wide): 87MM **Privately Held**
WEB: www.mercadolatinoinc.com
SIC: 5148 Vegetables, fresh
PA: Mercado Latino, Inc.
245 Baldwin Park Blvd
City Of Industry CA 91746
626 333-6862

(P-9418)
MOONLIGHT PACKING CORPORATION (PA)
Also Called: Moonlight Companies
17719 E Huntsman Ave, Reedley (93654-9205)
P.O. Box 846 (93654-0846)
PHONE..............................559 638-7799
Russell Tavlan, *President*
Tara Sondergaard, *CFO*
Ty Tavlan, *CFO*
Jim Jones, *Executive*
Jared Riley, *CTO*
EMP: 185 **EST:** 1992
SQ FT: 80,000
SALES (est): 443.1MM **Privately Held**
WEB: www.moonlightcompanies.com
SIC: 5148 4783 Fruits, fresh; packing & crating

5148 - Fresh Fruits & Vegetables Wholesale County (P-9419)

(P-9419)
MORADA PRODUCE COMPANY LP
500 N Jack Tone Rd, Stockton (95215-9725)
P.O. Box 659, Linden (95236-0659)
PHONE 209 546-0426
Henry Foppiano, *Partner*
Linda Jenkins, *Executive Asst*
Michael Van Breda, *Controller*
Ana Garibay, *Director*
Lance Kagehiro, *Manager*
◆ **EMP:** 1500 **EST:** 2003
SQ FT: 98,000
SALES (est): 221.8MM **Privately Held**
WEB: www.moradaproduce.com
SIC: 5148 Fresh fruits & vegetables

(P-9420)
NOR-CAL PRODUCE INC
2995 Oates St, West Sacramento (95691-5902)
P.O. Box 980188 (95798-0188)
PHONE 916 373-0830
Todd Achondo, *CEO*
▼ **EMP:** 130 **EST:** 1972
SQ FT: 85,000
SALES (est): 48.4MM **Publicly Held**
WEB: www.unfifresh.com
SIC: 5148 Fruits, fresh
PA: United Natural Foods, Inc.
313 Iron Horse Way
Providence RI 02908

(P-9421)
O G PACKING CO
Also Called: O-G Packing & Cold Storage Co
2097 Beyer Ln, Stockton (95215-2009)
PHONE 209 931-4392
Delano Gotelli, *CEO*
Denis Gogna, *Vice Pres*
Al J Gotelli, *Principal*
Faith Ellingsworth, *Opers Mgr*
Tom Gotelli, *Director*
◆ **EMP:** 35 **EST:** 1956
SQ FT: 200,000
SALES (est): 22.3MM **Privately Held**
WEB: www.growerdirect.net
SIC: 5148 Fruits, fresh

(P-9422)
OAKVILLE PRODUCE PARTNERS LLC
Also Called: Green Leaf Produce
453 Valley Dr, Brisbane (94005-1209)
PHONE 415 647-2991
William F Wilkinson, *Mng Member*
Frank Ballentine, *Vice Pres*
Alvin Padilla, *General Mgr*
Mark Natividad, *Controller*
Nick Salas, *Opers Mgr*
EMP: 150 **EST:** 1974
SQ FT: 32,000
SALES (est): 40.2MM **Privately Held**
SIC: 5148 5451 Fruits, fresh; vegetables, fresh; dairy products stores

(P-9423)
PERI & SONS FARMS CAL LLC (PA)
48845 W Nees Ave, Firebaugh (93622-9641)
P.O. Box 35, Yerington NV (89447-0035)
PHONE 775 463-4444
David J Peri,
▼ **EMP:** 35 **EST:** 2007
SALES (est): 8.8MM **Privately Held**
WEB: www.periandsons.com
SIC: 5148 Fresh fruits & vegetables

(P-9424)
PREMIER MUSHROOMS LP (PA)
2880 Niagara Ave, Colusa (95932)
PHONE 530 458-2700
John Ashbaugh, *Partner*
Rex Pugh, *CFO*
▲ **EMP:** 168 **EST:** 2006
SQ FT: 10,000
SALES (est): 33.3MM **Privately Held**
WEB: www.premiermushrooms.com
SIC: 5148 Fresh fruits & vegetables

(P-9425)
PRODUCE EXCHANGE INCORPORATED (DH)
7407 Southfront Rd, Livermore (94551-8224)
PHONE 925 454-8700
Marty Mazzanti, *Manager*
Samuel E Jones Jr, *President*
Martin Moreno, *Buyer*
Tami Weststeyn, *Buyer*
Alison Contois, *Sales Staff*
▲ **EMP:** 65 **EST:** 1980
SQ FT: 10,000
SALES (est): 10MM
SALES (corp-wide): 299.6MM **Privately Held**
WEB: www.tpeonline.com
SIC: 5148 Fruits, fresh
HQ: Lipman-Texas, Llc
11990 Shiloh Rd
Dallas TX 75228
214 367-6500

(P-9426)
READY PAC FOODS INC
125 Railroad Ave Ste 203, Danville (94526-3835)
PHONE 925 552-0400
EMP: 330
SALES (corp-wide): 2.6MM **Privately Held**
WEB: www.readypac.com
SIC: 5148 Fresh fruits & vegetables
HQ: Ready Pac Foods, Inc.
4401 Foxdale St
Irwindale CA 91706
626 856-8686

(P-9427)
ROHRER BROS INC
200 N 16th St Ste 600, Sacramento (95811-0697)
P.O. Box 731 (95812-0731)
PHONE 916 443-5921
Gary M Chipman, *CEO*
Jeff Granja, *Corp Secy*
▼ **EMP:** 35 **EST:** 1930
SQ FT: 28,000
SALES (est): 7.3MM **Privately Held**
WEB: www.rohrer-brothers-jobs.com
SIC: 5148 Fruits, fresh; vegetables, fresh

(P-9428)
SFFI COMPANY INC (PA)
Also Called: Simply Fresh Fruit
11020 White Rock Rd Ste 1, Rancho Cordova (95670-6402)
PHONE 323 586-0000
William T Sander, *President*
Bruce Spiro, *Vice Pres*
Jaxon Potter, *General Mgr*
Rafael Raya, *Purchasing*
Raul Moreno, *Plant Mgr*
▲ **EMP:** 174 **EST:** 1999
SALES (est): 30MM **Privately Held**
SIC: 5148 Fresh fruits & vegetables

(P-9429)
SIMPLY FRESH FRUIT INC
11020 White Rock Rd # 100, Rancho Cordova (95670-6402)
PHONE 323 586-0000
Gustavo Fernandez, *CEO*
William Sander, *President*
Jaxon Potter, *Vice Pres*
Bruce Spiro, *Vice Pres*
◆ **EMP:** 99 **EST:** 1983
SALES (est): 18.3MM
SALES (corp-wide): 30MM **Privately Held**
SIC: 5148 Fresh fruits & vegetables
PA: Sffi Company, Inc.
11020 White Rock Rd Ste 1
Rancho Cordova CA 95670
323 586-0000

(P-9430)
STANLEY PRODUCE CO INC
2088 Jerrold Ave, San Francisco (94124-1605)
PHONE 415 282-7510
Stanley Corriea Jr, *President*
Stanley A Corriea Sr, *CEO*
Oscar Martin, *Sales Staff*
EMP: 42 **EST:** 1941
SQ FT: 5,000
SALES (est): 4.9MM **Privately Held**
WEB: www.stanleyproduce.com
SIC: 5148 Fruits, fresh; vegetables, fresh

(P-9431)
STELLAR DISTRIBUTING INC
21801 Ave Ste 16, Madera (93637)
PHONE 559 664-8400
Paul Catania Jr, *President*
Robert Farnam, *CFO*
Lulu Cappelluti, *Officer*
Connie Gil, *Purchasing*
Kurt Cappelluti, *Manager*
◆ **EMP:** 350 **EST:** 1988
SQ FT: 30,000
SALES (est): 61.6MM **Privately Held**
WEB: www.cataniaworldwide.com
SIC: 5148 Vegetables, fresh; fruits, fresh

(P-9432)
SUNWEST FRUIT CO INC
755 E Manning Ave, Parlier (93648-2553)
PHONE 559 646-4000
Martin Britz, *President*
David Britz, *Vice Pres*
Bob Glassman, *Vice Pres*
Dean Thonesen, *Vice Pres*
McKenzie Dougherty, *Accountant*
◆ **EMP:** 40 **EST:** 1988
SQ FT: 40,000
SALES (est): 41.4MM
SALES (corp-wide): 104.2MM **Privately Held**
WEB: www.sunwestfruit.com
SIC: 5148 Fruits, fresh
PA: Britz, Inc.
3265 W Figarden Dr
Fresno CA 93711
559 448-8000

(P-9433)
TURLOCK FRUIT CO (PA)
500 S Tully Rd, Turlock (95380-5121)
P.O. Box 130 (95381-0130)
PHONE 209 634-7207
Donald J Smith, *President*
Stephen H Smith, *Admin Sec*
EMP: 41 **EST:** 1923
SQ FT: 1,500
SALES (est): 27.9MM **Privately Held**
WEB: www.turlockfruit.com
SIC: 5148 Fruits, fresh

(P-9434)
VEGIWORKS INC
6 Viewmont Ter, South San Francisco (94080-1570)
PHONE 415 643-8686
Shing Ho, *CFO*
Calvin Leong, *Vice Pres*
Phillip Woo, *Admin Sec*
Dale Forest, *Manager*
Christopher Hollins, *Manager*
EMP: 65 **EST:** 1992
SALES (est): 13.5MM **Privately Held**
WEB: www.vegiworks.com
SIC: 5148 Fresh fruits & vegetables

(P-9435)
VERITABLE VEGETABLE INC
1100 Cesar Chavez, San Francisco (94124-1214)
PHONE 415 641-3500
Maryjane Evans, *President*
Shira Tannor, *Officer*
Ruth Lalputan, *Administration*
Joshua Boneh, *Info Tech Mgr*
Keith Wall, *Business Mgr*
EMP: 57 **EST:** 1976
SQ FT: 8,000
SALES (est): 24.9MM **Privately Held**
WEB: www.veritablevegetable.com
SIC: 5148 Fruits, fresh

(P-9436)
WATSONVILLE COAST PRODUCE INC
275 Kearney Ext Frnt, Watsonville (95076-4463)
P.O. Box 490 (95077-0490)
PHONE 831 722-3851
Gary L Manfre, *CEO*
Douglas Peterson, *Treasurer*
John Burkett, *Vice Pres*
Frank L Capurro, *Vice Pres*
Melissa Contreras, *Human Resources*
EMP: 75 **EST:** 1952
SQ FT: 40,000
SALES (est): 32.2MM **Privately Held**
WEB: www.coastpro.com
SIC: 5148 Fruits, fresh

5149 Groceries & Related Prdts, NEC Wholesale

(P-9437)
ARTISAN BAKERS
21684 8th St E Ste 400, Sonoma (95476-2816)
PHONE 707 939-1765
Bill Dozier, *CEO*
Craig Ponsford, *President*
Elizabeth Ponsford, *Treasurer*
Sharon Ponsford, *Vice Pres*
Chris Jones, *Admin Sec*
EMP: 60 **EST:** 1992
SQ FT: 4,400
SALES (est): 18.6MM **Privately Held**
WEB: www.artisanbakers.com
SIC: 5149 5461 Bakery products; bakeries

(P-9438)
ASHBURY MARKET INC
Also Called: Raison D'Etre Bakery
179 Starlite St, South San Francisco (94080-6313)
PHONE 650 952-8889
Arnold E Wong, *President*
Richard Wong, *CEO*
Mary Wong, *CFO*
Janet Nakamura, *Manager*
EMP: 80 **EST:** 1993
SQ FT: 10,000
SALES (est): 21.6MM **Privately Held**
WEB: www.raisondetrebakery.com
SIC: 5149 Bakery products

(P-9439)
ASPIRE BAKERIES LLC
6500 Overlake Pl, Newark (94560-1083)
PHONE 510 494-1700
Ricardo Luna, *Prdtn Mgr*
Javier Urenda, *Maint Spvr*
EMP: 65
SALES (corp-wide): 1.7B **Privately Held**
WEB: www.aryzta.com
SIC: 5149 Bakery products
HQ: Aspire Bakeries Llc
350 N Orleans St 3001n
Chicago IL 60654
855 427-9982

(P-9440)
BAY BREAD LLC
Also Called: La Boulange
2325 Pine St, San Francisco (94115-2714)
PHONE 415 440-0356
Pascal Rigo, *Mng Member*
Fred Estrada,
Lori Goodman,
EMP: 70 **EST:** 2003
SALES (est): 27.6MM
SALES (corp-wide): 23.5B **Publicly Held**
WEB: www.laboulangebakery.com
SIC: 5149 Breading mixes
PA: Starbucks Corporation
2401 Utah Ave S
Seattle WA 98134
206 447-1575

(P-9441)
BORDENAVES MARIN BAKING
Also Called: Bordenaves
1512 4th St, San Rafael (94901-2713)
P.O. Box 150505 (94915-0505)
PHONE 415 453-2957
Fred Radwan,
EMP: 53 **EST:** 1997
SQ FT: 24,000
SALES (est): 12.1MM **Privately Held**
WEB: www.bordenavesbakery.com
SIC: 5149 Bakery products

(P-9442)
CARAVALI COFFEES INC (DH)
Also Called: Java City
1300 Del Paso Rd, Sacramento (95834-1168)
PHONE 916 565-5500
Micheal Dugadamn, *President*

PRODUCTS & SERVICES SECTION
5149 - Groceries & Related Prdts, NEC Wholesale County (P-9464)

▲ **EMP:** 69 **EST:** 1985
SALES (est): 6.8MM Privately Held
WEB: www.javacity.com
SIC: 5499 5149 Coffee; coffee, green or roasted
HQ: Cucina Holdings, Inc.
 1300 Del Paso Rd
 Sacramento CA 95834
 916 565-5500

(P-9443)
CHOOLJIAN BROS PACKING CO INC
3192 S Indianola Ave, Sanger (93657-9716)
P.O. Box 395 (93657-0395)
PHONE................559 875-5501
Michael Chuoolgin, *CEO*
Sandra Barr, *Admin Sec*
Darrell Smith, *Controller*
Dannie Cantos, *Director*
◆ **EMP:** 50 **EST:** 1967
SQ FT: 1,800
SALES (est): 18.9MM Privately Held
WEB: www.chooljianbrothers.com
SIC: 5149 Dried or canned foods

(P-9444)
CLOVER-STORNETTA FARMS INC (PA)
Also Called: Clover Sonoma
1800 S Mcdowell Blvd Ext, Petaluma (94954-6962)
P.O. Box 750369 (94975-0369)
PHONE................707 769-3282
Marcus Benedetti, *President*
Dan Benedetti, *Ch of Bd*
Gene Benedetti, *Vice Pres*
Mkulima Britt, *Vice Pres*
Mike Keifer, *Vice Pres*
EMP: 180 **EST:** 1977
SQ FT: 80,000
SALES (est): 111.5MM Privately Held
WEB: www.cloversonoma.com
SIC: 5149 5143 2026 Juices; dairy products, except dried or canned; milk & cream, except fermented, cultured & flavored

(P-9445)
COLUSA PRODUCE CORPORATION
1954 Progress Rd, Meridian (95957-9643)
PHONE................530 696-0121
Jim Wallace, *President*
Barbara Overton, *Office Mgr*
◆ **EMP:** 78 **EST:** 1990
SQ FT: 5,000
SALES (est): 26.9MM Privately Held
SIC: 5149 5159 5148 Spices & seasonings; broomcorn; fresh fruits & vegetables

(P-9446)
CORT YARD CREAMERY INC
Also Called: Leatherby's Family Creamery
7910 Antelope Rd, Citrus Heights (95610-2402)
PHONE................916 729-4021
Ronald Anderson, *President*
Carol Flynn, *Manager*
EMP: 45 **EST:** 1985
SQ FT: 5,000
SALES (est): 1MM Privately Held
WEB: www.leatherbys.net
SIC: 5812 5451 5149 Ice cream stands or dairy bars; ice cream (packaged); bakery products

(P-9447)
CREATIVE ENERGY FOODS INC
9957 Medford Ave Ste 4, Oakland (94603-2360)
PHONE................510 638-8668
Richard C Dwinell, *CEO*
George Jewell, *President*
Jacker Wong, *CFO*
Wesley Felton, *Principal*
Richard Barnes, *CIO*
◆ **EMP:** 95 **EST:** 1998
SQ FT: 105,000
SALES (est): 52.4MM Privately Held
WEB: www.creativeenergyfoods.com
SIC: 5149 2026 Health foods; dips, sour cream based

(P-9448)
DEL MONTE FOODS INC (HQ)
205 N Wiget Ln, Walnut Creek (94598-2458)
PHONE................925 949-2772
Greg Longstreet, *CEO*
Parag Scahdeva, *COO*
Paul Miller, *CFO*
Alfred Artis, *Treasurer*
Bibie Wu, *Chief Mktg Ofcr*
◆ **EMP:** 125 **EST:** 2013
SALES (est): 784.6MM Privately Held
WEB: www.delmonte.com
SIC: 5149 2033 Groceries & related products; canned fruits & specialties

(P-9449)
DTJ INC
Also Called: Crystal Springs Water Co
2151-B Delaware Ave, Santa Cruz (95060-5706)
PHONE................831 423-8956
Ross Markley, *CEO*
Teri Metter, *Treasurer*
Deborah Markley, *Admin Sec*
Jeanne Housek, *Asst Sec*
EMP: 35 **EST:** 1935
SQ FT: 17,400
SALES (est): 11.2MM Privately Held
SIC: 5149 Mineral or spring water bottling

(P-9450)
ENARTIS USA INC (PA)
Also Called: Enartis Vinquiry
7795 Bell Rd, Windsor (95492-8519)
PHONE................707 838-6312
Jose Santos, *President*
Libby Spencer, *Area Mgr*
Tyler Franzen, *Technical Staff*
Walter Jorge, *Technical Staff*
Jennifer Wyatt, *Human Res Mgr*
▲ **EMP:** 38 **EST:** 1979
SQ FT: 2,000
SALES (est): 14.4MM Privately Held
WEB: www.shop-usa.enartis.com
SIC: 5149 8734 Wine makers' equipment & supplies; food testing service

(P-9451)
FISCHL TIBOR (HQ)
Also Called: Goji Farm USA
1030 Winding Ridge Ct, Santa Rosa (95404-2563)
PHONE................707 529-9350
Tibor Fischl, *Owner*
EMP: 50 **EST:** 2013
SQ FT: 1,600
SALES (est): 257.3K Privately Held
WEB: www.gojifarmusa.com
SIC: 5149 0191 Tea; general farms, primarily crop

(P-9452)
GUAYAKI SSTNBLE RNFREST PDTS I (PA)
Also Called: Guayaki Yerba Mate
6782 Sebastopol Ave # 100, Sebastopol (95472-3880)
PHONE................888 482-9254
Christopher Mann, *CEO*
Mateo Matthew, *Vice Pres*
Steven Karr, *Creative Dir*
Kim Fetzer, *Office Mgr*
Maria Sandoval, *Accountant*
▲ **EMP:** 20 **EST:** 1999
SALES (est): 27.6MM Privately Held
SIC: 5149 2095 Beverages, except coffee & tea; coffee extracts

(P-9453)
HONG KONG EVRGRN TRDG CO INC
Also Called: Hi-Grade Foods Co
30988 San Benito St, Hayward (94544-7935)
P.O. Box 204, Millbrae (94030-0204)
PHONE................510 476-1881
Ming Lien Lue, *CEO*
Peter Lue, *Vice Pres*
◆ **EMP:** 35 **EST:** 1986
SQ FT: 100,000
SALES (est): 13.3MM Privately Held
SIC: 5149 5113 Groceries & related products; industrial & personal service paper

(P-9454)
IL FORNAIO (AMERICA) LLC (HQ)
Also Called: IL Fornaio Cucina Italiana
770 Tamalpais Dr Ste 208, Corte Madera (94925-1795)
PHONE................415 945-0500
Mike Beatrice, *CEO*
Michele Godina, *Partner*
Mike Beatrice, *CEO*
Jun Kawai, *Bd of Directors*
Shaun Maki, *Bd of Directors*
▲ **EMP:** 35 **EST:** 1982
SALES (est): 114MM
SALES (corp-wide): 7.3B Privately Held
WEB: www.ilfornaio.com
SIC: 5812 5813 5149 5461 Italian restaurant; drinking places; bakery products; bakeries; bread, cake & related products
PA: Roark Capital Group Inc.
 1180 Peachtree St Ne # 2500
 Atlanta GA 30309
 404 591-5200

(P-9455)
IRIS USA INC
3021 Boeing Way, Stockton (95206-4920)
PHONE................209 982-9100
Kenji Megero, *Manager*
Kenji Meguro, *Plant Mgr*
▲ **EMP:** 109 Privately Held
WEB: www.irisusainc.com
SIC: 5149 5099 5191 Dog food; luggage; soil, potting & planting
HQ: Iris Usa, Inc.
 13423 W Cactus Rd
 Surprise AZ 85379

(P-9456)
J & D MEAT COMPANY
Also Called: JD Food
4671 E Edgar Ave, Fresno (93725-1676)
P.O. Box 12051 (93776-2051)
PHONE................559 445-1123
Mark K Ford, *President*
Robert Maxey, *CFO*
Jon Trueblood, *General Mgr*
Steven Maxey, *Admin Sec*
Steve Lloyd, *Human Res Mgr*
EMP: 115 **EST:** 1974
SQ FT: 51,000
SALES (est): 90.1MM Privately Held
WEB: www.jdfood.com
SIC: 5149 5147 5148 5143 Groceries & related products; meats & meat products; fresh fruits & vegetables; dairy products, except dried or canned; packaged frozen goods

(P-9457)
JACMAR DDC LLC
Also Called: Jacmar Food Service Dist
3057 Promenade St, West Sacramento (95691-5941)
PHONE................916 372-9795
James A Dalpozzo, *Mng Member*
David Reid,
EMP: 55 **EST:** 2004
SQ FT: 100,000
SALES (est): 49.5MM
SALES (corp-wide): 259.9MM Privately Held
WEB: www.jacmar.com
SIC: 5149 Natural & organic foods
PA: The Jacmar Companies
 300 Baldwin Park Blvd
 City Of Industry CA 91746
 800 834-8806

(P-9458)
JAGPREET ENTERPRISES LLC
Also Called: Quick-N-Ezee Indian Foods
25823 Clawiter Rd, Hayward (94545-3217)
PHONE................510 336-8376
Sukhjeet K Singh, *CEO*
Cecilia Huffstutler, *Vice Pres*
Jyoti Arora, *Research*
Bonnie Chimni, *Opers Staff*
Dalbir Singh, *Director*
▲ **EMP:** 150 **EST:** 1992
SQ FT: 30,000
SALES (est): 30.2MM Privately Held
WEB: www.sukhis.com
SIC: 5149 Groceries & related products

(P-9459)
JAVA CITY (HQ)
717 Del Paso Rd, Sacramento (95834-7740)
PHONE................916 565-5500
Jeff Hill, *CEO*
Cheryl Dominguez, *CFO*
Paul Bork, *Admin Sec*
Frank Cardona, *Technical Staff*
Christina Baba, *Graphic Designe*
▲ **EMP:** 80 **EST:** 1984
SQ FT: 11,200
SALES (est): 40.3MM Privately Held
WEB: www.javacity.com
SIC: 5812 5149 Cafe; coffee, green or roasted

(P-9460)
KEHE DISTRIBUTORS LLC
4650 Newcastle Rd, Stockton (95215-9446)
PHONE................209 467-1962
EMP: 35
SALES (corp-wide): 3.5B Privately Held
WEB: www.kehe.com
SIC: 5149 Whol Groceries
PA: Kehe Distributors, Llc
 1245 E Diehl Rd Ste 200
 Naperville IL 60563
 630 343-0000

(P-9461)
KIKKOMAN SALES USA INC (HQ)
50 California St Ste 3600, San Francisco (94111-4760)
P.O. Box 420784 (94142-0784)
PHONE................415 956-7750
Yuzaburo Mogi, *CEO*
Nakamura Mitsunodu, *Treasurer*
Yuichi Nakagawa, *Senior VP*
Ken Saito, *Admin Sec*
Becky Philipp, *Admin Asst*
◆ **EMP:** 40 **EST:** 1957
SQ FT: 10,000
SALES (est): 129.5MM Privately Held
WEB: www.kikkomanusa.com
SIC: 5149 2035 Specialty food items; pickles, sauces & salad dressings

(P-9462)
L AND C COOK SPCALTY FOODS INC
Also Called: Truckee Sourdough Co
10607 W River St Ste 2f, Truckee (96161-0351)
P.O. Box 2706 (96160-2706)
PHONE................530 587-3939
Dianne C Nikkel, *President*
▲ **EMP:** 40 **EST:** 1981
SQ FT: 2,400
SALES (est): 13.3MM Privately Held
WEB: www.truckeesourdough.com
SIC: 5149 Bakery products

(P-9463)
LA TORTILLA FACTORY INC (PA)
3300 Westwind Blvd, Santa Rosa (95403-8273)
PHONE................707 586-4000
Samuel Carlos Tamayo, *CEO*
Carlos G Tamayo, *President*
Carlos Tamayo, *President*
Dave Davis, *COO*
Willie Tamayo, *Exec VP*
EMP: 280 **EST:** 1977
SALES (est): 79MM Privately Held
WEB: www.latortillafactory.com
SIC: 5149 2051 Specialty food items; bakery products; bread, cake & related products

(P-9464)
LETTIERI & CO LTD
120 Park Ln, Brisbane (94005-1312)
PHONE................415 657-3392
Frank Lettieri, *President*
Tony Lettieri, *COO*
Kelly Dalton, *Admin Mgr*
Tony Devincenzi, *Analyst*
Dino Lettieri, *Marketing Staff*
▲ **EMP:** 40 **EST:** 1988
SQ FT: 20,000

5149 - Groceries & Related Prdts, NEC Wholesale County (P-9465)

PRODUCTS & SERVICES SECTION

SALES (est): 17.2MM Privately Held
WEB: www.lettieriandco.com
SIC: 5149 Specialty food items

(P-9465)
MIGHTY LEAF TEA
100 Smith Ranch Rd # 120, San Rafael (94903-1979)
PHONE..................415 491-2650
Shiela Stanziale, CEO
Jill Portman, President
Bliss Dake, Vice Pres
▲ EMP: 65 EST: 1998
SQ FT: 5,000
SALES (est): 48.9MM
SALES (corp-wide): 177.9K Privately Held
WEB: www.peets.com
SIC: 5149 5499 Tea; tea
HQ: Peet's Coffee & Tea, Llc
    1400 Park Ave
    Emeryville CA 94608
    510 594-2100

(P-9466)
MOUNTANOS BROTHERS COFFEE CO (PA)
Also Called: Mountanos Family Coffee & Tea
1331 Commerce St, Petaluma (94954-1426)
P.O. Box 927, Redwood Valley (95470-0927)
PHONE..................707 774-8800
Michael S Mountanos, President
Melanie Mountanos, Comptroller
Matthew Kneisel, Plant Mgr
Dora Gomez, Manager
◆ EMP: 45 EST: 1981
SQ FT: 24,000
SALES (est): 26.1MM Privately Held
WEB: www.mfct.com
SIC: 5149 0711 5812 2095 Coffee, green or roasted; soil preparation services; eating places; roasted coffee

(P-9467)
NASSAU-SOSNICK DIST CO LLC (PA)
258 Littlefield Ave, South San Francisco (94080-6922)
PHONE..................650 952-2226
Jeff Sosnick, CEO
Martin Sosnick, President
Wayne Sosnick, Vice Pres
EMP: 61 EST: 2015
SALES (est): 141.5MM Privately Held
SIC: 5149 5145 5182 Groceries & related products; candy; wine

(P-9468)
NAVITAS LLC
Also Called: Navitas Naturals
15 Pamaron Way, Novato (94949-6231)
PHONE..................415 883-8116
Zachary Adelman, Mng Member
Ira Haber, COO
Greg Hingsbergen, Vice Pres
Judy Hemming, Creative Dir
John Schwering, General Mgr
◆ EMP: 50 EST: 2003
SALES (est): 21.3MM Privately Held
WEB: www.navitasorganics.com
SIC: 5149 Health foods

(P-9469)
NEW DESSERTS INC
Also Called: Just Desserts
5000 Fulton Dr, Fairfield (94534-1677)
PHONE..................415 780-6860
Michael Mendes, CEO
David Baffoni, Vice Pres
Dean Gold, Vice Pres
Leighton Mue, VP Finance
Patricia Seymour, Controller
EMP: 71 EST: 1974
SQ FT: 73,500
SALES (est): 30.4MM
SALES (corp-wide): 121.9MM Privately Held
SIC: 5149 2024 Bakery products; ice cream & frozen desserts
HQ: Rubicon Bakers Llc
    154 S 23rd St
    Richmond CA 94804
    510 779-3010

(P-9470)
OLLY PUBLIC BENEFIT CORP
415 Jackson St Fl 2, San Francisco (94111-1628)
PHONE..................415 412-0812
Brad Harrington, CEO
Gerry Chesser, COO
Eric Ryan, Founder
Taryn Forrelli, Vice Pres
Darci Rosenblum, Vice Pres
EMP: 105 EST: 2013
SQ FT: 1,974
SALES (est): 57.6MM
SALES (corp-wide): 59.9B Privately Held
WEB: www.olly.com
SIC: 5149 Diet foods
PA: Unilever Plc
    Unilever House
    London
    207 822-5252

(P-9471)
OTIS MCALLISTER INC (PA)
300 Frank H Ogawa Plz, Oakland (94612-2037)
PHONE..................415 421-6010
Royce A Nicolaisen, Ch of Bd
Everett C Golden III, President
Jim Hostetler, Vice Pres
John Koppel, Vice Pres
James Kochheiser, CIO
◆ EMP: 49 EST: 1892
SQ FT: 7,800
SALES (est): 46.1MM Privately Held
WEB: www.otismcallister.com
SIC: 5149 5141 Canned goods: fruit, vegetables, seafood, meats, etc.; groceries, general line

(P-9472)
PACIFIC COOKIE COMPANY INC (PA)
303 Potrero St Ste 40, Santa Cruz (95060-2899)
PHONE..................831 429-9709
Cara Pearson, President
Lawrence Pearson, COO
Michele Pearson, Vice Pres
Jon Cox, Sales Staff
Sharon McCourt, Manager
EMP: 35 EST: 1980
SQ FT: 6,000
SALES (est): 5MM Privately Held
WEB: www.pacificcookie.com
SIC: 5461 5149 2053 2052 Cookies; cookies; frozen bakery products, except bread; cookies & crackers

(P-9473)
PACIFIC CROWN PARTNERS LLC
Also Called: Triple Crown International
1100 W Shaw Ave Ste 116, Fresno (93711-3708)
PHONE..................559 900-1451
Cody Moore, Mng Member
EMP: 48
SALES (corp-wide): 9.8MM Privately Held
WEB: www.triplecrownintl.com
SIC: 5149 5159 Fruits, dried; nuts, unprocessed or shelled only
PA: Pacific Crown Partners Llc
    39128 Donigan Rd
    Brookshire TX 77423
    661 709-3155

(P-9474)
PASTA SHOP (PA)
Also Called: Market Hall Foods
5655 College Ave Ste 201, Oakland (94618-1583)
PHONE..................510 250-6005
Sara Wilson, Managing Prtnr
Anthony Wilson, Partner
Peter Wilson, Partner
Nel Da Silva, Executive
Taylor Black, Administration
▲ EMP: 80 EST: 1981
SQ FT: 4,500
SALES (est): 46.2MM Privately Held
WEB: www.rockridgemarkethall.com
SIC: 5149 5411 5812 5431 Pasta & rice; delicatessens; caterers; fruit & vegetable markets

(P-9475)
POMWONDERFUL LLC
900 Airport Blvd, Mendota (93640-2441)
PHONE..................310 966-5800
Larry Isonio, Branch Mgr
EMP: 100
SALES (corp-wide): 2B Privately Held
WEB: www.wonderful.com
SIC: 5149 5148 5085 Beverage concentrates; fruits, fresh; plastic bottles
HQ: Pomwonderful Llc
    11444 W Olympic Blvd
    Los Angeles CA 90064
    310 966-5800

(P-9476)
PRESSED JUICERY INC
3530 E Church Ave, Fresno (93725-1337)
PHONE..................559 777-8900
Hayden Slater, President
EMP: 17
SALES (corp-wide): 124.2MM Privately Held
WEB: www.pressed.com
SIC: 5149 2033 Water, distilled; fruit juices: packaged in cans, jars, etc.
PA: Pressed Juicery, Inc.
    4016 Wilshire Blvd
    Los Angeles CA 90010
    310 477-7171

(P-9477)
PRIMAL PET FOODS INC
2045 Mckinnon Ave, San Francisco (94124-1608)
PHONE..................415 642-7400
▲ EMP: 36
SALES (est): 7.4MM Privately Held
SIC: 5149 Whol Groceries

(P-9478)
PRINCE PEACE ENTERPRISES INC (PA)
751 N Canyons Pkwy, Livermore (94551-9479)
PHONE..................925 292-3888
Kenneth Yeung, President
Lolita Lim, Vice Pres
Billy Poon, General Mgr
Linda Lam, Sales Mgr
Eva Yen, Manager
◆ EMP: 46 EST: 1983
SQ FT: 72,774
SALES (est): 35.7MM Privately Held
WEB: www.popus.com
SIC: 5149 5122 Health foods; specialty food items; drugs, proprietaries & sundries

(P-9479)
PULMUONE USA INC
5755 Rossi Ln, Gilroy (95020-7063)
PHONE..................714 361-0806
▲ EMP: 290 Privately Held
WEB: www.pulmuonefoodsusa.com
SIC: 5149 Natural & organic foods
HQ: Pulmuone U.S.A., Inc.
    2315 Moore Ave
    Fullerton CA 92833

(P-9480)
RAYBERN FOODS LLC
Also Called: Raybern Quality Foods
3170 Crow Canyon Pl # 200, San Ramon (94583-1347)
PHONE..................925 302-7800
Rob Leibowitz, CEO
Rhondi Shigemura-Webst, Vice Pres
Jamie Viggiano, Manager
Wendy Howell, Assistant
Reynaldo Cariaga, Supervisor
EMP: 42 EST: 2010
SQ FT: 35,000
SALES (est): 21MM
SALES (corp-wide): 2.7B Privately Held
WEB: www.rayberns.com
SIC: 5149 2015 2051 5147 Sandwiches; poultry slaughtering & processing; bread, cake & related products; meats & meat products; packaged frozen goods; sausages & other prepared meats
PA: Premium Brands Holdings Corporation
    10991 Shellbridge Way Unit 100
    Richmond BC V6X 3
    604 656-3100

(P-9481)
RELS FOODS
3001 Academy Way, Sacramento (95815-1540)
PHONE..................916 927-7677
Tom Whitton, Manager
EMP: 35
SALES (corp-wide): 3.7MM Privately Held
SIC: 5149 Sandwiches
PA: Rel's Foods
    1814 Franklin St Ste 310
    Oakland CA 94612
    510 652-2747

(P-9482)
ROUTE 40 VENTURES INC
717 San Miguel Ln, Foster City (94404-3722)
PHONE..................650 743-0051
EMP: 17
SALES (est): 2.9MM Privately Held
WEB: www.route40ventures.com
SIC: 5149 2037 5145 Groceries And Related Products, Nec, Nsk

(P-9483)
SEMIFREDDIS INC (PA)
Also Called: Semifreddi's Bakery
1980 N Loop Rd, Alameda (94502-3540)
PHONE..................510 596-9930
Thomas Frainier, President
Jorge Blancas, General Mgr
Michael Rose, Admin Sec
Cary Weigle, Engrg Dir
Wendy Brace, Director
EMP: 110 EST: 1984
SQ FT: 36,000
SALES (est): 33.4MM Privately Held
WEB: www.semifreddis.com
SIC: 5149 5461 Bakery products; bakeries

(P-9484)
SHAMROCK FOODS COMPANY
856 National Dr, Sacramento (95834-1173)
PHONE..................602 819-1654
Mark Harris, Sales Associate
Joe Rodriguez, Sales Associate
Jeffrey Pigg, Accounts Exec
Jason Winans, Accounts Exec
EMP: 360
SALES (corp-wide): 3.8B Privately Held
WEB: www.shamrockfoods.com
SIC: 5149 Groceries & related products
PA: Shamrock Foods Company
    3900 E Camelback Rd # 300
    Phoenix AZ 85018
    602 477-2500

(P-9485)
SHAW BAKERS LLC
320b Shaw Rd Ste B, South San Francisco (94080-6623)
PHONE..................650 273-1440
Nicolas Bernadi, CEO
Darrell Smith, Mng Member
EMP: 170 EST: 2015
SALES (est): 10MM Privately Held
SIC: 5149 5142 2053 Bakery products; bakery products, frozen; frozen bakery products, except bread; cakes, bakery: frozen

(P-9486)
SHENG-KEE OF CALIFORNIA INC (PA)
Also Called: Sheng-Kee Bakery
1941 Irving St, San Francisco (94122-1713)
PHONE..................415 564-4800
Mark KAO, CEO
Hsaio-Yung KAO, President
Siau-Liang KAO, President
Gary Lo, Manager
◆ EMP: 50 EST: 1979
SQ FT: 5,000
SALES (est): 28.6MM Privately Held
SIC: 5461 5149 Cakes; cookies; bread; bakery products

▲ = Import ▼ = Export
◆ = Import/Export

PRODUCTS & SERVICES SECTION

5159 - Farm-Prdt Raw Mtrls, NEC Wholesale County (P-9508)

(P-9487)
SONOMA SPECIALTY FOODS INC
Also Called: Sonoma Gourmet
21684 8th St E Ste 100, Sonoma (95476-2816)
PHONE...................707 939-3700
William K Weber, *CEO*
EMP: 35 **EST:** 1996
SALES (est): 5.5MM **Privately Held**
SIC: 5149 Sauces

(P-9488)
SPECIALTY BAKING INC
Also Called: Specialty Baking Co.
3134 Capelaw Ct, San Jose (95135-1101)
PHONE...................408 298-6950
Robert Murillo Jr, *CEO*
Mark Murillo, *Treasurer*
Manual Escobar, *Vice Pres*
EMP: 70 **EST:** 1978
SQ FT: 10,000
SALES (est): 9MM **Privately Held**
WEB: www.specialtybaking.com
SIC: 5149 2051 Bakery products; bread, cake & related products

(P-9489)
STARWEST BOTANICALS LLC (PA)
161 Main Ave, Sacramento (95838-2080)
PHONE...................916 638-8100
Van Joerger, *President*
Mark Wendley, *Controller*
Steven Riccardelli, *VP Sls/Mktg*
Melissa Waters, *Mktg Dir*
Kayla Pellegrini, *Sales Staff*
◆ **EMP:** 93 **EST:** 1975
SQ FT: 68,400
SALES (est): 37.3MM **Privately Held**
WEB: www.starwest-botanicals.com
SIC: 5149 Tea

(P-9490)
SUMANOS BAKERY LLC
358 Locust St, Watsonville (95076-4514)
P.O. Box 144 (95077-0144)
PHONE...................831 722-5511
Raymundo Sumano,
EMP: 39 **EST:** 2002
SALES (est): 5.3MM **Privately Held**
WEB: www.sumanosbakery.com
SIC: 5149 Bakery products

(P-9491)
SUN HING FOODS INC (PA)
271 Harbor Way, South San Francisco (94080-6811)
PHONE...................650 583-8188
Trung Dang, *CEO*
John Lau, *Executive*
Virginia Teng, *Admin Sec*
Winnie Ho, *Human Res Mgr*
Ricky Cheung, *Sales Mgr*
◆ **EMP:** 35 **EST:** 1981
SQ FT: 40,000
SALES (est): 32.6MM **Privately Held**
WEB: www.sunhingfoods.com
SIC: 5149 Dried or canned foods

(P-9492)
SUN-MAID GROWERS CALIFORNIA (PA)
6795 N Palm Ave Ste 200, Fresno (93704-1088)
PHONE...................559 896-8000
Harry J Overly, *President*
Braden Bender, *CFO*
Richard Paumen, *Senior VP*
Kayhan Hazrati, *Vice Pres*
Rick Stark, *Admin Sec*
◆ **EMP:** 750 **EST:** 1912
SALES: 394.9MM **Privately Held**
WEB: www.sunmaid.com
SIC: 5149 Groceries & related products

(P-9493)
SUNSWEET GROWERS INC
23760 Loleta Ave, Corning (96021-9699)
P.O. Box 201 (96021-0201)
PHONE...................530 824-5376
Robert Safford, *Manager*
Dan Lima, *Manager*
EMP: 60

SALES (corp-wide): 244.8MM **Privately Held**
WEB: www.sunsweet.com
SIC: 5149 Fruits, dried
PA: Sunsweet Growers Inc.
901 N Walton Ave
Yuba City CA 95993
800 417-2253

(P-9494)
SUPER STORE INDUSTRIES
Also Called: Ssi
2800 W March Ln Ste 210, Stockton (95219-8200)
P.O. Box 549, Lathrop (95330-0549)
PHONE...................209 858-3365
Tom Hughes, *Branch Mgr*
Angela Mills-Dixon, *Human Resources*
Scott Sommerfeld, *Manager*
EMP: 400 **Privately Held**
WEB: www.ssica.com
SIC: 5149 5141 4225 Groceries & related products; groceries, general line; general warehousing & storage
PA: Super Store Industries
16888 Mckinley Ave
Lathrop CA 95330

(P-9495)
TOO GOOD GOURMET INC (PA)
2380 Grant Ave, San Lorenzo (94580-1806)
PHONE...................510 317-8150
Amie G Watson, *CEO*
Jennifer Finley, *President*
Alyssa Albatana, *Graphic Designe*
Joe Waldrep, *Plant Mgr*
Jade Burchett, *Marketing Staff*
▲ **EMP:** 99 **EST:** 1998
SQ FT: 50,000
SALES (est): 26.5MM **Privately Held**
WEB: www.toogoodgourmet.com
SIC: 5149 5461 2052 Cookies; crackers, cookies & bakery products; cookies; cookies

(P-9496)
TRAINA DRIED FRUIT INC
Also Called: Traina Foods
280 S 1st St, Patterson (95363-2822)
PHONE...................209 892-5472
Gina Szenasi, *Human Resources*
Carrie Taylor, *Sales Executive*
Jill Kazdin, *Sales Staff*
Paul Walker, *Sales Staff*
EMP: 160 **Privately Held**
WEB: www.trainafoods.com
SIC: 5149 Fruits, dried
PA: Traina Dried Fruit, Inc.
337 Lemon Ave
Patterson CA 95363

(P-9497)
TRAINA DRIED FRUIT INC (PA)
Also Called: Traina Foods
337 Lemon Ave, Patterson (95363-9634)
P.O. Box 157 (95363-0157)
PHONE...................209 892-5472
William Traina, *CEO*
Joseph Traina, *CFO*
Brent Bradley, *Vice Pres*
Justin A Traina, *Vice Pres*
Michelle Bettencourt, *Admin Sec*
◆ **EMP:** 80 **EST:** 1926
SQ FT: 5,000
SALES (est): 51.5MM **Privately Held**
WEB: www.trainafoods.com
SIC: 5149 Fruits, dried

(P-9498)
UB INC
Also Called: United Bakery and Company
1115 Shore St, West Sacramento (95691-3508)
P.O. Box 981194 (95798-1194)
PHONE...................916 374-8899
Tai Nguy, *CEO*
Mina Nguy, *CFO*
▲ **EMP:** 37 **EST:** 1991
SALES (est): 24.2MM **Privately Held**
WEB: www.unitedbakery.com
SIC: 5149 Bakery products

(P-9499)
WALTER C VOIGT INC
Also Called: Culligan
2479 S Orange Ave, Fresno (93725-1332)
PHONE...................559 233-3055
Sepp Becker, *President*
Christy Bowen, *Office Mgr*
EMP: 37 **EST:** 1949
SQ FT: 3,700
SALES (est): 4.7MM **Privately Held**
WEB: www.culliganfresnolindsay.com
SIC: 5999 5149 Water purification equipment; mineral or spring water bottling

5153 Grain & Field Beans Wholesale

(P-9500)
BUNGE MILLING INC
845 Kentucky Ave, Woodland (95695-2744)
PHONE...................530 666-1691
EMP: 72 **Privately Held**
WEB: www.bungenorthamerica.com
SIC: 5153 Grains
HQ: Bunge Milling, Inc.
1391 Timberlake Manor Pkw
Chesterfield MO 63017
314 292-2000

(P-9501)
CALIFORNIA CEREAL PRODUCTS INC (PA)
1267 14th St, Oakland (94607-2246)
PHONE...................510 452-4500
Robert Sterling Savely, *CEO*
Mark Graham, *President*
Sterling Savely, *Mfg Staff*
Nestor Pajuleras, *Products*
Phil Gunter, *Manager*
◆ **EMP:** 71 **EST:** 1994
SQ FT: 120,000
SALES (est): 44.2MM **Privately Held**
WEB: www.californiacereal.com
SIC: 5153 Grains

(P-9502)
FARMERS RICE COOPERATIVE
Also Called: Pacific Intl Rice Mills
845 Kentucky Ave, Woodland (95695-2744)
P.O. Box 652 (95776-0652)
PHONE...................530 666-1691
Melveryn Anderson, *President*
Scott Sherburne, *Vice Pres*
Robert Rogel, *Executive*
Jennifer Kalfsbeek, *Opers Staff*
Julie Lillywhite-Lagr, *Director*
EMP: 56
SALES (corp-wide): 71.8MM **Privately Held**
WEB: www.farmersrice.com
SIC: 5153 Grains
PA: Rice Farmers' Cooperative
2566 River Plaza Dr
Sacramento CA 95833
916 923-5100

(P-9503)
PACIFIC GRAIN & FOODS LLC (PA)
Also Called: Pacific Grain and Foods
4067 W Shaw Ave Ste 116, Fresno (93722-6214)
P.O. Box 3928, Pinedale (93650-3928)
PHONE...................559 276-2580
Lee Perkins, *President*
Karen Perkins, *Vice Pres*
Martha Prado, *Executive Asst*
Priscilla Lira, *President*
Rita Garcia, *Human Resources*
◆ **EMP:** 134 **EST:** 1982
SQ FT: 172,000
SALES (est): 51.2MM **Privately Held**
WEB: www.pacificgrainandfoods.com
SIC: 5153 7389 5149 Grains; packaging & labeling services; spices & seasonings

(P-9504)
PENCOM/DUALL THERMO PRODUCTS
1300 Industrial Rd Ste 21, San Carlos (94070-4141)
PHONE...................650 593-3288
William Gardiner, *President*
Deborah Gardiner, *Vice Pres*
Brian Tokumoto, *QA Dir*
Paul Lanagan, *Director*
Allan Bennett, *Manager*
EMP: 55 **EST:** 1978
SALES (est): 5.7MM **Privately Held**
WEB: www.pencomsf.com
SIC: 5153 Grains
PA: Peninsula Components, Inc.
1300 Industrial Rd Ste 21
San Carlos CA 94070

(P-9505)
PENNY NEWMAN GRAIN CO (PA)
2691 S Cedar Ave, Fresno (93725-2032)
P.O. Box 12147 (93776-2147)
PHONE...................559 448-8800
Mike Nicoletti, *CEO*
Jeff Barnes, *Vice Pres*
Marsha Waller, *Human Res Mgr*
William Slivkoff, *Production*
John Verwey, *Sales Staff*
◆ **EMP:** 35 **EST:** 1878
SQ FT: 10,000
SALES (est): 92MM **Privately Held**
WEB: www.penny-newman.com
SIC: 5153 Grains; wheat; barley; corn

5154 Livestock Wholesale

(P-9506)
R EMIGH LIVESTOCK
30 S 2nd St, Rio Vista (94571-1802)
P.O. Box 788 (94571-0788)
PHONE...................707 374-5585
Christine Mahoney, *President*
Richard M Emigh, *CEO*
Faye Emigh, *Admin Sec*
EMP: 70 **EST:** 1960
SQ FT: 400
SALES (est): 6.3MM **Privately Held**
WEB: www.emighlivestock.com
SIC: 5154 0212 Livestock; beef cattle except feedlots

5159 Farm-Prdt Raw Mtrls, NEC Wholesale

(P-9507)
IMPERIAL WESTERN PRODUCTS INC
3766 E Conejo Ave, Selma (93662-9655)
PHONE...................559 891-2600
Jeff Harger, *General Mgr*
Thomas Prokop, *Vice Pres*
EMP: 69
SQ FT: 25,948
SALES (corp-wide): 100.4MM **Privately Held**
WEB: www.imperialwesternproducts.com
SIC: 5159 5191 Cotton merchants & products; animal feeds
PA: Imperial Western Products, Inc., A California Corporation
86600 Avenue 54
Coachella CA 92236
760 398-0815

(P-9508)
KR SUBSIDIARY INC (DH)
Also Called: Young Pecan Company
1050 Diamond St, Stockton (95205-7020)
PHONE...................915 320-7033
James W Swink, *President*
Helen Watts, *Exec VP*
▼ **EMP:** 35 **EST:** 2006
SQ FT: 150,000
SALES (est): 84.8MM
SALES (corp-wide): 605MM **Privately Held**
WEB: www.nationalpecan.com
SIC: 5159 Pecan shellers

5159 - Farm-Prdt Raw Mtrls, NEC Wholesale County (P-9509)

HQ: Diamond Foods Holdings, Llc
1050 Diamond St
Stockton CA 95205
469 353-2993

(P-9509)
LODI NUT COMPANY INC
1230 S Fairmont Ave, Lodi (95240-5519)
PHONE..................................209 334-2081
Calvin Kelly Suess, *President*
Della Suess, *Treasurer*
Virgil Suess, *Vice Pres*
Verla Suess, *Admin Sec*
▲ EMP: 21 EST: 1949
SQ FT: 40,000
SALES (est): 4.3MM **Privately Held**
WEB: www.lodinews.com
SIC: **5159** 0723 2068 Nuts, unprocessed or shelled only; almond hulling & shelling services; walnut hulling & shelling services; tree nut crops market preparation services; salted & roasted nuts & seeds

(P-9510)
MINTURN HULLER COOPERATIVE INC
9080 S Minturn Rd, Chowchilla (93610-9317)
P.O. Box 760 (93610-0760)
PHONE..................................559 665-1185
Mark Wolfshorndl, *President*
Jeff Hamilton, *Treasurer*
Kitt Kahl, *Corp Secy*
Sterling Alexander, *Vice Pres*
Brad Schnoor, *Vice Pres*
EMP: 76 EST: 1966
SQ FT: 25,000
SALES (est): 24.8MM **Privately Held**
WEB: www.minturnhuller.com
SIC: **5159** 0723 Nuts & nut by-products; almond hulling & shelling services

(P-9511)
SELECT HARVEST USA LLC (PA)
Also Called: Spycher Brothers
14827 W Harding Rd, Turlock (95380-9012)
P.O. Box 3307 (95381-3307)
PHONE..................................209 668-2471
Robert L Nunes, *Mng Member*
Maria Medina, *Purchasing*
Paula Jones, *Marketing Staff*
Juan-Carlos Veraza, *Director*
Carol Baldwin, *Manager*
◆ EMP: 123 EST: 2008
SQ FT: 100,000
SALES (est): 47.6MM **Privately Held**
WEB: www.selectharvestusa.com
SIC: **5159** 0173 Nuts & nut by-products; almond grove

(P-9512)
VF MARKETING CORP
365 Ruggieri Way, Williams (95987-5155)
PHONE..................................530 473-2607
Garnett Vann, *President*
Jeff Schaap, *CFO*
William Vann, *Vice Pres*
Dorothy Murphy, *Admin Sec*
EMP: 42 EST: 2012
SALES (est): 16.4MM **Privately Held**
SIC: **5159** Nuts & nut by-products

5162 Plastics Materials & Basic Shapes Wholesale

(P-9513)
DONGALEN ENTERPRISES INC (PA)
Also Called: Interstate Plastics
330 Commerce Cir, Sacramento (95815-4213)
P.O. Box 130027 (95853-0027)
PHONE..................................916 422-3110
Larry Chavez, *President*
Cole Klokkevold, *CFO*
Bob Umphress, *Branch Mgr*
Mark Courtright, *General Mgr*
Terry Renzoni, *Prdtn Mgr*
▲ EMP: 50 EST: 1981
SQ FT: 33,000
SALES (est): 94.6MM **Privately Held**
WEB: www.interstateplastics.com
SIC: **5162** Plastics products

(P-9514)
MR PLASTICS
844 Doolittle Dr, San Leandro (94577-1020)
PHONE..................................510 895-0774
Mike Adelson, *President*
Angele Woodfin, *Sales Associate*
Norma Barajas, *Sales Staff*
▲ EMP: 25 EST: 1988
SQ FT: 24,000
SALES (est): 7.5MM **Privately Held**
WEB: www.mr-plastics.com
SIC: **5162** 2821 Plastics sheets & rods; plastics film; plastics materials; acrylic resins; acrylonitrile-butadiene-styrene resins (ABS resins)

(P-9515)
PEAK TECHNOLOGY ENTPS INC
Also Called: Peak Plastics
6951 Via Del Oro, San Jose (95119-1316)
PHONE..................................408 748-1102
Sharon Woo Griffoul, *CEO*
Matt Griffoul, *President*
Lotus Miranda, *Senior Buyer*
Rick Ornellas, *Director*
Miguel Martinez, *Supervisor*
▼ EMP: 38 EST: 1999
SQ FT: 15,000
SALES (est): 20.5MM **Privately Held**
WEB: www.peakfab.com
SIC: **5162** 3089 3599 Plastics materials & basic shapes; molding primary plastic; thermoformed finished plastic products; hose, flexible metallic; machine & other job shop work

5169 Chemicals & Allied Prdts, NEC Wholesale

(P-9516)
ALPHA DYNO NOBEL (PA)
Also Called: Alpha Explosives
3400 Nader Rd, Lincoln (95648)
PHONE..................................916 645-3377
Brad Langner, *CEO*
Gerald Hackler, *Opers Staff*
Richard Medina, *Supervisor*
▲ EMP: 29 EST: 1906
SQ FT: 40,000
SALES (est): 29.3MM **Privately Held**
WEB: www.alphaexplosives.com
SIC: **5169** 2892 Explosives; explosives

(P-9517)
E T HORN COMPANY
2135 Frederick St, Oakland (94606-5317)
P.O. Box 1238, La Mirada (90637-1238)
PHONE..................................510 532-8689
Beth Hillard, *Sales & Mktg Staff*
Yanely Linares, *Controller*
Marilou Picazo, *Purchasing*
Ella Pochay, *Marketing Staff*
Teresa Avalos, *Manager*
EMP: 127
SALES (corp-wide): 100.4MM **Privately Held**
WEB: www.imcdus.com
SIC: **5169** 5085 Industrial chemicals; industrial supplies
PA: E. T. Horn Company
16050 Canary Ave
La Mirada CA 90638
714 523-8050

(P-9518)
ENVIRO TECH CHEMICAL SVCS INC (PA)
500 Winmoore Way, Modesto (95358-5750)
PHONE..................................209 581-9576
Michael S Harvey, *President*
Michael B Archibald, *Vice Pres*
Jon Howarth, *Vice Pres*
Cynthia Harvey, *Administration*
Charlie Lucas, *Maintence Staff*
◆ EMP: 102 EST: 1991
SQ FT: 136,551
SALES: 64.4MM **Privately Held**
WEB: www.envirotech.com
SIC: **5169** 2842 Industrial chemicals; specialty cleaning preparations

(P-9519)
K R ANDERSON INC (PA)
Also Called: Krayden
18330 Sutter Blvd, Morgan Hill (95037-2841)
PHONE..................................408 825-1800
Dennis Wagner, *CEO*
Jim Caviglia, *Treasurer*
Samanthaa Wag Wagner, *General Mgr*
Doreen Oroshnik, *Administration*
Johnny Quilenderino, *QC Mgr*
▲ EMP: 55 EST: 1963
SQ FT: 60,000
SALES (est): 25.6MM **Privately Held**
WEB: www.krafab.com
SIC: **5169** Synthetic resins, rubber & plastic materials

(P-9520)
MG4 MANUFACTURING INC
370 N Wiget Ln Ste 200, Walnut Creek (94598-2452)
PHONE..................................925 295-9700
Cathy Hampton, *President*
▼ EMP: 97 EST: 1996
SQ FT: 42,000
SALES (est): 4.8MM
SALES (corp-wide): 14.2B **Publicly Held**
WEB: www.dupont.com
SIC: **5169** Chemicals & allied products
HQ: E. I. Du Pont De Nemours And Company
974 Centre Rd Bldg 735
Wilmington DE 19805
302 485-3000

(P-9521)
SAMIRIAN CHEMICALS INC
1999 S Bascom Ave Ste 515, Campbell (95008-2204)
PHONE..................................408 558-8282
Shei Huei Liao, *President*
Sam Liao, *CEO*
May Liao, *CFO*
Barney Daigle, *Sales Staff*
Mark Ramelb, *Manager*
◆ EMP: 48 EST: 1988
SQ FT: 3,000
SALES (est): 27.7MM **Privately Held**
WEB: www.samirian.com
SIC: **5169** Industrial chemicals

(P-9522)
SEAYU ENTERPRISES
236 West Portal Ave 399, San Francisco (94127-1423)
P.O. Box 16236 (94116-0236)
PHONE..................................415 566-9677
Quincy Yu, *President*
EMP: 15 EST: 2001
SALES (est): 4.8MM **Privately Held**
WEB: www.odorandstainremover.com
SIC: **5169** 2841 Chemicals & allied products; soap & other detergents

5171 Petroleum Bulk Stations & Terminals

(P-9523)
BOSCO OIL INC
Also Called: Valley Oil Co
785 Yuba Dr, Mountain View (94041-2402)
P.O. Box 1655 (94042-1655)
PHONE..................................650 967-2253
Robert Christiansen, *President*
Mike Eyre, *CFO*
Robert Buck, *Vice Pres*
Roberta Cummings, *Accounting Dir*
Mary Turnbull, *Accountant*
EMP: 45 EST: 1947
SQ FT: 5,000
SALES (est): 53.3MM **Privately Held**
WEB: www.valleyoil.com
SIC: **5171** Petroleum bulk stations

(P-9524)
GENERAL PETROLEUM CORPORATION
237 E Whitmore Ave, Modesto (95358-9411)
PHONE..................................209 537-1056
EMP: 70
SALES (corp-wide): 1.1B **Privately Held**
SIC: **5171** Petroleum Bulk Station
HQ: General Petroleum Corporation
19501 S Santa Fe Ave
Compton CA 90221
562 983-7300

(P-9525)
HUNT & SONS INC (PA)
5750 S Watt Ave, Sacramento (95829-9349)
P.O. Box 277670 (95827-7670)
PHONE..................................916 383-4868
R Dean Hunt, *President*
Audrey Hunt, *CEO*
Joshua Hunt, *Treasurer*
Warren H Hunt III, *Vice Pres*
Joe Hunt, *Admin Sec*
EMP: 46 EST: 1946
SQ FT: 10,000
SALES (est): 102.6MM **Privately Held**
WEB: www.huntnsons.com
SIC: **5541** 5171 Truck stops; petroleum bulk stations

(P-9526)
JIM JONAS INC
Also Called: Jonas Heating & Cooling
9125 Hwy 53, Lower Lake (95457)
P.O. Box 277 (95457-0277)
PHONE..................................707 994-5911
Russell Jonas, *Manager*
Tonya Jonas, *Admin Sec*
EMP: 35
SQ FT: 190
SALES (corp-wide): 25.5MM **Privately Held**
WEB: www.jonasenergy.com
SIC: **5171** 1711 Petroleum bulk stations; heating & air conditioning contractors
PA: Jim Jonas, Inc.
16445 Main St
Lower Lake CA 95457
707 994-5911

5172 Petroleum & Petroleum Prdts Wholesale

(P-9527)
ALL-POINTS PETROLEUM LLC
640 Noyes Ct, Benicia (94510-1229)
P.O. Box 2658, Grants Pass OR (97528-0240)
PHONE..................................707 745-1116
Ronald Myska,
Ralph Martin, *General Mgr*
Christine Botkin, *Admin Sec*
Carolyn Kunde, *Admin Sec*
Roger Mathews, *Info Tech Dir*
EMP: 61 EST: 1993
SQ FT: 4,000
SALES (est): 11.5MM **Privately Held**
WEB: www.allpointspetroleum.com
SIC: **5172** Gasoline

(P-9528)
AMERIGAS PROPANE LP
11030 White Rock Rd # 100, Rancho Cordova (95670-6011)
PHONE..................................916 852-7400
Fax: 916 631-3180
EMP: 100 **Publicly Held**
SIC: **5172** 7374 Whol Petroleum Products Data Processing/Preparation
HQ: Amerigas Propane, L.P.
460 N Gulph Rd Ste 100
King Of Prussia PA 19406

(P-9529)
AMYRIS FUELS LLC
5885 Hollis St Ste 100, Emeryville (94608-2405)
PHONE..................................510 450-0761
John G Melo,
Christine Ofori, *Officer*

PRODUCTS & SERVICES SECTION **5181 - Beer & Ale Wholesale County (P-9550)**

Sunil Chandran, *Vice Pres*
Thomas Krivas, *Vice Pres*
Benedict Tanjoco, *Manager*
EMP: 36 **EST:** 2008
SALES (est): 8.2MM
SALES (corp-wide): 173.1MM **Publicly Held**
WEB: www.amyris.com
SIC: 5172 Fuel oil
PA: Amyris, Inc.
 5885 Hollis St Ste 100
 Emeryville CA 94608
 510 450-0761

(P-9530)
BAY AREA/DIABLO PETROLEUM CO
1800 Sutter St, Concord (94520-2563)
P.O. Box 44550, San Francisco (94144-0001)
PHONE..................925 228-2222
Russell Mederios, *Manager*
EMP: 48
SALES (corp-wide): 90.4MM **Privately Held**
SIC: 5172 Gases, liquefied petroleum (propane)
HQ: Bay Area/Diablo Petroleum, Co.
 16580 Wedge Pkwy Ste 300
 Reno NV 89511
 925 228-2222

(P-9531)
CHEVRON TRADING LLC (HQ)
6001 Bollinger Canyon Rd, San Ramon (94583-5737)
PHONE..................925 842-1000
EMP: 228 **EST:** 2019
SALES (est): 23.6MM
SALES (corp-wide): 94.6B **Publicly Held**
WEB: www.chevron.com
SIC: 5172 Fuel oil
PA: Chevron Corporation
 6001 Bollinger Canyon Rd
 San Ramon CA 94583
 925 842-1000

(P-9532)
DASSELS PETROLEUM INC (PA)
Also Called: Pacific Pride
31 Wright Rd, Hollister (95023-9318)
PHONE..................831 636-5100
James P Dassel, *CEO*
Graham Mackie, *Vice Pres*
Mike Goode, *Manager*
Jan Fraser, *Supervisor*
EMP: 45 **EST:** 1939
SQ FT: 4,915
SALES (est): 17.5MM **Privately Held**
WEB: www.dassels.com
SIC: 5172 5531 Gasoline; butane gas; automotive & home supply stores

(P-9533)
FRONTIER PERFORMANCE LUBR INC
816 Black Diamond Way A, Lodi (95240-0728)
P.O. Box 1777 (95241-1777)
PHONE..................209 334-6353
Andrew F Miller, *President*
Jim Kasinger, *Vice Pres*
EMP: 45 **EST:** 1994
SQ FT: 10,000
SALES (est): 26.1MM **Privately Held**
WEB: www.frontierlubricants.com
SIC: 5172 Lubricating oils & greases

(P-9534)
J S WEST AND COMPANY (PA)
501 9th St, Modesto (95354-3420)
PHONE..................209 577-3221
Donald Garrison West, *President*
Mike West, *Vice Pres*
Samantha Ford, *Department Mgr*
Stephanie Vandoorn, *Office Mgr*
Timothy Waldvogel, *IT/INT Sup*
EMP: 131 **EST:** 1946
SALES (est): 83.7MM **Privately Held**
WEB: www.jswest.com
SIC: 5172 5211 5251 0723 Gases, liquefied petroleum (propane); lumber & other building materials; hardware; feed milling custom services; eggs & poultry

(P-9535)
PROPANE CNSTR & METER SVCS (PA)
1262 Dupont Ct, Manteca (95336-6003)
PHONE..................866 587-7411
Terry Ayres, *CEO*
EMP: 107 **EST:** 2003
SALES (est): 664.7K **Privately Held**
WEB: www.lpcams.com
SIC: 5984 5172 1321 Propane gas, bottled; gases, liquefied petroleum (propane); propane (natural) production

(P-9536)
RAMOS OIL CO INC (PA)
1515 S River Rd, West Sacramento (95691-2882)
P.O. Box 401 (95691-0401)
PHONE..................916 371-2570
Kent Ramos, *President*
Kyle Ramos, *President*
William Ramos, *President*
John Bailey, *CFO*
Jan Bard, *CFO*
EMP: 100 **EST:** 1951
SQ FT: 3,200
SALES (est): 182.8MM **Privately Held**
WEB: www.ramosoil.com
SIC: 5541 5172 Filling stations, gasoline; lubricating oils & greases

(P-9537)
ROBERT V JENSEN INC (PA)
Also Called: Rvj
4029 S Maple Ave, Fresno (93725-9357)
P.O. Box 12907 (93779-2907)
PHONE..................559 485-8210
William Jensen, *President*
Ron King, *CFO*
Mike Jensen, *Vice Pres*
Brenda Bridger, *Executive*
Deann Williams, *Controller*
EMP: 59 **EST:** 1974
SQ FT: 8,000
SALES (est): 49.5MM **Privately Held**
WEB: www.rvjensen.com
SIC: 5541 5172 Filling stations, gasoline; petroleum products

(P-9538)
SACRAMENTO INTL JET CTR INC
6133 Freeport Blvd, Sacramento (95822-3534)
PHONE..................916 428-8292
Scott Powell, *CEO*
Becky Watts, *Vice Pres*
Ihsan Mallah, *Admin Asst*
EMP: 75 **EST:** 2006
SALES (est): 14.1MM **Privately Held**
WEB: www.sacjet.com
SIC: 5172 4581 Aircraft fueling services; airport hangar rental

(P-9539)
STAN BOYETT & SON INC (PA)
Also Called: Boyett Petroleum
601 Mchenry Ave, Modesto (95350-5411)
PHONE..................209 577-6000
Dale Boyett, *President*
Laverne Couch, *COO*
Scott Castle, *Vice Pres*
Clark Nakamura, *Vice Pres*
John Duncan, *Executive*
EMP: 40
SQ FT: 10,000
SALES (est): 250.4MM **Privately Held**
WEB: www.boyett.net
SIC: 5172 Petroleum products

(P-9540)
TOM LOPES DISTRIBUTING INC (PA)
Also Called: Western States Oil
1790 S 10th St, San Jose (95112-4106)
P.O. Box 1307 (95109-1307)
PHONE..................408 292-1041
Steve Lopes, *President*
Greg Michael, *CFO*
Jeff Lopes, *Vice Pres*
Kathy Disalvo, *Office Admin*
Tonya Lopez, *Marketing Mgr*
▲ **EMP:** 40 **EST:** 1956
SQ FT: 8,000

SALES (est): 60.5MM **Privately Held**
WEB: www.lubeoil.com
SIC: 5172 Gasoline

(P-9541)
VALLEY PACIFIC PETRO SVCS INC (PA)
152 Frank West Cir # 100, Stockton (95206-4005)
PHONE..................209 948-9412
Norman Eugene Crum, *CEO*
Dan Elmer, *President*
Dale Heinze, *President*
Nathan Crum, *Vice Pres*
Diane E Crum, *Admin Sec*
EMP: 40 **EST:** 1954
SQ FT: 10,000
SALES (est): 110.6MM **Privately Held**
WEB: www.chevron.com
SIC: 5172 Gasoline

(P-9542)
VAN DE POL ENTERPRISES INC (PA)
4895 S Airport Way, Stockton (95206-3915)
P.O. Box 1107 (95201-1107)
PHONE..................209 465-3421
Lee Atwater, *Ch of Bd*
Paul Gosal, *Owner*
Ted Wysoki, *Owner*
Ronald M Vandepol, *CEO*
Scott Macewan, *CFO*
EMP: 75
SQ FT: 10,000
SALES (est): 131.8MM **Privately Held**
WEB: www.vandepol.us
SIC: 5172 Gasoline

5181 Beer & Ale Wholesale

(P-9543)
AUBURN ALEHOUSE LP
Also Called: Auburn Ale House
289 Washington St, Auburn (95603-5036)
PHONE..................530 885-2537
Brian Ford, *Owner*
EMP: 40 **EST:** 2006
SALES (est): 7.2MM **Privately Held**
WEB: www.auburnalehouse.com
SIC: 5181 2082 5921 5812 Beer & ale; beer (alcoholic beverage); wine & beer; American restaurant

(P-9544)
BAY AREA DISTRIBUTING CO INC
1061 Factory St, Richmond (94801-2161)
PHONE..................510 232-8554
Kenneth G Sodo, *President*
Michael Bosnich, *Vice Pres*
Kevin Brans, *Manager*
▲ **EMP:** 50 **EST:** 1973
SQ FT: 22,000
SALES (est): 14MM **Privately Held**
WEB: www.bayareadistributing.com
SIC: 5181 5149 Beer & other fermented malt liquors; mineral or spring water bottling; soft drinks

(P-9545)
BOTTOMLEY DISTRIBUTING CO INC
755 Yosemite Dr, Milpitas (95035-5463)
PHONE..................408 945-0660
Donald A Bottomley, *President*
Tony Sanfilippo, *Sales Mgr*
Michael Santos, *Sales Mgr*
Craig Shore, *Sales Mgr*
Jeremy Smith, *Sales Staff*
◆ **EMP:** 90 **EST:** 1965
SQ FT: 96,000
SALES (est): 24.7MM **Privately Held**
WEB: www.bottomleydistributing.com
SIC: 5181 Beer & other fermented malt liquors

(P-9546)
CAPITAL BEVERAGE COMPANY (PA)
2500 Del Monte St, West Sacramento (95691-3835)
P.O. Box 914 (95691-0914)
PHONE..................916 371-8164
Kenneth M Adamson, *President*
Charles Moulton, *CFO*
◆ **EMP:** 110 **EST:** 1960
SQ FT: 130,000
SALES (est): 15.4MM **Privately Held**
SIC: 5181 5182 5149 Beer & other fermented malt liquors; wine coolers, alcoholic; juices; mineral or spring water bottling

(P-9547)
CHRISSA IMPORTS LTD
Also Called: Spatten West
280 Harbor Way, South San Francisco (94080-6816)
P.O. Box 2161 (94083-2161)
PHONE..................650 877-8460
K D Hildebrandt, *CEO*
Christopher Hildebrandt, *President*
Andreas Hildebrandt, *Vice Pres*
Keith Tabayoyon, *General Mgr*
Socorro Tinoco, *Controller*
◆ **EMP:** 35 **EST:** 1965
SALES (est): 13.8MM **Privately Held**
WEB: www.chrissaimports.com
SIC: 5181 5182 5921 Beer & other fermented malt liquors; wine; wine

(P-9548)
COUCH DISTRIBUTING COMPANY INC
104 Lee Rd, Watsonville (95076-9448)
P.O. Box 50004 (95077-5004)
PHONE..................831 724-0649
George W Couch III, *CEO*
Bonte Eugene, *Exec VP*
Pieracci Louie, *Exec VP*
Geoffrey A Couch, *Vice Pres*
Geoffrey Couch, *Vice Pres*
▲ **EMP:** 160 **EST:** 1947
SQ FT: 72,000
SALES (est): 46.9MM **Privately Held**
WEB: www.couchdistributing.com
SIC: 5181 Beer & other fermented malt liquors

(P-9549)
DBI BEVERAGE SAN FRANCISCO
245 S Spruce Ave Ste 100, South San Francisco (94080-4597)
PHONE..................415 643-9900
David Ingram, *Ch of Bd*
Bob Stahl, *Co-President*
Stan J Butkowski, *Vice Pres*
Sergio Serrano, *District Mgr*
Bill Bahr, *General Mgr*
▲ **EMP:** 250 **EST:** 1934
SALES (est): 38.7MM
SALES (corp-wide): 125.5MM **Privately Held**
WEB: www.goldenbrands.com
SIC: 5181 5149 Beer & other fermented malt liquors; soft drinks; mineral or spring water bottling
PA: Dbi Beverage Inc.
 2 Ingram Blvd
 La Vergne TN 37089
 615 793-2337

(P-9550)
DONAGHY SALES INC
2363 S Cedar Ave, Fresno (93725-1078)
PHONE..................559 486-0901
Edward Donaghy, *CEO*
Janis Donaghy, *Admin Sec*
Lisa Valdez, *Human Resources*
Tanner Hargis, *Buyer*
Trevor Cisneros, *Manager*
▲ **EMP:** 675 **EST:** 1968
SQ FT: 75,000
SALES (est): 115.1MM **Privately Held**
WEB: www.donaghysales.com
SIC: 5181 Beer & other fermented malt liquors

5181 - Beer & Ale Wholesale County (P-9551)

(P-9551)
FRESNO BEVERAGE COMPANY INC
Also Called: Valley Wide Beverage Company
3525 S East Ave, Fresno (93725-9000)
PHONE..............................559 650-1500
Louis J Amendola, *CEO*
Michelle Smith, *Executive*
Rose Lewellon, *Admin Sec*
Tommy Wong, *Administration*
Kimberly Lester, *Controller*
◆ **EMP:** 180 **EST:** 1985
SQ FT: 140,000
SALES (est): 63.4MM **Privately Held**
WEB: www.valleywidebeverage.com
SIC: 5181 Beer & other fermented malt liquors

(P-9552)
HARBOR DISTRIBUTING LLC
Also Called: Golden Brands
3500 Carlin Dr, West Sacramento (95691-5872)
PHONE..............................916 373-5700
Kimberly Clift, *Branch Mgr*
EMP: 300 **Privately Held**
WEB: www.harbordistributingllc.com
SIC: 5181 Beer & other fermented malt liquors
HQ: Harbor Distributing, Llc
5901 Bolsa Ave
Huntington Beach CA 92647
714 933-2400

(P-9553)
HARBOR DISTRIBUTING LLC ◯
6450 Lockheed Dr, Redding (96002-9000)
PHONE..............................530 691-5811
Duke Reyes, *Mng Member*
EMP: 73 **EST:** 2021
SALES (est): 4.6MM **Privately Held**
SIC: 5181 Beer & ale

(P-9554)
MARKSTEIN BEV CO SACRAMENTO
Also Called: Markstein Beverage Company
60 Main Ave, Sacramento (95838-2034)
P.O. Box 15379 (95851-0379)
PHONE..............................916 920-3911
Hayden Markstein, *CEO*
Richard Markstein, *Ch of Bd*
Steve Markstein, *President*
Barbara Sady, *Administration*
Adam Strautman, *IT/INT Sup*
▲ **EMP:** 150 **EST:** 1974
SALES (est): 68.3MM **Privately Held**
WEB: www.marksteinbev.com
SIC: 5181 5149 Beer & other fermented malt liquors; soft drinks; mineral or spring water bottling

(P-9555)
MARKSTEIN SALES COMPANY
Also Called: Markstein Beverage Co
1645 Drive In Way, Antioch (94509-8507)
PHONE..............................925 755-1919
Laura Lee Markstein, *President*
Robert C Markstein, *CFO*
Keith Hammonds, *Manager*
▲ **EMP:** 130 **EST:** 1955
SQ FT: 5,000
SALES (est): 56.9MM **Privately Held**
WEB: www.marksteinsalescompany.com
SIC: 5181 Beer & other fermented malt liquors

(P-9556)
MATAGRANO INC
440 Forbes Blvd, South San Francisco (94080-2015)
P.O. Box 2588 (94083-2588)
PHONE..............................650 829-4829
Louis Matagrano, *President*
William Hill, *CFO*
Tom Haas, *Vice Pres*
Frank Matagrano Jr, *Vice Pres*
Scott Mills, *Controller*
▲ **EMP:** 175 **EST:** 1972
SQ FT: 100,000
SALES (est): 51.2MM **Privately Held**
WEB: www.matagrano.com
SIC: 5181 5149 Beer & other fermented malt liquors; mineral or spring water bottling; juices

(P-9557)
MORRIS DISTRIBUTING
3800a Lakeville Hwy, Petaluma (94954-5673)
P.O. Box 5699 (94955-5699)
PHONE..............................707 769-7294
Ronald L Morris, *CEO*
Joe Netter, *Corp Secy*
Michael Morton, *General Mgr*
Amanda Balenzuela, *Sales Staff*
Dan Dupree, *Sales Staff*
▲ **EMP:** 80 **EST:** 1933
SQ FT: 13,500
SALES (est): 21.2MM **Privately Held**
WEB: www.morrisdistributing.com
SIC: 5181 5149 Beer & other fermented malt liquors; mineral or spring water bottling; juices

(P-9558)
NOR-CAL BEVERAGE CO INC (PA)
2150 Stone Blvd, West Sacramento (95691-4049)
PHONE..............................916 372-0600
Shannon Deary-Bell, *President*
Donald Deary, *Ch of Bd*
Grant Deary, *President*
Tim Deary, *President*
Mike Montroni, *CFO*
◆ **EMP:** 280 **EST:** 1937
SQ FT: 152,000
SALES (est): 231.7MM **Privately Held**
WEB: www.ncbev.com
SIC: 5181 2086 Beer & other fermented malt liquors; soft drinks: packaged in cans, bottles, etc.

(P-9559)
NORTH COAST MERCANTILE CO INC (PA)
1115 W Del Norte St, Eureka (95501-2117)
PHONE..............................707 445-4910
Robert Hansen, *President*
Constance Hansen, *Vice Pres*
Lisa Hindley, *Admin Asst*
Bradley Bill, *Manager*
EMP: 39 **EST:** 1941
SQ FT: 21,000
SALES (est): 11MM **Privately Held**
WEB: www.ncmercantile.com
SIC: 5181 5182 Beer & other fermented malt liquors; wine

(P-9560)
REDDING DISTRIBUTING COMPANY
6450 Lockheed Dr, Redding (96002-9000)
P.O. Box 492515 (96049-2515)
PHONE..............................530 226-5700
David E Jensen, *President*
Jack S Studebaker, *Corp Secy*
Al Shufelberger, *Vice Pres*
Lewis Milligan, *General Mgr*
Brandon McDonald, *Sales Staff*
▲ **EMP:** 45 **EST:** 1960
SQ FT: 30,000
SALES (est): 12.5MM **Privately Held**
WEB: www.reddingdistributing.com
SIC: 5181 5182 5149 Ale; beer & other fermented malt liquors; wine coolers, alcoholic; soft drinks
HQ: Harbor Distributing, Llc
5901 Bolsa Ave
Huntington Beach CA 92647
714 933-2400

(P-9561)
REYES HOLDINGS LLC
Also Called: Golden Brands
1729 Seabright Ave Ste A, Santa Cruz (95062-2120)
PHONE..............................831 761-6400
David Reyes, *Branch Mgr*
EMP: 103 **Privately Held**
WEB: www.reyesholdings.com
SIC: 5181 5149 Beer & other fermented malt liquors; beverages, except coffee & tea
PA: Reyes Holdings, L.L.C.
6250 N River Rd Ste 9000
Rosemont IL 60018

(P-9562)
SACCANI DISTRIBUTING COMPANY
2600 5th St, Sacramento (95818-2899)
P.O. Box 1764 (95812-1764)
PHONE..............................916 441-0213
Gary Saccani, *President*
Steven Fishman, *Corp Secy*
Jill Saccani, *Vice Pres*
Roland Saccani, *Vice Pres*
Neal Banyard, *District Mgr*
▲ **EMP:** 90 **EST:** 1933
SQ FT: 40,000
SALES (est): 33.8MM **Privately Held**
WEB: www.saccanidist.com
SIC: 5181 5149 Beer & other fermented malt liquors; soft drinks

(P-9563)
T F LOUDERBACK INC
Also Called: Bay Area Beverage Company
700 National Ct, Richmond (94804-2008)
PHONE..............................510 965-6120
Thomas J Louderback, *President*
Ron Bishop, *CFO*
Chris Reed, *Division Mgr*
Todd Rovelstad, *Admin Sec*
Michael J Marver, *Controller*
◆ **EMP:** 102 **EST:** 1969
SQ FT: 65,000
SALES (est): 34.6MM **Privately Held**
WEB: www.bayareabev.com
SIC: 5181 5149 2037 2033 Beer & other fermented malt liquors; beverages, except coffee & tea; juices; frozen fruits & vegetables; canned fruits & specialties

(P-9564)
VARNI BROTHERS CORPORATION (PA)
Also Called: Stanislaus Distributing Co
400 Hosmer Ave, Modesto (95351-3920)
PHONE..............................209 521-1777
Michael Attilio Varni, *President*
Fred Varni, *Corp Secy*
John Salzman, *Maintence Staff*
Tony C Varni, *Manager*
◆ **EMP:** 80 **EST:** 1960
SQ FT: 80,000
SALES (est): 80.1MM **Privately Held**
WEB: www.vbcbottling.com
SIC: 5181 2086 5182 Beer & other fermented malt liquors; bottled & canned soft drinks; wine

---

5182 Wine & Distilled Alcoholic Beverages Wholesale

(P-9565)
ARROWHEAD MOUNTAIN WINERY CORP (PA)
2352 Thornsberry Rd, Sonoma (95476-4821)
PHONE..............................707 938-3254
Robert C Elster Jr, *Principal*
EMP: 42 **EST:** 2008
SALES (est): 880.7K **Privately Held**
WEB: www.arrowheadmountainwinery.com
SIC: 5182 Wine

(P-9566)
AV BRANDS INC
Also Called: Aveniu Brands
635 Broadway Ste 2, Sonoma (95476-7004)
PHONE..............................410 884-9463
Andrew Mansinne, *President*
◆ **EMP:** 50 **EST:** 2007
SQ FT: 7,000
SALES (est): 7.2MM **Privately Held**
SIC: 5182 Wine

(P-9567)
BEN MYERSON CANDY CO INC
Also Called: Wine Warehouse
912 Harbour Way S, Richmond (94804-3615)
P.O. Box 45616, San Francisco (94145-0616)
PHONE..............................510 236-2233
Michael Cimino, *Manager*
Trevor Thiret, *Exec VP*
Linda Myerson, *Vice Pres*
Keith Smith, *Vice Pres*
Alex Lopez, *Regional Mgr*
EMP: 67
SALES (corp-wide): 363.7MM **Privately Held**
WEB: www.winewarehouse.com
SIC: 5182 5181 Liquor; neutral spirits; beer & ale
PA: Ben Myerson Candy Co., Inc.
6550 E Washington Blvd
Commerce CA 90040
800 331-2829

(P-9568)
BENCHMARK WINE GROUP INC
445 Devlin Rd, NAPA (94558-6274)
PHONE..............................707 255-3500
David Parker, *CEO*
Lorielle Wiatr, *Executive Asst*
Jaimini Bhagwan, *Administration*
Harry Rindler, *Marketing Staff*
Beatrice Fernandez, *Sales Staff*
▲ **EMP:** 36 **EST:** 2002
SALES (est): 10MM **Privately Held**
WEB: www.benchmarkwine.com
SIC: 5182 Wine

(P-9569)
CANANDAIGUA WINE COMPANY INC
12667 Road 24, Madera (93637-9020)
PHONE..............................559 673-7071
Marvin Sands, *Ch of Bd*
Richard Sands, *President*
Thomas Howe, *Treasurer*
Lynn K Fetterman, *Vice Pres*
James P Finkle, *Vice Pres*
◆ **EMP:** 144 **EST:** 1937
SALES (est): 22.6MM
SALES (corp-wide): 8.6B **Publicly Held**
WEB: www.cbrands.com
SIC: 5182 Wine
PA: Constellation Brands, Inc.
207 High Point Dr # 100
Victor NY 14564
585 678-7100

(P-9570)
CENTRAL COAST WINE COMPANY (DH)
Also Called: Henry Wine Group, The
4301 Industrial Way, Benicia (94510-1227)
PHONE..............................707 745-8500
Ed Hogan, *President*
Julia Chalios, *District Mgr*
Brian Crowley, *District Mgr*
▲ **EMP:** 135 **EST:** 1980
SALES (est): 34.5MM
SALES (corp-wide): 542MM **Privately Held**
WEB: www.winebow.com
SIC: 5182 Wine coolers, alcoholic; wine

(P-9571)
CHAMBERS & CHAMBERS INC (PA)
511 Alexis Ct, NAPA (94558-7526)
PHONE..............................415 642-5500
Jack Paul Chambers, *Ch of Bd*
Suzanne Chambers Turley, *President*
Robert Rankin, *CFO*
Erik Hattevik, *Business Anlyst*
Daniel Kapp, *Engineer*
▲ **EMP:** 40 **EST:** 1976
SALES (est): 27.5MM **Privately Held**
WEB: www.chamberswines.com
SIC: 5182 Wine

(P-9572)
CONSTLLTION BRNDS US OPRTONS I
Also Called: Mission Bell Winery
12667 Road 24, Madera (93637-9020)
PHONE..............................559 485-0141
Michael Othites, *Branch Mgr*
Tim Pfeiff, *Senior Engr*
Leticia Motz, *Buyer*
John Prado, *Plant Engr*
Kent Lindgren, *Director*
EMP: 773
SALES (corp-wide): 8.6B **Publicly Held**
WEB: www.cbrands.com
SIC: 5182 Wine

▲ = Import ▼ = Export
◆ = Import/Export

PRODUCTS & SERVICES SECTION

5191 - Farm Splys Wholesale County (P-9594)

HQ: Constellation Brands U.S. Operations, Inc.
235 N Bloomfield Rd
Canandaigua NY 14424
585 396-7600

(P-9573)
DARCIE KENT WINERY LLC
Also Called: Almost Famous Wine Company
7000 Tesla Rd, Livermore (94550-9151)
PHONE....................925 443-5368
David Kent, Mng Member
EMP: 20 EST: 2020
SALES (est): 1.6MM Privately Held
SIC: 5182 2084 Wine & distilled beverages; wines, brandy & brandy spirits

(P-9574)
EPIC VENTURES INC (PA)
Also Called: Epic Wines & Spirits
200 Concourse Blvd, Santa Rosa (95403-8210)
PHONE....................844 824-0422
Bill Foley, CEO
John Reiter, Vice Pres
John Adams, Controller
Kevin Groom, Purchasing
Nicole Rizzo, Sales Associate
▲ EMP: 50 EST: 1995
SALES (est): 99.3MM Privately Held
SIC: 5182 Wine

(P-9575)
FOLIO WINE COMPANY LLC (PA)
Also Called: Folio Wine Company Imports
550 Gateway Dr Ste 220, NAPA (94558-7578)
PHONE....................707 256-2700
R Michael Mondavi, Mng Member
Jamie Conahan, Partner
Diane Garfield, Vice Pres
Chad Pare, Area Mgr
Liz Sathe, Area Mgr
▲ EMP: 40 EST: 2004
SALES (est): 34.1MM Privately Held
WEB: www.foliowine.com
SIC: 5182 Wine

(P-9576)
FOLIO WINE COMPANY LLC
1285 Dealy Ln, NAPA (94559-9706)
PHONE....................707 256-2757
Rick Choate, Branch Mgr
EMP: 65
SALES (corp-wide): 34.1MM Privately Held
WEB: www.foliowine.com
SIC: 5182 Wine
PA: Folio Wine Company, Llc
550 Gateway Dr Ste 220
Napa CA 94558
707 256-2700

(P-9577)
FRANK-LIN DISTILLERS PDTS LTD (PA)
2455 Huntington Dr, Fairfield (94533-9734)
PHONE....................408 259-8900
Frank J Maestri, President
Vince Maestri Jr, Exec VP
Mark S Pechusick, Exec VP
Lindley Maestri, Vice Pres
Michael Maestri, Vice Pres
◆ EMP: 110 EST: 1966
SQ FT: 54,216
SALES (est): 43.9MM Privately Held
WEB: www.frank-lin.com
SIC: 5182 2085 Wine; distilled & blended liquors

(P-9578)
FREIXENET USA INC
Also Called: Gloria Ferrer
23555 Arnold Dr, Sonoma (95476-9285)
P.O. Box 1949 (95476-1949)
PHONE....................707 996-7256
Jose Maria Ferrer, President
Eva Bertran, Exec VP
Jake Callinan, Accounting Mgr
David Brown, VP Mktg
Kevin Newby, Marketing Staff
▲ EMP: 54 EST: 1981
SQ FT: 4,000

SALES (est): 23.7MM
SALES (corp-wide): 176.2MM Privately Held
WEB: www.gloriaferrer.com
SIC: 5182 Wine
PA: Freixenet Sa
Plaza Joan Sala 2
Sant Sadurni D Anoia 08770
938 917-000

(P-9579)
HENRY WINE GROUP LLC (HQ)
Also Called: Henry Wine Group of C.A., The
4301 Industrial Way, Benicia (94510-1227)
PHONE....................707 745-8500
Ed Hogan, President
Kent Fitzgerald, CFO
Stephanie O'Brien, CFO
Amoreena Anker, Vice Pres
Chris Choate, Vice Pres
▲ EMP: 297 EST: 2003
SALES (est): 83.2MM
SALES (corp-wide): 542MM Privately Held
WEB: www.winebow.com
SIC: 5182 Wine
PA: The Winebow Group Llc
4800 Cox Rd Ste 300
Glen Allen VA 23060
804 752-3670

(P-9580)
MADISON VINEYARD HOLDINGS LLC
1 Kirkland Ranch Rd, American Canyon (94503-9697)
PHONE....................707 254-8673
▲ EMP: 40 EST: 2009
SQ FT: 50,000
SALES (est): 17.1MM Privately Held
SIC: 5182 5921 Whol Wine/Distilled Beverages Ret Alcoholic Beverages
PA: The Madison Companies Llc
5619 Dtc Pkwy Ste 800
Greenwood Village CO 80111
303 957-2000

(P-9581)
MAGAVE TEQUILA INC
6 Park Pl, Belvedere Tiburon (94920-1048)
PHONE....................415 515-3536
Michael Patane, CEO
▲ EMP: 50 EST: 2008
SALES (est): 5.5MM Privately Held
SIC: 5182 Liquor

(P-9582)
NEW PARROTT & CO
5565 Tesla Rd, Livermore (94550-9149)
PHONE....................925 456-2300
Eric Wente, CEO
Peter Chouinard, CFO
Rich Archer, Controller
◆ EMP: 114 EST: 1977
SALES (est): 2.3MM
SALES (corp-wide): 92.4MM Privately Held
WEB: www.wentevineyards.com
SIC: 5182 Wine; liquor
PA: Wente Bros.
5565 Tesla Rd
Livermore CA 94550
925 456-2300

(P-9583)
POPCORN DESIGN LLC
Also Called: Popcorn Wine Group
824a Healdsburg Ave, Healdsburg (95448-3613)
PHONE....................707 321-7982
David P Sayre, CEO
Jay M Behmke, CFO
Thomas Hinde, Manager
▲ EMP: 50 EST: 1995
SALES (est): 5.3MM Privately Held
WEB: www.popcornwine.com
SIC: 5182 Wine

(P-9584)
REGAL III LLC
Also Called: Regal Wine Co
421 Aviation Blvd, Santa Rosa (95403-1069)
PHONE....................707 836-2100
Donald M Hartford Jr, Mng Member
Edwin Abedi, Executive

Jenna Fletcher, Executive
Chris Cooke, District Mgr
Jessica Schaffer, Office Mgr
◆ EMP: 54 EST: 2010
SQ FT: 8,000
SALES (est): 7.2MM Privately Held
WEB: www.regalwineco.com
SIC: 5182 Wine

(P-9585)
SOUTHERN GLZERS WINE SPRITS WA
Also Called: Sgws of CA
33321 Dowe Ave, Union City (94587-2033)
P.O. Box 5001 (94587-8501)
PHONE....................510 477-5500
Wayne Chaplin, CEO
Steven Burrows, Senior VP
Christina Lara, Office Mgr
Carl Corsi, Technical Staff
Marc Meersman, Asst Controller
EMP: 350
SALES (corp-wide): 7.2B Privately Held
WEB: www.southernglazers.com
SIC: 5182 Wine
PA: Southern Glazer's Wine And Spirits, Llc
2400 Sw 145th Ave Ste 200
Miramar FL 33027
866 375-9555

(P-9586)
VARNI BROTHERS CORPORATION
Also Called: Stanislaus Distributing
416 Hosmer Ave, Modesto (95351-3920)
PHONE....................209 526-5513
Dianne Varni, Manager
EMP: 77
SQ FT: 2,000
SALES (corp-wide): 80.1MM Privately Held
WEB: www.vbcbottling.com
SIC: 5182 5181 Wine; beer & other fermented malt liquors
PA: Varni Brothers Corporation
400 Hosmer Ave
Modesto CA 95351
209 521-1777

(P-9587)
VINO FARMS LLC
1377 E Lodi Ave, Lodi (95240-0840)
PHONE....................209 334-6975
James Ledbetter,
John Ledbetter,
EMP: 700 EST: 2008
SQ FT: 5,000
SALES (est): 82MM Privately Held
WEB: www.vinofarms.net
SIC: 5182 Wine

(P-9588)
WINERY EXCHANGE INC (PA)
Also Called: Wx Brands
500 Redwood Blvd Ste 200, Novato (94947-6921)
PHONE....................415 382-6900
Peter Byck, CEO
Michael Lukan, CFO
John Gilmer, Senior VP
Peter Arbios, Vice Pres
Natasha Hayes, Vice Pres
▲ EMP: 50 EST: 1999
SQ FT: 8,300
SALES (est): 42.4MM Privately Held
SIC: 5182 Wine

(P-9589)
YOUNGS MARKET COMPANY LLC
850 Jarvis Dr, Morgan Hill (95037-2846)
PHONE....................408 782-3121
Ken Feroli, Manager
EMP: 70
SALES (corp-wide): 1.3B Privately Held
WEB: www.mdc-usa.com
SIC: 5182 Wine
HQ: Young's Market Company, Llc
14402 Franklin Ave
Tustin CA 92780
800 317-6150

(P-9590)
YOUNGS MARKET COMPANY LLC
1255 E Fortune Ave # 101, Fresno (93725-1950)
PHONE....................213 612-1216
Todd Mihaly, Manager
EMP: 70
SQ FT: 55,000
SALES (corp-wide): 1.3B Privately Held
WEB: www.mdc-usa.com
SIC: 5182 Wine; wine coolers, alcoholic; cocktails, alcoholic: premixed; brandy & brandy spirits
HQ: Young's Market Company, Llc
14402 Franklin Ave
Tustin CA 92780
800 317-6150

(P-9591)
YOUNGS MARKET COMPANY LLC
256 Sutton Pl Ste 106, Santa Rosa (95407-8163)
PHONE....................707 584-5170
Mark Delbenny, Manager
Richard Gilpin, Manager
EMP: 70
SALES (corp-wide): 1.3B Privately Held
WEB: www.mdc-usa.com
SIC: 5182 Wine
HQ: Young's Market Company, Llc
14402 Franklin Ave
Tustin CA 92780
800 317-6150

(P-9592)
YOUNGS MARKET COMPANY LLC
3620 Industrial Blvd # 10, West Sacramento (95691-6518)
PHONE....................916 617-4402
Jim Morris, Branch Mgr
Gary Matalucci, Vice Pres
Todd Kamla, Sales Staff
EMP: 70
SALES (corp-wide): 1.3B Privately Held
WEB: www.mdc-usa.com
SIC: 5182 Liquor; wine
HQ: Young's Market Company, Llc
14402 Franklin Ave
Tustin CA 92780
800 317-6150

5191 Farm Splys Wholesale

(P-9593)
ACTAGRO LLC (HQ)
4516 N Howard Ave, Kerman (93630-9644)
P.O. Box 309, Biola (93606-0309)
PHONE....................559 369-2222
Monty Bayer, CEO
Greg Crawford, COO
Terri West, CFO
Kirsten Burrows, Controller
Eric Scott, Supervisor
▲ EMP: 103 EST: 1997
SQ FT: 7,000
SALES (est): 159.2MM
SALES (corp-wide): 20.9B Privately Held
WEB: www.actagro.com
SIC: 5191 Fertilizer & fertilizer materials
PA: Nutrien Ltd
122 1st Ave S Suite 500
Saskatoon SK S7K 7
306 933-8500

(P-9594)
ASSOCIATED FEED & SUPPLY CO (PA)
Also Called: Farwest Trading
5213 W Main St, Turlock (95380-9413)
P.O. Box 2367 (95381-2367)
PHONE....................209 667-2708
Matt Swanson, President
Jim Hyer, Exec VP
Kurt Hertlein, Vice Pres
Bruce Freeby, Creative Dir
Michael Lopes, Controller
▲ EMP: 118 EST: 1971
SQ FT: 1,800
SALES (est): 136.2MM Privately Held
WEB: www.associatedfeed.com
SIC: 5191 Feed

5191 - Farm Splys Wholesale County (P-9595)

PRODUCTS & SERVICES SECTION

(P-9595)
BONNIE PLANTS INC
729 Green Valley Rd, Watsonville (95076-1226)
PHONE..................541 441-2847
EMP: 289
SALES (corp-wide): 1.1B Privately Held
WEB: www.bonnieplants.com
SIC: 5191 Farm supplies
HQ: Bonnie Plants, Inc.
1727 Highway 223
Union Springs AL 36089

(P-9596)
BRITZ FERTILIZERS INC
Also Called: Bsgs Five Points
21817 S Frsno Coalinga Rd, Five Points (93624)
P.O. Box 366 (93624-0366)
PHONE..................559 884-2421
Ken Walls, Manager
EMP: 47
SALES (corp-wide): 104.2MM Privately Held
SIC: 5191 Chemicals, agricultural; fertilizer & fertilizer materials
HQ: Britz Fertilizers Inc.
3265 W Figarden Dr
Fresno CA 93711
559 448-8000

(P-9597)
CUSTOM AG FORMULATORS INC (PA)
3430 S Willow Ave, Fresno (93725-9004)
P.O. Box 26104 (93729-6104)
PHONE..................559 435-1052
Gerald Steward, CEO
▼ EMP: 75 EST: 2010
SALES (est): 21.9MM Privately Held
WEB: www.customagformulators.com
SIC: 5191 Fertilizer & fertilizer materials

(P-9598)
E B STONE & SON INC
Also Called: Greenall
6111 Lambie Rd, Suisun City (94585-9789)
P.O. Box 550 (94585-0550)
PHONE..................707 426-2500
Bradford G Crandall, CEO
Bradford G Crandall Jr, President
Lynne Crandall, Admin Sec
EMP: 65 EST: 1918
SQ FT: 79,000
SALES (est): 32.6MM Privately Held
WEB: www.ebstone.org
SIC: 5191 2873 2875 3423 Fertilizer & fertilizer materials; nitrogenous fertilizers; fertilizers, mixing only; hand & edge tools

(P-9599)
GERMAINS SEED TECHNOLOGY INC
8333 Swanston Ln, Gilroy (95020-4517)
PHONE..................408 848-8120
Paul Mullan, CEO
Patrick Clode, Treasurer
Victoria Lawrence, Managing Dir
Catherine Farr, Admin Sec
Tina Fegan, Finance
◆ EMP: 39 EST: 1988
SALES (est): 19.6MM
SALES (corp-wide): 18.2B Privately Held
WEB: www.germains.com
SIC: 5191 Seeds: field, garden & flower
HQ: Germain's(U.K.)Limited
Hansa Road
King's Lynn PE30
155 377-4012

(P-9600)
HUNT & BEHRENS INC
Also Called: H & B
30 Lakeville St, Petaluma (94952-3125)
P.O. Box 2040 (94953-2040)
PHONE..................707 762-4594
Daniel J Figone, CEO
Dan Figone, President
Robert J Falco, Vice Pres
▼ EMP: 42 EST: 1921
SQ FT: 43,200
SALES (est): 23.3MM Privately Held
WEB: www.hbfeeds.com
SIC: 5191 5999 Feed; feed & farm supply

(P-9601)
JOHN TAYLOR FERTILIZERS CO (DH)
841 W Elkhorn Blvd, Rio Linda (95673-3097)
PHONE..................916 991-9840
Daniel R Vradenburg, CEO
EMP: 302 EST: 1949
SQ FT: 3,000
SALES (est): 3.4MM
SALES (corp-wide): 3.2B Privately Held
WEB: www.wilburellis.com
SIC: 5191 0711 Fertilizer & fertilizer materials; insecticides; fertilizer application services
HQ: Wilbur-Ellis Company Llc
345 California St Fl 27
San Francisco CA 94104
415 772-4000

(P-9602)
LIMAGRAIN SUNFLOWERS INC
71 W Kentucky Ave, Woodland (95695-5800)
P.O. Box 1866 (95776-1866)
PHONE..................530 661-0756
Ken Scarlett, President
Craig Sharp, Vice Pres
▼ EMP: 133 EST: 1997
SQ FT: 10,000
SALES (est): 4.6MM Privately Held
WEB: www.agreliantgenetics.com
SIC: 5191 Seeds: field, garden & flower
PA: Agreliant Genetics, Llc
1122 E 169th St
Westfield IN 46074

(P-9603)
LYMAN GROUP INC (PA)
201 East St, Woodland (95776-3523)
P.O. Box 279, Walnut Grove (95690-0279)
PHONE..................530 662-5442
Ernie Roncoroni, CEO
Larry Chillemi, CFO
Julie Newton, Vice Pres
Betty Murphy, Office Mgr
Joe Silveira, Admin Sec
▲ EMP: 35 EST: 1963
SQ FT: 10,000
SALES (est): 236.8MM Privately Held
WEB: www.growwest.com
SIC: 5191 Chemicals, agricultural; fertilizer & fertilizer materials

(P-9604)
M CALOSSO & SON
1947 E Miner Ave, Stockton (95205-4543)
PHONE..................209 466-8994
Susan Gay Calosso, President
Michael J Calosso, Corp Secy
EMP: 26 EST: 1924
SQ FT: 48,500
SALES (est): 20.7MM Privately Held
SIC: 5191 2441 5085 3993 Farm supplies; boxes, wood; box shooks; signs & advertising specialties; wood partitions & fixtures

(P-9605)
MAYFIELD EQUIPMENT COMPANY (PA)
Also Called: Rainbow Agricultural Services
235 E Perkins St, Ukiah (95482-4401)
PHONE..................707 462-2404
James Mayfield, President
John Mayfield Jr, Chairman
Mark Wedegaertner, Officer
Ted Mayfield, Vice Pres
Sandra Mayfield, Admin Sec
▲ EMP: 49 EST: 1940
SQ FT: 15,000
SALES (est): 17.3MM Privately Held
WEB: www.doitbest.com
SIC: 5251 5191 5211 Hardware; farm supplies; animal feeds; lumber & other building materials

(P-9606)
MID VALLEY AG SVCS INC (PA)
16401 E Highway 26, Linden (95236-9746)
P.O. Box 593 (95236-0593)
PHONE..................209 931-7600
Larry Beck, President
Pete Bulthuis, Vice Pres
EMP: 45
SQ FT: 14,000
SALES (est): 168.8MM Privately Held
WEB: www.midvalleyag.com
SIC: 5191 Chemicals, agricultural

(P-9607)
REDI-GRO CORPORATION
8909 Elder Creek Rd, Sacramento (95828-1806)
PHONE..................916 381-6063
Dennis Chan, President
Judy Kennedy, Vice Pres
▼ EMP: 43 EST: 1978
SQ FT: 14,000
SALES (est): 10.7MM Privately Held
WEB: www.redi-gro.com
SIC: 5191 Chemicals, agricultural

(P-9608)
SAKATA SEED AMERICA INC (HQ)
18095 Serene Dr, Morgan Hill (95037-2833)
P.O. Box 880 (95038-0880)
PHONE..................408 778-7758
David Armstrong, CEO
Koichi Matsunaga, Vice Pres
Margaret Camarillo, Admin Mgr
Isabel Fuenzalida, Executive Asst
Linda Garcia, Admin Asst
▲ EMP: 90 EST: 1977
SQ FT: 48,000
SALES (est): 108.4MM Privately Held
WEB: www.sakata.com
SIC: 5191 0182 Seeds: field, garden & flower; vegetable crops grown under cover

(P-9609)
SANTA CRUZ COMPOST COMPANY INC
71 Elkhorn Rd, Royal Oaks (95076-5447)
PHONE..................831 728-0113
Robert Bowers, President
Janice Bowers, Corp Secy
EMP: 42 EST: 1977
SQ FT: 1,200
SALES (est): 1.3MM Privately Held
WEB: www.tricountylandscapesupply.com
SIC: 5261 5191 Garden supplies & tools; top soil; soil, potting & planting; garden supplies

(P-9610)
SIERRA REFORESTATION COMPANY
Also Called: Reforestation Tech Intl
5355 Monterey Frontage Rd, Gilroy (95020-8033)
PHONE..................408 848-9604
Maria Anderson, President
John Anderson, Vice Pres
Christy Oneil, Technology
Cristina Najar, Opers Mgr
EMP: 40 EST: 1993
SALES (est): 10.4MM Privately Held
WEB: www.reforest.com
SIC: 5191 Fertilizer & fertilizer materials

(P-9611)
STANISLAUS FARM SUPPLY COMPANY (PA)
Also Called: Stan Farm
624 E Service Rd, Modesto (95358-9451)
PHONE..................209 538-7070
Nickolas J Biscay, CEO
Espiri Ixta, COO
Espiridion Ixta, CFO
Tony Weatherred, Vice Pres
Martin Bianchi, Purchasing
EMP: 61
SQ FT: 4,000
SALES (est): 55.5MM Privately Held
WEB: www.farmsupply.coop
SIC: 5191 Fertilizer & fertilizer materials; insecticides; seeds: field, garden & flower

(P-9612)
TENCATE ADVANCED COMPOSITE
2450 Cordelia Rd, Fairfield (94534-1651)
PHONE..................707 359-3400
EMP: 80
SALES (corp-wide): 1.1B Privately Held
WEB: www.toraytac.com
SIC: 5191 Garden supplies
HQ: Toray Advanced Composites Usa Inc.
18410 Butterfield Blvd
Morgan Hill CA 95037

(P-9613)
TREMONT GROUP INCORPORATED
Agrifarm Div
201 East St, Woodland (95776-3523)
PHONE..................530 662-5442
Scott Mansell, Manager
EMP: 17
SQ FT: 10,000
SALES (corp-wide): 236.8MM Privately Held
WEB: www.growwest.com
SIC: 5191 5261 2873 Chemicals, agricultural; fertilizer; nitrogenous fertilizers
HQ: The Tremont Group Incorporated
201 East St
Woodland CA 95776

(P-9614)
UNITED COMPOST & ORGANICS INC
Also Called: Foxfarm Soil & Fertilizer
2200 Bendixsen St, Samoa (95564-9524)
P.O. Box 787, Arcata (95518-0787)
PHONE..................707 443-4369
Mindy Brooks, Admin Asst
Brent Paton, Graphic Designe
Augustus Johnson, Purchasing
Melody Funk, Sales Staff
Kevin Lane, Sales Staff
EMP: 36 Privately Held
WEB: www.foxfarm.com
SIC: 5191 Fertilizer & fertilizer materials
PA: United Compost And Organics
8601 N Scottsdale Rd # 309
Scottsdale AZ 85253

(P-9615)
VOLOAGRI INC
41970 E Main St, Woodland (95776-9508)
PHONE..................805 547-9391
Alois Van Vliet, CEO
Robert Voreyer, CFO
Steve Strange, IT/INT Sup
Brian Avansino, Prdtn Mgr
Tiffany Cook, Senior Mgr
EMP: 150 EST: 2012
SALES (est): 24.9MM Privately Held
WEB: www.voloagri.com
SIC: 5191 Seeds: field, garden & flower

(P-9616)
WILBUR-ELLIS COMPANY LLC
2903 S Cedar Ave, Fresno (93725-2324)
P.O. Box 1286 (93715-1286)
PHONE..................559 442-1220
Doug Hudson, General Mgr
Corina Richards, Office Mgr
Phillip Paggi, Plant Mgr
Juan Rosales, Sales Staff
EMP: 57
SALES (corp-wide): 3.2B Privately Held
WEB: www.wilburellis.com
SIC: 5191 Fertilizer & fertilizer materials
HQ: Wilbur-Ellis Company Llc
345 California St Fl 27
San Francisco CA 94104
415 772-4000

(P-9617)
WILBUR-ELLIS COMPANY LLC (DH)
345 California St Fl 27, San Francisco (94104-2644)
PHONE..................415 772-4000
John P Thacher, Ch of Bd
Keith Beamer, President
Daniel R Vradenburg, President
Michael J Hunter, CFO
Alison J Amonette, Treasurer
EMP: 300 EST: 2016
SALES (est): 2.1B
SALES (corp-wide): 3.2B Privately Held
WEB: www.wilburellis.com
SIC: 5191 0711 Fertilizer & fertilizer materials; fertilizer application services

▲ = Import ▼=Export
◆ =Import/Export

PRODUCTS & SERVICES SECTION

5193 - Flowers, Nursery Stock & Florists' Splys Wholesale County (P-9640)

HQ: Wilbur-Ellis Holdings Ii, Inc.
345 California St Fl 27
San Francisco CA 94104
415 772-4000

(P-9618)
WILBUR-ELLIS HOLDINGS II INC (HQ)
345 California St Fl 27, San Francisco (94104-2644)
PHONE..................415 772-4000
John L Buckley, *President*
Michael J Hunter, *CFO*
John P Thacher, *Chairman*
Alison J Amonette, *Treasurer*
Anne E Cleary, *Vice Pres*
◆ **EMP:** 70 **EST:** 2015
SQ FT: 27,000
SALES (est): 3.1B
SALES (corp-wide): 3.2B **Privately Held**
WEB: www.wilburellis.com
SIC: 5999 5191 5169 Feed & farm supply; chemicals, agricultural; fertilizer & fertilizer materials; animal feeds; industrial chemicals
PA: Wilbur-Ellis Holdings, Inc.
345 California St Fl 27
San Francisco CA 94104
415 772-4000

5192 Books, Periodicals & Newspapers Wholesale

(P-9619)
SCHOLASTIC BOOK FAIRS INC
42001 Christy St, Fremont (94538-3163)
PHONE..................510 771-1700
Caesey Ryan, *Branch Mgr*
EMP: 57
SALES (corp-wide): 1.3B **Publicly Held**
WEB: www.scholasticbookfairs.com
SIC: 5192 Books
HQ: Scholastic Book Fairs, Inc.
1080 Greenwood Blvd
Lake Mary FL 32746
407 829-7300

(P-9620)
ZYANTE INC
Also Called: Zybooks
41 E Main St, Los Gatos (95030-6907)
PHONE..................510 541-4434
Smita Bakshi, *CEO*
Kathleen Hayes, *Vice Pres*
Alex Von Rosenberg, *Vice Pres*
Kate Gleeson, *Executive*
Maureen Schwartz, *Executive*
EMP: 91 **EST:** 2012
SALES (est): 13.7MM
SALES (corp-wide): 1.9B **Publicly Held**
WEB: www.zybooks.com
SIC: 5192 Newspapers
PA: John Wiley & Sons, Inc.
111 River St Ste 2000
Hoboken NJ 07030
201 748-6000

5193 Flowers, Nursery Stock & Florists' Splys Wholesale

(P-9621)
A TO Z TREE NURSERY INC (PA)
Also Called: Tree Movers
3225 Auto Mall Pkwy, Fremont (94538)
P.O. Box 320940, Los Gatos (95032-0115)
PHONE..................510 651-9021
Jon P Anderson, *President*
▲ **EMP:** 35 **EST:** 1973
SALES (est): 8.5MM **Privately Held**
WEB: www.treemovers.com
SIC: 5193 5261 0783 0782 Nursery stock; nursery stock, seeds & bulbs; removal services, bush & tree; lawn & garden services

(P-9622)
AGROMILLORA CALIFORNIA
Also Called: Wholesale Olive Tree Nursery
612 E Gridley Rd, Gridley (95948-9407)
PHONE..................530 846-0404
Clifford Bryan Little, *CEO*
Xabier Marques, *President*
Ed Henderson, *Opers Staff*
Martin Stockton, *Production*
Suman Sohal, *Manager*
▲ **EMP:** 35 **EST:** 2000
SALES (est): 15.4MM **Privately Held**
WEB: www.agromillora.com
SIC: 5193 Nursery stock

(P-9623)
ANNIES ANNUALS PERENNIALS LLC
801 Chesley Ave, Richmond (94801-2135)
PHONE..................510 215-3301
Annie Hayes,
Elayne Takemoto, *Manager*
EMP: 40 **EST:** 2001
SALES (est): 10.7MM **Privately Held**
WEB: www.anniesannuals.com
SIC: 5193 5261 Nursery stock; nurseries & garden centers

(P-9624)
ASA EDEN LLC
Also Called: Asa Floral
2044 Edison Ave, San Leandro (94577-1104)
PHONE..................510 653-7227
Peter Stair,
Jennifer Cerruti, *Admin Asst*
EMP: 45 **EST:** 1986
SQ FT: 25,000
SALES (est): 4.6MM **Privately Held**
WEB: www.asafloral.com
SIC: 5193 Flowers, fresh

(P-9625)
BALDOCCHI AND SONS INC
Also Called: Pacific Nurseries
2499 Hillside Blvd, Colma (94014-2882)
PHONE..................650 755-2330
Donald Baldocchi, *President*
Julie Baldocchi, *Vice Pres*
Jenny Lombardo, *Controller*
Don Schenone, *VP Opers*
Julia Saelee, *Sales Staff*
EMP: 35 **EST:** 1997
SQ FT: 6,000
SALES (est): 9.8MM **Privately Held**
SIC: 5193 Nursery stock

(P-9626)
BAY CITY FLOWER CO (PA)
2265 Cabrillo Hwy S, Half Moon Bay (94019-2250)
P.O. Box 186 (94019-0186)
PHONE..................650 726-5535
Harrison Higaki, *Ch of Bd*
Naomi Higaki, *Shareholder*
Sam Hasegawa, *CFO*
Sandee Loeffler, *Marketing Mgr*
Michael Hall, *Sales Mgr*
▲ **EMP:** 75 **EST:** 1910
SQ FT: 2,000
SALES (est): 57.2MM **Privately Held**
WEB: www.baycityflower.com
SIC: 5193 Flowers, fresh

(P-9627)
BLOOMS WHOLESALE NURSERY INC
15079 Trestle Glen Dr, Glen Ellen (95442-9635)
PHONE..................707 935-0606
Anthony Bloom, *Partner*
Peter Bloom, *Partner*
Annie Steendam, *Sales Mgr*
EMP: 40 **EST:** 1984
SQ FT: 2,000
SALES (est): 6.9MM **Privately Held**
WEB: www.bloomswholesalenursery.com
SIC: 5193 Nursery stock; flowers & nursery stock

(P-9628)
BUSHNELL GARDENS
Also Called: Bushnell's Landscape Creations
5255 Douglas Blvd, Granite Bay (95746-6204)
PHONE..................916 791-4199
David Bushnell, *Owner*
Shelby Bushnell, *Buyer*
EMP: 80 **EST:** 1979
SQ FT: 1,040
SALES (est): 14.9MM **Privately Held**
WEB: www.bushnellgardens.com
SIC: 5193 Nursery stock; landscape architects; lawn & garden services; landscape contractors; nurseries

(P-9629)
CAMFLOR INC
2364 Riverside Rd, Watsonville (95076-9430)
PHONE..................831 726-1330
Daniel Campos, *President*
Zandra Campos, *CFO*
Gil Campos, *Info Tech Mgr*
Javier Zamora, *Prdtn Mgr*
Carlos Cardoza, *Sales Mgr*
▲ **EMP:** 110 **EST:** 1986
SALES (est): 11.7MM **Privately Held**
WEB: www.camflor.com
SIC: 5193 Flowers, fresh

(P-9630)
CREATIVE PLANT DESIGN INC
1670 Las Plumas Ave Ste C, San Jose (95133-1677)
PHONE..................408 452-1444
Mary McCormick, *President*
Tammy Kraft, *Director*
Talia Leiva, *Accounts Mgr*
EMP: 17 **EST:** 1985
SALES (est): 4MM **Privately Held**
WEB: www.creativeplant.com
SIC: 5193 3999 7699 Flowers & nursery stock; plants, artificial & preserved; agricultural equipment repair services

(P-9631)
DEVIL MOUNTAIN WHL NURS LLC (PA)
9885 Alcosta Blvd, San Ramon (94583-3244)
PHONE..................925 829-6006
Pat Murphy, *Principal*
Drew McMillan, *CFO*
David Book, *Info Tech Mgr*
Kevin Kudla, *Info Tech Mgr*
Andrea Overton, *Controller*
EMP: 53 **EST:** 1995
SALES (est): 118.4MM **Privately Held**
WEB: www.devilmountainnursery.com
SIC: 5193 Nursery stock

(P-9632)
FISHERS NURSERY
24081 S Austin Rd, Ripon (95366-9646)
P.O. Box 657 (95366-0657)
PHONE..................209 599-3412
Jerry Fisher, *President*
Mary Fisher, *Corp Secy*
▲ **EMP:** 75 **EST:** 1968
SQ FT: 450,000
SALES (est): 22MM **Privately Held**
SIC: 5193 Nursery stock

(P-9633)
GREEN TREE NURSERY
Also Called: Linwood Nursery
23979 Lake Rd, La Grange (95329-9505)
PHONE..................209 874-9100
Jason Hall, *Partner*
EMP: 50 **EST:** 1966
SQ FT: 6,000
SALES (est): 16.4MM **Privately Held**
WEB: www.greentreenursery.com
SIC: 5193 Nursery stock

(P-9634)
HEADSTART NURSERY INC (PA)
4860 Monterey Rd, Gilroy (95020-9511)
PHONE..................408 842-3030
Steven H Costa, *President*
Don Christopher, *Vice Pres*
Randy Costa, *Vice Pres*
Doug Iten, *General Mgr*
Chris Peck, *General Mgr*
▲ **EMP:** 85 **EST:** 1977
SQ FT: 3,000
SALES (est): 51.6MM **Privately Held**
WEB: www.headstartnursery.com
SIC: 5193 5261 Plants, potted; nursery stock; nurseries & garden centers

(P-9635)
HIGH RANCH NURSERY INC
3800 Delmar Ave, Loomis (95650-9051)
P.O. Box 2262 (95650-2262)
PHONE..................916 652-9261
John C Nitta, *President*
Sarah Nitta, *Vice Pres*
Pauline Sakai, *Sales Associate*
Mark Nitta, *Facilities Mgr*
EMP: 40 **EST:** 1977
SQ FT: 5,000
SALES (est): 8.9MM **Privately Held**
WEB: www.hrnursery.com
SIC: 5193 Nursery stock

(P-9636)
MCCALLS NURSERIES INC
8151 E Olive Ave, Fresno (93737-9753)
PHONE..................559 255-7679
Steve McCall, *President*
Lisa McCall, *Corp Secy*
Denise Martin, *Vice Pres*
Brian McCall, *Prdtn Mgr*
John Foth, *Sales Mgr*
EMP: 45 **EST:** 1948
SQ FT: 6,000
SALES (est): 10.4MM **Privately Held**
WEB: www.mccallsnurseries.com
SIC: 5193 Nursery stock

(P-9637)
MT EDEN FLORAL COMPANY LLC (PA)
2124 Bering Dr, San Jose (95131-2013)
PHONE..................408 213-5777
Yoshimi Shibata, *Mng Member*
Alex Shibata, *Department Mgr*
Lena Ruan, *Controller*
Esmeralda Ruiz, *Purchasing*
Adeodato O Calderon, *Sales Staff*
EMP: 40 **EST:** 1952
SQ FT: 60,000
SALES (est): 11MM **Privately Held**
WEB: www.mteden.com
SIC: 5193 Flowers, fresh; florists' supplies

(P-9638)
NORMANS NURSERY INC
6250 N Escalon Bellota Rd, Linden (95236-9428)
P.O. Box 959 (95236-0959)
PHONE..................209 887-2033
Barbara Hayes, *Manager*
Nancy Norman, *COO*
Cheri Mayer, *Office Mgr*
Lena Loo, *Finance Mgr*
EMP: 120
SALES (corp-wide): 95.8MM **Privately Held**
WEB: www.normansnursery.com
SIC: 5193 0181 Nursery stock; nursery stock, growing of
PA: Norman's Nursery, Inc.
8665 Duarte Rd
San Gabriel CA 91775
626 285-9795

(P-9639)
SHIBATA FLORAL COMPANY (PA)
620 Brannan St, San Francisco (94107-1512)
PHONE..................415 495-8611
Toll Free:..................888 -
Eric L Shibata, *President*
▲ **EMP:** 35 **EST:** 1994
SQ FT: 40,000
SALES (est): 14.1MM **Privately Held**
WEB: www.shibatafc.com
SIC: 5193 Flowers, fresh

(P-9640)
SUNCREST NURSERIES INC
400 Casserly Rd, Watsonville (95076-9700)
PHONE..................831 728-2595
Stan Iversen, *President*
Maria Torres, *Executive*
Cassandra McAleer, *Administration*
Lisa Rulison, *Sales Staff*
Miguel Quintero, *Manager*
EMP: 55 **EST:** 1989
SQ FT: 1,000

5193 - Flowers, Nursery Stock & Florists' Splys Wholesale

SALES (est): 11.2MM **Privately Held**
WEB: www.suncrestnurseries.com
SIC: 5193 Nursery stock

(P-9641)
VILLAGE NURSERIES WHL LLC
6901 Bradshaw Rd, Sacramento (95829-9303)
PHONE..................916 993-2292
Steve Sawyer, *Branch Mgr*
EMP: 272
SALES (corp-wide): 61.2MM **Privately Held**
WEB: www.everde.com
SIC: 5193 Nursery stock
PA: Village Nurseries Wholesale, Llc
 1589 N Main St
 Orange CA 92867
 714 279-3100

(P-9642)
WINWARD INTERNATIONAL INC (PA)
Also Called: Winward Silks
42760 Albrae St, Fremont (94538-3390)
PHONE..................510 487-8686
Patrick Tai, *President*
Garrison Tai, *President*
Raymond Chiu, *Vice Pres*
Raymond Chu, *Sales Staff*
◆ EMP: 60 EST: 1977
SQ FT: 10,000
SALES (est): 24.6MM **Privately Held**
WEB: www.winwardsilks.com
SIC: 5193 5023 Artificial flowers; decorative home furnishings & supplies

5194 Tobacco & Tobacco Prdts Wholesale

(P-9643)
PACIFIC GROSERVICE INC
Also Called: Pitco Foods
567 Cinnabar St, San Jose (95110-2306)
PHONE..................408 727-4826
Pericles Navab, *Ch of Bd*
Azadeh Hariri, *Shareholder*
Esmael Maboudi, *Shareholder*
Parviz Maboudi, *Shareholder*
David Luttway, *President*
▲ EMP: 360 EST: 1982
SQ FT: 85,000
SALES (est): 84.6MM **Privately Held**
WEB: www.pitcofoods.com
SIC: 5194 5145 5141 5113 Tobacco & tobacco products; candy; groceries, general line; industrial & personal service paper; service establishment equipment

(P-9644)
PATTON MUSIC CO INC (PA)
Also Called: Patton Vending
1512 Princeton Ave, Modesto (95350-5728)
PHONE..................209 574-1101
James B Reed Jr, *President*
Christine A Reed, *Vice Pres*
Dan Kreutz, *Branch Mgr*
EMP: 50 EST: 1946
SQ FT: 100,000
SALES (est): 16MM **Privately Held**
SIC: 5993 5194 5962 7993 Cigarette store; cigarettes; sandwich & hot food vending machines; juke boxes; amusement machine rental, coin-operated

5199 Nondurable Goods, NEC Wholesale

(P-9645)
APPODEAL INC (PA)
575 Market St Fl 4, San Francisco (94105-5818)
PHONE..................415 996-6877
Pavel Golubev, *CEO*
Natalie Portier, *COO*
Wing Poon, *Marketing Mgr*
Gareth Lee, *Sales Mgr*
Seymour Ellis, *Sales Associate*
EMP: 88 EST: 2015
SALES (est): 29.8MM **Privately Held**
WEB: www.appodeal.com
SIC: 5199 Advertising specialties

(P-9646)
ART SUPPLY ENTERPRISES INC (PA)
Also Called: Macpherson's
1375 Ocean Ave, Emeryville (94608-1128)
PHONE..................800 289-9800
David Schofield, *CEO*
Tali Even-Kesef, *Graphic Designe*
Paulina Dong, *Analyst*
Mike Chen, *Accountant*
Cindy Harris, *Marketing Staff*
◆ EMP: 45 EST: 1906
SQ FT: 16,000
SALES (est): 87.3MM **Privately Held**
WEB: www.macphersonart.com
SIC: 5199 Artists' materials

(P-9647)
BONA FURTUNA LLC (PA)
20 N Santa Cruz Ave Ste B, Los Gatos (95030-5956)
PHONE..................800 380-8819
Stephen J Luczo,
EMP: 98 EST: 2015
SALES (est): 877.1K **Privately Held**
WEB: www.bonafurtuna.com
SIC: 5199 Nondurable goods

(P-9648)
CALVEY INCORPORATED
Also Called: Ernest Packaging Solutions
8670 Fruitridge Rd # 300, Sacramento (95826-9735)
PHONE..................916 681-4800
A Charles Wilson, *Chairman*
Tim Wilson, *President*
◆ EMP: 60 EST: 1946
SQ FT: 155,000
SALES (est): 31.6MM
SALES (corp-wide): 189.3MM **Privately Held**
WEB: www.ernestpackaging.com
SIC: 5199 Packaging materials; cat box litter
PA: Ernest Packaging
 5777 Smithway St
 Commerce CA 90040
 800 233-7788

(P-9649)
CENTRAL GARDEN & PET COMPANY (PA)
1340 Treat Blvd Ste 600, Walnut Creek (94597-7578)
PHONE..................925 948-4000
Timothy P Cofer, *CEO*
William E Brown, *Ch of Bd*
John E Hanson, *President*
Tara Stratinsky, *COO*
Nicholas Lahanas, *CFO*
▲ EMP: 35 EST: 1955
SALES (est): 2.7B **Publicly Held**
WEB: www.central.com
SIC: 5199 5191 Pet supplies; garden supplies

(P-9650)
CENTRAL GARDEN & PET COMPANY
38 Pheasant Run Pl, Danville (94506-5819)
PHONE..................925 964-9879
EMP: 31
SALES (corp-wide): 1.8B **Publicly Held**
SIC: 5999 5199 2048 Ret Misc Merchandise Whol Nondurable Goods Mfg Prepared Feeds
PA: Central Garden & Pet Company
 1340 Treat Blvd Ste 600
 Walnut Creek CA 94597
 925 948-4000

(P-9651)
CLOUDRADIANT CORP
Also Called: Enbiz International
1111 Di Napoli Dr, San Jose (95129-4014)
PHONE..................408 256-1527
Anil RAO, *President*
EMP: 726
SALES (corp-wide): 42.9MM **Privately Held**
SIC: 5199 8748 General merchandise, non-durable; business consulting
PA: Cloudradiant Corp.
 12 Fuchsia
 Lake Forest CA 92630
 408 256-1527

(P-9652)
CORK SUPPLY USA INC
531 Stone Rd, Benicia (94510-1113)
PHONE..................707 746-0353
James W Herwatt, *CEO*
Jochen Michalski, *President*
Miguel Mardel Correia, *CFO*
Lisa Kurtz, *CFO*
Art Danner, *Vice Pres*
◆ EMP: 35 EST: 1981
SQ FT: 24,000
SALES (est): 21MM **Privately Held**
WEB: www.corksupply.com
SIC: 5199 2499 2448 Packaging materials; corks, bottle; pallets, wood

(P-9653)
CROSSROAD SERVICES INC
2360 Alvarado St, San Leandro (94577-4314)
PHONE..................714 728-3915
Steven Scheiner, *President*
Feroun Khan, *Vice Pres*
Chris Whisler, *Vice Pres*
Christopher Boyle, *Software Dev*
EMP: 419 EST: 1984
SQ FT: 5,000 **Privately Held**
WEB: www.csimerchandising.com
SIC: 5199 Variety store merchandise

(P-9654)
D & K LEATHER CORPORATION
3001 Ponderosa Dr, Concord (94520-1667)
PHONE..................415 433-9320
Eum Park, *Principal*
EMP: 77
SALES (corp-wide): 165.2K **Privately Held**
SIC: 5199 Leather goods, except footwear, gloves, luggage, belting
PA: D & K Leather Corporation
 1420 Santa Monica Blvd
 Santa Monica CA
 310 838-8379

(P-9655)
DELAVE INC (PA)
Also Called: Delave Periodicals
311 E Reed St Apt 13, San Jose (95112-3886)
PHONE..................408 293-7200
Frank De La Cruz, *President*
Javier Vega, *Vice Pres*
Maria Rodraguez, *Sales Staff*
EMP: 65 EST: 1983
SQ FT: 40,000
SALES (est): 8.8MM **Privately Held**
SIC: 5994 5199 5611 Magazine stand; newsstand; advertising specialties; clothing, sportswear, men's & boys'

(P-9656)
EMERALD PACKAGING INC
Also Called: E P
33050 Western Ave, Union City (94587-2157)
PHONE..................510 429-5700
Kevin Kelly, *CEO*
James P Kelly Sr, *Ch of Bd*
James M Kelly Jr, *Exec VP*
Jim Kelly, *Vice Pres*
Maura Kelly Koberlein, *Vice Pres*
▲ EMP: 250 EST: 1963
SQ FT: 80,000
SALES (est): 100.2MM **Privately Held**
WEB: www.empack.com
SIC: 5199 Packaging materials

(P-9657)
EVERGREEN PACKAGING LLC
Also Called: Turlock Plant
1500 W Main St, Turlock (95380-3704)
PHONE..................209 664-3426
Ed Sanfrancisco, *Controller*
Deborah Amaya, *Safety Mgr*
EMP: 177 **Publicly Held**
WEB: www.evergreenpackaging.com
SIC: 5199 Packaging materials
HQ: Evergreen Packaging Llc
 5350 Poplar Ave Ste 600
 Memphis TN 38119

(P-9658)
FOAM DISTRIBUTORS INCORPORATED
Also Called: Foam Fabrication For Packaging
31009 San Antonio St, Hayward (94544-7903)
PHONE..................510 441-8377
Stephanie Wright, *Chairman*
Steve M Doyle, *CEO*
James Doyle, *General Mgr*
David Brown, *CTO*
Mark David, *Technology*
EMP: 75 EST: 1977
SQ FT: 72,000
SALES (est): 11.6MM **Privately Held**
WEB: www.foamdist.com
SIC: 5199 Packaging materials

(P-9659)
FREE STREAM MEDIA CORP (PA)
Also Called: Samba TV
123 Townsend St Fl 5, San Francisco (94107-1907)
PHONE..................415 854-0073
Ashwin Navin, *CEO*
Jackson Huynh, *COO*
Dan Ackerman, *Officer*
Chris Jantz, *Vice Pres*
Kris Magel, *Vice Pres*
EMP: 80 EST: 2008
SQ FT: 11,000
SALES (est): 48.3MM **Privately Held**
WEB: www.samba.tv
SIC: 5199 Advertising specialties

(P-9660)
GAMUS LLC
Also Called: GTS Distribution- Northern Cal
3286 Victor St, Santa Clara (95054-2317)
PHONE..................408 441-0170
Mike Cardoza, *Facilities Mgr*
Joe Fallon, *Vice Pres*
Phillip Hughes, *Sales Mgr*
Kevin Branvold, *Sales Staff*
Rob Bertrand, *Manager*
EMP: 48 **Privately Held**
WEB: www.gtsdistribution.com
SIC: 5199 2754 Gifts & novelties; cards, except greeting: gravure printing
PA: Gamus, Llc
 2822 119th St Sw Ste B
 Everett WA 98204

(P-9661)
HUHTAMAKI INC
8450 Gerber Rd, Sacramento (95828-3712)
PHONE..................916 688-4938
Carl Graf, *Opers Spvr*
David Clarke, *Maintence Staff*
EMP: 97
SALES (corp-wide): 3.9B **Privately Held**
WEB: www.huhtamaki.com
SIC: 5199 Packaging materials
HQ: Huhtamaki, Inc.
 9201 Packaging Dr
 De Soto KS 66018
 913 583-3025

(P-9662)
INTERPET USA LLC (HQ)
1340 Treat Blvd Ste 4600, Walnut Creek (94597-2101)
PHONE..................925 948-4000
Allen Simon, *Principal*
EMP: 50 EST: 2004
SALES (est): 2.4MM
SALES (corp-wide): 2.7B **Publicly Held**
WEB: www.central.com
SIC: 5199 Pet supplies
PA: Central Garden & Pet Company
 1340 Treat Blvd Ste 600
 Walnut Creek CA 94597
 925 948-4000

PRODUCTS & SERVICES SECTION
6021 - National Commercial Banks County (P-9685)

(P-9663)
INTERPRESS TECHNOLOGIES INC (HQ)
1120 Del Paso Rd, Sacramento (95834-7772)
PHONE..................916 929-9771
Roderick W Miner, *President*
Peter Fox, *President*
Rocio Galaz-Gomez, *Controller*
Patricia Maciel, *Manager*
◆ **EMP:** 50 **EST:** 1984
SQ FT: 20,000
SALES (est): 30MM **Privately Held**
WEB: www.interpresstechnologies.com
SIC: 5199 Packaging materials
PA: R. W. Miner Corporation
260 California St Ste 300
San Francisco CA 94111
415 781-2626

(P-9664)
ITALIAN AMERICAN CORP
Also Called: American Packaging Co
1515 Alvarado St, San Leandro (94577-2640)
PHONE..................510 877-9000
Kaye Leedham, *President*
Jim Thompson, *Sales Mgr*
George Schmitt, *Consultant*
▲ **EMP:** 42 **EST:** 1976
SQ FT: 103,000
SALES (est): 26.2MM
SALES (corp-wide): 1.3B **Privately Held**
WEB: www.nocalpackaging.kellyspicers.com
SIC: 5199 Packaging materials
HQ: Kelly Spicers Inc.
12310 Slauson Ave
Santa Fe Springs CA 90670

(P-9665)
KENNETH ALLEN RUSH
Also Called: Rush Advertising Specialties
3030 N Maroa Ave, Fresno (93704-5655)
PHONE..................559 224-3976
Kenneth Allen Rush, *Owner*
Michael Rush, *Vice Pres*
Chuck Mangini, *Sales Staff*
Matt McWhorter, *Sales Staff*
▲ **EMP:** 25 **EST:** 1976
SQ FT: 2,750
SALES (est): 9.7MM **Privately Held**
WEB: www.rushadvertising.com
SIC: 5199 2752 Advertising specialties; commercial printing, offset

(P-9666)
LIFESTREET CORPORATION
Also Called: Lifestreet Media
98 Battery St St 504, San Carlos (94070)
PHONE..................650 508-2220
Mitchell Wiesman, *CEO*
Patrick McNenny, *CFO*
EMP: 75 **EST:** 2008
SALES (est): 9.5MM **Privately Held**
WEB: www.lifestreet.com
SIC: 5199 Advertising specialties

(P-9667)
MISSION PETS INC
986 Mission St Fl 5, San Francisco (94103-2970)
PHONE..................415 904-9914
Carmine Petruzello, *CEO*
Jannita Hanson, *CFO*
Dan Brown, *Vice Pres*
Michelle Elliot, *Vice Pres*
Sarah Williamson, *Technical Staff*
▲ **EMP:** 50 **EST:** 1999
SQ FT: 10,000
SALES (est): 45MM **Privately Held**
WEB: www.mission-pets.com
SIC: 5199 Pet supplies

(P-9668)
PAK INC
6108 Lincoln Ave, Carmichael (95608-1722)
PHONE..................916 944-1428
Jae Pak, *Branch Mgr*
EMP: 79
SALES (corp-wide): 94.4K **Privately Held**
WEB: www.henrypak.com
SIC: 5199 Packaging materials
PA: Pak Inc
11116 Tuxford St
Sun Valley CA

(P-9669)
POLYVORE INC
701 First Ave, Sunnyvale (94089-1019)
PHONE..................650 968-1195
Jessica Lee, *CEO*
Pasha Sadri, *CTO*
Chihyu Chang, *Software Engr*
Yue Wu, *Software Engr*
Doug Nomura, *Technology*
EMP: 60 **EST:** 2007
SALES (est): 28.3MM
SALES (corp-wide): 2.1MM **Privately Held**
WEB: www.ssense.com
SIC: 5199 Advertising specialties
HQ: Atallah Group Inc
333 Rue Chabanel O Bureau 900
Montreal QC H2N 2
514 600-5818

(P-9670)
QUAKER PET GROUP INC
160 Mitchell Blvd, San Rafael (94903-2044)
PHONE..................415 721-7400
Kevin Fick, *CEO*
Mike Trott, *CFO*
▲ **EMP:** 100 **EST:** 2010
SQ FT: 11,000
SALES (est): 67MM
SALES (corp-wide): 1.2B **Privately Held**
WEB: www.worldwise.com
SIC: 5199 Pet supplies
HQ: Worldwise, Inc.
6 Hamilton Landing # 150
Novato CA 94949

(P-9671)
SMITH NEWS COMPANY INC
Also Called: Smith Novelty Company
460 9th St, San Francisco (94103-4411)
PHONE..................415 861-4900
Kenneth Glaser Jr, *President*
Stanley Glaser, *CFO*
Matt Kastner, *Creative Dir*
Greg Garlock, *Opers Mgr*
▲ **EMP:** 45 **EST:** 1885
SQ FT: 18,000
SALES (est): 12.3MM **Privately Held**
WEB: www.smithnovelty.com
SIC: 5199 Novelties, paper

(P-9672)
SUPERMARKET ASSOCIATES LLC
533 Boherty Ave, Modesto (95354)
P.O. Box 4278 (95352-4278)
PHONE..................209 529-2639
Robert M Piccinini, *Mng Member*
Trust Dated,
▲ **EMP:** 40 **EST:** 1983
SQ FT: 65,000
SALES (est): 13.3MM **Privately Held**
SIC: 5199 General merchandise, non-durable

(P-9673)
VOLKMAN SEED COMPANY INC
4319 Jessup Rd, Ceres (95307-9604)
P.O. Box 245 (95307-0245)
PHONE..................209 669-3040
Randall Steele, *President*
Lynda Blakemore, *Corp Secy*
▲ **EMP:** 44 **EST:** 1994
SQ FT: 30,000
SALES (est): 12.6MM **Privately Held**
SIC: 5199 5191 Pets & pet supplies; grass seed

(P-9674)
WAL-MARTCOM USA LLC (HQ)
Also Called: Walmart
850 Cherry Ave, San Bruno (94066-3031)
PHONE..................650 837-5000
Marc Lore, *CEO*
Jonathan Gourdet, *Partner*
Towfiq Mark, *President*
Gloria Guo, *Chairman*
Judith McKenna, *Exec VP*
◆ **EMP:** 45 **EST:** 2002
SALES (est): 521.7MM
SALES (corp-wide): 559.1B **Publicly Held**
WEB: www.corporate.walmart.com
SIC: 5961 5199 General merchandise, mail order; general merchandise, non-durable
PA: Walmart Inc.
702 Sw 8th St
Bentonville AR 72716
479 273-4000

(P-9675)
WALLYS NATURAL
Also Called: Wally's Natural Products
11837 Kemper Rd Ste 5, Auburn (95603-9067)
P.O. Box 5275 (95604-5275)
PHONE..................530 887-0396
Russell Shepard, *President*
Holly Sheppard, *VP Mktg*
Tracy Liggett-Burns, *Sales Staff*
Breeann Wollesen, *Manager*
▲ **EMP:** 21 **EST:** 1998
SQ FT: 1,600
SALES (est): 9.5MM **Privately Held**
WEB: www.wallysnatural.com
SIC: 5199 3999 Candles; candles

(P-9676)
WONDERTREATS INC
2200 Lapham Dr, Modesto (95354-3911)
PHONE..................209 521-8881
Jocelyn Yu Hall, *CEO*
Greg Hall, *President*
Aileen Ong, *Admin Asst*
Don Greenland, *Sales Mgr*
Victor Baez, *Director*
▲ **EMP:** 315 **EST:** 1992
SQ FT: 230,000
SALES (est): 51.1MM **Privately Held**
SIC: 5199 5947 Gift baskets; gift baskets

6021 National Commercial Banks

(P-9677)
BANC AMERICA LSG & CAPITL LLC (DH)
555 California St Fl 4, San Francisco (94104-1506)
PHONE..................415 765-7349
Eric Lundquist, *Managing Dir*
Daniel Monberg, *Vice Pres*
EMP: 150 **EST:** 1975
SALES (est): 426.5MM
SALES (corp-wide): 93.7B **Publicly Held**
WEB: www.bankofamerica.com
SIC: 6021 National commercial banks
HQ: Bank Of America, National Association
100 S Tryon St
Charlotte NC 28202
704 386-5681

(P-9678)
BANK AMERICA NATIONAL ASSN
444 Castro St Ste 100, Mountain View (94041-2071)
PHONE..................650 960-4701
Mary Williams, *Branch Mgr*
EMP: 35
SALES (corp-wide): 93.7B **Publicly Held**
WEB: www.bankofamerica.com
SIC: 6021 National commercial banks
HQ: Bank Of America, National Association
100 S Tryon St
Charlotte NC 28202
704 386-5681

(P-9679)
BANK AMERICA NATIONAL ASSN
1601 I St Frnt, Modesto (95354-1135)
P.O. Box 142 (95353-0142)
PHONE..................209 578-6006
EMP: 45
SALES (corp-wide): 93.7B **Publicly Held**
WEB: www.bankofamerica.com
SIC: 6021 Natl Commercial Banks
HQ: Bank Of America, National Association
100 S Tryon St
Charlotte NC 28202
704 386-5681

(P-9680)
BANK AMERICA NATIONAL ASSN
1300 Hilltop Dr, Redding (96003-3874)
PHONE..................530 226-6172
Trent Kinnier, *Manager*
EMP: 35
SALES (corp-wide): 93.7B **Publicly Held**
WEB: www.bankofamerica.com
SIC: 6021 National commercial banks
HQ: Bank Of America, National Association
100 S Tryon St
Charlotte NC 28202
704 386-5681

(P-9681)
CHASE INC (PA)
3754 W Holland Ave, Fresno (93722-7836)
PHONE..................559 277-2828
Bob Shiralian, *President*
Brandon Godbolt, *President*
Firouzeh Shiralian, *Principal*
Philip Slater, *Branch Mgr*
EMP: 90 **EST:** 1993
SALES (est): 35.7MM **Privately Held**
WEB: www.chase.com
SIC: 6021 National commercial banks

(P-9682)
CITIBANK FSB (HQ)
1 Sansome St, San Francisco (94104-4448)
PHONE..................415 627-6000
David A Brooks, *Ch of Bd*
Jay Compton, *President*
Edgar Ancona, *Treasurer*
Michael McCarthy, *Officer*
EMP: 300 **EST:** 1921
SQ FT: 20,000
SALES (est): 110.2MM
SALES (corp-wide): 88.8B **Publicly Held**
WEB: www.citigroup.com
SIC: 6021 National commercial banks
PA: Citigroup Inc.
388 Greenwich St Fl 38
New York NY 10013
212 559-1000

(P-9683)
CITIBANK FSB
2000 Irving St, San Francisco (94122-1716)
PHONE..................415 649-6971
EMP: 122
SALES (corp-wide): 88.8B **Publicly Held**
WEB: www.citigroup.com
SIC: 6021 National commercial banks
HQ: Citibank, F.S.B.
1 Sansome St
San Francisco CA 94104
415 627-6000

(P-9684)
JPMORGAN CHASE BANK NAT ASSN
6495 N Palm Ave Ste 101, Fresno (93704-1063)
PHONE..................559 449-0632
Peter Green, *Vice Pres*
Hrant Kargayan, *Vice Pres*
EMP: 223
SALES (corp-wide): 129.5B **Publicly Held**
WEB: www.chase.com
SIC: 6021 6029 National commercial banks; commercial banks
HQ: Jpmorgan Chase Bank, National Association
1111 Polaris Pkwy
Columbus OH 43240
614 436-3055

(P-9685)
MERRILL LYNCH PRCE FNNER SMITH
101 California St Fl 21, San Francisco (94111-5891)
PHONE..................415 676-2500
EMP: 198

6021 - National Commercial Banks County (P-9686)

PRODUCTS & SERVICES SECTION

SALES (corp-wide): 93.7B **Publicly Held**
SIC: 6021 National commercial banks
HQ: Merrill Lynch, Pierce, Fenner & Smith Incorporated
111 8th Ave
New York NY 10011
800 637-7455

(P-9686)
MUFG AMERICAS HOLDINGS CORP
1221 Broadway Fl 8, Oakland (94612-1837)
PHONE..................212 782-5911
Deborah Carbone, Analyst
Marjo Cruz, Analyst
EMP: 108 **Privately Held**
WEB: www.unionbank.com
SIC: 6021 National commercial banks
HQ: Mufg Americas Holdings Corporation
1251 Ave Of The Americas
New York NY 10020
212 782-6800

(P-9687)
MUFG UNION BANK NATIONAL ASSN (DH)
400 California St Fl 14, San Francisco (94104-1302)
PHONE..................415 705-7000
Norimichi Kanari, President
Kyota Omori, Ch of Bd
Mark W Midkiff, Vice Chairman
Timothy H Wennes, Vice Chairman
Patrick Nygren, President
▲ EMP: 1000 EST: 1864
SALES (est): 5.9B **Privately Held**
WEB: www.unionbank.com
SIC: 6021 National commercial banks
HQ: Mufg Americas Holdings Corporation
1251 Ave Of The Americas
New York NY 10020
212 782-6800

(P-9688)
PORREY PINES BANK INC
Also Called: Western Alliance Bank
1951 Webster St, Oakland (94612-2909)
PHONE..................510 899-7500
Larry Fountain, Manager
Dianne Williams, Manager
EMP: 151 EST: 2006
SALES (est): 626.1K
SALES (corp-wide): 1.3B **Publicly Held**
WEB: www.westernalliancebancorporation.com
SIC: 6021 National commercial banks
PA: Western Alliance Bancorporation
1 E Wshington St Ste 1400
Phoenix AZ 85004
602 389-3500

(P-9689)
SIX RIVERS NATIONAL BANK (HQ)
402 F St, Eureka (95501-1008)
PHONE..................707 443-8400
Fax: 707 443-3631
EMP: 51
SALES: 46.3MM
SALES (corp-wide): 206.7MM **Publicly Held**
SIC: 6021 National Commercial Bank
PA: Trico Bancshares
63 Constitution Dr
Chico CA 95973
530 898-0300

(P-9690)
SUMMIT BANK
2969 Broadway, Oakland (94611-5710)
PHONE..................510 839-8800
Shirley Nelson, Chairman
Steve Nelson, President
Tom Duryea, CEO
Mani Ganesamurthy, CFO
Denise Dodini, Ch Credit Ofcr
EMP: 40 EST: 1982
SALES (est): 2.8MM **Privately Held**
WEB: www.summitbanking.com
SIC: 6021 National commercial banks

(P-9691)
UNIONBANCAL MORTGAGE CORP
400 California St, San Francisco (94104-1302)
PHONE..................415 705-7350
William Baner, President
Elodia Soza, Officer
John Wied, Sr Exec VP
Jeff Bottenfield, Vice Pres
Paul Fisher, Vice Pres
EMP: 75 EST: 1993
SALES (est): 16.5MM **Privately Held**
WEB: www.unionbank.com
SIC: 6021 National commercial banks
HQ: Mufg Union Bank, National Association
400 California St Fl 14
San Francisco CA 94104
415 705-7000

(P-9692)
USI INSURANCE SERVICES NAT INC
39899 Balentine Dr # 200, Newark (94560-5355)
PHONE..................914 749-8500
EMP: 60 **Privately Held**
SIC: 6021 National commercial banks
HQ: Usi Insurance Services National, Inc.
150 N Michigan Ave # 3900
Chicago IL 60601
866 294-2571

(P-9693)
USI INSURANCE SERVICES NAT INC
1001 Galaxy Way Ste 300, Concord (94520-5758)
PHONE..................925 988-1700
Brian Heatherington, Director
Steven Lee, Vice Pres
EMP: 60 **Privately Held**
SIC: 6021 National commercial banks
HQ: Usi Insurance Services National, Inc.
150 N Michigan Ave # 3900
Chicago IL 60601
866 294-2571

(P-9694)
WELLS FARGO & COMPANY (PA)
420 Montgomery St, San Francisco (94104-1207)
PHONE..................866 249-3302
Steven D Black, Ch of Bd
Charles W Scharf, President
Kyle Hrancky, CEO
Scott E Powell, COO
Michael P Santomassimo, CFO
▲ EMP: 7035 EST: 1929
SQ FT: 400,000
SALES (est): 80.3B **Publicly Held**
WEB: www.wellsfargo.com
SIC: 6021 National commercial banks

(P-9695)
WELLS FARGO BANK NATIONAL ASSN
Merchant Paymnt A0347-023
1655 Grant St, Concord (94520-2600)
PHONE..................925 746-3718
EMP: 60
SQ FT: 57,192
SALES (corp-wide): 97.7B **Publicly Held**
SIC: 6021 National Commercial Bank
HQ: Wells Fargo Bank, National Association
101 N Phillips Ave
Sioux Falls SD 57103
605 575-6900

(P-9696)
WELLS FARGO INVESTMENTS LLC (DH)
420 Montgomery St Frnt, San Francisco (94104-1205)
PHONE..................415 396-7767
Charles W Daggs, President
Jeb Courtney, President
Susie McLeod, Officer
Lee Tune, Trust Officer
Stacey Anderson, Vice Pres
EMP: 474 EST: 2000
SALES (est): 918MM
SALES (corp-wide): 80.3B **Publicly Held**
WEB: www.wellsfargo.com
SIC: 6021 National commercial banks

(P-9697)
WFC HOLDINGS LLC (HQ)
420 Montgomery St, San Francisco (94104-1207)
PHONE..................415 396-7392
Richard M Kovacevich, Ch of Bd
Larry Salvati, Opers Staff
EMP: 200 EST: 1998
SQ FT: 750,000
SALES (est): 1.8B
SALES (corp-wide): 80.3B **Publicly Held**
WEB: www.wellsfargo.com
SIC: 6021 National commercial banks
PA: Wells Fargo & Company
420 Montgomery St
San Francisco CA 94104
866 249-3302

6022 State Commercial Banks

(P-9698)
AMERICAN RIVER BANK (PA)
1545 River Park Dr # 107, Sacramento (95815-4600)
P.O. Box 276300 (95827-6300)
PHONE..................916 565-6100
David T Taber, President
Gregory Patton, President
Mitchel Derenzo, CFO
Dennis Raymond,
Robert Barrett, Senior VP
EMP: 38 EST: 1983
SQ FT: 8,200
SALES: 29.4MM **Privately Held**
WEB: www.americanriverbank.com
SIC: 6022 State trust companies accepting deposits, commercial

(P-9699)
AVIDBANK (PA)
1732 N 1st St Fl 6, San Jose (95112-4544)
PHONE..................408 200-7390
Mark D Mordell, Chairman
Karen Amaya, President
Ronald E Oliveira, President
Jodie Tibbott, President
Steve Leen, CFO
EMP: 73 EST: 2003
SALES: 20.5MM **Privately Held**
WEB: www.avidbank.com
SIC: 6022 State trust companies accepting deposits, commercial

(P-9700)
AVIDBANK HOLDINGS INC
1732 N 1st St Fl 6, San Jose (95112-4544)
PHONE..................408 200-7390
Mark Mordell, CEO
Robert Holden, President
Geoff Butner, Ch Credit Ofcr
Mike Berrier, Officer
Ronald Oliveira, Officer
EMP: 107 EST: 2003 **Privately Held**
WEB: www.avidbank.com
SIC: 6022 State commercial banks

(P-9701)
BANCWEST CORPORATION
180 Montgomery St, San Francisco (94104-4205)
PHONE..................415 765-4800
Nandita Bakhshi, CEO
Mitchell Nishimoto, Vice Chairman
Panhia Crawford, Sr Corp Ofcr
Alana STA Ana, Officer
Natalie Bowers, Officer
EMP: 2310 EST: 2016
SALES (est): 56.9MM
SALES (corp-wide): 2.7B **Privately Held**
WEB: www.bankofthewest.com
SIC: 6022 State commercial banks
PA: Bnp Paribas
16 Boulevard Des Italiens
Paris 75009
825 334-335

(P-9702)
BANK OF MARIN
Also Called: Northgate Branch
4460 Redwood Hwy Ste 1, San Rafael (94903-1952)
PHONE..................415 472-2265
EMP: 78 **Publicly Held**
WEB: www.bankofmarin.com
SIC: 6022 State Commercial Banks
HQ: Bank Of Marin
504 Redwood Blvd Ste 100
Novato CA 94947

(P-9703)
BANK OF MARIN BANCORP (PA)
504 Redwood Blvd Ste 100, Novato (94947-6923)
P.O. Box 2039 (94948-2039)
PHONE..................415 763-4520
Russell A Colombo, CEO
Brian M Sobel, Ch of Bd
Timothy D Myers, President
Tani Girton, CFO
William H McDevitt Jr, Vice Ch Bd
EMP: 132 EST: 2007
SALES (est): 108.1MM **Publicly Held**
WEB: www.bankofmarin.com
SIC: 6022 State trust companies accepting deposits, commercial

(P-9704)
BANK OF ORIENT FOUNDATION (HQ)
100 Pine St Ste 600, San Francisco (94111-5108)
P.O. Box 2489 (94126-2489)
PHONE..................415 338-0668
Ernest L Go, Ch of Bd
Michael R Delucchi, COO
Carl Andersen, CFO
Lyle Deepe, Officer
Mark K McDonald, Exec VP
▲ EMP: 65 EST: 1970
SQ FT: 20,000
SALES: 45.9MM
SALES (corp-wide): 44.5MM **Privately Held**
WEB: www.bankorient.com
SIC: 6022 State trust companies accepting deposits, commercial
PA: Orient Bancorporation
100 Pine St Ste 600
San Francisco CA 94111
415 567-1554

(P-9705)
BANK OF SAN FRANCISCO
575 Market St Ste 900, San Francisco (94105-2823)
PHONE..................415 744-6700
Ed Obuchowski, CEO
Samuel Clonmell, President
Kathy Phan, President
Laura Catolico, Officer
Jollin Gonzales, Officer
EMP: 35
SALES: 17.5MM **Privately Held**
WEB: www.bankofsf.com
SIC: 6022 State trust companies accepting deposits, commercial

(P-9706)
BANK OF STOCKTON (HQ)
301 E Miner Ave, Stockton (95202-2501)
P.O. Box 1110 (95201-3003)
PHONE..................209 929-1600
Robert M Eberhardt, President
Kelly Christian, President
Douglass M Eberhardt, President
Kathryne Prather-Garza, President
Robin Price, President
EMP: 180
SQ FT: 15,000
SALES: 140.4MM **Privately Held**
WEB: www.bankofstockton.com
SIC: 6022 State trust companies accepting deposits, commercial

(P-9707)
BANK OF THE WEST (HQ)
180 Montgomery St # 1400, San Francisco (94104-4297)
PHONE..................415 765-4800
J Michael Shepherd, CEO
Randy Arnold, Partner

▲ = Import ▼ = Export
◆ = Import/Export

PRODUCTS & SERVICES SECTION
6022 - State Commercial Banks County (P-9730)

Vanessa Midgley, *Shareholder*
Mir Ali, *President*
Nicole Auyang, *President*
▲ **EMP:** 1000 **EST:** 1874
SQ FT: 30,000
SALES (est): 1.2B
SALES (corp-wide): 2.7B **Privately Held**
WEB: www.bankofthewest.com
SIC: 6022 State commercial banks
PA: Bnp Paribas
  16 Boulevard Des Italiens
  Paris 75009
  825 334-335

(P-9708)
BBVA USA
Also Called: Compass Bank
201 N Main St, Manteca (95336-4632)
PHONE 209 239-1381
Grace Henderson, *Branch Mgr*
EMP: 123
SALES (corp-wide): 18.2B **Publicly Held**
WEB: www.bbvausa.com
SIC: 6022 State commercial banks
HQ: Bbva Usa
  15 20th St S Ste 100
  Birmingham AL 35233
  205 297-1986

(P-9709)
BBVA USA
Also Called: Compass Bank
2427 W Hammer Ln, Stockton (95209-2367)
PHONE 209 473-6925
Gabriel Riley, *Branch Mgr*
EMP: 123
SALES (corp-wide): 18.2B **Publicly Held**
WEB: www.bbvausa.com
SIC: 6022 State commercial banks
HQ: Bbva Usa
  15 20th St S Ste 100
  Birmingham AL 35233
  205 297-1986

(P-9710)
BBVA USA
Also Called: Compass Bank
202 N Hunter St, Stockton (95202-2327)
PHONE 209 939-3288
Brian Stemen, *Branch Mgr*
EMP: 123
SALES (corp-wide): 18.2B **Publicly Held**
WEB: www.bbvausa.com
SIC: 6022 State commercial banks
HQ: Bbva Usa
  15 20th St S Ste 100
  Birmingham AL 35233
  205 297-1986

(P-9711)
BIG POPPY HOLDINGS INC
6580 Oakmont Dr Ste A, Santa Rosa (95409-5966)
PHONE 707 636-9020
Andrew Fuller, *Officer*
Steven Gill, *Vice Pres*
Sandra Kleinau, *Assistant VP*
EMP: 133 **Privately Held**
WEB: www.poppy.bank
SIC: 6022 State commercial banks
PA: Big Poppy Holdings, Inc.
  438 1st St Ste 100
  Santa Rosa CA 95401

(P-9712)
BIG POPPY HOLDINGS INC
9230 Old Redwood Hwy, Windsor (95492-9282)
PHONE 707 836-1588
Tania Gibbons, *Branch Mgr*
EMP: 133 **Privately Held**
WEB: www.poppy.bank
SIC: 6022 State commercial banks
PA: Big Poppy Holdings, Inc.
  438 1st St Ste 100
  Santa Rosa CA 95401

(P-9713)
CENTRAL VALLEY CMNTY BANCORP (PA)
7100 N Fincl Dr Ste 101, Fresno (93720)
PHONE 559 298-1775
James M Ford, *President*

Daniel J Doyle, *Ch of Bd*
David A Kinross, *CFO*
Patrick J Carman, *Ch Credit Ofcr*
Chad Bringe, *Officer*
EMP: 231 **EST:** 2000
SALES (est): 79.8MM **Publicly Held**
WEB: www.cvcb.com
SIC: 6022 State commercial banks

(P-9714)
CENTRAL VALLEY COMMUNITY BANK
Also Called: Folsom Lake Bank
905 Sutter St Ste 100, Folsom (95630-2479)
PHONE 916 985-8700
EMP: 50
SALES (corp-wide): 79.8MM **Publicly Held**
WEB: www.cvcb.com
SIC: 6022 State trust companies accepting deposits, commercial
HQ: Central Valley Community Bank
  7100 N Fincl Dr Ste 101
  Fresno CA 93720
  800 298-1775

(P-9715)
CENTRAL VALLEY COMMUNITY BANK (HQ)
7100 N Fincl Dr Ste 101, Fresno (93720)
PHONE 800 298-1775
Daniel J Doyle, *CEO*
James M Ford, *President*
David A Kinross, *CFO*
Thomas L Sommer, *Ch Credit Ofcr*
James Kim, *Exec VP*
EMP: 117 **EST:** 1979
SQ FT: 11,400
SALES: 75.4MM
SALES (corp-wide): 79.8MM **Publicly Held**
WEB: www.cvcb.com
SIC: 6022 State trust companies accepting deposits, commercial
PA: Central Valley Community Bancorp
  7100 N Fincl Dr Ste 101
  Fresno CA 93720
  559 298-1775

(P-9716)
FARMERS & MERCHANTS BANCORP (PA)
111 W Pine St, Lodi (95240-2110)
PHONE 209 367-2300
Kent A Steinwert, *Ch of Bd*
Mark K Olson, *CFO*
Kenneth W Smith, *Officer*
EMP: 330 **EST:** 1999
SALES (est): 174.3MM **Publicly Held**
WEB: www.fmbonline.com
SIC: 6022 State commercial banks

(P-9717)
FIRST NORTHERN BANK OF DIXON (HQ)
Also Called: FIRST NORTHERN COMMUNITY
  195 N 1st St, Dixon (95620-3025)
  P.O. Box 547 (95620-0547)
PHONE 707 678-4422
Owen J Onsum, *President*
Jeremiah Z Smith, *COO*
Louise A Walker, *CFO*
T Joe Danelson, *Ch Credit Ofcr*
Ryan Pyne, *Officer*
EMP: 59 **EST:** 1910
SQ FT: 14,000
SALES: 56.3MM **Publicly Held**
WEB: www.thatsmybank.com
SIC: 6022 State trust companies accepting deposits, commercial

(P-9718)
FIRST NORTHERN CMNTY BANCORP (PA)
195 N 1st St, Dixon (95620-3025)
P.O. Box 547 (95620-0547)
PHONE 707 678-3041
Richard Martinez, *Ch of Bd*
Javier Sanchez, *President*
Louise A Walker, *President*
Jeremiah Z Smith, *COO*
Kevin Spink, *CFO*
EMP: 64 **EST:** 2000

SALES (est): 56.6MM **Publicly Held**
WEB: www.thatsmybank.com
SIC: 6022 State commercial banks

(P-9719)
FIRST REPUBLIC BANK
750 Redwood Hwy Frontage, Mill Valley (94941-2483)
PHONE 415 389-0880
Vince Franceschi, *Branch Mgr*
Andrew Huang, *Associate Dir*
Heshmati Sam, *Managing Dir*
Phipps Stefani, *Managing Dir*
Theresa Samsotha, *Program Mgr*
EMP: 87
SALES (corp-wide): 4.5B **Publicly Held**
WEB: www.firstrepublic.com
SIC: 6022 State commercial banks
PA: First Republic Bank
  111 Pine St Fl 2
  San Francisco CA 94111
  415 392-1400

(P-9720)
FIRST REPUBLIC BANK
44 Montgomery St Ste 110, San Francisco (94104-4600)
PHONE 415 392-3888
Monica Brazil, *Manager*
Lynn Rueb, *Vice Pres*
Ron Tremblay, *Vice Pres*
John Williams, *Associate Dir*
Valerie Caveney, *Program Mgr*
EMP: 87
SALES (corp-wide): 4.5B **Publicly Held**
WEB: www.firstrepublic.com
SIC: 6022 State commercial banks
PA: First Republic Bank
  111 Pine St Fl 2
  San Francisco CA 94111
  415 392-1400

(P-9721)
FIRST REPUBLIC BANK
2550 Sand Hill Rd Ste 100, Menlo Park (94025-7095)
PHONE 650 233-8880
Gayle Nickel, *Branch Mgr*
Tina Chao, *Opers Staff*
Trish Cashman, *Director*
Jessica Gordon, *Manager*
EMP: 87
SALES (corp-wide): 4.5B **Publicly Held**
WEB: www.firstrepublic.com
SIC: 6022 State commercial banks
PA: First Republic Bank
  111 Pine St Fl 2
  San Francisco CA 94111
  415 392-1400

(P-9722)
FIRST REPUBLIC BANK
558 Presidio Blvd Ste A, San Francisco (94129-1186)
PHONE 415 561-2988
Leanne Bu, *Branch Mgr*
Michael Griffin, *Sr Trust Ofc*
Susie Cranston, *Exec VP*
Carol Highton, *Vice Pres*
William Terry, *Vice Pres*
EMP: 87
SALES (corp-wide): 4.5B **Publicly Held**
WEB: www.firstrepublic.com
SIC: 6022 State commercial banks
PA: First Republic Bank
  111 Pine St Fl 2
  San Francisco CA 94111
  415 392-1400

(P-9723)
FIRST REPUBLIC BANK
249 Main St, Pleasanton (94566-7322)
PHONE 925 846-8811
James Ott, *Branch Mgr*
Delia Teixeira, *Officer*
EMP: 87
SALES (corp-wide): 4.5B **Publicly Held**
WEB: www.firstrepublic.com
SIC: 6022 State commercial banks
PA: First Republic Bank
  111 Pine St Fl 2
  San Francisco CA 94111
  415 392-1400

(P-9724)
FIRST REPUBLIC BANK
224 Brookwood Rd, Orinda (94563-3015)
PHONE 925 254-8993
Dina Zapanta, *Branch Mgr*
EMP: 87
SALES (corp-wide): 4.5B **Publicly Held**
WEB: www.firstrepublic.com
SIC: 6022 State commercial banks
PA: First Republic Bank
  111 Pine St Fl 2
  San Francisco CA 94111
  415 392-1400

(P-9725)
FIRST REPUBLIC BANK
653 Irving St, San Francisco (94122-2401)
PHONE 415 564-8881
EMP: 87
SALES (corp-wide): 4.5B **Publicly Held**
WEB: www.firstrepublic.com
SIC: 6022 State commercial banks
PA: First Republic Bank
  111 Pine St Fl 2
  San Francisco CA 94111
  415 392-1400

(P-9726)
FIRST REPUBLIC BANK
1355 Market St Ste 140, San Francisco (94103-1337)
PHONE 415 487-0888
Matt Rose, *Program Mgr*
Mary Benavides, *Benefits Mgr*
Bran McNamee, *Director*
EMP: 87
SALES (corp-wide): 4.5B **Publicly Held**
WEB: www.firstrepublic.com
SIC: 6022 State commercial banks
PA: First Republic Bank
  111 Pine St Fl 2
  San Francisco CA 94111
  415 392-1400

(P-9727)
FIRST REPUBLIC BANK
405 Howard St Ste 110, San Francisco (94105-2665)
PHONE 415 975-3877
EMP: 87
SALES (corp-wide): 4.5B **Publicly Held**
WEB: www.firstrepublic.com
SIC: 6022 State commercial banks
PA: First Republic Bank
  111 Pine St Fl 2
  San Francisco CA 94111
  415 392-1400

(P-9728)
FIRST REPUBLIC BANK
401 San Antonio Rd Ste 68, Mountain View (94040-5310)
PHONE 650 383-2888
EMP: 87
SALES (corp-wide): 4.5B **Publicly Held**
WEB: www.firstrepublic.com
SIC: 6022 State commercial banks
PA: First Republic Bank
  111 Pine St Fl 2
  San Francisco CA 94111
  415 392-1400

(P-9729)
FIRST REPUBLIC BANK
1215 El Camino Real, Menlo Park (94025-4208)
PHONE 650 470-8888
Andrea Jefferson, *Manager*
EMP: 87
SALES (corp-wide): 4.5B **Publicly Held**
WEB: www.firstrepublic.com
SIC: 6022 State commercial banks
PA: First Republic Bank
  111 Pine St Fl 2
  San Francisco CA 94111
  415 392-1400

(P-9730)
FIRST REPUBLIC INV MGT INC
111 Pine St, San Francisco (94111-5602)
PHONE 415 296-5727
Angela Osborne, *Director*
Christopher J Wolfe, *CIO*
EMP: 50 **EST:** 2013

6022 - State Commercial Banks County (P-9731)

SALES (est): 9MM **Privately Held**
WEB: www.firstrepublic.com
SIC: **6022** State commercial banks

(P-9731)
FREMONT BANK (HQ)
39150 Fremont Blvd, Fremont (94538-1313)
P.O. Box 5101 (94537-5101)
PHONE..................510 505-5226
Morris Hyman, *Ch of Bd*
Andy Mastorakis, *President*
Bradford L Anderson, *CEO*
Patti Greenup, *COO*
Ron Wagner, *CFO*
EMP: 250 EST: 1964
SQ FT: 20,000
SALES (est): 274.1MM
SALES (corp-wide): 275.7MM **Privately Held**
WEB: www.fremontbank.com
SIC: **6022** State commercial banks
PA: Fremont Bancorporation
   39150 Fremont Blvd
   Fremont CA 94538
   510 792-2200

(P-9732)
FREMONT BANK
1679 Industrial Pkwy W, Hayward (94544-7046)
PHONE..................510 512-1900
Carrie Alejandre, *Manager*
Lou Scarpa, *Loan*
EMP: 82
SALES (corp-wide): 275.7MM **Privately Held**
WEB: www.fremontbank.com
SIC: **6022** State commercial banks
HQ: Fremont Bank
   39150 Fremont Blvd
   Fremont CA 94538
   510 505-5226

(P-9733)
FREMONT BANK
210 Railroad Ave, Danville (94526-3818)
PHONE..................925 314-1420
Guy Greco, *Manager*
Louis Scarpa, *Manager*
EMP: 82
SALES (corp-wide): 275.7MM **Privately Held**
WEB: www.fremontbank.com
SIC: **6022** State commercial banks
HQ: Fremont Bank
   39150 Fremont Blvd
   Fremont CA 94538
   510 505-5226

(P-9734)
GOLDEN PACIFIC BANK NAT ASSN (DH)
1409 28th St, Sacramento (95816-6404)
P.O. Box 2488, Marysville (95901-0089)
PHONE..................916 288-1069
Chuck Brooks, *President*
Lynn Baker, *President*
Tarra Victorino, *CFO*
Martha Cassi, *Officer*
Don McDonel, *Exec VP*
EMP: 38 EST: 1986
SQ FT: 1,640
SALES (est): 6.4MM
SALES (corp-wide): 536.9MM **Publicly Held**
WEB: www.goldenpacificbank.com
SIC: **6022** State commercial banks

(P-9735)
HERITAGE BANK OF COMMERCE (HQ)
224 Airport Pkwy Ste 100, San Jose (95110-2020)
PHONE..................408 947-6900
Walter Kaczmarek, *CEO*
Keith Wilton, *President*
Lawrence D McGovern, *CFO*
Michael Ong, *Ch Credit Ofcr*
John Angelesco, *Officer*
EMP: 120 EST: 1993
SQ FT: 36,000
SALES (est): 160.1MM
SALES (corp-wide): 160.3MM **Publicly Held**
WEB: www.heritagebankofcommerce.bank
SIC: **6022** State trust companies accepting deposits, commercial
PA: Heritage Commerce Corp
   224 Airport Pkwy Ste 100
   San Jose CA 95110
   408 947-6900

(P-9736)
HERITAGE COMMERCE CORP (PA)
224 Airport Pkwy Ste 100, San Jose (95110-1020)
PHONE..................408 947-6900
Walter T Kaczmarek, *President*
Jack W Conner, *Ch of Bd*
Keith A Wilton, *COO*
Lawrence D McGovern, *CFO*
Trisha Parnell, *Officer*
EMP: 57 EST: 1997
SQ FT: 35,547
SALES (est): 160.3MM **Publicly Held**
WEB: www.heritagecommercecorp.com
SIC: **6022** State commercial banks

(P-9737)
LIBERTY BANK (PA)
500 Linden Ave, South San Francisco (94080-2994)
P.O. Box 431 (94083-0431)
PHONE..................650 871-2400
Bruce K Farrell, *President*
John M Cullison, *Ch of Bd*
John B De Nault, *Ch of Bd*
Mike Dinicola, *President*
Ariella Fioranelli, *President*
EMP: 39
SALES: 11.8MM **Privately Held**
WEB: www.libertybk.com
SIC: **6022** State trust companies accepting deposits, commercial

(P-9738)
MECHANICS BANK (DH)
1111 Civic Dr Ste 290, Walnut Creek (94596-8203)
PHONE..................800 797-6324
John Decero, *President*
E Michael Downer, *Vice Chairman*
Suman Raj, *President*
Nathan Duda, *CFO*
Mark Borrecco, *Co-CEO*
EMP: 110 EST: 1905
SQ FT: 77,000
SALES: 682.1MM **Privately Held**
WEB: www.mechanicsbank.com
SIC: **6022** State commercial banks
HQ: Eb Acquisition Company Llc
   6565 Hillcrest Ave
   Dallas TX 75205
   214 871-5151

(P-9739)
MERCHANTS BANK OF COMMERCE (HQ)
1951 Churn Creek Rd, Redding (96002-0246)
PHONE..................530 224-7355
Randall S Eslick, *President*
Cathy Smallhouse, *President*
Brenda Truett, *President*
Linda J Miles, *CFO*
Patrick J Moty, *Ch Credit Ofcr*
EMP: 80 EST: 1982
SQ FT: 10,000
SALES (est): 63.8MM
SALES (corp-wide): 64.1MM **Privately Held**
WEB: www.mboc.com
SIC: **6022** State commercial banks
PA: Bank Of Commerce Holdings
   555 Capitol Mall Ste 1255
   Sacramento CA 95814
   800 421-2575

(P-9740)
ORIENT BANCORPORATION (PA)
Also Called: BANK OF THE ORIENT
100 Pine St Ste 600, San Francisco (94111-5108)
PHONE..................415 567-1554
Ernest Go, *Ch of Bd*
John Ing, *President*
May Ann Wong, *President*
Michael R Delucchi, *COO*
Lyle Deepe, *Officer*
EMP: 101 EST: 1971
SALES: 44.5MM **Privately Held**
WEB: www.bankorient.com
SIC: **6022** State trust companies accepting deposits, commercial

(P-9741)
PACIFIC COAST BANKERS BANK
1676 N Calif Blvd Ste 300, Walnut Creek (94596-4185)
PHONE..................415 399-1900
Steve Brown, *President*
Nino Petroni, *COO*
Eric Davis, *Senior VP*
Lavanya Chandrasekhar, *Vice Pres*
Patricio Morillo, *Vice Pres*
EMP: 60 EST: 1997
SALES: 80.5MM
SALES (corp-wide): 21.1MM **Privately Held**
WEB: www.pcbb.com
SIC: **6022** State commercial banks
PA: Pacific Coast Bankers' Bancshares
   1676 N Calif Blvd Ste 300
   Walnut Creek CA 94596
   415 399-1900

(P-9742)
PACIFIC STATE BANK (PA)
115 James Dr W Ste 140, Stockton (95207)
P.O. Box 6002, Arroyo Grande (93421-6002)
PHONE..................209 870-3200
Harold Hand, *Ch of Bd*
Rick Simas, *President*
Laura Maffei, *Vice Pres*
Linda Ogata, *Vice Pres*
EMP: 40 EST: 1987
SQ FT: 9,500
SALES (est): 7.5MM **Privately Held**
SIC: **6022** 6029 State commercial banks; commercial banks

(P-9743)
PLUMAS BANK (HQ)
35 S Lindan Ave, Quincy (95971-9122)
PHONE..................530 283-7305
Andrew J Rayback, *President*
Shane Holland, *President*
Gail Meskovsky, *President*
Richard L Belstock, *CFO*
Jeffrey T Moore, *Ch Credit Ofcr*
EMP: 35 EST: 1980
SALES (est): 47.4MM
SALES (corp-wide): 39.6MM **Publicly Held**
WEB: www.plumasbank.com
SIC: **6022** State trust companies accepting deposits, commercial
PA: Plumas Bancorp
   5050 Meadowood Mall Cir
   Reno NV 89502
   775 786-0907

(P-9744)
POPPY BANK (HQ)
438 1st St Ste 100, Santa Rosa (95401-6333)
PHONE..................707 636-9000
Kathy Pinkard, *CEO*
Jeanne Bauer, *President*
Andrew Hutchins, *COO*
Debbie Fakalata, *CFO*
Bryan Reed, *Ch Credit Ofcr*
EMP: 51 EST: 2004
SALES: 122.3MM **Privately Held**
WEB: www.poppy.bank
SIC: **6022** State trust companies accepting deposits, commercial

(P-9745)
RCB CORPORATION (PA)
Also Called: River City Bank
2485 Natomas Park Dr # 100, Sacramento (95833-2937)
P.O. Box 15247 (95851-0247)
PHONE..................916 567-2600
Stephen Fleming, *President*
Shawn Devlin, *Ch of Bd*
Anker Christensen, *CFO*
Jon Kelly, *Founder*
Pat McHone, *Ch Credit Ofcr*
EMP: 80 EST: 1981
SQ FT: 34,000
SALES (est): 106MM **Privately Held**
WEB: www.rivercitybank.com
SIC: **6022** State commercial banks

(P-9746)
RIVER CITY BANK (HQ)
2485 Natomas Park Dr # 100, Sacramento (95833-2975)
P.O. Box 15247 (95851-0247)
PHONE..................916 567-2600
Stephen A Fleming, *President*
Kerry Gordon, *Managing Prtnr*
Dan Franklin, *President*
Camille Lasky, *President*
Yulia Yevsukova, *President*
▲ EMP: 80 EST: 1973
SQ FT: 15,000
SALES: 104.7MM
SALES (corp-wide): 106MM **Privately Held**
WEB: www.rivercitybank.com
SIC: **6022** State commercial banks
PA: Rcb Corporation
   2485 Natomas Park Dr # 100
   Sacramento CA 95833
   916 567-2600

(P-9747)
SAVINGS BANK MENDOCINO COUNTY (PA)
Also Called: Sbmc
200 N School St, Ukiah (95482-4811)
P.O. Box 3600 (95482-3600)
PHONE..................707 462-6613
Stacy Starkey, *President*
Sharon Harshbarger, *President*
Charles B Mannon, *President*
Bruce Little, *CFO*
Ernie Wipf, *Bd of Directors*
▲ EMP: 130 EST: 1903
SALES: 46.7MM **Privately Held**
WEB: www.savingsbank.com
SIC: **6022** State trust companies accepting deposits, commercial

(P-9748)
SIERRA BANCORP
7029 N Ingram Ave Ste 101, Fresno (93650-1091)
PHONE..................559 449-8145
EMP: 82
SALES (corp-wide): 136.3MM **Publicly Held**
WEB: www.sierrabancorp.com
SIC: **6022** State Commercial Banks
PA: Sierra Bancorp
   86 N Main St
   Porterville CA 93257
   559 782-4900

(P-9749)
SUMMIT BANK FOUNDATION (HQ)
2969 Broadway, Oakland (94611-5710)
P.O. Box 898 (94604-0898)
PHONE..................510 839-8800
Thomas M Duryea, *CEO*
George Yang, *President*
Micheal Ziemann, *President*
Shirley W Nelson, *Chairman*
Kyle Woodstrom, *Officer*
EMP: 37 EST: 1982
SQ FT: 6,200
SALES: 13.5MM **Publicly Held**
WEB: www.summitbankfoundation.org
SIC: **6022** State commercial banks
PA: Summit Bancshares, Inc.
   2969 Broadway
   Oakland CA 94611
   510 839-8800

(P-9750)
SVB FINANCIAL GROUP (PA)
3003 Tasman Dr, Santa Clara (95054-1191)
PHONE..................408 654-7400
Greg W Becker, *President*
Roger F Dunbar, *Ch of Bd*
John China, *President*
Michael Descheneaux, *President*
Philip Cox, *COO*
EMP: 3003 EST: 1999

PRODUCTS & SERVICES SECTION
6036 - Savings Institutions, Except Federal County (P-9771)

SQ FT: 157,177
SALES (est): 4B Publicly Held
WEB: www.svb.com
SIC: 6022 State commercial banks

(P-9751)
TRICO BANCSHARES (PA)
63 Constitution Dr, Chico (95973-4937)
PHONE.................................530 898-0300
Richard P Smith, *Ch of Bd*
John S Fleshood, *COO*
Peter G Wiese, *CFO*
Michael W Koehnen, *Vice Ch Bd*
Craig Carney, *Ch Credit Ofcr*
EMP: 70 EST: 1981
SALES (est): 322.3MM Publicly Held
WEB: www.tcbk.com
SIC: 6022 State commercial banks

(P-9752)
WESTAMERICA BANCORPORATION (PA)
1108 5th Ave, San Rafael (94901-2916)
P.O. Box 1200, Suisun City (94585-1200)
PHONE.................................707 863-6000
David L Payne, *Ch of Bd*
Lisa Harman, *President*
Jesse Leavitt, *CFO*
John Thorson, *CFO*
Etta Allen, *Bd of Directors*
EMP: 195 EST: 1972
SALES (est): 211.4MM Publicly Held
WEB: www.westamerica.com
SIC: 6022 State commercial banks

(P-9753)
WESTAMERICA BANK (HQ)
1108 5th Ave, San Rafael (94901-2916)
P.O. Box 1200, Suisun City (94585-1200)
PHONE.................................707 863-6113
David L Payne, *Ch of Bd*
Audrey King, *President*
Jennifer Finger, *CFO*
E Joseph Bowler, *Treasurer*
Joseph Bowler, *Bd of Directors*
▲ EMP: 159 EST: 1972
SQ FT: 5,000
SALES: 211.3MM
SALES (corp-wide): 211.4MM Publicly Held
WEB: www.westamerica.com
SIC: 6022 State commercial banks
PA: Westamerica Bancorporation
1108 5th Ave
San Rafael CA 94901
707 863-6000

(P-9754)
WESTERN ALLIANCE BANK
Also Called: Bridge Bank
55 Almaden Blvd Ste 200, San Jose (95113-1619)
PHONE.................................408 423-8500
Lee Shodiss, *Vice Pres*
Sheetal Cordova, *Vice Pres*
Christine Egitto, *Vice Pres*
Maggie Hsu, *Vice Pres*
Randall Lee, *Vice Pres*
EMP: 70
SALES (corp-wide): 1.3B Publicly Held
WEB: www.westernalliancebancorporation.com
SIC: 6022 8742 State commercial banks; management consulting services
HQ: Western Alliance Bank
1 E Wshington St Ste 1400
Phoenix AZ 85004

6029 Commercial Banks, NEC

(P-9755)
AMALGAMATED BANK
Also Called: New Resource Bank
255 California St Ste 600, San Francisco (94111-4904)
PHONE.................................415 995-8157
Rich Hildebrand, *Vice Pres*
Suzanne Reicher, *Vice Pres*
Stephanie Meade, *Marketing Staff*
Nick Healey, *Manager*
Jenise Bermudez, *Assistant VP*
EMP: 45

SALES (corp-wide): 229.4MM Publicly Held
WEB: www.amalgamatedbank.com
SIC: 6029 Commercial banks
PA: Amalgamated Bank
275 7th Ave
New York NY 10001
212 895-8988

(P-9756)
FEDERAL LAND BNK ASSN NTHRN CA
3435 Silverbell Rd, Chico (95973-0386)
P.O. Box 929 (95927-0929)
PHONE.................................530 895-8698
Bruce Strickler, *President*
Daniel Stevenson, *Ch Credit Ofcr*
EMP: 84 EST: 1990
SQ FT: 4,000
SALES (est): 20MM Privately Held
SIC: 6029 Commercial banks

(P-9757)
FIRST REPUBLIC BANK (PA)
111 Pine St Fl 2, San Francisco (94111-5606)
PHONE.................................415 392-1400
James H Herbert II, *Ch of Bd*
Hafize Gaye Erkan, *President*
Jason C Bender, *COO*
Michael J Roffler, *CFO*
Katherine August-Dewilde, *Vice Ch Bd*
EMP: 332 EST: 1985
SALES (est): 4.5B Publicly Held
WEB: www.firstrepublic.com
SIC: 6029 Commercial banks

(P-9758)
LUTHER BURBANK CORPORATION (PA)
520 3rd St Fl 4, Santa Rosa (95401-6414)
PHONE.................................844 446-8201
Simone Lagomarsino, *President*
Victor S Trione, *Ch of Bd*
Laura Tarantino, *CFO*
William Fanter, *Exec VP*
Tammy Mahoney, *Exec VP*
EMP: 73 EST: 1991
SALES (est): 243.9MM Publicly Held
WEB: www.lutherburbanksavings.com
SIC: 6029 Commercial banks

(P-9759)
PATENT AND TRADEMARK OFFICE US
26 S 4th St, San Jose (95112-3526)
PHONE.................................831 332-7127
EMP: 95 Publicly Held
WEB: www.uspto.gov
SIC: 6029 Commercial banks
HQ: United States Patent And Trademark Office
600 Dulany St Ste 1
Alexandria VA 22314
571 272-4100

(P-9760)
PREMIER VALLEY BANK (HQ)
Also Called: HEARTLAND
255 E River Park Cir # 180, Fresno (93720-1574)
P.O. Box 778, Dubuque IA (52004-0778)
PHONE.................................559 438-2002
Mike Martinez, *President*
J Mike McGowan, *President*
Lo B Nestman, *President*
Thomas Sherman, *President*
Isaiah Bernal, *Officer*
EMP: 62 EST: 2015
SALES (est): 37.9MM Publicly Held
WEB: www.premiervalleybank.com
SIC: 6029 Commercial banks

(P-9761)
SILICON VALLEY BANK (HQ)
3003 Tasman Dr, Santa Clara (95054-1191)
PHONE.................................408 654-7400
Greg Becker, *CEO*
Michael Dreyer, *COO*
Cecilia Shea, *CFO*
Harry Kellogg, *Vice Ch Bd*
Michelle Draper, *Chief Mktg Ofcr*
EMP: 592 EST: 1983
SQ FT: 100,000

SALES (est): 2.8MM
SALES (corp-wide): 4B Publicly Held
WEB: www.svb.com
SIC: 6029 Commercial banks
PA: Svb Financial Group
3003 Tasman Dr
Santa Clara CA 95054
408 654-7400

(P-9762)
SVB ASSET MANAGEMENT
185 Berry St Ste 3000, San Francisco (94107-1799)
PHONE.................................408 654-7400
Lauri Moss, *CEO*
John China, *Technology*
Lisa Valerio, *Opers Staff*
Michael White, *Manager*
EMP: 44 EST: 2002
SALES (est): 35.4K
SALES (corp-wide): 4B Publicly Held
WEB: www.svb.com
SIC: 6029 Commercial banks
HQ: Silicon Valley Bank
3003 Tasman Dr
Santa Clara CA 95054
408 654-7400

(P-9763)
TRI COUNTIES BANK (HQ)
63 Constitution Dr, Chico (95973-4937)
PHONE.................................530 898-0300
William J Casey, *Ch of Bd*
Jason Cove, *Shareholder*
Suzanne Youngs, *Shareholder*
Alex A Vereschagin Jr, *Ch of Bd*
Michael Koehnen, *Vice Chairman*
EMP: 75 EST: 1974
SALES: 322.4MM
SALES (corp-wide): 322.3MM Publicly Held
WEB: www.tcbk.com
SIC: 6029 6163 Commercial banks; loan brokers
PA: Trico Bancshares
63 Constitution Dr
Chico CA 95973
530 898-0300

(P-9764)
TRI COUNTIES BANK
975 El Camino Real, South San Francisco (94080-3203)
PHONE.................................650 583-8450
EMP: 184
SALES (corp-wide): 322.3MM Publicly Held
WEB: www.tcbk.com
SIC: 6029 Commercial banks
HQ: Tri Counties Bank
63 Constitution Dr
Chico CA 95973
530 898-0300

(P-9765)
TRICO BANCSHARES
2844 F St, Eureka (95501-4423)
PHONE.................................707 476-0981
EMP: 37
SALES (corp-wide): 322.3MM Publicly Held
WEB: www.tcbk.com
SIC: 6029 Commercial banks
PA: Trico Bancshares
63 Constitution Dr
Chico CA 95973
530 898-0300

(P-9766)
TRICO BANCSHARES
880 E Cypress Ave, Redding (96002-1004)
P.O. Box 994630 (96099-4630)
PHONE.................................530 221-8400
Michael Cushman, *Manager*
EMP: 37
SALES (corp-wide): 322.3MM Publicly Held
WEB: www.tcbk.com
SIC: 6029 Commercial banks
PA: Trico Bancshares
63 Constitution Dr
Chico CA 95973
530 898-0300

(P-9767)
TRICO BANCSHARES
1327 South St, Redding (96001-1911)
PHONE.................................530 245-5930
Michelle Jordan, *Manager*
Steve Brown, *Manager*
EMP: 37
SALES (corp-wide): 322.3MM Publicly Held
WEB: www.tcbk.com
SIC: 6029 Commercial banks
PA: Trico Bancshares
63 Constitution Dr
Chico CA 95973
530 898-0300

6035 Federal Savings Institutions

(P-9768)
BBVA USA
2536 N Main St Ste 100, Walnut Creek (94597-3128)
PHONE.................................925 947-3434
Art Keogh, *Manager*
EMP: 123
SALES (corp-wide): 18.2B Publicly Held
WEB: www.bbvausa.com
SIC: 6035 Savings institutions, federally chartered
HQ: Bbva Usa
15 20th St S Ste 100
Birmingham AL 35233
205 297-1986

(P-9769)
CITIBANK FSB
590 Market St, San Francisco (94104-5322)
PHONE.................................415 817-9111
EMP: 122
SALES (corp-wide): 88.8B Publicly Held
WEB: www.citigroup.com
SIC: 6035 Federal savings banks
HQ: Citibank, F.S.B.
1 Sansome St
San Francisco CA 94104
415 627-6000

(P-9770)
EL DORADO SAVINGS BANK (PA)
4040 El Dorado Rd, Placerville (95667-5269)
P.O. Box 1208 (95667-1208)
PHONE.................................530 622-1492
Thomas Meuser, *Ch of Bd*
George Cook Jr, *President*
William H Blucher, *CFO*
William Buechler, *CFO*
Becky Holm, *Officer*
EMP: 55 EST: 1956
SQ FT: 37,779
SALES: 57.9MM Privately Held
WEB: www.eldoradosavingsbank.com
SIC: 6035 Federal savings & loan associations

6036 Savings Institutions, Except Federal

(P-9771)
EXCHANGE BANK (PA)
Also Called: Eb
545 4th St, Santa Rosa (95401-6323)
P.O. Box 403 (95402-0403)
PHONE.................................707 524-3000
Gary T Hartwick, *CEO*
Pam Maslak, *President*
William R Schrader, *President*
Audra Cavallero, *COO*
Bruce Decrona, *COO*
EMP: 135 EST: 1890
SQ FT: 50,000
SALES: 121.2MM Privately Held
WEB: www.exchangebank.com
SIC: 6036 8741 6022 State savings banks, not federally chartered; management services; state commercial banks

6036 - Savings Institutions, Except Federal

(P-9772)
LUTHER BURBANK SAVINGS (HQ)
500 3rd St, Santa Rosa (95401-6321)
P.O. Box 1783 (95402-1783)
PHONE.....................707 578-9216
John Biggs, *President*
Victor S Trione, *Ch of Bd*
Ken Hense, *President*
Danielle Norlund, *President*
Alex Stefani, *Exec VP*
EMP: 50
SQ FT: 11,000
SALES: 230.2MM **Publicly Held**
WEB: www.lutherbanksavings.com
SIC: 6036 6035 Savings & loan associations, not federally chartered; federal savings & loan associations

6061 Federal Credit Unions

(P-9773)
1ST PACIFIC CREDIT UNION (PA)
536 Santa Clara St, Vallejo (94590-5923)
P.O. Box 1552 (94590-0654)
PHONE.....................707 552-4550
Lawrence Tierney, *President*
EMP: 40 **EST:** 1936
SQ FT: 10,000
SALES (est): 5.8MM **Privately Held**
WEB: www.1stpacific.org
SIC: 6061 Federal credit unions

(P-9774)
1ST UNITED CREDIT UNION (PA)
5901 Gibraltar Dr, Pleasanton (94588-2718)
P.O. Box 11746 (94588-1746)
PHONE.....................800 649-0193
Victor Quint, *President*
Ed Renteria, *COO*
Shirley Sifuentes, *COO*
Victoria Pipkin, *CFO*
Ganga Radhakrishnan, *CFO*
▲ **EMP:** 60 **EST:** 1932
SQ FT: 20,000
SALES (est): 36.3MM **Privately Held**
WEB: www.1stunitedcu.org
SIC: 6061 Federal credit unions

(P-9775)
BAY FEDERAL CREDIT UNION (PA)
3333 Clares St, Capitola (95010-2564)
PHONE.....................831 479-6000
Dennis Osmer, *Chairman*
H Duane Smith, *Vice Chairman*
Michael Leung, *Treasurer*
Manny Escarcega, *Assoc VP*
Scott Nguyen, *Assoc VP*
EMP: 70 **EST:** 1957
SALES (est): 35.7MM **Privately Held**
WEB: www.bayfed.com
SIC: 6061 Federal credit unions

(P-9776)
CHEVRON FEDERAL CREDIT UNION (PA)
500 12th St Ste 200, Oakland (94607-4084)
P.O. Box 2069 (94604-2069)
PHONE.....................888 884-4630
James Mooney, *President*
Ron Thomas, *COO*
Janet Lee, *CFO*
Gina Lee, *Officer*
Lana Aliyev, *Business Anlyst*
EMP: 54 **EST:** 1935
SQ FT: 25,663
SALES: 236MM **Privately Held**
WEB: www.chevronfcu.org
SIC: 6061 Federal credit unions

(P-9777)
COAST CENTRAL CREDIT UNION (PA)
2650 Harrison Ave, Eureka (95501-3223)
PHONE.....................707 445-8801
Dean Christensen, *President*
Tom Noonan, *Treasurer*
Kristen Mainwaring, *Officer*
Mandy Marquez, *Officer*
Ed Christians, *Vice Pres*
EMP: 65 **EST:** 1932
SQ FT: 17,000
SALES: 43.2MM **Privately Held**
WEB: www.coastccu.org
SIC: 6061 Federal credit unions

(P-9778)
COAST CENTRAL CREDIT UNION
1968 Central Ave, McKinleyville (95519-3606)
PHONE.....................707 445-8801
Leah Morse, *Administration*
Amelia Calvert,
EMP: 43
SALES (corp-wide): 43.2MM **Privately Held**
WEB: www.coastccu.org
SIC: 6061 Federal credit unions
PA: Coast Central Credit Union Inc
2650 Harrison Ave
Eureka CA 95501
707 445-8801

(P-9779)
COMMONWEALTH CENTRAL CREDIT UN (PA)
5890 Silver Creek Vly Rd, San Jose (95138-1027)
P.O. Box 641690 (95164-1690)
PHONE.....................408 531-3100
Craig Weber, *CEO*
Kathleen Blas, *Analyst*
EMP: 69
SQ FT: 36,432
SALES: 20.4MM **Privately Held**
WEB: www.wealthcu.org
SIC: 6061 Federal credit unions

(P-9780)
COMMUNITY FIRST CREDIT UNION (PA)
1105 N Dutton Ave Ste A, Santa Rosa (95401-4683)
P.O. Box 6004 (95406-0004)
PHONE.....................707 546-6000
Todd Sheffield, *CEO*
David Rhoades, *CFO*
EMP: 134 **EST:** 1959
SALES (est): 23.4MM **Privately Held**
WEB: www.comfirstcu.org
SIC: 6061 Federal credit unions

(P-9781)
CONTRA COSTA FEDERAL CREDIT UN (PA)
Also Called: 1STNORCAL
1111 Pine St, Martinez (94553-1702)
P.O. Box 509 (94553-0144)
PHONE.....................925 228-7550
David Green, *President*
Lisa Homes, *Vice Pres*
EMP: 35 **EST:** 1949
SQ FT: 5,000
SALES: 16.5MM **Privately Held**
WEB: www.1stnorcalcu.org
SIC: 6061 Federal credit unions

(P-9782)
EDUCATIONAL EMPLOYEES CR UN (PA)
2222 W Shaw Ave, Fresno (93711-3419)
PHONE.....................559 437-7700
Barbara Thomas, *Chairman*
John Tinker, *Vice Chairman*
Elizabeth Dooley, *President*
Denda Matthews, *COO*
Rick Browning, *Treasurer*
EMP: 110
SQ FT: 44,000
SALES: 99.7MM **Privately Held**
WEB: www.myeecu.org
SIC: 6061 Federal credit unions

(P-9783)
EDUCATIONAL EMPLOYEES CR UN
3488 W Shaw Ave, Fresno (93711-3216)
P.O. Box 5242 (93755-5242)
PHONE.....................559 896-0222
Bruce L Barnett, *President*
Denda Matthews, *Vice Pres*
Christy Alkire, *Branch Mgr*
Joanne Lockhart, *Branch Mgr*
Argelia Martinez, *Branch Mgr*
EMP: 64
SALES (corp-wide): 99.7MM **Privately Held**
WEB: www.myeecu.org
SIC: 6061 Federal credit unions
PA: Educational Employees Credit Union
2222 W Shaw Ave
Fresno CA 93711
559 437-7700

(P-9784)
EDUCATIONAL EMPLOYEES CR UN
455 E Barstow Ave, Fresno (93710-6104)
PHONE.....................559 437-7700
Bruce L Barnett, *President*
Ben Canonoy, *Network Enginr*
Vanessa Lopez,
EMP: 64
SALES (corp-wide): 99.7MM **Privately Held**
WEB: www.myeecu.org
SIC: 6061 Federal credit unions
PA: Educational Employees Credit Union
2222 W Shaw Ave
Fresno CA 93711
559 437-7700

(P-9785)
EXCITE CREDIT UNION (PA)
265 Curtner Ave, San Jose (95125-1404)
P.O. Box 18460 (95158-8460)
PHONE.....................800 232-8669
Brian Dorcy, *CEO*
Ram Misra, *Bd of Directors*
Larry Carter, *Officer*
Kevin Alsup, *Vice Pres*
Sean Chambers, *Vice Pres*
EMP: 73 **EST:** 1952
SQ FT: 40,000
SALES (est): 19.9MM **Privately Held**
WEB: www.excitecu.org
SIC: 6061 Federal credit unions

(P-9786)
FINANCIAL CENTER CREDIT UNION
2405 S Airport Way, Stockton (95206-3318)
PHONE.....................209 462-2807
EMP: 38
SALES (corp-wide): 21.9MM **Privately Held**
SIC: 6061 Federal Credit Unions
PA: Financial Center Credit Union
18 S Center St
Stockton CA 95202
209 948-6024

(P-9787)
FINANCIAL CENTER CREDIT UNION (PA)
18 S Center St, Stockton (95202-2803)
P.O. Box 208005 (95208-9005)
PHONE.....................209 948-6024
Michael P Duffy, *CEO*
Dawn McMeans, *Principal*
EMP: 40 **EST:** 1954
SQ FT: 20,000
SALES: 12.8MM **Privately Held**
WEB: www.fccuburt.org
SIC: 6061 Federal credit unions

(P-9788)
FIRST TECHNOLOGY FEDERAL CR UN
19960 Stevens Creek Blvd, Cupertino (95014-2306)
PHONE.....................408 863-6240
Dennis Nakpil, *Manager*
EMP: 79
SALES (corp-wide): 637.1MM **Privately Held**
WEB: www.firsttechfed.com
SIC: 6061 Federal credit unions
PA: First Technology Federal Credit Union
2702 Orchard Pkwy
San Jose CA 95134
855 855-8805

(P-9789)
FIRST TECHNOLOGY FEDERAL CR UN (PA)
Also Called: First Tech Federal Credit Un
2702 Orchard Pkwy, San Jose (95134-2012)
PHONE.....................855 855-8805
Greg A Mitchell, *President*
Scott Jenner, *President*
Hank Sigmon, *CFO*
Monique Little,
Lisa Banner, *Senior VP*
EMP: 100
SALES: 480.8MM **Privately Held**
WEB: www.firsttechfed.com
SIC: 6061 Federal credit unions

(P-9790)
FIRST TECHNOLOGY FEDERAL CR UN
1011 Sunset Blvd Ste 210, Rocklin (95765-3782)
PHONE.....................855 855-8805
Greg A Mitchell, *CEO*
Marito Domingo, *Ch Invest Ofcr*
Tamera Jette, *Vice Pres*
Sandi Papenfuhs, *Vice Pres*
Edward Powers, *Vice Pres*
EMP: 79
SALES (corp-wide): 637.1MM **Privately Held**
WEB: www.firsttechfed.com
SIC: 6061 Federal credit unions
PA: First Technology Federal Credit Union
2702 Orchard Pkwy
San Jose CA 95134
855 855-8805

(P-9791)
FIRST US COMMUNITY CREDIT UN (PA)
580 University Ave # 100, Sacramento (95825-6528)
PHONE.....................916 576-5700
Carol Hauck, *CEO*
Richard Cochran, *President*
Brian W Doyle, *Chairman*
Richard D Cochran, *Treasurer*
Christopher Tatton, *Officer*
EMP: 40 **EST:** 1936
SQ FT: 10,000
SALES: 13.7MM **Privately Held**
WEB: www.firstus.org
SIC: 6061 Federal credit unions

(P-9792)
HERITAGE COMMUNITY CREDIT UN (PA)
10415 Old Placerville Rd, Sacramento (95827-2508)
P.O. Box 790, Rancho Cordova (95741-0790)
PHONE.....................916 364-1700
Ed Turk, *CEO*
Ron Delgado, *President*
Judy Flores, *CEO*
Brandon Ivie, *CFO*
Brian Allen, *Officer*
EMP: 44
SALES: 7.4MM **Privately Held**
WEB: www.heritageccu.com
SIC: 6061 Federal credit unions

(P-9793)
KEYPOINT CREDIT UNION (PA)
2805 Bowers Ave Ste 105, Santa Clara (95051-0972)
PHONE.....................408 731-4100
T Bradford Canfield, *CEO*
Timothy M Kramer, *President*
John Herrick, *CFO*
Keith Stattenfield, *Treasurer*
Raul Nieves, *Officer*
EMP: 123 **EST:** 1979
SQ FT: 60,715
SALES: 41.3MM **Privately Held**
WEB: www.kpcu.com
SIC: 6061 Federal credit unions

(P-9794)
MEMBERS 1ST CREDIT UNION (PA)
4710 Mountain Lakes Blvd, Redding (96003-1451)
PHONE.....................530 222-6060

PRODUCTS & SERVICES SECTION   6061 - Federal Credit Unions County (P-9815)

Mark Moore, *President*
Heidi Brown, *Officer*
Rudy Martinez, *Officer*
Judi Bartholomew, *Exec VP*
Noel Stratton, *Vice Pres*
EMP: 50 **EST:** 1936
SALES (est): 9.5MM **Privately Held**
WEB: www.m1cu.org
SIC: 6061 Federal credit unions

(P-9795)
MERCED SCHL EMPLOYEES FDRAL CR (PA)
Also Called: MSEFCU
1021 Olivewood Dr, Merced (95348-1218)
P.O. Box 1349 (95341-1349)
PHONE.................................209 383-5550
Nancy Deavours, *President*
Jennifer Riedeman, *Admin Sec*
Adrian Coronado, *Loan Officer*
Lisa Oberg, *Loan Officer*
Lori Smith, *Loan*
EMP: 52
SQ FT: 16,500
SALES: 16.5MM **Privately Held**
WEB: www.mercedschoolcu.org
SIC: 6061 Federal credit unions

(P-9796)
MERIWEST CREDIT UNION (PA)
5615 Chesbro Ave Ste 100, San Jose (95123-3057)
P.O. Box 530953 (95153-5353)
PHONE.................................408 363-3200
Toll Free:...................................877 -
Julie A Kirsch, *Principal*
Janet Grogan, *President*
Steven G Johnson, *CEO*
Christopher Owen, *CEO*
Brian Hennessey, *CFO*
EMP: 130 **EST:** 1961
SQ FT: 61,000
SALES: 58.4MM **Privately Held**
WEB: www.meriwest.com
SIC: 6061 Federal credit unions

(P-9797)
MOCSE FEDERAL CREDIT UNION
3600 Coffee Rd, Modesto (95355-1164)
PHONE.................................209 572-3600
Tracey Kerr, *President*
Charlie Rodgers, *CFO*
Justin Garcia, *Technical Staff*
Kathryn Dougherty, *Accounting Mgr*
EMP: 41 **EST:** 1959
SQ FT: 20,000
SALES: 8.5MM **Privately Held**
WEB: www.mocse.org
SIC: 6061 6062 Federal credit unions; state credit unions

(P-9798)
NOBLE CREDIT UNION (PA)
2580 W Shaw Ln Frnt, Fresno (93711-2776)
P.O. Box 8027 (93747-8027)
PHONE.................................559 252-5000
Karen B Cobb, *Ch of Bd*
Doug Papagni, *Chairman*
Linzie Daniel, *Treasurer*
Mary Ann Rogozinski, *Treasurer*
Robert Vandergon, *Vice Ch Bd*
EMP: 50
SQ FT: 12,000
SALES: 33.1MM **Privately Held**
WEB: www.noblecu.com
SIC: 6061 Federal credit unions

(P-9799)
NOBLE CREDIT UNION
2580 W Shaw Ln Frnt, Fresno (93711-2776)
P.O. Box 8027 (93747-8027)
PHONE.................................559 252-5000
Susan Ryan, *Manager*
EMP: 69
SALES (corp-wide): 33.1MM **Privately Held**
WEB: www.noblecu.com
SIC: 6061 Federal credit unions
PA: Noble Credit Union
2580 W Shaw Ln Frnt
Fresno CA 93711
559 252-5000

(P-9800)
OPERATING ENGINEERS LOCAL UN 3 (PA)
250 N Canyons Pkwy, Livermore (94551-9470)
P.O. Box 5073 (94551-5073)
PHONE.................................925 454-4000
Mike Donahue, *CEO*
Jenna Anderson, *Vice Pres*
Christina Boyd, *Vice Pres*
Deepak Godhwani, *Vice Pres*
Gabe Ybarrolaza, *Vice Pres*
EMP: 43 **EST:** 2005
SALES: 44.5MM **Privately Held**
WEB: www.oefederal.org
SIC: 6061 Federal credit unions

(P-9801)
PACIFIC SERVICE CREDIT UNION (PA)
3000 Clayton Rd, Concord (94519-2731)
P.O. Box 8191, Walnut Creek (94596-8191)
PHONE.................................888 858-6878
Jenna Lampson, *President*
Lawrence Labonte, *CFO*
David Sena, *Chairman*
Vicki Turano, *Treasurer*
Randal Cain, *Officer*
EMP: 76 **EST:** 1936
SQ FT: 23,689
SALES: 38MM **Privately Held**
WEB: www.pacificservice.org
SIC: 6061 Federal credit unions

(P-9802)
PATELCO CREDIT UNION (PA)
3 Park Pl, Dublin (94568-7983)
P.O. Box 8020, Pleasanton (94588-8601)
PHONE.................................800 358-8228
Erin Mendez, *CEO*
Sue Gruber, *CFO*
Richard Wada,
Brent Gifford, *Officer*
Sharon Tallon, *Officer*
EMP: 250 **EST:** 1936
SALES: 223.3MM **Privately Held**
WEB: www.patelco.org
SIC: 6061 Federal credit unions

(P-9803)
POLICE CREDIT UNION OF CAL (PA)
1250 Grundy Ln, San Bruno (94066-3032)
P.O. Box 1087 (94066-7087)
PHONE.................................415 242-2142
Eddie C Young, *CEO*
Rosalyn Reilly, *COO*
Jeffrey Ng, *Officer*
Kathleen Litman, *Vice Pres*
Michael Sordelli, *Principal*
EMP: 70 **EST:** 1958
SQ FT: 18,561
SALES: 28.8MM **Privately Held**
WEB: www.thepolicecu.org
SIC: 6061 Federal credit unions

(P-9804)
REDWOOD CREDIT UNION
1129 S Cloverdale Blvd A, Cloverdale (95425-4482)
PHONE.................................800 479-7928
Jose Alvarez, *Branch Mgr*
EMP: 42
SALES (corp-wide): 180.2MM **Privately Held**
WEB: www.redwoodcu.org
SIC: 6061 Federal credit unions
PA: Redwood Credit Union
3033 Cleveland Ave # 100
Santa Rosa CA 95403
707 545-4000

(P-9805)
REDWOOD CREDIT UNION (PA)
3033 Cleveland Ave # 100, Santa Rosa (95403-2126)
P.O. Box 6104 (95406-0104)
PHONE.................................707 545-4000
Brett Martinez, *President*
Sean Anderson, *Treasurer*
Judy James, *Bd of Directors*
Michelle Anderson,
Daniel Torres, *Officer*
EMP: 190 **EST:** 1950

SQ FT: 20,000
SALES (est): 180.2MM **Privately Held**
WEB: www.redwoodcu.org
SIC: 6061 Federal credit unions

(P-9806)
REDWOOD CREDIT UNION
1390 Market St, San Francisco (94102-5402)
PHONE.................................800 479-7928
Andrew Muir, *Analyst*
EMP: 42
SALES (corp-wide): 180.2MM **Privately Held**
WEB: www.redwoodcu.org
SIC: 6061 Federal credit unions
PA: Redwood Credit Union
3033 Cleveland Ave # 100
Santa Rosa CA 95403
707 545-4000

(P-9807)
REDWOOD CREDIT UNION
100 Van Ness Ave Fl 10, San Francisco (94102-5209)
PHONE.................................415 861-7928
Jacob Roberts, *Manager*
Jenn Holm, *Officer*
Kim Odeh, *Officer*
Michelle Walling, *Officer*
Kimberly Williams, *Senior VP*
EMP: 42
SALES (corp-wide): 180.2MM **Privately Held**
WEB: www.redwoodcu.org
SIC: 6061 Federal credit unions
PA: Redwood Credit Union
3033 Cleveland Ave # 100
Santa Rosa CA 95403
707 545-4000

(P-9808)
SAFE CREDIT UNION (PA)
2295 Iron Point Rd # 100, Folsom (95630-8767)
PHONE.................................916 979-7233
Dave Roughton, *CEO*
Robert E Logue, *Vice Chairman*
Jennifer M Santos, *President*
Janine Southwick, *President*
Michael Webber, *President*
EMP: 160 **EST:** 1940
SQ FT: 57,000
SALES: 100.5MM **Privately Held**
WEB: www.safecu.org
SIC: 6061 Federal credit unions

(P-9809)
SAFEAMERICA CREDIT UNION (PA)
6001 Gibraltar Dr, Pleasanton (94588-2707)
P.O. Box 11269 (94588-1269)
PHONE.................................925 734-4111
Barry Roach, *CEO*
Jason Chang, *Vice Chairman*
Chuck Dunbar, *CFO*
Frank Zampella, *Chairman*
Susan Walls, *Treasurer*
EMP: 45
SQ FT: 27,000
SALES: 17.7MM **Privately Held**
WEB: www.safeamerica.com
SIC: 6061 Federal credit unions

(P-9810)
SAN FRANCISCO FEDERAL CR UN (PA)
770 Golden Gate Ave Fl 1, San Francisco (94102-3194)
PHONE.................................415 775-5377
William Wolverton, *CEO*
Luenna Kim, *Ch of Bd*
Todd Rydstrom, *Vice Chairman*
Steve Ho, *COO*
William Smith, *Treasurer*
▲ **EMP:** 70
SQ FT: 35,500
SALES: 38.4MM **Privately Held**
WEB: www.sanfranciscofcu.com
SIC: 6061 Federal credit unions

(P-9811)
SAN FRANCISCO FIRE CREDIT UN (PA)
Also Called: SFFCU
3201 California St, San Francisco (94118-1903)
PHONE.................................415 674-4800
Darren Herrmann, *CEO*
Diana Dykstra, *President*
John E Sweeney, *Chairman*
Jennifer Ebert, *Officer*
Dennis Pecorella, *Officer*
EMP: 42
SQ FT: 20,000
SALES: 52.4MM **Privately Held**
WEB: www.sffirecu.org
SIC: 6061 Federal credit unions

(P-9812)
SAN MATEO CREDIT UNION
525 Middlefield Rd, Redwood City (94063-1853)
P.O. Box 910 (94064-0910)
PHONE.................................,....650 363-1725
Barry Jolette, *CEO*
Connie Paniagua, *CEO*
Jack Chinn, *CFO*
Jon Carlson, *Vice Pres*
Edith Munoz, *Branch Mgr*
EMP: 66
SALES (corp-wide): 49.2MM **Privately Held**
WEB: www.smcu.org
SIC: 6061 Federal credit unions
PA: San Mateo Credit Union
350 Convention Way # 300
Redwood City CA 94063
650 363-1725

(P-9813)
SAN MATEO CREDIT UNION (PA)
350 Convention Way # 300, Redwood City (94063-1435)
P.O. Box 910 (94064-0910)
PHONE.................................650 363-1725
Berry Jolette, *President*
Magda Gonzalez, *Ch of Bd*
Valerie Alsip, *COO*
Motley Snuth, *Treasurer*
Jasmen Avedian, *Officer*
▲ **EMP:** 55 **EST:** 1952
SQ FT: 18,300
SALES: 49.2MM **Privately Held**
WEB: www.smcu.org
SIC: 6061 Federal credit unions

(P-9814)
SAN MATEO CREDIT UNION
1515 S El Cmino Real Ste, San Mateo (94402)
P.O. Box 910, Redwood City (94064-0910)
PHONE.................................650 363-1725
Preston Monroe, *Principal*
Angelica Luna, *Officer*
Robert Carter, *Vice Pres*
David Capurro, *Administration*
EMP: 159 **EST:** 2008
SALES (est): 4.1MM
SALES (corp-wide): 49.2MM **Privately Held**
WEB: www.smcu.org
SIC: 6061 Federal credit unions
PA: San Mateo Credit Union
350 Convention Way # 300
Redwood City CA 94063
650 363-1725

(P-9815)
SANTA CLARA CNTY FDERAL CR UN
1641 N 1st St Ste 170, San Jose (95112-4521)
PHONE.................................408 282-0700
Michael Delmonico, *Branch Mgr*
Marco Denson, *Vice Pres*
Athena Atienza, *Credit Staff*
EMP: 55
SALES (corp-wide): 25.1MM **Privately Held**
WEB: www.sccfcu.org
SIC: 6061 Federal credit unions
PA: Santa Clara County Federal Credit Union (Inc)
1641 N 1st St Ste 245
San Jose CA 95112
408 282-0700

6061 Federal Credit Unions County

(P-9816)
SANTA CLARA CNTY FDERAL CR UN (PA)
1641 N 1st St Ste 245, San Jose (95112-4519)
PHONE................................408 282-0700
Mike Delmonico, *CEO*
Divine David, *Officer*
Margaret Czyz, *Vice Pres*
Michael Kadel, *Vice Pres*
Steve Naylor, *Vice Pres*
EMP: 55
SQ FT: 42,000
SALES: 28.4MM **Privately Held**
WEB: www.sccfcu.org
SIC: 6061 Federal credit unions

(P-9817)
SANTA CRUZ COMMUNITY CREDIT UN (PA)
324 Front St, Santa Cruz (95060-4502)
PHONE................................831 425-7708
Michael Meara, *Chairman*
Christina Cuevas, *Principal*
Reggie Knox, *Principal*
Ricardo Rocha, *Principal*
Howard Sherer, *Principal*
EMP: 35 **EST:** 1977
SQ FT: 6,500
SALES: 6.6MM **Privately Held**
WEB: www.scccu.org
SIC: 6061 Federal credit unions

(P-9818)
SCHOOLS FINANCIAL CREDIT UNION (PA)
1485 Response Rd Ste 126, Sacramento (95815-5261)
P.O. Box 11547, Santa Ana (92711-1547)
PHONE................................916 569-5400
James P Jordan III, *President*
Brenda Gipson, *COO*
Todd Devoogd, *CFO*
Tim Marriott, *CFO*
David Menker, *Vice Pres*
EMP: 150 **EST:** 1933
SQ FT: 56,000
SALES: 71.3MM **Privately Held**
WEB: www.schoolsfirstfcu.org
SIC: 6061 Federal credit unions

(P-9819)
SIERRA CENTRAL CREDIT UNION (PA)
1351 Harter Pkwy, Yuba City (95993-2604)
PHONE................................530 671-3009
John Cassidy, *CEO*
Lori Guertner, *President*
Steven Magallanes, *President*
Stephanie Dickinson, *CFO*
Ron Sweeney, *Exec VP*
EMP: 90 **EST:** 1955
SQ FT: 8,000
SALES: 43MM **Privately Held**
WEB: www.sierracentral.com
SIC: 6061 Federal credit unions

(P-9820)
SOLANO FIRST FEDERAL CREDIT UN
1000 Union Ave, Fairfield (94533-5516)
P.O. Box 5040 (94533-0682)
PHONE................................707 422-9626
Russell Hatch, *President*
EMP: 38 **EST:** 1956
SQ FT: 15,000
SALES: 4.5MM **Privately Held**
WEB: www.solanofirst.com
SIC: 6061 Federal credit unions

(P-9821)
STANFORD FEDERAL CREDIT UNION (PA)
Also Called: SFCU
1860 Embarcadero Rd # 200, Palo Alto (94303-3320)
P.O. Box 10690 (94303-0843)
PHONE................................650 725-1000
Jane S Duperrault, *Ch of Bd*
Tana Hutchison, *Treasurer*
Scott Ferguson, *Business Dir*
Valdemar Sandoval, *Branch Mgr*
Jerry L Jobe, *Admin Sec*
EMP: 61

SALES: 98.2MM **Privately Held**
WEB: www.sfcu.org
SIC: 6061 Federal credit unions

(P-9822)
STAR ONE CREDIT UNION (PA)
1306 Bordeaux Dr, Sunnyvale (94089-1005)
P.O. Box 3643 (94088-3643)
PHONE................................408 543-5202
Rick Heldebrant, *President*
Scott Dunlap, *Treasurer*
Patricia Gustafson, *Bd of Directors*
Nya Munday, *Officer*
Lynn Brubaker, *Vice Pres*
EMP: 107
SQ FT: 25,000
SALES: 245.9MM **Privately Held**
WEB: www.starone.org
SIC: 6061 Federal credit unions

(P-9823)
TECHNOLOGY CREDIT UNION (PA)
2010 N 1st St Ste 200, San Jose (95131-2024)
P.O. Box 1409 (95109-1409)
PHONE................................408 451-9111
Todd Harris, *CEO*
Wendy Cheney, *President*
Dean Davis, *President*
Barbara B Kamm, *CEO*
Doug Stoveland, *Ch Credit Ofcr*
EMP: 133 **EST:** 1960
SQ FT: 23,000
SALES: 118.5MM **Privately Held**
WEB: www.techcu.com
SIC: 6061 Federal credit unions

(P-9824)
TRAVIS CREDIT UNION (PA)
1 Travis Way, Vacaville (95687-3276)
P.O. Box 2069 (95696-2069)
PHONE................................707 449-4000
Patsy Vanouwerkerk, *CEO*
Deborah Aspling, *Vice Chairman*
Cynthia McGuire, *President*
Latanya Robinson, *President*
Tom Corio, *CFO*
EMP: 300
SQ FT: 12,000
SALES: 135.9MM **Privately Held**
WEB: www.traviscu.org
SIC: 6061 Federal credit unions

(P-9825)
UNCLE CREDIT UNION (PA)
2100 Las Positas Ct, Livermore (94551-7301)
PHONE................................925 447-5001
Harold Roundtree, *CEO*
Fidela Hernandez, *President*
Jim Ott, *President*
Wendy Zanotelli, *COO*
Gina Bloomfield, *CFO*
▲ **EMP:** 58
SQ FT: 17,000
SALES: 17.9MM **Privately Held**
WEB: www.unclecu.org
SIC: 6061 Federal credit unions

(P-9826)
VALLEY FIRST CREDIT UNION (PA)
1419 J St, Modesto (95354-1014)
P.O. Box 1411 (95353-1411)
PHONE................................209 549-8511
Hank Barrett, *Exec Dir*
Fred Cruz, *CEO*
Dennis Barta, *CFO*
Gary Hall, *Treasurer*
Jennifer Brown, *Vice Pres*
EMP: 79 **EST:** 1948
SQ FT: 14,000
SALES: 23.2MM **Privately Held**
WEB: www.valleyfirstcu.org
SIC: 6061 Federal credit unions

(P-9827)
VOCALITY COMMUNITY CREDIT UN
757 Redwood Dr, Garberville (95542-3116)
PHONE................................707 923-2012
Shon Wellborn, *President*
Sharon Toborg, *Vice Pres*
Valerie Johnston, *VP Finance*

Ember Meserve,
EMP: 42 **EST:** 1979
SQ FT: 6,100
SALES: 5.7MM **Privately Held**
WEB: www.vocalityccu.org
SIC: 6061 Federal credit unions

(P-9828)
YOLO FEDERAL CREDIT UNION (PA)
266 W Main St, Woodland (95695-3684)
P.O. Box 657 (95776-0657)
PHONE................................530 668-2700
Clyde Brooker, *President*
Crystal Salcedo,
EMP: 40
SQ FT: 15,500
SALES: 11MM **Privately Held**
WEB: www.yolofcu.org
SIC: 6061 Federal credit unions

6062 State Credit Unions

(P-9829)
GOLDEN 1 CREDIT UNION
5901 Sunrise Blvd, Citrus Heights (95610-6832)
PHONE................................916 732-2900
Michelle Larson, *Manager*
EMP: 51
SALES (corp-wide): 412MM **Privately Held**
WEB: www.golden1.com
SIC: 6062 6061 State credit unions, not federally chartered; federal credit unions
PA: Golden 1 Credit Union
8945 Cal Center Dr
Sacramento CA 95826
916 732-2900

(P-9830)
GOLDEN 1 CREDIT UNION
7770 College Town Dr, Sacramento (95826-2343)
PHONE................................916 732-2900
Wayne Moore, *Branch Mgr*
Cherrish Manzo,
EMP: 51
SALES (corp-wide): 412MM **Privately Held**
WEB: www.golden1.com
SIC: 6062 State credit unions, not federally chartered
PA: Golden 1 Credit Union
8945 Cal Center Dr
Sacramento CA 95826
916 732-2900

(P-9831)
GOLDEN 1 CREDIT UNION
1282 Stabler Ln Ste 640, Yuba City (95993-2625)
PHONE................................877 465-3361
Choni Weigman, *Manager*
EMP: 51
SALES (corp-wide): 412MM **Privately Held**
WEB: www.golden1.com
SIC: 6062 State credit unions, not federally chartered
PA: Golden 1 Credit Union
8945 Cal Center Dr
Sacramento CA 95826
916 732-2900

(P-9832)
GOLDEN 1 CREDIT UNION (PA)
8945 Cal Center Dr, Sacramento (95826-3239)
P.O. Box 15966 (95852-0966)
PHONE................................916 732-2900
Teresa Halleck, *President*
Alphonso Cosby, *Officer*
Barbara Heming, *Officer*
Andrew Zaragoza, *Officer*
Lisa Lemus, *Senior VP*
EMP: 400 **EST:** 1933
SQ FT: 100,000
SALES: 412MM **Privately Held**
WEB: www.golden1.com
SIC: 6062 State credit unions, not federally chartered

(P-9833)
GOLDEN 1 CREDIT UNION
Also Called: Unknown
2942 Main St, Susanville (96130-4730)
PHONE................................530 251-0205
EMP: 51
SALES (corp-wide): 412MM **Privately Held**
WEB: www.golden1.com
SIC: 6062 State credit unions, not federally chartered
PA: Golden 1 Credit Union
8945 Cal Center Dr
Sacramento CA 95826
916 732-2900

(P-9834)
GOLDEN 1 CREDIT UNION
1701 Santa Clara Dr # 120, Roseville (95661-2983)
PHONE................................916 784-9226
Tina Jeffries, *Manager*
EMP: 51
SALES (corp-wide): 412MM **Privately Held**
WEB: www.golden1.com
SIC: 6062 6061 State credit unions, not federally chartered; federal credit unions
PA: Golden 1 Credit Union
8945 Cal Center Dr
Sacramento CA 95826
916 732-2900

(P-9835)
PROVIDENT CREDIT UNION (PA)
303 Twin Dolphin Dr # 303, Redwood City (94065-1419)
P.O. Box 8007 (94063-0907)
PHONE................................650 508-0300
Maurice Schmid, *Chairman*
Ludelle Morrow, *President*
Iris Solano, *President*
Jim Ernest, *CEO*
Claudia Jimenez, *Officer*
EMP: 130 **EST:** 1951
SQ FT: 150,000
SALES: 84.3MM **Privately Held**
WEB: www.providentcu.org
SIC: 6062 State credit unions, not federally chartered

(P-9836)
SACRAMENTO CREDIT UNION (PA)
800 H St Ste 100, Sacramento (95814-2686)
P.O. Box 2351 (95812-2351)
PHONE................................916 444-6070
Toll Free:................................888
Bhavnesh Makin, *CEO*
James Batson, *CFO*
Jovanna Chavez, *Officer*
Christina Narain, *Officer*
Blake Cairney, *Vice Pres*
EMP: 64
SQ FT: 39,138
SALES: 22.1MM **Privately Held**
WEB: www.sactocu.org
SIC: 6062 6163 State credit unions, not federally chartered; loan brokers

6081 Foreign Banks, Branches & Agencies

(P-9837)
PARIBAS ASSET MANAGEMENT INC
1 Front St Fl 23, San Francisco (94111-5325)
PHONE................................415 772-1300
Bernard Digeon, *General Mgr*
William Liebscher, *President*
Rita Liu, *Officer*
Diane Cozian, *Vice Pres*
Michael Ueyama, *Vice Pres*
EMP: 147
SALES (corp-wide): 2.7B **Privately Held**
WEB: www.usa.bnpparibas
SIC: 6081 6021 Branches & agencies of foreign banks; national commercial banks

PRODUCTS & SERVICES SECTION

6141 - Personal Credit Institutions County (P-9858)

HQ: Paribas Asset Management, Inc.
787 7th Ave Fl 27
New York NY 10019

6082 Foreign Trade & Intl Banks

(P-9838)
PARIBAS ASSET MANAGEMENT INC
1 Front St Fl 23, San Francisco (94111-5325)
PHONE..................................415 772-1300
Francois Denis, *Principal*
William J La Herran, *Vice Pres*
EMP: 147
SALES (corp-wide): 2.7B **Privately Held**
WEB: www.usa.bnpparibas
SIC: 6082 Foreign trade & international banking institutions
HQ: Paribas Asset Management, Inc.
787 7th Ave Fl 27
New York NY 10019

6099 Functions Related To Deposit Banking, NEC

(P-9839)
ACFN FRANCHISED INC
4 N 2nd St Ste 1240, San Jose (95113-1329)
PHONE..................................888 794-2236
Jeffrey D Ker, *CEO*
Dana Kerr, *Admin Sec*
Gershon Yakir, *VP Opers*
EMP: 38 EST: 2002
SALES (est): 15MM **Privately Held**
WEB: www.acfn.info
SIC: 6099 Automated teller machine (ATM) network

(P-9840)
AIRBNB PAYMENTS INC
888 Brannan St, San Francisco (94103-4928)
PHONE..................................415 861-2325
David Bernstein, *CFO*
EMP: 39 EST: 2013
SALES (est): 4.7MM **Privately Held**
WEB: www.airbnbhell.com
SIC: 6099 Electronic funds transfer network, including switching

(P-9841)
AXCESS FINANCIAL SERVICES INC
4241 Florin Rd, Sacramento (95823-2535)
PHONE..................................916 424-4180
EMP: 36
SALES (corp-wide): 795.4MM **Privately Held**
WEB: www.axcess-financial.com
SIC: 6099 Check cashing agencies
HQ: Axcess Financial Services, Inc.
7755 Montgomery Rd # 400
Cincinnati OH 45236
513 336-7735

(P-9842)
AXCESS FINANCIAL SERVICES INC
3981 Foothills Blvd, Roseville (95747-7347)
PHONE..................................916 783-0173
EMP: 36
SALES (corp-wide): 795.4MM **Privately Held**
WEB: www.axcess-financial.com
SIC: 6099 Check cashing agencies
HQ: Axcess Financial Services, Inc.
7755 Montgomery Rd # 400
Cincinnati OH 45236
513 336-7735

(P-9843)
BEL AIR MART
Also Called: Bel Air Market 525
9435 Elk Grove Blvd, Elk Grove (95624-5013)
PHONE..................................916 714-6996
Gary Larrabee, *Manager*
EMP: 106
SALES (corp-wide): 2.1B **Privately Held**
WEB: www.raleys.com
SIC: 5411 4311 6099 Supermarkets, chain; U.S. Postal Service; money order issuance
HQ: Bel Air Mart
500 W Capitol Ave
West Sacramento CA

(P-9844)
BLACKHAWK NETWORK INC (DH)
6220 Stoneridge Mall Rd, Pleasanton (94588-3260)
PHONE..................................925 226-9990
Talbott Roche, *President*
Heather Krishnan, *Partner*
Jessica Madigan, *Partner*
Mike Gionfriddo, *President*
Ben King, *President*
EMP: 625 EST: 2005
SALES (est): 650.1MM
SALES (corp-wide): 2.2B **Privately Held**
WEB: www.blackhawknetwork.com
SIC: 6099 Electronic funds transfer network, including switching

(P-9845)
BLACKHAWK NETWORK HOLDINGS INC (HQ)
6220 Stoneridge Mall Rd, Pleasanton (94588-3260)
PHONE..................................925 226-9990
Talbott Roche, *President*
Jenna Clark, *Partner*
Stephanie Wilson, *Partner*
Nick Samurkas, *COO*
Charles O Garner, *CFO*
EMP: 500 EST: 2001
SQ FT: 149,000
SALES: 2.2B **Privately Held**
WEB: www.blackhawknetwork.com
SIC: 6099 Electronic funds transfer network, including switching
PA: Bhn Holdings, Inc.
6220 Stoneridge Mall Rd
Pleasanton CA 94588
925 226-9990

(P-9846)
CITCON USA LLC (PA)
2001 Gateway Pl Ste 410w, San Jose (95110-1039)
PHONE..................................888 254-4887
Chunbo Huang, *Mng Member*
Jing Jarrett, *Partner*
WEI Jiang, *President*
Alex Chen, *CTO*
Haitao Xin, *Vice Pres*
EMP: 50 EST: 2015
SALES (est): 6.3MM **Privately Held**
WEB: www.citcon.com
SIC: 6099 Electronic funds transfer network, including switching

(P-9847)
ESCROWCOM INC
180 Montgomery St Ste 650, San Francisco (94104-4208)
PHONE..................................949 635-3800
Matt Barrie, *CEO*
Greg Robinson, *Vice Pres*
Jason Whitlow, *CTO*
Michael Liedtke, *Engineer*
Sagar Yadav, *Sales Engr*
EMP: 50 EST: 1999
SQ FT: 5,590
SALES (est): 14.2MM **Privately Held**
WEB: www.escrow.com
SIC: 6099 4813 Escrow institutions other than real estate;
PA: Freelancer Limited
'grosvenor Place' Level 37 225 George Street
Sydney NSW 2000

(P-9848)
FINASTRA MERCHANT SERVICES INC (PA)
333 Bush St Fl 26, San Francisco (94104-2806)
PHONE..................................415 277-9900
Reuven Ben Menachem, *CEO*
Edward Ho, *President*
Don Suva, *CFO*
Bryan Schreiber, *Treasurer*
Mierzwa Dennis, *Vice Pres*
EMP: 60 EST: 1999
SQ FT: 14,000
SALES (est): 17.1MM **Privately Held**
WEB: www.finastra.com
SIC: 6099 Electronic funds transfer network, including switching

(P-9849)
NATIONAL DATA FUNDING LLC
462 Waterford Dr, Chico (95973-0318)
PHONE..................................530 343-1605
Richard Graeff, *COO*
EMP: 55 EST: 1986
SQ FT: 17,000
SALES (est): 16.3MM
SALES (corp-wide): 1.7B **Publicly Held**
WEB: www.first-american.net
SIC: 6099 Electronic funds transfer network, including switching
HQ: First American Payment Systems Lp
100 Throckmorton St # 1800
Fort Worth TX 76102

(P-9850)
XOOM CORPORATION
425 Market St Ste 1200, San Francisco (94105-5404)
PHONE..................................415 777-4800
John Kunze, *President*
Ryno Blignaut, *CFO*
Christopher G Ferro, *Ch Credit Ofcr*
Julian King, *Senior VP*
Bobby Aitkenhead, *Vice Pres*
EMP: 190 EST: 2001
SQ FT: 35,552
SALES (est): 99.3MM
SALES (corp-wide): 21.4B **Publicly Held**
WEB: www.xoom.com
SIC: 6099 Electronic funds transfer network, including switching
HQ: Paypal, Inc.
2211 N 1st St
San Jose CA 95131
877 981-2163

6111 Federal Credit Agencies

(P-9851)
FEDERAL HM LN BNK SAN FRNCISCO (PA)
333 Bush St Ste 2700, San Francisco (94104-2806)
PHONE..................................415 616-1000
John F Luikart, *Ch of Bd*
Eric Cicourel, *President*
Deb Eldridge, *President*
Gwen Hill, *President*
Jamie Leong, *President*
▲ EMP: 222 EST: 1932
SQ FT: 108,147
SALES (est): 1.1B **Privately Held**
WEB: www.fhlbsf.com
SIC: 6111 Federal & federally sponsored credit agencies

(P-9852)
FRESN-MDERA FDRAL LAND BNK ASS (HQ)
Also Called: Fresno-Madera Farm Credit
4635 W Spruce Ave, Fresno (93722-8425)
P.O. Box 13069 (93794-3069)
PHONE..................................559 277-7000
Thomas Brown, *President*
Doug Weber, *Ch Credit Ofcr*
EMP: 35 EST: 1917
SQ FT: 28,000
SALES (est): 10.2MM
SALES (corp-wide): 10.6MM **Privately Held**
WEB: www.fmfarmcredit.com
SIC: 6111 Federal Land Banks
PA: Fresno-Madera Farm Credit, Aca
4635 W Spruce Ave
Fresno CA
559 277-7000

(P-9853)
YOSEMITE FARM CREDIT ACA (PA)
806 W Monte Vista Ave, Turlock (95382-7242)
P.O. Box 3278 (95381-3278)
PHONE..................................209 667-2366
Leonard Van Eldern, *President*
Tracy Sparks, *CFO*
Ken Johnson, *Vice Pres*
Matt McNelis, *Vice Pres*
Neibeth Munoz, *Credit Staff*
EMP: 60 EST: 1917
SQ FT: 9,000
SALES: 108.4MM **Privately Held**
WEB: www.yosemitefarmcredit.com
SIC: 6111 Federal Land Banks

6141 Personal Credit Institutions

(P-9854)
CAMICO SERVICES INC
1800 Gateway Dr Ste 200, San Mateo (94404-4072)
PHONE..................................800 652-1772
Ricardo R Rosario, *President*
Edie Keating, *Business Anlyst*
Tim Huggins, *Manager*
Anna Fernandez, *Supervisor*
EMP: 39 EST: 1984
SALES (est): 8.3MM **Privately Held**
WEB: www.camico.com
SIC: 6141 Consumer finance companies

(P-9855)
CITIFINANCIAL CREDIT COMPANY
1054 Harter Pkwy Ste 4, Yuba City (95993-2653)
PHONE..................................530 671-7970
EMP: 135
SALES (corp-wide): 88.8B **Publicly Held**
SIC: 6141 Consumer finance companies
HQ: Citifinancial Credit Company
300 Saint Paul Pl Fl 3
Baltimore MD 21202
410 332-3000

(P-9856)
FEDERAL HM LN BNK SAN FRNCISCO
11050 White Rock Rd, Rancho Cordova (95670-6386)
PHONE..................................916 851-6900
Lawrence Parks, *Branch Mgr*
EMP: 35
SALES (corp-wide): 1.1B **Privately Held**
WEB: www.fhlbsf.com
SIC: 6141 6021 Personal credit institutions; national commercial banks
PA: Federal Home Loan Bank Of San Francisco
333 Bush St Ste 2700
San Francisco CA 94104
415 616-1000

(P-9857)
FLURISH INC
Also Called: Lendup
1750 Broadway 300, Oakland (94612-2106)
PHONE..................................855 253-6387
Sasha Orloff, *CEO*
Bill Donnelly, *Chief Mktg Ofcr*
Kathleen Fitzpatrick, *Vice Pres*
Robert Novick, *Vice Pres*
Jacob Rosenberg, *Admin Sec*
EMP: 80 EST: 2011
SALES (est): 26.1MM **Privately Held**
SIC: 6141 Consumer finance companies

(P-9858)
GLOBAL UPSIDE INC (PA)
4300 Stevens Creek Blvd # 270, San Jose (95129-1249)
PHONE..................................650 964-4820
Sangeeta Bhargava, *President*

6141 - Personal Credit Institutions County (P-9859)

Raghav Bhargava, *CFO*
Spencer Brown, *Officer*
EMP: 50 **EST:** 2008
SALES (est): 13.4MM **Privately Held**
WEB: www.globalupside.com
SIC: 6141 Consumer finance companies

(P-9859)
LENDINGCLUB CORPORATION (PA)
595 Market St Fl 4, San Francisco (94105-2807)
PHONE..................415 632-5600
Scott Sanborn, *CEO*
John C Morris, *Ch of Bd*
Thomas Casey, *CFO*
Valerie Kay, *Officer*
Brandon Pace, *Officer*
EMP: 973 **EST:** 2006
SALES (est): 314.7MM **Publicly Held**
WEB: www.lendingclub.com
SIC: 6141 7389 6153 Personal credit institutions; financial services; working capital financing

(P-9860)
METROMILE INC (PA)
425 Market St Ste 700, San Francisco (94105-5418)
PHONE..................888 242-5204
Dan Preston, *CEO*
David Friedberg, *Ch of Bd*
Mark Gundacker,
Jesse McKendry, *Vice Pres*
Lindsay Alexovich,
EMP: 118 **EST:** 2018 **Publicly Held**
WEB: www.metromile.com
SIC: 6141 Automobile loans, including insurance

(P-9861)
OPORTUN FINANCIAL CORPORATION (PA)
2 Circle Star Way, San Carlos (94070-6200)
PHONE..................650 810-8823
Raul Vazquez, *CEO*
Matthew Jenkins, *COO*
Jonathan Coblentz, *CFO*
Patrick Kirscht, *Ch Credit Ofcr*
David Needham,
EMP: 577 **EST:** 2005
SALES (est): 583.7MM **Publicly Held**
WEB: www.oportun.com
SIC: 6141 Personal credit institutions; automobile & consumer finance companies; financing: automobiles, furniture, etc., not a deposit bank

(P-9862)
TFC CREDIT CORP CALIFORNIA
Also Called: TFC Tuition Financing
2010 Crow Canyon Pl # 300, San Ramon (94583-1344)
P.O. Box 579 (94583-0579)
PHONE..................800 832-5626
Stephen A Breitbart, *President*
Paula Apsel, *Vice Pres*
Kathleen Altamura, *Mktg Coord*
EMP: 53 **EST:** 1970
SQ FT: 6,000
SALES (est): 13.3MM **Privately Held**
WEB: www.tfctuition.com
SIC: 6141 Personal credit institutions

(P-9863)
UPGRADE INC (PA)
275 Battery St Ste 2300, San Francisco (94111-3366)
PHONE..................347 776-1730
Renaud Laplanche, *CEO*
Jeff Bogan, *Founder*
Myles Reaz, *Ch Credit Ofcr*
Sudip Lahiri, *Officer*
Nii Dodoo, *Vice Pres*
EMP: 319 **EST:** 2016
SQ FT: 7,100
SALES (est): 20MM **Privately Held**
WEB: www.upgrade.com
SIC: 6141 Personal credit institutions

(P-9864)
UPSTART NETWORK INC
2950 S Del St Ste 300, San Mateo (94403)
P.O. Box 1503, San Carlos (94070-7503)
PHONE..................650 204-1000

Dave Girouard, *CEO*
Chantal Rapport, *Partner*
Annie Delgado, *Officer*
Sagar Mehta, *Vice Pres*
Paul Gu, *Principal*
EMP: 80 **EST:** 2012
SALES (est): 24.6MM **Privately Held**
WEB: www.upstart.com
SIC: 6141 Personal finance licensed loan companies, small

(P-9865)
W FS FINANCIAL INC
Also Called: Wells Fargo Dealer Services
10100 Trinity Pkwy # 400, Stockton (95219-7238)
PHONE..................209 955-7800
EMP: 35 **EST:** 2010
SALES (est): 3.1MM **Privately Held**
SIC: 6141 Personal Credit Institution

6153 Credit Institutions, Short-Term Business

(P-9866)
AFFIRM INC (HQ)
Also Called: Affirm Identity
650 California St Fl 12, San Francisco (94108-2716)
PHONE..................415 984-0490
Max Levchin, *CEO*
Rob Pfeifer, *Owner*
Kevin Bartels, *Partner*
Nanda Dubey, *Partner*
Chip Overstreet, *President*
EMP: 199 **EST:** 2003
SALES (est): 110.2MM
SALES (corp-wide): 870.4MM **Publicly Held**
WEB: www.affirm.com
SIC: 6153 Working capital financing
PA: Affirm Holdings, Inc.
650 California St Fl 12
San Francisco CA 94108
415 984-0490

(P-9867)
AFFIRM HOLDINGS INC (PA)
650 California St Fl 12, San Francisco (94108-2716)
PHONE..................415 984-0490
Max Levchin, *Ch of Bd*
Libor Michalek, *President*
Michael Linford, *CFO*
Sharda Caro Del Castillo,
Silvija Martincevic, *Officer*
EMP: 111 **EST:** 2012
SALES (est): 870.4MM **Publicly Held**
SIC: 6153 Working capital financing

(P-9868)
BANKAMERICA FINANCIAL INC
Also Called: Bank of America
315 Montgomery St, San Francisco (94104-1856)
PHONE..................415 622-3521
James A Dern, *President*
Lewis W Teel, *Ch of Bd*
Michael K Riley, *Treasurer*
Gabe Serna, *Assoc VP*
John Carson, *Senior VP*
EMP: 99 **EST:** 1990
SALES (est): 5.8MM
SALES (corp-wide): 93.7B **Publicly Held**
WEB: www.bankofamerica.com
SIC: 6153 6141 6282 Factors of commercial paper; consumer finance companies; investment advisory service
PA: Bank Of America Corporation
100 N Tryon St Ste 170
Charlotte NC 28202
704 386-5681

(P-9869)
BROKER SOLUTIONS INC
Also Called: New American Funding
55 S Market St Ste 1600, San Jose (95113-2327)
PHONE..................408 429-2085
Chris Macnaughton, *Manager*
EMP: 86 **Privately Held**
WEB: www.newamericanfunding.com
SIC: 6153 Working capital financing

PA: Broker Solutions, Inc.
14511 Myford Rd Ste 100
Tustin CA 92780

(P-9870)
FUNDING CIRCLE USA INC
Also Called: Endurance Lending Network
85 2nd St Ste 400, San Francisco (94105-3462)
PHONE..................855 385-5356
Sam Hodges, *Director*
Taimur Ahmed, *Partner*
Dawn Ruggeroli, *Partner*
Geeta Gopalan, *Bd of Directors*
Jerome Le Luel, *Officer*
EMP: 55 **EST:** 2014
SALES (est): 40.6MM
SALES (corp-wide): 325.3MM **Privately Held**
WEB: www.fundingcircle.com
SIC: 6153 Working capital financing
HQ: Funding Circle Ltd
71 Queen Victoria Street
London EC4V
207 401-9111

(P-9871)
FUNDING PACE GROUP LLC
750 University Ave # 240, Los Gatos (95032-7695)
PHONE..................844 873-7223
Robert Giles, *CEO*
Dianne Chervenka, *Vice Pres*
James Vergara, *CIO*
Natasha Casey, *Opers Staff*
Debi Gupta, *Opers Staff*
EMP: 45 **EST:** 2014
SALES (est): 5.4MM **Privately Held**
WEB: www.homerunfinancing.com
SIC: 6153 Working capital financing

(P-9872)
ORACLE CREDIT CORPORATION (DH)
500 Oracle Pkwy Fl 1, Redwood City (94065-1678)
PHONE..................650 506-7000
Jeffrey O Henley, *President*
EMP: 141 **EST:** 1988
SALES (est): 3.9MM
SALES (corp-wide): 40.4B **Publicly Held**
SIC: 6153 Mercantile financing

(P-9873)
PLAYSPAN LLC
2900 Gordon Ave Ste 201, Santa Clara (95051-0710)
P.O. Box 8999, San Francisco (94128-8999)
PHONE..................408 617-9155
Alfred F Kelly Jr, *President*
Julie Whitehead, *CFO*
Lex Bayer, *General Mgr*
Andrew Magruder, *CTO*
Tony Weber, *Opers Staff*
EMP: 56 **EST:** 2006
SQ FT: 3,500
SALES (est): 4MM **Publicly Held**
WEB: www.cybersource.com
SIC: 6153 Credit card services, central agency collection
PA: Visa Inc.
900 Metro Center Blvd
Foster City CA 94404

(P-9874)
PROSPER FUNDING LLC (HQ)
101 2nd St Fl 15, San Francisco (94105-3672)
PHONE..................415 593-5400
Stephan Vermut, *Principal*
Cheryl Law, *Chief Mktg Ofcr*
John Goldston, *Vice Pres*
Ryan Bosley, *Administration*
Christopher Lee, *Planning*
EMP: 62 **EST:** 2014
SALES (est): 52.1MM **Privately Held**
WEB: www.prosper.com
SIC: 6153 Working capital financing

(P-9875)
SEQUOIA RESIDENTIAL FUNDING
1 Belvedere Pl Ste 330, Mill Valley (94941-2493)
PHONE..................415 389-7373
George Bull, *CEO*
EMP: 90 **EST:** 2004
SALES (est): 21.9MM **Publicly Held**
WEB: www.redwoodtrust.com
SIC: 6153 7389 Working capital financing; financial services
PA: Redwood Trust, Inc.
1 Belvedere Pl Ste 300
Mill Valley CA 94941

(P-9876)
SIT FUNDING CORPORATION
44201 Nobel Dr, Fremont (94538-3178)
PHONE..................510 656-3333
Robert T Huang, *President*
EMP: 48 **EST:** 1998
SALES (est): 49MM
SALES (corp-wide): 24.6B **Publicly Held**
WEB: www.synnex.com
SIC: 6153 Working capital financing
PA: Td Synnex Corporation
44201 Nobel Dr
Fremont CA 94538
510 656-3333

(P-9877)
STANISLAUS CNTY TOBACCO FUNDNG
1010 10th St Ste 6400, Modesto (95354-0882)
PHONE..................209 525-6376
Gordon B Ford, *Principal*
EMP: 180 **EST:** 2007
SALES (est): 1.7MM
SALES (corp-wide): 1.2B **Privately Held**
WEB: www.stancounty.com
SIC: 6153 Working capital financing
PA: County Of Stanislaus
1010 10th St Ste 5100
Modesto CA 95354
209 525-6398

(P-9878)
WELLS FARGO COML DIST FIN LLC
3100 Zinfandel Dr Ste 255, Rancho Cordova (95670-6391)
PHONE..................916 636-2020
EMP: 138
SALES (corp-wide): 80.3B **Publicly Held**
SIC: 6153 Mercantile financing
HQ: Wells Fargo Commercial Distribution Finance, Llc
10 S Wacker Dr
Chicago IL 60606
847 747-6800

6159 Credit Institutions, Misc Business

(P-9879)
AMERICAN AGCREDIT FLCA (PA)
400 Aviation Blvd Ste 100, Santa Rosa (95403-1181)
P.O. Box 1120 (95402-1120)
PHONE..................707 545-1200
Ron Carli, *CEO*
Karen Carstens, *President*
Byron Enix, *President*
Becky Steckel, *President*
Christopher Call, *CFO*
EMP: 91 **EST:** 1925
SQ FT: 26,000
SALES (est): 157.8MM **Privately Held**
WEB: www.agloan.com
SIC: 6159 Agricultural credit institutions

(P-9880)
ATEL 12 LLC
600 California St Fl 6, San Francisco (94108-2733)
PHONE..................415 989-8800
Dean L Cash, *President*
Andrew Witherow, *President*
Paritosh K Choksi, *CFO*

PRODUCTS & SERVICES SECTION

6162 - Mortgage Bankers & Loan Correspondents County (P-9902)

Russell H Wilder, *Senior VP*
Vasco H Moaris, *Admin Sec*
EMP: 112 **EST:** 2007
SALES: 1.4MM **Privately Held**
WEB: www.atel.com
SIC: 6159 Machinery & equipment finance leasing
PA: Atel Associates 12, Llc
600 California St Fl 9
San Francisco CA 94108

(P-9881)
ATEL 14 LLC
600 California St Fl 6, San Francisco (94108-2733)
PHONE 415 989-8800
Dean L Cash, *President*
Paritosh K Choksi, *CFO*
Russell H Wilder, *Senior VP*
Vasco H Morais, *Admin Sec*
EMP: 36 **EST:** 2009
SALES (est): 2.7MM **Privately Held**
WEB: www.atel.com
SIC: 6159 Machinery & equipment finance leasing
PA: Atel Associates 14, Llc
600 California St Fl 9
San Francisco CA 94108

(P-9882)
ATEL ASSOCIATES 14 LLC (PA)
600 California St Fl 9, San Francisco (94108-2706)
PHONE 415 989-8800
Dean L Cash, *President*
Paritosh Choksi, *COO*
Paritosh K Choski, *CFO*
Samuel Schussler, *Senior VP*
Russell H Wilder, *Senior VP*
EMP: 95 **EST:** 2009
SALES (est): 2.7MM **Privately Held**
WEB: www.atel.com
SIC: 6159 Machinery & equipment finance leasing

(P-9883)
ATEL CAPITAL GROUP (PA)
Also Called: Leasing Equipment
600 Montgomery St Fl 9, San Francisco (94111-2711)
PHONE 800 543-2835
Dean L Cash, *CEO*
Welson Lau, *President*
Paritosh K Choksi, *CFO*
Russell Wilder, *Ch Credit Ofcr*
Pari Choksi, *Officer*
EMP: 80 **EST:** 1977
SALES (est): 83.6MM **Privately Held**
WEB: www.atel.com
SIC: 6159 Machinery & equipment finance leasing

(P-9884)
ATEL FINANCIAL SERVICES LLC (DH)
Also Called: Atel Capital Group
600 Montgomery St Fl 9, San Francisco (94111-2711)
PHONE 415 989-8800
A J Batt, *President*
Dean L Cash, *President*
Partichosh Choksi, *CFO*
Russell Wilder, *Senior VP*
Vasco Morais, *Admin Sec*
EMP: 62 **EST:** 2001
SALES (est): 10.8MM **Privately Held**
WEB: www.atel.com
SIC: 6159 6211 Machinery & equipment finance leasing; brokers, security
HQ: Atel Financial Corporation
600 Montgomery St Fl 9
San Francisco CA 94111
415 989-8800

(P-9885)
BANCORP FINANCIAL SERVICES INC (HQ)
9343 Tech Center Dr # 100, Sacramento (95826-2563)
P.O. Box 460, Red Bluff (96080-0460)
PHONE 916 641-2000
William Ellison, *CEO*
Curtis Dair, *CFO*
EMP: 62 **EST:** 1996

SQ FT: 8,100
SALES (est): 3.8MM
SALES (corp-wide): 1.4B **Publicly Held**
WEB: www.umpquabank.com
SIC: 6159 Loan institutions, general & industrial
PA: Umpqua Holdings Corporation
1 Sw Columbia St Ste 1200
Portland OR 97204
503 727-4100

(P-9886)
FARM CREDIT WEST
939 Live Oak Blvd, Yuba City (95991-4002)
P.O. Box 552 (95992-0552)
PHONE 530 671-1420
Gary Olson, *Manager*
Jacob Tidwell, *Officer*
Elise Pillote, *Vice Pres*
EMP: 56
SALES (corp-wide): 50.9MM **Privately Held**
WEB: www.farmcreditwest.com
SIC: 6159 7389 6111 Farm mortgage companies; auction, appraisal & exchange services; Federal Land Banks
PA: Farm Credit West
3755 Atherton Rd
Rocklin CA 95765
916 724-4800

(P-9887)
GAELCO LEASING INC (PA)
8656 Sparling Ln, Dixon (95620-9605)
PHONE 707 678-4404
David Nickum, *Administration*
EMP: 38 **EST:** 2017
SALES (est): 4.4MM **Privately Held**
WEB: www.gaelco.biz
SIC: 6159 Truck finance leasing

(P-9888)
NATIONS FIRST CAPITAL LLC
Also Called: Go Capital
516 Gibson Dr Ste 160, Roseville (95678-5792)
PHONE 855 396-3600
Evan Lang, *Mng Member*
Dan Summers,
EMP: 70 **EST:** 2013
SALES (est): 14.3MM **Privately Held**
WEB: www.gotruckcapital.com
SIC: 6159 Equipment & vehicle finance leasing companies

6162 Mortgage Bankers & Loan Correspondents

(P-9889)
A D BILICH INC
Also Called: Nationwide
11 Crow Canyon Ct Ste 100, San Ramon (94583-1981)
PHONE 925 820-5557
Tim Barnes, *President*
Anthony D Bilich, *Owner*
John Engstrom, *Officer*
Jason Cline, *Vice Pres*
Angela Bilich, *Admin Sec*
EMP: 63 **EST:** 1979
SQ FT: 4,000
SALES (est): 16.5MM **Privately Held**
WEB: www.preferredfinancial.com
SIC: 6162 6411 Mortgage bankers; insurance agents, brokers & service

(P-9890)
AMERICAN PACIFIC MORTGAGE CORP (PA)
Also Called: BIG VALLEY MORTGAGE
3000 Lava Ridge Ct # 200, Roseville (95661-2800)
PHONE 916 960-1325
Kurt Reisig, *CEO*
Nicky Cruz, *Partner*
Lisa Hill, *Partner*
Bill Lowman, *President*
David Mack, *COO*
EMP: 120 **EST:** 1996
SQ FT: 35,000
SALES (est): 335.1K **Privately Held**
WEB: www.apmortgage.com
SIC: 6162 Mortgage bankers

(P-9891)
BLEND INSURANCE AGENCY INC
415 Kearny St, San Francisco (94108-2803)
PHONE 650 550-4810
Crystal Sumner, *President*
Graham Carling, *Software Engr*
Rahul Grewal, *Software Engr*
Perry Huang, *Software Engr*
Alex Lew, *Software Engr*
EMP: 103 **EST:** 2018
SALES (est): 11.1MM **Privately Held**
WEB: www.blend.com
SIC: 6162 Loan correspondents

(P-9892)
CAL COAST FINANCIAL INC
39355 California St # 101, Fremont (94538-1447)
PHONE 510 683-9850
Roger Bakshi, *CEO*
EMP: 70 **EST:** 1990
SALES (est): 4.2MM **Privately Held**
WEB: www.calcoastmtg.com
SIC: 6162 Mortgage bankers & correspondents

(P-9893)
CAL COAST FINANCIAL CORP (PA)
5960 Stoneridge Dr # 101, Pleasanton (94588-2725)
PHONE 510 683-9850
Roger Bakshi, *CEO*
Naeem Wahab, *President*
Ritu Bhalla, *Officer*
Carlos Montecino, *Officer*
Sunny Bakshi, *Executive*
EMP: 73 **EST:** 1990
SALES (est): 12.8MM **Privately Held**
WEB: www.calcoastmtg.com
SIC: 6162 Mortgage bankers & correspondents

(P-9894)
CALIBER HOME LOANS INC
6600 Koll Center Pkwy, Pleasanton (94566-3256)
PHONE 925 417-3491
Tim Soldati, *Principal*
Karstin Hickerson, *Officer*
Wendy Werdmuller, *Loan*
Mary Story, *Consultant*
EMP: 37
SALES (corp-wide): 1.7B **Privately Held**
WEB: www.caliberhomeloans.com
SIC: 6162 Mortgage bankers & correspondents
HQ: Caliber Home Loans, Inc.
1525 S Belt Line Rd
Coppell TX 75019

(P-9895)
CALIBER HOME LOANS INC
2101 Forest Ave Ste 150, Chico (95928-7717)
PHONE 530 894-6418
Steven Cooley, *Branch Mgr*
EMP: 37
SALES (corp-wide): 1.7B **Privately Held**
WEB: www.caliberhomeloans.com
SIC: 6162 Mortgage bankers & correspondents
HQ: Caliber Home Loans, Inc.
1525 S Belt Line Rd
Coppell TX 75019

(P-9896)
CALIBER HOME LOANS INC
3700 Hilborn Rd Ste 700, Fairfield (94534-7997)
PHONE 707 432-1000
Sanjiv Das, *Principal*
David Wright, *Officer*
Jessica Nix, *Manager*
Heather Quinlan, *Manager*
EMP: 37
SALES (corp-wide): 1.7B **Privately Held**
WEB: www.caliberhomeloans.com
SIC: 6162 Mortgage bankers & correspondents

HQ: Caliber Home Loans, Inc.
1525 S Belt Line Rd
Coppell TX 75019

(P-9897)
CALIBER HOME LOANS INC
527 D St, Eureka (95501-0308)
PHONE 707 834-6094
Adam Freitas, *Loan*
EMP: 37
SALES (corp-wide): 1.7B **Privately Held**
WEB: www.caliberhomeloans.com
SIC: 6162 Mortgage bankers & correspondents
HQ: Caliber Home Loans, Inc.
1525 S Belt Line Rd
Coppell TX 75019

(P-9898)
CALIFORNIA MRTG ADVISORS INC
4304 Redwood Hwy 100, San Rafael (94903-2103)
PHONE 415 451-4888
Jack Terrell, *President*
Scott Baer, *CFO*
Bill Sockolov, *Officer*
Robert Lee, *Vice Pres*
EMP: 43 **EST:** 1993
SQ FT: 5,600
SALES (est): 4.2MM **Privately Held**
WEB: www.calmtg.com
SIC: 6162 Mortgage bankers; mortgage brokers, using own money

(P-9899)
CATALYST MORTGAGE
Also Called: Ignite Lending
3013 Douglas Blvd Ste 135, Roseville (95661-3899)
PHONE 916 283-9922
Brandon Haefele, *President*
Paige De Kleer, *Principal*
Courtney Kalsi, *Principal*
Tyler Burke, *Branch Mgr*
JP Tingey, *Controller*
EMP: 38 **EST:** 2005
SALES (est): 4MM **Privately Held**
WEB: www.catalystmortgage.com
SIC: 6162 Mortgage bankers

(P-9900)
CHASE MANHATTAN MORTGAGE CORP
560 Mission St Fl 2, San Francisco (94105-2915)
PHONE 858 605-3300
Cindy Dunks, *Manager*
EMP: 142
SALES (corp-wide): 129.5B **Publicly Held**
SIC: 6162 Mortgage bankers
HQ: Chase Manhattan Mortgage Corp
343 Thornall St Ste 7
Edison NJ 08837
732 205-0600

(P-9901)
CHASE MANHATTAN MORTGAGE CORP
2245 Mendocino Ave # 202, Santa Rosa (95403-3112)
PHONE 707 525-5060
Randy Blankenbaker, *Manager*
EMP: 142
SALES (corp-wide): 129.5B **Publicly Held**
SIC: 6162 Mortgage bankers & correspondents
HQ: Chase Manhattan Mortgage Corp
343 Thornall St Ste 7
Edison NJ 08837
732 205-0600

(P-9902)
CMG FINANCIAL SERVICES
3160 Crow Canyon Rd # 400, San Ramon (94583-1368)
PHONE 925 983-3073
Christopher M George, *CEO*
Nora Garcia, *Partner*
Raffie Kalajian, *President*
Cindy Brown, *Officer*

6162 - Mortgage Bankers & Loan Correspondents County (P-9903)

Peter Gilbert, *Officer*
EMP: 223 **EST:** 2003
SALES (est): 48.7MM **Privately Held**
WEB: www.cmgfi.com
SIC: 6162 Mortgage bankers & correspondents

(P-9903)
COMMERCE HOME MORTGAGE LLC
523 Capitola Ave, Capitola (95010-2824)
PHONE 831 460-0202
Peter Gaeckle, *Branch Mgr*
Mary Pennel, *Branch Mgr*
EMP: 97 **Privately Held**
WEB: www.changemtg.com
SIC: 6162 Mortgage bankers & correspondents
PA: Change Lending, Llc
16845 Von Karman Ave # 2
Irvine CA 92606

(P-9904)
COMMERCE HOME MORTGAGE LLC
970 Executive Way, Redding (96002-0630)
PHONE 530 282-1166
Gretchen Wilson, *Branch Mgr*
Olivia Glisson, *Advisor*
Heidi Meeks, *Advisor*
EMP: 97 **Privately Held**
WEB: www.changemtg.com
SIC: 6162 Mortgage bankers & correspondents
PA: Change Lending, Llc
16845 Von Karman Ave # 2
Irvine CA 92606

(P-9905)
FIRST PRIORITY FINANCIAL INC
3700 Hilborn Rd Ste 700, Fairfield (94534-7997)
PHONE 707 432-1000
Timothy Kearns, *President*
David Soldati, *CFO*
Kristin Calmerin, *Officer*
Michael Soldati, *Vice Pres*
Tana Tenold, *Admin Asst*
EMP: 300 **EST:** 1977
SQ FT: 4,500
SALES (est): 35.9MM **Privately Held**
WEB: www.joinfpf.com
SIC: 6162 Mortgage bankers & correspondents

(P-9906)
GENERAL MORTGAGE CAPITAL CORP (PA)
1350 Bayshore Hwy Ste 740, Burlingame (94010-1816)
PHONE 650 340-7800
Charles Zhao, *President*
Karen Liang, *Branch Mgr*
Simon Xie, *Technology*
EMP: 96 **EST:** 2005
SALES (est): 25.1MM **Privately Held**
WEB: www.gmccloan.com
SIC: 6162 Mortgage bankers

(P-9907)
GOLDEN EMPIRE MORTGAGE INC
601 University Ave # 105, Sacramento (95825-6775)
PHONE 916 576-7919
EMP: 49 **Privately Held**
WEB: www.gemcorp.com
SIC: 6162 Mortgage bankers
PA: Golden Empire Mortgage, Inc.
1200 Discovery Dr Ste 300
Bakersfield CA 93309

(P-9908)
GUARANTEED RATE INC
915 Highland Pointe Dr, Roseville (95678-5419)
PHONE 916 501-3919
EMP: 205 **Privately Held**
WEB: www.rate.com
SIC: 6162 Mortgage bankers & correspondents
PA: Guaranteed Rate, Inc.
3940 N Ravenswood Ave
Chicago IL 60613

(P-9909)
HOMEQ SERVICING CORPORATION (DH)
4837 Watt Ave, North Highlands (95660-5108)
PHONE 916 339-6192
Arthur Lyon, *President*
Keith G Becher, *COO*
Mark K Metz, *Admin Sec*
EMP: 1000 **EST:** 1967
SALES (est): 361.8MM
SALES (corp-wide): 960.9MM **Publicly Held**
WEB: www.homeq.com
SIC: 6162 6163 6111 6159 Mortgage bankers; agents, farm or business loan; Student Loan Marketing Association; automobile finance leasing
HQ: Ocwen Loan Servicing, Llc
1661 Worthington Rd # 100
West Palm Beach FL 33409
561 682-8000

(P-9910)
LAND HOME FINANCIAL SVCS INC (PA)
1355 Willow Way Ste 250, Concord (94520-8113)
PHONE 925 676-7038
Bradley Harold Waite, *CEO*
Angela Warren, *President*
David Waite, *CFO*
Evonne Coddington, *Officer*
Jennie Davis, *Officer*
EMP: 50 **EST:** 1988
SQ FT: 6,000
SALES (est): 61.7MM **Privately Held**
WEB: www.lhfs.com
SIC: 6162 Loan correspondents

(P-9911)
LENDUS LLC
Also Called: Venice Team, The
3240 Stone Valley Rd W, Alamo (94507-1555)
PHONE 925 295-9300
Jacqualyn Lush, *Partner*
Elena Cardoza, *COO*
Gary Scoma, *Ch Credit Ofcr*
Jonathan Shrum, *Officer*
Richard Walton, *Exec VP*
EMP: 720 **EST:** 2017
SALES (est): 79.4MM **Privately Held**
WEB: www.lend.us
SIC: 6162 Mortgage bankers & correspondents

(P-9912)
LENDUSA LLC (PA)
Also Called: RPM Mortgage
3240 Stone Valley Rd W, Alamo (94507-1555)
PHONE 925 295-9300
Holly Carter, *Partner*
Kier Evergreen, *Partner*
Katie Hartnett, *Partner*
Michelle Hoffman, *Partner*
Ofra Martin, *Partner*
EMP: 237 **EST:** 2017
SALES (est): 86.9MM **Privately Held**
WEB: www.rpm-mtg.com
SIC: 6162 Mortgage bankers & correspondents

(P-9913)
LOANDEPOTCOM LLC
1020 15th St Ste 20, Modesto (95354-1132)
PHONE 209 846-6400
Shareen Carnes, *Branch Mgr*
EMP: 639
SALES (corp-wide): 4.4B **Publicly Held**
WEB: www.loandepot.com
SIC: 6162 Mortgage bankers & correspondents
HQ: Loandepot.Com, Llc
26642 Towne Centre Dr
Foothill Ranch CA 92610

(P-9914)
LOANPAL LLC (PA)
Also Called: Paramount Equity
8781 Sierra College Blvd, Roseville (95661-5920)
PHONE 916 290-9999
Hayes Barnard, *President*
Araceli Munoz, *Partner*
Brittany Ritter, *Officer*
Shirley Sherrill, *Vice Pres*
Nicholas Saxton, *Business Dir*
EMP: 469 **EST:** 2003
SALES (est): 150.5MM **Privately Held**
WEB: www.goodleap.com
SIC: 6162 Mortgage bankers

(P-9915)
MASON MCDUFFIE MORTGAGE CORP (PA)
2010 Crow Canyon Pl # 400, San Ramon (94583-1344)
PHONE 925 242-4400
Marilyn Richardson, *CEO*
Jack Radin, *CFO*
Herb Tasker, *Chairman*
James Harrington, *Officer*
Tiffani Hom, *Officer*
EMP: 83 **EST:** 1887
SALES (est): 58.5MM **Privately Held**
WEB: www.mutualreverse.com
SIC: 6162 Mortgage bankers

(P-9916)
NATIONAL MORTGAGE INSUR CORP
2100 Powell St Fl 12, Emeryville (94608-1826)
PHONE 855 530-6642
Bradley Mize Shuster, *CEO*
Claudia J Merkle, *Exec VP*
Adam Pollitzer, *Exec VP*
Robert Smith, *Exec VP*
Joy Benner, *Vice Pres*
EMP: 44 **EST:** 2016
SALES (est): 19.3MM **Privately Held**
WEB: www.nationalmi.com
SIC: 6162 Mortgage bankers & correspondents

(P-9917)
NL INC (PA)
Also Called: Residential Pacific Mortgage
3240 Stone Valley Rd W, Alamo (94507-1555)
PHONE 925 295-9300
Robert Hirt, *CEO*
Tracey Hirt, *President*
Eva Noack, *CFO*
Scott Davis, *Vice Pres*
EMP: 35 **EST:** 1991
SQ FT: 14,000
SALES (est): 10.3MM **Privately Held**
SIC: 6162 Mortgage bankers & correspondents

(P-9918)
PARKSIDE LENDING LLC
180 Redwood St Ste 250, San Francisco (94102-3283)
PHONE 415 771-3700
Alan Sagatelyan, *Officer*
Linda Jacopetti, *Ch Credit Ofcr*
Helen Matoesian, *Officer*
Daniel Padilla, *Officer*
Adam Reuter, *Officer*
EMP: 60 **EST:** 2004
SQ FT: 5,097
SALES (est): 33MM **Privately Held**
WEB: www.parksidelending.com
SIC: 6162 Mortgage bankers & correspondents

(P-9919)
PERSONAL MORTGAGE GROUP LLC (HQ)
420 Montgomery St, San Francisco (94104-1207)
PHONE 415 396-0560
James Robinson, *Principal*
Patricia Ciulla, *Sales Mgr*
EMP: 62 **EST:** 2001

SALES (est): 30.7MM
SALES (corp-wide): 80.3B **Publicly Held**
WEB: www.wellsfargo.com
SIC: 6162 Mortgage bankers & correspondents
PA: Wells Fargo & Company
420 Montgomery St
San Francisco CA 94104
866 249-3302

(P-9920)
PNC MULTIFAMILY FINANCE INC (DH)
575 Market St Ste 2800, San Francisco (94105-5843)
PHONE 415 733-1500
Thomas Booher, *CEO*
EMP: 62 **EST:** 1987
SQ FT: 13,285
SALES (est): 1.8MM
SALES (corp-wide): 18.2B **Publicly Held**
SIC: 6162 Mortgage bankers

(P-9921)
PRIVATE MORTGAGE ADVISORS LLC
390 Diablo Rd Ste 100, Danville (94526-3432)
PHONE 408 754-1610
John Dutra, *President*
EMP: 37 **EST:** 2003
SALES (est): 10.1MM
SALES (corp-wide): 80.3B **Publicly Held**
WEB: www.wellsfargo.com
SIC: 6162 Mortgage bankers & correspondents
PA: Wells Fargo & Company
420 Montgomery St
San Francisco CA 94104
866 249-3302

(P-9922)
PROVIDENT FUNDING ASSOC LP
1235 N Dutton Ave Ste A, Santa Rosa (95401-4666)
PHONE 707 568-2420
Mark Mast, *Manager*
Jessica Ball, *Administration*
Richard Chiddix, *Manager*
EMP: 35 **Privately Held**
WEB: www.provident.com
SIC: 6162 Mortgage bankers
PA: Provident Funding Associates, L.P.
851 Traeger Ave Ste 100
San Bruno CA 94066

(P-9923)
PROVIDENT FUNDING ASSOC LP (PA)
851 Traeger Ave Ste 100, San Bruno (94066-3091)
P.O. Box 5914, Santa Rosa (95402-5914)
PHONE 650 652-1300
Doug Pica, *General Ptnr*
Michelle Blake, *Partner*
Craig Pica, *Partner*
Ralph Pica, *Partner*
Lori Pica, *COO*
EMP: 50 **EST:** 1992
SALES (est): 153.5MM **Privately Held**
WEB: www.provident.com
SIC: 6162 Mortgage bankers

(P-9924)
REAL ESTATE EQUITY EXCHANGE
Also Called: Unison
650 California St Fl 1800, San Francisco (94108-2722)
PHONE 415 992-4200
Thomas Stonholtz, *CEO*
Andrew Toby, *Vice Pres*
Erika Malykin, *Program Mgr*
Amanda Pindar, *Opers Staff*
Natalie Tunnard, *Marketing Staff*
EMP: 75 **EST:** 2013
SALES (est): 15.5MM **Privately Held**
WEB: www.unison.com
SIC: 6162 Mortgage bankers & correspondents

PRODUCTS & SERVICES SECTION

6163 - Loan Brokers County (P-9947)

(P-9925)
RENEW FINANCIAL CORP II
Also Called: Afc First Consumer Discount Co
555 12th St Ste 1650, Oakland (94607-3623)
PHONE.....................................610 433-7486
Peter J Krajsa, *CEO*
John M Hayes, *President*
Ken Yeager, *President*
Kirk Inglis, *CFO*
Laura Nelson, *CFO*
EMP: 220 **EST:** 1947
SALES (est): 9.7MM **Privately Held**
WEB: www.renewfinancial.com
SIC: 6162 6036 Bond & mortgage companies; savings institutions, not federally chartered
PA: Renew Financial Holdings Inc.
555 12th St Ste 1650
Oakland CA 94607

(P-9926)
SECURITY NAT MSTR HOLDG CO LLC (PA)
323 5th St, Eureka (95501-0305)
P.O. Box 1028 (95502-1028)
PHONE.....................................707 442-2818
Robin P Arkley II, *CEO*
EMP: 140 **EST:** 2002
SQ FT: 15,000
SALES (est): 114.4MM **Privately Held**
WEB: www.snsc.com
SIC: 6162 Mortgage bankers & correspondents

(P-9927)
SIERRA PACIFIC MORTGAGE CO INC (PA)
1180 Iron Point Rd # 200, Folsom (95630-8321)
PHONE.....................................916 932-1700
James Coffrini, *President*
Curtis Dair, *CFO*
Felecia Bowers, *Officer*
Gina Grant, *Officer*
Thomas Hull, *Officer*
EMP: 580 **EST:** 1986
SALES (est): 217.8MM **Privately Held**
WEB: www.sierrapacificmortgage.com
SIC: 6162 Mortgage bankers

(P-9928)
SKYLINE FINANCIAL SERVICES (PA)
2355 Gold Meadow Way # 160, Gold River (95670-6365)
PHONE.....................................818 995-1700
Ryan Morrow, *Principal*
EMP: 70 **EST:** 2009
SALES (est): 622.9K **Privately Held**
SIC: 6162 Mortgage bankers & correspondents

(P-9929)
SN SERVICING CORPORATION
1484 Haddington Dr, Folsom (95630-5312)
PHONE.....................................916 779-2200
Robin P Arkley II, *President*
Margaret Mackin, *Sr Project Mgr*
EMP: 47
SALES (corp-wide): 114.4MM **Privately Held**
WEB: www.snsc.com
SIC: 6162 Mortgage bankers & correspondents
HQ: Sn Servicing Corporation
3050 Westfork Dr
Baton Rouge LA 70816

(P-9930)
SN SERVICING CORPORATION
323 5th St, Eureka (95501-0305)
P.O. Box 35 (95502-0035)
PHONE.....................................707 445-9883
Robin P Arkley, *Principal*
Matt Deibler, *Officer*
John Clark, *Manager*
EMP: 47
SALES (corp-wide): 114.4MM **Privately Held**
WEB: www.snsc.com
SIC: 6162 6211 Mortgage bankers & correspondents; security brokers & dealers
HQ: Sn Servicing Corporation
3050 Westfork Dr
Baton Rouge LA 70816

(P-9931)
SOFI TECHNOLOGIES INC (PA)
234 1st St, San Francisco (94105-2624)
PHONE.....................................855 456-7634
Anthony Noto, *CEO*
Tom Hutton, *Ch of Bd*
Christopher Lapointe, *CFO*
Steven Freiberg, *Vice Ch Bd*
Lauren Stafford Webb, *Chief Mktg Ofcr*
EMP: 52 **EST:** 2011
SALES (est): 536.9MM **Publicly Held**
WEB: www.sofi.com
SIC: 6162 7389 Mortgage bankers & correspondents; financial services

(P-9932)
STEARNS HOLDINGS LLC
2600 E Bidwell St Ste 160, Folsom (95630-6449)
PHONE.....................................916 358-9170
EMP: 357
SALES (corp-wide): 167.7MM **Privately Held**
SIC: 6162 6141 Mortgage bankers & correspondents; personal credit institutions
PA: Stearns Holdings, Llc
401 E Corporate Dr # 150
Lewisville TX 75057
714 513-7273

(P-9933)
SUMMIT FUNDING INC
2241 Harvard St Ste 200, Sacramento (95815-3332)
PHONE.....................................916 571-3000
Todd Scrima, *CEO*
Lisa Cox, *Partner*
Tracy Fry, *Partner*
Judy Hutton, *Partner*
Steve Hatalla, *Officer*
EMP: 88 **EST:** 1997
SALES (est): 25.4MM **Privately Held**
WEB: www.summitfunding.net
SIC: 6162 Mortgage bankers & correspondents

(P-9934)
UPSTART HOLDINGS INC (PA)
2950 S Del St Ste 300, San Mateo (94403)
PHONE.....................................650 204-1000
Dave Girouard, *Ch of Bd*
Sanjay Datta, *CFO*
Anna M Counselman, *Senior VP*
Paul Gu, *Senior VP*
Alison Nicoll, *General Counsel*
EMP: 411 **EST:** 2013
SQ FT: 48,000
SALES (est): 233.4MM **Publicly Held**
WEB: www.upstart.com
SIC: 6162 Mortgage bankers & correspondents

(P-9935)
VITEK RE INDS GROUP INC (PA)
Also Called: Vitek Mortgage Group
2882 Prospect Park Dr # 10, Rancho Cordova (95670-6053)
PHONE.....................................916 486-6400
Harry Duncan, *President*
Philip Duncan, *CEO*
Kevin Muth, *CFO*
Jennika Royce, *Marketing Staff*
Sandy Smith, *Manager*
EMP: 40 **EST:** 1987
SQ FT: 3,200
SALES (est): 27.4MM **Privately Held**
SIC: 6162 6163 Mortgage bankers; mortgage brokers arranging for loans, using money of others

6163 Loan Brokers

(P-9936)
BLUEVINE CAPITAL INC
401 Warren St Ste 300, Redwood City (94063-1578)
PHONE.....................................888 216-9619
Eyal Lifshitz, *CEO*
Nicholas Zortea, *Partner*
Steve Allocca, *COO*
David Quinn, *CFO*
Brad Brodigan, *Ch Credit Ofcr*
EMP: 300 **EST:** 2013
SALES (est): 72.8MM **Privately Held**
WEB: www.bluevine.com
SIC: 6163 Agents, farm or business loan

(P-9937)
CHANGE LENDING LLC
100 Stony Point Rd # 290, Santa Rosa (95401-4117)
PHONE.....................................707 596-5111
Scott Simonich, *Branch Mgr*
Erin Hickey, *Regional Mgr*
EMP: 97 **Privately Held**
WEB: www.changemtg.com
SIC: 6163 Mortgage brokers arranging for loans, using money of others
PA: Change Lending, Llc
16845 Von Karman Ave # 2
Irvine CA 92606

(P-9938)
CMG MORTGAGE INC (PA)
3160 Crow Canyon Rd # 400, San Ramon (94583-1382)
PHONE.....................................619 554-1327
Christopher M George, *CEO*
Paul Akinmade, *Chief Mktg Ofcr*
Anthony Cimino, *Senior VP*
Todd L Hempstead, *Senior VP*
Paolo Gochangco, *Vice Pres*
EMP: 349 **EST:** 1993
SQ FT: 5,500
SALES (est): 132.2MM **Privately Held**
WEB: www.cmgfi.com
SIC: 6163 Mortgage brokers arranging for loans, using money of others

(P-9939)
E-LOAN INC (DH)
6230 Stoneridge Mall Rd, Pleasanton (94588-3260)
PHONE.....................................925 847-6200
Mark E Lefanowicz, *President*
EMP: 850 **EST:** 1992
SQ FT: 118,000
SALES (est): 191.9MM
SALES (corp-wide): 2.6B **Publicly Held**
WEB: www.eloan.com
SIC: 6163 6162 Mortgage brokers arranging for loans, using money of others; mortgage bankers & correspondents
HQ: Popular Finance Inc
326 Slud St El Snrial Con El Senorial Cond
Ponce PR 00716
787 844-2760

(P-9940)
GETRIGHT VENTURES INC
3675 Rocky Shore Ct, Vallejo (94591-6349)
PHONE.....................................510 402-4816
Joseph Pamplieda, *President*
Eddie E Bansag, *CFO*
EMP: 80 **EST:** 2004
SALES (est): 2.8MM **Privately Held**
SIC: 6163 Mortgage brokers arranging for loans, using money of others

(P-9941)
HMW AND JK ENTERPRISES INC (PA)
Also Called: Asia Pacific Groups
1290 24th Ave, San Francisco (94122-1615)
PHONE.....................................415 731-3100
Joseph Kong, *President*
Lydia Cuiting, *Vice Pres*
Hong Xiao, *Vice Pres*
Lindsay Allen, *Consultant*
EMP: 39 **EST:** 1987
SQ FT: 3,300
SALES (est): 500K **Privately Held**
SIC: 6163 6531 Mortgage brokers arranging for loans, using money of others; real estate brokers & agents

(P-9942)
IZT MORTGAGE INC (PA)
Also Called: Ameritech Mortgage
3011 Citrus Cir Ste 202, Walnut Creek (94598-2631)
P.O. Box 492239, Los Angeles (90049-8239)
PHONE.....................................925 946-1858
EMP: 50
SQ FT: 12,000
SALES (est): 11MM **Privately Held**
SIC: 6163 Loan Broker

(P-9943)
LIBERTY AMERICAN MORTGAGE CORP (PA)
193 Blue Ravine Rd # 240, Folsom (95630-4756)
PHONE.....................................916 780-3000
Frank A Sousa, *President*
William Templeton, *Ch of Bd*
Dan Martinelli, *COO*
Jennifer Robinson, *CFO*
Patrick White, *Chairman*
EMP: 92 **EST:** 1985
SQ FT: 18,000
SALES (est): 8MM **Privately Held**
SIC: 6163 6162 Mortgage brokers arranging for loans, using money of others; mortgage bankers

(P-9944)
PACIFIC UNION INTL INC
135 W Napa St Ste 200, Sonoma (95476-6632)
PHONE.....................................707 934-2300
Jill Silvas, *Branch Mgr*
Jeffrey Lokey, *Real Est Agnt*
Matt Sevenau, *Real Est Agnt*
EMP: 75 **Privately Held**
WEB: www.compass.com
SIC: 6163 Loan agents
PA: Pacific Union International, Inc.
1 Letterman Dr Bldg C
San Francisco CA 94129

(P-9945)
PROSPER MARKETPLACE INC (PA)
221 Main St Fl 3, San Francisco (94105-1906)
PHONE.....................................415 593-5400
David Kimball, *Ch of Bd*
Usama Ashraf, *President*
Edward R Buell III, *Admin Sec*
EMP: 325 **EST:** 2005
SQ FT: 50,000
SALES (est): 103.2MM **Privately Held**
WEB: www.prosper.com
SIC: 6163 Loan brokers

(P-9946)
ROOSTIFY INC
180 Howard St Ste 100, San Francisco (94105-6153)
PHONE.....................................888 908-2470
Rajesh Bhat, *CEO*
Eric Amblard, *CFO*
Syed Ijaz, *Ch Credit Ofcr*
Courtney Keating Chakarun, *Chief Mktg Ofcr*
Courtney Chakarun, *Chief Mktg Ofcr*
EMP: 40 **EST:** 2016
SALES (est): 7.2MM **Privately Held**
WEB: www.roostify.com
SIC: 6163 7372 Mortgage brokers arranging for loans, using money of others; application computer software; business oriented computer software

(P-9947)
SACRAMENTO 1ST MORTGAGE INC
Also Called: Comstock Mortgage
3626 Fair Oaks Blvd # 100, Sacramento (95864-7200)
PHONE.....................................916 486-6500
Craig Sardella, *President*
Alan Wackman, *COO*
Scott Fife, *Vice Pres*
Dennis Alger, *Executive*
EMP: 44 **EST:** 2003
SQ FT: 7,500

6163 - Loan Brokers County (P-9948) **PRODUCTS & SERVICES SECTION**

SALES (est): 3.6MM **Privately Held**
WEB: www.sacramento1stmortgage.com
SIC: **6163** Mortgage brokers arranging for loans, using money of others

(P-9948)
SHIELD COMMERCIAL INC (PA)
7311 Greenhaven Dr # 100, Sacramento (95831-3572)
PHONE 916 684-9093
Shan Padayachee, *President*
EMP: 79 EST: 2001
SALES (est): 205.1K **Privately Held**
WEB: www.shieldcommercialinc.com
SIC: **6163** Mortgage brokers arranging for loans, using money of others

(P-9949)
SOCIAL FINANCE INC (HQ)
Also Called: Sofi
234 1st St, San Francisco (94105-2624)
PHONE 415 930-4467
Anthony Noto, *CEO*
Alyssa Banks, *Partner*
Chris Lapointe, *CFO*
William Tanona, *Senior VP*
Kirk Chapman, *Vice Pres*
EMP: 160 EST: 2011
SQ FT: 20,000
SALES (est): 536.8MM
SALES (corp-wide): 536.9MM **Publicly Held**
WEB: www.sofi.com
SIC: **6163** Loan brokers
PA: Sofi Technologies, Inc.
   234 1st St
   San Francisco CA 94105
   855 456-7634

(P-9950)
SOCIAL FINANCE INC
375 Healdsburg Ave # 280, Healdsburg (95448-4150)
PHONE 707 473-9889
Chad Nelson, *Analyst*
EMP: 451
SALES (corp-wide): 536.9MM **Publicly Held**
WEB: www.sofi.com
SIC: **6163** Loan brokers
HQ: Social Finance, Inc.
   234 1st St
   San Francisco CA 94105
   415 930-4467

(P-9951)
VENTURE LENDING & LSG IX INC
104 La Mesa Dr Ste 102, Portola Valley (94028-7510)
PHONE 650 234-4300
Martin Eng, *Branch Mgr*
EMP: 46
SALES (corp-wide): 504.6K **Privately Held**
SIC: **6163** Loan brokers
PA: Venture Lending & Leasing Ix, Inc.
   1519 York Rd
   Lutherville MD

(P-9952)
W-STAR INVESTMENTS INC
2130 Ringwood Ave, San Jose (95131-1720)
PHONE 408 821-7678
Steven Wu, *President*
EMP: 50 EST: 2001
SQ FT: 3,000
SALES (est): 500K **Privately Held**
SIC: **6163 6531** Mortgage brokers arranging for loans, using money of others; real estate agents & managers

(P-9953)
WYMAC CAPITAL INC (PA)
2700 Ygnacio Valley Rd # 260, Walnut Creek (94598-3463)
PHONE 925 937-4300
Darrel Wiley, *President*
Russell McDonald, *Treasurer*
Liz Reese, *Loan*
Matthew Wiley, *Loan*
EMP: 39 EST: 1990
SQ FT: 16,000 **Privately Held**
WEB: www.wymac.com
SIC: **6163** 6211 Mortgage brokers arranging for loans, using money of others; syndicate shares (real estate, entertainment, equip.) sales

---

6211 Security Brokers & Dealers

(P-9954)
643 CAPITAL MANAGEMENT INC (PA)
2001 Broadway Fl 4th, Oakland (94612-2302)
PHONE 650 759-0599
EMP: 42 EST: 2017
SALES (est): 754.5K **Privately Held**
WEB: www.643capital.com
SIC: **6211** Security brokers & dealers

(P-9955)
ALAMO CAPITAL
201 N Civic Dr Ste 180, Walnut Creek (94596-8226)
PHONE 925 472-5700
Nancy Mullally, *CEO*
Bill Mullally, *President*
Ben Mullally, *Exec VP*
Matthew P Deane, *Senior VP*
Adam Gold, *Vice Pres*
EMP: 40 EST: 1987
SALES (est): 11.5MM **Privately Held**
WEB: www.alamocapital.com
SIC: **6211** Security brokers & dealers

(P-9956)
BAY CITY CAPITAL MGT LLC (PA)
3001 Bridgeway, Sausalito (94965-1405)
PHONE 415 676-3830
Fred Craves,
Doug Given, *Partner*
Carl Goldfischer, *Principal*
David Beierr, *Managing Dir*
Lionel Carnot, *Managing Dir*
EMP: 109 EST: 1996
SALES (est): 32.4MM **Publicly Held**
WEB: www.baycitycapital.com
SIC: **6211** Security brokers & dealers

(P-9957)
BBAM US LP
Also Called: Bbam Arcft Holdings 139 Labuan
50 California St Fl 14, San Francisco (94111-4683)
PHONE 415 267-1600
Steve Vissis, *CEO*
Greg Azzara, *COO*
Wesley Dick, *Manager*
Richard Strollo, *Manager*
Hassan Iftikhar, *Associate*
EMP: 320 EST: 1993
SALES (est): 37.3MM **Privately Held**
WEB: www.bbam.com
SIC: **6211** Investment bankers
HQ: Bbam Llc
   50 California St Fl 14
   San Francisco CA 94111
   415 267-1600

(P-9958)
BLACKSTONE TECHNOLOGY GROUP (PA)
33 New Montgomery St # 850, San Francisco (94105-4539)
PHONE 415 837-1400
David Mysona, *CEO*
Casey Courneen, *President*
Giles Kesteloot, *President*
Patrick James, *COO*
Rakesh Agrawal, *Exec VP*
EMP: 100 EST: 2000
SQ FT: 10,000
SALES (est): 55.1MM **Privately Held**
WEB: www.bstonetech.com
SIC: **6211** Security brokers & dealers

(P-9959)
BTIG LLC (PA)
Also Called: Baypoint Trading
600 Montgomery St Fl 6, San Francisco (94111-2708)
PHONE 415 248-2200
Scott Kovalik,
Matt Clark, *COO*
Brian Endres, *CFO*
Craig Habkirk, *Senior VP*
Andrea Alfonso, *Vice Pres*
EMP: 77 EST: 2003
SALES (est): 139.2MM **Privately Held**
WEB: www.wwwca01.btig.com
SIC: **6211** Investment firm, general brokerage

(P-9960)
CANACCORD GENUITY LLC
44 Montgomery St Ste 1600, San Francisco (94104-4703)
PHONE 415 229-7171
Corey Elliott, *Vice Pres*
Warren Thorpe, *Vice Pres*
Jason Mills, *Managing Dir*
Paul Morgan, *Managing Dir*
Laura Cooper, *Admin Asst*
EMP: 51
SALES (corp-wide): 921.4MM **Privately Held**
WEB: www.canaccordgenuity.com
SIC: **6211** Investment bankers
HQ: Canaccord Genuity Llc
   99 High St Ste 1200
   Boston MA 02110
   617 371-3900

(P-9961)
CASEY SECURITIES INC (PA)
301 Pine St, San Francisco (94104-3301)
PHONE 415 544-5030
Richard Casey, *Ch of Bd*
George Gasparini, *President*
Kathleen Gallagher, *Vice Pres*
Scott Nelson, *Vice Pres*
EMP: 67 EST: 1976
SQ FT: 800
SALES (est): 8.2MM **Privately Held**
SIC: **6211** Brokers, security; stock brokers & dealers

(P-9962)
CHARLES SCHWAB & CO INC (HQ)
211 Main St Fl 17, San Francisco (94105-1901)
P.O. Box 636009, Littleton CO (80163-6009)
PHONE 415 636-7000
Walt Bettinger, *CEO*
Danielle Schulman, *Officer*
Sarah Sontheimer, *Officer*
Tom D Seip, *Sr Exec VP*
Dawn G Lepore, *Exec VP*
EMP: 454 EST: 1971
SQ FT: 295,000
SALES (est): 5.6MM
SALES (corp-wide): 11.6B **Publicly Held**
WEB: www.schwab.com
SIC: **6211** Brokers, security; dealers, security; investment firm, general brokerage
PA: The Charles Schwab Corporation
   211 Main St Fl 17
   San Francisco CA 94105
   415 667-7000

(P-9963)
CHARLES SCHWAB CORPORATION (PA)
211 Main St Fl 17, San Francisco (94105-1901)
PHONE 415 667-7000
Walter W Bettinger II, *CEO*
Charles R Schwab, *Ch of Bd*
Rick Wurster, *President*
Joseph R Martinetto, *COO*
Peter B Crawford, *CFO*
EMP: 562 EST: 1986
SQ FT: 662,000
SALES (est): 11.6B **Publicly Held**
WEB: www.aboutschwab.com
SIC: **6211** 6091 6282 7389 Brokers, security; investment bankers; investment firm, general brokerage; nondeposit trust facilities; investment advice; investment advisory service; financial services

(P-9964)
CITIGROUP GLOBAL MARKETS INC
Also Called: Smith Barney
225 W Santa Clara St # 9, San Jose (95113-1723)
PHONE 408 947-2200
David Perez, *Manager*
Jeff Alkire, *Consultant*
Michael Napoli, *Consultant*
EMP: 75
SALES (corp-wide): 88.8B **Publicly Held**
WEB: www.citigroup.com
SIC: **6211** Security brokers & dealers; stock brokers & dealers
HQ: Citigroup Global Markets Inc.
   388 Greenwich St Fl 18
   New York NY 10013
   212 816-6000

(P-9965)
CONIFER FINANCIAL SERVICES LLC (HQ)
1 Ferry Building Ste 255, San Francisco (94111-4243)
PHONE 415 677-1500
Jack McDonald, *President*
Sal Campo, *COO*
EMP: 62 EST: 2014
SALES (est): 16.9MM
SALES (corp-wide): 4.6B **Publicly Held**
WEB: www.ssctech.com
SIC: **6211** Security brokers & dealers
PA: Ss&C Technologies Holdings, Inc.
   80 Lamberton Rd
   Windsor CT 06095
   860 298-4500

(P-9966)
CONIFER FUND SERVICES LLC
Also Called: Conifer Securities
1 Ferry Plz Ste 255, San Francisco (94111-4205)
PHONE 415 677-5979
Mark Friesen,
Gary Wu, *Vice Pres*
Julia Coulter, *Administration*
Michael Lau, *Info Tech Mgr*
Maureen Viola, *Technology*
EMP: 42 EST: 2009
SALES (est): 1.1MM **Privately Held**
WEB: www.ssctech.com
SIC: **6211** Security brokers & dealers

(P-9967)
EMBASSADOR PRIVATE SECURITIES
1341 Evans Ave, San Francisco (94124-1705)
PHONE 415 822-8811
Rj Hongisto, *Director*
Rj Hingisto, *Director*
David Culot, *Manager*
EMP: 55 EST: 2000
SQ FT: 4,500
SALES (est): 4.7MM **Privately Held**
WEB: www.ambassador-security.com
SIC: **6211** Security brokers & dealers

(P-9968)
FINTAN PARTNERS LLC
Also Called: Cantor Ftzgrald Asset MGT Hldn
203 Rdwood Shres Pkwy Ste, Redwood City (94065)
PHONE 650 687-3400
Alexander Klikoff,
Christopher Montclare,
EMP: 39 EST: 2005
SALES (est): 5.5MM
SALES (corp-wide): 778MM **Privately Held**
WEB: www.fintanpartners.com
SIC: **6211** Brokers, security
HQ: Cantor Fitzgerald Asset Management Holdings, Lc
   499 Park Ave
   New York NY 10022
   212 938-5000

(P-9969)
FOX PAINE & COMPANY LLC (PA)
2105 Woodside Rd Ste D, Woodside (94062-1153)
PHONE 650 235-2075

PRODUCTS & SERVICES SECTION

6211 - Security Brokers & Dealers County (P-9991)

Saul A Fox, *Mng Member*
Robert N Lowe Jr,
Dexter Paine,
EMP: 237 **EST:** 1997
SQ FT: 8,000
SALES (est): 38.8MM **Privately Held**
WEB: www.foxpaine.com
SIC: 6211 Investment firm, general brokerage

(P-9970)
FRANKLIN TMPLETON INV SVCS LLC (DH)
Also Called: Franklin Templeton Investment
3344 Quality Dr, Rancho Cordova (95670-7361)
P.O. Box 2258 (95741-2258)
PHONE..................................916 463-1500
Charles B Johnson, *Ch of Bd*
Basil Fox, *President*
Greg Johnson, *President*
Robert Smith, *Senior VP*
May Tong, *Senior VP*
EMP: 1200 **EST:** 1981
SQ FT: 40,000
SALES (est): 473.3MM
SALES (corp-wide): 5.5B **Publicly Held**
WEB: www.franklintempletonindia.com
SIC: 6211 6282 Traders, security; investment advisory service

(P-9971)
FREMONT MUTUAL FUNDS INC
333 Market St Ste 2600, San Francisco (94105-2127)
PHONE..................................800 548-4539
EMP: 55
SQ FT: 19,000
SALES (est): 4.8MM **Privately Held**
SIC: 6211 Security Brokers And Dealers, Nsk

(P-9972)
GENSTAR CAPITAL LLC (PA)
4 Embarcadero Ctr # 1900, San Francisco (94111-4106)
PHONE..................................415 834-2350
Richard Paterson, *Managing Dir*
Mark Hanson, *Partner*
Robert Sheehy, *Partner*
Dani Arrecis, *CFO*
Melissa Dickerson, *CFO*
▲ **EMP:** 35 **EST:** 1991
SQ FT: 10,000
SALES (est): 671.3MM **Privately Held**
WEB: www.gencap.com
SIC: 6211 3647 Investment firm, general brokerage; vehicular lighting equipment

(P-9973)
GI GP IV LLC (PA)
Also Called: GI Partners
188 The Embarcadero # 700, San Francisco (94105-1231)
PHONE..................................415 688-4800
Richard Magnuson, *Mng Member*
Roman Braslavsky, *Vice Pres*
Keith Collins, *Vice Pres*
Sendil Rajendran, *Vice Pres*
David Mace, *Managing Dir*
EMP: 50 **EST:** 2014
SALES (est): 85.7MM **Privately Held**
SIC: 6211 6512 Investment bankers; commercial & industrial building operation

(P-9974)
GRIGSBY & ASSOCIATES INC (PA)
2406 Saddleback Dr, Danville (94506-3116)
PHONE..................................214 522-4664
Calvin B Grigsby, *CEO*
Calvin Grigsby, *CEO*
Jonathan Robert Ceresa, *Sales Staff*
EMP: 88 **EST:** 1981
SQ FT: 10,000
SALES (est): 2MM **Privately Held**
SIC: 6211 Bond dealers & brokers

(P-9975)
HEIGHTS CAPITAL MANAGEMENT INC
101 California St # 3250, San Francisco (94111-5802)
PHONE..................................415 403-6500
Andrew Frost, *President*
Joe Wise, *Administration*
EMP: 64 **EST:** 1996
SALES (est): 592.9K **Privately Held**
SIC: 6211 Security brokers & dealers

(P-9976)
HOEFER & ARNETT INC (PA)
555 Market St Ste 1800, San Francisco (94105-2857)
PHONE..................................415 538-5700
Steve Didion, *President*
Kevin Daly, *Shareholder*
Bob Arnett, *Ch of Bd*
Art Raitano, *COO*
Phil Economopoulos, *Principal*
EMP: 36 **EST:** 1982
SALES (est): 4.3MM **Privately Held**
SIC: 6211 Brokers, security

(P-9977)
JMP GROUP INC (HQ)
600 Montgomery St # 1100, San Francisco (94111-2702)
PHONE..................................415 835-8900
Joseph A Jolson, *Ch of Bd*
Carter D Mack, *President*
Raymond S Jackson, *CFO*
Craig R Johnson, *Vice Ch Bd*
Kenneth Clausman, *Managing Dir*
EMP: 62 **EST:** 2000
SQ FT: 37,810
SALES (est): 127MM
SALES (corp-wide): 121.8MM **Publicly Held**
WEB: www.jmpg.com
SIC: 6211 Investment bankers
PA: Jmp Group Llc
600 Montgomery St # 1100
San Francisco CA 94111
415 835-8900

(P-9978)
JMP SECURITIES LLC (DH)
600 Montgomery St # 1100, San Francisco (94111-2713)
PHONE..................................415 835-8900
Mark Lehmann, *CEO*
Craig R Johnson, *Vice Chairman*
Carter D Mack, *President*
Thomas Wright, *COO*
Raymond S Jackson, *CFO*
EMP: 130 **EST:** 2001
SALES (est): 111.6MM
SALES (corp-wide): 121.8MM **Publicly Held**
WEB: www.jmpg.com
SIC: 6211 Investment bankers
HQ: Jmp Group Inc.
600 Montgomery St # 1100
San Francisco CA 94111
415 835-8900

(P-9979)
MAP ENERGY LLC
3000 El Camino Real, Palo Alto (94306-2100)
PHONE..................................650 324-9095
Jane Woodward,
Steve Hall, *Managing Prtnr*
Aaron Zubaty, *Managing Prtnr*
Radhika Nayak, *Vice Pres*
Aaron Van Boer, *Vice Pres*
EMP: 85 **EST:** 2018
SALES (est): 10.9MM **Privately Held**
WEB: www.map-energy.com
SIC: 6211 Security brokers & dealers

(P-9980)
MERRILL LYNCH PIERCE FENNER
333 Middlefield Rd, Menlo Park (94025-3552)
PHONE..................................650 473-7888
Fax: 650 473-7800
EMP: 75
SALES (corp-wide): 95.1B **Publicly Held**
SIC: 6211 Securities Brokerage
HQ: Merrill Lynch, Pierce, Fenner & Smith Incorporated
111 8th Ave
New York NY 10011
800 637-7455

(P-9981)
MERRILL LYNCH PIERCE FENNER
Also Called: Merrill Lynch Wealth MGT
560 S Winchester Blvd, San Jose (95128-2560)
PHONE..................................408 260-6001
Bill Yates, *Principal*
EMP: 85
SALES (corp-wide): 93.7B **Publicly Held**
WEB: www.ml.com
SIC: 6211 6411 Security brokers & dealers; insurance agents & brokers
HQ: Merrill Lynch, Pierce, Fenner & Smith Incorporated
111 8th Ave
New York NY 10011
800 637-7455

(P-9982)
MERRILL LYNCH PRCE FNNER SMITH
150 Parker St, Vacaville (95688-3914)
PHONE..................................925 988-2113
Ann Johnson, *Branch Mgr*
EMP: 85
SALES (corp-wide): 93.7B **Publicly Held**
WEB: www.ml.com
SIC: 6211 Security brokers & dealers
HQ: Merrill Lynch, Pierce, Fenner & Smith Incorporated
111 8th Ave
New York NY 10011
800 637-7455

(P-9983)
MERRILL LYNCH PRCE FNNER SMITH
292 Hemsted Dr Ste 100, Redding (96002-0946)
PHONE..................................530 223-3005
Gregory Debord, *Manager*
EMP: 85
SALES (corp-wide): 93.7B **Publicly Held**
WEB: www.ml.com
SIC: 6211 Security brokers & dealers
HQ: Merrill Lynch, Pierce, Fenner & Smith Incorporated
111 8th Ave
New York NY 10011
800 637-7455

(P-9984)
MERRILL LYNCH PRCE FNNER SMITH
3075b Hansen Way, Palo Alto (94304-1000)
PHONE..................................650 842-2440
Huert Chang, *Branch Mgr*
Michael Khaw, *Manager*
EMP: 85
SALES (corp-wide): 93.7B **Publicly Held**
WEB: www.ml.com
SIC: 6211 Security brokers & dealers
HQ: Merrill Lynch, Pierce, Fenner & Smith Incorporated
111 8th Ave
New York NY 10011
800 637-7455

(P-9985)
MERRILL LYNCH PRCE FNNER SMITH
555 California St Fl 9, San Francisco (94104-1512)
PHONE..................................415 955-3700
Jim Dullanty, *Branch Mgr*
Judy Klink, *Vice Pres*
Kelly Milligan, *Vice Pres*
Len Tallerico, *Vice Pres*
Davis Stephen, *Director*
EMP: 150
SALES (corp-wide): 93.7B **Publicly Held**
WEB: www.ml.com
SIC: 6211 6282 Security brokers & dealers; investment advice
HQ: Merrill Lynch, Pierce, Fenner & Smith Incorporated
111 8th Ave
New York NY 10011
800 637-7455

(P-9986)
MERRILL LYNCH PRCE FNNER SMITH
801 10th St Fl 7-1, Modesto (95354-2311)
PHONE..................................209 578-2600
Stanly Oneil, *Owner*
EMP: 85
SALES (corp-wide): 93.7B **Publicly Held**
WEB: www.ml.com
SIC: 6211 Security brokers & dealers
HQ: Merrill Lynch, Pierce, Fenner & Smith Incorporated
111 8th Ave
New York NY 10011
800 637-7455

(P-9987)
MERRILL LYNCH PRCE FNNER SMITH
2320 E Bidwell St Ste 100, Folsom (95630-3561)
PHONE..................................916 984-3200
Nancy Dian-Smith, *Manager*
EMP: 85
SALES (corp-wide): 93.7B **Publicly Held**
WEB: www.ml.com
SIC: 6211 Security brokers & dealers
HQ: Merrill Lynch, Pierce, Fenner & Smith Incorporated
111 8th Ave
New York NY 10011
800 637-7455

(P-9988)
MERRILL LYNCH PRCE FNNER SMITH
50 W San Fernando St 16, San Jose (95113-2429)
PHONE..................................408 283-3000
Patricia Williams, *Manager*
EMP: 85
SALES (corp-wide): 93.7B **Publicly Held**
WEB: www.ml.com
SIC: 6211 6282 Security brokers & dealers; investment advice
HQ: Merrill Lynch, Pierce, Fenner & Smith Incorporated
111 8th Ave
New York NY 10011
800 637-7455

(P-9989)
MERRILL LYNCH PRCE FNNER SMITH
Also Called: Merrill Lynch Prce Fnner Smith
555 Capitol Mall, Sacramento (95814-4504)
PHONE..................................916 648-6200
EMP: 85
SALES (corp-wide): 93.7B **Publicly Held**
WEB: www.ml.com
SIC: 6211 Security brokers & dealers
HQ: Merrill Lynch, Pierce, Fenner & Smith Incorporated
111 8th Ave
New York NY 10011
800 637-7455

(P-9990)
MERRILL LYNCH PRCE FNNER SMITH
4900 Hopyard Rd Ste 140, Pleasanton (94588-3345)
PHONE..................................925 227-6600
Uwe Ruttke, *Manager*
John Steiner, *Director*
EMP: 85
SALES (corp-wide): 93.7B **Publicly Held**
WEB: www.ml.com
SIC: 6211 Security brokers & dealers
HQ: Merrill Lynch, Pierce, Fenner & Smith Incorporated
111 8th Ave
New York NY 10011
800 637-7455

(P-9991)
MERRILL LYNCH PRCE FNNER SMITH
3255 W March Ln Ste 110, Stockton (95219-2353)
PHONE..................................209 472-3500
Philip B Benson, *Manager*
Frank Quacinella, *Manager*

6211 - Security Brokers & Dealers County (P-9992)

EMP: 85
SALES (corp-wide): 93.7B Publicly Held
WEB: www.ml.com
SIC: 6211 8742 Security brokers & dealers; financial consultant
HQ: Merrill Lynch, Pierce, Fenner & Smith Incorporated
111 8th Ave
New York NY 10011
800 637-7455

(P-9992)
MERRILL LYNCH PRCE FNNER SMITH
90 S E St Frnt, Santa Rosa (95404-6511)
PHONE.................................707 575-6374
Matthew Davis, Manager
EMP: 85
SALES (corp-wide): 93.7B Publicly Held
WEB: www.ml.com
SIC: 6211 Security brokers & dealers
HQ: Merrill Lynch, Pierce, Fenner & Smith Incorporated
111 8th Ave
New York NY 10011
800 637-7455

(P-9993)
MERRILL LYNCH PRCE FNNER SMITH
1331 N Calif Blvd Ste 400, Walnut Creek (94596-4561)
PHONE.................................925 945-4800
Michael Dunn, Branch Mgr
Susan Mazzetti, Assistant VP
EMP: 85
SALES (corp-wide): 93.7B Publicly Held
WEB: www.ml.com
SIC: 6211 8742 Security brokers & dealers; financial consultant
HQ: Merrill Lynch, Pierce, Fenner & Smith Incorporated
111 8th Ave
New York NY 10011
800 637-7455

(P-9994)
MERRILL LYNCH PRCE FNNER SMITH
101 California St Fl 24, San Francisco (94111-5898)
PHONE.................................415 274-7000
Jim Delancey, Branch Mgr
Christine Koh-Wong, Vice Pres
Andrew J Mayer, Manager
Claudia Denton, Advisor
EMP: 50
SALES (corp-wide): 93.7B Publicly Held
WEB: www.ml.com
SIC: 6211 6282 Stock brokers & dealers; investment advice
HQ: Merrill Lynch, Pierce, Fenner & Smith Incorporated
111 8th Ave
New York NY 10011
800 637-7455

(P-9995)
MERRILL LYNCH PRCE FNNER SMITH
5260 N Palm Ave Ste 100, Fresno (93704-2220)
P.O. Box 11217 (93772-1217)
PHONE.................................559 436-0919
Leonard Kirqorian, Sales/Mktg Dir
EMP: 85
SALES (corp-wide): 93.7B Publicly Held
WEB: www.ml.com
SIC: 6211 Security brokers & dealers
HQ: Merrill Lynch, Pierce, Fenner & Smith Incorporated
111 8th Ave
New York NY 10011
800 637-7455

(P-9996)
MERRILL LYNCH PRCE FNNER SMITH
101 S Ellsworth Ave Fl 4, San Mateo (94401-3956)
PHONE.................................650 579-3050
Peter Soltesz, Manager
Robert Haeusslein, Manager
EMP: 85

SALES (corp-wide): 93.7B Publicly Held
WEB: www.ml.com
SIC: 6211 Security brokers & dealers
HQ: Merrill Lynch, Pierce, Fenner & Smith Incorporated
111 8th Ave
New York NY 10011
800 637-7455

(P-9997)
MERRILL LYNCH PRCE FNNER SMITH
2 Belvedere Pl Ste 100, Mill Valley (94941-2486)
PHONE.................................415 289-8800
Rodney Williams, Marketing Staff
John Damico, Manager
William A Glenn, Advisor
Sean Heyman, Representative
EMP: 85
SALES (corp-wide): 93.7B Publicly Held
WEB: www.ml.com
SIC: 6211 Security brokers & dealers
HQ: Merrill Lynch, Pierce, Fenner & Smith Incorporated
111 8th Ave
New York NY 10011
800 637-7455

(P-9998)
MORGAN STANLEY & CO LLC
4309 Hacienda Dr Ste 200, Pleasanton (94588-2730)
PHONE.................................510 538-5203
EMP: 35
SALES (corp-wide): 43.6B Publicly Held
SIC: 6211 Security Broker/Dealer
HQ: Morgan Stanley & Co. Llc
1585 Broadway
New York NY 10036
212 761-4000

(P-9999)
MORGAN STNLEY SMITH BARNEY LLC
1400 Page Mill Rd, Palo Alto (94304-1177)
PHONE.................................650 496-4200
EMP: 68
SALES (corp-wide): 52B Publicly Held
WEB: www.morganstanley.com
SIC: 6211 Stock brokers & dealers
HQ: Morgan Stanley Smith Barney, Llc
1585 Broadway
New York NY 10036

(P-10000)
MORGAN STNLEY SMITH BARNEY LLC
1020 10th St, Modesto (95354-0850)
PHONE.................................209 526-3700
Marc Glass, Branch Mgr
EMP: 68
SALES (corp-wide): 52B Publicly Held
WEB: www.morganstanley.com
SIC: 6211 Stock brokers & dealers
HQ: Morgan Stanley Smith Barney, Llc
1585 Broadway
New York NY 10036

(P-10001)
MORGAN STNLEY SMITH BARNEY LLC
4309 Hacienda Dr Ste 200, Pleasanton (94588-2730)
PHONE.................................925 730-3800
Michael O'Connell, Manager
EMP: 68
SALES (corp-wide): 52B Publicly Held
WEB: www.morganstanley.com
SIC: 6211 Stock brokers & dealers
HQ: Morgan Stanley Smith Barney, Llc
1585 Broadway
New York NY 10036

(P-10002)
MORGAN STNLEY SMITH BARNEY LLC
225 W Santa Clara St # 9, San Jose (95113-1723)
PHONE.................................408 346-0105
David Perez, Branch Mgr
EMP: 68

SALES (corp-wide): 52B Publicly Held
WEB: www.morganstanley.com
SIC: 6211 Stock brokers & dealers
HQ: Morgan Stanley Smith Barney, Llc
1585 Broadway
New York NY 10036

(P-10003)
MORGAN STNLEY SMITH BARNEY LLC
5250 N Palm Ave, Fresno (93704-2218)
PHONE.................................559 431-5900
Roger Byrd, Branch Mgr
EMP: 68
SALES (corp-wide): 52B Publicly Held
WEB: www.morganstanley.com
SIC: 6211 Security brokers & dealers
HQ: Morgan Stanley Smith Barney, Llc
1585 Broadway
New York NY 10036

(P-10004)
MORGAN STNLEY SMITH BARNEY LLC
6004 La Madrona Dr, Scotts Valley (95060-1040)
PHONE.................................831 440-5200
Stephanie Tucker, Branch Mgr
EMP: 68
SALES (corp-wide): 52B Publicly Held
WEB: www.morganstanley.com
SIC: 6211 Security brokers & dealers
HQ: Morgan Stanley Smith Barney, Llc
1585 Broadway
New York NY 10036

(P-10005)
MORGAN STNLEY SMITH BARNEY LLC
555 California St Fl 35, San Francisco (94104-1615)
PHONE.................................415 984-6500
Greg M Desmond, Branch Mgr
EMP: 68
SALES (corp-wide): 52B Publicly Held
WEB: www.morganstanley.com
SIC: 6211 Security brokers & dealers
HQ: Morgan Stanley Smith Barney, Llc
1585 Broadway
New York NY 10036

(P-10006)
MORGAN STNLEY SMITH BARNEY LLC
2365 Iron Point Rd # 235, Folsom (95630-8711)
PHONE.................................916 983-8888
Jim Pugan, Branch Mgr
EMP: 68
SALES (corp-wide): 52B Publicly Held
WEB: www.morganstanley.com
SIC: 6211 Security brokers & dealers
HQ: Morgan Stanley Smith Barney, Llc
1585 Broadway
New York NY 10036

(P-10007)
POINT DIGITAL FINANCE INC
635 High St, Palo Alto (94301-1626)
P.O. Box 192 (94302-0192)
PHONE.................................650 460-8668
Edward Lim, CEO
Dulguun Bayaraa, Partner
Christine Dela Cruz-Siba, Opers Staff
Nicole Hoang, Opers Staff
Andrew Lee, Manager
EMP: 47 EST: 2014
SALES (est): 11.1MM Privately Held
WEB: www.point.com
SIC: 6211 Investment firm, general brokerage

(P-10008)
PORTSMOUTH FINANCIAL SERVICES
601 Montgomery St # 1950, San Francisco (94111-2691)
PHONE.................................415 543-8500
Ray Lent, Chairman
Walton Logan, Ch of Bd

Thomas Carcasio, President
Renee Amochaev, Vice Pres
Charles Lowrey, Vice Pres
EMP: 39 EST: 1983
SALES (est): 6.3MM Privately Held
WEB: www.portsmouthfinancial.com
SIC: 6211 6282 6411 Stock brokers & dealers; investment advice; insurance agents, brokers & service

(P-10009)
PREMIER FINANCIAL GROUP INC
725 6th St, Eureka (95501-1103)
PHONE.................................707 443-2741
Wayne O Caldwell, President
John Gloor, Principal
Ron Ross, Principal
Yvette Metz, Admin Sec
Cassi Anaya-Bishop, Administration
EMP: 35 EST: 1987
SQ FT: 2,200
SALES (est): 5.1MM Privately Held
WEB: www.premierfinancial.com
SIC: 6211 6411 6282 Investment firm, general brokerage; insurance agents & brokers; life insurance agents; investment advice

(P-10010)
ROBINHOOD MARKETS INC (PA)
85 Willow Rd, Menlo Park (94025-3656)
PHONE.................................844 428-5411
Vladimir Tenev, Ch of Bd
Gretchen Howard, COO
Jason Warnick, CFO
Baiju Bhatt, Ch Credit Ofcr
Daniel Gallagher,
EMP: 821 EST: 2013
SALES (est): 958.8MM Publicly Held
SIC: 6211 Stock brokers & dealers

(P-10011)
ROBINHOOD SECURITIES LLC
85 Willow Rd, Menlo Park (94025-3656)
PHONE.................................650 294-4857
Baiju Bhat, CEO
Kelly Hoppensteadt, Partner
Shiv Verma, Treasurer
David Favreau, Officer
Joe Binney, Vice Pres
EMP: 131 EST: 2016
SALES (est): 29.4MM
SALES (corp-wide): 958.8MM Publicly Held
WEB: www.robinhood.com
SIC: 6211 Stock brokers & dealers
PA: Robinhood Markets, Inc.
85 Willow Rd
Menlo Park CA 94025
844 428-5411

(P-10012)
SAGEPOINT FINANCIAL INC
4950 Hamilton Ave Ste 107, San Jose (95130-1748)
PHONE.................................408 374-4787
Tammy Leu, Branch Mgr
Suzanne Kwong, Advisor
Didi Guchiang, Agent
Michael Mulvrhill, Agent
EMP: 41
SALES (corp-wide): 651.5MM Privately Held
WEB: www.sagepointfinancial.com
SIC: 6211 Security brokers & dealers
HQ: Sagepoint Financial, Inc.
20 E Thomas Rd Ste 2000
Phoenix AZ 85012

(P-10013)
SIG STRUCTURED PRODUCTS LLLP
425 California St # 2450, San Francisco (94104-2102)
PHONE.................................415 951-3533
Greg Wedd, Manager
EMP: 40
SALES (corp-wide): 240.8MM Privately Held
WEB: www.sig.com
SIC: 6211 Security brokers & dealers

PA: Sig Structured Products, Lllp
401 E City Ave Ste 220
Bala Cynwyd PA 19004
610 617-2600

(P-10014)
STANDARD PACIFIC CAPITAL LLC
101 California St Fl 36, San Francisco (94111-5831)
PHONE..............................415 352-7100
EMP: 50
SQ FT: 9,000
SALES (est): 12.7MM Privately Held
WEB: www.standardpacific.com
SIC: 6211 Security Brokers And Dealers, Nsk

(P-10015)
STONE & YOUNGBERG LLC (PA)
1 Ferry Plz, San Francisco (94111-4212)
PHONE..............................415 445-2300
EMP: 130
SQ FT: 19,034
SALES (est): 35.7MM Privately Held
WEB: www.syllc.com
SIC: 6211 6282 Security Brokers And Dealers, Nsk

(P-10016)
THE CHARLES SCHWAB TRUST CO (HQ)
425 Market St Fl 7, San Francisco (94105-5405)
PHONE..............................415 371-0518
James McCool, *CEO*
Steven Scheid, *CFO*
Peter Kalafa, *Vice Pres*
Denise Kampf, *Vice Pres*
Nancy Larget, *Vice Pres*
EMP: 50 EST: 1992
SALES (est): 2.9MM
SALES (corp-wide): 11.6B Publicly Held
WEB: www.schwab.com
SIC: 6211 Brokers, security
PA: The Charles Schwab Corporation
211 Main St Fl 17
San Francisco CA 94105
415 667-7000

(P-10017)
THOMAS WEISEL PARTNERS LLC (DH)
1 Montgomery St Ste 3700, San Francisco (94104-5537)
PHONE..............................415 364-2500
Thomas Weisel,
Mark Baillie, *Vice Pres*
Tracy Beaver, *Vice Pres*
Michael Carr, *Vice Pres*
Wilson Lam, *Vice Pres*
EMP: 300 EST: 1998
SALES (est): 107.8MM
SALES (corp-wide): 3.7B Publicly Held
WEB: www.thomasweisel.com
SIC: 6211 Investment bankers

(P-10018)
THOMAS WSEL PARTNERS GROUP INC (HQ)
1 Montgomery St Fl 36, San Francisco (94104-5536)
PHONE..............................415 364-2500
Thomas W Weisel, *Ch of Bd*
Lionel F Conacher, *President*
Ryan Stroub, *CFO*
Shaugn S Stanley, *Officer*
Mark P Fisher, *General Counsel*
EMP: 65 EST: 1998
SQ FT: 140,400
SALES (est): 107.8MM
SALES (corp-wide): 3.7B Publicly Held
WEB: www.stifel.com
SIC: 6211 Security brokers & dealers
PA: Stifel Financial Corp.
501 N Broadway
Saint Louis MO 63102
314 342-2000

(P-10019)
VECTOR CAPITAL MANAGEMENT LP (PA)
1 Market St Ste 2300, San Francisco (94105-1414)
PHONE..............................415 293-5000
Alex Slusky, *CIO*
David Baylor, *COO*
James Murray, *CFO*
Dan Fletcher, *Vice Pres*
Stephen Goodman, *Vice Pres*
EMP: 364 EST: 1998
SQ FT: 8,000
SALES (est): 621MM Privately Held
WEB: www.vectorcapital.com
SIC: 6211 6799 Security brokers & dealers; venture capital companies

(P-10020)
VEEV GROUP INC
Also Called: Dragonfly Investments Group
777 Mariners Island Blvd # 15, San Mateo (94404-5008)
PHONE..............................650 292-0752
Amit Haller, *Principal*
Bella Kapsheev, *Vice Pres*
Tommy Katzenellenboge, *Vice Pres*
AMI Avrahami, *Principal*
Jennifer Watters, *Marketing Staff*
EMP: 210 EST: 2018
SALES (est): 49.7MM Privately Held
WEB: www.veev.com
SIC: 6211 Investment firm, general brokerage

(P-10021)
VIVO CAPITAL LLC (PA)
192 Lytton Ave, Palo Alto (94301-1046)
PHONE..............................650 688-0818
Frank Kung, *Managing Prtnr*
Vivian Chiau, *Vice Pres*
Gaurav Aggarwal, *Managing Dir*
Jack Nielsen, *Managing Dir*
Brittanie Montoya, *Administration*
EMP: 54 EST: 2005
SALES (est): 19.6MM Privately Held
WEB: www.vivocapital.com
SIC: 6211 Investment firm, general brokerage

(P-10022)
W R HAMBRECHT CO INC (PA)
Bay 3 Pier 1, San Francisco (94111)
PHONE..............................415 551-8600
William R Hambrecht, *Ch of Bd*
Jonathan Fayman, *CFO*
Clay Corbus, *Co-CEO*
EMP: 60 EST: 1998
SQ FT: 25,000
SALES (est): 20.5MM Privately Held
WEB: www.wrhambrecht.com
SIC: 6211 Investment bankers

(P-10023)
WELLS FARGO PRIME SERVICES LLC
45 Fremont St Ste 3000, San Francisco (94105-2256)
PHONE..............................415 848-0269
Stephan P Vermut,
Robert Garrett, *Senior Partner*
Regina O'Neill,
EMP: 65 EST: 2004
SALES (est): 41.6MM
SALES (corp-wide): 80.3B Publicly Held
WEB: www.merlinsecurities.com
SIC: 6211 Security brokers & dealers
HQ: Everen Capital Corporation
301 S College St
Charlotte NC 28202

6221 Commodity Contracts Brokers & Dealers

(P-10024)
ARTISAN PARTNERS LTD PARTNR
100 Pine St Ste 2950, San Francisco (94111-5200)
PHONE..............................415 283-2444
Vickey Harris, *Manager*
Charles Raz, *Technology*
Todd Forster, *Financial Analy*
Sam Sellers, *General Counsel*
Brooke-Lynn Orage, *Receptionist*
EMP: 52 Privately Held
WEB: www.artisanpartners.com
SIC: 6221 Commodity dealers, contracts
PA: Artisan Partners Limited Partnership
875 E Wsconsin Ave Ste 800
Milwaukee WI 53202

6231 Security & Commodity Exchanges

(P-10025)
NYSE ARCA INC
115 Sansome St, San Francisco (94104-3601)
PHONE..............................415 393-4000
Philip D Defeo, *CEO*
David Diamond, *CFO*
Paul N Koutoulas, *Exec VP*
Peter Armstrong, *Senior VP*
Hark Yip, *Senior VP*
▲ EMP: 177 EST: 1882
SALES (est): 11.3MM
SALES (corp-wide): 6B Publicly Held
WEB: www.nyse.com
SIC: 6231 Stock exchanges
HQ: Nyse Group, Inc.
11 Wall St
New York NY 10005

6282 Investment Advice

(P-10026)
ALLWORTH FINANCIAL LP
Also Called: Hanson McClain Advisors
135 Camino Dorado Ste 1, NAPA (94558-7531)
PHONE..............................888 577-2489
EMP: 90 Privately Held
WEB: www.allworthfinancial.com
SIC: 6282 Investment advisory service
PA: Allworth Financial, L.P.
8775 Folsom Blvd Ste 100
Sacramento CA 95826

(P-10027)
AMERICAN FINANCIAL NETWORK INC
2125 Oak Grove Rd, Walnut Creek (94598-2536)
PHONE..............................925 705-7710
EMP: 81
SALES (corp-wide): 99.2MM Privately Held
SIC: 6282 Investment Advice
PA: American Financial Network, Inc.
10 Pointe Dr Ste 330
Brea CA 92821
909 606-3905

(P-10028)
AMERICAN FINANCIAL NETWORK INC
3300 Tully Rd Ste C6, Modesto (95350-0849)
PHONE..............................209 238-3210
EMP: 44
SALES (corp-wide): 201.9MM Privately Held
WEB: www.afncorp.com
SIC: 6282 Investment advice
PA: American Financial Network, Inc.
10 Pointe Dr Ste 330
Brea CA 92821
909 606-3905

(P-10029)
ASSETMARK INC (HQ)
1655 Grant St Ste 1000, Concord (94520-2789)
PHONE..............................925 521-1040
Natalie Wolfsen, *CEO*
Michael Kim, *President*
Gary Zyla, *CFO*
Cathy Clauson, *Senior VP*
Jeff Bridge, *Vice Pres*
EMP: 50 EST: 1982
SQ FT: 15,000
SALES (est): 56MM
SALES (corp-wide): 432MM Publicly Held
WEB: www.assetmark.com
SIC: 6282 Manager of mutual funds, contract or fee basis
PA: Assetmark Financial Holdings, Inc.
1655 Grant St Fl 10
Concord CA 94520
925 521-2200

(P-10030)
ASSETMARK FINANCIAL INC (HQ)
1655 Grant St Fl 10, Concord (94520-2600)
PHONE..............................925 521-2200
Carrie Hansen, *COO*
Gary Zyla, *CFO*
Michael Kim, *Officer*
Natalie Wolfsen, *Officer*
Ted Angus, *Exec VP*
EMP: 484 EST: 1996
SALES (est): 141.8MM
SALES (corp-wide): 432MM Publicly Held
WEB: www.assetmark.com
SIC: 6282 Investment advice
PA: Assetmark Financial Holdings, Inc.
1655 Grant St Fl 10
Concord CA 94520
925 521-2200

(P-10031)
ASSETMARK FINCL HOLDINGS INC (PA)
1655 Grant St Fl 10, Concord (94520-2600)
PHONE..............................925 521-2200
Natalie Wolfsen, *CEO*
Xiaoning Jiao, *Ch of Bd*
Michael Kim, *President*
Carrie Hansen, *COO*
Gary Zyla, *CFO*
EMP: 62 EST: 2013
SQ FT: 96,944
SALES (est): 432MM Publicly Held
SIC: 6282 Investment advice

(P-10032)
BAILARD INC (HQ)
950 Tower Ln Ste 1900, Foster City (94404-2131)
PHONE..............................650 571-5800
Thomas E Bailard, *CEO*
Henry Newhall, *President*
Sonya Thadhani, *COO*
Barbara Bailey, *Vice Pres*
Eric Leve, *Ch Invest Ofcr*
EMP: 47 EST: 1969
SQ FT: 150,000
SALES (est): 19.5MM Privately Held
WEB: www.bailard.com
SIC: 6282 Investment advisory service
PA: B B & K Holdings
950 Tower Ln Ste 1900
Foster City CA 94404
650 571-5800

(P-10033)
BAKER AVENUE ASSET MGT LP (PA)
301 Battery St Fl 2, San Francisco (94111-3237)
PHONE..............................415 986-1110
Simon Baker, *Partner*
Bill Connor, *Partner*
Zuzanna Forrest, *Partner*
King Lip, *Partner*
Scott Stephens, *Partner*
EMP: 65 EST: 2004
SALES (est): 8.7MM Privately Held
WEB: www.bakerave.com
SIC: 6282 Investment advisory service

(P-10034)
BAM ADVISOR SERVICES LLC
Also Called: Loring Ward
10 Almaden Blvd Fl 15, San Jose (95113-2226)
PHONE..............................800 366-7266
Mike Ozburn, *Vice Pres*
Eric Rienhardt, *Vice Pres*
Tim Hacker, *Engineer*
Sara Buser, *Analyst*
Shane Schofield, *Director*

6282 - Investment Advice County (P-10035)

EMP: 60 Privately Held
WEB:
www.buckinghamstrategicpartners.com
SIC: **6282** Investment advisory service
PA: Bam Advisor Services, Llc
8182 Maryland Ave Ste 500
Saint Louis MO 63105

(P-10035)
BLUM CAPITAL PARTNERS T LP
909 Montgomery St Ste 400, San Francisco (94133-4652)
PHONE...............................415 645-0092
Richard C Blum, *Partner*
David Chung, *Partner*
John Park, *Partner*
James Su, *Partner*
Murray McCabe, *Managing Prtnr*
EMP: 48 EST: 1975
SQ FT: 8,100
SALES (est): 20.6MM Privately Held
WEB: www.blumcapital.com
SIC: **6282** Investment advisory service

(P-10036)
C2 FINANCIAL CORPORATION
3000 Citrus Cir Ste 118, Walnut Creek (94598-2694)
PHONE...............................925 938-1300
Star Darden, *Branch Mgr*
EMP: 162
SALES (corp-wide): 96.9MM Privately Held
WEB: www.c2financialcorp.com
SIC: **6282** Investment advice
PA: C2 Financial Corporation
10509 Vista Sorrento Pkwy # 200
San Diego CA 92121
858 312-4900

(P-10037)
C2 FINANCIAL CORPORATION
978 Burlingame Ave, Clovis (93612-0464)
PHONE...............................559 824-2300
EMP: 162
SALES (corp-wide): 96.9MM Privately Held
WEB: www.c2financialcorp.com
SIC: **6282** Investment advice
PA: C2 Financial Corporation
10509 Vista Sorrento Pkwy # 200
San Diego CA 92121
858 312-4900

(P-10038)
CALLAN LLC (PA)
600 Montgomery St Ste 800, San Francisco (94111-2710)
PHONE...............................415 974-5060
Ronald D Peyton, *CEO*
Gregory C Allen, *President*
Karen Witham, *President*
Ronald Peyton, *CEO*
James Callahan, *Exec VP*
EMP: 120 EST: 1973
SQ FT: 43,000
SALES (est): 58.5MM Privately Held
WEB: www.callan.com
SIC: **6282** **8742** Investment advisory service; banking & finance consultant

(P-10039)
CITICORP SELECT INVESTMENTS
250 University Ave Lbby, Palo Alto (94301-1725)
PHONE...............................650 353-2765
Betsy Bechtel, *Branch Mgr*
EMP: 49
SALES (corp-wide): 88.8B Publicly Held
SIC: **6282** **6211** Investment advisory service; flotation companies
HQ: Citicorp Select Investments Inc
1 Court Sq Fl 24 Flr 24
Long Island City NY 11101

(P-10040)
CITICORP SELECT INVESTMENTS
1 Sansome St Fl 22, San Francisco (94104-4433)
PHONE...............................415 658-4468
Jonathan Powell, *Manager*
EMP: 49
SALES (corp-wide): 88.8B Publicly Held
SIC: **6282** **6726** Investment advisory service; investment offices
HQ: Citicorp Select Investments Inc
1 Court Sq Fl 24 Flr 24
Long Island City NY 11101

(P-10041)
CLEANTECH GROUP INC (PA)
Also Called: Cleantech Network
33 New Montgomery St # 22, San Francisco (94105-4506)
PHONE...............................415 684-1020
Sheeraz Haji, *CEO*
Richard Youngman, *Managing Prtnr*
Todd Allmendinger, *Research*
Nicholas Parker, *Director*
Chris Sworder, *Associate*
EMP: 62 EST: 2007
SALES (est): 12MM Privately Held
WEB: www.cleantech.com
SIC: **6282** Investment advisory service

(P-10042)
CTHULHU VENTURES LLC (PA)
184 Bulkley Ave, Sausalito (94965-2161)
PHONE...............................415 444-9602
Jim Babcock, *CEO*
Christopher Hill, *CFO*
Regina Doody, *Controller*
EMP: 37 EST: 2009
SALES (est): 907.5K Privately Held
WEB: www.cthulhuventures.com
SIC: **6282** **6726** Investment advisory service; investment offices

(P-10043)
ENVESTMENT MANAGEMENT INC (HQ)
160 W Santa Clara St Fl 8, San Jose (95113-1700)
PHONE...............................408 962-7878
Siva Suresh, *CEO*
William Crager, *President*
Judd Bergman, *CEO*
Pete D'Arrigo, *CFO*
George Alvin, *Ch Credit Ofcr*
EMP: 40 EST: 1999
SQ FT: 9,000
SALES (est): 16.2MM
SALES (corp-wide): 998.2MM Publicly Held
WEB: www.envestnet.com
SIC: **6282** Investment advice
PA: Envestnet, Inc.
35 E Wacker Dr Ste 2400
Chicago IL 60601
312 827-2800

(P-10044)
FORWARD MANAGEMENT LLC
Also Called: Webster Investment Management
101 California St Fl 16, San Francisco (94111-6100)
P.O. Box 1345, Denver CO (80201-1345)
PHONE...............................415 869-6300
John Blaisdell, *CEO*
Jeffrey P Cusack, *President*
Robert S Naka, *Senior VP*
Joseph R Elefante, *Vice Pres*
Mark Guadagnini, *Vice Pres*
EMP: 100 EST: 1998
SQ FT: 22,000
SALES (est): 23.5MM
SALES (corp-wide): 66.6MM Privately Held
WEB: www.salientpartners.com
SIC: **6282** Investment advisory service
PA: Salient Partners, L.P.
4265 San Felipe St Fl 8
Houston TX 77027
713 993-4675

(P-10045)
FRANKLIN RESOURCES INC (PA)
1 Franklin Pkwy Bldg 920, San Mateo (94403-1906)
PHONE...............................650 312-2000
Jennifer M Johnson, *President*
Gregory E Johnson, *Ch of Bd*
Tara Jacques, *President*
Matthew Nicholls, *CFO*
Rupert H Johnson Jr, *Vice Ch Bd*
EMP: 1852 EST: 1947
SQ FT: 743,793
SALES (est): 5.5B Publicly Held
WEB: www.franklinresources.com
SIC: **6282** **6722** Investment advice; management investment, open-end; management investment funds, closed-end

(P-10046)
FRANKLIN TMPLETON INV SVCS LLC
5130 Hacienda Dr Fl 4, Dublin (94568-7598)
PHONE...............................925 875-2619
Priscilla Voyer, *Manager*
EMP: 138
SALES (corp-wide): 5.5B Publicly Held
SIC: **6282** Investment advisory service
HQ: Franklin Templeton Investor Services, Llc
3344 Quality Dr
Rancho Cordova CA 95670
916 463-1500

(P-10047)
FREMONT GROUP LLC (PA)
199 Fremont St Fl 19, San Francisco (94105-2261)
PHONE...............................415 284-8500
Deborah L Duncans,
Jeffrey W Jones, *Partner*
Scott R Earthy, *Managing Prtnr*
Claude J Zinngrabe Jr, *Managing Prtnr*
David R Covin, *COO*
EMP: 110 EST: 1995
SQ FT: 50,000
SALES (est): 35MM Privately Held
WEB: www.fremontgroup.com
SIC: **6282** Investment advisory service

(P-10048)
HIGHMARK CAPITAL MGT INC
350 California St Fl 22, San Francisco (94104-1435)
PHONE...............................800 582-4734
Earle Malm, *President*
Jeffrey L Klein, *Vice Pres*
Todd Lowenstein, *Vice Pres*
Bonnie Mullen, *Vice Pres*
Kevin Rowell, *Vice Pres*
EMP: 93 EST: 1998
SALES (est): 33MM Privately Held
WEB: www.unionbank.com
SIC: **6282** Investment advisory service
HQ: Mufg Union Bank, National Association
400 California St Fl 14
San Francisco CA 94104
415 705-7000

(P-10049)
INSIGHT WEALTH STRATEGIES LLC
5000 Executive Pkwy # 420, San Ramon (94583-4344)
PHONE...............................925 659-0251
David Chazin, *Mng Member*
Anthony Ortole, *Ch Credit Ofcr*
Anthony Ortale, *Officer*
Kristine Slear, *Admin Asst*
Nate Hintz, *Info Tech Mgr*
EMP: 45 EST: 2002
SQ FT: 14,000
SALES (est): 5MM Privately Held
WEB: www.insight2wealth.com
SIC: **6282** **7389** Investment advisory service; financial services

(P-10050)
MORGAN STNLEY SMITH BARNEY LLC
650 Castro St, Mountain View (94041-2055)
PHONE...............................650 316-6788
Mitchell Baker, *Branch Mgr*
EMP: 158
SALES (corp-wide): 52B Publicly Held
WEB: www.morganstanley.com
SIC: **8299** **6282** Educational services; investment advice
HQ: Morgan Stanley Smith Barney, Llc
1585 Broadway
New York NY 10036

(P-10051)
MORGAN STNLEY SMITH BARNEY LLC
2421 Buhne St, Eureka (95501-3206)
PHONE...............................707 443-3071
Edward Vaccaro, *Branch Mgr*
EMP: 90
SALES (corp-wide): 52B Publicly Held
WEB: www.morganstanley.com
SIC: **6282** Investment advisory service
HQ: Morgan Stanley Smith Barney, Llc
1585 Broadway
New York NY 10036

(P-10052)
NATIONAL FINANCIAL SVCS LLC
44 Montgomery St Ste 1900, San Francisco (94104-4706)
PHONE...............................415 912-2805
Jay Penn, *Principal*
Jim Dunn, *Vice Pres*
Robert Evans, *Vice Pres*
Diane Jackson, *Vice Pres*
Samantha Miller, *Vice Pres*
EMP: 917
SALES (corp-wide): 4.3B Privately Held
WEB: www.mybrokerageinfo.com
SIC: **6282** Investment advisory service
HQ: National Financial Services Llc
200 Seaport Blvd Ste 630
Boston MA 02210
800 471-0382

(P-10053)
OSTERWEIS CAPITAL MGT INC
1 Maritime Plz Ste 800, San Francisco (94111-3421)
PHONE...............................415 434-4441
John Osterweis, *President*
Lisa R Campos, *Vice Pres*
Shawn Eubanks, *Vice Pres*
Shawn M Eubanks, *Vice Pres*
Nael Fakhry, *Vice Pres*
EMP: 40 EST: 1983
SALES (est): 15.2MM Privately Held
WEB: www.osterweis.com
SIC: **6282** Investment advisory service

(P-10054)
PARALLEL ADVISORS LLC
150 Spear St Ste 950, San Francisco (94105-5154)
PHONE...............................866 627-6984
Jerry E Rendic, *Mng Mgr*
Stacey Blalock, *Opers Mgr*
Jake Schutt,
Julianne Jeffrey, *Client Mgr*
Joan Schriger, *Director*
EMP: 51 EST: 2006
SALES (est): 11MM Privately Held
WEB: www.paralleladvisors.com
SIC: **6282** Investment advisory service

(P-10055)
PERMIRA ADVISERS LLC
3000 Sand Hill Rd 1-170, Menlo Park (94025-7162)
PHONE...............................650 681-4701
Richard Sanders, *Branch Mgr*
Mia Olsson, *Executive Asst*
Peter Flynn, *Finance Dir*
Denise Gallagher, *Marketing Mgr*
Nina Suter, *Corp Comm Staff*
EMP: 366
SALES (corp-wide): 136.9MM Privately Held
WEB: www.permira.com
SIC: **6282** Investment advisory service
HQ: Permira Advisers Llc
320 Park Ave Fl 28
New York NY 10022
212 386-7480

(P-10056)
PROGRESS INVESTMENT MGT CO LLC
33 New Montgomery St # 19, San Francisco (94105-4506)
PHONE...............................415 512-3480
Thurman White, *President*
Janice M Osugi, *President*
Beverly Pasley-Harrison, *COO*
Mona Williams, *Exec VP*

PRODUCTS & SERVICES SECTION
6311 - Life Insurance Carriers County (P-10078)

Chau Nguyen, *Senior VP*
EMP: 35 **EST:** 1989
SQ FT: 12,703
SALES: 12.7MM **Privately Held**
SIC: 6282 Investment advisory service

(P-10057)
R & S INVESTMENTS LLC
1 Bush St Fl 9, San Francisco
(94104-4415)
PHONE 415 591-2700
G Randy Hecht, *Mng Member*
Robert Bird, *Partner*
Job Rivera, *Partner*
John Casconi, *President*
Matthew Fessler, *President*
EMP: 71 **EST:** 2000
SALES (est): 2.5MM
SALES (corp-wide): 775.3MM **Publicly Held**
WEB: www.investor.vcm.com
SIC: 6282 Investment advisory service
HQ: Victory Capital Management Inc.
4900 Tiedeman Rd Fl 4
Brooklyn OH 44144

(P-10058)
RAYA6 INVESTMENTS INC (PA)
1860 The Alameda, San Jose
(95126-1781)
PHONE 408 529-1269
Bhupen Magan, *CEO*
EMP: 65 **EST:** 2014
SALES (est): 368.9K **Privately Held**
SIC: 6282 Investment advice

(P-10059)
SAGEPOINT FINANCIAL INC
903 W Center St, Manteca (95337-7315)
PHONE 209 825-8888
EMP: 54
SALES (corp-wide): 651.5MM **Privately Held**
WEB: www.sagepointfinancial.com
SIC: 6282 Investment advice
HQ: Sagepoint Financial, Inc.
20 E Thomas Rd Ste 2000
Phoenix AZ 85012

(P-10060)
STANFORD INVESTMENT GROUP
2570 W El Cmino Real Ste, Mountain View
(94040)
PHONE 650 941-1717
Lisa Barnea, *Manager*
John Kirkpatrick, *Advisor*
EMP: 37 **EST:** 2000
SALES (est): 1MM **Privately Held**
WEB: www.aspiriant.com
SIC: 6282 Investment advisory service

(P-10061)
STEIN ROE INV COUNSEL INC
Also Called: Atlantic Trust Wlfare Prvate M
3 Embarcadero Ctr # 1600, San Francisco
(94111-4019)
PHONE 415 433-5844
Adrian Morazcsik, *Manager*
EMP: 47
SALES (corp-wide): 6.1B **Publicly Held**
WEB: www.sric.net
SIC: 6282 Investment advisory service
HQ: Roe Stein Investment Counsel Inc
181 W Madison St Ste 3600
Chicago IL 60602
312 368-7800

(P-10062)
TARRANT CAPITAL IP LLC (PA)
Also Called: Tpg Growth
345 California St # 3300, San Francisco
(94104-2606)
PHONE 415 743-1500
Karl Peterson, *President*
Jena Stebly, *Partner*
Art Heidrich, *Vice Pres*
Steven Pluss, *Vice Pres*
Mike Tepatti, *Vice Pres*
EMP: 3659 **EST:** 2007

SALES (est): 1.3B **Privately Held**
WEB: www.tpg.com
SIC: 6282 7372 Manager of mutual funds, contract or fee basis; prepackaged software

(P-10063)
THETOS ADVISORS LLC
268 Bush St, San Francisco (94104-3503)
PHONE 415 917-0485
EMP: 35 **EST:** 2016
SALES (est): 1.6MM **Privately Held**
SIC: 6282 Investment advice

(P-10064)
TIEDEMANN INVESTMENT GROUP LLC
Also Called: Tiedemann Wealth Management
101 California St, San Francisco
(94111-5802)
PHONE 415 762-2541
Michael Yelverton, *Principal*
Erik Christoffersen, *Managing Dir*
EMP: 45 **Privately Held**
WEB: www.tigfunds.com
SIC: 6282 6726 6719 Investment advisory service; investment offices; management investment funds, closed-end; investment holding companies, except banks
PA: Tiedemann Investment Group, Llc
520 Madison Ave Ste 2600
New York NY 10022

(P-10065)
TRANSAMERICA CBO I INC
600 Montgomery St Fl 16, San Francisco
(94111-2718)
PHONE 415 983-4000
EMP: 64
SALES (est): 2.2MM **Privately Held**
SIC: 6282 Investment Advisor
HQ: Transamerica Corporation
4333 Edgewood Rd Ne
Cedar Rapids IA 52411
319 398-8511

(P-10066)
USCF ADVISERS LLC
1999 Harrison St Ste 1530, Oakland
(94612-4730)
PHONE 510 522-9600
Nicholas Gerber,
Kevin Baum, *Ch Invest Ofcr*
Stuart Crumbaugh, *Principal*
EMP: 259 **EST:** 2013
SALES (est): 10.9MM **Publicly Held**
WEB: www.uscfinvestments.com
SIC: 6282 Investment advisory service
HQ: Wainwright Holdings, Inc.
103 Foulk Rd Ste 202
Wilmington DE 19803
302 656-1950

(P-10067)
VISTA EQITY PRTNERS FUND VI LP (PA)
4 Embarcadero Ctr Lbby 2, San Francisco
(94111-4132)
PHONE 415 765-6500
John McMillian, *Partner*
Jocelyn Powers, *Partner*
Nate Thompson, *Vice Pres*
Erin Broughton, *Associate Dir*
Anna Connelly, *Associate Dir*
EMP: 40 **EST:** 2016
SALES (est): 551.4MM **Privately Held**
WEB: www.vistaequitypartners.com
SIC: 6282 Investment advice

(P-10068)
WEALTHFRONT CORPORATION
261 Hamilton Ave, Palo Alto (94301-2533)
PHONE 650 249-4258
Andrew Rachleff, *President*
Avery Moon, *President*
Rick Foreman, *CFO*
Daniel Carroll, *Officer*
Ashley F Johnson, *Officer*
EMP: 25 **EST:** 2009
SQ FT: 3,000

SALES (est): 10.6MM **Privately Held**
WEB: www.wealthfront.com
SIC: 6282 7372 Investment advisory service; prepackaged software; publishers' computer software

(P-10069)
WELLS CAPITAL MANAGEMENT INC (DH)
525 Market St Fl 10, San Francisco
(94105-2718)
PHONE 415 396-8000
Kirk Heartman, *President*
Thomas M Omalley, *Exec VP*
Lucia Cronin, *Vice Pres*
David Van Hecke, *Vice Pres*
John Boldrick, *Principal*
EMP: 261 **EST:** 1997
SQ FT: 20,000
SALES (est): 215.2MM
SALES (corp-wide): 80.3B **Publicly Held**
WEB: www.wellsfargoassetmanagement.com
SIC: 6282 Investment advisory service
HQ: Wells Fargo Bank, National Association
1301 N Cliff Ave
Sioux Falls SD 57103
605 575-6900

(P-10070)
WELLS FARGO ASSET MGT INTL LLC
525 Market St Fl 10, San Francisco
(94105-2718)
PHONE 415 396-8000
Anthony Norris, *CEO*
Peter Wilson, *Manager*
EMP: 100 **EST:** 1991
SALES (est): 10.6MM **Privately Held**
WEB: www.wellsfargoassetmanagement.com
SIC: 6282 Investment advisory service

(P-10071)
WENTWORTH HAUSER & VIOLICH INC
301 Battery St Fl 4, San Francisco
(94111-3237)
PHONE 415 981-6911
Steve Rhone, *CEO*
Judith Stevens, *President*
Earl Bell, *CFO*
Phillip Fox, *Exec VP*
George Springman, *CIO*
EMP: 78 **EST:** 1937
SQ FT: 14,000
SALES (est): 13.9MM **Privately Held**
WEB: www.violichcapital.com
SIC: 6282 Investment advisory service
PA: Laird Norton Investment Management, Inc.
801 2nd Ave Ste 1300
Seattle WA 98104

(P-10072)
WETHERBY ASSET MANAGEMENT
580 California St Fl 8, San Francisco
(94104-1029)
PHONE 415 399-9159
Debra L Wetherby, *President*
Chris Hauswirth, *COO*
Allan Jacobi, *CFO*
Steve Janowsky, *Principal*
Nichole Perry, *Office Mgr*
EMP: 55 **EST:** 1990
SALES (est): 19.1MM **Privately Held**
WEB: www.wetherby.com
SIC: 6282 Investment advisory service

(P-10073)
WHITE GAZELLE INC (PA)
1220 Melody Ln Ste 150, Roseville
(95678-5195)
PHONE 916 718-0601
Christopher Reid, *Principal*
Yuri Pinko, *Sales Staff*
EMP: 46 **EST:** 2014
SALES (est): 2.8MM **Privately Held**
WEB: www.gazelle.com
SIC: 6282 Investment advice

(P-10074)
XULU INC
Also Called: Futureadvisor
505 Howard St Fl 4, San Francisco
(94105-3222)
PHONE 800 975-7199
Bo Lu, *CEO*
Jon Xu, *CTO*
Rafik Robeal, *Engineer*
Kim Correia, *Director*
Anna Wolf, *Director*
EMP: 40 **EST:** 2010
SALES (est): 11.1MM **Publicly Held**
WEB: www.blackrock.com
SIC: 6282 Investment advisory service
PA: Blackrock, Inc.
55 E 52nd St
New York NY 10055

6311 Life Insurance Carriers

(P-10075)
ALTERRA SPCALTY INSUR SVCS LTD
201 California St, San Francisco
(94111-5002)
PHONE 415 490-4615
EMP: 61
SALES (corp-wide): 9.7B **Publicly Held**
SIC: 6311 Life insurance
HQ: Alterra Specialty Insurance Services Limited
9020 Stony Point Pkwy # 32
Richmond VA 23235

(P-10076)
ASSOCIATED INDEMNITY CORP
1465 N Mcdowell Blvd # 100, Petaluma
(94954-6569)
P.O. Box 970, O Fallon MO (63366-0970)
PHONE 415 899-2000
D Andrew Torrance, *Chairman*
Jill E Paterson, *CFO*
Linda E Wright, *Treasurer*
Cynthia L Pevehouse, *Senior VP*
Bradley Harris, *Director*
EMP: 242 **EST:** 1922
SQ FT: 240,000
SALES (est): 2MM
SALES (corp-wide): 26.4B **Privately Held**
SIC: 6311 6321 6331 6351 Life insurance carriers; accident insurance carriers; fire, marine & casualty insurance & carriers; surety insurance
HQ: Fireman's Fund Insurance Company
1 Progress Point Pkwy # 200
O Fallon MO 63368
415 899-2000

(P-10077)
BUILDERS & TRADESMENS INSUR
6610 Sierra College Blvd, Rocklin
(95677-4306)
PHONE 916 772-9200
Norbert Hohlbein, *Principal*
Matt Horton, *Assoc VP*
Jeff Erickson, *Vice Pres*
Kimberli Powers, *Assistant*
EMP: 43 **EST:** 2006
SALES (est): 31.7MM **Privately Held**
WEB: www.my.btisinc.com
SIC: 6311 Life insurance

(P-10078)
PATRA CORPORATION (PA)
1107 Inv Blvd Ste 100, El Dorado Hills
(95762)
PHONE 415 595-9987
Dan Easterlin, *President*
Bob Murphy, *Officer*
Tony LI, *CTO*
Chanel Hradecky, *Accounts Mgr*
Ellen Ostler, *Accounts Mgr*
EMP: 203 **EST:** 2007
SALES (est): 205.7MM **Privately Held**
WEB: www.patracorp.com
SIC: 6311 Life insurance

6311 - Life Insurance Carriers County (P-10079)

(P-10079)
TANNER COMPANIES LLC (PA)
4670 Willow Rd Ste 250, Pleasanton (94588-8589)
P.O. Box 9105 (94566-9104)
PHONE....................925 463-9672
Steven J Tanner,
Amanda Eisenagel, *Marketing Staff*
Ron Hernbroth, *Mng Member*
Patrick M Stroud, *Mng Member*
EMP: 145 EST: 2000
SALES (est): 734.9K **Privately Held**
SIC: **6311** 6324 6371 Life insurance; hospital & medical service plans; group hospitalization plans; dental insurance; pensions

(P-10080)
TRANSAMERICA FINANCE CORP (DH)
600 Montgomery St Fl 16, San Francisco (94111-2718)
PHONE....................415 983-4000
Robert A Watson, *Ch of Bd*
James L Schoedinger, *President*
Robert R McDuff, *Treasurer*
Keith Mason, *Ch Credit Ofcr*
Thomas G Bastian, *Senior VP*
EMP: 180 EST: 1931
SALES (est): 124.8MM
SALES (corp-wide): 270.8MM **Privately Held**
WEB: www.transamerica.com
SIC: **6311** Life insurance
HQ: Transamerica Corporation
4333 Edgewood Rd
Cedar Rapids IA 52411
319 398-8511

6321 Accident & Health Insurance

(P-10081)
ALLIANZ REINSURANCE AMER INC
1465 N Mcdowell Blvd, Petaluma (94954-6569)
PHONE....................415 899-2000
Joe Beneducci, *President*
Susan Stein, *Director*
EMP: 542 EST: 1956
SQ FT: 240,000
SALES (est): 82.6MM
SALES (corp-wide): 26.4B **Privately Held**
WEB: www.allianz.ru
SIC: **6321** Reinsurance carriers, accident & health
HQ: Fireman's Fund Insurance Company
1 Progress Point Pkwy # 200
O Fallon MO 63368
415 899-2000

(P-10082)
BETA HEALTHCARE GROUP (PA)
1443 Danville Blvd, Alamo (94507-1911)
PHONE....................925 838-6070
Tom Wander, *CEO*
Abiy Moges, *CFO*
Daniel J Sevilla Jr, *CFO*
Michael Willard, *CFO*
Heather Gocke, *Vice Pres*
EMP: 45 EST: 1989
SQ FT: 10,000
SALES (est): 26.8MM **Privately Held**
WEB: www.betahg.com
SIC: **6321** Accident & health insurance carriers

(P-10083)
CAPITOL ADMINISTRATORS INC
10951 White Rock Rd # 100, Rancho Cordova (95670-6366)
PHONE....................916 669-2463
David Reynolds, *President*
David Yee, *CFO*
Connie Leier, *Analyst*
Ginger Regotti, *Director*
Mildred Hemmatijou, *Manager*
EMP: 35 EST: 1997

SALES (est): 11.3MM **Privately Held**
WEB: www.lucenthealth.com
SIC: **6321** 6411 Indemnity plans health insurance, except medical service; insurance agents, brokers & service

(P-10084)
DOCTORS COMPANY FOUNDATION
185 Greenwood Rd, NAPA (94558-7540)
PHONE....................800 421-2368
Richard E Anderson, *CEO*
Dave McHale, *Officer*
Devin O 'brien, *Vice Pres*
Brian Dalton, *VP Bus Dvlpt*
Adam Russell, *Analyst*
EMP: 755
SALES (est): 329.7MM **Privately Held**
WEB: www.thedoctors.com
SIC: **6321** Health insurance carriers

(P-10085)
HEALTHPOCKET INC
444 Castro St Ste 710, Mountain View (94041-2080)
PHONE....................800 984-8015
Bruce Telkamp, *CEO*
Julia Bringans, *Partner*
Sheldon Wang, *President*
Steve Zaleznick, *Exec Dir*
Michael Bass, *Technology*
EMP: 123 EST: 2012
SALES (est): 14.5MM
SALES (corp-wide): 381.8MM **Privately Held**
WEB: www.healthpocket.com
SIC: **6321** Health insurance carriers
PA: Benefytt Technologies, Inc.
15438 N Florida Ave # 201
Tampa FL 33613
877 376-5831

(P-10086)
SANTA CLARA COUNTY HEALTH AUTH
210 E Hacienda Ave, Campbell (95008-6617)
PHONE....................408 376-2000
Pamela Collier Bowman, *Director*
Gloria Ramirez, *Technology*
EMP: 40 EST: 2000
SALES (est): 17.3MM **Privately Held**
WEB: www.scfhp.com
SIC: **6321** Assessment associations, accident & health insurance

(P-10087)
SANTE HEALTH SYSTEM INC (PA)
Also Called: Sante Community Physicians
7370 N Palm Ave Ste 101, Fresno (93711-5782)
P.O. Box 1507 (93716-1507)
PHONE....................559 228-5400
Mateo F Desoto, *CEO*
Scott Wells, *President*
Juan Muro, *COO*
Chris Cheney, *Officer*
Wesley Qualls, *Officer*
EMP: 123 EST: 1994
SQ FT: 20,000
SALES (est): 171.9MM **Privately Held**
WEB: www.live5010.santehealth.net
SIC: **6321** 7371 Accident & health insurance; computer software development & applications

(P-10088)
WESTERN HEALTH ADVANTAGE
2349 Gateway Oaks Dr # 100, Sacramento (95833-4244)
PHONE....................916 567-1950
Garry Maisel, *President*
Rita Ruecker, *Treasurer*
Jeff Cinciarelli, *Officer*
Irene Sandoval, *Executive Asst*
David Walker, *Admin Asst*
EMP: 100 EST: 1995
SQ FT: 25,000
SALES (est): 726MM **Privately Held**
WEB: www.westernhealth.com
SIC: **6321** Health insurance carriers

6324 Hospital & Medical Svc Plans Carriers

(P-10089)
AETNA HEALTH CALIFORNIA INC (DH)
1401 Willow Pass Rd # 600, Concord (94520-7927)
PHONE....................925 543-9223
Kristen Ann Miranda, *CEO*
Tracy Louis Smith, *CFO*
Rick M Jelinek, *Exec VP*
Janet How, *Vice Pres*
Johnetta Semper, *Vice Pres*
EMP: 198 EST: 1979
SALES (est): 300.2MM
SALES (corp-wide): 268.7B **Publicly Held**
WEB: www.aetna.com
SIC: **6324** Health maintenance organization (HMO), insurance only

(P-10090)
ALAMEDA ALLIANCE FOR HEALTH
1240 S Loop Rd, Alameda (94502-7084)
PHONE....................510 747-4555
Ingrid Lamirault, *CEO*
Charles Nelson, *Surgery Dir*
Jamie Gavarrete, *Executive Asst*
Monica Tackitt, *Executive Asst*
Lemuel Francois, *Admin Asst*
EMP: 135 EST: 1993
SQ FT: 50,000
SALES (est): 86.8MM **Privately Held**
WEB: www.alamedaalliance.org
SIC: **6324** Health maintenance organization (HMO), insurance only

(P-10091)
ANTHEM INSURANCE COMPANIES INC
5260 N Palm Ave Ste 215, Fresno (93704-2216)
PHONE....................559 230-6200
EMP: 275
SALES (corp-wide): 121.8B **Publicly Held**
WEB: www.anthem.com
SIC: **6324** Hospital & medical service plans
HQ: Anthem Insurance Companies, Inc.
220 Virginia Ave
Indianapolis IN 46204
317 488-6000

(P-10092)
ANTHEM INSURANCE COMPANIES INC
2 Embarcadero Ctr # 1310, San Francisco (94111-3823)
PHONE....................415 617-1700
Deepa Jebaraj, *Master*
Natalie Chung, *Sr Consultant*
Sudha Jayachandran, *Director*
Sandra Sears, *Director*
Lonnie Wong, *Director*
EMP: 275
SALES (corp-wide): 121.8B **Publicly Held**
WEB: www.anthem.com
SIC: **6324** Hospital & medical service plans
HQ: Anthem Insurance Companies, Inc.
220 Virginia Ave
Indianapolis IN 46204
317 488-6000

(P-10093)
BLUE SHIELD CAL LF HLTH INSUR
4005 Manzanita Ave Ste 6, Carmichael (95608-1779)
P.O. Box 629015, El Dorado Hills (95762-9015)
PHONE....................800 660-3007
EMP: 1135
SALES (corp-wide): 17.6B **Privately Held**
WEB: www.blueshieldca.com
SIC: **6324** Hospital & medical service plans
HQ: Blue Shield Of California Life & Health Insurance Co
50 Beale St Ste 2000
San Francisco CA 94105
415 229-5000

(P-10094)
CALIFORNIA PHYSICIANS SERVICE
Also Called: Blue Sheild of California
2066 Camel Ln Apt 24, Walnut Creek (94596-5955)
PHONE....................925 927-7419
John Durst, *Branch Mgr*
EMP: 98
SALES (corp-wide): 17.6B **Privately Held**
WEB: www.blueshieldca.com
SIC: **6324** Hospital & medical service plans
PA: California Physicians' Service
601 12th St
Oakland CA 94607
510 607-2000

(P-10095)
CALIFORNIA PHYSICIANS SERVICE
6300 Canoga Ave, Woodland (95695)
PHONE....................530 668-2986
EMP: 98
SALES (corp-wide): 17.6B **Privately Held**
WEB: www.blueshieldca.com
SIC: **6324** Hospital & medical service plans
PA: California Physicians' Service
601 12th St
Oakland CA 94607
510 607-2000

(P-10096)
CALIFORNIA PHYSICIANS SERVICE (PA)
Also Called: Blue Shield of California
601 12th St, Oakland (94607-3885)
P.O. Box 272540, Chico (95927-2540)
PHONE....................510 607-2000
Paul Markovich, *President*
Karen Vigil, *CEO*
Sandra Clarke, *CFO*
Jeffrey Robertson, *Chief Mktg Ofcr*
Mary O 'hara, *Officer*
EMP: 900 EST: 1939
SQ FT: 120,000
SALES (est): 17.6B **Privately Held**
WEB: www.blueshieldca.com
SIC: **6324** Hospital & medical service plans

(P-10097)
CALIFORNIA PHYSICIANS SERVICE
4700 Bechelli Ln, Redding (96002-3506)
PHONE....................530 351-6115
EMP: 98
SALES (corp-wide): 17.6B **Privately Held**
WEB: www.blueshieldca.com
SIC: **6324** Hospital & medical service plans
PA: California Physicians' Service
601 12th St
Oakland CA 94607
510 607-2000

(P-10098)
CALIFORNIA PHYSICIANS SERVICE
Also Called: Blue Shield of California
1915 Laurel St, NAPA (94559-3225)
PHONE....................949 859-6303
Nancy Gyles, *Branch Mgr*
Liz Schrette, *Engineer*
EMP: 98
SALES (corp-wide): 17.6B **Privately Held**
WEB: www.blueshieldca.com
SIC: **6324** Hospital & medical service plans
PA: California Physicians' Service
601 12th St
Oakland CA 94607
510 607-2000

(P-10099)
CALIFORNIA PHYSICIANS SERVICE
Also Called: Blue Shield of California
10834 International Dr, Rancho Cordova (95670-7364)
PHONE....................916 350-7730
EMP: 98
SALES (corp-wide): 17.6B **Privately Held**
WEB: www.blueshieldca.com
SIC: **6324** Hospital & medical service plans

PRODUCTS & SERVICES SECTION
6324 - Hospital & Medical Svc Plans Carriers County (P-10120)

PA: California Physicians' Service
601 12th St
Oakland CA 94607
510 607-2000

(P-10100)
CALIFORNIA PHYSICIANS SERVICE
Also Called: Blue Shield of California
5250 N Palm Ave Ste 120, Fresno
(93704-2200)
PHONE..................559 440-4000
Mark Turley, *Director*
EMP: 98
SALES (corp-wide): 17.6B **Privately Held**
WEB: www.blueshieldca.com
SIC: 6324 Hospital & medical service plans
PA: California Physicians' Service
601 12th St
Oakland CA 94607
510 607-2000

(P-10101)
CENTENE CORPORATION
12033 Foundation Pl, Gold River
(95670-4502)
PHONE..................314 505-6689
Brandon Wilmesherr, *Technology*
Matthew Lew, *Engineer*
Randy Strebe, *Manager*
Ludi Zarick, *Manager*
EMP: 46 **Publicly Held**
WEB: www.centene.com
SIC: 6324 Hospital & medical service plans
PA: Centene Corporation
7700 Forsyth Blvd Ste 800
Saint Louis MO 63105

(P-10102)
CENTER FOR ELDERS INDEPENDENCE
Also Called: C E I
510 17th St Ste 400, Oakland
(94612-1570)
PHONE..................510 433-1150
Peter Szutu, *President*
EMP: 225 **EST:** 1981
SALES: 86.3MM **Privately Held**
WEB: www.cei.elders.org
SIC: 6324 Hospital & medical service plans

(P-10103)
DELTA DENTAL OF CALIFORNIA (PA)
560 Mission St Ste 1300, San Francisco
(94105-0938)
PHONE..................415 972-8300
Mike Castro, *President*
Miranda Horton, *Partner*
Jackie Kortz, *President*
Nilesh Patel, *COO*
Alicia Weber, *Acting CFO*
EMP: 487 **EST:** 1955
SQ FT: 241,000
SALES (est): 5.8B **Privately Held**
WEB: www.deltadentalins.com
SIC: 6324 Dental insurance

(P-10104)
DELTA DENTAL OF CALIFORNIA
Also Called: Delta Dental Plan
11155 International Dr, Sacramento
(95826)
PHONE..................916 853-7373
Dick Aracich, *Vice Pres*
Thomas Baltis, *Vice Pres*
Melissa Fullerton, *Vice Pres*
Joe Ruiz, *Vice Pres*
Roy Bybee, *Administration*
EMP: 48
SALES (corp-wide): 5.8B **Privately Held**
WEB: www.deltadental.com
SIC: 6324 Dental insurance
PA: Delta Dental Of California
560 Mission St Ste 1300
San Francisco CA 94105
415 972-8300

(P-10105)
DELTA DENTAL OF CALIFORNIA
7801 Folsom Blvd, Sacramento
(95826-2600)
PHONE..................916 381-4054
EMP: 48

SALES (corp-wide): 5.8B **Privately Held**
WEB: www.deltadental.com
SIC: 6324 Dental insurance
PA: Delta Dental Of California
560 Mission St Ste 1300
San Francisco CA 94105
415 972-8300

(P-10106)
HEALTH NET FEDERAL SVCS LLC (DH)
10730 International Dr, Rancho Cordova
(95670-7359)
P.O. Box 2890 (95741-2890)
PHONE..................916 935-5000
Thomas F Carrato, *President*
David Thomas, *Exec VP*
Kathy Fielding, *Vice Pres*
Fidel Ligsay, *Vice Pres*
Barbara Taylor, *Admin Sec*
EMP: 700 **EST:** 1989
SQ FT: 100,000
SALES (est): 536.4MM **Publicly Held**
WEB: www.healthnetfederalservices.com
SIC: 6324 Hospital & medical service plans
HQ: Health Net Of California, Inc.
7700 Forsyth Blvd
Saint Louis MO 63105
818 676-6775

(P-10107)
HEALTH NET PHARMACEUTICAL SVCS
2868 Prospect Park Dr, Rancho Cordova
(95670-6020)
PHONE..................800 977-7532
EMP: 232 **EST:** 2019
SALES (est): 18.2MM **Publicly Held**
WEB: www.healthnet.com
SIC: 6324 Hospital & medical service plans
PA: Centene Corporation
7700 Forsyth Blvd Ste 800
Saint Louis MO 63105

(P-10108)
HEALTH PLAN OF SAN JOAQUIN
7751 S Manthey Rd, French Camp
(95231-9802)
PHONE..................209 942-6300
Michael Schrader, *CEO*
Lakshmi Dhanvanthari, *Chief Mktg Ofcr*
Evert Hendrix, *Officer*
Nancy Raymond, *Officer*
Marc Radner, *Vice Pres*
EMP: 120 **EST:** 1994
SALES (est): 97.6MM **Privately Held**
WEB: www.hpsj.com
SIC: 6324 Health maintenance organization (HMO), insurance only

(P-10109)
KAISER FOUNDATION HOSPITALS
Also Called: Kaiser Foundation Health Plan
30116 Eigenbrodt Way, Union City
(94587-1225)
PHONE..................510 675-5777
Colleen McKeown, *Manager*
EMP: 104
SALES (corp-wide): 30.5B **Privately Held**
WEB: www.healthy.kaiserpermanente.org
SIC: 6324 Hospital & medical service plans
HQ: Kaiser Foundation Hospitals Inc
1 Kaiser Plz
Oakland CA 94612
510 271-6611

(P-10110)
KAISER FOUNDATION HOSPITALS
4785 N 1st St Fl 2, Fresno (93726-0513)
PHONE..................559 448-4620
Sung Jun, *Admin Asst*
Patrick Cloney, *Administration*
Michelle Olson, *Psychologist*
Wilson Chen, *Pediatrics*
Kamlesh K Sandhu, *Psychiatry*
EMP: 104
SALES (corp-wide): 30.5B **Privately Held**
WEB: www.kaisercenter.com
SIC: 6324 Hospital & medical service plans

HQ: Kaiser Foundation Hospitals Inc
1 Kaiser Plz
Oakland CA 94612
510 271-6611

(P-10111)
KAISER FOUNDATION HOSPITALS
Also Called: Kaiser Foundation Health Plan
9201 Big Horn Blvd, Elk Grove
(95758-1240)
PHONE..................916 478-5000
Calvin Tong-Fong, *Manager*
Brian Grabert, *Project Mgr*
Susan Y Wong, *Persnl Dir*
Katherine A Ceske, *Psychologist*
Mandy Cheung, *Pediatrics*
EMP: 104
SALES (corp-wide): 30.5B **Privately Held**
WEB: www.healthy.kaiserpermanente.org
SIC: 6324 Hospital & medical service plans
HQ: Kaiser Foundation Hospitals Inc
1 Kaiser Plz
Oakland CA 94612
510 271-6611

(P-10112)
KAISER FOUNDATION HOSPITALS
Also Called: Kaiser Foundation Health Plan
1761 Broadway St Ste 210, Vallejo
(94589-2227)
PHONE..................707 645-2720
Cynthia Chandler, *Director*
John Williams, *Vice Pres*
Odesser Maxie, *Prgrmr*
Gail Fahey,
EMP: 104
SALES (corp-wide): 30.5B **Privately Held**
WEB: www.healthy.kaiserpermanente.org
SIC: 6324 Hospital & medical service plans
HQ: Kaiser Foundation Hospitals Inc
1 Kaiser Plz
Oakland CA 94612
510 271-6611

(P-10113)
KAISER FOUNDATION HOSPITALS
Also Called: Kaiser Foundation Health Plan
820 Las Gallinas Ave, San Rafael
(94903-3410)
PHONE..................415 444-3522
Bob Johnson, *Branch Mgr*
Christine Hom, *Psychologist*
Haleh Kashani, *Psychologist*
John M Maas, *Psychologist*
EMP: 104
SALES (corp-wide): 30.5B **Privately Held**
WEB: www.healthy.kaiserpermanente.org
SIC: 6324 Hospital & medical service plans
HQ: Kaiser Foundation Hospitals Inc
1 Kaiser Plz
Oakland CA 94612
510 271-6611

(P-10114)
KAISER FOUNDATION HOSPITALS
Also Called: Kaiser Foundation Health Plan
255 W Macarthur Blvd, Oakland
(94611-5641)
PHONE..................510 752-7864
Albert Carver, *Branch Mgr*
EMP: 104
SALES (corp-wide): 30.5B **Privately Held**
WEB: www.healthy.kaiserpermanente.org
SIC: 6324 Hospital & medical service plans
HQ: Kaiser Foundation Hospitals Inc
1 Kaiser Plz
Oakland CA 94612
510 271-6611

(P-10115)
KAISER FOUNDATION HOSPITALS
Also Called: Kaiser Foundation Health Plan
4785 N 1st St, Fresno (93726-0513)
PHONE..................559 448-4555
Carolina Simunovic, *Dermatology*
Posada Carlos, *Pharmacist*
Trina Reilly, *Manager*
Bette Greer, *Assistant*
EMP: 104

SALES (corp-wide): 30.5B **Privately Held**
WEB: www.healthy.kaiserpermanente.org
SIC: 6324 Hospital & medical service plans
HQ: Kaiser Foundation Hospitals Inc
1 Kaiser Plz
Oakland CA 94612
510 271-6611

(P-10116)
KAISER FOUNDATION HOSPITALS
Also Called: Kaiser Foundation Health Plan
10305 Promenade Pkwy, Elk Grove
(95757-9400)
PHONE..................916 544-6000
Yewondwossen Kassa, *Family Practiti*
Jose Sumaquial, *Family Practiti*
Maninderjit Atwal, *Obstetrician*
EMP: 104
SALES (corp-wide): 30.5B **Privately Held**
WEB: www.healthy.kaiserpermanente.org
SIC: 6324 Hospital & medical service plans
HQ: Kaiser Foundation Hospitals Inc
1 Kaiser Plz
Oakland CA 94612
510 271-6611

(P-10117)
KAISER FOUNDATION HOSPITALS
Also Called: Kaiser Foundation Health Plan
27303 Sleepy Hollow Ave S, Hayward
(94545-4203)
PHONE..................510 454-1000
EMP: 85
SALES (corp-wide): 15.7B **Privately Held**
SIC: 6324 Hospital/Medical Service Plan
HQ: Kaiser Foundation Hospitals Inc
1 Kaiser Plz
Oakland CA 94612
510 271-6611

(P-10118)
KAISER FOUNDATION HOSPITALS
Also Called: San Ramon Medical Offices
2300 Camino Ramon, San Ramon
(94583-1354)
PHONE..................925 244-7600
Kathryn Mar, *Family Practiti*
Benedict Buenviaje, *Internal Med*
Kai Kai Lam, *Pediatrics*
EMP: 104
SALES (corp-wide): 30.5B **Privately Held**
WEB: www.kaisercenter.com
SIC: 6324 Hospital & medical service plans
HQ: Kaiser Foundation Hospitals Inc
1 Kaiser Plz
Oakland CA 94612
510 271-6611

(P-10119)
KAISER FOUNDATION HOSPITALS
Also Called: Kaiser Foundation Health Plan
975 Sereno Dr, Vallejo (94589-2441)
PHONE..................707 651-2311
Steve Allen, *Director*
Maung Myint, *Med Doctor*
EMP: 104
SALES (corp-wide): 30.5B **Privately Held**
WEB: www.healthy.kaiserpermanente.org
SIC: 6324 Hospital & medical service plans
HQ: Kaiser Foundation Hospitals Inc
1 Kaiser Plz
Oakland CA 94612
510 271-6611

(P-10120)
KAISER FOUNDATION HOSPITALS
Also Called: Vaxaville Medical Offices
1 Quality Dr, Vacaville (95688-9494)
PHONE..................707 624-4000
Murty Savitala, *Principal*
Adriana Weyandt, *Manager*
EMP: 104
SALES (corp-wide): 30.5B **Privately Held**
WEB: www.kaisercenter.com
SIC: 6324 Hospital & medical service plans
HQ: Kaiser Foundation Hospitals Inc
1 Kaiser Plz
Oakland CA 94612
510 271-6611

(PA)=Parent Co (HQ)=Headquarters (DH)=Div Headquarters
✪ = New Business established in last 2 years

6324 - Hospital & Medical Svc Plans Carriers County (P-10121)

(P-10121)
KAISER FOUNDATION HOSPITALS
Also Called: Kaiser Permanente
1795 2nd St, Berkeley (94710-1704)
PHONE..................510 559-5362
David Newkom, *Director*
Lindsay Williams, *Executive Asst*
David Delahoussaye, *Engineer*
Sarah Singleton, *Financial Analy*
Bejan Adly, *Supervisor*
EMP: 104
SALES (corp-wide): 30.5B **Privately Held**
WEB: www.kaisercenter.com
SIC: **6324** Health maintenance organization (HMO), insurance only
HQ: Kaiser Foundation Hospitals Inc
    1 Kaiser Plz
    Oakland CA 94612
    510 271-6611

(P-10122)
KAISER FOUNDATION HOSPITALS
Also Called: Kaiser Permanente Division RES
2000 Brdwy, Oakland (94612)
PHONE..................510 891-3400
Joe Shelby MD, *Director*
Leslie Litton, *Vice Pres*
Michelle Taylor, *Administration*
Viviana Stewart, *Planning*
Victoria Peckham, *Business Anlyst*
EMP: 104
SQ FT: 86,875
SALES (corp-wide): 30.5B **Privately Held**
WEB: www.kaisercenter.com
SIC: **6324** Hospital & medical service plans
HQ: Kaiser Foundation Hospitals Inc
    1 Kaiser Plz
    Oakland CA 94612
    510 271-6611

(P-10123)
KAISER FOUNDATION HOSPITALS
Also Called: Kaiser Foundation Health Plan
25 N Via Monte, Walnut Creek (94598-2510)
PHONE..................925 926-3000
Phil Newbold, *Principal*
Cynthia Boucher, *Vice Pres*
Kim Wood, *Project Mgr*
Mike Dachuk, *Technology*
Jitesh Mistry, *Engineer*
EMP: 70
SQ FT: 79,360
SALES (corp-wide): 30.5B **Privately Held**
WEB: www.healthy.kaiserpermanente.org
SIC: **6324** Hospital & medical service plans
HQ: Kaiser Foundation Hospitals Inc
    1 Kaiser Plz
    Oakland CA 94612
    510 271-6611

(P-10124)
KAISER FOUNDATION HOSPITALS
Also Called: Kaiser Foundation Health Plan
2071 Herndon Ave, Clovis (93611-6101)
PHONE..................559 324-5100
Angela H Kuo, *Med Doctor*
Wendy Gospodnetich, *Education*
Christiane George, *Family Practiti*
Rozanne Hug, *Family Practiti*
Toussaint Streat, *Family Practiti*
EMP: 104
SQ FT: 67,465
SALES (corp-wide): 30.5B **Privately Held**
WEB: www.healthy.kaiserpermanente.org
SIC: **6324** Hospital & medical service plans
HQ: Kaiser Foundation Hospitals Inc
    1 Kaiser Plz
    Oakland CA 94612
    510 271-6611

(P-10125)
KAISER FOUNDATION HOSPITALS
Also Called: Kaiser Foundation Health Plan
1840 Sierra Gardens Dr, Roseville (95661-2912)
PHONE..................916 784-4050
Don Vu, *Principal*
Joyce Lippe, *Pediatrics*
EMP: 104
SQ FT: 102,150
SALES (corp-wide): 30.5B **Privately Held**
WEB: www.healthy.kaiserpermanente.org
SIC: **6324** Hospital & medical service plans
HQ: Kaiser Foundation Hospitals Inc
    1 Kaiser Plz
    Oakland CA 94612
    510 271-6611

(P-10126)
KAISER FOUNDATION HOSPITALS
Also Called: Kaiser Foundation Health Plan
1033 3rd St, San Rafael (94901-3107)
PHONE..................415 482-6800
Mary Molander, *Branch Mgr*
EMP: 104
SALES (corp-wide): 30.5B **Privately Held**
WEB: www.healthy.kaiserpermanente.org
SIC: **6324** Hospital & medical service plans
HQ: Kaiser Foundation Hospitals Inc
    1 Kaiser Plz
    Oakland CA 94612
    510 271-6611

(P-10127)
KAISER FOUNDATION HOSPITALS
Also Called: Kaiser Foundation Health Plan
40595 Westlake Dr, Oakhurst (93644-9024)
PHONE..................559 658-8388
CHI Ly, *Principal*
EMP: 104
SALES (corp-wide): 30.5B **Privately Held**
WEB: www.healthy.kaiserpermanente.org
SIC: **6324** Hospital & medical service plans
HQ: Kaiser Foundation Hospitals Inc
    1 Kaiser Plz
    Oakland CA 94612
    510 271-6611

(P-10128)
KAISER FOUNDATION HOSPITALS
Also Called: Kaiser Foundation Health Plan
395 Hickey Blvd, Daly City (94015-2770)
PHONE..................650 301-5860
Arthur Chin, *Principal*
Elena Torello, *Internal Med*
Antonio Laranjo, *Nurse*
Samuel N Fallejo,
EMP: 104
SALES (corp-wide): 30.5B **Privately Held**
WEB: www.healthy.kaiserpermanente.org
SIC: **6324** Hospital & medical service plans
HQ: Kaiser Foundation Hospitals Inc
    1 Kaiser Plz
    Oakland CA 94612
    510 271-6611

(P-10129)
KAISER FOUNDATION HOSPITALS
Also Called: Kaiser Foundation Health Plan
3553 Whipple Rd, Union City (94587-1507)
PHONE..................510 675-2170
Mani Kammula, *Principal*
EMP: 104
SALES (corp-wide): 30.5B **Privately Held**
WEB: www.healthy.kaiserpermanente.org
SIC: **6324** Hospital & medical service plans
HQ: Kaiser Foundation Hospitals Inc
    1 Kaiser Plz
    Oakland CA 94612
    510 271-6611

(P-10130)
KAISER FOUNDATION HOSPITALS
Also Called: Kaiser Foundation Health Plan
2417 Naglee Rd, Tracy (95304-7324)
PHONE..................209 832-6339
EMP: 104
SALES (corp-wide): 30.5B **Privately Held**
WEB: www.healthy.kaiserpermanente.org
SIC: **6324** Hospital & medical service plans
HQ: Kaiser Foundation Hospitals Inc
    1 Kaiser Plz
    Oakland CA 94612
    510 271-6611

(P-10131)
KAISER FOUNDATION HOSPITALS
Also Called: Kaiser Foundation Health Plan
901 El Camino Real, San Bruno (94066-3009)
PHONE..................650 742-2100
Allen Wu, *Principal*
EMP: 104
SALES (corp-wide): 30.5B **Privately Held**
WEB: www.healthy.kaiserpermanente.org
SIC: **6324** Hospital & medical service plans
HQ: Kaiser Foundation Hospitals Inc
    1 Kaiser Plz
    Oakland CA 94612
    510 271-6611

(P-10132)
KAISER FOUNDATION HOSPITALS
Also Called: Kaiser Foundation Health Plan
3554 Round Barn Blvd, Santa Rosa (95403-0929)
PHONE..................707 571-3835
Jay Kelley, *Manager*
EMP: 104
SALES (corp-wide): 30.5B **Privately Held**
WEB: www.healthy.kaiserpermanente.org
SIC: **6324** Hospital & medical service plans
HQ: Kaiser Foundation Hospitals Inc
    1 Kaiser Plz
    Oakland CA 94612
    510 271-6611

(P-10133)
KAISER FOUNDATION HOSPITALS
Also Called: Kaiser Foundation Health Plan
3925 Old Redwood Hwy, Santa Rosa (95403-1719)
PHONE..................707 393-4033
Clay Wheeler, *Principal*
EMP: 104
SALES (corp-wide): 30.5B **Privately Held**
WEB: www.healthy.kaiserpermanente.org
SIC: **6324** Hospital & medical service plans
HQ: Kaiser Foundation Hospitals Inc
    1 Kaiser Plz
    Oakland CA 94612
    510 271-6611

(P-10134)
KAISER FOUNDATION HOSPITALS
Also Called: Kaiser Foundation Health Plan
1320 Standiford Ave, Modesto (95350-0726)
PHONE..................855 268-4096
Anita Vohra, *Principal*
EMP: 104
SALES (corp-wide): 30.5B **Privately Held**
WEB: www.healthy.kaiserpermanente.org
SIC: **6324** Hospital & medical service plans
HQ: Kaiser Foundation Hospitals Inc
    1 Kaiser Plz
    Oakland CA 94612
    510 271-6611

(P-10135)
KAISER FOUNDATION HOSPITALS
Also Called: Kaiser Foundation Health Plan
5900 State Farm Dr # 100, Rohnert Park (94928-2149)
PHONE..................707 206-3000
Noel Smith, *Branch Mgr*
Hana Clark, *Family Practiti*
Judith Heiler, *Family Practiti*
EMP: 104
SALES (corp-wide): 30.5B **Privately Held**
WEB: www.healthy.kaiserpermanente.org
SIC: **6324** Hospital & medical service plans
HQ: Kaiser Foundation Hospitals Inc
    1 Kaiser Plz
    Oakland CA 94612
    510 271-6611

(P-10136)
KAISER FOUNDATION HOSPITALS
Also Called: Kaiser Foundation Health Plan
969 Broadway, Oakland (94607-4017)
PHONE..................510 251-0121
Mary Sage, *Branch Mgr*
EMP: 104
SALES (corp-wide): 30.5B **Privately Held**
WEB: www.healthy.kaiserpermanente.org
SIC: **6324** Hospital & medical service plans
HQ: Kaiser Foundation Hospitals Inc
    1 Kaiser Plz
    Oakland CA 94612
    510 271-6611

(P-10137)
KAISER FOUNDATION HOSPITALS
Also Called: Kaiser Foundation Health Plan
2651 Highland Ave, Selma (93662-3392)
PHONE..................559 898-6000
Hong-Hanh Ton-Nu, *Principal*
EMP: 104
SQ FT: 37,081
SALES (corp-wide): 30.5B **Privately Held**
WEB: www.healthy.kaiserpermanente.org
SIC: **6324** Hospital & medical service plans
HQ: Kaiser Foundation Hospitals Inc
    1 Kaiser Plz
    Oakland CA 94612
    510 271-6611

(P-10138)
KAISER FOUNDATION HOSPITALS
Also Called: Kaiser Prmnnte Manteca Med Ctr
1777 W Yosemite Ave, Manteca (95337-5187)
PHONE..................209 825-3700
Anita Kennedy, *COO*
Corwin Harper, *Officer*
Lisa Dasko, *Controller*
Poonam Arora, *Family Practiti*
Noel Libuit, *Pathologist*
EMP: 104
SALES (corp-wide): 30.5B **Privately Held**
WEB: www.kaisercenter.com
SIC: **6324** Hospital & medical service plans
HQ: Kaiser Foundation Hospitals Inc
    1 Kaiser Plz
    Oakland CA 94612
    510 271-6611

(P-10139)
KAISER FOUNDATION HOSPITALS
Also Called: Kaiser Foundation Health Plan
2345 Fair Oaks Blvd, Sacramento (95825-4708)
PHONE..................916 973-5000
Jerry Newman, *Manager*
Natalie Bastiao, *Technician*
Ruby Chan, *Family Practiti*
Kimberly Laurenson, *Family Practiti*
SA Vang, *Family Practiti*
EMP: 104
SALES (corp-wide): 30.5B **Privately Held**
WEB: www.healthy.kaiserpermanente.org
SIC: **6324** Hospital & medical service plans
HQ: Kaiser Foundation Hospitals Inc
    1 Kaiser Plz
    Oakland CA 94612
    510 271-6611

(P-10140)
KAISER FOUNDATION HOSPITALS
Also Called: Kaiser Foundation Health Plan
5755 Cottle Rd, San Jose (95123-3640)
PHONE..................408 972-3376
Donald D Mordecai, *Branch Mgr*
Joseph Rico, *Buyer*
Kathleen Bonal, *Psychologist*
Lev Basin, *Psychiatry*
Kavitha Raja, *Psychiatry*
EMP: 104
SALES (corp-wide): 30.5B **Privately Held**
WEB: www.healthy.kaiserpermanente.org
SIC: **6324** 8011 6321 Hospital & medical service plans; offices & clinics of medical doctors; accident & health insurance
HQ: Kaiser Foundation Hospitals Inc
    1 Kaiser Plz
    Oakland CA 94612
    510 271-6611

PRODUCTS & SERVICES SECTION
6324 - Hospital & Medical Svc Plans Carriers County (P-10159)

(P-10141)
KAISER FOUNDATION HOSPITALS
Also Called: Kaiser Foundation Health Plan
7520 Arroyo Cir, Gilroy (95020-7303)
PHONE..................408 848-4600
Gary Zuselt, *Branch Mgr*
Robert Levan, *Family Practiti*
Tenagne Mekbeb, *Family Practiti*
Van Thai, *Family Practiti*
Ton Hoang, *Internal Med*
EMP: 104
SQ FT: 62,360
SALES (corp-wide): 30.5B **Privately Held**
WEB: www.healthy.kaiserpermanente.org
SIC: 6324 Hospital & medical service plans
HQ: Kaiser Foundation Hospitals Inc
1 Kaiser Plz
Oakland CA 94612
510 271-6611

(P-10142)
KAISER FOUNDATION HOSPITALS
Also Called: Kaiser Foundation Health Plan
7300 N Fresno St, Fresno (93720-2941)
PHONE..................559 448-4500
Jeffrey Collins, *Manager*
Karen Strauman, *Executive*
Domenic Previte, *Radiology Dir*
Scott Shimamoto, *Business Dir*
Michael Baldi, *Program Mgr*
EMP: 104
SALES (corp-wide): 30.5B **Privately Held**
WEB: www.healthy.kaiserpermanente.org
SIC: 6324 Hospital & medical service plans
HQ: Kaiser Foundation Hospitals Inc
1 Kaiser Plz
Oakland CA 94612
510 271-6611

(P-10143)
KAISER FOUNDATION HOSPITALS
Also Called: Kaiser Foundation Health Plan
1625 I St, Modesto (95354-1121)
P.O. Box 577680 (95357-7680)
PHONE..................209 557-1000
Larry Stump, *Director*
James Redula, *CIO*
Jennifer Razo, *Opers Staff*
Christina Hill, *Sales Associate*
Amardeep S Deol, *Obstetrician*
EMP: 104
SALES (corp-wide): 30.5B **Privately Held**
WEB: www.healthy.kaiserpermanente.org
SIC: 6324 Health maintenance organization (HMO), insurance only
HQ: Kaiser Foundation Hospitals Inc
1 Kaiser Plz
Oakland CA 94612
510 271-6611

(P-10144)
KAISER FUNDATION HLTH PLAN INC
4460 Hacienda Dr, Pleasanton (94588-2761)
PHONE..................510 271-5800
Linsey Dicks, *Manager*
Carol Davis-Smith, *Vice Pres*
Manish Vipani, *Vice Pres*
Christina Baldomero, *Executive Asst*
Ilana Soyferman, *Info Tech Mgr*
EMP: 100
SALES (corp-wide): 30.5B **Privately Held**
WEB: www.kpihp.org
SIC: 6324 Health maintenance organization (HMO), insurance only
PA: Kaiser Foundation Health Plan, Inc.
1 Kaiser Plz
Oakland CA 94612
510 271-5800

(P-10145)
LUMITY INC
71 E 3rd Ave, San Mateo (94401-4010)
PHONE..................844 258-6489
Tariq Hilaly, *CEO*
Senthil Nagarajan, *COO*
Jonathan Surridge, *CFO*
Aaron Huang, *Chief Mktg Ofcr*
Suzi Harstrick, *Vice Pres*
EMP: 53 **EST:** 2014
SALES (est): 19.2MM **Privately Held**
WEB: www.lumity.com
SIC: 6324 Hospital & medical service plans

(P-10146)
MANAGED HEALTH NETWORK (DH)
2370 Kerner Blvd, San Rafael (94901-5613)
P.O. Box 10207 (94912-0207)
PHONE..................415 460-8168
Jeffrey Bairstow, *CEO*
Jerry Coil, *President*
Steven Sell, *President*
Linda Brisbane, *COO*
Jonathan Wormhoudt, *COO*
EMP: 500
SQ FT: 97,314
SALES (est): 215MM **Publicly Held**
WEB: www.mhn.com
SIC: 6324 8099 8093 8011 Hospital & medical service plans; health maintenance organization (HMO), insurance only; medical services organization; specialty outpatient clinics; offices & clinics of medical doctors
HQ: Health Net, Llc
21650 Oxnard St Fl 25
Woodland Hills CA 91367
818 676-6000

(P-10147)
ON LOK SENIOR HEALTH SERVICES (PA)
Also Called: ON LOK LIFEWAYS
1333 Bush St, San Francisco (94109-5691)
PHONE..................415 292-8888
Robert Edmondson, *CEO*
Grace Li, *COO*
Sue Wong, *CFO*
Niewiarowski Chris, *Technology*
Eileen Kunz, *Director*
EMP: 570 **EST:** 1971
SQ FT: 40,000
SALES (est): 187.2MM **Privately Held**
WEB: www.onlok.org
SIC: 6324 8082 Health maintenance organization (HMO), insurance only; home health care services

(P-10148)
PARTNERSHIP HEALTH PLAN CAL
4665 Business Center Dr, Fairfield (94534-1675)
PHONE..................707 863-4100
Jack Horn, *CEO*
Liz Gibboney, *COO*
Gary Erickson, *CFO*
Mark Glickstein, *Associate Dir*
Jennifer Bush, *Executive Asst*
EMP: 290 **EST:** 1994
SQ FT: 75,000
SALES (est): 188.2MM **Privately Held**
WEB: www.partnershiphp.org
SIC: 6324 Health maintenance organization (HMO), insurance only

(P-10149)
PERMANENTE KAISER INTL (HQ)
Also Called: Kp International
1 Kaiser Plz, Oakland (94612-3610)
PHONE..................510 271-5910
Raymond J Baxter, *CEO*
Bill Marsh, *COO*
Kathy Lancaster, *CFO*
Tarek Salaway, *Senior VP*
Le Anne Trachok, *Senior VP*
EMP: 62 **EST:** 2009
SALES (est): 242.8MM
SALES (corp-wide): 30.5B **Privately Held**
WEB: www.kpcrest.net
SIC: 6324 Hospital & medical service plans
PA: Kaiser Foundation Health Plan, Inc.
1 Kaiser Plz
Oakland CA 94612
510 271-5800

(P-10150)
PERMANENTE MEDICAL GROUP INC
220 Oyster Point Blvd, South San Francisco (94080-1911)
PHONE..................650 827-6500
Milan Patel, *Branch Mgr*
Marcy Kaufman, *Oncology*
Laura Millender, *Oncology*
Deep Patel, *Oncology*
Joseph Song, *Oncology*
EMP: 279
SALES (corp-wide): 30.5B **Privately Held**
WEB: www.permanente.org
SIC: 6324 Hospital & medical service plans
HQ: The Permanente Medical Group Inc
1950 Franklin St Fl 18th
Oakland CA 94612
866 858-2226

(P-10151)
PERMANENTE MEDICAL GROUP INC
900 Veterans Blvd Ste 400, Redwood City (94063-1742)
PHONE..................650 598-2852
Diana Patino, *Principal*
EMP: 279
SALES (corp-wide): 30.5B **Privately Held**
WEB: www.permanente.org
SIC: 6324 Hospital & medical service plans
HQ: The Permanente Medical Group Inc
1950 Franklin St Fl 18th
Oakland CA 94612
866 858-2226

(P-10152)
PERMANENTE MEDICAL GROUP INC
1725 Eastshore Hwy, Berkeley (94710-1703)
PHONE..................510 559-5119
Susan Yee, *Administration*
Rita Routt, *Admin Sec*
Catina Marino, *Regional*
EMP: 279
SALES (corp-wide): 30.5B **Privately Held**
WEB: www.permanente.org
SIC: 6324 Hospital & medical service plans
HQ: The Permanente Medical Group Inc
1950 Franklin St Fl 18th
Oakland CA 94612
866 858-2226

(P-10153)
PERMANENTE MEDICAL GROUP INC
3555 Whipple Rd, Union City (94587-1507)
PHONE..................510 675-4010
Deana Medinas, *Director*
Joseph Racklin, *Psychologist*
EMP: 279
SALES (corp-wide): 30.5B **Privately Held**
WEB: www.permanente.org
SIC: 6324 Hospital & medical service plans
HQ: The Permanente Medical Group Inc
1950 Franklin St Fl 18th
Oakland CA 94612
866 858-2226

(P-10154)
SIERRA HEALTH SERVICES LLC
2423 W March Ln Ste 100, Stockton (95207-8250)
P.O. Box 7096 (95267-0096)
PHONE..................209 956-7725
Earl Ohgman, *Mng Member*
Cindy Birmingham,
Candice Almonte, *Director*
Gianelli Buensuceso CPC, *Director*
Zandra Padilla, *Director*
EMP: 36 **EST:** 1999
SALES (est): 30.6MM **Privately Held**
WEB: www.sierrahealth.net
SIC: 6324 8011 Hospital & medical service plans; specialized medical practitioners, except internal; physicians' office, including specialists

(P-10155)
SUPERIOR VISION SERVICES INC (DH)
Also Called: Versant Health
11090 White Rock Rd Ste 1, Rancho Cordova (95670-6082)
PHONE..................800 507-3800
Kirk Rothrock, *CEO*
Brian Silverberg, *CFO*
Kimberley Hess, *Senior VP*
Stephanie Lucas, *Senior VP*
Audrey Weinstein, *Senior VP*
EMP: 62 **EST:** 1993
SQ FT: 12,000
SALES (est): 57.1MM
SALES (corp-wide): 67.8B **Publicly Held**
WEB: www.superiorvision.com
SIC: 6324 Hospital & medical service plans
HQ: Versant Health, Inc.
881 Elkridge Landing Rd
Linthicum Heights MD 21090
800 243-1401

(P-10156)
VALLEY HEALTH PLAN
2480 N 1st St Ste 160, San Jose (95131-1014)
P.O. Box 26160 (95159-6160)
PHONE..................408 885-4760
Greg Price, *CEO*
Elizabeth Rodriguez, *Officer*
Grace Kieler, *Analyst*
Sean Tobin, *Manager*
EMP: 257 **EST:** 1986
SALES (est): 13MM **Privately Held**
WEB: www.valleyhealthplan.org
SIC: 6324 Hospital & medical service plans
PA: County Of Santa Clara
70 W Hedding St 2wing
San Jose CA 95110
408 299-5200

(P-10157)
VISION SERVICE PLAN INC (PA)
Also Called: C V S Optical Lab Div
3333 Quality Dr, Rancho Cordova (95670-9757)
PHONE..................916 851-5000
James Robinson Lynch, *CEO*
Laura Costa, *COO*
Donald J Ball Jr, *CFO*
Marvin Davenport, *Officer*
Gary Brooks, *Senior VP*
▲ **EMP:** 1600 **EST:** 1955
SQ FT: 300,000
SALES (est): 1.8B **Privately Held**
WEB: www.vspglobal.com
SIC: 6324 5048 Hospital & medical service plans; ophthalmic goods

(P-10158)
VIVIO HEALTH INC
1933 Davis St Ste 274, San Leandro (94577-1263)
PHONE..................925 365-6600
Pramod John, *Principal*
Mike Reisler, *Vice Pres*
J Tedesco, *Vice Pres*
Bhargav Raman, *Director*
EMP: 40 **EST:** 2016
SALES (est): 5.5MM **Privately Held**
WEB: www.viviohealth.com
SIC: 6324 Hospital & medical service plans

(P-10159)
VSP OPTICAL GROUP INC (PA)
3333 Quality Dr, Rancho Cordova (95670-7985)
PHONE..................916 851-4682
Don Oakley, *President*
David Dess, *Senior VP*
Eric Johannessen, *Vice Pres*
Suzie Mackenzie, *Vice Pres*
Laura Olson, *Vice Pres*
EMP: 328 **EST:** 2009
SALES (est): 34.2MM **Privately Held**
SIC: 6324 Hospital & medical service plans

6331 Fire, Marine & Casualty Insurance

(P-10160)
ACE USA INC
Also Called: West Chester
275 Battery St Ste 1500, San Francisco (94111-3334)
PHONE...................415 773-6500
EMP: 45
SALES (corp-wide): 17.4B Privately Held
SIC: 6331 Fire/Casualty Insurance Carrier
HQ: Ace Usa, Inc.
 436 Walnut St
 Philadelphia PA 19106
 215 923-5352

(P-10161)
ALLIANZ GLOBL RISKS US INSUR
Also Called: Allianz Insurance Company
1465 N Mcdowell Blvd, Petaluma (94954-6569)
PHONE...................415 899-3758
Lori Oaks, *Manager*
EMP: 400
SALES (corp-wide): 26.4B Privately Held
SIC: 6331 Fire, marine & casualty insurance
HQ: Allianz Global Risks Us Insurance Company
 2350 W Empire Ave
 Burbank CA 91504
 818 260-7500

(P-10162)
CALIFORNIA CASUALTY MGT CO (HQ)
Also Called: CALIFORNIA CASUALITY
1875 S Grant St Ste 800, San Mateo (94402-7030)
PHONE...................650 574-4000
Carl B Brown, *Ch of Bd*
Dan Marshall, *President*
Manik Peddada, *President*
Joseph L Volponi, *President*
Michael Ray, *CFO*
▲ EMP: 135 EST: 1917
SALES: 134.8MM
SALES (corp-wide): 239.8MM Privately Held
SIC: 6331 8741 Reciprocal interinsurance exchanges: fire, marine, casualty; management services
PA: California Casualty Indemnity Exchange
 1900 Almeda De Las Pulgas
 San Mateo CA 94403
 650 574-4000

(P-10163)
CALIFORNIA CSLTY FIRE INSUR CO
1900 Alameda De Las Pulga, San Mateo (94403-1295)
P.O. Box M (94402-0080)
PHONE...................650 574-4000
Thomas R Brown, *Chairman*
EMP: 41 EST: 1973
SQ FT: 90,000
SALES (est): 2.7MM
SALES (corp-wide): 239.8MM Privately Held
SIC: 6331 Workers' compensation insurance
PA: California Casualty Indemnity Exchange
 1900 Almeda De Las Pulgas
 San Mateo CA 94403
 650 574-4000

(P-10164)
CALIFORNIA CSLTY GEN INSUR CO (DH)
1900 Alameda De Las Pulga, San Mateo (94403-1295)
P.O. Box M (94402-0080)
PHONE...................650 574-4000
Thomas R Brown, *Ch of Bd*
Douglas Goldberg, *Vice Pres*
James Kauffman, *Vice Pres*
Kai G E Anderson, *Director*
EMP: 242 EST: 1977

SQ FT: 90,000
SALES (est): 3.8MM
SALES (corp-wide): 239.8MM Privately Held
WEB: www.calcas.com
SIC: 6331 Workers' compensation insurance; automobile insurance; property damage insurance; fire, marine & casualty insurance & carriers
HQ: California Casualty Insurance Company
 1875 S Grant St Ste 800
 San Mateo CA 94402
 800 800-9410

(P-10165)
CALIFRNIA CSLTY INDEMNITY EXCH (PA)
1900 Almeda De Las Pulgas, San Mateo (94402-1222)
PHONE...................650 574-4000
Thomas R Brown, *Chairman*
Mike Ray, *CFO*
Ian Small, *Vice Pres*
Yvette Jones, *Analyst*
Amy Grosso, *Marketing Staff*
EMP: 130 EST: 1914
SQ FT: 90,000
SALES: 239.8MM Privately Held
SIC: 6331 Workers' compensation insurance; automobile insurance; property damage insurance; fire, marine & casualty insurance & carriers

(P-10166)
COMPWEST INSURANCE COMPANY
100 Pringle Ave Ste 515, Walnut Creek (94596-3558)
PHONE...................415 593-5100
William J Mudge, *President*
Patrick Persse, *CFO*
Gene J Simpson, *Vice Pres*
Cyndi Kroop, *Regional Mgr*
Alice Pau, *Financial Analy*
EMP: 140 EST: 2004
SALES (est): 33.9MM Privately Held
WEB: www.compwestinsurance.com
SIC: 6331 Reciprocal interinsurance exchanges: fire, marine, casualty

(P-10167)
DEANS & HOMER (PA)
340 Pine St Fl 2, San Francisco (94104-3209)
P.O. Box 2839 (94126-2839)
PHONE...................415 421-8332
Winnifred Homer Smith, *President*
Micheal Torp, *Treasurer*
Dan L Beach, *Vice Pres*
William H Burdt, *Vice Pres*
Katherine K Costa, *Vice Pres*
EMP: 46
SQ FT: 7,500
SALES (est): 33.7MM Privately Held
WEB: www.deanshomer.com
SIC: 6331 Automobile insurance

(P-10168)
FEDERATED MUTUAL INSURANCE CO
Also Called: Federated Insurance
10850 Gold Center Dr # 100, Rancho Cordova (95670-6045)
PHONE...................916 631-0345
EMP: 35
SALES (corp-wide): 1.5B Privately Held
WEB: www.federatedinsurance.com
SIC: 6331 Fire/Casualty Insurance Carrier
PA: Federated Mutual Insurance Company
 121 E Park Sq
 Owatonna MN 55060
 507 455-5200

(P-10169)
GENERAL RE CORPORATION
555 California St # 3400, San Francisco (94104-1503)
PHONE...................415 781-1700
Katherine Auyers, *Sales/Mktg Mgr*
David Hurt, *Vice Pres*
EMP: 37

SALES (corp-wide): 245.5B Publicly Held
WEB: www.genre.com
SIC: 6331 Fire, marine & casualty insurance
HQ: General Re Corporation
 120 Long Ridge Rd
 Stamford CT 06902
 203 328-5000

(P-10170)
MERCURY INSURANCE COMPANY
Also Called: Mercury Insurance Group
104 Woodmere Rd, Folsom (95630-4705)
PHONE...................916 353-4859
Beverly Ramm, *Vice Pres*
EMP: 354
SALES (corp-wide): 3.7B Publicly Held
WEB: www.mercuryinsurance.com
SIC: 6331 6411 Fire, marine & casualty insurance; insurance claim processing, except medical
HQ: Mercury Insurance Company
 4484 Wilshire Blvd
 Los Angeles CA 90010
 323 937-1060

(P-10171)
METROMILE OPERATING COMPANY (PA)
425 Market St Ste 700, San Francisco (94105-5418)
PHONE...................888 244-1702
Dan Preston, *CEO*
Carrie Dolan, *CFO*
Bhanu Pullela, *Chief Mktg Ofcr*
Jose Mercado, *CTO*
Erick Hong, *Technical Staff*
EMP: 80 EST: 2013
SALES (est): 218.7MM Privately Held
WEB: www.metromile.com
SIC: 6331 Automobile insurance

(P-10172)
REPUBLIC INDEMNITY CO AMER
100 Pine St Fl 14, San Francisco (94111-5116)
P.O. Box 7878 (94120-7878)
PHONE...................415 981-3200
Darryl Yim, *Vice Pres*
James Frey, *Assistant*
EMP: 100 Publicly Held
WEB: www.republicindemnity.com
SIC: 6331 Workers' compensation insurance
HQ: Republic Indemnity Company Of America
 4500 Park Granada Ste 300
 Calabasas CA 91302
 818 990-9860

(P-10173)
SOVEREIGN GEN INSUR SVCS INC
501 W Weber Ave Ste 404, Stockton (95203-3176)
PHONE...................209 932-5200
Martin F Sullivan Sr, *CEO*
Fred Godinez, *President*
Martin Sullivan Sr, *CEO*
Steve Phillips, *COO*
Chad Hunter, *Vice Pres*
EMP: 38 EST: 1992
SQ FT: 6,000
SALES (est): 5.2MM Privately Held
SIC: 6331 6411 Fire, marine & casualty insurance; insurance agents & brokers

(P-10174)
STATE COMPENSATION INSUR FUND (PA)
Also Called: State Fund
333 Bush St Fl 8, San Francisco (94104-2806)
P.O. Box 8192, Pleasanton (94588-8792)
PHONE...................888 782-8338
Vern Steiner, *CEO*
Hilda Padua, *President*
Beatriz Sanchez, *COO*
Peter Guastamachio, *CFO*
Daniel J Sevilla Jr, *CFO*
EMP: 75 EST: 1914
SQ FT: 80,000

SALES (est): 2.7B Privately Held
WEB: www.statefundca.com
SIC: 6331 Workers' compensation insurance

(P-10175)
STATE COMPENSATION INSUR FUND
1030 Vaquero Cir, Vacaville (95688-8804)
PHONE...................415 565-1222
Maria C Castanares, *Principal*
Tony Durante, *Manager*
Rick Linton, *Supervisor*
EMP: 92
SALES (corp-wide): 2.7B Privately Held
WEB: www.statefundca.com
SIC: 6331 Workers' compensation insurance
PA: State Compensation Insurance Fund
 333 Bush St Fl 8
 San Francisco CA 94104
 888 782-8338

(P-10176)
STATE COMPENSATION INSUR FUND
Also Called: Oakland District Office
2955 Peralta Oaks Ct, Oakland (94605-5319)
PHONE...................510 577-3000
EMP: 200
SALES (corp-wide): 1.5B Privately Held
SIC: 6331 9651 6321 Fire/Casualty Insurance Rgltn Misc Coml Sectors Accident/Hlth Insurance
PA: State Compensation Insurance Fund
 333 Bush St Fl 8
 San Francisco CA 94104
 888 782-8338

(P-10177)
STATE COMPENSATION INSUR FUND
1533 Shumaker Way, San Jose (95131-2673)
PHONE...................408 656-7417
David Jeypaul, *Principal*
EMP: 92
SALES (corp-wide): 2.7B Privately Held
WEB: www.statefundca.com
SIC: 6331 Workers' compensation insurance
PA: State Compensation Insurance Fund
 333 Bush St Fl 8
 San Francisco CA 94104
 888 782-8338

(P-10178)
STATE COMPENSATION INSUR FUND
Also Called: Redding District Office
364 Knollcrest Dr, Redding (96002-0175)
P.O. Box 496049 (96049-6049)
PHONE...................888 782-8338
Michael Labeaux, *Manager*
EMP: 92
SALES (corp-wide): 2.7B Privately Held
WEB: www.statefundca.com
SIC: 6331 9651 Workers' compensation insurance; regulation, miscellaneous commercial sectors
PA: State Compensation Insurance Fund
 333 Bush St Fl 8
 San Francisco CA 94104
 888 782-8338

(P-10179)
STATE COMPENSATION INSUR FUND
Also Called: State Fund
1020 Vaquero Cir, Vacaville (95688-8804)
PHONE...................707 455-9900
EMP: 92
SALES (corp-wide): 2.7B Privately Held
WEB: www.statefundca.com
SIC: 6331 Workers' compensation insurance
PA: State Compensation Insurance Fund
 333 Bush St Fl 8
 San Francisco CA 94104
 888 782-8338

PRODUCTS & SERVICES SECTION

6361 - Title Insurance County (P-10199)

(P-10180)
STATE COMPENSATION INSUR FUND
1416 9th St, Sacramento (95814-5511)
PHONE.....................530 223-7000
EMP: 92
SALES (corp-wide): 2.7B Privately Held
WEB: www.statefundca.com
SIC: 6331 Workers' compensation insurance
PA: State Compensation Insurance Fund
333 Bush St Fl 8
San Francisco CA 94104
888 782-8338

(P-10181)
STATE COMPENSATION INSUR FUND
Also Called: Fresno District Office
10 E Rver Pk Pl E Ste 110, Fresno (93720)
PHONE.....................559 433-2700
John Putnam, District Mgr
Drake Gomez, Technician
Patrick Taylor, Consultant
Monica Segura, Underwriter
EMP: 92
SALES (corp-wide): 2.7B Privately Held
WEB: www.statefundca.com
SIC: 6331 9651 Workers' compensation insurance; insurance commission, government;
PA: State Compensation Insurance Fund
333 Bush St Fl 8
San Francisco CA 94104
888 782-8338

(P-10182)
STATE COMPENSATION INSUR FUND
Also Called: Group Insurance Programs
2300 River Plaza Dr # 150, Sacramento (95833-4243)
PHONE.....................916 263-8102
Grant Phillips, Manager
Wayne Burleson, Underwriter
EMP: 92
SALES (corp-wide): 2.7B Privately Held
WEB: www.statefundca.com
SIC: 6331 9651 Workers' compensation insurance; insurance commission, government;
PA: State Compensation Insurance Fund
333 Bush St Fl 8
San Francisco CA 94104
888 782-8338

(P-10183)
STATE COMPENSATION INSUR FUND
Also Called: Stockton District Office
3247 W March Ln Ste 110, Stockton (95219-2363)
PHONE.....................888 782-8338
Tom Clark, Manager
Philip Johnson, Executive
Gail Drzewiecki, Manager
Belinda Walker, Manager
Veronica Bedolla, Representative
EMP: 92
SALES (corp-wide): 2.7B Privately Held
WEB: www.statefundca.com
SIC: 6331 9651 6411 Workers' compensation insurance; insurance commission, government; ; insurance agents, brokers & service
PA: State Compensation Insurance Fund
333 Bush St Fl 8
San Francisco CA 94104
888 782-8338

(P-10184)
STATE COMPENSATION INSUR FUND
Also Called: Sacramento District Office
2275 Gateway Oaks Dr, Sacramento (95833-3224)
PHONE.....................916 924-5100
Gary Dunlap, Manager
Andreas Wacker, Senior VP
Darren Wong, Counsel
EMP: 92
SALES (corp-wide): 2.7B Privately Held
WEB: www.statefundca.com
SIC: 6331 9651 Workers' compensation insurance; insurance commission, government;
PA: State Compensation Insurance Fund
333 Bush St Fl 8
San Francisco CA 94104
888 782-8338

(P-10185)
STATE COMPENSATION INSUR FUND
Also Called: Eureka District Office
800 W Harris St Ste 37, Eureka (95503-3929)
PHONE.....................707 443-9721
Steve Mackey, Branch Mgr
EMP: 92
SALES (corp-wide): 2.7B Privately Held
WEB: www.statefundca.com
SIC: 6331 9651 Workers' compensation insurance; insurance commission, government;
PA: State Compensation Insurance Fund
333 Bush St Fl 8
San Francisco CA 94104
888 782-8338

(P-10186)
STATE COMPENSATION INSUR FUND
5880 Owens Dr, Pleasanton (94588-3900)
PHONE.....................925 523-5000
Patricia Smith, Manager
Harry Tang, Info Tech Mgr
Bhargav Patel, Software Dev
Madhavi Alluri, Programmer Anys
Amelita Castillo, Technician
EMP: 185
SALES (corp-wide): 2.7B Privately Held
WEB: www.statefundca.com
SIC: 6331 9441 Workers' compensation insurance; administration of social & manpower programs;
PA: State Compensation Insurance Fund
333 Bush St Fl 8
San Francisco CA 94104
888 782-8338

(P-10187)
STATE COMPENSATION INSUR FUND
5890 Owens Dr, Pleasanton (94588-3900)
PHONE.....................888 782-8338
Alicia Reyes, Principal
Frances Chan, Analyst
Sara Pretti, Human Resources
Stephanie Cruz, Manager
EMP: 92
SALES (corp-wide): 2.7B Privately Held
WEB: www.statefundca.com
SIC: 6331 Workers' compensation insurance
PA: State Compensation Insurance Fund
333 Bush St Fl 8
San Francisco CA 94104
888 782-8338

(P-10188)
SWISS RE SOLUTIONS HOLDG CORP
111 Sutter St Ste 400, San Francisco (94104-4509)
PHONE.....................415 834-2200
Ken Brandt, Manager
Karen Musto, Assistant VP
EMP: 126
SALES (corp-wide): 43.3B Privately Held
SIC: 6331 Property damage insurance
HQ: Swiss Re Solutions Holding Corporation
5200 Metcalf Ave
Overland Park KS 66202
913 676-5200

(P-10189)
UNITED STATES FIRE INSUR CO
1 Front St Ste 300, San Francisco (94111-5397)
PHONE.....................415 541-3249
Margaret Tsai, Branch Mgr
EMP: 60

SALES (corp-wide): 19.7B Privately Held
WEB: www.cfins.com
SIC: 6331 Property damage insurance
HQ: United States Fire Insurance Company
305 Madison Ave
Morristown NJ 07960
973 490-6600

(P-10190)
WORKERS CMPNSTION INSUR RTING (PA)
Also Called: WCIRB
1221 Broadway Ste 900, Oakland (94612-1995)
PHONE.....................888 229-2472
William Mudge, President
Dave Bellusci, Officer
David Bellusci, Senior VP
Brenda Keys, Senior VP
Timothy Benjamin, Vice Pres
EMP: 160
SQ FT: 31,000
SALES: 41MM Privately Held
WEB: www.wcirb.com
SIC: 6331 Insurance agents, brokers & service

6351 Surety Insurance Carriers

(P-10191)
ARCH US MI HOLDINGS INC (HQ)
Pmi Plaza 3003 Oak Rd, Walnut Creek (94597)
PHONE.....................800 909-4264
David Gansberg, President
Eugene Sunshine, Bd of Directors
Andrew Caughey, Vice Pres
Evan Harris, Vice Pres
Eric Pearson, Vice Pres
EMP: 224 EST: 2013
SALES (est): 1.9B Privately Held
WEB: www.archgroup.com
SIC: 6351 Mortgage guarantee insurance

(P-10192)
DOCTORS COMPANY INSURANCE SVCS
185 Greenwood Rd, NAPA (94558-7540)
P.O. Box 2900 (94558-0900)
PHONE.....................707 226-0100
Manuel F Puebla, Ch of Bd
Jack Meyer, President
EMP: 300 EST: 1994
SALES (est): 102.6MM
SALES (corp-wide): 760.2MM Privately Held
WEB: www.thedoctors.com
SIC: 6351 6331 Liability insurance; fire, marine & casualty insurance
PA: The Doctors' Company An Interinsurance Exchange
185 Greenwood Rd
Napa CA 94558
707 226-0100

(P-10193)
NMI HOLDINGS INC
2100 Powell St Fl 12th, Emeryville (94608-1894)
PHONE.....................855 530-6642
Bradley M Shuster, Ch of Bd
Claudia J Merkle, President
Adam Pollitzer, CFO
Lynn McCreary, Bd of Directors
Regina Muehlhauser, Bd of Directors
EMP: 299 EST: 2011
SQ FT: 47,000
SALES (est): 433.2MM Privately Held
WEB: www.nationalmi.com
SIC: 6351 Mortgage guarantee insurance

(P-10194)
XL SPECIALTY INSURANCE COMPANY
1340 Treat Blvd, Walnut Creek (94597-2101)
P.O. Box 8098 (94596-8098)
PHONE.....................925 942-6142
Jim Bily, Assistant VP
EMP: 325

SALES (corp-wide): 26.6MM Privately Held
WEB: www.axaxl.com
SIC: 6351 Surety insurance
HQ: Xl Specialty Insurance Company
10 N Martingale Rd # 220
Schaumburg IL 60173
847 517-2990

6361 Title Insurance

(P-10195)
BIDWELL TITLE AND ESCROW CO (PA)
500 Wall St, Chico (95928-5625)
P.O. Box 5173 (95927-5173)
PHONE.....................530 894-2612
Ladonna Joyner, President
Peggy Gaddini, Officer
Tracie Ularte, Officer
Trevor Joyner, Vice Pres
Valarie Welch, Administration
EMP: 35 EST: 1929
SQ FT: 6,642
SALES (est): 16.8MM Privately Held
WEB: www.bidwelltitle.com
SIC: 6361 6531 Title insurance; real estate agents & managers

(P-10196)
CHICAGO TITLE COMPANY
675 N 1st St Ste 400, San Jose (95112-5111)
PHONE.....................408 292-4212
Randy Couurk, Owner
Michelle Manaois, President
Linda Ancar, Officer
Lynn Cogliandro, Officer
Fawn Vinh, Officer
EMP: 114 EST: 2010
SALES (est): 12.9MM Privately Held
WEB: www.ctccommercialonline.com
SIC: 6361 Real estate title insurance

(P-10197)
CHICAGO TITLE INSURANCE CO
1500 E Hamilton Ave # 104, Campbell (95008-0809)
PHONE.....................408 371-4100
Mary Dm, Branch Mgr
Joette Joseph, Branch Mgr
Celia Ortega-Vasquez, Assistant
Vickie Sweeney, Assistant
EMP: 1511 Publicly Held
WEB: www.ctic.com
SIC: 6361 Real estate title insurance
HQ: Chicago Title Insurance Company
10 S Lasalle St Ste 2850
Chicago IL 60603
312 223-2402

(P-10198)
FIDELITY NAT HM WARRANTY CO
1850 Gateway Blvd Ste 400, Concord (94520-8446)
PHONE.....................925 356-0194
Bill Jensen, Manager
EMP: 150 Publicly Held
WEB: www.marycollinshomes.com
SIC: 6361 Title insurance
HQ: Fidelity National Home Warranty Company
2950 Buskirk Ave Ste 201
Walnut Creek CA

(P-10199)
FIRST AMERICAN TITLE INSUR CO (HQ)
330 Soquel Ave, Santa Cruz (95062-2300)
PHONE.....................714 250-3109
James Boxdell, Vice Pres
Tina Alvarez, Officer
Robert Baca, Officer
Christy Becknell, Officer
Devon Boyles, Officer
EMP: 3000
SQ FT: 98,000
SALES (est): 663.8MM Publicly Held
WEB: www.firstam.com
SIC: 6361 Real estate title insurance

6361 - Title Insurance County (P-10200) — PRODUCTS & SERVICES SECTION

(P-10200)
LAWYERS TITLE INSURANCE CORP
530 El Camino Real Ste A, San Carlos (94070-2454)
PHONE...................650 445-6300
Terri Haun, *Officer*
Latter Sarah, *Officer*
Lucy Tran, *Officer*
EMP: 174 **Publicly Held**
WEB: www.ltic.com
SIC: 6361 Real estate title insurance
HQ: Lawyers Title Insurance Corporation
601 Riverside Ave
Jacksonville FL 32204
888 866-3684

(P-10201)
LAWYERS TITLE INSURANCE CORP
20630 Patio Dr, Castro Valley (94546-5606)
PHONE...................510 733-2250
EMP: 174 **Publicly Held**
WEB: www.ltic.com
SIC: 6361 Real estate title insurance
HQ: Lawyers Title Insurance Corporation
601 Riverside Ave
Jacksonville FL 32204
888 866-3684

(P-10202)
MID VALLEY TITLE AND ESCROW CO (DH)
601 Main St, Chico (95928-5698)
P.O. Box 3039 (95927-3039)
PHONE...................530 893-5644
Daniel F Hunt, *President*
John Burghardt, *Corp Secy*
Jennifer Mackall, *Manager*
EMP: 85 **EST:** 1956
SQ FT: 8,500
SALES (est): 27.7MM **Publicly Held**
WEB: www.firstam.com
SIC: 6361 Title insurance
HQ: First American Title Insurance Company
1 First American Way
Santa Ana CA 92707
800 854-3643

(P-10203)
MOTHER LODE HOLDING CO
9085 Foothills Blvd, Roseville (95747-7130)
PHONE...................916 624-8141
Marsha A Emmett, *Branch Mgr*
EMP: 99 **Privately Held**
WEB: www.placertitle.com
SIC: 6361 Real estate title insurance
PA: Mother Lode Holding Co.
189 Fulweiler Ave
Auburn CA 95603

(P-10204)
MOTHER LODE HOLDING CO (PA)
189 Fulweiler Ave, Auburn (95603-4507)
PHONE...................530 887-2410
Jerry Adams, *CEO*
Marsha Emmett, *President*
David Philipp, *CFO*
Kim Akins, *Officer*
Tami Baker, *Officer*
EMP: 54 **EST:** 1987
SQ FT: 10,000
SALES (est): 344.4MM **Privately Held**
WEB: www.mlhc.com
SIC: 6361 6531 7389 Real estate title insurance; escrow agent, real estate; courier or messenger service

(P-10205)
NORTH AMERICAN ASSET DEV CORP (DH)
1855 Gateway Blvd Ste 650, Concord (94520-8454)
PHONE...................925 935-5599
Dan R Wentzel, *President*
Jeff Wright, *CFO*
EMP: 62 **EST:** 1991
SQ FT: 10,000
SALES (est): 488.8MM
SALES (corp-wide): 22.4B **Publicly Held**
WEB: www.natic.com
SIC: 6361 6531 Title insurance; escrow agent, real estate
HQ: Calatlantic Title Group, Llc
760 Nw 107th Ave Ste 400
Miami FL 33172
305 929-7799

(P-10206)
NORTH AMERICAN TITLE CO INC
175 Lennon Ln Ste 100, Walnut Creek (94598-2466)
PHONE...................925 935-0400
EMP: 70
SALES (corp-wide): 22.4B **Publicly Held**
WEB: www.natic.com
SIC: 6361 Title Insurance Carrier Title Abstract Office
HQ: North American Title Company, Inc.
1981 N Broadway Ste 100
Walnut Creek CA 94596
925 935-5599

(P-10207)
OLD REPUBLIC NAT TITLE INSUR
555 12th St, Oakland (94607-4046)
PHONE...................510 286-7798
Shokoufeh Amiri, *President*
Dick Hoium, *Sr Project Mgr*
EMP: 40
SALES (corp-wide): 7.1B **Publicly Held**
WEB: www.oldrepublictitle.com
SIC: 6361 Real estate title insurance
HQ: Old Republic National Title Insurance Company
400 2nd Ave S
Minneapolis MN 55401
612 371-1111

(P-10208)
OLD REPUBLIC TITLE COMPANY (DH)
275 Battery St Ste 1500, San Francisco (94111-3334)
PHONE...................415 421-3500
Rande K Yeager, *Ch of Bd*
Wayne Shupe, *President*
Dick Neves, *Treasurer*
Beth Becerra, *Officer*
Courtney Braunstein, *Officer*
EMP: 35 **EST:** 1969
SALES (est): 349.1MM
SALES (corp-wide): 7.1B **Publicly Held**
WEB: www.ortconline.com
SIC: 6361 6531 Real estate title insurance; escrow agent, real estate
HQ: Old Republic Title Insurance Group, Inc.
307 N Michigan Ave Fl 17
Chicago IL 60601
312 346-8100

(P-10209)
OLD RPBLIC TITLE INFO CONCEPTS
524 Gibson Dr, Roseville (95678-5799)
PHONE...................916 781-4100
Robert Matanane, *Senior VP*
Joe Ramos, *Vice Pres*
EMP: 231 **EST:** 1973
SQ FT: 15,000
SALES (est): 25.8MM
SALES (corp-wide): 7.1B **Publicly Held**
WEB: www.ortconline.com
SIC: 6361 6531 Real estate title insurance; escrow agent, real estate
HQ: Old Republic Title Holding Company, Inc.
275 Battery St Ste 1500
San Francisco CA 94111
415 421-3500

(P-10210)
TRANSCOUNTY TITLE CO (PA)
635 W 19th St, Merced (95340-4702)
PHONE...................209 383-4660
Robert Ayers, *President*
Nancy Bucio, *Officer*
Annette Heikkila, *Officer*
Yvonne Ayers, *Vice Pres*
Peggy Ayers, *Admin Sec*
EMP: 37 **EST:** 1984
SQ FT: 6,500
SALES (est): 11.6MM **Privately Held**
WEB: www.transcountytitle.com
SIC: 6361 6531 Real estate title insurance; real estate agents & managers; escrow agent, real estate

6371 Pension, Health & Welfare Funds

(P-10211)
ASSOCIATED PENSION CONS INC (PA)
2035 Forest Ave, Chico (95928-7620)
P.O. Box 1282 (95927-1282)
PHONE...................530 343-4233
Matt Blofsky, *President*
Marc Roberts, *Treasurer*
Sharon Vine, *Trust Officer*
Ethan Grodofsky, *Vice Pres*
Linda Madsen, *Vice Pres*
EMP: 51 **EST:** 1974
SQ FT: 20,000
SALES (est): 19.7MM **Privately Held**
WEB: www.e-apc.com
SIC: 6371 6411 Pension, health & welfare funds; pension & retirement plan consultants

(P-10212)
CALIFRNIA PUB EMPLYEES RTRMENT (DH)
400 Q St, Sacramento (95811-6201)
P.O. Box 942706 (94229-2706)
PHONE...................916 795-3000
Anne Stausboll, *CEO*
Henry Jones, *President*
Tiffany Davis, *Officer*
Ronald E Gene Reich, *Officer*
Kathie Vaughn, *Officer*
EMP: 1600 **EST:** 1932
SALES (est): 1.1B **Privately Held**
WEB: www.calpers.ca.gov
SIC: 6371 9441 Pension funds; administration of social & manpower programs;

(P-10213)
CALIFRNIA STATE TCHERS RTRMENT (DH)
Also Called: Cal Strs
100 Waterfront Pl, West Sacramento (95605-2807)
P.O. Box 15275, Sacramento (95851-0275)
PHONE...................800 228-5453
James D Mosman, *CEO*
Dana Dillon, *Ch of Bd*
Sharon Hendricks, *Ch of Bd*
Todd Golterman, *Technology*
EMP: 331 **EST:** 1913
SQ FT: 100,000
SALES: 24.7B **Privately Held**
WEB: www.calstrs.com
SIC: 6371 9441 Pension, health & welfare funds; administration of social & manpower programs

(P-10214)
CHELBAY SCHULER & CHELBAY (PA)
Also Called: United Administrative Services
6800 Santa Teresa Blvd # 100, San Jose (95119-1238)
P.O. Box 5057 (95150-5057)
PHONE...................408 288-4400
Robert J Bradley, *President*
David Andresen, *Corp Secy*
Sharon Crist, *Vice Pres*
Sandy Stephenson, *Vice Pres*
Alison Humphrey, *Executive Asst*
EMP: 100 **EST:** 1951
SQ FT: 35,000
SALES (est): 26.7MM **Privately Held**
WEB: www.uastpa.com
SIC: 6371 Pension funds

(P-10215)
HEALTH SVCS BNEFT ADMNSTRTORS (PA)
Also Called: Hsba
4160 Dublin Blvd, Dublin (94568-7735)
PHONE...................925 833-7300
Stanley R Fisher, *President*
Ronald Hall, *President*
Angela Rampone, *COO*
David Haumesser, *CFO*
Stephanie Chen, *Trust Officer*
EMP: 52 **EST:** 1989
SQ FT: 12,500
SALES (est): 17.9MM **Privately Held**
WEB: www.hsba.com
SIC: 6371 Union welfare, benefit & health funds

(P-10216)
LIPMAN INSUR ADMNISTRATORS INC (PA)
39420 Liberty St Ste 260, Fremont (94538-2297)
P.O. Box 5820 (94537-5820)
PHONE...................510 796-4676
Frederic J Lipman, *President*
Janet Sylvester, *CFO*
Margaret Epstein, *Admin Sec*
EMP: 60 **EST:** 1987
SQ FT: 14,000
SALES (est): 25.7MM **Privately Held**
WEB: www.lipmantpa.com
SIC: 6371 Union welfare, benefit & health funds

(P-10217)
PENSCO LLC (PA)
Also Called: Pensco Trust Company NH
275 Battery St Ste 1220, San Francisco (94111-3382)
P.O. Box 7576 (94120-7576)
PHONE...................415 274-5600
Kelly Rodriques, *CEO*
Scott K Rosebrook, *President*
Carol Foster, *CFO*
Mark Lee, *CFO*
John Beater, *Vice Pres*
EMP: 40 **EST:** 1989
SALES (est): 12.1MM **Privately Held**
WEB: www.pacificpremiertrust.com
SIC: 6371 Pension funds

(P-10218)
PUBLIC EMPLOYEES RETIREMENT
Also Called: Calpers
400 Q St, Sacramento (95811-6201)
PHONE...................916 795-3400
Russell Fong, *Branch Mgr*
Robert Borrelli, *Officer*
Tiffany Davis, *Officer*
Anne Eklund, *Officer*
Chris Lum, *Officer*
EMP: 331 **Privately Held**
WEB: www.calpers.ca.gov
SIC: 6371 9441 Pension funds; administration of social & manpower programs;
HQ: California Public Employees' Retirement System
400 Q St
Sacramento CA 95811

(P-10219)
WOODMONT REALTY ADVISORS INC
1050 Ralston Ave, Belmont (94002-2240)
PHONE...................650 592-3960
Ronald V Granville, *CEO*
Howard Friedman, *President*
Caryn Kali, *CFO*
Greg Perez, *Property Mgr*
EMP: 266 **EST:** 1987
SQ FT: 10,000
SALES (est): 4.5MM **Privately Held**
WEB: www.woodmontrealtyadvisors.com
SIC: 6371 Pension funds
PA: Woodmont Real Estate Services, L.P.
1050 Ralston Ave
Belmont CA 94002

6399 Insurance Carriers, NEC

(P-10220)
ROBERT W BAIRD & CO INC
360 Sierra College Dr # 200, Grass Valley (95945-5088)
PHONE...................530 271-3000
Jonathan H Lee, *Director*
Colin Sebastian, *Research*

EMP: 49 EST: 2009
SALES (est): 16.8MM Privately Held
WEB: www.rwbaird.com
SIC: 6399 Deposit insurance
PA: Baird Holding Company
   777 E Wisconsin Ave
   Milwaukee WI 53202

(P-10221)
SQUARETRADE INC (DH)
600 Harrison St Ste 400, San Francisco (94107-1370)
PHONE.............................415 541-1000
Ahmedulia Khaishgi, *President*
Mark Etnyre, *CFO*
Steve Abernethy, *Chairman*
Vince Tseng, *Officer*
EMP: 244 EST: 1999
SALES (est): 855.6MM Publicly Held
WEB: www.squaretrade.com
SIC: 6399 Warranty insurance, product; except automobile
HQ: Allstate Non Insurance Holdings Inc
   2775 Sanders Rd Ste D
   Northbrook IL 60062
   847 402-5000

(P-10222)
UNITRIN DIRECT INSURANCE CO (HQ)
80 Blue Ravine Rd Ste 200, Folsom (95630-4702)
PHONE.............................760 603-3276
Scott Carter, *President*
EMP: 62 EST: 2000
SALES (est): 37.1MM Publicly Held
WEB: www.kemper.com
SIC: 6399 Warranty insurance, automobile

6411 Insurance Agents, Brokers & Svc

(P-10223)
501(C INSURANCE PROGRAMS INC
Also Called: 501 C Services
400 Race St Ste 200, San Jose (95126-3519)
PHONE.............................408 216-9796
John F Huckstadt, *President*
Carmen Lucas, *Technology*
Maureen Marfell, *Human Res Dir*
Lea Ovrootsky, *Director*
Sonya Llewellyn, *Consultant*
EMP: 36 EST: 2001
SALES (est): 7.5MM Privately Held
WEB: www.501ctrust.org
SIC: 6411 Insurance agents, brokers & service

(P-10224)
ABD INSURANCE & FINCL SVCS INC (PA)
Also Called: Nationwide
777 Mariners Island Blvd # 250, San Mateo (94404-5008)
PHONE.............................650 488-8565
Brian M Hetherington, *CEO*
Kurt De Grosz, *President*
Carolyn Locke, *President*
Helen Yu, *COO*
Michael F McCloskey, *CFO*
EMP: 68 EST: 2009
SQ FT: 14,000
SALES (est): 83.5MM Privately Held
WEB: www.theabdteam.com
SIC: 6411 Insurance brokers

(P-10225)
ACCLAMATION INSURANCE MGT SVCS
4450 N Brawley Ave, Fresno (93722-3950)
P.O. Box 26597 (93729-6597)
PHONE.............................559 227-9891
Kenneth Wilkerson, *Manager*
Mark Denison, *Vice Pres*
Jeffrey Russo, *Vice Pres*
Maylynn Whatley, *Manager*
Ken Wilkerson, *Manager*
EMP: 78 Privately Held
WEB: www.aims4claims.com
SIC: 6411 Insurance agents

PA: Acclamation Insurance Management Services
   10445 Old Placerville Rd
   Sacramento CA 95827

(P-10226)
ACE USA
39300 Civic Center Dr # 290, Fremont (94538-2337)
PHONE.............................510 790-4695
EMP: 65
SALES (est): 3.8MM
SALES (corp-wide): 17.2B Privately Held
SIC: 6411 Insurance Agent/Broker
HQ: Ace Usa, Inc.
   436 Walnut St
   Philadelphia PA 19106
   215 923-5352

(P-10227)
ALAMEDA CNTY EMPLYEES RTRMENT
Also Called: Acera
475 14th St Ste 1000, Oakland (94612-1916)
PHONE.............................510 628-3000
Charles Conrad, *General Mgr*
Catherine Walker, *CEO*
Kathleen Foster, *Officer*
Grant Hughs, *Sr Invest Ofcr*
George Wood, *Vice Pres*
EMP: 70
SALES (est): 36.1MM Privately Held
WEB: www.acera.org
SIC: 6411 Pension & retirement plan consultants

(P-10228)
ALBANO DALE DUNN & LEWIS INSUR
9197 Greenback Ln Ste E, Orangevale (95662-4792)
P.O. Box 2470 (95662-7417)
PHONE.............................916 988-0214
Tony Albano, *President*
Lynn Peters, *President*
Brent Albano, *Corp Secy*
Anthony Albano, *Vice Pres*
Denise Triplett, *Broker*
▲ EMP: 39 EST: 1955
SQ FT: 4,500
SALES (est): 4.6MM Privately Held
WEB: www.addlins.com
SIC: 6411 Insurance agents

(P-10229)
AMBR INC (PA)
Also Called: American Medical Bill Review
1160 Industrial St, Redding (96002-0734)
P.O. Box 492710 (96049-2710)
PHONE.............................530 221-4759
William Hullinger, *CEO*
Kevin Bird, *Vice Pres*
Heather Oconner, *Office Mgr*
EMP: 44 EST: 1996
SQ FT: 9,800
SALES (est): 5.4MM Privately Held
SIC: 6411 Medical insurance claim processing, contract or fee basis

(P-10230)
AMES-GRENZ INSURANCE SVCS INC
3435 American River Dr C, Sacramento (95864-5797)
PHONE.............................916 486-2900
Larrie Grenz, *Owner*
Reggie Conley, *Vice Chairman*
Larrie N Grenz, *President*
Mary A Hathaway, *Vice Pres*
Carl Trexler, *Vice Pres*
EMP: 36 EST: 1970
SQ FT: 2,700
SALES (est): 5.8MM Privately Held
WEB: www.amesgrenz.com
SIC: 6411 Insurance agents

(P-10231)
AMWINS CONNECT INSUR SVCS LLC (PA)
1600 W Hillsdale Blvd, San Mateo (94402-3768)
PHONE.............................650 348-4131
Philip Lebherz, *Ch of Bd*

Peter Diaz, *Partner*
Becky Patel, *CEO*
Kevin Timone, *Senior VP*
Tamara Henderson, *Vice Pres*
EMP: 60 EST: 1976
SQ FT: 18,000
SALES (est): 57MM Privately Held
WEB: www.amwinsconnect.com
SIC: 6411 Insurance agents

(P-10232)
ANDREINI & COMPANY (PA)
Also Called: Nationwide
220 W 20th Ave, San Mateo (94403-1339)
PHONE.............................650 573-1111
Michael J Colzani, *CEO*
Craig Oden, *Managing Prtnr*
Jeff Tebow, *Managing Prtnr*
John Andreini, *President*
Dan Centoni, *COO*
EMP: 95 EST: 1951
SQ FT: 30,000
SALES (est): 41.2MM Privately Held
WEB: www.andreini.com
SIC: 6411 Insurance brokers; insurance agents

(P-10233)
ANFIELD INSURANCE SERVICE
433 California St Ste 820, San Francisco (94104-2012)
PHONE.............................415 439-5750
Noel Higgitt, *President*
Brad Wiley, *Admin Sec*
EMP: 85 EST: 1990
SQ FT: 1,700
SALES (est): 2.6MM Publicly Held
WEB: www.thehartford.com
SIC: 6411 Insurance agents
HQ: The Navigators Group Inc
   400 Atlantic St Fl 8
   Stamford CT 06901
   203 905-6090

(P-10234)
AON CONSULTING & INSUR SVCS
199 Fremont St Fl 14, San Francisco (94105-2253)
PHONE.............................415 486-7500
Judy Vukovich, *Senior VP*
Frank Blair, *Vice Pres*
Jeff Green, *Vice Pres*
Chris Heinicke, *Vice Pres*
Angela Mahoney, *Vice Pres*
EMP: 161 EST: 1988
SALES (est): 12.5MM
SALES (corp-wide): 102.6MM Privately Held
WEB: www.aon.com
SIC: 6411 8742 Insurance brokers; management consulting services
PA: Aon Consulting, Inc.
   200 E Randolph St Ll3
   Chicago IL 60601
   312 381-1000

(P-10235)
AON RISK INSURANCE SVCS W INC (DH)
Also Called: Nationwide
425 Market St Ste 2800, San Francisco (94105-2490)
PHONE.............................415 486-7000
Tom Rodell, *CEO*
Brandon Raaf, *Sr Consultant*
▲ EMP: 48 EST: 1966
SQ FT: 43,000
SALES (est): 26.1MM
SALES (corp-wide): 45.4B Privately Held
WEB: www.nationwide.com
SIC: 6411 Insurance brokers
HQ: Aon Corporation
   200 E Randolph St
   Chicago IL 60601
   312 381-1000

(P-10236)
ARCHWAY INSURANCE BROKERS LLC
Also Called: Nationwide
1731 Tech Dr Ste 250, San Jose (95110)
PHONE.............................408 441-2000
Gregory W Stewart, *President*
Greg Stewart, *Treasurer*
David Tuckness, *Vice Pres*

Rie Farr, *Executive*
Ellen Bertolucci, *Admin Asst*
EMP: 45 EST: 1975
SQ FT: 13,000
SALES (est): 13.3MM Privately Held
WEB: www.archwayinsurance.com
SIC: 6411 Insurance brokers

(P-10237)
ARGO INSURANCE BROKERS INC (HQ)
2300 Contra Costa Blvd # 375, Pleasant Hill (94523-3976)
P.O. Box 232017 (94523-6017)
PHONE.............................925 682-7001
Jerry Katopodis, *President*
Sandra Demartini, *Technology*
Cheryl Kough, *Technology*
William Ferree, *Producer*
Beth Lee, *Manager*
EMP: 40 EST: 2007
SALES (est): 7.1MM Privately Held
WEB: www.argoinsurance.com
SIC: 6411 Insurance agents; insurance brokers

(P-10238)
ASPIRE GENERAL INSURANCE CO
2721 Citrus Rd Ste B, Rancho Cordova (95742-6313)
P.O. Box 2426, Rancho Cucamonga (91729-2426)
PHONE.............................877 789-4742
Byron Storms, *CEO*
Brad Hinkle, *Officer*
Tyler Nicholson, *VP Mktg*
EMP: 40 EST: 1980
SALES (est): 6.3MM Privately Held
WEB: www.aspiregeneral.com
SIC: 6411 Insurance agents

(P-10239)
ASSOC CA WTR AGC/JT PW INS
Also Called: Acwa Jpia
2100 Professional Dr, Roseville (95661-3700)
P.O. Box 619082 (95661-9082)
PHONE.............................916 786-5742
Walter Sells, *CEO*
EMP: 45 EST: 1979
SQ FT: 7,000
SALES (est): 8.4MM Privately Held
WEB: www.acwajpia.com
SIC: 6411 9651 Insurance agents; insurance commission, government

(P-10240)
ASSURED INSURANCE TECHNOLOGIES
650 Page Mill Rd, Palo Alto (94304-1001)
PHONE.............................424 781-7123
Justin Lewis-Weber, *CEO*
EMP: 63 EST: 2019
SALES (est): 2.5MM Privately Held
SIC: 6411 Insurance agents, brokers & service

(P-10241)
ASSUREDPARTNERS INC
1455 Response Rd Ste 260, Sacramento (95815-5263)
PHONE.............................916 443-0200
EMP: 56 Privately Held
WEB: www.assuredpartners.com
SIC: 6411 Insurance agents
PA: Assuredpartners, Inc.
   200 Colonial Center Pkwy # 1
   Lake Mary FL 32746

(P-10242)
AT-BAY INC (PA)
196 Castro St Ste A, Mountain View (94041-2802)
PHONE.............................888 338-9522
Rotem Iram, *CEO*
Scott Gold, *Manager*
EMP: 48 EST: 2016
SALES (est): 2.7MM Privately Held
WEB: www.at-bay.com
SIC: 6411 Loss prevention services, insurance

6411 - Insurance Agents, Brokers & Svc County (P-10243)

(P-10243)
ATHENS INSURANCE SERVICE INC
Also Called: Athens Administrators
2552 Stanwell Dr Ste 100, Concord (94520-4851)
P.O. Box 4029 (94524-4029)
PHONE...................925 826-1000
James C Jenkins, *Ch of Bd*
James R Jenkins, *President*
Jane Catelani, *CFO*
Jodi Ellington, *CFO*
EMP: 250 **EST:** 1976
SALES (est): 38.8MM **Privately Held**
WEB: www.athensadmin.com
SIC: 6411 Insurance claim adjusters, not employed by insurance company

(P-10244)
BAINS WOODWARD INSUR SVCS INC
2260 Oro Dam Blvd E Ste C, Oroville (95966-6051)
PHONE...................530 534-6600
EMP: 70
SALES (corp-wide): 6.1MM **Privately Held**
WEB: www.saveproins.com
SIC: 6411 Insurance agents
HQ: Bains & Woodward Insurance Services Inc.
1557 Starr Dr Ste A
Yuba City CA 95993
530 923-2930

(P-10245)
BB&T INSURANCE SVCS CAL INC (DH)
Also Called: Armstrng/Robitaille Insur Svcs
4480 Willow Rd, Pleasanton (94588-8519)
PHONE...................925 463-9672
Mark Ruggles, *President*
Jo Brett, *Personnel*
Karen Smith, *Manager*
Kasey Johnson, *Accounts Exec*
EMP: 49 **EST:** 1981
SALES (est): 30.5MM
SALES (corp-wide): 24.4B **Publicly Held**
WEB: www.bbt.com
SIC: 6411 Insurance agents & brokers
HQ: Mcgriff Insurance Services, Inc.
3201 Beechleaf Ct Ste 200
Raleigh NC 27604
919 716-9907

(P-10246)
BENEFIT & RISK MANAGEMENT SVCS
80 Iron Point Cir Ste 200, Folsom (95630-8593)
P.O. Box 2140 (95763-2140)
PHONE...................916 467-1200
Matthew Allen Schafer, *CEO*
Shannon Baxter, *Officer*
Vanessa Pahlberg, *Vice Pres*
Luke Schafer, *Vice Pres*
Paul Schafer, *Vice Pres*
EMP: 130 **EST:** 1993
SQ FT: 15,000
SALES (est): 25.6MM **Privately Held**
WEB: www.brmsonline.com
SIC: 6411 Insurance brokers

(P-10247)
BENEFITSTREET INC
12677 Alcosta Blvd, San Ramon (94583-4423)
PHONE...................925 831-0800
Jerry Bramlett, *President*
Alex Hehmeyer, *Bd of Directors*
Michael Angel, *Exec VP*
Bill Klein, *Vice Pres*
Paul Warenski, *Vice Pres*
EMP: 96 **EST:** 1993
SALES (est): 10.2MM **Privately Held**
WEB: www.benefitstreet.com
SIC: 6411 Pension & retirement plan consultants

(P-10248)
BENETECH INC (PA)
3841 N Freeway Blvd # 185, Sacramento (95834-1948)
P.O. Box 348570 (95834-8570)
PHONE...................916 484-6811
Robert L Brandon, *President*
James Casalegno, *Senior VP*
Chuck Walker, *Senior VP*
Betsy G Beaumon, *Vice Pres*
Chris Blazek, *Vice Pres*
EMP: 60 **EST:** 1974
SQ FT: 20,000
SALES (est): 21MM **Privately Held**
WEB: www.benetechinc.com
SIC: 6411 Pension & retirement plan consultants

(P-10249)
BERKSHIRE HATHAWAY HOMESTATES (HQ)
1 California St Ste 600, San Francisco (94111-5403)
P.O. Box 881716 (94188-1716)
PHONE...................415 433-1650
Louis B Rovens, *President*
Dennis Halloran, *Technology*
Tracy Clark, *Technical Staff*
Matt Hausman, *Analyst*
Janice Post, *Broker*
EMP: 180
SQ FT: 51,000
SALES (est): 157.1MM
SALES (corp-wide): 245.5B **Publicly Held**
WEB: www.berkshirehathaway.com
SIC: 6411 Insurance claim processing, except medical
PA: Berkshire Hathaway Inc.
3555 Farnam St Ste 1140
Omaha NE 68131
402 346-1400

(P-10250)
BICKMORE AND ASSOCIATES INC (DH)
Also Called: Bickmore Risk Svcs Consulting
1750 Creekside Oaks Dr # 200, Sacramento (95833-3648)
PHONE...................916 244-1100
Greg L Trout, *CEO*
John Alltop, *President*
L Robert Kramer, *President*
Jeffrey C Grubbs, *COO*
Solomiya Murphy, *Admin Asst*
EMP: 70 **EST:** 1984
SQ FT: 25,500
SALES (est): 17.3MM **Privately Held**
SIC: 6411 Insurance information & consulting services
HQ: York Risk Services Group, Inc.
1 Upper Pond Rd Ste 4
Parsippany NJ 07054
973 404-1200

(P-10251)
BROWN BROWN INSUR BRKS SCRMNTO
Also Called: Powers and Company
5750 West Oaks Blvd # 140, Rocklin (95765-4000)
PHONE...................916 630-8643
Mike Pascke, *Regional VP*
Ronald Floyd, *Principal*
EMP: 38 **EST:** 2011
SALES (est): 10.1MM
SALES (corp-wide): 2.6B **Publicly Held**
WEB: www.bbsacramento.com
SIC: 6411 Insurance agents; life insurance agents
PA: Brown & Brown, Inc.
300 N Beach St
Daytona Beach FL 32114
386 252-9601

(P-10252)
BROWN BROWN INSUR SVCS CAL INC
5890 Stoneridge Dr # 209, Pleasanton (94588-5818)
PHONE...................925 416-1692
EMP: 39
SALES (corp-wide): 2.6B **Publicly Held**
WEB: www.bbnca.com
SIC: 6411 Insurance agents, brokers & service
HQ: Brown & Brown Insurance Services Of California, Inc.
3697 Mt Diablo Blvd # 100
Lafayette CA 94549
415 884-7400

(P-10253)
BUILDERS & TRADESMENS
6610 Sierra College Blvd, Rocklin (95677-4306)
PHONE...................916 772-9200
Norbert Hohlbein, *President*
Jeff Erickson, *Vice Pres*
Lisa Erickson, *Vice Pres*
Jeff Hohlbein, *Vice Pres*
Paul Hohlbein, *Vice Pres*
EMP: 75 **EST:** 1998
SQ FT: 15,000
SALES (est): 31.5MM
SALES (corp-wide): 5.9B **Privately Held**
WEB: www.my.btisinc.com
SIC: 6411 Insurance brokers; fire insurance underwriters' laboratories
HQ: Amtrust Financial Services, Inc.
59 Maiden Ln Fl 43
New York NY 10038

(P-10254)
C D SIMONIAN INSURANCE INC
Also Called: C D Simonian Insurance Agency
503 N 7th St, Fowler (93625-2331)
P.O. Box 370 (93625-0370)
PHONE...................559 834-5333
David Simonian, *President*
Harold J Simonian, *Shareholder*
Lois Gigliotti, *Office Mgr*
Mark Pryor, *Agent*
EMP: 41 **EST:** 1951
SQ FT: 3,000
SALES (est): 10.8MM **Privately Held**
WEB: www.simonianins.com
SIC: 6411 Insurance agents

(P-10255)
CAL INSURANCE AND ASSOC INC
Also Called: Nationwide
2311 Taraval St, San Francisco (94116-2253)
PHONE...................415 661-6500
Scott Hauge, *President*
Marc Dorneles, *President*
Richard Miller, *Corp Secy*
Joe Be Lotchi, *Vice Pres*
Danielle Kaminski, *Executive*
EMP: 94 **EST:** 1961
SQ FT: 8,000
SALES (est): 7.9MM **Privately Held**
WEB: www.mycalteam.com
SIC: 6411 Insurance agents

(P-10256)
CAL LAND TITLE
497 Walnut St, NAPA (94559-3102)
PHONE...................707 361-5760
Jonny Karpuk, *CEO*
EMP: 38 **EST:** 1963
SALES (est): 6MM
SALES (corp-wide): 7.1MM **Privately Held**
WEB: www.cal-land.com
SIC: 6411 7371 ; computer software development & applications
PA: First American Title Company Of Napa
497 Walnut St Ste A
Napa CA 94559
707 254-4500

(P-10257)
CALIFORNIA COASTAL INSURANCE (PA)
Also Called: CCI Financial and Insur Svcs
3000 Executive Pkwy # 300, San Ramon (94583-4255)
P.O. Box 5076 (94583-0976)
PHONE...................925 866-7050
James P Vawter, *President*
Michael Vawter, *Admin Sec*
EMP: 38 **EST:** 1969
SQ FT: 10,000
SALES (est): 40MM **Privately Held**
WEB: www.kemperhsc.com
SIC: 6411 Insurance agents

(P-10258)
CAMICO MUTUAL INSURANCE CO (PA)
1800 Gateway Dr Ste 200, San Mateo (94404-4072)
PHONE...................650 378-6874
Ricardo R Rosario, *President*
Robert P Evans, *Ch of Bd*
Jay H Stewart, *CFO*
Rachel Ehrlich, *Officer*
Judith Frederiksen, *Vice Pres*
EMP: 79 **EST:** 1986 **Privately Held**
WEB: www.camico.com
SIC: 6411 Professional standards services, insurance

(P-10259)
CAPAX MANAGEMENT & INSUR SVCS (DH)
Also Called: Nationwide
4335 N Star Way Ste D, Modesto (95356-8628)
P.O. Box 3231 (95353-3231)
PHONE...................209 526-3110
Joel W Geddes Jr, *President*
Nick Mascitelli, *Senior VP*
Don Barbe, *Vice Pres*
Patty Martino, *Vice Pres*
Alfred Sarina, *Admin Sec*
EMP: 45 **EST:** 1952
SQ FT: 14,800
SALES (est): 27.9MM **Privately Held**
WEB: www.capax.com
SIC: 6411 Insurance agents

(P-10260)
CBIZ INC
2300 Contra Costa Blvd, Pleasant Hill (94523-3918)
PHONE...................925 956-0505
Melania Budiman, *President*
EMP: 35 **Publicly Held**
WEB: www.cbiz.com
SIC: 6411 Pension & retirement plan consultants
PA: Cbiz, Inc.
6050 Oak Tree Blvd # 500
Cleveland OH 44131

(P-10261)
CIVIL SVC EMPLOYEES INSUR CO (PA)
Also Called: Cse Insurance Group
2121 N Calif Blvd Ste 900, Walnut Creek (94596-7381)
PHONE...................800 282-6848
Pierre Bize, *President*
Gardner Gray Jr, *Senior VP*
Wally San Miguel, *Vice Pres*
Diana Puig, *Vice Pres*
Jessica Wendland, *Executive Asst*
EMP: 39 **EST:** 1949
SQ FT: 60,000 **Privately Held**
WEB: www.cseinsurance.com
SIC: 6411 Insurance agents

(P-10262)
CLAIMS MANAGEMENT INC
1101 Crkside Rdg Dr, Roseville (95678-3567)
P.O. Box 619079 (95661-9079)
PHONE...................916 631-1250
Kathy Peterson, *President*
John Scott, *Senior Mgr*
Randa Graham, *Manager*
EMP: 37 **EST:** 1981
SQ FT: 23,000
SALES (est): 2.8MM **Privately Held**
WEB: www.cmiw.com
SIC: 6411 Insurance claim adjusters, not employed by insurance company

(P-10263)
CLAIMS SERVICES GROUP LLC (DH)
6111 Bollinger Canyon Rd # 2, San Ramon (94583-5186)
PHONE...................925 866-1100
EMP: 64 **EST:** 1979
SALES (est): 110.2MM
SALES (corp-wide): 1.1B **Privately Held**
WEB: www.solera.com
SIC: 6411 Medical insurance claim processing, contract or fee basis

(P-10264)
COALITION INC (PA)
1160 Battery St Ste 350, San Francisco (94111-1238)
PHONE...................833 866-1337

PRODUCTS & SERVICES SECTION
6411 - Insurance Agents, Brokers & Svc County (P-10283)

Joshua Motta, *CEO*
EMP: 54 EST: 2010
SALES (est): 10MM **Privately Held**
WEB: www.coalitioninc.com
SIC: 6411 6211 Insurance agents, brokers & service; security brokers & dealers

(P-10265)
COLDWELL BANKER
580 El Camino Real, San Carlos (94070-2412)
PHONE..................................650 596-5400
EMP: 80 EST: 2011
SALES (est): 5.7MM **Privately Held**
SIC: 6411 Insurance Agent/Broker

(P-10266)
COLLECTIVEHEALTH INC
Also Called: Collective Health
85 Bluxome St, San Francisco (94107-1605)
PHONE..................................650 376-3804
Ali Diab, *CEO*
Ken Hahn, *CFO*
Rajaie Batniji, *Officer*
Susan Dybbs, *Vice Pres*
Hope Kragh, *Vice Pres*
EMP: 410 EST: 2013
SQ FT: 6,000
SALES (est): 129.3MM **Privately Held**
WEB: www.collectivehealth.com
SIC: 6411 7379 7372 Medical insurance claim processing, contract or fee basis; ; business oriented computer software

(P-10267)
CSAA INSURANCE EXCHANGE (PA)
3055 Oak Rd, Walnut Creek (94597-2098)
P.O. Box 23392, Oakland (94623-0392)
PHONE..................................925 279-2300
Thomas Troy, *President*
Michael Zukerman, *Officer*
Stephen O'Connor, *CIO*
James Stewart, *Consultant*
EMP: 869 EST: 1914
SALES (est): 2B **Privately Held**
WEB: www.csaa-insurance.aaa.com
SIC: 6411 Insurance agents

(P-10268)
CSAA INSURANCE SERVICES INC (HQ)
Also Called: Csaa Insurance Group
3055 Oak Rd, Walnut Creek (94597-2098)
P.O. Box 23392, Oakland (94623-0392)
PHONE..................................925 279-3153
Thomas M Troy, *CEO*
Greg Meyer, *COO*
Michael Day, *CFO*
Paul Acevedo, *Exec VP*
Bob Valliere, *Exec VP*
EMP: 62 EST: 2015
SALES (est): 167.6MM
SALES (corp-wide): 2B **Privately Held**
WEB: www.csaa-insurance.aaa.com
SIC: 6411 Insurance agents, brokers & service
PA: Csaa Insurance Exchange
3055 Oak Rd
Walnut Creek CA 94597
925 279-2300

(P-10269)
CSAC EXCESS INSURANCE AUTH
75 Iron Point Cir Ste 200, Folsom (95630-8813)
PHONE..................................916 850-7300
Michael Fleming, *CEO*
Amy Chang, *Officer*
Jim Castle, *Sr Exec VP*
Ken Caldwell, *Exec VP*
Thomas Bryson, *Vice Pres*
EMP: 60 EST: 1979
SQ FT: 13,613
SALES (est): 10.5MM **Privately Held**
WEB: www.prismrisk.gov
SIC: 6411 Insurance agents

(P-10270)
D A FINANCIAL GROUP CALIFORNIA
Also Called: Nfp Advisors
3470 Mt Diablo Blvd A100, Lafayette (94549-3958)
PHONE..................................925 254-7100
Theodore Zouzounis, *President*
John Hohman, *Vice Pres*
John Pacelli, *Vice Pres*
Robert Sciutto, *Vice Pres*
Reg Street, *Vice Pres*
EMP: 52 EST: 1958
SALES (est): 4.3MM
SALES (corp-wide): 376.7MM **Privately Held**
WEB: www.nfp.com
SIC: 6411 Insurance brokers
HQ: Nfp Corp.
340 Madison Ave Fl 21
New York NY 10173
212 301-4000

(P-10271)
DENTISTS INSURANCE COMPANY (HQ)
Also Called: Tdic
1201 K St Ste 1600, Sacramento (95814-3925)
P.O. Box 1582 (95812-1582)
PHONE..................................916 443-4567
Mark Soeth, *President*
Peter Dubois, *Exec Dir*
Robyn Taylor, *Opers Staff*
Kelli Young, *Sales Staff*
Melanie Duval, *Director*
EMP: 118 EST: 1979
SQ FT: 12,000
SALES (est): 39.5MM **Privately Held**
WEB: www.cda.org
SIC: 6411 Insurance agents, brokers & service
PA: California Dental Association Inc
1201 K St Fl 14
Sacramento CA 95814
916 443-0505

(P-10272)
DIBUDUO DFENDIS INSUR BRKS LLC (PA)
Also Called: Nationwide
6873 N West Ave, Fresno (93711-4308)
P.O. Box 5479 (93755-5479)
PHONE..................................559 432-0222
Matt Defendis, *Partner*
Mike De Fendis, *Partner*
Tony Canizales, *Vice Pres*
Steve Ellsworth, *Vice Pres*
Chris Falco, *Vice Pres*
EMP: 93
SQ FT: 22,000
SALES (est): 47.7MM **Privately Held**
WEB: www.dibu.com
SIC: 6411 Insurance agents

(P-10273)
DOCTORS MANAGEMENT COMPANY (HQ)
185 Greenwood Rd, NAPA (94558-6270)
P.O. Box 2900 (94558-0900)
PHONE..................................707 226-0100
Richard E Anderson, *CEO*
Eugene M Bullis, *CFO*
Kenneth R Chrisman, *Exec VP*
William J Gallagher, *Senior VP*
Michael Yacob, *Principal*
EMP: 200 EST: 1976
SQ FT: 72,000
SALES (est): 232.2MM
SALES (corp-wide): 760.2MM **Privately Held**
WEB: www.thedoctors.com
SIC: 6411 Insurance information & consulting services
PA: The Doctors' Company An Interinsurance Exchange
185 Greenwood Rd
Napa CA 94558
707 226-0100

(P-10274)
DON RAMATICI INSURANCE INC
Also Called: Nationwide
731 Southpoint Blvd A, Petaluma (94954-1495)
PHONE..................................707 782-9200
Paul Ramatici, *President*
Tom Griffith, *Vice Pres*
John Ramatici, *Vice Pres*
Sioban Amazeen, *Manager*
Hank Corda, *Accounts Mgr*
EMP: 35 EST: 1956
SALES (est): 5.3MM **Privately Held**
WEB: www.ramaticiins.com
SIC: 6411 Insurance agents

(P-10275)
EDGEWOOD PARTNERS INSUR CTR (HQ)
Also Called: Nationwide
1 California St Ste 400, San Francisco (94111-5402)
P.O. Box 5900, San Mateo (94402-5900)
PHONE..................................415 356-3900
Peter Garvey, *CEO*
Karman Chan, *CFO*
Stephen Adkins, *Officer*
Michael Gonthier, *Officer*
Kevin Grady, *Officer*
EMP: 65 EST: 1994
SALES (est): 384.5MM
SALES (corp-wide): 660.3MM **Privately Held**
WEB: www.epicbrokers.com
SIC: 6411 Insurance brokers
PA: Epic Holdings Inc.
1390 Willow Pass Rd # 80
Concord CA 94520
650 295-4600

(P-10276)
EHEALTH INC (PA)
2625 Augustine Dr Ste 125, Santa Clara (95054-2956)
PHONE..................................650 584-2700
Scott N Flanders, *CEO*
Robert S Hurley, *President*
David K Francis, *COO*
Christine Janofsky, *CFO*
Derek N Yung, *CFO*
EMP: 206 EST: 1997
SQ FT: 32,492
SALES (est): 582.7MM **Publicly Held**
WEB: www.ehealthinsurance.com
SIC: 6411 Insurance agents; insurance agents & brokers; insurance information & consulting services

(P-10277)
EHEALTHINSURANCE SERVICES INC (HQ)
2625 Augustine Dr Ste 201, Santa Clara (95054-2956)
PHONE..................................650 584-2700
Ellen O Tausche, *Principal*
Rob Lapstuen, *President*
Bill Shaughnessy, *President*
Jiang Wu, *President*
Randall S Livingston, *Bd of Directors*
EMP: 100 EST: 1997
SALES (est): 257.4MM **Publicly Held**
WEB: www.ehealthmedicare.com
SIC: 6411 Insurance agents

(P-10278)
EMBROKER INSURANCE SVCS LLC (PA)
Also Called: Nationwide
24 Shotwell St, San Francisco (94103-3626)
PHONE..................................844 436-2765
Matthew Miller,
Brad Barkin, *Vice Pres*
Tom Demichael, *Vice Pres*
Charlie Hughes, *Vice Pres*
Thomas Mangan, *Vice Pres*
EMP: 149 EST: 2015
SALES (est): 25.8MM **Privately Held**
WEB: www.embroker.com
SIC: 6411 Insurance agents

(P-10279)
EMMETT W MCCRKLE INC INSUR SVC
Also Called: Maccorkle Insurance Service
700 Airport Blvd Ste 300, Burlingame (94010-1931)
PHONE..................................650 349-2364
Bernard Lauper, *President*
Pamela Lauper, *COO*
Keith Fujishige, *Vice Pres*
Marci Sheeran, *Executive*
Roy Folger, *Producer*
EMP: 35 EST: 1980
SQ FT: 6,000
SALES (est): 11.2MM
SALES (corp-wide): 772.2MM **Privately Held**
WEB: www.risk-strategies.com
SIC: 6411 Insurance brokers
PA: Rsc Insurance Brokerage, Inc.
160 Federal St Fl 4
Boston MA 02110
617 330-5700

(P-10280)
EPIC HOLDINGS INC (PA)
1390 Willow Pass Rd # 80, Concord (94520-5200)
PHONE..................................650 295-4600
John Hahn, *CEO*
Elaine Andrian, *CFO*
Dan R Francis, *Chairman*
David Thoke, *Exec VP*
Robin Brooks, *Vice Pres*
EMP: 81 EST: 2007
SALES (est): 660.3MM **Privately Held**
WEB: www.epicbrokers.com
SIC: 6411 Insurance brokers

(P-10281)
ESURANCE INSURANCE SVCS INC (HQ)
Also Called: PNC
650 Davis St, San Francisco (94111-1904)
PHONE..................................415 875-4500
Gary C Tolman, *CEO*
Jonathan Adkisson, *CFO*
Alan Gellman, *Chief Mktg Ofcr*
Eric Brandt, *Officer*
Kerian Bunch, *Vice Pres*
EMP: 104 EST: 1999
SQ FT: 10,000
SALES (est): 373MM **Publicly Held**
WEB: www.esurance.com
SIC: 6411 Insurance agents

(P-10282)
FARMERS INSURANCE EXCHANGE
2344 Merced St, San Leandro (94577-4209)
PHONE..................................510 895-6000
EMP: 288
SALES (corp-wide): 59.9B **Privately Held**
WEB: www.farmers.com
SIC: 6411 Insurance agents, brokers & service
HQ: Farmers Insurance Exchange
6301 Owensmouth Ave # 750
Woodland Hills CA 91367
888 327-6335

(P-10283)
FINANCIAL PACIFIC INSUR GROUP (DH)
Also Called: Financial Pacific Insurance Co
3880 Atherton Rd, Rocklin (95765-3700)
P.O. Box 292220, Sacramento (95829-2220)
PHONE..................................916 630-5000
Paul Ehrhardt, *President*
Artur A Terner, *CFO*
Robert Romanek, *Assistant VP*
Peggy Seale, *Underwriter*
EMP: 99 EST: 1993
SQ FT: 42,000
SALES (est): 21MM **Publicly Held**
WEB: www.ufginsurance.com
SIC: 6411 Insurance agents
HQ: Mercer Insurance Group, Inc.
10 N Hwy 31
Pennington NJ 08534
609 737-0426

6411 - Insurance Agents, Brokers & Svc County (P-10284)

(P-10284)
GALLAGHER BASSETT SERVICES INC
1451 River Park Dr # 220, Sacramento (95815-4507)
PHONE..................916 929-7581
EMP: 35
SALES (corp-wide): 7B Publicly Held
WEB: www.ajg.com
SIC: 6411 Insurance Agent/Broker
HQ: Gallagher Bassett Services, Inc.
2850 Golf Rd
Rolling Meadows IL 60008
630 773-3800

(P-10285)
GEICO GENERAL INSURANCE CO
5211 Madison Ave, Sacramento (95841-3053)
PHONE..................916 923-5050
EMP: 402
SALES (corp-wide): 245.5B Publicly Held
WEB: www.geico.com
SIC: 6411 Insurance agents
HQ: Geico General Insurance Company
1 Geico Plz
Washington DC 20076

(P-10286)
GEORGE HILLS COMPANY INC
3017 Gold Canal Dr 400, Rancho Cordova (95670-6129)
PHONE..................916 859-4800
Michael Kielty, President
Rodger Hayton, Branch Mgr
Chuck Torretta, Administration
Kim Santin, Finance
Robert Chalfant,
EMP: 161
SALES (corp-wide): 34.8MM Privately Held
WEB: www.georgehills.com
SIC: 6411 Insurance claim adjusters, not employed by insurance company
PA: George Hills Company, Inc.
3043 Gold Canal Dr # 200
Rancho Cordova CA 95670
916 859-4800

(P-10287)
GEOVERA SPECIALTY INSURANCE CO
1455 Oliver Rd, Fairfield (94534-3472)
PHONE..................707 863-3700
Karen Padovese, President
Kevin Nish, President
Robert Hagedorn, Vice Pres
Frank Lazzeroni, Vice Pres
Brian Prentice, Vice Pres
EMP: 60 EST: 1996
SALES (est): 17.3MM Privately Held
WEB: www.geovera.com
SIC: 6411 Insurance agents
PA: Geovera Holdings, Inc.
4820 Busineca Ctr Dr 20
Fairfield CA 94534

(P-10288)
GREGORY B BRAGG & ASSOCIATES
4512 Feather River Dr B, Stockton (95219-6563)
P.O. Box 619079, Roseville (95661-9079)
PHONE..................209 956-2119
Gregory B Bragg, Branch Mgr
EMP: 39 Privately Held
WEB: www.gbbragg.com
SIC: 6411 Insurance claim adjusters, not employed by insurance company
PA: Gregory B Bragg & Associates Inc
1 Sierra Gate Plz 250b
Roseville CA
916 783-0100

(P-10289)
GROSVENOR INV MGT US INC
155 Montgomery St Ste 611, San Francisco (94104-4111)
PHONE..................415 773-0275
John Ford, Principal
EMP: 80
SALES (corp-wide): 5.5B Publicly Held
SIC: 6411 Pension & retirement plan consultants
HQ: Grosvenor Investment Management Us Inc.
10 New King St Ste 214
White Plains NY 10604
914 683-3710

(P-10290)
HEALTH COMP ADMINISTRATORS (PA)
621 Santa Fe Ave, Fresno (93721-2724)
P.O. Box 45018 (93718-5018)
PHONE..................559 499-2450
Phillip Musson, President
Michael Bouskos, Vice Pres
Mike Bouskos, Vice Pres
Yer Xiong, Accountant
Vickie Houts, Nurse
EMP: 165 EST: 1994
SALES (est): 20.8MM Privately Held
WEB: www.healthcomp.com
SIC: 6411 Medical insurance claim processing, contract or fee basis

(P-10291)
HEALTHCOMP
Also Called: Healthcomp Administrators
621 Santa Fe Ave, Fresno (93721-2724)
P.O. Box 45018 (93718-5018)
PHONE..................559 499-2450
Phillip Musson, CEO
Michael Bouskos, CFO
Monique Bouskos, Vice Pres
Kelly Ferreira, Vice Pres
Justin Forton, Vice Pres
EMP: 260 EST: 1994
SQ FT: 50,000
SALES (est): 41.6MM Privately Held
WEB: www.healthcomp.com
SIC: 6411 Medical insurance claim processing, contract or fee basis

(P-10292)
HILB RGAL HOBBS INSUR SVCS INC (DH)
Also Called: Willis Hrh
525 Market St Ste 3400, San Francisco (94105-2742)
PHONE..................212 915-8084
Guy Numan, President
EMP: 41 EST: 1954
SQ FT: 12,500
SALES (est): 25.3MM Privately Held
WEB: www.willistowerswatson.com
SIC: 6411 Insurance brokers
HQ: Willis North America Inc.
200 Liberty St Fl 3
New York NY 10281
212 915-8888

(P-10293)
HIPPO ANALYTICS INC (PA)
Also Called: Hippo Insurance Service
150 Forest Ave, Palo Alto (94301-1614)
PHONE..................925 895-9184
Assaf Wand, President
Stewart Ellis, CFO
Eyal Navon, Founder
Sergio Iastrebner, Vice Pres
Anna Lee, Vice Pres
EMP: 277 EST: 2015
SALES (est): 25.1MM Privately Held
SIC: 6411 Insurance agents, brokers & service

(P-10294)
HUB INTRNTIONAL INSUR SVCS INC
Also Called: Nationwide
44 2nd St, San Francisco (94105-3440)
PHONE..................415 512-2100
Bruce Callander, Branch Mgr
Bill Ryan, Exec VP
Elaine Sy, Executive Asst
Irene Hughes, Sales Associate
Sabine De Lambert-Liop, Manager
EMP: 35 Privately Held
WEB: www.sweetandbaker.com
SIC: 6411 Insurance agents
HQ: Hub International Insurance Services Inc.
3390 University Ave # 300
Riverside CA 92501

(P-10295)
HUB INTRNTIONAL INSUR SVCS INC
Also Called: Der Manuel Insurance Group
548 W Cromwell Ave # 101, Fresno (93711-5714)
PHONE..................559 447-4600
Jonathan Wiebe, Admin Sec
Maria Hustedde, Admin Asst
Scott Armstrong, IT/INT Sup
Tina Heister, Technology
Britt Gosswiller, Broker
EMP: 71 Privately Held
WEB: www.dmig.com
SIC: 6411 Insurance agents
HQ: Hub International Insurance Services Inc.
3390 University Ave # 300
Riverside CA 92501

(P-10296)
INSPRO CORPORATION
Also Called: Risk Administration & MGT
2300 Clayton Rd Ste 1100, Concord (94520-2157)
PHONE..................925 685-1600
Grant Weaver, Managing Dir
Andrea Weaver, Shareholder
S Lee Nelson, Officer
EMP: 73 EST: 1982
SQ FT: 1,400
SALES (est): 9.8MM Privately Held
WEB: www.tmhcc.com
SIC: 6411 Insurance brokers
HQ: Hcc Insurance Holdings, Inc.
13403 Northwest Fwy
Houston TX 77040

(P-10297)
INSURNCE SVCS SAN FRNCISCO INC
Also Called: Nationwide
201 California St Ste 200, San Francisco (94111-5004)
PHONE..................415 788-9810
Thomas J Ryan III, President
Jason Cheung, Vice Pres
Cary White, Managing Dir
Thomas MEI, Admin Asst
Winston Velasco, Administration
EMP: 67 EST: 1989
SALES (est): 5.3MM Privately Held
WEB: www.isusf.com
SIC: 6411 Insurance agents

(P-10298)
INTERCARE SPCLTY RISK INSUR SV (PA)
Also Called: Isr Holdings
140 Diamond Creek Pl, Roseville (95747-6652)
PHONE..................916 757-1200
Kevin Hamm, President
EMP: 37 EST: 2008
SALES (est): 9.1MM Privately Held
SIC: 6411 Property & casualty insurance agent

(P-10299)
INTERWEST INSURANCE SVCS LLC (PA)
Also Called: Kemper Insurance
8950 Cal Center Dr Bldg 3, Sacramento (95826-3259)
PHONE..................916 488-3100
Tom Williams, Chairman
Thomas Williams, President
Keith Schuler, CEO
Nancy Luttenbacher, COO
Donald Pollard, CFO
EMP: 173 EST: 2014
SQ FT: 20,000
SALES (est): 150.2MM Privately Held
WEB: www.iwins.com
SIC: 6411 Insurance brokers

(P-10300)
INTERWEST INSURANCE SVCS LLC
Also Called: Nationwide
5 Sierra Gate Plz Fl 2nd, Roseville (95678-6637)
PHONE..................916 784-1008
Chelsea Rumolo, Accounts Mgr
Jazmin Villa, Accounts Mgr
EMP: 60
SALES (corp-wide): 150.2MM Privately Held
WEB: www.iwins.com
SIC: 6411 Insurance agents
PA: Interwest Insurance Services, Llc
8950 Cal Center Dr Bldg 3
Sacramento CA 95826
916 488-3100

(P-10301)
JAGDEEP SINGH INSUR AGCY INC
Also Called: Nationwide
4185 W Figarden Dr # 101, Fresno (93722-6069)
PHONE..................559 277-5580
Jagdeep Singh, President
EMP: 35 EST: 2010
SALES (est): 20MM Privately Held
WEB: www.jsinghagency.com
SIC: 6411 Insurance agents

(P-10302)
JAMES C JENKINS INSUR SVC INC
Also Called: Athens Insurance
1390 Willow Pass Rd, Concord (94520-5200)
PHONE..................925 798-3334
John Hahn, CEO
Peter Garvey, President
Karman Chan, CFO
Jason Del Grande, Vice Pres
Michael Gonthier,
EMP: 125 EST: 1977
SQ FT: 30,000
SALES (est): 37.2MM
SALES (corp-wide): 660.3MM Privately Held
WEB: www.epicbrokers.com
SIC: 6411 Insurance brokers
HQ: Edgewood Partners Insurance Center
1 California St Ste 400
San Francisco CA 94111

(P-10303)
JAMES G PARKER INSURANCE ASSOC (PA)
Also Called: Nationwide
1753 E Fir Ave, Fresno (93720-3840)
P.O. Box 3947 (93650-3947)
PHONE..................559 222-7722
James G Parker, President
Janice W Parker, Treasurer
Janice Parker, Treasurer
Leroy Berrett, Vice Pres
John Cleveland, Vice Pres
EMP: 70 EST: 1978
SQ FT: 13,000
SALES (est): 41.8MM Privately Held
WEB: www.jgparker.com
SIC: 6411 Insurance agents

(P-10304)
JOURNEY INC
2211 Plaza Dr Ste 100, Rocklin (95765-4420)
PHONE..................916 780-7000
Ronald Abram, President
Candice Niederberger, Commercial
EMP: 37 EST: 1996
SQ FT: 8,000
SALES (est): 4.7MM Privately Held
SIC: 6411 Insurance agents

(P-10305)
KASPICK & CO LLC (DH)
203 Redwood Shores Pkwy # 300, Redwood City (94065-1198)
PHONE..................650 585-4100
Lindy Sherwood, Mng Member
Sarah Devany, COO
C A Korthals, Officer
David Lyons, Officer
Colleen Mesec, Officer
EMP: 60 EST: 1989
SALES (est): 19.3MM
SALES (corp-wide): 32.6B Privately Held
WEB: www.kaspick.com
SIC: 6411 Insurance agents, brokers & service

2022 Northern California Business Directory and Buyers Guide

▲ = Import ▼ = Export
◆ = Import/Export

PRODUCTS & SERVICES SECTION
6411 - Insurance Agents, Brokers & Svc County (P-10325)

HQ: Teachers Insurance And Annuity Association-College Retirement Equities Fund
730 3rd Ave Ste 2a
New York NY 10017
212 490-9000

(P-10306)
KEMPER INDEPENDENCE INSUR CO
Also Called: Kemper Insurance
2565 Alluvial Ave Ste 182, Clovis (93611-9515)
PHONE..................559 326-2551
Dan Kumar, *Agent*
EMP: 36 **Publicly Held**
WEB: www.kemper.com
SIC: 6411 Insurance agents
HQ: Kemper Independence Insurance Company
12926 Gran Bay Pkwy W # 11
Jacksonville FL 32258
904 245-5600

(P-10307)
KONING & ASSOCIATES INC (PA)
1631 Willow St Ste 220, San Jose (95125-5108)
PHONE..................408 265-3800
Chris Koning, *President*
EMP: 50 **EST:** 1985
SALES (est): 6MM **Privately Held**
WEB: www.koning.us
SIC: 6411 7389 Insurance claim adjusters, not employed by insurance company; inspection & investigation services, insurance;

(P-10308)
LEAVITT PACIFIC INSUR BRKS INC
Also Called: Nationwide
1330 S Bascom Ave Ste A, San Jose (95128-4513)
PHONE..................408 288-6262
Bill Beck, *General Mgr*
EMP: 41 **EST:** 1978
SQ FT: 6,000
SALES (est): 3.6MM **Privately Held**
WEB: www.nationwide.com
SIC: 6411 Insurance brokers

(P-10309)
LIPMAN COMPANY INC
Also Called: TLC Insurance Administrators
3340 Walnut Ave Ste 290, Fremont (94538-2215)
PHONE..................510 796-4676
Frederic J Lipman, *President*
Janet Sylvester, *CFO*
Caroline Nelson, *Vice Pres*
Margaret Epstein, *Admin Sec*
Nora Johnson, *Administration*
EMP: 40 **EST:** 1994
SQ FT: 11,000
SALES (est): 975.9K
SALES (corp-wide): 25.7MM **Privately Held**
WEB: www.lipmanpa.com
SIC: 6411 Insurance claim adjusters, not employed by insurance company
PA: Lipman Insurance Administrators, Inc.
39420 Liberty St Ste 260
Fremont CA 94538
510 796-4676

(P-10310)
MAROEVICH OSHEA CGHLAN INSUR S
Also Called: Nationwide
44 Montgomery St Ste 1700, San Francisco (94104-4704)
PHONE..................415 957-0600
Van Maroevich, *CEO*
Gerald Clifford, *CFO*
Jerry Clifford, *CFO*
Steve Elkins, *Exec VP*
Peter Brown, *Senior VP*
EMP: 60 **EST:** 1969
SQ FT: 10,000
SALES (est): 11.7MM **Privately Held**
WEB: www.nationwide.com
SIC: 6411 Insurance brokers

(P-10311)
MC GRAW COMMERCIAL INSUR SVC (PA)
3601 Haven Ave, Menlo Park (94025-1064)
PHONE..................650 780-4800
Michael J Mc Graw, *President*
Joan D Mc Graw, *Corp Secy*
John M Mc Graw, *Vice Pres*
Susan Valencia, *Vice Pres*
EMP: 90 **EST:** 1984
SQ FT: 20,000
SALES (est): 7.9MM **Privately Held**
SIC: 6411 Insurance agents

(P-10312)
MEDICAL INSURANCE EXCHANGE CAL
6250 Claremont Ave, Oakland (94618-1324)
PHONE..................510 596-4935
Dr Bradford Cohn, *President*
Dr William Donald, *Vice Chairman*
Shelly Shaw, *Officer*
Tova Rabinowitz, *Executive Asst*
Dr Conrad Anderson, *Admin Sec*
EMP: 74 **EST:** 1975
SQ FT: 13,000
SALES (est): 10.6MM **Privately Held**
WEB: www.miec.com
SIC: 6411 Loss prevention services, insurance

(P-10313)
MEDICAL UNDERWRITERS CAL INC (PA)
Also Called: Medical Insurance Exchange
6250 Claremont Ave, Oakland (94618-1324)
PHONE..................510 428-9411
William K Scheuber, *President*
L Richard Mello, *Treasurer*
Ron Neupauer, *Vice Pres*
Annie Petrides, *Vice Pres*
Stephen Stimel, *Vice Pres*
EMP: 78 **EST:** 1975
SQ FT: 13,000
SALES (est): 24.8MM **Privately Held**
WEB: www.miec.com
SIC: 6411 Insurance agents

(P-10314)
MELITA-MCDONALD INSUR SVCS INC
Also Called: Melita Group, The
75 E Santa Clara St # 1200, San Jose (95113-1834)
P.O. Box 610520 (95161-0520)
PHONE..................408 882-0800
Paul Mifsud, *President*
Lisa McCormack, *Exec VP*
Greg Geme, *Vice Pres*
Greg St Geme, *Vice Pres*
Jodi Costello, *Technology*
EMP: 46 **EST:** 1993
SQ FT: 11,500
SALES (est): 5.1MM **Privately Held**
WEB: www.melitagroup.com
SIC: 6411 Insurance brokers

(P-10315)
MERCER CONSULTING GROUP INC
3 Embarkadero Ctr, Oakland (94619)
PHONE..................415 743-8510
Elmore Quiboloy, *COO*
Courtney Patt, *Manager*
EMP: 45
SALES (corp-wide): 17.2B **Publicly Held**
WEB: www.marshmclennan.com
SIC: 6411 Insurance brokers
HQ: Mercer Consulting Group, Inc.
1166 Ave Of The Americas
New York NY 10036
212 345-3829

(P-10316)
NATIONAL INSUR INSPTN SVCS INC
Also Called: Nationwide
1040 E Herndon Ave # 205, Fresno (93720-3158)
PHONE..................559 435-1117
Larry D Lewallen, *President*
Debra Lewallen, *Vice Pres*
Morgan Wood, *CTO*
Norma Ruiz, *Opers Mgr*
Robbie Greeley, *Client Mgr*
EMP: 43 **EST:** 2007
SQ FT: 4,400
SALES (est): 6.4MM **Privately Held**
WEB: www.nationalis.com
SIC: 6411 Insurance agents, brokers & service

(P-10317)
NETWORKED INSURANCE AGENTS LLC
Also Called: Nationwide
443 Crown Point Cir Ste A, Grass Valley (95945-9557)
PHONE..................800 682-8476
George Biancardi, *President*
Kelly McRae, *CFO*
Larry Oslie, *Exec VP*
Michael Carrington, *Senior VP*
Joe Stankowich, *Vice Pres*
EMP: 110 **EST:** 2013
SQ FT: 15,000
SALES (est): 16.6MM
SALES (corp-wide): 797.1MM **Privately Held**
WEB: www.amwins.com
SIC: 6411 Insurance agents
PA: Amwins Group, Inc.
4725 Piedmont Row Dr # 600
Charlotte NC 28210
704 749-2700

(P-10318)
NEWFRONT INSURANCE SVCS LLC (HQ)
Also Called: Nationwide
777 Mariners Island Blvd # 250, San Mateo (94404-5088)
PHONE..................415 754-3635
Spike Lipkin, *CEO*
Anna Beach, *Officer*
Garth Hamilton, *Officer*
Pallavi Devaraj, *Executive*
Debbie Obiacoro, *Executive*
EMP: 83 **EST:** 2017
SALES (est): 10.2MM
SALES (corp-wide): 83.5MM **Privately Held**
WEB: www.newfront.com
SIC: 6411 Insurance agents & brokers
PA: Abd Insurance & Financial Services, Inc.
777 Mariners Island Blvd # 250
San Mateo CA 94404
650 488-8565

(P-10319)
NEWPORT GROUP INC (PA)
1350 Treat Blvd Ste 300, Walnut Creek (94597-7959)
PHONE..................925 328-4540
Greg W Tschider, *CEO*
Nancy Worth, *COO*
John Matelis, *CFO*
Michael Dicenso, *Exec VP*
Martha Sadler, *Exec VP*
EMP: 201 **EST:** 1985
SALES (est): 194.6MM **Privately Held**
WEB: www.newportgroup.com
SIC: 6411 Pension & retirement plan consultants

(P-10320)
NEXT INSURANCE INC (PA)
490 California Ave # 300, Palo Alto (94306-1988)
P.O. Box 1027 (94302-1027)
PHONE..................855 222-5919
Melanie Chase, *Chief Mktg Ofcr*
Guy Goldstein, *President*
Sofya Pogreb, *COO*
Michelle Cheung, *Officer*
Christine Pfeiffer, *Opers Staff*
EMP: 474 **EST:** 2016
SALES (est): 131.5MM **Privately Held**
WEB: www.nextinsurance.com
SIC: 6411 Insurance agents

(P-10321)
NONPROFITS INSUR ALIANCE CAL
300 Panetta Ave, Santa Cruz (95060-6372)
P.O. Box 8507 (95061-8507)
PHONE..................831 459-0980
Pamela E Davis, *President*
Ren Agarwal, *Chief Mktg Ofcr*
Dave Gibson, *Officer*
Betty Johnson, *Vice Pres*
Melissa Yarnell, *Vice Pres*
EMP: 45
SALES: 72.7MM **Privately Held**
WEB: www.insurancefornonprofits.org
SIC: 6411 Insurance agents, brokers & service

(P-10322)
NORCAL MUTUAL INSURANCE CO (HQ)
575 Market St Fl 10, San Francisco (94105-2885)
PHONE..................415 735-2000
Ned Rand, *President*
Jaan Sidorov, *Bd of Directors*
Cobie Buchman, *Assoc VP*
Christoph Dugre, *Assoc VP*
Kevin Smith, *Assoc VP*
EMP: 285 **EST:** 1975
SALES (est): 308.9MM
SALES (corp-wide): 874.9MM **Publicly Held**
WEB: www.norcal-group.com
SIC: 6411 6331 Insurance agents; fire, marine & casualty insurance
PA: Proassurance Corporation
100 Brookwood Pl
Birmingham AL 35209
205 877-4400

(P-10323)
NORTHSTAR RISK MGT INSUR SVCS
Also Called: Kemper Insurance
1777 Botelho Dr Ste 360, Walnut Creek (94596-5084)
PHONE..................925 975-5900
Charlie Bates, *CEO*
David Costello, *President*
Michael Martin, *Exec VP*
Michael P Martin, *Exec VP*
Chris Thorndike, *Exec VP*
EMP: 40 **EST:** 1988
SQ FT: 4,200
SALES (est): 2.7MM **Privately Held**
WEB: www.northstar-ins.com
SIC: 6411 Insurance agents

(P-10324)
NORTHWEST ADMINISTRATORS INC
1000 Marina Blvd Ste 400, Brisbane (94005-1841)
PHONE..................650 570-7300
William Riker, *Principal*
Celeste Furlough, *Trust Officer*
Debra Rockafellow, *Trust Officer*
Walter Pentz, *Senior VP*
Kate Carroll, *Executive*
EMP: 48
SALES (corp-wide): 301.9MM **Privately Held**
WEB: www.nwadmin.com
SIC: 6411 Pension & retirement plan consultants
PA: Northwest Administrators, Inc.
2323 Eastlake Ave E
Seattle WA 98102
206 329-4900

(P-10325)
NORTHWEST INSURANCE AGENCY INC (PA)
Also Called: Nationwide
175 W College Ave, Santa Rosa (95401-6503)
P.O. Box 3539 (95402-3539)
PHONE..................707 573-1300
Charles L Bussman, *CEO*
Mary Fairow, *President*
Michael R Sullivan, *Chairman*
Manny Mello, *Corp Secy*
Dennis Stanley, *Vice Pres*
EMP: 45 **EST:** 1976
SQ FT: 8,500
SALES (est): 9.3MM **Privately Held**
WEB: www.gpins.com
SIC: 6411 Insurance agents; insurance brokers; property & casualty insurance agent

6411 - Insurance Agents, Brokers & Svc County (P-10326)

PRODUCTS & SERVICES SECTION

(P-10326)
OAK RIVER INSURANCE COMPANY
1 California St Ste 600, San Francisco (94111-5403)
P.O. Box 881236 (94188-1236)
PHONE..................800 661-6029
EMP: 254
SALES (corp-wide): 245.5B Publicly Held
WEB: www.bhhc.com
SIC: 6411 Insurance agents, brokers & service
HQ: Oak River Insurance Company
1314 Douglas St
Omaha NE 68102

(P-10327)
OLD REPUBLIC HM PROTECTION INC
2 Annabel Ln Ste 112, San Ramon (94583-1377)
P.O. Box 5017 (94583-0917)
PHONE..................925 866-1500
Frank Caballero, *President*
Pj Cochran, *Vice Pres*
Lorna Mello, *Vice Pres*
Gail Stevens, *Vice Pres*
Terry Toole, *Vice Pres*
EMP: 305 EST: 1974
SQ FT: 39,500
SALES (est): 240.7MM
SALES (corp-wide): 7.1B Publicly Held
WEB: www.orhp.com
SIC: 6411 Insurance agents, brokers & service
PA: Old Republic International Corporation
307 N Michigan Ave
Chicago IL 60601
312 346-8100

(P-10328)
ORBA INSURANCE SERVICES INC
Also Called: Orba Financial & Inter SEC
2339 Gold Mdal Way Ste 20, Rancho Cordova (95670)
PHONE..................916 858-1222
Gary Curry, *President*
Susan Curry, *Corp Secy*
EMP: 91 EST: 1979
SQ FT: 2,600
SALES (est): 6.7MM Privately Held
SIC: 6411 Insurance agents & brokers

(P-10329)
OWEN & COMPANY
1455 Response Rd Ste 260, Sacramento (95815-5263)
PHONE..................916 993-2700
Jere Owen, *President*
Roger De Lusignan, *COO*
Jennifer Robles, *CFO*
John Owen, *Treasurer*
Renee Nunes, *Chief Mktg Ofcr*
EMP: 57 EST: 1948
SQ FT: 4,741
SALES (est): 13.5MM Privately Held
WEB: www.owendunn.com
SIC: 6411 8111 Insurance brokers; legal services

(P-10330)
PEGASUS RISK MANAGEMENT INC (PA)
Also Called: Status Medical Management
642 Galaxy Way, Modesto (95356-9606)
P.O. Box 5038 (95352-5038)
PHONE..................209 574-2800
Ray Simon, *President*
Brian Bergstrom, *Vice Pres*
Toby Stime, *Vice Pres*
Paula Towe, *Vice Pres*
Jackie Smith,
EMP: 70 EST: 1995
SQ FT: 10,000
SALES (est): 12.3MM Privately Held
WEB: www.simon-companies.com
SIC: 6411 Insurance claim processing, except medical

(P-10331)
PENNBROOK INSURANCE SERVICE
300 Montgomery St Ste 450, San Francisco (94104-1906)
P.O. Box 26849 (94126-0849)
PHONE..................415 820-2200
Clayton Wiens, *President*
Henry Bender, *Controller*
Renae Cannon, *Broker*
John Engers, *Broker*
Clifford Wiens, *Personnel*
EMP: 43 EST: 1982
SQ FT: 5,200
SALES (est): 6.7MM Privately Held
WEB: www.kemperhsc.com
SIC: 6411 Insurance agents; insurance brokers

(P-10332)
PINNEY INSURANCE CENTER INC
2266 Lava Ridge Ct # 200, Roseville (95661-2856)
PHONE..................916 773-3800
R Jan Pinney, *President*
Katie Cumalat, *Vice Pres*
Tracy Meier, *Vice Pres*
Nancy Pinney, *Vice Pres*
David Cranfield, *Director*
EMP: 43 EST: 1972
SQ FT: 5,500
SALES (est): 18MM Privately Held
WEB: www.pinneyinsurance.com
SIC: 6411 Insurance agents

(P-10333)
PLANPRESCRIBER INC
440 E Middlefield Rd, Mountain View (94043-4006)
PHONE..................650 584-2700
Bruce A Telkamp, *CEO*
EMP: 243 EST: 2012
SALES (est): 927.4K Publicly Held
WEB: www.ehealthmedicare.com
SIC: 6411 Insurance agents, brokers & service
PA: Ehealth, Inc.
2625 Augustine Dr Ste 125
Santa Clara CA 95054

(P-10334)
POLYCOMP ADMINISTRATIVE SVCS
3000 Lava Ridge Ct # 130, Roseville (95661-2802)
PHONE..................916 773-3480
Pamela Constantino, *Systems Mgr*
Martha Poppy, *Manager*
EMP: 50
SQ FT: 4,500
SALES (corp-wide): 24.2MM Privately Held
WEB: www.futureplan.com
SIC: 6411 Pension & retirement plan consultants
PA: Polycomp Administrative Services, Inc.
16030 Ventura Blvd # 200
Encino CA 91436
818 716-0111

(P-10335)
PRIMARK BENEFITS
Also Called: Professional Retirement Svcs
1810 Gateway Dr Ste 230, San Mateo (94404-4083)
PHONE..................650 692-2043
Stephen Dobrow, *President*
Maria Topacio, *Administration*
Gregg Rubenstein, *Finance*
Debby Shaw, *Accountant*
Heather Thompson, *Sales Staff*
EMP: 46 EST: 1971
SALES (est): 5.7MM Privately Held
WEB: www.primarkbenefits.com
SIC: 6411 Pension & retirement plan consultants

(P-10336)
PROFESSIONAL INSUR ASSOC INC (PA)
Also Called: Nationwide
1100 Industrial Rd Ste 3, San Carlos (94070-4131)
P.O. Box 1266 (94070-1266)
PHONE..................650 592-7333
Paula Hammack, *President*
Devan Hammack, *Vice Pres*
Paul Hammack, *Vice Pres*
Anne Johnson, *Administration*
Jared Adams, *Business Mgr*
EMP: 50 EST: 1960
SQ FT: 9,000
SALES (est): 15.7MM Privately Held
WEB: www.nationwide.com
SIC: 6411 Insurance agents; insurance brokers

(P-10337)
PROSIGHT SPECLTY INSUR GRP INC
1425 N Mcdowell Blvd # 213, Petaluma (94954-6500)
PHONE..................707 324-5000
Jacob Combs, *Vice Pres*
Nestor Lopez, *Vice Pres*
Dexter Alcedo, *Executive*
Christine Howley, *Program Mgr*
John Fitzgerald, *Systems Dir*
EMP: 59
SALES (corp-wide): 816.1MM Privately Held
WEB: www.prosightspecialty.com
SIC: 6411 Insurance brokers
HQ: Prosight Specialty Insurance Group, Inc.
412 Mount Kemble Ave 300c
Morristown NJ 07960

(P-10338)
RIELLI INSUR & FINCL SVCS LL (PA)
Also Called: Nationwide
100 Howe Ave, Sacramento (95825-8202)
PHONE..................916 234-1490
Alison Rielli, *Principal*
Ronnie Harper, *Agent*
EMP: 38 EST: 2015
SALES (est): 625K Privately Held
WEB: www.teamrielli.com
SIC: 6411 Insurance agents

(P-10339)
RON FILICE ENTERPRISES INC
Also Called: Filice Insurance Agency
738 N 1st St Ste 202, San Jose (95112-6371)
PHONE..................408 294-0477
Ron Filice, *President*
Jeffrey Bader, *Ch of Bd*
Silvia G Lucero, *Officer*
Chuck Batchelder, *Vice Pres*
Mike Chavez, *Vice Pres*
EMP: 81 EST: 1989
SQ FT: 3,000
SALES (est): 14.9MM Privately Held
WEB: www.filice.com
SIC: 6411 Insurance agents

(P-10340)
SACRAMNTO HSING RDVLPMENT AGCY
630 I St Fl 3, Sacramento (95814-2404)
PHONE..................916 440-1376
La Shelle Dozier, *Branch Mgr*
Angela Hall, *Program Mgr*
Karen Wallace, *Regional Mgr*
Ranjit Rai, *CTO*
Kenneth Olson, *Technical Mgr*
EMP: 100
SALES (corp-wide): 48.9MM Privately Held
WEB: www.shra.org
SIC: 6411 Insurance agents, brokers & service
PA: Sacramento Housing And Redevelopment Agency
801 12th St
Sacramento CA 95814
916 440-1390

(P-10341)
SANDER JCOBS CSSYRE GRFFIN INC
Also Called: Nationwide
3200 Villa Ln, NAPA (94558-3017)
PHONE..................707 252-8822
Jeffrey Erickson, *President*
Debbie Thibodaux, *Accounting Mgr*
Bob Chovick, *Broker*
Cherie Bolyarde, *Personnel*
Bruce Cassayre, *Producer*
EMP: 37 EST: 1947
SQ FT: 4,400
SALES (est): 5.5MM Privately Held
WEB: www.sanderjacobs.com
SIC: 6411 Insurance agents

(P-10342)
SCC ESA DEPT OF RISK MGMT
Also Called: ESA Risk Management
2310 N 1st St Ste 202, San Jose (95131-1040)
PHONE..................408 441-4207
EMP: 65
SALES (est): 2.8MM Privately Held
WEB: www.esariskmanagement.com
SIC: 6411 Insurance Agent/Broker

(P-10343)
SEDGWICK CLAIMS MGT SVCS INC
1410 Rocky Ridge Dr Ste 3, Roseville (95661-2811)
P.O. Box 619066 (95661-9066)
PHONE..................916 771-2900
David Banta, *Principal*
Michael Fisher, *Director*
Anasheh Chaharmahali, *Manager*
EMP: 66 Privately Held
WEB: www.sedgwick.com
SIC: 6411 Insurance claim adjusters, not employed by insurance company
HQ: Sedgwick Claims Management Services, Inc.
8125 Sedgwick Way
Memphis TN 38125
901 415-7400

(P-10344)
SEDGWICK CLAIMS MGT SVCS INC
1600 Riviera Ave Ste 405, Walnut Creek (94596-7114)
PHONE..................925 988-1536
Lewis Lawrence, *Branch Mgr*
Michelle Lawler, *Litigation*
Shawn Hagist, *Director*
Black Stephanie, *Manager*
Megan Schroth, *Representative*
EMP: 66 Privately Held
WEB: www.sedgwick.com
SIC: 6411 Insurance claim adjusters, not employed by insurance company
HQ: Sedgwick Claims Management Services, Inc.
8125 Sedgwick Way
Memphis TN 38125
901 415-7400

(P-10345)
SEDGWICK CLAIMS MGT SVCS INC
2101 Webster St, Oakland (94612-3011)
PHONE..................510 302-3000
Athanasios Soha, *Branch Mgr*
William Etheridge, *President*
David Hocutt, *President*
Lesley Kochel, *Vice Pres*
Laura Giron, *Office Mgr*
EMP: 66 Privately Held
WEB: www.sedgwick.com
SIC: 6411 Insurance claim adjusters, not employed by insurance company
HQ: Sedgwick Claims Management Services, Inc.
8125 Sedgwick Way
Memphis TN 38125
901 415-7400

(P-10346)
SEDGWICK CLAIMS MGT SVCS INC
1851 Heritage Ln, Sacramento (95815-4926)
PHONE..................916 568-7394

PRODUCTS & SERVICES SECTION
6411 - Insurance Agents, Brokers & Svc County (P-10367)

EMP: 70
SALES (corp-wide): 14.9B **Publicly Held**
SIC: 6411 Insurance Agent/Broker
HQ: Sedgwick Claims Management Services, Inc.
8125 Sedgwick Way
Memphis TN 38125
901 415-7400

(P-10347)
SELECTQUOTE INSURANCE SERVICES (HQ)
1440 Broadway Ste 1000, Oakland (94612-2029)
PHONE 415 543-7338
Tim Danker, *CEO*
Bonnie Wilson, *Managing Prtnr*
Donald Hawks III, *Ch of Bd*
William Grant II, *COO*
Raffaele Sadun, *CFO*
EMP: 200 **EST:** 1984
SALES (est): 266.3MM
SALES (corp-wide): 937.8MM **Publicly Held**
WEB: www.selectquote.com
SIC: 6411 Insurance agents
PA: Selectquote, Inc.
6800 W 115th St Ste 2511
Overland Park KS 66211
913 274-1994

(P-10348)
SENTRY LIFE INSURANCE COMPANY
535 Main St Fl 2, Martinez (94553-1102)
PHONE 925 370-7339
EMP: 191
SALES (corp-wide): 3B **Privately Held**
WEB: www.sentry.com
SIC: 6411 Insurance agents, brokers & service
HQ: Sentry Life Insurance Company
1800 N Point Dr
Stevens Point WI 54481
715 346-6000

(P-10349)
SEQUOIA BNEFITS INSUR SVCS LLC (PA)
1850 Gateway Dr Ste 600, San Mateo (94404-4064)
PHONE 650 369-0200
Greg Golub,
Geoffrey Valentine, *Chairman*
Hall Kesmodel, *Officer*
Melissa Lightbody, *Officer*
Suzette Germano, *Vice Pres*
EMP: 69 **EST:** 2001
SQ FT: 2,000
SALES (est): 26.8MM **Privately Held**
WEB: www.sequoia.com
SIC: 6411 Insurance agents, brokers & service

(P-10350)
SEQUOIA INSURANCE COMPANY
P.O. Box 1510, Monterey (93942-1510)
PHONE 916 933-9524
EMP: 72 **Publicly Held**
SIC: 6411 Insurance Agent/Broker
HQ: Sequoia Insurance Company
31 Upper Ragsdale Dr
Monterey CA 44114
831 655-9612

(P-10351)
SHAW & PETERSEN INSURANCE INC
Also Called: Nationwide
1313 5th St, Eureka (95501-0660)
P.O. Box 1026 (95502-1026)
PHONE 707 443-0845
Maurice O Shaw Sr, *President*
Maurice O Shaw Jr, *Corp Secy*
Maurice Shaw, *General Mgr*
Pat Krebs, *Receptionist*
EMP: 50 **EST:** 1963
SQ FT: 3,000
SALES (est): 8.8MM **Privately Held**
WEB: www.gpins.com
SIC: 6411 Insurance agents

(P-10352)
SPECIALTY RISK SERVICES INC
6140 Stnrdge Mall Rd Ste, Pleasanton (94588)
PHONE 877 809-9478
Eric Hansen, *Principal*
EMP: 97 **Privately Held**
SIC: 6411 Insurance claim processing, except medical; loss prevention services, insurance
HQ: Specialty Risk Services, Inc.
100 Corporate Dr Ste 211
Windsor CT 06095

(P-10353)
STANDARD INSURANCE COMPANY
1600 Riviera Ave Ste 150, Walnut Creek (94596-7117)
PHONE 925 947-3950
Vicky Toroian, *Manager*
EMP: 38 **Privately Held**
WEB: www.standard.com
SIC: 6411 Insurance agents
HQ: Standard Insurance Company
920 Sw 6th Ave Ste 1100
Portland OR 97204
971 321-7000

(P-10354)
STATE FARM LIFE INSURANCE CO
Also Called: State Farm Insurance
11230 Gold Express Dr, Gold River (95670-4484)
PHONE 916 852-9491
Karen Egan, *Branch Mgr*
EMP: 38
SALES (corp-wide): 27.8B **Privately Held**
WEB: www.statefarm.com
SIC: 6411 Insurance agents & brokers
HQ: State Farm Life Insurance Company Inc
1 State Farm Plz
Bloomington IL 61701
309 766-2311

(P-10355)
STRACHOTA INSURANCE AGENCY
Also Called: Nationwide
2721 Citrus Rd Ste A, Rancho Cordova (95742-6313)
PHONE 951 676-2229
Angelica Barnett, *President*
Eddie Prieboy, *IT Specialist*
Ed Prieboy, *Technology*
Carrie Palmer, *Accounting Mgr*
Bobby Arban, *Broker*
EMP: 40 **EST:** 1931
SALES (est): 9.9MM
SALES (corp-wide): 22MM **Privately Held**
WEB: www.strachota.com
SIC: 6411 Insurance agents
PA: Inszone Insurance Services Llc
2721 Citrus Rd Ste A
Rancho Cordova CA 95742
833 819-5009

(P-10356)
SUNLAND INSURANCE AGENCY
4961 E Kings Canyon Rd, Fresno (93727-3812)
P.O. Box 779, Clovis (93613-0779)
PHONE 559 251-7861
Michael Denman, *Owner*
EMP: 797 **EST:** 1974
SALES (est): 2.1MM
SALES (corp-wide): 3.7B **Publicly Held**
WEB: www.sunlandinsurance.com
SIC: 6411 Insurance agents
HQ: Mercury Insurance Company
4484 Wilshire Blvd
Los Angeles CA 90010
323 937-1060

(P-10357)
TAPP LABEL HOLDING COMPANY LLC (PA)
580 Gateway Dr, NAPA (94558-7517)
PHONE 707 252-8300
David Bowyer, *Mng Member*
EMP: 59 **EST:** 2014

SQ FT: 24,000
SALES (est): 45.1MM **Privately Held**
WEB: www.tapptech.com
SIC: 6411 7389 Insurance agents & brokers; packaging & labeling services

---

(P-10358)
TDIC INSURANCE SOLUTIONS
1201 K St, Sacramento (95814-3918)
PHONE 800 733-0633
Mark Soeth, *President*
Peter Dubois, *Vice Chairman*
Bob Spinelli, *CEO*
Brynna Sely, *Agent*
EMP: 39 **EST:** 1982
SQ FT: 22,400
SALES (est): 7.6MM **Privately Held**
WEB: www.tdicinsurance.com
SIC: 6411 Insurance brokers
PA: Cda Holding Company, Inc.
1201 K St Ste 1400
Sacramento CA 95814

(P-10359)
THOITS INSURANCE SERVICE INC
Also Called: Kemper Insurance
160 W Santa Clara St # 1200, San Jose (95113-1733)
PHONE 408 792-5400
Paul Saich, *CEO*
Dean Middour, *President*
Eric Nielsen, *CFO*
Marianne Chow, *Vice Pres*
Derek Culligan, *Vice Pres*
EMP: 53 **EST:** 1999
SALES (est): 29.4MM
SALES (corp-wide): 376.7MM **Privately Held**
WEB: www.kemperhsc.com
SIC: 6411 Insurance brokers
HQ: Nfp Corp.
340 Madison Ave Fl 21
New York NY 10173
212 301-4000

(P-10360)
TRANSWSTERN INSUR ADMNISTRATOR (PA)
955 N St, Fresno (93721-2216)
P.O. Box 45019 (93718-5019)
PHONE 559 499-0285
Roger Boman, *President*
Son Le, *Info Tech Mgr*
Zachary Boman, *Marketing Staff*
Liliana Venegas, *Representative*
EMP: 41 **EST:** 1986
SALES (est): 8.4MM **Privately Held**
WEB: www.trans-western.com
SIC: 6411 Insurance claim processing, except medical

(P-10361)
TRAVELERS PROPERTY CSLTY CORP
Also Called: Travelers Insurance
401 Lennon Ln, Walnut Creek (94598-2508)
P.O. Box 13089, Sacramento (95813-3089)
PHONE 925 945-4000
Julie Weisert, *Branch Mgr*
Brian Gerritsen, *Director*
Nicholas McCarthy, *Accounts Mgr*
EMP: 241
SALES (corp-wide): 31.9B **Publicly Held**
WEB: www.travelers.com
SIC: 6411 Insurance agents
HQ: Travelers Property Casualty Corp.
1 Tower Sq 8ms
Hartford CT 06183

(P-10362)
TSM INSURANCE & FINCL SVCS INC
Also Called: Nationwide
1317 Oakdale Rd Ste 910, Modesto (95355-3369)
PHONE 209 524-6366
Tony Miligi, *President*
Lowell Clark, *Senior Partner*
Randy Clark, *Principal*
Mark Antrim, *Broker*
Cheyanne Cabral, *Personnel*

EMP: 56 **EST:** 1929
SQ FT: 6,800
SALES (est): 5.7MM **Privately Held**
WEB: www.tsminsurance.com
SIC: 6411 6282 Insurance agents; insurance brokers; investment advice

---

(P-10363)
US SCRIPT INC (HQ)
5 E River Park Pl E # 210, Fresno (93720-1560)
P.O. Box 26330 (93729-6330)
PHONE 559 244-3700
Robert Bagdasarian, *President*
Don Nagy, *Vice Pres*
Kevin Rhoades, *Vice Pres*
Troy Collins, *Executive*
Chris Moua, *Admin Asst*
EMP: 35 **EST:** 1999
SQ FT: 24,000
SALES (est): 33.4MM **Publicly Held**
WEB: www.redirect.envolvehealth.com
SIC: 6411 Medical insurance claim processing, contract or fee basis

---

(P-10364)
USI INSRNCE SVCS NTHRN CAL INC (DH)
2021 W March Ln Ste 3, Stockton (95207-6400)
PHONE 209 954-3900
Jon Bush, *President*
Diane Harris, *Vice Pres*
Diane Tondee, *Accounts Mgr*
EMP: 43 **EST:** 1860
SQ FT: 8,100
SALES (est): 23.3MM **Privately Held**
WEB: www.usi.com
SIC: 6411 Insurance agents

(P-10365)
VAN BEURDEN INSURANCE SVCS INC (PA)
Also Called: Kemper Insurance
1600 Draper St, Kingsburg (93631-1911)
P.O. Box 67 (93631-0067)
PHONE 559 634-7125
William J Van Beurden, *President*
Mike Beall, *Vice Pres*
Chris V Beurden, *Vice Pres*
Don Clark, *Vice Pres*
Jeanette Heinrichs, *Vice Pres*
EMP: 67 **EST:** 1934
SQ FT: 20,000
SALES (est): 25.4MM **Privately Held**
WEB: www.vanbeurden.com
SIC: 6411 Insurance agents

(P-10366)
WALTER R REINHARDT INSUR AGCY
Also Called: Nationwide
499 W Shaw Ave Ste 130, Fresno (93704-2516)
PHONE 559 226-4700
Walter R Reinhardt, *CEO*
Judy Reinhardt, *Corp Secy*
Camille Fisher, *General Mgr*
Jon Clague, *Producer*
Terry Moore, *Producer*
EMP: 40 **EST:** 1966
SQ FT: 5,000
SALES (est): 5.3MM **Privately Held**
WEB: www.reinhardtinsurance.com
SIC: 6411 Insurance agents; life insurance agents; property & casualty insurance agent

---

(P-10367)
WESPAC PLAN SERVICES LLC (DH)
4 Orinda Way Ste 100b, Orinda (94563-2507)
PHONE 510 740-4163
Renee T Szu, *President*
Nelson P Chia, *Exec VP*
Mark Dupont, *Vice Pres*
Kyle Gentile, *Vice Pres*
Wayne Lou, *Vice Pres*
EMP: 35 **EST:** 1977
SALES (est): 5.5MM
SALES (corp-wide): 1.2B **Publicly Held**
WEB: www.wespac.net
SIC: 6411 Pension & retirement plan consultants

6411 - Insurance Agents, Brokers & Svc County (P-10368)

(P-10368)
WESTERN NATIONAL LIFE INSUR CO
Also Called: AIG
1395 Creekside Dr, Walnut Creek (94596-7412)
PHONE.................925 946-5100
Elaine Woolery, *Manager*
EMP: 198
SALES (corp-wide): 43.7B **Publicly Held**
WEB: www.nationalwesternlife.com
SIC: 6411 Insurance agents, brokers & service
HQ: Western National Life Insurance Company
2929 Allen Pkwy Ste 3800
Houston TX 77019
713 522-1111

(P-10369)
WINTON IRLAND STROM GREEN INSU (PA)
Also Called: Nationwide
627 E Canal Dr, Turlock (95380-4022)
P.O. Box 3277 (95381-3277)
PHONE.................209 667-0995
Michael Ireland, *President*
Ted Green, *Vice Pres*
Jeff Quinn, *Vice Pres*
Karen Koch, *Human Res Dir*
Lupe Valeriano, *Personnel*
EMP: 80 **EST:** 1913
SQ FT: 10,000
SALES (est): 20.6MM **Privately Held**
WEB: www.wisg.com
SIC: 6411 Insurance brokers

(P-10370)
WM MICHAEL STEMLER INC (PA)
Also Called: DELTA HEALTH SYSTEMS
3244 Brookside Rd Ste 200, Stockton (95219-2384)
P.O. Box 1227 (95201-1227)
PHONE.................209 948-8483
William M Stemler, *CEO*
Richard Roge, *President*
Patti Silva, *Exec VP*
Gordon McDonald, *Opers Dir*
Corliss Loera, *Manager*
EMP: 110 **EST:** 1968
SQ FT: 30,100
SALES (est): 21.2MM **Privately Held**
WEB: www.deltahealthsystems.com
SIC: 6411 Medical insurance claim processing, contract or fee basis

(P-10371)
WM MICHAEL STEMLER INC
7110 N Fresno St Ste 350, Fresno (93720-2933)
PHONE.................559 228-4144
Robert Maes, *Vice Pres*
Lori Cravalho, *Manager*
EMP: 80
SALES (corp-wide): 21.2MM **Privately Held**
WEB: www.deltahealthsystems.com
SIC: 6411 Medical insurance claim processing, contract or fee basis
PA: Wm. Michael Stemler, Incorporated
3244 Brookside Rd Ste 200
Stockton CA 95219
209 948-8483

(P-10372)
WOODRUFF-SAWYER & CO (PA)
Also Called: Nationwide
50 California St Fl 12, San Francisco (94111-4646)
PHONE.................415 391-2141
Andy Barrengos, *Ch of Bd*
Zac Overbay, *COO*
Kristine Furrer, *Senior VP*
Stephen Gaitley, *Senior VP*
Charles Shoemaker, *Senior VP*
EMP: 240 **EST:** 1966
SQ FT: 54,000
SALES (est): 163.3MM **Privately Held**
WEB: www.woodruffsawyer.com
SIC: 6411 Insurance brokers

(P-10373)
YORK INSUR SRVCS GROUP - CA
1101 Creekside Ridge Dr, Roseville (95678-3567)
P.O. Box 619058 (95661-9058)
PHONE.................916 783-0100
Randall Smith, *Senior VP*
Lisa Plata, *Executive Asst*
Jeff Kimball, *Human Res Dir*
Alric Harper, *Facilities Mgr*
Wendy Scheller, *Manager*
EMP: 41 **EST:** 2010
SALES (est): 14MM **Privately Held**
SIC: 6411 Insurance agents
HQ: York Risk Services Group, Inc.
1 Upper Pond Rd Ste 4
Parsippany NJ 07054
973 404-1200

6512 Operators Of Nonresidential Bldgs

(P-10374)
2150 N FRST NVEL COWORKING LLC
2150 N 1st St, San Jose (95131-2020)
PHONE.................312 283-3683
William Bennnett,
Kayley Dicicco,
EMP: 75 **EST:** 2020
SALES (est): 2.5MM **Privately Held**
WEB: www.expansive.com
SIC: 6512 Commercial & industrial building operation

(P-10375)
8181 LLC
2570 W El Camino Real, Mountain View (94040-1306)
PHONE.................303 779-3053
EMP: 50 **EST:** 2017
SALES (est): 1.8MM
SALES (corp-wide): 404.9MM **Privately Held**
WEB: www.transwestern.com
SIC: 6512 Commercial & industrial building operation
PA: Transwestern Commercial Services, L.L.C.
1900 West Loop S Ste 1300
Houston TX 77027
713 270-7700

(P-10376)
ALLEN PROPERTY GROUP INC
347 Spreckels Dr, Aptos (95003-3923)
PHONE.................831 688-5100
Steven Allen, *Principal*
Karen Ramirez, *Agent*
EMP: 50 **EST:** 2008
SALES (est): 5.7MM **Privately Held**
WEB: www.alleninc.com
SIC: 6512 Nonresidential building operators

(P-10377)
BAY WEST SHWPLACE INVSTORS LLC (PA)
Also Called: Sheplace Design Center
2 Henry Adams St Ste 450, San Francisco (94103-5000)
PHONE.................415 490-5800
Bill Poland, *Manager*
Tim Threadway, *Chairman*
EMP: 50 **EST:** 1983
SALES (est): 7MM **Privately Held**
SIC: 6512 5712 Commercial & industrial building operation; furniture stores

(P-10378)
BPR PROPERTIES BERKELEY LLC
953 Industrial Ave # 100, Palo Alto (94303-4923)
PHONE.................650 424-1400
Bhupendra B Patel,
Shashank Parasnis, *Info Tech Dir*
Puja Gupta, *Director*
John Searby, *Director*
Lynne Reelfs, *Manager*
EMP: 130 **EST:** 2006
SALES (est): 15.9MM **Privately Held**
WEB: www.bprhotels.com
SIC: 6512 Nonresidential building operators

(P-10379)
BROADWAY SACRAMENTO
1419 H St, Sacramento (95814-1901)
PHONE.................916 446-5880
Laura Mattice, *Branch Mgr*
Stephanie Tabor, *CFO*
Andrea Izumi, *Accountant*
Patrick Burns, *Prdtn Mgr*
Gina Harrower, *Sales Mgr*
EMP: 165 **Privately Held**
WEB: www.broadwaysacramento.com
SIC: 6512 Theater building, ownership & operation
PA: Broadway Sacramento
1510 J St Ste 200
Sacramento CA 95814

(P-10380)
CALIFORNIA SCHOOL OF MECH ARTS
Also Called: Lick Wilmerding High School
755 Ocean Ave, San Francisco (94112-1856)
PHONE.................415 333-4021
Albert Adams, *Headmaster*
Paula McLaughlin, *Teacher*
EMP: 80 **EST:** 1895
SQ FT: 62,167
SALES (est): 31.2MM **Privately Held**
WEB: www.lwhs.org
SIC: 8211 6512 Preparatory school; commercial & industrial building operation

(P-10381)
CAMERON & LISA PALMER
Also Called: Cameron's Restaurant & Inn
1410 Cabrillo Hwy S, Half Moon Bay (94019-2243)
PHONE.................650 726-5705
Cameron Palmer, *Owner*
Lisa Palmer, *Manager*
EMP: 40 **EST:** 1983
SQ FT: 3,750
SALES (est): 1MM **Privately Held**
WEB: www.cameronsinn.com
SIC: 5812 6512 Family restaurants; non-residential building operators

(P-10382)
CANADIAN AMERICAN OIL CO INC (PA)
Also Called: Divisadero Touchless Car Wash
444 Divisadero St 100, San Francisco (94117-2211)
PHONE.................415 621-8676
Roy Shimek, *President*
▲ **EMP:** 100 **EST:** 1968
SQ FT: 5,000
SALES (est): 52.3MM **Privately Held**
WEB: www.bp.com
SIC: 5541 6512 6552 Filling stations, gasoline; commercial & industrial building operation; subdividers & developers

(P-10383)
CODDING ENTERPRISES LP (PA)
Also Called: Codding Construction
1400 Valley House Dr # 100, Rohnert Park (94928-4935)
P.O. Box 5800, Santa Rosa (95406-5800)
PHONE.................707 795-3550
Rick Freeman, *President*
EMP: 35 **EST:** 1960
SQ FT: 30,000
SALES (est): 21.6MM **Privately Held**
WEB: www.codding.com
SIC: 6512 1531 1542 1541 Shopping center, property operation only; commercial & industrial building operation; operative builders; commercial & office building, new construction; industrial buildings, new construction; warehouse construction

(P-10384)
COPPERFIELDS BOOKS INC (PA)
Also Called: Copperflds Petaluma Gold Bkstr
139 Edman Way, Sebastopol (95472-3454)
PHONE.................707 823-8991
Thomas Montan, *CEO*
Bernard M Brown, *Ch of Bd*
Paul Jaffe, *President*
Robert Brown, *Corp Secy*
Garth Haslam, *Info Tech Dir*
EMP: 40
SQ FT: 3,800
SALES (est): 15.2MM **Privately Held**
WEB: www.copperfieldsbooks.com
SIC: 5942 5932 6512 Books, religious; used merchandise stores; book stores, secondhand; commercial & industrial building operation

(P-10385)
DAVID D BOHANNON ORGANIZATION (PA)
Also Called: San Lorenzo Village Shopg Ctr
60 31st Ave, San Mateo (94403-3404)
PHONE.................650 345-8222
David D Bohannon II, *President*
Joseph Fede, *Officer*
Scott Bohannon, *Senior VP*
Ernest Lotti Jr, *Vice Pres*
Diane Sheardown, *Administration*
EMP: 60 **EST:** 1946
SQ FT: 5,000
SALES (est): 17.9MM **Privately Held**
WEB: www.ddbo.com
SIC: 6512 6552 Commercial & industrial building operation; subdividers & developers

(P-10386)
ESKATON (PA)
5105 Manzanita Ave Ste D, Carmichael (95608-0523)
PHONE.................916 334-0296
Todd Murch, *CEO*
Trevor Hammond, *COO*
William Pace, *CFO*
Sheri Peifer, *Officer*
Robert Brandi, *Vice Pres*
EMP: 100 **EST:** 1968
SQ FT: 27,000
SALES (est): 148.8MM **Privately Held**
WEB: www.eskaton.org
SIC: 6512 8051 Commercial & industrial building operation; convalescent home with continuous nursing care

(P-10387)
ESKATON
Also Called: Falconer House
5701 Falconer Way, Sacramento (95824-1517)
PHONE.................916 395-1722
Kim Delgado, *Exec Dir*
EMP: 137
SALES (corp-wide): 148.8MM **Privately Held**
WEB: www.eskaton.org
SIC: 6512 8051 Commercial & industrial building operation; convalescent home with continuous nursing care
PA: Eskaton
5105 Manzanita Ave Ste D
Carmichael CA 95608
916 334-0296

(P-10388)
FREMONT PROPERTIES INC
199 Fremont St Ste 1900, San Francisco (94105-2245)
PHONE.................415 284-8500
Allen Dachs, *CEO*
David Wall, *Exec VP*
Christopher Quiett, *Vice Pres*
Gry Faber, *Principal*
Suzanne Gagan, *Principal*
EMP: 50 **EST:** 1989
SALES (est): 9.7MM
SALES (corp-wide): 16.6MM **Privately Held**
WEB: www.fremontgroup.com
SIC: 6512 Nonresidential building operators
PA: Fremont Investors, Inc.
199 Fremont St Fl 19
San Francisco CA 94105
415 284-8500

▲ = Import ▼ = Export
◆ = Import/Export

PRODUCTS & SERVICES SECTION
6512 - Operators Of Nonresidential Bldgs County (P-10411)

(P-10389)
GALAXY PATTERSON ROAD LLC
2525 Patterson Rd, Riverbank (95367-2707)
PHONE...................209 863-9012
Frank Rimkus,
EMP: 53 EST: 2015
SALES (est): 1.8MM Privately Held
SIC: 6512 Nonresidential building operators

(P-10390)
GONGS MARKET OF SANGER INC (PA)
Also Called: Gong's Ventures
1825 Academy Ave, Sanger (93657-3798)
PHONE...................559 875-5576
William Gong, President
Bessie Gong Ohashi, Corp Secy
Thomas Gong, Vice Pres
EMP: 50 EST: 1964
SQ FT: 35,000
SALES (est): 5.3MM Privately Held
WEB: www.gongsmarket.com
SIC: 6512 Property operation, retail establishment

(P-10391)
GREENTREE PROPERTY MGT INC
1 Bush St Fl 9, San Francisco (94104-4415)
PHONE...................415 347-8600
Yat Pang Au, President
Lauren Covarrubias, Maintence Staff
Eric Lakin, Sr Project Mgr
Jay Pedde, Director
Jennifer Cosgrove, Manager
EMP: 50 EST: 2011
SALES (est): 5.2MM Privately Held
WEB: www.greentreepmco.com
SIC: 6512 Property operation, retail establishment

(P-10392)
HEALTH CARE WORKERS UNION (PA)
Also Called: Local 250 Health Care Wkrs Un
560 Thomas L Berkley Way, Oakland (94612-1602)
PHONE...................510 251-1250
Sal Rosselli, President
Sarah Steck, Opers Mgr
EMP: 70
SQ FT: 25,777
SALES (est): 11.7MM Privately Held
WEB: www.seiu-uhw.org
SIC: 6512 8631 Commercial & industrial building operation; labor unions & similar labor organizations

(P-10393)
JAPANESE CLTRAL CMNTY N CALI C
Also Called: Japanese Community Center
1840 Sutter St Ste 202, San Francisco (94115-3220)
PHONE...................415 567-5505
Paul Osake, Director
Erika Iwamura, Bd of Directors
Mika Shimizu, Office Mgr
Aya Ino, Corp Comm Staff
Lori Matoba, Deputy Dir
EMP: 36 EST: 1973
SALES (est): 2.5MM Privately Held
WEB: www.jcccnc.org
SIC: 6512 8399 Nonresidential building operators; community development groups

(P-10394)
JOHNSON SERVICE GROUP INC
950 S Bascom Ave, San Jose (95128-3536)
PHONE...................408 728-9510
Dina Romero, Manager
EMP: 1157
SALES (corp-wide): 50.1MM Privately Held
WEB: www.jsginc.com
SIC: 6512 Commercial & industrial building operation
PA: Johnson Service Group, Inc.
1 E Oakhill Dr Ste 200
Westmont IL 60559
630 590-6511

(P-10395)
MGP IX PROPERTIES LLC (PA)
425 California St # 1000, San Francisco (94104-2112)
PHONE...................415 693-9000
EMP: 44 EST: 2011
SALES (est): 1.8MM Privately Held
SIC: 6512 Nonresidential building operators

(P-10396)
MMI REALTY SERVICES INC
260 California St Fl 4, San Francisco (94111-4396)
PHONE...................415 288-6888
John Mendelsohn, Branch Mgr
EMP: 98
SALES (corp-wide): 5.2MM Privately Held
WEB: www.mmirealty.com
SIC: 6512 Shopping center, property operation only
PA: Mmi Realty Services, Inc.
99 S Lake Ave Ste 209
Pasadena CA 91101
626 577-8660

(P-10397)
NECSEL INTLLCTUAL PROPERTY INC (DH)
801 Ames Ave, Milpitas (95035-6322)
PHONE...................408 246-7555
William F Mackenzie, President
Dawn Penner, General Mgr
EMP: 36 EST: 2008
SALES (est): 14.3MM Privately Held
WEB: www.ushio.com
SIC: 6512 Property operation, retail establishment
HQ: Ushio America, Inc.
5440 Cerritos Ave
Cypress CA 90630
714 236-8600

(P-10398)
PACIFIC STHWEST CNFRNCE OF EVA
Also Called: Mission Springs Conf Cntr
1050 Lockhart Gulch Rd, Scotts Valley (95066-2934)
PHONE...................831 335-9133
Bryan Hayes, Director
Deanna Valencia, Controller
Rachel Lockridge, Sales Staff
Stacie D Burch, Education
Clement Ojugo, Director
EMP: 139
SQ FT: 15,000
SALES (corp-wide): 12.2MM Privately Held
WEB: www.pswc.org
SIC: 6512 Auditorium & hall operation
PA: Pacific Southwest Conference Of The Evangelical Covenant Church
1333 Willow Pass Rd # 212
Concord CA
925 677-2140

(P-10399)
PIER 39 LIMITED PARTNERSHIP (PA)
Beach Embarcadero Level 3, San Francisco (94133)
PHONE...................415 705-5500
Robert A Moor, General Ptnr
Molly M South, Partner
Scott Gentner, CFO
Lysa Lewin, Vice Pres
Frazer Thompson, Vice Pres
EMP: 60 EST: 1968
SQ FT: 200,000
SALES (est): 40MM Privately Held
WEB: www.pier39.com
SIC: 6512 Commercial & industrial building operation

(P-10400)
PREMIUM OUTLET PARTNERS LP
Folsom Premium Outlets
13000 Folsom Blvd Ste 309, Folsom (95630-8002)
PHONE...................916 985-0312
Brenda Sprouse, Branch Mgr
EMP: 94 Publicly Held
WEB: www.simon.com
SIC: 6512 Shopping center, property operation only
HQ: Premium Outlet Partners, L.P.
225 W Washington St
Indianapolis IN 46204

(P-10401)
PREMIUM OUTLET PARTNERS LP
Factory Stres/ Vcvlle Prmium O
321 Nut Tree Rd Ste 2, Vacaville (95687-3242)
PHONE...................707 448-3661
Larry Wallin, Manager
EMP: 94 Publicly Held
WEB: www.simon.com
SIC: 6512 Shopping center, property operation only
HQ: Premium Outlet Partners, L.P.
225 W Washington St
Indianapolis IN 46204

(P-10402)
PREMIUM OUTLET PARTNERS LP
Gilroy Premium Outlets
681 Leavesley Rd, Gilroy (95020-3647)
PHONE...................408 842-3729
Jennifer Bradley, Branch Mgr
Joanna Contreras, Office Admin
EMP: 94 Publicly Held
WEB: www.simon.com
SIC: 6512 Shopping center, property operation only
HQ: Premium Outlet Partners, L.P.
225 W Washington St
Indianapolis IN 46204

(P-10403)
RLW PROPERTIES LLC
1771 Castellina Dr, Brentwood (94513-6544)
PHONE...................925 418-5668
Lynn Tei, Principal
EMP: 100 EST: 2004
SALES (est): 3.4MM Privately Held
SIC: 6512 Nonresidential building operators

(P-10404)
SECURITY NAT PRPTS HOLDG LLC (HQ)
Also Called: Security National Funding Tr
323 5th St, Eureka (95501-0305)
P.O. Box 1028 (95502-1028)
PHONE...................707 476-2702
Robin P Arkley II,
EMP: 43 EST: 1998
SALES (est): 24.5MM
SALES (corp-wide): 114.4MM Privately Held
WEB: www.snsc.com
SIC: 6512 Nonresidential building operators
PA: Security National Master Holding Company Llc
323 5th St
Eureka CA 95501
707 442-2818

(P-10405)
SHORENSTEIN COMPANY LLC
235 Montgomery St Fl 15, San Francisco (94104-3102)
PHONE...................415 772-7000
Douglas Shorenstein,
Tony Calabrese, COO
Tom Hart, Exec VP
Lisa Lind, Senior VP
John Boynton, Vice Pres
EMP: 50 EST: 2003
SALES (est): 13.7MM Privately Held
WEB: www.shorenstein.com
SIC: 6512 Commercial & industrial building operation

(P-10406)
SHORENSTEIN PROPERTIES LLC (PA)
235 Montgomery St Fl 16, San Francisco (94104-3104)
PHONE...................415 772-7000
Douglas W Shorenstein, CEO
Glenn A Shannon, President
Thomas Cashin, Senior VP
D Drew Dowsett, Senior VP
Lisa Lind, Senior VP
EMP: 125 EST: 1924
SQ FT: 20,000
SALES (est): 294.8MM Privately Held
WEB: www.shorenstein.com
SIC: 6512 Commercial & industrial building operation

(P-10407)
SKYWALKER PROPERTIES LTD LLC (PA)
1 Letterman Dr Bldg B, San Francisco (94129-1494)
PHONE...................415 746-5059
George W Lucas,
Sheila Gibson, Info Tech Mgr
Sasha Krassovsky, Manager
EMP: 59 EST: 2003
SALES (est): 8.3MM Privately Held
SIC: 6512 Nonresidential building operators

(P-10408)
SLA LLC (PA)
245 Lytton Ave Ste 150, Palo Alto (94301-1472)
PHONE...................650 322-2600
Stephen Henry, Principal
EMP: 46 EST: 2016
SALES (est): 1.3MM Privately Held
SIC: 6512 Nonresidential building operators

(P-10409)
SOTOYOME MEDICAL BUILDING LLC
Also Called: Redwood Regional Medical Group
990 Sonoma Ave Ste 15, Santa Rosa (95404-4813)
PHONE...................707 525-4000
Harold Phillips,
Sharon Debenedetti, COO
EMP: 55 EST: 1976
SQ FT: 27,000
SALES (est): 9.8MM Privately Held
SIC: 6512 Commercial & industrial building operation

(P-10410)
SUNSET DEVELOPMENT COMPANY (PA)
Also Called: Bishop Ranch
2600 Camino Ramon Ste 201, San Ramon (94583-5000)
P.O. Box 640 (94583-0640)
PHONE...................925 277-1700
Alexander R Mehran, President
Alex Mehran Sr, Chairman
James Clancy, Exec VP
Edward Hagopian, Exec VP
David Claveau, Senior VP
EMP: 143 EST: 1954
SQ FT: 15,000
SALES (est): 41.4MM Privately Held
WEB: www.bishopranch.com
SIC: 6512 6552 6799 Commercial & industrial building operation; land subdividers & developers, commercial; real estate investors, except property operators; real property lessors

(P-10411)
TARIFF BUILDING ASSOCIATES LP (PA)
222 Kearny St Ste 200, San Francisco (94108-4537)
PHONE...................415 397-5572
Michael Depatie, CEO
Cheryl Lovelace, Vice Pres

6512 - Operators Of Nonresidential Bldgs County (P-10412)

Michael Thibodeau, *Info Tech Dir*
EMP: 60 **EST:** 1998
SALES (est): 5.1MM **Privately Held**
SIC: 6512 6513 Property operation, retail establishment; residential hotel operation

(P-10412)
TEGTMEIER ASSOCIATES INC
6701 Clark Rd, Paradise (95969-2833)
P.O. Box 1930 (95967-1930)
PHONE 530 872-7700
John Tegemeier, *President*
EMP: 58
SQ FT: 24,000
SALES (corp-wide): 1.7MM **Privately Held**
SIC: 6512 7841 5049 Theater building, ownership & operation; video disk/tape rental to the general public; theatrical equipment & supplies
PA: Tegtmeier Associates Inc.
14 Mansion Ct
Menlo Park CA 94025
650 847-1639

(P-10413)
TEN 15 INC
1015 Folsom St, San Francisco (94103-4016)
PHONE 415 431-1200
Ira J Sandler, *President*
Melissa Yeung, *Manager*
EMP: 80 **EST:** 1990
SQ FT: 15,000
SALES (est): 5.8MM **Privately Held**
WEB: www.1015.com
SIC: 5813 6512 Night clubs; auditorium & hall operation

(P-10414)
VIRGA INVESTMENT PROPERTY
430 S George Wash Blvd, Yuba City (95993-9154)
PHONE 530 755-4409
Larry S Virga, *Owner*
EMP: 143
SALES (est): 300K **Privately Held**
SIC: 6512 Nonresidential building operators

(P-10415)
WESTLAKE DEVELOPMENT GROUP LLC (PA)
520 S El Camino Real # 900, San Mateo (94402-1722)
PHONE 650 579-1010
T M Chang, *Mng Member*
William H C Chang,
EMP: 75 **EST:** 1972
SQ FT: 80,000
SALES (est): 17.8MM **Privately Held**
WEB: www.westlake-realty.com
SIC: 6512 6513 6531 Shopping center, property operation only; commercial & industrial building operation; apartment building operators; retirement hotel operation; real estate agents & managers

6513 Operators Of Apartment Buildings

(P-10416)
4TH & FOLSOM ASSOCIATES LP
201 Eddy St, San Francisco (94102-2715)
PHONE 415 417-3086
Donald S Falk, *Partner*
Hermandeep Kaur, *Partner*
EMP: 431 **EST:** 2019
SALES (est): 15.4MM **Privately Held**
WEB: www.tndc.org
SIC: 6513 Apartment building operators

(P-10417)
ASPEN APTS I
165 Eddy St, San Francisco (94102)
PHONE 415 673-5879
EMP: 99
SALES (est): 3.4MM **Privately Held**
SIC: 6513 Apartment Building Operator

(P-10418)
BAY VISTA SENIOR HOUSING
6120 Stnrdge Mall Rd 3rd, Pleasanton (94588)
PHONE 925 924-7100
Grace Chrisostomo, *Governor*
Linda Coleman, *Governor*
Andrew McDonald, *Governor*
Susan Tolentino, *Governor*
EMP: 704 **EST:** 2012
SALES: 336.6K
SALES (corp-wide): 25.9MM **Privately Held**
WEB: www.humangood.org
SIC: 6513 Retirement hotel operation
HQ: Humangood Affordable Housing
6120 Stoneridge Mall Rd # 100
Pleasanton CA 94588
925 924-7163

(P-10419)
BLANDING BOYER & ROCKWELL LLP
1676 N Calif Blvd Fl 3, Walnut Creek (94596-4144)
PHONE 925 954-0113
Steve Blanding, *Partner*
Ronald Boyer, *Senior Partner*
Steve Blading, *Partner*
Tom Rockwell, *Partner*
Gary Bong, *Treasurer*
EMP: 50 **EST:** 1969
SALES (est): 2.9MM **Privately Held**
SIC: 6513 Apartment building operators

(P-10420)
CALIFRNIA ODD FLLOWS HSING NAP (PA)
Also Called: Meadows of NAPA Valley
1800 Atrium Pkwy, NAPA (94559-4837)
PHONE 707 257-7885
Wayne Panchesson, *Exec Dir*
EMP: 100 **EST:** 1992
SQ FT: 219,000
SALES (est): 20.9MM **Privately Held**
SIC: 6513 8051 8322 Retirement hotel operation; convalescent home with continuous nursing care; old age assistance

(P-10421)
CALIFRNIA ODD FLLOWS HSING NAP
Also Called: Meadows Nappa Valley Care Ctr
1800 Atrium Pkwy, NAPA (94559-4837)
PHONE 707 257-7885
Wyane Panchesson, *Administration*
EMP: 68
SQ FT: 30,000
SALES (corp-wide): 20.9MM **Privately Held**
SIC: 6513 8051 Retirement hotel operation; skilled nursing care facilities
PA: California Odd Fellows Housing Of Napa, Incorporated
1800 Atrium Pkwy
Napa CA 94559
707 257-7885

(P-10422)
CASA SANDOVAL LLC
1200 Russell Way, Hayward (94541-7708)
PHONE 510 727-1700
Wai Tsin Chang,
Jess Barreto, *Maintence Staff*
EMP: 90 **EST:** 1995
SQ FT: 215,000
SALES (est): 10.9MM **Privately Held**
WEB: www.morningstarseniorliving.com
SIC: 6513 Retirement hotel operation

(P-10423)
CHANATE LDGE ASSOC A CAL LTD P
Also Called: The Chanate
3250 Chanate Rd, Santa Rosa (95404-1794)
PHONE 707 575-7503
Paul Roemer, *General Ptnr*
EMP: 41 **EST:** 1984
SALES (est): 1.1MM
SALES (corp-wide): 418.2MM **Privately Held**
WEB: www.sunriseseniorliving.com
SIC: 6513 Retirement hotel operation
HQ: Sunrise Senior Living, Llc
7902 Westpark Dr
Mc Lean VA 22102

(P-10424)
CHINATOWN CMNTY DEV CTR INC (PA)
1525 Grant Ave, San Francisco (94133-3323)
PHONE 415 984-1450
Susie Wong, *CEO*
Cindy Wu, *Planning*
Genise Choy, *Project Mgr*
Kim Piechota, *Project Mgr*
Olson Lee, *Human Resources*
EMP: 40
SQ FT: 3,000
SALES (est): 10.1MM **Privately Held**
WEB: www.chinatowncdc.org
SIC: 6513 6512 Apartment building operators; commercial & industrial building operation

(P-10425)
CHRISTIAN CHURCH HOMES (PA)
Also Called: Westlake Christian Terrace
303 Hegenberger Rd # 201, Oakland (94621-1419)
PHONE 510 632-6712
Donald Stump, *President*
Syd Najeeb, *COO*
Penny Ross, *Treasurer*
Lisa Dennis, *Vice Pres*
Nicole Ennix, *Vice Pres*
EMP: 40 **EST:** 1961
SQ FT: 5,480
SALES: 11.4MM **Privately Held**
WEB: www.cchno.org
SIC: 6513 6531 Retirement hotel operation; real estate managers

(P-10426)
CHRISTIAN CHURCH HOMES
Also Called: Sr. Thea Bowman Manor
6400 San Pablo Ave, Oakland (94608-1274)
PHONE 510 420-8802
Sharon Jacob, *Manager*
EMP: 44
SALES (corp-wide): 11.4MM **Privately Held**
WEB: www.cchno.org
SIC: 6513 Retirement hotel operation
PA: Christian Church Homes
303 Hegenberger Rd # 201
Oakland CA 94621
510 632-6712

(P-10427)
CHRISTIAN CHURCH HOMES
Also Called: Westlake Christian Terrace - E
251 28th St, Oakland (94611-6063)
PHONE 510 893-2998
John Jordan, *Branch Mgr*
EMP: 44
SALES (corp-wide): 11.4MM **Privately Held**
WEB: www.cchno.org
SIC: 6513 Retirement hotel operation
PA: Christian Church Homes
303 Hegenberger Rd # 201
Oakland CA 94621
510 632-6712

(P-10428)
DOMINICAN OAKS CORPORATION
3400 Paul Sweet Rd Ofc, Santa Cruz (95065-1559)
PHONE 831 462-6257
Patience Beck, *Finance Mgr*
Sister Julie Hyer, *President*
Brenda Bouch, *Executive*
Janet Thiel, *Executive*
Deborah Routley, *Administration*
EMP: 80 **EST:** 1986
SALES (est): 13.4MM **Privately Held**
WEB: www.dominicanoaks.com
SIC: 6513 Retirement hotel operation

(P-10429)
EAH ELENA GARDENS LP
Also Called: Elena Gardens Apartments
1902 Lakewood Dr, San Jose (95132-1409)
PHONE 415 295-8840
Cindy McAnally, *Principal*
EMP: 94
SALES: 3.1MM
SALES (corp-wide): 86MM **Privately Held**
WEB: www.eahhousing.org
SIC: 6513 Apartment building operators
PA: Eah Inc.
22 Pelican Way
San Rafael CA 94901
415 258-1800

(P-10430)
EAST BAY ASIAN LOCAL DEV CORP
1825 San Pablo Ave # 200, Oakland (94612-1517)
PHONE 510 267-1917
Jeremy Liu, *Exec Dir*
Israel Terriquez, *Manager*
April Gubatina, *Assistant*
EMP: 109 **EST:** 1975
SQ FT: 78,000
SALES (est): 24.4MM **Privately Held**
WEB: www.ebaldc.org
SIC: 6513 Apartment building operators

(P-10431)
EDEN HOUSING RESIDENT SVCS INC
22645 Grand St, Hayward (94541-5031)
PHONE 510 582-1460
Yolanda York, *Exec Dir*
EMP: 99
SALES (est): 887.3K **Privately Held**
WEB: www.edenhousing.org
SIC: 6513 Apartment building operators

(P-10432)
EDEN LODGE LP (HQ)
Also Called: Eden Housing Management
400 Springlake Dr, San Leandro (94578-4665)
PHONE 510 352-7008
Linda Mandolini, *Exec Dir*
EMP: 39 **EST:** 1978
SQ FT: 10,000
SALES (est): 3.5MM
SALES (corp-wide): 7MM **Privately Held**
WEB: www.edenhousing.org
SIC: 6513 Apartment building operators
PA: Eden Housing Management, Inc.
326 Ward St
Martinez CA 94553
510 582-1460

(P-10433)
ESSEX MANAGEMENT CORPORATION (HQ)
925 E Meadow Dr, Palo Alto (94303-4299)
PHONE 650 494-3700
Keith Guericke, *President*
Michael J Schall, *CFO*
John Eudy, *Exec VP*
Craig Zimmerman, *Exec VP*
Mark Mikl, *Vice Pres*
EMP: 62 **EST:** 1994
SALES (est): 13.4MM
SALES (corp-wide): 1.5B **Publicly Held**
WEB: www.essexapartmenthomes.com
SIC: 6513 Apartment building operators
PA: Essex Property Trust, Inc.
1100 Park Pl Ste 200
San Mateo CA 94403
650 655-7800

(P-10434)
ESSEX PROPERTY TRUST INC (PA)
1100 Park Pl Ste 200, San Mateo (94403-7107)
PHONE 650 655-7800
Michael J Schall, *President*
George M Marcus, *Ch of Bd*
Elisa Taylor, *President*
Angela L Kleiman, *COO*
Barb Pak, *CFO*
EMP: 316 **EST:** 1994
SQ FT: 39,600

PRODUCTS & SERVICES SECTION

6513 - Operators Of Apartment Buildings County (P-10457)

SALES (est): 1.5B **Publicly Held**
WEB: www.essexapartmenthomes.com
SIC: **6513** 6798 Apartment hotel operation; real estate investment trusts

(P-10435)
FAIRWOOD ASSOCIATES APTS
Also Called: Fairwood Apartments
8893 Fair Oaks Blvd Ofc, Carmichael (95608-2672)
PHONE..................................916 944-0152
Leeann Morein, *Principal*
Arthur F Evans, *Partner*
The National Housing Partnersh, *Partner*
Jennifer Hardee, *Principal*
Joanette Stiron, *Manager*
EMP: 99 **EST:** 1980
SALES (est): 500K **Publicly Held**
WEB: www.aimco.com
SIC: **6513** Apartment building operators
PA: Apartment Investment & Management Company
  4582 S Ulster St Ste 1450
  Denver CO 80237

(P-10436)
GREENBRAE MANAGEMENT INC (PA)
50 Bon A Shopg Ctr Ste 20, Greenbrae (94904)
PHONE..................................415 461-0200
Andrea Schultz, *President*
Iyana Christine Eshoo, *Corp Secy*
Niels Schultz, *Corp Secy*
Phil Simon, *Vice Pres*
Manda Slessor, *Director*
EMP: 45 **EST:** 1991
SQ FT: 5,000
SALES (est): 6.3MM **Privately Held**
WEB: www.bonair.com
SIC: **6513** 6512 6552 Apartment building operators; shopping center, property operation only; commercial & industrial building operation; subdividers & developers

(P-10437)
HIGNELL INCORPORATED
Also Called: Sierra Manor Apts
1836 Laburnum Ave, Chico (95926-2375)
PHONE..................................530 345-1965
Becky Nelson, *Branch Mgr*
EMP: 40
SALES (corp-wide): 19.2MM **Privately Held**
WEB: www.hignell.com
SIC: **6513** Apartment building operators
PA: Hignell, Incorporated
  1750 Humboldt Rd
  Chico CA 95928
  530 894-0404

(P-10438)
HILLCREST SENIOR HOUSING CORP
35 Hillcrest Dr, Daly City (94014-1098)
PHONE..................................650 757-1737
Susan Ruan, *Principal*
David A Grant, *Principal*
EMP: 528 **EST:** 2005
SALES (est): 873.1K
SALES (corp-wide): 25.9MM **Privately Held**
WEB: www.humangood.org
SIC: **6513** Retirement hotel operation
HQ: Humangood Affordable Housing
  6120 Stoneridge Mall Rd # 100
  Pleasanton CA 94588
  925 924-7163

(P-10439)
HUMANGOOD AFFORDABLE HOUSING
6120 Stoneridge Mall Rd, Pleasanton (94588-3296)
PHONE..................................925 924-7100
David A Grant, *Branch Mgr*
EMP: 59
SALES (corp-wide): 25.9MM **Privately Held**
WEB: www.humangood.org
SIC: **6513** Retirement hotel operation

HQ: Humangood Affordable Housing
  6120 Stoneridge Mall Rd # 100
  Pleasanton CA 94588
  925 924-7163

(P-10440)
HUMANGOOD NORCAL (HQ)
Also Called: American Baptist Homes of West
6120 Stnrdge Mall Rd Ste, Pleasanton (94588)
PHONE..................................925 924-7100
David B Ferguson, *CEO*
Christopher A Vito, *President*
Randy Stamper, *Chairman*
Sloan Bentley, *Senior VP*
Terese Farkas, *Senior VP*
EMP: 60 **EST:** 1955
SQ FT: 26,000
SALES (est): 173MM
SALES (corp-wide): 25.9MM **Privately Held**
WEB: www.humangood.org
SIC: **6513** Retirement hotel operation
PA: Humangood
  6120 Stoneridge Mall Rd
  Pleasanton CA 94588
  602 906-4024

(P-10441)
IRVINE APT COMMUNITIES LP
39 Rio Robles E, San Jose (95134-1629)
PHONE..................................408 943-1595
Donald Bren, *Branch Mgr*
EMP: 211
SALES (corp-wide): 1.4B **Privately Held**
WEB: www.irvinecompanyapartments.com
SIC: **6513** Apartment building operators
HQ: Irvine Apartment Communities, Lp
  110 Innovation Dr
  Irvine CA 92617

(P-10442)
JEWISH SENIOR LIVING GROUP
302 Silver Ave, San Francisco (94112-1510)
PHONE..................................415 562-2600
Daniel Ruth, *President*
Olga Strashnaya, *Info Tech Mgr*
Terrence Scott, *Controller*
Josh Moomaw, *Opers Staff*
Pam Biasotti, *Supervisor*
EMP: 60 **EST:** 2008
SALES (est): 8.9MM **Privately Held**
WEB: www.jewishseniorlivinggroup.org
SIC: **6513** Retirement hotel operation

(P-10443)
KAE PROPERTIES (PA)
2033 Miramonte Ave, San Leandro (94578-1535)
P.O. Box 2947, Castro Valley (94546-0947)
PHONE..................................510 276-2635
Kenneth A Evilsizor Jr, *Owner*
EMP: 46 **EST:** 1956
SQ FT: 10,000
SALES (est): 1.9MM **Privately Held**
SIC: **6513** Apartment hotel operation

(P-10444)
KISCO SENIOR LIVING LLC
Also Called: Drake Terrace
275 Los Ranchitos Rd, San Rafael (94903-3673)
PHONE..................................415 491-1935
Judy Lucous, *Director*
EMP: 62
SALES (corp-wide): 138.2MM **Privately Held**
WEB: www.kiscoseniorliving.com
SIC: **6513** Retirement hotel operation
PA: Senior Kisco Living Llc
  5790 Fleet St Ste 300
  Carlsbad CA 92008
  760 804-5900

(P-10445)
KISCO SENIOR LIVING LLC
1100 E Spruce Ave Ofc, Fresno (93720-3314)
PHONE..................................559 449-8070
EMP: 62
SALES (corp-wide): 138.2MM **Privately Held**
WEB: www.kiscoseniorliving.com
SIC: **6513** Retirement hotel operation

PA: Senior Kisco Living Llc
  5790 Fleet St Ste 300
  Carlsbad CA 92008
  760 804-5900

(P-10446)
KISCO SENIOR LIVING LLC
Also Called: Oak View Snoma Hlls Apartments
1350 Oak View Cir, Rohnert Park (94928-6411)
PHONE..................................707 585-1800
Kim Healis, *Manager*
EMP: 62
SALES (corp-wide): 138.2MM **Privately Held**
WEB: www.kiscoseniorliving.com
SIC: **6513** Retirement hotel operation
PA: Senior Kisco Living Llc
  5790 Fleet St Ste 300
  Carlsbad CA 92008
  760 804-5900

(P-10447)
KISCO SENIOR LIVING LLC
Also Called: KRC Los Altos
1174 Los Altos Ave Ofc, Los Altos (94022-1059)
PHONE..................................650 948-7337
Felora Lotfi, *Branch Mgr*
Angela Neale, *Vice Pres*
EMP: 62
SALES (corp-wide): 138.2MM **Privately Held**
WEB: www.kiscoseniorliving.com
SIC: **6513** Retirement hotel operation
PA: Senior Kisco Living Llc
  5790 Fleet St Ste 300
  Carlsbad CA 92008
  760 804-5900

(P-10448)
LIVERMORE SNIOR LVING ASSOC LP
Also Called: Leisure Care
900 E Stanley Blvd # 38, Livermore (94550-4089)
PHONE..................................925 371-2300
Mike Palmer, *General Mgr*
Laura Matteucci, *Records Dir*
Sue Harding, *Marketing Staff*
Alyssa Sturgill, *Education*
Patrick Nunez, *Food Svc Dir*
EMP: 37 **EST:** 2001
SALES (est): 11.5MM **Privately Held**
SIC: **6513** Retirement hotel operation

(P-10449)
MERCED A PARK CALIFORNIA LP
2020 W Kettleman Ln, Lodi (95242-4338)
PHONE..................................209 334-6565
EMP: 35
SALES (est): 1MM **Privately Held**
SIC: **6513** Commerical Building Owner

(P-10450)
MONTEREY PINE APARTMENTS
680 S 37th St, Richmond (94804-4207)
PHONE..................................510 215-1926
Brian Arnold, *Manager*
EMP: 89 **EST:** 2002
SALES (est): 312.9K
SALES (corp-wide): 37.6MM **Privately Held**
WEB: www.themontereypines.com
SIC: **6513** Apartment hotel operation
PA: A. F. Evans Company, Inc.
  2033 N Main St Ste 340
  Walnut Creek CA 94596
  510 891-9400

(P-10451)
OAK CREEK APARTMENTS
Also Called: Gerson Bakar & Associates
1600 Sand Hill Rd, Palo Alto (94304-2047)
PHONE..................................650 327-1600
Gerson Bakar, *Partner*
A S Wilsey, *General Ptnr*
EMP: 237 **EST:** 1968
SQ FT: 300,000
SALES (est): 1.7MM
SALES (corp-wide): 38.3MM **Privately Held**
WEB: www.oakcreekapts.com
SIC: **6513** Apartment hotel operation

PA: Jalson Co., Inc.
  201 Filbert St Ste 700
  San Francisco CA 94133
  415 391-1313

(P-10452)
OCONNER WOODS A CALIFORNIA
3400 Wagner Heights Rd, Stockton (95209-4843)
PHONE..................................209 956-3400
Scot Sinclair, *President*
EMP: 46 **EST:** 1990
SQ FT: 3,000
SALES (est): 1.2MM **Privately Held**
WEB: www.oconnorwoods.org
SIC: **6513** Retirement hotel operation
PA: St. Joseph's Regional Housing Corporation
  3400 Wagner Heights Rd
  Stockton CA 95209

(P-10453)
OCONNOR WOODS HOUSING CORP
3400 Wagner Heights Rd, Stockton (95209-4843)
PHONE..................................209 956-3400
Edward G Schoeder, *President*
Scot Sinclair, *Exec Dir*
Penny Mallette, *Director*
Dawn Shimel, *Director*
EMP: 100
SALES (est): 29.1MM **Privately Held**
WEB: www.oconnorwoods.org
SIC: **6513** Retirement hotel operation
PA: St. Joseph's Regional Housing Corporation
  3400 Wagner Heights Rd
  Stockton CA 95209

(P-10454)
PENINSULA VOLUNTEER PRPTS INC (PA)
800 Middle Ave, Menlo Park (94025-5121)
PHONE..................................650 326-2025
Michelle Knapik, *Exec Dir*
EMP: 37 **EST:** 1949
SQ FT: 25,000
SALES (est): 3.3MM **Privately Held**
WEB: www.penvol.org
SIC: **6513** Apartment building operators

(P-10455)
PREFERRED CORPORATE SVCS INC
Also Called: Master Suites
1769 E El Paso Ave, Fresno (93720-2790)
PHONE..................................559 765-6755
Sylvia Hines, *President*
Michelle Benge, *Bookkeeper*
Sandra Little, *Manager*
Emilio Voorhees, *Supervisor*
EMP: 51 **EST:** 2001
SALES (est): 2.8MM **Privately Held**
WEB: www.mastersuites.net
SIC: **6513** 7359 7011 Apartment building operators; appliance rental; hotels & motels; motels; vacation lodges; hotels

(P-10456)
PRESIDIO GATE APARTMENTS
2770 Lombard St, San Francisco (94123-2446)
PHONE..................................415 567-1050
Jorge Lima, *Maintence Staff*
Lucy Ascalon, *Nurse*
EMP: 68
SALES (corp-wide): 1.3MM **Privately Held**
WEB: www.covia.org
SIC: **6513** 7389 Retirement hotel operation; business services
PA: Presidio Gate Apartments
  2185 N Calif Blvd Ste 215
  Walnut Creek CA 94596
  925 956-7400

(P-10457)
RURAL CMMNITIES HSING DEV CORP (PA)
499 Leslie St, Ukiah (95482-5506)
PHONE..................................707 463-1975

(PA)=Parent Co (HQ)=Headquarters (DH)=Div Headquarters
✪ = New Business established in last 2 years

2022 Northern California Business Directory and Buyers Guide

473

6513 - Operators Of Apartment Buildings County (P-10458)

William Thompson, *CEO*
Angelica Figueroa, *Project Mgr*
Tom Simms, *Controller*
Erica Ramirez, *Sls & Mktg Exec*
Rebecca Neilson, *Director*
EMP: 59 **EST:** 1975
SQ FT: 2,400
SALES (est): 993.5K **Privately Held**
WEB: www.rchdc.org
SIC: 6513 6515 8742 Apartment building operators; mobile home site operators; real estate consultant

(P-10458)
SATELLITE FIRST COMMUNITIES LP (PA)
1835 Alcatraz Ave, Berkeley (94703-2714)
PHONE...........................510 647-0700
Susan Friedland, *Exec Dir*
EMP: 54 **EST:** 2008
SALES (est): 1.7MM **Privately Held**
SIC: 6513 Apartment building operators

(P-10459)
SILVERADO ORCHARDS LLC (PA)
Also Called: Management Associates
601 Pope St Ofc, Saint Helena (94574-1275)
P.O. Box 102 (94574-0102)
PHONE...........................707 963-1461
Alan Baldwin, *General Ptnr*
L Meade Baldwin, *General Ptnr*
EMP: 75 **EST:** 1975
SQ FT: 80,000
SALES (est): 6.4MM **Privately Held**
WEB: www.silveradoorchards.com
SIC: 6513 Retirement hotel operation

(P-10460)
SILVERWOOD MANAGEMENT INC (PA)
Also Called: Parks Silverwood
5150 Douglas Ln, Sebastopol (95472-2177)
PHONE...........................703 777-8322
Mark Silverwood, *Owner*
EMP: 59 **EST:** 2015
SALES (est): 2.5MM **Privately Held**
WEB: www.silverwoodcompanies.com
SIC: 6513 Apartment building operators

(P-10461)
SMITH RNCH HMES HMEOWNERS ASSN
500 Deer Valley Rd, San Rafael (94903-5504)
PHONE...........................415 492-4900
John Patrick Maura, *CEO*
EMP: 85 **EST:** 1989
SALES (est): 1.8MM **Privately Held**
SIC: 6513 Retirement hotel operation

(P-10462)
ST JSEPHS REGIONAL HSING CORP (PA)
3400 Wagner Heights Rd, Stockton (95209-4843)
PHONE...........................209 956-3400
Edward G Schroeder, *President*
EMP: 126 **EST:** 1979
SALES (est): 24.6MM **Privately Held**
SIC: 6513 8741 8052 Apartment building operators; hospital management; intermediate care facilities

(P-10463)
STONESFAIR FINANCIAL CORP
577 Airport Blvd Ste 700, Burlingame (94010-2024)
PHONE...........................650 347-0442
Karl E Bakhtiari, *President*
Emily Henry, *Asst Mgr*
EMP: 60 **EST:** 1993
SALES (est): 2.5MM **Privately Held**
WEB: www.stonesfairfinancial.com
SIC: 6513 6514 Apartment building operators; residential building, four or fewer units: operation

(P-10464)
TRAMMELL CROW RESIDENTIAL CO
Also Called: T C R
1810 Gateway Dr Ste 100, San Mateo (94404-2470)
PHONE...........................650 349-1224
Fax: 650 349-0343
EMP: 45
SALES (corp-wide): 51MM **Privately Held**
SIC: 6513 6552 6512 Apartment Building Operator Subdivider/Developer Nonresidential Building Operator
PA: Trammell Crow Residential Company
3889 Maple Ave Ste 200
Dallas TX 75219
214 922-8400

(P-10465)
TRULIA INC
116 New Montgomery St, San Francisco (94105-3607)
PHONE...........................415 648-4358
Oleg Salnik, *Branch Mgr*
Natalie Foote, *Officer*
Stephen Capezza, *Vice Pres*
Brian Lee, *Vice Pres*
Brandon Bro, *Sr Software Eng*
EMP: 666
SALES (corp-wide): 3.3B **Publicly Held**
WEB: www.trulia.com
SIC: 6513 Apartment building operators
HQ: Trulia, Inc.
535 Mission St Fl 7
San Francisco CA 94105

(P-10466)
VASONA MANAGEMENT INC
Also Called: Marina Breeze
13949 Doolittle Dr, San Leandro (94577-5548)
PHONE...........................510 352-8728
Willie Johnson, *Principal*
EMP: 58
SALES (corp-wide): 29.8MM **Privately Held**
WEB: www.vasonamgmt.com
SIC: 6513 Apartment building operators
PA: Vasona Management, Inc.
1500 E Hamilton Ave # 210
Campbell CA 95008
408 354-4200

(P-10467)
VINTAGE SENIOR MANAGEMENT INC
91 Napa Rd, Sonoma (95476-7691)
PHONE...........................707 595-0009
EMP: 40 **Privately Held**
WEB: www.vintagehousing.com
SIC: 6513 Retirement hotel operation
PA: Senior Vintage Management Inc
23 Corporate Plaza Dr # 190
Newport Beach CA 92660

(P-10468)
WILLOW GLEN VILLA A
1660 Gaton Dr, San Jose (95125-4534)
PHONE...........................408 266-1660
EMP: 70
SQ FT: 146,000
SALES: 3MM **Privately Held**
SIC: 6513 Retirement Complex

(P-10469)
WINNRESIDENTIAL LTD PARTNR
Also Called: Hci
255 Washington Rd, Chowchilla (93610-1909)
PHONE...........................559 665-9600
EMP: 43
SALES (corp-wide): 52.6MM **Privately Held**
WEB: www.winncompanies.com
SIC: 6513 Apartment building operators
PA: Winnresidential Limited Partnership
1 Wshngton Mall Ste 500
Boston MA 02108
617 742-4500

6514 Operators Of Dwellings, Except Apartments

(P-10470)
APARTMENT LIST INC
475 Brannan St Ste 410, San Francisco (94107-5421)
PHONE...........................415 817-1068
John Kobs, *CEO*
Evan Kahn, *Partner*
Matt Nemenman, *President*
Matthew Woods, *Officer*
Dennis Cogbill, *Vice Pres*
EMP: 43 **EST:** 2008
SALES (est): 11.3MM **Privately Held**
WEB: www.apartmentlist.com
SIC: 6514 Dwelling operators, except apartments

(P-10471)
EAH INC (PA)
Also Called: EAH HOUSING
22 Pelican Way, San Rafael (94901-5545)
PHONE...........................415 258-1800
Laura Hall, *President*
Cathy Macy, *CFO*
Alvin Bonnett, *Senior VP*
Welton Jordon, *Senior VP*
Karen Belanger, *Vice Pres*
EMP: 70 **EST:** 1968
SQ FT: 30,000
SALES (est): 86MM **Privately Held**
WEB: www.eahhousing.org
SIC: 6514 Residential building, four or fewer units: operation

(P-10472)
MENLO GATEWAY INC
Also Called: MIDPEN HOUSING
303 Vintage Park Dr # 250, Foster City (94404-1166)
PHONE...........................650 356-2900
Mark Battey, *Chairman*
Art Fatum, *CFO*
Mick Vergura, *CFO*
Lance Smith, *Vice Pres*
Peter Villareal, *Principal*
EMP: 99 **EST:** 1986
SALES (est): 45.9MM **Privately Held**
SIC: 6514 6513 Residential building, four or fewer units: operation; apartment building operators
PA: Stanford Mid-Peninsula Urban Coalition
303 Vintage Park Dr # 250
Foster City CA 94404

6515 Operators of Residential Mobile Home Sites

(P-10473)
MOBILEHOME COMMUNITIES AMERICA
Also Called: Chateau La Salle
2681 Monterey Hwy, San Jose (95111-3097)
PHONE...........................408 298-3230
Jodi Damon Cookson, *Manager*
EMP: 116
SALES (corp-wide): 8MM **Privately Held**
WEB: www.brandenburg-properties.com
SIC: 6515 Mobile home site operators
PA: Mobilehome Communities Of America
1122 Willow St Ste 200
San Jose CA 95125
408 279-5200

(P-10474)
R C ROBERTS & CO (PA)
Also Called: Sands Rv Resort
801 A St, San Rafael (94901-3010)
PHONE...........................415 456-8600
Barbel Roberts,
Cecil Yates, *COO*
Felix Gonzales, *Sales Mgr*
Niels Roberts,
Scott Roberts,
EMP: 216 **EST:** 1977
SQ FT: 3,000
SALES (est): 11MM **Privately Held**
WEB: www.djogradyconsultants.com
SIC: 6515 7011 6531 Mobile home site operators; resort hotel; real estate agents & managers

(P-10475)
WATERHOUSE MANAGEMENT CORP
500 Giuseppe Ct Ste 2, Roseville (95678-6305)
PHONE...........................916 772-4918
Kenneth Watershouse, *President*
Larry Richey, *Regional Mgr*
Lana Work, *Admin Asst*
EMP: 150 **EST:** 1997
SQ FT: 10,000
SALES (est): 7.2MM **Privately Held**
WEB: www.waterhousemgmt.com
SIC: 6515 Mobile home site operators

6519 Lessors Of Real Estate, NEC

(P-10476)
CALIFORNIA PARKING COMPANY (PA)
Also Called: Dnj Parking
768 Sansome St, San Francisco (94111-1704)
P.O. Box 2882 (94126-2882)
PHONE...........................415 781-4896
Richard Puccinelli, *President*
Ronald Britz, *Vice Pres*
Robert Puccinelli, *Vice Pres*
EMP: 63 **EST:** 1959
SQ FT: 1,300
SALES (est): 5MM **Privately Held**
WEB: www.californiaparking.com
SIC: 6519 6512 7521 Real property lessors; nonresidential building operators; parking lots

(P-10477)
CALIFORNIA SUITES (PA)
Also Called: Suiteamerica
4970 Windplay Dr, El Dorado Hills (95762-9659)
PHONE...........................916 941-7970
James Masten, *CEO*
Robin Masten, *President*
Guy Cook, *COO*
Kim Dunbar, *Executive*
Samantha Ellis, *Program Mgr*
EMP: 40 **EST:** 1990
SQ FT: 8,000
SALES (est): 21.7MM **Privately Held**
WEB: www.stayinns.com
SIC: 6519 Sub-lessors of real estate

(P-10478)
DREISBACH ENTERPRISES INC
2530 E 11th St, Oakland (94601-1425)
PHONE...........................510 533-6600
Ray Guy, *Branch Mgr*
EMP: 43
SALES (corp-wide): 41.5MM **Privately Held**
WEB: www.dreisbach.com
SIC: 6519 1541 4222 4225 Real property lessors; industrial buildings & warehouses; warehousing, cold storage or refrigerated; general warehousing & storage
PA: Dreisbach Enterprises, Inc.
575 Maritime St
Oakland CA 94607
510 533-6600

(P-10479)
FLEA MARKET INC
1590 Berryessa Rd Frnt, San Jose (95133-1096)
PHONE...........................408 453-1110
George Bumb, *President*
Brian Bumb, *President*
Jeff Bumb, *Vice Pres*
Tim Bumb, *Vice Pres*
Ted Palsgrove, *Security Dir*
EMP: 38 **EST:** 1960
SQ FT: 5,000
SALES (est): 5.4MM **Privately Held**
WEB: www.sjfm.com
SIC: 6519 Real property lessors

PRODUCTS & SERVICES SECTION

6531 - Real Estate Agents & Managers County (P-10503)

(P-10480)
FOOD SPECIALISTS INC
Also Called: Scott's Seafood Grill & Bar
2 Broadway, Oakland (94607-3748)
PHONE.....................510 444-3456
Raymond Gallagher, *President*
EMP: 340 **EST:** 1972
SALES (est): 16.5MM **Privately Held**
SIC: 5812 6519 Restaurant, family: independent; real property lessors

(P-10481)
LYON REALTY
4340 Golden Center Dr A, Placerville (95667-6254)
PHONE.....................530 295-4444
Michael Levedahl, *CFO*
Teresa Burroughs, *Broker*
Mary Meyer, *Broker*
Cathy Harrington, *Marketing Staff*
Janet Hubbard, *Director*
EMP: 110 **Privately Held**
WEB: www.golyon.com
SIC: 6519 6531 Real property lessors; real estate brokers & agents
PA: Lyon Realty
  2280 Del Paso Rd Ste 100
  Sacramento CA 95834

(P-10482)
MAXIMUS REAL ESTATE PARTNERS
1 Maritime Plz Ste 1900, San Francisco (94111-3509)
PHONE.....................415 584-4832
Robert Rosania, *CEO*
Fred Knapp, *Partner*
Seth Mallen, *Treasurer*
Mike Boyadjian, *Vice Pres*
Ron Kanter, *Info Tech Dir*
EMP: 100 **EST:** 2013
SALES (est): 11.8MM **Privately Held**
WEB: www.maximusrepartners.com
SIC: 6519 Sub-lessors of real estate

(P-10483)
MT EDEN NURSERY CO INC (PA)
2124 Bering Dr, San Jose (95131-2013)
PHONE.....................408 213-5777
Yoshimi Shibata, *President*
Esmeralda Ruiz, *Purchasing*
Lori Librero, *Sales Staff*
EMP: 50 **EST:** 1915
SALES (est): 2.3MM **Privately Held**
WEB: www.mteden.com
SIC: 6519 Farm land leasing

(P-10484)
PACIFIC YGNACIO CORPORATION
201 California St Ste 500, San Francisco (94111-5028)
PHONE.....................925 939-3275
Robin Andrews, *Manager*
EMP: 115 **EST:** 1998
SQ FT: 105,495
SALES (est): 1.9MM **Privately Held**
WEB: www.pacificeagleholdings.com
SIC: 6519 Real property lessors
PA: Pacific Eagle Holdings Corporation
  353 Sacramento St # 1788
  San Francisco CA 94111

(P-10485)
PEREZ FARMS LP
22001 E St, Crows Landing (95313)
P.O. Box 97 (95313-0097)
PHONE.....................209 837-4701
Ramon Perez, *Partner*
Mark Perez Est, *Partner*
Daniel J Perez, *Partner*
Earl Perez, *Partner*
Michael Perez, *Partner*
EMP: 35 **EST:** 1941
SALES (est): 3.4MM **Privately Held**
WEB: www.perezfarms.com
SIC: 6519 Farm land leasing; landholding office

(P-10486)
UNIVERSITY CAL SAN FRANCISCO
Also Called: Umspe
2120 N Winery Ave Ste 102, Fresno (93703-4809)
PHONE.....................559 251-3033
EMP: 39 **Privately Held**
WEB: www.ucsf.edu
SIC: 6519 Real property lessors
HQ: University Cal San Francisco
  513 Parnassus Ave 115f
  San Francisco CA 94143

6531 Real Estate Agents & Managers

(P-10487)
ACCO MANAGEMENT COMPANY
Also Called: Spring Creek Apartments
100 Buckingham Dr Ofc, Santa Clara (95051-7151)
PHONE.....................408 241-3000
Margie Misner, *Manager*
EMP: 102
SALES (corp-wide): 8.6MM **Privately Held**
WEB: www.greendaleapartments.com
SIC: 6531 6513 Real estate managers; apartment building operators
PA: Acco Management Company
  130 E Dana St
  Mountain View CA 94041
  650 961-8330

(P-10488)
ALICE GRAY
Also Called: Coldwell Banker Residential BR
36 Tiburon Blvd, Mill Valley (94941-2440)
PHONE.....................415 388-5060
EMP: 40
SALES (est): 1.4MM **Privately Held**
WEB: www.alicegray.com
SIC: 6531 Real Estate Agent/Manager

(P-10489)
AMERICAN MARKETING SYSTEMS INC
Also Called: Amsi Real Estate Services
2800 Van Ness Ave, San Francisco (94109-1426)
PHONE.....................800 747-7784
Zoya L Smithton, *Director*
Kate Barkauskas, *Office Mgr*
Heather Upton, *Office Mgr*
Robb Fleischer, *Director*
EMP: 75 **EST:** 1970
SQ FT: 8,000 **Privately Held**
WEB: www.amsires.com
SIC: 6531 Real estate brokers & agents

(P-10490)
AMERICANA VACATION RESORTS INC (PA)
1156 Ski Run Blvd Ste 1, South Lake Tahoe (96150-8885)
PHONE.....................530 544-8463
Edward J McCarthy, *President*
EMP: 37 **EST:** 1980
SALES (est): 3.1MM **Privately Held**
SIC: 6531 Real estate managers

(P-10491)
AMR APPRAISALS INC
Also Called: Got Appraisals
4000 Executive Pkwy # 230, San Ramon (94583-4257)
P.O. Box 2426 (94583-7426)
PHONE.....................925 400-6066
Joe M Reid, *President*
Nicole Stefani, *Business Mgr*
EMP: 54 **EST:** 2004
SALES (est): 5MM **Privately Held**
WEB: www.gotappraisals.com
SIC: 6531 Appraiser, real estate

(P-10492)
ARDENBROOK INC
Also Called: Ardenwood Rental Condominiums
5016 Paseo Padre Pkwy, Fremont (94555-3416)
PHONE.....................510 794-1020
Ben Cisneros, *Manager*
EMP: 62 **Privately Held**
WEB: www.ardenbrook.com
SIC: 6531 6513 Real estate agents & managers; apartment building operators
PA: Ardenbrook, Inc.
  4725 Thornton Ave
  Fremont CA 94536

(P-10493)
BARCELON ASSOCIATES MGT CORP
590 Lennon Ln Ste 110, Walnut Creek (94598-5923)
PHONE.....................925 627-7000
Mark Barcelon, *CEO*
Sandy Barcelon, *Co-CEO*
Sean Barcelon, *Director*
Rosewood Townhomes, *Supervisor*
EMP: 250 **EST:** 1979
SQ FT: 3,000
SALES (est): 10.4MM **Privately Held**
WEB: www.barcelon.com
SIC: 6531 Real estate managers

(P-10494)
BERKSHIRE HATHAWAY INC
43225 Mission Blvd, Fremont (94539-5826)
PHONE.....................510 651-6500
EMP: 40
SALES (corp-wide): 242.1B **Publicly Held**
SIC: 6531 Real Estate Agent/Manager
PA: Berkshire Hathaway Inc.
  3555 Farnam St Ste 1140
  Omaha NE 68131
  402 346-1400

(P-10495)
BPAZ HOLDINGS 2 LLC
1 Sansome St Ste 1500, San Francisco (94104-4449)
PHONE.....................972 354-6250
Matt Novak,
EMP: 50 **EST:** 2018
SALES (est): 8.8MM **Privately Held**
SIC: 6531 Real estate agents & managers
PA: Bkly Ptn Crps Idst Ptshp Llc
  1 Sansome St Ste 1500
  San Francisco CA 94104
  972 354-6250

(P-10496)
BROADWAY MANAGEMENT CO INC
8 Crow Canyon Ct Ste 100, San Ramon (94583-1985)
PHONE.....................925 820-7292
Joe Conron, *President*
Moshe Melamed, *Vice Pres*
Barbara Conde, *Regional Mgr*
William Conron, *Project Mgr*
Jim Lawson, *Controller*
EMP: 40 **EST:** 1965
SQ FT: 1,400
SALES (est): 3.9MM **Privately Held**
WEB: www.broadwaymanagement.com
SIC: 6531 Real estate managers

(P-10497)
BROSAMER & WALL LLC
1777 Oakland Blvd Ste 300, Walnut Creek (94596-4063)
PHONE.....................925 932-7900
Charles Wall, *Mng Member*
Cynthia Lundquist, *Controller*
Robert Brosamer,
EMP: 50 **EST:** 1999
SALES (est): 6.7MM **Privately Held**
WEB: www.brosamerwall.com
SIC: 6531 8711 Rental agent, real estate; construction & civil engineering

(P-10498)
BUNGALOW LIVING INC
1 Letterman Dr Ste Cp500, San Francisco (94129-1494)
PHONE.....................415 501-0981
Andrew Collins, *President*
Alex Halliday, *Vice Pres*
Bryan Connolly, *General Mgr*
Amy Beemer, *Opers Staff*
Bob Reish, *Opers Staff*
EMP: 82 **EST:** 2013
SALES (est): 9.5MM **Privately Held**
WEB: www.bungalow.com
SIC: 6531 Real estate agents & managers

(P-10499)
BUZZ OATES MANAGEMENT SERVICES
555 Capitol Mall Ste 900, Sacramento (95814-4606)
PHONE.....................916 381-3843
Phil Oates, *Chairman*
Larry Allbaugh, *President*
Mike Stodden, *CFO*
Kimberly Chambers, *Vice Pres*
EMP: 50 **EST:** 2001
SQ FT: 8,630
SALES (est): 3.8MM **Privately Held**
WEB: www.buzzoates.com
SIC: 6531 Real estate agent, commercial

(P-10500)
C L S WOODSIDE MGT GROUP (PA)
1620 N Carptr Rd Ste C28, Modesto (95351)
PHONE.....................209 577-4181
Carol Tougas, *Managing Prtnr*
Kerri Hunter, *Partner*
Jim McFaddin, *Opers Staff*
EMP: 40 **EST:** 1976
SQ FT: 3,500
SALES (est): 8.3MM **Privately Held**
WEB: www.woodside-management.com
SIC: 6531 Real estate managers

(P-10501)
CARITAS MANAGEMENT CORPORATION
1358 Valencia St, San Francisco (94110-3715)
PHONE.....................415 647-7191
Robert Zerrilla, *President*
Raysha Waters, *Property Mgr*
Cindy Fung, *Director*
Jessica Hickerson, *Director*
Deborah Madaris, *Supervisor*
EMP: 55 **EST:** 1981
SQ FT: 3,000
SALES (est): 12.4MM
SALES (corp-wide): 12.4MM **Privately Held**
WEB: www.caritasmanagement.com
SIC: 6531 Real estate managers
PA: Mission Housing Development Corporation
  474 Valencia St Ste 280
  San Francisco CA 94103
  415 864-6432

(P-10502)
CARLTON SENIOR LIVING INC
6915 Elk Grove Blvd, Elk Grove (95758-5526)
PHONE.....................916 714-2404
Kimberly Carlton, *Branch Mgr*
EMP: 77
SALES (corp-wide): 33.6MM **Privately Held**
WEB: www.carltonseniorliving.com
SIC: 6531 Real estate managers
PA: Senior Carlton Living Inc
  4071 Port Chicago Hwy # 130
  Concord CA 94520
  925 338-2434

(P-10503)
CARLTON SENIOR LIVING INC (PA)
Also Called: Intercontinental Services
4071 Port Chicago Hwy # 130, Concord (94520-1163)
PHONE.....................925 338-2434
Thomas McDonald, *Ch of Bd*
Philp Scott, *President*

6531 - Real Estate Agents & Managers County (P-10504)

Ruby Mac Donald, *Corp Secy*
EMP: 35
SALES (est): 33.6MM **Privately Held**
WEB: www.carltonseniorliving.com
SIC: 6531 3732 6552 Real estate managers; yachts, building & repairing; subdividers & developers

(P-10504)
CARLTON SENIOR LIVING INC
Also Called: Carlton Plaza of San Leandro
1000 E 14th St, San Leandro (94577-3787)
PHONE 510 636-0660
Harry Darrett, *Manager*
EMP: 77
SQ FT: 96,676
SALES (corp-wide): 33.6MM **Privately Held**
WEB: www.carltonseniorliving.com
SIC: 6531 Real estate agents & managers
PA: Senior Carlton Living Inc
  4071 Port Chicago Hwy # 130
  Concord CA 94520
  925 338-2434

(P-10505)
CASSIDY TRLY PROP MGT SN FRNCS
201 California St Ste 800, San Francisco (94111-5002)
PHONE 415 781-8100
EMP: 69 **EST:** 2010
SALES (est): 14MM
SALES (corp-wide): 5.7B **Privately Held**
SIC: 6531 Real Estate Agent/Manager
HQ: Cushman & Wakefield, Inc.
  225 W Wacker Dr Ste 3000
  Chicago IL 60606
  312 424-8000

(P-10506)
CBRE INC
500 Capitol Mall Ste 2400, Sacramento (95814-4752)
PHONE 916 446-6800
David Brennan, *Manager*
Bill Roohan, *Vice Chairman*
Keith Collins, *Exec VP*
John Maher, *Exec VP*
William Frain, *Senior VP*
EMP: 100 **Publicly Held**
WEB: www.cbre.com
SIC: 6531 Real estate agent, commercial
HQ: Cbre, Inc.
  400 S Hope St Ste 2500
  Los Angeles CA 90071
  213 613-3333

(P-10507)
CENTURY 21 WILDWOOD PROPERTIES
22910 Twain Harte Dr, Twain Harte (95383-9597)
PHONE 209 586-3258
Kimberly Darr, *President*
EMP: 36 **EST:** 1981
SQ FT: 1,700
SALES (est): 5.4MM **Privately Held**
WEB: www.century21wildwood.com
SIC: 6531 Real estate agent, residential

(P-10508)
CHIP ARASAN SYSTEMS INC
2150 N 1st St, San Jose (95131-2020)
PHONE 408 282-1616
Arasan Ganesan, *President*
Padamunnur RAO, *CFO*
Kevin K Yee, *Vice Pres*
Surender Sharma, *Senior Mgr*
Anand D Rajkumar, *Manager*
▼ **EMP:** 72 **EST:** 1995
SALES (est): 7.4MM **Privately Held**
WEB: www.arasan.com
SIC: 6531 7371 7379 Real estate agents & managers; computer software development; computer related consulting services
PA: Arasan Chip Technologies Limited
  Nagar
  Thoothukudi TN 62800

(P-10509)
CHRISTOPHER RANSOM LLC
1300 Clay St, Oakland (94612-1425)
P.O. Box 268 (94604-0268)
PHONE 510 345-9144
EMP: 76
SALES (est): 15MM **Privately Held**
SIC: 6531 Real Estate Agent/Manager

(P-10510)
CITISCAPE PRPRTY MGT GROUP LLC
3450 3rd St Ste 1a, San Francisco (94124-1444)
PHONE 415 401-2000
Kevin Wiley,
Wayne Lee, *CFO*
Terri Perozzi, *General Mgr*
Jack Gallagher, *Portfolio Mgr*
Katie Harnish, *Portfolio Mgr*
EMP: 96 **EST:** 1999
SQ FT: 11,000
SALES (est): 17.2MM **Privately Held**
WEB: www.citiscapesf.com
SIC: 6531 Real estate managers

(P-10511)
CLAY SHERMAN & CO (PA)
Also Called: S C Management
1111 Bayhill Dr Ste 450, San Bruno (94066-3054)
PHONE 650 952-2300
Fred W Concklin, *President*
Eric A Schwartz, *Ch of Bd*
Michael S Schwartz, *Ch of Bd*
Donald N Ravitch, *Chairman*
Victor J Richmond, *Senior VP*
EMP: 36 **EST:** 1870
SQ FT: 14,000
SALES (est): 10.3MM **Privately Held**
WEB: www.shermanclay.com
SIC: 6531 5736 6141 7359 Real estate managers; pianos; installment sales finance, other than banks; equipment rental & leasing

(P-10512)
CLEARCAPITALCOM INC
10266 Truckee Airport Rd, Truckee (96161-3310)
PHONE 530 550-2500
Duane Andrews, *CEO*
Simon Blackburn, *Exec VP*
Beth Buell, *Vice Pres*
David Cherner, *General Mgr*
Jennifer Lee, *Administration*
EMP: 140
SALES (corp-wide): 59.2MM **Privately Held**
WEB: www.clearcapital.com
SIC: 6531 Appraiser, real estate
PA: Clearcapital.Com, Inc.
  300 E 2nd St Ste 1405
  Reno NV 89501
  775 470-5656

(P-10513)
CLIMB REAL ESTATE (DH)
251 Rhode Island St Ste 1, San Francisco (94103-5131)
PHONE 415 431-8888
Chris Lim, *CEO*
Justina Ortiz, *Office Admin*
Carina Demeter, *Executive Asst*
Mark Cheoy, *CTO*
Teresa Larson, *Accountant*
EMP: 58 **EST:** 2010
SALES (est): 18.3MM **Publicly Held**
WEB: www.climbre.com
SIC: 6531 Real estate agent, residential; real estate brokers & agents

(P-10514)
COLDWELL BNKR AMRAL ASSOC RLTO
3775 Main St Ste E, Oakley (94561-5793)
PHONE 925 439-7400
EMP: 65
SALES (est): 1.6MM **Privately Held**
WEB: www.coldwellbanker.com
SIC: 6531 Real Estate Agents And Managers

(P-10515)
COLDWELL BNKR RESIDENTIAL BRKG (DH)
Also Called: Valley of California, Inc.
1855 Gateway Blvd Ste 750, Concord (94520-3290)
PHONE 925 275-3000
Bruce G Zipf, *CEO*
Avram Goldman, *President*
Bryce Johnson, *COO*
Melissa Huntsman, *Engineer*
Eric Peterson, *Analyst*
EMP: 100 **EST:** 1965
SALES (est): 48MM **Publicly Held**
WEB: www.aleksey.cbintouch.com
SIC: 6531 Real estate agent, residential

(P-10516)
COLDWELL BNKR RESIDENTIAL BRKG
1427 Chapin Ave, Burlingame (94010-4002)
PHONE 650 558-4200
Rachel Ni, *Branch Mgr*
Elaine Cosca, *Admin Mgr*
Stephan Marshall, *Asst Broker*
Donnamarie Baldwin, *Broker*
Nick Corcoleotes, *Sales Associate*
EMP: 50 **Publicly Held**
WEB: www.coldwellbanker.com
SIC: 6531 Real estate agent, residential
HQ: Coldwell Banker Residential Brokerage
  1855 Gateway Blvd Ste 750
  Concord CA 94520
  925 275-3000

(P-10517)
COLDWELL BNKR RESIDENTIAL BRKG
124 Rancho Del Mar, Aptos (95003-3913)
PHONE 831 462-9000
Spencer Hays, *Branch Mgr*
Richard Sternberg, *Asst Broker*
Keith Jackson, *Broker*
EMP: 50 **Publicly Held**
WEB: www.coldwellbanker.com
SIC: 6531 Real estate agent, residential
HQ: Coldwell Banker Residential Brokerage
  1855 Gateway Blvd Ste 750
  Concord CA 94520
  925 275-3000

(P-10518)
COLDWELL BNKR RESIDENTIAL BRKG
3340 Walnut Ave Ste 110, Fremont (94538-2215)
PHONE 510 608-7600
Mitchell Grisso, *Technology*
Emily Estrada, *Asst Broker*
Diane Petek, *Asst Broker*
Robert Brown, *Broker*
Molly Devinger, *Broker*
EMP: 50 **Publicly Held**
WEB: www.californiamoves.com
SIC: 6531 Real estate agent, residential
HQ: Coldwell Banker Residential Brokerage
  1855 Gateway Blvd Ste 750
  Concord CA 94520
  925 275-3000

(P-10519)
COLDWELL BNKR RSDNTIAL RE SVCS
500 Sir Frncis Drake Blvd, Greenbrae (94904-2347)
PHONE 415 461-2020
Kate Hamilton, *Manager*
EMP: 379 **Publicly Held**
WEB: www.coldwellbanker.com
SIC: 6531 Real estate agent, residential
HQ: Coldwell Banker Residential Real Estate Services, Inc.
  27742 Vista Del Lago # 1
  Mission Viejo CA 92692

(P-10520)
COLLIERS INTERNATIONAL
101 2nd St Ste 1100, San Francisco (94105-3652)
PHONE 415 788-3100
Herbert Damner Jr, *Partner*
Tony Crossley, *Exec VP*
Robert Gilley, *Exec VP*
Erika Elliott, *Vice Pres*
Matt Hurd, *Vice Pres*
EMP: 65 **EST:** 1979
SALES (est): 19.5MM
SALES (corp-wide): 2.7B **Privately Held**
WEB: www.ll-cre.com
SIC: 6531 Real estate agent, commercial
HQ: Colliers International New England, Llc
  160 Federal St Fl 11
  Boston MA 02110
  617 330-8000

(P-10521)
COMMUNITY MANAGEMENT SVCS INC
1935 Dry Creek Rd Ste 203, Campbell (95008-3631)
PHONE 408 559-1977
Tim Johnson, *President*
Diana Johnson, *CFO*
Marianne Hudkins, *Vice Pres*
Sue Thompson, *Executive*
Jill Grellman, *Accountant*
EMP: 45 **EST:** 1977
SQ FT: 8,800
SALES (est): 5.8MM **Privately Held**
WEB: www.communitymanagement.com
SIC: 6531 Real estate managers; condominium manager

(P-10522)
CONGREGATION EMANU-EL
Also Called: Home of Peace Cemetery
1299 El Camino Real, Colma (94014-3238)
PHONE 650 755-4700
James Carlson, *General Mgr*
EMP: 122
SALES (corp-wide): 12.1MM **Privately Held**
WEB: www.emanuelsf.org
SIC: 6531 Cemetery management service
PA: The Congregation Emanu-El
  2 Lake St
  San Francisco CA
  415 751-2535

(P-10523)
COOK REALTY INC
Also Called: Cook Realty Sales
4305 Freeport Blvd, Sacramento (95822-2045)
PHONE 916 451-6702
Frank Cook, *President*
Barbara Cook, *Corp Secy*
Trey Bonetti, *Vice Pres*
Vickie Hulbert, *Sales Staff*
Mindy Defenbaugh, *Agent*
EMP: 47 **EST:** 1976
SALES (est): 5.1MM **Privately Held**
WEB: www.cookrealty.net
SIC: 6531 Real estate agent, residential; real estate brokers & agents

(P-10524)
CORELOGIC INC
201 Spear St Fl 4, San Francisco (94105-1669)
PHONE 714 250-6400
EMP: 50
SALES (corp-wide): 1.8B **Publicly Held**
SIC: 6531 Real Estate Agent/Manager
PA: Corelogic, Inc.
  40 Pacifica Ste 900
  Irvine CA 92618
  949 214-1000

(P-10525)
CORINTHIAN REALTY LLC
3902 Smith St, Union City (94587-2616)
PHONE 510 487-8653
EMP: 60
SALES (est): 2.5MM **Privately Held**
SIC: 6531 Real Estate Agent/Manager

(P-10526)
CORTLANDT LIQUIDATING LLC
Also Called: Century 21 Showcase
13117 Highway 9, Boulder Creek (95006-9120)
PHONE 831 338-4500
John Carver, *Branch Mgr*
EMP: 56
SALES (corp-wide): 856.2MM **Privately Held**
WEB: www.century21.com
SIC: 6531 Real estate agent, residential

PRODUCTS & SERVICES SECTION
6531 - Real Estate Agents & Managers County (P-10549)

HQ: Cortlandt Liquidating Llc
22 Cortland St
New York NY 10007

(P-10527)
CUSHMAN & WAKEFIELD CAL INC (DH)
1 Maritime Plz Ste 900, San Francisco (94111-3412)
PHONE..................................408 275-6730
Joseph Stettinius Jr, *CEO*
Randy Borron, *President*
Robert Rudin, *Exec VP*
Sam Higgins, *Vice Pres*
Melissa Bach, *Exec Dir*
EMP: 110 **EST:** 1887
SQ FT: 26,500
SALES (est): 310.7MM
SALES (corp-wide): 7.8B **Privately Held**
WEB: www.cushmanwakefield.com
SIC: 6531 Real estate brokers & agents; real estate agent, commercial; real estate managers; appraiser, real estate
HQ: Cushman & Wakefield, Inc.
225 W Wacker Dr Ste 3000
Chicago IL 60606
312 424-8000

(P-10528)
CUSHMAN & WAKEFIELD CAL INC
1357 Hillcrest Dr, San Jose (95120-5618)
PHONE..................................408 572-4134
Robby Perrino, *Principal*
EMP: 546
SALES (corp-wide): 7.8B **Privately Held**
WEB: www.cushmanwakefield.com
SIC: 6531 Real estate agent, commercial
HQ: Cushman & Wakefield Of California, Inc.
1 Maritime Plz Ste 900
San Francisco CA 94111
408 275-6730

(P-10529)
CUSHMAN & WAKEFIELD CAL INC
555 12th St Ste 1400, Oakland (94607-4061)
PHONE..................................510 763-4900
Samuel C Swan, *Director*
EMP: 546
SALES (corp-wide): 7.8B **Privately Held**
WEB: www.cushmanwakefield.com
SIC: 6531 Real estate agent, commercial
HQ: Cushman & Wakefield Of California, Inc.
1 Maritime Plz Ste 900
San Francisco CA 94111
408 275-6730

(P-10530)
CUSHMAN & WAKEFIELD CAL INC
560 S Wnchester Blvd # 200, San Jose (95128-2500)
PHONE..................................408 436-5500
Joseph Cook II, *Principal*
EMP: 546
SALES (corp-wide): 7.8B **Privately Held**
WEB: www.cushmanwakefield.com
SIC: 6531 Real estate agent, commercial
HQ: Cushman & Wakefield Of California, Inc.
1 Maritime Plz Ste 900
San Francisco CA 94111
408 275-6730

(P-10531)
CUSHMAN & WAKEFIELD CAL INC
1333 N Calif Blvd Ste 550, Walnut Creek (94596-4557)
PHONE..................................925 935-0770
Jill Campbell, *Manager*
EMP: 546
SALES (corp-wide): 7.8B **Privately Held**
WEB: www.cushmanwakefield.com
SIC: 6531 Real estate agent, commercial
HQ: Cushman & Wakefield Of California, Inc.
1 Maritime Plz Ste 900
San Francisco CA 94111
408 275-6730

(P-10532)
CUSHMAN & WAKEFIELD CAL INC
2125 Hamilton Ave, San Jose (95125-5905)
PHONE..................................415 397-1700
Matt Chatham, *Director*
EMP: 546
SALES (corp-wide): 7.8B **Privately Held**
WEB: www.cushmanwakefield.com
SIC: 6531 Real estate agent, commercial
HQ: Cushman & Wakefield Of California, Inc.
1 Maritime Plz Ste 900
San Francisco CA 94111
408 275-6730

(P-10533)
CUSHMAN & WAKEFIELD CAL INC
455 Market St Ste 530, San Francisco (94105-2455)
PHONE..................................415 828-1923
Mary Husnagel, *Branch Mgr*
EMP: 546
SALES (corp-wide): 7.8B **Privately Held**
WEB: www.cushmanwakefield.com
SIC: 6531 Real estate agent, commercial
HQ: Cushman & Wakefield Of California, Inc.
1 Maritime Plz Ste 900
San Francisco CA 94111
408 275-6730

(P-10534)
CUSTOMER SERVICE REALTY (PA)
Also Called: Client First Home Loans
5330 Canton Ave, San Jose (95123)
PHONE..................................408 558-5000
Bryan Bonafetti, *President*
Janie Kelly, *Vice Pres*
Dave Bonafetti, *Principal*
Alora Frederick, *Agent*
Scott Raley, *Real Est Agnt*
EMP: 48 **EST:** 2003
SALES (est): 8.5MM **Privately Held**
WEB: www.csrrealestateservices.com
SIC: 6531 Real estate agents & managers

(P-10535)
DELEON REALTY INC
1717 Embarcadero Rd # 500, Palo Alto (94303-3357)
PHONE..................................650 543-8500
Michael Repka, *CEO*
Anthony Halawa, *Creative Dir*
Kimika Anjal, *Executive Asst*
Cynthia Masters, *Executive Asst*
Karen Fairburn, *Administration*
EMP: 37 **EST:** 2011
SALES (est): 5.6MM **Privately Held**
WEB: www.deleonrealty.com
SIC: 6531 Real estate agent, residential

(P-10536)
DENOVA HOME SALES INC
Also Called: Denova Homes
1500 Willow Pass Ct, Concord (94520-1009)
PHONE..................................925 852-0545
David Sanson, *President*
Joel Crawford, *CFO*
Lori Sanson, *Vice Pres*
Michael Evans, *Planning*
Cindi Walker, *Purchasing*
EMP: 84 **EST:** 1991
SQ FT: 1,850
SALES (est): 16.8MM **Privately Held**
WEB: www.denovahomes.com
SIC: 6531 Real estate brokers & agents

(P-10537)
DIABLO REALTY
Also Called: Pacific Mortgage Resources
975 Ygnacio Valley Rd, Walnut Creek (94596-3825)
PHONE..................................925 933-9300
Linda Jean Anderson, *President*
Moses Guillory, *Corp Secy*
EMP: 46 **EST:** 1977
SQ FT: 7,000
SALES (est): 5.2MM **Privately Held**
WEB: www.windermerediablo.withwre.com
SIC: 6531 6163 Real estate agent, residential; mortgage brokers arranging for loans, using money of others

(P-10538)
DICK JAMES & ASSOCIATES INC
Also Called: James Nevada Properties
2990 Lava Ridge Ct Ste 24, Roseville (95661-3057)
PHONE..................................916 332-7430
Michelle Amaral, *CFO*
EMP: 246 **EST:** 1998
SALES (est): 6.2MM **Privately Held**
SIC: 6531 Real estate managers

(P-10539)
DIEZ & LEIS RE GROUP INC
Also Called: Prudential Norcal Realty
5120 Manzanita Ave # 120, Carmichael (95608-0558)
PHONE..................................916 487-4287
Ron Leis, *President*
EMP: 926 **EST:** 1993
SQ FT: 10,000
SALES (est): 5.2MM
SALES (corp-wide): 57B **Publicly Held**
SIC: 6531 Real estate agent, residential
HQ: Brer Affiliates Llc
18500 Von Karman Ave # 4
Irvine CA 92612
949 794-7900

(P-10540)
DIVCO WEST RE SVCS INC
301 Howard St Ste 2100, San Francisco (94105-6616)
PHONE..................................415 284-5700
Stuart Shiff, *CEO*
Steve Dietsch, *CFO*
Marc Sternberg, *Officer*
Harshit Shah, *Managing Dir*
Paul Turek, *Managing Dir*
EMP: 40 **EST:** 2006
SALES (est): 10.2MM **Privately Held**
WEB: www.divcowest.com
SIC: 6531 Real estate managers

(P-10541)
DOUG ARNOLD REAL ESTATE INC (PA)
Also Called: Coldwell Banker
505 2nd St, Davis (95616-4618)
PHONE..................................530 758-3080
Doug Arnold, *President*
J David Taoramino, *Treasurer*
EMP: 50 **EST:** 1973
SQ FT: 7,000
SALES (est): 7.3MM **Privately Held**
WEB: www.coldwellbankerdougarnold.com
SIC: 6531 Real estate agent, residential

(P-10542)
DPPM INC
Also Called: Zephyr Real Estate
4040 24th St, San Francisco (94114-3716)
PHONE..................................415 695-7707
Fax: 415 695-1106
EMP: 80
SALES (corp-wide): 16.4MM **Privately Held**
SIC: 6531 Real Estate Agents And Managers
PA: Dppm, Inc.
850 7th St
San Francisco CA 94114
415 348-1212

(P-10543)
EGOMOTION CORP (PA)
Also Called: Zeus Living
888 Marin St Ste B, San Francisco (94124-1222)
PHONE..................................415 849-4662
Kulveer Taggar, *CEO*
Srinivas Panguluri, *COO*
Joseph Wong, *CTO*
Karolis Karalevicius, *Business Mgr*
Sara Katz, *Human Resources*
EMP: 50 **EST:** 2011
SALES (est): 10.9MM **Privately Held**
WEB: www.zeusliving.com
SIC: 6531 6514 6513 Real estate leasing & rentals; dwelling operators, except apartments; apartment building operators

(P-10544)
EMPIRE REALTY ASSOCIATES INC
380 Diablo Rd, Danville (94526-3468)
PHONE..................................925 217-5000
Judi Keenholtz, *CEO*
Jo Bender, *Real Est Agnt*
Tonya Colton, *Real Est Agnt*
Kay Sherwood, *Real Est Agnt*
Lindsey Sindayen, *Real Est Agnt*
EMP: 767 **EST:** 2002
SALES (est): 5.5MM **Privately Held**
WEB: www.empirerealty.com
SIC: 6531 Real estate agent, residential
PA: Pacific Union International, Inc.
1 Letterman Dr Bldg C
San Francisco CA 94129

(P-10545)
ETHAN CONRAD PROPERTIES INC (PA)
1300 National Dr Ste 100, Sacramento (95834-1981)
PHONE..................................916 779-1000
Ethan Conrad, *President*
Ken Miller, *COO*
Kenneth Miller, *CFO*
Chase Burke, *Vice Pres*
Race Merritt, *Vice Pres*
EMP: 95 **EST:** 2000
SQ FT: 45,063
SALES (est): 24.7MM **Privately Held**
WEB: www.ethanconradprop.com
SIC: 6531 Real estate agent, commercial

(P-10546)
EUGENE BURGER MANAGEMENT CORP (PA)
Also Called: Ebmc
6600 Hunter Dr, Rohnert Park (94928-2418)
PHONE..................................707 584-5123
Eugene J Burger, *Ch of Bd*
Stephen L Burger, *President*
Ronald Vaughn, *Senior VP*
Karen Brigg, *Vice Pres*
Lori E Burger, *Vice Pres*
EMP: 43 **EST:** 1969
SQ FT: 12,541
SALES (est): 40.7MM **Privately Held**
WEB: www.ebmc.com
SIC: 6531 6512 4225 Condominium manager; cooperative apartment manager; commercial & industrial building operation; warehousing, self-storage

(P-10547)
FELSON COMPANIES INC
1290 B St Ste 210, Hayward (94541-2996)
PHONE..................................510 538-1150
Joseph Felson, *President*
Joseph Lee Felson, *President*
Elliot Felson, *Corp Secy*
Victor Richard Felson, *Vice Pres*
Blake Felson, *Director*
EMP: 90 **EST:** 1955
SQ FT: 4,000
SALES (est): 12.9MM **Privately Held**
WEB: www.felson.com
SIC: 6531 Real estate managers

(P-10548)
FERGUSON & BREWER INV CO (PA)
2565 Zanella Way Ste C, Chico (95928-7170)
P.O. Box 69, Paradise (95967-0069)
PHONE..................................530 872-1810
Robert H Brewer, *Ch of Bd*
Thomas A Ferguson, *CEO*
Laurie Raucher, *Property Mgr*
Jan Johnson, *Manager*
Nicole Mills, *Manager*
EMP: 43 **EST:** 1983
SALES (est): 7MM **Privately Held**
WEB: www.fergusonandbrewer.com
SIC: 6531 Real estate managers

(P-10549)
FIVE POINT HOLDINGS LLC
1 Sansome St Ste 3200, San Francisco (94104-4436)
PHONE..................................415 344-8865
Leo Kij, *Branch Mgr*

6531 - Real Estate Agents & Managers County (P-10550)

PRODUCTS & SERVICES SECTION

Steve Sammartano, *Superintendent*
EMP: 35
SALES (corp-wide): 153.6MM **Publicly Held**
WEB: www.fivepoint.com
SIC: 6531 Real estate brokers & agents
PA: Five Point Holdings, Llc
15131 Alton Pkwy Ste 400
Irvine CA 92618
949 349-1000

(P-10550)
FLY WITH Y LLC
611 Gateway Blvd Ste 120, South San Francisco (94080-7066)
PHONE.....................844 435-9948
Waifung Sit, *Administration*
EMP: 51 **EST:** 2019
SALES (est): 3.7MM **Privately Held**
WEB: www.flywithyllc.wixsite.com
SIC: 6531 Real estate brokers & agents

(P-10551)
FLYNN PROPERTIES INC
225 Bush St Ste 1470, San Francisco (94104-4226)
PHONE.....................415 835-0225
Greg Flynn, *President*
Lorin Cortina, *CFO*
Genevieve Hancock, *General Mgr*
Anna Jones, *Admin Sec*
John Zook, *CTO*
EMP: 50 **EST:** 2000
SALES (est): 5.1MM **Privately Held**
WEB: www.flynnholdings.com
SIC: 6531 Real estate agent, commercial

(P-10552)
FPI MANAGEMENT INC
1124 F St, Davis (95616-2045)
PHONE.....................530 756-5332
EMP: 184
SALES (corp-wide): 249.9MM **Privately Held**
WEB: www.fpimgt.com
SIC: 6531 Real estate managers
PA: Fpi Management, Inc.
800 Iron Point Rd
Folsom CA 95630
916 357-5300

(P-10553)
FPI MANAGEMENT INC (PA)
800 Iron Point Rd, Folsom (95630-9004)
PHONE.....................916 357-5300
Dennis Treadaway, *President*
Ken Hunt, *Shareholder*
Gary Quattrin, *Shareholder*
Jennifer Briggs, *Vice Pres*
Gary Haugstad, *Vice Pres*
EMP: 50 **EST:** 1990
SQ FT: 18,000
SALES (est): 249.9MM **Privately Held**
WEB: www.fpimgt.com
SIC: 6531 Real estate managers

(P-10554)
FPI MANAGEMENT INC
Also Called: Hilltop Estates
131 Eureka St Ofc, Grass Valley (95945-6361)
PHONE.....................530 272-5274
Guy Strange, *Branch Mgr*
EMP: 184
SALES (corp-wide): 249.9MM **Privately Held**
WEB: www.fpimgt.com
SIC: 6531 6513 Real estate managers; apartment building operators
PA: Fpi Management, Inc.
800 Iron Point Rd
Folsom CA 95630
916 357-5300

(P-10555)
FUSION REAL ESTATE NETWORK INC
1300 National Dr Ste 170, Sacramento (95834-1991)
PHONE.....................916 448-3174
Gwen Scott, *President*
James Becker, *Vice Pres*
Helen Whitelaw, *Vice Pres*
Renee Wecker, *Exec Sec*
EMP: 90 **EST:** 2001
SQ FT: 4,400
SALES (est): 6.4MM **Privately Held**
WEB: www.hillcrestre.com
SIC: 6531 Real estate agent, residential

(P-10556)
GALLAGHER & LINDSEY INC (PA)
2424 Central Ave, Alameda (94501-4516)
P.O. Box 1286 (94501-0135)
PHONE.....................510 521-8181
Donald Lindsey, *President*
Suzanne Lindsay, *Vice Pres*
Terri Rafter, *Office Admin*
Joan Cecconi, *Broker*
Lisa Fowler, *Manager*
EMP: 48 **EST:** 1967
SQ FT: 3,500
SALES (est): 9.3MM **Privately Held**
WEB: www.glrealtor.com
SIC: 6531 Real estate agent, residential

(P-10557)
GAVIN ATWOOD COOMBS (PA)
Also Called: Rental Radar High-End
1400 Van Ness Ave, San Francisco (94109-4608)
PHONE.....................415 292-2384
Gavin A Coombs, *Owner*
Robert N Dadurka, *President*
George McNabb, *Officer*
Daniel McGue, *Exec VP*
John Antonini, *Vice Pres*
EMP: 67 **EST:** 2004
SALES (est): 16.8MM **Privately Held**
WEB: www.compass.com
SIC: 6531 Real estate brokers & agents

(P-10558)
GIC REAL ESTATE INC (DH)
1 Bush St Ste 1100, San Francisco (94104-4417)
PHONE.....................415 229-1800
Adam Gallistel, *CEO*
Deanna Ong, *Officer*
Sam Kim, *Director*
Betty Tay, *Director*
EMP: 60 **EST:** 1985
SQ FT: 10,000
SALES (est): 40.7MM **Privately Held**
WEB: www.gic.com.sg
SIC: 6531 6799 Real estate managers; real estate investors, except property operators

(P-10559)
GLENBOROUGH LLC (PA)
400 S El Camino Real # 1100, San Mateo (94402-1706)
PHONE.....................650 343-9300
Andrew Batinovich, *CEO*
Terri Garnick, *Senior VP*
EMP: 60 **EST:** 1995 **Privately Held**
WEB: www.glenborough.com
SIC: 6531 Real estate managers

(P-10560)
GLENMOOR REALTY INC
5255 Mowry Ave Ste L, Fremont (94538-1001)
P.O. Box 726 (94537-0726)
PHONE.....................510 793-4030
James L Reeder Sr, *President*
James L Reeder Jr, *President*
Robert H Reeder, *Vice Pres*
William J Rowe, *Vice Pres*
Ralph E Cotter, *Admin Sec*
EMP: 45 **EST:** 1951
SQ FT: 6,500
SALES (est): 1.7MM **Privately Held**
SIC: 6531 6512 6552 Real estate brokers & agents; nonresidential building operators; subdividers & developers

(P-10561)
GOLDEN RAIN FOUNDATION (PA)
Also Called: Rossmoor
1001 Golden Rain Rd, Walnut Creek (94595-2441)
P.O. Box 2070 (94595-0070)
PHONE.....................925 988-7700
Stephen Adams, *CEO*
Lyle Brown, *Vice Pres*
Mary Stuart, *Vice Pres*
Anne Paone, *Admin Sec*
Joe Bruzdzinksi, *Technology*
EMP: 300 **EST:** 1963
SQ FT: 5,000
SALES (est): 33.2MM **Privately Held**
WEB: www.rossmoor.com
SIC: 6531 8011 2711 7997 Real estate managers; offices & clinics of medical doctors; newspapers; golf club, membership

(P-10562)
GRANITE PEAK MANAGEMENT (PA)
Also Called: Squaw Valley Lodge
150 Alpine Meadows Rd 1, Alpine Meadows (96146-9880)
P.O. Box 3750, Olympic Valley (96146-3750)
PHONE.....................530 583-7545
Art Takaki, *President*
Evan Benjaminson, *Treasurer*
Jeff Chamberlin, *Vice Pres*
Michael Mumbert, *Controller*
Hayley Barnett, *Opers Mgr*
EMP: 40 **EST:** 1998
SQ FT: 1,000
SALES (est): 5.1MM **Privately Held**
WEB: www.granitepeakmanagement.com
SIC: 6531 Real estate leasing & rentals; condominium manager

(P-10563)
GRASS ROOTS REALTY
Also Called: Coldwell Banker
1012 Sutton Way, Grass Valley (95945-5181)
PHONE.....................530 273-7293
Rick Dejesus, *President*
Lisa Moore, *Opers Staff*
Darlene Mariani, *Consultant*
EMP: 47 **EST:** 1980
SALES (est): 5.5MM **Privately Held**
WEB: www.nevadacounty4sale.com
SIC: 6531 Real estate agent, residential

(P-10564)
GREENBRIAR MANAGEMENT COMPANY
Also Called: Greenbriar Homes Community
43160 Osgood Rd, Fremont (94539-5608)
PHONE.....................510 497-8200
Gilbert M Meyer, *CEO*
Carol Meyer, *Vice Pres*
EMP: 100 **EST:** 1984
SQ FT: 16,932
SALES (est): 5.7MM **Privately Held**
WEB: www.greenbriarhomessacramento.com
SIC: 6531 Cooperative apartment manager

(P-10565)
GROSVENOR PROPERTIES LTD
Also Called: Grosvenor House
899 Pine St Apt 103, San Francisco (94108-3027)
PHONE.....................415 421-1899
Paul Herbert, *Manager*
EMP: 303
SALES (corp-wide): 22.3MM **Privately Held**
WEB: www.grosvenorproperties.com
SIC: 6531 6513 7389 7011 Real estate managers; apartment hotel operation; relocation service; hotels
PA: Grosvenor Properties Ltd.
222 Front St Fl 7
San Francisco CA 94111
415 421-5940

(P-10566)
GRUBB CO INC
1960 Mountain Blvd, Oakland (94611-2894)
PHONE.....................510 339-0400
D J Grubb Jr, *President*
Laura Castillo, *Office Mgr*
Leslie Mullin, *Graphic Designe*
Sandra Vogl, *Asst Broker*
Sherry Benninger, *Broker*
EMP: 53 **EST:** 1967
SQ FT: 2,800
SALES (est): 13.4MM **Privately Held**
WEB: www.grubbco.com
SIC: 6531 Real estate agent, commercial

(P-10567)
GRUPE COMPANY (PA)
3255 W March Ln Ste 400, Stockton (95219-2352)
P.O. Box 7576 (95267-0576)
PHONE.....................209 473-6000
Frank A Passadore, *President*
Greenlaw Grupe Jr, *Ch of Bd*
Frank Passadore, *Vice Chairman*
Jeremys White, *COO*
Mark Fischer, *CFO*
EMP: 60 **EST:** 1960
SQ FT: 7,000
SALES (est): 65.6MM **Privately Held**
WEB: www.grupe.com
SIC: 6531 1542 Real estate agent, residential; commercial & office building, new construction

(P-10568)
GUARANTEE REAL ESTATE CORP
180 W Bullard Ave Ste 101, Clovis (93612-0998)
PHONE.....................559 321-6040
Kyle Chaney, *Branch Mgr*
EMP: 51
SALES (corp-wide): 245.5B **Publicly Held**
WEB: www.guarantee.com
SIC: 6531 Real estate brokers & agents
HQ: Guarantee Real Estate Corporation
3 E River Park Pl E
Fresno CA 93720
559 650-6000

(P-10569)
HAM DELLES COMPANY INC (PA)
386 Tesconi Ct, Santa Rosa (95401-4653)
PHONE.....................707 578-8840
Genie Delles, *Principal*
Andrea Ham, *CFO*
Chalyn Stone, *Admin Asst*
Suzanne Hutchison, *Accounting Mgr*
Jeff Hotchkiss, *Property Mgr*
EMP: 48 **EST:** 1989
SALES (est): 6.9MM **Privately Held**
WEB: www.hamdellescompany.com
SIC: 6531 Real estate agent, commercial; real estate managers

(P-10570)
HARSCH INVESTMENT REALTY LLC
32970 Alvarado Niles Rd # 740, Union City (94587-3194)
PHONE.....................510 475-0755
Susan Chun, *Branch Mgr*
John Gordon, *Vice Pres*
Traci Stout, *General Mgr*
Sherry Bowerman, *Administration*
Sucherrie Macaraeg, *Administration*
EMP: 37
SALES (corp-wide): 115.1MM **Privately Held**
WEB: www.harsch.com
SIC: 6531 Real estate managers
PA: Harsch Investment Realty, Llc
1121 Sw Salmon St Ste 500
Portland OR 97205
503 242-2900

(P-10571)
HAWTHRN/STONE RE INVSTMNTS INC
1704 Union St, San Francisco (94123-4407)
PHONE.....................415 441-8400
Rob Cassil, *President*
Kevin Cassil, *Vice Pres*
Andy Mehiel, *Manager*
EMP: 39 **EST:** 1973
SQ FT: 2,000
SALES (est): 1.7MM **Privately Held**
WEB: www.hawthornestone.com
SIC: 6531 Real estate agent, commercial; real estate managers

(P-10572)
HDC BUSINESS DEVELOPMENT INC (HQ)
Also Called: Chdc
3315 Airway Dr, Santa Rosa (95403-2005)
PHONE.....................707 523-1155

PRODUCTS & SERVICES SECTION
6531 - Real Estate Agents & Managers County (P-10594)

Chris Page, *President*
EMP: 62 EST: 1985
SQ FT: 15,000
SALES (est): 1.4MM
SALES (corp-wide): 14.4MM **Privately Held**
WEB: www.californiahumandevelopment.org
SIC: **6531** 3679 7374 5065 Real estate managers; electronic circuits; calculating service (computer); communication equipment; administrative services consultant
PA: California Human Development Corporation
3315 Airway Dr
Santa Rosa CA 95403
707 523-1155

(P-10573)
HE INC
Also Called: Hastings Enterprises
3 E 3rd Ave, San Mateo (94401-4279)
PHONE.................................650 794-1128
Newlin Hastings, *President*
Brian Beckham, *Vice Pres*
EMP: 56 EST: 1979
SQ FT: 2,500
SALES (est): 7MM **Privately Held**
WEB: www.pasowinerealestate.com
SIC: **6531** 6552 Real estate agent, commercial; land subdividers & developers, commercial

(P-10574)
HERITAGE REALTY
1107 S B St, San Mateo (94401-4314)
PHONE.................................650 349-9300
Terry Michaud, *Partner*
Jeff Mar, *Managing Dir*
John Elliot, *Broker*
Jennifer Ruiz, *Manager*
EMP: 36 EST: 1975
SQ FT: 500
SALES (est): 5.3MM **Privately Held**
WEB: www.heritagerealtysanmateo.com
SIC: **6531** Real estate agent, residential

(P-10575)
HILL & CO REAL ESTATE INC (HQ)
1880 Lombard St, San Francisco (94123-2981)
PHONE.................................415 921-6000
Joseph V Costello Jr, *President*
Eileen Mougeot, *Vice Pres*
Felicia Howell, *Admin Asst*
Khoi Vo, *Info Tech Dir*
Jay Costello, *Finance*
EMP: 40 EST: 1977
SALES (est): 14.6MM **Privately Held**
WEB: www.donnacooper.com
SIC: **6531** Real estate agent, residential

(P-10576)
HINES INTERESTS LTD PARTNR
1 Hacker Way Bldg 10, Menlo Park (94025-1456)
PHONE.................................650 518-6139
Melissa Perla, *Senior Mgr*
EMP: 170
SALES (corp-wide): 1.3B **Privately Held**
WEB: www.hines.com
SIC: **6531** Real estate agent, commercial
PA: Hines Interests Limited Partnership
2800 Post Oak Blvd Fl 48
Houston TX 77056
713 621-8000

(P-10577)
HOMEGAINCOM INC
12667 Alcosta Blvd # 200, San Ramon (94583-5272)
PHONE.................................925 983-2852
Tim Fagan, *CEO*
Mandy Grace, *CFO*
Addy Behrouzi, *Sales Mgr*
EMP: 65 EST: 1999
SQ FT: 13,000
SALES (est): 192.4K
SALES (corp-wide): 899.8K **Privately Held**
WEB: www.homegain.com
SIC: **6531** Real estate agent, residential

PA: One Planet Ops Inc.
1820 Bonanza St
Walnut Creek CA 94596
925 983-2800

(P-10578)
HUST BROTHERS INC (PA)
Also Called: Butte Auto
710 3rd St, Marysville (95901-5806)
P.O. Box 591 (95901-0015)
PHONE.................................530 743-1561
Roy E Lanza, *CEO*
Judi Hageman, *Treasurer*
Linda Holley, *Admin Sec*
Nicole Wolfe, *Admin Sec*
Gerald Jones, *Opers Staff*
EMP: 40 EST: 1919
SQ FT: 60,000
SALES: 6.6MM **Privately Held**
WEB: www.hust.com
SIC: **5531** 6531 5999 Automotive parts; real estate managers; welding supplies

(P-10579)
INSIGNIA/ESG HT PARTNERS INC
225 W Santa Clara St # 2, San Jose (95113-1723)
PHONE.................................408 288-2900
Pamela Cotta, *Manager*
EMP: 329 **Publicly Held**
SIC: **6531** Real estate agent, commercial
HQ: Insignia/Esg Hotel Partners, Inc.
11150 Santa Monica Blvd # 220
Los Angeles CA 90025

(P-10580)
INSIGNIA/ESG HT PARTNERS INC
101 California St, San Francisco (94111-5802)
PHONE.................................415 772-0123
EMP: 329 **Publicly Held**
SIC: **6531** Real estate agent, commercial
HQ: Insignia/Esg Hotel Partners, Inc.
11150 Santa Monica Blvd # 220
Los Angeles CA 90025

(P-10581)
INTERNET ESCROW SERVICES INC
180 Montgomery St Ste 650, San Francisco (94104-4208)
PHONE.................................888 511-8600
Robert Barrie, *CEO*
Marcus Calloway, *Managing Prtnr*
Neil Katz, *CFO*
Jackson Elsegood, *General Mgr*
EMP: 69 EST: 1999
SALES (est): 7.5MM **Privately Held**
WEB: www.escrow.com
SIC: **6531** Escrow agent, real estate
PA: Freelancer Limited
'grosvenor Place' Level 37 225 George Street
Sydney NSW 2000

(P-10582)
J M K INVESTMENTS INC
Also Called: Sunnyhills Apts
1724 Sunnyhills Dr, Milpitas (95035-2720)
PHONE.................................408 263-2626
Anna Wick, *Manager*
EMP: 43
SALES (corp-wide): 15.5MM **Privately Held**
WEB: www.jmkinvestments.com
SIC: **6531** 6513 Real estate agent, commercial; apartment building operators
PA: J M K Investments Inc
100 Saratoga Ave Ste 300
Santa Clara CA 95051
408 249-2500

(P-10583)
JAE PROPERTIES INC
801 1st St Ste F, Benicia (94510-5501)
P.O. Box 1027 (94510-4027)
PHONE.................................707 747-2861
Edmund Johnson, *President*
Cheryl Lewis Johnson, *Vice Pres*
Jonnie E Johnson, *Admin Sec*

Monet Roberson, *Admin Asst*
Olla Ellis, *Assistant*
EMP: 46 EST: 1973
SALES (est): 3MM **Privately Held**
WEB: www.jaeproperties.com
SIC: **6531** 6552 Real estate managers; subdividers & developers

(P-10584)
JMS REALTORS LTD (PA)
Also Called: Realty Concepts
575 E Alluvial Ave # 101, Fresno (93720-2822)
PHONE.................................559 490-1500
John M Shamshoian, *CEO*
Judy Kubale, *Executive Asst*
Lynette Baker, *Broker*
Wright Jan, *Broker*
Don Scordino, *Broker*
EMP: 172 EST: 1991
SALES (est): 14.8MM **Privately Held**
SIC: **6531** 7389 Selling agent, real estate; brokers, contract services

(P-10585)
JOHN STEWART COMPANY
191 Heritage Ln, Dixon (95620-4873)
PHONE.................................707 676-5660
EMP: 44
SALES (corp-wide): 118MM **Privately Held**
WEB: www.jsco.net
SIC: **6531** Real estate managers
PA: John Stewart Company
1388 Sutter St Ste 1100
San Francisco CA 94109
415 345-4400

(P-10586)
JOHN STEWART COMPANY
1455 Response Rd Ste 140, Sacramento (95815-5264)
PHONE.................................916 561-0323
Steve McElroy, *Director*
EMP: 44
SALES (corp-wide): 118MM **Privately Held**
WEB: www.jsco.net
SIC: **6531** 6552 6726 Real estate managers; subdividers & developers; investors syndicates
PA: John Stewart Company
1388 Sutter St Ste 1100
San Francisco CA 94109
415 345-4400

(P-10587)
JOHN STEWART COMPANY
104 Whispering Pines Dr # 200, Scotts Valley (95066-4799)
PHONE.................................831 438-5725
Mari Tustin, *Vice Pres*
EMP: 44
SALES (corp-wide): 118MM **Privately Held**
WEB: www.jsco.net
SIC: **6531** 6552 6726 Real estate managers; subdividers & developers; investors syndicates
PA: John Stewart Company
1388 Sutter St Ste 1100
San Francisco CA 94109
415 345-4400

(P-10588)
JOHN STEWART COMPANY (PA)
1388 Sutter St Ste 1100, San Francisco (94109-5454)
PHONE.................................415 345-4400
John K Stewart, *Chairman*
John Stewart, *General Ptnr*
Steve McElroy, *Owner*
Jack D Gardner, *CEO*
Noah Schwartz, *COO*
EMP: 80
SQ FT: 15,000
SALES (est): 118MM **Privately Held**
WEB: www.jsco.net
SIC: **6531** 6552 6726 Real estate managers; subdividers & developers; investors syndicates

(P-10589)
JOHN STEWART COMPANY
370 Valencia St, San Francisco (94103-3519)
PHONE.................................415 621-6258
John Stewart, *Principal*
EMP: 44
SALES (corp-wide): 118MM **Privately Held**
WEB: www.jsco.net
SIC: **6531** 6552 6726 Real estate managers; subdividers & developers; investors syndicates
PA: John Stewart Company
1388 Sutter St Ste 1100
San Francisco CA 94109
415 345-4400

(P-10590)
KAPPEL AND KAPPEL INC (PA)
Also Called: Kappel & Kappel Mortgage & Inv
355 Main St, Vacaville (95688-3907)
PHONE.................................707 446-0600
Steven T Kappel, *President*
Susan J Kappel, *Vice Pres*
Hong Buccat, *Broker*
Susan Truax, *Broker*
Barbara Elfers, *Sales Associate*
EMP: 35
SQ FT: 4,400
SALES (est): 1.1MM **Privately Held**
WEB: www.kappelgateway.com
SIC: **6531** Real estate agent, residential

(P-10591)
KAPPEL AND KAPPEL INC
Also Called: Kappel & Kappel Mortgage & Inv
1300 Oliver Rd Ste 105, Fairfield (94534-3431)
PHONE.................................707 429-2922
Dan Disano, *Manager*
EMP: 58
SALES (corp-wide): 1.1MM **Privately Held**
WEB: www.kappelgateway.com
SIC: **6531** Real estate agent, residential
PA: Kappel And Kappel Inc.
355 Main St
Vacaville CA 95688
707 446-0600

(P-10592)
KATIE MINOR
Also Called: Coldwell Banker
5980 Stoneridge Dr # 122, Pleasanton (94588-4518)
PHONE.................................925 847-2200
EMP: 35
SALES (est): 1.3MM **Privately Held**
SIC: **6531** Rl Este Agntresidntl

(P-10593)
KEEGAN & COPPIN COMPANY INC (PA)
Also Called: Keegan & Coppin Property MGT
1355 N Dutton Ave Ste 100, Santa Rosa (95401-7110)
PHONE.................................707 528-1400
Albert Coppin, *President*
Christopher Castellucci, *Partner*
Gilbert R Saydah, *Partner*
Jim Keegan Jr, *Vice Pres*
Chris Perez, *Network Enginr*
EMP: 43 EST: 1976
SQ FT: 13,000
SALES (est): 7.7MM **Privately Held**
WEB: www.keegancoppin.com
SIC: **6531** Real estate agent, commercial

(P-10594)
KIDDER MATHEWS CALIFORNIA INC (HQ)
101 Mission St Ste 1800, San Francisco (94105-1727)
PHONE.................................415 229-8888
Gordon Buchan, *President*
Michael Tobin, *Partner*
Jeffrey Lyon, *Ch of Bd*
Keith Kaiser, *Exec VP*
Jim Maggi, *Exec VP*
EMP: 36 EST: 2014
SQ FT: 9,422

6531 - Real Estate Agents & Managers County (P-10595)

SALES (est): 10.1MM
SALES (corp-wide): 140.6MM **Privately Held**
WEB: www.kidder.com
SIC: 6531 Real estate agent, commercial
PA: Kidder Mathews Inc.
  601 Union St Ste 4720
  Seattle WA 98101
  206 296-9600

(P-10595)
KIDDER MATHEWS INC
10 Almaden Blvd Ste 550, San Jose (95113-2262)
PHONE 408 970-9400
Jeffrey S Lyon, *Branch Mgr*
Michael Gschwend, *Partner*
Ben Garrett, *Assoc VP*
Craig Leiker, *Exec VP*
Kristopher Blais, *Vice Pres*
EMP: 36
SALES (corp-wide): 140.6MM **Privately Held**
WEB: www.kidder.com
SIC: 6531 Real estate agent, commercial
PA: Kidder Mathews Inc.
  601 Union St Ste 4720
  Seattle WA 98101
  206 296-9600

(P-10596)
KIDDER MATHEWS INC
101 Mission St Fl 21, San Francisco (94105-1712)
PHONE 415 229-8888
Jeffrey S Lyon, *Manager*
Calder Conrad, *Vice Pres*
EMP: 36
SALES (corp-wide): 140.6MM **Privately Held**
WEB: www.kidder.com
SIC: 6531 Real estate agent, commercial
PA: Kidder Mathews Inc.
  601 Union St Ste 4720
  Seattle WA 98101
  206 296-9600

(P-10597)
KLAIR REAL ESTATE INC
Also Called: Exit Realty Consultants
3018 E Svc Rd Ste 104105, Ceres (95307)
PHONE 209 484-8075
EMP: 120 **Privately Held**
WEB: www.exitrealty.com
SIC: 6531 Real estate agent, residential
PA: Klair Real Estate, Inc.
  600 E Main St Ste 300
  Turlock CA 95380

(P-10598)
LAPHAM COMPANY INC
Also Called: Lapham Company Management
4844 Telegraph Ave, Oakland (94609-2010)
PHONE 510 531-6000
Jon Shahoian, *President*
Jon M Shahoian, *President*
Tsegab Assefa, *Vice Pres*
EMP: 85 EST: 1947
SQ FT: 10,500
SALES (est): 7.9MM **Privately Held**
WEB: www.laphamcompany.com
SIC: 6531 Real estate agent, residential; real estate managers

(P-10599)
LEE & ASSOCIATES CENTRAL VLY
241 Frank West Cir # 300, Stockton (95206-4012)
PHONE 209 983-1111
Ernest J Pearson, *Chairman*
Thomas D Davis, *President*
Tim Martin, *Senior VP*
Mark Reckers, *Vice Pres*
EMP: 41 EST: 1993
SALES (est): 1.9MM **Privately Held**
WEB: www.lee-associates.com
SIC: 6531 Real estate agent, commercial

(P-10600)
LEMBI GROUP INC (PA)
2101 Market St, San Francisco (94114-1321)
PHONE 415 861-1111
Frank Lembi, *President*
Walter Lembi, *Vice Pres*
EMP: 92 EST: 1990
SALES (est): 42.4MM **Privately Held**
SIC: 6531 Real estate managers

(P-10601)
LILY DEVELOPMENT INC (PA)
Also Called: Pmz Real Estate
1230 E Orangeburg Ave A, Modesto (95350-4652)
P.O. Box 577005 (95357-7005)
PHONE 209 527-2010
Michael P Zagaris, *President*
Pmz Carpenter, *Admin Asst*
Tracey Long, *Finance Mgr*
Raelene Martins, *Controller*
Kally Fulke, *Broker*
EMP: 48 EST: 1986
SALES (est): 14.7MM **Privately Held**
SIC: 6531 Real estate agent, residential

(P-10602)
LOOPNET INC (HQ)
101 California St # 4300, San Francisco (94111-5802)
PHONE 415 243-4200
Richard J Boyle Jr, *CEO*
Thomas Byrne, *President*
Brent Stumme, *CFO*
Jason Greenman, *Senior VP*
Wayne Warthen, *Senior VP*
EMP: 204 EST: 1997
SQ FT: 46,157
SALES (est): 26.5MM
SALES (corp-wide): 1.6B **Publicly Held**
WEB: www.loopnet.com
SIC: 6531 Real estate agent, commercial
PA: Costar Group, Inc.
  1331 L St Nw Ste 2
  Washington DC 20005
  202 346-6500

(P-10603)
LYON REALTY
2220 Douglas Blvd Ste 100, Roseville (95661-3822)
PHONE 916 784-1500
Chris Sheffer, *Principal*
Suzanne Owen, *Sales Executive*
Wendy Jeans, *Mktg Dir*
Kathryn Lockhart, *Mktg Dir*
Sharon Cassulo, *Property Mgr*
EMP: 146 **Privately Held**
WEB: www.golyon.com
SIC: 6531 Real estate agent, residential
PA: Lyon Realty
  2280 Del Paso Rd Ste 100
  Sacramento CA 95834

(P-10604)
LYON REALTY
2580 Fair Oaks Blvd # 20, Sacramento (95825-7631)
PHONE 916 481-3840
Jim Waters, *Office Mgr*
William Lyon, *Vice Pres*
Marcia Tucker, *Executive*
Tina Sizemore, *Office Admin*
Adrianna Parrott, *Executive Asst*
EMP: 146 **Privately Held**
WEB: www.golyon.com
SIC: 6531 Real estate agent, residential
PA: Lyon Realty
  2280 Del Paso Rd Ste 100
  Sacramento CA 95834

(P-10605)
LYON REALTY
851 Pleasant Grove Blvd # 150, Roseville (95678-6177)
PHONE 916 787-7700
Cheree Hort, *Real Est Agnt*
EMP: 146 **Privately Held**
WEB: www.golyon.com
SIC: 6531 Real estate agent, residential
PA: Lyon Realty
  2280 Del Paso Rd Ste 100
  Sacramento CA 95834

(P-10606)
LYON REALTY
8814 Madison Ave, Fair Oaks (95628-3908)
PHONE 916 962-0111
EMP: 146 **Privately Held**
WEB: www.golyon.com
SIC: 6531 Selling agent, real estate
PA: Lyon Realty
  2280 Del Paso Rd Ste 100
  Sacramento CA 95834

(P-10607)
LYON REALTY
3900 Park Dr, El Dorado Hills (95762-4553)
PHONE 916 939-5300
Cathy Harrington, *Marketing Staff*
Lorrie Stern, *Sales Staff*
Tony Fennoy, *Agent*
Bud Griscom, *Real Est Agnt*
Steve Irwin, *Real Est Agnt*
EMP: 146 **Privately Held**
WEB: www.golyon.com
SIC: 6531 Real estate agent, residential
PA: Lyon Realty
  2280 Del Paso Rd Ste 100
  Sacramento CA 95834

(P-10608)
LYON REALTY (PA)
2280 Del Paso Rd Ste 100, Sacramento (95834-9701)
PHONE 916 574-8800
Patrick Shey, *President*
Rod Bouvia, *Broker*
Joann Kaleel, *Broker*
Andi Wagner, *Broker*
Tim Pierce, *Sales Associate*
EMP: 60 EST: 2007
SALES (est): 55.8MM **Privately Held**
WEB: www.golyon.com
SIC: 6531 6519 Real estate agent, residential; real property lessors

(P-10609)
M A D INC (PA)
Also Called: Century 21
3500 G St, Merced (95340-0691)
PHONE 209 383-6475
Michael Salvadori, *President*
Audrey Searcy, *Sales Staff*
EMP: 40 EST: 1976
SQ FT: 7,000
SALES (est): 5.7MM **Privately Held**
WEB: www.century21.com
SIC: 6531 Real estate agent, residential

(P-10610)
MARCUS MILLICHAP CORP RE SVCS (HQ)
2626 Hanover St, Palo Alto (94304-1132)
PHONE 650 391-1700
William Millichap, *Ch of Bd*
EMP: 60 EST: 1982
SQ FT: 12,509
SALES (est): 5MM
SALES (corp-wide): 201.9MM **Privately Held**
WEB: www.marcusmillichap.com
SIC: 6531 Real estate agent, commercial
PA: The Marcus & Millichap Company
  777 California Ave
  Palo Alto CA 94304
  650 494-1400

(P-10611)
MARCUS MLLCHAP RE INV SVCS INC
2626 Hanover St, Palo Alto (94304-1117)
PHONE 650 494-8900
EMP: 35
SALES (corp-wide): 62.6MM **Privately Held**
SIC: 6531 Real Estate Agents And Managers
HQ: Marcus & Millichap Real Estate Investment Services Of Indiana, Inc.
  2626 Hanover St
  Palo Alto CA 94304
  650 494-1400

(P-10612)
MARQUEZ & ASSOCIATES RE INC
1630 N Main St 196, Walnut Creek (94596-4609)
PHONE 510 863-0081
Lilia Marquez, *CEO*
EMP: 50 EST: 2005
SALES (est): 1.1MM **Privately Held**
WEB: www.marquezassociatesre.com
SIC: 6531 Real estate brokers & agents

(P-10613)
MARVIN GARDENS REAL PROPERTY
Also Called: Marvin Gardens Real Estate
7502 Fairmount Ave, El Cerrito (94530-3746)
PHONE 510 527-9111
Jackie Gray, *Manager*
Todd Hudson, *President*
Ron Egherman, *Treasurer*
Marion Henon, *Admin Sec*
Robert Bronson, *Professor*
EMP: 40 EST: 1989
SALES (est): 5MM **Privately Held**
WEB: www.redoakrealty.com
SIC: 6531 Real estate agent, residential

(P-10614)
MASON-MCDUFFIE REAL ESTATE INC (PA)
Also Called: Better Homes and Gardens
1555 Riviera Ave Ste E, Walnut Creek (94596-7321)
PHONE 925 924-4600
David Cobo, *Ch of Bd*
Edmond Krafchow, *President*
Michael Levedhl, *CFO*
John Auka, *Vice Pres*
Etta Brown, *Office Admin*
EMP: 40 EST: 1927
SQ FT: 5,000
SALES (est): 53.3MM **Privately Held**
WEB: www.bhr.com
SIC: 6531 Real estate agent, residential

(P-10615)
MASSINGHAM & ASSOC MGT INC (PA)
8000 Jarvis Ave 2, Newark (94560-1154)
PHONE 510 896-2634
Joe Price, *CEO*
Robert Rosenberg, *President*
Lisa Esposito, *COO*
Jeanne Waal, *Branch Mgr*
Robin Frybarger, *Human Resources*
EMP: 45 EST: 1978
SALES (est): 10.1MM **Privately Held**
SIC: 6531 7349 Real estate managers; building maintenance services

(P-10616)
MCCLELLAN REALTY LLC
3140 Peacekeeper Way, McClellan (95652-2508)
PHONE 916 965-7100
Frank Myers, *Principal*
Larry Kelley, *Principal*
EMP: 50 EST: 2020
SALES (est): 1MM **Privately Held**
WEB: www.mcclellanpark.com
SIC: 6531 Real estate brokers & agents

(P-10617)
MELISSA BRADLEY RE INC
3249 Browns Valley Rd, NAPA (94558-5424)
PHONE 707 258-3900
Carol Adler, *Branch Mgr*
EMP: 49
SALES (corp-wide): 27.4MM **Privately Held**
WEB: www.bradyharris.net
SIC: 6531 Real estate agent, residential
PA: Melissa Bradley Real Estate, Inc.
  55 Broadway Blvd
  Fairfax CA

(P-10618)
MELISSA BRADLEY RE INC
1401 4th St, Santa Rosa (95404-4015)
PHONE 707 536-0888
Robert Bradley, *Branch Mgr*

PRODUCTS & SERVICES SECTION
6531 - Real Estate Agents & Managers County (P-10640)

EMP: 49
SALES (corp-wide): 27.4MM **Privately Held**
WEB: www.bradyharris.net
SIC: 6531 Real estate brokers & agents
PA: Melissa Bradley Real Estate, Inc.
55 Broadway Blvd
Fairfax CA

(P-10619)
MELISSA BRADLEY RE INC
1690 Tiburon Blvd, Belvedere Tiburon (94920-2543)
PHONE...................................415 435-2705
Arlene Manalo, *Branch Mgr*
EMP: 49
SALES (corp-wide): 27.4MM **Privately Held**
WEB: www.bradyharris.net
SIC: 6531 Real estate agent, residential
PA: Melissa Bradley Real Estate, Inc.
55 Broadway Blvd
Fairfax CA

(P-10620)
MELISSA BRADLEY RE INC
1701 Novato Blvd Ste 100, Novato (94947-3002)
PHONE...................................415 209-1000
Julie Mello, *Branch Mgr*
Kirtis Donaldson, *Real Est Agnt*
Pamela S English, *Real Est Agnt*
EMP: 49
SALES (corp-wide): 27.4MM **Privately Held**
WEB: www.bradyharris.net
SIC: 6531 Real estate agent, residential
PA: Melissa Bradley Real Estate, Inc.
55 Broadway Blvd
Fairfax CA

(P-10621)
MELISSA BRADLEY RE INC
850 Sir Frncis Drake Blvd, San Anselmo (94960-1914)
PHONE...................................415 455-1080
Vince Sheehan, *Branch Mgr*
EMP: 49
SALES (corp-wide): 27.4MM **Privately Held**
WEB: www.bradyharris.net
SIC: 6531 Real estate brokers & agents
PA: Melissa Bradley Real Estate, Inc.
55 Broadway Blvd
Fairfax CA

(P-10622)
MERIDIAN MANAGEMENT GROUP
1145 Bush St, San Francisco (94109-5919)
PHONE...................................415 434-9700
Randall Chapman, *President*
Gil Dowd, *Vice Pres*
Russell Flynn, *Vice Pres*
James R Wilson, *Admin Sec*
Erin Lee, *Admin Asst*
EMP: 160 **EST:** 1984
SQ FT: 6,200
SALES (est): 16.8MM **Privately Held**
WEB: www.mmgprop.com
SIC: 6531 Real estate managers

(P-10623)
MOVE INC (HQ)
Also Called: Realsuite SM
3315 Scott Blvd, Santa Clara (95054-3139)
PHONE...................................408 558-7100
David Doctrow, *CEO*
Michael Lam, *COO*
Bryan Charap, *CFO*
Mickey Neuberger, *Chief Mktg Ofcr*
Kat Koutsantonis, *Officer*
EMP: 500 **EST:** 1993
SQ FT: 32,405
SALES (est): 142.4MM
SALES (corp-wide): 9.3B **Publicly Held**
WEB: www.move.com
SIC: 6531 Real estate listing services; multiple listing service, real estate
PA: News Corporation
1211 Ave Of The Americas
New York NY 10036
212 416-3400

(P-10624)
MOVE SALES INC (DH)
Also Called: Homestore Apartments & Rentals
3315 Scott Blvd, Santa Clara (95054-3139)
PHONE...................................805 557-2300
Steve Berkowitz, *CEO*
Maria Pietrosorte, *President*
Patricia Wehr, *Officer*
Terry Kontonickas, *Vice Pres*
Larry Peterson, *Vice Pres*
EMP: 75 **EST:** 1996
SALES (est): 36.3MM
SALES (corp-wide): 9.3B **Publicly Held**
WEB: www.move.com
SIC: 6531 Real estate brokers & agents
HQ: Move, Inc.
3315 Scott Blvd
Santa Clara CA 95054
408 558-7100

(P-10625)
MOVOTO LLC (HQ)
1900 S Norfolk St Ste 350, San Mateo (94403-1171)
PHONE...................................650 241-0910
Imtiyaz Haque, *CEO*
Mark Brandemuehl, *COO*
EMP: 50 **EST:** 2005
SALES (est): 10.5MM **Privately Held**
WEB: www.ojo.com
SIC: 6531 Real estate agent, residential
PA: Ojo Labs, Inc.
1007 S Congress Ave
Austin TX 78704
202 441-5391

(P-10626)
NANVAL INC
613 1st St, Brentwood (94513-1397)
PHONE...................................925 634-3200
Fred Valverda, *President*
Virginia Carranza, *Manager*
Tony King, *Manager*
Erma Payne, *Manager*
EMP: 60 **EST:** 1989
SALES (est): 2MM **Privately Held**
SIC: 6531 Real estate agent, residential

(P-10627)
NORCAL GOLD INC
Also Called: Re/Max Gold-Natomas
2081 Arena Blvd Ste 100, Sacramento (95834-2309)
PHONE...................................916 285-1000
Sterling Royal, *Principal*
Jerry Rivera, *Consultant*
EMP: 46 **Privately Held**
WEB: www.remax.com
SIC: 6531 Real estate agent, residential
PA: Norcal Gold, Inc.
5200 Sunrise Blvd Ste 5
Fair Oaks CA 95628

(P-10628)
NORCAL GOLD INC
Also Called: Re/Max
2365 Iron Point Rd # 200, Folsom (95630-8711)
PHONE...................................916 984-8778
Michael Kooken, *Manager*
Vince Sheehan, *Broker*
Jen Levea, *Sales Staff*
Tami Mellor, *Manager*
Todd Cackler, *Agent*
EMP: 46 **Privately Held**
WEB: www.remax.com
SIC: 6531 Real estate agent, residential
PA: Norcal Gold, Inc.
5200 Sunrise Blvd Ste 5
Fair Oaks CA 95628

(P-10629)
NORTHGATE TER CMNTY PARTNER LP
550 24th St, Oakland (94612-1757)
PHONE...................................510 465-9346
Fax: 510 465-0604
EMP: 50
SQ FT: 49,846
SALES (est): 1.8MM **Privately Held**
SIC: 6531 Real Estate Agent/Manager

(P-10630)
OBAYASHI USA LLC (HQ)
577 Airport Blvd Ste 600, Burlingame (94010-2057)
PHONE...................................650 952-4910
Kengo Shimada,
Tatsuya Inokuchi, *General Mgr*
Fumitaka Katafuchi, *General Mgr*
Savio Fernandes, *Info Tech Mgr*
Kenji Yamauchi, *Engineer*
EMP: 174 **EST:** 2002
SALES (est): 2.5B **Privately Held**
WEB: www.obayashi-na.com
SIC: 6531 Real estate agents & managers

(P-10631)
OCEAN SHORE BROKERAGE INC (PA)
248 Main St, Half Moon Bay (94019-7120)
PHONE...................................650 726-1100
Robert Ross, *Manager*
EMP: 40 **EST:** 1984
SQ FT: 3,500
SALES (est): 5.5MM **Privately Held**
WEB: www.coldwellbanker.com
SIC: 6531 Real estate agent, residential

(P-10632)
OPENDOOR LABS INC
Also Called: Opendoor Property
8880 Cal Center Dr # 400, Sacramento (95826-3222)
PHONE...................................888 352-7075
EMP: 51
SALES (corp-wide): 192.5MM **Privately Held**
WEB: www.opendoor.com
SIC: 6531 Buying agent, real estate
PA: Opendoor Labs Inc.
410 N Scottsdale Rd # 1600
Tempe AZ 85281
415 510-7213

(P-10633)
PACIFIC CITIES MANAGEMENT INC (PA)
Also Called: Westcal Management
6056 Rutland Dr Ste 1, Carmichael (95608-0514)
P.O. Box 417127, Sacramento (95841-7127)
PHONE...................................916 348-1188
Michael Force, *President*
EMP: 55 **EST:** 1992
SQ FT: 2,600
SALES (est): 6.4MM **Privately Held**
SIC: 6531 Real estate managers

(P-10634)
PACIFIC UNION CO
1550 Tiburon Blvd Ste U, Belvedere (94920-2516)
PHONE...................................415 789-8686
Kathleen Brady, *Real Est Agnt*
EMP: 55
SALES (corp-wide): 49MM **Privately Held**
WEB: www.compass.com
SIC: 6531 Real estate brokers & agents
PA: Pacific Union Co.
1699 Van Ness Ave 2
San Francisco CA 94109
415 929-7100

(P-10635)
PACIFIC UNION CO
Also Called: Pacific Union Residential Brkg
51 Moraga Way Ste 1, Orinda (94563-3037)
PHONE...................................925 258-0090
Linda Kaneko, *Vice Pres*
Solomon Mark, *Real Est Agnt*
EMP: 55
SALES (corp-wide): 49MM **Privately Held**
WEB: www.compass.com
SIC: 6531 Real estate agent, residential
PA: Pacific Union Co.
1699 Van Ness Ave 2
San Francisco CA 94109
415 929-7100

(P-10636)
PACIFIC UNION CO
1699 Van Ness Ave, San Francisco (94109-3608)
PHONE...................................415 474-6600
Linda Harrison, *Manager*
Craig Coulter, *COO*
Rick Laws, *Senior VP*
David Barca, *Vice Pres*
Jessica Frushtick, *Vice Pres*
EMP: 55
SALES (corp-wide): 49MM **Privately Held**
WEB: www.compass.com
SIC: 6531 6552 Real estate brokers & agents; subdividers & developers
PA: Pacific Union Co.
1699 Van Ness Ave 2
San Francisco CA 94109
415 929-7100

(P-10637)
PACIFIC UNION INTL INC
23 Ross Cmn, Ross (94957-9900)
PHONE...................................415 461-8686
Don Leisey, *Manager*
Nancy Dolinajec, *Office Mgr*
EMP: 60 **Privately Held**
WEB: www.compass.com
SIC: 6531 Real estate brokers & agents
PA: Pacific Union International, Inc.
1 Letterman Dr Bldg C
San Francisco CA 94129

(P-10638)
PACIFIC UNION INTL INC
1900 Mountain Blvd # 102, Oakland (94611-2800)
PHONE...................................510 338-1379
Crystal Franco, *Admin Asst*
Marvin Guzman, *Administration*
Robert James, *Administration*
Richerson Farnsworth, *Broker*
Jennifer Holderness, *Broker*
EMP: 60 **Privately Held**
WEB: www.compass.com
SIC: 6531 Real estate brokers & agents
PA: Pacific Union International, Inc.
1 Letterman Dr Bldg C
San Francisco CA 94129

(P-10639)
PACIFIC UNION INTL INC (PA)
1 Letterman Dr Bldg C, San Francisco (94129-2402)
PHONE...................................415 929-7100
Mark A McLaughlin, *President*
Jaime Pera, *CFO*
Felicia Chan, *Vice Pres*
Daniel Gillis, *Info Tech Dir*
Ted Bartlett, *Broker*
EMP: 397 **EST:** 2009
SQ FT: 12,000
SALES (est): 126.8MM **Privately Held**
WEB: www.compass.com
SIC: 6531 Real estate brokers & agents

(P-10640)
PACIFIC UNION RE GROUP (DH)
1699 Van Ness Ave 2, San Francisco (94109-3608)
PHONE...................................415 929-7100
Sandy Shaffer, *President*
Wright John, *Senior VP*
Ed Lynch, *Vice Pres*
Amy Bowes, *Office Mgr*
Aneel Sharma, *Office Mgr*
EMP: 80 **EST:** 1987
SQ FT: 700
SALES (est): 37.4MM
SALES (corp-wide): 2.1B **Privately Held**
WEB: www.compass.com
SIC: 6531 6163 8741 Real estate agent, commercial; mortgage brokers arranging for loans, using money of others; financial management for business
HQ: Gmac Home Services, Inc.
4 Walnut Grove Dr
Horsham PA 19044
215 682-4600

6531 - Real Estate Agents & Managers County (P-10641)

(P-10641)
PACIFIC UNION RESIDENTIAL BRKG
1900 Mountain Blvd # 102, Oakland (94611-2800)
PHONE..................510 339-6460
Pamela Hoffman, *President*
Cherie Blanco, *Opers Staff*
Bob Marks, *Advisor*
EMP: 41 EST: 1989
SALES (est): 1.6MM
SALES (corp-wide): 2.1B **Privately Held**
WEB: www.compass.com
SIC: 6531 Real estate agent, residential
HQ: Pacific Union Real Estate Group Ltd
1699 Van Ness Ave 2
San Francisco CA 94109

(P-10642)
PAPOLA ENTERPRISES INC
Also Called: Network Real Estate
167 S Auburn St, Grass Valley (95945-6516)
PHONE..................530 272-8885
William Papola Jr, *President*
Gail Williams, *Office Mgr*
Jim Bitto, *Broker*
Steve Johnstone, *Broker*
Brooke Realty, *Manager*
EMP: 62 EST: 1981
SALES (est): 10.8MM **Privately Held**
SIC: 6531 Real estate agent, residential; real estate managers

(P-10643)
PAUL M ZAGARIS REALTOR INC
1230 E Orangeburg Ave A, Modesto (95350-4652)
PHONE..................209 527-2010
Michael Zagaris, *President*
Paula Leffler, *Corp Secy*
Maria Mari, *Broker*
Rachel Maricich, *Broker*
Silvia Muro, *Real Est Agnt*
EMP: 36 EST: 1947
SQ FT: 9,000
SALES (est): 1.2MM **Privately Held**
SIC: 6531 Real estate agent, residential; real estate managers

(P-10644)
PEARSON REALTY ONE LLC (PA)
7480 N Palm Ave Ste 101, Fresno (93711-5501)
PHONE..................559 432-6200
John Stewart, *CEO*
Jon Daggett, *Vice Pres*
Mario Defrancesco, *Vice Pres*
Sullivan Grosz, *Vice Pres*
Bill Hopkins, *Vice Pres*
EMP: 40 EST: 1919
SQ FT: 12,000
SALES (est): 8.5MM **Privately Held**
WEB: www.pearsonrealty.com
SIC: 6531 Real estate agent, residential; appraiser, real estate

(P-10645)
PML MANAGEMENT CORPORATION
Also Called: Pml Estates Division
655 Mariners Island Blvd, San Mateo (94404-1059)
PHONE..................650 349-9113
Stephen A Fox, *President*
Greg Fox, *Vice Pres*
Virenea Monteiro, *Admin Asst*
EMP: 49 EST: 1976
SQ FT: 3,500
SALES (est): 3.7MM **Privately Held**
WEB: www.pmlmanagement.com
SIC: 6531 Real estate managers; condominium manager; real estate agent, residential

(P-10646)
PREMIER PROPERTIES INC
461 Beltrami Dr, Ukiah (95482-8747)
P.O. Box 1418 (95482-1418)
PHONE..................707 467-0300
Steven Gomes, *President*
EMP: 35 EST: 2000
SQ FT: 1,000

SALES (est): 1.3MM **Privately Held**
SIC: 6531 Real estate brokers & agents

(P-10647)
PREMIER VALLEY INC A CAL CORP
Also Called: Century 21
1351 Geer Rd Ste 103, Turlock (95380-3269)
PHONE..................209 667-6111
Teresa Moitoso, *Manager*
Cecilia Solorio-Smith, *Vice Pres*
Daniel Mueller, *Exec Dir*
Steve Senden, *Asst Broker*
Bella Daniel, *Broker*
EMP: 50
SALES (corp-wide): 11MM **Privately Held**
WEB: www.century21.com
SIC: 6531 Real estate agent, residential
PA: Premier Valley, Inc., A California Corporation
1414 E F St Bldg A
Oakdale CA 95361
209 847-6111

(P-10648)
PROFESSNAL FINCL INVESTORS INC
350 Ignacio Blvd Ste 300, Novato (94949-7202)
PHONE..................415 382-6001
Lewis Wallach, *President*
Michael Angelo Albanese Irrevo, *Shareholder*
Inez Bradley, *Manager*
EMP: 41 EST: 1983
SQ FT: 4,100
SALES (est): 6.3MM **Privately Held**
WEB: www.investpfi.com
SIC: 6531 8742 Rental agent, real estate; real estate consultant

(P-10649)
PROMETHEUS RE GROUP INC (PA)
1900 S Norfolk St Ste 150, San Mateo (94403-1161)
PHONE..................650 931-3400
Sanford N Diller, *CEO*
Bill Levia, *CFO*
Jackie Safier, *Exec VP*
Dan Emerson, *Senior VP*
John Ghio, *Vice Pres*
EMP: 140 EST: 1965
SALES (est): 232.1MM **Privately Held**
WEB: www.prometheusapartments.com
SIC: 6531 6552 Real estate managers; land subdividers & developers, commercial; land subdividers & developers, residential

(P-10650)
PROPERTY SCIENCES GROUP INC (PA)
395 Taylor Blvd Ste 250, Pleasant Hill (94523-2293)
PHONE..................925 246-7300
Paul Earle Chandler, *President*
David Kim, *Vice Pres*
Jim Goodrich, *Sales Staff*
Chad Martin, *Commercial*
EMP: 37 EST: 1984
SQ FT: 6,000
SALES (est): 11.9MM **Privately Held**
WEB: www.propsci.com
SIC: 6531 Appraiser, real estate

(P-10651)
PRUDENTIAL CALIFORNIA REALTY
677 Portola Dr, San Francisco (94127-1207)
PHONE..................415 664-9400
Steven Spears, *President*
Diana Smith, *Real Est Agnt*
EMP: 36 EST: 1978
SALES (est): 1.7MM **Privately Held**
WEB: www.pgim.com
SIC: 6531 Real estate agent, residential

(P-10652)
RAM COMMERCIAL ENTERPRISES INC
Also Called: Homepointe Property Management
5896 S Land Park Dr, Sacramento (95822-3311)
P.O. Box 221660 (95822-8660)
PHONE..................916 429-1205
Robert Machado, *President*
Cheryl Colburn, *Property Mgr*
Denise McCoy, *Property Mgr*
Eileen Stearman, *Property Mgr*
Michelle Wight, *Property Mgr*
EMP: 43 EST: 1997
SALES (est): 5MM **Privately Held**
WEB: www.propertymanagement-sacramento.com
SIC: 6531 Real estate managers

(P-10653)
REAL ESTATE AMERICA INC
2000 Powell St Ste 100, Emeryville (94608-1774)
P.O. Box 494846, Port Charlotte FL (33949-4846)
PHONE..................510 594-3100
Kareem K Macarthur, *President*
EMP: 55 **Privately Held**
SIC: 6531 Real estate brokers & agents
PA: Real Estate America, Inc.
10120 S Estrn Ave Ste 200
Henderson NV 89052

(P-10654)
REMAX GOLD ELITE
455 Lopes Rd Ste D, Fairfield (94534-1796)
PHONE..................707 422-4411
Don McDonald, *Executive Asst*
Kim Broders, *Vice Pres*
James Jensen, *Vice Pres*
Dana Tuggle, *Vice Pres*
Stewart Monique, *Executive*
EMP: 53 EST: 2007
SALES (est): 939.4K **Privately Held**
WEB: www.remaxgold.com
SIC: 6531 Real estate agent, residential

(P-10655)
ROSSMOOR REALTY
1641 Tice Valley Blvd, Walnut Creek (94595-1695)
PHONE..................925 932-1162
John Russell, *Owner*
Robert Seibert, *Vice Pres*
Eric Loranger, *Technology*
Lou Landgraf, *Graphic Designe*
Jo Cooper, *Financial Analy*
EMP: 40 EST: 1965
SQ FT: 1,500
SALES (est): 5.8MM **Privately Held**
WEB: www.rossmoorrealty.com
SIC: 6531 Real estate agent, residential

(P-10656)
S&J STADTLER INC
Also Called: Remax Accord
5980 Stoneridge Dr # 122, Pleasanton (94588-4518)
PHONE..................925 847-8900
Jerry Stadtler, *Owner*
EMP: 330
SALES (corp-wide): 22MM **Privately Held**
WEB: www.remax.com
SIC: 6531 Real estate agent, residential
PA: S&J Stadtler, Inc.
313 Sycamore Valley Rd W
Danville CA 94526
925 838-4100

(P-10657)
SACRAMNTO HSING RDVLPMENT AGCY
Also Called: Housing Auth of The Cy Scrmnto
801 12th St, Sacramento (95814-2947)
P.O. Box 1834 (95812-1834)
PHONE..................916 440-1399
Lashelle Dozier, *Exec Dir*
Cecette Hawkins, *Principal*
Russell Robertson, *Finance*
EMP: 100

SALES (corp-wide): 48.9MM **Privately Held**
WEB: www.shra.org
SIC: 6531 Real estate agents & managers
PA: Sacramento Housing And Redevelopment Agency
801 12th St
Sacramento CA 95814
916 440-1390

(P-10658)
SAN MAR PROPERTIES INC (PA)
Also Called: Valleywide Maintenance
6356 N Fresno St Ste 101, Fresno (93710-6870)
PHONE..................559 439-5500
Marc A Wilson, *President*
Angel Martin, *Partner*
Angel Jackson, *Vice Pres*
Sandra Wilson, *Vice Pres*
Stephanie Strobel, *Office Mgr*
EMP: 50 EST: 1981
SQ FT: 3,400
SALES (est): 9.8MM **Privately Held**
WEB: www.sanmarprop.com
SIC: 6531 7349 Real estate managers; real estate agent, commercial; building maintenance services

(P-10659)
SANTA ROSA & SONOMA CO REAL ES
1057 College Ave, Santa Rosa (95404-4128)
PHONE..................707 524-1124
EMP: 50
SALES (est): 2MM **Privately Held**
SIC: 6531 Real Estate Agent/Manager

(P-10660)
SAVILLS INC
150 California St Fl 14, San Francisco (94111-4555)
PHONE..................415 421-5900
Steve Baker, *Exec VP*
Royce Sharf, *Exec VP*
Aaron Hafliger, *Associate Dir*
Matt Hart, *Broker*
Trina Blas, *Opers Staff*
EMP: 36
SALES (corp-wide): 2.3B **Privately Held**
WEB: www.savills.us
SIC: 6531 Real estate agent, commercial
HQ: Savills Inc.
399 Park Ave Fl 11
New York NY 10022
212 326-1000

(P-10661)
SECURITY PACIFIC REAL ESTATE
3223 Blume Dr Ste 227, Richmond (94806-5782)
PHONE..................510 222-9772
Jack Burnes Sr, *Owner*
Ray Degennaro, *Agent*
EMP: 35 EST: 1965
SALES (est): 5MM **Privately Held**
WEB: www.jleonardrealestate.com
SIC: 6531 Real estate agents & managers

(P-10662)
SIDE INC
466 Brannan St, San Francisco (94107-1713)
PHONE..................650 930-0873
Edward Wu, *President*
Corey Alverson, *Creative Dir*
Armin Shahabi, *Principal*
Arthur Lai, *Admin Sec*
Rachel Moore, *Software Engr*
EMP: 47 EST: 2017
SALES (est): 8.1MM **Privately Held**
WEB: www.houseofkinoko.com
SIC: 6531 Real estate brokers & agents

(P-10663)
SNOWCREEK PROPERTY MANAGEMENT
Also Called: Snow Creek Resort
1254 Old Mammoth Rd, Mammoth Lakes (93546)
P.O. Box 1647 (93546-1647)
PHONE..................760 934-3333

PRODUCTS & SERVICES SECTION
6531 - Real Estate Agents & Managers County (P-10687)

Linda Dempsey, *Owner*
Julie Wright, *Vice Pres*
Sherry Wishney, *Broker*
Allison Page, *Real Est Agnt*
EMP: 50 **EST:** 2003
SALES (est): 7MM **Privately Held**
WEB: www.snowcreekresort.com
SIC: 6531 Time-sharing real estate sales, leasing & rentals

(P-10664)
SOLANO GATEWAY REALTY INC (PA)
2420 Martin Rd Ste 100, Fairfield (94534-8610)
PHONE 707 422-1725
Stephen C Spencer, *President*
Bev Dorsett, *Vice Pres*
Cathy Spencer, *Real Est Agnt*
EMP: 40 **EST:** 1972
SALES (est): 9MM **Privately Held**
WEB: www.gatewayrealty.com
SIC: 6531 Real estate agent, residential

(P-10665)
SOUTH COUNTY HOUSING CORP (PA)
16500 Monterey St Ste 120, Morgan Hill (95037-5193)
P.O. Box 4112, San Jose (95150-4112)
PHONE 510 582-1460
Dennis Lalor, *CEO*
John Cesare, *CFO*
Nestor Nu A EZ, *Finance*
EMP: 50 **EST:** 1979
SQ FT: 13,000
SALES (est): 113.4K **Privately Held**
WEB: www.scounty.org
SIC: 6531 Real estate agent, residential

(P-10666)
SUNMAR CORPORATION
Also Called: Century 21
474 E El Camino Real, Sunnyvale (94087-1938)
PHONE 408 249-5100
Bruce E Martin, *President*
EMP: 36 **EST:** 1981
SALES (est): 3.9MM **Privately Held**
WEB: www.century21.com
SIC: 6531 6163 Real estate agent, residential; mortgage brokers arranging for loans, using money of others

(P-10667)
T ROYAL MANAGEMENT (PA)
7419 N Cedar Ave Ste 102, Fresno (93720-3640)
PHONE 559 447-9887
David Michael Thomas, *CEO*
James Ganson, *Shareholder*
EMP: 55 **EST:** 1987
SQ FT: 5,000
SALES (est): 11.3MM **Privately Held**
WEB: www.royaltmanagement.com
SIC: 6531 Real estate managers

(P-10668)
TAHOE KEYS RESORT
Also Called: Reservation Bureau
599 Tahoe Keys Blvd B1, South Lake Tahoe (96150-3369)
P.O. Box 20088 (96151-1088)
PHONE 530 544-5397
Maria Herbert, *President*
Gigi Moran, *Vice Pres*
Lisa Underwood, *Vice Pres*
EMP: 41 **EST:** 1990
SQ FT: 7,000
SALES (est): 3.9MM **Privately Held**
WEB: www.tahoevacationguide.com
SIC: 6531 6513 Rental agent, real estate; apartment building operators

(P-10669)
TAHOE SEASONS RESORT TIME INTE
3901 Saddle Rd, South Lake Tahoe (96150-8707)
P.O. Box 16300 (96151-6300)
PHONE 530 541-6700
Michael Presley, *General Mgr*
EMP: 123 **EST:** 1983

SALES (est): 9.5MM **Privately Held**
WEB: www.tahoeseasons.com
SIC: 6531 7011 5813 5812 Time-sharing real estate sales, leasing & rentals; hotels & motels; drinking places; eating places

(P-10670)
TANDEM PROPERTIES INCORPORATED (PA)
3500 Anderson Rd, Davis (95616-7519)
PHONE 530 756-5075
John Whitcombe, *President*
Paul Makley, *Treasurer*
Bill Roe, *Vice Pres*
William Roe, *Vice Pres*
Carol Tavatli, *Bookkeeper*
EMP: 41 **EST:** 1965
SQ FT: 3,100
SALES (est): 6.3MM **Privately Held**
WEB: www.tandemproperties.com
SIC: 6531 Real estate managers

(P-10671)
TENDERLOIN HOUSING CLINIC INC (PA)
126 Hyde St, San Francisco (94102-3606)
PHONE 415 771-9850
Randall Shaw, *President*
David Virgo, *Info Tech Dir*
Steven Shubert, *Legal Staff*
Danny Smith, *Asst Director*
Michelle Duke, *Director*
EMP: 238 **EST:** 1980
SALES: 53.6MM **Privately Held**
WEB: www.thclinic.com
SIC: 6531 8111 Real estate agents & managers; legal services

(P-10672)
TERRY MEYER
Also Called: Coldwell Banker Residential RE
1712 Meridian Ave Ste C, San Jose (95125-5587)
PHONE 408 723-3300
EMP: 61
SALES (est): 1.7MM **Privately Held**
SIC: 6531 Real Estate Agent/Manager

(P-10673)
TRANS PACIFIC INC (PA)
Also Called: Masters Group, The
1610 Blossom Hill Rd 7c, San Jose (95124-6349)
P.O. Box 20094 (95160-0094)
PHONE 408 445-4455
Robert March, *CEO*
Linda March, *President*
Dionna Smith, *CFO*
EMP: 44 **EST:** 1982
SALES (est): 3.9MM **Privately Held**
WEB: www.emastersgrouppresidential.com
SIC: 6531 Real estate agents & managers

(P-10674)
TRI COMMERCIAL RE SVCS
1777 Oakland Blvd Ste 100, Walnut Creek (94596-4096)
PHONE 925 296-3300
Dick Sullivan, *Manager*
Edward Del Beccaro, *Exec VP*
Justin Flom, *Marketing Staff*
Mark Gedymin, *Manager*
EMP: 44 **Privately Held**
WEB: www.tricommercial.com
SIC: 6531 Real estate agent, commercial
PA: Tri Commercial Real Estate Services, Inc
 2001 Union St Ste 200
 San Francisco CA 94123

(P-10675)
TRI COMMERCIAL RE SVCS
2250 Douglas Blvd Ste 200, Roseville (95661-4207)
PHONE 916 677-8000
Ed Benoit, *Branch Mgr*
Anton Qiu, *COO*
Dennis Shorrock, *Vice Pres*
Greg Worman, *Info Tech Dir*
Jody Booras, *Manager*
EMP: 44 **Privately Held**
WEB: www.tricommercial.com
SIC: 6531 Real estate agent, commercial

PA: Tri Commercial Real Estate Services, Inc
 2001 Union St Ste 200
 San Francisco CA 94123

(P-10676)
TRIMONT LAND COMPANY (DH)
Also Called: Northstar-At-Tahoe
5001 Northstar Dr, Truckee (96161-4236)
P.O. Box 129 (96160-0129)
PHONE 530 562-1010
Robert A Katz, *CEO*
Michael Barkin, *CFO*
▲ **EMP:** 300 **EST:** 1966
SALES (est): 53.2MM **Publicly Held**
WEB: www.northstarcalifornia.com
SIC: 6531 7011 Real estate managers; ski lodge; resort hotel

(P-10677)
TRINITY MANAGEMENT SERVICES
1145 Market St Fl 12, San Francisco (94103-1568)
PHONE 415 864-1111
Connie Lam, *Controller*
Mike Nevotti, *Info Tech Dir*
Michael Nevotti, *Technology*
Trisha Marschke, *Property Mgr*
Jason Ortiz, *Maintence Staff*
EMP: 45 **EST:** 2011
SALES (est): 6.6MM **Privately Held**
WEB: www.trinitysf.com
SIC: 6531 Rental agent, real estate

(P-10678)
TROTTER-VOGEL REALTY INC
Also Called: Prudential
180 El Camino Real, San Bruno (94066-5552)
PHONE 650 589-1000
Michael Monozon, *CEO*
Lawrence L Franzella, *President*
Beth Anderson, *COO*
Brian F Boisson, *Vice Pres*
John L Gieseker, *Vice Pres*
EMP: 52 **EST:** 1959
SQ FT: 10,000
SALES (est): 6.2MM **Privately Held**
WEB: www.karonfranzella.com
SIC: 6531 Real estate agent, residential

(P-10679)
USA MULTIFAMILY MANAGEMENT INC
3200 Douglas Blvd Ste 200, Roseville (95661-4238)
PHONE 916 773-6060
Karen McCurdy, *President*
EMP: 130 **EST:** 1984
SQ FT: 5,020
SALES (est): 9.4MM
SALES (corp-wide): 1.1MM **Privately Held**
WEB: www.usapropfund.com
SIC: 6531 Real estate managers
PA: Usa Properties Fund, Inc.
 3200 Douglas Blvd Ste 200
 Roseville CA 95661
 916 773-6060

(P-10680)
WALSH VINEYARDS MANAGEMENT INC
1125 Golden Gate Dr, NAPA (94558-6188)
PHONE 707 255-1650
Tim Rodgers, *President*
Christopher Lynch, *CFO*
Vicki Thorpe, *Corp Secy*
Brian Shepard, *Vice Pres*
Joseph Walsh, *General Mgr*
EMP: 250 **EST:** 1980
SQ FT: 6,000
SALES (est): 28.3MM **Privately Held**
WEB: www.wvmgmt.com
SIC: 6531 Real estate managers

(P-10681)
WALTER E MC GUIRE RE INC (PA)
Also Called: McGuire Real Estate
2001 Lombard St, San Francisco (94123-2808)
PHONE 415 929-1500

EMP: 50
SQ FT: 10,000
SALES (est): 29.8MM **Privately Held**
WEB: www.mcguire.com
SIC: 6531 Real Estate Agents And Managers

(P-10682)
WALTER E MCGUIRE RE INC
Also Called: Raymond Brown Company
17 Bluxome St, San Francisco (94107-1605)
PHONE 415 296-0123
EMP: 50
SALES (corp-wide): 29.8MM **Privately Held**
WEB: www.mcguire.com
SIC: 6531 Real Estate Agent/Manager
PA: Walter E. Mc Guire Real Estate, Inc.
 2001 Lombard St
 San Francisco CA 94123
 415 929-1500

(P-10683)
WELLS & BENNETT REALTORS (PA)
1451 Leimert Blvd, Oakland (94602-1896)
PHONE 510 531-7000
Barton W Bennett, *Owner*
Jeannine Nelson, *Manager*
Tracy Lee L Butler, *Real Est Agnt*
EMP: 65 **EST:** 1924
SQ FT: 5,000
SALES (est): 8.8MM **Privately Held**
WEB: www.wellsandbennett.com
SIC: 6531 6512 Real estate agent, commercial; real estate managers; nonresidential building operators; commercial & industrial building operation

(P-10684)
WEST COAST PROPERTY MAINT LLC
714 Van Ness Ave, San Francisco (94102-3291)
PHONE 415 885-6970
Eric Andresen,
Kitty Davis, *Vice Pres*
Joy Flores, *Vice Pres*
Celena Juarez, *Executive Asst*
Chris Amerine, *Director*
EMP: 42 **EST:** 1957
SQ FT: 7,000
SALES (est): 2.7MM **Privately Held**
WEB: www.wcpm.com
SIC: 6531 Real estate managers

(P-10685)
WESTCO EQUITIES INC (PA)
Also Called: RPM Services
1625 E Shaw Ave Ste 116, Fresno (93710-8100)
PHONE 559 228-6788
Lee Brand, *President*
Ken Warkentin, *Vice Pres*
Dwayne Welch, *Vice Pres*
Jeanette Rodgers, *Supervisor*
EMP: 84 **EST:** 1979
SALES (est): 8.2MM **Privately Held**
WEB: www.west-co.com
SIC: 6531 1522 Real estate managers; real estate brokers & agents; remodeling, multi-family dwellings

(P-10686)
WESTLAKE REALTY GROUP INC (PA)
520 S El Cmino Real 9th F, San Mateo (94402)
PHONE 650 579-1010
M Gary Wong, *President*
Hanming Chen, *Accounting Mgr*
EMP: 98 **EST:** 2002
SALES (est): 8MM **Privately Held**
WEB: www.westlake-realty.com
SIC: 6531 Real estate agent, commercial

(P-10687)
WILLIAM L LYON & ASSOC INC
Also Called: Lyon & Associates Realtors
2801 J St, Sacramento (95816-4315)
PHONE 916 447-7878
Laure Woodgundlach, *Manager*
Deana Hegland, *Auditor*
Paul Brecher, *Broker*

6531 - Real Estate Agents & Managers County (P-10688)

Krystal Stewart, *VP Sales*
Elizabeth Weintraub, *Property Mgr*
EMP: 158
SALES (corp-wide): 164.4MM **Privately Held**
WEB: www.golyon.com
SIC: 6531 Real estate agent, residential
HQ: L Lyon William & Associates Inc
3640 Amrcn Rver Dr Ste 10
Sacramento CA 95864
916 978-4200

(P-10688)
WILLIAM L LYON & ASSOC INC
Also Called: Lyon Realtors
8814 Madison Ave, Fair Oaks (95628-3908)
PHONE.................................916 535-0356
Clay Sigg, *Manager*
Lisa McKee, *Broker*
Anthony Metz, *Agent*
EMP: 158
SALES (corp-wide): 164.4MM **Privately Held**
WEB: www.golyon.com
SIC: 6531 Real estate agent, residential
HQ: L Lyon William & Associates Inc
3640 Amrcn Rver Dr Ste 10
Sacramento CA 95864
916 978-4200

(P-10689)
XANDER MORTGAGE & REAL ESTATE
Also Called: Real Estate & Mortgage Broker
2520 W Shaw Ln Ste 106, Fresno (93711-2768)
PHONE.................................855 905-2575
Mohan Cheema, *President*
EMP: 71 **EST:** 2019
SALES (est): 3.4MM **Privately Held**
WEB: www.goxander.com
SIC: 6531 Real estate agents & managers

(P-10690)
ZAPLABS LLC (DH)
2000 Powell St Ste 700, Emeryville (94608-1805)
PHONE.................................510 735-2600
Lanny Baker, *CEO*
Eric L Mersch, *CFO*
Paul Leone, *Vice Pres*
Jaime Wison, *Vice Pres*
Larry Young, *Tech Recruiter*
▲ **EMP:** 62 **EST:** 2004
SQ FT: 23,803
SALES (est): 19.2MM **Publicly Held**
WEB: www.zaplabs.com
SIC: 6531 7375 Real estate brokers & agents; information retrieval services

(P-10691)
ZIPI INC
101 Creekside Ridge Ct # 2, Roseville (95678-3595)
PHONE.................................424 444-6700
Jesse Garcia, *CEO*
EMP: 37 **EST:** 2014
SALES (est): 1.6MM **Privately Held**
WEB: www.zipi.co
SIC: 6531 Real estate agents & managers

6541 Title Abstract Offices

(P-10692)
FIRST AMERICAN TITLE CO NAPA (PA)
497 Walnut St Ste A, NAPA (94559-3126)
P.O. Box 388 (94559-0388)
PHONE.................................707 254-4500
Jonny Karpuk, *CEO*
Heather Abshier, *Officer*
Diane Burton, *Officer*
Patty Campoyr, *Officer*
Liz Cooper, *Officer*
EMP: 38 **EST:** 1963
SQ FT: 1,460
SALES (est): 7.1MM **Privately Held**
WEB: www.firstamnapa.com
SIC: 6541 7371 Title search companies; title & trust companies; computer software development & applications

(P-10693)
MID VALLEY TITLE AND ESCROW CO
2295 Fther Rver Blvd Ste, Oroville (95965)
PHONE.................................530 533-6680
Angie Mastelotto, *Branch Mgr*
EMP: 43
SQ FT: 6,000 **Publicly Held**
WEB: www.firstam.com
SIC: 6541 6531 Title search companies; escrow agent, real estate
HQ: Mid Valley Title And Escrow Company
601 Main St
Chico CA 95928
530 893-5644

(P-10694)
STEWART TITLE OF SACRAMENTO (PA)
6700 Fair Oaks Blvd Ste B, Carmichael (95608-3812)
PHONE.................................916 484-6990
Robert Baker, *President*
James Boras, *Corp Secy*
Noble Barton, *Officer*
Sandra Berset, *Officer*
Joanna Herrod, *Officer*
EMP: 35 **EST:** 1979
SQ FT: 6,000
SALES (est): 11.8MM **Privately Held**
WEB: www.stewartsac.com
SIC: 6541 Title & trust companies

6552 Land Subdividers & Developers

(P-10695)
BAILEY CREEK INVSTORS A CAL LT (PA)
1766 Bidwell Ave, Chico (95926-9670)
PHONE.................................530 891-6753
Dennis Durkin, *General Ptnr*
Susy Durkin, *Partner*
EMP: 41 **EST:** 1991
SALES (est): 6.9MM **Privately Held**
SIC: 6552 Land subdividers & developers, commercial

(P-10696)
BOSTON PROPERTIES LTD PARTNR
4 Embarcadero Ctr Lvel, San Francisco (94111-4106)
PHONE.................................415 772-0700
Robert Pester, *Manager*
EMP: 61
SALES (corp-wide): 2.7B **Publicly Held**
WEB: www.bxp.com
SIC: 6552 6531 Land subdividers & developers, commercial; real estate agents & managers
HQ: Boston Properties Limited Partnership
800 Boylston St Ste 1900
Boston MA 02199
617 236-3300

(P-10697)
BROOKFELD BAY AREA HLDINGS LLC
Also Called: Brookfield Homes
500 La Gonda Way Ste 100, Danville (94526-1747)
PHONE.................................925 743-8000
John J J Ryan,
Laurie Craig, *CFO*
Randy Johnson, *Exec VP*
Dave Bartlett, *Vice Pres*
John O 'brien, *Vice Pres*
EMP: 60 **EST:** 2000
SALES (est): 11.8MM **Privately Held**
SIC: 6552 Land subdividers & developers, residential

(P-10698)
BURBANK HOUSING DEV CORP (PA)
1425 Corporate Cntr Pkwy, Santa Rosa (95407-5434)
PHONE.................................707 526-9782
David W Spilman, *CEO*
Charles A Cornell, *President*
John Lowry, *President*

Jeff Moline, *CFO*
Stuart W Martin, *Treasurer*
EMP: 155 **EST:** 1980
SALES: 15.4MM **Privately Held**
WEB: www.burbankhousing.org
SIC: 6552 Land subdividers & developers, residential

(P-10699)
CAMBRIDGE HOMES (HQ)
8080 N Palm Ave Ste 110, Fresno (93711-5797)
PHONE.................................559 447-3400
Steve Lutton, *President*
Steven White, *Principal*
EMP: 77 **EST:** 1992
SALES (est): 11.3MM
SALES (corp-wide): 22.4B **Publicly Held**
WEB: www.lennar.com
SIC: 6552 1521 Subdividers & developers; single-family housing construction
PA: Lennar Corporation
700 Nw 107th Ave Ste 400
Miami FL 33172
305 559-4000

(P-10700)
CARLTON SENIOR LIVING INC
Also Called: Chateau Pleasant Hill 2
2770 Pleasant Hill Rd Ofc, Concord (94523-2086)
PHONE.................................925 935-1660
Linda Jackson, *Manager*
EMP: 38
SALES (corp-wide): 33.6MM **Privately Held**
WEB: www.carltonseniorliving.com
SIC: 6552 Subdividers & developers
PA: Senior Carlton Living Inc
4071 Port Chicago Hwy # 130
Concord CA 94520
925 338-2434

(P-10701)
EDAW INC (HQ)
300 California St Fl 5, San Francisco (94104-1411)
PHONE.................................415 955-2800
Joseph E Brown, *CEO*
Jason Prior, *President*
Dana Waymire, *CFO*
Vaughan Davies, *Principal*
Jason Bowen, *Controller*
▲ **EMP:** 120 **EST:** 1939
SQ FT: 18,072
SALES (est): 34.1MM
SALES (corp-wide): 13.2B **Publicly Held**
WEB: www.aecom.com
SIC: 6552 0781 Subdividers & developers; landscape architects
PA: Aecom
13355 Noel Rd Ste 400
Dallas TX 75240
972 788-1000

(P-10702)
EVERGREEN CO
2485 Natomas Park Dr # 360, Sacramento (95833-2943)
PHONE.................................916 923-9000
Daniel M Cole, *Partner*
Ray Gundlach, *Partner*
Trey Gundlach, *Partner*
Dante V Petrocchi, *Partner*
Don Timmons, *Partner*
EMP: 35 **EST:** 1981
SALES (est): 5.4MM **Privately Held**
WEB: www.theevergreencompany.com
SIC: 6552 Subdividers & developers

(P-10703)
GRUPE COMMERCIAL COMPANY
Also Called: Grupe Huber Company
1203 N Grant St, Stockton (95202-1895)
P.O. Box 7576 (95267-0576)
PHONE.................................209 473-6000
Kevin Huber, *President*
Samantha Hola, *Administration*
EMP: 73 **EST:** 1989
SALES (est): 7.4MM
SALES (corp-wide): 65.6MM **Privately Held**
WEB: www.grupe.com
SIC: 6552 Land subdividers & developers, commercial

PA: The Grupe Company
3255 W March Ln Ste 400
Stockton CA 95219
209 473-6000

(P-10704)
HIGNELL INCORPORATED
Also Called: Courtyard Little Chico Creek
1770 Humboldt Rd, Chico (95928-8104)
PHONE.................................530 342-0707
Vicky Reed, *Administration*
Matthew Dietz, *Vice Pres*
Federico Martinez, *Business Dir*
Roy Strop, *Project Mgr*
Shane Ely, *Manager*
EMP: 80
SQ FT: 22,799
SALES (corp-wide): 19.2MM **Privately Held**
WEB: www.hignell.com
SIC: 6552 6531 Land subdividers & developers, commercial; real estate agents & managers
PA: Hignell, Incorporated
1750 Humboldt Rd
Chico CA 95928
530 894-0404

(P-10705)
LAHONTAN LLC
Also Called: Lahontan Golf Club
11253 Brockway Rd Ste 201, Truckee (96161-3360)
PHONE.................................530 550-2990
Nick Doran, *CFO*
Wendy Briggs, *Controller*
Martis Creek Corp,
Dmb Consolidated Holdings LLC,
Craig Boyle, *Manager*
EMP: 75 **EST:** 1996
SQ FT: 1,500
SALES (est): 3.5MM **Privately Held**
WEB: www.lahontangolf.com
SIC: 6552 6531 Land subdividers & developers, residential; real estate agents & managers

(P-10706)
LAND SERVICES LDSCP CONTRS INC
901 Brown Rd, Fremont (94539-7089)
PHONE.................................510 656-8101
John Ahner, *President*
Kari E Wood, *Office Mgr*
Dean Ritchie, *Manager*
EMP: 80 **EST:** 1980
SQ FT: 11,000
SALES (est): 5.3MM **Privately Held**
WEB: www.landservices.net
SIC: 6552 Subdividers & developers

(P-10707)
MARINSHIP DEV INTEREST LLC (PA)
1485 Bay Shore Blvd Ste 2, San Francisco (94124-3002)
PHONE.................................415 282-5160
Derek Smith, *Mng Member*
EMP: 39 **EST:** 2005
SALES (est): 2.8MM **Privately Held**
SIC: 6552 Subdividers & developers

(P-10708)
MEANY WILSON L P
4 Embarcadero Ctr # 3330, San Francisco (94111-4184)
PHONE.................................415 905-5300
Thomas P Sullivan, *Partner*
Kevin Griffith, *Project Mgr*
Brian Caruso, *Manager*
Alair Dias, *Manager*
Diana Singh, *Manager*
EMP: 50 **EST:** 2000
SQ FT: 22,000
SALES (est): 12.2MM **Privately Held**
WEB: www.wilsonmeany.com
SIC: 6552 6531 Land subdividers & developers, commercial; real estate agents & managers

▲ = Import ▼ = Export
◆ = Import/Export

PRODUCTS & SERVICES SECTION
6719 - Offices Of Holding Co's, NEC County (P-10731)

(P-10709)
MIDPEN HOUSING CORPORATION
303 Vintage Park Dr # 250, Foster City (94404-1166)
PHONE..................................650 356-2900
Mark Battey, *CEO*
Matthew O Franklin, *President*
Janine L Lind, *COO*
Janine Lind, *COO*
Kyle Attenhofer, *Vice Pres*
EMP: 300 **EST:** 1971
SQ FT: 20,000
SALES (est): 22.3MM **Privately Held**
WEB: www.midpen-housing.org
SIC: 6552 Land subdividers & developers, residential

(P-10710)
MOUNTAIN RETREAT INCORPORATED
111 Deerwood Rd Ste 100, San Ramon (94583-4445)
P.O. Box 178 (94583-0178)
PHONE..................................925 838-7780
EMP: 100 **EST:** 1976
SQ FT: 8,000
SALES (est): 5.7MM **Privately Held**
SIC: 6552 6531 Real Estate Development & Property Management

(P-10711)
OCEAN COLONY PARTNERS LLC
Also Called: Half Moon Bay Golf Links
2450 Cabrillo Hwy S # 200, Half Moon Bay (94019-2266)
PHONE..................................650 726-5764
William E Barrett, *Partner*
Bill Murray, *Comms Dir*
Clay Mallory, *Sales Staff*
Dan Miller, *Superintendent*
EMP: 175 **EST:** 1988
SQ FT: 6,000
SALES (est): 16.4MM **Privately Held**
SIC: 6552 7992 7389 Subdividers & developers; public golf courses; telephone services

(P-10712)
PACIFIC UNION HOMES INC (PA)
675 Hartz Ave Ste 300, Danville (94526-3859)
PHONE..................................925 314-3800
Jeffrey W Abramson, *President*
Todd Deutscher, *CFO*
Matt Tunney, *Vice Pres*
Tammy Reyes, *Admin Sec*
Summer Dunn, *Sales Staff*
EMP: 75 **EST:** 1996
SALES (est): 6.4MM **Privately Held**
SIC: 6552 Subdividers & developers

(P-10713)
RAYMUS DEVELOPMENT & SALES INC (PA)
544 E Yosemite Ave, Manteca (95336-5807)
PHONE..................................209 823-3148
Antone Raymus, *President*
Marie Raymus, *President*
EMP: 40 **EST:** 1945
SALES (est): 145.1K **Privately Held**
WEB: www.raymushomes.com
SIC: 6552 6531 6411 5963 Land subdividers & developers, residential; real estate brokers & agents; real estate managers; insurance agents, brokers & service; newspapers, home delivery, not by printers or publishers

(P-10714)
SIGNATURE PROPERTIES INC
4670 Willow Rd Ste 200, Pleasanton (94588-8588)
PHONE..................................925 463-1122
Mike Ghielmetti, *President*
Natasha Moldoveanu, *Sales Associate*
EMP: 39 **EST:** 1983
SQ FT: 24,000
SALES (est): 4.4MM **Privately Held**
WEB: www.sighomes.com
SIC: 6552 Subdividers & developers

(P-10715)
STEELWAVE INC (PA)
999 Baker Way Ste 200, San Mateo (94404-5047)
PHONE..................................650 571-2200
Barry S Diraimondo, *CEO*
C Preston Butcher, *President*
Meghan Fauss, *President*
Rick Wada, *Senior VP*
Melodie Borg, *Vice Pres*
EMP: 175 **EST:** 2004
SALES (est): 327.4MM **Privately Held**
WEB: www.steelwavellc.com
SIC: 6552 8741 6531 6512 Land subdividers & developers, commercial; land subdividers & developers, residential; financial management for business; real estate agents & managers; nonresidential building operators

(P-10716)
STEELWAVE LLC
999 Baker Way Ste 200, San Mateo (94404-5047)
PHONE..................................650 571-2200
Preston Butcher, *Mng Member*
Cristina Arcinas, *Vice Pres*
Monica Baytos, *Vice Pres*
McClure Charles, *Vice Pres*
Aaron Dwinell, *Vice Pres*
EMP: 1200 **EST:** 2003
SALES (est): 59.1MM **Privately Held**
WEB: www.steelwavellc.com
SIC: 6552 8741 6531 Land subdividers & developers, commercial; financial management for business; real estate agents & managers

(P-10717)
STERLING INTERNATIONAL GROUP
Also Called: Wyndham Garden Silicon Valley
399 Silicon Valley Blvd, San Jose (95138-1858)
PHONE..................................408 972-7800
Jaya Shingal, *Managing Dir*
EMP: 36 **EST:** 2020
SALES (est): 2.5MM **Privately Held**
WEB: www.wyndhamhotels.com
SIC: 6552 7011 Subdividers & developers; hotels & motels

(P-10718)
STONE BROS MANAGEMENT
Also Called: Stone Bros Security
5308 Sherwood Mall, Stockton (95207)
PHONE..................................209 952-7500
Max D Stone, *Partner*
EMP: 52
SALES (corp-wide): 12.8MM **Privately Held**
WEB: www.stonebros.com
SIC: 6552 Subdividers & developers
PA: Stone Bros Management
5250 Claremont Ave
Stockton CA 95207
209 478-1791

(P-10719)
UNIWELL CORPORATION
2233 Ventura St, Fresno (93721-2915)
PHONE..................................559 268-1000
Steve Klein, *Manager*
EMP: 122
SALES (corp-wide): 28.3MM **Privately Held**
WEB: www.holidayinn.com
SIC: 6552 Subdividers & developers
PA: Uniwell Corporation
21172 Figueroa St
Carson CA 90745
310 782-8888

(P-10720)
USA PROPERTIES FUND INC (PA)
3200 Douglas Blvd Ste 200, Roseville (95661-4238)
PHONE..................................916 773-6060
Geoffrey C Brown, *President*
Jonny Harmer, *CFO*
Kristen Hawkins, *Treasurer*
Steven Gall, *Exec VP*
Edward R Herzog, *Exec VP*
EMP: 122 **EST:** 1981
SQ FT: 10,500
SALES: 1.1MM **Privately Held**
WEB: www.usapropfund.com
SIC: 6552 6531 Subdividers & developers; real estate agents & managers

(P-10721)
WENDT CONSTRUCTION CO INC
1660 Newburg Rd, Fortuna (95540-2610)
PHONE..................................707 725-5641
Dennis Wendt, *President*
Ronald Brown, *Vice Pres*
Susan Long, *Admin Sec*
EMP: 40 **EST:** 1957
SQ FT: 10,000
SALES (est): 4MM **Privately Held**
WEB: www.wendtco.com
SIC: 6552 1521 Subdividers & developers; new construction, single-family houses

(P-10722)
WHITETHORN CONSTRUCTION CO
545 Shelter Cove Rd, Whitethorn (95589-8991)
P.O. Box 400 (95589-0400)
PHONE..................................707 986-7412
Robert Mc Kee Sr, *Owner*
EMP: 30 **EST:** 1963
SQ FT: 15,000
SALES (est): 2.6MM **Privately Held**
WEB: www.whitethornconstruction.com
SIC: 6552 5211 2426 Land subdividers & developers, commercial; lumber & other building materials; hardwood dimension & flooring mills

(P-10723)
WHITEVALE CO INC
Also Called: Burger King
180 Constitution Dr Ste 3, Menlo Park (94025-1137)
PHONE..................................650 324-1882
EMP: 80
SQ FT: 10,000
SALES (est): 1.2MM **Privately Held**
WEB: www.whitevalegolfclub.com
SIC: 5812 6552 Drive-In Fast Food & Developer

6553 Cemetery Subdividers & Developers

(P-10724)
CHAPEL OF CHIMES (DH)
Also Called: Alameda Chapel of The Chimes
32992 Mission Blvd, Hayward (94544-8277)
PHONE..................................510 471-3363
Andy Bryant, *President*
Gordon Swallow, *Treasurer*
Grant Pollard, *Sales Staff*
Rocio Regalado, *Director*
Lisa Rogers, *Manager*
EMP: 71 **EST:** 1965
SQ FT: 10,000
SALES (est): 167.8K
SALES (corp-wide): 62MM **Publicly Held**
WEB: www.hayward.chapelofthechimes.com
SIC: 6553 7261 Cemeteries, real estate operation; mausoleum operation; funeral home; crematory
HQ: Skylawn
32992 Mission Blvd
Hayward CA 94544
510 471-3363

(P-10725)
CHAPEL OF CHIMES
Also Called: Skylawn Memorial Park
100 Lifemark Rd, Redwood City (94062-4592)
P.O. Box 5070, San Mateo (94402-0070)
PHONE..................................650 349-4411
Rich McGown, *General Mgr*
Terry Deweese, *Site Mgr*
Amelia Gonzales, *Sales Mgr*
Joycelyn Van Hoof, *Manager*
Leticia Pizziconi, *Consultant*
EMP: 80
SALES (corp-wide): 62MM **Publicly Held**
WEB: www.hayward.chapelofthechimes.com
SIC: 6553 7261 Cemeteries, real estate operation; crematory
HQ: Chapel Of The Chimes
32992 Mission Blvd
Hayward CA 94544
510 471-3363

(P-10726)
CYPRESS LAWN CEMETERY ASSN
Also Called: CYPRESS LAWN MEMORIAL PARK
1370 El Camino Real, Colma (94014-3239)
P.O. Box 397 (94014-0397)
PHONE..................................650 755-0580
Kenneth E Varner, *CEO*
Barbara Dryg, *CFO*
Charles Arancia, *Director*
Kelly Chen, *Director*
EMP: 164 **EST:** 1892
SALES: 8.3MM **Privately Held**
WEB: www.cypresslawn.com
SIC: 6553 Cemeteries, real estate operation

(P-10727)
EAST LAWN INC (PA)
Also Called: East Lawn Memorial Park
4300 Folsom Blvd, Sacramento (95819-4401)
P.O. Box 19334 (95819-0334)
PHONE..................................916 732-2000
Alan Fisher, *President*
Steven Bartel, *CFO*
Steve Bartell, *Senior VP*
Shannon Beltram, *Admin Sec*
Shawntay Jones, *Admin Sec*
EMP: 45 **EST:** 1904
SALES (est): 11.8MM **Privately Held**
WEB: www.eastlawn.com
SIC: 6553 Cemeteries, real estate operation; mausoleum operation

6719 Offices Of Holding Co's, NEC

(P-10728)
BPAZ HOLDINGS 18 LLC
1 Sansome St Fl 15, San Francisco (94104-4448)
P.O. Box 2689 (94126-2689)
PHONE..................................972 354-6250
Rob Saidi, *Mng Member*
EMP: 60 **EST:** 2018 **Privately Held**
SIC: 6719 Holding companies

(P-10729)
BPAZ HOLDINGS 6 LLC
1 Sansome St Ste 1500, San Francisco (94104-4449)
PHONE..................................415 295-8080
Rob Saidi, *Vice Pres*
EMP: 80 **EST:** 2018 **Privately Held**
SIC: 6719 Holding companies

(P-10730)
CHASEN (USA) INC
19925 Stevns Crk Blvd, Cupertino (95014-2300)
PHONE..................................408 725-7571
Dixzyquo Nurman, *Principal*
EMP: 36 **EST:** 2016 **Privately Held**
WEB: www.chasen.com.sg
SIC: 6719 Investment holding companies, except banks

(P-10731)
COADNA HOLDINGS INC
1020 Stewart Dr, Sunnyvale (94085-3914)
PHONE..................................408 736-1100
Jim Yuan, *President*
Irene Yum, *CFO*
Oliver Lu, *Officer*
Tom LI, *Senior VP*
EMP: 80 **EST:** 2000
SALES (corp-wide): 3.1B **Publicly Held**
WEB: www.optical.communications.ii-vi.com
SIC: 6719 3661 Investment holding companies, except banks; fiber optics communications equipment

---

(PA)=Parent Co (HQ)=Headquarters (DH)=Div Headquarters
✣ = New Business established in last 2 years

6719 - Offices Of Holding Co's, NEC County (P-10732)

PA: Ii-Vi Incorporated
375 Saxonburg Blvd
Saxonburg PA 16056
724 352-4455

(P-10732)
CONDOR TRADING LP
600 Montgomery St Fl 6, San Francisco (94111-2708)
PHONE.................415 248-2200
Scott Kovalik, *CEO*
Brian Endres, *CFO*
Yojna Verma, *Senior VP*
EMP: 560 **EST:** 2002 **Privately Held**
SIC: 6719 Investment holding companies, except banks

(P-10733)
ETS-ESC HOLDINGS LLC
2001 Crow Canyon Rd # 110, San Ramon (94583-5368)
PHONE.................925 314-7100
Gary M Cappa, *President*
James Backman, *COO*
Charles Brice, *CFO*
EMP: 470 **EST:** 2017
SQ FT: 10,000
SALES (corp-wide): 533.8MM **Privately Held**
WEB: www.oneatlas.com
SIC: 6719 Investment holding companies, except banks
PA: Atlas Technical Consultants Llc
13215 Bee Cave Pkwy B230
Austin TX 78738
866 858-4499

(P-10734)
FINE CHEMICALS HOLDINGS CORP
Hwy 50 Hzel Ave Bldg 0501, Rancho Cordova (95741)
P.O. Box 1718 (95741-1718)
PHONE.................916 357-6880
Fraser Preston, *President*
John Sobchak, *CFO*
Michael Gallagher, *Corp Secy*
EMP: 450 **EST:** 2014 **Privately Held**
WEB: www.ampacfinechemicals.com
SIC: 6719 Investment holding companies, except banks

(P-10735)
GCM HOLDING CORPORATION
1350 Atlantic St, Union City (94587-2004)
PHONE.................510 475-0404
Seamus Meagher, *President*
Alex Volchek, *Engineer*
EMP: 300 **EST:** 2014 **Privately Held**
WEB: www.gogcm.com
SIC: 6719 8711 3444 3541 Investment holding companies, except banks; machine tool design; sheet metalwork; machine tools, metal cutting type
PA: Avista Capital Holdings, L.P.
65 E 55th St Fl 18
New York NY 10022

(P-10736)
GGC ADMINISTRATION LLC
Also Called: Golden Gate Capital
1 Embarcadero Ctr Fl 39, San Francisco (94111-3714)
PHONE.................415 983-2700
Stephan Scholl, *President*
EMP: 8590 **EST:** 2000 **Privately Held**
SIC: 6719 Personal holding companies, except banks

(P-10737)
HONOLUA BAY HOLDINGS LLC
Also Called: Quartz Hill Post Acute
2120 Benton Dr, Redding (96003-2151)
PHONE.................530 243-6317
Dan Gill, *Mng Member*
Kevin Galbasini,
Cameron Rosenhan,
EMP: 50 **EST:** 2019 **Privately Held**
WEB: www.quartzhillpostacute.com
SIC: 6719 Holding companies

(P-10738)
INDUSTRIAL GRWTH PARTNERS V LP
101 Mission St Ste 1500, San Francisco (94105-1731)
PHONE.................415 882-4550
Michael Beaumont, *Managing Prtnr*
EMP: 200 **EST:** 2016 **Privately Held**
WEB: www.igpequity.com
SIC: 6719 Investment holding companies, except banks

(P-10739)
INTERCTIVE FITNES HOLDINGS LLC
Also Called: Expresso
2225 Martin Ave Ste I, Santa Clara (95050-2713)
PHONE.................888 528-8589
William Stensrud, *Mng Member*
Brian Button, *CFO*
Bill Stensrud, *Chairman*
Ross Stensrud, *Chief Mktg Ofcr*
Mark Urlage, *Vice Pres*
EMP: 40 **EST:** 2009 **Privately Held**
WEB: www.ifholdings.com
SIC: 6719 Investment holding companies, except banks

(P-10740)
SPR OP CO INC
70 W Ohio Ave Ste H, Richmond (94804-2033)
PHONE.................510 232-5030
Matt Guelfi, *President*
Richard Olson, *CFO*
Scott Lowry, *Exec VP*
Matthew Guelfi, *Vice Pres*
Michael Guelfi, *Vice Pres*
EMP: 150 **EST:** 1975
SQ FT: 105,000 **Privately Held**
SIC: 6719 Investment holding companies, except banks

(P-10741)
STEELRVER INFRSTRCTURE PRTNERS (PA)
1 Harbor Dr Ste 101, Sausalito (94965-1433)
P.O. Box 751074, Petaluma (94975-1074)
PHONE.................415 512-1515
Christopher P Kinney, *Partner*
John Anderson, *Partner*
Chris Kinney, *Partner*
Dennis Mahoney, *Partner*
Austin Voss, *COO*
EMP: 200 **EST:** 2009
SALES (est): 149.5MM **Privately Held**
WEB: www.steelriverpartners.com
SIC: 6719 Investment holding companies, except banks

(P-10742)
THYCOTICCENTRIFY HOLDINGS INC
201 Rdwood Shres Pkwy St3, Redwood City (94065)
PHONE.................669 444-5200
Art Gilliland, *CEO*
EMP: 800 **EST:** 2018 **Privately Held**
SIC: 6719 7371 Investment holding companies, except banks; computer software development

(P-10743)
TRADESHIFT HOLDINGS INC (PA)
221 Main St Ste 250, San Francisco (94105-1907)
PHONE.................800 381-3585
Christian Lanng, *CEO*
Jigish Avalani, *President*
Jeppe Rindom, *CFO*
Peter Van Pruissen, *CFO*
Jeff Cooperman, *Vice Pres*
EMP: 80 **EST:** 2011
SALES (est): 102MM **Privately Held**
WEB: www.tradeshift.com
SIC: 6719 Investment holding companies, except banks

(P-10744)
TRANSAMERICA INTL HOLDINGS
600 Montgomery St Fl 16, San Francisco (94111-2718)
PHONE.................415 983-4000
EMP: 220 **Privately Held**
SIC: 6719 Holding Company
HQ: Transamerica Corporation
4333 Edgewood Rd Ne
Cedar Rapids IA 52411
319 398-8511

(P-10745)
TRESTLES HOLDINGS LLC
Also Called: Hillcrest Post Acute
450 Hayes Ln, Petaluma (94952-4010)
PHONE.................707 778-8686
Cameron Rosenhan, *Principal*
Kevin Galbasini, *Principal*
Dan Gill, *Principal*
EMP: 80 **EST:** 2016 **Privately Held**
SIC: 6719 8051 Holding companies; skilled nursing care facilities

(P-10746)
VISIONARY INTGRTION PRFSSNALS (PA)
Also Called: VIP
80 Iron Point Cir Ste 100, Folsom (95630-8592)
PHONE.................916 985-9625
Jonna Ward, *President*
Robert Sborofsky, *Software Dev*
Justin Sacks, *Project Mgr*
Katherine Stein, *Contract Mgr*
Amanda Zvolanek, *Marketing Staff*
EMP: 95 **EST:** 1996
SQ FT: 9,000
SALES (est): 65.2MM **Privately Held**
WEB: www.trustvip.com
SIC: 6719 Personal holding companies, except banks

(P-10747)
WEDRIVEU HOLDINGS INC (DH)
700 Airport Blvd Ste 250, Burlingame (94010-1937)
PHONE.................650 579-5800
Dennis Carlson, *CEO*
Erick Vanwagenen, *President*
Pat McConn, *CFO*
Tim Wayland, *Officer*
Shelly Marks, *Senior VP*
EMP: 40 **EST:** 2008
SALES (est): 45.9MM **Privately Held**
WEB: www.wedriveu.com
SIC: 6719 4729 Investment holding companies, except banks; transportation ticket offices

6722 Management Investment Offices

(P-10748)
BAY GROVE CAPITAL GROUP LLC (PA)
801 Montgomery St Fl 5, San Francisco (94133-5151)
PHONE.................415 229-7953
Kevin Marchetti, *Managing Prtnr*
Lizzy Kaler, *Vice Pres*
David Brandes, *Managing Dir*
Adam Forste, *Managing Dir*
Christen Chesel, *Executive Asst*
EMP: 50 **EST:** 2008
SALES (est): 2.7B **Privately Held**
WEB: www.bay-grove.com
SIC: 6722 Management investment, open-end

(P-10749)
BLACKROCK GLOBAL INVESTORS
400 Howard St, San Francisco (94105-2618)
PHONE.................415 670-2000
Patricia Dunn, *CEO*
Blake Grossman, *Principal*
Carter Lyons, *Principal*
EMP: 1100
SQ FT: 65,000
SALES (est): 107.2MM **Publicly Held**
WEB: www.blackrock.com
SIC: 6722 Money market mutual funds
PA: Blackrock, Inc.
55 E 52nd St
New York NY 10055

(P-10750)
BLACKROCK INSTNL TR NAT ASSN (HQ)
Also Called: Ishares
400 Howard St, San Francisco (94105-2618)
PHONE.................415 597-2000
Laurence D Fink, *CEO*
Robert S Kapito, *President*
James Parsons, *President*
EMP: 600 **EST:** 1973
SQ FT: 65,000
SALES: 1.4B **Publicly Held**
WEB: www.blackrock.com
SIC: 6722 Money market mutual funds

(P-10751)
BROADRACH CPITL PRTNERS FUND I
248 Homer Ave, Palo Alto (94301-2722)
PHONE.................650 331-2500
EMP: 1626 **EST:** 2014
SALES (est): 1.5MM
SALES (corp-wide): 46.7MM **Privately Held**
WEB: www.broadreachcp.com
SIC: 6722 Money market mutual funds
PA: Broadreach Capital Partners Llc
855 El Cmino Real Bldg 5
Palo Alto CA 94301
650 331-2500

(P-10752)
DIVCO WEST ACQUISITIONS LLC (PA)
301 Howard St Ste 2100, San Francisco (94105-6616)
PHONE.................415 284-5700
Stuart Shiff, *CEO*
Mike Carp, *President*
Steven Dietsch, *CFO*
Kenneth D Wong, *CFO*
Robert Mashaal, *Ch Invest Ofcr*
EMP: 41 **EST:** 2006
SALES (est): 36.4MM **Privately Held**
WEB: www.divcowest.com
SIC: 6722 Management investment, open-end

(P-10753)
DODGE & COX
555 California St Fl 40, San Francisco (94104-1503)
PHONE.................415 981-1710
Dana M Emery, *CEO*
Courtney Marques, *Partner*
John A Gunn, *Chairman*
Marian Z Baldauf, *Treasurer*
John Loll, *Treasurer*
EMP: 195 **EST:** 1930
SQ FT: 45,000
SALES (est): 58.3MM **Privately Held**
WEB: www.dodgeandcox.com
SIC: 6722 Money market mutual funds

(P-10754)
FARALLON CAPITAL PARTNERS LP (PA)
1 Maritime Plz Ste 2100, San Francisco (94111-3528)
PHONE.................415 421-2132
Chun R Ding, *Mng Member*
Jim Swerkes, *Managing Prtnr*
Paul Caldwell, *Exec Dir*
Wissam Charbel, *Managing Dir*
Colby Clark, *Managing Dir*
EMP: 80 **EST:** 2003
SQ FT: 8,000
SALES (est): 45.7MM **Privately Held**
WEB: www.faralloncapital.com
SIC: 6722 Money market mutual funds

6726 - Unit Investment Trusts, Face-Amount Certificate Offices

(P-10755)
FRANCISCO PARTNERS AGILITY LP (PA)
1 Letterman Dr Bldg C, San Francisco (94129-2402)
PHONE.................................415 418-2900
EMP: 110 EST: 2017
SALES (est): 20.7MM Privately Held
WEB: www.franciscopartners.com
SIC: 6722 Management investment, open-end

(P-10756)
FRANCISCO PARTNERS IV-A LP
1 Letterman Dr, San Francisco (94129-1494)
PHONE.................................415 418-2900
Dipanjan Deb, *CEO*
Chris Adams, *Partner*
Kim Moceri, *Partner*
Manny Rivelo, *Partner*
Dave Stevens, *Partner*
EMP: 43 EST: 2016
SALES (est): 7.1MM Privately Held
WEB: www.franciscopartners.com
SIC: 6722 Money market mutual funds

(P-10757)
FRANKLIN ADVISERS INC (HQ)
1 Franklin Pkwy, San Mateo (94403-1906)
PHONE.................................650 312-2000
Charles B Johnson, *Ch of Bd*
EMP: 656 EST: 1985
SQ FT: 120,000
SALES (est): 545.5MM
SALES (corp-wide): 5.5B Publicly Held
WEB: www.franklinresources.com
SIC: 6722 Money market mutual funds
PA: Franklin Resources, Inc.
   1 Franklin Pkwy Bldg 920
   San Mateo CA 94403
   650 312-2000

(P-10758)
FRANKLIN TEMPLETON INSTNL LLC (HQ)
1 Franklin Pkwy, San Mateo (94403-1906)
PHONE.................................650 312-2000
Crawford Cargon, *President*
EMP: 53 EST: 1983
SALES (est): 17.2MM
SALES (corp-wide): 5.5B Publicly Held
WEB: www.ftinstitutional.com
SIC: 6722 Money market mutual funds
PA: Franklin Resources, Inc.
   1 Franklin Pkwy Bldg 920
   San Mateo CA 94403
   650 312-2000

(P-10759)
FRANKLIN TEMPLETON SVCS LLC
1 Franklin Pkwy Bldg 970, San Mateo (94403-1906)
PHONE.................................650 312-3000
Martin L Flanagan, *President*
Charles B Johnson, *Ch of Bd*
EMP: 2500 EST: 1996
SALES (est): 527.8MM
SALES (corp-wide): 5.5B Publicly Held
WEB: www.franklinresources.com
SIC: 6722 Money market mutual funds
PA: Franklin Resources, Inc.
   1 Franklin Pkwy Bldg 920
   San Mateo CA 94403
   650 312-2000

(P-10760)
FRANKLIN TMPLETON INV SVCS LLC
3366 Quality Dr, Rancho Cordova (95670-7363)
PHONE.................................650 312-2000
Bavel Fox, *Branch Mgr*
EMP: 138
SALES (corp-wide): 5.5B Publicly Held
SIC: 6722 Money market mutual funds
HQ: Franklin Templeton Investor Services, Llc
   3344 Quality Dr
   Rancho Cordova CA 95670
   916 463-1500

(P-10761)
FTV MANAGEMENT COMPANY LP (PA)
Also Called: Financial Technology Ventures
555 California St # 2900, San Francisco (94104-1503)
PHONE.................................415 229-3000
Liron Gitig, *Partner*
Karen Derr Gilbert, *Partner*
Adam Hallquist, *Partner*
David Haynes, *Partner*
Tyler Krueger, *Partner*
EMP: 128 EST: 2007
SALES (est): 54.2MM Privately Held
WEB: www.ftvcapital.com
SIC: 6722 Money market mutual funds

(P-10762)
GENSTAR CAPITAL PARTNERS IX LP
4 Embarcadero Ctr # 1900, San Francisco (94111-4106)
PHONE.................................415 834-2350
James R Clark, *Partner*
EMP: 40
SALES (est): 5.3MM Privately Held
WEB: www.gencap.com
SIC: 6722 Money market mutual funds

(P-10763)
HALL CAPITAL PARTNERS LLC (PA)
1 Maritime Plz Fl 5, San Francisco (94111-3408)
PHONE.................................415 288-0544
Kathryn A Hall, *CEO*
John W Buoymaster, *President*
Morgan Plouff, *CEO*
William Powers, *COO*
Jeffrey Daems, *Vice Pres*
EMP: 72 EST: 1995
SQ FT: 6,000
SALES (est): 31.1MM Privately Held
WEB: www.hallcapital.com
SIC: 6722 Management investment, open-end

(P-10764)
ISHARES INC (PA)
400 Howard St, San Francisco (94105-2618)
PHONE.................................415 597-2000
Peter Blessing, *Ch of Bd*
Todd A McDonald, *Analyst*
Tyler Anthony, *Manager*
EMP: 755 EST: 1994
SALES (est): 65.7MM Privately Held
WEB: www.ishares.com
SIC: 6722 Money market mutual funds

(P-10765)
MELLON GLOBAL OPRTNTY FUND LLC
Also Called: Mellon Capital Management
50 Fremont St Ste 3900, San Francisco (94105-2240)
PHONE.................................415 546-6056
Linda T Lillard, *Officer*
Alfred Chu, *Vice Pres*
Thomas Durante, *Vice Pres*
Kristen Fontaine, *Vice Pres*
Brian Hock, *Vice Pres*
EMP: 44 EST: 2014
SALES (est): 2.8MM Privately Held
WEB: www.mellon.com
SIC: 6722 Money market mutual funds

(P-10766)
PACIFIC HEIGHTS ASSET MGT LLC (PA)
600 Montgomery St # 1700, San Francisco (94111-2719)
PHONE.................................415 398-8000
Michael Cuggino, *Principal*
Susan Freund, *Officer*
Jeannette Gough, *Administration*
James Andrews, *Finance*
Derek D Hyatt, *Analyst*
EMP: 40 EST: Pre 1900
SALES (est): 8.5MM Privately Held
WEB: www.permanentportfoliofunds.com
SIC: 6722 Money market mutual funds

(P-10767)
PW FUND B LP
7585 Longe St, Stockton (95206-4940)
PHONE.................................916 379-3852
EMP: 80 EST: 2017
SALES (est): 10.7MM Privately Held
SIC: 6722 Money market mutual funds

(P-10768)
RS INVESTMENT MANAGEMENT INC
Also Called: Rs Investments
1 Bush St Fl 9, San Francisco (94104-4415)
PHONE.................................415 591-2700
Terry R Otton, *Principal*
William J Wolfenden, *Principal*
Jim Shaughnessy, *Research*
Steve Bishop, *Portfolio Mgr*
EMP: 62 EST: 2006
SALES (est): 10MM
SALES (corp-wide): 775.3MM Publicly Held
WEB: www.investor.vcm.com
SIC: 6722 Money market mutual funds
HQ: Victory Capital Management Inc.
   4900 Tiedeman Rd Fl 4
   Brooklyn OH 44144

(P-10769)
STAMOS CAPITAL PARTNERS LP
2498 Sand Hill Rd, Menlo Park (94025-6940)
PHONE.................................650 233-5000
Peter Stamos, *CEO*
Jared Kanover, *COO*
John Russell, *Managing Dir*
James Chenault, *Executive Asst*
Adam Afshar, *Technology*
EMP: 55 EST: 2002
SALES (est): 11.1MM Privately Held
WEB: www.stamoscapital.com
SIC: 6722 Money market mutual funds

(P-10770)
STG IV GP LP (PA)
2475 Hanover St, Palo Alto (94304-1114)
PHONE.................................650 935-9500
William Chisholm,
Mahinder Mathrani, *Partner*
John Ouren, *Partner*
Min Fang, *Vice Pres*
Cindy Munn, *Vice Pres*
EMP: 280 EST: 2011
SALES (est): 23.2MM Privately Held
SIC: 6722

(P-10771)
VALUEACT CAPITAL MANAGEMENT LP
1 Letterman Dr Bldg D4th, San Francisco (94129-1494)
PHONE.................................415 249-1232
Mason Morfit, *CEO*
Jeffrey Williams Ubben, *Ch of Bd*
Olga Rohde, *Executive Asst*
Kelly Barlow, *Portfolio Mgr*
Brandon Boze, *Analyst*
EMP: 38 EST: 2005
SQ FT: 30,000 Privately Held
WEB: www.valueact.com
SIC: 6722 Money market mutual funds

(P-10772)
WESTBRDGE CPITL US ADVSORS LLC
400 S El Camino Real, San Mateo (94402-1704)
PHONE.................................650 645-6220
Sumir Chadha, *Managing Dir*
Sandeep Singhal, *Managing Dir*
Maria Cheeran, *Legal Staff*
EMP: 35 EST: 2016
SALES (est): 48.6MM Privately Held
WEB: www.westbridgeadvisors.com
SIC: 6722 Management investment, open-end
HQ: Westbridge Capital India Advisors Private Limited
   301, 3rd Floor, Campus 6a
   Bengaluru KA 56010

(P-10773)
WISDOMTREE CNADA QLTY DVDEND G
50 Fremont St Ste 3900, San Francisco (94105-2240)
PHONE.................................415 905-5448
EMP: 35 EST: 2017
SALES (est): 9MM
SALES (corp-wide): 15.8B Publicly Held
WEB: www.mellon.com
SIC: 6722 Money market mutual funds
HQ: Mellon Investments Corporation
   1 Boston Pl
   Boston MA 02108
   415 905-5448

6726 Unit Investment Trusts, Face-Amount Certificate Offices

(P-10774)
ATOMIC LABS LLC (PA)
1 Letterman Dr Ste 702, San Francisco (94129-1505)
PHONE.................................415 896-4148
Joshua Miller, *Mng Member*
Jack Howell, *Executive*
EMP: 56 EST: 2013
SALES (est): 72.6MM Privately Held
WEB: www.atomic.vc
SIC: 6726 Management investment funds, closed-end

(P-10775)
CRIMSON SV LLC (PA)
601 California St # 1450, San Francisco (94108-2834)
PHONE.................................415 970-5800
John Paul Ho, *Mng Member*
EMP: 82
SALES (est): 711.8K Privately Held
WEB: www.crimsoninvestment.com
SIC: 6726 Investment offices

(P-10776)
DCM MANAGEMENT INC
Also Called: D C M
2420 Sand Hill Rd Ste 200, Menlo Park (94025-6942)
PHONE.................................650 233-1400
Dixon R Doll, *President*
Carl Amdahl, *General Ptnr*
Thomas Blaisdell, *General Ptnr*
David Chao, *General Ptnr*
Dixon Doll, *General Ptnr*
EMP: 40 EST: 1996
SQ FT: 10,500
SALES (est): 12.5MM Privately Held
WEB: www.dcm.com
SIC: 6726 Investment offices

(P-10777)
FFL PARTNERS LLC (PA)
Also Called: F F L
1 Maritime Plz Fl 22, San Francisco (94111-3404)
PHONE.................................415 402-2100
Tully M Friedman, *CEO*
Martin Carter, *Partner*
Robert Eckert, *Partner*
Mark Laudy, *Partner*
Chris Harris, *Managing Prtnr*
EMP: 90 EST: 1997
SALES (est): 178.9MM Privately Held
WEB: www.fflpartners.com
SIC: 6726 Investment offices

(P-10778)
JASPER RIDGE PARTNERS
2885 Sand Hill Rd Ste 100, Menlo Park (94025-7022)
PHONE.................................650 494-4800
Maura Bowman, *Office Mgr*
Linda Assante, *Managing Prtnr*
Richard J Hayes, *Managing Prtnr*
Rozmin Ajanee, *Vice Pres*
Peter Harris, *Vice Pres*
EMP: 43 EST: 2012
SALES (est): 16.2MM Privately Held
WEB: www.jasperridge.com
SIC: 6726 Management investment funds, closed-end

6726 - Unit Investment Trusts, Face-Amount Certificate Offices County (P-10779)

(P-10779)
MCCOWN DE LEEUW & CO
950 Tower Ln Ste 800, Foster City (94404-2191)
PHONE 650 854-6000
George E McCown, *Partner*
David De Leeuw, *Partner*
Pamela Swain, *Executive Asst*
George McCown, *Opers Staff*
EMP: 24 EST: 1985
SQ FT: 5,255
SALES (est): 3MM **Privately Held**
WEB: www.aimlp.com
SIC: 6726 6799 2675 2672 Investment offices; investors; folders, filing, die-cut: made from purchased materials; adhesive papers, labels or tapes: from purchased material

(P-10780)
MILLENNIUM MANAGEMENT LLC
2 Embarcadero Ctr # 1640, San Francisco (94111-3908)
PHONE 415 844-4048
EMP: 314
SALES (corp-wide): 113MM **Privately Held**
WEB: www.mlp.com
SIC: 6726 Management investment funds, closed-end
PA: Millennium Management, Llc
399 Park Ave Bsmt Lc
New York NY 10022
212 841-4132

(P-10781)
SILVER LAKE PARTNERS LP (PA)
2775 Sand Hill Rd Ste 100, Menlo Park (94025-7085)
PHONE 650 233-8120
Jim Davidson, *Partner*
Yolande Jun, *Partner*
Ken Hao, *Chairman*
Egon Durban, *Co-CEO*
Greg Mondre, *Co-CEO*
EMP: 70 EST: 1999
SALES (est): 110.9MM **Privately Held**
SIC: 6726 Investment offices

(P-10782)
SILVER LAKE PARTNERS II LP
10080 N Wolfe Rd Sw3190, Cupertino (95014-2544)
PHONE 408 454-4732
Andy Wagner, *Branch Mgr*
EMP: 47 **Privately Held**
SIC: 6726 Investment offices
PA: Silver Lake Partners Ii, L.P.
2775 Sand Hill Rd Ste 100
Menlo Park CA 94025

(P-10783)
SILVER LAKE PARTNERS II LP
Also Called: Silver Lake Financial
1 Market Plz, San Francisco (94105-1101)
PHONE 415 293-4355
Roger Whittlin, *Manager*
Debbie Jones, *Vice Pres*
EMP: 47 **Privately Held**
SIC: 6726 Investment offices
PA: Silver Lake Partners Ii, L.P.
2775 Sand Hill Rd Ste 100
Menlo Park CA 94025

(P-10784)
SILVER LAKE TECH ASSOC LLC (HQ)
2725 Sand Hill Rd Ste 150, Menlo Park (94025-7056)
PHONE 650 233-8120
James Davidson,
Glenn Hutchins,
David Roux,
EMP: 62 EST: 1999
SQ FT: 12,500
SALES (est): 3.9MM **Privately Held**
SIC: 6726 Investment offices

6732 Education, Religious & Charitable Trusts

(P-10785)
CALIFRNIA MRTIME ACDEMY FNDTIO
200 Maritime Academy Dr, Vallejo (94590-8181)
PHONE 707 654-1000
Tom Cropper, *CEO*
Audun Aaberg, *President*
Beverly Byl, *Vice Pres*
Natalia Abrego, *Admin Asst*
Samantha Koekemoer, *Admin Asst*
EMP: 200 EST: 1972
SALES (est): 2.9MM **Privately Held**
WEB: www.csum.edu
SIC: 6732 Educational trust management

(P-10786)
CHALCEDON INC
Also Called: CHALCEDON FOUNDATION
3756 Highway 4, Vallecito (95251-9710)
P.O. Box 158 (95251-0158)
PHONE 209 736-4365
Mark Rushdoony, *President*
Martin Selbred, *Vice Pres*
Martin Selbrede, *Vice Pres*
Susan Burns, *Executive Asst*
Ford Schwartz, *Admin Sec*
EMP: 19 EST: 1965
SQ FT: 2,500
SALES (est): 975.1K **Privately Held**
WEB: www.chalcedon.edu
SIC: 6732 2721 Religious trust management; trade journals: publishing only, not printed on site; magazines: publishing only, not printed on site

(P-10787)
COMMUNITY PARTNERS INTL
580 California St Fl 16, San Francisco (94104-1068)
PHONE 510 225-9676
Si Thura, *Exec Dir*
Jim Baker, *Principal*
Thomas Lee, *Principal*
Linda Smith, *Principal*
Kalsang Tashi, *Principal*
EMP: 117 EST: 2011
SALES: 10.4MM **Privately Held**
WEB: www.cpintl.org
SIC: 6732 Trusts: educational, religious, etc.

(P-10788)
FOUNDATION FOR EDUCATIONAL ADM
1575 Bayshore Hwy Ste 300, Burlingame (94010-1616)
PHONE 916 444-3216
Wesley Apker, *Exec Dir*
Thomas Magner, *Director*
EMP: 45 EST: 1980
SQ FT: 5,000
SALES (est): 6.1MM **Privately Held**
SIC: 6732 8299 Charitable trust management; educational services

(P-10789)
OAKLAND PUBLIC EDUCATION FUND
520 3rd St Ste 109, Oakland (94607-3503)
P.O. Box 71005 (94612-7105)
PHONE 510 221-6968
Robert Spencer, *President*
Brian Stanley, *Exec Dir*
Sarah Price, *Admin Asst*
Nathan Bellet, *Database Admin*
Dolimer Rodriguez, *Project Mgr*
EMP: 95 EST: 2003
SALES (est): 34.4MM **Privately Held**
WEB: www.oaklandedfund.org
SIC: 6732 Trusts: educational, religious, etc.

(P-10790)
SEIU UHW-W & JOINT EMPLOYER ED (PA)
1000 Broadway Ste 675, Oakland (94607-4070)
PHONE 510 250-6800
Rebecca Hanson, *Exec Dir*
Jocelyn Cutay, *Finance*
Phoenix Lockett, *Deputy Dir*
Jill McCullough, *Asst Director*
Rachel Lupole, *Director*
EMP: 40 EST: 2009
SALES (est): 25.8MM **Privately Held**
WEB: www.theedfund.org
SIC: 6732 Educational trust management

(P-10791)
UNIVERSITY FNDTION CAL STATE U
400 W 1st St, Chico (95929-0001)
PHONE 530 898-5936
Gayle Hutchinson, *President*
Chengtu Hsieh, *Assoc Prof*
Connie Huyck, *Director*
Donna Deems, *Assistant*
EMP: 87 EST: 1940
SQ FT: 4,000
SALES (est): 11.4MM **Privately Held**
WEB: www.csuchico.edu
SIC: 6732 0191 Trusts: educational, religious, etc.; general farms, primarily crop

6733 Trusts Except Educational, Religious & Charitable

(P-10792)
CARPENTER FNDS ADMNSTRTIVE OFF
265 Hegenberger Rd # 100, Oakland (94621-1443)
PHONE 510 633-0333
David Lee, *CEO*
Maria Gonzalez, *Controller*
EMP: 79 EST: 1953
SQ FT: 60,956
SALES (est): 15MM **Privately Held**
WEB: www.carpenterfunds.com
SIC: 6733 Trusts, except educational, religious, charity: management

(P-10793)
COHESITY INC
1880 Fallen Leaf Ln, Los Altos (94024-6218)
PHONE 650 968-4470
Mohit Aron, *Principal*
Michael Cremen, *Officer*
Andy Dobrov, *Vice Pres*
Lorenzo Montesi, *Vice Pres*
Michael Porat, *Vice Pres*
EMP: 500
SALES (corp-wide): 221.1MM **Privately Held**
WEB: www.cohesity.com
SIC: 6733 Trusts
PA: Cohesity, Inc.
300 Park Ave Ste 1700
San Jose CA 95110
855 926-4374

(P-10794)
EL CAMINO HOSPITAL DISTRICT RE (PA)
Also Called: EL CAMINO HOSPITAL MOUNTAIN VI
2500 Grant Rd, Mountain View (94040-4378)
PHONE 650 940-7000
Darlene Balbas, *Principal*
Edwina Sequeira, *Lab Dir*
Tamara Stafford, *Education*
Linda Garza, *Food Svc Dir*
Dharshi Sivakumar, *Pediatrics*
EMP: 117 EST: 2010
SALES: 6.6K **Privately Held**
WEB: www.elcaminohealthcaredistrict.org
SIC: 6733 Trusts

(P-10795)
IRA SERVICES TRUST COMPANY
1160 Industrial Rd Ste 1, San Carlos (94070-4128)
P.O. Box 7080 (94070-7080)
PHONE 650 591-3335
Todd Yancey, *Bd of Directors*
Casey Smith, *Officer*
Gary R Shumm, *Admin Sec*
Michael Carrier, *CTO*
Saabreen Ahmed, *Project Mgr*
EMP: 40 EST: 2013
SALES (est): 8.7MM **Privately Held**
WEB: www.forgetrust.com
SIC: 6733 Trusts

(P-10796)
KAISER FOUNDATION HOSPITALS
Also Called: Martinez Medical Offices
200 Muir Rd, Martinez (94553-4672)
PHONE 925 372-1000
Bryan Fong, *Principal*
Erick Martinez, *Administration*
Pablo Baker, *Chief Engr*
Allen J Finley, *VP Mktg*
Sandra Seier, *Family Practiti*
EMP: 52
SALES (corp-wide): 30.5B **Privately Held**
WEB: www.kaisercenter.com
SIC: 6733 8011 Trusts; general & family practice, physician/surgeon
HQ: Kaiser Foundation Hospitals Inc
1 Kaiser Plz
Oakland CA 94612
510 271-6611

(P-10797)
KAISER FOUNDATION HOSPITALS
Also Called: Kaiser Permanente
3285 Claremont Way, NAPA (94558-3313)
PHONE 707 258-2500
Debby Bacon, *Branch Mgr*
Jonathan Hernandez, *Family Practiti*
Maung San, *Family Practiti*
Roxana Mundy, *Internal Med*
Linda Row, *Internal Med*
EMP: 52
SALES (corp-wide): 30.5B **Privately Held**
WEB: www.kaisercenter.com
SIC: 6733 8093 8062 Trusts, except educational, religious, charity: management; specialty outpatient clinics; general medical & surgical hospitals
HQ: Kaiser Foundation Hospitals Inc
1 Kaiser Plz
Oakland CA 94612
510 271-6611

(P-10798)
KAISER FOUNDATION HOSPITALS
Also Called: Sierra Gardens Medical Offices
1840 Sierra Gardens Dr, Roseville (95661-2912)
PHONE 916 784-5081
Michelle Mattison-Kelly, *Manager*
EMP: 52
SALES (corp-wide): 30.5B **Privately Held**
WEB: www.kaisercenter.com
SIC: 6733 Trusts
HQ: Kaiser Foundation Hospitals Inc
1 Kaiser Plz
Oakland CA 94612
510 271-6611

(P-10799)
MINISTRY SERVICES OF THE DAUGH
Also Called: Daughters Charity Health Sys
26000 Altamont Rd, Los Altos Hills (94022-4317)
PHONE 650 917-4500
Ernie Wallerstein, *CEO*
James F Dover, *President*
Carol Furgurson, *Administration*
EMP: 86 EST: 2014
SALES (est): 10MM **Privately Held**
WEB: www.daughtersofcharity.com
SIC: 6733 6732 Trusts; religious trust management

(P-10800)
UFCW & EMPLOYERS TRUST LLC (PA)
1000 Burnett Ave Ste 110, Concord (94520-2000)
PHONE 800 552-2400
Jody Osterweil, *Administration*
Timothy May, *CIO*
Ken Foulke, *Technology*
Ontiveros Claudia, *Accounting Mgr*
Norma Villa, *Payroll Mgr*

PRODUCTS & SERVICES SECTION

6798 - Real Estate Investment Trusts County (P-10820)

EMP: 110
SQ FT: 57,600
SALES: 555.4MM Privately Held
WEB: www.ufcwtrust.com
SIC: 6733 Trusts

(P-10801)
YOLO COUNTY CHILDRENS ALLIANCE
600 A St Ste Y, Davis (95616-3648)
PHONE.................................530 757-5558
Katie Villegas, *CEO*
EMP: 35 **EST:** 2002
SALES (est): 3.8MM Privately Held
WEB: www.yolokids.org
SIC: 6733 Trusts, except educational, religious, charity; management

6792 Oil Royalty Traders

(P-10802)
MAP ROYALTY INC (PA)
3000 El Cmino Real Ste 5, Palo Alto (94306)
PHONE.................................650 324-9095
Jane Woodward, *CEO*
Keith Davidge, *Senior VP*
Debbie Formhals, *Vice Pres*
Patrick Grammar, *Vice Pres*
Ellen Piamonte-Cleto, *Vice Pres*
EMP: 46 **EST:** 1989
SQ FT: 26,000
SALES (est): 22.1MM Privately Held
WEB: www.map-energy.com
SIC: 6792 Oil royalty traders

6794 Patent Owners & Lessors

(P-10803)
BB FRANCHISING LLC
Also Called: Brain Balance Franchising
1777 N Calif Blvd Ste 330, Walnut Creek (94596-4195)
PHONE.................................510 817-2786
Chip Miller, *CEO*
Erin Miller, *CFO*
Heidi Rose, *Chief Mktg Ofcr*
Stephanie Bourles, *CIO*
EMP: 60 **EST:** 2007
SQ FT: 3,000
SALES (est): 14.5MM
SALES (corp-wide): 14.8MM Privately Held
SIC: 6794 Franchises, selling or licensing
PA: Bb Holdings, Inc
    1777 N Calif Blvd Ste 330
    Walnut Creek CA 94596
    510 817-2786

(P-10804)
CENTRAL VALLEY PIZZA LLC
Also Called: Domino's
2930 Geer Rd Ste 174, Turlock (95382-1142)
PHONE.................................209 589-9633
Greg De Grandis, *Mng Member*
EMP: 35 **EST:** 2010
SQ FT: 150,000
SALES (est): 5MM Privately Held
WEB: www.centralvalleypump.com
SIC: 6794 5812 Franchises, selling or licensing; pizzeria, chain

(P-10805)
HEARTMATH LLC
14700 W Park Ave, Boulder Creek (95006-9673)
PHONE.................................831 338-8700
Bruce Cryer, *President*
Chris W Jacob, *COO*
Brian Kabaker, *CFO*
Doc Childre, *Chairman*
Howard Martin, *Exec VP*
◆ **EMP:** 50 **EST:** 1997
SQ FT: 9,500
SALES (est): 8.7MM Privately Held
WEB: www.heartmath.com
SIC: 8299 5961 6794 Educational services; computer equipment & electronics, mail order; patent owners & lessors

(P-10806)
LEES SANDWICHES INTL INC
660 E Gish Rd, San Jose (95112-2707)
PHONE.................................408 280-1595
Chieu Le, *Principal*
Loc Tran, *Executive Asst*
Jimmy Lee, *VP Sales*
EMP: 45 **EST:** 2002
SALES (est): 801.2K Privately Held
WEB: www.leessandwiches.com
SIC: 5812 6794 Sandwiches & submarines shop; franchises, selling or licensing

(P-10807)
MILANO RESTAURANTS INTL CORP (HQ)
Also Called: ME-N-ED'S PIZZERIA
6729 N Palm Ave Ste 200, Fresno (93704-1077)
PHONE.................................559 432-0399
John Ferdinandi, *President*
Stephanie Perger, *President*
A Thomas Ferdinandi Jr, *COO*
Thomas Ferdinandi, *COO*
Marta Gray, *CFO*
EMP: 407 **EST:** 1996
SQ FT: 2,800
SALES: 56.3K Publicly Held
WEB: www.milano-ri.com
SIC: 5812 6794 Pizzeria, chain; franchises, selling or licensing

(P-10808)
PAN PENNSYLVANIA LLC (HQ)
Also Called: Panera Bread
225 Bush St Ste 1800, San Francisco (94104-4211)
PHONE.................................415 903-2100
EMP: 86 **EST:** 2016
SALES (est): 11.1MM
SALES (corp-wide): 1.8B Privately Held
WEB: www.panerabread.com
SIC: 5812 6794 Cafe; franchises, selling or licensing
PA: Flynn Restaurant Group Lp
    225 Bush St Ste 1800
    San Francisco CA 94104
    415 903-2100

(P-10809)
PAN WASHINGTON LLC (HQ)
Also Called: Panera Bread
225 Bush St Ste 1800, San Francisco (94104-4211)
PHONE.................................415 903-2100
EMP: 40 **EST:** 2016
SALES (est): 9.8MM
SALES (corp-wide): 1.8B Privately Held
WEB: www.panamericangroup.com
SIC: 5812 6794 Cafe; franchises, selling or licensing
PA: Flynn Restaurant Group Lp
    225 Bush St Ste 1800
    San Francisco CA 94104
    415 903-2100

(P-10810)
RISK MANAGEMENT SOLUTIONS INC (HQ)
Also Called: RMS
7575 Gateway Blvd Ste 300, Newark (94560-1196)
PHONE.................................510 505-2500
Karen White, *CEO*
Paul Dali, *Ch of Bd*
Stephen Robertson, *CFO*
Moe Khosravy, *Exec VP*
Karl Armani, *Senior VP*
EMP: 140 **EST:** 1988
SALES (est): 153.7MM
SALES (corp-wide): 5.3B Publicly Held
WEB: www.rms.com
SIC: 6794 6411 Patent owners & lessors; insurance information & consulting services
PA: Moody's Corporation
    250 Greenwich St
    New York NY 10007
    212 553-0300

(P-10811)
ROUND TABLE PIZZA INC (DH)
1390 Willow Pass Rd # 300, Concord (94520-5250)
PHONE.................................925 969-3900
Robert McCourt, *President*
Matthew Dowling, *CFO*
Nick Fletcher, *Vice Pres*
Thomas Guilford, *Vice Pres*
Janell Muri, *Planning*
EMP: 65 **EST:** 1972
SQ FT: 18,000
SALES (est): 104.2MM
SALES (corp-wide): 176MM Publicly Held
WEB: www.roundtablepizza.com
SIC: 5812 6794 Pizzeria, chain; franchises, selling or licensing

(P-10812)
RPX CORPORATION (HQ)
4 Embarcadero Ctr Fl 40, San Francisco (94111-4100)
PHONE.................................866 779-7641
Dan McCurdy, *CEO*
Robert H Heath, *CFO*
Jon Knight, *Exec VP*
Mallun Yen, *Exec VP*
Martin E Roberts, *Senior VP*
EMP: 154 **EST:** 2008
SQ FT: 67,000
SALES: 330.4MM Privately Held
WEB: www.rpxcorp.com
SIC: 6794 8741 Patent owners & lessors; business management

(P-10813)
TENSILICA INC (HQ)
3393 Octavius Dr, Santa Clara (95054-3004)
P.O. Box 202769, Dallas TX (75320-2769)
PHONE.................................408 986-8000
Jack Guedj, *President*
Chris Carney, *CFO*
Keith Van Sickle, *CFO*
Ashish Dixia, *Senior VP*
Beatrice Fu, *Senior VP*
◆ **EMP:** 80 **EST:** 1998
SQ FT: 20,000
SALES (est): 29.6MM
SALES (corp-wide): 2.6B Publicly Held
WEB: www.ip.cadence.com
SIC: 6794 9621 Patent owners & lessors; licensing agencies
PA: Cadence Design Systems, Inc.
    2655 Seely Ave Bldg 5
    San Jose CA 95134
    408 943-1234

(P-10814)
TIVO CORPORATION (HQ)
2160 Gold St, San Jose (95002-3700)
PHONE.................................408 519-9100
David Shull, *President*
James E Meyer, *Ch of Bd*
Peter Halt, *CFO*
Raghavendra Rau, *Vice Ch Bd*
Pamela Sergeeff, *Ch Credit Ofcr*
EMP: 595 **EST:** 1997
SQ FT: 127,000
SALES (est): 668.1MM
SALES (corp-wide): 892MM Publicly Held
WEB: www.ir.tivo.com
SIC: 6794 7374 Patent owners & lessors; computer graphics service
PA: Xperi Holding Corporation
    3025 Orchard Pkwy
    San Jose CA 95134
    408 321-6000

6798 Real Estate Investment Trusts

(P-10815)
CANYON VIEW CAPITAL INC
331 Soquel Ave Ste 100, Santa Cruz (95062-2330)
PHONE.................................831 480-6335
Robert J Davidson, *CEO*
Alison Ruday, *Vice Pres*
Dennis Rimac, *Controller*
EMP: 80 **EST:** 2005
SALES (est): 60MM Privately Held
WEB: www.canyonviewcapital.com
SIC: 6798 Real estate investment trusts

(P-10816)
DIGITAL JAPAN LLC (HQ)
4 Embarcadero Ctr, San Francisco (94111-4106)
PHONE.................................415 738-6500
EMP: 57 **EST:** 2015
SALES: 7.3MM
SALES (corp-wide): 3.9B Privately Held
WEB: www.digitalrealty.com
SIC: 6798 Real estate investment trusts
PA: Digital Realty Trust, Inc.
    5707 Sw Pkwy Ste 2
    Austin TX 78735
    737 281-0101

(P-10817)
ESSEX PORTFOLIO LP (HQ)
Also Called: EPLP
1100 Park Pl Ste 200, San Mateo (94403-7107)
PHONE.................................650 655-7800
Michael J Schall, *President*
George M Marcus, *Ch of Bd*
Angela L Kleiman, *COO*
Barbara Pak, *CFO*
Adam W Berry, *Exec VP*
EMP: 316 **EST:** 1994
SALES (est): 1.5B Publicly Held
WEB: www.essexapartmenthomes.com
SIC: 6798 Real estate investment trusts
PA: Essex Property Trust, Inc.
    1100 Park Pl Ste 200
    San Mateo CA 94403
    650 655-7800

(P-10818)
FEDERAL REALTY INVESTMENT TR
Also Called: Santana Row
356 Santana Row Ste 1005, San Jose (95128-2034)
PHONE.................................408 551-4600
John Benbenuto, *Manager*
Jay Brinson, *Vice Pres*
Patrick Inaba, *Vice Pres*
Melissa Solis, *Vice Pres*
Madalena Moreau, *General Mgr*
EMP: 40
SQ FT: 95,953
SALES (corp-wide): 835.4MM Publicly Held
WEB: www.federalrealty.com
SIC: 6798 Realty investment trusts
PA: Federal Realty Investment Trust
    909 Rose Ave Ste 200
    North Bethesda MD 20852
    301 998-8100

(P-10819)
FOUR CORNERS PROPERTY TR INC (PA)
591 Redwood Hwy Frontage # 3215, Mill Valley (94941-6006)
PHONE.................................415 965-8030
William H Lenehan, *President*
John S Moody, *Ch of Bd*
Gerald R Morgan, *CFO*
James L Brat, *Admin Sec*
Carlos Mosqueda, *Asst Controller*
EMP: 199 **EST:** 2015
SALES (est): 170.9MM Publicly Held
WEB: www.fcpt.com
SIC: 6798 Real estate investment trusts

(P-10820)
GIC REAL ESTATE INC
1 Bush St Ste 1100, San Francisco (94104-4417)
PHONE.................................415 229-1800
Awa Thiam, *Administration*
EMP: 45 Privately Held
WEB: www.gic.com.sg
SIC: 6798 6531 Real estate investment trusts; real estate agents & managers
HQ: Gic Real Estate, Inc.
    1 Bush St Ste 1100
    San Francisco CA 94104
    415 229-1800

6798 - Real Estate Investment Trusts County (P-10821)

PRODUCTS & SERVICES SECTION

(P-10821)
KKR FINANCIAL CORPORATION (DH)
555 California St # 5000, San Francisco (94104-1503)
PHONE.....................................415 315-3620
David A Netjes, *COO*
EMP: 52 **EST:** 2004
SALES (est): 38.4MM **Publicly Held**
WEB: www.kkr.com
SIC: 6798 Real estate investment trusts

(P-10822)
PROLOGIS INC (PA)
Bay 1 Pier 1, San Francisco (94111)
PHONE.....................................415 394-9000
Hamid R Moghadam, *Ch of Bd*
Gary E Anderson, *COO*
Thomas S Olinger, *CFO*
Michael S Curless, *Ch Credit Ofcr*
Edward S Nekritz,
EMP: 460 **EST:** 1997
SALES (est): 4.4B **Publicly Held**
WEB: www.prologis.com
SIC: 6798 Real estate investment trusts

(P-10823)
PROLOGIS LP (HQ)
Bay 1 Pier 1, San Francisco (94111)
PHONE.....................................415 394-9000
Hamid R Moghadam, *Ch of Bd*
Lisa Maldonado, *Partner*
Thomas S Olinger, *CFO*
Oliver Bycroft, *Vice Pres*
Alan Sarjant, *Vice Pres*
EMP: 452 **EST:** 1997
SALES (est): 4.4B **Publicly Held**
WEB: www.prologis.com
SIC: 6798 Real estate investment trusts
PA: Prologis, Inc.
Bay 1 Pier 1
San Francisco CA 94111
415 394-9000

(P-10824)
QUAIL HILL INVESTMENTS INC
Also Called: Remax Value Properties
1124 Meridian Ave, San Jose (95125-4329)
PHONE.....................................408 978-9000
EMP: 110
SALES (est): 5.9MM **Privately Held**
WEB: www.colleenanddennisb.com
SIC: 6798 Real Estate Investment

(P-10825)
REDWOOD TRUST INC (PA)
1 Belvedere Pl Ste 300, Mill Valley (94941-2493)
PHONE.....................................415 389-7373
Christopher J Abate, *CEO*
Richard D Baum, *Ch of Bd*
Dashiell I Robinson, *President*
Collin L Cochrane, *CFO*
Debora Horvath, *Bd of Directors*
EMP: 138 **EST:** 1994
SALES (est): 96.5MM **Publicly Held**
WEB: www.redwoodtrust.com
SIC: 6798 Real estate investment trusts

(P-10826)
VANTAGE DATA CTRS MGT CO LLC (PA)
2820 Northwestern Pkwy, Santa Clara (95051-0904)
PHONE.....................................408 748-9830
Sureel Choksi, *President*
Chris Yetman, *COO*
David Renner, *CFO*
Joe Goldsmith, *Officer*
Lee Kestler, *Officer*
EMP: 40 **EST:** 2010
SQ FT: 19,000
SALES (est): 53.3MM **Privately Held**
WEB: www.vantage-dc.com
SIC: 6798 Real estate investment trusts

6799 Investors, NEC

(P-10827)
500 STARTUPS MANAGEMENT CO LLC
Also Called: Spacer.com
3478 Buskirk Ave Ste 1000, Pleasant Hill (94523-4378)
PHONE.....................................650 743-4738
Christine Tsai, *President*
Josh Curtis, *Partner*
Matt Ellsworth, *Partner*
Santiago Zavala, *Partner*
Vishal Harnal, *Managing Prtnr*
EMP: 120 **EST:** 2010
SALES (est): 75.6MM **Privately Held**
WEB: www.500.co
SIC: 6799 Investors
HQ: Spacer.Com.Au Pty Ltd
Level 3 55 Pyrmont Bridge Road
Pyrmont NSW 2009

(P-10828)
ABS CAPITAL PARTNERS III LP
101 California St Fl 24, San Francisco (94111-5898)
PHONE.....................................415 617-2800
John Mallon, *Branch Mgr*
Trisha Edmondson, *Executive Asst*
Liz Nightingale, *Executive Asst*
Shannon Flaherty, *Research*
Nick Irion, *Sr Associate*
EMP: 431 **Privately Held**
WEB: www.abscapital.com
SIC: 6799 Venture capital companies
PA: Abs Capital Partners Iii, L.P.
201 Intrntl Cir Ste 150
Cockeysville MD 21030

(P-10829)
ACCEL-KKR CAPITL PARTNERS V LP (PA)
2180 Sand Hill Rd Ste 300, Menlo Park (94025-6947)
PHONE.....................................650 289-2460
EMP: 411 **EST:** 2015
SALES (est): 9.6MM **Privately Held**
SIC: 6799 Investors

(P-10830)
ACCEL-KKR COMPANY LLC (PA)
2180 Sand Hill Rd Ste 300, Menlo Park (94025-6947)
PHONE.....................................650 289-2460
Thomas Barnds, *Mng Member*
Tom Barnds, *Managing Prtnr*
Rob Palumbo, *Managing Prtnr*
Herald Chen, *Bd of Directors*
Patrick Fallon, *Officer*
EMP: 737 **EST:** 2000
SQ FT: 7,000
SALES (est): 106.2MM **Privately Held**
WEB: www.accel-kkr.com
SIC: 6799 Venture capital companies

(P-10831)
AH PARALLEL FUND V LP
2865 Sand Hill Rd Ste 101, Menlo Park (94025-7022)
PHONE.....................................650 798-3900
Balaji Srinivasan, *Principal*
Martin Casado, *General Ptnr*
Connie Chan, *General Ptnr*
Jorge Conde, *General Ptnr*
Lars Dalgaard, *General Ptnr*
EMP: 40 **EST:** 2015
SALES (est): 15.6MM **Privately Held**
SIC: 6799 Investors

(P-10832)
ALTA PARTNERS MANAGEMENT CORP
1 Embarcadero Ctr Fl 37, San Francisco (94111-3628)
PHONE.....................................415 362-4022
Jean Deleage, *CEO*
Hilary Strain, *CFO*
Garrett P Gruener, *Vice Pres*
Daniel Janney, *Vice Pres*
Alix Marduel, *Vice Pres*
EMP: 42 **EST:** 1996
SQ FT: 7,000

SALES (est): 4.3MM **Privately Held**
WEB: www.altapartners.com
SIC: 6799 Venture capital companies

(P-10833)
ALTAMONT CAPITAL PARTNERS LLC (PA)
400 Hamilton Ave Ste 230, Palo Alto (94301-1834)
PHONE.....................................650 264-7750
Jesse Rogers, *Mng Member*
John Barr, *Partner*
Paul Harrington, *Partner*
Sharon Luboff, *Partner*
Kc Moylan, *Partner*
EMP: 375 **EST:** 2011
SALES (est): 615.2MM **Privately Held**
WEB: www.altamontcapital.com
SIC: 6799 Venture capital companies

(P-10834)
AMERICAN SECURITIES COMPANY
464 California St Ste 100, San Francisco (94104-1227)
PHONE.....................................415 396-4566
Michael Azevedo, *President*
EMP: 37 **EST:** 1968
SALES (est): 10.2MM
SALES (corp-wide): 80.3B **Publicly Held**
WEB: www.wellsfargo.com
SIC: 6799 Real estate investors, except property operators
HQ: Wells Fargo Bank, National Association
1301 N Cliff Ave
Sioux Falls SD 57103
605 575-6900

(P-10835)
BERTRAM CAPITAL MANAGEMENT LLC (PA)
950 Tower Ln Ste 1000, Foster City (94404-4244)
PHONE.....................................650 358-5000
Jeff Drazan,
Ingrid Swenson, *Partner*
Paul Price, *CEO*
Ivy Ono, *CFO*
Zoey Armstrong, *Ch Credit Ofcr*
EMP: 136 **EST:** 2006
SALES (est): 263.4MM **Privately Held**
WEB: www.bertramcapital.com
SIC: 6799 Venture capital companies

(P-10836)
BROADREACH CAPITL PARTNERS LLC (PA)
855 El Cmino Real Bldg 5, Palo Alto (94301)
PHONE.....................................650 331-2500
John A Foster, *Director*
Eli Khari,
Philip Flip F Maritz, *Director*
Craig G Vought, *Director*
EMP: 60 **EST:** 2002
SALES (est): 46.7MM **Privately Held**
WEB: www.broadreachcp.com
SIC: 6799 Investors

(P-10837)
BROADREACH CAPITL PARTNERS LLC
235 Montgomery St # 1018, San Francisco (94104-2902)
PHONE.....................................415 354-4640
John A Foster, *Branch Mgr*
EMP: 1161
SALES (corp-wide): 46.7MM **Privately Held**
WEB: www.broadreachcp.com
SIC: 6799 Investors
PA: Broadreach Capital Partners Llc
855 El Cmino Real Bldg 5
Palo Alto CA 94301
650 331-2500

(P-10838)
CENTURY PK CAPITL PARTNERS LLC
1010 Coleman Ave Ste 30, Menlo Park (94025-2339)
PHONE.....................................650 324-1956
Charles Roellig, *Manager*
Adam Zacuto, *Vice Pres*
Matt Minnaugh, *Business Dir*
Gina O 'donnell, *Controller*
EMP: 90 **Privately Held**
WEB: www.centuryparkcapital.com
SIC: 6799 Investors
PA: Century Park Capital Partners, Llc
2101 Rosecrans Ave # 4275
El Segundo CA 90245

(P-10839)
CROSSLINK CAPITAL INC
2180 Sand Hill Rd Ste 200, Menlo Park (94025-6959)
PHONE.....................................415 617-1800
Peter Van Camp, *CEO*
David Courtney, *General Ptnr*
Eric Chin, *Partner*
Michael Stark, *President*
Gerri Grossmann, *Treasurer*
EMP: 35 **EST:** 1999
SALES (est): 10.3MM **Privately Held**
WEB: www.crosslinkcapital.com
SIC: 6799 Venture capital companies

(P-10840)
CVF CAPITAL PARTNERS INC
Also Called: Central Valley Fund, The
1590 Drew Ave Ste 110, Davis (95618-7849)
PHONE.....................................530 757-7004
Jose C Blanco, *CEO*
Brad Triebsch, *Managing Prtnr*
Edward McNulty, *President*
Brian Hoblit, *CFO*
Chris Carleson, *Vice Pres*
EMP: 150 **EST:** 2012
SALES (est): 14.5MM **Privately Held**
WEB: www.cvfcapitalpartners.com
SIC: 6799 Investors

(P-10841)
D E SHAW VALENCE LLC
2735 Sand Hill Rd Ste 105, Menlo Park (94025-7126)
PHONE.....................................650 926-9460
Michael Lee, *Branch Mgr*
EMP: 186 **Privately Held**
WEB: www.deshaw.com
SIC: 6799 Investors
PA: D. E. Shaw Valence, L.L.C.
120 W 45th St Fl 39
New York NY 10036

(P-10842)
DFJ MANAGEMENT LLC
2882 Sand Hill Rd Ste 150, Menlo Park (94025-7057)
PHONE.....................................650 233-9000
Timothy C Draper, *Mng Member*
Randall Glein, *Partner*
Jennifer Kodner, *Partner*
Heidi Roizen, *Partner*
Jo Roizen, *Partner*
▲ **EMP:** 39 **EST:** 1992
SQ FT: 3,000
SALES (est): 20.8MM **Privately Held**
SIC: 6799 Venture capital companies

(P-10843)
EVENTURE CPITL PARTNERS II LLC
600 Montgomery St Fl 43, San Francisco (94111-2818)
PHONE.....................................415 869-5200
Mathias Schilling,
Thomas Gieselmann, *General Ptnr*
Andreas Haug, *General Ptnr*
Conrad Chu, *Partner*
Luis Hanemann, *Partner*
EMP: 42 **EST:** 2011
SALES (est): 9MM **Privately Held**
WEB: www.headline.com
SIC: 6799 Venture capital companies

(P-10844)
FIRST ROUND CAPITAL LLC
595 Pacific Ave Fl 4, San Francisco (94133-4685)
PHONE.....................................415 646-0072
Josh Kopelman, *Branch Mgr*
Cory Perkins, *Partner*
Monica Avila, *Executive Asst*
Breanna Manore, *Executive Asst*
EMP: 43 **Privately Held**

PRODUCTS & SERVICES SECTION

6799 - Investors, NEC County (P-10868)

WEB: www.firstround.com
SIC: 6799 Venture capital companies
PA: First Round Capital, Llc
4040 Locust St
Philadelphia PA 19104

(P-10845)
FOUNDATION CAPITAL LLC
550 High St Ste 300, Palo Alto (94301-1696)
PHONE...................................650 614-0500
Ted Meyer, Partner
Moldow Charles, General Ptnr
William Elmore, General Ptnr
Ashmeet Sidana, General Ptnr
Bill Elmore, Partner
EMP: 35 EST: 1995
SALES (est): 10MM Privately Held
WEB: www.foundationcapital.com
SIC: 6799 Venture capital companies

(P-10846)
FRANCISCO PARTNERS MGT LP (PA)
1 Letterman Dr Ste 410, San Francisco (94129-1495)
PHONE...................................415 418-2900
Dipanjan Deb, Managing Prtnr
Benjamin Ball, Partner
Mike Barry, Partner
Neil Garfinkel, Partner
David Golob, Partner
EMP: 50 EST: 1999
SQ FT: 15,000
SALES (est): 2.6B Privately Held
WEB: www.franciscopartners.com
SIC: 6799 7372 Venture capital companies; application computer software

(P-10847)
GENERATE CAPITAL INC
560 Davis St Ste 250, San Francisco (94111-2006)
PHONE...................................415 360-3063
Scott Jacobs, CEO
Steve Gossett, Partner
Jigar Shah, President
Nam Tran Nguyen, COO
Judy Bornstein, CFO
EMP: 52 EST: 2014
SALES (est): 14.6MM Privately Held
WEB: www.generatecapital.com
SIC: 6799 Venture capital companies

(P-10848)
GOBP HOLDINGS INC
2000 5th St, Berkeley (94710-1811)
PHONE...................................510 845-1999
EMP: 149 EST: 2018
SALES (est): 383K
SALES (corp-wide): 3.1B Publicly Held
WEB: www.groceryoutlet.com
SIC: 6799 Investors
PA: Grocery Outlet Holding Corp.
5650 Hollis St
Emeryville CA 94608
510 845-1999

(P-10849)
GOLDEN 85 INVESTMENTS CORP
Also Called: 85 C Bakery Cafe
878 W Benjamin Holt Dr, Stockton (95207-3652)
PHONE...................................209 242-2916
David Frost, Branch Mgr
EMP: 44
SALES (corp-wide): 4MM Privately Held
SIC: 5812 6799 Cafe; investors
PA: Golden 85 Investments Corp
1672 Mcgaw Ave
Irvine CA 92614
949 250-1688

(P-10850)
GOLDEN GATE PRIVATE EQUITY INC (PA)
Also Called: Golden Gate Capital
1 Embarcadero Ctr Fl 39, San Francisco (94111-3714)
PHONE...................................415 983-2706
David Dominik, Mng Member
Neale Attenborough, Partner
Arthur Baptist, Partner
Tushar Khadloya, Partner
Terence Kwan, Partner
EMP: 1505 EST: 2000
SQ FT: 7,800
SALES (est): 1.6B Privately Held
WEB: www.goldengatecap.com
SIC: 6799 3534 Investors; elevators & moving stairways

(P-10851)
GRANITE RICK CO
5225 Hellyer Ave Ste 220, San Jose (95138-1021)
PHONE...................................831 768-2000
Audrey Huff, Project Mgr
EMP: 222 EST: 2017
SALES (est): 4.2MM
SALES (corp-wide): 390.3MM Privately Held
WEB: www.graniterock.com
SIC: 6799 Investors
PA: Granite Rock Co.
350 Technology Dr
Watsonville CA 95076
831 768-2000

(P-10852)
GRYPHON INVESTORS INC (PA)
1 Maritime Plz Ste 2300, San Francisco (94111-3513)
PHONE...................................415 217-7400
R David Andrews, CEO
Mark Fuller, Vice Pres
Clint Kadolph, Vice Pres
Will McCallum, Vice Pres
Justin Saks, Vice Pres
▲ EMP: 1830 EST: 1995
SALES (est): 1.3B Privately Held
WEB: www.gryphon-inv.com
SIC: 6799 Venture capital companies

(P-10853)
HGGC LLC (PA)
1950 University Ave # 350, East Palo Alto (94303-2250)
PHONE...................................650 321-4910
Rich Lawson, Mng Member
Christopher Guinn, Partner
Les Brown, CFO
Niki Hall, Chief Mktg Ofcr
Gregory Benson, Officer
EMP: 253 EST: 2011
SALES (est): 562.3MM Privately Held
WEB: www.hggc.com
SIC: 6799 Commodity investors

(P-10854)
HORSLEY BRIDGE PARTNERS INC (PA)
505 Montgomery St # 2100, San Francisco (94111-2587)
PHONE...................................415 986-7733
Phillip Horsley, President
Kathryn Abbott, Managing Prtnr
Duane Phillips, CFO
Carol Christensen, Officer
Gary Bridge, Managing Dir
EMP: 39 EST: 1983
SQ FT: 10,834
SALES (est): 16.2MM Privately Held
WEB: www.horsleybridge.com
SIC: 6799 Venture capital companies

(P-10855)
HORSLEY BRIDGE PARTNERS LLC
505 Montgomery St # 2100, San Francisco (94111-2587)
PHONE...................................415 986-7733
Kathleen M Murphy,
EMP: 78 EST: 1997
SALES (est): 1.2MM Privately Held
WEB: www.horsleybridge.com
SIC: 6799 Venture capital companies

(P-10856)
INCUBE LABS LLC
518 Sycamore Dr, Milpitas (95035-7412)
PHONE...................................847 565-9506
EMP: 50
SALES (corp-wide): 29.6MM Privately Held
WEB: www.incubelabs.com
SIC: 6799 Venture capital companies

PA: Incube Labs, Llc
2051 Ringwood Ave
San Jose CA 95131
408 457-3700

(P-10857)
INDUSTRY VENTURES LLC (PA)
30 Hotaling Pl 3, San Francisco (94111-2201)
PHONE...................................415 273-4201
Hans D Swildens,
Robert May, COO
Nate Leung, Vice Pres
Amir Malayery, Vice Pres
Lindsay Sharma, Vice Pres
EMP: 72 EST: 2003
SALES (est): 8.2MM Privately Held
WEB: www.industryventures.com
SIC: 6799 Venture capital companies

(P-10858)
INSTITUTIONAL VENTURE PARTNERS
Also Called: Ivp
607 Front St, San Francisco (94111-1913)
PHONE...................................415 432-4660
Nikki Conte, Regional Mgr
EMP: 35
SALES (corp-wide): 3.6MM Privately Held
WEB: www.ivp.com
SIC: 6799 Venture capital companies
PA: Institutional Venture Partners
3000 Sand Hill Rd 2-250
Menlo Park CA 94025
650 854-0132

(P-10859)
KDR HOLDING INC (PA)
47448 Fremont Blvd, Fremont (94538-6503)
PHONE...................................510 230-2777
James F Brear, President
Barbara Martinez, Opers Mgr
Wilson Craig, Pub Rel Staff
EMP: 32 EST: 2015
SALES (est): 30.8MM Privately Held
SIC: 6799 7372 Investors; application computer software

(P-10860)
KHOSLA VENTURES LLC
2128 Sand Hill Rd, Menlo Park (94025-6903)
PHONE...................................650 376-8500
Kim Totah,
Samir Kaul, General Ptnr
Bruce Armstrong, Partner
Irene Au, Partner
Andrew Chung, Partner
EMP: 40 EST: 2006
SALES (est): 18.5MM Privately Held
WEB: www.khoslaventures.com
SIC: 6799 Venture capital companies

(P-10861)
KINGFISH GROUP INC (PA)
601 California St # 1250, San Francisco (94108-2817)
PHONE...................................650 980-0200
Christian Dubiel, President
Teresa Boland, Vice Pres
Vinayak Ghosh, Research
Akansha Jaiswal, Research
Mansi Lokhande, Research
EMP: 66 EST: 2008
SALES (est): 2.7MM Privately Held
WEB: www.kingfishgroup.com
SIC: 6799 Venture capital companies

(P-10862)
KLEINER PRKINS CFELD BYERS LLC (PA)
Also Called: Kpcb
2750 Sand Hill Rd, Menlo Park (94025-7020)
PHONE...................................650 233-2750
Mamoon Hamid, General Ptnr
William Hearst III, General Ptnr
Tom Jermoluk, General Ptnr
Bill Joy, General Ptnr
Noah Knauf, General Ptnr
EMP: 25 EST: 1984
SQ FT: 11,000

SALES (est): 86.2MM Privately Held
WEB: www.kleinerperkins.com
SIC: 6799 3691 Venture capital companies; storage batteries

(P-10863)
KOHLBERG KRAVIS ROBERTS CO LP
Also Called: K K R
2800 Sand Hill Rd Ste 200, Menlo Park (94025-7080)
PHONE...................................650 233-6560
Michael Michelson, Manager
Peggy Shaughnessy, Managing Dir
Sugiyama Isobelle, Executive Asst
Colleen Morse, Executive Asst
Ed Ruiz, Technology
EMP: 55 Publicly Held
WEB: www.kkr.com
SIC: 6799 Venture capital companies
HQ: Kohlberg Kravis Roberts & Co. L.P.
9 W 57th St Ste 4200
New York NY 10019
212 750-8300

(P-10864)
KPCB HOLDINGS INC (PA)
2750 Sand Hill Rd, Menlo Park (94025-7020)
PHONE...................................650 233-2750
Brook Byers, President
Scott Ryles, COO
Susan Biglieri, CFO
EMP: 37 EST: 1999
SALES (est): 10.3MM Privately Held
WEB: www.kleinerperkins.com
SIC: 6799 Venture capital companies

(P-10865)
M & H REALTY PARTNERS LP
353 Sacramento St Fl 21, San Francisco (94111-3620)
PHONE...................................415 693-9000
EMP: 70
SALES (est): 4.2MM Privately Held
SIC: 6799 Investors, Nec

(P-10866)
MAKENA CAPITAL MANAGEMENT LLC
2755 Sand Hill Rd Ste 200, Menlo Park (94025-7086)
PHONE...................................650 926-0510
William Miller, CFO
Luke Proskine, Managing Prtnr
Andre Cuerington, Managing Dir
Peter Dolan, Managing Dir
Jackson Garton, Managing Dir
EMP: 55 EST: 2005
SALES (est): 10.1MM Privately Held
WEB: www.makenacap.com
SIC: 6799 Investors

(P-10867)
MAYFIELD FUND
2484 Sand Hill Rd, Menlo Park (94025-6940)
PHONE...................................650 854-5560
Navin Chaddha, Partner
John Cocoziello, General Ptnr
Yogen Dalal, General Ptnr
Janice Robert, General Ptnr
Dado Banatao, Partner
EMP: 45 EST: 1969
SQ FT: 23,000
SALES (est): 10.8MM Privately Held
WEB: www.mayfield.com
SIC: 6799 Venture capital companies

(P-10868)
MDV MANAGEMENT COMPANY LLC
Also Called: Mohr Davidow Ventures
3000 Sand Hill Rd 3-290, Menlo Park (94025-7113)
PHONE...................................650 233-9301
William Davidow,
Jonathan Feiber,
Nancy Schoendorf,
Nancy J Schoendorf,
Linda Patane, Manager
EMP: 40 EST: 1983
SQ FT: 6,500
SALES (est): 8MM Privately Held
SIC: 6799 Venture capital companies

6799 - Investors, NEC County (P-10869)

(P-10869)
MORGENTHLER MGT PRTNERS VI LLC
Also Called: Morgenthaler Ventures
2710 Sand Hill Rd Ste 100, Menlo Park (94025-7140)
PHONE..................650 388-7600
Gary Morgenthaler, *Branch Mgr*
Ralph E Christoffersen, *Partner*
Rebecca Lynn, *Partner*
Al Stanley, *Partner*
Peter Taft, *Partner*
EMP: 2023
SALES (corp-wide): 166.4MM Privately Held
WEB: www.mpepartners.com
SIC: 6799 Venture capital companies
PA: Morgenthaler Management Partners Vi, Llc
600 Superior Ave E # 2500
Cleveland OH 44114
216 416-7500

(P-10870)
MSR HOTELS & RESORTS INC
Also Called: Embassy Suites- Santa Clara
2885 Lakeside Dr, Santa Clara (95054-2805)
PHONE..................408 496-6400
Teri Owens, *Branch Mgr*
EMP: 98
SALES (corp-wide): 52B Publicly Held
WEB: www.cnl.com
SIC: 6799 Investors
HQ: Msr Hotels & Resorts, Inc.
450 S Orange Ave
Orlando FL 32801
407 650-1000

(P-10871)
NATIONAL FINANCIAL SVCS LLC
1411 Chapin Ave, Burlingame (94010-4002)
PHONE..................650 343-6775
James Stevenson, *Principal*
Sajay Cherian, *Vice Pres*
Alexis Mitchell, *Vice Pres*
Kevin Roy, *Vice Pres*
Raymond Ruan, *Vice Pres*
EMP: 1146
SALES (corp-wide): 4.3B Privately Held
WEB: www.mybrokerageinfo.com
SIC: 6799 Investors
HQ: National Financial Services Llc
200 Seaport Blvd Ste 630
Boston MA 02210
800 471-0382

(P-10872)
NEW ENTERPRISE ASSOCIATES INC
2855 Sand Hill Rd, Menlo Park (94025-7022)
PHONE..................650 854-9499
Annie Pyle, *Office Mgr*
Tony Florence, *General Ptnr*
Albert Lee, *General Ptnr*
Stewart Alsop III, *Partner*
Colin Bryant, *Partner*
EMP: 40
SALES (corp-wide): 216.1MM Privately Held
WEB: www.nea.com
SIC: 6799 Venture capital companies
PA: New Enterprise Associates, Inc.
1954 Greenspring Dr # 600
Lutherville Timonium MD 21093
410 842-4000

(P-10873)
NUTRITION PARENT LLC (DH)
1950 University Ave # 350, East Palo Alto (94303-2250)
PHONE..................650 321-4910
Rich Lawson, *Principal*
EMP: 62 EST: 2017
SALES (est): 908.3MM
SALES (corp-wide): 319.3MM Privately Held
SIC: 6799 Investors
HQ: The Better Being Co Llc
222 S Main St Ste 1600
Salt Lake City UT 84101
435 655-6000

(P-10874)
OAK HILL CAPITAL MGT LLC
Also Called: Oak Hill Capital Partners
2775 Sand Hill Rd Ste 220, Menlo Park (94025-7085)
PHONE..................650 234-0500
Taylor Crandall, *Mng Member*
Karen Capparelli, *Executive Asst*
Tracey Garrett, *Executive Asst*
Steven B Gruber,
EMP: 4017 EST: 2004
SALES (est): 5.9MM
SALES (corp-wide): 395.4MM Privately Held
WEB: www.oakhill.com
SIC: 6799 Venture capital companies
PA: Oak Hill Capital Partners, L.P.
65 E 55th St Fl 32
New York NY 10022
212 527-8400

(P-10875)
PARTHENON CAPITAL LLC
4 Embarcadero Ctr # 2500, San Francisco (94111-4106)
PHONE..................415 913-3900
Robert Hood, *Principal*
Jill M Aiello, *Vice Pres*
Jim Chappell, *Vice Pres*
Lesly J Schlender, *Research*
Koopman Jim, *Asst Controller*
EMP: 1041
SALES (corp-wide): 214.1MM Privately Held
WEB: www.parthenoncapital.com
SIC: 6799 Venture capital companies
PA: Parthenon Capital, Llc
399 Boylston St Ste 28
Boston MA 02116
617 960-4000

(P-10876)
PLUG & PLAY LLC (PA)
Also Called: Plugandplaytechcenter.com
440 N Wolfe Rd, Sunnyvale (94085-3869)
PHONE..................408 524-1400
Saeed Amidi, *CEO*
Adam Antony, *Partner*
Alireza Masrour, *Managing Prtnr*
Chen Zhao, *Managing Prtnr*
Candace Widdoes, *COO*
EMP: 97 EST: 2004
SQ FT: 180,000
SALES (est): 20MM Privately Held
WEB: www.plugandplaytechcenter.com
SIC: 6799 7389 Investors; office facilities & secretarial service rental

(P-10877)
QATALYST GROUP LP (PA)
1 Maritime Plz Fl 24, San Francisco (94111-3404)
PHONE..................415 844-7700
Frank Quattrone, *CEO*
George Boutros, *Senior Partner*
Brian Cayne, *Principal*
Jeff Chang, *Education*
Karthik Ramakrishnan, *Internal Med*
EMP: 42 EST: 2008
SALES (est): 3.2MM Privately Held
WEB: www.qatalyst.com
SIC: 6799 Investors

(P-10878)
RECORE GROWTH INVESTMENTS INC
1116 Mcclaren Dr, Carmichael (95608-6116)
PHONE..................916 813-3798
Matthew Recore, *Branch Mgr*
EMP: 45
SALES (corp-wide): 505.1K Privately Held
SIC: 6799 Investors
PA: Recore Growth Investments Inc.
2398 Fair Oaks Blvd Ste 8
Sacramento CA 95825
916 389-2953

(P-10879)
RECURRENT ENRGY DEV HLDNGS LLC (DH)
3000 Oak Rd Ste 300, Walnut Creek (94597-7775)
PHONE..................415 675-1501
Yumin Liu, *President*
Joshua Goldstein, *Vice Pres*
Helen Shin, *Vice Pres*
Odessa Cooper, *Admin Sec*
EMP: 62 EST: 2009
SALES (est): 18.7MM
SALES (corp-wide): 3.4B Privately Held
WEB: www.recurrentenergy.com
SIC: 6799 Investors

(P-10880)
RED EAGLE VENTURES INC
338 Main St Unit 26b, San Francisco (94105-2172)
PHONE..................415 773-1800
David Pottruck, *Chairman*
David S Potruck, *President*
Colleen B McGill, *Officer*
EMP: 50 EST: 2007
SALES (est): 2.6MM Privately Held
WEB: www.redeagleventures.com
SIC: 6799 Venture capital companies

(P-10881)
SAINTS MANAGEMENT LLC (PA)
475 Sansome St Ste 1850, San Francisco (94111-3131)
PHONE..................415 773-2080
David Quinlivian, *Mng Member*
Kenneth B Sawyer,
Lilian Shackelford Murray, *Mng Member*
EMP: 47 EST: 2004
SALES (est): 67.4MM Privately Held
WEB: www.saintscapital.com
SIC: 6799 Venture capital companies

(P-10882)
SEQUOIA CAPITAL OPERATIONS LLC (PA)
2800 Sand Hill Rd Ste 101, Menlo Park (94025-7079)
PHONE..................650 854-3927
Donald Valentine, *General Ptnr*
Doug Leone, *General Ptnr*
Tom McMurray, *General Ptnr*
Bryan Schreier, *General Ptnr*
Thomas Stephenson, *General Ptnr*
EMP: 87 EST: 1963
SQ FT: 6,000
SALES (est): 58.8MM Privately Held
WEB: www.sequoiacap.com
SIC: 6799 Venture capital companies

(P-10883)
SIERRA VENTURES MANAGEMENT LLC
1400 Fashion Island Blvd, San Mateo (94404-2060)
PHONE..................650 854-1000
Martha Clarke Adamson, *CEO*
Jim Doehrman, *Partner*
Robert Walker, *Partner*
Jeffrey M Drazan, *Managing Dir*
Tim Guleri, *Managing Dir*
EMP: 43 EST: 1982
SQ FT: 9,300
SALES (est): 2.6MM Privately Held
WEB: www.sierraventures.com
SIC: 6799 Venture capital companies

(P-10884)
STARWOOD CAPITAL GROUP LLC
100 Pine St Ste 3000, San Francisco (94111-5216)
PHONE..................415 247-1220
Mark Davison, *Manager*
Sam Caven, *Vice Pres*
EMP: 173 Privately Held
WEB: www.starwoodcapital.com
SIC: 6799 Investors
PA: Starwood Capital Group, L.L.C.
591 W Putnam Ave
Greenwich CT 06830

(P-10885)
SUMMIT PARTNERS LP
200 Middlefield Rd # 200, Menlo Park (94025-4003)
PHONE..................650 614-6670
Bruce R Evans, *Manager*
Eunji Chung, *Vice Pres*
Craig D Frances, *Principal*
Yoon K Lee, *Investment Ofcr*
Max J Rich, *Analyst*
EMP: 1258 Privately Held
WEB: www.summitpartners.com
SIC: 6799 Venture capital companies
PA: Summit Partners, L.P.
222 Berkeley St Fl 18
Boston MA 02116

(P-10886)
SUNSTONE PARTNERS LLC
400 S El Cmino Real Ste 3, San Mateo (94402)
PHONE..................650 289-4400
Scott Hammack, *Partner*
Jeff Rich, *Partner*
Jennifer Gunn, *CFO*
Gustavo Alberelli, *Managing Dir*
Sterling Tai, *CIO*
EMP: 83 EST: 2004
SALES (est): 11.8MM Privately Held
WEB: www.sunstonepartners.com
SIC: 6799 Venture capital companies

(P-10887)
SUNSTONE PARTNERS MGT LLC
400 S El Cmino Real Ste 3, San Mateo (94402)
PHONE..................650 289-4400
Mike Biggee,
John Moragne, *Managing Dir*
Gus Alberelli,
Cynthia Snow, *Manager*
EMP: 65 EST: 2015
SALES (est): 2.9MM Privately Held
WEB: www.sunstonepartners.com
SIC: 6799 Venture capital companies

(P-10888)
SWANDER PACE CAPITAL LLC (PA)
101 Mission St Ste 1900, San Francisco (94105-1726)
PHONE..................415 477-8500
Andrew Richards, *CEO*
Heather Fraser, *COO*
Virginia Calvo, *CFO*
Alex Litt, *Senior VP*
Tara Hyland, *Vice Pres*
EMP: 567
SQ FT: 5,000
SALES (est): 62.1MM Privately Held
WEB: www.spcap.com
SIC: 6799 Venture capital companies

(P-10889)
TC PRPRTY MGT LTD A CAL LTD PR
1723 Oak Ave, Davis (95616-1004)
PHONE..................530 666-5799
Theodore Caldwell, *President*
EMP: 35 EST: 1987
SALES (est): 3MM Privately Held
SIC: 6799 6531 Real estate investors, except property operators; real estate managers

(P-10890)
TCMI INC (PA)
Also Called: Technology Crossover Ventures
250 Middlefield Rd, Menlo Park (94025-3560)
PHONE..................650 614-8200
Nari Ansari, *Principal*
Susan Clark, *General Ptnr*
Ric Fenton, *General Ptnr*
Jake Reynolds, *General Ptnr*
Jay Hoag, *President*
EMP: 50 EST: 1995
SQ FT: 2,700
SALES (est): 46.1MM Privately Held
WEB: www.tcv.com
SIC: 6799 Venture capital companies

(P-10891)
ULTIMATE CREATIONS LLC
516 W Shaw Ave Ste 200, Fresno (93704-2515)
PHONE..................559 221-4936
Duwayne Turner,
EMP: 51 EST: 2018
SALES (est): 2.8MM Privately Held
SIC: 6799 8742 Investors; real estate consultant

PRODUCTS & SERVICES SECTION

7011 - Hotels, Motels & Tourist Courts County (P-10918)

(P-10892)
VANTAGEPOINT CAPITAL PARTNERS (PA)
1111 Bayhill Dr Ste 220, San Bruno (94066-3198)
PHONE..................650 866-3100
Alan E Salzman, *Partner*
James Marver, *Partner*
Karen Eliadis, *CFO*
Richard Harroch, *Managing Dir*
Neil Wolff, *Managing Dir*
EMP: 68 **EST:** 1996
SALES (est): 8.8MM **Privately Held**
WEB: www.vpcp.com
SIC: 6799 Venture capital companies

(P-10893)
VANTAGEPOINT MANAGEMENT INC (PA)
Also Called: Vantagepoint Capital Partners
1111 Bayhill Dr Ste 220, San Bruno (94066-3198)
PHONE..................650 866-3100
Alan E Salzman, *CEO*
Harold Friedman, *CFO*
Tom Bevilacqua, *Managing Dir*
Jim Marver, *Managing Dir*
James D Marver, *Admin Sec*
EMP: 65 **EST:** 1996
SQ FT: 21,166
SALES (est): 7.2MM **Privately Held**
WEB: www.vpcp.com
SIC: 6799 Venture capital companies

(P-10894)
VIRGO INVESTMENT GROUP LLC
555 Twin Dolphin Dr # 61, Redwood City (94065-2129)
PHONE..................650 453-3627
Jesse Watson,
Flemming Bjoernslev, *Partner*
Rick Ray, *Partner*
Kyle Limberg, *Vice Pres*
Anthony Lubiano, *Vice Pres*
EMP: 50 **EST:** 2010
SALES (est): 7.9MM **Privately Held**
WEB: www.virgo-llc.com
SIC: 6799 Investors

(P-10895)
VISTA EQITY PRTNERS FUND III L (DH)
4 Embarcadero Ctr # 2000, San Francisco (94111-4106)
PHONE..................415 765-6500
Robert F Smith, *Partner*
Rares Barbu, *Partner*
Betty Hung, *Partner*
Ralph Debernardo, *Vice Pres*
Aaron Gupta, *Vice Pres*
EMP: 948 **EST:** 2007
SALES (est): 117.1MM
SALES (corp-wide): 1.6B **Privately Held**
WEB: www.vistaequitypartners.com
SIC: 6799 Venture capital companies

(P-10896)
WALDEN CAPITAL PARTNERSHIP
Also Called: Walden Vc
750 Battery St Ste 700, San Francisco (94111-1527)
PHONE..................415 391-7225
Arthur S Berliner, *General Ptnr*
George S Sarlo, *General Ptnr*
Rowena Baginski, *Executive*
Larry Marcus, *Managing Dir*
George Sarlo, *Managing Dir*
EMP: 47 **EST:** 1974
SQ FT: 6,000
SALES (est): 2.5MM **Privately Held**
WEB: www.waldenvc.com
SIC: 6799 Venture capital companies

(P-10897)
XOJET SALES LLC
2000 Sierra Point Pkwy # 200, Brisbane (94005-1846)
PHONE..................877 599-6538
Payman Vakil-Zadeh, *Advisor*
EMP: 36 **EST:** 2018
SALES (est): 6.1MM **Privately Held**
WEB: www.flyxo.com
SIC: 6799 Investors

(P-10898)
Y COMBINATOR MANAGEMENT LLC
335 Pioneer Way, Mountain View (94041-1505)
PHONE..................775 287-3519
Sam Altman,
Ali Rowghani, *Partner*
Laura Fiuza, *Officer*
Stephanie Simon, *Officer*
Jonathan Kau, *Software Engr*
EMP: 49 **EST:** 2014
SALES (est): 12.4MM **Privately Held**
WEB: www.ycombinator.com
SIC: 6799 Investment clubs

(P-10899)
YIHENG CAPITAL LLC (PA)
1 Montgomery St Ste 3450, San Francisco (94104-5532)
PHONE..................415 875-5600
Yuanshan Guo, *Principal*
Janet Ji, *CFO*
Sean Cumiskey, *Officer*
EMP: 76 **EST:** 2012
SALES (est): 278.9K **Privately Held**
WEB: www.yihengcapital.com
SIC: 6799 Investors

7011 Hotels, Motels & Tourist Courts

(P-10900)
15TH & L INVESTORS LLC
1121 15th St, Sacramento (95814-4011)
PHONE..................916 267-6805
Anthony R Giannoni, *Mng Member*
Shelly Moranville, *Mng Member*
EMP: 55 **EST:** 2000
SALES (est): 4.9MM **Privately Held**
SIC: 7011 Hotel, franchised

(P-10901)
1651 TIBURON HOTEL LLC
Also Called: Lodge At Tiburon
1651 Tiburon Blvd, Belvedere Tiburon (94920-2511)
PHONE..................401 946-4600
James Procaccianti,
EMP: 80 **EST:** 2019
SALES (est): 3.5MM **Privately Held**
WEB: www.lodgeattiburon.com
SIC: 7011 Hotels

(P-10902)
205 KENTUCKY STREET LLC
Also Called: Hotel Petaluma
205 Kentucky St, Petaluma (94952-2815)
PHONE..................707 559-3393
Satish Patel,
Shannon Kremer, *Sales Staff*
Colleen Marlow, *Sales Staff*
EMP: 35 **EST:** 1995
SALES (est): 1.4MM **Privately Held**
WEB: www.hotelpetaluma.com
SIC: 7011 Hotels

(P-10903)
28 SASF OWNER LLC
Also Called: Four Season
222 Sansome St, San Francisco (94104-2703)
PHONE..................415 276-9888
EMP: 39 **EST:** 2018
SALES (est): 1.5MM **Privately Held**
SIC: 7011 Hotels

(P-10904)
425 NORTH POINT STREET LLC
Also Called: Tuscan Inn
101 California St Ste 950, San Francisco (94111-5826)
PHONE..................800 648-4626
Jan Misch,
EMP: 49 **EST:** 2011
SALES (est): 395K **Privately Held**
WEB: www.hotelzoesf.com
SIC: 7011 Hotels

(P-10905)
4290 EL CAMINO PROPERTIES LP
Also Called: Cabana Hotel
4290 El Camino Real, Palo Alto (94306-4404)
PHONE..................650 857-0787
Bhupendra B Patel, *Owner*
Jenny Klemba-Friedman, *Sales Staff*
Elias Samonte, *Director*
EMP: 146 **EST:** 1996
SALES (est): 5.4MM **Privately Held**
WEB: www.cabanapaloalto.com
SIC: 7011 Hotels

(P-10906)
4961 NORTH CDR LLC
4961 N Cedar Ave, Fresno (93726-1062)
PHONE..................559 224-4200
Michael Mohr,
EMP: 56 **EST:** 2011
SALES (est): 930.1K **Privately Held**
SIC: 7011 Hotels & motels

(P-10907)
765 AIRPORT BOULEVARD PARTNR
Also Called: Hilton
765 Airport Blvd, Burlingame (94010-1921)
PHONE..................650 347-7800
Irving Chnag, *Partner*
Dennis Burton, *Partner*
EMP: 45 **EST:** 2000
SALES (est): 3.7MM **Privately Held**
WEB: www.hiltongrandvacations.com
SIC: 7011 Resort hotel

(P-10908)
A29 FUNDING LLC
Also Called: Holiday Inn
300 J St, Sacramento (95814-2210)
PHONE..................916 446-0100
Liz Tavernese, *Manager*
Gerald Hill, *Director*
Laquila Walker, *Director*
Kathy Rutledge, *Correspondent*
EMP: 247
SALES (corp-wide): 455.4MM **Privately Held**
WEB: www.holidayinn.com
SIC: 7011 Hotels & motels
PA: A29 Funding Llc
2398 E Cmlback Rd Ste 100
Scottsdale AZ 85260
678 762-0005

(P-10909)
ACCOR SERVICES US LLC (HQ)
Also Called: Fairmont Hotel
950 Mason St, San Francisco (94108-6000)
PHONE..................415 772-5000
April Schizley,
Michelle Gilman, *Executive*
Andrew McLaughlin, *General Mgr*
April Sheesley, *Executive Asst*
Emiko Shibuya, *Technology*
◆ **EMP:** 1000 **EST:** 2007
SQ FT: 2,100
SALES (est): 770.3MM
SALES (corp-wide): 627.9MM **Privately Held**
WEB: www.fairmont.com
SIC: 7011 Hotels
PA: Accor
82 Rue Henry Farman
Issy Les Moulineaux 92130
146 429-193

(P-10910)
ADOBE ROAD INVESTMENT GROUP
Also Called: Hampton Inn
520 Adobe Rd, Red Bluff (96080-9623)
PHONE..................530 529-4178
Floyd E Damschen, *Managing Prtnr*
Lillian Damschen, *Partner*
EMP: 37 **EST:** 2005
SQ FT: 56,000
SALES (est): 921.9K **Privately Held**
WEB: www.redbluffsuites.hamptoninn.com
SIC: 7011 Hotels & motels

(P-10911)
ADSWOOD TRS LLC
Also Called: Domain Hotel, The
1085 E El Camino Real, Sunnyvale (94087-3755)
PHONE..................408 247-0800
Justin Hart, *General Mgr*
EMP: 36 **EST:** 2017
SALES (est): 973.3K **Privately Held**
WEB: www.domainhotelsv.com
SIC: 7011 Hotels

(P-10912)
AJPJ II LLC
Also Called: Marriott
1140 Airport Park Blvd, Ukiah (95482-5997)
PHONE..................707 972-9563
Anil Bhula,
EMP: 143 **EST:** 1998
SALES (est): 1.4MM **Privately Held**
WEB: www.fairfield.marriott.com
SIC: 7011 Hotels & motels

(P-10913)
ALAMEDA HOSPITALITY LLC
Also Called: Hawthorn Suites
1628 Webster St, Alameda (94501-2134)
PHONE..................510 522-1000
Sandip B Jariwala, *Mng Member*
Archana S Jariwala,
EMP: 44 **EST:** 2003
SQ FT: 31,000
SALES (est): 4.7MM **Privately Held**
WEB: www.oaklandhs.com
SIC: 7011 7389 Hotels & motels; office facilities & secretarial service rental

(P-10914)
ALBION RIVER INN INCORPORATED
3790 N Highway 1, Albion (95410-9781)
P.O. Box 100 (95410-0100)
PHONE..................707 937-1919
Peter Wells, *President*
Flurry Healy, *Vice Pres*
EMP: 56 **EST:** 1979
SQ FT: 15,000
SALES (est): 1.5MM **Privately Held**
WEB: www.albionriverinn.com
SIC: 7011 Bed & breakfast inn

(P-10915)
ALOFT HOTEL SANTA CLARA
510 America Ctr Ct, Alviso (95002)
PHONE..................408 263-3900
Angelina Gibbs, *Sales Staff*
Teresa Soliz, *Supervisor*
EMP: 114 **EST:** 2017
SALES (est): 2.9MM **Privately Held**
WEB: www.marriott.com
SIC: 7011 Resort hotel

(P-10916)
ALOFT HT SAN FRANCISCO ARPRT
401 E Millbrae Ave, Millbrae (94030-3111)
PHONE..................650 443-5500
Jason Kwan, *Principal*
EMP: 60 **EST:** 2018
SALES (est): 3.1MM **Privately Held**
WEB: www.marriott.com
SIC: 7011 Hotels

(P-10917)
ALOFT SILICON VALLEY
8200 Gateway Blvd, Newark (94560-8000)
PHONE..................510 494-8800
Gregory Pearson, *President*
Jaime Puga, *Engineer*
Jason Ransom, *Director*
Veronica Celaya, *Supervisor*
EMP: 67 **EST:** 2016
SALES (est): 6.1MM **Privately Held**
WEB: www.marriott.com
SIC: 7011 Hotels

(P-10918)
ALPINE MEADOWS SKI AREA
Also Called: Alpine Meadows Ski Resort
2600 Alpine Meadows Rd, Alpine Meadows (96146-9854)
PHONE..................530 583-4232
John Cumming, *President*
Rick D Vaux, *CFO*

7011 - Hotels, Motels & Tourist Courts County (P-10919)

Nick Badami, *Admin Sec*
Christine Horvath, *Marketing Staff*
Jessica Richitelli, *Manager*
▲ **EMP:** 50 **EST:** 1959
SQ FT: 30,000
SALES (est): 11.8MM **Privately Held**
WEB: www.palisadestahoe.com
SIC: 7011 Ski lodge; resort hotel
HQ: The Squaw Valley Development Company
1960 Squaw Valley Rd
Olympic Valley CA 96146
530 452-6985

(P-10919)
ALPS GROUP INC
Also Called: Holiday Inn
1100 Cadillac Ct, Milpitas (95035-3056)
PHONE 760 500-4490
Saahil Khandwala, *President*
EMP: 35 **EST:** 2018
SALES (est): 1.5MM **Privately Held**
WEB: www.holidayinn.com
SIC: 7011 Hotels & motels

(P-10920)
ALTA MIRA RECOVERY CTRS LLC
Also Called: Alta Mira Hotel & Restaurant
125 Bulkley Ave, Sausalito (94965-2231)
PHONE 415 332-1350
Tom Adams, *Manager*
Ian Wolds, *Exec Dir*
Karen Spedowfski, *Director*
Phyllis Green, *Manager*
EMP: 89 **EST:** 1948
SQ FT: 5,000
SALES (est): 8.5MM **Privately Held**
WEB: www.altamirarecovery.com
SIC: 5812 7011 Eating places; bar (drinking places); hotels

(P-10921)
AMERICAN HOTEL INC
Also Called: Cardinal Hotel
235 Hamilton Ave, Palo Alto (94301-2530)
PHONE 650 323-5101
Stephanie Wansek, *Manager*
Bob Davis, *Manager*
EMP: 38 **EST:** 1924
SALES (est): 1.5MM **Privately Held**
WEB: www.cardinalhotel.com
SIC: 7011 Hotel, franchised; hotels

(P-10922)
AMERICAN PROPERTY MANAGEMENT
Also Called: Pleasanton Hilton Hotel
7050 Johnson Dr, Pleasanton (94588-3328)
PHONE 925 463-8000
Han-Ching Lin, *President*
Hui-Ying Chou, *Vice Pres*
EMP: 145 **EST:** 1985
SQ FT: 191,112
SALES (est): 8.2MM **Privately Held**
SIC: 7011 5813 5812 Resort hotel; drinking places; eating places

(P-10923)
AMIN-OAKLAND LLC
Also Called: Comfort Inn
8452 Edes Ave, Oakland (94621-1306)
PHONE 510 568-1500
Kanti Amin,
Mike Amin,
Urmilla Amin,
EMP: 40 **EST:** 1996
SQ FT: 65,000
SALES (est): 514K **Privately Held**
WEB: www.choicehotels.com
SIC: 7011 Hotels & motels

(P-10924)
ANDREWS HOTEL (PA)
624 Post St, San Francisco (94109-8222)
PHONE 415 563-6877
Harry Andrews, *Owner*
Cathy Cha, *General Mgr*
Raj Kapadia, *General Mgr*
EMP: 35 **EST:** 1966
SQ FT: 19,560
SALES (est): 1.6MM **Privately Held**
WEB: www.andrewshotel.info
SIC: 7011 6513 Hotels; apartment building operators

(P-10925)
ANKOOR FINANCIAL LLC
Also Called: Best Western Country
3930 County Rd 89, Dunnigan (95937)
P.O. Box 20836, San Jose (95160-0836)
PHONE 530 724-3471
Kishor Patel,
Ashwin Doshi,
Rajib Patel,
EMP: 42 **EST:** 2002
SALES (est): 369.4K **Privately Held**
WEB: www.bestwestern.com
SIC: 7011 Hotels & motels

(P-10926)
APPLE INNS INC
Also Called: Marina Inn
68 Monarch Bay Dr, San Leandro (94577-6427)
PHONE 510 895-1311
Audrey Velasquez, *Branch Mgr*
Peter Schultz, *President*
David Miller, *Vice Pres*
Michael Williams, *Manager*
EMP: 50 **EST:** 1985
SALES (est): 2.5MM **Privately Held**
WEB: www.slmarinainn.com
SIC: 7011 Motels

(P-10927)
APPLE SIX HOSPITALITY MGT
Also Called: Hilton Garden
670 Gateway Blvd, South San Francisco (94080-7014)
PHONE 650 872-1515
EMP: 40
SALES (est): 786.6K **Privately Held**
SIC: 7011 Hotels And Motels, Nsk

(P-10928)
ARETE HOTELS LLC
2229 Den Helder Dr, Modesto (95356-0729)
PHONE 209 602-7952
Kimberly Ali, *CEO*
Heather Houser, *Accountant*
EMP: 74 **EST:** 2017
SALES (est): 662.3K **Privately Held**
SIC: 7011 Resort hotel

(P-10929)
ARGONAUT HOTEL
495 Jefferson St, San Francisco (94109-1314)
PHONE 415 563-0800
Micheal Ditatie, *CEO*
Charlotte Dehaven, *Vice Pres*
Kathleen Reidenbach, *Vice Pres*
Joe Schwingler, *Vice Pres*
Celia Ghanem, *Finance*
EMP: 37 **EST:** 1998
SALES (est): 2.5MM **Privately Held**
WEB: www.argonauthotel.com
SIC: 7011 Resort hotel; hotels

(P-10930)
ART PICCADILLY SHAW LLC (PA)
Also Called: Piccadilly Inn Shaw
2305 W Shaw Ave, Fresno (93711-3411)
PHONE 559 348-5520
Ronald F Akin, *Manager*
EMP: 111 **EST:** 2004
SALES (est): 12.6MM **Privately Held**
WEB: www.hotel-piccadilly.com
SIC: 7011 Hotels

(P-10931)
ART PICCADILLY SHAW LLC
Also Called: Piccadilly Inn Airport
5115 E Mckinley Ave, Fresno (93727-2033)
PHONE 559 375-7760
Kathy Bell, *Branch Mgr*
EMP: 89
SALES (corp-wide): 12.6MM **Privately Held**
WEB: www.hotel-piccadilly.com
SIC: 7011 5813 5812 Hotels; drinking places; eating places
PA: Art Piccadilly Shaw Llc
2305 W Shaw Ave
Fresno CA 93711
559 348-5520

(P-10932)
ART PICCADILLY SHAW LLC
Piccadilly Inn-University
4961 N Cedar Ave, Fresno (93726-1062)
PHONE 559 224-4200
Theresa Cross, *Branch Mgr*
EMP: 89
SALES (corp-wide): 12.6MM **Privately Held**
WEB: www.hotel-piccadilly.com
SIC: 7011 Hotels
PA: Art Piccadilly Shaw Llc
2305 W Shaw Ave
Fresno CA 93711
559 348-5520

(P-10933)
ARVEE BROS INC
Also Called: Millwood Inn
1375 El Camino Real, Millbrae (94030-1410)
P.O. Box 970 (94030-0970)
PHONE 650 583-3935
Vijay R Patel, *President*
Reeta Patel, *Vice Pres*
EMP: 65 **EST:** 1953
SQ FT: 20,000
SALES (est): 1.6MM **Privately Held**
SIC: 7011 7389 Motels; office facilities & secretarial service rental

(P-10934)
ASHFORD TRS FREMONT LLC
Also Called: Fremont Marriott Silicon Vly
46100 Landing Pkwy, Fremont (94538-6437)
PHONE 510 413-3700
Deric Eubanks, *President*
EMP: 130 **EST:** 2019
SALES (est): 5.4MM **Privately Held**
WEB: www.marriott.com
SIC: 7011 Hotels & motels

(P-10935)
ATHARWA INVESTMENTS LLC
Also Called: Best Western
111 E March Ln, Stockton (95207-5854)
PHONE 209 474-3301
Ramesh Pitamber, *Mng Member*
Lucia Perez, *Manager*
EMP: 47 **EST:** 1985
SALES (est): 1MM **Privately Held**
WEB: www.bestwestern.com
SIC: 7011 Hotels & motels

(P-10936)
ATRIUM FINANCE I LP
Also Called: Holiday Inn
300 J St, Sacramento (95814-2210)
PHONE 916 446-0100
Liz Tavernese, *General Ptnr*
EMP: 297 **EST:** 2005
SALES (est): 2.5MM **Privately Held**
WEB: www.holidayinn.com
SIC: 7011 Hotels & motels
HQ: Atrium Hospitality Lp
12735 Morris Road Ext # 400
Alpharetta GA 30004
678 762-0005

(P-10937)
ATRIUM PLAZA LLC
Also Called: San Mateo Marriott
1770 S Amphlett Blvd, San Mateo (94402-2708)
PHONE 650 653-6000
Ron Anderhan,
Mario Urroz, *Info Tech Mgr*
Parwinder Kaur, *Finance*
Kathy Nicholl, *Human Res Dir*
Victor Acevedo, *Purch Agent*
EMP: 97 **EST:** 2000
SALES (est): 20MM **Privately Held**
WEB: www.marriott.com
SIC: 7011 Hotels

(P-10938)
AVR SAN JOSE DOWNTOWN HT LLC
Also Called: AC Hotel San Jose Downtown
350 W Santa Clara St, San Jose (95113-1501)
PHONE 408 924-0900
Mona Rigdon, *Principal*
Allan Rose, *Principal*
EMP: 60 **EST:** 2019

SALES (est): 2.9MM **Privately Held**
WEB: www.sanjose.org
SIC: 7011 Hotels

(P-10939)
AXIOM INC
Also Called: Axiom Hotel
28 Cyril Magnin St, San Francisco (94102-2838)
PHONE 415 392-9466
Garry Cox, *Principal*
Robel Seyoum, *Accounting Mgr*
Heiko Novak, *Marketing Staff*
Taylor Medina, *Sales Staff*
EMP: 45 **EST:** 2014
SALES (est): 3.3MM **Privately Held**
WEB: www.axiomhotel.com
SIC: 7011 Resort hotel; hotels

(P-10940)
B & W RESORT MARINA
964 Brannan Island Rd, Isleton (95641-9607)
PHONE 916 777-6161
Candice Kelp, *General Ptnr*
James A Deak, *Partner*
Joan Deak, *Partner*
Joseph Deak, *Partner*
Lewis Deak, *Partner*
EMP: 49 **EST:** 1946
SQ FT: 15,000
SALES (est): 1MM **Privately Held**
WEB: www.bandwresort.net
SIC: 7011 4493 Resort hotel; marinas

(P-10941)
B H R OPERATIONS LLC
Also Called: Crown Plaza
777 Bellew Dr, Milpitas (95035-7900)
PHONE 408 321-9500
Roy Escobar, *Mng Member*
Winnie Kwok, *General Mgr*
EMP: 5212 **EST:** 1987
SQ FT: 250,000
SALES (est): 2.2MM **Privately Held**
WEB: www.crowneplaza.com
SIC: 7011 Hotels
HQ: Bristol Hotel & Resorts Inc.
3 Ravinia Dr Ste 100
Atlanta GA 30346

(P-10942)
B K D HOLDINGS
Also Called: Hampton Inn
800 Mason St, Vacaville (95688-4643)
PHONE 650 704-3454
Divyefh B Patel, *Owner*
EMP: 36 **EST:** 1999
SALES (est): 826.8K **Privately Held**
WEB: www.hilton.com
SIC: 7011 Hotels & motels

(P-10943)
BALAJI ALAMEDA LLC
Also Called: Hampton Inn
1700 Harbor Bay Pkwy, Alameda (94502-3000)
PHONE 510 521-4500
Pravin Patel,
EMP: 35 **EST:** 2007
SALES (est): 1.5MM **Privately Held**
WEB: www.hilton.com
SIC: 7011 Hotels & motels

(P-10944)
BANCROFT CLUB
Also Called: Bancroft Hotel
2680 Bancroft Way, Berkeley (94704-1717)
PHONE 510 549-0152
Daryl Roff, *Owner*
Martin Ross, *Principal*
Scott Lorenz, *Manager*
EMP: 46 **EST:** 1993
SALES (est): 2.6MM **Privately Held**
WEB: www.bancrofthotel.com
SIC: 7011 Hotels

(P-10945)
BAVARIAN LION COMPANY CAL (PA)
Also Called: Flamingo Resort Hotel
2777 4th St, Santa Rosa (95405-4795)
PHONE 707 545-8530
Pierre Ehret, *President*
Roger Cardona, *Controller*

PRODUCTS & SERVICES SECTION

7011 - Hotels, Motels & Tourist Courts County (P-10970)

Dan Towers, *Sales Mgr*
Robert Bondanza, *Marketing Staff*
Ashley Barndt, *Sales Staff*
EMP: 200
SQ FT: 32,000
SALES (est): 15.2MM Privately Held
WEB: www.flamingoresort.com
SIC: 7011 7991 Resort hotel; health club

(P-10946) BEAR RIVER CASINO
Also Called: Bear River Casino Hotel
11 Bear Paws Way, Loleta (95551-9684)
PHONE 707 733-9644
John McGinnis, *Executive Asst*
Wendell Freeman, *Treasurer*
Edward Bowie, *Admin Sec*
Kevin Fox, *Administration*
Allen Rode, *Finance Dir*
EMP: 212 Privately Held
WEB: www.bearrivercasino.com
SIC: 7011 Casino hotel
PA: Bear River Casino
27 Bear River Dr
Loleta CA 95551

(P-10947) BEAR RIVER CASINO (PA)
Also Called: Bear River Gaming Agency
27 Bear River Dr, Loleta (95551-9646)
PHONE 707 733-9644
Crystal Ammons, *General Mgr*
John McGinnis, *General Mgr*
Scott Joachim, *Info Tech Dir*
Jesse Reeves, *Technical Staff*
Michelle August, *Financial Analy*
EMP: 74 **EST:** 2007
SQ FT: 5,000
SALES (est): 50MM Privately Held
WEB: www.bearrivercasino.com
SIC: 7011 Casino hotel

(P-10948) BEAR RIVER LAKE RESORT INC
Also Called: Gunter Enterprises
40800 State Highway 88, Pioneer (95666-9114)
PHONE 209 295-4868
Jon Frazier, *Partner*
Janette Frazier, *Partner*
Eddy Mc Intosh, *Partner*
Nancy Mc Intosh, *Partner*
EMP: 36 **EST:** 1966
SQ FT: 2,000
SALES (est): 812.8K Privately Held
WEB: www.bearrivercampground.com
SIC: 7011 7999 7699 Resort hotel; recreation equipment rental; snowmobile repair

(P-10949) BECKS MOTOR LODGE
2222 Market St, San Francisco (94114-1506)
PHONE 415 621-8212
Eugene Marty, *Partner*
Brittany Beck, *General Mgr*
EMP: 36 **EST:** 1937
SALES (est): 997.7K Privately Held
WEB: www.becksmotorlodge.com
SIC: 7011 Motels

(P-10950) BELMONT CORPORATION
Also Called: Best Western
901 Park Ave, South Lake Tahoe (96150-6938)
PHONE 530 542-1101
Wilson Williford, *President*
Eric Eyman, *Manager*
EMP: 83 **EST:** 1980
SALES (est): 1.5MM Privately Held
WEB: www.stationhouseinn.com
SIC: 7011 5012 Motels; automobiles & other motor vehicles

(P-10951) BERESFORD CORPORATION
Also Called: Beresford Arms, The
635 Sutter St, San Francisco (94102-1017)
PHONE 415 673-9900
Richard Osborn, *Branch Mgr*
EMP: 43
SALES (corp-wide): 5.3MM Privately Held
WEB: www.beresford.com
SIC: 7011 Hotels
PA: Beresford Corporation
582 Market St Ste 912
San Francisco CA 94104
415 981-7386

(P-10952) BERKELEY
2086 Allston Way, Berkeley (94704-1430)
PHONE 510 845-7300
Greg Maultin, *General Mgr*
Long Hu, *Research*
Catherine Supnet, *Marketing Staff*
EMP: 42 **EST:** 1998
SALES (est): 1.6MM Privately Held
WEB: www.berkeley.edu
SIC: 7011 Hotels & motels

(P-10953) BERKELEY DOWNTOWN HT OWNER LLC ✪
Also Called: Residnce Inn By Mrriot Brkeley
2121 Center St, Berkeley (94704)
PHONE 510 982-2100
Bruce Carlton, *Mng Member*
EMP: 75 **EST:** 2021
SALES (est): 233.5K Privately Held
SIC: 7011 Hotel, franchised

(P-10954) BEST WESTERN BAYSHORE INN
3500 Broadway, Eureka (95503-3810)
PHONE 707 268-8005
Mark Watson, *President*
Emily Manfredonia, *General Mgr*
EMP: 50 **EST:** 1997
SALES (est): 2.6MM Privately Held
WEB: www.bestwestern.com
SIC: 7011 Motels

(P-10955) BEST WESTERN CIVIC CTR MTR INN
364 9th St, San Francisco (94103-3836)
PHONE 415 621-2826
Hiten Patel, *Owner*
Eugene Marty, *Owner*
EMP: 49 **EST:** 1957
SQ FT: 12,000
SALES (est): 404.3K Privately Held
WEB: www.staysf.com
SIC: 7011 5812 Hotels & motels; coffee shop

(P-10956) BEST WESTERN HOTEL TOMO
1800 Sutter St, San Francisco (94115-3220)
PHONE 415 921-4000
Sean Salera, *CFO*
EMP: 48 **EST:** 2007
SALES (est): 1.2MM Privately Held
WEB: www.bestwestern.com
SIC: 7011 Hotels & motels
PA: Khp Iii Sf Sutter Llc
1800 Sutter St
San Francisco CA 94115
415 921-4000

(P-10957) BEST WESTERN INN INC
6020 Scotts Valley Dr, Scotts Valley (95066-3234)
PHONE 831 438-6666
Praful Patel, *President*
Robert Hogan, *President*
EMP: 35 **EST:** 1985
SQ FT: 25,600
SALES (est): 649K Privately Held
WEB: www.bestwestern.com
SIC: 7011 Hotels & motels

(P-10958) BEST WESTERN PLUS-HERITAGE INN
Also Called: Holiday Inn
111 E March Ln, Stockton (95207-5854)
PHONE 209 474-3301
Ganatra Vasant, *Mng Member*
EMP: 68 **EST:** 1999
SALES (est): 650.1K Privately Held
WEB: www.bestwestern.com
SIC: 7011 Hotels & motels

(P-10959) BEST WESTERN SILICON VLY INN
600 N Mathilda Ave, Sunnyvale (94085-3508)
PHONE 408 735-7800
Vimal Kumar, *President*
EMP: 44 **EST:** 1994
SQ FT: 50,000
SALES (est): 929.1K Privately Held
WEB: www.bestwesternsiliconvalley.com
SIC: 7011 Hotels & motels

(P-10960) BHR OPERATIONS LLC
Also Called: Holiday Inn
495 Bay St, San Francisco (94133-1860)
PHONE 415 771-9000
Sheila Martin, *General Mgr*
EMP: 103
SALES (corp-wide): 473MM Privately Held
WEB: www.holidayinn.com
SIC: 7011 Hotels & motels
HQ: Bhr Operations, L.L.C.
125 E John Carpenter Fwy
Irving TX 75062
972 444-4900

(P-10961) BHR TRS TAHOE LLC
Also Called: Ritz-Carlton Lake Tahoe, The
13031 Ritz Crlton Hghlnds, Truckee (96161-4306)
PHONE 530 562-3045
Chris Stevens, *Asst Mgr*
Tysen Gregersen, *Exec Dir*
Jennifer Sawyer, *Accountant*
Jodi Demko, *Sales Staff*
Natasha Bugosh, *Senior Mgr*
EMP: 248 **EST:** 2018
SALES (est): 20.5MM
SALES (corp-wide): 226.9MM Privately Held
WEB: www.ritzcarlton.com
SIC: 7011 Hotels
PA: Braemar Hotels & Resorts Inc.
14185 Dallas Pkwy # 1100
Dallas TX 75254
972 490-9600

(P-10962) BIG RIVER LTD-DESIGN
Also Called: Big River Lodge
44850 Comptche Ukiah Rd, Mendocino (95460-9007)
P.O. Box 487 (95460-0487)
PHONE 707 937-5615
Jeff Stanford, *Co-Owner*
Joan Stanford, *Co-Owner*
Claire Amanno, *Agent*
Alana Joaquin, *Agent*
EMP: 51 **EST:** 1968
SQ FT: 40,000
SALES (est): 7.8MM Privately Held
WEB: www.stanfordinn.com
SIC: 7011 5551 5941 5261 Resort hotel; canoes; kayaks; bicycle & bicycle parts; surfing equipment & supplies; nursery stock, seeds & bulbs; antiques; bathing suits; marine apparel

(P-10963) BLUE LAKE CASINO
777 Casino Way Blue Lk Blue Lake, Blue Lake (95525)
P.O. Box 1128 (95525-1128)
PHONE 707 668-5101
Eric Ramos, *President*
Michael Shackelford, *Manager*
Jennifer Wood, *Supervisor*
EMP: 100 **EST:** 2012
SALES (est): 6MM Privately Held
WEB: www.bluelakecasino.com
SIC: 7011 Casino hotel

(P-10964) BNP LODGING LLC
Also Called: Fresno Airport Hotel
1551 N Peach Ave, Fresno (93727-8507)
PHONE 559 251-5200
James Evans,
Ginka Petrova, *Opers Mgr*
EMP: 36 **EST:** 2007
SALES (est): 1.4MM Privately Held
SIC: 7011 Hotels

(P-10965) BODEGA BAY ASSOCIATES
Also Called: Bodega Bay Lodge
1100 Alma St Ste 106, Bodega Bay (94923)
PHONE 650 330-8888
Ellis J Alden,
EMP: 53 **EST:** 1971
SALES (est): 1.1MM Privately Held
WEB: www.bodegabaylodge.com
SIC: 7011 Motels

(P-10966) BONANZA INN MAGNUSON GRAND HT
1001 Clark Ave, Yuba City (95991-3399)
PHONE 530 674-8824
Rick Mangu, *Principal*
EMP: 71 **EST:** 1963
SQ FT: 80,000
SALES (est): 5.2MM Privately Held
SIC: 5812 7011 5813 Steak restaurant; hotels & motels; drinking places

(P-10967) BOREAL RIDGE CORPORATION
Also Called: Boreal Ski Area
19749 Boreal Ridge Rd, Soda Springs (95728)
P.O. Box 39, Truckee (96160-0039)
PHONE 530 426-1012
John Cumming, *President*
Jodi Church, *Vice Pres*
EMP: 110 **EST:** 1964
SQ FT: 10,000
SALES (est): 11.5MM
SALES (corp-wide): 325MM Privately Held
WEB: www.powdr.com
SIC: 7011 7999 Ski lodge; hotels; ski rental concession
PA: Powdr Corp.
1794 Olympic Pkwy Ste 210
Park City UT 84098
435 658-5500

(P-10968) BOURDOLAN 25 LUSK LLC
25 Lusk St, San Francisco (94107-7000)
PHONE 415 495-5875
Matthew Dolan,
Chad Bourdon, *Partner*
Cezar Kusik, *Partner*
EMP: 41 **EST:** 2010
SALES (est): 5.2MM Privately Held
WEB: www.25lusk.com
SIC: 7011 Hotels

(P-10969) BOYKIN MGT CO LTD LBLTY CO
Also Called: Radisson Inn
200 Marina Blvd, Berkeley (94710-1608)
PHONE 510 548-7920
Neil Pasan, *Manager*
EMP: 73
SALES (corp-wide): 38.6MM Privately Held
WEB: www.boykin.com
SIC: 7011 5812 5813 Hotels & motels; eating places; drinking places
PA: Boykin Management Company Limited Liability Company
8015 W Kenton Cir Ste 220
Huntersville NC 28078
704 896-2880

(P-10970) BRE SELECT HOTELS OPER LLC
Also Called: Hilton
1951 Taylor Rd, Roseville (95661-3008)
PHONE 916 773-7171
Jenn Mertz, *General Mgr*
EMP: 35
SALES (corp-wide): 241.3MM Privately Held
WEB: www.hiltongrandvacations.com
SIC: 7011 Hotels & motels

7011 - Hotels, Motels & Tourist Courts County (P-10971)

HQ: Bre Select Hotels Operating Llc
501 E Camino Real
Boca Raton FL 33432
973 503-9733

(P-10971)
BRE SELECT HOTELS OPER LLC
Also Called: Hilton
221 Iron Point Rd, Folsom (95630-9001)
PHONE 916 353-1717
Tracy Kopshy, *General Mgr*
EMP: 38
SALES (corp-wide): 241.3MM **Privately Held**
WEB: www.hiltongrandvacations.com
SIC: 7011 Hotels & motels
HQ: Bre Select Hotels Operating Llc
501 E Camino Real
Boca Raton FL 33432
973 503-9733

(P-10972)
BRE/JAPANTOWN OWNER LLC
Also Called: Hotel Kabuki
1625 Post St, San Francisco (94115-3603)
PHONE 415 922-3200
Craig Walterman, *General Mgr*
EMP: 100 **EST:** 2014
SALES (est): 8.9MM **Privately Held**
SIC: 7011 Hotels

(P-10973)
BRIDGE BAY RESORT & MARINA
10300 Bridge Bay Rd, Redding (96003-9419)
PHONE 530 275-3021
Howard Weinberg,
EMP: 75 **EST:** 2013
SALES (est): 11.8MM
SALES (corp-wide): 12.7MM **Privately Held**
WEB: www.bridgebayhouseboats.com
SIC: 7011 Resort hotel
PA: Peloria Marinas Investors Llc
2550 Via Tejon Ste 2b
Palos Verdes Estates CA 90274
310 363-7775

(P-10974)
BRISTOL HOTEL
Also Called: Best Western-Bristol Hotel
3341 S Bascom Ave, San Jose (95124)
PHONE 408 559-3330
Yann De Fabrique, *General Mgr*
EMP: 38 **EST:** 2000
SALES (est): 157.6K **Privately Held**
WEB: www.bristol-hotel.com
SIC: 7011 Hotels

(P-10975)
BROADMOOR HOTEL (PA)
Also Called: The Broadmoore
1499 Sutter St, San Francisco (94109-5417)
PHONE 415 776-7034
Irene Lieberman, *President*
Samuel Johnson, *Finance*
◆ **EMP:** 75 **EST:** 1969
SALES (est): 9MM **Privately Held**
WEB: www.broadmoorsf.com
SIC: 7011 Resort hotel

(P-10976)
BROADMOOR HOTEL
Gaylord Suites
1465 65th St Apt 274, Emeryville (94608-1168)
PHONE 415 673-8445
Tony Daviduskis, *Branch Mgr*
Susan G Wilson, *President*
Cassie Hernandez, *Director*
EMP: 72
SQ FT: 85,619
SALES (corp-wide): 9MM **Privately Held**
WEB: www.broadmoorsf.com
SIC: 7011 6513 Resort hotel; apartment hotel operation
PA: Broadmoor Hotel
1499 Sutter St
San Francisco CA 94109
415 776-7034

(P-10977)
BROADMOOR HOTEL
Also Called: Granada Hotel
1000 Sutter St, San Francisco (94109-5818)
PHONE 415 673-2511
Tony Daviduskis, *Manager*
EMP: 72
SALES (corp-wide): 9MM **Privately Held**
WEB: www.broadmoorsf.com
SIC: 7011 Resort hotel
PA: Broadmoor Hotel
1499 Sutter St
San Francisco CA 94109
415 776-7034

(P-10978)
BROMLEY PROPERTIES INC
Also Called: Best Western
1500 Santa Rosa Ave, Santa Rosa (95404-5428)
PHONE 707 546-4031
Donald H Bromley, *President*
Donna Renteria, *General Mgr*
EMP: 51 **EST:** 1971
SALES (est): 784.5K **Privately Held**
WEB: www.thegardeninn.com
SIC: 7011 5812 Motels; American restaurant

(P-10979)
BROOKDALE INN AND SPA
11570 Highway 9, Brookdale (95007-3009)
PHONE 831 588-6609
Pravin Patel, *Principal*
EMP: 57 **EST:** 1978
SQ FT: 110,000
SALES (est): 994.1K **Privately Held**
WEB: www.brookdalelodge.com
SIC: 7011 5813 5812 7389 Vacation lodges; cocktail lounge; eating places; convention & show services; wedding chapel, privately operated

(P-10980)
BUENA VISTA GAMING AUTHORITY
Also Called: Harrah's Northern California
4640 Coal Mine Rd, Ione (95640-9626)
PHONE 866 915-0777
JC Rieger, *General Mgr*
Rhad Reckamp, *Finance Dir*
EMP: 420 **EST:** 2019
SALES (est): 19.7MM **Privately Held**
SIC: 7011 Casino hotel

(P-10981)
BWDIXON LLC (PA)
1345 Commercial Way, Dixon (95620-2025)
PHONE 707 678-1400
Bharat Patel, *CEO*
EMP: 39 **EST:** 2017
SALES (est): 486.9K **Privately Held**
WEB: www.bestwesterndixon.com
SIC: 7011 Hotels

(P-10982)
CACHE CREEK CASINO RESORT
14455 State Highway 16, Brooks (95606-9707)
P.O. Box 65 (95606-0065)
PHONE 530 796-3118
Mark Pirruccello, *CFO*
Stephen Bailey, *Vice Pres*
Wendy Carter, *Vice Pres*
Bill Harland, *Vice Pres*
Kathleen Jackson, *Vice Pres*
EMP: 2000 **EST:** 2007
SALES (est): 105.7MM **Privately Held**
WEB: www.cachecreek.com
SIC: 7011 Casino hotel
PA: Yocha Dehe Wintun Nation, California
18960 County Rd 75 A
Brooks CA 95606
530 796-3400

(P-10983)
CALIFORNIA VACATION CLUB
Also Called: Riverpoint
500 Lincoln Ave, NAPA (94558-3611)
PHONE 707 252-4200
Don Wudtke, *President*
EMP: 39 **EST:** 1997
SALES (est): 789.2K **Privately Held**
WEB: www.riverpointeresort.com
SIC: 7011 Resort hotel

(P-10984)
CALIFRNIA PROPERTY OWNERS ASSN
Also Called: CALIFORNIA PINES LODGE
750 Shasta View Dr, Alturas (96101-7669)
PHONE 530 233-5842
Hank Drury, *Administration*
Robert H Ridenour, *President*
Edwin Price, *General Mgr*
Ed Price, *Manager*
EMP: 36 **EST:** 1968
SALES (est): 1.4MM **Privately Held**
WEB: www.californiapinespoa.org
SIC: 7011 Resort hotel

(P-10985)
CAMINO REAL GROUP LLC
Also Called: Aloft Mountain View
840 E El Camino Real, Mountain View (94040-2808)
PHONE 650 964-1700
Garrett Ritter,
Alexandra Tang, *General Mgr*
EMP: 50 **EST:** 1998
SALES (est): 1.2MM **Privately Held**
WEB: www.aloft-hotels-marriott.com
SIC: 7011 Hotels & motels

(P-10986)
CAMPBELL HHG HOTEL DEV LLP
Also Called: Courtyard By Mrrott San Jose C
655 Creekside Way, Campbell (95008-0636)
PHONE 408 626-9590
Brian Fox, *Managing Prtnr*
EMP: 57 **EST:** 2008
SALES (est): 1.1MM **Privately Held**
WEB: www.courtyard.marriott.com
SIC: 7011 7389 Hotels & motels; office facilities & secretarial service rental

(P-10987)
CANTERBURY HOTEL CORP
Also Called: Wyndham Cntrbury At San Frncsc
750 Sutter St, San Francisco (94109-6417)
PHONE 415 345-3200
Dean Lehr, *President*
Jacqueline W Lehr, *Ch of Bd*
Frederick T Smith, *Treasurer*
Jon Lehr, *Vice Pres*
EMP: 89 **EST:** 1932
SQ FT: 98,410
SALES (est): 4.5MM **Privately Held**
WEB: www.clubwyndham.wyndhamdestinations.com
SIC: 7011 5812 6531 Resort hotel; eating places; time-sharing real estate sales, leasing & rentals

(P-10988)
CAPITOL REGENCY LLC
Also Called: Hyatt Regency Sacramento
1209 L St, Sacramento (95814-3936)
PHONE 916 443-1234
Randy Verrue,
Brenda Kirian, *Sales Dir*
EMP: 360 **EST:** 1996
SALES (est): 24.8MM **Privately Held**
WEB: www.hyatt.com
SIC: 7011 Hotels & motels

(P-10989)
CARLTON HT PRPTS A CAL LTD PRT
1075 Sutter St, San Francisco (94109-5817)
PHONE 415 673-0242
Diane Feinstein, *Partner*
Richard Blum, *Partner*
Eileen Gartland, *Partner*
EMP: 83 **EST:** 1957
SQ FT: 76,000
SALES (est): 1.8MM **Privately Held**
SIC: 7011 5812 Hotels; eating places

(P-10990)
CARNEROS INN LLC
Also Called: Poumtjack Hotels
4048 Sonoma Hwy, NAPA (94559-9745)
PHONE 707 299-4880
Keith Rogal, *CEO*
Nick Monroe, *CFO*
Jonathan Vail, *Info Tech Mgr*
Christal Giomi, *Accounting Mgr*
Ariel Kirk, *Accountant*
EMP: 350
SQ FT: 50,000
SALES (est): 22.1MM **Privately Held**
WEB: www.thecarnerosinn.com
SIC: 7011 Resort hotel; hotels

(P-10991)
CARSON HOUSE INN
1209 4th St, Eureka (95501-0634)
PHONE 707 443-1601
Jack Mac Donald, *Partner*
Linda Mac Donald, *Partner*
EMP: 47 **EST:** 1964
SALES (est): 558.4K **Privately Held**
WEB: www.carterhouse.com
SIC: 7011 Motels

(P-10992)
CARTWRIGHT HOTEL
524 Sutter St, San Francisco (94102-1102)
PHONE 415 421-2865
Fred Wrapp, *Manager*
Steve Viscio, *General Mgr*
Ronnie Navas, *Manager*
EMP: 50 **EST:** 1916
SQ FT: 37,865
SALES (est): 1MM **Privately Held**
WEB: www.cartwrightunionsquare.com
SIC: 7011 Hotels

(P-10993)
CASA MADRONA HOTEL AND SPA LLC
801 Bridgeway, Sausalito (94965-2186)
PHONE 415 332-0502
John W Mays, *Executive*
Stefan Muhle, *General Mgr*
Brian Kelley, *Controller*
Jeremy Gaunt, *Human Res Mgr*
Darren Oliver, *Marketing Staff*
EMP: 1926 **EST:** 1951
SQ FT: 18,000
SALES (est): 8.7MM **Privately Held**
WEB: www.casamadrona.com
SIC: 7011 5812 Hotels; eating places
PA: Olympus Real Estate Corp
5080 Spectrum Dr
Addison TX 75001

(P-10994)
CASINO REAL INC
Also Called: Casino Real Card Room
1355 N Main St, Manteca (95336-3212)
PHONE 209 239-1455
Ernie Schmiedt, *Owner*
Dennis Williams, *General Mgr*
EMP: 39 **EST:** 1980
SALES (est): 1.1MM **Privately Held**
WEB: www.thecasinoreal.com
SIC: 7011 Casino hotel

(P-10995)
CASTLEHILL PROPERTIES INC (PA)
Also Called: Residnce Inn By Mrrott Stcktn
3240 W March Ln, Stockton (95219-2341)
PHONE 209 472-9800
Jeff Carpenter, *General Mgr*
EMP: 55 **EST:** 1997
SALES (est): 8.7MM **Privately Held**
WEB: www.residence-inn.marriott.com
SIC: 7011 Hotels & motels

(P-10996)
CASTLEHILL PROPERTIES INC
Also Called: Courtyard By Marriott Stockton
3252 W March Ln, Stockton (95219-2341)
PHONE 209 472-9700
Shawn Williams, *Manager*
EMP: 45
SALES (corp-wide): 8.7MM **Privately Held**
WEB: www.courtyard.marriott.com
SIC: 7011 Hotels & motels

PRODUCTS & SERVICES SECTION

7011 - Hotels, Motels & Tourist Courts County (P-11021)

PA: Castlehill Properties, Inc.
3240 W March Ln
Stockton CA 95219
209 472-9800

(P-10997)
CAVALLO POINT LLC (PA)
601 Murray Cir, Sausalito (94965)
PHONE 415 339-4700
Peter Heinmann, *Partner*
Brad Jacobs, *CEO*
Brendan Carlin, *Officer*
Lonny Watne, *Branch Mgr*
Dane Jackson, *Info Tech Dir*
EMP: 72 EST: 2007
SALES (est): 11MM **Privately Held**
WEB: www.cavallopoint.com
SIC: 7011 Hotels

(P-10998)
CB-1 HOTEL
Also Called: Four Seasons Hotel
757 Market St, San Francisco
(94103-2001)
PHONE 415 633-3838
Douglas Housley, *General Mgr*
Richard Barnes, *CIO*
Marian Luk, *Accountant*
Farrell Williams, *Sales Mgr*
Katie Distefano, *Sales Staff*
EMP: 99 EST: 2005
SQ FT: 59,300
SALES (est): 8.2MM **Privately Held**
SIC: 7011 Hotels

(P-10999)
CDC SAN FRANCISCO LLC
Also Called: Intercontinental San Francisco
888 Howard St, San Francisco
(94103-3011)
PHONE 415 616-6512
Peter Koehler,
Vivian Gonzales, *Manager*
Jose Pineda, *Manager*
EMP: 99 EST: 2007
SALES (est): 7.9MM **Privately Held**
WEB: www.icsanfrancisco.com
SIC: 7011 Hotels

(P-11000)
CH CUPERTINO OWNER LLC
Also Called: Cypress Hotel
10050 S De Anza Blvd, Cupertino
(95014-2128)
PHONE 408 253-8900
David Hayes, *Marketing Staff*
EMP: 64 EST: 2007
SALES (est): 2.8MM **Privately Held**
SIC: 7011 Hotels

(P-11001)
CHAMINADE LTD
Also Called: Chaminade At Santa Cruz
1 Chaminade Ln, Santa Cruz (95065-1524)
PHONE 831 475-5600
Tom O'Shea, *General Mgr*
James Birpo, *General Ptnr*
James Greggs, *General Ptnr*
Don Murchanson, *General Ptnr*
Scott Stillinger, *Human Resources*
EMP: 200 EST: 1979
SQ FT: 12,000
SALES (est): 10.3MM **Privately Held**
WEB: www.chaminade.com
SIC: 7011 Resort hotel

(P-11002)
CHANCELLOR HOTEL ASSOCIATES A
433 Powell St, San Francisco
(94102-1586)
PHONE 415 362-2004
Edgar Ross, *Partner*
Joseph Lacavera, *General Mgr*
Dan Boling, *Chief Engr*
Renato Marcos, *Controller*
Roanna McDaniel, *Sales Mgr*
EMP: 40 EST: 1938
SALES (est): 3.5MM **Privately Held**
WEB: www.chancellorhotel.com
SIC: 7011 5812 5813 Hotels; eating places; cocktail lounge

(P-11003)
CHESAPEAKE LODGING TRUST
Also Called: Le Meridien Hotel
333 Battery St Lbby, San Francisco
(94111-3234)
PHONE 415 296-2900
Joel Myers, *Director*
Craig Martin, *General Mgr*
Amgad Andrawos, *Finance*
Lisa Christiansen, *Finance*
Jorge Silva, *Finance*
EMP: 153 EST: 2007
SALES (est): 19.8MM **Privately Held**
WEB: www.le-meridien.marriott.com
SIC: 7011 7021 Hotels; lodging house, except organization

(P-11004)
CHICO LODGING LLC
Also Called: Courtyard Chico
2481 Carmichael Dr, Chico (95928-7132)
PHONE 318 635-8000
Megan Riley, *Principal*
EMP: 43
SALES (corp-wide): 1.1MM **Privately Held**
WEB: www.courtyardinchico.com
SIC: 7011 Hotels & motels
PA: Chico Lodging, L.L.C.
2390 Tower Dr
Monroe LA 71201
318 325-5561

(P-11005)
CHICO LODGING LLC
Also Called: Residence Inn Chico
2485 Carmichael Dr, Chico (95928-7132)
PHONE 530 894-5500
Dewey F Weaver Jr, *Branch Mgr*
EMP: 43
SALES (corp-wide): 1.1MM **Privately Held**
SIC: 7011 Hotels & motels
PA: Chico Lodging, L.L.C.
2390 Tower Dr
Monroe LA 71201
318 325-5561

(P-11006)
CHINA PEAK MOUNTAIN RESORT LLC
59265 Hwy 168, Lakeshore (93634)
P.O. Box 236 (93634-0236)
PHONE 559 233-2500
Tim Cohee, *CEO*
Rich Bailey, *Manager*
Roger Myers, *Manager*
Katrina Cross, *Supervisor*
EMP: 53 EST: 2010
SALES (est): 6.1MM **Privately Held**
WEB: www.skichinapeak.com
SIC: 7011 Resort hotel

(P-11007)
CHSP TRS FISHERMAN WHARF LLC
Also Called: Hyatt Fshrmans Wharf San Frncs
555 N Point St, San Francisco
(94133-1311)
PHONE 415 563-1234
Thomas Baltimore,
Matheaw Dicello,
Michael Kapoulis,
EMP: 500 EST: 2013
SALES (est): 31.1MM
SALES (corp-wide): 852MM **Publicly Held**
SIC: 7011 5813 5812 Hotels & motels; bars & lounges; eating places
HQ: Pk Domestic Sub Llc
4300 Wilson Blvd Ste 625
Arlington VA 22203

(P-11008)
CHUKCHANSI GOLD RESORT CASINO
711 Lucky Ln, Coarsegold (93614-8206)
PHONE 866 794-6946
Richard Williams, *Owner*
Elaine McFarland, *Social Dir*
Tim Bos, *Security Dir*
Robert St Onge, *Administration*
Lewis Chenot, *Business Anlyst*
EMP: 1400 EST: 2010
SQ FT: 489,000
SALES (est): 87.9MM **Privately Held**
WEB: www.chukchansigold.com
SIC: 7011 Casino hotel

(P-11009)
CIM/OAKLAND CITY CENTER LLC
Also Called: City Center Grill
1001 Broadway, Oakland (94607-4019)
PHONE 510 451-4000
John Mazzoni, *Manager*
Avraham Shemesh, *Principal*
Keith Montgomery, *Controller*
EMP: 99 EST: 2006
SALES (est): 5.4MM **Privately Held**
WEB: www.oaklandca.gov
SIC: 7011 Hotels & motels

(P-11010)
CLAREMONT HOTEL PROPERTIES LLC
Also Called: Claremont Ht Prpts Ltd Partnr
41 Tunnel Rd, Berkeley (94705-2429)
PHONE 510 843-3000
Len Czarnecki,
Michael Coughlin, *Finance*
Ana Macario, *Sales Staff*
Ashlee Fairbanks, *Director*
Stacey Parks, *Director*
EMP: 550 EST: 2008
SALES (est): 40.6MM
SALES (corp-wide): 627.9MM **Privately Held**
WEB: www.claremontresort.com
SIC: 7011 Resort hotel; hotels
HQ: Accor Services Us Llc
950 Mason St
San Francisco CA 94108
415 772-5000

(P-11011)
CLARION HOTEL SAN JOSE AIRPORT
1355 N 4th St, San Jose (95112-4783)
PHONE 408 453-5340
Ajay Shingal,
Ram Garg,
Mira Shingal,
EMP: 41 EST: 2008
SALES (est): 692K **Privately Held**
SIC: 7011 Hotels

(P-11012)
CLARION INN
Also Called: Clarion Hotel
1050 Burnett Ave, Concord (94520-5713)
PHONE 925 566-8820
Santokh Singh, *Principal*
Mary Ann Rhoe, *Manager*
EMP: 37 EST: 2011
SALES (est): 1.8MM **Privately Held**
WEB: www.choicehotels.com
SIC: 7011 Hotels & motels

(P-11013)
CLARION RESORT
2223 4th St, Eureka (95501-0820)
PHONE 707 442-3261
Scott Feil, *Owner*
EMP: 37 EST: 1992
SALES (est): 511.5K **Privately Held**
WEB: www.choicehotels.com
SIC: 7011 Hotels & motels

(P-11014)
CLAUDE LAMBERT
Also Called: Cornell Hotel
715 Bush St, San Francisco (94108-3402)
PHONE 415 421-3154
Claude Lambert, *Owner*
EMP: 65 EST: 1966
SQ FT: 18,720
SALES (est): 1.2MM **Privately Held**
WEB: www.cornellhotel.com
SIC: 7011 5812 Hotels; eating places

(P-11015)
CLOVIS HOTELS INC
Also Called: Fairfield Inn
50 N Clovis Ave, Clovis (93612-0301)
PHONE 559 323-8080
Dave Virk, *President*
EMP: 35 EST: 2009 **Privately Held**
WEB: www.fairfield.marriott.com
SIC: 7011 Hotels & motels

(P-11016)
CLUB ONE CASINO INC
3950 N Cedar Ave Ste 101, Fresno
(93726-5273)
PHONE 559 497-3000
Kyle R Kirkland, *President*
George Sarantos, *President*
Nicholas Johnson, *Info Tech Dir*
Jeremy Newman, *Mktg Dir*
EMP: 325 EST: 1995
SALES (est): 11.3MM **Privately Held**
WEB: www.clubonecasino.com
SIC: 7011 Casino hotel

(P-11017)
CLUB QUARTERS SAN FRANCISCO
424 Clay St, San Francisco (94111-3207)
PHONE 415 268-3606
Sanj Rai, *Manager*
Joeann La Madrid, *Sales Executive*
EMP: 38 EST: 2003
SALES (est): 765.4K **Privately Held**
SIC: 7011 Hotels

(P-11018)
CMP I FREMONT OWNER LP
Also Called: Courtyard Fremont Silicon Vly
47000 Lakeview Blvd, Fremont
(94538-6542)
PHONE 510 656-1800
Kerry Schiewek, *General Mgr*
Kerry Sehiewek, *General Mgr*
EMP: 55 EST: 2010
SALES (est): 988.3K
SALES (corp-wide): 196.3MM **Privately Held**
WEB: www.marriott.com
SIC: 7011 Hotels & motels
PA: Cmp I Owner-T, Llc
399 Park Ave Fl 18
New York NY 10022
212 547-2609

(P-11019)
CNCML A CALIFORNIA LTD PARTNR
Also Called: Plumpjack The
1920 Squaw Valley Rd, Olympic Valley
(96146-1030)
P.O. Box 2407 (96146-2407)
PHONE 530 583-1578
Hilary Newsom, *President*
Jeremy Scherer, *Vice Pres*
Milham D Wakin, *Vice Pres*
Steve Lamb, *General Mgr*
Patty Lewis, *Executive Asst*
EMP: 100 EST: 1975
SQ FT: 20,000
SALES (est): 5.2MM **Privately Held**
WEB: www.plumpjackinn.com
SIC: 7011 5812 Resort hotel; eating places

(P-11020)
CNI THL OPS LLC
Also Called: Fairfield Inn Roseville
1910 Taylor Rd, Roseville (95661-3008)
PHONE 916 772-3500
Jasmine Allop, *Manager*
EMP: 70
SALES (corp-wide): 9.6MM **Privately Held**
WEB: www.fairfield.marriott.com
SIC: 7011 Hotels
PA: Cni Thl Ops, Llc
515 S Flower St Fl 44
Los Angeles CA

(P-11021)
CNI THL OPS LLC
Also Called: Four Points Pleasanton
5115 Hopyard Rd, Pleasanton
(94588-3303)
PHONE 925 460-8800
Mona Rigdon, *Principal*
Keon Marvasti, *Principal*
Tom Buckley, *General Mgr*
EMP: 35 EST: 2017
SALES (est): 1.2MM **Privately Held**
WEB: www.marriott.com
SIC: 7011 Hotels & motels

7011 - Hotels, Motels & Tourist Courts County (P-11022)

(P-11022)
CNI THL OPS LLC
Also Called: Hampton Inn Rancho Cordova
10755 Gold Center Dr, Gold River
(95670-6038)
PHONE..................916 638-4800
Keon Marvasti, *Manager*
EMP: 70
SALES (corp-wide): 9.6MM **Privately Held**
WEB: www.hilton.com
SIC: **7011** Hotels & motels
PA: Cni Thl Ops, Llc
  515 S Flower St Fl 44
  Los Angeles CA

(P-11023)
CNI THL OPS LLC
Also Called: Courtyard Morgan Hill
18610 Madrone Pkwy, Morgan Hill
(95037-2837)
PHONE..................408 782-6034
Keon Marvasti, *Manager*
EMP: 70
SQ FT: 49,493
SALES (corp-wide): 9.6MM **Privately Held**
WEB: www.marriott.com
SIC: **7011** Hotels & motels
PA: Cni Thl Ops, Llc
  515 S Flower St Fl 44
  Los Angeles CA

(P-11024)
CNI THL OPS LLC
Also Called: Courtyard Roseville 2
301 Creekside Ridge Ct, Roseville
(95678-1994)
PHONE..................916 772-3404
Keon Marvasti, *Manager*
EMP: 35
SALES (corp-wide): 9.6MM **Privately Held**
WEB: www.marriott.com
SIC: **7011** Hotels & motels
PA: Cni Thl Ops, Llc
  515 S Flower St Fl 44
  Los Angeles CA

(P-11025)
CNI THL OPS LLC
Also Called: Courtyard Folsom
2575 Iron Point Rd, Folsom (95630-8708)
PHONE..................916 984-7624
Keon Marvasti, *Manager*
EMP: 35
SALES (corp-wide): 9.6MM **Privately Held**
WEB: www.ryanandholland.com
SIC: **7011** Hotel, franchised
PA: Cni Thl Ops, Llc
  515 S Flower St Fl 44
  Los Angeles CA

(P-11026)
COLUMBIA CITY HOTEL LLC
Also Called: Fallon Hotel
22768 Main St, Columbia (95310-9401)
P.O. Box 29041, Phoenix AZ (85038-9041)
PHONE..................209 532-5341
Dave Wood, *Manager*
EMP: 48 EST: 1856
SQ FT: 17,000
SALES (est): 1.1MM **Privately Held**
SIC: **7011** 5813 Hotels; bar (drinking places)

(P-11027)
COLUMBIA HOSPITALITY INC
665 Bush St, San Francisco (94108-3510)
PHONE..................415 362-8878
S C Huang, *Branch Mgr*
EMP: 89
SALES (corp-wide): 114.5MM **Privately Held**
WEB: www.bellharbor.com
SIC: **7011** Hotels
PA: Columbia Hospitality Inc
  2200 Alaskan Way Ste 200
  Seattle WA 98121
  206 441-6666

(P-11028)
COMFORT CALIFORNIA INC
Also Called: Comfort Inn
2775 Van Ness Ave, San Francisco
(94109-1423)
PHONE..................415 928-5000
Todd Symynuk, *Branch Mgr*
EMP: 149
SALES (corp-wide): 91.4MM **Privately Held**
WEB: www.choicehotels.com
SIC: **7011** Hotels & motels
HQ: Comfort California, Inc.
  8171 Maple Lawn Blvd # 380
  Fulton MD 20759

(P-11029)
COMFORT SUITES
Also Called: Comfort Inn
121 E Grand Ave, South San Francisco
(94080-4800)
PHONE..................650 589-7100
David R Lane, *CFO*
Steven Nokes, *Partner*
Richard Barnes, *CIO*
EMP: 45 EST: 2002
SQ FT: 5,000
SALES (est): 1.8MM **Privately Held**
WEB: www.sfosuites.com
SIC: **7011** Hotels & motels

(P-11030)
CONCEPT HOTELS LLC (PA)
260 Main St Ste E, Redwood City
(94063-1733)
PHONE..................650 600-8257
Bimal Patel, *President*
Maria Villanueva, *Manager*
EMP: 40 EST: 2015
SALES (est): 911.5K **Privately Held**
WEB: www.concepthotelgroup.com
SIC: **7011** Hotels

(P-11031)
CONCORD HOTEL LLC
Also Called: Crowne Plaza Concord
45 John Glenn Dr, Concord (94520-5604)
PHONE..................925 521-3751
Dave Warner,
Aaron Olson, *General Mgr*
Paul Policarpio, *Sales Dir*
Nedziba Ustovic, *Facilities Dir*
Cathy Jackson, *Director*
EMP: 95 EST: 2006
SALES (est): 5.5MM **Privately Held**
WEB: www.crowneplazaconcord.com
SIC: **7011** Hotels

(P-11032)
CONDIT INN GP LLC
Also Called: Inn At Morgan Hill The
16115 Condit Rd, Morgan Hill
(95037-9508)
PHONE..................408 779-7666
Joy Kaminoto, *Principal*
Lennar Corporation, *Mng Member*
EMP: 36 EST: 1994
SALES (est): 506.6K **Privately Held**
SIC: **7011** Motor inn

(P-11033)
CONVICT LAKE RESORT INC
2000 Convict Lake Rd, Crowley Lake
(93546-9718)
PHONE..................760 934-3800
Al Bentley, *CEO*
Joseph Thomkinson, *Shareholder*
Brian Balarsky, *CFO*
EMP: 38 EST: 1982
SQ FT: 22,000
SALES (est): 2.6MM **Privately Held**
WEB: www.convictlake.com
SIC: **5411 7011 5812 4493** Grocery stores; tourist camps, cabins, cottages & courts; eating places; marinas; bar (drinking places)

(P-11034)
CORAL REEF MOTEL LLC
Also Called: Coral Reef Motel & Suites
400 Park St, Alameda (94501-6231)
PHONE..................510 521-2330
Ray Moser, *President*
Eric Carlyle,
Alan H Davidson,
Angelo De Mattei,
Gayle Harlow,
EMP: 38 EST: 1977
SALES (est): 530.7K **Privately Held**
WEB: www.coralreefinn.com
SIC: **7011** Motels

(P-11035)
COURTYARD BY MARRIOTT
350 Hegenberger Rd, Oakland
(94621-1445)
PHONE..................510 568-7600
Mike Fleming, *Principal*
EMP: 38 EST: 2007
SALES (est): 2.9MM **Privately Held**
WEB: www.courtyard.marriott.com
SIC: **7011** Hotels & motels

(P-11036)
COURTYARD BY MARRIOTT
18090 San Ramon Vly Blvd, San Ramon
(94583-4405)
PHONE..................925 866-2900
Lisa Definney, *General Mgr*
Linda Robles, *Principal*
Erica Chasco, *Sales Mgr*
EMP: 109 EST: 2007
SALES (est): 2.1MM
SALES (corp-wide): 10.5B **Publicly Held**
WEB: www.courtyard.marriott.com
SIC: **7011** Hotels & motels
HQ: Courtyard Management Corporation
  10400 Fernwood Rd
  Bethesda MD 20817

(P-11037)
COURTYARD MANAGEMENT CORP
Also Called: Courtyard By Marriott
10605 N Wolfe Rd, Cupertino
(95014-0613)
PHONE..................408 252-9100
Mellisa Vela, *General Mgr*
Jennifer Han, *Manager*
Anika Raikar, *Manager*
EMP: 40
SALES (corp-wide): 10.5B **Publicly Held**
WEB: www.courtyard.marriott.com
SIC: **7011** Hotels & motels
HQ: Courtyard Management Corporation
  10400 Fernwood Rd
  Bethesda MD 20817

(P-11038)
COURTYARD MANAGEMENT CORP
Also Called: Courtyard By Marriott
140 E Shaw Ave, Fresno (93710-7608)
PHONE..................559 221-6000
Brandy Karoll, *Manager*
EMP: 85 EST: 2007
SALES (est): 1MM **Privately Held**
WEB: www.courtyard.marriott.com
SIC: **7011** Hotels & motels

(P-11039)
COURTYARD MANAGEMENT CORP
Also Called: Courtyard By Marriott
2500 Larkspur Landing Cir, Larkspur
(94939-1831)
PHONE..................415 925-1800
Sam Pahlazan, *Principal*
Sam Pahlavan, *General Mgr*
EMP: 64 EST: 2007
SALES (est): 2.1MM **Privately Held**
WEB: www.courtyard.marriott.com
SIC: **7011** Hotels & motels

(P-11040)
COURTYARD MANAGEMENT CORP
Also Called: Courtyard By Marriott
550 Shell Blvd, Foster City (94404-1634)
PHONE..................650 377-0600
Diana Peves, *Principal*
EMP: 38 EST: 2007
SALES (est): 998.4K **Privately Held**
WEB: www.courtyard.marriott.com
SIC: **7011 7389** Hotels & motels; office facilities & secretarial service rental

(P-11041)
CROWN MANAGEMENT SERVICES INC
Also Called: Green Shutter Plaza
22660 Main St, Hayward (94541-5112)
PHONE..................510 537-8470
Sanjay Bakshi, *CEO*
EMP: 48 EST: 1981
SALES (est): 712.2K **Privately Held**
SIC: **7011** Hotels & motels

(P-11042)
CUPERTINO HSPITALITY ASSOC LLC
Also Called: Hilton Garden Inn Cupertino
10741 N Wolfe Rd, Cupertino
(95014-0613)
PHONE..................408 777-8787
Melanie Strother, *Branch Mgr*
Rama Alvarez, *Manager*
EMP: 126
SALES (corp-wide): 1.2MM **Privately Held**
WEB: www.hiltongrandvacations.com
SIC: **7011** Hotels & motels
PA: Cupertino Hospitality Associates, Llc
  489 S El Camino Real
  San Mateo CA

(P-11043)
CUPERTINO LESSEE LLC
Also Called: Juniper Hotel
10050 S De Anza Blvd, Cupertino
(95014-2128)
PHONE..................908 253-8900
Peggy Chen, *General Mgr*
EMP: 120 EST: 2017
SALES (est): 19.5MM
SALES (corp-wide): 852MM **Publicly Held**
WEB: www.pkhotelsandresorts.com
SIC: **7011 5812** Hotels; American restaurant
PA: Park Hotels & Resorts Inc.
  1775 Tysons Blvd Fl 7
  Tysons VA 22102
  571 302-5757

(P-11044)
CY OAKLAND OPERATOR LLC
Also Called: Courtyard Oakland Downtown
988 Broadway, Oakland (94607-4064)
PHONE..................510 625-8282
Manish Bhakta, *Mng Member*
Austin Thull, *General Mgr*
EMP: 43 EST: 2015
SALES (est): 10MM **Privately Held**
SIC: **7011** Hotel, franchised

(P-11045)
CY SAC OPERATOR LLC
Also Called: Courtyard Sacramento-Midtown
4422 Y St, Sacramento (95817-2220)
PHONE..................916 455-6800
Colleen Jimenez,
Roshan Bhakta,
EMP: 67 EST: 2013 **Privately Held**
SIC: **7011** Hotels & motels

(P-11046)
DAYS INN
590 N Mathilda Ave, Sunnyvale
(94085-3504)
PHONE..................408 737-1177
Thelmonique Lowe, *Manager*
EMP: 39 **Publicly Held**
WEB: www.diyosemitepark.com
SIC: **7011** Hotels & motels
HQ: Days Inn
  1113 Airport Blvd
  South San Francisco CA 94080
  650 873-9300

(P-11047)
DAYS INN BY WYNDHAM SAN FRNCSC
2358 Lombard St, San Francisco
(94123-2602)
PHONE..................415 766-0678
EMP: 58 EST: 2019
SALES (est): 2MM
SALES (corp-wide): 1.3B **Publicly Held**
WEB: www.wyndhamhotels.com
SIC: **7011** Hotels

PRODUCTS & SERVICES SECTION

7011 - Hotels, Motels & Tourist Courts County (P-11070)

PA: Wyndham Hotels & Resorts, Inc.
22 Sylvan Way
Parsippany NJ 07054
973 753-6000

(P-11048)
DIAMOND MOUNTAIN CASINO
900 Skyline Dr, Susanville (96130-6071)
P.O. Box 1327 (96130-1327)
PHONE..................................530 252-1100
Campbell Jamieson, *General Mgr*
Bonnie Meyers, *COO*
Jill Ault, *Officer*
Jeff Shigut, *Officer*
Ted Cutler, *Exec Dir*
EMP: 135 EST: 1996
SQ FT: 24,000
SALES (est): 12MM **Privately Held**
WEB: www.dmcah.com
SIC: 7011 Casino hotel

(P-11049)
DINAHS GARDEN HOTEL INC
4261 El Camino Real, Palo Alto (94306-4405)
PHONE...................................650 493-2844
Julie Handley, *President*
Michael Simon, *Controller*
Jeannie Louie, *Sales Mgr*
Elena Isaykina, *Marketing Staff*
MEI Sausa, *Sales Staff*
EMP: 115 EST: 1956
SQ FT: 51,370
SALES (est): 7.4MM **Privately Held**
WEB: www.dinahshotel.com
SIC: 5812 7011 Eating places; hotels

(P-11050)
DJONT OPERATIONS LLC
Also Called: Embassy Suites
150 Anza Blvd, Burlingame (94010-1924)
PHONE...................................650 342-4600
Ernie Catanzaro, *General Mgr*
Hendrick Moy, *Sales Mgr*
Natalia Nikolaev, *Manager*
EMP: 120
SALES (corp-wide): 473MM **Privately Held**
WEB: www.hilton.com
SIC: 7011 Hotels & motels
HQ: Djont Operations, L.L.C.
125 E Houston St
San Antonio TX 78205

(P-11051)
DJONT OPERATIONS LLC
Also Called: Embassy Stes - Mlpts/Slcon Vly
901 E Calaveras Blvd, Milpitas (95035-5419)
PHONE...................................408 942-0400
Teri Owens, *General Mgr*
EMP: 120
SALES (corp-wide): 473MM **Privately Held**
WEB: www.hilton.com
SIC: 7011 Hotels & motels
HQ: Djont Operations, L.L.C.
125 E Houston St
San Antonio TX 78205

(P-11052)
DJONT/CMB SSF LEASING LLC
Also Called: Embassy Stes - So San Frncisco
250 Gateway Blvd, South San Francisco (94080-7018)
PHONE...................................650 589-3400
Rudy Ortiz, *General Mgr*
EMP: 47 EST: 2000
SALES (est): 1.9MM
SALES (corp-wide): 473MM **Privately Held**
WEB: www.hilton.com
SIC: 7011 Hotels & motels
HQ: Rangers Sub I, Llc
3 Bethesda Metro Ctr # 1000
Bethesda MD 20814

(P-11053)
DJONT/CMB SSF LEASING LLC
Also Called: Embassy Sites-So San Francisco
250 Gateway Blvd, South San Francisco (94080-7018)
PHONE...................................650 589-3400
Rudy Ortiz, *General Mgr*
Dee Bradford, *Executive*
EMP: 60 EST: 1989
SALES (est): 4.1MM
SALES (corp-wide): 473MM **Privately Held**
WEB: www.hilton.com
SIC: 7011 Hotels & motels
HQ: Rangers Sub I, Llc
3 Bethesda Metro Ctr # 1000
Bethesda MD 20814

(P-11054)
DNC PRKS RESORTS AT TENAYA INC (DH)
Also Called: Tenaya Lodge
1122 Highway 41, Fish Camp (93623-9600)
P.O. Box 159 (93623-0159)
PHONE...................................877 247-9241
Kevin T Kelly, *President*
Thomas Barney, *Vice Pres*
Ron Burnheimer, *Controller*
Shelly Keyser, *Sales Mgr*
EMP: 154 EST: 2001
SALES (est): 45.8MM
SALES (corp-wide): 2.9B **Privately Held**
WEB: www.tenayalodge.com
SIC: 7011 Resort hotel; hotels

(P-11055)
DNC PRKS RSRTS AT YOSEMITE INC
Also Called: Yosemite Concession Services
9001 Village Dr, Yosemite Ntpk (95389)
PHONE...................................209 372-1001
Dan Jensen, *President*
Paul Jensen, *Vice Pres*
Paul Jeppson, *Vice Pres*
Dan Lyle, *Director*
Alison Grove, *Manager*
EMP: 1100 EST: 1911
SALES (est): 50MM
SALES (corp-wide): 2.9B **Privately Held**
SIC: 7011 5399 5812 5947 Resort hotel; vacation lodges; country general stores; eating places; snack shop; gift shop; gasoline service stations; tours, conducted
HQ: Delaware North Companies Parks & Resorts, Inc.
250 Delaware Ave Ste 3
Buffalo NY 14202

(P-11056)
DODGE RIDGE CORPORATION
Also Called: Dodge Ridge Winter Sports Area
1 Dodge Ridge Rd, Pinecrest (95364)
P.O. Box 1188 (95364-0188)
PHONE...................................209 536-5300
Jason Reed, *CFO*
Kristin Taylor, *Finance Dir*
Erin Jensen, *Human Resources*
Kenneth Hurst, *Manager*
EMP: 350 EST: 1960
SQ FT: 10,000
SALES (est): 18.9MM **Privately Held**
WEB: www.dodgeridge.com
SIC: 7011 7033 Ski lodge; campgrounds

(P-11057)
DOMINION INTERNATIONAL INC
Also Called: Hampton Inn
2305 Longport Ct, Elk Grove (95758-7127)
PHONE...................................916 683-9545
Perry Ferrera, *General Mgr*
EMP: 40 EST: 2002
SALES (est): 1MM **Privately Held**
WEB: www.hilton.com
SIC: 7011 Hotels & motels

(P-11058)
DONNER LAKE VILLAGE RESORT
15695 Dnner Paca Rd Ste 1, Truckee (96161)
PHONE...................................530 587-6081
Evans Benjaminson, *General Mgr*
David Miller, *General Mgr*
EMP: 77 EST: 1974
SALES (est): 250.5K **Privately Held**
WEB: www.donnerlakevillage.com
SIC: 7011 Resort hotel

(P-11059)
DOUBLE EAGLE RESORT
Also Called: Double Eagle Resort & Spa
5587 Boulder Drv Hwy 158, June Lake (93529)
P.O. Box 736 (93529-0736)
PHONE...................................760 648-7004
Ron Black, *Owner*
Darla Ross, *General Mgr*
EMP: 45 EST: 1998
SALES (est): 3.7MM **Privately Held**
WEB: www.doubleeagle.com
SIC: 7011 Motels

(P-11060)
DRD HOSPITALITY INC
Also Called: Holiday Inn Express Manteca
179 Commerce Ave, Manteca (95336-5063)
PHONE...................................916 952-6552
Avtar Dhillon, *President*
Swinder Dhillon, *Vice Pres*
EMP: 40 EST: 2010
SALES (est): 1.3MM **Privately Held**
WEB: www.hiexpress.com
SIC: 7011 Hotels & motels

(P-11061)
DRD HOSPITALITY INC
Also Called: Holiday Inn
9950 Koa Ln, Elk Grove (95624-5009)
PHONE...................................916 952-6552
Avtar S Dhillon, *President*
EMP: 39 EST: 2008
SALES (est): 867.3K **Privately Held**
WEB: www.holidayinn.com
SIC: 7011 Hotels & motels

(P-11062)
DRY CREEK INN LTD PARTNERSHIP
Also Called: Best Western Dry Creek Inn
200 Dry Creek Rd, Healdsburg (95448-4779)
PHONE...................................707 433-0300
Aaron Crug, *Partner*
Krug Development Corporation, *General Ptnr*
Laura Osness, *Sales Staff*
Eric Markson, *Manager*
EMP: 66 EST: 1984
SQ FT: 46,439
SALES (est): 2.4MM **Privately Held**
WEB: www.drycreekinn.com
SIC: 7011 Hotels & motels

(P-11063)
DRY CREEK RANCHERIA
Also Called: Dry Creek Band of Pomo Indians
3250 Highway 128, Geyserville (95441-8908)
PHONE...................................707 857-1266
Doug Searles, *Manager*
Hans Winkler, *Controller*
EMP: 39 **Privately Held**
WEB: www.drycreekrancheria.com
SIC: 7011 Casino hotel
PA: Dry Creek Rancheria
1450 Arprt Blvd Ste 200a
Santa Rosa CA 95403

(P-11064)
DTRS ST FRANCIS LLC
Also Called: Westin St. Francis, The
335 Powell St, San Francisco (94102-1804)
PHONE...................................415 397-7000
Marc Swerdlow, *President*
Mark Zettl, *COO*
EMP: 100 EST: 1902
SALES (est): 12.6MM
SALES (corp-wide): 95.9MM **Privately Held**
WEB: www.westinstfrancis.com
SIC: 7011 Hotels & motels
HQ: Ultima Hospitality, L.L.C.
30 S Wacker Dr Ste 3600
Chicago IL 60606
312 948-4500

(P-11065)
E Z 8 MOTELS INC
Also Called: E-Z 8 Motel
1581 Concord Ave, Concord (94520-2314)
PHONE...................................925 674-0888
Randy Wilder, *Manager*
EMP: 35
SALES (corp-wide): 35MM **Privately Held**
WEB: www.ez8motels.com
SIC: 7011 Motels; hotels
PA: E Z 8 Motels Inc
2484 Hotel Circle Pl
San Diego CA 92108
619 291-8252

(P-11066)
E Z 8 MOTELS INC
Also Called: E-Z 8 Motel
5555 Cedar Ct, Newark (94560-4812)
PHONE...................................510 794-7775
Bud Coleman, *Manager*
EMP: 35
SALES (corp-wide): 35MM **Privately Held**
WEB: www.ez8motels.com
SIC: 7011 Motels
PA: E Z 8 Motels Inc
2484 Hotel Circle Pl
San Diego CA 92108
619 291-8252

(P-11067)
E Z 8 MOTELS INC
Also Called: E-Z 8 Motels
3550 El Camino Real, Santa Clara (95051-2136)
PHONE...................................408 246-3119
Nate Marlor, *Manager*
EMP: 35
SALES (corp-wide): 35MM **Privately Held**
WEB: www.ez8motels.com
SIC: 7011 Motels
PA: E Z 8 Motels Inc
2484 Hotel Circle Pl
San Diego CA 92108
619 291-8252

(P-11068)
EAGLE TRS 3 LLC
330 N Bayshore Blvd, San Mateo (94401-1235)
PHONE...................................650 418-2444
Michael Weinstock, *Mng Member*
EMP: 45
SALES (est): 688.9K **Privately Held**
SIC: 7011 Hotel, franchised

(P-11069)
EAGLE TRS 4 LLC
4800 Riverside Blvd, Sacramento (95822-1739)
PHONE...................................916 443-8400
Andrew Herenstein, *Mng Member*
EMP: 45
SALES (est): 174K **Privately Held**
SIC: 7011 Hotel, franchised

(P-11070)
EAST PALO ALTO HOTEL DEV INC
Also Called: Four Seasons Hotel Silicon Vly
2050 University Ave, East Palo Alto (94303-2248)
PHONE...................................650 566-1200
Tracy Mercer, *General Mgr*
EMP: 210 EST: 2005
SALES (est): 17.4MM **Privately Held**
SIC: 7011 7389 Resort hotel; office facilities & secretarial service rental

7011 - Hotels, Motels & Tourist Courts County (P-11071)

PRODUCTS & SERVICES SECTION

(P-11071)
EASUN INC
2001 Point West Way, Sacramento (95815-4702)
PHONE................916 929-8855
Benjamin Shih, *Director*
EMP: 38 **EST:** 2015
SALES (est): 778.2K **Privately Held**
SIC: 7011 Hotels & motels

(P-11072)
ECHO CHALET INC
9900 Echo Lakes Rd, Echo Lake (95721-9400)
PHONE................530 659-7207
Thomas R Fashinell, *President*
EMP: 25 **EST:** 1939
SQ FT: 4,200
SALES (est): 833.2K **Privately Held**
WEB: www.echochalet.com
SIC: 7011 4493 7694 5411 Resort hotel; marinas; motor repair services; grocery stores, independent; motor boat dealers

(P-11073)
ECONO LODGE
711 16th St, Sacramento (95814-2001)
PHONE................916 443-6631
Andy Patel, *Partner*
Babu Patel, *Partner*
EMP: 39 **EST:** 1975
SALES (est): 699.8K **Privately Held**
WEB: www.choicehotels.com
SIC: 7011 Hotels & motels

(P-11074)
EHT WSAC LLC
Also Called: Westin Sacramento
4800 Riverside Blvd, Sacramento (95822-1739)
PHONE................916 443-8400
Howard Wu, *Principal*
EMP: 50 **EST:** 2019
SALES (est): 2.5MM **Privately Held**
WEB: www.marriott.com
SIC: 7011 Hotels & motels

(P-11075)
EL PUEBLO MOTEL INC
Also Called: El Pueblo Inn
896 W Napa St, Sonoma (95476-6415)
PHONE................707 996-3651
Holly Bradbury, *President*
Wendy Watkins Stewar, *Vice Pres*
EMP: 53 **EST:** 1960
SQ FT: 45,000
SALES (est): 718.7K **Privately Held**
WEB: www.elpuebloinn.com
SIC: 7011 Motels

(P-11076)
EL RANCHO MOTEL INC
Also Called: Best Wstn El Rancho Inn Suites
1100 El Camino Real, Millbrae (94030-2098)
PHONE................650 588-8500
John C Wilms, *President*
Paul Wilms, *Vice Pres*
Art Schwass, *Technology*
EMP: 109 **EST:** 1948
SQ FT: 23,958
SALES (est): 1.4MM **Privately Held**
WEB: www.elranchoinn.com
SIC: 7011 5812 5813 7991 Motels; eating places; drinking places; physical fitness facilities

(P-11077)
ELIZABETHAN INN ASSOCIATES LP
Also Called: The Sterling Hotel
1935 Wright St Apt 231, Sacramento (95825-1191)
PHONE................916 448-1300
Sandra Wasserman, *Partner*
EMP: 37 **EST:** 1988
SQ FT: 15,000
SALES (est): 449.9K **Privately Held**
SIC: 7011 5812 7299 Resort hotel; ethnic food restaurants; banquet hall facilities

(P-11078)
ELK VALLEY CASINO INC
Also Called: Elk Valley Rancheria Cal
2500 Howland Hill Rd, Crescent City (95531-9241)
PHONE................707 464-1020
Dale Miller, *Ch of Bd*
Patti Ulbricht, *Admin Asst*
Shelly Woods, *Administration*
John Green, *Software Engr*
Kerri Vue, *Human Resources*
EMP: 107 **EST:** 1995
SQ FT: 35,000
SALES (est): 11.3MM **Privately Held**
WEB: www.elkvalleycasino.com
SIC: 7011 Casino hotel

(P-11079)
EMBARCADERO INN ASSOCIATES
Also Called: Hotel Griffon
155 Steuart St, San Francisco (94105-1206)
PHONE................415 495-2100
Edward Marinucci, *General Ptnr*
Pacific Union Investment Corpo, *General Ptnr*
Julia Umyarova, *Manager*
Mollie Warren, *Manager*
EMP: 57 **EST:** 1988
SALES (est): 2.6MM **Privately Held**
WEB: www.hotelgriffon.com
SIC: 7011 5812 Hotels; family restaurants

(P-11080)
EMBASSY INVESTMENTS LLC
Also Called: Courtyard Marriott
1350 Holiday Ln, Fairfield (94534-3449)
PHONE................707 422-4111
Sushil Patel, *Mng Member*
Edward Deloumr, *Mng Member*
Sheryl Coburn, *Manager*
EMP: 66 **EST:** 1998
SALES (est): 2.4MM **Privately Held**
WEB: www.courtyard.marriott.com
SIC: 7011 5813 5812 Hotels & motels; drinking places; eating places

(P-11081)
EMERALD INVESTMENTS INC
Also Called: Best Western
25 Heritage Ln, Chico (95926-1368)
PHONE................530 894-8600
Ramesh Pitamber, *President*
EMP: 35 **EST:** 2001
SALES (est): 1.7MM **Privately Held**
WEB: www.bwchico.com
SIC: 7011 Hotels & motels

(P-11082)
EPIC HOSPITALITY INC
Also Called: Holiday Inn
1859 Alamar Way, Fortuna (95540-8535)
PHONE................707 725-5500
Gina Thompson, *President*
EMP: 40 **EST:** 2010
SALES (est): 486.6K **Privately Held**
WEB: www.holidayinn.com
SIC: 7011 Hotels & motels

(P-11083)
EQUINOX HOTEL MANAGEMENT INC
Also Called: Aloha Beach Resort
2422 Lake St, San Francisco (94121-1117)
PHONE................415 668-6887
Abdul Suleman, *President*
Adam Suleman, *Exec VP*
EMP: 100 **EST:** 1995
SALES (est): 7.1MM **Privately Held**
WEB: www.equinoxhotels.com
SIC: 7011 6531 Hotels & motels; real estate managers

(P-11084)
ESPANAS MEXICAN RESTAURANT
Also Called: Canal Farm Motel
1460 E Pacheco Blvd, Los Banos (93635-4991)
PHONE................209 826-2741
Michael Amabile, *Partner*
Esther Amabile, *Partner*
EMP: 64 **EST:** 1967
SQ FT: 12,500
SALES (est): 3.4MM **Privately Held**
SIC: 5812 5813 7011 Mexican restaurant; bar (drinking places); motels

(P-11085)
ESTERLE LLC
Also Called: Travelodge By The Bay
1450 Lombard St, San Francisco (94123-3112)
PHONE................415 673-0691
Pierre Nebout,
Janet Nebout,
EMP: 38 **EST:** 1998
SQ FT: 30,412
SALES (est): 1.2MM **Privately Held**
WEB: www.travelodgesanfranciscobay.com
SIC: 7011 Motels

(P-11086)
EUREKA SUPER 8 MOTEL
1304 4th St, Eureka (95501-0605)
PHONE................707 443-3193
Shailesh Patel, *Owner*
Premabhi Patel, *Owner*
EMP: 49 **EST:** 1973
SQ FT: 26,000
SALES (est): 950.7K **Privately Held**
WEB: www.wyndhamhotels.com
SIC: 7011 5813 Hotels & motels; cocktail lounge

(P-11087)
EVERGREEN DSTNTION HLDINGS LLC
Also Called: Evergreen Lodge
33160 Evergreen Rd, Groveland (95321-9772)
PHONE................209 379-2606
Brian Anderluh,
Donna West, *Executive*
Joe Juszkiewicz, *General Mgr*
Joseph M Juszkiewicz, *General Mgr*
Nick Simon, *General Mgr*
EMP: 75
SQ FT: 6,000
SALES (est): 4.9MM **Privately Held**
WEB: www.evergreenlodge.com
SIC: 7011 5812 Resort hotel; eating places

(P-11088)
EXECUTIVE INN INC
Also Called: Ramada Inn Silicon Valley
1217 Wildwood Ave, Sunnyvale (94089-2701)
PHONE................408 245-5330
Roger Chang, *President*
Jeffry S C Chang, *President*
David C M Chang, *Admin Sec*
EMP: 97 **EST:** 1971
SQ FT: 15,400
SALES (est): 5.6MM **Privately Held**
WEB: www.ramadasv.com
SIC: 7011 Hotels & motels

(P-11089)
FAIRFIELD INN BY MRROTT VCVILLE
370 Orange Dr, Vacaville (95687-3205)
PHONE................707 469-0800
Francis Penalba, *General Mgr*
Helen Forbes, *General Mgr*
Michelle Bautista, *Manager*
Meghan O'Hara, *Asst Mgr*
EMP: 51 **EST:** 2006
SALES (est): 467.9K **Privately Held**
WEB: www.fairfield.marriott.com
SIC: 7011 Hotels & motels

(P-11090)
FAIRMONT HOTEL GUEST)
170 S Market St Lbby, San Jose (95113-2395)
PHONE................615 578-2670
Tonia Sanders, *Principal*
Myisha Harris, *Credit Mgr*
Justin Allbright, *Sales Staff*
Jeff Doane, *Sales Staff*
MO Halawani, *Director*
EMP: 56 **EST:** 2015
SALES (est): 3.1MM **Privately Held**
SIC: 7011 Hotels

(P-11091)
FAIRMONT HRITG PL GHRRDELLI SQ
900 N Point St Ste E204, San Francisco (94109-1192)
PHONE................415 268-9900
Karl Leutner, *Principal*
Jean Francois Vary, *General Mgr*
Kelly Conley, *Sales Staff*
EMP: 113 **EST:** 2008
SALES (est): 4.5MM **Privately Held**
WEB: www.ghirardellisq.com
SIC: 7011 Resort hotel

(P-11092)
FARMHOUSE INN & RESTAURANT LLC
7871 River Rd, Forestville (95436-9494)
PHONE................707 887-3300
Catheryn Bartllomei, *President*
Stanley Mazor, *Partner*
Geoff Kruth, *Officer*
Thelma Kroese, *Accounting Mgr*
Brian Gipson, *Sales Staff*
EMP: 45 **EST:** 1991
SALES (est): 4.5MM **Privately Held**
WEB: www.farmhouseinn.com
SIC: 7011 5812 Bed & breakfast inn; restaurant, family: independent

(P-11093)
FEDERTED INDANS GRTON RNCHERIA
Graton Resort & Casino
630 Park Ct, Rohnert Park (94928-7906)
PHONE................707 588-7100
Greg Sarris, *Branch Mgr*
EMP: 92 **Privately Held**
WEB: www.gratonrancheria.com
SIC: 7011 Casino hotel
PA: Federated Indians Of Graton Rancheria
6400 Redwood Dr Ste 300
Rohnert Park CA 94928
619 917-9566

(P-11094)
FELCOR UNION SQUARE LESSEE LLC
Also Called: Marriott - Un Sq San Francisco
480 Sutter St, San Francisco (94108-3901)
PHONE................415 398-8900
Carol Alcantara, *Planning*
Meridith Zelones, *Accounts Exec*
Llando Delago, *Supervisor*
EMP: 59 **EST:** 2014
SALES (est): 27.7MM
SALES (corp-wide): 473MM **Privately Held**
SIC: 7011 Hotels
HQ: Rangers Sub I, Llc
3 Bethesda Metro Ctr # 1000
Bethesda MD 20814

(P-11095)
FIRST ORLEANS HOTEL ASSOC LP
222 Kearny St Ste 200, San Francisco (94108-4537)
PHONE................415 397-5572
Michael Tepatie, *CEO*
St Charles Avenue LLC, *General Ptnr*
Thomas Latour, *Partner*
J Kirke Wrench, *Partner*
Steven Koehler, *Finance*
EMP: 200 **EST:** 1999
SALES (est): 4.2MM **Privately Held**
WEB: www.hotelmonaco.com
SIC: 7011 Hotels

(P-11096)
FLORENCE VILLA HOTEL
Also Called: The Villa Florence Hotel
225 Powell St, San Francisco (94102-2205)
PHONE................415 397-7700
Steve Miller, *General Mgr*
Andrea Murray, *General Mgr*
EMP: 200 **EST:** 1985
SALES (est): 10.9MM **Publicly Held**
WEB: www.villaflorence.com
SIC: 7011 5812 Hotels; eating places

PRODUCTS & SERVICES SECTION

7011 - Hotels, Motels & Tourist Courts County (P-11119)

PA: Pebblebrook Hotel Trust
4747 Bethesda Ave # 1100
Bethesda MD 20814

(P-11097)
FLORENCE VILLA HOTEL LLC
225 Powell St, San Francisco (94102-2205)
PHONE..................415 397-7700
Sue Hefty,
Marit Davey,
EMP: 53 EST: 2006
SALES (est): 137.7K **Privately Held**
WEB: www.villaflorence.com
SIC: **7011** Hotels

(P-11098)
FORGE-VDVICH MTL LTD PRTNR A C
Also Called: Cupertino Inn
10889 N De Anza Blvd, Cupertino (95014-0439)
PHONE..................408 996-7700
John Vidovich, *General Ptnr*
Stephen J Vidovich, *General Ptnr*
Marguerite Lambert, *Manager*
EMP: 59 EST: 1984
SQ FT: 8,323
SALES (est): 5.3MM **Privately Held**
WEB: www.cupertino-hotel.com
SIC: **7011** Hotels

(P-11099)
FORTUNA COUNTRY INN CORP
Also Called: Best Western
2025 Riverwalk Dr, Fortuna (95540-9552)
PHONE..................707 725-6822
Mark Watson, *President*
EMP: 41 EST: 1993
SALES (est): 519.3K **Privately Held**
WEB: www.bestwestern.com
SIC: **7011** Hotels & motels

(P-11100)
FOUNDERS MANAGEMENT II CORP
Also Called: Crowne Plaza Hotel
1221 Chess Dr, Foster City (94404-1173)
PHONE..................650 570-5700
Solomon Tsai, *Managing Dir*
Scott Castle, *General Mgr*
Deena Castle, *Sales Staff*
Martin Uiberlacker, *Manager*
▲ EMP: 275 EST: 1986
SQ FT: 280,000
SALES (est): 12.3MM **Privately Held**
WEB: www.eventscp.com
SIC: **7011 5812 5813** Hotels; eating places; bar (drinking places)

(P-11101)
FOUNTAINGROVE INN LLC
Also Called: Fountngrove Inn Conference Ctr
101 Fountaingrove Pkwy, Santa Rosa (95403-1777)
P.O. Box 12277 (95406-2277)
PHONE..................707 578-6101
Robert Miller,
Justin Hayman, *General Mgr*
Angelo Serro,
Brenda Alberigi, *Director*
Cecile Kraus, *Director*
EMP: 60 EST: 1986
SQ FT: 79,200
SALES (est): 6MM **Privately Held**
WEB: www.fountaingroveinn.com
SIC: **7011 5812** Resort hotel; eating places

(P-11102)
FOUR POINTS SAN JOSE DOWNTOWN
211 S 1st St, San Jose (95113-2702)
PHONE..................408 282-8800
Randy Zimmerman, *General Mgr*
EMP: 50 EST: 2010
SALES (est): 2.6MM **Privately Held**
WEB: www.marriott.com
SIC: **7011** Resort hotel; hotels

(P-11103)
FOUR SEASONS HOTEL INC
Also Called: Four Ssons Hotel-San Francisco
735 Market St Fl 6, San Francisco (94103-2034)
PHONE..................415 633-3441
Stan Bromley, *Branch Mgr*
Max Epps, *Officer*
Mariia Grishchenko, *Agent*
Josephine Garcia, *Supervisor*
EMP: 147
SALES (corp-wide): 55MM **Privately Held**
WEB: www.fourseasons.com
SIC: **7011** Resort hotel
HQ: Four Seasons Hotels Limited
1165 Leslie St
North York ON M3C 2
416 449-1750

(P-11104)
FOUR SISTERS INNS
Also Called: Inns At Sonoma
630 Broadway, Sonoma (95476-7002)
PHONE..................707 939-1340
Chapman Retterer, *Branch Mgr*
David Jessup, *General Mgr*
Lindsey Novitzke, *Marketing Staff*
Sharon Rooney, *Pub Rel Staff*
Joe Capaul, *Director*
EMP: 91
SALES (corp-wide): 24.2MM **Privately Held**
WEB: www.foursisters.com
SIC: **7011** Bed & breakfast inn
PA: Four Sisters Inns
460 Alma St Ste 100
Monterey CA 93940
831 649-0908

(P-11105)
FREMONT MARRIOTT
46100 Landing Pkwy, Fremont (94538-6437)
PHONE..................510 413-3700
John Ault, *General Mgr*
EMP: 39 EST: 2015
SALES (est): 2.7MM **Privately Held**
WEB: www.marriott.com
SIC: **7011** Hotels

(P-11106)
FRENCH REDWOOD INC
Also Called: Hotel Sfitel San Francisco Bay
223 Twin Dolphin Dr, Redwood City (94065-1414)
PHONE..................650 598-9000
EMP: 228
SALES (est): 7.7MM
SALES (corp-wide): 1B **Privately Held**
WEB: www.hbsaward.com
SIC: **7011 5813 5812** Hotel/Motel Operation Drinking Place Eating Place
PA: Accor
82 Rue Henry Farman
Issy Les Moulineaux 92130
146 429-193

(P-11107)
FRESNO AIRPORT HOTELS LLC
Also Called: Wyndham Garden Fresno Airport
5090 E Clinton Way, Fresno (93727-1506)
PHONE..................559 252-3611
Rohit Kumar, *President*
Leslie Beninga, *Director*
EMP: 65 EST: 2016
SALES (est): 3.6MM **Privately Held**
WEB: www.visitfresnocounty.org
SIC: **7011** Hotels

(P-11108)
FUN TO STAY LESSEE INC
165 Steuart St, San Francisco (94105-1206)
PHONE..................415 882-1300
Todd Metzeber, *General Mgr*
EMP: 40 EST: 2013
SALES (est): 1.4MM **Privately Held**
SIC: **7011 5812** Hotels & motels; Japanese restaurant

(P-11109)
G B COMMERCIAL LLC
Also Called: Four Pnts By Shrton Scrmnto In
4900 Duckhorn Dr, Sacramento (95834-2595)
PHONE..................916 263-9000
Gurmukh Gosal,
Kyle Pacheco, *Sales Mgr*
EMP: 74 EST: 2004
SQ FT: 83,000
SALES (est): 3.7MM **Privately Held**
WEB: www.marriott.com
SIC: **7011 6552** Hotels & motels; subdividers & developers

(P-11110)
G-ELK GROVE LP
Also Called: Holiday Inn
9175 W Stockton Blvd, Elk Grove (95758-8051)
PHONE..................916 478-9000
Clint Reed, *Partner*
Sean Woo, *CFO*
Tiffany Kintanar, *Sales Staff*
EMP: 57 EST: 2002
SALES (est): 1.6MM **Privately Held**
WEB: www.holidayinn.com
SIC: **7011** Hotels & motels

(P-11111)
GALLERIA PARK ASSOCIATES LLC
Also Called: Galleria Park Hotel
191 Sutter St, San Francisco (94104-4501)
PHONE..................415 781-3060
James Lim, *General Mgr*
Fred De Stefano, *Exec VP*
Stephen Muir, *Chief Engr*
Patrick De Almeida, *Finance*
Severine Michl, *Sales Staff*
EMP: 73 EST: 1984
SQ FT: 109,673
SALES (est): 9.3MM **Privately Held**
SIC: **7011 6512 5813 5812** Hotels; non-residential building operators; drinking places; eating places

(P-11112)
GARDEN CITY INC
Also Called: Garden City Casino & Rest
1887 Matrix Blvd, San Jose (95110-2309)
PHONE..................408 244-3333
Pete V Lunardi III, *CEO*
Eli Reinhard, *President*
Llene Brandon, *CFO*
Kathy Reiner, *CFO*
Simeon Shigg, *CFO*
EMP: 569 EST: 1974
SQ FT: 22,000
SALES (est): 29.1MM **Privately Held**
WEB: www.gardencitycasino.com
SIC: **7011** Casino hotel

(P-11113)
GEARY DARLING LESSEE INC
Also Called: Marker Hotel, The
501 Geary St, San Francisco (94102-1640)
PHONE..................415 292-0100
Alfred L Young, *CEO*
EMP: 150 EST: 2010
SQ FT: 20,000
SALES (est): 17.4MM **Publicly Held**
WEB: www.themarkersf.com
SIC: **7011 7991 5813 5812** Hotels; physical fitness facilities; drinking places; eating places; banquet hall facilities
PA: Pebblebrook Hotel Trust
4747 Bethesda Ave # 1100
Bethesda MD 20814

(P-11114)
GOLDEN GATE CNCIL AMRCN YUTH H
Also Called: Hostelling International
685 Ellis St, San Francisco (94109-8027)
PHONE..................415 474-5721
Patrick Rafferty, *Branch Mgr*
EMP: 36
SQ FT: 24,544
SALES (corp-wide): 6.2MM **Privately Held**
WEB: www.hiusa.org
SIC: **7011** Hostels

PA: Golden Gate Council Of American Youth Hostels, Inc.
425 Divisadero St Ste 307
San Francisco CA 94117
415 863-1444

(P-11115)
GOLDEN GATE CNCIL AMRCN YUTH H
Also Called: San Frncsco Intl Youth Hostel
240 Fort Mason, San Francisco (94123-1335)
PHONE..................415 771-7277
Jean Comasky, *Manager*
Christopher Bauman, *General Mgr*
EMP: 36
SALES (corp-wide): 6.2MM **Privately Held**
WEB: www.hiusa.org
SIC: **7011** Hostels
PA: Golden Gate Council Of American Youth Hostels, Inc.
425 Divisadero St Ste 307
San Francisco CA 94117
415 863-1444

(P-11116)
GRAND HYATT SF LLC
345 Stockton St, San Francisco (94108-4606)
PHONE..................415 398-1234
Sandra Micek, *Senior VP*
Martin Pfefferkorn, *Executive*
Heidi Hutcherson, *Social Dir*
Angela Jellum, *Social Dir*
Brittany Patterson, *Social Dir*
EMP: 48 EST: 2014
SALES (est): 860.5K **Publicly Held**
WEB: www.hyatt.com
SIC: **7011** Hotels
PA: Hyatt Hotels Corporation
150 N Riverside Plz Fl 8
Chicago IL 60606

(P-11117)
GRAND PRIX BELMONT LLC
Also Called: Hyatt Hse Blmnt/Redwood Shores
400 Concourse Dr, Belmont (94002-4125)
PHONE..................650 591-8600
Gregg Forde,
Triin Pops-Botero,
EMP: 50 EST: 2007
SALES (est): 1.1MM **Privately Held**
WEB: www.hyatt.com
SIC: **7011** Hotels

(P-11118)
GRANLIBAKKEN MANAGEMENT CO LTD
Also Called: Granlbakken Ski Racquet Resort
725 Granlibakken Rd, Tahoe City (96145-2370)
P.O. Box 6329 (96145-6329)
PHONE..................800 543-3221
Willem G C Parson, *President*
Norma Parson, *Treasurer*
Brandi Dalton, *Maintence Staff*
Shannon Liron, *Manager*
EMP: 60 EST: 1978
SALES (est): 7MM **Privately Held**
WEB: www.granlibakken.com
SIC: **7011** Resort hotel

(P-11119)
GREENHORN CREEK GUEST RANCH
2116 Greenhorn Rd, Quincy (95971)
PHONE..................530 283-0930
Ralph Wilburn, *President*
Patricia Wilburn, *Treasurer*
EMP: 36 EST: 2000
SQ FT: 200
SALES (est): 2.6MM **Privately Held**
WEB: www.greenhornranch.com
SIC: **7011 7032** Vacation lodges; dude ranch

(PA)=Parent Co (HQ)=Headquarters (DH)=Div Headquarters
◯ = New Business established in last 2 years

7011 - Hotels, Motels & Tourist Courts County (P-11120)

PRODUCTS & SERVICES SECTION

(P-11120)
GRM BYSHORE PROPERTY OWNER LLC
Also Called: Holiday Inn Ex San Frncsco - A
1250 Bayshore Hwy, Burlingame (94010-1805)
PHONE..................................650 347-2381
Andre Ferrigno, *Principal*
Alex Cerda, *Principal*
EMP: 35 EST: 2018
SALES (est): 1.1MM **Privately Held**
WEB: www.hiexpress.com
SIC: 7011 Hotels & motels

(P-11121)
GROSVENOR PROPERTIES LTD (PA)
222 Front St Fl 7, San Francisco (94111-4421)
PHONE..................................415 421-5940
Todd Werby, *President*
Susan Gallagher, *Exec VP*
Susanne Gallagher, *Exec VP*
Dan Croley, *Senior VP*
Steve Nokes, *Vice Pres*
EMP: 40 EST: 1972
SQ FT: 6,000
SALES (est): 22.3MM **Privately Held**
WEB: www.grosvenorproperties.com
SIC: 7011 Hotels & motels

(P-11122)
GROSVENOR PROPERTIES LTD
Also Called: Best Western
380 S Airport Blvd, South San Francisco (94080-6704)
PHONE..................................650 873-3200
Jim McGuire, *Manager*
Dan Croley, *Vice Pres*
Colin Stermer, *Info Tech Mgr*
Stella Yu, *Human Res Mgr*
David Huddleston, *Opers Mgr*
EMP: 160
SALES (corp-wide): 22.3MM **Privately Held**
WEB: www.grosvenorproperties.com
SIC: 7011 5813 5812 7299 Hotels & motels; drinking places; eating places; banquet hall facilities
PA: Grosvenor Properties Ltd.
222 Front St Fl 7
San Francisco CA 94111
415 421-5940

(P-11123)
HALF MOON BAY LODGE
Also Called: Best Wstn Half Moon Bay Lodge
2400 Cabrillo Hwy S, Half Moon Bay (94019-2253)
PHONE..................................650 726-9000
Keith Wesstlmann, *Manager*
Keith Wesselmann, *General Mgr*
EMP: 52 EST: 1976
SALES (est): 4.7MM **Privately Held**
WEB: www.halfmoonbaylodge.com
SIC: 7011 Bed & breakfast inn

(P-11124)
HAMLIN HOTEL LP
1525 Grant Ave, San Francisco (94133-3323)
PHONE..................................415 984-1450
Chinatown Com, *Principal*
EMP: 51 EST: 2001
SALES: 8.5MM **Privately Held**
WEB: www.chinatowncdc.org
SIC: 7011 Hotels

(P-11125)
HANDLERY HOTELS INC
Also Called: Handlery Union Square Hotel
351 Geary St, San Francisco (94102-1801)
PHONE..................................415 781-7800
John Handlery, *Manager*
EMP: 238
SALES (corp-wide): 18.7MM **Privately Held**
SIC: 7011 Resort hotel
PA: Handlery Hotels, Inc.
180 Geary St Ste 700
San Francisco CA 94108
415 781-4550

(P-11126)
HANFORD HOTELS
Also Called: La Quinta Inn
20777 Hesperian Blvd, Hayward (94541-5879)
PHONE..................................510 732-6300
Donald E Sodaro, *Principal*
EMP: 38 EST: 2008
SALES (est): 3.5MM **Privately Held**
WEB: www.wyndhamhotels.com
SIC: 7011 Hotels & motels

(P-11127)
HAPPY TEAM INC
Also Called: Holiday Inn
101 Clinton Rd, Jackson (95642-2601)
PHONE..................................209 257-1500
Atul Patel, *Branch Mgr*
EMP: 47
SALES (corp-wide): 4.2MM **Privately Held**
WEB: www.holidayinn.com
SIC: 7011 Hotels & motels
PA: Happy Team, Inc.
2449 Nalin Dr
Los Angeles CA 90077
858 748-7311

(P-11128)
HARBOR LITE LODGE LLC
120 N Harbor Dr, Fort Bragg (95437-5513)
PHONE..................................707 964-0221
Jason Hurst, *Managing Prtnr*
Barbara Hurst, *Partner*
Judith Moilanen, *Partner*
EMP: 38 EST: 1973
SALES (est): 768.5K **Privately Held**
WEB: www.harborlitelodge.com
SIC: 7011 Motels

(P-11129)
HARD ROCK CAFE INTL INC
Also Called: Hard Rock Ht Csino Scrmnto At
3317 Forty Mile Rd, Wheatland (95692-8803)
PHONE..................................530 633-6938
EMP: 75
SALES (corp-wide): 134MM **Privately Held**
WEB: www.hardrockhotels.com
SIC: 7011 5812 Casino hotel; eating places
PA: Hard Rock Cafe International, Inc.
1 Seminole Way
Fort Lauderdale FL 33314
228 437-6968

(P-11130)
HARSCH INVESTMENT REALTY LLC
Also Called: Claremont Rsort Spa Tennis CLB
41 Tunnel Rd, Berkeley (94705-2429)
PHONE..................................510 843-3000
Todd Shelling, *Director*
Phillip Durocher, *Vice Pres*
David Foster, *Vice Pres*
Robert Holland, *Vice Pres*
Linda Topping, *Vice Pres*
EMP: 119
SALES (corp-wide): 115.1MM **Privately Held**
WEB: www.harsch.com
SIC: 7011 7997 Hotels; swimming club, membership; tennis club, membership
PA: Harsch Investment Realty, Llc
1121 Sw Salmon St Ste 500
Portland OR 97205
503 242-2900

(P-11131)
HARVEST INN INVESTORS I LLC
1 Main St, Saint Helena (94574-2155)
PHONE..................................707 963-9463
Nathan Davis, *Vice Pres*
Cary L Neiman, *Managing Prtnr*
Matthew McElroy, *Director*
EMP: 62 EST: 1976
SALES (est): 7.1MM **Privately Held**
WEB: www.harvestinn.com
SIC: 7011 Motel, franchised; hotels

(P-11132)
HAWTHORN SUITES
321 Bercut Dr, Sacramento (95811-0103)
PHONE..................................916 441-1200
EMP: 39
SQ FT: 103,000
SALES (est): 605.4K **Privately Held**
SIC: 7011 Hotels And Motels, Nsk

(P-11133)
HAYES MANSION CONFERENCE CTR
200 Edenvale Ave, San Jose (95136-3309)
PHONE..................................408 226-3200
Vickie Leong, *Principal*
Jeff Carpenter, *General Mgr*
EMP: 140 EST: 1994
SALES (est): 7.7MM **Privately Held**
WEB: www.hayesmansion.com
SIC: 7011 Hotels

(P-11134)
HEALTH AND HUMN SVCS AGCY HHSA
Also Called: El Dorado County
3057 Briw Rd Ste A, Placerville (95667-5335)
PHONE..................................530 621-5834
EMP: 43 EST: 2015
SALES (est): 3.9MM **Privately Held**
WEB: www.edcgov.us
SIC: 7011 Hotels & motels

(P-11135)
HERITAGE INVSTMNTS CONCORD LLC
Also Called: Best Western Concord
4600 Clayton Rd, Concord (94521-7644)
PHONE..................................925 686-4466
Ramesh Pitamber, *Principal*
EMP: 38 EST: 1993
SALES (est): 1MM **Privately Held**
WEB: www.bwconcord.com
SIC: 7011 Hotels & motels

(P-11136)
HILL HOUSE ASSOCIATES
Also Called: Hill House of Mendocino
10701 Palette Dr, Mendocino (95460)
P.O. Box 625 (95460-0625)
PHONE..................................707 937-0554
Jamie Buckner, *Principal*
Lauren Hoops-Schmieg, *Exec Dir*
EMP: 39 EST: 1978
SQ FT: 15,000
SALES (est): 643.7K **Privately Held**
WEB: www.hillhouseinn.reservations.com
SIC: 7011 5812 Bed & breakfast inn; eating places

(P-11137)
HILL TOP HOSPITALITY LLC
8801 Folsom Blvd Ste 150, Sacramento (95826-3265)
PHONE..................................530 888-7441
Hossein Bozorgzad, *President*
Kenneth Poelman, *Managing Dir*
EMP: 45 EST: 2015
SALES (est): 1.2MM **Privately Held**
SIC: 7011 Hotel, franchised

(P-11138)
HILLSIDE INN INC
Also Called: Best Western Hillside Inn Mtl
2901 4th St, Santa Rosa (95409-4020)
PHONE..................................707 546-9353
Robert Coombs, *Treasurer*
Arlene Coombs, *President*
EMP: 36 EST: 1968
SQ FT: 10,000
SALES (est): 273.6K **Privately Held**
WEB: www.hillside-inn.com
SIC: 7011 Motels

(P-11139)
HILLTOP INN REDDING LLC
2300 Hilltop Dr, Redding (96002-0508)
PHONE..................................530 221-6100
Ed Rullman, *Mng Member*
Tracy Wahrlich,
Steve Gaines, *Mng Member*
Steven Wahrlich, *Mng Member*
EMP: 91 EST: 1977
SQ FT: 10,000
SALES (est): 3.7MM **Privately Held**
WEB: www.thehilltopinn.com
SIC: 7011 5812 5813 Hotels & motels; eating places; drinking places

(P-11140)
HILTON GARDEN IN SAN MATEO
Also Called: Hilton Garden Hotel
2000 Bridgepointe Pkwy, Foster City (94404-1586)
PHONE..................................650 522-9000
Derrick Hudson, *Manager*
EMP: 59
SALES (corp-wide): 3.6MM **Privately Held**
WEB: www.hilton.com
SIC: 7011 Hotels & motels
PA: Hilton Garden In San Mateo
2000 Bridgepointe Pkwy
Foster City CA 94404
650 522-9000

(P-11141)
HILTON GARDEN INN
510 Lewelling Blvd, San Leandro (94579-1803)
PHONE..................................510 346-5533
Burt Knewson, *Manager*
Susan Parkinson, *Auditor*
Anita Atkinson, *Human Resources*
David Schlesinger, *Director*
EMP: 51 EST: 2002
SALES (est): 4.9MM **Privately Held**
WEB: www.hilton.com
SIC: 7011 Hotels & motels

(P-11142)
HILTON GARDEN INNS MGT LLC
6070 Monterey Rd, Gilroy (95020-9502)
PHONE..................................408 840-7000
Toll Free:..................................866 -
Paula Hutchison, *Branch Mgr*
Eric Gebhardt, *Manager*
EMP: 100
SALES (corp-wide): 4.3B **Publicly Held**
WEB: www.hilton.com
SIC: 7011 Hotels & motels
HQ: Hilton Garden Inns Management Llc
7930 Jones Branch Dr
Mc Lean VA 22102
703 883-1000

(P-11143)
HILTON GARDEN INNS MGT LLC
2801 Constitution Dr Fl 2, Livermore (94551-7613)
PHONE..................................925 292-2000
Joan Baldon, *Manager*
EMP: 100
SALES (corp-wide): 4.3B **Publicly Held**
WEB: www.hilton.com
SIC: 7011 Hotels & motels
HQ: Hilton Garden Inns Management Llc
7930 Jones Branch Dr
Mc Lean VA 22102
703 883-1000

(P-11144)
HILTON SAN FRANCISCO FINCL DST
750 Kearny St, San Francisco (94108-1860)
PHONE..................................415 433-6600
Randall King, *Principal*
J San Miguel, *Asst Director*
EMP: 52 EST: 2006
SALES (est): 12.9MM **Privately Held**
WEB: www.hilton.com
SIC: 7011 Hotels

(P-11145)
HLT SAN JOSE LLC
Also Called: Doubletree Hotel
2050 Gateway Pl, San Jose (95110-1011)
PHONE..................................408 437-2103
David L Jackson, *Director*
EMP: 49 EST: 2007
SALES (est): 1.4MM **Privately Held**
WEB: www.hilton.com
SIC: 7011 Hotels & motels

(P-11146)
HMB INVESTORS LLC
Also Called: Wrc Huntington
1075 California St, San Francisco (94108-2251)
PHONE..................................415 474-5400
Michael Rosenfeld, *CEO*
John Cop, *President*
Karen Stevenson, *Sales Mgr*
Jane Lee, *Sales Staff*

Lauren Vojvoda, *Director*
EMP: 90 **EST:** 1941
SALES (est): 777.5K **Privately Held**
SIC: 7011 Hotels

(P-11147)
HOLBROOKE HOTEL LLC
212 W Main St, Grass Valley (95945-4788)
PHONE 530 273-2300
Micheal Nudelman,
James Obrien,
Donna Weaver,
EMP: 41 **EST:** 1951
SQ FT: 17,000
SALES (est): 1.3MM **Privately Held**
WEB: www.holbrooke.com
SIC: 5812 7011 5813 American restaurant; hotels; saloon

(P-11148)
HOLIDAY GARDEN WC CORP
Also Called: Holiday Inn Ex Walnut Creek
2730 N Main St, Walnut Creek (94597-2732)
PHONE 925 932-3332
Justin Saylor, *General Mgr*
Candice Kelly, *Marketing Staff*
EMP: 50 **EST:** 2018
SALES (est): 3.1MM **Privately Held**
WEB: www.hiexpress.com
SIC: 7011 Hotels & motels

(P-11149)
HOLIDAY INN EX HT & SUITES
1175 University Ave, Berkeley (94702-1605)
PHONE 510 548-1700
Jay Patel, *Partner*
EMP: 43 **EST:** 2000
SALES (est): 2.8MM **Privately Held**
WEB: www.holidayinn.com
SIC: 7011 Hotels & motels

(P-11150)
HOLIDAY INN EXPRESS
4525 Howard Rd, Westley (95387)
P.O. Box 307 (95387-0307)
PHONE 650 863-8771
Phyllis Simpson, *General Mgr*
EMP: 47 **EST:** 1996
SALES (est): 1.1MM **Privately Held**
WEB: www.holidayinn.com
SIC: 7011 Hotels & motels

(P-11151)
HOLIDAY INN EXPRESS
3961 Lake Tahoe Blvd, South Lake Tahoe (96150-8907)
PHONE 530 544-5900
John House, *Principal*
EMP: 74 **EST:** 1967
SQ FT: 38,000
SALES (est): 626K **Privately Held**
WEB: www.holidayinnexpress.com
SIC: 7011 Hotels & motels

(P-11152)
HOLIDAY INN EXPRESS
600 Riverside Ave, Santa Cruz (95060-5162)
PHONE 888 803-5176
Joe Ritchey, *Partner*
James Gilbert, *Partner*
EMP: 69 **EST:** 1985
SALES (est): 323.9K **Privately Held**
WEB: www.holidayinn.com
SIC: 7011 Hotels & motels

(P-11153)
HOLIDAY INN EXPRESS
28976 Plaza Dr, Gustine (95322-9767)
PHONE 209 826-8282
Mark Dudys, *Manager*
Steven Cavadias, *Partner*
Jerry Philipps, *Partner*
EMP: 39 **EST:** 1989
SALES (est): 2MM **Privately Held**
WEB: www.holidayinnexpress.com
SIC: 7011 Hotels & motels

(P-11154)
HOLIDAY INN EXPRESS & SUITES
650 W Shaw Ave, Clovis (93612-3211)
PHONE 559 297-0555
Bob Yoon, *Mng Member*

Johnnie Harris, *Sales Mgr*
EMP: 51 **EST:** 2012
SALES (est): 5.6MM **Privately Held**
WEB: www.holidayinn.com
SIC: 7011 Hotels & motels

(P-11155)
HOLIDAY INN EXPRESS MERCED
730 Motel Dr, Merced (95341-5151)
PHONE 209 383-0333
Kainth Brothers, *Principal*
EMP: 100 **EST:** 1992
SALES (est): 2.9MM **Privately Held**
WEB: www.holidayinn.com
SIC: 7011 Hotels & motels

(P-11156)
HOLIDAY INN GREAT AMERICA
4200 Great America Pkwy, Santa Clara (95054-1210)
PHONE 408 235-8900
Dan Ponder, *Manager*
Robert Hendricks, *General Mgr*
EMP: 67 **EST:** 1996
SQ FT: 56,264
SALES (est): 495.6K **Privately Held**
WEB: www.holidayinn.com
SIC: 7011 Resort hotel

(P-11157)
HOLIDAY INN SUITES
5046 N Barcus Ave, Fresno (93722-5057)
PHONE 559 277-5700
Sherry Choutchorru, *Manager*
EMP: 38 **EST:** 1998
SQ FT: 25,122
SALES (est): 187K **Privately Held**
WEB: www.holidayinn.com
SIC: 7011 Hotels & motels

(P-11158)
HOME AWAY INC
54432 Road 432, Bass Lake (93604-9762)
P.O. Box 149 (93604-0149)
PHONE 559 642-3121
Kyusun Choe, *President*
Sun Choe, *Admin Sec*
Christopher Talley, *Engineer*
EMP: 65 **EST:** 2004
SALES (est): 2.7MM **Privately Held**
SIC: 7011 Hotels & motels

(P-11159)
HOMEWOOD SUITES MANAGEMENT LLC
1103 Embarcadero, Oakland (94606-5122)
PHONE 510 663-2700
Jason Oliveras, *Manager*
EMP: 45
SALES (corp-wide): 4.3B **Publicly Held**
WEB: www.homewoodsuites3.hilton.com
SIC: 7011 Hotels & motels
HQ: Homewood Suites Management Llc
7930 Jones Branch Dr
Mc Lean VA 22102
703 883-1000

(P-11160)
HOMEWOOD VILLAGE RESORTS LLC
Also Called: Homewood Mountain Resort
5145 W Lake Blvd, Homewood (96141-9806)
P.O. Box 165 (96141-0165)
PHONE 530 525-2992
Todd Chapman, *CEO*
Lisa Nigon, *Mktg Dir*
Dave Paulson, *Maintence Staff*
Fred Scholz, *Maintence Staff*
Abby Groman, *Manager*
EMP: 50 **EST:** 2012
SALES (est): 5.2MM **Privately Held**
WEB: www.skihomewood.com
SIC: 7011 Ski lodge

(P-11161)
HOMWOOD SUITES BY HILTON
Also Called: Homewood Suites
6820 N Fresno St, Fresno (93710-3738)
PHONE 559 440-0801
Jason Boehm, *Principal*
EMP: 56 **EST:** 2008

SALES (est): 1.2MM **Privately Held**
WEB: www.homewoodsuites3.hilton.com
SIC: 7011 Hotels & motels

(P-11162)
HOST INTERNATIONAL INC
Also Called: Marriott
1661 Airport Blvd Ste 3e, San Jose (95110-1216)
PHONE 408 294-1702
Fax: 408 294-4260
EMP: 180
SALES (corp-wide): 9.4MM **Privately Held**
SIC: 7011 Hotels And Motels
HQ: Host International, Inc.
6905 Rockledge Dr Fl 1
Bethesda MD 20817
240 694-4100

(P-11163)
HOTEL DURANT A LTD PARTNERSHIP
Also Called: Henry's Pub
2600 Durant Ave, Berkeley (94704-1711)
PHONE 510 845-8981
Stephen Wahrlich, *General Ptnr*
Thunderbird Investors, *General Ptnr*
Tracy W Wahrlich Jr, *General Ptnr*
EMP: 100 **EST:** 1928
SQ FT: 57,730
SALES (est): 4.5MM **Privately Held**
WEB: www.hoteldurantberkeley.com
SIC: 7011 5812 5813 6512 Hotels; American restaurant; bar (drinking places); nonresidential building operators

(P-11164)
HOTEL HEALDSBURG LLC (PA)
25 Matheson St, Healdsburg (95448-4107)
PHONE 707 431-2800
Aziz Zhari, *Manager*
Fatimah Abdullah, *Sales Staff*
Most Rev Aziz Zhari, *Manager*
EMP: 77 **EST:** 2001
SQ FT: 57,500
SALES (est): 10.4MM **Privately Held**
WEB: www.hotelhealdsburg.com
SIC: 7011 Hotels

(P-11165)
HOTEL LA ROSE
308 Wilson St, Santa Rosa (95401-6245)
PHONE 707 284-2879
Claus Neumann, *President*
Debra Neumann, *General Mgr*
EMP: 52 **EST:** 1962
SALES (est): 997.5K **Privately Held**
WEB: www.hotellarose.com
SIC: 7011 5812 Hotels; eating places

(P-11166)
HOTEL LEGER LLC
83047 Main St, Burlingame (94010)
PHONE 209 286-1401
Ashley Canty, *Managing Prtnr*
Jane Canty, *Partner*
Ron Pitner, *Partner*
EMP: 37 **EST:** 1971
SQ FT: 17,000
SALES (est): 446.7K **Privately Held**
WEB: www.hotelleger.com
SIC: 7011 5813 5812 Hotel, franchised; bar (drinking places); restaurant, family: independent

(P-11167)
HOTEL MCINNIS MARIN LLC
Also Called: Embassy Suites
101 Mcinnis Pkwy, San Rafael (94903-2773)
PHONE 415 499-9222
Shawn Milburn, *Mng Member*
Hope Fuerniss,
EMP: 90 **EST:** 1990
SALES (est): 5.5MM **Privately Held**
WEB: www.hilton.com
SIC: 7011 6512 4729 5812 Hotels & motels; commercial & industrial building operation; passenger transportation arrangement; caterers

(P-11168)
HOTEL NAPA I OPCO L P
Also Called: Staybridge Suites NAPA
4775 Business Center Dr, Fairfield (94534-1916)
PHONE 707 863-0900
Denis J Olson,
Irish Kiocho, *General Mgr*
EMP: 67 **EST:** 2005
SALES (est): 1.5MM **Privately Held**
WEB: www.staybridgesuites.com
SIC: 7011 Hotels & motels

(P-11169)
HOTEL NAPA II OPCO LP
Also Called: Homewood Suites
4755 Business Center Dr, Fairfield (94534-1916)
PHONE 707 863-0300
Raymond Schulte, *Managing Prtnr*
EMP: 50 **EST:** 2016
SALES (est): 2.8MM **Privately Held**
WEB: www.homewoodsuites3.hilton.com
SIC: 7011 Hotels & motels

(P-11170)
HOTEL NIKKO SAN FRANCISCO INC
222 Mason St, San Francisco (94102-2115)
PHONE 415 394-1111
Vincent Rafanan, *CFO*
Anna Marie Presutti, *Vice Pres*
Randy Taradash, *General Mgr*
Chris Reyes, *Chief Engr*
Emmanuel Sakellarios, *Opers Staff*
EMP: 260 **EST:** 1984
SQ FT: 540,000
SALES (est): 38.5MM **Privately Held**
WEB: www.hotelnikkosf.com
SIC: 7011 5812 5813 7991 Resort hotel; eating places; bar (drinking places); health club; banquet hall facilities
HQ: Okura Nikko Hotel Management Co., Ltd.
2-10-4, Toranomon
Minato-Ku TKY 105-0

(P-11171)
HOTEL PRDOX AUTOGRAPH COLLECTN
611 Ocean St, Santa Cruz (95060-4005)
PHONE 831 425-7100
C Jones, *General Mgr*
Christopher Jones, *General Mgr*
Flavia Oliveira, *Sales Staff*
EMP: 41 **EST:** 2012
SALES (est): 6MM **Privately Held**
WEB: www.hotelparadox.com
SIC: 7011 Hotels

(P-11172)
HOTEL TONIGHT INC (PA)
888 Brannan St Fl 3, San Francisco (94103-4968)
PHONE 800 208-2949
Sam Shank, *CEO*
Jared Simon, *COO*
Tony Grimminck, *CFO*
Ray Elias, *Chief Mktg Ofcr*
Kelly Russell, *Office Mgr*
EMP: 253 **EST:** 2011
SALES (est): 22.5MM **Privately Held**
WEB: www.hoteltonight.com
SIC: 7011 Hotels

(P-11173)
HOTEL TONIGHT LLC (PA)
888 Brannan St Fl 3, San Francisco (94103-4968)
PHONE 248 525-3814
Tony Grimminck, *CFO*
Ray Elias, *Chief Mktg Ofcr*
Jatinder Singh, *CTO*
Kristin McManus, *Business Anlyst*
Emma Leggat, *Corp Comm Staff*
EMP: 51 **EST:** 2018
SALES (est): 1.9MM **Privately Held**
WEB: www.hoteltonight.com
SIC: 7011 Hotels

7011 - Hotels, Motels & Tourist Courts County (P-11174)

(P-11174)
HOTEL WHITCOMB
1231 Market St, San Francisco (94103-1405)
PHONE..................415 626-8000
Thomas Chan, *Controller*
Brittany Wimer, *Chief Acct*
Santiago Hernandez, *Finance*
Tyler Gard, *Opers Staff*
Mohamed Abdelmaksoud, *Facilities Dir*
EMP: 99 **EST:** 1988
SALES (est): 8.4MM **Privately Held**
WEB: www.hotelwhitcomb.com
SIC: 7011 Hotels

(P-11175)
HOTEL YOUNTVILLE LLC
6462 Washington St, Yountville (94599-1408)
PHONE..................707 967-7900
George Altamira, *President*
Michele Querin, *Sales Staff*
Kristin Takemoto, *Sales Staff*
Espinosa Fernando, *Facilities Dir*
Cassondra Rogers- Royael, *Director*
EMP: 40 **EST:** 1998
SALES (est): 5.2MM **Privately Held**
WEB: www.hotelyountville.com
SIC: 7011 Bed & breakfast inn; inns

(P-11176)
HUMBOLDT HOUSE INN LLC
Also Called: Best Western
701 Redwood Dr, Garberville (95542-3104)
PHONE..................707 923-2771
James O Johnson, *Partner*
Thomas Tobin, *Partner*
Wagner Family Trust, *Partner*
EMP: 41 **EST:** 1984
SALES (est): 1.3MM **Privately Held**
WEB: www.humboldthouseinn.com
SIC: 7011 Hotels & motels

(P-11177)
HUSKIES LESSEE LLC
Also Called: Sir Francis Drake Hotel
450 Powell St, San Francisco (94102-1504)
PHONE..................415 392-7755
John Price, *General Mgr*
EMP: 153 **EST:** 2010
SALES (est): 406.9K **Privately Held**
SIC: 7011 Hotels

(P-11178)
HV-HOUSTON DEVELOPMENT INC
Also Called: Marriott
11211 Point East Dr, Rancho Cordova (95742-6239)
PHONE..................916 638-1100
James Evans, *CFO*
Marco Filice, *General Mgr*
Rebecca Garcia, *Human Res Dir*
Christian Kershner, *Sales Mgr*
Robbie Garcia, *Sales Staff*
EMP: 40 **EST:** 1992
SQ FT: 30,000
SALES (est): 5MM **Privately Held**
WEB: www.marriott.com
SIC: 7011 Hotels & motels

(P-11179)
HWANG LLC
Also Called: La Quinta Inn San Jose
2585 Seaboard Ave, San Jose (95131-1006)
PHONE..................408 435-8800
Gemma Hwang,
Jason Cabral, *General Mgr*
Benji Fernandez, *Manager*
EMP: 80 **EST:** 1990
SALES (est): 3.1MM **Privately Held**
WEB: www.wyndhamhotels.com
SIC: 7011 Hotels & motels

(P-11180)
HYATT CORPORATION
Also Called: Grand Hyatt San Francisco
345 Stockton St, San Francisco (94108-4606)
PHONE..................415 848-6050
Steve Trent, *Manager*
Jordan Meisner, *Vice Pres*
Sara Frey, *Human Res Mgr*
Michael Scherbert, *Sales Staff*
Chelsea Hildreth, *Asst Director*
EMP: 477 **Publicly Held**
WEB: www.hyatt.com
SIC: 7011 5813 5812 6512 Hotels & motels; drinking places; eating places; non-residential building operators
HQ: Hyatt Corporation
150 N Riverside Plz
Chicago IL 60606
312 750-1234

(P-11181)
HYATT CORPORATION
Also Called: Hyatt House San Ramon
2323 San Ramon Vly Blvd, San Ramon (94583-1607)
PHONE..................925 743-1882
Pam Callahan, *Branch Mgr*
EMP: 316 **Publicly Held**
WEB: www.hyatt.com
SIC: 7011 Hotels
HQ: Hyatt Corporation
150 N Riverside Plz
Chicago IL 60606
312 750-1234

(P-11182)
HYATT CORPORATION
Also Called: Hyatt Hotel
55 S Mcdonnell Rd, San Francisco (94128-3102)
PHONE..................650 452-1234
Shun Matsumoto, *Manager*
EMP: 192 **Publicly Held**
WEB: www.hyatt.com
SIC: 7011 Hotels & motels
HQ: Hyatt Corporation
150 N Riverside Plz
Chicago IL 60606
312 750-1234

(P-11183)
HYATT CORPORATION
Also Called: Hyatt Regency San Francisco Ht
5 Embarcadero Ctr, San Francisco (94111-4800)
PHONE..................415 788-1234
Jerry Simmons, *General Mgr*
Harish Chand, *Admin Sec*
Valerie Saito, *Human Res Dir*
Judy Cronkhite, *Sales Dir*
Christopher Uy, *Sales Mgr*
EMP: 581 **Publicly Held**
WEB: www.hyatt.com
SIC: 7011 5812 5813 Hotels & motels; eating places; drinking places
HQ: Hyatt Corporation
150 N Riverside Plz
Chicago IL 60606
312 750-1234

(P-11184)
HYATT REGENCY SANTA CLARA
Also Called: Hyatt Hotel
5101 Great America Pkwy, Santa Clara (95054-1118)
PHONE..................408 200-1234
Peter Reice, *General Mgr*
Jeanne Muljadi-Reed, *Finance*
EMP: 66 **EST:** 2006
SALES (est): 13.2MM **Privately Held**
WEB: www.santaclara.org
SIC: 7011 Hotels & motels

(P-11185)
IA LODGING NAPA SOLANO TRS LLC
Also Called: NAPA Valley Marriott
3425 Solano Ave, NAPA (94558-2709)
PHONE..................707 253-8600
Amanda Hawkins-Vogel, *General Mgr*
Jeremy Spaulding, *Sales Staff*
Blossom Price, *Supervisor*
EMP: 210 **EST:** 2011
SQ FT: 200,000
SALES (est): 21.3MM **Publicly Held**
WEB: www.marriott.com
SIC: 7011 Resort hotel, franchised
PA: Xenia Hotels & Resorts, Inc.
200 S Orange Ave Ste 2700
Orlando FL 32801

(P-11186)
IAV INC
Also Called: Geyserville Inn
21714 Geyserville Ave, Geyserville (95441-9541)
PHONE..................707 857-4343
Dan Christensen Sr, *President*
Daniel Christensen, *CPA*
Danny Christensen Jr, *Manager*
EMP: 36 **EST:** 1997
SALES (est): 2.9MM **Privately Held**
WEB: www.geyservilleinn.com
SIC: 7011 Hotels

(P-11187)
IHMS (SF) LLC
Also Called: Campton Place, A Taj Hotel
340 Stockton St, San Francisco (94108-4609)
PHONE..................415 781-5555
Sanjay Jain,
Celia Arias, *General Mgr*
Naresh Kumar, *General Mgr*
Juanita Santos, *General Mgr*
Sunil Sunar, *General Mgr*
EMP: 150 **EST:** 2007
SALES (est): 20.9MM **Privately Held**
WEB: www.thepierreny.com
SIC: 7011 Hotels
HQ: International Hotel Management Services Inc.
2 E 61st St
New York NY 10065

(P-11188)
INN AT DEPOT HILL
250 Monterey Ave, Capitola (95010-3358)
PHONE..................831 462-3376
Dan Floyd, *Partner*
Suzanne Lankes, *Partner*
EMP: 36 **EST:** 1990
SQ FT: 5,000
SALES (est): 567.2K **Privately Held**
WEB: www.innatdepothill.com
SIC: 7011 Bed & breakfast inn

(P-11189)
INN AT JACK LONDON SQUARE LLC
Also Called: Z Hotel Jack London Square
1000 Marina Village Pkwy # 100, Alameda (94501-6457)
PHONE..................510 452-4565
Clyde R Gibb,
Kurt Helmke, *General Mgr*
Sam Nassif,
Joanne Mallari, *Manager*
Pitt Onkchareon, *Manager*
EMP: 38 **EST:** 1984
SALES (est): 2.5MM **Privately Held**
WEB: www.zhoteljacklondonsquare.com
SIC: 7011 Hotels

(P-11190)
INN AT OPERA A CAL LTD PARTNR
Also Called: Shell Vacations Club
333 Fulton St, San Francisco (94102-4423)
PHONE..................415 863-8400
Sean Pierson, *Principal*
EMP: 35 **EST:** 1985
SALES (est): 1MM **Privately Held**
WEB: www.sfopera.com
SIC: 7011 5812 6531 Resort hotel; eating places; time-sharing real estate sales, leasing & rentals

(P-11191)
INN AT SCOTTS VALLEY LLC
Also Called: Hilton
6001 La Madrona Dr, Scotts Valley (95060-1057)
PHONE..................831 440-1000
Rich Higdon, *Mng Member*
EMP: 94 **EST:** 1998
SQ FT: 130,000
SALES (est): 1.6MM **Privately Held**
WEB: www.hiltongrandvacations.com
SIC: 7011 Inns

(P-11192)
INN VENTURES INC
Also Called: Hilton Garden Inn Roseville
1951 Taylor Rd, Roseville (95661-3008)
PHONE..................916 773-7171
Greg Juceam, *COO*
Tabitha Christensen, *Manager*
Tracy Kopshy, *Manager*
EMP: 93 **EST:** 2005
SALES (est): 1MM **Privately Held**
WEB: www.innventures.com
SIC: 7011 Hotels & motels

(P-11193)
INNCAL INCORPORATED
Also Called: Super 8 Motel
2717 W March Ln, Stockton (95219-6572)
PHONE..................209 477-5576
Peggy Lindsey, *Branch Mgr*
Ryan Thompson, *Associate*
EMP: 55
SALES (corp-wide): 4.7MM **Privately Held**
WEB: www.wyndhamhotels.com
SIC: 7011 Hotels & motels
PA: Inncal, Incorporated
1919 Grand Canal Blvd B5
Stockton CA 95207
209 473-4667

(P-11194)
INTERCNTNNTAL HTELS SAN FRNCSC
Also Called: Intercntinental Hotels Resorts
888 Howard St, San Francisco (94103-3011)
PHONE..................415 616-6500
Peter Koehler, *General Mgr*
Connie Perez, *Pub Rel Mgr*
Tanish Kumar, *Sales Mgr*
Jennifer Dunn, *Sales Staff*
Thomas Sloneker, *Manager*
EMP: 150 **Privately Held**
WEB: www.icsanfrancisco.com
SIC: 7011 Hotels
HQ: Intercontinental Hotels Of San Francisco, Inc.
35016 Avenue D
Yucaipa CA 92399

(P-11195)
INTERNATIONAL HOTEL ASSOC LLC
Also Called: Windsor Tea Room, The
334 Mason St, San Francisco (94102-1707)
PHONE..................415 283-4832
Todd Irish, *General Mgr*
EMP: 40 **EST:** 1914
SQ FT: 56,000
SALES (est): 2.6MM **Privately Held**
WEB: www.kinggeorge.com
SIC: 7011 5812 Hotels; eating places

(P-11196)
INTERNTIONAL HT ASSOC NO 3 LLC
Also Called: Creekside Inn In Palo Alto
3400 El Camino Real, Palo Alto (94306-2702)
PHONE..................650 493-2411
Luis Carreno, *General Mgr*
Toya Barnette, *Human Res Mgr*
Kathleen Posadas, *Manager*
EMP: 57 **EST:** 1958
SQ FT: 43,000
SALES (est): 1.4MM **Privately Held**
WEB: www.creekside-inn.com
SIC: 7011 Hotels

(P-11197)
INTRAWEST NAPA RVRBEND HSPTLIT
Also Called: Westin Verasa NAPA
1314 Mckinstry St, NAPA (94559-1900)
PHONE..................408 829-4141
Don Shindle, *General Mgr*
Richard Barnes, *CIO*
Katarina Mezeiova, *Finance*
David Martin, *Accountant*
Karen Gartner, *Sales Mgr*
EMP: 64 **EST:** 2005

PRODUCTS & SERVICES SECTION
7011 - Hotels, Motels & Tourist Courts County (P-11220)

SALES (est): 12.9MM Privately Held
WEB: www.marriott.com
SIC: 7011 Hotels

(P-11198)
ISLAND HOSPITALITY MGT LLC
Also Called: Residence Inn By Marriott
6111 San Ignacio Ave, San Jose (95119-1389)
PHONE.................408 226-7676
Frank Machado, *Manager*
Maya Rhodes, *Executive*
Julissa Barragan, *General Mgr*
Francisco Cruz, *General Mgr*
EMP: 43
SALES (corp-wide): 451.7MM Privately Held
WEB: www.islandhospitality.com
SIC: 7011 Hotels & motels
PA: Island Hospitality Management, Llc
   222 Lakeview Ave Ste 200
   West Palm Beach FL 33401
   561 832-6132

(P-11199)
ISLAND HOSPITALITY MGT LLC
Residence Inn By Marriott
750 Lakeway Dr, Sunnyvale (94085-4011)
PHONE.................408 720-1000
Hugo Hernandez, *Branch Mgr*
Jenae Moore, *Marketing Staff*
EMP: 43
SALES (corp-wide): 451.7MM Privately Held
WEB: www.islandhospitality.com
SIC: 7011 Hotels & motels
PA: Island Hospitality Management, Llc
   222 Lakeview Ave Ste 200
   West Palm Beach FL 33401
   561 832-6132

(P-11200)
ISLAND HOSPITALITY MGT LLC
Also Called: Residence Inn By Marriott
2000 Winward Way, San Mateo (94404-2472)
PHONE.................650 574-4700
Omar Paredes, *Branch Mgr*
EMP: 43
SALES (corp-wide): 451.7MM Privately Held
WEB: www.islandhospitality.com
SIC: 7011 Hotels & motels
PA: Island Hospitality Management, Llc
   222 Lakeview Ave Ste 200
   West Palm Beach FL 33401
   561 832-6132

(P-11201)
ISLAND HOSPITALITY MGT LLC
Residence Inn By Marriott
1080 Stewart Dr, Sunnyvale (94085-3917)
PHONE.................408 720-8893
Kort Gursu, *Manager*
EMP: 43
SALES (corp-wide): 451.7MM Privately Held
WEB: www.islandhospitality.com
SIC: 7011 Hotels & motels
PA: Island Hospitality Management, Llc
   222 Lakeview Ave Ste 200
   West Palm Beach FL 33401
   561 832-6132

(P-11202)
ISLAND HOSPITALITY MGT LLC
Also Called: Hyatt Hse Blmnt/Redwood Shores
400 Concourse Dr, Belmont (94002-4125)
PHONE.................650 591-8600
Trinity Nguyen, *Branch Mgr*
Denise Eldrich, *General Mgr*
Alvin Magcale, *General Mgr*
EMP: 43
SALES (corp-wide): 451.7MM Privately Held
WEB: www.islandhospitality.com
SIC: 7011 Hotels
PA: Island Hospitality Management, Llc
   222 Lakeview Ave Ste 200
   West Palm Beach FL 33401
   561 832-6132

(P-11203)
ISLAND HOSPITALITY MGT LLC
Also Called: Residnce Inn Palo Alto Mtn Vie
1854 W El Camino Real, Mountain View (94040-2356)
PHONE.................650 940-1300
Andrew Allison, *Branch Mgr*
Thompson Mosher, *Vice Pres*
EMP: 43
SALES (corp-wide): 451.7MM Privately Held
WEB: www.islandhospitality.com
SIC: 7011 Hotels & motels
PA: Island Hospitality Management, Llc
   222 Lakeview Ave Ste 200
   West Palm Beach FL 33401
   561 832-6132

(P-11204)
JACK PLUMP INC
3138 Fillmore St, San Francisco (94123-3452)
PHONE.................415 346-5712
Rick Riess, *President*
Deeann Graffigna, *Vice Pres*
Emiley Thrasher, *Comms Mgr*
Rosie Gibson, *General Mgr*
Kevin Krueger, *General Mgr*
EMP: 46 EST: 1991
SALES (est): 205.6K Privately Held
WEB: www.plumpjack.com
SIC: 7011 Hotels

(P-11205)
JAI JAI MATA INC
Also Called: Comfort Suites
102 E Herndon Ave, Fresno (93720-2914)
PHONE.................559 435-5650
Narender Taneja, *President*
Amita Narender, *Vice Pres*
Mahesh Patel, *Manager*
EMP: 48 EST: 2000
SQ FT: 47,000
SALES (est): 795.5K Privately Held
WEB: www.choicehotels.com
SIC: 7011 Hotel, franchised

(P-11206)
JAI SHRI RAM HOSPITALI
Also Called: Holiday Inn
685 Manzanita Ct, Chico (95926-2359)
PHONE.................530 345-2491
Vinod Sharma, *Mng Member*
EMP: 79 EST: 2000
SALES (est): 2.2MM Privately Held
WEB: www.holidayinn.com
SIC: 7011 Hotels & motels

(P-11207)
JALARAM INVESTMENT LLC
Also Called: Days Inn Oakland Airport
8350 Edes Ave, Oakland (94621-1307)
PHONE.................510 568-1880
Amit Motawala, *Mng Member*
Sunil Patel,
EMP: 44 EST: 2005
SQ FT: 100,000
SALES (est): 964.7K Privately Held
WEB: www.wyndhamhotels.com
SIC: 7011 Hotels & motels

(P-11208)
JAME HOTEL CORPORATION
Also Called: Hotel California
405 Taylor St, San Francisco (94102-1701)
PHONE.................415 885-2500
Jack Schleifer, *President*
Jack Scheifer, *President*
Andy Wong, *Credit Mgr*
Mary Finn, *Asst Controller*
EMP: 65 EST: 1972
SQ FT: 40,000
SALES (est): 1.3MM Privately Held
SIC: 7011 Hotels

(P-11209)
JBEAR ASSOCIATES LLC
Also Called: Hotel Mark Twain
345 Taylor St, San Francisco (94102-2004)
PHONE.................415 673-2332
Jay Ellsworth,
EMP: 52 EST: 1998
SQ FT: 20,000
SALES (est): 1.1MM Privately Held
WEB: www.tildenhotel.com
SIC: 7011 6552 8741 Hotels; subdividers & developers; hotel or motel management

(P-11210)
JBR ASSOCIATES INC
Also Called: Holiday Inn
151 Lawrence Dr, Vacaville (95687-3201)
PHONE.................707 451-3500
Ravindra Patel, *CEO*
Jayantilal Patel, *CFO*
Bhupen Magen, *Admin Sec*
EMP: 53 EST: 2002
SQ FT: 53,620
SALES (est): 1.3MM Privately Held
WEB: www.holidayinn.com
SIC: 7011 Hotels & motels

(P-11211)
JJK HOTELS LP (PA)
Also Called: Red Lion Hotel Eureka
1929 4th St, Eureka (95501-0725)
PHONE.................707 441-4721
EMP: 63 EST: 2014
SALES (est): 2.9MM Privately Held
WEB: www.redlion.com
SIC: 7011 Hotels

(P-11212)
JOIE DE VIVRE HOSPITALITY LLC
210 E Main St, Los Gatos (95030-6107)
PHONE.................408 335-1700
EMP: 81
SALES (corp-wide): 138.4MM Privately Held
WEB: www.jdvhotels.com
SIC: 7011 Hotels
PA: Joie De Vivre Hospitality, Llc
   1750 Geary Blvd
   San Francisco CA 94115
   415 922-6000

(P-11213)
JOIE DE VIVRE HOSPITALITY LLC (PA)
Also Called: Kabuki Springs & Spa
1750 Geary Blvd, San Francisco (94115-3715)
PHONE.................415 922-6000
Stephen T Conley Jr, *CEO*
Daniel Korn, *Vice Pres*
Suzie Yang, *General Mgr*
Anne Conley, *Admin Sec*
Linda Vergil, *Accounting Mgr*
EMP: 50 EST: 2010
SALES (est): 138.4MM Privately Held
WEB: www.jdvhotels.com
SIC: 7011 Hotels

(P-11214)
JOIE DE VIVRE HOSPITALITY LLC
Also Called: Hotel Vitale
8 Mission St, San Francisco (94105-1227)
PHONE.................415 278-3700
Chip Conley, *Branch Mgr*
Paolo Alarcon, *CIO*
Rebeca Iavarone, *Sales Staff*
Monica Lostica, *Sales Staff*
Diane Wesley, *Sales Staff*
EMP: 81
SALES (corp-wide): 138.4MM Privately Held
WEB: www.jdvhotels.com
SIC: 7011 Hotels
PA: Joie De Vivre Hospitality, Llc
   1750 Geary Blvd
   San Francisco CA 94115
   415 922-6000

(P-11215)
JOIE DE VIVRE HOSPITALITY LLC
Also Called: Laurel Inn
444 Presidio Ave, San Francisco (94115-2004)
PHONE.................415 567-8467
Chip Conley, *President*
EMP: 81
SQ FT: 25,448
SALES (corp-wide): 138.4MM Privately Held
WEB: www.jdvhotels.com
SIC: 7011 Hotels
PA: Joie De Vivre Hospitality, Llc
   1750 Geary Blvd
   San Francisco CA 94115
   415 922-6000

(P-11216)
JOIE DE VIVRE HOSPITALITY LLC
Also Called: Acqua Hotel
555 Redwood Hwy Frontage, Mill Valley (94941-3007)
PHONE.................415 380-0400
Steve Conley, *President*
EMP: 81
SALES (corp-wide): 138.4MM Privately Held
WEB: www.jdvhotels.com
SIC: 7011 Hotels
PA: Joie De Vivre Hospitality, Llc
   1750 Geary Blvd
   San Francisco CA 94115
   415 922-6000

(P-11217)
JOIE DE VIVRE HOSPITALITY LLC
580 Geary St, San Francisco (94102-1650)
PHONE.................415 441-2700
Frank Okun, *General Mgr*
EMP: 81
SALES (corp-wide): 138.4MM Privately Held
WEB: www.jdvhotels.com
SIC: 7011 8741 Hotels; hotel or motel management
PA: Joie De Vivre Hospitality, Llc
   1750 Geary Blvd
   San Francisco CA 94115
   415 922-6000

(P-11218)
JOIE DE VIVRE HOSPITALITY LLC
Also Called: Hotel Del Sol
3100 Webster St, San Francisco (94123-3411)
PHONE.................415 921-5520
Steve Conley, *President*
EMP: 81
SALES (corp-wide): 138.4MM Privately Held
WEB: www.jdvhotels.com
SIC: 7011 Hotels
PA: Joie De Vivre Hospitality, Llc
   1750 Geary Blvd
   San Francisco CA 94115
   415 922-6000

(P-11219)
JOIE DE VIVRE HOSPITALITY LLC
Also Called: Phoenix Hotel
601 Eddy St, San Francisco (94109-7904)
PHONE.................415 776-1380
Steven Conley, *Principal*
Anderson Foote, *General Mgr*
EMP: 81
SALES (corp-wide): 138.4MM Privately Held
WEB: www.jdvhotels.com
SIC: 7011 Hotels
PA: Joie De Vivre Hospitality, Llc
   1750 Geary Blvd
   San Francisco CA 94115
   415 922-6000

(P-11220)
JOIE DE VIVRE HOSPITALITY LLC
Also Called: Hotel Avante
860 E El Camino Real, Mountain View (94040-2808)
PHONE.................650 940-1000
Fred Deftesano, *Vice Pres*
EMP: 81
SALES (corp-wide): 138.4MM Privately Held
WEB: www.jdvhotels.com
SIC: 7011 Hotels

7011 - Hotels, Motels & Tourist Courts County (P-11221)

PA: Joie De Vivre Hospitality, Llc
1750 Geary Blvd
San Francisco CA 94115
415 922-6000

(P-11221)
JOIE DE VIVRE HOSPITALITY LLC
Also Called: White Swan Inn, The
845 Bush St, San Francisco (94108-3312)
PHONE..................415 775-1755
Rebecca Levy, *Branch Mgr*
EMP: 81
SALES (corp-wide): 138.4MM **Privately Held**
WEB: www.jdvhotels.com
SIC: 7011 8741 Hotels; management services
PA: Joie De Vivre Hospitality, Llc
1750 Geary Blvd
San Francisco CA 94115
415 922-6000

(P-11222)
JOIE DE VIVRE HOSPITALITY INC
Also Called: Wild Palms Hotel & Bar
910 E Fremont Ave, Sunnyvale (94087-3702)
PHONE..................408 738-0500
Steven C Y Chen, *President*
Patricia Hayakawa, *Human Resources*
EMP: 57 EST: 1975
SQ FT: 80,000
SALES (est): 573.4K **Privately Held**
WEB: www.jdvhotels.com
SIC: 7011 Hotels

(P-11223)
JOIE DE VIVRE HOTELS
Also Called: Phoenix Inn, The
601 Eddy St, San Francisco (94109-7904)
PHONE..................415 776-1380
Steve Conley Sr, *Partner*
Paul Gasper, *Manager*
EMP: 51 EST: 1966
SQ FT: 20,000
SALES (est): 641.3K **Privately Held**
WEB: www.phoenixsf.com
SIC: 7011 Motels

(P-11224)
JRP HOSPITALITY INC
309 Prosperity Blvd, Chowchilla (93610-8498)
PHONE..................408 569-2911
Mahesh M Patel, *President*
Mahesh M Patel, *President*
Nick Patel, *Admin Sec*
EMP: 38 EST: 2006
SALES (est): 528.6K **Privately Held**
SIC: 7011 Hotels & motels

(P-11225)
K3 DEV LLC
Also Called: AC Hotel San Jose Snnyvale Cpr
725 S Fair Oaks Ave, Sunnyvale (94086-7915)
PHONE..................408 733-7950
Mayur Patel, *Principal*
Mona Rigdon, *Principal*
EMP: 80 EST: 2018
SALES (est): 2.8MM **Privately Held**
WEB: www.ac-hotels.marriott.com
SIC: 7011 Hotels

(P-11226)
K3 DEV LLC
Also Called: AC Hotel Sunnyvale
597 E El Camino Real, Sunnyvale (94087-1942)
PHONE..................408 733-7950
Mona Rigdon, *Principal*
Mayur Patel, *Principal*
EMP: 65 EST: 2019
SALES (est): 2.5MM **Privately Held**
WEB: www.ac-hotels.marriott.com
SIC: 7011 Hotels

(P-11227)
KAIDAN HOSPITALITY LP
Also Called: Red Lion Hotel Redding
1830 Hilltop Dr, Redding (96002-0212)
PHONE..................530 221-8700
Ken Galarowicz, *Controller*
EMP: 66 EST: 2014
SALES (est): 3.4MM **Privately Held**
WEB: www.redlion.com
SIC: 7011 Hotels & motels

(P-11228)
KHANNA ENTPS - II LTD PARTNR
Also Called: Crowne Plz Scramento Northeast
5321 Date Ave, Sacramento (95841-2512)
PHONE..................916 338-5800
Ravi Khanna, *Partner*
Anil Khanna, *Partner*
Ashwin Khanna, *Partner*
Rajesh Khanna, *Partner*
David Huber, *General Mgr*
EMP: 35 EST: 2004
SALES (est): 2.8MM **Privately Held**
WEB: www.ihg.com
SIC: 7011 Hotels & motels

(P-11229)
KHP III SF SUTTER LLC (PA)
Also Called: Hotel Tomo
1800 Sutter St, San Francisco (94115-3220)
PHONE..................415 921-4000
George Daneshgar,
EMP: 95 EST: 2006
SALES (est): 1.2MM **Privately Held**
WEB: www.bestwestern.com
SIC: 7011 Hotels

(P-11230)
KIMPTON HOTEL & REST GROUP LLC
Also Called: Serrano Hotel
405 Taylor St, San Francisco (94102-1701)
PHONE..................415 885-2500
John Turner, *General Mgr*
Barry Dorsey, *General Mgr*
Benjamin Malmquist, *General Mgr*
Sarah Mendoza, *Asst Controller*
Maricar Miller, *Finance*
EMP: 206 **Privately Held**
WEB: www.kimptonhotels.com
SIC: 7011 7299 Hotels; banquet hall facilities
HQ: Kimpton Hotel & Restaurant Group Llc
222 Kearny St Ste 200
San Francisco CA 94108
415 397-5572

(P-11231)
KIMPTON HOTEL & REST GROUP LLC (HQ)
222 Kearny St Ste 200, San Francisco (94108-4537)
PHONE..................415 397-5572
Mike Depatie, *CEO*
Donald Ogrady, *Owner*
Mike Defrino, *COO*
Niki Leondakis, *COO*
Ben Rowe, *CFO*
EMP: 100 EST: 1982
SALES (est): 606.5MM **Privately Held**
WEB: www.kimptonhotels.com
SIC: 7011 8741 6794 Hotels; hotel or motel management; franchises, selling or licensing

(P-11232)
KIMPTON HOTEL & REST GROUP LLC
Also Called: Tuscan Inn
425 N Point St, San Francisco (94133-1405)
PHONE..................415 561-1100
Jan Misch, *Manager*
EMP: 206 **Privately Held**
WEB: www.kimptonhotels.com
SIC: 7011 7299 5813 Hotels; banquet hall facilities; drinking places
HQ: Kimpton Hotel & Restaurant Group Llc
222 Kearny St Ste 200
San Francisco CA 94108
415 397-5572

(P-11233)
KIMPTON HOTEL & REST GROUP LLC
Also Called: Monticello Inn
127 Ellis St, San Francisco (94102-2109)
PHONE..................415 392-8800
Chris Holbrook, *General Mgr*
EMP: 206 **Privately Held**
WEB: www.kimptonhotels.com
SIC: 7011 Hotels
HQ: Kimpton Hotel & Restaurant Group Llc
222 Kearny St Ste 200
San Francisco CA 94108
415 397-5572

(P-11234)
KIMPTON HOTEL & REST GROUP LLC
Also Called: Pescatore
2455 Mason St, San Francisco (94133-1401)
PHONE..................415 561-1111
Leon Calahan, *Manager*
EMP: 206 **Privately Held**
WEB: www.kimptonhotels.com
SIC: 7011 Hotels
HQ: Kimpton Hotel & Restaurant Group Llc
222 Kearny St Ste 200
San Francisco CA 94108
415 397-5572

(P-11235)
KIMPTON HOTEL & REST GROUP LLC
Also Called: Hotel Monaco
501 Geary St, San Francisco (94102-1640)
PHONE..................415 292-0100
Jimmy Hord, *Manager*
EMP: 206 **Privately Held**
WEB: www.kimptonhotels.com
SIC: 7011 5812 Hotels; eating places
HQ: Kimpton Hotel & Restaurant Group Llc
222 Kearny St Ste 200
San Francisco CA 94108
415 397-5572

(P-11236)
KIROSH INC
Also Called: Holiday Inn
93 W El Camino Real, Mountain View (94040-2642)
PHONE..................650 595-2847
Dilip R Patel, *President*
Kirit Patel, *Treasurer*
Dina Patel, *Admin Sec*
EMP: 88 EST: 1963
SQ FT: 38,000
SALES (est): 1.2MM **Privately Held**
WEB: www.hotelstrata.com
SIC: 7011 Hotels & motels

(P-11237)
KMS FISHERMANS WHARF LP
Also Called: Tuscan Inn
425 N Point St, San Francisco (94133-1405)
PHONE..................415 561-1100
Laura Meith, *Director*
Jan Misch, *Partner*
EMP: 66 EST: 1990
SQ FT: 97,724
SALES (est): 1.7MM **Privately Held**
WEB: www.hotelzoesf.com
SIC: 7011 Hotel, franchised

(P-11238)
KOSMADI BROTHERS
Also Called: Holiday Inn
374 Ruggieri Way, Williams (95987-5155)
PHONE..................530 473-5120
Bob Patel, *Partner*
Harshad Patel, *Partner*
EMP: 55 EST: 1997
SALES (est): 675.8K **Privately Held**
WEB: www.hiexpress.com
SIC: 7011 Hotels & motels

(P-11239)
KUMAR HOTELS INC (PA)
Also Called: Holiday Inn
545 N Humboldt Ave, Willows (95988-3502)
PHONE..................530 934-8900
Pawan Kumar, *President*
EMP: 124 EST: 2005
SALES (est): 10.4MM **Privately Held**
WEB: www.holidayinn.com
SIC: 7011 Hotels & motels

(P-11240)
L-O SOMA HOTEL INC
Also Called: Argent Hotel, The
50 3rd St, San Francisco (94103-3106)
PHONE..................415 974-6400
Charles S Peck, *President*
Peter A Del Franco, *Exec VP*
Ronald A Silva, *Exec VP*
Michael Baier, *Managing Dir*
Jay Heidenreich, *Marketing Staff*
EMP: 3609 EST: 1998
SALES (est): 11.3MM
SALES (corp-wide): 935.4MM **Privately Held**
WEB: www.argentwork.com
SIC: 7011 5812 Hotels; eating places
HQ: Destination Residences Llc
10333 E Dry Creek Rd
Englewood CO 80112
303 799-3830

(P-11241)
LA QUINTA INN
8465 Enterprise Way, Oakland (94621-1317)
PHONE..................510 632-8900
Shailandra Devdhara, *President*
Balwantsinh Thakor, *Treasurer*
Nitin Shah, *Vice Pres*
Sajid Dadabhoai, *General Mgr*
Dilip Patel, *Director*
EMP: 99 EST: 2001
SQ FT: 76,000
SALES (est): 1.6MM **Privately Held**
WEB: www.wyndhamhotels.com
SIC: 7011 Hotels & motels

(P-11242)
LAFAYETTE PARK HOTEL CORP
3287 Mt Diablo Blvd, Lafayette (94549-4099)
PHONE..................925 283-3700
Tony Eichenberg, *Branch Mgr*
Linda Anderson, *Human Res Dir*
Christina Chohlis, *Sales Mgr*
Brett Brown, *Sales Staff*
Mirna Aguilar, *Supervisor*
EMP: 40
SALES (corp-wide): 28.9MM **Privately Held**
WEB: www.lafayetteparkhotel.com
SIC: 7011 7299 Resort hotel; banquet hall facilities
PA: Lafayette Park Hotel Corporation
1100 Alma St Ste 106
Menlo Park CA 94025
650 330-8888

(P-11243)
LAKE NATOMA LODGING LP
Also Called: Lake Natoma Inn
702 Gold Lake Dr, Folsom (95630-2559)
PHONE..................916 351-1500
Robert Leach, *Partner*
Rick Fenstermaker, *General Ptnr*
Kathy O'Connor, *Accounting Mgr*
Elizabeth Kuwabara, *Manager*
EMP: 80 EST: 1992
SQ FT: 82,000
SALES (est): 10.9MM **Privately Held**
WEB: www.lakenatomainn.com
SIC: 7011 Hotel, franchised; hotels

(P-11244)
LAKESHORE RESORT
Also Called: Lakeshore Supply
61953 Huntington Lake Rd, Lakeshore (93634)
P.O. Box 197 (93634-0197)
PHONE..................559 893-3193
Stephen Sherry, *Partner*
Melinda Sherry, *Partner*
Jessica Daugherty, *Manager*
Dan Rogers, *Manager*
EMP: 54 EST: 1927
SALES (est): 928.8K **Privately Held**
WEB: www.lakeshoreresort.net
SIC: 7011 Resort hotel

(P-11245)
LANAI GARDEN CORPORATION
Also Called: Lanai Garden Inn & Suites
1575 Tully Rd, San Jose (95122-2459)
PHONE..................408 929-8100
Ashok Thakrar, *General Mgr*
EMP: 37 EST: 2003

PRODUCTS & SERVICES SECTION
7011 - Hotels, Motels & Tourist Courts County (P-11270)

SQ FT: 25,341
SALES (est): 898.9K Privately Held
SIC: 7011 Hotels & motels

(P-11246)
LARKSPUR GROUP LLC
Also Called: Hampton Inn & Suites By Hilton
2160 Larkspur Ln, Redding (96002-0628)
PHONE.................................530 223-9344
David Grabal, Branch Mgr
EMP: 78
SALES (corp-wide): 1.3MM Privately Held
WEB: www.hilton.com
SIC: 7011 Hotels
PA: Larkspur Group Llc
   2160 Larkspur Ln
   Redding CA 96002
   530 224-1001

(P-11247)
LARKSPUR GROUP LLC (PA)
2160 Larkspur Ln, Redding (96002-0628)
PHONE.................................530 224-1001
Nona M Soltero, Administration
EMP: 55 EST: 2003
SALES (est): 1.3MM Privately Held
WEB: www.hilton.com
SIC: 7011 Hotels & motels

(P-11248)
LARKSPUR HSPTALITY DEV MGT LLC
1931 Taylor Rd, Roseville (95661-3008)
PHONE.................................916 773-1717
EMP: 48 Privately Held
WEB: www.larkspurhotels.com
SIC: 7011 Hotels
PA: Larkspur Hospitality Development And
   Management Company, Llc
   125 E Sir Frncis Drake Bl
   Larkspur CA 94939

(P-11249)
LARKSPUR HSPTALITY DEV MGT LLC
Also Called: Hilton Garden Inn Roseville
1951 Taylor Rd, Roseville (95661-3008)
PHONE.................................916 773-7171
Regina Bryant, Manager
EMP: 48 Privately Held
WEB: www.larkspurhotels.com
SIC: 7011 Hotels
PA: Larkspur Hospitality Development And
   Management Company, Llc
   125 E Sir Frncis Drake Bl
   Larkspur CA 94939

(P-11250)
LARKSPUR HSPTALITY DEV MGT LLC
Also Called: Larkspur Landing
121 Iron Point Rd, Folsom (95630-9000)
PHONE.................................916 355-1616
Regina Brent, General Mgr
EMP: 48 Privately Held
WEB: www.larkspurhotels.com
SIC: 7011 Hotels
PA: Larkspur Hospitality Development And
   Management Company, Llc
   125 E Sir Frncis Drake Bl
   Larkspur CA 94939

(P-11251)
LARKSPUR HSPTALITY DEV MGT LLC
Also Called: Larkspur Landing Home Sweet Ht
690 Gateway Blvd, South San Francisco (94080-7014)
PHONE.................................650 827-1515
David Holmes, General Mgr
EMP: 48 Privately Held
WEB: www.larkspurhotels.com
SIC: 7011 Hotels
PA: Larkspur Hospitality Development And
   Management Company, Llc
   125 E Sir Frncis Drake Bl
   Larkspur CA 94939

(P-11252)
LARKSPUR HSPTALITY DEV MGT LLC
Also Called: Larkspur Landing Hotel
555 Howe Ave, Sacramento (95825-8314)
PHONE.................................916 646-1212
Kimberley Babiasz, Manager
Tika Singh, General Mgr
Amanda Arabe, Office Mgr
Richard Barnes, CIO
Kim Baynard, Sales Staff
EMP: 48 Privately Held
WEB: www.larkspurhotels.com
SIC: 7011 Hotels
PA: Larkspur Hospitality Development And
   Management Company, Llc
   125 E Sir Frncis Drake Bl
   Larkspur CA 94939

(P-11253)
LARKSPUR HSPTALITY DEV MGT LLC
Also Called: Candlewood Pleasanton
5535 Johnson Ct, Pleasanton (94588-3309)
PHONE.................................925 463-1212
Jeff Durkin, Manager
EMP: 48 Privately Held
WEB: www.larkspurhotels.com
SIC: 7011 Hotels
PA: Larkspur Hospitality Development And
   Management Company, Llc
   125 E Sir Frncis Drake Bl
   Larkspur CA 94939

(P-11254)
LARKSPUR HSPTALITY DEV MGT LLC
Also Called: Sainte Claire, The
302 S Market St, San Jose (95113-2817)
PHONE.................................408 885-1234
Lisa Riedel, Manager
EMP: 48 Privately Held
WEB: www.hiltongrandvacations.com
SIC: 7011 Hotels
PA: Larkspur Hospitality Development And
   Management Company, Llc
   125 E Sir Frncis Drake Bl
   Larkspur CA 94939

(P-11255)
LARKSPUR HSPTALITY DEV MGT LLC
Also Called: Hilton Grdn Inn San Frncsco Ar
670 Gateway Blvd, South San Francisco (94080-7014)
PHONE.................................650 872-1515
Brian Fox, General Mgr
Tina Chircop, Sales Dir
EMP: 48 Privately Held
WEB: www.larkspurhotels.com
SIC: 7011 Hotels
PA: Larkspur Hospitality Development And
   Management Company, Llc
   125 E Sir Frncis Drake Bl
   Larkspur CA 94939

(P-11256)
LARKSPUR HSPTALITY DEV MGT LLC (PA)
125 E Sir Frncis Drake Bl, Larkspur (94939-1860)
PHONE.................................415 945-5000
Karl K Hoagland III, Mng Member
Tina Chircop, Sales Dir
Jim Hansen,
Thomas Hughes, Manager
Estela Lemus, Manager
EMP: 35 EST: 1996
SALES (est): 20.1MM Privately Held
WEB: www.hiltongrandvacations.com
SIC: 7011 Hotels

(P-11257)
LAS ALCOBAS HOTEL
1485 Main St Ste 201, Saint Helena (94574-1850)
PHONE.................................707 963-7000
Sylvester Kurtis, Sales Staff
EMP: 42 EST: 2016

SALES (est): 3.5MM Privately Held
SIC: 7011 Resort hotel

(P-11258)
LAUBERGE DE SONOMA LLC
29 E Macarthur St, Sonoma (95476-7615)
PHONE.................................707 938-2929
Chad Parson, Mng Member
EMP: 180 EST: 2017
SALES (est): 17MM Privately Held
SIC: 7011 Hotels

(P-11259)
LCOF LAKE TAHOE OPERATING LLC
Also Called: Beach Retreat & Lodge At Tahoe
3411 Lake Tahoe Blvd, South Lake Tahoe (96150-7919)
PHONE.................................530 541-6722
Glenn Gistis, Principal
EMP: 50 EST: 2018
SALES (est): 2.6MM Privately Held
SIC: 7011 Hotels & motels

(P-11260)
LEISURE SPORTS INC
Also Called: Renaissance Clubsport
2805 Jones Rd, Walnut Creek (94597-7848)
PHONE.................................925 938-3058
Brian Amador, General Mgr
Julio Garneff, Executive
Barbara Buckert, CTO
Amy Tye, Human Res Dir
Kevin Cabral, Mktg Dir
EMP: 260
SALES (corp-wide): 46.1MM Privately Held
WEB: www.leisuresportsinc.com
SIC: 7011 Hotels & motels
PA: Leisure Sports, Inc.
   225 Spring St
   Pleasanton CA 94566
   925 600-1966

(P-11261)
LET IT FLHO LESSEE INC
Also Called: Villa Florence Hotel
225 Powell St, San Francisco (94102-2205)
PHONE.................................415 397-7700
Garrin David, General Mgr
EMP: 40 EST: 2012
SALES (est): 386.9K Privately Held
WEB: www.villaflorence.com
SIC: 7011 Hotels

(P-11262)
LIONSGATE HT & CONFERENCE CTR
3410 Westover St, McClellan (95652-1005)
PHONE.................................916 643-6222
Lary Kelly, President
Laura Kennedy, COO
Marilou Will, Director
EMP: 77 EST: 2001
SALES (est): 3.1MM Privately Held
WEB: www.lionsgatehotel.com
SIC: 7011 Hotels

(P-11263)
LITTLE RIVER INN INC
Also Called: Little River Inn and Golf Crse
7901 N Highway 1, Little River (95456-9527)
P.O. Box B (95456-0430)
PHONE.................................707 937-5942
Charles D Hervilla, CEO
Susan Mc Kinney, Vice Pres
Cally Dym, General Mgr
Jim Shaw, Persnl Mgr
Connie Reynolds, Dean
EMP: 203 EST: 1939
SQ FT: 3,000
SALES (est): 9.9MM Privately Held
WEB: www.littleriverinn.com
SIC: 7011 5812 Bed & breakfast inn; American restaurant

(P-11264)
LL SUNNYVALE LP
Also Called: Sunnyvale Larkspur Landing
748 N Mathilda Ave, Sunnyvale (94085-3510)
PHONE.................................408 733-1212
Sue Hefty, Partner

EMP: 40 EST: 2008
SALES (est): 950K Privately Held
WEB: www.larkspurhotels.com
SIC: 7011 Hotels

(P-11265)
LODGE AT THE BEAR VALLEY INC
3 Bear Valley Rd, Bear Valley (95223-9997)
P.O. Box 5440 (95223-5440)
PHONE.................................209 753-2325
Charles J Toeniskoetter, President
Dan Breeding, Exec VP
EMP: 50 EST: 1990
SALES (est): 521.8K Privately Held
WEB: www.bearvalley.com
SIC: 7011 Resort hotel

(P-11266)
LODGEWORKS LP
1230 1st St, NAPA (94559-2930)
PHONE.................................707 690-9800
Michael Collins, Branch Mgr
EMP: 60
SALES (corp-wide): 47.2MM Privately Held
WEB: www.lodgeworks.com
SIC: 7011 Hotels & motels
PA: Lodgeworks, L.P.
   8100 E 22nd St N Bldg 500
   Wichita KS 67226
   316 681-5100

(P-11267)
LOK REDWOOD EMPIRE PRPTS INC
Also Called: Quality Inn
5100 Montero Way, Petaluma (94954-6535)
PHONE.................................707 584-8280
Kirkman Lok, CEO
Cynthia Lok, Admin Sec
EMP: 68 EST: 1985
SQ FT: 49,835
SALES (est): 1.1MM Privately Held
WEB: www.winecountryqi.com
SIC: 7011 Hotels & motels

(P-11268)
LONG MEADOW RANCH PARTNERS LP
Also Called: Farmstead Long Meadow Ranch
738 Main St, Saint Helena (94574-2005)
PHONE.................................707 963-4555
Brad Groper, Vice Pres
Adam White, Buyer
Adam Kim, Opers Staff
Kory Kovac, Production
Jennifer Didomizio, Sales Staff
EMP: 46 EST: 2018
SALES (est): 7.3MM Privately Held
WEB: www.longmeadowranch.com
SIC: 5812 7011 Eating places; hotels & motels

(P-11269)
LOS ALTOS HOTEL ASSOCIATES LLC
Also Called: Residence Inn By Marriott
4460 El Camino Real, Los Altos (94022-1003)
PHONE.................................650 559-7890
Arne M Sorenson, CEO
EMP: 41 EST: 2000
SALES (est): 1.8MM Privately Held
WEB: www.residence-inn.marriott.com
SIC: 7011 Hotels & motels

(P-11270)
LOTUS HOSPITALITY INC
Also Called: Double Tree By Hilton Sfo Arprt
275 S Airport Blvd, South San Francisco (94080-6703)
PHONE.................................650 873-3550
Ganendra M Singh, President
EMP: 38 EST: 1998
SALES (est): 7.1MM Privately Held
WEB: www.hilton.com
SIC: 7011 Hotels & motels

7011 - Hotels, Motels & Tourist Courts County (P-11271)

(P-11271)
LOTUS HOTELS INC
Also Called: Holiday Inn
2525 San Pablo Dam Rd, San Pablo (94806-3913)
PHONE....................510 965-1900
Bhupen Amin, *President*
Amit Modi, *Manager*
EMP: 57 **EST:** 1998
SQ FT: 50,000
SALES (est): 1.1MM **Privately Held**
WEB: www.lotushotels.com
SIC: 7011 Hotels & motels

(P-11272)
LOTUS HOTELS - UNION CITY LLC
Also Called: Holiday Inn
31140 Alvarado Niles Rd, Union City (94587-2701)
PHONE....................510 475-0600
Bhupen Amin, *President*
Tyrone Sanders, *Manager*
EMP: 45 **EST:** 2000
SQ FT: 50,000
SALES (est): 1MM **Privately Held**
WEB: www.holidayinn.com
SIC: 7011 Hotels & motels

(P-11273)
LOWE ENTERPRISES
Also Called: Squaw Creek Transportation
400 Squaw Creek Rd, Olympic Valley (96146-9778)
P.O. Box 3333 (96146-3333)
PHONE....................530 581-6628
Chris Tedesko, *Manager*
EMP: 46 **EST:** 1992
SALES (est): 335.7K **Privately Held**
SIC: 7011 Resort hotel

(P-11274)
LUCKY BEAR CASINO
Also Called: Lucky Bear Casino and Bingo
Hwy 96, Hoopa (95546)
P.O. Box 729 (95546-0729)
PHONE....................530 625-5198
Kim Dodge, *Manager*
EMP: 35 **EST:** 1995
SALES (est): 281.7K **Privately Held**
WEB: www.hoopa-nsn.gov
SIC: 7011 7999 Casino hotel; tourist attractions, amusement park concessions & rides

(P-11275)
LUCKY CHANCES INC
Also Called: Lucky Chances Casino
1700 Hillside Blvd, Colma (94014-2801)
PHONE....................650 758-2237
Rommel R Medina, *CEO*
Ruell Medina, *President*
Dustin Chase, *General Mgr*
Kyle Alegrete, *Opers Staff*
Ralph Baude, *Opers Staff*
EMP: 650 **EST:** 1998
SALES (est): 25MM **Privately Held**
WEB: www.luckychances.com
SIC: 7011 Casino hotel

(P-11276)
LYTTON RANCHERIA
Also Called: Casino San Pablo
13255 San Pablo Ave, San Pablo (94806-3907)
PHONE....................510 215-7888
Michael Gorczysnski, *General Mgr*
Cathi Hamel, *Principal*
Tamara Sullivan, *Exec Dir*
Richard Barnes, *CIO*
Sheri Lent, *Finance*
EMP: 547 **EST:** 1995
SALES (est): 39.8MM **Privately Held**
SIC: 7011 Casino hotel

(P-11277)
M ROTHROCK PROPERTIES INC
Also Called: Golden Key Motel
13450 Lincoln Way, Auburn (95603-3238)
PHONE....................530 885-6611
Susan Cole, *President*
EMP: 73 **EST:** 1963
SQ FT: 28,000
SALES (est): 1.6MM **Privately Held**
WEB: www.bestwestern.com
SIC: 7011 Hotels & motels

(P-11278)
M10 DEV LLC (PA)
750 San Antonio Rd, Palo Alto (94303-4625)
PHONE....................650 424-8991
Michael Lerman, *Manager*
Tiffany Marcelino, *Director*
EMP: 114 **EST:** 2013
SALES (est): 557.5K **Privately Held**
WEB: www.marriott.com
SIC: 7011 Hotels & motels

(P-11279)
M10 DEV LLC
Also Called: AC By Marriott Palo Alto
744 San Antonio Rd, Palo Alto (94303-4632)
PHONE....................650 565-8100
Michael Lerman, *General Mgr*
EMP: 43
SALES (corp-wide): 557.5K **Privately Held**
WEB: www.ac-hotels.marriott.com
SIC: 7011 Hotels & motels
PA: M10 Dev, Llc
750 San Antonio Rd
Palo Alto CA 94303
650 424-8991

(P-11280)
MACCALLUM HOUSE RESTAURANT
Also Called: Bed and Breakfast
45020 Albion St, Mendocino (95460)
P.O. Box 206 (95460-0206)
PHONE....................707 937-0289
Jed Ayes, *President*
Alan Kantor, *Executive*
EMP: 43 **EST:** 1993
SALES (est): 1MM **Privately Held**
WEB: www.maccallumhouse.com
SIC: 7011 Bed & breakfast inn

(P-11281)
MADRONA MNOR WINE CNTRY INN RE
1001 Westside Rd, Healdsburg (95448-9434)
PHONE....................707 433-4231
William R Konrad, *President*
Gertrude V Konrad,
EMP: 55 **EST:** 1983
SQ FT: 1,800
SALES (est): 5.6MM **Privately Held**
WEB: www.themadronahotel.com
SIC: 7011 5812 Bed & breakfast inn; Italian restaurant; Chinese restaurant; French restaurant; American restaurant

(P-11282)
MAMMOTH MOUNTAIN SKI AREA LLC (DH)
Also Called: Mammoth Mountain Inn
10001 Minaret Rd, Mammoth Lakes (93546)
P.O. Box 24 (93546-0024)
PHONE....................760 934-2571
Ron Cohen, *President*
David Cummings, *Partner*
Dick Flotho, *Officer*
Craig Albright, *Vice Pres*
Bruce Burton, *Vice Pres*
▲ **EMP:** 347 **EST:** 1951
SQ FT: 140,000
SALES (est): 125.6MM
SALES (corp-wide): 1.3B **Privately Held**
WEB: www.mammothmountain.com
SIC: 7011 5812 Ski lodge; resort hotel; eating places
HQ: Alterra Mountain Company
3501 Wazee St Ste 400
Denver CO 80216
303 749-8200

(P-11283)
MANTECA HAMPTON INN & SUITES
Also Called: Hampton By Hilton
1461 Bass Pro Dr, Manteca (95337-9503)
PHONE....................209 823-1926
EMP: 40
SALES (est): 1.1MM **Privately Held**
SIC: 7011 Hotels And Motels, Nsk

(P-11284)
MARIN SUITES HOTEL LLC
Also Called: Madera Village Suites
45 Tamal Vista Blvd, Corte Madera (94925-1144)
PHONE....................415 924-3608
Steven Zimmerman,
EMP: 63 **EST:** 1963
SQ FT: 50,000
SALES (est): 3.4MM **Privately Held**
WEB: www.marinsuites.com
SIC: 7011 Hotel, franchised

(P-11285)
MARK CARTER
Also Called: Carter House
301 L St, Eureka (95501-0571)
PHONE....................707 444-8062
Mark Carter, *Owner*
Christi Carter, *CIO*
Shannon Willison, *Controller*
Maja Jeramaz, *Export Mgr*
Steve Scott, *Opers Staff*
EMP: 38 **EST:** 1973
SALES (est): 6.8MM **Privately Held**
WEB: www.carterhouse.com
SIC: 7011 Hostels; bed & breakfast inn

(P-11286)
MARRIOTS TMBER LDGE AT LK THOE
4100 Lake Tahoe Blvd, South Lake Tahoe (96150-6965)
PHONE....................530 542-8416
Brain Reichle, *Asst Controller*
Brian Cinaer, *Controller*
EMP: 77 **EST:** 2002
SALES (est): 3.4MM **Privately Held**
WEB: www.tahoebeachretreat.com
SIC: 7011 Resort hotel

(P-11287)
MARRIOTT DOWNTOWN
55 4th St, San Francisco (94103-3156)
PHONE....................415 896-1600
Edward Sampson, *General Mgr*
Michael Lynch, *Executive*
Ken Hansen, *Finance*
Eric Hooper, *Sales Staff*
Shelby Hill, *Director*
EMP: 40 **EST:** 2011
SALES (est): 5MM **Privately Held**
SIC: 7011 Hotels

(P-11288)
MARUTIZ INC
Also Called: Comfort Inn
16225 Condit Rd, Morgan Hill (95037-9585)
PHONE....................408 778-3400
San K Panwala, *President*
EMP: 43 **EST:** 2004
SQ FT: 107,640
SALES (est): 812.1K **Privately Held**
WEB: www.comfortinnmorganhill.com
SIC: 7011 Hotels & motels

(P-11289)
MASON STREET OPCO LLC
Also Called: Fairmont San Francisco
950 Mason St, San Francisco (94108-6000)
PHONE....................415 772-5000
Seung Geon Kim, *President*
Kendall Hanson, *General Mgr*
Patrick Farrell, *Director*
Jacco Vanteeffelen, *Manager*
EMP: 850 **EST:** 2015
SQ FT: 750,000
SALES (est): 112MM
SALES (corp-wide): 627.9MM **Privately Held**
WEB: www.kashmirsanfrancisco.com
SIC: 7011 Hotels
HQ: Accor Services Us Llc
950 Mason St
San Francisco CA 94108
415 772-5000

(P-11290)
MAXS PARTNERSHIP A GEN PARTNR
Also Called: Courtyard By Marriott Merced
750 Motel Dr, Merced (95341-5151)
PHONE....................209 725-1221

Edwin Kainth, *Partner*
Sean Williams, *General Mgr*
EMP: 39 **EST:** 2001
SALES (est): 1.2MM **Privately Held**
WEB: www.courtyard.marriott.com
SIC: 7011 Hotels & motels

(P-11291)
MB HOSPTLITY SROSA AC 2018 LLC
Also Called: AC Hotel Santa Rosa Downtown
300 Davis St, Santa Rosa (95401-6265)
PHONE....................707 527-1075
Jeffrey Blackman, *Principal*
EMP: 35 **EST:** 2018
SALES (est): 1.6MM **Privately Held**
WEB: www.ac-hotels.marriott.com
SIC: 7011 Hotels & motels

(P-11292)
MCCLELLAN HOSPITALITY SVCS LLC
3140 Peacekeeper Way, McClellan (95652-2508)
PHONE....................916 965-7100
Larry Kelley,
Deborah Anderson, *Executive Asst*
Magee Duke, *Administration*
Douglas Hart,
EMP: 64 **EST:** 2004
SALES (est): 826.9K **Privately Held**
WEB: www.mcclellanpark.com
SIC: 7011 5812 Hotels & motels; caterers

(P-11293)
MEADOWOOD ASSOC A LTD PARTNR (PA)
Also Called: Meadowood Resort and Cntry CLB
900 Meadowood Ln, Saint Helena (94574-9620)
PHONE....................707 963-3646
Bob Ringstab, *Partner*
H William Harland, *Partner*
Jennifer Brunetti, *COO*
Lois Rothenberger, *CFO*
Karla Jensin, *Vice Pres*
EMP: 160 **EST:** 1957
SALES (est): 38.1MM **Privately Held**
WEB: www.meadowood.com
SIC: 5812 7011 7997 Eating places; resort hotel; country club, membership

(P-11294)
MENDOCINO HOTEL & RESORT CORP
Also Called: Mendocino Hotel & Grdn Suites
45080 Main St, Mendocino (95460-9203)
PHONE....................707 937-0511
Thomas Clark Kravis, *Owner*
Carlos Pena, *Executive*
Juan C Pena, *Executive*
Dan Clark, *Info Tech Mgr*
Cindy Rhinehart, *Data Proc Staff*
EMP: 80 **EST:** 1881
SQ FT: 12,500
SALES (est): 4MM **Privately Held**
SIC: 7011 5812 5813 7299 Hotels; eating places; bars & lounges; banquet hall facilities

(P-11295)
MENDOCINO ONSEN CORPORATION
Also Called: Orr Hot Springs
13201 Orr Springs Rd, Ukiah (95482-9021)
PHONE....................707 462-6277
James Leslie Williams, *President*
EMP: 41 **EST:** 1974
SALES (est): 617.5K **Privately Held**
WEB: www.orrhotsprings.org
SIC: 7011 Resort hotel

(P-11296)
MERCHANT VALLEY CORP
Also Called: Best Wstn Plus Clnga Inn Sites
1786 Jayne Ave, Coalinga (93210-9249)
PHONE....................916 410-2021
Sareena Merchant, *Principal*
Mike Merchant, *Principal*
EMP: 50 **EST:** 2017
SALES (est): 1.1MM **Privately Held**
WEB: www.bestwestern.com
SIC: 7011 Hotels & motels

PRODUCTS & SERVICES SECTION
7011 - Hotels, Motels & Tourist Courts County (P-11322)

(P-11297)
MERITAGE RESORT LLC
Also Called: Meritage Resort and Spa, The
875 Bordeaux Way, NAPA (94558-7524)
PHONE.................................707 251-1900
Timothy R Busch, *President*
David Ryan, *Managing Dir*
Janice Phillips, *Executive Asst*
Rashann Flores, *Hum Res Coord*
Tanya Torrence, *Human Res Mgr*
EMP: 350 **EST:** 2006
SALES (est): 40.1MM **Privately Held**
WEB: www.meritagecollection.com
SIC: 7011 Resort hotel

(P-11298)
MGM HOLIDAY INC
1004 S Claremont St, San Mateo (94402-1836)
PHONE.................................415 690-0020
Tianhong Zhao, *CEO*
EMP: 45 **EST:** 2012
SALES (est): 195.4K **Privately Held**
SIC: 7011 Hotels & motels

(P-11299)
MILE POST PROPERTIES LLC
Also Called: La Quinta Inn
1050 Van Ness Ave, San Francisco (94109-6934)
PHONE.................................415 673-4711
Fred Reed, *General Mgr*
EMP: 78 **EST:** 1994
SQ FT: 100,000
SALES (est): 823.7K **Privately Held**
WEB: www.wyndhamhotels.com
SIC: 7011 Hotels & motels

(P-11300)
MILL VALLEY INN INC
165 Throckmorton Ave, Mill Valley (94941-1909)
PHONE.................................415 389-6608
Patience Moore Zambrano, *President*
Judy Gilmore, *General Mgr*
Bryan Pourtabib, *Opers Staff*
Lisa Giffin, *Sales Dir*
EMP: 50 **EST:** 1994
SALES (est): 3.7MM **Privately Held**
WEB: www.millvalleyinn.com
SIC: 5813 7011 Drinking places; hotels

(P-11301)
MILLBRAE WCP HOTEL II LLC
Also Called: Aloft Sfo
401 E Millbrae Ave, Millbrae (94030-3111)
PHONE.................................650 443-5500
Marc Swerdlow, *President*
Mark Zettl, *COO*
EMP: 50 **EST:** 2005
SQ FT: 288,000
SALES (est): 5.3MM
SALES (corp-wide): 95.9MM **Privately Held**
WEB: www.aloft-hotels.marriott.com
SIC: 7011 Hotels
HQ: Ultima Hospitality, L.L.C.
30 S Wacker Dr Ste 3600
Chicago IL 60606
312 948-4500

(P-11302)
MILLENNIUM HOTEL INC
30073 Skylark Ct, Hayward (94544-6883)
PHONE.................................510 432-5665
Mahendra Bhukhan, *Administration*
EMP: 35 **EST:** 2014
SALES (est): 513.1K **Privately Held**
WEB: www.millenniumhotels.com
SIC: 7011 Hotels

(P-11303)
MILPITAS COURTYARD BY MARRIOTT
1480 Falcon Dr, Milpitas (95035-8047)
PHONE.................................408 719-1966
John W Marriott, *Owner*
J W Marriott, *Owner*
Iris Washington, *Admin Asst*
Zahid Bhatti, *Info Tech Mgr*
Jose-Antonio Sanchez, *Manager*
EMP: 45 **EST:** 1999
SALES (est): 10.4MM **Privately Held**
WEB: www.marriott.com
SIC: 7011 Hotels & motels

(P-11304)
MIRAMAR HOSPITALITY CONSULTING
Also Called: Hampton Inn
55 Tully Rd, San Jose (95122)
PHONE.................................408 298-7373
Rinko Patel, *Branch Mgr*
EMP: 40 **Privately Held**
WEB: www.miramarhospitality.com
SIC: 7011 Hotels & motels
PA: Miramar Hospitality Consulting
1100 Lincoln Ave Ste 265
San Jose CA 95125

(P-11305)
MISSION STUART HT PARTNERS LLC
Also Called: Hotel Vitale
8 Mission St, San Francisco (94105-1227)
PHONE.................................415 278-3700
Fax: 415 278-3750
EMP: 200
SALES (est): 10.8MM **Privately Held**
WEB: www.hotelvitale.com
SIC: 7011 Hotel/Motel Operation

(P-11306)
MODESTO HOSPITALITY LLC
Also Called: Doubltree By Hilton Ht Modesto
1150 9th St, Modesto (95354-0823)
PHONE.................................209 526-6000
EMP: 180 **EST:** 2006
SALES (est): 10.2MM **Privately Held**
WEB: www.hilton.com
SIC: 7011 Hotels & motels

(P-11307)
MODESTO HOSPITALITY LESSEE LLC
Also Called: Doubletree Hotel Modesto
1150 9th St Ste C, Modesto (95354-0857)
PHONE.................................209 526-6000
EMP: 99
SALES: 950K **Privately Held**
SIC: 7011 Hotel/Motel Operation

(P-11308)
MONO WIND CASINO
Also Called: Big Sandy Rancheria
37302 Rancheria Ln, Auberry (93602-9423)
P.O. Box 1060 (93602-1060)
PHONE.................................559 855-4350
Connie Lewis, *Principal*
Elizabeth D Kipp, *Principal*
Kerry Smith, *General Mgr*
Audra Bagdasarian, *Marketing Staff*
EMP: 75 **EST:** 1996
SALES (est): 10.9MM **Privately Held**
WEB: www.monowind.com
SIC: 7011 5812 Casino hotel; restaurant, family; independent

(P-11309)
MONTCLAIR HOTELS MB LLC
Also Called: Holiday Inn
1050 Burnett Ave, Concord (94520-5713)
PHONE.................................925 687-5500
Stephanie Mullen, *General Mgr*
EMP: 300 **Privately Held**
WEB: www.holidayinn.com
SIC: 7011 Hotels & motels
PA: Montclair Hotels Mb, Llc
6600 Mannheim Rd
Rosemont IL 60018

(P-11310)
MONTICELLO HOTEL LLC
Also Called: Hotel Abri
127 Ellis St, San Francisco (94102-2109)
PHONE.................................415 392-8800
Sue Hefty,
Marit Davey,
EMP: 42 **EST:** 2009
SALES (est): 2MM **Privately Held**
WEB: www.hotelabrisf.com
SIC: 7011 7389 Resort hotel; office facilities & secretarial service rental

(P-11311)
MOROSIN ENTERPRISES INC
Also Called: La Hacienda Inn Hotel
2275 Winchester Blvd, Campbell (95008-3426)
PHONE.................................408 354-0300
Russell Stanley, *President*
EMP: 91 **EST:** 1955
SALES (est): 411.8K **Privately Held**
WEB: www.enterprise.com
SIC: 7011 6519 Hotels; real property lessors

(P-11312)
MOSSER VCTRIAN HT ARTS MUS INC (HQ)
Also Called: Mosser Hotel, The
308 Jessie St, San Francisco (94103-3002)
PHONE.................................415 986-4400
Charles Mosser, *President*
Adam Nicholson, *Administration*
Carol Rohan, *Manager*
EMP: 40 **EST:** 1980
SQ FT: 40,000
SALES (est): 15.9MM
SALES (corp-wide): 17.3MM **Privately Held**
WEB: www.themosser.com
SIC: 7011 5812 Hotels; American restaurant
PA: Property Management Merchandise
308 Jessie St
San Francisco CA 94103
415 284-9000

(P-11313)
MOSSER VCTRIAN HT ARTS MUS INC
Also Called: Annabelles Bar & Bistro
68 4th St, San Francisco (94103-3102)
PHONE.................................415 777-1200
Greg Quinn, *Manager*
EMP: 120
SALES (corp-wide): 17.3MM **Privately Held**
WEB: www.themosser.com
SIC: 5812 7011 American restaurant; hotels & motels
HQ: Mosser Victorian Hotel Of Arts And Music, Inc.
308 Jessie St
San Francisco CA 94103
415 986-4400

(P-11314)
MOUNTAIN HOME INN
810 Panoramic Hwy, Mill Valley (94941-1765)
PHONE.................................415 381-9000
Ed Cunningham, *General Ptnr*
Burton Smith, *General Ptnr*
EMP: 57 **EST:** 1981
SALES (est): 3.1MM **Privately Held**
WEB: www.mtnhomeinn.com
SIC: 7011 5812 5813 Bed & breakfast inn; cafe; drinking places

(P-11315)
MOUNTAIN RESORTS INC
Also Called: Trinity Alps Resort
1750 Trinity Alps Rd, Trinity Center (96091-9400)
PHONE.................................530 286-2205
Morgan Langan, *President*
Margo Gray, *Vice Pres*
EMP: 47 **EST:** 1924
SALES (est): 1MM **Privately Held**
WEB: www.trinityalpsresort.com
SIC: 7011 5399 5812 5813 Tourist camps, cabins, cottages & courts; country general stores; restaurant, family; independent; bar (drinking places); riding stable

(P-11316)
MSR HOTELS & RESORTS INC
Also Called: Sheraton
1100 N Mathilda Ave, Sunnyvale (94089-1206)
PHONE.................................408 745-6000
Randy Langley, *Manager*
EMP: 256

SALES (corp-wide): 52B **Publicly Held**
WEB: www.sheraton.marriott.com
SIC: 7011 Hotels & motels
HQ: Msr Hotels & Resorts, Inc.
450 S Orange Ave
Orlando FL 32801
407 650-1000

(P-11317)
MURPHYS HISTORIC HOTEL
457 Main St, Murphys (95247-9628)
PHONE.................................209 728-3444
Dorian Saught, *Owner*
Goss Brian, *Vice Pres*
EMP: 56 **EST:** 1856
SQ FT: 4,000
SALES (est): 1.3MM **Privately Held**
WEB: www.murphyshotel.com
SIC: 7011 5812 5813 7389 Resort hotel; eating places; drinking places; hotel & motel reservation service

(P-11318)
NANA ENTERPRISES
Also Called: Travelodge
707 Rdwood Hwy Frntage Rd, Mill Valley (94941-2538)
PHONE.................................415 383-0340
Ebrahim Nana, *President*
Ilias Nana, *President*
Ilyas Nana, *Treasurer*
Ebrahim M Nana, *Vice Pres*
▲ **EMP:** 83 **EST:** 1977
SQ FT: 40,000
SALES (est): 4.2MM **Privately Held**
WEB: www.millvalley.com
SIC: 7011 Hotels & motels

(P-11319)
NAPA ES LEASING LLC
Also Called: Embassy Suites
1075 California Blvd, NAPA (94559-1061)
PHONE.................................707 253-9540
Reynaldo Zertuche, *General Mgr*
EMP: 53 **EST:** 2014
SALES (est): 1.4MM
SALES (corp-wide): 473MM **Privately Held**
WEB: www.hilton.com
SIC: 7011 Hotels & motels
HQ: Rangers Sub I, Llc
3 Bethesda Metro Ctr # 1000
Bethesda MD 20814

(P-11320)
NAPA MILL LLC
500 Main St Ste 208, NAPA (94559-3353)
PHONE.................................707 251-8500
Sara Brooks, *Branch Mgr*
Karen Kaminski, *Accounting Mgr*
Melodie Hilton, *Marketing Staff*
EMP: 35
SALES (corp-wide): 5.4MM **Privately Held**
WEB: www.napariverinn.com
SIC: 7011 Motels
PA: Napa Mill Llc
1567 Silver Trl
Napa CA 94558
707 252-9372

(P-11321)
NAPA MOTEL AND RESTAURANT
Also Called: Best Western
100 Soscol Ave, NAPA (94559-4010)
P.O. Box 515 (94559-0515)
PHONE.................................707 257-1930
Tom Cudd Jr, *Partner*
Tyler Cudd, *Partner*
Rosa Chavez, *Mktg Dir*
Bret Cudd, *Manager*
EMP: 35 **EST:** 1983
SQ FT: 7,000
SALES (est): 1MM **Privately Held**
WEB: www.innatthevines.com
SIC: 7011 Hotels & motels

(P-11322)
NAPA RIVER INN
500 Main St, NAPA (94559-3353)
PHONE.................................707 251-8500
Harry T Price, *Partner*
Harry Price, *Partner*
Linda Price, *Partner*

7011 - Hotels, Motels & Tourist Courts County (P-11323)

Armando Ortiz, *Division Mgr*
Ellen Sitter, *Admin Sec*
▲ **EMP:** 60 **EST:** 1999
SALES (est): 4.7MM **Privately Held**
WEB: www.napariverinn.com
SIC: 7011 Hotels

(P-11323)
NAPA VALLEY BREWING CO INC
Also Called: Calistoga Inn
1250 Lincoln Ave, Calistoga (94515-1741)
PHONE.................................707 942-4101
Michael Dunsford, *President*
Susan Dunsford, *Treasurer*
Cortez Manger, *Manager*
EMP: 63 **EST:** 1974
SQ FT: 8,800
SALES (est): 1.7MM **Privately Held**
WEB: www.calistogainn.com
SIC: 5812 7011 5813 Chicken restaurant; resort hotel; bar (drinking places)

(P-11324)
NAPA VALLEY LODGE LP
Also Called: Bodega Bay Lodge
103 Coast Highway 1, Bodega Bay (94923-9723)
PHONE.................................707 875-3525
Ellis Alden, *Owner*
EMP: 65
SALES (corp-wide): 6.1MM **Privately Held**
WEB: www.napavalleylodge.com
SIC: 7011 Vacation lodges
PA: Napa Valley Lodge L.P.
2230 Madison St
Yountville CA 94599
707 944-2468

(P-11325)
NASA AMES RESEARCH CENTER
Nasa Exch Lodge 19 Mccord St Nasa Exchange Lod, Mountain View (94035)
PHONE.................................650 604-4620
Julia Horner, *Manager*
EMP: 35 **Publicly Held**
SIC: 7011 Hotels & motels
HQ: Nasa Ames Research Center
Nasa Ames Research Ctr
Moffett Field CA 94035
650 604-1110

(P-11326)
NATIONAL 9 MOTELS INC
1500 Broadway, Placerville (95667-5905)
PHONE.................................530 622-3884
Patel Vinot, *Branch Mgr*
EMP: 35
SQ FT: 7,616
SALES (corp-wide): 1.7MM **Privately Held**
WEB: www.national9inns.com
SIC: 7011 Motels
PA: National 9 Motels Inc
9571 S 700 E Ste 202
Sandy UT 84070
801 208-0537

(P-11327)
NATIONAL HISTORIC REST INC
Also Called: National Hotel & Restaurant
18187 Main St, Jamestown (95327-9748)
P.O. Box 502 (95327-0502)
PHONE.................................209 984-3446
Stephen A Willey, *General Mgr*
Don R Hazelwood, *President*
Michael Willey, *Vice Pres*
Julie M Adams, *Manager*
Heather Parkhurst, *Manager*
EMP: 51 **EST:** 1946
SALES (est): 689.4K **Privately Held**
WEB: www.national-hotel.com
SIC: 7011 5813 5812 Hotels; bar (drinking places); eating places

(P-11328)
NICKS COVE INC
23240 Ca 1, Marshall (94940)
PHONE.................................415 663-1033
Ruth Gibson, *Owner*
Dustin Moore, *Manager*
Erikka Newton, *Manager*
EMP: 70 **EST:** 1973
SQ FT: 1,000
SALES (est): 3.4MM **Privately Held**
WEB: www.nickscove.com
SIC: 7011 Hotels; bed & breakfast inn

(P-11329)
NOB HILL PROPERTIES INC
Also Called: Big Four Restaurant
1075 California St, San Francisco (94108-2281)
PHONE.................................415 474-5400
John Cope, *President*
Newton Cope Sr, *Ch of Bd*
Newton Cope Jr, *Vice Pres*
Daniel Davee, *Sr Software Eng*
Sreyas Vengilat, *Software Engr*
EMP: 280 **EST:** 1940
SALES (est): 14.2MM **Privately Held**
WEB: www.huntingtonhotel.com
SIC: 7011 5812 Hotels; eating places

(P-11330)
NOBLE AEW VINEYARD CREEK LLC
Also Called: Hyatt Hotel
170 Railroad St, Santa Rosa (95401-6266)
PHONE.................................707 284-1234
Josephine Redrico, *Principal*
EMP: 37 **EST:** 2008 **Privately Held**
WEB: www.vineyardcreek.hyatt.com
SIC: 7011 Hotels & motels

(P-11331)
NORTHERN QUEEN INC
Also Called: Northern Queen Inn
400 Railroad Ave, Nevada City (95959-2868)
PHONE.................................530 265-4492
Roy J Ramey, *President*
Jacqueline Ramey, *Corp Secy*
Colleen Flores, *Vice Pres*
Diane Mansfield, *Systems Mgr*
EMP: 41 **EST:** 1978
SQ FT: 32,000
SALES (est): 558.4K **Privately Held**
WEB: www.northernqueeninn.com
SIC: 7011 6552 Motels; subdividers & developers

(P-11332)
NOVATO MANAGEMENT GROUP INC
Also Called: Days Inn
8141 Redwood Blvd, Novato (94945-1403)
PHONE.................................415 897-7111
Heng Ta Chiang, *Partner*
Peter Chiang, *Partner*
Grace Wong, *Partner*
EMP: 53 **EST:** 1957
SQ FT: 40,000
SALES (est): 1.5MM **Privately Held**
WEB: www.wyndhamhotels.com
SIC: 7011 5812 Motels; Chinese restaurant

(P-11333)
NOVATO TRAVELODGE
7600 Redwood Blvd, Novato (94945-1409)
PHONE.................................415 892-7500
Simon MA, *Partner*
Ying Wang MA, *Partner*
EMP: 36 **EST:** 1989
SQ FT: 39,204
SALES (est): 368.4K **Privately Held**
WEB: www.wyndhamhotels.com
SIC: 7011 Hotels & motels

(P-11334)
NOYO VISTA INC
Also Called: Super 8 Motel
888 S Main St, Fort Bragg (95437-5316)
PHONE.................................707 964-4003
Tara Wagner, *President*
EMP: 46 **EST:** 1983
SALES (est): 472.2K **Privately Held**
WEB: www.wyndhamhotels.com
SIC: 7011 Hotels & motels

(P-11335)
OAKLAND RENAISSANCE ASSOCIATES
Also Called: Oakland Mrriott Hotels Resorts
1001 Broadway, Oakland (94607-4019)
PHONE.................................510 451-4000
EMP: 375 **Privately Held**
WEB: www.marriott.com
SIC: 7011 Hotels & motels
PA: Oakland Renaissance Associates
388 9th St Ste 222
Oakland CA 94607

(P-11336)
OCCIDENTAL UNION HOTEL INC
3731 Main St, Occidental (95465)
P.O. Box 427 (95465-0427)
PHONE.................................707 874-3444
Barbara Gonnella, *Treasurer*
Daniel Gonnella, *President*
Frank Gonnella, *Treasurer*
EMP: 42 **EST:** 2013
SQ FT: 2,500
SALES (est): 1.9MM **Privately Held**
WEB: www.unionhoteloccidental.com
SIC: 5812 7011 5921 Pizza restaurants; motels; liquor stores

(P-11337)
OCEAN PCF INVSTORS A CAL LTD P
Also Called: Ocean Pacific Lodge
301 Pacific Ave, Santa Cruz (95060-4922)
PHONE.................................831 457-1234
Peter Patel, *Manager*
EMP: 37 **Privately Held**
WEB: www.theoceanpacificlodge.com
SIC: 7011 Motels
PA: Ocean Pacific Investors, A California Limited Partnership
751 1st St Ste B
Gilroy CA 95020

(P-11338)
OMNI HOTELS CORPORATION
500 California St, San Francisco (94104-1001)
PHONE.................................415 677-9494
Michael Casey, *Branch Mgr*
Molly Cohen, *Human Resources*
Aimee King, *Marketing Staff*
Kelsey Angel, *Sales Staff*
Brett Howard, *Sales Staff*
EMP: 53 **Privately Held**
WEB: www.omnihotels.com
SIC: 7011 Hotels & motels
HQ: Omni Hotels Corporation
4001 Maple Ave Ste 500
Dallas TX 75219
972 871-5600

(P-11339)
ONE NOB HILL ASSOCIATES LLC
Also Called: Intercontinental Mark Hopkins
999 California St, San Francisco (94108-2250)
PHONE.................................415 392-3434
Mary Ann Gonzales, *General Mgr*
EMP: 86 **EST:** 2014
SALES (est): 4.5MM **Privately Held**
WEB: www.sfmarkhopkins.com
SIC: 7011 Hotels & motels

(P-11340)
ONTARIO AIRPORT HOTEL CORP
Also Called: Hilton
4949 Great America Pkwy, Santa Clara (95054-1216)
PHONE.................................408 562-6709
James Evans, *CFO*
Kathya Inga, *Human Res Dir*
Michele Knipe, *Marketing Staff*
Michele Chalupa, *Sales Staff*
▲ **EMP:** 127 **EST:** 2004
SQ FT: 169,768
SALES (est): 13.8MM **Privately Held**
WEB: www.hiltonsantaclara.com
SIC: 7011 Hotels

(P-11341)
ORCHARD INTL GROUP INC (PA)
Also Called: Orchard Hotel
665 Bush St, San Francisco (94108-3510)
PHONE.................................415 362-8878
S C Huang, *President*
Robert Huang, *CEO*
Darlene Chhem, *Sales Staff*
EMP: 99 **EST:** 1991
SQ FT: 60,000
SALES (est): 9MM **Privately Held**
WEB: www.theorchardhotel.com
SIC: 7011 Hotels

(P-11342)
PAAR HOSPITALITY INC
500 W A St, Hayward (94541-4843)
PHONE.................................510 828-3585
EMP: 57 **Privately Held**
SIC: 7011 Hotels & motels
PA: Paar Hospitality Inc
25569 Gold Ridge Dr
Castro Valley CA 94552

(P-11343)
PACIFIC BEACH HOUSE LLC (PA)
Also Called: Beach House Ht - Half Moon Bay
4100 Cabrillo Hwy N, Half Moon Bay (94019-5219)
P.O. Box 129 (94019-0129)
PHONE.................................650 712-0220
Dana Daho, *General Mgr*
Charlotte Papedis, *General Mgr*
EMP: 46 **EST:** 1997
SQ FT: 5,007
SALES (est): 11MM **Privately Held**
WEB: www.beach-house.com
SIC: 7011 7999 Resort hotel; bathing beach, non-membership

(P-11344)
PACIFIC HOTEL DEV VENTR LP
Also Called: Sheraton Palo Alto
625 El Camino Real, Palo Alto (94301-2301)
PHONE.................................650 347-8260
Clement Chen, *Vice Pres*
Keiko Freese, *Manager*
EMP: 200 **EST:** 1998
SALES (est): 21.8MM **Privately Held**
WEB: www.phmhotels.com
SIC: 7011 Hotels

(P-11345)
PACIFIC HOTEL MANAGEMENT LLC
Also Called: Hawthorn Suites Fremont Newark
39270 Cedar Blvd, Newark (94560-5024)
PHONE.................................510 791-7700
Nicole Harris,
Nicole Mass, *Manager*
EMP: 159
SALES (corp-wide): 56.8MM **Privately Held**
WEB: www.phmhotels.com
SIC: 7011 Hotels
PA: Pacific Hotel Management, Llc
400 S El Cmino Real Ste 2
San Mateo CA 94402
650 347-8260

(P-11346)
PACIFIC HOTEL MANAGEMENT LLC
Also Called: Sheraton
1603 Powell St, Emeryville (94608-2436)
PHONE.................................510 547-7888
Michelle Sims, *Owner*
Michael Chu, *Auditor*
Sabeen Afzal, *Hum Res Coord*
Erin Divine, *Sales Mgr*
Amar Chawla, *Manager*
EMP: 159
SALES (corp-wide): 56.8MM **Privately Held**
WEB: www.phmhotels.com
SIC: 7011 Hotels & motels
PA: Pacific Hotel Management, Llc
400 S El Cmino Real Ste 2
San Mateo CA 94402
650 347-8260

(P-11347)
PACIFIC HOTEL MANAGEMENT LLC
Also Called: Courtyard By Marriott
3150 Garrity Way, Richmond (94806-1983)
PHONE.................................510 262-0700
Curt Newport, *Branch Mgr*
EMP: 159

PRODUCTS & SERVICES SECTION

7011 - Hotels, Motels & Tourist Courts County (P-11372)

SALES (corp-wide): 56.8MM Privately Held
WEB: www.phmhotels.com
SIC: 7011 7389 Hotels; office facilities & secretarial service rental
PA: Pacific Hotel Management, Llc
400 S El Cmino Real Ste 2
San Mateo CA 94402
650 347-8260

(P-11348)
PACIFIC HOTEL MANAGEMENT LLC
Also Called: Sheraton
625 El Camino Real, Palo Alto (94301-2301)
PHONE.................................650 328-2800
Jim Rebosio, *General Mgr*
Annie Tepe, *Social Dir*
Justo Morales, *Chief Engr*
Sagir Ahmed, *Controller*
Anne Stroul, *Marketing Staff*
EMP: 159
SALES (corp-wide): 56.8MM Privately Held
WEB: www.phmhotels.com
SIC: 7011 Hotels
PA: Pacific Hotel Management, Llc
400 S El Cmino Real Ste 2
San Mateo CA 94402
650 347-8260

(P-11349)
PACIFIC LODGING GROUP
Also Called: Bodega Coast Inn
521 Hwy 1, Bodega (94922)
PHONE.................................707 875-2217
Solo Patel, *Owner*
Kanti Patel, *Partner*
EMP: 46 EST: 1987
SQ FT: 32,000
SALES (est): 543.2K Privately Held
WEB: www.bodegacoastinn.com
SIC: 7011 Motels

(P-11350)
PACIFICA HOTEL COMPANY
Also Called: Best Western Half Moon Bay
2400 Cabrillo Hwy S, Half Moon Bay (94019-2253)
PHONE.................................650 726-9000
Curt Picillo, *Manager*
EMP: 39
SALES (corp-wide): 61.3MM Privately Held
WEB: www.pacificahotels.com
SIC: 7011 Hotels
HQ: Pacifica Hotel Company
39 Argonaut
Aliso Viejo CA 92656
805 957-0095

(P-11351)
PALO ALTO INN
Also Called: Days Inn
4238 El Camino Real, Palo Alto (94306-4404)
PHONE.................................650 493-4222
Suresh Patel, *Owner*
EMP: 56 EST: 1973
SQ FT: 5,000
SALES (est): 1.3MM Privately Held
WEB: www.wyndhamhotels.com
SIC: 7011 Hotels & motels

(P-11352)
PARC 55 LESSEE LLC
Also Called: Hilton
55 Cyril Magnin St, San Francisco (94102-2812)
PHONE.................................415 392-8000
EMP: 56 EST: 2014
SALES (est): 255.6MM
SALES (corp-wide): 852MM Publicly Held
WEB: www.parc55hotel.com
SIC: 7011 Hotels
PA: Park Hotels & Resorts Inc.
1775 Tysons Blvd Fl 7
Tysons VA 22102
571 302-5757

(P-11353)
PARCO LLC
Also Called: Neptune Palace Hotel
1546 Webster St, Alameda (94501-3340)
P.O. Box 295 (94501-9395)
PHONE.................................510 865-0100
Steve Case, *Mng Member*
Veronica Case,
EMP: 39 EST: 1997
SQ FT: 13,895
SALES (est): 340.1K
SALES (corp-wide): 1.2B Privately Held
WEB: www.daetwyler.com
SIC: 7011 Hotels
PA: Datwyler Fuhrungs Ag
Gotthardstrasse 31
Altdorf UR 6460
418 751-100

(P-11354)
PARK HOTELS & RESORTS INC
Also Called: Hilton
1 Hegenberger Rd, Oakland (94621-1405)
P.O. Box 2549 (94614-0549)
PHONE.................................510 635-5000
Mark Clement, *General Mgr*
Lillian Virdure, *Telecom Exec*
EMP: 114
SALES (corp-wide): 852MM Publicly Held
WEB: www.hilton.com
SIC: 7011 5813 5812 Hotels & motels; drinking places; eating places
PA: Park Hotels & Resorts Inc.
1775 Tysons Blvd Fl 7
Tysons VA 22102
571 302-5757

(P-11355)
PARK PLAZA HOTEL
150 Hegenberger Rd, Oakland (94621-1422)
PHONE.................................510 635-5300
Tracy W Wahrlich Jr, *President*
Carl T Doughty, *General Ptnr*
Bert Taprizi, *General Ptnr*
Stephen Wahrlich, *General Ptnr*
EMP: 38 EST: 1985
SALES (est): 590.5K Privately Held
SIC: 7011 Hotel, franchised

(P-11356)
PARK PLAZA SAN JOSE ARPRT LLC
1355 N 4th St, San Jose (95112-4714)
PHONE.................................408 453-5340
Noor Billawala,
EMP: 41 EST: 2003
SALES (est): 954.5K Privately Held
SIC: 7011 Hotel, franchised

(P-11357)
PARK US LESSEE HOLDINGS LLC
Also Called: Doubltree By Hlton Ht Snoma Wi
1 Doubletree Dr, Rohnert Park (94928-1336)
PHONE.................................707 887-7838
EMP: 90 EST: 2017
SALES (est): 2.1MM Privately Held
SIC: 7011 Hotels & motels

(P-11358)
PARLIAMENT INC (PA)
1307 El Centro Ave, Oakland (94602-1817)
PHONE.................................415 702-0624
Peter Sims, *Principal*
EMP: 40 EST: 2017
SALES (est): 83K Privately Held
SIC: 7011 Motels

(P-11359)
PARMAR ASHOK
Also Called: Super 8 Motel
1855 W Cleveland Ave, Madera (93637-9283)
PHONE.................................559 661-1131
Ashok Parmar, *Partner*
Pravin Parmar, *Partner*
Umesh Parmar, *Partner*
EMP: 65 EST: 1991
SQ FT: 25,000
SALES (est): 685.3K Privately Held
WEB: www.wyndhamhotels.com
SIC: 7011 Hotels & motels

(P-11360)
PASADENA HOTEL DEV VENTR LP
Also Called: Sheraton Pasadena
400 S El Camino Real # 200, San Mateo (94402-1704)
PHONE.................................650 347-8260
June Chen,
Cathy Sampognaro, *Human Res Dir*
Barbara Chen,
Clement Chen III,
Trust Under The Will of Clemen,
EMP: 92 EST: 1975
SALES (est): 722.8K Privately Held
SIC: 7011 5812 Hotels & motels; eating places

(P-11361)
PASATIEMPO III INVESTMENTS
Also Called: Inn At Pasatiempo
555 Highway 17, Santa Cruz (95060-1812)
PHONE.................................831 423-5000
Richard Gregerson, *General Ptnr*
Christina Gibson, *Manager*
EMP: 53 EST: 1956
SALES (est): 731.2K Privately Held
WEB: www.innatpasatiempo.com
SIC: 7011 5812 Hotels & motels; eating places

(P-11362)
PELICAN INN
10 Pacific Way, Muir Beach (94965-9729)
PHONE.................................415 383-6000
Edward Cunningham, *Partner*
EMP: 59 EST: 1979
SQ FT: 6,000
SALES (est): 1MM Privately Held
WEB: www.pelicaninn.com
SIC: 7011 5812 Resort hotel; eating places

(P-11363)
PEPPER TREE INN
Also Called: Rodeway Inn
645 N Lake Blvd, Tahoe City (96145-2274)
PHONE.................................530 583-3711
Thomas Brown, *Manager*
Billy Decaneo, *Manager*
EMP: 61
SQ FT: 18,609
SALES (corp-wide): 5.4MM Privately Held
WEB: www.peppertreetahoe.com
SIC: 7011 Motels
PA: Pepper Tree Inn
106 Bluebonnet Ln Unit 13
Scotts Valley CA

(P-11364)
PETALUMA PROPERTIES INC
Also Called: Best Western Petaluma Inn
200 S Mcdowell Blvd, Petaluma (94954-3506)
PHONE.................................707 763-0994
Richard L Myers, *President*
Victor Decarli, *Vice Pres*
EMP: 55 EST: 1960
SQ FT: 20,000
SALES (est): 1MM Privately Held
WEB: www.petalumahomes.com
SIC: 7011 Hotels & motels

(P-11365)
PHF RUBY LLC
Also Called: Marriott Vacaltion Club Pulse
2620 Jones St, San Francisco (94133-1306)
PHONE.................................415 885-4700
Jose L Torres,
Anthony Kai Chiu Ceng,
EMP: 159 EST: 1988
SALES (est): 7.6MM Privately Held
WEB: www.marriott.com
SIC: 7011 Hotel, franchised

(P-11366)
PICCADILLY HOSPITALITY LLC
Also Called: Piccadilly Inn Shaw
2305 W Shaw Ave, Fresno (93711-3411)
PHONE.................................559 348-5520
Mu-Pien Chien, *President*
Gene Chien, *Vice Pres*
EMP: 48 EST: 2012
SALES (est): 1MM Privately Held
WEB: www.hotel-piccadilly.com
SIC: 7011 Resort hotel; hotels

(P-11367)
PICCADILLY INN AIRPORT
5115 E Mckinley Ave, Fresno (93727-2093)
PHONE.................................559 375-7760
Sheenal Patel,
Puja Singh,
EMP: 42 EST: 2013
SALES (est): 3.5MM Privately Held
WEB: www.piccadillyairport.com
SIC: 7011 Resort hotel

(P-11368)
PINE & POWELL PARTNERS LLC
Also Called: Stanford Court Hotel
905 California St, San Francisco (94108-2201)
PHONE.................................415 989-3500
Naveen Kakarla,
Rose Rivera, *Administration*
Bryan Terris, *Engineer*
Ada Yan, *Finance*
Cliff Lee, *Human Resources*
EMP: 99 EST: 2014
SQ FT: 287,000
SALES (est): 6.9MM Privately Held
WEB: www.stanfordcourt.com
SIC: 7011 Hotels & motels

(P-11369)
PINECREST LAKE RESORT
421 Pinecrest Lake Rd, Pinecrest (95364)
P.O. Box 1216 (95364-0216)
PHONE.................................209 965-3411
Roland Webb, *Owner*
Laurie Cashman, *General Mgr*
Caitie Campodonico, *Receptionist*
EMP: 37 EST: 1976
SQ FT: 1,000
SALES (est): 691.5K Privately Held
WEB: www.pinecrestlakeresort.com
SIC: 7011 Resort hotel

(P-11370)
PINES RESORTS OF CALIFORNIA (PA)
Also Called: Ducey's On The Lake
54449 Road 432, Bass Lake (93604-9762)
P.O. Box 109 (93604-0109)
PHONE.................................559 642-3121
Stephen R Welch, *Vice Pres*
Rudolph Schulte, *President*
James H Franzen, *Corp Secy*
Tom Smith, *Exec Dir*
EMP: 120 EST: 1974
SQ FT: 20,000
SALES (est): 13.1MM Privately Held
WEB: www.basslake.com
SIC: 5812 7011 5411 5813 Restaurant, family: independent; tourist camps, cabins, cottages & courts; resort hotel; grocery stores, independent; cocktail lounge

(P-11371)
PLEASANT CANYON HOTEL INC
Also Called: Residence Inn By Marriott
11920 Dublin Canyon Rd, Pleasanton (94588-2818)
PHONE.................................925 847-0535
James Evans, *CFO*
Alexis Belardes-Flores, *Agent*
Jee Howard, *Agent*
EMP: 50 EST: 1996
SQ FT: 98,496
SALES (est): 5.8MM Privately Held
WEB: www.marriott.com
SIC: 7011 Hotels & motels

(P-11372)
PLEASANTON PROJECT OWNER LLC
Also Called: Marriott
11950 Dublin Canyon Rd, Pleasanton (94588-2818)
PHONE.................................925 847-7592
Warren Field, *CEO*
Takako Smith, *Finance Dir*
EMP: 40 EST: 2016

7011 - Hotels, Motels & Tourist Courts County (P-11373)

SALES (est): 10.1MM
SALES (corp-wide): 173.4MM **Privately Held**
WEB: www.marriott.com
SIC: 7011 Hotels & motels
PA: Pyramid Advisors Limited Partnership
1 Post Office Sq Ste 19
Boston MA 02109
617 202-2033

(P-11373)
PONDEROSA GARDEN MOTEL INC
7010 Skyway, Paradise (95969-3910)
PHONE 888 727-3423
Johan Klempa, *President*
Sandra Klempa, *Corp Secy*
EMP: 53 **EST:** 1979
SQ FT: 12,800
SALES (est): 1MM **Privately Held**
WEB: www.ponderosagardensmotel.com
SIC: 7011 Motels

(P-11374)
POST ST RNSSNCE PRTNERS A CAL
Also Called: Prescott Hotel, The
545 Post St, San Francisco (94102-1228)
PHONE 415 563-0303
John Dern, *President*
EMP: 1080 **EST:** 1987
SALES (est): 18.9MM **Privately Held**
WEB: www.viceroyhotelsandresorts.com
SIC: 7011 Resort hotel; hotels
HQ: Kimpton Hotel & Restaurant Group Llc
222 Kearny St Ste 200
San Francisco CA 94108
415 397-5572

(P-11375)
PR RANCHO HOTEL LLC
11260 Point East Dr, Rancho Cordova (95742-6232)
PHONE 916 638-4141
Viorica Sanchevici, *Principal*
Guneet Bajwa, *Principal*
Cosmin Nicula, *General Mgr*
EMP: 53 **EST:** 2016
SALES (est): 1.4MM **Privately Held**
SIC: 7011 Hotels

(P-11376)
PRESIDIO HOTEL GROUP LLC
Also Called: Fairfield Inn
10713 White Rock Rd, Rancho Cordova (95670-6031)
PHONE 916 631-7500
Sushil Patel, *Branch Mgr*
EMP: 107
SALES (corp-wide): 6.9MM **Privately Held**
WEB: www.presidioco.com
SIC: 7011 Hotels & motels
PA: Presidio Hotel Group, Llc
1011 10th St
Sacramento CA 95814
707 429-6000

(P-11377)
PRZM LLC
Also Called: Acqua Hotel The
555 Rdwood Hwy Frntage Rd, Mill Valley (94941-3007)
PHONE 415 380-0400
Justin Slake, *General Mgr*
Justine Slake, *General Mgr*
EMP: 40 **EST:** 2008
SALES (est): 2.9MM **Privately Held**
SIC: 7011 Hotels

(P-11378)
PSAS INC
3400 Mccall Ave Ste 100, Selma (93662-2560)
PHONE 559 896-1443
Dwight G Nelson, *President*
EMP: 46 **EST:** 1989
SQ FT: 2,000
SALES (est): 379.9K **Privately Held**
SIC: 7011 5541 5947 5812 Hotels; filling stations, gasoline; gift shop; American restaurant

(P-11379)
QUALITY INN AND SUITES
2315 Pentland Way, San Jose (95148-4028)
PHONE 806 335-1561
Vikramjit Singh,
Kuldip Deol,
EMP: 57 **EST:** 2003
SQ FT: 261,360
SALES (est): 368.5K **Privately Held**
WEB: www.choicehotels.com
SIC: 7011 Hotels & motels

(P-11380)
RAILROAD PARK INC
100 Railroad Park Rd, Dunsmuir (96025-2604)
PHONE 530 235-2300
Mark Lilley, *President*
EMP: 37 **EST:** 2016
SALES (est): 1.4MM **Privately Held**
WEB: www.rrpark.com
SIC: 7011 5812 7033 Resort hotel; restaurant, family; independent; campgrounds

(P-11381)
RAMADA LIMITED
Also Called: Ramada Inn
1286 Twin View Blvd, Redding (96003-1500)
PHONE 530 246-2222
Minaxi Patel, *Partner*
EMP: 41 **EST:** 1999
SALES (est): 250.4K **Privately Held**
WEB: www.ramadainn.net
SIC: 7011 Hotels & motels

(P-11382)
RAMKABIR LLC
Also Called: La Quinta Inn Suites Airport W
1390 El Camino Real, Millbrae (94030-1411)
PHONE 650 952-3200
Arvind Desai, *Mng Member*
Amar Desai,
Indumati Desai,
▲ **EMP:** 152 **EST:** 1988
SALES (est): 9.2MM **Privately Held**
WEB: www.wyndhamhotels.com
SIC: 7011 Hotels & motels

(P-11383)
RAP INVESTORS LP
Also Called: Beachcomber Motel
1111 N Main St, Fort Bragg (95437-8132)
PHONE 707 964-2402
Pam Omante, *Partner*
Robert Hunt, *Partner*
EMP: 43 **EST:** 1972
SALES (est): 1MM **Privately Held**
WEB: www.thebeachcombermotel.com
SIC: 7011 Motels

(P-11384)
RAPS DUBLIN LLC
Also Called: La Quinta Inn
6275 Dublin Blvd, Dublin (94568-7573)
PHONE 925 828-9393
Arvin Patel, *Owner*
Wayne Goldberg, *CEO*
Ron Gapol, *Manager*
EMP: 40 **EST:** 1999
SALES (est): 5.8MM **Privately Held**
WEB: www.wyndhamhotels.com
SIC: 7011 Hotels & motels

(P-11385)
RAPS HOSPITALITY GROUP
Also Called: Holiday Inn
5977 Mowry Ave, Newark (94560-5005)
PHONE 510 795-7995
Gary Ghandi, *Manager*
EMP: 122
SQ FT: 59,499
SALES (corp-wide): 15MM **Privately Held**
WEB: www.rapshotels.com
SIC: 7011 Hotels & motels
PA: Raps Hospitality Group
229 Kings Ct
San Carlos CA 94070
650 596-8520

(P-11386)
RECP/WNDSOR SCRAMENTO VENTR LP
Also Called: Windsor Capital Hotel Group
4422 Y St, Sacramento (95817-2220)
PHONE 916 455-6800
Mike Cryan, *CEO*
Recp Windsor Rim Sacramento GP, *General Ptnr*
EMP: 42 **EST:** 2005
SALES (est): 548.3K **Privately Held**
WEB: www.courtyard.marriott.com
SIC: 7011 Hotels

(P-11387)
RED BEAR INC
Also Called: Rose Hotel
807 Main St, Pleasanton (94566-6070)
PHONE 925 846-8802
Mike Madden, *CEO*
Tom Walker, *Sales Mgr*
Vishakha Bhadra, *Manager*
Phylis A Grisham, *Manager*
EMP: 37 **EST:** 2001
SALES (est): 724.3K **Privately Held**
WEB: www.rosehotel.net
SIC: 7011 Hotels

(P-11388)
RED FOX CASINO
200 Cahto Dr, Laytonville (95454)
P.O. Box 1763 (95454-1763)
PHONE 707 984-6800
Corey James, *Manager*
EMP: 35 **EST:** 1997
SALES (est): 735.8K **Privately Held**
WEB: www.redfoxcasino.com
SIC: 7011 Casino hotel

(P-11389)
REDDING RANCHERIA
Also Called: Win River Resort & Casino
2100 Redding Rancheria Rd, Redding (96001-5530)
PHONE 530 245-9161
Bob Boyles, *Manager*
Christopher Decamp, *Technical Staff*
Sherry Bates, *Manager*
EMP: 51 **Privately Held**
WEB: www.reddingrancheria-nsn.gov
SIC: 7011 Hotels
PA: Redding Rancheria
2000 Redding Rancheria Rd
Redding CA 96001

(P-11390)
REDDING RANCHERIA (PA)
2000 Redding Rancheria Rd, Redding (96001-5528)
PHONE 530 225-8979
Tracy Edward, *CEO*
Stacey Carman, *COO*
Christi Hines, *CFO*
Tamra Olson, *CFO*
Morgan Watkins, *Executive*
EMP: 60 **EST:** 1922
SQ FT: 16,360
SALES (est): 36.5MM **Privately Held**
WEB: www.reddingrancheria-nsn.gov
SIC: 7011 Hotels & motels

(P-11391)
REDDING RNCHRIA ECNMIC DEV COR
Also Called: Win-River Casino
2100 Redding Rancheria Rd, Redding (96001-5530)
PHONE 530 243-3377
Redding Rancheria Tribe, *Principal*
Christi Ross, *CFO*
Wayne Erickson, *Officer*
Chad Bartlett, *Vice Pres*
Esteban Pizano, *Vice Pres*
EMP: 310 **EST:** 1993
SQ FT: 3,000
SALES (est): 25.8MM **Privately Held**
WEB: www.reddingrancheria-nsn.gov
SIC: 7011 Casino hotel

(P-11392)
REDDING SUPER 8 MOTEL INC
5175 Churn Creek Rd, Redding (96002-3915)
PHONE 530 221-8881

PRODUCTS & SERVICES SECTION

Eugene Graff, *President*
Milo Graff, *Vice Pres*
Cliff Visscher, *Admin Sec*
EMP: 54 **EST:** 1988
SQ FT: 12,000
SALES (est): 394.7K **Privately Held**
WEB: www.wyndhamhotels.com
SIC: 7011 Hotels & motels

(P-11393)
REMINGTON LDGING HSPTALITY LLC
Bardessono Hotel
6526 Yount St, Yountville (94599-1270)
PHONE 877 932-5333
Phillip G Sherburne, *Branch Mgr*
John Wymann, *Sales Mgr*
Ashley Nicho, *Sales Staff*
EMP: 84 **Privately Held**
WEB: www.remingtonhotels.com
SIC: 7011 Hotels
HQ: Remington Lodging & Hospitality Llc
14185 Dallas Pkwy # 1150
Dallas TX 75254

(P-11394)
RENAISSANCE HOTEL HOLDINGS INC
1325 Broadway, Sonoma (95476-7505)
PHONE 707 935-6600
Dave Dalquist, *General Mgr*
Rick Eldridge, *Finance*
Citlalli Solis, *Human Res Mgr*
Steve Dunnegan, *Opers Staff*
Denelle Sala, *Sales Staff*
EMP: 38 **EST:** 1961
SALES (est): 518.7K **Privately Held**
WEB: www.renaissance-hotels.marriott.com
SIC: 7011 Hotels

(P-11395)
RENAISSANCE HOTEL OPERATING CO
Also Called: Marriott
905 California St, San Francisco (94108-2201)
PHONE 415 989-3500
Bill Love, *Branch Mgr*
Teresa Crooks, *Administration*
Rory Kagan, *Regl Sales Mgr*
Cinthya Costakis, *Sales Staff*
EMP: 141
SALES (corp-wide): 10.5B **Publicly Held**
WEB: www.renaissance-hotels.marriott.com
SIC: 7011 Hotels & motels
HQ: Renaissance Hotel Operating Company
10400 Fernwood Rd
Bethesda MD 20817

(P-11396)
RENESON HOTELS INC (PA)
Also Called: Carriage Inn
2700 Junipero Serra Blvd, Daly City (94015-1634)
PHONE 650 449-5353
Alrene Flynn, *Chairman*
Garrett Grialou, *President*
Doug Sherer, *CFO*
Diane Grialou, *Admin Sec*
Jennifer Wade-Yeo, *Human Res Dir*
▲ **EMP:** 100 **EST:** 1957
SALES (est): 28.4MM **Privately Held**
WEB: www.renesonhotels.com
SIC: 7011 Hotels & motels

(P-11397)
RENESON HOTELS INC
Also Called: Hotel Britton
112 7th St, San Francisco (94103-2809)
PHONE 415 621-7001
Norman Onaga, *General Mgr*
EMP: 203
SALES (corp-wide): 28.4MM **Privately Held**
WEB: www.renesonhotels.com
SIC: 7011 Resort hotel
PA: Reneson Hotels, Inc.
2700 Junipero Serra Blvd
Daly City CA 94015
650 449-5353

PRODUCTS & SERVICES SECTION

7011 - Hotels, Motels & Tourist Courts County (P-11422)

(P-11398)
RESERVATION RANCH (PA)
356 Sarina Rd N, Smith River (95567-9458)
P.O. Box 75 (95567-0075)
PHONE...................707 487-3516
Henry L Westbrook III, *Partner*
EMP: 38 EST: 1930
SQ FT: 2,000
SALES (est): 3.6MM **Privately Held**
SIC: 7011 0241 Hotels & motels; dairy heifer replacement farm

(P-11399)
RESIDENCE INN BY MARRIOTT
5322 N Diana St, Fresno (93710-6700)
PHONE...................559 222-8900
Juliee May, *Manager*
EMP: 58 EST: 2007
SALES (est): 1.2MM **Privately Held**
WEB: www.residence-inn.marriott.com
SIC: 7011 Hotels & motels

(P-11400)
RESIDENCE INN BY MARRIOTT LLC
800 E San Carlos Ave, San Carlos (94070-2611)
PHONE...................650 637-5500
EMP: 44 EST: 1987
SALES (est): 4.1MM **Privately Held**
WEB: www.residence-inn.marriott.com
SIC: 7011 Hotels & motels

(P-11401)
RESIDENCE INN BY MARRIOTT LLC
1850 Freedom Way, Roseville (95678-6269)
PHONE...................888 484-1695
EMP: 40
SALES (corp-wide): 10.5B **Publicly Held**
WEB: www.marriott.com
SIC: 7011 Hotels & motels
HQ: Residence Inn By Marriott, Llc
10400 Fernwood Rd
Bethesda MD 20817

(P-11402)
RESIDENCE INN BY MARRIOTT LLC
Also Called: Residnce Inn By Mrrott Nwark S
35466 Dumbarton Ct, Newark (94560-1100)
PHONE...................510 739-6000
Melody Lanthorn-Gale, *Manager*
EMP: 40
SALES (corp-wide): 10.5B **Publicly Held**
WEB: www.marriott.com
SIC: 7011 Hotels & motels
HQ: Residence Inn By Marriott, Llc
10400 Fernwood Rd
Bethesda MD 20817

(P-11403)
RESIDENCE INN BY MARRIOTT LLC
Also Called: Residnce Inn San Frncsco Arprt
1350 Veterans Blvd, South San Francisco (94080-1954)
PHONE...................650 837-9000
Edward Busch, *Branch Mgr*
Margaux Esplana, *Sales Mgr*
EMP: 40
SALES (corp-wide): 10.5B **Publicly Held**
WEB: www.marriott.com
SIC: 7011 Hotels & motels
HQ: Residence Inn By Marriott, Llc
10400 Fernwood Rd
Bethesda MD 20817

(P-11404)
RESIDENCE INN BY MARRIOTT LLC
700 Ellinwood Way, Pleasant Hill (94523-4700)
PHONE...................925 689-1010
JC Medina, *Principal*
EMP: 40
SALES (corp-wide): 10.5B **Publicly Held**
WEB: www.marriott.com
SIC: 7011 Hotels & motels
HQ: Residence Inn By Marriott, Llc
10400 Fernwood Rd
Bethesda MD 20817

(P-11405)
RESIDNCE INN SAN JOSE NRTH/SLC
656 America Center Ct, San Jose (95002-2500)
PHONE...................408 758-9550
Alice Sheets Marriott,
EMP: 50 EST: 2019
SALES (est): 788.4K **Privately Held**
SIC: 7011 Hotel, franchised

(P-11406)
RESORT AT INDIAN SPRINGS LLC
Also Called: Indian Springs Resort & Spa
1712 Lincoln Ave, Calistoga (94515-1113)
PHONE...................707 709-2434
Patricia Merchant, *Mng Member*
Eric Muth, *Sales Mgr*
Pat Merchant,
John Merchant, *Mng Member*
EMP: 150 EST: 1861
SALES (est): 13.6MM **Privately Held**
WEB: www.indianspringscalistoga.com
SIC: 7011 5812 Resort hotel; restaurant, family: independent

(P-11407)
RI HERITG INN ROSEVILLE LLC
Also Called: Residence Inn By Marriott
1850 Freedom Way, Roseville (95678-6269)
PHONE...................916 780-1850
Heather Hilton, *Principal*
EMP: 40 EST: 2018
SALES (est): 1MM **Privately Held**
WEB: www.heritagehotelroseville.com
SIC: 7011 Hotels & motels

(P-11408)
RICHMOND HOTELS LLC
Also Called: Surestay
915 W Cutting Blvd, Richmond (94804-2027)
PHONE...................510 237-3000
Adra Stencil, *Principal*
Adra Stunstle, *Regional Mgr*
EMP: 60 EST: 1999
SALES (est): 636.8K **Privately Held**
SIC: 7011 Hotels

(P-11409)
RITZ-CARLTON SAN FRANCISCO
600 Stockton St, San Francisco (94108-2311)
PHONE...................415 296-7465
Hossein Vetry, *Director*
EMP: 51 EST: 1991
SALES (est): 8.7MM **Privately Held**
WEB: www.ritzcarlton.com
SIC: 7011 Hotels

(P-11410)
RITZ-CARLTON HOTEL COMPANY LLC
Also Called: Ritz-Carlton San Francisco
600 Stockton St, San Francisco (94108-2386)
PHONE...................415 773-6168
Edward Madey, *Manager*
Jo-Anne Hill, *President*
Trevor Warman, *Executive*
Nickolas Tice, *General Mgr*
Julie Lytle, *Executive Asst*
EMP: 500
SALES (corp-wide): 10.5B **Publicly Held**
WEB: www.ritzcarlton.com
SIC: 7011 Hotels
HQ: The Ritz-Carlton Hotel Company Llc
10400 Fernwood Rd
Bethesda MD 20817
301 380-3000

(P-11411)
RIVER RANCH
Also Called: Truckee River Ranch
2285 River Rd, Tahoe City (96145-2158)
P.O. Box 197 (96145-0197)
PHONE...................530 583-4264
Dennis Nevin, *Partner*
Peter Friedrichsen, *Vice Pres*
EMP: 54 EST: 1968
SQ FT: 10,000
SALES (est): 1.2MM **Privately Held**
WEB: www.riverranchlodge.com
SIC: 5812 5813 7011 American restaurant; bar (drinking places); hotels

(P-11412)
RIVER ROCK ENTERTAINMENT AUTH
Also Called: River Rock Casino
3250 Highway 128, Geyserville (95441-8908)
P.O. Box 607 (95441-0607)
PHONE...................707 857-2777
David Fendrick, *CEO*
Joseph R Callahan, *CFO*
Yola Bawlec, *Exec Sec*
Jerry Arretche, *Manager*
EMP: 616 EST: 2002
SALES (est): 20.7MM **Privately Held**
WEB: www.riverrockcasino.com
SIC: 7011 Casino hotel

(P-11413)
RLJ C SAN FRANCISCO LESSEE LP
Also Called: Courtyard By Mrrott San Frncsc
761 Post St, San Francisco (94109-6105)
PHONE...................415 346-3800
Sherrie Carreno, *General Mgr*
Howard Isaacson, *Vice Pres*
EMP: 45 EST: 2013
SQ FT: 55,699
SALES (est): 4MM **Privately Held**
WEB: www.courtyard.marriott.com
SIC: 7011 Hotels & motels
PA: The Rlj Companies Llc
3 Bethesda Ctr Ste 1000
Bethesda MD 20814

(P-11414)
RLJHGN EMERYVILLE LESSEE LP
Also Called: Hilton
1800 Powell St, Emeryville (94608-1808)
PHONE...................510 658-9300
Mark Burden, *CEO*
Jeff Virgil, *CFO*
EMP: 69 EST: 2004
SQ FT: 476
SALES (est): 2.8MM **Privately Held**
WEB: www.hilton.com
SIC: 7011 Hotels & motels

(P-11415)
ROCKLIN LODGING GROUP LLC
Also Called: Staybridge Suites
6664 Lonetree Blvd, Rocklin (95765-3737)
PHONE...................916 761-7500
C Lamont, *Mng Member*
EMP: 51 EST: 2007
SALES (est): 1.5MM **Privately Held**
WEB: www.staybridgesuites.com
SIC: 7011 Hotels & motels

(P-11416)
ROLLING HILLS CASINO
2655 Everett Freeman Way, Corning (96021-9000)
PHONE...................530 528-3500
Austen Brauker, *Train & Dev Mgr*
Jessica Linn, *Sales Staff*
Vue Chue, *Manager*
Robyn Mueller, *Manager*
Parry Salsi, *Manager*
EMP: 101
SALES (est): 13.9MM **Privately Held**
WEB: www.rollinghillscasino.com
SIC: 7011 Casino hotel

(P-11417)
ROMAN SPA HOT SPRNG RESORT LLC
1300 Washington St, Calistoga (94515-1442)
PHONE...................707 942-4441
Michael Quast, *Mng Member*
Wendy Hiller, *Executive*
Quast Elyse, *Marketing Staff*
Elyse Quast, *Marketing Staff*
EMP: 45 EST: 1975
SQ FT: 5,000
SALES (est): 2.9MM **Privately Held**
WEB: www.romanspahotsprings.com
SIC: 7011 Resort hotel

(P-11418)
ROPPONG-THOE LP A CAL LTD PRTN
Also Called: Lake Tahoe Resort Hotel
4130 Lake Tahoe Blvd, South Lake Tahoe (96150-6965)
PHONE...................530 544-5400
Kunihiro Nakayabu, *Managing Prtnr*
Masaru Saito, *Managing Prtnr*
John Steinbach, *General Mgr*
EMP: 200 EST: 2000
SALES (est): 16.9MM **Privately Held**
WEB: www.tahoeresorthotel.com
SIC: 7011 Resort hotel; hotels

(P-11419)
ROSE GRAMMAS GARDEN INN
Also Called: Rose Garden Inn
2740 Telegraph Ave, Berkeley (94705-1131)
PHONE...................510 549-2145
Kathy Kuhner, *Partner*
Indu Patel, *Partner*
EMP: 46 EST: 1979
SQ FT: 15,000
SALES (est): 644.8K **Privately Held**
WEB: www.rosegardeninn.com
SIC: 7011 Bed & breakfast inn

(P-11420)
ROSEWOOD HOTELS & RESORTS LLC
Also Called: Rosewood Sand Hill Hotel
2825 Sand Hill Rd, Menlo Park (94025-7022)
PHONE...................650 561-1500
James Chung, *Manager*
Michael Casey, *Managing Dir*
Philip Meyer, *Managing Dir*
Anthony Gutierrez, *Office Spvr*
Maxim Klassen, *Info Tech Dir*
EMP: 300 EST: 1997
SALES (est): 25.5MM **Privately Held**
WEB: www.rosewoodhotels.com
SIC: 7011 Resort hotel; hotels

(P-11421)
ROYAL GORGE NORDIC SKI RESORT (PA)
Also Called: Royal Grge Cross Cntry Ski Rso
9411 Hillside Rd, Soda Springs (95728)
P.O. Box 1100 (95728-1100)
PHONE...................530 426-3871
John Slouber, *President*
Frances Wiesel, *Admin Sec*
EMP: 120 EST: 1971
SQ FT: 50,000
SALES (est): 4.7MM **Privately Held**
WEB: www.royalgorge.com
SIC: 7011 Resort hotel

(P-11422)
RP/KINETIC PARC 55 OWNER LLC
Also Called: Parc 55 Hotel
55 Cyril Magnin St, San Francisco (94102-2812)
PHONE...................415 392-8000
Steve Barick,
Joeann Lamadrid, *President*
Peter Beheda, *Senior VP*
Gary Gutierrez, *Vice Pres*
Rob Gauthier, *General Mgr*
EMP: 126 EST: 2006
SALES (est): 264.6MM
SALES (corp-wide): 6.1B **Publicly Held**
WEB: www.parc55hotel.com
SIC: 7011 Hotels

7011 - Hotels, Motels & Tourist Courts County (P-11423)

PA: Blackstone Inc.
345 Park Ave
New York NY 10154
212 583-5000

(P-11423)
RUNNING CREEK CASINO
635 E State Highway 20, Upper Lake (95485-8793)
P.O. Box 788 (95485-0788)
PHONE 707 275-9209
Mike Caryl, *Finance Dir*
Albert Menchaca, *Marketing Mgr*
Terry Orin, *Director*
Stacy Bethel, *Manager*
Kathleen Treppa, *Manager*
EMP: 170 **EST:** 2011
SALES (est): 14.8MM **Privately Held**
WEB: www.runningcreekcasino.com
SIC: 7011 5812 Casino hotel; eating places

(P-11424)
S R H H INC
Also Called: Radisson Inn
1085 E El Camino Real, Sunnyvale (94087-3755)
PHONE 408 247-0800
Donald Bramer, *President*
Gaylon Patterson, *Treasurer*
John Branagh, *Admin Sec*
▲ **EMP:** 42 **EST:** 1985
SQ FT: 150,000
SALES (est): 284.4K **Privately Held**
WEB: www.radissonhotelgroup.com
SIC: 7011 5812 5813 Hotels & motels; American restaurant; cocktail lounge

(P-11425)
SACRAMENTO 49ER TRAVEL PLAZA
2828 El Centro Rd, Sacramento (95833-9602)
PHONE 916 927-4774
Tristen Griffith, *President*
Terrace Rust, *Vice Pres*
Darrell Carlson, *Maintence Staff*
EMP: 125 **EST:** 1976
SQ FT: 27,000
SALES (est): 11.5MM **Privately Held**
WEB: www.sacramento49er.com
SIC: 7011 5331 5812 5541 Motels; variety stores; restaurant, family: independent; truck stops

(P-11426)
SAGE HOSPITALITY RESOURCES LLC
Also Called: Homewood Stes Hlton Sfo Arprt
2000 Shoreline Ct, Brisbane (94005-1802)
PHONE 650 589-1600
Gina Merz, *Branch Mgr*
EMP: 159
SALES (corp-wide): 286.2MM **Privately Held**
WEB: www.sagehospitalitygroup.com
SIC: 7011 Hotels & motels
PA: Sage Hospitality Resources L.L.C.
1575 Welton St Ste 300
Denver CO 80202
303 595-7200

(P-11427)
SAINT ORRES CORPORATION
Also Called: St Orres Restaurant & Inn
36601 S Highway 1, Gualala (95445-8583)
P.O. Box 523 (95445-0523)
PHONE 707 884-3335
Eric Black, *President*
Rosemary Campiformio, *Vice Pres*
EMP: 35 **EST:** 1973
SQ FT: 9,000
SALES (est): 997.3K **Privately Held**
WEB: www.saintorres.com
SIC: 7011 5812 Bed & breakfast inn; eating places

(P-11428)
SAK HOSPITALITY INC
Also Called: Hampton Inn Vallejo
1596 Fairgrounds Dr, Vallejo (94589-2080)
PHONE 707 554-9655
Sukhdev Patel, *President*
Sangita Patel, *Vice Pres*
Kalpesh Patel, *Admin Sec*
EMP: 51 **EST:** 1993

SQ FT: 42,916
SALES (est): 1.5MM **Privately Held**
WEB: www.hilton.com
SIC: 7011 Hotels & motels

(P-11429)
SALT LAKE HOTEL ASSOCIATES LP (PA)
222 Kearny St Ste 200, San Francisco (94108-4537)
PHONE 415 397-5572
Tom Lataur, *President*
EMP: 111 **EST:** 1997
SALES (est): 12.2MM **Privately Held**
SIC: 7011 Hotels

(P-11430)
SAM BENNION
Also Called: Hillsdale Inn
477 E Hillsdale Blvd, San Mateo (94403-2822)
PHONE 650 341-3461
Samuel H Bennion, *Partner*
Earl Garr, *Partner*
EMP: 52 **EST:** 1971
SALES (est): 658.5K **Privately Held**
WEB: www.hillsdaleinn.com
SIC: 7011 5813 5812 Motels; bar (drinking places); restaurant, family: independent

(P-11431)
SAN BENITO HOUSE INC
445 Main St, Half Moon Bay (94019-1749)
PHONE 650 726-3425
Greg Regan, *President*
Carol Jean Regan-Mickelsen, *Treasurer*
EMP: 41 **EST:** 1977
SQ FT: 4,000
SALES (est): 622.9K **Privately Held**
WEB: www.sanbenitohouse.com
SIC: 7011 5813 Bed & breakfast inn; bar (drinking places)

(P-11432)
SAN FRANCISCO C & C INC
1050 Van Ness Ave, San Francisco (94109-6934)
PHONE 415 673-4711
Lee Hufford, *Branch Mgr*
EMP: 45
SALES (corp-wide): 9.2MM **Privately Held**
WEB: www.marriott.com
SIC: 7011 Hotels
PA: San Francisco C & C
2165 Lombard St
San Francisco CA 94123
702 249-5995

(P-11433)
SAN FRANCISCO HOTEL ASSOCIATES
Also Called: Masa's
650 Bush St, San Francisco (94108-3509)
PHONE 415 392-4666
Michael Lennon, *Partner*
EMP: 44 **EST:** 1982
SQ FT: 46,067
SALES (est): 799.3K **Privately Held**
WEB: www.masasrestaurant.com
SIC: 7011 5812 Hotels; French restaurant

(P-11434)
SAN FRANCISCO HOTEL GROUP LLC
Also Called: Loews Regency San Francisco
222 Sansome St, San Francisco (94104-2703)
PHONE 415 276-9888
Yue-Tin Chang, *President*
Jonathan Tisch, *Chairman*
Tracy Lee, *Controller*
▲ **EMP:** 109 **EST:** 1989
SALES (est): 14.9MM
SALES (corp-wide): 12.5B **Publicly Held**
WEB: www.loewshotels.com
SIC: 7011 Resort hotel
HQ: Loews Hotels Holding Corporation
667 Madison Ave
New York NY 10065
212 521-2000

(P-11435)
SAN JOSE AIRPORT GARDEN HOTEL
1740 N 1st St, San Jose (95112-4508)
PHONE 408 793-3300
EMP: 99
SALES (est): 2.2MM **Privately Held**
SIC: 7011 Hotel/Motel Operation

(P-11436)
SAN JOSE AIRPORT HOTEL LLC
Also Called: Holiday Inn
1740 N 1st St, San Jose (95112-4508)
PHONE 408 793-3939
Manou Mobedshahi, *Mng Member*
Vijay Bhatia, *General Mgr*
Andy Evers, *General Mgr*
Harry Engineer,
Dilkhush Engineer, *Manager*
EMP: 230 **EST:** 1996
SALES (est): 13.9MM **Privately Held**
WEB: www.sanjose.com
SIC: 7011 Hotels & motels

(P-11437)
SAN JOSE HHG HOTEL DEV LP
Also Called: Springhill Stes San Jose Arprt
10 Skyport Dr, San Jose (95110-1354)
PHONE 408 650-0590
Patricia Santini, *Partner*
Kevin Keefer, *Principal*
EMP: 44 **EST:** 2015
SQ FT: 215,834
SALES (est): 1MM **Privately Held**
SIC: 7011 Hotels

(P-11438)
SAN JOSE HHG HOTEL DEV LP
Also Called: Residence Inn San Jose Airport
10 Skyport Dr, San Jose (95110-1354)
PHONE 650 868-4911
Patricia Santini, *Principal*
EMP: 36 **EST:** 2015
SALES (est): 682.9K **Privately Held**
SIC: 7011 Hotels & motels

(P-11439)
SAN JOSE LESSEE LLC
Also Called: Doubletree By Hilton San Jose
2050 Gateway Pl, San Jose (95110-1011)
PHONE 408 453-4000
Missoon Kong, *General Mgr*
Rowan Tejada, *Finance*
Agnes Abrenica, *Manager*
Reanna Graettinger, *Manager*
EMP: 99 **EST:** 2017
SALES (est): 8.3MM
SALES (corp-wide): 852MM **Publicly Held**
WEB: www.hilton.com
SIC: 7011 Hotels & motels
HQ: Park Us Lessee Holdings Inc.
1600 Tysons Blvd Ste 1000
Mc Lean VA 22102
703 883-1052

(P-11440)
SAN JOSE RESIDENCE CLUB INC
Also Called: Mother Olson's Inn
72 N 5th St, San Jose (95112-5417)
PHONE 408 998-0223
Keith A Watt, *President*
Keith Watt, *President*
EMP: 48 **EST:** 1960
SALES (est): 460K **Privately Held**
WEB: www.sanjose.com
SIC: 7011 Hotels

(P-11441)
SAN RAFAEL HILLCREST LLC
Also Called: Four Points San Rafael
1010 Northgate Dr, San Rafael (94903-2502)
PHONE 415 479-8800
Beth Gamble,
EMP: 51 **EST:** 2012
SQ FT: 50,000
SALES (est): 4.7MM **Privately Held**
WEB: www.marriott.com
SIC: 7011 Hotels

(P-11442)
SANTA CLARA SUITES LP
Also Called: Hawthorn Suites
2455 El Camino Real, Santa Clara (95051-3001)
PHONE 408 241-6444
Fax: 408 241-6446
EMP: 41
SQ FT: 48,500
SALES (est): 2MM **Privately Held**
SIC: 7011 Hotels And Motels

(P-11443)
SANTA CRUZ HT ASSOC A CAL LTD
Also Called: West Coast Santa Cruz Hotel
175 W Cliff Dr, Santa Cruz (95060-5438)
PHONE 831 426-4330
Brian Corbell, *President*
Jenny Hernandez, *Sales Staff*
EMP: 67 **EST:** 1964
SALES (est): 507.2K **Privately Held**
WEB: www.santacruz.com
SIC: 7011 Resort hotel

(P-11444)
SANTA CRUZ SEASIDE COMPANY
Also Called: Sea & Sand Inn
201 W Cliff Dr, Santa Cruz (95060-6144)
PHONE 831 427-3400
Lisa Morley, *Manager*
EMP: 507
SALES (corp-wide): 55.2MM **Privately Held**
WEB: www.scseaside.com
SIC: 7011 Motels
PA: Santa Cruz Seaside Company Inc
400 Beach St
Santa Cruz CA 95060
831 423-5590

(P-11445)
SANTANA ROW HOTEL PARTNERS LP
355 Santana Row, San Jose (95128-2049)
PHONE 408 551-0010
Bonnie Best, *General Mgr*
EMP: 200 **Privately Held**
WEB: www.hotelvalencia-santanarow.com
SIC: 7011 Hotels
PA: Santana Row Hotel Partners Lp
4400 Post Oak Pkwy Ste 16
Houston TX 77027

(P-11446)
SAWHNEY PROPERTIES LP (PA)
Also Called: Ramada Inn
156 Las Quebradas, Alamo (94507-1741)
PHONE 925 837-0932
Dinesh Sawhney, *Mng Member*
EMP: 49 **EST:** 2003
SALES (est): 2.6MM **Privately Held**
WEB: www.wyndhamhotels.com
SIC: 7011 Hotels & motels

(P-11447)
SC HOTEL PARTNERS LLC
Also Called: Hotel Adagio
550 Geary St, San Francisco (94102-1650)
PHONE 415 775-5000
Paul Frentsos, *Manager*
Lonnie Shotwell, *Auditor*
Tiffany Andrade, *Opers Staff*
EMP: 66 **EST:** 2001
SALES (est): 8.3MM **Privately Held**
WEB: www.hoteladagiosf.com
SIC: 7011 Resort hotel; hotels

(P-11448)
SEACLIFF INN INC
Also Called: Best Western
7500 Old Dominion Ct, Aptos (95003-3807)
PHONE 831 661-4671
Frank Giuliani, *President*
T J Scott, *Treasurer*
Norm BEI, *Vice Pres*
Coleen Giuliani, *Admin Sec*
Nikki Castro, *Human Res Dir*
EMP: 90 **EST:** 1985
SQ FT: 60,000

PRODUCTS & SERVICES SECTION
7011 - Hotels, Motels & Tourist Courts County (P-11473)

SALES (est): 5.6MM
SALES (corp-wide): 61.3MM **Privately Held**
WEB: www.seacliffinn.com
SIC: 7011 Hotels & motels
HQ: Pacifica Hotel Company
39 Argonaut
Aliso Viejo CA 92656
805 957-0095

(P-11449)
SEAL SAN LEANDRO LLC
510 Lewelling Blvd, San Leandro (94579-1803)
PHONE..................510 343-8105
Sheenal Patel, *Mng Member*
EMP: 35 EST: 2019
SALES (est): 1MM **Privately Held**
SIC: 7011 Hotels & motels

(P-11450)
SEASCAPE BEACH ASSOCIATION
1 Seascape Resort Dr, Aptos (95003-5854)
P.O. Box 408 (95001-0408)
PHONE..................831 688-6800
Joan Nixon, *Owner*
Lee Ann Hein, *General Mgr*
Larry Tompkins, *Controller*
Judy Heckerman, *Regl Sales Mgr*
Brittany Chinevere, *Sales Staff*
EMP: 41 EST: 2010
SALES (est): 115.5K **Privately Held**
WEB: www.seascaperesort.com
SIC: 7011 Resort hotel

(P-11451)
SEASCAPE RESORT OWNERS ASSN
1 Seascape Resort Dr, Aptos (95003-5854)
PHONE..................831 688-6800
Bob Perasso, *CEO*
Gregory Steelman, *Controller*
Dottie Bella, *Sales Mgr*
Kelly Kerr, *Manager*
Angela Marks, *Manager*
EMP: 82 EST: 2008
SALES (est): 11.9MM **Privately Held**
WEB: www.seascaperesort.com
SIC: 7011 Resort hotel

(P-11452)
SEASCAPE RSORT LTD A CAL LTD P
Also Called: Sanderlings
19 Seascape Vlg, Aptos (95003-6102)
PHONE..................831 662-7120
Mark Holcomb, *General Ptnr*
EMP: 116 EST: 1989
SQ FT: 45,000
SALES (est): 1MM **Privately Held**
WEB: www.sanderlingsrestaurant.com
SIC: 7011 Resort hotel

(P-11453)
SELECT HOTELS GROUP LLC
Also Called: Hyatt House San Ramon
2323 San Ramon Vly Blvd, San Ramon (94583-1607)
PHONE..................925 743-1882
Pam Callahan, *General Mgr*
EMP: 37 **Publicly Held**
WEB: www.hyatt.com
SIC: 7011 Hotels
HQ: Select Hotels Group, L.L.C.
71 S Wacker Dr Ste 2500
Chicago IL 60606
312 750-1234

(P-11454)
SELECT HOTELS GROUP LLC
Also Called: Hyatt Hse Emryvll/San Frncsco
5800 Shellmound St, Emeryville (94608-1966)
PHONE..................510 601-5880
Alan Mass, *General Mgr*
EMP: 37
SQ FT: 16,424 **Publicly Held**
WEB: www.hyatt.com
SIC: 7011 Hotels
HQ: Select Hotels Group, L.L.C.
71 S Wacker Dr Ste 2500
Chicago IL 60606
312 750-1234

(P-11455)
SELECT HOTELS GROUP LLC
Also Called: Hyatt Pl Fremont/Silicon Vly
3101 W Warren Ave, Fremont (94538-6428)
PHONE..................510 623-6000
John McEngee, *Manager*
EMP: 37 **Publicly Held**
WEB: www.hyatt.com
SIC: 7011 Hotels & motels
HQ: Select Hotels Group, L.L.C.
71 S Wacker Dr Ste 2500
Chicago IL 60606
312 750-1234

(P-11456)
SELECT HOTELS GROUP LLC
Also Called: Hyatt House Santa Clara
3915 Rivermark Plz, Santa Clara (95054-4156)
PHONE..................408 486-0800
Mike Lamarche, *General Mgr*
EMP: 37 **Publicly Held**
WEB: www.santaclara.org
SIC: 7011 Hotels
HQ: Select Hotels Group, L.L.C.
71 S Wacker Dr Ste 2500
Chicago IL 60606
312 750-1234

(P-11457)
SELECT HOTELS GROUP LLC
Also Called: Hyatt House Rancho Cordova
11260 Point East Dr, Rancho Cordova (95742-6232)
PHONE..................916 638-4141
Brett Tmekei, *General Mgr*
EMP: 37 **Publicly Held**
WEB: www.hyatt.com
SIC: 7011 Hotels
HQ: Select Hotels Group, L.L.C.
71 S Wacker Dr Ste 2500
Chicago IL 60606
312 750-1234

(P-11458)
SELECT HOTELS GROUP LLC
Also Called: Hyatt Pl Sacramento/Roseville
220 Conference Center Dr, Roseville (95678-1388)
PHONE..................916 781-6400
Sulynn Jew, *Branch Mgr*
Julie Carpenter, *Vice Pres*
EMP: 37 **Publicly Held**
WEB: www.hyatt.com
SIC: 7011 Hotels & motels
HQ: Select Hotels Group, L.L.C.
71 S Wacker Dr Ste 2500
Chicago IL 60606
312 750-1234

(P-11459)
SELECT HOTELS GROUP LLC
Also Called: Hyatt Hse San Jose Silicon Vly
75 Headquarters Dr, San Jose (95134-1357)
PHONE..................408 324-1155
Mike Lamarche, *General Mgr*
EMP: 37 **Publicly Held**
WEB: www.hyatt.com
SIC: 7011 Hotels
HQ: Select Hotels Group, L.L.C.
71 S Wacker Dr Ste 2500
Chicago IL 60606
312 750-1234

(P-11460)
SELVI-VIDOVICH LP
Also Called: Grand Hotel The
865 W El Camino Real, Sunnyvale (94087-1154)
PHONE..................408 720-8500
John Vidovich, *Managing Prtnr*
Al Selvi, *Partner*
Raul Suarez, *CIO*
Christine Tran, *Sales Staff*
EMP: 63 EST: 2000
SQ FT: 90,805
SALES (est): 3.5MM **Privately Held**
WEB: www.svgrandhotel.com
SIC: 7011 Hotels

(P-11461)
SERENITY NOW LESSEE INC
Also Called: Hotel Spero Jspers Crnr Tap Ki
405 Taylor St, San Francisco (94102-1701)
PHONE..................415 885-2500
Alfred L Young, *CEO*
Joseph Dickey, *Associate Dir*
Benjamin Malmquist, *General Mgr*
Liezel Cruz, *Human Res Mgr*
Jordan Baldry, *Sales Mgr*
EMP: 44 EST: 2013
SALES (est): 5.1MM **Privately Held**
WEB: www.hotelspero.com
SIC: 7011 Hotels

(P-11462)
SERVICE HOSPITALITY LLC
1050 Burnett Ave, Concord (94520-5713)
PHONE..................925 566-8820
Maryann Rhoe,
EMP: 70 EST: 2017
SALES (est): 1.4MM **Privately Held**
SIC: 7011 Seasonal hotel

(P-11463)
SETHI CONGLOMERATE LLC
Also Called: Comfort Inn
5455 W Shaw Ave, Fresno (93722-5035)
PHONE..................559 275-2374
J P Sethi,
M L Sethi,
Ravi Sethi,
EMP: 39 EST: 1998
SQ FT: 30,661
SALES (est): 653.7K **Privately Held**
WEB: www.choicehotels.com
SIC: 7011 Hotels & motels

(P-11464)
SF MARRIOTT MARQUIS
780 Mission St, San Francisco (94103-3113)
PHONE..................415 896-1600
Kristine Van, *Executive*
Chuck Passioni, *General Mgr*
Mildred Guerra, *Admin Asst*
Regina Lassiter, *Accountant*
Lisa Lucas-Yap, *Human Res Dir*
EMP: 35 EST: 2015
SALES (est): 3.2MM **Privately Held**
WEB: www.sfviewlounge.com
SIC: 7011 Hotels

(P-11465)
SFD PARTNERS LLC
Also Called: Sir Francis Drake Hotel
450 Powell St, San Francisco (94102-1504)
PHONE..................415 392-7755
John Price, *General Mgr*
EMP: 260 EST: 1928
SALES (est): 1.7MM **Privately Held**
SIC: 7011 5812 5813 7389 Hotels; eating places; drinking places; hotel & motel reservation service

(P-11466)
SG DOWNTOWN LLC
Also Called: Kimpton Hotels
500 J St Fl 4, Sacramento (95814-2323)
PHONE..................916 545-7100
Mike Defrino, *CEO*
Kathleen Reidenbach, *Ch Credit Ofcr*
EMP: 40 EST: 2014
SALES (est): 2.5MM **Privately Held**
WEB: www.kimptonhotels.com
SIC: 7011 Hotels

(P-11467)
SHERATON LLC
2500 Mason St, San Francisco (94133-1450)
PHONE..................415 362-5500
Jim Sega, *Manager*
EMP: 58
SALES (corp-wide): 10.5B **Publicly Held**
WEB: www.sheraton.marriott.com
SIC: 7011 Hotels & motels
HQ: The Sheraton Llc
1111 Westchester Ave
White Plains NY 10604
800 328-6242

(P-11468)
SHERATON LLC
Also Called: Marriott
5030 Scotts Valley Dr, Scotts Valley (95066-4210)
PHONE..................831 438-1500
EMP: 58
SALES (corp-wide): 10.5B **Publicly Held**
WEB: www.sheraton.marriott.com
SIC: 7011 Hotels & motels
HQ: The Sheraton Llc
1111 Westchester Ave
White Plains NY 10604
800 328-6242

(P-11469)
SHERATON LLC
1230 J St 13th, Sacramento (95814-2907)
PHONE..................916 447-1700
Gunter Stannius, *Manager*
EMP: 58
SALES (corp-wide): 10.5B **Publicly Held**
WEB: www.sheraton.marriott.com
SIC: 7011 Hotels & motels
HQ: The Sheraton Llc
1111 Westchester Ave
White Plains NY 10604
800 328-6242

(P-11470)
SHERATON RDDING HT AT SNDIAL B
820 Sundial Bridge Dr, Redding (96001-0978)
PHONE..................530 364-2800
Marjorie Culley, *General Mgr*
Krista Mires, *Sales Mgr*
EMP: 100 EST: 2018
SALES (est): 3.2MM **Privately Held**
WEB: www.sheraton.marriott.com
SIC: 7011 Hotels & motels

(P-11471)
SHERWOOD VALLEY RANCHERIA
Also Called: Sherwood Vlley Rnchria Casino
100 Kawi Pl, Willits (95490-4674)
PHONE..................707 459-7330
Kani Neves, *Manager*
EMP: 75 **Privately Held**
WEB: www.svrcasino.com
SIC: 7011 Casino hotel
PA: Sherwood Valley Rancheria
190 Sherwood Hill Dr
Willits CA 95490
707 459-9690

(P-11472)
SHINGLE SPRNG TRBAL GMING AUTH
Also Called: Red Hawk Casino
1 Red Hawk Pkwy, Placerville (95667-8639)
PHONE..................530 677-7000
Nicholas Fonseca, *Ch of Bd*
Tyrone Huff, *CFO*
Sandy Campbell, *Treasurer*
Miguel Colon, *Officer*
Sebastian Gutierrez, *Officer*
EMP: 1200 EST: 2008
SQ FT: 278,000
SALES (est): 57.3MM **Privately Held**
WEB: www.redhawkcasino.com
SIC: 7011 Casino hotel
PA: Shingle Springs Rancheria
5168 Honpie Rd
Placerville CA 95667

(P-11473)
SHIVA ENTERPRISES INC
Also Called: Holiday Inn
2834 El Camino Real, Redwood City (94061-4002)
PHONE..................650 366-2000
Vijay Patel, *President*
H L Patel, *Treasurer*
Tina Patel, *Vice Pres*
EMP: 108 EST: 1975
SQ FT: 20,000
SALES (est): 1.3MM **Privately Held**
WEB: www.hiexpress.com
SIC: 7011 Hotels & motels

7011 - Hotels, Motels & Tourist Courts County (P-11474)

PRODUCTS & SERVICES SECTION

(P-11474)
SHOKAWAH CASINO
Also Called: Hopland Sho-Ka-Wah Casino
13101 Nokomis Rd, Hopland (95449-9793)
PHONE....................707 744-1395
Donna Sallady, *Principal*
Chase Matisse, *Technical Staff*
EMP: 41 EST: 2009
SALES (est): 5.8MM **Privately Held**
WEB: www.shokawah.com
SIC: 7011 Casino hotel

(P-11475)
SHYAM LODGING GROUP II LLC
Also Called: Hampton Inn
2700 Junipero Serra Blvd, Daly City (94015-1634)
PHONE....................650 755-7500
Raman Patel,
Hasahukh Patel,
EMP: 38 EST: 1998
SALES (est): 805.5K **Privately Held**
WEB: www.hilton.com
SIC: 7011 Hotels & motels

(P-11476)
SIDJON CORPORATION
Also Called: Livermore Casino
3571 1st St, Livermore (94551-4901)
PHONE....................925 606-6135
Sidney Ahn, *CEO*
Kristen Salisbury, *Opers Staff*
EMP: 57 EST: 2007
SQ FT: 15,000
SALES (est): 2MM **Privately Held**
SIC: 7011 Casino hotel

(P-11477)
SIERRA AT TAHO SKI RESORTS
1111 Sierra At Tahoe Rd, Twin Bridges (95735-9505)
PHONE....................530 659-7519
John Rice, *President*
George Gillette, *President*
Helen Behn, *Admin Mgr*
EMP: 104 EST: 1996
SALES (est): 1.2MM **Privately Held**
WEB: www.sierraattahoe.com
SIC: 7011 Resort hotel

(P-11478)
SIERRA NEVADA LODGE
164 Old Mammoth Rd, Mammoth Lakes (93546-6000)
P.O. Box 918 (93546-0918)
PHONE....................760 934-2515
Paul Payne, *Partner*
David Dahl, *Partner*
Jess Karell, *Sales Staff*
EMP: 57 EST: 1996
SALES (est): 1.3MM **Privately Held**
WEB: www.thesierranevadaresort.com
SIC: 7011 Resort hotel

(P-11479)
SIERRA PCF HOTELS & RESORTS
Also Called: Squaw Valley Lodge
201 Squaw Peak Rd, Olympic Valley (96146-1020)
P.O. Box 2364 (96146-2364)
PHONE....................530 583-5500
Arthur R Takaki, *Vice Pres*
EMP: 60 EST: 1990
SQ FT: 5,000
SALES (est): 820.5K **Privately Held**
WEB: www.squawvalleylodge.com
SIC: 7011 Resort hotel

(P-11480)
SIERRA SUMMIT INC
59265 Hwy 168, Lakeshore (93634)
P.O. Box 236 (93634-0236)
PHONE....................559 233-2500
Richard C Kun, *President*
Alan Macquoid, *Treasurer*
Robert Law, *Vice Pres*
Ken Wood, *Admin Sec*
EMP: 663 EST: 1977
SQ FT: 5,000
SALES (est): 1.4MM
SALES (corp-wide): 59.8MM **Privately Held**
WEB: www.skichinapeak.com
SIC: 7011 Ski lodge; resort hotel

PA: Snow Summit Ski Corporation
880 Summit Blvd
Big Bear Lake CA 92315
909 866-5766

(P-11481)
SILVERADO RSORT SVCS GROUP LLC
1600 Atlas Peak Rd, NAPA (94558-1425)
PHONE....................707 257-0200
Tim Wall, *Mng Member*
John Brovelli, *Executive*
John Evans, *General Mgr*
Mario Garcia, *General Mgr*
Hing Ting, *Finance*
EMP: 450 EST: 2010
SALES (est): 49.5MM **Privately Held**
WEB: www.silveradoresort.com
SIC: 7011 Resort hotel

(P-11482)
SING SENG HING CO LTD
Also Called: Baldwin Hotel
1020 Clement St, San Francisco (94118-2113)
PHONE....................415 781-2220
Eddie Tang, *Vice Pres*
Danny Ho, *Manager*
EMP: 37 EST: 1989
SQ FT: 23,100
SALES (est): 539.8K **Privately Held**
SIC: 7011 Hotels

(P-11483)
SISKIYOU DEVELOPMENT COMPANY
Also Called: HI Lo Motel
88 S Weed Blvd, Edgewood (96094-2607)
PHONE....................530 938-2731
Shawn Zanni, *Manager*
EMP: 65
SALES (corp-wide): 30.8MM **Privately Held**
WEB: www.sisdevco.com
SIC: 7011 Motels
PA: Siskiyou Development Company, Inc.
79 S Weed Blvd Ste 2
Weed CA 96094
530 938-2904

(P-11484)
SITA RAM LLC
Also Called: Best Western Amador Inn
200 S State Highway 49, Jackson (95642-2548)
PHONE....................209 223-0211
Kumar Sharma,
Puwan Kumar,
EMP: 42 EST: 1983
SQ FT: 8,000
SALES (est): 340.3K **Privately Held**
WEB: www.bestwestern.com
SIC: 7011 5812 5813 7991 Hotels & motels; eating places; bar (drinking places); physical fitness facilities

(P-11485)
SIX CONTINENTS HOTELS INC
Also Called: Inter Continental
2819 E Hamilton Ave, Fresno (93721-3208)
PHONE....................559 272-7840
EMP: 74 **Privately Held**
WEB: www.ihg.com
SIC: 7011 Hotels
HQ: Six Continents Hotels, Inc
35016 Avenue D
Yucaipa CA 92399
770 604-5000

(P-11486)
SIX CONTINENTS HOTELS INC
Also Called: Holiday Inn
50 8th St, San Francisco (94103-1409)
PHONE....................415 626-6103
Gino Lazzara, *General Mgr*
EMP: 160 **Privately Held**
WEB: www.holidayinn.com
SIC: 7011 5813 5812 6512 Hotels; drinking places; eating places; nonresidential building operators
HQ: Six Continents Hotels, Inc
35016 Avenue D
Yucaipa CA 92399
770 604-5000

(P-11487)
SIX CS ENTERPRISES INC
Also Called: Best Western Tree Hse Mtr Inn
111 Morgan Way, Mount Shasta (96067-2557)
PHONE....................530 926-3101
James Cottrel, *President*
EMP: 45 EST: 1974
SALES (est): 1.3MM **Privately Held**
WEB: www.bestwestern.com
SIC: 7011 5812 5813 Hotels; eating places; bar (drinking places)

(P-11488)
SJ 1ST STREET HOTEL LLC
Also Called: Holiday Inn San Js-Silicon Vly
1350 N 1st St, San Jose (95112-4709)
PHONE....................408 453-6200
Fred Wong, *Principal*
EMP: 45 EST: 2012
SALES (est): 1.6MM **Privately Held**
WEB: www.holidayinn.com
SIC: 7011 Hotels

(P-11489)
SMITH RIVER LUCKY 7 CASINO
350 N Indian Rd, Smith River (95567-9474)
PHONE....................707 487-7777
Terry Westrick, *Partner*
Debbie Morris, *Accountant*
Rachel Ochoa, *Human Res Mgr*
Jeffrey Dunlap, *Supervisor*
EMP: 119 EST: 1997
SALES (est): 7MM **Privately Held**
WEB: www.lucky7casino.com
SIC: 7011 Casino hotel

(P-11490)
SONESTA INTL HOTELS CORP
Also Called: Clift Royal Sonesta Hotel, The
495 Geary St, San Francisco (94102-1222)
PHONE....................415 929-2393
EMP: 305
SALES (corp-wide): 449.1MM **Privately Held**
WEB: www.sonesta.com
SIC: 7011 Hotels & motels
PA: Sonesta International Hotels Corporation
255 Washington St Ste 270
Newton MA 02458
770 923-1775

(P-11491)
SONOMA HOTEL OPERATOR INC
Also Called: Fairmont Snoma Mission Inn Spa
100 Boyes Blvd, Sonoma (95476-3678)
P.O. Box 1447 (95476-1447)
PHONE....................707 938-9000
Rick Corcoran, *General Mgr*
Anson Fung, *Info Tech Mgr*
Heckert Astrid, *Finance*
Nina Hayes, *Finance*
Karen Roenau, *Purch Agent*
EMP: 310
SALES (corp-wide): 627.9MM **Privately Held**
SIC: 7011 Hotels
HQ: Sonoma Hotel Operator, Llc
50 Rockefeller Plz
New York NY

(P-11492)
SONOMA HOTEL PARTNERS LP
Also Called: Sheraton Sonoma Cnty Petaluma
745 Baywood Dr, Petaluma (94954-5388)
PHONE....................707 283-2888
Scott Satterfield, *General Mgr*
Kimberly Sowinski, *Executive*
Shannon Keaney, *General Mgr*
Taylor Moore, *Finance*
Helen Cho, *Controller*
EMP: 95 EST: 1999
SQ FT: 134,732
SALES (est): 14.6MM **Privately Held**
WEB: www.marriott.com
SIC: 7011 Hotels

(P-11493)
SONESTA SELECT SAN JOSE ARPRT
Also Called: Courtyard By Marriott
1727 Technology Dr, San Jose (95110-1310)
PHONE....................408 441-6111
Mir Said, *Manager*
John Southwell, *General Mgr*
EMP: 40 EST: 2007
SALES (est): 2.3MM **Privately Held**
WEB: www.sanjose.org
SIC: 7011 Hotels & motels

(P-11494)
SOUTHBOURNE INC
Also Called: Campton Place Hotel
340 Stockton St, San Francisco (94108-4609)
PHONE....................415 781-5555
Reymond Dixon, *Director*
Maria Conlon, *Administration*
EMP: 168 EST: 1983
SALES (est): 4.9MM **Privately Held**
WEB: www.camptonplace.com
SIC: 7011 Hotels
PA: Taj Hotels
Nandafata Aral Korpana
Wardha MH

(P-11495)
SPRING MOUNTAIN HOTEL LLC (PA)
1485 Main St Ste 201, Saint Helena (94574-1850)
PHONE....................530 304-5619
EMP: 124 EST: 2013
SALES (est): 366K **Privately Held**
SIC: 7011 Hotels

(P-11496)
SQUAW CREEK ASSOCIATES LLC
Also Called: Resort At Squaw Creek
400 Squaw Creek Rd, Alpine Meadows (96146-9778)
P.O. Box 3333, Olympic Valley (96146-3333)
PHONE....................530 581-6624
Andrea Baltzegar,
Andre Priemer, *General Mgr*
Terry Ozanich, *Controller*
Claudia Martinello, *Manager*
Robert Sackett, *Manager*
EMP: 600 EST: 1990
SALES (est): 48.1MM **Privately Held**
WEB: www.destinationhotels.com
SIC: 7011 Resort hotel

(P-11497)
SQUAW VALLEY DEVELOPMENT CO (HQ)
Also Called: Squaw Valley Ski
1960 Squaw Valley Rd, Olympic Valley (96146-1030)
P.O. Box 2007 (96146-2007)
PHONE....................530 452-6985
Andrew D Wirth, *CEO*
Lori Pommerenck, *Treasurer*
Rodney Jones, *Vice Pres*
Mark Daly, *Engineer*
Stephanie Phillips, *Accountant*
EMP: 40 EST: 1948
SALES (est): 49.7MM **Privately Held**
WEB: www.palisadestahoe.com
SIC: 7011 5812 5813 7929 Hostels; ski lodge; eating places; bar (drinking places); entertainment service

(P-11498)
SQUAW VALLEY SKI CORPORATION (DH)
1960 Squaw Valley Rd, Olympic Valley (96146-1030)
P.O. Box 2007 (96146-2007)
PHONE....................530 583-6985
Alexander C Cushing, *Ch of Bd*
Mike Livak, *President*
Nancy R Wendt, *President*
Andy Wirth, *President*
Mike Degroff, *Vice Pres*
EMP: 243 EST: 1974
SQ FT: 200,000

SALES (est): 25.3MM **Privately Held**
WEB: www.palisadestahoe.com
SIC: 7011 Resort hotel
HQ: The Squaw Valley Development Company
1960 Squaw Valley Rd
Olympic Valley CA 96146
530 452-6985

(P-11499)
ST REGIS SAN FRANCISCO HT LLC
125 3rd St, San Francisco (94103-3107)
PHONE..................................415 284-4000
Henry Hofilena, *Finance*
Roger Huldi, *General Mgr*
EMP: 56 **EST:** 1999
SALES (est): 10.6MM
SALES (corp-wide): 10.5B **Publicly Held**
WEB: www.marriott.com
SIC: 7011 Hotels
PA: Marriott International, Inc.
10400 Fernwood Rd
Bethesda MD 20817
301 380-3000

(P-11500)
STANFORD HOTELS CORPORATION
Also Called: Hilton Santa Clara
4949 Great America Pkwy, Santa Clara (95054-1216)
PHONE..................................408 330-0001
Peter Dolton, *Manager*
EMP: 75 **Privately Held**
WEB: www.stanfordhotels.com
SIC: 7011 Hotels
PA: Stanford Hotels Corporation
433 California St Ste 700
San Francisco CA 94104

(P-11501)
STANFORD HOTELS CORPORATION (PA)
433 California St Ste 700, San Francisco (94104-2011)
PHONE..................................415 398-3333
Lawrence Lui, *President*
Gary Hauck, *COO*
James Evans, *CFO*
Henry Perez, *General Mgr*
Amy Matabuena, *Administration*
◆ **EMP:** 50 **EST:** 1987
SQ FT: 12,000
SALES (est): 35.1MM **Privately Held**
WEB: www.stanfordhotels.com
SIC: 7011 Hotels

(P-11502)
STANFORD PARK HOTEL
100 El Camino Real, Menlo Park (94025-5292)
PHONE..................................650 322-1234
Ellis Alden, *Partner*
Western Lodging Flume Corpor, *Partner*
Patrick Lane, *Manager*
EMP: 212 **EST:** 1984
SQ FT: 122,000
SALES (est): 12.1MM **Privately Held**
WEB: www.stanfordparkhotel.com
SIC: 7011 5813 5812 Resort hotel; drinking places; eating places

(P-11503)
STARLIGHT ROOM HARRY DENTONS
191 Sutter St, San Francisco (94104-4501)
PHONE..................................415 392-7755
Harry Denton, *Owner*
EMP: 40 **EST:** 2010
SALES (est): 46.7K **Privately Held**
SIC: 7011 Hotels

(P-11504)
STARWOOD HTLS & RSRTS WRLDWDE
335 Powell St, San Francisco (94102-1804)
PHONE..................................415 397-7000
Joe Burger, *Manager*
EMP: 300

SALES (corp-wide): 10.5B **Publicly Held**
WEB: www.marriott.com
SIC: 7011 5812 Hotels & motels; eating places
HQ: Starwood Hotels & Resorts Worldwide, Llc
1 Star Pt
Stamford CT 06902
203 964-6000

(P-11505)
STARWOOD HTLS & RSRTS WRLDWDE
2 New Montgomery St, San Francisco (94105-3402)
PHONE..................................415 512-1111
T Staramelino, *Business Mgr*
EMP: 195
SALES (corp-wide): 10.5B **Publicly Held**
WEB: www.marriott.com
SIC: 7011 Hotels & motels
HQ: Starwood Hotels & Resorts Worldwide, Llc
1 Star Pt
Stamford CT 06902
203 964-6000

(P-11506)
STATELINE TRAVELODGE INC
4011 Lake Tahoe Blvd, South Lake Tahoe (96150-6930)
PHONE..................................530 544-6000
Manfred C Lohr, *President*
K Lohr, *Owner*
EMP: 37 **EST:** 1974
SQ FT: 80,000
SALES (est): 124.1K **Privately Held**
WEB: www.wyndhamhotels.com
SIC: 7011 Hotels & motels

(P-11507)
STAY CAL SAN JOSE LLC
Also Called: Row Hotel, The
2404 Stevens Creek Blvd, San Jose (95128-1652)
PHONE..................................408 275-2147
EMP: 56
SALES (corp-wide): 739.2K **Privately Held**
SIC: 7011 Hotels
PA: Stay Cal San Jose, Llc
2110 S El Camino Real
San Mateo CA
408 293-5000

(P-11508)
STAYBRIDGE SUITES
900 Hamlin Ct, Sunnyvale (94089-1401)
PHONE..................................408 745-1515
EMP: 40
SALES (est): 480.6K **Privately Held**
SIC: 7011 Hotel/Motel Operation

(P-11509)
STEUART STREET VENTURE LP
Also Called: Harbor Court Hotel
191 Sutter St, San Francisco (94104-4501)
PHONE..................................415 882-1300
Taimy Bomey, *Manager*
Bay Area Hotel Assoc, *General Ptnr*
EMP: 63 **EST:** 1989
SALES (est): 4.6MM **Privately Held**
WEB: www.harborcourthotel.com
SIC: 7011 Resort hotel

(P-11510)
STOCKTON HOTEL LTD
Also Called: Hilton
2323 Grand Canal Blvd, Stockton (95207-6554)
PHONE..................................209 957-9090
Robert Hong, *General Ptnr*
Edward Hazard, *General Ptnr*
Claude Viergutz, *General Mgr*
Lilly McIntyre, *Controller*
EMP: 92 **EST:** 1980
SALES (est): 3.8MM **Privately Held**
WEB: www.visitstockton.org
SIC: 7011 Hotel, franchised

(P-11511)
STRAWBERRY INN
31888 Hwy 108, Strawberry (95375)
PHONE..................................209 965-3662
Mary Sutherland, *Partner*
Brian Sutherland, *Partner*

EMP: 37 **EST:** 1939
SQ FT: 1,200
SALES (est): 471K **Privately Held**
WEB: www.strawberryinn.com
SIC: 5812 5813 7011 Restaurant, family: independent; bar (drinking places); vacation lodges

(P-11512)
SUGAR BOWL CORPORATION
629 Sugar Bowl Rd, Norden (95724)
P.O. Box 5 (95724-0005)
PHONE..................................530 426-9000
Nancy Bechtle, *Ch of Bd*
Warren Haellman, *Shareholder*
Robert H Kautz, *President*
Bonny Bavetta, *CFO*
Dan Kingsley, *Treasurer*
▲ **EMP:** 100 **EST:** 1937
SQ FT: 30,000
SALES (est): 27.5MM **Privately Held**
WEB: www.sugarbowl.com
SIC: 7011 Resort hotel

(P-11513)
SUGAR BOWL SKI RESORT
629 Sugar Bowl Rd, Norden (95724)
P.O. Box 5 (95724-0005)
PHONE..................................530 426-3651
Steven Beatie, *Vice Pres*
Mike Roth, *Info Tech Dir*
Kim Canton, *Human Res Dir*
EMP: 39 **EST:** 2006
SALES (est): 8.8MM **Privately Held**
WEB: www.sugarbowl.com
SIC: 7011 Resort hotel

(P-11514)
SUISUN CITY HOTEL LLC
Also Called: Hampton Inn
212 Sutter St Fl 3, San Francisco (94108-4423)
PHONE..................................707 429-0900
Hartmut Ott, *General Mgr*
Teresa Muniaerts, *Manager*
Hartmut White, *Manager*
EMP: 37 **EST:** 2009
SALES (est): 4.7MM **Privately Held**
WEB: www.hilton.com
SIC: 7011 Hotels & motels

(P-11515)
SUMMIT HOTEL TRS 115 LLC (PA)
Also Called: Four Pnts By Shrton Ht Stes Sa
264 S Airport Blvd, South San Francisco (94080-6701)
PHONE..................................650 624-3700
EMP: 177 **EST:** 2017
SALES (est): 5.6MM **Privately Held**
WEB: www.sheraton.marriott.com
SIC: 7011 Hotels

(P-11516)
SUNDIAL RESTAURANT
808 Mchenry Ave, Modesto (95350-5443)
PHONE..................................209 524-0808
Stanley C Galas, *Partner*
Norman Galas, *Partner*
EMP: 42 **EST:** 1958
SQ FT: 25,000
SALES (est): 624.6K **Privately Held**
SIC: 5813 5812 7011 Bar (drinking places); eating places; motels

(P-11517)
SUNNYSIDE RESORT
1850 W Lake Blvd, Tahoe City (96145-2302)
P.O. Box 5969 (96145-5969)
PHONE..................................530 583-7200
Sandy Saxton, *President*
J Robert Thibaut, *Vice Pres*
EMP: 39 **EST:** 1987
SALES (est): 2.4MM **Privately Held**
WEB: www.sunnysidelodge.com
SIC: 7011 5812 5813 Resort hotel; American restaurant; bar (drinking places)

(P-11518)
SUNRISE HOSPITALITY INC
Also Called: Hampton Inn
2060 Freeway Dr, Woodland (95776-9504)
PHONE..................................916 419-4440
Arvind Patel, *President*
EMP: 48 **Privately Held**

WEB: www.hilton.com
SIC: 7011 Hotels & motels

(P-11519)
SUNRISE PALACE INC
Also Called: Hyatt Place Vacaville
610 Orange Dr, Vacaville (95687-3101)
PHONE..................................707 469-2323
Mona Rigdon, *Principal*
Jeevanpreet Sidhu, *Principal*
EMP: 36 **EST:** 2019
SALES (est): 2.5MM **Privately Held**
WEB: www.hyatt.com
SIC: 7011 Hotels & motels

(P-11520)
SUPER 8 MOTEL
511 N Main St, Alturas (96101-3459)
PHONE..................................530 233-3545
Thalia Ellena, *Partner*
Jack Ellena, *Partner*
Jacquie Ellena, *Partner*
Thaila Ellena, *Partner*
C D Nelson MD, *Partner*
EMP: 50 **EST:** 1973
SALES (est): 347.3K **Privately Held**
WEB: www.wyndhamhotels.com
SIC: 7011 Hotels & motels

(P-11521)
SUPERB HOSPITALITY LLC
Also Called: Fairfield Inn
216 W Ventura Ct, Kingsburg (93631-1753)
PHONE..................................559 897-8840
Gurbax R Marwah, *Mng Member*
EMP: 38 **EST:** 2007
SALES (est): 571.3K **Privately Held**
WEB: www.fairfield.marriott.com
SIC: 7011 Hotels & motels

(P-11522)
SVI HEALDSBURG LLC
Also Called: Hotel Trio
110 Dry Creek Rd, Healdsburg (95448-4702)
PHONE..................................707 433-4000
Scott Satterfield, *General Mgr*
EMP: 40
SALES (corp-wide): 2.9MM **Privately Held**
WEB: www.healdsburg.com
SIC: 7011 Hotels
PA: Svi Healdsburg, Llc
3334 E Coast Hwy Ste 410
Corona Del Mar CA 92625
949 566-0000

(P-11523)
SWISS HOTEL GROUP INC
18 W Spain St, Sonoma (95476-5601)
PHONE..................................707 938-2884
Henry Marioni, *President*
EMP: 67 **EST:** 1929
SQ FT: 6,350
SALES (est): 826.6K **Privately Held**
WEB: www.swisshotelsonoma.com
SIC: 7011 5813 5812 Hotels; bar (drinking places); steak restaurant

(P-11524)
SYCAMORE HOSPITALITY CORP (PA)
433 California St, San Francisco (94104-2016)
PHONE..................................415 398-3333
Lawrence Lui, *President*
EMP: 49 **EST:** 2008
SALES (est): 565.4K **Privately Held**
WEB: www.domainsnext.com
SIC: 7011 Hotels & motels

(P-11525)
TABLE MOUNTAIN CASINO
8184 Table Mountain Rd, Friant (93626)
P.O. Box 445 (93626-0445)
PHONE..................................559 822-7777
Frances Dandy, *Senior VP*
Ted Thay, *COO*
Troy Benne, *CFO*
Courtney Wenleder, *CFO*
Mark Solomon, *Exec Dir*
EMP: 1000 **EST:** 1987
SQ FT: 30,000

7011 - Hotels, Motels & Tourist Courts County (P-11526)

SALES (est): 51.4MM **Privately Held**
WEB: www.tmcasino.com
SIC: **7011** Casino hotel

(P-11526)
TAHOE BEACH & SKI CLUB
3601 Lake Tahoe Blvd, South Lake Tahoe (96150-8915)
PHONE..................................530 541-6220
Roy Fraser, *President*
Tamara Hollingsworth, *Manager*
EMP: 60 EST: 1970
SALES (est): 2.9MM **Privately Held**
WEB: www.tahoebeachandski.com
SIC: **7011** 6513 Resort hotel; apartment hotel operation

(P-11527)
TAHOE CRSS-CNTRY SKI EDCATN AS
925 Country Club Dr, Tahoe City (96145-1930)
P.O. Box 7260 (96145-7260)
PHONE..................................530 583-5475
Jim Robins, *Owner*
Ben Grasseschi, *Exec Dir*
EMP: 36 EST: 1999
SQ FT: 3,000
SALES (est): 519.4K **Privately Held**
WEB: www.tahoexc.org
SIC: **7011** Resort hotel

(P-11528)
TERA SAHARA INC
536 E Cypress Ave, Redding (96002-0106)
PHONE..................................530 223-1600
Maninder Jit Bath, *President*
EMP: 39 EST: 2000
SALES (est): 742.1K **Privately Held**
SIC: **7011** Hotels & motels

(P-11529)
TERRE DU SOLEIL LTD
Also Called: Auberge Du Soleil
180 Rutherford Hill Rd, Rutherford (94573)
P.O. Box B (94573-0902)
PHONE..................................707 963-1211
George Goeggel, *General Ptnr*
Robert Harmon, *General Ptnr*
Bradley Reynolds, *General Ptnr*
Claude Rouas, *General Ptnr*
Kris Margerum, *Director*
EMP: 280 EST: 1981
SQ FT: 20,000
SALES (est): 24.6MM **Privately Held**
WEB: www.aubergeresorts.com
SIC: **7011** 5812 Resort hotel; French restaurant

(P-11530)
TERRITORY DESIGNS INC
Also Called: Gray Eagle Lodge
5000 Gold Lake Rd, Blairsden (96103)
PHONE..................................530 836-2511
David Bret Smith, *President*
EMP: 40 EST: 1924
SQ FT: 5,000
SALES (est): 500K **Privately Held**
WEB: www.grayeaglelodge.com
SIC: **7011** Tourist camps, cabins, cottages & courts

(P-11531)
THE INN
Also Called: El Monte Motor Inn
3555 Clayton Rd, Concord (94519-2421)
PHONE..................................925 682-1601
Adrian Karris, *Partner*
Betty Karris, *Partner*
EMP: 52 EST: 1978
SALES (est): 962.6K **Privately Held**
WEB: www.visitconcordca.com
SIC: **7011** Hotels

(P-11532)
THUNDRBIRD LDGE FRMONT A CAL L
Also Called: Best Western Garden Court Inn
5400 Mowry Ave, Fremont (94538-1049)
PHONE..................................510 792-4300
Martin Fox, *Executive Asst*
Thunderbird Properties, *General Ptnr*
EMP: 42 EST: 1974
SQ FT: 200

SALES (est): 1.1MM **Privately Held**
WEB: www.gardencourtinn.com
SIC: **7011** Motels

(P-11533)
TIBURON HOTEL LLC
Also Called: Lodge At Tiburon, The
1651 Tiburon Blvd, Belvedere Tiburon (94920-2511)
PHONE..................................415 435-5996
Mike Schuminsky, *Mng Member*
EMP: 36 EST: 2009
SALES (est): 4.4MM **Privately Held**
WEB: www.lodgeattiburon.com
SIC: **7011** 7389 Hotels; office facilities & secretarial service rental

(P-11534)
TIBURON LODGE LTD
1651 Tiburon Blvd, Belvedere Tiburon (94920-2511)
PHONE..................................415 435-3133
Mike Schuminsky, *General Ptnr*
Phillip Schuminsky, *Ltd Ptnr*
Mike Schuminsky Childrens Trus, *Ltd Ptnr*
Richard Pearce, *Vice Pres*
Tom Maddox, *Project Mgr*
▲ EMP: 96 EST: 1969
SQ FT: 40,000
SALES (est): 1.4MM **Privately Held**
WEB: www.lodgeattiburon.com
SIC: **7011** 5812 5813 Motels; eating places; bar (drinking places)

(P-11535)
TIDES CENTER
124 Turk St, San Francisco (94102-3926)
PHONE..................................415 359-9401
EMP: 331 **Privately Held**
WEB: www.tides.org
SIC: **7011** Hotels & motels
PA: The Tides Center
The Prsdio 1014 Trney Ave The Presidio
San Francisco CA 94129

(P-11536)
TIMBER COVE INN
21780 N Coast Hwy 1, Jenner (95450)
PHONE..................................707 847-3231
Richard Hojohn, *Owner*
EMP: 50 EST: 1967
SQ FT: 35,000
SALES (est): 7.6MM **Privately Held**
WEB: www.timbercoveresort.com
SIC: **7011** 5812 Motel, franchised; eating places

(P-11537)
TODAYS HOTEL CORPORATION
835 Airport Blvd Ste 288, Burlingame (94010-1922)
PHONE..................................415 447-3005
Tee Fong Zen, *CEO*
EMP: 50 EST: 1991
SALES (est): 680.6K **Privately Held**
WEB: www.goldengatewayhotel.com
SIC: **7011** Hotels

(P-11538)
TODAYS HOTEL CORPORATION (PA)
Also Called: Holiday Inn
1500 Van Ness Ave, San Francisco (94109-4606)
PHONE..................................415 441-4000
Ming Nin Zen, *President*
EMP: 242 EST: 1991
SALES (est): 41.4MM **Privately Held**
WEB: www.goldengatewayhotel.com
SIC: **7011** Hotels & motels

(P-11539)
TRADEWINDS LODGE (PA)
Also Called: Cliff House Restaurant
400 S Main St, Fort Bragg (95437-4806)
PHONE..................................707 964-4761
Dominic Affinito, *Partner*
EMP: 65 EST: 1965
SQ FT: 19,000

SALES (est): 3.2MM **Privately Held**
SIC: **7011** 5812 5813 6512 Motels; restaurant, family: independent; seafood restaurants; bars & lounges; commercial & industrial building operation; land subdividers & developers, commercial; land subdividers & developers, residential

(P-11540)
TREVI PARTNERS A CALIF LP
Also Called: Tollhouse Hotel
140 S Santa Cruz Ave, Los Gatos (95030-6702)
PHONE..................................408 395-7070
Marie Tallman, *Manager*
Aimee Avalon, *Sales Mgr*
Nicole Brennan, *Director*
Jason Bogan, *Manager*
EMP: 39 **Privately Held**
WEB: www.trivalleyhotel.com
SIC: **7011** 5812 Hotels; eating places
HQ: Trevi Partners, A Calif. L.P.
6680 Regional St
Dublin CA 94568
925 828-7750

(P-11541)
TREVI PARTNERS A CALIF LP (HQ)
Also Called: Holiday Inn
6680 Regional St, Dublin (94568-2916)
PHONE..................................925 828-7750
Micheal McDavid, *General Mgr*
EMP: 154 EST: 1979
SALES (est): 17.4MM **Privately Held**
WEB: www.trivalleyhotel.com
SIC: **7011** Hotels & motels

(P-11542)
TREVI PARTNERS A CALIF LP
Also Called: Holiday Inn
1250 Old Bayshore Hwy, Burlingame (94010-1805)
PHONE..................................650 347-2381
Steven Dodaro, *Manager*
EMP: 39 **Privately Held**
WEB: www.hiexpress.com
SIC: **7011** Hotels & motels
HQ: Trevi Partners, A Calif. L.P.
6680 Regional St
Dublin CA 94568
925 828-7750

(P-11543)
TREVI PARTNERS A CALIF LP (PA)
5955 Coronado Ln, Pleasanton (94588-8518)
PHONE..................................925 225-4000
Michael Madden, *Partner*
EMP: 120 EST: 2002
SALES (est): 29.4MM **Privately Held**
WEB: www.bestwestern.com
SIC: **7011** Hotels & motels

(P-11544)
TREVI PARTNERS A CALIF LP
Also Called: Holiday Inn
160 Shoreline Hwy, Mill Valley (94941-3610)
PHONE..................................415 332-5700
Jeffery Perry, *Manager*
EMP: 39 **Privately Held**
WEB: www.hiexpress.com
SIC: **7011** Hotels & motels
HQ: Trevi Partners, A Calif. L.P.
6680 Regional St
Dublin CA 94568
925 828-7750

(P-11545)
TRIGILD INTERNATIONAL INC
Also Called: Howard Johnson
2731 Bechelli Ln, Redding (96002-1924)
PHONE..................................530 223-1935
Mike Bath, *General Mgr*
EMP: 68
SALES (corp-wide): 20.6MM **Privately Held**
WEB: www.trigild.com
SIC: **7011** Hotels & motels
PA: Trigild International, Inc.
3323 Carmel Mountain Rd # 2
San Diego CA 92121
858 720-6700

(P-11546)
TURLOCK HOSPITALITY LLC
Also Called: Candlewood Suites
1000 Powers Ct, Turlock (95380-8455)
PHONE..................................209 250-1501
EMP: 48 **Privately Held**
WEB: www.ihg.com
SIC: **7011** Hotels
PA: Turlock Hospitality, Llc
9500 Aquafina Ct
Elk Grove CA

(P-11547)
TWIN LAKES RESORT
10316 Twin Lakes Rd, Bridgeport (93517-8134)
P.O. Box 636 (93517-0636)
PHONE..................................760 932-7751
Steve Marti, *President*
EMP: 35 EST: 1971
SALES (est): 1MM **Privately Held**
WEB: www.twinlakesresort.com
SIC: **7011** Tourist camps, cabins, cottages & courts

(P-11548)
TWIN PINE CASINO & HOTEL
22223 Rancheria Rd Hwy 29, Middletown (95461)
P.O. Box 789 (95461-0789)
PHONE..................................707 987-0197
Moke Simon, *Chairman*
Brian Latona, *Info Tech Dir*
Dan Dziubanski, *Technician*
Kenn Stump, *Technology*
Darrell Yee, *Technical Staff*
EMP: 87 EST: 2006
SALES (est): 10.5MM **Privately Held**
WEB: www.twinpine.com
SIC: **5813** 7011 Drinking places; casino hotel

(P-11549)
TYME MAIDU TRIBE-BERRY CREEK
Also Called: Gold Country Casino
4020 Olive Hwy, Oroville (95966-5527)
PHONE..................................530 538-4560
Jim E Tribal, *CEO*
Leatha C Tribal, *Treasurer*
Jeff Fields, *Officer*
Grant Townsend, *Vice Pres*
Debra A Tribal, *Vice Pres*
EMP: 519 EST: 1996
SALES (est): 55.5MM **Privately Held**
WEB: www.goldcountrycasino.com
SIC: **7011** Casino hotel

(P-11550)
UNITED AUBURN INDIAN COMMUNITY
Also Called: Thunder Valley Casino
1200 Athens Ave, Lincoln (95648-9328)
PHONE..................................916 408-7777
Scott Garawitz, *Branch Mgr*
Michael Kuhn, *President*
Nancy Yang, *President*
Sean Dunne, *Officer*
Kevin Simington, *Officer*
EMP: 1182 **Privately Held**
WEB: www.auburnrancheria.com
SIC: **7011** Casino hotel
PA: United Auburn Indian Community
10720 Indian Hill Rd
Auburn CA 95603

(P-11551)
UNIWELL FRESNO HOTEL LLC
Also Called: Doubletree By Hilton Fresno
2233 Ventura St, Fresno (93721-2915)
PHONE..................................559 268-1000
Steve Klein,
Wendy Niles, *Sales Executive*
Kristine Bacon, *Manager*
Kris Doyle, *Manager*
EMP: 59 EST: 1998
SALES (est): 8.4MM **Privately Held**
WEB: www.fresnoconferencehotel.com
SIC: **7011** Hotels

PRODUCTS & SERVICES SECTION
7011 - Hotels, Motels & Tourist Courts County (P-11578)

(P-11552)
VACA VALLEY INN
1050 Orange Dr, Vacaville (95687-3112)
PHONE.................707 446-8888
John Dreyfous, Partner
Pat Mitchell, Vice Pres
Jeff Whitehead, Area Mgr
James Hope, General Mgr
Kapila Senanayake, General Mgr
EMP: 64 EST: 1985
SQ FT: 45,000
SALES (est): 424.1K Privately Held
SIC: 7011 Motel, franchised

(P-11553)
VALUE PLACE HOTEL
550 Hawkcrest Cir, Sacramento (95835-2033)
PHONE.................916 688-1330
Robert J Dailey, Principal
EMP: 55 EST: 2009
SALES (est): 178.1K Privately Held
WEB: www.allstays.com
SIC: 7011 Hotels

(P-11554)
VAN NESS HOTEL INC
1050 Van Ness Ave, San Francisco (94109-6934)
PHONE.................415 673-4711
John M Scheurer, President
EMP: 65 EST: 2003
SALES (est): 744.5K Privately Held
SIC: 7011 Hotels

(P-11555)
VANMALI INC
251 El Camino Real, San Carlos (94070-2405)
PHONE.................650 576-9134
Narendra Dahya, Principal
EMP: 35 EST: 2005
SALES (est): 468.8K Privately Held
SIC: 7011 Hotels & motels

(P-11556)
VENTUR HOSPITALITY LLC (PA)
855 Burnett Ave Apt 7, San Francisco (94131-1574)
PHONE.................415 279-8688
James Burkhouse, Principal
EMP: 53 EST: 2008
SALES (est): 220.9K Privately Held
SIC: 7011 Hotels & motels

(P-11557)
VIEIRAS RESORT
15476 State Highway 160, Isleton (95641-9736)
PHONE.................916 777-6661
Sylvia Vieira, President
Kevis Chavier, Corp Secy
Rick Viera, Vice Pres
EMP: 48 EST: 1970
SQ FT: 2,000
SALES (est): 1MM Privately Held
WEB: www.vieirasresort.com
SIC: 7011 Resort hotel

(P-11558)
VILLA INN
Also Called: Cafe Villa
1600 Lincoln Ave, San Rafael (94901-1931)
PHONE.................415 456-4975
Romain Cherbero, President
Norma Cherbero, Corp Secy
Marcel Balestierm, Vice Pres
Roland Cherbero, Vice Pres
EMP: 45 EST: 1972
SQ FT: 10,000
SALES (est): 760.8K Privately Held
WEB: www.villainn.com
SIC: 7011 5812 Motels; American restaurant

(P-11559)
VILLAGE INN OWNERS ASSOCIATION
Also Called: Olympic Village Inn
1909 Chamonix Pl, Olympic Valley (96146-1033)
P.O. Box 2395 (96146-2395)
PHONE.................530 581-6000
Alan Traenker, President
EMP: 51 EST: 1983
SQ FT: 45,000
SALES (est): 2.4MM Privately Held
WEB: www.olympicvillageinn.com
SIC: 7011 Resort hotel

(P-11560)
VINTNERS INN
4350 Barnes Rd, Santa Rosa (95403-1514)
PHONE.................707 575-7350
Donald Carano,
Sonia Kalinski, Office Mgr
Jessica Adams, Sales Staff
Elena Reynoso, Sales Staff
Alison Abbott, Director
EMP: 100 EST: 2000
SQ FT: 30,670
SALES (est): 9.8MM Privately Held
WEB: www.vintnersresort.com
SIC: 7011 Motels

(P-11561)
VIPA HOSPITALITY INC
Also Called: Comfort Inn
2025 W Orangeburg Ave, Modesto (95350-3741)
PHONE.................209 544-2000
Suresh Chandra, President
EMP: 37 EST: 2004
SQ FT: 28,596
SALES (est): 337.8K Privately Held
WEB: www.choicehotels.com
SIC: 7011 Hotels

(P-11562)
VIRGIN HTELS SAN FRANCISCO LLC
250 4th St, San Francisco (94103-3109)
PHONE.................415 534-6500
Alexander Jomant, Director
Jasmine Tomelden, Sales Mgr
EMP: 40 EST: 2013
SALES (est): 6.3MM Privately Held
WEB: www.virginhotels.com
SIC: 7011 Hotels
HQ: Virgin Management Limited
The Battleship Building
London
207 313-2000

(P-11563)
VISHNU HOTEL LLC
Also Called: Comfort Inn
25921 Industrial Blvd, Hayward (94545-2995)
PHONE.................650 508-1800
Nick Dahya, Principal
EMP: 37 EST: 1999
SQ FT: 50,000
SALES (est): 572.6K Privately Held
WEB: www.choicehotels.com
SIC: 7011 Hotels & motels

(P-11564)
VWI CONCORD LLC
Also Called: Hilton Concord
1970 Diamond Blvd, Concord (94520-5718)
PHONE.................925 827-2000
Jack Hlavac, General Mgr
Jim Dunbar, Officer
Rocelita Aragon, Manager
EMP: 130 EST: 2008
SALES (est): 12.5MM Privately Held
SIC: 7011 Hotels & motels

(P-11565)
WARREN RESORTS INC
Also Called: El Bonita Motel
195 Main St, Saint Helena (94574-2156)
PHONE.................707 251-8687
Pierrette Pherene, Manager
EMP: 57
SALES (corp-wide): 4.1MM Privately Held
WEB: www.elbonita.com
SIC: 7011 Motels
PA: Warren Resorts, Inc.
575 River Pkwy
Idaho Falls ID 83402
208 523-2242

(P-11566)
WARWICK CALIFORNIA CORPORATION
Also Called: Warwick Hotel San Francisco
490 Geary St, San Francisco (94102-1223)
PHONE.................415 992-3809
Richard Chiu, President
Joseph Tung, Vice Pres
EMP: 107 EST: 1912
SQ FT: 23,386
SALES (est): 2.1MM
SALES (corp-wide): 2.6MM Privately Held
WEB: www.warwickhotels.com
SIC: 7011 7299 Hotels; banquet hall facilities
PA: Warwick Holdings S.A.
Rue Eugene Ruppert 6
Luxembourg 2453

(P-11567)
WASHINGTON INN ASSOCIATES
495 10th St, Oakland (94607-4012)
PHONE.................510 452-1776
Kenneth C Rupenthal, General Ptnr
Lillian Rupenthal, General Ptnr
Jason Martinez, Sales Staff
EMP: 80 EST: 1987
SQ FT: 25,000
SALES (est): 610.8K Privately Held
WEB: www.thewashingtoninn.com
SIC: 7011 Hotels

(P-11568)
WELCOME GROUP INC
Also Called: Fairfield Inn By Marr
1780 Tribute Rd, Sacramento (95815-4402)
PHONE.................916 920-5300
Tammy Boland, Vice Pres
EMP: 77
SALES (corp-wide): 4.3MM Privately Held
WEB: www.welcomegroupinc.com
SIC: 7011 Hotels & motels
PA: Welcome Group, Inc.
222 N Pacific Coast Hwy # 2222
El Segundo CA 90245
860 741-2211

(P-11569)
WELCOME NATOMAS LLC
2618 Gateway Oaks Dr, Sacramento (95833)
PHONE.................916 649-1300
Amar Shokeen, CEO
Genii Reynolds, Director
Denia Phillips, Manager
EMP: 40 EST: 2018
SALES (est): 599.4K Privately Held
SIC: 7011 Hotels & motels

(P-11570)
WEST COAST PROPERTY MANAGEMENT
Also Called: Best Western
400 Valley Way, Milpitas (95035-4136)
PHONE.................408 263-5566
Susan Truong, Manager
EMP: 52 EST: 1988
SQ FT: 40,000
SALES (est): 1.5MM Privately Held
WEB: www.bwbrooksideinn.com
SIC: 7011 Hotels & motels

(P-11571)
WEST HOTEL PARTNERS LP
Also Called: Hilton
300 Almaden Blvd, San Jose (95110-2703)
PHONE.................408 947-4450
John Southwell, Branch Mgr
Michelle Rowden, Sales Mgr
EMP: 231 Privately Held
WEB: www.hilton.com
SIC: 7011 7371 6512 5813 Hotels & motels; custom computer programming services; nonresidential building operators; drinking places; eating places
PA: West Hotel Partners, L.P.
11828 La Grange Ave # 20
Los Angeles CA 90025

(P-11572)
WEST SAN CRLOS HT PARTNERS LLC
Also Called: Hyatt Place San Jose/Downtown
282 Almaden Blvd, San Jose (95113-2003)
PHONE.................408 998-0400
F Matthew Dinapoli,
Tina Castaneda, Administration
EMP: 60 EST: 2010
SALES (est): 6.6MM Privately Held
WEB: www.hyatt.com
SIC: 7011 Hotels

(P-11573)
WESTIN MONACHE
50 Hillside Dr, Mammoth Lakes (93546-9681)
P.O. Box 388 (93546-0004)
PHONE.................760 934-0400
Erin Heilman, Sales Mgr
Cammon Wilders, Manager
EMP: 46 EST: 2010
SALES (est): 3.7MM Privately Held
WEB: www.marriott.com
SIC: 7011 Resort hotel

(P-11574)
WESTPOST BERKELEY LLC
Also Called: Doubltree By Hilton Brkley Mrin
200 Marina Blvd, Berkeley (94710-1608)
PHONE.................510 548-7920
Moez Mangalgi, Mng Member
Mohan Persaud, Controller
EMP: 39 EST: 2011
SALES (est): 2.6MM Privately Held
WEB: www.doubletreeberkeleymarina.com
SIC: 7011 Hotels

(P-11575)
WH PLEASANTON HOTEL LP
Also Called: Sheraton
5990 Stoneridge Mall Rd, Pleasanton (94588-3229)
PHONE.................925 463-3330
Michael Murray, General Ptnr
EMP: 38 EST: 2017
SALES (est): 8.2MM Privately Held
WEB: www.marriott.com
SIC: 7011 Hotels & motels

(P-11576)
WHARF
Also Called: Wharf Restaurant & Anchr Lodge
32260 N Harbor Dr, Fort Bragg (95437-5546)
P.O. Box 1429 (95437-1429)
PHONE.................707 964-4283
Tom Wisdom, Partner
Jay Gray, Partner
EMP: 86 EST: 1952
SQ FT: 8,500
SALES (est): 1.5MM Privately Held
WEB: www.silversatthewharf.com
SIC: 5812 5813 7011 Seafood restaurants; bar (drinking places); motels

(P-11577)
WHARF MOTEL CORP
Also Called: Wharf Inn, The
2601 Mason St, San Francisco (94133-1209)
PHONE.................415 673-7411
Toll Free:.................877
Jay Shah, General Mgr
Varnum Paul, President
Michael Laplante, General Mgr
EMP: 55 EST: 1959
SALES (est): 602.9K Privately Held
WEB: www.wharfinn.com
SIC: 7011 Motels

(P-11578)
WIN RIVER HOTEL CORPORATION
Also Called: Hilton
5050 Bechelli Ln, Redding (96002-3539)
PHONE.................530 226-5111
Glen Howard, President
EMP: 457 EST: 2004
SALES (est): 7.4MM Privately Held
WEB: www.hiltongrandvacations.com
SIC: 7011 Hotels & motels

7011 - Hotels, Motels & Tourist Courts County (P-11579)   PRODUCTS & SERVICES SECTION

PA: Redding Rancheria
2000 Redding Rancheria Rd
Redding CA 96001

(P-11579)
WINE & ROSES LLC
Also Called: Wine & Roses Hotel and Rest
2505 W Turner Rd, Lodi (95242-4643)
PHONE..................................209 334-6988
Russ Munson, *Mng Member*
Ann Forshey, *Human Res Dir*
Erin Stacher, *Sales Mgr*
Emily Hetzner, *Sales Staff*
Kathy Munson,
EMP: 190 EST: 1999
SQ FT: 22,000
SALES (est): 10.6MM **Privately Held**
WEB: www.winerose.com
SIC: 5812 7011 7299 5813 American restaurant; hotels & motels; hotels; banquet hall facilities; bars & lounges

(P-11580)
WOODSPRING SUITES SACRAMENTO
550 Hawkcrest Cir, Sacramento (95835-2033)
PHONE..................................916 688-1330
EMP: 36 EST: 2019
SALES (est): 75.5K **Privately Held**
WEB: www.woodspring.com
SIC: 7011 Hotels

(P-11581)
WORLDMARK CLUB
3927 E State Hwy 20, Nice (95464-8647)
PHONE..................................707 274-0118
Bennet Posman, *Branch Mgr*
EMP: 66
SALES (corp-wide): 1.3B **Publicly Held**
WEB: www.worldmark.wyndhamdestinations.com
SIC: 7011 Resort hotel
HQ: Worldmark, The Club
9805 Willows Rd Ne
Redmond WA 98052

(P-11582)
WORLDMARK CLUB
Also Called: Worldmark Club At Bass Lake
53134 Road 432, Bass Lake (93604-9768)
PHONE..................................559 642-6780
Vaden Savage, *Branch Mgr*
EMP: 66
SALES (corp-wide): 1.3B **Publicly Held**
WEB: www.worldmark.wyndhamdestinations.com
SIC: 7011 6531 Resort hotel; time-sharing real estate sales, leasing & rentals
HQ: Worldmark, The Club
9805 Willows Rd Ne
Redmond WA 98052

(P-11583)
Y & Y PROPERTY MANAGEMENT INC
3110 N Blackstone Ave, Fresno (93703-1018)
PHONE..................................559 226-2110
Bob Yoon, *President*
Renee McCoy, *Manager*
EMP: 44 EST: 1972
SQ FT: 62,893
SALES (est): 724.1K **Privately Held**
SIC: 7011 Hotels & motels

(P-11584)
YANGS BROTHERS INTL CORP
Also Called: Woodcrest Hotel
5415 Stevens Creek Blvd, Santa Clara (95051-7202)
PHONE..................................408 446-9636
Lien Shan Yang, *President*
Rebecca Chao, *Assistant*
EMP: 103 EST: 1985
SQ FT: 36,000
SALES (est): 1.4MM **Privately Held**
WEB: www.woodcresthotel.com
SIC: 7011 Hotel, franchised

(P-11585)
YHB SAN FRANCISCO LLC
Also Called: Pickwick Hotel The
85 5th St, San Francisco (94103-1812)
PHONE..................................415 421-7500
Fred Kleisner, *CEO*
Fred Adriano, *General Mgr*
Allen Allgood, *Director*
EMP: 105 EST: 1926
SALES (est): 9.6MM **Privately Held**
WEB: www.pickwickhotel.com
SIC: 7011 Hotels

(P-11586)
YORK HOTEL GROUP LLC
940 Sutter St, San Francisco (94109-6025)
PHONE..................................415 885-6800
Trinidad Rosas,
EMP: 35 EST: 2003
SQ FT: 84,000
SALES (est): 284.1K **Privately Held**
SIC: 7011 Hotels

(P-11587)
ZENIQUE HOTEL MANAGEMENT LLC
800 Airport Blvd Ste 418, Burlingame (94010-1929)
PHONE..................................650 483-9968
Rupesh Patel, *Mng Member*
Michael Day, *Controller*
Angela Cangiamilla, *Sales Staff*
Aaron Penry, *Director*
Krista Brughelli, *Manager*
EMP: 39 EST: 2015
SALES (est): 3.3MM **Privately Held**
WEB: www.zeniquehotels.com
SIC: 7011 Hotels

7021 Rooming & Boarding Houses

(P-11588)
AISHA ACADEMY
706 S Pershing Ave, Stockton (95203-3243)
P.O. Box 4638, Inglewood (90309-4638)
PHONE..................................310 908-1962
Kelvin Williams, *Exec Dir*
Krystal Williams, *CFO*
EMP: 99 EST: 2014
SQ FT: 139,800
SALES (est): 16.7K **Privately Held**
WEB: www.aishaacademy23.org
SIC: 7021 Rooming & boarding houses

(P-11589)
GUM MOON RESIDENCE HALL
Also Called: Gum Moon RES Hall
940 Washington St, San Francisco (94108-1114)
PHONE..................................415 421-8827
Michelle Mah, *President*
EMP: 40 EST: 1969
SQ FT: 16,768
SALES (est): 1.7MM **Privately Held**
WEB: www.gummoon.org
SIC: 7021 Furnished room rental

(P-11590)
HOPE HOSPICE INC
6377 Clark Ave Ste 100, Dublin (94568-3024)
PHONE..................................925 829-8770
Helen Meier, *Exec Dir*
Raul Perez,
Elsei Yeh-Arling,
Patty Hefner, *Director*
Jennifer Pettley, *Director*
EMP: 122 EST: 1981
SQ FT: 1,500
SALES (est): 14.7MM **Privately Held**
WEB: www.hopehospice.com
SIC: 7021 5943 Rooming & boarding houses; stationery stores

(P-11591)
INTERNATIONAL HOUSE
Also Called: INTERNATIONAL HOUSE AT U C BER
2299 Piedmont Ave Ste 535, Berkeley (94720-2392)
PHONE..................................510 642-9490
Robert M Berdahl, *Ch of Bd*
Joseph Lurie, *Exec Dir*
Jeff Royal, *Research*
Avery Yoon, *Graphic Designe*
Shankar Sastry, *Engineer*
EMP: 162 EST: 1928
SQ FT: 100,000
SALES (est): 21.2MM **Privately Held**
SIC: 7021 Rooming & boarding houses

(P-11592)
MIDPEN PROPERTY MGT CORP
Also Called: Carroll Inn
174 Carroll St Ofc, Sunnyvale (94086-6293)
PHONE..................................408 773-8014
Ted Wilson, *Manager*
EMP: 38 **Privately Held**
WEB: www.midpen-housing.org
SIC: 7021 Rooming & boarding houses
HQ: Midpen Property Management Corporation
303 Vintage Park Dr # 250
Foster City CA 94404
650 356-2900

(P-11593)
RICHARDSON CAMP RESORT INC (PA)
Also Called: Beacon Restaurant
1900 Jameson Beach Rd, South Lake Tahoe (96150)
PHONE..................................530 542-6570
Bob Hassett, *President*
EMP: 45 EST: 1923
SQ FT: 1,310
SALES (est): 6.1MM **Privately Held**
WEB: www.camprichardson.com
SIC: 7021 5812 7011 7033 Lodging house, except organization; eating places; tourist camps, cabins, cottages & courts; campgrounds; trailer park; filling stations, gasoline; convenience stores

(P-11594)
SAN BNITO CNTY CMNTY SVCS DEV
1101 San Felipe Rd, Hollister (95023-2819)
PHONE..................................831 636-5524
Jeffrey C Jeffers, *Exec Dir*
Fernando Gonzalez, *Ch of Bd*
Jeff Conway, *Vice Chairman*
EMP: 45 EST: 1984
SQ FT: 2,000
SALES (est): 2.1MM **Privately Held**
WEB: www.csdcsbc.org
SIC: 7021 7519 Rooming & boarding houses;

(P-11595)
WORLDWIDE CORPORATE HOUSING LP
Also Called: Oakwood Worldwide
10183 Croydon Way Ste E, Sacramento (95827-2103)
PHONE..................................916 631-3777
Tauna Renau, *Manager*
EMP: 119
SALES (corp-wide): 75.7MM **Privately Held**
WEB: www.oakwood.com
SIC: 7021 Furnished room rental
HQ: Worldwide Corporate Housing, Lp
1 World Trade Ctr # 2400
Long Beach CA 90831
562 473-7371

7032 Sporting & Recreational Camps

(P-11596)
ADVENTRES RLLING CROSS-COUNTRY
Also Called: Adventures Cross-Country
242 Rdwood Hwy Frntage Rd, Mill Valley (94941-6613)
PHONE..................................415 332-5075
Scott A Von Eschen, *President*
Kristin V Eschen, *Opers Mgr*
Margo Brookfield,
Lisa Halsted, *Director*
Emily Rosser, *Director*
EMP: 46 EST: 1983
SQ FT: 2,500
SALES (est): 1.4MM **Privately Held**
SIC: 7032 Summer camp, except day & sports instructional

(P-11597)
ALLIANCE RDWODS CNFRNCE GRUNDS
Also Called: Sonoma Canopy Tours
6250 Bohemian Hwy, Occidental (95465-9105)
PHONE..................................707 874-3507
Jim Blake, *CEO*
James Blake, *Exec Dir*
Caitlin Bishop, *Executive Asst*
Jon Maves, *Pastor*
Abby Abrahams, *Manager*
EMP: 115 EST: 1979
SQ FT: 1,392
SALES (est): 10.3MM **Privately Held**
WEB: www.allianceredwoods.com
SIC: 7032 Recreational camps; youth camps; Bible camp

(P-11598)
CALIFRNIA STHERN BPTST CNVNTIO
Also Called: Southern Bptst Jnness Pk Encmp
29005 Highway 108, Long Barn (95335-9737)
PHONE..................................209 965-3735
Rod Goodmon, *Director*
Bob Veach, *Manager*
EMP: 83
SQ FT: 23,904
SALES (corp-wide): 18.6MM **Privately Held**
WEB: www.csbc.com
SIC: 8661 7032 Religious organizations; sporting & recreational camps
PA: California Southern Baptist Convention
678 E Shaw Ave
Fresno CA 93710
559 229-9533

(P-11599)
CAMPBELL CHRISTIAN SCHOOL
1075 W Campbell Ave, Campbell (95008-1753)
PHONE..................................408 370-4900
Shawn Stewart, *Superintendent*
Jordan Smith, *Ch of Bd*
Brian Kinnett, *Facilities Mgr*
Sheri Agers, *Teacher*
Sunny Ahrens, *Teacher*
EMP: 89 EST: 1967
SALES (est): 7.4MM **Privately Held**
WEB: www.campbellchristian.org
SIC: 8211 7032 Private elementary school; summer camp, except day & sports instructional

(P-11600)
CITY BEACH INC
4020 Technology Pl, Fremont (94538-6362)
PHONE..................................408 654-9330
Aaron Benning, *Principal*
Amber Biddle, *Manager*
EMP: 40
SALES (corp-wide): 3.9MM **Privately Held**
SIC: 7032 Sporting & recreational camps
PA: City Beach, Inc.
4949 E Red Range Way
Cave Creek AZ 85331
510 651-2500

(P-11601)
EXPLORING NEW HORIZONS INC
6265 Highway 9, Felton (95018-9710)
P.O. Box 1514 (95018-1514)
PHONE..................................831 338-3013
Tracey Weiss, *Branch Mgr*
EMP: 38 **Privately Held**
WEB: www.exploringnewhorizons.org
SIC: 7032 Sporting & recreational camps
PA: Exploring New Horizons
6265 Highway 9
Felton CA 95018

PRODUCTS & SERVICES SECTION
7041 - Membership-Basis Hotels County (P-11623)

(P-11602) GALILEO LEARNING LLC (PA)
1021 3rd St, Oakland (94607-2507)
PHONE..................................510 595-7293
Glen E Tripp,
Sarah Marie Lewallen, *Vice Pres*
Carol Liao, *Finance*
Shauna Clements, *Opers Staff*
Mimi Gordon, *Opers Staff*
EMP: 39 EST: 2002
SQ FT: 10,000
SALES (est): 10.4MM **Privately Held**
WEB: www.galileo-camps.com
SIC: 7032 Sporting & recreational camps

(P-11603) HUME LAKE CHRISTIAN CAMPS INC
64144 Hume Lake Rd Ofc, Miramonte (93628-9600)
PHONE..................................559 305-7770
Genie Coe, *Accountant*
Aubrie Wright, *Executive Asst*
Cameron Cadiz, *Administration*
Amy Northrop, *Administration*
Michelle Wilcox, *Administration*
EMP: 43
SALES (corp-wide): 11.6MM **Privately Held**
WEB: www.hume.org
SIC: 7032 Bible camp
PA: Hume Lake Christian Camps Inc
5545 E Hedges Ave
Fresno CA 93727
559 305-7770

(P-11604) INTERNAL DRIVE
Also Called: ID Tech Camps
910 E Hamilton Ave # 300, Campbell (95008-0645)
P.O. Box 111720 (95011-1720)
PHONE..................................408 871-2227
Pete Ingram Cauchi, *President*
Meredith Ruble, *CFO*
Ricky Bennett, *Vice Pres*
Jimmy Hill, *Vice Pres*
Robby Little, *Vice Pres*
EMP: 323 EST: 1999
SQ FT: 10,000
SALES (est): 23.3MM **Privately Held**
WEB: www.idtech.com
SIC: 7032 Youth camps

(P-11605) INTERNTNAL CH OF FRSQARE GOSPL
Also Called: Old Oak Ranch
15250 Old Oak Ranch Rd, Sonora (95370-8317)
PHONE..................................209 532-4295
Jeffrey Fitch, *Branch Mgr*
Palma Fitch, *Office Mgr*
EMP: 36
SQ FT: 28,451
SALES (corp-wide): 175.9MM **Privately Held**
WEB: www.foursquare.org
SIC: 7032 8361 Boys' camp; girls' camp; rehabilitation center, residential; health care incidental
PA: International Church Of The Foursquare Gospel
1910 W Sunset Blvd
Los Angeles CA 90026
213 989-4234

(P-11606) JEWISH CMNTY CTR SAN FRANCISCO (PA)
3200 California St, San Francisco (94118-1994)
PHONE..................................415 292-1200
Barry Finesone, *President*
Diane Walters, *CFO*
David Green, *Officer*
Andrew Ergas, *Exec Dir*
Matt Epstein, *Security Dir*
EMP: 243 EST: 1878
SQ FT: 35,000
SALES (est): 29.6MM **Privately Held**
WEB: www.jccsf.org
SIC: 8211 7032 8322 Preparatory school; youth camps; individual & family services

(P-11607) JOPLIN INC (PA)
Also Called: Plantation Farm Camp
34285 Kruse Ranch Rd, Cazadero (95421-9610)
PHONE..................................707 847-3494
John Chakan, *President*
Kelly Marston, *Director*
EMP: 39 EST: 1952
SALES (est): 500K **Privately Held**
WEB: www.farmcampca.com
SIC: 7032 Dude ranch

(P-11608) KENNOLYN CAMP INC
8205 Glen Haven Rd, Soquel (95073-9588)
PHONE..................................831 479-6714
Pam Caldwell, *General Mgr*
Kenneth Caldwell, *Treasurer*
EMP: 36 EST: 1946
SALES (est): 4.1MM **Privately Held**
WEB: www.kennolycamps.com
SIC: 7032 Summer camp, except day & sports instructional

(P-11609) MOUNT HERMON ASSOCIATION INC (PA)
Also Called: Christian Conference Grounds
37 Conference Dr, Mount Hermon (95041-3002)
PHONE..................................831 335-4466
Roger E Williams, *Exec Dir*
Bryan Hayes, *Vice Pres*
Ron Demolar, *Associate Dir*
Roger Williams, *Exec Dir*
Kelsey Paterson, *Administration*
EMP: 90 EST: 1906
SQ FT: 10,000
SALES (est): 10.2MM **Privately Held**
WEB: www.mounthermon.org
SIC: 7032 5942 Bible camp; books, religious

(P-11610) SHASTA COUNTY OFFICE EDUCATION
Also Called: Camp Latieze
1644 Magnolia Ave, Redding (96001-1513)
PHONE..................................530 225-0285
Fax: 530 225-0329
EMP: 35
SALES (corp-wide): 26.3MM **Privately Held**
SIC: 7032 Sport/Recreation Camp
PA: Shasta County Office Of Education
1644 Magnolia Ave
Redding CA 96001
530 225-0200

(P-11611) SILVER SPUR CHRISTIAN CAMP
17301 Silver Spur Dr, Tuolumne (95379-9638)
PHONE..................................209 928-4248
Stephen Johnson, *Director*
Marie Johnson, *Administration*
EMP: 46 EST: 1965
SALES (est): 2.5MM **Privately Held**
WEB: www.silverspur.com
SIC: 7032 7011 Recreational camps; hotels & motels

(P-11612) TRUST FOR HIDDEN VILLA
26870 Moody Rd, Los Altos Hills (94022-4209)
PHONE..................................650 949-8650
Chris Overington, *Director*
Jesse Dolan, *Property Mgr*
Wesley Mills, *Property Mgr*
Marc Sidel, *Deputy Dir*
Nikki Bryant, *Director*
EMP: 35 EST: 1945
SALES (est): 3.2MM **Privately Held**
WEB: www.hiddenvilla.org
SIC: 7032 7011 7389 Summer camp, except day & sports instructional; hostels; welcoming services

(P-11613) UNITED CMPS CNFRENCES RETREATS (PA)
Also Called: Uccr
1304 Sthpint Blvd Ste 200, Petaluma (94954)
PHONE..................................707 762-3220
Mike Carr, *President*
Matthew Compton-Clark, *COO*
Tina Heck, *Director*
EMP: 50 EST: 1969
SQ FT: 1,700
SALES (est): 2.7MM **Privately Held**
WEB: www.uccr.org
SIC: 7032 Recreational camps; youth camps

(P-11614) UNITED CMPS CNFRENCES RETREATS
Also Called: Montepoyon Camp
220 Cloister Ln, Aptos (95003-2910)
PHONE..................................831 684-0148
Michael Petrov, *Manager*
Saxton Pope, *Owner*
EMP: 47
SALES (corp-wide): 2.7MM **Privately Held**
WEB: www.uccr.org
SIC: 7032 7011 Sporting & recreational camps; hotels & motels
PA: United Camps Conferences & Retreats, Inc
1304 Sthpint Blvd Ste 200
Petaluma CA 94954
707 762-3220

(P-11615) WESTERN CAMPS INC
Also Called: Wonder Valley Resort
6450 Elwood Rd, Sanger (93657-9047)
P.O. Box 71 (93657-0071)
PHONE..................................559 787-2551
Roy Oken, *President*
Stanford Oken, *Ch of Bd*
Larry Oken, *General Mgr*
Carrie Gross, *Office Mgr*
Nancy Nighbert, *Admin Sec*
EMP: 40 EST: 1967
SQ FT: 200,000
SALES (est): 5.4MM **Privately Held**
WEB: www.wondervalley.com
SIC: 7032 7011 7389 Sporting & recreational camps; resort hotel; convention & show services

(P-11616) WINNARAINBOW INC (PA)
Also Called: CAMP WINNARAINBOW
1301 Henry St, Berkeley (94709-1928)
P.O. Box 1359, Laytonville (95454-1359)
PHONE..................................510 525-4304
Jahanara Romney, *Director*
Dr Larry Brilliant, *Treasurer*
Hugh Romney, *Co-Director*
EMP: 38 EST: 1973
SALES: 866.8K **Privately Held**
WEB: www.campwinnarainbow.org
SIC: 7032 Summer camp, except day & sports instructional

7033 Trailer Parks & Camp Sites

(P-11617) CASINI ENTERPRISES INC
Also Called: Casini Ranch Family Campground
22855 Moscow Rd, Duncans Mills (95430)
P.O. Box 22 (95430-0022)
PHONE..................................707 865-2255
Paul Casini, *President*
EMP: 45 EST: 1961
SALES (est): 1.5MM **Privately Held**
WEB: www.casiniranch.com
SIC: 7033 4212 0212 Campgrounds; liquid haulage, local; beef cattle except feedlots

(P-11618) COMMUNITY RECREATION CENTER
Also Called: City of Santa Clara
969 Kiely Blvd, Santa Clara (95051-5099)
PHONE..................................408 615-3140
Marilyn Dippell, *Superintendent*
Cheri Fulk, *Supervisor*
EMP: 35 EST: 1998
SALES (est): 642.4K **Privately Held**
WEB: www.santaclaraca.gov
SIC: 7033 Recreational vehicle parks

(P-11619) LAWSONS LANDING INC
137 Marine View Dr, Dillon Beach (94929)
P.O. Box 67 (94929-0067)
PHONE..................................707 878-2443
Michael J Lawson, *President*
Tad E Vogler, *Shareholder*
Carl V Vogler, *Vice Pres*
Nancy Vogler, *Admin Sec*
EMP: 35 EST: 1995
SQ FT: 4,000
SALES (est): 3.4MM **Privately Held**
WEB: www.lawsonslanding.com
SIC: 7033 Campgrounds

(P-11620) SAN FRNCSCO NORTH/PETALUMA KOA
20 Rainsville Rd, Petaluma (94952-8121)
PHONE..................................707 763-1492
William Wood, *President*
Judith Wood, *Corp Secy*
EMP: 50 EST: 1975
SQ FT: 2,000
SALES (est): 3.8MM **Privately Held**
WEB: www.koa.com
SIC: 7033 4119 Campgrounds; sightseeing bus

(P-11621) SONOMA COUNTY REGIONAL PARKS
2300 County Center Dr A120, Santa Rosa (95403-3029)
PHONE..................................707 527-2041
Jim Angelo, *Director*
Elizabeth Tyree, *Principal*
Sandi Funke, *Program Mgr*
Pam McBride, *Admin Asst*
Carson Hunter, *Park Mgr*
EMP: 69 EST: 1970
SALES (est): 814K **Privately Held**
WEB: www.sonomacountyparksfoundation.org
SIC: 7033 Recreational vehicle parks

(P-11622) STOCKTON DELTA RESORT LLC
14900 W Highway 12, Lodi (95242-9514)
PHONE..................................209 369-1041
Chelsea Bossenbroek,
EMP: 40 EST: 2006
SALES (est): 2.4MM
SALES (corp-wide): 1.4B **Publicly Held**
WEB: www.towerparkresort.com
SIC: 7033 Campgrounds
PA: Sun Communities, Inc.
27777 Franklin Rd Ste 200
Southfield MI 48034
248 208-2500

7041 Membership-Basis Hotels

(P-11623) 1849 HOMEOWNERS ASSOCIATION
Also Called: 1849 Condominiums Rentals
826 Lakeview Blvd, Mammoth Lakes (93546-6164)
P.O. Box 835 (93546-0835)
PHONE..................................760 934-7525
Dave McCoy, *Founder*
EMP: 38 EST: 1972
SQ FT: 60
SALES (est): 582.6K **Privately Held**
WEB: www.1849mountainrentals.com
SIC: 7041 8641 Residence club, organization; homeowners' association

(P-11624)
BERKELEY STUDENT COOP INC
2424 Ridge Rd, Berkeley (94709-1212)
PHONE.....................510 848-1936
Janette E Stokley, *Exec Dir*
Palmer Buchholz, *President*
Marjorie Greene, *CFO*
Bryan Goodwin, *Vice Pres*
Chris Kelley, *Human Res Mgr*
EMP: 100 **EST:** 1934
SQ FT: 18,000
SALES (est): 12.3MM **Privately Held**
WEB: www.bsc.coop
SIC: 7041 Boarding house, organization

(P-11625)
HEART CONSCIOUSNESS CHURCH INC (PA)
Also Called: Harbin Hot Springs
18424 Harbin Springs Rd, Middletown (95461-9687)
P.O. Box 782 (95461-0782)
PHONE.....................707 987-2477
Robert F Hartley, *President*
Suzie Lecavalier, *Treasurer*
Julie Adams, *Vice Pres*
Sajjad Mahmud, *Vice Pres*
EMP: 110 **EST:** 1975
SQ FT: 4,000
SALES (est): 4.8MM **Privately Held**
WEB: www.harbin.org
SIC: 7041 Membership-basis organization hotels

7211 Power Laundries, Family & Commercial

(P-11626)
AMERICAN ETC INC
Also Called: Royal Laundry
1140 San Mateo Ave, South San Francisco (94080-6602)
PHONE.....................650 873-5353
Kenn T Edwards, *CEO*
Don Luckenbach, *President*
Elie Karch, *Vice Pres*
Martha A Guzman, *Controller*
Nuvia Urena, *Accounts Mgr*
▲ **EMP:** 325 **EST:** 1964
SQ FT: 70,000
SALES (est): 14.1MM **Privately Held**
WEB: www.royallaundry.net
SIC: 7211 Power laundries, family & commercial

7212 Garment Pressing & Cleaners' Agents

(P-11627)
ECMS INC (HQ)
1809 Peralta St, Oakland (94607-1638)
PHONE.....................510 986-0131
Paul F Curtis, *CEO*
EMP: 40 **EST:** 2005
SALES (est): 1.1MM
SALES (corp-wide): 102.7MM **Privately Held**
WEB: www.ecmsinc.biz
SIC: 7212 Pickup station, laundry & drycleaning
PA: L.N. Curtis And Sons
185 Lennon Ln 110
Walnut Creek CA 94598
510 839-5111

(P-11628)
FCSI INC
Also Called: Alex's Dry Cleaning Valet
628 Lindaro St, San Rafael (94901-3936)
PHONE.....................415 457-8000
Alex Najafi, *President*
EMP: 29 **EST:** 2010
SALES (est): 3.6MM **Privately Held**
WEB: www.alexdryclean.net
SIC: 7212 7372 Pickup station, laundry & drycleaning; application computer software

(P-11629)
PARK AVENUE CLEANERS INC
2529 N Tracy Blvd, Tracy (95376-1768)
PHONE.....................209 914-1265
Gurtej Brar, *President*
EMP: 38 **EST:** 1996
SALES (est): 2.3MM **Privately Held**
WEB: www.parkavenuecleaners.co
SIC: 7212 3582 Laundry & drycleaner agents; commercial laundry equipment

7213 Linen Sply

(P-11630)
ALSCO INC
1009 Factory St, Richmond (94801-2166)
PHONE.....................510 237-9634
EMP: 84
SALES (corp-wide): 658.7MM **Privately Held**
SIC: 7213 Linen Supply Service
PA: Alsco Inc.
505 E South Temple
Salt Lake City UT 84102
801 328-8831

(P-11631)
ARAMARK UNF & CAREER AP LLC
Also Called: Aramark Uniform Services
1419 National Dr, Sacramento (95834-1946)
PHONE.....................916 286-4100
Gary Koolhof, *Principal*
Sergio Balderas, *District Mgr*
Arturo Covartubias, *District Mgr*
Justin Norred, *District Mgr*
Franz Wiegand, *District Mgr*
EMP: 99 **EST:** 2007
SALES (est): 8.4MM **Publicly Held**
WEB: www.aramarkuniform.com
SIC: 7213 Uniform supply
PA: Aramark
2400 Market St
Philadelphia PA 19103

(P-11632)
CINTAS CORPORATION NO 3
1877 Industrial Dr, Stockton (95206-4975)
PHONE.....................209 922-0500
Randy Galvin, *Branch Mgr*
Marcy Rosario, *Human Resources*
Preston Graham, *Production*
Richard McDowell, *Sales Mgr*
David Bousquet, *Director*
EMP: 117
SALES (corp-wide): 7.1B **Publicly Held**
WEB: www.cintas.com
SIC: 5699 5713 7213 7359 Uniforms; floor covering stores; uniform supply; equipment rental & leasing
HQ: Cintas Corporation No. 3
6800 Cintas Blvd
Mason OH 45040

(P-11633)
CINTAS CORPORATION NO 3
1229 California Ave, Pittsburg (94565-4112)
PHONE.....................925 692-5860
Bruce Meators, *Branch Mgr*
Melissa Uniforms, *Sales Staff*
Matt Wheeler, *Sales Staff*
EMP: 117
SALES (corp-wide): 7.1B **Publicly Held**
WEB: www.cintas.com
SIC: 5699 5713 7213 7359 Uniforms; floor covering stores; uniform supply; equipment rental & leasing
HQ: Cintas Corporation No. 3
6800 Cintas Blvd
Mason OH 45040

(P-11634)
CITY TOWEL & DUST SERVICE INC
Also Called: Sunset Linen Service
3016 Dutton Ave, Santa Rosa (95407-7886)
PHONE.....................707 542-0391
Michael Erwin, *President*
EMP: 79 **EST:** 1959
SQ FT: 5,000
SALES (est): 4.8MM **Privately Held**
WEB: www.sunsetlinen.com
SIC: 7213 7211 Uniform supply; linen supply, non-clothing; laundry collecting & distributing outlet

(P-11635)
KAHN RENNAISSANCE LLC
640 Bailey Rd Ste 509, Bay Point (94565-4306)
PHONE.....................510 260-3161
David Chulu, *Director*
Ophelia Chulu, *Vice Pres*
EMP: 112
SALES (est): 73.2K **Privately Held**
SIC: 7213 6798 Linen supply, clothing; real estate investment trusts

(P-11636)
LACE HOUSE LDRY & LIN SUP INC
949 Lindberg Ln, Petaluma (94952-3356)
P.O. Box 221 (94953-0221)
PHONE.....................707 763-1515
Daniel G Libarle, *President*
Melinda Pillow, *Officer*
Emily Marie Libarle, *Vice Pres*
EMP: 45 **EST:** 1910
SQ FT: 25,000
SALES (est): 4.6MM **Privately Held**
WEB: www.lacehouselinen.com
SIC: 7213 Uniform supply

(P-11637)
MEDICAL LINEN SERVICE INC
Also Called: Complete Linen Services
290 S Maple Ave, South San Francisco (94080-6304)
PHONE.....................650 873-1221
Steve Bruni, *President*
Patrice Bruni, *Treasurer*
Colin Morf, *Vice Pres*
Kathy Lobos, *Admin Asst*
EMP: 100 **EST:** 1986
SQ FT: 14,000
SALES (est): 5.7MM **Privately Held**
WEB: www.completelinen.com
SIC: 7213 Linen supply

(P-11638)
MISSION LINEN SUPPLY
Also Called: Mission Linen & Uniform Svc
7520 Reese Rd, Sacramento (95828-3707)
PHONE.....................916 423-3179
Peppy Secaile, *Manager*
Irving Dungca, *Area Mgr*
EMP: 74
SALES (corp-wide): 161.2MM **Privately Held**
WEB: www.missionlinen.com
SIC: 7213 7218 Uniform supply; industrial launderers
PA: Mission Linen Supply
717 E Yanonali St
Santa Barbara CA 93103
805 730-3620

(P-11639)
MISSION LINEN SUPPLY
Also Called: Mission Linen & Uniform Svc
136 Coyado Ave, Modesto (95350-5813)
PHONE.....................209 523-6758
Ken McDaniel, *General Mgr*
Michael Callaway, *General Mgr*
Mike Callaway, *Site Mgr*
EMP: 74
SALES (corp-wide): 161.2MM **Privately Held**
WEB: www.missionlinen.com
SIC: 7213 Uniform supply
PA: Mission Linen Supply
717 E Yanonali St
Santa Barbara CA 93103
805 730-3620

(P-11640)
MISSION LINEN SUPPLY
Also Called: Mission Linen Supply & Svcs
1401 Summer St, Eureka (95501-2246)
PHONE.....................707 443-8681
Jack Anderson, *General Mgr*
EMP: 74
SALES (corp-wide): 161.2MM **Privately Held**
WEB: www.missionlinen.com
SIC: 7213 Uniform supply
PA: Mission Linen Supply
717 E Yanonali St
Santa Barbara CA 93103
805 730-3620

(P-11641)
MISSION LINEN SUPPLY
Also Called: Mission Linen & Uniform Svc
2555 S Orange Ave, Fresno (93725-1398)
PHONE.....................559 268-0647
Allen Gregory, *Manager*
Joslyn Buckner, *Manager*
EMP: 74
SALES (corp-wide): 161.2MM **Privately Held**
WEB: www.missionlinen.com
SIC: 7213 Uniform supply
PA: Mission Linen Supply
717 E Yanonali St
Santa Barbara CA 93103
805 730-3620

(P-11642)
MISSION LINEN SUPPLY
Also Called: Mission Linen & Uniform Svc
1001 Whipple Rd, Hayward (94544-7926)
PHONE.....................510 401-5904
Bill Cacheco, *Manager*
EMP: 74
SALES (corp-wide): 161.2MM **Privately Held**
WEB: www.missionlinen.com
SIC: 7213 Uniform supply
PA: Mission Linen Supply
717 E Yanonali St
Santa Barbara CA 93103
805 730-3620

(P-11643)
MISSION LINEN SUPPLY
Also Called: Mission Linen & Uniform Svc
550 Florida St, San Francisco (94110-1960)
PHONE.....................510 429-7305
EMP: 120
SALES (corp-wide): 161.2MM **Privately Held**
WEB: www.missionlinen.com
SIC: 7213 7218 Linen Supply Services Industrial Launderer
PA: Mission Linen Supply
717 E Yanonali St
Santa Barbara CA 93103
805 730-3620

(P-11644)
MISSION LINEN SUPPLY
Also Called: Mission Linen & Uniform Svc
1340 W 7th St, Chico (95928-4907)
PHONE.....................530 342-4110
Nick Katzenstein, *Manager*
Angela Wipf, *Office Mgr*
EMP: 74
SALES (corp-wide): 161.2MM **Privately Held**
WEB: www.missionlinen.com
SIC: 7213 5699 Uniform supply; uniforms & work clothing
PA: Mission Linen Supply
717 E Yanonali St
Santa Barbara CA 93103
805 730-3620

(P-11645)
RFID CORPORATION
701 Willow Pass Rd Ste 10, Pittsburg (94565-1803)
PHONE.....................925 473-9978
John Burskens, *Plant Mgr*
EMP: 190 **Publicly Held**
WEB: www.angelica.com
SIC: 7213 Uniform supply
HQ: Rfid Corporation
1901 S Meyers Rd Ste 630
Oakbrook Terrace IL 60181
678 823-4100

(P-11646)
SHASTA LINEN SUPPLY INC
1931 E St, Sacramento (95811-1192)
PHONE.....................916 443-5966
Thomas Hammer Jr, *President*

PRODUCTS & SERVICES SECTION

7218 - Industrial Launderers County (P-11667)

EMP: 48 EST: 1920
SQ FT: 15,000
SALES (est): 2.9MM Privately Held
WEB: www.shastalinensupply.com
SIC: 7213 Uniform supply

(P-11647)
YOSEMITE LINEN SUPPLY INC
3330 E Church Ave, Fresno (93725-1339)
P.O. Box 2697 (93745-2697)
PHONE..................................559 233-2654
Bill Bakos, *President*
John Masten, *President*
Billy Bakos, *Vice Pres*
Ray Sanchez, *Manager*
EMP: 46 EST: 1945
SQ FT: 16,640
SALES (est): 5MM Privately Held
WEB: www.yosemitelinen.com
SIC: 7213 Table cover supply; towel supply; uniform supply

7215 Coin Operated Laundries & Cleaning

(P-11648)
CROTHALL SERVICES GROUP
8190 Murray Ave, Gilroy (95020-4605)
PHONE..................................909 991-4887
EMP: 620
SALES (corp-wide): 26B Privately Held
WEB: www.crothall.com
SIC: 7215 Coin-operated laundries & cleaning
HQ: Crothall Services Group
   1500 Liberty Ridge Dr # 210
   Chesterbrook PA 19087

(P-11649)
GBK CORPORATION (PA)
Also Called: Hardware Express
2245 Eureka Way, Redding (96001-0313)
P.O. Box 992107 (96099-2107)
PHONE..................................530 241-2337
Martin Kalsbeek, *CEO*
Gary Kalsbeek, *President*
Terry Grafe, *CFO*
Mike Wood, *Store Mgr*
Beverly Kalsbeek, *Admin Sec*
EMP: 49 EST: 1981
SQ FT: 48,400
SALES (est): 10.1MM Privately Held
WEB: www.helpfulace.com
SIC: 5251 7215 Builders' hardware; laundry, coin-operated

(P-11650)
SACRAMENTO LAUNDRY COMPANY INC
3750 Pell Cir, Sacramento (95838-2528)
PHONE..................................916 930-0330
Julia Pooler, *CEO*
Keith Pooler, *Principal*
Ariel Carvajal, *Prdtn Mgr*
Susan Carr, *Opers Staff*
Marc Kuder, *Sales Staff*
EMP: 49 EST: 2010
SALES (est): 5.2MM Privately Held
WEB: www.saclaundry.com
SIC: 7215 Laundry, coin-operated

(P-11651)
WASH MLTFMILY LDRY SYSTEMS LLC
1104 S Parallel Ave, Fresno (93702-4046)
PHONE..................................559 233-0595
EMP: 19
SALES (corp-wide): 53.5MM Privately Held
WEB: www.wash.com
SIC: 7215 5084 3582 Coin-Operated Laundry Whol Industrial Equipment Mfg Commercial Laundry Equipment
PA: Wash Multifamily Laundry Systems, Llc
   100 N Pacific Coast Hwy
   El Segundo CA 90245
   310 643-8491

7216 Dry Cleaning Plants, Except Rug Cleaning

(P-11652)
FASHION CLEANERS (PA)
318 Montecillo Dr, Walnut Creek (94595-2660)
PHONE..................................925 672-5505
Lawrence Lim, *President*
EMP: 40 EST: 1965
SALES (est): 1.1MM Privately Held
WEB: www.fashion-cleaners.com
SIC: 7216 Cleaning & dyeing, except rugs

(P-11653)
GILLESPIES CARPET CENTER INC
Also Called: Abbey Carpet
360 Chadbourne Rd, Fairfield (94534-9636)
PHONE..................................707 427-3773
Russell D Hoover, *President*
Rhonda Labarga, *Bookkeeper*
Tempest Hoover, *Manager*
EMP: 50 EST: 1934
SQ FT: 15,000
SALES (est): 8.6MM Privately Held
WEB: www.fairfield.abbeycarpet.com
SIC: 5713 7216 7217 Carpets; curtain cleaning & repair; carpet & upholstery cleaning

(P-11654)
INTER-CITY CLEANERS
438 S Airport Blvd, South San Francisco (94080-6908)
PHONE..................................650 875-9200
Hans Gelfand, *Co-Owner*
Vera Gelfand, *Co-Owner*
EMP: 68 EST: 1962
SQ FT: 9,000
SALES (est): 4MM Privately Held
WEB: www.intercitymetrocleaners.com
SIC: 7216 7219 Cleaning & dyeing, except rugs; laundry, except power & coin-operated

(P-11655)
RATNAKAR & SONS (PA)
Also Called: Great American Dry Cleaners
2145 Rumrill Blvd Ste A, San Pablo (94806-3469)
PHONE..................................510 236-6280
Ankit Vakharia, *President*
EMP: 38 EST: 2012
SALES (est): 994.9K Privately Held
SIC: 7216 Cleaning & dyeing, except rugs

(P-11656)
SNOW CLEANERS INC (PA)
38 W Sonora St, Stockton (95203-3414)
P.O. Box 1849 (95201-1849)
PHONE..................................209 547-1454
Harold Turner, *President*
Lorraine T Turner, *Corp Secy*
EMP: 42 EST: 1952
SALES (est): 1.5MM Privately Held
WEB: www.snowcleaners.com
SIC: 7216 7212 7219 7699 Cleaning & dyeing, except rugs; garment pressing; fur garment cleaning, repairing & storage; leather goods, cleaning & repair

7217 Carpet & Upholstery Cleaning

(P-11657)
C & S DRAPERIES INC
Also Called: Coit Restoration Services
4210 Kiernan Ave, Modesto (95356-9758)
PHONE..................................209 466-5371
Pete Bakker, *CEO*
Helen Bakker, *CEO*
Don Camping, *Sales Staff*
EMP: 150 EST: 1975
SQ FT: 50,000
SALES (est): 9.1MM Privately Held
WEB: www.coit.com
SIC: 7217 Carpet & furniture cleaning on location; carpet & rug cleaning plant; carpet & rug cleaning & repairing plant

(P-11658)
CLEANRITE INC
2684 State Highway 32 # 100, Chico (95973-8699)
PHONE..................................800 870-0030
Dan Andreasen, *Branch Mgr*
Vincent Linares, *Branch Mgr*
Peter Sprague, *Branch Mgr*
Trevor Deadmond, *Project Mgr*
Dave Degrasse, *Project Mgr*
EMP: 43
SALES (corp-wide): 30.8MM Privately Held
WEB: www.cleanrite-buildrite.com
SIC: 7217 Carpet & furniture cleaning on location
PA: Cleanrite, Inc.
   2684 Highway 32 Ste 100
   Chico CA 95973
   530 891-0333

(P-11659)
CLEANRITE INC
5601 Cedars Rd Ste I, Redding (96001-4467)
PHONE..................................530 246-4886
Eric Martin, *Manager*
EMP: 43
SALES (corp-wide): 30.8MM Privately Held
WEB: www.cleanrite-buildrite.com
SIC: 7217 Carpet & upholstery cleaning
PA: Cleanrite, Inc.
   2684 Highway 32 Ste 100
   Chico CA 95973
   530 891-0333

(P-11660)
COIT SERVICES INC
865 Hinckley Rd, Burlingame (94010-1502)
PHONE..................................650 697-6190
Jesse Ramirez, *Project Mgr*
Hank Shubin, *Project Mgr*
Jackie Hajati, *Business Mgr*
Steve Singerman, *Business Mgr*
Carol Towner, *Business Mgr*
EMP: 63
SALES (corp-wide): 22.6MM Privately Held
WEB: www.coit.com
SIC: 7217 7216 7221 7699 Upholstery cleaning on customer premises; curtain cleaning & repair; photographic studios, portrait; sewing machine repair shop; upholstery materials; packaging & labeling services
PA: Coit Services, Inc.
   897 Hinckley Rd
   Burlingame CA 94010
   650 697-5471

(P-11661)
COIT SERVICES INC
3499 Business Dr, Sacramento (95820-2160)
PHONE..................................916 731-7006
Obert L Kearn, *President*
EMP: 63
SALES (corp-wide): 22.6MM Privately Held
WEB: www.coit.com
SIC: 7217 7216 Upholstery cleaning on customer premises; curtain cleaning & repair
PA: Coit Services, Inc.
   897 Hinckley Rd
   Burlingame CA 94010
   650 697-5471

(P-11662)
WHITE MGIC CLG RESTORATION INC
1024 Shary Ct, Concord (94518-2409)
PHONE..................................925 935-4449
Daniel Hayward, *CEO*
Paul Hayward, *COO*
EMP: 46 EST: 1973
SQ FT: 19,000
SALES (est): 2.8MM Privately Held
WEB: www.white-magic.com
SIC: 7217 7349 1799 Carpet & upholstery cleaning on customer premises; janitorial service, contract basis; post-disaster renovations

7218 Industrial Launderers

(P-11663)
CINTAS CORPORATION NO 3
220 Demeter St, East Palo Alto (94303-1303)
PHONE..................................650 589-4300
EMP: 35
SALES (corp-wide): 7.1B Publicly Held
WEB: www.cintas.com
SIC: 7218 Industrial uniform supply
HQ: Cintas Corporation No. 3
   6800 Cintas Blvd
   Mason OH 45040

(P-11664)
MISSION LINEN SUPPLY
Also Called: Mission Linen & Uniform Svc
7524 Reese Rd, Sacramento (95828-3707)
PHONE..................................916 423-3135
Ed Morrow, *Manager*
EMP: 74
SALES (corp-wide): 161.2MM Privately Held
WEB: www.missionlinen.com
SIC: 7218 7213 Industrial launderers; uniform supply
PA: Mission Linen Supply
   717 E Yanonali St
   Santa Barbara CA 93103
   805 730-3620

(P-11665)
NU WEST TEXTILE GROUP LLC
1910 Mark Ct 100, Concord (94520-8529)
P.O. Box 6206 (94524-1206)
PHONE..................................925 676-1414
Kathy Gonzalez, *Controller*
Kristina Long, *Marketing Staff*
Gary Gonzalez, *Director*
Ryan Gonzalez, *Director*
Tim Stites, *Manager*
EMP: 38 EST: 2000
SQ FT: 12,500
SALES (est): 4.8MM Privately Held
WEB: www.nuwestlinens.com
SIC: 7218 7213 Industrial launderers; linen supply, clothing

(P-11666)
PRUDENTIAL OVERALL SUPPLY
1429 N Milpitas Blvd, Milpitas (95035-3197)
PHONE..................................408 263-3464
Jerry Brigham, *Manager*
Tom Orr, *Opers Staff*
John Uribe, *Production*
Laurie Lecair, *Manager*
Donna Aguilar, *Supervisor*
EMP: 131
SALES (corp-wide): 158.2MM Privately Held
WEB: www.prudentialuniforms.com
SIC: 5699 7218 7213 Uniforms; industrial launderers; uniform supply
PA: Prudential Overall Supply
   1661 Alton Pkwy
   Irvine CA 92606
   949 250-4855

(P-11667)
PRUDENTIAL OVERALL SUPPLY
Also Called: Prudential Cleanroom Services
1437 N Milpitas Blvd, Milpitas (95035-3154)
PHONE..................................408 719-0886
Tim Bleigh, *Manager*
Kelli Cather, *Office Mgr*
Chelsi Craig, *Office Mgr*
Sandra Quezada, *Office Mgr*
Michelle Singleterry, *Admin Sec*
EMP: 39
SQ FT: 30,201
SALES (corp-wide): 158.2MM Privately Held
WEB: www.prudentialuniforms.com
SIC: 7218 Wiping towel supply
PA: Prudential Overall Supply
   1661 Alton Pkwy
   Irvine CA 92606
   949 250-4855

7218 - Industrial Launderers County (P-11668)
PRODUCTS & SERVICES SECTION

(P-11668)
PRUDENTIAL OVERALL SUPPLY
1260 E North Ave, Fresno (93725-1930)
PHONE 559 264-8231
Rick Ponce, *Branch Mgr*
Nicole Palmer, *Regional Mgr*
Zach Guilds, *General Mgr*
Mark Willis, *General Mgr*
Carlos Paniagua, *Office Mgr*
EMP: 39
SQ FT: 42,704
SALES (corp-wide): 158.2MM **Privately Held**
WEB: www.prudentialuniforms.com
SIC: 7218 7213 Industrial launderers; linen supply
PA: Prudential Overall Supply
    1661 Alton Pkwy
    Irvine CA 92606
    949 250-4855

(P-11669)
PRUDENTIAL OVERALL SUPPLY
545 Jefferson Blvd Ste 5, West Sacramento (95605-2374)
PHONE 916 372-7466
Ron Pharres, *Manager*
Ron Leal, *Sales Staff*
Chris Miller, *Sales Staff*
EMP: 39
SALES (corp-wide): 158.2MM **Privately Held**
WEB: www.prudentialuniforms.com
SIC: 7218 Industrial launderers
PA: Prudential Overall Supply
    1661 Alton Pkwy
    Irvine CA 92606
    949 250-4855

(P-11670)
SPECIALIZED LAUNDRY SVCS INC
Also Called: 1st Class Laundry Services
33485 Western Ave, Union City (94587-3201)
PHONE 510 487-8297
Jefferey Lee Schlagel, *CEO*
Jeylobb Schlagel, *Manager*
EMP: 165 EST: 2006
SQ FT: 24,000
SALES (est): 7.3MM **Privately Held**
WEB: www.1stclasslaundry.net
SIC: 7218 Industrial launderers

7219 Laundry & Garment Svcs, NEC

(P-11671)
PENINOU FRENCH LDRY & CLRS INC (PA)
101 S Maple Ave, South San Francisco (94080-6303)
PHONE 800 392-2532
Todd Edwards, *CEO*
EMP: 90 EST: 1903
SQ FT: 25,000
SALES (est): 5.3MM **Privately Held**
WEB: www.peninou.com
SIC: 7219 7216 French hand laundry; drycleaning collecting & distributing agency

7221 Photographic Studios, Portrait

(P-11672)
BAY PHOTO INC
2959 Park Ave Ste A, Soquel (95073-2863)
PHONE 831 475-6090
Larry Abitbol, *Principal*
EMP: 137
SALES (corp-wide): 215.4MM **Privately Held**
WEB: www.bayphoto.com
SIC: 7221 Photographer, still or video
HQ: Bay Photo, Inc.
    920 Disc Dr
    Scotts Valley CA
    831 475-6686

(P-11673)
HAYWARD AREA RECREATION & PARK
Also Called: PHOTO CENTRAL GALLERY DARK ROO
1099 E St, Hayward (94541-5210)
PHONE 510 881-6721
Geri Jordahl, *Director*
Mike Koslosky, *Principal*
Thomas Vigil, *Maintence Staff*
Barbara Alcantar, *Instructor*
Ryan Howard, *Director*
EMP: 41 EST: 2001
SALES (est): 1.4MM **Privately Held**
WEB: www.truenortheditions.com
SIC: 7221 Photographer, still or video

(P-11674)
IYP INC
Also Called: Imagine Your Photos
46595 Landing Pkwy, Fremont (94538-6421)
PHONE 305 593-1211
James Peng, *CEO*
Michael A Rosenberg, *President*
EMP: 50 EST: 2004
SALES (est): 2.4MM **Privately Held**
WEB: www.iypstore.com
SIC: 7221 Photographer, still or video

7231 Beauty Shops

(P-11675)
BEAUTY BAZAR INC
Also Called: La Belle Days Spas and Salons
36 Stanford Shopping Ctr, Palo Alto (94304-1423)
PHONE 650 326-8522
Vella Schner, *Owner*
EMP: 90
SALES (corp-wide): 4MM **Privately Held**
SIC: 7231 5999 Cosmetology & personal hygiene salons; toiletries, cosmetics & perfumes
PA: Beauty Bazar, Inc.
    36 Stanford Shopping Ctr
    Palo Alto CA 94304
    415 699-3575

(P-11676)
BUENA VISTA BUSINESS SVCS LP
Also Called: Great Clips
1276 Lincoln Ave Ste 107, San Jose (95125-3008)
PHONE 908 452-9002
Ray Solnik, *General Ptnr*
EMP: 71 EST: 2008
SALES (est): 1.4MM **Privately Held**
WEB: www.bvbs.us
SIC: 7231 Unisex hair salons

(P-11677)
CHANGING FUTURE OUTCOME
372 Hanover St A41, San Francisco (94112-4305)
PHONE 415 901-7000
Stuart Finger, *Vice Pres*
Dieundonne Kamga, *Manager*
EMP: 50 EST: 2015
SALES (est): 122.9K **Privately Held**
SIC: 7231 Beauty shops

(P-11678)
CINTA SALON INC
23 Grant Ave Fl 2, San Francisco (94108-5844)
PHONE 415 989-1000
Jacinta M Gibbons, *President*
Mariela Bermudez, *Sales Executive*
EMP: 46 EST: 2007
SALES (est): 3.5MM **Privately Held**
WEB: www.cinta.com
SIC: 7231 7371 Cosmetology & personal hygiene salons; computer software development & applications

(P-11679)
CLASS ACT HAIR & NAIL SALON
2795 Bechelli Ln, Redding (96002-1924)
PHONE 530 223-3442
EMP: 69
SALES (est): 598.4K **Privately Held**
SIC: 7231 Beauty Shop

(P-11680)
DYBECK INC (PA)
Also Called: Supercuts
7094 N Cedar Ave, Fresno (93720-3300)
PHONE 559 299-7696
James Dyer, *President*
Becky Dyer, *Vice Pres*
EMP: 37 EST: 1980
SALES (est): 1.2MM **Privately Held**
WEB: www.supercuts.com
SIC: 7231 Hairdressers

(P-11681)
GF CARNEROS TENANT LLC
Also Called: Carneros Resort and Spa
4048 Sonoma Hwy, NAPA (94559-9745)
PHONE 707 299-4900
Monda Rigdon,
Frederick Fennikoh, *General Mgr*
Leigh Sharkey, *Sales Mgr*
Anne Elcon, *Marketing Staff*
Jeffrey Peterson, *Marketing Staff*
EMP: 50 EST: 2016
SALES (est): 5MM **Privately Held**
WEB: www.carnerosresort.com
SIC: 7231 Cosmetology & personal hygiene salons

(P-11682)
GINO MORENA ENTERPRISES LLC (PA)
Also Called: Onyx
111 Starlite St, South San Francisco (94080-6398)
PHONE 800 227-6905
Meryl Morena, *Mng Member*
Molly Duke, *General Mgr*
Adrianna Morena,
Rex Morena, *Mng Member*
Belinda Gonzalez, *Manager*
EMP: 35 EST: 1943
SALES (est): 66.6MM **Privately Held**
WEB: www.ginomorena.com
SIC: 7231 Hairdressers

(P-11683)
GROVES/EDEN CORPORATION (PA)
Also Called: Supercuts
534 S Del Puerto Ave, Patterson (95363-9306)
PHONE 209 894-2481
Ronald Groves, *President*
EMP: 134 EST: 1987
SALES (est): 2.4MM **Privately Held**
WEB: www.supercuts.com
SIC: 7231 Unisex hair salons

(P-11684)
H2O PLUS LLC
727 Sansome St Fl 2, San Francisco (94111-1734)
PHONE 415 964-5100
John Melk, *Branch Mgr*
EMP: 40 **Privately Held**
WEB: www.h2oplus.com
SIC: 7231 Beauty shops
PA: H2o Plus, Llc
    111 Sutter St Fl 22
    San Francisco CA 94104

(P-11685)
HEADWAY TECHNOLOGIES INC
39639 Leslie St Apt 135, Fremont (94538-2245)
PHONE 425 503-2131
Hemlata Bhandari, *Branch Mgr*
EMP: 705 **Privately Held**
WEB: www.headway.com
SIC: 7231 Beauty shops
HQ: Headway Technologies, Inc.
    682 S Hillview Dr
    Milpitas CA 95035
    408 934-5300

(P-11686)
J M D ENTERPRISES (PA)
Also Called: Supercuts
1434 N Main St, Walnut Creek (94596-4651)
PHONE 925 935-4780
Dianne Chavannes, *President*
EMP: 99 EST: 1989
SQ FT: 1,200
SALES (est): 1.4MM **Privately Held**
WEB: www.supercuts.com
SIC: 7231 Unisex hair salons

(P-11687)
JOSEPH COZZA SALON INC (PA)
77 Maiden Ln Fl 2, San Francisco (94108-5417)
PHONE 415 433-3030
Joseph Bisazza, *President*
Joseph Cozza, *Corp Secy*
James Bondoc, *Manager*
▲ EMP: 45 EST: 1995
SALES (est): 2.3MM **Privately Held**
WEB: www.blakecharlessalons.com
SIC: 7231 Hairdressers

(P-11688)
JUUT MIDWEST INC
Also Called: Juut Salonspa
240 University Ave, Palo Alto (94301-1711)
PHONE 650 328-4067
David Wagner, *Owner*
Michelle Cabalic, *Asst Mgr*
EMP: 46
SALES (corp-wide): 24.3MM **Privately Held**
WEB: www.juut.com
SIC: 7231 Hairdressers
HQ: Juut Midwest, Inc.
    310 Groveland Ave
    Minneapolis MN 55403

(P-11689)
MACYS INC
22 4th St Fl 7, San Francisco (94103-3141)
PHONE 415 951-5700
EMP: 51
SALES (corp-wide): 24.8B **Publicly Held**
SIC: 5311 5621 7231 Department Store Ret Women's Clothing Beauty Shop
PA: Macy's, Inc.
    7 W 7th St
    Cincinnati OH 10001
    513 579-7000

(P-11690)
MARIN BEAUTY COMPANY (PA)
Also Called: Marin Buty Cmpny-Beauty Sups S
417 3rd St, San Rafael (94901-3548)
PHONE 415 454-4500
Sheri Dunne, *President*
EMP: 35 EST: 1988
SQ FT: 2,000
SALES (est): 4.7MM **Privately Held**
WEB: www.marinbeautycompany.com
SIC: 5999 7231 Hair care products; unisex hair salons

(P-11691)
PENNEY OPCO LLC
Also Called: JC Penney
1695 Arden Way, Sacramento (95815-4004)
PHONE 916 564-0315
Wayne Schlaefli, *Manager*
EMP: 80
SQ FT: 200,000
SALES (corp-wide): 1.9B **Privately Held**
SIC: 5311 7231 Department stores, non-discount; beauty shops
HQ: Penney Opco Llc
    6501 Legacy Dr
    Plano TX 75024
    972 431-4746

(P-11692)
PENNEY OPCO LLC
Also Called: JC Penney
4915 Claremont Ave, Stockton (95207-5707)
PHONE 209 951-1110
Ralph Carino, *Manager*
EMP: 80
SALES (corp-wide): 1.9B **Privately Held**
SIC: 5311 7231 7221 5995 Department stores, non-discount; beauty shops; photographic studios, portrait; optical goods stores
HQ: Penney Opco Llc
    6501 Legacy Dr
    Plano TX 75024
    972 431-4746

▲ = Import ▼ = Export
◆ = Import/Export

PRODUCTS & SERVICES SECTION

7299 - Miscellaneous Personal Svcs, NEC County (P-11714)

(P-11693)
PENNEY OPCO LLC
Also Called: JC Penney
1932 E 20th St, Chico (95928-6342)
PHONE.................530 899-8160
Dave Oliver, *Manager*
EMP: 80
SALES (corp-wide): 1.9B **Privately Held**
SIC: 5311 7231 5961 Department stores, non-discount; beauty shops; catalog & mail-order houses
HQ: Penney Opco Llc
  6501 Legacy Dr
  Plano TX 75024
  972 431-4746

(P-11694)
PMCA BAKERSFIELD LLC
Also Called: Paul Mitchell School Fresno
5091 N Fresno St Ste 104, Fresno (93710-7617)
PHONE.................559 224-2700
Erik Pedersen,
D'Ann Evans,
EMP: 35 **EST:** 2007
SALES (est): 1MM **Privately Held**
SIC: 7231 Cosmetology school

(P-11695)
SUPERBROWARD LLC
Also Called: Supercuts
1222 Broadway, Burlingame (94010-3424)
PHONE.................650 348-4881
Rachel Hara, *Manager*
EMP: 103
SALES (corp-wide): 2MM **Privately Held**
WEB: www.supercuts.com
SIC: 7231 Unisex hair salons
PA: Superbroward Llc
  9000 Main Ave Ste B4
  Bakersfield CA 93309
  661 664-8790

(P-11696)
TODD DIPIETRO SALON (PA)
520 Washington St, San Francisco (94111-2904)
PHONE.................415 397-0177
Kim R Todd, *Owner*
Andrew Todd, *Partner*
Jason White-Chagnon, *Instructor*
Debi Alley, *Director*
Jocelyn Abarca, *Manager*
EMP: 40 **EST:** 1988
SQ FT: 6,000
SALES (est): 6.4MM **Privately Held**
WEB: www.dipietrotodd.com
SIC: 7231 Hairdressers

(P-11697)
YOSH FOR HAIR (PA)
Also Called: Yosh For Hair Gina Khan
173 Maiden Ln, San Francisco (94108-5301)
PHONE.................415 989-7704
Georgina Khan, *Owner*
EMP: 36 **EST:** 1970
SQ FT: 3,500
SALES (est): 1MM **Privately Held**
WEB: www.salonninesf.com
SIC: 7231 Hairdressers

7241 Barber Shops

(P-11698)
GINO MORENA ENTERPRISES LLC
Also Called: Barber Beale
Bldg 2434, Marysville (95903)
PHONE.................530 788-0053
Marilia Asaco, *Branch Mgr*
EMP: 294
SALES (corp-wide): 66.6MM **Privately Held**
WEB: www.ginomorena.com
SIC: 7241 7231 Barber shops; beauty shops
PA: Gino Morena Enterprises, Llc
  111 Starlite St
  South San Francisco CA 94080
  800 227-6905

7261 Funeral Svcs & Crematories

(P-11699)
DUGGANS SERRA MORTUARY
500 Westlake Ave, Daly City (94014-1927)
PHONE.................650 756-4500
Daniel Duggan, *President*
Teresa Proano, *President*
Maureen Duggan, *Treasurer*
William Duggan, *Vice Pres*
Joey Duggan, *Director*
EMP: 53 **EST:** 1961
SQ FT: 5,500
SALES (est): 10.3MM **Privately Held**
WEB: www.duggans-serra.com
SIC: 7261 Funeral home

(P-11700)
SACRAMENTO MEMORIAL LAWN
Also Called: Sacramnto Grdn Chapel Mortuary
6100 Stockton Blvd, Sacramento (95824-4011)
PHONE.................916 421-1171
David Anderson, *President*
Patrick J Brown, *Shareholder*
Buck Kamphausen, *Shareholder*
William Brodovsky, *Corp Secy*
EMP: 36 **EST:** 1921
SQ FT: 6,000
SALES (est): 10.4MM **Privately Held**
WEB: www.smlfh.com
SIC: 7261 Funeral home; crematory

7291 Tax Return Preparation Svcs

(P-11701)
ANDERSEN TAX LLC
2121 S El Camino Real # 1100, San Mateo (94403-1855)
PHONE.................650 289-5700
Estrella Salguero, *Marketing Staff*
Christie Cornejo, *Associate*
Bobby Ramirez, *Associate*
EMP: 53
SALES (corp-wide): 83.3MM **Privately Held**
WEB: www.andersen.com
SIC: 7291 Tax return preparation services
PA: Andersen Tax Llc
  333 Bush St Ste 1700
  San Francisco CA 94104
  415 764-2700

(P-11702)
M E PRIGMORE & CO (PA)
Also Called: H & R Block
22922 Huston Ave, Twain Harte (95383-9641)
PHONE.................530 223-6672
M E Prigmore, *President*
EMP: 36 **EST:** 1990
SQ FT: 2,000
SALES (est): 1.5MM **Privately Held**
WEB: www.hrblock.ca
SIC: 7291 Tax return preparation services

(P-11703)
TAXRESOURCES INC (PA)
Also Called: Taxaudit.com
600 Coolidge Dr Ste 300, Folsom (95630-4211)
PHONE.................877 369-7827
Mark D Olander, *CEO*
Kurt Lee, *CFO*
Dave E Du Val, *Vice Pres*
Nancy K Farwell, *Vice Pres*
Jane T Smith, *Vice Pres*
EMP: 120 **EST:** 1988
SQ FT: 3,000
SALES (est): 13.9MM **Privately Held**
WEB: www.taxaudit.com
SIC: 7291 Tax return preparation services

7299 Miscellaneous Personal Svcs, NEC

(P-11704)
360 VIANSA LLC
Also Called: Viansa Winery & Italian Mkt Pl
25200 Arnold Dr, Sonoma (95476-9222)
PHONE.................707 935-4700
Samuel J Sebastiani Sr,
Victoria Sebastiani,
Victoria Campbell, *Director*
▲ **EMP:** 27 **EST:** 1986
SQ FT: 1,500
SALES (est): 3.6MM **Privately Held**
WEB: www.viansa.com
SIC: 5921 5499 5947 7299 Wine; gourmet food stores; gift shop; wedding chapel, privately operated; wines

(P-11705)
AMERICAN CONSERVATORY THEATER (PA)
30 Grant Ave Fl 7, San Francisco (94108-5880)
PHONE.................415 749-2228
Heather Kitchen, *Exec Dir*
Hillary Bray, *Vice Pres*
Peter Davey, *Treasurer*
Peter Pastreich, *Trustee*
Coralyn Bond, *Executive Asst*
EMP: 121 **EST:** 1966
SALES (est): 25MM **Privately Held**
WEB: www.act-sf.org
SIC: 5999 8299 7299 6512 Theater programs; dramatic school; costume rental; theater building, ownership & operation

(P-11706)
BABYCENTER LLC (DH)
163 Freelon St, San Francisco (94107-1624)
PHONE.................415 537-0900
Mary Baker,
Stephanie Galli, *Regional Mgr*
Brian Coan, *Software Dev*
Erin Stuart, *Software Dev*
Olivia Ng, *Production*
EMP: 69 **EST:** 2001
SALES (est): 25.5MM
SALES (corp-wide): 82.5B **Publicly Held**
WEB: www.babycenter.com
SIC: 7299 5999 Information services, consumer; infant furnishings & equipment
HQ: Johnson & Johnson Consumer Inc.
  199 Grandview Rd
  Skillman NJ 08558
  908 874-1000

(P-11707)
BELCAMPO GROUP INC
Also Called: Belcampo Meat
329 N Phillipe Ln, Yreka (96097-9413)
PHONE.................530 842-5200
Anya Sernald, *President*
EMP: 70
SALES (corp-wide): 21.9MM **Privately Held**
WEB: www.belcampo.com
SIC: 7299 5421 Butcher service, processing only; meat markets, including freezer provisioners
PA: Belcampo Group, Inc.
  65 Webster St
  Oakland CA 94607
  510 250-7810

(P-11708)
BUCKINGHAM PROPERTY MANAGEMENT
Also Called: Coventry Cove Apartments
12609 Moffatt Ln, Fresno (93730-9704)
PHONE.................559 322-1105
Cher Cha, *Principal*
Nora Barrera, *Area Mgr*
Katie Miller, *Manager*
EMP: 70
SALES (corp-wide): 25.2MM **Privately Held**
WEB: www.buckinghampm.com
SIC: 7299 Apartment locating service
PA: Buckingham Property Management Inc
  601 Pollasky Ave Ste 201
  Clovis CA 93612
  559 452-8250

(P-11709)
CALIFORNIA SUN INC
8265 Sierra College Blvd, Roseville (95661-9403)
PHONE.................916 789-1034
Michael Blore, *Branch Mgr*
EMP: 80 **Privately Held**
WEB: www.californiasun.com
SIC: 7299 Tanning salon
PA: California Sun, Inc.
  2630 Sierra Meadows Dr
  Rocklin CA 95677

(P-11710)
CAPS OAK STREET BAR AND GRILL
144 Oak St, Brentwood (94513-1335)
PHONE.................925 634-1025
Vasilios Karadais, *President*
Steve Capozzo, *President*
EMP: 41 **EST:** 1995
SQ FT: 4,400
SALES (est): 610.3K **Privately Held**
WEB: www.capsrestaurant.com
SIC: 5812 7299 Grills (eating places); banquet hall facilities

(P-11711)
CATTLEMENS
Also Called: Cattleman's Restaurant
2000 Taylor Rd, Roseville (95678-1901)
PHONE.................916 782-5587
Anne Rae, *General Mgr*
John Frenzel, *Officer*
Mindy Johnson, *Human Res Dir*
Paula Krey-Baker, *Human Resources*
David Russell, *Opers Mgr*
EMP: 95
SALES (corp-wide): 46.3MM **Privately Held**
WEB: www.cattlemens.com
SIC: 5812 7299 5813 Steak restaurant; banquet hall facilities; cocktail lounge
PA: Cattlemens
  250 Dutton Ave
  Santa Rosa CA 95407
  707 528-1040

(P-11712)
CINTAS CORPORATION NO 3
777 139th Ave, San Leandro (94578-3218)
PHONE.................510 352-6330
Brian Delbecq, *General Mgr*
Jeffrey Foht, *Sales Staff*
EMP: 35
SQ FT: 25,000
SALES (corp-wide): 7.1B **Publicly Held**
WEB: www.cintas.com
SIC: 7299 2326 Clothing rental services; men's & boys' work clothing
HQ: Cintas Corporation No. 3
  6800 Cintas Blvd
  Mason OH 45040

(P-11713)
CONSUMER CR CNSLING SVC SAN FR (PA)
Also Called: Balance
1655 Grant St Ste 1300, Concord (94520-2789)
PHONE.................888 456-2227
Rico Delgadillo, *CEO*
EMP: 60 **EST:** 1969
SQ FT: 14,000
SALES (est): 8.8MM **Privately Held**
WEB: www.balancepro.org
SIC: 7299 Debt counseling or adjustment service, individuals

(P-11714)
DARATEL LTD (PA)
Also Called: Fuddruckers
1975 Diamond Blvd E260, Concord (94520-5792)
PHONE.................925 825-1443
George Almeida, *Owner*
Rebecca Almeida, *Owner*
Maripaz Morando, *Opers Staff*
EMP: 40 **EST:** 1991
SQ FT: 11,000

7299 - Miscellaneous Personal Svcs, NEC County (P-11715)

SALES (est): 3.2MM **Privately Held**
WEB: www.fuddruckers.com
SIC: 5812 5813 7299 Restaurant, family: chain; cocktail lounge; banquet hall facilities

(P-11715)
EJS PIZZA CO
Also Called: Round Table Pizza
9500 Greenback Ln Ste 1, Folsom (95630-2091)
PHONE 916 989-1133
Kevin Reduk, *Manager*
EMP: 59 **Privately Held**
WEB: www.roundtablepizza.com
SIC: 5812 7299 Pizzeria, chain; banquet hall facilities
PA: Ej's Pizza Co.
8755 Sierra College Blvd B
Roseville CA 95661

(P-11716)
EL CHARRO MEXICAN DINING
16 Saint Louis Ln, Pleasant Hill (94523-1139)
PHONE 925 283-2345
Dave Shields, *Owner*
EMP: 36 **EST:** 1947
SALES (est): 1.2MM **Privately Held**
WEB: www.elcharrolafayette.com
SIC: 5812 7299 Mexican restaurant; banquet hall facilities

(P-11717)
EVENTS MANAGEMENT INC
Also Called: McCalls Catering
1798 Bryant St, San Francisco (94110-1406)
PHONE 415 487-9114
Stephen Denison, *President*
Arnie Ertola, *Managing Prtnr*
Ruedi Schneider, *Shareholder*
Dan McCall, *CEO*
Lee Gregory, *Exec VP*
EMP: 300 **EST:** 1984
SALES (est): 25.4MM **Privately Held**
WEB: www.mccallssf.com
SIC: 5812 5813 7299 Caterers; bar (drinking places); party planning service

(P-11718)
EVEREST WTRPRFING RSTRTION INC
1270 Missouri St, San Francisco (94107-3310)
PHONE 415 282-9800
Keith Goldstein, *President*
Mark Murray, *Vice Pres*
Andrina Howell, *Administration*
Arleen Campos, *Opers-Prdtn-Mfg*
Seth Acharya, *Sales Staff*
EMP: 64 **EST:** 1999
SQ FT: 5,000
SALES (est): 5.4MM **Privately Held**
WEB: www.everestsf.com
SIC: 7299 Home improvement & renovation contractor agency

(P-11719)
FREEDOM FINANCIAL NETWORK LLC (PA)
Also Called: Freedom Debt Relief
1875 S Grant St Ste 400, San Mateo (94402-2676)
PHONE 650 393-6619
Bradford Stroh,
Ralph L Leung, *CFO*
Rich Ransom, *CFO*
Megan Hanley, *Chief Mktg Ofcr*
Jon Pedley, *Exec VP*
EMP: 560 **EST:** 2002
SQ FT: 20,000
SALES (est): 72.3MM **Privately Held**
WEB: www.freedomfinancialnetwork.com
SIC: 7299 Debt counseling or adjustment service, individuals

(P-11720)
IBERIA CATERING INC
Also Called: Patio Espanol Restaurant
139 20th Ave, San Francisco (94121-1307)
PHONE 415 587-5117
EMP: 35

SALES (est): 1.1MM **Privately Held**
WEB: www.iberiacatering.com
SIC: 5812 7299 Eating Place Misc Personal Services

(P-11721)
IMPACT DESTINATIONS & EVENTS
Also Called: Impact Events
26338 Esperanza Dr, Los Altos Hills (94022-2653)
PHONE 415 766-4170
Dan Houdek, *President*
Alexis Van Meeteren, *Manager*
EMP: 50 **EST:** 2011
SALES (est): 736.3K **Privately Held**
WEB: www.impacteventsdmc.com
SIC: 7299 Party planning service

(P-11722)
JASPER HALL LLC
Also Called: August Hall & Fifth Arrow
420 Mason St, San Francisco (94102-1706)
PHONE 415 872-5745
Nathan Valentine, *Manager*
Chad Donnelly, *Manager*
Scott Murphy, *Manager*
EMP: 75 **EST:** 2018
SALES (est): 762.8K **Privately Held**
SIC: 7299 Banquet hall facilities

(P-11723)
JN PROJECTS INC
Also Called: Hellosign
333 Brannan St, San Francisco (94107-1810)
PHONE 415 766-0273
Joseph H Walla, *CEO*
MAI Ton, *Vice Pres*
Jack Dauer, *Executive*
Mike Petrosyan, *Executive*
John Spaetzel, *Sr Software Eng*
EMP: 100 **EST:** 2010
SALES (est): 12.4MM **Publicly Held**
WEB: www.hellosign.com
SIC: 7299 Personal document & information services
PA: Dropbox, Inc.
1800 Owens St Ste 200
San Francisco CA 94158

(P-11724)
LARK CREEK INN PRTNERS L P A C
234 Magnolia Ave, Larkspur (94939-2099)
PHONE 415 924-7767
Michael D Dellar, *President*
Bradley M Ogden, *General Ptnr*
Michael Dellar, *CIO*
EMP: 42 **EST:** 1972
SQ FT: 3,000
SALES (est): 1.1MM **Privately Held**
WEB: www.tavernatlarkcreek.com
SIC: 5812 5813 7299 Restaurant, family: independent; bar (drinking places); banquet hall facilities

(P-11725)
MICHAAEL S HENSLEY
Also Called: Hensly Event Resources
180 W Hill Pl, Brisbane (94005-1216)
PHONE 650 692-7007
Michael Hensley, *President*
Javier Guardado, *Opers Staff*
Agustin Hernandez, *Manager*
Arnie Kelber, *Accounts Mgr*
Joe Dempsey, *Consultant*
EMP: 120 **EST:** 1992
SALES (est): 5.4MM **Privately Held**
WEB: www.hensleyeventresources.com
SIC: 7299 5947 Party planning service; party favors

(P-11726)
PALO ALTO HLLS GOLF CNTRY CLB
3000 Alexis Dr, Palo Alto (94304-1303)
PHONE 650 948-1800
Padmanabhan Srinagesh, *CEO*
Josh Rumsey, *General Mgr*
Ani Markarian, *Admin Sec*
Marian Paragas, *Controller*
Chloe Callahan, *Merchandising*

EMP: 75 **EST:** 1958
SQ FT: 25,000
SALES (est): 10.3MM **Privately Held**
WEB: www.pahgcc.com
SIC: 7299 7997 Banquet hall facilities; golf club, membership

(P-11727)
PRAETORIAN USA
Also Called: Praetorian Event Services
228 Windsor River Rd, Windsor (95492-9206)
PHONE 707 780-3018
Kathy J Kingman, *President*
EMP: 35 **EST:** 2008
SALES (est): 2.9MM **Privately Held**
WEB: www.praetorianusa.com
SIC: 7299 7389 Party planning service;

(P-11728)
PTS PROVIDERS INC
3130 Crow Canyon Pl # 210, San Ramon (94583-1346)
PHONE 925 553-3763
Michael Zumbo, *President*
Jeff Stevenson, *Vice Pres*
EMP: 38 **EST:** 2018
SALES (est): 1.4MM **Privately Held**
WEB: www.ptsproviders.com
SIC: 7299 Miscellaneous personal service

(P-11729)
RISTORANTI PIEMONTESI INC
Also Called: Palio D'Asti
640 Sacramento St, San Francisco (94111-2510)
PHONE 415 395-9800
Dan Scherotter, *President*
EMP: 55 **EST:** 1988
SQ FT: 6,500
SALES (est): 4.9MM **Privately Held**
WEB: www.paliosf.com
SIC: 5812 7299 Italian restaurant; banquet hall facilities

(P-11730)
SOIREE VALET PARKING SERVICE
1470 Howard St, San Francisco (94103-2523)
PHONE 415 284-9700
Jamie Dyos, *President*
Katie Dyos, *Business Dir*
Artem Shestopalov, *Production*
EMP: 76 **EST:** 1989
SQ FT: 3,000 **Privately Held**
WEB: www.soireevalet.com
SIC: 7299 7521 Valet parking; automobile parking

(P-11731)
TEN LIFESTYLE MGT USA INC (DH)
33 New Montgomery St # 10, San Francisco (94105-4506)
PHONE 415 625-1900
Alex Cheatle, *CEO*
Malcolm Berry, *President*
Andrew Long, *COO*
David Porter, *Managing Dir*
Kerry Anderson, *Corp Comm Staff*
EMP: 119 **EST:** 2012
SALES (est): 2MM
SALES (corp-wide): 59.6MM **Privately Held**
WEB: www.tenlifestylegroup.com
SIC: 7299 Apartment locating service

(P-11732)
THINK OUTSIDE BOX INC
Also Called: Randy Peters Catrg & Event Plg
105 Vernon St, Roseville (95678-2630)
PHONE 916 726-2339
Lisa Peters, *President*
Randy Peters, *Vice Pres*
Kendal Bond-Seidl, *Sales Staff*
EMP: 36 **EST:** 2007 **Privately Held**
SIC: 7299 5812 Banquet hall facilities; contract food services

(P-11733)
U P C INC
165 Channing Ave, Palo Alto (94301-2409)
PHONE 650 462-2010
Susan Nightingale, *President*
EMP: 102 **EST:** 1989

SALES (est): 7MM **Privately Held**
SIC: 7299 Massage parlor & steam bath services

(P-11734)
VICS TRADER RESTAURANTS INC
9 Anchor Dr, Emeryville (94608-1510)
PHONE 510 653-3400
Andrew Rubini, *Manager*
EMP: 53
SQ FT: 8,000
SALES (corp-wide): 7.1MM **Privately Held**
WEB: www.tradervicsemeryville.com
SIC: 5812 7299 Eating places; banquet hall facilities
PA: Trader Vic's Restaurants, Incorporated
978 Howe Rd
Martinez CA 94553
925 675-6400

(P-11735)
VISA INC
1 Market St Ste 600, San Francisco (94105-1307)
PHONE 415 805-4000
Charles W Scharf, *CEO*
Jeff Allison, *Vice Pres*
Jennifer Como, *Vice Pres*
Matthew Friend, *Vice Pres*
Kevin Jacques, *Vice Pres*
EMP: 36 **EST:** 2007
SALES (est): 9.9MM **Privately Held**
WEB: www.usa.visa.com
SIC: 7299 Visa procurement service

(P-11736)
WATERCOURSE WAY
Also Called: Water Course Way
165 Channing Ave, Palo Alto (94301-2409)
PHONE 650 462-2000
John Roberts, *Partner*
Watercourse Way, *Partner*
EMP: 120 **EST:** 1981
SALES (est): 5.1MM **Privately Held**
WEB: www.watercourseway.com
SIC: 7299 Massage parlor

7311 Advertising Agencies

(P-11737)
3Q DIGITAL INC (HQ)
155 Bovet Rd Ste 480, San Mateo (94402-3136)
PHONE 650 539-4124
David Rodnitzky, *CEO*
Maury Domengeaux, *President*
Julia Hu, *COO*
Steve Schlossareck, *COO*
Brian Bennett, *Chief Mktg Ofcr*
EMP: 109 **EST:** 2009
SALES (est): 24MM **Privately Held**
WEB: www.3qdigital.com
SIC: 7311 8742 Advertising consultant; marketing consulting services
PA: 3q Digital Holdings, Inc.
25 E Washington St # 509
Chicago IL 60602
650 539-4124

(P-11738)
AGI PUBLISHING INC (PA)
Also Called: Valley Yellow Pages
1850 N Gateway Blvd # 152, Fresno (93727-1600)
PHONE 559 251-8888
Sieg A Fischer, *CEO*
Michael Schilling, *Treasurer*
Dominic D'Innocenti, *Vice Pres*
Dominick Innocenti, *Vice Pres*
Janet Avers, *Executive*
EMP: 50 **EST:** 1985
SQ FT: 19,000
SALES (est): 43.9MM **Privately Held**
WEB: www.myyp.com
SIC: 7311 Advertising agencies

(P-11739)
AMOBEE INC (DH)
100 Redwood Shores Pkwy # 300, Redwood City (94065-1253)
PHONE 650 353-4399
Nick Brien, *CEO*

PRODUCTS & SERVICES SECTION

7311 - Advertising Agencies County (P-11761)

Domenic Venuto, *COO*
Craig Foster, *CFO*
Steve Hoffman, *CFO*
Mark Liao, *CFO*
EMP: 309 **EST:** 2005
SALES (est): 341.7MM **Privately Held**
WEB: www.amobee.com
SIC: 7311 Advertising agencies

(P-11740)
BARRETT SF
250 Sutter St Ste 200, San Francisco (94108-4451)
PHONE.................................415 986-2960
Abby John, *CEO*
Jillian Davis, *Partner*
Conor Duignan, *Partner*
Michael Reardon, *Accounting Mgr*
Nash Rachel, *Finance*
EMP: 50 **EST:** 2015
SALES (est): 5.6MM **Privately Held**
WEB: www.barrettsf.com
SIC: 7311 Advertising consultant

(P-11741)
BRANDVIA ALLIANCE INC (PA)
2159 Bering Dr, San Jose (95131-2014)
PHONE.................................408 955-0500
James Childers, *President*
Diane Garretson, *Partner*
Falle Hutton, *Partner*
Cindy Kahl, *Partner*
Don Williams, *Partner*
◆ **EMP:** 174 **EST:** 2003
SQ FT: 21,000
SALES (est): 35MM **Privately Held**
WEB: www.brandvia.com
SIC: 7311 Advertising agencies

(P-11742)
BRITE MEDIA LLC (PA)
Also Called: Britevision Media
350 Frank Ogawa Plz Ste 3, Oakland (94612)
PHONE.................................877 479-7777
Andrew Brown, *Mng Member*
Andrew Knopf, *Exec VP*
Bruce Friedman,
Jeffrey Robinson, *Manager*
EMP: 182 **EST:** 2014
SALES (est): 25.4MM **Privately Held**
WEB: www.britevision.com
SIC: 7311 Advertising consultant

(P-11743)
BUTLER SHINE STERN PRTNERS LLC
Also Called: Bssp
20 Liberty Ship Way, Sausalito (94965-3312)
PHONE.................................415 331-6049
Greg Stern,
Dennis Moore, *CFO*
Chris Cummings, *Officer*
Matthew Curry, *Officer*
Stella Lin, *Vice Pres*
EMP: 139 **EST:** 2003
SALES (est): 39.7MM **Privately Held**
WEB: www.bssp.com
SIC: 7311 Advertising consultant

(P-11744)
CHRISTENSEN ADVERTISING
Also Called: Chrisad
11 Professional Ctr Pkwy, San Rafael (94903-2702)
PHONE.................................415 924-8575
John R Christensen, *General Ptnr*
Ann Christensen, *Partner*
Adria Green, *Executive*
Duprel Nave-Kilpatrick, *Administration*
Christopher Guidry, *Info Tech Mgr*
EMP: 35 **EST:** 1980
SQ FT: 4,000
SALES (est): 6MM **Privately Held**
WEB: www.chrisad.com
SIC: 7311 Advertising consultant

(P-11745)
CIASOM LLC (PA)
Also Called: Mosaic
1040 Richard Ave, Santa Clara (95050-2816)
PHONE.................................408 560-2990
Jason Azevedo,
Jim Brasil, *Engineer*

Keven Azevedo,
Steve Hermosillo,
EMP: 45 **EST:** 2011
SQ FT: 68,000
SALES (est): 11.4MM **Privately Held**
WEB: www.mosaic-sf.com
SIC: 7311 Advertising agencies

(P-11746)
CLEVER GIRLS COLLECTIVE INC
2415 San Rmon Vly Blvd St, San Ramon (94583-5381)
PHONE.................................408 676-6428
Cat Lincoln, *CEO*
Sheila Tabuena, *Engineer*
Monica Padilla, *Sales Associate*
Kristina Hollis, *Sales Staff*
Robin Johnson, *Program Dir*
EMP: 36 **EST:** 2009
SALES (est): 5.6MM **Privately Held**
WEB: www.realclever.com
SIC: 7311 Advertising agencies

(P-11747)
COMPASS MARKETING INC
3447 Mt Diablo Blvd, Lafayette (94549-3911)
PHONE.................................925 299-7878
Paul Schweibinz, *President*
Joanne Schweibinz, *Vice Pres*
Weaver Sonny Toledano, *Manager*
Beth McDermott, *Supervisor*
EMP: 35 **EST:** 1983
SQ FT: 5,000
SALES (est): 2.9MM **Privately Held**
WEB: www.compassad.com
SIC: 7311 Advertising agencies

(P-11748)
D AUGUSTINE & ASSOCIATES
Also Called: Augustine Ideas
3017 Douglas Blvd Ste 200, Roseville (95661-3837)
PHONE.................................916 774-9600
Debra Augustine, *CEO*
Robert Nelson, *COO*
Michael Mezzanotte, *Creative Dir*
Samantha Burns, *Graphic Designe*
Sandy Forseth, *Human Res Dir*
EMP: 52 **EST:** 1996
SALES (est): 13MM **Privately Held**
WEB: www.augustineideas.com
SIC: 7311 Advertising consultant

(P-11749)
DDB WORLDWIDE
600 California St Fl 7, San Francisco (94108-2731)
PHONE.................................415 732-3600
Mary Moudry, *President*
ARI Weiss, *Officer*
Tom Browning, *Vice Pres*
Ryan De Leon, *Administration*
Paul Colman, *Opers Staff*
EMP: 160
SALES (corp-wide): 13.1B **Publicly Held**
WEB: www.ddb.com
SIC: 7311 Advertising consultant
HQ: Ddb Worldwide Communications Group Llc
   195 Broadway Fl 7
   New York NY 10007
   212 415-2000

(P-11750)
DOREMUS & COMPANY
720 California St Fl 6, San Francisco (94108-2478)
PHONE.................................415 273-7800
Garrett Lawrence, *Manager*
Bennett Miller, *Creative Dir*
Sal Allababidi, *Info Tech Mgr*
Adriana Ngau, *Director*
Alice Wang, *Manager*
EMP: 46
SALES (corp-wide): 13.1B **Publicly Held**
WEB: www.doremus.com
SIC: 7311 7319 Advertising consultant; sky writing
HQ: Doremus & Company
   1285 Ave Of The Amrcas Fl
   New York NY, 10019
   212 366-3076

(P-11751)
ELANCE INC (HQ)
2625 Augustine Dr Ste 601, Santa Clara (95054-2956)
PHONE.................................650 316-7500
Stephane Kasriel, *President*
Brian Kinion, *CFO*
Raymond Lane, *Bd of Directors*
Rich Pearson, *Chief Mktg Ofcr*
Lars Asbjornsen, *Vice Pres*
EMP: 239 **EST:** 1998
SQ FT: 20,000
SALES (est): 52.3MM
SALES (corp-wide): 373.6MM **Publicly Held**
WEB: www.elance.com
SIC: 7311 Advertising consultant
PA: Upwork Inc.
   2625 Augustine Dr Fl 6th
   Santa Clara CA 95054
   650 316-7500

(P-11752)
ELEVEN INC
500 Sansome St Ste 100, San Francisco (94111-3213)
PHONE.................................415 707-1111
Courtney Buechert, *CEO*
Ted Bluey, *Partner*
Michael Borosky, *Partner*
Alison Fowler, *Partner*
Jarett Hausske, *Partner*
EMP: 120 **EST:** 1999
SALES (est): 22MM **Privately Held**
WEB: www.eleveninc.com
SIC: 7311 Advertising consultant

(P-11753)
EVB LLC
Also Called: Evolution Bureau
29 Park Way, Piedmont (94611-3928)
PHONE.................................415 281-3950
Daniel Stein, *CEO*
Jody La Point, *Financial Exec*
Daniel Steim,
EMP: 40 **EST:** 1999
SALES (est): 9.5MM
SALES (corp-wide): 13.1B **Publicly Held**
WEB: www.evb.com
SIC: 7311 Advertising consultant
HQ: Das Holdings, Inc.
   437 Madison Ave
   New York NY 10022
   212 415-3700

(P-11754)
FORTY FOUR GROUP LLC (PA)
Also Called: Origaudio
600 San Ramon Valley Blvd # 200, Danville (94526-4021)
PHONE.................................949 407-6360
Michael Szymczak,
Casey Ouye, *Graphic Designe*
Anh Hoang, *Opers Staff*
Chris Jackson, *Opers Staff*
Jasmine Lee, *Opers Staff*
▲ **EMP:** 56 **EST:** 2009
SQ FT: 2,000
SALES (est): 6.4MM **Privately Held**
SIC: 7311 Advertising agencies

(P-11755)
GIANT CREATIVE STRATEGY LLC
1700 Montgomery St # 485, San Francisco (94111-1025)
PHONE.................................415 655-5200
Steven Gold, *CEO*
Adam Gelling, *President*
Jeff Nemy, *CFO*
Eric Steckelman, *Officer*
Jodi Allen, *Exec VP*
EMP: 150 **EST:** 2002
SQ FT: 24,000
SALES (est): 36MM
SALES (corp-wide): 5.8MM **Privately Held**
WEB: www.giantagency.com
SIC: 7311 Advertising agencies
PA: Huntsworth Limited
   Holborn Gate
   London WC2A

(P-11756)
GODFREY DADICH PARTNERS LLC
140 New Montgomery St # 7, San Francisco (94105-3705)
PHONE.................................415 217-2800
Gary Cole, *Mng Member*
Kysa Ludviksen, *CEO*
Sydney Arkin, *Creative Dir*
Joel Mendoza, *Accountant*
Kirsten Golden, *Prdtn Dir*
EMP: 42 **EST:** 2003
SALES (est): 7.8MM **Privately Held**
WEB: www.godfreydadich.com
SIC: 7311 Advertising consultant

(P-11757)
GOODBY SLVERSTEIN PARTNERS INC
720 California St, San Francisco (94108-2440)
PHONE.................................415 392-0669
Rich Silverstein, *CEO*
James Horner, *Partner*
Brian McPherson, *Managing Prtnr*
Robert Riccardi, *Managing Prtnr*
Derek Robson, *Managing Prtnr*
EMP: 200 **EST:** 1983
SQ FT: 60,000
SALES (est): 42.4MM
SALES (corp-wide): 13.1B **Publicly Held**
WEB: www.goodbysilverstein.com
SIC: 7311 Advertising consultant
PA: Omnicom Group Inc.
   280 Park Ave Fl 31w
   New York NY 10017
   212 415-3600

(P-11758)
GREEN RUSH GROUP INC
714 N San Mateo Dr, San Mateo (94401-2224)
PHONE.................................650 762-5474
Paul Warshaw, *CEO*
Rachel Shipp, *Vice Pres*
William Lambert, *Director*
▼ **EMP:** 35 **EST:** 2014
SALES (est): 4.9MM **Privately Held**
WEB: www.greenrush.com
SIC: 7311 8741 Advertising agencies; business management

(P-11759)
GUMAS ADVERTISING LLC
Also Called: Adsmart Digital Prepress
99 Shotwell St, San Francisco (94103-3625)
PHONE.................................415 621-7575
John Gumas, *President*
Janice Herwegh,
Keone Moore, *Director*
EMP: 37 **EST:** 1984
SQ FT: 5,000
SALES (est): 8.3MM **Privately Held**
WEB: www.gumas.com
SIC: 7311 Advertising consultant

(P-11760)
HOFFMAN/LEWIS (PA)
Also Called: H&L Partners
100 Webster St Ste 100 # 100, Oakland (94607-3724)
PHONE.................................415 434-8500
Josh Nichol, *CEO*
Mark Schaeffer, *President*
Andrea Alfano, *COO*
Trey Curtola, *Vice Pres*
Chris Kilcullen, *Vice Pres*
EMP: 46 **EST:** 1985
SQ FT: 17,200
SALES (est): 23.7MM **Privately Held**
WEB: www.buyatoyota.com
SIC: 7311 Advertising consultant

(P-11761)
HORN GROUP INC
101 Montgomery St Fl 15, San Francisco (94104-4147)
PHONE.................................415 905-4000
Sabrina Horn, *President*
Todd Cadley, *Exec VP*
Katie Neuman, *Senior VP*
Smita Topolski, *Vice Pres*
Michelle Sieling, *Account Dir*
EMP: 50 **EST:** 1993

(PA)=Parent Co (HQ)=Headquarters (DH)=Div Headquarters
✪ = New Business established in last 2 years

7311 - Advertising Agencies County (P-11762)

SQ FT: 13,000
SALES (est): 10MM Privately Held
WEB: www.finnpartners.com
SIC: 7311 Advertising agencies

(P-11762)
HVSF TRANSITION LLC
Also Called: Heat
1100 Sansome St, San Francisco
(94111-1205)
PHONE..............................415 477-1999
John Elder, *President*
Mike Elliott, *Office Mgr*
Phil Van Buren, *Director*
EMP: 318 **EST:** 1996
SQ FT: 12,000
SALES (est): 2.2MM
SALES (corp-wide): 768.6K Privately Held
WEB: www.deloitte.com
SIC: 7311 Advertising consultant
HQ: Deloitte Consulting Llp
30 Rockefeller Plz
New York NY 10112
212 492-4000

(P-11763)
INMOBI INC (HQ)
475 Brannan St Ste 420, San Francisco
(94107-5421)
PHONE..............................650 269-5173
Naveen Tewari, *CEO*
Shan Zhou, *Partner*
Sachin Kanodia, *President*
Vasuta Agarwal, *Senior VP*
Sameer Sondhi, *Vice Pres*
EMP: 91 **EST:** 2008
SALES (est): 58.7MM Privately Held
WEB: www.inmobi.com
SIC: 7311 Advertising agencies

(P-11764)
INPOWERED INC
129 Marina Blvd, San Francisco
(94123-1202)
PHONE..............................415 796-7800
Peymanr Nilforoush, *CEO*
Pirouz Nilforoush, *President*
Ann Marinovich, *Officer*
Timothy Carey, *Vice Pres*
Erin Conover, *Office Mgr*
EMP: 41 **EST:** 2012
SALES (est): 6.7MM Privately Held
WEB: www.inpowered.ai
SIC: 7311 Advertising agencies

(P-11765)
KINESSO LLC
600 Battery St, San Francisco
(94111-1817)
PHONE..............................415 262-5900
Ian Johnson, *General Mgr*
Andy Butters, *Partner*
Arun Kumar, *Officer*
Jason Chambers, *Vice Pres*
John George, *Vice Pres*
EMP: 120
SALES (corp-wide): 9B Publicly Held
WEB: www.matterkind.com
SIC: 7311 Advertising consultant
HQ: Kinesso, Llc
100 W 33rd St Fl 8
New York NY 10001

(P-11766)
LEAD GENIUS
2054 University Ave, Berkeley
(94704-2687)
PHONE..............................415 969-2915
Santosh Sharan, *COO*
Brett McBee-Wise, *Vice Pres*
Derek Rahn, *Vice Pres*
Austin Brewin, *Exec Dir*
Roman Gladkov, *Software Engr*
EMP: 35 **EST:** 2015
SALES (est): 1.9MM Privately Held
SIC: 7311 Advertising agencies

(P-11767)
LIFE STREET CORPORATION
981 Industrial Rd Ste D, San Carlos
(94070-4150)
PHONE..............................415 757-0497
Paul Kennedy, *Principal*
EMP: 35 **EST:** 2014

SALES (est): 1.2MM Privately Held
WEB: www.lifestreet.com
SIC: 7311 Advertising agencies

(P-11768)
M/H VCCP LLC (HQ)
220 Sansome St Fl 15, San Francisco
(94104-2321)
PHONE..............................415 255-6363
John Muhtazyik, *Mng Member*
Allen Yu, *Creative Dir*
Henry Fernandez, *Business Dir*
Georgia Mahaffie, *Business Dir*
Cara Orlowski, *Business Dir*
EMP: 37 **EST:** 2010
SQ FT: 3,200
SALES (est): 5.5MM
SALES (corp-wide): 172.5MM Privately Held
WEB: www.mtzhf.com
SIC: 7311 Advertising consultant
PA: Vccp Group Llp
Po Box 70693
London SW1P
207 592-9331

(P-11769)
MCCANN-ERICKSON CORPORATION (HQ)
135 Main St Fl 21, San Francisco
(94105-1812)
PHONE..............................415 348-5600
Don Hov, *CFO*
Gillian Derario, *Accounts Exec*
EMP: 100 **EST:** 1982
SQ FT: 37,000
SALES (est): 23.4MM
SALES (corp-wide): 9B Publicly Held
WEB: www.interpublic.com
SIC: 7311 Advertising agencies
PA: The Interpublic Group Of Companies Inc
909 3rd Ave
New York NY 10022
212 704-1200

(P-11770)
MEKANISM INC (PA)
570 Pacific Ave, San Francisco
(94133-4608)
PHONE..............................415 908-4000
Jason Harris, *CEO*
Peter Caban, *Partner*
Tommy Means, *Partner*
Pete Caban, *CEO*
Michael Zlatoper, *Exec VP*
EMP: 50 **EST:** 1999
SALES (est): 20.7MM Privately Held
WEB: www.mekanism.com
SIC: 7311 Advertising agencies

(P-11771)
MERING HOLDINGS (PA)
1700 I St Ste 210, Sacramento
(95811-3018)
PHONE..............................916 441-0571
David Mering, *CEO*
Colm Conn, *Senior Partner*
Gregory Carson, *Partner*
Lori Bartle, *President*
Debi Huston, *COO*
EMP: 80 **EST:** 1984
SQ FT: 11,000
SALES (est): 23.1MM Privately Held
WEB: www.mering.com
SIC: 7311 Advertising consultant

(P-11772)
METRIC THEORY LLC
311 California St Ste 200, San Francisco
(94104-2604)
PHONE..............................415 659-8600
Ken Baker, *CEO*
Adam Edwards, *Ch Credit Ofcr*
Jeremy Brown, *Chief Mktg Ofcr*
Jeff Buenrostro,
Brian Jones, *Senior VP*
EMP: 124 **EST:** 2012
SALES (est): 14.3MM
SALES (corp-wide): 455.6MM Privately Held
WEB: www.metrictheory.com
SIC: 7311 Advertising consultant

HQ: Mightyhive, Inc.
394 Pacific Ave Ste B100
San Francisco CA 94111
888 727-9742

(P-11773)
MILITARY ADVANTAGE INC (DH)
Also Called: Military.com
799 Market St Fl 7, San Francisco
(94103-2045)
PHONE..............................415 820-3434
Christopher Michel, *CEO*
Jim Roesing, *CFO*
Ann Dwane, *Vice Pres*
Ed Petrus, *Vice Pres*
EMP: 114 **EST:** 1999
SQ FT: 3,000
SALES (est): 9.1MM
SALES (corp-wide): 24.5B Privately Held
WEB: www.military.com
SIC: 7311 Advertising agencies
HQ: Monster Worldwide, Inc.
133 Boston Post Rd
Weston MA 02493
978 461-8000

(P-11774)
MYPOINTSCOM LLC (HQ)
Also Called: My Points.com
44 Montgomery St Ste 1050, San Francisco
(94104-4621)
PHONE..............................415 615-1100
Jeff Goldstein, *CFO*
Mark Harrington, *Exec VP*
Edward Zinser, *Exec VP*
Mv Krishnamurthy, *Senior VP*
Tripti Thakur, *Vice Pres*
EMP: 60 **EST:** 1996
SALES (est): 7MM
SALES (corp-wide): 35.5MM Privately Held
WEB: www.mypoints.com
SIC: 7311 Advertising agencies
PA: Prodege, Llc
2030 E Maple Ave Ste 200
El Segundo CA 90245
310 294-9599

(P-11775)
OGILVY PUB RLTONS WRLDWIDE LLC
1530 J St, Sacramento (95814-2052)
PHONE..............................916 231-7700
Suanne Buggy, *Vice Pres*
Heidi Johnson, *Vice Pres*
EMP: 38
SALES (corp-wide): 15.9B Privately Held
WEB: www.ogilvy.com
SIC: 7311 Advertising agencies
HQ: Ogilvy Public Relations Worldwide Llc
636 11th Ave
New York NY 10036
212 880-5200

(P-11776)
ONE PLANET OPS INC (PA)
Also Called: Buyerlink
1820 Bonanza St, Walnut Creek
(94596-8490)
PHONE..............................925 983-2800
Payam Zamani, *CEO*
David Wittenkamp, *CFO*
Chris Mancini, *Chief Mktg Ofcr*
Mike Wienick, *Exec VP*
David Greene, *Vice Pres*
EMP: 121 **EST:** 2001
SALES (est): 899.8K Privately Held
WEB: www.oneplanetgroup.com
SIC: 7311 Advertising agencies

(P-11777)
PEREIRA & ODELL LLC (PA)
1265 Battery St Fl 4, San Francisco
(94111-1101)
PHONE..............................415 284-9916
Nancy Daum, *CFO*
Anthony Hay, *General Ptnr*
Pj Pereira, *Officer*
Joshua F Brandau, *Vice Pres*
Chris Wilcox, *Vice Pres*
EMP: 92 **EST:** 2007
SALES (est): 12MM Privately Held
WEB: www.pereiraodell.com
SIC: 7311 Advertising consultant

(P-11778)
QUOTIENT TECHNOLOGY INC (PA)
400 Logue Ave, Mountain View
(94043-4019)
PHONE..............................650 605-4600
Steven R Boal, *Ch of Bd*
Scott Raskin, *President*
Pamela Strayer, *CFO*
Glenn Smith, *Vice Pres*
Jeffrey Bolar, *Administration*
EMP: 847 **EST:** 1998
SQ FT: 42,000
SALES (est): 445.8MM Publicly Held
WEB: www.quotient.com
SIC: 7311 Advertising agencies

(P-11779)
RETAIL RADIO INC
7921 Kingswood Dr Ste A3, Citrus Heights
(95610-7710)
PHONE..............................916 415-9446
William Louie, *CEO*
Shawn Cash, *Director*
Randy Craig, *Director*
EMP: 43 **EST:** 2007
SQ FT: 4,100
SALES (est): 2.3MM Privately Held
WEB: www.spectrio.com
SIC: 7311 Advertising agencies

(P-11780)
RUNYON SALTZMAN INC
Also Called: Rse
2020 L St Ste 100, Sacramento
(95811-4260)
PHONE..............................916 446-9900
Christopher Holben, *President*
Estelle Saltzman, *Ch of Bd*
Paul McClure, *Vice Pres*
Scott Rose, *Vice Pres*
Vicky Lelash, *Managing Dir*
EMP: 65 **EST:** 1960
SQ FT: 14,000 Privately Held
WEB: www.rs-e.com
SIC: 7311 8743 Advertising consultant; public relations & publicity

(P-11781)
RYAN PARTNERSHIP LLC (PA)
100 Montgomery St # 1500, San Francisco
(94104-4331)
PHONE..............................415 289-1110
Mark Modesto,
Greg Carter, *Chief Mktg Ofcr*
Kelly McCarthy, *Admin Asst*
Jon Blaskovich, *Info Tech Dir*
Hillary Shipp, *Manager*
EMP: 372 **EST:** 2012
SALES (est): 37.2MM Privately Held
WEB: www.ryanidirect.com
SIC: 7311 Advertising agencies

(P-11782)
SHARETHIS INC (PA)
3000 El Cmino Real Ste 5, Palo Alto
(94306)
PHONE..............................650 641-0191
Dana Hayes Jr, *CEO*
Tim Schigel, *Ch of Bd*
Matt Gallatin, *CFO*
Ann Kennedy, *Senior VP*
Paul Lentz, *Senior VP*
EMP: 50
SALES (est): 15.9MM Privately Held
WEB: www.sharethis.com
SIC: 7311 7313 7372 Advertising consultant; electronic media advertising representatives; prepackaged software

(P-11783)
SIEGEL & GALE LLC
650 California St Fl 10, San Francisco
(94108-2714)
PHONE..............................415 955-1250
Sven Seger, *Branch Mgr*
EMP: 50
SALES (corp-wide): 13.1B Publicly Held
WEB: www.siegelgale.com
SIC: 7311 Advertising consultant
HQ: Siegel & Gale Llc
195 Broadway Fl 17
New York NY 10007
212 453-0400

PRODUCTS & SERVICES SECTION
7313 - Radio, TV & Publishers Adv Reps County (P-11806)

(P-11784)
SIERRA WEATHERIZATION CO INC
43 E Main St Ste B, Los Gatos (95030-6907)
PHONE..............................408 354-1900
Peter Hofmann, *President*
Amy Diffenderfer, *Corp Secy*
EMP: 37 **EST:** 1987
SALES (est): 4.4MM **Privately Held**
SIC: 7311 Advertising agencies

(P-11785)
SIZMEK DSP INC (PA)
1900 Seaport Blvd, Redwood City (94063-5587)
PHONE..............................650 595-1300
EMP: 37 **EST:** 2008
SALES (est): 582.3K **Privately Held**
SIC: 7311 Advertising agencies

(P-11786)
SIZMEK DSP INC
Also Called: Rocket Fuel
1455 Market St Ste 2100, San Francisco (94103-1331)
PHONE..............................415 757-2300
Devon Morehead, *Branch Mgr*
Barry Miller, *Executive*
Eduardo Moreno, *Software Dev*
Zoujin Ouyang, *Engineer*
David Feinstein, *Manager*
EMP: 51 **Privately Held**
SIC: 7311 Advertising agencies
HQ: Sizmek Dsp, Inc.
2000 Seaport Blvd Ste 400
Redwood City CA 94063

(P-11787)
STOTT OUTDOOR ADVERTISING
700 Fortress St, Chico (95973-9012)
P.O. Box 7209 (95927-7209)
PHONE..............................888 342-7868
Jim Moravec, *Partner*
Chris Zukin, *Partner*
Joe Zukin, *Partner*
John Zukin, *Partner*
Mike Zukin, *Partner*
EMP: 47 **EST:** 1947
SALES (est): 7.5MM **Privately Held**
WEB: www.stottoutdoor.com
SIC: 7311 7312 Advertising agencies; outdoor advertising services

(P-11788)
SWIRL INC
Also Called: Swirl McGarrybowen
1620 Montgomery St # 220, San Francisco (94111-1016)
PHONE..............................415 276-8300
Martin Lauber, *Chairman*
Ryan Lindholm, *President*
Wayne Esplana, *CFO*
Greg Fischer, *Exec VP*
Greg Johnson, *Exec VP*
EMP: 60 **EST:** 1997
SALES (est): 22.7MM **Privately Held**
WEB: www.dentsumb.com
SIC: 7311 Advertising agencies
HQ: Dentsu Mcgarry Bowen Llc
601 W 26th St Rm 1150
New York NY 10001
212 598-2900

(P-11789)
TAPJOY INC (PA)
353 Sacramento St Ste 600, San Francisco (94111-3604)
PHONE..............................415 766-6900
Steve Wadsworth, *President*
Brett Nicholson, *COO*
Matthew Service, *COO*
Al Wood, *CFO*
George Garrick, *Chairman*
EMP: 50 **EST:** 2007
SALES (est): 19.8MM **Privately Held**
WEB: www.tapjoy.com
SIC: 7311 Advertising agencies

(P-11790)
THREE MRKTERS CMMNCTONS GROUP
Also Called: Three Marketeers Advertising
6399 San Ignacio Ave, San Jose (95119-1215)
PHONE..............................408 293-3233
Jeffrey Holmes, *President*
Mike Nguyen, *Graphic Designe*
Rita Gunderson, *Director*
Jennifer McClenon, *Manager*
EMP: 42 **EST:** 1986
SQ FT: 43,000
SALES (est): 3.6MM **Privately Held**
WEB: www.3marketeers.com
SIC: 7311 Advertising consultant

(P-11791)
TM SLEEVES LLC
475 14th St Ste 200, Oakland (94612-1936)
PHONE..............................415 374-8210
Bruce Friedman, *Mng Member*
Arthur Baer,
Tm Holdco LLC,
EMP: 88 **EST:** 2000
SQ FT: 2,000
SALES (est): 3.2MM
SALES (corp-wide): 25.4MM **Privately Held**
WEB: www.britevision.com
SIC: 7311 Advertising agencies
PA: Brite Media Llc
350 Frank Ogawa Plz Ste 3
Oakland CA 94612
877 479-7777

(P-11792)
TRACTION CORPORATION
1349 Larkin St, San Francisco (94109-4717)
PHONE..............................415 962-5800
Adam Kleinberg, *CEO*
Paul Giese, *Partner*
Theo Fanning, *President*
Ginger Piscitello, *CFO*
Paul Giese, *Admin Sec*
EMP: 36 **EST:** 2003
SQ FT: 6,000
SALES (est): 6.1MM **Privately Held**
WEB: www.tractionco.com
SIC: 7311 8742 Advertising consultant; marketing consulting services

(P-11793)
UHURU NETWORK LLC
100 Pine St Ste 1250, San Francisco (94111-5235)
PHONE..............................415 745-3616
Peter Lang, *CEO*
Vanessa Rodriguez, *President*
EMP: 38 **EST:** 2010
SALES (est): 2.5MM **Privately Held**
WEB: www.uhurunetwork.com
SIC: 7311 8742 Advertising agencies; marketing consulting services

(P-11794)
VENABLES/BELL & PARTNERS LLC
Also Called: Vbp Orange
201 Post St Fl 2, San Francisco (94108-5027)
PHONE..............................415 288-3300
Kate Jeffers, *President*
Erich Pfeifer, *Creative Dir*
Anne Louise Petterss, *Office Mgr*
Glen Leach, *CTO*
Glenn Leach, *Opers Staff*
EMP: 190 **EST:** 2001
SQ FT: 30,000
SALES (est): 42.4MM **Privately Held**
WEB: www.venablesbell.com
SIC: 7311 Advertising consultant

(P-11795)
VUNGLE INC (PA)
1255 Battery St Ste 500, San Francisco (94111-1167)
PHONE..............................415 800-1400
Jeremy Bond, *CEO*
Colin Behr, *Vice Pres*
Jeremy Bondy, *Vice Pres*
Nicola Holmes, *Office Mgr*
Agnes Wysocka, *Office Mgr*
EMP: 101 **EST:** 2011
SQ FT: 4,500
SALES (est): 43.4MM **Privately Held**
WEB: www.vungle.com
SIC: 7311 7319 7313 Advertising consultant; display advertising service; electronic media advertising representatives

(P-11796)
YUME INC (HQ)
601 Montgomery St # 1600, San Francisco (94111-2603)
PHONE..............................650 591-9400
Ted Hastings, *President*
Dan Slivjanovski, *COO*
Ed Reginelli, *CFO*
Frank Barbieri, *Officer*
Michael Hudes, *Officer*
EMP: 495 **EST:** 2004
SQ FT: 20,400
SALES (est): 160.4MM **Privately Held**
WEB: www.tremorinternational.com
SIC: 7311 Advertising consultant

7312 Outdoor Advertising Svcs

(P-11797)
OUTFRONT MEDIA LLC
2512 River Plaza Dr, Sacramento (95833)
PHONE..............................209 466-5021
Fax: 209 466-6013
EMP: 20
SALES (corp-wide): 1.5B **Publicly Held**
SIC: 7312 3993 Outdoor Advertising Services Mfg Signs/Advertising Specialties
HQ: Outfront Media Llc
405 Lexington Ave Fl 14
New York NY 10174
212 297-6400

(P-11798)
VOLTA CHARGING LLC
155 De Haro St, San Francisco (94103-5121)
PHONE..............................415 735-5169
Scott Mercer, *CEO*
Chris Wendel, *President*
Debra Crow, *CFO*
Dr Abdellah Cherkaoui, *Senior VP*
Jon Michaels, *Senior VP*
EMP: 70 **EST:** 2015
SQ FT: 8,250
SALES (est): 11.8MM
SALES (corp-wide): 25.7MM **Publicly Held**
WEB: www.voltacharging.com
SIC: 7312 7694 Outdoor advertising services; electric motor repair
HQ: Volta Industries, Inc.
155 De Haro St
San Francisco CA 94103
415 583-3805

7313 Radio, TV & Publishers Adv Reps

(P-11799)
4INFO INC
4 N 2nd St Ste 1150, San Jose (95113-1308)
PHONE..............................650 350-4800
Tim Jenkins, *CEO*
Ray Colwell, *Officer*
Michelle Estabrook, *Vice Pres*
Peters Ryan, *Vice Pres*
Mari Tangredi, *Vice Pres*
EMP: 39 **EST:** 2003
SQ FT: 12,000
SALES (est): 5.3MM **Privately Held**
SIC: 7313 Electronic media advertising representatives

(P-11800)
ADSWIZZ INC (DH)
210 S Ellsworth Ave, San Mateo (94401-4074)
P.O. Box 1689 (94401-0914)
PHONE..............................408 674-4355
Alexis Van De Wyer, *CEO*
Philippe A Leroux, *COO*
Bruno Nieuwenhuys, *CTO*
Kate Gerwe, *Marketing Staff*
Kevin W Chen, *General Counsel*
EMP: 79 **EST:** 2010
SALES (est): 60.5K
SALES (corp-wide): 9.3B **Publicly Held**
WEB: www.adswizz.com
SIC: 7313 Radio advertising representative
HQ: Pandora Media, Llc
2100 Franklin St Ste 700
Oakland CA 94612
510 451-4100

(P-11801)
APPSFLYER LTD
111 New Montgomery St, San Francisco (94105-3605)
PHONE..............................415 636-9430
Armando Osuna, *Partner*
Sha Liang, *Partner*
Vrushali Khatav, *President*
Sunil Bhagwan, *Vice Pres*
Cecilia Xu, *Business Dir*
EMP: 80 **EST:** 2015
SALES (est): 8.1MM **Privately Held**
WEB: www.appsflyer.com
SIC: 7313 Electronic media advertising representatives

(P-11802)
BRITE MEDIA GROUP LLC (PA)
Also Called: Gsa Media
50 1st St Ste 600, San Francisco (94105-2429)
PHONE..............................877 479-7777
Art Baer,
EMP: 39 **EST:** 2005
SALES (est): 22.5MM **Privately Held**
SIC: 7313 Electronic media advertising representatives

(P-11803)
JAYLANEENTERTAINMENT CORP
585 Fernando Dr, Novato (94945-3333)
PHONE..............................707 820-2773
EMP: 65 **EST:** 2016
SALES (est): 941.1K **Privately Held**
SIC: 7313 Advertising Representative

(P-11804)
ONE PUTT
Also Called: One Putt Broadcasting
1415 Fulton St, Fresno (93721-1609)
PHONE..............................559 497-5118
John Ostlund, *Partner*
Chris Pacheco, *Partner*
Kevin O'Rorke, *Vice Pres*
Jesus Sepulveda, *Internal Med*
Jason Squires, *Director*
EMP: 36 **EST:** 2012
SQ FT: 10,500
SALES (est): 2.5MM **Privately Held**
WEB: www.kjwl.com
SIC: 7313 Television & radio time sales

(P-11805)
PAC-12 ENTEPRISES LLC
360 3rd St Ste 300, San Francisco (94107-2163)
PHONE..............................415 580-4200
Lydia Murphy Stevens, *President*
Jamie Zaninovich, *COO*
Ron McQuate, *CFO*
Woodie Dixon, *Senior VP*
Lisa Brand, *Vice Pres*
EMP: 120 **EST:** 1915
SQ FT: 11,000
SALES (est): 533.7MM **Privately Held**
WEB: www.pac-12.com
SIC: 7313 Electronic media advertising representatives

(P-11806)
ROI DNA INC
156 Cascade Dr, Fairfax (94930-2106)
PHONE..............................831 238-2514
Matt Quirie, *Principal*
Michelle Harburn, *COO*
Larry Vollmer, *CIO*
Max Shpungin, *Senior Mgr*
Meredith Heins, *Manager*
EMP: 41 **EST:** 2012
SALES (est): 3.7MM **Privately Held**
WEB: www.roidna.com
SIC: 7313 Electronic media advertising representatives

7313 - Radio, TV & Publishers Adv Reps County (P-11807)

(P-11807)
TRAVELZOO INC
800 W El Camino Real, Mountain View (94040-2567)
PHONE..................................650 316-6956
Chris Loughlin, *CEO*
Ralph Bartel, *President*
Wayne Lee, *CFO*
Hamid Vossoughi, *Software Engr*
Jim Allen, *Credit Staff*
EMP: 81 **EST:** 2005
SALES (est): 20.2MM
SALES (corp-wide): 53.6MM **Publicly Held**
WEB: www.travelzoo.com
SIC: 7313 Electronic media advertising representatives
PA: Travelzoo
590 Madison Ave Fl 35
New York NY 10022
212 484-4900

(P-11808)
ZENREACH INC (HQ)
1 Letterman Dr Bldg C, San Francisco (94129-2402)
PHONE..................................415 612-1900
Jack Abraham, *CEO*
Jeff Boughton, *Partner*
Joe Wylezik, *Partner*
Nitin Duggal, *Officer*
Jonas Hedberg, *Vice Pres*
EMP: 167 **EST:** 2011
SQ FT: 1,300
SALES (corp-wide): 72.6MM **Privately Held**
WEB: www.zenreach.com
SIC: 7313 Electronic media advertising representatives
PA: Atomic Labs, Llc
1 Letterman Dr Ste 702
San Francisco CA 94129
415 896-4148

7319 Advertising, NEC

(P-11809)
ATHLETIC MEDIA COMPANY (PA)
332 Pine St Ph, San Francisco (94104-3233)
PHONE..................................415 891-7354
Alex Mather, *CEO*
Paul Fichtenbaum, *Officer*
Balen Gore, *CTO*
Dom Luszczyszyn, *Author*
Marc Carig, *Agent*
EMP: 463 **EST:** 2015
SALES (est): 41.9MM **Privately Held**
WEB: www.theathletic.com
SIC: 7319 Media buying service

(P-11810)
BAY AREA NEWS GROUP E BAY LLC (HQ)
6270 Houston Pl Ste A, Dublin (94568-3161)
PHONE..................................925 302-1683
William D Singleton,
Dilasha Dharia, *Financial Analy*
Daniel Roderick, *Recruiter*
Peggy Labo, *Advt Staff*
Joseph J Lodovic IV,
EMP: 50 **EST:** 2007
SALES (est): 15.1MM
SALES (corp-wide): 17.6MM **Privately Held**
SIC: 7319 Media buying service
PA: California Newspapers Partnership
4 N 2nd St Ste 700
San Jose CA 95113
408 920-5333

(P-11811)
CBS INTERACTIVE INC (DH)
Also Called: Cbsi
235 2nd St, San Francisco (94105-3124)
PHONE..................................415 344-2000
Jarl Mohn, *Ch of Bd*
Eric Foote, *Partner*
Barry Briggs, *President*
Jim Lanzone, *President*
Domenic Dimeglio, *Exec VP*
EMP: 600 **EST:** 1992
SQ FT: 283,000
SALES (est): 787.3MM
SALES (corp-wide): 25.3B **Publicly Held**
WEB: www.cbsinteractive.com
SIC: 7319 7375 4832 Distribution of advertising material or sample services; on-line data base information retrieval; radio broadcasting stations
HQ: Viacomcbs Inc.
1515 Broadway
New York NY 10036
212 258-6000

(P-11812)
CONTEXTLOGIC INC (PA)
Also Called: Wish
1 Sansome St Fl 33, San Francisco (94104-4436)
PHONE..................................415 795-8061
Piotr Szulczewski, *CEO*
Tarek Fahmy, *Senior VP*
Thomas Chuang, *Vice Pres*
Eugene Sapozhnikov, *Administration*
Tao Lin, *Sr Software Eng*
EMP: 397 **EST:** 2010
SALES (est): 2.5B **Publicly Held**
WEB: www.wish.com
SIC: 7319 4813 5961 Shopping news, advertising & distributing service; ; television, home shopping

(P-11813)
LEGGETT & PLATT INCORPORATED
Beeline Group
31023 Huntwood Ave, Hayward (94544-7007)
PHONE..................................510 487-8063
Fax: 510 441-1782
EMP: 100
SALES (corp-wide): 3.7B **Publicly Held**
SIC: 7319 Advertising Services
PA: Leggett & Platt, Incorporated
1 Leggett Rd
Carthage MO 64836
417 358-8131

(P-11814)
ND SYSTEMS INC
5750 Hellyer Ave, San Jose (95138-1000)
PHONE..................................408 776-0085
Jim Ciardella, *CFO*
Trina Ciraulo, *COO*
EMP: 49 **EST:** 1979
SALES (est): 1MM **Privately Held**
WEB: www.ndssi.com
SIC: 7319 Display advertising service

(P-11815)
ODWALLA INC
2996 Alvarado St F, San Leandro (94577-5706)
PHONE..................................510 559-6840
EMP: 38
SALES (corp-wide): 33B **Publicly Held**
WEB: www.coca-cola.com
SIC: 7319 Shopping news, advertising & distributing service
HQ: Odwalla, Inc.
1 Coca Cola Plz Nw
Atlanta GA 30313
479 721-6260

(P-11816)
SAVE MART SUPERMARKETS DISC
6797 N Milburn Ave, Fresno (93722-2132)
PHONE..................................559 261-4123
Rick Hancock, *Manager*
EMP: 85
SALES (corp-wide): 414.7K **Privately Held**
WEB: www.thesavemartcompanies.com
SIC: 5411 7319 Supermarkets, chain; shopping news, advertising & distributing service
PA: Save Mart Supermarkets Disc
1800 Standiford Ave
Modesto CA 95350
209 577-1600

(P-11817)
SHARETHROUGH INC (PA)
170 Columbus Ave Ste 280, San Francisco (94133-5146)
PHONE..................................415 644-0054
Dan Greenberg, *CEO*
AVI Brown, *Vice Pres*
Shannon Espinola, *Vice Pres*
Jillian Kranz, *Vice Pres*
Lauren Wray, *Vice Pres*
EMP: 35 **EST:** 2008
SALES (est): 10.1MM **Privately Held**
WEB: www.sharethrough.com
SIC: 7319 Distribution of advertising material or sample services

(P-11818)
TUBI INC
Also Called: Tubitv
315 Montgomery St Fl 16, San Francisco (94104-1837)
PHONE..................................415 504-3505
Farhad Massoudi, *CEO*
Chris Bishko, *CFO*
Michael Ahiakpor,
Marios Assiotis, *Officer*
Mark Rotblat, *Officer*
EMP: 39 **EST:** 2009
SALES (est): 7MM
SALES (corp-wide): 12.9B **Publicly Held**
WEB: www.fox.com
SIC: 7319 7313 Transit advertising services; radio, television, publisher representatives
PA: Fox Corporation
1211 Ave Of The Americas
New York NY 10036
212 852-7000

(P-11819)
TURN INC (DH)
901 Marshall St Ste 200, Redwood City (94063-2026)
PHONE..................................650 353-4399
Bill Demas, *President*
Alexander Knudsen, *Partner*
Maureen Lee, *Partner*
Joe Nemeth, *CFO*
Joshua Koran, *Senior VP*
EMP: 270 **EST:** 2004
SQ FT: 14,000
SALES (est): 68.5MM **Privately Held**
WEB: www.amobee.com
SIC: 7319 Display advertising service

(P-11820)
VERVE GROUP INC
350 Marine Pkwy Ste 220, Redwood City (94065-5223)
PHONE..................................760 536-8350
Remco Westermann, *CEO*
EMP: 60 **EST:** 2020
SALES (est): 1.5MM **Privately Held**
SIC: 7319 Advertising

7322 Adjustment & Collection Svcs

(P-11821)
ACCESS CAPITAL SERVICES INC (PA)
1625 E Shaw Ave Ste 137, Fresno (93710-8100)
P.O. Box 16187 (93755-6187)
PHONE..................................559 627-5221
Chris Lardiere, *President*
EMP: 53 **EST:** 1993
SQ FT: 6,500
SALES (est): 2.1MM **Privately Held**
WEB: www.acscollectors.com
SIC: 7322 Collection agency, except real estate

(P-11822)
FRESNO CREDIT BUREAU
Also Called: Creditors Bureau of California
757 L St, Fresno (93721-2904)
P.O. Box 942 (93714-0942)
PHONE..................................559 650-7177
Carol L Capriotti, *President*
John Smoot, *Vice Pres*
Patty Grace, *Admin Sec*
EMP: 45 **EST:** 1945
SQ FT: 10,000
SALES (est): 2.4MM **Privately Held**
WEB: www.creditorsbureau.com
SIC: 7322 Collection agency, except real estate

(P-11823)
H&H RESOLUTION LLC
151 Bernal Rd Ste 6, San Jose (95119-1306)
PHONE..................................408 362-2293
Daniel Oditt, *Mng Member*
EMP: 100 **EST:** 2008
SALES (est): 1.5MM **Privately Held**
SIC: 7322 Collection agency, except real estate

(P-11824)
INVESTMENT RETRIEVERS INC
950 Glenn Dr Ste 160, Folsom (95630-3196)
P.O. Box 4733, El Dorado Hills (95762-0023)
PHONE..................................916 941-8851
James Kiley, *CEO*
Joel I Cohen, *President*
Sammy F Cemo, *Treasurer*
George Bottley, *Portfolio Mgr*
Orlando Evans, *Portfolio Mgr*
EMP: 45 **EST:** 2001
SALES (est): 6.5MM **Privately Held**
WEB: www.investment-retrievers.com
SIC: 7322 Collection agency, except real estate

(P-11825)
K B R INC (PA)
Also Called: Rash Curtis & Associates
190 S Orchard Ave A200, Vacaville (95688-3647)
P.O. Box 5790 (95696-5790)
PHONE..................................707 454-2000
Terrence Paff, *CEO*
Natasha L Paff, *Corp Secy*
Natasha Paff, *Officer*
Nick Keith, *Analyst*
Karmin Keith, *Human Res Dir*
EMP: 62 **EST:** 1977
SALES (est): 6.5MM **Privately Held**
WEB: www.rashcurtis.com
SIC: 7322 Collection agency, except real estate

(P-11826)
OPTIO SOLUTIONS LLC
Also Called: Qualia Collection Services
1444 N Mcdowell Blvd, Petaluma (94954-6515)
PHONE..................................800 360-2827
Chris Schumacher, *CEO*
Brad Lantz, *Vice Pres*
Bradley Lantz, *Vice Pres*
Ronald Roonzani, *Vice Pres*
Zach Eskelson, *Analyst*
EMP: 263 **EST:** 2007
SALES (est): 11.7MM **Privately Held**
WEB: www.optiosolutions.com
SIC: 7322 Collection agency, except real estate

(P-11827)
PERFORMANT RECOVERY INC
Also Called: DCS
17080 S Harlan Rd, Lathrop (95330-8739)
PHONE..................................209 858-3500
James Tracey, *Principal*
Lauren Homer, *Auditor*
Celeste Vargas, *Senior Mgr*
Carol Winston, *Supervisor*
EMP: 118 **Publicly Held**
WEB: www.performantpayments.com
SIC: 7322 Collection agency, except real estate
HQ: Performant Recovery, Inc.
333 N Canyons Pkwy # 100
Livermore CA 94551
209 858-3994

(P-11828)
PERFORMANT RECOVERY INC (HQ)
333 N Canyons Pkwy # 100, Livermore (94551-9478)
PHONE..................................209 858-3994
Lisa Im, *CEO*
Harold T Leach, *President*
Ian A Johnston, *Treasurer*
Julie Snyder, *Surgery Dir*
David Louttit, *Software Engr*
EMP: 447 **EST:** 1976
SQ FT: 31,000

PRODUCTS & SERVICES SECTION

7334 - Photocopying & Duplicating Svcs County (P-11851)

SALES: 131.2MM **Publicly Held**
WEB: www.performantpayments.com
SIC: 7322 8742 7371 Collection agency, except real estate; financial consultant; custom computer programming services

(P-11829)
PREMIERE CREDIT NORTH AMER LLC
17054 S Harlan Rd, Lathrop (95330-8739)
PHONE 844 897-2901
EMP: 120 **Publicly Held**
WEB: www.premierecredit.com
SIC: 7322 Collection agency, except real estate
HQ: Premiere Credit Of North America Llc
2002 Wellesley Blvd # 100
Indianapolis IN 46219

(P-11830)
PROFESSIONAL BUREAU OF COLLECT
9675 Elk Grove Florin Rd, Elk Grove (95624-2225)
PHONE 916 685-3399
Travis Justus, *Branch Mgr*
EMP: 115 **Privately Held**
WEB: www.pbccorp.com
SIC: 7322 Collection agency, except real estate
PA: Professional Bureau Of Collections Of Maryland, Inc.
5295 Dtc Pkwy
Greenwood Village CO 80111

(P-11831)
TRUE NORTH AR LLC (DH)
Also Called: Eos Healthcare
100 Wood Hllow Dr Ste 200, Novato (94945)
P.O. Box 981041, Boston MA (02298-1041)
PHONE 800 700-0220
Manoj Sharma, *CEO*
David Espinda, *Director*
EMP: 50 **EST:** 1969
SALES (est): 2.2MM
SALES (corp-wide): 177.9K **Privately Held**
WEB: www.truenorthar.com
SIC: 7322 Collection agency, except real estate

7323 Credit Reporting Svcs

(P-11832)
CHECKR INC
1 Montgomery St Ste 2400, San Francisco (94104-5524)
PHONE 844 824-3257
Daniel Yanisse, *CEO*
Kristen Faris, *Vice Pres*
Todd Freedman, *Vice Pres*
Freddy Metoyer, *Executive*
Jonathan Perichon, *Principal*
EMP: 164 **EST:** 2014
SALES (est): 30.9MM **Privately Held**
WEB: www.checkr.com
SIC: 7323 Credit investigation service

(P-11833)
CORELOGIC INC
Also Called: Corelogic Info Solutions
11010 White Rock Rd, Rancho Cordova (95670-6361)
PHONE 916 431-2146
Christine Christian, *Branch Mgr*
Danielle Mire, *Manager*
Patricia Bales, *Supervisor*
EMP: 95
SALES (corp-wide): 1.6B **Privately Held**
WEB: www.corelogic.com
SIC: 7323 Credit reporting services
HQ: Corelogic, Inc.
40 Pacifica Ste 900
Irvine CA 92618
866 873-3651

7331 Direct Mail Advertising Svcs

(P-11834)
ABS DIRECT INC
4724 Enterprise Way, Modesto (95356-8717)
PHONE 209 545-6090
Todd L Thomas, *CEO*
Elaine Thomas, *President*
Hank Vanderveen, *COO*
Pamela Bizzini, *Admin Sec*
Todd Thomas, *Info Tech Mgr*
EMP: 35 **EST:** 1983
SQ FT: 18,800
SALES (est): 5.7MM **Privately Held**
WEB: www.absdirectinc.com
SIC: 7331 7389 Mailing service; advertising, promotional & trade show services

(P-11835)
ACE MAILING & DATA PROCESSING
2736 16th St, San Francisco (94103-4216)
PHONE 415 863-4223
Royce Dyer, *Partner*
Gwendolyn Kaplan, *Partner*
Matthew Kaplan, *Manager*
Ron Ross, *Manager*
EMP: 38 **EST:** 1977
SQ FT: 12,000
SALES (est): 3.5MM **Privately Held**
WEB: www.acemailingsf.com
SIC: 7331 2752 Mailing service; commercial printing, lithographic

(P-11836)
BUSINESS SERVICES NETWORK
1275 Fairfax Ave Ste 103, San Francisco (94124-1759)
PHONE 415 282-8161
Harry Yue, *President*
Cindy Yue, *Vice Pres*
EMP: 72 **EST:** 1984
SQ FT: 31,120
SALES (est): 5MM **Privately Held**
WEB: www.bsnc.com
SIC: 7331 2752 7374 Mailing service; commercial printing, offset; data processing service

(P-11837)
GOODE PRINTING AND MAILING LLC
Also Called: Goode Company, The
361 Blodgett St, Cotati (94931-8700)
PHONE 707 588-8028
Michael Sanabria, *CEO*
Bryan Neill, *Vice Pres*
Scott Worden, *Vice Pres*
Laura Goode,
William Goode,
EMP: 44 **EST:** 2006
SALES (est): 10.5MM **Privately Held**
WEB: www.thegoodeco.com
SIC: 7331 2759 2752 Mailing service; commercial printing; commercial printing, lithographic

(P-11838)
INFOGROUP INC
951 Mariners Island Blvd # 130, San Mateo (94404-1558)
PHONE 650 389-0700
Fax: 650 389-0707
EMP: 75
SALES (corp-wide): 151.6MM **Privately Held**
SIC: 7331 2741 Direct Mail Advertising Services Misc Publishing
PA: Infogroup Inc.
1020 E 1st St
Papillion NE 68005
402 836-4500

(P-11839)
MAILING SYSTEMS INC
Also Called: M S I
2431 Mercantile Dr Ste A, Rancho Cordova (95742-6252)
P.O. Box 429 (95741-0429)
PHONE 916 266-2285
Michael R Lebeck, *CEO*
Balina Gnaytk, *CFO*
Joe Szemesi, *Vice Pres*
Kim Durham, *Executive*
Dave Baker, *Opers Staff*
▲ **EMP:** 48 **EST:** 1991
SQ FT: 100,000
SALES (est): 12.5MM **Privately Held**
WEB: www.msimail.net
SIC: 7331 Mailing service

(P-11840)
RECALL MASTERS INC
740 Tunbridge Rd, Danville (94526-4338)
PHONE 650 434-5211
Christopher J Miller, *Branch Mgr*
Helena Lucia, *Senior Engr*
Dave Slicer, *Regl Sales Mgr*
Jeff Tampe, *Regl Sales Mgr*
Angelique Appleton, *Client Mgr*
EMP: 39
SALES (corp-wide): 6.5MM **Privately Held**
WEB: www.recallmasters.com
SIC: 7331 Direct mail advertising services
PA: Recall Masters Inc.
23131 Verdugo Dr
Laguna Hills CA

(P-11841)
SAN JOSE MAILING INC
Also Called: GLOBE BUSINESS SERVICE'S
1445 Monterey Hwy, San Jose (95110-3618)
PHONE 408 971-1911
William Wilson, *President*
Stanley Barrios, *Vice Pres*
Alicia Sanchez, *Executive*
EMP: 21 **EST:** 1982
SQ FT: 20,000
SALES (est): 102.8K **Privately Held**
WEB: www.sanjosemailing.com
SIC: 7331 2752 Mailing service; commercial printing, lithographic

(P-11842)
VALASSIS DIRECT MAIL INC
6955 Mowry Ave, Newark (94560-4924)
PHONE 510 505-6500
Debra Robinson, *Manager*
Hannah Livianu, *Director*
EMP: 90 **Publicly Held**
SIC: 7331 Mailing service
HQ: Valassis Direct Mail, Inc.
235 Great Pond Dr
Windsor CT 06095
800 437-0479

(P-11843)
VALASSIS DIRECT MAIL INC
1601 Response Rd Ste 100, Sacramento (95815-5257)
PHONE 916 923-2398
Joseph Nix, *Branch Mgr*
EMP: 90 **Publicly Held**
SIC: 7331 Mailing service
HQ: Valassis Direct Mail, Inc.
235 Great Pond Dr
Windsor CT 06095
800 437-0479

7334 Photocopying & Duplicating Svcs

(P-11844)
ALL-AMERICAN PRTG SVCS CORP (PA)
1324 Rand St, Petaluma (94954-1138)
PHONE 707 762-2500
Darren Keffury, *President*
Alan Brayton, *Vice Pres*
Mike Mannion, *Manager*
EMP: 29
SQ FT: 17,500
SALES (est): 4.5MM **Privately Held**
WEB: www.allamericanprinting.com
SIC: 7334 2752 Photocopying & duplicating services; commercial printing, offset

(P-11845)
COMPEX LEGAL SERVICES LLC
1225 Pear Ave 110, Mountain View (94043-1431)
PHONE 650 833-0460
Steve Martin, *Managing Prtnr*
EMP: 158 **Privately Held**
WEB: www.cpxlegal.com
SIC: 7334 7389 Photocopying & duplicating services; document embossing
PA: Compex Legal Services Llc
920 Main St Ste 115
Kansas City MO 64105

(P-11846)
FRYES PRINTING INC
1050 Lincoln Ave, NAPA (94558-4914)
PHONE 707 253-1114
Kevin Frye, *President*
Rob Frye, *Production*
Richard Westbrook, *Sales Staff*
Cindy Turner, *Manager*
EMP: 24 **EST:** 1981
SQ FT: 10,000
SALES (est): 3MM **Privately Held**
WEB: www.fryesprinting.com
SIC: 7334 2752 Blueprinting service; commercial printing, lithographic

(P-11847)
GRAPHIC REPRODUCTION (PA)
1381 Franquette Ave B1, Concord (94520-5298)
PHONE 925 674-0900
Rose Walker, *CEO*
Walt J Walker, *President*
EMP: 53 **EST:** 1991
SALES (est): 3MM **Privately Held**
SIC: 7334 Photocopying & duplicating services

(P-11848)
OFFICEMAX NORTH AMERICA INC
1465 Shaw Ave, Clovis (93611-4056)
PHONE 559 298-0164
Armando Alvarez, *Administration*
EMP: 46
SALES (corp-wide): 9.7B **Publicly Held**
SIC: 7334 5112 Photocopying & duplicating services; office supplies
HQ: Officemax North America, Inc.
263 Shuman Blvd Ste 145
Naperville IL 60563
630 717-0791

(P-11849)
PACIFIC COPY AND PRINT
1700 N Market Blvd # 107, Sacramento (95834-1932)
PHONE 916 928-8434
Darren Herbert, *President*
Corina Workman, *Corp Secy*
Keith Lowe, *Vice Pres*
Krystal Del Carlo, *Prdtn Mgr*
Mary Hucklebridge, *Production*
EMP: 20 **EST:** 1991
SALES (est): 2.7MM **Privately Held**
WEB: www.pacificcopy.com
SIC: 7334 2752 Blueprinting service; commercial printing, lithographic

(P-11850)
SAC CITY BLUE INC
Also Called: Signature Reprographics
620 Sunbeam Ave, Sacramento (95811-0437)
PHONE 916 454-0800
Jason Cable, *President*
Stanley Rutledge, *Vice Pres*
Ray Stone, *Vice Pres*
Bridget Rutledge,
Debbie Marquez, *Manager*
EMP: 42 **EST:** 2002
SQ FT: 10,000
SALES (est): 6.9MM **Privately Held**
SIC: 7334 Blueprinting service

(P-11851)
SAN JOSE BLUPRT SVC & SUP CO
821 Martin Ave, Santa Clara (95050-2903)
PHONE 408 295-5770
David Dignam, *President*

7334 - Photocopying & Duplicating Svcs

Bernice E Cowherd, *Treasurer*
Miles Cowherd, *Vice Pres*
EMP: 150
SQ FT: 10,000
SALES (est): 6.6MM **Privately Held**
SIC: 5999 7334 Drafting equipment & supplies; blueprinting service

(P-11852)
SPEEDWAY COPY SYSTEMS INC
Also Called: Speedway Digital Printing
275 E L St, Benicia (94510-3238)
PHONE.....................................415 495-4330
Harry Newhall Jr, *President*
Gerard Burnett, *Corp Secy*
Fletcher Reid, *Facilities Mgr*
EMP: 24 EST: 1969
SALES (est): 3.2MM **Privately Held**
WEB: www.speedwayprinting.com
SIC: 7334 2752 Photocopying & duplicating services; commercial printing, offset

(P-11853)
V A ANDERSON ENTERPRISES INC
2680 Bishop Dr Ste 140, San Ramon (94583-4453)
PHONE.....................................925 866-6150
Fax: 925 866-6664
EMP: 73
SALES (corp-wide): 8.3MM **Privately Held**
SIC: 7334 Photocopying Services
PA: V. A. Anderson Enterprises, Inc.
400 Atlas St
Brea CA 92821
714 990-6100

7335 Commercial Photography

(P-11854)
ARC DOCUMENT SOLUTIONS INC (PA)
12657 Alcosta Blvd # 200, San Ramon (94583-4433)
PHONE.....................................925 949-5100
Kumar Suriyakumar, *Ch of Bd*
Kumarakulasingam Suriyakumar, *Ch of Bd*
Dilantha Wijesuriya, *COO*
Jorge Avalos, *CFO*
Joe Fox, *Division VP*
EMP: 25 EST: 1997
SALES (est): 289.4MM **Publicly Held**
WEB: www.e-arc.com
SIC: 7335 7334 7372 7334 Photographic studio, commercial; computer graphics service; prepackaged software; blueprinting service

(P-11855)
VEER INCORPORATED (PA)
690 Airpark Rd, NAPA (94558-7516)
PHONE.....................................877 297-7900
Brad Zumwalt, *President*
EMP: 63 EST: 2002
SQ FT: 7,000
SALES (est): 3.1MM **Privately Held**
WEB: www.veer.com
SIC: 7335 Commercial photography

7336 Commercial Art & Graphic Design

(P-11856)
99DESIGNS INC (PA)
2201 Broadway Ste 815, Oakland (94612-3024)
P.O. Box 3330 (94609-0330)
PHONE.....................................415 539-1088
Patrick Llewellyn, *CEO*
David Kaplan, *CFO*
Pamela Webber, *Chief Mktg Ofcr*
Eva Missling, *Vice Pres*
Michael Tibben, *Vice Pres*
EMP: 117 EST: 2011
SQ FT: 14,000
SALES (est): 14.9MM **Privately Held**
WEB: www.99designs.com
SIC: 7336 Graphic arts & related design

(P-11857)
ABC IMAGING OF WASHINGTON
679 Bryant St, San Francisco (94107-1612)
PHONE.....................................415 869-1669
Richard Adinolfi, *VP Sales*
Kenny Kast, *Manager*
Michael Weisend, *Manager*
EMP: 23
SALES (corp-wide): 124.9MM **Privately Held**
WEB: www.abcimaging.com
SIC: 7336 2759 Graphic arts & related design; commercial printing
PA: Abc Imaging Of Washington, Inc
5290 Shawnee Rd Ste 300
Alexandria VA 22312
202 429-8870

(P-11858)
CONCORD GRAPHIC ARTS INC
Also Called: C G A
3270 Monument Way, Concord (94518-2406)
PHONE.....................................925 682-9670
John J Yust, *President*
Lisa Boldischar, *Bookkeeper*
EMP: 30 EST: 1963
SQ FT: 11,000
SALES (est): 1.4MM **Privately Held**
WEB: www.concordgraphicarts.com
SIC: 7336 2752 Commercial art & graphic design; commercial printing, offset

(P-11859)
DIXON CORP
35182 Santiago St, Fremont (94536-4557)
PHONE.....................................510 366-6697
Thomas Dixon, *CEO*
EMP: 49
SALES (est): 58.9K **Privately Held**
SIC: 7336 Commercial art & graphic design

(P-11860)
FORM & FICTION LLC (PA)
1935 Lawton St, San Francisco (94122-3221)
PHONE.....................................415 802-2000
Howard Cao, *President*
Ferris Plock,
Kelly Tunstall,
EMP: 48 EST: 2016
SALES (est): 1.3MM **Privately Held**
WEB: www.form-fiction.com
SIC: 7336 5947 Commercial art & graphic design; gift, novelty & souvenir shop

(P-11861)
FROG DESIGN INC (DH)
427 Brannan St, San Francisco (94107-1715)
PHONE.....................................415 442-4804
Andy Zimmerman, *CEO*
Michelle Pliner, *Partner*
Toshi Mogi, *President*
Craig Ayers, *CFO*
Thomas Sutton, *Officer*
▲ EMP: 295 EST: 1982
SALES (est): 52.9MM
SALES (corp-wide): 387.8MM **Privately Held**
WEB: www.frogdesign.com
SIC: 7336 Graphic arts & related design

(P-11862)
G3 ENTERPRISES INC
Also Called: Label Division
2612 Crows Landing Rd, Modesto (95358-9400)
PHONE.....................................209 341-5265
Tom Gallow, *Branch Mgr*
Miriam Torrison, *Research*
Salvador Ramirez, *Technical Staff*
Shang-Lin Tsou, *Technical Staff*
Bruce Boyd, *Engineer*
EMP: 35
SALES (corp-wide): 116.5MM **Privately Held**
WEB: www.g3enterprises.com
SIC: 7336 2752 Commercial art & graphic design; commercial printing, lithographic
PA: G3 Enterprises, Inc.
502 E Whitmore Ave
Modesto CA 95358
209 341-7515

(P-11863)
GEL PAK LLC
31398 Huntwood Ave, Hayward (94544-7818)
PHONE.....................................510 576-2220
Jeanne Beacham, *Principal*
Priya Anand, *Admin Asst*
Rajesh Varma, *CTO*
Philip Shue, *Controller*
Ginger Demello, *Prdtn Mgr*
EMP: 75 EST: 1997
SALES (est): 12.9MM
SALES (corp-wide): 25.8MM **Privately Held**
WEB: www.gelpak.com
SIC: 7336 Package design
PA: Delphon Industries, Llc
31398 Huntwood Ave
Hayward CA 94544
510 576-2220

(P-11864)
HARDING MKTG CMMUNICATIONS INC (PA)
Also Called: Harding & Associates
377 S Daniel Way, San Jose (95128-5120)
PHONE.....................................408 345-4545
James F Harding, *CEO*
Maria Richard, *CFO*
EMP: 70 EST: 1981
SQ FT: 10,000
SALES (est): 9.9MM **Privately Held**
WEB: www.hardingmarketing.com
SIC: 7336 Graphic arts & related design

(P-11865)
IDEO LP (PA)
780 High St, Palo Alto (94301-2420)
PHONE.....................................650 289-3400
Sandy Speicher, *CEO*
Lynda Deakin, *Partner*
Charles Hayes, *Partner*
Thomas Overtun, *Partner*
Jane Suri, *Partner*
EMP: 135 EST: 1978
SALES (est): 39.4MM **Privately Held**
WEB: www.ideo.com
SIC: 7336 7389 8711 Commercial art & graphic design; design, commercial & industrial; engineering services

(P-11866)
LANDOR ASSOCIATES INTL LTD (DH)
360 3rd St 5, San Francisco (94107-2154)
PHONE.....................................415 365-1700
Lois Jacobs, *CEO*
Cheryl Giovannoni, *President*
Gabriel Miller, *President*
Ran Wadleigh, *CFO*
Craig Branigan, *Chairman*
EMP: 200 EST: 1942
SALES (est): 52MM
SALES (corp-wide): 15.9B **Privately Held**
WEB: www.landor.com
SIC: 7336 Graphic arts & related design

(P-11867)
MATTER LLC
22 Shotwell St, San Francisco (94103-3626)
PHONE.....................................415 589-7036
Max Burton, *CEO*
EMP: 35 EST: 2014
SALES (est): 4.4MM **Privately Held**
WEB: www.matterglobal.com
SIC: 7336 Commercial art & graphic design
PA: Accenture Public Limited Company
1 Grand Canal Square
Dublin D02 P

(P-11868)
MEDIA PRINT SERVICES INC
Also Called: Snap Pack Mail
10012 Del Almendra Dr, Oakdale (95361-9258)
PHONE.....................................866 935-5077
Becky Gould, *President*
Marshall Gould, *Owner*
Becky McGinty, *Vice Pres*
Kathy Royer, *Vice Pres*
EMP: 16 EST: 2005

SALES (est): 6.5MM **Privately Held**
SIC: 7336 2752 7389 Commercial art & graphic design; commercial printing, lithographic;

(P-11869)
METADESIGN INC
2001 The Embarcadero, San Francisco (94133-5200)
PHONE.....................................415 627-0790
EMP: 35
SQ FT: 12,000
SALES (est): 209.9K
SALES (corp-wide): 29.8MM **Privately Held**
WEB: www.metadesign.com
SIC: 7336 Commercial Art And Graphic Design
HQ: Mms Usa Investments, Inc.
2701 Queens Plz N
Long Island City NY 11101

(P-11870)
MINDSHARE DESIGN INC (PA)
Also Called: Savicom
475 14th St Ste 250, Oakland (94612-1933)
PHONE.....................................510 904-6900
Meredith Crawford, *CEO*
Reza Richard Sirafinejad, *Director*
Bill Schmidt, *Manager*
EMP: 25 EST: 1996
SQ FT: 7,300
SALES (est): 2.7MM **Privately Held**
WEB: www.mindsharedesign.com
SIC: 7336 7372 7371 Graphic arts & related design; prepackaged software; custom computer programming services

(P-11871)
NEVER BORING DESIGN ASSOCIATES
1016 14th St, Modesto (95354-1002)
PHONE.....................................209 526-9136
David Boring, *Owner*
Kit Lloyd, *Mktg Dir*
Ron Posey, *Advt Staff*
Dan Zampa, *Director*
Christina Kekai, *Assistant*
EMP: 25 EST: 1983
SQ FT: 2,500
SALES (est): 3MM **Privately Held**
WEB: www.neverboring.com
SIC: 7336 3993 7311 Graphic arts & related design; signs & advertising specialties; advertising agencies

(P-11872)
ON TARGET MARKETING
Also Called: Image Masters
429 Grogan Ave, Merced (95341-6401)
PHONE.....................................209 723-1691
Tim O'Neill, *President*
Marilyn O'Neill, *Vice Pres*
Holly Lourenco, *Marketing Staff*
Becky Albright, *Director*
Tong Chang, *Manager*
EMP: 20 EST: 1988
SQ FT: 5,000
SALES (est): 3.3MM **Privately Held**
WEB: www.imagemasters.com
SIC: 7336 2396 2759 7311 Graphic arts & related design; screen printing on fabric articles; promotional printing; advertising consultant

(P-11873)
STRATEGIC MATERIALS INC
299 Beck Ave, Fairfield (94533-6804)
PHONE.....................................707 452-3362
Humberto Perez, *Branch Mgr*
EMP: 35
SALES (corp-wide): 474MM **Privately Held**
WEB: www.smi.com
SIC: 7336 Chart & graph design
HQ: Strategic Materials, Inc.
17220 Katy Fwy Ste 150
Houston TX 77094

PRODUCTS & SERVICES SECTION
7342 - Disinfecting & Pest Control Svcs County (P-11896)

(P-11874)
TRANS PACIFIC DIGITAL INC
Also Called: Techart
1629b Irving St, San Francisco (94122-1813)
PHONE....................................415 362-1110
Diane Burns, *President*
EMP: 17 EST: 1983
SALES (est): 896K **Privately Held**
WEB: www.transpacificdigital.com
SIC: 7336 2791 Graphic arts & related design; typesetting, computer controlled

(P-11875)
YOUNG & RUBICAM LLC
Landor Associates
1001 Front St, San Francisco (94111-1424)
PHONE....................................415 365-1700
Courtney Reseer, *Director*
Craig Branigan, *President*
Rob Horius, *CFO*
Roth Hayes, *Chief Mktg Ofcr*
Paige Delacey, *Officer*
EMP: 170
SALES (corp-wide): 15.9B **Privately Held**
WEB: www.vmlyr.com
SIC: 7336 8742 Commercial art & graphic design; marketing consulting services
HQ: Young & Rubicam Llc
3 Columbus Cir Frnt 3 # 3
New York NY 10019
212 210-3000

7338 Secretarial & Court Reporting Svcs

(P-11876)
FEDERAL SOLUTIONS GROUP
2303 Camino Ramon, San Ramon (94583-1392)
PHONE....................................510 775-9068
Selina Singh, *CEO*
EMP: 40 EST: 2003
SALES (est): 1.6MM **Privately Held**
WEB: www.fedsolutionsgroup.com
SIC: 7338 Formal writing services

7342 Disinfecting & Pest Control Svcs

(P-11877)
A-PRO PEST CONTROL INC
75 Cristich Ln, Campbell (95008-5403)
PHONE....................................408 559-0933
Charles Payton, *President*
William Cress, *Vice Pres*
EMP: 37 EST: 1985
SQ FT: 2,000
SALES (est): 1.3MM **Privately Held**
WEB: www.bootstrapjs.info
SIC: 7342 Pest control in structures; pest control services

(P-11878)
ADVANCED IPM
205 Kenroy Ln, Roseville (95678-4201)
PHONE....................................916 759-1570
Adrienne Sederquist, *CEO*
Brock Peck, *Director*
Kimberly Ervin, *Manager*
Garette Rochester, *Accounts Mgr*
EMP: 50 EST: 2018
SALES (est): 2.8MM **Privately Held**
WEB: www.advancedipm.com
SIC: 7342 Pest control in structures

(P-11879)
AREA WIDE EXTERMINATORS INC
2239 Country Club Blvd, Stockton (95204-4803)
PHONE....................................209 464-4731
Carole Smith, *President*
Albert Smith, *Vice Pres*
Daniel Smith, *Vice Pres*
Terry Purpur, *Admin Sec*
EMP: 41 EST: 1979
SQ FT: 3,000
SALES (est): 1MM **Privately Held**
WEB: www.areawidepest.com
SIC: 7342 Exterminating & fumigating

(P-11880)
BUSINESS INDUSTRY & ENVMT INC
Also Called: North American Pest Management
3720 Madison Ave 210, North Highlands (95660-5024)
PHONE....................................916 481-0268
David L Lovenvirth, *CEO*
Ann C Lovenvirth, *Shareholder*
Charles Lanman, *President*
Aja Barragan, *Controller*
AMI Fetter, *Director*
EMP: 51 EST: 1978
SQ FT: 5,000
SALES (est): 7.1MM **Privately Held**
SIC: 7342 Pest control in structures; termite control

(P-11881)
CLARK PEST CTRL STOCKTON INC
1370 Merced Ave, Merced (95341-5330)
PHONE....................................209 826-6051
Don Harris, *Branch Mgr*
EMP: 40
SALES (corp-wide): 2.1B **Publicly Held**
WEB: www.clarkpest.com
SIC: 7342 Pest control in structures
HQ: Clark Pest Control Of Stockton, Inc.
555 N Guild Ave
Lodi CA 95240
209 368-7152

(P-11882)
CLARK PEST CTRL STOCKTON INC
595 Pomona Dr, Brentwood (94513-6948)
PHONE....................................209 483-4043
EMP: 40
SALES (corp-wide): 2.1B **Publicly Held**
WEB: www.clarkpest.com
SIC: 7342 Pest control in structures
HQ: Clark Pest Control Of Stockton, Inc.
555 N Guild Ave
Lodi CA 95240
209 368-7152

(P-11883)
CLARK PEST CTRL STOCKTON INC (HQ)
555 N Guild Ave, Lodi (95240-0809)
P.O. Box 1480 (95241-1480)
PHONE....................................209 368-7152
Gary Rollins, *CEO*
Rosemary Lopez, *Administration*
Elizabeth Victor-Martinez, *Administration*
Marcos Hernandez, *Sales Staff*
John Dohmen,
EMP: 70 EST: 1950
SQ FT: 2,500
SALES (est): 85.4MM
SALES (corp-wide): 2.1B **Publicly Held**
WEB: www.clarkpest.com
SIC: 7342 Pest control in structures; termite control
PA: Rollins, Inc.
2170 Piedmont Rd Ne
Atlanta GA 30324
404 888-2000

(P-11884)
CLARK PEST CTRL STOCKTON INC
1288 Garden Hwy, Yuba City (95991-7502)
PHONE....................................530 235-6101
Dave Shumake, *Manager*
Micah Taylor, *Technician*
Michael Wiliams, *Manager*
EMP: 40
SALES (corp-wide): 2.1B **Publicly Held**
WEB: www.clarkpest.com
SIC: 7342 Pest control in structures
HQ: Clark Pest Control Of Stockton, Inc.
555 N Guild Ave
Lodi CA 95240
209 368-7152

(P-11885)
CLARK PEST CTRL STOCKTON INC
480 E Service Rd, Modesto (95358-9491)
PHONE....................................209 524-6384
Ron Fair, *Manager*
Debra Posada, *Admin Asst*
EMP: 40
SALES (corp-wide): 2.1B **Publicly Held**
WEB: www.clarkpest.com
SIC: 7342 Pest control in structures
HQ: Clark Pest Control Of Stockton, Inc.
555 N Guild Ave
Lodi CA 95240
209 368-7152

(P-11886)
CLARK PEST CTRL STOCKTON INC
4045 Nelson Ave Ste B, Concord (94520-1215)
PHONE....................................925 935-5077
Chris Aguniga, *General Mgr*
EMP: 40
SQ FT: 2,000
SALES (corp-wide): 2.1B **Publicly Held**
WEB: www.clarkpest.com
SIC: 7342 Pest control in structures
HQ: Clark Pest Control Of Stockton, Inc.
555 N Guild Ave
Lodi CA 95240
209 368-7152

(P-11887)
CLARK PEST CTRL STOCKTON INC
5822 Roseville Rd, Sacramento (95842-3071)
PHONE....................................916 925-7000
Steven Adams, *Manager*
Robin Crowley-Swehla, *Admin Asst*
Patrick Cleary, *Technician*
Nathan Pops, *Manager*
EMP: 40
SQ FT: 3,100
SALES (corp-wide): 2.1B **Publicly Held**
WEB: www.clarkpest.com
SIC: 7342 Pest control in structures
HQ: Clark Pest Control Of Stockton, Inc.
555 N Guild Ave
Lodi CA 95240
209 368-7152

(P-11888)
CLARK PEST CTRL STOCKTON INC
811 U Banks, Vacaville (95688)
PHONE....................................707 446-9748
Ron Gardner, *Manager*
EMP: 40
SQ FT: 1,300
SALES (corp-wide): 2.1B **Publicly Held**
WEB: www.clarkpest.com
SIC: 7342 Pest control in structures
HQ: Clark Pest Control Of Stockton, Inc.
555 N Guild Ave
Lodi CA 95240
209 368-7152

(P-11889)
CLARK PEST CTRL STOCKTON INC
429 Mono Way, Sonora (95370-5234)
PHONE....................................209 532-3464
Baron Mc Donnald, *Manager*
EMP: 40
SALES (corp-wide): 2.1B **Publicly Held**
WEB: www.clarkpest.com
SIC: 7342 Pest control in structures; termite control
HQ: Clark Pest Control Of Stockton, Inc.
555 N Guild Ave
Lodi CA 95240
209 368-7152

(P-11890)
CLARK PEST CTRL STOCKTON INC
4816 Clowes St, Stockton (95210-3506)
P.O. Box 1480, Lodi (95241-1480)
PHONE....................................209 474-3204
Joe Dinubilo, *Manager*
Irma Prescott, *COO*
Jared Bitton, *Branch Mgr*
Michael Clark, *Technician*
Alex Prutsos, *Technician*
EMP: 40
SALES (corp-wide): 2.1B **Publicly Held**
WEB: www.clarkpest.com
SIC: 7342 Pest control in structures
HQ: Clark Pest Control Of Stockton, Inc.
555 N Guild Ave
Lodi CA 95240
209 368-7152

(P-11891)
CLARK PEST CTRL STOCKTON INC
485 Oneill Ave, Belmont (94002-4004)
PHONE....................................650 596-1270
Joe Clark, *President*
EMP: 40
SALES (corp-wide): 2.1B **Publicly Held**
WEB: www.clarkpest.com
SIC: 7342 Pest control in structures
HQ: Clark Pest Control Of Stockton, Inc.
555 N Guild Ave
Lodi CA 95240
209 368-7152

(P-11892)
CLARK PEST CTRL STOCKTON INC
2030 Fortune Dr Ste 100, San Jose (95131-1835)
PHONE....................................408 866-2278
Joe Gatto, *Manager*
EMP: 40
SALES (corp-wide): 2.1B **Publicly Held**
WEB: www.clarkpest.com
SIC: 7342 Pest control in structures
HQ: Clark Pest Control Of Stockton, Inc.
555 N Guild Ave
Lodi CA 95240
209 368-7152

(P-11893)
CLARK PEST CTRL STOCKTON INC
2313 Research Dr, Livermore (94550-3824)
PHONE....................................925 449-6203
Dave Erichsen, *Manager*
EMP: 40
SALES (corp-wide): 2.1B **Publicly Held**
WEB: www.clarkpest.com
SIC: 7342 Pest control in structures
HQ: Clark Pest Control Of Stockton, Inc.
555 N Guild Ave
Lodi CA 95240
209 368-7152

(P-11894)
CLARK PEST CTRL STOCKTON INC
4045 Nelson Ave, Concord (94520-1215)
PHONE....................................925 757-5890
Chris Aguniga, *Branch Mgr*
Brian Oistad, *Technician*
Tim Hootman, *Commercial*
EMP: 40
SALES (corp-wide): 2.1B **Publicly Held**
WEB: www.clarkpest.com
SIC: 7342 Pest control in structures
HQ: Clark Pest Control Of Stockton, Inc.
555 N Guild Ave
Lodi CA 95240
209 368-7152

(P-11895)
CLARK PEST CTRL STOCKTON INC
11285 White Rock Rd, Rancho Cordova (95742-6504)
PHONE....................................916 635-7770
Robert Golubski, *Manager*
EMP: 40
SALES (corp-wide): 2.1B **Publicly Held**
WEB: www.clarkpest.com
SIC: 7342 Pest control in structures
HQ: Clark Pest Control Of Stockton, Inc.
555 N Guild Ave
Lodi CA 95240
209 368-7152

(P-11896)
CLARK PEST CTRL STOCKTON INC
Also Called: Clark Pest Control 11
3215 Brickway Blvd, Santa Rosa (95403-8261)
PHONE....................................707 571-0414
Brad Abansino, *Manager*
Beto Rangel, *Technician*
EMP: 40

7342 - Disinfecting & Pest Control Svcs County (P-11897)

SALES (corp-wide): 2.1B **Publicly Held**
WEB: www.clarkpest.com
SIC: 7342 Pest control in structures; exterminating & fumigating
HQ: Clark Pest Control Of Stockton, Inc.
555 N Guild Ave
Lodi CA 95240
209 368-7152

(P-11897)
CLEANRITE INC
814 Striker Ave Ste B, Sacramento (95834-2475)
PHONE.................................916 381-1321
Eric Martin, *Branch Mgr*
EMP: 43
SALES (corp-wide): 30.8MM **Privately Held**
WEB: www.cleanrite-buildrite.com
SIC: 7342 7217 Disinfecting services; carpet & upholstery cleaning
PA: Cleanrite, Inc.
2684 Highway 32 Ste 100
Chico CA 95973
530 891-0333

(P-11898)
CRANE ACQUISITION INC
Also Called: Crane Pest Control
2700 Geary Blvd, San Francisco (94118-3406)
PHONE.................................415 922-1666
Harold Stein, *President*
Harry J Cynkus, *Treasurer*
Eugene Iarocci, *Admin Sec*
EMP: 516 EST: 1930
SQ FT: 6,000
SALES (est): 11.9MM
SALES (corp-wide): 2.1B **Publicly Held**
WEB: www.rollins.com
SIC: 7342 Exterminating & fumigating; pest control services
PA: Rollins, Inc.
2170 Piedmont Rd Ne
Atlanta GA 30324
404 888-2000

(P-11899)
GODFATHERS EXTERMINATOR INC
Also Called: California Amercn Exterminator
13350 W Park Ave Ste E, Boulder Creek (95006-9333)
P.O. Box 129 (95006-0129)
PHONE.................................831 338-4800
Ray Schwerdtfeger, *President*
Michael Schwerdtfeger, *Treasurer*
Sharon Schwerdtfeger, *Vice Pres*
Tami Stuparich, *Vice Pres*
Michelle Meschi, *Admin Mgr*
EMP: 38 EST: 1968
SQ FT: 800
SALES (est): 1.3MM **Privately Held**
WEB: www.calamericanext.com
SIC: 7342 Pest control in structures

(P-11900)
HOMEGUARD INCORPORATED (PA)
Also Called: Redrocks Fumigation
510 Madera Ave, San Jose (95112-2918)
PHONE.................................408 993-1900
James Steffenson Jr, *President*
Jim Hessling, *Treasurer*
Gilbert Fregoso, *Officer*
Christopher Benne, *General Mgr*
Dominic D'Ambrosio, *General Mgr*
▲ EMP: 56
SQ FT: 6,000
SALES (est): 11.6MM **Privately Held**
WEB: www.homeguard.com
SIC: 7342 Pest control in structures

(P-11901)
LUIS A AGURTO
Also Called: Pestec Exterminator Co
1555 Yosemite Ave Ste 46, San Francisco (94124-3272)
P.O. Box 2393, Antioch (94531-2393)
PHONE.................................925 238-0744
Luis A Agurto, *President*
EMP: 40 EST: 1985
SALES (est): 3.3MM **Privately Held**
SIC: 7342 Pest control in structures

(P-11902)
MADERA CNTY MSQITO VCTOR CTRL
3105 Airport Dr, Madera (93637-8704)
PHONE.................................559 662-8880
Leonard Irby, *District Mgr*
Chris Munoz, *Technician*
Alex Scalzo, *Manager*
EMP: 36 EST: 1947
SQ FT: 900
SALES (est): 3.8MM **Privately Held**
WEB: www.maderamosq.org
SIC: 7342 Pest control services

(P-11903)
MCCAULEY BROTHERS INC (PA)
Also Called: Garden Plus Pest Control
6678 Owens Dr Ste 100, Pleasanton (94538-3324)
PHONE.................................925 439-1000
Sean McCauley, *President*
Glen McCauley, *Vice Pres*
EMP: 35 EST: 2007
SQ FT: 20,000
SALES (est): 1.9MM **Privately Held**
SIC: 7342 Pest control in structures

(P-11904)
MILLENNIUM TERMITE & PEST
9900 Horn Rd Ste 5, Sacramento (95827-1996)
PHONE.................................707 673-1050
Robert Erickson, *President*
EMP: 40 EST: 1999
SQ FT: 10,000
SALES (est): 3.7MM **Privately Held**
WEB: www.mtpest.com
SIC: 7342 1521 Pest control in structures; single-family housing construction

(P-11905)
NATURAL ORANGE INC
Also Called: Planet Orange
434 Park Ave, San Jose (95110-2614)
PHONE.................................408 963-6868
Nathan Cocozza, *President*
Patrick Becker, *Vice Pres*
Scott Mendenhall, *Vice Pres*
Mathew Warwick, *Vice Pres*
Keeley Horton, *Finance*
EMP: 68 EST: 2008
SQ FT: 17,000
SALES (est): 6.3MM **Privately Held**
WEB: www.planetorange.com
SIC: 7342 Pest control in structures; termite control

(P-11906)
NEIGHBORLY PEST MANAGEMENT INC
324 Riverside Ave, Roseville (95678-3198)
PHONE.................................916 782-3767
Kathryn Roberts, *President*
Monica Gollmyer, *Treasurer*
Rod Gollmyer, *Vice Pres*
Elliott Roberts, *Vice Pres*
Rick Stiles, *Sales Staff*
EMP: 53 EST: 1978
SALES (est): 4MM **Privately Held**
WEB: www.neighborlypest.com
SIC: 7342 Pest control in structures

(P-11907)
ROYCE CORPORATION (PA)
Also Called: Aei Termite Pest Control
4970 Salida Blvd, Salida (95368-9403)
P.O. Box 586 (95368-0586)
PHONE.................................209 545-0789
Michael Rogers, *President*
Robert Capdeville, *Vice Pres*
EMP: 55 EST: 1980
SQ FT: 6,500
SALES (est): 4.7MM **Privately Held**
SIC: 7342 Termite control

(P-11908)
TERMINIX COMPANY LLC
5451 Industrial Way, Benicia (94510-1010)
PHONE.................................800 480-8439
John Testa, *Branch Mgr*
EMP: 40
SALES (corp-wide): 1.9B **Publicly Held**
WEB: www.terminix.com
SIC: 7342 Pest control services
HQ: The Terminix Company Llc
150 Peabody Pl
Memphis TN 38103
901 597-1400

(P-11909)
TWIN TERMITE AND PEST CTRL INC
3720 Madison Ave Ste 100, North Highlands (95660-5024)
PHONE.................................916 344-8946
Kyle Finley, *CEO*
Frank Siino, *Vice Pres*
Chase Johnson, *Branch Mgr*
Doug Johnson, *Branch Mgr*
Jason Molina, *Branch Mgr*
EMP: 45 EST: 2017
SALES (est): 5.6MM **Privately Held**
WEB: www.twintermite.com
SIC: 7342 Pest control in structures

(P-11910)
WEED ENTERPRISES INC
Also Called: Proven Termite Solution
662 Giguere Ct Ste F, San Jose (95133-1744)
PHONE.................................408 929-1992
James Weed, *President*
Aubrey Malave, *Executive*
EMP: 43 EST: 1994
SQ FT: 6,000
SALES (est): 2.9MM **Privately Held**
WEB: www.proventermitesolutions.com
SIC: 7342 Pest control in structures; pest control services

(P-11911)
WILDLIFE CONTROL TECH INC
Also Called: Wildlife Product
2501 N Sunnyside Ave, Fresno (93727-1329)
PHONE.................................559 490-2262
Colleen M Martin, *President*
Lee R Martin, *Vice Pres*
EMP: 41 EST: 1978
SQ FT: 2,500
SALES (est): 1MM **Privately Held**
WEB: www.wildlife-control.com
SIC: 7342 Pest control in structures; bird proofing

7349 Building Cleaning & Maintenance Svcs, NEC

(P-11912)
ABM ELCTRCAL LTG SOLUTIONS INC
6940 Koll Center Pkwy # 100, Pleasanton (94566-3100)
PHONE.................................408 399-3030
EMP: 65
SALES (corp-wide): 5.9B **Publicly Held**
SIC: 7349 Lighting maintenance service
HQ: Abm Electrical & Lighting Solutions, Inc.
14201 Franklin Ave
Tustin CA 92780
866 226-2838

(P-11913)
ACME BUILDING MAINT CO INC (DH)
941 Catherine St, Alviso (95002)
PHONE.................................408 263-5911
Richard Sanchez, *President*
Henry Sanchez, *Ch of Bd*
Solomon Wong, *Treasurer*
EMP: 80 EST: 1970
SQ FT: 8,000
SALES (est): 54MM
SALES (corp-wide): 5.9B **Publicly Held**
WEB: www.gcaservices.com
SIC: 7349 Janitorial service, contract basis; building component cleaning service
HQ: Gca Services Group, Inc.
1350 Euclid Ave Ste 1500
Cleveland OH 44115
800 422-8760

(P-11914)
AHTNA FACILITY SERVICES INC
3100 Beacon Blvd, West Sacramento (95691-3483)
PHONE.................................916 375-0199
Brenda Rebne, *President*
Meghann Hurt, *Project Mgr*
Elizabeth Robertson, *Manager*
EMP: 150
SALES (corp-wide): 479.5MM **Privately Held**
WEB: www.ahtna.com
SIC: 7349 Janitorial service, contract basis
HQ: Ahtna Facility Services, Incorporated
110 W 38th Ave Ste 200e
Anchorage AK 99503

(P-11915)
ALLIED JANITORIAL MAINT INC
16925 S Harlan Rd Ste 205, Lathrop (95330-8780)
P.O. Box 40, French Camp (95231-0040)
PHONE.................................209 992-6687
Lee Mortera, *President*
EMP: 35 EST: 2017
SALES (est): 980K **Privately Held**
WEB: www.alliedjanitors.com
SIC: 7349 Janitorial service, contract basis

(P-11916)
ALVAREZ INDUSTRIES
116 Hubbard St, Santa Cruz (95060-2938)
P.O. Box 1527 (95061-1527)
PHONE.................................831 423-5515
Sixto Alvarez, *CEO*
EMP: 49 EST: 2004
SALES (est): 1.5MM **Privately Held**
WEB: www.mycleanbldg.com
SIC: 7349 5087 0782 Janitorial service, contract basis; janitors' supplies; landscape contractors

(P-11917)
AMERI-KLEEN
Also Called: Ameri-Kleen Building Services
313 W Beach St, Watsonville (95076-4508)
P.O. Box 2167 (95077-2167)
PHONE.................................831 722-8888
Marisol Tavera, *Branch Mgr*
EMP: 190 **Privately Held**
WEB: www.ameri-kleen.com
SIC: 7349 Building maintenance services
PA: Ameri-Kleen
119 W Beach St
Watsonville CA 95076

(P-11918)
AMERICAN BLDG MAINT CO OF ILL
44870 Osgood Rd, Fremont (94539-6101)
PHONE.................................510 573-1618
EMP: 487
SALES (corp-wide): 5.9B **Publicly Held**
SIC: 7349 Janitorial service, contract basis
HQ: American Building Maintenance Co Of Illinois, Inc
420 Taylor St 200
San Francisco CA 94102
415 351-4386

(P-11919)
AMERICAN BLDG MAINT CO-WEST (HQ)
75 Broadway Ste 111, San Francisco (94111-1423)
PHONE.................................415 733-4000
Henrik Slipsager, *President*
Douglas Bowlus, *Treasurer*
Harry H Kahn, *Admin Sec*
Gary Haslam, *Business Mgr*
EMP: 150 EST: 1986
SALES (est): 29.5MM
SALES (corp-wide): 5.9B **Publicly Held**
WEB: www.abm.com
SIC: 7349 Janitorial service, contract basis
PA: Abm Industries Incorporated
1 Liberty Plz Fl 7
New York NY 10006
212 297-0200

PRODUCTS & SERVICES SECTION

7349 - Building Cleaning & Maintenance Svcs, NEC County (P-11944)

(P-11920)
AMERICAN BUILDING MAINT CO NY
101 California St, San Francisco (94111-5802)
PHONE.....................415 733-4000
Henrik Slipsager, *President*
Douglas Bowlus, *Treasurer*
Scott Salmirs, *Exec VP*
EMP: 66 **EST:** 1975
SALES (est): 1.7MM
SALES (corp-wide): 5.9B **Publicly Held**
WEB: www.abm.com
SIC: 7349 Janitorial service, contract basis
PA: Abm Industries Incorporated
1 Liberty Plz Fl 7
New York NY 10006
212 297-0200

(P-11921)
AMERICAN BUILDING SERVICE INC
4578 Crow Canyon Pl, Castro Valley (94552-4804)
P.O. Box 32, San Leandro (94577-0003)
PHONE.....................510 483-5120
Rui Donaldo Teixeira Canha, *President*
EMP: 100 **EST:** 1988
SALES (est): 3.3MM **Privately Held**
WEB: www.absbayarea.com
SIC: 7349 Janitorial service, contract basis

(P-11922)
ATTAINIT
2555 3rd St Ste 100, Sacramento (95818-1100)
PHONE.....................916 325-7800
EMP: 44
SALES (est): 2.3MM **Privately Held**
WEB: www.attainit.net
SIC: 7349 Building Maintenance Services, Nec, Nsk

(P-11923)
B&R MAINTENANCE INC
90 S Spruce Ave Ste Us, South San Francisco (94080-4567)
P.O. Box 77348, San Francisco (94107-0348)
PHONE.....................650 589-0331
Carlos M Beltran, *President*
EMP: 45 **EST:** 2012
SQ FT: 1,500
SALES (est): 2.6MM **Privately Held**
WEB: www.bandrmaintenance.org
SIC: 7349 Janitorial service, contract basis

(P-11924)
BARBARA-HOFFMAN INC
Also Called: Star Industries
3780 Happy Ln Ste A, Sacramento (95827-9733)
PHONE.....................916 635-9767
Dale Hoffman, *President*
Nancy Barton, *Data Proc Staff*
Susana Williams, *Sales Mgr*
Michael Lahlouh, *Manager*
EMP: 55 **EST:** 1984
SALES (est): 1.4MM **Privately Held**
WEB: www.starindustries.net
SIC: 7349 Janitorial service, contract basis

(P-11925)
BAY CONTRACT MAINTENANCE INC
1129 Airport Blvd, South San Francisco (94080-1821)
PHONE.....................650 737-5902
Pedro Rivera, *Owner*
Aracely Rivera, *Principal*
Jorge Rivera, *Technology*
EMP: 40
SALES (est): 2MM **Privately Held**
WEB: www.baycontract.com
SIC: 7349 Janitorial service, contract basis

(P-11926)
BILLING SERVICES PLUS DBA APEX
70 Dorman Ave, San Francisco (94124-1809)
PHONE.....................415 604-3515
Gina Gregori, *Principal*
EMP: 99 **EST:** 2016
SQ FT: 300

SALES (est): 2.1MM **Privately Held**
SIC: 7349 Building & office cleaning services; building cleaning service

(P-11927)
BISSELL BROTHERS JANITORIAL
Also Called: Bissell Bros Bldg Maint Servic
3207 Luyung Dr, Rancho Cordova (95742-6862)
PHONE.....................916 635-1852
David Bissell, *CEO*
EMP: 80 **EST:** 1980
SQ FT: 2,400
SALES (est): 924.8K **Privately Held**
WEB: www.cleaningcrew.com
SIC: 7349 Janitorial service, contract basis

(P-11928)
BORA BORA RESIDENTIAL COML CLE
3135 Clayton Rd Ste 208, Concord (94519-2796)
PHONE.....................925 243-5992
Monica Galli, *CEO*
EMP: 35 **EST:** 2019
SALES (est): 1MM **Privately Held**
WEB: www.cleaningserviceconcordca.com
SIC: 7349 Janitorial service, contract basis

(P-11929)
BRILLIANT GENERAL MAINT INC (PA)
Also Called: Bgm
954 Chestnut St, San Jose (95110-1504)
PHONE.....................408 287-6708
Daniel Montes, *CEO*
Anna Corona, *Regional Mgr*
Adalet Aguiar, *Opers Mgr*
Eleuterio Pacheco, *Opers Mgr*
Daniel H Montes, *Marketing Staff*
EMP: 185 **EST:** 1983
SQ FT: 6,000
SALES (est): 10.2MM **Privately Held**
WEB: www.rcc-bgm.com
SIC: 7349 Building maintenance, except repairs; janitorial service, contract basis

(P-11930)
BUILDING & FACILITIES SVCS LLC (PA)
Also Called: Complete Building Services
63 Bovet Rd Ste 334, San Mateo (94402-3104)
PHONE.....................650 458-9083
William Miranda,
Anthony Venturi,
Jaylene Poirier, *Manager*
EMP: 173 **EST:** 2005
SALES (est): 8.9MM **Privately Held**
WEB: www.completebuildingserv.com
SIC: 7349 Janitorial service, contract basis

(P-11931)
BUILDING SERVICES/SYSTEM INC
2575 Stanwell Dr, Concord (94520-4888)
PHONE.....................925 688-1234
Sam Martinovich, *Principal*
Sam Mardinovich, *Principal*
EMP: 35 **EST:** 2009
SALES (est): 1.2MM **Privately Held**
WEB: www.bsminc.com
SIC: 7349 Janitorial service, contract basis

(P-11932)
CALEDONIAN BUILDING SVCS INC
47 Rickenbacker Cir, Livermore (94551-7212)
PHONE.....................925 803-3500
James Sherry, *President*
Stephen Sherry, *Vice Pres*
EMP: 39 **EST:** 1996
SALES (est): 4.3MM **Privately Held**
WEB: www.caledonianservices.com
SIC: 7349 Window cleaning

(P-11933)
CAPPSTONE INC
1699 Valencia St, San Francisco (94110-5012)
PHONE.....................415 821-6757
Cori Chipman, *CEO*

Michael Henriques, *COO*
Cameron Mahoney, *CFO*
Nicholas D Mettler, *Principal*
Adriana Rico, *Personnel Assit*
EMP: 150 **EST:** 2012
SALES (est): 6.5MM **Privately Held**
WEB: www.nomoredirt.com
SIC: 7349 Janitorial service, contract basis

(P-11934)
CEPHAS ENTERPRISES INC
Also Called: ServiceMaster
1365 Lowrie Ave, South San Francisco (94080-6403)
PHONE.....................650 244-0310
Steve Vandenverg, *President*
David Decker, *President*
EMP: 35 **EST:** 1967
SQ FT: 15,000
SALES (est): 232.3K **Privately Held**
WEB: www.servicemaster.com
SIC: 7349 1799 Building maintenance services; post-disaster renovations

(P-11935)
CJ MODEL HOME MAINTENANCE INC
240 Spring St, Pleasanton (94566-6626)
P.O. Box 5547 (94566-1547)
PHONE.....................925 485-3280
Carrie Wevill, *President*
Richard Wevill, *Admin Sec*
EMP: 70 **EST:** 1990
SQ FT: 2,200
SALES (est): 2.9MM **Privately Held**
WEB: www.cjsmodelhome.com
SIC: 7349 Building component cleaning service

(P-11936)
CLEANAIR IMAGE INC
Also Called: SERVPRO Belmont / San Carlos
2334 Stagecoach Rd Ste J, Stockton (95215-7939)
P.O. Box 422, San Carlos (94070-0422)
PHONE.....................510 352-2480
Roy Drake, *President*
Clayton A Barry, *Vice Pres*
EMP: 54 **EST:** 2004
SALES (est): 6.1MM **Privately Held**
WEB: www.servprostockton.com
SIC: 7349 Building maintenance services

(P-11937)
COUNTY OF SAN JOAQUIN
Also Called: Facilities MGT Div Bldg Maint
4520 W Eight Mile Rd, Stockton (95209-8701)
PHONE.....................209 468-3357
Rex Grayson, *Branch Mgr*
EMP: 64
SALES (corp-wide): 1.2B **Privately Held**
WEB: www.sjgov.org
SIC: 9111 7349 County supervisors' & executives' offices; building maintenance, except repairs
PA: County Of San Joaquin
44 N San Joaquin St # 640
Stockton CA 95202
209 468-3203

(P-11938)
CROWN BUILDING MAINTENANCE CO
1832 Tribute Rd Ste H, Sacramento (95815-4309)
PHONE.....................916 920-9556
Jeff Marquis, *Principal*
Claudia Mondragon, *Office Mgr*
EMP: 285
SALES (corp-wide): 270.5MM **Privately Held**
WEB: www.ableserve.com
SIC: 7349 1623 Janitorial service, contract basis; water, sewer & utility lines
PA: Crown Building Maintenance Co.
868 Folsom St
San Francisco CA 94107
415 981-8070

(P-11939)
CROWN BUILDING MAINTENANCE CO
235 Pine St Ste 600, San Francisco (94104-2745)
PHONE.....................303 680-3713
Dan Jaster, *Branch Mgr*
EMP: 285
SALES (corp-wide): 270.5MM **Privately Held**
WEB: www.ableserve.com
SIC: 7349 8711 Janitorial service, contract basis; engineering services
PA: Crown Building Maintenance Co.
868 Folsom St
San Francisco CA 94107
415 981-8070

(P-11940)
CROWN BUILDING MAINTENANCE CO
Also Called: Able Building Maintenance
1143 N Market Blvd Ste 3, Sacramento (95834-1913)
PHONE.....................415 546-6534
EMP: 285
SALES (corp-wide): 270.5MM **Privately Held**
WEB: www.ableserve.com
SIC: 7349 Janitorial service, contract basis
PA: Crown Building Maintenance Co.
868 Folsom St
San Francisco CA 94107
415 981-8070

(P-11941)
DAVE CALHOUN AND ASSOC LLC
2575 Stanwell Dr Ste 100, Concord (94520-4838)
PHONE.....................925 688-1234
Sam Martinovich, *CEO*
Dave Calhoun, *President*
Don Debeaumont, *Vice Pres*
Missy Calhoun, *Administration*
Robanne Olson, *Accounts Exec*
EMP: 195 **EST:** 1985
SALES (est): 7.1MM **Privately Held**
SIC: 7349 Janitorial service, contract basis

(P-11942)
DCS ASPHALT MAINTENANCE
1470 Warrington Rd, Santa Rosa (95404-9781)
P.O. Box 2622, Rohnert Park (94927-2622)
PHONE.....................415 577-6705
Donny Edward Costa, *CEO*
EMP: 37 **EST:** 2014
SALES (est): 220.4K **Privately Held**
SIC: 7349 Building maintenance services

(P-11943)
DELTA TECH SERVICE INC (PA)
397 W Channel Rd, Benicia (94510-1117)
PHONE.....................707 745-2080
Curtis S Johnson, *President*
G Leslie Johnson, *Shareholder*
Greg Niemuth, *CFO*
Gregg Niemuth, *Officer*
Karna Davis, *Vice Pres*
EMP: 35 **EST:** 1970
SQ FT: 6,000
SALES (est): 20.4MM **Privately Held**
WEB: www.deltatechservice.com
SIC: 7349 Cleaning service, industrial or commercial; chemical cleaning services

(P-11944)
DMS FACILITY SERVICES INC
Also Called: D M S
3137 Skyway Ct, Fremont (94539-5910)
PHONE.....................510 656-9400
Loren Dotts, *Manager*
Jhovana Montes, *Relations*
EMP: 1245
SALES (corp-wide): 29MM **Privately Held**
WEB: www.dmsfacilityservices.com
SIC: 7349 0782 Building maintenance, except repairs; lawn & garden services
PA: Dms Facility Services, Inc.
1040 Arroyo Dr
South Pasadena CA 91030
626 305-8500

7349 - Building Cleaning & Maintenance Svcs, NEC County (P-11945)

(P-11945)
ELEMENTS MOUNTAIN COMPANY
17356 Northwoods Blvd, Truckee (96161-6045)
PHONE.................................530 582-0300
EMP: 42 EST: 2018
SALES (est): 3.1MM Privately Held
WEB: www.elementsmtn.co
SIC: 7349 Building & office cleaning services

(P-11946)
ENVIRONMENT CONTROL
3065 N Sunnyside Ave # 101, Fresno (93727-1344)
PHONE.................................559 456-9791
Dick Johns, Partner
Kit Seals, Partner
Johan Johnson, Data Proc Staff
Patricia Cardenas, Human Res Dir
Terry Williams, Sales Mgr
EMP: 43 EST: 1967
SALES (est): 1.7MM Privately Held
WEB: www.environmentcontrol.com
SIC: 7349 Janitorial service, contract basis

(P-11947)
EXCEL BUILDING SERVICES LLC
1061 Serpentine Ln Ste H, Pleasanton (94566-4793)
PHONE.................................925 474-1080
Jennifer Fabrique, CEO
Jack Fabrique, President
Steve Sui, CFO
Scott Henley, Exec VP
Joe Persico, Vice Pres
EMP: 1300 EST: 1998
SQ FT: 5,000
SALES (est): 39.4MM Privately Held
WEB: www.excelbuildingservices.com
SIC: 7349 Janitorial service, contract basis

(P-11948)
FACILITY MASTERS INC (PA)
1604 Kerley Dr, San Jose (95112-4815)
PHONE.................................408 436-9090
Ramsin Bitmansour, CEO
James Machado, President
Osvaldo Almeida, Vice Pres
EMP: 230 EST: 1980
SQ FT: 7,000
SALES (est): 14MM Privately Held
WEB: www.facilitymasters.com
SIC: 7349 Janitorial service, contract basis

(P-11949)
FAIRFLD-SISUN UNIFIED SCHL DST
Also Called: Maintance
1650 Fairfield Ave, Fairfield (94533-3770)
PHONE.................................707 421-4253
Bill R Bucerevich, Director
EMP: 52
SALES (corp-wide): 274.7MM Privately Held
WEB: www.fsusd.org
SIC: 8211 7349 Public elementary & secondary schools; building maintenance services
PA: Fairfield-Suisun Unified School District
2490 Hilborn Rd
Fairfield CA 94534
707 399-5000

(P-11950)
FLAGSHIP AIRPORT SERVICES INC (HQ)
1050 N 5th St Ste E, San Jose (95112-4400)
PHONE.................................408 977-0155
David Pasek, Principal
Mark Cornish, Vice Pres
Jim Mikacich, Vice Pres
Rick Olesek, Vice Pres
Marion Terrell, Vice Pres
EMP: 454 EST: 2003
SQ FT: 40,000
SALES (est): 26.2MM Privately Held
WEB: www.flagshipinc.com
SIC: 7349 Janitorial service, contract basis

(P-11951)
FLAGSHIP ENTERPRISES HOLDG INC (PA)
1050 N 5th St Ste E, San Jose (95112-4400)
PHONE.................................408 977-0155
David M Pasek, President
Bill Benson, Senior VP
Bread Bakers, Admin Asst
Jackelyn Segura, Administration
Chad Jones, Engineer
EMP: 115 EST: 2009
SALES (est): 165.7MM Privately Held
WEB: www.flagshipinc.com
SIC: 7349 Janitorial service, contract basis

(P-11952)
FLAIR BUILDING SERVICES INC
Also Called: Flair Building Maintenance
3470 Edward Ave, Santa Clara (95054-2130)
PHONE.................................408 987-4040
Oscar Pena, President
Shirely McEvoy, Treasurer
EMP: 90 EST: 1976
SQ FT: 2,400
SALES (est): 1.7MM Privately Held
WEB: www.flairbuildingsvcs.com
SIC: 7349 Janitorial service, contract basis

(P-11953)
FLUOR FACILITY & PLANT SVCS
124 Blossom Hill Rd Ste H, San Jose (95123-2397)
PHONE.................................408 256-1333
Brett Heckel, Finance
Bob McAuley, Design Engr
Sam Marjiya, Engineer
Patty Richardson, Controller
EMP: 125
SALES (corp-wide): 15.6B Publicly Held
SIC: 7349 Building maintenance services
HQ: Fluor Facility & Plant Services, Inc
3 Polaris Way
Aliso Viejo CA

(P-11954)
FRANKS JANITORIAL SERVICE
2400 Oak St, NAPA (94559-2295)
PHONE.................................707 226-1848
Frank M Bozzini, President
Del Bozzini, Vice Pres
EMP: 47 EST: 1958
SQ FT: 1,500
SALES (est): 1.2MM Privately Held
WEB: www.franksjanitorial.com
SIC: 7349 Janitorial service, contract basis

(P-11955)
FULL SERVICE JANITORIAL INC
Also Called: Universal Janitorial Maint
350 Piercy Rd, San Jose (95138-1401)
PHONE.................................408 227-0600
Kevin Bridgeman, President
Trudi Bridgeman, Vice Pres
EMP: 45 EST: 1989
SQ FT: 5,500
SALES (est): 2.8MM Privately Held
WEB: www.universaljanitorial.com
SIC: 7349 Janitorial service, contract basis

(P-11956)
FULL SERVICE MAINTENANCE INC
Also Called: Universal Maintenance
350 Piercy Rd, San Jose (95138-1401)
PHONE.................................408 227-2400
Mike Burke, President
Andrew Ajluni, President
Dan Zajac, Vice Pres
EMP: 40 EST: 1984
SQ FT: 1,600
SALES (est): 4.9MM Privately Held
WEB: www.universalmaintenance.com
SIC: 7349 Janitorial service, contract basis

(P-11957)
GENESIS BUILDING SERVICES INC
Also Called: GBS Pest Control
916 S Claremont St, San Mateo (94402-1834)
P.O. Box 25360 (94402-5360)
PHONE.................................650 375-5935
Teresa Reif, President
Moira O'connell, Accounts Exec
EMP: 67 EST: 2004
SQ FT: 5,000
SALES (est): 4.7MM Privately Held
WEB: www.2genesis.com
SIC: 7349 Janitorial service, contract basis

(P-11958)
GREEN LIVING PLANET LLC
Also Called: Shine Facility Services
44 Montgomery St 4-101, San Francisco (94104-4602)
PHONE.................................415 715-4718
Luis Ramirez, Mng Member
EMP: 75 EST: 2011
SALES (est): 3.9MM Privately Held
WEB: www.shinefacilityservices.com
SIC: 7349 Janitorial service, contract basis

(P-11959)
HARPERS MODEL HOME SERVICES
Also Called: Harper's Model Homes Services
4900 Cothrin Ranch Rd, Shingle Springs (95682-7526)
P.O. Box 5527, El Dorado Hills (95762-0010)
PHONE.................................916 335-0282
Karen Harper, President
Garay Harper, Admin Sec
EMP: 40 EST: 1959
SQ FT: 1,600
SALES (est): 1MM Privately Held
SIC: 7349 Building cleaning service

(P-11960)
HARRIS LORENZO
Also Called: Janico Building Services
4704 Roseville Rd Ste 112, North Highlands (95660-5173)
PHONE.................................916 993-5863
Lorenzo Harris, Owner
Yolanda Harris, Co-Owner
Ramon Cofield, Area Spvr
EMP: 40 EST: 1985
SQ FT: 1,833
SALES (est): 1.8MM Privately Held
WEB: www.janicoservices.com
SIC: 7349 Janitorial service, contract basis

(P-11961)
IMPEC GROUP INC (PA)
3350 Scott Blvd Bldg 8, Santa Clara (95054-3108)
PHONE.................................408 330-9350
Raffy Espiritu, President
Kevin Manning, Exec VP
Christina Hudnall, Senior VP
Christine Chen, Vice Pres
Jason Fang, Admin Sec
EMP: 225 EST: 1991
SQ FT: 5,000
SALES (est): 15.9MM Privately Held
WEB: www.impecgroup.com
SIC: 7349 Janitorial service, contract basis

(P-11962)
INNOLUX OPTOELECTRONIC INC
Also Called: CHI MEI Optelectronics USA Inc
101 Metro Dr Ste 510, San Jose (95110-1343)
PHONE.................................408 573-8438
Junichi Ishii, CEO
Michelle MA, Accountant
Robert Meerten, Sr Project Mgr
Charles Darwin, Director
▲ EMP: 55 EST: 2002
SQ FT: 55,000
SALES (est): 9.2MM Privately Held
WEB: www.innolux.com
SIC: 7349 Janitorial service, contract basis
PA: Innolux Corporation
No. 160, Kesyue Rd., Hsinchu Science Park,
Chunan Chen MIA 35053

(P-11963)
JAMES FURULI INVESTMENT CO
Also Called: Environmental Dynamics
1320 Commerce St Ste T, Petaluma (94954-1470)
PHONE.................................707 778-7102
Jim Furuli, President
EMP: 55 EST: 1979
SQ FT: 1,100
SALES (est): 1.7MM Privately Held
WEB: www.envdynamics.com
SIC: 7349 1542 5087 Janitorial service, contract basis; building maintenance, except repairs; commercial & office building contractors; janitors' supplies

(P-11964)
JANI-KING OF CALIFORNIA INC
5050 Hopyard Rd Ste 225, Pleasanton (94588-3394)
PHONE.................................925 688-1120
Michael Dawson, Branch Mgr
Helen Nelson, Executive
EMP: 37
SALES (corp-wide): 122.1MM Privately Held
WEB: www.janiking.com
SIC: 7349 Janitorial service, contract basis
HQ: Jani-King Of California, Inc
16885 Dallas Pkwy
Addison TX 75001
972 991-0900

(P-11965)
JMEKM ENTERPRISES
Also Called: Perfect Shine Housekeeping
1072 S De Anza Blvd, San Jose (95129-3500)
PHONE.................................866 370-0419
EMP: 37
SALES: 926K Privately Held
WEB: www.perfectshinehousekeeping.com
SIC: 7349 Building Maintenance Svc

(P-11966)
LEWIS & TAYLOR LLC
Also Called: Lewis & Taylor Bldg Svc Contrs
440 Bryant St, San Francisco (94107-1303)
PHONE.................................415 781-3496
Michael L Milstein, President
Howard Sturdevant, Accounting Mgr
Mayela Ortiz, Human Res Mgr
Juan Vargas, Opers Dir
EMP: 150 EST: 1945
SQ FT: 4,000
SALES (est): 6.4MM Privately Held
WEB: www.lewistaylor.com
SIC: 7349 Janitorial service, contract basis; window cleaning; chemical cleaning services

(P-11967)
LITTLE GIANT BLDG MAINT INC (PA)
Also Called: Lg
1485 Bay Shore Blvd # 117, San Francisco (94124-4008)
PHONE.................................415 508-0282
David Dellanini, President
EMP: 74 EST: 1962
SQ FT: 1,000
SALES (est): 11.2MM Privately Held
SIC: 7349 Janitorial service, contract basis; building & office cleaning services; window cleaning

(P-11968)
LITTLE GIANT BLDG MAINT INC
15 Brooks Pl, Pacifica (94044-4403)
PHONE.................................415 508-0282
David Dellanini, President
EMP: 176
SALES (corp-wide): 11.2MM Privately Held
SIC: 7349 7217 Window cleaning; carpet & upholstery cleaning
PA: Little Giant Building Maintenance, Inc.
1485 Bay Shore Blvd # 117
San Francisco CA 94124
415 508-0282

(P-11969)
M & C RESTORATION INC
Also Called: ServiceMaster
11229 Mccourtney Rd, Grass Valley (95949-7412)
PHONE.................................530 273-1957
Charles R Heaps, President
April Stock, Principal
EMP: 56 EST: 1995
SQ FT: 3,000

PRODUCTS & SERVICES SECTION
7349 - Building Cleaning & Maintenance Svcs, NEC County (P-11994)

SALES (est): 301.5K **Privately Held**
WEB: www.servicemaster.com
SIC: 7349 5719 7217 1799 Building maintenance services; vertical blinds; carpet & furniture cleaning on location; post-disaster renovations; window blind repair services

(P-11970)
MELGAR FACILITY MAINT LLC (PA)
Also Called: Melgar Janitorial Solutions
6980 Santa Teresa Blvd, San Jose (95119-1393)
PHONE....................408 657-0110
Audelino Melgar Jr, *President*
Janet Herring, *Chief Mktg Ofcr*
Isaac Seymour, *Finance Mgr*
Jimmy Wooley, *Opers Staff*
Bertila Melgar,
EMP: 376 **EST:** 1986
SALES (est): 13.8MM **Privately Held**
WEB: www.mfmindustries.com
SIC: 7349 Janitorial service, contract basis

(P-11971)
MELIN ENTERPRISES INC
Also Called: ServiceMaster
812 W 18th St, Merced (95340-4605)
P.O. Box 2192 (95344-0192)
PHONE....................209 726-9182
David Melin, *President*
EMP: 70 **EST:** 2006
SALES (est): 4.2MM **Privately Held**
WEB: www.servicemaster.com
SIC: 7349 Building maintenance services

(P-11972)
MILLARD GROUP INC
1950 E 20th St, Chico (95928-6369)
PHONE....................530 899-7299
EMP: 187
SALES (corp-wide): 246.1MM **Privately Held**
WEB: www.millardgroup.com
SIC: 7349 Janitorial service, contract basis
PA: The Millard Group Inc
8140 River Dr
Morton Grove IL 60053
847 674-4100

(P-11973)
MILLER CREEK SCHOOL DISTRICT
Also Called: Dixie SC Dst Maint Dept
121 Marinwood Ave, San Rafael (94903-1521)
PHONE....................415 492-3776
Tim Walsh, *Director*
EMP: 142
SALES (corp-wide): 29.4MM **Privately Held**
SIC: 8211 7349 Public elementary school; school custodian, contract basis
PA: Miller Creek School District Inc
380 Nova Albion Way
San Rafael CA 94903
415 492-3700

(P-11974)
MISSION LINEN SUPPLY
6590 Central Ave, Newark (94560-3933)
PHONE....................510 996-3416
EMP: 99
SALES (corp-wide): 161.2MM **Privately Held**
WEB: www.missionlinen.com
SIC: 7349 7213 7211 Janitorial service, contract basis; linen supply; power laundries, family & commercial
PA: Mission Linen Supply
717 E Yanonali St
Santa Barbara CA 93103
805 730-3620

(P-11975)
MORENO & ASSOCIATES INC
782 Auzerais Ave, San Jose (95126-3503)
PHONE....................408 924-0353
Ernie Moreno, *President*
Paul Lima, *Vice Pres*
Alfredo Cortez, *Opers Spvr*
Rafael Merino, *Manager*
EMP: 60 **EST:** 1993

SALES (est): 6MM **Privately Held**
WEB: www.morenoclean.com
SIC: 7349 Janitorial service, contract basis

(P-11976)
MTNA INC
2855 S Elm Ave, Fresno (93706-5462)
PHONE....................559 354-9639
Ramon Haya, *Manager*
EMP: 40
SALES (corp-wide): 4MM **Privately Held**
SIC: 7349 Janitorial service, contract basis
PA: Mtna, Inc.
8950 Rochester Ave # 150
Rancho Cucamonga CA 91730
909 484-4332

(P-11977)
NAPA VALLEY UNIFIED SCHOOL DST
Also Called: Maintenance Office
1616 Lincoln Ave, NAPA (94558-4859)
PHONE....................707 253-3520
Don Evans, *Administration*
Mike Mansuy, *Officer*
EMP: 45
SALES (corp-wide): 246.9MM **Privately Held**
WEB: www.nvusd.k12.ca.us
SIC: 8211 7349 Public elementary & secondary schools; building maintenance services
PA: Napa Valley Unified School District
2425 Jefferson St
Napa CA 94558
707 253-3715

(P-11978)
NETWORK FCILTY SVCS GROUP LLC
Also Called: Network Fsg
48273 Lakeview Blvd, Fremont (94538-6519)
PHONE....................510 256-6035
EMP: 45 **EST:** 2012
SQ FT: 2,500
SALES (est): 770K **Privately Held**
SIC: 7349 Building Maintenance Services

(P-11979)
NEXSENTIO INC
1346 Ridder Park Dr, San Jose (95131-2313)
PHONE....................408 392-9249
Danielle Bunel, *President*
Rene Velazquez, *Vice Pres*
EMP: 54 **EST:** 2006
SALES (est): 15.5MM **Privately Held**
WEB: www.nexsentio.com
SIC: 7349 7299 Janitorial service, contract basis; handyman service

(P-11980)
NORTH COAST CLEANING SVCS INC
211 7th St, Eureka (95501-1701)
P.O. Box 177 (95502-0177)
PHONE....................707 269-0838
Dave Toor, *President*
Charles Powell, *President*
EMP: 50 **EST:** 1981
SALES (est): 3.9MM **Privately Held**
WEB: www.northcoastcleaning.com
SIC: 7349 Janitorial service, contract basis

(P-11981)
NOVA COMMERCIAL COMPANY INC (PA)
24683 Oneil Ave, Hayward (94544-1627)
P.O. Box 759 (94543-0759)
PHONE....................510 728-7000
Janice Slade, *Vice Pres*
Gabriela Gonzalez, *Executive*
Sophia Silva, *Principal*
Eleanor Anglin, *Opers Staff*
Larry Gillis, *Opers Staff*
EMP: 133 **EST:** 1968
SQ FT: 8,544
SALES (est): 7.5MM **Privately Held**
WEB: www.novacommercial.us
SIC: 7349 Janitorial service, contract basis

(P-11982)
OPTIMA BUILDING SERVICES MAINT
210 Mountain View Ave, Santa Rosa (95407-8203)
PHONE....................707 586-6640
Adolfo Mendoza, *President*
EMP: 100 **EST:** 2000
SALES (est): 2.6MM **Privately Held**
WEB: www.optimabuildingservices.com
SIC: 7349 Janitorial service, contract basis

(P-11983)
PACIFIC RESTORATION INC
Also Called: SERVPRO OF PETALUMA ROHNERT PA
373 Blodgett St, Cotati (94931-8700)
PHONE....................707 588-8226
Jesus Espinal, *President*
Jenny Villena, *Owner*
EMP: 45 **EST:** 2005
SALES (est): 10.3MM **Privately Held**
WEB: www.pacificrestoration.net
SIC: 7349 Building maintenance services

(P-11984)
PERFORMNCE FIRST BLDG SVCS INC (PA)
789 E Brokaw Rd, San Jose (95112-1014)
PHONE....................408 441-4632
Alvaro S Cuevas, *Principal*
EMP: 63 **EST:** 2009
SALES (est): 1.2MM **Privately Held**
WEB: www.perfirst.com
SIC: 7349 Janitorial service, contract basis

(P-11985)
POLARIS BUILDING MAINT INC
2580 Wyandotte St Ste E, Mountain View (94043-2366)
PHONE....................650 964-9400
Frank Schwarb, *President*
Roger Gomez, *Vice Pres*
EMP: 80 **EST:** 1983
SQ FT: 2,700
SALES (est): 3.2MM **Privately Held**
WEB: www.polarisbuildingmaintenance.net
SIC: 7349 Janitorial service, contract basis; building maintenance, except repairs

(P-11986)
PREMIER FLOOR CARE INC (PA)
390 Carrol Ct Ste C, Brentwood (94513-7376)
PHONE....................925 679-4901
Cedric Moore, *President*
EMP: 95 **EST:** 2000
SALES (est): 3.7MM **Privately Held**
WEB: www.premierfloorcare.com
SIC: 7349 3589 Janitorial service, contract basis; commercial cleaning equipment

(P-11987)
PROPERTY MAINTENANCE COMPANY (PA)
Also Called: Dkd Property Management
255 W Julian St Ste 301, San Jose (95110-2406)
PHONE....................408 297-7849
Sue Williams, *President*
EMP: 101 **EST:** 1979
SQ FT: 6,000
SALES (est): 2.6MM **Privately Held**
WEB: www.dkdproperties.com
SIC: 7349 Building maintenance, except repairs

(P-11988)
RAINBOW - BRITE INDUS SVCS LLC
Also Called: Santa Rosa Indian Cmnty of Snt
463 E Salmon River Dr, Fresno (93730-0860)
PHONE....................559 925-2580
Diana Tutson-Snowden, *CEO*
EMP: 925 **EST:** 2000
SALES (est): 453.1K **Privately Held**
WEB: www.rainbowbriteservices.com
SIC: 7349 Janitorial service, contract basis

PA: Santa Rosa Indian Community Of The Santa Rosa Rancheria
16835 Alkali Dr
Lemoore CA 93245
559 924-1278

(P-11989)
RESTORATION CLEAN UP CO INC (PA)
198 Harbor Ct, Pittsburg (94565-5063)
PHONE....................800 500-4310
Dean Miller, *CEO*
EMP: 39 **EST:** 2005
SQ FT: 29,600
SALES (est): 4.2MM **Privately Held**
WEB: www.thecleanupco.com
SIC: 7349 Building maintenance services

(P-11990)
RUBICON ENTERPRISES INC
Also Called: RUBICON PROGRAMS
2500 Bissell Ave, Richmond (94804-1815)
PHONE....................510 235-1516
Richard Aubry PHD, *Exec Dir*
EMP: 44 **EST:** 1995
SALES: 1.5MM **Privately Held**
WEB: www.rubiconprograms.org
SIC: 7349 8322 8331 Building maintenance services; social service center; job training & vocational rehabilitation services

(P-11991)
RUBICON PROGRAMS INCORPORATED (PA)
2500 Bissell Ave, Richmond (94804-1815)
PHONE....................510 235-1516
Jane Fischberg, *President*
Adrienne Kimball, *Officer*
Hallie Friedman, *Administration*
Alexander Pfeifer-Rosenblum, *Development*
Dechen Naga, *Accounting Mgr*
EMP: 66 **EST:** 1973
SQ FT: 14,500
SALES: 15.1MM **Privately Held**
WEB: www.rubiconprograms.org
SIC: 7349 8322 8331 Building maintenance services; social service center; job training & vocational rehabilitation services

(P-11992)
SANITATION PROCESS CONTROL LLC
24 W Jamestown St Apt 307, Stockton (95207-7231)
PHONE....................510 909-4910
Gonzalo De La Cruz, *President*
EMP: 50 **EST:** 2013
SALES (est): 2.6MM **Privately Held**
WEB: www.saniprocess.com
SIC: 7349 Janitorial service, contract basis

(P-11993)
SANTA CLARA VALLEY CORPORATION
Also Called: Swenson Developers and Contrs
715 N 1st St Ste 27, San Jose (95112-6309)
PHONE....................408 947-1100
Case Swenson, *President*
Lisa Swenson, *Admin Sec*
Heather Solis, *Project Mgr*
Kevin Young, *Project Mgr*
Aaron Gallaty, *Sales Staff*
EMP: 85 **EST:** 1974
SQ FT: 1,200
SALES (est): 8.6MM **Privately Held**
WEB: www.wewillrentforyou.com
SIC: 7349 0782 7623 7699 Building maintenance, except repairs; janitorial service, contract basis; lawn services; refrigeration service & repair; elevators: inspection, service & repair

(P-11994)
SBM MANAGEMENT SERVICES LP
5241 Arnold Ave, McClellan (95652-1025)
PHONE....................866 855-2211
Charles Somers, *CEO*
Ken Silva, *CFO*
Marcos Salvi, *Chief Mktg Ofcr*
Roger Dau, *Exec VP*

7349 - Building Cleaning & Maintenance Svcs, NEC County (P-11995)

Paul Emperador, *Exec VP*
EMP: 300 **EST:** 2007
SALES (est): 71.7MM **Privately Held**
WEB: www.sbmmanagement.com
SIC: 7349 Janitorial service, contract basis

(P-11995)
SBM SITE SERVICES LLC (PA)
Also Called: S B M
5241 Arnold Ave, McClellan (95652-1025)
PHONE 916 922-7600
Charles Somers, *Mng Member*
Ron Alvarado, *Partner*
Ronald Alvarado, *Partner*
Carina O'Brien, *CFO*
Ken Silva, *Officer*
EMP: 100 **EST:** 1994
SQ FT: 25,000
SALES (est): 104.2MM **Privately Held**
WEB: www.sbmmanagement.com
SIC: 7349 Janitorial service, contract basis

(P-11996)
SERVICE BY MEDALLION
Also Called: Medallion Cnstr Clean-Up
411 Clyde Ave, Mountain View (94043-2209)
PHONE 650 625-1010
Roland H Strick, *CEO*
Elias Nacif, *Vice Pres*
Roland F Strick, *Vice Pres*
Trino Cardenas, *District Mgr*
Ruben Lopez, *District Mgr*
EMP: 620 **EST:** 1978
SQ FT: 7,000
SALES (est): 45.9MM **Privately Held**
WEB: www.servicebymedallion.com
SIC: 7349 Janitorial service, contract basis

(P-11997)
SERVPRO OF MENDOCINO
3001 S State St Ste 5, Ukiah (95482-6966)
PHONE 707 462-3848
Doug Bridges, *Principal*
EMP: 50 **EST:** 2017
SALES (est): 991.4K **Privately Held**
WEB: www.servpro.com
SIC: 7349 Building maintenance services

(P-11998)
SIGNATURE BUILDING MAINT INC
4005 Clipper Ct, Fremont (94538-6540)
P.O. Box 110340, Campbell (95011-0340)
PHONE 408 377-8066
Anna Murphy, *President*
Jeff Lolyd, *CFO*
Patrick Murphy, *General Mgr*
Tony Reyes, *Admin Sec*
Joel Everidge, *Superintendent*
EMP: 80
SALES (est): 3MM **Privately Held**
WEB: www.signaturefacilities.com
SIC: 7349 Janitorial service, contract basis

(P-11999)
SIGNIFICANT CLEANING SVCS LLC
148 E Virginia St Ste 1, San Jose (95112-5881)
PHONE 408 559-5959
Larry Lovaglia,
Anthony Lovaglia, *Business Mgr*
Eduardo Cardoza, *Opers Mgr*
Nelson Celada, *Facilities Mgr*
Juan Almazo, *Supervisor*
EMP: 105 **EST:** 1988 **Privately Held**
WEB: www.significantcleaning.com
SIC: 7349 Cleaning service, industrial or commercial

(P-12000)
SONOMA VALLEY UNIFIED SCHL DST
18751 Railroad Ave, Sonoma (95476-4570)
PHONE 707 935-4291
Eric Muller, *Manager*
EMP: 51
SALES (corp-wide): 71.9MM **Privately Held**
WEB: www.sonomaschools.org
SIC: 8211 7349 Public elementary school; building maintenance services

PA: Sonoma Valley Unified School District
17850 Railroad Ave
Sonoma CA 95476
707 935-6000

(P-12001)
SPENCER BUILDING MAINTENANCE
10457 Old Placerville Rd # 10, Sacramento (95827-2508)
PHONE 916 922-1900
Aaron D Spencer, *President*
Gordon Platt, *Business Mgr*
Jose Yanez, *Opers Staff*
Julie Bizal, *Manager*
Aracely Gonzalez, *Supervisor*
EMP: 307 **EST:** 1997
SQ FT: 5,000
SALES (est): 14MM **Privately Held**
WEB: www.spencerservices.com
SIC: 7349 Janitorial service, contract basis

(P-12002)
SUMMIT BUILDING SERVICES INC
1128 Willow Pass Ct, Concord (94520-1006)
PHONE 925 827-9500
Matt Colchico, *CEO*
Seth Pitzer, *Office Mgr*
Teri Forde, *Clerk*
EMP: 100 **EST:** 1996
SALES (est): 7.1MM **Privately Held**
SIC: 7349 Janitorial service, contract basis

(P-12003)
SUPERIOR BUILDINGS SVCS INC
1070 Horizon Dr Ste I, Fairfield (94533-1604)
PHONE 707 429-3000
Bill Perry, *Owner*
EMP: 45 **EST:** 1978
SALES (est): 1.1MM **Privately Held**
WEB: www.sbsjanitorial.com
SIC: 7349 Janitorial service, contract basis

(P-12004)
SWA SERVICES GROUP INC
64 Bonaventura Dr, San Jose (95134-2123)
PHONE 408 938-8678
Solomon Wong, *CEO*
Carrie Li, *Vice Pres*
Nancy Cortes, *Human Resources*
EMP: 45 **EST:** 2000
SALES (est): 1.5MM **Privately Held**
WEB: www.swagreen.com
SIC: 7349 Janitorial service, contract basis

(P-12005)
TOTAL QUALITY MAINTENANCE INC
895 Commercial St, Palo Alto (94303-4906)
PHONE 650 846-4700
Peter Vesanovic, *President*
Dee Vesanovic, *Admin Sec*
EMP: 180 **EST:** 1997
SQ FT: 2,000
SALES (est): 8.2MM **Privately Held**
WEB: www.tqm.bz
SIC: 7349 Janitorial service, contract basis

(P-12006)
TRASHLOGIC LLC
5740 Windmill Way Ste 17, Carmichael (95608-1379)
PHONE 916 900-4008
Lainika Johnson, *CEO*
EMP: 35 **EST:** 2016
SQ FT: 1,350
SALES (est): 1.8MM **Privately Held**
WEB: www.trashlogic.com
SIC: 7349 Janitorial service, contract basis

(P-12007)
TRINITY BUILDING SERVICES
1071 Sneath Ln, San Bruno (94066-2311)
PHONE 650 873-2121
Mike A Boschetto, *President*
EMP: 59 **EST:** 1987
SALES (est): 2.4MM **Privately Held**
WEB: www.trinityservices.com
SIC: 7349 Janitorial service, contract basis

(P-12008)
UNITED BUILDING MAINT INC
8211 Sierra College Blvd, Roseville (95661-9404)
PHONE 916 772-8101
Valerie Lynne Sherman, *CEO*
Ruy Couto, *Vice Pres*
Paula Fischer, *Vice Pres*
Stephanie Kearns, *Manager*
Vianney Tinoco, *Supervisor*
EMP: 225 **EST:** 2007
SQ FT: 2,500
SALES (est): 4.3MM **Privately Held**
WEB: www.unitedfullservice.com
SIC: 7349 Janitorial service, contract basis

(P-12009)
UNITED CONTRACT SERVICES INC
1161 Ringwood Ct Ste 170, San Jose (95131-1758)
PHONE 408 577-0105
Cyrus K Anvari, *President*
▲ **EMP:** 40 **EST:** 1991
SALES (est): 3.4MM **Privately Held**
WEB: www.ucsteam.com
SIC: 7349 Janitorial service, contract basis

(P-12010)
UNIVERSAL BLDG SVCS & SUP CO
Also Called: Universal Building Svc & Sup
1318 Ross St, Petaluma (94954-6526)
PHONE 707 781-7434
Leonard Bruso, *Owner*
EMP: 92
SALES (corp-wide): 34.4MM **Privately Held**
WEB: www.ubsco.com
SIC: 7349 Janitorial service, contract basis
PA: Universal Building Services And Supply Co.
3120 Pierce St
Richmond CA 94804
510 527-1078

(P-12011)
UNIVERSAL BLDG SVCS & SUP CO (PA)
3120 Pierce St, Richmond (94804-5996)
PHONE 510 527-1078
Grace Brusseau, *CEO*
Leonard Brusseau, *President*
Glen Sondag, *Vice Pres*
Garrett Pringle, *Executive*
James Hulburd, *Managing Dir*
EMP: 250
SQ FT: 20,000
SALES (est): 34.4MM **Privately Held**
WEB: www.ubsco.com
SIC: 7349 5087 5169 Janitorial service, contract basis; janitors' supplies; chemicals & allied products

(P-12012)
UNIVERSAL BLDG SVCS & SUP CO
421 N Buchanan Cir, Pacheco (94553-5142)
PHONE 925 934-5533
Frank Batra, *Controller*
EMP: 92
SALES (corp-wide): 34.4MM **Privately Held**
WEB: www.ubsco.com
SIC: 7349 Janitorial service, contract basis
PA: Universal Building Services And Supply Co.
3120 Pierce St
Richmond CA 94804
510 527-1078

(P-12013)
UNIVERSAL BLDG SVCS & SUP CO
430 Roberson Ln, San Jose (95112-1125)
PHONE 408 995-5111
Su Miles, *Branch Mgr*
EMP: 92
SALES (corp-wide): 34.4MM **Privately Held**
WEB: www.ubsco.com
SIC: 7349 Janitorial service, contract basis

PA: Universal Building Services And Supply Co.
3120 Pierce St
Richmond CA 94804
510 527-1078

(P-12014)
UNIVERSAL SITE SERVICES INC (PA)
760 E Capitol Ave, Milpitas (95035-6812)
PHONE 800 647-9337
Gina Vella, *President*
Joseph Vella, *Vice Pres*
Ricardo Alimorong, *Regional Mgr*
Ken Koch, *Regional Mgr*
Kevin Parker, *Regional Mgr*
EMP: 107 **EST:** 1958
SQ FT: 20,000 **Privately Held**
WEB: www.universalsiteservices.com
SIC: 7349 4959 0782 Building maintenance, except repairs; road, airport & parking lot maintenance services; lawn services

7352 Medical Eqpt Rental & Leasing

(P-12015)
TIMBERLAKE CORPORATION
Also Called: Timberlake Medical Gas Supply
8322 Ferguson Ave, Sacramento (95828-0902)
PHONE 916 423-2198
Steve Vinci, *General Mgr*
Nadine Cassella, *Accounts Mgr*
EMP: 73 **EST:** 1982
SALES (est): 9.5MM
SALES (corp-wide): 13.2B **Privately Held**
WEB: www.sutterhealth.org
SIC: 5999 7352 Medical apparatus & supplies; medical equipment rental
HQ: Sutter Ambulatory Care Corp
1 Capitol Mall Ste 390
Sacramento CA 95814
916 733-8800

7353 Heavy Construction Eqpt Rental & Leasing

(P-12016)
AMERICAN CRANE RENTAL INC
17800 Comconex Rd, Manteca (95336-8121)
P.O. Box 308, Escalon (95320-0308)
PHONE 209 838-8815
Keith Powell, *CEO*
Denise Powell, *CFO*
Everett Powell, *Vice Pres*
Nic Belletto, *Project Mgr*
Gary Rich, *Accounting Mgr*
EMP: 65 **EST:** 2002
SALES (est): 27.7MM **Privately Held**
WEB: www.americancranerental.net
SIC: 7353 Cranes & aerial lift equipment, rental or leasing

(P-12017)
CAITCON LLC
2001 Crow Canyon Rd # 110, San Ramon (94583-5368)
PHONE 925 314-7100
Gary Cappa, *Principal*
EMP: 564 **EST:** 2008
SALES (est): 1.3MM
SALES (corp-wide): 468.2MM **Publicly Held**
WEB: www.boxwoodmc.com
SIC: 7353 Heavy construction equipment rental
PA: Atlas Technical Consultants, Inc.
13215 Bee Cave Pkwy B230
Austin TX 78738
512 851-1501

(P-12018)
CALIFRNIA HIGH RACH EQP RNTL I
531 Bitritto Way, Modesto (95356-9237)
P.O. Box 578519 (95357-8519)
PHONE 209 577-0515
Thomas Randall, *CEO*

PRODUCTS & SERVICES SECTION

7359 - Equipment Rental & Leasing, NEC County (P-12042)

Paige Airington, *Accounts Mgr*
EMP: 41 **EST:** 2000
SALES (est): 8.3MM **Privately Held**
WEB: www.cahighreach.com
SIC: 7353 Heavy construction equipment rental

(P-12019)
CALIFRNIA SRVYING DRFTG SUP IN (PA)
Also Called: CSDS
4733 Auburn Blvd, Sacramento (95841-3601)
PHONE...............................916 344-0232
Bruce Gandelman, *CEO*
Tom Cardenas, *President*
Mike Woodel, *Vice Pres*
Dan Soldavini, *Principal*
Dan Cooney, *Graphic Designe*
EMP: 49 **EST:** 1986
SQ FT: 17,500
SALES (est): 27.9MM **Privately Held**
WEB: www.csdsinc.com
SIC: 7353 3993 5082 5045 Heavy construction equipment rental; displays & cutouts, window & lobby; general construction machinery & equipment; printers, computer; drafting supplies; printers & plotters

(P-12020)
FAIRFIELD RENTAL SERVICE INC
Also Called: All Star Rentals
2525 Clay Bank Rd, Fairfield (94533-1656)
PHONE...............................707 422-2270
Kenton De Vries, *President*
EMP: 16 **EST:** 1963
SQ FT: 12,000
SALES (est): 2.5MM **Privately Held**
WEB: www.allstarrents.com
SIC: 7353 7359 3273 Heavy construction equipment rental; rental store, general; ready-mixed concrete

(P-12021)
GALENA EQUIPMENT RENTAL LLC
Also Called: Biggie Crane and Ritting
10700 Bigge St, San Leandro (94577-1032)
PHONE...............................510 638-8100
Brock Settlemier,
Reid Settlemier,
Weston Settlemier,
EMP: 86 **EST:** 1999
SALES (est): 3.5MM **Privately Held**
WEB: www.bigge.com
SIC: 7353 Cranes & aerial lift equipment, rental or leasing

(P-12022)
SHEEDY DRAYAGE CO (PA)
1215 Michigan St, San Francisco (94107-3518)
P.O. Box 77004 (94107-0004)
PHONE...............................415 648-7171
Don Russell, *Chairman*
Richard Battaini, *President*
Michael A Battaini, *CEO*
Peter Hogan, *Corp Secy*
▲ **EMP:** 80 **EST:** 1925
SQ FT: 25,000
SALES (est): 21.2MM **Privately Held**
WEB: www.sheedycrane.com
SIC: 7353 Cranes & aerial lift equipment, rental or leasing

(P-12023)
SILLER AND SILLER CONSTRUCTION
13286 Vineyard Ln, Penn Valley (95946)
P.O. Box 430 (95946-0430)
PHONE...............................916 893-3462
Neal Mac Arthur Siller, *Principal*
EMP: 16 **EST:** 2017
SALES (est): 1.8MM **Privately Held**
WEB: www.sillerconstruction.com
SIC: 7353 1611 1442 Heavy construction equipment rental; general contractor, highway & street construction; construction sand & gravel

(P-12024)
SUMMIT CRANE INC
892 Aldridge Rd, Vacaville (95688-9282)
P.O. Box 6714 (95696-6714)
PHONE...............................707 448-6740
Cheryl Posthuma, *Principal*
EMP: 43 **EST:** 2009
SALES (est): 1.3MM **Privately Held**
WEB: www.summitcrane.net
SIC: 7353 Cranes & aerial lift equipment, rental or leasing

7359 Equipment Rental & Leasing, NEC

(P-12025)
(A) TOOL SHED INC (PA)
Also Called: A Tool Shed Equipment Rentals
3700 Soquel Ave, Santa Cruz (95062-1774)
PHONE...............................831 477-7133
Robert Pedersen, *President*
Lars Pedersen, *Vice Pres*
EMP: 48 **EST:** 1945
SQ FT: 2,500
SALES (est): 26.2MM **Privately Held**
WEB: www.atoolshed.com
SIC: 7359 Tool rental

(P-12026)
A & A PORTABLES INC
201 Roscoe Rd, Modesto (95357-1828)
PHONE...............................209 524-0401
Bill King, *CEO*
Michael King, *Admin Sec*
Dan Markkula, *Manager*
EMP: 39 **EST:** 1960
SQ FT: 6,000
SALES (est): 4.8MM **Privately Held**
WEB: www.unitedsiteservices.com
SIC: 7359 5082 3448 7699 Portable toilet rental; contractors' materials; prefabricated metal buildings; septic tank cleaning service

(P-12027)
ADDLIFE
1190 Kern Ave, Sunnyvale (94085-3907)
PHONE...............................650 556-9430
Lorie Townsend, *President*
Mandi Wight, *Branch Mgr*
Rita Zamacona, *Director*
Suzette Upchurch, *Manager*
Karine Murray, *Supervisor*
EMP: 35 **EST:** 1981
SQ FT: 11,000
SALES (est): 3.4MM **Privately Held**
WEB: www.addlife.com
SIC: 7359 Live plant rental

(P-12028)
AFTER-PARTY2 INC
22674 Broadway A, Sonoma (95476-8217)
PHONE...............................408 457-1187
EMP: 74 **Publicly Held**
SIC: 7359 Party supplies rental services
HQ: After-Party2, Inc.
901 W Hillcrest Blvd
Inglewood CA 90301
310 202-0011

(P-12029)
ARENA STUART RENTALS INC
454 S Abbott Ave, Milpitas (95035-5258)
PHONE...............................408 856-3232
Michael Berman, *President*
EMP: 150 **EST:** 2018
SALES (est): 4.1MM **Privately Held**
WEB: www.stuartrental.com
SIC: 5947 7359 Party favors; party supplies rental services; dishes, silverware, tables & banquet accessories rental; rental store, general; tent & tarpaulin rental

(P-12030)
BA LEASING & CAPITAL CORP (DH)
555 California St Fl 4, San Francisco (94104-1506)
PHONE...............................415 765-1804
Richard Harris, *President*
K Thomas Rose, *COO*

Rod Hurd, *Treasurer*
Oliver James Warner, *Vice Pres*
EMP: 130 **EST:** 1955
SALES (est): 44.7MM
SALES (corp-wide): 93.7B **Publicly Held**
SIC: 7359 Equipment rental & leasing
HQ: Banc Of America Leasing & Capital, Llc
555 California St Fl 4
San Francisco CA 94104
415 765-7349

(P-12031)
BAY CITIES CRANE & RIGGING INC (PA)
Also Called: Bragg Crane & Rigging
457 Parr Blvd, Richmond (94801-1133)
PHONE...............................510 232-7222
Marilynn Bragg, *President*
Mary Ann Pool, *Corp Secy*
Jon Elliff, *Opers Mgr*
Edward Gray, *Sales Staff*
Barry Baldwin, *Manager*
EMP: 49 **EST:** 1970
SQ FT: 10,000
SALES (est): 5.9MM **Privately Held**
WEB: www.braggcompanies.com
SIC: 7359 7353 Equipment rental & leasing; cranes & aerial lift equipment, rental or leasing

(P-12032)
BRIGHT EVENT RENTALS LLC
22674 Broadway Ste A, Sonoma (95476-8217)
PHONE...............................310 202-0011
Matt Wiltshire, *Manager*
EMP: 52
SALES (corp-wide): 34.4MM **Privately Held**
WEB: www.bright.com
SIC: 7359 Party supplies rental services
PA: Bright Event Rentals, Llc
1640 W 190th St Ste A
Torrance CA 90501
310 202-0011

(P-12033)
CAI INTERNATIONAL INC (PA)
1 Market Plz Ste 2400, San Francisco (94105-1102)
PHONE...............................415 788-0100
Timothy B Page, *President*
David G Remington, *Ch of Bd*
Steven J Garcia,
Camille G Cutino, *Senior VP*
Daniel J Hallahan, *Senior VP*
▼ **EMP:** 39 **EST:** 1989
SALES (est): 294MM **Publicly Held**
WEB: www.capps.com
SIC: 7359 Shipping container leasing

(P-12034)
CENTRAL VALLEY PARTY SUPPLY
Also Called: Grand Events
3250 Dale Rd Ste I, Modesto (95356-0578)
PHONE...............................209 569-0399
Ray Pogue, *Principal*
EMP: 50 **EST:** 1991
SQ FT: 37,000
SALES (est): 3.7MM **Privately Held**
WEB: www.thepartyguys.party
SIC: 7359 Party supplies rental services

(P-12035)
CONCORD JET SERVICE INC
3000 Oak Rd Ste 200, Walnut Creek (94597-4506)
P.O. Box 907, Concord (94522-0907)
PHONE...............................925 825-2980
Kenneth Hoffman, *President*
Goy Fuller, *Principal*
Dewayne Herrman, *Manager*
EMP: 50 **EST:** 1988
SALES (est): 8MM **Privately Held**
WEB: www.concordjetcenter.com
SIC: 7359 Aircraft rental

(P-12036)
CONTRACTORS SCAFFOLD SUP INC
229 Harbor Way, South San Francisco (94080-6811)
PHONE...............................650 871-8190

Mark Tessum, *President*
Janet Vergara, *Treasurer*
Karen Tessum, *Vice Pres*
EMP: 53 **EST:** 1936
SQ FT: 15,000
SALES (est): 1.1MM **Privately Held**
WEB: www.contractorsscaffold.com
SIC: 7359 5082 Equipment rental & leasing; scaffolding

(P-12037)
CP OPCO LLC
Also Called: Classic Party Rentals
22674 Broadway A, Sonoma (95476-8217)
PHONE...............................707 253-2332
EMP: 59
SALES (corp-wide): 1.9MM **Privately Held**
SIC: 7359 Equipment Rental/Leasing
HQ: Cp Opco, Llc
901 W Hillcrest Blvd A
Inglewood CA 90301
310 966-4900

(P-12038)
CP OPCO LLC
Also Called: Classic Party Rentals
22674 Broadway A, Sonoma (95476-8217)
PHONE...............................650 652-0300
Fax: 650 697-9090
EMP: 59
SALES (corp-wide): 1.9MM **Privately Held**
SIC: 7359 Equipment Rental/Leasing
HQ: Cp Opco, Llc
901 W Hillcrest Blvd A
Inglewood CA 90301
310 966-4900

(P-12039)
CP OPCO LLC
Also Called: Classic Party Rentals
22674 Broadway A, Sonoma (95476-8217)
PHONE...............................916 444-6120
EMP: 40
SALES (corp-wide): 1.9MM **Privately Held**
SIC: 7359 Equipment Rental/Leasing
HQ: Cp Opco, Llc
901 W Hillcrest Blvd A
Inglewood CA 90301
310 966-4900

(P-12040)
ENCORE EVENTS RENTALS INC
1001 American Way, Windsor (95492-7760)
PHONE...............................707 431-3500
Bridget Doherty, *CEO*
Janice Griffin, *Accounting Mgr*
Kendall Burger, *Marketing Mgr*
Brian Rankin, *Warehouse Mgr*
Hannah Oliva, *Consultant*
EMP: 100 **EST:** 2010
SALES (est): 8.5MM **Privately Held**
WEB: www.encoreeventsrentals.com
SIC: 7359 Party supplies rental services

(P-12041)
FARWEST SANITATION AND STORAGE
2625 E 18th St, Antioch (94509-7230)
PHONE...............................925 686-1625
Federico Alex Rodriguez, *President*
Alex F Rodriguez, *President*
Jacqueline McCosker, *Treasurer*
Lola Rodriguez, *Admin Sec*
EMP: 39 **EST:** 1999
SQ FT: 4,000
SALES (est): 5.7MM **Privately Held**
WEB: www.unitedsiteservices.com
SIC: 7359 Portable toilet rental

(P-12042)
GOODWIN-COLE COMPANY INC
8320 Belvedere Ave, Sacramento (95826-5902)
PHONE...............................916 381-8888
Roger B Gilleland, *President*
Jackie Kirkwood, *Vice Pres*
Gloria Richey, *Products*
Scott Pierce, *Sales Staff*
EMP: 20 **EST:** 1888
SQ FT: 17,000

7359 - Equipment Rental & Leasing, NEC County (P-12043)   PRODUCTS & SERVICES SECTION

SALES (est): 3.2MM **Privately Held**
WEB: www.goodwincole.com
SIC: **7359** 2394 5999 2591 Tent & tarpaulin rental; tents: made from purchased materials; awnings; drapery hardware & blinds & shades

(P-12043)
HANSON & FITCH INC
3458 Enterprise Ave, Hayward (94545-3219)
P.O. Box 175, Danville (94526-0175)
PHONE..........................408 778-0499
Todd Fitch, *President*
Kristin Fitch, *CFO*
Kari Funaro, *Sales Staff*
EMP: 35 EST: 2006
SALES (est): 4.3MM **Privately Held**
WEB: www.hansonfitch.com
SIC: **7359** Portable toilet rental

(P-12044)
HD SUPPLY FACILITIES MAINT LTD
2754 W Winton Ave, Hayward (94545-1120)
PHONE..........................510 783-4019
Craig Bohlen, *Asst Mgr*
EMP: 69
SALES (corp-wide): 132.1B **Publicly Held**
WEB: www.hdsupply.com
SIC: **7359** Equipment rental & leasing
HQ: Hd Supply Facilities Maintenance, Ltd.
3400 Cumberland Blvd Se
Atlanta GA 30339
770 852-9000

(P-12045)
HEADWAY TECHNOLOGIES INC
678 S Hillview Dr, Milpitas (95035-5457)
PHONE..........................408 934-5660
EMP: 470 **Privately Held**
WEB: www.headway.com
SIC: **7359** Sound & lighting equipment rental
HQ: Headway Technologies, Inc.
682 S Hillview Dr
Milpitas CA 95035
408 934-5300

(P-12046)
HOLZMUELLER CORPORATION
Also Called: Holzmueller Productions
1000 25th St, San Francisco (94107-3509)
P.O. Box 880970 (94188-0970)
PHONE..........................415 826-8383
Richard P Gentschel, *President*
Carol Gentschel, *Vice Pres*
Richard Board, *Project Mgr*
Michael Hamlin, *Sales Mgr*
Damon Hope, *Manager*
EMP: 50 EST: 1902
SQ FT: 30,000
SALES (est): 9.3MM **Privately Held**
WEB: www.holzmueller.com
SIC: **7359** 5719 1731 Sound & lighting equipment rental; lighting fixtures; electrical work

(P-12047)
HOME DEPOT USA INC
Also Called: Home Depot, The
4000 Alameda Ave, Oakland (94601-3934)
PHONE..........................510 533-7379
EMP: 150
SALES (corp-wide): 132.1B **Publicly Held**
WEB: www.homedepot.com
SIC: **5211** 7359 Ret Lumber/Building Materials Equipment Rental/Leasing
HQ: Home Depot U.S.A., Inc.
2455 Paces Ferry Rd Se
Atlanta GA 30339

(P-12048)
HOME DEPOT USA INC
Also Called: Home Depot, The
2675 E Bidwell St, Folsom (95630-6404)
PHONE..........................916 983-0401
EMP: 200

SALES (corp-wide): 132.1B **Publicly Held**
WEB: www.homedepot.com
SIC: **5211** 7359 Ret Lumber/Building Materials Equipment Rental/Leasing
HQ: Home Depot U.S.A., Inc.
2455 Paces Ferry Rd Se
Atlanta GA 30339

(P-12049)
I-5 RENTALS INC
8443 Commercial Way, Redding (96002-3902)
PHONE..........................530 226-8081
Daniel P Haugus, *President*
EMP: 40 EST: 1995
SQ FT: 5,000
SALES (est): 14.3MM **Privately Held**
WEB: www.i5rentals.com
SIC: **7359** Stores & yards equipment rental

(P-12050)
J M EQUIPMENT COMPANY INC (PA)
Also Called: John Deere Authorized Dealer
321 Spreckels Ave, Manteca (95336-6007)
PHONE..........................209 522-3271
Ray Azevedo, *CEO*
Dave Baiocchi, *President*
Ed Henriquez, *President*
Vincent C Victorine, *CFO*
Audie Burgan, *Vice Pres*
▲ EMP: 80 EST: 1936
SQ FT: 7,000
SALES (est): 44.5MM **Privately Held**
WEB: www.jmequipment.com
SIC: **7359** 5084 5999 Equipment rental & leasing; materials handling machinery; farm equipment & supplies; farm machinery; farm tractors

(P-12051)
LA CASA VENTURES INC
Also Called: Casaone
1900 Powell St Ste 150, Emeryville (94608-1837)
PHONE..........................415 272-3147
Shashank Shankaranarayana, *CEO*
Madhusudan Kagwad, *Founder*
EMP: 35 EST: 2017
SALES (est): 2.6MM **Privately Held**
WEB: www.casaone.com
SIC: **7359** Equipment rental & leasing; furniture rental; rental store, general

(P-12052)
LEWIS RENTS INC
15740 Hesperian Blvd, San Lorenzo (94580-1536)
PHONE..........................510 276-3080
Fax: 510 278-9333
EMP: 35 EST: 1953
SQ FT: 13,000
SALES (est): 4.1MM **Privately Held**
SIC: **7359** 7513 Equipment Rental/Leasing Truck Rental/Leasing

(P-12053)
MACQURIE ARCFT LSG SVCS US INC
2 Embarcadero Ctr Ste 200, San Francisco (94111-3801)
PHONE..........................415 829-6600
John R Willingham, *CEO*
Jeffrey Buckio, *Exec VP*
Harry Forsythe, *Exec VP*
Matt Corley, *Vice Pres*
Bruce Hogarth, *Vice Pres*
EMP: 60 EST: 2006
SALES (est): 19.1MM
SALES (corp-wide): 585.6MM **Privately Held**
SIC: **7359** Aircraft rental
HQ: Macquarie Airfinance (No 2) Limited
South Bank House
Dublin 4

(P-12054)
MERRIMAK CAPITAL COMPANY LLC
64 Digital Dr, Novato (94949-5704)
PHONE..........................415 475-4100
Mary Kariotis, *Mng Member*

Marsha Quinn, *Exec VP*
Janice Crouse, *Administration*
Nicole Siegel, *Finance*
Dana Breaux, *Controller*
EMP: 40 EST: 1991
SQ FT: 11,000
SALES (est): 52.1MM **Privately Held**
WEB: www.merrimak.com
SIC: **7359** 6159 Equipment rental & leasing; machinery & equipment finance leasing; truck finance leasing

(P-12055)
NATIONAL CNSTR RENTALS INC
1300 Business Center Dr, San Leandro (94577-2242)
PHONE..........................510 563-4000
Marco Lopez, *Manager*
EMP: 31
SALES (corp-wide): 123.1MM **Privately Held**
WEB: www.rentnational.com
SIC: **7359** 3496 Portable toilet rental; miscellaneous fabricated wire products
HQ: National Construction Rentals, Inc.
15319 Chatsworth St
Mission Hills CA 91345
818 221-6000

(P-12056)
NEFF CORPORATION
Also Called: Lewis Rents
15740 Hesperian Blvd, San Lorenzo (94580-1536)
PHONE..........................510 276-3080
EMP: 35
SALES (corp-wide): 8.5B **Publicly Held**
SIC: **7359** 7513 Equipment Rental/Leasing Truck Rental/Leasing
HQ: Neff Corporation
12802 Tampa Oaks Blvd # 350
Temple Terrace FL 33637
888 458-2768

(P-12057)
OHANA PARTNERS INC (PA)
Also Called: Stuart Rental Company
454 S Abbott Ave, Milpitas (95035-5258)
PHONE..........................408 856-3232
Michael Berman, *CEO*
Andrew Sutton, *Exec VP*
R Andrew Sutton, *Vice Pres*
Clara Ayala, *Controller*
Juan Rodriguez, *Production*
▲ EMP: 99 EST: 2002
SALES (est): 15MM **Privately Held**
SIC: **7359** 5947 Party supplies rental services; tent & tarpaulin rental; gifts & novelties

(P-12058)
PARKMERCED INVESTORS LLC
3711 19th Ave, San Francisco (94132-2641)
PHONE..........................877 243-5544
Bruce Ward,
Ralph Arnold, *CIO*
Gayle Mustanich, *Accountant*
Michael Clark, *Sales Associate*
Elizabeth Kershaw, *Legal Staff*
EMP: 50 EST: 2005
SALES (est): 4.7MM **Privately Held**
WEB: www.parkmerced.com
SIC: **7359** Lawn & garden equipment rental

(P-12059)
RENTOKIL NORTH AMERICA INC
Also Called: Ambius
3481 Arden Rd, Hayward (94545-3905)
PHONE..........................510 265-1949
Marj Vonnel, *Vice Pres*
Iryna Krasnobaieva, *Sales Staff*
Rigo Beltran, *Supervisor*
EMP: 36
SALES (corp-wide): 3.7B **Privately Held**
SIC: **7359** Live plant rental
HQ: Rentokil North America, Inc.
1125 Berkshire Blvd # 15
Wyomissing PA 19610
610 372-9700

(P-12060)
RIVERVIEW SYSTEMS GROUP INC
1101 Cadillac Ct, Milpitas (95035-3055)
PHONE..........................408 347-3700
Evan Williams, *CEO*
Christopher A Thorne, *President*
Kathryn C Thorne, *Admin Sec*
Melissa York, *Admin Sec*
Jon Hunter, *Info Tech Dir*
EMP: 50 EST: 1987
SQ FT: 26,000
SALES (est): 11.4MM **Privately Held**
WEB: www.riverview.com
SIC: **5999** 7359 Audio-visual equipment & supplies; audio-visual equipment & supply rental

(P-12061)
ROCKINS EQUIPMENT COMPANY
Also Called: Morgan's
2233 San Ramon Vly Blvd, San Ramon (94583-1209)
P.O. Box 127 (94583-0127)
PHONE..........................925 837-7296
Steven Staats, *President*
Mark Staats, *Treasurer*
Marta Ramirez, *Office Admin*
Dave Mekeel, *Sales Associate*
EMP: 50 EST: 1990
SQ FT: 2,500
SALES (est): 6.2MM **Privately Held**
SIC: **7359** Equipment rental & leasing

(P-12062)
SABA DECOR RENTALS LLC (PA)
4451 Vincente St, Fremont (94536-4516)
PHONE..........................510 449-4890
Jino Joseph, *Principal*
EMP: 41 EST: 2016
SALES (est): 593.4K **Privately Held**
WEB: www.sabadecorrentals.com
SIC: **7359** Party supplies rental services

(P-12063)
SEACASTLE INC
4000 Executive Pkwy # 240, San Ramon (94583-4257)
PHONE..........................925 480-3000
Kathleen Francis, *Vice Pres*
EMP: 148 **Privately Held**
WEB: www.seacubecontainers.com
SIC: **7359** Equipment rental & leasing
PA: Seacastle, Inc
123 Tice Blvd
Woodcliff Lake NJ 07677

(P-12064)
TEXTAINER EQUIPMENT MGT US LTD (DH)
650 California St Fl 16, San Francisco (94108-2720)
PHONE..........................415 434-0551
Ernest Furtado, *CFO*
Robert Pedersen, *Exec VP*
Brian Hogan, *Vice Pres*
Michael Samsel, *Vice Pres*
Robert Warner, *Info Tech Dir*
EMP: 55
SQ FT: 15,000
SALES (est): 11.7MM **Privately Held**
WEB: www.textainer.com
SIC: **7359** Shipping container leasing
HQ: Textainer Group Holdings Ltd
650 California St Fl 16
San Francisco CA 94108
415 434-0551

(P-12065)
UNITED SITE SERVICES CAL INC
3408 Hillcap Ave, San Jose (95136-1306)
PHONE..........................408 295-2263
Frank Youngblood, *President*
Terence P Moriarty, *CFO*
Jim Youngblood, *Exec VP*
Dan Youngblood, *Vice Pres*
Horace Booth, *Opers Mgr*
EMP: 200 EST: 2004

PRODUCTS & SERVICES SECTION
7361 - Employment Agencies County (P-12088)

SALES (est): 26.2MM
SALES (corp-wide): 568.3MM **Privately Held**
WEB: www.unitedsiteservices.com
SIC: 7359 Portable toilet rental
PA: United Site Services, Inc.
118 Flanders Rd
Westborough MA 01581
508 594-2655

(P-12066)
WINE COUNTRY PTY & EVENTS LLC (PA)
22674 Broadway Ste A, Sonoma (95476-8217)
PHONE..................707 940-6060
Marshall Bauer, *Owner*
Loren Marple, *General Mgr*
Ellen Finley, *Accountant*
Paul Conway, *Director*
▲ EMP: 83 EST: 2003
SALES (est): 6.1MM **Privately Held**
WEB: www.bright.
SIC: 7359 Party supplies rental services

7361 Employment Agencies

(P-12067)
40 HRS INC
Also Called: 40 Hours Staffing
1669 Flanigan Dr, San Jose (95121-1682)
PHONE..................408 414-0158
Bryan Phan, *President*
Nancy Nghia, *General Mgr*
Van Ngo, *Recruiter*
Danny Tran, *Cust Mgr*
Fanny Liao, *Accounts Mgr*
EMP: 1000 EST: 2006
SQ FT: 3,000
SALES (est): 37.2MM **Privately Held**
WEB: www.40hrs.us
SIC: 7361 Executive placement

(P-12068)
ACCOUNTBLE HLTHCARE STFFING IN
Also Called: Hrn Services
7777 Greenback Ln Ste 205, Citrus Heights (95610-5800)
PHONE..................916 286-7667
Tina Wilson, *Branch Mgr*
EMP: 244
SALES (corp-wide): 123.1MM **Privately Held**
WEB: www.ahcstaff.com
SIC: 7361 Nurses' registry
PA: Accountable Healthcare Staffing, Inc.
999 W Yamato Rd Ste 210
Boca Raton FL 33431
561 235-7810

(P-12069)
ACCOUNTBLE HLTHCARE STFFING IN
Also Called: Hrn Services
1999 S Bascom Ave Ste 590, Campbell (95008-2236)
PHONE..................408 377-9960
Mary Begin, *Branch Mgr*
EMP: 244
SALES (corp-wide): 123.1MM **Privately Held**
WEB: www.ahcstaff.com
SIC: 7361 Nurses' registry
PA: Accountable Healthcare Staffing, Inc.
999 W Yamato Rd Ste 210
Boca Raton FL 33431
561 235-7810

(P-12070)
ADVANCE STAFFING INC
2060 Walsh Ave Ste 101, Santa Clara (95050-2568)
P.O. Box 391447, Mountain View (94039-1447)
PHONE..................408 205-6154
Jose Badillo, *President*
Nelly Hau, *Bookkeeper*
EMP: 300 EST: 2007
SALES (est): 9MM **Privately Held**
WEB: www.advance-staffing.com
SIC: 7361 Employment agencies

(P-12071)
AKRAYA INC
2933 Bunker Hill Ln # 100, Santa Clara (95054-1149)
PHONE..................408 907-6400
Sonu Ratra, *President*
Amar Panchal, *Chairman*
Keshava Kumar, *Principal*
Abhijaat Shrivastava, *Tech Recruiter*
Pallavi Bhujbal, *Technical Staff*
EMP: 48 EST: 2001
SALES (est): 17.2MM **Privately Held**
WEB: www.akraya.com
SIC: 7361 8711 7379 Executive placement; engineering services; computer related consulting services

(P-12072)
ALLIANCE FOR WORKFORCE DEV INC
76 Crescent St, Quincy (95971-9118)
P.O. Box 3750 (95971-3750)
PHONE..................530 283-3933
Gary Corderman, *Director*
EMP: 43 EST: 1980
SALES (est): 6.6MM **Privately Held**
WEB: www.afwd.org
SIC: 7361 Employment agencies

(P-12073)
ALOIS LLC
Also Called: Alois Staffing
548 Market St Ste 47970, San Francisco (94104-5401)
PHONE..................215 297-4492
Farhad Wadia, *CEO*
Kinjal Desai, *COO*
Chaitali Parekh, *Executive*
Muntazir Tinwala, *Tech Recruiter*
Amit Pandey, *Technical Staff*
EMP: 150 EST: 2016
SALES (est): 20MM **Privately Held**
WEB: www.aloisstaffing.com
SIC: 7361 7389 Employment agencies;

(P-12074)
ALPHA AGENCY INC
Also Called: Stars Agency, The
23 Grant Ave Fl 4, San Francisco (94108-5846)
PHONE..................415 421-6272
Lynn Claxon, *President*
Nate Tico, *Vice Pres*
Stephanie Parks, *Controller*
Hannah Karen,
EMP: 43 EST: 1986
SQ FT: 2,700
SALES (est): 5.3MM **Privately Held**
SIC: 7361 7922 7363 Model registry; talent agent, theatrical; modeling service

(P-12075)
ATR INTERNATIONAL INC (PA)
2804 Mission College Blvd # 120, Santa Clara (95054-1842)
PHONE..................408 328-8000
Jerry Brenholz, *Ch of Bd*
Andrea Brenholz, *President*
Maria C Novoa Brenholz, *CFO*
Angelique Alvarez, *Officer*
Laura Curtin, *Vice Pres*
▲ EMP: 45 EST: 1988
SALES: 73.2MM **Privately Held**
WEB: www.atrinternational.com
SIC: 7361 Labor contractors (employment agency)

(P-12076)
BALANCE STAFFING WORKFORCE LLC
2800 N Cherryland Ave, Stockton (95215-2263)
PHONE..................209 215-4188
John Moss, *Mng Member*
EMP: 40
SALES (est): 82.8K **Privately Held**
WEB: www.balancestaffing.com
SIC: 7361 Employment agencies

(P-12077)
BARRETT BUSINESS SERVICES INC
1840 Gateway Dr, San Mateo (94404-4027)
PHONE..................650 653-7588
EMP: 3049
SALES (corp-wide): 880.8MM **Publicly Held**
WEB: www.bbsi.com
SIC: 7361 Employment agencies
PA: Barrett Business Services Inc
8100 Ne Parkway Dr # 200
Vancouver WA 98662
360 828-0700

(P-12078)
BAY AREA TECHWORKERS (PA)
2000 Crow Canyon Pl # 150, San Ramon (94583-4633)
PHONE..................925 359-2200
Don Peed, *CEO*
Mark Thompson, *CFO*
Paris Arey, *Senior VP*
HB Drake, *Vice Pres*
Rob Olsen, *Vice Pres*
EMP: 1399 EST: 1998
SQ FT: 8,609
SALES (est): 70.8MM **Privately Held**
WEB: www.techworkers.com
SIC: 7361 Placement agencies

(P-12079)
CAREER GROUP INC
345 California St # 1650, San Francisco (94104-2652)
PHONE..................415 781-8188
Michael B Levine, *CEO*
EMP: 150
SALES (corp-wide): 50.8MM **Privately Held**
WEB: www.careergroupcompanies.com
SIC: 7361 Executive placement
PA: Career Group, Inc.
10100 Santa Monica Blvd # 900
Los Angeles CA 90067
310 277-8188

(P-12080)
CLC INCORPORATED (PA)
3001 Lava Ridge Ct # 250, Roseville (95661-2838)
PHONE..................916 789-7600
Brad Barron, *President*
Doug Abbott, *Senior VP*
Daniel Davis, *Vice Pres*
Mike Hackett, *Vice Pres*
Duncan Hay, *Vice Pres*
EMP: 50 EST: 1986
SQ FT: 20,000
SALES (est): 11.3MM **Privately Held**
WEB: www.clchomeoffice.com
SIC: 7361 Employment agencies

(P-12081)
CROSSROADS DIVERSFD SVCS INC
7011 Sylvan Rd Ste A, Citrus Heights (95610-3800)
PHONE..................916 676-2540
Danny Marquez, *Principal*
Kimberly Speers, *Director*
EMP: 53
SALES (corp-wide): 12.4MM **Privately Held**
WEB: www.prideindustries.com
SIC: 7361 Executive placement
PA: Crossroads Diversified Services, Inc.
10030 Foothills Blvd
Roseville CA 95747
916 457-1900

(P-12082)
CVPARTNERS INC (HQ)
655 Montgomery St # 1200, San Francisco (94111-2635)
PHONE..................415 543-8600
Kent Gray, *President*
Danny Spagnola, *Branch Mgr*
Michal Krasnopolski, *IT/INT Sup*
Kimberly Ward, *Finance*
Sarah Baltzer, *Recruiter*
EMP: 161 EST: 2001
SALES (est): 28.1MM
SALES (corp-wide): 153.3MM **Privately Held**
WEB: www.cvpartnersinc.com
SIC: 7361 Executive placement

PA: Addison Professional Financial Search Llc
125 S Wacker Dr Fl 27
Chicago IL 60606
312 424-0300

(P-12083)
DAVID POWELL INC (PA)
3190 Clearview Way # 100, San Mateo (94402-3751)
P.O. Box 620109, Woodside (94062-0109)
PHONE..................650 357-6000
David L Powell, *President*
Nicole Lee, *Controller*
EMP: 51 EST: 1976
SQ FT: 4,500
SALES (est): 5MM **Privately Held**
WEB: www.davidpowell.com
SIC: 7361 8741 Executive placement; financial management for business

(P-12084)
DO ARELLANES HOLDINGS
Also Called: Itsourcetek, Inc.
899 Northgate Dr Ste 304, San Rafael (94903-3667)
P.O. Box 127, Kentfield (94914-0127)
PHONE..................415 472-5700
Brian M Arellanes, *CEO*
Jean Dubois, *Vice Pres*
Walter Jones, *Executive*
EMP: 35 EST: 2006
SQ FT: 1,200
SALES (est): 3.2MM **Privately Held**
WEB: www.itsourcetek.com
SIC: 7361 7371 Executive placement; computer software systems analysis & design, custom
PA: Lynx Technology Partners, Inc.
244 5th Ave Ste 1220
New York NY 10001
800 314-0455

(P-12085)
DYNAMIC STAFFING INC (PA)
920 Reserve Dr Ste 150, Roseville (95678-1382)
PHONE..................916 773-3900
Michael J Reale, *President*
Keri J Case, *COO*
Steve Saucedo, *CFO*
Keri Case, *Officer*
Christine Selman, *Technology*
EMP: 140 EST: 1996
SQ FT: 2,768
SALES (est): 13.7MM **Privately Held**
SIC: 7361 Employment agencies

(P-12086)
ELITECARE MEDICAL STAFFING LLC
761 E Locust Ave Ste 103, Fresno (93720-3023)
PHONE..................559 438-7700
Steve Poggi,
Stacey Green, *Opers Staff*
EMP: 60 EST: 2002
SALES (est): 3MM **Privately Held**
WEB: www.elitecare.net
SIC: 7361 Nurses' registry

(P-12087)
FANEUIL INC
5012 Dudley Blvd, McClellan (95652-1029)
PHONE..................757 722-4095
EMP: 489 **Publicly Held**
WEB: www.faneuil.com
SIC: 7361 Employment agencies
HQ: Faneuil, Inc.
2 Eaton St Ste 1002
Hampton VA 23669

(P-12088)
FIRST CALL NURSING SVCS INC
1313 N Milpitas Blvd # 15, Milpitas (95035-3180)
PHONE..................408 262-1533
Franklin Camillo, *CEO*
Celina Salazar-Camillo, *President*
Celina Camillo, *General Mgr*
EMP: 37 EST: 1988
SALES (est): 1.4MM **Privately Held**
WEB: www.firstcallnursingservices.com
SIC: 7361 Nurses' registry

7361 - Employment Agencies County (P-12089)

(P-12089)
FLEXCARE LLC
Also Called: Flexcare Medical Staffing
532 Gibson Dr Ste 100, Roseville
(95678-5878)
PHONE...............................866 564-3589
Nate Porter, *Mng Member*
Zoyah Khan, *Info Tech Mgr*
Brayden Giacomini, *Analyst*
Karisa Stahle, *Human Resources*
Mike Arrcyo, *Recruiter*
EMP: 1000 **EST:** 2007
SALES (est): 48.7MM **Privately Held**
WEB: www.flexcarestaff.com
SIC: 7361 Employment agencies

(P-12090)
FOWLER LABOR SERVICE INC
633 W Fresno St, Fowler (93625-9697)
PHONE...............................559 834-3723
Fax: 559 834-5949
EMP: 300
SQ FT: 3,250
SALES (est): 8.8MM **Privately Held**
SIC: 7361 0783 Employment Agency Shrub/Tree Services

(P-12091)
GARY D NELSON ASSOCIATES INC (PA)
Also Called: Nelson Staffing Solutions
19080 Lomita Ave, Sonoma (95476-5453)
P.O. Box 1546 (95476-1546)
PHONE...............................707 935-6113
Jack Unroe, *Principal*
Gary D Nelson, *Ch of Bd*
Mark Nelson, *President*
Joan Van Donge, *President*
Donna Farrugia, *CEO*
EMP: 45 **EST:** 1970
SQ FT: 16,000
SALES (est): 65.4MM **Privately Held**
WEB: www.nelsonjobs.com
SIC: 7361 Executive placement

(P-12092)
GENERAL SERVICES CAL DEPT
Also Called: Procurement Div
707 3rd St Fl 1, West Sacramento (95605-2811)
P.O. Box 989052 (95798-9052)
PHONE...............................916 376-5330
Mariel Dennis, *Manager*
EMP: 36 **Privately Held**
WEB: www.ca.gov
SIC: 7361 9199 Employment agencies; general government administration
HQ: California Department Of General Services
707 3rd St
West Sacramento CA 95605

(P-12093)
GLASSDOOR INC (HQ)
50 Beale St Ste 1600, San Francisco (94105-1825)
PHONE...............................415 275-7411
Fiona McLaren, *CEO*
Christian Sutherland-Wong, *President*
Robert Hohman, *CEO*
James S Cox, *CFO*
Moody Glasgow, *Chief Mktg Ofcr*
EMP: 197 **EST:** 2007
SQ FT: 2,000
SALES (est): 111MM **Privately Held**
WEB: www.glasscoortalentsolutions.com
SIC: 7361 7375 7371 Employment agencies; on-line data base information retrieval; computer software development & applications

(P-12094)
GRANITE SOLUTIONS GROUPE INC (PA)
235 Montgomery St Ste 430, San Francisco (94104-2907)
P.O. Box 3399, Diamond Springs (95619-3399)
PHONE...............................415 963-3999
Daniel Hector L'Abbe, *CEO*
Ann Bauer, *CFO*
John Henning, *Chief Mktg Ofcr*
Michael Lacson, *Exec Dir*
Fannie Yao, *Accounting Mgr*
EMP: 208 **EST:** 1998
SQ FT: 3,582
SALES (est): 19.1MM **Privately Held**
WEB: www.granitesolutionsgroupe.com
SIC: 7361 8742 Executive placement; management consulting services

(P-12095)
HARVEST TECHNICAL SERVICE INC
1839 Ygnacio Valley Rd # 390, Walnut Creek (94598-3214)
PHONE...............................925 937-4874
Judy Fick, *President*
Chris Fick, *Admin Sec*
Carla Adcock, *Administration*
Jen Lindsey, *Recruiter*
Powell Samantha, *Recruiter*
EMP: 150 **EST:** 1997
SQ FT: 1,000
SALES (est): 7.8MM **Privately Held**
WEB: www.harvtech.com
SIC: 7361 Executive placement

(P-12096)
HAWTHORNE GROUP INC
1010 Cameraco Dr Ste 108, Cameron Park (95682-7984)
PHONE...............................530 672-1330
Steven Mc Gimsey, *President*
Diane Mc Gimsey, *CFO*
EMP: 44 **EST:** 1983
SALES (est): 2.7MM **Privately Held**
WEB: www.hawthornegroup.org
SIC: 7361 Nurses' registry

(P-12097)
HIRE UP STAFFING SERVICE
155 E Shaw Ave Ste 108, Fresno (93710-7619)
PHONE...............................559 579-1331
Rebecca Abell, *President*
Leah Perez, *Branch Mgr*
Carrie Bryson, *Controller*
Ashley Tristao, *Director*
Carolyn Basinger, *Manager*
EMP: 450 **EST:** 2010
SALES (est): 15.7MM **Privately Held**
WEB: www.hireupss.com
SIC: 7361 Executive placement

(P-12098)
IDC TECHNOLOGIES INC (PA)
920 Hillview Ct Ste 250, Milpitas (95035-4560)
PHONE...............................408 376-0212
Prateek Gattani, *CEO*
Maneesh Singh, *President*
Yogen Malvia, *CFO*
Muntazir Zargar, *Executive*
Naveen Panwar, *CIO*
EMP: 191 **EST:** 2003
SQ FT: 4,000
SALES (est): 78.2MM **Privately Held**
WEB: www.idctechnologies.com
SIC: 7361 Placement agencies

(P-12099)
IITJOBS INC
1340 S De Anza Blvd # 208, San Jose (95129-4644)
PHONE...............................510 509-9368
Shobhan Shah, *President*
Sudha Burle, *Tech Recruiter*
EMP: 66 **EST:** 2006
SALES (est): 873.2K **Privately Held**
WEB: www.iitjobs.com
SIC: 7361 Executive placement

(P-12100)
INFOTECH CONSULTING LLC
Also Called: Infotech Global Services
340 Pine St Ste 504, San Francisco (94104-3211)
PHONE...............................415 986-5400
Brad Miller, *Mng Member*
Susan Woodrum, *Bookkeeper*
Disha Savaria, *Recruiter*
EMP: 48 **EST:** 2008
SQ FT: 2,500
SALES (est): 7MM **Privately Held**
WEB: www.infotechglobalservices.com
SIC: 7361 8748 Executive placement; systems analysis & engineering consulting services

(P-12101)
JOSEPHINES PROF STAFFING INC (PA)
Also Called: Josephine's Personnel Services
2158 Ringwood Ave, San Jose (95131-1720)
PHONE...............................408 943-0111
Josephine Hughes, *President*
Victoria Picard, *Administration*
EMP: 225 **EST:** 1988
SQ FT: 4,000
SALES (est): 13.1MM **Privately Held**
WEB: www.jps-inc.com
SIC: 7361 8742 8721 7363 Placement agencies; management consulting services; accounting, auditing & bookkeeping; help supply services

(P-12102)
JUSTICE UNITED STATES DEPT
2500 Tulare St Ste 4401, Fresno (93721-1331)
PHONE...............................559 251-4040
Brian Enos, *Branch Mgr*
EMP: 46 **Publicly Held**
WEB: www.justice.gov
SIC: 7361 Employment agencies
HQ: United States Department Of Justice
950 Pennsylvania Ave Nw
Washington DC 20530
202 514-2201

(P-12103)
LEADSTACK INC
611 Gateway Blvd Ste 120, South San Francisco (94080-7066)
PHONE...............................628 200-3063
Kazi Ahmed, *CEO*
EMP: 64 **EST:** 2016
SALES (est): 7.2MM **Privately Held**
WEB: www.leadstackinc.com
SIC: 7361 Employment agencies

(P-12104)
LENSA INC (PA)
541 Jefferson Ave Ste 100, Redwood City (94063-1700)
PHONE...............................415 528-8467
Pal Megyeri, *CTO*
Tim Heston, *Director*
EMP: 36 **EST:** 2018
SALES (est): 421.9K **Privately Held**
WEB: www.lensa.com
SIC: 7361 Employment agencies

(P-12105)
MANAGMENT RCRTERS GRASS VLY IN
Also Called: Retail Search Group
426 Sutton Way Ste 108, Grass Valley (95945-5300)
PHONE...............................530 432-1966
Dave Campeas, *President*
Kim Franchi, *Partner*
Edara Mitchell, *Vice Pres*
Christine Bauch, *Planning*
Steve Olson, *Finance*
EMP: 42 **EST:** 1997
SQ FT: 1,700
SALES (est): 2.8MM
SALES (corp-wide): 41.7MM **Privately Held**
WEB: www.retailsearchgroup.com
SIC: 7361 Executive placement
PA: Princeton Search L.L.C.
23 Orchard Rd Ste 103
Skillman NJ 08558
609 924-3444

(P-12106)
MARATHON STAFFING SOLUTIONS
2950 Beacon Blvd Ste 45, West Sacramento (95691-5031)
PHONE...............................978 649-6230
Chris Panagiotopoulos, *Principal*
Suzanne Deshler, *Principal*
Athena Panagiotakos, *Principal*
EMP: 99 **EST:** 2016
SALES (est): 1.9MM **Privately Held**
WEB: www.marathonstaffing.com
SIC: 7361 Employment agencies

(P-12107)
MATRIX RESOURCES INC
1 Embarcadero Ctr Ste 500, San Francisco (94111-3610)
PHONE...............................415 644-0642
Valarie Harrison, *Accounts Exec*
EMP: 69
SALES (corp-wide): 186.5MM **Privately Held**
WEB: www.matrixres.com
SIC: 7361 Employment agencies
PA: Matrix Resources, Inc.
400 Perimeter Center Ter
Atlanta GA 30346
770 677-2400

(P-12108)
MID VALLEY LABOR SERVICES INC
19358 Avenue 18 1/2, Madera (93637-9709)
P.O. Box 899 (93639-0899)
PHONE...............................559 661-6390
Samuel Mascarenas, *President*
Ben Mascarenas, *CFO*
EMP: 39 **EST:** 1962
SQ FT: 2,132
SALES (est): 3.5MM **Privately Held**
SIC: 7361 Labor contractors (employment agency)

(P-12109)
MYA SYSTEMS INC (PA)
351 California St Fl Mezz, San Francisco (94104)
PHONE...............................877 679-0952
Eyal Grayevsky, *CEO*
Braydan Young, *President*
Jay Murphy, *Vice Pres*
Mike Pauletich, *Vice Pres*
Jonathan Krueger, *Program Mgr*
EMP: 49 **EST:** 2011
SALES (est): 4.8MM **Privately Held**
WEB: www.mya.com
SIC: 7361 Placement agencies

(P-12110)
NETPACE INC
5000 Executive Pkwy # 530, San Ramon (94583-4210)
PHONE...............................925 543-7760
Omar Khan, *President*
Valerie Schilling, *Vice Pres*
Jaya Suresh, *Executive*
Rudy Aguirre, *Creative Dir*
Feroz Gul, *Software Engr*
EMP: 123 **EST:** 1996
SQ FT: 4,000
SALES (est): 9.3MM **Privately Held**
WEB: www.netpace.com
SIC: 7361 7363 7371 Employment agencies; temporary help service; custom computer programming services

(P-12111)
NETPOLARITY INC
900 E Campbell Ave, Campbell (95008-2366)
PHONE...............................408 971-1100
Haixia Zhang, *CEO*
David Chuang, *President*
Cathleen Lariviere, *General Mgr*
Kyle Davis, *Tech Recruiter*
Jessica Mendoza, *Tech Recruiter*
EMP: 150 **EST:** 2000
SQ FT: 5,000
SALES (est): 25.4MM **Privately Held**
WEB: www.netpolarity.com
SIC: 7361 Executive placement

(P-12112)
NORTHWEST STFFING RSOURCES INC
Also Called: Resource Staffing Group
100 Howe Ave, Sacramento (95825-8202)
PHONE...............................916 960-2668
Windy Richard, *Manager*
Samantha Frieders, *Accounts Exec*
EMP: 2196
SALES (corp-wide): 19.5MM **Privately Held**
WEB: www.nwstaffing.com
SIC: 7361 7363 Labor contractors (employment agency); temporary help service

PRODUCTS & SERVICES SECTION
7361 - Employment Agencies County (P-12136)

PA: Northwest Staffing Resources, Inc.
851 Sw 6th Ave Ste 300
Portland OR 97204
503 323-9190

(P-12113)
OFFICEWORKS INC
300 Frank H Ste 269, Oakland (94612)
PHONE...................................510 444-2161
EMP: 85
SALES (corp-wide): 28.6MM **Privately Held**
WEB: www.officeworksrx.com
SIC: 7361 Employment agencies
PA: Officeworks, Inc.
3200 E Guasti Rd Ste 100
Ontario CA 91761
909 606-4100

(P-12114)
ONLINE TECHNICAL SERVICES INC (PA)
1901 S Bascom Ave # 1460, Campbell (95008-2215)
PHONE...................................408 378-1100
Hans Lemcke, *Ch of Bd*
Sean Anderson, *COO*
Brenton Hanlon, *Director*
Jim Piazza, *Director*
EMP: 40 **EST:** 1988
SQ FT: 1,000
SALES (est): 5.2MM **Privately Held**
WEB: www.onlinetechnical.com
SIC: 7361 Executive placement

(P-12115)
OUTSOURCE CONSULTING SVCS INC (PA)
Also Called: Ocsi.co
7901 Okport St N Bldg Ste, Oakland (94621)
PHONE...................................510 986-0686
Sandra O Floyd, *President*
Kit Floyd, *Finance Other*
EMP: 41 **EST:** 1994
SALES (est): 6.4MM **Privately Held**
WEB: www.ocsi.co
SIC: 7361 Employment agencies

(P-12116)
PACIFIC NETSOFT INC (PA)
Also Called: Clarity Consultants
910 E Hamilton Ave # 400, Campbell (95008-0610)
PHONE...................................800 330-6558
Herbert Tieger, *CEO*
Cristina Mendonca, *Vice Pres*
Christina Ngo, *Vice Pres*
Angie Devine, *Business Mgr*
Jeffrey Lawrence, *Business Mgr*
EMP: 40
SQ FT: 20,000
SALES (est): 18.4MM **Privately Held**
WEB: www.clarityconsultants.com
SIC: 7361 Executive placement

(P-12117)
PARADIGM STAFFING SOLUTIONS
1970 Broadway Ste 615, Oakland (94612-2218)
PHONE...................................510 663-7860
Fax: 510 663-7866
EMP: 50
SALES (est): 2.3MM **Privately Held**
WEB: www.parastaffing.com
SIC: 7361 Employment Agency

(P-12118)
PDS TECH INC
1798 Tech Dr Ste 130, San Jose (95110)
PHONE...................................408 916-4848
EMP: 188
SALES (corp-wide): 262.4MM **Privately Held**
WEB: www.pdstech.com
SIC: 7361 Employment agencies
PA: Pds Tech, Inc.
300 E John Carpenter Fwy # 700
Irving TX 75062
214 647-9600

(P-12119)
PEAK TECHNICAL SERVICES INC
1885 De La Cruz Blvd, Santa Clara (95050-3000)
PHONE...................................855 650-7325
Ashley Samuel, *Manager*
EMP: 242
SALES (corp-wide): 47.7MM **Privately Held**
WEB: www.peaktechnical.com
SIC: 7361 Employment agencies
PA: Peak Technical Services, Inc.
583 Epsilon Dr
Pittsburgh PA 15238
412 696-1080

(P-12120)
PEOPLE SCIENCES INC
951 Mrners Lsland Blvd St, San Mateo (94404)
PHONE...................................888 924-1004
Christine Nichlos, *CEO*
Lindsey Roundtree, *Client Mgr*
Aliza Zaffar, *Manager*
EMP: 50
SALES (corp-wide): 11.6MM **Privately Held**
WEB: www.people-science.com
SIC: 7361 Executive placement
PA: People Sciences, Inc.
595 Shrewsbury Ave # 102
Shrewsbury NJ 07702
888 924-1004

(P-12121)
PREMIER STAFFING INC (PA)
Also Called: Premier Talent Partners
3595 Mt Diablo Blvd # 340, Lafayette (94549-3849)
PHONE...................................415 362-2211
Sara Menke, *CEO*
Shellie Roanhaus, *CEO*
Matt Ruport, *COO*
Amanda Stevens, *Managing Dir*
Lito Abiva, *Info Tech Dir*
EMP: 66 **EST:** 1998
SQ FT: 5,400
SALES (est): 17.4MM **Privately Held**
WEB: www.premiertalentpartners.com
SIC: 7361 Executive placement

(P-12122)
PRIVATE INDUSTRY CNCL SLNO CTY (PA)
Also Called: Workforce Dev Bd Solano Cnty
500 Chadbourne Rd, Fairfield (94534-9656)
PHONE...................................707 864-3370
Heather Henry, *Exec Dir*
Taffy Della-Cioppa, *Principal*
Robert Bloom, *Exec Dir*
EMP: 49 **EST:** 1984
SALES (est): 4.2MM **Privately Held**
SIC: 7361 8331 Employment agencies; job training & vocational rehabilitation services

(P-12123)
R&D CONSULTING GROUP INC
Also Called: R & D Partners
920 Main St, Redwood City (94063-1996)
PHONE...................................415 697-2585
Nancy Baltzer, *CEO*
Ryan Maano, *Recruiter*
Anthony Scuorzo, *Sales Staff*
John Applewhite, *Manager*
Georgene Nathan, *Manager*
EMP: 125 **EST:** 2012
SALES (est): 8.2MM **Privately Held**
WEB: www.r-dpartners.com
SIC: 7361 Labor contractors (employment agency)

(P-12124)
RAMCO ENTERPRISES LP
585 Auto Center Dr, Watsonville (95076-3764)
PHONE...................................831 722-3370
EMP: 558
SALES (corp-wide): 92.8MM **Privately Held**
WEB: www.ramcoenterpriseslp.com
SIC: 7361 Employment agencies
PA: Ramco Enterprises, L.P.
710 La Guardia St
Salinas CA 93905
831 758-5272

(P-12125)
RANDSTAD PROFESSIONALS US LLC
Also Called: Randstad Finance & Accounting
111 Anza Blvd Ste 202, Burlingame (94010-1910)
PHONE...................................650 343-5111
Shannon Guzzetta, *Branch Mgr*
Anna Santiago, *HR Admin*
EMP: 86
SALES (corp-wide): 24.5B **Privately Held**
WEB: www.randstadusa.com
SIC: 7361 Executive placement
HQ: Randstad Professionals Us, Llc
150 Presidential Way Fl 4
Woburn MA 01801

(P-12126)
RANDSTAD PROFESSIONALS US LLC
Also Called: Accountants International
2033 Gateway Pl Ste 120, San Jose (95110-3713)
PHONE...................................408 573-1111
Rona Patroni, *Branch Mgr*
EMP: 86
SALES (corp-wide): 24.5B **Privately Held**
WEB: www.randstadusa.com
SIC: 7361 Executive placement
HQ: Randstad Professionals Us, Llc
150 Presidential Way Fl 4
Woburn MA 01801

(P-12127)
REACTION SEARCH INTL INC (PA)
5000 Executive Pkwy # 450, San Ramon (94583-4282)
PHONE...................................925 275-0727
Robert Ls Boroff, *CEO*
Whitney Campitiello, *Exec Dir*
Joe St Leger, *Managing Dir*
Chris Dowdy, *Prgrmr*
Gabriela Valdez, *Project Mgr*
EMP: 79 **EST:** 2004
SALES (est): 4.8MM **Privately Held**
WEB: www.reactionsearch.com
SIC: 7361 Executive placement

(P-12128)
RIVER CITY STAFFING INC
3301 Watt Ave Ste 100, Sacramento (95821-3616)
PHONE...................................916 485-1588
Cindy Bunker, *President*
Doug Bunker, *Vice Pres*
EMP: 40 **EST:** 1998
SQ FT: 2,800
SALES (est): 3.4MM **Privately Held**
WEB: www.rivercitystaffing.com
SIC: 7361 Executive placement

(P-12129)
RIVIERA PARTNERS LLC (PA)
1 Blackfield Dr Ste 2, Belvedere Tiburon (94920-2053)
PHONE...................................877 748-4372
Will Hunsinger, *Mng Member*
Dirk Cleveland, *Senior Partner*
Austin Brizendine, *Managing Prtnr*
Edie Dykstra, *Vice Pres*
Majed Itani, *Vice Pres*
EMP: 53 **EST:** 2002
SALES (est): 12.8MM **Privately Held**
WEB: www.rivierapartners.com
SIC: 7361 Executive placement

(P-12130)
ROBERT HALF INTERNATIONAL INC
Also Called: Office Team
2613 Camino Ramon, San Ramon (94583-4289)
PHONE...................................925 913-1000
Max Messner, *Manager*
Marisa Ellis, *Vice Pres*
Mark Grimse, *Vice Pres*
Daisy Chase, *Executive*
Jolynn Conway-James, *Exec Dir*
EMP: 50
SALES (corp-wide): 5.1B **Publicly Held**
WEB: www.roberthalf.com
SIC: 7361 7363 Placement agencies; temporary help service
PA: Robert Half International Inc.
2884 Sand Hill Rd Ste 200
Menlo Park CA 94025
650 234-6000

(P-12131)
ROY CARRINGTON INC
Also Called: Human Resource Solutions
13804 Bosc Dr, Chico (95973-8506)
PHONE...................................530 893-2100
Roy Carrington, *President*
EMP: 75 **EST:** 1980
SALES (est): 1MM **Privately Held**
SIC: 7361 8721 Executive placement; accounting, auditing & bookkeeping

(P-12132)
SAGE GROUP
33 Falmouth St, San Francisco (94107-1046)
PHONE...................................415 512-8200
Cara France, *CEO*
Alina Warda, *President*
Chris Yelton, *President*
Lauren Cousin, *Marketing Staff*
Rebekah Smith, *Sr Associate*
EMP: 100 **EST:** 2016
SALES (est): 14.9MM
SALES (corp-wide): 22.4MM **Privately Held**
WEB: www.thesagegroup.com
SIC: 7361 Employment agencies
PA: 24 Seven, Llc
41 Madison Ave Fl 37
New York NY 10010
212 966-4426

(P-12133)
SAMUEL HALE LLC
2365 Iron Point Rd # 190, Folsom (95630-8713)
PHONE...................................916 235-1477
Michael Dimanno, *CEO*
Desiree Frees, *General Mgr*
EMP: 2500 **EST:** 2016
SALES (est): 20.3MM **Privately Held**
WEB: www.samuelhale.com
SIC: 7361 Employment agencies

(P-12134)
SE SCHER CORPORATION
Also Called: Acrobat Staffing
6731 Five Star Blvd Ste C, Rocklin (95677-2680)
PHONE...................................916 632-1363
Steve Scher, *CEO*
Brigitte Tribble, *Vice Pres*
Niana Dela Cruz, *Administration*
Amanda Mergelmeyer, *Administration*
Marisela Segura, *Human Resources*
EMP: 663
SALES (corp-wide): 19.8MM **Privately Held**
SIC: 7361 Employment agencies
PA: S.E. Scher Corporation
303 Hegenberger Rd # 300
Oakland CA 94621
415 431-8826

(P-12135)
SEEDIF INC
85 Tamalpais Ave, Mill Valley (94941-1033)
PHONE...................................408 930-3446
Shannon Nguyen, *President*
EMP: 50 **EST:** 2017
SALES (est): 3MM **Privately Held**
WEB: www.seedif.com
SIC: 7361 Executive placement

(P-12136)
SILICON VLY TECHNICAL STAFFING (PA)
Also Called: Svs Group
2336 Harrison St, Oakland (94612-3712)
PHONE...................................510 923-9898
Eugene Lupario, *President*
Steve Allen, *Treasurer*
Kirsten Erwin, *Branch Mgr*
Cynthia Harper, *Recruiter*
Kathleen Souza, *Recruiter*

7361 - Employment Agencies County (P-12137)

EMP: 41 EST: 1996
SQ FT: 4,000
SALES (est): 11.4MM **Privately Held**
WEB: www.svsjobs.com
SIC: **7361** Executive placement

(P-12137)
SISKIYOU OPPORTUNITY CENTER
Also Called: Yreka Employment Services
321 N Gold St, Yreka (96097-2307)
P.O. Box 594 (96097-0594)
PHONE...................530 842-4110
Bryan Taylor, *Supervisor*
EMP: 40
SALES (corp-wide): 2.6MM **Privately Held**
WEB: www.siskiyouoc.org
SIC: **7361** Employment agencies
PA: Siskiyou Opportunity Center Inc
1516 S Mount Shasta Blvd
Mount Shasta CA 96067
530 926-4698

(P-12138)
SPEC PERSONNEL LLC
Also Called: Spec. Personnel
433 Airport Blvd Ste 310, Burlingame (94010-2010)
PHONE...................408 727-8000
EMP: 77
SALES (corp-wide): 26.4MM **Privately Held**
WEB: www.speconthejob.com
SIC: **7361** Employment agencies
PA: Spec Personnel, Llc
4625 Creekstone Dr # 130
Durham NC 27703
203 254-9935

(P-12139)
SPEC PERSONNEL LLC
Also Called: Spectra
1900 La Fytte St Unit 125, Santa Clara (95050)
PHONE...................408 727-8000
Andrew Bergen, *Branch Mgr*
EMP: 77
SALES (corp-wide): 26.4MM **Privately Held**
WEB: www.speconthejob.com
SIC: **7361** Employment agencies
PA: Spec Personnel, Llc
4625 Creekstone Dr # 130
Durham NC 27703
203 254-9935

(P-12140)
STAR H-R
1822 Jefferson St, NAPA (94559-1618)
PHONE...................707 265-9911
EMP: 422
SALES (corp-wide): 37.4MM **Privately Held**
WEB: www.starhr.com
SIC: **7361** Executive placement
PA: Star H-R
3820 Cypress Dr Ste 2
Petaluma CA 94954
707 762-4447

(P-12141)
STAR H-R
105 E 1st St, Cloverdale (95425-3701)
PHONE...................707 894-4404
EMP: 422
SALES (corp-wide): 37.4MM **Privately Held**
WEB: www.starhr.com
SIC: **7361** Employment agencies
PA: Star H-R
3820 Cypress Dr Ste 2
Petaluma CA 94954
707 762-4447

(P-12142)
STAR H-R (PA)
Also Called: Star Staffing
3820 Cypress Dr Ste 2, Petaluma (94954-6964)
PHONE...................707 762-4447
Carla Shevchuk, *President*
Lisa A Rogelstad, *Vice Pres*
Teresa Castillo, *Branch Mgr*
Jennifer Kraus, *Recruiter*
Ciera Pratt, *Marketing Mgr*

EMP: 1218 EST: 1998
SALES (est): 37.4MM **Privately Held**
WEB: www.starhr.com
SIC: **7361** Employment agencies

(P-12143)
STAT NURSING SERVICES INC (PA)
2740 Van Ness Ave Ste 210, San Francisco (94109-0216)
PHONE...................415 673-9791
Kathleen Cleary, *President*
Charles Duck, *CEO*
Mark Deal, *Plant Mgr*
EMP: 372 EST: 1979
SQ FT: 3,600
SALES (est): 8.7MM **Privately Held**
WEB: www.statrn.com
SIC: **7361** Nurses' registry

(P-12144)
STRAIGHT EDGE STVDORE SVCS INC (PA)
9769 Dawn Way, Windsor (95492-8879)
PHONE...................707 837-8564
Robert A Hall, *President*
Leslie Hall, *CFO*
EMP: 52 EST: 2005
SQ FT: 680
SALES (est): 3.8MM **Privately Held**
WEB: www.straightedgestaffing.com
SIC: **7361** Labor contractors (employment agency)

(P-12145)
TALENT SPACE INC
1650 The Alameda, San Jose (95126-2307)
PHONE...................408 330-1900
Lisa Flores, *President*
Debbie Minardi, *Partner*
Lynda Beauchesne, *Accounts Exec*
EMP: 80 EST: 2004
SALES (est): 6.1MM **Privately Held**
WEB: www.svtalentspace.com
SIC: **7361** Placement agencies

(P-12146)
TEKBERRY INC
3763 Shillingford Pl, Santa Rosa (95404-7666)
P.O. Box 9222 (95405-1222)
PHONE...................707 313-5345
Ed Hamilton, *CEO*
Greg Scott, *Recruiter*
Karen Partovi, *Manager*
EMP: 400 EST: 2005
SALES (est): 25MM **Privately Held**
WEB: www.tekberry.com
SIC: **7361** Placement agencies

(P-12147)
TRINET USA INC
1 Park Pl Ste 600, Dublin (94568-7983)
PHONE...................510 352-5000
Burton Goldfield, *CEO*
EMP: 99 EST: 2017
SALES (est): 22.6MM **Publicly Held**
WEB: www.trinet.com
SIC: **7361** Employment agencies
PA: Trinet Group, Inc.
1 Park Pl Ste 600
Dublin CA 94568

(P-12148)
UNITED TEMP SERVICES INC
694 Albanese Cir, San Jose (95111-1001)
PHONE...................408 472-4309
EMP: 100
SALES (est): 1.5MM **Privately Held**
SIC: **7361** **7363** Employment Agency Help Supply Services

(P-12149)
UPWORK INC (PA)
2625 Augustine Dr Fl 6th, Santa Clara (95054-2956)
PHONE...................650 316-7500
Thomas Layton, *Ch of Bd*
Stephane Kasriel, *President*
Brian Kinion, *CFO*
Hayden Brown, *Officer*
Elizabeth TSE, *Senior VP*
EMP: 197 EST: 2013
SQ FT: 32,000

SALES (est): 373.6MM **Publicly Held**
WEB: www.upwork.com
SIC: **7361** Executive placement

(P-12150)
VALLEY HEALTH CARE SYSTEMS INC
Also Called: Valley Healthcare Staffing
1300 National Dr Ste 140, Sacramento (95834-1981)
PHONE...................916 505-4112
Sejal Shah, *CEO*
Jason Beck, *President*
Lisa Baker, *Vice Pres*
Wright Philip, *Administration*
Steve Swan, *CTO*
EMP: 150 EST: 2002
SQ FT: 5,000
SALES (est): 11.4MM
SALES (corp-wide): 33.9MM **Privately Held**
WEB: www.totalmed.com
SIC: **7361** Nurses' registry
PA: Totalmed Inc.
221 W College Ave
Appleton WI 54911
866 288-8001

(P-12151)
VIDHWAN INC (PA)
Also Called: E-Solutions
2 N Market St Ste 400, San Jose (95113-1213)
PHONE...................408 289-8200
Priyanka Singh, *President*
Rohit Manhas, *Partner*
Priyanka Gupta, *Partner*
Ashish Pandey, *Executive*
Shiv Singh, *Administration*
EMP: 1746 EST: 2003
SQ FT: 2,000
SALES (est): 200MM **Privately Held**
WEB: www.e-solutionsinc.com
SIC: **7361** **8742** Employment agencies; construction project management consultant; personnel management consultant

(P-12152)
WOLT COM INC
Also Called: Woltcom
2300 Tech Pkwy Ste 8, Hollister (95023)
PHONE...................940 271-4703
Less Than, *Branch Mgr*
EMP: 199
SALES (corp-wide): 13.8MM **Privately Held**
WEB: www.woltcom.com
SIC: **7361** Employment agencies
PA: Woltcom, Inc.
2300 Tech Pkwy Ste 8
Hollister CA 95023
831 638-4900

(P-12153)
WONOLO INC
535 Mission St Fl 14, San Francisco (94105-3253)
PHONE...................415 766-7692
Yong Kim, *CEO*
Asher Brustein, *COO*
Margot Moellenberg, *CFO*
Beatrice Pang, *Vice Pres*
Shayla Navin, *Executive*
EMP: 85 EST: 2014
SQ FT: 7,500
SALES (est): 15.8MM **Privately Held**
WEB: www.wonolo.com
SIC: **7361** Labor contractors (employment agency)

(P-12154)
ZENITH TALENT CORPORATION
6030 Hellyer Ave, San Jose (95138-1018)
PHONE...................408 300-0531
Sunil Bagai, *CEO*
Shailendra Kumar, *Partner*
Bhanu Pandey, *Partner*
Shane Lewis, *Tech Recruiter*
Yashasvi Agrawal, *Recruiter*
EMP: 35 EST: 2012
SALES (est): 6.8MM **Privately Held**
WEB: www.crowdstaffing.com
SIC: **7361** Executive placement

(P-12155)
ZOE HOLDING COMPANY INC
2143 Hurley Way, Sacramento (95825-3253)
PHONE...................916 646-3100
Ryan Johnson, *Branch Mgr*
Adam Reed, *Recruiter*
Michael Jurczak, *Accounts Mgr*
EMP: 90
SALES (corp-wide): 36.9MM **Privately Held**
WEB: www.zoeholding.com
SIC: **7361** Employment agencies
PA: Zoe Holding Company, Inc.
7025 N Scottsdale Rd # 200
Scottsdale AZ 85253
602 508-1883

7363 Help Supply Svcs

(P-12156)
ADECCO EMPLOYMENT SERVICES
1231 W Robinhood Dr, Stockton (95207-5506)
PHONE...................209 474-0443
Alice Prouty, *Branch Mgr*
EMP: 70
SALES (corp-wide): 775.3MM **Privately Held**
WEB: www.adeccousa.com
SIC: **7363** Temporary help service
HQ: Adecco Employment Services, Inc
175 Broadhollow Rd
Melville NY 11747
631 844-7100

(P-12157)
ADVANTAGE WORKFORCE SVCS LLC
39 Stillman St, San Francisco (94107-1309)
PHONE...................415 212-6464
Sumir Meghani,
EMP: 125 EST: 2019
SALES (est): 4.5MM **Privately Held**
SIC: **7363** Temporary help service

(P-12158)
AJILON LLC
2055 Gateway Pl Ste 300, San Jose (95110-1015)
PHONE...................408 367-2592
EMP: 242
SALES (corp-wide): 775.3MM **Privately Held**
SIC: **7363** Temporary help service
HQ: Ajilon Llc
175 Broadhollow Rd
Melville NY 11747
631 844-7800

(P-12159)
ARCADIA SERVICES INC
4340 Redwood Hwy Ste 123, San Rafael (94903-2104)
PHONE...................248 352-7530
John E Elliott II, *Branch Mgr*
EMP: 47
SALES (corp-wide): 26.5MM **Privately Held**
WEB: www.arcadiahomecare.com
SIC: **7363** **8082** Medical help service; home health care services
PA: Arcadia Services, Inc.
20750 Civic Center Dr # 100
Southfield MI 48076
248 352-7530

(P-12160)
ASCENT SERVICES GROUP INC
1001 Galaxy Way Ste 408, Concord (94520-5758)
PHONE...................925 627-4900
Joseph Nordlinger, *President*
Richard Lawrence, *CFO*
W Todd Peterson, *CFO*
Sudhir Sahu, *Chairman*
Max Levine, *Exec VP*
EMP: 450 EST: 2012
SQ FT: 7,000

PRODUCTS & SERVICES SECTION

7363 - Help Supply Svcs County (P-12183)

SALES (est): 59.9MM
SALES (corp-wide): 605.6MM **Privately Held**
WEB: www.ascentsg.com
SIC: 7363 7379 Help supply services; computer related consulting services
PA: American Cybersystems, Inc.
2400 Meadowbrook Pkwy
Duluth GA 30096
770 493-5588

(P-12161)
BEHAVIORAL INTERVENTION ASSN
Also Called: B I A
2354 Powell St A, Emeryville (94608-1738)
PHONE 510 652-7445
Hilary Stubblefield, *Exec Dir*
Fred Baldi, *COO*
Deanne Detmers, *Program Dir*
Hilary S Baldi, *Director*
EMP: 50 **EST:** 1993
SALES (est): 5.2MM **Privately Held**
WEB: www.bia4autism.org
SIC: 7363 Domestic help service

(P-12162)
CHILDCARE CAREERS LLC
2000 Sierra Point Pkwy # 702, Brisbane (94005-1845)
PHONE 650 372-0211
Jason Jones,
Ryan Rios, *Human Resources*
Sandra Shilhanek, *Recruiter*
Sabah Raza, *Opers Staff*
Chrystal Rhee, *Opers Staff*
EMP: 1000 **EST:** 2010
SQ FT: 6,300
SALES (est): 48.7MM **Privately Held**
WEB: www.childcarecareers.net
SIC: 7363 7361 Temporary help service; teachers' agency

(P-12163)
CLEARPATH MANAGEMENT GROUP INC
1928 Old Middlefield Way A, Mountain View (94043-2574)
PHONE 650 691-4140
Rocio Hernandez, *Client Mgr*
EMP: 35
SALES (corp-wide): 23.6MM **Privately Held**
WEB: www.1099oremployee.com
SIC: 7363 Temporary help service
PA: Clearpath Management Group, Inc.
1215 W Center St Ste 102
Manteca CA 95337
209 239-8700

(P-12164)
CLEARPATH WORKFORCE MGT INC
1215 W Center St Ste 102, Manteca (95337-4280)
P.O. Box 1930 (95336-1156)
PHONE 209 239-8700
Renee Fink, *CEO*
Sandi Silva, *COO*
Natasha Giordano, *CFO*
Judy Gnade, *CFO*
Jason Posel, *Senior VP*
EMP: 173 **EST:** 2001
SQ FT: 3,171
SALES (corp-wide): 23.6MM **Privately Held**
WEB: www.1099oremployee.com
SIC: 7363 Temporary help service
PA: Clearpath Management Group, Inc.
1215 W Center St Ste 102
Manteca CA 95337
209 239-8700

(P-12165)
CLP RESOURCES INC
1000 Sunrise Ave Ste 8a, Roseville (95661-5471)
PHONE 916 788-0300
EMP: 60
SALES (corp-wide): 2.1B **Publicly Held**
SIC: 7363 Temporary Construction Help
HQ: Clp Resources, Inc.
1015 A St
Tacoma WA 98402
775 321-8000

(P-12166)
CLP RESOURCES INC
4460 Redwood Hwy Ste 14, San Rafael (94903-1953)
PHONE 415 446-7000
EMP: 50
SALES (corp-wide): 2.1B **Publicly Held**
SIC: 7363 Temporary Construction Help
HQ: Clp Resources, Inc.
1015 A St
Tacoma WA 98402
775 321-8000

(P-12167)
COAST PERSONNEL SERVICES INC (PA)
2295 De La Cruz Blvd, Santa Clara (95050-3020)
P.O. Box 328 (95052-0328)
PHONE 408 653-2100
Larry K Bunker, *CEO*
Michael Avidano, *Vice Pres*
Larry Broun, *Vice Pres*
Vance Tiller, *Vice Pres*
Vangie Fuentes, *Program Mgr*
EMP: 1895 **EST:** 1987
SQ FT: 7,500
SALES (est): 38.4MM **Privately Held**
WEB: www.coastjobs.com
SIC: 7363 Temporary help service

(P-12168)
COUNTY OF STANISLAUS
Also Called: C C S Medical Service
1325 Sonoma Ave, Modesto (95355-3922)
PHONE 209 558-8118
Christine Edwards, *Principal*
EMP: 49
SALES (corp-wide): 1.2B **Privately Held**
WEB: www.stancounty.com
SIC: 9431 7363 ; medical help service
PA: County Of Stanislaus
1010 10th St Ste 5100
Modesto CA 95354
209 525-6398

(P-12169)
ENCORE TECHNICAL STAFFING LLC (PA)
1134 Crane St Ste 216, Menlo Park (94025-4329)
PHONE 541 396-1885
Dan Wooldridge, *Mng Member*
Jennifer Heebink,
Cheryl Wooldridge,
Katie Roberts, *Director*
EMP: 35 **EST:** 1998
SQ FT: 2,000
SALES (est): 4.4MM **Privately Held**
WEB: www.lowmargins.com
SIC: 7363 Temporary help service

(P-12170)
EPN ENTERPRISES INC
Also Called: 24/7 Medstaff
1900 Point West Way # 171, Sacramento (95815-4705)
PHONE 888 788-5424
Edward Navales, *President*
Tammie Newell, *Contract Mgr*
Danielle Courtney, *Recruiter*
EMP: 70 **EST:** 2008
SALES (est): 5.4MM **Privately Held**
WEB: www.247medstaff.com
SIC: 7363 8099 Temporary help service; medical services organization

(P-12171)
EXPRESS PERSONNEL SERVICES
870 W Onstott Frontage Rd E, Yuba City (95991-3500)
PHONE 530 671-9202
Tina Williams, *President*
Carey Campbell, *Treasurer*
Chad Purdy, *Senior VP*
Betty Malinowski, *Vice Pres*
Jane McHann, *Vice Pres*
EMP: 72 **EST:** 1985
SALES (est): 1.2MM **Privately Held**
WEB: www.expresspros.com
SIC: 7363 Temporary help service

(P-12172)
FELTON INSTITUTE (PA)
Also Called: FAMILY SERVICE AGENCY OF SAN F
1500 Franklin St, San Francisco (94109-4523)
PHONE 415 474-7310
Albert Gilbert III, *President*
Marvin L Davis, *CFO*
Michael Gaston, *CFO*
Robert W Bennet, *Principal*
Michael Hofman, *Principal*
EMP: 70 **EST:** 1898
SQ FT: 14,000
SALES (est): 31.9MM **Privately Held**
WEB: www.felton.org
SIC: 7363 Help supply services

(P-12173)
GOODWILL SILICON VALLEY LLC (PA)
1080 N 7th St, San Jose (95112-4425)
PHONE 408 998-5774
Michael E Fox, *CEO*
Frank Kent, *CEO*
Christopher King, *COO*
Christopher Baker, *CFO*
Dale Achabal, *Treasurer*
▲ **EMP:** 100 **EST:** 1937
SQ FT: 180,000
SALES (est): 46.5MM **Privately Held**
WEB: www.goodwillsv.org
SIC: 7363 5932 Help supply services; used merchandise stores

(P-12174)
GOODWILL SILICON VALLEY LLC
550 Tres Pnos Rd Frnt Frn, Hollister (95023)
PHONE 831 634-0960
Lucy Gonzalez, *Manager*
EMP: 43
SALES (corp-wide): 46.5MM **Privately Held**
WEB: www.goodwillsv.org
SIC: 7363 5932 Help supply services; used merchandise stores
PA: Goodwill Of Silicon Valley, Llc
1080 N 7th St
San Jose CA 95112
408 998-5774

(P-12175)
GOODWILL SILICON VALLEY LLC
7098 Santa Teresa Blvd, San Jose (95139-1348)
PHONE 408 281-1449
Vicki Stevenson, *Branch Mgr*
EMP: 43
SALES (corp-wide): 46.5MM **Privately Held**
WEB: www.goodwillsv.org
SIC: 7363 5932 Help supply services; used merchandise stores
PA: Goodwill Of Silicon Valley, Llc
1080 N 7th St
San Jose CA 95112
408 998-5774

(P-12176)
INTERCTIVE MED SPECIALISTS INC
252 Waterside Cir, San Rafael (94903-2795)
PHONE 415 472-4204
Jaleh Ebrahimi, *President*
Oranous Ebrahimi, *Treasurer*
Ghazaleh Ebrahimi, *Vice Pres*
Oranus Ebrahimi, *Vice Pres*
Ory Shirazi, *Vice Pres*
EMP: 70 **EST:** 1994
SALES (est): 2.8MM **Privately Held**
WEB: www.imsspecialists.com
SIC: 7363 Medical help service

(P-12177)
JOHN PAUL USA (PA)
575 Market St Ste 720, San Francisco (94105-2837)
PHONE 415 905-6088
Paul McKnight, *CEO*
David Amsellem, *CEO*
Amber Treshnell, *CEO*
Aurore Lami, *Officer*
Romain Latimier, *Officer*
EMP: 192 **EST:** 1987
SALES (est): 27.8MM **Privately Held**
WEB: www.johnpaul.com
SIC: 7363 Help supply services

(P-12178)
LANDMARK EVENT STAFFING
1965 Adams Ave, San Leandro (94577-1005)
PHONE 510 632-9000
Peter Kranske, *Branch Mgr*
EMP: 1095 **Privately Held**
WEB: www.landmarkeventstaff.com
SIC: 7363 Help supply services
PA: Landmark Event Staffing Services, Inc.
4131 Harbor Walk Dr
Fort Collins CO 80525

(P-12179)
LANE SAFETY CO INC
340 W Channel Rd Ste F, Benicia (94510-1160)
PHONE 707 746-4820
Marion Gizzi, *President*
EMP: 46 **EST:** 1991
SQ FT: 10,000
SALES (est): 2.9MM **Privately Held**
WEB: www.lanesafetycoinc.business.site
SIC: 7363 3669 Help supply services; transportation signaling devices

(P-12180)
MAXIM HEALTHCARE SERVICES INC
Also Called: Sacramento Staffing
1050 Fulton Ave Ste 230, Sacramento (95825-4299)
PHONE 916 614-9539
Manpreet Singh, *Branch Mgr*
EMP: 92 **Privately Held**
WEB: www.maximhealthcare.com
SIC: 7363 Medical help service
PA: Maxim Healthcare Services, Inc.
7227 Lee Deforest Dr
Columbia MD 21046

(P-12181)
MAXIM HEALTHCARE SERVICES INC
Also Called: San Frncisco Staffing Staffing
6475 Christie Ave Ste 350, Emeryville (94608-2260)
PHONE 510 873-0700
J Cronte, *Manager*
Mike Palomino, *Business Mgr*
Hailey Dell'immagine, *Recruiter*
Judy Bender,
EMP: 92 **Privately Held**
WEB: www.maximhealthcare.com
SIC: 7363 7361 Medical help service; nurses' registry
PA: Maxim Healthcare Services, Inc.
7227 Lee Deforest Dr
Columbia MD 21046

(P-12182)
MAXIM HEALTHCARE SERVICES INC
Also Called: Fresno Staffing
5066 N Fresno St Ste 103, Fresno (93710-7615)
PHONE 559 224-0299
Tina Roberts, *Manager*
EMP: 92 **Privately Held**
WEB: www.maximhealthcare.com
SIC: 7363 8082 Medical help service; home health care services
PA: Maxim Healthcare Services, Inc.
7227 Lee Deforest Dr
Columbia MD 21046

(P-12183)
MAXIM HEALTHCARE SERVICES INC
Also Called: Roseville Home Healthcare
151 N Sunrise Ave Ste 905, Roseville (95661-2929)
PHONE 916 771-7444
Andrew Brusaschetti, *Manager*

7363 - Help Supply Svcs County (P-12184)

EMP: 92 **Privately Held**
WEB: www.maximhealthcare.com
SIC: 7363 8082 Medical help service; home health care services
PA: Maxim Healthcare Services, Inc.
7227 Lee Deforest Dr
Columbia MD 21046

(P-12184)
MAXIM HEALTHCARE SERVICES INC
Also Called: San Mateo Staffing
1101 S Wnchster Blvd Ste, San Mateo (94403)
PHONE................................410 910-1500
Jeff Nugent, *Manager*
EMP: 92 **Privately Held**
WEB: www.maximhealthcare.com
SIC: 7363 Medical help service
PA: Maxim Healthcare Services, Inc.
7227 Lee Deforest Dr
Columbia MD 21046

(P-12185)
MERITAGE MEDICAL NETWORK
4 Hamilton Landing # 100, Novato (94949-8256)
PHONE................................415 884-1840
Joel Criste, *CEO*
EMP: 89 **EST:** 1993
SALES (est): 6.4MM **Privately Held**
WEB: www.marinclinic.org
SIC: 7363 Pilot service, aviation

(P-12186)
OPHELIA QUINONES
Also Called: Best Event Staffing Team
223 S 22nd St, San Jose (95116-2726)
PHONE................................408 757-1718
Ophelia Quinones, *Owner*
EMP: 50 **EST:** 2016
SALES (est): 2MM **Privately Held**
SIC: 7363 Help supply services

(P-12187)
PLANT MAINTENANCE INC
Also Called: Temporary Plant Cleaners
1330 Arnold Dr Ste 147, Martinez (94553-6538)
P.O. Box 48 (94553-0115)
PHONE................................925 228-3285
Tim Hollz, *President*
Kenneth B Johnson, *Vice Pres*
EMP: 90 **EST:** 1996
SQ FT: 2,800
SALES (est): 2.3MM
SALES (corp-wide): 37.7MM **Privately Held**
WEB: www.montmech.com
SIC: 7363 Industrial help service
PA: Monterey Mechanical Co.
8275 San Leandro St
Oakland CA 94621
510 632-3173

(P-12188)
PLUS GROUP INC
3300 Tully Rd Ste B1, Modesto (95350-0848)
PHONE................................209 342-9022
Knowledge Hardy, *Manager*
EMP: 296 **Privately Held**
WEB: www.theplusgroup.com
SIC: 7363 7361 Temporary help service; employment agencies
PA: The Plus Group Inc
7425 Janes Ave Ste 201
Woodridge IL 60517

(P-12189)
PLUS GROUP INC
Also Called: Jobs Plus
2551 San Ramon Valley Blv, San Ramon (94583-1661)
PHONE................................925 831-8551
Patrick O'Donnell, *Branch Mgr*
Kelly Karmer, *Recruiter*
EMP: 296 **Privately Held**
WEB: www.theplusgroup.com
SIC: 7363 7361 Temporary help service; executive placement

PA: The Plus Group Inc
7425 Janes Ave Ste 201
Woodridge IL 60517

(P-12190)
PROJECT HIRED (PA)
2505 Eaton Ave, San Carlos (94070-4438)
PHONE................................408 557-0880
Marie Bernard, *CEO*
Deb Huff, *Bd of Directors*
Jeff Jacobs, *Bd of Directors*
Gwen Ford, *Exec Dir*
Janice Tone, *Administration*
EMP: 69 **EST:** 1978
SALES: 2.4MM **Privately Held**
WEB: www.projecthired.org
SIC: 7363 7361 Temporary help service; employment agencies

(P-12191)
REAL TIME INFORMATION SVCS INC
Also Called: Real-Time Staffing Services
191 W Shaw Ave Ste 106, Fresno (93704-2826)
PHONE................................559 222-6456
Aijaz Ahmed, *CEO*
EMP: 50 **EST:** 1998
SALES (est): 7.7MM **Privately Held**
WEB: www.realtimeca.com
SIC: 7363 Temporary help service

(P-12192)
ROBERT HALF INTERNATIONAL INC (PA)
2884 Sand Hill Rd Ste 200, Menlo Park (94025-7059)
PHONE................................650 234-6000
M Keith Waddell, *Vice Chairman*
Gary Pittman, *Partner*
Harold M Messmer Jr, *Ch of Bd*
Paul F Gentzkow, *President*
Garrett Mathison, *President*
▲ **EMP:** 100 **EST:** 1948
SALES (est): 5.1B **Publicly Held**
WEB: www.roberthalf.com
SIC: 7363 7361 8748 8721 Temporary help service; placement agencies; business consulting; auditing services

(P-12193)
SE SCHER CORPORATION
1585 The Alameda, San Jose (95126-2310)
PHONE................................408 844-0772
William Friedeberg,
Griffin Long, *Manager*
EMP: 663
SALES (corp-wide): 19.8MM **Privately Held**
SIC: 7363 Help supply services
PA: S.E. Scher Corporation
303 Hegenberger Rd # 300
Oakland CA 94621
415 431-8826

(P-12194)
SFN GROUP INC
919 E Hillsdale Blvd, Foster City (94404-2112)
PHONE................................650 348-4967
Dayna Miller, *Branch Mgr*
EMP: 715
SALES (corp-wide): 24.5B **Privately Held**
WEB: www.spherion.com
SIC: 7363 Temporary help service
HQ: Sfn Group, Inc.
2050 Spectrum Blvd
Fort Lauderdale FL 33309
954 308-7600

(P-12195)
SFN GROUP INC
401 River Oaks Pkwy, San Jose (95134-1916)
PHONE................................408 526-0115
Chris Van Groningen, *Branch Mgr*
EMP: 715
SALES (corp-wide): 24.5B **Privately Held**
WEB: www.spherion.com
SIC: 7363 Temporary help service
HQ: Sfn Group, Inc.
2050 Spectrum Blvd
Fort Lauderdale FL 33309
954 308-7600

(P-12196)
SFN GROUP INC
Also Called: Spherion Staffing Group
3050 Bictor Ave Ste A, Redding (96002)
PHONE................................530 222-3434
Sheryl Lakowski, *Branch Mgr*
EMP: 715
SALES (corp-wide): 24.5B **Privately Held**
WEB: www.spherion.com
SIC: 7363 Temporary help service
HQ: Sfn Group, Inc.
2050 Spectrum Blvd
Fort Lauderdale FL 33309
954 308-7600

(P-12197)
SFN GROUP INC
Also Called: Spherion Technology Svcs Group
3825 Hopyard Rd Ste 270, Pleasanton (94588-2958)
PHONE................................925 847-8500
Beth Vanier, *Exec Dir*
EMP: 715
SALES (corp-wide): 24.5B **Privately Held**
WEB: www.spherion.com
SIC: 7363 Temporary help service
HQ: Sfn Group, Inc.
2050 Spectrum Blvd
Fort Lauderdale FL 33309
954 308-7600

(P-12198)
SFN GROUP INC
Also Called: Spherion Hr Consulting
2150 N 1st St Ste 230, San Jose (95131-2020)
PHONE................................408 452-4845
Jeanne Palmer, *Branch Mgr*
EMP: 715
SALES (corp-wide): 24.5B **Privately Held**
WEB: www.spherion.com
SIC: 7363 Temporary help service
HQ: Sfn Group, Inc.
2050 Spectrum Blvd
Fort Lauderdale FL 33309
954 308-7600

(P-12199)
SFN GROUP INC
1 Meyer Plz, Vallejo (94590-5925)
PHONE................................707 551-2719
Elizabeth Childs, *Branch Mgr*
EMP: 715
SALES (corp-wide): 24.5B **Privately Held**
WEB: www.spherion.com
SIC: 7363 Temporary help service
HQ: Sfn Group, Inc.
2050 Spectrum Blvd
Fort Lauderdale FL 33309
954 308-7600

(P-12200)
SHIFAMED LLC
745 Camden Ave Ste A, Campbell (95008-4146)
PHONE................................408 364-1242
Omar Salahiah, *Owner*
Debbie White, *Vice Pres*
Mariam Maghribi, *VP Bus Dvlpt*
Creag Trautman, *General Mgr*
Irene Tan, *Office Admin*
EMP: 20 **EST:** 2010
SALES (est): 3.6MM **Privately Held**
WEB: www.shifamed.com
SIC: 7363 3841 Medical help service; medical instruments & equipment, blood & bone work

(P-12201)
STAY SAFE SOLUTIONS INC
3140 Peacekeeper Way 101a, McClellan (95652-2508)
PHONE................................916 640-1300
Kenny D Shoemake, *President*
EMP: 42 **EST:** 2009
SQ FT: 31,558
SALES (est): 3.6MM **Privately Held**
WEB: www.staysafesolutions.com
SIC: 7363 5047 Help supply services; medical & hospital equipment

(P-12202)
TRANSFORCE INC
965 E Yosemite Ave Ste 7, Manteca (95336-5943)
PHONE................................209 952-2573
EMP: 50
SALES (est): 2.7MM **Privately Held**
SIC: 7363 Help Supply Services

(P-12203)
VACAVILLE CONDOLESCENT AND REH
585 Nut Tree Ct, Vacaville (95687-3353)
PHONE................................707 449-8000
Joseph M Niccoli Jr, *President*
EMP: 150 **EST:** 2003
SALES (est): 7MM **Privately Held**
WEB: www.vacavilleurgentcare.com
SIC: 7363 Medical help service

(P-12204)
VOLT MANAGEMENT CORP
Also Called: Volt Workforce Solutions
7330 N Palm Ave Ste 105, Fresno (93711-5768)
PHONE................................559 435-1255
Scott Giroux, *Branch Mgr*
EMP: 75
SALES (corp-wide): 822MM **Publicly Held**
WEB: www.arctern.com
SIC: 7363 7361 Temporary help service; employment agencies
HQ: Volt Management Corp.
2401 N Glassell St
Orange CA 92865

(P-12205)
VOLT MANAGEMENT CORP
Also Called: Volt Workforce Solutions
1544 Eureka Rd Ste 150, Roseville (95661-3093)
PHONE................................916 923-0454
Tim Chapman, *Branch Mgr*
EMP: 75
SALES (corp-wide): 822MM **Publicly Held**
WEB: www.arctern.com
SIC: 7363 Temporary help service
HQ: Volt Management Corp.
2401 N Glassell St
Orange CA 92865

(P-12206)
VOLT MANAGEMENT CORP
Also Called: Volt Workforce Solutions
3558 Deer Park Dr 2, Stockton (95219-2350)
PHONE................................209 952-5627
Scott Giroux, *Branch Mgr*
EMP: 75
SALES (corp-wide): 822MM **Publicly Held**
WEB: www.arctern.com
SIC: 7363 Temporary help service
HQ: Volt Management Corp.
2401 N Glassell St
Orange CA 92865

(P-12207)
VOLT MANAGEMENT CORP
Also Called: Volt Workforce Solutions
3700 Old Redwood Hwy # 1, Santa Rosa (95403-5738)
PHONE................................707 547-1660
Tim Chapman, *Branch Mgr*
Lauren Griffin, *Vice Pres*
EMP: 75
SALES (corp-wide): 822MM **Publicly Held**
WEB: www.arctern.com
SIC: 7363 Temporary help service
HQ: Volt Management Corp.
2401 N Glassell St
Orange CA 92865

(P-12208)
WEAVE INC (PA)
1900 K St Ste 200, Sacramento (95811-4187)
PHONE................................916 448-2321
Beth Hassett, *Exec Dir*

PRODUCTS & SERVICES SECTION
7371 - Custom Computer Programming Svcs County (P-12230)

Garry Maisel, *Ch of Bd*
Kelly Chavez, *CFO*
Priya Batra, *Principal*
Neil Forester, *Principal*
EMP: 95 **EST:** 1977
SALES: 5.9MM **Privately Held**
WEB: www.weaveinc.org
SIC: 7363 8322 Domestic help service; individual & family services

(P-12209)
WEST VALLEY ENGINEERING INC (PA)
Also Called: West Valley Staffing Group
390 Potrero Ave, Sunnyvale (94085-4116)
PHONE.................................408 735-1420
Michael F Williams, *President*
Teresa Kossayian, *CFO*
Korina Loera, *Program Mgr*
Yolanda Alva, *Admin Asst*
Douglas Griffith, *Administration*
EMP: 1152 **EST:** 1969
SALES (est): 46.8MM **Privately Held**
WEB: www.westvalley.com
SIC: 7363 Temporary help service

(P-12210)
YOUTH UPRISING
8711 Macarthur Blvd, Oakland (94605-4000)
P.O. Box 5380 (94605-0380)
PHONE.................................510 777-9909
Y'Anad Burrell, *Mng Member*
Olive Simmons, *CEO*
John Payne, *CFO*
Laneva Johnson, *Executive Asst*
Omana Imani, *Director*
EMP: 51 **EST:** 2004
SALES (est): 3.4MM **Privately Held**
WEB: www.youthuprising.org
SIC: 7363 8299 Medical help service; educational services

7371 Custom Computer Programming Svcs

(P-12211)
22ND CENTURY TECHNOLOGIES INC
6203 San Ignacio Ave # 1, San Jose (95119-1371)
PHONE.................................866 537-9191
Satvinder Singh, *President*
EMP: 435
SALES (corp-wide): 356MM **Privately Held**
WEB: www.tscti.com
SIC: 7371 Computer software systems analysis & design, custom
PA: 22nd Century Technologies Inc.
 8251 Greensboro Dr # 900
 Mc Lean VA 22102
 732 537-9191

(P-12212)
24I UNIT MEDIA INC
1633 Bayshore Hwy Ste 338, Burlingame (94010-1515)
PHONE.................................818 802-9995
EMP: 180
SALES (est): 42.8K **Privately Held**
WEB: www.24i.com
SIC: 7371 Custom Computer Programing

(P-12213)
2K MARIN INC
10 Hamilton Landing, Novato (94949-8207)
PHONE.................................646 536-2898
Strauss Zelnick, *President*
EMP: 44 **EST:** 2007
SALES (est): 3.1MM **Publicly Held**
WEB: www.take2games.com
SIC: 7371 Custom computer programming services
PA: Take-Two Interactive Software, Inc.
 110 W 44th St
 New York NY 10036

(P-12214)
314E CORPORATION (PA)
6701 Koll Center Pkwy # 34, Pleasanton (94566-8061)
PHONE.................................510 371-6736
Abhishek Begerhotta, *President*
Matthew Rusch, *Assoc VP*
Casey Post, *Senior VP*
Jibu George, *Vice Pres*
Archit Trivedi, *Business Anlyst*
EMP: 157 **EST:** 2004
SQ FT: 10,078
SALES (est): 13.2MM **Privately Held**
WEB: www.314e.com
SIC: 7371 Computer software development

(P-12215)
3K TECHNOLOGIES LLC
1114 Cadillac Ct, Milpitas (95035-3058)
PHONE.................................408 716-5900
Sireesha Chittabbathini,
Ram Sethuraman, *Partner*
Upender Reddy, *Tech Recruiter*
Krishna Chittabbathini,
Kishore Gobireddy, *Manager*
EMP: 105
SQ FT: 2,000
SALES: 13.8MM **Privately Held**
WEB: www.3ktechnologies.com
SIC: 7371 Custom computer programming services

(P-12216)
4D INC
95 S Market St Ste 240, San Jose (95113-2311)
PHONE.................................408 557-4600
Laurent Ribardiere, *CEO*
Phillipe Berthault, *CFO*
Ricardo Mello, *Vice Pres*
Doris Beaulieu, *Admin Sec*
Jean Laguerre, *QA Dir*
EMP: 101 **EST:** 2000
SALES (est): 10MM
SALES (corp-wide): 937.3K **Privately Held**
WEB: www.us.4d.com
SIC: 7371 7372 Computer software development; prepackaged software
HQ: 4d
 Entree 4 Parc Des Erables
 Le Pecq 78230
 130 539-200

(P-12217)
6WIND USA INC
2445 Augustine Dr Ste 150, Santa Clara (95054-3032)
PHONE.................................408 816-1366
Eric Carmes, *President*
Fengtian Guo, *Software Engr*
Charlie Ashton, *VP Mktg*
Mike Erickson, *Sales Staff*
Karim McHirki, *Director*
EMP: 88 **EST:** 2008
SALES (est): 6.4MM **Privately Held**
WEB: www.6wind.com
SIC: 7371 Computer software development

(P-12218)
AARKI INC (PA)
530 Lakeside Dr Ste 260, Sunnyvale (94085-4064)
PHONE.................................408 382-1180
Sid Bhatt, *President*
Ed Battle, *COO*
Kim Carlson, *Vice Pres*
Pyong Kim, *Vice Pres*
Naoki Kobayashi, *Vice Pres*
EMP: 101 **EST:** 2007
SALES (est): 29.7MM **Privately Held**
WEB: www.aarki.com
SIC: 7371 5199 Computer software development; advertising specialties

(P-12219)
ABACUS SERVICE CORPORATION
1725 23rd St, Sacramento (95816-7100)
PHONE.................................916 288-8948
Michelle Reuter, *Branch Mgr*
EMP: 300

SALES (corp-wide): 29.9MM **Privately Held**
WEB: www.abacusservice.com
SIC: 7371 Custom computer programming services
PA: Abacus Service Corporation
 25925 Telg Rd Ste 206
 Southfield MI
 248 324-9200

(P-12220)
ABBYY USA SOFTWARE HOUSE INC (DH)
890 Hillview Ct Ste 300, Milpitas (95035-4574)
PHONE.................................408 457-9777
Ding Yuan Tang, *CEO*
Arthur Whipple, *President*
Jay Hood, *COO*
Sheryl Lodolce, *CFO*
Gregory Lipich, *Officer*
EMP: 105 **EST:** 2000
SQ FT: 31,000
SALES (est): 25.4MM **Privately Held**
WEB: www.abbyy.com
SIC: 7371 Computer software development

(P-12221)
ABELISK INC (PA)
Also Called: Argos Software
7060 N Fresno St Ste 210, Fresno (93720-2984)
PHONE.................................559 227-1000
Alan R Thodey, *President*
Christopher Pierce, *Network Enginr*
Michael Parrilli, *VP Sales*
Ali Al-Abbasi, *Director*
Pauline Montgomery, *Director*
EMP: 24 **EST:** 1979
SQ FT: 10,000
SALES (est): 2.8MM **Privately Held**
WEB: www.argosoftware.com
SIC: 7371 7372 Computer software development; prepackaged software

(P-12222)
ABJAYON INC
42808 Christy St Ste 228, Fremont (94538-3116)
PHONE.................................510 824-3260
Anita Bolinjkar, *CEO*
Neeraj Datta, *CFO*
EMP: 250 **EST:** 2007
SALES (est): 3MM **Privately Held**
WEB: www.abjayon.com
SIC: 7371 Computer software development

(P-12223)
ABZOOBA INC (DH)
1551 Mccarthy Blvd # 204, Milpitas (95035-7437)
PHONE.................................650 453-8760
Vivek Vipul, *CEO*
Arnab Bose, *Officer*
Navin Ahuja, *Vice Pres*
Pushpal Bhattacharya, *Vice Pres*
Riti Chowdhury, *Executive*
EMP: 119 **EST:** 2010
SALES (est): 17.3MM **Privately Held**
WEB: www.abzooba.com
SIC: 7371 Computer software development

(P-12224)
ACCESS SYSTEMS AMERICAS INC
3965 Freedom Cir Ste 200, Santa Clara (95054-1293)
PHONE.................................408 400-3000
Kiyo Oishi, *CEO*
Jeanne Seeley, *CFO*
Michael Kelley, *Vice Pres*
Sawako Takemoto, *Vice Pres*
Michimasa Uematsu, *Vice Pres*
EMP: 78 **EST:** 2001
SQ FT: 71,000
SALES (est): 3.5MM **Privately Held**
WEB: www.access-company.com
SIC: 7371 7372 Computer software development; prepackaged software
PA: Access Co.,Ltd.
 3, Kandaneribeicho
 Chiyoda-Ku TKY 101-0

(P-12225)
ACCU-IMAGE INC
330 Tennant Ave, Morgan Hill (95037-5443)
PHONE.................................408 736-9066
Anne Bennett, *President*
Lawrence C Bennett, *CEO*
Lawrence Bennet, *Representative*
EMP: 44 **EST:** 1988
SALES (est): 4.7MM **Privately Held**
WEB: www.accu-image.com
SIC: 7371 7374 Computer software development; optical scanning data service

(P-12226)
ACHIEVO CORPORATION (PA)
1400 Terra Bella Ave E, Mountain View (94043-3062)
PHONE.................................925 498-8864
EMP: 66
SALES (est): 52MM **Privately Held**
SIC: 7371 Custom Computer Programming Services, Nsk

(P-12227)
ACTUATE CORPORATION (HQ)
951 Mariners Island Blvd # 7, San Mateo (94404-1561)
PHONE.................................650 645-3000
Mark J Barrenechea, *President*
John Doolittle, *CFO*
Adam Howatson, *Chief Mktg Ofcr*
Gordon A Davies, *Officer*
Jonathan Hunter, *Exec VP*
EMP: 490 **EST:** 1993
SQ FT: 58,000
SALES (est): 111.1MM
SALES (corp-wide): 3.1B **Privately Held**
WEB: www.opentext.com
SIC: 7371 Computer software development
PA: Open Text Corporation
 275 Frank Tompa Dr
 Waterloo ON N2L 0
 519 888-7111

(P-12228)
ADDEPAR INC (PA)
303 Bryant St, Mountain View (94041-1552)
PHONE.................................855 464-6268
Eric Poirier, *CEO*
Karen White, *President*
Stephen Snyder, *CFO*
Joe Lonsdale, *Chairman*
Natalie Sunderland, *Chief Mktg Ofcr*
EMP: 85 **EST:** 2009
SALES (est): 21.4MM **Privately Held**
WEB: www.addepar.com
SIC: 7371 Computer software development

(P-12229)
ADVANCED SOFTWARE DESIGN INC
Also Called: Advanced Software Dynamics
58 Van Tassel Ln, Orinda (94563-1136)
PHONE.................................925 457-8540
Manu Chatterjee, *CEO*
Sonali Singh, *President*
Shikha Chatterjee, *VP Opers*
EMP: 59 **EST:** 1981
SALES (est): 3MM **Privately Held**
WEB: www.asdglobal.com
SIC: 7371 7373 8711 8742 Computer software development; computer integrated systems design; engineering services; management consulting services

(P-12230)
ADVANTAGE ROUTE SYSTEMS INC
3201 Liberty Square Pkwy, Turlock (95380-9665)
PHONE.................................209 632-1122
David Kroutil, *President*
Dianne Kroutil, *Corp Secy*
Richard Giubbini, *Software Engr*
Cameron Anderson, *Prgrmr*
Seth Jaggers, *Technical Staff*
EMP: 40 **EST:** 1994
SALES (est): 6.1MM **Privately Held**
WEB: www.advantageroute.com
SIC: 7371 Computer software development

7371 - Custom Computer Programming Svcs County (P-12231)

(P-12231)
ADVANTECH CORPORATION (HQ)
380 Fairview Way, Milpitas (95035-3062)
P.O. Box 45895, San Francisco (94145-0895)
PHONE......................................408 519-3800
Ke-Cheng Liu, *CEO*
Chaney Ho, *President*
Eric Chen, *Vice Pres*
Deryu Yin, *Vice Pres*
Mike Voss, *Executive*
▲ **EMP:** 300 **EST:** 1987
SQ FT: 100,000
SALES (est): 512.8MM **Privately Held**
WEB: www.advantech.com
SIC: 7371 Computer software systems analysis & design, custom

(P-12232)
ADVENT SOFTWARE INC (HQ)
Also Called: SS&c Advent
600 Townsend St Fl 4, San Francisco (94103-4945)
PHONE......................................415 543-7696
David Peter Hess Jr, *President*
Stephanie Dimarco, *Ch of Bd*
James Cox, *CFO*
Todd Gottula, *Exec VP*
Chris Momsen, *Exec VP*
EMP: 740 **EST:** 1995
SQ FT: 158,264
SALES (est): 130MM
SALES (corp-wide): 4.6B **Publicly Held**
WEB: www.advent.com
SIC: 7371 7373 7372 6722 Custom computer programming services; computer integrated systems design; systems software development services; computer systems analysis & design; prepackaged software; management investment, open-end
PA: Ss&C Technologies Holdings, Inc.
80 Lamberton Rd
Windsor CT 06095
860 298-4500

(P-12233)
AERA TECHNOLOGY INC (PA)
707 California St, Mountain View (94041-2005)
PHONE......................................408 524-2222
Ram Mohan, *President*
Paul Crayford, *Partner*
Fred Fontes, *Partner*
Valerie Preston, *Partner*
Travis Adlman, *CFO*
EMP: 104 **EST:** 1999
SALES (est): 15.7MM **Privately Held**
WEB: www.aeratechnology.com
SIC: 7371 Computer software development

(P-12234)
AFFINITY INC
Also Called: Project Affinity
121 2nd St Fl 6, San Francisco (94105-3611)
PHONE......................................650 380-9305
EMP: 35
SALES (est): 583.1K **Privately Held**
SIC: 7371 Custom Computer Programming Services, Nsk

(P-12235)
AGARI DATA INC (DH)
950 Tower Ln Ste 2000, Foster City (94404-4255)
PHONE......................................650 627-7667
Patrick R Peterson, *CEO*
Armen Najarian, *Chief Mktg Ofcr*
Ramon Peypoch,
John Giacomini, *Officer*
Sabina Knotter-Finney, *Vice Pres*
EMP: 155 **EST:** 2010
SALES (est): 23.2MM
SALES (corp-wide): 562.3MM **Privately Held**
WEB: www.agari.com
SIC: 7371 Computer software systems analysis & design, custom
HQ: Help/Systems, Llc
6455 City West Pkwy
Eden Prairie MN 55344
952 933-0609

(P-12236)
AISERA INC
1121 San Antonio Rd C202, Palo Alto (94303-4311)
PHONE......................................650 667-4308
Sudhakar Muddu, *President*
Fred Patton, *CFO*
Puru Amradkar, *Vice Pres*
Kim Del Fierro, *Vice Pres*
Robert Hirst, *General Mgr*
EMP: 52 **EST:** 2018
SALES (est): 2.8MM **Privately Held**
WEB: www.aisera.com
SIC: 7371 Computer software development

(P-12237)
AL STOCKWELL INC
405 14th St Fl 7, Oakland (94612-2715)
PHONE......................................510 269-7423
Paul Morell McDonald, *CEO*
Ashwath Rajan, *President*
Kelli Sousa, *Sales Staff*
EMP: 40 **EST:** 2016
SALES (est): 2.8MM **Privately Held**
SIC: 7371 Computer software development & applications

(P-12238)
ALIEN TECHNOLOGY LLC
845 Embedded Way Ste 100, San Jose (95138-1091)
PHONE......................................408 782-3900
Damon Bramble, *General Mgr*
EMP: 72 **Privately Held**
WEB: www.alientechnology.com
SIC: 7371 Computer software development
PA: Alien Technology, Llc
845 Embedded Way Ste 100
San Jose CA 95138

(P-12239)
ALL TURTLES CORPORATION (PA)
1266 Harrison St, San Francisco (94103-4406)
PHONE......................................609 352-3172
Phil Libin, *CEO*
Jon Cifuentes, *Marketing Staff*
EMP: 50 **EST:** 2017
SALES (est): 2.1MM **Privately Held**
WEB: www.all-turtles.com
SIC: 7371 Computer software development & applications

(P-12240)
ALLDRAGON INTERNATIONAL INC
4285 Payne Ave 10028, San Jose (95117-3324)
PHONE......................................408 410-6248
Tom Gong, *CEO*
Connie Kang, *President*
EMP: 50 **EST:** 2009
SALES (est): 150K **Privately Held**
WEB: www.alldragon.com
SIC: 7371 Computer software development & applications

(P-12241)
ALLIANCE INFO TECH CMPT SFTWR (PA)
Also Called: Allianceit
7041 Koll Center Pkwy # 140, Pleasanton (94566-3196)
PHONE......................................925 462-9787
Purushothama Polkampalli, *President*
Kalyani Mokkapati, *Managing Dir*
Nihanth Krishna, *Opers Mgr*
Hrinish Patalay, *Manager*
EMP: 15 **EST:** 2011
SQ FT: 2,000
SALES (est): 2.8MM **Privately Held**
WEB: www.allianceit.com
SIC: 7371 8748 7379 7372 Computer software development; systems engineering consultant, ex. computer or professional; data processing consultant; prepackaged software

(P-12242)
ALPHA NET CONSULTING LLC
3080 Olcott St Ste C235, Santa Clara (95054-3281)
PHONE......................................408 330-0896
Gurderpinder Dhillon,
Surjit Bedi, *Technical Staff*
Karan Sharma, *Technical Staff*
Kamal Kishore, *Engineer*
Peter Bostwick, *Opers Staff*
EMP: 85 **EST:** 1999
SQ FT: 1,500
SALES (est): 8.1MM **Privately Held**
WEB: www.anetcorp.com
SIC: 7371 Custom computer programming services

(P-12243)
ALPHABET INC (PA)
1600 Amphitheatre Pkwy, Mountain View (94043-1351)
PHONE......................................650 253-0000
Sundar Pichai, *CEO*
Stephen Merritt, *Partner*
John L Hennessy, *Ch of Bd*
Ruth M Porat, *CFO*
Arjan Dijk, *Vice Pres*
EMP: 541 **EST:** 1998
SALES (est): 182.5B **Publicly Held**
WEB: www.abc.xyz
SIC: 7371 Computer software development & applications

(P-12244)
ALPHONSO INC (PA)
331 Castro St Ste 200, Mountain View (94041-1205)
PHONE......................................415 223-2112
Raghu Kodige, *CEO*
Serge Matta, *President*
Sandeep Beotra, *CFO*
Tom Perchinsky, *Exec VP*
Michael Mercede, *Vice Pres*
EMP: 40 **EST:** 2013
SALES (est): 45MM **Privately Held**
WEB: www.lgads.tv
SIC: 7371 Computer software development

(P-12245)
ALTAPACIFIC INC
Also Called: Alta PCF Tech Solutions Group
1525 E Shaw Ave Ste 201, Fresno (93710-8005)
PHONE......................................559 439-5700
Alex Metson, *President*
Matt Johnson, *CFO*
EMP: 27 **EST:** 1996
SQ FT: 5,000
SALES (est): 3.8MM **Privately Held**
WEB: www.altapacific.com
SIC: 7371 3825 3699 8999 Computer software development; network analyzers; security devices; communication services

(P-12246)
AMBER HOLDINGS INC
Also Called: Vista Equity Partners Fund III
150 California St, San Francisco (94111-4500)
PHONE......................................415 765-6500
Robert F Smith, *President*
Brian N Sheth, *Vice Pres*
EMP: 82 **EST:** 1995
SALES (est): 6.7MM
SALES (corp-wide): 1.6B **Privately Held**
WEB: www.vistaequitypartners.com
SIC: 7371 Computer software development
HQ: Vista Equity Partners Fund Iii, L.P.
4 Embarcadero Ctr # 2000
San Francisco CA 94111

(P-12247)
AMDOCS BCS INC
1104 Investment Blvd, El Dorado Hills (95762-5710)
PHONE......................................916 934-7000
EMP: 336
SALES: 557.9K
SALES (corp-wide): 3.5B **Privately Held**
SIC: 7371 7389 7374 Computer Programming Svc Business Services Data Processing/Prep
HQ: Amdocs, Inc.
1390 Timberlake Manor Pkw
Chesterfield MO 63017
314 212-7000

(P-12248)
AMICK BROWN LLC (PA)
2500 Old Crow Canyon Rd, San Ramon (94583-1623)
PHONE......................................925 820-2000
Karen Gildea, *Managing Prtnr*
Anitha Brown, *Managing Prtnr*
Jenna Rosdahl, *Human Res Mgr*
Claudia Espinoza, *Recruiter*
Alyanna Espina, *Marketing Staff*
EMP: 51 **EST:** 2010
SQ FT: 1,669
SALES (est): 7MM **Privately Held**
WEB: www.amickbrown.com
SIC: 7371 Computer software development

(P-12249)
AMP TECHNOLOGIES LLC
445 Melrose Ct, San Ramon (94582-5103)
PHONE......................................877 442-2824
Neel Naicker, *CEO*
Arvind Sathyamoorthy, *CTO*
EMP: 140 **EST:** 2011
SALES (est): 7.8MM **Privately Held**
WEB: www.theampwebsite.com
SIC: 7371 Computer software development & applications

(P-12250)
AMPLITUDE INC (PA)
Also Called: Amplitude Analytics
201 3rd St Ste 200, San Francisco (94103-3143)
PHONE......................................650 988-5131
Spenser Skates, *CEO*
Hoang Vuong, *CFO*
Jennifer Johnson, *Officer*
Matt Heinz, *Risk Mgmt Dir*
Curtis Liu, *CTO*
EMP: 489 **EST:** 2012
SALES (est): 102.4MM **Publicly Held**
WEB: www.amplitude.com
SIC: 7371 Computer software development

(P-12251)
AMZN MOBILE LLC
525 Market St Fl 19, San Francisco (94105-2728)
PHONE......................................925 348-4580
EMP: 500 **EST:** 2007
SALES (est): 18.6MM **Publicly Held**
WEB: www.amazon.com
SIC: 7371 Software programming applications
PA: Amazon.Com, Inc.
410 Terry Ave N
Seattle WA 98109

(P-12252)
ANAND SOFTWARE INC
4719 Quail Lakes Dr, Stockton (95207-5267)
PHONE......................................209 287-1708
EMP: 99
SALES: 3MM **Privately Held**
SIC: 7371 7373 Custom Computer Programing Computer Systems Design

(P-12253)
ANATOMAGE INC (PA)
303 Almaden Blvd Ste 100, San Jose (95110-2721)
PHONE......................................408 885-1474
Jack Choi, *CEO*
Jeff Mar, *Engineer*
Nick Nguyen, *Accountant*
Megan Cheek, *Human Res Dir*
Natalie Carlson, *Human Res Mgr*
▲ **EMP:** 81 **EST:** 2006
SALES (est): 26MM **Privately Held**
WEB: www.anatomage.com
SIC: 7371 Computer software development

PRODUCTS & SERVICES SECTION **7371 - Custom Computer Programming Svcs County (P-12275)**

(P-12254)
ANGAD CORP
950 Tower Ln Ste 1975, Foster City (94404-2791)
PHONE.................................650 743-0461
Mayank Bawa, *CEO*
EMP: 48 **EST:** 2014
SALES (est): 3.5MM **Privately Held**
SIC: 7371 Software programming applications

(P-12255)
ANGAZA DESIGN INC
315 Montgomery St Fl 10, San Francisco (94104-1823)
PHONE.................................415 993-5595
Lesley Marincola, *CEO*
EMP: 70 **EST:** 2010
SALES (est): 5.1MM **Privately Held**
WEB: www.angaza.com
SIC: 7371 Computer software development

(P-12256)
ANIMOTO LLC
333 Kearny St Fl 6, San Francisco (94108-3269)
P.O. Box 320428 (94132-0428)
PHONE.................................415 987-3139
Bradley C Jefferson, *CEO*
Russell G Keefe, *CFO*
Kristen Connor, *Vice Pres*
Vivian Sakovich, *VP Finance*
EMP: 60 **EST:** 2006
SQ FT: 15,000
SALES (est): 3.8MM **Privately Held**
SIC: 7371 Computer software development

(P-12257)
APACHE DESIGN INC (HQ)
Also Called: Apache Computer Retail
2645 Zanker Rd, San Jose (95134-2136)
PHONE.................................408 457-2000
Andrew T Yang, *CEO*
Emily Chang, *CFO*
Yanfei Gu, *Software Engr*
Abhishek Yadav, *Research*
Zhigang Feng, *Technical Staff*
EMP: 138 **EST:** 2001
SALES (est): 3MM
SALES (corp-wide): 1.6B **Publicly Held**
WEB: www.jac-designs.com
SIC: 7371 Computer software systems analysis & design, custom
PA: Ansys, Inc.
2600 Ansys Dr
Canonsburg PA 15317
724 746-3304

(P-12258)
APIGEE CORPORATION
1600 Amphitheatre Pkwy, Mountain View (94043-1351)
PHONE.................................408 343-7300
Chet Kapoor, *CEO*
Tim Wan, *CFO*
Eric Cross, *Officer*
Ed Anuff, *Vice Pres*
Srinivasulu Grandhi, *Vice Pres*
EMP: 374 **EST:** 2004
SQ FT: 41,000
SALES (est): 56.5MM
SALES (corp-wide): 182.5B **Publicly Held**
WEB: www.cloud.google.com
SIC: 7371 Computer software development & applications
HQ: Google Llc
1600 Amphitheatre Pkwy
Mountain View CA 94043
650 253-0000

(P-12259)
APOLLO GRAPH INC
37 Oceanview Dr, Pittsburg (94565-1356)
PHONE.................................206 225-9488
Geoffrey Schmidt, *CEO*
Catrina Zhang, *CFO*
Matthew Debergalis, *Treasurer*
Zoltan Olah, *Director*
EMP: 35 **EST:** 2011

SALES (est): 4.2MM
SALES (corp-wide): 300K **Privately Held**
WEB: www.apollographql.com
SIC: 7371 Computer software development & applications
PA: Tiny Capital Ltd
524 Yates St Unit 101
Victoria BC V8W 1
604 369-2553

(P-12260)
APP ANNIE INC (DH)
23 Geary St Ste 8, San Francisco (94108-5751)
PHONE.................................844 277-2664
Bertrand Schmitt, *CEO*
Toshi Kameoka, *Partner*
Xiaojun LI, *Partner*
Kelly Numerov, *Partner*
Ted Krantz, *President*
EMP: 437 **EST:** 2012
SALES (est): 54.9MM
SALES (corp-wide): 177.3K **Privately Held**
WEB: www.appannie.com
SIC: 7371 Computer software development; computer software development & applications

(P-12261)
APPDYNAMICS LLC (HQ)
303 2nd St Fl 8, San Francisco (94107-1366)
PHONE.................................415 442-8400
David Wadhwani, *President*
Daniel J Wright, *Senior VP*
Maricris Rebutiaco, *Vice Pres*
Dan Wright, *Vice Pres*
Marty Galvin, *Executive*
EMP: 1104 **EST:** 2008
SQ FT: 83,500
SALES (est): 176.3MM
SALES (corp-wide): 49.8B **Publicly Held**
WEB: www.appdynamics.com
SIC: 7371 Computer software development
PA: Cisco Systems, Inc.
170 W Tasman Dr
San Jose CA 95134
408 526-4000

(P-12262)
APPLIED INTUITION INC (PA)
145 E Dana St, Mountain View (94041-1507)
PHONE.................................630 935-8986
Qasar Younis, *CEO*
Asad Iqbal, *General Mgr*
Peter Ludwig, *CTO*
Marc Andreessen,
EMP: 39 **EST:** 2017
SALES (est): 2MM **Privately Held**
WEB: www.appliedintuition.com
SIC: 7371 Computer software development

(P-12263)
APPLITOOLS INC
155 Bovet Rd Ste 600, San Mateo (94402-3143)
PHONE.................................650 680-1000
Gil Sever, *CEO*
Linda Kobara, *Vice Pres*
Jeff Lewis, *Vice Pres*
Moshe Milman, *Vice Pres*
Daniel Levy, *CIO*
EMP: 41 **EST:** 2015
SQ FT: 1,000
SALES (est): 4MM **Privately Held**
WEB: www.applitools.com
SIC: 7371 Computer software development
PA: Applitools Ltd
3 Shoham
Ramat Gan 52500

(P-12264)
APPSFLYER INC
100 1st St Ste 2500, San Francisco (94105-3082)
PHONE.................................408 367-9938
Brian Quinn, *President*
Lior Leiba, *Surgery Dir*
Geon Basa, *Analyst*
Lisa Pogue, *Human Res Dir*

Orlee Maimon, *Opers Staff*
EMP: 42 **EST:** 2018
SALES (est): 2.7MM **Privately Held**
WEB: www.appsflyer.com
SIC: 7371 Computer software development

(P-12265)
APTELIGENT INC
1100 La Avenida St Ste A, Mountain View (94043-1453)
PHONE.................................415 371-1402
Zane Rowe, *CFO*
Scott Bajtos, *COO*
Sanjay Poonen, *COO*
Raghu Raghuram, *COO*
Rajiv Ramaswami, *COO*
EMP: 60 **EST:** 2011
SALES (est): 8.9MM
SALES (corp-wide): 11.7B **Publicly Held**
WEB: www.apteligent.com
SIC: 7371 Computer software development
PA: Vmware, Inc.
3401 Hillview Ave
Palo Alto CA 94304
650 427-5000

(P-12266)
AQUERA INC
2100 Geng Rd Ste 210, Palo Alto (94303-3307)
PHONE.................................650 618-6442
Reed Henry, *CEO*
Jerry Waldorf, *Officer*
EMP: 40 **EST:** 2017
SALES (est): 2.9MM **Privately Held**
WEB: www.aquera.com
SIC: 7371 Computer software development

(P-12267)
ARCHIPELAGO ANALYTICS HOLDINGS (PA)
165 Buena Vista Ave E, San Francisco (94117-4156)
PHONE.................................415 696-4896
Hemant Shah, *CEO*
EMP: 48 **EST:** 2019
SALES (est): 1.3MM **Privately Held**
WEB: www.onarchipelago.com
SIC: 7371 Computer software development & applications

(P-12268)
ARCSOFT INC (PA)
46605 Fremont Blvd, Fremont (94538-6410)
PHONE.................................510 440-9901
Michael Deng, *President*
David Nagel, *Ch of Bd*
Todd Peters, *President*
Robert Mjaseth, *COO*
Jennifer Pang, *CFO*
▲ **EMP:** 696 **EST:** 1994
SQ FT: 26,000
SALES (est): 56.9MM **Privately Held**
WEB: www.arcsoft.com
SIC: 7371 5734 Computer software development; computer & software stores

(P-12269)
ARCTOUCH LLC
1001 Front St, San Francisco (94111-1424)
PHONE.................................415 944-2000
Eric Shapiro, *CEO*
Jeremy Stephan, *Partner*
Rodrigo Valentim, *COO*
Adam Fingerman, *Officer*
Chris Loeper, *Exec VP*
EMP: 200 **EST:** 2009
SALES (est): 22.8MM
SALES (corp-wide): 15.9B **Privately Held**
WEB: www.arctouch.com
SIC: 7371 Computer software development & applications
HQ: Grey Global Group Llc
200 5th Ave Fl 5
New York NY 10010
212 546-2000

(P-12270)
ARIA SYSTEMS INC (PA)
100 Pine St Ste 2450, San Francisco (94111-5230)
PHONE.................................415 852-7250

Tom Dibble, *President*
Rick Lund, *CFO*
Brendan O'brien, *Officer*
Arun Thakur, *Officer*
Allison Barlaz, *Senior VP*
▼ **EMP:** 174 **EST:** 2003
SALES (est): 29.9MM **Privately Held**
WEB: www.ariasystems.com
SIC: 7371 Computer software development

(P-12271)
ARICENT NA INC (DH)
Also Called: Altran
3979 Freedom Cir Ste 950, Santa Clara (95054-1294)
PHONE.................................408 324-1800
Dominique Cerutti, *CEO*
EMP: 58 **EST:** 2004
SALES (est): 10.5MM
SALES (corp-wide): 387.8MM **Privately Held**
WEB: www.capgemini-engineering.com
SIC: 7371 Computer software development
HQ: Altran Usa Holdings, Inc.
451 D St
Boston MA 02210
617 449-9790

(P-12272)
ARICENT US INC (DH)
Also Called: Aricent Technologies
3979 Freedom Cir Ste 950, Santa Clara (95054-1294)
PHONE.................................408 329-7400
Frank Kern, *CEO*
Doreen Lorenzo, *President*
David Freedman, *CFO*
Masood Amin, *Vice Pres*
Scott Houghton, *Vice Pres*
EMP: 50 **EST:** 2006
SALES (est): 120.7MM
SALES (corp-wide): 387.8MM **Privately Held**
WEB: www.capgemini-engineering.com
SIC: 7371 Computer software development
HQ: Altran Usa Holdings, Inc.
451 D St
Boston MA 02210
617 449-9790

(P-12273)
ARICENT US INC
303 Twin Dolphin Dr # 600, Redwood City (94065-1497)
PHONE.................................650 632-4310
Sudip Nandy, *Branch Mgr*
Randy Tornes, *Partner*
Bob Wyan, *Partner*
Eric Johnson, *CFO*
Camie Shelmire, *Officer*
EMP: 123
SALES (corp-wide): 387.8MM **Privately Held**
WEB: www.capgemini-engineering.com
SIC: 7371 Computer software development
HQ: Aricent Us Inc.
3979 Freedom Cir Ste 950
Santa Clara CA 95054

(P-12274)
ARRCUS INC
2077 Gateway Pl Ste 400, San Jose (95110-1085)
PHONE.................................408 884-1965
Shekar Ayyar, *Ch of Bd*
Arthi Ayyangar, *Vice Pres*
Mitesh Kanjariya, *Technical Staff*
Cathy Xu, *Technical Staff*
EMP: 37 **EST:** 2016
SALES (est): 5.7MM **Privately Held**
WEB: www.arrcus.com
SIC: 7371 Computer software development

(P-12275)
ARXAN TECHNOLOGIES INC
760 Market St Ste 709, San Francisco (94102-2401)
PHONE.................................301 968-4290
James Love, *Officer*
Krish Kalkiraj, *Senior VP*

7371 - Custom Computer Programming Svcs County (P-12276)

PRODUCTS & SERVICES SECTION

Rusty Carter, *Vice Pres*
Michael Kelley, *Vice Pres*
Jessie Angulo, *VP Human Res*
EMP: 39
SALES (corp-wide): 19.3MM **Privately Held**
WEB: www.digital.ai
SIC: 7371 Computer software development
PA: Arxan Technologies, Inc.
    52 3rd Ave
    Burlington MA 01803
    415 247-0900

(P-12276)
ASCENDIFY CORPORATION
30 Castlewood Dr, Pleasanton (94566-9728)
PHONE.................................415 528-5503
Matt Hendrickson, *CEO*
Jason Ball, *Vice Pres*
Kelly King, *Vice Pres*
Derek Mercer, *Vice Pres*
Lauren Smith, *Vice Pres*
EMP: 50 EST: 2012
SALES (est): 5.1MM **Privately Held**
WEB: www.ascendify.com
SIC: 7371 Computer software development

(P-12277)
ASCENSION LABS INC
Also Called: Ascend.io
541 Cowper St, Palo Alto (94301-1835)
PHONE.................................650 898-9798
Sean Knapp, *CEO*
Tom Weeks, *Officer*
Riley Nagel, *CIO*
EMP: 41 EST: 2016
SALES (est): 2.8MM **Privately Held**
SIC: 7371 Computer software development & applications

(P-12278)
ASSURX INC
18525 Sutter Blvd Ste 150, Morgan Hill (95037-2899)
PHONE.................................408 778-1376
Tamar June, *CEO*
Eric Cooper, *Vice Pres*
Sal Lucido, *Executive*
Chris Harness, *Office Mgr*
Brian Harness, *Administration*
EMP: 70 EST: 1993
SQ FT: 1,200
SALES (est): 5.7MM **Privately Held**
WEB: www.assurx.com
SIC: 7371 7372 Computer software development; prepackaged software

(P-12279)
ASTUTE BUSINESS SOLUTIONS
11501 Dublin Blvd Ste 200, Dublin (94568-2827)
PHONE.................................925 997-3267
Sudhir Mehandru, *Vice Pres*
Arvind Rajan, *President*
Joe Finlinson, *CTO*
Kavitha Mani, *Accountant*
Supriya Prabhakara, *Senior Mgr*
EMP: 152 EST: 2006
SQ FT: 2,530
SALES (est): 12.2MM **Privately Held**
WEB: www.beastute.com
SIC: 7371 Computer software development

(P-12280)
ATCG TECHNOLOGY SOLUTIONS INC (HQ)
785 Orchard Dr Ste 150, Folsom (95630-5559)
PHONE.................................916 850-2620
Brent Kelton, *CEO*
Paul Freudenberg, *President*
Marvin Soohoo, *COO*
Maria WEI, *Exec VP*
EMP: 50 EST: 2011
SALES (est): 1MM **Publicly Held**
WEB: www.enveric.com
SIC: 7371 Computer software development

(P-12281)
ATEMPO AMERICAS INC (DH)
2465 E Byshore Rd Ste 400, Palo Alto (94303)
PHONE.................................650 494-2600
Thierry Flajoliet, *CEO*
Fabrice De Salaberry, *COO*
Neal Ater, *Vice Pres*
Stephen Terlizzi, *Marketing Staff*
EMP: 50 EST: 1992
SALES (est): 22.8MM
SALES (corp-wide): 35.3K **Privately Held**
WEB: www.atempo.com
SIC: 7371 7379 Computer software development; computer related maintenance services

(P-12282)
ATLAZ INC
10721 Fair Oaks Blvd, Fair Oaks (95628-7212)
PHONE.................................415 671-6142
EMP: 70 EST: 2015
SALES (est): 1.2MM **Privately Held**
SIC: 7371 Custom Computer Programing

(P-12283)
ATOPTECH INC
2111 Tasman Dr, Santa Clara (95054-1027)
PHONE.................................408 550-2600
Jue-Hsien Chern, *CEO*
Don-Min Tsou, *President*
EMP: 40 EST: 2003
SQ FT: 15,000
SALES (est): 4.4MM **Privately Held**
WEB: www.avatar-da.com
SIC: 7371 Computer software development

(P-12284)
ATRENTA INC (HQ)
690 E Middlefield Rd, Mountain View (94043-4010)
PHONE.................................408 453-3333
Ajoy K Bose, *President*
Bert Clement, *COO*
Ajoy Bose, *Exec VP*
Yuan Lu, *Vice Pres*
Yunshan Zhu, *Vice Pres*
EMP: 70 EST: 1995
SQ FT: 8,000
SALES (est): 46.3MM
SALES (corp-wide): 3.6B **Publicly Held**
WEB: www.synopsys.com
SIC: 7371 Computer software development
PA: Synopsys, Inc.
    690 E Middlefield Rd
    Mountain View CA 94043
    650 584-5000

(P-12285)
AUTO CLERK INC
1981 N Broadway Ste 430, Walnut Creek (94596-3829)
P.O. Box 398840, San Francisco (94139-8840)
PHONE.................................925 284-1005
Gary Gibb, *President*
Charlotte Gibb, *Exec VP*
Edward Bear, *Vice Pres*
Tony Miller, *Prgrmr*
Mohammed Hansia, *Opers Staff*
EMP: 32 EST: 1984
SQ FT: 2,500
SALES (est): 2.6MM **Privately Held**
WEB: www.autoclerk.com
SIC: 7371 7372 5734 Computer software development; prepackaged software; software, business & non-game

(P-12286)
AUTOMATION ANYWHERE INC (PA)
633 River Oaks Pkwy, San Jose (95134-1907)
P.O. Box 640007 (95164-0007)
PHONE.................................888 484-3535
Mihir Shukla, *CEO*
Sridhar Gunapu, *President*
Riadh Dridi, *Chief Mktg Ofcr*
Chris Riley, *Officer*
Neeraj Gokhale, *Exec VP*
EMP: 500 EST: 2003
SQ FT: 14,000
SALES (est): 456MM **Privately Held**
WEB: www.automationanywhere.com
SIC: 7371 5045 Computer software writing services; computer software

(P-12287)
AUTOMATION TECHNOLOGY INC
2001 Gateway Pl Ste 100w, San Jose (95110-1046)
PHONE.................................408 350-7020
Arvind Agarwal, *President*
Rana Ghosh, *Vice Pres*
Dipak Patel, *Vice Pres*
Robert Wann, *Vice Pres*
Neelo Agarwal, *Office Mgr*
EMP: 24 EST: 1989
SQ FT: 10,000
SALES (est): 1MM
SALES (corp-wide): 3.6B **Privately Held**
WEB: www.intertek.com
SIC: 7371 7372 Computer software development; prepackaged software
PA: Intertek Group Plc
    33 Cavendish Square
    London W1G 0
    207 396-3400

(P-12288)
AUTOMOTIVEMASTERMIND INC
201 Mission St Fl 10, San Francisco (94105-8101)
PHONE.................................646 679-3441
Marco G Schnabl, *President*
Jaclyn Brizzi, *Partner*
Suzanne Reimer, *Partner*
Matt Wilmsen, *Partner*
Eric Daniels, *CFO*
EMP: 80 EST: 2012
SALES (est): 7.1MM
SALES (corp-wide): 948.2MM **Privately Held**
WEB: www.automotivemastermind.com
SIC: 7371 Software programming applications
HQ: Markit North America, Inc.
    450 W 33rd St Fl 5
    New York NY 10001
    212 931-4900

(P-12289)
AUTONOMIC LLC (PA)
3251 Hillview Ave 200, Palo Alto (94304-1202)
PHONE.................................650 823-1806
Gavin Sherry,
Julie Davies, *COO*
Amy Wengler, *CFO*
EMP: 66 EST: 2016
SQ FT: 8,700
SALES (est): 14.5MM **Privately Held**
WEB: www.autonomic.ai
SIC: 7371 Software programming applications

(P-12290)
AUTOX TECHNOLOGIES INC
441 W Trimble Rd, San Jose (95131-1036)
PHONE.................................650 492-8869
Jianxiong Xiao, *CEO*
EMP: 38 EST: 2016
SALES (est): 500K **Privately Held**
SIC: 7371 Software programming applications

(P-12291)
AVANQUEST PUBLISHING USA INC (HQ)
Also Called: Vcom
7031 Koll Center Pkwy # 150, Pleasanton (94566-3133)
PHONE.................................925 474-1700
Roger Bloxberg, *CEO*
William Gilsing, *Sales Mgr*
EMP: 69 EST: 1988
SALES (est): 2.9MM
SALES (corp-wide): 1.8MM **Privately Held**
WEB: www.claranova.com
SIC: 7371 Computer software development
PA: Claranova S.E.
    Avanquest Blue Squad Bvrp Software
    Immeuble Vision Defense
    La Garenne Colombes 92250
    962 557-603

(P-12292)
AVANTA INC (HQ)
1470 Civic Ct Ste 309, Concord (94520-5230)
PHONE.................................925 818-4760
Mark Fedin, *CEO*
Elena Florova, *Vice Pres*
EMP: 50 EST: 2018
SALES (est): 3.8MM
SALES (corp-wide): 769.9K **Privately Held**
WEB: www.avanta.co
SIC: 7371 Computer software development & applications

(P-12293)
AVEGANT CORP
37 E 4th Ave 1, San Mateo (94401-4004)
PHONE.................................800 270-0760
Joerg Tewes, *CEO*
Annie Rogaski, *COO*
Richard Kerris, *Chief Mktg Ofcr*
Tang Edward, *Officer*
Eric Trabold, *VP Business*
EMP: 46 EST: 2014
SALES (est): 2.7MM **Privately Held**
WEB: www.avegant.com
SIC: 7371 Computer software development

(P-12294)
AZUMIO INC (PA)
255 Shoreline Dr Ste 130, Redwood City (94065-1425)
PHONE.................................719 310-3774
Bojan Bostjancic, *President*
Tom Xu,
Jennifer Grenz, *Vice Pres*
Bojan Kahvedzic, *Vice Pres*
Eric Huynh, *Sr Project Mgr*
EMP: 102 EST: 2011
SALES (est): 5.8MM **Privately Held**
WEB: www.azumio.com
SIC: 7371 Computer software development

(P-12295)
AZUMO LLC
3130 Alpine Rd Ste 288, Portola Valley (94028-7541)
PHONE.................................415 610-7002
Chike Agbai, *CEO*
EMP: 125 EST: 2016
SALES (est): 3.3MM **Privately Held**
WEB: www.azumo.com
SIC: 7371 Custom computer programming services

(P-12296)
BALBIX INC
3031 Tisch Way Ste 800, San Jose (95128-2532)
PHONE.................................866 936-3180
Gaurav Banga, *President*
Rich Campagna, *Chief Mktg Ofcr*
Shelly Morales, *Officer*
Chris Griffith, *Vice Pres*
Sumanth Maram, *Engineer*
EMP: 64 EST: 2015
SALES (est): 6MM **Privately Held**
WEB: www.balbix.com
SIC: 7371 Computer software development

(P-12297)
BAY DYNAMICS INC
1320 Ridder Park Dr, San Jose (95131-2313)
PHONE.................................415 912-3130
Feris Rifai, *CEO*
Gautam Aggarwal, *Chief Mktg Ofcr*
Bill Holzendorf, *Vice Pres*
Steve Poulson, *Vice Pres*
Jean Lau, *Administration*
EMP: 50 EST: 2014
SALES (est): 8.6MM
SALES (corp-wide): 23.8B **Publicly Held**
WEB: www.broadcom.com
SIC: 7371 Computer software development
PA: Broadcom Inc.
    1320 Ridder Park Dr
    San Jose CA 95131
    408 433-8000

PRODUCTS & SERVICES SECTION
7371 - Custom Computer Programming Svcs County (P-12318)

(P-12298)
BAYONE SOLUTIONS
4637 Chabot Dr Ste 250, Pleasanton (94588-2752)
PHONE.............................408 930-1600
Yogesh Virmani, *CEO*
Rahul Sharma, *President*
Pawan Tripathi, *Executive*
Anurag Dixit, *CIO*
Vikas Kumar, *IT/INT Sup*
EMP: 130 **EST:** 2012
SALES (est): 10MM **Privately Held**
WEB: www.bayone.com
SIC: 7371 7379 Custom computer programming services; computer related consulting services

(P-12299)
BEA SYSTEMS INC (HQ)
2315 N 1st St, San Jose (95131-1010)
PHONE.............................650 506-7000
Alfred S Chuang, *Ch of Bd*
Alan Button, *Partner*
Ted Kimes, *President*
Mark T Carges, *Exec VP*
Richard Geraffo, *Exec VP*
EMP: 1000 **EST:** 1995
SQ FT: 236,000
SALES (est): 160.7MM
SALES (corp-wide): 40.4B **Publicly Held**
WEB: www.oracle.com
SIC: 7371 7372 Computer software development; prepackaged software
PA: Oracle Corporation
2300 Oracle Way
Austin TX 78741
737 867-1000

(P-12300)
BEEZWAX DATATOOLS INC
200 Frank H Ogawa Plz 7th, Oakland (94612-2005)
PHONE.............................510 835-4483
Julian Nadel, *President*
Abe Zaidi, *Program Mgr*
Jules Bowie, *Project Mgr*
Tony Nguyen, *Manager*
Rachel Nisbeth, *Accounts Mgr*
EMP: 49 **EST:** 2004
SQ FT: 2,500
SALES (est): 7MM **Privately Held**
WEB: www.beezwax.net
SIC: 7371 Computer software development

(P-12301)
BENTLEY SYSTEMS INCORPORATED
1600 Riviera Ave Ste 300, Walnut Creek (94596-3570)
PHONE.............................925 933-2525
EMP: 80
SALES (corp-wide): 854.3MM **Privately Held**
SIC: 7371 8711 Custom Computer Programing Engineering Services
PA: Bentley Systems, Incorporated
685 Stockton Dr
Exton PA 19341
610 458-5000

(P-12302)
BIRST INC
45 Fremont St Ste 1800, San Francisco (94105-2219)
PHONE.............................415 766-4800
Jay Larson, *CEO*
Samuel Wolff, *CFO*
Carl Tsukamura, *Chief Mktg Ofcr*
Brad Peters, *Officer*
Paul Staelin, *Officer*
EMP: 300 **EST:** 2005
SQ FT: 36,171
SALES (est): 43.6MM
SALES (corp-wide): 36.9B **Privately Held**
WEB: www.birst.com
SIC: 7371 Computer software development
HQ: Infor, Inc.
641 Ave Of The Americas # 4
New York NY 10011
646 336-1700

(P-12303)
BITALIGN INC
Also Called: Grio
95 Minna St Fl 4, San Francisco (94105-3029)
PHONE.............................415 395-9525
Douglas Kadlecek, *CEO*
Bradley Johnson, *CFO*
Robert Jarrell, *Creative Dir*
Mike Mulvey, *Creative Dir*
Debby George, *Office Mgr*
EMP: 60 **EST:** 2006
SALES (est): 10.2MM **Privately Held**
SIC: 7371 Computer software development

(P-12304)
BITTORRENT INC
612 Howard St Ste 400, San Francisco (94105-3944)
PHONE.............................408 641-4219
Aseem Mohanty, *President*
Sam Hariri, *Officer*
Chris Verzello, *Vice Pres*
Robert McDonald, *Sr Software Eng*
Eric Klinker, *CTO*
EMP: 50 **EST:** 2017
SALES (est): 2MM **Privately Held**
WEB: www.bittorrent.com
SIC: 7371 Computer software development

(P-12305)
BOKU INC (PA)
Also Called: Mobillcash
660 Market St Ste 400, San Francisco (94104-5004)
P.O. Box 190725 (94119-0725)
PHONE.............................415 375-3160
Mark J Britto, *CEO*
Ron Hirson, *President*
Keith Butcher, *CFO*
Gillian Davies, *CFO*
Christian Hinrichs, *CFO*
EMP: 76 **EST:** 2008
SALES (est): 34.5MM **Privately Held**
WEB: www.boku.com
SIC: 7371 7322 Computer software development & applications; collection agency, except real estate

(P-12306)
BORDERX LAB INC (PA)
111 W Evelyn Ave Ste 202, Sunnyvale (94086-6140)
PHONE.............................408 746-5462
Xuehua Shen, *CEO*
Jeff Unze, *VP Bus Dvlpt*
Richard Barnes, *CIO*
Dezheng Xu, *Software Engr*
Lily Zhang, *Accountant*
EMP: 55 **EST:** 2014
SALES (est): 6.7MM **Privately Held**
WEB: www.borderxlab.com
SIC: 7371 Computer software development & applications

(P-12307)
BRAIN TECHNOLOGIES INC
400 S El Cmino Real Ste 2, San Mateo (94402)
P.O. Box 938 (94403-0538)
PHONE.............................650 918-2245
Sheng Yue, *CEO*
Gleb Kuznetsov, *Officer*
EMP: 315 **EST:** 2015
SALES (est): 14.2MM **Privately Held**
WEB: www.xahuateng.com
SIC: 7371 Computer software development & applications
PA: Xi'an Huateng Photoelectricity Co., Ltd.
Incubation Zone, Floor 3, Comprehensive Office Building, Interne
Xian 71004

(P-12308)
BRIENCE INC (DH)
Also Called: A Development Stage Company
128 Spear St Fl 3, San Francisco (94105-5147)
PHONE.............................415 974-5300
Roderick McGeary, *Ch of Bd*
James Drumright, *COO*
Stephen E Recht, *CFO*
Keyur Patel, *Officer*
Mark Losh, *Senior VP*
EMP: 90 **EST:** 2000
SQ FT: 15,000
SALES (est): 24.3MM **Privately Held**
WEB: www.brience.com
SIC: 7371 Computer software development & applications

(P-12309)
BRIGHTEDGE TECHNOLOGIES INC (PA)
989 E Hillsdale Blvd # 3, Foster City (94404-2113)
PHONE.............................800 578-8023
Jim Yu, *President*
Krish Kumar, *COO*
Jim Emerich, *CFO*
Jeffrey Bakus, *Vice Pres*
Joshua Crossman, *Vice Pres*
EMP: 134 **EST:** 2007
SALES (est): 84.4MM **Privately Held**
WEB: www.brightedge.com
SIC: 7371 5045 Computer software development; computers, peripherals & software

(P-12310)
BRIGHTERION INC
123 Mission St Ste 1700, San Francisco (94105-5133)
PHONE.............................415 986-5600
Akli Adjaoute, *CEO*
Jeff Muschick, *Vice Pres*
Kurt Schwabe, *Marketing Mgr*
EMP: 62 **EST:** 1999
SALES (est): 5.8MM
SALES (corp-wide): 15.3B **Publicly Held**
WEB: www.brighterion.com
SIC: 7371 Computer software development
PA: Mastercard Incorporated
2000 Purchase St
Purchase NY 10577
914 249-2000

(P-12311)
BRIGHTTALK INC (HQ)
703 Market St Ste 15, San Francisco (94103-2150)
PHONE.............................415 625-1500
Paul Heald, *President*
John Eichhorn, *CFO*
Jeff Wheeler, *CFO*
David Pitta, *Chief Mktg Ofcr*
Vasu Ramachandra, *Exec VP*
EMP: 37 **EST:** 2006
SALES (est): 15.8MM
SALES (corp-wide): 38.9MM **Privately Held**
WEB: www.brighttalk.com
SIC: 7371 Computer software development & applications

(P-12312)
BRILLIO LLC
5201 Great America Pkwy # 100, Santa Clara (95054-1157)
PHONE.............................800 317-0575
Sandhya Balakrishnan, *Partner*
Farooq Ahmad, *Managing Prtnr*
Greg Morton, *Managing Prtnr*
Piyush Pandya, *Managing Prtnr*
Ashish Mahadwar, *COO*
EMP: 664 **Privately Held**
WEB: www.brillio.com
HQ: Brillio, Llc
399 Thornall St Fl 1
Edison NJ 08837
800 317-0575

(P-12313)
BRISTLECONE INCORPORATED
10 Almaden Blvd Ste 600, San Jose (95113-2226)
PHONE.............................650 386-4000
Nirav Patel, *President*
Rajesh Raghuvanshi, *Partner*
Charlie Bienvenu, *Managing Prtnr*
Rajan Venkateswaran, *Assoc VP*
Naresh Hingorani, *Vice Pres*
EMP: 1300 **EST:** 1998
SQ FT: 10,000
SALES (est): 84.8MM **Privately Held**
WEB: www.bristlecone.com
SIC: 7371 8742 Software programming applications; management consulting services
PA: Mahindra And Mahindra Limited
Mahindra Towers, 5th Floor,
Mumbai MH 40001

(P-12314)
BUILDINGMINDS INC (PA)
1200 Seaport Blvd, Redwood City (94063-5537)
PHONE.............................973 397-6510
Thomas Sparno, *Principal*
EMP: 49 **EST:** 2018
SALES (est): 5MM **Privately Held**
SIC: 7371 Computer software development & applications

(P-12315)
BUILTIO LLC
49 Geary St Ste 238, San Francisco (94108-5727)
PHONE.............................415 255-5955
Nishant Patel, *CEO*
Spencer Hulsey, *Business Mgr*
EMP: 40 **EST:** 2018
SALES (est): 4.5MM
SALES (corp-wide): 987.3MM **Privately Held**
WEB: www.softwareag.com
SIC: 7371 Computer software development
PA: Software Ag
Uhlandstr. 12
Darmstadt HE 64297
615 192-0

(P-12316)
BUYCOINS INC ✪
2261 Market St, San Francisco (94114-1612)
PHONE.............................650 278-7402
Timi Ajiboye, *CEO*
Ire Aderinokun, *COO*
Tomiwa Lasebikan,
EMP: 45 **EST:** 2021
SALES (est): 1.1MM **Privately Held**
SIC: 7371 Computer software development & applications

(P-12317)
BYND LLC
100 Montgomery St # 1102, San Francisco (94104-4331)
PHONE.............................415 944-2293
Nicholas Rappolt, *CEO*
Michael Euphrat, *Partner*
Matthew Iliffe, *Partner*
Charlie Lyons, *Managing Prtnr*
Sam Smith, *Managing Prtnr*
EMP: 100 **EST:** 2004
SALES (est): 15MM
SALES (corp-wide): 435.2MM **Privately Held**
WEB: www.bynd.com
SIC: 7371 Computer software development & applications
PA: Next Fifteen Communications Group Plc
75 Bermondsey Street
London SE1 3
207 908-6444

(P-12318)
CADENT TECH INC (HQ)
4 N 2nd St Ste 1100, San Jose (95113-1308)
PHONE.............................408 642-6400
Nick Troiano, *CEO*
Stephanie Mitchko-Beale, *COO*
Jonathan Batt, *CFO*
Vinod Vijayan, *Vice Pres*
Melanie Nottingham, *Marketing Staff*
EMP: 55 **EST:** 2015
SQ FT: 10,000
SALES (est): 9.8MM **Privately Held**
WEB: www.cadent.tv
SIC: 7371 Computer software development & applications

(PA)=Parent Co (HQ)=Headquarters (DH)=Div Headquarters
✪ = New Business established in last 2 years

7371 - Custom Computer Programming Svcs County (P-12319) — PRODUCTS & SERVICES SECTION

(P-12319)
CAKE CORPORATION
Also Called: Sysco Labs
1528 S El Cmino Real Ste, San Mateo (94402)
PHONE..................650 215-7777
Mani Kulasooriya, *CEO*
Brian Beach, *Senior VP*
Shanil Fernando, *Vice Pres*
Paul Kelaita, *Vice Pres*
Jim O'Connor, *Vice Pres*
▲ EMP: 100 EST: 2010
SALES (est): 22.6MM
SALES (corp-wide): 52.8B **Publicly Held**
WEB: www.trycake.com
SIC: 7371 Computer software development & applications
PA: Sysco Corporation
   1390 Enclave Pkwy
   Houston TX 77077
   281 584-1390

(P-12320)
CAL-SIERRA TECHNOLOGIES INC
39055 Hastings St Ste 103, Fremont (94538-1518)
PHONE..................510 742-9996
Steve Mandell, *President*
John Gustafson, *Executive*
Donna Soutar, *Exec Dir*
Kim Bailey, *Admin Asst*
Laurie Collanton, *Accounting Mgr*
EMP: 46 EST: 1999
SALES (est): 9MM **Privately Held**
WEB: www.calsierra.com
SIC: 7371 7379 Computer software development; computer related consulting services

(P-12321)
CALLIDUS SOFTWARE INC (DH)
Also Called: Calliduscloud
2700 Camino Ramon 400, San Ramon (94583-5004)
PHONE..................925 251-2200
Leslie Stretch, *President*
Roxanne Oulman, *CFO*
Andres Botero, *Chief Mktg Ofcr*
Mary Ainsworth,
Richey Gupta, *Officer*
▲ EMP: 693 EST: 1996
SALES: 206.7MM
SALES (corp-wide): 32.3B **Publicly Held**
WEB: cx.sap.com
SIC: 7371 7372 Custom computer programming services; business oriented computer software
HQ: Hybris Gesellschaft Mit Beschrankter Haftung
   Nymphenburger Str. 86
   Munchen BY 80636
   898 906-50

(P-12322)
CALLSIGN INC (PA)
2225 E Bayshore Rd, Palo Alto (94303-3220)
PHONE..................650 320-1710
Zia Hayat, *Principal*
Ian Welch, *COO*
Patrick Imbach, *CFO*
Amir Nooriala, *Ch Credit Ofcr*
Sarah Whipp, *Chief Mktg Ofcr*
EMP: 35 EST: 2011
SALES (est): 5MM **Privately Held**
WEB: www.calisign.com
SIC: 7371 4813 Computer software development;

(P-12323)
CALYX TECHNOLOGY INC (PA)
Also Called: Calyx Software
6475 Camden Ave Ste 207, San Jose (95120-2848)
PHONE..................408 997-5525
Greg Ellis, *CEO*
Doug Chang, *President*
Dennis Boggs, *Exec VP*
Bob Dougherty, *Exec VP*
MEI Liu, *Database Admin*
EMP: 35 EST: 1991
SQ FT: 1,000
SALES (est): 14MM **Privately Held**
WEB: www.calyxsoftware.com
SIC: 7371 Computer software development; computer software development & applications

(P-12324)
CAMPAIGN MONITOR USA INC (DH)
55 2nd St Ste 1925, San Francisco (94105-3450)
PHONE..................888 533-8098
Alex Bard, *CEO*
Sharon Strauss, *Officer*
Ethan Zoubek, *Officer*
Dustin Finkle, *Project Dir*
Andrew Hosmer, *Sales Engr*
EMP: 99 EST: 2014
SALES (est): 8.5MM **Privately Held**
WEB: www.campaignmonitor.com
SIC: 7371 Computer software development

(P-12325)
CAPTIVATEIQ INC
480 2nd St Ste 100, San Francisco (94107-1429)
PHONE..................650 930-0619
Teng Conway, *CEO*
Mark Schopmeyer, *CEO*
Hubert Wong, *Engineer*
Christian Borrelli, *Sales Staff*
Kap Ravindra, *Accounts Exec*
EMP: 95 EST: 2017
SALES (est): 6.4MM **Privately Held**
WEB: www.captiveiq.com
SIC: 7371 Computer software systems analysis & design, custom

(P-12326)
CARBONFIVE INCORPORATED
Also Called: Carbon Five
585 Howard St Fl 2, San Francisco (94105-4677)
PHONE..................415 546-0500
Don Thompson, *COO*
Courtney Hemphill, *Partner*
David Hendee, *Partner*
Mike Wynholds, *CEO*
Amanda Prince, *Vice Pres*
EMP: 62 EST: 2001
SALES (est): 7.4MM **Privately Held**
WEB: www.carbonfive.com
SIC: 7371 Computer software development

(P-12327)
CASAHL TECHNOLOGY INC
2400 Cmino Rmon Bldg K St, San Ramon (94583)
PHONE..................925 328-2828
Harry Wong, *President*
Linda Wong, *Exec VP*
Lara Mayugba, *Sr Software Eng*
Wesley Wong, *Info Tech Mgr*
Karim Senussi, *Technical Staff*
EMP: 40 EST: 1993
SALES (est): 2.9MM **Privately Held**
WEB: www.casahl.com
SIC: 7371 Computer software development

(P-12328)
CASETEXT INC
330 Townsend St Ste 100, San Francisco (94107-1655)
PHONE..................317 407-0790
Jacob Heller, *CEO*
Laura Safdie, *COO*
Anand Upadhye, *VP Bus Dvlpt*
Can Babaoglu, *Director*
Valerie McConnell, *Director*
EMP: 38 EST: 2015
SALES (est): 1.1MM **Privately Held**
WEB: www.casetext.com
SIC: 7371 7379 Computer software development & applications; computer related services

(P-12329)
CASTLE GLOBAL INC
Also Called: Hive
575 Market St Fl 15, San Francisco (94105-5815)
PHONE..................401 523-9531
Kevin Guo, *CEO*
Dmitri Kareman, *CTO*
EMP: 120 EST: 2013
SALES (est): 10.8MM **Privately Held**
WEB: www.thehive.ai
SIC: 7371 Computer software development

(P-12330)
CATAMORPHIC CO (PA)
Also Called: Launchdarkly
1999 Harrison St Ste 1100, Oakland (94612-4708)
PHONE..................415 579-3275
Edith Ellen Harbaugh, *CEO*
Scott Raney, *Bd of Directors*
Keith Messick, *Vice Pres*
Penny Foster, *Executive*
Richard Guzzo, *Executive*
EMP: 199 EST: 2014
SQ FT: 5,000
SALES (est): 12.8MM **Privately Held**
WEB: www.launchdarkly.com
SIC: 7371 Software programming applications

(P-12331)
CATAPHORA INC (PA)
3425 Edison Way, Menlo Park (94025-1813)
P.O. Box 2007 (94026-2007)
PHONE..................650 622-9840
Elizabeth B Charnock, *President*
EMP: 60 EST: 2002
SQ FT: 25,000
SALES (est): 7.9MM **Privately Held**
WEB: www.cataphora.com
SIC: 7371 Computer software development

(P-12332)
CENTRIFY CORPORATION (PA)
Also Called: Thycoticcentrify
201 Rdwood Shres Pkwy Ste, Redwood City (94065)
P.O. Box 60428, Sunnyvale (94088-0428)
PHONE..................669 444-5200
Art Gilliland, *CEO*
Linlin LI, *Vice Pres*
Jeremy Stieglitz, *Vice Pres*
Dean Thompson, *Vice Pres*
Ally Zwahlen, *Vice Pres*
EMP: 654 EST: 2004
SQ FT: 8,300
SALES (est): 144.7MM **Privately Held**
WEB: www.centrify.com
SIC: 7371 Computer software development

(P-12333)
CERTENT INC (HQ)
1548 Eureka Rd Ste 100, Roseville (95661-3083)
PHONE..................925 730-4300
Gordon Rausser, *Ch of Bd*
Michael Boese, *President*
Jorge Martin, *CEO*
Ryan Stroub, *CFO*
Satish Adettiwar, *Vice Pres*
EMP: 36 EST: 2002
SALES (est): 52MM
SALES (corp-wide): 96.7MM **Privately Held**
WEB: www.insightsoftware.com
SIC: 7371 Computer software development
PA: Insightsoftware.Com, Inc.
   8529 Six Forks Rd Ste 400
   Raleigh NC 27615
   919 703-2183

(P-12334)
CETEC AUTOMATION INC
553 Pilgrim Dr Ste A, Foster City (94404-1248)
PHONE..................650 570-7557
EMP: 20
SQ FT: 2,700
SALES (est): 1.9MM **Privately Held**
SIC: 7371 7372 Custom Computer Programing Prepackaged Software Services

(P-12335)
CHARTBOOST INC (HQ)
1 Sansome St Fl 21, San Francisco (94104-4402)
PHONE..................415 493-0727
Rich Izzo, *CEO*
Adam Mosqueda, *Partner*
Eswar Kondapavuluri, *CIO*
Sean Fannan, *CTO*
Geoff Heeren, *Engineer*
EMP: 222 EST: 2011
SALES (est): 27.6MM
SALES (corp-wide): 1.9B **Publicly Held**
WEB: www.chartboost.com
SIC: 7371 Computer software development & applications
PA: Zynga Inc.
   699 8th St
   San Francisco CA 94103
   855 449-9642

(P-12336)
CHATTERBUG INC (PA)
995 Market St, San Francisco (94103-1702)
PHONE..................415 957-9000
EMP: 43 EST: 2017
SALES (est): 630.9K **Privately Held**
WEB: www.chatterbug.com
SIC: 7371 Computer software development & applications

(P-12337)
CHELSIO COMMUNICATIONS INC
735 N Pastoria Ave, Sunnyvale (94085-2918)
PHONE..................408 962-3600
Kianoosh Naghshineh, *President*
William Delaney, *CFO*
Danny Gur, *Vice Pres*
Mehdi Mohtashemi, *Vice Pres*
Kun Taek Yim, *Vice Pres*
EMP: 130 EST: 1997
SALES (est): 19.5MM **Privately Held**
WEB: www.chelsio.com
SIC: 7371 Computer software systems analysis & design, custom
PA: Chelsio Communications Private Limited
   2 Floor, Uniworth Plaza,
   Bengaluru KA 56002

(P-12338)
CITRIX SYSTEMS INC
4988 Great America Pkwy, Santa Clara (95054-1200)
PHONE..................408 790-8000
Klaus Oerstermann, *Principal*
Brad Adams, *Partner*
Huzaifah Saifee, *Partner*
Roger Shambaugh, *Partner*
Donna Goldstein, *Vice Pres*
EMP: 95 **Publicly Held**
WEB: www.citrix.com
SIC: 7371 Computer software development
PA: Citrix Systems, Inc.
   851 W Cypress Creek Rd
   Fort Lauderdale FL 33309

(P-12339)
CITRUSBITS INC
5994 W Las Psts Blvd, Pleasanton (94588-8509)
PHONE..................925 452-6012
Harry Lee, *CEO*
Luke Waites, *Vice Pres*
Zarak Afridi, *Marketing Staff*
EMP: 50 EST: 2007
SQ FT: 3,000
SALES (est): 5.9MM **Privately Held**
WEB: www.citrusbits.com
SIC: 7371 Computer software systems analysis & design, custom

(P-12340)
CLARIS INTERNATIONAL INC (HQ)
1 Apple Park Way 104-1g, Cupertino (95014-0642)
PHONE..................408 987-7000
Dominique Philippe Goupil, *President*
Bill Epling, *CFO*
Chung Le, *Vice Pres*
Scott Lewis, *Vice Pres*
Ann Monroe, *Vice Pres*
EMP: 230 EST: 1987
SQ FT: 128,000

PRODUCTS & SERVICES SECTION
7371 - Custom Computer Programming Svcs County (P-12362)

SALES (est): 65.7MM
SALES (corp-wide): 365.8B **Publicly Held**
WEB: www.claris.com
SIC: 7371 Computer software development; and applications
PA: Apple Inc.
1 Apple Park Way
Cupertino CA 95014
408 996-1010

(P-12341)
CLICK LABS INC
315 Montgomery St Fl 8, San Francisco (94104-1803)
PHONE..................415 658-5227
Samar Singla, *CEO*
Sarah Terrazas, *Vice Pres*
Kristine Willems, *Sales Mgr*
Rubal Singh, *Manager*
EMP: 36 **EST:** 2012
SALES (est): 3.6MM **Privately Held**
WEB: www.click-labs.com
SIC: 7371 Computer software development

(P-12342)
CLOUDELY INC (PA)
2880 Zanker Rd Ste 203, San Jose (95134-2122)
PHONE..................800 797-8608
Chris Holmes, *Technical Staff*
EMP: 35 **EST:** 2018
SALES (est): 2.9MM **Privately Held**
WEB: www.cloudely.com
SIC: 7371 Computer software development

(P-12343)
CLOUDPASSAGE INC
180 Townsend St Fl 3, San Francisco (94107-2589)
PHONE..................800 838-4098
Carson Sweet, *Officer*
Steve Shevick, *CFO*
Mitch Bishop, *Chief Mktg Ofcr*
David Appelbaum, *Officer*
Brian Harmon, *Exec VP*
EMP: 80 **EST:** 2009
SQ FT: 10,000
SALES (est): 13MM
SALES (corp-wide): 50MM **Privately Held**
WEB: www.cloudpassage.com
SIC: 7371 Computer software development
PA: Fidelis Cybersecurity, Inc.
4500 East West Hwy # 400
Bethesda MD 20814
301 652-7190

(P-12344)
CLOUDPEOPLE GLOBAL
2485 Notre Dame Blvd, Chico (95928-7161)
PHONE..................530 591-7028
Sean Worthington, *President*
EMP: 50 **EST:** 2018
SALES (est): 1.2MM **Privately Held**
SIC: 7371 Computer software development & applications

(P-12345)
CLUSTRIX INC
699 Veterans Blvd, Redwood City (94063-1408)
PHONE..................415 501-9560
Mike Azevedo, *CEO*
Robin Purohit, *President*
Thomas Muise, *CFO*
Mark Sarbiewski, *Chief Mktg Ofcr*
Scott Sullivan, *Vice Pres*
EMP: 29 **EST:** 2006
SALES (est): 6.9MM
SALES (corp-wide): 7.8MM **Privately Held**
WEB: www.mariadb.com
SIC: 7371 3577 Computer software development; computer peripheral equipment
PA: Mariadb Usa, Inc.
68 Willow Rd
Menlo Park CA 94025
855 562-7423

(P-12346)
COBALT ROBOTICS INC
2121 S El Cmino Real Ste, San Mateo (94403)
PHONE..................650 315-4314
Travis Deyle, *CEO*
Kina Tua, *Executive Asst*
Dennis Cui, *Engineer*
EMP: 100 **EST:** 2016
SALES (est): 12.9MM **Privately Held**
WEB: www.cobaltrobotics.com
SIC: 7371 Computer software development & applications

(P-12347)
CODE GREEN NETWORKS INC
385 Moffett Park Dr # 105, Sunnyvale (94089-1218)
PHONE..................408 498-8413
Daniel Udoutch, *President*
Randy Spratt, *Exec VP*
Rhett Ohlson, *Vice Pres*
Sudhakar Ravi, *CTO*
EMP: 48 **EST:** 2004
SQ FT: 25,000
SALES (est): 3.1MM
SALES (corp-wide): 562.3MM **Privately Held**
WEB: www.digitalguardian.com
SIC: 7371 Computer software development
HQ: Digital Guardian, Inc.
275 Wyman St Ste 250
Waltham MA 02451
781 788-8180

(P-12348)
CODILITY US INC
1355 Market St Ste 488, San Francisco (94103-1337)
PHONE..................415 568-5055
Rachel Whitehead, *Principal*
George Brueggeman, *Executive*
Andrew Knowles, *Opers Staff*
Khalilah Daniels, *Sales Engr*
Sally Lee, *Marketing Staff*
EMP: 150 **EST:** 2015
SALES (est): 12.2MM **Privately Held**
WEB: www.codility.com
SIC: 7371 Computer software development & applications

(P-12349)
COGNICIAN INC (HQ)
535 Mission St Ste 1628, San Francisco (94105-2997)
PHONE..................858 997-6732
Barry Kayton, *CEO*
Patrick Kayton, *CFO*
Michael Leeman, *Admin Sec*
Jeff Kayton, *Marketing Staff*
Nicole Petersen, *Sr Project Mgr*
EMP: 46 **EST:** 2011
SALES (est): 9.4MM **Privately Held**
WEB: www.cognician.com
SIC: 7371 Computer software development

(P-12350)
COGNITIVECLOUDS SOFTWARE INC
5433 Ontario Cmn, Fremont (94555-2930)
PHONE..................415 234-3611
Prasanna Gopinath, *Principal*
EMP: 70 **EST:** 2017
SALES (est): 2.4MM **Privately Held**
WEB: www.cognitiveclouds.com
SIC: 7371 Computer software development

(P-12351)
COHESITY INC (PA)
300 Park Ave Ste 1700, San Jose (95110-2774)
PHONE..................855 926-4374
Mohit Aron, *CEO*
Junichi Iwakami, *President*
Robert Salmon, *COO*
Robert Odonovan, *CFO*
Lynn Lucas, *Chief Mktg Ofcr*
EMP: 500
SQ FT: 98,000
SALES (est): 221.1MM **Privately Held**
WEB: www.cohesity.com
SIC: 7371 Custom computer programming services

(P-12352)
COMMURE INC (PA)
376 Brannan St, San Francisco (94107-1830)
PHONE..................415 741-1114
Brent Dover, *CEO*
EMP: 82 **EST:** 2017
SQ FT: 11,500
SALES (est): 33.2MM **Privately Held**
WEB: www.commure.com
SIC: 7371 Computer software development

(P-12353)
COMPUTER POWER SFTWR GROUP INC (PA)
Also Called: Cpsg
716 Figueroa St, Folsom (95630-2514)
PHONE..................916 985-4445
David M Saykally, *President*
EMP: 17
SQ FT: 4,000
SALES (est): 9.1MM **Privately Held**
WEB: www.cpsoftwaregroup.com
SIC: 7371 7372 Computer software development; prepackaged software

(P-12354)
CONCORD WORLDWIDE INC
177 Post St Ph Ste 910, San Francisco (94108-4712)
PHONE..................415 689-5488
Mathieu Lhoumeau, *CEO*
Matt Benjamin, *Executive*
Lauren Nute, *Executive*
Florian Parain, *CTO*
Jill Myers, *Marketing Staff*
EMP: 65 **EST:** 2014
SQ FT: 2,700
SALES (est): 4.2MM **Privately Held**
WEB: www.concordnow.com
SIC: 7371 Computer software development

(P-12355)
CORBIN WILLITS SYSTEMS INC
3755 Washington Blvd # 204, Fremont (94538-4978)
PHONE..................510 979-5600
Roland Willits, *President*
Joyce McFarland, *Controller*
EMP: 15 **EST:** 1976
SQ FT: 8,000
SALES (est): 1.4MM **Privately Held**
WEB: www.corbinwillitssystems.com
SIC: 7371 7372 Computer software development; prepackaged software

(P-12356)
CORE MOBILITY INC (PA)
2023 Stierlin Ct 2, Mountain View (94043-4761)
PHONE..................650 603-6600
EMP: 45
SALES (est): 15.3MM **Privately Held**
WEB: www.coremobility.com
SIC: 7371 Software Development

(P-12357)
COREOS LLC
101 New Montgomery St # 5, San Francisco (94105-3624)
PHONE..................888 733-4281
Alexander Polvi, *CEO*
Kelly Tenn, *Comms Mgr*
Brandon Philips, *CTO*
Yifan Gu, *Software Engr*
David Hunt, *Director*
EMP: 52 **EST:** 2012
SALES (est): 8.4MM
SALES (corp-wide): 73.6B **Publicly Held**
WEB: www.redhat.com
SIC: 7371 Computer software development
HQ: Red Hat, Inc.
100 E Davie St
Raleigh NC 27601

(P-12358)
COUCHBASE INC (PA)
3250 Olcott St, Santa Clara (95054-3026)
PHONE..................650 417-7500
Matthew M Cain, *President*
Gregory N Henry, *CFO*
Margaret Chow,
Denis Murphy, *Senior VP*
Thomas Dong, *Vice Pres*
EMP: 595 **EST:** 2008
SQ FT: 46,000
SALES (est): 103.2MM **Publicly Held**
WEB: www.couchbase.com
SIC: 7371 7372 Computer software development; business oriented computer software

(P-12359)
COVEO SOFTWARE CORP
44 Montgomery St, San Francisco (94104-4602)
PHONE..................800 635-5476
Louis Tetu, *CEO*
Laurent Simoneau, *President*
Benoit Hogue, *CEO*
John Lavigueur, *CFO*
Mark Floisand, *Officer*
EMP: 64 **EST:** 2005
SQ FT: 2,000
SALES (est): 17.2MM
SALES (corp-wide): 14.4MM **Privately Held**
WEB: www.coveo.com
SIC: 7371 8748 Computer software development; business consulting
PA: Coveo Solutions Inc
3175 Ch Des Quatre-Bourgeois Bureau 200
Quebec QC G1W 2
418 263-1111

(P-12360)
COVERITY LLC (HQ)
185 Berry St Ste 6500, San Francisco (94107-1728)
PHONE..................415 321-5200
Anthony Bettencourt, *President*
Jennifer Johnson, *Chief Mktg Ofcr*
Dave Peterson, *Chief Mktg Ofcr*
Matt Green, *Officer*
John E Calonico Jr, *Vice Pres*
EMP: 80 **EST:** 2002
SALES (est): 39.3MM
SALES (corp-wide): 3.6B **Publicly Held**
WEB: www.synopsys.com
SIC: 7371 7372 Computer software development; prepackaged software
PA: Synopsys, Inc.
690 E Middlefield Rd
Mountain View CA 94043
650 584-5000

(P-12361)
CROSS MATCH INC
6607 Kaiser Dr, Fremont (94555-3608)
PHONE..................650 474-4000
Vito Fabbrizio, *Vice Pres*
Kathryn Hutton, *Vice Pres*
Jeff Parker, *Vice Pres*
Chris Trytten, *Marketing Staff*
EMP: 102
SALES (corp-wide): 10.1B **Privately Held**
SIC: 7371 Computer software development
HQ: Cross Match, Inc.
3950 Rca Blvd Ste 5001
Palm Beach Gardens FL 33410
561 622-1650

(P-12362)
CROSSINSTALL INC
Also Called: Cross Install
650 California St Fl 30, San Francisco (94108-2611)
PHONE..................415 425-5929
Jeff Marshall, *CEO*
Victor Perez, *Executive*
Angela Gioukaris, *Manager*
EMP: 44 **EST:** 2013
SQ FT: 4,000
SALES (est): 4.2MM
SALES (corp-wide): 3.7B **Publicly Held**
WEB: www.mopub.com
SIC: 7371 8742 Computer software development & applications; marketing consulting services
PA: Twitter, Inc.
1355 Market St Ste 900
San Francisco CA 94103
415 222-9670

7371 - Custom Computer Programming Svcs County (P-12363) — PRODUCTS & SERVICES SECTION

(P-12363)
CROSSLINK PROF TAX SLTIONS LLC (PA)
16916 S Harlan Rd, Lathrop (95330-8737)
P.O. Box 611, Tracy (95378-0611)
PHONE.................................209 835-2720
Reynold Sbrilli, *Officer*
Reynold F Sbrilli, *CEO*
Brett Klutch, *COO*
Stephanie Tesfazghi, *CFO*
Rey Sbrilli, *Officer*
EMP: 74 **EST:** 1974
SALES (est): 22.4MM **Privately Held**
WEB: www.crosslinktax.com
SIC: 7371 Software programming applications

(P-12364)
CRYSTALGRAPHICS INC
Also Called: Crystal Graphics
1999 S Bascom Ave Ste 700, Campbell (95008-2205)
PHONE.................................800 394-0700
Dennis E Ricks, *President*
Alok Mohan, *Ch of Bd*
George Meyers, *Info Tech Mgr*
Sachi Matsumura, *VP Opers*
EMP: 17 **EST:** 1986
SQ FT: 2,000
SALES (est): 1.5MM **Privately Held**
WEB: www.crystalgraphics.com
SIC: 7371 Computer software development; 7372 prepackaged software

(P-12365)
CSC COVANSYS CORPORATION
34740 Tuxedo Cmn, Fremont (94555-2746)
PHONE.................................510 304-3430
Chris Pensy, *Manager*
EMP: 287
SALES (corp-wide): 17.7B **Publicly Held**
SIC: 7371 Computer software development
HQ: Csc Covansys Corporation
3170 Fairview Park Dr
Falls Church VA 22042
703 876-1000

(P-12366)
CURATED INC
638 4th St, San Francisco (94107-1602)
PHONE.................................415 855-1825
Peter Ombres, *Mng Member*
Eduardo Vivsa, *President*
EMP: 65 **EST:** 2017
SALES (est): 5.3MM **Privately Held**
SIC: 7371 5941 Computer software development & applications; sporting goods & bicycle shops

(P-12367)
CUREBASE INC
145 Gardenside Dr Apt 9, San Francisco (94131-1384)
PHONE.................................248 978-3541
Thomas Lemberg, *CEO*
EMP: 44 **EST:** 2017
SALES (est): 1MM **Privately Held**
WEB: www.web.curebase.com
SIC: 7371 Computer software development & applications

(P-12368)
CYBERNET SOFTWARE SYSTEMS INC
75 E Santa Clara St # 900, San Jose (95113-1842)
PHONE.................................972 792-7597
Harvey Steve, *Branch Mgr*
EMP: 497 **Privately Held**
SIC: 7371 Computer software development
HQ: Cybernet Software Systems Inc
18111 Preston Rd Ste 400
Dallas TX 75252
408 615-5700

(P-12369)
CYRAL INC
691 S Milpitas Blvd # 212, Milpitas (95035-5478)
PHONE.................................310 689-8512
Manav Mital, *CEO*
EMP: 35
SALES (est): 583.1K **Privately Held**
SIC: 7371 Software programming applications

(P-12370)
DASHER TECHNOLOGIES INC (HQ)
675 Campbell Tech Pkwy, Campbell (95008-5092)
PHONE.................................408 409-2607
Laurie M Dasher, *CEO*
Al Chien, *President*
Marcus Hodge, *Executive*
John Galatea, *VP Sales*
Michael Skipper, *Sales Staff*
EMP: 42 **EST:** 1998
SQ FT: 16,000
SALES (est): 24.3MM
SALES (corp-wide): 516.5MM **Privately Held**
WEB: www.dasher.com
SIC: 7371 Computer software development
PA: Converge Technology Solutions Corp
161 Bay St Suite 2325
Toronto ON M5J 2
416 360-3995

(P-12371)
DATABRICKS INC (PA)
160 Spear St Fl 13, San Francisco (94105-1546)
PHONE.................................415 494-7672
Ali Ghodsi, *CEO*
Brian Dirking, *Partner*
Denis Dubeau, *Partner*
Mark Lobree, *Partner*
Allen Smolinski, *Partner*
EMP: 55 **EST:** 2013
SQ FT: 18,000
SALES (est): 103.7MM **Privately Held**
WEB: www.databricks.com
SIC: 7371 Computer software development

(P-12372)
DATAMAX SOFTWARE GROUP INC
Also Called: Rfgen Software
1101 Inv Blvd Ste 250, El Dorado Hills (95762)
PHONE.................................916 939-4065
Tom Eddinger, *CEO*
Robert Brice, *President*
Dustin Caudell, *Vice Pres*
Stan Schoch, *Vice Pres*
Judie Lew, *Program Mgr*
EMP: 47 **EST:** 1995
SQ FT: 12,000
SALES (est): 14.7MM **Privately Held**
WEB: www.rfgen.com
SIC: 7371 5734 Computer software development; computer peripheral equipment

(P-12373)
DATAMEER INC (PA)
535 Mission St Ste 2602, San Francisco (94105-3260)
PHONE.................................650 286-9100
Stefan Groschupf, *CEO*
Nikhil Kumar, *Partner*
George Shahid, *CFO*
Steve Dille, *Chief Mktg Ofcr*
Lance Walter, *Chief Mktg Ofcr*
EMP: 129 **EST:** 2009
SALES (est): 6MM **Privately Held**
WEB: www.datameer.com
SIC: 7371 Computer software development

(P-12374)
DATASELF CORP
1200 Franklin Mall, Santa Clara (95050-4807)
PHONE.................................888 910-9802
Joni Girardi, *CEO*
Lori Wright, *Technical Staff*
Gabriela Piccoli, *Marketing Staff*
EMP: 20 **EST:** 2005
SALES (est): 1.6MM **Privately Held**
WEB: www.dataself.com
SIC: 7371 7372 Software programming applications; publishers' computer software

(P-12375)
DATASTAX INC (PA)
3975 Freedom Cir Fl 4, Santa Clara (95054-1241)
PHONE.................................650 389-6000
Chet Kapoor, *CEO*
Don Dixon, *CFO*
Karl Van Den Bergh, *Chief Mktg Ofcr*
Martin Van Ryswyk, *Exec VP*
Debbie Murray, *Vice Pres*
EMP: 866 **EST:** 2010
SALES (est): 130MM **Privately Held**
WEB: www.datastax.com
SIC: 7371 Computer software development

(P-12376)
DCM TECHNOLOGIES INC
Also Called: D C M Data Systems
39159 Paseo Padre Pkwy # 303, Fremont (94538-1698)
PHONE.................................510 494-2321
Janakiram Kaki, *Vice Pres*
EMP: 35 **EST:** 1982
SALES (est): 2.5MM **Privately Held**
WEB: www.dcminfotech.com
SIC: 7371 Computer software systems analysis & design, custom
PA: Baap Technologies India Private Limited
No. 7
Coimbatore TN

(P-12377)
DEALERTRACK CLLTRAL MGT SVCS I
Also Called: Fdi Collateral Management
9750 Goethe Rd, Sacramento (95827-3500)
PHONE.................................916 368-5300
Mark O'Neil, *CEO*
Daniel L Wollenberg, *President*
Beverly Devine, *Exec VP*
Tony Panganiban, *Vice Pres*
Don Hearth, *Sr Software Eng*
EMP: 220 **EST:** 1992
SQ FT: 84,900
SALES (est): 31MM
SALES (corp-wide): 1.6MM **Privately Held**
WEB: www.us.dealertrack.com
SIC: 7371 Computer software development
HQ: Trivin, Inc.
115 Pohegaunt Dr Ste 201
Groton CT 06340
860 448-3177

(P-12378)
DEEP NORTH INC (PA)
303 Twin Dolphin Dr # 600, Redwood City (94065-1422)
PHONE.................................650 781-1550
Michael Adair, *CEO*
Casey Swan, *Senior VP*
Nate Angara, *Vice Pres*
Prakash Atawale, *Vice Pres*
Rohan Sanil, *Vice Pres*
EMP: 60 **EST:** 2016
SALES (est): 2.8MM **Privately Held**
WEB: www.deepnorth.com
SIC: 7371 Computer software development

(P-12379)
DELPHIX CORP (PA)
1400 Saport Blvd Ste 200a, Redwood City (94063)
PHONE.................................650 494-1645
Chris Cook, *President*
Suzanne Eger, *Partner*
Stewart Grierson, *CFO*
Monika Sain, *Chief Mktg Ofcr*
Jedidiah Yueh, *Officer*
EMP: 47 **EST:** 2008
SQ FT: 18,000
SALES (est): 14.6MM **Privately Held**
WEB: www.delphix.com
SIC: 7371 Computer software development

(P-12380)
DEMANDFORCE INC
600 Harrison St Ste 601, San Francisco (94107-1390)
PHONE.................................800 246-9853
Richard E Berry, *President*
Keith Conte, *CFO*
Tim McLean, *Chief Mktg Ofcr*
Olga Braylovskiy, *Vice Pres*
Jonathan Tucker, *Vice Pres*
EMP: 35 **EST:** 2003
SQ FT: 10,000
SALES (est): 5.7MM
SALES (corp-wide): 188.1MM **Privately Held**
WEB: www.demandforce.com
SIC: 7371 Computer software development; computer software development & applications
PA: Autodata Solutions Group, Inc.
909 N Pacific Coast Hwy # 11
El Segundo CA 90245
310 280-4000

(P-12381)
DEMANDTEC LLC
1 Franklin Pkwy Bldg 910, San Mateo (94403-1906)
PHONE.................................914 499-1900
Daniel R Fishback, *President*
William R Phelps, *COO*
Mark A Culhane, *CFO*
Michael A Bromme, *Senior VP*
EMP: 340 **EST:** 1999
SQ FT: 82,000
SALES (est): 28.7MM
SALES (corp-wide): 73.6B **Publicly Held**
WEB: www.ibm.com
SIC: 7371 Computer software development
PA: International Business Machines Corporation
1 New Orchard Rd Ste 1 # 1
Armonk NY 10504
914 499-1900

(P-12382)
DENODO TECHNOLOGIES INC (PA)
525 University Ave Ste 31, Palo Alto (94301-1906)
PHONE.................................650 566-8833
Angel Vina, *President*
Ravi Shankar, *Officer*
Suresh Chandrasekaran, *Exec VP*
Anastasio Molano, *Vice Pres*
Gary Ryan, *Business Dir*
EMP: 76 **EST:** 2006
SALES (est): 17.7MM **Privately Held**
WEB: www.denodo.com
SIC: 7371 Computer software development

(P-12383)
DENSITY INC
369 Sutter St, San Francisco (94108-4301)
PHONE.................................888 990-2253
Andrew Farah, *CEO*
Ben Redfield, *Co-Owner*
Steve Vondeak, *Co-Owner*
Victoria Rudakova, *Sr Software Eng*
Keith Mok, *Software Engr*
EMP: 50 **EST:** 2013
SALES (est): 8.7MM **Privately Held**
WEB: www.density.io
SIC: 7371 Computer software development

(P-12384)
DESIGNIT NORTH AMERICA INC
Also Called: Cooper Software, Inc.
450 Sansome St Fl 9, San Francisco (94111-3306)
PHONE.................................415 267-3500
Alan Cooper, *CEO*
Sue Cooper, *CEO*
Jim Dibble, *Associate Dir*
Steve Calde, *Managing Dir*
Nate Clinton, *Managing Dir*
EMP: 35 **EST:** 1987
SQ FT: 1,000
SALES (est): 7MM **Privately Held**
WEB: www.designit.com
SIC: 7371 Computer software development

PRODUCTS & SERVICES SECTION
7371 - Custom Computer Programming Svcs County (P-12407)

PA: Wipro Limited
Doddakannelli, Sarjapur Road,
Bengaluru KA 56003

(P-12385)
DEVICE ANYWHERE
777 Mariners Isl Blvd # 250, San Mateo (94404-5008)
PHONE..................650 655-6400
EMP: 68
SALES (est): 4.2MM **Privately Held**
SIC: 7371 Custom Computer Programing

(P-12386)
DEVONWAY INC (PA)
601 California St Ste 210, San Francisco (94108-2833)
PHONE..................415 904-4000
Chris Moustakas, *President*
Sally White, *President*
Matt Sacks, *Vice Pres*
Wade Watts, *Vice Pres*
Don Fitzgerald, *Software Dev*
EMP: 56 EST: 2007
SALES (est): 5.3MM **Privately Held**
WEB: www.devonway.com
SIC: 7371 7372 Computer software development; business oriented computer software

(P-12387)
DGN TECHNOLOGIES INC (PA)
46500 Fremont Blvd # 708, Fremont (94538-6467)
PHONE..................510 252-0346
Ranvir Singh, *President*
Manpreet Bajaj, *Vice Pres*
Tony Sodhi, *VP Bus Dvlpt*
Taj Singh, *Technical Staff*
Puneet Kahlon, *Manager*
EMP: 228 EST: 2003
SQ FT: 1,863
SALES: 37.7MM **Privately Held**
WEB: www.dgntechnologies.com
SIC: 7371 8748 Computer software development; systems engineering consultant, ex. computer or professional

(P-12388)
DIAMOND TOUCH INC
Also Called: Vinsuite
1625 Trancas St Unit 2280, NAPA (94558-7704)
PHONE..................707 253-7450
Thomas Bronson, *President*
Mark Rosenberg, *COO*
Lindy Dresser, *Administration*
Carlos Galarce, *CIO*
Blake Sinclair, *Info Tech Mgr*
EMP: 66 EST: 2001
SALES (est): 4.6MM **Privately Held**
WEB: www.granburysolutions.com
SIC: 7371 Computer software development & applications

(P-12389)
DICOM SYSTEMS INC
119 University Ave, Los Gatos (95030-6010)
PHONE..................415 684-8790
Dmitriy Tochilnik, *CEO*
Anna Koval, *President*
Florent Saint-Clair, *Exec VP*
Tanya Wehr, *Marketing Staff*
EMP: 15 EST: 2008
SALES (est): 1MM **Privately Held**
WEB: www.dcmsys.com
SIC: 7371 7372 Computer software development; prepackaged software

(P-12390)
DIGITAL CHOCOLATE INC
1855 S Grant St Ste 200, San Mateo (94402-7017)
PHONE..................650 372-1600
Trip Hawkins, *Ch of Bd*
Cheryl Dalrymple, *CFO*
EMP: 27 EST: 2003
SALES (est): 2.2MM **Privately Held**
SIC: 7371 2741 Computer software development; miscellaneous publishing

(P-12391)
DIGITAL ONUS INC (PA)
84 W Santa Clara St # 74, San Jose (95113-1815)
PHONE..................408 228-3490
Surinder S Chawla, *CEO*
Deena W Dukle, *Shareholder*
Viridiana De La Garza, *Shareholder*
Arvin Narula, *Exec VP*
Emilio Ojeda, *Practice Mgr*
EMP: 106 EST: 2015
SALES (est): 5.9MM **Privately Held**
WEB: www.digitalonus.com
SIC: 7371 7379 Software programming applications; computer related consulting services

(P-12392)
DIGITE INC
21060 Homestead Rd # 220, Cupertino (95014-0204)
PHONE..................408 418-3834
Suhas S Patil, *Ch of Bd*
Sridhar Auynam, *CEO*
Raghunath Basavanahalli, *Senior VP*
Sudipta Lahiri, *Senior VP*
Mahesh Singh, *Senior VP*
EMP: 150 EST: 1998
SQ FT: 1,400
SALES (est): 15.1MM **Privately Held**
WEB: www.digite.com
SIC: 7371 Computer software development

(P-12393)
DIRECTLY INC
333 Bryant St Ste 250, San Francisco (94107-1443)
PHONE..................650 714-7334
Michael De La Cruz, *CEO*
Shaun Donnelly, *Vice Pres*
Jean Tessier, *Vice Pres*
Peter Thalman, *Executive*
Richard Barnes, *CIO*
EMP: 63 EST: 2015
SALES (est): 2MM **Privately Held**
WEB: www.directly.com
SIC: 7371 Computer software development & applications

(P-12394)
DISCORD INC
444 De Haro St Ste 200, San Francisco (94107-2578)
PHONE..................650 389-2453
Jason Citron, *CEO*
Cory Cumming, *Office Mgr*
Donald Chen, *Software Engr*
Kodie Goodwin, *Software Engr*
Mason Sciotti, *Technical Staff*
EMP: 150 EST: 2014
SALES (est): 22.9MM **Privately Held**
WEB: www.discord.com
SIC: 7371 Computer software development & applications

(P-12395)
DISPLAYLINK CORP (HQ)
1251 Mckay Dr, San Jose (95131-1709)
PHONE..................650 838-0481
Graham Okeeffe, *CEO*
Adrian Den Heever, *Vice Pres*
Jonathan Jeacocke, *Vice Pres*
Ian Stacey, *Vice Pres*
Prince Joveluro, *Software Engr*
EMP: 16 EST: 2003
SALES: 5.8MM
SALES (corp-wide): 1.3B **Publicly Held**
WEB: www.synaptics.com
SIC: 7371 7372 Computer software development & applications; prepackaged software
PA: Synaptics Incorporated
1251 Mckay Dr
San Jose CA 95131
408 904-1100

(P-12396)
DNFCS INC (PA)
2150 N 1st St Ste 400, San Jose (95131-2043)
PHONE..................510 201-9809
Patrick Howell, *CEO*
EMP: 38 EST: 2017

SALES (est): 2.3MM **Privately Held**
WEB: www.dnfcs.com
SIC: 7371 8742 Computer software systems analysis & design, custom; computer software development & applications; management consulting services

(P-12397)
DO BIG THINGS LLC
147 Buckelew St, Sausalito (94965-1148)
P.O. Box 128, Mill Valley (94942-0128)
PHONE..................415 806-3423
Cheryl Contee, *CEO*
Tova Vance, *COO*
Ryanne Brown, *Vice Pres*
Dionna Humphrey, *Vice Pres*
Cassie Tangney, *Vice Pres*
EMP: 35 EST: 2017
SALES (est): 2.2MM **Privately Held**
WEB: www.dobigthings.today
SIC: 7371 Software programming applications

(P-12398)
DOCKER INC (PA)
3790 Corina Way 1052, Palo Alto (94303-4504)
P.O. Box 61180 (94306-6180)
PHONE..................800 764-4847
Scott Johnston, *CEO*
Gary Gilbert, *Partner*
Dan Guzman, *Partner*
Dan Powers, *Partner*
Eric Bardin, *CFO*
EMP: 360 EST: 2010
SALES (est): 47MM **Privately Held**
WEB: www.docker.com
SIC: 7371 Computer software development

(P-12399)
DORADO SOFTWARE INC
Also Called: Visiworks Software
4805 Golden Foothill Pkwy, El Dorado Hills (95762-9651)
PHONE..................916 673-1100
Timothy Sebring, *President*
Justin Flemer, *Vice Pres*
Roger Hosier, *Vice Pres*
Ed Kucala, *Vice Pres*
Bill Acevedo, *Info Tech Mgr*
EMP: 80 EST: 1997
SALES (est): 9.5MM **Privately Held**
WEB: www.doradosoftware.com
SIC: 7371 Computer software development

(P-12400)
DOXIMITY INC
500 3rd St Ste 510, San Francisco (94107-6803)
PHONE..................650 549-4330
Jeffrey Tangney, *CEO*
Kristen Venettone, *Partner*
Richard R Deluca, *Partner*
Anna Bryson, *CFO*
Joseph Kleine, *Ch Credit Ofcr*
EMP: 713 EST: 2010
SQ FT: 23,000
SALES (est): 206.9MM **Privately Held**
WEB: www.doximity.com
SIC: 7371 Custom computer programming services

(P-12401)
DPP TECH INC
1390 Market St Ste 200, San Francisco (94102-5404)
PHONE..................415 754-9170
Puran Moorjani, *President*
Bob McLauchlan, *Vice Pres*
Sonal Pradhan, *Technical Staff*
EMP: 37 EST: 2002
SALES (est): 3.8MM **Privately Held**
WEB: www.dpptech.com
SIC: 7371 Computer software development

(P-12402)
DREMIO CORPORATION (PA)
3970 Freedom Cir Ste 110, Santa Clara (95054-1298)
PHONE..................408 882-3569
Tomer Shiran, *CEO*
Mike Lombard, *Sales Staff*

Alex Ciunciusky, *Director*
Kim Pegnato, *Consultant*
EMP: 31 EST: 2015
SALES (est): 4.1MM **Privately Held**
WEB: www.dremio.com
SIC: 7371 7372 Computer software development; business oriented computer software

(P-12403)
DRISHTI TECHNOLOGIES INC
1975 W El Cmino Real Ste, Mountain View (94040)
PHONE..................669 273-9090
Prasad Akell, *CEO*
Srida Joisa, *CFO*
Michael Robertson, *Principal*
EMP: 110 EST: 2017
SALES (est): 6.9MM **Privately Held**
WEB: www.drishti.com
SIC: 7371 Custom computer programming services

(P-12404)
DRIVEWYZE INC
398 Primrose Rd, Burlingame (94010-4005)
PHONE..................888 988-1590
Brian Heath, *CEO*
Laura Colwill, *CFO*
Fred Ko, *Admin Sec*
Doug Johnson, *Marketing Staff*
Charles Buffone, *Senior Mgr*
EMP: 35 EST: 2012
SALES (est): 3.3MM
SALES (corp-wide): 56.6MM **Privately Held**
WEB: www.drivewyze.com
SIC: 7371 Software programming applications
PA: Intelligent Imaging Systems, Inc
6325 Gateway Blvd Nw Suite 170
Edmonton AB T6H 5
780 461-3355

(P-12405)
DTEX SYSTEMS INC
19630 Allendale Ave # 22, Saratoga (95070-7799)
P.O. Box 3210 (95070-1210)
PHONE..................408 418-3786
Christy Wyatt, *CEO*
Bahman Mahbod, *COO*
Debbie Tuck, *CFO*
Steve Holton, *Officer*
Steve Hewitt, *Vice Pres*
EMP: 50 EST: 2014
SALES (est): 3.6MM **Privately Held**
WEB: www.dtexsystems.com
SIC: 7371 Computer software development

(P-12406)
DUETTO RESEARCH INC
333 Bush St Fl 12, San Francisco (94104-2866)
PHONE..................415 968-9389
Patrick Bosworth, *Ch of Bd*
Marissa McAfee, *Senior Partner*
David Woolenberg, *President*
Greg Stanger, *CFO*
Jeff MA, *Senior VP*
EMP: 66 EST: 2012
SALES (est): 5.8MM **Privately Held**
WEB: www.duettocloud.com
SIC: 7371 Computer software development

(P-12407)
DYNAMIC GRAPHICS INC (PA)
1015 Atlantic Ave, Alameda (94501-1154)
PHONE..................510 522-0700
Arthur Paradis, *President*
Tamara Paradis, *Corp Secy*
Agnis Kaugars, *Sr Software Eng*
Rick Schnell, *Sr Software Eng*
Robin Gowen, *Info Tech Mgr*
EMP: 25 EST: 1969
SQ FT: 23,000
SALES (est): 3.4MM **Privately Held**
WEB: www.dgi.com
SIC: 7371 7372 Computer software development; prepackaged software

7371 - Custom Computer Programming Svcs County (P-12408)   PRODUCTS & SERVICES SECTION

(P-12408)
DYNED INTERNATIONAL INC (PA)
1350 Bayshore Hwy Ste 850, Burlingame (94010-1843)
P.O. Box 50970, Palo Alto (94303-0676)
PHONE.................................650 375-7011
P Lance Knowles, *President*
Ian Adam, *CEO*
Hoa Tran, *CFO*
Andrew Blasky, *Director*
Thomas Kingery, *Accounts Mgr*
EMP: 83 EST: 1987
SQ FT: 4,800
SALES (est): 2.9MM Privately Held
WEB: www.dyned.com
SIC: 7371 Computer software development

(P-12409)
E LA CARTE INC
Also Called: Sales Mkt Mfg Smart Dining Sys
810 Hamilton St, Redwood City (94063-1624)
PHONE.................................650 468-0680
Rajat Suri, *President*
Mark Belinsky, *COO*
Sarah Garner, *Office Mgr*
Dan Smith, *Opers Staff*
David Fedoronko, *Sales Staff*
EMP: 60 EST: 2008
SALES (est): 15.5MM Privately Held
WEB: www.presto.com
SIC: 5734 7371 Computer software & accessories; computer software development

(P-12410)
E-BASE TECHNOLOGIES INC (PA)
39159 Paseo Padre Pkwy # 206, Fremont (94538-1623)
PHONE.................................510 790-2547
Madhavi L Tatineni, *CEO*
Vithal Dandi, *President*
Vinai Kolli, *Vice Pres*
EMP: 49 EST: 2000
SQ FT: 1,750
SALES (est): 5.1MM Privately Held
WEB: www.ebasetek.com
SIC: 7371 8748 Computer software development; systems engineering consultant, ex. computer or professional

(P-12411)
ECONOSOFT INC
2375 Zanker Rd Ste 250, San Jose (95131-1143)
PHONE.................................408 442-3663
Chander Shaiker, *President*
Aditya Abhiraj, *Technical Staff*
Ronak Dhawan, *Business Mgr*
Abu Taurab, *Business Mgr*
Ishani Kalra, *Sales Mgr*
EMP: 72 EST: 2000
SALES (est): 1.1MM
SALES (corp-wide): 18.3MM Privately Held
WEB: www.econosoftinc.com
SIC: 7371 Computer software systems analysis & design, custom
PA: Ace Technologies, Inc.
2375 Zanker Rd Ste 250
San Jose CA 95131
408 324-1203

(P-12412)
EDEN TECHNOLOGIES INC
54 Jeff Adachi Way, San Francisco (94103-4714)
PHONE.................................800 754-3166
Joseph Du Bey, *CEO*
Lauren Peterson, *Partner*
Camille Merritt, *Vice Pres*
Keran Sangha, *Regional Mgr*
Otto Chen, *Software Engr*
EMP: 57 EST: 2014
SALES (est): 5.1MM Privately Held
WEB: www.edenworkplace.com
SIC: 7371 Computer software development

(P-12413)
EFRONT FINANCIAL SOLUTIONS INC
135 Main St Ste 1330, San Francisco (94105-1843)
PHONE.................................415 653-3239
Tarek Chouman, *CEO*
Matthew Bagley, *CFO*
Thibaut De Laval, *Chief Mktg Ofcr*
Sevgi Eason, *Vice Pres*
Alan Erickson, *Executive*
EMP: 88 EST: 2008
SALES (est): 3.3MM Privately Held
SIC: 7371 Computer software development & applications

(P-12414)
EHEALTHINSURANCE SERVICES INC
Also Called: Ehealth Insurance.com
11919 Foundation Pl # 100, Gold River (95670-4537)
PHONE.................................916 608-6101
Robert Hurley, *Branch Mgr*
Phillip Morelock, *Officer*
Katerina Sidorovich, *Vice Pres*
Kyle Hammer, *Business Dir*
Derek Streich, *Business Dir*
EMP: 200 Publicly Held
WEB: www.ehealthmedicare.com
SIC: 7371 Computer software development
HQ: Ehealthinsurance Services, Inc.
2625 Augustine Dr Ste 201
Santa Clara CA 95054
650 584-2700

(P-12415)
EINFOCHIPS INC (HQ)
2025 Gateway Pl Ste 270, San Jose (95110-1007)
PHONE.................................408 496-1882
Pratul Shroff, *CEO*
Raj Sirohi, *COO*
Sribash Dey, *Exec VP*
Bharath Aitha, *Vice Pres*
Saurabh Desai, *Vice Pres*
EMP: 148 EST: 1998
SQ FT: 6,178
SALES (est): 26.6MM
SALES (corp-wide): 28.6B Publicly Held
WEB: www.einfochips.com
SIC: 7371 7373 Computer software development; systems software development services; computer systems analysis & design; computer-aided system services; computer-aided design (CAD) systems service
PA: Arrow Electronics, Inc.
9201 E Dry Creek Rd
Centennial CO 80112
303 824-4000

(P-12416)
ELASTIC BEAM LLC
497 Seaport Ct Ste 101, Redwood City (94063-5598)
PHONE.................................925 963-8122
Bernard Harguindeguy, *CEO*
EMP: 35 EST: 2014
SALES (est): 2.4MM
SALES (corp-wide): 147.7MM Privately Held
WEB: www.pingidentity.com
SIC: 7371 Computer software development
PA: Ping Identity Corporation
1001 17th St Ste 100
Denver CO 80202
303 468-2900

(P-12417)
ELASTIC PROJECTS INC
Also Called: Abstract
255 Golden Gate Ave, San Francisco (94102-3709)
PHONE.................................415 857-1593
Josh Brewer, *CEO*
Kevin Smith, *CTO*
Andrew Rossi, *Director*
Frank Wong, *Manager*
EMP: 100 EST: 2016
SQ FT: 8,000
SALES (est): 3.5MM Privately Held
WEB: www.abstract.com
SIC: 7371 Computer software systems analysis & design, custom

(P-12418)
ELECTRONEEK ROBOTICS INC ✪
611 Gateway Blvd Ste 120, South San Francisco (94080-7066)
PHONE.................................650 600-9550
Sergey Yudovskiy, *CEO*
EMP: 80 EST: 2021
SALES (est): 3.5MM Privately Held
SIC: 7371 Software programming applications

(P-12419)
ELLATION LLC (DH)
Also Called: Crunchyroll
444 Bush St, San Francisco (94108-3731)
PHONE.................................415 796-3560
Tom Pickett, *CEO*
Pierre Cadena, *Senior VP*
Thomas Overton, *Vice Pres*
SAE Song, *Vice Pres*
Kenneth Williams, *Vice Pres*
EMP: 199 EST: 2015
SALES (est): 22.7MM Privately Held
WEB: www.sony.com
SIC: 7371 5932 Computer software development & applications; used merchandise stores

(P-12420)
EMANIO INC (PA)
832 Bancroft Way, Berkeley (94710-2236)
PHONE.................................510 849-9300
K G Charles Harris, *CEO*
Richard Schwab, *Sales Staff*
EMP: 124 EST: 2005
SALES (est): 10.8MM Privately Held
WEB: www.emanio.com
SIC: 7371 5045 Computer software development; computer software

(P-12421)
EMERGENT PAYMENTS INC
Also Called: Live Gamer
2445 Augustine Dr Ste 460, Santa Clara (95054-3098)
PHONE.................................646 867-7200
Mitchell Davis, *Ch of Bd*
Andrew Schneider, *President*
Joe Podulka, *CFO*
Rossini Zumwalt, *Officer*
Christopher Donahue, *Senior VP*
EMP: 60 EST: 2007
SALES (est): 4.4MM Privately Held
WEB: www.emergentafrica.com
SIC: 7371 Computer software development & applications

(P-12422)
EMERSON COLLECTIVE LLC
555 Bryant St Ste 259, Palo Alto (94301-1704)
P.O. Box 10196 (94303-0996)
PHONE.................................650 422-2152
Laurene Powell Jobs, *President*
Arne Duncan, *Managing Prtnr*
Dan Tangherlini, *CFO*
Amy Low, *Managing Dir*
Rochelle Greene, *Executive Asst*
EMP: 110 EST: 2011
SALES (est): 8.4MM Privately Held
WEB: www.emersoncollective.com
SIC: 8299 7371 Educational services; computer software development & applications

(P-12423)
EMETER CORPORATION
4000 E 3rd Ave Ste 400, Foster City (94404-4827)
PHONE.................................650 227-7770
Lisa Caswell, *President*
Guido Frantzen, *CFO*
Werner Wenning, *Chairman*
Lothar Herrmann, *Exec VP*
Chris King, *Risk Mgmt Dir*
EMP: 130 EST: 1998
SQ FT: 30,000
SALES (est): 18.1MM
SALES (corp-wide): 67.4B Privately Held
WEB: www.siemens.com
SIC: 7371 Computer software development
HQ: Siemens Industry, Inc.
1000 Deerfield Pkwy
Buffalo Grove IL 60089
847 215-1000

(P-12424)
EMILYKATE LLC
Also Called: Lifearound2angels
8336 Valdez Ave, Sacramento (95828-0938)
PHONE.................................916 761-6261
Simon Leung,
Ningzi Sun, *President*
EMP: 19 EST: 2017
SALES (est): 738.4K Privately Held
SIC: 7371 2844 2841 2842 Computer software development & applications; bath salts; soap & other detergents; disinfectants, household or industrial plant

(P-12425)
ENVOY INC (PA)
410 Townsend St Ste 410 # 410, San Francisco (94107-1581)
PHONE.................................415 787-7871
Laurentiu Gadea, *CEO*
Nina Raczkowski, *Office Mgr*
Brian Ko, *Software Engr*
Kamal Mohamed, *Engineer*
Jillian Smith, *Marketing Mgr*
EMP: 46 EST: 2013
SALES (est): 5.1MM Privately Held
WEB: www.envoy.com
SIC: 7371 Computer software development & applications

(P-12426)
EPIC CREATIONS INC
702 Marshall St Ste 280, Redwood City (94063-1823)
PHONE.................................650 918-7327
Suren Markosian, *CEO*
Tim Ditlow, *Vice Pres*
Kevin Donahue, *Co-Founder*
Ryan Alejandro, *Web Dvlpr*
Honoka Eguchi, *Project Mgr*
EMP: 112 EST: 2012
SALES (est): 8.3MM Privately Held
WEB: www.getepic.com
SIC: 7371 Computer software development & applications
PA: Think & Learn Private Limited
Ibc Knowledge Park, 4/1, 2nd Floor, Tower D,
Bengaluru KA 56002

(P-12427)
ERT OPERATING COMPANY
5615 Scotts Valley Dr # 150, Scotts Valley (95066-3492)
PHONE.................................412 390-3000
Douglas Engfer, *President*
EMP: 667
SALES (corp-wide): 1.5MM Privately Held
WEB: www.ert.com
SIC: 7371 Computer software development
HQ: Ert Operating Company
1818 Market St Ste 1000
Philadelphia PA 19103
215 972-0420

(P-12428)
ESSENTIAL PRODUCTS INC
380 Portage Ave, Palo Alto (94306-2244)
PHONE.................................650 300-0000
Andrew E Rubin, *CEO*
Niccolo De Masi, *President*
Meena Srinivasan, *CFO*
Matt Hershenson, *Co-Founder*
Ron Cheung, *Program Mgr*
EMP: 82 EST: 2015
SALES (est): 9.7MM Privately Held
WEB: www.essential.com
SIC: 7371 Computer software systems analysis & design, custom

▲ = Import ▼=Export
◆ =Import/Export

7371 - Custom Computer Programming Svcs County (P-12450)

(P-12429)
ESTUATE INC
830 Hillview Ct Ste 280, Milpitas (95035-4564)
PHONE................................408 946-0002
Prakash Balebail, *President*
Nagaraja Kini, *CFO*
Gopal K Vasudeva, *Administration*
Richard Barnes, *CIO*
Balaji Narayan, *Software Engr*
EMP: 67 **EST:** 2005
SQ FT: 2,558
SALES (est): 12.3MM **Privately Held**
WEB: www.estuate.com
SIC: 7371 Computer software development

(P-12430)
ETECH-360 INC
1141 Folsom St, San Francisco (94103-3931)
PHONE................................714 900-3486
John Fries, *CFO*
Christina Durum, *CEO*
Amanda Gutierrez, *Principal*
She'ma Zabid, *Principal*
EMP: 551
SALES (est): 17MM **Privately Held**
WEB: www.360s2g.com
SIC: 7371 Custom computer programming services

(P-12431)
EVEREST CONSULTING GROUP INC
39650 Mission Blvd, Fremont (94539-3000)
PHONE................................510 494-8440
EMP: 85
SALES (corp-wide): 21.4MM **Privately Held**
WEB: www.everestconsulting.net
SIC: 7371 Software Consulting
PA: Everest Consulting Group Inc.
3840 Park Ave Ste 203
Edison NJ 08820
732 548-2700

(P-12432)
EVERGENT TECHNOLOGIES INC
1250 Borregas Ave, Sunnyvale (94089-1309)
PHONE................................877 897-1240
Vijay Sajja, *CEO*
Bill Woods, *Exec VP*
Craig Barberich, *Vice Pres*
Ashok Bhaskar, *Vice Pres*
Bruce Lampert, *Vice Pres*
EMP: 325 **EST:** 2003
SQ FT: 2,000
SALES (est): 5MM **Privately Held**
WEB: www.evergent.com
SIC: 7371 Computer software development

(P-12433)
EVERNOTE CORPORATION (PA)
Also Called: Skitch
305 Walnut St, Redwood City (94063-1731)
PHONE................................650 216-7700
Chris O'Neill, *CEO*
Linda Kozlowski, *COO*
Jeff Shotts, *CFO*
Hitoshi Hokamura, *Chairman*
Justina Altiere, *Vice Pres*
▲ **EMP:** 384 **EST:** 2004
SALES (est): 96.9MM **Privately Held**
WEB: www.evernote.com
SIC: 7371 Computer software development

(P-12434)
EVIDATION HEALTH INC
Also Called: Achievemint
400 Concar Dr Rm 3-109, San Mateo (94402-2681)
PHONE................................650 727-5557
Deborah Kilpatrick, *CEO*
Christine Lemke, *CEO*
Sam Marwaha, *Ch Credit Ofcr*
Maggie Sandoval, *Planning*
Rob Kitson, *Sr Software Eng*
EMP: 292 **EST:** 2014
SALES (est): 18.3MM **Privately Held**
WEB: www.evidation.com
SIC: 7371 8742 Computer software development & applications; hospital & health services consultant

(P-12435)
EVIDENTIO INC (HQ)
7901 Stoneridge Dr # 150, Pleasanton (94588-3677)
PHONE................................855 933-1337
Mark McLaughlin, *CEO*
EMP: 85 **EST:** 2013
SQ FT: 5,000
SALES (est): 8MM
SALES (corp-wide): 4.2B **Publicly Held**
WEB: www.paloaltonetworks.com
SIC: 7371 Computer software systems analysis & design, custom
PA: Palo Alto Networks Inc.
3000 Tannery Way
Santa Clara CA 95054
408 753-4000

(P-12436)
EVOLVEWARE INC
4677 Old Ironsides Dr # 240, Santa Clara (95054-1825)
P.O. Box 2297, Sunnyvale (94087-0297)
PHONE................................408 748-8301
Miten Marfatia, *President*
Sanjay Sule, *Software Dev*
EMP: 78 **EST:** 2000
SQ FT: 1,200
SALES (est): 3.8MM **Privately Held**
WEB: www.evolveware.com
SIC: 7371 Computer software development

(P-12437)
EXIGEN (USA) INC (PA)
Also Called: Exigen Group
345 California St Fl 22, San Francisco (94104-2606)
PHONE................................415 402-2600
Greg Shenkman, *CEO*
Alec Miloslavsky, *Ch of Bd*
Alex Kolt, *President*
Steve James, *Exec VP*
Glenn Lim, *Exec VP*
EMP: 320 **EST:** 1993
SQ FT: 26,000
SALES (est): 47.7MM **Privately Held**
WEB: www.eisgroup.com
SIC: 7371 Computer software development

(P-12438)
EXPANSE LLC
Also Called: Expanse, Inc.
425 Market St Fl 8, San Francisco (94105-2465)
PHONE................................415 590-0129
Timothy Junio, *CEO*
Daniel Quinlan, *CFO*
Tom Barsi, *Vice Pres*
Matt Kraning, *CTO*
EMP: 180 **EST:** 2012
SALES (est): 19.2MM
SALES (corp-wide): 4.2B **Publicly Held**
WEB: www.expanse.co
SIC: 7371 Computer software development & applications
PA: Palo Alto Networks Inc.
3000 Tannery Way
Santa Clara CA 95054
408 753-4000

(P-12439)
EXTRAVIEW CORPORATION
100 Enterprise Way C210, Scotts Valley (95066-3248)
PHONE................................831 461-7100
Carl A Koppel, *President*
Denise Hendsbee, *Engineer*
Rob Campbell, *Manager*
EMP: 45 **EST:** 2004
SQ FT: 10,000
SALES (est): 2.9MM **Privately Held**
WEB: www.extraview.com
SIC: 7371 Computer software development

(P-12440)
EXTREME NETWORKS INC
3585 Monroe St, Santa Clara (95051-7774)
PHONE................................630 288-3665
Robert A Perry, *Branch Mgr*
Charles Carinalli, *Bd of Directors*
Sandy Kakaio, *Admin Asst*
Araceli Vega, *Administration*
Patricia Jones, *Info Tech Mgr*
EMP: 51 **Publicly Held**
WEB: www.extremenetworks.com
SIC: 7371 Computer software development
PA: Extreme Networks, Inc.
6480 Via Del Oro
San Jose CA 95119

(P-12441)
EYECARELIVE INC
5201 Great America Pkwy, Santa Clara (95054-1122)
PHONE................................415 329-7848
Rajesh Ramchandani, *CEO*
William Lard, *CEO*
Beth Samenuk, *Sales Staff*
Nicole Derubertis, *Manager*
EMP: 37 **EST:** 2016
SALES (est): 3.5MM **Privately Held**
WEB: www.eyecarelive.com
SIC: 7371 Computer software development & applications

(P-12442)
FALKONRY INC
10020 N De Anza Blvd, Cupertino (95014-2213)
PHONE................................408 761-7108
Nikunj R Mehta, *CEO*
Pratibha Mehta, *Treasurer*
Uday Kamath, *Officer*
Sanket Amberkar, *Vice Pres*
Mark Gorenberg, *Principal*
EMP: 55 **EST:** 2013
SQ FT: 3,900
SALES (est): 4.9MM **Privately Held**
WEB: www.falkonry.com
SIC: 7371 7372 Software programming applications; application computer software

(P-12443)
FAMOUS SOFTWARE II LLC (PA)
8080 N Palm Ave Ste 210, Fresno (93711-5797)
PHONE................................559 438-3600
Kirk Parrish, *Human Res Mgr*
Meya Moua, *Business Anlyst*
Natalie Kaita, *Sales Mgr*
Jordan Long, *Sales Staff*
Nick Calderon, *Manager*
EMP: 53 **EST:** 1975
SQ FT: 8,300
SALES (est): 14.4MM **Privately Held**
WEB: www.famoussoftware.com
SIC: 7371 7372 Computer software development; business oriented computer software

(P-12444)
FASTLY INC (PA)
475 Brannan St Ste 300, San Francisco (94107-5420)
P.O. Box 78266 (94107-8266)
PHONE................................844 432-7859
Joshua Bixby, *CEO*
Artur Bergman, *Ch of Bd*
Ronald W Kisling, *CFO*
Paul Luongo, *Senior VP*
Brett Shirk, *Risk Mgmt Dir*
EMP: 748 **EST:** 2011
SQ FT: 71,343
SALES (est): 290.8MM **Publicly Held**
WEB: www.fastly.com
SIC: 7371 Computer software development; computer software development & applications

(P-12445)
FCS SOFTWARE SOLUTIONS LIMITED
2375 Zanker Rd Ste 250, San Jose (95131-1143)
PHONE................................408 324-1203
Dalip Kumar, *President*
Janak Sharma, *Director*
EMP: 131 **EST:** 2001
SALES (est): 5.2MM **Privately Held**
WEB: www.fcsltd.com
SIC: 7371 Computer software development
PA: Fcs Software Solutions Limited
Plot No 83 Fcs House
Noida UP 20130

(P-12446)
FEEDZAI INC
1875 S Grant St Ste 950, San Mateo (94402-7015)
PHONE................................650 649-9486
Nuno Sebastiao, *CEO*
Marcus Bragg, *Officer*
Ruela Margarida, *Officer*
Phong Rock, *Senior VP*
Pedro Barata, *Vice Pres*
EMP: 500 **EST:** 2012
SALES (est): 5MM **Privately Held**
WEB: www.feedzai.com
SIC: 7371 Computer software development

(P-12447)
FICTIV INC
168 Welsh St, San Francisco (94107-5513)
PHONE................................415 580-2509
David Evans, *CEO*
Nathan Evans, *CFO*
Rodney Chiu, *Vice Pres*
Andy Sherman, *Executive*
Miriam Rene, *Office Mgr*
EMP: 120 **EST:** 2013
SQ FT: 1,000
SALES (est): 14.9MM **Privately Held**
WEB: www.fictiv.com
SIC: 7371 3089 Computer software development; air mattresses, plastic

(P-12448)
FIELDWIRELABS INC
85 2nd St Fl 6, San Francisco (94105-3464)
PHONE................................415 234-3050
EMP: 39 **EST:** 2016
SALES (est): 3.5MM **Privately Held**
WEB: www.fieldwire.com
SIC: 7371 Computer software development

(P-12449)
FIGMA INC (PA)
760 Market St Fl 10, San Francisco (94102-2300)
PHONE................................888 236-4310
Dylan Field, *CEO*
John Fuetsch, *Sr Software Eng*
Rudi Chen, *Software Eng*
Ryan Kaplan, *Software Engr*
Davy Mao, *Software Engr*
EMP: 98 **EST:** 2012
SALES (est): 6.8MM **Privately Held**
WEB: www.figma.com
SIC: 7371 Computer software development

(P-12450)
FIME USA INC
1737 N 1st St Ste 410, San Jose (95112-4641)
PHONE................................408 228-4040
Xavier Girngiendominici, *Director*
Christian Damour, *Senior Mgr*
Pascal Richard, *Sr Consultant*
Edouard Baroin, *Director*
Bruno Daval, *Director*
EMP: 42 **EST:** 2014
SALES (est): 5.6MM
SALES (corp-wide): 1.1MM **Privately Held**
WEB: www.fime.com
SIC: 7371 7379 Computer software development; computer related consulting services
HQ: Fime
2 6
Antony 92160
141 984-820

7371 - Custom Computer Programming Svcs County (P-12451)   PRODUCTS & SERVICES SECTION

(P-12451)
FINANCIALFORCECOM INC (DH)
595 Market St Ste 2700, San Francisco (94105-2840)
PHONE..................866 743-2220
Scott Brown, *President*
Natalie Cripe, *Partner*
Aaron Koenderman, *Partner*
Burton M Goldfield, *Ch of Bd*
Joe Fuca, *President*
EMP: 642 **EST:** 2009
SALES (est): 103.9MM
SALES (corp-wide): 257.2K Privately Held
WEB: www.financialforce.com
SIC: 7371 Computer software development

(P-12452)
FINLINK INC (PA)
Also Called: Mbanq
241 Center St Ste B, Healdsburg (95448-4401)
PHONE..................888 999-5467
Vlad Lounegov, *CEO*
Karlo Kosina, *Vice Pres*
Javier Valverde, *Vice Pres*
Lars Rottweiler, *CTO*
EMP: 101 **EST:** 2016
SQ FT: 1,000
SALES (est): 5MM Privately Held
WEB: www.mbanq.com
SIC: 7371 Computer software development

(P-12453)
FIXSTREAM NETWORKS INC
2001 Gateway Pl Ste 520w, San Jose (95110-1065)
PHONE..................408 921-0200
Sameer Padhye, *CEO*
Enzo Signore, *Chief Mktg Ofcr*
Raju Desai, *Vice Pres*
Rosario Greenbaum, *Vice Pres*
Brian Deisenroth, *Regl Sales Mgr*
EMP: 45 **EST:** 2013
SQ FT: 5,500
SALES (est): 8.8MM Privately Held
WEB: www.resolve.io
SIC: 7371 Computer software development
PA: Tech Mahindra Limited
Plot No. 1, Phase Iii
Pune MH 41105

(P-12454)
FLEXON TECHNOLOGIES INC
7901 Stoneridge Dr # 390, Pleasanton (94588-4532)
PHONE..................925 398-8280
Sanjay Madhwal, *President*
Gary Virklon, *Sales Staff*
EMP: 121 **EST:** 2015
SQ FT: 75,000
SALES (est): 9.7MM Privately Held
WEB: www.flexontechnologies.com
SIC: 7371 Computer software development

(P-12455)
FLICKR INC
390 Fremont St, San Francisco (94105-2316)
PHONE..................650 265-0396
Don Makaskill, *CEO*
Eric Willis, *President*
EMP: 50 **EST:** 2018
SALES (est): 3.9MM Privately Held
WEB: www.flickr.com
SIC: 7371 Computer software development & applications

(P-12456)
FLOCK IS INC
350 Townsend St Ste 402, San Francisco (94107-1683)
PHONE..................415 851-2376
Sarvraj Singh, *CEO*
Ketan Deshmukh, *Software Engr*
Sahil Haria, *Marketing Staff*
Kelly Stojka, *Sales Staff*
EMP: 35 **EST:** 2014

SALES (est): 3.2MM
SALES (corp-wide): 3.3B Publicly Held
WEB: www.helloflock.com
SIC: 7371 Computer software development & applications; computer software development
PA: Paychex, Inc.
911 Panorama Trl S
Rochester NY 14625
585 385-6666

(P-12457)
FLUID INC (DH)
1611 Telegraph Ave # 400, Oakland (94612-2150)
PHONE..................877 343-3240
Vanessa Cartwright, *CEO*
Tamir Scheinok, *COO*
Bridget Fahrland, *Vice Pres*
Kyle Montgomery, *Vice Pres*
Antun Karlovac, *Director*
EMP: 56 **EST:** 1990
SQ FT: 7,000
SALES (est): 15MM
SALES (corp-wide): 166.7MM Privately Held
WEB: www.fluidapp.com
SIC: 7371 Computer software development
HQ: Astound Commerce Corporation
1611 Telegraph Ave # 400
Oakland CA 94612
800 591-4710

(P-12458)
FLUXX LABS INC
67 Carmel St, San Francisco (94117-4332)
PHONE..................408 981-7080
Kristy Gannon, *CEO*
Kerrin Mitchell, *COO*
Jill Richards, *Chief Mktg Ofcr*
Denis Brennan, *Executive*
Madeline Duva, *Principal*
EMP: 66 **EST:** 2010
SALES (est): 9.3MM Privately Held
WEB: www.fluxx.io
SIC: 7371 Computer software development

(P-12459)
FLYEX INC
4000 E 3rd Ave Ste 650, Foster City (94404-4830)
PHONE..................650 646-3339
Venkat Pasupuleti, *President*
EMP: 35
SALES (est): 583.1K Privately Held
SIC: 7371 Computer software development & applications

(P-12460)
FORESCOUT TECHNOLOGIES INC (PA)
190 W Tasman Dr, San Jose (95134-1700)
PHONE..................408 213-3191
Wael Mohamed, *CEO*
Theresia Gouw, *Ch of Bd*
Christopher Harms, *CFO*
David G Dewalt, *Vice Ch Bd*
Jason Pishotti, *Ch Credit Ofcr*
EMP: 1108 **EST:** 2000
SQ FT: 95,950
SALES: 336.8MM Privately Held
WEB: www.forescout.com
SIC: 7371 Computer software development

(P-12461)
FORTEX TECHNOLOGIES INC (PA)
203 Rdwood Shres Pkwy Ste, Redwood City (94065)
PHONE..................650 591-8822
Daniel Chen, *President*
Anya Aratovskaya, *Vice Pres*
Richard Perona, *Vice Pres*
Yu Zhi, *Vice Pres*
EMP: 89 **EST:** 2005
SALES (est): 4.6MM Privately Held
WEB: www.fortex.com
SIC: 7371 Computer software development

(P-12462)
FRONT PORCH INC (PA)
905 Mono Way, Sonora (95370-5206)
PHONE..................209 288-5500
Zach Britton, *CEO*
Zachary Britton, *President*
Cheri Oteri, *CEO*
Robert Hohne Jr, *CFO*
Ned Sudduth, *Vice Pres*
▼ **EMP:** 60
SQ FT: 1,022
SALES (est): 8.6MM Privately Held
WEB: www.frontporch.com
SIC: 7371 Computer software development

(P-12463)
FUJITSU AMERICA INC
5000 Executive Pkwy # 290, San Ramon (94583-4210)
PHONE..................925 327-0050
Ron Prather, *Manager*
EMP: 50 Privately Held
WEB: www.fujitsu.com
SIC: 7371 Computer software systems analysis & design, custom
HQ: Fujitsu America Inc
2821 Telecom Pkwy
Richardson TX 75082
408 746-6000

(P-12464)
FULLCONTACT INC
Also Called: Mattermark
535 Mission St Fl 14, San Francisco (94105-3253)
PHONE..................415 366-6587
Alex Lee, *Engineer*
Chris Rodriguez, *Opers Staff*
EMP: 22
SALES (corp-wide): 28.7MM Privately Held
WEB: www.fullcontact.com
SIC: 7371 7372 Computer software development; application computer software
PA: Fullcontact Inc.
1615 Platte St Ste 3-163
Denver CO 80202
888 330-6943

(P-12465)
FULLPOWER TECHNOLOGIES INC
1200 Pacific Ave Ste 300, Santa Cruz (95060-3946)
PHONE..................831 459-0447
Philippe Kahn, *CEO*
Norman Cheung, *CFO*
Benjamin Kohler-Crowe, *Software Engr*
Taylor Stratton, *Technology*
Laura Roppel, *Accountant*
EMP: 36 **EST:** 2005
SQ FT: 130,000
SALES (est): 6.6MM Privately Held
WEB: www.fullpower.com
SIC: 7371 Custom computer programming services

(P-12466)
FULLSTACK LABS LLC (PA)
9719 Village Center Dr # 100, Granite Bay (95746-6499)
PHONE..................415 609-2453
David Jackson, *CEO*
Ricardo Berdejo, *Sr Software Eng*
Jeison Berdugo, *Sr Software Eng*
Shawn Cheng, *Sr Software Eng*
Pablo Cordero, *Sr Software Eng*
EMP: 47 **EST:** 2013
SALES (est): 3.5MM Privately Held
WEB: www.fullstacklabs.co
SIC: 7371 Computer software development

(P-12467)
FUSIONONE INC
55 Almaden Blvd Ste 500, San Jose (95113-1612)
PHONE..................408 282-1200
Mike Mulica, *CEO*
Rick Onyon, *Ch of Bd*
Ed Battle, *CFO*
Jay Burrell, *Exec VP*
Alexander Tsarkov, *Vice Pres*
EMP: 46 **EST:** 1998
SQ FT: 13,000

SALES (est): 1.2MM Publicly Held
WEB: www.synchronoss.com
SIC: 7371 Custom computer programming services
PA: Synchronoss Technologies, Inc.
200 Crossing Blvd Fl 8
Bridgewater NJ 08807

(P-12468)
FUTURE DIAL INCORPORATED
392 Potrero Ave, Sunnyvale (94085-4116)
PHONE..................408 245-8880
George C Huang, *CEO*
Sung L Choi, *President*
Steve Chan, *CEO*
Alejandro Magana, *Chairman*
Christopher Callahan, *Vice Pres*
▲ **EMP:** 80 **EST:** 1999
SQ FT: 8,000
SALES (est): 9.2MM Privately Held
WEB: www.futuredial.com
SIC: 7371 Computer software development

(P-12469)
GAINSIGHT INC
350 Bay St Ste 100, San Francisco (94133-1998)
PHONE..................888 623-8562
Nick Mehta, *CEO*
Igor Beckerman, *CFO*
Dan Steinman, *Ch Credit Ofcr*
Carol Mahoney,
Allison Pickens, *Officer*
EMP: 430 **EST:** 2013
SALES (est): 58.1MM Privately Held
WEB: www.gainsight.com
SIC: 7371 Computer software development; computer software development & applications

(P-12470)
GATSBY INC
2055 Center St Apt 311, Berkeley (94704-1271)
PHONE..................650 468-0587
Samuel Bhagwat, *Principal*
Maddie Wolf, *Vice Pres*
Kyle Mathews, *Principal*
EMP: 50 **EST:** 2017
SALES (est): 2.8MM Privately Held
WEB: www.gatsbyjs.com
SIC: 7371 Computer software development & applications

(P-12471)
GENERAL MOTORS LLC
955 Benecia Ave, Sunnyvale (94085-2805)
PHONE..................408 529-6794
Danny Jiang, *Director*
EMP: 48 Publicly Held
WEB: www.gm.com
SIC: 7371 Computer software development & applications
HQ: General Motors Llc
300 Renaissance Ctr L1
Detroit MI 48243

(P-12472)
GENIUM INC
2955 Campus Dr Ste 110, San Mateo (94403-2563)
PHONE..................415 935-3593
Alexander Ledovskiy, *CEO*
Alex Iceman, *Exec Dir*
EMP: 150 **EST:** 2013
SQ FT: 40,000
SALES (est): 4MM Privately Held
SIC: 7371 8742 Computer software development; human resource consulting services

(P-12473)
GETFEEDBACK INC
1 Curiosity Way, San Mateo (94403-2396)
PHONE..................888 684-8821
Kraig Swensrud, *CEO*
Alan Macdougall, *Software Dev*
Jonathan Unson, *Recruiter*
Jeff Rice, *Sales Staff*
Kenny Zhang, *Sales Staff*
EMP: 60 **EST:** 2013

PRODUCTS & SERVICES SECTION
7371 - Custom Computer Programming Svcs County (P-12494)

SALES (est): 7.5MM
SALES (corp-wide): 375.6MM Publicly Held
WEB: www.getfeedback.com
SIC: 7371 Computer software development & applications
HQ: Momentive Inc.
1 Curiosity Way
San Mateo CA 94403
650 543-8400

(P-12474)
GIGSTER INC
301 Howard St Ste 1800, San Francisco (94105-6614)
PHONE....................941 888-4447
Andy Tryba, CEO
Andy Cuthill, CFO
Chanda Dharap, Vice Pres
Steve Pollock, Vice Pres
Jarad Gilmore, Engineer
EMP: 200 EST: 2013
SALES (est): 10.4MM
SALES (corp-wide): 15.5MM Privately Held
WEB: www.gigster.com
SIC: 7371 Computer software development
PA: Ionic Partners, Llc
500 W 5th St Ste 1010
Austin TX

(P-12475)
GINGERIO INC
116 New Montgomery St # 5, San Francisco (94105-3607)
PHONE....................408 455-0574
Russell Gla, CEO
Karan Singh, COO
Michelle Patruno, Office Mgr
Francisco Saldaa, Software Engr
Tim Wilson, Engineer
EMP: 62 EST: 2011
SALES (est): 6.1MM Privately Held
WEB: www.ginger.io
SIC: 7371 Computer software development & applications

(P-12476)
GLADLY SOFTWARE INC
60 29th St Ste 125, San Francisco (94110-4929)
PHONE....................650 387-8485
Yolanda Ruiz, VP Finance
Bruno Bergher, Vice Pres
Mike McCarron, Vice Pres
Michael Wolfe, Vice Pres
Gemma Ragozzine, Sr Software Eng
EMP: 60 EST: 2014
SALES (est): 3.7MM Privately Held
WEB: www.gladly.com
SIC: 7371 Computer software development

(P-12477)
GLASSBEAM INC
2033 Gateway Pl Ste 658, San Jose (95110-3709)
P.O. Box 610 (95002-0610)
PHONE....................408 740-4600
Puneet Pandit, CEO
Taneli Otala, CTO
Yohan Kim, Business Mgr
David Sawatzke, Marketing Staff
Cheryl Elliott, Manager
EMP: 97 EST: 2004
SALES (est): 5.4MM Privately Held
WEB: www.glassbeam.com
SIC: 7371 Computer software development

(P-12478)
GLOBAL TOUCHPOINTS INC
3017 Douglas Blvd Ste 300, Roseville (95661-3850)
PHONE....................916 878-5954
Naren Kini, CEO
Udayan Chanda, President
Sandhya Shenoy, Treasurer
Seema Chanda, Admin Sec
EMP: 94 EST: 2004
SALES (est): 15MM Privately Held
WEB: www.touchpointsinc.com
SIC: 7371 Computer software development; computer software development & applications; computer systems analysis & design; systems integration services

(P-12479)
GLOBALLOGIC INC (HQ)
1741 Tech Dr Ste 400, San Jose (95110)
PHONE....................408 273-8900
Shashank Samant, CEO
Betsy Atkins, Ch of Bd
Nitesh Banga, COO
Jim Dellamore, COO
Scott Brubaker, CFO
EMP: 213 EST: 2000
SALES (est): 406.5MM Privately Held
WEB: www.globallogic.com
SIC: 7371 7373 7379 Computer software development; systems engineering, computer related; computer related consulting services

(P-12480)
GLOBANT LLC (HQ)
875 Howard St Fl 3, San Francisco (94103-3027)
PHONE....................877 215-5230
Martin Migoya, CEO
Juan Pereyra, Partner
Gabriel Praino, President
Juan Urthiague, CFO
Andres Angelani, Officer
EMP: 543 EST: 2003
SALES (est): 100MM
SALES (corp-wide): 2.6MM Privately Held
WEB: www.globant.com
SIC: 7371 Computer software development

(P-12481)
GONGIO INC
265 Cmbrdge Ave Ste 60717, Palo Alto (94306)
PHONE....................415 412-0214
Amit Bendov, CEO
EMP: 36 EST: 2017
SALES (est): 5.3MM Privately Held
WEB: www.gong.io
SIC: 7371 Computer software development

(P-12482)
GOOD TECHNOLOGY CORPORATION (HQ)
3001 Bishop Dr Ste 400, San Ramon (94583-5005)
PHONE....................408 352-9102
Christy Wyatt, President
Geri Charnin, Partner
Ronald J Fior, CFO
Barry Schuler, Bd of Directors
Lynn Lucas, Chief Mktg Ofcr
EMP: 160 EST: 2014
SQ FT: 80,000
SALES (est): 77.2MM
SALES (corp-wide): 1B Privately Held
WEB: www.blackberry.com
SIC: 7371 7382 Computer software development; protective devices, security
PA: Blackberry Limited
2200 University Ave E
Waterloo ON N2K 0
519 888-7465

(P-12483)
GOOGLE LLC
345 Spear St Fl 2-4, San Francisco (94105-1673)
PHONE....................415 546-3149
Brad Green, Branch Mgr
Lem Diaz, Partner
Amelia Antrim, Sr Software Eng
Angus Kong, Sr Software Eng
Sandeep Dinesh, Software Dev
EMP: 40
SALES (corp-wide): 182.5B Publicly Held
WEB: www.google.com
SIC: 7371 7375 Computer software development & applications; data base information retrieval
HQ: Google Llc
1600 Amphitheatre Pkwy
Mountain View CA 94043
650 253-0000

(P-12484)
GOOGLE LLC (HQ)
1600 Amphitheatre Pkwy, Mountain View (94043-1351)
P.O. Box 2050 (94042-2050)
PHONE....................650 253-0000
Sundar Pichai, CEO
Laura Driussi, Partner
Marina Gardiner, Partner
Obadiah Greenberg, Partner
Scott Beaumont, President
▲ EMP: 250 EST: 1998
SQ FT: 4,800,000
SALES (est): 2.1B
SALES (corp-wide): 182.5B Publicly Held
WEB: www.google.com
SIC: 7371 7375 Computer software development; data base information retrieval
PA: Alphabet Inc.
1600 Amphitheatre Pkwy
Mountain View CA 94043
650 253-0000

(P-12485)
GOVERNMENT APP SOLUTIONS INC
980 9th St Ste 1601, Sacramento (95814-2719)
PHONE....................833 538-2220
Gagan Johal, Principal
William Kroske, Principal
Steven Nguyen, Principal
Paul Sohal, Principal
EMP: 40 EST: 2018
SALES (est): 849.4K Privately Held
SIC: 7371 Computer software development & applications

(P-12486)
GRACENOTE INC (DH)
2000 Powell St Ste 1500, Emeryville (94608-1820)
PHONE....................510 428-7200
Stephen White, President
Amilcar Perez, Officer
Eric Allen, Senior VP
Tal Ball, Senior VP
Desmond Cussen, Senior VP
EMP: 264 EST: 1999
SALES (est): 51.2MM
SALES (corp-wide): 3.3B Privately Held
WEB: www.gracenote.com
SIC: 7371 Software programming applications

(P-12487)
GRAPPA SOFTWARE INC
1470 Civic Ct Ste 309, Concord (94520-5230)
PHONE....................925 818-4760
Mark Fedin, CEO
Elena Florova, Vice Pres
EMP: 52 EST: 2019
SALES (est): 11.5MM Privately Held
SIC: 7371 Computer software development

(P-12488)
GREE INTERNATIONAL INC
275 Battery St Ste 1700, San Francisco (94111-3369)
PHONE....................415 409-5200
Naoki Aoyagi, CEO
Andrew Sheppard, COO
Shanti Bergel, Senior VP
Takeshi Nakano, Director
EMP: 250 EST: 2011
SALES (est): 28MM Privately Held
WEB: www.gree-corp.com
SIC: 7371 Computer software development & applications; computer software systems analysis & design, custom; software programming applications
PA: Gree, Inc.
6-10-1, Roppongi
Minato-Ku TKY 106-0

(P-12489)
GREE INTERNATIONAL ENTRMT INC
185 Berry St Ste 590, San Francisco (94107-9105)
PHONE....................415 409-5200
Andrew Sheppard, CEO
Ryotaro Shima, COO
Shanti Bergel, Senior VP
Yoshikazu Tanaka, Director
EMP: 220 EST: 2016
SALES (est): 16.4MM Privately Held
WEB: www.corp.gree.net
SIC: 7371 Computer software development & applications
PA: Gree, Inc.
6-10-1, Roppongi
Minato-Ku TKY 106-0

(P-12490)
GRID NET INC (PA)
909 Montgomery St Ste 104, San Francisco (94133-4625)
PHONE....................415 419-6632
Ray Bell, CEO
Marck Gorszwick, Engineer
Mark Bowlby, Controller
Dan Laffin, Director
EMP: 47 EST: 2006
SQ FT: 4,000
SALES (est): 5.1MM Privately Held
WEB: www.aetheros.com
SIC: 7371 Software programming applications; computer software development & applications

(P-12491)
GROQ INC
400 Castro St Ste 600, Mountain View (94041-2008)
PHONE....................650 521-9007
Jonathan Ross, CEO
Dinesh Maheshwari, CTO
Sander Arts, Marketing Staff
EMP: 186 EST: 2016
SQ FT: 3,900
SALES (est): 16MM Privately Held
WEB: www.groq.com
SIC: 7371 Computer software development

(P-12492)
GROUP AVANTICA INC
Also Called: Avantica Technologies
2680 Bayshore Pkwy Ste 4, Mountain View (94043-1011)
PHONE....................650 248-9678
Mario Chaves, CEO
Luis C Chaves, President
Marcela Chaverri, CFO
Kenneth Jimnez, Sr Software Eng
Orlando Elizondo, Software Engr
EMP: 48 EST: 2001
SALES (est): 993.3K Privately Held
WEB: www.avantica.com
SIC: 7371 Computer software development

(P-12493)
GT NEXUS INC (DH)
1111 Broadway Ste 700, Oakland (94607-4172)
PHONE....................510 808-2222
Sean Feeney, CEO
Jamie Halloran, Partner
Guy Rey-Herme, COO
Andreas Stinnes, Exec VP
John Urban, Exec VP
EMP: 59 EST: 2015
SALES (est): 16MM
SALES (corp-wide): 36.9B Privately Held
WEB: www.gtnexus.com
SIC: 7371 Computer software development
HQ: Infor, Inc.
641 Ave Of The Americas # 4
New York NY 10011
646 336-1700

(P-12494)
H2OAI INC
Also Called: H2o.ai
2307 Leghorn St, Mountain View (94043-1609)
PHONE....................650 429-8337

7371 - Custom Computer Programming Svcs County (P-12495)

PRODUCTS & SERVICES SECTION

Srisatish Ambati, *CEO*
Allison Washburn, *CEO*
Raman Kapur, *CFO*
Ingrid Burton, *Chief Mktg Ofcr*
David Armstrong, *Senior VP*
EMP: 103 **EST:** 2011
SALES (est): 14.5MM **Privately Held**
WEB: www.h2o.ai
SIC: 7371 Computer software development

(P-12495)
HACKEREARTH INC (PA)
550 Bryant St Ste 2k, San Francisco (94107-1217)
PHONE..........................650 461-4192
Sachin Gupta, *President*
Avinash Kodical, *Sales Staff*
EMP: 118 **EST:** 2014
SALES (est): 11.2MM **Privately Held**
SIC: 7371 Custom computer programming services

(P-12496)
HANDPICK INC (PA)
215 Red Rock Way Apt 206j, San Francisco (94131-1724)
PHONE..........................415 859-8955
Payman Nejati, *CEO*
EMP: 49 **EST:** 2013
SALES (est): 1.5MM **Privately Held**
WEB: www.handpick.com
SIC: 7371 Computer software development

(P-12497)
HASHICORP INC (PA)
101 2nd St Ste 700, San Francisco (94105-3648)
PHONE..........................415 301-3250
Dave McJannet, *CEO*
Eric Schwindt, *Partner*
Scott Raney, *Bd of Directors*
Armon Dadgar, *Officer*
Mitchell Hashimoto, *Officer*
EMP: 1098 **EST:** 2013
SQ FT: 17,881
SALES (est): 69.4MM **Publicly Held**
WEB: www.hashicorp.com
SIC: 7371 Computer software development

(P-12498)
HASHICORP FEDERAL INC
101 2nd St Ste 700, San Francisco (94105-3648)
PHONE..........................415 672-0721
Dave McJannate, *CEO*
Joanna Liu, *Accountant*
EMP: 1000 **EST:** 2020
SALES (est): 11.4MM **Privately Held**
SIC: 7371 Software programming applications

(P-12499)
HELPWARE INC (PA)
548 Market St, San Francisco (94104-5401)
PHONE..........................949 273-2824
Alexander Tereshchenko, *CIO*
EMP: 35 **EST:** 2019
SALES (est): 738.8K **Privately Held**
WEB: www.helpware.com
SIC: 7371 Computer software development & applications

(P-12500)
HEWLETT PACKARD
3000 Hanover St, Palo Alto (94304-1185)
PHONE..........................650 857-1501
EMP: 1835
SALES (est): 98.4MM **Privately Held**
SIC: 7371 Custom Computer Programing

(P-12501)
HONEYBOOK INC
539 Bryant St 200, San Francisco (94107-1269)
PHONE..........................770 403-9234
Oz Eliyahu, *CEO*
John Kramer, *COO*
Tina Hoang-To, *Officer*
Maya Wolkoon, *General Mgr*
Elad Gelman, *Software Engr*
EMP: 55 **EST:** 2012
SALES (est): 1MM **Privately Held**
WEB: www.honeybook.com
SIC: 7371 Computer software development

(P-12502)
HONOR TECHNOLOGY INC (PA)
2151 Salvio St Ste 310, Concord (94520-2460)
PHONE..........................415 999-0555
Seth Sternberg, *CEO*
Jill Dellich, *Partner*
Mara Perman, *Partner*
Juliet Nyatta, *COO*
Mike Price, *Senior VP*
EMP: 64 **EST:** 2014
SALES (est): 102.5MM **Privately Held**
WEB: www.joinhonor.com
SIC: 7371 Computer software development

(P-12503)
HOUZZ INC (PA)
285 Hamilton Ave Fl 4, Palo Alto (94301-2540)
PHONE..........................650 326-3000
ADI Tatarko, *CEO*
Alon Cohen, *President*
Richard Wong, *CFO*
Liza Hausman, *Vice Pres*
Jerry Kingkade, *Vice Pres*
▼ **EMP:** 91 **EST:** 2008
SALES (est): 62.8MM **Privately Held**
WEB: www.houzz.com
SIC: 7371 Computer software development

(P-12504)
HUMANAPI INC
951 Mariners Island Blvd # 300, San Mateo (94404-1560)
PHONE..........................650 542-9800
Andrei Pop, *CEO*
Reuben Reyes, *Software Engr*
Zorah Mardesich, *Technical Staff*
Stephanie Wilson, *Opers Staff*
Cecilia Hewett, *Mng Member*
EMP: 60 **EST:** 2013
SALES (est): 10.6MM **Privately Held**
WEB: www.humanapi.co
SIC: 7371 Computer software development & applications

(P-12505)
HUMU INC (PA)
100 View St Ste 101, Mountain View (94041-1374)
PHONE..........................669 241-4868
Laszlo Bock, *CEO*
Kat Slump, *Software Engr*
Jake Goldwasser, *Manager*
Jessica Wisdom, *Manager*
EMP: 72 **EST:** 2017
SALES (est): 2.2MM **Privately Held**
WEB: www.humu.com
SIC: 7371 Computer software development

(P-12506)
HUSTLE INC
595 Market St Ste 920, San Francisco (94105-2814)
PHONE..........................415 851-4878
Robert Lindsay, *CEO*
Ysiad Ferreiras, *COO*
Zach Fang, *Technology*
Tamilla Mirzoyva, *Marketing Staff*
Gino Donati, *Sales Staff*
EMP: 46 **EST:** 2014
SALES (est): 3.4MM **Privately Held**
WEB: www.hustle.com
SIC: 7371 Computer software development & applications

(P-12507)
HYLAND LLC
12919 Earhart Ave, Auburn (95602-9538)
PHONE..........................440 788-5045
Bill Premier, *CEO*
EMP: 15
SALES (corp-wide): 1.2B **Privately Held**
WEB: www.hyland.com
SIC: 7371 7372 Computer software development; prepackaged software
HQ: Hyland Llc
18103 W 106th St Ste 200
Olathe KS 66061
440 788-5045

(P-12508)
HYPERGRID INC
425 Tasso St, Palo Alto (94301-1545)
PHONE..........................650 316-5524
Manoj Nair, *CEO*
Bob Taccini, *CFO*
Said Syed, *Vice Pres*
Michael Tan, *Vice Pres*
John Kim, *Principal*
EMP: 64 **EST:** 2009
SALES (est): 10.7MM **Privately Held**
WEB: www.cloudsphere.com
SIC: 7371 5045 Computer software development; computers, peripherals & software

(P-12509)
HYTRUST INC (HQ)
1975 W El Cmino Real Ste, Mountain View (94040)
PHONE..........................650 681-8100
John De Santis, *CEO*
Eric Chiu, *President*
Mercy Caprara, *CFO*
Fred Kost, *Senior VP*
Ashwin Krishnan, *Senior VP*
EMP: 67 **EST:** 2007
SQ FT: 12,000
SALES (est): 23.3MM
SALES (corp-wide): 800MM **Privately Held**
WEB: www.hytrust.com
SIC: 7371 Computer software development
PA: Entrust Corporation
1187 Park Pl
Shakopee MN 55379
952 933-1223

(P-12510)
ILLUMIO INC
920 De Guigne Dr, Sunnyvale (94085-3900)
PHONE..........................669 800-5000
Andrew Rubin, *CEO*
Anup Singh, *CFO*
Bobby Guhasarkar, *Chief Mktg Ofcr*
Shay Mowlem, *Chief Mktg Ofcr*
Kathleen Swift, *Officer*
EMP: 140 **EST:** 2012
SALES (est): 11MM **Privately Held**
WEB: www.illumio.com
SIC: 7371 Computer software development

(P-12511)
IMMECOR
1650 Northpoint Pkwy C, Santa Rosa (95407-5043)
PHONE..........................707 636-2550
Hai Giang, *Principal*
Nhon Tran, *Principal*
Shawn Pongkhamsing, *Production*
James Foley, *Sales Staff*
EMP: 36
SALES (est): 1MM **Privately Held**
WEB: www.immecor.com
SIC: 7371 7373 Custom computer programming services; computer integrated systems design

(P-12512)
IMPERVA INC (HQ)
1 Curiosity Way Ste 203, San Mateo (94403-2396)
PHONE..........................650 345-9000
Pam Murphy, *CEO*
Charles Goodman, *Partner*
Mary Spooner, *Partner*
Mike Burns, *CFO*
Nanhi Singh, *Ch Credit Ofcr*
EMP: 864 **EST:** 2002
SALES: 321.7MM **Privately Held**
WEB: www.imperva.com
SIC: 7371 6799 Computer software development; venture capital companies

(P-12513)
IMUSTI INC (PA)
48371 Fremont Blvd # 103, Fremont (94538-6554)
PHONE..........................510 453-1864
Samir Khandwala, *CEO*
Ganesh Laxman, *CTO*
EMP: 54 **EST:** 2010
SALES (est): 1.4MM **Privately Held**
WEB: www.imusti.com
SIC: 7371 Computer software development & applications

(P-12514)
IN FRONT ENTERPRISES
1877 Redwood Rd, Hercules (94547-1336)
P.O. Box 5642 (94547-5642)
PHONE..........................510 799-9018
EMP: 45 **EST:** 1992
SALES (est): 3.4MM **Privately Held**
SIC: 7371 Custom Computer Programing

(P-12515)
INCOGNIA US INC
2479 E Byshore Rd Ste 150, East Palo Alto (94303)
PHONE..........................650 463-9280
Andr Ferraz, *CEO*
Andrie Ferraz, *CEO*
John Lindner, *Risk Mgmt Dir*
EMP: 100
SALES (est): 1.3MM **Privately Held**
WEB: www.incognia.com
SIC: 7371 Software programming applications

(P-12516)
INDUS CORPORATION
1275 Columbus Ave, San Francisco (94133-1301)
PHONE..........................415 202-1830
EMP: 60
SALES (corp-wide): 2.5B **Publicly Held**
SIC: 7371 7372 7373 7379 Provider Of Information Technologies Solutions
HQ: Indus Corporation
1515 Wilson Blvd Ste 1100
Arlington VA 22209
703 506-6700

(P-12517)
INFLUXDATA INC
799 Market St Ste 400, San Francisco (94103-2001)
PHONE..........................415 295-1901
Jim Walsh, *Senior VP*
Brian Mullen, *Vice Pres*
Jonathan Brough, *Executive*
Anders Ranum, *Managing Dir*
Adam Anthony, *Software Dev*
EMP: 105 **EST:** 2012
SALES (est): 7.2MM **Privately Held**
WEB: www.influxdata.com
SIC: 7371 Computer software development

(P-12518)
INFOWORKSIO INC
490 California Ave # 200, Palo Alto (94306-1900)
PHONE..........................408 899-4687
Buno Pati, *CEO*
David Dorman, *Ch of Bd*
Amar Arsikere,
Brian Ferguson, *Vice Pres*
Chid Kollengode, *Vice Pres*
EMP: 55 **EST:** 2014
SALES (est): 3.3MM **Privately Held**
WEB: www.infoworks.io
SIC: 7371 Computer software development

(P-12519)
INFRRD INC
2001 Gateway Pl Ste 301e, San Jose (95110-1012)
PHONE..........................844 446-3773
Amit Jnagal, *CEO*
Anoop Halgeri, *Vice Pres*
EMP: 35 **EST:** 2016
SALES (est): 3MM **Privately Held*
WEB: www.infrrd.ai
SIC: 7371 Computer software systems analysis & design, custom

▲ = Import ▼ = Export
◆ = Import/Export

PRODUCTS & SERVICES SECTION **7371 - Custom Computer Programming Svcs County (P-12541)**

(P-12520)
INNOMEDIA INC
1901 Mccarthy Blvd, Milpitas (95035-7427)
PHONE..................................408 943-8604
Nan-Sheng Lin, *President*
Wymond Choy, *Vice Pres*
Jonah Ninger, *Vice Pres*
Kai WA Ng, *Principal*
Sherwin Lee, *Info Tech Dir*
▲ **EMP:** 38 **EST:** 1995
SQ FT: 23,000
SALES (est): 6.3MM **Privately Held**
WEB: www.innomedia.com
SIC: 7371 4813 Computer software systems analysis & design, custom; computer software development; voice telephone communications

(P-12521)
INNOMINDS SOFTWARE INC (PA)
2055 Junction Ave Ste 122, San Jose (95131-2115)
PHONE..................................408 434-6463
Divakar Tantravahi, *CEO*
Kanakesh Pyla, *Assoc VP*
Manohar Mahavadi, *Senior VP*
SAI P Koppolu, *Vice Pres*
Murali Ramanathan, *Vice Pres*
EMP: 44 **EST:** 1998
SQ FT: 1,100
SALES (est): 15MM **Privately Held**
WEB: www.innominds.com
SIC: 7371 Computer software development

(P-12522)
INNOSYS INCORPORATED
Also Called: Keyspan
1555 3rd Ave, Walnut Creek (94597-2604)
PHONE..................................510 594-1034
Michael Ridenhour, *President*
Vic Pectol, *CFO*
Eric Welch, *Vice Pres*
Risa Baumrind, *Analyst*
EMP: 30 **EST:** 1972
SQ FT: 10,000
SALES (est): 2.5MM **Privately Held**
WEB: www.innosys.com
SIC: 7371 3577 Computer software development; computer peripheral equipment

(P-12523)
INNOVACCER INC (PA)
535 Mission St Fl 18, San Francisco (94105-3256)
PHONE..................................650 479-4891
Deepak Murthy, *President*
David K Nace, *Chief Mktg Ofcr*
David Nace, *Chief Mktg Ofcr*
J Thomas Matthews, *Vice Pres*
Jeff McHugh, *Vice Pres*
EMP: 359 **EST:** 2014
SALES (est): 26.1MM **Privately Held**
WEB: www.innovaccer.com
SIC: 7371 Computer software development

(P-12524)
INSPIRA INC
4125 Blackford Ave # 255, San Jose (95117-1711)
PHONE..................................408 247-9500
Ravindra Gudapati, *President*
Namrata Karmakar, *Manager*
EMP: 42 **EST:** 1997
SQ FT: 2,908
SALES (est): 3.2MM **Privately Held**
WEB: www.inspira.com
SIC: 7371 Software programming applications

(P-12525)
INSTABUG INC
855 El Cmino Real St Ste, Palo Alto (94301)
PHONE..................................650 422-9555
Moataz Soliman, *CTO*
EMP: 65 **EST:** 2013
SALES (est): 3.8MM **Privately Held**
WEB: www.instabug.com
SIC: 7371 Computer software development

(P-12526)
INSTANT SYSTEMS INC
Also Called: Instantsys
447 King Ave, Fremont (94536-1516)
PHONE..................................510 657-8100
Vipin K Chawla, *President*
Uzay Takaoglu, *Vice Pres*
Sweety Gupta, *Software Dev*
Sunal Dhawan, *Software Engr*
Ajay Soni, *Software Engr*
▲ **EMP:** 90 **EST:** 2004
SALES (est): 7MM **Privately Held**
WEB: www.instantsys.com
SIC: 7371 7372 Custom computer programming services; computer software development & applications; business oriented computer software

(P-12527)
INSTART LOGIC INC
3945 Freedom Cir Ste 560, Santa Clara (95054-1269)
PHONE..................................888 576-3166
EMP: 35
SALES (est): 4MM **Privately Held**
SIC: 7371 Computer software development

(P-12528)
INTAPP US INC (HQ)
3101 Park Blvd, Palo Alto (94306-2233)
PHONE..................................650 852-0400
John Hall, *CEO*
Stuart Douglass, *President*
Daniel Harsell, *President*
Kelvyn Stirk, *President*
Dan Tacone, *President*
EMP: 200 **EST:** 2005
SALES: 186.8MM
SALES (corp-wide): 214.6MM **Publicly Held**
WEB: www.intapp.com
SIC: 7371 7372 Computer software development & applications; business oriented computer software
PA: Intapp, Inc.
3101 Park Blvd
Palo Alto CA 94306
650 852-0400

(P-12529)
INTELENEX INC (HQ)
2455 Bennett Valley Rd C2, Santa Rosa (95404-5663)
PHONE..................................415 367-4871
David Krauthamer, *Partner*
Jared Willson, *COO*
EMP: 50 **EST:** 2005
SQ FT: 32,008
SALES (est): 4.8MM
SALES (corp-wide): 148.8MM **Publicly Held**
WEB: www.emtecinc.com
SIC: 7371 Computer software development
PA: Emtec, Inc.
9454 Philips Hwy Ste 8
Jacksonville FL 32256
973 376-4242

(P-12530)
INTELLISWIFT SOFTWARE INC (PA)
Also Called: Magagnini
39600 Balentine Dr # 200, Newark (94560-5304)
PHONE..................................510 490-9240
Parag Patel, *CEO*
Keyur Karnik, *Vice Pres*
Mahesh Shinde, *Executive*
Bob Patel, *Principal*
Anna Ashcraft, *Regional Mgr*
EMP: 225 **EST:** 2001
SQ FT: 5,200
SALES (est): 42.5MM **Privately Held**
WEB: www.intelliswift.com
SIC: 7371 Computer software development

(P-12531)
INTELLISYNC CORPORATION (HQ)
313 Fairchild Dr, Mountain View (94043-2215)
PHONE..................................650 625-2185
Woodson Hobbs, *President*
Clyde Foster, *COO*
David Eichler, *CFO*
Robert Gerber, *Chief Mktg Ofcr*
Blair Hankins, *Technology*
EMP: 55 **EST:** 1993
SQ FT: 33,821
SALES (est): 26.3MM
SALES (corp-wide): 25.8B **Privately Held**
WEB: www.nokia.com
SIC: 7371 7372 Computer software development; prepackaged software
PA: Nokia Oyj
Karakaari 7
Espoo 02610
104 488-000

(P-12532)
INTERCOM INC
55 2nd St Fl 4, San Francisco (94105-4560)
PHONE..................................831 920-7088
Eoghan McCabe, *CEO*
Des Traynor, *Officer*
Paul Adams, *Vice Pres*
Richard Archbold, *Vice Pres*
Gabriel Madureira, *Vice Pres*
EMP: 300 **EST:** 1983
SALES (est): 25.9MM **Privately Held**
WEB: www.intercom.com
SIC: 7371 Computer software development

(P-12533)
INTERNATIONAL BUS MCHS CORP
Also Called: IBM
555 Bailey Ave, San Jose (95141-1003)
PHONE..................................408 463-2000
Lou Gerstner, *Manager*
Kevin Foster, *Partner*
Jeffrey Fara, *Executive*
Peter Whitney, *Executive*
Qiuhong Sun, *Software Engr*
EMP: 1500
SALES (corp-wide): 73.6B **Publicly Held**
WEB: www.ibm.com
SIC: 7371 7372 5961 Computer software development; prepackaged software; catalog & mail-order houses
PA: International Business Machines Corporation
1 New Orchard Ste 1 # 1
Armonk NY 10504
914 499-1900

(P-12534)
INTERNATIONAL MICRO DESIGN INC
Also Called: Health Financial Systems
8109 Laguna Blvd, Elk Grove (95758-7946)
PHONE..................................888 216-6041
Rebecca Dolin, *CEO*
Chuck Briggs, *Officer*
Linda Briggs, *Vice Pres*
Eric Swanson, *General Mgr*
EMP: 44 **EST:** 1983
SALES (est): 3.8MM **Privately Held**
WEB: www.hfssoft.com
SIC: 7371 Computer software writing services

(P-12535)
INTERTRUST TECHNOLOGIES CORP (PA)
920 Stewart Dr, Sunnyvale (94085-3921)
PHONE..................................408 616-1600
Talal G Shamoon, *CEO*
Anahita Poonegar, *Chief Mktg Ofcr*
David P Maher, *Exec VP*
Tim Schaaff, *Exec VP*
Gilles Boccon Gibod, *Senior VP*
EMP: 45 **EST:** 1990
SQ FT: 58,000
SALES (est): 20.7MM **Privately Held**
WEB: www.intertrust.com
SIC: 7371 Computer software development; computer software development & applications

(P-12536)
INTIME INFOTECH INC
39962 Cedar Blvd Ste 185, Newark (94560-5326)
PHONE..................................650 396-4319
EMP: 47
SALES (corp-wide): 9.3MM **Privately Held**
WEB: www.intime-info.com
SIC: 7371 Custom computer programming services
PA: Intime Infotech Inc
4490 Ladner St
Fremont CA 94538
510 449-9965

(P-12537)
INTRINSYX TECHNOLOGIES CORP
350 N Akron Rd M S 19 102 Ms, Moffett Field (94035)
PHONE..................................650 210-9220
Arshad Mian, *CEO*
Dr Ghazala Mian, *CFO*
EMP: 42 **EST:** 2000
SQ FT: 600
SALES (est): 1.1MM **Privately Held**
WEB: www.intrinsyx.com
SIC: 7371 Computer software development

(P-12538)
IPTOR SUPPLY CHAIN SYSTEMS USA (DH)
Also Called: I B S
915 Highland Pointe Dr # 250, Roseville (95678-5419)
PHONE..................................916 542-2820
Doug Braun, *CEO*
Christian Paulsson, *COO*
Fredrik Sandelin, *CFO*
David Rode, *Vice Pres*
Hiten Varia, *Vice Pres*
EMP: 153 **EST:** 1978
SQ FT: 55,000
SALES (est): 48.2MM
SALES (corp-wide): 7.8B **Privately Held**
WEB: www.iptor.com
SIC: 7371 5045 Computer software development; computer software
HQ: Iptor Supply Chain Systems Ab
Hemvarnsgatan 11
Solna 171 5
862 723-00

(P-12539)
IRDETO USA INC (DH)
3255 Scott Blvd Ste 3-101, Santa Clara (95054-3012)
PHONE..................................818 508-2313
Barry Douglas Coleman, *CEO*
Loefie Engelbrecht, *President*
Gram Kill, *President*
Keddy Perry, *President*
Osama Hussain, *Officer*
EMP: 63 **EST:** 2000
SALES (est): 20.7MM **Privately Held**
WEB: www.irdeto.com
SIC: 7371 Computer software development

(P-12540)
IRONCLAD INC (PA)
71 Stevenson St Ste 600, San Francisco (94105-2966)
PHONE..................................855 999-4766
Jason Boehmig, *CEO*
Jen Paau, *COO*
Jennifer Paau, *COO*
Leyla Seka, *COO*
Helen Wang, *CFO*
EMP: 163 **EST:** 2014
SALES (est): 16.2MM **Privately Held**
WEB: www.ironcladapp.com
SIC: 7371 Computer software development & applications

(P-12541)
ISCS INC
100 Great Oaks Blvd # 100, San Jose (95119-1462)
PHONE..................................408 362-3000
Andy J Scurto, *President*
Myron Meier, *President*
Andy Scurto, *President*
Tim Shelton, *CFO*
Larry Chlebeck, *Vice Pres*
EMP: 201 **EST:** 1994
SQ FT: 11,000

7371 - Custom Computer Programming Svcs County (P-12542)

SALES (est): 29.4MM
SALES (corp-wide): 743.2MM **Publicly Held**
WEB: www.guidewire.com
SIC: 7371 Software programming applications
PA: Guidewire Software, Inc.
2850 S Del St Ste 400
San Mateo CA 94403
650 357-9100

(P-12542)
ISHERIFF INC
555 Twin Dolphin Dr # 135, Redwood City (94065-2129)
PHONE..................650 412-4300
Paul Lipman, *CEO*
Jon Botter, *President*
Eric Jenny, *CFO*
Marcus Smith, *CFO*
James Socas, *Chairman*
EMP: 235 EST: 2011
SALES (est): 29.1MM **Privately Held**
WEB: www.isheriff.com
SIC: 7371 Software programming applications
PA: Mimecast Uk Limited
Floor 4
London

(P-12543)
IVALUA INC (HQ)
805 Veterans Blvd Ste 203, Redwood City (94063-1736)
PHONE..................650 930-9710
Daniel Olivier Amzallag, *CEO*
John McAdoo, *CFO*
Alex Saric, *Chief Mktg Ofcr*
Amol Joshi, *Vice Pres*
Dawn Gershinzon, *Executive*
EMP: 38 EST: 2001
SQ FT: 4,000
SALES (est): 21.3MM
SALES (corp-wide): 62.2MM **Privately Held**
WEB: www.ivalua.com
SIC: 7371 Computer software development
PA: Ivalua
102 Avenue De Paris
Massy 91300
164 865-454

(P-12544)
IX LAYER INC
440 N Wolfe Rd, Sunnyvale (94085-3869)
PHONE..................408 594-7586
Pouria Sanae, *CEO*
EMP: 48 EST: 2017
SALES (est): 6.9MM **Privately Held**
WEB: www.ixlayer.com
SIC: 7371 Computer software development

(P-12545)
IXSYSTEMS INC (PA)
Also Called: Ix Systems
2490 Kruse Dr, San Jose (95131-1234)
PHONE..................408 943-4100
Mike Lauth, *CEO*
Andrew Madrid, *COO*
Valerie Burniece, *CFO*
Morgan Littlewood, *Senior VP*
Matt Finney, *Vice Pres*
EMP: 59 EST: 1991
SQ FT: 20,000
SALES (est): 36.5MM **Privately Held**
WEB: www.ixsystems.com
SIC: 7371 Computer software development

(P-12546)
JETSTREAM SOFTWARE INC
2550 N 1st St Ste 420, San Jose (95131-1038)
PHONE..................408 766-1775
Anthony Lai, *Mng Member*
Atoka Sema, *Software Engr*
Kun Lu, *Engineer*
Glenn Skinner, *Engineer*
EMP: 45 EST: 2018
SALES (est): 2.6MM **Privately Held**
WEB: www.jetstreamsoft.com
SIC: 7371 Computer software development

(P-12547)
JIANGSU JUWANG INFO TECH CO (PA)
195 Recino St, Fremont (94539-3835)
PHONE..................510 967-3729
Song Han, *Owner*
EMP: 45 EST: 2014
SALES (est): 2.2MM **Privately Held**
SIC: 7371 Computer software development & applications

(P-12548)
JIFF INC (HQ)
150 Spear St Ste 400, San Francisco (94105-1500)
PHONE..................415 829-1400
Mike Leonard, *Exec VP*
Matt Kirchstein, *Sr Software Eng*
Ed Lopez, *Technology*
Masooma Badar, *Controller*
Lisa Giacinti, *Director*
EMP: 400 EST: 2011
SALES (est): 108.6MM **Publicly Held**
WEB: www.castlighthealth.com
SIC: 7371 Computer software development

(P-12549)
JIGHI INC
2005 De La Cruz Blvd # 295, Santa Clara (95050-3031)
PHONE..................408 332-1262
Mack Coulibaly, *CEO*
Karim Arana, *Principal*
EMP: 41 EST: 2012
SALES (est): 2.5MM **Privately Held**
WEB: www.jighi.com
SIC: 7371 8748 8742 7379 Computer software development; telecommunications consultant; management information systems consultant; computer related consulting services;

(P-12550)
JOVEO INC (PA)
1047 Whipple Ave Ste B, Redwood City (94062-1414)
PHONE..................408 896-9030
Kshitij Jain, *CEO*
Kevin Bunce, *Partner*
Krishna Gopal Bajpai, *CFO*
Jim Dwyer, *Vice Pres*
Shehzad Karkhanawala, *Vice Pres*
EMP: 51 EST: 2016
SQ FT: 3,000
SALES (est): 5.1MM **Privately Held**
WEB: www.joveo.com
SIC: 7371 Computer software development

(P-12551)
JUMIO CORPORATION (HQ)
395 Page Mill Rd Ste 150, Palo Alto (94306-2067)
PHONE..................650 424-8545
Robert Prigge, *CEO*
Kenton Chow, *CFO*
Colby Moosman, *CFO*
Bala Kumar, *Officer*
Christian Schwaiger, *Officer*
EMP: 35 EST: 2016
SALES (est): 30.6MM
SALES (corp-wide): 30.7MM **Privately Held**
WEB: www.jumio.com
SIC: 7371 Computer software development
PA: Jumio Holdings, Inc.
2711 Centerville Rd # 400
Wilmington DE 19808
650 424-8545

(P-12552)
JUMPSHOT INC
333 Bryant St Ste 240, San Francisco (94107-1443)
P.O. Box 78071 (94107-8071)
PHONE..................415 212-9250
Deren Baker, *CEO*
Hong Tsui, *Vice Pres*
Michael Perlman, *Risk Mgmt Dir*
Chris Wasik, *Controller*
Jessica Miranda, *Human Resources*
EMP: 85 EST: 2015
SALES (est): 6.1MM **Privately Held**
SIC: 7371 Computer software development

(P-12553)
KABAM INC (HQ)
575 Market St Ste 2450, San Francisco (94105-2896)
PHONE..................604 256-0054
Seungwon Lee, *President*
Nick Earl, *President*
Jangwon Seo, *CFO*
Paxton R Cooper, *Senior VP*
Doug Inamine, *Senior VP*
EMP: 645 EST: 2006
SALES (est): 120.7MM **Privately Held**
WEB: www.kabam.com
SIC: 7371 Computer software development & applications

(P-12554)
KAIZEN TECHNOLOGY PARTNERS LLC
981 Mission St, San Francisco (94103-2912)
PHONE..................415 515-1909
Lori Jensen, *Partner*
Ted Ritchie, *Info Tech Dir*
Cassell Tim, *VP Opers*
Arthur Chambers, *Mng Member*
Dao Jensen, *Mng Member*
EMP: 20 EST: 2013
SALES (est): 5.8MM **Privately Held**
WEB: www.oakrocket.com
SIC: 7371 7372 8748 Computer software systems analysis & design, custom; business oriented computer software; systems engineering consultant, ex. computer or professional

(P-12555)
KALLIDUS INC
Also Called: Skava
555 Mission St Ste 1950, San Francisco (94105-0924)
PHONE..................877 554-2176
Arish Ali, *President*
Khurram Khan, *Officer*
Jeanne Mariani, *Vice Pres*
Gaurav Mahajan, *Program Mgr*
Gretchen Jones, *Executive Asst*
EMP: 100 EST: 2002
SALES (est): 10.9MM **Privately Held**
WEB: www.infosys.com
SIC: 7371 Computer software development
PA: Infosys Limited
Plot No. 44 & 97a, Electronics City
Bengaluru KA 56010

(P-12556)
KANRAD TECHNOLOGIES INC
4340 Stevens Creek Blvd, San Jose (95129-1102)
PHONE..................408 615-8880
Sundar Kannan, *President*
Swami Nathan, *Vice Pres*
EMP: 35 EST: 1997
SALES (est): 3.1MM **Privately Held**
WEB: www.kantime.com
SIC: 7371 Computer software development

(P-12557)
KAZEON SYSTEMS INC
2841 Mission College Blvd, Santa Clara (95054-1838)
PHONE..................650 641-8100
Fax: 650 641-8195
EMP: 80
SQ FT: 24,000
SALES (est): 3.9MM **Privately Held**
WEB: www.kazeon.com
SIC: 7371 7379 Custom Computer Programing Computer Related Services

(P-12558)
KEEP TRUCKIN INC (PA)
55 Hawthorne St Ste 400, San Francisco (94105-3910)
PHONE..................855 434-3564
Shoaib Makani, *CEO*
Obaid Khan, *President*
Brice Kittinger, *Executive*
Chandrika Iyer, *Sr Software Eng*
Brindha Ramasamy, *Sr Software Eng*
EMP: 50 EST: 2013
SALES (est): 80MM **Privately Held**
WEB: www.keeptruckin.com
SIC: 7371 Computer software development & applications

(P-12559)
KEY BUSINESS SOLUTIONS INC (PA)
4738 Duckhorn Dr, Sacramento (95834-2592)
PHONE..................916 646-2080
Rajan Gutta, *President*
Malou Catanyag, *Technical Staff*
Naresh Chowdary, *Opers Staff*
EMP: 48 EST: 1999
SQ FT: 1,000
SALES (est): 4.9MM **Privately Held**
WEB: www.keybusinessglobal.com
SIC: 7371 Computer software systems analysis & design, custom

(P-12560)
KMS TECHNOLOGY INC (PA)
6098 Kingsmill Ter, Dublin (94568-7778)
PHONE..................925 828-1906
Vu Lam, *President*
Uyen Le, *Executive*
Kaushal Amin, *CTO*
Dat Quach, *Technology*
EMP: 36 EST: 2009
SALES (est): 768K **Privately Held**
WEB: www.kms-technology.com
SIC: 7371 Computer software development

(P-12561)
KONG INC
Also Called: Kong Hq
251 Post St Ste 200, San Francisco (94108-5021)
PHONE..................415 754-9283
Harriet K Rohde, *CEO*
Ken Kim, *VP Bus Dvlpt*
Jeremy Balian, *General Mgr*
Marco Palladino, *CTO*
Maria Bujold, *Opers Staff*
EMP: 38 EST: 1978
SALES (est): 3.3MM **Privately Held**
WEB: www.konghq.com
SIC: 7371 Computer software development

(P-12562)
KONG INC
150 Spear St Ste 1600, San Francisco (94105-1541)
PHONE..................415 754-9283
Augusto Marietti, *CEO*
Reza Shafii, *Vice Pres*
Richard Barnes, *CIO*
Darren Jennings, *Technician*
Hernando Buitrago, *Opers Staff*
EMP: 50 EST: 2009
SALES (est): 5.7MM **Privately Held**
WEB: www.konghq.com
SIC: 7371 Computer software development

(P-12563)
KPI PARTNERS INC
39899 Balentine Dr # 375, Newark (94560-5355)
PHONE..................510 818-9480
Kusal Swarnaker, *President*
Sid Goel, *Partner*
Vikas Agrawal, *Vice Pres*
EMP: 45 EST: 2007
SQ FT: 200
SALES (est): 8.1MM **Privately Held**
WEB: www.kpipartners.com
SIC: 7371 Computer software development

(P-12564)
KRISH COMPUSOFT SERVICES INC
1525 Mccarthy Blvd # 212, Milpitas (95035-7451)
PHONE..................855 527-7890
Parthive Zaveri, *CEO*
Vishal Shukla, *CEO*
Parthiv Zaveri, *Manager*
EMP: 200 EST: 2012
SQ FT: 550

PRODUCTS & SERVICES SECTION
7371 - Custom Computer Programming Svcs County (P-12586)

SALES: 1MM **Privately Held**
WEB: www.kcsitglobal.com
SIC: 7371 7379 Computer software development; computer related consulting services
PA: Krish Compusoft Services Private Limited
  801, Pelican House , Gcci Compound Ahmedabad GJ 38000

(P-12565)
KUGGA INC
  1841 Sunnyvale Ave, Walnut Creek (94597-1811)
  PHONE 925 639-0721
  Yifan Ren, *CEO*
EMP: 60 **EST:** 2017
SALES (est): 1.2MM **Privately Held**
SIC: 7371 Computer software development & applications

(P-12566)
LADDER FINANCIAL INC
  555 University Ave, Palo Alto (94301-1911)
  P.O. Box 456, Menlo Park (94026-0456)
  PHONE 844 533-7206
  Jamie Hale, *President*
  Christine Lara, *Accounting Mgr*
  Ken Quan, *Director*
EMP: 35 **EST:** 2015
SALES (est): 5MM **Privately Held**
WEB: www.ladderlife.com
SIC: 7371 7372 Computer software development & applications; software programming applications; application computer software

(P-12567)
LANDACORP INC
  500 Orient St Ste 110, Chico (95928-5672)
  PHONE 530 891-0853
  Rishabh Mehrotra, *CEO*
  Mark Rapoport, *COO*
  Marlene McCurdy, *Senior VP*
  Brandon Raines, *Senior VP*
EMP: 27 **EST:** 1999
SQ FT: 21,000
SALES (est): 1MM
SALES (corp-wide): 958.4MM **Publicly Held**
WEB: www.landacorp.com
SIC: 7371 7379 7372 Computer software development; computer related consulting services; prepackaged software
PA: Exlservice Holdings, Inc.
  320 Park Ave Fl 29
  New York NY 10022
  212 277-7100

(P-12568)
LARK TECHNOLOGIES INC
  2570 W El Cmino Real Ste, Mountain View (94040)
  PHONE 650 300-1750
  Julia Hu, *CEO*
  Dave Fiore, *CFO*
  Rosemary Ku, *Chief Mktg Ofcr*
  Vadim Axelrod, *Vice Pres*
  Kevin Delury, *Vice Pres*
EMP: 53 **EST:** 2010
SALES (est): 5.7MM **Privately Held**
WEB: www.lark.com
SIC: 7371 Software programming applications

(P-12569)
LARSON AUTOMATION INC
  960 Rincon Cir, San Jose (95131-1313)
  PHONE 408 432-4800
  Wayne Larson, *President*
  Cecilia Gold, *Office Mgr*
  Homer Jones, *Administration*
  Darren Schwald, *Engineer*
  Robert Mitchell, *Consultant*
EMP: 55 **EST:** 1993
SQ FT: 2,850
SALES (est): 5.5MM **Privately Held**
WEB: www.larsonautomation.com
SIC: 7371 Computer software development

(P-12570)
LAXMI GROUP INC
  Also Called: Importers Software
  4701 Patrick Henry Dr # 25, Santa Clara (95054-1863)
  PHONE 408 329-7733
EMP: 60
SALES (est): 6.4MM **Privately Held**
SIC: 7371 7363 Custom Computer Programming Services, Nsk

(P-12571)
LEANTAAS INC
  471 El Cmino Real Ste 230, Santa Clara (95050)
  PHONE 650 409-3501
  Mohan Giridharadas, *CEO*
  Lloyd Martin, *CFO*
  Michael Concordia, *Vice Pres*
  Kelly Brambila, *Office Mgr*
  Brad Ledbetter, *Sr Software Eng*
EMP: 171 **EST:** 2010
SQ FT: 500
SALES (est): 20MM **Privately Held**
WEB: www.leantaas.com
SIC: 7371 Computer software development

(P-12572)
LEAPYEAR TECHNOLOGIES INC
  612 Howard St, San Francisco (94105-3905)
  PHONE 510 542-9193
  Colton Jang, *Administration*
  Ishaan Nerurkar, *CEO*
  Richard Barber, *Vice Pres*
  Christopher Hockenbrocht, *Chief Engr*
  Enrique Salem, *President*
EMP: 50 **EST:** 2016
SALES (est): 5.1MM **Privately Held**
WEB: www.leapyear.io
SIC: 7371 7372 Computer software systems analysis & design, custom; business oriented computer software

(P-12573)
LEVER INC
  1125 Mission St, San Francisco (94103-1514)
  PHONE 415 458-2731
  Sarah Nahm, *CEO*
  Laura Marino, *Senior VP*
  Mike Bailen, *Vice Pres*
  Jessica Green, *Vice Pres*
  Kenneth Choo, *Executive*
EMP: 100
SALES (est): 10MM **Privately Held**
WEB: www.lever.co
SIC: 7371 Computer software development & applications

(P-12574)
LIGHTBEND INC
  625 Market St Ste 1000, San Francisco (94105-3312)
  PHONE 877 989-7372
  Mark Brewer, *Ch of Bd*
  Hywel Evans, *Partner*
  Steve Bean, *CFO*
  Martin Odersky, *Chairman*
  Jonas Bon R, *Officer*
EMP: 72 **EST:** 2010
SALES (est): 12.6MM **Privately Held**
WEB: www.lightbend.com
SIC: 7371 Computer software development

(P-12575)
LILT INC (PA)
  550 15th St Ste 39, San Francisco (94103-5032)
  P.O. Box 20391, Palo Alto (94309-0391)
  PHONE 650 530-7180
  William Green, *CEO*
  Zack Kass, *Vice Pres*
  Meredith Chandler, *Executive*
  Josephine Pang, *Opers Staff*
  Katherine Przybus, *Manager*
EMP: 78 **EST:** 2015
SALES (est): 6MM **Privately Held**
WEB: www.lilt.com
SIC: 7371 Computer software development

(P-12576)
LINDEN RESEARCH INC
  Also Called: Linden Lab
  945 Battery St, San Francisco (94111-1305)
  P.O. Box 2374 (94126-2374)
  PHONE 415 243-9000
  Ebbe Altberg, *CEO*
  Bill Gurley, *Partner*
  Bob Komin, *COO*
  Malcolm Dunne, *CFO*
  John Zdanowski, *CFO*
EMP: 330 **EST:** 1999
SALES (est): 39.9MM **Privately Held**
WEB: www.lindenlab.com
SIC: 7371 Computer software development

(P-12577)
LIVERMORE SOFTWARE TECH LLC (HQ)
  7374 Las Positas Rd, Livermore (94551-5110)
  P.O. Box 712 (94551-0712)
  PHONE 925 449-2500
  John Hallquist, *CEO*
  Russell Sims, *Principal*
  Nathan Hallquist, *CTO*
  Jennifer Xu, *Info Tech Mgr*
  Philip Ho, *Webmaster*
EMP: 96 **EST:** 1987
SALES (est): 9.9MM
SALES (corp-wide): 1.6B **Publicly Held**
WEB: www.ansys.com
SIC: 7371 8742 Computer software development; industry specialist consultants
PA: Ansys, Inc.
  2600 Ansys Dr
  Canonsburg PA 15317
  724 746-3304

(P-12578)
LOC-AID TECHNOLOGIES INC (PA)
  Also Called: Locaid
  101 Clay St, San Francisco (94111-2033)
  PHONE 415 666-2370
  Rip Gerber, *President*
  Thomas Stahl, *COO*
  Carolyn Hodge, *Chief Mktg Ofcr*
  David Allen, *Senior VP*
  Jeff Allyn, *Senior VP*
EMP: 41 **EST:** 2005
SALES (est): 10.8MM **Privately Held**
WEB: www.locationsmart.com
SIC: 7371 Computer software development

(P-12579)
LOCALMIND CORP
  300 Brannan St Ste 201, San Francisco (94107-1870)
  PHONE 858 382-4809
  Lenny Rachitsky, *CEO*
  Beau Haugh, *CTO*
EMP: 1830 **EST:** 2011
SALES (est): 248.1K
SALES (corp-wide): 3.3B **Publicly Held**
WEB: www.airbnb.com
SIC: 7371 Computer software systems analysis & design, custom
PA: Airbnb, Inc.
  888 Brannan St Fl 3
  San Francisco CA 94103
  415 510-4027

(P-12580)
LOGIGEAR CORPORATION (PA)
  Also Called: Softgear Technologies
  1730 S Amphlett Blvd, San Mateo (94402-2707)
  PHONE 650 572-1400
  Hung Nguyen, *President*
  Laura Fese, *Vice Pres*
  Michael Hackett, *Vice Pres*
  Pranav Mundi, *Vice Pres*
  Sunny Nair, *Vice Pres*
EMP: 559 **EST:** 1996
SALES (est): 37.1MM **Privately Held**
WEB: www.logigear.com
SIC: 7371 Computer software development

(P-12581)
LOHIKA SYSTEMS INC
  1825 S Grant St Ste 400, San Mateo (94402-7039)
  PHONE 650 636-6993
  Daniel Dargham, *President*
  Michael Makishima, *CFO*
  Valentyna Stetska, *Engineer*
EMP: 65 **EST:** 2001
SALES (est): 7.9MM
SALES (corp-wide): 387.8MM **Privately Held**
WEB: www.lohika.com
SIC: 7371 Computer software development
HQ: Altran Technologies
  76 Avenue Kleber
  Paris 75116

(P-12582)
LOOKER DATA SCIENCES INC (DH)
  101 Church St Fl 4, Santa Cruz (95060-3963)
  PHONE 831 244-0340
  Frank Bien, *CEO*
  Lloyd Tabb, *Ch of Bd*
  Rob Ward, *Bd of Directors*
  Nick Caldwell,
  Pedro Arellano, *Vice Pres*
EMP: 56 **EST:** 2012
SALES (est): 17.9MM
SALES (corp-wide): 182.5B **Publicly Held**
WEB: www.looker.com
SIC: 7371 Custom computer programming services
HQ: Google Llc
  1600 Amphitheatre Pkwy
  Mountain View CA 94043
  650 253-0000

(P-12583)
LUCAS LEARNING LTD
  5858 Lucas Valley Rd, Nicasio (94946-9703)
  PHONE 415 662-1927
  Gordon Radley, *President*
  George Lucas, *Ch of Bd*
  Micheline Chau, *CFO*
EMP: 37 **EST:** 1996
SALES (est): 5.1MM
SALES (corp-wide): 65.3B **Publicly Held**
WEB: www.edutopia.org
SIC: 7371 Computer software development
HQ: Lucasfilm Ltd.
  1110 Gorgas Ave Bldg C-Hr
  San Francisco CA 94129
  415 623-1000

(P-12584)
LUCID VR INC (PA)
  63 Bettencourt Way, Milpitas (95035-4141)
  PHONE 408 391-0506
  Han Jin, *CEO*
  Adam Rowell, *CTO*
EMP: 78 **EST:** 2015
SALES (est): 5.4MM **Privately Held**
WEB: www.lucidinside.com
SIC: 7371 Computer software development

(P-12585)
LUMA HEALTH INC
  3 E 3rd Ave, San Mateo (94401-4279)
  PHONE 415 741-3377
  Adnan Iqbal, *CEO*
  Marina Hardof, *CFO*
  Tashfeen Ekram, *Chief Mktg Ofcr*
  Ramesh Munnangi, *Business Dir*
  Aditya Bansod, *CTO*
EMP: 50 **EST:** 2015
SALES (est): 5MM **Privately Held**
WEB: www.lumahealth.io
SIC: 7371 Software programming applications

(P-12586)
LUMEDX CORPORATION (PA)
  555 12th St Ste 2060, Oakland (94607-3695)
  PHONE 510 419-1000
  Allyn Mc Auley, *President*
  Laurel Shearer, *Exec VP*

7371 - Custom Computer Programming Svcs County (P-12587)

PRODUCTS & SERVICES SECTION

Corkey Christensen, *Vice Pres*
Cheryl Iseberg, *Vice Pres*
Gwen Korney, *Vice Pres*
EMP: 18 **EST:** 1984
SQ FT: 15,000
SALES (est): 11.6MM **Privately Held**
WEB: www.lumedx.com
SIC: 7371 7372 Computer software development; prepackaged software

(P-12587)
LUMIN DIGITAL LLC
3001 Bishop Dr Ste 110, San Ramon (94583-5005)
PHONE................................727 561-2227
Charles Fagan III,
Brian Caldarelli,
Jeff Chambers,
EMP: 95 **EST:** 2019
SALES (est): 1MM **Privately Held**
WEB: www.pscu.com
SIC: 7371 Computer software development

(P-12588)
LUMINA NETWORKS INC (PA)
2077 Gateway Pl Ste 500, San Jose (95110-1085)
PHONE................................800 430-7321
Andrew Coward, *CEO*
Nitin Serro, *COO*
Benjamin Hickey, *Ch Credit Ofcr*
Ben Hickey, *Officer*
Raj Serro, *Exec VP*
EMP: 26 **EST:** 2017
SQ FT: 17,000
SALES (est): 2.4MM **Privately Held**
WEB: www.luminanetworks.com
SIC: 7371 7372 Software programming applications; business oriented computer software

(P-12589)
M NEXON INC
6121 Hollis St Ste 6, Emeryville (94608-2078)
PHONE................................805 448-3351
EMP: 65 **EST:** 2011
SALES (est): 4.1MM **Privately Held**
WEB: www.nexon.com
SIC: 7371 Software programming applications

(P-12590)
MAANA INC (PA)
524 Hamilton Ave Ste 201, Palo Alto (94301-2079)
PHONE................................888 956-2262
Babur Ozden, *CEO*
Mandi Browning, *Executive Asst*
Nova Chamberlain, *Opers Mgr*
Julia Ochinero, *VP Mktg*
Chase Westlye, *Manager*
EMP: 97 **EST:** 2012
SALES (est): 510.5K **Privately Held**
WEB: www.sparkcognition.com
SIC: 7371 Computer software development

(P-12591)
MACHINE ZONE INC (HQ)
Also Called: Epic War
1050 Page Mill Rd, Palo Alto (94304-1019)
PHONE................................650 320-1678
Kristen Dumont, *CEO*
Tony Koinov, *President*
Eric Brown, *CFO*
Dan Nash, *CFO*
Deepak Gupta, *Officer*
EMP: 73 **EST:** 2008
SALES (est): 20.1MM **Publicly Held**
WEB: www.mz.com
SIC: 7371 Computer software development

(P-12592)
MAGMA DESIGN AUTOMATION INC (HQ)
1650 Tech Dr Ste 100, San Jose (95110)
PHONE................................408 565-7500
Rajeev Madhavan, *CEO*
Noriaki Kikuchi, *President*
Peter S Teshima, *CFO*
Saiyed Atiq Raza, *Bd of Directors*
Gregory C Walker, *Senior VP*
▲ **EMP:** 410 **EST:** 1997

SQ FT: 106,854
SALES (est): 66.8MM
SALES (corp-wide): 3.6B **Publicly Held**
WEB: www.synopsys.com
SIC: 7371 7373 Computer software development; computer integrated systems design
PA: Synopsys, Inc.
690 E Middlefield Rd
Mountain View CA 94043
650 584-5000

(P-12593)
MAKERSIGHTS INC
435 Pacific Ave Ste 350, San Francisco (94133-4662)
PHONE................................415 658-7709
Matthew Field, *President*
Amy Sullivan, *Vice Pres*
Mike Mullins, *Engineer*
EMP: 40 **EST:** 2016
SALES (est): 2.6MM **Privately Held**
WEB: www.makersights.com
SIC: 7371 Computer software development

(P-12594)
MAPLELABS INC
1248 Reamwood Ave, Sunnyvale (94089-2225)
PHONE................................408 743-4414
Pramod Murthy, *President*
EMP: 190 **EST:** 2014
SALES (est): 6MM **Privately Held**
WEB: www.maplelabs.com
SIC: 7371 Custom computer programming services
PA: Xoriant Corporation
1248 Reamwood Ave
Sunnyvale CA 94089

(P-12595)
MARKETO INC (DH)
901 Mariners Island Blvd # 200, San Mateo (94404-1573)
PHONE................................650 376-2300
Steve Lucas, *CEO*
Jane Truch, *Partner*
Jamie Anderson, *President*
Kate Fitzgerald, *President*
Brady Holcomb, *President*
EMP: 739 **EST:** 2006
SQ FT: 102,670
SALES (est): 169.9MM
SALES (corp-wide): 12.8B **Publicly Held**
WEB: www.marketo.com
SIC: 7371 7372 Computer software development; prepackaged software
HQ: Milestone Holdco, Inc.
901 Mariners Island Blvd
San Mateo CA 94404
650 376-2300

(P-12596)
MARKLOGIC CORPORATION (PA)
999 Skyway Rd Ste 200, San Carlos (94070-2722)
PHONE................................650 655-2300
Jeffrey Casale, *CEO*
Peter Norman, *CFO*
David Ponzini, *Exec VP*
Stephen Buxton, *Vice Pres*
Adrian Carr, *Vice Pres*
EMP: 435 **EST:** 2004
SQ FT: 40,000
SALES (est): 294.2MM **Privately Held**
WEB: www.marklogic.com
SIC: 7371 Computer software development

(P-12597)
MARVEL PARENT LLC (HQ)
1950 University Ave # 350, East Palo Alto (94303-2250)
PHONE................................650 321-4910
Scott E Landers, *President*
EMP: 50 **EST:** 2019
SALES (est): 246.7MM
SALES (corp-wide): 562.3MM **Privately Held**
WEB: www.hggc.com
SIC: 7371 7372 Custom computer programming services; prepackaged software

PA: Hggc, Llc
1950 University Ave # 350
East Palo Alto CA 94303
650 321-4910

(P-12598)
MATTERMOST INC (PA)
530 Lytton Ave Fl 2, Palo Alto (94301-1541)
PHONE................................650 667-8512
Ian Tien, *CEO*
Ken Olofsen, *Vice Pres*
Steve Green, *General Mgr*
Tim Quock, *Finance Dir*
Hanna Park, *Opers Staff*
EMP: 123 **EST:** 2011
SALES (est): 13MM **Privately Held**
WEB: www.mattermost.com
SIC: 7371 Computer software development

(P-12599)
MAXIMUM GAMES INC (PA)
590 Ygnacio Valley Rd # 220, Walnut Creek (94596-3889)
PHONE................................925 708-3242
Christina Seelye, *CEO*
Thierry Bonnefoi, *CFO*
Shane Bierwith, *Exec VP*
Derek Neal, *Vice Pres*
Steve Powell, *Managing Dir*
EMP: 22 **EST:** 2009
SQ FT: 2,500
SALES (est): 3.5MM **Privately Held**
WEB: www.maximumgames.com
SIC: 7371 3944 Custom computer programming services; video game machines, except coin-operated

(P-12600)
MAXPLORE TECHNOLOGIES INC
4450 Rosewood Dr Ste 200, Pleasanton (94588-3061)
PHONE................................925 621-1400
Sam Mukherjee, *Principal*
EMP: 100 **EST:** 2011
SALES (est): 1.7MM **Privately Held**
SIC: 7371 Computer software development

(P-12601)
MEDIAJEL INC (PA)
1601 N Main St Ste 101, Walnut Creek (94596-4685)
PHONE................................925 393-0444
Jacob Litke, *CEO*
Sadie Reyes, *President*
Chris Andrews, *Officer*
Guillermo Bravo, *Officer*
Ben Malone, *Vice Pres*
EMP: 39 **EST:** 2017
SALES (est): 500K **Privately Held**
WEB: www.mediajel.com
SIC: 7371 Computer software development & applications

(P-12602)
MEMVERGE INC
1525 Mccarthy Blvd # 218, Milpitas (95035-7453)
PHONE................................408 605-0841
Charles Fan, *CEO*
Yue LI, *CTO*
Frank Berry, *VP Mktg*
EMP: 60 **EST:** 2017
SALES (est): 3.8MM **Privately Held**
WEB: www.memverge.com
SIC: 7371 Computer software development

(P-12603)
MENLO SECURITY INC (PA)
800 W El Cmino Real Ste 2, Mountain View (94040)
PHONE................................650 614-1705
Amir Ben-Efraim, *CEO*
Todd Vender, *President*
David Eckstein, *CFO*
Young-SAE Song, *Chief Mktg Ofcr*
Lennart Van Den Ende, *Vice Pres*
EMP: 74 **EST:** 2006
SALES (est): 13.1MM **Privately Held**
WEB: www.menlosecurity.com
SIC: 7371 7382 Computer software development; security systems services

(P-12604)
METASWITCH NETWORKS
1751 Harbor Bay Pkwy # 125, Alameda (94502-3001)
PHONE................................415 513-1500
John Lazar, *CEO*
Thomas L Cronan III, *CFO*
Roger Heinz, *Officer*
Graeme Macarthur, *Exec VP*
Chris Todd, *Exec VP*
EMP: 50 **EST:** 2008
SALES (est): 8.6MM
SALES (corp-wide): 722.7K **Privately Held**
WEB: www.metaswitch.com
SIC: 7371 Computer software development
HQ: Metaswitch Limited
33 Genotin Road
Enfield MIDDX EN1 2
208 366-1177

(P-12605)
METREO INC
3500 W Bayshore Rd, Palo Alto (94303-4228)
PHONE................................650 935-9400
Dafney Carmeli, *President*
Craig Harding, *Corp Secy*
John Dionisio, *Vice Pres*
Kelly Ireland, *Vice Pres*
Pamela Kline Smith, *VP Mktg*
EMP: 665 **EST:** 2000
SQ FT: 10,000
SALES (est): 1.5MM
SALES (corp-wide): 191.2MM **Privately Held**
WEB: www.metreo.com
SIC: 7371 Computer software development
PA: Symphony Technology Group, L.L.C.
428 University Ave
Palo Alto CA 94301
650 935-9500

(P-12606)
MIGHTYHIVE INC (HQ)
394 Pacific Ave Ste B100, San Francisco (94111-1712)
PHONE................................888 727-9742
Peter Kim, *CEO*
Jayne Babine, *Partner*
Christopher S Martin, *COO*
Christopher Martin, *Bd of Directors*
Leah Kim, *Chief Mktg Ofcr*
EMP: 79 **EST:** 2012
SALES (est): 30MM
SALES (corp-wide): 455.6MM **Privately Held**
WEB: www.mightyhive.com
SIC: 7371 8742 7311 Computer software development; marketing consulting services; advertising agencies

(P-12607)
MINDSOURCE INC
995 Montague Expy Ste 121, Milpitas (95035-6827)
PHONE................................650 314-6400
David Clark, *President*
Gabriel Meza, *CFO*
Puneet Sehgal, *Business Dir*
Victor Kumar, *Tech Recruiter*
Sowmya Gullapalli, *Technical Staff*
EMP: 55 **EST:** 1994
SALES (est): 5.4MM **Privately Held**
WEB: www.mindsource.com
SIC: 7371 7372 Computer software development; application computer software

(P-12608)
MINERVA NETWORKS INC (PA)
1600 Technology Dr Fl 8, San Jose (95110-1382)
PHONE................................800 806-9594
Mauro Bonomi, *President*
Dr Jean-Georges Fritsch, *COO*
Mike Davies, *CFO*
John Doerner, *CFO*
John Campos, *Vice Pres*
EMP: 99 **EST:** 1992
SQ FT: 25,600
SALES (est): 15.8MM **Privately Held**
WEB: www.minervanetworks.com
SIC: 7371 Software programming applications

PRODUCTS & SERVICES SECTION
7371 - Custom Computer Programming Svcs County (P-12630)

(P-12609)
MINIO INC
530 University Ave Ste B, Palo Alto (94301-1935)
PHONE 844 356-4646
Anand Babu Periasamy, *CEO*
Garima Kapoor, *CFO*
Jonathan Symonds, *Chief Mktg Ofcr*
Daniel Valdivia, *Engineer*
EMP: 42 **EST:** 2014
SALES (est): 2.9MM **Privately Held**
WEB: www.min.io
SIC: 7371 Computer software development

(P-12610)
MIRROR PLUS TECHNOLOGIES INC
Also Called: ARC USA
45545 Northport Loop E, Fremont (94538-6461)
PHONE 510 403-2400
Rahul Roy, *President*
EMP: 90 **EST:** 1996
SALES (est): 2.1MM
SALES (corp-wide): 289.4MM **Publicly Held**
WEB: www.ryansallans.com
SIC: 7371 Computer software development
HQ: American Reprographics Company, L.L.C.
1981 N Broadway Ste 385
Walnut Creek CA 94596
925 949-5100

(P-12611)
MISTRAL SOLUTIONS INC (HQ)
Also Called: Mistral Software
43092 Christy St, Fremont (94538-3183)
PHONE 408 705-2240
Anees Ahmed, *CEO*
Satish RAO, *Business Dir*
Ashish Singh, *General Mgr*
Thejas Gupta, *Business Mgr*
Raja Subramanian, *Manager*
EMP: 85 **EST:** 2001
SQ FT: 1,700
SALES (est): 7.4MM **Privately Held**
WEB: www.mistralsolutions.com
SIC: 7371 Computer software development

(P-12612)
MIXPANEL INC (PA)
1 Front St Ste 2800, San Francisco (94111-5385)
PHONE 415 688-4001
Suhail M Doshi, *President*
Meka Asonye, *Vice Pres*
Michelle Denman, *Vice Pres*
Cassie Gamm, *Vice Pres*
Andy Boyer, *Executive*
EMP: 49 **EST:** 2009
SALES (est): 20.7MM **Privately Held**
WEB: www.mixpanel.com
SIC: 7371 Computer software systems analysis & design, custom; computer software development & applications

(P-12613)
MOBACK INC
226 Airport Pkwy Ste 320, San Jose (95110-3700)
PHONE 510 565-6672
Devkumar R Gandhi, *CEO*
Vijay Kumar, *VP Bus Dvlpt*
Uday Nayak, *General Mgr*
EMP: 45 **EST:** 2012
SALES (est): 3MM **Privately Held**
WEB: www.moback.com
SIC: 7371 5045 Computer software development; accounting machines using machine readable programs

(P-12614)
MOBILEDGEX INC (HQ)
333 W San Carlos St # 600, San Jose (95110-2731)
PHONE 707 364-8830
Jason Hoffman, *CEO*
Leah Maher, *CFO*
Ulf Andersson, *Senior VP*
Lev Shvarts, *Software Engr*
Vikram Siwach, *Manager*
EMP: 50 **EST:** 2017
SALES (est): 20MM
SALES (corp-wide): 119.4B **Privately Held**
WEB: www.mobiledgex.com
SIC: 7371 Computer software development
PA: Deutsche Telekom Ag
Friedrich-Ebert-Allee 140
Bonn NW 53113
228 181-0

(P-12615)
MODIS INC
1750 Creekside Oaks Dr # 225, Sacramento (95833-3647)
PHONE 800 467-4448
Stefanie Janof, *Branch Mgr*
Salvatore Arrigo, *Manager*
James Chow, *Manager*
EMP: 179
SALES (corp-wide): 775.3MM **Privately Held**
WEB: www.modis.com
SIC: 7371 Computer software systems analysis & design, custom
HQ: Modis, Inc.
10151 Deerwood Park Blvd
Jacksonville FL 32256
904 360-2300

(P-12616)
MODIS INC
135 Main St Ste 1040, San Francisco (94105-1818)
PHONE 415 896-5566
Michael Terozzi, *Branch Mgr*
Cori Luu, *Manager*
EMP: 179
SALES (corp-wide): 775.3MM **Privately Held**
WEB: www.modis.com
SIC: 7371 Computer software systems analysis & design, custom
HQ: Modis, Inc.
10151 Deerwood Park Blvd
Jacksonville FL 32256
904 360-2300

(P-12617)
MODIS INC
2055 Gateway Pl Ste 300, San Jose (95110-1015)
PHONE 408 441-7144
Steven Ranson, *Director*
Lane Greever, *Senior VP*
Jeffrey Marts, *Vice Pres*
Todd Weneck, *Vice Pres*
Justin Mas, *Managing Dir*
EMP: 179
SALES (corp-wide): 775.3MM **Privately Held**
WEB: www.modis.com
SIC: 7371 Computer software systems analysis & design, custom
HQ: Modis, Inc.
10151 Deerwood Park Blvd
Jacksonville FL 32256
904 360-2300

(P-12618)
MOJIO USA INC
300 Orchard Cy Dr Ste 100, Campbell (95008)
PHONE 604 868-0804
Kenny Hawk, *CEO*
Shannon Rusk, *Controller*
Carlos Beccar, *Marketing Staff*
Karlo Ilagan, *Manager*
Vishal Karnik, *Manager*
EMP: 40 **EST:** 2014
SALES (est): 4MM **Privately Held**
WEB: www.moj.io
SIC: 7371 Computer software development

(P-12619)
MOMENTIVE GLOBAL INC
3050 S Delaware St, San Mateo (94403-2392)
PHONE 503 225-1202
EMP: 727
SALES (corp-wide): 375.6MM **Publicly Held**
WEB: www.surveymonkey.com
SIC: 7371 Custom computer programming services; custom computer programming services; computer software systems analysis & design, custom; computer software writing services
PA: Momentive Global Inc.
1 Curiosity Way
San Mateo CA 94403
650 543-8400

(P-12620)
MOMENTIVE GLOBAL INC (PA)
Also Called: Surveymonkey
1 Curiosity Way, San Mateo (94403-2396)
PHONE 650 543-8400
Alexander Lurie, *CEO*
David A Ebersman, *Ch of Bd*
Thomas E Hale, *President*
Justin Coulombe, *CFO*
Lora D Blum,
EMP: 580 **EST:** 1999
SQ FT: 199,000
SALES (est): 375.6MM **Publicly Held**
WEB: www.surveymonkey.com
SIC: 7371 Custom computer programming services; custom computer programming services; computer software systems analysis & design, custom; computer software writing services

(P-12621)
MOTION MATH INC
582 Market St Ste 511, San Francisco (94104-5306)
PHONE 415 590-2961
Jacob Klein, *CEO*
Gabriel Adauto, *CTO*
EMP: 772 **EST:** 2010
SALES (est): 1MM
SALES (corp-wide): 587.7MM **Privately Held**
WEB: www.curriculumassociates.com
SIC: 7371 Computer software development & applications
PA: Curriculum Associates, Llc
153 Rangeway Rd
North Billerica MA 01862
978 667-8000

(P-12622)
MOVOCASH INC
530 Lytton Ave Fl 2, Palo Alto (94301-1541)
PHONE 650 722-3990
Eric A Solis, *CEO*
Charles Young, *Opers Staff*
EMP: 50 **EST:** 2014
SALES (est): 5.4MM **Privately Held**
WEB: www.movo.cash
SIC: 7371 Computer software development

(P-12623)
MOZILLA FOUNDATION (PA)
2 Harrison St Ste 175, San Francisco (94105-6130)
PHONE 650 903-0800
Mark Surman, *CEO*
Joanne Nagel, *Partner*
Jascha Kaykas-Wolff, *Chief Mktg Ofcr*
Ashley Boyd, *Vice Pres*
Deborah N Cohen, *Vice Pres*
EMP: 288 **EST:** 2003
SALES (est): 28.3MM **Privately Held**
WEB: www.mozilla.org
SIC: 7371 Computer software development

(P-12624)
MROADIE LLC
721 Colorado Ave Ste 101, Palo Alto (94303-3973)
PHONE 650 300-4320
Artem Kozel, *Mng Member*
Maksym Bezzub,
EMP: 35 **EST:** 2015
SALES (est): 1.4MM **Privately Held**
WEB: www.mobileroadie.com
SIC: 7371 Computer software development & applications

(P-12625)
MSHIFT INC
39899 Balentine Dr # 235, Newark (94560-5358)
PHONE 408 437-2740
Scott Moeller, *CEO*
Jeff Chen, *Vice Pres*
Alan Finke, *Vice Pres*
Jacqueline Snell, *Vice Pres*
Tien Ha, *Administration*
EMP: 50 **EST:** 1999
SALES (est): 5.5MM **Privately Held**
WEB: www.mshift.com
SIC: 7371 Computer software development & applications

(P-12626)
N MODEL INC (PA)
Also Called: Model N
777 Mariners Island Blvd, San Mateo (94404-5008)
PHONE 650 610-4600
Jason Blessing, *CEO*
Baljit Dail, *Ch of Bd*
John Ederer, *CFO*
Suresh Kannan,
Laura Selig, *Officer*
EMP: 482 **EST:** 1999
SQ FT: 35,000
SALES (est): 161MM **Publicly Held**
WEB: www.modeln.com
SIC: 7371 Computer software development; computer software development & applications

(P-12627)
NETBASE SOLUTIONS INC (PA)
Also Called: Netbase Quid
3945 Freedom Cir Ste 730, Santa Clara (95054-1272)
PHONE 650 810-2100
Peter M Caswell, *CEO*
Bob Goodson, *President*
Bob Ciccone, *COO*
David Pefley, *CFO*
Paige Leidig, *Chief Mktg Ofcr*
EMP: 138 **EST:** 2004
SALES (est): 29MM **Privately Held**
WEB: www.netbasequid.com
SIC: 7371 Computer software development

(P-12628)
NETPULSE INC (PA)
560 Fletcher Dr, Atherton (94027-6414)
PHONE 415 643-0223
Bryan Arp, *CEO*
Thomas Proulx, *Chairman*
Alex Peacock, *Vice Pres*
Kelly Caviglia, *Marketing Staff*
Neil Tejwani, *Manager*
EMP: 46 **EST:** 2001
SALES (est): 5.1MM **Privately Held*
WEB: www.egym.com
SIC: 7371 4813 Computer software development;

(P-12629)
NEURON FUEL INC
Also Called: Tynker
280 Hope St, Mountain View (94041-1308)
PHONE 408 537-3966
Srivinas Mandyam, *CTO*
Krishna Vidati, *CEO*
Brandon Aragones, *Sales Staff*
Kevin Elgan, *Director*
EMP: 25 **EST:** 2011
SALES (est): 2.7MM **Privately Held**
WEB: www.tynker.com
SIC: 7371 7372 Computer software development; educational computer software

(P-12630)
NEUSTAR INC
300 Lakeside Dr Ste 1500, Oakland (94612-3553)
PHONE 510 500-1000
Ted Prince, *Vice Pres*
Jose Delgado, *Financial Analy*
Andrew Chan, *Director*
Oscar Moncada, *Accounts Mgr*
EMP: 39

7371 - Custom Computer Programming Svcs County (P-12631)

SALES (corp-wide): 606.2MM **Privately Held**
WEB: www.home.neustar
SIC: **7371** 7379 Computer software development; computer related consulting services
HQ: Neustar, Inc.
 1906 Reston Metro Plz # 5
 Reston VA 20190
 571 434-5400

(P-12631)
NINTHDECIMAL INC (PA)
150 Post St Ste 500, San Francisco (94108-4720)
PHONE.................................415 264-1849
Michael Fordyce, *CEO*
David Staas, *President*
Jeff Stephens, *CFO*
Amy Caplan, *Senior VP*
Brian Kilmer, *Senior VP*
EMP: 110 EST: 2003
SQ FT: 7,487
SALES (est): 16.5MM **Privately Held**
WEB: www.ninthdecimal.com
SIC: **7371** Computer software development

(P-12632)
NISUM TECHNOLOGIES INC
71 Stevenson St Ste 446, San Francisco (94105-2934)
PHONE.................................714 619-7989
EMP: 603
SALES (corp-wide): 23.4MM **Privately Held**
WEB: www.nisum.com
SIC: **7371** Computer software development
PA: Nisum Technologies, Inc.
 500 S Kraemer Blvd # 301
 Brea CA
 714 579-7979

(P-12633)
NISUM TECHNOLOGIES INC
46231 Landing Pkwy, Fremont (94538-6407)
PHONE.................................714 579-7979
EMP: 603
SALES (corp-wide): 23.4MM **Privately Held**
WEB: www.nisum.com
SIC: **7371** Computer software development
PA: Nisum Technologies, Inc.
 500 S Kraemer Blvd # 301
 Brea CA
 714 579-7979

(P-12634)
NITRO SOFTWARE INC
150 Spear St Ste 1850, San Francisco (94105-1564)
PHONE.................................415 632-4894
Sam Chandler, *President*
Gina O Reilly, *COO*
Peter Bardwick, *CFO*
Bardwick Peter, *CFO*
Richard Wenzel, *Treasurer*
▼ EMP: 125 EST: 2007
SALES (est): 26MM **Privately Held**
WEB: www.gonitro.com
SIC: **7371** Computer software development
PA: Nitro Software Limited
 Level 7 330 Collins Street
 Melbourne VIC 3000

(P-12635)
NIXEL INC
2225 E Byshore Rd Ste 200, Palo Alto (94303)
PHONE.................................650 618-9516
EMP: 35
SALES (est): 583.1K **Privately Held**
SIC: **7371** Custom Computer Programing

(P-12636)
NOMIS SOLUTIONS INC (PA)
611 Gateway Blvd Fl 2, South San Francisco (94080-7040)
PHONE.................................650 588-9800
Frank Rohde, *CEO*
Johnathan Bant, *Partner*

Christopher Mondfrans, *CFO*
Richard Whittow, *CFO*
Stephen Clark, *Chief Mktg Ofcr*
▼ EMP: 108 EST: 2002
SALES (est): 37.4MM **Privately Held**
WEB: www.nomissolutions.com
SIC: **5734** 7371 Software, business & non-game; computer software development & applications

(P-12637)
NOODLE ANALYTICS INC
Also Called: Noodle.ai
115 Sansome St Fl 8, San Francisco (94104-3609)
PHONE.................................415 412-2139
Stephen Pratt, *CEO*
Gail Moody-Byrd, *Chief Mktg Ofcr*
Deepinder Dhingra,
Chelsea Hardaway, *Officer*
Steve Moskovitz, *Marketing Staff*
EMP: 100 EST: 2016
SALES (est): 10MM **Privately Held**
WEB: www.noodle.ai
SIC: **7371** Computer software development & applications

(P-12638)
NOREDINK CORP
118 2nd St Fl 3, San Francisco (94105-3620)
PHONE.................................617 308-4549
EMP: 76
SALES (est): 323K **Privately Held**
WEB: www.noredink.com
SIC: **7371** Custom Computer Programing

(P-12639)
NTT CLOUD INFRASTRUCTURE INC (DH)
Also Called: Dimension Data Cloud
5201 Great America Pkwy, Santa Clara (95054-1122)
PHONE.................................408 567-2000
Graham McNeill Jefferson, *CEO*
Ray Solnik, *President*
Bryan Tolls, *CFO*
Richard Dym, *Chief Mktg Ofcr*
Don Green, *Senior VP*
EMP: 75 EST: 2002
SALES (est): 32.1MM **Privately Held**
WEB: www.dimensiondata.com
SIC: **7371** Computer software development

(P-12640)
NUNA INCORPORATED
Also Called: Nuna Health
370 Townsend St, San Francisco (94107-1607)
PHONE.................................415 942-5200
Jini Kim, *CEO*
Michael Stephenson, *Officer*
Mark Krempley, *Top Exec*
Louise Briguglio, *Vice Pres*
Neil Austin, *Business Dir*
EMP: 100 EST: 2010
SQ FT: 25,000 **Privately Held**
WEB: www.nuna.com
SIC: **7371** Computer software development

(P-12641)
OBERON MEDIA INC (PA)
1100 La Avenida St Ste A, Mountain View (94043-1453)
PHONE.................................646 367-2020
David Lebow, *CEO*
Tal Kerret, *Ch of Bd*
Bob Hayes, *COO*
Don Ryan, *COO*
Pat Barry, *CFO*
EMP: 98 EST: 2003
SQ FT: 24,000
SALES (est): 25.6MM **Privately Held**
WEB: www.iwin.com
SIC: **7371** Computer software development

(P-12642)
OBJECTIVE SYSTEMS INTEGRATORS (HQ)
Also Called: OSI
2365 Iron Point Rd # 170, Folsom (95630-8713)
PHONE.................................916 467-1500

Mounir Ladki, *Principal*
Bob Franzetta, *CFO*
Cheri Simko, *Vice Pres*
Gene McKinlay, *Business Dir*
Bill Burdgick, *Sr Software Eng*
EMP: 50 EST: 1996
SQ FT: 14,000
SALES (est): 37.9MM
SALES (corp-wide): 4.6MM **Privately Held**
WEB: www.mycom-osi.com
SIC: **7371** Computer software development

(P-12643)
OC ACQUISITION LLC (HQ)
500 Oracle Pkwy, Redwood City (94065-1677)
PHONE.................................650 506-7000
Dorian Daley, *President*
Brian Kerr, *Partner*
Eric Ball, *Treasurer*
Nora O 'leary-roseb, *Software Dev*
James Cheng, *Software Engr*
EMP: 53 EST: 2011
SALES (est): 1.4B
SALES (corp-wide): 40.4B **Publicly Held**
WEB: www.oracle.com
SIC: **7371** 7372 Computer software development; business oriented computer software
PA: Oracle Corporation
 2300 Oracle Way
 Austin TX 78741
 737 867-1000

(P-12644)
ODOO INC
250 Executive Park Blvd # 3400, San Francisco (94134-3349)
PHONE.................................650 691-3277
Fabrice Henrion, *President*
Alessandro Mazzocchetti, *CFO*
Elizabeth Sanchez, *Executive*
Phuong Luu, *Security Dir*
Antony Lesuisse, *CTO*
EMP: 46 EST: 2015
SALES (est): 8.2MM
SALES (corp-wide): 51.8MM **Privately Held**
WEB: www.odoo.com
SIC: **7371** Computer software development
PA: Odoo
 Chaussee De Namur 40
 Ramillies 1367
 818 137-00

(P-12645)
ONBOARDIQ INC
Also Called: Fountain
275 Sacramento St Ste 300, San Francisco (94111-3855)
PHONE.................................480 433-1197
Sean Behr, *President*
Rachel Weinstein, *Marketing Staff*
Ian Powell, *Accounts Exec*
EMP: 60 EST: 2014
SALES (est): 10MM **Privately Held**
WEB: www.get.fountain.com
SIC: **7371** Custom computer programming services

(P-12646)
ONDOT SYSTEMS INC
1731 Tech Dr Ste 700, San Jose (95110)
PHONE.................................408 316-2379
Bharghavan Vaduvur, *CEO*
Nathan Lali, *CFO*
Cathy Wilkins, *Manager*
EMP: 40 EST: 2015
SALES (est): 10.5MM
SALES (corp-wide): 14.8B **Publicly Held**
WEB: www.ondotsystems.com
SIC: **7371** Computer software systems analysis & design, custom
HQ: Ondot Systems India Private Limited
 No.3155, Srinivasam Tower, 3rd Floor, Bengaluru KA 56003

(P-12647)
ONE INC SOFTWARE CORPORATION (PA)
620 Coolidge Dr Ste 200, Folsom (95630-3183)
PHONE.................................866 343-6940
Christopher W Ewing, *President*
Tim Tyannikov, *COO*
Sarah Owen,
Steve Hall, *Vice Pres*
Krystyna Kravchuk, *Vice Pres*
EMP: 218 EST: 2009
SALES (est): 28.5MM **Privately Held**
WEB: www.oneinc.com
SIC: **7371** Custom computer programming services

(P-12648)
ONFLEET INC
703 Market St Fl 20, San Francisco (94103-2102)
PHONE.................................650 283-7547
Khaled Naim, *CEO*
Mikel Carmenes, *Principal*
Elissa Malmquist, *Manager*
EMP: 71 EST: 2012
SALES (est): 7MM **Privately Held**
WEB: www.onfleet.com
SIC: **7371** Computer software development

(P-12649)
OOMNITZA INC (PA)
414 Brannan St, San Francisco (94107-1714)
PHONE.................................415 525-3949
Arthur Lozinski, *CEO*
Ettehad Ramin, *VP Bus Dvlpt*
Tung Isaac, *Software Engr*
Julia Thomas, *Manager*
Lorin Bartlett, *Accounts Exec*
EMP: 68 EST: 2014
SALES (est): 2.5MM **Privately Held**
WEB: www.oomnitza.com
SIC: **7371** Computer software development & applications

(P-12650)
OOYALA INC (HQ)
2099 Gateway Pl Ste 600, San Jose (95110-1048)
PHONE.................................650 961-3400
Jonathan Huberman, *CEO*
Jay Fulcher, *President*
Duane Bell, *CFO*
David Wilson, *CFO*
Jeremy Cath, *Vice Pres*
EMP: 494 EST: 2007
SALES (est): 107.6MM **Privately Held**
WEB: www.ooyala.dalet.com
SIC: **7371** Software programming applications
PA: Ooyala Holdings, Inc.
 2099 Gateway Pl Ste 600
 San Jose CA 95110
 650 961-3400

(P-12651)
OPEN TEXT INC (HQ)
Also Called: Hightail
2950 S Delaware St # 400, San Mateo (94403-2580)
PHONE.................................650 645-3000
Michael Delaney, *Partner*
Louis Goldner, *Partner*
Jacquie Ebert, *Vice Chairman*
Mark J Barrenechea, *CEO*
Gordon Davies, *Officer*
EMP: 109 EST: 1989
SALES (est): 519.2MM
SALES (corp-wide): 3.1B **Privately Held**
WEB: www.opentext.com
SIC: **7371** Computer software development
PA: Open Text Corporation
 275 Frank Tompa Dr
 Waterloo ON N2L 0
 519 888-7111

(P-12652)
OPENMIND TECHNOLOGIES INC (PA)
3984 Washington Blvd # 183, Fremont (94538-4954)
PHONE.................................866 536-2324

▲ = Import ▼ =Export
◆ =Import/Export

PRODUCTS & SERVICES SECTION **7371 - Custom Computer Programming Svcs County (P-12676)**

Kiran Bharatsingh Bhalla, *CEO*
Pankaj Bhasin, *General Mgr*
Joe Fernandes, *Technical Staff*
Dave Anu, *Manager*
EMP: 65 EST: 2005
SALES (est): 530.1K Privately Held
WEB: www.openmindtechno.com
SIC: 7371 8742 7373 Computer software development; computer software systems analysis & design, custom; computer software development & applications; software programming applications; management consulting services; systems software development services

(P-12653)
OPINR INC
Also Called: Vetted
20824 Pamela Way, Saratoga (95070-6031)
PHONE..................646 207-3000
Jagmeet Lamba, *CEO*
Dudley Brundige, *CFO*
Jared Ezzell, *Ch Credit Ofcr*
EMP: 60 EST: 2013
SALES (est): 6.5MM Privately Held
WEB: www.getcerta.com
SIC: 7371 8742 Computer software systems analysis & design, custom; computer software development & applications; management consulting services

(P-12654)
OPSHUB INC
1000 Elwell Ct Ste 101, Palo Alto (94303-4306)
PHONE..................650 701-1800
Sandeep Jain, *CEO*
Ranjana Prashar, *Finance*
EMP: 31 EST: 2010
SALES (est): 564.6K Privately Held
WEB: www.opshub.com
SIC: 7371 7372 Computer software development; prepackaged software; application computer software

(P-12655)
ORACLE CORPORATION
75 Hawthorne St Ste 2000, San Francisco (94105-3919)
PHONE..................415 541-9462
Julian J Brandes, *Principal*
Eugene Flyash, *Director*
EMP: 200
SALES (corp-wide): 40.4B Publicly Held
WEB: www.oracle.com
SIC: 7371 8748 Custom computer programming services; business consulting
PA: Oracle Corporation
    2300 Oracle Way
    Austin TX 78741
    737 867-1000

(P-12656)
ORGANZTONAL PRFMCE SYSTEMS INC
Also Called: Ops1
1393 Oak Ave, Los Altos (94024-5768)
PHONE..................650 968-7032
James J Hill Jr, *CEO*
Aiko Hill, *CFO*
Tom Moore, *Vice Pres*
Kie Hill, *Accounts Exec*
EMP: 35 EST: 2003 Privately Held
WEB: www.ops1.com
SIC: 7371 7379 8741 7374 Computer software development; computer related consulting services; administrative management; data processing & preparation

(P-12657)
ORIDUS INC
46335 Landing Pkwy, Fremont (94538-6407)
PHONE..................510 796-1111
EMP: 35
SALES (est): 2.9MM Privately Held
WEB: www.oridus.com
SIC: 7371 Custom Computer Programing

(P-12658)
ORIGIN SYSTEMS INC
209 Redwood Shores Pkwy, Redwood City (94065-1175)
PHONE..................650 628-1500
EMP: 270
SQ FT: 175,000
SALES (est): 9.1MM
SALES (corp-wide): 4.5B Publicly Held
SIC: 7371 Custom Computer Programing
PA: Electronic Arts Inc.
    209 Redwood Shores Pkwy
    Redwood City CA 94065
    650 628-7272

(P-12659)
OSISOFT LLC (HQ)
Also Called: OSI Software
1600 Alvarado St, San Leandro (94577-2600)
PHONE..................510 297-5800
J Kennedy, *Principal*
Gary Zies S, *Officer*
Jenny Linton, *Exec VP*
Ronan De Hooge, *Senior VP*
Kimthu Doan, *Senior VP*
▲ EMP: 418 EST: 1980
SQ FT: 55,000
SALES (est): 181.8MM Privately Held
WEB: www.osisoft.com
SIC: 7371 7372 7373 Computer software development; application computer software; computer integrated systems design

(P-12660)
OTTERAI INC
800 W El Cmino Real Ste 1, Mountain View (94040)
PHONE..................650 250-6322
Sam Liang, *CEO*
Yun Fu, *Vice Pres*
Simon Lau, *Vice Pres*
Seamus McAteer, *General Mgr*
Chang Chen, *Teacher*
EMP: 29 EST: 2016
SALES (est): 3.8MM Privately Held
WEB: www.otter.ai
SIC: 7371 7372 7373 Computer software development & applications; application computer software; systems integration services

(P-12661)
OUTRIGHT INC
100 Mathilda Pl Ste 100 # 100, Sunnyvale (94086-6019)
PHONE..................918 926-6578
Kevin Reeth, *President*
EMP: 846 EST: 2008
SALES (est): 1.2MM
SALES (corp-wide): 88.2MM Privately Held
WEB: www.outright.com
SIC: 7371 Computer software development
PA: Yam Special Holdings, Inc.
    15475 N 84th St
    Scottsdale AZ 85260
    480 505-8800

(P-12662)
OVEROPS INC
44 Montgomery St Ste 1050, San Francisco (94104-4621)
PHONE..................415 767-1250
Rod Squires, *CEO*
Bob Kemper, *Vice Pres*
Bob Patel, *Vice Pres*
Jeff Miller, *Risk Mgmt Dir*
David Zhu,
EMP: 50 EST: 2011
SALES (est): 5.1MM Privately Held
WEB: www.overops.com
SIC: 7371 Custom computer programming services

(P-12663)
PACHAMA INC
2261 Market St Ste 4303, San Francisco (94114-1612)
PHONE..................650 338-9394
Diego Saez Gil, *CEO*
EMP: 30 EST: 2018
SALES (est): 8MM Privately Held
SIC: 7371 7372 Software programming applications; application computer software

(P-12664)
PAGEBITES INC
395 Page Mill Rd, Palo Alto (94306-2065)
PHONE..................650 353-0546
Ralph Harik, *CEO*
Laurette Hartigan, *CFO*
EMP: 40 EST: 2015
SALES (est): 3MM Privately Held
SIC: 7371 Computer software development & applications

(P-12665)
PALANTIR TECHNOLOGIES INC PAC
100 Hamilton Ave Ste 300, Palo Alto (94301-1651)
PHONE..................650 833-9460
David Glazer, *Officer*
Lori Baylor, *Administration*
Danielle Kramer, *Software Engr*
Glenn Sheasby, *Software Engr*
James Shuster, *Software Engr*
EMP: 55 EST: 2011
SALES (est): 5.8MM Privately Held
WEB: www.palantir.com
SIC: 7371 Computer software development

(P-12666)
PALANTIR USG INC (HQ)
635 Waverley St, Palo Alto (94301-2550)
PHONE..................650 815-0200
Akash Jain, *President*
EMP: 50 EST: 2008
SQ FT: 4,000
SALES (est): 2.7MM
SALES (corp-wide): 1B Publicly Held
WEB: www.palantir.com
SIC: 7371 Computer software development
PA: Palantir Technologies Inc.
    1555 Blake St Ste 250
    Denver CO 80202
    720 358-3679

(P-12667)
PANASAS INC (PA)
2680 N 1st St Ste 150, San Jose (95134-2042)
PHONE..................408 215-6800
Faye Pairman, *President*
Tom Shea, *COO*
Stephanie Vinella, *CFO*
Jim Donovan, *Chief Mktg Ofcr*
Barbara Murphy, *Chief Mktg Ofcr*
▲ EMP: 100 EST: 2000
SQ FT: 20,000
SALES (est): 23.5MM Privately Held
WEB: www.panasas.com
SIC: 7371 Computer software development

(P-12668)
PANTHEON SYSTEMS INC (PA)
717 California St, San Francisco (94108-2455)
PHONE..................855 927-9387
Zachary Rosen, *CEO*
Cara Kalnow, *Partner*
David Strauss, *Founder*
Mark Etchin, *Vice Pres*
Eric Hamer, *Executive*
EMP: 93
SALES (est): 12.2MM Privately Held
WEB: www.pantheon.io
SIC: 7371 Computer software development

(P-12669)
PARACOSMA INC
2081 Norris Rd, Walnut Creek (94596-5446)
PHONE..................650 924-9896
Kenneth Ehrhart, *President*
EMP: 75 EST: 2016
SALES (est): 1.5MM Privately Held
SIC: 7371 7379 Computer software development & applications; computer related consulting services

(P-12670)
PARSABLE INC (PA)
115 Sansome St Ste 500, San Francisco (94104-3616)
PHONE..................888 681-2119
Yan-David Erlich, *CEO*
Ryan Junee, *President*
Michael Chou,
Jason Kalira, *Vice Pres*
Scott McMullan, *Vice Pres*
EMP: 151 EST: 2013
SALES (est): 3.7MM Privately Held
WEB: www.parsable.com
SIC: 7371 7374 Computer software development; data processing & preparation

(P-12671)
PARTICLE INDUSTRIES INC
126 Post St Fl 4, San Francisco (94108-4704)
PHONE..................415 316-1024
Zachary Supalla, *Officer*
Stephanie Rich, *Vice Pres*
Richard Whitney, *Vice Pres*
William Hart, *General Mgr*
David Middlecamp, *Sr Software Eng*
EMP: 82 EST: 2011
SQ FT: 2,300
SALES (est): 9.4MM Privately Held
WEB: www.particle.io
SIC: 7371 Computer software development

(P-12672)
PATIENTSAFE SOLUTIONS INC (PA)
525 Race St Ste 150, San Jose (95126-3497)
PHONE..................858 746-3100
Si Luo, *CEO*
Bill Roof, *President*
Mark Young, *COO*
Balaji Sekar, *CFO*
Loren Tarmo, *CFO*
EMP: 81 EST: 2000
SALES (est): 15MM Privately Held
WEB: www.patientsafesolutions.com
SIC: 7371 Software programming applications

(P-12673)
PATREON INC (PA)
600 Townsend St Ste 500, San Francisco (94103-5696)
PHONE..................415 967-2735
Jack Conte, *CEO*
Monica Malhotra, *Planning*
Sean Choe, *Sr Software Eng*
Fiona Manzella, *Software Engr*
Jeffrey Sun, *Software Engr*
EMP: 183 EST: 2013
SALES (est): 16.4MM Privately Held
WEB: www.patreon.com
SIC: 7371 Computer software development & applications

(P-12674)
PAYSTACK INC
201 Spear St Ste 1100, San Francisco (94105-6164)
PHONE..................415 941-8102
Olusola Akinlade, *CEO*
Ezra Olubi, *President*
EMP: 70
SQ FT: 8,698
SALES (est): 6.2MM Privately Held
WEB: www.paystack.com
SIC: 7371 Computer software development

(P-12675)
PEARL BLACK INC
100 Pine St Ste 475, San Francisco (94111-5120)
PHONE..................415 640-4987
EMP: 35
SQ FT: 6,000
SALES (est): 1.3MM Privately Held
SIC: 7371 Software Programming Applications

(P-12676)
PENCIL AND PIXEL INC
Also Called: Modsy
340 Brannan St Ste 500, San Francisco (94107-1892)
PHONE..................510 422-5036
Shanna Tellerman, *CEO*
John Howard, *Engineer*
Nicolas Richard, *Engineer*
Rachael Tellerman, *Marketing Staff*
Sarah Frazee, *Manager*

7371 - Custom Computer Programming Svcs County (P-12677)   PRODUCTS & SERVICES SECTION

EMP: 120 **EST:** 2015
SALES (est): 11.3MM **Privately Held**
WEB: www.modsy.com
SIC: 7371 Computer software development

(P-12677)
PEOPLEAI INC
475 Brannan St Ste 320, San Francisco (94107-5420)
P.O. Box 1366, San Carlos (94070-7366)
PHONE..................888 997-3675
Oleg Rogynskyy, *CEO*
Art Harding, *COO*
Thomas Wyatt,
Dana Ray, *Senior VP*
John Gilman, *Risk Mgmt Dir*
EMP: 92
SQ FT: 14,794
SALES (est): 5MM **Privately Held**
WEB: www.people.ai
SIC: 7371 Computer software development & applications

(P-12678)
PERFECT WORLD ENTRMT INC
100 Redwood Shores Pkwy # 200, Redwood City (94065-1253)
PHONE..................650 590-7700
Alan Chen, *CEO*
Yan Ji, *Vice Pres*
Bill Wang, *Vice Pres*
Carol Quito, *Comms Dir*
Jack Lau, *Office Mgr*
EMP: 150 **EST:** 2007
SQ FT: 10,000
SALES (est): 27MM **Privately Held**
WEB: www.perfectworld.com
SIC: 7371 Computer software development & applications
HQ: Perfect World Co., Ltd.
701-14, Floor 7, Building 5, No.1 Courtyard, Shangdi E. Road, Ha Beijing 10010

(P-12679)
PERNIXDATA INC
1740 Tech Dr Ste 150, San Jose (95110)
PHONE..................408 724-8413
Poojan Kumar, *CEO*
Sridhar Devarapalli, *Vice Pres*
Harjot Gill, *Vice Pres*
Mike Munoz, *Risk Mgmt Dir*
EMP: 75 **EST:** 2012
SALES (est): 9.2MM **Publicly Held**
WEB: www.nutanix.com
SIC: 7371 Computer software development
PA: Nutanix, Inc.
1740 Tech Dr Ste 150
San Jose CA 95110

(P-12680)
PERSISTENT SYSTEMS INC (HQ)
2055 Laurelwood Rd # 210, Santa Clara (95054-2727)
PHONE..................408 216-7010
Anand Deshpande, *CEO*
Albert Tabachnik, *Partner*
Jitendra Gokhale, *President*
Atul Khadilkar, *President*
Sudhir Kulkarni, *President*
EMP: 65 **EST:** 2001
SQ FT: 25,500
SALES (est): 172MM **Privately Held**
WEB: www.persistent.com
SIC: 7371 Computer software development

(P-12681)
PERSISTENT TLCOM SOLUTIONS INC
Also Called: Persistant Systems
2055 Laurelwood Rd # 210, Santa Clara (95054-2729)
PHONE..................408 216-7010
Dr Anand Suresh Deshpande, *CEO*
Jitendra Gokhale, *President*
Hari Haran, *President*
Atul Khadilkar, *President*
Sudhir Kulkarni, *President*
EMP: 50 **EST:** 2012
SQ FT: 25,500

SALES (est): 13.2MM **Privately Held**
WEB: www.persistent.com
SIC: 7371 Computer software development
HQ: Persistent Systems Inc.
2055 Laurelwood Rd # 210
Santa Clara CA 95054
408 216-7010

(P-12682)
PERSONAGRAPH CORPORATION
920 Stewart Dr Ste 100, Sunnyvale (94085-3923)
PHONE..................408 616-1600
Mandar Shinde, *CEO*
Jason Davis, *Treasurer*
William Rainey, *Admin Sec*
EMP: 55 **EST:** 2012
SQ FT: 1,500
SALES (est): 5.1MM **Privately Held**
WEB: www.intertrust.com
SIC: 7371 Computer software development

(P-12683)
PHILIPS HLTHCARE INFRMTICS INC (DH)
4430 Rosewood Dr Ste 200, Pleasanton (94588-3050)
PHONE..................650 293-2300
Deborah Disanzo, *CEO*
Davidi Gilo, *Ch of Bd*
Oran Muduroglu, *President*
Douglas Sinclair, *CFO*
Dana Cambra, *Vice Pres*
EMP: 50 **EST:** 1998
SQ FT: 31,523
SALES (est): 111.7MM
SALES (corp-wide): 133.6MM **Privately Held**
WEB: www.usa.philips.com
SIC: 7371 Computer software development & applications
HQ: Philips North America Llc
222 Jacobs St Fl 3
Cambridge MA 02141
978 659-3000

(P-12684)
PHOTON INFOTECH INC
100 Century Center Ct # 502, San Jose (95112-4536)
PHONE..................408 417-0600
Srinivas Balasubramanian, *CEO*
Mukund Balasubramanian, *Officer*
Muhamad Daud, *Exec VP*
Karthick Mani, *Vice Pres*
Suresh Muvva, *Technical Staff*
EMP: 58 **Privately Held**
WEB: www.photon.in
SIC: 7371 Computer software development
HQ: Photon Infotech Inc.
12300 Ford Rd Ste 270
Dallas TX 75234
408 416-1685

(P-12685)
PIVOTAL SOFTWARE INC (HQ)
Also Called: Pivotal Labs
875 Howard St Fl 5, San Francisco (94103-3021)
PHONE..................415 777-4868
Robert Mee, *CEO*
Paul Maritz, *Ch of Bd*
William Cook, *President*
Cynthia Gaylor, *CFO*
Andrew Cohen, *Senior VP*
EMP: 2923 **EST:** 2013
SQ FT: 66,510
SALES (est): 657.4MM **Publicly Held**
WEB: www.tanzu.vmware.com
SIC: 7371 Computer software development

(P-12686)
PIXLEE INC
625 Market St Ste 900, San Francisco (94105-3311)
PHONE..................718 753-5307
George So, *President*
Tahima Begum, *Vice Pres*
Atoosa Grey, *Teacher*
Dayo Oyekanmi, *Manager*
EMP: 46 **EST:** 2012

SALES (est): 5.6MM **Privately Held**
WEB: www.pixlee.com
SIC: 7371 Computer software development & applications

(P-12687)
PLAYPHONE INC
3031 Tisch Way Ste 110pw, San Jose (95128-2584)
PHONE..................408 261-6200
Takahito Yasuki, *Chairman*
Ron Czerny, *CEO*
Bhaskar Roy,
Rick Liu, *Officer*
Ata Ivanov, *Exec VP*
EMP: 61 **EST:** 2005
SALES (est): 13.3MM **Privately Held**
WEB: www.playphone.com
SIC: 7371 Computer software development

(P-12688)
PMDSOFT INC
345 California St Ste 600, San Francisco (94104-2657)
PHONE..................800 587-4989
Philippe D'Offay, *CEO*
Mark Janveaux, *Vice Pres*
Adam Kenney, *Vice Pres*
Veronica Alfert, *Executive*
Chris Bui, *Executive*
EMP: 59 **EST:** 1998
SALES (est): 6.7MM **Privately Held**
WEB: www.pmd.com
SIC: 7371 Computer software development

(P-12689)
POLARIS NETWORKS INCORPORATED
14856 Holden Way, San Jose (95124-4515)
PHONE..................408 625-7273
Buddhadeb Biswas, *CEO*
EMP: 100 **EST:** 2003
SQ FT: 2,000
SALES (est): 6.5MM **Privately Held**
WEB: www.polarisnetworks.net
SIC: 7371 7373 Computer software development; computer integrated systems design

(P-12690)
POLARIS WIRELESS INC
301 N Whisman Rd, Mountain View (94043-3969)
PHONE..................408 492-8900
Manlio Allegra, *President*
Victor C Chun, *CFO*
John Cinicolo, *Vice Pres*
Anand Dubey, *Surgery Dir*
Victor Hwang, *Principal*
EMP: 50 **EST:** 2001
SALES (est): 13MM **Privately Held**
WEB: www.polariswireless.com
SIC: 7371 8711 Computer software development; engineering services

(P-12691)
PONYAI INC
3501 Gateway Blvd, Fremont (94538-6585)
PHONE..................510 906-8868
Jun Peng, *CEO*
Tiancheng Lou, *Principal*
Philip Mao,
EMP: 333 **EST:** 2016
SQ FT: 50,000
SALES (est): 34.5MM
SALES (corp-wide): 1.2MM **Privately Held**
WEB: www.pony.ai
SIC: 7371 Computer software development
PA: Guangzhou Pony.Ai Technology Co., Ltd.
Room 1201, No.1 Mingzhu Street, Hengli Town, Nansha District (Of Guangzhou 51145

(P-12692)
PORTWORX INC
650 Castro St Ste 400, Mountain View (94041-2081)
PHONE..................650 386-0766

Murli Thirumale, *CEO*
Vinod Jayaraman, *Engineer*
Goutham RAO, *Chief Engr*
Joe Gardiner, *Director*
EMP: 90 **EST:** 2015
SALES (est): 5.8MM **Publicly Held**
WEB: www.portworx.com
SIC: 7371 Software programming applications
PA: Pure Storage, Inc.
650 Castro St Ste 400
Mountain View CA 94041

(P-12693)
POSTMAN INC
55 2nd St Ste 300, San Francisco (94105-3495)
PHONE..................415 796-6470
Abhinav Asthana, *President*
Tracy Segur, *Manager*
EMP: 60 **EST:** 2015
SALES (est): 8.3MM **Privately Held**
WEB: www.postman.com
SIC: 7371 Computer software development

(P-12694)
POSTX CORPORATION
3 Results Way, Cupertino (95014-5924)
PHONE..................408 861-3500
Cayce Ullman, *President*
A T Thomas, *Ch of Bd*
Claudia Brown, *Senior VP*
John Dumper, *Vice Pres*
Scott Olechowski, *Vice Pres*
EMP: 50 **EST:** 1994
SQ FT: 25,000
SALES (est): 3.5MM **Privately Held**
WEB: www.postx.com
SIC: 7371 Computer software development

(P-12695)
POYNT CO
4151 Middlefield Rd 2, Palo Alto (94303-4753)
PHONE..................650 600-8849
Osama Bedier, *CEO*
Rishi Taparia, *Vice Pres*
Vinod Mahalingam, *Engineer*
Bo Wang, *Engineer*
Khalid Zaheer, *Engineer*
EMP: 35
SALES (est): 1.9MM **Privately Held**
WEB: www.poynt.com
SIC: 7371 8731 Computer software development; computer (hardware) development

(P-12696)
PRIMARY DIAGNOSTICS INC
595 Pacific Ave Fl 4, San Francisco (94133-4685)
PHONE..................619 356-3701
Andrew Kobylinski, *CEO*
EMP: 50 **EST:** 2020
SALES (est): 25MM **Privately Held**
WEB: www.primary.health
SIC: 7371 Software programming applications

(P-12697)
PRIMARYDATA INC (PA)
4300 El Camino Realste100, Los Altos (94022)
PHONE..................650 422-3800
Lance Smith, *CEO*
Rick White, *Chief Mktg Ofcr*
David Flynn, *CTO*
John Cagle, *Engineer*
EMP: 45 **EST:** 2010
SQ FT: 7,500
SALES (est): 1MM **Privately Held**
SIC: 7371 Computer software development

(P-12698)
PRIVACERA INC
39300 Civic Center Dr # 140, Fremont (94538-2324)
PHONE..................510 413-7300
Balaji Ganesan, *CEO*
Don Bosco Durai, *Vice Pres*
EMP: 67 **EST:** 2016

PRODUCTS & SERVICES SECTION
7371 - Custom Computer Programming Svcs County (P-12721)

SALES (est): 6.4MM **Privately Held**
WEB: www.privacera.com
SIC: 7371 Computer software development

(P-12699)
PRIYO INC
605 Tumbleweed Cmn, Fremont (94539-6810)
PHONE..................408 248-2507
Atm Zakaria, *CEO*
Abul Nuruzzaman, *CFO*
EMP: 50
SALES (est): 60K **Privately Held**
SIC: 7371 Computer software development & applications

(P-12700)
PROACTIVE TECHNICAL SVCS INC (HQ)
2350 Mission College Blvd # 246, Santa Clara (95054-1532)
PHONE..................408 531-6040
Nitin Seth, *CEO*
Ashish Choudhary, *President*
Anant Pandey, *Finance*
EMP: 46 **EST:** 2004
SQ FT: 350
SALES (est): 4.9MM
SALES (corp-wide): 67.4MM **Privately Held**
WEB: www.incedoinc.com
SIC: 7371 Computer software development
PA: Incedo Inc.
  170 Wood Ave S
  Iselin NJ 08830
  408 531-6040

(P-12701)
PROJECT AFFINITY INC
170 Columbus Ave, San Francisco (94133-5119)
PHONE..................415 606-7649
Ray Zhou, *CEO*
Shubham Goel, *Founder*
Jess Dolnick, *Sales Staff*
Paul Hlatky, *Sales Staff*
EMP: 84 **EST:** 2014
SALES (est): 6.6MM **Privately Held**
WEB: www.affinity.co
SIC: 7371 Computer software development & applications

(P-12702)
PROMISE NETWORK INC
436 14th St Ste 920, Oakland (94612-2725)
PHONE..................877 717-7664
Phaedra Ellislamkins, *CEO*
Diana Frappier, *Principal*
EMP: 40 **EST:** 2017
SALES (est): 1.2MM **Privately Held**
WEB: www.joinpromise.com
SIC: 7371 Custom computer programming services

(P-12703)
PROOV INC
2345 Yale St Fl 1, Palo Alto (94306-1449)
PHONE..................847 715-8218
Toby Olshanetsky, *CEO*
Alexey Sapozhnikov, *Co-Founder*
Yossi Ben Harosh, *General Mgr*
EMP: 35
SALES (est): 7MM **Privately Held**
SIC: 7371 Computer software systems analysis & design, custom

(P-12704)
PROPELPLM INC
451 El Camino Real # 110, Santa Clara (95050-4376)
PHONE..................408 755-3780
Raymond Hein, *CEO*
Rachel Jang, *Partner*
Carmine Napolitano, *CFO*
Be 'anka Ashaolu, *Vice Pres*
September Higham, *Vice Pres*
EMP: 75 **EST:** 2015
SALES (est): 5.2MM **Privately Held**
WEB: www.propelplm.com
SIC: 7371 Computer software development

(P-12705)
PROSPANCE INC (PA)
4221 Bus Ctr Dr Ste 1, Fremont (94538)
PHONE..................925 415-2394
Manish Bhardwaj, *President*
Kirk Muhlenbruck, *President*
Peter Anand, *CFO*
Manpreet Bajaj, *Vice Pres*
Rajesh Sinha, *Vice Pres*
EMP: 78 **EST:** 2009
SQ FT: 2,400
SALES (est): 9.8MM **Privately Held**
WEB: www.prospanceinc.com
SIC: 7371 Computer software development

(P-12706)
PROTOMINDS INC
1551 Mccarthy Blvd # 103, Milpitas (95035-7437)
PHONE..................408 684-6363
Venkatesh Kirupakaran, *President*
Keerthipati Raghava Sridhar Ra, *CEO*
EMP: 40 **EST:** 2017
SALES (est): 3MM **Privately Held**
WEB: www.protominds.com
SIC: 7371 Computer software development

(P-12707)
PROVECTUS IT INC
125 University Ave # 290, Palo Alto (94301-1280)
PHONE..................650 787-3207
Nikolay Antonov, *COO*
EMP: 561 **EST:** 2014
SALES (est): 18.9MM **Privately Held**
WEB: www.provectus.com
SIC: 7371 Computer software development

(P-12708)
PUBMATIC INC (PA)
3 Lagoon Dr Ste 180, Redwood City (94065-5155)
PHONE..................650 331-3485
Rajeev K Goel, *CEO*
Amar K Goel, *Ch of Bd*
Mukul Kumar, *President*
Steven Pantelick, *CFO*
Jeffrey K Hirsch, *Ch Credit Ofcr*
EMP: 327 **EST:** 2006
SQ FT: 3,500
SALES (est): 148.7MM **Publicly Held**
WEB: www.pubmatic.com
SIC: 7371 Custom computer programming services

(P-12709)
PUBNUB INC (PA)
60 Francisco St, San Francisco (94133-2104)
PHONE..................415 223-7552
Todd Greene, *CEO*
Stephen Blum, *COO*
Russ Lemelin, *CFO*
Green Jeff, *Vice Pres*
Doron Sherman, *Vice Pres*
EMP: 176 **EST:** 2011
SALES (est): 10.2MM **Privately Held**
WEB: www.pubnub.com
SIC: 7371 Computer software development

(P-12710)
PULSE SECURE LLC (DH)
2700 Zanker Rd Ste 200, San Jose (95134-2140)
PHONE..................408 372-9600
Sudhakar Ramakrishna, *CEO*
Doug Erickson, *Partner*
James Hebler, *Partner*
Nicole Kensicki, *Partner*
Jeffrey C Key, *CFO*
EMP: 85 **EST:** 2014
SALES (est): 19.5MM
SALES (corp-wide): 5.6MM **Privately Held**
WEB: www.pulsesecure.net
SIC: 7371 4899 Computer software development; communication signal enhancement network system
HQ: Ivanti, Inc.
  10377 S Jordan Gtwy # 110
  South Jordan UT 84095
  801 208-1500

(P-12711)
PULSE SYSTEMS INC (DH)
438 Listowe Dr, Folsom (95630-6204)
PHONE..................316 636-5900
Charles Walls, *CEO*
James Isaac, *President*
Elias Hourani, *COO*
Samuel Ambrose, *Chief Mktg Ofcr*
Tana Goering, *Chief Mktg Ofcr*
EMP: 70 **EST:** 1982
SALES (est): 16MM
SALES (corp-wide): 8MM **Privately Held**
WEB: www.pulseinc.com
SIC: 7371 Computer software development

(P-12712)
QRS CORPORATION (DH)
1400 Marina Way S, Richmond (94804-3747)
PHONE..................510 215-5000
Elizabeth Fetter, *President*
Sean Salehi, *President*
David B Cooper Jr, *CFO*
Jack Parsons, *CFO*
Ray Rike, *Senior VP*
EMP: 70 **EST:** 1984
SQ FT: 63,000
SALES (est): 64.7MM
SALES (corp-wide): 3.1B **Privately Held**
SIC: 7371 8742 7375 Custom computer programming services; management consulting services; information retrieval services
HQ: Inovis Usa, Inc.
  11720 Amberpark Dr # 400
  Alpharetta GA 30009
  770 521-2284

(P-12713)
QUADRIGA INC
Also Called: Taller Technologies
1 Sansome St Ste 3500, San Francisco (94104-4436)
PHONE..................650 270-6326
Lucas E Fuller, *CEO*
Adrian Robles, *Opers Staff*
Adrian Marini, *Manager*
EMP: 70 **EST:** 2008
SALES (est): 3MM **Privately Held**
SIC: 7371 Custom computer programming services

(P-12714)
QUALYS INC (PA)
919 E Hillsdale Blvd Fl 4, Foster City (94404-2112)
PHONE..................650 801-6100
Sumedh S Thakar,
Sandra E Bergeron, *Ch of Bd*
Joo MI Kim, *CFO*
Jeffrey Hank, *Bd of Directors*
Rima Touma-Bruno, *Officer*
EMP: 1506 **EST:** 1999
SQ FT: 76,922
SALES (est): 362.9MM **Publicly Held**
WEB: www.qualys.com
SIC: 7371 7372 Custom computer programming services; software programming applications; prepackaged software

(P-12715)
QUANTCAST CORPORATION (PA)
795 Folsom St Fl 5, San Francisco (94107-4226)
PHONE..................800 293-5706
Konrad Feldman, *President*
Christina Cubeta, *Senior Partner*
Stephen Collins, *President*
Michael Kamprath, *President*
Julio Pekarovic, *CFO*
EMP: 57 **EST:** 2005
SALES (est): 260.7MM **Privately Held**
WEB: www.quantcast.com
SIC: 7371 7372 Computer software development & applications; publishers' computer software

(P-12716)
QUANTITATIVE MED SYSTEMS INC (DH)
Also Called: Q M S
1900 Powell St Ste 810, Emeryville (94608-1813)
PHONE..................510 654-9200
John A Sargent, *President*
Melissa Gabriel, *Managing Dir*
Jackie Wong, *Sr Software Eng*
Robert Khokhlov, *Info Tech Mgr*
Michelle Huang, *Engineer*
EMP: 50 **EST:** 1976
SQ FT: 2,500
SALES (est): 14.1MM
SALES (corp-wide): 3.9B **Privately Held**
WEB: www.constellationhb.com
SIC: 7371 Computer software development

(P-12717)
QUESTRA CORPORATION (PA)
3200 Bridge Pkwy Ste 101, Redwood City (94065-1197)
PHONE..................650 632-4011
Emil Wang, *President*
Yvette MA, *CFO*
Kaj Van De Loo, *Vice Pres*
Pranav Mohindroo, *Vice Pres*
Walt Rossi, *Vice Pres*
EMP: 43 **EST:** 2000
SQ FT: 10,000
SALES (est): 3.7MM **Privately Held**
WEB: www.questra.com
SIC: 7371 Computer software development & applications

(P-12718)
QUICKEN INC
3760 Haven Ave Ste C, Menlo Park (94025-1382)
PHONE..................650 564-3399
Eric Dunn, *CEO*
EMP: 120 **EST:** 2015
SQ FT: 10,000
SALES (est): 100MM **Privately Held**
WEB: www.quicken.com
SIC: 7371 Computer software development & applications
PA: Hig Capital Management, Inc.
  1450 Brickell Ave Fl 31
  Miami FL 33131

(P-12719)
QUID LLC (PA)
3960 Freedom Cir Ste 200, Santa Clara (95054-1450)
PHONE..................415 813-5300
Bob Goodson, *CEO*
Sinohe Terrero, *COO*
Dan Buczaczer, *Chief Mktg Ofcr*
Vasudev Bailey, *Senior VP*
Michael Milner, *Vice Pres*
EMP: 124 **EST:** 2006
SALES (est): 24.8MM **Privately Held**
WEB: www.netbasequid.com
SIC: 7371 7372 Computer software development; prepackaged software

(P-12720)
QUIP INC
50 Fremont St Ste 300, San Francisco (94105-2231)
PHONE..................877 544-7847
Bret Taylor, *CEO*
Patrick Moran, *Chief Mktg Ofcr*
Mihai Parparita, *Software Dev*
Kevin Gibbs, *Software Engr*
Alexys Flores, *Technical Staff*
EMP: 44 **EST:** 2012
SALES (est): 3.3MM **Privately Held**
WEB: www.quip.com
SIC: 7371 Computer software development

(P-12721)
QUOORI INC (PA)
44 Montgomery St Ste 3150, San Francisco (94104-4818)
PHONE..................707 393-8305
Andreas Poliza, *CEO*
Peter Markatos, *Principal*
Khurram Than, *Principal*
EMP: 36 **EST:** 2018

7371 - Custom Computer Programming Svcs County (P-12722)

SALES (est): 238.1K **Privately Held**
WEB: www.quoori.com
SIC: **7371** Computer software development & applications

(P-12722)
RAI TECHNOLOGY INCORPORATED
4104 24th St 385, San Francisco (94114-3615)
PHONE....................................415 252-9393
David Ashbuner, *President*
Cameron Momtaz, *COO*
EMP: 45 EST: 2003
SALES (est): 1.2MM **Privately Held**
WEB: www.raitechnology.com
SIC: **7371** Computer software systems analysis & design, custom

(P-12723)
RAINFOREST QA INC
5675 W Cog Hill Ter, Dublin (94568-1166)
PHONE....................................650 866-1407
Fred Stevens Smith, *CEO*
Russell Smith, *President*
Heather Doshay, *Vice Pres*
Chris Yin, *Vice Pres*
Sara Yiu, *Executive Asst*
EMP: 120 EST: 2014
SALES (est): 10.2MM **Privately Held**
WEB: www.rainforestqa.com
SIC: **7371** Computer software development; software programming applications

(P-12724)
RANCHER LABS INC (DH)
10050 N Wolfe Rd Sw127, Cupertino (95014-2519)
PHONE....................................650 521-6902
Sheng Liang, *President*
Will Chan, *Vice Pres*
Bala Gopalan, *Vice Pres*
Shannon Williams, *Vice Pres*
Rajashree Mandaogane, *Software Engr*
EMP: 58 EST: 2014
SALES (est): 8MM
SALES (corp-wide): 943K **Privately Held**
WEB: www.rancher.com
SIC: **7371** Computer software development
HQ: Suse Software Solutions Germany Gmbh
Maxfeldstr. 5
Nurnberg BY 90409
911 740-5377

(P-12725)
RAPIDAPI
2 Shaw Aly Fl 4, San Francisco (94105-0905)
PHONE....................................650 575-7633
Iddo Gino, *CEO*
Sasha Pesic, *Officer*
Alex Walling, *Software Dev*
EMP: 74 EST: 2020
SALES (est): 5.2MM **Privately Held**
WEB: www.rapidapi.com
SIC: **7371** Custom computer programming services

(P-12726)
RAPIDBIZAPPSCOM LLC
1525 Mccarthy Blvd # 110, Milpitas (95035-7451)
PHONE....................................408 647-3050
Satish Penmetsa, *CEO*
Zachary Savit, *Sales Staff*
Krishna Kunam,
Hima Bindu Mudunuru,
EMP: 20 EST: 2010
SQ FT: 500
SALES (est): 820.7K **Privately Held**
WEB: www.groundhogapps.com
SIC: **7371 7372 7373** Computer software development; business oriented computer software; systems software development services

(P-12727)
RAYDIANT
1 Letterman Dr 3500, San Francisco (94129-1494)
PHONE....................................888 966-5188
Bobby Marhamat, *CEO*
EMP: 53 EST: 2016

SALES (est): 7.5MM **Privately Held**
WEB: www.raydiant.com
SIC: **7371** Software programming applications

(P-12728)
READY PRICE LLC
5671 Santa Teresa Blvd, San Jose (95123-6512)
PHONE....................................408 357-0931
Richard Soukoulis, *CEO*
EMP: 723 EST: 2005
SALES (est): 1MM
SALES (corp-wide): 563.7MM **Privately Held**
WEB: www.readyprice.com
SIC: **7371 6162** Computer software development & applications; mortgage bankers & correspondents
PA: Situsamc Holdings Corporation
5065 Westheimer Rd 700e
Houston TX 77056
713 328-4400

(P-12729)
REAL-TIME INNOVATIONS INC (PA)
Also Called: R T I
232 E Java Dr, Sunnyvale (94089-1318)
PHONE....................................408 990-7400
Stanley Schneider, *CEO*
Supreet Oberoi, *President*
Jim Suggs, *COO*
Jody Schneider, *CFO*
Jody G Schneider, *CFO*
EMP: 60 EST: 1986
SQ FT: 1,000
SALES (est): 24.6MM **Privately Held**
WEB: www.rti.com
SIC: **7371 7379** Computer software development; computer related consulting services

(P-12730)
RECALL MANAGEMENT INC
2610 Crow Canyon Rd # 120, San Ramon (94583-1547)
PHONE....................................877 386-8186
Mohammed Halim, *Principal*
EMP: 48 EST: 2011
SALES (est): 1.2MM **Privately Held**
WEB: www.managerecalls.com
SIC: **7371** Computer software development

(P-12731)
RECIPROCITY INC
548 Market St 73905, San Francisco (94104-5401)
PHONE....................................415 851-8667
Kenneth Lynch, *CEO*
Michael Knighten, *Vice Pres*
Chet Jacobs, *Executive*
Bernard Van Ulden, *Executive*
Korina Lealiiee, *Office Mgr*
EMP: 50 EST: 2010
SQ FT: 5,300
SALES (est): 5.1MM **Privately Held**
WEB: www.reciprocity.com
SIC: **7371** Computer software systems analysis & design, custom

(P-12732)
RED CONDOR INC
1300 Valley House Dr # 115, Rohnert Park (94928-4927)
PHONE....................................707 569-7419
Ron Longo, *President*
EMP: 42 EST: 2003
SALES (est): 1MM **Privately Held**
WEB: www.redcondor.com
SIC: **7371** Computer software development

(P-12733)
RED RIVER CONSULTING SVCS INC (HQ)
1030 R St, Sacramento (95811-6500)
PHONE....................................916 383-9005
Martin R McGartland, *President*
Veronica Westlund, *COO*
Amanda Radmand, *Administration*
Jeff Drewes, *CTO*
Catherine Baganz, *Business Anlyst*
EMP: 44 EST: 1998

SALES (est): 144.5K **Privately Held**
WEB: www.redriver.com
SIC: **7371 7379** Computer software development;

(P-12734)
REDACTED INC
350 Rhode Island St # 240, San Francisco (94103-5188)
PHONE....................................415 858-2719
Max Kelly, *CEO*
Ralph Logan, *Exec VP*
Michelle Paulson, *General Counsel*
EMP: 75 EST: 2015
SALES (est): 4.4MM **Privately Held**
WEB: www.redacted.com
SIC: **7371** Computer software systems analysis & design, custom

(P-12735)
REDIS INC
700 E El Cmino Real Ste 1, Mountain View (94040)
PHONE....................................415 930-9666
Ofer Bengal, *CEO*
Manish Gupta, *Chief Mktg Ofcr*
Itai Raz, *Officer*
Elad Ash, *Vice Pres*
Lisa Contini, *Vice Pres*
EMP: 439 EST: 2013
SALES (est): 29.8MM **Privately Held**
WEB: www.redis.com
SIC: **7371** Computer software development
PA: Redis Ltd
94 Alon Yigal
Tel Aviv-Jaffa
-

(P-12736)
REDTAIL TECHNOLOGY INC
3131 Fite Cir, Sacramento (95827-1801)
PHONE....................................800 206-5030
Brian T McLaughlin, *CEO*
Christopher Gonzales, *Partner*
Gary Curry, *President*
Andrew Hernandez, *COO*
Susan Curry, *Treasurer*
EMP: 80 EST: 2003
SALES (est): 18.9MM **Privately Held**
WEB: www.corporate.redtailtechnology.com
SIC: **7371** Computer software development

(P-12737)
REFLEKTION INC (PA)
1825 S Grant St Ste 900, San Mateo (94402-2675)
PHONE....................................650 293-0800
Rajeev Madhavan, *CEO*
Ray Villeneuve, *President*
Kurt Heinemann, *Chief Mktg Ofcr*
Vivek Gupta, *Vice Pres*
Sanjay Jain, *Vice Pres*
EMP: 49 EST: 2012
SALES (est): 7.8MM **Privately Held**
WEB: www.reflektion.com
SIC: **7371** Computer software systems analysis & design, custom

(P-12738)
REFLEKTIVE INC
123 Townsend St Ste 300, San Francisco (94107-1938)
PHONE....................................203 886-9240
David Laszewski, *Officer*
Travis Wentling, *CFO*
Jennifer Toton, *Chief Mktg Ofcr*
Marc Caltabiano,
Barbara Competello, *Officer*
EMP: 199 EST: 2013
SALES (est): 925K
SALES (corp-wide): 175.9MM **Privately Held**
WEB: www.reflektive.com
SIC: **7371** Computer software development; computer software systems analysis & design, custom
HQ: Learning Technologies Group Inc.
300 5th Ave
Waltham MA 02451
781 530-2000

(P-12739)
RELTIO INC (PA)
100 Marine Pkwy Ste 275, Redwood City (94065-5234)
PHONE....................................855 360-3282
Manish Sood, *CEO*
Greg Durken, *Partner*
Satish Ramakrishnan, *Exec VP*
Greg Ladd, *Vice Pres*
James McMurray, *Vice Pres*
EMP: 150 EST: 2011
SQ FT: 6,242
SALES (est): 45.6MM **Privately Held**
WEB: www.reltio.com
SIC: **7371** Custom computer programming services

(P-12740)
REMIX SOFTWARE INC
1128 Howard St, San Francisco (94103-3914)
PHONE....................................415 900-4332
EMP: 85
SALES (est): 10.4MM
SALES (corp-wide): 12.3MM **Privately Held**
WEB: www.remix.com
SIC: **7371** Custom Computer Programming Services, Nsk
PA: Via Transportation, Inc.
160 Varick St Fl 4
New York NY
619 731-0710

(P-12741)
REPLICON SOFTWARE INC (PA)
3 Lagoon Dr Ste 130, Redwood City (94065-1566)
PHONE....................................650 286-9200
Raj Narayanaswamy, *CEO*
Peter Kinash, *CFO*
Suresh Kuppahally, *Exec VP*
Brent Sapiro, *Exec VP*
Scott Bales, *Vice Pres*
EMP: 42 EST: 2006
SALES (est): 7.7MM **Privately Held**
WEB: www.replicon.com
SIC: **7371 7372** Computer software development; prepackaged software

(P-12742)
REPRESENT DEVELOPMENT
650 University Ave Unit 3, Berkeley (94710-1935)
PHONE....................................510 944-1938
Aaron Clark, *CEO*
EMP: 40 EST: 2018
SALES (est): 1.2MM **Privately Held**
WEB: www.representdev.com
SIC: **7371 7389** Custom computer programming services; business services

(P-12743)
RESOLVE SYSTEMS LLC (PA)
300 Orchard Cy Dr Ste 110, Campbell (95008)
PHONE....................................949 325-0120
Martin B Savitt, *CEO*
Jim Livergood, *President*
Vijay Kurkal, *COO*
Dan Jackson, *Officer*
Larry Lien, *Senior VP*
EMP: 65 EST: 2000
SALES (est): 20.7MM **Privately Held**
WEB: www.resolve.io
SIC: **7371** Computer software development

(P-12744)
RESONATE I INC (PA)
90 Great Oaks Blvd Ste 20, San Jose (95119-1314)
PHONE....................................408 545-5500
Kishore Khandavalli, *CEO*
Peter R Watkins, *Ch of Bd*
Richard Hornstein, *CFO*
David Wheatley, *CFO*
Christopher Marino, *Founder*
EMP: 160 EST: 1995
SQ FT: 38,000
SALES (est): 13.8MM **Privately Held**
WEB: www.resonatenetworks.com
SIC: **7371 7372** Computer software development; business oriented computer software

PRODUCTS & SERVICES SECTION **7371 - Custom Computer Programming Svcs County (P-12768)**

(P-12745)
RESPONSYS INC (DH)
Also Called: Responsys.com
1100 Grundy Ln Ste 300, San Bruno (94066-3066)
PHONE.....................650 745-1700
Daniel D Springer, *CEO*
Christian A Paul, *CFO*
Scott V Olrich, *Chief Mktg Ofcr*
Julian Ong, *Senior VP*
Michael Della Penna, *Senior VP*
EMP: 645 EST: 1998
SQ FT: 72,000
SALES (est): 105.9MM
SALES (corp-wide): 40.4B **Publicly Held**
WEB: www.oracle.com
SIC: **7371** 7372 Computer software development; business oriented computer software
HQ: Oc Acquisition Llc
  500 Oracle Pkwy
  Redwood City CA 94065
  650 506-7000

(P-12746)
RETAIL PRO INTERNATIONAL LLC (PA)
Also Called: Retail Pro Software
400 Plaza Dr Ste 200, Folsom (95630-4746)
PHONE.....................916 605-7200
Kerry Lemos, *CEO*
William Colley, *Senior VP*
Shaff Kassam, *Vice Pres*
Peter Latona, *Vice Pres*
Amit Lohia, *Vice Pres*
EMP: 69 EST: 1985
SQ FT: 7,500
SALES (est): 13.6MM **Privately Held**
WEB: www.retailpro.com
SIC: **7371** 7372 Computer software development; prepackaged software

(P-12747)
RETAILNEXT INC (PA)
60 S Market St Ste 310, San Jose (95113-2351)
PHONE.....................408 884-2162
Alexei Agratchev, *CEO*
Michael Manlapas, *President*
Kenton D Chow, *COO*
David Tognotti, *CFO*
Andrew Skarupa, *CFO*
EMP: 155 EST: 2007
SALES (est): 41.9MM **Privately Held**
WEB: www.retailnext.net
SIC: **7371** Computer software development

(P-12748)
REVINATE INC
1 Letterman Dr Bldg C, San Francisco (94129-2402)
PHONE.....................415 671-4703
Jay Ashton, *Principal*
Peter Fenton, *General Ptnr*
Wayne Huang, *President*
Daniel Brewer, *Vice Pres*
JD Cain, *Vice Pres*
EMP: 51 EST: 2010
SALES (est): 11.5MM **Privately Held**
WEB: www.revinate.com
SIC: **7371** Computer software development

(P-12749)
RHP SOFT INC
5700 Stnrdge Mall Rd Ste, Pleasanton (94588)
PHONE.....................925 353-1629
Haritha Polakala, *CEO*
Rushendra Kanchi, *Vice Pres*
EMP: 38 EST: 2011
SQ FT: 1,000
SALES (est): 2.5MM **Privately Held**
WEB: www.rhpsoft.com
SIC: **7371** 7379 Computer software systems analysis & design, custom; computer related consulting services

(P-12750)
RHYTHMONE LLC
800 W El Camino Real, Mountain View (94040-2567)
PHONE.....................650 961-9024
EMP: 70

SALES (corp-wide): 214.9MM **Privately Held**
SIC: **7371** Mobile Video Technology And Advertising Platform Software And Services
HQ: Rhythmone, Llc
  1 Market St Ste 1810
  San Francisco CA 94111
  415 655-1450

(P-12751)
RIGHTWARE INC
470 Ramona St, Palo Alto (94301-1707)
PHONE.....................408 502-1017
Ville Ilves, *President*
EMP: 56
SALES (corp-wide): 399.2MM **Privately Held**
WEB: www.rightware.com
SIC: **7371** Software programming applications
HQ: Rightware Inc.
  850 Stephenson Hwy # 308
  Troy MI 48083
  877 775-2694

(P-12752)
ROADSTER INC
300 De Haro St Ste 334, San Francisco (94103-5165)
PHONE.....................833 568-5968
Andrew Moss, *CEO*
EMP: 750 EST: 2013
SALES (est): 5.2MM
SALES (corp-wide): 1.6B **Publicly Held**
WEB: www.roadster.com
SIC: **7371** Computer software development & applications
PA: Cdk Global, Inc.
  1950 Hassell Rd
  Hoffman Estates IL 60169
  847 397-1700

(P-12753)
ROKU HOLDINGS INC (HQ)
1701 Junction Ct Ste 100, San Jose (95112-1030)
PHONE.....................408 556-9391
EMP: 56 EST: 2019
SALES (est): 668.9K **Publicly Held**
WEB: www.roku.com
SIC: **7371** Computer software development & applications

(P-12754)
SAAMA TECHNOLOGIES INC (PA)
900 E Hamilton Ave # 200, Campbell (95008-0664)
PHONE.....................408 371-1900
Ken Coleman, *Ch of Bd*
Benzi Mathew, *Partner*
Suresh Katta, *President*
Simon Ho, *CFO*
Scott Kleinberg, *CFO*
EMP: 237 EST: 1997
SQ FT: 10,000
SALES (est): 58.7MM **Privately Held**
WEB: www.saama.com
SIC: **7371** Computer software development

(P-12755)
SAFE SECURITIES INC
3000 El Cmino Real Bldg 4, Palo Alto (94306)
PHONE.....................650 398-3669
Saket Modi, *CEO*
EMP: 200 EST: 2018
SALES (est): 13.7MM **Privately Held**
SIC: **7371** Computer software development

(P-12756)
SALT SECURITY INC
3921 Fabian Way, Palo Alto (94303-4640)
PHONE.....................650 254-6580
Roey Eliyahu, *CEO*
Michael Nicosia, *COO*
Yaron Hagai, *Vice Pres*
Ahuvy Mrad, *Human Resources*
Chris Westphal, *Marketing Staff*
EMP: 65 EST: 2019

SALES (est): 5.3MM **Privately Held**
WEB: www.salt.security
SIC: **7371** Computer software development

(P-12757)
SALTMINE USA INC
601 California St Fl 4, San Francisco (94108-2809)
PHONE.....................408 464-3631
Shagufta Anurag, *CEO*
EMP: 35 EST: 2018
SALES (est): 4.6MM **Privately Held**
WEB: www.saltmine.com
SIC: **7371** Computer software development

(P-12758)
SAMSUNG SDS AMERICA INC
2665 N 1st St Ste 110, San Jose (95134-2033)
PHONE.....................408 638-8800
Jh Kim, *Manager*
Tyler Lee, *Administration*
Kevin Gould, *Counsel*
EMP: 72 **Privately Held**
WEB: www.samsungsds.com
SIC: **7371** Computer software development
HQ: Samsung Sds America, Inc.
  100 Challenger Rd Ste 102
  Ridgefield Park NJ 07660
  201 807-5950

(P-12759)
SANO INTELLIGENCE INC
1155 Bryant St, San Francisco (94103-4336)
PHONE.....................408 483-6518
Ashwin Pushpala, *CEO*
Matthew Chapman, *Vice Pres*
Erika Cashman, *Office Mgr*
Dan Girellini, *Software Engr*
EMP: 64 EST: 2011
SALES (est): 3.3MM
SALES (corp-wide): 6.3MM **Privately Held**
WEB: www.onedrop.today
SIC: **7371** Computer software systems analysis & design, custom
PA: Informed Data Systems Inc.
  166 Mercer St Apt 2
  New York NY 10012
  917 442-8626

(P-12760)
SAP LABS LLC
3475 Deer Creek Rd, Palo Alto (94304-1316)
PHONE.....................650 849-4000
Ben Frommherz, *Manager*
Robert Buehler, *Partner*
Beth Glasstetter, *Partner*
Kristin Albright, *Vice Pres*
Darryl Gray, *Vice Pres*
EMP: 53
SALES (corp-wide): 32.3B **Publicly Held**
WEB: www.sap.com
SIC: **7371** Computer software development
HQ: Sap Labs, Llc
  3410 Hillview Ave
  Palo Alto CA 94304

(P-12761)
SAT CORPORATION (DH)
3200 Patrick Henry Dr # 1, Santa Clara (95054-1875)
PHONE.....................402 208-9200
Eric Demarco, *CEO*
Deanna Lund, *CEO*
Laura Siegal, *Treasurer*
Phil Carrai, *Vice Pres*
Michael Fink, *Vice Pres*
EMP: 56 EST: 1989
SQ FT: 15,000
SALES (est): 15.3MM **Publicly Held**
WEB: www.kratosdefense.com
SIC: **7371** Computer software development
HQ: Integral Systems, Inc.
  10680 Treena St Ste 600
  San Diego CA 92131
  443 539-5330

(P-12762)
SATMETRIX SYSTEMS INC
555 Twin Dolphin Dr # 36, Redwood City (94065-2129)
PHONE.....................650 227-8300
Richard Owen, *President*
Brian Curry, *COO*
Raymond Yue, *CFO*
Jennifer Wang, *Executive Asst*
Steffan Martell, *Director*
EMP: 250 EST: 1996
SALES (est): 28MM **Privately Held**
WEB: www.satmetrix.com
SIC: **7371** Software programming applications

(P-12763)
SCALE AI INC (PA)
155 5th St Fl 6, San Francisco (94103-2919)
PHONE.....................650 294-8644
Alexander Wa-Ng, *CEO*
Sarah Niyogi, *Admin Sec*
Brad Porter, *CTO*
EMP: 197 EST: 2016
SALES (est): 19.3MM **Privately Held**
WEB: www.scale.com
SIC: **7371** 8748 Custom computer programming services; systems analysis or design

(P-12764)
SCALIO LLC
548 Market St Pmb 21933, San Francisco (94104-5401)
PHONE.....................408 835-0640
Bradley Greenwood, *CEO*
EMP: 42 EST: 2011
SALES (est): 1.7MM **Privately Held**
WEB: www.scal.io
SIC: **7371** Software programming applications

(P-12765)
SCHOOLCITY INC
462 Joshua Way, Sunnyvale (94086-6521)
PHONE.....................408 638-8438
Vaseem Anjum, *President*
Saarah Anjum, *CIO*
Sumitra Chari, *Human Resources*
Omar Ali, *Sales Staff*
Julia Sterne, *Manager*
EMP: 46 EST: 1999 **Privately Held**
WEB: www.illuminateed.com
SIC: **7371** Computer software development

(P-12766)
SCIMAGE INC
4916 El Cmino Real Ste 20, Los Altos (94022)
PHONE.....................650 694-4858
SAI P Raya PHD, *President*
Mahdavi Raya, *CFO*
Matthew Wolkenmuth, *Program Mgr*
Estelle Amarandos, *Administration*
Tiffany Tran, *Administration*
EMP: 47 EST: 1994
SQ FT: 10,000
SALES (est): 6.6MM **Privately Held**
WEB: www.scimage.com
SIC: **7371** Computer software development

(P-12767)
SCIO TECHNOLOGIES INC
2650 Birch St Ste 150, Palo Alto (94306-2071)
PHONE.....................408 203-0518
Arvind Jain, *CEO*
EMP: 50 EST: 2019
SALES (est): 975.8K **Privately Held**
SIC: **7371** Computer software development & applications

(P-12768)
SCREENBEAM INC (PA)
220 Devcon Dr, San Jose (95112-4210)
PHONE.....................800 752-7820
Dean Chang, *CEO*
Chuong Vu, *Vice Pres*
Alison Maxson, *Marketing Staff*
Carlyn Fernandez, *Sales Staff*
Rodney Lopez, *Sales Staff*
EMP: 59 EST: 2019

7371 - Custom Computer Programming Svcs County (P-12769)

SALES (est): 7MM **Privately Held**
WEB: www.screenbeam.com
SIC: **7371** Computer software development

(P-12769)
SECURITI INC
3031 Tisch Way Ste 502, San Jose (95128-2531)
PHONE..................................408 401-1160
Rehan Jalil, *CEO*
EMP: 200 **EST**: 2018
SALES (est): 11.7MM **Privately Held**
SIC: **7371** Custom computer programming services

(P-12770)
SELECTIVA SYSTEMS INC
2051 Junction Ave Ste 225, San Jose (95131-2114)
PHONE..................................408 297-1336
Milind Gokarn, *CEO*
Savinder Singh, *Officer*
Archana Gokarn, *Admin Sec*
Mythri Ramakrishna, *Business Anlyst*
Tania Chanda, *Analyst*
EMP: 39 **EST**: 1999
SALES (est): 2.6MM **Privately Held**
WEB: www.selectiva.com
SIC: **7371** **7372** Computer software systems analysis & design, custom; publishers' computer software

(P-12771)
SENSORY INC (PA)
Also Called: Fluent Speech Technologies
4701 Patrick Henry Dr # 7, Santa Clara (95054-1863)
PHONE..................................408 625-3302
Todd Mozer, *CEO*
Stan Louie, *President*
Forrest Mozer, *Chairman*
Jim Gilbreath, *Vice Pres*
Bill Teasley, *Vice Pres*
EMP: 58 **EST**: 1994
SQ FT: 10,000
SALES (est): 9MM **Privately Held**
WEB: www.sensory.com
SIC: **7371** Custom computer programming services

(P-12772)
SENTIENT TECHNOLOGIES USA LLC
611 Mission St Fl 6, San Francisco (94105-3536)
PHONE..................................415 422-9886
Antoine Blondeau, *CEO*
Julian Tandler, *President*
Fabrice Fischer, *CFO*
Peter Harrigan,
Babak Hodjat,
EMP: 50 **EST**: 2008
SALES (est): 6.5MM **Privately Held**
WEB: www.evolv.ai
SIC: **7371** Computer software development
PA: Sentient Technologies (Hk) Limited
    Dominion Ctr
    Wan Chai HK

(P-12773)
SERVICEMAX INC (PA)
4450 Rosewood Dr Ste 200, Pleasanton (94588-3061)
PHONE..................................925 965-7859
Neil Barua, *CEO*
Kimberly Forseth, *Partner*
Sean Ryan, *Partner*
Tony Zingale, *Ch of Bd*
Scott Berg, *COO*
EMP: 120 **EST**: 1999
SALES (est): 103MM **Privately Held**
WEB: www.servicemax.com
SIC: **7371** Computer software development

(P-12774)
SHAPE SECURITY INC (HQ)
800 W El Cmino Real Ste 2, Mountain View (94040)
PHONE..................................650 399-0400
Tamara Macduff, *CFO*
Reena Choudhry, *Vice Pres*
Marc Hansen, *Vice Pres*
Hasan Imam, *Vice Pres*
Sudhir Kandula, *Vice Pres*
EMP: 184 **EST**: 2012
SALES (est): 25MM **Publicly Held**
WEB: www.shapesecurity.com
SIC: **7371** Computer software development

(P-12775)
SHARPSWITCH INC
2655 Hill Park Dr, San Jose (95124-1735)
PHONE..................................866 633-6944
Brandon Ringer, *Exec Dir*
EMP: 54 **EST**: 2011
SALES (est): 3.6MM **Privately Held**
WEB: www.sharpswitch.com
SIC: **7371** **7373** **7372** Computer software systems analysis & design, custom; software programming applications; systems software development services; business oriented computer software

(P-12776)
SHEEBA DULEEP
Also Called: Wemakeiot
28850 Dixon St Apt 408, Hayward (94544-5589)
PHONE..................................267 250-9106
Sheeba Duleep, *Owner*
EMP: 50
SALES (est): 772K **Privately Held**
SIC: **7371** Software programming applications

(P-12777)
SHIFT FINANCE LLC
2500 Market St, San Francisco (94114-1915)
PHONE..................................541 335-9245
EMP: 565 **EST**: 2016
SALES (est): 500.6K
SALES (corp-wide): 195.7MM **Publicly Held**
WEB: www.shift.com
SIC: **7371** Computer software development & applications
PA: Shift Technologies, Inc.
    2525 16th St Ste 316
    San Francisco CA 94103
    815 575-6739

(P-12778)
SHIFT3 TECHNOLOGIES LLC
700 Van Ness Ave, Fresno (93721-2912)
PHONE..................................559 560-3300
Jake Soberal, *CEO*
Irma Olguin Jr, *CEO*
Greg Goforth, *Exec Dir*
Mario Soberal, *Exec Dir*
Coby Fielding, *Software Dev*
EMP: 35 **EST**: 2017
SALES (est): 2.7MM **Privately Held**
WEB: www.shift3tech.com
SIC: **7371** Computer software development

(P-12779)
SHOPIFY (USA) INC
33 New Montgomery St # 75, San Francisco (94105-4506)
PHONE..................................415 944-7572
Russell Jones, *CEO*
Carl Rivera, *General Mgr*
Vee McClure, *Technical Staff*
Gabriela Annacone, *Marketing Staff*
Kit Shopify, *Marketing Staff*
EMP: 70 **EST**: 2014
SALES (est): 7.2MM
SALES (corp-wide): 1.5B **Privately Held**
WEB: www.shopify.jp
SIC: **7371** Computer software development
PA: Shopify Inc
    151 Oconnor St
    Ottawa ON K2P 2
    613 241-2828

(P-12780)
SHOPKICK INC
273a S Railroad Ave, San Mateo (94401-3339)
PHONE..................................650 763-8727
Cyriac Roeding, *CEO*
Alexis Rask, *CFO*
Gina Waterman, *Assoc VP*
James Weinberg, *Vice Pres*
Heather Skae, *Executive*
EMP: 70 **EST**: 2009
SALES (est): 11.7MM **Privately Held**
WEB: www.shopkick.com
SIC: **7371** Computer software development
PA: Trax Technology Solutions Pte. Ltd.
    65 Chulia Street
    Singapore 04951

(P-12781)
SHOPSTYLE INC (DH)
160 Spear St Ste 1900, San Francisco (94105-1548)
PHONE..................................415 908-2200
Seth Spitzer, *Administration*
Wynter Finley, *Producer*
Gianna Ferraro, *Mktg Coord*
Matthew Livingston, *Director*
EMP: 119 **EST**: 2006
SALES (est): 28.5MM **Privately Held**
WEB: www.shopstyle.com
SIC: **7371** Computer software development & applications

(P-12782)
SHORELINE LABS INC
315 Montgomery St, San Francisco (94104-1856)
PHONE..................................415 630-6212
Isaac Madan, *CEO*
Rohan Sathe, *Admin Sec*
EMP: 50 **EST**: 2019
SALES (est): 2.3MM **Privately Held**
WEB: www.shoreline.com
SIC: **7371** Computer software development & applications

(P-12783)
SIERRAWARE LLC
1042 Westchester Dr, Sunnyvale (94087-2047)
PHONE..................................408 337-6400
Kasey Cross, *Mng Member*
Melinda Mason, *Manager*
EMP: 35 **EST**: 2011
SALES (est): 1MM **Privately Held**
WEB: www.sierraware.com
SIC: **7371** Computer software development

(P-12784)
SIFT SCIENCE INC (PA)
123 Mission St Ste 2000, San Francisco (94105-1592)
PHONE..................................855 981-7438
Jason Tan, *CEO*
Marc Olesen, *President*
Richard Gardner, *Vice Pres*
Lauren Shapiro, *Executive*
Brittany Dean, *Executive Asst*
EMP: 64 **EST**: 2011
SALES (est): 7.6MM **Privately Held**
WEB: www.sift.com
SIC: **7371** Computer software development

(P-12785)
SILICON VALLEY COMMERCE LLC
16 Jessie St, San Francisco (94105-2782)
PHONE..................................888 507-8266
Patrick Xie, *VP Bus Dvlpt*
EMP: 71
SALES (corp-wide): 10.4MM **Privately Held**
SIC: **7371** Custom computer programming services
PA: Silicon Valley Commerce Llc
    1466 Us Highway 395 N
    Gardnerville NV 89410
    888 507-8266

(P-12786)
SILICON VALLEY SFTWR GROUP LLC
74 Tehama St, San Francisco (94105-3110)
PHONE..................................844 946-7874
Matt Swanson,
Eric Leppo, *COO*
Dylan Steinman, *Opers Staff*
Mike Andler, *Senior Mgr*
Gustavo Huber, *Senior Mgr*
EMP: 50 **EST**: 2013

SALES: 2.4MM **Privately Held**
WEB: www.svsg.co
SIC: **7371** Computer software systems analysis & design, custom

(P-12787)
SINGLESTORE INC (PA)
534 4th St, San Francisco (94107-1621)
PHONE..................................855 463-6775
Raj Verma, *CEO*
Matt Ocko, *Managing Prtnr*
Jerry Held, *Chairman*
Gary Orenstein, *Officer*
Mick Charles, *Vice Pres*
EMP: 46 **EST**: 2011
SALES (est): 11.1MM **Privately Held**
WEB: www.singlestore.com
SIC: **7371** Computer software development

(P-12788)
SINGULAR LABS INC (PA)
2345 Yale St Fl 1, Palo Alto (94306-1449)
PHONE..................................415 999-8368
Gadi Elishayov, *CEO*
Susan Kuo, *COO*
Vince Cortese, *Officer*
Viviana Notcovich, *Vice Pres*
Rob Pohlman, *Software Engr*
EMP: 37 **EST**: 2014
SALES (est): 5.1MM **Privately Held**
WEB: www.singular.net
SIC: **7371** Computer software development

(P-12789)
SIX APART LTD (HQ)
180 Townsend St Fl 3, San Francisco (94107-2589)
PHONE..................................415 738-5100
Christopher J Alden, *CEO*
Mena Trott, *President*
Andrew Anker, *Exec VP*
Aaron P Bailey, *Senior VP*
Michael Sippey, *Vice Pres*
EMP: 50 **EST**: 2002
SALES (est): 2.2MM **Privately Held**
WEB: www.movabletype.com
SIC: **7371** **5734** Computer software development; software, computer games

(P-12790)
SKILLNET SOLUTIONS INC (PA)
1901 S Bascom Ave Ste 600, Campbell (95008-2209)
PHONE..................................408 522-3600
Vidya Damle, *CEO*
Saroj Damle, *President*
Jack Grover, *Vice Pres*
Satin Gandhi, *Software Engr*
Mahesh Joshi, *Consultant*
EMP: 89 **EST**: 1996
SQ FT: 10,000
SALES: 25.5MM **Privately Held**
WEB: www.skillnetinc.com
SIC: **7371** **7379** Computer software development; computer related consulting services

(P-12791)
SKIRE INC
500 Oracle Pkwy, Redwood City (94065-1677)
PHONE..................................650 289-2600
Massy Mendipour, *CEO*
Steve Apfelberg, *Chief Mktg Ofcr*
EMP: 46 **EST**: 1999
SALES (est): 9.7MM
SALES (corp-wide): 40.4B **Publicly Held**
WEB: www.skire.com
SIC: **7371** Computer software development
PA: Oracle Corporation
    2300 Oracle Way
    Austin TX 78741
    737 867-1000

(P-12792)
SKUPOS INC (PA)
1462 Pine St, San Francisco (94109-4720)
PHONE..................................303 718-4805
Mike Glassman, *Ch Credit Ofcr*
Scott Latham, *Engineer*
David Hewlett, *Marketing Staff*
William Hamblen, *Manager*
Mounika Reddy, *Manager*

PRODUCTS & SERVICES SECTION
7371 - Custom Computer Programming Svcs County (P-12814)

EMP: 110 EST: 2016
SALES (est): 13.8MM **Privately Held**
WEB: www.skupos.com
SIC: 7371 Computer software development

(P-12793)
SKYBOX SECURITY INC (PA)
2077 Gateway Pl Ste 200, San Jose (95110-1016)
PHONE 408 441-8060
Gideon Cohen, *CEO*
Charlie Velasquez, *CFO*
Rob Rosiello, *Exec VP*
Ron Davidson, *Vice Pres*
Moti Dror, *Vice Pres*
EMP: 79 EST: 2002
SALES (est): 22.2MM **Privately Held**
WEB: www.skyboxsecurity.com
SIC: 7371 Computer software development

(P-12794)
SKYCATCH INC
38350 Fremont Blvd # 203, Fremont (94536-6060)
PHONE 415 504-3929
Christian Sanz, *CEO*
Cormac Eubanks, *Vice Pres*
Lisa Hu, *Vice Pres*
Eli Kagan, *Creative Dir*
Alex Ramirez, *Sr Software Eng*
EMP: 45 EST: 2013
SALES (est): 7.8MM **Privately Held**
WEB: www.skycatch.com
SIC: 7371 Computer software development

(P-12795)
SKYLITE NETWORKS
761 Mabury Rd Ste 75, San Jose (95133-1018)
PHONE 403 934-9349
EMP: 70
SALES (est): 108.8K **Privately Held**
WEB: www.skylite.com
SIC: 7371 Custom Computer Programing

(P-12796)
SLI SYSTEMS INC
333 W San Carlos St # 1250, San Jose (95110-2726)
PHONE 408 255-2487
Michael Grantham, *Branch Mgr*
Dinh Mac, *Sales Staff*
Tracy Roman, *Sales Staff*
Eric Rosa, *Sales Staff*
Frank Barajas, *Manager*
EMP: 59 **Privately Held**
WEB: www.sli-systems.com
SIC: 7371 Computer software development
PA: S.L.I. Systems, Inc.
    268 Bush St Ste 3900
    San Francisco CA

(P-12797)
SLIDERULE LABS INC (PA)
Also Called: Springboard
22 Battery St Ste 1100, San Francisco (94111-5525)
PHONE 646 748-0378
Parul Gupta, *Vice Pres*
Vince Huang, *Vice Pres*
Jonathan Heyne, *General Mgr*
Zishan Ahmad, *Engineer*
Rimil Dey, *Engineer*
EMP: 188 EST: 2013
SALES (est): 9.8MM **Privately Held**
WEB: www.springboard.com
SIC: 7371 Computer software development & applications

(P-12798)
SMART ERP SOLUTIONS INC (PA)
3875 Hopyard Rd Ste 180, Pleasanton (94588-8505)
PHONE 925 271-0200
Doris Wong, *CEO*
Ramesh B Panchagnula, *President*
Raghu Yelluru, *Officer*
Tom Rumberg, *Vice Pres*
David Testa, *Vice Pres*
EMP: 68 EST: 2005

SQ FT: 6,000
SALES (est): 16.9MM **Privately Held**
WEB: www.smarterp.com
SIC: 7371 5734 7372 8742 Computer software development; computer software development & applications; software, business & non-game; prepackaged software; application computer software; management consulting services

(P-12799)
SMARTNEWS INTERNATIONAL INC
144 2nd St, San Francisco (94105-3716)
PHONE 628 444-3000
Ken Suzuki, *President*
Bernie Davis, *Partner*
Jodi Donner, *Partner*
Kaisei Hamamoto, *CEO*
Atsuo Fujimura, *Senior VP*
EMP: 53 EST: 2014
SALES (est): 5.4MM **Privately Held**
WEB: www.smartnews.com
SIC: 7371 Software programming applications

(P-12800)
SMARTRECRUITERS INC (PA)
225 Bush St Ste 300, San Francisco (94104-4257)
PHONE 415 659-9130
Jerome Ternynck, *CEO*
Jeremy Johnson, *CFO*
Bjorn Eriksson, *Chief Mktg Ofcr*
Bob Memmer, *Officer*
Racher Orston, *Officer*
EMP: 396 EST: 2010
SALES (est): 109.2MM **Privately Held**
WEB: www.smartrecruiters.com
SIC: 7371 Computer software development & applications

(P-12801)
SNAPDOCS INC
100 Montgomery St # 2400, San Francisco (94104-4356)
PHONE 415 967-0136
Aaron King, *President*
Christian Hjorth, *Vice Pres*
Kirk Schmink, *Vice Pres*
Jason Latimer, *Executive*
Nick Purchio, *Executive*
EMP: 50 EST: 2013
SALES (est): 6.9MM **Privately Held**
WEB: www.snapdocs.com
SIC: 7371 Computer software development & applications

(P-12802)
SOFA HOLDCO DEV LLC
Also Called: Software Dev & Technical Svc
470 S Market St, San Jose (95113-2819)
PHONE 847 713-0680
Donald Scott, *CEO*
EMP: 55 EST: 2016
SALES (est): 8MM **Privately Held**
SIC: 7371 Computer software development & applications

(P-12803)
SOFTSOL RESOURCES INC (HQ)
42808 Christy St Ste 100, Fremont (94538-3156)
PHONE 510 824-2000
Srini Madala, *President*
Kumar Talluri, *Vice Pres*
Kris Yalavarthy, *Vice Pres*
Santhosh Latikar, *Tech Recruiter*
Krishna Magam, *Tech Recruiter*
▲ EMP: 100 EST: 1993
SALES (est): 12.2MM **Privately Held**
WEB: www.softsol.com
SIC: 7371 Computer software development

(P-12804)
SOLIX TECHNOLOGIES INC (PA)
4701 Patrick Henry Dr # 2001, Santa Clara (95054-1864)
PHONE 408 654-6405
SAI Gundavelli, *CEO*
Kishore Gadiraju, *Vice Pres*
Rishi Kumar, *Vice Pres*
Ramanand Prasad, *Info Tech Mgr*
Kausthubha Ippagunta, *Analyst*

▼ EMP: 60
SQ FT: 17,000
SALES (est): 10MM **Privately Held**
WEB: www.solix.com
SIC: 7371 Computer software development

(P-12805)
SOLVVY INC
1200 Park Pl Ste 350, San Mateo (94403-2498)
PHONE 650 246-9685
Rory O'Driscoll, *Principal*
Kaan Ersun, *Vice Pres*
Yulia Savitskaya, *Vice Pres*
Tom Schmidt, *Vice Pres*
Jared Betteridge, *Software Engr*
EMP: 39 EST: 2013
SALES (est): 5.7MM **Privately Held**
WEB: www.solvvy.com
SIC: 7371 Computer software development

(P-12806)
SONATA SOFTWARE NORTH AMER INC (HQ)
39300 Civic Center Dr # 270, Fremont (94538-2337)
PHONE 510 791-7220
P Srikar Reddy, *President*
Ravi Aithal, *Partner*
Prasanna Oke, *CFO*
N E Devasahayam, *Assoc VP*
N Sridhara, *Assoc VP*
EMP: 66 EST: 1992
SALES (est): 25.7MM **Privately Held**
WEB: www.sonata-software.com
SIC: 7371 Computer software development

(P-12807)
SONY CORPORATION OF AMERICA
Sony Interactive Studios Amer
2207 Bridgepointe Pkwy, Foster City (94404-5060)
PHONE 650 655-8000
Kelly Flock, *Manager*
Julie Currie, *Vice Pres*
Mary Yee, *Vice Pres*
Tina Barnes, *Program Mgr*
Tracy Seifert, *Executive Asst*
EMP: 200 **Privately Held**
WEB: www.sony.com
SIC: 7371 Computer software development
HQ: Sony Corporation Of America
    25 Madison Ave Fl 27
    New York NY 10010

(P-12808)
SOUNDHOUND INC (PA)
Also Called: Mobile Application
5400 Betsy Ross Dr, Santa Clara (95054-1101)
PHONE 408 441-3200
Keyvan Mohajer, *CEO*
Nitesh Sharan, *CFO*
Amir Arbabi, *Vice Pres*
Seyed Majid Emami, *Vice Pres*
Steve Emberland, *Vice Pres*
EMP: 59 EST: 2005
SQ FT: 61,000
SALES (est): 24.4MM **Privately Held**
WEB: www.soundhound.com
SIC: 7371 Software programming applications

(P-12809)
SPERASOFT INC
2033 Gateway Pl Ste 500, San Jose (95110-3712)
PHONE 408 715-6615
Igor Efremov, *CEO*
Alexei Kudriashov, *CFO*
Maxim Oleynikov, *Sr Software Eng*
Alexander Alexandrov, *Project Mgr*
Vyacheslav Adadurov, *Technical Staff*
EMP: 375 EST: 2005
SQ FT: 15,000

SALES (est): 16MM
SALES (corp-wide): 441.7MM **Privately Held**
WEB: www.sperasoft.com
SIC: 7371 Software programming applications
HQ: Keywords International Limited
    Whelan House
    Dublin D18 T

(P-12810)
SPLASH DATA INC
Also Called: Salexo Software
155 N Santa Cruz Ave # 210, Los Gatos (95030-5946)
PHONE 408 355-4508
Morgan Slain, *Principal*
EMP: 15 EST: 2006
SALES (est): 1.1MM **Privately Held**
WEB: www.splashdata.com
SIC: 7371 7372 Computer software development; application computer software

(P-12811)
SPLASHTOP INC (PA)
1054 S De Anza Blvd Ste 2, San Jose (95129-3553)
PHONE 408 861-1088
Mark Lee, *President*
Alexander Draaijer, *General Mgr*
Philip Sheu, *CTO*
Claire Marinucci, *Sales Staff*
Annie Chen, *Director*
EMP: 48 EST: 2006
SALES (est): 7.1MM **Privately Held**
WEB: www.splashtop.com
SIC: 7371 Computer software development

(P-12812)
SPLICE MACHINE INC (PA)
44 Tehama St, San Francisco (94105-3110)
PHONE 650 678-8985
Monte Zweben, *CEO*
Krishnan Parasuraman, *Vice Pres*
Sara Schrage, *Vice Pres*
Mark Sirek, *Software Engr*
Jun Yuan, *Software Engr*
EMP: 219 EST: 2013
SALES (est): 6.3MM **Privately Held**
WEB: www.splicemachine.com
SIC: 7371 7374 Software programming applications; data entry service

(P-12813)
SPRINGSOFT USA INC (HQ)
700 E Middlefield Rd, Mountain View (94043-4024)
PHONE 650 584-5000
Johnson Teng, *CEO*
Jerry Wang, *CFO*
Yu-Chin Hsu, *Vice Pres*
EMP: 40 EST: 1996
SALES (est): 24.9MM
SALES (corp-wide): 3.6B **Publicly Held**
WEB: www.synopsys.com
SIC: 7371 Computer software systems analysis & design, custom
PA: Synopsys, Inc.
    690 E Middlefield Rd
    Mountain View CA 94043
    650 584-5000

(P-12814)
SRS CONSULTING INC
39465 Paseo Padre Pkwy # 1100, Fremont (94538-5349)
PHONE 510 252-0625
Sangeetha Chowhan, *CEO*
Shankar Chowhan, *President*
Vinod Gonepally, *Tech Recruiter*
EMP: 258 EST: 2002
SQ FT: 1,250
SALES (est): 14.6MM **Privately Held**
WEB: www.srsconsultinginc.com
SIC: 7371 7379 Computer software development; software programming applications; computer related consulting services

7371 - Custom Computer Programming Svcs County (P-12815)   PRODUCTS & SERVICES SECTION

(P-12815)
STANDARD EULER INC
Also Called: Flair
479 Jessie St, San Francisco
(94103-1832)
PHONE..................954 261-6679
Daniel Myers, *President*
Andrew Dai, *Director*
EMP: 50 EST: 2014
SALES (est): 4.3MM **Privately Held**
WEB: www.flair.co
SIC: 7371 8731 7389 Computer software development & applications; computer (hardware) development;

(P-12816)
STARSHIP TECHNOLOGIES INC
535 Mission St Fl 19, San Francisco
(94105-2997)
PHONE..................844 445-5333
Dalis Raducanu, *Opers Staff*
EMP: 36 EST: 2018
SALES (est): 4.5MM **Privately Held**
WEB: www.starship.xyz
SIC: 7371 Computer software development & applications

(P-12817)
STARTUP FARMS INTL LLC
Also Called: Sufi
45690 Northport Loop E, Fremont
(94538-6477)
PHONE..................510 440-0110
Jasvir Gill, *President*
Kaval Kaur,
EMP: 350 EST: 2006
SALES (est): 8.7MM **Privately Held**
WEB: www.startupfarms.com
SIC: 7371 Computer software development

(P-12818)
STELLAR LABS INC
1325 Howard Ave Pmb 412, Burlingame
(94010-4212)
PHONE..................818 578-4078
Vicki Nakata, *CEO*
Dave Fox, *Ch of Bd*
Noel Villamil, *VP Finance*
Blake O 'rafferty, *Senior Mgr*
EMP: 45 EST: 2014
SALES (est): 4.8MM **Privately Held**
WEB: www.stellar.aero
SIC: 7371 Custom computer programming services

(P-12819)
STEPPECHANGE LLC
900 Uccelli Dr Apt 9301, Redwood City
(94063-3051)
PHONE..................415 279-7638
Igor Neyman, *CEO*
EMP: 70 EST: 2010
SALES (est): 2.1MM **Privately Held**
WEB: www.steppechange.com
SIC: 7371 Computer software development

(P-12820)
STRANDS LABS INC
Also Called: Strands Finance
999 Baker Way Ste 430, San Mateo
(94404-1581)
PHONE..................415 398-4333
EMP: 50
SALES (est): 3.1MM **Privately Held**
SIC: 7371 Custom Computer Programming

(P-12821)
STRATEDGE INC (PA)
2410 Camino Ramon Ste 235, San Ramon
(94583-4324)
PHONE..................925 236-2022
Ravi Pangal, *President*
Shilpa RAO, *Human Resources*
EMP: 47 EST: 1998
SQ FT: 700
SALES (est): 5.4MM **Privately Held**
WEB: www.stratedge.us.com
SIC: 7371 Computer software development

(P-12822)
STREAMLINE DEVELOPMENT LLC
Also Called: Streamline Solutions
100 Smith Ranch Rd # 124, San Rafael
(94903-1900)
PHONE..................415 499-3355
Laurence Snyder, *CEO*
Walter Franz, *CFO*
EMP: 46 EST: 1984
SQ FT: 9,000
SALES (est): 9.9MM
SALES (corp-wide): 1B **Privately Held**
WEB: www.efi.com
SIC: 7371 Computer software development
HQ: Electronics For Imaging, Inc.
    6453 Kaiser Dr
    Fremont CA 94555

(P-12823)
STREAMSETS INC (PA)
150 Spear St Ste 300, San Francisco
(94105-1754)
PHONE..................415 851-1018
Girish Pancha, *CEO*
Jobi George, *Partner*
Shekhar Iyer, *President*
Mark Ramsey, *Senior VP*
Arvind Prabhakar, *CTO*
EMP: 50 EST: 2014
SALES (est): 6.4MM **Privately Held**
WEB: www.streamsets.com
SIC: 7371 7372 Software programming applications; business oriented computer software

(P-12824)
STREAMVECTOR INC (PA)
4701 Patrick Henry Dr # 2, Santa Clara
(95054-1819)
PHONE..................415 870-8395
Lokesh Anand, *President*
Piyush Khemka, *Vice Pres*
EMP: 169 EST: 2014
SALES (est): 18.2MM **Privately Held**
SIC: 7371 Computer software development

(P-12825)
STRIIM INC (PA)
575 Middlefield Rd, Palo Alto (94301-2150)
PHONE..................425 894-1998
Ali Kutay, *President*
Codin Pora, *Partner*
Kevin Colon, *Vice Pres*
Michelle Monica, *Executive Asst*
Eben Bedford, *Administration*
EMP: 49 EST: 2012
SALES (est): 1MM **Privately Held**
WEB: www.striim.com
SIC: 7371 Computer software development

(P-12826)
STRIPE INC (PA)
Also Called: Stripe Payments Company
510 Townsend St, San Francisco
(94103-4918)
PHONE..................888 963-8955
Patrick Collison, *CEO*
Dawn Lambeth, *Partner*
John Collison, *President*
Sterling Kahn, *Executive*
James Wu, *CIO*
EMP: 285 EST: 2009
SALES (est): 616.1MM **Privately Held**
WEB: www.stripe.com
SIC: 7371 Computer software development & applications

(P-12827)
STRIVR LABS INC
3520 Thomas Rd Ste C, Santa Clara
(95054-2048)
PHONE..................650 656-9987
Derek Belch, *CEO*
Aneesh Kulkarni, *Vice Pres*
Tom Bronikowski, *Executive*
Rosstin Murphy, *Engineer*
Ken Wolfe, *Engineer*
EMP: 140 EST: 2015

SALES (est): 20.7MM **Privately Held**
WEB: www.strivr.com
SIC: 7371 Computer software development & applications

(P-12828)
STRUCTIONSITE INC
248 3rd St, Oakland (94607-4375)
PHONE..................510 340-9515
Matthew Daly, *CEO*
Brianna Williams, *Senior Mgr*
Chris Jervey, *Director*
Michael Koski, *Accounts Exec*
EMP: 35 EST: 2016
SALES (est): 3.1MM **Privately Held**
WEB: www.structionsite.com
SIC: 7371 7389 Computer software development & applications;

(P-12829)
STYRA INC
1800 Broadway St Ste 1, Redwood City
(94063-2044)
PHONE..................415 200-8871
Ettori Pierre, *CEO*
Stan Lagun, *Sr Software Eng*
Magnus MA, *Sr Software Eng*
Richard Barnes, *CIO*
Andy Curtis, *Software Engr*
EMP: 36 EST: 2017
SALES (est): 2MM **Privately Held**
WEB: www.styra.com
SIC: 7371 Custom computer programming services

(P-12830)
SUCCESSFACTORS INC
1500 Fashion Island Blvd, San Mateo
(94404-1597)
PHONE..................650 645-2000
Greg Tomb, *CEO*
Kara Wilson, *Chief Mktg Ofcr*
Jackie Ato, *Executive*
Kristin Gaw, *Admin Sec*
Sarat Polavarapu, *Sr Software Eng*
EMP: 53 EST: 2001
SALES (est): 2.3MM **Privately Held**
WEB: www.successfactors.nl
SIC: 7371 Computer software development

(P-12831)
SUGARCRM INC (PA)
10050 N Wolfe Rd Sw2130, Cupertino
(95014-2528)
PHONE..................877 842-7276
Larry Augustin, *Ch of Bd*
Craig Charlton, *CEO*
Andrew Chmyz, *CFO*
John Donaldson, *CFO*
Steve Valenzuela, *CFO*
EMP: 110 EST: 2004
SQ FT: 40,000
SALES (est): 83.2MM **Privately Held**
WEB: www.sugarcrm.com
SIC: 7371 Computer software development

(P-12832)
SUKI AI INC
1823 El Cmino Real Unit A, Redwood City
(94063)
PHONE..................650 549-8959
Punit Singh Soni, *CEO*
Mahlet Getachew, *General Counsel*
EMP: 40 EST: 2016
SALES (est): 3MM **Privately Held**
WEB: www.suki.ai
SIC: 7371 Computer software development & applications

(P-12833)
SUMO LOGIC INC (PA)
305 Main St Fl 3, Redwood City
(94063-1729)
PHONE..................650 810-8700
Ramin Sayar, *President*
Sydney Carey, *CFO*
Suku Krishnaraj Chettiar, *Chief Mktg Ofcr*
Dione Hedgpeth, *Officer*
Jim Hoppe, *Vice Pres*
EMP: 708 EST: 2010
SQ FT: 37,000

SALES: 202.6MM **Publicly Held**
WEB: www.sumologic.com
SIC: 7371 Computer software development

(P-12834)
SUNGARD BI-TECH INC (DH)
890 Fortress St, Chico (95973-9023)
PHONE..................530 891-5281
Aaron Johnson, *President*
Bruce Langston, *CFO*
EMP: 50 EST: 1981
SALES (est): 10.2MM
SALES (corp-wide): 12.5B **Publicly Held**
SIC: 7371 Computer software development
HQ: Fis Capital Markets Us Llc
    601 Riverside Ave
    Jacksonville FL 32204
    877 776-3706

(P-12835)
SUPER EVIL MEGA CORP
119a S B St, San Mateo (94401-3908)
PHONE..................650 787-2505
Robert Daly, *CEO*
Kristian Federstrale, *COO*
Patrick O 'callahan, *Creative Dir*
Alexander Wallisch, *Sr Software Eng*
Tommy Krul, *CTO*
EMP: 40 EST: 2012
SALES (est): 5.3MM **Privately Held**
WEB: www.superevilmegacorp.com
SIC: 7371 Computer software development & applications

(P-12836)
SYBASE 365 LLC
1 Sybase Dr, Dublin (94568-7976)
PHONE..................925 236-5000
David Tan, *Administration*
Kshitiz Bhattarai, *Software Dev*
Joe Love, *Engineer*
Jody KAO, *Manager*
Scott Boman, *Consultant*
EMP: 67 EST: 2000
SALES (est): 5.2MM
SALES (corp-wide): 32.3B **Publicly Held**
WEB: www.sybase.com
SIC: 7371 Computer software development
HQ: Sap America, Inc.
    3999 West Chester Pike
    Newtown Square PA 19073
    610 661-1000

(P-12837)
SYMANTEC OPERATING CORPORATION (HQ)
350 Ellis St, Mountain View (94043-2202)
PHONE..................650 527-8000
Scott C Taylor, *President*
Jake Christensen, *Engineer*
EMP: 746 EST: 2011
SALES (est): 24.1MM
SALES (corp-wide): 2.5B **Publicly Held**
WEB: www.nortonlifelock.com
SIC: 7371 Computer software development & applications
PA: Nortonlifelock Inc.
    60 E Rio Salado Pkwy # 1
    Tempe AZ 85281
    650 527-8000

(P-12838)
SYMPHONY METREO INC
2475 Hanover St, Palo Alto (94304-1114)
PHONE..................650 935-9500
Tal Ball, *CEO*
EMP: 1126 EST: 2007
SALES (est): 4.8MM
SALES (corp-wide): 191.2MM **Privately Held**
WEB: www.stgpartners.com
SIC: 7371 Computer software development
PA: Symphony Technology Group, L.L.C.
    428 University Ave
    Palo Alto CA 94301
    650 935-9500

PRODUCTS & SERVICES SECTION
7371 - Custom Computer Programming Svcs County (P-12862)

(P-12839)
SYNACTIVE INC (PA)
2253 Harbor Bay Pkwy, Alameda (94502-3026)
P.O. Box 4609, San Mateo (94404-0609)
PHONE.................................650 341-3310
Thomas C Ewe, *President*
Cynthia Goco-Nakar, *President*
Damian Shanoian, *Finance*
Colin Branch, *Sales Staff*
Umang Desai, *Director*
EMP: 43 **EST:** 1998
SALES (est): 5.7MM **Privately Held**
WEB: www.liquid-ui.com
SIC: 7371 Computer software development

(P-12840)
SYNARC INC (DH)
Also Called: Bioclinica
777 Mariners Island Blvd # 550, San Mateo (94404-5048)
PHONE.................................415 817-8900
Claus Christiansen, *CEO*
Harry K Genant, *Chairman*
Thomas T Fuerst, *Officer*
Thomas Fuerst, *Officer*
Todd Kisner, *Vice Pres*
EMP: 153 **EST:** 1998
SALES (est): 35.7MM
SALES (corp-wide): 1.5MM **Privately Held**
WEB: www.bioclinica.com
SIC: 7371 Computer software development & applications

(P-12841)
SYNERGEX INTERNATIONAL CORP
2355 Gold Meadow Way # 200, Gold River (95670-6326)
PHONE.................................916 635-7300
Michele C Wong, *CEO*
Serena Channel, *Partner*
Vigfus A Asmundson, *Shareholder*
Georgia Petersen, *Shareholder*
Thomas J Powers, *Shareholder*
EMP: 55 **EST:** 1976
SALES (est): 10.3MM **Privately Held**
WEB: www.synergex.com
SIC: 7371 Computer software development

(P-12842)
SYNOPHIC SYSTEMS INC
19925 Stevens Creek Blvd, Cupertino (95014-2300)
PHONE.................................408 459-7676
Kondal Balusu, *CEO*
EMP: 500 **EST:** 2010
SALES (est): 25MM **Privately Held**
WEB: www.synophic.com
SIC: 7371 7373 4899 Computer software systems analysis & design, custom; software programming applications; systems engineering, computer related; local area network (LAN) systems integrator; communication signal enhancement network system

(P-12843)
SYNOVA INTERACTIVE GROUP INC
1400 Marsten Rd, Burlingame (94010-2418)
PHONE.................................650 513-1058
EMP: 45
SALES (est): 1.2MM **Privately Held**
SIC: 7371 Custom Computer Programing

(P-12844)
SYSDIG INC (PA)
135 Main St Fl 21, San Francisco (94105-1812)
PHONE.................................415 872-9473
Suresh Vasudevan, *CEO*
Larry Castro, *CFO*
Janet Matsuda, *Chief Mktg Ofcr*
Keegan Riley, *Officer*
Adityashnkar Kini, *Vice Pres*
EMP: 218 **EST:** 2013
SALES (est): 24.2MM **Privately Held**
WEB: www.sysdig.com
SIC: 7371 Computer software development

(P-12845)
SYSOREX INTERNATIONAL INC (PA)
335 E Middlefield Rd, Mountain View (94043-4003)
PHONE.................................408 702-2167
Abdul Salam Quresihi, *President*
Amy Hughes, *Accounting Mgr*
EMP: 37 **EST:** 1971
SQ FT: 4,377
SALES: 62.9MM **Privately Held**
WEB: www.inpixon.com
SIC: 7371 Computer software development

(P-12846)
TACTAI TECHNOLOGIES INC
150 Mathilda Pl Ste 104, Sunnyvale (94086-6010)
PHONE.................................844 439-8228
Chockalingam Ganapathi, *CEO*
Trevor Templar, *Officer*
Mark Masters, *Vice Pres*
Vijay Jegan, *CTO*
Clement Paulraj, *Sales Staff*
EMP: 46 **EST:** 2011
SALES (est): 5.5MM **Privately Held**
WEB: www.tact.ai
SIC: 7371 Software programming applications

(P-12847)
TALARI NETWORKS INC (HQ)
4230 Leonard Stocking Dr, Santa Clara (95054-1777)
PHONE.................................408 689-0400
Patrick Sweeney, *CEO*
Emerick Woods, *President*
Kevin Gavin, *Chief Mktg Ofcr*
Adrian Tate, *Vice Pres*
Cristina Fortuna, *Exec Sec*
EMP: 62 **EST:** 2007
SALES (est): 19.9MM
SALES (corp-wide): 40.4B **Publicly Held**
WEB: www.oracle.com
SIC: 7371 Computer software development
PA: Oracle Corporation
   2300 Oracle Way
   Austin TX 78741
   737 867-1000

(P-12848)
TAMTRON CORPORATION (DH)
6203 San Ignacio Ave # 110, San Jose (95119-1371)
PHONE.................................408 323-3303
Fax: 408 246-5415
EMP: 60
SQ FT: 2,600
SALES (est): 3.8MM
SALES (corp-wide): 1.3B **Privately Held**
SIC: 7371 Computer Software Development
HQ: Impac Medical Systems, Inc
   100 Mathilda Pl Fl 5
   Sunnyvale CA 94086
   408 830-8000

(P-12849)
TANGIBLE PLAY INC (HQ)
195 Page Mill Rd Ste 105, Palo Alto (94306-2073)
PHONE.................................650 667-1693
Pramod Sharma, *CEO*
Garrett Hipple, *CIO*
Jerome Scholler, *CTO*
Ariel Zekelman, *Senior Mgr*
Kay Hsi, *Manager*
EMP: 101 **EST:** 2013
SALES (est): 48.3MM **Privately Held**
WEB: www.tangibleplay.com
SIC: 7371 3944 Software programming applications; board games, children's & adults'

(P-12850)
TASK HELP LLC
1390 Market St Ste 200, San Francisco (94102-5404)
PHONE.................................833 229-0726
Etop Udo,
EMP: 68 **EST:** 2019

SALES (est): 9.6MM **Privately Held**
WEB: www.task.help
SIC: 7371 Software programming applications

(P-12851)
TAULIA INC (PA)
95 3rd St, San Francisco (94103-3103)
PHONE.................................415 376-8280
Cedric Bru, *CEO*
Tina Ngo, *Partner*
Archana Sridhar, *Partner*
Jonathan Lowenhar, *President*
Rik Thorbecke, *CFO*
EMP: 182 **EST:** 2009
SALES (est): 40.2MM **Privately Held**
WEB: www.taulia.com
SIC: 7371 Computer software development

(P-12852)
TAVANT TECHNOLOGIES INC (PA)
3965 Freedom Cir Ste 750, Santa Clara (95054-1285)
PHONE.................................408 519-5400
Sarvesh Mahesh, *CEO*
Sanjay Shah, *Partner*
Sesha Devana, *CFO*
Venkata Devana, *CFO*
Raj Menon, *Chief Mktg Ofcr*
EMP: 2273 **EST:** 2000
SALES (est): 118.8MM **Privately Held**
WEB: www.tavantengage.com
SIC: 7371 Computer software development

(P-12853)
TECHEXCEL INC (PA)
3675 Mt Diablo Blvd # 330, Lafayette (94549-3792)
PHONE.................................925 871-3900
Tieren Zhou, *President*
James Zhou, *CFO*
Rickard Jonsson, *Vice Pres*
Tingjin Xu, *Software Engr*
Prince Huang, *Opers Staff*
EMP: 51 **EST:** 1995
SQ FT: 11,187
SALES (est): 10MM **Privately Held**
WEB: www.techexcel.com
SIC: 7371 Computer software development

(P-12854)
TEKRELIANCE LLC
46560 Fremont Blvd # 302, Fremont (94538-6482)
PHONE.................................732 829-7585
Umang Kathrani, *President*
Chirag Kathrani, *Vice Pres*
EMP: 35 **EST:** 2006
SALES (est): 3.2MM **Privately Held**
WEB: www.tekreliance.com
SIC: 7371 Software programming applications

(P-12855)
TEKREVOL LLC
39899 Balentine Dr # 200, Newark (94560-5355)
PHONE.................................832 426-3532
Abeer Raza, *Partner*
Joshua Crane, *CIO*
Estes Saville, *Sales Mgr*
Asim Rais, *Mng Member*
Paul Adams, *Manager*
EMP: 55
SALES (est): 1.1MM **Privately Held**
WEB: www.tekrevol.com
SIC: 7371 Computer software development & applications

(P-12856)
TELESTREAM LLC (PA)
848 Gold Flat Rd, Nevada City (95959-3208)
PHONE.................................530 470-1300
Daniel Castles, *CEO*
Scott Puopolo, *CEO*
Mark Cuny, *CFO*
Chris Osika, *Chief Mktg Ofcr*
Barbara Dehart, *Vice Pres*
▲ **EMP:** 120 **EST:** 1998

SALES (est): 91.4MM **Privately Held**
WEB: www.telestream.net
SIC: 7371 Computer software development & applications

(P-12857)
TELLAPART INC (HQ)
1355 Market St 5, San Francisco (94103-1307)
PHONE.................................415 222-9670
Josh McFarland, *President*
Wade Chambers, *President*
EMP: 70 **EST:** 2009
SALES (est): 351.7K
SALES (corp-wide): 3.7B **Publicly Held**
WEB: www.twitter.com
SIC: 7371 Computer software development
PA: Twitter, Inc.
   1355 Market St Ste 900
   San Francisco CA 94103
   415 222-9670

(P-12858)
TEMUJIN LABS INC
Also Called: Findora
444 High St Ste 300, Palo Alto (94301-1671)
PHONE.................................650 850-9037
Kevin Wong, *President*
Charles Lu, *Principal*
EMP: 50 **EST:** 2019
SALES (est): 1.4MM **Privately Held**
SIC: 7371 Custom computer programming services

(P-12859)
TESCRA
3130 Crow Canyon Pl # 205, San Ramon (94583-1346)
PHONE.................................925 242-0100
Chhabi Gupta, *CEO*
Manoj Gupta, *COO*
Annie Thomas, *Recruiter*
Shaikh Rafiq, *Asst Mgr*
Karan Babblu, *Consultant*
EMP: 40 **EST:** 2002
SALES (est): 5.5MM **Privately Held**
WEB: www.tescra.com
SIC: 7371 Computer software development

(P-12860)
TESLARATI LLC
11040 Bollinger Canyon Rd, San Ramon (94582-4969)
PHONE.................................323 405-7657
Gene Liu, *CEO*
EMP: 18 **EST:** 2016
SALES (est): 1.1MM **Privately Held**
WEB: www.teslarati.com
SIC: 7371 2741 Computer software development & applications;

(P-12861)
THIRD PILLAR SYSTEMS INC (PA)
703 Market St Ste 700, San Francisco (94103-2116)
PHONE.................................650 346-3108
Pankaj Chowdhry, *President*
EMP: 42 **EST:** 1999
SQ FT: 11,516
SALES (est): 4.9MM **Privately Held**
SIC: 7371 Computer software systems analysis & design, custom

(P-12862)
THISMOMENT INC
690 Market St Unit 1101, San Francisco (94104-5123)
PHONE.................................415 200-4730
Vince Broady, *CEO*
Raffy Kaloustian, *President*
Trey Walker, *President*
John Walliser, *President*
Steve Bach, *CFO*
EMP: 135 **EST:** 2008
SQ FT: 15,000
SALES (est): 12.6MM **Privately Held**
WEB: www.thismoment.com
SIC: 7371 Computer software development

7371 - Custom Computer Programming Svcs County (P-12863)

(P-12863)
THOUGHT STREAM LLC
Also Called: Bluescape
303 Twin Dolphin Dr Fl 6, Redwood City (94065-1497)
PHONE..................650 567-4550
Peter Jackson, *CEO*
Scott Poulton, *Ch of Bd*
Rick Tywoniak, *Chief Mktg Ofcr*
Josh Ulm, *Vice Pres*
Mt Robertson, *VP Business*
EMP: 49 **EST:** 2012
SALES (est): 6.1MM
SALES (corp-wide): 1.8B **Privately Held**
WEB: www.bluescape.com
SIC: 7371 Computer software development
HQ: Haworth, Inc.
1 Haworth Ctr
Holland MI 49423
616 393-3000

(P-12864)
THREATMETRIX INC
160 W Santa Clara St # 1, San Jose (95113-1701)
PHONE..................408 200-5700
Reed Taussig, *President*
Frank Teruel, *CFO*
Armen Najarian, *Chief Mktg Ofcr*
Paul Abbey, *Officer*
Alisdair Faulkner, *Officer*
EMP: 165 **EST:** 2008
SQ FT: 10,000
SALES (est): 31.3MM
SALES (corp-wide): 9.4B **Privately Held**
WEB: www.risk.lexisnexis.com
SIC: 7371 7374 7382 Computer software development & applications; computer processing services; security systems services
HQ: Lexisnexis Risk Solutions Inc.
1000 Alderman Dr
Alpharetta GA 30005
678 694-6000

(P-12865)
TIBCO SOFTWARE INC (HQ)
3307 Hillview Ave, Palo Alto (94304-1204)
PHONE..................650 846-1000
Dan Streetman, *CEO*
Sumati Natarajan, *Partner*
Armin Jabs, *COO*
Matt Quinn, *COO*
Tom Berquist, *CFO*
EMP: 470 **EST:** 1985
SQ FT: 292,000
SALES (est): 613.1MM
SALES (corp-wide): 885.6MM **Privately Held**
WEB: www.tibco.com
SIC: 7371 7373 Computer software development; systems integration services
PA: Balboa Intermediate Holdings Llc
3307 Hillview Ave
Palo Alto CA 94304
650 846-1000

(P-12866)
TIGHTDB INC
Also Called: Realm
100 Forest Ave, Palo Alto (94301-1612)
PHONE..................415 766-2020
Alexander Stigsen, *CEO*
Paul Kopacki, *Chief Mktg Ofcr*
Bjarne Christiansen, *Principal*
EMP: 60 **EST:** 2011
SALES (est): 3.2MM **Privately Held**
WEB: www.tightdb.com
SIC: 7371 Computer software development & applications

(P-12867)
TOM SAWYER SOFTWARE CORP (PA)
1997 El Dorado Ave, Berkeley (94707-2441)
PHONE..................510 208-4370
Brendan P Madden, *CEO*
Jay Cheung, *Officer*
Tina Lim, *Admin Mgr*
Joshua Feingold, *CTO*
Nancy Adams, *Technical Staff*
EMP: 43 **EST:** 1991
SQ FT: 6,264
SALES (est): 6.3MM **Privately Held**
WEB: www.tomsawyer.com
SIC: 7371 Computer software development

(P-12868)
TONICAI INC
548 Market St, San Francisco (94104-5401)
PHONE..................415 340-0330
Ian Coe, *CEO*
EMP: 40 **EST:** 2018
SALES (est): 2.9MM **Privately Held**
WEB: www.tonic.ai
SIC: 7371 Computer software development

(P-12869)
TOOLWIRE INC
6754 Bernal Ave Ste 740, Pleasanton (94566-1235)
PHONE..................925 227-8500
John Valencia, *President*
David Clarke, *Founder*
John Catanzaro, *Vice Pres*
Cameron Crowe, *Vice Pres*
Joseph White, *Technical Staff*
EMP: 56 **EST:** 1999
SALES (est): 21.7MM **Privately Held**
WEB: www.spaceslearning.com
SIC: 7371 Computer software development

(P-12870)
TORR INDUSTRIES INC
4564 Caterpillar Rd, Redding (96003-1418)
PHONE..................530 247-6909
Timothy Orr, *Owner*
Clyde Orr, *Vice Pres*
Amanda Runciman, *Engineer*
EMP: 38 **EST:** 2007
SALES (est): 6.5MM **Privately Held**
WEB: www.torrindustries.com
SIC: 7371 7692 Software programming applications; welding repair

(P-12871)
TRACEABLE INC
548 Market St Ste 83903, San Francisco (94104-5401)
PHONE..................855 346-7233
Jyoti Bansal, *CEO*
Arisa Nakamura, *Manager*
EMP: 50 **EST:** 2018
SALES (est): 2.7MM **Privately Held**
SIC: 7371 Software programming applications

(P-12872)
TRAFORM INC
49016 Milmont Dr, Fremont (94538-7301)
PHONE..................650 387-5536
Sathiya Thulasidas, *CEO*
EMP: 35 **EST:** 2016
SALES (est): 2.6MM **Privately Held**
WEB: www.traform.com
SIC: 7371 Custom computer programming services

(P-12873)
TRANSCENSE INC (PA)
1864 Fell St, San Francisco (94117-2021)
PHONE..................415 867-7230
Thibault Duchemin, *CFO*
EMP: 49 **EST:** 2015
SALES (est): 583.9K **Privately Held**
SIC: 7371 Computer software development & applications

(P-12874)
TRAY IO INC (PA)
25 Stillman St Ste 200, San Francisco (94107-1379)
PHONE..................415 418-3570
Ajeeth Kumar, *Principal*
Jennifer Shum Chang, *Partner*
Paul Fung, *Partner*
Shibani Mehta, *Admin Sec*
Philip Childers, *CIO*
EMP: 68 **EST:** 2012
SALES (est): 3.3MM **Privately Held**
WEB: www.tray.io
SIC: 7371 Computer software development & applications

(P-12875)
TREASURE DATA INC (HQ)
800 W El Cmino Real Ste 1, Mountain View (94040)
PHONE..................866 899-5386
Hiro Yoshikawa, *CEO*
Dan Weirich, *CFO*
Daniel Weirich, *CFO*
Kiyoto Tamura, *Ch Credit Ofcr*
Rob Glickman, *Chief Mktg Ofcr*
EMP: 98 **EST:** 2011
SALES (est): 28.4MM **Privately Held**
WEB: www.treasuredata.com
SIC: 7371 7374 Custom computer programming services; optical scanning data service

(P-12876)
TRIESTEN TECHNOLOGIES LLC (PA)
320 Channing Way Apt 121, San Rafael (94903-2622)
PHONE..................916 719-6150
Ssiram Thirupakkuzhi, *Mng Member*
EMP: 135 **EST:** 2009
SALES (est): 3MM **Privately Held**
WEB: www.triesten.com
SIC: 7371 Custom computer programming services; software programming applications

(P-12877)
TRUE NORTH
8 Cadiz Cir, Redwood City (94065-1333)
PHONE..................650 207-9800
Alexander Gonikman, *CEO*
EMP: 65 **EST:** 2018
SALES (est): 1.3MM **Privately Held**
SIC: 7371 Computer software development

(P-12878)
TRYFACTA INC
Also Called: Systems America Public Sector
4637 Chabot Dr Ste 100, Pleasanton (94588-2753)
PHONE..................408 419-9200
Ratika Tyagi, *CEO*
EMP: 351 **EST:** 1996
SALES (est): 42.7MM **Privately Held**
WEB: www.tryfacta.ai
SIC: 7371 7361 7373 8748 Computer software systems analysis & design, custom; labor contractors (employment agency); systems software development services; systems engineering consultant, ex. computer or professional

(P-12879)
TURING VIDEO
1730 S El Cmino Real Ste, San Mateo (94402)
PHONE..................877 730-8222
Xing Zhong, *President*
Jiang Lei, *Finance*
EMP: 70 **EST:** 2017
SALES (est): 4.3MM **Privately Held**
WEB: www.turingvideo.com
SIC: 7371 Computer software development & applications

(P-12880)
TURINGSENSE INC (PA)
4675 Stevens Creek Blvd # 101, Santa Clara (95051-6763)
P.O. Box 2190 (95055-2190)
PHONE..................408 887-7833
Limin He, *Principal*
Pietro Garofalo, *Vice Pres*
EMP: 43 **EST:** 2015
SALES (est): 1.2MM **Privately Held**
WEB: www.turingsense.com
SIC: 7371 Computer software development & applications

(P-12881)
TWIN HEALTH INC
2525 Charleston Rd # 104, Mountain View (94043-1635)
PHONE..................970 215-8300
Jahangir Mohammed, *CEO*
Eric Carlson, *CFO*
EMP: 50 **EST:** 2018
SALES (est): 3.1MM **Privately Held**
SIC: 7371 Computer software development & applications

(P-12882)
UBERTAL INC
Also Called: Ubertal Technology
1730 S Amphlett Blvd # 250, San Mateo (94402-2723)
PHONE..................650 542-8100
Xianghong Kang,
Pavan Kochar, *CEO*
Monica Foyer, *Vice Pres*
Vince Xu, *Vice Pres*
Zoe Liang, *Human Resources*
EMP: 40 **EST:** 2011
SALES (est): 2.9MM **Privately Held**
WEB: www.ubertal.com
SIC: 7371 7361 Computer software development; placement agencies

(P-12883)
UBICS INC
1050 Bridgeway, Sausalito (94965-2173)
PHONE..................415 289-1400
Vijay Mallya, *Branch Mgr*
EMP: 140 **Privately Held**
WEB: www.ubics.com
SIC: 7371 Custom computer programming services
PA: Ubics, Inc.
400 Sthpinte Blvd Ste 425
Canonsburg PA 15317

(P-12884)
UBISOFT INC (DH)
625 3rd St, San Francisco (94107-1901)
PHONE..................415 547-4000
Laurent Detoc, *President*
Spencer Audet, *Partner*
Frederick Duguet, *CFO*
Marc Fortier, *Vice Pres*
Nao Higo, *Vice Pres*
▲ **EMP:** 623 **EST:** 1991
SALES (est): 341.8MM
SALES (corp-wide): 2.6B **Privately Held**
WEB: www.ubisoft.com
SIC: 7371 Computer software writing services

(P-12885)
UDELV INC
1826 Rollins Rd Ste 100, Burlingame (94010-2215)
PHONE..................650 376-3785
Daniel Laury, *CEO*
Anchan Saxena, *Engineer*
Edward Knudsen, *Director*
Andrew Phavichitr, *Director*
EMP: 30 **EST:** 2016
SALES (est): 2.9MM **Privately Held**
WEB: www.udelv.com
SIC: 7371 3711 Computer software development & applications; motor vehicles & car bodies

(P-12886)
ULTIMO SOFTWARE SOLUTIONS INC
33268 Central Ave 2, Union City (94587-2010)
PHONE..................408 943-1490
Venkatasubhash Pasumarthy, *President*
Smita Pasumarthi, *CFO*
Saurabh Srivastava, *Consultant*
EMP: 127 **EST:** 2002
SQ FT: 4,000
SALES (est): 7.1MM **Privately Held**
WEB: www.ultimosoft.com
SIC: 7371 Computer software development

(P-12887)
ULTRASENSE SYSTEMS INC (PA)
2025 Gateway Pl Ste 156, San Jose (95110-1000)
PHONE..................408 391-5734
MO Maghsoudnia, *President*
EMP: 38 **EST:** 2018
SALES (est): 3.7MM **Privately Held**
WEB: www.ultrasensesys.com
SIC: 7371 Computer software development

▲ = Import ▼ = Export
◆ = Import/Export

7371 - Custom Computer Programming Svcs County (P-12911)

(P-12888)
UNITY SOFTWARE INC (PA)
30 3rd St, San Francisco (94103-3104)
PHONE..............................415 539-3162
John Riccitiello, *Ch of Bd*
Jackie Jones, *Partner*
Kimberly Jabal, *CFO*
Roelof Botha, *Bd of Directors*
Clive Downie, *Chief Mktg Ofcr*
EMP: 334 **EST:** 2004
SQ FT: 53,000
SALES (est): 772.4MM **Publicly Held**
WEB: www.unity.com
SIC: 7371 7372 Computer software development; prepackaged software

(P-12889)
UPLIFT INC
440 N Wolfe Rd, Sunnyvale (94085-3869)
PHONE..............................408 396-3374
Brian Barth, *CEO*
Kunal Shah, *Finance*
Brian Louie, *Analyst*
Rob Borden, *Marketing Staff*
EMP: 61 **EST:** 2014
SALES (est): 6.2MM **Privately Held**
WEB: www.uplift.com
SIC: 7371 Computer software development & applications

(P-12890)
UPTIMA INC
55 E Empire St, San Jose (95112-5309)
PHONE..............................408 933-9505
Bill Butler, *CEO*
EMP: 40 **EST:** 2016
SALES (est): 5.3MM **Privately Held**
WEB: www.uptima.com
SIC: 7371 Custom computer programming services

(P-12891)
UPWORK GLOBAL INC (HQ)
655 Montgomery St Ste 490, San Francisco (94111-2676)
PHONE..............................650 316-7500
Stephane Kasriel, *CEO*
Brian Kinion, *CFO*
Brian Levey, *Officer*
Matt McDonald, *Vice Pres*
Leslie Taylor, *Executive Asst*
EMP: 49 **EST:** 2003
SALES (est): 26.9MM
SALES (corp-wide): 373.6MM **Publicly Held**
WEB: www.upwork.com
SIC: 7371 2741 Computer software development & applications; miscellaneous publishing
PA: Upwork Inc.
2625 Augustine Dr Fl 6th
Santa Clara CA 95054
650 316-7500

(P-12892)
USER ZOOM INC
10 Almaden Blvd Ste 250, San Jose (95113-2226)
PHONE..............................408 533-8619
Alfonso De La Nuez, *CEO*
Xavier Mestres, *COO*
Arthur Moan, *Vice Pres*
Matthew Paulus, *Vice Pres*
Matt Paulus, *Executive*
EMP: 80 **EST:** 2007
SALES (est): 10.7MM **Privately Held**
WEB: www.userzoom.com
SIC: 7371 Computer software development

(P-12893)
VAGARO INC
4120 Dublin Blvd Ste 250, Dublin (94568-7765)
PHONE..............................800 919-0157
Fred Helou, *CEO*
Cheryl Pursell, *Technical Staff*
John Zukoski, *Finance*
Alexa Mitchell, *Sales Executive*
Carina King, *Marketing Staff*
EMP: 78 **EST:** 2009
SALES (est): 7.2MM **Privately Held**
WEB: www.vagaro.com
SIC: 7371 Custom computer programming services

(P-12894)
VARITE INC (PA)
111 N Market St Ste 730, San Jose (95113-1108)
PHONE..............................408 977-0700
Adarsh Katyal, *President*
Kanwar Singh, *Senior VP*
Purushotam Sharma, *Opers Staff*
Deepak Kumar, *Manager*
Amit Rai, *Manager*
EMP: 39 **EST:** 2000
SQ FT: 1,200
SALES (est): 6.7MM **Privately Held**
WEB: www.varite.com
SIC: 7371 Computer software development

(P-12895)
VAST SYSTEMS TECHNOLOGY CORP
700 E Middlefield Rd, Mountain View (94043-4024)
PHONE..............................650 584-5000
Alain Labat, *President*
Kyle Park, *CFO*
EMP: 36 **EST:** 1998
SALES (est): 9MM
SALES (corp-wide): 3.6B **Publicly Held**
WEB: www.synopsys.com
SIC: 7371 Computer software development
PA: Synopsys, Inc.
690 E Middlefield Rd
Mountain View CA 94043
650 584-5000

(P-12896)
VCOMPLY TECHNOLOGIES INC
75 E Santa Clara St Fl 6, San Jose (95113-1827)
PHONE..............................650 319-8842
Harsh Kariwala, *CEO*
EMP: 100 **EST:** 2016
SALES (est): 5.3MM **Privately Held**
WEB: www.v-comply.com
SIC: 7371 Computer software development

(P-12897)
VEEAR PROJECTS
4695 Chabot Dr Ste 108, Pleasanton (94588-2787)
PHONE..............................415 827-1671
Raj Khaware, *CEO*
EMP: 54 **EST:** 2004
SALES (est): 5MM **Privately Held**
WEB: www.veearprojects.com
SIC: 7371 Custom computer programming services

(P-12898)
VENDINI INC (PA)
201 1st St Ste 111, Petaluma (94952-4291)
PHONE..............................415 693-9611
Mark Tacchi, *President*
Michael Farrow, *CFO*
Susan Hollingshead,
Keith Goldberg, *Officer*
Thao Le, *Executive*
EMP: 79 **EST:** 2002
SALES (est): 17.1MM **Privately Held**
WEB: www.vendini.com
SIC: 7371 Computer software development

(P-12899)
VENDIO SERVICES INC (PA)
1510 Fashion Island Blvd, San Mateo (94404-1596)
PHONE..............................650 293-3500
Rodrigo Sales, *CEO*
Mike Effle, *Vice Pres*
EMP: 79 **EST:** 1999
SQ FT: 8,000
SALES (est): 10.4MM **Privately Held**
WEB: www.vendio.com
SIC: 7371 Computer software development

(P-12900)
VERITAS TECHNOLOGIES LLC (DH)
2625 Augustine Dr, Santa Clara (95054-2956)
PHONE..............................866 837-4827
Greg Hughes, *CEO*
Mick Lopez, *CFO*
Todd Forsythe, *Chief Mktg Ofcr*
Ben Gibson, *Chief Mktg Ofcr*
Matt Cain,
EMP: 200 **EST:** 2014
SALES (est): 191.9MM
SALES (corp-wide): 2.9B **Publicly Held**
WEB: www.veritas.com
SIC: 7371 7375 Computer software development & applications; information retrieval services; data base information retrieval

(P-12901)
VERITAS US INC
2625 Augustine Dr, Santa Clara (95054-2956)
PHONE..............................650 933-1000
Greg Huges, *CEO*
Mark Dentinger, *Exec VP*
Sophie Ames, *Vice Pres*
Todd Forsythe, *Vice Pres*
EMP: 200 **EST:** 2014
SALES (est): 1.2B **Privately Held**
WEB: www.veritas.com
SIC: 7371 Computer software development & applications

(P-12902)
VERSA NETWORKS INC (PA)
6001 America Center Dr # 400, San Jose (95002-2562)
PHONE..............................408 385-7660
Kulvinder Ahuja, *CEO*
Kelly Ahuja, *CEO*
Apurva Mehta, *Founder*
Kumar Mehta, *Founder*
Robert McBride, *Senior VP*
EMP: 316 **EST:** 2012
SQ FT: 37,000
SALES (est): 50.2MM **Privately Held**
WEB: www.versa-networks.com
SIC: 7371 Computer software development

(P-12903)
VIDA HEALTH INC
100 Montgomery St Ste 750, San Francisco (94104-4302)
PHONE..............................415 989-1017
Stephanie Tilenius, *CEO*
Cynthia Mark, *Ch Credit Ofcr*
Randy Forman, *Officer*
Craig Foster, *Vice Pres*
Kevin Knight, *Vice Pres*
EMP: 100 **EST:** 2013
SALES (est): 7.8MM **Privately Held**
WEB: www.vida.com
SIC: 7371 Computer software development & applications

(P-12904)
VIM INC
548 Market St Pmb 84904, San Francisco (94104-5401)
PHONE..............................844 843-5381
Oron Afek, *CEO*
Mike Leonard, *Officer*
Asaf David, *CTO*
EMP: 80 **EST:** 2015
SALES (est): 3.3MM **Privately Held**
WEB: www.getvim.com
SIC: 7371 Computer software development

(P-12905)
VINETI INC
633 Howard St, San Francisco (94105-3903)
P.O. Box 427397 (94142-7397)
PHONE..............................415 704-8730
Amy Duross, *CEO*
Joe Depinto, *Ch Credit Ofcr*
Heidi M Hagen, *Bd of Directors*
Christophe Suchet,
Heidi Hagen, *Officer*
EMP: 63 **EST:** 2016
SALES (est): 6MM **Privately Held**
WEB: www.vineti.com
SIC: 7371 Computer software development

(P-12906)
VIRTUAL INSTRUMENTS CORP (PA)
Also Called: Virtana
2363 Bering Dr, San Jose (95131-1125)
PHONE..............................408 579-4000
Kash Shaikh, *President*
Lorie Ross, *Partner*
Ray Villeneuve, *President*
Philippe Vincent, *CEO*
Lisa Alger, *COO*
EMP: 55 **EST:** 2008
SALES (est): 27.2MM **Privately Held**
WEB: www.virtana.com
SIC: 7371 7379 Computer software development; computer related consulting services

(P-12907)
VIRTUNET LLC
Also Called: Virtunet Systems
1900 S Norfolk St Ste 300, San Mateo (94403-1165)
PHONE..............................650 847-8633
Parag Patkar, *Partner*
EMP: 64 **EST:** 2010
SQ FT: 1,000
SALES (est): 3.9MM **Privately Held**
WEB: www.virtunetsystems.com
SIC: 7371 Computer software development

(P-12908)
VISIONONE INC (PA)
Also Called: Showare Ticketing
5260 N Palm Ave Ste 229, Fresno (93704-2217)
PHONE..............................559 432-8000
Bruno Boehi, *CEO*
Regina Williams, *CFO*
Joe Wettstead, *Vice Pres*
Ralph Fasi, *Principal*
Rhonda Manfredo, *Office Mgr*
EMP: 36 **EST:** 1998
SALES (est): 5MM **Privately Held**
WEB: www.v-1.com
SIC: 7371 Computer software development

(P-12909)
VISISTAT INC
Also Called: Kickfire
2290 N 1st St Ste 102, San Jose (95131-2017)
PHONE..............................408 725-9370
Stephen Oachs, *President*
Michael Choy, *CFO*
Tina Bean, *Vice Pres*
Tim Lucarini, *Executive*
Hoa Brothers, *Software Dev*
EMP: 35 **EST:** 2005
SQ FT: 9,208
SALES (est): 6.5MM **Privately Held**
WEB: www.id.kickfire.com
SIC: 7371 Computer software development

(P-12910)
VISUAL CONCEPTS ENTERTAINMENT
10 Hamilton Landing, Novato (94949-8207)
PHONE..............................415 479-3634
Gregory Thomas, *President*
Scott Patterson, *Vice Pres*
Chad Riggleman, *Recruiter*
Derek Hefflinger, *Producer*
Dave Zdyrko, *Producer*
EMP: 67 **EST:** 1988
SALES (est): 8MM **Publicly Held**
WEB: www.vcentertainment.com
SIC: 7371 Computer software development
PA: Take-Two Interactive Software, Inc.
110 W 44th St
New York NY 10036

(P-12911)
VISUAL SUPPLY COMPANY (PA)
Also Called: Vsco
1500 Broadway Ste 300, Oakland (94612-2078)
PHONE..............................847 721-9285
Joel Flory, *CEO*
Bryan Mason, *COO*

7371 - Custom Computer Programming Svcs County (P-12912)

Tesa Aragones, *Chief Mktg Ofcr*
Greg Lutze, *Officer*
Wayne Wu, *Officer*
EMP: 76 **EST:** 2011
SQ FT: 50,000
SALES (est): 22.4MM **Privately Held**
WEB: www.vsco.co
SIC: 7371 Computer software development

(P-12912)
VIVIDO LABS INC (PA)
3350 Scott Blvd Bldg 201, Santa Clara (95054-3126)
PHONE..................................408 692-5002
Greg Tomb, *President*
Ravi Melgiri, *COO*
EMP: 191 **EST:** 2009
SALES (est): 6.4MM **Privately Held**
WEB: www.vividolabs.com
SIC: 7371 7379 Computer software development; computer related consulting services

(P-12913)
VM SERVICES INC (DH)
1621 Barber Ln, Milpitas (95035-7455)
PHONE..................................510 744-3720
Chin Tong Wong, *CEO*
Johnathon Nguyen, *Technician*
▲ **EMP:** 120 **EST:** 1996
SALES (est): 83MM **Privately Held**
WEB: www.venturemfg-usa.com
SIC: 7371 Computer software development

(P-12914)
VM SERVICES INC
6723 Mowry Ave, Newark (94560-4927)
PHONE..................................510 744-3720
EMP: 90 **Privately Held**
WEB: www.venturemfg-usa.com
SIC: 7371 Computer software development
HQ: Vm Services, Inc.
1621 Barber Ln
Milpitas CA 95035
510 744-3720

(P-12915)
VOSSLOH SIGNALING LLC
Also Called: Apex Rail Automation
12799 Loma Rica Dr, Grass Valley (95945-9552)
PHONE..................................530 272-8194
David Ruskauff, *President*
EMP: 29 **EST:** 2020
SALES (est): 1.3MM **Privately Held**
WEB: www.vossloh-north-america.com
SIC: 7371 3679 Computer software systems analysis & design, custom; electronic circuits

(P-12916)
WAITWHILE INC
1407 Funston Ave, San Francisco (94122-3511)
PHONE..................................888 983-0869
Christoffer Klemming, *CEO*
Jonas Klemming, *Admin Sec*
EMP: 35 **EST:** 2016
SALES (est): 1.3MM **Privately Held**
WEB: www.waitwhile.com
SIC: 7371 7372 Computer software development & applications; application computer software

(P-12917)
WALKME INC (PA)
71 Stevenson St Ste 2000, San Francisco (94105-2981)
PHONE..................................855 492-5563
Dan Adika, *CEO*
Rephael Sweary, *President*
Amir Farhi, *Officer*
Shane Orlick, *Officer*
Eyal Cohen, *Exec VP*
EMP: 57 **EST:** 2012
SALES (est): 9.9MM **Privately Held**
WEB: www.walkme.com
SIC: 7371 Computer software development

(P-12918)
WEBEVENTS LLC
Also Called: Webevents Global
3706 Atherton Rd 100, Rocklin (95765-3717)
PHONE..................................916 784-9456
Karis Takiya, *Mng Member*
Fred Takiya, *Info Tech Mgr*
Hooman Behnia, *Software Dev*
Jamie Lamport, *Software Dev*
Julie Ramirez, *Software Dev*
EMP: 40 **EST:** 2002
SALES (est): 3MM **Privately Held**
WEB: www.webeventsglobal.com
SIC: 7371 Computer software development & applications

(P-12919)
WERIDE CORP
2630 Orchard Pkwy, San Jose (95134-2020)
PHONE..................................408 645-7118
Qing Lu, *CEO*
EMP: 36 **EST:** 2017
SALES (est): 6.8MM **Privately Held**
WEB: www.weride.ai
SIC: 7371 Computer software development

(P-12920)
WHITERABBITAI INC
3930 Freedom Cir Ste 101, Santa Clara (95054-1246)
PHONE..................................408 215-8876
Rakesh Mathur, *President*
Maureen O'Connor, *President*
Jason Su, *President*
EMP: 60 **EST:** 2018
SALES (est): 5.4MM **Privately Held**
WEB: www.whiterabbit.ai
SIC: 7371 Computer software development & applications

(P-12921)
WIDEORBIT LLC (PA)
1160 Battery St Ste 300, San Francisco (94111-1212)
PHONE..................................415 675-6700
Eric Mathewson, *CEO*
Lee Bell, *Partner*
Nathan Gans, *COO*
Mark Moeder, *COO*
Margaret McCarthy, *CFO*
EMP: 88 **EST:** 1999
SQ FT: 9,000
SALES (est): 45MM **Privately Held**
WEB: www.wideorbit.com
SIC: 7371 Computer software development

(P-12922)
WILLIAM STUCKY & ASSOC INC
6059 Sycamore Ter, Pleasanton (94566-3870)
PHONE..................................415 788-2441
William Stucky, *President*
Andrew Lim, *Senior VP*
Rosanne Doyle, *Vice Pres*
Ted Maung, *Info Tech Mgr*
Hendra Richard, *Analyst*
EMP: 20 **EST:** 1989
SALES (est): 3.5MM **Privately Held**
WEB: www.idsgrp.com
SIC: 7371 7372 Computer software development; business oriented computer software

(P-12923)
WINMAX SYSTEMS CORPORATION
1900 Mccarthy Blvd # 301, Milpitas (95035-7436)
PHONE..................................408 894-9000
Suparna Bhattacharya, *President*
Bhattacharya Pam, *COO*
Reema Bains, *Vice Pres*
Vinnie Bandla, *Executive*
Savi Chandra, *Tech Recruiter*
EMP: 55 **EST:** 2005
SQ FT: 1,900
SALES (est): 6MM **Privately Held**
WEB: www.winmaxcorp.com
SIC: 7371 8742 Computer software development; management consulting services

(P-12924)
WIXCOM INC
500 Terry A Francois Blvd # 600, San Francisco (94158-2355)
PHONE..................................415 329-4610
Avishai Abrahami, *CEO*
Ido Gaver, *Partner*
Nir Zohar, *COO*
Lior Shemesh, *CFO*
Sonny Yu, *CFO*
EMP: 52 **EST:** 2008
SALES (est): 12.3MM **Privately Held**
WEB: www.wix.com
SIC: 7371 Computer software development
PA: Wix.Com Ltd
40 Nemal Tel Aviv
Tel Aviv-Jaffa

(P-12925)
WIZELINE INC (PA)
1 Market Plz Fl 36, San Francisco (94105-1120)
PHONE..................................888 386-9493
Bismarck Lepe, *CEO*
Daniele Lasher, *CEO*
Anthony Conte, *CFO*
Sung Kim, *Vice Pres*
Michael Patsalos-Fox, *Principal*
EMP: 647 **EST:** 2013
SALES (est): 40.5MM **Privately Held**
WEB: www.wizeline.com
SIC: 7371 Computer software development

(P-12926)
WONDER WORKSHOP INC (PA)
Also Called: Play-I
116c E 25th Ave, San Mateo (94403-2351)
PHONE..................................408 785-7981
Vikas Gupta, *CEO*
Jonathan Boustania, *Technical Staff*
Anna Ong, *Accountant*
Bryan Miller, *Manager*
EMP: 32 **EST:** 2012
SALES (est): 2MM **Privately Held**
WEB: www.makewonder.com
SIC: 7371 3944 5092 5945 Computer software development & applications; games, toys & children's vehicles; toys & hobby goods & supplies; hobby, toy & game shops

(P-12927)
WORKDAY INC (PA)
6110 Stoneridge Mall Rd, Pleasanton (94588-3211)
PHONE..................................925 951-9000
Aneel Bhusri, *Ch of Bd*
Stuart Noun, *Managing Prtnr*
Robynne D Sisco, *President*
James J Bozzini, *COO*
Luciano Fernandez, *Co-CEO*
EMP: 7134 **EST:** 2005
SALES (est): 4.3B **Publicly Held**
WEB: www.workday.com
SIC: 7371 7374 Custom computer programming services; computer software development; data processing & preparation

(P-12928)
WORKSTREAM TECHNOLOGIES INC
521 7th St, San Francisco (94103-4709)
PHONE..................................415 767-1006
Huang Hui Lim, *CEO*
Ruoyu Wang, *CTO*
EMP: 76 **EST:** 2016
SALES (est): 7.4MM **Privately Held**
SIC: 7371 Computer software development & applications

(P-12929)
WSO2 INC (PA)
3080 Olcott St Ste C220, Santa Clara (95054-3281)
PHONE..................................650 745-4499
Sanjiva Weerawarana, *CEO*
Mokshika Dissanayake, *Officer*
Fernando Arditti, *Vice Pres*
Nuwan Dias, *Vice Pres*
Ricardo Diniz, *Vice Pres*
EMP: 36 **EST:** 2005
SALES: 39.4MM **Privately Held**
WEB: www.wso2.com
SIC: 7371 Computer software development

(P-12930)
XACTLY CORPORATION (HQ)
505 S Market St, San Jose (95113-2827)
PHONE..................................408 977-3132
Christopher W Cabrera, *CEO*
L Evan Ellis Jr, *President*
Joseph C Consul, *CFO*
Elizabeth Salomon, *CFO*
Scott R Broomfield, *Chief Mktg Ofcr*
EMP: 331 **EST:** 2005
SALES: 95.4MM
SALES (corp-wide): 140.9MM **Privately Held**
WEB: www.xactlycorp.com
SIC: 7371 7372 Software programming applications; prepackaged software
PA: Excalibur Parent, Llc
300 Park Ave Ste 1700
San Jose CA 95110
408 977-3132

(P-12931)
XYTHOS SOFTWARE INC
655 Montgomery St Fl 16, San Francisco (94111-2684)
PHONE..................................415 248-3800
▲ **EMP:** 60
SALES (est): 3.3MM **Privately Held**
WEB: www.xythosondemand.com
SIC: 7371 Custom Computer Programming Services, Nsk

(P-12932)
YOUMASK INC
Also Called: Mymaskmovement.org/ My Mask
730 Serra St Apt 408, Stanford (94305-7239)
PHONE..................................818 282-2496
Jesse Chang, *Exec Dir*
EMP: 40 **EST:** 2020
SALES (est): 904K **Privately Held**
SIC: 7371 Computer software development & applications

(P-12933)
YVAAI INC (PA)
Also Called: Yva.ai
2445 Augustine Dr Ste 150, Santa Clara (95054-3032)
PHONE..................................650 704-5503
David Yan, *CEO*
EMP: 66 **EST:** 2016
SALES (est): 9.2MM **Privately Held**
WEB: www.yva.ai
SIC: 7371 Computer software development

(P-12934)
ZAZMIC INC (PA)
Also Called: Computer
79 Coleridge St, San Francisco (94110-5155)
PHONE..................................415 728-1621
Yann Kronberg, *Officer*
Julie Sanders, *Chief Mktg Ofcr*
Omer Khawar, *Senior VP*
Irina Dubonos, *Director*
EMP: 237 **EST:** 2012
SALES (est): 9.6MM **Privately Held**
WEB: www.zazmic.com
SIC: 7371 7389 Computer software development;

(P-12935)
ZEDEDA INC (PA)
160 W Santa Clara St # 775, San Jose (95113-1759)
PHONE..................................408 550-5531
Said Ouissal, *CEO*
Joel Vincent, *Chief Mktg Ofcr*
Jason Shepherd, *Vice Pres*
Prosenjit Pal, *Managing Dir*
Amanda Fein-Tower, *Opers Staff*
EMP: 54 **EST:** 2016
SALES (est): 4.8MM **Privately Held**
WEB: www.zededa.com
SIC: 7371 Computer software development

PRODUCTS & SERVICES SECTION

7372 - Prepackaged Software County (P-12960)

(P-12936)
ZEESOFT INC (PA)
14891 Vine St, Saratoga (95070-6338)
PHONE.................................408 247-2987
Jitendra Maheshwari, *President*
EMP: 47 **EST:** 1992
SQ FT: 600
SALES (est): 528.6K **Privately Held**
SIC: 7371 Computer software development

(P-12937)
ZENPUT INC
548 Market St, San Francisco (94104-5401)
PHONE.................................800 537-0227
Vladislav Rikhter, *CEO*
David Karel, *Chief Mktg Ofcr*
Tim Olshansky, *VP Engrg*
Kimberly Heldman, *Opers Staff*
David Mostovoy, *Marketing Mgr*
EMP: 40 **EST:** 2014
SALES (est): 3.6MM **Privately Held**
WEB: www.zenput.com
SIC: 7371 Computer software development

(P-12938)
ZENSAR TECHNOLOGIES INC
555 E El Camino Real, Sunnyvale (94087-1929)
PHONE.................................408 469-5408
EMP: 2266 **Privately Held**
WEB: www.zensar.com
SIC: 7371 Computer software development
HQ: Zensar Technologies, Inc.
55 W Monroe St Ste 1200
Chicago IL 60603

(P-12939)
ZIGNAL LABS INC
600 California St Fl 18, San Francisco (94108-2711)
PHONE.................................415 683-7871
Bob Deppisch, *Director*
Josh Ginsberg, *CEO*
Chris Krook, *CFO*
David Atlas, *Chief Mktg Ofcr*
Jennifer Granston, *Officer*
EMP: 60 **EST:** 2011
SALES (est): 8.4MM **Privately Held**
WEB: www.zignallabs.com
SIC: 7371 Computer software development & applications

(P-12940)
ZIPLINE INTERNATIONAL INC
495 Pine Ave, Half Moon Bay (94019-1605)
PHONE.................................508 340-3291
Peter Winn, *CEO*
Nick Hu, *Managing Dir*
Daniel Marfo, *General Mgr*
Div Arora, *Engineer*
Sven Blaser, *Engineer*
EMP: 114 **EST:** 2006
SALES (est): 6.3MM **Privately Held**
SIC: 7371 Computer software development & applications

(P-12941)
ZL TECHNOLOGIES INC (PA)
860 N Mccarthy Blvd # 10, Milpitas (95035-5110)
PHONE.................................408 240-8989
Kon Leong, *President*
Jin Chang, *General Mgr*
Richard Barnes, *CIO*
Ramesh Velampalayam, *Software Dev*
Derek Hollowood, *Software Engr*
EMP: 64 **EST:** 1999
SQ FT: 1,860
SALES (est): 13.4MM **Privately Held**
WEB: www.zlti.com
SIC: 7371 5045 Computer software systems analysis & design, custom; computer software

(P-12942)
ZOOM VIDEO COMMUNICATIONS INC (PA)
55 Almaden Blvd Fl 6, San Jose (95113-1608)
PHONE.................................888 799-9666
Eric S Yuan, *Ch of Bd*
Aparna Bawa, *COO*
Kelly Steckelberg, *CFO*
Janine Pelosi, *Chief Mktg Ofcr*
Damien Hooper-Campbell, *Officer*
EMP: 1561 **EST:** 2011
SQ FT: 66,000
SALES: 2.6B **Publicly Held**
WEB: www.zoom.us
SIC: 7371 Computer software development

(P-12943)
ZSCALER INC (PA)
120 Holger Way, San Jose (95134-1376)
PHONE.................................408 533-0288
Jagtar S Chaudhry, *Ch of Bd*
Remo Canessa, *CFO*
Robert Schlossman,
Dali Rajic, *Risk Mgmt Dir*
Amit Sinha, *CTO*
EMP: 1874 **EST:** 2007
SQ FT: 172,000
SALES: 673.1MM **Publicly Held**
WEB: www.zscaler.com
SIC: 7371 7372 Computer software development; prepackaged software

7372 Prepackaged Software

(P-12944)
4D SIGHT INC
2150 Shattuck Ave, Berkeley (94704-1345)
PHONE.................................415 425-1321
Erhan Ciris, *CEO*
EMP: 25 **EST:** 2020
SALES (est): 913.7K **Privately Held**
SIC: 7372 Application computer software

(P-12945)
ABAQUS INC
972 N California Ave, Palo Alto (94303-3405)
PHONE.................................415 496-9436
Shailendra Jain, *CEO*
Ayush Kapahi, *Partner*
John Benger, *CFO*
EMP: 40 **EST:** 2007
SALES (est): 3.6MM **Privately Held**
WEB: www.mygeotracking.com
SIC: 7372 5734 Business oriented computer software; software, business & non-game

(P-12946)
ACCELA INC (PA)
2633 Camino Ramon Ste 500, San Ramon (94583-9149)
PHONE.................................925 659-3200
Gary Kovacs, *CEO*
Greg Pappas, *Partner*
Mark Jung, *Ch of Bd*
Maury Blackman, *CEO*
Ed Daihl, *CEO*
EMP: 150 **EST:** 1979
SALES (est): 95.1MM **Privately Held**
WEB: www.accela.com
SIC: 7372 Business oriented computer software

(P-12947)
ACCELERANCE INC
303 Twin Dolphin Dr # 60, Redwood City (94065-1497)
PHONE.................................650 472-3785
Stephan A Mezak, *Principal*
Katie Tolchin, *Partner*
Bobby Dewrell, *Vice Pres*
Michael McAuliffe, *Managing Dir*
Meghan Heflin, *Research*
EMP: 16 **EST:** 2001
SALES (est): 1.1MM **Privately Held**
WEB: www.accelerance.com
SIC: 7372 Prepackaged software

(P-12948)
ACCELERITE (PA)
2055 Laurelwood Rd, Santa Clara (95054-2729)
PHONE.................................408 216-7010
Nara Rajagopalan, *CEO*
Jeff Rowland, *Vice Pres*
Vinayak Datar, *Mng Officer*
James Longo, *Analyst*
Frans Wilbrink, *Sales Staff*
EMP: 92 **EST:** 2014
SALES (est): 1MM **Privately Held**
WEB: www.accelerite.com
SIC: 7372 Prepackaged software

(P-12949)
ACCORDENT TECHNOLOGIES INC
1846 Schooldale Dr, San Jose (95124-1136)
PHONE.................................310 374-7491
EMP: 16
SALES (corp-wide): 856.9MM **Publicly Held**
SIC: 7372 Prepackaged Software Services
HQ: Accordent Technologies, Inc.
300 N Cntntl Blvd Ste 200
El Segundo CA
310 374-7491

(P-12950)
ACCOUNTMATE SOFTWARE CORP (PA)
1445 Technology Ln Ste A5, Petaluma (94954-7613)
PHONE.................................707 774-7500
David Dierke, *Principal*
David Render, *COO*
Tommy Tan, *CTO*
Rosemarie Dasig, *Applctn Conslt*
Rosalie Lang, *Accounting Mgr*
▲ **EMP:** 44 **EST:** 1984
SQ FT: 8,700
SALES (est): 4.2MM **Privately Held**
WEB: www.accountmate.com
SIC: 7372 Business oriented computer software

(P-12951)
ADAPTIVE INSIGHTS LLC (HQ)
2300 Geng Rd Ste 100, Palo Alto (94303-3352)
PHONE.................................650 528-7500
Thomas F Bogan, *CEO*
James D Johnson, *CFO*
Connie Dewitt, *Chief Mktg Ofcr*
Michael A Schmitt, *Chief Mktg Ofcr*
Fred Gewant, *Officer*
EMP: 200
SALES: 106.5MM **Publicly Held**
WEB: www.adaptiveplanning.com
SIC: 7372 Business oriented computer software

(P-12952)
ADARA INC (PA)
2625 Middlefield Rd # 827, Palo Alto (94306-2516)
PHONE.................................408 876-6360
Layton Han, *CEO*
Yukari Bista, *Partner*
Elizabeth Harz, *President*
Frank Teruel, *COO*
Arnold Gee, *Officer*
EMP: 224 **EST:** 2005
SALES (est): 61MM **Privately Held**
WEB: www.adara.com
SIC: 7372 Business oriented computer software

(P-12953)
ADDAPPT INC
15680 Loma Vista Ave, Los Gatos (95032-3635)
PHONE.................................408 402-5468
Mrinal Desai, *Principal*
EMP: 15 **EST:** 2012
SALES (est): 151.1K **Privately Held**
WEB: www.addappt.com
SIC: 7372 Prepackaged software

(P-12954)
ADMI INC
18525 Sutter Blvd Ste 290, Morgan Hill (95037-8102)
PHONE.................................408 776-0060
Allen D Moyer, *President*
Michael Collins, *Manager*
Pamela Tallada, *Manager*
EMP: 42 **EST:** 2007
SALES (est): 4.9MM **Privately Held**
WEB: www.admii.com
SIC: 7372 Operating systems computer software

(P-12955)
ADOBE INC
321 Park Ave, San Jose (95110-2704)
PHONE.................................408 536-6000
Arun Ananthararaman, *Engineer*
EMP: 34
SALES (corp-wide): 12.8B **Publicly Held**
WEB: www.adobe.com
SIC: 7372 Prepackaged software
PA: Adobe Inc.
345 Park Ave
San Jose CA 95110
408 536-6000

(P-12956)
ADOBE INC (PA)
345 Park Ave, San Jose (95110-2704)
PHONE.................................408 536-6000
Shantanu Narayen, *Ch of Bd*
John Murphy, *CFO*
Scott Belsky, *Officer*
Gloria Chen, *Officer*
Ann Lewnes, *Officer*
EMP: 600 **EST:** 1982
SQ FT: 1,100,000
SALES (est): 12.8B **Publicly Held**
WEB: www.adobe.com
SIC: 7372 Prepackaged software; application computer software

(P-12957)
ADOBE MACROMEDIA SOFTWARE LLC (HQ)
601 Townsend St, San Francisco (94103-5247)
PHONE.................................415 832-2000
Bruce R Chizen,
Murray Demo,
Shantanu Narayen,
▲ **EMP:** 1421 **EST:** 1992
SQ FT: 210,000
SALES (est): 158.4MM
SALES (corp-wide): 12.8B **Publicly Held**
WEB: www.adobe.com
SIC: 7372 Prepackaged software; publishers' computer software; educational computer software; home entertainment computer software
PA: Adobe Inc.
345 Park Ave
San Jose CA 95110
408 536-6000

(P-12958)
ADS SOLUTIONS
10 Commercial Blvd # 208, Novato (94949-6107)
PHONE.................................415 897-3700
Kenneth Levin, *President*
Ann Grace, *Software Dev*
Donna Robertson, *Software Dev*
Kerry Hardesty,
EMP: 19 **EST:** 1984
SALES (est): 2.2MM **Privately Held**
WEB: www.adssolutions.com
SIC: 7372 Application computer software; business oriented computer software

(P-12959)
ADVISOR SOFTWARE INC (PA)
2185 N Calif Blvd Ste 290, Walnut Creek (94596-7389)
PHONE.................................925 299-7782
Andrew Rudd, *CEO*
Neal Ringquist, *President*
Neil Osborne, *CFO*
Michelle Farmer, *Officer*
Erik Jepson, *Officer*
EMP: 25
SALES (est): 6.7MM **Privately Held**
WEB: www.advisorpartners.com
SIC: 7372 Business oriented computer software

(P-12960)
AFRESH TECHNOLOGIES INC
116 New Montgomery St # 4, San Francisco (94105-3607)
PHONE.................................805 551-9245
Matthew Schwartz, *CEO*
Nathan Fenner, *COO*
Volodymyr Kuleshov, *CTO*
EMP: 100 **EST:** 2017
SQ FT: 1,400

7372 - Prepackaged Software County (P-12961)

PRODUCTS & SERVICES SECTION

SALES (est): 8.3MM **Privately Held**
WEB: www.afresh.com
SIC: 7372 Business oriented computer software

(P-12961)
AGGRIGATOR INC
350 W Beach St, Watsonville (95076-4547)
PHONE.................................831 728-2824
Douglas Peterson, *CEO*
Gerard Rego, *CEO*
Doug Peterson, *Bd of Directors*
Margarita Quihuis, *Bd of Directors*
Benjamin Warr, *Bd of Directors*
EMP: 20 **EST:** 2014
SALES (est): 1.9MM **Privately Held**
WEB: www.aggrigator.com
SIC: 7372 5148 0139 5411 Business oriented computer software; fresh fruits & vegetables; food crops; grocery stores

(P-12962)
AGILEPOINT INC (PA)
1916 Old Middlefield Way, Mountain View (94043-2555)
PHONE.................................650 968-6789
Jesse Shiah, *President*
Bryan Chandler, *COO*
Kelvin Wang, *General Mgr*
Choyling Poan, *Software Engr*
Meenakshi Nadimuthu, *Engineer*
EMP: 114 **EST:** 2003
SQ FT: 2,000
SALES (est): 12MM **Privately Held**
WEB: www.agilepoint.com
SIC: 7372 Business oriented computer software

(P-12963)
AGILOFT INC
460 Seaport Ct Ste 200, Redwood City (94063-5548)
PHONE.................................650 587-8615
Colin Earl, *CEO*
Richard Morgan, *Vice Pres*
May Quock, *Vice Pres*
Christian Thun, *Vice Pres*
Diana Banks, *Executive*
EMP: 46 **EST:** 1991
SQ FT: 3,200
SALES (est): 11.8MM **Privately Held**
WEB: www.agiloft.com
SIC: 7372 Business oriented computer software

(P-12964)
AHA LABS INC
20 Gloria Cir, Menlo Park (94025-3556)
PHONE.................................650 575-1425
Brian De Haaff, *CEO*
Melissa Hopkins, *Vice Pres*
Jay Margolis, *Sr Software Eng*
Yuko Takegoshi, *Sr Software Eng*
John Bohn, *Software Dev*
EMP: 100 **EST:** 2013
SALES (est): 5.7MM **Privately Held**
WEB: www.aha.io
SIC: 7372 Business oriented computer software

(P-12965)
AHOY-HOY INC (PA)
6116 N Rockridge Blvd, Oakland (94618-1813)
PHONE.................................415 669-6902
Ivan Ivanovich Kanevski, *Owner*
EMP: 26 **EST:** 2018
SALES (est): 172.9K **Privately Held**
SIC: 7372 Prepackaged software

(P-12966)
AKOONU INC
350 Townsend St Ste 402, San Francisco (94107-1683)
PHONE.................................844 425-6668
Sean Noonan, *CFO*
EMP: 16 **EST:** 2018
SALES (est): 976.7K **Privately Held**
WEB: www.akoonu.com
SIC: 7372 Prepackaged software

(P-12967)
AKTANA INC (PA)
207 Powell St Fl 8, San Francisco (94102-2205)
PHONE.................................888 707-3125
David Ehrlich, *CEO*
Pini Ben-or, *Officer*
Marc-David Cohen, *Officer*
Dmitri Daveynis, *Senior VP*
Manny Triggiano, *Senior VP*
EMP: 374 **EST:** 2008
SALES (est): 52MM **Privately Held**
WEB: www.aktana.com
SIC: 7372 Prepackaged software

(P-12968)
ALATION INC (PA)
3 Lagoon Dr Ste 300, Redwood City (94065-1567)
P.O. Box 1216 (94064-1216)
PHONE.................................650 779-4440
Satyen Sangani, *CEO*
Joy Wolken, *Partner*
Eric Chan, *CFO*
Max Ochoa, *CFO*
Tracy Eiler, *Chief Mktg Ofcr*
EMP: 53 **EST:** 2012
SALES (est): 7.7MM **Privately Held**
WEB: www.alation.com
SIC: 7372 Application computer software

(P-12969)
ALERTENTERPRISE INC
4350 Starboard Dr, Fremont (94538-6434)
PHONE.................................510 440-0840
Jasvir Gill, *CEO*
Kaval Kaur, *COO*
Ehsan Hameed, *Vice Pres*
Willem Ryan, *Vice Pres*
Azizur Rahman, *VP Bus Dvlpt*
EMP: 140 **EST:** 2007
SQ FT: 24,000
SALES (est): 14.6MM **Privately Held**
WEB: www.alertenterprise.com
SIC: 7372 Prepackaged software

(P-12970)
ALGO TECHNOLOGIES INC
2025 Geri Ln, Hillsborough (94010-6321)
PHONE.................................608 332-9716
EMP: 16 **EST:** 2018
SALES (est): 423.2K **Privately Held**
SIC: 7372 Application computer software

(P-12971)
ALGOLIA INC (PA)
Also Called: Seaurchin. Io.
301 Howard St Ste 300, San Francisco (94105-6620)
PHONE.................................415 366-9672
Nicolas Dessaigne, *CEO*
Iain Hassall, *CFO*
Ashley Stirrup, *Chief Mktg Ofcr*
Jean-Louis Baffier, *Officer*
Julien Lemoine, *Officer*
EMP: 59 **EST:** 2014
SALES (est): 9.2MM **Privately Held*
WEB: www.algolia.com
SIC: 7372 Prepackaged software

(P-12972)
ALIENVAULT LLC (DH)
1100 Park Pl Ste 300, San Mateo (94403-7108)
P.O. Box 25237 (94402-5237)
PHONE.................................650 713-3333
Barmak Meftah, *President*
J Alberto Yepez, *Ch of Bd*
Chris Murphy, *President*
Brian Robins, *CFO*
Rita Selvaggi, *Chief Mktg Ofcr*
EMP: 299 **EST:** 2009
SALES (est): 43.2MM
SALES (corp-wide): 171.7B **Publicly Held**
WEB: www.cybersecurity.att.com
SIC: 7372 Business oriented computer software
HQ: Alienvault, Inc.
1100 Park Pl Ste 300
San Mateo CA 94403
650 713-3333

(P-12973)
ALIVECOR INC (PA)
189 Bernardo Ave Ste 100, Mountain View (94043-5139)
PHONE.................................650 396-8650
Priya Abani, *CEO*
Jim Jenkins, *Officer*
Jacqueline Shreibati, *Officer*
Sharon Tracy, *Vice Pres*
Julie Aguas, *Engineer*
EMP: 51 **EST:** 2012
SALES (est): 12.3MM **Privately Held**
WEB: www.woodleyequipment.com
SIC: 7372 Application computer software

(P-12974)
ALKIRA INC
2811 Mission College Blvd F, Santa Clara (95054-1884)
PHONE.................................408 654-9696
EMP: 19 **EST:** 2018
SALES (est): 2.5MM **Privately Held**
WEB: www.alkira.com
SIC: 7372 Prepackaged software

(P-12975)
ALLDATA LLC
9650 W Taron Dr Ste 100, Elk Grove (95757-8197)
PHONE.................................916 684-5200
Stephen Odland,
Doug Wines, *Vice Pres*
Paul Burkett, *Administration*
Pete Chuong, *Administration*
Clifford Peerson, *IT/INT Sup*
EMP: 400 **EST:** 1986
SQ FT: 35,000
SALES (est): 102.6MM
SALES (corp-wide): 12.6B **Publicly Held**
WEB: www.support.alldata.com
SIC: 7372 Business oriented computer software
PA: Autozone, Inc.
123 S Front St
Memphis TN 38103
901 495-6500

(P-12976)
ANDAPT INC (PA)
950 S Bascom Ave Ste 3012, San Jose (95128-3539)
PHONE.................................408 931-4898
Kapil Shankar, *CEO*
Anton Bakker, *Exec VP*
Zaryab Hamavand, *Vice Pres*
Giovanni Garcea, *VP Engrg*
Jonas Pollack, *Sales Staff*
EMP: 31 **EST:** 2015
SALES (est): 917.3K **Privately Held**
WEB: www.andapt.com
SIC: 7372 Prepackaged software

(P-12977)
APORETO INC
10 Almaden Blvd Ste 400, San Jose (95113-2226)
PHONE.................................408 472-7648
Jason Schmitt, *CEO*
Gregg Holzrichter, *Chief Mktg Ofcr*
Hussain Al-Shorafa, *Vice Pres*
Mike Casey, *Vice Pres*
Sunil Sampat, *Risk Mgmt Dir*
EMP: 57 **EST:** 2016
SALES (est): 5.2MM **Privately Held**
SIC: 7372 Prepackaged software

(P-12978)
APPDIRECT INC (PA)
650 California St Fl 25, San Francisco (94108-2606)
PHONE.................................415 852-3924
Nicolas Desmarais, *Ch of Bd*
Daniel Saks, *President*
Michael Difilippo, *CFO*
Andy Sen, *Officer*
Mark Beebe, *Vice Pres*
EMP: 51 **EST:** 2009
SQ FT: 10,000
SALES (est): 32.6MM **Privately Held**
WEB: www.appdirect.com
SIC: 7372 7371 Application computer software; computer software development & applications

(P-12979)
APPEX NETWORKS CORPORATION
4010 Moorpark Ave Ste 212, San Jose (95117-1843)
PHONE.................................408 973-7898
Yongdong Wang, *CEO*
EMP: 21 **EST:** 2007
SALES (est): 1.8MM **Privately Held**
WEB: www.appexnetworks.com
SIC: 7372 Prepackaged software
HQ: Beijing Huaxia Chuangxin Technology Co., Ltd.
601, Floor 6, Suite C, Building 24,
No.68 Courtyard, Beiqing Roa
Beijing 10009

(P-12980)
APPLIED EXPERT SYSTEMS INC
Also Called: AES
999 Commercial St Ste 201, Palo Alto (94303-4909)
P.O. Box 50927 (94303-0673)
PHONE.................................650 617-2400
Catherine H Liu, *President*
David Cheng, *Vice Pres*
Mark Nguyen, *Research*
David Billing, *Technology*
▲ **EMP:** 38 **EST:** 1991
SALES (est): 2.6MM **Privately Held**
WEB: www.aesclever.com
SIC: 7372 Business oriented computer software

(P-12981)
APPLOVIN CORPORATION (PA)
1100 Page Mill Rd, Palo Alto (94304-1047)
PHONE.................................800 839-9646
Adam Foroughi, *Ch of Bd*
Herald Chen, *President*
Katie Jansen, *Chief Mktg Ofcr*
Victoria Valenzuela,
Cheryl Chua, *Office Mgr*
EMP: 484 **EST:** 2011
SQ FT: 72,812
SALES: 1.4B **Publicly Held**
WEB: www.applovin.com
SIC: 7372 Prepackaged software

(P-12982)
APPORTO CORPORATION
200 Hamilton Ave, Palo Alto (94301-2529)
PHONE.................................650 326-0920
Anthony Awaida, *CEO*
Heather Wasserlein, *Manager*
EMP: 20 **EST:** 2011
SALES (est): 1.3MM **Privately Held**
WEB: www.apporto.com
SIC: 7372 Prepackaged software

(P-12983)
APPVANCE INC
3080 Olcott St Ste B240, Santa Clara (95054-3278)
PHONE.................................408 871-0122
John Hubinger, *Ch of Bd*
Kevin Parker, *Vice Pres*
EMP: 41 **EST:** 2014
SALES (est): 2.5MM **Privately Held**
WEB: www.appvance.com
SIC: 7372 Prepackaged software

(P-12984)
APTIV DIGITAL LLC
2160 Gold St, San Jose (95002-3700)
PHONE.................................818 295-6789
Neil Jones, *President*
Jim Meyer, *Bd of Directors*
Timj Clark, *Vice Pres*
Williamh Guggina, *Vice Pres*
Wendyf Miller, *Vice Pres*
EMP: 85 **EST:** 1996
SALES (est): 12.3MM
SALES (corp-wide): 892MM **Publicly Held**
SIC: 7372 Home entertainment computer software
HQ: Rovi Guides, Inc.
2233 N Ontario St Ste 100
Burbank CA 91504

(P-12985)
ARANGODB INC
548 Market St 61436, San Francisco (94104-5401)
PHONE.................................415 992-7801
Claudius Weinberger, *CEO*
Mark Ekstrom, *Risk Mgmt Dir*
Frank Celler, *CTO*
EMP: 20 **EST:** 2017

▲ = Import ▼ = Export
◆ = Import/Export

PRODUCTS & SERVICES SECTION

7372 - Prepackaged Software County (P-13008)

SALES (est): 1.3MM **Privately Held**
WEB: www.arangodb.com
SIC: 7372 Application computer software

(P-12986)
AREA 1 SECURITY INC
15 N Ellsworth Ave # 102, San Mateo (94401-2864)
PHONE 650 924-1637
Patrick Sweeney, *CEO*
Oren Falkowitz, *Ch of Bd*
Hussain Al-Shorafa, *Officer*
Steve Pataky, *Risk Mgmt Dir*
Dominic Yip, *Engineer*
EMP: 65 EST: 2014
SALES (est): 8.5MM **Privately Held**
WEB: www.area1security.com
SIC: 7372 Prepackaged software

(P-12987)
ARIBA INC (DH)
3420 Hillview Ave, Palo Alto (94304-1355)
PHONE 650 849-4000
Alex Atzberger, *CEO*
Marc Malone, *CFO*
Marcell Vollmer, *Officer*
Anthony Dellano, *Vice Pres*
Jason Wolf, *Vice Pres*
EMP: 105 EST: 1996
SQ FT: 86,000
SALES (est): 204.3MM
SALES (corp-wide): 32.3B **Publicly Held**
WEB: www.support.ariba.com
SIC: 7372 Business oriented computer software
HQ: Sap America, Inc.
3999 West Chester Pike
Newtown Square PA 19073
610 661-1000

(P-12988)
ARISTA NETWORKS
1390 Market St Ste 800, San Francisco (94102-5303)
PHONE 408 547-5725
Ita Brennan, *CFO*
Christophe Metivier, *Vice Pres*
Kumar Narayanan, *Surgery Dir*
Krithika Balan, *Software Engr*
Ajay Chhatwal, *Software Engr*
EMP: 17 EST: 2018
SALES (est): 1MM **Privately Held**
WEB: www.arista.com
SIC: 7372 Prepackaged software

(P-12989)
ATHOC INC (DH)
3001 Bishop Dr Ste 400, San Ramon (94583-5005)
PHONE 925 242-5660
Guy Miasnik, *President*
Douglas Doyle, *Officer*
Nita White-Ivy, *Officer*
Aviv Siegel, *Exec VP*
Ly Tran, *Exec VP*
EMP: 55 EST: 1999
SALES (est): 21.6MM
SALES (corp-wide): 1B **Privately Held**
WEB: www.blackberry.com
SIC: 7372 Prepackaged software
HQ: Blackberry Corporation
3001 Bishop Dr
San Ramon CA 94583
972 650-6126

(P-12990)
ATLASSIAN INC (DH)
350 Bush St Fl 13, San Francisco (94104-2879)
PHONE 415 701-1110
Scott Farquhar, *CEO*
Doug Burgum, *Ch of Bd*
Jay Simons, *President*
Murray Demo, *CFO*
Alex Estevez, *CFO*
EMP: 94 EST: 2005
SALES: 5MM **Privately Held**
WEB: www.bitbucket.org
SIC: 7372 Business oriented computer software

(P-12991)
ATTAINIA INC
1503 Grant Rd Ste 200, Mountain View (94040-3270)
PHONE 866 288-2464
Dianna Sovine, *VP Mktg*
John Longo, *VP Sales*
Dennis Murdock, *Director*
Randall Bates, *Manager*
Nathan Chestnut, *Manager*
EMP: 17 EST: 2016
SALES (est): 675.5K **Privately Held**
WEB: www.attainia.com
SIC: 7372 Prepackaged software

(P-12992)
ATYPON SYSTEMS LLC (PA)
5201 Great America Pkwy # 215, Santa Clara (95054-1177)
PHONE 408 988-1240
Marty Picco, *General Mgr*
Colin Caprani, *Partner*
Chao Zhang, *Partner*
Steve Castro, *CFO*
Himanshu Jhamb, *Vice Pres*
EMP: 60 EST: 1996
SQ FT: 6,000
SALES (est): 12MM **Privately Held**
WEB: www.atypon.com
SIC: 7372 Application computer software

(P-12993)
AUGMEDIX INC (PA)
111 Sutter St Ste 1300, San Francisco (94104-4541)
PHONE 888 669-4885
Emmanuel Krakaris, *President*
Gerard Van Hamel Platerink, *Ch of Bd*
Sandra Breber, *COO*
Paul Ginocchio, *CFO*
Jonathan Hawkins, *Risk Mgmt Dir*
EMP: 558 EST: 2020
SALES (est): 16.4MM **Publicly Held**
WEB: www.augmedix.com
SIC: 7372 Prepackaged software

(P-12994)
AURORA INNOVATION INC
77 Stillman St, San Francisco (94107-1309)
PHONE 646 725-4999
Christopher Paul Urmson, *CEO*
EMP: 69
SALES (corp-wide): 545.8MM **Privately Held**
WEB: www.aurora.tech
SIC: 7372 Utility computer software
PA: Aurora Operations, Inc.
280 Bernardo Ave
Mountain View CA 94043
888 583-9506

(P-12995)
AURORA OPERATIONS INC (PA)
280 Bernardo Ave, Mountain View (94043-5238)
PHONE 888 583-9506
Christopher Urmson, *CEO*
William Mouat, *Vice Pres*
Randy Reibel, *Vice Pres*
Sterling Anderson, *Principal*
Huy Nguyen, *Executive Asst*
EMP: 1275 EST: 2016
SALES (est): 545.8MM **Privately Held**
WEB: www.aurora.tech
SIC: 7372 Utility computer software

(P-12996)
AUTHENTICA SOLUTIONS LLC (PA)
717 Market St Ste 300, San Francisco (94103-2109)
PHONE 614 296-6479
Russell Long, *CEO*
Lori Nelson, *COO*
Gene Garcia, *CTO*
EMP: 19 EST: 2013
SALES (est): 2.5MM **Privately Held**
WEB: www.brightbytes.net
SIC: 7372 8299 Educational computer software; educational services

(P-12997)
AUTODESK INC
1 Market St, San Francisco (94105-1420)
PHONE 415 356-0700
Chris Bradshaw, *Branch Mgr*
Damon Dieckmeyer, *Partner*
Jim Lynch, *Vice Pres*
Molly Zoeller, *Vice Pres*
Evan Casey, *Executive*
EMP: 61
SALES (corp-wide): 3.7B **Publicly Held**
WEB: www.autodesk.com
SIC: 7372 Application computer software
PA: Autodesk, Inc.
111 Mcinnis Pkwy
San Rafael CA 94903
415 507-5000

(P-12998)
AUTODESK INC (PA)
111 Mcinnis Pkwy, San Rafael (94903-2700)
PHONE 415 507-5000
Andrew Anagnost, *President*
Stacy J Smith, *Ch of Bd*
Deborah L Clifford, *CFO*
Pascal W Di Fronzo,
Steve M Blum, *Risk Mgmt Dir*
◆ EMP: 400 EST: 1982
SQ FT: 162,000
SALES: 3.7B **Publicly Held**
WEB: www.autodesk.com
SIC: 7372 Prepackaged software; application computer software

(P-12999)
AUTODESK GLOBAL INC (HQ)
1111 Mcinnis Pkwy, San Rafael (94903)
PHONE 415 507-5000
EMP: 319 EST: 2016
SALES (est): 1MM
SALES (corp-wide): 3.7B **Publicly Held**
WEB: www.autodesk.com
SIC: 7372 Business oriented computer software
PA: Autodesk, Inc.
111 Mcinnis Pkwy
San Rafael CA 94903
415 507-5000

(P-13000)
AUTOGRID SYSTEMS INC (PA)
255 Shoreline Dr Ste 350, Redwood City (94065-1435)
PHONE 650 461-9038
Amit Narayan, *CEO*
Dave Garcia, *Vice Pres*
Saaransh Gulati, *Sr Software Eng*
Brett Langston, *Sr Software Eng*
Utkarsh Dalal, *Software Engr*
EMP: 17 EST: 2010
SALES (est): 3.3MM **Privately Held**
WEB: www.auto-grid.com
SIC: 7372 Business oriented computer software

(P-13001)
AUTONOMY INC (HQ)
1 Market Plz F1 19, San Francisco (94105-1103)
PHONE 415 243-9955
Antonio Neri, *CEO*
Chris Hsu, *COO*
Tim Stonesifer, *CFO*
John Hinshaw, *Ch Credit Ofcr*
Martin Fink, *Exec VP*
EMP: 34 EST: 1996
SQ FT: 10,000
SALES (est): 14.4MM
SALES (corp-wide): 26.9B **Publicly Held**
WEB: www.hpe.com
SIC: 7372 Business oriented computer software
PA: Hewlett Packard Enterprise Company
11445 Compaq Center W Dr
Houston TX 77070
650 687-5817

(P-13002)
AVATIER CORPORATION (PA)
4733 Chabot Dr Ste 201, Pleasanton (94588-3971)
P.O. Box 12124 (94588-2124)
PHONE 925 217-5170
Nelson Cicchitto, *CEO*
Nelson A Cicchitto, *CEO*
Phil Ferreira, *Vice Pres*
Sarah Gylling, *Executive Asst*
Kelly Gibson, *Software Dev*
EMP: 21 EST: 1995
SQ FT: 5,500
SALES (est): 9MM **Privately Held**
WEB: www.avatier.com
SIC: 7372 7373 Business oriented computer software; systems software development services

(P-13003)
AWAKE SECURITY INC
5453 Great America Pkwy, Santa Clara (95054-3645)
PHONE 833 292-5348
Rahul Kashyap, *CEO*
Rajdeep Wadhwa, *Vice Pres*
Paul Young, *Software Dev*
Dana Ellingen, *Technical Staff*
Mark Calkins, *Sales Dir*
EMP: 36 EST: 2014
SALES (est): 4.2MM **Privately Held**
WEB: www.awakesecurity.com
SIC: 7372 Prepackaged software

(P-13004)
AYEHU INC (HQ)
Also Called: Ayehu Software Technologies
99 Almaden Blvd Fl 6, San Jose (95113-1610)
PHONE 800 652-5601
Gabby Nizri, *CEO*
Rami Lipman, *Bd of Directors*
Peter Lee, *Vice Pres*
Daniel Cohen, *CPA*
Evelyn Kotler, *VP Mktg*
EMP: 52 EST: 2016
SALES (est): 6.5MM **Privately Held**
WEB: www.resolve.io
SIC: 7372 Business oriented computer software

(P-13005)
AZUL SYSTEMS INC (PA)
385 Moffett Park Dr # 115, Sunnyvale (94089-1217)
PHONE 650 230-6500
Scott Sellers, *President*
Anya Chernyak, *Vice Pres*
Michael J Field, *Vice Pres*
George W Gould, *Vice Pres*
Eric Graber, *Vice Pres*
EMP: 164 EST: 2002
SALES (est): 27.7MM **Privately Held**
WEB: www.azul.com
SIC: 7372 Operating systems computer software

(P-13006)
BADGER MAPS INC
539 Broadway, San Francisco (94133-4521)
PHONE 415 592-5909
Steven Benson, *CEO*
Doug Ybarra, *Business Mgr*
Timothy Jernigan, *Marketing Staff*
Sonia Joseph, *Marketing Staff*
Christina Wong, *Marketing Staff*
EMP: 40 EST: 2012
SQ FT: 1,000
SALES (est): 5MM **Privately Held**
WEB: www.badgermapping.com
SIC: 7372 Application computer software

(P-13007)
BADGEVILLE INC
805 Veterans Blvd Ste 307, Redwood City (94063-1737)
PHONE 650 323-6668
Jon Shalowitz, *President*
Stephanie Vinella, *CFO*
Karen Hsu, *Vice Pres*
Andy Pederson, *Vice Pres*
Roel Stalman, *Vice Pres*
EMP: 28 EST: 2010
SALES (est): 2.2MM **Privately Held**
SIC: 7372 Prepackaged software

(P-13008)
BAFFLE INC
2811 Mission College Blvd F, Santa Clara (95054-1884)
PHONE 408 663-6737
Ameesh Divatia, *CEO*
Harold Byun, *Vice Pres*
Priyadarshan Kolte, *CTO*
EMP: 30 EST: 2015
SQ FT: 10,000

7372 - Prepackaged Software County (P-13009)

SALES (est): 2.6MM **Privately Held**
WEB: www.baffle.io
SIC: 7372 Application computer software

(P-13009)
BARRA LLC (HQ)
Also Called: Msci Barra
2100 Milvia St, Berkeley (94704-1861)
PHONE.....................510 548-5442
Kamal Duggirala, *CEO*
Andrew Rudd, *Ch of Bd*
Aamir Sheikh, *President*
Greg Stockett, *CFO*
Sue Gledhill, *Vice Pres*
▲ EMP: 280 EST: 1975
SQ FT: 35,000
SALES (est): 97.4MM **Publicly Held**
WEB: www.msci.com
SIC: 7372 8741 6282 Business oriented computer software; financial management for business; investment advisory service

(P-13010)
BARRACUDA NETWORKS INC (DH)
3175 Winchester Blvd, Campbell (95008-6557)
PHONE.....................408 342-5400
Hatem Naguib, *CEO*
William D Jenkins Jr, *President*
Dustin Driggs, *CFO*
Erin Hintz, *Chief Mktg Ofcr*
Diane Honda, *Officer*
EMP: 225 EST: 2003
SQ FT: 61,400
SALES: 352.6MM **Privately Held**
WEB: www.barracuda.com
SIC: 7372 7373 Prepackaged software; computer integrated systems design
HQ: Barracuda Holdings, Llc
3175 Winchester Blvd
Campbell CA 95008
408 342-5400

(P-13011)
BEAMERY INC (PA)
353 Sacramento St Ste 800, San Francisco (94111-3608)
PHONE.....................866 473-7136
Abakar Saidov, *President*
Phlipp Becker, *CFO*
Andrew Wedge, *Vice Pres*
Jan Hammer, *Director*
Alistair Mitchell, *Director*
EMP: 82 EST: 2014
SALES (est): 7.5MM **Privately Held**
WEB: www.beamery.com
SIC: 7372 Prepackaged software

(P-13012)
BEATS MUSIC LLC
235 2nd St, San Francisco (94105-3124)
PHONE.....................415 590-5104
Timothy Cook, *CEO*
EMP: 95 EST: 2012
SALES (est): 21.4MM
SALES (corp-wide): 365.8B **Publicly Held**
WEB: www.apple.com
SIC: 7372 Prepackaged software
PA: Apple Inc.
1 Apple Park Way
Cupertino CA 95014
408 996-1010

(P-13013)
BEE CONTENT DESIGN INC
450 Townsend St, San Francisco (94107-1510)
PHONE.....................888 962-4587
Massimo Arrigoni, *CEO*
Guido Boulay, *Business Dir*
EMP: 51 EST: 2011
SQ FT: 500
SALES (est): 6.4MM **Privately Held**
WEB: www.mailup.com
SIC: 7372 7371 Operating systems computer software; software programming applications

(P-13014)
BEHAVIOSEC USA INC
535 Mission St Fl 14, San Francisco (94105-3253)
PHONE.....................833 248-6732
Neil Costigan, *CEO*

Josh Pouliot, *CFO*
Ingo Deutschmann, *Vice Pres*
Olov Renberg, *Vice Pres*
EMP: 40 EST: 2011
SALES (est): 3.1MM **Privately Held**
WEB: www.behaviosec.com
SIC: 7372 Application computer software

(P-13015)
BELKASOFT LLC
702 San Conrado Ter # 1, Sunnyvale (94085-2534)
PHONE.....................650 272-0384
Yuri Gubanov,
Mikhail Pliskin, *Manager*
EMP: 35 EST: 2017
SALES (est): 3.2MM **Privately Held**
WEB: www.belkasoft.com
SIC: 7372 7389 5045 Application computer software; ; computers, peripherals & software

(P-13016)
BENTO TECHNOLOGIES INC
Also Called: Bento Merge Enterprises
221 Main St Ste 1325, San Francisco (94105-1946)
P.O. Box 10929, Chicago IL (60610-0929)
PHONE.....................415 887-2028
Guido Schulz, *CEO*
Farhan Ahmad, *Ch of Bd*
Sean Anderson, *CFO*
Paula Bachman, *CFO*
Jonathan Su, *Vice Pres*
EMP: 28 EST: 2014
SQ FT: 2,628
SALES (est): 2.5MM **Privately Held**
WEB: www.bentoforbusiness.com
SIC: 7372 Business oriented computer software

(P-13017)
BIG SWITCH NETWORKS LLC
5453 Great America Pkwy, Santa Clara (95054-3645)
PHONE.....................650 322-6510
Douglas Murray, *President*
Jeffrey Wang, *President*
Seamus Hennessy, *CFO*
Wendell Laidley, *CFO*
Gregg Holzrichter, *Chief Mktg Ofcr*
EMP: 180 EST: 2010
SALES (est): 27.3MM **Publicly Held**
WEB: www.arista.com
SIC: 7372 Prepackaged software
PA: Arista Networks, Inc.
5453 Great America Pkwy
Santa Clara CA 95054

(P-13018)
BILLCOM LLC (HQ)
1800 Embarcadero Rd, Palo Alto (94303-3308)
P.O. Box 370, Alviso (95002-0370)
PHONE.....................650 353-3301
Rene Lacerte, *CEO*
Salvador Chavez, *Partner*
Priya Daftary, *Partner*
Jennifer Mohoney, *Partner*
Mark Orttung, *COO*
EMP: 140 EST: 2006
SALES (est): 129.4MM
SALES (corp-wide): 238.2MM **Publicly Held**
WEB: www.bill.com
SIC: 7372 Application computer software
PA: Bill.Com Holdings, Inc.
6220 America Center Dr # 100
San Jose CA 95002
650 621-7700

(P-13019)
BILLCOM HOLDINGS INC (PA)
6220 America Center Dr # 100, San Jose (95002-2563)
P.O. Box 370, Alviso (95002-0370)
PHONE.....................650 621-7700
Rene Lacerte, *CEO*
Carole Amos, *Partner*
Jennifer Mohoney, *Partner*
Mark Orttung, *COO*
John Rettig, *CFO*
EMP: 300 EST: 2006
SQ FT: 48,200

SALES (est): 238.2MM **Publicly Held**
WEB: www.bill.com
SIC: 7372 Prepackaged software

(P-13020)
BINTI INC
1212 Broadway Ste 200, Oakland (94612-1930)
PHONE.....................844 424-6844
Felicia Curcuru, *CEO*
Allison Lacker, *Software Engr*
Sen Lu, *Software Engr*
Tina Parija, *Software Engr*
Rahul Patel, *Software Engr*
EMP: 23 EST: 2014
SALES (est): 1.7MM **Privately Held**
WEB: www.binti.com
SIC: 7372 7389 Business oriented computer software;

(P-13021)
BITZER MOBILE INC
4230 Leonard Stocking Dr, Santa Clara (95054-1777)
PHONE.....................866 603-8392
Naeem Zafar, *President*
Ali Ahmed, *CTO*
EMP: 38 EST: 2010
SQ FT: 2,000
SALES (est): 3MM
SALES (corp-wide): 40.4B **Publicly Held**
WEB: www.oracle.com
SIC: 7372 Business oriented computer software
PA: Oracle Corporation
2300 Oracle Way
Austin TX 78741
737 867-1000

(P-13022)
BIZ PERFORMANCE SOLUTIONS INC
Also Called: Bizps
840 Loma Vista St, Moss Beach (94038-9721)
PHONE.....................408 844-4284
David Mosher, *CEO*
Ken Matusow, *COO*
EMP: 15 EST: 2010
SALES (est): 1MM **Privately Held**
WEB: www.bizps.com
SIC: 7372 8711 Application computer software; consulting engineer

(P-13023)
BLACKBERRY CORPORATION (HQ)
3001 Bishop Dr, San Ramon (94583-5005)
PHONE.....................972 650-6126
John Chen, *CEO*
Mangesh Belkhode, *Software Dev*
Esviandvytwo Jones, *Software Dev*
Rita Labde, *Software Dev*
Trung Pham, *Software Dev*
▲ EMP: 1221 EST: 1999
SALES (est): 508.5MM
SALES (corp-wide): 1B **Privately Held**
WEB: www.blackberry.com
SIC: 7372 Prepackaged software
PA: Blackberry Limited
2200 University Ave E
Waterloo ON N2K 0
519 888-7465

(P-13024)
BLAMELESS INC
500 University Ave, Palo Alto (94301-1901)
PHONE.....................425 749-8859
Muhammad Ashar Rizqi, *CEO*
EMP: 21 EST: 2018
SALES (est): 1MM **Privately Held**
WEB: www.blameless.com
SIC: 7372 Prepackaged software

(P-13025)
BLEND LABS INC
415 Kearny St, San Francisco (94108-2803)
PHONE.....................650 550-4810
Timothy J Mayopoulos, *President*
Ritesh Paspulati, *IT/INT Sup*
Marc Greenberg, *Finance*
Jonathan Lachman, *Opers Staff*
Justin Schuster, *Marketing Staff*
EMP: 577 EST: 2012
SQ FT: 47,000

SALES (est): 96MM **Privately Held**
WEB: www.blend.com
SIC: 7372 Business oriented computer software

(P-13026)
BLOCKFREIGHT INC
535 Mission St Fl 14, San Francisco (94105-3253)
PHONE.....................415 815-3924
Julian Smith, *Founder*
EMP: 20 EST: 2017
SALES (est): 1.3MM **Privately Held**
WEB: www.blockfreight.com
SIC: 7372 7371 Business oriented computer software; computer software development & applications

(P-13027)
BLUE COAT LLC
350 Ellis St, Mountain View (94043-2202)
PHONE.....................408 220-2200
Michael Fey, *President*
Thomas Seifert, *CFO*
Fran Rosch, *Exec VP*
Scott Taylor, *Exec VP*
Balaji Yelamanchili, *Exec VP*
EMP: 1583 EST: 2015
SALES (est): 149.7MM
SALES (corp-wide): 2.5B **Publicly Held**
WEB: www.broadcom.com
SIC: 7372 Prepackaged software
PA: Nortonlifelock Inc.
60 E Rio Salado Pkwy # 1
Tempe AZ 85281
650 527-8000

(P-13028)
BLUE COAT SYSTEMS LLC (HQ)
420 N Mary Ave, Sunnyvale (94085-4121)
PHONE.....................650 527-8000
Michael Fey, *President*
Donald W Alford, *President*
David Yntemai, *President*
Nicholas R Noviello, *CFO*
Thomas Seifert, *CFO*
▲ EMP: 620 EST: 1996
SQ FT: 234,000
SALES (est): 50.7MM
SALES (corp-wide): 2.5B **Publicly Held**
WEB: www.nortonlifelock.com
SIC: 7372 Prepackaged software
PA: Nortonlifelock Inc.
60 E Rio Salado Pkwy # 1
Tempe AZ 85281
650 527-8000

(P-13029)
BLUEDATA SOFTWARE INC
3979 Freedom Cir Ste 850, Santa Clara (95054-1452)
PHONE.....................650 450-4067
Kumar Sreekanti, *CEO*
Thomas Phelan, *COO*
Amit Parikh, *CFO*
Shane Margraves, *Vice Pres*
EMP: 17 EST: 2012
SALES (est): 3.8MM
SALES (corp-wide): 26.9B **Publicly Held**
WEB: www.hpe.com
SIC: 7372 Prepackaged software
PA: Hewlett Packard Enterprise Company
11445 Compaq Center W Dr
Houston TX 77070
650 687-5817

(P-13030)
BLUESHIFT LABS INC
433 California St Ste 600, San Francisco (94104-2010)
PHONE.....................844 258-3735
Vijay Chittoor, *President*
Travis Adlman, *CFO*
Subramanyam Mallela, *Treasurer*
Mehul Shah, *Admin Sec*
Michael Ruescher, *Software Dev*
EMP: 176 EST: 2014
SQ FT: 5,000
SALES (est): 14.4MM **Privately Held**
WEB: www.blueshift.com
SIC: 7372 Business oriented computer software

PRODUCTS & SERVICES SECTION

7372 - Prepackaged Software County (P-13056)

(P-13031)
BLUESTACK SYSTEMS INC
2105 S Bascom Ave Ste 380, Campbell (95008-3278)
PHONE.................................408 412-9439
Rosen Sharma, *President*
Hue Harguindeguy, *CFO*
Jay Vaishnav, *Senior VP*
Ben Armstrong, *Vice Pres*
Dan Liu, *Business Dir*
EMP: 39 **EST:** 2008
SALES (est): 3.3MM **Privately Held**
WEB: www.bluestacks.com
SIC: 7372 Application computer software

(P-13032)
BONSAI AI INC
2150 Shattuck Ave # 1200, Berkeley (94704-1357)
PHONE.................................510 900-1112
EMP: 42
SQ FT: 1,445
SALES (est): 49.3K
SALES (corp-wide): 110.3B **Publicly Held**
SIC: 7372 Prepackaged Software Services
PA: Microsoft Corporation
1 Microsoft Way
Redmond WA 98052
425 882-8080

(P-13033)
BOX INC (PA)
900 Jefferson Ave, Redwood City (94063-1837)
PHONE.................................877 729-4269
Aaron Levie, *Ch of Bd*
Stephanie Carullo, *COO*
Dylan Smith, *CFO*
Dan Levin, *Bd of Directors*
Diego Dugatkin, *Officer*
EMP: 1769 **EST:** 2005
SQ FT: 340,000
SALES: 770.7MM **Publicly Held**
WEB: www.box.com
SIC: 7372 Application computer software

(P-13034)
BREAKTIME STUDIOS INC (PA)
100 Montgomery St # 1900, San Francisco (94104-4331)
PHONE.................................415 290-4900
Matthew Davie, *CEO*
Sean Phinney, *COO*
Gary Gee, *Controller*
EMP: 42 **EST:** 2011
SALES (est): 4.8MM **Privately Held**
WEB: www.breaktimestudios.com
SIC: 7372 Application computer software

(P-13035)
BRIGHTIDEA INCORPORATED
255 California St # 1100, San Francisco (94111-4927)
PHONE.................................415 814-1387
EMP: 25
SALES (corp-wide): 8.6MM **Privately Held**
SIC: 7372 Prepackaged Software
PA: Brightidea Incorporated
25 Pacific Ave
San Francisco CA
415 814-3817

(P-13036)
BRILLIANT WORLDWIDE INC
200 Pine St Fl 8, San Francisco (94104-2707)
PHONE.................................650 468-2966
Suyeon Khim, *CEO*
Jim Pekarek, *Sr Software Eng*
Maryann Vellanikaran, *VP Engrg*
Skylar Zhang, *Senior Mgr*
Josh Silverman, *Director*
EMP: 27 **EST:** 2012
SALES (est): 2.4MM **Privately Held**
WEB: www.brilliant.org
SIC: 7372 Educational computer software

(P-13037)
BROADLY INC
409 13th St Fl 3, Oakland (94612-2607)
PHONE.................................510 400-6039
Joshua Melick, *CEO*
Krystal Nguyen, *Vice Pres*
Brad McCready, *Executive*
Kieu Tran, *Software Dev*
Pascal Balthrop, *Software Engr*
EMP: 42 **EST:** 2014
SALES (est): 4.8MM **Privately Held**
WEB: www.broadly.com
SIC: 7372 Business oriented computer software

(P-13038)
BUGSNAG INC
110 Sutter St Fl 10, San Francisco (94104-4027)
PHONE.................................415 484-8664
Kirti Dewan, *Vice Pres*
John Skubel, *Vice Pres*
Nicole Broadstock, *Office Mgr*
Mike Bull, *Sr Software Eng*
Ben Ibinson, *Sr Software Eng*
EMP: 45 **EST:** 2013
SALES (est): 2.9MM **Privately Held**
WEB: www.bugsnag.com
SIC: 7372 Application computer software

(P-13039)
BUOY LABS INC
Also Called: Resideo Buoy
125 Mcpherson St, Santa Cruz (95060-5883)
PHONE.................................855 481-7112
Keri Waters, *CEO*
EMP: 16 **EST:** 2015
SALES (est): 1.5MM
SALES (corp-wide): 5B **Publicly Held**
WEB: www.resideo.com
SIC: 7372 Prepackaged software
PA: Resideo Technologies, Inc.
901 E 6th St
Austin TX 78702
512 726-3500

(P-13040)
BUYERSROAD INC
3000 Executive Pkwy # 315, San Ramon (94583-4325)
PHONE.................................937 313-4466
Steve Harris, *CEO*
Dave R Taylor, *Chief Mktg Ofcr*
EMP: 15 **EST:** 2017
SALES (est): 728.2K **Privately Held**
WEB: www.experience.com
SIC: 7372 Prepackaged software

(P-13041)
BVRP AMERICA INC
Also Called: Avanquest Software USA
7031 Koll Center Pkwy # 15, Pleasanton (94566-3128)
PHONE.................................303 450-1139
Robert Lang, *President*
Craig Senick, *Sales Staff*
EMP: 36 **EST:** 2004
SALES (est): 5.2MM
SALES (corp-wide): 1.8MM **Privately Held**
WEB: www.claranova.com
SIC: 7372 Prepackaged software
PA: Claranova S.E.
Avanquest Blue Squad Bvrp Software
Immeuble Vision Defense
La Garenne Colombes 92250
962 557-603

(P-13042)
C3 DELAWARE INC
1300 Seaport Blvd Ste 500, Redwood City (94063-5592)
PHONE.................................650 503-2200
Patricia A House, *Owner*
Huanwen Chen, *Engineer*
Martin Tobiczyk, *Accounting Mgr*
EMP: 19 **EST:** 2013
SALES (est): 3.2MM **Privately Held**
WEB: www.c3.ai
SIC: 7372 Business oriented computer software

(P-13043)
C3AI INC (PA)
1300 Seaport Blvd Ste 500, Redwood City (94063-5592)
PHONE.................................650 503-2200
Thomas M Siebel, *Ch of Bd*
David Barter, *CFO*
Patricia A House, *Vice Ch Bd*
Bruce Cleveland, *Chief Mktg Ofcr*
Houman Behzadi,
EMP: 209 **EST:** 2009
SALES: 183.2MM **Publicly Held**
WEB: www.c3.ai
SIC: 7372 Prepackaged software; business oriented computer software

(P-13044)
CA INC
3965 Freedom Cir Fl 6, Santa Clara (95054-1286)
PHONE.................................800 225-5224
Ashok Reddy, *General Mgr*
Alf Abuhajleh, *Director*
EMP: 166
SALES (corp-wide): 23.8B **Publicly Held**
WEB: www.broadcom.com
SIC: 7372 Business oriented computer software
HQ: Ca, Inc.
520 Madison Ave
New York NY 10022
800 225-5224

(P-13045)
CADENCE DESIGN SYSTEMS INC (PA)
2655 Seely Ave Bldg 5, San Jose (95134-1931)
PHONE.................................408 943-1234
Lip-Bu Tan, *CEO*
John B Shoven, *Ch of Bd*
Anirudh Devgan, *President*
John M Wall, *CFO*
Alinka Flaminia,
▲ **EMP:** 700 **EST:** 1982
SALES (est): 2.6B **Publicly Held**
WEB: www.cadence.com
SIC: 7372 Prepackaged software; application computer software

(P-13046)
CALMCOM INC (PA)
77 Geary St 3, San Francisco (94108-5723)
PHONE.................................415 278-0991
Alexander Tew, *CEO*
Tony Hsieh, *Vice Pres*
Chase Ward, *Engineer*
Jacob Lindman, *Finance*
Bazzani Nikki, *Marketing Mgr*
EMP: 39 **EST:** 2012
SALES (est): 20MM **Privately Held**
SIC: 7372 Application computer software

(P-13047)
CALYPTO DESIGN SYSTEMS INC
2099 Gateway Pl Ste 550, San Jose (95110-1051)
PHONE.................................408 850-2300
Sanjiv Kaul, *President*
Chris Mausler, *CFO*
EMP: 34 **EST:** 2002
SALES (est): 1.2MM **Privately Held**
SIC: 7372 Prepackaged software

(P-13048)
CANARY TECHNOLOGIES CORP
450 9th St Fl 1, San Francisco (94103-4411)
PHONE.................................415 578-1414
Satjot Sawhney, *CEO*
Dhiraj Singh, *Vice Pres*
Harman Narula, *Administration*
Gurtej Gill, *Opers Staff*
Austin Kroll, *Sales Staff*
EMP: 22 **EST:** 2017
SALES (est): 1.8MM **Privately Held**
WEB: www.canarytechnologies.com
SIC: 7372 Business oriented computer software

(P-13049)
CANTO INC
625 Market St Ste 600, San Francisco (94105-3308)
PHONE.................................415 495-6545
Jack McGannon, *CEO*
Cory Schmidt, *Marketing Staff*
Anthony Hurtado, *Advisor*
Robert Mackey, *Accounts Exec*
James Wanbaugh, *Accounts Exec*
EMP: 60 **EST:** 2019
SALES (est): 5.4MM **Privately Held**
WEB: www.canto.com
SIC: 7372 Prepackaged software

(P-13050)
CARE ZONE INC
Also Called: Carezone
121 Capp St Ste 200, San Francisco (94110-1885)
P.O. Box 150, San Mateo (94401-0150)
PHONE.................................206 707-9127
Jonathan Schwartz, *CEO*
Walter Smith, *Vice Pres*
Victor Ilyukevich, *Software Dev*
Lito Nicolai, *Software Dev*
EMP: 50 **EST:** 2010
SALES (est): 5.3MM **Privately Held**
WEB: www.carezone.com
SIC: 7372 Application computer software

(P-13051)
CASEMAKER INC
1680 Civic Center Dr Frnt, Santa Clara (95050-4146)
PHONE.................................408 261-8265
Jui-Long Liu, *President*
Linda Franklin, *Director*
EMP: 16 **EST:** 1991
SQ FT: 11,000
SALES (est): 1.6MM **Privately Held**
WEB: www.casemaker.com
SIC: 7372 7371 Application computer software; custom computer programming services

(P-13052)
CASPIO INC (PA)
1286 Kifer Rd Ste 107, Sunnyvale (94086-5326)
PHONE.................................650 691-0900
Frank Zamani, *CEO*
Steven Leung, *Vice Pres*
Spring Babb, *Admin Sec*
Noah Ismen, *Info Tech Dir*
Caren Vito, *Technical Staff*
EMP: 22 **EST:** 2000
SALES (est): 7.3MM **Privately Held**
WEB: www.caspio.com
SIC: 7372 Business oriented computer software

(P-13053)
CATO NETWORKS INC
3031 Tisch Way, San Jose (95128-2541)
PHONE.................................646 975-9243
Shlomo Kramer, *CEO*
Tomer Wald, *CFO*
Steven Krausz, *Vice Pres*
Gur Shatz, *CTO*
Ofir Agasi, *Director*
EMP: 31 **EST:** 2015
SALES (est): 11.6MM **Privately Held**
WEB: www.catonetworks.com
SIC: 7372 Application computer software

(P-13054)
CELIGO INC (PA)
1820 Gateway Dr Ste 260, San Mateo (94404-4068)
PHONE.................................650 579-0210
Jan K Arendtsz, *CEO*
Matt Nawrocki, *Vice Pres*
Laura Sherman, *Administration*
Brad Thomas, *CIO*
Tim Brocato, *Web Dvlpr*
EMP: 198 **EST:** 2008
SALES (est): 17.9MM **Privately Held**
WEB: www.celigo.com
SIC: 7372 Business oriented computer software

(P-13055)
CELLFUSION INC (PA)
2033 Gateway Pl Fl 5, San Jose (95110-3709)
PHONE.................................650 347-4000
Kersten Ellerbrock, *President*
EMP: 45 **EST:** 1999
SALES (est): 267.8K **Privately Held**
WEB: www.cellfusion.com
SIC: 7372 Business oriented computer software

(P-13056)
CELONA INC
10080 N Wolfe Rd Sw3250, Cupertino (95014-2556)
PHONE.................................408 839-7625
Rajeev Shah, *CEO*
EMP: 20 **EST:** 2019

7372 - Prepackaged Software County (P-13057) — PRODUCTS & SERVICES SECTION

SALES (est): 3.1MM **Privately Held**
SIC: 7372 Application computer software

(P-13057)
CENTRA SOFTWARE INC
Also Called: Field Sales Office
1840 Gateway Dr Fl 2, San Mateo
(94404-4027)
PHONE..................650 378-1363
David Allen, *Branch Mgr*
EMP: 30
SALES (corp-wide): 238.9K **Privately Held**
SIC: 7372 7379 Business oriented computer software; computer related consulting services
HQ: Centra Software Inc
430 Bedford St Ste 220
Lexington MA 02420

(P-13058)
CENTRL INC
257 Castro St Ste 215, Mountain View (94041-1287)
PHONE..................650 641-7092
Sanjeev Dheer, *CEO*
Chris Marino, *COO*
Mike Kaufman, *Vice Pres*
Serge Rubinstein, *VP Mktg*
Rupali Chopra, *General Counsel*
EMP: 33 EST: 2015
SALES (est): 3.6MM **Privately Held**
WEB: www.oncentrl.com
SIC: 7372 Application computer software

(P-13059)
CERTAIN INC (PA)
75 Hawthorne St Ste 550, San Francisco (94105-3938)
PHONE..................415 353-5330
Peter Micciche, *CEO*
Brian Bailard, *Officer*
Gerard Larios, *Vice Pres*
Meg Canepa, *Office Mgr*
Steven Wong, *Administration*
EMP: 50 EST: 1994
SALES (est): 11.9MM **Privately Held**
WEB: www.certain.com
SIC: 7372 Prepackaged software

(P-13060)
CETAS INC
3260 Hillview Ave, Palo Alto (94304-1220)
PHONE..................847 530-5785
Lavanya Katla, *CEO*
EMP: 15 EST: 2018
SALES (est): 628.2K **Privately Held**
WEB: www.cetas.ai
SIC: 7372 Business oriented computer software

(P-13061)
CHECK POINT SOFTWARE TECH INC (HQ)
959 Skyway Rd Ste 300, San Carlos (94070-2723)
PHONE..................650 628-2000
John Slavitt, *CEO*
Lisa Williams, *Partner*
Marius Nacht, *Ch of Bd*
Rafael Alegre, *President*
Jerry Ungerman, *President*
▲ EMP: 120 EST: 1996
SALES (est): 250.2MM **Privately Held**
WEB: www.checkpoint.com
SIC: 7372 Operating systems computer software

(P-13062)
CHEMSW INC
2480 Burskirk Ste 300, Pleasant Hill (94523)
PHONE..................707 864-0845
Brian Stafford, *President*
Patrick Spink, *Vice Pres*
EMP: 16 EST: 1991
SQ FT: 2,600
SALES (est): 2.1MM
SALES (corp-wide): 2B **Privately Held**
WEB: www.chemsw.com
SIC: 7372 Prepackaged software
HQ: Dassault Systemes Biovia Corp.
5005 Wateridge Vista Dr
San Diego CA 92121

(P-13063)
CHIA NETWORK INC
44 Montgomery St Ste 2310, San Francisco (94104-4711)
PHONE..................628 222-5925
Gene Hoffman, *President*
Bram Cohen, *CEO*
Mitch Edwards, *CFO*
Vishal Kapoor, *Senior VP*
EMP: 16 EST: 2017
SALES (est): 1MM **Privately Held**
WEB: www.chia.net
SIC: 7372 Prepackaged software

(P-13064)
CHIP ESTIMATE CORPORATION
Also Called: Chipestimate.com
2655 Seely Ave, San Jose (95134-1931)
PHONE..................408 943-1234
J George Janac, *Principal*
Adam Traidman, *General Mgr*
Paul Rose, *IT/INT Sup*
Ryan Badger, *Engineer*
EMP: 43 EST: 2003
SALES (est): 7.2MM
SALES (corp-wide): 2.6B **Publicly Held**
WEB: www.chipestimate.com
SIC: 7372 Application computer software
PA: Cadence Design Systems, Inc.
2655 Seely Ave Bldg 5
San Jose CA 95134
408 943-1234

(P-13065)
CIPHERCLOUD INC (HQ)
2581 Junction Ave Ste 200, San Jose (95134-1923)
PHONE..................408 687-4350
James Dolce, *CEO*
Simon Pius, *CFO*
Pravin Kothari, *Exec VP*
Robert Bartolomeo, *Vice Pres*
Harnish Kanani, *Vice Pres*
EMP: 90 EST: 2010
SQ FT: 21,800
SALES (est): 69.5MM **Privately Held**
WEB: www.ingeniux.lookout.com
SIC: 7372 Business oriented computer software

(P-13066)
CIRCLE INTERNET SERVICES INC (PA)
Also Called: Circleci
201 Spear St Fl 12, San Francisco (94105-1635)
PHONE..................707 731-4912
EMP: 23
SALES (est): 6MM **Privately Held**
WEB: www.circleci.com
SIC: 7372 Prepackaged Software Services

(P-13067)
CISCO SYSTEMS LLC (HQ)
170 W Tasman Dr, San Jose (95134-1706)
PHONE..................650 989-6500
Scott Weiss, *CEO*
Tom Peterson, *President*
Craig Collins, *CFO*
Bob Kavner, *Chairman*
Kelly Bodnar Battles, *Vice Pres*
EMP: 260 EST: 2000
SALES (est): 100.2MM
SALES (corp-wide): 49.8B **Publicly Held**
WEB: www.cisco.com
SIC: 7372 5045 Prepackaged software; computers, peripherals & software
PA: Cisco Systems, Inc.
170 W Tasman Dr
San Jose CA 95134
408 526-4000

(P-13068)
CLEAR SKYE INC
2340 Powell St Ste 325, Emeryville (94608-1738)
PHONE..................415 619-5001
John Milburn, *CEO*
Vahan Galachyan, *COO*
EMP: 25 EST: 2015
SALES (est): 1.4MM **Privately Held**
WEB: www.clearskye.com
SIC: 7372 Prepackaged software

(P-13069)
CLEARSLIDE INC (DH)
45 Fremont St Fl 32, San Francisco (94105-2258)
PHONE..................877 360-3366
Dustin Grosse, *CEO*
Jim Benton, *Officer*
Sandra Wright, *Vice Pres*
Lawrence Bruhmuller, *Engineer*
Janelle Pon, *Hum Res Coord*
EMP: 94 EST: 2009
SALES (est): 21.5MM
SALES (corp-wide): 621MM **Privately Held**
WEB: www.clearslide.com
SIC: 7372 Business oriented computer software
HQ: Corel Corporation
1600 Carling Ave Suite 200
Ottawa ON K1Z 8
613 728-8200

(P-13070)
CLEARWELL SYSTEMS INC
350 Ellis St, Mountain View (94043-2202)
PHONE..................877 253-2793
Aaref Hilaly, *CEO*
Anup Singh, *CFO*
Venkat Rangan, *CTO*
▼ EMP: 110 EST: 2004
SQ FT: 17,000
SALES (est): 32.1MM
SALES (corp-wide): 2.5B **Publicly Held**
WEB: www.clearwellsystems.com
SIC: 7372 Business oriented computer software
PA: Nortonlifelock Inc.
60 E Rio Salado Pkwy # 1
Tempe AZ 85281
650 527-8000

(P-13071)
CLIMATE CORPORATION (DH)
Also Called: Climate Fieldview
201 3rd St Ste 1010, San Francisco (94103-3129)
PHONE..................415 363-0500
Mike Stern, *CEO*
Greg Smirin, *COO*
Dana Greene, *Exec Officer*
Ranjeeta Singh,
Avery Moon, *Vice Pres*
EMP: 50 EST: 2006
SALES (est): 29MM
SALES (corp-wide): 48.9B **Privately Held**
WEB: www.climate.com
SIC: 7372 5045 Prepackaged software; computer software
HQ: Monsanto Company
800 N Lindbergh Blvd
Saint Louis MO 63167
314 694-1000

(P-13072)
CLIOSOFT INC
39500 Stevenson Pl # 110, Fremont (94539-3102)
PHONE..................510 790-4732
Srinath Anantharaman, *President*
Michael Henrie, *Sr Software Eng*
Mahendra Khalsa, *Software Engr*
Sriram Rajamanohar, *Software Engr*
Prathna Sekar, *Engineer*
▲ EMP: 36 EST: 1997
SALES (est): 3.4MM **Privately Held**
WEB: www.cliosoft.com
SIC: 7372 Prepackaged software

(P-13073)
CLONETAB INC
1660 W Linne Rd Ste 214, Tracy (95377-8027)
PHONE..................209 292-5663
Hema Meka, *CEO*
Bharathi Meka, *CFO*
EMP: 39 EST: 2011
SALES (est): 1.7MM **Privately Held**
WEB: www.clonetab.com
SIC: 7372 Prepackaged software

(P-13074)
CLOUD9 CHARTS INC
1528 Webster St, Oakland (94612-3314)
PHONE..................510 507-3661
Jay Gopalakrishn, *CEO*
Jay Gopalakrishnan, *CEO*
EMP: 15 EST: 2014
SALES (est): 903K **Privately Held**
SIC: 7372 Prepackaged software

(P-13075)
CLOUDCAR INC
2560 N 1st St Ste 100, San Jose (95131-1041)
PHONE..................650 946-1236
Philipp Popov, *CEO*
Bruce Leak, *COO*
Albert Jordan, *Vice Pres*
Ashley Fahey, *Office Mgr*
Danh Le, *CIO*
EMP: 48 EST: 2010
SALES (est): 4.4MM **Privately Held**
WEB: www.cloudcar.com
SIC: 7372 Prepackaged software

(P-13076)
CLOUDERA INC (PA)
5470 Great America Pkwy, Santa Clara (95054-3644)
PHONE..................650 362-0488
Robert Bearden, *President*
Nicholas Graziano, *Ch of Bd*
Robert Carey, *President*
James Frankola, *CFO*
Jim Frankola, *CFO*
EMP: 2588 EST: 2008
SALES (est): 869.2MM **Privately Held**
WEB: www.cloudera.com
SIC: 7372 Prepackaged software

(P-13077)
CLOUDFLARE INC (PA)
101 Townsend St, San Francisco (94107-1934)
PHONE..................888 993-5273
Matthew Prince, *CEO*
Michelle Zatlyn, *President*
Thomas Seifert, *CFO*
Clint Fulmer, *Executive*
Douglas Kramer, *Admin Sec*
EMP: 1580 EST: 2009
SQ FT: 81,000
SALES (est): 431MM **Publicly Held**
WEB: www.cloudflare.com
SIC: 7372 Prepackaged software

(P-13078)
CLOUDJEE INC
1975 W El Cmino Real 30, Mountain View (94040)
PHONE..................866 660-6099
Samir Ghosh, *CEO*
Vinay Murthy, *VP Bus Dvlpt*
Brian Yurkus, *Contractor*
EMP: 20 EST: 2012
SQ FT: 3,000
SALES (est): 1.1MM **Privately Held**
WEB: www.cloudjee.com
SIC: 7372 7371 Business oriented computer software; application computer software; computer software development

(P-13079)
CLOUDSHIELD TECHNOLOGIES LLC
212 Gibraltar Dr, Sunnyvale (94089-1324)
PHONE..................408 331-6640
Randy Brumfield, *Senior VP*
Timothy Laehy, *CFO*
Todd Beine, *CTO*
EMP: 115 EST: 2000
SQ FT: 35,000
SALES (est): 15MM
SALES (corp-wide): 37MM **Privately Held**
WEB: www.lookingglasscyber.com
SIC: 7372 8741 8742 Prepackaged software; business management; business consultant
PA: Lookingglass Cyber Solution, Inc.
10740 Parkridge Blvd # 200
Reston VA 20191
703 351-1000

(P-13080)
CLOUDSIMPLE INC
1600 Amphitheatre Pkwy, Mountain View (94043-1351)
PHONE..................412 568-3487
Gururaj Pangal, *CEO*
EMP: 78 EST: 2016

▲ = Import ▼ = Export
◆ = Import/Export

7372 - Prepackaged Software County (P-13103)

SALES (est): 25MM
SALES (corp-wide): 182.5B **Publicly Held**
WEB: www.google.com
SIC: 7372 Application computer software
HQ: Google Llc
  1600 Amphitheatre Pkwy
  Mountain View CA 94043
  650 253-0000

(P-13081)
COBALT LABS INC (PA)
575 Market St Fl 4, San Francisco (94105-5818)
PHONE...................415 651-7028
Esben Friis Jensen, *Founder*
Jacob Hansen, *CEO*
Caleb Sima, *Vice Pres*
Chris Tilton, *Vice Pres*
Scott Marcelo, *Executive*
EMP: 19 **EST:** 2017
SALES (est): 1.8MM **Privately Held**
WEB: www.cobalt.io
SIC: 7372 Prepackaged software

(P-13082)
CODEFAST INC
21170 Canyon Oak Way, Cupertino (95014-6572)
PHONE...................408 687-4700
Nick Barens, *President*
EMP: 21 **EST:** 2004
SALES (est): 1MM
SALES (corp-wide): 3.6B **Publicly Held**
WEB: www.synopsys.com
SIC: 7372 Business oriented computer software
HQ: Coverity Llc
  185 Berry St Ste 6500
  San Francisco CA 94107
  415 321-5200

(P-13083)
COLABO INC
751 Laurel St Ste 840, San Carlos (94070-3113)
PHONE...................650 288-6649
Yoav Dembak, *CEO*
David Popkin, *Director*
EMP: 34 **EST:** 2013
SALES (est): 2.6MM **Privately Held**
WEB: www.colabo.com
SIC: 7372 Prepackaged software

(P-13084)
COLLABORATIVE DRG DISCOVERY INC
Also Called: Molecular Databank
1633 Bayshore Hwy Ste 342, Burlingame (94010-1515)
PHONE...................650 204-3084
Barry Bunin, *President*
Alex Clark, *Research*
Lixin Liu, *Accountant*
Sheryl Thompson, *Sales Executive*
Frank Cole, *Sales Staff*
EMP: 35 **EST:** 2004
SALES (est): 5MM **Privately Held**
WEB: www.collaborativedrug.com
SIC: 7372 Prepackaged software

(P-13085)
COLORTOKENS INC (PA)
2101 Tasman Dr Ste 201, Santa Clara (95054-1020)
P.O. Box K, Sunnyvale (94087-0106)
PHONE...................408 341-6030
Rajesh Parekh, *President*
Vats Srivatsan, *President*
Debra Krapivkin, *Executive Asst*
Navin Leon, *Web Dvlpr*
Scott Emo, *Marketing Staff*
EMP: 48 **EST:** 2015
SALES (est): 5.7MM **Privately Held**
WEB: www.colortokens.com
SIC: 7372 Business oriented computer software

(P-13086)
COMPOSE INC
273 S Railroad Ave Ste A, San Mateo (94401-3339)
PHONE...................415 574-7038
Kurt Mackey, *CEO*
EMP: 19 **EST:** 2011

SALES (est): 618.3K
SALES (corp-wide): 73.6B **Publicly Held**
WEB: www.app.compose.io
SIC: 7372 Application computer software
PA: International Business Machines Corporation
  1 New Orchard Rd Ste 1 # 1
  Armonk NY 10504
  914 499-1900

(P-13087)
COMPOSITE SOFTWARE LLC (DH)
755 Sycamore Dr, Milpitas (95035-7411)
PHONE...................800 553-6387
Jim Green, *CEO*
Jon Bode, *CFO*
David Besemer, *CTO*
Phil Theodore, *Manager*
Matthew Lee, *Consultant*
EMP: 74 **EST:** 2002
SQ FT: 14,000
SALES (est): 31.2MM
SALES (corp-wide): 885.6MM **Privately Held**
WEB: www.tibco.com
SIC: 7372 Prepackaged software

(P-13088)
CONCENTRIC SOFTWARE INC
4750 Blue Ridge Dr, San Jose (95129-4303)
PHONE...................408 816-7068
Karthik Krishnan, *CEO*
Paul Landry, *Technology*
EMP: 25 **EST:** 2018
SALES (est): 1.6MM **Privately Held**
SIC: 7372 Prepackaged software

(P-13089)
CONDECO SOFTWARE INC (HQ)
2105 S Bascom Ave Ste 150, Campbell (95008-3276)
PHONE...................917 677-7600
Martin Brooker, *Officer*
Craig Goldberg, *Technical Staff*
Curtis King, *Consultant*
EMP: 16 **EST:** 2010
SALES (est): 10.2MM
SALES (corp-wide): 47.8MM **Privately Held**
WEB: www.condecosoftware.com
SIC: 7372 Business oriented computer software
PA: Condeco Group Limited
  8th Floor
  London E14 9
  207 001-2020

(P-13090)
CONFLUENT INC (PA)
899 W Evelyn Ave, Mountain View (94041-1225)
PHONE...................800 439-3207
Edward Kreps, *CEO*
Erica Schultz, *President*
Steffan Tomlinson, *CFO*
EMP: 1469 **EST:** 2014
SQ FT: 75,475
SALES (est): 236.5MM **Publicly Held**
WEB: www.confluent.io
SIC: 7372 Application computer software; business oriented computer software; utility computer software

(P-13091)
CONTACTUAL INC
810 W Maude Ave, Sunnyvale (94085-2910)
PHONE...................650 292-4408
Mansour Salame, *CEO*
David Sohm, *President*
Jeff Williams, *COO*
Jonathan Ive, *Officer*
David Chen, *Vice Pres*
EMP: 80 **EST:** 2000
SQ FT: 5,000
SALES (est): 8.2MM
SALES (corp-wide): 532.3MM **Publicly Held**
WEB: www.contactual.com
SIC: 7372 Prepackaged software
PA: 8x8, Inc.
  675 Creekside Way
  Campbell CA 95008
  408 727-1885

(P-13092)
CONTRACT WRANGLER INC
1840 Gateway Dr Ste 300, San Mateo (94404-4030)
PHONE...................408 472-6898
John Gengarella, *Administration*
Harry Register, *Chairman*
Nick Mandelstein, *Vice Pres*
Brian Ascher, *Director*
Neil Peretz, *Director*
EMP: 35 **EST:** 2016
SQ FT: 2,000
SALES (est): 3MM **Privately Held**
WEB: www.contractwrangler.com
SIC: 7372 Prepackaged software

(P-13093)
CORALTREE INC
6120 Hellyer Ave Ste 100, San Jose (95138-1065)
PHONE...................408 215-1441
Tiruvali Srinivasan, *CEO*
Chris Wise, *Director*
Alison Garcia, *Manager*
EMP: 20 **EST:** 2009
SALES (est): 2.4MM **Privately Held**
SIC: 5734 7372 Software, business & non-game; prepackaged software

(P-13094)
COUNTER HOSPITALITY GROUP LLC
Also Called: Heirloom
8398 N Fresno St Ste 101, Fresno (93720-1599)
PHONE...................559 228-9735
Kevin Koligian,
EMP: 85 **EST:** 2019
SALES (est): 6.5MM **Privately Held**
SIC: 5812 7372 American restaurant; application computer software

(P-13095)
COUPA SOFTWARE INCORPORATED (PA)
1855 S Grant St, San Mateo (94402-7016)
PHONE...................650 931-3200
Robert Bernshteyn, *Ch of Bd*
Todd Ford, *President*
Anthony Tiscornia, *CFO*
Mark Riggs, *Ch Credit Ofcr*
Robert Glenn, *Exec VP*
EMP: 1445 **EST:** 2006
SQ FT: 69,220
SALES: 541.6MM **Publicly Held**
WEB: www.coupa.com
SIC: 7372 Business oriented computer software

(P-13096)
COURSERA INC (PA)
381 E Evelyn Ave, Mountain View (94041-1530)
PHONE...................650 963-9884
Jeffrey N Maggioncalda, *President*
Giovanni Dubois, *Partner*
Andrew Y Ng, *Ch of Bd*
Ken Hahn, *CFO*
Kenneth R Hahn, *CFO*
EMP: 776 **EST:** 2011
SALES (est): 293.5MM **Publicly Held**
WEB: www.coursera.org
SIC: 7372 Prepackaged software

(P-13097)
CROWDCIRCLE INC
Also Called: Healthcrowd
1810 Gateway Dr Ste 200, San Mateo (94404-4062)
PHONE...................206 853-7560
Neng Bing Doh, *CEO*
Nick Reutell, *Principal*
Julia Miura, *Office Mgr*
Minglun Gu, *Sr Software Eng*
Srivani Ganti, *CIO*
EMP: 50 **EST:** 2010
SALES (est): 5MM **Privately Held**
WEB: www.healthcrowd.com
SIC: 7372 Prepackaged software

(P-13098)
CROWDSTRIKE HOLDINGS INC (PA)
150 Mathilda Pl Ste 300, Sunnyvale (94086-6012)
PHONE...................888 512-8906
George Kurtz, *President*
Gerhard Watzinger, *Ch of Bd*
Michael Carpenter, *President*
Shawn Henry, *President*
Colin Black, *COO*
EMP: 120 **EST:** 2011
SQ FT: 30,331
SALES: 874.4MM **Publicly Held**
WEB: www.ir.crowdstrike.com
SIC: 7372 7379 Prepackaged software; computer related maintenance services

(P-13099)
CRYSTAL DYNAMICS INC (DH)
1400a Saport Blvd Ste 300, Redwood City (94063)
PHONE...................650 421-7600
Philip Rogers, *CEO*
Robert Dyer, *President*
John Horsley, *Vice Pres*
John Miller, *Vice Pres*
Tore Blystad, *Creative Dir*
EMP: 88 **EST:** 1992
SQ FT: 26,000
SALES (est): 20.5MM **Privately Held**
WEB: www.crystald.com
SIC: 7372 Business oriented computer software
HQ: Square Enix Limited
  240 Blackfriars Road
  London SE1 8
  208 636-3000

(P-13100)
CUMULUS NETWORKS INC (PA)
185 E Dana St, Mountain View (94041-1507)
PHONE...................650 383-6700
Jame Rivers, *CEO*
Nolan Leake, *Co-Owner*
Reza Malekzadeh, *Vice Pres*
Jason Martin, *Vice Pres*
Edward Leake, *Principal*
EMP: 124 **EST:** 2010
SALES (est): 24MM **Privately Held**
WEB: www.nvidia.com
SIC: 7372 7371 Publishers' computer software; computer software development

(P-13101)
CURACUBBY INC
2120 University Ave, Berkeley (94704-1026)
PHONE...................415 200-3373
Rosauro Lugos, *Principal*
Surya Voinar, *Sales Staff*
EMP: 17 **EST:** 2016
SALES (est): 1.8MM **Privately Held**
WEB: www.curacubby.com
SIC: 7372 Prepackaged software

(P-13102)
CYARA INC (PA)
805 Veterans Blvd Ste 105, Redwood City (94063-1750)
PHONE...................650 549-8522
Alok Kulkarni, *CEO*
James Isaacs, *President*
Mark Verbeck, *CFO*
Matt Melymuka, *Vice Pres*
Bonny Malik, *Exec Dir*
EMP: 172 **EST:** 2016
SALES (est): 17.6MM **Privately Held**
WEB: www.cyara.com
SIC: 7372 Application computer software

(P-13103)
CYBER INC
4000 Executive Pkwy # 250, San Ramon (94583-4257)
PHONE...................925 242-0777
EMP: 17 **EST:** 1998
SALES (est): 1.2MM **Privately Held**
WEB: www.cyberinc.com
SIC: 7372 Business oriented computer software

7372 - Prepackaged Software County (P-13104)

PA: Aurionpro Solutions Limited
Synergia It Park, Plot No-R-270, T.T.C.
Industrial Estate,
Navi Mumbai MH 40070

(P-13104)
CYBERINC CORPORATION (HQ)
Also Called: Aurionpro
4000 Executive Pkwy # 250, San Ramon
(94583-4257)
PHONE....................................925 242-0777
Samir Shah, *CEO*
Nirav Shah, *COO*
Balaji Desikamani, *Vice Pres*
Rajiv Raghunarayan, *Vice Pres*
Romi Randhawa, *Security Dir*
EMP: 30 **EST:** 2005
SQ FT: 3,000
SALES (est): 6.1MM **Privately Held**
WEB: www.aurionpro.com
SIC: 7372 7371 Business oriented computer software; custom computer programming services

(P-13105)
CYLANCE INC (DH)
3001 Bishop Dr Ste 400, San Ramon
(94583-5005)
PHONE....................................949 375-3380
Stuart McClure, *CEO*
Lorri Bondi, *Partner*
Dan Satinoff, *Partner*
Rick Stojak, *Partner*
Patrick Wood, *Partner*
EMP: 887 **EST:** 2012
SALES (est): 200MM
SALES (corp-wide): 1B **Privately Held**
WEB: www.blackberry.com
SIC: 7372 Application computer software
HQ: Blackberry Corporation
3001 Bishop Dr
San Ramon CA 94583
972 650-6126

(P-13106)
DADO INC
248 3rd St Ste 938, Oakland (94607-4375)
PHONE....................................510 364-6263
Jacob Olsen, *CEO*
EMP: 20
SALES (est): 200K **Privately Held**
SIC: 7372 Publishers' computer software

(P-13107)
DATA ADVANTAGE GROUP INC
145 Natoma St Fl 5, San Francisco
(94105-3733)
PHONE....................................415 947-0400
Geoffrey Rayner, *CEO*
Gregory Blumstein, *President*
Belen Jimenez, *Office Mgr*
EMP: 15 **EST:** 1999
SQ FT: 2,200
SALES (est): 2MM **Privately Held**
WEB: www.dag.com
SIC: 7372 Prepackaged software

(P-13108)
DATAFOX INTELLIGENCE INC
475 Sansome St Fl 15, San Francisco
(94111-3166)
PHONE....................................415 969-2144
Bastiaan Janmaat, *CEO*
Michael Dorsey, *COO*
Lisa Kinard, *Office Mgr*
Hunter Fox, *Software Engr*
Stacy Huang, *Software Engr*
EMP: 18 **EST:** 2013
SALES (est): 2.5MM **Privately Held**
SIC: 7372 Business oriented computer software

(P-13109)
DATAVISOR INC
967 N Shoreline Blvd, Mountain View
(94043-1932)
PHONE....................................408 331-9886
Yinglian Xie, *CEO*
Jon Sakoda, *General Ptnr*
David Cassady, *Vice Pres*
Ron Bernal, *Principal*
Fang Yu, *Principal*
EMP: 75 **EST:** 2014
SALES (est): 563.7K **Privately Held**
WEB: www.datavisor.com
SIC: 7372 Business oriented computer software

(P-13110)
DATERA INC
2811 Mission College Blvd F, Santa Clara
(95054-1884)
PHONE....................................844 432-8372
Guy Churchward, *CEO*
Marc Fleischmann, *President*
Andrew Komar, *Technical Staff*
Richard Ens, *Engineer*
Zach Roros, *Sales Dir*
EMP: 58 **EST:** 2013
SALES (est): 6.7MM **Privately Held**
WEB: www.datera.io
SIC: 7372 Business oriented computer software

(P-13111)
DCATALOG INC
956 Larkspur Ave, Sunnyvale
(94086-8634)
PHONE....................................408 824-5648
Michael Raviv, *President*
Costa Bakouros, *Sales Staff*
EMP: 20 **EST:** 2012
SALES (est): 300K **Privately Held**
WEB: www.dcatalog.com
SIC: 7372 Application computer software

(P-13112)
DEEM INC (DH)
1330 Broadway Fl 7, Oakland
(94612-2503)
PHONE....................................415 590-8300
John F Rizzo, *President*
David Shiba, *CFO*
Eddie Bridgers, *Senior VP*
Todd Kaiser, *Senior VP*
Neil Markey, *Senior VP*
▲ **EMP:** 65 **EST:** 2001
SQ FT: 133,000
SALES (est): 102.3MM
SALES (corp-wide): 6.8B **Privately Held**
WEB: www.deem.com
SIC: 7372 Prepackaged software
HQ: Enterprise Holdings, Inc.
600 Corporate Park Dr
Saint Louis MO 63105
314 512-5000

(P-13113)
DEEP LABS INC (PA)
101 2nd St Ste 375, San Francisco
(94105-3670)
PHONE....................................877 504-4544
Scott Edington, *CEO*
Michael Dreyer, *Officer*
EMP: 42 **EST:** 2016
SQ FT: 1,500
SALES (est): 3.1MM **Privately Held**
WEB: www.deep-labs.com
SIC: 7372 Business oriented computer software

(P-13114)
DEMANDBASE INC (PA)
680 Folsom St Ste 400, San Francisco
(94107-2159)
PHONE....................................415 683-2660
Gabe Rogol, *CEO*
Peter Isaacson, *Chief Mktg Ofcr*
Alan Fletcher, *Officer*
Fatima Khan, *Officer*
Landon Pearson, *Officer*
EMP: 104 **EST:** 2005
SALES (est): 62.3MM **Privately Held**
WEB: www.demandbase.com
SIC: 7372 Business oriented computer software

(P-13115)
DENALI SOFTWARE INC (HQ)
2655 Seely Ave, San Jose (95134-1931)
PHONE....................................408 943-1234
Sanjay Srivastava, *President*
R Mark Gogolewski, *CFO*
EMP: 36 **EST:** 1995
SQ FT: 10,000
SALES (est): 13MM
SALES (corp-wide): 2.6B **Publicly Held**
WEB: www.denali.com
SIC: 7372 Application computer software
PA: Cadence Design Systems, Inc.
2655 Seely Ave Bldg 5
San Jose CA 95134
408 943-1234

(P-13116)
DIGITS FINANCIAL INC
1015 Fillmore St, San Francisco
(94115-4709)
PHONE....................................814 634-4487
Katya Valadzko, *CEO*
EMP: 20 **EST:** 2018
SALES (est): 1.5MM **Privately Held**
WEB: www.digits.com
SIC: 7372 Business oriented computer software

(P-13117)
DO DINE INC
Also Called: Multani Logistics
24052 Mission Blvd, Hayward
(94544-1017)
PHONE....................................510 583-7546
Bikramjit Singh, *CEO*
EMP: 15 **EST:** 2014
SQ FT: 5,000
SALES (est): 1.4MM **Privately Held**
WEB: www.dodine.com
SIC: 7372 Business oriented computer software

(P-13118)
DOCSEND INC
351 California St # 1200, San Francisco
(94104-2412)
PHONE....................................888 258-5951
Russell Heddleston, *CEO*
Anthony Cassanego, *CFO*
Kate Gollogly, *Vice Pres*
David Koslow, *Admin Sec*
Russ Heddleston, *CIO*
EMP: 96 **EST:** 2013
SALES (est): 5.4MM **Publicly Held**
WEB: www.docsend.com
SIC: 7372 Business oriented computer software
PA: Dropbox, Inc.
1800 Owens St Ste 200
San Francisco CA 94158

(P-13119)
DOCUSIGN INC (PA)
221 Main St Ste 1550, San Francisco
(94105-1947)
PHONE....................................415 489-4940
Daniel D Springer, *CEO*
Mary Agnes Wilderotter, *Ch of Bd*
Scott V Olrich, *COO*
Cynthia Gaylor, *CFO*
Loren Alhadeff, *Officer*
EMP: 300 **EST:** 2003
SQ FT: 211,000
SALES: 1.4B **Publicly Held**
WEB: www.docusign.com
SIC: 7372 Prepackaged software

(P-13120)
DOMICO SOFTWARE
1220 Oakland Blvd Ste 300, Walnut Creek
(94596-8409)
PHONE....................................510 841-4155
Glenn Hunter, *President*
EMP: 15 **EST:** 1984
SQ FT: 4,000
SALES (est): 1.2MM **Privately Held**
WEB: www.domico.com
SIC: 7372 7371 Prepackaged software; custom computer programming services

(P-13121)
DOMINO DATA LAB INC (PA)
548 Market St 72800, San Francisco
(94104-5401)
P.O. Box 78062 (94107-8062)
PHONE....................................415 570-2425
Nick Elprin, *CEO*
Dennis Sevilla, *CFO*
Lisa Brummel, *Bd of Directors*
Michelle Arieta, *Vice Pres*
Tim Babcock, *Vice Pres*
EMP: 123 **EST:** 2012
SALES: 27.1MM **Privately Held**
WEB: www.dominodatalab.com
SIC: 7372 Business oriented computer software

(P-13122)
DORADO NETWORK SYSTEMS CORP
Also Called: Corelogic Dorado
555 12th St Ste 1100, Oakland
(94607-4049)
PHONE....................................650 227-7300
Dain Ehring, *CEO*
Karen Camp, *CFO*
Adam Springer, *Vice Pres*
Dave Parker, *VP Bus Dvlpt*
Rob Carpenter PHD, *CTO*
EMP: 140 **EST:** 1998
SQ FT: 19,000
SALES (est): 29.6MM
SALES (corp-wide): 1.6B **Privately Held**
WEB: www.dorado.ca
SIC: 7372 Application computer software
HQ: Corelogic, Inc.
40 Pacifica Ste 900
Irvine CA 92618
866 873-3651

(P-13123)
DOUBLEDUTCH INC (DH)
44 Tehama St Ste 504, San Francisco
(94105-3110)
PHONE....................................800 748-9024
Lawrence Coburn, *Officer*
Brad Roberts, *CFO*
Lucian Beebe, *Vice Pres*
Matthew Ziegler, *Marketing Staff*
Bryan Collins, *Manager*
EMP: 234 **EST:** 1984
SALES (est): 30.1MM
SALES (corp-wide): 1.2B **Privately Held**
WEB: www.doubledutch.me
SIC: 7372 Application computer software
HQ: Cvent, Inc.
1765 Grnsboro Stn Pl Fl 7
Tysons Corner VA 22102
703 226-3500

(P-13124)
DRIVEAI INC
365 Ravendale Dr, Mountain View
(94043-5217)
P.O. Box 57, Los Altos (94023-0057)
PHONE....................................408 693-0765
Sameep Tandon, *CEO*
Swati Dube, *Co-Owner*
Brody Huval, *Co-Owner*
Jeff Kinske, *Co-Owner*
Joel Pazhayampallil, *Co-Owner*
EMP: 150 **EST:** 2015
SALES (est): 11.2MM **Privately Held**
SIC: 7372 Prepackaged software

(P-13125)
DRIVER INC
438 Shotwell St, San Francisco
(94110-1914)
PHONE....................................415 999-4960
Will Polkinghorn, *CEO*
Tet Matsuguchi, *Engineer*
EMP: 85 **EST:** 2011
SALES (est): 7.4MM **Privately Held**
WEB: www.driver.xyz
SIC: 7372 Educational computer software

(P-13126)
DRIVESCALE INC
1320 Hillview Dr, Menlo Park (94025-5513)
PHONE....................................408 849-4651
Gene Banman, *CEO*
Denise Shiffman, *Officer*
Sk Vinod, *Vice Pres*
Alvin Eugene Banman, *Principal*
Satya Nishtala, *Principal*
EMP: 38 **EST:** 2013
SALES (est): 2.1MM **Privately Held**
WEB: www.drivescale.com
SIC: 7372 Application computer software

(P-13127)
DROPBOX INC (PA)
1800 Owens St Ste 200, San Francisco
(94158-2533)
PHONE....................................415 857-6800
Andrew W Houston, *Ch of Bd*
Tahsin Islam, *Partner*
Timothy Young, *President*
Olivia Nottebohm, *COO*
Timothy Regan, *CFO*
EMP: 2422 **EST:** 2007

PRODUCTS & SERVICES SECTION
7372 - Prepackaged Software County (P-13151)

SALES (est): 1.9B **Publicly Held**
WEB: www.dropbox.com
SIC: 7372 Prepackaged software

(P-13128)
DRUVA INC (HQ)
800 W California Ave # 100, Sunnyvale (94086-3608)
PHONE..................................650 241-3501
Jaspreet Singh, *CEO*
Ashley Frizzell, *Partner*
Makenzi McHam, *Partner*
Mahesh Patel, *CFO*
Matt Lindeman, *Ch Credit Ofcr*
EMP: 57 **EST:** 2010
SALES (est): 21.3MM **Privately Held**
WEB: www.druva.com
SIC: 7372 Business oriented computer software

(P-13129)
DUDA MOBILE INC
577 College Ave, Palo Alto (94306-1433)
PHONE..................................855 790-0003
Itia Sadan, *CEO*
Adam Ferris, *Partner*
Sarah Carpenter, *CFO*
Joann Avina, *Accountant*
Elaine Flynn, *Marketing Mgr*
EMP: 72 **EST:** 2011
SALES (est): 5.8MM **Privately Held**
WEB: www.duda.co
SIC: 7372 Application computer software

(P-13130)
ECRIO INC
19925 Stevns Crk Blvd, Cupertino (95014-2300)
PHONE..................................408 973-7290
Randy Granovetter, *CEO*
Tad Bogdan, *COO*
Nagesh Challa, *Officer*
Ted Goldstein, *Officer*
Lina Martin, *Vice Pres*
EMP: 90 **EST:** 1998
SALES (est): 7.1MM **Privately Held**
WEB: www.ecrio.com
SIC: 7372 Prepackaged software

(P-13131)
EDCAST INC (PA)
1901 Old Middlefield Way, Mountain View (94043-2556)
PHONE..................................650 823-3511
Karl Mehta, *CEO*
Karthik Nagaraj, *Vice Pres*
Linda Neff, *Vice Pres*
Ramin Mahmoodi, *Engineer*
Jake Grodin, *Director*
EMP: 24 **EST:** 2013
SALES (est): 4MM **Privately Held**
WEB: www.edcast.com
SIC: 7372 Educational computer software

(P-13132)
EDMODO INC (DH)
400 Concar Dr, San Mateo (94402-2681)
PHONE..................................310 614-6868
Nic Borg, *CEO*
Manish Kothari, *General Mgr*
Stephen Fisico, *Software Engr*
Tiffany Coleman, *Human Res Mgr*
Anya Ramamurthy, *Marketing Staff*
EMP: 30 **EST:** 2009
SALES (est): 10.9MM **Privately Held**
WEB: www.support.edmodo.com
SIC: 7372 Educational computer software

(P-13133)
EDMODO INC
Edmodo World
400 Concar Dr, San Mateo (94402-2681)
PHONE..................................202 489-8129
Susan Shinoff, *General Counsel*
EMP: 30 **Privately Held**
WEB: www.support.edmodo.com
SIC: 7372 Educational computer software
HQ: Edmodo, Inc.
400 Concar Dr
San Mateo CA 94402
310 614-6868

(P-13134)
EDUCATION ELEMENTS INC
101 Hickey Blvd Ste A, South San Francisco (94080-1177)
PHONE..................................650 440-7860
Anthony Kim, *CEO*
Noah Dougherty, *Partner*
Andrea Goetchius, *Partner*
Jill Thompson, *Partner*
Angela Chubb, *Managing Prtnr*
EMP: 44 **EST:** 2010
SALES (est): 6.7MM **Privately Held**
WEB: www.edelements.com
SIC: 7372 Educational computer software

(P-13135)
EGAIN CORPORATION (PA)
1252 Borregas Ave, Sunnyvale (94089-1309)
PHONE..................................408 636-4500
Ashutosh Roy, *Ch of Bd*
Eric Smit, *Officer*
Promod Narang, *Senior VP*
Todd Woodstra, *Senior VP*
John Carpenter, *Vice Pres*
EMP: 419 **EST:** 1997
SQ FT: 42,541
SALES: 78.2MM **Publicly Held**
WEB: www.egain.com
SIC: 7372 7371 Prepackaged software; application computer software; custom computer programming services

(P-13136)
EIGHTFOLD AI INC (PA)
2625 Augustine Dr Fl 6th, Santa Clara (95054-2956)
PHONE..................................650 265-7380
Eightfold Garg, *CEO*
Ashutosh Garg, *CEO*
Gaurav Gupta, *Engineer*
Rupa Veerapuneni, *Director*
EMP: 119 **EST:** 2016
SALES (est): 11.5MM **Privately Held**
WEB: www.eightfold.ai
SIC: 7372 Prepackaged software

(P-13137)
EIS GROUP INC
731 Sansome St Fl 4, San Francisco (94111-1723)
PHONE..................................415 402-2622
Alec Miloslavsky, *CEO*
Sergiy Synyanskyy, *CFO*
Rowshi Pejooh, *Exec VP*
Slava Kritov, *Senior VP*
Linette Atterbury, *Vice Pres*
EMP: 128 **EST:** 2008
SQ FT: 16,803
SALES (est): 31.4MM **Privately Held**
WEB: www.eisgroup.com
SIC: 7372 Business oriented computer software

(P-13138)
ELECTRONIC ARTS INC (PA)
Also Called: EA
209 Redwood Shores Pkwy, Redwood City (94065-1175)
PHONE..................................650 628-1500
Andrew Wilson, *CEO*
Lawrence F Probst III, *Ch of Bd*
Blake Jorgensen, *COO*
Mary Lou Biancalana, *Chief Mktg Ofcr*
Christopher Bruzzo, *Chief Mktg Ofcr*
▲ **EMP:** 475 **EST:** 1982
SALES (est): 5.5B **Publicly Held**
WEB: www.ea.com
SIC: 7372 Home entertainment computer software

(P-13139)
ELEKTA INC
100 Mathilda Pl Fl 5, Sunnyvale (94086-6017)
PHONE..................................408 830-8000
Jaya Bhardwaj, *Sr Software Eng*
Sanjay Bari, *Software Dev*
Derek Lane, *Software Dev*
John Whitmer, *Software Engr*
Anelia Tritchkova, *Project Mgr*
EMP: 40
SALES (corp-wide): 1.4B **Privately Held**
WEB: www.elekta.com
SIC: 7372 Business oriented computer software; computer integrated systems design
HQ: Elekta, Inc.
400 Perimeter Center Ter
Atlanta GA 30346
770 300-9725

(P-13140)
ELEVATE LABS LLC
1390 Market St Ste 200, San Francisco (94102-5404)
PHONE..................................415 875-9817
Jesse Pickard,
Ryan Garver, *Software Engr*
EMP: 22 **EST:** 2014
SALES (est): 1.9MM **Privately Held**
WEB: www.elevateapp.com
SIC: 7372 Application computer software

(P-13141)
ENABLENCE SYSTEMS INC (HQ)
Also Called: Pannaway
2933 Bayview Dr, Fremont (94538-6520)
PHONE..................................510 226-8900
Gary Davis, *President*
Robert Monaco, *COO*
Boris Grek, *Vice Pres*
Dan Shmitt, *Director*
▲ **EMP:** 58 **EST:** 2002
SALES (est): 10.9MM
SALES (corp-wide): 1.4MM **Privately Held**
WEB: www.enablence.com
SIC: 7372 Application computer software
PA: Enablence Technologies Inc
390 March Rd Suite 119
Kanata ON K2K 0
613 656-2850

(P-13142)
ENACT SYSTEMS INC
6200 Stnrdge Mall Rd Ste, Pleasanton (94588)
PHONE..................................510 828-2701
Deep Chakraborty, *CEO*
Manasij Kar, *COO*
Thomas King, *CFO*
Matthew Cheney, *Chairman*
Manish Anand, *Exec VP*
EMP: 19 **EST:** 2014
SALES (est): 1MM **Privately Held**
WEB: www.enact-systems.com
SIC: 7372 Business oriented computer software

(P-13143)
ENGAGIO INC
181 2nd Ave Ste 200, San Mateo (94401-3816)
PHONE..................................650 265-2264
Jon Miller, *CEO*
Heidi Bullock, *Chief Mktg Ofcr*
Cheryl Chavez, *Officer*
Inger Rarick, *Vice Pres*
Nick Feeney, *Executive*
EMP: 50 **EST:** 2015
SALES (est): 6.9MM **Privately Held**
WEB: www.demandbase.com
SIC: 7372 Business oriented computer software
PA: Demandbase, Inc.
680 Folsom St Ste 400
San Francisco CA 94107

(P-13144)
ENTCO HOLDINGS INC
3000 Hanover St, Palo Alto (94304-1112)
PHONE..................................650 687-5817
EMP: 25 **EST:** 2004
SALES (est): 2MM **Privately Held**
WEB: www.microfocus.com
SIC: 7372 7379 3572 Prepackaged software; computer related maintenance services; computer storage devices
PA: Micro Focus International Plc
The Lawn
Newbury BERKS

(P-13145)
EOS SOFTWARE INC
900 E Hamilton Ave # 100, Campbell (95008-0664)
PHONE..................................408 439-2903
Mohit Doshi, *Mng Member*
Naveen Pasumarthi, *Vice Pres*
EMP: 50 **EST:** 2004
SQ FT: 500
SALES (est): 3.1MM **Privately Held**
WEB: www.eossoftware.com
SIC: 7372 Business oriented computer software

(P-13146)
EPICOR SOFTWARE CORPORATION
4120 Dublin Blvd Ste 300, Dublin (94568-7759)
PHONE..................................925 361-9900
EMP: 101 **Privately Held**
WEB: www.epicor.com
SIC: 7372 Prepackaged Software Services
PA: Epicor Software Corporation
804 Las Cimas Pkwy # 200
Austin TX 78746

(P-13147)
EPIGNOSIS LLC
315 Montgomery St Fl 9, San Francisco (94104-1858)
PHONE..................................646 797-2799
Dimitrios Tsigkos,
EMP: 21 **EST:** 2012
SALES (est): 600.6K **Privately Held**
WEB: www.epignosishq.com
SIC: 7372 Application computer software

(P-13148)
ERIDE INC
1 Letterman Dr Ste 310, San Francisco (94129-1411)
PHONE..................................415 848-7800
Arthur Woo, *President*
Gary L Fischer, *CFO*
W Bradley Stewart, *Vice Pres*
Paul McBurney, *CTO*
EMP: 18 **EST:** 1999
SQ FT: 5,000
SALES (est): 2.7MM **Privately Held**
WEB: www.eride.com
SIC: 7372 Business oriented computer software
PA: Furuno Electric Co., Ltd.
9-52, Ashiharacho
Nishinomiya HYO 662-0

(P-13149)
ESMART SOURCE INC
Also Called: Rfid4u
5159 Commercial Cir Ste H, Concord (94520-8503)
P.O. Box 5366 (94524-0366)
PHONE..................................408 739-3500
Sanjiv Dua, *CEO*
Sam Patadia, *Vice Pres*
Anu Dua, *Technology*
EMP: 15 **EST:** 1999
SALES (est): 1.9MM **Privately Held**
WEB: www.rfid4u.com
SIC: 7372 7373 Business oriented computer software; local area network (LAN) systems integrator

(P-13150)
ESPRESSIVE INC
5201 Great America Pkwy # 110, Santa Clara (95054-1122)
PHONE..................................408 753-8766
Criss Marshall, *Marketing Staff*
Anthony Evans, *Manager*
EMP: 44 **EST:** 2016
SALES (est): 3.6MM **Privately Held**
WEB: www.espressive.com
SIC: 7372 Application computer software

(P-13151)
EVOLPHIN SOFTWARE INC (PA)
6101 Bollinger Canyon Rd # 3, San Ramon (94583-5108)
PHONE..................................888 386-4114
Brian Ahearn, *CEO*
Rahul Bhargava, *CTO*
Tomas Sudnius, *Finance Mgr*

7372 - Prepackaged Software County (P-13152)   PRODUCTS & SERVICES SECTION

EMP: 29 EST: 2010
SALES (est): 3.1MM **Privately Held**
WEB: www.evolphin.com
SIC: 7372 Business oriented computer software

(P-13152)
EVOLV TECHNOLOGY SOLUTIONS INC (PA)
611 Mission St Fl 6, San Francisco (94105-3536)
PHONE..........................415 444-9040
Michael Scharff, *CEO*
EMP: 32 EST: 2019
SALES (est): 4.1MM **Privately Held**
WEB: www.evolv.ai
SIC: 7372 Prepackaged software

(P-13153)
EXABLOX CORPORATION
1156 Sonora Ct, Sunnyvale (94086-5308)
PHONE..........................408 773-8477
Douglas Brockett, *CEO*
Ramesh Iyer Balan, *Vice Pres*
Ramesh Balan, *Vice Pres*
Shridar Subramanian, *Risk Mgmt Dir*
Meagan Banning, *Office Mgr*
EMP: 32 EST: 2010
SALES (est): 3MM **Privately Held**
WEB: www.storagecraft.com
SIC: 7372 Prepackaged software
PA: Storagecraft Technology Corporation
380 W Data Dr
Draper UT 84020

(P-13154)
EXACTTARGET LLC (HQ)
415 Mission St Fl 3, San Francisco (94105-2504)
PHONE..........................415 901-7000
Marc Benioff, *Ch of Bd*
Andrew J Kofoid, *COO*
Steven A Collins, *CFO*
Timothy B Kopp, *Chief Mktg Ofcr*
Traci M Dolan,
EMP: 50 EST: 2000
SQ FT: 66,536
SALES (est): 612MM
SALES (corp-wide): 17.1B **Publicly Held**
WEB: www.salesforce.com
SIC: 7372 Business oriented computer software
PA: Salesforce.Com, Inc.
415 Mission St Fl 3
San Francisco CA 94105
415 901-7000

(P-13155)
EXADEL INC (PA)
1340 Treat Blvd Ste 375, Walnut Creek (94597-7590)
PHONE..........................925 363-9510
Fima Katz, *CEO*
Lev Shur, *President*
Alex Kreymer, *COO*
Elena Krukovskaya, *Officer*
Dmitry Binunsky, *Vice Pres*
EMP: 108 EST: 1995
SALES (est): 28.9MM **Privately Held**
WEB: www.exadel.com
SIC: 7372 Application computer software

(P-13156)
EXPANDABLE SOFTWARE INC (PA)
900 Lafayette St Ste 400, Santa Clara (95050-4925)
PHONE..........................408 261-7880
Tony Nevshemal, *CEO*
Bob Swedroe, *CEO*
David Kearney, *CFO*
Gerald G Lass, *Founder*
Gerald Lass, *Vice Pres*
EMP: 40 EST: 1983
SQ FT: 10,000
SALES (est): 6.1MM **Privately Held**
WEB: www.expandable.com
SIC: 7372 7371 Prepackaged software; custom computer programming services

(P-13157)
FACILITRON INC (PA)
485 Alberto Way Ste 210, Los Gatos (95032-5476)
PHONE..........................800 272-2962

Jeff Benjamin, *CEO*
Cheryl Galloway, *Education*
Kristina Kirkland, *Manager*
Hao Liu, *Manager*
Bridget Borrison, *Accounts Mgr*
EMP: 23 EST: 2014
SQ FT: 3,000
SALES (est): 2.8MM **Privately Held**
WEB: www.facilitron.com
SIC: 7372 Business oriented computer software

(P-13158)
FAIR ISAAC INTERNATIONAL CORP (HQ)
200 Smith Ranch Rd, San Rafael (94903-5551)
PHONE..........................415 446-6000
Thomas G Grudnowski, *President*
Cheryl St John, *Cust Svc Dir*
EMP: 600 EST: 1979
SALES (est): 151.1MM
SALES (corp-wide): 1.2B **Publicly Held**
WEB: www.fico.com
SIC: 7372 Business oriented computer software
PA: Fair Isaac Corporation
181 Metro Dr Ste 700
San Jose CA 95110
408 535-1500

(P-13159)
FAMSOFT CORPORATION
44946 Osgood Rd, Fremont (94539-6110)
PHONE..........................510 683-3940
Fahim Rahman, *CEO*
Fareeha Rahman, *President*
EMP: 26 EST: 1995
SQ FT: 2,500
SALES (est): 1.7MM **Privately Held**
WEB: www.famsoft.com
SIC: 7372 7361 8243 7373 Prepackaged software; employment agencies; data processing schools; computer integrated systems design; custom computer programming services

(P-13160)
FIORANO SOFTWARE INC
230 California Ave # 103, Palo Alto (94306-1637)
PHONE..........................650 326-1136
Atul Saini, *CEO*
Madhav Vodnala, *President*
Anjali Saini, *CFO*
William La Forge, *Vice Pres*
Tony George, *Manager*
◆ EMP: 85 EST: 1993
SALES (est): 5.9MM **Privately Held**
WEB: www.fiorano.com
SIC: 7372 7371 Prepackaged software; custom computer programming services; computer software development

(P-13161)
FIRST ADVNTAGE TLENT MGT SVCS
Also Called: Findly
98 Battery St Ste 400, San Francisco (94111-5512)
PHONE..........................415 446-3930
Rob Stubblefield, *CFO*
Denis Lowe, *Engineer*
EMP: 33 EST: 2007
SQ FT: 4,000
SALES (est): 1MM **Privately Held**
SIC: 7372 Business oriented computer software

(P-13162)
FIRSTUP INC (PA)
123 Mission St Fl 25, San Francisco (94105-5139)
PHONE..........................415 655-2700
Gary Nakamura, *CEO*
Peter C Horan, *Chairman*
Gregory Shove, *Chairman*
Brad Kingsbury, *Vice Pres*
Brian McDowell, *Vice Pres*
EMP: 122 EST: 2010
SALES (est): 9.8MM **Privately Held**
WEB: www.socialchorus.com
SIC: 7372 Business oriented computer software

(P-13163)
FITSTAR INC
80 Langton St, San Francisco (94103-3916)
PHONE..........................415 409-8348
Mike Maser, *CEO*
EMP: 49 EST: 2004
SALES (est): 3.1MM
SALES (corp-wide): 182.5B **Publicly Held**
WEB: www.fitbit.com
SIC: 7372 Application computer software
HQ: Fitbit Llc
199 Fremont St Fl 14
San Francisco CA 94105

(P-13164)
FIVE9 INC (PA)
3001 Bishop Dr Ste 350, San Ramon (94583-5005)
PHONE..........................925 201-2000
Rowan Trollope, *CEO*
Erin Wilker, *Partner*
Michael Burkland, *Ch of Bd*
Daniel Burkland, *President*
Barry Zwarenstein, *CFO*
EMP: 854 EST: 2001
SQ FT: 104,000
SALES (est): 328MM **Publicly Held**
WEB: www.five9.com
SIC: 7372 7374 Prepackaged software; data processing & preparation

(P-13165)
FLEXPORT INC (PA)
760 Market St Fl 8, San Francisco (94102-2300)
PHONE..........................415 231-5252
Ryan Petersen, *CEO*
Emma Shiflett, *Partner*
Sandy Manders, *CFO*
Sudhanshu Priyadarshi, *CFO*
Paige Delacey,
EMP: 624 EST: 2013
SALES (est): 232.1MM **Privately Held**
WEB: www.flexport.com
SIC: 7372 4731 Business oriented computer software; freight transportation arrangement

(P-13166)
FLIPCAUSE INC
101 Broadway Fl 3, Oakland (94607-3755)
PHONE..........................800 523-1950
Emerson Valiao, *CEO*
Darya Gorlova, *Director*
Chris Valiao, *Director*
Sean Wheeler, *Director*
Joe Flynn, *Manager*
EMP: 15 EST: 2014
SALES (est): 3.5MM **Privately Held**
WEB: www.flipcause.com
SIC: 7372 Prepackaged software

(P-13167)
FLYWHEEL SOFTWARE INC
816 Hamilton St, Redwood City (94063-1624)
PHONE..........................650 260-1700
Steve Humphreys, *CEO*
Sachin Kansal, *Chief Engr*
Mark Towfiq, *Chief Engr*
Anagha Dutt, *Controller*
Brogan Keane, *Marketing Staff*
EMP: 21 EST: 2009
SALES (est): 1.3MM **Privately Held**
WEB: www.flywheel.com
SIC: 7372 Application computer software

(P-13168)
FOLIO3 SOFTWARE INC
1301 Shoreway Rd Ste 160, Belmont (94002-4158)
PHONE..........................650 802-8668
Peggy Chen, *Principal*
Peggy H Chen, *Principal*
Charles Thevenet, *Consultant*
EMP: 22 EST: 2006
SALES (est): 1.3MM **Privately Held**
WEB: www.folio3.com
SIC: 7372 Prepackaged software

(P-13169)
FOODLINK ONLINE LLC
475 Alberto Way Ste 100, Los Gatos (95032-5480)
PHONE..........................408 395-7280
EMP: 20
SQ FT: 5,000
SALES (est): 2.7MM **Privately Held**
WEB: www.foodlinkonline.com
SIC: 7372 Prepackaged Software Services

(P-13170)
FORENSIC LOGIC INC
712 Bancroft Rd 423, Walnut Creek (94598-1531)
PHONE..........................415 810-2114
Robert L Batty, *CEO*
Dave Dunlap, *COO*
Bradford Davis, *VP Bus Dvlpt*
Rob Cassetti, *Risk Mgmt Dir*
Alex Emmons, *Software Dev*
EMP: 25 EST: 2003
SQ FT: 1,000
SALES (est): 547.8K **Privately Held**
WEB: www.forensiclogic.com
SIC: 7372 Application computer software

(P-13171)
FORGE GLOBAL INC (PA)
415 Mission St Ste 5510, San Francisco (94105-2615)
PHONE..........................415 881-1612
Kelly Rodriques, *CEO*
Samvit Ramadurgam, *President*
Mark Lee, *CFO*
John-Paul Teutonico, *Ch Credit Ofcr*
Jose Cobos, *Officer*
EMP: 148 EST: 2015
SALES (est): 16.6MM **Privately Held**
WEB: www.forgeglobal.com
SIC: 7372 Business oriented computer software

(P-13172)
FORGEROCK US INC (HQ)
201 Mission St Ste 2900, San Francisco (94105-1858)
PHONE..........................415 599-1100
John Fernandez, *Mng Member*
Robert Humphrey, *Chief Mktg Ofcr*
Lasse Andresen, *CTO*
EMP: 73 EST: 2010
SQ FT: 15,744
SALES (est): 38.5MM
SALES (corp-wide): 127.6MM **Publicly Held**
WEB: www.forgerock.com
SIC: 7372 5045 Prepackaged software; computer software
PA: Forgerock, Inc.
201 Mission St Ste 2900
San Francisco CA 94105
415 599-1100

(P-13173)
FORMATION INC
Also Called: Formation Systems
315 Montgomery St Fl 10, San Francisco (94104-1823)
PHONE..........................650 257-2277
Christian Hansen, *CEO*
Christian Selchau-Hansen, *CEO*
Max Dame, *Vice Pres*
Ammon Haggerty, *Vice Pres*
Erica Sabalones, *Administration*
EMP: 87 EST: 2017
SALES (est): 8.7MM **Privately Held**
WEB: www.formation.ai
SIC: 7372 Business oriented computer software

(P-13174)
FORTANIX INC (PA)
800 W El Cmino Real Ste 1, Mountain View (94040)
PHONE..........................650 943-2484
Ambuj Kumar, *CEO*
Bobbie Myers, *Executive*
Andy Leiserson, *Chief*
EMP: 102 EST: 2016
SALES (est): 7.6MM **Privately Held**
WEB: www.fortanix.com
SIC: 7372 Prepackaged software

▲ = Import ▼ = Export
◆ = Import/Export

PRODUCTS & SERVICES SECTION
7372 - Prepackaged Software County (P-13198)

(P-13175)
FORTEZZA IRIDIUM HOLDINGS INC
150 California St, San Francisco (94111-4500)
PHONE..................................415 765-6500
Robert F Smith, *President*
EMP: 836 **EST:** 2006
SALES (est): 40.2MM **Privately Held**
WEB: www.vistaequitypartners.com
SIC: 7372 Business oriented computer software
PA: Vista Equity Fund Ii Lp
150 California St Fl 19
San Francisco CA 94111

(P-13176)
FORWARD NETWORKS INC
2390 Mission College Blvd, Santa Clara (95054-1530)
PHONE..................................844 393-6389
David Erickson, *CEO*
Nikhil Ashok Handigol, *CFO*
Denis Maynard, *Officer*
Brandon Heller, *Admin Sec*
Sivasankar Radhakrishnan, *Technical Staff*
EMP: 75 **EST:** 2013
SALES: 4MM **Privately Held**
WEB: www.forwardnetworks.com
SIC: 7372 8748 Application computer software; business oriented computer software; utility computer software; systems engineering consultant, ex. computer or professional

(P-13177)
FOXPASS INC
548 Market St, San Francisco (94104-5401)
PHONE..................................415 805-6350
Aren Sandersen, *CEO*
Erin Sandersen, *President*
Travis Theune, *Director*
EMP: 15 **EST:** 2015
SALES (est): 1.6MM **Privately Held**
WEB: www.foxpass.com
SIC: 7372 Prepackaged software

(P-13178)
FRAMEHAWK INC
650 Townsend St Ste 325, San Francisco (94103-6200)
PHONE..................................415 371-9110
EMP: 15
SALES (est): 852.7K **Publicly Held**
WEB: www.citrix.com
SIC: 7372 Application computer software
PA: Citrix Systems, Inc.
851 W Cypress Creek Rd
Fort Lauderdale FL 33309

(P-13179)
FRANZ INC
3685 Mt Diablo Blvd # 300, Lafayette (94549-6884)
PHONE..................................510 452-2000
Jans Aasman, *CEO*
Kevin Layer, *COO*
John Foderar, *Treasurer*
Craig Norvell, *Vice Pres*
Sheng-Chuan Wu, *Vice Pres*
EMP: 25 **EST:** 1984
SQ FT: 5,000
SALES (est): 3.2MM **Privately Held**
WEB: www.franz.com
SIC: 7372 7371 Prepackaged software; computer software development

(P-13180)
FRESHWORKS INC (PA)
2950 S Del St Ste 201, San Mateo (94403)
PHONE..................................650 513-0514
Rathna Girish Mathrubootham, *Ch of Bd*
Tyler Sloat, *CFO*
Stacey Epstein, *Chief Mktg Ofcr*
Srinivasagopalan Ramamurthy,
Jose Morales, *Risk Mgmt Dir*
EMP: 29 **EST:** 2010
SQ FT: 20,000
SALES (est): 249.6MM **Publicly Held**
WEB: www.freshworks.com
SIC: 7372 Prepackaged software

(P-13181)
FRONTAPP INC
1455 Market St Fl 19, San Francisco (94103-1332)
PHONE..................................415 680-3048
Mathilde Collin, *CEO*
Laurent Perrin, *CTO*
Alan Gou, *Software Engr*
Lemuel Chan, *Technical Staff*
Evan Ostroski, *Engineer*
EMP: 71 **EST:** 2014
SALES (est): 5MM **Privately Held**
WEB: www.front.com
SIC: 7372 Application computer software

(P-13182)
FUSION MPHC HOLDING CORP (HQ)
6800 Koll Center Pkwy, Pleasanton (94566-7045)
PHONE..................................925 201-2500
Paul Millie, *CFO*
EMP: 50 **EST:** 2007
SALES (est): 279.3MM
SALES (corp-wide): 844.2MM **Privately Held**
WEB: www.fusionconnect.com
SIC: 7372 6719 Business oriented computer software; investment holding companies, except banks
PA: Fusion Connect, Inc.
210 Interstate North Pkwy
Atlanta GA 30339
212 201-2400

(P-13183)
FUZEBOX SOFTWARE CORPORATION (HQ)
150 Spear St Ste 900, San Francisco (94105-5118)
PHONE..................................415 692-4800
David Obrand, *CEO*
Charlie Newark-French, *President*
Mark Stubbs, *CFO*
Jeffrey Henley, *Bd of Directors*
Manuel Rivelo, *Bd of Directors*
EMP: 55 **EST:** 2015
SQ FT: 16,000
SALES (est): 24MM **Privately Held**
WEB: www.fuze.com
SIC: 7372 Application computer software

(P-13184)
GATE-OR-DOOR INC
14811 Leroy Ave, Ripon (95366-9417)
PHONE..................................209 751-4881
James Bickle, *Principal*
EMP: 17 **EST:** 2011
SALES (est): 1MM **Privately Held**
SIC: 7372 Operating systems computer software

(P-13185)
GE DIGITAL LLC (HQ)
2623 Camino Ramon, San Ramon (94583-9130)
PHONE..................................925 242-6200
H Lawrence Culp Jr, *Ch of Bd*
David L Joyce, *Vice Chairman*
Cyndi Mackenzie, *Executive Asst*
Neeta Nair, *Executive Asst*
Danny Truong, *Software Engr*
EMP: 278 **EST:** 2015
SALES (est): 61.4MM
SALES (corp-wide): 79.6B **Publicly Held**
WEB: www.ge.com
SIC: 7372 Business oriented computer software
PA: General Electric Company
5 Necco St
Boston MA 02210
617 443-3000

(P-13186)
GE DIGITAL LLC
2700 Camino Ramon, San Ramon (94583-5004)
PHONE..................................925 242-6200
Chad Wirt, *Opers Mgr*
Kate Shaw, *Senior Mgr*
Philippa Sinnerton, *Senior Mgr*
EMP: 22

SALES (corp-wide): 79.6B **Publicly Held**
WEB: www.ge.com
SIC: 7372 Prepackaged software; business oriented computer software
HQ: Ge Digital Llc
2623 Camino Ramon
San Ramon CA 94583
925 242-6200

(P-13187)
GENESYS CLOUD SERVICES INC (HQ)
Also Called: Genesys Telecom Labs
2001 Junipero Serra Blvd, Daly City (94014-3891)
PHONE..................................650 466-1100
Paul Segre, *Ch of Bd*
Tom Eggemeier, *President*
Tony Bates, *CEO*
Jim Ren, *Officer*
Jim Rene, *Officer*
EMP: 450 **EST:** 1990
SQ FT: 156,000
SALES (est): 930MM
SALES (corp-wide): 136.9MM **Privately Held**
WEB: www.genesys.com
SIC: 7372 Business oriented computer software
PA: Permira Advisers Llp
80 Pall Mall
London SW1Y
207 632-1000

(P-13188)
GINSBERG HOLDCO INC
3300 Olcott St, Santa Clara (95054-3005)
PHONE..................................408 831-4000
Paul A Hooper, *CEO*
Rex S Jackson, *CFO*
Kim Decarlis, *Chief Mktg Ofcr*
Shehzad T Merchant, *CTO*
EMP: 500 **EST:** 2017
SQ FT: 105,600
SALES (est): 30.4MM **Privately Held**
SIC: 7372 3577 Prepackaged software; computer peripheral equipment

(P-13189)
GITLAB INC (PA)
268 Bush St 350, San Francisco (94104-3503)
PHONE..................................415 829-2854
Sytse Sijbrandij, *Ch of Bd*
Brian Robins, *CFO*
Robin J Schulman,
Michael McBride, *Risk Mgmt Dir*
Eric Johnson, *CTO*
EMP: 18 **EST:** 2011
SALES (est): 152.1MM **Publicly Held**
WEB: www.about.gitlab.com
SIC: 7372 Prepackaged software

(P-13190)
GLASSLAB INC
209 Redwood Shores Pkwy, Redwood City (94065-1175)
PHONE..................................415 244-5584
Jessica Lindl, *Exec Dir*
Granetta Blevins, *CFO*
Michael John, *Managing Dir*
Michelle Riconscente, *Managing Dir*
Ben Dapkiewicz, *Technology*
EMP: 24 **EST:** 2014
SALES (est): 4.2MM **Privately Held**
SIC: 7372 8748 Educational computer software; educational consultant

(P-13191)
GLOBAL GRID FOR LEARNING PBC (PA)
1101 Marina Village Pkwy # 201, Alameda (94501-3579)
PHONE..................................888 904-9773
Robert Iskander, *President*
Julian Mobbs, *CEO*
Wallace Reeves, *Vice Pres*
Larry Smith, *Vice Pres*
Perry Smithson, *Vice Pres*
EMP: 18 **EST:** 2013
SALES (est): 5MM **Privately Held**
WEB: www.gg4l.com
SIC: 7372 Educational computer software

(P-13192)
GLU MOBILE INC (PA)
875 Howard St Ste 100, San Francisco (94103-3032)
PHONE..................................415 800-6100
Nick Earl, *President*
Masaho Ninomiya, *Partner*
Niccolo De Masi, *Ch of Bd*
Eric R Ludwig, *COO*
Ben Smith, *Bd of Directors*
EMP: 412 **EST:** 2001
SQ FT: 57,000
SALES: 540.5MM **Privately Held**
WEB: www.glu.com
SIC: 7372 Prepackaged software

(P-13193)
GLYNTAI INC
Also Called: Wattzon
705 N Shoreline Blvd, Mountain View (94043-3208)
PHONE..................................650 386-6932
Martha Amram, *CEO*
Dave Smith, *Software Dev*
David Nelson, *Senior Mgr*
EMP: 18 **EST:** 2008
SALES (est): 1.6MM **Privately Held**
WEB: www.glynt.ai
SIC: 7372 Application computer software

(P-13194)
GO RISK VISION
845 Stewart Dr Ste D, Sunnyvale (94085-4504)
PHONE..................................925 271-8227
Keith Higgins, *Principal*
Jean Dube, *Vice Pres*
Michael West, *Vice Pres*
Cassandra Ho, *Surgery Dir*
Sergei Nikolaev, *Info Tech Mgr*
EMP: 18 **EST:** 2016
SALES (est): 712.7K **Privately Held**
SIC: 7372 Prepackaged software

(P-13195)
GOALSR INC
933 Berryessa Rd Ste 10, San Jose (95133-1006)
PHONE..................................650 453-5844
Vidyadhar Handragal, *President*
Divya Krishnaswamy, *CEO*
EMP: 19 **EST:** 2014
SALES (est): 500K **Privately Held**
WEB: www.goalsr.com
SIC: 7372 7371 Application computer software; computer software systems analysis & design, custom; computer software development; computer software development & applications

(P-13196)
GOTTS PARTNERS LP
Also Called: Gott's Roadside
1344 Adams St, Saint Helena (94574-1938)
P.O. Box 1226 (94574-1179)
PHONE..................................415 213-2992
Clay Walker, *President*
EMP: 50 **EST:** 1999
SALES (est): 3.1MM **Privately Held**
WEB: www.gotts.com
SIC: 5812 7372 Fast-food restaurant, chain; application computer software

(P-13197)
GREMLIN INC
55 S Market St Ste 1205, San Jose (95113-2324)
PHONE..................................408 214-9885
Kolton Andrus, *CEO*
Matthew Fornaciari, *Shareholder*
Valerie Mah, *Executive Asst*
Ana M Medina, *Engineer*
Cory Barnard, *Sales Staff*
EMP: 40 **EST:** 2016
SALES (est): 3MM **Privately Held**
WEB: www.gremlin.com
SIC: 7372 8742 Prepackaged software; management consulting services

(P-13198)
GRID DYNAMICS HOLDINGS INC (PA)
5000 Executive Pkwy # 520, San Ramon (94583-4282)
PHONE..................................650 523-5000

7372 - Prepackaged Software County (P-13199)

Leonard Livschitz, *CEO*
Lloyd Carney, *Ch of Bd*
Yury Gryzlov, *COO*
Anil Doradla, *CFO*
Max Martynov, *CTO*
EMP: 217 **EST:** 2006
SALES (est): 111.2MM **Publicly Held**
WEB: www.griddynamics.com
SIC: 7372 Prepackaged software

(P-13199)
GRIDGAIN SYSTEMS INC (PA)
1065 E Hillsdale Blvd # 410, Foster City (94404-1615)
PHONE 650 241-2281
Abe Kleinfeld, *President*
Eoin Connor, *CFO*
Eoin Oconnor, *CFO*
Max Herrmann, *Exec VP*
Andy Sacks, *Exec VP*
EMP: 130 **EST:** 2010
SALES (est): 22.8MM **Privately Held**
WEB: www.gridgain.com
SIC: 7372 Prepackaged software

(P-13200)
GUARDIAN ANALYTICS INC
2465 Latham St Ste 200, Mountain View (94040-4792)
PHONE 650 383-9200
Laurent Pacalin, *President*
Vinny Alvino, *CFO*
Hue Harguindeguy, *CFO*
Avner Amram, *Vice Pres*
Dennis Concannon, *Vice Pres*
EMP: 27 **EST:** 2005
SALES (est): 9MM **Privately Held**
WEB: www.guardiananalytics.com
SIC: 7372 Prepackaged software

(P-13201)
GUAVUS INC (HQ)
2125 Zanker Rd, San Jose (95131-2109)
PHONE 650 243-3400
Anukool Lakhina, *CEO*
Michael Crane, *President*
Ty Nam, *COO*
Edan Kabatchnik, *Vice Pres*
Ankur Singhal, *Sr Software Eng*
EMP: 52 **EST:** 2006
SALES (est): 18.6MM
SALES (corp-wide): 279.3MM **Privately Held**
WEB: www.guavus.com
SIC: 7372 7371 Prepackaged software; computer software development & applications
PA: Thales
Tour Carpe Diem Esplanade Nord
Courbevoie 92400
157 778-000

(P-13202)
GUIDEWIRE SOFTWARE INC (PA)
2850 S Del St Ste 400, San Mateo (94403)
PHONE 650 357-9100
Michael Rosenbaum, *CEO*
Marcus S Ryu, *Ch of Bd*
Priscilla Hung, *President*
Jeff Cooper, *CFO*
James Winston King,
EMP: 2148 **EST:** 2001
SQ FT: 189,000
SALES (est): 743.2MM **Publicly Held**
WEB: www.guidewire.com
SIC: 7372 Business oriented computer software

(P-13203)
GUPSHUP INC (PA)
415 Jackson St, San Francisco (94111-1626)
PHONE 415 506-9095
Beerud Dilip Sheth, *CEO*
Gaurav Kachhawa, *Officer*
Nirmesh Mehta, *Vice Pres*
Kunal Patke, *Vice Pres*
Salim Akhtar, *Manager*
EMP: 379 **EST:** 2004
SALES (est): 3.1MM **Privately Held**
WEB: www.gupshup.io
SIC: 7372 Prepackaged software

(P-13204)
GUSTO INC (PA)
525 20th St, San Francisco (94107-4345)
PHONE 800 936-0383
Joshua D Reeves, *CEO*
Ashley Prince, *Partner*
Nate Watson, *Partner*
Lexi Reese, *COO*
Mike Dinsdale, *CFO*
EMP: 250 **EST:** 2011
SALES (est): 103.6MM **Privately Held**
WEB: www.gusto.com
SIC: 7372 Business oriented computer software

(P-13205)
HAZELCAST INC (PA)
2 W 5th Ave Ste 300, San Mateo (94402-2002)
PHONE 650 521-5453
Kelly Herrell, *CEO*
Wilson Chris, *Vice Pres*
Kevin Cox, *Vice Pres*
John Desjardins, *Vice Pres*
Mustafa Sancar, *Software Dev*
EMP: 68 **EST:** 2012
SQ FT: 30,000
SALES (est): 9MM **Privately Held**
WEB: www.hazelcast.com
SIC: 7372 7371 Publishers' computer software; computer software systems analysis & design, custom

(P-13206)
HEALTH GORILLA INC (PA)
228 Hamilton Ave, Palo Alto (94301-2583)
PHONE 844 446-7455
Steven Yaskin, *CEO*
Terence Cullen, *CFO*
Sam Godwin, *Vice Pres*
Sergio Wagner, *Vice Pres*
Heena Shah, *Manager*
EMP: 119 **EST:** 2014
SALES (est): 10.5MM **Privately Held**
WEB: www.healthgorilla.com
SIC: 7372 8011 Application computer software; health maintenance organization

(P-13207)
HEARSAY SOCIAL INC (PA)
600 Harrison St Ste 120, San Francisco (94107-1389)
PHONE 888 399-2280
Clara Shih, *CEO*
Michael H Lock, *President*
Steve Garrity, *COO*
Pete Godbole, *CFO*
William Salisbury, *CFO*
EMP: 196 **EST:** 2009
SALES (est): 51.8MM **Privately Held**
WEB: www.hearsaysystems.com
SIC: 7372 Publishers' computer software

(P-13208)
HEIRLOOM COMPUTING INC
3000 Dnville Blvd Ste 148, Alamo (94507)
PHONE 510 709-7245
Gary Crook, *CEO*
Kevin Moultrup, *COO*
Edward Abbati, *CFO*
Graham Cunningham, *General Mgr*
Mark Haynie, *Senior Mgr*
EMP: 20 **EST:** 2010
SALES (est): 1.4MM **Privately Held**
WEB: www.heirloomcomputing.com
SIC: 7372 Prepackaged software

(P-13209)
HEROKU INC
1 Market St Ste 300, San Francisco (94105-1315)
PHONE 650 704-6107
Tod Nielsen, *CEO*
Paul Kopacki, *Chief Mktg Ofcr*
Michael Schiff, *Vice Pres*
Abe Pursell, *VP Business*
Loren Fraser, *Executive*
EMP: 30 **EST:** 2007
SALES (est): 6.8MM
SALES (corp-wide): 17.1B **Publicly Held**
WEB: www.heroku.com
SIC: 7372 Application computer software
PA: Salesforce.Com, Inc.
415 Mission St Fl 3
San Francisco CA 94105
415 901-7000

(P-13210)
HIGHER ONE PAYMENTS INC
Also Called: Cashnet
80 Swan Way Ste 200, Oakland (94621-1439)
PHONE 510 769-9888
Dan Peterson, *President*
Chuck Haddock, *Senior VP*
Mark Tancil, *Vice Pres*
Pat Kinlough, *Executive*
EMP: 158 **EST:** 1983
SQ FT: 4,500
SALES (est): 3.3MM
SALES (corp-wide): 157.9MM **Privately Held**
WEB: www.transactcampus.com
SIC: 7372 Business oriented computer software
HQ: Higher One, Inc.
22601 N 19th Ave Ste 130
Phoenix AZ 85027

(P-13211)
HOONUIT LLC (DH)
Also Called: Atomic Training
150 Parkshore Dr, Folsom (95630-4710)
PHONE 320 631-5900
Paul Hesser, *CEO*
Lisa Barnett, *CEO*
Clay Anderson, *CFO*
Teseresa Giese, *CFO*
Jeff Watson, *Vice Pres*
EMP: 45 **EST:** 16
SALES (est): 25.8MM
SALES (corp-wide): 1.6B **Privately Held**
WEB: www.infobase.com
SIC: 7372 Educational computer software
HQ: Powerschool Group Llc
150 Parkshore Dr
Folsom CA 95630
916 288-1588

(P-13212)
HOOPLA SOFTWARE INC
84 W Santa Clara St # 460, San Jose (95113-1820)
PHONE 408 498-9600
Michael Smalls, *CEO*
Cathleen Candia, *Executive Asst*
Christine Hao, *Engineer*
Joshua Benedetto, *Marketing Staff*
Greg Rockwell, *Manager*
EMP: 38 **EST:** 2008
SALES (est): 5.1MM **Privately Held**
WEB: www.hoopla.net
SIC: 7372 Application computer software

(P-13213)
HORTONWORKS INC (HQ)
5470 Great America Pkwy, Santa Clara (95054-3644)
PHONE 408 916-4121
Scott Aronson, *Risk Mgmt Dir*
Peter Fenton, *General Ptnr*
Ali Bajwa, *Partner*
Cynthia Girdler, *Partner*
Linda Morales, *Partner*
EMP: 725 **EST:** 2011
SQ FT: 92,000
SALES (est): 229.5MM
SALES (corp-wide): 869.2MM **Privately Held**
WEB: www.cloudera.com
SIC: 7372 Application computer software
PA: Cloudera, Inc.
5470 Great America Pkwy
Santa Clara CA 95054
650 362-0488

(P-13214)
HPE ENTERPRISES LLC (HQ)
6280 America Center Dr, San Jose (95002-2563)
PHONE 650 857-5817
Sheena Campbell, *Partner*
Alberto Corona, *Partner*
Patricia Gill-Thielen, *Partner*
Todd Vorsanger, *Partner*
Ian Reid, *Officer*
EMP: 4993 **EST:** 2015
SALES (est): 513.1MM
SALES (corp-wide): 26.9B **Publicly Held**
WEB: www.hpe.com
SIC: 7372 7379 3572 Prepackaged software; computer related maintenance services; computer storage devices
PA: Hewlett Packard Enterprise Company
11445 Compaq Center W Dr
Houston TX 77070
650 687-5817

(P-13215)
HPI CCHGPII LLC
1501 Page Mill Rd, Palo Alto (94304-1126)
PHONE 650 687-5817
Dion J Weisler,
EMP: 24 **EST:** 2015
SALES (est): 2.5MM
SALES (corp-wide): 56.6B **Publicly Held**
WEB: www.hp.com
SIC: 7372 7379 3572 Prepackaged software; computer related maintenance services; computer storage devices
PA: Hp Inc.
1501 Page Mill Rd
Palo Alto CA 94304
650 857-1501

(P-13216)
HULFT INC (PA)
1820 Gateway Dr Ste 120, San Mateo (94404-2471)
PHONE 650 393-4930
Masahiro Maruyama, *President*
Takashi Watanuki, *CEO*
Adam K Erickson, *Vice Pres*
Javier Fernandez, *Software Engr*
Vivian Shic, *Marketing Staff*
EMP: 63 **EST:** 2016
SALES (est): 600.7K **Privately Held**
WEB: www.hulftinc.com
SIC: 7372 Prepackaged software

(P-13217)
HUMANCONCEPTS LLC
3 Harbor Dr Ste 200, Sausalito (94965-1491)
PHONE 650 581-2500
Martin Sacks,
Hanif Ismail,
Kathleen Jensen,
Luis Rivera,
EMP: 40 **EST:** 2000
SQ FT: 6,500
SALES (est): 11.3MM
SALES (corp-wide): 238.9K **Privately Held**
WEB: www.cornerstoneondemand.com
SIC: 7372 Application computer software
HQ: Saba Software, Inc.
4120 Dublin Blvd Ste 200
Dublin CA 94568
877 722-2101

(P-13218)
HVR SOFTWARE INC (PA)
135 Main St Ste 850, San Francisco (94105-8117)
PHONE 415 655-6361
Anthony Williams, *President*
Anthony Brooks-Williams, *President*
Kyle Klopfer, *CFO*
Jonathan Weiss, *Officer*
Chris Lawless, *Senior VP*
EMP: 44 **EST:** 2013
SQ FT: 3,000
SALES (est): 5MM **Privately Held**
WEB: www.hvr-software.com
SIC: 7372 Business oriented computer software

(P-13219)
HVR SOFTWARE USA INC
44 Montgomery St Ste 3, San Francisco (94104-4618)
PHONE 415 489-3427
Anthony Brooks Williams, *CEO*
Kyle Klopfer, *CFO*
Jonathan Weiss, *CFO*
Mark Van De Wiel, *CTO*
Steve Sheil, *Chief*
EMP: 62 **EST:** 2014
SALES (est): 6.3MM **Privately Held**
WEB: www.hvr-software.com
SIC: 7372 Business oriented computer software

PRODUCTS & SERVICES SECTION

7372 - Prepackaged Software County (P-13242)

(P-13220)
I MANAGEPROPERTY INC
Also Called: Peak Property Management Sftwr
1400 Shattuck Ave Ste 2, Berkeley (94709-1485)
PHONE..................510 665-0665
Zorba Libeberman, *President*
Joesph Gaspardone, *CFO*
Lisa Putnam, *Officer*
EMP: 20 **EST:** 1994
SQ FT: 3,000
SALES (est): 983.5K **Privately Held**
WEB: www.enterpret.com
SIC: 7372 Prepackaged software

(P-13221)
I T M SOFTWARE CORP
1030 W Maude Ave, Sunnyvale (94085-2812)
PHONE..................650 864-2500
Kenneth Coleman, *CEO*
Tom Niermann, *Founder*
Steve O'Conner, *Vice Pres*
Christina Ellwood, *Principal*
Jorge Helmer, *VP Finance*
EMP: 16 **EST:** 2002
SQ FT: 18,600
SALES (est): 450.5K **Privately Held**
SIC: 7372 Prepackaged software

(P-13222)
ICE MORTGAGE TECHNOLOGY INC (HQ)
Also Called: Ellie Mae
4420 Rosewood Dr Ste 500, Pleasanton (94588-3059)
PHONE..................855 224-8572
Jonathan Corr, *President*
Dan Madden, *CFO*
Susan Chenoweth Beermann, *Chief Mktg Ofcr*
Selim Aissi, *Officer*
Brian Brown, *Exec VP*
EMP: 770 **EST:** 1997
SQ FT: 280,680
SALES: 480.2MM
SALES (corp-wide): 6B **Publicly Held**
WEB: www.icemortgagetechnology.com
SIC: 7372 7371 Prepackaged software; computer software systems analysis & design, custom; computer software development & applications
PA: Intercontinental Exchange, Inc.
5660 New Northside Dr # 3
Atlanta GA 30328
770 857-4700

(P-13223)
IFWE INC (DH)
848 Battery St, San Francisco (94111-1504)
PHONE..................415 946-1850
Dash Gopinath, *CEO*
Greg Tseng, *CEO*
Jeremy Zorn, *Senior VP*
Victoria Diaz, *Vice Pres*
Devin Dworak, *Vice Pres*
▼ **EMP:** 107 **EST:** 2005
SQ FT: 13,000
SALES (est): 22.4MM
SALES (corp-wide): 4.7B **Privately Held**
WEB: www.secure.tagged.com
SIC: 7372 Application computer software
HQ: The Meet Group Inc
100 Union Square Dr
New Hope PA 18938
215 862-1162

(P-13224)
IMPAC MEDICAL SYSTEMS INC (HQ)
Also Called: Elekta / Impac Medical Systems
100 Mathilda Pl Fl 5, Sunnyvale (94086-6017)
PHONE..................408 830-8000
Fax: 408 830-8003
EMP: 40
SQ FT: 35,000
SALES (est): 61.6MM
SALES (corp-wide): 1.3B **Privately Held**
WEB: www.impac.com
SIC: 7372 7373 Prepackaged Software Services Computer Systems Design
PA: Elekta Ab (Publ)
Kungstensgatan 18
Stockholm 113 5
858 725-400

(P-13225)
IMPLY DATA INC (PA)
1633 Old Byshore Hwy Ste, Burlingame (94010)
PHONE..................415 685-8187
Fang Jin Yang, *CEO*
Anthony Russo, *CFO*
Gian Merlino, *Exec VP*
Andy Sacks, *Exec VP*
Chris Andres, *Vice Pres*
EMP: 139 **EST:** 2015
SQ FT: 1,000
SALES (est): 10MM **Privately Held**
WEB: www.imply.io
SIC: 7372 Business oriented computer software

(P-13226)
INBENTA TECHNOLOGIES INC (PA)
440 N Wolfe Rd, Sunnyvale (94085-3869)
PHONE..................408 213-8771
Jordi Torras, *CEO*
Ferran Saurina, *COO*
Fadi Zananiri, *Officer*
Luc Truntzler, *Associate Dir*
Ramon Hak, *Managing Dir*
EMP: 20 **EST:** 2011
SALES (est): 3.8MM **Privately Held**
WEB: www.inbenta.com
SIC: 7372 Application computer software

(P-13227)
INCOUNTRY INC
2443 Fillmore St 380-1, San Francisco (94115-1814)
PHONE..................415 323-0322
EMP: 62
SALES (corp-wide): 231.5K **Privately Held**
SIC: 7372 Application computer software
PA: Incountry, Inc.
4023 Kennett Pike # 5037
Wilmington DE 19807
415 323-0322

(P-13228)
INDIUM SOFTWARE INC
19925 Stevns Crk Blvd, Cupertino (95014-2300)
PHONE..................408 501-8844
Harsha Nutalapati, *CEO*
Vijay Shankar Balaji, *President*
Shailesh Khanapur, *Assoc VP*
Arun Kumar, *Assoc VP*
Satish Pala, *Senior VP*
EMP: 40 **EST:** 2006
SALES (est): 10.6MM **Privately Held**
WEB: www.indiumsoft.com
SIC: 7372 Prepackaged software
HQ: Indium Software (India) Limited
2nd Floor Vds House,
Chennai TN 60008

(P-13229)
INDIVIDUAL SOFTWARE INC
3049 Independence Dr E, Livermore (94551-7673)
PHONE..................925 734-6767
Jo-L Hendrickson, *President*
Diane Dietzler, *Vice Pres*
Steve Jeong, *Creative Dir*
Christy Paulson, *Engineer*
Paul Hendrickson, *Materials Mgr*
EMP: 48 **EST:** 1981
SALES (est): 10MM **Privately Held**
WEB: www.individualsoftware.com
SIC: 7372 7371 Prepackaged software; custom computer programming services

(P-13230)
INFOR PUBLIC SECTOR INC (DH)
11092 Sun Center Dr, Rancho Cordova (95670-6109)
PHONE..................916 921-0883
Charles Hansen, *CEO*
Mark Watts, *President*
Ashley Hart, *Chief Mktg Ofcr*
Bob Benstead, *Principal*
EMP: 160 **EST:** 1983
SQ FT: 28,000
SALES (est): 56.7MM
SALES (corp-wide): 36.9B **Privately Held**
WEB: www.infor.com
SIC: 7372 Application computer software
HQ: Infor (Us), Llc
641 Ave Of The Americas
New York NY 10011
866 244-5479

(P-13231)
INFORMATICA HOLDCO INC
2100 Seaport Blvd, Redwood City (94063-5596)
PHONE..................650 385-5000
Amit Walia, *CEO*
Brad Lewis, *Vice Pres*
Ansa Sekharan, *Vice Pres*
Vineet Walia, *Vice Pres*
Steven Fleishman, *Technical Staff*
EMP: 4897 **EST:** 2015
SALES (est): 480.3MM **Privately Held**
WEB: www.informatica.com
SIC: 7372 Prepackaged software

(P-13232)
INFORMATICA INC
2100 Seaport Blvd, Redwood City (94063-5596)
PHONE..................650 385-5000
Amit Walia, *CEO*
Bruce Chizen, *Ch of Bd*
Eric Brown, *CFO*
Ansa Sekharan, *Ch Credit Ofcr*
Jitesh Ghai,
EMP: 5249 **EST:** 1993
SQ FT: 290,000
SALES (est): 26.7MM **Privately Held**
SIC: 7372 Prepackaged software

(P-13233)
INFORMATICA INTERNATIONAL INC (DH)
2100 Seaport Blvd, Redwood City (94063-5596)
PHONE..................650 385-5000
Sohaib Abbasi, *President*
Art Demaio, *Vice Pres*
Steve Jensen, *Vice Pres*
Mark Pellowski, *Vice Pres*
Emilio Valdes, *Vice Pres*
EMP: 242 **EST:** 2005
SALES (est): 13MM
SALES (corp-wide): 136.9MM **Privately Held**
WEB: www.informatica.com
SIC: 7372 Prepackaged software

(P-13234)
INFORMATICA LLC (DH)
2100 Seaport Blvd, Redwood City (94063-5596)
PHONE..................650 385-5000
Amit Walia, *CEO*
Tracey Newell, *President*
Charles Hardison, *COO*
Eric Brown, *CFO*
Bradford Lewis,
EMP: 1472 **EST:** 1999
SQ FT: 290,000
SALES (est): 519.8MM
SALES (corp-wide): 136.9MM **Privately Held**
WEB: www.informatica.com
SIC: 7372 Prepackaged software
HQ: Permira Advisers Llc
320 Park Ave Fl 28
New York NY 10022
212 386-7480

(P-13235)
INFOSTAR LLC (PA)
779 Sunny Brook Way, Pleasanton (94566-3821)
PHONE..................650 288-6717
Dipam S Patel, *Principal*
EMP: 19 **EST:** 2015
SALES (est): 441.6K **Privately Held**
SIC: 7372 Educational computer software

(P-13236)
INKTOMI CORPORATION (HQ)
701 First Ave, Sunnyvale (94089-1019)
PHONE..................650 653-2800
David Peterschmidt, *Ch of Bd*
Randy Gottfried, *CFO*
EMP: 25 **EST:** 1996
SQ FT: 177,000
SALES (est): 107.8MM **Privately Held**
WEB: www.robgeo.net
SIC: 7372 7371 Application computer software; custom computer programming services

(P-13237)
INMAGE SYSTEMS INC
1065 La Avenida St, Mountain View (94043-1421)
PHONE..................408 200-3840
Debbie Button, *CEO*
John Ferraro, *President*
Marty Bradford, *CFO*
EMP: 99 **EST:** 2001
SALES (est): 17.8MM
SALES (corp-wide): 168B **Publicly Held**
WEB: www.microsoft.com
SIC: 7372 Business oriented computer software
PA: Microsoft Corporation
1 Microsoft Way
Redmond WA 98052
425 882-8080

(P-13238)
INSITESOURCE INC
203 Carol Ct, Alamo (94507-2862)
PHONE..................510 263-9157
EMP: 16 **EST:** 2014
SALES (est): 157.5K **Privately Held**
SIC: 7372 Prepackaged software

(P-13239)
INSTAGIS INC (PA)
218 9th St, San Francisco (94103-3807)
PHONE..................415 527-6636
Julian Garcia, *CEO*
Jean Coleman, *Principal*
EMP: 17 **EST:** 2013
SALES (est): 977.8K **Privately Held**
WEB: www.instagis.com
SIC: 7372 7374 Prepackaged software; data processing service

(P-13240)
INSYNC SOFTWARE INC
181 Metro Dr Ste 540, San Jose (95110-1346)
PHONE..................408 352-0600
Ravi Panja, *CEO*
Srinivas Surabhi, *Engineer*
Chris Foley, *Director*
EMP: 38 **EST:** 2003
SALES (est): 2.8MM
SALES (corp-wide): 248.4MM **Privately Held**
WEB: www.orbcomm.com
SIC: 7372 Prepackaged software
HQ: Orbcomm Inc.
395 W Passaic St Ste 325
Rochelle Park NJ 07662
703 433-6300

(P-13241)
INTERACTIVE SOLUTIONS INC (DH)
Also Called: Web Traffic School
283 4th St Ste 301, Oakland (94607-4320)
P.O. Box 209 (94604-0209)
PHONE..................510 214-9002
Isaak Tsifrin, *CEO*
Gary Golduber, *President*
Gary Tsifrin, *COO*
Mercy Gitue, *Human Res Mgr*
EMP: 67 **EST:** 1987
SQ FT: 14,000
SALES: 13.3MM
SALES (corp-wide): 1.1B **Privately Held**
WEB: www.edriving.com
SIC: 7372 Prepackaged software
HQ: Edriving Llc
1255 Treat Blvd Ste 300
Walnut Creek CA 94597
800 243-4008

(P-13242)
INTERMDIA CLOUD CMMNCTIONS INC
100 Mathilda Pl Ste 600, Sunnyvale (94086-6081)
PHONE..................650 641-4000
Michael J Gold, *President*

7372 - Prepackaged Software County (P-13243)   PRODUCTS & SERVICES SECTION

Jonathan S McCormick, *COO*
Jason H Veldhuis, *CFO*
EMP: 1064 **EST:** 1993
SQ FT: 19,600
SALES: 251.6MM **Privately Held**
WEB: www.intermedia.net
SIC: 7372 Prepackaged software
PA: Ivy Parent Holdings, Llc
    70 W Madison St Ste 4600
    Chicago IL 60602
    312 895-1000

(P-13243)
INTERSHOP COMMUNICATIONS INC
461 2nd St Apt 151, San Francisco (94107-1498)
PHONE.................................415 844-1500
Jochen Moll, *CEO*
Peter Mark Droste, *Ch of Bd*
Eckhard Pfeiffer, *Chairman*
Hans W Gutsch, *Treasurer*
Ralf Maennlein, *Exec Dir*
EMP: 20 **EST:** 1996
SQ FT: 2,700
SALES (est): 4.4MM
SALES (corp-wide): 39.7MM **Privately Held**
WEB: www.intershop.com
SIC: 7372 7375 Prepackaged software; information retrieval services
PA: Intershop Communications Ag
    Steinweg 10
    Jena TH 07743
    364 150-0

(P-13244)
INTUIT FINANCING INC
Also Called: Quickbooks Capital
2700 Coast Ave, Mountain View (94043-1140)
PHONE.................................605 944-6000
Brad D Smith, *President*
EMP: 50 **EST:** 2013
SALES (est): 5.4MM
SALES (corp-wide): 9.6B **Publicly Held**
WEB: www.intuit.com
SIC: 7372 Business oriented computer software
PA: Intuit Inc.
    2700 Coast Ave
    Mountain View CA 94043
    650 944-6000

(P-13245)
INTUIT INC (PA)
2700 Coast Ave, Mountain View (94043-1140)
P.O. Box 7850 (94039-7850)
PHONE.................................650 944-6000
Sasan K Goodarzi, *President*
Jennifer Johnston, *Partner*
Marianne Madrigal, *Partner*
Vanessa Valenzuela, *Partner*
Brad D Smith, *Ch of Bd*
EMP: 70 **EST:** 1983
SQ FT: 712,000
SALES: 9.6B **Publicly Held**
WEB: www.intuit.com
SIC: 7372 Prepackaged software; business oriented computer software

(P-13246)
INTUIT INC
2535 Garcia Ave, Mountain View (94043-1111)
PHONE.................................650 944-6000
Connie Berg, *Branch Mgr*
Linda-Maria Vasquez, *Partner*
Hardy Suzanne, *President*
Ashok Srivastava, *Officer*
Alex Balazs, *Senior VP*
EMP: 128
SALES (corp-wide): 9.6B **Publicly Held**
WEB: www.intuit.com
SIC: 7372 Business oriented computer software
PA: Intuit Inc.
    2700 Coast Ave
    Mountain View CA 94043
    650 944-6000

(P-13247)
INVOICE 2GO LLC (DH)
2317 Broadway St Fl 2, Redwood City (94063-1674)
PHONE.................................650 300-5180
Mark Lenhard, *CEO*
Sean Deorsey, *CFO*
Madeleine Lux, *Office Mgr*
Angela Dickinson, *Marketing Staff*
Rucha Fulay, *Director*
EMP: 140 **EST:** 2014
SALES (est): 25.9MM
SALES (corp-wide): 238.2MM **Publicly Held**
WEB: www.invoice.2go.com
SIC: 7372 Prepackaged software
HQ: Bill.Com, Llc
    1800 Embarcadero Rd
    Palo Alto CA 94303
    650 353-3301

(P-13248)
IPOLIPO INC
Also Called: Jifflenow
440 N Wolfe Rd, Sunnyvale (94085-3869)
PHONE.................................408 916-5290
Hari Shetty, *President*
Uday Bellary, *CFO*
Chopra Anil, *Software Dev*
Bodhayan Prashanth, *Engineer*
Jagdish Upadhyay, *Marketing Staff*
EMP: 75 **EST:** 2006
SALES (est): 6.6MM **Privately Held**
WEB: www.jifflenow.com
SIC: 7372 Application computer software

(P-13249)
ITAPP INC
4633 Old Ironsides Dr # 280, Santa Clara (95054-1807)
PHONE.................................415 786-3455
Brajesh Goyal, *Principal*
EMP: 19 **EST:** 2013
SALES (est): 1MM **Publicly Held**
WEB: www.servicenow.com
SIC: 7372 Prepackaged software
PA: Servicenow, Inc.
    2225 Lawson Ln
    Santa Clara CA 95054

(P-13250)
ITTAVI INC
Also Called: Supportpay
1100 La Avenida St Ste A, Mountain View (94043-1453)
PHONE.................................866 246-4408
Sheri Atwood, *CEO*
Floyd Nikki, *Opers Mgr*
EMP: 25 **EST:** 2011
SALES (est): 1.7MM **Privately Held**
WEB: www.supportpay.com
SIC: 7372 7373 7371 8748 Business oriented computer software; systems software development services; custom computer programming services; systems engineering consultant, ex. computer or professional

(P-13251)
JAUNT INC
Also Called: Jaunt Xr
951 Mariners Island Blvd # 500, San Mateo (94404-1589)
PHONE.................................650 618-6579
George Kliavkoff, *CEO*
Fabrice Cantou, *CFO*
Mitzi Reaugh, *Vice Pres*
Jean-Paul Colaco, *Risk Mgmt Dir*
Arthur Van Hoff, *CTO*
EMP: 28 **EST:** 1999
SALES (est): 1.6MM **Privately Held**
WEB: www.jauntxr.com
SIC: 7372 7371 Application computer software; computer software development & applications

(P-13252)
JEMSTEP INC
5150 El Camino Real B16, Los Altos (94022-1550)
PHONE.................................650 966-6500
Kevin Cimring, *CEO*
Simon Roy, *President*
Matthew Rennie, *Engineer*
Mark Richards, *Products*

EMP: 20 **EST:** 2008
SALES (est): 2.9MM
SALES (corp-wide): 6.1B **Publicly Held**
WEB: www.intelliflo.com
SIC: 7372 Business oriented computer software
HQ: Invesco North American Holdings Inc
    1555 Peachtree St Ne # 18
    Atlanta GA 30309
    404 892-0896

(P-13253)
JETLORE LLC
1528 S El Cmino Real Ste, San Mateo (94402)
PHONE.................................650 485-1822
Eldar Sadikov, *CEO*
Brian Yamasaki, *President*
Montse Medina, *COO*
Thomas Lai, *Officer*
EMP: 24 **EST:** 2011
SQ FT: 6,700
SALES (est): 6MM
SALES (corp-wide): 21.4B **Publicly Held**
WEB: www.paypal.com
SIC: 7372 Application computer software
PA: Paypal Holdings, Inc.
    2211 N 1st St
    San Jose CA 95131
    408 967-1000

(P-13254)
JFROG LTD (PA)
270 E Caribbean Dr, Sunnyvale (94089-1007)
PHONE.................................408 329-1540
Shlomi Ben Haim, *Ch of Bd*
Jacob Shulman, *CFO*
Sagi Dudai, *Exec VP*
Tali Notman, *Risk Mgmt Dir*
Yoav Landman, *CTO*
EMP: 57 **EST:** 2008
SQ FT: 49,000
SALES (est): 150.8MM **Publicly Held**
WEB: www.jfrog.com
SIC: 7372 Prepackaged software

(P-13255)
JISEKI HEALTH INC
10 Rollins Rd Ste 209, Millbrae (94030-3129)
PHONE.................................408 763-7264
Tushar Vasisht, *CEO*
Susan Bowen, *COO*
Chandra Nagaraja, *CTO*
EMP: 22 **EST:** 2014
SALES (est): 2MM **Privately Held**
WEB: www.jisekihealth.com
SIC: 7372 Business oriented computer software

(P-13256)
JIVE SOFTWARE INC
735 Emerson St, Palo Alto (94301-2411)
PHONE.................................503 295-3700
Susan Ridgeon, *Technician*
Haneen Abu-Khater, *Engineer*
Dolan Halbrook, *Engineer*
Samuel Wolf, *Engineer*
Nilan Roy, *Finance*
EMP: 19 **EST:** 2019
SALES (est): 568.7K **Privately Held**
WEB: www.jivesoftware.com
SIC: 7372 Prepackaged software

(P-13257)
JOMU MIST INCORPORATED
Also Called: Myvr.com
309 Chapman Dr, Corte Madera (94925-1508)
PHONE.................................415 448-7273
Jonathan Murray, *CEO*
EMP: 15 **EST:** 2010
SALES (est): 10MM **Privately Held**
SIC: 7372 Prepackaged software

(P-13258)
JUMIO SOFTWARE & DEV LLC
1971 Landings Dr, Mountain View (94043-0806)
PHONE.................................650 388-0264
EMP: 30
SALES (est): 1.2MM
SALES (corp-wide): 16.9MM **Privately Held**
SIC: 7372 Prepackaged Software Services

PA: Jumio Inc
    268 Lambert Ave
    Palo Alto CA
    650 424-8545

(P-13259)
KANA SOFTWARE INC (HQ)
Also Called: Verint
2550 Walsh Ave Ste 120, Santa Clara (95051-1345)
PHONE.................................650 614-8300
Mark Duffell, *CEO*
William A Bose, *President*
Brett White, *President*
Jeff Wylie, *CFO*
James Norwood, *Chief Mktg Ofcr*
EMP: 100 **EST:** 1999
SQ FT: 40,000
SALES (est): 116.5MM **Publicly Held**
WEB: www.verint.com
SIC: 7372 Application computer software

(P-13260)
KBA2 INC
Also Called: Crowdoptic
55 New Montgomery St # 606, San Francisco (94105-3433)
PHONE.................................415 528-5500
Jon Fisher, *CEO*
Tony Wu, *CFO*
James Redfield, *Vice Pres*
Luke Harris, *Director*
EMP: 22 **EST:** 2010
SQ FT: 2,500
SALES (est): 803.2K **Privately Held**
WEB: www.crowdoptic.com
SIC: 7372 Application computer software

(P-13261)
KERIO TECHNOLOGIES INC
111 W Saint John St # 1100, San Jose (95113-1107)
PHONE.................................409 880-7011
Jozef Belvon, *Systems Dir*
Alan Hughes, *CFO*
Kevin Davy, *Technical Staff*
Marirose Landicho-Rasay, *Accountant*
Yvette Graff, *Marketing Staff*
EMP: 18 **EST:** 2017
SALES (est): 506.9K **Privately Held**
WEB: www.gfi.com
SIC: 7372 Prepackaged software

(P-13262)
KETERA TECHNOLOGIES INC (DH)
3055 Olin Ave Ste 2200, San Jose (95128-2066)
PHONE.................................408 572-9500
Steve Savignano, *CEO*
Tom Foody, *CFO*
Leslie Cedar, *Vice Pres*
Mike Gardner, *Vice Pres*
Percival Tieng, *CTO*
EMP: 30 **EST:** 2000
SALES (est): 11MM
SALES (corp-wide): 6.8B **Privately Held**
WEB: www.deem.com
SIC: 7372 Prepackaged software
HQ: Deem, Inc.
    1330 Broadway Fl 7
    Oakland CA 94612
    415 590-8300

(P-13263)
KEVALA INC
55 Francisco St Ste 350, San Francisco (94133-2112)
PHONE.................................415 712-7829
Aram Shumavon, *CEO*
Laura Wang, *Manager*
EMP: 30 **EST:** 2016
SALES (est): 2.8MM **Privately Held**
SIC: 7372 Application computer software

(P-13264)
KHAN ACADEMY INC
1200 Villa St Ste 200, Mountain View (94041-2922)
P.O. Box 1630 (94042-1630)
PHONE.................................650 336-5426
Salman Khan, *Exec Dir*
Shantanu Sinha, *President*
Michael Johnson, *CFO*
Kristen Dicerbo, *Officer*
Marta Kosarchyn, *Officer*

PRODUCTS & SERVICES SECTION
7372 - Prepackaged Software County (P-13290)

EMP: 85 EST: 2009
SALES: 46.2MM **Privately Held**
WEB: www.khanacademy.org
SIC: 7372 Educational computer software

(P-13265)
KINETIC FARM INC
210 Industrial Rd Ste 102, San Carlos (94070-2395)
PHONE..................650 503-3279
EMP: 17 EST: 2010
SALES (est): 1.2MM **Privately Held**
SIC: 7372 Prepackaged Software Services

(P-13266)
KLOUDGIN INC
440 N Wolfe Rd, Sunnyvale (94085-3869)
PHONE..................877 256-8303
Vikram Takru, *CEO*
Dharmesh Sethi, *CFO*
Justin Foley, *Officer*
Ram Gupta, *Officer*
Venkat Venkatasubraman, *Senior VP*
EMP: 175 EST: 2010
SALES (est): 13.1MM **Privately Held**
WEB: www.kloudgin.com
SIC: 7372 Business oriented computer software

(P-13267)
KNO INC
2200 Mission College Blvd, Santa Clara (95054-1537)
PHONE..................408 844-8120
Ronald D Dickel, *CEO*
Babur Habib, *CTO*
EMP: 70 EST: 1998
SQ FT: 35,000
SALES (est): 43MM
SALES (corp-wide): 77.8B **Publicly Held**
WEB: www.intel.com
SIC: 7372 Educational computer software
PA: Intel Corporation
 2200 Mission College Blvd
 Santa Clara CA 95054
 408 765-8080

(P-13268)
KPISOFT INC
50 California St Ste 1500, San Francisco (94111-4612)
PHONE..................415 439-5228
EMP: 80
SQ FT: 4,000
SALES (est): 3MM **Privately Held**
WEB: www.kpisoft.com
SIC: 7372 Prepackaged Software Services

(P-13269)
KRANEM CORPORATION
560 S Wnchester Blvd # 5, San Jose (95128-2560)
PHONE..................650 319-6743
Ajay Batheja, *Ch of Bd*
Edward Miller, *CFO*
Luigi Caramico, *Vice Pres*
Christopher L Rasmussen, *Admin Sec*
EMP: 190
SALES: 8.3MM **Privately Held**
SIC: 7372 Business oriented computer software

(P-13270)
KWAN SOFTWARE ENGINEERING INC
Also Called: Veripic
849 Lakechime Dr, Sunnyvale (94089-2541)
PHONE..................408 496-1200
John Kwan, *President*
Jean Joe, *COO*
Ryan Ruiz, *Info Tech Mgr*
Aaron Cho, *Software Engr*
EMP: 32 EST: 1997
SALES (est): 4.6MM **Privately Held**
SIC: 7372 Business oriented computer software

(P-13271)
LABELBOX INC (PA)
510 Treat Ave, San Francisco (94110-2014)
PHONE..................415 294-0791
Manu Sharma, *President*
Carolyn Goldenberg, *Executive*
Jackie Ricci, *Principal*
Audrey Smith, *Director*
EMP: 29 EST: 2018
SALES: 2MM **Privately Held**
WEB: www.labelbox.com
SIC: 7372 Prepackaged software

(P-13272)
LASERBEAM SOFTWARE LLC
1647 Willow Pass Rd # 40, Concord (94520-2611)
PHONE..................925 459-2595
Patrick Durall, *CEO*
EMP: 16 EST: 2004
SALES (est): 533.2K **Privately Held**
WEB: www.laserbeamsoftware.com
SIC: 7372 Application computer software

(P-13273)
LASTLINE INC (PA)
3401 Hillview Ave, Palo Alto (94304-1320)
PHONE..................877 671-3239
John Dilullo, *CEO*
Ananth Avva, *CFO*
Claire Trimble, *Chief Mktg Ofcr*
Christopher Kruegel, *Officer*
Bert Rankin, *Officer*
EMP: 198 EST: 2009
SALES (est): 50.1MM **Privately Held**
WEB: www.lastline.com
SIC: 7372 Prepackaged software

(P-13274)
LATTICE DATA INC
801 El Camino Real, Menlo Park (94025-4807)
PHONE..................650 800-7262
Andy Jacques, *CEO*
EMP: 20 EST: 2015
SQ FT: 5,700
SALES (est): 3MM
SALES (corp-wide): 365.8B **Publicly Held**
WEB: www.lattice.com
SIC: 7372 Business oriented computer software
PA: Apple Inc.
 1 Apple Park Way
 Cupertino CA 95014
 408 996-1010

(P-13275)
LCR-DIXON CORPORATION
2048 Union St Apt 4, San Francisco (94123-4118)
P.O. Box 812, Bel Air MD (21014-0812)
PHONE..................404 307-1695
Suzy SOO, *CEO*
Jeffrey Bleachler, *COO*
Donna Miller, *Technology*
Amy Eller, *Manager*
Greg Polek, *Manager*
EMP: 17 EST: 2006
SALES (est): 1.3MM
SALES (corp-wide): 374.6MM **Publicly Held**
WEB: www.lcrdixon.com
SIC: 7372 Application computer software
PA: Vertex, Inc.
 2301 Renaissance Blvd
 King Of Prussia PA 19406
 800 355-3500

(P-13276)
LEEYO SOFTWARE INC (HQ)
2841 Junction Ave Ste 201, San Jose (95134-1938)
PHONE..................408 988-5800
Jagan Reddy, *CEO*
Jeffery Pickett, *Ch of Bd*
Michael Compton, *CFO*
Karthikeyan Ramamoorthy, *Vice Pres*
Sudarsan Umashankar, *Vice Pres*
EMP: 41
SALES (est): 14.4MM **Publicly Held**
WEB: www.leeyo.com
SIC: 7372 Business oriented computer software

(P-13277)
LEVEL LABS LP
Also Called: Unshackled
530 Lytton Ave Lbby, Palo Alto (94301-1539)
PHONE..................408 499-6839
Manan Mehta, *Managing Prtnr*
Nitin Pachisia, *Mng Member*
Maria Salamanca, *Associate*
EMP: 17 EST: 2014
SALES (est): 1.1MM **Privately Held**
SIC: 7372 Application computer software

(P-13278)
LIVEACTION INC (PA)
960 San Antonio Rd # 200, Palo Alto (94303-4931)
PHONE..................415 837-3303
Darren Kimura, *CEO*
R Brooks Borcherding, *President*
Dana Matsunaga, *President*
Ulrica Menares, *Vice Pres*
Vishwas Puttasubbappa, *Vice Pres*
EMP: 35 EST: 2008
SALES (est): 5.7MM **Privately Held**
WEB: www.liveaction.com
SIC: 7372 Business oriented computer software

(P-13279)
LOGICOOL INC
1825 De La Cruz Blvd # 201, Santa Clara (95050-3012)
PHONE..................408 907-1344
EMP: 30
SALES (est): 2.9MM **Privately Held**
SIC: 7372 Prepackaged Software Srvcs

(P-13280)
LOGINEXT SOLUTIONS INC
5002 Spring Crest Ter, Fremont (94536-6525)
PHONE..................339 244-0380
Dhruvil Sanghvi, *CEO*
Manisha Raisinghani, *Chief Engr*
EMP: 100 EST: 2014
SALES (est): 5.1MM **Privately Held**
WEB: www.loginextsolutions.com
SIC: 7372 7371 7379 8243 Prepackaged software; computer software systems analysis & design, custom; computer software development & applications; software programming applications; computer related consulting services; software training, computer

(P-13281)
LORE IO INC
557 Croyden Ct, Sunnyvale (94087-3367)
PHONE..................415 691-9680
Digvijay Lamba, *CEO*
Nataly Menares, *Software Dev*
Theo Shih, *Software Engr*
Samuel Ling, *Sales Mgr*
EMP: 25 EST: 2015
SALES (est): 1.6MM **Privately Held**
WEB: www.getlore.io
SIC: 7372 Prepackaged software

(P-13282)
LOTUSFLARE INC
2880 Lakeside Dr Ste 331, Santa Clara (95054-2826)
PHONE..................626 695-5634
Surendra Gadodia, *CEO*
Hansen Zuo, *CIO*
Brennan McDonald, *Business Mgr*
Nick Thakkar, *Director*
Roslyn Lee, *Manager*
EMP: 24 EST: 2012
SALES (est): 3.2MM **Privately Held**
WEB: www.lotusflare.com
SIC: 7372 Business oriented computer software

(P-13283)
LOYALTY JUGGERNAUT INC
5216 Ashley Way, San Jose (95135-1261)
PHONE..................650 283-5081
Shyam Shah, *Principal*
EMP: 15 EST: 2015
SALES (est): 126.4K **Privately Held**
WEB: www.lji.io
SIC: 7372 Prepackaged software

(P-13284)
LPA INSURANCE AGENCY INC
Also Called: Sat
3800 Watt Ave Ste 147, Sacramento (95821-2676)
PHONE..................916 286-7850
Michael Winkel, *President*
EMP: 55 EST: 1983
SALES (est): 17.1MM
SALES (corp-wide): 12.5B **Publicly Held**
SIC: 7372 Application computer software
HQ: Fis Capital Markets Us Llc
 601 Riverside Ave
 Jacksonville FL 32204
 877 776-3706

(P-13285)
LYNX SOFTWARE TECHNOLOGIES INC (PA)
855 Embedded Way, San Jose (95138-1030)
PHONE..................408 979-3900
Inder Singh, *Chairman*
Gurjot Singh, *President*
Keith Shea, *Risk Mgmt Dir*
Julie Gutierrez, *Admin Asst*
Yuri Bakalov, *Sr Software Eng*
EMP: 52
SQ FT: 30,000
SALES (est): 15.1MM **Privately Held**
WEB: www.lynx.com
SIC: 7372 Business oriented computer software

(P-13286)
MACHINE ZONE LLC
2225 E Byshore Rd Ste 200, East Palo Alto (94303)
PHONE..................650 320-1678
Ed Lu,
Marc Silos, *IT/INT Sup*
Jeremy Goble, *QC Mgr*
Jerome Turnbull, *Marketing Staff*
EMP: 61 EST: 2013
SALES (est): 11.6MM **Privately Held**
WEB: www.mz.com
SIC: 7372 Publishers' computer software

(P-13287)
MAGNET SYSTEMS INC
2300 Geng Rd Ste 100, Palo Alto (94303-3352)
P.O. Box 320805, Los Gatos (95032-0113)
PHONE..................650 329-5904
Alfred Chuang, *CEO*
Elizabeth Vera, *Executive Asst*
EMP: 34 EST: 2008
SALES (est): 518.9K **Privately Held**
WEB: www.magnet.com
SIC: 7372 Application computer software

(P-13288)
MALIKCO LLC
2121 N Calif Blvd Ste 290, Walnut Creek (94596-7351)
PHONE..................925 974-3555
Stephynie R Malik, *CEO*
◆ EMP: 27 EST: 2004
SQ FT: 1,000
SALES (est): 1.3MM **Privately Held**
WEB: www.malikco.com
SIC: 7372 Operating systems computer software

(P-13289)
MALWAREBYTES INC
3979 Freedom Cir Fl 12, Santa Clara (95054-1256)
PHONE..................408 852-4336
Marcin Kleczynski, *CEO*
Steve Smith, *Partner*
Rj Singh, *President*
Thomas R Fox, *CFO*
Mark Harris, *CFO*
EMP: 600 EST: 2009
SALES (est): 103.5MM **Privately Held**
WEB: www.malwarebytes.com
SIC: 7372 Prepackaged software

(P-13290)
MANTICORE GAMES INC
1390 Buckingham Way, Hillsborough (94010-7307)
PHONE..................650 799-6145
Frederic Descamps, *Principal*
Danny Lin, *Vice Pres*
EMP: 21 EST: 2017
SALES (est): 651.3K **Privately Held**
WEB: www.manticoregames.com
SIC: 7372 Prepackaged software

7372 - Prepackaged Software County (P-13291) PRODUCTS & SERVICES SECTION

(P-13291)
MAPBOX INC
50 Beale St Ste 900, San Francisco (94105-1863)
PHONE..................................202 250-3633
Eric Gundersen, *CEO*
Paige Zeigler, *CEO*
Roy Ng, *COO*
SAI Sriskandarajah, *Vice Pres*
Will White, *Vice Pres*
EMP: 36 EST: 2013
SALES (est): 6.1MM **Privately Held**
WEB: www.mapbox.com
SIC: 7372 Application computer software

(P-13292)
MARK/SPACE INC (PA)
654 N Santa Cruz Ave C, Los Gatos (95030-4360)
PHONE..................................408 399-5300
Brian Hall, *President*
EMP: 61 EST: 2002
SALES (est): 474.5K **Privately Held**
WEB: www.markspace.com
SIC: 7372 Prepackaged software

(P-13293)
MARQETA INC
180 Grand Ave Ste 600, Oakland (94612-3746)
PHONE..................................888 462-7738
Jason Gardner, *Ch of Bd*
Philip Faix, *CFO*
Vidya Peters, *Chief Mktg Ofcr*
Seth Weissman,
Kevin Doerr, *Officer*
EMP: 509 EST: 2010
SQ FT: 63,284
SALES (est): 290.2MM **Privately Held**
WEB: www.marqeta.com
SIC: 7372 Prepackaged software

(P-13294)
MASTER OF CODE GLOBAL
541 Jefferson Ave Ste 104, Redwood City (94063-1700)
PHONE..................................650 200-8490
Dmytro Hrytsenko, *Administration*
EMP: 15 EST: 2014
SALES (est): 1.3MM **Privately Held**
WEB: www.masterofcode.com
SIC: 7372 Prepackaged software

(P-13295)
MATRIX LOGIC CORPORATION
1380 East Ave Ste 124240, Chico (95926-7349)
PHONE..................................415 893-9877
Stephen C Page, *President*
Roberto Villongco, *Engineer*
EMP: 31 EST: 1994
SQ FT: 1,500
SALES (est): 2.9MM **Privately Held**
WEB: www.matrix-logic.com
SIC: 7372 Business oriented computer software

(P-13296)
MATTERPORT INC (PA)
352 E Java Dr, Sunnyvale (94089-1328)
PHONE..................................650 641-2241
Raymond J Pittman, *Ch of Bd*
James D Fay, *CFO*
Seth Finkel, *Vice Pres*
Jon Maron, *Vice Pres*
Jay Remley, *Risk Mgmt Dir*
EMP: 36 EST: 2011
SQ FT: 28,322
SALES (est): 61.2MM **Publicly Held**
SIC: 7372 Prepackaged software

(P-13297)
MAXIMUS HOLDINGS INC
2475 Hanover St, Palo Alto (94304-1114)
PHONE..................................650 935-9500
Dominic Gallello, *CEO*
Jim Johnson, *CFO*
EMP: 793 EST: 2009
SALES (est): 6.4MM
SALES (corp-wide): 191.2MM **Privately Held**
WEB: www.stgpartners.com
SIC: 7372 Prepackaged software
PA: Symphony Technology Group, L.L.C.
428 University Ave
Palo Alto CA 94301
650 935-9500

(P-13298)
MCAFEE LLC (HQ)
6220 America Center Dr, San Jose (95002-2563)
PHONE..................................888 847-8766
Peter Leav, *President*
Jean-Claude Broido, *President*
Tom Miglis, *President*
Michael Berry, *CFO*
Ling MEI, *Officer*
▲ EMP: 3058 EST: 1992
SQ FT: 208,000
SALES (est): 808.4MM
SALES (corp-wide): 1.5B **Publicly Held**
WEB: www.mcafee.com
SIC: 7372 Application computer software
PA: Mcafee Corp.
6220 America Center Dr
San Jose CA 95002
866 622-3911

(P-13299)
MCAFEE CORP (PA)
6220 America Center Dr, San Jose (95002-2563)
PHONE..................................866 622-3911
Peter Leav, *President*
Venkat Bhamidipati, *CFO*
Terry Hicks, *Exec VP*
Gagan Singh, *Exec VP*
EMP: 254 EST: 2017
SQ FT: 85,000
SALES (est): 1.5B **Publicly Held**
WEB: www.mcafee.com
SIC: 7372 7382 Prepackaged software; security systems services

(P-13300)
MCAFEE FINANCE 1 LLC (DH)
2821 Mission College Blvd, Santa Clara (95054-1838)
P.O. Box 3128, Alviso (95002-3128)
PHONE..................................888 847-8766
Christopher Young, *CEO*
Michael Berry, *CFO*
EMP: 50 EST: 2017
SALES (est): 11.3MM
SALES (corp-wide): 333.4MM **Privately Held**
WEB: www.mcafee.com
SIC: 7372 Prepackaged software
HQ: Foundation Technology Worldwide Llc
2200 Mission College Blvd
Santa Clara CA 95054
888 847-8766

(P-13301)
MCAFEE FINANCE 2 LLC
2821 Mission College Blvd, Santa Clara (95054-1838)
P.O. Box 3128, Alviso (95002-3128)
PHONE..................................888 847-8766
EMP: 604 EST: 2016
SALES (est): 4.3MM
SALES (corp-wide): 333.4MM **Privately Held**
WEB: www.mcafee.com
SIC: 7372 Prepackaged software
HQ: Mcafee Finance 1, Llc
2821 Mission College Blvd
Santa Clara CA 95054
888 847-8766

(P-13302)
MCAFEE SECURITY LLC
2821 Mission College Blvd, Santa Clara (95054-1838)
P.O. Box 3128, Alviso (95002-3128)
PHONE..................................866 622-3911
Michael Decesare, *President*
Bob Kelly, *CFO*
Edward Hayden, *Senior VP*
Louis Riley, *Senior VP*
EMP: 52 EST: 2006
SQ FT: 208,000
SALES (est): 3.9MM
SALES (corp-wide): 1.5B **Publicly Held**
WEB: www.mcafee.com
SIC: 7372 Application computer software
HQ: Mcafee, Llc
6220 America Center Dr
San Jose CA 95002

(P-13303)
MEDALLIA INC (PA)
575 Market St Ste 1850, San Francisco (94105-5803)
PHONE..................................650 321-3000
Leslie J Stretch, *President*
Borge Hald, *Ch of Bd*
Roxanne M Oulman, *CFO*
Jimmy C Duan, *Ch Credit Ofcr*
Sarika Khanna, *Exec VP*
EMP: 145 EST: 2000
SALES (est): 477.2MM **Privately Held**
WEB: www.medallia.com
SIC: 7372 8732 Business oriented computer software; market analysis, business & economic research

(P-13304)
MEDITAB SOFTWARE INC
1420 River Park Dr, Sacramento (95815-4506)
P.O. Box 255687 (95865-5687)
PHONE..................................510 201-0130
Paragi Patel, *CEO*
Kunal Shah, *President*
Rajesh Patel, *Technology*
Ronak Kotecha, *Regl Sales Mgr*
EMP: 69 EST: 2002
SALES (est): 16.1MM **Privately Held**
WEB: www.meditab.com
SIC: 7372 Business oriented computer software
PA: Meditab Software (India) Private Limited
Officeno. 219/A, 2nd Floor,
Ahmedabad GJ 38006

(P-13305)
MEDRIO INC (PA)
345 California St Ste 325, San Francisco (94104-2658)
PHONE..................................415 963-3700
Nicole Latimer, *CEO*
Nathan Weems, *CFO*
Richard H Scheller, *Exec VP*
Mike Lewis, *Vice Pres*
Hannah Mooney, *Program Mgr*
EMP: 109 EST: 2006
SALES (est): 10.6MM **Privately Held**
WEB: www.medrio.com
SIC: 7372 Business oriented computer software

(P-13306)
METRICSTREAM INC (PA)
Also Called: Complianceonline
6201 America Center Dr # 240, San Jose (95002-2563)
P.O. Box 246, Alviso (95002-0246)
PHONE..................................650 620-2955
Bruce Dahlgren, *CEO*
Shanti Panditharadyula, *President*
Gaurave Kapoor, *COO*
Mike Strambi, *CFO*
Gunjan Sinha, *Chairman*
EMP: 150 EST: 1999
SALES (est): 169.8MM **Privately Held**
WEB: www.metricstream.com
SIC: 7372 Application computer software

(P-13307)
MICROMEGA SYSTEMS INC
2 Fifer Ave Ste 120, Corte Madera (94925-1153)
PHONE..................................415 924-4700
Charles Bornheim, *President*
Anand Rama, *Technical Staff*
EMP: 19 EST: 1979
SQ FT: 3,300
SALES (est): 1.1MM **Privately Held**
WEB: www.micromegasystems.com
SIC: 7372 7371 7379 Business oriented computer software; custom computer programming services; computer software development; computer related consulting services

(P-13308)
MICROSOFT CORPORATION
680 Vaqueros Ave, Sunnyvale (94085-3523)
PHONE..................................650 964-7200
EMP: 61
SALES (corp-wide): 143B **Publicly Held**
WEB: www.microsoft.com
SIC: 7372 Prepackaged Software Services
PA: Microsoft Corporation
1 Microsoft Way
Redmond WA 98052
425 882-8080

(P-13309)
MINDSNACKS INC
1390 Market St Ste 200, San Francisco (94102-5404)
PHONE..................................415 875-9817
Jesse Pickard, *CEO*
Bryan Schreier, *Principal*
Aydin Senkut, *Principal*
Darren McNally, *Manager*
EMP: 30 EST: 2010
SALES (est): 3.4MM **Privately Held**
WEB: www.elevateapp.com
SIC: 7372 Application computer software

(P-13310)
MINDTICKLE INC (PA)
115 Sansome St Ste 700, San Francisco (94104-3620)
PHONE..................................973 400-1717
Krishna Depura, *CEO*
Gopkiran RAO, *Officer*
Jeff Santelices, *Officer*
Dan Coady, *Vice Pres*
Ahmed Hedayat, *Vice Pres*
EMP: 37 EST: 2011
SALES (est): 3.6MM **Privately Held**
WEB: www.mindtickle.com
SIC: 7372 Business oriented computer software

(P-13311)
MINT SOFTWARE INC
280 Hope St, Mountain View (94041-1308)
P.O. Box 7850 (94039-7850)
PHONE..................................650 944-6000
Aaron T Patzer, *President*
Rob Hayes, *Partner*
David K Michaels, *President*
EMP: 59 EST: 2006
SQ FT: 5,000
SALES (est): 2.6MM
SALES (corp-wide): 9.6B **Publicly Held**
WEB: www.intuit.com
SIC: 7372 Business oriented computer software
PA: Intuit Inc.
2700 Coast Ave
Mountain View CA 94043
650 944-6000

(P-13312)
MIXAMO INC
2415 3rd St Ste 239, San Francisco (94107-3177)
PHONE..................................415 255-7455
EMP: 25
SALES (est): 1.6MM
SALES (corp-wide): 7.3B **Publicly Held**
SIC: 7372 Prepackaged Software Services
PA: Adobe Systems Incorporated
345 Park Ave
San Jose CA 95110
408 536-6000

(P-13313)
MLY TECHNIX CORP
2005 De La Cruz Blvd, Santa Clara (95050-3013)
PHONE..................................650 384-1456
George Moser, *Principal*
Randy Linn, *Principal*
EMP: 26 EST: 2005
SQ FT: 6,000
SALES (est): 1.3MM **Privately Held**
SIC: 7372 Utility computer software

(P-13314)
MOJO NETWORKS INC (PA)
5453 Great America Pkwy, Santa Clara (95054-3645)
PHONE..................................650 961-1111
Rick Wilmer, *CEO*

▲ = Import ▼ = Export
◆ = Import/Export

PRODUCTS & SERVICES SECTION
7372 - Prepackaged Software County (P-13336)

Tushar Saxena, *Partner*
Mike Anthofer, *CFO*
Freddy Mangum, *Chief Mktg Ofcr*
Jatin Parekh, *Vice Pres*
EMP: 149 **EST:** 2003
SALES (est): 33.2MM **Privately Held**
WEB: www.arista.com
SIC: 7372 Prepackaged software

(P-13315)
MONTAVISTA SOFTWARE LLC (DH)
2315 N 1st St Fl 4, San Jose (95131-1010)
PHONE.................................408 572-8000
Art Landro, *President*
Sanjay Uppal, *CFO*
Jason B Wacha, *Vice Pres*
James Ready, *CTO*
EMP: 100 **EST:** 1999
SALES (est): 14.3MM
SALES (corp-wide): 682.9MM **Privately Held**
WEB: www.mvista.com
SIC: 7372 Prepackaged software

(P-13316)
MOVEWORKS INC (PA)
1277 Terra Bella Ave, Mountain View (94043-1843)
PHONE.................................408 435-5100
Bhavin Shah, *CEO*
Ankoor Shah, *Software Engr*
Vaibhav Nivargi, *Chief Engr*
Anastasia Kaverina, *Analyst*
Dave Uppal, *Manager*
EMP: 103 **EST:** 2016
SQ FT: 818
SALES (est): 14.1MM **Privately Held**
WEB: www.moveworks.com
SIC: 7372 7371 Business oriented computer software; custom computer programming services

(P-13317)
MULESOFT INC
50 Fremont St Ste 300, San Francisco (94105-2231)
PHONE.................................415 229-2009
Greg Schott, *CEO*
Emily Fisher, *CEO*
Matt Langdon, *CFO*
Vidya Peters, *Chief Mktg Ofcr*
Mark Dao, *Officer*
EMP: 841 **EST:** 2006
SQ FT: 41,500
SALES: 187.7MM
SALES (corp-wide): 17.1B **Publicly Held**
WEB: www.mulesoft.com
SIC: 7372 7371 Prepackaged software; computer software development
PA: Salesforce.Com, Inc.
 415 Mission St Fl 3
 San Francisco CA 94105
 415 901-7000

(P-13318)
MURSION INC (PA)
1 California St Ste 1550, San Francisco (94111-5450)
PHONE.................................415 746-9631
Mark Atkinson, *CEO*
Fran Rodriguez, *Partner*
John Streblow, *Partner*
Arjun Nagendran, *Vice Pres*
Christina Yu, *Vice Pres*
EMP: 59 **EST:** 2014
SQ FT: 3,600
SALES (est): 7MM **Privately Held**
WEB: www.mursion.com
SIC: 7372 Educational computer software; publishers' computer software

(P-13319)
MUX INC (PA)
1182 Market St Ste 425, San Francisco (94102-4990)
PHONE.................................510 402-2257
Jonathan Dahl, *CEO*
Becca Axvig, *President*
Salman Kothari, *COO*
Venus Najeeb, *Office Mgr*
Jacqui Manzi, *Sr Software Eng*
EMP: 17 **EST:** 2015
SALES (est): 2.3MM **Privately Held**
WEB: www.mux.com
SIC: 7372 Application computer software

(P-13320)
MYENERSAVE INC
Also Called: Bidgely
440 N Wolfe Rd, Sunnyvale (94085-3869)
PHONE.................................408 464-6385
Abhay Gupta, *CEO*
Tim Clark, *Vice Pres*
Colin Gibbs, *Vice Pres*
Preeth Kumar, *Marketing Staff*
Sophia Wen, *Marketing Staff*
EMP: 15 **EST:** 2011
SALES (est): 198.6K **Privately Held**
WEB: www.bidgely.com
SIC: 7372 Utility computer software

(P-13321)
NCOUP INC (PA)
825 Corporate Way, Fremont (94539-6115)
PHONE.................................510 739-4010
John S McLlwain, *President*
Kamar Aulakh, *COO*
Stefi Panit, *Project Mgr*
Rehan Anwar, *Engineer*
EMP: 23 **EST:** 1994
SALES (est): 5.7MM **Privately Held**
SIC: 7372 Publishers' computer software

(P-13322)
NESTGSV SILICON VALLEY LLC
Also Called: Gsvlabs
2955 Campus Dr Ste 100, San Mateo (94403-2539)
PHONE.................................650 421-2000
Alexander Wright, *COO*
Fareeha Ahmed, *Software Engr*
Margaret Diesel, *Controller*
Gina Hornung, *Marketing Staff*
Slater McLean, *Director*
EMP: 15 **EST:** 2012
SALES (est): 15.6MM **Privately Held**
SIC: 7372 Prepackaged software

(P-13323)
NET OPTICS INC
Also Called: Ixia
5301 Stevens Creek Blvd, Santa Clara (95051-7201)
PHONE.................................408 737-7777
Thomas B Miller, *CEO*
Robert Shaw, *President*
Dennis Omanoff, *COO*
Burt Podbere, *CFO*
Nadine Matityahu, *Corp Secy*
EMP: 85 **EST:** 1997
SQ FT: 39,000
SALES (est): 35.9MM
SALES (corp-wide): 4.2B **Publicly Held**
WEB: www.support.ixiacom.com
SIC: 7372 Operating systems computer software
HQ: Ixia
 26601 Agoura Rd
 Calabasas CA 91302
 818 871-1800

(P-13324)
NETLIFY
610 22nd St Ste 315, San Francisco (94107-3163)
PHONE.................................925 922-0921
Aaronekia Williams, *Principal*
Lauren Sell, *Vice Pres*
David Wells, *Technical Mgr*
Tegan Barry, *Producer*
Brandi Bergstrom, *Manager*
EMP: 39 **EST:** 2017
SALES (est): 2.7MM **Privately Held**
WEB: www.netlify.com
SIC: 7372 Prepackaged software

(P-13325)
NETSKOPE INC (PA)
2445 Augustine Dr Fl 3, Santa Clara (95054-3032)
PHONE.................................800 979-6988
Sanjay Beri, *CEO*
Andrew Del Matto, *CFO*
Jason Clark, *Officer*
David Fairman, *Officer*
Chris Andrews, *Senior VP*
EMP: 630 **EST:** 2012
SQ FT: 62,086
SALES (est): 450MM **Privately Held**
WEB: www.netskope.com
SIC: 7372 7371 Application computer software; computer software development

(P-13326)
NETSUITE INC (DH)
Also Called: Oracle
2955 Campus Dr Ste 100, San Mateo (94403-2539)
PHONE.................................650 627-1000
Dorian Daley, *President*
Evan Goldberg, *Exec VP*
Jim McGeever, *Exec VP*
Sanjay Bulchandani, *Senior VP*
Brian Chess, *Senior VP*
EMP: 3614 **EST:** 1998
SQ FT: 165,000
SALES (est): 781.2MM
SALES (corp-wide): 40.4B **Publicly Held**
WEB: www.netsuite.com
SIC: 7372 Business oriented computer software
HQ: Oc Acquisition Llc
 500 Oracle Pkwy
 Redwood City CA 94065
 650 506-7000

(P-13327)
NETSUITE INC
500 Oracle Pkwy, Redwood City (94065-1677)
PHONE.................................650 627-1000
Sam Levy, *Vice Pres*
Diorez Bermudez, *Technical Mgr*
Don Blanding, *Technical Mgr*
Amod Deshpande, *Technical Mgr*
Karen Pensyl, *Technical Mgr*
EMP: 18 **EST:** 2016
SALES (est): 1MM **Privately Held**
WEB: www.netsuite.com
SIC: 7372 Prepackaged software

(P-13328)
NEW GENERATION SOFTWARE INC
Also Called: N G S
3835 N Freeway Blvd # 200, Sacramento (95834-1954)
PHONE.................................916 920-2200
Bernard B Gough, *CEO*
John O'Sullivan, *Executive*
Jeff Pearson, *Marketing Staff*
EMP: 45 **EST:** 1982
SQ FT: 10,000
SALES (est): 6.4MM **Privately Held**
WEB: www.ngsi.com
SIC: 7372 Application computer software; utility computer software

(P-13329)
NEW RELIC INC (PA)
188 Spear St Fl 11, San Francisco (94105-1752)
PHONE.................................650 777-7600
Lewis Cirne, *CEO*
Hope Cochran, *Ch of Bd*
Kristy Friedrichs, *COO*
Mark Sachleben, *CFO*
William Staples,
EMP: 1997 **EST:** 2007
SQ FT: 73,000
SALES (est): 667.6MM **Publicly Held**
WEB: www.newrelic.com
SIC: 7372 Prepackaged software; application computer software

(P-13330)
NEXENTA BY DDN INC
2025 Gateway Pl Ste 160, San Jose (95110-1059)
PHONE.................................408 791-3300
Tarkan Maner, *CEO*
EMP: 40 **EST:** 2019
SALES (est): 2.6MM
SALES (corp-wide): 214.7MM **Privately Held**
WEB: www.nexenta.com
SIC: 7372 Prepackaged software
PA: Datadirect Networks, Inc.
 9351 Deering Ave
 Chatsworth CA 91311
 818 700-7600

(P-13331)
NEXGATE INC
433 Airport Blvd Ste 303, Burlingame (94010-2010)
PHONE.................................650 762-9890
Devin Redmond, *Vice Pres*
Joe Ferrara, *Senior VP*
Dan Nadir, *Vice Pres*
Ray Kruck, *Principal*
Rich Sutton, *Principal*
EMP: 21 **EST:** 2011
SALES (est): 1MM
SALES (corp-wide): 1B **Privately Held**
WEB: www.proofpoint.com
SIC: 7372 7382 Business oriented computer software; security systems services
PA: Proofpoint, Inc.
 925 W Maude Ave
 Sunnyvale CA 94085
 408 517-4710

(P-13332)
NEXTROLL INC (PA)
Also Called: Adroll
2300 Harrison St Fl 2, San Francisco (94110-2013)
PHONE.................................877 723-7655
Robin Bordoli, *President*
Peter Krivkovich, *COO*
Aaron Bell,
Amy Lebold, *Exec VP*
Mee Patrick, *Vice Pres*
EMP: 691 **EST:** 2006
SALES (est): 203.9MM **Privately Held**
WEB: www.nextroll.com
SIC: 7372 Prepackaged software

(P-13333)
NIMBULA INC
4230 Leonard Stocking Dr, Santa Clara (95054-1777)
PHONE.................................800 633-0738
Christopher C Pinkham, *CEO*
Willem V Biljon, *Vice Pres*
EMP: 19 **EST:** 2009
SALES (est): 392.2K **Privately Held**
WEB: www.oracle.com
SIC: 7372 Prepackaged software

(P-13334)
NOK NOK LABS INC
2890 Zanker Rd Ste 203, San Jose (95134-2118)
PHONE.................................650 433-1300
Phil Dunkelberger, *CEO*
Rajiv Dholakia, *Vice Pres*
Todd Thiemann, *Vice Pres*
David Wiener, *Vice Pres*
Matthew Lourie, *Surgery Dir*
EMP: 16 **EST:** 2011
SALES (est): 1.6MM **Privately Held**
WEB: www.noknok.com
SIC: 7372 Business oriented computer software

(P-13335)
NOMINUM INC
3355 Scott Blvd Fl 3, Santa Clara (95054-3127)
PHONE.................................650 381-6000
Garry Messiana, *CEO*
Gopala Tumuluri, *COO*
Bob Verheecke, *CFO*
Pete Wisowaty, *Exec VP*
Srini Avirneni, *Senior VP*
EMP: 126 **EST:** 1999
SQ FT: 15,000
SALES (est): 25.2MM
SALES (corp-wide): 3.2B **Publicly Held**
WEB: www.akamai.com
SIC: 7372 Prepackaged software
PA: Akamai Technologies, Inc.
 145 Broadway
 Cambridge MA 02142
 617 444-3000

(P-13336)
NUTANIX INC (PA)
1740 Tech Dr Ste 150, San Jose (95110)
PHONE.................................408 216-8360
Rajiv Ramaswami, *President*
David Sangster, *COO*
Duston M Williams, *CFO*
Tarkan Maner, *Ch Credit Ofcr*
Julie O 'brien, *Chief Mktg Ofcr*
EMP: 623 **EST:** 2009
SQ FT: 436,000
SALES: 1.3B **Publicly Held**
WEB: www.nutanix.com
SIC: 7372 7371 Prepackaged software; computer software development

7372 - Prepackaged Software County (P-13337)

(P-13337)
NUTSTAR SOFTWARE LLC
1460 W 18th St, Merced (95340-4403)
PHONE..........................209 250-1324
Frank Ramos, *President*
EMP: 15 EST: 2012
SALES (est): 675.5K **Privately Held**
WEB: www.nutstar.net
SIC: 7372 Prepackaged software

(P-13338)
NYANSA INC
430 Cowper St Ste 250, Palo Alto (94301-1579)
PHONE..........................650 446-7818
Abe Ankumah, *CEO*
Daniel Kan, *Vice Pres*
Jason Reese, *Executive*
Anand Srinivas, *CTO*
Jason Wan, *Engineer*
EMP: 45 EST: 2013
SALES (est): 3MM
SALES (corp-wide): 11.7B **Publicly Held**
WEB: www.nyansa.com
SIC: 7372 Application computer software
PA: Vmware, Inc.
3401 Hillview Ave
Palo Alto CA 94304
650 427-5000

(P-13339)
OKTA INC (PA)
100 1st St Ste 600, San Francisco (94105-3513)
PHONE..........................888 722-7871
Todd McKinnon, *Ch of Bd*
Ona Allison, *Partner*
Sagnik Nandy, *President*
Charles Race, *President*
J Frederic Kerrest, *COO*
EMP: 2668 EST: 2009
SQ FT: 266,366
SALES: 835.4MM **Publicly Held**
WEB: www.okta.com
SIC: 7372 7371 Prepackaged software; software programming applications

(P-13340)
OMNISCI INC (PA)
100 Montgomery St Ste 500, San Francisco (94104-4373)
PHONE..........................415 997-2814
Jon Kondo, *CEO*
David Besemer, *Vice Pres*
Ray Falcione Jr, *Vice Pres*
Herfini Haryono, *Vice Pres*
Allison Searle, *Vice Pres*
EMP: 89 EST: 2013
SQ FT: 2,000
SALES (est): 7.1MM **Privately Held**
WEB: www.omnisci.com
SIC: 7372 Business oriented computer software

(P-13341)
ON24 INC (PA)
50 Beale St Fl 8, San Francisco (94105-1863)
PHONE..........................415 369-8000
Sharat Sharan, *President*
Steven Vattuone, *CFO*
Jayesh Sahasi, *Exec VP*
Shalini Mitha, *Vice Pres*
Leo Ryan, *Vice Pres*
EMP: 350 EST: 1998
SQ FT: 31,182
SALES (est): 156.9MM **Publicly Held**
WEB: www.on24.com
SIC: 7372 Business oriented computer software

(P-13342)
ONELOGIN INC (DH)
848 Bttery St San Frncsco San Francisco, San Francisco (94111)
PHONE..........................415 645-6830
Bradford Brooks, *CEO*
Chelsea Wadsworth, *Senior Partner*
Nathan Chan, *Partner*
Mackenzie Conarro, *Partner*
Diana Ellis, *Partner*
EMP: 175 EST: 2009
SQ FT: 44,461
SALES (est): 68.5MM
SALES (corp-wide): 2.6B **Privately Held**
WEB: www.onelogin.com
SIC: 7372 Prepackaged software
HQ: One Identity Llc
4 Polaris Way
Aliso Viejo CA 92656
949 754-8000

(P-13343)
ONESIGNAL INC
2850 S Delaware St # 201, San Mateo (94403-2575)
PHONE..........................408 506-0701
George Deglin, *President*
Long Vo, *COO*
Josh Wetzel, *Officer*
Richard Barnes, *CIO*
Karima Wagner, *CIO*
EMP: 69 EST: 2011
SALES (est): 6.5MM **Privately Held**
WEB: www.onesignal.com
SIC: 7372 Business oriented computer software

(P-13344)
OPENTV INC (DH)
Also Called: Nagra
275 Sacramento St, San Francisco (94111-3810)
PHONE..........................415 962-5000
EMP: 150
SALES (est): 70.7MM
SALES (corp-wide): 827.2MM **Privately Held**
WEB: www.nagra.com
SIC: 7372 Prepackaged Software

(P-13345)
OPENWAVE MOBILITY INC (DH)
400 Seaport Ct Ste 104, Redwood City (94063-2799)
PHONE..........................650 480-7200
John Paul Giere, *President*
Poh Sim Gan, *CFO*
Matt Halligan, *Vice Pres*
Dean Liming, *Vice Pres*
Martin Davidson, *Software Engr*
EMP: 67 EST: 2012
SALES (est): 11.7MM
SALES (corp-wide): 105.8MM **Privately Held**
WEB: www.owmobility.com
SIC: 7372 Prepackaged software
HQ: Enea Software Ab
Jan Stenbecks Torg 17
Kista 164 4
850 714-000

(P-13346)
OPERA SOFTWARE AMERICAS LLC
1875 S Grant St Ste 750, San Mateo (94402-2670)
PHONE..........................650 625-1262
Lars Boilesen, *CEO*
John Metzger, *President*
Erik C Harrell, *CFO*
Mahi De Silva, *Exec VP*
Tristine Jew, *Analyst*
EMP: 77 EST: 2006
SALES (est): 4.4MM **Privately Held**
SIC: 7372 Prepackaged software
PA: Opera Limited
Maples Corporate Services Limited
George Town GR CAYMAN

(P-13347)
OPSCRUISE INC
5255 Stevens Creek Blvd, Santa Clara (95051-6664)
PHONE..........................916 204-4369
Scott Fulton, *CEO*
Aloke Guha, *CTO*
EMP: 30 EST: 2018
SALES (est): 5MM **Privately Held**
SIC: 7372 Prepackaged software

(P-13348)
OPSMATIC LLC
188 Spear St Ste 1200, San Francisco (94105-1749)
PHONE..........................650 777-7600
Jim Stoneham, *CEO*
Gil Lawson, *Vice Pres*
EMP: 15 EST: 2013
SALES (corp-wide): 317K **Publicly Held**
WEB: www.newrelic.com
SIC: 7372 Application computer software
PA: New Relic, Inc.
188 Spear St Fl 11
San Francisco CA 94105

(P-13349)
OPSVEDA INC
4030 Moorpark Ave Ste 107, San Jose (95117-1848)
PHONE..........................408 628-0461
Sanjiv Gupta, *President*
Harsh Vardhan Pant, *Vice Pres*
Dinesh Somani, *Vice Pres*
EMP: 25 EST: 2010
SALES (est): 1.9MM **Privately Held**
WEB: www.opsveda.com
SIC: 7372 7371 Business oriented computer software; computer software development

(P-13350)
OPTIMUM SOLUTIONS GROUP LLC
419 Ponderosa Ct, Lafayette (94549-1812)
PHONE..........................415 954-7100
G John Houtary,
Lisa Massman,
EMP: 20 EST: 1999
SQ FT: 3,300
SALES (est): 790.1K
SALES (corp-wide): 1.3B **Privately Held**
WEB: www.optimumsolutions.com
SIC: 7372 7371 8243 7374 Prepackaged software; computer software systems analysis & design, custom; data processing schools; computer graphics service
PA: Kpmg Llp
345 Park Ave
New York NY 10154
212 758-9700

(P-13351)
ORACLE AMERICA INC
Also Called: Sun Microsystems
1001 Sunset Blvd, Rocklin (95765-3702)
PHONE..........................303 272-6473
Mark Kulaga, *Branch Mgr*
Arieh Markel, *Software Engr*
EMP: 15
SALES (corp-wide): 40.4B **Publicly Held**
WEB: www.oracle.com
SIC: 7372 Prepackaged software
HQ: Oracle America, Inc.
500 Oracle Pkwy
Redwood City CA 94065
650 506-7000

(P-13352)
ORACLE CORPORATION
1001 Sunset Blvd, Rocklin (95765-3702)
PHONE..........................916 315-3500
Chris Wilson, *Branch Mgr*
Eric Kinnoin, *Vice Pres*
Marion Smith, *Executive Asst*
Kathy Potter, *Admin Sec*
Ric Walz-Smith, *Info Tech Dir*
EMP: 500
SALES (corp-wide): 40.4B **Publicly Held**
WEB: www.oracle.com
SIC: 7372 7371 Business oriented computer software; custom computer programming services
PA: Oracle Corporation
2300 Oracle Way
Austin TX 78741
737 867-1000

(P-13353)
ORACLE INTERNATIONAL CORP (HQ)
500 Oracle Pkwy, Redwood City (94065-1677)
PHONE..........................650 506-7000
Dorian Daley, *CEO*
Silvia Questore, *Manager*
EMP: 50 EST: 2001
SALES (est): 11.7MM
SALES (corp-wide): 40.4B **Publicly Held**
WEB: www.oracle.com
SIC: 7372 Prepackaged software
PA: Oracle Corporation
2300 Oracle Way
Austin TX 78741
737 867-1000

(P-13354)
ORACLE TAIWAN LLC (HQ)
500 Oracle Pkwy, Redwood City (94065-1677)
PHONE..........................650 506-7000
EMP: 39 EST: 2018
SALES (est): 6.4MM
SALES (corp-wide): 40.4B **Publicly Held**
WEB: www.oracle.com
SIC: 7372 Prepackaged software
PA: Oracle Corporation
2300 Oracle Way
Austin TX 78741
737 867-1000

(P-13355)
ORACLE TALEO LLC (HQ)
4140 Dublin Blvd Ste 400, Dublin (94568-7757)
PHONE..........................925 452-3000
Dorian Daley, *President*
Eric Ball, *CFO*
Guy Gauvin, *Exec VP*
Neil Hudspith, *Exec VP*
Jason Blessing, *Senior VP*
EMP: 100 EST: 1999
SQ FT: 47,500
SALES (est): 142.8MM
SALES (corp-wide): 40.4B **Publicly Held**
WEB: www.oracle.com
SIC: 7372 Business oriented computer software
PA: Oracle Corporation
2300 Oracle Way
Austin TX 78741
737 867-1000

(P-13356)
ORB INTELLIGENCE INC
1900 Camden Ave, San Jose (95124-2942)
PHONE..........................650 391-4298
Maria Grineva, *CEO*
Leonid Shvechikov, *Engineer*
EMP: 23 EST: 2014
SALES (est): 5MM
SALES (corp-wide): 1.7B **Publicly Held**
WEB: www.dnb.com
SIC: 7372 Prepackaged software
HQ: Dun & Bradstreet, Inc
101 John F Kennedy Pkwy # 5
Short Hills NJ 07078
973 921-5500

(P-13357)
OREILLY ALPHATECH VENTURES II
101a Clay St, San Francisco (94111-2033)
PHONE..........................707 827-7000
Richard Mark Soley, *Principal*
Denise Kiley, *Vice Pres*
Stuart Silcox, *Executive*
Katy Lavallee, *Software Engr*
Subathra Thanabalan, *Software Engr*
EMP: 21 EST: 2011
SALES (est): 1.2MM **Privately Held**
SIC: 7372 Publishers' computer software

(P-13358)
OUTREACH CORPORATION
Also Called: Sales & Marketing
600 California St Fl 7, San Francisco (94108-2731)
PHONE..........................888 938-7356
Theron Glenny, *Accounts Exec*
EMP: 16
SALES (corp-wide): 49.1MM **Privately Held**
WEB: www.outreach.io
SIC: 7372 Business oriented computer software
PA: Outreach Corporation
333 Elliott Ave W Ste 500
Seattle WA 98119
206 235-3672

(P-13359)
PACTUM AI INC
800 W El Cmino Real Ste 1, Mountain View (94040)
PHONE..........................669 289-9041
Martin Rand, *CEO*

PRODUCTS & SERVICES SECTION

7372 - Prepackaged Software County (P-13381)

Kaspar Korjus,
Kristjan Korjus, *CTO*
EMP: 30 **EST:** 2019
SALES (est): 1.9MM **Privately Held**
WEB: www.pactum.com
SIC: 5734 7372 Software, business & non-game; business oriented computer software

(P-13360)
PAGERDUTY INC (PA)
600 Townsend St Ste 200, San Francisco (94103-4959)
PHONE.................................844 800-3889
Jennifer Tejada, *Ch of Bd*
Casey Culler, *Partner*
Timm Hoyt, *Partner*
Howard Wilson, *CFO*
Dave Justice, *Officer*
EMP: 768 **EST:** 2010
SQ FT: 59,000
SALES: 213.5MM **Publicly Held**
WEB: www.pagerduty.com
SIC: 7372 Prepackaged software

(P-13361)
PANDORA DATA SYSTEMS INC
10 Victor Sq Ste 250, Scotts Valley (95066-3562)
PHONE.................................831 429-8900
James C Felich, *CEO*
EMP: 51 **EST:** 1992
SQ FT: 4,200
SALES (est): 970.9K **Publicly Held**
WEB: www.omnicell.com
SIC: 7372 Application computer software
PA: Omnicell, Inc.
590 E Middlefield Rd
Mountain View CA 94043

(P-13362)
PARALLEL MACHINES INC
Also Called: Parallelm
2445 Augustine Dr Ste 150, Santa Clara (95054-3032)
PHONE.................................669 467-2638
Sivan Metzger, *CEO*
Michal Kirshner, *CFO*
Amar Mudrankit, *Sr Software Eng*
EMP: 20 **EST:** 2015
SALES (est): 1.4MM
SALES (corp-wide): 132.6MM **Privately Held**
WEB: www.datarobot.com
SIC: 7372 Business oriented computer software
PA: Datarobot, Inc.
225 Franklin St Fl 13
Boston MA 02110
617 765-4500

(P-13363)
PAXATA INC
1800 Seaport Blvd 1, Redwood City (94063-5543)
PHONE.................................650 542-7897
Prakasa Nanduri, *CEO*
David Brewster, *Co-Owner*
Piet Loubser, *Senior VP*
Nenshad Bardoliwalla, *Vice Pres*
Manu Chadha, *Vice Pres*
EMP: 90 **EST:** 2012
SALES (est): 9MM
SALES (corp-wide): 132.6MM **Privately Held**
WEB: www.datarobot.com
SIC: 7372 Business oriented computer software
PA: Datarobot, Inc.
225 Franklin St Fl 13
Boston MA 02110
617 765-4500

(P-13364)
PAYJOY INC (PA)
655 4th St, San Francisco (94107-1601)
PHONE.................................888 632-1922
Douglas Ricket, *CEO*
Deepak Murthy, *President*
Gib Lopez, *COO*
Brad Pennington, *Officer*
Juan Castro-Zumaeta, *VP Finance*
EMP: 68 **EST:** 2015
SALES (est): 10.9MM **Privately Held**
WEB: www.payjoy.com
SIC: 7372 7389 6141 Business oriented computer software; financial services; personal credit institutions

(P-13365)
PDF SOLUTIONS INC (PA)
2858 De La Cruz Blvd, Santa Clara (95050-2619)
PHONE.................................408 280-7900
John K Kibarian, *President*
Adnan Raza, *CFO*
Kimon Michaels, *Exec VP*
EMP: 293 **EST:** 1992
SQ FT: 20,800
SALES (est): 88MM **Publicly Held**
WEB: www.pdf.com
SIC: 7372 7371 Prepackaged software; computer software development

(P-13366)
PEOPLE CENTER INC
Also Called: Rippling
2443 Fillmore St 380-7, San Francisco (94115-1814)
PHONE.................................415 737-5780
Parker Conrad, *CEO*
Stefan Nilsson, *Vice Pres*
Persona Sankaranarayana, *CTO*
Matt Plank, *VP Sales*
Cesca Fleischer, *Marketing Staff*
EMP: 50 **EST:** 2016
SQ FT: 4,000
SALES (est): 1MM **Privately Held**
WEB: www.rippling.com
SIC: 7372 Business oriented computer software

(P-13367)
PERFORMANCE MATTERS LLC (DH)
150 Parkshore Dr, Folsom (95630-4710)
PHONE.................................801 453-0136
Adam J Klaber, *CEO*
Woody Dillaha, *President*
Jeanette Haren,
Kathy Lee, *Exec VP*
Eric Jensen, *CTO*
EMP: 45 **EST:** 2000
SALES (est): 10.4MM
SALES (corp-wide): 1.6B **Privately Held**
WEB: www.peopleadmin.com
SIC: 7372 Educational computer software
HQ: Peopleadmin, Inc.
805 Las Cimas Pkwy # 400
Austin TX 78746
877 637-5800

(P-13368)
PERKVILLE INC
344 Thomas L Berkley Way # 111, Oakland (94612-3577)
PHONE.................................510 808-5668
Adam Easterling, *CTO*
Ria Cruz, *Director*
EMP: 24 **EST:** 2010
SALES (est): 1.8MM **Privately Held**
WEB: www.perkville.com
SIC: 7372 Business oriented computer software

(P-13369)
PHANTOM CYBER CORPORATION
2479 E Byshore Rd Ste 185, Palo Alto (94303)
PHONE.................................650 208-5151
Oliver Friedrichs, *CEO*
Jackie Kruger, *Partner*
Tim Driscoll, *CFO*
C Morey, *Vice Pres*
Clarence Morey, *Vice Pres*
EMP: 30 **EST:** 2014
SALES (est): 5.3MM
SALES (corp-wide): 2.2B **Publicly Held**
WEB: www.splunk.com
SIC: 7372 7371 Prepackaged software; computer software development & applications
PA: Splunk Inc.
270 Brannan St
San Francisco CA 94107
415 848-8400

(P-13370)
PILLAR DATA SYSTEMS INC
2840 Junction Ave, San Jose (95134-1922)
PHONE.................................408 503-4000
Michael L Workman, *CEO*
Nancy Holleran, *President*
Edward Hayes, *CFO*
Warren Webster, *Treasurer*
Adrian Jones, *Senior VP*
EMP: 409 **EST:** 1993
SQ FT: 80,000
SALES: 53.1MM
SALES (corp-wide): 40.4B **Publicly Held**
WEB: www.oracle.com
SIC: 7372 Prepackaged software
PA: Oracle Corporation
2300 Oracle Way
Austin TX 78741
737 867-1000

(P-13371)
PLANFUL INC (HQ)
555 Twin Dolphin Dr # 40, Redwood City (94065-2129)
PHONE.................................650 249-7100
Grant Halloran, *CEO*
Jim Eberlin, *President*
Dan Fletcher, *CFO*
Shane Hansen, *CFO*
Rown Tonkin, *Chief Mktg Ofcr*
EMP: 120 **EST:** 2000
SALES (est): 58.5MM **Privately Held**
WEB: www.planful.com
SIC: 7372 Application computer software

(P-13372)
PLANGRID INC (HQ)
Also Called: Loupe
2111 Mission St Ste 400, San Francisco (94110-6349)
P.O. Box 194087 (94119-4087)
PHONE.................................800 646-0796
Tracy Young, *CEO*
George Hu, *COO*
Michael Galvin, *CFO*
David Cain, *Chief Mktg Ofcr*
Linda Keala, *Officer*
EMP: 84 **EST:** 2011
SQ FT: 16,000
SALES (est): 16MM
SALES (corp-wide): 3.7B **Publicly Held**
WEB: www.construction.autodesk.com
SIC: 7372 Application computer software
PA: Autodesk, Inc.
111 Mcinnis Pkwy
San Rafael CA 94903
415 507-5000

(P-13373)
PLAYFIRST INC
160 Spear St Fl 13, San Francisco (94105-1546)
PHONE.................................415 738-4600
Mari Jean Baker, *CEO*
John R Welch, *President*
Jim Wandrey, *CFO*
Becky Hughes, *Vice Pres*
Becky A Hughes, *Vice Pres*
EMP: 24 **EST:** 2004
SALES (est): 1.1MM
SALES (corp-wide): 540.5M **Privately Held**
WEB: www.playfirst.com
SIC: 7372 Prepackaged software
PA: Glu Mobile Inc.
875 Howard St Ste 100
San Francisco CA 94103
415 800-6100

(P-13374)
PLUSAI INC
20401 Stevens Creek Blvd, Cupertino (95014-2225)
PHONE.................................408 508-4758
David Wanqian Liu, *CEO*
EMP: 100 **EST:** 2016
SALES (est): 12.2MM **Privately Held**
WEB: www.plus.ai
SIC: 7372 Application computer software

(P-13375)
PLUTOSHIFT INC
530 Lytton Ave Fl 2, Palo Alto (94301-1541)
PHONE.................................213 400-2104
Prateek Joshi, *CEO*
EMP: 18 **EST:** 2015
SALES (est): 1.2MM **Privately Held**
WEB: www.plutoshift.com
SIC: 7372 Prepackaged software

(P-13376)
POLARION SOFTWARE INC
1001 Marina Village Pkwy # 403, Alameda (94501-6401)
PHONE.................................877 572-4005
Frank Schrder, *CEO*
George Briner, *CFO*
Stefano Rizzo, *Senior VP*
Nikolay Entin, *Vice Pres*
Jiri Walek, *Vice Pres*
EMP: 90 **EST:** 2005
SALES (est): 6.8MM **Privately Held**
WEB: www.polarion.plm.automation.siemens.com
SIC: 7372 Prepackaged software

(P-13377)
POPOUT INC
Also Called: Shippo
731 Market St Ste 200, San Francisco (94103-2005)
PHONE.................................415 691-7447
Laura Behrens Wu, *CEO*
Carl Burkhard, *Partner*
Sergio Sicairos, *Executive*
Dan Dai, *Software Engr*
Aaron Wong, *Software Engr*
EMP: 86 **EST:** 2013
SALES (est): 7.6MM **Privately Held**
WEB: www.goshippo.com
SIC: 7372 Business oriented computer software

(P-13378)
POPULUS TECHNOLOGIES INC
177 Post St Ste 200, San Francisco (94108-4700)
PHONE.................................415 364-8048
Regina Clewlow, *CEO*
Ashley Bernstein,
Charles Hudson,
EMP: 23 **EST:** 2017
SALES (est): 1MM **Privately Held**
SIC: 7372 Prepackaged software

(P-13379)
POSHMARK INC (PA)
203 Rdwood Shres Pkwy Fl Flr 8, Redwood City (94065)
PHONE.................................650 262-4771
Manish Chandra, *Ch of Bd*
Nina Du, *Partner*
John McDonald, *COO*
William Ingham,
Anan Kashyap, *Officer*
EMP: 499 **EST:** 2011
SQ FT: 75,876
SALES (est): 262MM **Publicly Held**
WEB: www.poshmark.com
SIC: 7372 5611 5621 Application computer software; men's & boys' clothing stores; clothing accessories: men's & boys'; clothing, sportswear, men's & boys'; women's clothing stores

(P-13380)
POWERSCHOOL GROUP LLC (HQ)
150 Parkshore Dr, Folsom (95630-4710)
PHONE.................................916 288-1588
Hardeep Gulati, *CEO*
Mark Oldemeyer, *CFO*
Rebecca Baker, *Vice Pres*
SAI Rangarajan, *Vice Pres*
Mike Rhein, *Vice Pres*
EMP: 125 **EST:** 2015
SALES (est): 265.1MM
SALES (corp-wide): 1.6B **Privately Held**
WEB: www.powerschool.com
SIC: 7372 Prepackaged software
PA: Vista Equity Partners Management, Llc
401 Congress Ave Ste 3100
Austin TX 78701
415 765-6500

(P-13381)
POWERSCHOOL HOLDINGS INC
150 Parkshore Dr, Folsom (95630-4710)
PHONE.................................877 873-1550
Hardeep Gulati, *CEO*

7372 - Prepackaged Software County (P-13382)
PRODUCTS & SERVICES SECTION

Maulik Datanwala, *COO*
Eric Shander, *CFO*
Anthony Miller, *Chief Mktg Ofcr*
Marcy Daniel,
EMP: 2905 **EST:** 2020
SQ FT: 61,338
SALES (est): 133.6MM **Privately Held**
SIC: 7372 Prepackaged software

(P-13382)
POWWOW INC
71 Stevenson St Ste 400, San Francisco (94105-0908)
PHONE...................877 800-4381
Jonathan Kaplan, *CEO*
Andrew Cohen, *Officer*
Kausik Dasgupta, *Engineer*
Paul Gallico, *Accounts Mgr*
EMP: 24 **EST:** 2012
SALES (est): 6.9MM **Privately Held**
WEB: www.powwowmobile.com
SIC: 7372 Business oriented computer software
PA: Magic Software Enterprises Ltd.
1 Yahadut Canada
Or Yehuda 60375

(P-13383)
PREDICTSPRING INC
447 Rinconada Ct, Los Altos (94022-3808)
PHONE...................650 917-9052
Nitin Mangtani, *Principal*
Sandilya Garimella, *Vice Pres*
Alex Martinovic, *Software Engr*
Viswanth Chadalawada, *Engineer*
Martin Chiu, *Engineer*
EMP: 21 **EST:** 2013
SALES (est): 5.2MM **Privately Held**
WEB: www.predictspring.com
SIC: 7372 Prepackaged software

(P-13384)
PREDII INC
283 Margarita Ave, Palo Alto (94306-2823)
PHONE...................415 269-1146
Tilak Kasturi, *CEO*
Raonak Ahmad, *Vice Pres*
Mark Seng, *Vice Pres*
Doyle Irvin, *Marketing Mgr*
EMP: 20 **EST:** 2013
SALES (est): 14MM **Privately Held**
WEB: www.predii.com
SIC: 7372 7389 Business oriented computer software;

(P-13385)
PREZI INC (PA)
450 Bryant St, San Francisco (94107-1303)
PHONE...................415 398-8012
Peter Arvai, *CEO*
Jim Szafranski, *COO*
Narayan Menon, *CFO*
Chris Ford, *Vice Pres*
Stefanie Grossman, *Vice Pres*
EMP: 27 **EST:** 2009
SQ FT: 1,600
SALES (est): 6.2MM **Privately Held**
WEB: www.prezi.com
SIC: 7372 Business oriented computer software

(P-13386)
PRO UNLIMITED INC (PA)
1 Post St Ste 375, San Francisco (94104-5262)
PHONE...................561 994-9500
Kevin Akeroyd, *CEO*
Ellie Doost, *Partner*
Ben Barstow, *CFO*
Jessica Kane, *Officer*
Gregg Spratto, *Officer*
EMP: 58 **EST:** 1992
SALES (est): 686.3MM **Privately Held**
WEB: www.prounlimitedglobalsolutions.com
SIC: 7372 8741 Application computer software; business oriented computer software; personnel management

(P-13387)
PROCESSWEAVER INC
5201 Great America Pkwy # 300, Santa Clara (95054-1140)
PHONE...................510 648-1420

Venu Naladala, *Prgrmr*
John Burns, *Sales Staff*
Pritesh Shah, *Director*
EMP: 17 **EST:** 2019
SALES (est): 529.2K **Privately Held**
SIC: 7372 Prepackaged software

(P-13388)
PROJECTOR IS INC
Also Called: Screenmeet.com
130 11th Ave, San Francisco (94118-1107)
PHONE...................917 972-5553
Ben Lilienthal, *President*
Lou Guercia, *COO*
Eugene Abovsky, *Admin Sec*
Aleksei Loginov, *Engineer*
EMP: 30 **EST:** 2015
SALES (est): 4MM **Privately Held**
WEB: www.screenmeet.com
SIC: 7372 Prepackaged software

(P-13389)
PROVIDE INC
268 Bush St 2921, San Francisco (94104-3503)
PHONE...................877 341-0617
Daniel Titcomb, *CEO*
James Bachmeier, *COO*
Tony Shishima, *Officer*
Andrew Bennett,
Tony Bako, *CTO*
EMP: 39 **EST:** 2013
SALES (est): 6.3MM
SALES (corp-wide): 8.4B **Publicly Held**
WEB: www.getprovide.com
SIC: 7372 Prepackaged software; business oriented computer software
PA: Fifth Third Bancorp
38 Fountain Square Plz
Cincinnati OH 45202
800 972-3030

(P-13390)
PROXIMEX CORPORATION
300 Santana Row Ste 200, San Jose (95128-2443)
PHONE...................408 215-9000
Jack Smith, *CEO*
James A Barth, *CFO*
Diane M Z Robinette, *Vice Pres*
Ken Prayoon Cheng, *CTO*
EMP: 41 **EST:** 2004
SALES (est): 6.3MM **Publicly Held**
WEB: www.proximex.com
SIC: 7372 Business oriented computer software
HQ: Johnson Controls Security Solutions Llc
6600 Congress Ave
Boca Raton FL 33487
561 264-2071

(P-13391)
PUNCHH INC ◆
1875 S Grant St Ste 810, San Mateo (94402-7048)
PHONE...................415 623-4466
Jitendra Gupta, *CEO*
Anish Mehta, *CFO*
Kim Decarolis, *Vice Pres*
Kellen Johnson, *Technical Staff*
Xin Heng, *Director*
EMP: 71 **EST:** 2021
SALES (est): 13.2MM **Privately Held**
WEB: www.punchh.com
SIC: 7372 Prepackaged software
PA: Punchh Tech India Private Limited
Sanghi Building, Mezzanine Floor
Jaipur RJ 30200

(P-13392)
PURE STORAGE INC (PA)
650 Castro St Ste 400, Mountain View (94041-2081)
PHONE...................800 379-7873
Charles Giancarlo, *Ch of Bd*
Kevan Krysler, *CFO*
Scott Dietzen, *Vice Ch Bd*
John Colgrove, *CTO*
▲ **EMP:** 3548 **EST:** 2009
SALES: 1.6B **Publicly Held**
WEB: www.purestorage.com
SIC: 7372 3572 Prepackaged software; computer storage devices

(P-13393)
QUALIO INC
268 Bush St, San Francisco (94104-3503)
PHONE...................415 795-7331
Robert Fenton, *CEO*
EMP: 35 **EST:** 2017
SALES (est): 2.7MM **Privately Held**
WEB: www.qualio.com
SIC: 7372 Prepackaged software

(P-13394)
QUANTAL INTERNATIONAL INC
455 Market St Ste 1200, San Francisco (94105-2441)
PHONE...................415 644-0754
Terry Marsh, *President*
Jeff Rogers, *COO*
Paul Pfleiderer, *CFO*
Indro Fedrigo, *Vice Pres*
EMP: 26 **EST:** 1992
SQ FT: 7,000
SALES (est): 2.7MM **Privately Held**
WEB: www.quantal.com
SIC: 7372 6282 Business oriented computer software; investment advisory service

(P-13395)
QUESTIVITY INC
1680 Civic Center Dr # 209, Santa Clara (95050-4660)
PHONE...................408 615-1781
Humayun Sohel, *President*
Muhammad Jafri, *Network Enginr*
Madhu Reddy, *Network Enginr*
Gajendra Karle, *Network Tech*
Gurwinder Singh, *Technology*
EMP: 15 **EST:** 1999
SQ FT: 1,180
SALES (est): 4.5MM **Privately Held**
WEB: www.questivity.com
SIC: 7372 7361 Prepackaged software; employment agencies

(P-13396)
QUMU INC (DH)
1100 Grundy Ln Ste 110, San Bruno (94066-3072)
PHONE...................650 396-8530
Jim Stewart, *CFO*
John Poole, *Vice Pres*
Scott Smith, *Vice Pres*
Michele Thomas, *Vice Pres*
Balaji Vijayaraghavan, *QA Dir*
EMP: 50 **EST:** 2002
SQ FT: 13,000
SALES (est): 11.1MM
SALES (corp-wide): 81.3MM **Publicly Held**
WEB: www.qumu.com
SIC: 7372 Business oriented computer software
HQ: Qumu Corporation
400 S 4th St Ste 401
Minneapolis MN 55415
612 638-9100

(P-13397)
QWILT INC
275 Shoreline Dr Ste 510, Redwood City (94065-1413)
PHONE...................866 824-8009
Alon Maor, *CEO*
Yoni Mizrahi, *CFO*
Yuval Shahar, *Chairman*
Nimrod Cohen, *Vice Pres*
Yoav Gressel, *Vice Pres*
EMP: 45 **EST:** 2010
SALES (est): 4.7MM **Privately Held**
WEB: www.qwilt.com
SIC: 7372 Business oriented computer software

(P-13398)
R-QUEST TECHNOLOGIES LLC
4710 Oak Hill Rd, Placerville (95667-9104)
PHONE...................530 621-9916
Larry Robertson, *President*
Jim Filkins, *VP Sales*
EMP: 15 **EST:** 1994
SQ FT: 3,500
SALES (est): 968.9K **Privately Held**
WEB: www.r-quest.com
SIC: 7372 Prepackaged software

(P-13399)
RADIANT LOGIC INC (HQ)
75 Rowland Way Ste 300, Novato (94945-5060)
PHONE...................415 209-6800
Joe Sander, *CEO*
Dieter Shuller, *Officer*
Carol Mannella, *Office Mgr*
Kim Macrez, *Sr Software Eng*
Nicolas Guyot, *Software Dev*
EMP: 103 **EST:** 1995
SQ FT: 10,718
SALES: 37.9MM **Privately Held**
WEB: www.radiantlogic.com
SIC: 7372 8742 Prepackaged software; management consulting services
PA: Moon Buyer, Inc.
251 Little Falls Dr
Wilmington DE 19808
302 636-5401

(P-13400)
READ IT LATER INC
Also Called: Pocket
233 Sansome St Ste 1200, San Francisco (94104-2300)
PHONE...................415 692-6111
Nathan Weiner, *CEO*
Blake Boznanski, *Partner*
Jeshua Borges, *Software Dev*
Meredith Folsom, *Manager*
Amber Milner, *Manager*
EMP: 34 **EST:** 2011
SALES (est): 5MM
SALES (corp-wide): 28.3MM **Privately Held**
WEB: www.getpocket.com
SIC: 7372 Application computer software
HQ: Mozilla Corporation
2 Harrison St Ste 175
San Francisco CA 94105

(P-13401)
REALSCOUT INC
480 Ellis St Ste 203, Mountain View (94043-2204)
PHONE...................650 397-6500
Arthur Kaneko, *CEO*
Andrew S Flanchner, *President*
Sergio Lopez, *Admin Asst*
Vedrana Kavalar, *Marketing Mgr*
Dane Dismuke,
EMP: 15 **EST:** 2012
SQ FT: 500
SALES (est): 1.7MM **Privately Held**
WEB: www.realscout.com
SIC: 7372 Business oriented computer software

(P-13402)
REDSEAL INC
1600 Technology Dr Fl 4, San Jose (95110-1382)
PHONE...................408 641-2200
Bryan Barney, *CEO*
Ray Rothrock, *CEO*
Julie Parrish, *COO*
Greg Straughn, *CFO*
Gordon Adams, *Officer*
EMP: 145 **EST:** 2004
SQ FT: 6,500
SALES (est): 60.2MM **Privately Held**
WEB: www.blank.flywheelsites.com
SIC: 7372 Prepackaged software

(P-13403)
RELATIONALAI INC
2120 University Ave, Berkeley (94704-1026)
PHONE...................650 307-8776
Molham Aref, *President*
EMP: 19 **EST:** 2018
SALES (est): 6.6MM **Privately Held**
WEB: www.relational.ai
SIC: 7372 Prepackaged software

(P-13404)
REMEDLY INC
407 Sansome St Fl 4, San Francisco (94111-3104)
PHONE...................650 265-8449
Victor Gane, *Principal*
Sara Bayer, *Director*
Susan Reed, *Director*
Gabriel Francisco, *Manager*

PRODUCTS & SERVICES SECTION
7372 - Prepackaged Software County (P-13429)

EMP: 16 EST: 2017
SALES (est): 1.4MM Privately Held
WEB: www.remedly.com
SIC: 7372 Prepackaged software

(P-13405)
REPUTATIONCOM INC (PA)
1400 A Sport Blvd Ste 401, Redwood City (94063)
PHONE.................................800 888-0924
Joe Fuca, CEO
Amir Jafari, CFO
Jason Grier, Ch Credit Ofcr
Rebecca Biestman, Chief Mktg Ofcr
Shannon Nash,
EMP: 439 EST: 2006
SQ FT: 21,454
SALES (est): 100MM Privately Held
WEB: www.reputation.com
SIC: 7372 7371 Business oriented computer software; operating systems computer software; computer software development & applications

(P-13406)
RESCALE INC
33 New Montgomery St # 950, San Francisco (94105-4554)
PHONE.................................855 737-2253
Joris Poort, President
Devin Blase, Vice Pres
Gabriel Broner, Vice Pres
Gerhard Esterhuizen, Vice Pres
Edward Hsu, Vice Pres
EMP: 62 EST: 2011
SALES (est): 7MM Privately Held
WEB: www.rescale.com
SIC: 7372 Application computer software

(P-13407)
RETAIL SOLUTIONS INCORPORATED (HQ)
100 Century Center Ct # 800, San Jose (95112-4537)
PHONE.................................650 390-6100
Andrew Appel, President
Peter Rieman, COO
Richard Welling, Program Mgr
Michael Renzi, Administration
Fangjing Wang, Sr Software Eng
EMP: 30 EST: 1997
SALES (est): 47.5MM
SALES (corp-wide): 550.6MM Privately Held
WEB: www.retailsolutions.com
SIC: 7372 Business oriented computer software
PA: Information Resources, Inc.
  203 N Lasalle St Ste 1500
  Chicago IL 60601
  312 726-1221

(P-13408)
RETAIL ZIPLINE INC
2370 Market St Ste 436, San Francisco (94114-1696)
PHONE.................................510 390-4904
Melissa Wong, CEO
Deri McCrea, Officer
EMP: 82 EST: 2014
SALES (est): 7.4MM Privately Held
WEB: www.getzipline.com
SIC: 7372 Business oriented computer software

(P-13409)
REVJET
981 Industrial Rd Ste D, San Carlos (94070-4150)
PHONE.................................650 508-2215
Patrick McNenny, Vice Pres
David Mackay, Officer
Bradley McKeon, Vice Pres
Andriy Gusyev, Engrg Dir
Natasha Daty, Human Res Mgr
EMP: 110 EST: 2017
SALES (est): 6.8MM Privately Held
WEB: www.revjet.com
SIC: 7372 Application computer software

(P-13410)
REVUP SOFTWARE INC
101 Redwood Shores Pkwy # 125, Redwood City (94065-1176)
PHONE.................................415 231-2315
Steve Spinner, CEO

EMP: 20 EST: 2016
SALES (est): 592.8K Privately Held
SIC: 7372 Prepackaged software

(P-13411)
RIVERMEADOW SOFTWARE INC
2107 N 1st St Ste 660, San Jose (95131-2005)
PHONE.................................408 217-6498
Richard Scannell, Principal
Denise Maher, Executive Asst
Greg Dennis, CTO
Emma Tompkins, Marketing Staff
John Merryman, Director
EMP: 17 EST: 2013
SALES (est): 402.4K Privately Held
WEB: www.rivermeadow.com
SIC: 7372 Business oriented computer software

(P-13412)
ROBLOX CORPORATION (PA)
970 Park Pl, San Mateo (94403-1907)
PHONE.................................888 858-2569
David Baszucki, Ch of Bd
Michael Guthrie, CFO
Mike Guthrie, CFO
Matthew Curtis, Vice Pres
Claus Moberg, Vice Pres
EMP: 898 EST: 1989
SQ FT: 300,000
SALES (est): 923.8MM Privately Held
WEB: www.corp.roblox.com
SIC: 7372 Prepackaged software

(P-13413)
ROLLAPP INC (PA)
530 Lytton Ave Fl 2, Palo Alto (94301-1541)
PHONE.................................650 617-3372
Dmitry Dakhnovsky, Principal
Dima Malenko, CTO
EMP: 23 EST: 2012
SALES (est): 1.1MM Privately Held
WEB: www.rollapp.com
SIC: 7372 Prepackaged software

(P-13414)
RUNA INC
2 W 5th Ave Ste 300, San Mateo (94402-2002)
PHONE.................................508 253-5000
Ashok Narasimhan, CEO
EMP: 30 EST: 2006
SALES (est): 3.4MM Privately Held
WEB: www.staples.com
SIC: 7372 Business oriented computer software
HQ: Staples, Inc.
  500 Staples Dr
  Framingham MA 01702
  508 253-5000

(P-13415)
RYPPLE
577 Howard St Fl 3, San Francisco (94105-4635)
PHONE.................................888 479-7753
EMP: 15
SALES (est): 1.1MM Privately Held
SIC: 7372 Prepackaged Software Services

(P-13416)
RYSIGO TECHNOLOGIES CORP (PA)
119 Lyon St Apt A, San Francisco (94117-2291)
PHONE.................................408 621-9274
Suhail Maqsood, President
Magesh Mylbagana, CTO
EMP: 49 EST: 2008 Privately Held
WEB: www.rysigo.com
SIC: 7372 8748 7371 7373 Prepackaged software; systems engineering consultant, ex. computer or professional; custom computer programming services; systems engineering, computer related; computer related consulting services

(P-13417)
S-MATRIX CORPORATION
1594 Myrtle Ave, Eureka (95501-1654)
PHONE.................................707 441-0404
Richard Verseput, President
George Cooney, Vice Pres
Ed Kallen, QC Mgr

Bill Merkle, Manager
EMP: 21 EST: 1985
SALES (est): 1.8MM Privately Held
WEB: www.smatrix.com
SIC: 7372 7371 Business oriented computer software; software programming applications

(P-13418)
S2C INC
1754 Tech Dr Ste 206, San Jose (95110)
PHONE.................................408 213-8818
Mon Ren Chene, CEO
Chenglun Chang, President
Rob Van Blommestein, Vice Pres
Lawrence Liang, Executive
EMP: 15 EST: 2006
SALES (est): 545K Privately Held
WEB: www.s2ceda.com
SIC: 5734 7372 Computer software & accessories; prepackaged software

(P-13419)
SABA SOFTWARE INC (DH)
4120 Dublin Blvd Ste 200, Dublin (94568-7759)
PHONE.................................877 722-2101
Phil Saunders, President
Jeff Lautenbach, President
Chirag Shah, CFO
Theresa Damato, Chief Mktg Ofcr
Ajay Awatramani,
EMP: 100 EST: 1997
SQ FT: 36,000
SALES (est): 122.5MM
SALES (corp-wide): 238.9K Privately Held
WEB: www.cornerstoneondemand.com
SIC: 7372 7371 Application computer software; computer software development & applications

(P-13420)
SAFETYCHAIN SOFTWARE INC (PA)
7599 Redwood Blvd Ste 205, Novato (94945-7706)
PHONE.................................415 233-9474
Walter Smith, Principal
Noah Logan, Officer
David Detweiler, Vice Pres
Clara Gavriliuc, Vice Pres
Eric Hansen, Vice Pres
EMP: 44 EST: 2012
SALES (est): 5.3MM Privately Held
WEB: www.safetychain.com
SIC: 7372 Business oriented computer software

(P-13421)
SAFEXAI INC (PA)
Also Called: Banjo
833 Main St, Redwood City (94063-1901)
PHONE.................................650 425-6376
Justin R Lindsey, CEO
Ryan Johnson, Vice Pres
Katie Vellucci, Executive Asst
Rish Mehta, Engineer
Peck Jennifer, Consultant
EMP: 15 EST: 2010
SALES (est): 4.9MM Privately Held
WEB: www.ban.jo
SIC: 7372 Prepackaged software

(P-13422)
SAGE MICROELECTRONICS CORP
910 Campisi Way Ste 2a, Campbell (95008-2351)
PHONE.................................408 680-0060
Chris Tsu, Principal
EMP: 16 EST: 2015
SALES (est): 96.2K Privately Held
SIC: 7372 Prepackaged software

(P-13423)
SALESFORCECOM INC (PA)
415 Mission St Fl 3, San Francisco (94105-2504)
PHONE.................................415 901-7000
Marc Benioff, Ch of Bd
Alexandre Dayon, President
Mark Hawkins, President
Gavin Patterson, President
Srinivas Tallapragada, President
EMP: 600 EST: 1999

SALES (est): 17.1B Publicly Held
WEB: www.salesforce.com
SIC: 7372 7375 Business oriented computer software; information retrieval services

(P-13424)
SAP LABS LLC (DH)
3410 Hillview Ave, Palo Alto (94304-1395)
PHONE.................................650 849-4000
Heinz Roggenkemper, Mng Member
Anita Franzke, Vice Pres
David Hu, Vice Pres
Ralf Malek, Vice Pres
Almer Podbicanin, Vice Pres
◆ EMP: 300 EST: 1996
SQ FT: 200,000
SALES (est): 199.4MM
SALES (corp-wide): 32.3B Publicly Held
WEB: www.sap.com
SIC: 7372 Prepackaged software
HQ: Sap America, Inc.
  3999 West Chester Pike
  Newtown Square PA 19073
  610 661-1000

(P-13425)
SAQQARA SYSTEMS INC
2833 Junction Ave Ste 100, San Jose (95134-1920)
PHONE.................................408 325-8241
EMP: 30
SQ FT: 13,000
SALES (est): 970.4K Privately Held
WEB: www.saqqara.com
SIC: 7372 Prepackaged Software Services

(P-13426)
SARS SOFTWARE PRODUCTS INC
3589 Jerald Ct, Castro Valley (94546-3049)
P.O. Box 653, Mill Valley (94942-0653)
PHONE.................................415 226-0040
Joanne Fields Doty, President
James Doty, Vice Pres
Brian Dobbie, Marketing Staff
EMP: 17 EST: 1986
SALES (est): 808.6K Privately Held
WEB: www.sarsgrid.com
SIC: 7372 Prepackaged software

(P-13427)
SASS LABS INC
Also Called: Allyo
121 W Washington Ave # 209, Sunnyvale (94086-1101)
PHONE.................................404 731-7284
Ankit Somani, President
Sahil Sahni, Vice Pres
EMP: 20 EST: 2017
SALES (est): 3.4MM
SALES (corp-wide): 2.9B Publicly Held
WEB: www.hirevue.com
SIC: 7372 Application computer software
HQ: Hirevue, Inc.
  10876 S Rver Front Pkwy S
  South Jordan UT 84095
  801 316-2910

(P-13428)
SCHOOL INNOVATIONS ACHIEVEMENT (PA)
5200 Golden Foothill Pkwy, El Dorado Hills (95762-9610)
PHONE.................................916 933-2290
Jeffrey C Williams, CEO
Gemma Ball, Partner
Susan Cook, COO
Joe Steele, CFO
Meredith Baker, Vice Pres
EMP: 95 EST: 2003
SQ FT: 25,000
SALES (est): 14.8MM Privately Held
WEB: www.sia-us.com
SIC: 7372 8742 Prepackaged software; management consulting services

(P-13429)
SCIENTIFIC LEARNING CORP
300 Frank H Ogawa Plz # 600, Oakland (94612-2056)
PHONE.................................510 444-3500
Louise Dube, Vice Pres
Chris Brookhart, Vice Pres
Joan Ferguson, Program Mgr
Vickie Bottero, Executive Asst

7372 - Prepackaged Software County (P-13430) PRODUCTS & SERVICES SECTION

Robert Collett, *Administration*
EMP: 21
SALES (corp-wide): 113.9MM **Privately Held**
WEB: www.scilearn.com
SIC: 7372 7371 Prepackaged software; computer software development
HQ: Scientific Learning Corporation
501 Grant St Ste 1075
Pittsburgh PA 15219

(P-13430)
SCOPE TECHNOLOGIES US INC (PA)
575 Market St Fl 4, San Francisco (94105-5818)
PHONE 855 207-2673
Scott Montgomerie, *CEO*
David Nedohin, *President*
Keshav Sahoo, *Vice Pres*
Brent Hensley, *Marketing Staff*
Hadley Sowerby, *Sales Staff*
EMP: 33 **EST:** 2014
SALES (est): 741.8K **Privately Held**
WEB: www.scopear.com
SIC: 7372 Application computer software

(P-13431)
SEAL SOFTWARE INCORPORATED (HQ)
1990 N Calif Blvd Ste 500, Walnut Creek (94596-3743)
PHONE 650 938-7325
Ulf Zetterberg, *CEO*
David Gingell, *Chief Mktg Ofcr*
Rich Bohne, *Risk Mgmt Dir*
Jim Wagner, *Security Dir*
EMP: 17 **EST:** 2013
SALES (est): 6.5MM
SALES (corp-wide): 1.4B **Publicly Held**
WEB: www.docusign.com
SIC: 7372 Prepackaged software
PA: Docusign, Inc.
221 Main St Ste 1550
San Francisco CA 94105
415 489-4940

(P-13432)
SECPOD TECHNOLOGIES
303 Twin Dolphin Dr Fl 6, Redwood City (94065-1497)
PHONE 405 385-9890
Chandrashekhar Basavanna, *CEO*
Greg Pottebaum, *VP Bus Dvlpt*
EMP: 40 **EST:** 2017
SALES (est): 1.8MM **Privately Held**
WEB: www.sanernow.com
SIC: 7372 Prepackaged software

(P-13433)
SECURE COMPUTING CORPORATION (DH)
3965 Freedom Cir 4, Santa Clara (95054-1206)
PHONE 408 979-2020
Daniel Ryan, *President*
Richard Scott, *Ch of Bd*
Timothy J Steinkopf, *CFO*
Atri Chatterjee, *Senior VP*
Michael J Gallagher, *Senior VP*
EMP: 40 **EST:** 1996
SQ FT: 10,895
SALES (est): 65.8MM
SALES (corp-wide): 1.5B **Publicly Held**
WEB: www.securecomputing.com
SIC: 7372 Prepackaged software

(P-13434)
SECURLY INC (HQ)
111 N Market St Ste 400, San Jose (95113-1101)
P.O. Box 3216, Los Altos (94024-0216)
PHONE 855 732-8759
Vinay Mahadik, *CEO*
Scott Cohn, *Senior VP*
Anders Johnsson, *Vice Pres*
David Huson, *Executive*
Hayden Jesserer, *Executive*
EMP: 88 **EST:** 2012
SALES (est): 13.7MM
SALES (corp-wide): 1.6B **Privately Held**
WEB: www.securly.com
SIC: 7372 Educational computer software

PA: Golden Gate Private Equity Incorporated
1 Embarcadero Ctr Fl 39
San Francisco CA 94111
415 983-2706

(P-13435)
SEMOTUS INC
Also Called: Hiplink Software
20 S Santa Cruz Ave # 300, Los Gatos (95030-6827)
PHONE 408 667-2046
Anthony Lapine, *Ch of Bd*
Pamela Lapine, *President*
Brad Steinberg, *Sales Mgr*
Frank Williams, *Sales Mgr*
EMP: 20 **EST:** 2008
SQ FT: 4,000
SALES (est): 2.7MM **Privately Held**
WEB: www.hiplink.com
SIC: 7372 7371 8243 Prepackaged software; computer software systems analysis & design, custom; operator training, computer

(P-13436)
SEMOTUS SOLUTIONS INC
20 S Santa Cruz Ave # 300, Los Gatos (95030-6827)
PHONE 408 367-1745
Anthony N La Pine, *Principal*
Jeff Greer, *Technical Staff*
Bradley Lance, *Engineer*
Dion Warrender, *Manager*
EMP: 17 **EST:** 2008
SALES (est): 674.7K **Privately Held**
WEB: www.semotussolutions.com
SIC: 7372 Prepackaged software

(P-13437)
SENTINELONE INC (PA)
444 Castro St Ste 400, Mountain View (94041-2053)
PHONE 855 868-3733
Tomer Weingarten, *Ch of Bd*
Nicholas Warner, *COO*
David Bernhardt, *CFO*
Daniel Bernard, *Chief Mktg Ofcr*
Keenan Conder,
EMP: 670 **EST:** 2013
SQ FT: 10,000
SALES (est): 93MM **Publicly Held**
WEB: www.sentinelone.com
SIC: 7372 7382 Prepackaged software; protective devices, security

(P-13438)
SEPASOFT INC
1262 Hawks Flight Ct # 190, El Dorado Hills (95762-9803)
PHONE 916 939-1684
Thomas Andrew Hechtman, *President*
Roxann Hechtman, *CFO*
Roxanna Hechtman, *CFO*
Keith Adair, *Engineer*
EMP: 22 **EST:** 2003
SQ FT: 2,955
SALES (est): 993.6K **Privately Held**
WEB: www.sepasoft.com
SIC: 7372 Prepackaged software

(P-13439)
SEQUENT SOFTWARE INC
4699 Old Ironsides Dr # 470, Santa Clara (95054-1861)
PHONE 650 419-2713
Andrew Weinstein, *CEO*
Robb Duffield, *CEO*
Raaj Shah, *CFO*
Lance Johnson, *Officer*
John Kirst, *Officer*
EMP: 17 **EST:** 2010
SALES (est): 4MM **Privately Held**
WEB: www.sequent.com
SIC: 7372 Application computer software

(P-13440)
SERRA SYSTEMS INC (HQ)
126 Mill St, Healdsburg (95448-4438)
PHONE 707 433-5104
Paul Deas, *President*
Pamela Deas, *Corp Secy*
Steven Deas, *Vice Pres*
EMP: 17 **EST:** 1984
SQ FT: 7,000

SALES (est): 3.5MM
SALES (corp-wide): 91MM **Privately Held**
WEB: www.serra.com
SIC: 7372 Business oriented computer software
PA: E & M Electric And Machinery, Inc.
126 Mill St
Healdsburg CA 95448
707 433-5578

(P-13441)
SERVICEAIDE INC (PA)
1762 Tech Dr Ste 116, San Jose (95110)
PHONE 650 206-8988
Wai Wong, *President*
Sam Acchione, *CFO*
Yip Ly, *Officer*
Chandra Swarna, *Vice Pres*
Rich Graves, *Director*
EMP: 43 **EST:** 2016
SALES (est): 11.9MM **Privately Held**
WEB: www.serviceaide.com
SIC: 7372 Application computer software

(P-13442)
SESAME SOFTWARE INC (PA)
5201 Great America Pkwy, Santa Clara (95054-1122)
PHONE 408 550-7999
Richard D Banister, *President*
Michael Hoydic, *Accounting Mgr*
Steven Hoydic, *Sales Staff*
Tom Hawkes, *Director*
Caleb McLain, *Director*
EMP: 21 **EST:** 1988
SALES (est): 5.1MM **Privately Held**
WEB: www.sesamesoftware.com
SIC: 7372 Business oriented computer software

(P-13443)
SHOTSPOTTER INC
7979 Gateway Blvd Ste 210, Newark (94560-1158)
PHONE 510 794-3100
Ralph A Clark, *President*
Pascal Levensohn, *Ch of Bd*
Alan R Stewart, *CFO*
Gary T Bunyard, *Senior VP*
Joseph O Hawkins, *Senior VP*
EMP: 157 **EST:** 2001
SALES (est): 45.7MM **Privately Held**
WEB: www.shotspotter.com
SIC: 7372 7382 Prepackaged software; security systems services

(P-13444)
SIGHT MACHINE INC
243 Vallejo St, San Francisco (94111-1511)
PHONE 888 461-5739
Jon Sobel, *CEO*
John Stone, *President*
Syed Hoda, *Chief Mktg Ofcr*
Jeff Chalmers, *Vice Pres*
Kurt Demaagd, *Vice Pres*
EMP: 60 **EST:** 2013
SQ FT: 6,500
SALES (est): 6.7MM **Privately Held**
WEB: www.sightmachine.com
SIC: 7372 Business oriented computer software

(P-13445)
SIMPPLR INC
3 Twin Dolphin Dr Ste 160, Redwood City (94065-1604)
PHONE 650 396-2646
Dhiraj Sharma, *CEO*
Piyush Rajput, *Officer*
Ted Sapountzis, *Vice Pres*
Sam Keninger, *Marketing Staff*
Hani Khan, *Marketing Staff*
EMP: 130 **EST:** 2014
SALES (est): 12.1MM **Privately Held**
WEB: www.simpplr.com
SIC: 7372 Business oriented computer software

(P-13446)
SLACK TECHNOLOGIES LLC (HQ)
500 Howard St Ste 100, San Francisco (94105-3031)
PHONE 415 902-5526
Stewart Butterfield, *Ch of Bd*

Allen Shim, *CFO*
Graham Smith, *Bd of Directors*
Tamar Yehoshua,
Sean Catlett, *Officer*
EMP: 1632 **EST:** 2009
SQ FT: 228,998
SALES (est): 902.6MM
SALES (corp-wide): 17.1B **Publicly Held**
WEB: www.slack.com
SIC: 7372 Business oriented computer software
PA: Salesforce.Com, Inc.
415 Mission St Fl 3
San Francisco CA 94105
415 901-7000

(P-13447)
SMARSH INC
Also Called: Actiance
900 Veterans Blvd Fl 5, Redwood City (94063-1715)
PHONE 650 631-6300
Anthony West, *CTO*
Todd Heythaler, *Vice Pres*
Razvan Pop, *Engineer*
Jithesh Vadi, *Engineer*
Kim Him, *Opers Staff*
EMP: 150
SALES (corp-wide): 293.9MM **Privately Held**
WEB: www.smarsh.com
SIC: 7372 8742 Prepackaged software; management consulting services
HQ: Smarsh Inc.
851 Sw 6th Ave Ste 800
Portland OR 97204
866 762-7741

(P-13448)
SMARTLOGIC SEMAPHORE INC
111 N Market St Ste 365, San Jose (95113-1101)
PHONE 408 213-9500
Rupert Bentley, *President*
Noelle McMullen, *COO*
Matthieu Jonglez, *CTO*
David Mott, *Consultant*
EMP: 32 **EST:** 2010
SALES (est): 1.8MM **Privately Held**
WEB: www.smartlogic.com
SIC: 7372 Business oriented computer software

(P-13449)
SNAPLOGIC INC (PA)
1825 S Grant St Ste 550, San Mateo (94402-2719)
PHONE 888 494-1570
Gaurav Dhillon, *CEO*
Robert J Parker, *CFO*
David Downing, *Chief Mktg Ofcr*
Dayle Hall, *Chief Mktg Ofcr*
George Mogannam, *Officer*
EMP: 139 **EST:** 2006
SALES (est): 37.7MM **Privately Held**
WEB: www.snaplogic.com
SIC: 7372 Business oriented computer software

(P-13450)
SNAPWIZ INC
Also Called: Edulastic
39300 Civic Center Dr # 310, Fremont (94538-2338)
PHONE 510 328-3277
Madhu Narasa, *CEO*
Jeff Bork, *Ch of Bd*
Satish Kumar, *COO*
Mangal Jain, *Software Engr*
EMP: 120 **EST:** 2010
SALES (est): 11.9MM **Privately Held**
WEB: www.edulastic.com
SIC: 7372 Educational computer software

(P-13451)
SOFTWARE DEVELOPMENT INC
Also Called: Mi9
5000 Hopyard Rd Ste 160, Pleasanton (94588-3352)
PHONE 925 847-8823
Michael Burge, *President*
Ernie Eichenbaum, *COO*
Kurt Bloxdorf, *Vice Pres*
Wikus Van Dyk, *Vice Pres*
Neal Kaiser, *Exec Dir*
EMP: 25 **EST:** 1979

PRODUCTS & SERVICES SECTION
7372 - Prepackaged Software County (P-13474)

SQ FT: 8,400
SALES (est): 7.2MM
SALES (corp-wide): 161.2K Privately Held
WEB: www.mi9retail.com
SIC: 7372 7379 Prepackaged software; computer related consulting services
PA: Mi9 Business Intelligence Systems Inc
  245 Yorkland Blvd Suite 301
  North York ON M2J 4
  416 491-1483

(P-13452)
SOFTWARE LICENSING CONSULTANTS
Also Called: SLC
12030 Donner Pass Rd # 1, Truckee (96161-4989)
PHONE.................................925 371-1277
Edgardo Ramirez, Principal
Evan Boyd, VP Bus Dvlpt
Brandi Addington, Finance
Ray Negrin, Accounts Mgr
EMP: 35 EST: 2003
SALES (est): 3.4MM Privately Held
WEB: www.slccorporation.com
SIC: 7372 5087 Prepackaged software; janitors' supplies

(P-13453)
SOLIDCORE SYSTEMS INC (DH)
3965 Freedom Cir, Santa Clara (95054-1206)
PHONE.................................408 387-8400
Anne Bonaparte, President
David Walker, Senior VP
Steve Albertolle, Vice Pres
Monico Mallari, Vice Pres
Terry Schwab, Vice Pres
EMP: 100 EST: 2003
SQ FT: 2,000
SALES (est): 20.3MM
SALES (corp-wide): 1.5B Publicly Held
WEB: www.mcafee.com
SIC: 7372 Prepackaged software

(P-13454)
SONY BIOTECHNOLOGY INC
1730 N 1st St Fl 2, San Jose (95112-4642)
PHONE.................................800 275-5963
James Graziadei, President
Narayan Prabhu, CFO
Peter Kim, Admin Sec
EMP: 65 EST: 2003
SALES (est): 12.8MM Privately Held
WEB: www.sonybiotechnology.com
SIC: 7372 3699 Prepackaged software; laser systems & equipment
HQ: Sony Corporation Of America
  25 Madison Ave Fl 27
  New York NY 10010

(P-13455)
SPACE TIME INSIGHT INC (HQ)
1850 Gateway Dr Ste 125, San Mateo (94404-4082)
P.O. Box 729, Bolton MA (01740-0729)
PHONE.................................650 513-8550
Rob Schilling, CEO
Tony Tibshirani, CEO
William Tamblyn, CFO
Bryan Hughes, Officer
Steve Lawrence, Vice Pres
EMP: 46 EST: 2003
SALES (est): 12.5MM
SALES (corp-wide): 25.8B Privately Held
WEB: www.space-timeinsight.com
SIC: 7372 Business oriented computer software
PA: Nokia Oyj
  Karakaari 7
  Espoo 02610
  104 488-000

(P-13456)
SPLUNK INC (PA)
270 Brannan St, San Francisco (94107-2007)
PHONE.................................415 848-8400
Douglas S Merritt, President
Graham V Smith, Ch of Bd
Shawn Bice, President
Teresa Carlson, President
Jason E Child, CFO
EMP: 160 EST: 2003
SQ FT: 182,000
SALES: 2.2B Publicly Held
WEB: www.splunk.com
SIC: 7372 Prepackaged software; business oriented computer software

(P-13457)
SPLUNK SERVICES CAYMAN LTD (HQ)
270 Brannan St, San Francisco (94107-2007)
PHONE.................................415 848-8400
EMP: 69
SALES (est): 2MM
SALES (corp-wide): 2.2B Publicly Held
WEB: www.splunk.com
SIC: 7372 Prepackaged software
PA: Splunk Inc.
  270 Brannan St
  San Francisco CA 94107
  415 848-8400

(P-13458)
SPOTINST INC
600 California St Fl 11, San Francisco (94108-2727)
PHONE.................................415 223-1333
Eran Grabiner, Officer
Grant Lee, Vice Pres
Kevin McGrath, CTO
EMP: 38 EST: 2017
SALES (est): 5.3MM Privately Held
WEB: www.spot.io
SIC: 7372 Prepackaged software
PA: Spotinst Ltd
  9 Ahad Haam
  Tel Aviv-Jaffa 65251

(P-13459)
SPOTON COMPUTING INC
Also Called: Stanza
550 Sutter St, San Francisco (94102-1102)
PHONE.................................650 293-7464
Smita Saxena, CEO
EMP: 28 EST: 2012
SALES (est): 2.3MM Privately Held
WEB: www.spoton.com
SIC: 7372 Business oriented computer software

(P-13460)
SQUARE INC (PA)
1455 Market St Ste 600, San Francisco (94103-1332)
PHONE.................................415 375-3176
Jack Dorsey, Ch of Bd
Amrita Ahuja, CFO
David Grodsky, Officer
Raul Moreno, Officer
Dj Ortua, Trust Officer
EMP: 50 EST: 2009
SQ FT: 469,056
SALES: 9.5B Publicly Held
WEB: www.squareup.com
SIC: 7372 Prepackaged software

(P-13461)
SQUELCH INC
3945 Freedom Cir Ste 560, Santa Clara (95054-1269)
PHONE.................................650 241-2700
Jayaram Bhat, CEO
Janette Chock, CFO
Janette Schock, CFO
Giorgiana Gottlied, Vice Pres
Dan Morris, Vice Pres
EMP: 30 EST: 2017
SALES (est): 2.9MM Privately Held
WEB: www.squelch.io
SIC: 7372 Application computer software

(P-13462)
SRA OSS INC
2114 Ringwood Ave, San Jose (95131-1715)
PHONE.................................408 855-8200
RAO Papolu, President
EMP: 58 EST: 2005
SALES (est): 5.1MM Privately Held
WEB: www.sraoss.com
SIC: 7372 Publishers' computer software
HQ: Software Research Associates, Inc.
  2-32-8, Minamiikebukuro
  Toshima-Ku TKY 171-0

(P-13463)
STACKLA INC
548 Market St, San Francisco (94104-5401)
PHONE.................................415 789-3304
Damien Mahoney, CEO
Peter Cassaidy,
Chris Lesperance, General Mgr
Mallory Walsh, VP Mktg
Hannah Morris, Marketing Staff
EMP: 65 EST: 2014
SALES (est): 9MM Privately Held
WEB: www.stackla.com
SIC: 7372 Application computer software

(P-13464)
STACKROX INC (PA)
100 View St Ste 204, Mountain View (94041-1374)
PHONE.................................650 489-6769
Kamal Shah, President
WEI Dang, Vice Pres
Ali Golshan, CTO
Robby Cochran, Technical Staff
Linda Song, Technical Staff
EMP: 20 EST: 2014
SALES (est): 3.5MM Privately Held
WEB: www.stackrox.com
SIC: 7372 Application computer software

(P-13465)
STALKER SOFTWARE INC
Also Called: Communigate Systems
6 Tara View Rd, Belvedere Tiburon (94920-1522)
PHONE.................................415 569-2280
Vladimir Butenko, President
Naomi Nealon, Vice Pres
Naomi Nelson, Vice Pres
Joseph Pestana, Vice Pres
JP Pestana, Vice Pres
EMP: 50 EST: 1993
SALES (est): 5.4MM Privately Held
SIC: 7372 7371 Prepackaged software; custom computer programming services

(P-13466)
STANDARD COGNITION CORP (PA)
965 Mission St Fl 7, San Francisco (94103-2955)
PHONE.................................415 324-4156
Prena Patel, Administration
Jordan Fisher, CEO
Michael Suswal, COO
Anthony Lutz, CFO
Elizabeth Mashal, Sr Software Eng
EMP: 78 EST: 2017
SALES (est): 8.7MM Privately Held
WEB: www.standard.ai
SIC: 7372 Business oriented computer software

(P-13467)
STEP MOBILE INC
120 Hawthorne Ave, Palo Alto (94301-1000)
PHONE.................................203 913-9229
CJ McDonald, CEO
EMP: 35 EST: 2018
SALES (est): 100K Privately Held
WEB: www.step.com
SIC: 7372 Application computer software

(P-13468)
STORM8 INC
Also Called: Storm8 Entertainment
2400 Bridge Pkwy Ste 2, Redwood City (94065-1166)
PHONE.................................650 596-8600
Perry Tam, CEO
Steve Parkis, President
Jeff Witt, President
Laura Yip, Officer
Man Hay Tam, Vice Pres
EMP: 16 EST: 2009
SALES (est): 3.5MM Privately Held
WEB: www.storm8.com
SIC: 7372 Prepackaged software
PA: Stillfront Group Ab (Publ)
  Kungsgatan 38
  Stockholm 111 3

(P-13469)
STRYDER CORP (PA)
Also Called: Handshake
225 Bush St Fl 12, San Francisco (94104-4254)
P.O. Box 40770 (94140-0770)
PHONE.................................415 981-8400
Garrett Lord, Ch of Bd
Randy Bitting, Officer
Lamar Newbill, Executive
Ben Christensen, Principal
Scott Ringwelski, Principal
EMP: 99 EST: 2014
SALES (est): 16.1MM Privately Held
SIC: 7372 7371 7379 Educational computer software; application computer software; business oriented computer software; computer software development & applications; computer related consulting services

(P-13470)
SUBTLE MEDICAL INC
883 Santa Cruz Ave # 205, Menlo Park (94025-4608)
PHONE.................................650 397-8709
Miriam Murase, President
Tao Zhang, Director
EMP: 22 EST: 2017
SALES (est): 2.1MM Privately Held
WEB: www.subtlemedical.com
SIC: 7372 Prepackaged software

(P-13471)
SUCCESSFACTORS INC (DH)
Also Called: Success Factors
3410 Hillview Ave, Palo Alto (94304-1395)
PHONE.................................650 212-1296
Price Shawn, President
Mike Ettling, President
Matt Leone, COO
Klein Christian, CFO
Christian Klein, CFO
EMP: 815 EST: 2001
SALES (est): 201.5MM
SALES (corp-wide): 32.3B Publicly Held
WEB: www.successfactors.com
SIC: 7372 Prepackaged software
HQ: Sap America, Inc.
  3999 West Chester Pike
  Newtown Square PA 19073
  610 661-1000

(P-13472)
SUN MICROSYSTEMS INTL INC (HQ)
500 Oracle Pkwy, Redwood City (94065-1677)
PHONE.................................650 506-7000
Dorian Daley, CEO
Gregory Hilbrich, CFO
Brian S Higgins, Admin Sec
Brian Tauscher, Manager
EMP: 471 EST: 1995
SALES (est): 20.4MM
SALES (corp-wide): 40.4B Publicly Held
WEB: www.oracle.com
SIC: 7372 Prepackaged software
PA: Oracle Corporation
  2300 Oracle Way
  Austin TX 78741
  737 867-1000

(P-13473)
SUPPLYSHIFT
215 River St, Santa Cruz (95060-2770)
PHONE.................................831 824-4326
Supplyshift Gershenson, CEO
EMP: 62 EST: 2012
SALES (est): 5.4MM Privately Held
WEB: www.supplyshift.net
SIC: 7372 Business oriented computer software

(P-13474)
SWIFTCOMPLY US OPCO INC
6701 Koll Center Pkwy # 25, Pleasanton (94566-8061)
PHONE.................................650 430-4341
Michael O'Dwyer, CEO
EMP: 17
SALES (corp-wide): 1.6MM Privately Held
WEB: www.swiftcomply.com
SIC: 7372 7379 Prepackaged software; data processing consultant

7372 - Prepackaged Software County (P-13475)
PRODUCTS & SERVICES SECTION

PA: Swiftcomply Us Opco, Inc.
405 E D St Ste D
Petaluma CA 94952
800 761-4999

(P-13475)
SWIFTSTACK INC (HQ)
Also Called: Nvidia
423 Central Ave, Menlo Park (94025-2804)
PHONE.................................408 486-2000
Don Jaworski, *CEO*
Anders Tjernlund, *COO*
Randall Jackson, *Vice Pres*
Paul McLean, *Program Mgr*
Stephen Jones, *Engineer*
EMP: 62 **EST:** 2011
SALES (est): 14.7MM **Publicly Held**
WEB: www.swiftstack.com
SIC: 7372 Business oriented computer software; application computer software

(P-13476)
SWISSCOM CLOUD LAB LTD
675 Forest Ave, Palo Alto (94301-2624)
PHONE.................................404 316-9160
Christa Christine Marzouk, *Administration*
EMP: 31 **EST:** 2013
SALES (est): 11.2MM
SALES (corp-wide): 5.1B **Privately Held**
WEB: www.swisscom.ch
SIC: 7372 Prepackaged software
HQ: Swisscom Ag
Alte Tiefenaustrasse 6
Worblaufen BE 3048
582 219-911

(P-13477)
SWITCHBOARD SOFTWARE INC
268 Bush St, San Francisco (94104-3503)
PHONE.................................415 425-3660
EMP: 15 **EST:** 2019
SALES (est): 352.3K **Privately Held**
WEB: www.switchboard-software.com
SIC: 7372 Prepackaged software

(P-13478)
SYBASE INC (DH)
1 Sybase Dr, Dublin (94568-7976)
PHONE.................................925 236-5000
John S Chen, *President*
Pramod Iyengar, *President*
Jeffrey G Ross, *CFO*
Raj Nathan, *Chief Mktg Ofcr*
Daniel R Carl, *Vice Pres*
▲ **EMP:** 40 **EST:** 1984
SQ FT: 406,000
SALES (est): 271.8MM
SALES (corp-wide): 32.3B **Publicly Held**
WEB: www.sap.com
SIC: 7372 Prepackaged software
HQ: Sap America, Inc.
3999 West Chester Pike
Newtown Square PA 19073
610 661-1000

(P-13479)
SYCLE LLC (PA)
480 Green St, San Francisco (94133-4029)
PHONE.................................888 881-7925
Ridge Sampson, *CEO*
Nancy Girouard, *CFO*
Brier Casey, *Executive Asst*
Jamie Urborg, *Marketing Staff*
Nick Weber, *Sales Staff*
EMP: 53 **EST:** 2006
SALES (est): 1.1MM **Privately Held**
WEB: www.sycle.net
SIC: 7372 Prepackaged software

(P-13480)
SYNOPSYS INC (PA)
690 E Middlefield Rd, Mountain View (94043-4033)
PHONE.................................650 584-5000
Aart J De Geus, *Ch of Bd*
CHI-Foon Chan, *President*
Sassine Ghazi, *COO*
Trac Pham, *CFO*
Joseph W Logan, *Officer*
EMP: 500 **EST:** 1986
SQ FT: 341,000
SALES (est): 3.6B **Publicly Held**
WEB: www.synopsys.com
SIC: 7372 7371 Prepackaged software; computer software development

(P-13481)
SYNPLICITY INC (HQ)
690 E Middlefield Rd, Mountain View (94043-4010)
PHONE.................................650 584-5000
Gary Meyers, *President*
Alisa Yaffa, *Ch of Bd*
Andrew Dauman, *President*
John J Hanlon, *CFO*
Andrew Haines, *Senior VP*
EMP: 160 **EST:** 1994
SQ FT: 66,212
SALES (est): 52.1MM
SALES (corp-wide): 3.6B **Publicly Held**
WEB: www.synopsys.com
SIC: 7372 Prepackaged software
PA: Synopsys, Inc.
690 E Middlefield Rd
Mountain View CA 94043
650 584-5000

(P-13482)
SYNQY CORPORATION
3380 Vincent Rd Ste A, Pleasant Hill (94523-4324)
PHONE.................................925 407-2601
Michael Weissman, *CEO*
Michael Toepel, *Vice Pres*
John Hoye, *VP Bus Dvlpt*
Nikolaus Chanda, *Admin Sec*
EMP: 15 **EST:** 2013
SALES (est): 1.3MM **Privately Held**
WEB: www.synqy.com
SIC: 7372 Business oriented computer software

(P-13483)
TALENA INC
2860 Zanker Rd Ste 109, San Jose (95134-2119)
PHONE.................................408 649-6338
Justin Lau, *Administration*
Jay Desai, *Vice Pres*
Faizan Khan, *Software Dev*
EMP: 17 **EST:** 2013
SALES (est): 2.9MM **Privately Held**
WEB: www.cohesity.com
SIC: 7372 Prepackaged software

(P-13484)
TALIX INC
660 3rd St Ste 302, San Francisco (94107-1921)
PHONE.................................628 220-3885
Dean Stephens, *CEO*
Ashmi Shah, *CFO*
Shahyan Currimbhoy,
Bob Hetchler, *Senior VP*
Tim England, *Vice Pres*
EMP: 59 **EST:** 2014
SALES (est): 6.4MM **Privately Held**
WEB: www.talix.com
SIC: 7372 Application computer software
PA: Edifecs, Inc.
1756 114th Ave Se Ste 100
Bellevue WA 98004

(P-13485)
TALKDESK INC (PA)
388 Market St Ste 1300, San Francisco (94111-5316)
P.O. Box 40, Riverton UT (84065-0019)
PHONE.................................864 642-5230
Tiago Paiva, *CEO*
Marco Costa, *COO*
Sydney Carey, *CFO*
Cristina Fonseca, *Treasurer*
Kathie Johnson, *Chief Mktg Ofcr*
EMP: 999 **EST:** 2011
SALES (est): 100.2MM **Privately Held**
WEB: www.academy.talkdesk.com
SIC: 7372 Application computer software; business oriented computer software

(P-13486)
TANOSHI INC
505 14th St Fl 9, Oakland (94612-1406)
PHONE.................................949 677-5261
Bradley Wayne Johnston, *CEO*
EMP: 18 **EST:** 2017
SALES (est): 1.6MM **Privately Held**
WEB: www.tanoshikidscomputers.com
SIC: 7372 Prepackaged software

(P-13487)
TAPINGO INC (DH)
39 Stillman St, San Francisco (94107-1309)
PHONE.................................415 283-5222
Daniel Almog, *CEO*
Ryann Starks, *Partner*
Brian Madigan, *Vice Pres*
Jeff Macdonald, *Finance Mgr*
Gerardo Ojeda, *Opers Staff*
EMP: 77 **EST:** 2012
SQ FT: 4,300
SALES (est): 11.8MM
SALES (corp-wide): 2.4B **Privately Held**
WEB: www.home.tapingo.com
SIC: 7372 Prepackaged software
HQ: Grubhub Inc.
111 W Washington St # 2100
Chicago IL 60602
877 585-7878

(P-13488)
TECHNICAL SALES INTL LLC (HQ)
910 Pleasant Grove Blvd, Roseville (95678-6193)
PHONE.................................866 493-6337
Tammy Ford, *CEO*
Brenda Brill, *Accountant*
Cedric Green, *Opers Mgr*
Rebecca Foletta, *Mktg Dir*
Nathan Moore, *Regl Sales Mgr*
EMP: 50 **EST:** 2002
SALES (est): 1.4MM **Privately Held**
WEB: www.tsi-software.com
SIC: 7372 Application computer software

(P-13489)
TELLUS SOLUTIONS INC
3350 Scott Blvd Bldg 34a, Santa Clara (95054-3105)
PHONE.................................408 850-2942
Sara Jain, *President*
Jinesh Jain, *Vice Pres*
Christopher Raja, *Tech Recruiter*
Gandhi Sunar, *Technology*
Ajay Baira, *Recruiter*
EMP: 38 **EST:** 2005
SALES (est): 4.2MM **Privately Held**
WEB: www.tellussol.com
SIC: 7372 7371 7373 Prepackaged software; custom computer programming services; computer integrated systems design

(P-13490)
TEND INSIGHTS INC
46567 Fremont Blvd, Fremont (94538-6409)
PHONE.................................510 619-9289
Herman Yau, *CEO*
Patrick Meyer, *Exec VP*
Stanley Wong, *IT/INT Sup*
Bin LI, *Engineer*
▲ **EMP:** 28 **EST:** 2008
SQ FT: 7,000
SALES (est): 5.2MM **Privately Held**
WEB: www.tendinsights.com
SIC: 5731 7372 Video cameras & accessories; prepackaged software

(P-13491)
THOUGHTSPOT INC (PA)
1900 Camden Ave Ste 101, San Jose (95124-2944)
PHONE.................................800 508-7008
Sudheesh Nair, *CEO*
Toni Adams, *Partner*
Malery Lassen, *Partner*
Ajeet Singh, *Ch of Bd*
David Freeman, *Senior VP*
EMP: 451 **EST:** 2012
SALES (est): 86.2MM **Privately Held**
WEB: www.thoughtspot.com
SIC: 7372 Business oriented computer software

(P-13492)
THOUSANDEYES LLC (HQ)
Also Called: Thousandeyes, Inc.
201 Mission St Ste 1700, San Francisco (94105-8102)
PHONE.................................415 513-4526
Mohit Lad, *CEO*
Paul Kizakevich, *Vice Pres*
Prabha Krishna, *Vice Pres*
Matt Piercy, *Vice Pres*
David Stokey, *Vice Pres*
EMP: 72 **EST:** 2010
SALES (est): 17.4MM
SALES (corp-wide): 49.8B **Publicly Held**
WEB: www.thousandeyes.com
SIC: 7372 Business oriented computer software
PA: Cisco Systems, Inc.
170 W Tasman Dr
San Jose CA 95134
408 526-4000

(P-13493)
TIBCO SOFTWARE FEDERAL INC
3301 Hillview Ave, Palo Alto (94304-1204)
PHONE.................................703 208-3900
Richard L Mortin, *CEO*
Joseph Kijewski, *Vice Pres*
EMP: 30 **EST:** 2010
SALES (est): 5.5MM
SALES (corp-wide): 885.6MM **Privately Held**
WEB: www.tibco.com
SIC: 7372 Application computer software
HQ: Tibco Software Inc.
3307 Hillview Ave
Palo Alto CA 94304

(P-13494)
TINYCO INC
225 Bush St Ste 1900, San Francisco (94104-4292)
PHONE.................................415 644-8101
Saleman Ali, *CEO*
Jayme Dedona, *Software Engr*
Ivy Wong, *Marketing Staff*
Hannah Culver, *Manager*
EMP: 125 **EST:** 2011
SALES (est): 26.1MM
SALES (corp-wide): 59.5MM **Privately Held**
WEB: www.jamcity.com
SIC: 5734 7372 7371 Software, computer games; application computer software; software programming applications
PA: Jam City, Inc.
3562 Eastham Dr
Culver City CA 90232
310 205-4800

(P-13495)
TOPGUEST INC
Also Called: Ezrez Software
601 Montgomery St Fl 17, San Francisco (94111-2621)
PHONE.................................646 415-9402
EMP: 20
SALES (est): 841K **Privately Held**
WEB: www.topguest.com
SIC: 7372 Prepackaged Software Services
PA: Switchfly, Inc.
1550 Market St Ste 350
Denver CO 80202

(P-13496)
TOTALREWARDS SOFTWARE INC
2208 Plaza Dr Ste 100, Rocklin (95765-4418)
PHONE.................................916 632-1000
Raymond Odonnell, *CEO*
Elijah Blanton, *Technical Mgr*
Preeti Custer, *Manager*
EMP: 19 **EST:** 2006
SALES (est): 533.4K **Privately Held**
WEB: www.totalrewardssoftware.com
SIC: 7372 Prepackaged software

(P-13497)
TRIZIC INC
60 E Sir Francis Drake Bl, Larkspur (94939-1713)
PHONE.................................415 366-6583
Andrew Sievers, *CEO*
Iain Kennedy, *COO*
Jonas Kloiber, *Vice Pres*
Pete Chiccino, *General Mgr*
Vanessa Torney, *Office Mgr*
EMP: 40 **EST:** 2014

▲ = Import ▼ = Export
◆ = Import/Export

PRODUCTS & SERVICES SECTION

7372 - Prepackaged Software County (P-13521)

SALES (est): 6MM **Privately Held**
WEB: www.harvestsw.com
SIC: 7372 Business oriented computer software

(P-13498)
TROV INC (PA)
347 Hartz Ave, Danville (94526-3307)
PHONE..................925 478-5500
Scott Walchek, *CEO*
Michael Pearson, *Admin Sec*
Daniel Spangler, *Engineer*
Max Donnelly, *Analyst*
David Canavan, *Controller*
EMP: 18 **EST:** 2012
SQ FT: 4,972
SALES (est): 7.5MM **Privately Held**
WEB: www.trov.com
SIC: 7372 Application computer software

(P-13499)
TUBEMOGUL INC
1250 53rd St Ste 1, Emeryville (94608-2965)
PHONE..................510 653-0126
Brett Wilson, *President*
Robert Gatto, *COO*
Ron Will, *CFO*
Keith Eadie, *Chief Mktg Ofcr*
Paul Joachim, *Officer*
EMP: 577 **EST:** 2007
SQ FT: 49,000
SALES (est): 119.1MM
SALES (corp-wide): 12.8B **Publicly Held**
WEB: www.adobe.com
SIC: 7372 Application computer software
PA: Adobe Inc.
 345 Park Ave
 San Jose CA 95110
 408 536-6000

(P-13500)
TWILIO INC (PA)
101 Spear St Fl 1, San Francisco (94105-1580)
PHONE..................415 390-2337
Jeffrey Lawson, *Ch of Bd*
George Hu, *COO*
Khozema Shipchandler, *CFO*
Eyal Manor,
Karyn Smith, *Admin Sec*
EMP: 2272 **EST:** 2008
SQ FT: 259,416
SALES (est): 1.7B **Publicly Held**
WEB: www.twilio.com
SIC: 7372 Prepackaged software; business oriented computer software

(P-13501)
TYPEKIT INC
601 Townsend St, San Francisco (94103-5247)
PHONE..................415 596-6319
Jeffrey Veen, *Principal*
Tim Brown, *Manager*
EMP: 24 **EST:** 2011
SALES (est): 2.6MM
SALES (corp-wide): 12.8B **Publicly Held**
WEB: www.fonts.adobe.com
SIC: 7372 Operating systems computer software
PA: Adobe Inc.
 345 Park Ave
 San Jose CA 95110
 408 536-6000

(P-13502)
UCLASS INC
901 Mission St Ste 105, San Francisco (94103-3062)
PHONE..................630 520-8553
Zachary E Ringelstein, *CEO*
EMP: 15 **EST:** 2012
SALES (est): 697K
SALES (corp-wide): 125.4MM **Privately Held**
WEB: www.renaissance.com
SIC: 7372 Educational computer software
PA: Renaissance Learning, Inc.
 2911 Peach St
 Wisconsin Rapids WI 54494
 715 424-3236

(P-13503)
UJET INC
201 3rd St Ste 950, San Francisco (94103-3182)
PHONE..................855 242-8538
Anand Janefalkar, *CEO*
Jeff Nichols, *CFO*
Vasili Triant, *Officer*
Jennifer Reilly, *Opers Mgr*
Joerg Habermeier, *Director*
EMP: 112 **EST:** 2015
SALES (est): 6MM **Privately Held**
WEB: www.ujet.cx
SIC: 7372 Prepackaged software

(P-13504)
UNCOUNTABLE INC (PA)
300 Kansas St, San Francisco (94103-5169)
P.O. Box 77625 (94107-0625)
PHONE..................650 208-5949
Noel Hollingsworth, *CEO*
William Tashman, *Principal*
Ryan Kuang, *Software Engr*
Yijun Guo, *Engineer*
AVI Kejriwal, *Engineer*
EMP: 20 **EST:** 2016
SALES (est): 1.1MM **Privately Held**
WEB: www.uncountable.com
SIC: 7372 Application computer software

(P-13505)
UNIFI SOFTWARE INC
1810 Gateway Dr Ste 380, San Mateo (94404-4063)
PHONE..................732 614-9522
Matt Mosman, *CEO*
Rob Carlson, *President*
Intekhab Nazeer, *CFO*
Mike Asher, *Bd of Directors*
Bill Serino, *Risk Mgmt Dir*
EMP: 25 **EST:** 2015
SALES (est): 2.6MM **Privately Held**
WEB: www.boomi.com
SIC: 7372 Business oriented computer software

(P-13506)
UNIVERSAL MCLOUD USA CORP
580 California St, San Francisco (94104-1000)
PHONE..................613 222-5904
Russ McMeekin, *CEO*
Michael Sicuro, *CFO*
Gino Lander, *Executive*
Darren Anderson, *Exec VP*
Whitney Weller, *Vice Pres*
EMP: 15 **EST:** 2016
SALES (est): 2.2MM
SALES (corp-wide): 20.5MM **Privately Held**
WEB: www.magcloud.com
SIC: 7372 Business oriented computer software
PA: Mcloud Technologies Corp
 550-510 Burrard St
 Vancouver BC V6C 3
 866 420-1781

(P-13507)
UNTANGLE HOLDINGS INC (PA)
25 Metro Dr Ste 210, San Jose (95110-1338)
PHONE..................408 598-4299
Scott Devens, *CEO*
Lori Booroojian, *CFO*
Amy Abatangle, *Chief Mktg Ofcr*
Dirk Morris, *Officer*
Timur Kovalev, *CTO*
EMP: 45 **EST:** 2016
SALES (est): 5.5MM **Privately Held**
WEB: www.untangle.com
SIC: 7372 Prepackaged software

(P-13508)
UPGUARD INC (PA)
723 N Shoreline Blvd, Mountain View (94043-3208)
PHONE..................888 882-3223
Alan Sharp-Paul, *CEO*
Mike Baukes, *President*
Spiro Spiroski, *Officer*
Ann Beaver, *Vice Pres*
EMP: 30 **EST:** 2012
SQ FT: 13,800
SALES (est): 8.8MM **Privately Held**
WEB: www.upguard.com
SIC: 7372 Business oriented computer software

(P-13509)
USERTESTING INC (PA)
144 Townsend St, San Francisco (94107-1900)
PHONE..................650 567-5616
Andy Macmillan, *Ch of Bd*
Matt Zelen, *COO*
Jon Pexton, *CFO*
Michelle Huff, *Chief Mktg Ofcr*
David A Satterwhite, *Risk Mgmt Dir*
EMP: 79 **EST:** 2007
SQ FT: 45,000
SALES (est): 102.2MM **Publicly Held**
WEB: www.usertesting.com
SIC: 7372 Prepackaged software

(P-13510)
VALIANTICA INC (PA)
940 Saratoga Ave Ste 290, San Jose (95129-3417)
PHONE..................408 694-3803
Peiwei MI, *President*
Dharmagna Trivedi, *CFO*
Neel Vora, *Vice Pres*
Puja Gupta, *Tech Recruiter*
Reena Sah, *Human Resources*
EMP: 34 **EST:** 2007
SALES (est): 3MM **Privately Held**
WEB: www.valiantica.com
SIC: 7372 Business oriented computer software

(P-13511)
VARMOUR NETWORKS INC (PA)
270 3rd St, Los Altos (94022-3617)
PHONE..................650 564-5100
Jia-Jyi Roger Lian, *CEO*
Demetrios Lazarikos, *Officer*
Jeff Jennings, *Senior VP*
Rich Noguera, *Vice Pres*
Colin Ross, *Executive*
EMP: 74 **EST:** 2011
SALES (est): 17.8MM **Privately Held**
WEB: www.varmour.com
SIC: 7372 Prepackaged software

(P-13512)
VCOGNITION TECHNOLOGIES INC
230 42nd Ave, San Mateo (94403-5002)
PHONE..................415 374-0189
Krishna Motukuri, *CEO*
EMP: 35 **EST:** 2014
SALES (est): 2.7MM **Privately Held**
SIC: 7372 Business oriented computer software

(P-13513)
VEEVA SYSTEMS INC (PA)
4280 Hacienda Dr, Pleasanton (94588-2719)
PHONE..................925 452-6500
Peter P Gassner, *CEO*
Gordon Ritter, *Ch of Bd*
Thomas D Schwenger, *President*
Brent Bowman, *CFO*
E Nitsa Zuppas, *Chief Mktg Ofcr*
EMP: 3098 **EST:** 2007
SALES: 1.4B **Publicly Held**
WEB: www.veeva.com
SIC: 7372 7371 7379 Prepackaged software; software programming applications; computer related consulting services

(P-13514)
VELODYNE LIDAR INC (PA)
5521 Hellyer Ave, San Jose (95138-1017)
PHONE..................669 275-2251
Anand Gopalan, *CEO*
Michael Dee, *Ch of Bd*
Jim Barnhart, *COO*
Andrew Hamer, *CFO*
Sally Frykman, *Chief Mktg Ofcr*
EMP: 201 **EST:** 1983
SQ FT: 205,000
SALES (est): 95.3MM **Publicly Held**
WEB: www.velodynelidar.com
SIC: 7372 Prepackaged software

(P-13515)
VERANA HEALTH INC
600 Harrison St Ste 250, San Francisco (94107-2899)
PHONE..................415 215-4440
Miki Kapoor, *CEO*
Marie-Eve Piche, *CFO*
Matthew Roe, *Officer*
Hylton Kalvaria, *Vice Pres*
Ed Kanner, *Vice Pres*
EMP: 48 **EST:** 2008
SALES (est): 6.6MM **Privately Held**
SIC: 7372 Prepackaged software

(P-13516)
VERITAS SOFTWARE GLOBAL LLC
1600 Plymouth St, Mountain View (94043-1203)
PHONE..................650 335-8000
EMP: 15 **EST:** 2011
SALES (est): 1.3MM **Privately Held**
SIC: 7372 Prepackaged Software Services

(P-13517)
VERSANT CORPORATION (DH)
500 Arguello St Ste 200, Redwood City (94063-1567)
PHONE..................650 232-2400
Bernhard Woebker, *President*
Jerry Wong, *CFO*
Robert Greene, *Vice Pres*
Ismail Gazarin, *CIO*
Johannes Riedinger, *Manager*
EMP: 58 **EST:** 1988
SQ FT: 6,800
SALES (est): 19.5MM **Privately Held**
WEB: www.actian.com
SIC: 7372 Prepackaged software

(P-13518)
VINDICIA INC
2988 Campus Dr Ste 300, San Mateo (94403-2531)
PHONE..................650 264-4700
Kris Nagel, *CEO*
Mark Elrod, *Exec VP*
Irwin Jacobson, *Exec VP*
Jack Bullock, *Senior VP*
Steve Booth, *Vice Pres*
EMP: 135 **EST:** 2003
SQ FT: 9,000
SALES (est): 42MM
SALES (corp-wide): 3.5B **Privately Held**
WEB: www.vindicia.com
SIC: 7372 Business oriented computer software
HQ: Amdocs, Inc.
 1390 Tmberlake Manor Pkwy
 Chesterfield MO 63017
 314 212-7000

(P-13519)
VINTELLUS INC
19918 Wellington Ct, Saratoga (95070-3813)
PHONE..................510 972-4710
Sivakumar Sundaresan, *CEO*
EMP: 16 **EST:** 2018
SALES (est): 763.2K **Privately Held**
WEB: www.vintellus.com
SIC: 7372 Business oriented computer software

(P-13520)
VISUALON INC
1475 S Bascom Ave Ste 103, Campbell (95008-0628)
PHONE..................408 645-6618
Andy Lin, *President*
Bill Lin, *Senior VP*
Sean Torsney, *Senior VP*
Shawn O'Farrell, *Vice Pres*
Keeley Pat, *Sales Staff*
EMP: 22 **EST:** 2003
SALES (est): 724K **Privately Held**
WEB: www.visualon.com
SIC: 7372 Prepackaged software

(P-13521)
VIV LABS INC
60 S Market St Ste 900, San Jose (95113-2372)
PHONE..................650 268-9837
Dag Kittlaus, *CEO*
Sangmok Han, *Engineer*

7372 - Prepackaged Software County (P-13522)

EMP: 31 EST: 2012
SALES (est): 2.8MM Privately Held
WEB: www.samsung.com
SIC: 7372 Utility computer software
PA: Samsung Electronics Co., Ltd.
129 Samsung-Ro, Yeongtong-Gu
Suwon 16677

(P-13522)
VMWARE INC (PA)
3401 Hillview Ave, Palo Alto (94304-1383)
PHONE..................650 427-5000
Raghu Raghuram, CEO
Michael Dell, Ch of Bd
Sumit Dhawan, President
Sanjay Poonen, COO
Zane Rowe, CFO
▲ EMP: 18411 EST: 1998
SQ FT: 1,604,769
SALES: 11.7B Publicly Held
WEB: www.vmware.com
SIC: 7372 Prepackaged software

(P-13523)
VNOMIC INC
19925 Stevns Crk Blvd # 100, Cupertino (95014-2384)
PHONE..................408 641-3810
Allen Bannon, CEO
Alle Bannon, CEO
Derek Palma, Vice Pres
EMP: 37 EST: 2009
SALES (est): 2.7MM Privately Held
WEB: www.vnomic.com
SIC: 7372 Business oriented computer software

(P-13524)
WAGGL INC (PA)
1750 Bridgeway Ste B103, Sausalito (94965-1900)
PHONE..................415 399-9949
Michael Papay, CEO
Mila Stoupnikova, Controller
Julia Winn, Marketing Mgr
Allie Behr, Marketing Staff
Alex Kinnebrew, Marketing Staff
EMP: 60 EST: 2014
SALES (est): 6.4MM Privately Held
WEB: www.waggl.com
SIC: 7372 Application computer software

(P-13525)
WATERFALL
25 Division St Ste 205, San Francisco (94103-5234)
P.O. Box 77408 (94107-0408)
PHONE..................866 251-1200
EMP: 19 EST: 2018
SALES (est): 799.9K Privately Held
SIC: 7372 Business oriented computer software

(P-13526)
WEBGILITY INC
575 Market St Ste 1900, San Francisco (94105-2815)
PHONE..................415 640-7906
Parag K Mamnani, CEO
Billy Leung, Senior VP
Bill Gargiulo, Vice Pres
Michael Nisbet, Vice Pres
Shea Shatto, Vice Pres
EMP: 27 EST: 2014
SALES (est): 1.1MM Privately Held
WEB: www.webgility.com
SIC: 7372 Prepackaged software

(P-13527)
WIDE AREA MANAGEMENT SVCS INC
Also Called: W A M S
3226 Scott Blvd, Santa Clara (95054-3007)
PHONE..................408 327-1260
Thomas Shaw, President
Gary Rose, Vice Pres
EMP: 22 EST: 1995
SQ FT: 8,000
SALES (est): 4.7MM Privately Held
SIC: 7372 Prepackaged software
HQ: Fortify Infrastructure Services, Inc.
2340 Walsh Ave Ste A
Santa Clara CA 95051

(P-13528)
WIND RIVER SYSTEMS INC (HQ)
500 Wind River Way, Alameda (94501-1162)
PHONE..................510 748-4100
Kevin Dallas, CEO
Scot Morrision, President
Barry R Mainz, COO
Richard Kraber, CFO
Bryan Leblanc, CFO
EMP: 1035 EST: 1981
SQ FT: 273,000
SALES (est): 575.4MM Privately Held
WEB: www.windriver.com
SIC: 7372 7373 Application computer software; systems software development services

(P-13529)
WIRE US INC
650 Clfornia St Ste 6-129, San Francisco (94108)
PHONE..................415 602-6260
Morten Brogger, CEO
Dylan Riley, Vice Pres
EMP: 15
SALES (est): 305.2K Privately Held
SIC: 7372 Prepackaged software

(P-13530)
WIREX SYSTEMS
100 S Murphy Ave Ste 200, Sunnyvale (94086-6118)
PHONE..................408 799-4498
Tomer Saban, CEO
Ravit Peled, Admin Mgr
EMP: 35 EST: 2015
SALES (est): 2MM Privately Held
WEB: www.wirexsystems.com
SIC: 7372 Prepackaged software

(P-13531)
WORKBOARD INC (PA)
487 Seaport Ct Ste 100, Redwood City (94063-2730)
PHONE..................650 294-4480
Deidre Paknad, CEO
Diedre Paknad, CEO
Karim Damji, CFO
Stuart Crabb, Officer
Mike Hipp, Vice Pres
EMP: 221 EST: 2013
SALES (est): 18.3MM Privately Held
WEB: www.workboard.com
SIC: 7372 Business oriented computer software

(P-13532)
WORKSPOT INC (PA)
1901 S Bascom Ave Ste 900, Campbell (95008-2250)
PHONE..................888 426-8113
Amitabh Sinha, President
Maryam Alexandrian-Adams, COO
Aidan Cullen, CFO
Michele Borovac, Chief Mktg Ofcr
Prasad Krothapalli, Vice Pres
EMP: 27 EST: 2012
SALES (est): 4.4MM Privately Held
WEB: www.workspot.com
SIC: 7372 Business oriented computer software

(P-13533)
XCELMOBILITY INC
2225 E Byshore Rd Ste 200, Palo Alto (94303)
PHONE..................650 320-1728
Zhixiong WEI, Ch of Bd
LI Ouyang, CFO
Ying Yang, Admin Sec
EMP: 98 EST: 2007
SALES (est): 6.4MM Privately Held
WEB: www.xcelmobility.com
SIC: 7372 7999 Business oriented computer software; gambling & lottery services

(P-13534)
XIMAD INC
Also Called: Zimad
21 Airport Blvd Ste B, South San Francisco (94080-6518)
PHONE..................415 222-9909
Dmitry Belotserkovsky, President
Olga Ivanova, Marketing Staff

Oleg Muza, Director
EMP: 40 EST: 2010
SALES (est): 4.7MM Privately Held
WEB: www.zimad.com
SIC: 7372 Application computer software

(P-13535)
XINET LLC (HQ)
2560 9th St Ste 312, Berkeley (94710-2557)
PHONE..................510 845-0555
Scott Seebass, President
EMP: 98 EST: 1991
SQ FT: 9,000
SALES (est): 1.2MM
SALES (corp-wide): 391.6K Privately Held
WEB: www.ignitetech.com
SIC: 7372 7371 Prepackaged software; custom computer programming services
PA: North Plains Systems Corp
510 Front St W
Toronto ON M5V 3
416 345-1900

(P-13536)
XOLVIO LLC
18 Bartol St, San Francisco (94133-4501)
PHONE..................415 857-1317
Sam Hatoum, CEO
EMP: 16 EST: 2015
SALES (est): 858K Privately Held
WEB: www.xolv.io
SIC: 7372 8748 7371 Prepackaged software; business consulting; custom computer programming services; software programming applications

(P-13537)
XPANSIV DATA SYSTEMS INC
3041 Fulton St, Berkeley (94705-1804)
PHONE..................415 915-5124
Joe Madden, CEO
John Melby, President
Michael Burstein, CFO
Ben McAllister, Vice Pres
Sarah McGee, Vice Pres
EMP: 49 EST: 2016
SALES (est): 5.4MM Privately Held
WEB: www.xpansiv.com
SIC: 7372 Prepackaged software
PA: Xpansiv Limited
Suite 2 Level 8 28-34 O'connell Street
Sydney NSW 2000

(P-13538)
YERTLEWORKS LLC
5470 Great America Pkwy, Santa Clara (95054-3644)
PHONE..................408 916-4121
Robert Bearden, Ch of Bd
EMP: 22 EST: 2012
SALES (est): 593.8K
SALES (corp-wide): 869.2MM Privately Held
WEB: www.cloudera.com
SIC: 7372 Prepackaged software
HQ: Hortonworks, Inc.
5470 Great America Pkwy
Santa Clara CA 95054

(P-13539)
YOURPEOPLE INC
Also Called: Zenefits
50 Beale St, San Francisco (94105-1813)
PHONE..................888 249-3263
Parker Conrad, CEO
Erin Case, Partner
Lauren Perales, Partner
Avinash Anand, President
David Sacks, CEO
EMP: 700 EST: 2004
SALES (est): 158.4MM Privately Held
WEB: www.zenefits.com
SIC: 7372 8741 6411 Business oriented computer software; administrative management; insurance brokers

(P-13540)
YUJA INC
84 W Santa Clara St # 690, San Jose (95113-1809)
PHONE..................888 257-2278
Ajit Singh, President

Nannette Don, Sales Staff
James Zhang, Director
Kline Boudreau, Manager
Boudreau Kline, Manager
EMP: 125 EST: 2013
SALES (est): 11.1MM Privately Held
WEB: www.yuja.com
SIC: 7372 Prepackaged software

(P-13541)
ZENTERA SYSTEMS INC
97 E Brokaw Rd Ste 360, San Jose (95112-1031)
PHONE..................408 436-4811
Jaushin Lee, CEO
Mike Ichiriu, Vice Pres
John Michaels, Executive
Belinda Shih, Office Mgr
EMP: 16 EST: 2012
SQ FT: 2,834
SALES (est): 1.7MM Privately Held
WEB: www.zentera.net
SIC: 7372 Business oriented computer software

(P-13542)
ZIRA GROUP INC
400 Concar Dr, San Mateo (94402-2681)
PHONE..................650 701-7026
EMP: 27
SALES (est): 72K Privately Held
WEB: www.lightapp.com
SIC: 7372 Prepackaged Software Services
PA: Lightapp Technologies Ltd
144 Alon Yigal
Tel Aviv-Jaffa 67443

(P-13543)
ZOOMIFIER CORPORATION (PA)
5776 Stnrdge Mall Rd Ste, Pleasanton (94588)
PHONE..................800 255-5303
Chetan Saiya, CEO
Hina Saiya, Controller
EMP: 424 EST: 2011
SALES (est): 13.6MM Privately Held
WEB: www.zoomifier.com
SIC: 7372 Business oriented computer software

(P-13544)
ZUORA INC (PA)
101 Redwood Shores Pkwy # 100, Redwood City (94065-6131)
PHONE..................800 425-1281
Tien Tzuo, Ch of Bd
Sunil Khurana, Partner
Marc Diouane, President
Tyler R Sloat, CFO
Tom Krackeler, Ch Credit Ofcr
EMP: 300 EST: 2007
SQ FT: 100,000
SALES: 305.4MM Publicly Held
WEB: www.zuora.com
SIC: 7372 Business oriented computer software

(P-13545)
ZYRION INC
440 N Wolfe Rd, Sunnyvale (94085-3869)
PHONE..................408 524-7424
EMP: 75
SQ FT: 6,000
SALES (est): 4.7MM Privately Held
SIC: 7372 Computer Software Development
PA: Kaseya Global Ireland Limited
Commerzbank House
Dublin

7373 Computer Integrated Systems Design

(P-13546)
1000 SANSOME ASSOCIATES LLC
Also Called: Cibo
1000 Sansome St Ste 200, San Francisco (94111-1346)
PHONE..................415 233-8357
Lou Lacourte, CEO
Jim Magill, Partner

PRODUCTS & SERVICES SECTION
7373 - Computer Integrated Systems Design County (P-13567)

Peter Sapienza, *Partner*
Bob Skubic, *Officer*
Warner Witt, *Info Tech Dir*
EMP: 36 **EST:** 2010
SQ FT: 8,000
SALES (est): 3.6MM **Privately Held**
WEB: www.ciboglobal.com
SIC: 7373 7311 8742 Computer integrated systems design; computer systems analysis & design; advertising agencies; new products & services consultants

(P-13547)
10UP INC (PA)
2765 Carradale Dr, Roseville (95661-4089)
PHONE 888 571-7130
Jacob Goldman, *Owner*
Vasken Hauri, *Vice Pres*
Taylor Lovett, *Vice Pres*
Ricky L Whittemore, *Associate Dir*
Katie Wilkerson, *Associate Dir*
EMP: 94 **EST:** 2012
SQ FT: 1,300
SALES (est): 6.3MM **Privately Held**
WEB: www.10up.com
SIC: 7373 Systems software development services

(P-13548)
AAE SYSTEMS INC
5150 El Cmino Real Ste B3, Los Altos (94022)
P.O. Box 1088 (94023-1088)
PHONE 408 732-1710
Javed Husain, *President*
Jim Knecht, *IT/INT Sup*
Lidia Ivorra, *Manager*
EMP: 15 **EST:** 1984
SALES (est): 2.4MM **Privately Held**
WEB: www.aaesys.com
SIC: 7373 3663 Turnkey vendors, computer systems; radio & TV communications equipment

(P-13549)
ACTIVEVIDEO NETWORKS LLC (DH)
333 W San Carlos St # 90, San Jose (95110-2726)
PHONE 408 931-9200
Jeff Miller, *President*
Sangita Verma, *President*
Chris Linden, *COO*
Matt Andrade, *CFO*
Greg Brown, *Vice Pres*
EMP: 75 **EST:** 1988
SALES (est): 11.5MM **Publicly Held**
WEB: www.activevideo.com
SIC: 7373 Computer integrated systems design

(P-13550)
ACUMEN LLC
Also Called: Medric
500 Airport Blvd Ste 100, Burlingame (94010-1980)
PHONE 650 558-8882
Thomas Macurdy, *Mng Member*
Dale Ragone, *Managing Prtnr*
David Barnes, *Administration*
Kelly Macurdy, *Administration*
Nick Rose, *Administration*
EMP: 166 **EST:** 1996
SALES (est): 21.2MM **Privately Held**
WEB: www.acumenllc.com
SIC: 7373 7379 8742 Systems software development services; computer related consulting services; data processing consultant; management consulting services; administrative services consultant

(P-13551)
AEROHIVE NETWORKS INC (HQ)
1011 Mccarthy Blvd, Milpitas (95035-7920)
PHONE 408 510-6100
Ed Meyercord, *President*
John Payne, *Bd of Directors*
Conway Rulon-Miller, *Bd of Directors*
Christopher Schaepe, *Bd of Directors*
Alan Amrod, *Vice Pres*
▲ **EMP:** 528 **EST:** 2006

SALES: 154.9MM **Publicly Held**
WEB: www.extremenetworks.com
SIC: 7373 Computer integrated systems design

(P-13552)
AMSNET INC (PA)
502 Commerce Way, Livermore (94551-7812)
PHONE 925 245-6100
Robert Tocci, *CEO*
Diana Monaghan, *Executive*
Joe Moomau, *Admin Sec*
Mary Johnson, *Accountant*
Angela Amaral, *Personnel Assit*
EMP: 50
SQ FT: 15,000
SALES: 69.5MM **Privately Held**
WEB: www.ams.net
SIC: 7373 1731 7378 Systems integration services; computer installation; computer maintenance & repair

(P-13553)
APTTUS CORPORATION (PA)
1840 Gateway Dr Ste 300, San Mateo (94404-4030)
PHONE 650 445-7700
Frank Holland, *CEO*
Carlos Enriquez, *Partner*
Charles Mackenna, *Partner*
Shailesh Powdwal, *Partner*
David Murphy, *Ch of Bd*
EMP: 716 **EST:** 2012
SALES (est): 172.4MM **Privately Held**
WEB: www.conga.com
SIC: 7373 Systems software development services

(P-13554)
ARYAKA NETWORKS INC (PA)
1850 Gateway Dr Ste 500, San Mateo (94404-4064)
PHONE 888 692-7925
Matthew Carter, *CEO*
Aidan Cullen, *CFO*
Brad Kinnish, *CFO*
Karen Freitag, *Officer*
Olen Scott, *Senior VP*
EMP: 374 **EST:** 2008
SALES (est): 78.1MM **Privately Held**
WEB: www.aryaka.com
SIC: 7373 8748 Systems software development services; telecommunications consultant

(P-13555)
ASA COMPUTERS INC
48761 Kato Rd, Fremont (94538-7313)
PHONE 650 230-8000
Arvind Bhargava, *President*
Chris Terry, *President*
Umesh Bhargava, *Vice Pres*
Anu Bhargava, *VP Finance*
Kamal Madhani, *Controller*
▲ **EMP:** 45 **EST:** 1989
SQ FT: 7,000
SALES (est): 23.5MM **Privately Held**
WEB: www.asacomputers.com
SIC: 7373 5045 5734 Systems integration services; computers, peripherals & software; computer & software stores

(P-13556)
ASD GLOBAL INC
1371 Oakland Blvd Ste 100, Walnut Creek (94596-8407)
PHONE 925 975-0690
James Eccleston, *President*
Manu Chatterjee, *Ch of Bd*
Shikha Chatterjee, *Vice Pres*
Salig Chada, *VP Bus Dvlpt*
Arun Varma, *Engineer*
EMP: 36 **EST:** 2001
SQ FT: 1,800
SALES (est): 377.6K **Privately Held**
WEB: www.asdglobal.com
SIC: 7373 Computer integrated systems design

(P-13557)
ATAC (PA)
2770 De La Cruz Blvd, Santa Clara (95050-2624)
PHONE 408 736-2822
Mark Cochran, *Chairman*

Scott Simcox, *President*
Charles Winkleman, *CFO*
Joe A Isaacs, *Vice Pres*
Jason Bertino, *Program Mgr*
EMP: 65 **EST:** 1979
SQ FT: 31,000
SALES: 23.4MM **Privately Held**
WEB: www.atac.com
SIC: 7373 7376 7379 8711 Computer integrated systems design; computer facilities management; computer related maintenance services; engineering services; physical research, noncommercial

(P-13558)
AZUGA INC (DH)
42840 Christy St Ste 205, Fremont (94538-3154)
PHONE 888 790-0715
Anan Rani, *CEO*
Subash Gopalkrishnan, *CFO*
Subash Gopalkrishnan, *CFO*
Nate Bryer, *Vice Pres*
Scott Clymer, *Vice Pres*
▲ **EMP:** 361 **EST:** 2012
SQ FT: 1,800 **Privately Held**
WEB: www.azuga.com
SIC: 7373 Computer integrated systems design
HQ: Bridgestone Americas, Inc.
    200 4th Ave S Ste 100
    Nashville TN 37201
    615 937-1000

(P-13559)
BACKBONE SOFTWARE INC
490 43rd St Unit 132, Oakland (94609-2138)
PHONE 415 993-2468
Rajesh Chandran, *CEO*
EMP: 40 **EST:** 2018
SALES (est): 963.8K **Privately Held**
SIC: 7373 Systems software development services

(P-13560)
BAY SYSTEMS CONSULTING INC (PA)
3600 W Byshore Rd Ste 204, Palo Alto (94303)
PHONE 650 960-3310
Jasmine Ali, *President*
Asim Mughal, *Vice Pres*
Sam Mughal, *Vice Pres*
Doug Zipzer, *Vice Pres*
Harold Harvey, *Director*
EMP: 35 **EST:** 1997
SQ FT: 1,400
SALES (est): 7.1MM **Privately Held**
WEB: www.baysystemsinc.com
SIC: 7373 Systems integration services

(P-13561)
BEEZY INC (PA)
548 Market St 76279, San Francisco (94104-5401)
PHONE 510 567-7110
Jordi Plana, *President*
Yvonne Sandner, *CFO*
Mike Hicks, *Chief Mktg Ofcr*
Matt Moalem, *Vice Pres*
Rahil Jivani, *Principal*
EMP: 72 **EST:** 2013
SALES (est): 500K **Privately Held**
WEB: www.beezy.net
SIC: 7373 Systems software development services

(P-13562)
CADENT INC
Also Called: Orthocad
2560 Orchard Pkwy, San Jose (95131-1033)
PHONE 408 470-1000
Timothy Mack, *President*
Roger Blanchette, *CFO*
▲ **EMP:** 130 **EST:** 1999
SQ FT: 24,000
SALES (est): 12.4MM
SALES (corp-wide): 2.4B **Publicly Held**
WEB: www.itero.com
SIC: 7373 Computer systems analysis & design

HQ: Cadent Holdings, Inc.
    2560 Orchard Pkwy
    San Jose CA

(P-13563)
CALSOFT LABS INC (HQ)
Also Called: Acl Digital
2890 Zanker Rd Ste 200, San Jose (95134-2118)
PHONE 408 755-3000
Ramandeep Singh, *CEO*
Dirk Leifer, *Managing Prtnr*
SAI Satyam, *CFO*
Rajat Sethi, *Assoc VP*
Paul Elisii, *Vice Pres*
EMP: 158 **EST:** 2011
SALES (est): 26.3MM
SALES (corp-wide): 603.3MM **Privately Held**
WEB: www.acldigital.com
SIC: 7373 Systems software development services
PA: Alten
    40 Avenue Andre Morizet
    Boulogne Billancourt 92100
    146 056-673

(P-13564)
CAYLYM TECHNOLOGIES INTL LLC
Also Called: Caylym Holdings
5340 E Home Ave, Fresno (93727-2104)
PHONE 209 322-9596
John Kim, *Exec Dir*
Janis Ringheiser, *Human Resources*
Garrett Miller, *Sales Staff*
Jim Wilson, *Government*
Michael Phillips, *Legal Staff*
EMP: 21 **EST:** 2009
SQ FT: 2,000
SALES (est): 2.8MM **Privately Held**
WEB: www.caylym.com
SIC: 7373 0851 2653 Computer systems analysis & design; fire fighting services, forest; boxes, corrugated: made from purchased materials; pallets, corrugated: made from purchased materials

(P-13565)
CELESTIX NETWORKS INC
4125 Hopyard Rd Ste 225, Pleasanton (94588-8534)
P.O. Box 255, San Ramon (94583-0255)
PHONE 510 668-0700
Yong Thye Lin, *CEO*
Gabriele Sartori, *CTO*
Bobby Chen, *Finance Dir*
Yong Ping Lin, *Director*
▲ **EMP:** 70 **EST:** 1999
SQ FT: 9,000
SALES (est): 10.8MM **Privately Held**
WEB: www.celestix.com
SIC: 7373 Systems software development services; systems engineering, computer related; systems integration services; local area network (LAN) systems integrator
PA: Celestix Networks Pte Ltd
    62 Ubi Road 1
    Singapore 40873

(P-13566)
CEREBRAS SYSTEMS INC
1237 E Arques Ave, Sunnyvale (94085-4701)
PHONE 650 933-4980
Andrew Feldman, *CEO*
Michael James, *CFO*
Rebecca Boyden, *Vice Pres*
Dhiraj Mallick, *Vice Pres*
Gary Lauterbach, *Admin Sec*
EMP: 150 **EST:** 2016
SALES (est): 16MM **Privately Held**
WEB: www.cerebras.net
SIC: 7373 7389 Systems software development services;

(P-13567)
CHOUINARD & MYHRE INC
655 Redwood Hwy Frontage # 102, Mill Valley (94941-3034)
PHONE 415 480-3636
Steve Giondomenica, *President*
Peter Bussi, *COO*

7373 - Computer Integrated Systems Design County (P-13568)

John Wondolowski, *CTO*
Ken Slaugh, *Technology*
Vanessa Nudd, *Manager*
EMP: 30 **EST:** 1976
SQ FT: 4,000
SALES (est): 8.1MM **Privately Held**
WEB: www.solutions-ii.com
SIC: 7373 7371 7372 Value-added resellers, computer systems; computer software development; prepackaged software
PA: Solutions-Ii, Inc.
8822 Ridgeline Blvd # 250
Highlands Ranch CO 80129

(P-13568)
CLOUDIAN INC
177 Bovet Rd Ste 450, San Mateo (94402-3119)
PHONE 650 227-2380
Michael TSO, *CEO*
Grant Jacobson, *Partner*
Michael Morgan, *CFO*
Jon Toor, *Chief Mktg Ofcr*
Paul Turner, *Chief Mktg Ofcr*
EMP: 38 **EST:** 2001
SALES (est): 10.2MM **Privately Held**
WEB: www.cloudian.com
SIC: 7373 Systems software development services
PA: Cloudian K.K.
2-11-6, Shibuya
Shibuya-Ku TKY 150-0

(P-13569)
CNET NETWORKS INC
235 2nd St, San Francisco (94105-3100)
PHONE 415 344-2000
Mehdi Maghsoodnia, *Bd of Directors*
David Bricker, *Partner*
Debbie Andrews, *Vice Pres*
Eric Schuldt, *Vice Pres*
James Symington, *Vice Pres*
EMP: 620
SALES (est): 21MM
SALES (corp-wide): 25.3B **Publicly Held**
WEB: www.cnet.com
SIC: 7373 7371 Systems software development services; computer software development & applications
HQ: Cbs Interactive Inc.
235 2nd St
San Francisco CA 94105

(P-13570)
COGNIX AUTOMATION INC
4900 Hopyard Rd Ste 100, Pleasanton (94588-7101)
PHONE 925 464-8822
Prasad Dasari, *President*
EMP: 50 **EST:** 2017
SALES (est): 1.6MM **Privately Held**
SIC: 7373 Office computer automation systems integration

(P-13571)
COMGLOBAL SYSTEMS INC (DH)
1315 Dell Ave, Campbell (95008-6609)
PHONE 619 321-6000
Fax: 408 374-5209
EMP: 68
SQ FT: 600
SALES (est): 14.9MM
SALES (corp-wide): 335.6MM **Privately Held**
WEB: www.comglobal.com
SIC: 7373 Computer Systems Design
HQ: Analex Corporation
11091 Sunset Hills Rd # 200
Reston VA 20171
703 956-8243

(P-13572)
CONDUENT STATE LCAL SLTONS INC
455 The Embarcadero # 103, San Francisco (94111-2023)
PHONE 415 486-2409
Marilyn Malakowsky, *Manager*
Craig Moore, *Manager*
EMP: 940
SALES (corp-wide): 4.1B **Publicly Held**
SIC: 7373 7379 Computer integrated systems design;
HQ: Conduent State & Local Solutions, Inc.
12410 Milestone Center Dr
Germantown MD 20876
301 820-4200

(P-13573)
CONTENT GURU INC
900 E Hamilton Ave # 510, Campbell (95008-0664)
PHONE 408 559-3988
Sean Taylor, *President*
EMP: 300 **EST:** 2005
SALES (est): 21.8MM
SALES (corp-wide): 52.2MM **Privately Held**
WEB: www.contentguru.com
SIC: 7373 Computer integrated systems design
PA: Redwood Technologies Group Ltd
Radius Court
Bracknell BERKS RG12
134 485-2350

(P-13574)
DARKTRACE INC (PA)
555 Mission St Ste 3225, San Francisco (94105-0946)
PHONE 415 229-9100
Nicole Eagan, *Officer*
Cathy Graham, *CFO*
Karina Alves, *Executive*
Holly Biegel, *Executive*
Hanna Bixler, *Executive*
EMP: 81 **EST:** 2016
SALES (est): 8.8MM **Privately Held**
WEB: www.darktrace.com
SIC: 7373 Computer integrated systems design

(P-13575)
DATA DOMAIN LLC
2421 Mission College Blvd, Santa Clara (95054-1214)
PHONE 408 980-4800
Frank Slootman, *President*
Michael P Scarpelli, *CFO*
Nick Bacica, *Senior VP*
Daniel R McGee, *Senior VP*
David L Schneider, *Senior VP*
EMP: 777 **EST:** 2001
SQ FT: 200,000
SALES (est): 79.8MM **Publicly Held**
WEB: www.delltechnologies.com
SIC: 7373 Computer integrated systems design
HQ: Emc Corporation
176 South St
Hopkinton MA 01748
508 435-1000

(P-13576)
DELEGATA CORPORATION
2450 Venture Oaks Way # 40, Sacramento (95833-3292)
PHONE 916 609-5400
Kais Menoufy, *President*
Moataz Hussein, *Opers Staff*
Romy Haddad, *Marketing Mgr*
Kevin Malone, *Chief*
Bob Martinez, *Director*
EMP: 100 **EST:** 2000
SQ FT: 5,000
SALES (est): 6.3MM **Privately Held**
WEB: www.delegata.com
SIC: 7373 Computer integrated systems design

(P-13577)
DIGITALIST USA LTD
611 Gateway Blvd Ste 120, South San Francisco (94080-7066)
PHONE 949 278-1354
Jo Javier, *Vice Pres*
EMP: 1000 **EST:** 2010
SALES (est): 41.5MM **Privately Held**
WEB: www.digitalist.global
SIC: 7373 8731 Systems software development services; computer (hardware) development
PA: Digitalist Group Oyj
Pohjoisesplanadi 35a
Helsinki 00100

(P-13578)
DILIGENTE TECHNOLOGIES LLC
2350 Mission College Blvd, Santa Clara (95054-1532)
PHONE 510 304-0852
Rohita Joshi, *Mng Member*
Diana Caldera, *Accounts Mgr*
Deeksha Marwaha, *Accounts Mgr*
EMP: 500 **EST:** 2010
SALES (est): 19.5MM **Privately Held**
WEB: www.diligentetechnologies.com
SIC: 7373 7379 Computer integrated systems design; systems software development services; computer related maintenance services

(P-13579)
DROISYS INC (PA)
46540 Fremont Blvd # 516, Fremont (94538-6487)
PHONE 408 874-8333
Sanjiv Goyal, *President*
Kelman Dow, *Managing Prtnr*
Rahul Agarwal, *Vice Pres*
Archit Rathore, *General Mgr*
George Swapn, *General Mgr*
EMP: 333 **EST:** 2003
SQ FT: 3,374
SALES (est): 15.5MM **Privately Held**
WEB: www.droisys.com
SIC: 7373 7371 7379 Systems software development services; systems integration services; custom computer programming services; computer software writing services; computer related consulting services

(P-13580)
EERO LLC
660 3rd St Fl 4, San Francisco (94107-1921)
PHONE 415 738-7972
Nicholas Weaver, *CEO*
Justin Chien, *Mfg Staff*
Zoz Cuccias, *Corp Comm Staff*
EMP: 40 **EST:** 2014
SALES (est): 5.9MM **Publicly Held**
WEB: www.eero.com
SIC: 7373 3669 5731 Computer integrated systems design; intercommunication systems, electric; consumer electronic equipment
PA: Amazon.Com, Inc.
410 Terry Ave N
Seattle WA 98109

(P-13581)
ELEMENT ANALYTICS INC
564 Market St Ste 316, San Francisco (94104-5407)
PHONE 415 483-0310
EMP: 36
SALES (est): 799.8K **Privately Held**
WEB: www.elementanalytics.com
SIC: 7373 Computer Integrated Systems Design, Nsk

(P-13582)
EMR CPR LLC
32970 Alvarado Niles Rd # 736, Union City (94587-3194)
PHONE 408 471-6804
Edward Ohara, *CEO*
David Ohara, *COO*
David O 'hara, *Officer*
Mohammed Najjar, *IT/INT Sup*
Luis Vega, *Manager*
EMP: 412 **EST:** 2012
SALES (est): 25.6MM **Privately Held**
WEB: www.emrcpr.com
SIC: 7373 7374 Systems engineering, computer related; systems integration services; local area network (LAN) systems integrator; data entry service; data verification service

(P-13583)
ENQUERO INC
Also Called: Enquero, A Genpact Company
1551 Mccarthy Blvd # 207, Milpitas (95035-7437)
PHONE 408 406-3203
Arvinder Pal Singh, *CEO*
Krishna Chidambaram, *Partner*
Nishant Puri, *Partner*
Hemant Asher, *CFO*
Snigdha Priyadarshini, *CIO*
EMP: 80 **EST:** 2014
SALES (est): 1.9MM **Privately Held**
WEB: www.enquero.com
SIC: 7373 7379 Systems software development services;
HQ: Genpact Llc
1155 Ave Of The Amrcas Fl
New York NY 10036
212 896-6600

(P-13584)
EPSON RESEARCH AND DEV INC (DH)
214 Devcon Dr, San Jose (95112-4210)
PHONE 408 952-6000
Eishi Momosaki, *President*
Katsuhiko Baba, *CFO*
Kai-Ping Yin, *Senior VP*
EMP: 62 **EST:** 1997
SALES (est): 1.9MM **Privately Held**
WEB: www.epson.com
SIC: 7373 Computer integrated systems design

(P-13585)
EVERFLOW TECHNOLOGIES INC
530 Showers Dr Ste 7-302, Mountain View (94040-4740)
PHONE 408 479-9405
Sam Darawish, *Principal*
Olga Sadkova, *Vice Pres*
Curt Frieden, *VP Bus Dvlpt*
Drew Johnson, *Executive*
Jonathan Blais, *Principal*
EMP: 40 **EST:** 2016
SALES (est): 2.7MM **Privately Held**
WEB: www.everflow.io
SIC: 7373 Systems software development services

(P-13586)
EXCELFORE CORPORATION (PA)
39650 Liberty St Ste 255, Fremont (94538-2283)
PHONE 510 868-2500
Shrinath Acharya, *CEO*
Balakrishnan Anoop, *Vice Pres*
Anoop Balakrishnan, *Vice Pres*
Richard Barnes, *Vice Pres*
Shiro Ninomiya, *Senior Engr*
EMP: 48 **EST:** 2008
SALES (est): 7.9MM **Privately Held**
WEB: www.excelfore.com
SIC: 7373 Systems software development services

(P-13587)
EXPERIAN HEALTH INC
2233 Watt Ave Ste 275, Sacramento (95825-0570)
PHONE 415 716-6633
Milton Boyd, *Branch Mgr*
Denise Svetich, *Business Anlyst*
Spiro Kalapodis, *Director*
EMP: 86
SALES (corp-wide): 5.3B **Privately Held**
SIC: 7373 Computer integrated systems design
HQ: Experian Health, Inc.
720 Cool Springs Blvd # 200
Franklin TN 37067

(P-13588)
FINSIX CORPORATION
3565 Haven Ave Ste 1, Menlo Park (94025-1065)
P.O. Box 2224 (94026-2224)
PHONE 650 285-6400
Vanessa Green, *CEO*
David Schaezler, *CFO*
Joseph Scarci, *Vice Pres*
Kathyrn Gerrish, *Office Mgr*
Garet Gamache, *Electrical Engi*
EMP: 30 **EST:** 2010
SALES (est): 4.1MM **Privately Held**
WEB: www.finsix.com
SIC: 7373 3679 8731 Systems integration services; electronic loads & power supplies; electronic research

PRODUCTS & SERVICES SECTION
7373 - Computer Integrated Systems Design County (P-13610)

(P-13589)
FIREEYE INTERNATIONAL LLC (HQ)
601 Mccarthy Blvd, Milpitas (95035-7932)
PHONE.................................408 321-6300
EMP: 55 EST: 2011
SALES (est): 986.5K Publicly Held
WEB: www.fireeye.com
SIC: 7373 Computer integrated systems design

(P-13590)
FORCE10 NETWORKS GLOBAL INC
Also Called: Dell
350 Holger Way, San Jose (95134-1362)
PHONE.................................800 289-3355
Michael Dell, CEO
James Hanley, President
Luu Nguyen, President
Sachi Sambandan, President
Robert Tatnall, President
▲ EMP: 582
SQ FT: 97,000
SALES (est): 65.1MM Publicly Held
WEB: www.force10networks.com
SIC: 7373 Computer integrated systems design
HQ: Dell Inc.
    1 Dell Way
    Round Rock TX 78682
    800 289-3355

(P-13591)
FORMAC INC
3155 Kearney St Ste 210, Fremont (94538-2268)
PHONE.................................510 379-9027
Ram Danda, President
Praveen Maddipatla, Vice Pres
Prasha Ganga, Manager
EMP: 148 EST: 2013
SQ FT: 1,500
SALES (est): 16.3MM Privately Held
WEB: www.formacinc.com
SIC: 7373 7372 Systems engineering, computer related; business oriented computer software

(P-13592)
FRANCISCO PARTNERS GP III LP (HQ)
Also Called: FP
1 Letterman Dr Bldg C, San Francisco (94129-2402)
PHONE.................................415 418-2900
Dipanjan Deb, Managing Prtnr
Chris Adams, Partner
Ben Ball, Partner
Peter Christodoulo, Partner
Neil Garfinkel, Partner
EMP: 60 EST: 2000
SALES (est): 105.4MM
SALES (corp-wide): 2.6B Privately Held
WEB: www.franciscopartners.com
SIC: 7373 7372 Systems integration services; prepackaged software
PA: Francisco Partners Management, L.P.
    1 Letterman Dr Ste 410
    San Francisco CA 94129
    415 418-2900

(P-13593)
FUJITSU COMPUTER PDTS AMER INC (HQ)
1250 E Arques Ave, Sunnyvale (94085-5401)
PHONE.................................800 626-4686
Etsuro Sato, President
Victor Kan, COO
Motoyasu Matsuzaki, CFO
Scott Francis, Vice Pres
Glenn Wood, Vice Pres
▲ EMP: 340 EST: 1991
SQ FT: 75,335
SALES (est): 68.4MM Privately Held
WEB: www.scanners.us.fujitsu.com
SIC: 7373 Computer integrated systems design

(P-13594)
FUJITSU CONSULTING (CANADA) (PA)
1250 E Arques Ave, Sunnyvale (94085-5401)
PHONE.................................732 549-4100
Richard Deranleau, CEO
Hitoshi Matsumoto, VP Bus Dvlpt
Anthony Doye, Principal
EMP: 166 EST: 2001
SALES (est): 3.1MM Privately Held
SIC: 7373 Systems integration services

(P-13595)
FUJITSU CONSULTING LLC (DH)
1250 E Arques Ave, Sunnyvale (94085-5401)
PHONE.................................408 746-6000
Anthony Doye, CEO
Hemchand Basva, Executive
EMP: 51 EST: 2000
SALES (est): 4.6MM Privately Held
WEB: www.fujitsu.com
SIC: 7373 Systems integration services
HQ: Fujitsu America Inc
    2821 Telecom Pkwy
    Richardson TX 75082
    408 746-6000

(P-13596)
FUJITSU RETIREMENT MGT INC (DH)
1250 E Arques Ave, Sunnyvale (94085-5401)
PHONE.................................408 746-6000
Anthony Doye, CEO
Josh Napua, Vice Pres
EMP: 370 EST: 1977
SALES (est): 1MM Privately Held
WEB: www.fujitsu.com
SIC: 7373 Systems integration services
HQ: Fujitsu America Inc
    2821 Telecom Pkwy
    Richardson TX 75082
    408 746-6000

(P-13597)
GLODYNE TECHNOSERVE INC (PA)
2700 Augustine Dr Ste 190, Santa Clara (95054)
PHONE.................................408 340-5017
Annand Sarnaaik, Principal
Haneef Sheikh, President
EMP: 1438 EST: 2006
SALES (est): 30.2MM Privately Held
SIC: 7373 Computer integrated systems design

(P-13598)
GLUWARE INC (PA)
Also Called: Glue Networks Group
2020 L St Ste 130, Sacramento (95811-4260)
PHONE.................................916 877-8224
Jeff Gray, CEO
Hamish Butler, COO
Matthew Dittoe, Senior VP
Alan Grahame, Vice Pres
Patrick Milo, Creative Dir
EMP: 40 EST: 2007
SQ FT: 4,000
SALES (est): 4.6MM Privately Held
WEB: www.gluware.com
SIC: 7373 Systems software development services

(P-13599)
GOBIG INC
3185 Kipling St, Palo Alto (94306-3009)
PHONE.................................415 513-3029
Joachim Klein, COO
EMP: 50 EST: 2018
SALES (est): 902.6K Privately Held
SIC: 7373 Systems software development services

(P-13600)
GRAMMARLY INC (PA)
548 Market St Ste 35410, San Francisco (94104-5401)
PHONE.................................888 318-6146
Brad Hoover, CEO
Andy Chen, CFO
Valerie Bass, Executive
Woodrow Lin, Principal
Dorian Stone, General Mgr
EMP: 227 EST: 2009
SQ FT: 9,000
SALES (est): 66.4MM Privately Held
WEB: www.grammarly.com
SIC: 7373 8299 Systems software development services; educational services

(P-13601)
GRIDBRIGHT INC
618 Oakshire Pl, Alamo (94507-2326)
P.O. Box 830 (94507-0830)
PHONE.................................925 899-9025
Alireza Vojdani, CEO
Stephen Callahan, Senior VP
Tom Servas, Vice Pres
Travis Rouillard, CTO
David Razavi, Engineer
EMP: 18 EST: 2013
SALES (est): 1.4MM Privately Held
WEB: www.gridbright.com
SIC: 7373 7372 7371 8711 Computer integrated systems design; prepackaged software; custom computer programming services; engineering services

(P-13602)
GROUPWARE TECHNOLOGY INC (DH)
541 Division St, Campbell (95008-6905)
PHONE.................................408 540-0090
Mike Thompson, CEO
Scott Sutter, Officer
Josh Avila, Vice Pres
John Barnes, Vice Pres
Samara Halterman, Vice Pres
EMP: 50 EST: 1992
SQ FT: 14,000
SALES (est): 167.7MM
SALES (corp-wide): 212.5MM Privately Held
WEB: www.trace3.com
SIC: 7373 5045 Computer-aided system services; computers, peripherals & software; computer software
HQ: Trace3, Llc
    7565 Irvine Center Dr # 20
    Irvine CA 92618
    949 333-2300

(P-13603)
HANDS-ON MOBILE INC (PA)
208 Utah St Ste 300, San Francisco (94103-4890)
PHONE.................................415 580-6400
Jonathan Sacks, CEO
Dan Kranzler, Ch of Bd
Dave Arnold, President
Niccolo De Masi, President
Kevin Dent, President
EMP: 50 EST: 2001
SALES (est): 29.5MM Privately Held
WEB: www.handsonbayarea.org
SIC: 7373 Computer system selling services

(P-13604)
HARMAN CNNCTED SVCS HOLDG CORP (DH)
636 Ellis St, Mountain View (94043-2207)
PHONE.................................650 623-9400
Sanjay Dhawan, President
Luigi Sanna, President
Pradeep Chaudhry, CFO
Kapil Arora, Assoc VP
Subash A K RAO, Exec VP
EMP: 1821 EST: 2012
SALES (est): 35.5MM Privately Held
WEB: www.services.harman.com
SIC: 7373 Systems software development services
HQ: Harman International Industries Incorporated
    400 Atlantic St
    Stamford CT 06901
    203 328-3500

(P-13605)
HARMAN CONNECTED SERVICES INC (DH)
636 Ellis St, Mountain View (94043-2207)
PHONE.................................650 623-9400
Sanjay Dhawan, President
Supreetha Agnes, Manager
Raghunath Puthanveetil, Manager
Sylwia Salek, Manager
Sunistha Singh, Manager
EMP: 50 EST: 2002
SALES (est): 34.3MM Privately Held
WEB: www.services.harman.com
SIC: 7373 Systems software development services
HQ: Harman Connected Services Holding Corp.
    636 Ellis St
    Mountain View CA 94043
    650 623-9400

(P-13606)
HASURA INC
355 Bryant St Unit 403, San Francisco (94107-4143)
PHONE.................................833 690-2124
Tanmai Gopal, CEO
EMP: 43 EST: 2019
SALES (est): 2.7MM Privately Held
SIC: 7373 Systems software development services

(P-13607)
HEARTFLOW INC (PA)
1400 Seaport Blvd Bldg B, Redwood City (94063-5594)
PHONE.................................650 241-1221
Dana G Mead Jr, President
Yoshiki Kawabata, President
Baird Radford, CFO
John Stevens, Chairman
Michael Buck, Ch Credit Ofcr
EMP: 69 EST: 2007
SQ FT: 3,400
SALES (est): 22.8MM Privately Held
WEB: www.heartflow.com
SIC: 7373 Systems software development services

(P-13608)
HID GLOBAL SAFE INC
6607 Kaiser Dr, Fremont (94555-3608)
PHONE.................................408 453-1008
Stefan Widing, CEO
Rodney Glass, COO
Laura Crumbley, CFO
Neena Jain, Program Mgr
Jane Lee, Program Mgr
EMP: 55 EST: 2005
SALES (est): 14.6MM
SALES (corp-wide): 10.1B Privately Held
WEB: www.hidglobal.com
SIC: 7373 7371 Systems software development services; computer software development & applications
HQ: Hid Global Corporation
    611 Center Ridge Dr
    Austin TX 78753

(P-13609)
HSQ TECHNOLOGY A CORPORATION
26227 Research Pl, Hayward (94545-3725)
PHONE.................................510 259-1334
Harold K Spence, President
Clarence Weber, Vice Pres
James Wilkinson, Vice Pres
Vasile Papadopol, Software Engr
Brad Needham, Project Mgr
EMP: 44 EST: 1979
SQ FT: 25,000
SALES (est): 13.5MM
SALES (corp-wide): 3B Privately Held
WEB: www.hsq.com
SIC: 7373 Turnkey vendors, computer systems
HQ: Railworks Transit Systems, Inc.
    5 Penn Plz
    New York NY 10001

(P-13610)
INDUSYS TECHNOLOGY INC
210 Baypointe Pkwy, San Jose (95134-1621)
PHONE.................................408 321-2888
Tony Lau, President
Chien Yuan Ku, CFO
EMP: 40 EST: 1989
SQ FT: 67,000

7373 - Computer Integrated Systems Design County (P-13611)

SALES (est): 4.2MM **Privately Held**
WEB: www.itiworldwide.com
SIC: **7373** 5045 7378 7379 Computer integrated systems design; computers, peripherals & software; computer & data processing equipment repair/maintenance; computer data escrow service

(P-13611)
INFINITE SOLUTIONS INC (PA)
1687 Eureka Rd Ste 200, Roseville (95661-2816)
PHONE...................916 641-0500
Ganapathy Murugesh, *President*
Rani Murugesh, *CEO*
EMP: 45 EST: 1997
SALES (est): 3.3MM **Privately Held**
WEB: www.4infinitesolutions.com
SIC: **7373** Systems software development services

(P-13612)
INSIGNIA
Also Called: Grande Vitesse Systems
390 Fremont St, San Francisco (94105-2316)
PHONE...................415 777-0320
Jano Avanessian, *President*
Wendy Avanessian, *Shareholder*
Rene Young, *CFO*
EMP: 36 EST: 1987
SQ FT: 15,000
SALES (est): 1.1MM **Privately Held**
WEB: www.gvsnet.com
SIC: **7373** 3572 5734 Systems integration services; disk drives, computer; computer & software stores

(P-13613)
IP INFUSION INC (HQ)
3965 Freedom Cir Ste 200, Santa Clara (95054-1293)
PHONE...................408 400-1900
Koichi Narasaki, *Chairman*
Amit Chatterjee, *President*
Kiyo Oishi, *CEO*
Atsushi Ogata, *COO*
Shane Rigby, *COO*
EMP: 53 EST: 1999
SQ FT: 11,900
SALES (est): 11.9MM **Privately Held**
WEB: www.ipinfusion.com
SIC: **7373** Systems software development services

(P-13614)
IS INC
Also Called: Innovative Solutions
2554 Millcreek Dr, Sacramento (95833-3612)
PHONE...................916 920-1700
Janice Crawford, *CEO*
Richard S Crawford, *President*
Ann Crawford, *Corp Secy*
Michael Crawford, *Vice Pres*
▲ EMP: 50 EST: 1982
SQ FT: 25,000
SALES (est): 3.2MM **Privately Held**
WEB: www.isinc.com
SIC: **7373** 8243 5734 Value-added resellers, computer systems; systems software development services; software training, computer; computer & software stores

(P-13615)
JOSEPH SYSTEMS INC
Also Called: J4 Systems
2521 Warren Dr Ste A, Rocklin (95677-2179)
P.O. Box 2757 (95677-8463)
PHONE...................916 303-7200
Jeanette Joseph, *CEO*
John Joseph, *President*
Lydia Beal, *Controller*
EMP: 38 EST: 1994
SQ FT: 10,200
SALES (est): 6.3MM **Privately Held**
SIC: **7373** 7374 5045 Systems software development services; computer graphics service; computers, peripherals & software

(P-13616)
JUNIPER NETWORKS INC
Also Called: Proof of Concept Poc Lab
1137 Innovation Way B, Sunnyvale (94089-1228)
PHONE...................408 745-2000
Florin A Oprescu, *Principal*
Mariano Camacho, *Partner*
David Carr, *Vice Pres*
Kevin Hutchins, *Vice Pres*
Vijay Talati, *Vice Pres*
EMP: 2000 **Publicly Held**
WEB: www.juniper.net
SIC: **7373** 7372 Computer integrated systems design; prepackaged software
PA: Juniper Networks, Inc.
1133 Innovation Way
Sunnyvale CA 94089

(P-13617)
JUNIPER NETWORKS (US) INC (HQ)
1133 Innovation Way, Sunnyvale (94089-1228)
PHONE...................408 745-2000
Rami Rahim, *CEO*
Scott Kriens, *Ch of Bd*
Michael Ward, *Officer*
Anthony Cioffi, *Senior VP*
Siddharth Tuli, *Software Engr*
EMP: 139 EST: 2000
SALES (est): 34.2MM **Publicly Held**
WEB: www.juniper.net
SIC: **7373** Computer integrated systems design

(P-13618)
JUNIPER NETWORKS INTL LLC
1133 Innovation Way, Sunnyvale (94089-1228)
PHONE...................408 745-2000
Rami Rahim, *CEO*
EMP: 16 EST: 2016
SALES (est): 1.3MM **Publicly Held**
WEB: www.juniper.net
SIC: **7373** 7372 Computer integrated systems design; prepackaged software
PA: Juniper Networks, Inc.
1133 Innovation Way
Sunnyvale CA 94089

(P-13619)
KETOS INC
420 S Hillview Dr, Milpitas (95035-5464)
PHONE...................408 550-2162
Meenakshi Sankaran, *CEO*
Kim Speiser, *Senior VP*
Jay Shah, *Software Engr*
Ermias Leggesse, *Research*
Cris Ancheta, *Engineer*
EMP: 55 EST: 2015
SALES (est): 2MM **Privately Held**
WEB: www.ketos.co
SIC: **7373** 3823 Computer integrated systems design; industrial instrmnts msrmnt display/control process variable

(P-13620)
KG OLDCO INC (HQ)
2270 Martin Ave, Santa Clara (95050-2704)
PHONE...................408 980-8550
Jeff Kaiser, *CEO*
Jason Gress, *President*
Rick Chapman, *Vice Pres*
Peter Johnson, *Vice Pres*
Mitchell Sharp, *Vice Pres*
EMP: 50 EST: 1993
SQ FT: 13,130
SALES (est): 44.8MM
SALES (corp-wide): 76.4MM **Privately Held**
WEB: www.intervision.com
SIC: **7373** 8712 Systems integration services; computer systems analysis & design; architectural services
PA: Netelligent Corporation
16401 Swingley Ridge Rd
Chesterfield MO 63017
314 392-6900

(P-13621)
KLOVES INC (PA)
6203 San Ignacio Ave # 1, San Jose (95119-1371)
PHONE...................408 768-5966
Sarika Arora, *CEO*
Kamal Arora, *Principal*
Ariel Bautista, *Personnel Assit*
Matt Potts, *Manager*
EMP: 39 EST: 2010
SALES (est): 5.2MM **Privately Held**
WEB: www.klovesinc.com
SIC: **7373** Systems software development services

(P-13622)
LACEWORK INC (PA)
6201 America Center Dr # 200, San Jose (95002-2563)
PHONE...................888 292-5027
Dan Hubbard, *CEO*
Johnny Chen, *Vice Pres*
Ryan McCurdy, *Vice Pres*
Daniel Simon, *Sales Staff*
EMP: 351 EST: 2015
SALES (est): 14.3MM **Privately Held**
WEB: www.lacework.com
SIC: **7373** Computer integrated systems design

(P-13623)
LAMBDATEST INC
1390 Market St Ste 200, San Francisco (94102-5404)
PHONE...................866 430-7087
Asad Khan, *CEO*
Jay Singh, *COO*
Vipul Verma, *Senior VP*
Madhusudan Laxmanrao, *Vice Pres*
Syed Shayanur Rahman, *Engineer*
EMP: 210 EST: 2017
SALES (est): 13.9MM **Privately Held**
WEB: www.lambdatest.com
SIC: **7373** Computer systems analysis & design

(P-13624)
LANLOGIC INC (HQ)
248 Rickenbacker Cir, Livermore (94551-7615)
PHONE...................925 273-2300
Dan Ferguson, *President*
Wilma Smith, *CFO*
Alfredo Rodriguez, *Sr Ntwrk Engine*
Bayani Natividad, *Network Enginr*
Russell Feagley, *IT/INT Sup*
EMP: 35 EST: 1996
SQ FT: 6,000
SALES (est): 11.6MM **Privately Held**
WEB: www.lanlogic.com
SIC: **7373** 4813 Computer integrated systems design;
PA: Addressable Networks, Inc.
3170 Orthello Way
Santa Clara CA 95051
408 241-7446

(P-13625)
LATTICE ENGINES INC (DH)
1820 Gateway Dr Ste 200, San Mateo (94404-4059)
PHONE...................877 460-0010
Shashi Upadhyay, *CEO*
Timothy Carruthers, *President*
Kent McCormick, *President*
Howie Shohet, *CFO*
Michael McCarroll, *Officer*
EMP: 104 EST: 2010
SALES (est): 22.8MM
SALES (corp-wide): 1.7B **Publicly Held**
WEB: www.dnb.com
SIC: **7373** 7372 Computer system selling services; business oriented computer software

(P-13626)
LILIEN LLC (HQ)
17 E Sir Francis Drake Bl, Larkspur (94939-1708)
PHONE...................415 389-7500
Geoffrey I Lilien, *Mng Member*
Eric Borsky, *President*
Wendy Lounderman, *Officer*
Dhruv Gulati,
Wilson Lochridge,
EMP: 42 EST: 2006
SQ FT: 6,200
SALES (est): 904.3K
SALES (corp-wide): 62.9MM **Privately Held**
WEB: www.lilien.com
SIC: **7373** Computer integrated systems design
PA: Sysorex International, Inc
335 E Middlefield Rd
Mountain View CA 94043
408 702-2167

(P-13627)
LOOKOUT INC (PA)
Also Called: Flexilis
275 Battery St Ste 200, San Francisco (94111-3379)
PHONE...................650 241-2358
James Dolce, *Ch of Bd*
Zachary McCraw, *Partner*
Mark Nasiff, *COO*
Deborah Wolf, *Chief Mktg Ofcr*
Missy Ballew, *Officer*
EMP: 448 EST: 2005
SALES (est): 258.2MM **Privately Held**
WEB: www.lookout.com
SIC: **7373** Systems software development services

(P-13628)
LUCID DESIGN GROUP INC
55 Harrison St 200, Oakland (94607-3790)
PHONE...................510 907-0400
Will Coleman, *CEO*
Vladisoav Shunturov, *President*
Shelly Davenport, *Vice Pres*
Chris Fry, *Vice Pres*
Jeff McCarthy, *Vice Pres*
EMP: 80 EST: 2004
SALES (est): 13.9MM
SALES (corp-wide): 3.4B **Publicly Held**
WEB: www.buildingos.com
SIC: **7373** Systems software development services
PA: Acuity Brands, Inc.
1170 Peachtree St Ne # 23
Atlanta GA 30309
404 853-1400

(P-13629)
LUCIDWORKS INC (PA)
235 Montgomery St Ste 500, San Francisco (94104-2908)
PHONE...................415 329-6515
Will Hayes, *CEO*
Richard Gold, *Partner*
Earle Gregory, *COO*
Reade Frank, *CFO*
Ellen Petry Leanse, *Officer*
EMP: 281 EST: 2007
SALES (est): 17.3MM **Privately Held**
WEB: www.lucidworks.com
SIC: **7373** Systems software development services

(P-13630)
MACKEVISION LLC
1255 Treat Blvd Ste 250, Walnut Creek (94597-7997)
PHONE...................248 656-6566
Armin Pohl, *CEO*
Lindy Brodeur, *CFO*
Stefanie Griepentrog, *Corp Comm Staff*
EMP: 120 EST: 2007
SQ FT: 8,000
SALES (est): 10.7MM **Privately Held**
WEB: www.mackevision.com
SIC: **7373** Computer-aided design (CAD) systems service
HQ: Mackevision Medien Design Gmbh
Forststr. 7
Stuttgart BW 70174
711 933-0480

(P-13631)
MATRIXX SOFTWARE INC (PA)
1098 Fster Cy Blvd Ste 10, Foster City (94404)
PHONE...................408 215-9344
Glo Gordon, *CEO*
Milan Parikh, *CFO*
Bill Highstreet, *Officer*
Martin Savitt, *Officer*
Nick Cole, *Vice Pres*
EMP: 278 EST: 2008

PRODUCTS & SERVICES SECTION
7373 - Computer Integrated Systems Design County (P-13654)

SALES (est): 42MM **Privately Held**
WEB: www.matrixx.com
SIC: 7373 Systems software development services

(P-13632)
MILESTONE TECHNOLOGIES INC (PA)
3101 Skyway Ct, Fremont (94539-5910)
PHONE................................510 651-2454
Sameer Kishore, *CEO*
Anish Shah, *CFO*
Arlene Laborde, *Officer*
Olivier Crene, *Senior VP*
Nadia Dessouki, *Vice Pres*
EMP: 2509 EST: 1997
SQ FT: 6,500
SALES (est): 275MM **Privately Held**
WEB: www.milestone.tech
SIC: 7373 7374 Computer integrated systems design; data processing & preparation

(P-13633)
MINDWARE PERTECH INC (HQ)
Also Called: Mindteck USA
5820 Stnrdge Mall Rd Ste, Pleasanton (94588)
PHONE................................925 251-1550
Atar Sen Mittal, *President*
Nawroz Salam, *Senior VP*
EMP: 40 EST: 1994
SALES (est): 281.9K **Privately Held**
SIC: 7373 8748 Systems software development services; systems engineering consultant, ex. computer or professional

(P-13634)
MIST SYSTEMS INC
1601 S De Anza Blvd # 248, Cupertino (95014-5347)
PHONE................................408 326-0346
Sujai Hajela, *CEO*
Brett Galloway, *Ch of Bd*
Laura Perrone, *CFO*
Bob Friday, *CTO*
EMP: 125 EST: 2014
SALES (est): 18MM **Publicly Held**
WEB: www.mist.com
SIC: 7373 Local area network (LAN) systems integrator
PA: Juniper Networks, Inc.
1133 Innovation Way
Sunnyvale CA 94089

(P-13635)
MOBICA US INC
2570 N 1st St Fl 2, San Jose (95131-1035)
PHONE................................650 450-6654
Marcin Kloda, *CEO*
Rafael Janczyk, *COO*
Jenny Vang, *Office Mgr*
Anna Orlova, *Administration*
Radoslaw Dumanski, *Technical Staff*
EMP: 900 EST: 2012
SALES (est): 54MM
SALES (corp-wide): 52MM **Privately Held**
WEB: www.mobica.com
SIC: 7373 Systems software development services
HQ: Mobica Limited
Crown House
Wilmslow SK9 1

(P-13636)
MOZILLA CORPORATION (HQ)
2 Harrison St Ste 175, San Francisco (94105-6130)
PHONE................................650 903-0800
Mitchell Baker, *CEO*
Denelle Dixon, *COO*
Jascha Kaykaswolff, *Chief Mktg Ofcr*
Michael Deangelo, *Officer*
Mark Mayo, *Officer*
EMP: 508 EST: 2005
SALES (est): 28.3MM **Privately Held**
WEB: www.mozilla.org
SIC: 7373 Systems software development services
PA: Mozilla Foundation
2 Harrison St Ste 175
San Francisco CA 94105
650 903-0800

(P-13637)
MPA NETWORKS INC
9 Vasilakos Ct, Menlo Park (94025-5946)
PHONE................................650 566-8800
Michael Price, *President*
Joe Dito, *COO*
William Gandolph, *Network Enginr*
Alex Revel, *Network Enginr*
EMP: 42 EST: 1982
SALES (est): 4.9MM **Privately Held**
WEB: www.mpa.com
SIC: 7373 7371 Local area network (LAN) systems integrator; custom computer programming services

(P-13638)
MY ALLY INC
1000 Elwell Ct Ste 105, Palo Alto (94303-4306)
PHONE................................650 387-9118
Deepti Yenireddy, *CEO*
Carter Perez, *Vice Pres*
EMP: 70 EST: 2015
SALES (est): 5MM **Privately Held**
WEB: www.myally.ai
SIC: 7373 Systems software development services

(P-13639)
NEW DEAL DESIGN LLC
1265 Battery St 5, San Francisco (94111-1101)
PHONE................................415 399-0405
Gad Amit, *President*
Julie Connors, *Technology*
Adam Flynn, *Manager*
Hillary Hayden, *Manager*
EMP: 35 EST: 2000
SQ FT: 10,000
SALES (est): 4.8MM **Privately Held**
WEB: www.newdealdesign.com
SIC: 7373 Computer integrated systems design

(P-13640)
NORTHROP GRUMMAN SYSTEMS CORP
Also Called: Technical Services
P.O. Box 81, Moffett Field (94035-0081)
PHONE................................650 604-6056
James R Blount, *Manager*
EMP: 133 **Publicly Held**
WEB: www.northropgrumman.com
SIC: 7373 7374 Computer systems analysis & design; computer processing services
HQ: Northrop Grumman Systems Corporation
2980 Fairview Park Dr
Falls Church VA 22042
703 280-2900

(P-13641)
NS SOLUTION USA CORP
2000 Almeda De Las Pulgas, San Mateo (94403-1269)
PHONE................................650 627-1500
Masaki Chihara, *President*
EMP: 45 EST: 1997
SALES (est): 7.1MM **Privately Held**
WEB: www.nssol.nipponsteel.com
SIC: 7373 Computer integrated systems design
HQ: Ns Solutions Corporation
1-17-1, Toranomon
Minato-Ku TKY 105-0

(P-13642)
O2 MICRO INC
3118 Patrick Henry Dr, Santa Clara (95054-1850)
PHONE................................408 987-5920
Lynn Lin, *CEO*
Sterling Du, *President*
Yung Lin, *Officer*
Johnny Chiang, *Vice Pres*
William KAO, *Vice Pres*
EMP: 100
SQ FT: 37,000
SALES (est): 15.5MM **Privately Held**
WEB: www.ir.o2micro.com
SIC: 7373 Computer integrated systems design
PA: O2micro International Limited
The Grand Pavillion
George Town GR CAYMAN

(P-13643)
OMNITROL NETWORKS INC
4580 Auto Mall Pkwy Ste 1, Fremont (94538-3994)
PHONE................................408 919-1100
Raj Saksena, *CEO*
EMP: 50 EST: 2004
SQ FT: 5,000
SALES (est): 5.6MM **Privately Held**
WEB: www.omnitrol.com
SIC: 7373 7371 Systems integration services; computer software systems analysis & design, custom

(P-13644)
ONCORE CONSULTING LLC
3100 Zinfandel Dr Ste 250, Rancho Cordova (95670-6062)
PHONE................................916 461-3584
Lee Bennett, *Principal*
Paul Hester, *Sr Software Eng*
Kevin Peter, *Sr Software Eng*
Kris Royston, *Software Engr*
Nick Bennett, *Business Anlyst*
EMP: 46 EST: 2011
SQ FT: 2,100
SALES: 50.7MM **Privately Held**
WEB: www.oncorellc.com
SIC: 7373 7371 Computer integrated systems design; custom computer programming services

(P-13645)
OTO ANALYTICS INC
Also Called: Womply
548 Market St Ste 73871, San Francisco (94104-5401)
PHONE................................310 683-0000
Toby Scammell, *CEO*
Crystal Stephens, *Sales Staff*
EMP: 454 EST: 2011
SALES (est): 51.7MM **Privately Held**
WEB: www.womply.com
SIC: 7373 Computer integrated systems design

(P-13646)
PANZURA LLC
2880 Stevens Creek Blvd, San Jose (95128-4622)
PHONE................................408 457-8504
Jill Stelfox, *CEO*
Rich Weber, *President*
Judy Kopa, *CFO*
Jason Luehrs, *CFO*
Preethy Padman, *Vice Pres*
EMP: 150 EST: 2020
SALES (est): 31.3MM **Privately Held**
WEB: www.panzura.com
SIC: 7373 5734 Computer integrated systems design; computer software & accessories

(P-13647)
PERCOLATA CORPORATION
3630 El Camino Real, Palo Alto (94306-2743)
PHONE................................650 308-4980
EMP: 22
SQ FT: 3,000
SALES (est): 225.4K **Privately Held**
WEB: www.percolata.com
SIC: 7373 3661 Computer Integrated Systems Design, Nsk

(P-13648)
PIXIM INC
1730 N 1st St, San Jose (95112-4642)
PHONE................................650 934-0550
Chris Adams, *CEO*
Randy Strahan, *President*
John Monti, *Vice Pres*
EMP: 51 EST: 2003
SQ FT: 13,560
SALES (est): 4.1MM **Privately Held**
SIC: 7373 7361 Local area network (LAN) systems integrator; employment agencies

(P-13649)
PLUME DESIGN INC
Also Called: Plume Wifi
290 California Ave # 200, Palo Alto (94306-1618)
PHONE................................408 498-5512
Fahri Diner, *CEO*
Andrew Hartland, *CFO*
Kenny Chen, *Engineer*
John McGirr, *Accounts Mgr*
Adam Hotchkiss, *Editor*
EMP: 54 EST: 2015
SQ FT: 4,500
SALES (est): 4.4MM **Privately Held**
WEB: www.plume.com
SIC: 7373 Systems engineering, computer related

(P-13650)
PLURIS INC
10455 Bandley Dr, Cupertino (95014-1900)
PHONE................................408 863-9920
Joseph S Kennedy, *Ch of Bd*
Warren Roddy, *Senior VP*
David Cox, *Vice Pres*
Bulent Erbilgin, *Vice Pres*
Dan Keller, *Vice Pres*
EMP: 220 EST: 1996
SQ FT: 38,000
SALES (est): 17.7MM **Privately Held**
WEB: www.pluris.com
SIC: 7373 Computer integrated systems design

(P-13651)
PUSH INC
757 N Main St, Jackson (95642-9767)
P.O. Box 1807, Sutter Creek (95685-1807)
PHONE................................209 257-1100
Philip Howe, *President*
Lisa Howe, *Vice Pres*
Lisa E Howe, *Vice Pres*
EMP: 35 EST: 1995
SQ FT: 4,000
SALES (est): 4.5MM **Privately Held**
WEB: www.pushei.com
SIC: 7373 Turnkey vendors, computer systems

(P-13652)
QOLSYS INC (HQ)
1900 The Alameda, San Jose (95126-1404)
PHONE................................855 476-5797
David Lewis Pulling, *CEO*
Prasad Vindla, *Principal*
Cole Hackett, *CIO*
Bryan Herr, *CIO*
Jason Horton, *CIO*
EMP: 139 EST: 2010
SALES (est): 16.3MM **Publicly Held**
WEB: www.qolsys.com
SIC: 7373 Systems software development services

(P-13653)
QSOLV INC
440 N Wolfe Rd Ste 26, Sunnyvale (94085-3869)
PHONE................................408 429-0918
Sujaya Viswanathan, *CEO*
Shell Scripting, *Partner*
Shyam Gopal, *President*
Albert Fong, *Director*
EMP: 112 EST: 1997
SALES (est): 5.6MM **Privately Held**
WEB: www.qsolv-inc.com
SIC: 7373 7379 7371 Computer systems analysis & design; computer related consulting services; software programming applications

(P-13654)
QUANTELA INC (PA)
691 S Milpitas Blvd # 217, Milpitas (95035-5476)
PHONE................................650 479-3700
AMR Salem, *CEO*
Del White, *Senior VP*
EMP: 97 EST: 2011
SQ FT: 500
SALES (est): 8.5MM **Privately Held**
WEB: www.quantela.com
SIC: 7373 Computer integrated systems design

7373 - Computer Integrated Systems Design County (P-13655)

(P-13655)
R SYSTEMS INC (HQ)
5000 Windplay Dr Ste 5, El Dorado Hills (95762-9319)
PHONE..................................916 939-9696
Satinder Sing Rekhi, *CEO*
Ashok Bhatia, *Vice Pres*
Amit Gupta, *Vice Pres*
Kannan Natarajan, *Vice Pres*
Harpreet Rekhi, *Vice Pres*
EMP: 100 **EST:** 1993
SQ FT: 7,000
SALES: 23.5MM **Privately Held**
WEB: www.rsystems.com
SIC: 7373 Systems software development services

(P-13656)
RAVENSWOOD SOLUTIONS INC (HQ)
3065 Skyway Ct, Fremont (94539-5909)
PHONE..................................650 241-3661
Kipp Peppel, *President*
Peter Kuebler, *CFO*
Kathy Keyser, *Principal*
Ernesto Lozano Jr, *Principal*
Charlene Galanty, *Exec Dir*
EMP: 98 **EST:** 2015
SQ FT: 12,878
SALES (est): 550MM
SALES (corp-wide): 461.4MM **Privately Held**
WEB: www.ravenswoodsolutions.com
SIC: 7373 7379 3679 8711 Systems engineering, computer related; computer related maintenance services; antennas, receiving; engineering services
PA: Sri International
333 Ravenswood Ave
Menlo Park CA 94025
650 859-2000

(P-13657)
REBEL GIRLS INC
421 Elm Ave, Larkspur (94939-2042)
PHONE..................................808 398-2258
Jes Wolfe, *CEO*
EMP: 50 **EST:** 2012
SALES (est): 2.2MM **Privately Held**
SIC: 7373 Computer integrated systems design

(P-13658)
SABLE COMPUTER INC
Also Called: Kis
48383 Fremont Blvd # 122, Fremont (94538-6591)
PHONE..................................510 403-7500
Sean M Canevaro, *CEO*
Susan Canevaro, *CFO*
Michael Florence, *Executive*
Christian Grejsen, *Executive*
Dana Fuller, *CIO*
EMP: 35
SQ FT: 6,900
SALES (est): 15MM **Privately Held**
WEB: www.kiscc.com
SIC: 7373 Computer systems analysis & design

(P-13659)
SAMSARA INC (PA)
350 Rhode Island St # 400, San Francisco (94103-5188)
PHONE..................................415 985-2400
Sanjit Biswas, *CEO*
EMP: 1624 **EST:** 2015
SALES (est): 700.8MM **Privately Held**
WEB: www.samsara.com
SIC: 7373 Computer systems analysis & design; systems engineering, computer related

(P-13660)
SAUCE LABS INC (PA)
116 New Montgomery St # 3, San Francisco (94105-3639)
PHONE..................................855 677-0001
Aled Miles, *CEO*
Paul Joachim, *CFO*
Justin Dolly, *Officer*
Matt Bruun, *Senior VP*
Matt Wyman, *Senior VP*
EMP: 88 **EST:** 2008

SALES (est): 58.2MM **Privately Held**
WEB: www.saucelabs.com
SIC: 7373 Systems software development services

(P-13661)
SCALEFLUX INC
97 E Brokaw Rd Ste 260, San Jose (95112-1032)
PHONE..................................408 628-2291
Hao Zhong, *CEO*
Yong Peng, *Vice Pres*
Fei Sun, *Vice Pres*
Thad Omura, *VP Bus Dvlpt*
Richard Barnes, *CIO*
EMP: 60 **EST:** 2014
SALES (est): 6.5MM **Privately Held**
WEB: www.scaleflux.com
SIC: 7373 Systems engineering, computer related

(P-13662)
SELLIGENT INC (HQ)
1300 Island Dr Ste 200, Redwood City (94065-5171)
PHONE..................................650 421-4255
John Hernandez, *CEO*
Frank Addante, *President*
Tricia Robinson-Pridemore, *President*
Chris Botting, *COO*
Steve Pantelick, *CFO*
EMP: 122 **EST:** 2013
SALES (est): 25.9MM
SALES (corp-wide): 562.3MM **Privately Held**
WEB: www.hggc.com
SIC: 7373 Systems software development services
PA: Hggc, Llc
1950 University Ave # 350
East Palo Alto CA 94303
650 321-4910

(P-13663)
SILVACO INC (PA)
Also Called: Invarian
2811 Mission College Blvd # 6, Santa Clara (95054-1884)
PHONE..................................408 567-1000
Babak Taheri, *CEO*
David L Dutton, *Vice Chairman*
Howard Hideshima, *CFO*
Ken Myers, *CFO*
Iliya Pesic, *Chairman*
EMP: 162 **EST:** 2004
SALES (est): 21.9MM **Privately Held**
WEB: www.silvaco.com
SIC: 7373 Office computer automation systems integration

(P-13664)
SINGTEL ENTERPRISE SEC US INC (HQ)
901 Marshall St Ste 125, Redwood City (94063-2026)
PHONE..................................650 508-6800
Chang York Chye, *CEO*
Greg Smith, *Engineer*
Mike Janke, *Accounts Exec*
EMP: 50 **EST:** 2015
SALES (est): 240.9MM **Privately Held**
WEB: www.singtel.com
SIC: 7373 7372 Systems integration services; prepackaged software

(P-13665)
SIXGILL LLC (PA)
Also Called: Plainsight
548 Market St 22409, San Francisco (94104-5401)
PHONE..................................424 322-2009
Phil Ressler, *CEO*
Jeff Ester, *Vice Pres*
Alan Field,
Jonathon Ziskind,
Russell Ziskind,
EMP: 38 **EST:** 2008
SALES (est): 3.9MM **Privately Held**
SIC: 7373 Systems software development services

(P-13666)
SONICWALL INC (PA)
1033 Mccarthy Blvd, Milpitas (95035-7920)
PHONE..................................888 557-6642
Bill Conner, *President*

John Todd, *COO*
Ravi Chopra, *CFO*
David Chamberlin, *Chief Mktg Ofcr*
Joe Nguyenle, *Officer*
▲ **EMP:** 948 **EST:** 1991
SQ FT: 86,000
SALES (est): 153.9MM **Privately Held**
WEB: www.sonicwall.com
SIC: 7373 Systems software development services

(P-13667)
SOUL MACHINES INC
44 Tehama St Ste 411, San Francisco (94105-3110)
PHONE..................................649 283-0863
Greg Cross, *Director*
Chris Liu, *Director*
Mark Sagar, *Director*
EMP: 75 **EST:** 2017
SALES (est): 2.1MM **Privately Held**
SIC: 7373 Systems software development services

(P-13668)
SPOTLINE INC
226 Airport Pkwy Ste 450, San Jose (95110-3701)
PHONE..................................408 768-1664
Vinesh Goyal, *COO*
Sid Sahoo, *CEO*
Don Lamure, *Vice Pres*
Gus Nathan, *Vice Pres*
Kevin Taylor, *Program Mgr*
EMP: 35 **EST:** 2016
SALES (est): 6.5MM **Privately Held**
WEB: www.spotline.com
SIC: 7373 Computer integrated systems design

(P-13669)
STRIPE HEAVY INDUSTRIES INC (HQ)
510 Townsend St, San Francisco (94103-4918)
PHONE..................................877 887-7815
Eduardo Pereda, *Vice Pres*
Jonathan Kuhn, *Program Mgr*
Adrienne Dreyfus, *Software Dev*
Clinton Blackburn, *Software Engr*
James Boelen, *Software Engr*
EMP: 50 **EST:** 2015
SALES (est): 19.7MM **Privately Held**
WEB: www.stripe.com
SIC: 7373 Systems software development services

(P-13670)
SYCOMP A TECHNOLOGY CO INC (PA)
Also Called: Sycomp Computer Services
950 Tower Ln Ste 1785, Foster City (94404-4257)
PHONE..................................877 901-7416
Michael Symons, *CEO*
Scott Greco, *Executive*
Jean A Symons, *Principal*
Ruben Lee, *Sales Staff*
Vanessa Nudd, *Director*
EMP: 45 **EST:** 1994
SQ FT: 10,000
SALES (est): 52.3MM **Privately Held**
WEB: www.sycomp.com
SIC: 7373 7389 Computer integrated systems design; document storage service

(P-13671)
SYNAPSE DESIGN AUTOMATION INC (DH)
2200 Laurelwood Rd, Santa Clara (95054-1515)
PHONE..................................408 850-9527
Satish Bagalkotkar, *CEO*
EMP: 64 **EST:** 2003
SALES (est): 13.5MM **Privately Held**
WEB: www.synapse-da.com
SIC: 7373 Computer integrated systems design

(P-13672)
SYSOREX USA (HQ)
101 Larkspur Landing Cir # 120, Larkspur (94939-1749)
PHONE..................................415 389-7500
Nadir Ali, *CEO*

Amy Hughes, *Accounting Mgr*
EMP: 50 **EST:** 1984
SQ FT: 2,800
SALES (est): 16.4MM
SALES (corp-wide): 9.3MM **Publicly Held**
WEB: www.inpixon.com
SIC: 7373 Systems integration services
PA: Inpixon
2479 E Byshore Rd Ste 195
Palo Alto CA 94303
408 702-2167

(P-13673)
SYSTEM INTEGRATORS INC (HQ)
Also Called: Netlinx Publishing Solutions
1740 N Market Blvd, Sacramento (95834-1997)
PHONE..................................916 830-2400
Paul Donlan, *President*
Allan Katzen, *Vice Pres*
Paul Nartey, *Manager*
EMP: 140 **EST:** 1973
SQ FT: 70,000
SALES (est): 20.5MM
SALES (corp-wide): 177.9K **Privately Held**
WEB: www.systemintegrators.net
SIC: 7373 7372 7371 Computer integrated systems design; prepackaged software; custom computer programming services
PA: Net-Linx Ag
Kathe-Kollwitz-Ufer 76-79
Dresden SN
351 318-750

(P-13674)
TALEND INC (HQ)
800 Bridge Pkwy Ste 200, Redwood City (94065-1156)
PHONE..................................650 539-3200
Mike Tuchen, *CEO*
Laurent Bride, *COO*
Thomas Tuchscherer, *CFO*
John Brennan, *Bd of Directors*
Nanci Caldwell, *Bd of Directors*
EMP: 339 **EST:** 2007
SQ FT: 1,200
SALES (est): 77.3MM
SALES (corp-wide): 110.8MM **Privately Held**
WEB: www.talend.com
SIC: 7373 Computer systems analysis & design; systems integration services

(P-13675)
TATA ELXSI LTD (HQ)
4677 Old Ironsides Dr # 315, Santa Clara (95054-1809)
PHONE..................................408 894-8282
Madhukar Dev, *President*
Kalpana Patel, *Office Mgr*
Vargheese Baby, *Technical Staff*
Thomas George, *Sales Mgr*
EMP: 50 **EST:** 1998
SALES (est): 12.8MM **Privately Held**
WEB: www.tataelxsi.com
SIC: 7373 Computer integrated systems design

(P-13676)
TD SYNNEX CORPORATION (PA)
44201 Nobel Dr, Fremont (94538-3178)
PHONE..................................510 656-3333
Richard T Hume, *CEO*
Dennis Polk, *Ch of Bd*
Marshall Witt, *CFO*
Robert Kalsow-Ramos, *Vice Ch Bd*
Simon Leung, *Senior VP*
◆ **EMP:** 150 **EST:** 1980
SALES (est): 24.6B **Publicly Held**
WEB: www.synnex.com
SIC: 5734 7373 Computer & software stores; computer peripheral equipment; computer integrated systems design

(P-13677)
TENDDO INC
101 California St # 2710, San Francisco (94111-5802)
PHONE..................................415 295-4849
Raj Tyagi, *Principal*
EMP: 37 **EST:** 2009

▲ = Import ▼ = Export
◆ = Import/Export

PRODUCTS & SERVICES SECTION
7374 - Data & Computer Processing & Preparation County (P-13699)

SALES (est): 2.3MM **Privately Held**
WEB: www.tenddo.com
SIC: **7373** Computer integrated systems design

(P-13678)
TEQTRON INC
256 Snider Ct, Livermore (94550-8030)
PHONE..................................925 583-5411
Sid Nandi, *President*
Nandita Sinha, *CFO*
Abhaishek Nandi, *Admin Sec*
Dinesh Prabhu, *Sr Software Eng*
Dorina Dimulescu, *Analyst*
EMP: 43
SQ FT: 3,000
SALES: 5.3MM **Privately Held**
WEB: www.teqtron.com
SIC: **7373** Systems software development services

(P-13679)
TP-LINK RESEARCH INST USA CORP
245 Charcot Ave, San Jose (95131-1107)
PHONE..................................408 618-5478
Mingyuan LI, *CEO*
Matthew Liu, *CFO*
David WEI, *Opers Staff*
Michelle Johnson, *Marketing Staff*
Winfred Shu, *Director*
EMP: 17 EST: 2013
SALES (est): 1MM **Privately Held**
SIC: **7373** 3825 7379 Local area network (LAN) systems integrator; network analyzers; computer related maintenance services

(P-13680)
TRADESHIFT INC (HQ)
Also Called: Trade Shift APS
612 Howard St Ste 100, San Francisco (94105-3927)
PHONE..................................800 381-3585
Christian Lanng, *President*
Jeppe Rindom, *CFO*
Amer Moorhead,
Roy Anderson,
Sarika Garg, *Officer*
EMP: 212 EST: 2012
SALES (est): 18.3MM
SALES (corp-wide): 102MM **Privately Held**
WEB: www.tradeshift.com
SIC: **7373** Local area network (LAN) systems integrator
PA: Tradeshift Holdings Inc.
   221 Main St Ste 250
   San Francisco CA 94105
   800 381-3585

(P-13681)
TRICENTIS USA CORP
2570 W El Cmino Real Ste, Mountain View (94040)
PHONE..................................650 383-8329
Mike Vandivrer, *CFO*
Michael Hentze, *President*
Sandeep Johri, *CEO*
Brent Remai, *Chief Mktg Ofcr*
Dave Keil, *Officer*
EMP: 300 EST: 2011
SALES (est): 46.9MM
SALES (corp-wide): 50.7MM **Privately Held**
WEB: www.tricentis.com
SIC: **7373** Computer integrated systems design
PA: Tricentis Gmbh
   Leonard-Bernstein-StraBe 10
   Wien 1220
   126 324-09

(P-13682)
TRINITY TECHNOLOGY GROUP INC
2015 J St Ste 105, Sacramento (95811-3124)
PHONE..................................916 779-0201
Randall E Duart, *CEO*
Timothy Purdy, *CFO*
Jane Duart, *Treasurer*
Stephen Williamson, *Vice Pres*
Lexie Metzler, *Executive Asst*
EMP: 67 EST: 1999
SQ FT: 2,800

SALES (est): 14.8MM **Privately Held**
SIC: **7373** Systems software development services

(P-13683)
TRUEPOINT SOLUTIONS LLC (PA)
3262 Penryn Rd Ste 100b, Loomis (95650-8050)
PHONE..................................916 259-1293
Kent Johnson,
Keith Hobday,
Robert Strouse,
EMP: 29 EST: 2004
SQ FT: 1,800
SALES (est): 7.1MM **Privately Held**
WEB: www.truepointsolutions.com
SIC: **7373** 7372 Turnkey vendors, computer systems; value-added resellers, computer systems; application computer software; business oriented computer software

(P-13684)
UBIQUITI NETWORKS INC
2580 Orchard Pkwy, San Jose (95131-1059)
PHONE..................................408 942-3085
Robert J Pera, *CEO*
Alex Evangelatos, *Vice Pres*
John Holvey, *Vice Pres*
Laura Kiernan, *Vice Pres*
Benjamin Moore, *VP Bus Dvlpt*
EMP: 79 EST: 2014
SALES (est): 5.9MM **Publicly Held**
WEB: www.ui.com
SIC: **7373** 5045 7372 Local area network (LAN) systems integrator; computer software; prepackaged software
PA: Ubiquiti Inc.
   685 3rd Ave Fl 27
   New York NY 10017

(P-13685)
UNITEK INC
Also Called: Interket Enterprise
41350 Christy St, Fremont (94538-3115)
P.O. Box 14823 (94539-1823)
PHONE..................................510 623-8544
Philip Kim, *CEO*
EMP: 65 EST: 1995
SQ FT: 20,000
SALES (est): 9.6MM **Privately Held**
WEB: www.unitekinc.com
SIC: **7373** 3679 3672 Turnkey vendors, computer systems; electronic circuits; printed circuit boards

(P-13686)
UXREACTOR INC
5870 Stnrdge Mall Rd Ste, Pleasanton (94588)
PHONE..................................888 897-3228
Satyam Kantamneni, *Ch of Bd*
EMP: 45 EST: 2015
SALES (est): 2.8MM **Privately Held**
WEB: www.uxreactor.com
SIC: **7373** Computer integrated systems design

(P-13687)
VERTISYSTEM INC
39300 Civic Center Dr # 160, Fremont (94538-5397)
PHONE..................................510 794-8099
Shaloo Jeswani, *Owner*
Rakesh Sadhwani, *President*
Deebali Syed, *Vice Pres*
Chavi Vijay, *Accounting Mgr*
Hariom Bisopia, *Manager*
EMP: 200 EST: 2008
SQ FT: 2,744
SALES (est): 11MM **Privately Held**
WEB: www.vertisystem.com
SIC: **7373** Systems software development services

(P-13688)
VIEWPINT GVRNMENT SLUTIONS INC
955 Charter St, Redwood City (94063-3109)
PHONE..................................617 577-9000
Nasser Hajo, *CEO*
Bassil Silver, *COO*

Alex Pajusi, *CTO*
Tom Crosby, *Business Mgr*
Rachel Keyser, *Director*
EMP: 39 EST: 1995
SALES (est): 1.7MM **Privately Held**
WEB: www.viewpointbeacon.com
SIC: **7373** Computer integrated systems design
PA: Opengov, Inc.
   6525 Crown Blvd # 41340
   San Jose CA 95160

(P-13689)
WIPRO LLC
Also Called: Wipro Technologies
425 National Ave Ste 200, Mountain View (94043-1399)
PHONE..................................650 316-3555
Sridhar Ranasubbu, *Finance*
Rishad Premji, *Officer*
Jaswinder Singh, *Officer*
Biplab Adhya, *Vice Pres*
Harmeet Chauhan, *Vice Pres*
EMP: 45 **Privately Held**
WEB: www.wipro.com
SIC: **7373** 3571 Turnkey vendors, computer systems; mainframe computers; personal computers (microcomputers)
HQ: Wipro, Llc
   2 Tower Center Blvd # 2200
   East Brunswick NJ 08816

(P-13690)
Z-AXIS TECH SOLUTIONS INC (PA)
1754 Tech Dr Ste 224, San Jose (95110)
PHONE..................................408 263-8038
Srinivasa Sharma, *President*
▼ EMP: 77 EST: 2007
SALES (est): 6.3MM **Privately Held**
WEB: www.zaxistech.com
SIC: **7373** 7363 7371 7389 Computer integrated systems design; help supply services; custom computer programming services; translation services

(P-13691)
ZENITH INFOTECH LIMITED
39675 Cedar Blvd Ste 240b, Newark (94560-8541)
PHONE..................................510 687-1943
EMP: 145
SALES: 7.5MM **Privately Held**
WEB: www.zenithinfotech.com
SIC: **7373** Software Development
PA: Zenith Infotech Limited
   29 & 30 Zenith House
   Mumbai MH 40009

7374 Data & Computer Processing & Preparation

(P-13692)
AIRCARGO COMMUNITIES INC
41 Margaret Ave, Brisbane (94005-1651)
P.O. Box 2154, South San Francisco (94083-2154)
PHONE..................................650 952-9050
Mario Kovatchev, *CEO*
EMP: 20 EST: 2005
SALES (est): 356K **Privately Held**
WEB: www.aircargocommunities.com
SIC: **7374** 4212 4512 4731 Data processing & preparation; local trucking, without storage; air transportation, scheduled; freight transportation arrangement; directories: publishing only, not printed on site;

(P-13693)
APPLIED BIOSYSTEMS INC
850 Lincoln Centre Dr, Foster City (94404-1128)
PHONE..................................800 327-3002
Prabhu Sampath, *Managing Dir*
Dan Didier, *Director*
Renaldo Juanso, *Director*
Daniel Langston, *Director*
Amie Ingold, *Manager*
EMP: 47 EST: 2014

SALES (est): 3.6MM **Privately Held**
WEB: www.thermofisher.com
SIC: **7374** Data entry service

(P-13694)
AUTOMATIC DATA PROCESSING INC
Also Called: ADP
505 San Marin Dr Ste A110, Novato (94945-1302)
PHONE..................................415 899-7300
EMP: 130
SALES (corp-wide): 11.6B **Publicly Held**
SIC: **7374** Data Processing/Preparation
PA: Automatic Data Processing, Inc.
   1 Adp Blvd Ste 1
   Roseland NJ 07068
   973 974-5000

(P-13695)
BAYTECH WEBS INC
1798 Tech Dr Ste 178, San Jose (95110)
PHONE..................................408 533-8519
Howard Yeh, *President*
Maxine Wang, *Director*
Chloe Teng, *Manager*
EMP: 43 EST: 2001
SQ FT: 5,000
SALES (est): 4MM **Privately Held**
WEB: www.baytechdigital.com
SIC: **7374** 7311 7336 2741 Computer graphics service; advertising agencies; commercial art & graphic design; ; computer software development; systems software development services

(P-13696)
BETAWAVE CORPORATION (PA)
706 Mission St Fl 10, San Francisco (94103-3170)
PHONE..................................415 738-8706
Tabreez Verjee, *President*
James Moloshok, *Ch of Bd*
Matt Freeman, *Vice Ch of Bd*
Mark Oltarsh, *Officer*
Lennox L Vernon,
EMP: 45 EST: 2005
SQ FT: 10,000 **Publicly Held**
WEB: www.betawave.com
SIC: **7374** Computer graphics service

(P-13697)
BLEACHER REPORT INC
609 Mission St, San Francisco (94105-3506)
PHONE..................................415 777-5505
Mike Jacobsen, *CFO*
Miguel Deavila, *Vice Pres*
Bennett Spector, *Vice Pres*
Alex Vargas, *Vice Pres*
Joe Yanarella, *Vice Pres*
EMP: 51 EST: 2007
SALES (est): 3MM **Privately Held**
WEB: www.bleacherreport.com
SIC: **7374** Computer graphics service

(P-13698)
BMI IMAGING SYSTEMS INC (PA)
1115 E Arques Ave, Sunnyvale (94085-3904)
PHONE..................................916 924-6666
William D Whitney, *CEO*
Janice Harrison, *Corp Secy*
Mark Hoffman, *Officer*
Jim Modrall, *Officer*
Brad Penfold, *Vice Pres*
EMP: 45 EST: 1952
SQ FT: 16,000
SALES (est): 9MM **Privately Held**
WEB: www.bmiimaging.com
SIC: **7374** 5044 7334 Optical scanning data service; microfilm equipment; photocopying & duplicating services

(P-13699)
BRANCH METRICS INC (PA)
1400 Sport Blvd Bldg Bfl, Redwood City (94063)
PHONE..................................650 209-6491
Michael Molinet, *President*
Navid Zolfaghari, *Partner*
Michael Hindman, *Creative Dir*
Michelle Lerner, *Business Dir*
Gavriel Plotke, *Sr Software Eng*
EMP: 334 EST: 2013

7374 - Data & Computer Processing & Preparation County (P-13700)

SALES (est): 42.1MM **Privately Held**
WEB: www.branch.io
SIC: 7374 Data processing service

(P-13700)
BUSINESS RECOVERY SERVICES INC
Also Called: Bank Up
130 Marina Village Pkwy # 2, Alameda (94501-1082)
PHONE..................510 522-9700
Sharon David, *President*
Tim Holmes, *Exec VP*
Jeffrey Kirkland, *CTO*
Jeff Kirkland, *Software Dev*
Mark Vose, *Sales Staff*
EMP: 51 EST: 1998
SQ FT: 6,000
SALES (est): 5MM **Privately Held**
WEB: www.bank-up.com
SIC: 7374 Data processing service

(P-13701)
CALIFORNIA DEPARTMENT TECH
Also Called: Teale Data Center
10860 Gold Center Dr # 100, Rancho Cordova (95670-6024)
PHONE..................916 464-3747
Carlos Ramos, *Exec Dir*
EMP: 50 **Privately Held**
WEB: www.ca.gov
SIC: 7374 9199 Data processing & preparation; general government administration;
HQ: California Department Of Technology
1325 J St Ste 1600
Sacramento CA 95814

(P-13702)
CASTLIGHT HEALTH INC (PA)
150 Spear St Ste 400, San Francisco (94105-1500)
PHONE..................415 829-1400
Maeve O'Meara, *CEO*
Bryar Roberts, *Ch of Bd*
Will Bondurant, *CFO*
Dena Bravata, *Chief Mktg Ofcr*
Richa Gupta,
EMP: 442 EST: 2008
SQ FT: 31,000
SALES (est): 146.7MM **Publicly Held**
WEB: www.my.castlighthealth.com
SIC: 7374 7372 Data processing & preparation; prepackaged software

(P-13703)
CLICKTALE INC (PA)
2 Embarcadero Ctr, San Francisco (94111-3823)
PHONE..................800 807-2117
Tuval Chomut, *CEO*
Tal Schwartz, *Ch of Bd*
Nir Ackerman, *CFO*
Geoff Galat, *Chief Mktg Ofcr*
Yaron Chattah, *Vice Pres*
EMP: 52 EST: 2012
SALES (est): 25MM **Privately Held**
WEB: www.contentsquare.com
SIC: 7374 Data processing service

(P-13704)
CRUX INFORMATICS INC (PA)
201 California St # 1300, San Francisco (94111-5015)
PHONE..................415 614-4400
Philip Brittan, *CEO*
Larry Leibowitz, *President*
Marie Sonde, *CFO*
Mark Etherington, *CTO*
Sushmita Paul, *Engineer*
EMP: 39 EST: 2017
SALES (est): 4.2MM **Privately Held**
WEB: www.cruxinformatics.com
SIC: 7374 4813 Data processing service;

(P-13705)
CYBERSOURCE CORPORATION (HQ)
900 Metro Center Blvd, Foster City (94404-2172)
P.O. Box 8999, San Francisco (94128-8999)
PHONE..................650 432-7350
Alfred F Kelly Jr, *President*
Scott R Cruickshank, *President*
Steven D Pellizzer, *CFO*
Robert J Ford, *Exec VP*
Perry Dembner, *Senior VP*
EMP: 735 EST: 1998
SALES (est): 153.9MM **Publicly Held**
WEB: www.cybersource.com
SIC: 7374 Data processing service

(P-13706)
D E M ENTERPRISES INC
Also Called: Webtyme Design & Hosting
15 S Bayshore Blvd, San Mateo (94401-2045)
PHONE..................650 401-6200
Don Mahnke, *President*
▲ EMP: 40 EST: 1998
SALES (est): 1.7MM **Privately Held**
WEB: www.abctrans.com
SIC: 7374 4119 6512 Computer graphics service; limousine rental, with driver; commercial & industrial building operation

(P-13707)
DECISION MINDS
1525 Mccarthy Blvd # 224, Milpitas (95035-7451)
PHONE..................408 309-8051
Murali Pabbisetty, *Owner*
Balati Ratagocalan, *Co-Owner*
Balaji Sundaramoorthy, *Technology*
Vidhya Sridaran, *Opers Mgr*
Rajesh Gogumalla, *Senior Mgr*
EMP: 135 EST: 2013
SALES (est): 10MM **Privately Held**
WEB: www.decisionminds.com
SIC: 7374 Data entry service

(P-13708)
DIRECT COMMERCE INC
25 Martling Rd, San Anselmo (94960-1172)
PHONE..................415 288-9700
Bruce Hanavan, *President*
Hoda Kemp, *COO*
Alan Flohr, *Vice Pres*
Leela Gill, *Vice Pres*
Durbin Tadish, *Sr Software Eng*
EMP: 38 EST: 2000
SALES (est): 5.2MM **Privately Held**
WEB: www.directcommerce.com
SIC: 7374 Data processing service

(P-13709)
DYNAMIC SIGNAL INC (PA)
851 Traeger Ave Ste 200, San Bruno (94066-3037)
PHONE..................650 231-2550
Russ Fradin, *CEO*
Yang Chao, *CFO*
David Honig, *Vice Pres*
Samantha Kirk, *Vice Pres*
Joelle Gropper Kaufman, *Risk Mgmt Dir*
EMP: 316 EST: 2010
SALES (est): 4MM **Privately Held**
WEB: www.dynamicsignal.com
SIC: 7374 Data processing & preparation

(P-13710)
EDATA SOLUTIONS INC
2450 Peralta Blvd Ste 202, Fremont (94536-3826)
PHONE..................510 574-5380
Manan Kothari, *CEO*
EMP: 1000 EST: 2014
SALES (est): 4.7MM **Privately Held**
SIC: 7374 7371 Data processing service; computer software development & applications

(P-13711)
EQUINIX INC (PA)
1 Lagoon Dr Ste 400, Redwood City (94065-1564)
PHONE..................650 598-6000
Charles Meyers, *President*
Yash Soni, *Partner*
Peter Van Camp, *Ch of Bd*
Robert Busz, *CEO*
Keith Taylor, *CFO*
EMP: 220 EST: 1998
SALES (est): 6B **Publicly Held**
WEB: www.equinix.com
SIC: 7374 6798 Computer processing services; real estate investment trusts

(P-13712)
EVERYCARONLINE INC
4040 Moorpark Ave Ste 128, San Jose (95117-1802)
PHONE..................650 284-0497
Saad Laraki, *President*
EMP: 40
SQ FT: 3,000
SALES (est): 518.5K **Privately Held**
WEB: www.v12software.com
SIC: 7374 Data processing & preparation

(P-13713)
FIERCE WOMBAT GAMES INC
910 E Hamilton Ave Fl 6, Campbell (95008-0655)
PHONE..................408 745-5400
Jonathan Buckheit, *CEO*
EMP: 50 EST: 2010
SQ FT: 10,000
SALES (est): 50MM **Privately Held**
SIC: 7374 7371 Computer graphics service; computer software development & applications

(P-13714)
FIGURE EIGHT TECHNOLOGIES INC
940 Howard St, San Francisco (94103-4114)
PHONE..................415 471-1920
Lukas Biewald, *CEO*
Christopher Van Pelt, *COO*
Ryan Ferrier, *Vice Pres*
Benjamin Kearns, *Vice Pres*
Alyssa Simpson Rochwerger, *Vice Pres*
EMP: 60 EST: 2008
SQ FT: 8,400
SALES (est): 7.5MM **Privately Held**
WEB: www.appen.com
SIC: 7374 Computer graphics service

(P-13715)
FORSYS INC
691 S Milpitas Blvd # 213, Milpitas (95035-5478)
PHONE..................408 409-2567
Jayaprasad Vejendla, *President*
Ryan Madsen, *Vice Pres*
Sindhu Mansanpally, *Principal*
Vijay Kiran, *Senior Mgr*
Prasanth Veera, *Director*
EMP: 39 EST: 2015
SQ FT: 3,000
SALES (est): 1.2MM **Privately Held**
WEB: www.forsysinc.com
SIC: 7374 Data processing & preparation

(P-13716)
GLINT INC
1000 W Maude Ave, Sunnyvale (94085-2810)
PHONE..................650 817-7240
Jim Barnett, *CEO*
Dennis Jang, *CFO*
Jim Bell, *Chief Mktg Ofcr*
Marc Maloy, *Officer*
Mary Poppen, *Officer*
EMP: 100 EST: 2013
SALES (est): 12.6MM
SALES (corp-wide): 168B **Publicly Held**
WEB: www.glintinc.com
SIC: 7374 Data processing & preparation
HQ: Linkedin Corporation
1000 W Maude Ave
Sunnyvale CA 94085
650 687-3600

(P-13717)
HEWLETT PACKARD ENTERPRISE CO
4555 Great America Pkwy, Santa Clara (95054-1243)
PHONE..................408 914-2390
Antonio F Neri, *Branch Mgr*
EMP: 600
SALES (corp-wide): 26.9B **Publicly Held**
WEB: www.hpe.com
SIC: 7374 Data processing service
PA: Hewlett Packard Enterprise Company
11445 Compaq Center W Dr
Houston TX 77070
650 687-5817

(P-13718)
HOUSECANARY INC (PA)
201 Spear St, San Francisco (94105-1630)
PHONE..................866 729-7770
Jeremy Sicklick, *CEO*
Jeff Somers, *President*
Martin Morzynski, *Chief Mktg Ofcr*
Niti Bashambu,
Julia Davis, *Executive Asst*
EMP: 442 EST: 2014
SALES (est): 20.1MM **Privately Held**
WEB: www.housecanary.com
SIC: 7374 Computer processing services

(P-13719)
HP HEWLETT PACKARD GROUP LLC
1501 Page Mill Rd, Palo Alto (94304-1126)
PHONE..................650 857-1501
Charles V Bergh, *Ch of Bd*
EMP: 71 EST: 2015
SALES (est): 10.5MM
SALES (corp-wide): 56.6B **Publicly Held**
WEB: www.hp.com
SIC: 7374 Data processing service
PA: Hp Inc.
1501 Page Mill Rd
Palo Alto CA 94304
650 857-1501

(P-13720)
I MERIT INC (PA)
Also Called: I Merit USA
985 University Ave Ste 8, Los Gatos (95032-7639)
PHONE..................650 777-7857
Radha R Basu, *CEO*
Deb Dutta Ganguly, *President*
Anupam Biswas, *Officer*
Anirban R Chowdhury, *Vice Pres*
Jeff Mills, *General Mgr*
EMP: 35
SALES (est): 9.5MM **Privately Held**
WEB: www.imerit.net
SIC: 7374 Data processing & preparation

(P-13721)
I MERIT INC
14435c Big Basin Way, Saratoga (95070-6008)
PHONE..................504 226-2427
Rahda Basu, *CEO*
Malay Pal, *General Mgr*
Jai Natarajan, *VP Mktg*
Subham Chetry, *Marketing Staff*
Lauren Robinson, *Director*
EMP: 1965
SALES (corp-wide): 9.5MM **Privately Held**
WEB: www.imerit.net
SIC: 7374 Data processing & preparation
PA: I Merit Inc.
985 University Ave Ste 8
Los Gatos CA 95032
650 777-7857

(P-13722)
INFLECTION RISK SOLUTIONS LLC
Also Called: Goodhire
555 Twin Dolphin Dr # 63, Redwood City (94065-2129)
PHONE..................650 618-9910
Micheal Steven Grossman, *CEO*
Max Wesman, *COO*
Jared Waterman, *CFO*
Heather Capps, *Director*
Michael Rock, *Manager*
EMP: 169 EST: 2011
SQ FT: 7,095
SALES (est): 39MM
SALES (corp-wide): 33.2MM **Privately Held**
WEB: www.goodhire.com
SIC: 7374 Data processing & preparation
PA: Inflection.Com, Inc.
303 Twin Dolphin Dr # 600
Redwood City CA 94065
650 618-9910

PRODUCTS & SERVICES SECTION
7374 - Data & Computer Processing & Preparation County (P-13746)

(P-13723)
INKO INDUSTRIAL CORPORATION
695 Vaqueros Ave, Sunnyvale (94085-3524)
PHONE..................................408 830-1040
George Kuo, *President*
Teresa Kuo, *Executive*
Charlie Chau, *Facilities Mgr*
Wilson Yin, *Manager*
▲ **EMP:** 100 **EST:** 1983
SQ FT: 80,000
SALES (est): 11.1MM **Privately Held**
WEB: www.pellicle-inko.com
SIC: 7374 Computer graphics service

(P-13724)
LIVERAMP HOLDINGS INC (PA)
225 Bush St Ste 1700, San Francisco (94104-4248)
PHONE..................................866 352-3267
Scott E Howe, *CEO*
Clark M Kokich, *Ch of Bd*
Anneka R Gupta, *President*
Warren C Jenson, *President*
Diego Panama, *Officer*
EMP: 315 **EST:** 2005
SALES: 443MM **Publicly Held**
WEB: www.liveramp.com
SIC: 7374 Data processing & preparation

(P-13725)
LUNDI INC
548 Market St, San Francisco (94104-5401)
PHONE..................................415 735-0101
Jonathan Romley, *CEO*
EMP: 47
SALES (est): 937.7K **Privately Held**
SIC: 7374 Data processing & preparation

(P-13726)
MAINTENANCENET LLC
170 W Tasman Dr, San Jose (95134-1700)
PHONE..................................408 526-4000
Mark T Gorman,
Steven Merten, *Vice Pres*
Evan Sloves,
EMP: 89 **EST:** 2003
SALES (est): 15.8MM
SALES (corp-wide): 49.8B **Publicly Held**
WEB: www.cisco.com
SIC: 7374 Computer graphics service
PA: Cisco Systems, Inc.
170 W Tasman Dr
San Jose CA 95134
408 526-4000

(P-13727)
MARIN SOFTWARE INCORPORATED (PA)
123 Mission St Fl 27, San Francisco (94105-1681)
PHONE..................................415 399-2580
Christopher Lien, *Ch of Bd*
Robert Bertz, *CFO*
Wister Walcott, *Exec VP*
Masaru Ogi, *Vice Pres*
Douglas Pan, *Vice Pres*
EMP: 206 **EST:** 2006
SQ FT: 43,000
SALES (est): 29.9MM **Publicly Held**
WEB: www.marinsoftware.com
SIC: 7374 7372 Data processing & preparation; prepackaged software; business oriented computer software

(P-13728)
MERCHANT SERVICES INC (PA)
1 S Van Ness Ave Fl 5, San Francisco (94103-5416)
PHONE..................................817 725-0900
Lorraine Stimmell, *CEO*
Le Tran-Tl, *Senior VP*
Brian Belknap, *Regional Mgr*
Beth Dobyns, *Human Res Mgr*
Melanie Doherty, *Sales Associate*
EMP: 400 **EST:** 1996
SQ FT: 58,336
SALES (est): 20.2MM **Privately Held**
WEB: www.merchantsvcs.com
SIC: 7374 Data processing service

(P-13729)
MICRO FOCUS LLC (DH)
4555 Great America Pkwy, Santa Clara (95054-1243)
PHONE..................................801 861-7000
Christopher P Hsu,
Tony Delalama, *Vice Pres*
Bill Vollers, *Principal*
Denise Santos, *Program Mgr*
Linda Briggs, *Executive Asst*
EMP: 309 **EST:** 2007
SALES (est): 207.7MM **Privately Held**
WEB: www.microfocus.com
SIC: 7374 Data processing service

(P-13730)
MICRO HOLDING CORP
1 Maritime Plz Fl 12, San Francisco (94111-3404)
PHONE..................................415 788-5111
Warren Hellman, *President*
EMP: 49 **EST:** 2010
SALES (est): 2.7MM **Privately Held**
WEB: www.hf.com
SIC: 7374 7389 Computer graphics service; advertising, promotional & trade show services
PA: Hellman & Friedman Llc
415 Mission St Fl 57
San Francisco CA 94105

(P-13731)
MILESTONE INTERNET MKTG INC (PA)
3001 Oakmead Village Dr # 100, Santa Clara (95051-0833)
PHONE..................................408 492-9055
Benu Aggarwal, *President*
Dev Kurbur, *Senior VP*
Steve Fitzgerald, *Vice Pres*
Ravikanth Kasamsetty, *Vice Pres*
Erik Newton, *Vice Pres*
EMP: 152 **EST:** 2004
SALES (est): 10.4MM **Privately Held**
WEB: www.milestoneinternet.com
SIC: 7374 7336 Computer graphics service; commercial art & graphic design

(P-13732)
MOCANA CORPORATION
1735 N 1st St Ste 306, San Jose (95112-4511)
PHONE..................................415 617-0055
James Isaacs, *CEO*
Dinese Christopher, *Partner*
Najib Khouri-Haddad, *President*
Jeanne Angelo-Pardo, *CFO*
Hope Frank, *Chief Mktg Ofcr*
EMP: 100 **EST:** 2002
SALES (est): 15.5MM **Privately Held**
WEB: www.mocana.com
SIC: 7374 7379 Computer graphics service;

(P-13733)
MOMENTIVE INC (HQ)
Also Called: Surveymonkey Inc.
1 Curiosity Way, San Mateo (94403-2396)
PHONE..................................650 543-8400
Zander Lurie, *CEO*
David Ebersman, *Ch of Bd*
Tom Hale, *President*
Tim Maly, *COO*
Debbie Clifford, *CFO*
EMP: 50 **EST:** 1999
SQ FT: 200,000
SALES (est): 63.7MM
SALES (corp-wide): 375.6MM **Publicly Held**
WEB: www.surveymonkey.com
SIC: 7374 8732 Data processing service; survey service: marketing, location, etc.
PA: Momentive Global Inc.
1 Curiosity Way
San Mateo CA 94403
650 543-8400

(P-13734)
MOTIF INC (DH)
300 N Bayshore Blvd, San Mateo (94401-1235)
PHONE..................................917 903-5485
Kaushal Mehta, *CEO*
EMP: 203 **EST:** 2000

SALES (est): 8.3MM **Publicly Held**
WEB: www.ttec.com
SIC: 7374 Data processing service
HQ: Ttec Services Corporation
9197 S Peoria St
Englewood CO 80112
303 397-8100

(P-13735)
NEW CCH LLC (PA)
Also Called: Element Critical
1 Sansome St Ste 1500, San Francisco (94104-4449)
PHONE..................................855 234-6493
Ken Parent, *CEO*
Wayne Dietrich, *COO*
Bryan Chong, *Senior VP*
Michael Frank, *Vice Pres*
Mike Frank, *Vice Pres*
EMP: 96 **EST:** 2017
SALES (est): 6.7MM **Privately Held**
WEB: www.elementcritical.com
SIC: 7374 Data processing & preparation

(P-13736)
NGDATA US INC (PA)
71 Stevenson St Ste 400, San Francisco (94105-0908)
PHONE..................................415 655-6732
Luc Burgelman, *CEO*
Jens Ponnet, *Vice Pres*
Philippe Oellibrandt, *Human Res Mgr*
Jurgen Desmedt, *Marketing Staff*
EMP: 49 **EST:** 2013
SALES (est): 383.1K **Privately Held**
SIC: 7374 Data processing & preparation

(P-13737)
OOMA INC (PA)
525 Almanor Ave Ste 200, Sunnyvale (94085-3542)
PHONE..................................650 566-6600
Eric B Stang, *Ch of Bd*
Shig Hamamatsu, *CFO*
Namrata Sabharwal, *CFO*
Bill Pearce, *Bd of Directors*
Daniel Furse, *Vice Pres*
▲ **EMP:** 308 **EST:** 2003
SQ FT: 33,400
SALES (est): 168.9MM **Publicly Held**
WEB: www.ooma.com
SIC: 7374 4813 Data processing & preparation;

(P-13738)
PAYPAL GLOBAL HOLDINGS INC (HQ)
303 Bryant St, Mountain View (94041-1552)
PHONE..................................408 967-1000
Chen Christopher, *President*
Donna Slegg, *Executive Asst*
Tina Contis-Quinn, *Admin Asst*
Michael Poon, *Software Dev*
Uday Govekar, *Software Engr*
EMP: 3622 **EST:** 2003
SALES (est): 12.4MM
SALES (corp-wide): 21.4B **Publicly Held**
WEB: www.paypal.com
SIC: 7374 4813 Data processing & preparation; telephone communication, except radio
PA: Paypal Holdings, Inc.
2211 N 1st St
San Jose CA 95131
408 967-1000

(P-13739)
PAYYOURPEOPLE LLC
303 2nd St Towe Ste 401, San Francisco (94107-1366)
PHONE..................................415 914-7110
Parker Conrad, *Mng Member*
EMP: 46 **EST:** 2015
SQ FT: 30,000
SALES (est): 2.2MM **Privately Held**
WEB: www.zenefits.com
SIC: 7374 Data processing & preparation

(P-13740)
PEGATRON USA INC (HQ)
800 Corporate Way B, Fremont (94539-6106)
PHONE..................................510 580-4276
Jerry Yeh, *Vice Pres*
EMP: 52 **EST:** 2008

SALES (est): 3.3MM **Privately Held**
WEB: www.pegatroncorp.com
SIC: 7374 Data processing service

(P-13741)
PEOPLE DATA LABS INC
455 Market St Ste 1670, San Francisco (94105-2472)
PHONE..................................415 568-8415
Sean Thorne, *CEO*
Henry Nevue, *President*
Daniel Amaya, *CTO*
EMP: 80 **EST:** 2015
SALES (est): 5.9MM **Privately Held**
WEB: www.peopledatalabs.com
SIC: 7374 Data processing & preparation

(P-13742)
PINTEREST INC (PA)
505 Brannan St, San Francisco (94107-1610)
PHONE..................................415 762-7100
Baron Brown, *Partner*
Jessica Hoenes, *Partner*
Emily Knight, *Partner*
Madi McClenney, *Partner*
Brittany Mohr, *Partner*
EMP: 2246 **EST:** 2008
SQ FT: 339,000
SALES (est): 1.6B **Publicly Held**
WEB: www.about.pinterest.com
SIC: 7374 Data processing & preparation

(P-13743)
PLANET LABS INC (PA)
645 Harrison St Fl 4, San Francisco (94107-3624)
PHONE..................................415 829-3313
William Marshall, *CEO*
Amandeep Dali, *Partner*
Leeza Frantz, *Partner*
Nikki Hampton, *Partner*
Shireen Khan, *Partner*
EMP: 396 **EST:** 2010
SQ FT: 25,000
SALES (est): 93.8MM **Privately Held**
WEB: www.planet.com
SIC: 7374 Data processing service

(P-13744)
POSTINI INC (PA)
510 Veterans Blvd, Redwood City (94063-1122)
PHONE..................................650 482-5130
Scott Petry, *Principal*
EMP: 37 **EST:** 2010
SALES (est): 511.4K **Privately Held**
SIC: 7374 Data processing & preparation

(P-13745)
PROOFPOINT INC (PA)
925 W Maude Ave, Sunnyvale (94085-2802)
PHONE..................................408 517-4710
Gary Steele, *Ch of Bd*
Paul Auvil, *CFO*
David Knight, *Exec VP*
Ashan Willy, *Exec VP*
Michael Laudon, *Vice Pres*
EMP: 1667 **EST:** 2002
SQ FT: 242,400
SALES (est): 1B **Privately Held**
WEB: www.proofpoint.com
SIC: 7374 Data processing & preparation

(P-13746)
PROTECTIVE BUSINESS & HEALTH
Also Called: Pbs Paymaster Sales & Service
3785 Brickway Blvd # 200, Santa Rosa (95403-9033)
PHONE..................................845 354-5372
Jay Levine, *President*
Shane Gerhardt, *Web Dvlpr*
Jessica Lewis, *Software Dev*
Lenore Messler, *Graphic Designe*
Kayla Keller, *Marketing Staff*
EMP: 90 **EST:** 1978
SALES (est): 2.7MM **Privately Held**
WEB: www.iconsultendo.com
SIC: 7374 8742 Computer graphics service; marketing consulting services

7374 - Data & Computer Processing & Preparation County (P-13747)

(P-13747)
QUALITY INV PRPTS SCRMENTO LLC
Also Called: Quality Tech Svcs Sacramento
1100 N Market Blvd, Sacramento (95834-1931)
PHONE..................916 679-2100
EMP: 78
SALES (est): 1.4MM
SALES (corp-wide): 446.5MM **Privately Held**
SIC: 7374 Data Processing/Preparation
HQ: Qualitytech, Lp
12851 Foster St
Overland Park KS 66213

(P-13748)
R/GA MEDIA GROUP INC
55 Marinero Cir Apt 204, Belvedere Tiburon (94920-1677)
PHONE..................415 624-2000
Stepthen Plumlee, *Exec VP*
EMP: 58
SALES (corp-wide): 9B **Publicly Held**
WEB: www.rga.com
SIC: 7374 Computer graphics service
HQ: R/Ga Media Group, Inc.
450 W 33rd St Fl 12
New York NY 10001
212 946-4000

(P-13749)
RACKSPACE HOSTING INC
Also Called: Datapipe
650 Castro St Ste 270, Mountain View (94041-2057)
PHONE..................201 792-1918
Eric Trimmer, *Administration*
Darriane Taberer, *Software Dev*
Daniel Morgan, *Technician*
Charles Colletti, *Marketing Staff*
Alana Gillespie, *Counsel*
EMP: 276
SALES (corp-wide): 2.7B **Publicly Held**
WEB: www.rackspace.com
SIC: 7374 7371 Data processing & preparation; custom computer programming services
HQ: Rackspace Technology Global, Inc.
1 Fanatical Pl
San Antonio TX 78218

(P-13750)
RACKSPACE HOSTING INC
Also Called: Datapipe
150 S 1st St Ste 289, San Jose (95113-2611)
PHONE..................201 792-1918
EMP: 276
SALES (corp-wide): 2.7B **Publicly Held**
WEB: www.rackspace.com
SIC: 7374 Data entry service
HQ: Rackspace Technology Global, Inc.
1 Fanatical Pl
San Antonio TX 78218

(P-13751)
RAZVI INC
Also Called: Copy Rite
824 La Gonda Way, Danville (94526-1709)
PHONE..................925 242-1200
Asad Razvi, *President*
Joseph Dashiell, *Manager*
EMP: 20 EST: 1985
SALES (est): 3MM **Privately Held**
WEB: www.copyrite.net
SIC: 7374 2759 Computer graphics service; commercial printing

(P-13752)
REVENUE SOLUTIONS INC
2995 Fthills Blvd Ste 110, Roseville (95747)
PHONE..................916 780-8741
Chris Marakas, *Principal*
EMP: 285
SALES (corp-wide): 50.7MM **Privately Held**
WEB: www.revenuesolutionsinc.com
SIC: 7374 Data processing service

PA: Revenue Solutions, Inc.
42 Winter St Ste 36
Pembroke MA 02359
781 826-1546

(P-13753)
RINGCENTRAL INC (PA)
20 Davis Dr, Belmont (94002-3002)
PHONE..................650 472-4100
Vladimir Shmunis, *Ch of Bd*
Monique Proffitt, *Partner*
Anand Eswaran, *President*
David Sipes, *COO*
Mitesh Dhruv, *CFO*
▲ EMP: 80 EST: 1999
SQ FT: 110,000
SALES (est): 902.8MM **Publicly Held**
WEB: www.ringcentral.com
SIC: 7374 4899 Data processing & preparation; data communication services

(P-13754)
ROLLBAR INC (PA)
665 3rd St Ste 150, San Francisco (94107-1926)
PHONE..................415 366-3254
Brian Rue, *CEO*
Michael Davis, *Risk Mgmt Dir*
David Basoco, *Engineer*
Gianina Borcean, *Engineer*
Letania Ferreira, *Engineer*
EMP: 56 EST: 2012
SALES (est): 8.1MM **Privately Held**
WEB: www.rollbar.com
SIC: 7374 Data processing service

(P-13755)
RUBRIK INC (PA)
3495 Deer Creek Rd, Palo Alto (94304-1316)
PHONE..................650 300-5862
Bipul Sinha, *CEO*
Asheem Chandna, *Partner*
Dan Rogers, *President*
Arvind Jain, *Founder*
Arvind Nithrakashyap, *Founder*
EMP: 1545 EST: 2013
SQ FT: 54,000
SALES (est): 178.9MM **Privately Held**
WEB: www.rubrik.com
SIC: 7374 7371 7372 Data processing & preparation; computer software development & applications; application computer software

(P-13756)
SHIPT
701 Pine St Apt 43, San Francisco (94108-3150)
PHONE..................408 592-1029
David E Toomey, *Owner*
Tarek Barnes, *Engineer*
EMP: 1180 EST: 2017
SALES (est): 30.8MM **Privately Held**
WEB: www.shipt.com
SIC: 7374 Data processing & preparation

(P-13757)
SHOPPINGCOM INC
199 Fremont St Fl 4, San Francisco (94105-6634)
PHONE..................650 616-6500
Gautam Thakar, *CEO*
Amir Ashkenazi, *President*
Hendrik Krampe, *CFO*
Robert J Krolik, *CFO*
EMP: 230 EST: 1997
SALES (est): 22.1MM **Publicly Held**
WEB: www.fr.shopping.com
SIC: 7374 Data processing & preparation
PA: Ebay Inc.
2025 Hamilton Ave
San Jose CA 95125

(P-13758)
SIGNALFX INC (HQ)
3098 Olsen Dr, San Jose (95128-2048)
PHONE..................888 958-5950
Karthik Rau, *CEO*
Stephen Tsuchiyama, *Partner*
Mark Resnick, *CFO*
Mark Cranney, *Ch Credit Ofcr*
Tom Butta, *Chief Mktg Ofcr*
EMP: 49 EST: 2013

SALES (est): 10.4MM
SALES (corp-wide): 2.2B **Publicly Held**
WEB: www.splunk.com
SIC: 7374 Computer graphics service
PA: Splunk Inc.
270 Brannan St
San Francisco CA 94107
415 848-8400

(P-13759)
SKAEL INC
535 Mission St Fl 14, San Francisco (94105-3253)
PHONE..................415 653-9433
Baba Nadimpalli, *CEO*
Ragu Mantatikar, *Vice Pres*
EMP: 71 EST: 2016
SALES (est): 4.4MM **Privately Held**
WEB: www.skael.com
SIC: 7374 Data processing service

(P-13760)
SPLIT SOFTWARE INC (PA)
10 California St, Redwood City (94063-1513)
PHONE..................650 399-0005
Brian Bell, *CEO*
Trevor Stuart, *President*
Adil Aijaz, *CEO*
Joy Ebertz, *Engineer*
Tom Branch, *Sales Dir*
EMP: 129 EST: 2015
SALES (est): 9MM **Privately Held**
WEB: www.split.io
SIC: 7374 Data processing service

(P-13761)
STREETLINE INC (DH)
393 Vintage Park Dr # 140, Foster City (94404-1140)
PHONE..................650 242-3400
Manny Krakaris, *President*
Mark Noworolski, *CTO*
EMP: 56 EST: 2005
SQ FT: 10,000
SALES (est): 10.8MM
SALES (corp-wide): 1.1B **Privately Held**
WEB: www.streetline.com
SIC: 7374 Data processing & preparation
HQ: Kapsch Trafficcom Ag
Am Euro Platz 2
Wien 1120
508 110-

(P-13762)
SWEETRUSH INC
363 Valencia St Apt 4, San Francisco (94103-3570)
PHONE..................415 647-1956
Arthur Schwartzberg, *President*
Andrei Hedstrom, *CFO*
Krisa Brillantes, *Creative Dir*
Shane Donahue, *Creative Dir*
Sara Olsen, *CIO*
EMP: 37 EST: 2001
SALES (est): 2.5MM **Privately Held**
WEB: www.sweetrush.com
SIC: 7374 8243 Computer graphics service; operator training, computer

(P-13763)
TELSTRA INCORPORATED
575 Market St Ste 1650, San Francisco (94105-5815)
PHONE..................415 243-3430
Wirawan Krisman, *CFO*
Troy Drake, *Vice Pres*
Przemek Zajic, *Vice Pres*
Cory Carr, *Office Mgr*
Thomas Schultz, *Engineer*
EMP: 35 **Privately Held**
WEB: www.telstra.com.au
SIC: 7374 Computer graphics service
HQ: Telstra Incorporated
40 Wall St Fl 44
New York NY 10005
877 835-7872

(P-13764)
TIGERGRAPH INC (PA)
3 Twin Dolphin Dr Ste 160, Redwood City (94065-1604)
PHONE..................650 206-8888
Like Gao, *Vice Pres*
Mingxi Wu, *Vice Pres*
Michael Shaler, *VP Business*

Jing Qin, *Software Engr*
Chengjie Qin, *Research*
EMP: 40 EST: 2018
SALES (est): 4.5MM **Privately Held**
WEB: www.tigergraph.com
SIC: 7374 Computer graphics service

(P-13765)
TRIB3COM INC (PA)
Also Called: Tribe Dynamics
4 Embarcadero Ctr Ste 780, San Francisco (94111-4102)
PHONE..................415 562-5561
Jonathan Namnath, *CEO*
Krisna Sorathia, *Vice Pres*
Natasha Avery, *Research*
Grace Chao, *Research*
Bryan Jacobs, *Engineer*
EMP: 79 EST: 2012
SALES (est): 1.2MM **Privately Held**
WEB: www.tribedynamics.com
SIC: 7374 Computer graphics service

(P-13766)
TRULIA INC (HQ)
535 Mission St Fl 7, San Francisco (94105-3223)
PHONE..................415 648-4358
Peter Flint, *CEO*
Lloyd Frink, *President*
Jeff McConathy, *President*
Paul Levine, *COO*
Prashant Aggarwal, *CFO*
EMP: 357 EST: 2014
SQ FT: 32,000
SALES (est): 261.3MM
SALES (corp-wide): 3.3B **Publicly Held**
WEB: www.trulia.com
SIC: 7374 Data processing & preparation
PA: Zillow Group, Inc.
1301 2nd Ave Fl 31
Seattle WA 98101
206 470-7000

(P-13767)
VITESSE LLC
1601 Willow Rd, Menlo Park (94025-1452)
PHONE..................650 543-4800
Christopher R Gardner, *CEO*
EMP: 3000 EST: 2010
SALES (est): 77.3MM
SALES (corp-wide): 85.9B **Publicly Held**
WEB: www.facebook.com
SIC: 7374 Data processing service
PA: Meta Platforms, Inc.
1601 Willow Rd
Menlo Park CA 94025
650 543-4800

(P-13768)
VOICEBASE INC (PA)
2081 Center St, Berkeley (94704-1204)
PHONE..................415 886-7799
Walter Bachtiger, *CEO*
Ed Salay, *CFO*
Jeff Shukis, *CTO*
Matt Aquino, *Sales Engr*
JP Whitford, *Sales Staff*
EMP: 41 EST: 2010
SALES (est): 5.1MM **Privately Held**
WEB: www.voicebase.com
SIC: 7374 8748 Data processing & preparation; telecommunications consultant

(P-13769)
WANDERA INC
220 Sansome St Fl 14, San Francisco (94104-2729)
PHONE..................408 667-5489
Eldar Tuvey, *CEO*
Roy Tuvey, *President*
Ben Oxnam, *COO*
Garry Scott, *Vice Pres*
Jim Walker, *Vice Pres*
EMP: 50 EST: 2012
SALES (est): 23.6MM
SALES (corp-wide): 269.4MM **Publicly Held**
WEB: www.wandera.com
SIC: 7374 Data processing service
PA: Jamf Holding Corp.
100 Wshngton Ave S Ste 11
Minneapolis MN 55401
612 605-6625

PRODUCTS & SERVICES SECTION
7375 - Information Retrieval Svcs County (P-13792)

(P-13770)
WEBENERTIA INC
1570 The Alameda Ste 330, San Jose (95126-2334)
P.O. Box 334 (95103-0334)
PHONE..................................408 246-0000
Steve Ohaninas, *President*
Isaias Reyes, *Web Dvlpr*
Jatinder Verma, *Web Dvlpr*
Devinder Bhardwaj, *Prgrmr*
Kaitlyn Bounds, *Opers Staff*
EMP: 35 **EST:** 1998
SQ FT: 6,000
SALES (est): 3.7MM **Privately Held**
WEB: www.webenertia.com
SIC: 7374 7311 Computer graphics service; advertising agencies

(P-13771)
WEPAY INC
350 Convention Way # 200, Redwood City (94063-1435)
PHONE..................................855 469-3729
Bill Clerico, *CEO*
Tina Hsiao, *COO*
Steve Pellizzer, *CFO*
Rich Aberman, *Security Dir*
EMP: 39 **EST:** 2008
SQ FT: 18,850
SALES (est): 13.6MM
SALES (corp-wide): 129.5B **Publicly Held**
WEB: www.go.wepay.com
SIC: 7374 8721 Computer processing services; payroll accounting service
PA: Jpmorgan Chase & Co.
   383 Madison Ave
   New York NY 10179
   212 270-6000

(P-13772)
YAHOO CV LLC (HQ)
701 First Ave, Sunnyvale (94089-1019)
PHONE..................................408 349-3300
Terry Semel, *Mng Member*
Patricia Cuthbert, *Controller*
EMP: 325 **EST:** 2006
SALES (est): 20.2MM **Privately Held**
SIC: 7374 Data processing & preparation

(P-13773)
YELLOWBRICK DATA INC (PA)
250 Cambridge Ave Ste 301, Palo Alto (94306-1556)
PHONE..................................877 492-3282
David Lawler, *CEO*
Jim Dawson, *COO*
Brian Bulkowski, *CTO*
Jeff Boudreaux, *Director*
EMP: 260 **EST:** 2015
SALES (est): 10MM **Privately Held**
WEB: www.yellowbrick.com
SIC: 7374 Data processing service

(P-13774)
ZENIQ INC
47 Lusk St, San Francisco (94107-1730)
PHONE..................................415 562-6367
Srihari Kumar, *CEO*
Tapas Majumdar, *COO*
Anindo Mukherjee, *CTO*
Mike Cabot, *Sales Staff*
EMP: 36 **EST:** 2015
SALES (est): 579.1K
SALES (corp-wide): 6.7MM **Privately Held**
WEB: www.6sense.com
SIC: 7374 7371 Computer processing services; computer software development & applications
PA: 6 Sense Insights, Inc.
   450 Mission St Ste 201
   San Francisco CA 94105
   415 212-9225

(P-13775)
ZYNGA INC (PA)
699 8th St, San Francisco (94103-4901)
PHONE..................................855 449-9642
Frank Gibeau, *CEO*
Dmitriy Makiyevskiy, *Partner*
Mark Pincus, *Ch of Bd*
Bernard Kim, *President*
Matthew S Bromberg, *COO*
EMP: 242 **EST:** 2007
SQ FT: 669,000
SALES (est): 1.9B **Publicly Held**
WEB: www.zynga.com
SIC: 7374 7372 Data processing & preparation; application computer software

7375 Information Retrieval Svcs

(P-13776)
22 MILES INC
1595 Mccarthy Blvd, Milpitas (95035-7424)
PHONE..................................408 933-3000
Joey Zhao, *President*
Yu Zhao, *President*
Thomas Strade, *COO*
Tomer Mann, *Exec VP*
Jeffery Tan, *Info Tech Dir*
EMP: 20 **EST:** 2007
SALES (est): 2.5MM **Privately Held**
WEB: www.22miles.com
SIC: 7375 7371 7372 On-line data base information retrieval; custom computer programming services; business oriented computer software

(P-13777)
23ANDME INC (HQ)
223 N Mathilda Ave, Sunnyvale (94086-4830)
PHONE..................................650 961-7152
Anne Wojcicki, *CEO*
Grace Moeller, *Partner*
Katie Murray, *Partner*
Andy Page, *President*
Dean Schorno, *CFO*
EMP: 357 **EST:** 2006
SALES (est): 106.6MM **Publicly Held**
WEB: www.23andme.com
SIC: 7375 Information retrieval services
PA: 23andme Holding Co.
   223 N Mathilda Ave
   Sunnyvale CA 94086
   650 938-6300

(P-13778)
AERIAL TOPCO LP (PA)
1 Embarcadero Ctr Ste 390, San Francisco (94111-3753)
PHONE..................................415 983-2700
EMP: 37 **EST:** 2015
SALES (est): 606.2MM **Privately Held**
SIC: 7375 4899 Information retrieval services; data communication services

(P-13779)
BACKBLAZE INC
500 Ben Franklin Ct, San Mateo (94401-4045)
PHONE..................................650 352-3738
Gleb Budman, *Ch of Bd*
Frank Patchel, *CFO*
Tim Nufire, *Ch Credit Ofcr*
Brian Wilson, *CTO*
EMP: 228 **EST:** 2007
SALES (est): 53.7MM **Privately Held**
WEB: www.backblaze.com
SIC: 7375 Information retrieval services

(P-13780)
BLACKHAWK ENGAGEMENT SOLUTION
6220 Stoneridge Mall Rd, Pleasanton (94588-3260)
PHONE..................................925 226-9990
Colette Smith, *Surgery Dir*
William Arnold, *Administration*
Cody Frederick, *Sr Software Eng*
Robert Boeck, *Software Engr*
Robert Wright, *Technology*
EMP: 92 **EST:** 1999
SALES (est): 50.4MM
SALES (corp-wide): 2.2B **Privately Held**
WEB: www.blackhawknetwork.com
SIC: 7375 Information retrieval services
HQ: Blackhawk Network Holdings, Inc.
   6220 Stoneridge Mall Rd
   Pleasanton CA 94588

(P-13781)
CENTRRO INC (PA)
2418 Teal Ln, Alameda (94501-5482)
PHONE..................................510 891-7500
Ike Eze, *President*

Tuyen Vo, *Vice Pres*
Sumul Shah, *Technical Staff*
EMP: 37 **EST:** 2006
SQ FT: 1,500
SALES (est): 7.3MM **Privately Held**
SIC: 7375 Information retrieval services

(P-13782)
CHANGEORG INC (PA)
383 Rhode Island St # 300, San Francisco (94103-5178)
PHONE..................................415 817-1840
Benj Rattay, *CEO*
Jennifer Dulski, *President*
Benj Rattray, *CEO*
Rahoul Seth, *CFO*
BEC Wilson, *Officer*
EMP: 114 **EST:** 2006
SQ FT: 10,000 **Privately Held**
WEB: www.change.org
SIC: 7375 On-line data base information retrieval

(P-13783)
DATABASE SPECIALISTS INC (DH)
580 California St 500, San Francisco (94104-1000)
PHONE..................................415 344-0500
David Wolff, *CEO*
EMP: 76 **EST:** 1997
SQ FT: 200
SALES (est): 939.6K
SALES (corp-wide): 2.7B **Publicly Held**
WEB: www.dbspecialists.com
SIC: 7375 Remote data base information retrieval
HQ: Tricore Solutions, Llc
   141 Longwater Dr Ste 100
   Norwell MA 02061
   617 774-5200

(P-13784)
DIABLO CREEK INFORMATION LLC
4057 Port Chicago Hwy # 100, Concord (94520-1164)
PHONE..................................925 330-3200
Michelle Le-Cheung, *Principal*
EMP: 35 **EST:** 2017
SALES (est): 2.4MM **Privately Held**
WEB: www.diablocreekgc.com
SIC: 7375 On-line data base information retrieval

(P-13785)
DIGITAL INSIGHT CORPORATION (HQ)
Also Called: Intuit Financial Services
1300 Seaport Blvd Ste 300, Redwood City (94063-5591)
PHONE..................................818 879-1010
Jeffrey E Stiefler, *President*
Christina Johnson, *Partner*
Joseph M McDoniel, *Exec VP*
Tom Shen, *Exec VP*
Robert R Surridge, *Senior VP*
▲ **EMP:** 200 **EST:** 1997
SQ FT: 46,000
SALES (est): 111.2MM
SALES (corp-wide): 6.2B **Publicly Held**
WEB: www.ncr.com
SIC: 7375 7372 7371 Information retrieval services; prepackaged software; custom computer programming services
PA: Ncr Corporation
   864 Spring St Nw
   Atlanta GA 30308
   937 445-5000

(P-13786)
DRIVESAVERS INC
Also Called: Drivesavers Data Recovery
400 Bel Marin Keys Blvd, Novato (94949-5642)
PHONE..................................415 382-2000
Jay Hagan, *CEO*
Scott Moyer, *President*
Dave Bradley, *Executive*
David Bradley, *Executive*
Michael Hall, *CIO*
EMP: 90 **EST:** 1990
SQ FT: 4,400
SALES (est): 20MM **Privately Held**
WEB: www.drivesaversdatarecovery.com
SIC: 7375 Information retrieval services

(P-13787)
EBRARY
161 E Evelyn Ave, Mountain View (94041-1510)
PHONE..................................650 475-8700
Christopher Warnock, *CEO*
Kevin Sayar, *President*
EMP: 69 **EST:** 1999
SQ FT: 28,000
SALES (est): 10MM
SALES (corp-wide): 964.5MM **Privately Held**
WEB: www.ebrary.com
SIC: 7375 Information retrieval services
HQ: Proquest Llc
   789 E Eisenhower Pkwy
   Ann Arbor MI 48108
   734 761-4700

(P-13788)
FACEBOOK
1105 Hamilton Ct, Menlo Park (94025-1424)
PHONE..................................650 823-7128
Xin Huang, *Software Engr*
Boyang Zhang, *Software Engr*
Neeraj Bahl, *Network Enginr*
Pratap Prabhu, *Engineer*
Courtney Igo, *Marketing Mgr*
EMP: 59 **EST:** 2014
SALES (est): 7.5MM **Privately Held**
SIC: 7375 Information retrieval services

(P-13789)
FACEBOOK PARK TOWER
250 Howard St, San Francisco (94105-1803)
PHONE..................................949 725-8637
EMP: 4000 **EST:** 2019
SALES (est): 107.9MM
SALES (corp-wide): 85.9B **Publicly Held**
WEB: www.facebook.com
SIC: 7375 Information retrieval services
PA: Meta Platforms, Inc.
   1601 Willow Rd
   Menlo Park CA 94025
   650 543-4800

(P-13790)
FANDOM INC (PA)
Also Called: Wikia
130 Sutter St Ste 400, San Francisco (94104-4015)
PHONE..................................415 762-0780
Perkins Miller, *CEO*
Ed Lu, *CFO*
Kyle Cooney, *Vice Pres*
Nate Hunt, *Vice Pres*
Marc Steir, *Vice Pres*
EMP: 59 **EST:** 2006
SALES (est): 13.4MM **Privately Held**
WEB: www.fandom.com
SIC: 7375 On-line data base information retrieval

(P-13791)
HEALTHLINE NETWORKS INC
660 3rd St, San Francisco (94107-1927)
PHONE..................................415 281-3100
West Shell, *CEO*
Lisa Wong, *Partner*
Dean Stephens, *President*
David Kopp, *Exec VP*
Terry Lynn, *Vice Pres*
EMP: 40 **EST:** 1996
SQ FT: 10,000
SALES (est): 22.4MM **Privately Held**
WEB: www.healthline.com
SIC: 7375 On-line data base information retrieval

(P-13792)
HOOTSUITE MEDIA US INC
535 Mission St Fl 14, San Francisco (94105-3253)
PHONE..................................206 519-5705
Ryan Holmes, *CEO*
Sujeet Kini, *CFO*
Stefan Krepiakevich, *Vice Pres*
Ryan Donovan, *CTO*
Gary Tauss, *Marketing Staff*
EMP: 47 **EST:** 2015

7375 - Information Retrieval Svcs County (P-13793)

PRODUCTS & SERVICES SECTION

SALES (est): 5.9MM
SALES (corp-wide): 207.8MM **Privately Held**
WEB: www.hootsuite.com
SIC: 7375 Information retrieval services
PA: Hootsuite Inc
  111 5th Ave E Suite 300
  Vancouver BC V5T 4
  604 681-4668

(P-13793)
HURRICANE ELECTRIC LLC (PA)
760 Mission Ct, Fremont (94539-8204)
PHONE.....................510 580-4100
  Michael Leber, *Mng Member*
  Alfred Alejandrino, *Software Dev*
  Cole Bite, *Technician*
  Rob Mosher, *Engineer*
  Leinnan Roylo, *Accountant*
▲ EMP: 40
SQ FT: 43,000
SALES (est): 17.2MM **Privately Held**
WEB: www.he.net
SIC: 7375 4813 Information retrieval services;

(P-13794)
IAC SEARCH & MEDIA INC (HQ)
Also Called: Ask.com
555 12th St Ste 500, Oakland (94607-3699)
PHONE.....................510 985-7400
  Doug Leeds, *CEO*
  George S Lichter, *President*
  Shane McGilloway, *COO*
  Dominic Butera, *CFO*
  Steven J Sordello, *CFO*
EMP: 200 EST: 1996
SQ FT: 76,000
SALES (est): 109.4MM
SALES (corp-wide): 3B **Publicly Held**
WEB: www.iac.com
SIC: 7375 On-line data base information retrieval
PA: Iac/Interactivecorp
  555 W 18th St
  New York NY 10011
  212 314-7300

(P-13795)
INTERNET ARCHIVE
300 Funston Ave, San Francisco (94118-2116)
PHONE.....................415 561-6767
  Brewster Kahle, *Director*
  Kyrie Whitsett, *Partner*
  Mills Andrea, *Program Mgr*
  Caitlin Olson, *Executive Asst*
  Giovanni Damiola, *Software Dev*
EMP: 173 EST: 1996
SALES: 17.8MM **Privately Held**
WEB: www.archive.org
SIC: 7375 On-line data base information retrieval

(P-13796)
JEPPESEN DATAPLAN INC
225 W Santa Clara St # 1600, San Jose (95113-1752)
PHONE.....................408 961-2825
  Mark Van Tine, *President*
  Jepson Fuller, *CFO*
  Ted Glogovac, *Manager*
EMP: 1486 EST: 1974
SQ FT: 20,000
SALES (est): 16MM
SALES (corp-wide): 58.1B **Publicly Held**
WEB: www.jeppesen.com
SIC: 7375 Information retrieval services
HQ: Boeing Digital Solutions, Inc.
  55 Inverness Dr E
  Englewood CO 80112
  303 799-9090

(P-13797)
JIFF INC
1999 Harrison St Ste 2070, Oakland (94612-3583)
PHONE.....................510 844-4139
  Wendy Kinney, *Vice Pres*
EMP: 127 **Publicly Held**
WEB: www.castlighthealth.com
SIC: 7375 On-line data base information retrieval

HQ: Jiff, Inc.
  150 Spear St Ste 400
  San Francisco CA 94105
  415 829-1400

(P-13798)
LINKEDIN CORPORATION (HQ)
1000 W Maude Ave, Sunnyvale (94085-2810)
PHONE.....................650 687-3600
  Steve Sordello, *CFO*
  Michelle Forker, *Partner*
  Joe Hanson, *Partner*
  Jian Lu, *President*
  Maria Robinson, *President*
EMP: 4788 EST: 2002
SQ FT: 373,000
SALES (est): 1.7B
SALES (corp-wide): 168B **Publicly Held**
WEB: www.linkedin.com
SIC: 7375 On-line data base information retrieval
PA: Microsoft Corporation
  1 Microsoft Way
  Redmond WA 98052
  425 882-8080

(P-13799)
LOGIK SYSTEMS INC (PA)
Also Called: Logikcull
111 Sutter St, San Francisco (94104-4545)
PHONE.....................844 363-3347
  Andy Wilson, *CEO*
  Colin Bryant, *Partner*
  Sheng Yang, *Officer*
  Paul Drobot, *Vice Pres*
  Michelle Price, *Vice Pres*
EMP: 85 EST: 2007
SALES (est): 8.8MM **Privately Held**
WEB: www.logikcull.com
SIC: 7375 Information retrieval services

(P-13800)
META PLATFORMS INC (PA)
Also Called: Facebook
1601 Willow Rd, Menlo Park (94025-1452)
PHONE.....................650 543-4800
  Mark Zuckerberg, *Ch of Bd*
  Sheryl K Sandberg, *COO*
  David M Wehner, *CFO*
  Christopher K Cox, *Officer*
  David B Fischer, *Officer*
EMP: 800 EST: 2004
SALES (est): 85.9B **Publicly Held**
WEB: www.facebook.com
SIC: 7375 On-line data base information retrieval

(P-13801)
NEEVA INC
100 View St Ste 204, Mountain View (94041-1374)
PHONE.....................408 220-9086
  Sridhar Ramaswamy, *CEO*
  Lara Moore, *Project Mgr*
  Cosmos Nicolaou, *Director*
  Vivek Raghunathan, *Director*
EMP: 65 EST: 2018
SALES (est): 6.8MM **Privately Held**
WEB: www.neeva.com
SIC: 7375 Information retrieval services

(P-13802)
NEXTDOORCOM INC (PA)
875 Stevenson St Ste 100, San Francisco (94103-0906)
PHONE.....................415 236-0000
  Nirav Tolia, *CEO*
  Prakash Janakiraman, *Vice Pres*
  Sarah Leary, *Vice Pres*
  Dan Masquelier, *Vice Pres*
  Liliya Kuzmina, *Office Mgr*
EMP: 96 EST: 2011
SALES (est): 19.5MM **Privately Held**
WEB: www.nextdoor.com
SIC: 7375 On-line data base information retrieval

(P-13803)
PERFORMANT FINANCIAL CORP (PA)
333 N Canyons Pkwy # 100, Livermore (94551-9480)
PHONE.....................925 960-4800
  Lisa C Im, *Ch of Bd*
  Harold T Leach Jr, *Ch Credit Ofcr*

  Ian A Johnston, *Vice Pres*
  Simeon M Kohl, *Vice Pres*
EMP: 496 EST: 1976
SQ FT: 50,000
SALES (est): 155.9MM **Publicly Held**
WEB: www.performantcorp.com
SIC: 7375 Information retrieval services

(P-13804)
PLAID INC (PA)
1098 Harrison St, San Francisco (94103-4521)
PHONE.....................415 799-1354
  George Zachary Perret, *President*
  Kalee Hasselbach, *COO*
  Katie Van Vaerenbergh, *Executive Asst*
  William Hockey, *CTO*
  Austin Gibbons, *Software Engr*
EMP: 109 EST: 2012
SALES (est): 25.9MM **Privately Held**
WEB: www.plaid.com
SIC: 7375 Information retrieval services

(P-13805)
PROCTORU INC
3687 Old Sta, Pleasanton (94588)
PHONE.....................205 870-8122
  Stephanie Dille, *Chief Mktg Ofcr*
  Matt Jaeh, *Officer*
  Steve Morgan, *Vice Pres*
  Thomas Miller, *Sr Software Eng*
  Ashley Norris, *Ch Acad Ofcr*
EMP: 106
SALES (corp-wide): 18.9MM **Privately Held**
WEB: www.proctoru.com
SIC: 7375 Information retrieval services
PA: Proctoru, Inc.
  2200 Riverchase Ctr # 600
  Hoover AL 35244
  925 273-7588

(P-13806)
QUORA INC
650 Castro St Ste 450, Mountain View (94041-2026)
PHONE.....................650 485-2464
  Adam D Angelo, *CEO*
  Kelly Battles, *CFO*
  Steven Trieu, *CFO*
  Jascha Kaykas-Wolff, *Chief Mktg Ofcr*
  Alex Salkever, *Vice Pres*
EMP: 50 EST: 2009
SALES (est): 3.6MM **Privately Held**
WEB: www.quora.com
SIC: 7375 Information retrieval services

(P-13807)
SALON MEDIA GROUP INC (PA)
870 Market St Ste 442, San Francisco (94102-3018)
PHONE.....................415 870-7566
  Richard Macwilliams, *CEO*
  John Warnock, *Ch of Bd*
  Trevor Calhoun, *CFO*
  David Daley, *Chief*
  D Watkins, *Editor*
▲ EMP: 41 EST: 1995
SQ FT: 2,405 **Publicly Held**
WEB: www.salon.com
SIC: 7375 7383 On-line data base information retrieval; news feature syndicate; news pictures, gathering & distributing

(P-13808)
SCRIBD INC (PA)
460 Bryant St Fl 1, San Francisco (94107-2595)
PHONE.....................415 896-9890
  John Adler, *CEO*
  Jared Fliesler, *COO*
  Eric Shoup, *COO*
  Sabeen Minns, *Vice Pres*
  Andrew Weinstein, *Vice Pres*
EMP: 59 EST: 2007
SALES (est): 24.9MM **Privately Held**
WEB: www.scribd.com
SIC: 7375 Information retrieval services

(P-13809)
SPIRE GLOBAL SUBSIDIARY INC (HQ)
251 Rhode Island St Ste 2, San Francisco (94103-5131)
PHONE.....................415 356-3400
  Peter Platzer, *CEO*

  Carl Harris, *COO*
  Theresa Condor, *Exec VP*
  Kamal Arafeh, *Senior VP*
  Johnny Truong, *Vice Pres*
EMP: 148 EST: 2012
SALES (est): 26MM
SALES (corp-wide): 0 **Publicly Held**
WEB: www.spire.com
SIC: 7375 On-line data base information retrieval
PA: Spire Global, Inc.
  12020 Sunrise Valley Dr # 1
  Reston VA 20191
  571 500-2236

(P-13810)
TINTRI INC
303 Ravendale Dr, Mountain View (94043-5228)
PHONE.....................650 810-8200
  Kieran Harty, *CTO*
  Mario Blandini, *Chief Mktg Ofcr*
  Scott Buchanan, *Chief Mktg Ofcr*
  Doug Kahn, *Exec VP*
  Tom Cashman, *Vice Pres*
EMP: 445 EST: 2008
SQ FT: 127,000
SALES (est): 66.6MM
SALES (corp-wide): 214.7MM **Privately Held**
WEB: www.tintri.com
SIC: 7375 7374 Data base information retrieval; data processing & preparation
PA: Datadirect Networks, Inc.
  9351 Deering Ave
  Chatsworth CA 91311
  818 700-7600

(P-13811)
VESTEK SYSTEMS INC (DH)
425 Market St Fl 6, San Francisco (94105-2470)
PHONE.....................415 344-6000
EMP: 79
SQ FT: 18,000
SALES (est): 4MM
SALES (corp-wide): 104.8MM **Privately Held**
SIC: 7375 Information Retrieval Services

(P-13812)
YELP INC (PA)
140 New Montgomery St # 900, San Francisco (94105-3822)
PHONE.....................415 908-3801
  Jeremy Stoppelman, *CEO*
  Andrew Bernardi, *Partner*
  Evaggelos Bonanno, *Partner*
  Gus Chapdelaine, *Partner*
  Jacqueline Cherkas, *Partner*
EMP: 93 EST: 2004
SALES (est): 872.9MM **Publicly Held**
WEB: www.yelp.com
SIC: 7375 On-line data base information retrieval

(P-13813)
ZYME SOLUTIONS INC (PA)
240 Twin Dolphin Dr Ste D, Redwood City (94065-1403)
PHONE.....................650 585-2258
  Chandran Sankaran, *President*
  Adam Brenner, *Senior VP*
  Edward Dimbero, *Senior VP*
  Azza Hararah, *Vice Pres*
  Ashish Shete, *VP Engrg*
EMP: 100 EST: 2004
SALES (est): 19.6MM **Privately Held**
WEB: www.e2open.com
SIC: 7375 Information retrieval services

7376 Computer Facilities Management Svcs

(P-13814)
GLOBAL BLUE DVBE INC
4470 Yankee Hill Rd # 160, Rocklin (95677-1631)
PHONE.....................916 632-2583
  Dave Hornbeck, *President*
  Michael Terpstra, *Vice Pres*
EMP: 75 EST: 2011

▲ = Import ▼ = Export
♦ = Import/Export

PRODUCTS & SERVICES SECTION

7379 - Computer Related Svcs, NEC County (P-13835)

SALES (est): 5.3MM **Privately Held**
WEB: www.gbdvbe.com
SIC: 7376 7379 7371 Computer facilities management; computer related consulting services; computer software development & applications

(P-13815)
HCL AMERICA INC (DH)
330 Potrero Ave, Sunnyvale (94085-4194)
PHONE 408 733-0480
Shiv Nadar, *Director*
Victoria Bond, *Partner*
Manish Anand, *CEO*
Raghu R Lakshmanan, *Exec VP*
Gregory Emmert, *Vice Pres*
EMP: 200 **EST:** 1988
SQ FT: 31,000
SALES: 3.3B **Privately Held**
WEB: www.hcl.com
SIC: 7376 7371 8741 Computer facilities management; computer software development; management services

(P-13816)
NTT GLBAL DATA CTRS AMRCAS INC (DH)
Also Called: Raging Wire
1625 National Dr, Sacramento (95834-2901)
P.O. Box 348060 (95834-8060)
PHONE 916 286-3000
Douglas S Adams, *President*
Joel Stone, *COO*
Kevin Dalton, *Senior VP*
Joe Goldsmith, *Senior VP*
Judi A Lee, *Senior VP*
▲ **EMP:** 275 **EST:** 2000
SALES (est): 106.7MM **Privately Held**
WEB: www.ragingwire.com
SIC: 7376 8748 Computer facilities management; telecommunications consultant

(P-13817)
ZAG TECHNICAL SERVICES INC
645 River Oaks Pkwy, San Jose (95134-1907)
PHONE 408 383-2000
Greg Gatzke, *President*
Andrew Benjamin, *Administration*
Adam Kempton, *Administration*
Stephen Lucero, *Info Tech Dir*
Albert Brown, *Project Mgr*
EMP: 47 **EST:** 1998
SQ FT: 10,000
SALES (est): 7.4MM **Privately Held**
WEB: www.zagtech.com
SIC: 7376 Computer facilities management

7378 Computer Maintenance & Repair

(P-13818)
ALCHEMY CAFE INC (PA)
746 French Gulch Rd, Murphys (95247-9762)
PHONE 925 825-8400
Ken Eysel, *CEO*
Lorrie K Eysel, *President*
Brian Noble, *Manager*
EMP: 25 **EST:** 1989
SQ FT: 11,000
SALES (est): 4.4MM **Privately Held**
WEB: www.aristadoes.com
SIC: 7378 3861 Computer peripheral equipment repair & maintenance; photographic equipment & supplies

(P-13819)
CLICKAWAY CORPORATION
Also Called: Verizon Wreless Authorized Ret
457 E Mcglincy Ln Ste 1, Campbell (95008-4939)
PHONE 408 626-9400
Rick Sutherland, *President*
Oliver Rowen, *Exec VP*
Thomas Vu, *Vice Pres*
Farias Sal, *Store Mgr*
Susanna Simonyan, *Controller*
EMP: 35 **EST:** 2002
SQ FT: 3,000
SALES (est): 5.2MM **Privately Held**
WEB: www.clickaway.com
SIC: 7378 Computer maintenance & repair

(P-13820)
COKEVA INC
Also Called: Applied Materials
9000 Foothills Blvd, Roseville (95747-4411)
PHONE 916 462-6001
Ann D Nguyen, *CEO*
Dominick Derosa, *CFO*
Kevin Nguyen, *Vice Pres*
Lee Nguyen, *Vice Pres*
Qui Nguyen, *Vice Pres*
▲ **EMP:** 181 **EST:** 1990
SQ FT: 175,000
SALES (est): 28.9MM **Privately Held**
WEB: www.cokeva.com
SIC: 7378 Computer maintenance & repair

(P-13821)
DST OUTPUT CALIFORNIA INC
5220 Rbert J Mathews Pkwy, El Dorado Hills (95762-5705)
PHONE 916 939-4617
Kenneth Taylor, *Manager*
Rick Filarski, *Vice Pres*
Adam Miller, *Admin Asst*
Rosa Binder, *Sr Software Eng*
Zane Pearson, *Software Engr*
EMP: 132 **EST:** 2004
SALES (est): 39MM **Publicly Held**
WEB: www.broadridge.com
SIC: 7378 Computer maintenance & repair
HQ: Broadridge Customer Communications, Llc
2600 Southwest Blvd
Kansas City MO 64108

(P-13822)
ESL TECHNOLOGIES INC
8875 Washington Blvd B, Roseville (95678-6214)
PHONE 916 677-4500
Donna Kwidzinski, *CEO*
Tjeu Blommaert, *President*
▲ **EMP:** 350 **EST:** 1996
SQ FT: 100,000
SALES (est): 24.2MM
SALES (corp-wide): 355.8K **Privately Held**
SIC: 7378 Computer peripheral equipment repair & maintenance
HQ: Teleplan Holding Usa, Inc.
8875 Washington Blvd
Roseville CA 95678
916 677-4500

(P-13823)
TECH SERVICE 2 U INC
Also Called: Tech 2 U
1590 Howe Ave, Sacramento (95825-3358)
PHONE 888 931-0942
John Worthington, *CEO*
Todd Fiore, *CIO*
ARI Azad, *CTO*
EMP: 37 **EST:** 2008
SALES (est): 5MM **Privately Held**
WEB: www.tech2u.com
SIC: 7378 Computer & data processing equipment repair/maintenance

(P-13824)
TELEPLAN SERVICE SOLUTIONS INC
8875 Washington Blvd B, Roseville (95678-6214)
PHONE 916 677-4500
Russell Sproull, *CEO*
Pk Bala, *COO*
Jan Piet Valk, *CFO*
Jack Rockwood, *Vice Pres*
Chris Tejeda, *Business Dir*
▲ **EMP:** 75 **EST:** 2000
SALES (est): 21.2MM
SALES (corp-wide): 355.8K **Privately Held**
WEB: www.reconext.com
SIC: 7378 Computer maintenance & repair
HQ: Teleplan Holding Usa, Inc.
8875 Washington Blvd
Roseville CA 95678
916 677-4500

(P-13825)
TUSA INC (PA)
Also Called: Terix Computer Service
986 Walsh Ave, Santa Clara (95050-2649)
PHONE 888 848-3749
Bernd Appleby, *CEO*
EMP: 105 **EST:** 2016
SALES (est): 30MM **Privately Held**
SIC: 7378 Computer maintenance & repair

7379 Computer Related Svcs, NEC

(P-13826)
247AI INC (PA)
2001 All Programable # 200, San Jose (95124-4356)
PHONE 650 385-2247
Pallipuram V Kannan, *Ch of Bd*
Bruce Weiss, *Partner*
Rohan Ganeson, *COO*
Bill Robbins, *COO*
Brent Bowman, *CFO*
EMP: 8937 **EST:** 2000
SQ FT: 5,000
SALES (est): 372.6MM **Privately Held**
WEB: www.247.ai
SIC: 7379

(P-13827)
A10 NETWORKS INC (PA)
2300 Orchard Pkwy, San Jose (95131-1017)
PHONE 408 325-8668
Dhrupad Trivedi, *Ch of Bd*
Brian Becker, *CFO*
Matthew Bruening, *Exec VP*
Robert Cochran, *Exec VP*
Ross Wheeler, *Vice Pres*
▲ **EMP:** 719 **EST:** 2004
SQ FT: 116,381
SALES (est): 225.5MM **Publicly Held**
WEB: www.a10networks.com
SIC: 7379 7372 Computer related maintenance services; prepackaged software; utility computer software

(P-13828)
ACCELLION INC
1804 Embarcadero Rd # 200, Palo Alto (94303-3318)
PHONE 650 485-4300
Rebecca Soler, *Vice Pres*
Yaron Galant, *Vice Pres*
Jeremy Fong, *Vice Pres*
Ryan Gallagher, *Vice Pres*
Rajeev Gupta, *Vice Pres*
EMP: 150 **EST:** 1997
SQ FT: 11,145
SALES (est): 27MM **Privately Held**
WEB: www.accellion.com
SIC: 7379 Computer related maintenance services

(P-13829)
ACCRETE SOLUTIONS LLC
3350 Scott Blvd Bldg 34a, Santa Clara (95054-3105)
PHONE 877 849-5838
Sanjay Minocha, *President*
EMP: 290 **EST:** 2008
SALES (est): 10.7MM **Privately Held**
WEB: www.accretehitechsolutions.com
SIC: 7379 8742 7373 Computer related consulting services; management consulting services; systems integration services

(P-13830)
ACER AMERICA CORPORATION (DH)
1730 N 1st St Ste 400, San Jose (95112-4642)
PHONE 408 533-7700
Greg Prendergast, *CEO*
Tanuja Palsule, *Partner*
Ming Wang, *COO*
Nga Ly, *Treasurer*
Harish Kohli, *Officer*
◆ **EMP:** 100 **EST:** 1976
SALES (est): 103.9MM **Privately Held**
WEB: www.acer.com
SIC: 7379
HQ: Gateway, Inc.
7565 Irvine Center Dr # 150
Irvine CA 92618
949 471-7000

(P-13831)
ADROIT RESOURCES INC (HQ)
46231 Landing Pkwy, Fremont (94538-6407)
PHONE 510 344-8797
Mausami Kakkar, *CEO*
Prashant Sharma, *President*
Imtiaz Mohammady, *CEO*
Ahmed Lakhani, *Technical Staff*
EMP: 42 **EST:** 2011
SALES (est): 7.1MM
SALES (corp-wide): 23.4MM **Privately Held**
WEB: www.adroitresources.com
SIC: 7379
PA: Nisum Technologies, Inc.
500 S Kraemer Blvd # 301
Brea CA
714 579-7979

(P-13832)
ADVANCED BUS INTEGRATORS INC
Also Called: ABI Mastermind R
8413 Jackson Rd Ste C, Sacramento (95826-3914)
PHONE 916 381-3809
David Schwartz, *President*
Eric Hoffman, *COO*
Todd Linhart, *Treasurer*
Tim Whitehouse, *Vice Pres*
Aaron Dukovich, *Comms Mgr*
EMP: 45 **EST:** 1990
SALES (est): 6.3MM **Privately Held**
WEB: www.abico.com
SIC: 7379 5734 Data processing consultant; computer & software stores

(P-13833)
ADVANTIS GLOBAL INC (PA)
20 Sunnyside Ave Ste E, Mill Valley (94941-1928)
PHONE 415 612-3338
Bryan Barber, *CEO*
Jeff Taylor, *COO*
Shaun Porter, *CFO*
Randi Haaker, *Vice Pres*
Jeanne Bay, *Tech Recruiter*
EMP: 110 **EST:** 2007
SALES (est): 40MM **Privately Held**
WEB: www.advantisglobal.com
SIC: 7379 Computer related consulting services;

(P-13834)
AGILIANCE INC (PA)
845 Stewart Dr Ste D, Sunnyvale (94085-4504)
P.O. Box 961, San Ramon (94583-5961)
PHONE 408 200-0400
Joe Fantuzzi, *President*
Cassandra Ho, *CFO*
Keith Higgins, *Chief Mktg Ofcr*
Martin Jaffe, *Surgery Dir*
Kevin Barcellos, *Engineer*
EMP: 49 **EST:** 2005
SQ FT: 8,000
SALES (est): 5MM **Privately Held**
SIC: 7379 7376 7373 Computer related consulting services; computer facilities management; computer integrated systems design

(P-13835)
AGRIAN INC (PA)
352 W Spruce Ave, Clovis (93611-8705)
PHONE 559 437-5700
Nishan Majarian, *CEO*
Richard Machado, *President*
Joseph Middione, *COO*
Nick Morrow, *Vice Pres*
Peter Brandt, *CTO*
EMP: 90 **EST:** 2004
SQ FT: 3,500
SALES (est): 9.1MM **Privately Held**
WEB: www.agrian.com
SIC: 7379

7379 - Computer Related Svcs, NEC County (P-13836)

(P-13836)
AKSHAYA INC (PA)
415 Boulder Ct Ste 100, Pleasanton (94566-8321)
PHONE..................925 914-7395
Swaroop Antoo, *CEO*
Praveen Goud, *IT/INT Sup*
Ramya Parthasarathy, *Tech Recruiter*
EMP: 128 **EST:** 2012
SQ FT: 3,145
SALES (est): 20MM **Privately Held**
WEB: www.akshaya-inc.com
SIC: 7379 Computer related consulting services

(P-13837)
ALLIANZ TECHNOLOGY AMERICA INC
Also Called: Allianz Global Corporate &
1 Belvedere Dr, Mill Valley (94941-2418)
PHONE..................415 899-4110
Axel Shell, *CEO*
Olav Spiegel, *COO*
Michael Schiebel, *CFO*
Ryan Gibson, *Admin Sec*
Jean-Francois Landreau, *Technology*
EMP: 120 **EST:** 2013
SQ FT: 15,000
SALES (est): 29.1MM
SALES (corp-wide): 26.4B **Privately Held**
SIC: 7379
HQ: Allianz Technology International B.V.
Keizersgracht 484
Amsterdam 1017
205 569-715

(P-13838)
ALTEXSOFT INC
6590 Lockheed Dr, Redding (96002-9013)
PHONE..................877 777-9097
Oleksandr Medovoi, *President*
EMP: 146
SALES (corp-wide): 6.6MM **Privately Held**
WEB: www.altexsoft.com
SIC: 7379 Computer related consulting services
PA: Altexsoft Inc.
41829 Albrae St 111
Fremont CA 94538
877 777-9097

(P-13839)
ANAPLAN INC (PA)
50 Hawthorne St, San Francisco (94105-3902)
PHONE..................415 742-8199
Frank Calderoni, *President*
Pankaj Tibrewal, *Partner*
Vikas Mehta, *CFO*
David H Morton Jr, *CFO*
Simon Tucker, *Officer*
EMP: 1077 **EST:** 2008
SQ FT: 55,000
SALES: 447.7MM **Publicly Held**
WEB: www.anaplan.com
SIC: 7379

(P-13840)
APN SOFTWARE SERVICES INC (PA)
39899 Balentine Dr # 385, Newark (94560-5391)
PHONE..................510 623-5050
Aslam Chandiwalli, *President*
Mayur Paranjpe, *Business Dir*
Joe Kulkarni, *Business Anlyst*
Wasif Rehman, *Tech Recruiter*
Sachin Solanki, *Technology*
EMP: 128 **EST:** 1996
SQ FT: 3,500
SALES (est): 12.7MM **Privately Held**
WEB: www.apninc.com
SIC: 7379 Computer related consulting services

(P-13841)
APOLENT CORPORATION (PA)
2570 N 1st St Ste 200, San Jose (95131-1037)
PHONE..................408 203-6828
Anupama Awadhwa, *President*
Brijendra Sharma, *Treasurer*
Dinesh Kumar, *Vice Pres*
Achint Wadhwa, *Administration*
Matt Kieffer, *Sales Staff*
EMP: 44 **EST:** 2004 **Privately Held**
WEB: www.apolent.com
SIC: 7379 Computer related consulting services

(P-13842)
APPLIED SYSTEMS ENGRG INC
2105 S Bascom Ave Ste 155, Campbell (95008-3276)
PHONE..................408 364-0500
Prasanth Gopalakrishnan, *CEO*
Janet Hogan, *Executive*
Layla Daryan, *General Mgr*
Eva Ulett, *Sales Associate*
EMP: 16 **EST:** 1982
SALES (est): 4.2MM **Privately Held**
WEB: www.ase-systems.com
SIC: 7379 7371 3577 3663 Computer related consulting services; computer software development; computer peripheral equipment; decoders, computer peripheral equipment; mobile communication equipment
HQ: Kalkitech, Inc.
9900 Westpark Dr Ste 283
Houston TX 77063

(P-13843)
APSTRA INC (HQ)
1137 Innovation Way, Sunnyvale (94089-1228)
PHONE..................650 307-3245
Rami Rahim, *CEO*
Jeff Jones, *Vice Pres*
Herb Schneider, *VP Engrg*
Mari Clapp, *Marketing Staff*
Peter Lavington, *Sales Staff*
EMP: 70 **EST:** 2014
SALES (est): 12.7MM **Publicly Held**
WEB: www.apstra.com
SIC: 7379 Computer related consulting services

(P-13844)
ARCHERHALL LLC (PA)
2081 Arena Blvd Ste 200, Sacramento (95834-2309)
PHONE..................916 449-2820
Dave Wilkinson, *President*
Lucas Mageno, *Co-Owner*
Dave Baer, *General Mgr*
◆ **EMP:** 44 **EST:** 2007
SALES (est): 6.1MM **Privately Held**
WEB: www.capitol-digital.com
SIC: 7379 Data processing consultant

(P-13845)
ASANA INC (PA)
633 Folsom St Ste 100, San Francisco (94107-3600)
PHONE..................415 525-3888
Dustin Moskovitz, *Ch of Bd*
Anne Raimondi, *COO*
Tim Wan, *CFO*
Eleanor Lacey, *Admin Sec*
EMP: 1075 **EST:** 2008
SQ FT: 88,000
SALES: 227MM **Publicly Held**
WEB: www.asana.com
SIC: 7379 7372 Computer related consulting services; prepackaged software

(P-13846)
ASTOUND COMMERCE CORPORATION (HQ)
1611 Telegraph Ave # 400, Oakland (94612-2150)
PHONE..................800 591-4710
Igor Gorin, *CEO*
Roman Martynenko, *CFO*
Vanessa Cartwright, *Officer*
Sebastian Klare, *Vice Pres*
Josh Murack, *Vice Pres*
EMP: 402 **EST:** 2011
SQ FT: 4,636
SALES: 131.3MM
SALES (corp-wide): 166.7MM **Privately Held**
WEB: www.astoundcommerce.com
SIC: 7379 Computer related maintenance services
PA: Astound Holding Corporation
1111 Bayhill Dr Ste 425
San Bruno CA 94066
800 591-4710

(P-13847)
ATTACKIQ INC (PA)
171 Main St 656, Los Altos (94022-2912)
PHONE..................858 228-0864
Brett D Galloway, *CEO*
Danielle Murcray, *CFO*
Stephan Chenette, *Founder*
Carl Wright, *Officer*
Christopher Kennedy, *Vice Pres*
EMP: 117 **EST:** 2015
SALES (est): 7.1MM **Privately Held**
WEB: www.attackiq.com
SIC: 7379

(P-13848)
AVG TECHNOLOGIES USA INC (DH)
2100 Powell St, Emeryville (94608-1826)
PHONE..................978 319-4460
Gary Kovacs, *CEO*
John Little, *CFO*
Petra Sokolova, *CFO*
Justin Crowe, *Manager*
EMP: 45 **EST:** 2003
SQ FT: 3,500
SALES (est): 18.7MM
SALES (corp-wide): 892.9MM **Privately Held**
WEB: www.avg.com
SIC: 7379 7371 Disk & diskette recertification service; computer software development
HQ: Avg Technologies Uk Limited
7th Floor
London WC1V
800 652-4940

(P-13849)
AVIATRIX SYSTEMS INC
2901 Tasman Dr Ste 109, Santa Clara (95054-1137)
PHONE..................844 262-3100
Nick Sturiale, *Managing Prtnr*
Pankaj Manlik, *President*
Chee Kiong, *Vice Pres*
James Winebrenner, *Vice Pres*
Liming Xiang, *Vice Pres*
EMP: 61 **EST:** 2014
SALES (est): 7.1MM **Privately Held**
WEB: www.aviatrix.com
SIC: 7379 Computer related consulting services

(P-13850)
BAIDU USA LLC
1195 Bordeaux Dr, Sunnyvale (94089-1210)
PHONE..................669 224-6400
Lydia Liu, *Mng Member*
Paul Liu, *Principal*
Jiazhuo Wang, *Research*
EMP: 187 **EST:** 2010
SALES (est): 38.5MM **Privately Held**
WEB: www.usa.baidu.com
SIC: 7379
HQ: Baidu Japan Inc.
6-10-1, Roppongi
Minato-Ku TKY 106-0

(P-13851)
BANDPAGE INC
Also Called: Rootmusic
901 Cherry Ave, San Bruno (94066-2914)
PHONE..................415 800-6614
EMP: 38
SQ FT: 3,300
SALES (est): 4.2MM
SALES (corp-wide): 110.8B **Publicly Held**
WEB: www.rootmusic.com
SIC: 7379 Computer Related Services Telephone Communications
HQ: Loon, Llc
1600 Amphitheatre Pkwy
Mountain View CA 94043
650 623-4000

(P-13852)
BASIC SOLUTIONS CORP
46724 Fremont Blvd, Fremont (94538-6538)
PHONE..................510 573-3658
Jang Badesha, *Managing Dir*
Rohit Ghai, *Financial Analy*
Abheet Dhillon, *Sr Project Mgr*
Sunny Saggu, *Account Dir*
EMP: 108 **EST:** 2005
SALES (est): 21.8MM **Privately Held**
WEB: www.basicsolutions.com
SIC: 7379 Computer related maintenance services

(P-13853)
BCT CONSULTING INC (PA)
7910 N Ingram Ave Ste 101, Fresno (93711-5828)
PHONE..................559 579-1400
Eric Rawn, *President*
Chris Rawn, *Vice Pres*
Gabriel De La Cerda, *Administration*
Grant Robison, *Administration*
Eric Swisher, *Administration*
EMP: 38 **EST:** 1996
SALES (est): 8.1MM **Privately Held**
WEB: www.bctconsulting.com
SIC: 7379 7373 Computer related consulting services; local area network (LAN) systems integrator

(P-13854)
BEECHWOOD COMPUTING LIMITED (PA)
4677 Old Ironsides Dr, Santa Clara (95054-1809)
PHONE..................408 496-2900
Maurice Ryan, *President*
Jey Kumar, *COO*
Kapil Saigal, *Vice Pres*
V Radhakrishnan, *Manager*
EMP: 179 **EST:** 1992
SQ FT: 800
SALES (est): 8.4MM **Privately Held**
WEB: www.beechwoodcomputing.com
SIC: 7379 Computer related consulting services

(P-13855)
BERKELEY COMMUNICATIONS CORP
801 Addison St, Berkeley (94710-2053)
PHONE..................510 644-1599
Timothy Naple, *CEO*
Craig Stelmach, *CEO*
Andrew Atherton, *IT/INT Sup*
Matthew Houseman, *Mktg Dir*
Greg Orciuch, *Counsel*
▲ **EMP:** 45 **EST:** 2001
SQ FT: 50,000
SALES (est): 6.3MM **Privately Held**
WEB: www.berkcom.com
SIC: 7379 5961 7373 Computer related maintenance services; computer related consulting services; computer equipment & electronics, mail order; computer integrated systems design

(P-13856)
BEYONDID INC
535 Mission St Fl 14, San Francisco (94105-3253)
PHONE..................415 878-6210
Arun Shrestha, *CEO*
Charles Fortune, *COO*
Neeraj Methi, *Vice Pres*
Sanjay Shah, *Vice Pres*
Sasi Kelam, *Engineer*
EMP: 65 **EST:** 2018
SALES (est): 5.3MM **Privately Held**
WEB: www.beyondid.com
SIC: 7379 Computer related consulting services

(P-13857)
BIARCA INC (PA)
333 W San Carlos St # 600, San Jose (95110-2731)
PHONE..................408 564-4465
Subhashini Rajana, *CEO*
Kris Rajana, *President*
EMP: 74 **EST:** 2016

▲ = Import ▼ = Export
◆ = Import/Export

PRODUCTS & SERVICES SECTION
7379 - Computer Related Svcs, NEC County (P-13880)

SALES (est): 3.7MM **Privately Held**
WEB: www.biarca.io
SIC: 7379 7371 Computer related consulting services; custom computer programming services

(P-13858)
BUGCROWD INC (PA)
921 Front St Ste 100, San Francisco (94111-1417)
PHONE.................................650 260-8443
Ashish Gupta, *CEO*
Mark Oconnor, *CFO*
Andy Burtis, *Chief Mktg Ofcr*
Justin Beachler, *Trust Officer*
Logan Harris, *Trust Officer*
EMP: 157 **EST:** 2013
SALES (est): 7.6MM **Privately Held**
WEB: www.bugcrowd.com
SIC: 7379 Computer related consulting services

(P-13859)
CALIFORNIA DEPARTMENT TECH (DH)
Also Called: Dts
1325 J St Ste 1600, Sacramento (95814-2941)
P.O. Box 1810, Rancho Cordova (95741-1810)
PHONE.................................916 319-9223
Marybel Batjer, *Admin Sec*
Sergei Ludanov, *Manager*
EMP: 149 **EST:** 1978
SALES (est): 48.2MM **Privately Held**
WEB: www.ca.gov
SIC: 7379

(P-13860)
CAPGEMINI AMERICA INC
427 Brannan St, San Francisco (94107-1715)
PHONE.................................415 796-6777
EMP: 100
SALES (corp-wide): 387.8MM **Privately Held**
WEB: www.capgemini.com
SIC: 7379
HQ: Capgemini America, Inc.
79 5th Ave Fl 3
New York NY 10003
212 314-8000

(P-13861)
CBX TECHNOLOGIES INC
642 N L St Apt B, Livermore (94551-2861)
PHONE.................................510 729-7130
Christian D'Andrade, *President*
EMP: 35 **EST:** 1998
SQ FT: 2,108
SALES (est): 3.2MM **Privately Held**
WEB: www.cbxtech.com
SIC: 7379 Computer related consulting services; computer related maintenance services

(P-13862)
CENTERRA SOLUTIONS INC
368 Fairview Way, Milpitas (95035-3062)
PHONE.................................408 791-6188
Venkat Bussa, *CEO*
Syed Nawaz, *COO*
EMP: 40 **EST:** 2017
SALES (est): 1.4MM **Privately Held**
WEB: www.centerrasolutions.com
SIC: 7379

(P-13863)
CENTRAL BUSINESS SOLUTIONS INC
37600 Central Ct Ste 214, Newark (94560-3456)
PHONE.................................510 573-5500
Anjul Katare, *President*
Arvind Gokhale, *Executive*
Preetha Roy, *Executive*
Akash Kumar, *Tech Recruiter*
Digendra Singh, *Tech Recruiter*
EMP: 70 **EST:** 2000
SALES (est): 6.7MM **Privately Held**
WEB: www.cbsinfosys.com
SIC: 7379

(P-13864)
CERIUM SYSTEMS INC
1735 Tech Dr Ste 575, San Jose (95110)
PHONE.................................408 623-0787
Rajendra Boya, *Finance*
Rashmi Kumari, *Human Resources*
Venkat Arunarthi, *Director*
EMP: 79 **EST:** 2014
SALES (est): 5.4MM **Privately Held**
WEB: www.cerium-systems.com
SIC: 7379
PA: Tech Mahindra Cerium Private Limited
157/A, 3rd Floor Sector-5, Outer Ring Road
Bengaluru KA 56010

(P-13865)
CIVICACTIONS INC
3527 Mt Diablo Blvd # 269, Lafayette (94549-3815)
PHONE.................................510 408-7510
Henry Poole, *President*
Jonathan Bourland, *Engineer*
Julie Kramer, *Engineer*
Sam Lerner, *Engineer*
Daniel Schiavone, *Engineer*
EMP: 70 **EST:** 2009
SALES (est): 15MM **Privately Held**
WEB: www.civicactions.com
SIC: 7379 Computer related consulting services

(P-13866)
CLEAN POWER RESEARCH LLC
1541 Third St, NAPA (94559-2808)
PHONE.................................707 258-2765
Tom Hoff,
Eric Pak, *Software Engr*
Thomas Hoff, *Research*
Jennifer Gough, *Manager*
Ben Norris, *Consultant*
EMP: 49 **EST:** 1999
SALES (est): 5.4MM **Privately Held**
WEB: www.cleanpower.com
SIC: 7379 7371 Computer related consulting services; computer software development & applications

(P-13867)
CLOUD DESTINATIONS INC
2603 Camino Ramon Ste 200, San Ramon (94583-9137)
PHONE.................................510 715-7044
Vinayaga Dharmaraj, *CEO*
EMP: 50 **EST:** 2016
SALES (est): 3.2MM **Privately Held**
WEB: www.clouddestinations.com
SIC: 7379 Computer related consulting services

(P-13868)
CLOUDINARY INC
3400 Central Expy Ste 110, Santa Clara (95051-0703)
PHONE.................................650 772-1833
Itai Lahan, *CEO*
Scott Doughman, *Senior VP*
Edan Gottlib, *CIO*
Nitzan Jaitman, *Software Dev*
Gil Noy, *Software Dev*
EMP: 81 **EST:** 2015
SALES (est): 7.8MM **Privately Held**
WEB: www.cloudinary.com
SIC: 7379
PA: Cloudinary Ltd
20 Bart Aharon
Petah Tikva

(P-13869)
CLOUDIOUS LLC (PA)
2833 Junction Ave Ste 206, San Jose (95134-1920)
PHONE.................................732 666-2468
Vinoth Subramaniyan, *Mng Member*
Pravin Selvaraj, *Partner*
Subash Yammada, *Managing Prtnr*
Deepika Komma, *Human Res Mgr*
Kumar Govindarajan, *Recruiter*
EMP: 224 **EST:** 2016
SQ FT: 1,000

SALES (est): 18MM **Privately Held**
WEB: www.cloudious.com
SIC: 7379 Computer related consulting services

(P-13870)
CLOUDPHYSICS INC
2010 El Camino Real, Santa Clara (95050-4051)
PHONE.................................650 646-4616
Richard Sexton, *CEO*
John Beck III, *Partner*
John Blumenthal, *Vice Pres*
Jim Kleckner, *Vice Pres*
Mark Spurlock, *Vice Pres*
EMP: 40 **EST:** 2011
SALES (est): 5.6MM
SALES (corp-wide): 26.9B **Publicly Held**
WEB: www.cloudphysics.com
SIC: 7379
PA: Hewlett Packard Enterprise Company
11445 Compaq Center W Dr
Houston TX 77070
650 687-5817

(P-13871)
CLOUDWICK TECHNOLOGIES INC (PA)
39899 Balentine Dr # 350, Newark (94560-5395)
PHONE.................................650 346-5788
Maninder Chhabra, *CEO*
Chris Mische, *Vice Pres*
George Davy, *Administration*
Riyan Mohammed, *Software Dev*
Sowmya Varre, *Software Dev*
EMP: 88 **EST:** 2012
SQ FT: 6,000
SALES (est): 20.3MM **Privately Held**
WEB: www.cloudwick.com
SIC: 7379 Computer related consulting services

(P-13872)
COMERIT INC
2201 Francisco Dr 140-2, El Dorado Hills (95762-3713)
PHONE.................................888 556-5990
Greg Clark, *Senior Partner*
Jeff Johnston, *Senior Partner*
David Caspillo, *Vice Pres*
Karthi Kumar, *CIO*
Cathy Simko, *Manager*
EMP: 42 **EST:** 2008
SQ FT: 3,500
SALES (est): 3.1MM **Privately Held**
WEB: www.comerit.com
SIC: 7379

(P-13873)
COMITY DESIGNS INC
41 Marvin Ave, Los Altos (94022-3709)
PHONE.................................415 967-1530
Dushyant Pandya, *CEO*
Piyush Pandya, *CTO*
EMP: 100 **EST:** 2005
SALES (est): 13.4MM **Privately Held**
WEB: www.comitydesigns.com
SIC: 7379 Computer related consulting services
HQ: Brillio, Llc
399 Thornall St Fl 1
Edison NJ 08837
800 317-0575

(P-13874)
CONCENTRIX CORPORATION
44201 Nobel Dr, Fremont (94538-3178)
PHONE.................................510 668-3717
John Vitalie, *Branch Mgr*
Sean Carney, *Vice Pres*
Brandon Hubbs, *Vice Pres*
Murali Jayaraman, *Vice Pres*
Jason Karloff, *Vice Pres*
EMP: 40
SALES (corp-wide): 3B **Publicly Held**
WEB: www.concentrix.com
SIC: 7379 8742 7331 7311 Computer related maintenance services; management consulting services; direct mail advertising services; advertising agencies
HQ: Concentrix Solutions Corporation
3750 Monroe Ave
Pittsford NY 14534

(P-13875)
COYOTE CREEK CONSULTING INC
1057 Cochrane Rd, Morgan Hill (95037-9079)
PHONE.................................408 383-9200
Michael R Faster, *CEO*
Jimmy Areias, *Executive*
Nick Howser, *Executive*
Joe Allesi, *Engineer*
Logan Hawkes, *Engineer*
EMP: 45 **EST:** 1998
SALES (est): 8.2MM **Privately Held**
WEB: www.coyotecrk.com
SIC: 7379

(P-13876)
CROWDSTRIKE INC (HQ)
150 Mathilda Pl Ste 300, Sunnyvale (94086-6012)
PHONE.................................888 512-8906
George Kurtz, *CEO*
Michael Carpenter, *President*
Shawn Henry, *President*
Colin Black, *COO*
Marianne Budnick, *Chief Mktg Ofcr*
EMP: 167 **EST:** 2011
SQ FT: 16,000
SALES (est): 209.1MM
SALES (corp-wide): 874.4MM **Publicly Held**
WEB: www.crowdstrike.com
SIC: 7379 Computer related maintenance services
PA: Crowdstrike Holdings, Inc.
150 Mathilda Pl Ste 300
Sunnyvale CA 94086
888 512-8906

(P-13877)
CRYPTOGRAPHY RESEARCH INC
4453 N 1st St, San Jose (95134-1260)
PHONE.................................408 462-8000
Rahul Mather, *President*
Jerome Nadel, *Chief Mktg Ofcr*
Benjamin Jun, *Exec VP*
Christopher Rodgers, *Exec VP*
Simon Blake-Wilson, *Vice Pres*
EMP: 40 **EST:** 1998
SQ FT: 5,000
SALES (est): 6.9MM **Publicly Held**
WEB: www.rambus.com
SIC: 7379
PA: Rambus Inc.
4453 N 1st St Ste 100
San Jose CA 95134

(P-13878)
DECLARA INC
977 Commercial St, Palo Alto (94303-4908)
PHONE.................................877 216-0604
Ramona Pierson, *CEO*
Debra Chrapaty, *Executive*
Nelson Gonzalez, *Security Dir*
EMP: 68 **EST:** 2012
SQ FT: 3,000
SALES (est): 4.8MM **Privately Held**
WEB: www.declara.com
SIC: 7379 Data processing consultant

(P-13879)
DEPLABS INC
2872 Ygnacio Valley Rd # 24, Walnut Creek (94598-3534)
PHONE.................................415 456-5600
Sergii Ostapenko, *CEO*
EMP: 65 **EST:** 2005
SALES (est): 2.7MM **Privately Held**
WEB: www.miracommerce.com
SIC: 7379 8748 7371 Computer related consulting services; systems analysis & engineering consulting services; software programming applications

(P-13880)
DHYAN INFOTECH INC
Also Called: Dhyan Networks and Tech Inc
160 Stanford Ave, Fremont (94539-6092)
PHONE.................................510 589-7875
Ram Kumar, *CEO*
EMP: 45 **EST:** 2005

7379 - Computer Related Svcs, NEC County (P-13881)

SALES (est): 1.9MM **Privately Held**
WEB: www.dhyan.com
SIC: 7379 Computer related consulting services

(P-13881)
DIGITAL FOUNDRY INC
1707 Tiburon Blvd, Belvedere Tiburon (94920-2513)
PHONE.................................415 789-1600
Bradley W Stauffer, *President*
Robert Fraik, *Chairman*
Bonnie Albin Fraik, *Vice Pres*
Andrew Lee, *Software Engr*
Brandon Levinger, *Software Engr*
EMP: 50 **EST:** 1992
SQ FT: 7,500
SALES (est): 5.3MM **Privately Held**
WEB: www.digitalfoundry.com
SIC: 7379 7371 Computer related consulting services; computer software development & applications

(P-13882)
DIRECTAPPS INC (PA)
Also Called: Direct Technology
3009 Douglas Blvd Ste 300, Roseville (95661-3895)
PHONE.................................916 787-2200
Rick Nelson, *CEO*
Federico Michanie, *President*
Casey Stenzel, *CFO*
John Sercu, *Treasurer*
Kim Green, *Officer*
EMP: 125 **EST:** 1995
SQ FT: 19,000
SALES: 115.2MM **Privately Held**
WEB: www.directtechnology.com
SIC: 7379

(P-13883)
DISCOPYLABS
Also Called: Dcl
48819 Kato Rd, Fremont (94539-8070)
PHONE.................................510 651-5100
Norman Tu, *CEO*
▲ **EMP:** 49 **EST:** 1982
SALES (est): 885.6K **Privately Held**
WEB: www.dclcorp.com
SIC: 7379

(P-13884)
DVBE TECHNOLOGY GROUP
333 University Ave # 200, Sacramento (95825-6531)
PHONE.................................916 565-7610
Richard McKinnon, *CEO*
Sharon Kropf, *Vice Pres*
Tom Amato, *Advisor*
EMP: 45 **EST:** 2016
SALES (est): 3.8MM **Privately Held**
WEB: www.dvbetg.com
SIC: 7379 Computer related consulting services

(P-13885)
EDGEWATER NETWORKS INC
5225 Hellyer Ave Ste 100, San Jose (95138-1021)
PHONE.................................408 351-7200
David G Norman, *CEO*
Steve Pattison, *COO*
John Macario, *Senior VP*
Rumus Sakya, *Senior VP*
Jason Luehrs, *Vice Pres*
▲ **EMP:** 75 **EST:** 2002
SALES (est): 15.7MM
SALES (corp-wide): 843.8MM **Publicly Held**
WEB: www.info.rbbn.com
SIC: 7379 Computer related consulting services
PA: Ribbon Communications Inc.
6500 Chase Oaks Blvd Ste
Plano TX 75023
978 614-8100

(P-13886)
ENCLIPSE CORP
2410 Camino Ramon Ste 320, San Ramon (94583-4370)
PHONE.................................866 261-3503
Dan Genovaldi, *Technical Staff*
EMP: 35
SALES (corp-wide): 5.4MM **Privately Held**
WEB: www.enclipse.com
SIC: 7379
PA: Enclipse Corp.
1895 Plaza Dr Ste 120
Saint Paul MN 55122
612 384-6940

(P-13887)
ENDSIGHT
1440 4th St Ste B, Berkeley (94710-1315)
PHONE.................................510 280-2019
Michael Chaput, *CEO*
Brandon Galvin, *Executive*
Robert Gillette, *IT Executive*
Derek Tietze, *Technician*
Matt Isola, *Technical Staff*
EMP: 80 **EST:** 2004
SALES (est): 12.3MM **Privately Held**
WEB: www.endsight.net
SIC: 7379 Computer related consulting services

(P-13888)
ENEXUS GLOBAL INC
39510 Paseo Padre Pkwy # 390, Fremont (94538-2368)
PHONE.................................510 936-4044
Dinesh Puri, *President*
Ridhima Puri, *Principal*
EMP: 74 **EST:** 2015
SALES (est): 4.4MM **Privately Held**
WEB: www.enexusglobal.com
SIC: 7379 Computer related services

(P-13889)
ENJOY TECHNOLOGY INC (PA)
3240 Hillview Ave, Palo Alto (94304-1201)
PHONE.................................650 488-7676
Ron Johnson, *CEO*
Ed Park, *CFO*
Melissa McNamee, *Officer*
Kunal Malik, *CTO*
Ryan Faraday, *Info Tech Mgr*
EMP: 331 **EST:** 2014
SALES (est): 38.2MM **Publicly Held**
WEB: www.enjoy.com
SIC: 7379 Computer related maintenance services

(P-13890)
ENTERPRISE NTWRKING SLTONS INC
2860 Gold Tailings Ct, Rancho Cordova (95670-6106)
P.O. Box 123, Fair Oaks (95628-0123)
PHONE.................................916 369-7567
Paul Smitham, *President*
James Perkins, *Sr Ntwrk Engine*
Greg Brown, *Engineer*
Chris Retter, *Engineer*
Tyrone Benson, *Senior Engr*
EMP: 61 **EST:** 1999
SALES (est): 23.1MM **Privately Held**
WEB: www.ens-inc.com
SIC: 7379 Computer related consulting services

(P-13891)
ESG CONSULTING INC (PA)
Also Called: Executive System Group
4040 Clipper Ct, Fremont (94538-6540)
PHONE.................................408 970-8595
Sal Shafi, *President*
Ali Shafi, *Managing Prtnr*
Sara Refaat, *Recruiter*
Susan Slakey, *Director*
EMP: 45 **EST:** 1986
SALES (est): 11.9MM **Privately Held**
WEB: www.esginc.com
SIC: 7379

(P-13892)
ETOUCH SYSTEMS CORP
39899 Balentine Dr # 200, Newark (94560-5355)
PHONE.................................510 795-4800
Aniruddha Gadre, *CEO*
Amit Shah, *Vice Pres*
Santharam Chimili, *Sr Software Eng*
Rob Nelson, *Sr Software Eng*
Siddhartha Chakravarty, *Info Tech Mgr*
EMP: 600 **EST:** 1996
SQ FT: 12,800

SALES (est): 52.5MM
SALES (corp-wide): 1.3B **Privately Held**
WEB: www.virtusa.com
SIC: 7379
HQ: Virtusa Corporation
132 Turnpike Rd Ste 300
Southborough MA 01772
508 389-7300

(P-13893)
EVENTBRITE INC (PA)
155 5th St Fl 7, San Francisco (94103-2919)
PHONE.................................415 692-7779
Julia Hartz, *CEO*
Kevin Hartz, *Ch of Bd*
Charles Baker, *CFO*
Shane Crehan, *Officer*
Pat Poels, *Senior VP*
EMP: 331 **EST:** 2003
SQ FT: 48,812
SALES (est): 106MM **Publicly Held**
WEB: www.eventbrite.com
SIC: 7379

(P-13894)
EVENTBRITE INTERNATIONAL INC (PA)
155 5th St Fl 7, San Francisco (94103-2919)
PHONE.................................415 692-7779
EMP: 36 **EST:** 2013
SALES (est): 32.1K **Privately Held**
SIC: 7379

(P-13895)
EXTEND INC (PA)
301 Howard St Ste 1410, San Francisco (94105-6610)
PHONE.................................650 270-9184
Woodrow Levin, *CEO*
EMP: 48 **EST:** 2019
SALES (est): 5MM **Privately Held**
WEB: www.extend.co
SIC: 7379

(P-13896)
FAB-9 CORPORATION
5400 Hellyer Ave, San Jose (95138-1019)
PHONE.................................408 667-2448
Viet Tran, *President*
Bien Vo, *Vice Pres*
Bert Bustamante, *Technical Staff*
Kim Luu, *Accountant*
EMP: 65 **EST:** 2008
SALES (est): 5.7MM **Privately Held**
WEB: www.fab-9.com
SIC: 7379 Computer related maintenance services

(P-13897)
FORTIFY INFRSTRUCTURE SVCS INC (DH)
2340 Walsh Ave Ste A, Santa Clara (95051-1328)
PHONE.................................408 850-3119
Rajkumar Velagapudi, *President*
Madhuri Kakarla, *COO*
EMP: 50 **EST:** 2009
SALES (est): 7.1MM **Privately Held**
WEB: www.mphasis.com
SIC: 7379 Computer related consulting services
HQ: Mphasis Corporation
460 Park Ave S Rm 1101
New York NY 10016
212 686-6655

(P-13898)
FRESHDESK INC (HQ)
1250 Bayhill Dr Ste 315, San Bruno (94066-3096)
PHONE.................................866 832-3090
Girish Mathrubootham, *CEO*
Sukumar Ramachandran, *Vice Pres*
Francesco Rovetta, *Vice Pres*
Anand Venkatraman, *Vice Pres*
Justin Poet, *General Mgr*
EMP: 35 **EST:** 2014
SALES (est): 12.8MM
SALES (corp-wide): 249.6MM **Publicly Held**
WEB: www.freshdesk.com
SIC: 7379 Computer related consulting services

PA: Freshworks Inc.
2950 S Del St Ste 201
San Mateo CA 94403
650 513-0514

(P-13899)
FUTURE STATE
415 Mission St Ste 3300, San Francisco (94105-5422)
PHONE.................................925 956-4200
Julie Sweet, *President*
Venice Blue, *Director*
Elizabeth Rutherfurd, *Manager*
Maria Capote, *Assistant*
Trey Graham, *Consultant*
EMP: 126 **EST:** 1988
SALES (est): 19.2MM **Privately Held**
WEB: www.futurestate.com
SIC: 7379 8742 Data processing consultant; management consulting services
HQ: Accenture Inc.
161 N Clark St Ste 1100
Chicago IL 60601
312 693-0161

(P-13900)
GLOBAL AUTOMATION INC (PA)
Also Called: Dinostor
1388 Terra Bella Ave, Mountain View (94043-1836)
P.O. Box 1810 (94042-1810)
PHONE.................................650 316-5900
Srini Sankaran, *President*
Paul Arieckal, *Officer*
Carol Dettoni, *Vice Pres*
Kevin Fendrick, *Program Mgr*
Gail Chadwell, *Director*
EMP: 40 **EST:** 1993
SQ FT: 6,000 **Privately Held**
WEB: www.globalautomationinc.com
SIC: 7379 7372 Computer related consulting services; prepackaged software

(P-13901)
GLOBAL SOFTWARE RESOURCES INC (PA)
Also Called: G S R
4447 Stoneridge Dr Ste 1, Pleasanton (94588-8325)
PHONE.................................925 249-2200
Prem J Hinduja, *President*
Arun Epuri, *Sr Software Eng*
Satya Pappur, *Sr Software Eng*
Richard Barnes, *CIO*
Fred Valdez, *Info Tech Mgr*
EMP: 35 **EST:** 1992
SALES (est): 11.7MM **Privately Held**
WEB: www.showcase.gsr-inc.com
SIC: 7379 7371 Computer related consulting services; custom computer programming services

(P-13902)
GLOBAL TECHNOLOGY SERVICES INC
Also Called: Biztek Innovations
6120 Hellyer Ave Ste 100, San Jose (95138-1065)
PHONE.................................408 333-9639
Neelima Singireddy, *President*
EMP: 40 **EST:** 1998
SQ FT: 3,000
SALES (est): 1MM **Privately Held**
WEB: www.biztekinnovations.com
SIC: 7379

(P-13903)
GRID DYNAMICS INTL LLC (HQ)
5000 Executive Pkwy # 520, San Ramon (94583-4282)
PHONE.................................650 523-5000
Leonard Livschitz, *CEO*
Bohdana Kohut, *Partner*
Anil Doradla, *CFO*
Chris Munson, *Officer*
Max Martynov, *Vice Pres*
EMP: 368 **EST:** 2006
SQ FT: 1,700
SALES (est): 2.5MM
SALES (corp-wide): 111.2MM **Publicly Held**
WEB: www.griddynamics.com
SIC: 7379 Computer related consulting services

PRODUCTS & SERVICES SECTION
7379 - Computer Related Svcs, NEC County (P-13926)

PA: Grid Dynamics Holdings, Inc.
5000 Executive Pkwy # 520
San Ramon CA 94583
650 523-5000

(P-13904)
HACKERONE INC (PA)
22 4th St Fl 5, San Francisco (94103-3173)
PHONE.................................415 891-0777
Marten Mickos, *CEO*
Elizabeth Brittain, *CFO*
Marjorie Janiewicz, *Officer*
Rana Robillard, *Officer*
Debbie Chang, *Vice Pres*
EMP: 273 **EST:** 2013
SQ FT: 16,374
SALES (est): 32.1MM **Privately Held**
WEB: www.hackerone.com
SIC: 7379 Computer related maintenance services

(P-13905)
HEXAWARE TECHNOLOGIES INC
2603 Camino Ramon Ste 200, San Ramon (94583-9137)
PHONE.................................609 409-6950
EMP: 422 **Privately Held**
WEB: www.hexaware.com
SIC: 7379 7374 Computer related consulting services; computer processing services
HQ: Hexaware Technologies, Inc.
101 Wood Ave S Ste 600
Iselin NJ 08830

(P-13906)
HOMESTAR SYSTEMS INC
Also Called: Izmocars
251 Post St Ste 302, San Francisco (94108-5020)
PHONE.................................415 323-4008
Tej Soni, *CEO*
Layton Judd, *Principal*
Chris Daniels, *Director*
David Hyde, *Director*
Rod Lampart, *Director*
EMP: 85 **EST:** 2003
SALES (est): 7.5MM **Privately Held**
WEB: www.izmocars.com
SIC: 7379 Computer related consulting services

(P-13907)
HUMBOLDT DEV LLC
2804 Gateway Oaks Dr # 100, Sacramento (95833-4345)
PHONE.................................213 295-2890
Eric Walker, *Mng Member*
EMP: 57
SALES (est): 9.3MM **Privately Held**
SIC: 7379 7371 Computer related services; computer software development & applications

(P-13908)
ICE CONSULTING INC (PA)
1900 Mccarthy Blvd # 300, Milpitas (95035-7436)
PHONE.................................408 701-5700
Muhammad Uzair Sattar, *CEO*
Fred Care, *Info Tech Dir*
Reginald Mercado, *IT/INT Sup*
Alex Yarochkin, *IT/INT Sup*
Duong Bao, *Engineer*
EMP: 100 **EST:** 2007
SALES (est): 5.1MM **Privately Held**
WEB: www.iceconsulting.com
SIC: 7379 7373 7371 Computer related consulting services; computer integrated systems design; computer software systems analysis & design, custom

(P-13909)
INCALUS INC
41829 Albrae St Ste 212, Fremont (94538-3144)
PHONE.................................510 209-4064
Ashok Shetty, *CEO*
EMP: 50 **EST:** 2006
SALES (est): 5MM **Privately Held**
WEB: www.incalus.com
SIC: 7379 Computer related consulting services

(P-13910)
INFOBAHN SOFTWORLD INC (PA)
2010 N 1st St Ste 470, San Jose (95131-2039)
PHONE.................................408 855-9616
Maneesha Chandra, *CEO*
Nitin Chandra, *President*
SRI Vardhan, *Tech Recruiter*
Nick Kapur, *Technology*
Priti Sarma, *Accounting Mgr*
EMP: 150
SALES (est): 16.1MM **Privately Held**
WEB: www.infobahnsw.com
SIC: 7379 7371 Computer related consulting services; computer software development

(P-13911)
INFOGAIN CORPORATION (PA)
485 Alberto Way Ste 100, Los Gatos (95032-5476)
PHONE.................................408 355-6000
Sunil Bhatia, *CEO*
Eddie Chandhok, *President*
Ayan Mukerji, *President*
Kapil K Nanda, *President*
Brian Rogan, *President*
▲ **EMP:** 186 **EST:** 1990
SQ FT: 14,487
SALES (est): 74.6MM **Privately Held**
WEB: www.infogain.com
SIC: 7379 7373 8742 8748 Computer related consulting services; computer integrated systems design; management information systems consultant; systems engineering consultant, ex. computer or professional; data processing & preparation; electrical work

(P-13912)
INFOSTRETCH CORPORATION (PA)
3200 Patrick Henry Dr # 2, Santa Clara (95054-1875)
PHONE.................................408 727-1100
Rutesh Shah, *CEO*
Pinakin Sheth, *CFO*
Ashok Karania, *Vice Pres*
Manish Mistry, *Vice Pres*
Kinjan Shah, *Vice Pres*
EMP: 39 **EST:** 2004
SQ FT: 11,844
SALES (est): 14.3MM **Privately Held**
WEB: www.infostretch.com
SIC: 7379 8711 8742 Computer hardware requirements analysis; computer related consulting services; engineering services; quality assurance consultant

(P-13913)
INFOTECH SOURCING
2069 Green St, San Francisco (94123-4812)
PHONE.................................415 986-5400
Brad Miller, *CEO*
Christian Bernardini, *IT/INT Sup*
EMP: 38 **EST:** 2018
SALES (est): 2MM **Privately Held**
WEB: www.infotechsourcing.com
SIC: 7379 Computer related consulting services

(P-13914)
INFOVIE INC
1390 Market St Ste 200, San Francisco (94102-5404)
PHONE.................................551 214-8745
Rahul Guha, *CEO*
Devlina Guha, *Admin Sec*
Vivek Boray, *Director*
EMP: 35 **EST:** 2015
SQ FT: 500
SALES (est): 3MM **Privately Held**
WEB: www.infovie.com
SIC: 7379 Computer related consulting services

(P-13915)
INNOVA SOLUTIONS INC
3211 Scott Blvd Ste 202, Santa Clara (95054-3009)
PHONE.................................408 889-2020
Rajiv Sardana, *CEO*
Rich Marino, *Officer*
Fadi Baaklini, *Vice Pres*
Steven Craig, *Vice Pres*
Srinivas Kommalapati, *Vice Pres*
EMP: 1100
SQ FT: 4,656
SALES (est): 57.2MM
SALES (corp-wide): 631.3MM **Privately Held**
WEB: www.innovasolutions.com
SIC: 7379 Computer related consulting services
PA: American Cybersystems, Inc.
2400 Meadowbrook Pkwy
Duluth GA 30096
770 493-5588

(P-13916)
INPIXON (PA)
2479 E Byshore Rd Ste 195, Palo Alto (94303)
P.O. Box 174, Catharpin VA (20143-0174)
PHONE.................................408 702-2167
Nadir Ali, *CEO*
Soumya Das, *Chief Mktg Ofcr*
Tyler Hoffman, *Officer*
Wendy Loundermon, *Officer*
David Westgate, *Exec VP*
EMP: 45 **EST:** 1999
SQ FT: 4,377
SALES (est): 9.3MM **Publicly Held**
WEB: www.inpixon.com
SIC: 7379 7371 Computer related consulting services; computer software development

(P-13917)
INTELLIPRO GROUP INC
3120 Scott Blvd 301, Santa Clara (95054-3326)
PHONE.................................408 200-9891
Grace MA, *CEO*
Tina Truong, *Vice Pres*
Shivani Sharma, *Tech Recruiter*
John Truong, *Recruiter*
Mu Bai, *Opers Staff*
EMP: 380 **EST:** 2009
SALES (est): 16.2MM **Privately Held**
WEB: www.intelliprogroup.com
SIC: 7379 Computer related consulting services

(P-13918)
INTERNET-JOURNALS LLC
Also Called: Berkeley Electronic Press
2100 Milvia St Ste 300, Berkeley (94704-1862)
PHONE.................................510 665-1200
Jean-Gabriel Bankier, *CEO*
Jennifer Todd, *CIO*
Doug Cannon, *Sales Mgr*
Aaron Doran, *Consultant*
Anne Luca, *Consultant*
EMP: 89 **EST:** 1999
SALES (est): 2.3MM
SALES (corp-wide): 9.4B **Privately Held**
WEB: www.sendarestauracion.com
SIC: 7379
HQ: Elsevier Inc.
230 Park Ave Fl 8
New York NY 10169
212 989-5800

(P-13919)
INTROLLIGENT INC (PA)
1425 River Park Dr # 401, Sacramento (95815-4524)
PHONE.................................916 436-8889
Shaik Mujeeb, *CEO*
Satish Mudaliar, *VP Sales*
EMP: 49 **EST:** 2011
SALES (est): 2.8MM **Privately Held**
WEB: www.introlligent.com
SIC: 7379 Computer related consulting services

(P-13920)
INXEPTION CORPORATION
185 Valley Dr, Brisbane (94005-1340)
PHONE.................................888 852-4783
Farzad Dibachi, *President*
Josh Allen, *President*
Mark Moore, *COO*
J Judd, *Vice Pres*
Jennifer Roberts, *Vice Pres*
EMP: 150 **EST:** 2017
SALES (est): 46.1MM **Privately Held**
WEB: www.inxeption.com
SIC: 7379 4213 5961 ; automobiles, transport & delivery;

(P-13921)
IP INTERNATIONAL INC
Also Called: Info Plus International
1510 Fashion Island Blvd # 104, San Mateo (94404-1596)
PHONE.................................650 403-7800
Margaret Schaninger, *President*
Agustin Ramirez, *CFO*
EMP: 50 **EST:** 1986
SQ FT: 2,500
SALES (est): 6.5MM **Privately Held**
WEB: www.infoplusintl.com
SIC: 7379 8748 Computer related consulting services; business consulting

(P-13922)
ITALENT CORPORATION (PA)
Also Called: Italent Digital
300 Orchard Cy Dr Ste 136, Campbell (95008)
PHONE.................................408 496-6200
Renee Lalonde, *Partner*
Fred Walters, *General Ptnr*
Mark W Ciotek, *Ch of Bd*
Caleb Hernandez, *CFO*
Leslie Ottavi, *Exec VP*
EMP: 140 **EST:** 2002
SQ FT: 200,000
SALES (est): 15.6MM **Privately Held**
WEB: www.italentcorp.com
SIC: 7379 Computer related consulting services

(P-13923)
ITCO SOLUTIONS INC
1003 Whitehall Ln, Redwood City (94061-3687)
P.O. Box 610090 (94061-0090)
PHONE.................................650 367-0514
Ryan Edwards, *Director*
Chris Middleton, *Vice Pres*
Zane Edwards, *CIO*
Surendra Goud, *Technology*
Harpreet Sandhu, *Technology*
EMP: 295 **EST:** 1997
SALES (est): 10.5MM **Privately Held**
WEB: www.itcosolutions.com
SIC: 7379

(P-13924)
ITRENEW INC (HQ)
7575 Gateway Blvd Ste 100, Newark (94560-1194)
PHONE.................................408 744-9600
Aidin Aghamiri, *CEO*
Brandon Manley, *COO*
Colin Fisher, *CFO*
Andrew Perlmutter, *Officer*
Erik Riedel, *Senior VP*
▲ **EMP:** 39 **EST:** 2002
SQ FT: 72,000
SALES (est): 28.5MM **Privately Held**
WEB: www.itrenew.com
SIC: 7379 7378 ; computer maintenance & repair
PA: Intercept Parent, Inc.
110 E 59th St Fl 24
New York NY 10022
212 223-1383

(P-13925)
IXERV AMERICAS INC
785 Orchard Dr Ste 140, Folsom (95630-5558)
P.O. Box 120178, San Antonio TX (78212-9378)
PHONE.................................786 542-9744
Luke Marson, *President*
Vikram Bhagdev, *CEO*
Adam Hilger, *Risk Mgmt Dir*
EMP: 35 **EST:** 2016
SALES (est): 2.3MM **Privately Held**
WEB: www.ixerv.com
SIC: 7379 Computer related consulting services

(P-13926)
JADE GLOBAL INC (PA)
1731 Tech Dr Ste 350, San Jose (95110)
PHONE.................................408 899-7200
Karan Yaramada, *CEO*

7379 - Computer Related Svcs, NEC County (P-13927)

Rama Karanam, *CFO*
Manoj Machiwal, *Assoc VP*
Sudipta Bhattacharjee, *Exec VP*
Arun Menon, *Exec VP*
EMP: 96 **EST:** 2003
SQ FT: 2,200
SALES (est): 45.3MM **Privately Held**
WEB: www.jadeglobal.com
SIC: 7379 Computer related consulting services

(P-13927)
JOYENT INC
655 Montgomery St # 1600, San Francisco (94111-2684)
PHONE 415 400-0600
Eric Hahm, *Principal*
Will Gorman, *Software Engr*
Wyatt Preul, *Engineer*
Lo-An Le, *Accountant*
EMP: 120 **EST:** 2005
SQ FT: 11,408
SALES (est): 36.5MM **Privately Held**
WEB: www.joyent.com
SIC: 7379 Computer related consulting services
HQ: Samsung Semiconductor, Inc.
3655 N 1st St
San Jose CA 95134
408 544-4000

(P-13928)
KENNA SECURITY INC (HQ)
3945 Freedom Cir Ste 300, Santa Clara (95054-1266)
PHONE 855 474-7546
Karim Toubba, *CEO*
Alaina Ross, *Executive Asst*
Ed Bellis, *CTO*
Brian Kavanagh, *Engineer*
Jason Williams, *Engineer*
EMP: 129 **EST:** 2009
SALES (est): 15.4MM
SALES (corp-wide): 49.8B **Publicly Held**
WEB: www.kennasecurity.com
SIC: 7379
PA: Cisco Systems, Inc.
170 W Tasman Dr
San Jose CA 95134
408 526-4000

(P-13929)
KINETIX TECHNOLOGY SVCS LLC
2261 Market St Ste 4163, San Francisco (94114-1612)
PHONE 650 454-8850
Pratap Mukherjee, *CEO*
Rodger Keesee, *President*
Don Darby, *COO*
Mark Adams, *CTO*
Michael Gilmore, *Network Enginr*
EMP: 40 **EST:** 2005
SQ FT: 1,200
SALES (est): 5.2MM **Privately Held**
WEB: www.kinetix.com
SIC: 7379

(P-13930)
LEADSPACE INC (DH)
445 Bush St Ste 900, San Francisco (94108-3730)
PHONE 855 532-3772
Alex Yoder, *CEO*
Douglas Bewsher, *CEO*
Ed Schaffer, *CFO*
Oren Yardeni, *Vice Pres*
Jennifer Pieh Barker, *Executive*
EMP: 38 **EST:** 2012
SALES (est): 10.5MM **Privately Held**
WEB: www.leadspace.com
SIC: 7379 Computer related consulting services

(P-13931)
LITTLETHINGS INC
642 Harrison St Fl 3, San Francisco (94107-1323)
PHONE 917 364-9277
Joseph Speiser, *CEO*
Gretchen Tibbits, *President*
Evan Gotlib, *Senior VP*
Michael Brumenschenkel, *Vice Pres*
Michael Lackman, *Vice Pres*
EMP: 95 **EST:** 2011

SALES (est): 35MM **Privately Held**
SIC: 7379

(P-13932)
LOGICTIER INC
7 41st Ave 76, San Mateo (94403-5105)
PHONE 650 235-6600
EMP: 200
SALES (est): 7.2MM **Privately Held**
SIC: 7379 1731 Computer Related Services, Nec, Nsk

(P-13933)
MAXONIC INC
2542 S Bascom Ave Ste 190, Campbell (95008-5542)
PHONE 408 739-4900
Ajay Narain, *CEO*
Nitin Khanna, *President*
Tracia Chan, *Regional Mgr*
Jhankar Chanda, *Tech Recruiter*
Mani Maganti, *Tech Recruiter*
EMP: 65 **EST:** 2002
SQ FT: 3,499 **Privately Held**
WEB: www.maxonic.com
SIC: 7379 7371 Computer related consulting services; computer software development & applications

(P-13934)
MCV GROUP INC (PA)
7045 N Fruit Ave, Fresno (93711-0761)
PHONE 559 431-3142
Stephen Cornwell, *Principal*
EMP: 41 **EST:** 2009
SALES (est): 297.3K **Privately Held**
SIC: 7379 Computer related services

(P-13935)
MERAKI LLC (HQ)
Also Called: Cisco Meraki
500 Terry A Francois Blvd, San Francisco (94158-2354)
PHONE 415 632-5800
Sanjit Biswas,
Eam Lo, *Sr Software Eng*
Jose De Castro, *CTO*
Avery Dinauer, *Technology*
Christopher Mar, *Technical Staff*
▲ **EMP:** 303 **EST:** 2006
SQ FT: 1,500
SALES (est): 128.3MM
SALES (corp-wide): 49.8B **Publicly Held**
WEB: www.meraki.cisco.com
SIC: 7379 Computer related consulting services
PA: Cisco Systems, Inc.
170 W Tasman Dr
San Jose CA 95134
408 526-4000

(P-13936)
MESSAGESOLUTION INC
7080 Donlon Way Ste 216, Dublin (94568-2789)
PHONE 925 833-8000
Shuzhen Zhang, *Vice Pres*
EMP: 95 **EST:** 2004
SALES (est): 13MM **Privately Held**
WEB: www.messagesolution.com
SIC: 5734 7379 7371 Computer & software stores; computer related maintenance services; custom computer programming services; computer software development & applications

(P-13937)
METABYTE INC
Also Called: Hotdoodle.com
43238 Christy St, Fremont (94538-3171)
PHONE 510 494-9700
Manu Mehta, *CEO*
Saumya Balakrishnan, *Technical Staff*
Suresh Kallichetti, *Technical Staff*
Michael Garcia, *Business Mgr*
Vijay Parjan, *Finance*
EMP: 100 **EST:** 1993
SALES (est): 14MM **Privately Held**
WEB: www.metabyte.com
SIC: 7379

(P-13938)
MONSOON COMMERCE INC
1250 45th St Ste 100, Emeryville (94608-2924)
PHONE 510 594-4500

Kanth Gopalpur, *CEO*
Genny Rapp, *Associate Dir*
EMP: 76 **Privately Held**
WEB: www.monsooninc.com
SIC: 7379
HQ: Monsoon, Inc.
733 Sw 2nd Ave Ste 215
Portland OR 97204
503 239-1055

(P-13939)
MSRCOSMOS LLC (PA)
5250 Claremont Ave # 249, Stockton (95207-5700)
PHONE 925 218-6919
Saijyothsnadevi Kondapi, *CEO*
Jim Mulholland, *Officer*
Malathi Raj, *Vice Pres*
Sivagopal Madadugula, *Security Dir*
Rajesh Panja, *Business Mgr*
EMP: 40 **EST:** 2008
SQ FT: 650
SALES (est): 7.6MM **Privately Held**
WEB: www.msrcosmos.com
SIC: 7379 Computer related consulting services

(P-13940)
MULTIVEN INC
303 Twin Dolphin Dr # 600, Redwood City (94065-1497)
P.O. Box 394, San Carlos (94070-0394)
PHONE 408 828-2715
EMP: 50
SQ FT: 2,000
SALES (est): 2.2MM **Privately Held**
WEB: www.multiven.com
SIC: 7379 Computer Related Services, Nec, Nsk

(P-13941)
MURPHY MCKAY & ASSOCIATES INC
1990 N Calif Blvd Fl 8th, Walnut Creek (94596-7261)
PHONE 925 283-9555
David D McKay, *Ch of Bd*
Timothy J Murphy, *President*
Norma Marquez, *Supervisor*
EMP: 50 **EST:** 1992
SALES (est): 7.3MM **Privately Held**
WEB: www.murphymckay.com
SIC: 7379 Computer related consulting services

(P-13942)
NAGARRO INC (HQ)
Also Called: Projistics
2001 Gateway Pl Ste 100w, San Jose (95110-1046)
PHONE 408 436-6170
Vikram Sehgal, *President*
Vaibhav Gadodia, *Vice Pres*
Kapil Nagpal, *Vice Pres*
Kanchan Ray, *Vice Pres*
Jhalak Tyagi, *Software Engr*
EMP: 1856 **EST:** 1999
SQ FT: 3,000
SALES (est): 143.3MM
SALES (corp-wide): 508.9MM **Privately Held**
WEB: www.nagarro.com
SIC: 7379 Computer related consulting services
PA: Nagarro Se
Einsteinstr. 172
Munchen BY 81677
899 984-210

(P-13943)
NCC GROUP INC (HQ)
123 Mission St Ste 1020, San Francisco (94105-5126)
PHONE 415 268-9300
Rob Cotton, *President*
Craig Motta, *President*
Craig Foster, *CFO*
John Collins, *Vice Pres*
Vicki Gurney, *Executive*
EMP: 90 **EST:** 2005
SQ FT: 12,000
SALES (est): 56.1MM **Privately Held**
WEB: www.nccgroup.com
SIC: 7379 Computer data escrow service

(P-13944)
NCC GROUP SECURITY SVCS INC (DH)
650 California St # 2950, San Francisco (94108-2702)
PHONE 415 293-0808
Rob Cotton, *President*
Darren Maloney, *Treasurer*
Felicity Brandwood, *Admin Sec*
Joshua Welt, *Engineer*
Kusum Pandey, *Sr Project Mgr*
EMP: 46 **EST:** 2007
SALES (est): 8.6MM **Privately Held**
SIC: 7379 Computer related consulting services

(P-13945)
NETENRICH INC (PA)
2590 N 1st St Ste 300, San Jose (95131-1021)
PHONE 408 436-5900
Raju Chekuri, *President*
Courtney Cook, *Partner*
Satish Raj, *Partner*
Satish Raju, *Partner*
Bala Muppaneni, *President*
EMP: 159 **EST:** 2003
SALES (est): 17.1MM **Privately Held**
WEB: www.netenrich.com
SIC: 7379 Computer related consulting services

(P-13946)
NEWSMARKET INC (DH)
75 Broadway Ste 202, San Francisco (94111-1423)
PHONE 917 861-3797
Rob Beynon, *CEO*
Mark Toogood, *CFO*
Steven Bainnson, *Vice Pres*
Bhoomi Patel, *Director*
EMP: 40 **EST:** 2017
SQ FT: 3,000
SALES (est): 44.4MM
SALES (corp-wide): 42.4MM **Privately Held**
WEB: www.thenewsmarket.com
SIC: 7379 Computer related consulting services
HQ: Dma Media Limited
40 Linhope Street
London NW1 6
207 432-2800

(P-13947)
NEXIENT LLC (PA)
8000 Jarvis Ave Ste 200, Newark (94560-1155)
PHONE 415 992-7277
Mark Orttung, *CEO*
Victoria Papa, *Partner*
Khalil Virji, *Partner*
Neeraj Gupta, *Ch of Bd*
Tanmoy Chowdhury, *CFO*
EMP: 297 **EST:** 2009
SQ FT: 4,000
SALES (est): 45MM **Privately Held**
WEB: www.nexient.com
SIC: 7379

(P-13948)
NEXTLABS INC (PA)
3 E 3rd Ave Ste 223, San Mateo (94401-4280)
PHONE 650 577-9101
Keng Lim, *President*
Patrick Ball, *Senior VP*
Garrick Ballantine, *Vice Pres*
Krista Kendall, *Vice Pres*
Rajesh Rengarethinam, *Vice Pres*
EMP: 48 **EST:** 2003
SALES (est): 23.5MM **Privately Held**
WEB: www.nextlabs.com
SIC: 7379 Computer related consulting services

(P-13949)
NORLAND GROUP INC
3350 Scott Blvd Ste 6501, Santa Clara (95054-3125)
PHONE 408 855-8255
Mayling Liang, *President*
Reginald Malla, *Recruiter*
▲ **EMP:** 105 **EST:** 1996
SQ FT: 2,200

PRODUCTS & SERVICES SECTION

7379 - Computer Related Svcs, NEC County (P-13970)

SALES (est): 7.9MM **Privately Held**
WEB: www.norlandgroup.com
SIC: **7379** 7361 Computer related consulting services; employment agencies

(P-13950)
NSFOCUS INCORPORATED (HQ)
2520 Mission College Blvd # 130, Santa Clara (95054-1238)
P.O. Box 110010, Campbell (95011-0010)
PHONE.................................408 907-6638
Jiye Shen, *CEO*
Jens Andreassen, *COO*
Allan Thompson, *COO*
Andre Mello, *Vice Pres*
Marc Macalino, *Technology*
EMP: 43 EST: 2010
SALES (est): 6.3MM **Privately Held**
WEB: www.nsfocusglobal.com
SIC: **7379** Computer related consulting services

(P-13951)
NTM CONSULTING SERVICES INC
39300 Civic Center Dr # 250, Fremont (94538-2338)
PHONE.................................510 744-3901
Naji T Mourad, *CFO*
Najwa Mourad, *Vice Pres*
Christa Chavez, *Sales Staff*
John Mallory, *Director*
EMP: 20 EST: 1990
SALES (est): 3.3MM **Privately Held**
WEB: www.cayuse.com
SIC: **7379** 7372 ; application computer software

(P-13952)
NTT SCRITY APPSEC SLUTIONS INC (DH)
1741 Tech Dr Ste 300, San Jose (95110)
PHONE.................................408 343-8300
Craig Hinkley, *CEO*
Terry Murphy, *CFO*
Kevin Flynn, *Vice Pres*
Tanya Gay, *Vice Pres*
David Gerry, *Vice Pres*
EMP: 54 EST: 2002
SALES (est): 25MM **Privately Held**
WEB: www.whitehatsec.com
SIC: **7379**

(P-13953)
OPAL SOFT INC
Also Called: Opalsoft
1288 Kifer Rd Ste 201, Sunnyvale (94086-5326)
PHONE.................................408 267-2211
Omprakash Choudhary, *President*
Alkesh Choudhary, *CFO*
Peter Luyten, *Administration*
Carl Swift, *Administration*
John Wood, *Network Mgr*
EMP: 80 EST: 1997
SQ FT: 2,450 **Privately Held**
WEB: www.opalsoft.com
SIC: **7379** 8748 7371 8713 ; business consulting; custom computer programming services; computer software systems analysis & design, custom; surveying services; photogrammetric engineering; data processing & preparation; service bureau, computer; computer facilities management

(P-13954)
ORACLE SYSTEMS CORPORATION (HQ)
500 Oracle Pkwy, Redwood City (94065-1677)
PHONE.................................650 506-7000
Safra A Catz, *CEO*
Lawrence J Ellison, *Ch of Bd*
Jeffrey O Henley, *Ch of Bd*
Mark V Hurd, *President*
Mark Hurd, *CEO*
EMP: 2300 EST: 1987
SQ FT: 2,200,000
SALES (est): 1.4B
SALES (corp-wide): 40.4B **Publicly Held**
WEB: www.oracle.com
SIC: **7379** 8243 7372 Data processing consultant; software training, computer; business oriented computer software
PA: Oracle Corporation
2300 Oracle Way
Austin TX 78741
737 867-1000

(P-13955)
ORB ENTERPRISES INC
Also Called: Spiceorb
320 Crscent Vlg Cir Unit, San Jose (95134)
PHONE.................................669 281-9994
Shradha Chhajed, *CEO*
EMP: 51 EST: 2019
SALES (est): 2MM **Privately Held**
SIC: **7379**

(P-13956)
OSKI TECHNOLOGY INC (PA)
2099 Gateway Pl Ste 560, San Jose (95110-1051)
PHONE.................................408 216-7728
Craig Shirley, *President*
Vigyan Singhal, *Ch of Bd*
David Parry, *COO*
Gurudutt Bansal, *Vice Pres*
Roger Sabbagh, *Vice Pres*
EMP: 37 EST: 2005
SALES (est): 5.5MM **Privately Held**
WEB: www.oskitechnology.com
SIC: **7379** Computer related maintenance services

(P-13957)
PATTERN TAP LLC
55 N 3rd St, Campbell (95008-2070)
PHONE.................................408 341-0600
Bryan Zmijewski,
EMP: 55 EST: 2012
SALES (est): 246.3K **Privately Held**
WEB: www.zurb.com
SIC: **7379** Computer related consulting services
PA: Zurb, Inc.
100 W Rincon Ave
Campbell CA 95008

(P-13958)
PCG TECHNOLOGY SOLUTIONS LLC
2150 River Plaza Dr # 380, Sacramento (95833-3883)
PHONE.................................916 565-8090
William Mosakowski, *President*
Daniel Heaney, *Treasurer*
EMP: 112 EST: 1996
SALES (est): 12.3MM
SALES (corp-wide): 761.5MM **Privately Held**
WEB: www.publicconsultinggroup.com
SIC: **7379** 8748 8742 8322 Computer related consulting services; business consulting; management consulting services; disaster service
PA: Public Consulting Group Holdings, Inc.
148 State St Fl 10
Boston MA 02109
617 426-2026

(P-13959)
PERFORMANCE TECH PARTNERS LLC
500 Capitol Mall Ste 2350, Sacramento (95814-4760)
PHONE.................................800 787-4143
John Podlipnik,
Jeff Forderer, *Vice Pres*
Scott Metzger, *Managing Dir*
Tiffany Liou, *Admin Asst*
Danny Roozen, *Software Dev*
EMP: 106 EST: 2004
SALES (est): 14.1MM **Privately Held**
WEB: www.ptpinc.com
SIC: **7379**

(P-13960)
POWER BUSINESS TECHNOLOGY LLC
1020 Winding Creek Rd, Roseville (95678-7041)
PHONE.................................844 769-3729
Edward Roe, *President*
Bryan Davis, *Vice Pres*
Timothy Ramsay, *Executive*
Scott Orlando, *Sales Staff*
Andy Alsweet, *Manager*
EMP: 45 EST: 2019
SALES (est): 3.1MM **Privately Held**
WEB: www.powercopiers.com
SIC: **7379** Computer related consulting services

(P-13961)
PRAETORIAN GROUP (PA)
Also Called: Policeone Academy
200 Green St Ste 200 # 200, San Francisco (94111-1356)
PHONE.................................415 962-8310
Mike Herning, *Ch of Bd*
Alex Ford, *CEO*
Jon Hughes, *Vice Pres*
Ryan Houghtelling, *Info Tech Dir*
Anthony Weems, *Engineer*
EMP: 44 EST: 2000
SALES (est): 11.9MM **Privately Held**
WEB: www.lexipol.com
SIC: **7379**

(P-13962)
PRIMITIVE LOGIC INC
130 Battery St Fl 3, San Francisco (94111-4905)
PHONE.................................415 391-8080
Jill P Reber, *CEO*
Kevin Moos, *President*
Anisha Weber, *COO*
Mike McDermott, *Senior VP*
Andy Lin, *Vice Pres*
EMP: 63 EST: 1996
SALES (est): 8.7MM **Privately Held**
WEB: www.primitivelogic.com
SIC: **7379** Computer related consulting services

(P-13963)
PROJECT PARTNERS LLC (PA)
520 Purissima St, Half Moon Bay (94019-1931)
PHONE.................................650 712-6200
Randy Egger, *Mng Member*
Rebecca Portela, *Vice Pres*
Rob Sulzinger, *Admin Asst*
Suresh Padmanabhan, *Administration*
Chirag Gupta, *Software Engr*
EMP: 35 EST: 1997
SQ FT: 1,500
SALES (est): 5.4MM **Privately Held**
WEB: www.projectp.com
SIC: **7379**

(P-13964)
QT COMPANY
Also Called: Qtcom Helsinki Nasdaq
2350 Mission College Blvd # 1020, Santa Clara (95054-1563)
PHONE.................................408 906-8400
Juha Varelius, *President*
JP Miemi, *Vice Pres*
Jennifer Lau, *Executive*
Mika Palsi, *Admin Sec*
Michael Aubin, *VP Sales*
EMP: 40 EST: 2011
SQ FT: 5,000
SALES (est): 7.8MM
SALES (corp-wide): 93.9MM **Privately Held**
WEB: www.qt.io
SIC: **5734** 7379 Software, business & non-game; computer related consulting services
HQ: The Qt Company Oy
Bertel Jungin Aukio 3a
Espoo 02600
988 618-040

(P-13965)
QUANTIFIND INC
444 High St Ste 101, Palo Alto (94301-1671)
PHONE.................................650 561-4937
ARI Tuchman PHD, *President*
Paul Emery, *Vice Pres*
Adam Mulliken, *Vice Pres*
Lance Rutter, *Vice Pres*
Ryan Lecompte, *Engineer*
EMP: 50 EST: 2013
SALES (est): 7.2MM **Privately Held**
WEB: www.quantifind.com
SIC: **7379**

(P-13966)
QUEST MEDIA & SUPPLIES INC (PA)
9000 Fthills Blvd Ste 100, Roseville (95747)
P.O. Box 910 (95678-0910)
PHONE.................................916 338-7070
Timothy Burke, *CEO*
David Noel, *Partner*
Cindy P Burke, *President*
Kathy Campbell, *COO*
Francine Walrath, *CFO*
EMP: 92
SQ FT: 9,500
SALES: 159.4MM **Privately Held**
WEB: www.questsys.com
SIC: **7379** Computer related consulting services

(P-13967)
R S SOFTWARE INDIA LIMITED
1900 Mccarthy Blvd # 103, Milpitas (95035-7436)
PHONE.................................408 382-1200
Rajnit Jain, *President*
Bibek Das, *Vice Pres*
Subroto Mallick, *Info Tech Mgr*
Raghav Jain, *Regl Sales Mgr*
Garry Singer, *Regl Sales Mgr*
EMP: 96 EST: 1992
SQ FT: 3,100
SALES (est): 11MM **Privately Held**
WEB: www.rssoftware.com
SIC: **7379** 7371 Computer related consulting services; computer software development
PA: R S Software (India) Limited
A - 2, Fmc Fortuna,234 3a,
Kolkata WB 70002

(P-13968)
REALTIMEBOARD INC (PA)
Also Called: Miro Software
201 Spear St Ste 1100, San Francisco (94105-6164)
PHONE.................................415 669-8098
Andrey Khusid, *CEO*
Aj Josephson, *Vice Pres*
Minnie Chan, *Office Mgr*
Melissa Halim, *Marketing Staff*
Anna Savina, *Marketing Staff*
EMP: 158 EST: 2017
SALES (est): 10.7MM **Privately Held**
WEB: www.miro.com
SIC: **7379** 7371 ; computer software development & applications

(P-13969)
RISKALYZE INC (PA)
470 Nevada St Ste 110, Auburn (95603-3751)
PHONE.................................530 748-1660
Aaron Klein, *CEO*
Kyle Van Pelt, *Partner*
Micaela Pope, *CEO*
Andrew Palmer, *CFO*
Kathleen Parker, *CFO*
EMP: 118 EST: 2011
SALES (est): 9.6MM **Privately Held**
WEB: www.riskalyze.com
SIC: **7379**

(P-13970)
SAGE INTACCT INC (HQ)
300 Park Ave Ste 1400, San Jose (95110-2774)
PHONE.................................408 878-0900
Meg Deering, *Senior Partner*
Tonya Bush, *Partner*
Susan Vincent, *Partner*
Robert Kleinschmidt, *President*
Scott Lumish, *President*
EMP: 47 EST: 2005
SQ FT: 6,000
SALES (est): 26.3MM
SALES (corp-wide): 2.4B **Privately Held**
WEB: www.marketplace.intacct.com
SIC: **7379** 7371 Computer related consulting services; custom computer programming services
PA: The Sage Group Plc.
North Park Avenue
Newcastle-Upon-Tyne NE13
800 923-0344

7379 - Computer Related Svcs, NEC County (P-13971)

(P-13971)
SERVALAN ENTERPRISES INC
261 Wilson Ave, Novato (94947-4218)
PHONE.............................415 899-1880
EMP: 35
SALES (est): 25MM Privately Held
SIC: 7379 Computer Related Services

(P-13972)
SERVICENOW INC (PA)
2225 Lawson Ln, Santa Clara (95054-3311)
PHONE.............................408 501-8550
William R McDermott, President
Frederic B Luddy, Ch of Bd
Gina Mastantuono, CFO
Chirantan Desai, Officer
Jacqui Canney, Officer
EMP: 45 EST: 2004
SQ.FT: 608,000
SALES (est): 4.5B Publicly Held
WEB: www.servicenow.com
SIC: 7379 7372 Computer related maintenance services; prepackaged software

(P-13973)
SERVICENOW DELAWARE LLC (HQ)
2225 Lawson Ln, Santa Clara (95054-3311)
PHONE.............................408 501-8550
Frank Slootman, President
EMP: 506 EST: 2011
SALES (est): 611.7K Publicly Held
WEB: www.servicenow.com
SIC: 7379 7372 Computer related maintenance services; prepackaged software

(P-13974)
SHOWPAD INC (HQ)
301 Howard St Ste 500, San Francisco (94105-6603)
PHONE.............................415 800-2033
Pieterjan Bouten, CEO
Lenz Briana, President
Jason Holmes, President
Alan Gurock, Senior VP
Chris De Mol, Vice Pres
EMP: 237 EST: 2013
SALES (est): 35.2MM
SALES (corp-wide): 36.2MM Privately Held
WEB: www.showpad.com
SIC: 7379 Computer related maintenance services
PA: Showpad
    Moutstraat 62
    Gent 9000
    230 939-17

(P-13975)
SIMILITY LLC
2211 N 1st St, San Jose (95131-2021)
PHONE.............................650 351-7592
Rahul Pangam, CEO
EMP: 80 EST: 2014
SALES (est): 14MM
SALES (corp-wide): 21.4B Publicly Held
WEB: www.simility.com
SIC: 7379
PA: Paypal Holdings, Inc.
    2211 N 1st St
    San Jose CA 95131
    408 967-1000

(P-13976)
SIZMEK DSP INC (HQ)
2000 Seaport Blvd Ste 400, Redwood City (94063-5584)
PHONE.............................650 595-1300
Mark Grether, CEO
Stephen Snyder, CFO
Eric Duerr, Chief Mktg Ofcr
Jennifer Trzepacz, Exec VP
Richard Song, Risk Mgmt Dir
EMP: 681 EST: 2008
SALES (est): 456.2MM Privately Held
WEB: www.advertising.amazon.com
SIC: 7379 7371 Computer related consulting services; computer software development & applications

(P-13977)
SKYSLOPE INC
825 K St Fl 2, Sacramento (95814-3547)
PHONE.............................916 833-2390
Tyler Smith, CEO
Dave Hiller, Partner
Michael Barreiro, Vice Pres
Ryan Taylor, Vice Pres
Mark Christen, Executive
EMP: 100 EST: 2010
SQ FT: 23,000
SALES (est): 5.8MM Publicly Held
WEB: www.auth.skyslope.com
SIC: 7379
PA: Fidelity National Financial, Inc.
    601 Riverside Ave Fl 4
    Jacksonville FL 32204

(P-13978)
SMARTEK21 LLC
530 Lytton Ave Fl 2, Palo Alto (94301-1541)
PHONE.............................650 617-3221
EMP: 276 Privately Held
WEB: www.smartek21.com
SIC: 7379 Computer related consulting services
PA: Smartek21, Llc
    12910 Ttem Lk Blvd Ne Ste
    Kirkland WA 98034

(P-13979)
SOAPROJECTS INC (PA)
495 N Whisman Rd Ste 100, Mountain View (94043-5725)
PHONE.............................650 960-9900
Manpreet Grover, CEO
Joe Talley, Partner
Yuko Wakasugi, Partner
Bryon McDougall, Bd of Directors
Evangeline Sotelo, Admin Asst
EMP: 51 EST: 2004
SALES (est): 21.4MM Privately Held
WEB: www.soaprojects.com
SIC: 7379 8721 8742 Computer related consulting services; accounting, auditing & bookkeeping; management consulting services; financial consultant

(P-13980)
SPRINGML INC
6200 Stnrdge Mall Rd Ste, Pleasanton (94588)
PHONE.............................916 316-1566
Charles Landry, CEO
Prabu Palanisamy, President
Piyush Malik, Senior VP
Peter Harlan, Vice Pres
Jon Kennett, Vice Pres
EMP: 80 EST: 2015
SQ FT: 1,200
SALES (est): 8.5MM Privately Held
WEB: www.springml.com
SIC: 7379 7371 Computer related consulting services; computer software development & applications

(P-13981)
STELLA TECHNOLOGY INCORPORATED
450 S Abel St Unit 360832, Milpitas (95036-4034)
PHONE.............................402 350-1681
Christopher Henkenius, CEO
David Jones, President
Krishna Khadloya, President
Sandra Sarnoff, COO
Salim Kizaraly, CFO
EMP: 90 EST: 2012
SALES (est): 5.2MM Privately Held
WEB: www.stellatechnology.com
SIC: 7379

(P-13982)
STOTTLER HENKE ASSOCIATES INC (PA)
Also Called: Shai
1650 S Amphlett Blvd # 300, San Mateo (94402-2516)
PHONE.............................650 931-2700
Richard Stottler, President
Andrea Henke, Admin Sec
Sowmya Ramachandran, Research
Emilio Remolina, Research
Robert Richards, VP Sls/Mktg
EMP: 40 EST: 1988
SQ FT: 8,017
SALES (est): 7.9MM Privately Held
WEB: www.stottlerhenke.com
SIC: 7379 Computer related consulting services

(P-13983)
SUNERA TECHNOLOGIES INC
691 S Milpitas Blvd, Milpitas (95035-5476)
PHONE.............................510 474-2616
Prashanth Abbagani, Vice Pres
Sagar Peruka, Executive
Aravind Kotte, Associate Dir
Prasanna Kuma Reddy, Sr Software Eng
Raviteja Gaadhi, Technology
EMP: 48 Privately Held
WEB: www.suneratech.com
SIC: 7379 Computer related consulting services
PA: Sunera Technologies Inc
    631 E Big Beaver Rd # 105
    Troy MI 48083

(P-13984)
SYNACK INC
1600 Seaport Blvd Ste 170, Redwood City (94063-5599)
PHONE.............................855 796-2251
Jay Kaplan, CEO
Albert Lee, Executive
Teresa Allen, Admin Asst
Patricia Kingston, Administration
Armando Sandoval, Project Leader
EMP: 111 EST: 2013
SALES (est): 10.9MM Privately Held
WEB: www.synack.com
SIC: 7379 Computer related maintenance services; computer related consulting services

(P-13985)
SYSTECH INTEGRATORS INC
2050 Gateway Pl, San Jose (95110-1011)
PHONE.............................408 441-2700
Sam Tyagi, CEO
Rajeev Tyagi, COO
EMP: 57 EST: 2001
SALES (est): 2.7MM Privately Held
WEB: www.softtek.com
SIC: 7379 Computer related consulting services
HQ: Valores Corporativos Softtek, S.A. De C.V.
    Jaime Balmes No. 11 Torre C Piso 6
    Ciudad De Mexico CDMX 11520

(P-13986)
SYSTEMS INTGRTION SLUTIONS INC (PA)
Also Called: SIS
1255 Treat Blvd Ste 100, Walnut Creek (94597-7969)
PHONE.............................925 465-7400
Dennis Sechrest, Ch of Bd
Gerald Heath Jr, President
Peter W Ling, CEO
Doris Munoz, Vice Pres
John Peeke-Vout, Vice Pres
EMP: 40 EST: 1990
SQ FT: 16,000
SALES (est): 24.2MM Privately Held
WEB: www.sisinc.com
SIC: 7379

(P-13987)
TACIT KNOWLEDGE INC (HQ)
5000 Executive Pkwy # 520, San Ramon (94583-4210)
PHONE.............................415 694-4322
Todd Everett, President
Ben Wade, CFO
Bret Piontek, Technical Staff
Michael Scholz, Products
Rob Rene, Sales Staff
EMP: 91 EST: 2011
SALES (est): 8.3MM
SALES (corp-wide): 111.2MM Publicly Held
WEB: www.tacitknowledge.com
SIC: 7379
PA: Grid Dynamics Holdings, Inc.
    5000 Executive Pkwy # 520
    San Ramon CA 94583
    650 523-5000

(P-13988)
TACTUS TECHNOLOGY INC
47509 Seabridge Dr, Fremont (94538-6546)
PHONE.............................510 244-3968
Perry Constantine, CEO
Bob Pape, CFO
Bobby Sabhlok, Vice Pres
Justin Virgili PHD, Vice Pres
Micah Yairi, CTO
EMP: 125 EST: 2008
SALES (est): 9.1MM Privately Held
WEB: www.tactustechnology.com
SIC: 7379 Computer related consulting services

(P-13989)
TALVIEW INC (PA)
400 Concar Dr, San Mateo (94402-2681)
PHONE.............................830 484-6221
Sanjoe Tom Jose, CEO
EMP: 199 EST: 2017
SALES (est): 10.8MM Privately Held
WEB: www.talview.com
SIC: 7379

(P-13990)
TAOS MOUNTAIN LLC (PA)
121 Daggett Dr, San Jose (95134-2110)
PHONE.............................408 324-2800
Hamilton Yu, CEO
Ricardo Urrutia, Ch of Bd
Jeff Lucchesi, COO
Mary Hale, CFO
Ken Grohe, Officer
EMP: 335 EST: 1989
SQ FT: 45,000
SALES (est): 46.8MM Privately Held
WEB: www.taos.com
SIC: 7379 Computer related consulting services

(P-13991)
TATA AMERICA INTL CORP
Also Called: Tata Consulting Services
5201 Great America Pkwy, Santa Clara (95054-1122)
PHONE.............................408 569-5845
S K Bhattacharjee, Manager
Sunil Chauhan, Partner
Thomas Ehrich, Business Dir
Chiradip Das, Program Mgr
William Domeika, Info Tech Dir
EMP: 35 Privately Held
WEB: www.ex-ngn.com
SIC: 7379 Computer related consulting services
HQ: Tata America International Corporation
    101 Park Ave Fl 26
    New York NY 10178
    212 557-8038

(P-13992)
TECHNOLOGY SERVICES CAL DEPT
Also Called: Office of Technology
3101 Gold Camp Dr, Rancho Cordova (95670-6099)
PHONE.............................916 464-3747
Amy Tom, Branch Mgr
Pam Haase, Data Proc Staff
EMP: 200 Privately Held
WEB: www.ca.gov
SIC: 7379
HQ: California Department Of Technology
    1325 J St Ste 1600
    Sacramento CA 95814

(P-13993)
TECTURA CORPORATION (PA)
951 Old County Rd 2-317, Belmont (94002-2773)
PHONE.............................650 273-4249
Duane W Bell, CEO
Dave Kempski, CFO
▲ EMP: 50 EST: 2001
SALES (est): 40.4MM Privately Held
WEB: www.tectura.com
SIC: 7379 Computer related consulting services

PRODUCTS & SERVICES SECTION
7379 - Computer Related Svcs, NEC County (P-14016)

(P-13994)
TECTURA INTL HOLDINGS INC
333 Twin Dolphin Dr # 750, Redwood City (94065-1401)
PHONE..................650 585-5500
Terrence L Petzelka, *President*
Clarence Classen, *Technical Staff*
EMP: 96 EST: 2004
SALES (est): 3.5MM
SALES (corp-wide): 40.4MM **Privately Held**
WEB: www.tectura.com
SIC: 7379 Computer related consulting services
PA: Tectura Corporation
   951 Old County Rd 2-317
   Belmont CA 94002
   650 273-4249

(P-13995)
TEKION CORP
12647 Alcosta Blvd, San Ramon (94583-4439)
PHONE..................925 399-5569
Jayaprakash Vijayan, *CEO*
Jose Morales, *Partner*
Chuck Trelow, *Partner*
Christopher Upright, *Partner*
Napoleon Rumteen, *Senior VP*
EMP: 130 EST: 2016
SALES (est): 262K **Privately Held**
WEB: www.tekion.com
SIC: 7379 7374 Data processing consultant; ; data processing & preparation; data entry service; data processing service

(P-13996)
TEKVALLEY CORPORATION
4695 Chabot Dr Ste 200, Pleasanton (94588-2756)
PHONE..................925 558-2275
Seema Chawla, *CEO*
Mac Chellappam, *Partner*
Vardan Vengurlekar, *Software Dev*
EMP: 42 EST: 2000
SALES (est): 2.6MM **Privately Held**
WEB: www.tekvalley.com
SIC: 7379 Computer related consulting services

(P-13997)
THALES ESECURITY INC (HQ)
Also Called: AES Networks
2125 Zanker Rd, San Jose (95131-2109)
PHONE..................408 433-6000
Alan Kessler, *President*
Wayne Lewandowski, *President*
Greg Paulsen, *CFO*
Michael Coffield, *Vice Pres*
Brian Hartpence, *Vice Pres*
▼ EMP: 79 EST: 2001
SALES (est): 39.3MM
SALES (corp-wide): 279.3MM **Privately Held**
WEB: www.cpl.thalesgroup.com
SIC: 7379 Computer related maintenance services
PA: Thales
   Tour Carpe Diem Esplanade Nord
   Courbevoie 92400
   157 778-000

(P-13998)
TOPTAL LLC
548 Market St Ste 36879, San Francisco (94104-5401)
PHONE..................888 604-3188
David Camp, *Chief Mktg Ofcr*
Carlos Aguirre, *Vice Pres*
Hector Angulo, *Vice Pres*
Mike Dowhan, *Vice Pres*
Joellen Ferrer, *Vice Pres*
EMP: 438
SALES (corp-wide): 24.5MM **Privately Held**
WEB: www.toptal.com
SIC: 7379 Computer related consulting services
PA: Toptal, Llc
   2810 N Church St # 36879
   Wilmington DE 19802
   650 843-9206

(P-13999)
TRADEBEAM INC
303 Twin Dolphin Dr # 600, Redwood City (94065-1497)
PHONE..................650 653-4800
Fax: 650 653-4801
EMP: 100
SQ FT: 26,000
SALES (est): 4.8MM
SALES (corp-wide): 481.7MM **Privately Held**
WEB: www.tradebeam.com
SIC: 7379 Computer Related Services
HQ: Cdc Software, Inc.
   4325 Alexander Dr
   Alpharetta GA 30022

(P-14000)
TRESL INC (PA)
855 El Cmino Real Ste 125, Palo Alto (94301)
PHONE..................650 868-2862
John Chao, *Principal*
EMP: 48 EST: 2016
SALES (est): 1.1MM **Privately Held**
WEB: www.tresl.co
SIC: 7379 Computer related services

(P-14001)
TRIANZ LLC (HQ)
2350 Mission College Blvd, Santa Clara (95054-1532)
PHONE..................408 387-5800
Srikanth Manchala, *President*
Ira Horowitz, *Partner*
Lalit Kumar, *Partner*
Pradeep Sahu, *Partner*
Andy Singh, *Partner*
EMP: 120
SQ FT: 18,000
SALES: 88.9MM **Privately Held**
WEB: www.trianz.com
SIC: 7379

(P-14002)
TRIFACTA INC (PA)
575 Market St Ste 1100, San Francisco (94105-5816)
PHONE..................415 429-7570
Adam Wilson, *CEO*
Vijay Balasubramaniam, *Partner*
Sachin Chawla, *President*
Paul Staelin, *Officer*
Richard Barnes, *Vice Pres*
EMP: 91 EST: 2012
SQ FT: 3,000
SALES (est): 10.4MM **Privately Held**
WEB: www.trifacta.com
SIC: 7379 7374 Data processing consultant; data processing & preparation

(P-14003)
TSS LINK INC
2099 Gateway Pl Ste 310, San Jose (95110-1017)
PHONE..................408 745-7875
Jim Arnold, *CEO*
EMP: 35 EST: 2005
SALES (est): 1.4MM
SALES (corp-wide): 19.5B **Publicly Held**
WEB: www.avnet.com
SIC: 7379
PA: Avnet, Inc.
   2211 S 47th St
   Phoenix AZ 85034
   480 643-2000

(P-14004)
VCINITY INC (PA)
Also Called: Vcinity Ultimate Access
2055 Gateway Pl Ste 650, San Jose (95110-1084)
PHONE..................408 841-4700
Harry Carr, *CEO*
Mohsen Moazami, *Ch of Bd*
Russel Davis, *COO*
Michael McDonald, *CFO*
Mike McDonald, *CFO*
EMP: 37 EST: 1998
SQ FT: 12,100
SALES (est): 8.6MM **Privately Held**
WEB: www.vcinity.io
SIC: 7379 Computer hardware requirements analysis

(P-14005)
VECTOR STEALTH HOLDINGS II LLC (PA)
456 Montgomery St Fl 19, San Francisco (94104-1233)
PHONE..................415 293-5000
Alexander R Slusky, *Mng Member*
EMP: 37 EST: 2007
SALES (est): 25.3MM **Privately Held**
WEB: www.vectorcapital.com
SIC: 7379 Computer related maintenance services

(P-14006)
VISA COMMERCE SOLUTIONS INC
900 Metro Center Blvd, Foster City (94404-2172)
PHONE..................650 432-3200
Alfred F Kelly Jr, *President*
Terry Angelos, *COO*
Daniel Greenberg, *Chief Mktg Ofcr*
Oliver Jenkyn, *Exec VP*
Bill Sheedy, *Exec VP*
EMP: 35 EST: 2006
SQ FT: 17,600
SALES (est): 17.1MM **Publicly Held**
WEB: www.usa.visa.com
SIC: 7379
PA: Visa Inc.
   900 Metro Center Blvd
   Foster City CA 94404

(P-14007)
VISIONARY INTGRTION PRFSSNALS (HQ)
Also Called: Visionary Intgrtion Prfssonals
80 Iron Point Cir Ste 100, Folsom (95630-8592)
PHONE..................916 985-9625
Jonna Ward, *CEO*
Patti Bennion, *CFO*
Jeff Bettcher, *Officer*
Patrick Quarry, *Officer*
Steve Carpenter, *Vice Pres*
EMP: 95 EST: 2005
SQ FT: 9,000
SALES (est): 38.9MM **Privately Held**
WEB: www.trustvip.com
SIC: 7379 8742 Computer related maintenance services; management consulting services

(P-14008)
WAVE COMPUTING INC (PA)
780 Montague Expy Ste 308, San Jose (95131-1317)
PHONE..................408 412-8645
Sanjai Kohli, *CEO*
Mike Uhler, *COO*
Dennis Bencala, *CFO*
Lee Flanagin, *Senior VP*
Paul Alpern, *Vice Pres*
EMP: 56 EST: 2008
SALES (est): 53.2MM **Privately Held**
WEB: www.mips.com
SIC: 7379 7374 Computer data escrow service; data processing service

(P-14009)
WAZUH INC (PA)
1021 Lenor Way, San Jose (95128-4111)
PHONE..................844 349-2984
Santiago Gonzalez-Bassett, *CEO*
EMP: 149 EST: 2015
SALES (est): 8.4MM **Privately Held**
WEB: www.wazuh.com
SIC: 7379 Computer related consulting services

(P-14010)
WORK TRUCK SOLUTIONS INC
2485 Notre Dame Blvd # 3, Chico (95928-7161)
PHONE..................855 987-4544
Kathryn Schifferle, *CEO*
Gretchen Krugler, *CFO*
Keith Nordin, *Vice Pres*
Randy Ledbetter, *Software Engr*
John Austin, *Manager*
EMP: 80 EST: 2011
SALES (est): 4.6MM **Privately Held**
WEB: www.worktrucksolutions.com
SIC: 7379 Computer related services

(P-14011)
WYNDGATE TECHNOLOGIES
4925 Robert J Mathews Pkw, El Dorado Hills (95762-5700)
PHONE..................916 404-8400
Michael Ruxnin, *Ch of Bd*
Tom Marcinek, *COO*
Morgan Polcheni, *Vice Pres*
EMP: 35 EST: 1989
SALES (est): 3.2MM
SALES (corp-wide): 988.4MM **Publicly Held**
WEB: www.wyndgate.com
SIC: 7379 7371 7372 Computer related consulting services; custom computer programming services; prepackaged software
HQ: Global Med Technologies, Inc.
   4925 Robert J Mathews Pkw
   El Dorado Hills CA 95762

(P-14012)
X2NSAT
1310 Redwood Way Ste C, Petaluma (94954-6514)
PHONE..................707 664-5700
Karen Cividanes, *Program Mgr*
Audrey Arcuri, *Executive Asst*
Adolfo Duarte, *Info Tech Dir*
Michelle Stewart, *Accountant*
Shelley Caiati, *Controller*
▲ EMP: 35 EST: 1997
SALES (est): 8.3MM **Privately Held**
WEB: www.x2n.com
SIC: 7379

(P-14013)
XANTRION INCORPORATED
651 Thomas L Berkley Way, Oakland (94612-1344)
PHONE..................510 272-4701
Tom Snyder, *COO*
Anne Bisagno, *President*
George Babichev, *Administration*
Sean Cameron, *Administration*
Christian Kelly, *CTO*
EMP: 50 EST: 2000
SQ FT: 10,000
SALES (est): 14.6MM **Privately Held**
WEB: www.xantrion.com
SIC: 7379 ; computer related services

(P-14014)
XCOMMERCE INC (HQ)
Also Called: Magento
345 Park Ave, San Jose (95110-2704)
PHONE..................310 954-8012
Mark Lavelle, *President*
Meagan Dollins, *Partner*
Craig Jackson, *Partner*
Amy Schade, *Partner*
Phillip Depaul, *CFO*
▼ EMP: 629 EST: 2010
SQ FT: 4,000
SALES (est): 113.5MM
SALES (corp-wide): 12.8B **Publicly Held**
WEB: www.magento.com
SIC: 7379 5961 ; catalog sales
PA: Adobe Inc.
   345 Park Ave
   San Jose CA 95110
   408 536-6000

(P-14015)
XORIANT CORPORATION (PA)
1248 Reamwood Ave, Sunnyvale (94089-2225)
PHONE..................408 743-4400
Girish Gaitonde, *CEO*
Mehul Agarwal, *Partner*
Mandar Joshi, *Partner*
Jayson Taylor, *Partner*
Hari Haran, *President*
EMP: 120 EST: 1990
SALES: 236.4MM **Privately Held**
WEB: www.xoriant.com
SIC: 7379 7371 Computer related consulting services; computer software development

(P-14016)
YAANA TECHNOLOGIES LLC
542 Gibralter Dr, Milpitas (95035-6315)
PHONE..................650 996-2927

7379 - Computer Related Svcs, NEC County (P-14017)

Rajesh Puri,
Jeffrey Zellmer, *CFO*
Vaibhav Sharma, *Vice Pres*
Roger Magana, *Administration*
Dave Grootwassink, *CTO*
EMP: 45 **EST:** 2007
SALES (est): 6.3MM **Privately Held**
WEB: www.yaanatech.com
SIC: 7379 Computer related consulting services

(P-14017)
YAMMER INC
410 Townsend St, San Francisco (94107-1537)
PHONE................................415 796-7400
Keith R Dolliver, *CEO*
Dee Anna McPherson, *Vice Pres*
EMP: 160 **EST:** 2008
SALES (est): 33.4MM
SALES (corp-wide): 168B **Publicly Held**
WEB: www.yammer.com
SIC: 7379 Computer related maintenance services
PA: Microsoft Corporation
1 Microsoft Way
Redmond WA 98052
425 882-8080

(P-14018)
ZINIER INC
3182 Campus Dr Ste 333, San Mateo (94403-3123)
PHONE................................787 504-4826
Prateek Chakravarty, *CEO*
EMP: 150 **EST:** 2018
SALES (est): 3MM **Privately Held**
WEB: www.zinier.com
SIC: 7379 Computer related maintenance services

(P-14019)
ZIONTECH SOLUTIONS INC
1900 Mccarthy Blvd # 100, Milpitas (95035-7436)
PHONE................................408 434-6001
Hymavathi Anumandla, *President*
Ashok Anumandla, *CEO*
Hymavathi Pentaparthi, *Principal*
Soma Krishna, *Software Dev*
Lavakumar Gourishetty, *Technical Staff*
EMP: 45 **EST:** 2008
SALES (est): 6MM **Privately Held**
WEB: www.ziontech.com
SIC: 7379

(P-14020)
ZIPPEDI INC
1633 Bayshore Hwy Ste 335, Burlingame (94010-1538)
PHONE................................858 353-9743
Luis Vera, *CEO*
EMP: 37 **EST:** 2018
SALES (est): 2.4MM **Privately Held**
WEB: www.zippedi.com
SIC: 7379

(P-14021)
ZULTYS INC
785 Lucerne Dr, Sunnyvale (94085-3848)
PHONE................................408 328-0450
Neil Lichtman, *CEO*
David Termondt, *CFO*
Steve Francis, *Officer*
Pavel Matsienok, *Vice Pres*
Michael Troflianin, *Vice Pres*
▲ **EMP:** 40 **EST:** 2006
SQ FT: 20,000
SALES (est): 9.8MM **Privately Held**
WEB: www.zultys.com
SIC: 7379

7381 Detective & Armored Car Svcs

(P-14022)
A1 PROTECTIVE SERVICES INC
5 Thomas Mellon Cir, San Francisco (94134-2501)
PHONE................................415 467-7200
Paula Jones, *President*
EMP: 84 **EST:** 1998
SQ FT: 900 **Privately Held**
WEB: www.a1prosecurity.com
SIC: 7381 Security guard service

(P-14023)
A1 PROTECTIVE SERVICES LLC
7000 Franklin Blvd # 410, Sacramento (95823-1820)
PHONE................................916 421-3000
Paula Jones,
Brajah Norris,
EMP: 50 **EST:** 2017
SALES (est): 2.7MM **Privately Held**
WEB: www.a1prosecurity.com
SIC: 7381 Security guard service

(P-14024)
A3 SMART HOME LP
2440 Camino Ramon Ste 200, San Ramon (94583-4326)
PHONE................................925 830-4777
Yolanda Zara, *CFO*
Adela Wekselblatt, *Finance Mgr*
Sonny Hoang, *Counsel*
Clifton Wayne Jordan, *Director*
Anne Chechile, *Manager*
EMP: 51 **EST:** 1998
SALES (est): 5.6MM **Privately Held**
WEB: www.a3smarthome.com
SIC: 7381 Guard services

(P-14025)
ABC SECURITY SERVICE INC (PA)
1840 Embarcadero, Oakland (94606-5220)
P.O. Box 1709 (94604-1709)
PHONE................................510 436-0666
Ana Chretien, *President*
Roger Chretien, *Vice Pres*
Maria Salazar, *Regional Mgr*
EMP: 215 **EST:** 1968
SQ FT: 17,000
SALES (est): 6.8MM **Privately Held**
WEB: www.abcsecurityservice.us
SIC: 7381 Security guard service

(P-14026)
AIRBORNE SECURITY PATROL INC (PA)
10481 Grant Line Rd # 175, Elk Grove (95624-9722)
PHONE................................916 394-2400
Cedric Young Sr, *President*
Reginald Harris, *Executive*
EMP: 80 **EST:** 1988
SALES (est): 1MM **Privately Held**
WEB: www.airbornesecuritypatrol.com
SIC: 7381 Security guard service

(P-14027)
ALL PHASE SECURITY INC
Also Called: Sj Lighting
2959 Promenade St Ste 200, West Sacramento (95691-6400)
P.O. Box 980363 (95798-0363)
PHONE................................916 919-3859
Kenneth Garrett, *CEO*
Martin Flatley, *Chairman*
Ronda Ritchie, *Vice Pres*
EMP: 83 **EST:** 1994
SQ FT: 8,000
SALES (est): 2.5MM
SALES (corp-wide): 592.4MM **Privately Held**
WEB: www.allphasesecurity.com
SIC: 7381 Security guard service; detective services
HQ: Universal Protection Service, Lp
1551 N Tustin Ave Ste 650
Santa Ana CA 92705
714 619-9700

(P-14028)
AMERICAN CSTM PRIVATE SEC INC
446 E Vine St Ste A, Stockton (95202-1116)
P.O. Box 8513 (95208-0513)
PHONE................................209 369-1200
Rajesh Patti, *President*
Carl Murray, *Vice Pres*
EMP: 50 **EST:** 2008
SQ FT: 1,100
SALES (est): 3.5MM **Privately Held**
WEB: www.customofficers.com
SIC: 7381 Security guard service

(P-14029)
AMERIGUARD SECURITY SVCS INC
Also Called: AGS
5470 W Spruce Ave Ste 102, Fresno (93722-2115)
PHONE................................559 271-5984
Lawrence Garcia, *President*
Michael Pettersen, *Officer*
Lillian Flores, *Vice Pres*
Neveen Musleh, *Admin Asst*
Harlan Hartman, *Opers Mgr*
EMP: 63 **EST:** 2002
SQ FT: 6,000
SALES (est): 6.7MM **Privately Held**
WEB: www.ameriguardsecurity.com
SIC: 7381 Detective services

(P-14030)
ANI PRIVATE SEC & PATROL INC
4122 Broadway, Oakland (94611-5112)
PHONE................................510 652-6833
Kamorudeen Animashaun, *President*
EMP: 39 **EST:** 1992
SALES (est): 779.7K **Privately Held**
WEB: www.anisecurity.net
SIC: 7381 Security guard service

(P-14031)
ARMED GUARD PRIVATE SEC INC
50 Landing Cir, Chico (95973-7873)
PHONE................................530 751-3218
Adam Stricker, *CEO*
Michelle Greene, *CFO*
EMP: 85 **EST:** 2018
SALES (est): 2.8MM **Privately Held**
WEB: www.armedguard.net
SIC: 7381 Security guard service

(P-14032)
ARMOR BRER PROTECTIVE SVCS INC
2701 Del Paso Rd Ste 130, Sacramento (95835-2306)
PHONE................................833 692-2774
Terry Brown, *CEO*
Will Goldsborough, *COO*
EMP: 50 **EST:** 2004
SALES (est): 2MM **Privately Held**
SIC: 7381 7389 Protective services, guard; security guard service; private investigator; personal investigation service

(P-14033)
ARMOROUS
1360 19th Hole Dr Ste 207, Windsor (95492-7717)
PHONE................................707 387-4400
Eric Hanson, *President*
EMP: 96 **EST:** 2018
SALES (est): 6MM **Privately Held**
WEB: www.armorous.com
SIC: 7381 Security guard service; private investigator

(P-14034)
ATLAS PRIVATE SECURITY INC
888 N 1st St Ste 222, San Jose (95112-6314)
PHONE................................408 613-0668
Robert Foster, *Principal*
EMP: 50 **EST:** 2016
SALES (est): 3.2MM **Privately Held**
WEB: www.atlasps.org
SIC: 7381 Security guard service

(P-14035)
BACO REALTY CORPORATION
6310 Stockton Blvd, Sacramento (95824-4003)
PHONE................................916 974-9898
EMP: 85
SALES (corp-wide): 43MM **Privately Held**
WEB: www.bacorealty.com
SIC: 7381 Guard services
PA: Baco Realty Corporation
51 Federal St Ste 202
San Francisco CA 94107
415 281-3700

(P-14036)
BARBIER SECURITY GROUP
20 Galli Dr 9-10, Novato (94949-5735)
PHONE................................415 747-8473
Harry Evan Barbier, *President*
Elizabeth Ramirez, *Executive Asst*
Pedro Sanchez, *Admin Asst*
Blotzer Kyle, *Opers Spvr*
Kyle Blotzer, *Opers Staff*
EMP: 150 **EST:** 2011
SALES (est): 10.5MM **Privately Held**
WEB: www.barbiersecuritygroup.com
SIC: 7381 Security guard service

(P-14037)
BAYER PROTECTIVE SERVICES INC
3436 Amrcn Rver Dr Ste 10, Sacramento (95864)
PHONE................................916 486-5800
Bryon A Bayer, *President*
Bryon Bayer, *President*
EMP: 147 **EST:** 1995
SQ FT: 1,600
SALES (est): 609.3K
SALES (corp-wide): 13.5MM **Privately Held**
WEB: www.bayerprotectiveservices.com
SIC: 7381 Security guard service
PA: First Security Services
850 San Jose Ave Ste 128
Clovis CA 93612
559 297-1444

(P-14038)
BLACK BEAR SECURITY SVCS INC
Also Called: Montana Investigation
2016 Oakdale Ave Ste B, San Francisco (94124-2041)
PHONE................................415 559-5159
Moura Borisova, *President*
EMP: 47 **EST:** 1995
SQ FT: 3,000
SALES (est): 3.1MM **Privately Held**
WEB: www.blackbearsecurity.com
SIC: 7381 7382 Security guard service; security systems services

(P-14039)
BORGENS & BORGENS INC
Also Called: Delta Protective Services
141 E Acacia St Ste D, Stockton (95202-1400)
P.O. Box 8633 (95208-0633)
PHONE................................209 547-2980
L D Borgens, *President*
K R Borgens, *Vice Pres*
EMP: 37 **EST:** 1993
SQ FT: 2,475
SALES (est): 2.5MM **Privately Held**
SIC: 7381 Security guard service

(P-14040)
C & C SECURITY PATROL INC (PA)
4615 Enterprise Cmn, Fremont (94538-6345)
PHONE................................510 713-1260
Hermenegildo Couoh, *CEO*
Marcel Lopez, *Vice Pres*
Wayne Spalding, *VP Human Res*
Danny Bui, *Manager*
Tri Bui, *Manager*
EMP: 105 **EST:** 1996
SALES (est): 7.8MM **Privately Held**
WEB: www.ccsecuritypatrol.com
SIC: 7381 Security guard service

(P-14041)
CALIFORNIA SECURITY SVCS INC (PA)
Also Called: Elite Universal Security
5548 Feather River Blvd, Olivehurst (95961-6612)
PHONE................................530 749-0280
Monty Hecker, *President*
Linda Hahn, *CFO*
Mike Hahn, *Vice Pres*
Debra Hecker, *Admin Sec*
EMP: 40 **EST:** 2002
SQ FT: 5,000
SALES (est): 6.4MM **Privately Held**
WEB: www.elite.api-academy.com
SIC: 7381 Security guard service

PRODUCTS & SERVICES SECTION
7381 - Detective & Armored Car Svcs County (P-14066)

(P-14042)
CALIFORNIA SECURITY SVCS INC
Also Called: Elite Universal Security
35 Heritage Ln Ste 6, Chico (95926-1313)
PHONE...................530 899-3751
Monty Hecker, *President*
EMP: 38
SALES (corp-wide): 6.4MM **Privately Held**
WEB: www.elite.api-academy.com
SIC: 7381 Security guard service
PA: California Security Services, Inc.
  5548 Feather River Blvd
  Olivehurst CA 95961
  530 749-0280

(P-14043)
CLOUDKNOX SECURITY INC
333 Camarillo Ter Ste 3, Sunnyvale (94085-2019)
PHONE...................408 647-5515
Balaji Parimi, *Administration*
Raj Mallempati, *COO*
Michael Ratte, *Accounts Mgr*
EMP: 45 EST: 2017
SALES (est): 5.7MM **Privately Held**
WEB: www.cloudknox.io
SIC: 7381 Guard services

(P-14044)
COMPREHENSIVE SEC SVCS INC (PA)
10535 E Stockton Blvd G, Elk Grove (95624-9758)
P.O. Box 246719, Sacramento (95824-6719)
PHONE...................916 683-3605
Bashir A Choudry, *President*
Jamal-Eddine Kabbaj, *Exec VP*
Omar Choudhry, *Director*
EMP: 75 EST: 1989
SQ FT: 3,300 **Privately Held**
WEB: www.comprehensivesecurity.net
SIC: 7381 7382 Security guard service; security systems services

(P-14045)
CONSOLDTED PROTECTIVE SVCS INC
3307 Watt Ave Ste 3, Sacramento (95821-3630)
PHONE...................916 483-2500
Varinder Bhupal, *CEO*
EMP: 40 EST: 2008
SALES (est): 1.1MM **Privately Held**
WEB: www.consolidatedprotectiveservices.com
SIC: 7381 Security guard service

(P-14046)
COOKE & ASSOCIATES INC (PA)
145 Town And Country Dr # 108, Danville (94526-3963)
PHONE...................408 842-0602
Harry Arruda, *CEO*
EMP: 48 EST: 2002
SALES (est): 2.5MM **Privately Held**
WEB: www.cookepi.com
SIC: 7381 6211 Protective services, guard; securities flotation companies

(P-14047)
COURTESY SECURITY INC
Also Called: Securelion Security
2252 Erie Ct, Tracy (95304-5803)
PHONE...................888 572-5545
Ajmal Boomwal, *Principal*
EMP: 60 EST: 2016
SALES (est): 1.2MM **Privately Held**
WEB: www.securelionsecurity.com
SIC: 7381 Security guard service

(P-14048)
COVENANT AVIATION SECURITY LLC
1000 Marina Blvd Ste 100, Brisbane (94005-1839)
P.O. Box 280440, San Francisco (94128-0440)
PHONE...................650 219-3473
Brian O Apos, *Manager*
Geraldine White, *Opers Staff*
Rex Pillai, *Assoc Pastor*
Zachary Hollenbach, *Director*
Patrick Sinozich, *Director*
EMP: 635
SALES (corp-wide): 57.4MM **Privately Held**
WEB: www.covenantsecurity.com
SIC: 7381 Security guard service
HQ: Covenant Aviation Security, Llc
  156 Tamarack Ave
  Naperville IL 60540
  630 771-0800

(P-14049)
CPS SECURITY SOLUTIONS INC
799 Fletcher Ln Ste 201, Hayward (94544-1057)
PHONE...................510 806-7227
EMP: 56 **Privately Held**
SIC: 7381 Security guard service
PA: Cps Security Solutions, Inc.
  3400 E Airport Way
  Long Beach CA 90806

(P-14050)
CREATIVE SECURITY COMPANY INC
150 S Autumn St Ste B, San Jose (95110-2515)
PHONE...................408 295-2600
Charles Wall, *President*
Brian Wall, *Vice Pres*
Mike Mattocks, *Security Dir*
Kristina Davidson, *Accounting Mgr*
Jeff Spillers, *Accounts Mgr*
EMP: 350 EST: 1999
SQ FT: 12,000
SALES (est): 22.2MM **Privately Held**
WEB: www.creativesecurity.com
SIC: 7381 Security guard service; private investigator

(P-14051)
CRIMETEK SECURITY
3448 N Golden State Blvd, Turlock (95382-9709)
P.O. Box 845 (95381-0845)
PHONE...................209 668-6208
Edward Esmaili, *President*
Ed Esmaili, *Partner*
Rosy Esmaili, *Partner*
Randall Turner, *Officer*
Joseph Givargis, *Manager*
EMP: 67 EST: 1999
SQ FT: 2,200
SALES (est): 6.1MM **Privately Held**
WEB: www.crimetek.com
SIC: 7381 Security guard service; guard services

(P-14052)
CYPRESS PRIVATE SECURITY LP (DH)
478 Tehama St, San Francisco (94103-4141)
P.O. Box 1322, Ross (94957-1322)
PHONE...................866 345-1277
Kes Narbutas, *CEO*
Juan Infante, *Officer*
Walter Coupland, *Accounts Mgr*
Ernest Dayce, *Supervisor*
Nalisa Torres, *Supervisor*
EMP: 304 EST: 1996
SQ FT: 3,500
SALES (est): 32.3MM
SALES (corp-wide): 8.6B **Privately Held**
WEB: www.cypress-security.com
SIC: 7381 Security guard service
HQ: Universal Services Of America, Lp
  1551 N Tustin Ave Fl 6
  Santa Ana CA 92705
  866 877-1965

(P-14053)
DELTA HAWKEYE SECURITY INC
7400 Shoreline Dr Ste 2, Stockton (95219-5498)
PHONE...................209 957-3333
Dallas Faulkner, *Vice Pres*
Frank Passadore, *President*
Brian Millin, *Vice Pres*
EMP: 73 EST: 1996
SQ FT: 2,000
SALES (est): 2.6MM
SALES (corp-wide): 65.6MM **Privately Held**
WEB: www.deltahawkeye.com
SIC: 7381 Security guard service
PA: The Grupe Company
  3255 W March Ln Ste 400
  Stockton CA 95219
  209 473-6000

(P-14054)
DELTA PERSONNEL SERVICES INC
Also Called: Guardian Security Agency
1820 Galindo St Ste 3, Concord (94520-2447)
PHONE...................925 356-3034
Judith Travers, *CEO*
Heather Travers, *Vice Pres*
EMP: 80 EST: 1983
SQ FT: 4,300
SALES (est): 8.7MM **Privately Held**
WEB: www.guardiansecurityagency.com
SIC: 7381 Security guard service

(P-14055)
ENTERPRISE PROTECTIVE SVCS INC (PA)
777 1st St, Gilroy (95020-4918)
PHONE...................408 840-2680
Armand Aranda, *President*
EMP: 44 EST: 2006
SALES (est): 2MM **Privately Held**
SIC: 7381 Security guard service

(P-14056)
FIRST ALARM SEC & PATROL INC
1801 Oakland Blvd Ste 315, Walnut Creek (94596-7017)
PHONE...................925 295-1260
EMP: 337 **Privately Held**
WEB: www.firstalarm.com
SIC: 7381 Security guard service
PA: First Alarm Security & Patrol, Inc.
  1731 Tech Dr Ste 800
  San Jose CA 95110

(P-14057)
FIRST ALARM SEC & PATROL INC
1240 Briggs Ave, Santa Rosa (95401-4760)
PHONE...................707 584-1110
EMP: 337 **Privately Held**
WEB: www.firstalarm.com
SIC: 7381 Security guard service
PA: First Alarm Security & Patrol, Inc.
  1731 Tech Dr Ste 800
  San Jose CA 95110

(P-14058)
FIRST ALARM SEC & PATROL INC (PA)
Also Called: First Security Services
1731 Tech Dr Ste 800, San Jose (95110)
PHONE...................408 866-1111
Cal Horton, *President*
Jarl E Saal, *Chairman*
Teresa Larkin, *Officer*
Larry Gowin, *Executive*
Billy Hall, *Security Dir*
EMP: 250 EST: 1989
SALES (est): 39.5MM **Privately Held**
WEB: www.firstalarm.com
SIC: 7381 Security guard service

(P-14059)
FIRSTCALL (PA)
Also Called: Steele Corp SEC Advisory Svcs
1 Sansome St Ste 3500, San Francisco (94104-4436)
PHONE...................415 781-4300
Kenneth Kurtz, *CEO*
Kristen Lombardo, *Executive Asst*
EMP: 138 EST: 1989
SQ FT: 5,000
SALES (est): 49MM **Privately Held**
WEB: www.wwsteele.com
SIC: 7381 8742 8748 Security guard service; management consulting services; agricultural consultant

(P-14060)
G4S SECURE SOLUTIONS (USA)
1 Annabel Ln Ste 208, San Ramon (94583-4360)
PHONE...................925 543-0008
EMP: 119
SALES (corp-wide): 11.8B **Privately Held**
SIC: 7381 Detective/Armored Car Services
HQ: G4s Secure Solutions (Usa) Inc
  1395 University Blvd
  Jupiter FL 33458
  561 622-5656

(P-14061)
G4S TCHNOLOGY HOLDINGS USA INC
3073 Teagarden St, San Leandro (94577-5720)
PHONE...................510 633-1300
Lisa Vanverveek, *Branch Mgr*
EMP: 331 **Privately Held**
WEB: www.g4s.com
SIC: 7381 Security guard service
HQ: G4s Technology Holdings (Usa) Inc.
  1395 University Blvd
  Jupiter FL 33458

(P-14062)
GARDA CL WEST INC
1650 Northpoint Pkwy B, Santa Rosa (95407-5043)
PHONE...................707 591-0282
EMP: 39
SALES (corp-wide): 145.8MM **Privately Held**
SIC: 7381 Armored car services
HQ: Garda Cl West, Inc.
  1612 W Pico Blvd
  Los Angeles CA 90015
  213 383-3611

(P-14063)
GARDA CL WEST INC
1320 Willow Rd, Menlo Park (94025-1516)
PHONE...................650 617-4548
Richard Irvin, *Branch Mgr*
EMP: 39
SALES (corp-wide): 145.8MM **Privately Held**
SIC: 7381 Armored car services
HQ: Garda Cl West, Inc.
  1612 W Pico Blvd
  Los Angeles CA 90015
  213 383-3611

(P-14064)
GEIL ENTERPRISES INC
Also Called: CIS Security
1945 N Helm Ave Ste 102, Fresno (93727-1670)
PHONE...................559 495-3000
Sam Geil, *CEO*
Ryan Geil, *President*
Matias Smith, *Human Res Mgr*
Doug Cutts, *Sales Mgr*
Rose Membrila, *Representative*
EMP: 540 EST: 1986
SQ FT: 10,000
SALES (est): 27.9MM **Privately Held**
WEB: www.geilenterprises.com
SIC: 7381 7349 Protective services, guard; janitorial service, contract basis; building maintenance, except repairs

(P-14065)
GLOBAL DEFENSE GROUP LLC
Also Called: Inteltec Alarm Technologies
395 S State Highway 65 A-271, Lincoln (95648-9325)
PHONE...................530 510-5204
EMP: 40
SALES (est): 586K **Privately Held**
WEB: www.globaldefensegroup.us
SIC: 7381 7382 9711 Detective/Armored Car Services Security Systems Services National Security

(P-14066)
GUARDSMARK LLC
1601 Bayshore Hwy Ste 350, Burlingame (94010-1522)
PHONE...................650 652-9130
EMP: 145

7381 - Detective & Armored Car Svcs County (P-14067)

PRODUCTS & SERVICES SECTION

SALES (corp-wide): 928.7MM **Privately Held**
SIC: **7381** Detective/Armored Car Services
HQ: Guardsmark, Llc
6363 Poplar Ave Ste 300
Memphis TN 92705
901 761-2288

(P-14067)
HAL-MAR-JAC ENTERPRISES
Also Called: McCoy's Patrol Service
1044 Potrero Cir, Suisun City (94585-4139)
PHONE.................415 467-1470
EMP: 110
SALES (est): 2.3MM **Privately Held**
SIC: **7381** Detective/Armored Car Services

(P-14068)
HG HOLDINGS INC
Also Called: Sia Security Services
924 Enterprise Dr, Sacramento (95825-3902)
PHONE.................916 944-2828
Paul Ioanidis, *CEO*
Earl Rotes, *COO*
Earl Roets, *CFO*
Netza Saavedra, *Officer*
EMP: 41 **EST:** 1994
SALES (est): 1.2MM **Privately Held**
WEB: www.siasecurityservices.com
SIC: **7381** Security guard service

(P-14069)
HIGHCOM SECURITY SERVICES
1900 Webster St Ste B, Oakland (94612-2946)
PHONE.................510 893-7600
Sammy Joselewitz, *President*
Jackie Nunez-Smith, *Human Resources*
Uri Brodetzki, *Director*
Eileen Williams, *Assistant*
EMP: 60 **EST:** 2005
SALES (est): 5.2MM **Privately Held**
WEB: www.highcomsecurityservices.com
SIC: **7381** 8742 Security guard service; management consulting services

(P-14070)
HYLTON SECURITY INC
2045 Hallmark Dr Ste 6, Sacramento (95825-2224)
PHONE.................916 442-1000
David J Hylton, *President*
Mindy A Hylton, *Senior VP*
EMP: 40 **EST:** 2006
SALES (est): 3.6MM **Privately Held**
WEB: www.hyltonsecurity.com
SIC: **7381** Security guard service

(P-14071)
IUNLIMITED INCORPORATED
7801 Folsom Blvd Ste 203, Sacramento (95826-2620)
P.O. Box 276390 (95827-6390)
PHONE.................916 218-6198
Todd M Tano, *CEO*
Keith Jacobs, *President*
Jeffrey Walters, *Officer*
Justin Brunette, *Vice Pres*
Leonard Watson, *Opers Mgr*
EMP: 115 **EST:** 2006
SALES (est): 12.8MM
SALES (corp-wide): 30.7MM **Privately Held**
WEB: www.iunlimited.net
SIC: **7381** Private investigator
PA: Insight Service Group, Inc.
55 Ferncroft Rd Ste 300
Danvers MA 01923
800 278-0550

(P-14072)
KP RESEARCH SERVICES INC
11818 Kemper Rd, Auburn (95603-9500)
PHONE.................530 878-5390
Suzanna Grant, *CEO*
EMP: 50 **EST:** 1999
SALES (est): 2.2MM **Privately Held**
WEB: www.kpresearchservices.com
SIC: **7381** 9221 Private investigator; bureau of criminal investigation, government

(P-14073)
LEGION CORPORATION (PA)
784 Geary St, San Francisco (94109-7302)
PHONE.................800 750-0062
Joseph Shelley, *CEO*
Francois De La Roche, *COO*
EMP: 61 **EST:** 2012
SALES (est): 5MM **Privately Held**
WEB: www.legioncorporation.com
SIC: **7381** Security guard service

(P-14074)
LOSS PREVENTION GROUP INC
524 7th St, Oakland (94607-3913)
PHONE.................510 836-6011
Mark White, *CEO*
John Stretch, *Instructor*
Mamadou Ndom, *Relations*
EMP: 38 **EST:** 2006
SALES (est): 3.9MM **Privately Held**
WEB: www.lpgca.com
SIC: **7381** Security guard service

(P-14075)
MARINA SECURITY SERVICES INC
465 California St Ste 609, San Francisco (94104-1816)
PHONE.................415 773-2300
Sam Tadesse, *CEO*
Behailu Mekbib, *CEO*
Ana Espinola, *Manager*
EMP: 115 **EST:** 1997
SALES (est): 4.6MM **Privately Held**
WEB: www.marinasecurityservices.com
SIC: **7381** Security guard service

(P-14076)
MONUMENT SECURITY INC
24301 Suthland Dr Ste 312, Hayward (94545)
PHONE.................510 430-3540
EMP: 150 **Privately Held**
SIC: **7381** Detective/Armored Car Services
PA: Monument Security, Inc.
4926 43rd St Ste 10
Mcclellan CA 95652

(P-14077)
MONUMENT SECURITY INC (PA)
4926 43rd St Ste 10, McClellan (95652-2618)
P.O. Box 399, North Highlands (95660-0399)
PHONE.................916 564-4234
EMP: 150
SQ FT: 2,500
SALES (est): 36.3MM **Privately Held**
SIC: **7381** Detective/Armored Car Services

(P-14078)
NATIONAL SECURITY INDUSTRIES
Also Called: National Security Santa Cruz
501 Mission St Ste 1a, Santa Cruz (95060-3661)
PHONE.................831 425-2052
James Clarke, *Branch Mgr*
EMP: 73 **Privately Held**
WEB: www.nationalsecurityind.com
SIC: **7381** Security guard service
PA: National Security Industries
940 Park Ave Frnt Frnt
San Jose CA 95126

(P-14079)
NATIONAL SECURITY INDUSTRIES (PA)
940 Park Ave Frnt Frnt, San Jose (95126-3074)
PHONE.................408 371-6505
Micheal Gerami, *President*
EMP: 226 **EST:** 1995
SQ FT: 1,900
SALES (est): 11.6MM **Privately Held**
WEB: www.nationalsecurityind.com
SIC: **7381** Security guard service

(P-14080)
NORTHWEST PROTECTIVE SERVICE (PA)
1163 Chess Dr Ste I, Foster City (94404-1119)
P.O. Box 25332, San Mateo (94402-5332)
PHONE.................650 345-8500
Brian Magee, *President*
Lawrence Pelzner, *Treasurer*
Debbie Gonzales, *Office Mgr*
EMP: 59 **EST:** 1988
SQ FT: 15,000
SALES (est): 2MM **Privately Held**
SIC: **7381** Security guard service; private investigator

(P-14081)
ONTEL SECURITY SERVICES INC
2125 Wylie Dr Ste 11, Modesto (95355-3847)
P.O. Box 579730 (95357-9730)
PHONE.................209 521-0200
David Ackerman, *CEO*
David McCann, *COO*
Michael Ackerman, *CFO*
Roberta Gray, *Treasurer*
Latrisha Avila, *Officer*
EMP: 71 **EST:** 2006
SQ FT: 2,500 **Privately Held**
WEB: www.ontelsecurity.com
SIC: **7381** Security guard service

(P-14082)
ORION SECURITY PATROL INC
675 E Gish Rd, San Jose (95112-2708)
PHONE.................408 287-4411
Yooshieh Gahramani, *President*
Harry L Stice, *Vice Pres*
Ed Trumbull, *Vice Pres*
EMP: 450 **EST:** 1997
SALES (est): 9.8MM **Privately Held**
WEB: www.orionsecurity.com
SIC: **7381** Security guard service
PA: Yosh Enterprises, Inc.
675 E Gish Rd
San Jose CA 95112

(P-14083)
OVERTON SECURITY SERVICES INC
39300 Civic Center Dr # 370, Fremont (94538-2338)
PHONE.................510 791-7380
Andrew Overton, *President*
Vicki Greiner, *CFO*
Paul Baria, *Officer*
Sandra Overton, *Vice Pres*
Jonathan Casillas, *Security Dir*
EMP: 215 **EST:** 2007
SALES (est): 15.6MM **Privately Held**
WEB: www.overtonsecurity.com
SIC: **7381** Security guard service

(P-14084)
PALADIN PRTCTION SPCALISTS INC
Also Called: Paladin Private Security
320 Commerce Cir, Sacramento (95815-4213)
PHONE.................916 331-3175
Louis G Aljens, *CEO*
Matthew Carroll, *Vice Pres*
M Scott Johnson, *Vice Pres*
EMP: 135 **EST:** 2003
SALES (est): 8.1MM **Privately Held**
SIC: **7381** Security guard service

(P-14085)
PATROL SOLUTIONS LLC
6060 Sunrise Vista Dr # 1, Citrus Heights (95610-7053)
PHONE.................916 919-6079
Klinton Kehoe, *CEO*
Clinton Kehoe, *Mng Member*
EMP: 135 **EST:** 2011
SALES (est): 5.2MM **Privately Held**
WEB: www.patrolsolutions.com
SIC: **7381** Protective services, guard

(P-14086)
PERSONAL PROTECTIVE SVCS INC (PA)
398 Beach Rd Fl 2, Burlingame (94010-2004)
P.O. Box 14007, Oakland (94614-2007)
PHONE.................650 344-3302
Stan Teets, *President*
EMP: 96 **EST:** 1993
SQ FT: 1,500
SALES (est): 5.5MM **Privately Held**
WEB: www.personalprotective.com
SIC: **7381** Protective services, guard; private investigator

(P-14087)
PRE-EMPLOYCOM INC
3655 Meadow View Dr, Redding (96002-9715)
P.O. Box 491570 (96049-1570)
PHONE.................800 300-1821
Robert V Mather, *President*
Micah Page, *Sales Staff*
Jamee Dawson, *Manager*
EMP: 100 **EST:** 1993
SQ FT: 10,500
SALES (est): 10.4MM **Privately Held**
WEB: www.pre-employ.com
SIC: **7381** Private investigator

(P-14088)
PRIVATE EYES INC (PA)
2700 Ygnacio Valley Rd # 10, Walnut Creek (94598-3455)
PHONE.................925 927-3333
Sandra James, *President*
EMP: 43 **EST:** 1999
SQ FT: 6,000
SALES (est): 6.6MM **Privately Held**
WEB: www.privateeyesbackgroundchecks.com
SIC: **7381** Private investigator

(P-14089)
PROBE INFORMATION SERVICES INC
3835 N Freeway Blvd # 228, Sacramento (95834-1955)
P.O. Box 418429 (95841-8429)
PHONE.................916 676-1826
Ross O Stewart, *President*
Christy Watkins, *Regional Mgr*
Emily Wingo-Schneider, *Human Resources*
Nicole Ross, *Assistant*
Sheri Ewing-Mcdonald, *Supervisor*
EMP: 101 **EST:** 1992 **Privately Held**
WEB: www.probeinfo.com
SIC: **7381** Private investigator

(P-14090)
PROFESSNAL TCHNCAL SEC SVCS IN (PA)
Also Called: Protech
625 Market St Fl 9, San Francisco (94105-3302)
PHONE.................415 243-2100
Sergio Reyes, *President*
Mike Harrison, *President*
Debra Reyes, *Vice Pres*
Thomas Petersen, *Admin Sec*
Jason Daugherty, *Opers Staff*
EMP: 286 **EST:** 1994
SQ FT: 1,800
SALES (est): 10.2MM **Privately Held**
WEB: www.protechbayarea.com
SIC: **7381** Security guard service

(P-14091)
PROFESSNAL TCHNCAL SEC SVCS IN
1970 Broadway Ste 840, Oakland (94612-2299)
PHONE.................510 645-9200
EMP: 112
SALES (corp-wide): 10.2MM **Privately Held**
WEB: www.protechbayarea.com
SIC: **7381** Security guard service
PA: Professional Technical Security Services, Inc.
625 Market St Fl 9
San Francisco CA 94105
415 243-2100

(P-14092)
RCI ASSOCIATES
5030 Business Center Dr # 280, Fairfield (94534-6884)
PHONE.................866 668-4732
Mitchell Brooks, *CEO*
Mitchell A Brooks, *CEO*
Chris Rippee, *COO*
Richard Ches, *CFO*
EMP: 45 **EST:** 2010
SQ FT: 938

PRODUCTS & SERVICES SECTION

7382 - Security Systems Svcs County (P-14117)

SALES (est): 1.5MM **Privately Held**
WEB: www.rciassociatesinc.com
SIC: 7381 Protective services, guard

(P-14093)
SECURITAS SEC SVCS USA INC
505 Montgomery St, San Francisco (94111-6529)
PHONE...............................510 568-6818
EMP: 188
SALES (corp-wide): 11.5B **Privately Held**
WEB: www.securitasinc.com
SIC: 7381 Detective/Armored Car Services
HQ: Securitas Security Services Usa, Inc.
9 Campus Dr Ste 25
Parsippany NJ 07054
973 267-5300

(P-14094)
SECURITY INDUST SPCIALISTS INC
2880 Stevens Creek Blvd, San Jose (95128-4622)
PHONE...............................408 247-0100
Keith Jacobs, *Officer*
Ted Bosetti, *Controller*
Chris Cesena, *VP Opers*
Jesse Antonio, *Supervisor*
EMP: 210
SALES (corp-wide): 143.8MM **Privately Held**
WEB: www.sis.us
SIC: 7381 5065 Guard services; security control equipment & systems
PA: Security Industry Specialists, Inc.
6071 Bristol Pkwy
Culver City CA 90280
310 215-5100

(P-14095)
SECURITY MGT GROUP INTL INC
3353 Alder Canyon Way, Antelope (95843-4996)
PHONE...............................925 521-1500
Mitchell Brooke, *Branch Mgr*
EMP: 44
SALES (corp-wide): 2MM **Privately Held**
SIC: 7381 Guard services
PA: Security Management Group International, Inc.
4170 Larchmont Dr
El Paso TX 79902
925 521-1500

(P-14096)
SILICON VLY SEC & PATROL INC (PA)
1131 Luchessi Dr Ste 2, San Jose (95118-3770)
PHONE...............................408 267-1539
Ray Higdon, *CEO*
Lisa Higdon, *President*
Gary Mills, *Vice Pres*
Julianne Hinson, *Finance Mgr*
Stephanie Bownas, *Human Res Mgr*
EMP: 150 EST: 1994
SQ FT: 4,000
SALES (est): 11.4MM **Privately Held**
WEB: www.svsp.com
SIC: 7381 Security guard service

(P-14097)
SINTEX SECURITY SERVICES INC
501 Bangs Ave Ste D, Modesto (95356-8978)
PHONE...............................209 543-9044
Jerry Sterner, *President*
EMP: 75 EST: 1993
SQ FT: 2,500
SALES (est): 3.8MM **Privately Held**
WEB: www.sintexsecurity.com
SIC: 7381 Security guard service

(P-14098)
SOS SECURITY INCORPORATED
26250 Industrial Blvd # 48, Hayward (94545-2922)
PHONE...............................510 782-4900
Michael Boone, *Vice Pres*
EMP: 61
SALES (corp-wide): 97.7MM **Privately Held**
WEB: www.sossecurity.com
SIC: 7381 Security guard service; detective agency
PA: Sos Security Incorporated
1915 Us Highway 46 Ste 1
Parsippany NJ 07054
973 402-6600

(P-14099)
STAR PROTECTION AGENCY LLC
Also Called: Star Protection Agency CA
8201 Edgewater Dr Ste 102, Oakland (94621-2021)
PHONE...............................510 635-1732
Edward Lynd, *Branch Mgr*
EMP: 92
SALES (corp-wide): 25.7MM **Privately Held**
WEB: www.starprotectionagency.net
SIC: 7381 7389 Security guard service; personal investigation service
PA: Star Protection Agency Llc
846 S Hotel St Ste 200
Honolulu HI 96813
808 532-3911

(P-14100)
STRATEGIC THREAT MGT INC
2504 Verne Roberts Cir # 1, Antioch (94509-7917)
P.O. Box 2657 (94531-2657)
PHONE...............................925 775-4777
Charlene Mochizuki-Treat, *President*
EMP: 40 EST: 2005
SALES (est): 2.9MM **Privately Held**
WEB: www.strategicthreat.com
SIC: 7381 Security guard service

(P-14101)
TALOS SECURE GROUP INC
110 Railroad Ave Ste B, Suisun City (94585-1791)
PHONE...............................707 927-5432
Robert Smith, *CEO*
Michael Grabski, *COO*
Christopher Charo, *CFO*
EMP: 38 EST: 2013
SQ FT: 2,100
SALES (est): 2.6MM **Privately Held**
WEB: www.talossecuregroup.com
SIC: 7381 Security guard service

(P-14102)
TRIUMPH PROTECTION GROUP INC
853 Cotting Ct Ste D, Vacaville (95688-8701)
P.O. Box 852 (95696-0852)
PHONE...............................800 224-0286
Jeffrey Fields, *CEO*
Jose Flores, *Area Mgr*
Nick Torres, *Area Mgr*
Igor Boyko, *Opers Mgr*
Steve Johnson, *Marketing Staff*
EMP: 150 EST: 2013
SQ FT: 2,200
SALES: 5.9MM **Privately Held**
WEB: www.triumphprotection.com
SIC: 7381 Security guard service

(P-14103)
UNITED SEC SPECIALISTS INC (PA)
275 Saratoga Ave Ste 200, Santa Clara (95050-6669)
PHONE...............................408 431-0691
Kyle Madej, *CEO*
EMP: 210 EST: 2017
SALES (est): 4.6MM **Privately Held**
WEB: www.usselite.com
SIC: 7381 Guard services

(P-14104)
UNITED SEC SPECIALISTS INC
2010 El Camino Real, Santa Clara (95050-4051)
PHONE...............................408 878-5720
Henry Sierra, *Branch Mgr*
EMP: 40

SALES (corp-wide): 4.6MM **Privately Held**
WEB: www.usselite.com
SIC: 7381 Guard services
PA: United Security Specialists, Inc.
275 Saratoga Ave Ste 200
Santa Clara CA 95050
408 431-0691

(P-14105)
UNIVERSAL PROTECTION SVC LP
Also Called: Prestige Protection
2415 San Ramon Vly Blvd, San Ramon (94583-5381)
PHONE...............................805 496-4401
EMP: 61
SALES (corp-wide): 741.7MM **Privately Held**
SIC: 7381 Detective/Armored Car Services
HQ: Universal Protection Service, Lp
1551 N Tustin Ave Ste 650
Santa Ana CA 92705
714 619-9700

(P-14106)
UNIVERSAL SERVICES AMERICA LP
777 N 1st St Ste 150, San Jose (95112-6347)
PHONE...............................408 993-1965
Darryl Coleman, *Branch Mgr*
EMP: 999
SALES (corp-wide): 8.6B **Privately Held**
WEB: www.legacy.aus.com
SIC: 7381 Security guard service
HQ: Universal Services Of America, Lp
1551 N Tustin Ave Fl 6
Santa Ana CA 92705
866 877-1965

(P-14107)
VIGILANT PRIVATE SECURITY
2100 N Winery Ave Ste 102, Fresno (93703-4813)
PHONE...............................559 800-7233
Alena Trybunalava, *CEO*
EMP: 70 EST: 2013
SALES (est): 2.5MM **Privately Held**
WEB: www.vigilantprivatesecurity.com
SIC: 7381 Security guard service

(P-14108)
W S B & ASSOCIATES INC
150 Executive Park Blvd # 4700, San Francisco (94134-3303)
PHONE...............................510 444-6266
EMP: 100 **Privately Held**
SIC: 7381 Security Guard Service
PA: W S B & Associates Inc
1390 Market St Ste 314
San Francisco CA 94134

(P-14109)
W S B & ASSOCIATES INC
150 Executive Park Blvd # 4700, San Francisco (94134-3341)
PHONE...............................415 864-3510
Bobby Sisk, *CEO*
EMP: 177 EST: 1994
SALES (est): 9.5MM **Privately Held**
WEB: www.wsbassociates.net
SIC: 7381 Security guard service

(P-14110)
WADE CASEY
Also Called: Crime Prevention Patrol
1648 Kathleen Ave Ste A, Sacramento (95815-1815)
P.O. Box 245982 (95824-5982)
PHONE...............................916 395-9996
Wade Casey, *Owner*
Elizabeth Casey, *Partner*
EMP: 92 EST: 1985
SQ FT: 1,500
SALES (est): 1.1MM **Privately Held**
SIC: 7381 Protective services, guard

(P-14111)
WARDEN SECURITY ASSOCIATES INC
353 E 10th St Ste 730, Gilroy (95020-6572)
PHONE...............................408 722-6463

Juan Haro, *Principal*
EMP: 67
SALES (corp-wide): 443.8K **Privately Held**
WEB: www.wardensecurityassociates.com
SIC: 7381 Guard services
PA: Warden Security Associates, Inc.
544 Vermont St
San Jose CA

(P-14112)
YOSH ENTERPRISES INC (PA)
Also Called: Paramount Investigations
675 E Gish Rd, San Jose (95112-2708)
PHONE...............................408 287-4411
Yosh Gahramani, *President*
EMP: 187 EST: 1983
SQ FT: 6,800
SALES (est): 14.6MM **Privately Held**
SIC: 7381 6531 8742 0782 Security guard service; private investigator; real estate managers; industrial & labor consulting services; lawn & garden services

7382 Security Systems Svcs

(P-14113)
3SCALE INC (PA)
995 Market St, San Francisco (94103-1702)
PHONE...............................415 349-5187
Steven Willmott, *CEO*
Anna Grzywiska, *Hum Res Coord*
Laine Fuller, *VP Sales*
EMP: 49 EST: 2009
SALES (est): 5.8MM **Privately Held**
WEB: www.3scale.net
SIC: 7382 Security systems services

(P-14114)
3VR SECURITY INC
1 Kaiser Plz Ste 1030, Oakland (94612-3601)
PHONE...............................415 513-4577
Robert A Shipp, *CEO*
Charles F Ryan III, *CFO*
Masayuki Karahashi, *Senior VP*
James Hudson, *Vice Pres*
Loretta Pendenza, *Controller*
EMP: 90 EST: 2002
SALES (est): 12.9MM **Publicly Held**
WEB: www.identiv.com
SIC: 7382 Protective devices, security
PA: Identiv, Inc.
2201 Walnut Ave Ste 100
Fremont CA 94538

(P-14115)
ABM SECURITY SERVICES INC
830 Riverside Pkwy Ste 30, West Sacramento (95605-1505)
PHONE...............................916 614-9571
Steve Cader, *Manager*
EMP: 62
SALES (corp-wide): 5.9B **Publicly Held**
SIC: 7382 7381 5063 Security systems services; security guard services; alarm systems
HQ: Abm Security Services, Inc.
3800 Buffalo Speedway # 325
Houston TX 77098
713 928-5344

(P-14116)
ACALVIO TECHNOLOGIES INC
2520 Mission College Blvd # 110, Santa Clara (95054-1238)
PHONE...............................408 931-6160
Nat Natraj, *President*
Rick Moy, *Marketing Staff*
Divya Valmiki, *Marketing Staff*
Eric Farnham, *Sales Staff*
EMP: 52 EST: 2015
SQ FT: 4,166
SALES (est): 2.5MM **Privately Held**
WEB: www.acalvio.com
SIC: 7382 Security systems services

(P-14117)
ACCELDATA INC
3031 Tisch Way, San Jose (95128-2541)
PHONE...............................650 450-3423
Rohit Choudhary, *CEO*
EMP: 110 EST: 2018

7382 - Security Systems Svcs County (P-14118)

SALES (est): 10MM **Privately Held**
WEB: www.acceldata.io
SIC: 7382 Security systems services

(P-14118)
ADMIRAL SECURITY SERVICES INC
2151 Salvio St Ste 260, Concord (94520-2406)
PHONE..................888 471-1128
Mohamed S Ahmed, *CEO*
Youssef Abdallah, *President*
EMP: 400 EST: 2004
SQ FT: 3,500
SALES (est): 19.6MM **Privately Held**
WEB: www.admiralsecurityservices.com
SIC: 7382 7381 Security systems services; protective services, guard; security guard service; guard services

(P-14119)
ALCATRAZ AI INC
1808 El Camino Real, Redwood City (94063-2111)
P.O. Box 247 (94064-0247)
PHONE..................650 600-0197
Tina D'Agostin, *CEO*
Vince Gaydarzhiev, *President*
Chris Kennedy, *Vice Pres*
EMP: 53 EST: 2016
SALES (est): 2.9MM **Privately Held**
WEB: www.alcatraz.ai
SIC: 7382 Security systems services

(P-14120)
AMERICOM CENTRAL STATION INC
1355 Fairfax Ave Ste 6, San Francisco (94124-1742)
PHONE..................415 550-7100
William Cereske, *CEO*
Manuel Escobar, *President*
Greg Miller, *CFO*
Michael Williams, *Vice Pres*
Mike Williams, *Marketing Staff*
EMP: 51 EST: 1994
SALES (est): 660.8K **Privately Held**
WEB: www.americomcs.com
SIC: 7382 5063 Burglar alarm maintenance & monitoring; burglar alarm systems

(P-14121)
ANOMALI INCORPORATED
808 Winslow St, Redwood City (94063-1608)
PHONE..................408 800-4050
Hugh Njemanze, *CEO*
Drew Hamer, *CFO*
Steve Herrod, *Bd of Directors*
Dan Barahona, *Chief Mktg Ofcr*
WEI Huang, *Officer*
EMP: 100 EST: 2013
SALES (est): 23.7MM **Privately Held**
WEB: www.anomali.com
SIC: 7382 Security systems services

(P-14122)
ARKOSE LABS HOLDINGS INC (PA)
250 Montgomery St # 1000, San Francisco (94104-3421)
PHONE..................415 917-8701
Kevin Gosschalk, *CEO*
Mark Resnick, *COO*
Glen Arrowsmith, *Vice Pres*
Patrice Boffa, *Vice Pres*
David Senecal, *Vice Pres*
EMP: 124 EST: 2017
SQ FT: 7,652
SALES (est): 10.9MM **Privately Held**
WEB: www.arkoselabs.com
SIC: 7382 Security systems services

(P-14123)
CALIFORNIA SECURITY ALARMS INC (PA)
2440 Camino Ramon Ste 200, San Ramon (94583-4326)
P.O. Box 5164 (94583-5164)
PHONE..................800 669-7779
Roger Carr, *President*
Harry Thrash, *Info Tech Mgr*
Keith Thorne, *Technical Mgr*
Tim Wolfskill, *Sales Dir*
EMP: 35 EST: 1970
SQ FT: 10,000
SALES (est): 4.2MM **Privately Held**
SIC: 7382 1731 Burglar alarm maintenance & monitoring; confinement surveillance systems maintenance & monitoring; electrical work

(P-14124)
CHRONICLE LLC (HQ)
250 Mayfield Ave, Mountain View (94043-4124)
PHONE..................650 214-5199
Ben Heben, *CFO*
Jan Kang,
EMP: 62 EST: 2018
SALES (est): 10MM
SALES (corp-wide): 182.5B **Publicly Held**
WEB: www.chronicle.security
SIC: 7382 Security systems services
PA: Alphabet Inc.
1600 Amphitheatre Pkwy
Mountain View CA 94043
650 253-0000

(P-14125)
CORINTHIAN INTL PRKG SVCS INC
Also Called: Corinthian Parking Services
19925 Stevns Crk Blvd, Cupertino (95014-2300)
PHONE..................408 867-7275
Todd Fedde, *CEO*
Douglas E Knapp, *CEO*
Ronnie Aguilar, *Sales Staff*
Kyle Baldasano, *Director*
Jonathan Covey, *Manager*
EMP: 500 EST: 1997
SQ FT: 6,000
SALES (est): 32.6MM **Privately Held**
WEB: www.corinthiantransportation.com
SIC: 7382 Security systems services

(P-14126)
DEEP SENTINEL CORP
1249 Quarry Ln Ste 147, Pleasanton (94566-8446)
PHONE..................415 858-4688
David L Selinger, *CEO*
Thara Edson, *CFO*
Bari Abdul, *Chief Mktg Ofcr*
EMP: 50 EST: 2016
SALES (est): 5.3MM **Privately Held**
WEB: www.deepsentinel.com
SIC: 7382 Security systems services

(P-14127)
DENALECT INC
Also Called: Denalect Alarm Company
1309 Pine St, Walnut Creek (94596-3628)
P.O. Box 5208 (94596-1208)
PHONE..................925 935-2680
Rod Uffindell, *President*
Eugenia Stevenson, *Admin Sec*
Cheryl Johnston, *Manager*
EMP: 60 EST: 1969
SQ FT: 4,800
SALES (est): 1.6MM **Privately Held**
WEB: www.denalect.com
SIC: 7382 Burglar alarm maintenance & monitoring; fire alarm maintenance & monitoring

(P-14128)
DIAMOND COMMUNICATIONS INC
124 S C St Ste C, Madera (93638-3605)
P.O. Box 328 (93639-0328)
PHONE..................559 673-5925
Michael Isaac Tarin, *President*
Gloria Molina, *Opers Staff*
Connie Tarin, *Director*
EMP: 50 EST: 1967
SQ FT: 3,000
SALES (est): 2.5MM **Privately Held**
WEB: www.diamonddci.com
SIC: 7382 5065 7389 5063 Burglar alarm maintenance & monitoring; mobile telephone equipment; telephone equipment; communication equipment; telephone answering service; fire alarm systems

(P-14129)
DIGITAL SHADOWS INC (PA)
3046a Polk St, San Francisco (94109-1010)
PHONE..................888 889-4143
Alastair Ewan Paterson, *CEO*
Maria Mastakas, *Vice Pres*
Kyndal Clemons, *Executive Asst*
Jamie Baggott, *Software Dev*
Christos Rigas, *Software Dev*
EMP: 148 EST: 2015
SALES (est): 14.6MM **Privately Held**
WEB: www.digitalshadows.com
SIC: 7382 Security systems services

(P-14130)
ELITE SECURITY GROUP INC
640 Bailey Rd 124, Bay Point (94565-4306)
PHONE..................925 597-8852
Robert Shane Taylor, *CEO*
EMP: 40 EST: 2016
SQ FT: 1,000
SALES (est): 2.8MM **Privately Held**
WEB: www.eliteprotection.biz
SIC: 7382 Security systems services

(P-14131)
EMAGINED SECURITY INC
2816 San Simeon Way, San Carlos (94070-3611)
PHONE..................415 944-2977
David Sockol, *President*
Julianna Sockol, *Info Tech Mgr*
Cory Dixon, *Consultant*
EMP: 50 EST: 2002
SALES (est): 8.8MM **Privately Held**
WEB: www.emagined.com
SIC: 7382 Security systems services

(P-14132)
EXABEAM INC (PA)
1051 E Hillsdale Blvd # 400, Foster City (94404-1640)
PHONE..................844 392-2326
Michael Decesare, *President*
Manish Sarin, *CFO*
Tim Matthews, *Chief Mktg Ofcr*
James Anderson, *Vice Pres*
Gareth Cox, *Vice Pres*
EMP: 174 EST: 2013
SALES (est): 22.3MM **Privately Held**
WEB: www.exabeam.com
SIC: 7382 7379 Security systems services;

(P-14133)
FIRST ALARM (PA)
1111 Estates Dr, Aptos (95003-3572)
PHONE..................831 476-1111
Jarl E Saal, *Chairman*
David Hood, *President*
Douglas Castro, *Officer*
Jon Dallimonti, *Officer*
Justin Hames, *Officer*
EMP: 120 EST: 1982
SQ FT: 14,000
SALES (est): 51.4MM **Privately Held**
WEB: www.firstalarm.com
SIC: 7382 Burglar alarm maintenance & monitoring

(P-14134)
FIRST ALARM SEC & PATROL INC
5250 Claremont Ave, Stockton (95207-5700)
PHONE..................209 473-1110
EMP: 337 **Privately Held**
WEB: www.firstalarm.com
SIC: 7382 5063 Security systems services; transformers & transmission equipment
PA: First Alarm Security & Patrol, Inc.
1731 Tech Dr Ste 800
San Jose CA 95110

(P-14135)
GUARD FORCE INC
Also Called: Guard Force International
6135 Tam O Shanter Dr 2, Stockton (95210-3303)
P.O. Box 284, Austin TX (78767-0284)
PHONE..................951 233-0206
Gordon Brooks, *President*
EMP: 50 EST: 2010
SALES (est): 1.1MM **Privately Held**
WEB: www.guardforceint.com
SIC: 7382 7381 Protective devices, security; guard services

(P-14136)
HOFFMANS ELECTRONIC SYSTEMS
Also Called: Alarmwatch
2301 Aviation Dr, Atwater (95301-5120)
P.O. Box 879, Merced (95341-0879)
PHONE..................209 723-2667
Barbara Hoffman, *Owner*
Matt Hoffman, *Vice Pres*
Karen Falconer,
EMP: 58 EST: 1979
SQ FT: 10,000
SALES (est): 6MM **Privately Held**
WEB: www.hoffmansecurity.com
SIC: 7382 Security systems services

(P-14137)
IGUARD SECURITY SERVICES INC (PA)
2850 Stevens Creek Blvd, San Jose (95128-4615)
PHONE..................650 714-1884
Christopher Mike Edwards, *Principal*
EMP: 48 EST: 2016
SALES (est): 475.2K **Privately Held**
WEB: www.iguardss.com
SIC: 7382 Security systems services

(P-14138)
KIMBERLITE CORPORATION (PA)
Also Called: Sonitrol Security Systems
3621 W Beechwood Ave, Fresno (93711-0648)
P.O. Box 9189 (93791-9189)
PHONE..................559 264-9730
Joey RAO Russell, *CEO*
Marselle Nikkel, *CFO*
Kenneth Berry, *Vice Pres*
Brian Petrille, *Vice Pres*
Marcos Reyes, *Vice Pres*
EMP: 58 EST: 1986
SQ FT: 3,500
SALES (est): 12.9MM **Privately Held**
WEB: www.sonitrolsecurity.com
SIC: 7382 Burglar alarm maintenance & monitoring

(P-14139)
MATSON ALARM CO INC (PA)
581 W Fllbrook Ave Ste 10, Fresno (93711)
PHONE..................559 438-8000
Larry E Matson, *President*
Mike Matson, *Vice Pres*
EMP: 49 EST: 1980
SQ FT: 1,000
SALES (est): 9.4MM **Privately Held**
WEB: www.matsonalarm.com
SIC: 7382 Security systems services

(P-14140)
MCAFEE PUBLIC SECTOR LLC (DH)
6220 America Center Dr, San Jose (95002-2563)
PHONE..................888 847-8766
David Weigand, *Vice Pres*
Ellen V McLean, *Program Mgr*
Jaime Burbach Mustard, *Program Mgr*
Carl Delsey, *Software Engr*
Bernardo Martinez, *Software Engr*
EMP: 50 EST: 2015
SALES (est): 38.6MM
SALES (corp-wide): 1.5B **Publicly Held**
WEB: www.mcafee.com
SIC: 7382 Protective devices, security

(P-14141)
NATIONAL PRO SECURITY SVCS INC
9306 International Blvd, Oakland (94603-1404)
P.O. Box 1654, San Leandro (94577-0165)
PHONE..................877 392-2340
Brandon F Ellis, *President*
Joy Baucom, *CFO*
Michael Edwards, *Admin Sec*
Joseph Lee Dancey Jr, *VP Sales*
EMP: 48 EST: 2013

PRODUCTS & SERVICES SECTION

7384 - Photofinishing Labs County (P-14163)

SALES (est): 1.2MM **Privately Held**
WEB:
www.nationalprosecurityservices.com
SIC: 7382 Security systems services

(P-14142)
NOZOMI NETWORKS INC (HQ)
575 Market St Ste 3650, San Francisco (94105-5823)
PHONE 800 314-6114
Edgard Capdevielle, *CEO*
Phil Page, *Partner*
Kim Legelis, *Chief Mktg Ofcr*
Andrea Carcano,
Obbe Knoop, *Vice Pres*
EMP: 84 EST: 2016
SALES (est): 18.2MM
SALES (corp-wide): 654.3K **Privately Held**
WEB: www.nozominetworks.com
SIC: 7382 Security systems services
PA: Nozomi Holding Sagl
  Centro Alfa
  Mendrisio TI 6850
  916 470-406

(P-14143)
PACIFIC WEST SECURITY INC
Also Called: Sonitrol
1587 Schallenberger Rd, San Jose (95131-2434)
PHONE 801 748-1034
Paul Schumate, *President*
Sandra Oswalt, *Corp Secy*
Jeffrey Lippert, *Info Tech Dir*
Joanie Andrews, *Director*
EMP: 60 EST: 1986
SQ FT: 8,000
SALES (est): 10.1MM **Privately Held**
WEB: www.sonitrolsv.com
SIC: 7382 1731 Burglar alarm maintenance & monitoring; fire detection & burglar alarm systems specialization

(P-14144)
PROGUARD SECURITY SERVICES
300 Montgomery St Ste 813, San Francisco (94104-1910)
PHONE 415 672-0786
EMP: 35 EST: 2016
SALES (est): 4.2MM **Privately Held**
WEB: www.proguardsecurityservices.com
SIC: 7382 Security systems services

(P-14145)
SACRAMENTO CONTROL SYSTEMS INC
11249 Sunco Dr Ste 3, Rancho Cordova (95742-7504)
PHONE 916 638-0788
Robert R Rice Sr, *President*
Wilma Rice, *Treasurer*
Robert J Rice, *Vice Pres*
Pat Macdonald, *Controller*
Chris Dragoo, *Manager*
EMP: 57 EST: 1969
SQ FT: 14,000
SALES (est): 4MM **Privately Held**
WEB: www.saccontrolsys.com
SIC: 7382 Fire alarm maintenance & monitoring

(P-14146)
SAFEBREACH INC
111 W Evelyn Ave Ste 117, Sunnyvale (94086-6127)
PHONE 408 743-5279
Guy Bejerano, *CEO*
Ken Smith, *Officer*
Yotam Ben Ezra, *Vice Pres*
Nattu Nachimuthu, *Vice Pres*
Itzhak Kotler, *CTO*
EMP: 42 EST: 2015
SQ FT: 1,000
SALES (est): 5.1MM **Privately Held**
WEB: www.safebreach.com
SIC: 7382 Security systems services
PA: Safebreach Ltd
  18 Caro Yosef
  Tel Aviv-Jaffa

(P-14147)
SECURITY ALARM FING ENTPS INC
2440 Camino Ramon Ste 200, San Ramon (94583-4326)
P.O. Box 5164 (94583-5164)
PHONE 925 830-4786
EMP: 70
SQ FT: 20,000
SALES (est): 10.7MM **Privately Held**
WEB: www.a3smarthome.com
SIC: 7382 6141 Security Systems Services

(P-14148)
SKYHIGH NETWORKS INC
900 E Hamilton Ave # 400, Campbell (95008-0670)
PHONE 408 564-0278
Christopher D Young, *CEO*
Michael Berry, *CFO*
Allison Cerra, *Chief Mktg Ofcr*
Dawn Smith,
John Giamatteo, *Exec VP*
EMP: 99 EST: 2011
SALES (est): 17.1MM
SALES (corp-wide): 1.5B **Publicly Held**
WEB: www.mcafee.com
SIC: 7382 Security systems services
HQ: Mcafee, Llc
  6220 America Center Dr
  San Jose CA 95002

(P-14149)
SONITROL OF SACRAMENTO LLC
1334 Blue Oaks Blvd, Roseville (95678-7014)
PHONE 916 724-1170
Jorgen Heide, *CEO*
John Hanes, *Shareholder*
John McChesney, *Shareholder*
Ron Files, *President*
Richard Ahrens, *CFO*
EMP: 39 EST: 1979
SQ FT: 9,600
SALES (est): 6.1MM **Privately Held**
WEB: www.sonitrolca.com
SIC: 7382 Burglar alarm maintenance & monitoring

(P-14150)
TOTAL MONITORING SERVICES INC
2440 Glendale Ln, Sacramento (95825-2418)
PHONE 916 480-4828
Timothy M Sproul, *President*
Richard Barnes, *Technology*
Tiffany Romero, *Controller*
Donna Smith, *Manager*
Candice Fazekas, *Supervisor*
EMP: 41 EST: 2002
SALES (est): 2.8MM **Privately Held**
WEB: www.tmscentral.com
SIC: 7382 Burglar alarm maintenance & monitoring; fire alarm maintenance & monitoring

(P-14151)
TURNER CAMERA SEC SYSTEMS INC
Also Called: Don Turner and Associates
120 W Shields Ave, Fresno (93705-4101)
PHONE 559 486-3466
Donald A Turner, *President*
Michael Garaffa, *Office Mgr*
Terry Campbell, *Sales Executive*
EMP: 190 EST: 1972
SQ FT: 3,700
SALES (est): 17.5MM **Privately Held**
WEB: www.turnersecurityfresno.com
SIC: 7382 Security systems services

(P-14152)
VECTRA AI INC (PA)
550 S Wnchester Blvd # 200, San Jose (95128-2579)
PHONE 408 326-2020
Hitesh Sheth, *President*
Gerard Bauer, *Vice Pres*
Andrew Bryan, *Vice Pres*
Didi Dayton, *Vice Pres*
Kevin Moore, *Vice Pres*
EMP: 36 EST: 2010
SALES (est): 8.5MM **Privately Held**
WEB: www.vectra.ai
SIC: 7382 Security systems services

(P-14153)
VERKADA INC (PA)
405 E 4th Ave, San Mateo (94401-3311)
PHONE 833 837-5232
Filip Kaliszan, *CEO*
James Ren, *CFO*
Kameron Rezai, *Officer*
Ryan Bettencourt, *Vice Pres*
Idan Koren, *Vice Pres*
EMP: 398 EST: 2016
SALES (est): 104.2MM **Privately Held**
WEB: www.verkada.com
SIC: 7382 Security systems services

7383 News Syndicates

(P-14154)
GIGA OMNI MEDIA INC
1613a Lyon St, San Francisco (94115-2414)
PHONE 415 974-6355
Paul Walborsky, *CEO*
Adell Cairns, *Research*
Adrian Escarcega, *Business Mgr*
Jon Collins, *Analyst*
John Baltisberger, *Production*
EMP: 75 EST: 2010
SALES (est): 5.4MM **Privately Held**
WEB: www.gigaom.com
SIC: 7383 News pictures, gathering & distributing; press service

(P-14155)
MARKETWATCH INC (DH)
Also Called: C B S Marketwatch
201 California St Fl 13, San Francisco (94111-5002)
PHONE 415 439-6400
Larry S Kramer, *Ch of Bd*
Kathleen B Yates, *President*
Paul Mattison, *CFO*
William Bishop, *Exec VP*
Doug Appleton, *Admin Sec*
EMP: 51 EST: 1997
SQ FT: 24,000
SALES (est): 30MM
SALES (corp-wide): 9.3B **Publicly Held**
WEB: www.big-chart.com
SIC: 7383 News ticker service
HQ: Dow Jones & Company, Inc.
  1211 Avenue Of The Americ
  New York NY 10036
  609 627-2999

(P-14156)
MELTWATER NEWS US INC (DH)
465 California St Fl 11, San Francisco (94104-1826)
P.O. Box 123408, Dallas TX (75312-3408)
PHONE 415 829-5900
Jorn Lyseggen, *CEO*
Adam Dealy, *COO*
Martin Hernandez, *CFO*
Karthik Kumar, *Vice Pres*
Ambera Cruz, *Business Dir*
EMP: 54 EST: 2007
SALES (est): 25.8MM
SALES (corp-wide): 359.7MM **Privately Held**
WEB: www.meltwater.com
SIC: 7383 News syndicates

7384 Photofinishing Labs

(P-14157)
LONGS DRUG STORES CAL INC
388 Elm Ave, Auburn (95603-4525)
PHONE 530 823-0922
Fax: 530 823-9305
EMP: 45
SQ FT: 28,256
SALES (corp-wide): 177.5B **Publicly Held**
SIC: 5912 5331 7384 5999 Ret Drugs/Sundries Variety Store Photofinish Laboratory Ret Misc Merchandise

HQ: Longs Drug Stores California Inc.
  1 Cvs Dr
  Woonsocket RI 02895
  925 937-1170

(P-14158)
LONGS DRUG STORES CAL INC
4424 Treat Blvd, Concord (94521-2704)
PHONE 925 676-4700
Fax: 925 691-1540
EMP: 40
SALES (corp-wide): 177.5B **Publicly Held**
SIC: 5912 7384 5999 Ret Drugs/Sundries Photofinishing Laboratory Ret Misc Merchandise
HQ: Longs Drug Stores California Inc.
  1 Cvs Dr
  Woonsocket RI 02895
  925 937-1170

(P-14159)
LONGS DRUG STORES CAL INC
Also Called: CVS
1005 Sutton Way, Grass Valley (95945-5182)
PHONE 530 272-6611
EMP: 39
SALES (corp-wide): 177.5B **Publicly Held**
SIC: 5912 5331 7384 5999 Ret Drugs/Sundries Variety Store Photofinish Laboratory Ret Misc Merchandise Ret Records/Cd's/Tapes
HQ: Longs Drug Stores California Inc.
  1 Cvs Dr
  Woonsocket RI 02895
  925 937-1170

(P-14160)
LONGS DRUG STORES CAL INC
63 Lincoln Blvd, Lincoln (95648-9389)
PHONE 916 408-0209
Fax: 916 408-0252
EMP: 50
SALES (corp-wide): 177.5B **Publicly Held**
SIC: 5912 5331 7384 5999 Ret Drugs/Sundries Variety Store Photofinish Laboratory Ret Misc Merchandise
HQ: Longs Drug Stores California Inc.
  1 Cvs Dr
  Woonsocket RI 02895
  925 937-1170

(P-14161)
LONGS DRUG STORES CAL INC
Also Called: CVS
2511 Somersville Rd, Antioch (94509-4408)
PHONE 925 754-4600
Fax: 925 706-1985
EMP: 40
SQ FT: 28,130
SALES (corp-wide): 177.5B **Publicly Held**
SIC: 5912 5331 5946 5941 Ret Drugs/Sundries Variety Store Ret Cameras/Photo Supply Ret Sport Goods/Bicycles
HQ: Longs Drug Stores California Inc.
  1 Cvs Dr
  Woonsocket RI 02895
  925 937-1170

(P-14162)
LONGS DRUG STORES CAL INC
851 Cherry Ave Ste 10, San Bruno (94066-2953)
PHONE 650 873-9363
Fax: 650 873-0576
EMP: 65
SALES (corp-wide): 177.5B **Publicly Held**
SIC: 5912 5331 7384 Ret Drugs/Sundries Variety Store Photofinishing Laboratory
HQ: Longs Drug Stores California Inc.
  1 Cvs Dr
  Woonsocket RI 02895
  925 937-1170

(P-14163)
LONGS DRUG STORES CAL INC
929 Sierra St, Kingsburg (93631-1512)
PHONE 559 897-0116
Fax: 559 897-4329

7384 - Photofinishing Labs County (P-14164)

EMP: 39
SQ FT: 21,122
SALES (corp-wide): 177.5B **Publicly Held**
SIC: **5912** 7384 5999 Ret Drugs/Sundries Photofinishing Laboratory Ret Misc Merchandise
HQ: Longs Drug Stores California Inc.
1 Cvs Dr
Woonsocket RI 02895
925 937-1170

(P-14164)
LONGS DRUG STORES CAL INC
5333 Elkhorn Blvd, Sacramento (95842-2526)
PHONE..................916 334-7170
Fax: 916 332-3274
EMP: 39
SALES (corp-wide): 177.5B **Publicly Held**
SIC: **5912** 5331 7384 5999 Ret Drugs/Sundries Variety Store Photofinish Laboratory Ret Misc Merchandise
HQ: Longs Drug Stores California Inc.
1 Cvs Dr
Woonsocket RI 02895
925 937-1170

(P-14165)
LONGS DRUG STORES CAL INC
7465 Rush Rver Dr Ste 500, Sacramento (95831)
PHONE..................916 391-1200
Fax: 916 391-1379
EMP: 60
SALES (corp-wide): 177.5B **Publicly Held**
SIC: **5912** 7384 5999 Ret Drugs/Sundries Photofinishing Laboratory Ret Misc Merchandise
HQ: Longs Drug Stores California Inc.
1 Cvs Dr
Woonsocket RI 02895
925 937-1170

(P-14166)
LONGS DRUG STORES CAL INC
4785 Granite Dr, Rocklin (95677-2853)
PHONE..................916 624-8288
EMP: 40
SQ FT: 42,770
SALES (corp-wide): 177.5B **Publicly Held**
SIC: **5912** 7384 5999 Ret Drugs/Sundries Photofinishing Laboratory Ret Misc Merchandise
HQ: Longs Drug Stores California Inc.
1 Cvs Dr
Woonsocket RI 02895
925 937-1170

(P-14167)
LONGS DRUG STORES CAL INC
230 Atlantic Ave, Pittsburg (94565-5222)
PHONE..................925 439-7288
Fax: 925 432-4342
EMP: 39
SALES (corp-wide): 177.5B **Publicly Held**
SIC: **5912** 5331 7384 5999 Ret Drugs/Sundries Variety Store Photofinish Laboratory Ret Misc Merchandise
HQ: Longs Drug Stores California Inc.
1 Cvs Dr
Woonsocket RI 02895
925 937-1170

(P-14168)
LONGS DRUG STORES CAL INC
560 Center Ave, Martinez (94553-4600)
PHONE..................925 370-8075
Fax: 925 370-0713
EMP: 40
SQ FT: 22,916
SALES (corp-wide): 177.5B **Publicly Held**
SIC: **5912** 7384 5999 Ret Drugs/Sundries Photofinish Laboratory Ret Misc Merchandise
HQ: Longs Drug Stores California Inc.
1 Cvs Dr
Woonsocket RI 02895
925 937-1170

(P-14169)
LONGS DRUG STORES CAL INC
2140 Grass Valley Hwy, Auburn (95603-2522)
PHONE..................530 885-8783
Fax: 530 885-2501
EMP: 40
SQ FT: 26,790
SALES (corp-wide): 177.5B **Publicly Held**
SIC: **5912** 5331 7384 5999 Ret Drugs/Sundries Variety Store Photofinish Laboratory Ret Misc Merchandise
HQ: Longs Drug Stores California Inc.
1 Cvs Dr
Woonsocket RI 02895
925 937-1170

(P-14170)
LONGS DRUG STORES CAL INC
3625 Mt Diablo Blvd, Lafayette (94549-3711)
PHONE..................925 284-7177
Fax: 925 284-2056
EMP: 35
SALES (corp-wide): 177.5B **Publicly Held**
SIC: **5912** 7384 5999 Ret Drugs/Sundries Photofinish Laboratory Ret Misc Merchandise
HQ: Longs Drug Stores California Inc.
1 Cvs Dr
Woonsocket RI 02895
925 937-1170

(P-14171)
LONGS DRUG STORES CAL INC
8861 Greenback Ln, Orangevale (95662-4058)
PHONE..................916 989-2212
Fax: 916 987-5989
EMP: 40
SALES (corp-wide): 177.5B **Publicly Held**
SIC: **5912** 7384 5999 Ret Drugs/Sundries Photofinishing Laboratory Ret Misc Merchandise
HQ: Longs Drug Stores California Inc.
1 Cvs Dr
Woonsocket RI 02895
925 937-1170

(P-14172)
LONGS DRUG STORES CAL INC
5090 Foothills Blvd, Roseville (95747-6517)
PHONE..................916 783-1350
Fax: 916 783-1360
EMP: 45
SQ FT: 25,405
SALES (corp-wide): 177.5B **Publicly Held**
SIC: **5912** 7384 5999 Ret Drugs/Sundries Photofinishing Laboratory Ret Misc Merchandise
HQ: Longs Drug Stores California Inc.
1 Cvs Dr
Woonsocket RI 02895
925 937-1170

(P-14173)
LONGS DRUG STORES CAL LLC
201 W Napa St Ste 35, Sonoma (95476-6643)
PHONE..................707 938-4734
Ron Bastianon, *Manager*
EMP: 208
SQ FT: 24,651
SALES (corp-wide): 268.7B **Publicly Held**
WEB: www.cvs.com
SIC: **5912** 5331 7384 7331 Drug stores; variety stores; photofinishing laboratory; mailing service
HQ: Longs Drug Stores California L.L.C.
1 Cvs Dr
Woonsocket RI 02895

(P-14174)
LONGS DRUG STORES CAL LLC
Also Called: CVS
348 Gellert Blvd, Daly City (94015-2611)
PHONE..................650 994-0752
Dave Fryslie, *Manager*
EMP: 208
SALES (corp-wide): 268.7B **Publicly Held**
WEB: www.cvs.com
SIC: **5912** 7384 5999 Drug stores; variety stores; photofinishing laboratory; toiletries, cosmetics & perfumes
HQ: Longs Drug Stores California L.L.C.
1 Cvs Dr
Woonsocket RI 02895

(P-14175)
LONGS DRUG STORES CAL LLC
300 Merced Mall, Merced (95348-2432)
PHONE..................209 723-3292
William Rifenburg, *Sales/Mktg Mgr*
EMP: 208
SALES (corp-wide): 268.7B **Publicly Held**
WEB: www.cvs.com
SIC: **5912** 5331 7384 5999 Drug stores; variety stores; photofinishing laboratory; toiletries, cosmetics & perfumes
HQ: Longs Drug Stores California L.L.C.
1 Cvs Dr
Woonsocket RI 02895

(P-14176)
LONGS DRUG STORES CAL LLC
6197 Sunrise Blvd, Citrus Heights (95610-6834)
PHONE..................916 726-4433
Lon Mackie, *Manager*
EMP: 208
SALES (corp-wide): 268.7B **Publicly Held**
WEB: www.cvs.com
SIC: **5912** 5331 7384 5999 Drug stores; variety stores; photofinishing laboratory; cosmetics
HQ: Longs Drug Stores California L.L.C.
1 Cvs Dr
Woonsocket RI 02895

(P-14177)
LONGS DRUG STORES CAL LLC
5040 Laguna Blvd, Elk Grove (95758-4147)
PHONE..................916 684-6811
Ross Sall, *Manager*
EMP: 208
SALES (corp-wide): 268.7B **Publicly Held**
WEB: www.cvs.com
SIC: **5912** 7384 5999 Drug stores; photofinishing laboratory; toiletries, cosmetics & perfumes
HQ: Longs Drug Stores California L.L.C.
1 Cvs Dr
Woonsocket RI 02895

(P-14178)
LONGS DRUG STORES CAL LLC
738 Bancroft Rd, Walnut Creek (94598-1531)
PHONE..................925 938-7616
Steve Ross, *Manager*
EMP: 208
SALES (corp-wide): 268.7B **Publicly Held**
WEB: www.cvs.com
SIC: **5912** 5331 7384 5999 Drug stores; variety stores; photofinishing laboratory; toiletries, cosmetics & perfumes
HQ: Longs Drug Stores California L.L.C.
1 Cvs Dr
Woonsocket RI 02895

(P-14179)
LONGS DRUG STORES CAL LLC
2900 Standiford Ave, Modesto (95350-0167)
PHONE..................209 522-1047
Ron Nanau, *Manager*
EMP: 208
SQ FT: 28,718
SALES (corp-wide): 268.7B **Publicly Held**
WEB: www.cvs.com
SIC: **5912** 5331 7384 7331 Drug stores; variety stores; photofinishing laboratory; mailing service
HQ: Longs Drug Stores California L.L.C.
1 Cvs Dr
Woonsocket RI 02895

(P-14180)
LONGS DRUG STORES CAL LLC
5408 Ygnacio Valley Rd, Concord (94521-3836)
PHONE..................925 672-0547
Scott Bradley, *Office Mgr*
EMP: 208
SALES (corp-wide): 268.7B **Publicly Held**
WEB: www.cvs.com
SIC: **5912** 5331 7384 5999 Drug stores; variety stores; photofinishing laboratory; toiletries, cosmetics & perfumes
HQ: Longs Drug Stores California L.L.C.
1 Cvs Dr
Woonsocket RI 02895

(P-14181)
PHOTOWORKS INC
2077 Market St, San Francisco (94114-1315)
PHONE..................415 626-6800
Mike Josepher, *President*
EMP: 37 EST: 1987
SQ FT: 1,000
SALES (est): 2.7MM **Privately Held**
WEB: www.photoworkssf.com
SIC: **7384** Photofinishing laboratory

(P-14182)
SHUTTERFLY LLC (HQ)
2800 Bridge Pkwy Ste 100, Redwood City (94065-1193)
PHONE..................650 610-5200
Ryan O'Hara, *President*
Nicki Deuel, *Partner*
Randy Hart, *President*
James Hilt, *President*
Dwayne Black, *COO*
EMP: 301 EST: 1999
SQ FT: 100,000
SALES (est): 1.9B **Privately Held**
WEB: www.shutterflyinc.com
SIC: **7384** 5946 Photofinishing laboratory; film developing & printing; camera & photographic supply stores; cameras; photographic supplies
PA: Photo Holdings, Llc
2800 Bridge Pkwy
Redwood City CA 94065
650 610-5200

(P-14183)
SNAPFISH LLC (HQ)
100 Montgomery St # 1430, San Francisco (94104-4357)
PHONE..................415 979-3703
Jasbir Patel, *President*
Anthony Beckley, *CIO*
Igor Koval, *Software Dev*
Nik Gajare, *Manager*
EMP: 65 EST: 2015
SALES (est): 85.6MM
SALES (corp-wide): 143MM **Privately Held**
WEB: www.snapfish.com
SIC: **7384** Photofinishing laboratory
PA: District Photo, Inc.
10501 Rhode Island Ave
Beltsville MD 20705
301 595-5300

(P-14184)
WALGREEN CO
Also Called: Walgreens
1979 Mission St, San Francisco (94103-3404)
PHONE..................415 558-8749
EMP: 35
SALES (corp-wide): 139.5B **Publicly Held**
SIC: **5912** 7384 Drug Stores And Proprietary Stores
HQ: Walgreen Co.
200 Wilmot Rd Ste 2002
Deerfield IL 60015
847 940-2500

7389 Business Svcs, NEC

(P-14185)
280 CAPMARKETS LLC (PA)
220 Montgomery St # 1060, San Francisco (94104-3563)
PHONE....................628 231-2390
Gurinder Ahluwalia, *CEO*
David Rudd, *President*
Heather Hall, *CFO*
Prescott Nasser, *CTO*
EMP: 47 **EST:** 2016
SQ FT: 3,375
SALES (est): 4.2MM **Privately Held**
WEB: www.insperex.com
SIC: 7389 Financial services

(P-14186)
2DREAM INC
5729 Sonoma Dr Ste Z, Pleasanton (94566-7782)
PHONE....................650 943-2366
Hongfei Yin, *Principal*
EMP: 70 **EST:** 2017
SALES (est): 1.9MM **Privately Held**
WEB: www.2dreaminc.com
SIC: 7389

(P-14187)
35-A DISTRICT AG ASSN ✪
5007 Fairgrounds Rd, Mariposa (95338-9435)
PHONE....................209 966-2432
Brian Bullis, *General Mgr*
EMP: 50 **EST:** 2021
SALES (est): 680K **Privately Held**
SIC: 7389 Business services

(P-14188)
4LEAF INC (PA)
2126 Rheem Dr, Pleasanton (94588-2775)
PHONE....................925 462-5959
Kevin Duggan, *President*
Mike Leontiades, *Opers Staff*
Michael Renner, *Director*
EMP: 51 **EST:** 2001
SALES (est): 9.7MM **Privately Held**
WEB: www.4leafinc.com
SIC: 7389 Building inspection service

(P-14189)
5 PALMS LLC
800 S B St Fl 1, San Mateo (94401-4271)
PHONE....................650 457-0539
Stella Ohayon,
EMP: 212 **EST:** 2014
SALES (est): 74.3MM **Privately Held**
WEB: www.5palms.co
SIC: 7389 5083 3523 ; agricultural machinery & equipment; farm machinery & equipment

(P-14190)
A F EVANS COMPANY INC
Also Called: Byron Park
1700 Tice Valley Blvd Ofc, Walnut Creek (94595-1654)
PHONE....................925 937-1700
Kirsten Korhsege, *Manager*
EMP: 59
SALES (corp-wide): 37.6MM **Privately Held**
SIC: 7389 Personal service agents, brokers & bureaus
PA: A. F. Evans Company, Inc.
2033 N Main St Ste 340
Walnut Creek CA 94596
510 891-9400

(P-14191)
AAA RESTAURANT FIRE CTRL INC
Also Called: AAA Fire Protection Service
30113 Union City Blvd, Union City (94587-1511)
P.O. Box 3626, Hayward (94540-3626)
PHONE....................510 786-9555
Brent Patterson, *President*
Jeanne Patterson, *Treasurer*
Karen Patterson, *Treasurer*
Brian Patterson, *Vice Pres*
Jessica Troche, *Manager*
EMP: 90 **EST:** 1974
SQ FT: 10,000
SALES (est): 11MM **Privately Held**
SIC: 7389 Fire extinguisher servicing

(P-14192)
ABI DOCUMENT SUPPORT SVCS LLC
11010 White Rock Rd Ste 1, Rancho Cordova (95670-6361)
PHONE....................909 793-0613
Maggie Dragna, *Branch Mgr*
EMP: 79 **Privately Held**
SIC: 7389 5044 Microfilm recording & developing service; office equipment
HQ: Abi Document Support Services, Llc
3534 E Sunshine St Ste L
Springfield MO 65809

(P-14193)
ABSOLUTDATA TECHNOLOGIES INC
1320 Harbor Bay Pkwy # 170, Alameda (94502-6578)
PHONE....................510 748-9922
Anil Kaul, *President*
Rangan Bandyopadhyay, *Vice Pres*
Sudeshna Datta, *Vice Pres*
Chris Diener, *Vice Pres*
Suhale Kapoor, *Vice Pres*
EMP: 75 **EST:** 2004
SQ FT: 1,600
SALES (est): 8.6MM **Privately Held**
WEB: www.absolutdata.com
SIC: 7389 7374 Personal service agents, brokers & bureaus; data processing service

(P-14194)
ACCT HOLDINGS LLC
5949 Fair Oaks Blvd, Carmichael (95608-5221)
PHONE....................916 971-1981
EMP: 594
SALES (corp-wide): 540.5MM **Privately Held**
WEB: www.juliprun.com
SIC: 7389 Telemarketing services
PA: Acct Holdings Llc
1235 Westlakes Dr Ste 160
Berwyn PA 19312
610 695-0500

(P-14195)
ACCURATE FIRESTOP INC
1057 Serpentine Ln Ste A, Pleasanton (94566-8465)
PHONE....................510 886-1169
Gabrielle Lucatero, *Principal*
Javier Lucatero, *Principal*
Gicel Leanos, *Administration*
Monica Guzman, *Project Mgr*
Colleen Ussery, *Purchasing*
EMP: 150 **EST:** 1995
SALES (est): 10.7MM **Privately Held**
WEB: www.accuratefirestop.com
SIC: 7389 Fire protection service other than forestry or public

(P-14196)
ADMINISTRATIVE SYSTEMS INC
1651 Response Rd Ste 350, Sacramento (95815-5255)
P.O. Box 15437 (95851-0437)
PHONE....................916 563-1121
Donald J Robinson, *President*
Geraldine M Fong, *Corp Secy*
Keith Crane, *Vice Pres*
James R Powell, *Vice Pres*
EMP: 75 **EST:** 1972
SALES (est): 6.7MM **Privately Held**
WEB: www.asipay.com
SIC: 7389 Personal service agents, brokers & bureaus

(P-14197)
AIRBNB INC (PA)
888 Brannan St Fl 3, San Francisco (94103-4968)
PHONE....................415 510-4027
Brian Chesky, *Ch of Bd*
Dave Stephenson, *CFO*
Sloane Lehman, *Executive*
Nathan Blecharczyk, *Security Dir*
Divya Kumaraiah, *Program Mgr*
EMP: 1032 **EST:** 2008
SQ FT: 951,500
SALES (est): 3.3B **Publicly Held**
WEB: www.airbnb.com
SIC: 7389 Reservation services

(P-14198)
ALLENS PRESS CLIPPING BUREAU (PA)
55 New Montgomery St # 31, San Francisco (94105-3412)
PHONE....................415 392-2353
John McCombs, *Owner*
EMP: 42 **EST:** 1888
SQ FT: 900
SALES (est): 2.2MM **Privately Held**
WEB: www.allenspress.4t.com
SIC: 7389 Press clipping service

(P-14199)
ALOM TECHNOLOGIES CORPORATION (PA)
48105 Warm Springs Blvd, Fremont (94539-7498)
PHONE....................510 360-3600
Hannah Kain, *President*
Jack Sexton, *CFO*
Lisa Dolan, *Vice Pres*
Tami Strickland, *Executive*
Tony Chiu, *Info Tech Dir*
▲ **EMP:** 141 **EST:** 1997
SQ FT: 300,000
SALES (est): 40.8MM **Privately Held**
WEB: www.alom.com
SIC: 7389 4783 7374 7331 Packaging & labeling services; packing goods for shipping; data processing & preparation; direct mail advertising services

(P-14200)
AMPLE INC
100 Hooper St Ste 25, San Francisco (94107-3918)
PHONE....................617 504-3557
Khaled Hassounah, *CEO*
Harsh Jain, *Engineer*
Ankit Srivastava, *Engineer*
Eric Miller, *Senior Engr*
Marianella Cateriano, *Finance Dir*
EMP: 70 **EST:** 2014
SALES (est): 5MM **Privately Held**
WEB: www.ample.com
SIC: 7389

(P-14201)
ANDPAK INC (PA)
Also Called: Zip-Chem Products
400 Jarvis Dr Ste A, Morgan Hill (95037-8106)
PHONE....................408 776-1072
Dick Varien, *CEO*
Jack Douglass, *CEO*
Chuck Pottier, *Vice Pres*
Dennis Wagner, *Vice Pres*
Will Mattson, *Admin Sec*
EMP: 49 **EST:** 1978
SQ FT: 50,000
SALES (est): 19.9MM **Privately Held**
WEB: www.andpak.com
SIC: 7389 Packaging & labeling services

(P-14202)
APPLEBY & COMPANY INC (PA)
2828 N Wishon Ave, Fresno (93704-5579)
PHONE....................559 222-8402
Steven James Appleby, *CEO*
Rachel Appleby, *Treasurer*
Kaylyn Lasko, *Marketing Staff*
EMP: 42 **EST:** 1960
SQ FT: 4,000
SALES (est): 6MM **Privately Held**
WEB: www.applebyco.com
SIC: 7389 7381 Microfilm recording & developing service; private investigator

(P-14203)
ART SIGN COMPANY
732 Kevin Ct, Oakland (94621-4040)
PHONE....................510 632-6353
Reeder K Walsh, *President*
Paul H Ewen, *CEO*
James M Curtis, *CFO*
EMP: 24 **EST:** 1945
SQ FT: 12,000
SALES (est): 1.6MM **Privately Held**
WEB: www.theartsigncompany.com
SIC: 7389 3993 Sign painting & lettering shop; signs & advertising specialties

(P-14204)
ASSAY TECHNOLOGY INC
1382 Stealth St, Livermore (94551-9356)
PHONE....................925 461-8880
Charles Manning, *CEO*
William R Gerth, *CFO*
Michael P Zagaris, *Chairman*
Michelle Serrao, *CTO*
Karina Abreckov, *Accounting Mgr*
EMP: 24 **EST:** 1981
SQ FT: 17,000
SALES (est): 7.7MM **Privately Held**
WEB: www.assaytech.com
SIC: 7389 3826 2899 2813 Inspection & testing services; analytical instruments; chemical preparations; industrial gases

(P-14205)
ASSURED RELOCATION INC
50 Woodside Plz Ste 441, Redwood City (94061-2500)
PHONE....................888 670-9700
Janette Macdonell, *President*
Pat Persse, *CFO*
Christie Nikki, *Opers Mgr*
Meg Lenihan, *Regl Sales Mgr*
Cheri Zorzoli, *Regl Sales Mgr*
EMP: 40
SALES (est): 4.8MM **Privately Held**
WEB: www.assuredrelocation.com
SIC: 7389 Relocation service

(P-14206)
ATEL CORPORATION
600 Montgomery St Ste 900, San Francisco (94111-2711)
PHONE....................415 989-8800
Dean L Cash, *President*
Vasco Morais, *Exec VP*
Samuel Schussler, *Vice Pres*
Toni Martinez, *Asst Mgr*
Sam Cash, *Associate*
EMP: 61 **EST:** 2018
SQ FT: 2,000
SALES (est): 7.2MM **Privately Held**
WEB: www.atel.com
SIC: 7389 Office facilities & secretarial service rental
PA: Atel Capital Group
600 Montgomery St Fl 9
San Francisco CA 94111

(P-14207)
AUCTIONS BY BAY INC
Also Called: Michaans Auctions
2701 Monarch St, Alameda (94501-7457)
P.O. Box 489 (94501-9589)
PHONE....................510 740-0220
Allen C Michaan, *President*
Cameron Bradley, *COO*
EMP: 39 **EST:** 2001
SALES (est): 5.8MM **Privately Held**
WEB: www.alamedapointantiquesfaire.com
SIC: 7389 Auctioneers, fee basis; auction, appraisal & exchange services

(P-14208)
AUGMEDIX OPERATING CORPORATION
111 Sutter St Fl 13, San Francisco (94104-4541)
PHONE....................855 720-2929
Manny Krakaris, *CEO*
Damar Brown, *Network Enginr*
Christopher Alfaro, *Technical Staff*
Brett Parsons, *Engineer*
Sarah Bruce, *Accounting Mgr*
EMP: 92 **EST:** 2013
SALES (est): 10.1MM
SALES (corp-wide): 16.4MM **Publicly Held**
WEB: www.augmedix.com
SIC: 7389 Handwriting analysis
PA: Augmedix, Inc.
111 Sutter St Ste 1300
San Francisco CA 94104
888 669-4885

(P-14209)
AVICENATECH CORP (PA)
1130 Independence Ave, Mountain View (94043-1604)
PHONE....................919 376-6258
EMP: 56 **EST:** 2019

7389 - Business Svcs, NEC County (P-14210)

PRODUCTS & SERVICES SECTION

SALES (est): 593K **Privately Held**
WEB: www.avicena.tech
SIC: 7389 Business services

(P-14210)
AVITAS SYSTEMS INC
2882 Sand Hill Rd Ste 240, Menlo Park
(94025-7057)
PHONE..............................650 233-3900
Kenneth Alferez,
EMP: 51 EST: 2017
SQ FT: 6,000
SALES (est): 2.6MM **Privately Held**
SIC: 7389 Industrial & commercial equipment inspection service; petroleum refinery inspection service; pipeline & power line inspection service

(P-14211)
BAD BOYS BAIL BONDS INC (PA)
595 Park Ave Ste 200, San Jose
(95110-2641)
PHONE..............................408 298-3333
Clifford J Stanley, *President*
Craig A Stanley, *Vice Pres*
Craig Stanley, *Vice Pres*
Robert Venn, *General Mgr*
George Wallace, *General Mgr*
▲ EMP: 75 EST: 1998
SQ FT: 3,000
SALES (est): 16MM **Privately Held**
WEB: www.badboysbailbonds.com
SIC: 7389 Bail bonding

(P-14212)
BAY AREA TRAFFIC SOLUTIONS INC
44800 Industrial Dr, Fremont (94538-6433)
PHONE..............................510 657-2543
Rafael De La Cruz, *President*
Martha Ochoa, *Administration*
Monica Rojas, *Human Resources*
Ramon Guizar, *Manager*
Tammy Ta, *Manager*
EMP: 225
SALES (est): 11.4MM **Privately Held**
WEB: www.batstrafficsolutions.com
SIC: 7389 Flagging service (traffic control)

(P-14213)
BEIGENE USA INC
1900 Powell St Ste 500, Emeryville
(94608-1812)
PHONE..............................619 733-1842
Morita Pagan, *Associate Dir*
Sammy Zheng, *IT/INT Sup*
Stefanie Schneider, *Marketing Staff*
Shyamala Sivasubramanian, *Senior Mgr*
Anasuya Mohanty, *Director*
EMP: 85 **Privately Held**
WEB: www.beigene.com
SIC: 7389 Personal service agents, brokers & bureaus
HQ: Beigene Usa, Inc.
    55 Cambrdge Pkwy Ste 700w
    Cambridge MA 02142
    781 801-1887

(P-14214)
BENEFICENT TECHNOLOGY INC
Also Called: Benetech
480 California Ave # 201, Palo Alto
(94306-1623)
PHONE..............................650 644-3400
James R Fruchterman, *CEO*
Betsy Beaumon, *President*
Anh Bui, *Vice Pres*
Jane Poole, *Vice Pres*
Chirag Amin, *Program Mgr*
EMP: 50 EST: 2001
SALES: 12.9MM **Privately Held**
WEB: www.benetech.org
SIC: 7389 Personal service agents, brokers & bureaus

(P-14215)
BEST CHOICE LLC
22568 Mssion Blvd Ste 344, Hayward
(94541)
PHONE..............................510 862-4989
EMP: 46

SALES (corp-wide): 1MM **Privately Held**
SIC: 7389 Personal service agents, brokers & bureaus
PA: Best Choice Llc
    750 El Camino Real
    Tustin CA

(P-14216)
BEYOND POOL CARE INC (PA)
7911 Redwood Dr Ste 201, Cotati
(94931-3074)
PHONE..............................707 535-6463
Ernesto M Ibarra, *Owner*
EMP: 61 EST: 2018
SALES (est): 1.9MM **Privately Held**
WEB: www.beyondpoolcare.com
SIC: 7389 Swimming pool & hot tub service & maintenance

(P-14217)
BLACK KNIGHT INFOSERV LLC
601 California St Ste 980, San Francisco
(94108-2800)
PHONE..............................415 989-9800
EMP: 160
SALES (corp-wide): 1.2B **Publicly Held**
WEB: www.blackknightinc.com
SIC: 7389 7374 Financial services; data processing & preparation
HQ: Black Knight Infoserv, Llc
    601 Riverside Ave
    Jacksonville FL 32204

(P-14218)
BRADFORD MESSENGER SERVICE
4955 E Andersen Ave # 118, Fresno
(93727-1543)
PHONE..............................559 252-0775
EMP: 60
SQ FT: 1,500
SALES (est): 1.6MM **Privately Held**
SIC: 7389 Business Services, Nec, Nsk

(P-14219)
BREX INC (PA)
Also Called: Brex Technologies
110 S Park St, San Francisco
(94107-1809)
PHONE..............................650 250-6428
Henrique Dubugras, *CEO*
Michael Tannenbaum, *CFO*
Pedro Franceschi, *Co-CEO*
Cosmin Nicolaescu, *Vice Pres*
Phil Nachum, *Software Engr*
EMP: 423 EST: 2017
SALES (est): 50MM **Privately Held**
WEB: www.brex.com
SIC: 7389 7371 Financial services; computer software development & applications

(P-14220)
BUMBLEBEE SPACES INC (PA)
1004 Treat Ave, San Francisco
(94110-3322)
PHONE..............................415 624-3785
Sankarshan Murthy, *CEO*
EMP: 38 EST: 2020
SALES (est): 4.5MM **Privately Held**
WEB: www.bumbleespaces.com
SIC: 7389 Design services

(P-14221)
C P SHADES INC
2633 Ashby Ave, Berkeley (94705-2229)
PHONE..............................510 647-9605
EMP: 154
SALES (corp-wide): 29.1MM **Privately Held**
WEB: www.cpshades.com
SIC: 7389 Design services
PA: C P Shades, Inc.
    403 Coloma St
    Sausalito CA 94965
    415 331-4581

(P-14222)
C R MARTIN AUCTIONEERS INC
Also Called: Harvey Clars State Actn Gllery
5644 Telegraph Ave, Oakland
(94609-1708)
PHONE..............................510 428-0100
Redge Martin, *CEO*

Carole Martin, *Exec VP*
Julie Bai, *Controller*
Rick Unruh, *Director*
EMP: 35 EST: 1996
SQ FT: 17,800
SALES (est): 19MM **Privately Held**
WEB: www.clars.com
SIC: 7389 Auctioneers, fee basis

(P-14223)
CALIFORNIA HLTH COLLABORATIVE (PA)
1680 W Shaw Ave, Fresno (93711-3504)
P.O. Box 25609 (93729-5609)
PHONE..............................559 221-6315
Gary Erickson, *Chairman*
Stephen Ramirez, *Exec Dir*
Stephanie Chandler, *Program Mgr*
Marisol Zamora, *Program Mgr*
Lourdes Rosencrans, *Admin Asst*
EMP: 68 EST: 1982
SQ FT: 11,400
SALES: 10.6MM **Privately Held**
WEB: www.healthcollaborative.org
SIC: 7389 Fund raising organizations

(P-14224)
CASHEDGE INC
525 Almanor Ave Ste 150, Sunnyvale
(94085-3545)
PHONE..............................408 541-3900
McKenzie Lyons, *Principal*
EMP: 100
SALES (corp-wide): 14.8B **Publicly Held**
WEB: www.fiserv.com
SIC: 7389 Financial services
HQ: Cashedge Inc.
    255 Fiserv Dr
    Brookfield WI 53045
    262 879-5000

(P-14225)
CISCO SYSTEMS CAPITAL CORP (HQ)
170 W Tasman Dr, San Jose (95134-1706)
PHONE..............................610 386-5870
Kristine A Snow, *President*
David A Rogan, *President*
Prat Bhatt, *Treasurer*
David K Holland, *Treasurer*
John T Chambers, *Principal*
EMP: 1546 EST: 1996
SALES (est): 428.2MM
SALES (corp-wide): 49.8B **Publicly Held**
WEB: www.cisco.com
SIC: 7389 Financial services
PA: Cisco Systems, Inc.
    170 W Tasman Dr
    San Jose CA 95134
    408 526-4000

(P-14226)
CISCO WEBEX LLC (HQ)
Also Called: Webex.com
170 W Tasman Dr, San Jose (95134-1706)
PHONE..............................408 435-7000
Subrah S Iyar,
Tony Ni,
Blair Christie, *Senior VP*
Jeffrey Schmidt, *Vice Pres*
Praful Shah, *Vice Pres*
EMP: 1108 EST: 1995
SQ FT: 160,000
SALES (est): 199.1MM
SALES (corp-wide): 49.8B **Publicly Held**
WEB: www.webex.com
SIC: 7389 4813 Teleconferencing services; data telephone communications; voice telephone communications
PA: Cisco Systems, Inc.
    170 W Tasman Dr
    San Jose CA 95134
    408 526-4000

(P-14227)
CITY OF LODI (PA)
221 W Pine St, Lodi (95240-2089)
P.O. Box 3006 (95241-1910)
PHONE..............................209 333-6700
Bob Johnson, *Mayor*
Dale Eubanks, *Officer*
Michael Manetti, *Officer*
Adriana Granados, *Admin Asst*
Cari Shates, *Administration*
EMP: 60 EST: 1906
SQ FT: 6,320

SALES: 77.5MM **Privately Held**
WEB: www.lodi.gov
SIC: 7389

(P-14228)
CITY RISE LLC
18826 N Lwer Ste Escrmnt, Woodbridge
(95258)
PHONE..............................209 334-2703
Nicole Beadles, *Manager*
EMP: 100
SALES (corp-wide): 1.5MM **Privately Held**
WEB: www.cityrisesafety.com
SIC: 7389 Flagging service (traffic control)
PA: City Rise, Llc
    1225 S Sacramento St
    Lodi CA 95240
    209 333-0807

(P-14229)
CLEARXCHANGE LLC
275 Sacramento St 400, San Francisco
(94111-3810)
PHONE..............................415 813-4801
Andrew Cecere, *Ch of Bd*
EMP: 99 EST: 2011
SALES (est): 333.5K **Privately Held**
WEB: www.clearxchange.com
SIC: 7389 Financial services
PA: Early Warning Services, Llc
    16552 N 90th St Ste 100
    Scottsdale AZ 85260

(P-14230)
CLICKHOUSE INC ◆
4113 Alpine Rd, Portola Valley
(94028-8042)
PHONE..............................408 915-6542
Aaron Katz, *CEO*
EMP: 38 EST: 2021
SALES (est): 824.8K **Privately Held**
SIC: 5734 7389 Software; business & non-game;

(P-14231)
COASTAL INTL HOLDINGS LLC (PA)
3 Harbor Dr Ste 211, Sausalito
(94965-1491)
PHONE..............................415 339-1700
Bruce Green, *Mng Member*
EMP: 157 EST: 2014
SALES (est): 28MM **Privately Held**
SIC: 7389 1542 1522 Trade show arrangement; nonresidential construction; residential construction

(P-14232)
COMPASS GROUP USA INC
Also Called: Canteen Refreshment Services
20929 Cabot Blvd, Hayward (94545-1155)
PHONE..............................510 259-0416
Larry Rich, *Branch Mgr*
Sal Ochoa, *Warehouse Mgr*
Richard Heavingham, *Cust Mgr*
EMP: 157
SALES (corp-wide): 26B **Privately Held**
WEB: www.compass-usa.com
SIC: 7389 Coffee service
HQ: Compass Group Usa, Inc.
    2400 Yorkmont Rd
    Charlotte NC 28217

(P-14233)
COMPUMAIL INFORMATION SVCS INC
4057 Port Chicago Hwy # 300, Concord
(94520-1160)
P.O. Box 6756 (94524-1756)
PHONE..............................925 689-7100
Monte G Bish, *President*
Frank Fribley, *CFO*
Christine Fribley, *Officer*
Stephanie Kaster, *Officer*
Bill Kohrummel, *Exec VP*
▲ EMP: 75 EST: 1992
SQ FT: 22,000
SALES (est): 13.3MM **Privately Held**
WEB: www.compumailinc.com
SIC: 7389 Printers' services: folding, collating

PRODUCTS & SERVICES SECTION
7389 - Business Svcs, NEC County (P-14258)

(P-14234)
CONCENTRIX CORPORATION (PA)
44111 Nobel Dr, Fremont (94538-3173)
PHONE..................800 747-0583
Christopher Caldwell, *President*
Ralph Hulett, *Partner*
Kathryn Hayley, *Ch of Bd*
Andre Valentine, *CFO*
Guy Brosseau, *Exec VP*
EMP: 38779 **EST:** 2004
SALES (est): 3B **Publicly Held**
WEB: www.concentrix.com
SIC: 7389 8748 7374 ; business consulting; data processing service

(P-14235)
CORDELIA WINERY LLC (PA)
2650 Cordelia Rd, Fairfield (94534-9732)
PHONE..................707 286-1764
EMP: 35 **EST:** 2013
SALES (est): 496.4K **Privately Held**
SIC: 7389 Business services

(P-14236)
CORELOGIC INC
555 12th St Ste 1100, Oakland (94607-4049)
PHONE..................925 676-0225
Fax: 925 687-0615
EMP: 35
SALES (corp-wide): 1.5B **Publicly Held**
SIC: 7389 Property Tax Service
PA: Corelogic, Inc.
  40 Pacifica Ste 900
  Irvine CA 92618
  949 214-1000

(P-14237)
COROVAN
901 16th St, San Francisco (94107-2430)
PHONE..................415 934-1600
Robert Schmitz, *President*
Thomas Schmitz, *President*
Jack Appleton, *Marketing Staff*
David Blair, *Manager*
Michael Kading, *Consultant*
EMP: 49 **EST:** 1996
SALES (est): 1.3MM **Privately Held**
WEB: www.corovan.com
SIC: 7389 Document storage service

(P-14238)
COUNTY OF SAN JOAQUIN
Also Called: Building Inspection Division
1810 E Hazelton Ave, Stockton (95205-6232)
PHONE..................209 468-3123
Jaime Perez, *Branch Mgr*
EMP: 64
SALES (corp-wide): 1.2B **Privately Held**
WEB: www.sjgov.org
SIC: 9111 7389 County supervisors' & executives' offices; building inspection service
PA: County Of San Joaquin
  44 N San Joaquin St # 640
  Stockton CA 95202
  209 468-3203

(P-14239)
CREDIT KARMA LLC (HQ)
1100 Broadway Ste 1800, Oakland (94607-4192)
PHONE..................415 510-5059
Kenneth Lin, *CEO*
EMP: 748 **EST:** 2020
SALES: 185.7MM
SALES (corp-wide): 9.6B **Publicly Held**
WEB: www.creditkarma.com
SIC: 7389 Credit card service
PA: Intuit Inc.
  2700 Coast Ave
  Mountain View CA 94043
  650 944-6000

(P-14240)
CREDO SEMICONDUCTOR INC
1600 Technology Dr Fl 5, San Jose (95110-1382)
PHONE..................408 664-9329
William Brennan, *CEO*
Haoli Qian, *President*
Dan Fleming, *CFO*
Yifei Dai, *Vice Pres*
Michael G Lampe, *Vice Pres*
EMP: 28 **EST:** 2015
SALES (est): 3.3MM **Privately Held**
WEB: www.credosemi.com
SIC: 7389 3674 Design services; integrated circuits, semiconductor networks, etc.

(P-14241)
CRISIS SPPORT SVCS ALMEDA CNTY
Also Called: CSS
6117 Mrtin Lther King Jr, Oakland (94609-1240)
P.O. Box 3120 (94609-0120)
PHONE..................510 420-2460
Nancy A Salamy, *Director*
Elisay Digiuseppe, *Officer*
Nancy Salamy, *Exec Dir*
Mercedes Coleman, *Director*
Andrea Henderson, *Director*
EMP: 35 **EST:** 1966
SALES: 3MM **Privately Held**
WEB: www.crisissupport.org
SIC: 7389 8322 Speakers' bureau; general counseling services

(P-14242)
CTC SERVICES INC
3144 Venture Dr Ste 100, Lincoln (95648-9348)
PHONE..................916 434-0195
Mason Stoll, *President*
Tony Woods, *General Mgr*
EMP: 35 **EST:** 2000
SALES (est): 1.7MM **Privately Held**
WEB: www.ctcservicesinc.com
SIC: 7389 Personal service agents, brokers & bureaus

(P-14243)
CUBEWARE INC
1735 Technology Dr # 430, San Jose (95110-1313)
PHONE..................650 847-8345
EMP: 45
SALES (est): 2MM **Privately Held**
SIC: 7389 Business Services At Non-Commercial Site

(P-14244)
CULLIGAN PARTNERS LTD PARTNRS
3700 S El Camino Real, San Mateo (94403-4423)
PHONE..................650 573-1500
Thomas J Culligan, *President*
David Guisti, *Director*
Tom Culligan, *Associate*
EMP: 40 **EST:** 1946
SALES (est): 2.5MM **Privately Held**
SIC: 7389 Water softener service

(P-14245)
CURRENT TV LLC
118 King St, San Francisco (94107-1905)
PHONE..................415 995-8328
David Bohrman,
Guy Barbaro,
Mark Golmon,
Paul Hollerbach,
Joel Hyatt,
EMP: 200 **EST:** 2004
SQ FT: 27,000
SALES (est): 42.6MM **Privately Held**
WEB: www.aljazeera.com
SIC: 7389 Field audits, cable television
HQ: Al Jazeera Media Network
  Qatar Television Building Khalifa Street
  Doha

(P-14246)
CUTLER GROUP LP
101 Montgomery St Ste 700, San Francisco (94104-4125)
PHONE..................415 645-6745
Trent Cutler, *Managing Prtnr*
Anand Prakash, *Partner*
Walter Parng, *Managing Prtnr*
Doug Patterson, *Officer*
Steve Juno, *Managing Dir*
EMP: 50 **EST:** 1994
SALES (est): 8.5MM **Privately Held**
WEB: www.cutlergrouplp.com
SIC: 7389 Financial services

(P-14247)
DAN FITZGERALD & ASSOC INC
2910 State Highway 32 # 2200, Chico (95973-8678)
P.O. Box 4438 (95927-4438)
PHONE..................530 592-6500
Dan Fitzgerald, *President*
Joshua Eaton, *CFO*
Bonnie Fitzgerald, *Vice Pres*
EMP: 48 **EST:** 1979
SALES (est): 2.1MM **Privately Held**
WEB: www.safegassurvey.com
SIC: 7389 Pipeline & power line inspection service

(P-14248)
DECIMAL INC
Also Called: Ubiquity
1160 Battery St Ste 350, San Francisco (94111-1238)
PHONE..................855 980-6612
Chad Parks, *President*
Christopher Jasinski, *Partner*
Mary Torgerson, *COO*
Boris Chen, *Vice Pres*
John Farmakis, *Vice Pres*
EMP: 82 **EST:** 2000
SQ FT: 5,000
SALES (est): 11MM **Privately Held**
WEB: www.myubiquity.com
SIC: 7389 Financial services

(P-14249)
DEDICATED MANAGEMENT GROUP LLC
3876 E Childs Ave, Merced (95341-9520)
PHONE..................209 385-0694
EMP: 141
SALES (corp-wide): 15.7MM **Privately Held**
SIC: 7389 Business Services
PA: Dedicated Management Group Llc
  3651 Mars Hill Rd Ste 400
  Watkinsville GA 30677
  404 564-1201

(P-14250)
DELPHI PRODUCTIONS INC (PA)
Also Called: Group Delphi
950 W Tower Ave, Alameda (94501-5049)
PHONE..................510 748-7494
Justin Hersh, *President*
Pete Bowes, *CFO*
Pam Faaland, *Bd of Directors*
Rachel Mee, *Officer*
Kyle Wood, *Senior VP*
EMP: 102 **EST:** 1987
SQ FT: 148,000
SALES (est): 35.6MM **Privately Held**
WEB: www.groupdelphi.com
SIC: 7389 Trade show arrangement

(P-14251)
DENIOS RSVLLE FRMRS MKT ACTN I
2013 Opportunity Dr, Roseville (95678-3023)
PHONE..................916 782-2704
Jeff Ronten, *CEO*
Ken Denio, *President*
Marilee Denio, *Corp Secy*
Alani Bauer, *Accounting Mgr*
EMP: 120 **EST:** 1947
SQ FT: 18,212
SALES (est): 10.3MM **Privately Held**
WEB: www.deniosmarket.com
SIC: 7389 Flea market

(P-14252)
DEROUEN ENTERPRISES LLC
1547 Palos Verdes Mall, Walnut Creek (94597-2228)
PHONE..................925 360-5743
EMP: 53
SALES (corp-wide): 229.1K **Privately Held**
SIC: 7389 Personal service agents, brokers & bureaus
PA: Derouen Enterprises Llc
  4337 Machado Dr
  Concord CA 94521
  925 360-5743

(P-14253)
DFA OF CALIFORNIA
1050 Diamond St, Stockton (95205-7020)
P.O. Box 1727 (95201-1727)
PHONE..................209 465-2289
Debra Pennell, *Principal*
EMP: 62 **Privately Held**
WEB: www.dfaofcalifornia.com
SIC: 7389 Inspection & testing services
PA: Dfa Of California
  710 Striker Ave
  Sacramento CA 95834
  916 561-5900

(P-14254)
DIABLO VLY COLLEGE FOUNDATION (PA)
321 Golf Club Rd, Pleasant Hill (94523-1544)
PHONE..................925 685-1230
Mark G Edelstein, *President*
Katherine Guptill, *CEO*
Carol Hilton, *Vice Pres*
Anna Chuon, *Admin Sec*
Marta Gillen, *Admin Asst*
EMP: 1581 **EST:** 1975
SQ FT: 1,000
SALES: 737.3K **Privately Held**
WEB: www.dvc.edu
SIC: 7389 8221 Fund raising organizations; colleges universities & professional schools

(P-14255)
DIRECT LINE INC
Also Called: Direct Line Tele Response
2847 Shattuck Ave, Berkeley (94705-1037)
PHONE..................510 843-3900
Ruth Goldenburg, *President*
Ken Goldenberg, *Vice Pres*
Larry Goldenberg, *Vice Pres*
Constance Masinga-Loville, *Administration*
John Freire, *Technology*
EMP: 35 **EST:** 1979
SQ FT: 3,500
SALES (est): 5.3MM **Privately Held**
WEB: www.directlineinc.com
SIC: 7389 Telephone answering service

(P-14256)
DISTINCTIVE CORPORATION
14413 Big Basin Way, Saratoga (95070-6008)
PHONE..................408 568-5598
EMP: 37
SALES (corp-wide): 918.2K **Privately Held**
SIC: 7389 Personal service agents, brokers & bureaus
PA: Distinctive Corporation
  707 1st St
  Gilroy CA 95020
  408 219-1922

(P-14257)
EAST BAY INNOVATIONS
2450 Washington Ave # 240, San Leandro (94577-5996)
PHONE..................510 618-1580
Tom Heinz, *Exec Dir*
Kiera Swan, *Payroll Mgr*
Tamy Ratto, *Opers Staff*
Bruce Rhoads, *Teacher*
Leroy Harris, *Instructor*
EMP: 60 **EST:** 1993
SALES: 8.7MM **Privately Held**
WEB: www.eastbayinnovations.org
SIC: 7389 Personal service agents, brokers & bureaus

(P-14258)
ECONOLITE
Also Called: Traffic Signal Maintenance
4120 Business Center Dr, Fremont (94538-6354)
PHONE..................408 577-1733
Ron Hernandez, *Office Mgr*
Bill Weber, *Vice Pres*
Maral Hawa, *Mktg Coord*
EMP: 20 **EST:** 2012
SALES (est): 561.9K **Privately Held**
WEB: www.econolite.com
SIC: 7389 3812 Flagging service (traffic control); air traffic control systems & equipment, electronic

7389 - Business Svcs, NEC County (P-14259) — PRODUCTS & SERVICES SECTION

(P-14259)
ECONTACTLIVE INC
Also Called: Telecontact Resource Services
6436 Oakdale Rd, Riverbank (95367-9648)
PHONE..................................209 548-4300
Julie Hutchings, *CEO*
June Griffith, *Vice Pres*
David Schwerdtfeger, *Administration*
David Schwerd, *Info Tech Mgr*
Barbee Hummel, *Training Spec*
EMP: 83 **EST:** 1993
SQ FT: 42,000
SALES: 4MM **Privately Held**
WEB: www.econtactlive.com
SIC: 7389 Telemarketing services

(P-14260)
EDG INTERIOR ARCH & DESIGN INC (PA)
Also Called: E D G
7 Hamilton Landing # 200, Novato (94949-8209)
PHONE..................................415 454-2277
Jennifer Johanson, *CEO*
Eric Engstrom, *President*
David Barth, *CFO*
Sarah Lauffer, *General Mgr*
Laurene Schlosser, *Executive Asst*
EMP: 59 **EST:** 1987
SQ FT: 12,500
SALES (est): 11.2MM **Privately Held**
WEB: www.edgdesign.com
SIC: 7389 8712 Interior designer; architectural services

(P-14261)
ELATION HEALTH INC
530 Divisadero St Ste 872, San Francisco (94117-2213)
PHONE..................................415 213-5164
Conan Fong, *Principal*
Kyna Fong, *Principal*
Arjun Sanyal, *Software Engr*
Darren Tan, *Software Engr*
Eric Rivera, *Opers Mgr*
EMP: 67 **EST:** 2008
SQ FT: 5,000
SALES (est): 12.5MM **Privately Held**
WEB: www.elationhealth.com
SIC: 7389

(P-14262)
EMAGIA CORPORATION
4701 P Henry Dr Bldg 20, Santa Clara (95054)
PHONE..................................408 654-6575
Veena Gundavelli, *CEO*
Swetha Polamreddy, *Marketing Staff*
EMP: 50 **EST:** 1998
SALES (est): 3.4MM **Privately Held**
WEB: www.emagia.com
SIC: 7389 Financial services

(P-14263)
EMBURSE LLC
548 Market St 27197, San Francisco (94104-5401)
PHONE..................................415 766-2012
Roger Gu,
Sunil Kayiti, *CTO*
Danielle Camarata, *Controller*
Shelby Aitkenhead, *Opers Staff*
Chris Xia, *Manager*
EMP: 40 **EST:** 2014
SALES: 12.2MM
SALES (corp-wide): 19.1MM **Privately Held**
WEB: www.emburse.com
SIC: 7389 Credit card service
PA: Certify, Inc.
320 Cumberland Ave
Portland ME 04101
207 773-6100

(P-14264)
ENGINE NO 1 LP
710 Sansome St, San Francisco (94111-1704)
PHONE..................................628 251-1222
Jennifer Grancio, *CEO*
Sandra Kim-Suk, *CFO*
Elli Kavros, *Managing Dir*
Vince Chang, *Controller*
EMP: 35 **EST:** 2020
SALES (est): 1.9MM **Privately Held**
SIC: 7389 Financial services

(P-14265)
EPIC TECH INC (PA)
12177 Bus Park Dr Ste 10, Truckee (96161-3342)
PHONE..................................877 627-2215
Scott Ruzich, *CEO*
EMP: 69 **EST:** 2019
SALES (est): 355.6K **Privately Held**
WEB: www.epictech.com
SIC: 7389 Design services

(P-14266)
EQUILAR INC
1100 Marshall St, Redwood City (94063-2595)
PHONE..................................877 441-6090
David Chun, *CEO*
Timothy Ranzetta, *President*
Song Huang, *Exec VP*
Curtis Householder, *Executive*
Niranjan Samant, *Managing Dir*
EMP: 218 **EST:** 2000
SALES (est): 16.1MM **Privately Held**
WEB: www.equilar.com
SIC: 7389 Financial services

(P-14267)
EREPUBLIC INC (PA)
Also Called: Government Technology
100 Blue Ravine Rd, Folsom (95630-4509)
PHONE..................................916 932-1300
Dennis McKenna, *CEO*
Margaret Mohr, *Chief Mktg Ofcr*
Phil Bertolini, *Vice Pres*
John Flynn, *Vice Pres*
Dee Pearson, *Vice Pres*
EMP: 120 **EST:** 1984
SQ FT: 36,000
SALES (est): 23.8MM **Privately Held**
WEB: www.erepublic.com
SIC: 7389 2759 2721 Convention & show services; publication printing; magazines; printing; periodicals

(P-14268)
EXCEL RESTORATION INC
1369 E Waldon Way, Fresno (93730-3572)
PHONE..................................559 903-8902
Anthony Taffera, *Branch Mgr*
EMP: 92 **Privately Held**
SIC: 7389 Personal service agents, brokers & bureaus
PA: Excel Restoration, Inc.
2304 Perseus Ct
Bakersfield CA

(P-14269)
EXPO MARKETING & SERVICES INC
Also Called: Expo Decor
3714 N Valentine Ave, Fresno (93722-4457)
P.O. Box 9321 (93791-9321)
PHONE..................................559 495-3300
Mario A Viramontes, *CEO*
Thomas Thatcher, *President*
Connie Viramontes, *Corp Secy*
Amanda Bunch, *Relations*
EMP: 35 **EST:** 1990
SQ FT: 10,000
SALES (est): 7.1MM **Privately Held**
WEB: www.exporentals.com
SIC: 7389 Advertising, promotional & trade show services; convention & show services

(P-14270)
FAIR ISAAC CORPORATION (PA)
Also Called: Fico
181 Metro Dr Ste 700, San Jose (95110-1346)
PHONE..................................408 535-1500
William J Lansing, *CEO*
Tom Johnson, *Senior Partner*
Braden R Kelly, *Ch of Bd*
Michael I McLaughlin, *CFO*
Richard S Deal, *Officer*
▲ **EMP:** 175 **EST:** 1956
SQ FT: 55,000
SALES (est): 1.2B **Publicly Held**
WEB: www.fico.com
SIC: 7389 7372 8748 Financial services; business oriented computer software; business consulting

(P-14271)
FEDEX CORPORATION
50 Cypress Ln, Brisbane (94005-1217)
PHONE..................................415 657-0403
EMP: 50
SALES (corp-wide): 47.4B **Publicly Held**
SIC: 7389 Business Services
PA: Fedex Corporation
942 Shady Grove Rd S
Memphis TN 38120
901 818-7500

(P-14272)
FIGURE TECHNOLOGIES INC (PA)
650 California St Fl 2700, San Francisco (94108-2608)
PHONE..................................888 819-6388
Michael Cagney, *CEO*
Asiff Hirji, *President*
Wendy Harrington, *Chief Mktg Ofcr*
Melissa Howle, *Executive Asst*
EMP: 280 **EST:** 2018
SALES (est): 23.7MM **Privately Held**
WEB: www.figure.com
SIC: 7389 Financial services

(P-14273)
FIRE RECOVERY USA LLC
2271 Lava Ridge Ct # 120, Roseville (95661-3065)
PHONE..................................916 200-3999
Greg Schmidt, *Mng Member*
Justin Powell, *Director*
EMP: 59 **EST:** 2008
SALES (est): 5.2MM **Privately Held**
WEB: www.firerecoveryusa.com
SIC: 7389 Fire protection service other than forestry or public

(P-14274)
FIRE SYSTEM SOLUTIONS INC
4277 W Richert Ave # 103, Fresno (93722-6337)
PHONE..................................559 275-4894
Obed Guerrero, *President*
Ben Fitzgerald, *Shareholder*
Jorge Moran, *Shareholder*
EMP: 35 **EST:** 2012
SALES (est): 4.1MM **Privately Held**
WEB: www.firesystemsolutions.com
SIC: 7389 Fire protection service other than forestry or public

(P-14275)
FONG & CHAN ARCHITECT INC
Also Called: Fong & Chan Architects
1361 Bush St, San Francisco (94109-5611)
PHONE..................................415 931-8600
Chiu Lin TSE-Chan, *President*
David Fong, *Treasurer*
Sharlene Chan, *Office Mgr*
Christina Yueh, *Planning*
Richard Barnes, *CIO*
EMP: 36 **EST:** 1982
SQ FT: 21,000
SALES (est): 9.7MM **Privately Held**
WEB: www.fca-arch.com
SIC: 7389 8712 Interior design services; architectural services

(P-14276)
FOUNDERS FUND LLC
1 Letterman Dr Ste 500, San Francisco (94129-1496)
PHONE..................................415 359-1922
Peter Thiel,
Ken Howery, *Partner*
Luke Nosek, *Managing Prtnr*
Lauren Vance, *Vice Pres*
Cassandra Beresini, *Executive Asst*
EMP: 38 **EST:** 2008
SALES (est): 9.4MM **Privately Held**
WEB: www.foundersfund.com
SIC: 7389 Fund raising organizations

(P-14277)
FOUR STAR RECOVERY INC
1228 Doker Dr, Modesto (95351-1587)
P.O. Box 3532 (95352-3532)
PHONE..................................209 524-2854
Cheryl Goodban, *President*
Brian Chapman, *Vice Pres*
Robert Goodban, *Admin Sec*
EMP: 37 **EST:** 1992
SQ FT: 20,000
SALES (est): 1.2MM **Privately Held**
SIC: 7389 Automobile recovery service

(P-14278)
FRANCISCO PARTNERS VI LP (PA)
1 Letterman Dr Bldg Cs, San Francisco (94129-1494)
PHONE..................................415 418-2900
EMP: 128
SALES (est): 501.9K **Privately Held**
SIC: 7389 Business services

(P-14279)
FRESNO METRO FLOOD CTRL DST
5469 E Olive Ave, Fresno (93727-2541)
PHONE..................................559 456-3292
Bob Van Wyk, *General Mgr*
Esther Schwandt, *Bd of Directors*
Jerry Lakeman, *Principal*
Alan E Hofmann, *General Mgr*
Robert McIntyre, *Info Tech Dir*
EMP: 75 **EST:** 1955
SQ FT: 12,965
SALES (est): 9MM **Privately Held**
WEB: www.fresnofloodcontrol.com
SIC: 7389 Personal service agents, brokers & bureaus

(P-14280)
FUTURE FAST INC
5081 W Brown Ave, Fresno (93722-0439)
PHONE..................................559 813-0113
EMP: 58
SALES (corp-wide): 83.1K **Privately Held**
SIC: 7389
PA: Future Fast, Inc
5928 E Grove Ave
Fresno CA
559 813-0113

(P-14281)
FUTURE INNOVATIONS INC
Also Called: Calwest Steel Detailing
4495 Stoneridge Dr, Pleasanton (94588-8326)
PHONE..................................925 485-2000
Mark Frohnen, *President*
Robert Sprenkel, *Corp Secy*
Bob Sprenkel, *Admin Sec*
Sue Caswell, *Project Mgr*
Joshua Wood, *Project Mgr*
EMP: 21 **EST:** 1979
SQ FT: 8,000
SALES (est): 4.1MM **Privately Held**
WEB: www.cwsteeldetailing.com
SIC: 7389 8711 3441 Drafting service, except temporary help; structural engineering; fabricated structural metal

(P-14282)
GENGO INC
204 E 2nd Ave 736, San Mateo (94401-3904)
PHONE..................................650 585-4390
EMP: 50
SALES (est): 855.8K **Privately Held**
WEB: www.gengo.com
SIC: 7389 Business Services

(P-14283)
GLF INTEGRATED POWER INC (PA)
4500 Great America Pkwy, Santa Clara (95054-1283)
PHONE..................................408 239-4326
Ni Sun, *Administration*
Stephen Bryson, *Vice Pres*
EMP: 41 **EST:** 2015
SALES (est): 577.3K **Privately Held**
WEB: www.glfipower.com
SIC: 7389 Personal service agents, brokers & bureaus

(P-14284)
GLOBAL INNOVATION PARTNERS LLC
Also Called: GI Partners
188 The Embarcadero # 700, San Francisco (94105-1231)
PHONE..................................650 233-3600
Rick Magnuson, *Mng Member*
Amy Kendig, *Admin Asst*
Ben Krant, *Analyst*

PRODUCTS & SERVICES SECTION
7389 - Business Svcs, NEC County (P-14310)

EMP: 37 **EST:** 2000
SALES (est): 7.1MM Privately Held
WEB: www.gipartners.com
SIC: 7389 Brokers, business: buying & selling business enterprises

(P-14285)
GO WEST HOLDINGS LLC
795 Folsom St, San Francisco (94107-1243)
PHONE 888 670-0080
EMP: 145
SALES (est): 2MM Privately Held
SIC: 7389 Business Services

(P-14286)
GOLDENSPEAR LLC
Also Called: Artificial Intelligence Lab
729b Douglass St, San Francisco (94114-3150)
PHONE 415 643-0100
Santos M Soto III, *CEO*
EMP: 43 **EST:** 2015
SALES (est): 1.2MM Privately Held
SIC: 7389 Inspection & testing services

(P-14287)
GOOGLE PAYMENT CORP
Also Called: Google Checkout
1600 Amphitheatre Pkwy, Mountain View (94043-1351)
PHONE 650 253-0000
EMP: 50
SALES (est): 6.6MM
SALES (corp-wide): 74.9B Publicly Held
SIC: 7389 Business Services
HQ: Google Inc.
1600 Amphitheatre Pkwy
Mountain View CA 94043
650 253-0000

(P-14288)
GORDON AND SCHWENKMEYER INC
1860 Howe Ave Ste 300, Sacramento (95825-1098)
PHONE 916 569-1740
Brett Carter, *Exec VP*
Gerri Taylor, *Opers Staff*
Elena Rowland, *Director*
EMP: 170
SALES (corp-wide): 7.3MM Privately Held
WEB: www.gsitel.com
SIC: 7389 Personal service agents, brokers & bureaus
PA: Gordon And Schwenkmeyer, Inc.
20300 S Vt Ave Ste 210
Torrance CA 90502
310 615-2300

(P-14289)
GRANITE PAYMENT ALLIANCE LLC (PA)
3400 Douglas Blvd Ste 150, Roseville (95661-4281)
PHONE 916 580-6285
Wayne Keddy, *Principal*
George Cutlip, *Exec VP*
Jon Aronson, *Vice Pres*
Audrey Blackmon, *Vice Pres*
Kathy Oakes, *Vice Pres*
EMP: 49 **EST:** 2008
SALES (est): 3.5MM Privately Held
WEB: www.taluspay.com
SIC: 7389 Credit card service

(P-14290)
GRAPHIANT INC (PA)
760 Navajo Way, Fremont (94539-7132)
PHONE 510 676-5916
Khalid Raza, *Principal*
EMP: 45 **EST:** 2020
SALES (est): 1MM Privately Held
SIC: 7389 Business services

(P-14291)
GRM INFRMTION MGT SVCS SAN FRN
Also Called: Simmba/Grm
41099 Boyce Rd, Fremont (94538-2434)
PHONE 888 907-9687
Patrick McKillop,
Maurice Ebanks, *General Mgr*
Carlos Gudino, *Inv Control Mgr*

Javi Levanovsky,
Mohisie Mana,
EMP: 40 **EST:** 1997
SQ FT: 220,000
SALES (est): 2.5MM Privately Held
SIC: 7389 Document storage service

(P-14292)
HANSON & FITCH INC
342 Railroad Ave, Danville (94526-3820)
P.O. Box 175 (94526-0175)
PHONE 800 847-7037
Todd L Fitch, *Principal*
Diana Mason, *Principal*
EMP: 52 **EST:** 2006
SALES (est): 3MM Privately Held
WEB: www.hansonfitch.com
SIC: 7389 Decoration service for special events

(P-14293)
HAROLD A STEUBER ENTPS INC
553 Martin Ave, Rohnert Park (94928-2091)
PHONE 707 586-5205
Chuck Erly, *Branch Mgr*
Trish Schneider, *Manager*
EMP: 38
SALES (corp-wide): 22.9MM Privately Held
WEB: www.associatedcoffee.com
SIC: 7389 Coffee service
PA: Harold A. Steuber Enterprises, Inc.
600 Mccormick St
San Leandro CA
510 567-1620

(P-14294)
HARTMANN STUDIOS INC
1150 Brickyard Cove Rd # 202, Point Richmond (94801-4181)
PHONE 510 232-5030
Thomas J Mahoney, *CEO*
Mary Popplewell, *Office Mgr*
Sophia Kassab, *Project Mgr*
Lesley Mendoza, *Project Mgr*
Tim Desmond, *Technical Staff*
EMP: 150 **EST:** 2018
SALES (est): 11.4MM
SALES (corp-wide): 107.4MM Privately Held
WEB: www.hartmannstudios.com
SIC: 7389 Convention & show services
PA: Ita Group, Inc
4600 Westown Pkwy Ste 100
West Des Moines IA 50266
515 326-3400

(P-14295)
HEALTHY LIVING ENTERPRISE INC
Also Called: Togo's and Baskin
900 E Bidwell St Ste 700, Folsom (95630-3347)
PHONE 916 296-0228
Jothi M Periasamy, *Director*
EMP: 40 **EST:** 2019
SALES (est): 1.2MM Privately Held
SIC: 7389 Business services

(P-14296)
HERBS POOL SERVICE INC
3769 Redwood Hwy, San Rafael (94903-3998)
PHONE 415 479-4040
Sandra Louise Scott, *CEO*
EMP: 55 **EST:** 1958
SQ FT: 3,000
SALES (est): 6.4MM Privately Held
WEB: www.herbspoolservice.com
SIC: 7389 Swimming pool & hot tub service & maintenance

(P-14297)
HIGHERRING
17 Seadrift Lndg, Belvedere Tiburon (94920-2240)
PHONE 415 272-6948
Michelle Hirons, *CEO*
EMP: 49 **EST:** 2017
SALES (est): 1.5MM Privately Held
WEB: www.higherring.com
SIC: 7389 Telephone answering service

(P-14298)
HOOD EXHIBITS
1001 Canal Blvd Ste C, Richmond (94804-3524)
PHONE 510 965-9999
David R Hood, *President*
▲ **EMP:** 36 **EST:** 1994
SALES (est): 2.4MM Privately Held
SIC: 7389 Exhibit construction by industrial contractors

(P-14299)
HOOVER INSTITUTION
434 Galvez Mall, Stanford (94305-6003)
PHONE 650 723-0603
John Raisian, *Director*
Jenny Mayfield, *President*
Amy Zegart, *Managing Dir*
Victor Hanson, *Teacher*
Christopher Dauer, *Director*
EMP: 200 **EST:** 1920
SALES (est): 12.8MM Privately Held
WEB: www.hoover.org
SIC: 7389 Personal service agents, brokers & bureaus

(P-14300)
ICON EXHIBITS LLC
Also Called: Group Delphi
950 W Tower Ave, Alameda (94501-5049)
PHONE 260 482-8700
Justin Hersh, *CEO*
Sara Ost, *Chief Mktg Ofcr*
Matt Fortney, *Vice Pres*
Ian Lantz, *Info Tech Mgr*
Michael Snively, *Project Mgr*
EMP: 39 **EST:** 2000
SALES (est): 13.1MM Privately Held
WEB: www.groupdelphi.com
SIC: 7389 Trade show arrangement; exhibit construction by industrial contractors
PA: Delphi Productions, Inc.
950 W Tower Ave
Alameda CA 94501

(P-14301)
INDEPNDNT ONLNE DSTRIBUTION (PA)
Also Called: Ioda
539 Bryant St Ste 303, San Francisco (94107-1269)
PHONE 415 777-4632
Bradley Navin, *CEO*
EMP: 65 **EST:** 2006
SALES (est): 699.8K Privately Held
SIC: 7389 Music distribution systems

(P-14302)
INGENIOUS PACKAGING GROUP (HQ)
Also Called: Tapp Label
580 Gateway Dr, NAPA (94558-7517)
PHONE 707 252-8300
Raymond Schwartz, *Mng Member*
Natalie Morrell, *Business Dir*
Arel Segura, *QC Mgr*
David Bowyer,
EMP: 50 **EST:** 2015
SQ FT: 24,000
SALES (est): 45.1MM Privately Held
WEB: www.tapptech.com
SIC: 7389 Packaging & labeling services
PA: Tapp Label Holding Company, Llc
580 Gateway Dr
Napa CA 94558
707 252-8300

(P-14303)
INNOVATIVE SILICON INC
4800 Great America Pkwy # 500, Santa Clara (95054-1221)
P.O. Box 391657, Mountain View (94039-1657)
PHONE 408 572-8700
EMP: 80
SQ FT: 11,000
SALES (est): 3.4MM Privately Held
WEB: www.innovativesilicon.com
SIC: 7389 Business Services, Nec, Nsk

(P-14304)
INSTABASE INC (PA)
220 Montgomery St Ste 991, San Francisco (94104-3415)
PHONE 213 453-0488
Anant Bhardwaj, *CEO*
Kerry Chang, *Research*
Georgia Rust, *Technical Staff*
EMP: 145 **EST:** 2016
SALES (est): 3.1MM Privately Held
WEB: www.about.instabase.com
SIC: 7389 Personal service agents, brokers & bureaus

(P-14305)
INSTITUTIONAL VENTR MGT X LLC
3000 Sand Hill Rd Bldg 2, Menlo Park (94025-7113)
PHONE 650 854-0132
Norman Fogelsong, *Mng Member*
Sandy Miller,
EMP: 48 **EST:** 2000
SQ FT: 8,000
SALES (est): 729.7K Privately Held
WEB: www.ivp.com
SIC: 7389 Financial services

(P-14306)
INTERIOR PLANT DESIGN
1950 Monterey Hwy, San Jose (95112-6118)
PHONE 408 286-1367
Cydney Gates, *President*
Cindy Wilson, *Office Mgr*
EMP: 35 **EST:** 1972
SQ FT: 5,000
SALES (est): 3.5MM Privately Held
WEB: www.interiorplantdesign.com
SIC: 7389 5992 Plant care service; plants, potted

(P-14307)
INTERIOR SPECIALISTS INC
1164 National Dr Ste 10, Sacramento (95834-1925)
PHONE 916 779-1666
Steve Conte, *Executive*
Lance Blackmore, *Opers Staff*
EMP: 36
SALES (corp-wide): 629.1MM Privately Held
WEB: www.interiorlogicgroup.com
SIC: 7389 Interior designer
HQ: Interior Specialists, Inc.
1630 Faraday Ave
Carlsbad CA 92008
760 929-6700

(P-14308)
INTERIOR SPECIALISTS INC
4511 Willow Rd, Pleasanton (94588-2769)
PHONE 925 416-0408
Amy Meckfessel, *Manager*
EMP: 36
SALES (corp-wide): 629.1MM Privately Held
WEB: www.interiorlogicgroup.com
SIC: 7389 Interior designer
HQ: Interior Specialists, Inc.
1630 Faraday Ave
Carlsbad CA 92008
760 929-6700

(P-14309)
INTERPAC TECHNOLOGIES INC
Also Called: Interpac Distribution Center
260 N Pioneer Ave, Woodland (95776-5934)
PHONE 530 662-6363
Roderick W Miner, *President*
Corinne Christenson, *Vice Pres*
Stephen Cosenza, *Manager*
▲ **EMP:** 75 **EST:** 2000
SALES (est): 8.2MM Privately Held
WEB: www.interpactechnologies.com
SIC: 7389 Packaging & labeling services

(P-14310)
IROC
Also Called: Inititive Rvtlztion Cmmunities
20993 Foothill Blvd 208, Hayward (94541-1511)
PHONE 510 706-8669
C Tony Amaral, *Owner*
EMP: 45 **EST:** 1989

7389 - Business Svcs, NEC County (P-14311)

SQ FT: 1,000
SALES (est): 1.5MM Privately Held
SIC: 7389 0711 Filling pressure containers; soil preparation services

(P-14311)
ISI INSPECTION SERVICES INC (PA)
1798 University Ave, Berkeley (94703-1514)
PHONE 510 900-2101
Leslie A Sakai, *President*
Ed King, *Exec VP*
Kasandra Horcasitas, *Admin Asst*
Antoine Megevand, *Project Mgr*
Tobin Gaut, *Research*
EMP: 70 **EST:** 1995
SQ FT: 9,700
SALES (est): 13MM Privately Held
WEB: www.inspectionservices.net
SIC: 7389 Inspection & testing services

(P-14312)
JAMES TAYLOR ROBERTS INC
9000 Highway 128, Philo (95466-9530)
P.O. Box 86 (95466-0086)
PHONE 707 895-2500
James Roberts, *President*
EMP: 35 **EST:** 1996
SQ FT: 4,400
SALES (est): 751.1K Privately Held
SIC: 7389 5712 Interior design services; furniture stores

(P-14313)
JIM DOBBAS INC (PA)
Also Called: J D I
300 Taylor Rd, Newcastle (95658-9601)
P.O. Box 177 (95658-0177)
PHONE 916 663-3363
Donald Dobbas, *President*
EMP: 43 **EST:** 1964
SQ FT: 1,500
SALES (est): 9.5MM Privately Held
SIC: 7389 7353 5088 Salvaging of damaged merchandise, service only; heavy construction equipment rental; railroad equipment & supplies

(P-14314)
JOPARI SOLUTIONS INC
1855 Gateway Blvd Ste 500, Concord (94520-3277)
PHONE 925 459-5200
John Stevens II, *CEO*
John Gilmartin, *COO*
Tom Turi, *Chief Mktg Ofcr*
Scott A Hefner, *Senior VP*
Grady Fields, *Sr Software Eng*
EMP: 65
SALES (est): 8.7MM Privately Held
WEB: www.jopari.com
SIC: 7389 Financial services

(P-14315)
KASRA INVESTMENTS LLC
1480 Saratoga Ave, Saratoga (95070-3612)
PHONE 408 464-0074
Koushyar Keyhan, *Branch Mgr*
EMP: 39 Privately Held
SIC: 7389 Personal service agents, brokers & bureaus
PA: Kasra Investments Llc
929 E El Camino Real
Sunnyvale CA

(P-14316)
KEN FULK INC
310 7th St, San Francisco (94103-4030)
PHONE 415 285-1164
Jim Fraser, *CEO*
Mara Okita, *Controller*
Chanchira Chunephisal, *Internal Med*
Nina Castro, *Director*
Fadi Alnumaani, *Assistant*
EMP: 36 **EST:** 2006
SALES (est): 4MM Privately Held
WEB: www.kenfulk.com
SIC: 7389 Interior design services

(P-14317)
KING-REYNOLDS VENTURES LLC
Also Called: Costanoa
2001 Rossi Rd, Pescadero (94060-9732)
PHONE 650 879-2136
John King,
Trevor Bridge, *General Mgr*
Thomas Reynolds,
Sharon Carpenter, *Manager*
Greg Glasgow, *Manager*
EMP: 69 **EST:** 2003
SALES (est): 8.7MM Privately Held
WEB: www.costanoa.com
SIC: 7389 Financial services

(P-14318)
KOUNTABLE INC (PA)
321 Pacific Ave Fl 3, San Francisco (94111-1701)
PHONE 310 613-5481
Chris Hale, *CEO*
Cherry Allen, *Exec VP*
Ian Goudy, *Exec VP*
Maika Hemphill, *Vice Pres*
Herb Kelsey, *CTO*
EMP: 84 **EST:** 2014
SALES (est): 7.4MM Privately Held
WEB: www.kountable.com
SIC: 7389 Financial services

(P-14319)
LANDOR LLC
Also Called: Landor Associates
360 3rd St 5, San Francisco (94107-2154)
PHONE 415 365-1700
Lois Jacobs, *CEO*
Peter Harleman, *Vice Chairman*
James Bruce, *CFO*
Carol-Ann White, *Officer*
Thomas Hutchings, *Creative Dir*
EMP: 54 **EST:** 2002
SALES (est): 1.7MM
SALES (corp-wide): 15.9B Privately Held
WEB: www.landor.com
SIC: 7389 8742 Financial services; management consulting services
PA: Wpp Plc
13 Castle Street
Jersey JE1 1
207 282-4600

(P-14320)
LENDUP CARD SERVICES INC
225 Bush St Ste 1150, San Francisco (94104-4275)
PHONE 855 253-6387
Sasha Orloff, *CEO*
EMP: 208 **EST:** 2014
SALES (est): 3.5MM Privately Held
SIC: 7389 Financial services

(P-14321)
LESLIE HEAVY HAUL LLC
18971 Hess Ave, Sonora (95370-9724)
P.O. Box 4581 (95370-1581)
PHONE 209 840-1664
Colleen Leslie, *Mng Member*
EMP: 25 **EST:** 2005
SALES (est): 2.5MM Privately Held
SIC: 7389 2411 4213 8322 ; timber, cut at logging camp; heavy hauling; disaster service; forestry services

(P-14322)
LIBERTY PACKING COMPANY LLC
Also Called: Morning Star
12045 Ingomar Grade, Los Banos (93635-9796)
PHONE 209 826-7100
Chris Rufer, *President*
Jorge Azevedo, *Engineer*
Kelley Ider,
EMP: 40
SQ FT: 100,000
SALES (corp-wide): 102.8MM Privately Held
WEB: www.morningstarco.com
SIC: 7389 Labeling bottles, cans, cartons, etc.
PA: Liberty Packing Company, Llc
724 Main St
Woodland CA 95695
209 826-7100

(P-14323)
LOON LLC
100 Mayfield Ave, Mountain View (94043-4122)
PHONE 310 625-3449
Eleister Westgrath, *CEO*
Amanda Proctor, *Partner*
Justin Garofoli, *Sr Software Eng*
Diego Giorgini, *Sr Software Eng*
Dennis Kempin, *Sr Software Eng*
EMP: 200 **EST:** 2000
SALES (est): 10MM Privately Held
SIC: 7389

(P-14324)
LOYAL3 HOLDINGS INC
150 California St Ste 400, San Francisco (94111-4566)
P.O. Box 26027 (94126-6027)
PHONE 415 981-0700
Barry L Schneider, *CEO*
James Iry, *President*
Peter Coleman, *CFO*
Dana Schmidt, *Ch Credit Ofcr*
Jeff Modisett, *Officer*
EMP: 80 **EST:** 2008
SQ FT: 8,900
SALES (est): 6.8MM Privately Held
WEB: www.loyal3.com
SIC: 7389 Financial services

(P-14325)
LUNAR DESIGN INCORPORATED (HQ)
537 Hamilton Ave, Palo Alto (94301-2012)
PHONE 415 252-4388
Jeff Smith, *CEO*
John Edson, *President*
Gerard Furbershaw, *COO*
EMP: 47 **EST:** 2008
SQ FT: 9,000
SALES (est): 8.1MM
SALES (corp-wide): 2B Privately Held
WEB: www.lunar.com
SIC: 7389 Design, commercial & industrial
PA: Mckinsey & Company, Inc.
3 World Trade Ctr
New York NY 10007
212 446-7000

(P-14326)
M PARK INC
630 W Railroad Ave, Orange Cove (93646)
P.O. Box 10 (93646-0010)
PHONE 559 626-5057
Hyun J Kim, *President*
◆ **EMP:** 35 **EST:** 2004
SQ FT: 30,000
SALES (est): 3MM Privately Held
WEB: www.mparkinc.com
SIC: 7389 Packaging & labeling services

(P-14327)
MAILBOXES AND BUS SVCS INC
Also Called: UPS
2443 Fair Oaks Blvd, Sacramento (95825-7684)
PHONE 916 971-4957
William Neal, *CEO*
Jennifer Tillman, *Vice Pres*
EMP: 36 **EST:** 1990
SALES (est): 1.9MM Privately Held
WEB: www.theupsstore.com
SIC: 7389 Mailbox rental & related service

(P-14328)
MANUFACTURING RESOURCE CORP
Also Called: M R C
44853 Fremont Blvd, Fremont (94538-6318)
PHONE 510 438-9600
Bhavesh J Desai, *President*
Harshad Patel, *CFO*
EMP: 40 **EST:** 1994
SQ FT: 16,250
SALES (est): 1MM
SALES (corp-wide): 3.1MM Privately Held
WEB: www.m-r-c.com
SIC: 7389 3953 Packaging & labeling services; stencils, painting & marking

PA: Emarcee Llc
45375 Onondaga Dr
Fremont CA 94539
510 687-0153

(P-14329)
MASSDROP INC (PA)
1390 Market St Ste 200, San Francisco (94102-5404)
PHONE 415 340-2999
Steve El-Hage, *CEO*
Tony Meneghetti, *CFO*
Anne Morrissey, *Vice Pres*
Eric Stender, *Sr Software Eng*
Jasper Chan, *CTO*
EMP: 69 **EST:** 2012
SALES (est): 16.5MM Privately Held
WEB: www.drop.com
SIC: 7389 Design services

(P-14330)
METRICUS INC
P.O. Box 458 (94302-0458)
PHONE 650 328-2500
EMP: 119
SALES (est): 3.1MM Privately Held
WEB: www.metricus.com
SIC: 7389 Jury Research

(P-14331)
MIGO MONEY INC
3739 Balboa St Ste 1101, San Francisco (94121-2605)
PHONE 415 906-4040
Ekechi Nwokah, *CEO*
Derek White, *Principal*
EMP: 61 **EST:** 2013
SALES (est): 14MM Privately Held
WEB: www.migo.money
SIC: 7389 Financial services

(P-14332)
MISSION LANE LLC (PA)
101 2nd St Ste 350, San Francisco (94105-3669)
P.O. Box 105286, Atlanta GA (30348-5286)
PHONE 408 505-3081
Shane Holdaway, *CEO*
Monika Mantri, *President*
EMP: 66 **EST:** 2018 Privately Held
WEB: www.missionlane.com
SIC: 7389 Credit card service

(P-14333)
MOZILLA CORP (PA)
273 Pescadero Ct, Milpitas (95035-3018)
PHONE 408 946-2311
Nelson B Bolyard, *Principal*
EMP: 35 **EST:** 2011
SALES (est): 456.7K Privately Held
WEB: www.mozilla.org
SIC: 7389

(P-14334)
MTR TRANSPORTATION INC
1524 Hyde St, San Francisco (94109-3114)
PHONE 415 928-3279
Kin Keong Tam, *Branch Mgr*
EMP: 41
SALES (corp-wide): 103.9K Privately Held
SIC: 7389 Personal service agents, brokers & bureaus
PA: Mtr Transportation Inc
1065 Sneath Ln
San Bruno CA
650 872-3833

(P-14335)
MULTIVISION INC (DH)
Also Called: Bacon's Multivision
66 Franklin St Fl 3, Oakland (94607-3728)
PHONE 510 740-5600
Babak Farahi, *President*
EMP: 70 **EST:** 2002
SALES (est): 10MM
SALES (corp-wide): 671.3MM Privately Held
WEB: www.cision.com
SIC: 7389 Press clipping service
HQ: Cision Us Inc.
130 E Randolph St Fl 7
Chicago IL 60601
312 922-2400

▲ = Import ▼=Export
◆ =Import/Export

PRODUCTS & SERVICES SECTION
7389 - Business Svcs, NEC County (P-14358)

(P-14336)
MUSCOLINO INVENTORY SVC INC
1620 N Carptr Rd Ste D50, Modesto (95351)
PHONE..................209 576-8469
Fax: 209 576-8469
EMP: 50
SALES (corp-wide): 67MM Privately Held
SIC: 7389 Business Services
HQ: Muscolino Inventory Service, Inc.
320 W Chestnut Ave
Monrovia CA 91016
626 357-8600

(P-14337)
NEFAB PACKAGING WEST LLC
8477 Central Ave, Newark (94560-3431)
PHONE..................408 678-2516
Fredrik Solspher,
EMP: 60 EST: 2014
SALES (est): 7.9MM
SALES (corp-wide): 585.7MM Privately Held
WEB: www.nefab.com
SIC: 7389 Packaging & labeling services
HQ: Nefab Companies, Inc.
204 Airline Dr Ste 100
Coppell TX 75019
866 332-4425

(P-14338)
NES FINANCIAL CORP
50 W San Fernando St # 300, San Jose (95113-2416)
PHONE..................800 339-1031
Michael Halloran, CEO
Tom Steipp, President
Kevin Walkup, President
John Hart, CFO
Rick McEachern, Chief Mktg Ofcr
EMP: 40 EST: 2005
SALES (est): 5.4MM Privately Held
WEB: www.nesfinancial.com
SIC: 7389 Financial services

(P-14339)
NEW SCHOOLS VENTURE FUND
1616 Franklin St 2, Oakland (94612-2829)
PHONE..................415 615-6860
Stacey Childress, CEO
Jessica Ball, Partner
Derrick Johnson, Partner
Ariana Valenzuela, Partner
Heather McManus, Officer
EMP: 44 EST: 1998
SQ FT: 4,000
SALES: 56.2MM Privately Held
WEB: www.newschools.org
SIC: 7389 8742 Fund raising organizations; management consulting services

(P-14340)
NOVATO FIRE PROTECTION DIST
95 Rowland Way, Novato (94945-5001)
PHONE..................415 878-2690
Daniel Hom, Finance
Shannon Wager, Analyst
Marc Revere, Fire Chief
Zita Konik, Director
Jeanne Villa, Manager
EMP: 90 EST: 1926
SALES (est): 5.2MM Privately Held
WEB: www.novatofire.org
SIC: 7389 Fire protection service other than forestry or public

(P-14341)
NUCOMPASS MOBILITY SVCS INC (PA)
6800 Koll Center Pkwy # 10, Pleasanton (94566-7045)
PHONE..................925 734-3434
Dave Marron, CEO
Ronald Whitmill, COO
Stephen Chen, Senior VP
Lesley Dehoney, Vice Pres
Cara Skourtis, Vice Pres
EMP: 40 EST: 2009
SALES (est): 14.8MM Privately Held
WEB: www.nucompass.com
SIC: 7389 Relocation service

(P-14342)
NYACK INC
Also Called: Nyack Shell
1 Nyack Rd, Emigrant Gap (95715)
PHONE..................530 389-8212
Stewart P Wells, CEO
Grant Wells, Vice Pres
Stewart M Wells, Site Mgr
EMP: 38 EST: 1951
SQ FT: 14,000
SALES (est): 16.6MM Privately Held
WEB: www.nyackshell.com
SIC: 5541 5411 7389 5812 Filling stations, gasoline; convenience stores, independent; post office contract stations; coffee shop

(P-14343)
OMIC USA INC CALIFORNIA
1984 Del Paso Rd Ste 166, Sacramento (95834-7727)
PHONE..................916 285-8700
Takashi Nagasaka, President
Katsuhiro Toyoizumi, Manager
EMP: 38 EST: 1992
SQ FT: 2,600
SALES: 3.3MM Privately Held
WEB: www.omicnet.com
SIC: 7389 Building inspection service; inspection & testing services
PA: Overseas Merchandise Inspection Co., Ltd.
15-6, Nihombashikabutocho
Chuo-Ku TKY 103-0

(P-14344)
ON THE SPOT TRANSPORTATION LLC
10277 Jennick Way, Elk Grove (95757-1603)
PHONE..................317 379-6692
Charles Oyoo, COO
Alex Kiruja, CEO
EMP: 50 EST: 2017
SALES (est): 1.2MM Privately Held
SIC: 7389

(P-14345)
ON-SITE MANAGER INC (DH)
307 Orchard Cy Dr Ste 110, Campbell (95008)
PHONE..................866 266-7483
Jake Harrington, CEO
Monte Jones, President
Denise Demonbreun, Executive Asst
Scott Jones, CTO
Brian Nguyen, Software Dev
EMP: 50 EST: 1999
SALES (est): 21.6MM Privately Held
WEB: www.on-site.com
SIC: 7389 Tenant screening service
HQ: Realpage, Inc.
2201 Lakeside Blvd
Richardson TX 75082
972 820-3000

(P-14346)
OPENTABLE INC (HQ)
1 Montgomery St Ste 700, San Francisco (94104-4536)
PHONE..................415 344-4200
Debby SOO, CEO
Matthew Roberts, Ch of Bd
Jeff McCombs, CFO
I Duncan Robertson, CFO
Scott Day, Vice Pres
EMP: 588 EST: 1998
SQ FT: 50,965
SALES (est): 166.1MM
SALES (corp-wide): 6.8B Publicly Held
WEB: www.opentable.com
SIC: 7389 Restaurant reservation service
PA: Booking Holdings Inc.
800 Connecticut Ave
Norwalk CT 06854
203 299-8000

(P-14347)
OPUS 2 INTERNATIONAL INC
100 Pine St Ste 775, San Francisco (94111-5126)
PHONE..................888 960-3117
Graham Smith-Bernal, CEO
Clare Foley, Vice Pres
Taryn Auchecorne, Business Dir
Kenneth Poliran, Administration
Steve Fleming, CTO
EMP: 50 EST: 2012
SALES (est): 4.4MM Privately Held
WEB: www.opus2.com
SIC: 7389 Automobile recovery service

(P-14348)
OSTERHOUT GROUP INC
Also Called: Osterhout Design Group
200 Brannan St Apt 326, San Francisco (94107-6025)
PHONE..................415 644-4000
Ralph F Osterhout, President
Dave Halpin, Vice Pres
Jordan Torres, Internal Med
Manuel Sanchez, Director
EMP: 50 EST: 1999
SALES (est): 9.6MM Privately Held
SIC: 7389 Design, commercial & industrial

(P-14349)
OURARING INC
60 Francisco St, San Francisco (94133-2104)
PHONE..................734 660-5566
Harpreet Rai, General Mgr
EMP: 62 EST: 2018
SALES (est): 4.6MM Privately Held
SIC: 7389 Business services

(P-14350)
PACIFIC COAST COMPANIES INC
10600 White Rock Rd # 100, Rancho Cordova (95670-6294)
P.O. Box 419074 (95741-9074)
PHONE..................916 631-6500
David J Lucchetti, President
Dale Waldschmitt, COO
Joshua Kimerer, CFO
Daniel Yanagihara, Vice Pres
Ken Kerrick, CIO
EMP: 125 EST: 2003
SALES (est): 65.1MM
SALES (corp-wide): 1.1B Privately Held
WEB: www.paccoast.com
SIC: 7389 8742 Legal & tax services; human resource consulting services
PA: Pacific Coast Building Products, Inc.
10600 White Rock Rd # 100
Rancho Cordova CA 95670
916 631-6500

(P-14351)
PACIFIC MEDICAL INC (PA)
1700 N Chrisman Rd, Tracy (95304-9314)
P.O. Box 149 (95378-0149)
PHONE..................800 726-9180
John M Petlansky, CEO
Jeffrey Leonard, CFO
James Parsons,
Jerry Doll, Vice Pres
Bob McCune, Vice Pres
EMP: 141 EST: 1988
SQ FT: 18,000
SALES (est): 90.6MM Privately Held
WEB: www.pacmedical.com
SIC: 7389 7352 Brokers, contract services; medical equipment rental

(P-14352)
PACKLANE INC
548 Market St 90143, San Francisco (94105-5401)
PHONE..................855 289-7687
Miriam Brafman, CEO
Karen Goeller, Opers Mgr
Jimmy Chang, Mfg Staff
EMP: 40 EST: 2015
SALES (est): 5MM Privately Held
WEB: www.packlane.com
SIC: 7389 Textile folding & packing services

(P-14353)
PATRICK K WILLIS AND CO INC
Also Called: American Recovery Service
5118 Rbert J Mathews Pkwy, El Dorado Hills (95762-5703)
PHONE..................800 398-6480
David Baker, Senior VP
Steven Schelk, Officer
Cortney Osborne, Senior VP
Christian Beyer, Vice Pres
Cortney Cea, Opers Staff
EMP: 300 EST: 1984
SQ FT: 10,000
SALES (est): 24.8MM Privately Held
WEB: www.americanrecoveryservice.com
SIC: 7389 Repossession service

(P-14354)
PATTI ROSCOE & ASSOCIATES INC (PA)
Also Called: PRA Destination Mangement
508 Gibson Dr Ste 120, Roseville (95678-5797)
PHONE..................760 496-0540
Patricia Roscoe, President
Denise Dornfeld, Vice Pres
Monica Eastes, Executive
Jeffrey Ohara, Admin Sec
Jolanta Pomiotlo, Technology
EMP: 40 EST: 1981
SQ FT: 2,500
SALES (est): 10.3MM Privately Held
SIC: 7389 Convention & show services

(P-14355)
PAYMENT RESERVATIONS INC
Also Called: Pay Certify
59 N Santa Cruz Ave Ste Q, Los Gatos (95030-5931)
PHONE..................480 770-9064
Chase Harmer, CEO
Steve Mays, CTO
Cameron Clayton, Technical Staff
EMP: 45 EST: 2014
SALES (est): 4MM Privately Held
WEB: www.profitpay.io
SIC: 7389 Financial services

(P-14356)
PAYPAL INC
18930 Newsom Ave, Cupertino (95014-3618)
PHONE..................408 967-3256
Srinivas Vadhri, Principal
Jianmin Wu, Software Engr
Anurag Sinha, Engineer
EMP: 389
SALES (corp-wide): 21.4B Publicly Held
WEB: www.paypal.com
SIC: 7389 Credit card service
HQ: Paypal, Inc.
2211 N 1st St
San Jose CA 95131
877 981-2163

(P-14357)
PAYPAL INC
Also Called: Braintree
1895 El Camino Real, Palo Alto (94306-1151)
PHONE..................877 434-2894
Archana Puri, Manager
EMP: 389
SALES (corp-wide): 21.4B Publicly Held
WEB: www.paypal.com
SIC: 7389 7374 Credit card service; data processing service
HQ: Paypal, Inc.
2211 N 1st St
San Jose CA 95131
877 981-2163

(P-14358)
PAYPAL INC
Also Called: Braintree
123 Townsend St Fl 6, San Francisco (94107-1944)
PHONE..................415 947-0834
Carolyn Mellor, Vice Pres
Chirdeep Gupta, Risk Mgmt Dir
Praveen Sridharan, Program Mgr
Mary Manasan-Oeschge, Executive Asst
Shrinivasan Ganapathy, Sr Software Eng
EMP: 389
SALES (corp-wide): 21.4B Publicly Held
WEB: www.paypal.com
SIC: 7389 7374 Credit card service; data processing service
HQ: Paypal, Inc.
2211 N 1st St
San Jose CA 95131
877 981-2163

7389 - Business Svcs, NEC County (P-14359)

(P-14359)
PAYPAL INC
Also Called: Hyperwallet
123 Townsend St Fl 6, San Francisco (94107-1944)
PHONE..................................855 449-3737
Brent Warrington, *Manager*
Tomas Likar, *Vice Pres*
EMP: 389
SALES (corp-wide): 21.4B **Publicly Held**
WEB: www.paypal.com
SIC: 7389 Credit card service
HQ: Paypal, Inc.
   2211 N 1st St
   San Jose CA 95131
   877 981-2163

(P-14360)
PAYPAL INC (HQ)
2211 N 1st St, San Jose (95131-2021)
P.O. Box 7397, Redlands (92375-0397)
PHONE..................................877 981-2163
Daniel H Schulman, *President*
Daniel Schulman, *President*
Jonathan Auerbach, *Vice Pres*
Tomer Barel, *Vice Pres*
Patrick Dupuis, *Vice Pres*
◆ **EMP:** 1632 **EST:** 1998
SALES (est): 1B
SALES (corp-wide): 21.4B **Publicly Held**
WEB: www.paypal.com
SIC: 7389 Credit card service
PA: Paypal Holdings, Inc.
   2211 N 1st St
   San Jose CA 95131
   408 967-1000

(P-14361)
PAYPAL DATA SERVICES INC
2211 N 1st St, San Jose (95131-2021)
PHONE..................................408 376-7400
John D Muller, *CEO*
EMP: 45 **EST:** 2009
SALES (est): 5.4MM **Privately Held**
WEB: www.paypal.com
SIC: 7389 Credit card service

(P-14362)
PAYPAL HOLDINGS INC (PA)
2211 N 1st St, San Jose (95131-2021)
PHONE..................................408 967-1000
Daniel H Schulman, *President*
John J Donahoe, *Ch of Bd*
John D Rainey, *CFO*
John Rainey, *CFO*
Mark Britto, *Officer*
EMP: 2187 **EST:** 2015
SQ FT: 700,000
SALES (est): 21.4B **Publicly Held**
WEB: www.paypal.com
SIC: 7389 6099 7374 Financial services; automated clearinghouses; clearinghouse associations, bank or check; electronic funds transfer network, including switching; data processing & preparation; data processing service

(P-14363)
PENINSULA FLOORS INC
1070 Sixth Ave Ste 150, Belmont (94002-3893)
PHONE..................................650 593-5825
EMP: 40
SALES (est): 2.1MM **Privately Held**
SIC: 7389 Interior design services

(P-14364)
PHOENIX AMERCN FINCL SVCS INC (HQ)
2401 Kerner Blvd, San Rafael (94901-5569)
PHONE..................................415 485-4500
Gus Constantin, *President*
Andrew Gregson, *CFO*
Justin Deitrick, *Senior VP*
Robyn Holloway, *Vice Pres*
Joseph Horgan, *Vice Pres*
EMP: 49 **EST:** 2001
SQ FT: 60,000
SALES (est): 11.5MM
SALES (corp-wide): 40MM **Privately Held**
WEB: www.phxa.com
SIC: 7389 Personal service agents, brokers & bureaus

PA: Phoenix American Incorporated
2401 Kerner Blvd
San Rafael CA 94901
415 485-4500

(P-14365)
PINNACLE SOLUTIONS INC
Also Called: Acme Printing Co
1700 Mchenry Ave Ste 45, Modesto (95350-4327)
PHONE..................................209 523-8300
Steven L Gold, *CEO*
Paul Draper, *Shareholder*
Pinder Basi, *CFO*
Austin King, *Software Engr*
Nolan Morford, *Analyst*
EMP: 59 **EST:** 1983
SQ FT: 23,000
SALES (est): 13.9MM **Privately Held**
WEB: www.psiprints.com
SIC: 7389 8713 2752 Embroidering of advertising on shirts, etc.; advertising, promotional & trade show services; ; commercial printing, offset

(P-14366)
PIPE AND PLANT SOLUTIONS INC
225 3rd St, Oakland (94607-4309)
PHONE..................................888 978-8264
William Gilmartin IV, *CEO*
Corbin Marr, *General Mgr*
Heath Pope, *Project Mgr*
Tony Kingston, *Project Engr*
Jason Houlberg, *Production*
EMP: 45
SALES (est): 8.7MM **Privately Held**
WEB: www.pipeandplant.com
SIC: 7389 Personal service agents, brokers & bureaus

(P-14367)
PIVOT INTERIORS INC (PA)
3355 Scott Blvd Ste 110, Santa Clara (95054-3138)
PHONE..................................408 432-5600
Toll Free:.................................888 -
Kenneth Baugh, *President*
Bradley Bransen, *Vice Pres*
Patrick Donlon, *Vice Pres*
Anthony Jenkinson, *Vice Pres*
Harvey Van Baan, *Vice Pres*
▲ **EMP:** 192 **EST:** 1973
SQ FT: 24,000
SALES (est): 91.3MM **Privately Held**
WEB: www.pivotinteriors.com
SIC: 5712 7389 7299 Office furniture; interior design services; home improvement & renovation contractor agency

(P-14368)
PIVOTAL CONNECTIONS
75 E Santa Clara St # 14, San Jose (95113-1827)
PHONE..................................408 484-6200
Elise Cutini, *CEO*
Glenda Castro, *COO*
Jane Machin, *CFO*
Melissa Johns, *Exec VP*
John Hogan, *Vice Pres*
EMP: 35 **EST:** 1987
SALES (est): 4.3MM **Privately Held**
WEB: www.pivotalnow.org
SIC: 7389 Fund raising organizations

(P-14369)
PLAN DESIGN CONSULTANTS INC
1111 Triton Dr Ste 201, Foster City (94404-1217)
PHONE..................................650 341-3322
James D Carlson, *CEO*
Linda Carlson, *Shareholder*
Paul D Carlson, *CFO*
Judith Bono, *Vice Pres*
Houry Viola, *Vice Pres*
EMP: 39 **EST:** 1975
SQ FT: 6,000
SALES (est): 4.1MM **Privately Held**
WEB: www.plandesign.com
SIC: 7389 Financial services

(P-14370)
PRAXIS ASSOCIATES INC
332 Georgia St, Vallejo (94590-5907)
PHONE..................................707 551-8200

Michael Thomas Ort, *CEO*
Robert W Volker, *COO*
EMP: 37 **EST:** 2004
SALES (est): 3.5MM **Privately Held**
WEB: www.praxisfiber.com
SIC: 7389 3229 Design services; telephone services; fiber optics strands

(P-14371)
PRECISION IDEO INC
780 High St, Palo Alto (94301-2420)
PHONE..................................650 688-3400
Tim Brown, *President*
Duane Bray, *Partner*
Fred Dust, *Partner*
Tom Eich, *Partner*
Whitney Mortimer, *Partner*
EMP: 400 **EST:** 1992
SALES (est): 29.2MM **Privately Held**
WEB: www.ideo.com
SIC: 7389 Design services

(P-14372)
PREVENT LIFE SAFETY SVCS INC
448 Commerce Way Ste B, Livermore (94551-5213)
PHONE..................................925 667-2088
Carol D Cohan, *President*
Jodi Clem, *Vice Pres*
Jeff Norman, *Executive*
Nicolai Laguatan, *Technician*
Catherine Sharani, *Human Res Dir*
EMP: 50 **EST:** 2004
SALES (est): 9.1MM **Privately Held**
WEB: www.prevent-lss.com
SIC: 7389 Fire protection service other than forestry or public

(P-14373)
PRIMA NOCE PACKING INC
16461 E Comstock Rd, Linden (95236-9608)
P.O. Box 1298 (95236-1298)
PHONE..................................209 932-8800
Timothy Sambado, *President*
◆ **EMP:** 45 **EST:** 2007
SALES (est): 2.7MM **Privately Held**
WEB: www.premiumwalnuts.com
SIC: 7389 Packaging & labeling services

(P-14374)
PRIME FINANCE PARTNERS I LP (PA)
600 Montgomery St # 1700, San Francisco (94111-2719)
PHONE..................................415 986-2415
John C Atwater, *Partner*
Shawn Cully, *Managing Dir*
Brian Schneider, *Managing Dir*
George Sieverding, *Analyst*
David Godin, *Director*
EMP: 45 **EST:** 2008
SALES (est): 3.9MM **Privately Held**
WEB: www.primefinance.com
SIC: 7389 Financial services

(P-14375)
PROFESSIONAL EXCHANGE SVC
4747 N 1st St Ste 140, Fresno (93726-0517)
P.O. Box 1071 (93714-1071)
PHONE..................................559 229-6249
Cynthia Downing, *CEO*
Peggy Matsoura, *CFO*
Russell Nakaguchio, *Corp Secy*
Paul Bateman, *Principal*
Ashleigh Servadio, *Exec Dir*
EMP: 50 **EST:** 1980
SQ FT: 3,700
SALES (est): 7.8MM **Privately Held**
WEB: www.pesc.com
SIC: 7389 Telephone answering service

(P-14376)
PROGRAM PLG PROFESSIONALS INC
71 Stevenson St Ste 825, San Francisco (94105-2942)
PHONE..................................415 692-5870
Beverly Barnett, *Branch Mgr*
Joe Bailey, *Exec Dir*
Priyan Rathnayake, *Sr Ntwrk Engine*
Susan Davis, *Facilities Mgr*

Regina Lingerfelt, *Sr Consultant*
EMP: 109
SALES (corp-wide): 603.3MM **Privately Held**
WEB: www.migso-pcubed.com
SIC: 7389 Interior design services
HQ: Program Planning Professionals, Inc.
   1340 Eisenhower Pl
   Ann Arbor MI 48108
   734 741-7770

(P-14377)
PROPLUS DESIGN SOLUTIONS INC (PA)
2025 Gateway Pl Ste 130, San Jose (95110-1005)
PHONE..................................408 459-6128
Lianfeng Yang, *Vice Pres*
Zhijian MA, *CEO*
Yutao MA, *Vice Pres*
Esther Reeves, *Administration*
EMP: 119 **EST:** 2007
SALES (est): 7.2MM **Privately Held**
WEB: www.proplussolutions.com
SIC: 7389 Design services

(P-14378)
PUNCTUS TEMPORIS TRANSLATIONS
5201 Great America Pkwy, Santa Clara (95054-1122)
PHONE..................................510 309-0888
Jessica Cade, *Owner*
EMP: 50
SALES (est): 641.1K **Privately Held**
WEB: www.punctustemptrans.com
SIC: 7389 Translation services

(P-14379)
QUALIFIED DIGITAL LLC
813 Folger Ave Unit 8, Berkeley (94710-2800)
PHONE..................................518 727-3997
Jacqueline Saleem, *CEO*
Linda Schumacher, *Director*
EMP: 42 **EST:** 2017
SALES (est): 1.2MM **Privately Held**
SIC: 7389 Business services

(P-14380)
QUINSTREET INC (PA)
950 Tower Ln Ste 600, Foster City (94404-4253)
PHONE..................................650 578-7700
Douglas Valenti, *Ch of Bd*
Gregory Wong, *CFO*
Martin J Collins, *Ch Credit Ofcr*
Brett Moses, *Senior VP*
Andreja Stevanovic, *Senior VP*
EMP: 50 **EST:** 1999
SQ FT: 63,998
SALES: 578.4MM **Publicly Held**
WEB: www.quinstreet.com
SIC: 7389 7372 Advertising, promotional & trade show services; prepackaged software; business oriented computer software

(P-14381)
R&R SECURITY SOLUTIONS INC
Also Called: Signal 88 SEC Contra Costa
1975 Diamond Blvd E160, Concord (94520-5792)
PHONE..................................925 494-9000
Roger Estrada, *CEO*
EMP: 42 **EST:** 2017
SQ FT: 200
SALES (est): 1.5MM **Privately Held**
WEB: www.signal88.com
SIC: 7389 7381 Notary publics; guard services

(P-14382)
RABIN WORLDWIDE INC
21 Locust Ave 2a, Mill Valley (94941-2852)
PHONE..................................415 522-5700
Richard Reese, *President*
Micheal Bank, *Vice Pres*
Chelsea Greiwe, *Vice Pres*
Brian J Hayes, *Vice Pres*
Kendra Marshall, *Vice Pres*
▼ **EMP:** 62 **EST:** 1966

PRODUCTS & SERVICES SECTION

7389 - Business Svcs, NEC County (P-14407)

SALES (est): 4.2MM **Privately Held**
WEB: www.rabin.com
SIC: 7389 Auctioneers, fee basis

(P-14383)
RENEW FINANCIAL GROUP LLC
555 12th St Ste 1650, Oakland (94607-3623)
PHONE.................................888 996-0523
Joanna Karger, *Director*
Joel Eckhause, *COO*
Russ Hayden, *Vice Pres*
Scott Henderson, *Vice Pres*
Danika Snodgrass, *Administration*
EMP: 37 **EST:** 2016
SALES (est): 5.5MM **Privately Held**
WEB: www.renewfinancial.com
SIC: 7389 Financial services

(P-14384)
RESTAURANT ASSETS & DESIGN INC (PA)
3031 Stanford Ranch Rd, Rocklin (95765-5554)
PHONE.................................916 532-1377
Alan S Reed, *Principal*
EMP: 39 **EST:** 2016
SALES (est): 393.5K **Privately Held**
WEB: www.restaurantassetsanddesign.com
SIC: 7389 Design services

(P-14385)
REYES GROUP ENTERPRISES INC (PA)
1975 Mendocino Ave, Santa Rosa (95401-3630)
PHONE.................................415 524-5909
Hector Alexander Chavez, *Principal*
EMP: 46 **EST:** 2008
SALES (est): 672.1K **Privately Held**
SIC: 7389 Business services

(P-14386)
RGIS LLC
4320 Stevens Creek Blvd, San Jose (95129-1202)
PHONE.................................408 243-9141
EMP: 65
SALES (corp-wide): 5.1B **Publicly Held**
SIC: 7389 Business Services
HQ: Rgis, Llc
  2000 Taylor Rd
  Auburn Hills MI 48326
  248 651-2511

(P-14387)
RGIS LLC
20 Landing Cir Ste 100, Chico (95973-7889)
PHONE.................................530 898-1015
EMP: 65
SALES (corp-wide): 6.1B **Publicly Held**
SIC: 7389 Business Services
HQ: Rgis, Llc
  2000 Taylor Rd
  Auburn Hills MI 48326
  248 651-2511

(P-14388)
RHUMBIX INC
1169 Howard St, San Francisco (94103-3952)
PHONE.................................435 764-3014
Zachary Scheel, *CEO*
Drew Dewalt, *CFO*
Caspar Yen, *Vice Pres*
Emily Stember, *Executive Asst*
Guy Skillett, *CIO*
EMP: 59 **EST:** 2014
SALES (est): 5MM **Privately Held**
WEB: www.rhumbix.com
SIC: 7389 8748 8711 8742 ; business consulting; building construction consultant; personnel management consultant; commercial physical research

(P-14389)
RIVER CITY AUTO RECOVERY INC
3401 Fitzgerald Rd, Rancho Cordova (95742-6815)
PHONE.................................916 851-1100
EMP: 71

SQ FT: 15,000
SALES (est): 2.2MM
SALES (corp-wide): 577MM **Privately Held**
SIC: 7389 Automobile Repossession
PA: United Road Services, Inc.
  10701 Middlebelt Rd
  Romulus MI 48170
  734 946-3232

(P-14390)
RL LIQUIDATORS LLC
221 Richards Blvd, Sacramento (95811-0216)
PHONE.................................916 747-7762
Larry Morgan, *Principal*
Ryan Babineau, *CFO*
Aubrey Robinson, *District Mgr*
Xavier Bradley, *Marketing Staff*
EMP: 38 **EST:** 2011
SALES (est): 4.9MM **Privately Held**
WEB: www.rlliquidators.com
SIC: 7389 Auctioneers, fee basis

(P-14391)
ROAD SAFETY INC
4335 Pacific St Ste A, Rocklin (95677-2104)
PHONE.................................916 543-4600
Jason Bamberg, *President*
Melissa L Bamberg, *President*
Anthony Cancilla, *COO*
Andrea West, *Human Res Dir*
EMP: 120 **EST:** 2008
SQ FT: 6,000
SALES (est): 10.1MM **Privately Held**
WEB: www.roadsafetyinc.net
SIC: 7389 Flagging service (traffic control)

(P-14392)
RWS LIFE SCIENCES INC
555 Montgomery St Ste 720, San Francisco (94111-2570)
PHONE.................................415 981-5890
Jingyi Isaacs, *Project Mgr*
Anas Soumadi, *Project Mgr*
Amanda Wiley, *Project Mgr*
Kenneth Ip, *Finance*
Julia Ngo, *Accountant*
EMP: 36 **Privately Held**
SIC: 7389 Translation services
HQ: Rws Life Sciences Inc.
  101 E River Dr
  East Hartford CT 06108
  860 727-6000

(P-14393)
SACRAMENTO MUNICPL UTILITY DST
Also Called: Smud Financing Authority
14295 Clay East Rd, Herald (95638-9770)
PHONE.................................916 732-5743
EMP: 302
SALES (corp-wide): 1.5B **Privately Held**
WEB: www.smud.org
SIC: 7389 Financial services
PA: Sacramento Municipal Utility District
  6201 S St
  Sacramento CA 95817
  916 452-3211

(P-14394)
SAMSUNG PAY INC
Also Called: Loop
665 Clyde Ave, Mountain View (94043-2235)
PHONE.................................617 279-0520
William Graylin, *CEO*
Ty Shipman, *Vice Pres*
Paolo Lupi, *General Mgr*
Jennifer Ting, *Executive Asst*
John Kim, *Research*
EMP: 30 **EST:** 2007
SALES (est): 10.9MM **Privately Held**
SIC: 7389 3577 7372 Credit card service; computer peripheral equipment; prepackaged software

(P-14395)
SAN FRANCISCO FOUNDATION
1 Embarcadero Ctr # 1400, San Francisco (94111-3703)
PHONE.................................415 733-8500
Sandra Hernandez MD, *Director*
Galen Maness, *COO*
Ophelia B Basgal, *Chairman*

Robert Friedman, *Chairman*
Andrew Ballard, *Trustee*
EMP: 60 **EST:** 1948
SQ FT: 22,000
SALES (est): 341.4MM **Privately Held**
WEB: www.sff.org
SIC: 7389 Fund raising organizations

(P-14396)
SAN FRANCISCO TRAVEL ASSN
Also Called: Ss Travel
1 Front St Ste 2900, San Francisco (94111-5333)
PHONE.................................415 974-6900
Joe D'Alessandro, *President*
Terry Lewis, *Vice Chairman*
Tina Wu, *CFO*
Bill Poland, *Treasurer*
Monetta White, *Bd of Directors*
EMP: 70 **EST:** 1909
SQ FT: 15,000
SALES (est): 32.5MM **Privately Held**
WEB: www.sftravel.com
SIC: 7389 Convention & show services; tourist information bureau

(P-14397)
SANTA CLARA CONVENTION CENTER
5001 Great America Pkwy, Santa Clara (95054-1119)
PHONE.................................408 748-7000
Donald C Riccardi, *General Mgr*
Philip Ortega, *Officer*
Jazmin La Vigne, *Administration*
June Suzuki, *Administration*
Ali Terzian, *Chief Engr*
▲ **EMP:** 103 **EST:** 1986
SQ FT: 238,000
SALES (est): 10.4MM **Privately Held**
WEB: www.santaclara.org
SIC: 7389 Convention & show services; tourist information bureau

(P-14398)
SARPA-FELDMAN ENTERPRISES INC
Also Called: Progressive Solutions
650 N King Rd, San Jose (95133-1715)
PHONE.................................408 982-1790
Mark E Sarpa, *CEO*
Scott R Feldman, *CFO*
Scott Feldman, *CFO*
Trang Nguyen, *Accountant*
▲ **EMP:** 56 **EST:** 1990
SQ FT: 13,000
SALES (est): 9.9MM **Privately Held**
SIC: 7389 Printing broker

(P-14399)
SCANDINAVIAN GALLERIES LLC
4127 Dry Creek Rd, NAPA (94558-9720)
PHONE.................................650 862-8432
Andreas Meijer, *Branch Mgr*
EMP: 41 **Privately Held**
SIC: 7389 Personal service agents, brokers & bureaus
PA: Scandinavian Galleries Llc
  Mountain View CA
  -

(P-14400)
SCOTTS VLY FIRE PROTECTION DST
Also Called: Scotts Valley Fire District
7 Erba Ln, Scotts Valley (95066-4103)
PHONE.................................831 438-0211
Mike McMurray, *Fire Chief*
Daron Pisciotta, *Vice Pres*
Alicia Walton, *Admin Sec*
Nick Owens, *Engineer*
Garrett Grigg,
EMP: 52 **EST:** 1956
SALES (est): 2.8MM **Privately Held**
WEB: www.scottsvalleyfire.com
SIC: 7389 Fire protection service other than forestry or public

(P-14401)
SEACA PACKAGING INC
3194 E Manning Ave Ste 2, Fowler (93625-9785)
PHONE.................................559 813-9030
Gary Vetsch, *Regional Mgr*

EMP: 40
SALES (corp-wide): 67.1MM **Privately Held**
WEB: www.seattlebox.com
SIC: 7389 Packaging & labeling services
HQ: Seaca Packaging, Inc.
  23400 71st Pl S
  Kent WA 98032

(P-14402)
SECURITY CLASSIFICATION INC
2339 Gold Meadow Way, Gold River (95670-4467)
PHONE.................................707 301-6052
Ted Golshanara, *Manager*
Harold Curtis, *Chairman*
David Curtis, *Security Mgr*
Andrea Curtis, *Mng Member*
Chyree Curtis, *Mng Member*
EMP: 35 **EST:** 2017
SALES (est): 1.2MM **Privately Held**
SIC: 7389 7381 8741 6111 Automobile recovery service; guard services; financial management for business; Export/Import Bank; processing service, gas; consumer buying service

(P-14403)
SHUMS CODA ASSOCIATES INC
5776 Stnrdge Mall Rd Ste, Pleasanton (94588)
PHONE.................................925 463-0651
David Basinger, *CEO*
EMP: 75 **EST:** 2006
SALES (est): 1.7MM **Privately Held**
SIC: 7389 Business services

(P-14404)
SIGNET TESTING LABS INC
498 N 3rd St, Sacramento (95811-0215)
PHONE.................................916 374-0754
EMP: 75
SALES (corp-wide): 26.3MM **Privately Held**
WEB: www.signettesting.com
SIC: 7389 Inspection & testing services
HQ: Signet Testing Laboratories, Inc.
  3526 Breakwater Ct
  Hayward CA 94545

(P-14405)
SIGOS LLC (HQ)
20813 Stevns Crk Blvd # 200, Cupertino (95014-2194)
PHONE.................................650 535-0599
Richard Einsiedl,
Mel Kadkhodai, *Business Dir*
Maria Barroga, *Engineer*
Peter Philips, *Opers Staff*
Goce Talaganov, *Senior Mgr*
EMP: 43 **EST:** 2015
SALES (est): 12.2MM **Privately Held**
WEB: www.mobileum.com
SIC: 7389 Inspection & testing services

(P-14406)
SMART WORLD LLC
Also Called: Steri-Tek
48225 Lakeview Blvd, Fremont (94538-6519)
PHONE.................................510 933-9700
Larry Nichols, *CEO*
Abdelrahman Almulla, *Senior VP*
Ray Johal, *Opers Mgr*
Jordan Fujioka, *QC Mgr*
Eric Nakagawa, *Manager*
EMP: 49 **EST:** 2014
SQ FT: 3,600
SALES (est): 4.6MM **Privately Held**
WEB: www.steri-tek.com
SIC: 7389 3841 Product sterilization service; anesthesia apparatus

(P-14407)
SMITH-EMERY SAN FRANCISCO INC
1940 Oakdale Ave, San Francisco (94124-2004)
P.O. Box 880550 (94188-0550)
PHONE.................................415 642-7326
James E Partridge, *President*
Helen Choe, *CFO*
Alfreda Lee, *Office Mgr*

7389 - Business Svcs, NEC County (P-14408)

PRODUCTS & SERVICES SECTION

Siobhan Ruck, *Executive Asst*
Joel Nadler, *Director*
EMP: 47 **EST:** 2007
SQ FT: 10,160
SALES (est): 7.6MM **Privately Held**
WEB: www.smithemery.com
SIC: 7389 8711 Inspection & testing services; engineering services

(P-14408)
SOLID SOLUTIONS 24/7 INC
7700 14th Ave, Sacramento (95820-3668)
PHONE................................916 800-1847
Ryan Moore, *Principal*
EMP: 55 **EST:** 2013
SALES (est): 2.7MM **Privately Held**
WEB: www.solidsolutions247inc.com
SIC: 7389 Repossession service

(P-14409)
SOMAM INC
Also Called: Integrated Designs By Somam
6011 N Fresno St Ste 130, Fresno (93710-5292)
PHONE................................559 436-0881
Pete Mogensen, *Vice Pres*
Mark T Oba, *President*
Peter Mogensen, *CFO*
Larry Miller, *Vice Pres*
Justo Padron, *Vice Pres*
EMP: 45 **EST:** 1956
SQ FT: 10,000
SALES (est): 4.9MM **Privately Held**
WEB: www.integrateddesigns.com
SIC: 7389 8711 8712 Interior design services; contractors' disbursement control; engineering services; architectural services

(P-14410)
SONY INTERACTIVE ENTRMT LLC (HQ)
Also Called: Smss
2207 Bridgepointe Pkwy, Foster City (94404-5060)
PHONE................................310 981-1500
Jim Ryan,
Kazuhiko Takeda, *CFO*
Greg Yip, *Administration*
Josh Aeria, *Info Tech Mgr*
Matt Miller, *MIS Staff*
EMP: 483 **EST:** 2016
SALES (est): 985MM **Privately Held**
WEB: www.sie.com
SIC: 7389 Music distribution systems

(P-14411)
SOUTH PARK PLEATING INC
Also Called: Pleats Plus
867 Isabella St, Oakland (94607-3429)
PHONE................................510 625-8050
EMP: 22
SQ FT: 25,000
SALES (est): 1.2MM **Privately Held**
SIC: 7389 2339 Business Services Mfg Women's/Misses' Outerwear

(P-14412)
STANISLAUS CONSOL FIRE PROT (PA)
3324 Topeka St, Riverbank (95367-2330)
PHONE................................209 869-7470
Lyn Rambo, *Chief*
Kim Mossman, *Admin Asst*
Randall Bradley, *Fire Chief*
EMP: 48 **EST:** 1995
SQ FT: 1,560
SALES (est): 5.5MM **Privately Held**
WEB: www.scfpd.us
SIC: 7389 Fire protection service other than forestry or public

(P-14413)
STANLEE R GATTI DESIGNS
1208 Howard St, San Francisco (94103-2712)
PHONE................................415 558-8384
Stanlee R Gatti, *President*
EMP: 50 **EST:** 1993
SQ FT: 12,102
SALES (est): 4MM **Privately Held**
WEB: www.stanleegatti.com
SIC: 7389 Design services

(P-14414)
STERICYCLE INC
Also Called: Shred-It
5060 Forni Dr, Concord (94520-8584)
PHONE................................650 212-2332
Ken Hafner, *Branch Mgr*
Cory Johnson, *Sales Mgr*
Laurie Tortorici, *Sales Staff*
EMP: 39
SALES (corp-wide): 2.6B **Publicly Held**
WEB: www.stericycle.com
SIC: 7389 Document & office record destruction
PA: Stericycle, Inc.
   2355 Waukegan Rd Ste 300
   Bannockburn IL 60015
   847 367-5910

(P-14415)
STERLING HSA INC
475 14th St Ste 120, Oakland (94612-1900)
P.O. Box 71107 (94612-7207)
PHONE................................800 617-4729
Cora M Tellez, *President*
Duarte Vatista, *COO*
Mark Maltun, *CFO*
Chris Bettner, *Exec VP*
Pat Straughn, *Vice Pres*
EMP: 50 **EST:** 2004
SALES (est): 5.2MM **Privately Held**
WEB: www.sterlingadministration.com
SIC: 7389 Financial services

(P-14416)
STORM WTR INSPTN MINT SVCS INC
3361 Walnut Blvd Ste 110, Brentwood (94513-4489)
P.O. Box 1627, Discovery Bay (94505-7627)
PHONE................................925 516-8966
Ric Campos, *Principal*
Ethan Purkey, *Manager*
EMP: 40
SQ FT: 2,000
SALES (est): 7MM **Privately Held**
WEB: www.swimsclean.com
SIC: 7389 Inspection & testing services

(P-14417)
STRATHMOORE PRESS INC
Also Called: Warwick, Mal & Associates
2550 9th St Ste 103, Berkeley (94710-2551)
PHONE................................510 843-8888
Mal Warwick, *President*
Katie Dunne, *Executive*
Arturo Luna, *Web Dvlpr*
Brett Monzel, *Web Dvlpr*
EMP: 42 **EST:** 1996
SALES (est): 2.1MM **Privately Held**
SIC: 7389 Brokers, business: buying & selling business enterprises

(P-14418)
STREAMGUYS INC
Also Called: Streamguys.com
2212 Jacoby Creek Rd, Bayside (95524-9376)
P.O. Box 828, Arcata (95518-0828)
PHONE................................707 667-9479
Kiriki Delany, *President*
Jonathan Speaker, *COO*
EMP: 37 **EST:** 2004
SALES (est): 5MM **Privately Held**
WEB: www.streamguys.com
SIC: 7389 4813 Music & broadcasting services;

(P-14419)
SUN LIGHT & POWER
1035 Folger Ave, Berkeley (94710-2819)
PHONE................................510 845-2997
Gary Gerber, *President*
Troy Tyler, *COO*
Harry Payne, *Vice Pres*
Aurora Meerjans, *Project Mgr*
Devin Curry, *Technical Staff*
EMP: 70 **EST:** 1975
SQ FT: 10,000
SALES (est): 17MM **Privately Held**
WEB: www.sunlightandpower.com
SIC: 7389 1796 3433 Design services; power generating equipment installation; solar heaters & collectors

(P-14420)
SUTTER CONNECT LLC
2000 Powell St Ste 100, Emeryville (94608-1774)
PHONE................................510 596-4700
Tom Bacci, *Manager*
EMP: 182
SALES (corp-wide): 13.2B **Privately Held**
WEB: www.sutterphysicianservices.org
SIC: 7389 Personal service agents, brokers & bureaus
HQ: Sutter Physician Services
   10470 Old Placerville Rd
   Sacramento CA 95827

(P-14421)
SYMPHONY COMM SVCS HLDINGS LLC (PA)
640 W California Ave # 200, Sunnyvale (94086-3624)
PHONE................................650 733-6660
Brad Levy, *CEO*
Ben Chrnelich, *President*
Fred Stemmelin, *President*
Eran Barack, *COO*
Eric Chao, *Creative Dir*
EMP: 192 **EST:** 2014
SALES (est): 50.5MM **Privately Held**
WEB: www.symphony.com
SIC: 7389 8742 7373 Financial services; financial consultant; systems integration services

(P-14422)
SYNDICATE CORP
Also Called: Gymguyz Santa Clara Valley
350 N 2nd St Apt 131, San Jose (95112-4096)
PHONE................................408 740-5565
Shannon Sevor, *CEO*
Fermen Smith, *COO*
EMP: 45 **EST:** 2019
SALES (est): 1.1MM **Privately Held**
SIC: 7389

(P-14423)
SYNERGY MACHINES LLC
3152 San Gabriel Way, Union City (94587-2810)
PHONE................................408 676-9696
Navdeep Singh, *Principal*
EMP: 50 **EST:** 2014
SALES (est): 1.3MM **Privately Held**
WEB: www.synergymachines.us
SIC: 7389

(P-14424)
TACTICAL TELESOLUTIONS INC
2121 N Calif Blvd Ste 260, Walnut Creek (94596-3572)
PHONE................................415 788-8808
Laura Hylton, *President*
Eric Wicklund, *CFO*
Kurt Stenzel, *Vice Pres*
Kathy O'toole, *Technology*
Kema Riley, *Technology*
EMP: 130 **EST:** 1991
SQ FT: 15,000
SALES (est): 8.2MM **Privately Held**
WEB: www.ttstechnique.com
SIC: 7389 Telemarketing services

(P-14425)
TALENTBURST INC
575 Market St Ste 3025, San Francisco (94105-5840)
PHONE................................415 813-4011
Tanvi Kharbanda, *Technical Staff*
Vineet Dayal, *Manager*
Kashif Abidi, *Asst Mgr*
EMP: 65
SALES (corp-wide): 21.1MM **Privately Held**
WEB: www.talentburst.com
SIC: 7389 7375 Check validation service; information retrieval services
PA: Talentburst, Inc.
   679 Worcester St Ste 1
   Natick MA 01760
   508 628-7516

(P-14426)
TD SYNNEX CORPORATION
44131 Nobel Dr, Fremont (94538-3173)
PHONE................................510 688-3507
EMP: 71
SALES (corp-wide): 24.6B **Publicly Held**
WEB: www.synnex.com
SIC: 7389 Telemarketing services
PA: Td Synnex Corporation
   44201 Nobel Dr
   Fremont CA 94538
   510 656-3333

(P-14427)
TEAM SAN JOSE
408 Almaden Blvd, San Jose (95110-2709)
PHONE................................408 295-9600
Dave Costain, *COO*
Janette Divol, *CFO*
Ihab Sabry, *CFO*
Janette Sutton, *CFO*
Vijay Sammeta, *Vice Pres*
EMP: 900 **EST:** 2003
SQ FT: 300,000
SALES (est): 39MM **Privately Held**
WEB: www.sanjose.org
SIC: 7389 Convention & show services

(P-14428)
TEESPRING INC (PA)
2430 3rd St, San Francisco (94107-3111)
PHONE................................855 833-7774
Walker Williams, *CEO*
Morrie Eisenberg, *President*
Robert Chatwani, *Risk Mgmt Dir*
Jack Farina, *CIO*
Evan Stites-Clayton, *CTO*
EMP: 145 **EST:** 2014
SALES (est): 41.3MM **Privately Held**
WEB: www.teespring.com
SIC: 7389 5699 2253 Apparel designers, commercial; T-shirts, custom printed; T-shirts & tops, knit

(P-14429)
TELE-DIRECT COMMUNICATIONS INC
4741 Madison Ave Ste 200, Sacramento (95841-2580)
PHONE................................916 348-2170
A James Puff, *Chairman*
Thomas Coshow, *CEO*
Sandra Coggeshall, *Exec VP*
Deneen Barajas, *Human Res Mgr*
Jamei Puff, *Sales/Mktg Mgr*
EMP: 45 **EST:** 1961
SQ FT: 6,000
SALES (est): 7.1MM **Privately Held**
WEB: www.teledirect.com
SIC: 7389 5999 Telemarketing services; telephone & communication equipment

(P-14430)
TELECOM INC
2201 Broadway Ste 103, Oakland (94612-3028)
PHONE................................510 873-8283
Jon Martin, *President*
Lani Stackel, *Mktg Dir*
EMP: 100 **EST:** 1993
SALES (est): 8.4MM **Privately Held**
WEB: www.telecominc.com
SIC: 7389 4813 8742 Telemarketing services; data telephone communications; marketing consulting services

(P-14431)
TENCUE PRODUCTIONS LLC
Also Called: Tencue, An Opus Company
1250 Addison St Ste 110, Berkeley (94702-1782)
PHONE................................510 841-3000
Miriam Agrell, *Officer*
Kristin Leimkuhler, *General Ptnr*
Maria Rohlsson, *Executive Asst*
Matt Agrell, *Info Tech Mgr*
Jeff Kalafus, *Technical Staff*
EMP: 40 **EST:** 2000
SQ FT: 1,500
SALES (est): 8.5MM
SALES (corp-wide): 68.9MM **Privately Held**
WEB: www.tencue.com
SIC: 7389 Convention & show services
PA: Opus Solutions, Llc
   9000 Sw Nimbus Ave
   Beaverton OR 97008
   971 223-0777

PRODUCTS & SERVICES SECTION

7389 - Business Svcs, NEC County (P-14456)

(P-14432)
TESORO GOLDEN EAGLE REFIN
150 Solano Way, Pacheco (94553-1465)
PHONE...................925 370-3249
Gregory J Goff, *CEO*
Steven Sterin, *CFO*
Keith Casey, *Vice Pres*
Charles S Parrish, *Vice Pres*
EMP: 39 **EST:** 2009
SALES (est): 2.5MM **Privately Held**
SIC: 7389 Petroleum refinery inspection service

(P-14433)
TEXAS INSTRUMENTS SUNNYVALE
165 Gibraltar Ct, Sunnyvale (94089-1301)
PHONE...................408 541-9900
EMP: 50
SQ FT: 12,070
SALES (est): 1.6MM
SALES (corp-wide): 15.7B **Publicly Held**
SIC: 7389 Business Services, Nec, Nsk
PA: Texas Instruments Incorporated
12500 Ti Blvd
Dallas TX 75243
214 479-3773

(P-14434)
THOMPSON & RICH CRANE SERVICE
2373 E Mariposa Rd, Stockton (95205-7811)
P.O. Box 30035 (95213-0035)
PHONE...................209 465-3161
EMP: 50 **EST:** 1988
SALES (est): 2.5MM **Privately Held**
SIC: 7389 Crane & Aerial Lift Service

(P-14435)
TMC FINANCING
1720 Broadway Fl 3, Oakland (94612-2155)
PHONE...................415 989-8855
Barbara Morrison, *President*
Christina Johnson, *President*
Ron Lien, *President*
Pat Grech, *Officer*
Lisa Lucero, *Officer*
EMP: 65 **EST:** 2012
SALES (est): 6MM **Privately Held**
WEB: www.tmcfinancing.com
SIC: 7389 6141 Financial services; personal credit institutions

(P-14436)
TOUCHOFMODERN INC
30063 Ahern Ave, Union City (94587-1234)
PHONE...................888 868-1232
EMP: 155
SALES (corp-wide): 59.7MM **Privately Held**
WEB: www.touchofmodern.com
SIC: 7389 Interior design services
PA: Touchofmodern, Inc.
1025 Sansome St
San Francisco CA 94111
415 230-0750

(P-14437)
TRAFFIC MANAGEMENT INC
1277 Old Bayshore Hwy, San Jose (95112-2800)
PHONE...................408 279-9900
Troy Vander Voste, *Branch Mgr*
EMP: 36 **Privately Held**
WEB: www.trafficmanagement.com
SIC: 7389 8741 Flagging service (traffic control); business management
PA: Traffic Management, Inc.
4900 Arprt Plz Dr Ste 300
Long Beach CA 90815

(P-14438)
TRAFFIC MANAGEMENT INC
Also Called: TMI
690 Quinn Ave, San Jose (95112-2635)
PHONE...................877 763-5999
Tina Becker, *Branch Mgr*
EMP: 36 **Privately Held**
WEB: www.trafficmanagement.com
SIC: 7389 8741 Flagging service (traffic control); management services
PA: Traffic Management, Inc.
4900 Arprt Plz Dr Ste 300
Long Beach CA 90815

(P-14439)
TRANSPAK INC (PA)
520 Marburg Way, San Jose (95133-1619)
PHONE...................408 254-0500
Arlene Inch, *Chairman*
Bob Lally, *President*
Bert Inch, *CEO*
Ray Horner, *COO*
Chris Lee, *CFO*
◆ **EMP:** 118 **EST:** 1969
SALES: 187.9MM **Privately Held**
WEB: www.transpak.com
SIC: 7389 Packaging & labeling services

(P-14440)
TRAVELATOR INC
Also Called: Travelbank
2710 Gateway Oaks Dr # 150, Sacramento (95833-3505)
P.O. Box 838, Daly City (94017-0838)
PHONE...................415 322-9265
Duke Chung, *CEO*
Reid Williams, *CTO*
Steven Zafrani, *Software Dev*
Sara Abad, *Director*
EMP: 50 **EST:** 2015
SALES (est): 2.6MM **Privately Held**
SIC: 7389 Business services

(P-14441)
TRILLIANT NETWORKS INC (PA)
1100 Island Dr Ste 201, Redwood City (94065-5187)
PHONE...................650 204-5050
Andy White, *Principal*
Mike Mortimer, *Exec VP*
Norma Formanek, *Senior VP*
Ryan Gerbrandt, *Senior VP*
Paul Karr, *Senior VP*
EMP: 65 **EST:** 2004
SALES (est): 30.1MM **Privately Held**
WEB: www.trilliant.com
SIC: 7389 Meter readers, remote

(P-14442)
TRINET GROUP INC (PA)
1 Park Pl Ste 600, Dublin (94568-7983)
PHONE...................510 352-5000
Burton M Goldfield, *CEO*
David C Hodgson, *Ch of Bd*
Olivier Kohler, *COO*
Kelly Tuminelli, *CFO*
Samantha Wellington,
EMP: 2700 **EST:** 1988
SALES (est): 4B **Publicly Held**
WEB: www.trinet.com
SIC: 7389

(P-14443)
TRINITY PACKING COMPANY INC (PA)
18700 E South Ave, Reedley (93654-9711)
P.O. Box 28905, Fresno (93729-8905)
PHONE...................559 433-3785
David E White, *CEO*
Brian Hiett, *Vice Pres*
Lance Shebelut, *Vice Pres*
Bonnie Carrillo, *Accountant*
Faten Salem, *Materials Mgr*
▲ **EMP:** 300 **EST:** 2009
SALES (est): 27MM **Privately Held**
WEB: www.trinityfruit.com
SIC: 7389 Packaging & labeling services

(P-14444)
TRINITY PACKING COMPANY INC
7612 S Reed Ave, Reedley (93654-9712)
PHONE...................559 743-3913
Sam Gomez, *Branch Mgr*
EMP: 300
SALES (corp-wide): 27MM **Privately Held**
WEB: www.trinityfruit.com
SIC: 7389 Packaging & labeling services
PA: Trinity Packing Company, Inc.
18700 E South Ave
Reedley CA 93654
559 433-3785

(P-14445)
TRUE LINK FINANCIAL INC (PA)
47 Maiden Ln, San Francisco (94108-5401)
P.O. Box 581 (94104-0581)
PHONE...................800 299-7646
Kai Stinchcombe, *CEO*
Claire McDonnell, *COO*
Isaac Elias, *VP Engrg*
David Fritsch, *Engineer*
Coulter King, *Opers Staff*
EMP: 90 **EST:** 2014
SALES (est): 4.4MM **Privately Held**
WEB: www.truelinkfinancial.com
SIC: 7389 Financial services

(P-14446)
UBER TECHNOLOGIES INC (PA)
1515 3rd St, San Francisco (94158-2211)
PHONE...................415 612-8582
Dara Khosrowshahi, *CEO*
Ronald Sugar, *Ch of Bd*
Stacey Speizer, *CEO*
Nelson Chai, *CFO*
Derek Anthony West,
EMP: 9000 **EST:** 2009
SQ FT: 2,500,000
SALES (est): 11.1B **Publicly Held**
WEB: www.uber.com
SIC: 7389 4119 Drive-a-way automobile service; local passenger transportation

(P-14447)
UMBA INC
1714 Stockton St, San Francisco (94133-2930)
PHONE...................914 426-1771
Tiernan Kennedy, *CEO*
EMP: 37 **EST:** 2019
SALES (est): 176.9K **Privately Held**
SIC: 7389 Financial services

(P-14448)
UNITED PARCEL SERVICE INC
Also Called: UPS
3331 Industrial Dr Ste C, Santa Rosa (95403-2062)
PHONE...................678 339-3171
Karen Geerdes, *Manager*
EMP: 61
SALES (corp-wide): 84.6B **Publicly Held**
WEB: www.ups.com
SIC: 7389 Mailing & messenger services
HQ: United Parcel Service, Inc.
55 Glenlake Pkwy
Atlanta GA 30328
404 828-6000

(P-14449)
UNITED PARCEL SERVICE INC
Also Called: UPS
222 Mason St, San Francisco (94102-2115)
PHONE...................415 837-1929
EMP: 61
SALES (corp-wide): 84.6B **Publicly Held**
WEB: www.ups.com
SIC: 7389 Mailing & messenger services
HQ: United Parcel Service, Inc.
55 Glenlake Pkwy
Atlanta GA 30328
404 828-6000

(P-14450)
UNITED PARCEL SERVICE INC
Also Called: UPS
1746 D St, South Lake Tahoe (96150-6227)
PHONE...................800 742-5877
EMP: 61
SALES (corp-wide): 84.6B **Publicly Held**
WEB: www.ups.com
SIC: 7389 Mailing & messenger services
HQ: United Parcel Service, Inc.
55 Glenlake Pkwy
Atlanta GA 30328
404 828-6000

(P-14451)
UNITED PARCEL SERVICE INC
Also Called: UPS
48921 Warm Springs Blvd, Fremont (94539-7767)
PHONE...................800 742-5877
EMP: 61
SALES (corp-wide): 84.6B **Publicly Held**
WEB: www.ups.com
SIC: 7389 Mailing & messenger services
HQ: United Parcel Service, Inc.
55 Glenlake Pkwy
Atlanta GA 30328
404 828-6000

(P-14452)
UNITY COURIER SERVICE INC
1645 Parkway Blvd Ste A, West Sacramento (95691-5052)
PHONE...................916 246-0390
Terry Ragsdale, *Manager*
EMP: 143
SALES (corp-wide): 44.9MM **Privately Held**
WEB: www.unitycourier.com
SIC: 7389 Courier or messenger service
PA: Unity Courier Service, Inc.
3231 Fletcher Dr
Los Angeles CA 90065
323 255-9800

(P-14453)
V3 SYSTEMS SCRTYAUTOMATION INC
4925 Robert J Matthews Pa, El Dorado Hills (95762-5700)
PHONE...................916 543-1543
Adam Watts, *President*
Hilary Touey, *Human Res Mgr*
Sayed Seyar, *Opers Staff*
Ben Billings, *Manager*
Alexis Crayn, *Manager*
EMP: 20 **EST:** 2013
SALES (est): 1.5MM **Privately Held**
WEB: www.v3electric.com
SIC: 7389 5065 3699 Personal service agents, brokers & bureaus; security control equipment & systems; security devices

(P-14454)
VALLEY INVENTORY SERVICE INC
1180 Horizon Dr Ste B, Fairfield (94533-1693)
P.O. Box 503 (94533-0050)
PHONE...................707 422-6050
Jeffrey J Link, *President*
Veronica Link, *President*
Darian Dixon, *Info Tech Dir*
Alice Ballardo, *Opers Mgr*
Michelle Gutierrez, *Manager*
EMP: 61 **EST:** 1970
SALES (est): 4MM **Privately Held**
WEB: www.valleycount.com
SIC: 7389 Inventory computing service

(P-14455)
VISA INC (PA)
900 Metro Center Blvd, Foster City (94404-2775)
P.O. Box 8999, San Francisco (94128-8999)
PHONE...................650 432-3200
Alfred F Kelly Jr, *Ch of Bd*
Ryan McInerney, *President*
Rajat Taneja, *President*
Vasant M Prabhu, *CFO*
Lynne Biggar, *Exec VP*
EMP: 2000 **EST:** 1958
SALES: 24.1B **Publicly Held**
WEB: www.usa.visa.com
SIC: 7389 Credit card service

(P-14456)
VISA TECH & OPERATIONS LLC (DH)
900 Metro Center Blvd, Foster City (94404-2172)
P.O. Box 8999, San Francisco (94128-8999)
PHONE...................650 432-3200
Alfred F Kelly Jr, *CEO*
Una Somerville, *Exec VP*
Mark Crager, *Vice Pres*
Kate Kristensen, *Vice Pres*
Russell Zink, *Vice Pres*
EMP: 217 **EST:** 2000
SALES (est): 523.1MM **Publicly Held**
WEB: www.usa.visa.com
SIC: 7389 Financial services

(PA)=Parent Co (HQ)=Headquarters (DH)=Div Headquarters
✿ = New Business established in last 2 years

7389 - Business Svcs, NEC County (P-14457)

HQ: Visa U.S.A. Inc.
900 Metro Center Blvd
Foster City CA 94404
650 432-3200

(P-14457)
VITAL FARMLAND HOLDINGS LLC
3 Corte Las Casas, Belvedere Tiburon (94920-2012)
PHONE..................................415 465-2400
Craig Wichner, *Mng Member*
EMP: 54 **EST:** 2009
SALES (est): 938.8K Privately Held
WEB: www.farmlandlp.com
SIC: 7389 Financial services

(P-14458)
WALLIS FASHIONS INC
1100 8th Ave, Oakland (94606-3613)
PHONE..................................510 763-8018
Fax: 510 832-6882
EMP: 110
SALES (est): 5.2MM Privately Held
WEB: www.wallisfashions.com
SIC: 7389 Sewing Contractor

(P-14459)
WAVELABS TECHNOLOGIES INC (PA)
691 S Milpitas Blvd # 217, Milpitas (95035-5476)
PHONE..................................408 203-7670
Mansoor Ali Khan, *CEO*
Vineel Nalla,
EMP: 98 **EST:** 2018
SALES (est): 1.1MM Privately Held
SIC: 7389 Personal service agents, brokers & bureaus

(P-14460)
WBE TRAFFIC CONTROL INC
5150 Fair Oaks Blvd Ste 1, Carmichael (95608-5758)
PHONE..................................707 771-5870
Charity Cornet-Barnhart, *CEO*
Rita Reyes-Small, *Opers Staff*
EMP: 53 **EST:** 2018
SALES (est): 4.7MM Privately Held
WEB: www.wbetc.com
SIC: 7389 Flagging service (traffic control)

(P-14461)
WBI INVENTORY SERVICE INC (PA)
Also Called: MSI Inventory Service
7609 Greenback Ln, Citrus Heights (95610-6616)
PHONE..................................916 729-1147
Troy Waller, *President*
Tyler Adams, *Business Mgr*
EMP: 45 **EST:** 1999
SQ FT: 1,300
SALES (est): 1.5MM Privately Held
SIC: 7389 Inventory computing service

(P-14462)
WEST COAST LEGAL SERVICE INC
1925 Winchester Blvd # 20, Campbell (95008-1037)
PHONE..................................408 938-6520
Donald Russi, *President*
Susan Wertz, *Admin Sec*
EMP: 50 **EST:** 1972
SALES (est): 4.6MM Privately Held
WEB: www.westcoastlegal.com
SIC: 7389 Legal & tax services; process serving service

(P-14463)
WORLD OF CHANGE INC
2941 Shadow Brook Ln, Redding (96001-5717)
PHONE..................................352 495-3300
EMP: 40
SALES (est): 1.8MM Privately Held
WEB: www.world-of-change.org
SIC: 7389 Aerial Mapping

(P-14464)
WYRE INC
660 4th St Pmb 462, San Francisco (94107-1618)
PHONE..................................415 374-7356
Michael Dunworth, *CEO*
Javier Caceres, *CFO*
Jonathan Summerton, *Vice Pres*
Marvin Rivera, *Engineer*
Monika Mantri, *Controller*
EMP: 45 **EST:** 2013
SALES (est): 8.1MM Privately Held
WEB: www.sendwyre.com
SIC: 7389 Financial services

(P-14465)
YAPSTONE INC (PA)
Also Called: Rentpayment.com
2121 N Calif Blvd Ste 400, Walnut Creek (94596-7305)
PHONE..................................866 289-5977
Tom Villante, *Ch of Bd*
Kelly Kay, *President*
Bryan Murphy, *President*
Mary Hentges, *CFO*
John Malnar, *CFO*
EMP: 124 **EST:** 1999
SALES (est): 33.4MM Privately Held
WEB: www.yapstone.com
SIC: 7389 Credit card service

(P-14466)
YC CABLE USA INC (HQ)
44061 Nobel Dr, Fremont (94538-3162)
PHONE..................................510 824-2788
Gary Hsu, *President*
KAO Y Fang, *Shareholder*
Jimmy Kuang, *Engineer*
Ronnie Xu, *Engineer*
Bill Haas, *QC Mgr*
▲ **EMP:** 70
SQ FT: 45,000
SALES (est): 23.1MM Privately Held
WEB: www.yccable.com
SIC: 7389 3643 Field audits, cable television; power line cable

(P-14467)
ZOCA ROSEVILLE INC
Also Called: Zocalo
1182 Rsville Pkwy Ste 110, Roseville (95678)
PHONE..................................916 788-0303
Ernesto Jimenez, *President*
EMP: 55
SALES (est): 1MM Privately Held
SIC: 7389 Business services

7513 Truck Rental & Leasing, Without Drivers

(P-14468)
ASHBY LUMBER COMPANY (PA)
Also Called: Ashby Lumber Concord
824 Ashby Ave, Berkeley (94710-2897)
PHONE..................................510 843-4832
Kathleen Brown, *CEO*
Jeffrey O'Hogan, *President*
Arlene Bongiorno, *CFO*
Nadya Cook, *Office Mgr*
Emily Brown, *Info Tech Mgr*
EMP: 55
SQ FT: 10,000
SALES (est): 28.9MM Privately Held
WEB: www.ashbylumber.com
SIC: 5211 5251 7513 Millwork & lumber; wallboard (composition) & paneling; flooring, wood; doors, storm: wood or metal; builders' hardware; tools, hand; tools, power; door locks & lock sets; truck rental & leasing, no drivers

(P-14469)
GLOBAL RENTAL CO INC
Also Called: Global Equipment Rental Co
325 Industrial Way, Dixon (95620-9763)
PHONE..................................707 693-2520
Pete Garcia, *Manager*
EMP: 133
SQ FT: 4,000
SALES (corp-wide): 1.2B Privately Held
WEB: www.globalrental.com
SIC: 7513 Truck rental & leasing, no drivers
HQ: Global Rental Co., Inc.
33 Inverness Center Pkwy # 250
Hoover AL 35242

(P-14470)
LTS RENTALS LLC (PA)
927 Black Diamond Way, Lodi (95240-0738)
P.O. Box 1120 (95241-1120)
PHONE..................................209 334-4100
Dennis Altnow, *Mng Member*
Jim Musgrave, *Exec VP*
Don Altnow,
Danielle Bakey, *Manager*
EMP: 35 **EST:** 1957
SQ FT: 25,000
SALES (est): 27.4MM Privately Held
WEB: www.tigerlines.com
SIC: 7513 4212 Truck rental, without drivers; local trucking, without storage

(P-14471)
MISSION VLY FORD TRCK SLS INC
Also Called: Mission Vly Ford Strlng Trcks
780 E Brokaw Rd, San Jose (95112-1007)
P.O. Box 611150 (95161-1150)
PHONE..................................408 933-2300
Ernest A Speno, *President*
Jeffrey A Speno, *President*
Jeff Speno, *Vice Pres*
Yuliko Hopkins, *Office Mgr*
Christine Werner, *Finance Mgr*
EMP: 80 **EST:** 1986
SQ FT: 90,000
SALES (est): 25.6MM Privately Held
WEB: www.missionvalleyford.com
SIC: 5511 5531 7513 7538 Automobiles, new & used; truck equipment & parts; truck leasing, without drivers; truck rental, without drivers; general truck repair

(P-14472)
PAGE ONE AUTOMOTIVE (PA)
211 S Hill Dr Ste D, Brisbane (94005-1263)
PHONE..................................415 467-1000
Terrance Page, *President*
Melissa Taylor, *CFO*
Chris Williams, *Vice Pres*
Erin Kemp, *General Mgr*
Cheyenne Lewis, *Opers Mgr*
EMP: 39 **EST:** 1993
SALES (est): 5.1MM Privately Held
WEB: www.pageoneauto.com
SIC: 7513 Truck rental & leasing, no drivers

(P-14473)
U HAUL CO OF SACRAMENTO INC (HQ)
Also Called: U-Haul
1650 El Camino Ave, Sacramento (95815-2796)
PHONE..................................916 929-2215
Frank Staudaunras, *President*
Cecilia Owens, *Executive Asst*
EMP: 40 **EST:** 1975
SALES (est): 4MM
SALES (corp-wide): 4.5B Publicly Held
WEB: www.uhaul.com
SIC: 7513 7359 Truck rental & leasing, no drivers; equipment rental & leasing
PA: Amerco
5555 Kietzke Ln Ste 100
Reno NV 89511
775 688-6300

(P-14474)
U-HAUL CO OF CALIFORNIA (DH)
44511 S Grimmer Blvd, Fremont (94538-6309)
PHONE..................................800 528-0463
Dave Adams, *President*
EMP: 150 **EST:** 1971
SALES (est): 152.1MM
SALES (corp-wide): 4.5B Publicly Held
WEB: www.uhaul.com
SIC: 7513 7519 4226 Truck rental & leasing, no drivers; trailer rental; special warehousing & storage
HQ: U-Haul International, Inc.
2727 N Central Ave
Phoenix AZ 85004
602 263-6011

(P-14475)
WINNRESIDENTIAL LTD PARTNR
2350 W Shaw Ave Ste 148, Fresno (93711-3400)
PHONE..................................559 435-3434
EMP: 213
SALES (corp-wide): 52.6MM Privately Held
WEB: www.winncompanies.com
SIC: 7513 Truck rental & leasing, no drivers
PA: Winnresidential Limited Partnership
1 Wshngton Mall Ste 500
Boston MA 02108
617 742-4500

7514 Passenger Car Rental

(P-14476)
ENTERPRISE RENT-A-CAR CO
50 Elmira St, San Francisco (94124-1911)
PHONE..................................415 330-0290
EMP: 37
SALES (corp-wide): 6.8B Privately Held
WEB: www.enterprise.com
SIC: 7514 7359 Passenger car rental; equipment rental & leasing
HQ: Enterprise Rent-A-Car Co Of San Francisco, Llc
2633 Camino Ramon Ste 400
San Ramon CA 94583
925 464-5100

(P-14477)
ENTERPRISE RNT—CAR SAN FRNCSC
Also Called: National Rent A Car
687 Folsom St, San Francisco (94107-1313)
PHONE..................................415 882-9440
Farzaneh Younchi, *Manager*
EMP: 37
SALES (corp-wide): 6.8B Privately Held
WEB: www.enterprise.com
SIC: 7514 Rent-a-car service
HQ: Enterprise Rent-A-Car Co Of San Francisco, Llc
2633 Camino Ramon Ste 400
San Ramon CA 94583
925 464-5100

(P-14478)
ENTERPRISE RNT—CAR SAN FRNCSC
2800 N State St, Ukiah (95482-3028)
PHONE..................................707 462-2200
Carey Bell, *Branch Mgr*
EMP: 37
SALES (corp-wide): 6.8B Privately Held
WEB: www.enterprise.com
SIC: 7514 Passenger car rental
HQ: Enterprise Rent-A-Car Co Of San Francisco, Llc
2633 Camino Ramon Ste 400
San Ramon CA 94583
925 464-5100

(P-14479)
ENTERPRISE RNT—CAR SAN FRNCSC
2940 Hilltop Mall Rd, Richmond (94806-1902)
PHONE..................................510 223-6444
Reggie Venable, *General Mgr*
EMP: 37
SALES (corp-wide): 6.8B Privately Held
WEB: www.enterprise.com
SIC: 7514 Passenger car rental
HQ: Enterprise Rent-A-Car Co Of San Francisco, Llc
2633 Camino Ramon Ste 400
San Ramon CA 94583
925 464-5100

(P-14480)
ENTERPRISE RNT—CAR SAN FRNCSC
3030 Broadway, Oakland (94611-5713)
PHONE..................................510 271-4160
Christine Miller, *Manager*
EMP: 37
SQ FT: 760

PRODUCTS & SERVICES SECTION
7521 - Automobile Parking Lots & Garages County (P-14501)

SALES (corp-wide): 6.8B Privately Held
WEB: www.enterprise.com
SIC: 7514 Passenger car rental
HQ: Enterprise Rent-A-Car Co Of San Francisco, Llc
2633 Camino Ramon Ste 400
San Ramon CA 94583
925 464-5100

(P-14481)
ENTERPRISE RNT—CAR SAN FRNCSC
780 Mcdonnell Rd, San Francisco (94128-3103)
PHONE..................650 697-9200
Charlie Tippett, Branch Mgr
EMP: 37
SALES (corp-wide): 6.8B Privately Held
WEB: www.enterprise.com
SIC: 7514 Passenger car rental
HQ: Enterprise Rent-A-Car Co Of San Francisco, Llc
2633 Camino Ramon Ste 400
San Ramon CA 94583
925 464-5100

(P-14482)
ENTERPRISE RNT—CAR SAN FRNCSC
Also Called: Hertz
1659 Airport Blvd Ste 7, San Jose (95110-1234)
PHONE..................408 450-6000
EMP: 37
SALES (corp-wide): 6.8B Privately Held
WEB: www.enterprise.com
SIC: 7514 Rent-a-car service
HQ: Enterprise Rent-A-Car Co Of San Francisco, Llc
2633 Camino Ramon Ste 400
San Ramon CA 94583
925 464-5100

(P-14483)
ENTERPRISE RNT—CAR SCRMNTO LL
6320 Mcnair Cir, Sacramento (95837-1118)
PHONE..................916 576-3164
Alfred Husary, Manager
EMP: 118
SALES (corp-wide): 6.8B Privately Held
WEB: www.enterprise.com
SIC: 7514 Rent-a-car service
HQ: Enterprise Rent-A-Car Company Of Sacramento, Llc
150 N Sunrise Ave
Roseville CA 95661

(P-14484)
ENTERPRISE RNT—CAR SCRMNTO LL
7034 Rossmore Ln, El Dorado Hills (95762-7126)
PHONE..................916 934-0783
Natalie Boney, Manager
EMP: 118
SALES (corp-wide): 6.8B Privately Held
WEB: www.enterprise.com
SIC: 7514 Rent-a-car service
HQ: Enterprise Rent-A-Car Company Of Sacramento, Llc
150 N Sunrise Ave
Roseville CA 95661

(P-14485)
ENTERPRISE RNT—CAR SCRMNTO LL
3216 Palm St, McClellan (95652-2510)
PHONE..................916 648-1725
Susan M Irwin, Vice Pres
EMP: 118
SALES (corp-wide): 6.8B Privately Held
WEB: www.enterprise.com
SIC: 7514 Rent-a-car service
HQ: Enterprise Rent-A-Car Company Of Sacramento, Llc
150 N Sunrise Ave
Roseville CA 95661

(P-14486)
ENTERPRISE RNT—CAR SCRMNTO LL (DH)
150 N Sunrise Ave, Roseville (95661-2905)
PHONE..................916 787-4500
Pamela Nicholson, President
Susan Irwin, Vice Pres
Bryan Boeldt, Sales Executive
Jon Palsha, Manager
Alexandra Woolley, Manager
▲ EMP: 50 EST: 1989
SALES (est): 113.8MM
SALES (corp-wide): 6.8B Privately Held
WEB: www.enterprise.com
SIC: 7514 5511 Rent-a-car service; automobiles, new & used
HQ: Enterprise Holdings, Inc.
600 Corporate Park Dr
Saint Louis MO 63105
314 512-5000

(P-14487)
ENTERPRISE RNT—CAR SCRMNTO LL
217 E Cypress Ave, Redding (96002-0111)
PHONE..................530 223-0700
Daniel Patrie, Manager
Michael Amundson, Manager
Kenneth Greig, Manager
EMP: 118
SALES (corp-wide): 6.8B Privately Held
WEB: www.enterprise.com
SIC: 7514 Rent-a-car service
HQ: Enterprise Rent-A-Car Company Of Sacramento, Llc
150 N Sunrise Ave
Roseville CA 95661

(P-14488)
FOX RENT A CAR INC
Also Called: Fox Rent-A-Car & Truck
7600 Earhart Rd Ste 9o, Oakland (94621-4558)
PHONE..................408 210-2208
Greta Randev, Manager
EMP: 68
SALES (corp-wide): 7.7MM Privately Held
WEB: www.foxrentacar.com
SIC: 7514 Rent-a-car service
HQ: Fox Rent A Car, Inc.
5500 W Century Blvd
Los Angeles CA 90045

(P-14489)
GETAROUND INC (PA)
55 Green St Fl 4, San Francisco (94111-1412)
PHONE..................866 438-2768
Sam Zaid, CEO
Sylvano Carrasco, Vice Pres
Gaston Kelly, General Mgr
James Schappler, General Mgr
Nick Tenekedes, General Mgr
EMP: 118 EST: 2009
SALES (est): 48.2MM Privately Held
WEB: www.getaround.com
SIC: 7514 Rent-a-car service

(P-14490)
TRACY AUTO LP
Also Called: Tracy Toyota
2895 Naglee Rd, Tracy (95304-7307)
PHONE..................209 834-1111
Keena Turner, Partner
Ronnie Lott, Partner
Miranda Jacinto, Administration
Landon Cotton, Sales Staff
Deborah Pryor-Bruns, Manager
EMP: 68 EST: 1999
SALES (est): 27.6MM Privately Held
WEB: www.tracytoyota.com
SIC: 5511 7514 Automobiles, new & used; rent-a-car service

7515 Passenger Car Leasing

(P-14491)
FORD STORE MORGAN HILL INC
17045 Condit Rd, Morgan Hill (95037-3301)
PHONE..................408 782-8201
Timothy Paulus, President
Alex Garcia, Partner
Ashley Valletta, General Mgr
Marcell Tongco, Finance Mgr
Stephen Ngo, Finance
EMP: 70 EST: 2004
SALES (est): 28.2MM Privately Held
WEB: www.fordstoremorganhill.com
SIC: 5511 5521 Automobiles, new & used; used car dealers; passenger car leasing

(P-14492)
LITHIA MOTORS INC
Also Called: Lithia Ford Mzda Suzuki Fresno
195 E Auto Center Dr, Fresno (93710-5100)
PHONE..................559 435-8400
Ron Kirby, Manager
Dylan Demaio, Technology
Devin Rogers, Finance Mgr
Majerle Gutches, Accountant
Jeff Nock, Sales Mgr
EMP: 150
SALES (corp-wide): 13.1B Publicly Held
WEB: www.quicklane.com
SIC: 5511 7515 5521 7538 Automobiles, new & used; passenger car leasing; used car dealers; general automotive repair shops
PA: Lithia Motors, Inc.
150 N Bartlett St
Medford OR 97501
541 776-6401

(P-14493)
NICHOLAS K CORPORATION
Also Called: Ford Store San Leandro
1111 Marina Blvd, San Leandro (94577-3364)
PHONE..................510 352-2000
Robert Knezevich, CEO
Wahid Khawja, General Mgr
Esko Ashraf, Finance Dir
Ron Delapaz, Finance Mgr
Tomasz Kaliski, Finance Mgr
EMP: 109 EST: 1954
SQ FT: 60,000
SALES (est): 70.5MM Privately Held
WEB: www.lincoln.com
SIC: 5511 7515 Automobiles, new & used; pickups, new & used; passenger car leasing

(P-14494)
NIELLO IMPORTS
Also Called: Niello Acura Porsche
150 Automall Dr, Roseville (95661-3031)
PHONE..................916 334-6300
EMP: 100 EST: 1969
SQ FT: 32,000
SALES (est): 37.3MM Privately Held
SIC: 5511 7515 Ret New & Used Autos

(P-14495)
TED STEVENS INC
Also Called: Marin Acura
5860 Paradise Dr, Corte Madera (94925-1203)
P.O. Box 218 (94976-0218)
PHONE..................415 927-5664
Theodore Stevens, President
Debi Stevens-Byrnes, General Mgr
Kristin Fenn, Administration
Jean-Pierre Kabbara, Finance Dir
Jacki Carey, Accountant
EMP: 101 EST: 1985
SALES (est): 35.3MM Privately Held
WEB: www.marinacura.com
SIC: 5511 7515 Automobiles, new & used; pickups, new & used; trucks, tractors & trailers: new & used; vans, new & used; passenger car leasing

(P-14496)
WESTRUP-SADLER INC
Also Called: Reliable Pntiac Cdllac Bick GM
400 Automall Dr, Roseville (95661-3020)
PHONE..................916 783-2077
Bruce W Westrup, President
Joy H Westrup, Corp Secy
David Klein, Parts Mgr
EMP: 75 EST: 1969
SQ FT: 41,000
SALES (est): 2.7MM Privately Held
WEB: www.gm.com
SIC: 5511 7515 Automobiles, new & used; trucks, tractors & trailers: new & used; passenger car leasing

7521 Automobile Parking Lots & Garages

(P-14497)
ABM INDUSTRY GROUPS LLC
414 J St, Sacramento (95814-2311)
P.O. Box 915 (95812-0915)
PHONE..................916 443-9094
Joe Riney, Manager
Michael Nghiem, Site Mgr
Rey Agustin, Sales Executive
EMP: 36
SALES (corp-wide): 5.9B Publicly Held
WEB: www.abm.com
SIC: 7521 Parking lots
HQ: Abm Industry Groups, Llc
14141 Southwest Fwy # 477
Sugar Land TX 77478
855 226-3676

(P-14498)
ACE PARKING MANAGEMENT INC
1901 Harrison St Ste 102, Oakland (94612-3589)
PHONE..................510 589-2313
EMP: 53
SALES (corp-wide): 257.4MM Privately Held
WEB: www.aceparking.com
SIC: 7521 Parking lots
PA: Ace Parking Management, Inc.
645 Ash St
San Diego CA 92101
619 233-6624

(P-14499)
ACE PARKING MANAGEMENT INC
235 Montgomery St Lbby, San Francisco (94104-2912)
PHONE..................415 398-1900
Matt Griesheimer, Principal
Douglas Sherwood, Principal
Ronald Gonzalez, Area Mgr
EMP: 53
SALES (corp-wide): 257.4MM Privately Held
WEB: www.aceparking.com
SIC: 7521 Parking lots
PA: Ace Parking Management, Inc.
645 Ash St
San Diego CA 92101
619 233-6624

(P-14500)
ACE PARKING MANAGEMENT INC
900 13th St, Sacramento (95814-2924)
PHONE..................916 497-0222
EMP: 53
SALES (corp-wide): 257.4MM Privately Held
WEB: www.aceparking.com
SIC: 7521 Parking lots
PA: Ace Parking Management, Inc.
645 Ash St
San Diego CA 92101
619 233-6624

(P-14501)
ACE PARKING MANAGEMENT INC
1330 Broadway Ste 915, Oakland (94612-2503)
PHONE..................510 251-0509
EMP: 53
SALES (corp-wide): 257.4MM Privately Held
WEB: www.aceparking.com
SIC: 7521 Parking lots
PA: Ace Parking Management, Inc.
645 Ash St
San Diego CA 92101
619 233-6624

7521 - Automobile Parking Lots & Garages County (P-14502)

(P-14502)
ACE PARKING MANAGEMENT INC
415 Taylor St, San Francisco (94102-1701)
PHONE..................................415 749-1949
Tom Abdul, *Owner*
EMP: 53
SALES (corp-wide): 257.4MM **Privately Held**
WEB: www.aceparking.com
SIC: 7521 Parking lots
PA: Ace Parking Management, Inc.
   645 Ash St
   San Diego CA 92101
   619 233-6624

(P-14503)
ACE PARKING MANAGEMENT INC
1776 Sacramento St, San Francisco (94109-3685)
PHONE..................................415 674-1799
Kavarian Charles, *Branch Mgr*
EMP: 53
SALES (corp-wide): 257.4MM **Privately Held**
WEB: www.aceparking.com
SIC: 7521 Parking lots
PA: Ace Parking Management, Inc.
   645 Ash St
   San Diego CA 92101
   619 233-6624

(P-14504)
ACE PARKING MANAGEMENT INC
2050 Gateway Pl, San Jose (95110-1011)
PHONE..................................408 437-2185
Gregory V Wolcott, *Administration*
EMP: 53
SALES (corp-wide): 257.4MM **Privately Held**
WEB: www.aceparking.com
SIC: 7521 Parking lots
PA: Ace Parking Management, Inc.
   645 Ash St
   San Diego CA 92101
   619 233-6624

(P-14505)
ACE PARKING MANAGEMENT INC
350 Bush St, San Francisco (94104-2804)
PHONE..................................415 421-8800
EMP: 53
SALES (corp-wide): 257.4MM **Privately Held**
WEB: www.aceparking.com
SIC: 7521 Parking lots
PA: Ace Parking Management, Inc.
   645 Ash St
   San Diego CA 92101
   619 233-6624

(P-14506)
ACE PARKING MANAGEMENT INC
2185 N Calif Blvd Ste 212, Walnut Creek (94596-3566)
PHONE..................................925 295-3283
Greg Kibizoff, *Principal*
EMP: 53
SALES (corp-wide): 257.4MM **Privately Held**
WEB: www.aceparking.com
SIC: 7521 Parking lots
PA: Ace Parking Management, Inc.
   645 Ash St
   San Diego CA 92101
   619 233-6624

(P-14507)
AIRPORT PARKING SERVICE INC
Also Called: Skypark
630 N San Mateo Dr, San Mateo (94401-2328)
PHONE..................................650 875-6655
Kim Kasser, *President*
Joseph Galligan, *Ch of Bd*
Helen Galligan, *Admin Sec*
Shirley Krouse, *Admin Sec*
Susan D Porto, *Cust Mgr*
EMP: 75 EST: 1987
SALES (est): 9.7MM **Privately Held**
WEB: www.skypark.com
SIC: 7521 Parking lots

(P-14508)
ANZA PARKING CORPORATION
Also Called: Anza Park & Sky
615 Airport Blvd, Burlingame (94010-1913)
PHONE..................................650 348-8800
Jonathan Wu, *President*
Amy Chung, *Vice Pres*
Kevin Huang, *General Mgr*
EMP: 40 EST: 1993
SALES (est): 3.1MM **Privately Held**
WEB: www.anzaparking.com
SIC: 7521 Parking lots; parking structure

(P-14509)
CENTRAL PARKING CORPORATION
1624 Franklin St Ste 722, Oakland (94612-2823)
PHONE..................................510 832-7227
EMP: 100
SALES (corp-wide): 1.5B **Publicly Held**
SIC: 7521 Automobile Parking
HQ: Central Parking Corporation
   507 Mainstream Dr
   Nashville TN 37228
   615 297-4255

(P-14510)
CENTRAL PARKING SYSTEM INC
716 10th St Ste 101, Sacramento (95814-1807)
PHONE..................................916 441-1074
EMP: 60
SALES (corp-wide): 1.5B **Publicly Held**
SIC: 7521 Automobile Parking Management Services
HQ: Central Parking System, Inc.
   1225 I St Nw Ste C100
   Washington DC 20005
   202 496-9650

(P-14511)
CLASSIC PARKING INC
34 S Autumn St, San Jose (95110-2513)
P.O. Box 720781 (95172-0781)
PHONE..................................408 278-1444
Richard Flores, *CFO*
EMP: 690 **Privately Held**
WEB: www.classicparking.com
SIC: 7521 Parking garage
PA: Classic Parking, Inc.
   3208 Royal St
   Los Angeles CA 90007

(P-14512)
HARSCH INVESTMENT REALTY LLC
Downtown Center Garage
325 Mason St, San Francisco (94102-1709)
PHONE..................................415 673-6757
Benny Hunag, *Systems Mgr*
EMP: 37
SALES (corp-wide): 115.1MM **Privately Held**
WEB: www.harsch.com
SIC: 7521 Parking garage
PA: Harsch Investment Realty, Llc
   1121 Sw Salmon St Ste 500
   Portland OR 97205
   503 242-2900

(P-14513)
IMPERIAL PARKING (US) LLC
Also Called: City Park
1740 Cesar Chavez Fl 2, San Francisco (94124-1134)
PHONE..................................415 495-3909
Tim Leonoudakis, *Branch Mgr*
Edgar Matias, *Supervisor*
EMP: 650
SALES (corp-wide): 1.7B **Privately Held**
WEB: www.impark.com
SIC: 7521 Parking lots; parking garage
HQ: Imperial Parking (U.S.), Llc
   216 Haddon Ave Ste 400
   Haddon Township NJ 08108

(P-14514)
PACIFIC PARK MANAGEMENT INC
989 Franklin St, Oakland (94607-4470)
PHONE..................................510 836-7730
EMP: 85 **Privately Held**
WEB: www.pacificparkonline.com
SIC: 7521 Parking lots
PA: Pacific Park Management Inc
   311 California St Ste 310
   San Francisco CA 94104

(P-14515)
PARK N FLY LLC
101 Terminal Ct, South San Francisco (94080-6508)
PHONE..................................650 877-8438
Elise Rames, *Branch Mgr*
EMP: 37
SQ FT: 200
SALES (corp-wide): 3.3MM **Privately Held**
WEB: www.pnf.com
SIC: 7521 Parking lots
HQ: Park 'n Fly, Llc.
   2060 Mount Paran Rd Nw # 207
   Atlanta GA 30327
   404 264-1000

7532 Top, Body & Upholstery Repair & Paint Shops

(P-14516)
AHO ENTERPRISES INC
Also Called: Superior Body Shop
956 Bransten Rd, San Carlos (94070-4029)
PHONE..................................650 593-1019
Issa Aho, *President*
Frank Perez, *General Mgr*
EMP: 44 EST: 1986
SQ FT: 35,000
SALES (est): 2.9MM **Privately Held**
SIC: 7532 7538 Body shop, automotive; paint shop, automotive; general automotive repair shops

(P-14517)
ANTHONYS AUTO CRAFT INC (PA)
111 Verdi St, San Rafael (94901-4714)
PHONE..................................415 456-7591
Roy Carnevale, *President*
Diana Carnevale, *Corp Secy*
Jean-Pierre Saint-Louis, *Technician*
EMP: 56 EST: 1968
SALES (est): 3.6MM **Privately Held**
WEB: www.anthonysautocraft.com
SIC: 7532 Body shop, automotive; paint shop, automotive

(P-14518)
ART HILD BODY AND FRAME INC
Also Called: Hild Collision Center
1579 E Cypress Ave, Redding (96002-1322)
PHONE..................................530 222-6828
Carl Hild, *President*
Kevin Hanaoka, *Executive*
Steve Fuller, *Consultant*
Tyler Hild, *Consultant*
Duane Pierce, *Consultant*
EMP: 45 EST: 1957
SQ FT: 4,200 **Privately Held**
WEB: www.hildcollisioncenter.com
SIC: 7532 Body shop, automotive

(P-14519)
AUTOWEST COLLISION REPAIRS INC
1729 Junction Ave, San Jose (95112-1010)
PHONE..................................408 392-1200
Bobby Ali, *President*
Tammee Magahiz, *Office Mgr*
Keri Christie, *Admin Sec*
Emily Nguyen, *Accountant*
Richard Theobald, *Accounts Mgr*
EMP: 37 EST: 1987
SQ FT: 28,000
SALES (est): 6MM **Privately Held**
WEB: www.awcollision.com
SIC: 7532 Collision shops, automotive; lettering & painting services; exterior repair services

(P-14520)
B & J BODY SHOP INC (PA)
11000 Folsom Blvd, Rancho Cordova (95670-6102)
PHONE..................................916 635-4400
Richard Johnson, *President*
Steven Messner, *Vice Pres*
Sonja Warner, *Supervisor*
EMP: 39 EST: 1975
SQ FT: 15,000
SALES (est): 3MM **Privately Held**
WEB: www.bjbody.com
SIC: 7532 Body shop, automotive; paint shop, automotive

(P-14521)
CALIBER BODYWORKS TEXAS INC
Also Called: Caliber Collision Centers
3517 Hillcap Ave, San Jose (95136-1391)
PHONE..................................408 972-0300
Abel Silva, *Branch Mgr*
EMP: 100
SALES (corp-wide): 824.4MM **Privately Held**
WEB: www.calibercollision.com
SIC: 7532 Body shop, automotive
PA: Caliber Bodyworks Of Texas, Inc.
   2941 Lake Vista Dr
   Lewisville TX 75067
   469 948-9500

(P-14522)
CALIBER BODYWORKS TEXAS INC
Also Called: Calliber Collision
125 E Auto Center Dr, Fresno (93710-5100)
PHONE..................................559 435-9900
Sterling Killoin, *Manager*
EMP: 47
SALES (corp-wide): 824.4MM **Privately Held**
WEB: www.calibercollision.com
SIC: 7532 Body shop, automotive
PA: Caliber Bodyworks Of Texas, Inc.
   2941 Lake Vista Dr
   Lewisville TX 75067
   469 948-9500

(P-14523)
CANEPA GROUP INC
Also Called: Canepa Design
4900 Scotts Valley Dr, Scotts Valley (95066-4208)
PHONE..................................831 430-9940
Bruce Canapa, *CEO*
Candace Ebert, *Business Mgr*
▲ EMP: 41 EST: 2011
SALES (est): 7MM **Privately Held**
WEB: www.canepa.com
SIC: 7532 Antique & classic automobile restoration

(P-14524)
DENHAM SJ INC (PA)
772 N Market St, Redding (96003-3606)
P.O. Box 990326 (96099-0326)
PHONE..................................530 241-1756
Randy Denham, *President*
Denise Denham, *Corp Secy*
Ryan Denham, *Vice Pres*
Erin Brown, *Administration*
Michael Feehan, *CIO*
EMP: 38 EST: 1937
SQ FT: 7,500
SALES (est): 25.2MM **Privately Held**
WEB: www.sjdenhamcollision.com
SIC: 5511 7532 Automobiles, new & used; collision shops, automotive

(P-14525)
GERMAN MOTORS CORPORATION (PA)
Also Called: BMW of San Francisco
1675 Howard St, San Francisco (94103-2526)
PHONE..................................415 590-3773
Henry Schmitt, *CEO*

▲ = Import ▼ = Export
◆ = Import/Export

PRODUCTS & SERVICES SECTION
7538 - General Automotive Repair Shop County (P-14548)

Michael Greening, *Corp Secy*
Ralph Macia, *Vice Pres*
Michele Schmitt, *Vice Pres*
Eric Schmitt, *General Mgr*
▲ **EMP:** 239 **EST:** 1964
SQ FT: 112,000
SALES (est): 109.2MM **Privately Held**
WEB: www.sfgermanmotors.com
SIC: 5511 7532 Automobiles, new & used; top & body repair & paint shops

(P-14526)
HAYES FAMILY ENTERPRISES INC
Also Called: Hayes Brothers Collision
9141 Elkmont Dr, Elk Grove (95624-9706)
PHONE 916 686-8454
Ron Chase, *Manager*
EMP: 58
SALES (corp-wide): 4.9MM **Privately Held**
WEB: www.hayesbrothers.net
SIC: 7532 Body shop, automotive
PA: Hayes Family Enterprises, Inc.
925 Tuscan Ln
Sacramento CA 95864
916 456-3368

(P-14527)
KENYON CONSTRUCTION INC
364 Bellevue Ave, Santa Rosa (95407-7711)
PHONE 707 528-1906
Michael Bray, *Manager*
EMP: 55
SALES (corp-wide): 88.1MM **Privately Held**
WEB: www.kenyonweb.com
SIC: 7532 Exterior repair services
PA: Kenyon Construction, Inc.
4001 W Indian School Rd
Phoenix AZ 85019
602 484-0080

(P-14528)
KRAFTS BODY SHOP
6100 Soquel Ave, Santa Cruz (95062-1948)
PHONE 831 476-2440
Daniel R Kraft, *President*
Janice D Kraft, *Vice Pres*
EMP: 36 **EST:** 1964
SALES (est): 5.2MM **Privately Held**
WEB: www.kraftsbodyshop.com
SIC: 7532 Body shop, automotive

(P-14529)
L J INC
Also Called: Francis Classic Cars
2420 E Mckinley Ave, Fresno (93703-3009)
PHONE 559 485-1413
Jeff Francis, *President*
EMP: 40 **EST:** 1981
SQ FT: 1,000
SALES (est): 6.6MM **Privately Held**
WEB: www.franciscollision.com
SIC: 7532 5531 Body shop, automotive; automotive accessories

(P-14530)
MIKE ROSES AUTO BODY INC (PA)
Also Called: Mikes Auto Body
2260 Via De Mercados, Concord (94520-4920)
PHONE 925 689-1739
Michael Rose, *President*
Ragen Rose, *CFO*
Rick Rehm, *Manager*
John Crosthwaite, *Parts Mgr*
EMP: 35 **EST:** 1972
SQ FT: 20,000
SALES (est): 11.6MM **Privately Held**
WEB: www.mikesautobody.com
SIC: 7532 Body shop, automotive; paint shop, automotive

(P-14531)
PAN AMERICAN BODY SHOP INC (PA)
555 Burke Ln, San Jose (95112-4102)
PHONE 408 289-8745
Melchor Louis Alonso Jr, *President*
Melchor Alonso Sr, *Treasurer*
Gayle Alonso, *Admin Sec*

Melissa Leaman,
Will Galeas, *Parts Mgr*
EMP: 36 **EST:** 1980
SQ FT: 32,000
SALES (est): 9.9MM **Privately Held**
WEB: www.pabody.com
SIC: 7532 Collision shops, automotive; body shop, automotive

(P-14532)
SHING TAI CORPORATION
Also Called: Carrera Auto Body
1160 Battery St, San Francisco (94111-1213)
PHONE 415 986-2944
Jim Tsai, *President*
EMP: 44 **EST:** 1997
SALES (est): 1.6MM **Privately Held**
SIC: 7532 Body shop, automotive

(P-14533)
SOLANO COLLISION INC
3267 Sonoma Blvd, Vallejo (94590-2911)
PHONE 707 644-4044
Tom Canavesio, *President*
Cathy Cerin, *Vice Pres*
EMP: 40 **EST:** 1974
SQ FT: 28,000
SALES (est): 3MM **Privately Held**
WEB: www.calibercollision.com
SIC: 7532 Body shop, automotive

(P-14534)
SPORTSMOBILE WEST
3631 S Bagley Ave, Fresno (93725-2441)
PHONE 559 233-8267
Alan Feld, *President*
Liz Feld, *Vice Pres*
Brian Furrow, *Sales Staff*
▲ **EMP:** 49 **EST:** 1989
SQ FT: 60,000
SALES (est): 7.2MM **Privately Held**
WEB: www.sportsmobile.com
SIC: 7532 3792 3716 Van conversion; travel trailers & campers; motor homes

(P-14535)
STYMEIST AUTO BODY INC
Also Called: Steve Stymeist Auto Bdy & Pntg
3948 State Highway 49, Placerville (95667-6320)
PHONE 530 622-7588
Steve Stymeist, *Owner*
Rod Emmons, *Director*
Rich Demarco, *Manager*
EMP: 38 **EST:** 1986
SQ FT: 13,000
SALES (est): 2.8MM **Privately Held**
WEB: www.stymeistautobody.com
SIC: 7532 7539 Body shop, automotive; paint shop, automotive; frame repair shops, automotive

(P-14536)
TGIF BODY SHOP INC
4595 Enterprise St, Fremont (94538-7605)
PHONE 510 490-1342
Richard W Mello, *CEO*
Kathy Mello, *Vice Pres*
EMP: 30 **EST:** 1980
SQ FT: 20,000
SALES (est): 1.1MM **Privately Held**
WEB: www.tgifauto.com
SIC: 7532 3479 Body shop, automotive; coating of metals & formed products

7534 Tire Retreading & Repair Shops

(P-14537)
AAA SIGNS INC
Also Called: Total Tire Recycling
1834 Auburn Blvd, Sacramento (95815-1908)
PHONE 916 568-3456
Gary Matranga, *President*
Danny L Matranga, *Officer*
Steve Horrell, *Sales Associate*
Steve Horell, *Sales Staff*
EMP: 54 **EST:** 1973

SALES (est): 4.9MM **Privately Held**
WEB: www.aaacraneservice.com
SIC: 7534 Tire retreading & repair shops; cranes & aerial lift equipment, rental or leasing

(P-14538)
NEW PRIDE CORPORATION
333 Hegenberger Rd # 307, Oakland (94621-1420)
PHONE 636 937-5200
EMP: 37 **Privately Held**
SIC: 7534 Tire Retreading/Repair
HQ: New Pride Tire, Inc.
333 Hegenberger Rd # 705
Oakland CA 94621
510 567-8800

(P-14539)
RUBBER DUST INC (PA)
Also Called: J & O'S Commercial Tire Center
533 S 13th St, Richmond (94804-3702)
PHONE 510 237-6344
Charlie T Talbot, *CEO*
John A Talbot, *President*
Bonnie Talbot, *Corp Secy*
Edward Talbot, *Vice Pres*
▼ **EMP:** 38 **EST:** 1969
SQ FT: 40,000
SALES (est): 8.2MM **Privately Held**
SIC: 7534 7538 Tire repair shop; general automotive repair shops

7537 Automotive Transmission Repair Shops

(P-14540)
INTERNTNAL TRQUE CNVERTERS INC
Also Called: I T C
712 N Abby St, Fresno (93701-1051)
PHONE 559 266-7471
Raffi Hagi Pilavian, *CEO*
EMP: 38 **EST:** 1975
SQ FT: 3,000
SALES (est): 2.2MM **Privately Held**
WEB: www.itcfresno.com
SIC: 7537 5013 Automotive transmission repair shops; automotive supplies & parts

(P-14541)
PDQ AUTOMATIC TRANSM PARTS INC
8380 Tiogawoods Dr, Sacramento (95828-5048)
PHONE 916 681-7701
John G Hicks Jr, *President*
John Hicks Sr, *Treasurer*
Tracy Hicks, *Vice Pres*
Amy Hicks, *Admin Sec*
▲ **EMP:** 62 **EST:** 1971
SQ FT: 33,600
SALES (est): 8.7MM **Privately Held**
WEB: www.pdqparts.com
SIC: 7537 Automotive transmission repair shops

(P-14542)
SLAUSON TRANSMISSION PARTS
9675 Oconnell Rd, Sebastopol (95472-9621)
PHONE 310 768-2099
Kirk Wilson, *President*
Malcolm Bader, *Vice Pres*
▲ **EMP:** 35 **EST:** 1963
SALES (est): 1.1MM **Privately Held**
WEB: www.slauson-transmissionparts.com
SIC: 7537 Automotive transmission repair shops

7538 General Automotive Repair Shop

(P-14543)
AANW INC
Also Called: Bay Area Airstream Adventures
2400 Cordelia Rd, Fairfield (94534-4218)
PHONE 707 428-1623
Theodore Davis, *President*
Eric Winston, *CFO*

Steve Perry, *General Mgr*
Tim Levake, *Technician*
Brian Crayne, *Sales Mgr*
EMP: 43 **EST:** 2013
SALES (est): 6.5MM
SALES (corp-wide): 28.6MM **Privately Held**
WEB: www.bayareaairstream.com
SIC: 5561 7538 Recreational vehicle dealers; recreational vehicle parts & accessories; recreational vehicle repairs
PA: Aanw Holdings, Llc
16250 Se Evelyn St
Clackamas OR 97015
503 882-2647

(P-14544)
ALBANY FORD INC (PA)
Also Called: Albany Subaru
718 San Pablo Ave, Albany (94706-1131)
PHONE 510 528-1244
John Nakamura, *President*
Laurie Bush, *CFO*
Janice Isaac, *Regional Mgr*
Donald Val Strough, *Admin Sec*
Darcie Roderick, *Finance Mgr*
EMP: 60 **EST:** 1990
SQ FT: 20,000
SALES (est): 27.8MM **Privately Held**
WEB: www.ford.com
SIC: 5511 7538 Automobiles, new & used; general automotive repair shops

(P-14545)
ALIGNTECH
2820 Orchard Pkwy, San Jose (95134-2019)
PHONE 714 605-7114
EMP: 43 **EST:** 2004
SALES (est): 407.8K **Privately Held**
SIC: 7538 General truck repair

(P-14546)
AUBURN ASSOCIATES INC
Also Called: Auburn Honda
1801 Grass Valley Hwy, Auburn (95603-2853)
P.O. Box 5460 (95604-5460)
PHONE 530 823-7234
Jay Cooper, *President*
Tom Cline, *General Mgr*
David Jones, *General Mgr*
Connie Shumway, *Office Mgr*
Leanne Marshall, *Administration*
EMP: 70 **EST:** 1979
SQ FT: 38,000
SALES (est): 20.6MM **Privately Held**
WEB: www.honda.com
SIC: 5511 7538 5531 Automobiles, new & used; general automotive repair shops; automotive parts

(P-14547)
BAE SYSTEMS SRRA DTROIT DESL A (HQ)
1755 Adams Ave, San Leandro (94577-1001)
PHONE 510 635-8991
Cindy Bergstrom, *President*
Wade Sperry, *Vice Pres*
EMP: 95 **EST:** 1982
SQ FT: 45,000
SALES (est): 14.5MM
SALES (corp-wide): 137.7MM **Privately Held**
WEB: www.valleypowersystems.com
SIC: 7538 5084 5085 Diesel engine repair: automotive; engines & parts, diesel; industrial supplies
PA: Bae Systems Resolution Inc.
1000 La St Ste 4950
Houston TX 77002
713 868-7700

(P-14548)
BERBERIAN BROS INC
Also Called: Volvo
3755 West Ln, Stockton (95204-2431)
P.O. Box 8790 (95208-0790)
PHONE 209 944-5514
Brian Marricci, *Manager*
Christina Cochran, *Admin Asst*
Tuyet Tran, *Finance Mgr*
Denisa N Hammond,
Bryan Martucci, *Manager*
EMP: 62

7538 - General Automotive Repair Shop County (P-14549)

SALES (corp-wide): 14.1MM **Privately Held**
WEB: www.volvocars.com
SIC: 5511 7538 Automobiles, new & used; engine repair
PA: Berberian Bros., Inc.
    5200 N Palm Ave Ste 203
    Fresno CA 93704
    559 230-0134

(P-14549)
BIG VALLEY FORD INC
Also Called: Quick Lane
3282 Auto Center Cir, Stockton (95212-2836)
P.O. Box 690398 (95269-0398)
PHONE 209 870-4400
Paul Joseph Umdenstock, *President*
Darlene Gibbons, *Corp Secy*
Paul Umdenstock, *Executive*
Joan Detmering, *Office Mgr*
Jesus Ambriz, *Sales Mgr*
EMP: 150 **EST:** 1982
SQ FT: 10,000
SALES (est): 53.1MM **Privately Held**
WEB: www.bigvalleyford.biz
SIC: 5511 7538 Automobiles, new & used; general automotive repair shops

(P-14550)
BRIDGESTONE AMERICAS
Also Called: GCR Tires & Service 853
4575 Pacheco Blvd, Martinez (94553-2233)
PHONE 925 372-9056
David Schembri, *Manager*
EMP: 72 **Privately Held**
WEB: www.bridgestoneamericas.com
SIC: 5531 7538 Automotive tires; general truck repair
HQ: Bridgestone Americas Tire Operations, Llc
    200 4th Ave S Ste 100
    Nashville TN 37201
    615 937-1000

(P-14551)
CARONS SERVICE CENTER INC
Also Called: Caron's Auto Supply
4301 Castleglen Way, Fair Oaks (95628-6729)
PHONE 916 444-3713
EMP: 15
SALES: 100K **Privately Held**
SIC: 7538 5013 5531 3599 General Auto Repair

(P-14552)
CENTRAL VALLEY GMC (PA)
Also Called: Affinity Truck Center
2707 S East Ave, Fresno (93725-1906)
P.O. Box 1188 (93715-1188)
PHONE 559 334-3496
Douglas L Howard, *CEO*
Gary Howard, *President*
James Pollack, *Vice Pres*
Bob Blanchard, *Technician*
Kent Pollack, *Finance Mgr*
EMP: 58 **EST:** 1978
SQ FT: 30,000
SALES (est): 35.2MM **Privately Held**
WEB: www.affinitytruck.com
SIC: 5511 5531 7538 Automobiles, new & used; truck equipment & parts; general truck repair

(P-14553)
CENTRAL VALLEY TRLR REPR INC
Also Called: Cvtr
2974 S East Ave, Fresno (93725-1911)
P.O. Box 12427 (93777-2427)
PHONE 559 233-8444
Michael L Shuemake, *President*
Christine Shuemake, *CFO*
Lou Shuemake, *Vice Pres*
Lance Brodie, *Finance Mgr*
Leslie Lantis, *Finance*
EMP: 80
SQ FT: 24,000
SALES (est): 40.9MM **Privately Held**
WEB: www.cvtr.com
SIC: 5511 7538 7539 5531 Trucks, tractors & trailers: new & used; general truck repair; trailer repair; truck equipment & parts

(P-14554)
CHASE CHEVROLET CO INC
Also Called: Chase Chvrlet Chevy Trck World
6441 Holman Rd, Stockton (95212-2703)
P.O. Box 8349 (95208-0349)
PHONE 209 475-6600
John W Chase, *President*
Cesar Villa, *Partner*
Ron Bearian, *Vice Pres*
Alex Robinson, *Department Mgr*
Amy Clark, *Controller*
EMP: 100 **EST:** 1944
SALES (est): 42.2MM **Privately Held**
WEB: www.chasechevrolet.com
SIC: 5511 5531 7538 5521 Automobiles, new & used; automotive parts; general automotive repair shops; used car dealers

(P-14555)
COURTESY MOTORS AUTO CTR INC
Also Called: Volvo
2520 Cohasset Rd, Chico (95973-1399)
PHONE 530 345-9444
Ron Faria, *President*
Stephen W Wade, *CEO*
John Bishop, *General Mgr*
Lois Phelps, *Business Mgr*
Bill Magnotta, *Sales Staff*
EMP: 100 **EST:** 1975
SQ FT: 30,000
SALES (est): 33.3MM **Privately Held**
WEB: www.chicocourtesy.com
SIC: 5511 7538 7532 Automobiles, new & used; general automotive repair shops; top & body repair & paint shops

(P-14556)
D O NERONDE INC
Also Called: Grass Valley Nissan
1650 Grass Valley Hwy, Auburn (95603-2855)
PHONE 530 823-6591
Donald O Neronde Sr, *President*
Donald Neronde Jr, *Admin Sec*
EMP: 54 **EST:** 1978
SALES (est): 5.8MM **Privately Held**
WEB: www.lincoln.com
SIC: 5511 7538 5531 Automobiles, new & used; general automotive repair shops; automotive parts

(P-14557)
DIAMOND SALES & SERVICES INC
1505 N 4th St, San Jose (95112-4607)
P.O. Box 5879 (95150-5879)
PHONE 408 263-8997
Armand Kunde, *President*
Mary Hughes, *Vice Pres*
Mike Kunde, *Vice Pres*
EMP: 36 **EST:** 1967
SQ FT: 7,500
SALES (est): 1.1MM **Privately Held**
WEB: www.diamondsales.com
SIC: 7538 5511 General truck repair; trucks, tractors & trailers: new & used

(P-14558)
DUBLIN VOLKSWAGEN
6085 Scarlett Ct, Dublin (94568-3102)
P.O. Box 9099, San Jose (95157-0099)
PHONE 925 829-0800
Craig Perry, *General Mgr*
EMP: 75 **EST:** 1997
SQ FT: 22,161
SALES (est): 20.1MM
SALES (corp-wide): 9.7B **Publicly Held**
WEB: www.dublinvolkswagen.com
SIC: 5511 7538 Automobiles, new & used; general automotive repair shops
PA: Sonic Automotive, Inc.
    4401 Colwick Rd
    Charlotte NC 28211
    704 566-2400

(P-14559)
ELM FORD INC (PA)
Also Called: Elm Ford
346 Main St, Woodland (95695-3205)
PHONE 530 662-2817
E B Landis, *President*
William E Landis Sr, *President*
John Thornburg, *Sales Associate*
EMP: 36 **EST:** 1946

SQ FT: 18,000
SALES (est): 19MM **Privately Held**
WEB: www.ford.com
SIC: 5511 7538 5531 Automobiles, new & used; general automotive repair shops; automotive parts

(P-14560)
ENVIRNMENTAL TRNSP SPECIALISTS
Also Called: University Honda
4343 Chiles Rd, Davis (95618-4342)
PHONE 916 442-4971
Douglas Malinoff, *President*
Tami Anderson, *Sales Staff*
Tevin Schindler, *Sales Staff*
Jeff Schindler, *Manager*
Kirk Theis, *Parts Mgr*
EMP: 63 **EST:** 1978
SQ FT: 21,000
SALES (est): 12.4MM **Privately Held**
WEB: www.shottenkirkdavishonda.com
SIC: 5511 7538 5531 Automobiles, new & used; general automotive repair shops; automotive parts

(P-14561)
ESPARZA INC
Also Called: Firestone
1500 Sycamore Ave, Atwater (95301-3944)
PHONE 209 358-4944
Henry Esparza Sr, *President*
Jennie Esparza, *Corp Secy*
Byron Davidson, *Manager*
EMP: 48 **EST:** 1979
SQ FT: 3,000
SALES (est): 4.8MM **Privately Held**
WEB: www.bridgestoneamericas.com
SIC: 5531 7538 5411 Automotive tires; general automotive repair shops; convenience stores, independent

(P-14562)
FAA CONCORD T INC
Also Called: Concord Toyota
1090 Concord Ave, Concord (94520-5601)
PHONE 925 682-7131
Thomas A Price, *President*
W Bruce Bercovich, *Admin Sec*
Barry Collins, *Technician*
Vanessa Wenneker, *Technician*
Shawn White, *Technician*
EMP: 85 **EST:** 1970
SQ FT: 25,000
SALES (est): 29.5MM
SALES (corp-wide): 9.7B **Publicly Held**
WEB: www.concordtoyota.com
SIC: 5511 7538 5531 5521 Automobiles, new & used; general automotive repair shops; automotive & home supply stores; used car dealers
PA: Sonic Automotive, Inc.
    4401 Colwick Rd
    Charlotte NC 28211
    704 566-2400

(P-14563)
FLT INC
Also Called: Folsom Lake Toyota
12747 Folsom Blvd, Folsom (95630-8097)
PHONE 916 355-1500
Charles G Peterson, *President*
Jeff Bear, *General Mgr*
Pam Peterson, *Admin Sec*
Jim Miller, *Sales Staff*
Tim Stockwell, *Cust Mgr*
EMP: 125 **EST:** 1990
SALES (est): 10.9MM **Publicly Held**
WEB: www.toyota.com
SIC: 7538 5511 7532 5531 General automotive repair shops; automobiles, new & used; pickups, new & used; body shop, automotive; automotive parts; automobiles, used cars only
PA: Group 1 Automotive, Inc.
    800 Gessner Rd Ste 500
    Houston TX 77024

(P-14564)
FREEMAN MOTORS INC
Also Called: Freeman Toyota Rent-A-Car
2875 Corby Ave, Santa Rosa (95407-7878)
P.O. Box 1704 (95402-1704)
PHONE 707 542-1791
Stephen C Freeman, *CEO*

Betty E Freeman, *Corp Secy*
Donald E Woodruff, *Vice Pres*
Saul Chait, *Sales Staff*
Jim Ferguson, *Sales Staff*
EMP: 185 **EST:** 1961
SQ FT: 65,000
SALES (est): 18.7MM **Privately Held**
WEB: www.freemanmotors.com
SIC: 5511 7538 Automobiles, new & used; pickups, new & used; trucks, tractors & trailers: new & used; vans, new & used; general automotive repair shops

(P-14565)
FRESNO CHRYSLER JEEP INC
Also Called: Fresno Chrysler Ddge Jeep Ram
6162 N Blackstone Ave, Fresno (93710-5010)
PHONE 559 431-4000
Timothy Allen Finegan, *President*
Tim Finegan Sr, *President*
Tim Finegan Jr, *Vice Pres*
Annette Diggs, *Business Mgr*
Shirzad Shafi, *Sales Staff*
EMP: 85 **EST:** 1976
SQ FT: 5,000
SALES (est): 26.6MM **Privately Held**
WEB: www.fresnochryslerjeep.com
SIC: 5511 5531 7538 Automobiles, new & used; automotive parts; general automotive repair shops

(P-14566)
GILROY IM AUTOMOTIVE LLC
Also Called: Gilroy Buck GMC
6600 Automall Pkwy, Gilroy (95020-7142)
PHONE 408 713-3200
Gurusankar Sankararaman, *Principal*
Jayaprakash Vijayan, *Principal*
EMP: 40 **EST:** 2019
SALES (est): 1.4MM **Privately Held**
WEB: www.gilroybuickgmc.com
SIC: 7538 General automotive repair shops

(P-14567)
GOLD RUSH CHEVROLET INC
Also Called: Gold Rush Chevrolet-Subaru
570 Grass Valley Hwy, Auburn (95603-3832)
P.O. Box 6865 (95604-6865)
PHONE 530 885-0471
Steve Snyder, *President*
Scott Taylor, *Corp Secy*
Sharron Snyder, *Vice Pres*
Allen Hansen, *Sales Mgr*
Greg Levengood, *Manager*
EMP: 55 **EST:** 1986
SQ FT: 13,024
SALES (est): 20.7MM **Privately Held**
WEB: www.goldrushchevy.com
SIC: 5511 7538 5531 5521 Automobiles, new & used; general automotive repair shops; automotive parts; automobiles, used cars only

(P-14568)
GOLDEN GATE FREIGHTLINER INC (HQ)
Also Called: Golden Gate Truck Center
8200 Baldwin St, Oakland (94621-1910)
P.O. Box 6038 (94603-0038)
PHONE 559 486-4310
Gary L Howard, *President*
Brian Nicholson, *CFO*
Doug Howard, *Vice Pres*
Damion Rosby, *Sales Staff*
Russ Davison, *Manager*
EMP: 122 **EST:** 1977
SQ FT: 50,000
SALES (est): 97.6MM
SALES (corp-wide): 100.3MM **Privately Held**
WEB: www.freightliner.com
SIC: 5511 5531 7538 Trucks, tractors & trailers: new & used; truck equipment & parts; general truck repair
PA: Fresno Truck Center
    2727 E Central Ave
    Fresno CA 93725
    559 486-4310

PRODUCTS & SERVICES SECTION

7538 - General Automotive Repair Shop County (P-14589)

(P-14569)
GOODYEAR COML TIRE & SVC CTRS
Also Called: Goodyear Coml Tire & Svc Ctrs
3085 W Capitol Ave, West Sacramento (95691-2912)
PHONE.....................479 788-6400
Nicholas Stone, *Manager*
EMP: 221
SALES (corp-wide): 12.3B **Publicly Held**
WEB: www.goodyearctsc.com
SIC: 5531 7538 Automotive tires; general automotive repair shops
HQ: Goodyear Commercial Tire And Service Centers
1000 S 21st St
Fort Smith AR 72901
479 788-6400

(P-14570)
HARVEY & MADDING INC
Also Called: Dublin Honda
6300 Dublin Blvd, Dublin (94568-7657)
PHONE.....................925 828-8030
Kenneth C Harvey, *CEO*
Brenda S Harvey, *Vice Pres*
Jim Bailey, *General Mgr*
Luis Abreckov, *Finance Mgr*
Paula Glauber, *Controller*
EMP: 100 EST: 1977
SQ FT: 332,576
SALES (est): 85.4MM **Privately Held**
WEB: www.dublinhonda.com
SIC: 5511 7538 5015 5013 Automobiles, new & used; general automotive repair shops; motor vehicle parts, used; motor vehicle supplies & new parts

(P-14571)
HAYWARD FORD INC
1111 Marina Blvd, San Leandro (94577-3364)
PHONE.....................510 352-2000
Robert Knezevich, *President*
James Blakely, *Corp Secy*
EMP: 45 EST: 1991
SALES (est): 4.1MM **Privately Held**
WEB: www.ford.com
SIC: 5511 7538 7515 7513 Automobiles, new & used; pickups, new & used; vans, new & used; general automotive repair shops; passenger car leasing; truck rental & leasing, no drivers; automotive & home supply stores; motor vehicle supplies & new parts

(P-14572)
J & S OPERATIONS LLC
Also Called: Fremont Ford
39700 Balentine Dr, Newark (94560-5374)
PHONE.....................510 360-7165
Mahendra Patel,
Mike Patel, *Executive*
Michael Pollom, *General Mgr*
Angelina Rivera, *Office Mgr*
Tiffany Shenave, *Office Mgr*
EMP: 73 EST: 2005
SALES (est): 9MM **Privately Held**
WEB: www.quicklane.com
SIC: 5511 5531 7538 Automobiles, new & used; trucks, tractors & trailers: new & used; automotive accessories; automotive parts; automotive tires; general automotive repair shops

(P-14573)
J M FREMONT MOTORS LLC
43191 Boscell Rd, Fremont (94538-3106)
PHONE.....................510 403-3700
Fletcher Jones III, *CEO*
Keith May, *President*
EMP: 65
SALES (est): 70MM **Privately Held**
SIC: 5511 7538 5531 Automobiles, new & used; general automotive repair shops; automotive parts

(P-14574)
JOHN L SLLIVAN INVESTMENTS INC (PA)
Also Called: Roseville Toyota
6200 Northfront Rd, Livermore (94551-9507)
PHONE.....................916 969-5911
John L Sullivan, *President*
Steve Ruckels, *Corp Secy*
David Rodgers, *Vice Pres*
Lahoma Caudill, *Finance Mgr*
Dan Gentry, *Finance Mgr*
EMP: 220 EST: 1980
SQ FT: 15,000
SALES (est): 64MM **Privately Held**
WEB: www.toyota.com
SIC: 5511 7538 Automobiles, new & used; pickups, new & used; general automotive repair shops

(P-14575)
LARRY HOPKINS INC
Also Called: Larry Hopkins Honda
1048 W El Camino Real, Sunnyvale (94087-1024)
PHONE.....................408 720-1888
Steven E Hopkins, *President*
Terry Hopkins, *Shareholder*
Mike Serviss, *Technician*
Habib Qasimi, *Sales Staff*
EMP: 100 EST: 1947
SQ FT: 13,000
SALES (est): 25.9MM **Privately Held**
WEB: www.honda.com
SIC: 5511 7538 5531 5521 Automobiles, new & used; general automotive repair shops; automotive & home supply stores; used car dealers

(P-14576)
LITHIA MAZDA OF FRESNO
5200 N Blackstone Ave, Fresno (93710-6704)
PHONE.....................559 256-0700
Imran Mirza, *General Mgr*
EMP: 50 EST: 2014
SALES (est): 14.3MM **Privately Held**
WEB: www.fresnomazda.com
SIC: 5511 5531 7538 Automobiles, new & used; automotive parts; general automotive repair shops

(P-14577)
MANTECA FORD-MERCURY INC
Also Called: Quick Lane
555 N Main St, Manteca (95336-3926)
P.O. Box 2185 (95336-1160)
PHONE.....................209 239-3561
Phil Waterford, *President*
EMP: 45 EST: 1957
SQ FT: 5,000
SALES (est): 17.1MM **Privately Held**
WEB: www.mantecafm.com
SIC: 5511 7538 Automobiles, new & used; general automotive repair shops

(P-14578)
MELE ENTERPRISES INC
Also Called: Yuba City Honda
399 State Highway 99, Yuba City (95993-5652)
P.O. Box 512 (95992-0512)
PHONE.....................530 674-7900
Arthur J Mele, *President*
Joellen Jimerson, *Corp Secy*
Thomas Hoskins, *Consultant*
EMP: 35 EST: 1970
SQ FT: 10,000
SALES (est): 9MM **Privately Held**
WEB: www.honda.com
SIC: 5511 7538 5531 Automobiles, new & used; general automotive repair shops; automotive parts

(P-14579)
NIELLO IMPORTS II INC
Also Called: Neillo Audi
2350 Auburn Blvd, Sacramento (95821-1756)
PHONE.....................916 480-2800
Richard L Neillo Jr, *President*
EMP: 150 EST: 2005
SALES (est): 43.2MM **Privately Held**
WEB: www.niello.com
SIC: 5511 7538 Automobiles, new & used; general automotive repair shops

(P-14580)
NORTH VALLEY FLEET SVCS INC (PA)
3115 Coke St, West Sacramento (95691-3003)
P.O. Box 980006 (95798-0006)
PHONE.....................916 374-8850
Chan Sao GI, *CEO*
Jon Cruz, *Manager*
Jeff Lee, *Manager*
Mike Ram, *Manager*
Lester Gonzalez, *Parts Mgr*
EMP: 18 EST: 2004
SALES (est): 5.3MM **Privately Held**
WEB: www.nvisuzutrucks.com
SIC: 7538 3537 5012 3715 General truck repair; industrial trucks & tractors; trucks, commercial; truck trailers; trucks, tractors & trailers: new & used

(P-14581)
PAN PACIFIC RV CENTERS INC (PA)
252 Yettner Rd, French Camp (95231-9769)
P.O. Box 1300 (95231-1300)
PHONE.....................209 234-2000
Josef D Shields, *President*
Sherry Shields, *Treasurer*
Matt Jones, *Sales Mgr*
EMP: 35 EST: 1976
SQ FT: 25,000
SALES (est): 14.1MM **Privately Held**
WEB: www.panpacificrv.com
SIC: 5561 7538 Camper & travel trailer dealers; recreational vehicle repairs

(P-14582)
PAPE TRUCKS INC
Also Called: Pape' Kenworth
2892 E Jensen Ave, Fresno (93706-5111)
P.O. Box 407, Eugene OR (97440-0407)
PHONE.....................559 268-4344
Charles Davis, *General Mgr*
Matt Packer, *Sales Staff*
Veronica Pez,
Dan Hertel, *Director*
Joe Federico, *Manager*
EMP: 77 **Privately Held**
WEB: www.papekenworth.com
SIC: 7538 5511 5531 General truck repair; trucks, tractors & trailers: new & used; truck equipment & parts
HQ: Pape' Trucks, Inc.
355 Goodpasture Island Rd
Eugene OR 97401

(P-14583)
PERFORMANCE CHEVROLET INC
8757 Auburn Folsom Rd, Granite Bay (95746-0350)
P.O. Box 41469, Sacramento (95841-0469)
PHONE.....................916 338-7300
John A McMichael, *CEO*
Valerie McMichael, *Vice Pres*
Donna Jannuzio, *CIO*
Christopher Littlefield, *Finance Mgr*
Vincent Flores, *Foreman/Supr*
EMP: 109 EST: 1965
SALES (est): 21.5MM **Privately Held**
WEB: www.futurechevyofsac.com
SIC: 5511 7538 7532 5531 Automobiles, new & used; pickups, new & used; general automotive repair shops; body shop, automotive; body shop, trucks; automotive parts; truck equipment & parts; used car dealers

(P-14584)
PRICE-SIMMS FORD LLC
Also Called: Ford Lincoln Fairfield
3050 Auto Mall Ct, Fairfield (94534-4184)
PHONE.....................707 421-3300
Adam Simms,
Taylor Steffenie, *Administration*
Dennis Tokunaga, *IT/INT Sup*
Heather Vladislavich, *Business Mgr*
David Dupart, *Sales Dir*
EMP: 70 EST: 2010
SALES (est): 38.5MM **Privately Held**
WEB: www.fordfairfield.com
SIC: 5511 7538 Automobiles, new & used; general automotive repair shops

(P-14585)
QUALITY CYLINDER HEAD REPAIR
Also Called: Quality Diesel
2434 Evergreen Ave, West Sacramento (95691-3012)
P.O. Box 425 (95691-0425)
PHONE.....................916 371-4302
Jeff Learn, *President*
Jeffrey Learn, *President*
Steve Learn, *President*
▲ EMP: 20 EST: 1960
SQ FT: 12,000
SALES (est): 1MM **Privately Held**
WEB: www.qualitydieselmachine.com
SIC: 7538 5013 5531 3714 Diesel engine repair: automotive; automotive supplies & parts; automotive parts; motor vehicle parts & accessories

(P-14586)
REDWOOD GENERAL TIRE SVC CO
1630 Broadway St, Redwood City (94063-2402)
P.O. Box 5037 (94063-0037)
PHONE.....................650 369-0351
Alpio Barbara, *President*
Darlene Barbara, *Corp Secy*
Dennis Reiser, *General Mgr*
▲ EMP: 35 EST: 1957
SQ FT: 50,000
SALES (est): 10.5MM **Privately Held**
WEB: www.redwoodgeneraltire.com
SIC: 5531 7538 Automotive tires; general automotive repair shops

(P-14587)
RIVERVIEW INTL TRCKS LLC (PA)
2445 Evergreen Ave, West Sacramento (95691-3011)
P.O. Box 716 (95691-0716)
PHONE.....................916 372-8541
Lyle Bassett, *Managing Prtnr*
Pat Sawyer, *Sales Staff*
Eric Bassett,
EMP: 76 EST: 1945
SQ FT: 25,000
SALES (est): 35.9MM **Privately Held**
WEB: www.riverviewinternational.com
SIC: 5511 5531 7538 7532 Trucks, tractors & trailers: new & used; truck equipment & parts; general truck repair; body shop, trucks; truck rental & leasing, no drivers

(P-14588)
SANBORN CHEVROLET INC
Also Called: Sanborn Collision Center
1210 S Cherokee Ln, Lodi (95240-5994)
P.O. Box 1057 (95241-1057)
PHONE.....................209 334-5000
Kini Sanborn, *President*
Laura Lott, *Human Resources*
John Portschller, *Opers Staff*
Duane Fiene, *Sales Mgr*
Mike Moreland, *Director*
EMP: 88 EST: 1971
SQ FT: 31,500
SALES (est): 38.1MM **Privately Held**
WEB: www.sanbornchevrolet.com
SIC: 5511 7538 7532 5521 Automobiles, new & used; general automotive repair shops; body shop, automotive; automobiles, used cars only

(P-14589)
SANTA CLARA IMPORTED CARS INC
Also Called: Honda of Motor Creek
4590 Stevens Creek Blvd, San Jose (95129-1105)
PHONE.....................408 247-2550
Donald L Lucas, *CEO*
Scott Lucas, *President*
Norm Turner, *Vice Pres*
Stephanie Agricola, *Finance Dir*
Mike Djahra, *Sales Staff*
EMP: 58 EST: 1969
SQ FT: 4,000

7538 - General Automotive Repair Shop County (P-14590)

SALES (est): 23.9MM
SALES (corp-wide): 9.7B **Publicly Held**
WEB: www.hondaofstevenscreek.com
SIC: **5511** 7538 Automobiles, new & used; general automotive repair shops
PA: Sonic Automotive, Inc.
4401 Colwick Rd
Charlotte NC 28211
704 566-2400

(P-14590)
SANTA ROSA CITY OF
Also Called: Public Works-Garage
55 Stony Point Rd, Santa Rosa (95401-4446)
PHONE.................................707 543-3882
George Marion, *Branch Mgr*
Chuck Hammond, *Administration*
EMP: 36
SALES (corp-wide): 220.5MM **Privately Held**
WEB: www.srcity.org
SIC: **7538** 7699 General automotive repair shops; aircraft & heavy equipment repair services
PA: Santa Rosa, City Of
45 Stony Point Rd
Santa Rosa CA 95401
707 543-3010

(P-14591)
SEBRING-WEST AUTOMOTIVE
Also Called: Carquest Auto Parts
1744 N Blackstone Ave, Fresno (93703-2910)
PHONE.................................559 266-9378
Anthony J Pasco Jr, *Owner*
Frank Geisler, *Sales Staff*
EMP: 50 EST: 1971
SQ FT: 20,000
SALES (est): 5.7MM **Privately Held**
WEB: www.sebringwestauto.com
SIC: **5531** 7538 Automotive parts; general automotive repair shops

(P-14592)
SIEMENS MOBILITY INC
5301 Price Ave, McClellan (95652-2401)
PHONE.................................916 621-2700
Christopher Maynard, *Vice Pres*
Tracy Quintanar, *Executive Asst*
Brenda Billoups, *Buyer*
Michael Hutchens, *Opers Mgr*
Jason Shankland, *Cust Mgr*
EMP: 100
SALES (corp-wide): 67.4B **Privately Held**
SIC: **7538** 3743 General truck repair; train cars & equipment, freight or passenger
HQ: Siemens Mobility, Inc.
1 Penn Plz Ste 1100
New York NY 10119
212 672-4000

(P-14593)
SOUTH CNTY CHRYSLER-JEEP-DODGE
Also Called: South County Chrysler Dodge
455 Automall Dr, Gilroy (95020-7101)
PHONE.................................408 842-8244
Michael S Greenwood, *President*
Angela Greenwood, *Partner*
Christie Obata, *Office Admin*
Calvin Pham, *Finance Mgr*
Wayne Lew, *Finance*
EMP: 50 EST: 1962
SQ FT: 24,000
SALES (est): 31.1MM **Privately Held**
WEB: www.chrysler.com
SIC: **5511** 7538 5531 Automobiles, new & used; general automotive repair shops; automotive parts; automotive accessories

(P-14594)
TAYLOR MOTORS INC
2525 Churn Creek Rd, Redding (96002-1198)
PHONE.................................530 222-1200
Howard L Taylor, *President*
Donna L Taylor, *Vice Pres*
EMP: 48 EST: 1968
SQ FT: 10,000
SALES (est): 8.8MM **Privately Held**
WEB: www.taylormotorsredding.com
SIC: **5511** 7538 5531 7532 Automobiles, new & used; trucks, tractors & trailers: new & used; general automotive repair shops; automotive parts; body shop, automotive; body shop, trucks

(P-14595)
TEAMROSS INC
Also Called: Team Superstores
301 Auto Mall Pkwy, Vallejo (94591-3870)
PHONE.................................707 643-9000
Kenneth B Ross, *President*
Trish Gress, *Treasurer*
Michael Drinker, *Vice Pres*
EMP: 80 EST: 1995
SQ FT: 57,000
SALES (est): 13.2MM **Privately Held**
WEB: www.chevrolet.com
SIC: **7538** 5511 General automotive repair shops; automobiles, new & used

(P-14596)
THOMPSONS AUTO & TRCK CTR INC (PA)
140 Forni Rd, Placerville (95667-5332)
PHONE.................................530 295-5700
Ronald Thompson, *President*
Jeff Thompson, *Vice Pres*
Tim Stockwell, *General Mgr*
Susan Weiss, *Office Mgr*
Betty Thompson, *Admin Sec*
EMP: 40 EST: 1989
SALES (est): 11MM **Privately Held**
WEB: www.thompsonsauto.com
SIC: **5511** 7538 Automobiles, new & used; general automotive repair shops

(P-14597)
TIFFANY MOTOR COMPANY
Also Called: Greenwood Ford
300 Gateway Dr, Hollister (95023-3069)
P.O. Box 740 (95024-0740)
PHONE.................................831 637-4461
Michael Steven Greenwood, *CEO*
Charlotte Cabral, *Officer*
Jon Deluca, *Sales Mgr*
Don Huse, *Sales Staff*
Robby McGavin, *Sales Staff*
EMP: 35
SQ FT: 4,000
SALES (est): 18MM **Privately Held**
WEB: www.teamgreenwoodford.com
SIC: **5511** 7538 Automobiles, new & used; general automotive repair shops

(P-14598)
TIRE STORE 40 INC
Also Called: Big O Tires
220 W Main St, Woodland (95695-3684)
PHONE.................................530 662-9106
Mark R Werum, *President*
Paul Day, *Co-Owner*
EMP: 35 EST: 1978
SQ FT: 5,000
SALES (est): 1.7MM **Privately Held**
WEB: www.bigotires.com
SIC: **5531** 7538 Automotive tires; general automotive repair shops

(P-14599)
TOSCALITO ENTERPRISES INC (PA)
Also Called: Toscalito Tire & Automotive
668 Irwin St, San Rafael (94901-3941)
PHONE.................................415 456-2324
Vincent Ippolito, *CEO*
Kathy Bolds, *Office Mgr*
Mario Waters, *Store Mgr*
Craig Schulz, *Manager*
Dave Steacy, *Manager*
EMP: 36 EST: 1972
SQ FT: 7,000
SALES (est): 11.4MM **Privately Held**
WEB: www.toscalito.com
SIC: **7538** 5531 General automotive repair shops; automotive tires

(P-14600)
TOYOTA-SUNNYVALE INC (PA)
898 W El Camino Real, Sunnyvale (94087-1153)
PHONE.................................408 245-6640
Adam Simms, *President*
Tom Price, *Vice Pres*
Kevin Pang, *General Mgr*
Janet Kim, *Finance Dir*
Najaf Ali, *Finance Mgr*
EMP: 70 EST: 1959
SQ FT: 35,000
SALES (est): 74.3K **Privately Held**
WEB: www.toyotasunnyvale.com
SIC: **7538** 5511 5521 5531 General automotive repair shops; automobiles, new & used; used car dealers; automotive & home supply stores

(P-14601)
TRACY FORD
Also Called: Mercury
3500 Auto Plaza Way, Tracy (95304-7327)
PHONE.................................209 879-4700
Briane Nokes, *Owner*
Mary Eileen Morri, *Corp Secy*
Jeffrey P Morri, *Vice Pres*
Bobby Dell 'aringa, *Finance Mgr*
Joe Snelling, *Sales Mgr*
EMP: 48 EST: 1970
SQ FT: 35,000
SALES (est): 19.2MM **Privately Held**
WEB: www.tracyford.com
SIC: **5511** 7538 Automobiles, new & used; general automotive repair shops

(P-14602)
WALNUT CREEK ASSOCIATES 2 INC
Also Called: Walnut Creek Honda
1707 N Main St, Walnut Creek (94596-4104)
P.O. Box 5500 (94596-1500)
PHONE.................................925 934-0530
David Robb, *President*
Terri Stuart, *Treasurer*
Ralph Robb, *Vice Pres*
Nancy Robb, *Admin Sec*
George Enriquez, *Technician*
EMP: 86 EST: 1964
SALES (est): 25.7MM **Privately Held**
WEB: www.walnutcreekhonda.com
SIC: **5511** 7538 Automobiles, new & used; general automotive repair shops

(P-14603)
WEATHERFORD MOTORS INC
Also Called: Weatherford BMW
1967 Market St, Concord (94520-2626)
PHONE.................................510 654-8280
Luis Garcia, *CEO*
Mitsunori Umebayashi, *President*
Gino Maynetto, *Business Mgr*
Dan Swanson, *Business Mgr*
Eleni Wright, *Business Mgr*
EMP: 112 EST: 1971
SQ FT: 23,000
SALES (est): 47.1MM **Privately Held**
WEB: www.weatherfordbmw.com
SIC: **5511** 7538 Automobiles, new & used; general automotive repair shops
HQ: Sojitz Corporation Of America
1120 Ave Of The Amrcas Fl
New York NY 10036
212 704-6500

(P-14604)
WESLEY B LASHER INV CORP (PA)
Also Called: Lasher Wes ADI/ Ddg/Volkswagen
5800 Florin Rd, Sacramento (95823-2301)
PHONE.................................916 290-8500
Mark Lasher, *President*
Scott Lasher, *CFO*
EMP: 100 EST: 1955
SQ FT: 10,000
SALES (est): 48.5MM **Privately Held**
WEB: www.dodge.com
SIC: **5511** 7538 5521 Automobiles, new & used; general automotive repair shops; used car dealers

(P-14605)
WHEELER AUTO GROUP INC
Also Called: Wheeler Chevrolet
350 Colusa Ave, Yuba City (95991-4201)
P.O. Box 1150 (95992-1150)
PHONE.................................530 673-3765
Michael Wheeler, *President*
David W Wheeler, *Vice Pres*
Ellen J Wheeler, *Admin Sec*
Teya Traylor, *Consultant*
EMP: 65 EST: 1960
SQ FT: 6,250
SALES (est): 14.9MM **Privately Held**
WEB: www.yubacityquicklube.com
SIC: **5531** 7538 5511 5012 Automotive parts; automobile & truck equipment & parts; truck equipment & parts; general automotive repair shops; automobiles, new & used; automobiles & other motor vehicles; top & body repair & paint shops

(P-14606)
YOURMECHANIC INC
20 Park Rd Ste H, Burlingame (94010-4443)
PHONE.................................800 701-6230
Maddy Martin, *General Mgr*
Patrick Mederos, *Partner*
Paul Bruso, *Vice Pres*
Jefferey Peterson, *Sr Software Eng*
Steven Rowe, *Human Resources*
EMP: 93 EST: 2015
SALES (est): 9.4MM **Privately Held**
WEB: www.yourmechanic.com
SIC: **7538** 6794 General automotive repair shops; franchises, selling or licensing

7539 Automotive Repair Shops, NEC

(P-14607)
BONANDER PONTIAC INC (PA)
Also Called: Bonander Pontiac-Buick-Gmc
231 S Center St, Turlock (95380-4995)
PHONE.................................209 632-8871
Donald E Bonander, *President*
Jesse Pena, *CFO*
Bob Houck, *Branch Mgr*
Tim Koehn, *General Mgr*
Jerry Russell, *General Mgr*
EMP: 60 EST: 1937
SQ FT: 15,000
SALES (est): 58.8MM **Privately Held**
WEB: www.bonanderbuickgmc.com
SIC: **5511** 7539 5012 Automobiles, new & used; automotive repair shops; trailers for trucks, new & used

(P-14608)
CCM PARTNERSHIP
Also Called: Big O Tires
7121 Dublin Blvd, Dublin (94568-3020)
PHONE.................................925 829-1950
Greg Mitchell, *Managing Prtnr*
Bruce Cherry, *Managing Prtnr*
EMP: 42 EST: 1987
SALES (est): 4.4MM **Privately Held**
WEB: www.bigotires.com
SIC: **5531** 7539 Automotive tires; brake repair, automotive; shock absorber replacement; wheel alignment, automotive

(P-14609)
FUTURE FORD OF CONCORD LLC
Also Called: Future Ford Lncoln Mrcury Cnco
2285 Diamond Blvd, Concord (94520-5705)
PHONE.................................925 686-5000
Gary Steven Pleau, *Mng Member*
Pragnesh Khalasi, *IT/INT Sup*
Alex Golter, *Finance Dir*
Fabian Ugwueze, *Finance Dir*
Carlo Perez, *Finance Mgr*
EMP: 80 EST: 2004
SALES (est): 32.3MM **Privately Held**
WEB: www.futurefordofconcord.com
SIC: **5511** 7539 Automobiles, new & used; automotive repair shops

(P-14610)
GENERAL TRAILER INC
2150 E Fremont St, Stockton (95205-5022)
PHONE.................................209 948-6090
Al Fernandes, *President*
Julie Fernandes, *Corp Secy*
EMP: 36 EST: 1976
SQ FT: 10,000
SALES (est): 1.3MM **Privately Held**
WEB: www.generaltrailers.com
SIC: **7539** 5521 5013 Trailer repair; trucks, tractors & trailers: used; truck parts & accessories

PRODUCTS & SERVICES SECTION

7542 - Car Washes County (P-14633)

(P-14611)
HALREC INC
Also Called: Stevens Creek Toyota
4202 Stevens Creek Blvd, San Jose (95129-1336)
P.O. Box 9099 (95157-0099)
PHONE 408 984-1234
Harold Cornelius, *Ch of Bd*
Mark Feldman, *CFO*
Stephen C Cornelius, *Vice Pres*
Ray Khandan, *General Mgr*
Jojo Agutos, *Finance Mgr*
EMP: 250 **EST:** 1966
SQ FT: 11,500
SALES (est): 71.8MM **Privately Held**
WEB: www.stevenscreektoyota.com
SIC: 5511 7539 7538 7532 Automobiles, new & used; automotive repair shops; general automotive repair shops; top & body repair & paint shops

(P-14612)
HIGH SUMMIT LLC
Also Called: Special Events
174 Lawrence Dr Ste A, Livermore (94551-5150)
PHONE 925 605-2900
Weston Cook,
EMP: 50 **EST:** 2007
SALES (est): 3.8MM **Privately Held**
SIC: 7539 Automotive repair shops

(P-14613)
JACK L HUNT INC
Also Called: Jack Hunt Automotive
1714 4th St, San Rafael (94901-2717)
PHONE 415 453-1611
Jack L Hunt III, *President*
Barbara Hunt, *Vice Pres*
Bradley F Hunt, *Vice Pres*
EMP: 41 **EST:** 1927
SQ FT: 8,000
SALES (est): 1.5MM **Privately Held**
WEB: www.rhodwork.net
SIC: 7539 5511 Brake repair, automotive; carburetor repair; electrical services; automobiles, new & used

(P-14614)
JARVIS & JARVIS INC
Also Called: Goodyear
1520 Fitzgerald Dr, Pinole (94564-2229)
PHONE 510 222-0431
Douglas Jarvis, *President*
▲ **EMP:** 43 **EST:** 1974
SQ FT: 4,000
SALES (est): 1.3MM **Privately Held**
WEB: www.goodyear.com
SIC: 5531 7539 Automotive tires; automotive repair shops; wheel alignment, automotive; brake repair, automotive; shock absorber replacement

(P-14615)
JOHN L SULLIVAN CHEVROLET INC
350 Automall Dr, Roseville (95661-3019)
P.O. Box 1028 (95678-8028)
PHONE 916 782-1343
John L Sullivan, *President*
Steve Ruckels, *Treasurer*
Steve A Ruckels, *Corp Secy*
David Rogers, *Vice Pres*
Terry Rouda, *Business Mgr*
EMP: 150 **EST:** 1950
SQ FT: 70,000
SALES (est): 29.6MM **Privately Held**
WEB: www.johnlsullivanchevrolet.com
SIC: 5511 7539 5531 5521 Automobiles, new & used; pickups, new & used; automotive repair shops; automotive & home supply stores; used car dealers

(P-14616)
PEP BOYS MANNY MOE JACK OF CAL
4490 W Shaw Ave, Fresno (93722-6210)
PHONE 559 276-7501
Javier Gasca, *Manager*
EMP: 37 **Publicly Held**
WEB: www.pepboys.com
SIC: 5531 7539 Automotive accessories; automotive parts; automotive repair shops

HQ: The Pep Boys Manny Moe & Jack Of California
3111 W Allegheny Ave
Philadelphia PA 19132
215 430-9095

(P-14617)
PRO STAR AUTO SERVICE INC
355 Sango Ct, Milpitas (95035-6837)
PHONE 408 942-3330
Ted Dickson, *President*
Mike Dickson, *Vice Pres*
EMP: 36 **EST:** 1993
SQ FT: 12,500
SALES (est): 2.4MM **Privately Held**
SIC: 7539 Automotive repair shops

(P-14618)
PUTNAM MOTORS INC
Also Called: Putnam Lexus
390 Convention Way, Redwood City (94063-1405)
P.O. Box 2219 (94064-2219)
PHONE 650 381-3152
Marty Putnam, *President*
Ellen Beller, *Corp Secy*
Jory Hite, *General Mgr*
Tony Lagalo, *Finance Mgr*
Joshua Mojtahedi, *Finance Mgr*
▼ **EMP:** 75 **EST:** 1989
SALES (est): 32MM **Privately Held**
WEB: www.putnamlexus.com
SIC: 5511 7539 Automobiles, new & used; automotive repair shops

(P-14619)
QUALITY MOTOR CARS STOCKTON
Also Called: Acura of Stockton
2222 E Hammer Ln, Stockton (95210-4123)
PHONE 209 476-1640
S Robert Zamora, *President*
Paul C Wondries, *CEO*
Robert R Wondries, *Vice Pres*
EMP: 53 **EST:** 1987
SQ FT: 23,000
SALES (est): 42MM **Privately Held**
WEB: www.hyundaiusa.com
SIC: 5511 7539 Automobiles, new & used; automotive air conditioning repair

(P-14620)
RPM LUXURY AUTO SALES INC
Also Called: Lexus of Roseville
300 Automall Dr, Roseville (95661-3019)
P.O. Box 41529, Sacramento (95841-0529)
PHONE 916 783-9111
Roger Karker, *Branch Mgr*
Patrick McKeehan, *General Mgr*
Charlie Hunt, *Business Mgr*
Dennis Tachera, *Finance Mgr*
Gary Singh, *Sales Staff*
EMP: 106
SALES (corp-wide): 83.3MM **Privately Held**
WEB: www.lexusofsacramento.com
SIC: 5511 7539 7538 Automobiles, new & used; automotive repair shops; general automotive repair shops
PA: Rpm Luxury Auto Sales, Inc.
2600 Fulton Ave
Sacramento CA 95821
916 485-3987

(P-14621)
RUTTER ARMEY INC
Also Called: Armey, Rutter
2684 S Cherry Ave, Fresno (93706-5420)
P.O. Box 1585 (93716-1585)
PHONE 559 237-1866
Robert Armey, *President*
Toni Rosendahl, *Corp Secy*
EMP: 27 **EST:** 1941
SQ FT: 32,000
SALES (est): 1.5MM **Privately Held**
WEB: www.rutterarmey.com
SIC: 7539 3471 Machine shop, automotive; plating & polishing

(P-14622)
SAN FRANCISCO CITY & COUNTY
200 Paul Ave B, San Francisco (94124-3100)
PHONE 415 550-4600

EMP: 110 **Privately Held**
SIC: 7539 9311 7538 Automotive Repair Finance/Tax/Money Policy General Auto Repair
PA: City & County Of San Francisco
1 Dr Carlton B Goodlett P
San Francisco CA 94102
415 554-7500

(P-14623)
SIERRA CHEVROLET INC
Also Called: Winner Chevrolet
1624 S Canyon Way, Colfax (95713-9033)
P.O. Box 1240 (95713-1240)
PHONE 530 346-8313
David C Gard, *President*
Stephanie Gard, *Vice Pres*
EMP: 53 **EST:** 1953
SQ FT: 10,000
SALES (est): 7.3MM **Privately Held**
WEB: www.winnerchevy.com
SIC: 5511 7539 5531 5561 Automobiles, new & used; automotive repair shops; automotive parts; travel trailers: automobile, new & used

(P-14624)
SOUTHWICK INC (PA)
Also Called: Toyota of Berkeley
2400 Shattuck Ave, Berkeley (94704-2023)
PHONE 510 845-2530
Timothy Southwick Sr, *President*
Susan Southwick, *Vice Pres*
Timothy Southwick Jr, *Vice Pres*
Nikitovich Pete, *Executive*
Tim Southwick, *General Mgr*
EMP: 35 **EST:** 1962
SQ FT: 5,000
SALES (est): 22.1MM **Privately Held**
WEB: www.toyotaofberkeley.com
SIC: 5511 7539 Automobiles, new & used; pickups, new & used; automotive repair shops

(P-14625)
STINSON ENTERPRISES INC
Also Called: Modesto Scion World
4513 Mchenry Ave, Modesto (95356-9546)
P.O. Box 576725 (95357-6725)
PHONE 209 529-2933
Lynn H Stinson, *President*
Kevin H Stinson, *Vice Pres*
EMP: 125 **EST:** 1969
SQ FT: 45,000
SALES (est): 18.2MM **Privately Held**
SIC: 5511 7539 Automobiles, new & used; automotive repair shops

(P-14626)
TOWNE MOTOR COMPANY
Also Called: Towne Ford Sales
1601 El Camino Real, Redwood City (94063-2107)
P.O. Box 670 (94064-0670)
PHONE 650 366-5744
Benjamin Kopf Jr, *President*
Robert Kopf, *Corp Secy*
Marian Kopf, *Vice Pres*
Kent Inouye, *Consultant*
▼ **EMP:** 102 **EST:** 1926
SQ FT: 40,000
SALES (est): 32.9MM **Privately Held**
WEB: www.towneford.com
SIC: 5511 7539 7549 Automobiles, new & used; automotive repair shops; automotive customizing services, non-factory basis

(P-14627)
VALLEY TIRE AND BRAKE OF SANTA (PA)
1688 Piner Rd, Santa Rosa (95403-1985)
PHONE 707 544-3420
John McGill, *President*
Eric Offenpacher, *General Mgr*
Asher Nathan, *Bookkeeper*
Chris Edwards, *Asst Mgr*
Edgar Melendez, *Asst Mgr*
EMP: 35 **EST:** 1968
SQ FT: 15,000
SALES (est): 3MM **Privately Held**
SIC: 5531 7539 Automotive tires; tune-up service, automotive; brake repair, automotive; front end repair, automotive

7542 Car Washes

(P-14628)
AUTO WORLD CAR WASH LLC
15951 Los Gatos Blvd, Los Gatos (95032-3428)
PHONE 408 345-6532
EMP: 1597
SALES (est): 2.7MM
SALES (corp-wide): 66.5MM **Privately Held**
SIC: 7542 Carwash
PA: California Secured Investments, Llc
14225 Lora Dr Apt 96
Los Gatos CA

(P-14629)
BLUE BEACON USA LP
Also Called: Blue Beacon Truck Wash
3000 Highway 99w, Corning (96021)
P.O. Box 291 (96021-0291)
PHONE 530 824-0474
Phil Ryan, *Branch Mgr*
EMP: 46
SALES (corp-wide): 38MM **Privately Held**
WEB: www.bluebeacon.com
SIC: 7542 Truck wash
PA: Blue Beacon U.S.A., L.P.
500 Graves Blvd
Salina KS 67401
785 825-2221

(P-14630)
BLUEWAVE EXPRESS LLC (PA)
2175 Francisco Blvd E G, San Rafael (94901-5524)
PHONE 877 503-0008
Bill Poland,
Stratt Poland, *Vice Pres*
Craig Turner,
Charles Ballard, *Manager*
EMP: 43 **EST:** 2011
SALES (est): 10.5MM **Privately Held**
WEB: www.bluewaveexpress.com
SIC: 7542 Washing & polishing, automotive

(P-14631)
BOWIE ENTERPRISES (PA)
Also Called: Chevron
4411 N Blackstone Ave, Fresno (93726-1904)
PHONE 559 227-6221
David Bowie, *President*
James M Bowie, *Ch of Bd*
Karen Bowie, *Treasurer*
Kathryn Bowie, *Admin Sec*
Robin Irvin, *Info Tech Dir*
EMP: 60 **EST:** 1966
SQ FT: 7,700
SALES (est): 14.8MM **Privately Held**
WEB: www.redcarpetcarwash.com
SIC: 7542 5541 Carwash, automatic; filling stations, gasoline

(P-14632)
BOWIE ENTERPRISES
Also Called: Red Carpet Car Wash
801 W Shaw Ave, Clovis (93612-3218)
PHONE 559 292-6565
EMP: 95
SALES (corp-wide): 14.8MM **Privately Held**
WEB: www.redcarpetcarwash.com
SIC: 7542 Washing & polishing, automotive
PA: Bowie Enterprises
4411 N Blackstone Ave
Fresno CA 93726
559 227-6221

(P-14633)
CANADIAN AMERICAN OIL CO INC
Also Called: Berkeley Touchless Carwash
444 Divisadero St 100, San Francisco (94117-2211)
PHONE 510 644-8229
EMP: 35
SALES (corp-wide): 110.1MM **Privately Held**
WEB: www.berkeleytouchless.com
SIC: 7542 Carwash

(PA)=Parent Co (HQ)=Headquarters (DH)=Div Headquarters
✿ = New Business established in last 2 years

7542 - Car Washes County (P-14634)

PA: Canadian American Oil Co Inc
444 Divisadero St 100
San Francisco CA 94117
415 621-8676

(P-14634)
CANADIAN AMERICAN OIL CO INC
Also Called: Divisadero Touchless Carwash
444 Divisadero St, San Francisco (94117-2211)
PHONE....................415 621-8676
Cory Merritt, *General Mgr*
EMP: 56
SALES (corp-wide): 52.3MM **Privately Held**
WEB: www.bp.com
SIC: 7542 Carwashes
PA: Canadian American Oil Co Inc
444 Divisadero St 100
San Francisco CA 94117
415 621-8676

(P-14635)
CANEPAS CAR WASH
Also Called: Chevron
6230 Pacific Ave, Stockton (95207-3712)
PHONE....................209 478-5516
Steven Canepa, *Branch Mgr*
EMP: 35
SALES (corp-wide): 4.7MM **Privately Held**
WEB: www.chevron.com
SIC: 7542 5947 5541 Carwashes; gift shop; filling stations, gasoline
PA: Canepa's Car Wash
642 N Hunter St
Stockton CA 95202
209 951-9772

(P-14636)
CHARLES FENLEY ENTERPRISES (PA)
Also Called: California 5 Minute Car Wash
1121 Oakdale Rd Ste 7, Modesto (95355-4000)
P.O. Box 577200 (95357-7200)
PHONE....................209 576-0381
Michael Fenley, *President*
Brandon Fenley, *Vice Pres*
Lee Garner, *Vice Pres*
Flora Anderson, *Manager*
EMP: 40 **EST:** 1963
SQ FT: 1,800
SALES (est): 8.2MM **Privately Held**
WEB: www.fiveminutecarwash.com
SIC: 7542 5541 5948 Carwash, automatic; carwash, self-service; filling stations, gasoline; luggage, except footlockers & trunks; leather goods, except luggage & shoes

(P-14637)
CHARLES FENLEY ENTERPRISES
Also Called: Chevron
1109 Oakdale Rd, Modesto (95355-4065)
P.O. Box 577200 (95357-7200)
PHONE....................209 523-2832
Gene Rooney, *Manager*
EMP: 41
SALES (corp-wide): 8.2MM **Privately Held**
WEB: www.fiveminutecarwash.com
SIC: 7542 5541 5948 7549 Carwash, automatic; filling stations, gasoline; luggage, except footlockers & trunks; leather goods, except luggage & shoes; lubrication service, automotive
PA: Charles Fenley Enterprises
1121 Oakdale Rd Ste 7
Modesto CA 95355
209 576-0381

(P-14638)
CHARLES FENLEY ENTERPRISES
1115 Oakdale Rd, Modesto (95355-4065)
PHONE....................209 576-0381
Flora Anderson, *Manager*
EMP: 41

SALES (corp-wide): 8.2MM **Privately Held**
WEB: www.fiveminutecarwash.com
SIC: 7542 5541 5948 Carwash, automatic; carwash, self-service; filling stations, gasoline; luggage, except footlockers & trunks
PA: Charles Fenley Enterprises
1121 Oakdale Rd Ste 7
Modesto CA 95355
209 576-0381

(P-14639)
DUCKYS CAR WASH (PA)
1301 Old County Rd, San Carlos (94070-5201)
PHONE....................650 637-1301
Rick Theobald,
Sue E Alfano, *Controller*
EMP: 40 **EST:** 2006
SQ FT: 1,500
SALES (est): 4.7MM **Privately Held**
WEB: www.duckysexpress.com
SIC: 7542 Washing & polishing, automotive

(P-14640)
EDWARDS & ANDERSON INC (PA)
3649 Jamison Way, Castro Valley (94546-4303)
PHONE....................510 581-0230
Jerry Anderson, *Principal*
Carol Anderson, *Admin Sec*
EMP: 61 **EST:** 1988
SALES (est): 1.1MM **Privately Held**
SIC: 7542 Carwashes

(P-14641)
HUTCHS CAR WASHES INC
17945 Hesperian Blvd, San Lorenzo (94580-3070)
PHONE....................510 538-9274
Jill Jackson, *Manager*
EMP: 35
SALES (corp-wide): 5.7MM **Privately Held**
WEB: www.hutchscarwashes.com
SIC: 7542 5541 Carwash, automatic; filling stations, gasoline
PA: Hutch's Car Washes, Inc
6355 S Mccarran Blvd
Reno NV 89509
775 827-2224

(P-14642)
JACK ANTHONY INDUSTRIES INC
Also Called: 7 Flags Car Wash
108 Elmira Rd, Vacaville (95687-4701)
PHONE....................707 448-0104
Tom Ignatieff, *Manager*
Thomas Wieck, *Manager*
EMP: 40
SALES (corp-wide): 10.1MM **Privately Held**
WEB: www.7flagscarwash.com
SIC: 7542 Carwash, automatic
PA: Jack Anthony Industries, Inc.
145 Valle Vista Ave Ste A
Vallejo CA 94590
707 642-2143

(P-14643)
JACK ANTHONY INDUSTRIES INC
Also Called: 7 Flags Car Wash - Fairfield
2270 N Texas St, Fairfield (94533-2102)
PHONE....................707 426-2000
Charles Booker, *Branch Mgr*
EMP: 40
SALES (corp-wide): 10.1MM **Privately Held**
WEB: www.7flagscarwash.com
SIC: 7542 Carwash, automatic
PA: Jack Anthony Industries, Inc.
145 Valle Vista Ave Ste A
Vallejo CA 94590
707 642-2143

(P-14644)
JACK ANTHONY INDUSTRIES INC
Also Called: 7 Flags Car Wash - Plaza
135 Valle Vista Ave, Vallejo (94590-2951)
PHONE....................707 557-5353
Mary Ann Desuyo, *Branch Mgr*
EMP: 40
SALES (corp-wide): 10.1MM **Privately Held**
WEB: www.7flagscarwash.com
SIC: 7542 Carwash, automatic
PA: Jack Anthony Industries, Inc.
145 Valle Vista Ave Ste A
Vallejo CA 94590
707 642-2143

(P-14645)
JACKS CAR WASH 3
6745 N West Ave, Fresno (93711-4304)
PHONE....................559 438-8201
EMP: 60 **EST:** 2003
SALES (est): 1.2MM **Privately Held**
SIC: 7542 5947 5812 Carwash, self-service; gift shop; coffee shop

(P-14646)
JKF AUTO SERVICE INC
Also Called: Five Star Auto Repair and Wash
6818 Five Star Blvd, Rocklin (95677-2660)
PHONE....................916 315-0555
Jeff Finerman, *President*
Karen W Finerman, *Vice Pres*
EMP: 60 **EST:** 1993
SALES (est): 1.3MM **Privately Held**
WEB: www.fivestarrocklin.com
SIC: 7542 7549 7539 Washing & polishing, automotive; lubrication service, automotive; automotive repair shops

(P-14647)
LARK AVENUE CAR WASH
Also Called: Lark Ave Classic Car Wash
16500 Lark Ave, Los Gatos (95032-2505)
PHONE....................408 356-2525
Brett Kott, *Manager*
EMP: 72
SALES (corp-wide): 62.4MM **Privately Held**
WEB: www.classiccarwash.com
SIC: 7542 Washing & polishing, automotive
PA: Lark Avenue Car Wash
871 E Hamilton Ave
Campbell CA 95008
408 371-2414

(P-14648)
LARK AVENUE CAR WASH
Also Called: Chevron
5005 Almaden Expy, San Jose (95118-2049)
P.O. Box 5993 (95150-5993)
PHONE....................408 371-2565
Chuck Mina, *Manager*
EMP: 72
SQ FT: 7,859
SALES (corp-wide): 62.4MM **Privately Held**
WEB: www.classiccarwash.com
SIC: 7542 Washing & polishing, automotive
PA: Lark Avenue Car Wash
871 E Hamilton Ave
Campbell CA 95008
408 371-2414

(P-14649)
LARK AVENUE CAR WASH
Also Called: Chevron
981 E Hamilton Ave, Campbell (95008-0648)
PHONE....................408 377-2525
Mike Davis, *Principal*
EMP: 72
SALES (corp-wide): 62.4MM **Privately Held**
WEB: www.classiccarwash.com
SIC: 7542 Washing & polishing, automotive
PA: Lark Avenue Car Wash
871 E Hamilton Ave
Campbell CA 95008
408 371-2414

(P-14650)
LOZANO INC
Also Called: Lozano Car Wash
2690 W El Camino Real, Mountain View (94040-1117)
PHONE....................650 941-0590
Manuel J Lozano, *President*
Claudia Rozriduez, *Manager*
EMP: 107 **EST:** 1961
SQ FT: 500
SALES (est): 6.1MM **Privately Held**
WEB: www.yessicalozano.com
SIC: 7542 Carwash, automatic

(P-14651)
PETROLEUM SALES INC (PA)
1475 2nd St, San Rafael (94901-2754)
PHONE....................415 256-1600
Ben Shimek, *President*
EMP: 120 **EST:** 1969
SALES (est): 13.5MM **Privately Held**
WEB: www.shineology.com
SIC: 7542 5541 Carwashes; gasoline service stations

(P-14652)
SWARTOUT INC
Also Called: Belmont Car Wash
5594 E Belmont Ave, Fresno (93727-2616)
PHONE....................559 252-4441
Jose Chavez, *Manager*
EMP: 55
SALES (corp-wide): 11.2MM **Privately Held**
WEB: www.belmontcarwash.net
SIC: 7542 Washing & polishing, automotive
PA: Swartout, Inc.
1754 E Bullard Ave # 107
Fresno CA
559 432-5200

(P-14653)
VINTAGE CAR WASH INC
Also Called: The Peddler
1801 Standiford Ave, Modesto (95350-0182)
PHONE....................209 572-1215
Patti Giameanco, *Manager*
EMP: 40
SALES (corp-wide): 2.6MM **Privately Held**
SIC: 7542 Carwash, automatic
PA: Vintage Car Wash, Inc.
3531 Carver Rd
Modesto CA 95356
209 523-8100

7549 Automotive Svcs, Except Repair & Car Washes

(P-14654)
ALLIED LUBE INC
Also Called: Jiffy Lube
17010 Walnut Grove Dr, Morgan Hill (95037-4437)
PHONE....................408 779-8969
Paul Delacruz, *Branch Mgr*
EMP: 80 **Privately Held**
WEB: www.jiffylube.com
SIC: 7549 Lubrication service, automotive
PA: Allied Lube, Inc.
27240 La Paz Rd
Mission Viejo CA 92692

(P-14655)
AMERICAN CRIER EQP TRLR SLS LL
2285 E Date Ave, Fresno (93706-5426)
PHONE....................559 442-1500
Tom Pistacchio, *Mng Member*
Phillip J Sweet, *President*
David Sweet, *Corp Secy*
Richard Hutchison Jr, *Mng Member*
Dolores Pistacchio, *Mng Member*
EMP: 25 **EST:** 2011
SQ FT: 36,000
SALES (est): 2.9MM **Privately Held**
WEB: www.americancarrierequipment.com
SIC: 7549 3715 Trailer maintenance; truck trailers

PRODUCTS & SERVICES SECTION

7622 - Radio & TV Repair Shops County (P-14679)

(P-14656)
AMERIT FLEET SOLUTIONS INC (HQ)
1331 N Calif Blvd Ste 150, Walnut Creek (94596-4535)
PHONE...............................877 512-6374
Dan Williams, *CEO*
Amein Punjani, *COO*
Matt Lavay, *CFO*
Kevin Clark, *Exec VP*
Natalie Kathain, *Vice Pres*
EMP: 100 **EST:** 2010
SALES (est): 94.9MM **Privately Held**
WEB: www.ameritfleetsolutions.com
SIC: 7549 4785 Inspection & diagnostic service, automotive; transportation inspection services

(P-14657)
AUTO EX TOWING & RECOVERY LLC
2594 Oakdale Ave, San Francisco (94124-1520)
PHONE...............................415 846-2262
Vladimir Mikshansky, *Branch Mgr*
EMP: 20
SALES (corp-wide): 3.3MM **Privately Held**
WEB: www.autoexpresstow.com
SIC: 7549 3715 3531 4212 Towing services; truck trailers; construction machinery; local trucking, without storage
PA: Auto Express Towing & Recovery Llc
154 E Hillsdale Blvd
San Mateo CA 94403
415 407-8977

(P-14658)
CAPITOLA IMPORTS INC
Also Called: Toyota of Santa Cruz
4200 Auto Plaza Dr, Capitola (95010-2073)
PHONE...............................831 462-4200
Charles L Canfield, *President*
EMP: 140 **EST:** 1985
SALES (est): 25.4MM **Privately Held**
WEB: www.santacruztoyota.com
SIC: 5511 7549 Automobiles, new & used; automotive maintenance services

(P-14659)
COVEY AUTO EXPRESS INC (PA)
Also Called: Pacific Towing
1444 El Pinal Dr, Stockton (95205-2642)
PHONE...............................253 826-0461
Michael D Covey, *President*
Kathy Covey, *Vice Pres*
EMP: 148 **EST:** 1986
SQ FT: 19,000
SALES (est): 21.5MM **Privately Held**
WEB: www.coveyautoinc.com
SIC: 7549 Towing service, automotive; towing services

(P-14660)
GUYNN INC (PA)
Also Called: Jiffy Lube
2452 Notre Dame Blvd, Chico (95928-7136)
PHONE...............................530 566-9292
Richard Guynn, *President*
EMP: 39 **EST:** 2004
SQ FT: 15,246
SALES (est): 2.1MM **Privately Held**
WEB: www.chicooilchange.com
SIC: 7549 Lubrication service, automotive

(P-14661)
HORIZON GLOBAL AMERICAS INC
Also Called: Cequent Towing Products
3181 S Willow Ave Ste 104, Fresno (93725-9460)
PHONE...............................559 266-9000
Sam Weissman, *Manager*
EMP: 211
SALES (corp-wide): 661.2MM **Publicly Held**
WEB: www.horizonglobal.com
SIC: 7549 Towing services
HQ: Horizon Global Americas Inc.
47912 Halyard Dr Ste 100
Plymouth MI 48170

(P-14662)
JACK JAMES TOW SVC
549 C St, Hayward (94541-5027)
PHONE...............................510 581-1950
Barbara Johnson, *President*
Richard Johnson, *Vice Pres*
EMP: 40 **EST:** 1946
SQ FT: 9,900
SALES (est): 1.3MM **Privately Held**
WEB: www.jackjamestow.com
SIC: 7549 Towing service, automotive; towing services

(P-14663)
JAMESTOWN MOTOR CORPORATION
Also Called: Sierra Motors
18475 5th Ave, Jamestown (95327-9378)
P.O. Box 1879 (95327-1879)
PHONE...............................209 984-5272
John Alexander, *President*
Angela Ciabatti, *Info Tech Dir*
Mike Enzi, *Sales Staff*
Kris Keezer, *Sales Staff*
EMP: 45 **EST:** 2001
SQ FT: 25,000
SALES (est): 19.2MM **Privately Held**
WEB: www.sierramotors.net
SIC: 5511 7549 Automobiles, new & used; automotive maintenance services

(P-14664)
LITHIA OF WALNUT CREEK INC
Also Called: Diablo Subaru of Walnut Creek
2646 N Main St, Walnut Creek (94597-2728)
PHONE...............................925 937-6900
Bryan Deboer, *President*
Sidney Deboer, *Admin Sec*
EMP: 50 **EST:** 2013
SALES (est): 22.5MM
SALES (corp-wide): 13.1B **Publicly Held**
WEB: www.subaru.com
SIC: 5511 7549 Automobiles, new & used; do-it-yourself garages
PA: Lithia Motors, Inc.
150 N Bartlett St
Medford OR 97501
541 776-6401

(P-14665)
MOC PRODUCTS COMPANY INC
9840 Kitty Ln, Oakland (94603-1070)
PHONE...............................510 635-1230
George Logan, *Branch Mgr*
EMP: 59
SALES (corp-wide): 73.9MM **Privately Held**
WEB: www.mocproducts.com
SIC: 7549 Automotive maintenance services
PA: Moc Products Company, Inc.
12306 Montague St
Pacoima CA 91331
818 794-3500

(P-14666)
MOTOR BODY COMPANY INC
455 Sunol St, San Jose (95126-3750)
PHONE...............................408 993-9555
Stan Alongi, *President*
Mark Alongi, *Admin Sec*
EMP: 37 **EST:** 1926
SQ FT: 5,025
SALES (est): 1.2MM **Privately Held**
WEB: www.motorbody.com
SIC: 7549 Towing service, automotive

(P-14667)
OIL CHANGER INC
780 San Antonio Rd, Palo Alto (94303-4613)
PHONE...............................650 494-8353
Daniel Ramirez, *Manager*
EMP: 67
SALES (corp-wide): 28.3MM **Privately Held**
WEB: www.oilchangers.com
SIC: 7549 Lubrication service, automotive
HQ: Oil Changer, Inc.
4511 Willow Rd Ste 1
Pleasanton CA 94588

(P-14668)
OIL CHANGER INC
Also Called: Oil Changer 303
2880 Skyline Dr, Pacifica (94044-2100)
PHONE...............................650 355-7233
Jason Manasselian, *Branch Mgr*
EMP: 67
SALES (corp-wide): 28.3MM **Privately Held**
WEB: www.oilchangers.com
SIC: 7549 Lubrication service, automotive
HQ: Oil Changer, Inc.
4511 Willow Rd Ste 1
Pleasanton CA 94588

(P-14669)
OIL CHANGER INC
Also Called: Oil Changer 304
1247 Portola Ave, Livermore (94551-1623)
PHONE...............................925 447-3346
Mark Lucas, *Manager*
EMP: 67
SALES (corp-wide): 28.3MM **Privately Held**
WEB: www.oilchangers.com
SIC: 7549 Lubrication service, automotive
HQ: Oil Changer, Inc.
4511 Willow Rd Ste 1
Pleasanton CA 94588

(P-14670)
PEP BOYS MANNY MOE JACK OF CAL
5135 Auburn Blvd, Sacramento (95841-2704)
PHONE...............................916 331-4880
Craig R Weckman, *Manager*
Craig Weckman, *Manager*
EMP: 37 **Publicly Held**
WEB: www.pepboys.com
SIC: 5531 7549 Automotive parts; automotive maintenance services
HQ: The Pep Boys Manny Moe & Jack Of California
3111 W Allegheny Ave
Philadelphia PA 19132
215 430-9095

(P-14671)
PEP BOYS MANNY MOE JACK OF CAL
10899 Folsom Blvd, Rancho Cordova (95670-5023)
PHONE...............................916 638-4808
Alaro Ruiz, *General Mgr*
EMP: 37 **Publicly Held**
WEB: www.pepboys.com
SIC: 5531 7549 Automotive parts; automotive maintenance services
HQ: The Pep Boys Manny Moe & Jack Of California
3111 W Allegheny Ave
Philadelphia PA 19132
215 430-9095

(P-14672)
PIERCEY HM LLC
Also Called: Piercey Honda
920 Thompson St, Milpitas (95035-6296)
PHONE...............................408 324-7400
Tom A Chadwell, *President*
EMP: 50 **EST:** 2018
SALES (est): 22MM
SALES (corp-wide): 114.1MM **Privately Held**
WEB: www.pierceyhonda.com
SIC: 5511 5531 7549 Automobiles, new & used; automotive parts; automotive maintenance services
PA: Piercey Management Services, Inc.
16901 Millikan Ave
Irvine CA 92606
949 379-3701

(P-14673)
R LANCE & SONS CO INC
6776 Patterson Pass Rd, Livermore (94550-9580)
PHONE...............................925 245-8884
R Lance Ruckteschler, *President*
Jason Ruckteschler, *Shareholder*
Katherine Ruckteschler, *Corp Secy*
Jeffery Ruckteschler, *General Mgr*
EMP: 36 **EST:** 1975
SQ FT: 20,000
SALES (est): 5MM **Privately Held**
WEB: www.rlanceandsons.com
SIC: 7549 Towing service, automotive

(P-14674)
REEVES ENTERPRISES INC
Also Called: Mike's Towing Service
229 Bangs Ave, Modesto (95356-8900)
PHONE...............................209 529-5698
Randahl R Reeves, *President*
Mike Reeves, *Vice Pres*
EMP: 37 **EST:** 1965
SQ FT: 8,625
SALES (est): 1.2MM **Privately Held**
SIC: 7549 7538 7513 Towing service, automotive; general automotive repair shops; truck rental & leasing, no drivers

(P-14675)
ROADRUNNER TOW INC
Also Called: Roadrunner Towing
1950 Walters Ct, Fairfield (94533-2763)
PHONE...............................707 434-9560
Jim Inglebright, *President*
Valerie Inglebright, *Vice Pres*
Robert Inglebright, *Admin Sec*
EMP: 36 **EST:** 1980
SQ FT: 500
SALES (est): 1.2MM **Privately Held**
WEB: www.roadrunnertow.com
SIC: 7549 Towing service, automotive

(P-14676)
TEGSCO LLC (PA)
Also Called: Autoreturn
450 7th St, San Francisco (94103-4532)
PHONE...............................415 865-8200
Ray Krouse,
Drew Griffin, *Partner*
Brian Serrano, *Partner*
Nolan Walker, *Partner*
Jay Atkins, *Vice Pres*
EMP: 58 **EST:** 2002
SQ FT: 15,000
SALES (est): 6.1MM **Privately Held**
WEB: www.autoreturn.com
SIC: 7549 Towing service, automotive

(P-14677)
TULA TECHNOLOGY INC (PA)
2460 Zanker Rd, San Jose (95131-1126)
PHONE...............................408 383-9447
Adya S Tripathi, *Ch of Bd*
R Scott Bailey, *CEO*
Chester J Silvestri, *CEO*
Michael Hasley, *CFO*
John Fuerst, *Vice Pres*
EMP: 89 **EST:** 2008
SALES (est): 10.4MM **Privately Held**
WEB: www.tulatech.com
SIC: 7549 8711 Fuel system conversion, automotive; engineering services

(P-14678)
WEBER MOTORS FRESNO INC
Also Called: BMW Fresno
7171 N Palm Ave, Fresno (93650-1082)
PHONE...............................559 447-6700
Yrma Rico, *President*
Al Monjazeb, *CEO*
Shahram Mihantajouh, *Vice Pres*
Jazmine Tchouboukjian, *Admin Asst*
Ahmed Abdalla, *Finance Mgr*
EMP: 65 **EST:** 1970
SQ FT: 17,000
SALES (est): 25.1MM **Privately Held**
WEB: www.bmwfresno.com
SIC: 5511 7549 7538 Automobiles, new & used; automotive maintenance services; general automotive repair shops

7622 Radio & TV Repair Shops

(P-14679)
COMTECH COMMUNICATIONS INC
120 Main Ave Ste J, Sacramento (95838-2043)
PHONE...............................800 377-7422
Steve Muir, *President*
Bob Dowdle, *Admin Sec*

7622 - Radio & TV Repair Shops

Jerry Nelson, *Director*
EMP: 43 **EST:** 1994
SQ FT: 8,400
SALES (est): 3.6MM **Privately Held**
WEB: www.comtechcom.net
SIC: 5731 7622 Radios, two-way, citizens' band, weather, short-wave, etc.; radio repair & installation

(P-14680)
DELTA WIRELESS INC
Also Called: Delta Network Solutions
1700 W Fremont St, Stockton (95203-2039)
PHONE 209 948-9611
David Naasz, *Manager*
EMP: 41 **Privately Held**
WEB: www.deltawireless.com
SIC: 7622 Radio repair shop
PA: Delta Wireless, Inc.
1170 National Dr Ste 60
Sacramento CA 95834

(P-14681)
PHILIPS NORTH AMERICA LLC
Also Called: Philips Consumer Electronics
681 E Brokaw Rd, San Jose (95112-1005)
PHONE 408 436-8566
Mike Bates, *Principal*
EMP: 40
SALES (corp-wide): 133.6MM **Privately Held**
WEB: www.usa.philips.com
SIC: 7622 Stereophonic equipment repair; video repair
HQ: Philips North America Llc
222 Jacobs St Fl 3
Cambridge MA 02141
978 659-3000

7623 Refrigeration & Air Conditioning Svc & Repair Shop

(P-14682)
BAY POINT CONTROL INC
Also Called: Marina Mechanical
799 Thornton St, San Leandro (94577-2628)
PHONE 510 614-3500
James R Hussey, *CEO*
David Mann, *Vice Pres*
Shelley Hussey, *Admin Sec*
Jim Swanson, *Project Mgr*
Rhonda Scott, *Controller*
EMP: 48 **EST:** 1980
SQ FT: 10,000
SALES (est): 16.3MM **Privately Held**
WEB: www.marinam.com
SIC: 7623 1711 Refrigeration repair service; plumbing, heating, air-conditioning contractors; warm air heating & air conditioning contractor

(P-14683)
BROWER MECHANICAL INC
Also Called: Honeywell Authorized Dealer
4060 Alvis Ct, Rocklin (95677-4012)
PHONE 530 749-0808
Jeff Brower, *President*
Duane Knickerbocker, *Vice Pres*
Troy Bagwell, *General Mgr*
EMP: 75 **EST:** 1980
SQ FT: 5,000
SALES (est): 17.9MM **Privately Held**
WEB: www.browermechanical.com
SIC: 7623 7629 Air conditioning repair; electrical household appliance repair

(P-14684)
CARRIER CORPORATION
Also Called: Carrier Commercial Service
1168 National Dr Ste 60, Sacramento (95834-1979)
PHONE 916 928-9500
Craig Sweeney, *Branch Mgr*
EMP: 50
SALES (corp-wide): 17.4B **Publicly Held**
WEB: www.rtx.com
SIC: 7623 Air conditioning repair
HQ: Carrier Corporation
13995 Pasteur Blvd
Palm Beach Gardens FL 33418
800 379-6484

(P-14685)
CITY MECHANICAL INC
724 Alfred Nobel Dr, Hercules (94547-1805)
PHONE 510 724-9088
Russell Will Jr, *CEO*
Ronald Tinkey, *Treasurer*
EMP: 70 **EST:** 1989
SALES (est): 13.6MM **Privately Held**
WEB: www.citymechanical.com
SIC: 7623 1711 Refrigeration service & repair; heating systems repair & maintenance; ventilation & duct work contractor

(P-14686)
COMMERCIAL MECHANICAL SVC INC (PA)
Also Called: C M Service
981 Bing St, San Carlos (94070-5321)
PHONE 650 610-8440
Thomas Fewell, *President*
EMP: 40 **EST:** 1982
SALES (est): 2.9MM **Privately Held**
WEB: www.commercialmechanicalservice.com
SIC: 7623 Refrigeration repair service; air conditioning repair

(P-14687)
ESTES COMMERCIAL RFRGN INC
Also Called: Estes Refrigeration
1400 Potrero Ave, Richmond (94804-3750)
PHONE 510 232-5464
Michael J Doninelli, *President*
Mark Doninelli, *Vice Pres*
EMP: 35 **EST:** 1953
SALES (est): 7.2MM **Privately Held**
WEB: www.estesrefrigeration.com
SIC: 7623 1711 Refrigeration repair service; warm air heating & air conditioning contractor; refrigeration contractor

(P-14688)
PRIBUSS ENGINEERING INC
523 Mayfair Ave, South San Francisco (94080-4509)
PHONE 650 588-0447
Bayardo Chamorro, *CEO*
John Pribuss, *CFO*
Selina Pribuss, *Office Mgr*
Ali Saremi, *Project Mgr*
Nel Lukovsky, *Credit Mgr*
EMP: 70 **EST:** 1968
SQ FT: 16,000
SALES (est): 17.9MM **Privately Held**
WEB: www.c7c.bbb.myftpupload.com
SIC: 7623 1711 Refrigeration service & repair; plumbing, heating, air-conditioning contractors; fire sprinkler system installation; warm air heating & air conditioning contractor

(P-14689)
VLY AIR COND & RPR
825 S Topeka Ave, Fresno (93721-2406)
PHONE 559 237-2123
Tobbie Viglion, *CEO*
EMP: 70 **EST:** 2015
SALES (est): 1.2MM **Privately Held**
WEB: www.valleyairrepair.com
SIC: 7623 Refrigeration service & repair

7629 Electrical & Elex Repair Shop, NEC

(P-14690)
ASM AMERICA INC
97 E Brokaw Rd Ste 100, San Jose (95112-4209)
PHONE 408 451-0830
Doug Traina, *Manager*
EMP: 122
SALES (corp-wide): 1.5B **Privately Held**
WEB: www.asm.com
SIC: 5999 7629 Electronic parts & equipment; electronic equipment repair
HQ: Asm America, Inc.
3440 E University Dr
Phoenix AZ 85034
602 470-5700

(P-14691)
CABLECOM LLC
5337 Luce Ave, McClellan (95652-2440)
PHONE 916 891-2400
EMP: 50
SALES (corp-wide): 3.2B **Publicly Held**
WEB: www.cablecomllc.us
SIC: 7629 1731 Telecommunication equipment repair (except telephones); telephone & telephone equipment installation
HQ: Cablecom Llc
8602 Maltby Rd
Woodinville WA 98072
360 668-1300

(P-14692)
CABLECOM LLC
Also Called: Cable Com
5745 E Fountain Way, Fresno (93727-7815)
PHONE 559 412-8720
EMP: 50
SALES (corp-wide): 3.2B **Publicly Held**
WEB: www.cablecomllc.us
SIC: 7629 1731 Electrical repair shops; electrical work
HQ: Cablecom Llc
8602 Maltby Rd
Woodinville WA 98072
360 668-1300

(P-14693)
COMMUNICATIONS & PWR INDS LLC
Microwave Pwr Pdts Div - Ecnco
1318 Commerce Ave, Woodland (95776-5908)
PHONE 530 662-7553
EMP: 73 **Privately Held**
WEB: www.cpii.com
SIC: 7629 3671 Electrical repair shops; vacuum tubes
HQ: Communications & Power Industries Llc
811 Hansen Way
Palo Alto CA 94304

(P-14694)
COOKS COMMUNICATIONS CORP
160 N Broadway St, Fresno (93701-1506)
PHONE 559 233-8818
Robert D Cook, *President*
Peggy Cook, *Treasurer*
Donald Cook, *Corp Comm Staff*
Paul Lambert, *Manager*
Craig Steitz, *Parts Mgr*
EMP: 27 **EST:** 1947
SQ FT: 16,000
SALES (est): 7.3MM **Privately Held**
WEB: www.cookscom.com
SIC: 5999 7629 4812 5065 Telephone equipment & systems; telephone set repair; radio telephone communication; cellular telephone services; electronic parts & equipment; radio & TV communications equipment

(P-14695)
EXTRATEAM, INC.
7031 Koll Center Pkwy # 250, Pleasanton (94566-3134)
PHONE 925 398-4400
EMP: 45
SALES (corp-wide): 1.8B **Privately Held**
WEB: www.extrateam.com
SIC: 7629 8748 Telecommunication equipment repair (except telephones); telecommunications consultant
HQ: Convergeone Government Solutions, Llc
350 Clark Dr Ste 120
Budd Lake NJ 07828

(P-14696)
FL SERVICE TEAM INC
2491 Alluvial Ave Ste 440, Clovis (93611-9587)
PHONE 559 647-5120

Jeff Hartman, *CEO*
EMP: 40 **EST:** 2013
SQ FT: 400
SALES (est): 3MM **Privately Held**
WEB: www.flserviceteam.com
SIC: 7629 5999 Business machine repair, electric; business machines & equipment

(P-14697)
FOLSOM LAKE APPLIANCE INC
8146 Greenback Ln Ste 102, Fair Oaks (95628-2551)
PHONE 916 985-3426
Scott McConnell, *CEO*
Krystle McConnell, *Principal*
Gary Hoff, *Technician*
EMP: 70 **EST:** 2005
SQ FT: 3,300
SALES (est): 6.6MM **Privately Held**
WEB: www.lakeappliancerepair.com
SIC: 7629 Electrical household appliance repair

(P-14698)
FORMAX LLC
Also Called: Formax Technologies
305 S Soderquist Rd, Turlock (95380-5130)
PHONE 800 800-1822
Ryan Lindsay, *Branch Mgr*
EMP: 35
SALES (corp-wide): 17.9MM **Privately Held**
WEB: www.formax.com
SIC: 7629 5044 Business machine repair, electric; office equipment
PA: Formax Llc
1 Education Way
Dover NH 03820
603 749-5807

(P-14699)
GDSA-LINCOLN INC (PA)
Also Called: Weco Aerospace Systems
1501 Aviation Blvd, Lincoln (95648-9388)
PHONE 916 645-8961
William Weygandt, *President*
Robert Weygandt, *CFO*
Kathleen Weygandt, *Admin Sec*
▲ **EMP:** 55 **EST:** 1971
SQ FT: 7,800
SALES (est): 3.2MM **Privately Held**
WEB: www.lincoln.com
SIC: 7629 5088 Aircraft electrical equipment repair; aircraft equipment & supplies

(P-14700)
ICRACKED INC (DH)
690 Broadway St, Redwood City (94063-3103)
PHONE 877 700-0349
Adam Forsythe, *CEO*
David Merenbach, *CFO*
▲ **EMP:** 40 **EST:** 2010
SQ FT: 24,000
SALES (est): 10.9MM **Publicly Held**
WEB: www.icracked.com
SIC: 7629 5961 Electronic equipment repair; electronic kits & parts, mail order

(P-14701)
JJR ENTERPRISES INC (HQ)
Also Called: Caltronics Business Systems
10491 Old Placerville Rd # 150, Sacramento (95827-2533)
PHONE 916 363-2666
Frank Gaspari, *CEO*
Daniel Reilly, *President*
Karen Roscher, *CFO*
Mike Murdoch, *Vice Pres*
Mark Demee, *Branch Mgr*
EMP: 95 **EST:** 1975
SQ FT: 30,000
SALES (est): 32.2MM **Privately Held**
WEB: www.caltronics.net
SIC: 7629 5044 7359 Business machine repair, electric; office equipment; equipment rental & leasing

(P-14702)
NSG TECHNOLOGY INC
Also Called: Hon Hai Precision Industry
1705 Junction Ct Ste 200, San Jose (95112-1023)
PHONE 408 547-8770
Ted Dubbs, *CEO*

PRODUCTS & SERVICES SECTION

7692 - Welding Repair County (P-14725)

Edgardo Blanchet, *Vice Pres*
Lee Nguyen, *VP Bus Dvlpt*
Aaron Tsai, *Executive*
Fabiola Elizalde, *Program Mgr*
▲ **EMP:** 429 **EST:** 1995
SALES (est): 96.1MM **Privately Held**
WEB: www.nsgtechnology.com
SIC: 7629 Electronic equipment repair
HQ: Maxwell Holdings Limited
 C/O Vistra (Cayman) Limited
 George Town GR CAYMAN

(P-14703)
PRECISION MEASUREMENTS INC
Also Called: PMI
1630 Zanker Rd, San Jose (95112-1114)
PHONE..................408 733-8600
Richard Ayala, *CEO*
Carlos Valdez, *Vice Pres*
Fernando Loza, *Manager*
Oscar Martinez, *Accounts Mgr*
EMP: 47 **EST:** 1985
SQ FT: 11,000
SALES (est): 9.2MM **Privately Held**
WEB: www.pmi-cal.com
SIC: 7629 7699 Electrical measuring instrument repair & calibration; mechanical instrument repair

(P-14704)
SCREEN SPE USA LLC (DH)
Also Called: Dns Electronics
820 Kifer Rd Ste B, Sunnyvale (94086-5200)
PHONE..................408 523-9140
Laszlo Mikulas, *President*
James Beard, *Senior VP*
Scott Prengle, *Vice Pres*
Duane Sutton, *Vice Pres*
Sam Garcia, *Technical Staff*
▲ **EMP:** 177 **EST:** 1984
SQ FT: 28,400
SALES (est): 37.5MM **Privately Held**
WEB: www.screen.co.jp
SIC: 7629 3559 Electrical repair shops; semiconductor manufacturing machinery
HQ: Screen North America Holdings, Inc.
 150 Innovation Dr Ste A
 Elk Grove Village IL 60007
 847 870-7400

(P-14705)
SIMCO ELECTRONICS (PA)
3131 Jay St Ste 100, Santa Clara (95054-3336)
PHONE..................408 734-9750
Brian Kenna, *CEO*
Sam Klooster, *Vice Pres*
Apoorva Anupindi, *Marketing Staff*
Michael Watts, *Director*
Mark Bohmier, *Manager*
EMP: 75 **EST:** 1962
SQ FT: 24,222
SALES (est): 44.3MM **Privately Held**
WEB: www.simco.com
SIC: 7629 8734 5045 7379 Electrical repair shops; calibration & certification; computer software; computer related consulting services; computer related maintenance services

(P-14706)
STAR MICROWAVE SERVICE CORP
41458 Christy St, Fremont (94538-5105)
P.O. Box 6006 (94538-0606)
PHONE..................510 651-8096
Luis Beas, *President*
Marilu Beas, *CFO*
John Saefke, *Vice Pres*
Francisco Cornejo, *Prdtn Mgr*
Orlando Garcia, *Sales Staff*
EMP: 40 **EST:** 1991
SQ FT: 25,000
SALES (est): 4.1MM **Privately Held**
WEB: www.starmicrowave.com
SIC: 7629 5065 Telecommunication equipment repair (except telephones); telephone & telegraphic equipment

7631 Watch, Clock & Jewelry Repair

(P-14707)
ADVANCE SERVICES INC
8021 Kern Ave, Gilroy (95020-4051)
PHONE..................408 767-2797
Vanessa Valencia, *Manager*
EMP: 2348 **Privately Held**
WEB: www.advanceservices.com
SIC: 7631 Watch, clock & jewelry repair
PA: Advance Services, Inc.
 12702 Wsport Pkwy Ste 201
 La Vista NE 68138

7641 Reupholstery & Furniture Repair

(P-14708)
A-1 MODULAR INC
1514 Mono Ave, San Leandro (94578-2078)
PHONE..................408 393-8808
Law Dawna J Cilluffo DC, *Administration*
EMP: 45 **EST:** 2015
SALES (est): 2MM **Privately Held**
SIC: 7641 Office furniture repair & maintenance

7692 Welding Repair

(P-14709)
B W PADILLA INC
Also Called: Brian's Welding
197 Ryland St, San Jose (95110-2241)
PHONE..................408 275-9834
Brian Wade Padilla, *CEO*
Diana Padilla, *Vice Pres*
EMP: 24 **EST:** 1991
SALES (est): 2.2MM **Privately Held**
WEB: www.brianswelding.com
SIC: 7692 Welding repair

(P-14710)
BALL RIG WELDING LLC
4801 Fther Rver Blvd Ste, Oroville (95965)
PHONE..................530 990-5795
Maurice Frank Ball, *Principal*
EMP: 22 **EST:** 2015
SALES (est): 1.6MM **Privately Held**
WEB: www.ballrigwelding.com
SIC: 7692 Welding repair

(P-14711)
CAL CUSTOM ENTERPRISES INC
792 Durham Dayton Hwy, Durham (95938-9519)
P.O. Box 42 (95938-0042)
PHONE..................530 774-2621
Gar Norlund, *Principal*
EMP: 15 **EST:** 2015
SALES (est): 536.2K **Privately Held**
WEB: www.calcustomenterprises.com
SIC: 7692 Welding repair

(P-14712)
DENTONIS WELDING WORKS INC (PA)
Also Called: Dentonis Spring and Suspension
801 S Airport Way, Stockton (95205-6901)
PHONE..................209 464-4930
David B Dentoni II, *CEO*
Donna Dentoni, *Treasurer*
Dan Dentoni, *Vice Pres*
Anthony Miranda, *Sales Mgr*
Gary Kiedrowski, *Manager*
EMP: 45
SQ FT: 1,000
SALES (est): 10.2MM **Privately Held**
WEB: www.dentoni.com
SIC: 7692 3599 5531 7539 Welding repair; machine shop, jobbing & repair; automotive parts; automotive springs, rebuilding & repair

(P-14713)
HESTER FABRICATION INC
20876 Corsair Blvd, Hayward (94545-1012)
PHONE..................530 227-6867
Daniel Hester, *Principal*
Janette Salas, *Office Mgr*
Daniel Wiggins, *Engineer*
EMP: 38 **EST:** 2014
SALES (est): 2MM **Privately Held**
WEB: www.hesterfabrication.com
SIC: 7692 Welding repair

(P-14714)
INTEGRATED MFG TECH INC
1477 N Milpitas Blvd, Milpitas (95035-3160)
PHONE..................510 659-9770
Andy Luong, *CEO*
EMP: 28 **Privately Held**
WEB: www.imt-intl.com
SIC: 7692 Welding repair
HQ: Integrated Manufacturing Technologies, Inc.
 45473 Warm Springs Blvd
 Fremont CA 94539
 408 934-5879

(P-14715)
JABIL SILVER CREEK INC
4050 Technology Pl, Fremont (94538-6362)
PHONE..................669 255-2900
John P Wolfe, *CEO*
Rita Wolfe, *Vice Pres*
▲ **EMP:** 115 **EST:** 1992
SALES (est): 23.2MM
SALES (corp-wide): 29.2B **Publicly Held**
WEB: www.jabil.com
SIC: 7692 3674 3498 3317 Welding repair; semiconductors & related devices; fabricated pipe & fittings; steel pipe & tubes; engineering services
PA: Jabil Inc.
 10560 Dr Mrtn Lther King
 Saint Petersburg FL 33716
 727 577-9749

(P-14716)
KNISLEY WELDING INC
Also Called: Knisley Aircraft Exhaust
3450 Swetzer Rd, Loomis (95650-9581)
PHONE..................916 652-5891
Bill Knisley, *President*
Curtis Knisley, *Vice Pres*
EMP: 20 **EST:** 1975
SQ FT: 15,000
SALES (est): 1.7MM **Privately Held**
WEB: www.knisleyexhaust.com
SIC: 7692 Welding repair

(P-14717)
MORRIS WELDING CO INC
11210 Socrates Mine Rd, Middletown (95461)
P.O. Box 567 (95461-0567)
PHONE..................707 987-1114
Sonnie Young, *President*
Judy Morris, *Corp Secy*
EMP: 21 **EST:** 1971
SQ FT: 6,000
SALES (est): 899.1K **Privately Held**
SIC: 7692 1623 Welding repair; water, sewer & utility lines

(P-14718)
NEVADA HEAT TREATING LLC (PA)
Also Called: California Brazing
37955 Central Ct Ste D, Newark (94560-3466)
PHONE..................510 790-2300
Richard T Penrose, *Corp Secy*
Rosie Tullis, *Admin Asst*
Grant Pocklington, *Engineer*
Bob Houghtelling, *Plant Mgr*
Mark Leonard, *Mfg Staff*
◆ **EMP:** 37 **EST:** 2002
SQ FT: 45,000
SALES (est): 42MM **Privately Held**
WEB: www.californiabrazing.com
SIC: 7692 3398 3599 Brazing; metal heat treating; air intake filters, internal combustion engine, except auto

(P-14719)
PT WELDING INC
1960 E Main St, Woodland (95776-6202)
PHONE..................530 406-0267
Patrick Trafician, *CEO*
Omar Limon, *Purchasing*
EMP: 18 **EST:** 2004
SALES (est): 1.4MM **Privately Held**
WEB: www.ptweldinginc.com
SIC: 7692 Welding repair

(P-14720)
RYLAND CUSTOM WELDING INC
1815 Monterey Hwy, San Jose (95112-6117)
PHONE..................408 781-2509
Jose Gallegos, *CEO*
EMP: 32 **EST:** 2008
SALES (est): 1.2MM **Privately Held**
SIC: 7692 Welding repair

(P-14721)
SHANNON SIDE WELDING INC (PA)
214 Shaw Rd Ste I, South San Francisco (94080-6614)
PHONE..................415 408-3219
Patrick M Sheedy, *CEO*
EMP: 49 **EST:** 2010
SALES (est): 1.2MM **Privately Held**
WEB: www.shannonsidewelding.com
SIC: 7692 Welding repair

(P-14722)
SMITH SONS WLDG & FABRICATION
2216 Cement Hill Rd, Fairfield (94533-2668)
PHONE..................707 437-3027
Greg Smith, *President*
EMP: 15 **EST:** 2014
SALES (est): 544.1K **Privately Held**
WEB: www.smithandsonswelding.com
SIC: 7692 Welding repair

(P-14723)
TC STEEL
464 Sonoma Mountain Rd, Petaluma (94954-9579)
PHONE..................707 773-2150
Tom Cleary, *President*
Kim Cleary, *CFO*
EMP: 17 **EST:** 1989
SALES (est): 1.8MM **Privately Held**
WEB: www.tcsteel.us
SIC: 7692 3449 5051 7389 Welding repair; miscellaneous metalwork; structural shapes, iron or steel; scrap steel cutting

(P-14724)
THOMAS MANUFACTURING CO LLC
1308 W 8th Ave, Chico (95926-3002)
PHONE..................530 893-8940
Carolyn Dauterman,
Thomas Dauterman,
▲ **EMP:** 16 **EST:** 1996
SQ FT: 55,000
SALES (est): 2.5MM **Privately Held**
WEB: www.thomasmfg.com
SIC: 7692 5083 3599 Welding repair; agricultural machinery & equipment; machine shop, jobbing & repair

(P-14725)
THOMAS WELDING & MACHINE INC
1308 W 8th Ave, Chico (95926-3002)
PHONE..................530 893-8940
Thomas Danterman, *CEO*
Carolyn Sue Dauterman, *Vice Pres*
EMP: 25 **EST:** 1970
SQ FT: 55,000
SALES (est): 2.3MM **Privately Held**
WEB: www.thomasmfg.com
SIC: 7692 5083 3599 Welding repair; agricultural machinery & equipment; machine shop, jobbing & repair

7692 - Welding Repair County (P-14726)

PRODUCTS & SERVICES SECTION

(P-14726)
YOSEMITE WELDING & MFG INC
647 Galaxy Way, Modesto (95356-9606)
PHONE..................................209 874-6140
Antony Konefat, *Principal*
Anthony Konefat, *Executive*
EMP: 19 EST: 2015
SALES (est): 1.8MM **Privately Held**
WEB: www.yosemitewelding.info
SIC: 7692 Welding repair

7694 Armature Rewinding Shops

(P-14727)
ARROW ELECTRIC MOTOR SERVICE
645 Broadway St, Fresno (93721-2890)
PHONE..................................559 266-0104
Larry Kragh, *President*
Geri Kragh, *Corp Secy*
Janice Sanders, *Office Mgr*
Kimberly Hall, *Admin Sec*
Clarence Kragh, *Marketing Staff*
EMP: 28 EST: 1936
SQ FT: 25,000
SALES (est): 2.2MM **Privately Held**
WEB: www.arrowelectricmotor.com
SIC: 7694 Electric motor repair

(P-14728)
AUL CORP (PA)
1250 Main St Ste 300, NAPA (94559-2622)
PHONE..................................707 257-9700
Jimmy Atkinson, *President*
Jose Fleites, *COO*
Dennis Mara, *CFO*
Glenn Schreuder, *Treasurer*
Paul McCarthy, *Senior VP*
EMP: 33 EST: 1989
SQ FT: 8,500
SALES (est): 10.6MM **Privately Held**
WEB: www.aulcorp.com
SIC: 7694 7549 Motor repair services; automotive maintenance services

(P-14729)
EANDM
126 Mill St, Healdsburg (95448-4438)
PHONE..................................707 473-3137
Stephanie Clark, *Principal*
Paul Deas, *CFO*
Dan Mossberg, *Office Admin*
Ryan Caven, *Software Dev*
Myles Fisette, *Buyer*
EMP: 15 EST: 2017
SALES (est): 4.1MM **Privately Held**
WEB: www.eandm.com
SIC: 7694 Electric motor repair

(P-14730)
STANLEY ELECTRIC MOTOR CO INC
222 N Wilson Way, Stockton (95205-4506)
PHONE..................................209 464-7321
Bradley Oneto, *President*
Beverly Oneto, *Accounting Mgr*
Pete Mamalis, *Controller*
Keota Sounthone, *Purch Mgr*
Jeff Andresen, *Sales Mgr*
EMP: 27 EST: 1936
SALES (est): 4.7MM **Privately Held**
SIC: 7694 5063 Electric motor repair; motors, electric

(P-14731)
VINCENT ELECTRIC COMPANY (PA)
Also Called: Vincent Electic Motor Company
8383 Baldwin St, Oakland (94621-1925)
PHONE..................................510 639-4500
Ronald Vincent, *Ch of Bd*
Thomas R Marvin, *President*
Sarah Beckwich, *Treasurer*
Nancy Vincent Marvin, *Admin Sec*
John Piekar, *Human Res Mgr*
EMP: 29 EST: 1932
SQ FT: 27,000
SALES (est): 3.3MM **Privately Held**
WEB: www.vincentelectric.com
SIC: 7694 5063 Electric motor repair; motors, electric

7699 Repair Shop & Related Svcs, NEC

(P-14732)
A & S MOTORCYCLE PARTS INC
Also Called: A & S BMW Motorcycles
1125 Orlando Ave Ste A, Roseville (95661-5264)
PHONE..................................916 726-7334
Randy Felice, *President*
Adrian Felice, *Treasurer*
Jamie Ormsby, *Technician*
Drew Williamson, *Technician*
Tim Whalen, *Manager*
EMP: 45 EST: 1968
SQ FT: 25,000
SALES (est): 15.9MM **Privately Held**
WEB: www.ascycles.com
SIC: 5511 7699 Automobiles, new & used; motorcycle repair service

(P-14733)
ADONAI ENTERPRISES INC (PA)
Also Called: Mathews Mechanical
7752 Enterprise Dr, Newark (94560-3409)
PHONE..................................510 475-9950
Jeffrey R Mathews, *President*
Jared B Mathews, *Treasurer*
Brenda L Mathews, *Vice Pres*
Bobby Bahmani, *Engineer*
Mark Frederick, *Engineer*
EMP: 35 EST: 1991
SQ FT: 10,000
SALES (est): 9.9MM **Privately Held**
WEB: www.mathmec.com
SIC: 7699 5084 Industrial machinery & equipment repair; conveyor systems; cranes, industrial; stackers, industrial

(P-14734)
AL-TAR SERVICES INC
823 Kifer Rd, Sunnyvale (94086-5204)
P.O. Box 1929, Evergreen CO (80437-1929)
PHONE..................................866 522-3499
Melissa Mia Castro, *President*
Dustin Castro, *COO*
Bob Nugent, *Business Dir*
Tom Digirolamo, *Technician*
Grant Wise, *Manager*
EMP: 54 EST: 1986
SQ FT: 15,000
SALES (est): 13.1MM **Privately Held**
WEB: www.al-tar.com
SIC: 7699 Laboratory instrument repair

(P-14735)
ALLIED CRANE INC
855 N Parkside Dr, Pittsburg (94565-3734)
PHONE..................................925 427-9200
David Costa, *CEO*
Jameila Haynes, *Admin Asst*
Vanessa Surrell, *Administration*
Sandy Cariel, *Accountant*
Maria Marinaro, *Purch Mgr*
EMP: 22 EST: 1977
SQ FT: 35,000
SALES (est): 6.5MM **Privately Held**
WEB: www.alliedcrane.us
SIC: 7699 3536 Industrial machinery & equipment repair; hoists, cranes & monorails

(P-14736)
ANKAR CYCLES INC
Also Called: Faultline Harley-Davidson
151 Hegenberger Rd, Oakland (94621-1407)
PHONE..................................510 657-7200
Faye Hall, *President*
Dan Roesler, *Vice Pres*
Carolyn Duranowski, *Marketing Staff*
EMP: 51 EST: 1965
SQ FT: 24,000
SALES (est): 31MM **Privately Held**
WEB: www.harley-davidson.com
SIC: 5511 7699 Automobiles, new & used; motorcycle repair service

(P-14737)
ARCLINE ELVTION SVCS HLDNGS LL
4 Embarcadero Ctr # 3460, San Francisco (94111-4106)
PHONE..................................860 805-2025
Mark Boelhouwer, *Mng Member*
Angelo Messina, *CFO*
EMP: 1000 EST: 2020
SALES (est): 4.9MM
SALES (corp-wide): 653.4MM **Privately Held**
WEB: www.arcline.com
SIC: 7699 Elevators: inspection, service & repair
PA: Arcline Investment Management Lp
    4 Embarcadero Ctr # 3460
    San Francisco CA 94111
    415 801-4570

(P-14738)
ATG-WCI INC (DH)
Also Called: Numotion
1650 Tribute Rd, Sacramento (95815-4400)
PHONE..................................916 489-3651
Jerry Knight, *President*
EMP: 104 EST: 1987
SQ FT: 16,200
SALES (est): 2.4MM
SALES (corp-wide): 491.3MM **Privately Held**
WEB: www.numotion.com
SIC: 7699 5999 Hospital equipment repair services; convalescent equipment & supplies

(P-14739)
B2 MACHINING LLC
4255 Business Center Dr, Fremont (94538-6357)
PHONE..................................510 668-1360
Bryan Bach, *Mng Member*
EMP: 17 EST: 2014
SQ FT: 7,300
SALES (est): 1.5MM **Privately Held**
WEB: www.b2machining.com
SIC: 7699 3449 Industrial machinery & equipment repair; miscellaneous metalwork

(P-14740)
BAY MARINE BOATWORKS INC
310 W Cutting Blvd, Richmond (94804-2018)
PHONE..................................510 237-0140
Erik Mattson, *President*
William Elliott, *Principal*
Kim Desenberg, *Project Mgr*
Ricardo Gutierrez, *Sales Staff*
Jamie Figueroa, *Supervisor*
▲ EMP: 36 EST: 2004
SQ FT: 500
SALES (est): 5MM
SALES (corp-wide): 75.4MM **Privately Held**
WEB: www.sbm.baymaritime.com
SIC: 7699 Boat repair
PA: Bay Ship & Yacht Co.
    2900 Main St Ste 2100
    Alameda CA 94501
    510 337-9122

(P-14741)
BAY VAVE SERVICE & ENGINEERING
3948 Teal Ct, Benicia (94510-1202)
PHONE..................................925 849-8600
Steve Teeter, *President*
EMP: 54 EST: 1972
SQ FT: 15,000
SALES (est): 283K
SALES (corp-wide): 53.6MM **Privately Held**
WEB: www.bay-valve.com
SIC: 7699 5085 Valve repair, industrial; valves & fittings
PA: Bay Valve Service & Engineering, Llc
    4385 S 133rd St
    Tukwila WA 98168
    206 782-7800

(P-14742)
CLEAN ROOFING
1445 Koll Cir Ste 109, San Jose (95112-4611)
PHONE..................................408 472-7378
Micah D Johnson, *President*
Jeff Ritchie, *Principal*
Randy Zeckman, *Principal*
EMP: 35 EST: 2019
SALES (est): 2.4MM **Privately Held**
WEB: www.cleanroofing.com
SIC: 7699 Cleaning services

(P-14743)
CNC SOLUTIONS INC
1011 Pecten Ct, Milpitas (95035-6804)
PHONE..................................408 586-8236
Timothy Bumb, *CEO*
Jim Selway, *Sales Associate*
EMP: 38 EST: 2002
SALES (est): 4.4MM **Privately Held**
WEB: www.cncsolutions.biz
SIC: 7699 Industrial machinery & equipment repair

(P-14744)
DESIGN MACHINE AND MFG
2491 Simpson St, Kingsburg (93631-9501)
PHONE..................................559 897-7374
Abe Wiabe, *Owner*
Abe Wiebe, *Managing Prtnr*
John Zweigle, *General Mgr*
Trent Miller, *Engineer*
EMP: 50 EST: 2014
SALES (est): 1.5MM **Privately Held**
WEB: www.designmachinemfg.com
SIC: 7699 Industrial machinery & equipment repair

(P-14745)
DOLK TRACTOR COMPANY
Also Called: Kubota Authorized Dealer
242 N Front St, Rio Vista (94571-1420)
P.O. Box 756 (94571-0756)
PHONE..................................707 374-6438
Rodney Dolk, *President*
Victoria Dolk, *Corp Secy*
Eric Dolk, *Vice Pres*
EMP: 39 EST: 1948
SQ FT: 13,000
SALES (est): 1.1MM **Privately Held**
WEB: www.dolktractorcompany.com
SIC: 7699 5999 5261 5083 Farm machinery repair; farm machinery; farm tractors; lawn & garden equipment; farm & garden machinery

(P-14746)
ENERGY PERFORMANCE INTL
3844 Lynwood Way, Sacramento (95864-0777)
PHONE..................................916 995-1511
Rikki Christensen, *Principal*
Rikki Christiansen, *COO*
Michael Demayo, *Executive*
EMP: 50 EST: 2007
SALES (est): 877.4K **Privately Held**
WEB: www.energyperformanceinternational.com
SIC: 7699 Repair services

(P-14747)
EXPRESS SEWER & DRAIN INC
3300 Fitzgerald Rd, Rancho Cordova (95742-6809)
PHONE..................................916 858-0220
William E Heinselman, *President*
Sang Tran, *CFO*
Laura Gallagher, *Office Mgr*
Dan Snow, *Controller*
EMP: 43 EST: 2011
SALES (est): 8.3MM **Privately Held**
WEB: www.expresssewer.com
SIC: 7699 Sewer cleaning & rodding

(P-14748)
F M G ENTERPRISES
Also Called: Fmg Vacuum Pump & Blower Repr
1125 Memorex Dr, Santa Clara (95050-2840)
PHONE..................................408 982-0110
Gary Govola, *CEO*
Mike Silva, *President*
Tracy Govola, *Treasurer*
Chris Long, *Vice Pres*

▲ = Import ▼ =Export
◆ =Import/Export

PRODUCTS & SERVICES SECTION
7699 - Repair Shop & Related Svcs, NEC County (P-14771)

Angelynne Johnson, *Accountant*
▲ **EMP:** 40 **EST:** 1985
SQ FT: 20,500
SALES (est): 6.3MM **Privately Held**
WEB: www.fmgvacpump.com
SIC: 7699 Industrial machinery & equipment repair

(P-14749)
FLUID TECH HYDRAULICS INC
8432 Tiogawoods Dr, Sacramento (95828-5046)
PHONE 916 681-0888
Stephen A Sparks, *President*
Matt Barajas, *Sales Staff*
Russ Myers, *Sales Staff*
EMP: 37 **EST:** 1989
SQ FT: 43,000
SALES (est): 3MM **Privately Held**
WEB: www.fluidtechhydraulics.com
SIC: 7699 5084 3599 Hydraulic equipment repair; hydraulic systems equipment & supplies; machine & other job shop work

(P-14750)
GMR NORTHERN CALIFORNIA LLC
Also Called: Green Mattress Recycling
7150 Patterson Pass Rd G, Livermore (94550-8302)
PHONE 925 294-9074
Jonathan Nasser, *President*
Nicole Tilley, *Manager*
EMP: 37 **EST:** 2018
SALES (est): 1.9MM **Privately Held**
SIC: 7699 Mattress renovating & repair shop

(P-14751)
GREAT AMERICAN PLUMBING CO INC
Also Called: Fifteen Dollar Sewer Drain Svc
166 Graham Ave, San Jose (95110-3110)
P.O. Box 26942 (95159-6942)
PHONE 408 279-1515
Mark Mc Giniss, *President*
Beryl Blackstone, *Vice Pres*
Oanh Lai, *Bookkeeper*
EMP: 40 **EST:** 1981
SQ FT: 6,000
SALES (est): 3.2MM **Privately Held**
SIC: 7699 Sewer cleaning & rodding

(P-14752)
GYMDOC INC
Also Called: Gym Doctors
3488 Arden Rd, Hayward (94545-3906)
PHONE 510 886-4321
Daniel Daneshvar, *CEO*
Emil Liggett, *Opers Staff*
Tim Hilton, *Manager*
EMP: 15 **EST:** 1991
SALES (est): 1.3MM **Privately Held**
WEB: www.gymdoc.com
SIC: 7699 3949 Recreational sporting equipment repair services; exercise equipment

(P-14753)
HARLEY-DAVIDSON FRESNO INC
4345 W Shaw Ave, Fresno (93722-6205)
PHONE 559 275-8586
Richard Miller, *President*
Monte E Miller, *Treasurer*
Debbie Miller, *Admin Sec*
Rich Miller, *Data Proc Exec*
Daniel Lopez, *Software Dev*
EMP: 36 **EST:** 1955
SQ FT: 18,000
SALES (est): 10MM **Privately Held**
WEB: www.hdfresno.com
SIC: 5571 7699 5699 Motorcycle dealers; motorcycle parts & accessories; motorcycle repair service; T-shirts, custom printed; leather garments

(P-14754)
HAVENS FOR TOTAL SECURITY INC
Also Called: Edwards Lock and Safe
459 N Blackstone Ave, Fresno (93701-1918)
PHONE 559 432-7600
G Haven Young, *Owner*
EMP: 35 **EST:** 1974
SALES (est): 2.6MM **Privately Held**
WEB: www.havensfts.com
SIC: 7699 Locksmith shop

(P-14755)
HYDRATECH LLC (HQ)
453 Pollasky Ave Ste 106, Clovis (93612-1178)
PHONE 559 233-0876
John J McMahon Jr
Ginny Zhou, *Executive*
Gurinder Khaira, *Engineer*
Taylor Kolb, *Engineer*
Angelica Almaguer, *Human Resources*
▲ **EMP:** 83 **EST:** 1987
SALES (est): 8.5MM
SALES (corp-wide): 467.9MM **Privately Held**
WEB: www.hydratechcylinders.com
SIC: 7699 Hydraulic equipment repair
PA: Ligon Industries, Llc
1927 1st Ave N Ste 500
Birmingham AL 35203
205 322-3302

(P-14756)
INLAND BUSINESS MACHINES INC (DH)
1326 N Market Blvd, Sacramento (95834-1912)
PHONE 916 928-0770
Liz Stafford, *President*
EMP: 68 **EST:** 1977
SALES (est): 15.5MM
SALES (corp-wide): 7B **Publicly Held**
WEB: www.inlandbusiness.us
SIC: 7699 5044 5999 Printing trades machinery & equipment repair; office equipment; photocopy machines

(P-14757)
KONE INC
15021 Wicks Blvd, San Leandro (94577-6621)
PHONE 510 351-5141
Drew Furman, *Branch Mgr*
Joe Harmeyer, *General Mgr*
Brad Lay, *Manager*
EMP: 25
SALES (corp-wide): 11.7B **Privately Held**
WEB: www.kone.us
SIC: 7699 3534 1796 Elevators: inspection, service & repair; elevators & moving stairways; installing building equipment
HQ: Kone Inc.
4225 Naperville Rd # 400
Lisle IL 60532
630 577-1650

(P-14758)
KONE INC
Also Called: Empire Elevator
1031 Laurel Ct, Sebastopol (95472-4140)
PHONE 707 778-2247
Tina Costa, *General Mgr*
EMP: 25
SALES (corp-wide): 11.7B **Privately Held**
WEB: www.kone.us
SIC: 7699 3534 1796 Elevators: inspection, service & repair; escalators, passenger & freight; elevator installation & conversion
HQ: Kone Inc.
4225 Naperville Rd # 400
Lisle IL 60532
630 577-1650

(P-14759)
LAMASSU UTILITY SERVICES INC
536 Stone Rd Ste D, Benicia (94510-1170)
P.O. Box 345, Loomis (95650-0345)
PHONE 707 750-5130
Adhab Mahmood Abdullah, *CEO*
EMP: 35 **EST:** 2017
SALES (est): 5.3MM **Privately Held**
WEB: www.lamassu.us
SIC: 7699 1623 7389 Sewer cleaning & rodding; water, sewer & utility lines; sewer inspection service

(P-14760)
LASERTEC USA INC (HQ)
2107 N 1st St Ste 210, San Jose (95131-2056)
PHONE 408 437-1441
Masashi Sunako, *President*
Haruhiko Kusunose, *Principal*
Osamu Okabayashi, *Principal*
Shu Uchiyama, *Principal*
Teruyo Matsugami, *Administration*
EMP: 49 **EST:** 1986
SALES (est): 6.1MM **Privately Held**
WEB: www.lasertecusah.openfos.com
SIC: 7699 5065 Professional instrument repair services; semiconductor devices

(P-14761)
M TEK CORPORATION
169 Borland Ave, Auburn (95603-4921)
PHONE 530 888-9609
Gordon Mason, *CEO*
EMP: 20 **EST:** 2005
SALES (est): 2.1MM **Privately Held**
WEB: www.mtekcorporation.com
SIC: 7699 3559 Industrial machinery & equipment repair; semiconductor manufacturing machinery

(P-14762)
MACS EQUIP REPAIR
3690 S Madera Ave, Kerman (93630-9000)
PHONE 559 846-6534
Macky Puckett, *Owner*
EMP: 39 **EST:** 2011
SALES (est): 2.1MM **Privately Held**
SIC: 7699 5999 Farm machinery repair; farm machinery

(P-14763)
MECHANICAL ANALYSIS/REPAIR INC
Also Called: Martech
142 N Cluff Ave, Lodi (95240-3104)
PHONE 209 333-8478
Richard Alan Leddy, *CEO*
Mike Donatelli, *Corp Secy*
Robert Delemos, *Vice Pres*
Barbara Pera, *Manager*
EMP: 45 **EST:** 1993
SQ FT: 12,000
SALES (est): 8.6MM **Privately Held**
WEB: www.mar-tech.com
SIC: 7699 5063 Industrial machinery & equipment repair; motors, electric

(P-14764)
MEL RAPTON INC
Also Called: Mel Rapton Honda
2329 Fulton Ave, Sacramento (95825-0374)
PHONE 916 514-4050
Katina Rapton, *General Mgr*
Ahmad Atassi, *Sales Mgr*
Pat Silva, *Sales Mgr*
Tommy Yanguas, *Sales Associate*
Farhad Atai, *Sales Staff*
EMP: 132
SALES (corp-wide): 55.6MM **Privately Held**
WEB: www.melraptonhonda.com
SIC: 5511 7699 Automobiles, new & used; battery service & repair
PA: Mel Rapton, Inc.
3630 Fulton Ave
Sacramento CA 95821
916 436-8364

(P-14765)
MKS INSTRUMENTS INC
3625 Peterson Way, Santa Clara (95054-2809)
PHONE 408 750-0300
Bob Hays, *Sales/Mktg Mgr*
John D Dunn, *Vice Pres*
Terence Hollister, *Engineer*
Yakov Rabiner, *Engineer*
Sebastian Peck, *Marketing Mgr*
EMP: 21
SQ FT: 5,007
SALES (corp-wide): 2.3B **Publicly Held**
WEB: www.mksinst.com
SIC: 7699 8741 3823 Ship boiler & tank cleaning & repair, contractors; management services; industrial instrmnts msrmnt display/control process variable
PA: Mks Instruments, Inc.
2 Tech Dr Ste 201
Andover MA 01810
978 645-5500

(P-14766)
N & S TRACTOR CO (PA)
600 S St 59, Merced (95341-6543)
P.O. Box 910 (95341-0910)
PHONE 209 383-5888
Arthur R Nutcher, *CEO*
Clark Bird, *CFO*
Mary Wallace, *Corp Secy*
Stephanie Nutcher, *Vice Pres*
Bob Souza, *General Mgr*
▲ **EMP:** 60 **EST:** 1954
SQ FT: 8,700
SALES (est): 28.5MM **Privately Held**
WEB: www.nstractor.com
SIC: 7699 5083 Farm machinery repair; agricultural machinery & equipment

(P-14767)
NGCW INC
Also Called: Scuderia West
69 Duboce Ave, San Francisco (94103-1231)
PHONE 415 621-7223
Don Lemelin, *President*
Crystal Garr, *Human Res Mgr*
EMP: 38 **EST:** 1991
SQ FT: 18,000
SALES (est): 3MM **Privately Held**
WEB: www.scuderiawest.com
SIC: 5571 7699 Motorcycle parts & accessories; motorcycle repair service

(P-14768)
NIACC-AVITECH TECHNOLOGIES INC (PA)
245 W Dakota Ave, Clovis (93612-5608)
PHONE 559 291-2500
Jeff Andrews, *CEO*
Thomas S Irwin, *Treasurer*
Todd Rose, *General Mgr*
Elizabeth R Letendre, *Admin Sec*
Van Vang, *Technician*
EMP: 80
SALES (est): 13.7MM **Privately Held**
WEB: www.heico.com
SIC: 7699 3471 Aircraft flight instrument repair; plating of metals or formed products

(P-14769)
OVERMILLER INC
Also Called: Roto-Rooter
195 Mason Cir, Concord (94520-1213)
PHONE 925 798-2122
Billy Joe Bristol, *President*
Mardell A Bristol, *Vice Pres*
EMP: 53 **EST:** 1956
SQ FT: 12,000
SALES (est): 4.6MM **Privately Held**
WEB: www.rotorooter.com
SIC: 7699 1711 Sewer cleaning & rodding; plumbing contractors

(P-14770)
PROPAK LOGISTICS INC
2650 Industrial Blvd B, West Sacramento (95691-3837)
PHONE 479 478-7828
EMP: 37 **Privately Held**
WEB: www.propak.com
SIC: 7699 Pallet repair
PA: Propak Logistics, Inc.
1100 Garrison Ave
Fort Smith AR 72901

(P-14771)
RAYMOND HANDLING CONCEPTS CORP (DH)
Also Called: Rhcc
41400 Boyce Rd, Fremont (94538-3113)
PHONE 510 745-7500
James Wilcox, *President*
Donald Jones, *Vice Pres*
Al Seiler, *Vice Pres*
Steven Koel, *VP Sales*
David Donatelli, *Sales Staff*
EMP: 60 **EST:** 1987
SQ FT: 32,000

7699 - Repair Shop & Related Svcs, NEC County (P-14772)

SALES (est): 61.6MM **Privately Held**
WEB: www.raymondhandling.com
SIC: **7699** 5084 7359 7629 Industrial machinery & equipment repair; materials handling machinery; equipment rental & leasing; electrical repair shops
HQ: The Raymond Corporation
22 S Canal St
Greene NY 13778
607 656-2311

(P-14772)
RICHMOND SANITARY SERVICE INC (HQ)
Also Called: Crockett Garbage Service
3260 Blume Dr Ste 100, Richmond (94806-1960)
P.O. Box 4100 (94804-0100)
PHONE.....................510 262-7100
Richard Granzella, *President*
Dennis Varni, *CFO*
Mario Acquilino, *Vice Pres*
Pina Barbiere, *Principal*
Loyd Bonfante, *Principal*
▲ **EMP:** 200 **EST:** 1924
SALES (est): 22.3MM
SALES (corp-wide): 10.1B **Publicly Held**
WEB: www.ci.richmond.ca.us
SIC: **7699** Septic tank cleaning service
PA: Republic Services, Inc.
18500 N Allied Way # 100
Phoenix AZ 85054
480 627-2700

(P-14773)
ROTO ROOTER SERVICE
Also Called: Roto-Rooter
3840 Bayshore Blvd, Brisbane (94005-1403)
PHONE.....................415 656-2130
Arnold Galarza, *Partner*
Bertha Galarza, *Partner*
EMP: 63 **EST:** 1959
SALES (est): 6.5MM **Privately Held**
WEB: www.rotorooter.com
SIC: **7699** Sewer cleaning & rodding

(P-14774)
RS CALIBRATION SERVICES INC
1047 Serpentine Ln # 500, Pleasanton (94566-4786)
PHONE.....................925 462-4217
Ralph Sabiel, *President*
Michele Rediger, *CFO*
Debbie Sabiel, *Treasurer*
Jon Deguzman, *Technician*
Dina Lueth, *Technician*
EMP: 50 **EST:** 1996
SQ FT: 5,000
SALES (est): 11.4MM **Privately Held**
SIC: **7699** 8734 Professional instrument repair services; calibration & certification

(P-14775)
SECURITY CENTRAL INC
Also Called: Reed Brothers Security
2950 Alvarado St Ste D, San Leandro (94577-5738)
PHONE.....................510 652-2477
Ronald Reed, *President*
Randall Reed, *Treasurer*
Michael Salk, *Vice Pres*
Robert Ferguson, *Manager*
Nicolas Rojas, *Manager*
EMP: 42 **EST:** 1990
SQ FT: 19,000
SALES (est): 9.6MM **Privately Held**
WEB: www.reedbrotherssecurity.com
SIC: **7699** 5099 3446 5999 Locksmith shop; locks & lock sets; fences or posts, ornamental iron or steel; electronic parts & equipment; security systems services; solar heating equipment

(P-14776)
SWAN ASSOCIATES INCORPORATED
4680 E 2nd St Ste H, Benicia (94510-1018)
PHONE.....................707 746-1989
Robert Mathews, *President*
EMP: 37 **EST:** 1976

SALES (est): 5.5MM **Privately Held**
WEB: www.swan-associates.com
SIC: **7699** 5084 Industrial equipment services; compressors, except air conditioning

(P-14777)
SWECO PRODUCTS INC (PA)
8949 Colusa Hwy, Sutter (95982-9321)
P.O. Box 259 (95982-0259)
PHONE.....................530 673-8949
Maria Jesus Ziegenmeyer, *CEO*
Raymond Ziegenmeyer, *President*
Michael Ziegenmeyer, *COO*
Julie Shepherd, *CFO*
Bobby Ziegenmeyer, *Exec VP*
▲ **EMP:** 38 **EST:** 1946
SQ FT: 65,000
SALES (est): 8.1MM **Privately Held**
WEB: www.swecoproducts.com
SIC: **7699** 3599 5082 Farm machinery repair; custom machinery; construction & mining machinery

(P-14778)
TK ELEVATOR CORPORATION
30984 Santana St, Hayward (94544-7058)
PHONE.....................510 476-1900
Homer Guerra, *Principal*
Patty Stone, *Human Res Dir*
Ed Persico, *Manager*
EMP: 40
SALES (corp-wide): 1B **Privately Held**
WEB: www.tkelevator.com
SIC: **7699** Elevators: inspection, service & repair
HQ: Tk Elevator Corporation
11605 Haynes Bridge Rd
Alpharetta GA 30009
678 319-3240

(P-14779)
TK ELEVATOR CORPORATION
2140 Zanker Rd, San Jose (95131-2113)
PHONE.....................408 392-0910
Joe Annino, *Manager*
Rhonda Emerson, *Branch Mgr*
EMP: 40
SALES (corp-wide): 1B **Privately Held**
WEB: www.tkelevator.com
SIC: **7699** Elevators: inspection, service & repair
HQ: Tk Elevator Corporation
11605 Haynes Bridge Rd
Alpharetta GA 30009
678 319-3240

(P-14780)
UNITED CALIFORNIA GLASS & DOOR
745 Cesar Chavez, San Francisco (94124-1211)
PHONE.....................415 824-8500
Judith Ticktin, *President*
Steve Montoya, *Project Mgr*
Harold Ticktin, *Manager*
▲ **EMP:** 70 **EST:** 1991
SQ FT: 31,000 **Privately Held**
WEB: www.ucgd.com
SIC: **7699** 1793 Door & window repair; glass & glazing work

(P-14781)
UNIVERSAL PLANT SVCS NTHRN CAL (HQ)
505 Lopes Rd Ste D, Fairfield (94534-6893)
PHONE.....................707 864-0100
Bradley T Jones, *CEO*
Stewart Jones, *President*
Reagan Busbee, *COO*
EMP: 40 **EST:** 2004
SALES (est): 2.3MM
SALES (corp-wide): 502.8MM **Privately Held**
WEB: www.universalplant.com
SIC: **7699** Industrial machinery & equipment repair
PA: Jones Industrial Holdings, Inc.
806 Seaco Ct
Deer Park TX 77536
281 479-6000

(P-14782)
UNIVERSITY ART CENTER INC (PA)
2550 El Camino Real, Redwood City (94061-3813)
PHONE.....................650 328-3500
Lauretta Cappiello, *CEO*
Cornelia Pendleton, *Treasurer*
Todd Ayers, *General Mgr*
Virginia Biondi, *Admin Sec*
Liz Moreno, *Technology*
EMP: 57 **EST:** 1965
SQ FT: 24,000
SALES (est): 10.9MM **Privately Held**
WEB: www.universityart.com
SIC: **7699** 5947 5999 Picture framing, custom; gift shop; artists' supplies & materials

(P-14783)
VENTEX CORP
2153 Otoole Ave Ste 10, San Jose (95131-1331)
PHONE.....................408 436-2929
Brett Pearson, *CEO*
Jay Bukant, *Vice Pres*
Jessica Oleksy, *Accounts Mgr*
▲ **EMP:** 26 **EST:** 1994
SQ FT: 10,000
SALES (est): 3.2MM **Privately Held**
WEB: www.ventexcorp.com
SIC: **7699** 3559 Industrial machinery & equipment repair; semiconductor manufacturing machinery

(P-14784)
WCR INCORPORATED
4636 E Drummond Ave, Fresno (93725-1601)
PHONE.....................559 266-8374
Jeff Simpson, *Principal*
Paul Dorn, *CIO*
Melissa Carter, *Sales Mgr*
EMP: 26
SQ FT: 12,656
SALES (corp-wide): 34.8MM **Privately Held**
WEB: www.wcrhx.com
SIC: **7699** 7629 3443 Metal reshaping & replating services; electrical repair shops; fabricated plate work (boiler shop)
PA: Wcr Incorporated
2377 Commerce Center Blvd
Fairborn OH 45324
937 223-0703

(P-14785)
WESTBROOK ENTERPRISES INC
Also Called: Harley-Davidson
1000 Arden Way, Sacramento (95815-3204)
PHONE.....................916 929-4680
Jay Westbrook, *President*
Christine Westbrook, *Vice Pres*
Kayla Barkell, *Asst Controller*
Alan Casner, *Sales Mgr*
EMP: 65 **EST:** 1950
SQ FT: 15,000
SALES (est): 12.6MM **Privately Held**
WEB: www.hdsac.com
SIC: **5571** 7699 Motorcycles; motorcycle repair service

7812 Motion Picture & Video Tape Production

(P-14786)
ATV VIDEO CENTER INC
Also Called: All Things Video
2424 Glendale Ln, Sacramento (95825-2418)
P.O. Box 3228, Hayden ID (83835-3228)
PHONE.....................916 973-9100
Gary Jones, *President*
Gary A Jones, *President*
Dave Hull, *Vice Pres*
Hysha Verthein, *General Mgr*
Robert Leven, *Sales Mgr*
EMP: 42 **EST:** 2000
SQ FT: 10,000

SALES (est): 3.1MM **Privately Held**
WEB: www.atv.net
SIC: **7812** 7819 7359 5065 Video tape production; video tape or disk reproduction; audio-visual equipment & supply rental; closed circuit television

(P-14787)
CONCORD VERANDA CINEMA LLC
Also Called: Veranda Luxe Cinema
2035 Diamond Blvd Ste 150, Concord (94520-5701)
P.O. Box 750595, Petaluma (94975-0595)
PHONE.....................707 762-0990
EMP: 142 **EST:** 2016
SALES (est): 2.6MM **Privately Held**
WEB: www.cinemawest.com
SIC: **7812** 7832 Motion picture production; motion picture theaters, except drive-in

(P-14788)
CYBERNET ENTERTAINMENT LLC (PA)
1800 Mission St, San Francisco (94103-3502)
PHONE.....................415 865-0230
Peter Ackworth, *Mng Member*
Matt Slusarenko, *Director*
Courtney Turner, *Manager*
EMP: 114 **EST:** 1998
SALES (est): 9.2MM **Privately Held**
WEB: www.cybernetentertainment.com
SIC: **7812** Video production

(P-14789)
DACAST
1175 Folsom St, San Francisco (94103-3930)
PHONE.....................510 619-4857
Stephane Roulland, *President*
Michael Cloward, *Executive*
Mihhail Danilenko, *Business Anlyst*
Michael Alagao, *Technical Staff*
Mary-Ann Concepcion, *Technical Staff*
EMP: 41 **EST:** 2010
SALES (est): 5.3MM **Privately Held**
WEB: www.dacast.com
SIC: **7812** Video production

(P-14790)
EVENT AND LABOR SERVICES
340 Bonair Siding Rd, Stanford (94305-7208)
PHONE.....................650 723-2285
Larry Davidson, *Director*
Sandy Meyer, *Vice Pres*
Cori Bossenberry, *Human Resources*
EMP: 107 **EST:** 1940
SQ FT: 18,000
SALES (est): 1.2MM **Privately Held**
SIC: **7812** Audio-visual program production

(P-14791)
FRANCIS FORD COPPOLA INC
Also Called: American Zoetrope
916 Kearny St, San Francisco (94133-5107)
PHONE.....................415 788-7500
Francis Ford Coppola, *Ch of Bd*
Anahid Nazarian, *Producer*
EMP: 67 **EST:** 1991
SALES (est): 5.5MM **Privately Held**
SIC: **7812** Motion picture production & distribution; television film production

(P-14792)
INDUSTRIAL LGHT MGIC VNCVER LL
1110 Gorgas Ave, San Francisco (94129-1406)
PHONE.....................415 292-4671
Steve Condiotti, *CEO*
Alex Aponte, *COO*
Nicole Letaw, *COO*
Sarah Derby, *Vice Pres*
Khuyen Dang, *Executive*
▲ **EMP:** 105 **EST:** 2011
SALES (est): 11.6MM
SALES (corp-wide): 65.3B **Publicly Held**
WEB: www.ilm.com
SIC: **7812** Motion picture & video production

PRODUCTS & SERVICES SECTION
7832 - Motion Picture Theaters, Except Drive-In County (P-14815)

HQ: Lucasfilm Ltd.
1110 Gorgas Ave Bldg C-Hr
San Francisco CA 94129
415 623-1000

(P-14793)
LUCASFILM LTD (DH)
Also Called: Lucasfilm Coml Productions
1110 Gorgas Ave Bldg C-Hr, San Francisco (94129-1406)
P.O. Box 29901 (94129-0901)
PHONE..................................415 623-1000
Kathleen Kennedy, *President*
Stephen Arnold, *CFO*
Lauri Aultman, *Vice Pres*
Lori Aultman, *Vice Pres*
Candice Campos, *Vice Pres*
▲ **EMP:** 250 **EST:** 1971
SALES (est): 190.3MM
SALES (corp-wide): 65.3B **Publicly Held**
WEB: www.lucasfilm.com
SIC: 7812 6794 Motion picture production & distribution; patent owners & lessors

(P-14794)
NEW PARADIGM PRODUCTIONS INC (PA)
Also Called: Edelman Productions
39 Mesa St Ste 212, San Francisco (94129-1019)
PHONE..................................415 924-8000
Steve Edelman, *President*
EMP: 100 **EST:** 1981
SQ FT: 8,500
SALES (est): 2.5MM **Privately Held**
WEB: www.edelmanproductions.com
SIC: 7812 Video production

(P-14795)
PIXAR (DH)
Also Called: Pixar Animation Studios
1200 Park Ave, Emeryville (94608-3677)
PHONE..................................510 922-3000
James W Morris, *CEO*
Ann Mather, *CFO*
John Lasseter, *Exec VP*
Pamela Kerwin, *Vice Pres*
Nathan Waters, *Vice Pres*
▲ **EMP:** 797 **EST:** 1985
SQ FT: 247,000
SALES (est): 122.6MM
SALES (corp-wide): 65.3B **Publicly Held**
WEB: www.pixar.com
SIC: 7812 7372 7371 Cartoon motion picture production; commercials, television; tape or film; prepackaged software; computer software development

(P-14796)
THRESHER CMMNCTONS PRDCTVITY I
234 E Caribbean Dr, Sunnyvale (94089-1007)
PHONE..................................408 780-3066
John Howard Nickel, *CEO*
EMP: 88 **EST:** 1998
SALES (est): 8.1MM
SALES (corp-wide): 165.6MM **Privately Held**
WEB: www.rahisystems.com
SIC: 7812 Audio-visual program production
PA: Rahi Systems Inc
  48303 Fremont Blvd
  Fremont CA 94538
  510 651-2205

(P-14797)
TICOMI PRODUCTION INC
6350 Stoneridge Mall Rd, Pleasanton (94588-8052)
PHONE..................................925 399-5117
EMP: 45 **EST:** 2007
SALES (est): 2.6MM **Privately Held**
SIC: 7812 Motion Picture/Video Production

(P-14798)
VUMEDI INC
555 12th St Ste 500, Oakland (94607-3699)
PHONE..................................650 450-2603
Roman Giverts, *CEO*
Ryan Martin, *Partner*
Katarina Jeanneau, *Controller*
Whitney Tilton, *Director*
Jennifer Hays, *Manager*
EMP: 63 **EST:** 2008

SALES (est): 5.9MM **Privately Held**
WEB: www.vumedi.com
SIC: 7812 Video production

(P-14799)
YES VIDEOCOM INC (PA)
2805 Bowers Ave Ste 230, Santa Clara (95051-0971)
PHONE..................................408 907-7600
Michael Chang, *CEO*
Bo Morris, *Vice Pres*
Mike Fales, *Controller*
Jexter Reynante, *Prdtn Mgr*
Kathy Camat, *Director*
▲ **EMP:** 152 **EST:** 1999
SQ FT: 36,000
SALES (est): 21MM **Privately Held**
WEB: www.yesvideo.com
SIC: 7812 Motion picture production

7819 Services Allied To Motion Picture Prdtn

(P-14800)
ATOMIC FICTION INC (HQ)
Also Called: Method Studios
160 Pacific Ave Ste 204, San Francisco (94111-1976)
PHONE..................................510 488-6641
Kevin Baillie, *CEO*
Ryan Tudhope, *Ch Credit Ofcr*
Amanda Belo, *Executive Asst*
Patrick Cardin, *Administration*
Sean Whitacre, *Engineer*
EMP: 43 **EST:** 2009
SALES (est): 12.7MM **Privately Held**
WEB: www.methodstudios.com
SIC: 7819 Visual effects production

(P-14801)
BAY AREA VIDEO COALITION INC
Also Called: Bavc
2727 Mariposa St Fl 2, San Francisco (94110-1401)
PHONE..................................415 861-3282
Ken Ikeda, *Director*
Paula S Arrigoni, *Exec Dir*
Alec Raffin, *Exec Dir*
Brittney Reaume, *Admin Asst*
Nilofar Gardezi, *Analyst*
EMP: 55 **EST:** 1977
SQ FT: 25,000
SALES: 5.3MM **Privately Held**
WEB: www.bavc.org
SIC: 7819 8249 Video tape or disk reproduction; vocational schools

(P-14802)
NETFLIX STUDIOS LLC (HQ)
100 Winchester Cir, Los Gatos (95032-1815)
PHONE..................................408 540-3700
Reed Hastings, *Ch of Bd*
EMP: 523 **EST:** 2013
SALES (est): 56.5MM **Publicly Held**
WEB: www.netflix.com
SIC: 7819 7841 Sound (effects & music production), motion picture; video tape rental; video disk/tape rental to the general public

7822 Motion Picture & Video Tape Distribution

(P-14803)
BLEACHER REPORT INC
153 Kearny St Fl 2, San Francisco (94108-4808)
PHONE..................................415 777-5505
Dave Finocchio, *CEO*
Sam Toles, *Officer*
Josh Abrams, *Vice Pres*
Bill McCandless, *Vice Pres*
Rich Calacci, *Principal*
EMP: 42 **EST:** 2007

SALES (est): 4.3MM
SALES (corp-wide): 171.7B **Publicly Held**
WEB: www.bleacherreport.com
SIC: 7822 4833 4841 7812 Motion picture distribution; television broadcasting stations; cable television services; motion picture production
HQ: Turner Broadcasting System, Inc.
  1 Cnn Ctr Nw 14sw
  Atlanta GA 30303
  404 827-1500

7832 Motion Picture Theaters, Except Drive-In

(P-14804)
BRENDEN THEATRE CORPORATION
531 Davis St, Vacaville (95688-4632)
PHONE..................................707 469-0180
Tim Kruse, *Branch Mgr*
EMP: 79 **Privately Held**
WEB: www.brendentheatres.com
SIC: 7832 Exhibitors, itinerant: motion picture
PA: Brenden Theatre Corporation
  1985 Willow Pass Rd Ste C
  Concord CA 94520

(P-14805)
BRENDEN THEATRE CORPORATION
1021 10th St Frnt, Modesto (95354-0888)
PHONE..................................209 491-7770
Saul Trujllo, *General Mgr*
EMP: 79 **Privately Held**
WEB: www.brendentheatres.com
SIC: 7832 Exhibitors, itinerant: motion picture
PA: Brenden Theatre Corporation
  1985 Willow Pass Rd Ste C
  Concord CA 94520

(P-14806)
BRENDEN THEATRE CORPORATION (PA)
1985 Willow Pass Rd Ste C, Concord (94520-2533)
PHONE..................................925 677-0462
John Brenden, *President*
EMP: 189 **EST:** 1989
SQ FT: 70,000
SALES (est): 37.5MM **Privately Held**
WEB: www.brendentheatres.com
SIC: 7832 Motion picture theaters, except drive-in

(P-14807)
CAMPUS POINTE CINEMAS OPER LLC
Also Called: Maya Fresno Cinemas
3090 E Campus Pointe Dr, Fresno (93710-7526)
PHONE..................................213 805-5333
EMP: 45
SALES (est): 701.4K **Privately Held**
SIC: 7832 Motion picture theaters, except drive-in

(P-14808)
CENTURY THEATRES INC
Also Called: Century 14
109 Plaza Dr, Vallejo (94591-3703)
PHONE..................................707 648-3456
EMP: 237 **Publicly Held**
WEB: www.cinemark.com
SIC: 7832 Motion picture theaters, except drive-in
HQ: Century Theatres, Inc
  3900 Dallas Pkwy Ste 500
  Plano TX 75093
  972 665-1000

(P-14809)
CENTURY THEATRES INC
Also Called: Capitol Drive-In
3630 Hillcap Ave, San Jose (95136-1344)
PHONE..................................408 226-2251
Teresa Dinh, *Manager*
EMP: 237 **Publicly Held**

WEB: www.cinemark.com
SIC: 7832 Motion picture theaters, except drive-in
HQ: Century Theatres, Inc
  3900 Dallas Pkwy Ste 500
  Plano TX 75093
  972 665-1000

(P-14810)
EDWARDS THEATRES CIRCUIT INC
Also Called: Fairfield Stadium Cinema
1549 Gateway Blvd, Fairfield (94533-6902)
PHONE..................................707 432-2121
EMP: 62 **Privately Held**
SIC: 7832 Motion picture theaters, except drive-in
HQ: Edwards Theatres Circuit, Inc.
  300 Newport Center Dr
  Newport Beach CA 92660
  949 640-4600

(P-14811)
IMAX CORPORATION
Also Called: Hackworth Imax Dome
201 S Market St, San Jose (95113-2008)
PHONE..................................408 294-8324
EMP: 80
SALES (corp-wide): 137MM **Privately Held**
WEB: www.thetech.org
SIC: 7832 Motion picture theaters, except drive-in
HQ: Imax Corporation
  12582 Millennium
  Los Angeles CA 90094

(P-14812)
MAYA PITTSBURG CINEMAS LLC
Also Called: Maya Cinemas Pittsburg
4085 Century Blvd, Pittsburg (94565-7105)
PHONE..................................213 805-5333
Heidi Garcia, *Opers Mgr*
EMP: 50 **EST:** 2012
SALES (est): 1.3MM **Privately Held**
SIC: 7832 Motion picture theaters, except drive-in

(P-14813)
MERCURY AIR CARGO INC
648 West Field Rd, San Francisco (94128-3101)
PHONE..................................650 588-5440
Karen Self, *Manager*
EMP: 43
SALES (corp-wide): 455.2MM **Privately Held**
WEB: www.mercuryaircargo.com
SIC: 7832 Exhibitors for airlines, motion picture
HQ: Mercury Air Cargo, Inc.
  2780 Skypark Dr Ste 300
  Torrance CA 90505
  310 258-6100

(P-14814)
NORTH AMERICAN CINEMAS INC
Also Called: Airport Cinemas 12
409 Aviation Blvd, Santa Rosa (95403-1069)
PHONE..................................707 571-1412
Nicholas Mann, *General Mgr*
EMP: 356 **Privately Held**
WEB: www.santarosacinemas.com
SIC: 7832 Motion picture theaters, except drive-in
PA: North American Cinemas, Inc.
  816 4th St
  Santa Rosa CA 95404

(P-14815)
PETALUMA CINEMAS LLC
Also Called: Boulevard Cinemas
515 E Washington St, Petaluma (94952-3217)
PHONE..................................707 762-0990
David Corkill, *Principal*
EMP: 37 **EST:** 2003
SALES (est): 790.4K **Privately Held**
SIC: 7832 Motion picture theaters, except drive-in

7832 - Motion Picture Theaters, Except Drive-In

(P-14816)
PREMIERE CINEMAS
641 Mccray St, Hollister (95023-4032)
PHONE..........................831 638-1800
Alfred Silva Jr, *President*
David Taliaferro, *Treasurer*
Tamra Koll, *Officer*
Craig Tankersly, *General Mgr*
Ted Intravia, *Admin Sec*
EMP: 35 **EST:** 1994
SALES (est): 2.7MM **Privately Held**
WEB: www.premierecinemas.net
SIC: 7832 Motion picture theaters, except drive-in

(P-14817)
READING INTERNATIONAL INC
2508 Land Park Dr, Sacramento (95818-2224)
PHONE..........................916 442-0985
EMP: 42
SALES (corp-wide): 77.8MM **Publicly Held**
WEB: www.readingrdi.com
SIC: 7832 Motion picture theaters, except drive-in
PA: Reading International, Inc.
5995 Sepulveda Blvd # 300
Culver City CA 90230
213 235-2240

(P-14818)
SYUFY CENTURY CORPORATION (PA)
Also Called: Century Theatres
150 Pelican Way, San Francisco (94102)
PHONE..........................415 448-8300
Raymond W Syufy, *President*
EMP: 52 **EST:** 1990
SALES (est): 744.4K **Privately Held**
SIC: 7832 Motion picture theaters, except drive-in

7833 Drive-In Motion Picture Theaters

(P-14819)
CENTURY THEATRES INC
Also Called: Century Laguna 16
9349 Big Horn Blvd, Elk Grove (95758-7934)
PHONE..........................916 683-5290
EMP: 237 **Publicly Held**
WEB: www.cinemark.com
SIC: 7833 7832 Drive-in motion picture theaters; motion picture theaters, except drive-in
HQ: Century Theatres, Inc
3900 Dallas Pkwy Ste 500
Plano TX 75093
972 665-1000

(P-14820)
CENTURY THEATRES INC
Also Called: Century 20
1010 Great Mall Dr, Milpitas (95035-8034)
PHONE..........................408 942-7441
EMP: 237 **Publicly Held**
WEB: www.cinemark.com
SIC: 7833 7832 Drive-in motion picture theaters; motion picture theaters, except drive-in
HQ: Century Theatres, Inc
3900 Dallas Pkwy Ste 500
Plano TX 75093
972 665-1000

(P-14821)
CENTURY THEATRES INC
Also Called: Plaza 7
445 Downtown Plz, Sacramento (95814-3322)
PHONE..........................916 442-7000
EMP: 42 **Publicly Held**
WEB: www.centurytheatres.com
SIC: 7833 7832 Drive-In Theater Motion Picture Theater
HQ: Century Theatres, Inc
3900 Dallas Pkwy Ste 500
Plano TX 75093
972 665-1000

(P-14822)
CENTURY THEATRES INC
825 Middlefield Rd, Redwood City (94063-1627)
PHONE..........................866 322-4547
EMP: 237 **Publicly Held**
SIC: 7833 Drive-in motion picture theaters
HQ: Century Theatres, Inc
3900 Dallas Pkwy Ste 500
Plano TX 75093
972 665-1000

(P-14823)
CENTURY THEATRES INC
3200 Klose Way, Richmond (94806-5792)
PHONE..........................510 758-9626
Makisha Jones, *Manager*
EMP: 237 **Publicly Held**
WEB: www.cinemark.com
SIC: 7833 7832 Drive-in motion picture theaters; motion picture theaters, except drive-in
HQ: Century Theatres, Inc
3900 Dallas Pkwy Ste 500
Plano TX 75093
972 665-1000

(P-14824)
CENTURY THEATRES INC
125 Crescent Dr, Pleasant Hill (94523-5503)
PHONE..........................925 681-2000
EMP: 42 **Publicly Held**
WEB: www.cinemark.com
SIC: 7833 7832 Drive-in motion picture theaters; motion picture theaters, except drive-in
HQ: Century Theatres, Inc
3900 Dallas Pkwy Ste 500
Plano TX 75093
972 665-1000

(P-14825)
CENTURY THEATRES INC
Also Called: Century Presidio
2340 Chestnut St, San Francisco (94123-2610)
PHONE..........................415 776-2388
Pamela Knopp, *Manager*
EMP: 237 **Publicly Held**
WEB: www.cinemark.com
SIC: 7833 7832 Drive-in motion picture theaters; motion picture theaters, except drive-in
HQ: Century Theatres, Inc
3900 Dallas Pkwy Ste 500
Plano TX 75093
972 665-1000

(P-14826)
CENTURY THEATRES INC
Also Called: Century Cinema
1500 N Shoreline Blvd, Mountain View (94043-1314)
PHONE..........................650 961-3828
Luis Alvarez, *Asst Mgr*
EMP: 237 **Publicly Held**
WEB: www.cinemark.com
SIC: 7833 7832 Drive-in motion picture theaters; motion picture theaters, except drive-in
HQ: Century Theatres, Inc
3900 Dallas Pkwy Ste 500
Plano TX 75093
972 665-1000

(P-14827)
CENTURY THEATRES INC
Also Called: Hyatt Cinema 3
1304 Bayshore Hwy, Burlingame (94010-1803)
PHONE..........................650 340-1516
EMP: 42 **Publicly Held**
WEB: www.centurytheatres.com
SIC: 7833 7832 Drive-In Theater Motion Picture Theater
HQ: Century Theatres, Inc
3900 Dallas Pkwy Ste 500
Plano TX 75093
972 665-1000

(P-14828)
CENTURY THEATRES INC
Also Called: Century Cinema
41 Tamal Vista Blvd, Corte Madera (94925-1144)
PHONE..........................415 924-6505
EMP: 38 **Publicly Held**
WEB: www.centurytheatres.com
SIC: 7833 7832 Drive-In Theater Motion Picture Theater
HQ: Century Theatres, Inc
3900 Dallas Pkwy Ste 500
Plano TX 75093
972 665-1000

(P-14829)
CENTURY THEATRES INC
Also Called: Cinedome 9
6233 Garfield Ave, Sacramento (95841-2010)
PHONE..........................916 332-2622
Sayward Gray, *Branch Mgr*
EMP: 237 **Publicly Held**
WEB: www.cinemark.com
SIC: 7833 7832 Drive-in motion picture theaters; motion picture theaters, except drive-in
HQ: Century Theatres, Inc
3900 Dallas Pkwy Ste 500
Plano TX 75093
972 665-1000

(P-14830)
CENTURY THEATRES INC
Also Called: Empire Cinema
85 West Portal Ave, San Francisco (94127-1303)
PHONE..........................415 661-2539
Robert Morgan, *Manager*
EMP: 237 **Publicly Held**
WEB: www.cinemark.com
SIC: 7833 7832 Drive-in motion picture theaters; motion picture theaters, except drive-in
HQ: Century Theatres, Inc
3900 Dallas Pkwy Ste 500
Plano TX 75093
972 665-1000

(P-14831)
CENTURY THEATRES INC
Also Called: Sacramento Drive In
9616 Oates Dr, Sacramento (95827-1607)
PHONE..........................916 363-6572
Raymond Syufy, *Branch Mgr*
EMP: 237 **Publicly Held**
WEB: www.cinemark.com
SIC: 7833 7832 Drive-in motion picture theaters; motion picture theaters, except drive-in
HQ: Century Theatres, Inc
3900 Dallas Pkwy Ste 500
Plano TX 75093
972 665-1000

7841 Video Tape Rental

(P-14832)
NETFLIX INC
121 Albright Way, Los Gatos (95032-1801)
PHONE..........................408 540-3700
Laura Day, *Partner*
Eric Ruiz, *Partner*
Sarah Comfort, *COO*
Richard Barton, *Bd of Directors*
Zach Ragatz, *Admin Sec*
EMP: 2000 **Publicly Held**
WEB: www.netflix.com
SIC: 7841 Video disk/tape rental to the general public
PA: Netflix, Inc.
100 Winchester Cir
Los Gatos CA 95032

(P-14833)
NETFLIX INC (PA)
100 Winchester Cir, Los Gatos (95032-1815)
PHONE..........................408 540-3700
Reed Hastings, *Ch of Bd*
Spencer Neumann, *CFO*
David Hyman,
Greg Peters,
Jessica Neal, *Officer*
EMP: 166 **EST:** 1998
SALES (est): 25B **Publicly Held**
WEB: www.netflix.com
SIC: 7841 2741 Video disk/tape rental to the general public;

(P-14834)
POWERVISION INC
298 Harbor Blvd, Belmont (94002-4017)
PHONE..........................650 620-9948
Barry Cheskin, *CEO*
S Arieh Zak, *Senior VP*
Bryan Flaherty, *Vice Pres*
Henry Wu, *Vice Pres*
Greg Matthews, *Principal*
EMP: 46 **EST:** 1990
SALES (est): 12.1MM
SALES (corp-wide): 6.8B **Privately Held**
WEB: www.powervision.com
SIC: 5735 7841 Video discs & tapes, pre-recorded; video disk/tape rental to the general public
HQ: Alcon, Inc.
1132 Ferris Rd
Amelia OH 45102
513 722-1037

7922 Theatrical Producers & Misc Theatrical Svcs

(P-14835)
AMERICAN CNSRVTORY THTRE FNDTI (PA)
Also Called: A C T
415 Geary St, San Francisco (94102-1222)
PHONE..........................415 834-3200
Jennifer Bielstein, *Exec Dir*
David Engelmann, *Treasurer*
Heather Kitchen, *Exec Dir*
Christopher Herold, *Director*
Carey Perloff, *Director*
▲ **EMP:** 92 **EST:** 1986
SQ FT: 40,000
SALES (est): 25.4MM **Privately Held**
WEB: www.act-sf.org
SIC: 7922 8299 Employment agency: theatrical, radio & television; dramatic school

(P-14836)
BELLA CIRCUS
231 Mullen Ave, San Francisco (94110-5331)
PHONE..........................415 205-8355
Abigail Munn, *Exec Dir*
EMP: 44
SALES (est): 741.3K **Privately Held**
WEB: www.circusbella.org
SIC: 7922 Theatrical producers & services

(P-14837)
BERKELEY REPERTORY THEATRE (PA)
2025 Addison St, Berkeley (94704-1103)
PHONE..........................510 204-8901
Susan Medak, *Managing Dir*
Tony Taccone, *Managing Dir*
Kate Horton, *Executive Asst*
John Horton, *CIO*
Suzanne Pettigrew, *Controller*
▲ **EMP:** 76 **EST:** 1967
SQ FT: 20,000
SALES: 12.3MM **Privately Held**
WEB: www.berkeleyrep.org
SIC: 7922 Legitimate live theater producers

(P-14838)
BNNV LLC
1030 Main St, NAPA (94559-2641)
PHONE..........................707 880-2300
Kenneth Tesler, *Mng Member*
EMP: 35 **EST:** 2016
SALES (est): 1.1MM **Privately Held**
SIC: 5812 7922 Eating places; concert management service

(P-14839)
BROADWAY BY BAY
1972 2nd Ave, Walnut Creek (94597-2563)
P.O. Box 728, San Carlos (94070-0728)
PHONE..........................650 579-5565
Waren Doan, *President*

PRODUCTS & SERVICES SECTION
7922 - Theatrical Producers & Misc Theatrical Svcs County (P-14862)

Alicia Jeffrey, *Director*
Alexis Lazear, *Director*
EMP: 140 **EST:** 1967
SQ FT: 1,600
SALES (est): 4.8MM **Privately Held**
WEB: www.bbbay.org
SIC: 7922 Ticket agency, theatrical

(P-14840)
BROADWAY SACRAMENTO (PA)
Also Called: Music Circus
1510 J St Ste 200, Sacramento (95814-2099)
PHONE..................................916 446-5880
Richard Lewis, *President*
Elisabeth Thomas, *Pub Rel Mgr*
Matt Hessburg, *Marketing Staff*
Michael Foster, *Sales Staff*
Marissa Eng, *Education*
▲ **EMP:** 150 **EST:** 1951
SQ FT: 7,000
SALES (est): 17.7MM **Privately Held**
WEB: www.broadwaysacramento.com
SIC: 7922 Theatrical companies

(P-14841)
CABRILLO CMNTY CLLEGE DST FING (PA)
Also Called: Cabrillo College
6500 Soquel Dr, Aptos (95003-3119)
PHONE..................................831 479-6100
Dlaurel Jones, *President*
MO Hassan, *Ch of Bd*
Laurel Jones, *President*
Cynthia Siegel, *Treasurer*
Brian King, *Vice Pres*
EMP: 980
SQ FT: 8,000
SALES: 71.9MM **Privately Held**
WEB: www.cabrillo.edu
SIC: 8222 7922 8221 Community college; theatrical producers & services; colleges universities & professional schools

(P-14842)
CALIFORNIA SHAKESPEARE THEATER (PA)
Also Called: Cal Shakes
100 Clfrnia Shkspear Thte, Orinda (94563)
PHONE..................................510 548-3422
Eric Ting, *Exec Dir*
Jay Yamada, *Treasurer*
Sk Kerastas, *Producer*
Naomi Arnst, *Director*
Derik Cowan, *Director*
EMP: 223 **EST:** 1974
SALES (est): 4.3MM **Privately Held**
WEB: www.calshakes.org
SIC: 7922 Plays, road & stock companies

(P-14843)
CALIFORNIA STATE UNIV LONG BCH
Also Called: Theatre Department
5201 N Maple Ave, Fresno (93740-0001)
PHONE..................................559 278-2216
Melissa Gibson, *Administration*
EMP: 205 **Privately Held**
WEB: www.csulb.edu
SIC: 8299 7922 8221 9411 Dramatic school; theatrical producers & services; university; administration of educational programs;
HQ: California State University, Long Beach
1250 N Bellflower Blvd
Long Beach CA 90840
562 985-4111

(P-14844)
CENTRAL VLY CTR FOR ARTS INC (PA)
Also Called: GALLO CENTER FOR THE ARTS
1000 I St, Modesto (95354-2381)
PHONE..................................209 338-2100
Robert Fores, *Chairman*
Tony Accurso, *Web Dvlpr*
Sarah Hosner, *Production*
Annie Benisch, *Marketing Staff*
Doug Hosner, *Marketing Staff*
EMP: 44 **EST:** 2001
SALES: 1.1MM **Privately Held**
WEB: www.galloarts.org
SIC: 7922 Ticket agency, theatrical

(P-14845)
CHRISTIAN EVANG CHRCHES AMER I
Also Called: Patten Christian Schools
2433 Coolidge Ave, Oakland (94601-2630)
PHONE..................................510 533-8300
Bebe Patten, *President*
Dr Gary Moncher, *President*
Anna Jean Pyle, *Treasurer*
EMP: 45 **EST:** 1945
SQ FT: 25,000
SALES (est): 5.3MM **Privately Held**
WEB: www.thecathedral.us
SIC: 8211 7922 8661 2711 Private combined elementary & secondary school; television program, including commercial producers; Covenant & Evangelical Church; newspapers: publishing only, not printed on site

(P-14846)
DIABLO BALLET
1646 N Calif Blvd Ste 109, Walnut Creek (94596-4113)
P.O. Box 4700 (94596-0700)
PHONE..................................925 943-1775
Miriam Leigh, *President*
Julie Hahn, *Manager*
EMP: 48 **EST:** 1994
SALES: 952.3K **Privately Held**
WEB: www.diabloballet.org
SIC: 7922 Theatrical companies

(P-14847)
GOLD CLUB INC
Also Called: Gold Club Centerfolds
11363 Folsom Blvd, Rancho Cordova (95742-6224)
PHONE..................................916 442-3111
Mark Boiles, *Manager*
Mark Boyles, *Manager*
EMP: 47 **EST:** 1995
SALES (est): 4.4MM **Privately Held**
WEB: www.centerfoldsadultstore.com
SIC: 7922 Theatrical companies

(P-14848)
I CAN DO THAT THEATRE COMPANY
194 Diablo Rd, Danville (94526-3303)
PHONE..................................415 264-2518
Shayna Ronen, *Exec Dir*
EMP: 35 **EST:** 2016
SALES (est): 412.4K **Privately Held**
WEB: www.icandothatpac.org
SIC: 7922 8699 Theatrical companies; charitable organization

(P-14849)
JOHN GORE ORGANIZATION INC
255 S B St, San Mateo (94401-4017)
PHONE..................................650 340-0469
EMP: 51
SALES (corp-wide): 555.1MM **Privately Held**
WEB: www.johngore.com
SIC: 7922 Entertainment promotion
PA: The John Gore Organization Inc
1619 Broadway Fl 9
New York NY 10019
917 421-5400

(P-14850)
LUCAS DIGITAL LTD (DH)
3155 Kerner Blvd, San Rafael (94901-5410)
P.O. Box 3000 (94912-3000)
PHONE..................................415 258-2000
James Morris, *President*
EMP: 500 **EST:** 1993
SALES (est): 3.5MM
SALES (corp-wide): 65.3B **Publicly Held**
WEB: www.lucasfilm.com
SIC: 7922 7819 Theatrical producers & services; sound (effects & music production), motion picture
HQ: Lucasfilm Ltd.
1110 Gorgas Ave Bldg C-Hr
San Francisco CA 94129
415 623-1000

(P-14851)
LUTHER BURBANK MEM FOUNDATION
50 Mark West Springs Rd, Santa Rosa (95403-1457)
PHONE..................................707 546-3600
Richard Nowlin, *Exec Dir*
Gene Soldani, *Info Tech Mgr*
Mark Desaulnier, *Marketing Staff*
Timothy Rogers, *Chief*
J David Siembieda, *Director*
EMP: 74 **EST:** 1978
SQ FT: 120,000
SALES (est): 7.4MM **Privately Held**
WEB: www.lutherburbankcenter.org
SIC: 7922 8299 6519 Performing arts center production; music & drama schools; real property lessors

(P-14852)
NEWPORT TELEVISION LLC
4880 N 1st St, Fresno (93726-0514)
PHONE..................................559 761-0243
EMP: 288
SALES (corp-wide): 26.5MM **Privately Held**
WEB: www.newporttv.com
SIC: 7922 Television program, including commercial producers
PA: Newport Television Llc
460 Nichols Rd Ste 250
Kansas City MO 64112
816 751-0200

(P-14853)
ODC THEATER
351 Shotwell St, San Francisco (94110-1324)
PHONE..................................415 863-6606
Carma Zisman, *Exec Dir*
Malia Connor, *Admin Asst*
Jason Dinneen, *Technical Staff*
Edgar Mendez, *Marketing Staff*
Lindsay Leonard, *Associate*
EMP: 55 **EST:** 1978
SQ FT: 10,000
SALES (est): 907K
SALES (corp-wide): 5.3MM **Privately Held**
WEB: www.odc.dance
SIC: 7922 7911 Theatrical companies; dance studio & school
PA: Odc
351 Shotwell St
San Francisco CA 94110
415 863-6606

(P-14854)
OPERA SAN JOSE INC
2149 Paragon Dr, San Jose (95131-1312)
PHONE..................................408 437-4450
Irene Dalis, *Exec Dir*
George Crow, *President*
Khori Dastoor, *Bd of Directors*
Matthew Vandercook, *Managing Dir*
Larry Hancock, *General Mgr*
EMP: 62 **EST:** 1977
SQ FT: 25,000
SALES: 4.5MM **Privately Held**
WEB: www.operasj.com
SIC: 7922 7929 Opera company; entertainers & entertainment groups

(P-14855)
PARAMOUNT THEATRE OF ARTS INC
2025 Broadway, Oakland (94612-2303)
PHONE..................................510 893-2300
Leslee Stewart, *Director*
EMP: 60 **EST:** 1986
SQ FT: 37,000
SALES: 3.5MM **Privately Held**
WEB: www.paramounttheatre.com
SIC: 7922 Performing arts center production

(P-14856)
PETER A KUZINICH
Also Called: Pink Poodle
328 S Bascom Ave, San Jose (95128-2207)
PHONE..................................408 292-3686
Peter A Kuzinich, *Owner*
EMP: 36 **EST:** 1963
SQ FT: 2,250

SALES (est): 2.3MM **Privately Held**
SIC: 7922 5942 Burlesque company; book stores

(P-14857)
PHOEBUS CO INC
Also Called: Phoebus Lighting
2800 3rd St, San Francisco (94107-3502)
PHONE..................................415 550-0770
John A Tedesco, *President*
Michael E Garrett, *Vice Pres*
EMP: 18 **EST:** 1973
SQ FT: 50,000
SALES (est): 459.7K **Privately Held**
WEB: www.pheobus.com
SIC: 7922 3646 Lighting, theatrical; commercial indusl & institutional electric lighting fixtures

(P-14858)
PLAYWRIGHTS FOUNDATION INC
1616 16th St Ste 350, San Francisco (94103-5164)
PHONE..................................415 626-2176
Amy Mueller, *Director*
Linda Brewer, *President*
Jill Maclean, *Producer*
Michelle Bank, *Manager*
Maddie Gaw, *Manager*
EMP: 73 **EST:** 1978
SQ FT: 1,200
SALES (est): 378.3K **Privately Held**
WEB: www.playwrightsfoundation.org
SIC: 7922 Legitimate live theater producers

(P-14859)
SACRAMENTO THEATRE COMPANY
1419 H St, Sacramento (95814-1901)
PHONE..................................916 446-7501
Daniel Brunner, *Ch of Bd*
Michael Laun, *Exec Dir*
Shelly Sandford, *Office Mgr*
Alan Almeida, *Opers Staff*
Kendra Lewis, *Med Doctor*
EMP: 57 **EST:** 1942
SALES (est): 1.8MM **Privately Held**
WEB: www.sactheatre.org
SIC: 7922 Legitimate live theater producers

(P-14860)
SACRAMENTO THEATRICAL LTG LTD
Also Called: S T L
410 N 10th St, Sacramento (95811-0310)
PHONE..................................916 447-3258
John W Cox, *CEO*
Kaye Newton, *Vice Pres*
Christina Cox-Lohrey, *Executive Asst*
Steven Rhetta, *Prdtn Mgr*
Bobbie Odehnal, *Manager*
EMP: 65 **EST:** 1947
SALES (est): 10MM **Privately Held**
WEB: www.stlltd.com
SIC: 7922 5063 Equipment rental, theatrical; lighting fixtures

(P-14861)
SAN FRANCISCO BALLET ASSN
455 Franklin St, San Francisco (94102-4471)
PHONE..................................415 865-2000
Glenn McCoy, *CEO*
Kim Carim, *CFO*
Donald B Paterson, *CFO*
J Stuart Francis, *Treasurer*
Jennifer Peterian, *Treasurer*
▲ **EMP:** 250 **EST:** 1933
SQ FT: 70,000
SALES: 3.7MM **Privately Held**
WEB: www.sfballet.org
SIC: 7922 7911 Ballet production; dance studio & school

(P-14862)
SAN FRANCISCO OPERA ASSN
301 Van Ness Ave, San Francisco (94102-4509)
PHONE..................................415 861-4008
John A Gunn, *Chairman*
Karl O Mills, *Vice Chairman*
Keith B Geeslin, *President*

7922 - Theatrical Producers & Misc Theatrical Svcs County (P-14863)

David Gockley, CEO
Michael Simpson, CFO
▲ EMP: 1050 EST: 1932
SALES (est): 27.2MM Privately Held
WEB: www.sfopera.com
SIC: 7922 Legitimate live theater producers

(P-14863)
SIERRA REPERTORY THEATRE INC
13891 Mono Way, Sonora (95370-8864)
P.O. Box 3030 (95370-3030)
PHONE.................................209 532-0502
Dennis Jones, President
Sara Jones, Managing Dir
Cat Loudermilk, Executive Asst
Erika Ervin, Director
Ryan Kessler, Director
EMP: 37 EST: 1980
SQ FT: 6,000
SALES (est): 5.4MM Privately Held
WEB: www.sierrarep.org
SIC: 7922 Legitimate live theater producers

(P-14864)
STEVE SILVER PRODUCTIONS INC
678 Green St Ste 2, San Francisco (94133-3846)
PHONE.................................415 421-4284
EMP: 94
SALES (corp-wide): 3.7MM Privately Held
SIC: 7922 Theatrical Production
PA: Silver Steve Productions Inc
470 Columbus Ave Ste 204
San Francisco CA 94133
415 421-4284

(P-14865)
THEATREWORKS SILICON VALLEY
350 Twin Dolphin Dr, Redwood City (94065-1457)
PHONE.................................650 517-5870
Phil Santora, Director
Lynn Davis, Associate Dir
Syche Phillips, Associate Dir
Frank Sarmiento, Technical Staff
Stevenb Mannshardt, Opers Mgr
EMP: 47 EST: 1970
SQ FT: 32,000
SALES (est): 9.8MM Privately Held
WEB: www.theatreworks.org
SIC: 7922 Legitimate live theater producers

(P-14866)
UPTOWN THEATRE
1350 Third St, NAPA (94559-2902)
PHONE.................................707 259-0123
Tim Herman,
EMP: 56 EST: 2020
SALES (est): 1.2MM Privately Held
WEB: www.uptowntheatrenapa.com
SIC: 7922 Theatrical companies

7929 Bands, Orchestras, Actors & Entertainers

(P-14867)
ARAMARK SPT & ENTRMT GROUP LLC
525 W Santa Clara St, San Jose (95113-1520)
PHONE.................................408 999-5735
John Heberden, Principal
Benedict Cipponeri, Controller
EMP: 312 Publicly Held
WEB: www.aramark.com
SIC: 7929 Entertainers & entertainment groups
HQ: Aramark Sports And Entertainment Group, Llc
2400 Market St
Philadelphia PA 19103
215 238-3000

(P-14868)
ARAMARK SPT & ENTRMT GROUP LLC
5001 Great America Pkwy, Santa Clara (95054-1119)
PHONE.................................408 748-7030
Jerry McCarthy, Manager
Rick Huking, Site Mgr
EMP: 312 Publicly Held
WEB: www.aramark.com
SIC: 7929 Entertainment service
HQ: Aramark Sports And Entertainment Group, Llc
2400 Market St
Philadelphia PA 19103
215 238-3000

(P-14869)
BERKELEY SYMPHONY ORCHESTRA
1919 Addison St Ste 104, Berkeley (94704-1142)
PHONE.................................510 841-2800
Gary Ginstling, Exec Dir
James Kleinmann, Exec Dir
Mollie Budiansky, Marketing Staff
Cindy Hickox, Marketing Staff
Ren Mandel, Manager
EMP: 50 EST: 1972
SALES (est): 950.1K Privately Held
WEB: www.berkeleysymphony.org
SIC: 7929 Symphony orchestras

(P-14870)
BOUNCE A RAMA INC
1450 Great Mall Dr, Milpitas (95035-8038)
PHONE.................................510 754-8799
Rick Tran, President
Daniel Dang, Info Tech Mgr
EMP: 52 EST: 2005
SALES (est): 3.7MM Privately Held
WEB: www.bounce-a-rama.com
SIC: 5812 7929 Pizza restaurants; entertainment service

(P-14871)
DREAMALLIANCE ENTRMT INC (PA)
20236 Santa Maria Ave, Castro Valley (94546-4226)
PHONE.................................510 270-8693
Le Tong, Manager
EMP: 42 EST: 2017
SALES (est): 290.6K Privately Held
WEB: www.dreameggsfc.com
SIC: 7929 Entertainers & entertainment groups

(P-14872)
I TROVATORI OPERA INC
2097 Olivera Rd Apt C, Concord (94520-5473)
PHONE.................................925 246-9360
Sonia E Harden Lemke, President
Temirzhan Yerzhanov, Vice Pres
Kelly Benjamson, Admin Sec
EMP: 35
SALES (est): 2.3K Privately Held
SIC: 7929 Classical music groups or artists

(P-14873)
KINGS VIEW
126 N D St, Madera (93638-3235)
PHONE.................................559 673-0167
EMP: 47
SALES (corp-wide): 26.8MM Privately Held
WEB: www.kingsview.org
SIC: 7929 Entertainment service
PA: Kings View
7170 N Fincl Dr Ste 110
Fresno CA 93720
559 256-0100

(P-14874)
PM ENTERTAINMENT CORP
Also Called: Pure Nightclub
146 S Murphy Ave, Sunnyvale (94086-6112)
PHONE.................................408 732-2121
Michael Shihua Hu, Administration
Peter Lin, CEO
Michael Hu, Admin Sec
EMP: 40 EST: 2012
SALES (est): 768.4K Privately Held
SIC: 7929 5813 Entertainers & entertainment groups; drinking places

(P-14875)
SAN FRANCISCO PERFORMANCES INC
500 Sutter St Ste 710, San Francisco (94102-1198)
PHONE.................................415 398-6449
Ruth Felt, President
Jorena De Pedro, Marketing Staff
Will Crockett, Sales Staff
B Wilson, Senior Mgr
Christine Lim, Director
EMP: 39 EST: 1979
SQ FT: 2,750
SALES (est): 2.4MM Privately Held
WEB: www.sfperformances.org
SIC: 7929 7922 Symphony orchestras; theatrical producers & services

(P-14876)
SAN FRANCISCO SYMPHONY (PA)
201 Van Ness Ave, San Francisco (94102-4585)
PHONE.................................415 552-8000
Brent Assink, CEO
James Kirk, CFO
Mark Koenig, CFO
Liz Pesch, CFO
Victor Steeb, Officer
▲ EMP: 178 EST: 1911
SALES: 65.3MM Privately Held
WEB: www.sfsymphony.org
SIC: 7929 Symphony orchestras

(P-14877)
SAN FRNCSCO CNSERVATORY OF MUS
Also Called: SFCM
50 Oak St, San Francisco (94102-6011)
PHONE.................................415 864-7326
David H Stull, President
Basma Edrees, Partner
Jonathan Kretschmer, Partner
Colin Murdoch, President
Kathryn Wittenmyer, CFO
EMP: 200 EST: 1917
SQ FT: 80,000
SALES: 65.9MM Privately Held
WEB: www.sfcm.edu
SIC: 8299 7929 Music school; entertainers & entertainment groups

(P-14878)
SOLID GOLD INC
Also Called: Gold Club, The
650 Howard St, San Francisco (94105-3916)
PHONE.................................415 536-0300
Donaldson Molinari, Manager
Elizabeth Furnelli, President
David Lou, Manager
EMP: 81 EST: 1994
SQ FT: 10,000
SALES (est): 1.4MM Privately Held
WEB: www.goldclubsf.com
SIC: 5812 5813 7929 Eating places; bar (drinking places); entertainment service

(P-14879)
SONY INTERACTIVE ENTRMT LLC
2207 Brindgepointe Pkwy, San Mateo (94404)
PHONE.................................650 655-8000
Fumihiko Kanagawa, Manager
Colby Turner, Administration
Jeremy Lunsford, Sr Ntwrk Engine
Stephen Townsend, Technology
Michael Huggins, Director
EMP: 100 Privately Held
WEB: www.playstation.com
SIC: 7929 Entertainment service
HQ: Sony Interactive Entertainment Llc
2207 Bridgepointe Pkwy
Foster City CA 94404
310 981-1500

(P-14880)
STREAMRAY INC (PA)
Also Called: Hotbox
910 E Hamilton Ave Fl 6, Campbell (95008-0655)
PHONE.................................408 745-5449
Mallorie Burak, CEO
EMP: 80 EST: 2008
SALES (est): 366.5K Privately Held
SIC: 7929 Entertainment group

(P-14881)
STRIKING DISTANCE STUDIOS INC
6111 Bollinger Canyon Rd # 150, San Ramon (94583-5103)
PHONE.................................925 355-5131
Glen Schofield, CEO
EMP: 50 EST: 2019
SALES (est): 4.2MM Privately Held
SIC: 7929 Entertainment group

(P-14882)
UBI SOFT ENTERTAINMENT
625 3rd St Fl 3, San Francisco (94107-1918)
PHONE.................................415 547-4000
Yves Guillemot, President
Fondy Les, Vice Pres
Brenda Panagrossi, Vice Pres
Jean Decant, Creative Dir
Victor Fajardo, Admin Mgr
EMP: 61 EST: 2011
SALES (est): 14.9MM
SALES (corp-wide): 2.6B Privately Held
WEB: www.ubisoft.com
SIC: 7929 Entertainers & entertainment groups
PA: Ubisoft Entertainment
2 Rue Du Chene Heleuc
Carentoir 56910

(P-14883)
WONDERFUL UNION LLC
1909 H St, Sacramento (95811-3107)
P.O. Box 160967 (95816-0967)
PHONE.................................916 526-0285
Edmond Meehan, Mng Member
Brice Turner, Business Dir
Gail Charles, Accounting Dir
Greg Patterson,
Jenny Quan,
EMP: 41 EST: 2013
SALES (est): 2.5MM Privately Held
WEB: www.wonderfulunion.com
SIC: 7929 Entertainment service

(P-14884)
YANKA INDUSTRIES INC
Also Called: Masterclass
660 4th St Ste 443, San Francisco (94107-1618)
PHONE.................................855 981-8208
David Jeremy Rogier, CEO
Mark Williamson, COO
Paul Bankhead, Officer
Tamara Jordan, Sr Software Eng
Valen Tong, CTO
EMP: 61 EST: 2012
SALES (est): 10MM Privately Held
WEB: www.masterclass.com
SIC: 7929 7812 Entertainment service; video production

7933 Bowling Centers

(P-14885)
BAY COUNTIES INVESTMENTS INC
Also Called: Castro Village Bowl
3501 Village Dr, Castro Valley (94546-5617)
PHONE.................................510 538-8100
Carl D Phippin, President
Bradley D Rudnick, Corp Secy
Pamela J Phippin, Vice Pres
EMP: 37 EST: 1959
SQ FT: 29,000
SALES (est): 1.3MM Privately Held
WEB: www.castrovillage.com
SIC: 7933 5813 5812 Ten pin center; bar (drinking places); snack bar

PRODUCTS & SERVICES SECTION 7941 - Professional Sports Clubs & Promoters County (P-14910)

(P-14886)
BDP BOWL INC
Also Called: Classic Bowling Center
900 King Plz, Daly City (94015-4450)
PHONE 650 878-0300
Robert Devincenzi, *President*
Richard J Bocci, *Treasurer*
Steve Devincenzi, *General Mgr*
Steven Devinchenzi, *Admin Sec*
Steve Devinchenzi, *Sales Executive*
EMP: 72 EST: 1984
SQ FT: 50,000
SALES (est): 4.4MM **Privately Held**
WEB: www.classicbowling.com
SIC: 7933 Ten pin center

(P-14887)
BOWLERO CORP
6450 N Blackstone Ave, Fresno (93710-3501)
PHONE 201 797-5400
EMP: 65
SALES (corp-wide): 530.3MM **Publicly Held**
WEB: www.bowlero.com
SIC: 7933 Ten pin center
PA: Bowlero Corp.
   222 W 44th St
   New York NY 10036
   212 777-2214

(P-14888)
BOWLERO CORP
300 Park St, Alameda (94501-6230)
PHONE 510 523-6767
EMP: 65
SALES (corp-wide): 530.3MM **Publicly Held**
WEB: www.bowlmor.com
SIC: 7933 Ten pin center
PA: Bowlero Corp.
   222 W 44th St
   New York NY 10036
   212 777-2214

(P-14889)
DOUBLE DECKER CORPORATION
Also Called: Double Decker Lanes
300 Golf Course Dr, Rohnert Park (94928-1758)
PHONE 707 585-0226
James Decker III, *President*
Susan Decker, *Vice Pres*
Dennis Ganduglia, *General Mgr*
Curtis Woods, *Asst Mgr*
EMP: 37 EST: 1962
SQ FT: 44,000
SALES (est): 1.3MM **Privately Held**
WEB: www.doubledeckerlanes.com
SIC: 7933 Ten pin center

(P-14890)
FIRESIDE LANES INC
7901 Auburn Blvd, Citrus Heights (95610-1404)
PHONE 916 725-2101
Steve Cook, *President*
EMP: 35 EST: 1987
SQ FT: 1,000
SALES (est): 519.2K **Privately Held**
WEB: www.stevecooksfiresidelanes.com
SIC: 5813 5812 7933 Cocktail lounge; cafe; bowling centers; ten pin center

(P-14891)
FOLSOM RECREATION CORP
Also Called: Lake Bowl
511 E Bidwell St, Folsom (95630-3118)
PHONE 916 983-4411
Wally Dreher, *President*
Sue Dreher, *Vice Pres*
Jeremy Dreher, *General Mgr*
Carly Dreher, *Bookkeeper*
Monica Dreher, *Manager*
EMP: 67 EST: 1960
SQ FT: 18,000
SALES (est): 3.4MM **Privately Held**
WEB: www.flb365.com
SIC: 7933 Ten pin center

(P-14892)
FOURTH STREET BOWL INC
1441 N 4th St, San Jose (95112-4716)
PHONE 408 453-5555
Ken Nakatsu, *President*
Cathie Judy, *General Mgr*
EMP: 37 EST: 1975
SQ FT: 31,450
SALES (est): 2.4MM **Privately Held**
WEB: www.4thstreetbowl.com
SIC: 7933 5813 5812 Ten pin center; bar (drinking places); coffee shop

(P-14893)
FREMONT SPORTS INC
Also Called: Cloverleaf Bowl
40645 Fremont Blvd Ste 3, Fremont (94538-4368)
P.O. Box 1456 (94538-0145)
PHONE 510 656-4411
EMP: 50
SQ FT: 40,000
SALES: 46.3K **Privately Held**
WEB: www.cloverleafbowl.com
SIC: 7933 5812 5813 Bowling Alley Food Bar & Cocktail Lounge

(P-14894)
GRANADA BOWL INC
1620 Railroad Ave, Livermore (94550-3129)
PHONE 925 447-5600
Dennis Fanucchi, *President*
Sandra Crane, *Treasurer*
Angela Fanucchi, *Vice Pres*
Tom Crane, *General Mgr*
EMP: 43 EST: 1964
SQ FT: 35,000
SALES (est): 2.5MM **Privately Held**
WEB: www.granadabowl.com
SIC: 7933 5813 7999 5941 Ten pin center; cocktail lounge; billiard parlor; bowling equipment & supplies

(P-14895)
HARVEST PARK BOWL
5000 Balfour Rd, Brentwood (94513-4001)
PHONE 925 516-1221
Jim Wangeman, *General Ptnr*
Natalie Paris, *Director*
Kevin Dexheimer, *Manager*
Sherry Mackenzie, *Manager*
EMP: 65 EST: 1994
SQ FT: 30,000
SALES (est): 3MM **Privately Held**
WEB: www.bowlero.com
SIC: 7933 Ten pin center

(P-14896)
PACIFIC AVENUE BOWL
Also Called: Spares & Strikes Bowling Sup
5939 Pacific Ave, Stockton (95207-4703)
PHONE 209 477-0267
Brian Nakashima, *President*
Robert Bell, *Administration*
Ryan Jimenez, *Administration*
Julianne Nakashima, *VP Finance*
Laura Clark, *Manager*
EMP: 46 EST: 1958
SQ FT: 33,660
SALES (est): 5.1MM **Privately Held**
WEB: www.pacificbowl.com
SIC: 7933 Ten pin center

(P-14897)
PINSETTERS INC
Also Called: Country Club Lanes
2600 Watt Ave, Sacramento (95821-6296)
PHONE 916 488-7545
Greg Kassis, *Ch of Bd*
Dave Haness, *President*
Jim Kassis, *Corp Secy*
Dave Kassis, *Vice Pres*
Kerry Kassis, *Vice Pres*
EMP: 74 EST: 1958
SQ FT: 70,000
SALES (est): 1.1MM **Privately Held**
WEB: www.countryclublanes.com
SIC: 7933 5812 5813 Ten pin center; snack bar; bar (drinking places)

(P-14898)
RAGERS RECREATIONAL ENTPS
Also Called: Yosemite Lanes
2301 Yosemite Blvd, Modesto (95354-3004)
PHONE 209 522-2452
Jim Gordin, *President*
Tina Fadelgo, *Bookkeeper*
EMP: 46 EST: 1961
SQ FT: 32,000
SALES (est): 2.5MM **Privately Held**
WEB: www.yosemitelanes.com
SIC: 7933 5812 5813 Ten pin center; restaurant, family: independent; bar (drinking places)

(P-14899)
SERRA BOWL INC (PA)
701 Price St, Daly City (94014-2133)
PHONE 415 626-2626
Rex Golobic, *President*
EMP: 38 EST: 1958
SQ FT: 43,000
SALES (est): 1.2MM **Privately Held**
WEB: www.serrabowl.com
SIC: 7933 5813 5812 7993 Ten pin center; bar (drinking places); snack bar; amusement arcade

(P-14900)
SPARE-TIME INC
429 W Lockeford St, Lodi (95240-2058)
PHONE 209 371-0241
Dennis Kaufman, *Principal*
EMP: 278
SALES (corp-wide): 53MM **Privately Held**
SIC: 7933 Ten pin center
PA: Spare-Time, Inc.
   11344 Coloma Rd Ste 350
   Gold River CA 95670
   916 859-5910

(P-14901)
STARS RECREATION CENTER LP
155 Browns Valley Pkwy, Vacaville (95688-3011)
PHONE 707 455-7827
Ernest E Sousa, *Partner*
Kenneth Sousa, *Partner*
EMP: 43 EST: 1998
SQ FT: 65,000
SALES (est): 2.1MM **Privately Held**
WEB: www.starsrecreation.com
SIC: 7933 Ten pin center

(P-14902)
STRIKES UNLIMITED INC
5681 Lonetree Blvd, Rocklin (95765-3735)
PHONE 916 626-3600
Kari Pegram, *CEO*
Armando Pacheco, *General Mgr*
Prakash Chandra, *Controller*
Annette Turek, *Human Res Dir*
EMP: 90 EST: 2011
SQ FT: 54,000
SALES (est): 5.1MM **Privately Held**
WEB: www.strikesrocklin.com
SIC: 7933 5812 Ten pin center; eating places

7941 Professional Sports Clubs & Promoters

(P-14903)
ATHLETICS INVESTMENT GROUP LLC (PA)
Also Called: Oakland Athletics
7000 Coliseum Way Ste 3, Oakland (94621-1917)
P.O. Box 2220 (94621-0120)
PHONE 510 638-4900
Lewis N Wolff, *Mng Member*
Andy Szabo, *Partner*
Dan Kantrovitz, *Vice Pres*
Ashwin Puri, *Vice Pres*
David Rinetti, *Vice Pres*
EMP: 177 EST: 1901
SALES (est): 52.9MM **Privately Held**
WEB: www.mlb.com
SIC: 7941 Baseball club, professional & semi-professional

(P-14904)
CITY VIEW AT METREON
135 4th St Ste 4000, San Francisco (94103-3060)
PHONE 415 369-6142
Patricia Sokol, *Admin Asst*
EMP: 47 EST: 2014
SALES (est): 537.8K **Privately Held**
WEB: www.cityviewmetreon.com
SIC: 7941 Stadium event operator services
HQ: Starwood Retail Partners, Llc
   1 E Wacker Dr Ste 3600
   Chicago IL 60601
   312 242-3200

(P-14905)
FORTY NINERS FOOTBALL CO LLC
Also Called: San Francisco 49ers
4949 Mrie P Debartolo Way, Santa Clara (95054-1156)
PHONE 408 562-4949
Denise Debartolo York, *Principal*
Paraag Marathe, *COO*
Brano Perkovich, *Ch Invest Ofcr*
Robert Alberino, *Vice Pres*
Russ Butler, *Vice Pres*
EMP: 99 EST: 1971
SALES (est): 37.4MM **Privately Held**
WEB: www.49ers.com
SIC: 7941 Football club

(P-14906)
FORTY NINERS SC STADIUM CO LLC
4949 Mrie P Debartolo Way, Santa Clara (95054-1156)
PHONE 408 562-4949
▲ EMP: 37 EST: 2012
SALES (est): 1.7MM **Privately Held**
SIC: 7941 Football club

(P-14907)
GOLDEN STATE WARRIORS LLC
1 Warriors Way, San Francisco (94158-2254)
PHONE 415 388-0100
Christopher Cohan, *Mng Member*
Michelle Libby, *COO*
Robert Rowell, *Officer*
John Beaven, *Vice Pres*
David Kelly, *Vice Pres*
EMP: 100 EST: 1962
SALES: 4.6MM **Privately Held**
WEB: www.warriors.com
SIC: 7941 Basketball club

(P-14908)
GYMSTARS GYMNASTICS INC (PA)
1740 W Hammer Ln, Stockton (95209-2922)
PHONE 209 955-7595
Roberto Tanon, *President*
Casey Tanon, *Corp Secy*
Jim Stars, *Principal*
EMP: 37 EST: 1999
SALES (est): 2.7MM **Privately Held**
WEB: www.gymstars.com
SIC: 7941 7999 7991 7911 Sports field or stadium operator, promoting sports events; gymnastic instruction, non-membership; athletic club & gymnasiums, membership; dance instructor & school services

(P-14909)
KINGS ARENA LTD PARTNERSHIP
Also Called: Maloof Sport Entertainment
1 Sports Pkwy, Sacramento (95834-2300)
PHONE 916 928-0000
Gavin Maloof, *Managing Prtnr*
John Rinehart, *Partner*
John Thomas, *Partner*
EMP: 60 EST: 1992
SALES (est): 10.9MM **Privately Held**
SIC: 7941 Boxing & wrestling arena

(P-14910)
LEVI STADIUM
4900 Mrie P Debartolo Way, Santa Clara (95054-1100)
PHONE 408 757-1156
EMP: 39 EST: 2015
SALES (est): 9.8MM **Privately Held**
WEB: www.levisstadium.com
SIC: 7941 Football club

7941 - Professional Sports Clubs & Promoters County (P-14911)

PRODUCTS & SERVICES SECTION

(P-14911)
SACRAMENTO KINGS LTD PARTNR
Also Called: Maloof Sports & Entertainment
1 Sports Pkwy, Sacramento (95834-2301)
PHONE..................916 928-0000
John Rinehart, *Partner*
Jozee Perrelli, *Manager*
EMP: 40 **EST:** 1978
SQ FT: 500,000
SALES (est): 11.4MM **Privately Held**
SIC: 7941 5812 6512 Sports field or stadium operator, promoting sports events; contract food services; nonresidential building operators

(P-14912)
SACRAMNTO RVER CATS BSBAL CLB
400 Ball Park Dr, West Sacramento (95691-2824)
PHONE..................916 376-4700
Art Savage,
Angela Kroeker, *Executive Asst*
Brittney Broberg, *Info Tech Mgr*
Madeline Strika, *Controller*
Joe Carlucci, *Opers Staff*
EMP: 50 **EST:** 1999
SALES (est): 15.1MM **Privately Held**
WEB: www.rivercats.com
SIC: 7941 Baseball club, professional & semi-professional
PA: River City Baseball Investment Group Llc
400 Ball Park Dr
West Sacramento CA 95691
916 376-4700

(P-14913)
SAN FRANCISCO FORTY NINERS (PA)
4949 Mrie P Debartolo Way, Santa Clara (95054-1156)
PHONE..................408 562-4949
Denise Debartolo York, *Ch of Bd*
Peter Harris, *President*
Andy Dolich, *COO*
Larry Macneil, *CFO*
Harpreet Basran, *Vice Pres*
EMP: 120 **EST:** 1948
SQ FT: 50,000
SALES: 5.6MM **Privately Held**
WEB: www.49ers.com
SIC: 7941 Football club

(P-14914)
SAN JOSE SHARKS LLC (PA)
Also Called: HP Pavillion At San Jose
525 W Santa Clara St, San Jose (95113-1500)
PHONE..................408 999-6810
Greg Jamison, *President*
Michael Ford, *Partner*
Flavil Hampsten, *Officer*
Neda Tabatabaie, *Vice Pres*
Andrei Losche, *Admin Mgr*
EMP: 169 **EST:** 1990
SALES (est): 29.3MM **Privately Held**
WEB: www.sapcenter.com
SIC: 7941 Ice hockey club

(P-14915)
SC HOCKEY FRANCHISE CORP
Also Called: Stockton Thunder
248 W Fremont St, Stockton (95203-2800)
PHONE..................209 373-1500
Brad Rowbotham, *CEO*
Dave Piecuch, *President*
Bill Davidson, *CFO*
Brandon Weiss, *Comms Dir*
Tess Jaurigue, *Finance*
EMP: 77 **EST:** 2005
SALES (est): 5MM **Privately Held**
WEB: www.stocktonheat.com
SIC: 7941 Sports field or stadium operator, promoting sports events

(P-14916)
SHARKS SPORTS & ENTRMT LLC
Also Called: SSE Merchandise
525 W Santa Clara St, San Jose (95113-1520)
PHONE..................408 287-7070
Hasso Plattner, *Mng Member*
Gary Parrish, *Officer*
Brian Towers, *Vice Pres*
Charles Faas, *Executive*
Kyle Stake, *Executive*
EMP: 800 **EST:** 1999
SALES (est): 77MM **Privately Held**
WEB: www.sharkssports.net
SIC: 7941 Sports field or stadium operator, promoting sports events

7948 Racing & Track Operations

(P-14917)
PACIFIC RACING ASSOCIATION
Also Called: Golden Gate Fields
1100 Eastshore Hwy, Albany (94710-1002)
P.O. Box 6027 (94706-0027)
PHONE..................510 559-7300
Frank Stronach, *President*
Patrick Mackey, *Admin Sec*
Juan Leon, *Info Tech Mgr*
Bob Hemmer, *Analyst*
Sheri Espique, *Sales Staff*
EMP: 140 **EST:** 1941
SALES (est): 63MM **Privately Held**
WEB: www.goldengatefields.com
SIC: 7948 Horses, racing

(P-14918)
SPEEDWAY SONOMA LLC
Also Called: Infineon Raceway
Hwy 37 N, Sonoma (95476)
PHONE..................707 938-8448
Bruton Smith,
Sarah Grasal,
▲ **EMP:** 60 **EST:** 2000
SALES (est): 16.9MM
SALES (corp-wide): 461.9MM **Privately Held**
WEB: www.sonomaraceway.com
SIC: 7948 Automotive race track operation
HQ: Speedway Motorsports, Llc
5555 Concord Pkwy S
Concord NC 28027
-

7991 Physical Fitness Facilities

(P-14919)
24 HOUR FITNESS USA INC
Also Called: Benjamin Holt Sport Club
3137 W Benjamin Holt Dr, Stockton (95219-3703)
PHONE..................209 951-5999
EMP: 35
SALES (corp-wide): 433.6MM **Privately Held**
SIC: 7991 Physical Fitness Facilities
HQ: 24 Hour Fitness Usa, Inc.
12647 Alcosta Blvd # 500
San Ramon CA 92011
925 543-3100

(P-14920)
24 HOUR FITNESS USA INC
Also Called: Capitol Sport Club
375 N Capitol Ave Ste A, San Jose (95133-1900)
PHONE..................408 923-2639
EMP: 35
SALES (corp-wide): 433.6MM **Privately Held**
SIC: 7991 Physical Fitness Facilities
HQ: 24 Hour Fitness Usa, Inc.
12647 Alcosta Blvd # 500
San Ramon CA 92011
925 543-3100

(P-14921)
24 HOUR FITNESS USA INC
Also Called: San Mateo Sport Club
500 El Camino Real, Burlingame (94010-5159)
PHONE..................650 343-7922
EMP: 50
SALES (corp-wide): 433.6MM **Privately Held**
SIC: 7991 Physical Fitness Facilities

(P-14922)
24 HOUR FITNESS USA INC
Also Called: Berkeley Sport Club
1775 Solano Ave, Berkeley (94707-2209)
PHONE..................510 524-4583
EMP: 43
SALES (corp-wide): 433.6MM **Privately Held**
SIC: 7991 Physical Fitness Facilities
HQ: 24 Hour Fitness Usa, Inc.
12647 Alcosta Blvd # 500
San Ramon CA 92011
925 543-3100

(P-14923)
ADDISN-PNZAK JWISH CMNTY CTR S
14855 Oka Rd Ste 201, Los Gatos (95032-1956)
PHONE..................408 358-3636
Nate Stein, *CEO*
Stuart Phillips, *CFO*
Maya Jacobson, *Program Mgr*
Erin McMahon, *General Mgr*
Sierra Burt, *Administration*
EMP: 236 **EST:** 1973
SALES (est): 8.2MM **Privately Held**
WEB: www.apjcc.org
SIC: 7991 8299 Physical fitness facilities; educational services

(P-14924)
ALMADEN VALLEY ATHLETIC CLUB
Also Called: Avac
5400 Camden Ave, San Jose (95124-5897)
PHONE..................408 445-4900
Joseph Shank, *General Ptnr*
Court Aquatic Sports, *General Ptnr*
EMP: 70 **EST:** 1974
SQ FT: 20,000
SALES (est): 6.9MM **Privately Held**
WEB: www.avac.us
SIC: 7991 Health club

(P-14925)
AMADEUS SPA NAPA VLY MARRIOTT
3425 Solano Ave, NAPA (94558-2709)
PHONE..................707 254-3330
Michael George, *Manager*
Alison Skoglund, *Finance*
Christine Ahlberg, *Marketing Staff*
Diane Stonework, *Director*
Jaime Tyner, *Manager*
EMP: 40 **EST:** 2002
SALES (est): 2MM **Privately Held**
WEB: www.marriott.com
SIC: 7991 Spas

(P-14926)
ARDEN HILLS COUNTRY CLUB INC
1220 Arden Hills Ln, Sacramento (95864-5378)
PHONE..................916 482-6111
Jeralyn Favero, *President*
Brett Favero, *Admin Sec*
Kathy Cameron, *Sales Mgr*
Paige Ricci,
Chris Floyd, *Director*
EMP: 60 **EST:** 1985
SALES (est): 6.5MM **Privately Held**
WEB: www.ardenhills.club
SIC: 5812 5813 7991 Eating places; caterers; drinking places; physical fitness facilities

(P-14927)
B A M I INC
Also Called: 24 Hour In Motion Fitness
1293 E 1st Ave, Chico (95926-1548)
PHONE..................530 343-5678
Carleton J Sommer, *President*
Chris Conway, *General Mgr*
Lance Baxman, *Accountant*
Emily Arroyo, *Director*
Ryan Flenner, *Director*
EMP: 93 **EST:** 1987
SQ FT: 19,400
SALES (est): 7MM **Privately Held**
WEB: www.inmotionfitness.com
SIC: 7991 Health club

(P-14928)
BACK STREET FITNESS INC
Also Called: Health Quest
3175 California Blvd, NAPA (94558-3307)
PHONE..................707 254-7200
Anthony Giovannoni, *President*
Lisa Ghisletta, *Sales Staff*
Mary Schaffer, *Director*
Peter Garaventa, *Manager*
EMP: 50 **EST:** 1989
SALES (est): 3.9MM **Privately Held**
WEB: www.napahealthquest.com
SIC: 7991 Health club

(P-14929)
BEST SUPPLEMENT GUIDE LLC (PA)
Also Called: Fitness Systems
512 N Cherokee Ln, Lodi (95240-2401)
PHONE..................209 366-2800
Sean Covell, *CEO*
Mary Elizabeth Halouzka, *Admin Sec*
EMP: 41 **EST:** 2008
SALES (est): 2.5MM **Privately Held**
WEB: www.fitlodi.com
SIC: 7991 Health club

(P-14930)
BLADIUM INC (PA)
Also Called: Bladium Sports Clubs
800 W Tower Ave Bldg 40, Alameda (94501-5048)
PHONE..................510 814-4999
Brad C Shook, *President*
David Walsh, *CFO*
Kelsey McKeon, *Manager*
EMP: 60 **EST:** 1994
SQ FT: 115,000
SALES (est): 8.5MM **Privately Held**
WEB: www.bladiumalameda.com
SIC: 7991 Health club

(P-14931)
BODIES IN MOTION
351 San Andreas Dr, Novato (94945-1206)
PHONE..................415 897-2185
Chuk Trieve, *Branch Mgr*
EMP: 38 **Privately Held**
WEB: www.bodiesinmotion.com
SIC: 7991 Exercise facilities
PA: Bodies In Motion
16663 Roscoe Blvd
North Hills CA 91343

(P-14932)
BODY KINETICS (PA)
1530 Center Rd Ste 11, Novato (94947-4089)
PHONE..................415 895-5965
Michael Hover-Jenkins, *Owner*
Katie Doolittle, *Executive*
Kevin Hamilton, *General Mgr*
Cheryl Hamilton, *Manager*
EMP: 45 **EST:** 2011
SALES (est): 1.6MM **Privately Held**
WEB: www.bodykinetics.com
SIC: 7991 Health club

(P-14933)
C BIG CORPORATION
Also Called: Big C Athletic Club
1381 Galaxy Way, Concord (94520-4932)
P.O. Box 5277 (94524-0277)
PHONE..................925 671-2110
Ronald Dawson, *Principal*
Lisa Morgan Hugman, *President*
Nick Schweickert, *Principal*
Beach Sandy, *Mktg Coord*
Rayona Arteaga, *Director*
EMP: 64 **EST:** 1978
SQ FT: 70,000
SALES (est): 7.5MM **Privately Held**
WEB: www.thebigc.com
SIC: 5812 7991 Cafe; health club

(P-14934)
CALISTOGA SPA INC
Also Called: Calistoga Spa Hot Springs
1006 Washington St, Calistoga (94515-1499)
PHONE..................707 942-6269

▲ = Import ▼ = Export
◆ = Import/Export

PRODUCTS & SERVICES SECTION
7991 - Physical Fitness Facilities County (P-14959)

Bradley L Barrett, *President*
Diane Barrett, *Admin Sec*
EMP: 65 **EST:** 1967
SQ FT: 50,000
SALES (est): 5.3MM **Privately Held**
WEB: www.calistogaspa.com
SIC: 7991 Spas

(P-14935)
CAPITAL ATHLETIC CLUB INC
1515 8th St, Sacramento (95814-5503)
PHONE 916 442-3927
Ken Hoffman, *President*
Jonna Edwinson, *Director*
Sabin Morris, *Director*
EMP: 47 **EST:** 1996
SQ FT: 52,000
SALES (est): 3.3MM **Privately Held**
WEB: www.capitalac.com
SIC: 7991 Health club

(P-14936)
CLUB AT LOS GATOS INC
14428 Big Basin Way Ste A, Saratoga (95070-6010)
PHONE 408 867-5110
David S Wilson, *CEO*
EMP: 60 **EST:** 2015
SALES (est): 1.4MM **Privately Held**
SIC: 7991 Physical fitness clubs with training equipment

(P-14937)
CLUB CORP INCORPORATED
Also Called: Delta Valley Athletic Club
120 Guthrie Ln, Brentwood (94513-4037)
PHONE 925 240-2990
Matthew Ellison, *President*
Lisa Flores, *Accountant*
Priya Nykan, *Director*
Shelly Tosh, *Manager*
Vicky Zakoian, *Manager*
EMP: 100 **EST:** 2003
SALES (est): 2.7MM **Privately Held**
WEB: www.deltavac.com
SIC: 7991 Physical fitness facilities

(P-14938)
CLUB SPORT OF FREMONT
46650 Landing Pkwy, Fremont (94538-6420)
PHONE 510 226-8500
Angela Grissar, *Business Mgr*
Guin Cloninger, *Partner*
Polin Huynh, *Sales Mgr*
Kimberly Digiacomo, *Director*
Michele Koenemann, *Director*
EMP: 35 **EST:** 1999
SALES (est): 5.3MM **Privately Held**
WEB: www.clubsports.com
SIC: 7991 Health club

(P-14939)
CLUBSPORT SAN RAMON LLC
Also Called: Oakwood Athletic Club
4000 Mt Diablo Blvd, Lafayette (94549-3498)
PHONE 925 283-4000
Michael Reardon, *Manager*
EMP: 90
SQ FT: 63,749 **Privately Held**
WEB: www.clubsportsr.com
SIC: 7991 7997 Athletic club & gymnasiums, membership; membership sports & recreation clubs
PA: Clubsport San Ramon, Llc
350 Bollinger Canyon Ln
San Ramon CA 94582

(P-14940)
CLUBSPORT SAN RAMON LLC (PA)
Also Called: Spa At Club Sport
350 Bollinger Canyon Ln, San Ramon (94582-4592)
PHONE 925 735-1182
Dennis Garrison,
John Moore, *Partner*
Al Schaffer, *Partner*
Shabnam Nawabi, *Program Mgr*
Mike Reardon, *General Mgr*
EMP: 170 **EST:** 1989
SQ FT: 70,000
SALES (est): 12.4MM **Privately Held**
WEB: www.clubsportsr.com
SIC: 7991 Health club

(P-14941)
COURT HOUSE ATHLETIC CLUB (PA)
2514 Bell Rd, Auburn (95603-2502)
PHONE 530 885-1964
Art Chappell Jr, *Owner*
Danielle Covert, *Manager*
EMP: 45 **EST:** 1980
SQ FT: 22,000
SALES (est): 1.9MM **Privately Held**
WEB: www.cacfit.com
SIC: 7991 Health club

(P-14942)
CRUNCH LLC
Also Called: Crunch Fitness
1725 Union St, San Francisco (94123-4406)
PHONE 415 346-0222
Victor Banda, *Branch Mgr*
Waylon Korpi, *General Mgr*
EMP: 59 **Privately Held**
WEB: www.crunch.com
SIC: 7991 Physical fitness facilities
PA: Crunch, Llc
220 W 19th St
New York NY 10011

(P-14943)
CRUNCH LLC
1190 Saratoga Ave, San Jose (95129-3438)
PHONE 650 257-8000
Saeid Ghafouri, *CEO*
EMP: 59 **Privately Held**
WEB: www.crunch.com
SIC: 7991 Physical fitness facilities
PA: Crunch, Llc
220 W 19th St
New York NY 10011

(P-14944)
CRUNCH LLC
Also Called: Crunch Fitness
61 New Montgomery St, San Francisco (94105-3438)
PHONE 415 543-1110
Ben Vadi, *Branch Mgr*
Polly Lesaguis, *General Mgr*
EMP: 59 **Privately Held**
WEB: www.crunch.com
SIC: 7991 Physical fitness facilities
PA: Crunch, Llc
220 W 19th St
New York NY 10011

(P-14945)
CRUNCH LLC
Also Called: Embarcadero, The
345 Spear St Ste 104, San Francisco (94105-1659)
PHONE 415 495-1939
Mahogany Lenard, *Branch Mgr*
Erick Draque, *General Mgr*
Adam Toma, *General Mgr*
Rachel Stinar, *Training Spec*
Mark Arpaia, *Manager*
EMP: 59 **Privately Held**
WEB: www.crunch.com
SIC: 7991 Health club
PA: Crunch, Llc
220 W 19th St
New York NY 10011

(P-14946)
DECATHLON CLUB INC
3250 Central Expy, Santa Clara (95051-0873)
PHONE 408 738-2582
Kayte Bandcraft, *Manager*
EMP: 57 **EST:** 1978
SQ FT: 100,000
SALES (est): 1.4MM **Privately Held**
SIC: 7991 5812 Physical fitness clubs with training equipment; eating places

(P-14947)
EPG GYM LLC
401 Cypress St, Fort Bragg (95437-5409)
PHONE 707 964-6290
James W Gay,
EMP: 37 **EST:** 2017
SALES (est): 638K **Privately Held**
SIC: 7991 Athletic club & gymnasiums, membership

(P-14948)
EQUINOX-76TH STREET INC
301 Pine St, San Francisco (94104-3301)
PHONE 415 398-0747
Patrick Ahern, *Manager*
Sara Spear, *District Mgr*
Kurt Baughn, *Personnel*
Alisa Grant, *Personnel*
Zelda Curry, *Opers Mgr*
EMP: 72
SALES (corp-wide): 2B **Privately Held**
SIC: 7991 Health club
HQ: Equinox-76th Street, Inc.
895 Broadway Fl 3
New York NY 10003

(P-14949)
EXECUTIVES OUTLET INC
Also Called: Decathalon Club
1 Lombard St Lbby, San Francisco (94111-1127)
PHONE 415 433-6044
James Gerber, *President*
Sandra Hoeffer, *Vice Pres*
Mindy Steiner, *Vice Pres*
David Smith, *Admin Sec*
EMP: 54 **EST:** 1977
SQ FT: 100,000
SALES (est): 728.9K **Privately Held**
SIC: 7991 7997 Athletic club & gymsiums, membership; racquetball club, membership
PA: Bay Club Holdings Iii, Llc
1 Lombard St Lbby
San Francisco CA 94111

(P-14950)
FIFER STREET FITNESS INC
Also Called: Gold's Gym Marin
2 Fifer Ave Ste 250, Corte Madera (94925-1155)
PHONE 415 927-4653
Sebastyen Jackovics, *President*
Zsolt Jackovics, *Treasurer*
Judy Jackovics, *Admin Sec*
EMP: 47 **EST:** 1989
SQ FT: 13,000
SALES (est): 732.2K **Privately Held**
WEB: www.fitnesssf.com
SIC: 7991 Physical fitness facilities

(P-14951)
GOLD STAR GYMNASTICS
240 S Whisman Rd, Mountain View (94041-1516)
PHONE 650 694-7827
Pamela Evans, *President*
Crystal Coates, *Office Mgr*
Kim Coates, *Manager*
EMP: 40 **EST:** 1997
SALES (est): 1.4MM **Privately Held**
WEB: www.goldstargym.com
SIC: 7991 7911 Physical fitness facilities; dance studios, schools & halls

(P-14952)
HEALTHSPORT LTD A LTD PARTNR (PA)
Also Called: Healthsport-Arcata
300 Dr Martin Luther, Arcata (95521)
PHONE 707 822-3488
Susan Johnson, *Partner*
Sam Murray, *Site Mgr*
David Bingham,
EMP: 110 **EST:** 1991
SQ FT: 24,560
SALES (est): 7.6MM **Privately Held**
WEB: www.healthsport.com
SIC: 7991 Health club

(P-14953)
IN-SHAPE HEALTH CLUBS LLC (PA)
Also Called: In-Shape City
6507 Pacific Ave 344, Stockton (95207-3717)
PHONE 209 472-2231
Francesca Schuler, *CEO*
Gina Aaron, *Vice Pres*
Rob Farrens, *Vice Pres*
Rachelle Gardette, *Regional Mgr*
Joe Schillace, *Area Mgr*
EMP: 50 **EST:** 1961
SQ FT: 60,000
SALES (est): 84.8MM **Privately Held**
WEB: www.inshape.com
SIC: 7991 Health club

(P-14954)
J&T CRENSHAW INC
Also Called: Get Fit Modesto
2801 Mchenry Ave, Modesto (95350-2328)
PHONE 209 606-8256
Jonathan Crenshaw, *Principal*
Tara Crenshaw, *President*
Carisah Lee, *Mktg Dir*
Heather Sutton, *Nutritionist*
EMP: 43 **EST:** 2017
SALES (est): 626.7K **Privately Held**
SIC: 7991 Physical fitness facilities

(P-14955)
JEFF STOVER INC
Also Called: Chico Sports Club
260 Cohasset Rd Ste 190, Chico (95926-2282)
PHONE 530 345-9427
Jeff Stover, *President*
Scott Hillard, *Partner*
EMP: 53 **EST:** 1989
SQ FT: 11,000
SALES (est): 6.1MM **Privately Held**
WEB: www.chicosportsclub.com
SIC: 7991 7997 Health club; membership sports & recreation clubs

(P-14956)
LAVENDER HILL SPA
1015 Foothill Blvd, Calistoga (94515-1711)
PHONE 707 942-4495
EMP: 35
SALES (est): 1.2MM **Privately Held**
SIC: 7991 Physical Fitness Facility

(P-14957)
LEISURE SPORTS INC
Also Called: Clubsport of Fremont
46650 Landing Pkwy, Fremont (94538-6420)
PHONE 510 226-8500
Dan Detrick, *General Mgr*
Michelle Litwin, *Executive Asst*
Leslie Davis, *Training Spec*
EMP: 100
SALES (corp-wide): 46.1MM **Privately Held**
WEB: www.leisuresportsinc.com
SIC: 7991 Athletic club & gymnasiums, membership
PA: Leisure Sports, Inc.
225 Spring St
Pleasanton CA 94566
925 600-1966

(P-14958)
LIFE TIME INC
1435 E Roseville Pkwy, Roseville (95661-3066)
PHONE 916 472-2000
Jennifer Hallahan, *Branch Mgr*
EMP: 103
SALES (corp-wide): 948.3MM **Privately Held**
WEB: www.lifetime.life
SIC: 7991 Health club
HQ: Life Time, Inc.
2902 Corporate Pl
Chanhassen MN 55317

(P-14959)
LIVE FIT GYM INC (PA)
301 Fell St, San Francisco (94102-5146)
P.O. Box 640746 (94164-0746)
PHONE 415 525-4364
Milton Warren Obrien, *President*

7991 - Physical Fitness Facilities County (P-14960)

Andrew Springer, *Manager*
EMP: 52 **EST:** 2009
SALES (est): 5MM **Privately Held**
WEB: www.livefitgym.com
SIC: 7991 Athletic club & gymnasiums, membership

(P-14960)
LIVERMORE VALLEY TENNIS CLUB
2000 Arroyo Rd, Livermore (94550-6027)
PHONE..................925 443-7700
Kim Fuller, *General Ptnr*
Roy Rasmussen, *General Ptnr*
Margot Green, *Principal*
Deborah Shore, *Bookkeeper*
Ann Ekay, *Director*
EMP: 59 **EST:** 1972
SQ FT: 51,758
SALES (est): 6.4MM **Privately Held**
WEB: www.lvtc.com
SIC: 7991 5941 Athletic club & gymnasiums, membership; sporting goods & bicycle shops; tennis goods & equipment

(P-14961)
LOS GATOS SWIM AND RACQUET CLB
Also Called: Lgsrc
14700 Oka Rd, Los Gatos (95032-1998)
PHONE..................408 356-2136
S Denevi, *Treasurer*
Shelli Denevi, *Treasurer*
Ron Denevi, *Vice Pres*
Deborah Rothschild, *Director*
EMP: 51 **EST:** 1955
SQ FT: 14,000
SALES (est): 5.3MM **Privately Held**
WEB: www.lgsrc.com
SIC: 7991 7997 Health club; tennis club, membership

(P-14962)
MARINER SQUARE ATHLETIC INC
2227 Mariner Square Loop, Alameda (94501-1021)
PHONE..................510 523-8011
Kathy Wagner, *President*
Diana Thomas, *General Mgr*
Lolla Miller, *Director*
Galen Lewis, *Manager*
EMP: 51 **EST:** 1975
SQ FT: 60,000
SALES (est): 7MM **Privately Held**
WEB: www.marinersq.com
SIC: 7991 7997 Athletic club & gymnasiums, membership; membership sports & recreation clubs

(P-14963)
NAKOMA RESORT LLC
Also Called: Nakoma Golf Resort
348 Bear Run, Clio (96106)
PHONE..................530 832-5067
Dariel D Garner, *President*
Margaret Garner, *Treasurer*
Margaret M Garner, *Corp Secy*
Wes Hull, *Manager*
EMP: 50 **EST:** 1998
SQ FT: 22,000
SALES (est): 5.4MM **Privately Held**
WEB: www.nakomaresort.com
SIC: 5812 7991 7011 Eating places; spas; vacation lodges

(P-14964)
PRECOR INCORPORATED
Also Called: Precor Home Fitness
1164 Galleria Blvd, Roseville (95678-4122)
PHONE..................916 788-8334
EMP: 55
SALES (corp-wide): 1.8B **Publicly Held**
WEB: www.precor.com
SIC: 7991 Physical fitness facilities
HQ: Precor Incorporated
    20031 142nd Ave Ne
    Woodinville WA 98072
    425 486-9292

(P-14965)
PRIME TIME ATHLETIC CLUB INC
1730 Rollins Rd, Burlingame (94010-2297)
PHONE..................650 204-3662

John Michael, *President*
John T Michael, *Vice Pres*
Richard Barnes, *CIO*
Jerry Bruton, *Sales Staff*
Cathy Firkins, *Director*
EMP: 101 **EST:** 1979
SQ FT: 35,000
SALES (est): 6.4MM **Privately Held**
WEB: www.primetimeathleticclub.com
SIC: 7991 Health club

(P-14966)
R THUNDER INC (PA)
Also Called: Fitness Together
15711 Watts Valley Rd, Sanger (93657-9253)
PHONE..................559 974-2203
Andrew J Polterock, *President*
Robert Johnson, *Vice Pres*
EMP: 37 **EST:** 2007
SALES (est): 888.4K **Privately Held**
WEB: www.fitnesstogether.com
SIC: 7991 Physical fitness facilities

(P-14967)
REDWOOD HEALTH CLUB (PA)
3101 S State St, Ukiah (95482-6938)
PHONE..................707 468-0441
Rob Marthe Deomont, *Partner*
EMP: 70 **EST:** 1979
SQ FT: 20,000
SALES (est): 1.6MM **Privately Held**
WEB: www.redwoodhealthclubofukiah.com
SIC: 7991 7997 5812 5813 Health club; racquetball club, membership; tennis club, membership; snack bar; drinking places

(P-14968)
RIEKES CTR FOR HUMN ENHNCEMENT
3455 Edison Way, Menlo Park (94025-1813)
PHONE..................650 364-2509
Gary Riekes, *General Ptnr*
Richard Claire, *CFO*
Robbie Merrill, *CIO*
Judy Butler, *Accountant*
Linc Holland, *Opers Staff*
EMP: 52 **EST:** 2010
SALES (est): 4.2MM **Privately Held**
WEB: www.riekes.org
SIC: 7991 Physical fitness facilities

(P-14969)
SALUTARY SPORTS CLUBS INC
Also Called: Millennium Sports Club
3250 Rncho Slano Pkwy Ste, Fairfield (94534)
PHONE..................707 438-2582
Tom Martin, *Manager*
EMP: 41
SALES (corp-wide): 5.2MM **Privately Held**
SIC: 7991 Athletic club & gymnasiums, membership
PA: Salutary Sports Clubs, Inc.
    3442 Browns Valley Rd # 100
    Vacaville CA 95688
    707 446-2350

(P-14970)
SALUTARY SPORTS CLUBS INC
Also Called: Sports Club of El Dorado
4242 Sports Club Dr, Shingle Springs (95682-9546)
P.O. Box 659 (95682-0659)
PHONE..................530 677-5705
Don Lynd, *Manager*
EMP: 41
SALES (corp-wide): 5.2MM **Privately Held**
SIC: 7991 Physical fitness facilities
PA: Salutary Sports Clubs, Inc.
    3442 Browns Valley Rd # 100
    Vacaville CA 95688
    707 446-2350

(P-14971)
SAN FRANCISCO TENNIS CLUB
645 5th St, San Francisco (94107-1516)
PHONE..................415 777-9000
Jim Hinckley, *President*
Thomas Kanar, *Corp Secy*
Jeff Janke, *Vice Pres*
EMP: 71 **EST:** 1976

SQ FT: 300,000
SALES (est): 11MM
SALES (corp-wide): 1B **Privately Held**
WEB: www.bayclubs.com
SIC: 7991 7997 5813 Physical fitness facilities; membership sports & recreation clubs; drinking places
HQ: Clubcorp Usa, Inc.
    3030 Lyndon B Johnson Fwy
    Dallas TX 75234
    972 243-6191

(P-14972)
SONORA SPORT & FITNES CTR INC (PA)
13760 Mono Way, Sonora (95370-8889)
PHONE..................209 532-1202
Tim Gallagher, *President*
Carole Canepa, *Shareholder*
Rick Canepa, *Shareholder*
Roger Canepa, *Shareholder*
Tiffeni Larsson, *Manager*
EMP: 42 **EST:** 1990
SQ FT: 80,000
SALES (est): 2.9MM **Privately Held**
WEB: www.sonorafitness.com
SIC: 7991 Health club

(P-14973)
SOUTH YUBA CLUB INC
130 W Berryhill Dr, Grass Valley (95945-5835)
PHONE..................530 470-9100
Phil Carville, *Treasurer*
Mike Carville, *President*
Belinda Rash-Carville, *Admin Sec*
John Hendrickson, *Personnel*
Amanda Helmuth, *Training Spec*
EMP: 45 **EST:** 1999
SALES (est): 5.7MM **Privately Held**
WEB: www.southyubaclub.com
SIC: 7991 Health club

(P-14974)
SPA FITNESS CENTER INC
1100 41st Ave, Capitola (95010-3931)
PHONE..................831 476-7373
Harry Jenkins, *Owner*
EMP: 99
SALES (corp-wide): 2.4MM **Privately Held**
WEB: www.spafitness.com
SIC: 7991 Spas
PA: Spa Fitness Center, Inc
    1200 41st Ave Ste C
    Capitola CA 95010
    831 462-2004

(P-14975)
SPA FITNESS CENTER INC
25 Penny Ln, Watsonville (95076-3058)
PHONE..................831 722-3895
Harry Jennings, *Owner*
EMP: 99
SALES (corp-wide): 2.4MM **Privately Held**
WEB: www.spafitness.com
SIC: 7991 Health club
PA: Spa Fitness Center, Inc
    1200 41st Ave Ste C
    Capitola CA 95010
    831 462-2004

(P-14976)
SPA RADIANCE ASSOCIATES INC
3011 Fillmore St, San Francisco (94123-4009)
PHONE..................415 346-6281
Angelina Umansky, *Owner*
EMP: 40 **EST:** 1998
SALES (est): 2.9MM **Privately Held**
WEB: www.sparadiance.com
SIC: 7991 Spas

(P-14977)
SPARE-TIME INC
Also Called: Natomas Racquet Club
2450 Natomas Park Dr, Sacramento (95833-2938)
PHONE..................916 649-0909
Joe Rose, *Manager*
EMP: 56
SALES (corp-wide): 53MM **Privately Held**

PA: Spare-Time, Inc.
    11344 Coloma Rd Ste 350
    Gold River CA 95670
    916 859-5910

(P-14978)
SPARE-TIME INC
Also Called: Rio Del Oro Racquet Club
119 Scripps Dr, Sacramento (95825-6305)
PHONE..................916 488-8100
Dana Rose, *Manager*
EMP: 56
SALES (corp-wide): 53MM **Privately Held**
SIC: 7991 7999 7997 Health club; tennis services & professionals; tennis club, membership
PA: Spare-Time, Inc.
    11344 Coloma Rd Ste 350
    Gold River CA 95670
    916 859-5910

(P-14979)
TALMADGE & TALMADGE INC
Also Called: World Gym Fitness Centers
290 De Haro St, San Francisco (94103-5124)
PHONE..................415 703-9650
Joseph Talmadge, *President*
Robin Talmadge, *Treasurer*
Arlene Robin Talmadge, *Vice Pres*
Mary Diaz, *Admin Sec*
EMP: 64 **EST:** 1990
SALES (est): 4.1MM **Privately Held**
WEB: www.worldgym.com
SIC: 7991 Health club

(P-14980)
TEMPO INTERACTIVE INC
Also Called: Coretech Fitness
575 7th Ave, San Francisco (94118-3818)
PHONE..................415 964-2975
Moawia Eldeeb, *CEO*
EMP: 41 **EST:** 2014
SALES (est): 9.5MM **Privately Held**
WEB: www.tempo.fit
SIC: 7991 Athletic club & gymnasiums, membership

(P-14981)
TENNIS EVERYONE INCORPORATED
Also Called: Rolling Hills Club
351 San Andreas Dr, Novato (94945-1206)
PHONE..................415 897-2185
Chuk Trieve, *President*
Andrea Pozzi, *Officer*
Susie McLoughlin, *Personnel*
Megan Brown, *Director*
Bobbie Bukszar, *Director*
EMP: 38 **EST:** 1973
SQ FT: 19,000
SALES (est): 1.8MM **Privately Held**
WEB: www.rollinghillsclub.com
SIC: 7991 Health club

(P-14982)
TURLOCK HLTH & FITNES CTR INC
Also Called: Los Banos Racquet Club
1520 Racquet Club Dr, Los Banos (93635-3840)
PHONE..................209 826-6011
Karen Arburua, *General Mgr*
EMP: 36
SALES (corp-wide): 3MM **Privately Held**
WEB: www.brendaathletics.com
SIC: 7991 7997 Health club; racquetball club, membership
PA: Turlock Health & Fitness Center, Inc.
    201 Tampa St
    Turlock CA 95382
    209 668-3838

(P-14983)
TURLOCK HLTH & FITNES CTR INC
Also Called: Modesto Fitness & Racquet
200 Norwegian Ave, Modesto (95350-3519)
PHONE..................209 571-2582
Phil Madarago, *Manager*
EMP: 36
SQ FT: 25,000

PRODUCTS & SERVICES SECTION
7992 - Public Golf Courses County (P-15008)

SALES (corp-wide): 3MM **Privately Held**
WEB: www.brendaathletics.com
SIC: 7991 Health club
PA: Turlock Health & Fitness Center, Inc.
201 Tampa St
Turlock CA 95382
209 668-3838

(P-14984)
TWIN ARBORS LLC
1900 S Hutchins St, Lodi (95240-6116)
PHONE..................................209 334-4897
David Claxton, *Mng Member*
EMP: 38 EST: 2018
SALES (est): 750K **Privately Held**
SIC: 7991 Athletic club & gymnasiums, membership

(P-14985)
WALSH GROUP INC
Also Called: Sun Oaks Tennis & Fitness
3135 Agassi Ln, Redding (96002-9548)
PHONE..................................530 221-4405
Jo Campbell, *Principal*
Jeremiah Walsh, *Principal*
Matthew Perdue, *Personnel*
Angie Baker, *Director*
EMP: 95 EST: 2016
SQ FT: 217,800
SALES (est): 1.2MM **Privately Held**
SIC: 7991 Health club

7992 Public Golf Courses

(P-14986)
ALTA SIERRA COUNTRY CLUB INC
11897 Tammy Way, Grass Valley (95949-6626)
PHONE..................................530 273-2041
Del Clement, *President*
Jim Hansen, *Treasurer*
Doug Bulman, *Vice Pres*
Carl Guastaferro, *Admin Sec*
EMP: 50 EST: 1963
SQ FT: 21,500
SALES (est): 5.1MM **Privately Held**
WEB: www.altasierracc.com
SIC: 7992 Public golf courses

(P-14987)
ANTIOCH PUBLIC GOLF CORP
Also Called: LONE TREE GOLF COURSE
4800 Golf Course Rd, Antioch (94531-8012)
P.O. Box 2115 (94531-2115)
PHONE..................................925 706-4220
Ollie Anderson, *President*
Abdon Aguilar, *Manager*
Crystal Biggs, *Relations*
EMP: 58
SALES: 2.8MM **Privately Held**
WEB: www.lonetreegolfcourse.com
SIC: 7992 5941 7999 5812 Public golf courses; golf goods & equipment; golf driving range; restaurant, family: independent

(P-14988)
BAILEY CREEK INVESTORS A CALI
Also Called: Bailey Creek Golf Course
433 Durkin Dr, Westwood (96137-9611)
PHONE..................................530 259-4653
Keith Hughes, *Branch Mgr*
Lyndsey Ohland, *Marketing Staff*
Kevin Hughes, *Director*
EMP: 40
SALES (corp-wide): 6.9MM **Privately Held**
WEB: www.baileycreek.com
SIC: 7992 Public golf courses
PA: Bailey Creek Investors, A California Limited Partnership
1766 Bidwell Ave
Chico CA 95926
530 891-6753

(P-14989)
BRIDGES AT GALE RANCH LLC
Also Called: Bridges Golf Club, The
9000 S Gale Ridge Rd, San Ramon (94582-9174)
PHONE..................................925 735-4253
Joey Pickavance, *Manager*
Sonal Yadav, *General Mgr*
Sandy Tijero, *Director*
Robby Henderson, *Asst Supt*
EMP: 90 EST: 1999
SALES (est): 4.8MM **Privately Held**
WEB: www.thebridgesgolf.com
SIC: 7992 Public golf courses

(P-14990)
BROOKTRAILS RESORT GOLF COURSE
24860 Birch St, Willits (95490-9475)
PHONE..................................707 459-6761
Mike Chapman, *General Mgr*
Ron Runberg, *Principal*
EMP: 42 EST: 1962
SALES (est): 744.1K **Privately Held**
WEB: www.btcsd.org
SIC: 7992 Public golf courses

(P-14991)
COUNTY OF SACRAMENTO
Also Called: Sacramento Golf Course
4103 Eagles Nest Rd, Sacramento (95830)
PHONE..................................916 575-4653
Asa Jennings, *Manager*
EMP: 44
SALES (corp-wide): 3.1B **Privately Held**
WEB: www.saccounty.net
SIC: 7992 9512 Public golf courses; recreational program administration, government;
PA: County Of Sacramento
700 H St Ste 7650
Sacramento CA 95814
916 874-8515

(P-14992)
COUNTY OF SACRAMENTO
Also Called: Parks and Recreation Dept
6341 Tarshes Dr, Carmichael (95608-5324)
PHONE..................................916 482-9792
Rich Sizelove, *Superintendent*
EMP: 44
SALES (corp-wide): 3.1B **Privately Held**
WEB: www.saccounty.net
SIC: 7992 9512 Public golf courses; recreational program administration, government;
PA: County Of Sacramento
700 H St Ste 7650
Sacramento CA 95814
916 874-8515

(P-14993)
COURSECO INC
Also Called: NAPA Golf Course At Kennedy Pk
2295 Streblow Dr, NAPA (94558-6211)
PHONE..................................707 255-4333
Tom Sims, *Branch Mgr*
Russ Erickson, *Vice Pres*
Sandy Marfin, *Human Resources*
Shawn Silva, *Opers Staff*
EMP: 429 **Privately Held**
WEB: www.courseco.com
SIC: 7992 Public golf courses
PA: Courseco, Inc.
5341 Old Redwood Hwy # 202
Petaluma CA 94954

(P-14994)
COYOTE CREEK GOLF CLUB
1 Coyote Creek Golf Dr, Morgan Hill (95037-9052)
P.O. Box 2527 (95038-2527)
PHONE..................................408 463-1400
Stephan Vigiano, *General Mgr*
Don Leone, *Director*
Gabby Mariscal, *Manager*
EMP: 49 EST: 1999
SQ FT: 12,000
SALES (est): 3.7MM **Privately Held**
WEB: www.coyotecreekgolf.com
SIC: 7992 5812 5941 Public golf courses; eating places; sporting goods & bicycle shops

(P-14995)
CRESTA BLANCA GOLF LLC
Also Called: Course At Wente Vineyards, The
5050 Arroyo Rd, Livermore (94550-9645)
PHONE..................................925 456-2475
Carolyn Wente,
David Howerton,
Earl Kemp,
EMP: 74 EST: 1998
SALES (est): 5.5MM **Privately Held**
WEB: www.wentevineyards.com
SIC: 7992 Public golf courses

(P-14996)
CRYSTAL SPRINGS GOLF PARTNERS
Also Called: Crystal Springs Golf Course
6650 Golf Course Dr, Burlingame (94010-6543)
PHONE..................................650 342-4188
Tom Issak, *President*
John Teleshek, *CFO*
Brian Wilcox, *General Mgr*
Natalia Aldana, *Director*
EMP: 50 EST: 1996
SALES (est): 5.2MM **Privately Held**
WEB: www.playcrystalsprings.com
SIC: 7992 Public golf courses

(P-14997)
DARKHORSE GOLF CLUB
24150 Darkhorse Dr, Auburn (95602-8612)
PHONE..................................530 269-7900
E M West, *President*
EMP: 39 EST: 1997
SQ FT: 5,000
SALES (est): 1.8MM **Privately Held**
WEB: www.darkhorsegolf.com
SIC: 7992 Public golf courses

(P-14998)
DAVIS GOLF COURSE INC
24439 Fairway Dr, Davis (95616-9706)
P.O. Box 928 (95617-0928)
PHONE..................................530 756-0647
EMP: 40
SQ FT: 3,780
SALES: 1.3MM **Privately Held**
WEB: www.davisgolfcourse.com
SIC: 7992 5941 5812 7999 Public Golf Course Ret Sport Goods/Bicycles Eating Place Amusement/Recreation Svc

(P-14999)
EAGLE VNES VNYRDS GOLF CLB LLC
580 S Kelly Rd, American Canyon (94503-5600)
P.O. Box 2398, NAPA (94558-0239)
PHONE..................................707 257-4470
Tokutaro Umezawa,
Nobu Mizuhara, *Executive*
David Koo, *Sales Staff*
Michael Stirling, *Director*
John Walsh, *Director*
EMP: 70 EST: 2010
SALES (est): 5.7MM **Privately Held**
WEB: www.eaglevinesgolfclub.com
SIC: 7992 Public golf courses

(P-15000)
EBIT-GOLF INC
Also Called: Riverside Golf Course
7492 N Bryan Ave, Fresno (93722-9302)
PHONE..................................559 275-5900
Thomas Isaak, *President*
Adam Pohll, *General Mgr*
Jake Kawaguchi, *Opers Staff*
EMP: 53 EST: 1989
SQ FT: 1,000
SALES (est): 2MM **Privately Held**
SIC: 7992 5812 5941 Public golf courses; coffee shop; golf goods & equipment

(P-15001)
EMPIRE GOLF INC
Also Called: Ancil Hoffman Golf Course
6700 Tarshes Dr, Carmichael (95608-5325)
PHONE..................................916 482-3284
Rod Metzler, *President*
EMP: 43 **Privately Held**
WEB: www.empiregolf.com
SIC: 7992 Public golf courses
PA: Empire Golf Inc.
5341 Old Redwood Hwy # 202
Petaluma CA

(P-15002)
FOUNTAIN GROVE GOLF & ATHC CLB
1525 Fountaingrove Pkwy, Santa Rosa (95403-1778)
PHONE..................................707 701-3050
Greg Sabens, *Manager*
EMP: 75
SQ FT: 33,000
SALES: 25.6MM **Privately Held**
WEB: www.thefountaingroveclub.com
SIC: 7992 7299 5941 7997 Public golf courses; banquet hall facilities; golf goods & equipment; golf club, membership

(P-15003)
FOX TAIL GOLF COURSE
100 Golf Course Dr, Rohnert Park (94928-1735)
PHONE..................................707 584-7766
Jon Lafever, *Manager*
EMP: 62 EST: 2001
SALES (est): 8.4MM **Privately Held**
SIC: 7992 Public golf courses

(P-15004)
INDIAN VALLEY GOLF CLUB INC
3035 Novato Blvd, Novato (94947-1002)
P.O. Box 351 (94948-0351)
PHONE..................................415 897-1118
Jeff Mc Andrew, *President*
Fermin Vergara, *Vice Pres*
Jeff McAndrews, *Exec Dir*
EMP: 50 EST: 1957
SQ FT: 4,000
SALES (est): 5.2MM **Privately Held**
WEB: www.indianvalleygolfclub.com
SIC: 7992 5941 Public golf courses; golf goods & equipment

(P-15005)
LA CONTENTA INVESTORS LTD
Also Called: La Contenta Golf Club
1653 S Highway 26, Valley Springs (95252-8328)
PHONE..................................209 772-1081
C Ryan Voorhees, *Partner*
Rod L Metzler, *General Ptnr*
Jessica Hughart, *Director*
Clark Bentz, *Manager*
EMP: 31 EST: 1986
SALES (est): 2.1MM **Privately Held**
WEB: www.lacontentagolf.com
SIC: 7992 5941 2599 Public golf courses; golf goods & equipment; bar, restaurant & cafeteria furniture

(P-15006)
LAKE OF PINES ASSOCIATION
Also Called: Lake of The Pines Homeowners
11665 Lakeshore N, Auburn (95602-8325)
PHONE..................................530 268-1141
Edwin Vitrano, *General Mgr*
Donna Lowenthal, *Finance Mgr*
Sislei Goldsmith, *Accountant*
Amy Davis, *Human Res Mgr*
Sean Bothelio, *Opers Mgr*
EMP: 50 EST: 1967
SALES (est): 8.2MM **Privately Held**
WEB: www.lop.org
SIC: 7992 Public golf courses

(P-15007)
LAKE SHSTINA GOLF CNTRY CLB IN
5925 Country Club Dr, Weed (96094-9687)
PHONE..................................530 938-3201
Chris Pappas, *President*
Gene Fink, *Vice Pres*
Myron Everhart, *Admin Sec*
EMP: 64 EST: 1980
SQ FT: 7,200
SALES (est): 709.8K **Privately Held**
WEB: www.lakeshastinagolf.com
SIC: 5813 5941 5812 7992 Bar (drinking places); golf goods & equipment; eating places; public golf courses

(P-15008)
LINCOLN HILLS GOLF CLUB
1005 Sun City Ln, Lincoln (95648-8443)
PHONE..................................916 543-9200
Marker Brian, *President*
John Reuer, *Manager*

7992 - Public Golf Courses County (P-15009)

Jason Wolf, *Superintendent*
EMP: 45 **EST:** 1999
SALES (est): 5.1MM **Privately Held**
WEB: www.lincolnhillsgolfclub.com
SIC: 7992 7997 Public golf courses; golf club, membership

(P-15009)
MACE MEADOW GOLF CNTRY CLB INC
26570 Fairway Dr, Pioneer (95666-9176)
P.O. Box 1350 (95666-1350)
PHONE 209 295-7020
Ronald Rumback, *President*
Greg Standridge, *Agent*
EMP: 35 **EST:** 1977
SQ FT: 6,600
SALES (est): 1.4MM **Privately Held**
WEB: www.macemeadows.com
SIC: 7992 5813 7997 Public golf courses; bars & lounges; golf club, membership

(P-15010)
MCINNIS PARK GOLF CENTER LTD (PA)
14 Commercial Blvd # 119, Novato (94949-6140)
PHONE 415 492-1800
Catherine Munson, *General Ptnr*
Donald Ham, *Partner*
Robert Kaplan, *Partner*
EMP: 47 **EST:** 1992
SQ FT: 100
SALES (est): 2.8MM **Privately Held**
WEB: www.mcinnisparkgolfcenter.com
SIC: 7992 7999 5812 5941 Public golf courses; golf services & professionals; baseball batting cage; Italian restaurant; golf, tennis & ski shops

(P-15011)
METROPOLITAN GOLF LINKS
10505 Doolittle Dr, Oakland (94603-1029)
PHONE 510 569-5555
Gary Ingram, *Director*
John Landers, *Principal*
Jerry Krause, *Opers Staff*
Gene Bakkum, *Director*
Rich Marik, *Director*
EMP: 37 **EST:** 2003
SALES (est): 2.5MM **Privately Held**
SIC: 7992 Public golf courses

(P-15012)
MORTON GOLF LLC
3645 Fulton Ave, Sacramento (95821-1808)
PHONE 916 481-4653
Kathleen Morton, *CPA*
Haggin Kawaguchi, *Buyer*
Bill Dixon, *Opers Staff*
David Blaise, *Nurse*
EMP: 57 **EST:** 2001
SALES (est): 5.3MM **Privately Held**
WEB: www.mortongolfsales.com
SIC: 7992 Public golf courses

(P-15013)
MORTON GOLF MANAGEMENT LLC
Also Called: Haggin Oaks Golf Shop
3645 Fulton Ave, Sacramento (95821-1808)
PHONE 916 481-4653
Terry Daubert,
Daya Kraemer, *Executive*
Tom Morton, *Exec Dir*
Andrew Wilson, *General Mgr*
Earl Kiyan, *Info Tech Dir*
EMP: 100 **EST:** 1932
SQ FT: 13,800
SALES (est): 17.2MM **Privately Held**
WEB: www.hagginoaks.com
SIC: 7992 5941 5813 5812 Public golf courses; golf goods & equipment; drinking places; eating places

(P-15014)
MOTHERLODE INVESTORS LLC
Also Called: Greenlaw Grupe Jr Operating Co
711 Mccauley Ranch Rd, Angels Camp (95222-9562)
PHONE 209 736-8112
EMP: 85
SALES (est): 2.4MM **Privately Held**
SIC: 7992 Public Golf Course

(P-15015)
OAKMONT GOLF CLUB INC
7025 Oakmont Dr, Santa Rosa (95409-6301)
PHONE 707 538-2454
John Yacobellis, *Director*
EMP: 80 **EST:** 1963
SQ FT: 4,000
SALES (est): 3.8MM **Privately Held**
WEB: www.classic.cybergolf.com
SIC: 7992 7997 5941 Public golf courses; golf club, membership; golf goods & equipment

(P-15016)
POPPY RIDGE INC
Also Called: Poppy Ridge Golf Course
4280 Greenville Rd, Livermore (94550-9720)
PHONE 925 456-8229
Paul Porter, *President*
Brett Armstrong, *General Mgr*
Melissa Johnson, *Accountant*
Jennifer Barbara, *Marketing Mgr*
Abigail Crandall, *Director*
EMP: 49 **EST:** 1992
SALES (est): 12MM **Privately Held**
WEB: www.poppyridgegolf.com
SIC: 7992 Public golf courses
PA: Poppy Holding, Inc.
3200 Lopez Rd
Pebble Beach CA 93953

(P-15017)
PORTLOCK INTERNATIONAL LTD
Also Called: Castle Oaks Golf Club
1000 Castle Oaks Dr, Ione (95640-4521)
PHONE 209 274-0167
Frank Hahn, *President*
EMP: 38 **EST:** 1992
SQ FT: 7,500
SALES (est): 836.5K **Privately Held**
WEB: www.castleoaksgolf.com
SIC: 7992 Public golf courses

(P-15018)
RANCHO DEL REY GOLF CLUB INC
5250 Green Sands Ave, Atwater (95301-9527)
PHONE 209 358-7131
Spalding Wathen, *President*
Jim Billiter, *Manager*
EMP: 35 **EST:** 1969
SQ FT: 2,000
SALES (est): 1.3MM **Privately Held**
WEB: www.ranchordr.com
SIC: 7992 5941 Public golf courses; golf goods & equipment

(P-15019)
RAWITSER GOLF SHOP MIKE
Also Called: San Jose Municipal Golf Course
1560 Oakland Rd, San Jose (95131-2430)
PHONE 408 441-4653
Mike Rawitser, *President*
Berne Finch, *Director*
EMP: 44 **EST:** 1967
SQ FT: 2,500
SALES (est): 627.3K **Privately Held**
SIC: 7992 Public golf courses

(P-15020)
RIDGE GOLF COURSE LLC
Also Called: Lanterns At The Ridge
2020 Golf Course Rd, Auburn (95602-9526)
PHONE 530 888-7122
Kevin Williams, *Manager*
Patrick Doppelmayr, *General Mgr*
Art Whitney, *General Mgr*
David Williams, *General Mgr*
EMP: 77 **EST:** 1997
SQ FT: 26,477
SALES (est): 7.3MM **Privately Held**
WEB: www.ridgegc.com
SIC: 7992 5941 Public golf courses; sporting goods & bicycle shops

(P-15021)
ROOSTER RUN GOLF CLUB INC
2301 E Washington St, Petaluma (94954-3897)
PHONE 707 778-1211
Rob Watson, *President*
John Nice, *Vice Pres*
EMP: 42 **EST:** 1998
SALES (est): 2.8MM **Privately Held**
WEB: www.roosterrun.com
SIC: 7992 5812 Public golf courses; eating places

(P-15022)
RUBY HILL GOLF CLUB LLC
3400 W Ruby Hill Dr, Pleasanton (94566-3604)
PHONE 925 417-5840
Jim Ghielmetti,
Chef Harold, *Executive*
Eric Jacobsen, *General Mgr*
Michael Rood, *General Mgr*
Sara Wood, *General Mgr*
EMP: 81 **EST:** 1994
SALES (est): 9MM **Privately Held**
WEB: www.rubyhill.com
SIC: 7992 Public golf courses

(P-15023)
SAN JUAN OAKS LLC
Also Called: San Juan Oaks Golf Club
3825 Union Rd, Hollister (95023-9135)
PHONE 831 636-6113
Kenneth Gimelli,
Darien Rovella, *Director*
EMP: 80 **EST:** 1994
SQ FT: 1,800
SALES (est): 6.2MM **Privately Held**
WEB: www.sanjuanoaks.com
SIC: 7992 5941 5812 5813 Public golf courses; golf goods & equipment; eating places; bar (drinking places); banquet hall facilities

(P-15024)
SANTA TERESA GOLF CLUB LP
Also Called: Santa Teresa Golf Center
260 Bernal Rd, San Jose (95119-1809)
PHONE 408 225-2650
Mike Rawitser, *Partner*
Lawrence Lobue, *General Ptnr*
Victor Lobue, *General Ptnr*
John Mc Enery III, *General Ptnr*
Rudy Steadler, *General Ptnr*
EMP: 39 **EST:** 1962
SQ FT: 5,300
SALES (est): 1.9MM **Privately Held**
WEB: www.santateresagolf.com
SIC: 7992 Public golf courses

(P-15025)
SGM INC
Also Called: Diablo Grande Golf Resort
9521 Morton Davis Dr, Patterson (95363-8610)
P.O. Box 788, Chowchilla (93610-0788)
PHONE 559 665-4462
Jeffrey A Christansen, *CEO*
EMP: 38 **EST:** 1996
SALES (est): 1.1MM **Privately Held**
SIC: 7992 Public golf courses

(P-15026)
SHERWOOD FOREST GOLF CLUB INC
79 N Frankwood Ave, Sanger (93657-9593)
PHONE 559 787-2611
Randy Hansen, *President*
Carol Hansen, *President*
EMP: 40 **EST:** 1968
SQ FT: 5,000
SALES (est): 1MM **Privately Held**
WEB: www.sherwoodforestgolfclub.com
SIC: 7992 5941 5699 Public golf courses; golf goods & equipment; sports apparel

(P-15027)
SISKIYOU LAKE GOLF RESORT INC
Also Called: Mount Shasta Resort
1000 Siskiyou Lake Blvd, Mount Shasta (96067-9482)
PHONE 530 926-3030
John Cullison, *President*
John Fryer, *Director*
EMP: 80 **EST:** 1991
SALES (est): 5MM **Privately Held**
WEB: www.mountshastaresort.com
SIC: 7992 5941 7011 5812 Public golf courses; golf goods & equipment; tourist camps, cabins, cottages & courts; American restaurant

(P-15028)
SPRING HILLS GOLF COURSE
Also Called: Spring Hills Golf Shop
501 Spring Hills Dr, Watsonville (95076-9789)
P.O. Box 493, Freedom (95019-0493)
PHONE 831 724-1404
Amy Preaseau, *Owner*
Hank Schimpler, *Owner*
Doris Schimpler, *Partner*
EMP: 36 **EST:** 1965
SQ FT: 2,500
SALES (est): 2.5MM **Privately Held**
WEB: www.springhillsgolf.com
SIC: 7992 5812 5941 Public golf courses; snack bar; golf goods & equipment

(P-15029)
SPRING VALLEY GOLF COURSE INC
Also Called: Spring Valley Pro Shop
3441 Calaveras Rd, Milpitas (95035-7214)
PHONE 408 262-1722
Rick Jetter, *President*
Richard Stewart, *Corp Secy*
Jeff Rockwood, *General Mgr*
EMP: 40 **EST:** 1956
SQ FT: 2,000
SALES (est): 2.9MM **Privately Held**
WEB: www.springvalleygolfcourse.com
SIC: 7992 5941 Public golf courses; golf goods & equipment

(P-15030)
SRI GOLF INC
Also Called: Woodcreek Golf Club
5880 Woodcreek Oaks Blvd, Roseville (95747-6787)
PHONE 916 771-4649
George Marshall, *President*
Dan Biever, *Vice Pres*
EMP: 46 **EST:** 1995
SQ FT: 3,500
SALES (est): 1.1MM **Privately Held**
WEB: www.golfroseville.com
SIC: 7992 Public golf courses

(P-15031)
STONETREE GOLF LLC
Also Called: Stonetree Management
9 Stonetree Ln, Novato (94945-3541)
PHONE 415 209-6744
Warren Spieker, *Partner*
Bill Bunce, *Partner*
Dennis Singleton, *Partner*
EMP: 50 **EST:** 1999
SALES (est): 5.2MM **Privately Held**
WEB: www.bayclubs.com
SIC: 7992 5941 5812 Public golf courses; golf, tennis & ski shops; family restaurants

(P-15032)
SUN CITY RSVLLE CMNTY ASSN INC (PA)
Also Called: Timber Creek Golf Course
7050 Del Webb Blvd, Roseville (95747-8040)
PHONE 916 774-3880
Dewolfe Emory, *CEO*
Earl Wiklund, *Exec Dir*
James Martin, *Finance*
Freda Kosterman, *Accountant*
Derek Zachman, *Marketing Staff*
EMP: 180 **EST:** 1994
SALES: 12.4MM **Privately Held**
WEB: www.suncityroseville.org
SIC: 7992 5812 Public golf courses; eating places; caterers

PRODUCTS & SERVICES SECTION
7997 - Membership Sports & Recreation Clubs County (P-15055)

(P-15033)
TAYMAN PARK GOLF GROUP INC
Also Called: Healdsburg Golf Club
927 S Fitch Mountain Rd, Healdsburg (95448-4609)
P.O. Box 448, Petaluma (94953-0448)
PHONE..................707 433-4275
James Stewart, *CEO*
Frank Johnson, *Manager*
EMP: 35 **EST:** 1999
SALES (est): 1.5MM **Privately Held**
WEB: www.healdsburggolfclub.com
SIC: 7992 Public golf courses

(P-15034)
TRADITIONS GOLF LLC
Also Called: Cinnabar Hills Golf Club
23600 Mckean Rd, San Jose (95141-1001)
PHONE..................408 323-5200
Bill Baron,
D Scott Hoyt, *General Mgr*
Lee Brandenburg,
Paul Pugh,
EMP: 100 **EST:** 1998
SQ FT: 25,000
SALES (est): 7.5MM **Privately Held**
WEB: www.cinnabarhills.com
SIC: 7992 Public golf courses

(P-15035)
VB GOLF LLC
Also Called: Mariner's Point Golf Course
2401 E 3rd Ave, Foster City (94404-1067)
PHONE..................650 573-7888
Chris Aliaga, *Manager*
Sergio Garcia, *Partner*
William Verbrugge, *Partner*
Christopher Aliaga, *Executive*
Mick Soli, *Exec Dir*
EMP: 39 **EST:** 1995
SALES (est): 4.6MM **Privately Held**
WEB: www.marinerspoint.com
SIC: 7992 Public golf courses

(P-15036)
WINDSOR GOLF CLUB INC
1340 19th Hole Dr, Windsor (95492-6829)
PHONE..................707 838-7888
Charlie Gibson, *General Mgr*
Larry Wasm, *Treasurer*
Brove O'Brien, *Vice Pres*
Alex Wright, *Principal*
Tami Sullberg, *General Mgr*
EMP: 48 **EST:** 1989
SALES (est): 4.6MM **Privately Held**
WEB: www.windsorgolf.com
SIC: 7992 5941 Public golf courses; golf goods & equipment

7993 Coin-Operated Amusement Devices & Arcades

(P-15037)
GAMEPLAY INC
50 California St Ste 1500, San Francisco (94111-4612)
PHONE..................415 617-1550
Michael Sassi, *President*
EMP: 50 **EST:** 2019
SALES (est): 372.2K **Privately Held**
SIC: 7993 Video game arcade

(P-15038)
MOORETOWN RANCHERIA
Also Called: Feather Falls Casino
3 Alverda Dr, Oroville (95966-9379)
PHONE..................530 533-3885
Tom Yarbrough, *General Mgr*
Ronald Bert, *Vice Pres*
Nicole Taylor, *CIO*
Scott Nash, *Manager*
EMP: 340 **Privately Held**
WEB: www.mooretownrancheria-nsn.gov
SIC: 7993 7999 Gambling establishments operating coin-operated machines; gambling establishment
PA: Mooretown Rancheria
1 Alverda Dr
Oroville CA 95966

(P-15039)
PELICANTUNES INC
3950 Valley Ave Ste A, Pleasanton (94566-4868)
PHONE..................925 838-8484
Peter Casas, *President*
EMP: 15 **EST:** 2012
SALES (est): 508.6K **Privately Held**
WEB: www.pelicantunes.com
SIC: 7993 5941 3944 Juke boxes; pool & billiard tables; darts & dart games

7996 Amusement Parks

(P-15040)
CEDAR FAIR LP
Auntie Anne's
4701 Great America Pkwy, Santa Clara (95054-1287)
P.O. Box 1776 (95052-1776)
PHONE..................408 988-1776
David Mannix, *Systems Mgr*
Danny Messinger, *Area Mgr*
Luwanna Le, *Finance*
Carl Ewaskowitz, *Sales Executive*
Jason Soyster, *Marketing Staff*
EMP: 120
SALES (corp-wide): 181.5MM **Publicly Held**
WEB: www.cedarfair.com
SIC: 7996 5461 Theme park, amusement; pretzels
PA: Cedar Fair, L.P.
1 Cedar Point Dr
Sandusky OH 44870
419 626-0830

(P-15041)
FAIRYTALE TOWN INC
3901 Land Park Dr, Sacramento (95822-1270)
PHONE..................916 808-7462
Kathryn Fleming, *Exec Dir*
Becky Bitter, *Bd of Directors*
Kathy Fleming, *Exec Dir*
Sarah Thomas, *Program Mgr*
Steve Caudle, *Manager*
EMP: 53 **EST:** 1958
SALES (est): 7MM **Privately Held**
WEB: www.fairytaletown.org
SIC: 7996 Theme park, amusement

(P-15042)
GILROY GARDENS FAMILY THEME PK
3050 Hecker Pass Rd, Gilroy (95020-9411)
PHONE..................408 840-7100
Michael Bonfante, *Director*
Barb Granter, *President*
Stephanie Anderson, *Office Mgr*
Patti Stephens, *Controller*
Zach Cohen, *Opers Staff*
EMP: 204 **EST:** 1998
SALES (est): 14.2MM **Privately Held**
WEB: www.gilroygardens.org
SIC: 7996 Theme park, amusement

(P-15043)
ISLAND WATER PARK INC
6099 W Barstow Ave, Fresno (93723-9372)
PHONE..................559 277-6800
Richard Ehrlich, *President*
Terry Mackey, *General Mgr*
Deserae Padilla, *Info Tech Mgr*
Janine St Lucia, *Finance*
Danielle Briseno, *Sales Staff*
EMP: 47 **EST:** 1998
SQ FT: 15,000
SALES (est): 4.1MM **Privately Held**
WEB: www.islandwaterpark.com
SIC: 7996 Theme park, amusement

(P-15044)
PARC WATERWORLD LLC
Also Called: Waterworld California
1950 Waterworld Pkwy, Concord (94520-2602)
PHONE..................925 609-1364
Randal H Drew,
EMP: 322 **EST:** 2007
SALES (est): 3.2MM
SALES (corp-wide): 133.3MM **Privately Held**
WEB: www.waterworldcalifornia.com
SIC: 7996 Theme park, amusement
PA: Parc Management, Llc
8649 Baypine Rd Ste 101
Jacksonville FL 32256
904 732-7272

(P-15045)
PARK MANAGEMENT CORP
Also Called: Cold Stone Creamery
1001 Fairgrounds Dr, Vallejo (94589-4001)
PHONE..................707 643-6722
Dale Kaetzel, *President*
Don McCoy, *President*
Sherry Martinez, *VP Opers*
William Charles, *Maintence Staff*
Jodi Davenport, *Director*
▲ **EMP:** 221 **EST:** 1997
SALES (est): 40.4MM
SALES (corp-wide): 356.5MM **Publicly Held**
WEB: www.sixflags.com
SIC: 7996 Theme park, amusement
PA: Six Flags Entertainment Corp
1000 Ballpark Way Ste 400
Arlington TX 76011
972 595-5000

(P-15046)
SANTA CRUZ SEASIDE COMPANY (PA)
400 Beach St, Santa Cruz (95060-5416)
PHONE..................831 423-5590
Charles L Canfield, *President*
Jo Anne Dlott, *Vice Pres*
Bryan Wall, *Exec Dir*
Regina Smith, *Managing Dir*
Patricia Isaak, *Admin Asst*
▲ **EMP:** 299 **EST:** 1915
SQ FT: 8,000
SALES (est): 55.2MM **Privately Held**
WEB: www.scseaside.com
SIC: 7996 7011 7933 6531 Pier, amusement; motels; bowling centers; real estate agents & managers

(P-15047)
YANACO INC
Also Called: Waterworks Park
151 N Boulder Dr, Redding (96003-4607)
PHONE..................530 246-9550
Joe Murphy, *President*
EMP: 176 **EST:** 2005
SQ FT: 1,000
SALES (est): 5.2MM **Privately Held**
WEB: www.waterworkspark.com
SIC: 7996 Amusement parks

7997 Membership Sports & Recreation Clubs

(P-15048)
AIRPORT CLUB
Also Called: Airport Health Club
432 Aviation Blvd, Santa Rosa (95403-1069)
PHONE..................707 528-2582
Bob Page, *President*
Vickie Morse, *Corp Secy*
Russell Tow, *Vice Pres*
EMP: 87 **EST:** 1990
SQ FT: 44,000
SALES (est): 8.4MM **Privately Held**
WEB: www.airportclub.com
SIC: 7997 7991 Membership sports & recreation clubs; physical fitness facilities

(P-15049)
ALMADEN GOLF & COUNTRY CLUB
6663 Hampton Dr, San Jose (95120-5536)
PHONE..................408 323-4812
Robert Osshalem, *General Mgr*
Kobi Brown, *Controller*
Primo Rodriguez, *Director*
Adrienne Simpson, *Director*
EMP: 60 **EST:** 1954
SQ FT: 26,000
SALES: 5.8MM **Privately Held**
WEB: www.almadengcc.org
SIC: 7997 Country club, membership; golf club, membership

(P-15050)
ALPINE HLLS TNNIS SWMMING CLB
4139 Alpine Rd, Portola Valley (94028-8042)
PHONE..................650 851-1591
Dolores V Johnson, *General Mgr*
Cherie Billings, *President*
Jerry Angelo, *Treasurer*
Steve Scharbough, *Vice Pres*
V Johnson, *General Mgr*
EMP: 35 **EST:** 1957
SALES: 5.9MM **Privately Held**
WEB: www.alpinehills.us
SIC: 7997 5812 5813 Tennis club, membership; swimming club, membership; eating places; cocktail lounge

(P-15051)
AMERICAN GOLF CORPORATION
Also Called: Oakhurst Country Club
1001 Peacock Creek Dr, Clayton (94517-2201)
PHONE..................925 672-9737
Craig Wong, *General Mgr*
EMP: 100 **Publicly Held**
WEB: www.americangolf.com
SIC: 7997 Golf club, membership
HQ: American Golf Corporation
10670 N Cntl Expy Ste 700
Dallas TX 75231
310 664-4000

(P-15052)
ANTIOCH ROTARY CLUB
324 G St, Antioch (94509-1255)
P.O. Box 692 (94509-0069)
PHONE..................925 757-1800
Richard McDaniel, *President*
EMP: 50 **EST:** 2010
SALES: 111.6K **Privately Held**
WEB: www.antiochrotaryclub.com
SIC: 7997 Membership sports & recreation clubs

(P-15053)
ARDEN LITTLE LEAGUE SNACK BAR (PA)
1150 Eastern Ave, Sacramento (95864-5308)
PHONE..................916 359-6379
Mike Peterson, *Principal*
EMP: 40 **EST:** 1996
SALES (est): 78.9K **Privately Held**
WEB: www.ardenlittleleague.com
SIC: 7997 Baseball club, except professional & semi-professional

(P-15054)
BAY CLUB AMERICA INC
Also Called: Pacific Athletic Club
1 Lombard St Ste 201, San Francisco (94111-1128)
PHONE..................415 781-1874
James Gerber, *President*
EMP: 111 **EST:** 1990
SQ FT: 10,000
SALES (est): 4MM **Privately Held**
WEB: www.bayclubs.com
SIC: 7997 Membership sports & recreation clubs
PA: Bay Club Holdings Iii, Llc
1 Lombard St Lbby
San Francisco CA 94111

(P-15055)
BAY CLUB GOLDEN GATEWAY LLC
Also Called: Golden Gtwy Tennis & Swim CLB
370 Drumm St, San Francisco (94111-2010)
PHONE..................415 616-8800
Broc Stevens, *General Mgr*
Rachel Ruperto, *President*
Meagan McCray, *Vice Pres*
David Smith, *Admin Sec*
Rebecca Baker, *Manager*

7997 - Membership Sports & Recreation Clubs County (P-15056)

EMP: 50 EST: 1992
SQ FT: 8,000
SALES (est): 6.6MM Privately Held
WEB: www.bayclubs.com
SIC: 7997 7999 7991 Tennis club, membership; swimming club, membership; swimming instruction; health club
PA: Bay Club Holdings Iii, Llc
    1 Lombard St Lbby
    San Francisco CA 94111

(P-15056)
BAY CLUB PENINSULA LLC
Also Called: Bay Sport
200 Redwood Shores Pkwy, Redwood City (94065-1100)
PHONE..............................650 593-2800
Ingrid Fripo, *Exec Dir*
Fernando Chilvarguer, *Exec VP*
Pete Jones, *Exec VP*
Ben Shearer, *Exec VP*
Jennifer Beaton, *Vice Pres*
EMP: 35 EST: 2009
SALES (est): 1.1MM Privately Held
SIC: 7997 Membership sports & recreation clubs

(P-15057)
BAYWOOD GOLF AND COUNTRY CLUB
3600 Buttermilk Ln, Arcata (95521-6999)
PHONE..............................707 822-3686
Mark Hayden, *General Mgr*
Kyle McKeown, *Asst Mgr*
EMP: 78 EST: 1956
SQ FT: 10,000
SALES (est): 5.1MM Privately Held
WEB: www.baywoodgcc.com
SIC: 7997 Country club, membership

(P-15058)
BEAU PRE CORPORATION
Also Called: Beau Pre Golf Course
1777 Norton Rd, McKinleyville (95519-9456)
PHONE..............................707 839-2342
Don Harling, *Director*
Donald Harling, *President*
Linda Harling, *Corp Secy*
EMP: 38 EST: 1965
SQ FT: 6,000
SALES (est): 1MM Privately Held
SIC: 7997 5812 Golf club, membership; eating places

(P-15059)
BERKELEY COUNTRY CLUB
7901 Cutting Blvd, El Cerrito (94530-1877)
P.O. Box 2636 (94530-5636)
PHONE..............................510 233-7550
Richard Pettler, *President*
Ken Kipp, *Treasurer*
Charles Ibbotson, *Vice Pres*
Ryan Wilson, *General Mgr*
Bob Langbein, *Admin Sec*
EMP: 166 EST: 1920
SQ FT: 12,000
SALES (est): 10MM Privately Held
WEB: www.berkeleycountryclub.com
SIC: 7997 Country club, membership

(P-15060)
BIG LGUE DREAMS CONSULTING LLC
20155 Viking Way, Redding (96003-8293)
PHONE..............................530 223-1177
Brandi Merkel, *Principal*
EMP: 138
SALES (corp-wide): 52.4MM Privately Held
WEB: www.bigleaguedreams.com
SIC: 7997 Baseball club, except professional & semi-professional
PA: Big League Dreams Consulting, Llc
    16333 Fairfield Ranch Rd
    Chino Hills CA 91709
    909 287-1700

(P-15061)
BIRDS LNDING HNTING PRSRVE INC
2099 Collinsville Rd, Rio Vista (94571)
PHONE..............................707 374-5092
Bob Cirillo, *President*

Rick Cirillo, *Treasurer*
Ernest Kallgren, *Vice Pres*
EMP: 46 EST: 1971
SQ FT: 3,500
SALES (est): 1.1MM Privately Held
WEB: www.birdslanding.net
SIC: 7997 Hunting club, membership

(P-15062)
BLACKHAWK COUNTRY CLUB
599 Blackhawk Club Dr, Danville (94506-4522)
PHONE..............................925 736-6500
Michael G Burton, *CEO*
Larry Marx, *President*
Kevin Dunne, *COO*
Matt Teuscher, *Personnel*
Debbie Schnitter, *Buyer*
EMP: 230 EST: 1987
SQ FT: 35,743
SALES (est): 17.2MM Privately Held
WEB: www.blackhawkcc.org
SIC: 7997 7992 5812 Golf club, membership; tennis club, membership; public golf courses; eating places

(P-15063)
BOYS & GIRLS CLB OF PENINSULA
401 Pierce Rd, Menlo Park (94025-1240)
PHONE..............................650 322-6255
Peter Fortenbaugh, *Exec Dir*
Tina Syer, *Officer*
Haliday Douglas, *Vice Pres*
Cindy McIntyre, *Finance Dir*
James Harris, *Opers Staff*
EMP: 60
SQ FT: 2,000
SALES (est): 15.5MM Privately Held
WEB: www.bgcp.org
SIC: 7997 Membership sports & recreation clubs

(P-15064)
BREAKFAST CLUB AT MIDTOWN
1432 W San Carlos St # 8, San Jose (95126-3217)
PHONE..............................408 280-0688
Spiro Tsaboukos, *Principal*
EMP: 38 EST: 2015
SALES (est): 541.8K Privately Held
WEB: www.essexapartmenthomes.com
SIC: 7997 Membership sports & recreation clubs

(P-15065)
BROOKSIDE COUNTRY CLUB
3603 Saint Andrews Dr, Stockton (95219-1868)
PHONE..............................209 956-6200
Barney Kramer, *CEO*
New England Life, *Partner*
Max Reed, *Controller*
Jason Tewart, *Director*
EMP: 70 EST: 1991
SQ FT: 5,000
SALES (est): 6MM Privately Held
WEB: www.brooksidegolf.net
SIC: 7997 7999 5941 5812 Country club, membership; swimming club, membership; tennis club, membership; golf driving range; golf goods & equipment; eating places

(P-15066)
BURLINGAME COUNTRY CLUB
80 New Place Rd, Hillsborough (94010-6499)
PHONE..............................650 696-8100
Ralston P Roberts, *CEO*
Gavin Havrilenko, *Director*
Ryan Cashen, *Manager*
Jon McCarthy, *Superintendent*
EMP: 89 EST: 1893
SALES (est): 12.7MM Privately Held
WEB: www.burlingamecc.org
SIC: 7997 Country club, membership

(P-15067)
CABRILLO FITNESS CLUB
6200 Soquel Dr, Aptos (95003-3118)
PHONE..............................831 475-5979
William Rose, *Partner*
EMP: 40 EST: 1978
SQ FT: 15,000

SALES (est): 588.8K Privately Held
WEB: www.cabrillo.edu
SIC: 7997 Racquetball club, membership

(P-15068)
CALIFRNIA GOLF CLB SAN FRNCSCO
844 W Orange Ave, South San Francisco (94080-3125)
PHONE..............................650 588-9021
Jon McGovern, *CEO*
Junaid Sheikh, *Treasurer*
Henry Bullock, *Vice Pres*
Gregory Spencer, *Exec Dir*
Glenn Smickley, *General Mgr*
EMP: 74 EST: 1918
SQ FT: 30,000
SALES (est): 15.7MM Privately Held
WEB: www.calclub.org
SIC: 7997 Country club, membership

(P-15069)
CAMERON PARK COUNTRY CLUB INC
3201 Royal Dr, Cameron Park (95682-8559)
PHONE..............................530 672-9840
J Poindexter, *Manager*
Jack Mehl, *President*
Mark Carson, *CEO*
Don Seese, *CFO*
Joe William, *Vice Pres*
EMP: 60 EST: 1979
SQ FT: 50,000
SALES (est): 3.6MM Privately Held
WEB: www.cameronparkcc.com
SIC: 7997 Country club, membership

(P-15070)
CASTLEWOOD COUNTRY CLUB
707 Country Club Cir, Pleasanton (94566-9743)
PHONE..............................925 846-2871
Jerry Olson, *CEO*
Rick Hankins, *President*
Jerry Olsen, *CEO*
Tom Rutherford, *General Mgr*
John Vest, *General Mgr*
EMP: 167 EST: 1954
SQ FT: 55,000
SALES (est): 12.2MM Privately Held
WEB: www.castlewoodcc.org
SIC: 7997 Country club, membership

(P-15071)
CATTA VERDERA COUNTRY CLUB LLC
1111 Catta Verdera, Lincoln (95648-9649)
PHONE..............................916 645-7200
Christopher R Steele, *Mng Member*
Jeff Wilson, *General Mgr*
Tiffanie Blaylock, *Buyer*
Paul Shorts, *Director*
Christina Addiego, *Manager*
EMP: 90 EST: 2004
SQ FT: 196,020
SALES (est): 7.5MM Privately Held
WEB: www.cattaverdera.com
SIC: 7997 Golf club, membership; country club, membership

(P-15072)
CHARDONNAY/ CLUB SHAKESPEARE
Also Called: Chardonnay Golf Club
2555 Jamieson Canyon Rd, NAPA (94558)
PHONE..............................707 257-1900
Jack Barry, *President*
EMP: 35 EST: 1989
SQ FT: 24,000
SALES (est): 1.9MM Privately Held
WEB: www.chardonnaygolfclub.com
SIC: 7997 Golf club, membership

(P-15073)
CITY CLUB LLC
Also Called: City Club of San Francisco
155 Sansome St Fl 9, San Francisco (94104-3687)
PHONE..............................415 362-2480
Martin Brown, *Owner*
Brian Reed, *President*
Jorge Covarrubias, *Bookkeeper*
Erica Faliano, *Sales Staff*
Taylor Ingraham, *Sales Staff*

EMP: 47 EST: 1988
SQ FT: 25,000
SALES (est): 6.8MM Privately Held
WEB: www.cityclubsf.com
SIC: 7997 8641 5812 Membership sports & recreation clubs; civic social & fraternal associations; caterers

(P-15074)
CLAREMONT COUNTRY CLUB
5295 Broadway Ter, Oakland (94618-1498)
PHONE..............................510 653-6789
Harold Peter Smith, *CEO*
Warren Chip Brown, *President*
Richard W Kraber, *Treasurer*
Thomas C Crosby, *Vice Pres*
Alec Churchward, *General Mgr*
EMP: 85 EST: 1903
SQ FT: 479,160
SALES (est): 11.4MM Privately Held
WEB: www.claremontcountryclub.com
SIC: 7997 Country club, membership

(P-15075)
COLD SPRINGS GOLF & CNTRY CLB
6500 Clubhouse Dr, Placerville (95667-9350)
PHONE..............................530 622-4567
Kevin Earl, *General Mgr*
Tyler Brown, *Director*
EMP: 46 EST: 1960
SQ FT: 5,000
SALES (est): 1.6MM Privately Held
WEB: www.coldspringsgolf.com
SIC: 7997 5812 5813 Golf club, membership; eating places; bar (drinking places)

(P-15076)
CONTRA COSTA COUNTRY CLUB
801 Golf Club Rd, Pleasant Hill (94523-1101)
PHONE..............................925 798-7135
Bill Wampler, *Manager*
Sharman Quinn, *Director*
Brian Wong, *Director*
Ryan Maher, *Superintendent*
EMP: 69 EST: 1925
SQ FT: 20,000
SALES (est): 7.5MM Privately Held
WEB: www.contracostacc.org
SIC: 7997 5812 5813 Golf club, membership; American restaurant; drinking places

(P-15077)
COPPER RIVER COUNTRY CLUB LP (PA)
2140 E Clubhouse Dr, Fresno (93730-7020)
P.O. Box 25850 (93729-5850)
PHONE..............................559 434-5200
William R Tatham Sr, *Partner*
Renne Antognoli, *Partner*
Michael F Tatham, *Partner*
William T Tatham Jr, *Partner*
Michael CCM, *General Mgr*
EMP: 50 EST: 1994
SALES (est): 5.1MM Privately Held
WEB: www.copperrivercountryclub.com
SIC: 7997 Golf club, membership

(P-15078)
CORDEVALLE GOLF CLUB LLC
1 Cordevalle Club Dr, San Martin (95046-9472)
PHONE..............................408 695-4500
Earl Wilson,
EMP: 1158 EST: 1999
SALES (est): 6.8MM
SALES (corp-wide): 567.4MM Privately Held
WEB: www.cordevalle.com
SIC: 7997 Golf club, membership
PA: Discovery Land Company, Llc
    14605 N 73rd St
    Scottsdale AZ 85260
    480 624-5200

(P-15079)
COURTSIDE TENNIS CLUB
Also Called: Courtside Club
14675 Winchester Blvd, Los Gatos (95032-1890)
PHONE..............................408 395-7111

PRODUCTS & SERVICES SECTION

7997 - Membership Sports & Recreation Clubs County (P-15102)

James Hinckley, *President*
Jim Gerber, *President*
Liza Maminski, *Info Tech Dir*
EMP: 80 **EST:** 1982
SQ FT: 100,000
SALES (est): 6.4MM
SALES (corp-wide): 1B Privately Held
WEB: www.bayclubs.com
SIC: 7997 7991 5812 Tennis club, membership; physical fitness facilities; eating places
HQ: Clubcorp Usa, Inc.
3030 Lyndon B Johnson Fwy
Dallas TX 75234
972 243-6191

(P-15080)
CROW CANYON MANAGEMENT CORP
Also Called: CROW CANYON COUNTRY CLUB
711 Silver Lake Dr, Danville (94526-6241)
P.O. Box 819012, Dallas TX (75381-9012)
PHONE 925 735-5700
Eric Jacobsen, *President*
John Beckert, *President*
EMP: 57 **EST:** 1982
SQ FT: 55,000
SALES (est): 44.4K
SALES (corp-wide): 1B Privately Held
WEB: www.crowcanyonjta.com
SIC: 7997 7991 5941 5813 Country club, membership; physical fitness facilities; sporting goods & bicycle shops; drinking places; eating places
HQ: Clubcorp Usa, Inc.
3030 Lyndon B Johnson Fwy
Dallas TX 75234
972 243-6191

(P-15081)
CS-PLEASANTON LLC
Also Called: Clubsport of Pleasanton
7090 Johnson Dr, Pleasanton (94588-3328)
PHONE 925 463-2822
Steve Gilmour, *President*
EMP: 559 **EST:** 2002
SALES (est): 5.6MM
SALES (corp-wide): 46.1MM Privately Held
WEB: www.leisuresportsinc.com
SIC: 7997 Membership sports & recreation clubs
PA: Leisure Sports, Inc.
225 Spring St
Pleasanton CA 94566
925 600-1966

(P-15082)
DE ANZA CUPERTINO AQUATICS
Also Called: Daca
1080 S De Anza Blvd Ste B, San Jose (95129-3554)
PHONE 408 446-5600
Pete Raykovich, *President*
Tarolyn Robertson, *Administration*
EMP: 45
SALES (est): 4.6MM Privately Held
WEB: www.daca.org
SIC: 7997 Swimming club, membership

(P-15083)
DEL NORTE CLUB INC
3040 Becerra Way, Sacramento (95821-3915)
PHONE 916 483-5111
Frank Martins, *President*
EMP: 42 **EST:** 1957
SALES (est): 839.8K Privately Held
WEB: www.delnorteclub.com
SIC: 7997 5812 Country club, membership; tennis club, membership; snack bar

(P-15084)
DEL PASO COUNTRY CLUB
3333 Marconi Ave, Sacramento (95821-6293)
PHONE 916 489-3681
Chris Shanks, *Controller*
Eric Hatzenbiler, *CEO*
Jeremy Gregory, *General Mgr*
EMP: 105
SALES: 7.6MM Privately Held
WEB: www.delpasocc.org
SIC: 7997 5941 5812 Country club, membership; sporting goods & bicycle shops; eating places

(P-15085)
DEL RIO GOLF & COUNTRY CLUB
Also Called: BRIGHTON
801 Stewart Rd, Modesto (95356-9639)
PHONE 209 341-2414
John Bellizzi, *Principal*
Duncan Reno, *COO*
Jay Ward, *Admin Sec*
Sergio Gonzalez,
Renee Smith, *Manager*
EMP: 112 **EST:** 1946
SQ FT: 48,000
SALES: 8.3MM Privately Held
WEB: www.delriocountryclub.com
SIC: 7997 5941 Country club, membership; golf club, membership; tennis club, membership; sporting goods & bicycle shops

(P-15086)
DIABLO COUNTRY CLUB
Also Called: Golf Pro. Shop
1700 Clubhouse Rd, Diablo (94528)
PHONE 925 837-4221
Larry Marx, *General Mgr*
Frank Cordeiro, *COO*
Bruce Pruitt, *General Mgr*
Rose Mitchell, *Admin Asst*
Jason Oleson, *Corp Comm Staff*
EMP: 50 **EST:** 1912
SQ FT: 38,199
SALES (est): 11.8MM Privately Held
WEB: www.diablocc.org
SIC: 7997 Country club, membership

(P-15087)
EAGLE RIDGE GOLF CNTRY CLB LLC
Also Called: Eagle Ridge Golf Club
2951 Club Dr, Gilroy (95020-3043)
PHONE 408 846-4531
Mark Gurnow, *Mng Member*
Brian McCrae, *Superintendent*
EMP: 53 **EST:** 1999
SALES (est): 8.8MM Privately Held
WEB: www.eagleridgegc.com
SIC: 7997 7992 5812 Country club, membership; public golf courses; eating places

(P-15088)
EL MACERO COUNTRY CLUB INC
44571 Clubhouse Dr, El Macero (95618-1073)
PHONE 530 753-3363
Steven Backman, *General Mgr*
EMP: 60 **EST:** 1962
SQ FT: 21,000
SALES (est): 3.8MM Privately Held
WEB: www.elmacerocc.org
SIC: 7997 5941 5812 5813 Golf club, membership; golf goods & equipment; American restaurant; bar (drinking places)

(P-15089)
ENCINAL YACHT CLUB
1251 Pacific Marina, Alameda (94501-1117)
PHONE 510 522-3272
Geoff Naleway, *General Mgr*
EMP: 40 **EST:** 1892
SQ FT: 6,000
SALES (est): 3.1MM Privately Held
WEB: www.encinal.org
SIC: 7997 Yacht club, membership

(P-15090)
FOREST PARK CABANA CLUB
2911 Pruneridge Ave, Santa Clara (95051-5652)
P.O. Box 2151 (95055-2151)
PHONE 408 244-1884
Jo Ann Frink, *President*
EMP: 50
SALES: 448.6K Privately Held
WEB: www.forestparkcabanaclub.com
SIC: 7997 Swimming club, membership

(P-15091)
FORT WASH GOLF & CNTRY CLB
Also Called: Fort, The
10272 N Millbrook Ave, Fresno (93730-3400)
PHONE 559 434-1702
Dean Pryor, *President*
Bruce Waltz, *President*
EMP: 95 **EST:** 1923
SALES: 4.5MM Privately Held
WEB: www.fortwashingtoncc.org
SIC: 7997 5813 5812 Golf club, membership; cocktail lounge; American restaurant

(P-15092)
FREMONT HILLS COUNTRY CLUB
12889 Viscaino Pl, Los Altos Hills (94022-2519)
PHONE 650 948-8261
Scott Dominie, *General Mgr*
Bob Blasing, *General Mgr*
Rick Cabasal, *General Mgr*
Vinnie Vieira, *Director*
Laura Gerst, *Manager*
EMP: 40 **EST:** 1957
SQ FT: 13,000
SALES: 3.5MM Privately Held
WEB: www.fremonthills.com
SIC: 7997 Country club, membership

(P-15093)
FRESNO BASEBALL CLUB LLC
Also Called: Fresno Grizzlies Baseball
1800 Tulare St, Fresno (93721-2505)
PHONE 559 320-4487
Chris Cummings, *General Ptnr*
Michael Baker, *Managing Prtnr*
Kimberlee Autry, *Officer*
Veronica Morales, *Executive*
Gary Hanson, *Opers Staff*
EMP: 40 **EST:** 1991
SALES (est): 8.3MM Privately Held
WEB: www.fresnogrizzlies.com
SIC: 7997 Baseball club, except professional & semi-professional

(P-15094)
GLENROCK GROUP
Also Called: Golf Club At Boulder Ridge
1000 Old Quarry Rd, San Jose (95123-2454)
PHONE 408 323-9900
Glenda Garcia, *Vice Pres*
Rocke Garcia, *President*
EMP: 38 **EST:** 2001
SALES (est): 623.1K Privately Held
WEB: www.bayclubs.com
SIC: 7997 Membership sports & recreation clubs

(P-15095)
GRANITE BAY GOLF CLUB INC
9600 Golf Club Dr, Granite Bay (95746-6721)
PHONE 916 791-5379
Bob Kunz, *General Mgr*
EMP: 76 **EST:** 1992
SQ FT: 1,440
SALES (est): 11.2MM
SALES (corp-wide): 1B Privately Held
WEB: www.granitebayclub.com
SIC: 7997 5812 7299 Golf club, membership; eating places; wedding chapel, privately operated
HQ: Clubcorp Usa, Inc.
3030 Lyndon B Johnson Fwy
Dallas TX 75234
972 243-6191

(P-15096)
GREEN VALLEY COUNTRY CLUB
35 Country Club Dr, Fairfield (94534-1305)
PHONE 707 864-1101
Tom Snell, *President*
EMP: 75 **EST:** 1950
SALES: 5.9MM Privately Held
WEB: www.greenvalleycc.com
SIC: 7997 Country club, membership

(P-15097)
GREENHORN CREEK ASSOCIATES LP (PA)
Also Called: Greenhorn Creek Golf Course
711 Mccauley Ranch Rd, Angels Camp (95222-9562)
PHONE 209 729-8111
Greenlaw Grupe, *Owner*
Barden Stevenot, *General Ptnr*
James Watson, *General Ptnr*
Karen Watson, *General Ptnr*
EMP: 55 **EST:** 1994
SALES (est): 2.5MM Privately Held
WEB: www.greenhorncreek.com
SIC: 7997 6552 Golf club, membership; subdividers & developers

(P-15098)
HIDDENBROOK GOLF CLUB (PA)
Also Called: Hiddenbrook Pro Shop
1095 Hddnbroke Pkwy Ste A, Vallejo (94591)
PHONE 707 558-0330
Jhon Goodman, *President*
David Schajatovic, *Sales Mgr*
EMP: 68 **EST:** 1991
SALES (est): 6.8MM Privately Held
WEB: www.hiddenbrookegolf.com
SIC: 7997 5941 Golf club, membership; golf, tennis & ski shops

(P-15099)
HOOVER LITTLE LEAGUE STOCKT
P.O. Box 7191 (95267-0191)
PHONE 209 467-7271
EMP: 53 **EST:** 2002
SALES: 69.8K Privately Held
SIC: 7997 Outdoor field clubs

(P-15100)
K9 ACTIVITY CLUB INC (PA)
4340 Occidental Rd, Santa Rosa (95401-5645)
PHONE 707 569-1394
Alicia M Collins, *President*
EMP: 42 **EST:** 2014
SALES (est): 585.3K Privately Held
WEB: www.k9activityclub.com
SIC: 7997 Membership sports & recreation clubs

(P-15101)
LA RINCONADA COUNTRY CLUB INC (PA)
Also Called: LA RINCONADA GOLF AND COUNTRY
14595 Clearview Dr, Los Gatos (95032-1799)
PHONE 408 395-4181
Steve Vindasius, *CEO*
Mac Niven, *General Mgr*
Janett Antle, *Admin Asst*
Ingrid Firpo, *Director*
Rachelle Reali, *Director*
EMP: 190 **EST:** 1938
SQ FT: 100,000
SALES: 8.4MM Privately Held
WEB: www.larinconadacc.com
SIC: 7997 5813 5812 Country club, membership; bar (drinking places); eating places

(P-15102)
LADERA OAKS
Also Called: Ladera Oaks Swim & Tennis Club
3249 Alpine Rd, Portola Valley (94028-7522)
PHONE 650 854-3101
Jim Gorman, *Manager*
Brian Laporte, *President*
Kimberly Wilcox, *Finance Mgr*
Gina Grasso, *Manager*
EMP: 56 **EST:** 1958
SQ FT: 13,400
SALES (est): 8.3MM Privately Held
WEB: www.laderaoaks.com
SIC: 7997 Country club, membership; swimming club, membership; tennis club, membership

7997 - Membership Sports & Recreation Clubs County (P-15103)

(P-15103)
LAHONTAN GOLF CLUB
12700 Lodgetrail Dr, Truckee (96161-5125)
PHONE..................................530 550-2400
Jon Madonna, *President*
Kelly Gold, *Branch Mgr*
Jeffrey Cobain, *General Mgr*
Steve Harris, *Admin Sec*
Zach Alling, *Buyer*
EMP: 150
SQ FT: 500,000
SALES (est): 10.3MM **Privately Held**
WEB: www.lahontangolf.com
SIC: 7997 Golf club, membership

(P-15104)
LAKE MERCED GOLF CLUB
2300 Junipero Serra Blvd, Daly City (94015-1630)
PHONE..................................650 755-2233
Dale Holub, *CEO*
Nick Bailey, *General Mgr*
Matthew Dachowski, *Superintendent*
Michael Perry, *Supervisor*
EMP: 75 EST: 1922
SQ FT: 38,000
SALES (est): 7MM **Privately Held**
WEB: www.lmgc.org
SIC: 7997 5813 Country club, membership; golf club, membership; tennis club, membership; bars & lounges

(P-15105)
LOS ALTOS GOLF AND COUNTRY CLUB
1560 Country Club Dr, Los Altos (94024-5907)
PHONE..................................650 947-3100
Bill Schneider, *President*
Grace Ikan, *Accountant*
Paul Sossaman, *Facilities Mgr*
James Callahan, *Director*
EMP: 70 EST: 1921
SALES: 14.1MM **Privately Held**
WEB: www.lagcc.com
SIC: 7997 Country club, membership

(P-15106)
MARIN COUNTRY CLUB INC
500 Country Club Dr, Novato (94949-5896)
PHONE..................................415 382-6700
Ryan Wilson, *CEO*
Greg French, *General Mgr*
Michelle Sand, *Administration*
Christine Maxwell, *Accounting Mgr*
Linda Mortarotti, *Buyer*
EMP: 75 EST: 1976
SQ FT: 5,000
SALES: 9.7MM **Privately Held**
WEB: www.marincountryclub.com
SIC: 7997 5812 Country club, membership; golf club, membership; tennis club, membership; swimming club, membership; eating places

(P-15107)
MAYACAMA GOLF CLUB LLC
1240 Mayacama Club Dr, Santa Rosa (95403-8251)
PHONE..................................707 569-2900
Johnathan Wilhelm, *Managing Prtnr*
Jonathan Wilhelm, *Managing Prtnr*
Greg Brown, *General Mgr*
Bryan Bell, *CIO*
Robert Stenger, *Accountant*
EMP: 120 EST: 1999
SQ FT: 5,000
SALES (est): 21.7MM **Privately Held**
WEB: www.mayacama.com
SIC: 7997 Golf club, membership

(P-15108)
MEADOW CLUB
1001 Bolinas Rd, Fairfax (94930-2200)
P.O. Box 129 (94978-0129)
PHONE..................................415 453-3274
John Grehan, *General Mgr*
Anita Law, *Manager*
Kevin Hauschel, *Superintendent*
EMP: 81 EST: 1927
SQ FT: 3,000
SALES (est): 9.4MM **Privately Held**
WEB: www.meadowclub.com
SIC: 7997 Country club, membership

(P-15109)
MENLO CIRCUS CLUB
190 Park Ln, Atherton (94027-4194)
PHONE..................................650 322-4616
Steve De Laet, *CEO*
Nora B Stent, *President*
Matt Quinlan, *CFO*
Susie Frimel, *Admin Sec*
Melissa Gottshall, *Human Res Dir*
EMP: 70 EST: 1923
SQ FT: 14,000
SALES (est): 10.7MM **Privately Held**
WEB: www.menlocircusclub.com
SIC: 7997 Country club, membership

(P-15110)
MENLO COUNTRY CLUB
2300 Woodside Rd, Woodside (94062-1132)
P.O. Box 729, Redwood City (94064-0729)
PHONE..................................650 369-2342
Chris Robinson, *General Mgr*
Bobby Poole, *Instructor*
Alex Martinez, *Manager*
Ariana Sacchi, *Manager*
Alicia Frolli, *Clerk*
EMP: 74 EST: 2011
SALES (est): 17.4MM **Privately Held**
WEB: www.menlocc.com
SIC: 7997 Country club, membership

(P-15111)
METROPOLITAN CLUB
640 Sutter St, San Francisco (94102-1097)
PHONE..................................415 673-0600
Clint Prescott, *General Mgr*
Kayne Maynard, *President*
Margaret Handelman, *Treasurer*
Gibbs Freeman, *General Mgr*
Anapaula Muniz, *General Mgr*
EMP: 65 EST: 1915
SQ FT: 101,662
SALES (est): 5.6MM **Privately Held**
WEB: www.metropolitanclubsf.org
SIC: 7997 Membership sports & recreation clubs

(P-15112)
MORAGA CNTRY CLB HMOWNERS ASSN
1600 Saint Andrews Dr, Moraga (94556-1194)
PHONE..................................925 376-2200
Frank Meln, *General Mgr*
Ron Haas, *COO*
Mick Nissen, *Finance*
Tony Capobianco, *Facilities Mgr*
Meghan Cullen, *Director*
EMP: 100 EST: 1973
SQ FT: 10,000
SALES (est): 10.8MM **Privately Held**
WEB: www.moragacc.com
SIC: 7997 Country club, membership

(P-15113)
NAPA GOLF ASSOCIATES LLC
Also Called: Chardnnay Golf CLB Vnyrds - NA
2555 Jameson Canyon Rd, NAPA (94558)
P.O. Box 3779 (94558-0377)
PHONE..................................707 257-1900
Kenneth E Laird,
Gus Gianulias,
Jim Gianulias,
EMP: 84 EST: 2005
SQ FT: 24,000
SALES (est): 8.7MM
SALES (corp-wide): 1B **Privately Held**
WEB: www.chardonnaygolfclub.com
SIC: 7997 Golf club, membership
HQ: Clubcorp Usa, Inc.
3030 Lyndon B Johnson Fwy
Dallas TX 75234
972 243-6191

(P-15114)
NAPA VALLEY COUNTRY CLUB
3385 Hagen Rd, NAPA (94558-3849)
PHONE..................................707 252-1111
Todd Jeffrey Meginness, *CEO*
Todd Meginness, *COO*
George Reve, *Treasurer*
Mike Wilson, *Vice Pres*
Patrick Smorra, *Admin Sec*
▲ EMP: 87 EST: 1923
SQ FT: 8,000
SALES (est): 17MM **Privately Held**
WEB: www.napavalleycc.com
SIC: 7997 5813 5812 Country club, membership; bar (drinking places); eating places

(P-15115)
NOR-WALL INC
Also Called: Cal Courts
3909 Walnut Dr, Eureka (95503-6281)
PHONE..................................707 445-5445
Agetha Nord, *President*
Glen Wallace, *President*
EMP: 50 EST: 1982
SALES (est): 3.7MM **Privately Held**
SIC: 7997 Tennis club, membership; racquetball club, membership

(P-15116)
NORTH RIDGE COUNTRY CLUB
7600 Madison Ave, Fair Oaks (95628-3400)
PHONE..................................916 967-5717
Dennis Tootelian, *CEO*
Rink Sanford, *General Mgr*
Lee Scarlett, *Director*
EMP: 75 EST: 1952
SQ FT: 5,000
SALES (est): 5.7MM **Privately Held**
WEB: www.northridgegolf.com
SIC: 7997 Country club, membership; golf club, membership

(P-15117)
OAK FLAT GOLF COMPANY LLC
9521 Morton Davis Dr, Patterson (95363-8610)
PHONE..................................209 892-4653
Russel Newman,
Josh Clay, *General Mgr*
Laura Aaron, *Merchandise Mgr*
Megan Martens, *Director*
EMP: 36 EST: 1996
SALES (est): 302.1K **Privately Held**
SIC: 7997 Golf club, membership

(P-15118)
OAKDALE GOLF AND COUNTRY CLUB
243 N Stearns Rd, Oakdale (95361-9247)
PHONE..................................209 847-2984
Tom Brennan, *President*
Alicia Hawkins, *Admin Asst*
Doreen Kirk, *Accountant*
Chris Carroll, *Director*
Joey Torres, *Superintendent*
EMP: 55 EST: 1960
SQ FT: 12,000
SALES (est): 3.9MM **Privately Held**
WEB: www.oakdalegcc.com
SIC: 7997 Country club, membership

(P-15119)
OAKLAND HILLS TENNIS CLUB INC
5475 Redwood Rd, Oakland (94619-3119)
PHONE..................................510 531-3300
James Walter Thompson Jr, *President*
Michelle Lafferty, *Vice Pres*
Eileen Thompson, *Admin Sec*
Kathleen Boyle, *Bookkeeper*
EMP: 41 EST: 1974
SQ FT: 12,500
SALES (est): 3MM **Privately Held**
WEB: www.oaklandhills.com
SIC: 7997 Tennis club, membership

(P-15120)
OLYMPIC CLUB
665 Sutter St, San Francisco (94102-1017)
PHONE..................................415 676-1412
Andrew Clark, *Bd of Directors*
Sharon Zimmerman, *Human Res Mgr*
Mark Anderson, *Opers Staff*
Gary Crook, *Athletic Dir*
Chris Lancerini,
EMP: 109
SALES (corp-wide): 58.9MM **Privately Held**
WEB: www.olyclub.com
SIC: 7997 Golf club, membership
PA: The Olympic Club
524 Post St
San Francisco CA 94102
415 345-5100

(P-15121)
ORINDA COUNTRY CLUB
315 Camino Sobrante, Orinda (94563-1899)
PHONE..................................925 254-4313
Jeff Bause, *President*
George Parker, *General Mgr*
Dawn Kelly, *Human Res Mgr*
Sean Piper, *Facilities Mgr*
Steve Haufler, *Athletic Dir*
EMP: 90 EST: 1924
SALES: 13MM **Privately Held**
WEB: www.orindacc.org
SIC: 7997 Country club, membership

(P-15122)
PETALUMA GOLF AND COUNTRY CLUB
1500 Country Club Dr, Petaluma (94952-5271)
PHONE..................................707 762-7041
Mike Johnson, *President*
Jack King, *President*
EMP: 56 EST: 1922
SQ FT: 6,000
SALES (est): 3.2MM **Privately Held**
WEB: www.petalumagolfandcountryclub.com
SIC: 7997 Golf club, membership

(P-15123)
PLUMAS LAKE GOLF AND CNTRY CLB
1551 Country Club Rd, Marysville (95901)
PHONE..................................530 742-3201
Keith Brown, *President*
Thomas Ponciano, *Treasurer*
Ron McCardy, *Vice Pres*
Kim Crother, *Admin Sec*
EMP: 41 EST: 1926
SQ FT: 6,000
SALES (est): 2.4MM **Privately Held**
WEB: www.plumaslake.com
SIC: 7997 5812 5813 5941 Golf club, membership; cafe; bar (drinking places); golf goods & equipment; sports professionals

(P-15124)
RAFAEL RACQUET CLUB INC
Also Called: Rafael Racquet & Swim Club
95 Racquet Club Dr, San Rafael (94901-1073)
P.O. Box 151362 (94915-1362)
PHONE..................................415 456-5522
Shana Tierre, *President*
Bill Johnson, *President*
Tom Litonovich, *Treasurer*
Michael Jantza, *Vice Pres*
Julio Montoya, *Facilities Mgr*
EMP: 46 EST: 1960
SQ FT: 25,000
SALES (est): 5.9MM **Privately Held**
WEB: www.rafaelracquetclub.com
SIC: 7997 Tennis club, membership; swimming club, membership

(P-15125)
RANCHO MURIETA COUNTRY CLUB
7000 Alameda Dr, Rancho Murieta (95683-9148)
PHONE..................................916 354-2400
Robert Wright, *CEO*
Vince Lepera, *President*
Buzz Breedlove, *Treasurer*
Dick Stenstrom, *Vice Pres*
Chris Pasek, *Admin Sec*
EMP: 90 EST: 1973
SQ FT: 40,000
SALES (est): 11.3MM **Privately Held**
WEB: www.ranchomurietacc.com
SIC: 7997 Country club, membership

(P-15126)
REDWOOD EMPIRE GOLF CNTRY CLB
352 Country Club Dr, Fortuna (95540-9212)
PHONE..................................707 725-5194
Greg Senestraro, *President*
Keith Demello, *President*
EMP: 60 EST: 1956
SQ FT: 2,000

PRODUCTS & SERVICES SECTION

7997 - Membership Sports & Recreation Clubs County (P-15150)

SALES: 869.7K *Privately Held*
WEB: www.redwoodempiregolf.com
SIC: 7997 5813 Country club, membership; bar (drinking places)

(P-15127)
RICHMOND COUNTRY CLUB
1 Markovich Ln, Richmond (94806-1825)
PHONE..................510 231-2241
Mac Niven, *General Mgr*
EMP: 57 EST: 1924
SQ FT: 30,000
SALES (est): 5.3MM *Privately Held*
WEB: www.myrichmondcc.com
SIC: 7997 Country club, membership

(P-15128)
RIVERVIEW GOLF AND COUNTRY CLB
4200 Bechelli Ln, Redding (96002-3533)
PHONE..................530 224-2254
Ralph Storch, *President*
Ralph Storch, *President*
Beth Havsgaard, *Director*
Ashli Helstrom, *Director*
EMP: 72 EST: 1947
SQ FT: 30,000
SALES: 3.3MM *Privately Held*
WEB: www.riverviewgolf.net
SIC: 7997 5812 5813 Country club, membership; eating places; bar (drinking places)

(P-15129)
ROLLING HILLS CLUB INC
351 San Andreas Dr, Novato (94945-1299)
PHONE..................415 897-2185
Linda Scharninghausen, *Finance*
Bobbie Bukszar, *Director*
Winnie Comfort, *Director*
Kathy Hart, *Director*
Chris Kretchmer, *Director*
EMP: 41 EST: 2010
SALES (est): 1.4MM *Privately Held*
WEB: www.rollinghillsclub.com
SIC: 7997 Membership sports & recreation clubs

(P-15130)
ROUND HILL COUNTRY CLUB
3169 Roundhill Rd, Alamo (94507-1735)
PHONE..................925 934-8211
Bruce Rarter, *President*
Greg Gonsalves, *COO*
Brian Plopner, *CFO*
Michael McDonald, *Vice Pres*
Charu Fitzgerald, *Human Res Dir*
EMP: 134 EST: 1959
SQ FT: 20,000
SALES (est): 17.9MM *Privately Held*
WEB: www.rhcountryclub.com
SIC: 7997 5813 5812 7371 Country club, membership; bar (drinking places); American restaurant; computer software development & applications

(P-15131)
ROUND HILL COUNTRY CLUB
Also Called: Rh
3169 Roundhill Rd, Alamo (94507-1735)
PHONE..................925 934-8211
Debby Grauman, *CEO*
Greg Tachiera, *CEO*
Matthew Straub, *Comms Mgr*
Charu Fitzgerald, *Human Res Dir*
Marcel Steigerwald, *Merchandising*
EMP: 50 EST: 1965
SALES (est): 10.2MM *Privately Held*
WEB: www.rhcountryclub.com
SIC: 7997 Country club, membership

(P-15132)
SAN FRANCISCO GOLF CLUB
1310 Junipero Serra Blvd, San Francisco (94132-2995)
PHONE..................415 469-4104
Michael E Myers, *CEO*
Gordon Dean, *CEO*
Margaret Viera, *Manager*
EMP: 45 EST: 1895
SALES (est): 7.7MM *Privately Held*
WEB: www.sfgcpar4.com
SIC: 7997 5812 5813 Golf club, membership; eating places; bar (drinking places)

(P-15133)
SAN FRANCISCO YACHT CLUB
98 Beach Rd, Belvedere Tiburon (94920-2300)
P.O. Box 379 (94920-0379)
PHONE..................415 435-9133
Robert Heller, *President*
Rob Dubuc, *Director*
Barbi Loy, *Manager*
Evelyne Swinscoe-Byer, *Manager*
EMP: 40 EST: 1869
SQ FT: 90,000
SALES (est): 6.3MM *Privately Held*
WEB: www.sfyc.org
SIC: 7997 Yacht club, membership

(P-15134)
SAN JOAQUIN COUNTRY CLUB
3484 W Bluff Ave, Fresno (93711-0199)
PHONE..................559 439-3483
Jeffrey Newman, *President*
Lee Castro, *General Mgr*
Tina Solis, *Administration*
Tommy Masters, *Opers Staff*
Melissa Allen, *Manager*
EMP: 63 EST: 1961
SQ FT: 39,615
SALES (est): 5MM *Privately Held*
WEB: www.sjcc.cc
SIC: 7997 5812 5813 Country club, membership; American restaurant; bar (drinking places)

(P-15135)
SAN JOSE COUNTRY CLUB
15571 Alum Rock Ave, San Jose (95127-2799)
PHONE..................408 258-4901
Chris Simpson, *General Mgr*
Michael Comerate, *General Mgr*
Jason Green, *General Mgr*
Ozzie Arauzo, *Technician*
Laura Pesavento, *Marketing Staff*
EMP: 70 EST: 1898
SQ FT: 24,000
SALES: 5.6MM *Privately Held*
WEB: www.sanjosecountryclub.org
SIC: 7997 7299 Ice sports; color consultant

(P-15136)
SAN JUAN SOCCER CLUB
11151 Trade Center Dr # 20, Rancho Cordova (95670-6292)
PHONE..................916 365-2801
Bashar Nazanda, *President*
Mireya Wathen-Mayorga, *Athletic Dir*
EMP: 38 EST: 2009 *Privately Held*
WEB: www.sanjuansoccer.org
SIC: 7997 Membership sports & recreation clubs

(P-15137)
SARATOGA COUNTRY CLUB INC
21990 Prospect Rd, Saratoga (95070-6541)
PHONE..................408 253-0340
Joe Callan, *General Mgr*
EMP: 76 EST: 1958
SQ FT: 12,000
SALES (est): 10MM *Privately Held*
WEB: www.saratogacc.com
SIC: 7997 Country club, membership; swimming club, membership; tennis club, membership

(P-15138)
SCOTT VLY SWIMMING TENNIS CLB
50 Underhill Rd, Mill Valley (94941-1438)
PHONE..................415 383-3483
Daniel Miller, *Manager*
Chris Ventris, *General Mgr*
Aaron Larson, *Bookkeeper*
Azzaddine Kachkach, *Personnel*
Laurent Lecellier, *Director*
EMP: 66 EST: 1967
SQ FT: 4,000
SALES: 2.4MM *Privately Held*
WEB: www.svstc.com
SIC: 7997 Swimming club, membership

(P-15139)
SEQUOIA WOOD COUNTRY CLUB
1000 Cypress Point Dr, Arnold (95223)
P.O. Box 930 (95223-0930)
PHONE..................209 795-1000
Norm Kestner, *President*
Bob Russell, *General Mgr*
EMP: 61 EST: 1968
SQ FT: 13,000
SALES (est): 2.3MM *Privately Held*
WEB: www.sequoiawoods.com
SIC: 7997 5812 5813 Golf club, membership; eating places; bar (drinking places)

(P-15140)
SEQUOYAH COUNTRY CLUB
Also Called: Sequoyah Golf Shop
4550 Heafey Rd, Oakland (94605-4699)
PHONE..................510 632-2900
John Farquhar, *President*
Cammy Fitzpatrick, *Buyer*
Santos Mejia, *Maint Spvr*
Bob Bodman, *Director*
Christopher Ford, *Director*
EMP: 125 EST: 1913
SQ FT: 20,000
SALES (est): 11.5MM *Privately Held*
WEB: www.sequoyahcc.com
SIC: 5941 7997 5812 5813 Golf goods & equipment; golf club, membership; American restaurant; bar (drinking places)

(P-15141)
SERRANO ASSOCIATES LLC
5005 Serrano Pkwy, El Dorado Hills (95762-7511)
PHONE..................916 939-3333
Kevitt Sale, *Manager*
Mia McDonald, *Sales Staff*
Jennifer Galistatus, *Director*
Nancy Provines, *Manager*
EMP: 72 *Privately Held*
WEB: www.parkerdevco.com
SIC: 7997 5941 5813 5812 Golf club, membership; sporting goods & bicycle shops; drinking places; eating places
PA: Serrano Associates, Llc
    4525 Serrano Pkwy Ste 100
    El Dorado Hills CA 95762

(P-15142)
SERRANO COUNTRY CLUB INC
5005 Serrano Pkwy P, El Dorado Hills (95762-7511)
PHONE..................916 933-5005
Dean Cummings, *President*
Steve Rimack, *Engineer*
Lauri Davis, *Accounting Mgr*
Cindy Koch, *Marketing Staff*
Ken Zinky, *Facilities Mgr*
EMP: 105 EST: 1995
SALES (est): 8MM *Privately Held*
WEB: www.serranocountryclub.org
SIC: 7997 Country club, membership

(P-15143)
SIERRA VIEW COUNTRY CLUB
105 Alta Vista Ave, Roseville (95678-1647)
P.O. Box 676 (95678-0676)
PHONE..................916 782-3741
Barry Macdonald, *CEO*
Steve Rainwater, *President*
Jerry Rief, *Administration*
Traci Burres, *Controller*
Belinda Kiefer,
EMP: 75 EST: 1958
SQ FT: 5,000
SALES (est): 5.9MM *Privately Held*
WEB: www.sierraviewcc.org
SIC: 7997 5812 5813 Golf club, membership; American restaurant; bar (drinking places)

(P-15144)
SILICON VALLEY CAPITAL (DH)
Also Called: Silicon Valley Capital Club
50 W San Fernando St Bsmt, San Jose (95113-2439)
PHONE..................408 971-9300
Michael Comerata, *General Mgr*
EMP: 95 EST: 1990
SQ FT: 14,272
SALES (est): 5.8MM
SALES (corp-wide): 1B *Privately Held*
WEB: www.sanjoseclub.com
SIC: 7997 Membership sports & recreation clubs
HQ: Clubcorp Usa, Inc.
    3030 Lyndon B Johnson Fwy
    Dallas TX 75234
    972 243-6191

(P-15145)
SILVER CREEK VLY CNTRY CLB INC
5460 Country Club Pkwy, San Jose (95138-2215)
PHONE..................408 239-5775
Rene Devos, *General Mgr*
Andy Moshier, *Vice Pres*
Janice Graves, *Executive*
Steven Backman, *General Mgr*
Barrett Eiselman, *General Mgr*
EMP: 121 EST: 1992
SALES (est): 20.1MM *Privately Held*
WEB: www.scvcc.com
SIC: 7997 5941 Country club, membership; sporting goods & bicycle shops

(P-15146)
SILVERADO RESORT AND SPA
1600 Atlas Peak Rd, NAPA (94558-1425)
PHONE..................707 257-0200
Setsuo Okawa, *CEO*
Isao Okawa, *Ch of Bd*
EMP: 600 EST: 1968
SQ FT: 2,000
SALES (est): 28.9MM *Privately Held*
WEB: www.silveradoresort.com
SIC: 7997 Country club, membership
HQ: Silverado Napa Corp
    1600 Atlas Peak Rd
    Napa CA 94558

(P-15147)
SOLANO ATHLETIC CLUBS INC (PA)
3006 Hillside Ct, Fairfield (94533-1349)
PHONE..................707 422-2858
Barry Young, *President*
EMP: 45 EST: 1985
SALES (est): 806.9K *Privately Held*
WEB: www.solanoathleticclub.com
SIC: 7997 Membership sports & recreation clubs

(P-15148)
SONOMA NATIONAL GOLF CLUB
17700 Arnold Dr, Sonoma (95476-4018)
PHONE..................707 939-4100
Lance Iwanaka, *Office Mgr*
Brian Simpson, *General Mgr*
Nicole Arends, *Associate*
EMP: 53 EST: 1927
SALES (est): 1MM *Privately Held*
WEB: www.sonomagolfclub.com
SIC: 7997 Golf club, membership

(P-15149)
SPARE-TIME INC
Also Called: Broadstone Raquet Club
820 Halidon Way, Folsom (95630-8406)
PHONE..................916 983-9180
Gavin Russo, *General Mgr*
EMP: 78
SALES (corp-wide): 53MM *Privately Held*
SIC: 7997 7991 Racquetball club, membership; health club
PA: Spare-Time, Inc.
    11344 Coloma Rd Ste 350
    Gold River CA 95670
    916 859-5910

(P-15150)
SPARE-TIME INC
Also Called: Twin Arbors Athletic Club
1900 S Hutchins St, Lodi (95240-6116)
PHONE..................209 334-4897
Dennis Kaufman, *Manager*
EMP: 78
SALES (corp-wide): 53MM *Privately Held*
SIC: 7997 7991 Racquetball club, membership; health club

7997 - Membership Sports & Recreation Clubs County (P-15151)

PA: Spare-Time, Inc.
11344 Coloma Rd Ste 350
Gold River CA 95670
916 859-5910

(P-15151)
SPARE-TIME INC
Also Called: Johnson Ranch Racquet Club
2501 Eureka Rd, Roseville (95661-6400)
PHONE..........................916 782-2600
Tim Munson, *General Mgr*
EMP: 78
SQ FT: 21,584
SALES (corp-wide): 53MM **Privately Held**
SIC: 7997 Racquetball club, membership
PA: Spare-Time, Inc.
11344 Coloma Rd Ste 350
Gold River CA 95670
916 859-5910

(P-15152)
SPARE-TIME INC
Also Called: Gold River Racquet Club
2201 Gold Rush Dr, Gold River (95670-4466)
PHONE..........................916 638-7001
Mike Burchett, *General Mgr*
EMP: 78
SALES (corp-wide): 53MM **Privately Held**
SIC: 7997 Racquetball club, membership
PA: Spare-Time, Inc.
11344 Coloma Rd Ste 350
Gold River CA 95670
916 859-5910

(P-15153)
SPARE-TIME INC
Also Called: Laguna Creek Racquet Club
9570 Racquet Ct, Elk Grove (95758-4349)
PHONE..........................916 859-5910
Kimberley Miller, *Manager*
EMP: 78
SALES (corp-wide): 53MM **Privately Held**
SIC: 7997 7999 7991 Racquetball club, membership; racquetball club, non-membership; health club
PA: Spare-Time, Inc.
11344 Coloma Rd Ste 350
Gold River CA 95670
916 859-5910

(P-15154)
SPRING CREEK GOLF & CNTRY CLB
1580 Spring Creek Dr, Ripon (95366-2268)
PHONE..........................209 599-3258
Dave Erb, *President*
Don Berg, *President*
Mike Garcia, *Vice Pres*
Marius Dingu, *Manager*
EMP: 38
SQ FT: 8,000
SALES: 3.9MM **Privately Held**
WEB: www.springcreekcc.com
SIC: 7997 Country club, membership

(P-15155)
ST FRANCIS YACHT CLUB
700 Marina Blvd, San Francisco (94123-1044)
PHONE..........................415 563-6363
Jim Diepenbrock, *CEO*
Anna Hoit, *Comms Mgr*
Noel Omilia, *MIS Mgr*
Paul Koojoolian, *Controller*
Penelope Smith,
◆ **EMP:** 110 **EST:** 1922
SQ FT: 20,000
SALES: 18.5MM **Privately Held**
WEB: www.stfyc.com
SIC: 7997 4493 Yacht club, membership; marinas

(P-15156)
STONEBRAE LP
Also Called: TPC Stonebrae
222 Country Club Dr, Hayward (94542-7927)
PHONE..........................510 728-7878
Lisa Hinman, *General Mgr*
Erin Crawford, *Project Mgr*
EMP: 40 **EST:** 2004

SALES (est): 2MM **Privately Held**
WEB: www.stonebrae.com
SIC: 7997 Country club, membership

(P-15157)
SUNNYSIDE COUNTRY CLUB
Also Called: University Sequoia
5704 E Butler Ave, Fresno (93727-5499)
PHONE..........................559 255-6871
Steve Menchinella, *Manager*
Jason Zeller, *Manager*
EMP: 85 **EST:** 1911
SQ FT: 24,250
SALES (est): 9.6MM **Privately Held**
WEB: www.sunnyside-cc.com
SIC: 7997 Country club, membership

(P-15158)
TABLE MOUNTAIN GOLF CLUB INC
Also Called: Table Mountain Golf Course
2700 Oro Dam Blvd W, Oroville (95965-9210)
PHONE..........................530 533-3922
Mike McGee, *President*
Don Bargo, *Treasurer*
Mike Murphy, *Vice Pres*
EMP: 35
SQ FT: 3,000
SALES: 1.1MM **Privately Held**
WEB: www.tablemountaingolf.com
SIC: 7997 7992 5941 5812 Golf club, membership; public golf courses; golf goods & equipment; eating places; cocktail lounge

(P-15159)
TEAL BEND GOLF CLUB INC
7200 Garden Hwy, Sacramento (95837-9314)
PHONE..........................916 922-5209
James Hinckley, *President*
Kevin Williams, *General Mgr*
EMP: 53 **EST:** 1996
SQ FT: 4,500
SALES (est): 4.7MM
SALES (corp-wide): 1B **Privately Held**
WEB: www.tealbendgolf.com
SIC: 7997 5812 Golf club, membership; eating places
HQ: Clubcorp Usa, Inc.
3030 Lyndon B Johnson Fwy
Dallas TX 75234
972 243-6191

(P-15160)
THE WOODBRIDGE GOLF CNTRY CLB
800 E Woodbridge Rd, Woodbridge (95258-9628)
P.O. Box 806 (95258-0806)
PHONE..........................209 369-2371
Jerry Leonard, *CEO*
Ernie Micelli, *General Mgr*
EMP: 79 **EST:** 1924
SQ FT: 20,000
SALES: 3.9MM **Privately Held**
WEB: www.woodbridgegcc.com
SIC: 7997 Country club, membership

(P-15161)
TIBURON PENINSULA CLUB
1600 Mar West St, Belvedere Tiburon (94920-1830)
PHONE..........................415 789-7900
Gerry Pang, *Principal*
Juliana Inferrera, *COO*
Julie Coulston, *General Mgr*
Brent Rodenbeck, *Director*
Nathaniel Parker, *Manager*
EMP: 50
SQ FT: 6,674
SALES: 6.8MM **Privately Held**
WEB: www.tiburonpc.org
SIC: 7997 Swimming club, membership; tennis club, membership

(P-15162)
TURLOCK GOLF AND COUNTRY CLUB (PA)
10532 Golf Rd, Turlock (95380)
PHONE..........................209 634-5471
Michael Blevins, *General Mgr*
EMP: 44 **EST:** 1947
SQ FT: 1,440

SALES (est): 8.3MM **Privately Held**
WEB: www.tgccmembers.com
SIC: 7997 5941 5812 Golf club, membership; golf goods & equipment; eating places

(P-15163)
UNIVERSITY CLUB OF SF LLC
800 Powell St, San Francisco (94108-2006)
PHONE..........................415 781-0900
Isabel Moore, *President*
Joe Boone, *Treasurer*
Wells Blaxter, *Vice Pres*
Hank Carrico, *General Mgr*
Neal Vohr, *General Mgr*
EMP: 40 **EST:** 1890
SQ FT: 5,000
SALES (est): 6.2MM **Privately Held**
WEB: www.uclubsf.org
SIC: 7997 Membership sports & recreation clubs

(P-15164)
VALLEY-HI COUNTRY CLUB
9595 Franklin Blvd, Elk Grove (95758-9532)
PHONE..........................916 684-2120
Edgar Gill, *CEO*
Nick West, *Principal*
Judi Santiago, *Office Mgr*
Holzman John, *Technology*
Stephanie White, *Sales Mgr*
EMP: 134 **EST:** 1958
SQ FT: 20,000
SALES (est): 17.5MM **Privately Held**
WEB: www.valleyhicc.com
SIC: 7997 Country club, membership

(P-15165)
VILLAGES GOLF AND COUNTRY CLUB
Also Called: Villages, The
5000 Cribari Ln, San Jose (95135-1397)
PHONE..........................408 274-4400
Virginia Fanelli, *CEO*
Tim Sutherland, *General Mgr*
Luann Busse, *Admin Asst*
Elissa Caruso, *Administration*
Jim White, *Finance Dir*
EMP: 170
SALES (est): 15.1MM **Privately Held**
WEB: www.thevillagesgcc.com
SIC: 7997 Country club, membership

(P-15166)
W C GARCIA & ASSOCIATES INC
Also Called: Sun Oaks Racquet Club
3452 Argyle Rd, Redding (96002-9513)
PHONE..........................530 221-4405
W C Garcia, *President*
Julie Garcia, *Vice Pres*
Lewis Pasquinelli, *Admin Sec*
Jo Campbell, *Instructor*
Angie Baker, *Director*
EMP: 35 **EST:** 1986
SQ FT: 2,500
SALES (est): 803K **Privately Held**
WEB: www.sunoaks.com
SIC: 7997 Tennis club, membership; racquetball club, membership; swimming club, membership

(P-15167)
WILCOX OAKS GOLF CLUB
20995 Wilcox Rd, Red Bluff (96080-8060)
P.O. Box 127 (96080-0127)
PHONE..........................530 527-7087
Roy Christ, *President*
EMP: 39 **EST:** 1948
SALES (est): 1.1MM **Privately Held**
WEB: www.wilcoxoaksgolfclub.com
SIC: 7997 Golf club, membership

(P-15168)
YUBA CITY RACQUET CLUB INC
825 Jones Rd, Yuba City (95991-6124)
PHONE..........................530 673-6900
Judie Jacoby, *President*
Terry Townsend, *Maintenance Dir*
▲ **EMP:** 46 **EST:** 1975
SQ FT: 40,000

SALES (est): 4.9MM **Privately Held**
WEB: www.ycrc.com
SIC: 7997 7991 Tennis club, membership; health club

7999 Amusement & Recreation Svcs, NEC

(P-15169)
ADRIENNE MATTOS SWIM SCHL INC (PA)
2203 Mariner Square Loop, Alameda (94501-1021)
PHONE..........................866 633-4147
Adrienne L Mattos, *CEO*
Heidi Moore, *COO*
Matthew Mitchell, *Manager*
EMP: 50 **EST:** 2006
SALES (est): 2.5MM **Privately Held**
WEB: www.aquatechswim.com
SIC: 7999 Swimming instruction

(P-15170)
ALAMEDA COUNTY AG FAIR ASSN
Also Called: Alameda County Fair
4501 Pleasanton Ave, Pleasanton (94566-7001)
PHONE..........................925 426-7600
Rick Pickering, *CEO*
Randy Maggie, *CFO*
Richard Sims, *Maintence Staff*
Tiffany Burrow, *Superintendent*
Candice Browning, *Supervisor*
EMP: 75 **EST:** 1939
SQ FT: 125,000
SALES: 24.5MM **Privately Held**
WEB: www.alamedacountyfair.com
SIC: 7999 Agricultural fair

(P-15171)
ALPENGLOW EXPEDITIONS LLC ❂
1985 Squaw Valley Rd # 23, Olympic Valley (96146-1090)
P.O. Box 3122 (96146-3122)
PHONE..........................877 873-5376
Logan Talbott,
EMP: 46 **EST:** 2021
SALES (est): 1.4MM **Privately Held**
WEB: www.alpenglowexpeditions.com
SIC: 7999 Tour & guide services

(P-15172)
AMBROSE RECREATION & PARK DST
3105 Willow Pass Rd, Bay Point (94565-3149)
PHONE..........................925 458-1601
Travis Stombaugh, *General Mgr*
Gloria Magleby, *Ch of Bd*
Veronica Washington, *Planning*
Judy Dawson,
Greg Enholm, *Director*
EMP: 38 **EST:** 1952
SALES (est): 2.7MM **Privately Held**
WEB: www.ambroserec.org
SIC: 7999 Recreation services

(P-15173)
AMERICAN WHTWTER EXPDTIONS INC
6019 New River Rd, Coloma (95613)
P.O. Box 455 (95613-0455)
PHONE..........................530 642-0804
Jon Osgood, *President*
EMP: 49
SALES (corp-wide): 2.5MM **Privately Held**
WEB: www.americanwhitewater.com
SIC: 7999 Rafting tours
PA: American Whitewater Expeditions, Inc.
11530 Oro Vista Ave
Sunland CA 91040
818 352-3205

(P-15174)
ART OF YOGA PROJECT
330 Twin Dolphin Dr # 13, Redwood City (94065-1454)
PHONE..........................650 924-9222
Lisa Pedersen, *Exec Dir*
Noelle Kaplan, *Director*

Jessica A Nuzzo, *Director*
EMP: 45 EST: 2003
SALES: 706.1K Privately Held
WEB: www.theartofyogaproject.org
SIC: 7999 8641 8999 Yoga instruction; youth organizations; artist

(P-15175)
ARTICHOKE JOES
Also Called: Artichoke Joe's Casino
659 Huntington Ave, San Bruno (94066-3608)
PHONE.................................650 589-8812
Dennis J Sammut, *CEO*
Helen Sammut, *Corp Secy*
Peter Ishaq, *Officer*
Susi Watt, *Manager*
Joseph Sammut, *Contractor*
EMP: 330 EST: 1916
SALES (est): 24.6MM Privately Held
WEB: www.artichokejoes.com
SIC: 7999 5812 5813 Game parlor; eating places; tavern (drinking places)

(P-15176)
ASSOC STUDENTS UNIVERSITY CA (PA)
Also Called: A S U C, Berkeley
Bancroft Way 400 Eshleman St Bancroft W, Berkeley (94704)
PHONE.................................510 642-5420
Thomas Cordi, *Exec Dir*
Dedasan Permalul MD, *Owner*
EMP: 250 EST: 1887
SQ FT: 20,000
SALES: 1.9MM Privately Held
WEB: www.asuc.org
SIC: 8299 7999 Educational services; billiard parlor

(P-15177)
ASSOCTED STDNTS CAL STATE UNIV (PA)
101 Hazel St Rm 218, Chico (95928)
PHONE.................................530 898-6815
Susan Jennings, *Exec Dir*
EMP: 600 EST: 1942
SQ FT: 55,000
SALES: 18MM Privately Held
WEB: www.as.csuchico.edu
SIC: 5942 5812 7999 7991 College book stores; contract food services; recreation center; physical fitness facilities

(P-15178)
BALANCED ROCK INC
Also Called: West Valley Gymnastics School
1190 Dell Ave Ste I, Campbell (95008-6614)
PHONE.................................408 374-8692
Mark Young, *President*
Evamarie Schmeer, *Office Spvr*
Kristina Williams, *Program Dir*
EMP: 54 EST: 1981
SALES (est): 6.7MM Privately Held
SIC: 7999 Gymnastic instruction, non-membership

(P-15179)
BALLOONS ABOVE VALLEY LTD
603 California Blvd, NAPA (94559-3131)
PHONE.................................707 253-2222
Bob Barbarick, *Owner*
EMP: 38 EST: 1986
SQ FT: 5,000
SALES (est): 2.6MM Privately Held
WEB: www.balloonrides.com
SIC: 7999 Hot air balloon rides

(P-15180)
BAY AREA MOTORCYCLE TRAINING
5100 Clayton Rd 311, Concord (94521-3139)
PHONE.................................925 677-7408
EMP: 40
SALES (est): 675.5K Privately Held
WEB: www.motorcycleschool.com
SIC: 7999 5571 Amusement/Recreation Services Ret Motorcycles

(P-15181)
BAY AREA SEATING SERVICE INC
Also Called: Bass Tickets
1855 Gateway Blvd Ste 630, Concord (94520-3200)
PHONE.................................925 671-4000
W Thomas Gimple, *President*
Doug Levenson, *Exec VP*
EMP: 300 EST: 1974
SQ FT: 18,000
SALES (est): 5MM
SALES (corp-wide): 434.8MM Privately Held
WEB: www.tickets.com
SIC: 7999 Ticket sales office for sporting events, contract
HQ: California Tickets.Com Inc.
    555 Anton Blvd Fl 11
    Costa Mesa CA 92626
    714 327-5400

(P-15182)
BEAR VALLEY SKI CO
Also Called: Bear Valley Mountain Resort
2280 State Rte 207, Bear Valley (95223)
P.O. Box 5038 (95223-5038)
PHONE.................................209 753-2301
Tim Bottomley, *CEO*
Barbara Moreci, *Maintence Staff*
EMP: 325 EST: 1991
SQ FT: 70,000
SALES (est): 20.7MM
SALES (corp-wide): 98.7MM Privately Held
WEB: www.bearvalley.com
SIC: 7999 5941 Recreation services; ski rental concession; ski instruction; skiing equipment
PA: Skyline Investments Inc
    36 King St E Suite 700
    Toronto ON M5C 2
    416 368-2565

(P-15183)
BLACK OAK CASINO
19400 Tuolumne Rd N, Tuolumne (95379-9696)
PHONE.................................209 928-9300
Ron Patel, *General Mgr*
Michael Cox, *Treasurer*
James Hodge, *General Mgr*
Ronaldo Pascual, *General Mgr*
James Canon, *Administration*
EMP: 99 EST: 2000
SQ FT: 168,000
SALES (est): 22MM Privately Held
WEB: www.blackoakcasino.com
SIC: 7999 Gambling establishment
PA: Tuolumne Me-Wuk Tribal Council
    19595 Mi Wu St
    Tuolumne CA 95379

(P-15184)
BVK GAMING INC
3466 Broadway St, American Canyon (94503-1263)
P.O. Box 10078 (94503-0078)
PHONE.................................707 644-8853
Brian Altizer, *Admin Sec*
Von Altizer, *President*
EMP: 90 EST: 2005
SALES (est): 1.8MM Privately Held
SIC: 7999 Card rooms

(P-15185)
CABLE CAR PARTNERS LLC (PA)
Also Called: Classic Sightseeing Adventures
190 Napoleon St, San Francisco (94124-1016)
PHONE.................................415 922-2425
Chris Herschend, *Mng Member*
EMP: 44 EST: 2008
SALES (est): 1.3MM Privately Held
WEB: www.classiccablecars.com
SIC: 7999 Tourist attractions, amusement park concessions & rides; tour & guide services

(P-15186)
CALIFORNIA GRAND CASINO
5988 Pacheco Blvd, Pacheco (94553-5608)
PHONE.................................925 685-8397
Lamar W Wilkinson, *President*
EMP: 82 EST: 1979
SQ FT: 15,000
SALES (est): 7.2MM Privately Held
WEB: www.californiagrandcasino.com
SIC: 5813 5812 7999 Bar (drinking places); eating places; gambling establishment

(P-15187)
CAMERON PARK FIREFIGHTERS ASSN
Also Called: Fire Dept
3200 Country Club Dr, Cameron Park (95682-8631)
PHONE.................................530 677-6190
Tammy Mefford, *General Mgr*
Felicity Carlson, *Director*
Holly Morrison, *Director*
Tina Helm, *Supervisor*
EMP: 77 EST: 1961
SQ FT: 10,000
SALES (est): 2.7MM Privately Held
WEB: www.cameronpark.org
SIC: 7999 Recreation services

(P-15188)
CAPITOL CASINO
411 N 16th St, Sacramento (95811-0516)
PHONE.................................916 446-0700
Clarke Rosa, *President*
EMP: 107 EST: 1991
SQ FT: 7,500
SALES (est): 6.3MM Privately Held
WEB: www.capitol-casino.com
SIC: 7999 5813 Card rooms; cocktail lounge

(P-15189)
CARMICHAEL RECREATION & PK DST
5750 Grant Ave, Carmichael (95608-3779)
PHONE.................................916 485-5322
Ronald D Cuppy, *Administration*
EMP: 54 EST: 1946
SALES (est): 123K Privately Held
WEB: www.carmichaelpark.com
SIC: 7999 Recreation center

(P-15190)
CENTRAL VALLEY GAMING LLC
Also Called: Turlock Poker Room
2321 W Main St Ste C, Turlock (95380-9485)
PHONE.................................209 668-1010
Joe Fernandez,
Pattie Filippini, *Manager*
EMP: 19 EST: 2004
SALES (est): 3.6MM Privately Held
SIC: 7999 3944 Gambling establishment; poker chips

(P-15191)
CHER-AE HEIGHTS INDIAN CMNTY
Also Called: Cher Ae Heights Casino
27 Scenic Dr, Trinidad (95570-9767)
P.O. Box 610 (95570-0610)
PHONE.................................707 677-3611
Ron Dadouin, *Manager*
EMP: 196 Privately Held
WEB: www.cheraeheightscasino.com
SIC: 7999 7011 Card rooms; casino hotel
PA: Cher-Ae Heights Indian Community
    1 Cher Ae Ln
    Trinidad CA 95570
    707 677-0211

(P-15192)
CHICO AREA RECREATION & PK DST (PA)
Also Called: Dorothy Johnson Center
545 Vallombrosa Ave, Chico (95926-4037)
PHONE.................................530 895-4711
Mary Cahill, *General Mgr*
Jason Miller, *Administration*
Heather Childs, *Finance Mgr*
Heidi Raddliffe, *Finance Asst*
Ryan Arnold, *Mktg Coord*
EMP: 129 EST: 1947

SQ FT: 27,000
SALES (est): 9.5MM Privately Held
WEB: www.chicorec.com
SIC: 7999 8322 Recreation services; individual & family services

(P-15193)
CIRCUS CENTER
755 Frederick St, San Francisco (94117-2755)
PHONE.................................415 759-8123
B Kendall, *Exec Dir*
Arthur Hong, *Bd of Directors*
Parry Kendall, *Exec Dir*
Tracey Shababo, *Program Mgr*
Katie Whitcraft, *General Mgr*
EMP: 46 EST: 1985
SALES (est): 2.7MM Privately Held
WEB: www.circuscenter.org
SIC: 7999 8299 Circus company; airline training

(P-15194)
COMMUNITY SKATING INC
Also Called: WINTER LODGE
3009 Middlefield Rd, Palo Alto (94306-2529)
PHONE.................................650 493-4566
Linda Jensen, *Exec Dir*
Linda Stebbins, *Financial Exec*
Meghan Bay, *Instructor*
EMP: 37 EST: 1956
SQ FT: 3,000
SALES (est): 1.5MM Privately Held
WEB: www.winterlodge.com
SIC: 7999 Roller skating rink operation; skating instruction, ice or roller

(P-15195)
CONCESSIONAIRES URBAN PARK (PA)
Also Called: Angel Island Co
2150 Main St Ste 5, Red Bluff (96080-2372)
PHONE.................................530 529-1512
John W Koeberer, *CEO*
Kris Koeberer, *Vice Pres*
Pamela Koeberrer Pitts, *Vice Pres*
Jeff Porter, *General Mgr*
Dina Del Dotto, *Director*
EMP: 300 EST: 1981
SQ FT: 2,800
SALES (est): 25.8MM Privately Held
WEB: www.basecamphospitality.com
SIC: 7999 5941 5812 Beach & water sports equipment rental & services; fishing equipment; snack bar

(P-15196)
CONCESSIONAIRES URBAN PARK
Also Called: Camanche Recreation-North
2000 Camanche Rd Ofc Ofc, Ione (95640-9420)
PHONE.................................209 763-5121
Chris Cantwell, *Branch Mgr*
EMP: 81
SALES (corp-wide): 25.8MM Privately Held
WEB: www.basecamphospitality.com
SIC: 7999 7032 Beach & water sports equipment rental & services; recreational camps
PA: Urban Park Concessionaires
    2150 Main St Ste 5
    Red Bluff CA 96080
    530 529-1512

(P-15197)
CONCESSIONAIRES URBAN PARK
Also Called: Camanche Nrthshore Str/Cffee S
2000 Camanche Rd Ofc Ofc, Ione (95640-9420)
PHONE.................................209 763-5166
Chris Cantwell, *Branch Mgr*
EMP: 81
SALES (corp-wide): 25.8MM Privately Held
WEB: www.basecamphospitality.com
SIC: 7999 5941 5812 Beach & water sports equipment rental & services; fishing equipment; snack bar

7999 - Amusement & Recreation Svcs, NEC County (P-15198)   PRODUCTS & SERVICES SECTION

PA: Urban Park Concessionaires
2150 Main St Ste 5
Red Bluff 96080
530 529-1512

(P-15198)
CONCESSIONAIRES URBAN PARK
34600 Ardenwood Blvd, Fremont (94555-3645)
PHONE..................530 529-1596
Michele Silva Lane, *Branch Mgr*
EMP: 81
SALES (corp-wide): 25.8MM **Privately Held**
WEB: www.basecamphospitality.com
SIC: 7999 5941 5812 Beach & water sports equipment rental & services; fishing equipment; snack bar
PA: Urban Park Concessionaires
2150 Main St Ste 5
Red Bluff CA 96080
530 529-1512

(P-15199)
CONCESSIONAIRES URBAN PARK
Also Called: Ranch At Little Hills, The
18013 Bollinger Canyon Rd, San Ramon (94583-1501)
PHONE..................530 529-1513
Michele Silva Lane, *Manager*
EMP: 81
SALES (corp-wide): 25.8MM **Privately Held**
WEB: www.basecamphospitality.com
SIC: 7999 5941 5812 Beach & water sports equipment rental & services; fishing equipment; snack bar
PA: Urban Park Concessionaires
2150 Main St Ste 5
Red Bluff CA 96080
530 529-1512

(P-15200)
COSUMNES COMMUNITY SVCS DST
9355 E Stockton Blvd, Elk Grove (95624-9476)
PHONE..................916 405-7150
Rod Brewer, *President*
Rich Lozano, *Vice Pres*
EMP: 387 **EST:** 1985
SQ FT: 10,000
SALES (est): 60MM **Privately Held**
WEB: www.yourcsd.com
SIC: 7999 Recreation services

(P-15201)
DESTINY ARTS CENTER
970 Grace Ave, Oakland (94608-2784)
PHONE..................510 597-1619
Cristy Johnson, *Exec Dir*
Cristy Johnson-Limon, *Exec Dir*
Archie Nagraj, *Exec Dir*
Razavi Nasim, *Business Mgr*
Eden Feil, *Finance*
EMP: 50 **EST:** 1995
SALES: 2.3MM **Privately Held**
WEB: www.destinyarts.org
SIC: 7999 7911 Martial arts school; golf professionals; dance studio & school

(P-15202)
EL DORADO HILLS CMNTY SVCS DST
1021 Harvard Way, El Dorado Hills (95762-4353)
PHONE..................916 933-6624
Kevin Loewen, *CEO*
Terry Crumpley, *Bd of Directors*
Noelle Mattock, *Vice Pres*
Brent Dennis, *General Mgr*
Kevin Loewen, *General Mgr*
EMP: 173 **EST:** 1962
SQ FT: 18,500
SALES (est): 9.3MM **Privately Held**
WEB: www.eldoradohillscsd.org
SIC: 7999 Recreation center

(P-15203)
FEATHER RVER RECREATION PK DST
1875 Feather River Blvd, Oroville (95965-5701)
PHONE..................530 533-2011
Vicky Smith, *Chairman*
Victoria Teague, *Executive Asst*
Victoria Coots, *Director*
Gary Emberland, *Director*
Teresa Bachellerie, *Relations*
EMP: 76 **EST:** 1953
SQ FT: 3,000
SALES (est): 2.9MM **Privately Held**
WEB: www.frrpd.org
SIC: 7999 Recreation center

(P-15204)
FOOTLOOSE INCORPORATED
Also Called: Footloose Sports
3043 Main St, Mammoth Lakes (93546-6075)
P.O. Box 1929 (93546-1929)
PHONE..................760 934-2400
Silver Chesak, *President*
Zachary Yates, *Vice Pres*
EMP: 35 **EST:** 1979
SQ FT: 15,000
SALES (est): 3.9MM **Privately Held**
WEB: www.footloosesports.com
SIC: 5941 7999 3949 Skiing equipment; bicycle rental; ski rental concession; snow skiing equipment & supplies, except skis

(P-15205)
FUNTOPIA INC
3700 Brookstone Dr, Turlock (95382-9290)
PHONE..................510 246-3098
Sukhdeep Garcha, *Administration*
EMP: 60 **EST:** 2019
SALES (est): 1.2MM **Privately Held**
SIC: 7999 Tourist attractions, amusement park concessions & rides

(P-15206)
GLAD ENTERTAINMENT INC (PA)
Also Called: Blackbeard's Family Fun Center
4055 N Chestnut Ave, Fresno (93726-4701)
PHONE..................559 292-9000
Greg Florer, *President*
Don Jackley, *Corp Secy*
Judy Nielsen, *Executive*
EMP: 70 **EST:** 1977
SQ FT: 12,000
SALES (est): 5MM **Privately Held**
WEB: www.blackbeards.com
SIC: 7999 Miniature golf course operation; baseball batting cage; waterslide operation; amusement concession

(P-15207)
GLASSHOUSE SJ LLC
Also Called: Glass House, The
84 W Santa Clara St # 10, San Jose (95113-1815)
PHONE..................408 606-8148
EMP: 36 **EST:** 2013
SALES (est): 2MM **Privately Held**
WEB: www.tghsj.com
SIC: 7999 Amusement & recreation

(P-15208)
GOLFLAND ENTRMT CTRS INC
Also Called: Milpitas Golfland
1199 Jacklin Rd, Milpitas (95035-3421)
PHONE..................408 263-4330
Maracio Ceron, *Manager*
EMP: 163
SALES (corp-wide): 14.1MM **Privately Held**
WEB: www.golfland.com
SIC: 7999 7993 5812 Miniature golf course operation; video game arcade; pizzeria, independent
PA: Golfland Entertainment Centers, Inc.
155 W Hampton Ave
Mesa AZ 85210
408 739-1971

(P-15209)
GREATER VALLEJO RECREATION DST
395 Amador St, Vallejo (94590-6320)
PHONE..................707 648-4600
William Pendergast III, *Ch of Bd*
Jazsmine Alzate, *Technician*
Rosa Ringseth, *Mktg Dir*
Dana Asbury, *Assistant*
Dayna Asbury, *Assistant*
EMP: 84 **EST:** 1944
SQ FT: 5,000
SALES (est): 12MM **Privately Held**
WEB: www.gvrd.org
SIC: 7999 Recreation services

(P-15210)
HEAD OVER HEELS
Also Called: Head Over Heels Athletic Art
4701 Doyle St Ste F, Emeryville (94608-2909)
PHONE..................510 655-1265
Bebe Bertolet, *Exec Dir*
Kathleen Macchia-Myhre, *Exec Dir*
EMP: 36 **EST:** 1977
SALES (est): 2.5MM **Privately Held**
WEB: www.hohathleticarts.com
SIC: 7999 Gymnastic instruction, non-membership

(P-15211)
IGT INTERACTIVE INC (DH)
Also Called: Ubet.com
300 California St Fl 8, San Francisco (94104-1416)
PHONE..................415 625-8300
Paul Miltenberger, *CEO*
Ken Lathorp, *COO*
Paul Mathews, *Admin Sec*
EMP: 84 **EST:** 2000
SALES (est): 10.9MM
SALES (corp-wide): 3.1B **Privately Held**
WEB: www.igt.com
SIC: 7999 Gambling establishment
HQ: International Game Technology Inc
6355 S Buffalo Dr
Las Vegas NV 89113
702 669-7777

(P-15212)
JTS SPORTS SERVICES INC
10556 Industrial Ave # 130, Roseville (95678-6232)
PHONE..................916 390-0829
Michael Sypolt, *President*
EMP: 35 **EST:** 2002
SQ FT: 13,000
SALES (est): 1.7MM **Privately Held**
SIC: 7999 Sports instruction, schools & camps

(P-15213)
KINGSBARNS GOLF LINKS LLC
239 Main St Ste E, Pleasanton (94566-8202)
PHONE..................800 441-1391
James Tong,
Garry Forrester, *Opers Staff*
EMP: 101 **EST:** 1997
SALES (est): 264.4K **Privately Held**
SIC: 7999 Golf services & professionals

(P-15214)
KONOCTI VISTA CASINO (PA)
2755 Mission Rancheria Rd, Lakeport (95453-9612)
P.O. Box 57, Finley (95435-0057)
PHONE..................707 262-1900
Sam Dornham, *General Mgr*
EMP: 219 **EST:** 1994
SALES (est): 10.7MM **Privately Held**
WEB: www.konocti-vista-casino.com
SIC: 7999 Gambling establishment

(P-15215)
LA PETITE BALEEN (PA)
775 Main St, Half Moon Bay (94019-1924)
PHONE..................650 726-7166
John S Kolbisen, *President*
Irene Kolbisen, *Vice Pres*
Lizzy Platero, *Office Mgr*
Aprile Uhland, *Director*
EMP: 40 **EST:** 1979
SQ FT: 3,500
SALES (est): 8.1MM **Privately Held**
WEB: www.swimlpb.com
SIC: 7999 7991 Swimming instruction; physical fitness facilities

(P-15216)
LEWIS & LEWIS INC
Also Called: The Cameo Club
5757 Pacific Ave 5, Stockton (95207-5100)
PHONE..................209 474-1777
David Lewis, *President*
Alexis Galbraith, *Executive*
Ronald J Knicker Bocker, *Agent*
EMP: 35 **EST:** 1995
SALES (est): 1MM **Privately Held**
WEB: www.lewisandlewisinc.com
SIC: 7999 Card rooms

(P-15217)
LIMELIGHT BAR AND CAFE LLC
Also Called: Limelight Bar & Cafe
1014 Alhambra Blvd, Sacramento (95816-5213)
PHONE..................916 446-2208
John Mikacich,
Barbara Mikacich, *Treasurer*
Wendelin Will,
EMP: 39 **EST:** 1972
SQ FT: 2,400
SALES (est): 1MM **Privately Held**
WEB: www.limelightcardroom.com
SIC: 5813 7999 5812 5699 Bar (drinking places); card & game services; American restaurant; T-shirts, custom printed

(P-15218)
LIVERMORE AREA RCRATION PK DST (PA)
4444 East Ave, Livermore (94550-5053)
PHONE..................925 373-5700
Tim Barry, *General Mgr*
David Furst, *Bd of Directors*
Jill Kirk, *Division Mgr*
Mathew Fuzie, *General Mgr*
Paulina Belmontes, *Marketing Staff*
EMP: 253 **EST:** 1947
SQ FT: 71,000
SALES (est): 40.5K **Privately Held**
WEB: www.larpd.org
SIC: 7999 Recreation services

(P-15219)
MEADOWOOD ASSOCIATES LP
Also Called: NAPA Valley Reserve, The
900 Silverado Trl N, Saint Helena (94574)
PHONE..................707 968-3190
William Harlan, *Ltd Ptnr*
Crystal Herrick, *Administration*
▲ **EMP:** 54 **EST:** 2000
SALES (est): 1.1MM **Privately Held**
WEB: www.meadowood.com
SIC: 7999 Golf services & professionals

(P-15220)
MOORETOWN RANCHERIA (PA)
Also Called: Feather Falls Casino
1 Alverda Dr, Oroville (95966-9379)
PHONE..................530 533-3625
Gary Archuleta, *Ch of Bd*
Kayla Lobo, *Treasurer*
Melvin Jackson, *Vice Pres*
Julie McIntosh, *Principal*
Penny Palmer, *Admin Sec*
EMP: 50 **EST:** 1989
SALES (est): 25.9MM **Privately Held**
WEB: www.mooretownrancheria-nsn.gov
SIC: 7999 5993 Gambling establishment; cigar store

(P-15221)
MOTHER LODE RIVER TRIPS LTD
6280 State Highway 49, Lotus (95651-9704)
P.O. Box 456, Coloma (95613-0456)
PHONE..................530 626-4187
Scott Underwood, *President*
Penny Gonzales, *Office Mgr*
Dick Wright, *Sales Mgr*
EMP: 42 **EST:** 1971
SQ FT: 800
SALES (est): 1.2MM **Privately Held**
WEB: www.malode.com
SIC: 7999 4725 Rafting tours; tour operators

PRODUCTS & SERVICES SECTION
7999 - Amusement & Recreation Svcs, NEC County (P-15245)

(P-15222)
NAPA VALLEY WINE TRAIN LLC (HQ)
Also Called: NAPA Valley Railroad Co
1275 Mckinstry St, NAPA (94559-1925)
PHONE.................707 253-2160
Anthony J Giaccio,
Vincent M De Deminico Jr, *Vice Pres*
Paula Maietta, *Human Resources*
Diana Evensen, *Purchasing*
Robin McKee, *Sales Mgr*
▲ **EMP:** 125 **EST:** 1984
SQ FT: 20,000
SALES (est): 20.5MM **Privately Held**
WEB: www.winetrain.com
SIC: 7999 5812 4011 4119 Scenic railroads for amusement; eating places; railroads, line-haul operating; local passenger transportation

(P-15223)
NEW COLUSA INDIAN BINGO
Also Called: Colusa Casino Resort
3770 State Highway 45, Colusa (95932-4021)
PHONE.................530 458-8844
Steve Gonzales, *Principal*
Fred Pina, *Vice Pres*
Dennis Pinney, *Info Tech Mgr*
Alonzo Becerra, *Technician*
Ricardo Cardona, *Technology*
EMP: 450 **EST:** 1986
SALES (est): 20.6MM **Privately Held**
WEB: www.colusacasino.com
SIC: 7999 Card & game services

(P-15224)
OC SAILING CLUB INC
Also Called: Olympic Circle Sailing Club
1 Spinnaker Way, Berkeley (94710-1612)
PHONE.................510 843-4200
EMP: 65
SQ FT: 5,000
SALES (est): 3.4MM **Privately Held**
WEB: www.ocscsailing.com
SIC: 7999 5651 Instructor And Boat Charter

(P-15225)
PARC MANAGEMENT LLC
Also Called: Waterworld USA
1950 Waterworld Pkwy, Concord (94520-2602)
PHONE.................925 609-1364
Steve Mayer, *Manager*
EMP: 45
SALES (corp-wide): 133.3MM **Privately Held**
WEB: www.parcentertainment.com
SIC: 7999 Picnic ground operation
PA: Parc Management, Llc
8649 Baypine Rd Ste 101
Jacksonville FL 32256
904 732-7272

(P-15226)
PEAK ATTRACTIONS LLC (PA)
350 Bay St Ste 370, San Francisco (94133-1966)
PHONE.................415 981-6300
James Hutton, *Mng Member*
Patrick O'Brien,
Stephen Molloy, *Manager*
EMP: 41 **EST:** 1996
SQ FT: 2,000
SALES (est): 4.9MM **Privately Held**
WEB: www.playerssf.com
SIC: 5812 7999 7993 Eating places; recreation center; amusement arcade

(P-15227)
PLAYWORKS EDUCATION ENERGIZED
380 Washington St, Oakland (94607-3800)
PHONE.................510 893-4180
Jill Vialet, *Branch Mgr*
EMP: 58 **Privately Held**
WEB: www.playworks.org
SIC: 7999 Recreation services
PA: Playworks Education Energized
638 3rd St
Oakland CA 94607

(P-15228)
PLAYWORKS EDUCATION ENERGIZED (PA)
638 3rd St, Oakland (94607-3551)
PHONE.................510 893-4180
Jill Vialet, *President*
Elizabeth Cushing, *President*
David Carroll, *CFO*
Phillis Carte, *CFO*
Amanda Casey, *CFO*
EMP: 50 **EST:** 1996
SALES (est): 32.4MM **Privately Held**
WEB: www.playworks.org
SIC: 7999 Recreation services

(P-15229)
PUTT-PUTT OF MODESTO INC (PA)
Also Called: Funworks
4307 Coffee Rd, Modesto (95357-0810)
PHONE.................209 578-4386
Ross Briles, *President*
Marie Briles, *Treasurer*
Anthony Gonsalves, *Vice Pres*
Angela Phan, *Accountant*
Tiffannie Raney, *Manager*
EMP: 59 **EST:** 1969
SQ FT: 17,000
SALES (est): 4.8MM **Privately Held**
WEB: www.funworksfuncompany.com
SIC: 5812 7999 Snack bar; miniature golf course operation; go-cart raceway operation & rentals; baseball batting cage

(P-15230)
RECREATION & PK DST ORANGEVALE
6826 Hazel Ave, Orangevale (95662-3445)
PHONE.................916 988-4373
Craig Foell, *Administration*
Greg Foell, *Administration*
EMP: 43 **EST:** 1983
SALES (est): 1MM **Privately Held**
WEB: www.ovparks.com
SIC: 7999 Recreation services

(P-15231)
REDWOOD EMPIRE ICE OPRTONS LLC (PA)
Also Called: Snoopy's Galary and Gift Shop
1667 W Steele Ln, Santa Rosa (95403-2625)
PHONE.................707 546-7147
Jean F Schulz,
Andrea Ewing, *Manager*
EMP: 65 **EST:** 1968
SQ FT: 40,000
SALES (est): 5.6MM **Privately Held**
WEB: www.snoopyshomeice.com
SIC: 7999 5947 5812 Ice skating rink operation; gift shop; coffee shop

(P-15232)
ROSEVILLE GOLFLAND LTD PARTNR
Also Called: Golfland-Sunsplash
1893 Taylor Rd, Roseville (95661-3008)
PHONE.................916 784-1273
Fred Kenney, *Partner*
EMP: 81 **EST:** 2000
SALES (est): 5MM **Privately Held**
WEB: www.golfland.com
SIC: 7999 Tourist attractions, amusement park concessions & rides; miniature golf course operation

(P-15233)
ROSEVILLE SPORTWORLD
Also Called: Skatetown
1009 Orlando Ave, Roseville (95661-5230)
PHONE.................916 783-8550
Scott Slavensky, *President*
Althea Slavensky, *Shareholder*
Frank Slavensky, *Shareholder*
Kerry Slavensky, *Corp Secy*
Susan Sweetser, *Marketing Staff*
EMP: 45 **EST:** 1997
SQ FT: 61,679
SALES (est): 5.4MM **Privately Held**
WEB: www.skatetown.biz
SIC: 7999 5941 Ice skating rink operation; skating equipment

(P-15234)
SAN FRANCISCO PERFORMING ARTS
893 Folsom St, San Francisco (94107-1122)
PHONE.................415 621-6600
EMP: 35
SALES (est): 1.8MM **Privately Held**
SIC: 7999 Amusement/Recreation Services

(P-15235)
SAN FRANCISCO ZOOLOGICAL SOC
1 Zoo Rd, San Francisco (94132-1098)
PHONE.................415 753-7080
Tanya Peterson, *CEO*
Robert Pedrero, *Chairman*
Elizabeth Romero, *Controller*
Brenda Olivera, *Human Resources*
EMP: 222 **EST:** 1954
SQ FT: 2,000
SALES (est): 20.5MM **Privately Held**
WEB: www.sfzoo.org
SIC: 7999 Concession operator; amusement ride; fund raising organizations

(P-15236)
SAN MATEO CNTY EXPO FAIR ASSN
Also Called: San Mateo County Expo Center
2495 S Delaware St, San Mateo (94403-1902)
PHONE.................650 574-3247
Chris Carpenter, *General Mgr*
Charlene King, *Officer*
Francois Hurstel, *Info Tech Mgr*
Thomas Ames, *Director*
Jim Fetter, *Manager*
▲ **EMP:** 50 **EST:** 1938
SQ FT: 225,000 **Privately Held**
WEB: www.smcec.co
SIC: 7999 6512 Exhibition operation; exposition operation; fair; nonresidential building operators

(P-15237)
SANTA CLARA CNTY FAIR GRNDS MG
Also Called: Santa Clara County FMC
344 Tully Rd, San Jose (95111-1913)
PHONE.................408 494-3100
Delana Romero, *Exec Dir*
Howard Thomas, *CFO*
Tom Muller, *General Mgr*
Arshad Rashid, *Administration*
Debbie Abad, *Accounting Mgr*
EMP: 80 **EST:** 1995
SQ FT: 125,000
SALES (est): 11.3MM **Privately Held**
WEB: www.thefairgrounds.org
SIC: 7999 Fair

(P-15238)
SANTA ROSA CITY OF
Also Called: Ridgeway Swim Center
455 Ridgway Ave, Santa Rosa (95401-4323)
PHONE.................707 543-3421
Tiffany Kuhn, *Branch Mgr*
EMP: 36
SALES (corp-wide): 220.5MM **Privately Held**
WEB: www.srcity.org
SIC: 7999 9121 Swimming pool, non-membership; city council
PA: Santa Rosa, City Of
45 Stony Point Rd
Santa Rosa CA 95401
707 543-3010

(P-15239)
SCANDIA SPORTS INC
Also Called: Scandia Family Fun Center
5070 Hillsdale Blvd, Sacramento (95842-3520)
PHONE.................916 331-5757
Paul Wood, *Manager*
EMP: 48
SALES (corp-wide): 2.9MM **Privately Held**
WEB: www.scandiafun.com
SIC: 7999 Miniature golf course operation; recreation center; trampoline operation
PA: Scandia Sports, Inc.
4607 Wardman Bullock Rd
Rancho Cucamonga CA 91739
909 380-4489

(P-15240)
SELF-HELP FOR ELDERLY
Also Called: Lady Shaw Activity Center
1483 Mason St, San Francisco (94133-4283)
PHONE.................415 677-7581
Karon Ho, *Manager*
EMP: 72
SALES (corp-wide): 27.9MM **Privately Held**
WEB: www.selfhelpelderly.org
SIC: 7999 8322 Recreation services; senior citizens' center or association
PA: Self-Help For The Elderly
731 Sansome St Ste 100
San Francisco CA 94111
415 677-7600

(P-15241)
SENOR SISIG
2277 Shafter Ave, San Francisco (94124-1918)
P.O. Box 883094 (94188-3094)
PHONE.................415 608-5048
Evan Kidera, *CEO*
Lejla Borovac, *Opers Staff*
EMP: 60 **EST:** 2009
SALES (est): 3.3MM **Privately Held**
WEB: www.senorsisig.com
SIC: 7999 Concession operator

(P-15242)
SILVERTHORN RESORT ASSOC LP
Also Called: Silverton Rsrt-Mrina-Bar Grill
16250 Silverthorn Rd, Redding (96003-9777)
PHONE.................530 275-1571
Walt Schneider, *Partner*
Mark Hansen, *Partner*
Ray Merlo, *Partner*
Lewie Pugh, *Exec VP*
Sarah Eaton, *Executive Asst*
EMP: 40 **EST:** 1993
SQ FT: 4,000
SALES (est): 5.1MM **Privately Held**
WEB: www.silverthornresort.com
SIC: 7999 5812 Houseboat rentals; American restaurant

(P-15243)
SOLANO COUNTY FAIR ASSOCIATION
900 Fairgrounds Dr, Vallejo (94589-4003)
PHONE.................707 551-2000
Kim Myrman, *General Mgr*
Amy Andrade, *Admin Asst*
EMP: 68 **EST:** 1949
SQ FT: 61,400
SALES (est): 2.8MM **Privately Held**
WEB: www.scfair.com
SIC: 7999 7948 7299 Fair; agricultural fair; exhibition operation; horse race track operation; facility rental & party planning services

(P-15244)
SOUTHGATE RECREATION & PK DST
Also Called: Rizal Community Center
7320 Florin Mall Dr, Sacramento (95823-3255)
PHONE.................916 421-7275
Jeremy Yee, *Manager*
EMP: 56
SALES (corp-wide): 13.9MM **Privately Held**
WEB: www.southgaterecandpark.net
SIC: 7999 Recreation services
PA: Southgate Recreation & Park District
6000 Orange Ave
Sacramento CA 95823
916 428-1171

(P-15245)
SPLASH SWIM SCHOOL INC
2411 Old Crow Canyon Rd, San Ramon (94583-1240)
PHONE.................925 838-7946
Elisabeth Claytor, *President*

7999 - Amusement & Recreation Svcs, NEC County (P-15246)

D Christian Claytor, *Admin Sec*
EMP: 42 **EST:** 2004
SQ FT: 7,310
SALES (est): 2.4MM **Privately Held**
WEB: www.splashswimschool.com
SIC: 7999 Swimming instruction

(P-15246)
STEVEN I KLOTZ
Also Called: Redwood Empire Gymnastics
434 Payran St Ste D, Petaluma (94952-5922)
PHONE.....................707 763-5010
Fax: 707 763-5542
EMP: 35
SALES (est): 800K **Privately Held**
WEB: www.regymnastics.com
SIC: 7999 Amusement/Recreation Services

(P-15247)
SUB SEA SYSTEMS INC
6524 Commerce Way Ste A, Diamond Springs (95619-9479)
PHONE.....................530 626-0100
Mike Stafford, *Chairman*
Melissa Mayfield, *CFO*
Tiffany Bishop, *Technician*
Christina Azbill, *Graphic Designe*
Terrie Carrozzella, *Manager*
◆ **EMP:** 43 **EST:** 1986
SQ FT: 8,000
SALES (est): 6.1MM **Privately Held**
WEB: www.subseasystems.com
SIC: 7999 Scuba & skin diving instruction

(P-15248)
SUTTERS PLACE INC (PA)
Also Called: Bay 101
1801 Bering Dr, San Jose (95112-4207)
PHONE.....................408 451-8888
Timothy Bumb, *CEO*
Michael Rapp, *CFO*
Ronald Werner, *Vice Pres*
Vince Shaw, *General Mgr*
David Imhof, *Office Mgr*
EMP: 639 **EST:** 1911
SQ FT: 80,000
SALES (est): 29MM **Privately Held**
WEB: www.bay101.com
SIC: 5812 5813 7999 Eating places; bar (drinking places); card rooms

(P-15249)
TECHNIQUE GYMNASTICS INC
11345 Folsom Blvd, Rancho Cordova (95742-6224)
PHONE.....................916 635-7900
Alice Welch, *President*
Whitney Slater, *Instructor*
EMP: 40 **EST:** 1996
SQ FT: 38,000
SALES (est): 2.7MM **Privately Held**
WEB: www.techniquegym.com
SIC: 7999 7911 Gymnastic instruction, non-membership; dance studios, schools & halls

(P-15250)
TICKETWEB LLC
685 Market St Ste 200, San Francisco (94105-4203)
PHONE.....................415 901-0210
EMP: 50
SALES (est): 1.2MM
SALES (corp-wide): 10.3B **Publicly Held**
WEB: www.ticketweb.com
SIC: 7999 Amusement/Recreation Services
HQ: Ticketmaster L.L.C.
 7060 Hollywood Blvd Fl 4
 Los Angeles CA 90028
 323 441-7236

(P-15251)
TONAL SYSTEMS INC
617 Bryant St, San Francisco (94107-1612)
PHONE.....................855 698-6625
Aly Orady, *CEO*
Max Lapides, *Engineer*
Mark McNally, *Engineer*
Gabriel Peal, *Engineer*
David Zimmer, *Engineer*
EMP: 65 **EST:** 2015

SALES (est): 16.7MM **Privately Held**
SIC: 7999 Physical fitness instruction

(P-15252)
TOPGOLF MEDIA LLC (DH)
100 California St Ste 650, San Francisco (94111-4531)
PHONE.....................214 377-0615
Ken May,
EMP: 52 **EST:** 2008
SALES (est): 5.2MM
SALES (corp-wide): 1.5B **Publicly Held**
WEB: www.topgolfmedia.com
SIC: 7999 Golf driving range
HQ: Topgolf International, Inc.
 8750 N Cntl Expy Ste 1200
 Dallas TX 75231
 214 377-0663

(P-15253)
TOTAL BODY FITNESS
Also Called: Tbf Travel
5209 Blaze Ct, Rocklin (95677-4443)
PHONE.....................916 202-3006
William Driskill, *Partner*
Mark Shaw, *Partner*
EMP: 44 **EST:** 1991
SALES (est): 505.7K **Privately Held**
WEB: www.totalbodyfitness.com
SIC: 7999 7941 Physical fitness instruction; sports field or stadium operator, promoting sports events

(P-15254)
TOUCHSTONE CLIMBING INC (PA)
Also Called: Mission Cliffs Rock Climbing
2295 Harrison St, San Francisco (94110-2036)
PHONE.....................415 550-0515
Mark Melvin, *President*
Debra Melvin, *Treasurer*
Vaughn Medford, *General Mgr*
Noah Ruiz, *Info Tech Mgr*
Heather Bellgreen, *Marketing Staff*
EMP: 56 **EST:** 1994
SQ FT: 10,000
SALES (est): 20.2MM **Privately Held**
WEB: www.touchstoneclimbing.com
SIC: 7999 7991 7997 5941 Recreation services; health club; membership sports & recreation clubs; specialty sport supplies

(P-15255)
TOWN OF DANVILLE
420 Front St, Danville (94526-3404)
PHONE.....................925 314-3400
Craig Bowen, *Branch Mgr*
Diane Friedmann, *Manager*
EMP: 41
SALES (corp-wide): 42.3MM **Privately Held**
WEB: www.danville.ca.gov
SIC: 7999 Recreation center
PA: Town Of Danville
 510 La Gonda Way
 Danville CA 94526
 925 314-3311

(P-15256)
TREES OF MYSTERY
Also Called: Motel Trees
15500 Us Highway 101 N, Klamath (95548-9351)
P.O. Box 96 (95548-0096)
PHONE.....................707 482-2251
Marylee Smith, *President*
Debbie Thompson, *President*
Brenda Lopez, *Office Mgr*
John Thompson, *Admin Sec*
EMP: 48 **EST:** 1946
SQ FT: 9,000
SALES (est): 949.7K **Privately Held**
WEB: www.treesofmystery.net
SIC: 7999 5947 7011 Tourist attraction, commercial; gift shop; motels

(P-15257)
TRICKS GYMNASTICS INC (PA)
4070 Cavitt Stallman Rd, Granite Bay (95746-9460)
PHONE.....................916 791-4496
Vern Taylor, *President*
Kenny Aldana, *Manager*
EMP: 35 **EST:** 1990

SQ FT: 10,000
SALES (est): 2.7MM **Privately Held**
WEB: www.tricksgym.com
SIC: 7999 7911 Gymnastic instruction, non-membership; dance instructor & school services

(P-15258)
TRUCKEE DNNER RCREATION PK DST
10981 Truckee Way, Truckee (96161-2904)
PHONE.....................530 582-7720
Steve Randall, *General Mgr*
Peter Werbel, *Chairman*
Anne Collin, *Admin Sec*
Kevin Murphy, *Admin Sec*
Elaina Deyo, *Admin Asst*
EMP: 100 **EST:** 1962
SQ FT: 10,000
SALES (est): 10.4MM **Privately Held**
WEB: www.tdrpd.org
SIC: 7999 Recreation services

(P-15259)
TWENTY FIRST DISTRICT AG ASSN (DH)
Also Called: Big Fresno Fair, The
1121 S Chance Ave, Fresno (93702-3707)
PHONE.....................559 650-3247
John Alkire, *CEO*
EMP: 35 **EST:** 1884
SQ FT: 7,000
SALES (est): 9.9MM **Privately Held**
WEB: www.fresnofair.com
SIC: 7999 7948 Agricultural fair; exposition operation; off-track betting; horse race track operation

(P-15260)
TWIN CREEKS SUNNYVALE INC
969 E Caribbean Dr, Sunnyvale (94089-1111)
PHONE.....................408 734-0888
Ray H Collishaw, *President*
Dale Cote, *Vice Pres*
EMP: 65 **EST:** 1983
SALES (est): 1.3MM **Privately Held**
WEB: www.twin-creeks.com
SIC: 5812 7999 7991 American restaurant; recreation center; physical fitness facilities

(P-15261)
UNITED SPORTSMEN INCORPORATED
4700 Evora Rd, Concord (94520-1002)
PHONE.....................925 676-1963
Dan Fowler, *President*
EMP: 37 **EST:** 1960
SQ FT: 3,300
SALES (est): 1.6MM **Privately Held**
WEB: www.unitedsportsmen.com
SIC: 7999 Shooting range operation

(P-15262)
VOLUME SERVICES INC
Also Called: Centerplate
24 Willie Mays Plz, San Francisco (94107-2134)
PHONE.....................415 972-1500
Angie Perrilliat, *General Mgr*
EMP: 135
SALES (corp-wide): 158.5MM **Privately Held**
WEB: www.us.sodexo.com
SIC: 7999 Concession operator
HQ: Volume Services, Inc.
 2187 Atlantic St Ste 6
 Stamford CT 06902

(P-15263)
WINCHESTER MYSTERY HOUSE LLC
525 S Winchester Blvd, San Jose (95128-2588)
PHONE.....................408 247-2101
Ray K Farris II,
Casey Flom, *Controller*
Charles Miranda, *Marketing Staff*
Vakerue Bovone,
Michael Taffe, *Manager*
EMP: 90 **EST:** 1923
SQ FT: 44,000

SALES (est): 8.8MM **Privately Held**
WEB: www.winchestermysteryhouse.com
SIC: 7999 Tourist attraction, commercial

(P-15264)
YARD HOUSE RESTAURANTS LLC
2005 Diamond Blvd, Concord (94520-5701)
PHONE.....................925 602-0523
EMP: 133 **Publicly Held**
WEB: www.yardhouse.com
SIC: 7999 Recreation services
HQ: Yard House Restaurants, Llc
 7700 Irvine Center Dr # 300
 Irvine CA 92618
 800 336-5336

(P-15265)
YOGA SOURCE PARTNERS LLC
Also Called: Yogasource
16185 Los Gatos Blvd, Los Gatos (95032-4568)
PHONE.....................408 402-9642
Linda McGrath, *Mng Member*
Steve McGrath, *Mng Member*
EMP: 100 **EST:** 2002
SALES (est): 3.4MM **Privately Held**
WEB: www.oneyogasource.com
SIC: 7999 Yoga instruction

8011 Offices & Clinics Of Doctors Of Medicine

(P-15266)
1LIFE HEALTHCARE INC (PA)
Also Called: One Medical
1 Embarcadero Ctr # 1900, San Francisco (94111-3723)
PHONE.....................415 814-0927
Amir Dan Rubin, *Ch of Bd*
Bjorn B Thaler, *CFO*
Andrew S Diamond, *Chief Mktg Ofcr*
Lisa A Mango, *Admin Sec*
Stuart Parmenter, *CTO*
EMP: 483 **EST:** 2002
SQ FT: 60,874
SALES (est): 380.2MM **Publicly Held**
WEB: www.onemedical.com
SIC: 8011 Primary care medical clinic

(P-15267)
A B C PEDIATRICS
50 S San Mateo Dr Ste 260, San Mateo (94401-3859)
PHONE.....................650 579-6500
Patricia Soong, *Partner*
Jeanne Beymer, *Partner*
Alger Chapmin, *Partner*
EMP: 39 **EST:** 1958
SQ FT: 4,000
SALES (est): 3.1MM **Privately Held**
WEB: www.abcped.com
SIC: 8011 Pediatrician

(P-15268)
ACTION URGENT CARE INC (PA)
1375 Blossom Hill Rd # 49, San Jose (95118-3806)
PHONE.....................408 440-8335
Garick Hismatullin, *CEO*
Genevieve La Cross, *COO*
EMP: 88 **EST:** 2012
SALES (est): 25.3MM **Privately Held**
WEB: www.actionurgentcare.com
SIC: 8011 Freestanding emergency medical center

(P-15269)
ADVANCED CRDVSCLAR SPCLSTS INC
2490 Hospital Dr Ste 311, Mountain View (94040-4126)
PHONE.....................650 962-4690
Dominic Curatola, *President*
EMP: 42 **EST:** 1990
SQ FT: 3,000
SALES (est): 6.5MM **Privately Held**
WEB: www.acs-mv.com
SIC: 8011 Cardiologist & cardio-vascular specialist

8011 - Offices & Clinics Of Doctors Of Medicine County (P-15294)

(P-15270)
AGE DEFY DERMATOLOGY WELLNESS
Also Called: Age Defying Dermatology
3803 S Bascom Ave Ste 200, Campbell (95008-7317)
P.O. Box 320038, Los Gatos (95032-0100)
PHONE..................................408 559-0988
EMP: 35
SALES (est): 5.3MM **Privately Held**
SIC: 8011 Medical Doctor's Office

(P-15271)
ALEXA ALBORZI DDS MDS INC (PA)
235 N San Mateo Dr # 300, San Mateo (94401-2672)
PHONE..................................650 342-4171
Alexa Alborzi, *Principal*
EMP: 41 **EST:** 2006
SALES (est): 6.3MM **Privately Held**
WEB: www.alborzismiles.com
SIC: 8011 8021 Offices & clinics of medical doctors; offices & clinics of dentists

(P-15272)
ALGOMEDICA INC (PA)
440 N Wolfe Rd, Sunnyvale (94085-3869)
PHONE..................................650 857-0116
Jagdish C Vij, *President*
Ramesh Neelmegh, *Vice Pres*
EMP: 42 **EST:** 2015
SALES (est): 907.8K **Privately Held**
WEB: www.algomedica.com
SIC: 8011 Radiologist

(P-15273)
ALLERGY ASTHMA ASSOC SNTA CLAR (PA)
4050 Moorpark Ave, San Jose (95117-1840)
PHONE..................................408 243-2700
Minoru Yamate MD, *President*
Alan Goldsobel MD, *Treasurer*
Authur Biedermann MD, *Vice Pres*
Patricia Cunnane, *Exec Dir*
James D Wolfe MD, *Admin Sec*
EMP: 45 **EST:** 1975
SALES (est): 13.6MM **Privately Held**
WEB: www.allergycare.com
SIC: 8011 Allergist

(P-15274)
ALLIANCE MEDICAL CENTER INC
1381 University St, Healdsburg (95448-3314)
PHONE..................................707 431-8234
Beatrice Bostick, *CEO*
Abraham Daniels, *Ch of Bd*
Jack Neureuter, *CEO*
Eric Ziedrich, *Bd of Directors*
Priscilla Contreras, *Marketing Staff*
EMP: 99 **EST:** 1975
SALES (est): 16.4MM **Privately Held**
WEB: www.alliancemed.org
SIC: 8011 Clinic, operated by physicians

(P-15275)
ALPINE ALLRGY ASTHMA ASSOC INC
Also Called: Auburn Dermatology Center
3254 Professional Dr, Auburn (95602-2412)
PHONE..................................530 888-1016
Michael McCormick, *Principal*
EMP: 51 **Privately Held**
WEB: www.alpineallergy.com
SIC: 8011 Allergist; dermatologist
PA: Alpine Allergy And Asthma Associates, Inc.
300 Sierra College Dr # 235
Grass Valley CA 95945

(P-15276)
ALTA BATES SUMMIT FOUNDATION
2450 Ashby Ave Ste 601, Berkeley (94705-2066)
PHONE..................................510 204-1667
James H Hickman, *President*
EMP: 51 **EST:** 1975
SALES (est): 2MM **Privately Held**
SIC: 8011 Offices & clinics of medical doctors

(P-15277)
ALTOS PEDIA ASSOC A PROF CORP
842 Altos Oaks Dr, Los Altos (94024-5403)
PHONE..................................650 941-0550
Dr Penny Loeb, *President*
Dr Maryann Zetes, *Vice Pres*
Dr Deborah Babcock, *Principal*
Dr Julie Chen, *Principal*
Dr Donna Chaet, *Admin Sec*
EMP: 35 **EST:** 1978
SQ FT: 4,230
SALES (est): 2.6MM **Privately Held**
SIC: 8011 Pediatrician

(P-15278)
AMARANTH MEDICAL INC
600 California St Fl 6, San Francisco (94108-2733)
PHONE..................................650 965-3830
Fred Schwarzer, *CEO*
Kamal Ramzipoor, *General Mgr*
EMP: 47 **EST:** 2006
SALES (est): 10.6MM **Privately Held**
WEB: www.amaranthmedical.com
SIC: 8011 Medical centers

(P-15279)
ANESTHSIA ANLGSIA MED GROUP IN
Also Called: Santa Rosa Ansthesia Med Group
2455 Bennett Valley Rd C2, Santa Rosa (95404-5663)
PHONE..................................707 522-1800
Eric Hodes, *President*
Jim Robello, *CEO*
Melissa Stewart, *Manager*
EMP: 37 **EST:** 1991
SQ FT: 2,832
SALES (est): 7.5MM **Privately Held**
WEB: www.aamgi.com
SIC: 8011 Anesthesiologist

(P-15280)
ANESTHSIA CONS OF FRSNO A MED
Also Called: Medical Blling Intgration Svcs
7417 N Cedar Ave, Fresno (93720-3637)
PHONE..................................559 436-0871
Donna Schroyer, *Manager*
John Jin, *Anesthesiology*
John Sturman, *Anesthesiology*
EMP: 98 **EST:** 1987
SQ FT: 2,500
SALES (est): 9.5MM **Privately Held**
WEB: www.anesthesiafresno.com
SIC: 8011 Anesthesiologist

(P-15281)
ANIMUS INC (PA)
Also Called: Alpine Animal Hospital
34501 7th St, Union City (94587-3673)
PHONE..................................800 306-7910
Mandeep Ghumman, *President*
EMP: 125 **EST:** 2005
SALES (est): 10.3MM **Privately Held**
WEB: www.animusvetgroup.com
SIC: 8011 8062 Offices & clinics of medical doctors; general medical & surgical hospitals

(P-15282)
ASIAN HEALTH SERVICES (PA)
101 8th St, Oakland (94607-4707)
PHONE..................................510 986-6800
Sherry Hirota, *CEO*
My Chan, *Analyst*
Lilybell Nakamura, *Human Resources*
Francesca Gibson, *Personnel Assit*
Angela Harris, *Opers Staff*
EMP: 147 **EST:** 1973
SQ FT: 30,000
SALES (est): 63MM **Privately Held**
WEB: www.asianhealthservices.org
SIC: 8011 Clinic, operated by physicians

(P-15283)
ASSOCIATED FMLY PHYSICIANS INC
8110 Timberlake Way, Sacramento (95823-5401)
PHONE..................................916 689-4111
David Kosh MD, *President*
Hope Kosh, *Vice Pres*
Tamie Forester, *Administration*
EMP: 98 **EST:** 1990
SALES (est): 12MM **Privately Held**
WEB: www.familymd.com
SIC: 8011 General & family practice, physician/surgeon

(P-15284)
ASSOCIATES IN WOMENS HLTH CARE
2 Medical Plaza Dr # 205, Roseville (95661-3043)
PHONE..................................916 782-2229
Harold Burton, *Principal*
Nancy McDonough, *Property Mgr*
Blake Lambourne, *Med Doctor*
Richard J Leach, *Med Doctor*
Denise L Sweeney, *Director*
EMP: 43 **EST:** 2001
SALES (est): 1.9MM **Privately Held**
WEB: www.aiwhc.com
SIC: 8011 Offices & clinics of medical doctors

(P-15285)
ASSOCTED INTRNAL MDCINE MED GR (PA)
5800 Hollis St, Emeryville (94608-2016)
PHONE..................................510 465-6700
Dean J Nickles, *President*
Marci Gottlieb, *Internal Med*
▲ **EMP:** 46 **EST:** 1990
SALES (est): 10.3MM **Privately Held**
WEB: www.stanfordhealthcare.org
SIC: 8011 General & family practice, physician/surgeon

(P-15286)
ATWATER MEDICAL GROUP
Also Called: Carter W Neal MD
1775 3rd St, Atwater (95301-3608)
PHONE..................................209 358-5611
W N Carter MD, *Partner*
Eric Disbrow MD, *Partner*
William Nation MD, *Partner*
Steven L Taggart MD, *Partner*
EMP: 53 **EST:** 1977
SQ FT: 3,000
SALES (est): 9.3MM **Privately Held**
WEB: www.atwatermedical.com
SIC: 8011 General & family practice, physician/surgeon

(P-15287)
BAY AREA COMMUNITY HEALTH (PA)
40910 Fremont Blvd, Fremont (94538-4375)
PHONE..................................510 770-8040
Zettie Page III, *CEO*
EMP: 146 **EST:** 1972
SALES (est): 47.6MM **Privately Held**
WEB: www.tri-cityhealth.org
SIC: 8011 Clinic, operated by physicians

(P-15288)
BAY AREA OBSTETRICS GYNECOLOGY
1850 Sullivan Ave Ste 550, Daly City (94015-2234)
PHONE..................................650 756-2404
Anna Powell, *Manager*
Stephen J Scheifele MD, *President*
Norman V Wheeler MD, *Vice Pres*
Shelley Zaglin MD, *Vice Pres*
Alberto A Consiglieri MD, *Admin Sec*
EMP: 35 **EST:** 1958
SQ FT: 7,200
SALES (est): 6.4MM **Privately Held**
WEB: www.baogmds.com
SIC: 8011 Gynecologist

(P-15289)
BAY AREA PDATRIC MED GROUP INC
Also Called: Mullikin Medical Center
123 S San Mateo Dr, San Mateo (94401-3804)
PHONE..................................650 343-4200
Diane Suwabe, *Branch Mgr*
EMP: 53
SALES (corp-wide): 5.9MM **Privately Held**
WEB: www.wbomg.com
SIC: 8011 Pediatrician
PA: Bay Area Pediatric Medical Group, Inc.
901 Campus Dr Ste 111
Daly City CA 94015
650 992-4200

(P-15290)
BAY AREA SRGCAL SPCLSTS INC A
2637 Shadelands Dr, Walnut Creek (94598-2512)
PHONE..................................925 350-4044
David M Pittman, *CEO*
Michael Duffy, *Vice Pres*
Emily Wrich, *Project Mgr*
Ramona Parvaneh, *VP Finance*
Carla Toledanes, *Controller*
EMP: 187 **EST:** 2006
SALES (est): 21.8MM **Privately Held**
WEB: www.bassmedicalgroup.com
SIC: 8011 General & family practice, physician/surgeon

(P-15291)
BAY IMAGING CONS MED GROUP INC (PA)
2125 Oak Grove Rd Ste 200, Walnut Creek (94598-2520)
PHONE..................................925 296-7150
Anton C Pogany, *Director*
Linda Womack, *Officer*
Reed Smoller, *Info Tech Dir*
Debbie Morgan, *Human Res Mgr*
Amy W Lai, *Pediatrics*
EMP: 80 **EST:** 1985
SQ FT: 4,500
SALES (est): 17.1MM **Privately Held**
WEB: www.bicrad.com
SIC: 8011 Radiologist

(P-15292)
BAY MEDICAL MANAGEMENT LLC
2125 Oak Grove Rd Ste 200, Walnut Creek (94598-2520)
PHONE..................................925 296-7150
Mary Gerard, *Mng Member*
Keith Tao, *Partner*
Ruby Chang, *Ch of Bd*
David Martin, *Admin Asst*
Graciela Paguirigan, *Administration*
EMP: 160 **EST:** 1992
SALES (est): 45.5MM **Privately Held**
WEB: www.bicrad.com
SIC: 8011 Radiologist

(P-15293)
BAY VALLEY MEDICAL GROUP INC (PA)
319 Diablo Rd Ste 105, Danville (94526-3428)
PHONE..................................510 785-5000
Shelley A Horwitz, *CEO*
Roland J Wong, *Ch of Bd*
Eric S Kohleriter, *President*
Cristina Hernandez,
Misha Roitshteyn, *Director*
EMP: 93 **EST:** 1954
SALES (est): 12.7MM **Privately Held**
WEB: www.stanfordhealthcare.org
SIC: 8011 Physicians' office, including specialists

(P-15294)
BAYCHILDRENS PHYSICIANS
747 52nd St, Oakland (94609-1809)
PHONE..................................510 428-3460
Pamela Friedman, *Principal*
EMP: 41 **EST:** 2008
SALES (est): 23.7MM **Privately Held**
WEB: www.ubcp.org
SIC: 8011 Physicians' office, including specialists

8011 - Offices & Clinics Of Doctors Of Medicine County (P-15295)

PRODUCTS & SERVICES SECTION

(P-15295)
BAYSPORT INC
Also Called: Baysport Physical Therapy
200 Redwood Shores Pkwy, Redwood City (94065-1100)
PHONE.................................650 593-2800
Doug Emery, *Manager*
Brian Schonfeld, *Director*
EMP: 157 **Privately Held**
WEB: www.baysport.com
SIC: 8011 8741 Sports medicine specialist, physician; management services
PA: Baysport, Inc.
  14830 Los Gatos Blvd # 101
  Los Gatos CA 95032

(P-15296)
BERKELEY PEDIATRIC MED GROUP
1650 Walnut St, Berkeley (94709-1606)
PHONE.................................510 848-2566
Ragna Boynton MD, *Partner*
James G Cuthbertson MD, *Partner*
Annemary Franks MD, *Partner*
Howard Gruber MD, *Partner*
Eydie Talavera, *Administration*
EMP: 35 **EST:** 1942
SQ FT: 5,000
SALES (est): 12.1MM **Privately Held**
WEB: www.berkeleypediatrics.com
SIC: 8011 Pediatrician

(P-15297)
BERKLEY CRDOVASCULAR MED GROUP
2450 Ashby Ave Ste 2785, Berkeley (94705-2067)
PHONE.................................510 204-1691
Fax: 510 204-5422
EMP: 39
SALES (est): 1.5MM **Privately Held**
WEB: www.bcvmg.com
SIC: 8011 Medical Doctor's Office

(P-15298)
BETTY K NG
1490 Mason St, San Francisco (94133-4222)
PHONE.................................415 364-7600
Betty C King, *Principal*
Troy Williams, *Nursing Mgr*
John Applegarth, *Network Mgr*
Dan Schwager, *Director*
EMP: 36 **EST:** 2013
SALES (est): 330.3K **Privately Held**
SIC: 8011 Offices & clinics of medical doctors

(P-15299)
BIO BEHAVIORAL MEDICAL CLINICS
1060 W Sierra Ave 105, Fresno (93711-2063)
PHONE.................................559 437-1111
Mateo F De Soto MD, *President*
Kenneth Steinbach MD, *Vice Pres*
Aleksandr Vydro, *Med Doctor*
EMP: 42 **EST:** 1987
SQ FT: 1,300
SALES (est): 5.3MM **Privately Held**
WEB: www.bbmc-inc.com
SIC: 8011 8049 Psychiatric clinic; clinical psychologist

(P-15300)
BOLTON RSNBAUM BRNSTEN PDTRIC
3838 California St Rm 111, San Francisco (94118-1504)
PHONE.................................415 666-1860
Brock D Bernsten MD, *Partner*
Caroline Wright MD, *Partner*
EMP: 39 **EST:** 1989
SALES (est): 4.9MM **Privately Held**
WEB: www.tcpediatrics.com
SIC: 8011 Pediatrician

(P-15301)
BRETT V CRTIS MD A PROF CORP I
Also Called: Medical Center of Marin
101 Casa Buena Dr, Corte Madera (94925-1762)
PHONE.................................415 924-4525
Brett V Curtis, *CEO*
Brett Cuirtis MD, *CEO*
Warren L Cipa DC, *COO*
Warren Cipa, *CFO*
Brett Curtis, *Bd of Directors*
EMP: 49 **EST:** 1981
SQ FT: 2,400
SALES (est): 4.7MM **Privately Held**
WEB: www.mcomarin.com
SIC: 8011 Specialized medical practitioners, except internal

(P-15302)
BRIAN D HOPKINS MD
Also Called: Bass Medical Group
365 Lennon Ln Ste 250, Walnut Creek (94598-5915)
PHONE.................................925 378-4517
Brian D Hopkins, *Principal*
Keshav Pandurangi, *Surgeon*
EMP: 40 **EST:** 2016
SALES (est): 10.6MM **Privately Held**
SIC: 8011 Physicians' office, including specialists; surgeon

(P-15303)
BROOKSIDE CMNTY HLTH CTR INC (PA)
Also Called: Mahony, John MD
2023 Vale Rd, San Pablo (94806-3834)
PHONE.................................510 215-9092
Joseph Gomes, *President*
Cheryl Johnson, *Exec Dir*
EMP: 66 **EST:** 1995
SALES (est): 11MM **Privately Held**
WEB: www.lifelongmedical.org
SIC: 8011 Clinic, operated by physicians

(P-15304)
BROWN & TOLAND MEDICAL GROUP
2100 Webster St Ste 117, San Francisco (94115-2374)
PHONE.................................415 923-3015
Carol Louie, *Office Mgr*
Sunny Kim, *Office Mgr*
Julie J Huh, *Obstetrician*
Neal S Birnbaum, *Rheumtlgy Spec*
Pedro Ruiz, *Rheumtlgy Spec*
EMP: 120
SALES (corp-wide): 121.9MM **Privately Held**
WEB: www.brownandtoland.com
SIC: 8011 Orthopedic physician
HQ: Brown & Toland Physician Services Organization, Inc.
  1221 Broadway Ste 700
  Oakland CA 94612
  415 972-4162

(P-15305)
BROWN & TOLAND MEDICAL GROUP
3905 Sacramento St # 301, San Francisco (94118-1636)
PHONE.................................415 752-8038
Jeanne David, *Office Mgr*
Nancy Chorne, *Pediatrics*
William Todd, *Podiatrist*
Thomas Engel, *Med Doctor*
Yasuko Fukuda, *Med Doctor*
EMP: 120
SALES (corp-wide): 121.9MM **Privately Held**
WEB: www.brownandtoland.com
SIC: 8011 Physicians' office, including specialists
HQ: Brown & Toland Physician Services Organization, Inc.
  1221 Broadway Ste 700
  Oakland CA 94612
  415 972-4162

(P-15306)
BROWN TLAND PHYSCN SVCS ORGNZT (HQ)
1221 Broadway Ste 700, Oakland (94612-1898)
P.O. Box 72710 (94612-8910)
PHONE.................................415 972-4162
Kelly Robison, *CEO*
Elisa Johnson, *Officer*
Rodolfo Mendoza, *Officer*
Jackie Bright, *Senior VP*
Nancy Griest, *Senior VP*
EMP: 240 **EST:** 1997
SQ FT: 8,000
SALES (est): 121.9MM **Privately Held**
WEB: www.brownandtoland.com
SIC: 8011 Medical centers
PA: Altais Clinical Services
  601 12th St Fl 22
  Oakland CA 94607
  415 902-4461

(P-15307)
CALIFORNIA DEPT OF PUB HLTH
Also Called: Genetic Dsase Screening Program
850 Marina Bay Pkwy F175, Richmond (94804-6403)
PHONE.................................510 231-7408
James Harmon, *Branch Mgr*
Sarit Gulati, *Technician*
Leslie Gaffney, *Sales Mgr*
Michael Fortunka, *Associate*
Kathryn Williams, *Associate*
EMP: 171 **Privately Held**
WEB: www.cdph.ca.gov
SIC: 8011 9431 Offices & clinics of medical doctors; administration of public health programs
HQ: The California Department Of Public Health
  1615 Capitol Ave
  Sacramento CA 95814
  916 558-1784

(P-15308)
CALIFORNIA EAR INSTITUTE INC
844 Portola Rd, Portola Valley (94028-7207)
PHONE.................................650 494-1000
Joseph B Roberson Jr, *CEO*
Joseph Roberson, *Executive*
Terri Cott, *General Mgr*
Monica Hellner, *Info Tech Dir*
Spencer Kirkland, *Network Mgr*
EMP: 37 **EST:** 1972
SALES (est): 4.7MM **Privately Held**
WEB: www.californiaearinstitute.com
SIC: 8011 Ears, nose & throat specialist: physician/surgeon

(P-15309)
CALIFORNIA EYE INSTITUTE
Low Vsion Dept St Agnes H, Fresno (93720)
PHONE.................................559 449-5000
Kathy Ploszaj, *Administration*
Eye Medical Center, *Shareholder*
Gary R Fogg MD, *Shareholder*
Saint Agnes Hospital, *Shareholder*
Larry R Lawrence MD, *Shareholder*
EMP: 180 **EST:** 1984
SQ FT: 59,000
SALES (est): 1.5K **Privately Held**
WEB: www.caleyeinstitute.com
SIC: 8011 Ophthalmologist

(P-15310)
CALIFORNIA SKIN INSTITUTE
6399 San Ignacio Ave, San Jose (95119-1215)
PHONE.................................650 969-5600
EMP: 51 **EST:** 2018
SALES (est): 18.9MM **Privately Held**
WEB: www.californiaskininstitute.com
SIC: 8011 Dermatologist

(P-15311)
CALIFRNIA CNCER ASSOC FOR RES (PA)
Also Called: CCARE
7130 N Millbrook Ave, Fresno (93720-3347)
P.O. Box 25100 (93729-5100)
PHONE.................................800 456-5860
Michael J Moffett, *CEO*
Irene Lustria, *Officer*
Alicia Shell, *Opers Staff*
Dina Ibrahim, *Hematology*
Amardeep Aulakh, *Internal Med*
EMP: 92 **EST:** 1993
SALES: 44.8K **Privately Held**
WEB: www.ccare.com
SIC: 8011 Oncologist

(P-15312)
CALIFRNIA CNCER CARE A MED GRO
1350 S Eliseo Dr Ste 200, Greenbrae (94904-2018)
PHONE.................................415 925-5000
Kent Adler, *President*
Myron Turbow, *President*
Bradley Ekstrand, *Hematology*
Jelena KAO, *Hematology*
Karen Chee, *Oncology*
EMP: 94 **EST:** 1978
SQ FT: 5,000
SALES (est): 10.3MM **Privately Held**
WEB: www.ucsfhealth.org
SIC: 8011 Oncologist; hematologist

(P-15313)
CALIFRNIA CRDVSCLAR CONS MED A (PA)
2333 Mowry Ave, Fremont (94538-1625)
PHONE.................................510 796-0222
Ashit Jain, *CEO*
Priscilla Ching, *Nurse Practr*
EMP: 84 **EST:** 2003
SALES (est): 12.6MM **Privately Held**
WEB: www.cccma.org
SIC: 8011 Cardiologist & cardio-vascular specialist

(P-15314)
CALIFRNIA EMRGNCY PHYSCANS MED
2100 Powell St Ste 400, Emeryville (94608-1826)
PHONE.................................510 350-2777
Theo Koury MD, *President*
EMP: 50 **EST:** 1975
SALES (est): 1.2MM **Privately Held**
SIC: 8011 Physicians' office, including specialists

(P-15315)
CALIFRNIA FRNSIC MED GROUP INC
200 E Hackett Rd, Modesto (95358-9415)
PHONE.................................209 525-5670
L Cottrel, *Principal*
EMP: 110
SALES (corp-wide): 33.7MM **Privately Held**
SIC: 8011 Primary care medical clinic
PA: California Forensic Medical Group, Incorporated
  1283 Murfreesboro Pike # 500
  Nashville TN 37217
  831 649-8994

(P-15316)
CALIFRNIA PSYCHTRIC TRNSITIONS
9234n Hinton Ave, Delhi (95315-8200)
P.O. Box 339 (95315-0339)
PHONE.................................209 667-9304
John T Hackett MD, *President*
EMP: 61 **EST:** 1995
SQ FT: 25,000
SALES (est): 22.5MM **Privately Held**
WEB: www.cptmhrc.com
SIC: 8011 Psychiatric clinic

(P-15317)
CAMARENA HEALTH (PA)
344 E 6th St, Madera (93638-3631)
P.O. Box 299 (93639-0299)
PHONE.................................559 664-4000

PRODUCTS & SERVICES SECTION
8011 - Offices & Clinics Of Doctors Of Medicine County (P-15339)

Paulo A Soares, *CEO*
Margarita Medina, *CFO*
Patty Thompson, *Treasurer*
Martha Cardona, *Bd of Directors*
Calvin Crane, *Bd of Directors*
EMP: 193 **EST:** 1980
SQ FT: 25,311
SALES (est): 45.4MM **Privately Held**
WEB: www.camarenahealth.org
SIC: 8011 Health maintenance organization

(P-15318)
CAPITAL EYE MEDICAL GROUP
6620 Coyle Ave Ste 408, Carmichael (95608-6338)
P.O. Box 279, Roseville (95661-0279)
PHONE....................916 241-9378
Mitra Ayazifar, *President*
EMP: 74 **EST:** 2011
SALES (est): 2.4MM
SALES (corp-wide): 40.5MM **Privately Held**
WEB: www.granitepointeeyecare.com
SIC: 8011 Surgeon
PA: Nvision Laser Eye Centers Inc.
   75 Enterprise Ste 200
   Aliso Viejo CA 92656
   877 455-9942

(P-15319)
CAPITAL OBGYN (PA)
77 Cadillac Dr Ste 230, Sacramento (95825-5480)
PHONE....................916 920-2082
Thomas E Melchione, *Principal*
EMP: 71 **EST:** 2006
SALES (est): 1.4MM **Privately Held**
WEB: www.capitalobgyn.com
SIC: 8011 Obstetrician; gynecologist

(P-15320)
CAPITOL INTRVENTIONAL CRDIOLGY
6347 Coyle Ave, Carmichael (95608-0438)
PHONE....................916 967-0115
Scott B Baron MD, *Partner*
Daniel Fisher MD, *Partner*
Jonathan Hamphill MD, *Partner*
EMP: 47 **EST:** 2000
SALES (est): 5.1MM **Privately Held**
SIC: 8011 Cardiologist & cardio-vascular specialist

(P-15321)
CARDIAC SURGERY WEST MED CORP
3941 J St Ste 270, Sacramento (95819-3633)
PHONE....................916 733-6850
Dr Steven Rossiter, *Partner*
John Dein, *Partner*
Allen Morris, *Partner*
Frank Slachman, *Partner*
EMP: 45 **EST:** 1964
SALES (est): 1.9MM **Privately Held**
SIC: 8011 Surgeon; thoracic physician

(P-15322)
CARDIO VASCULAR ASSOCIATES
Also Called: Heart Group, The
1313 E Herndon Ave # 203, Fresno (93720-3306)
PHONE....................559 439-6808
Robert Chambers MD, *Partner*
James Lee, *Partner*
Dale Merrill, *Partner*
Delpinder Sandhu MD, *Partner*
John Telles, *Partner*
EMP: 91 **EST:** 1994
SALES (est): 7.9MM **Privately Held**
SIC: 8011 Cardiologist & cardio-vascular specialist

(P-15323)
CARDIOVASCULAR CONS MED GROUP
5201 Norris Canyon Rd # 220, San Ramon (94583-5411)
PHONE....................925 277-1900
Leigh Bultman, *Manager*
Mark Nathan, *Med Doctor*
EMP: 36

SALES (corp-wide): 16.6MM **Privately Held**
SIC: 8011 Physicians' office, including specialists
PA: Cardiovascular Consultants Medical Group Inc
   365 Hawthorne Ave Ste 201
   Oakland CA 94609
   925 274-2860

(P-15324)
CARDIOVASCULAR CONS MED GROUP
Also Called: East Bay Arrhythmia Elctrphysl
20126 Stanton Ave Ste 100, Castro Valley (94546-5270)
PHONE....................510 537-3556
Wanna Ingrim, *Manager*
EMP: 36
SALES (corp-wide): 16.6MM **Privately Held**
SIC: 8011 Physicians' office, including specialists
PA: Cardiovascular Consultants Medical Group Inc
   365 Hawthorne Ave Ste 201
   Oakland CA 94609
   925 274-2860

(P-15325)
CARDIOVASCULAR CONSULTANTS HEA
1207 E Herndon Ave, Fresno (93720-3235)
PHONE....................559 432-4303
Kevin J Boran, *President*
William E Hanks MD, *Treasurer*
Sue Morrow, *Office Mgr*
Lianna Sheesley, *Office Mgr*
Donald Gregory MD, *Admin Sec*
EMP: 67 **EST:** 1980
SQ FT: 17,000
SALES (est): 11.5MM **Privately Held**
WEB: www.cvcfresno.com
SIC: 8011 Cardiologist & cardio-vascular specialist

(P-15326)
CARDIVSCLAR ASSOC OF PENINSULA
Also Called: Cardiovascular Assoc of Peninsu
1501 Trousdale Dr Fl 2, Burlingame (94010-4506)
PHONE....................650 652-8600
George H Cohen MD, *Partner*
Samuel Chan MD, *Partner*
Tak Poon MD, *Partner*
Stephen E Pope MD, *Partner*
Michael Rabbino MD, *Partner*
EMP: 47 **EST:** 1975
SQ FT: 3,600
SALES (est): 2.7MM **Privately Held**
SIC: 8011 Cardiologist & cardio-vascular specialist

(P-15327)
CAREMARK RX LLC
Also Called: Mullikin Medical Center
800 Douglas Rd, Stockton (95207-3607)
PHONE....................209 957-7050
EMP: 50
SALES (corp-wide): 184.7B **Publicly Held**
SIC: 8011 Medical Center
HQ: Caremark Rx, Inc.
   445 Great Circle Rd
   Nashville TN 37228

(P-15328)
CAREONSITE INC
1805 Arnold Dr, Martinez (94553-4182)
PHONE....................562 437-0381
Lindsey Baker, *Regional Mgr*
Joseph Gamble, *Technician*
Blake Manai, *Opers Staff*
Angelo Cruz, *Supervisor*
EMP: 70
SALES (corp-wide): 23MM **Privately Held**
WEB: www.tangandcompany.com
SIC: 8011 Occupational & industrial specialist, physician/surgeon
PA: Careonsite, Inc.
   1250 Pacific Ave
   Long Beach CA 90813
   562 437-0831

(P-15329)
CARES COMMUNITY HEALTH
Also Called: Pharmacy At Cares, The
1500 21st St, Sacramento (95811-5216)
PHONE....................916 443-3299
Christy Ward, *CEO*
Richard Soohoo, *Ch of Bd*
Kathleen Marshall, *COO*
Bob Styron, *CFO*
Nicole Machado, *Officer*
EMP: 105 **EST:** 1989
SALES (est): 40.2MM **Privately Held**
WEB: www.onecommunityhealth.com
SIC: 8011 8299 Offices & clinics of medical doctors; educational services

(P-15330)
CASTLE FAMILY HEALTH CTRS INC (PA)
3605 Hospital Rd Ste H, Atwater (95301-5173)
PHONE....................209 381-2000
Edward H Lujano, *CEO*
Bill Able, *CFO*
Fily Cale, *Executive Asst*
Madelyn Finister, *Analyst*
Mario Tenorio, *Materials Mgr*
EMP: 94 **EST:** 2006
SALES: 24.4MM **Privately Held**
WEB: www.cfhc.care
SIC: 8011 Clinic, operated by physicians

(P-15331)
CASTLE MEDICAL CENTER
2100 Douglas Blvd, Roseville (95661-3804)
P.O. Box 619085 (95661-9085)
PHONE....................808 263-5182
Susan Steffey, *Lab Dir*
Adnan Chowdhury, *Administration*
Helene Waihee, *Mktg Coord*
Wiley Brunel, *Surgeon*
Donna Awana, *Director*
EMP: 39 **EST:** 2017
SALES (est): 8.1MM **Privately Held**
WEB: www.adventisthealth.org
SIC: 8011 Medical centers

(P-15332)
CC CO HEALTH CNTR INFORMATION
Also Called: Pittsburgh Health Center
2311 Loveridge Rd, Pittsburg (94565-5117)
P.O. Box 2523, Martinez (94553-0317)
PHONE....................925 431-2300
Waynette Mason, *General Mgr*
Karen Alingog, *Family Practiti*
Nathan Brooks, *Family Practiti*
Craig Desoer, *Family Practiti*
Scott Loeliger, *Family Practiti*
EMP: 86 **EST:** 2002
SALES (est): 10.8MM **Privately Held**
WEB: www.cchealth.org
SIC: 8011 Offices & clinics of medical doctors; physicians' office, including specialists

(P-15333)
CENTRAL ANSTHSIA SVC EXCH MED
Also Called: Case Medical Group
3315 Watt Ave, Sacramento (95821-3600)
P.O. Box 660910 (95866-0910)
PHONE....................916 481-6800
David Downs MD, *President*
Vince Isso, *Officer*
Dan Bodily, *Anesthesiology*
Charles Boudreaux, *Anesthesiology*
Deborah Brauer, *Anesthesiology*
EMP: 80 **EST:** 1986
SALES (est): 11.1MM **Privately Held**
WEB: www.casemedgroup.com
SIC: 8011 Group health association

(P-15334)
CENTRAL CAL EAR NOSE THROAT ME
Also Called: Ent Facial Surgery Center
1351 E Spruce Ave, Fresno (93720-3342)
PHONE....................559 432-3724
Marvin Beil MD, *Partner*
Allan Evans MD, *Partner*
Brent Lanier MD, *Partner*
Jerry Moore MD, *Partner*
Oscar Tamez MD, *Partner*

EMP: 169 **EST:** 1977
SQ FT: 24,000
SALES: 22.8MM **Privately Held**
WEB: www.ccent.com
SIC: 8011 8049 5999 Eyes, ears, nose & throat specialist: physician/surgeon; audiologist; hearing aids

(P-15335)
CENTRAL CAL FCLTY MED GROUP IN
Also Called: University Surgical Associates
2335 E Kashian Ln Ste 220, Fresno (93701-2211)
PHONE....................559 435-6600
Jenny Eastman, *Branch Mgr*
EMP: 67
SALES (corp-wide): 54.7MM **Privately Held**
WEB: www.universitymds.com
SIC: 8011 Internal medicine, physician/surgeon
PA: Central California Faculty Medical Group, Inc.
   2625 E Divisadero St
   Fresno CA 93721
   559 453-5200

(P-15336)
CENTRAL CAL FCLTY MED GROUP IN
2335 E Kashian Ln, Fresno (93701-2230)
PHONE....................559 266-4100
Christopher Bauer, *Psychologist*
EMP: 67
SALES (corp-wide): 54.7MM **Privately Held**
WEB: www.universitymds.com
SIC: 8011 Surgeon
PA: Central California Faculty Medical Group, Inc.
   2625 E Divisadero St
   Fresno CA 93721
   559 453-5200

(P-15337)
CENTRAL CAL FCLTY MED GROUP IN
2828 Fresno St Ste 203, Fresno (93721-1327)
PHONE....................559 320-1090
Alan Kelton, *Internal Med*
Simon Paul, *Internal Med*
Nargis Naheed, *Med Doctor*
EMP: 67
SALES (corp-wide): 54.7MM **Privately Held**
WEB: www.universitymds.com
SIC: 8011 Internal medicine, physician/surgeon
PA: Central California Faculty Medical Group, Inc.
   2625 E Divisadero St
   Fresno CA 93721
   559 453-5200

(P-15338)
CENTRAL CAL FCLTY MED GROUP IN
Also Called: Pulmonary Sleep Disorders Ctr
6311 N Fresno St, Fresno (93710-5290)
PHONE....................559 435-4700
Lois Ceja, *Manager*
Devin Nugent, *Officer*
Valerie Araki, *Human Res Mgr*
Christopher Bauer, *Psychologist*
Khorsheda Ali, *Obstetrician*
EMP: 67
SALES (corp-wide): 54.7MM **Privately Held**
WEB: www.universitymds.com
SIC: 8011 Pulmonary specialist, physician/surgeon
PA: Central California Faculty Medical Group, Inc.
   2625 E Divisadero St
   Fresno CA 93721
   559 453-5200

(P-15339)
CENTRAL CALIFORNIA FACULTY MED (PA)
2625 E Divisadero St, Fresno (93721-1431)
PHONE....................559 453-5200

8011 - Offices & Clinics Of Doctors Of Medicine County (P-15340)

Karl Van Gundy, *CEO*
Robert Frediani, *COO*
Randall Stern, *Treasurer*
Paul Simon, *Executive*
Paramjeet Gill, *Principal*
EMP: 100 **EST:** 1979
SQ FT: 19,053
SALES (est): 54.7MM **Privately Held**
WEB: www.universitymds.com
SIC: 8011 Medical centers

(P-15340)
CENTRAL VALLEY INDIAN HLTH INC (PA)
2740 Herndon Ave, Clovis (93611-6813)
PHONE..................................559 299-2578
Chuck Fowler, *CEO*
Julie A Ramsey, *COO*
Julie Ramsey, *Executive*
Arthur Hugues, *Software Dev*
Gurpal S Bains, *Finance*
EMP: 74 **EST:** 1974
SQ FT: 14,000
SALES (est): 27.6MM **Privately Held**
WEB: www.cvih.org
SIC: 8011 8021 8042 8093 Clinic, operated by physicians; dental clinic; offices & clinics of optometrists; substance abuse clinics (outpatient)

(P-15341)
CEP AMERICA - ANESTHESIA PC
2100 Powell St Ste 400, Emeryville (94608-1826)
PHONE..................................510 350-2842
Theo Koury, *President*
David Birdsall, *CEO*
Christine Doyle, *Director*
EMP: 50 **EST:** 2017
SALES (est): 4.9MM **Privately Held**
WEB: www.cepamerica.com
SIC: 8011 Anesthesiologist

(P-15342)
CEP AMERICA - ILLINOIS LLP ◆
2100 Powell St Ste 400, Emeryville (94608-1826)
PHONE..................................510 350-2777
Philip Piccinini, *Partner*
EMP: 60 **EST:** 2021
SALES (est): 1.4MM **Privately Held**
SIC: 8011 Physicians' office, including specialists

(P-15343)
CEP AMERICA - INTENSIVISTS PC
2100 Powell St Ste 400, Emeryville (94608-1826)
PHONE..................................510 350-2777
Theo Koury, *President*
EMP: 50 **EST:** 2015
SALES (est): 1.1MM **Privately Held**
WEB: www.cepamerica.com
SIC: 8011 Physicians' office, including specialists

(P-15344)
CEP AMERICA - KANSAS LLC ◆
2100 Powell St Ste 400, Emeryville (94608-1826)
PHONE..................................510 350-2777
Theo Koury,
EMP: 50 **EST:** 2021
SALES (est): 1.6MM **Privately Held**
WEB: www.cepamerica.com
SIC: 8011 Physicians' office, including specialists

(P-15345)
CEP AMERICA LLC
Also Called: Vituity
2100 Powell St 400, Emeryville (94608-1826)
PHONE..................................510 350-2691
Theo Koury,
Greg Simsarian, *Senior Partner*
Jaime Rivas, *Partner*
David Birdsall, *Officer*
Phillip Piccinini, *Vice Pres*
EMP: 90 **EST:** 2011

SALES (est): 4.1MM **Privately Held**
WEB: www.cepamerica.com
SIC: 8011 Offices & clinics of medical doctors

(P-15346)
CEP AMRC-LLNOIS HSPTALISTS LLP
2100 Powell St Ste 400, Emeryville (94608-1826)
PHONE..................................510 350-2777
Wesley A Curry, *President*
EMP: 40 **EST:** 2014
SALES (est): 989.2K **Privately Held**
SIC: 8011 Physicians' office, including specialists

(P-15347)
CHAPA-DE INDIAN HLTH PRGRAM IN (PA)
11670 Atwood Rd, Auburn (95603-9522)
PHONE..................................530 887-2800
Lisa Davies, *President*
Sierk Haitsma, *CFO*
Darla Clark, *Officer*
Debbie Arvay, *Practice Mgr*
Crystal Miller, *Executive Asst*
EMP: 85 **EST:** 1970
SQ FT: 65,000
SALES (est): 60.9MM **Privately Held**
WEB: www.chapa-de.org
SIC: 8011 8322 8021 8042 Clinic, operated by physicians; outreach program; multi-service center; dentists' office; orthodontist; offices & clinics of optometrists; dietician

(P-15348)
CHICO IMMDATE CARE MED CTR INC (PA)
376 Vallombrosa Ave, Chico (95926-3900)
PHONE..................................530 891-1676
Bradley M Smith, *CEO*
David Ricci, *Accountant*
EMP: 50 **EST:** 1983
SQ FT: 4,000
SALES (est): 7.1MM **Privately Held**
WEB: www.chicoicmc.com
SIC: 8011 Clinic, operated by physicians

(P-15349)
CHINESE COMMUNITY HEALTH PLAN
Also Called: Cchp
445 Grant Ave Ste 700, San Francisco (94108-3250)
PHONE..................................415 955-8800
Edward Chow, *Director*
Larry Loo, *COO*
Wil Yu, *COO*
Jacqueline Zheng, *Division Mgr*
Farrah Tang, *Admin Asst*
EMP: 40 **EST:** 1986
SALES (est): 141.4MM
SALES (corp-wide): 207.6B **Privately Held**
WEB: www.cchca.com
SIC: 8011 Health maintenance organization
PA: Chinese Hospital Association
  845 Jackson St
  San Francisco CA 94133
  415 982-2400

(P-15350)
CLINICA SIERRA VISTA
2790 S Elm Ave, Fresno (93706-5435)
PHONE..................................559 457-5200
Auther Adams, *Obstetrician*
Kami K Jow, *Pediatrics*
Kami Jow, *Pediatrics*
Bill Dixon, *Physician Asst*
EMP: 41
SALES (corp-wide): 134.9MM **Privately Held**
WEB: www.clinicasierravista.org
SIC: 8011 Clinic, operated by physicians
PA: Clinica Sierra Vista
  1430 Truxtun Ave Ste 400
  Bakersfield CA 93301
  661 635-3050

(P-15351)
CLINICA SIERRA VISTA
1945 N Fine Ave Ste 100, Fresno (93727-1528)
PHONE..................................559 457-5292
Stephen W Schilling, *Branch Mgr*
EMP: 41
SALES (corp-wide): 134.9MM **Privately Held**
WEB: www.clinicasierravista.org
SIC: 8011 Clinic, operated by physicians
PA: Clinica Sierra Vista
  1430 Truxtun Ave Ste 400
  Bakersfield CA 93301
  661 635-3050

(P-15352)
CLINICA SIERRA VISTA
Also Called: Fresno - Rgnal Med Cmnty Hlth
2505 E Divisadero St # 100, Fresno (93721-1416)
PHONE..................................559 457-5500
Elaine Cantu, *Manager*
Beatriz Gonzalez, *Nursing Dir*
EMP: 41
SQ FT: 9,132
SALES (corp-wide): 134.9MM **Privately Held**
WEB: www.clinicasierravista.org
SIC: 8011 Clinic, operated by physicians
PA: Clinica Sierra Vista
  1430 Truxtun Ave Ste 400
  Bakersfield CA 93301
  661 635-3050

(P-15353)
CLOVIS ONCOLOGY INC
499 Illinois St Ste 230, San Francisco (94158-2519)
PHONE..................................415 409-5440
P J Mahaffy, *President*
Thomas Harding, *Exec VP*
Breanna Burkart, *Vice Pres*
Sara Sullivan, *Vice Pres*
Sean Carr, *Associate Dir*
EMP: 74 **Publicly Held**
WEB: www.clovisoncology.com
SIC: 8011 Oncologist
PA: Clovis Oncology, Inc.
  5500 Flatiron Pkwy # 100
  Boulder CO 80301

(P-15354)
COLUSA INDIAN CMNTY COUNCIL
3720 State Highway 45, Colusa (95932-4027)
PHONE..................................530 458-5787
Oscar Serrano, *Engineer*
Gina Dorenzo, *Accountant*
EMP: 266 **Privately Held**
WEB: www.syix.com
SIC: 8011 Medical centers
PA: Colusa Indian Community Council
  3730 State Highway 45 B
  Colusa CA 95932

(P-15355)
COLUSA INDIAN CMNTY COUNCIL
3710 Highway 45 Ste A, Colusa (95932-4026)
PHONE..................................530 458-5501
Mark Burg, *Administration*
EMP: 266 **Privately Held**
WEB: www.syix.com
SIC: 8011 Medical centers
PA: Colusa Indian Community Council
  3730 State Highway 45 B
  Colusa CA 95932

(P-15356)
COMMUNICARE HEALTH CENTERS
2051 John Jones Rd, Davis (95616-9701)
P.O. Box 1260 (95617-1260)
PHONE..................................530 758-2060
Melissa Marshall, *CEO*
Carolina Apicella, *CFO*
Jeff Novick, *Info Tech Dir*
Yvonne Page, *Technician*
Jessica Guerrero, *Accountant*

EMP: 200 **EST:** 1973
SALES (est): 28MM **Privately Held**
WEB: www.communicarehc.org
SIC: 8011 Clinic, operated by physicians

(P-15357)
COMMUNITY MEDICAL CENTER
Also Called: Esparto Family Practice
131 W A St Ste 1, Dixon (95620-3437)
P.O. Box 846 (95620-0846)
PHONE..................................209 944-4705
Mike Kirkpatrick, *Exec Dir*
Linda Winn, *Office Mgr*
Bob Chapnick, *Director*
EMP: 40 **EST:** 1972
SALES (est): 956K **Privately Held**
WEB: www.communitymedicalcenters.org
SIC: 8011 Health maintenance organization

(P-15358)
COMMUNITY MEDICAL CENTERS INC
Also Called: Channel Medical Center
701 E Channel St, Stockton (95202-2628)
P.O. Box 779 (95201-0779)
PHONE..................................209 944-4700
Alice Souligen, *Manager*
Jennifer Martinez, *Pediatrics*
Rick Beronilla, *Physician Asst*
Aziz Khambati, *Med Doctor*
Sarah Taft, *Director*
EMP: 39
SALES (corp-wide): 87.1MM **Privately Held**
WEB: www.communitymedicalcenters.org
SIC: 8011 Clinic, operated by physicians
PA: Community Medical Centers Inc
  7210 Murray Dr
  Stockton CA 95210
  209 373-2800

(P-15359)
COMMUNITY MEDICAL CENTERS INC
1031 Waterloo Rd, Stockton (95205-4256)
PHONE..................................209 940-5600
EMP: 39
SALES (corp-wide): 87.1MM **Privately Held**
WEB: www.communitymedicalcenters.org
SIC: 8011 Clinic, operated by physicians
PA: Community Medical Centers Inc
  7210 Murray Dr
  Stockton CA 95210
  209 373-2800

(P-15360)
COMMUNITY MEDICAL CENTERS INC
721 Calaveras St, Lodi (95240-0628)
PHONE..................................209 331-8019
Michael H Kirkpatrick, *CEO*
EMP: 39
SALES (corp-wide): 87.1MM **Privately Held**
WEB: www.communitymedicalcenters.org
SIC: 8011 Clinic, operated by physicians
PA: Community Medical Centers Inc
  7210 Murray Dr
  Stockton CA 95210
  209 373-2800

(P-15361)
COMMUNITY MEDICAL CENTERS INC
600 Nut Tree Rd Ste 260, Vacaville (95687-4686)
PHONE..................................707 359-1800
Kathleen Marshall, *Branch Mgr*
Bee Xiong, *Analyst*
Roberta Dunham, *Manager*
EMP: 39
SALES (corp-wide): 87.1MM **Privately Held**
WEB: www.communitymedicalcenters.org
SIC: 8011 Clinic, operated by physicians
PA: Community Medical Centers Inc
  7210 Murray Dr
  Stockton CA 95210
  209 373-2800

PRODUCTS & SERVICES SECTION
8011 - Offices & Clinics Of Doctors Of Medicine County (P-15386)

(P-15362)
COMMUNITY MEDICAL CENTERS INC
Also Called: Woodbridge Medical Group
2401 W Turner Rd Ste 450, Lodi (95242-2191)
PHONE..................209 368-2212
Diane Babazazo, *Branch Mgr*
EMP: 39
SALES (corp-wide): 87.1MM **Privately Held**
WEB: www.communitymedicalcenters.org
SIC: **8011** Clinic, operated by physicians
PA: Community Medical Centers Inc
7210 Murray Dr
Stockton CA 95210
209 373-2800

(P-15363)
COMMUNITY MEDICAL CENTERS INC
7210 Murray Dr, Stockton (95210-3339)
P.O. Box 779 (95201-0779)
PHONE..................209 373-2800
Michael H Kirkpatrick, *Principal*
Maged L Yacoub, *Med Doctor*
EMP: 39
SALES (corp-wide): 87.1MM **Privately Held**
WEB: www.communitymedicalcenters.org
SIC: **8011** Clinic, operated by physicians
PA: Community Medical Centers Inc
7210 Murray Dr
Stockton CA 95210
209 373-2800

(P-15364)
CONCENTRA MEDICAL CENTER
Also Called: Concentra Medical Center A Med
2970 Hilltop Mall Rd # 2, Richmond (94806-1947)
PHONE..................909 558-2273
Tanya Naquin, *Principal*
EMP: 142 EST: 2011
SQ FT: 1,600
SALES (est): 10.8MM
SALES (corp-wide): 5B **Publicly Held**
WEB: www.concentra.com
SIC: **8011** Medical centers
HQ: Concentra Health Services Inc
5080 Spectrum Dr Ste 500w
Addison TX 75001

(P-15365)
CONTRA CSTA RGONAL MED CTR AUX
2500 Alhambra Ave, Martinez (94553-3156)
PHONE..................925 370-5000
Jo-Ann Lee, *CEO*
Kristina Jadrich, *Manager*
EMP: 70 EST: 1969
SALES (est): 6.5MM **Privately Held**
WEB: www.cchealth.org
SIC: **8011** Medical centers

(P-15366)
COPPERTOWER FAMILY MEDICAL CTR
Also Called: Alexander Valley Healthcare
100 W 3rd St, Cloverdale (95425-3204)
PHONE..................707 894-4229
Debbie Howell, *CEO*
Jenine Rose, *CFO*
EMP: 50 EST: 1988
SQ FT: 2,700
SALES (est): 5.8MM **Privately Held**
WEB: www.alexandervalleyhealthcare.org
SIC: **8011** Clinic, operated by physicians

(P-15367)
COUNTY OF SACRAMENTO
Also Called: Del Paso Health Center
7001 East Pkwy A, Sacramento (95823-2501)
PHONE..................916 875-5701
Pamela Bonacci, *Manager*
EMP: 49
SALES (corp-wide): 3.1B **Privately Held**
WEB: www.saccounty.net
SIC: **8011** 9431 Medical centers; administration of public health programs;
PA: County Of Sacramento
700 H St Ste 7650
Sacramento CA 95814
916 874-8515

(P-15368)
COUNTY OF SAN JOAQUIN
Also Called: Children Health Care
1414 N California St, Stockton (95202-1515)
PHONE..................209 468-2385
Barbara Miller, *Branch Mgr*
EMP: 48
SALES (corp-wide): 1.2B **Privately Held**
WEB: www.sjgov.org
SIC: **8011** 9431 Pediatrician; communicable disease program administration, government
PA: County Of San Joaquin
44 N San Joaquin St # 640
Stockton CA 95202
209 468-3203

(P-15369)
COUNTY OF SAN JOAQUIN
Also Called: Healthy Beginning
1414 N California St Fl 1, Stockton (95202-1515)
PHONE..................209 468-3983
Faye Jacobs, *Branch Mgr*
Anh Le, *Vice Pres*
Fay Jacobs, *Office Mgr*
EMP: 48
SALES (corp-wide): 1.2B **Privately Held**
WEB: www.sjgov.org
SIC: **8011** 9111 Gynecologist; county supervisors' & executives' offices
PA: County Of San Joaquin
44 N San Joaquin St # 640
Stockton CA 95202
209 468-3203

(P-15370)
COUNTY OF SAN MATEO
Also Called: San Mateo Medical Center
222 W 39th Ave, San Mateo (94403-4364)
PHONE..................650 208-3480
EMP: 1265
SALES (corp-wide): 1.7B **Privately Held**
WEB: www.smchealth.org
SIC: **8011** Clinic, operated by physicians
PA: County Of San Mateo
555 County Ctr Fl 4
Redwood City CA 94063
650 363-4123

(P-15371)
COUNTY OF STANISLAUS
Also Called: Stanislaus Health Svcs Agcy
1209 Woodrow Ave Ste B10, Modesto (95350-1273)
PHONE..................209 558-5312
Samantha Phillips, *Office Mgr*
Christopher Grover, *Med Doctor*
EMP: 74
SALES (corp-wide): 1.2B **Privately Held**
WEB: www.stancounty.com
SIC: **8011** General & family practice, physician/surgeon
PA: County Of Stanislaus
1010 10th St Ste 5100
Modesto CA 95354
209 525-6398

(P-15372)
COURT STREET SURGERY CENTER
2184 Court St, Redding (96001-2530)
PHONE..................530 246-4444
David Hankin MD, *President*
William Heyerman MD, *President*
EMP: 48 EST: 1999
SALES (est): 4.1MM **Privately Held**
WEB: www.csscr.com
SIC: **8011** Surgeon

(P-15373)
DAVIS COMMUNITY CLINIC (PA)
Also Called: Davis Cmnty Clnic Dntl Program
2040 Sutter Pl, Davis (95616-6201)
P.O. Box 1260 (95617-1260)
PHONE..................530 758-2060
Sherry Cauchois, *Exec Dir*
Aileen Barandas, *Officer*
EMP: 100 EST: 1972
SQ FT: 5,000
SALES (est): 9.9MM **Privately Held**
WEB: www.communicarehc.org
SIC: **8011** Clinic, operated by physicians

(P-15374)
DEL PUERTO HEALTH CARE DST
Also Called: Del Puerto Health Center
875 E St, Patterson (95363-2670)
P.O. Box 187 (95363-0187)
PHONE..................209 892-9100
Margo Arnold, *Administration*
Jose Rodriguez, *Family Practiti*
Ali Wahid, *Med Doctor*
Paul Willette, *Director*
Suzie Benitez, *Manager*
EMP: 64 EST: 1948
SQ FT: 25,000
SALES (est): 5.1MM **Privately Held**
WEB: www.dphealth.org
SIC: **8011** Medical centers

(P-15375)
DELTA RADIOLOGY MEDICAL GROUP
1031 S Fairmont Ave, Lodi (95240-5165)
PHONE..................209 334-4416
Frank Michael Hartwick, *CEO*
Walter C Tim MD, *Corp Secy*
Claudia Reed, *Controller*
EMP: 88 EST: 1948
SQ FT: 3,420
SALES (est): 3.1MM **Privately Held**
WEB: www.deltarad.com
SIC: **8011** Radiologist

(P-15376)
DENNIS ZAI MD INC
3903 Lone Tree Way, Antioch (94509-6249)
PHONE..................925 754-8710
Dennis Zai MD, *President*
Cindy Zai, *CFO*
EMP: 42 EST: 1983
SQ FT: 1,033
SALES (est): 2.6MM **Privately Held**
SIC: **8011** General & family practice, physician/surgeon

(P-15377)
DEVRON H CHAR MD
Also Called: U C S F Medical Center
45 Castro St Ste 309, San Francisco (94114-1032)
PHONE..................415 522-0700
Devron H Char MD, *Owner*
Aquila Yeargin, *COO*
Novikov Yelena, *Admin Asst*
Michael Kilpatrick, *Engineer*
Patricia Gunderson, *Analyst*
EMP: 61 EST: 2002
SALES (est): 10.4MM **Privately Held**
WEB: www.tumori.org
SIC: **8011** Physicians' office, including specialists

(P-15378)
DIABLO CRDIOLGY MED GROUP INC
Also Called: Diablo Cardiology Med Group
1450 Treat Blvd, Walnut Creek (94597-2168)
PHONE..................925 933-6981
Platt Ryan MD, *President*
Tseng Hennesy, *General Ptnr*
Robert Deutscher MD, *President*
Gene A Voelkel MD, *Treasurer*
Lambert Chee MD, *Admin Sec*
EMP: 35 EST: 1970
SQ FT: 3,000
SALES (est): 438.2K **Privately Held**
WEB: www.johnmuirhealth.com
SIC: **8011** Cardiologist & cardio-vascular specialist; internal medicine, physician/surgeon

(P-15379)
DIABLO VALLEY EYE MEDICAL CTR
Also Called: Diablo Valley Eye Center
112 La Casa Via Ste 260, Walnut Creek (94598-3058)
PHONE..................925 934-6300
Vicki Burkart, *Administration*
EMP: 35 EST: 1974
SALES (est): 2.7MM **Privately Held**
WEB: www.diablovalleyeye.com
SIC: **8011** Ophthalmologist

(P-15380)
DIGESTIVE DISEASE CONSULTANTS
1187 E Herndon Ave # 101, Fresno (93720-3166)
PHONE..................559 440-0450
Cindi Ginn, *Manager*
Patrick D Ginn, *Med Doctor*
Carmelina Sanchez, *Supervisor*
EMP: 37 EST: 2001
SALES (est): 5.7MM **Privately Held**
SIC: **8011** Gastronomist

(P-15381)
DIGNITY HEALTH
Also Called: Mercy San Juan Surgery Center
1380 Lead Hill Blvd # 110, Roseville (95661-2997)
PHONE..................916 965-1936
EMP: 42 **Privately Held**
WEB: www.dignityhealth.org
SIC: **8011** Medical Doctor's Office
HQ: Dignity Health
185 Berry St Ste 300
San Francisco CA 94107
415 438-5500

(P-15382)
DIRECT URGENT CARE INC
2920 Telegraph Ave, Berkeley (94705-2031)
PHONE..................510 686-3621
Caesar Djavaherian, *CEO*
EMP: 36 EST: 2011
SALES (est): 13.1MM **Privately Held**
WEB: www.directurgentcare.com
SIC: **8011** Freestanding emergency medical center

(P-15383)
DONALDSON ARTHUR M D INC
Also Called: Sonora Eye Surgery Center
940 Sylva Ln Ste G, Sonora (95370-5969)
PHONE..................209 532-0966
Gerard Ardron MD, *President*
Darrell Wrortz, *Principal*
EMP: 57 EST: 1977
SQ FT: 3,000
SALES (est): 8.3MM **Privately Held**
WEB: www.donaldsoneyecare.com
SIC: **8011** Ophthalmologist

(P-15384)
DOS PALOS MEMORIAL HOSP INC
Also Called: Dos Palos Mem Rur Hlth Clinic
2118 Marguerite St, Dos Palos (93620-2339)
PHONE..................209 392-6121
Fax: 209 392-8872
EMP: 60
SQ FT: 16,000
SALES (est): 2.7MM **Privately Held**
SIC: **8011** 8051 Medical Doctor's Office Skilled Nursing Care Facility

(P-15385)
EAST BAY CARDIOLOGY MED GROUP
Also Called: Weiland, David S MD
2101 Vale Rd Ste 201, San Pablo (94806-3845)
PHONE..................510 233-9300
Anton Steven MD, *Partner*
Evelyn Hooker, *Manager*
EMP: 40 EST: 1993
SALES (est): 2MM **Privately Held**
SIC: **8011** Cardiologist & cardio-vascular specialist

(P-15386)
EAST BAY NEPHROLOGY
2089 Vale Rd Ste 32, San Pablo (94806-3850)
PHONE..................510 235-1057
Ellen Morrissey, *Principal*
Monte Wu, *Nephrology*
EMP: 50 EST: 2011
SALES (est): 1.5MM **Privately Held**
WEB: www.ebnmg.org
SIC: **8011** Nephrologist

8011 - Offices & Clinics Of Doctors Of Medicine County (P-15387)

(P-15387)
EBSC LP
Also Called: Surgery Center of Health South
3875 Telegraph Ave, Oakland
(94609-2428)
PHONE 510 547-2244
Judy Rich, *Administration*
EMP: 67 **EST:** 1986
SQ FT: 12,500
SALES (est): 9.1MM **Privately Held**
WEB: www.thesurgerycenter.net
SIC: 8011 Surgeon

(P-15388)
EL DORADO COUNTY HEALTH DEPT
Also Called: County of El Dorado
931 Spring St, Placerville (95667-4543)
PHONE 530 621-6100
Lori Walker, *CFO*
EMP: 94 **EST:** 1998
SALES (est): 10.3MM **Privately Held**
WEB: www.edcgov.us
SIC: 8011 Primary care medical clinic

(P-15389)
ELICA HEALTH CENTERS
3701 J St Ste 201, Sacramento (95816-5542)
PHONE 916 454-2345
Tamara Miroshniehenko, *Branch Mgr*
Tatyana Flek, *COO*
Irina Gerez, *COO*
Scott Needle, *Chief Mktg Ofcr*
Laton Fuller, *Info Tech Mgr*
EMP: 45
SALES (corp-wide): 35.3MM **Privately Held**
WEB: www.elicahealth.org
SIC: 8011 Clinic, operated by physicians
PA: Elica Health Centers
1860 Howe Ave Ste 455
Sacramento CA 95825
916 569-8484

(P-15390)
ELICA HEALTH CENTERS
155 15th St, West Sacramento (95691-3737)
PHONE 916 275-3747
Olga Gerez, *Branch Mgr*
Tamara Miroshnichenko, *Director*
Nina Tecson, *Director*
EMP: 45
SALES (corp-wide): 35.3MM **Privately Held**
WEB: www.elicahealth.org
SIC: 8011 Clinic, operated by physicians
PA: Elica Health Centers
1860 Howe Ave Ste 455
Sacramento CA 95825
916 569-8484

(P-15391)
ERIC LADENHEIM MD INC
Also Called: Ladenheim Dialysis Access Ctrs
6145 N Thesta St, Fresno (93710-5266)
PHONE 559 446-1065
Eric Ladenheim MD, *President*
James Lee, *Principal*
Sid Agrawal, *Director*
Rick Gonzalez, *Manager*
EMP: 37 **EST:** 2003
SALES (est): 9MM **Privately Held**
WEB: www.ladenheim.net
SIC: 8011 Offices & clinics of medical doctors

(P-15392)
EVERYDAY HEALTH CARE FRESNO
392 S Richelle Ave, Fresno (93727-8113)
PHONE 559 225-4706
Dale Derby, *Partner*
Murtaza Mandviwala, *CIO*
Alex Silver, *Project Mgr*
Kevin Montgomery, *Opers Staff*
Alan Rosenthal, *Osteopathy*
EMP: 40 **EST:** 1980
SALES (est): 1.6MM **Privately Held**
WEB: www.everydayhc.com
SIC: 8011 Freestanding emergency medical center

(P-15393)
EYE CARE INSTITUTE
1017 2nd St, Santa Rosa (95404-6608)
PHONE 707 546-9800
Gary A Barth MD, *President*
Daniel Barth MD, *President*
Gary Barth MD, *Corp Secy*
Bruce Abramson, *Vice Pres*
Bruce Abramson Od, *Vice Pres*
EMP: 89 **EST:** 1955
SQ FT: 5,000
SALES (est): 10.2MM **Privately Held**
WEB: www.see-eci.com
SIC: 8011 Ophthalmologist

(P-15394)
EYE MDCAL CLNIC SNTA CLARA VLY
220 Meridian Ave, San Jose (95126-2903)
PHONE 408 869-3400
John H Sullivan MD, *Partner*
Roderick Biswell MD, *Partner*
Robert Massey, *Partner*
Conor O Malley MD, *Partner*
EMP: 52 **EST:** 1946
SQ FT: 8,000
SALES (est): 4.5MM **Privately Held**
WEB: www.eyemedicalclinic.com
SIC: 8011 Ophthalmologist

(P-15395)
EYE MEDICAL CLINIC FRESNO INC
Also Called: Eye Medical Center of Fresno
1360 E Herndon Ave # 301, Fresno (93720-3326)
PHONE 559 486-5000
Richard H Whitten Jr, *CEO*
George Bertolucci M, *President*
Carolyn Sakauye, *Bd of Directors*
Esmeralda Garcia, *Executive*
Carmen Mares, *Office Mgr*
EMP: 55 **EST:** 1971
SQ FT: 12,000
SALES (est): 10.8MM **Privately Held**
WEB: www.emcfresno.com
SIC: 8011 8042 Ophthalmologist; offices & clinics of optometrists

(P-15396)
EYE Q VISION CARE
2339 W Cleveland Ave, Madera (93637-8764)
PHONE 559 673-8055
EMP: 36 **Privately Held**
WEB: www.eyeqvc.com
SIC: 8011 General & family practice, physician/surgeon
PA: Eye Q Vision Care
7075 N Sharon Ave
Fresno CA 93720

(P-15397)
EYE Q VISION CARE (PA)
7075 N Sharon Ave, Fresno (93720-3329)
PHONE 559 486-2000
Scott Bridgeman, *CEO*
Allison Benard, *Officer*
Sarah Jaimenez, *Administration*
Rebecca Merle, *Human Res Mgr*
Kim Nguyen,
EMP: 175 **EST:** 2007
SALES (est): 20.7MM **Privately Held**
WEB: www.eyeqvc.com
SIC: 8011 8042 8031 Ophthalmologist; offices & clinics of optometrists; offices & clinics of osteopathic physicians

(P-15398)
FAMILY HEALTH CARE MED GROUP
1320 Celeste Dr, Modesto (95355-2408)
PHONE 209 527-6900
J M Shiovitz, *Partner*
Scott Goodreau, *Partner*
Tom M Gray, *Partner*
Royland Nyegaaro, *Partner*
Jim M Shiovitz, *Partner*
EMP: 38 **EST:** 1982
SALES (est): 4.4MM **Privately Held**
WEB: www.fhcmodesto.md
SIC: 8011 General & family practice, physician/surgeon

(P-15399)
FAMILY HEALTHCARE NETWORK
12586 Ave 408, Orange Cove (93646)
PHONE 559 528-2804
Annamarie Gonzalez, *Family Practiti*
EMP: 114
SALES (corp-wide): 209.5MM **Privately Held**
WEB: www.fhcn.org
SIC: 8011 8021 8031 Clinic, operated by physicians; offices & clinics of dentists; offices & clinics of osteopathic physicians
PA: Family Healthcare Network
305 E Center Ave
Visalia CA 93291
559 737-4700

(P-15400)
FAMILY MED GROUP SAN LEANDRO
Also Called: Gelston, Willis L MD
13851 E 14th St Ste 102, San Leandro (94578-2628)
PHONE 510 351-2100
Willis Gilston, *Partner*
Kenneth R Harley MD, *Partner*
Bruce A Robertson MD, *Partner*
Christi Cheng, *Med Doctor*
EMP: 55 **EST:** 1940
SALES (est): 5.5MM **Privately Held**
WEB: www.fmgsl.com
SIC: 8011 General & family practice, physician/surgeon

(P-15401)
FAMILY MEDICAL GROUP
Also Called: Knapp, James C MD
911 E Tuolumne Rd, Turlock (95382-1543)
PHONE 209 668-4101
James Maclaren MD, *Partner*
Ronald Johanson MD, *Partner*
Thomas Wilson MD, *Partner*
Scott Hennes, *Family Practiti*
Rafael Soria, *Family Practiti*
EMP: 72 **EST:** 1980
SALES (est): 10.3MM **Privately Held**
WEB: www.fmgturlock.com
SIC: 8011 General & family practice, physician/surgeon

(P-15402)
FAMILY PHYSCANS INC A MED CORP
1530 N Township Rd, Yuba City (95993-8527)
PHONE 530 671-2020
Christen Miller, *CEO*
J David Miller Do, *President*
EMP: 71 **EST:** 1963
SQ FT: 3,800
SALES (est): 7.4MM **Privately Held**
SIC: 8011 General & family practice, physician/surgeon

(P-15403)
FAMILY PLG ASSOC MED GROUP
Also Called: Allred Edward C
165 N Clark St, Fresno (93701-2108)
PHONE 559 233-8657
Linda Rivera, *Manager*
EMP: 36
SQ FT: 8,976
SALES (corp-wide): 39.7MM **Privately Held**
WEB: www.fpamg.net
SIC: 8011 8093 Clinic, operated by physicians; birth control clinic
PA: Family Planning Associates Medical Group
3050 E Airport Way
Long Beach CA 90806
213 738-7283

(P-15404)
FAMILY PLG ASSOC MED GROUP
2030 Coffee Rd Ste A1, Modesto (95355-2498)
PHONE 209 578-0443
Edward C Allred, *Director*
EMP: 36
SALES (corp-wide): 39.7MM **Privately Held**
WEB: www.fpamg.net
SIC: 8011 8093 General & family practice, physician/surgeon; family planning clinic
PA: Family Planning Associates Medical Group
3050 E Airport Way
Long Beach CA 90806
213 738-7283

(P-15405)
FEATHER RIVER SURGERY CENTER
370 Del Norte Ave Ste 101, Yuba City (95991-4142)
PHONE 530 751-4800
Bill Pace, *CFO*
Michael Wiltermood, *COO*
David McDonald, *Director*
EMP: 183 **EST:** 1994
SQ FT: 12,000
SALES (est): 175.8K
SALES (corp-wide): 26.9MM **Privately Held**
WEB: www.rideoutUrology.org
SIC: 8011 Ambulatory surgical center; plastic surgeon
PA: Freemont Rideout Health Group
989 Plumas St
Yuba City CA 95991
530 751-4010

(P-15406)
FERTILITY PHYSICIANS NORTHE (PA)
2581 Samaritan Dr Ste 302, San Jose (95124-4112)
PHONE 408 356-5000
David Adamson, *Principal*
EMP: 76 **EST:** 2008
SALES (est): 448.8K **Privately Held**
WEB: www.fpnc.com
SIC: 8011 Fertility specialist, physician

(P-15407)
FOLSOM SURGERY CENTER INC
Also Called: Folsom Outpatient Surgery Ctr
1651 Creekside Dr Ste 100, Folsom (95630-3833)
PHONE 916 673-1990
Guy Guilfoy, *President*
Jay Hendrickson, *Vice Pres*
Ellie Marek, *Admin Sec*
EMP: 89 **EST:** 2000
SALES (est): 10.6MM **Privately Held**
WEB: www.folsom-sc.com
SIC: 8011 Surgeon

(P-15408)
FREMONT AMBLTORY SRGERY CTR LP
Also Called: Fremont Surgery Center
39350 Civic Center Dr, Fremont (94538-2343)
PHONE 510 456-4600
John Mazoros, *General Ptnr*
EMP: 80 **EST:** 1986
SQ FT: 19,000
SALES (est): 24.3MM **Privately Held**
WEB: www.fremontsurgerycenter.com
SIC: 8011 Surgeon

(P-15409)
FRESNO IMAGING CENTER (PA)
6191 N Thesta St, Fresno (93710-5266)
PHONE 559 447-2600
Jason Barr, *Administration*
Leo Shishmanian MD, *Administration*
Danielle Selleck, *Manager*
EMP: 48 **EST:** 1985
SQ FT: 15,000
SALES (est): 14.6MM **Privately Held**
WEB: www.radnet.com
SIC: 8011 Radiologist

(P-15410)
GARDNER FAMILY HLTH NETWRK INC
Also Called: Wic
3030 Alum Rock Ave, San Jose (95127-2807)
PHONE 408 254-5197
Kim Potter, *Director*

PRODUCTS & SERVICES SECTION
8011 - Offices & Clinics Of Doctors Of Medicine County (P-15433)

Tina Raei, *Family Practiti*
Giselle Sadorra, *Psychologist*
Manuel Yaniz, *Psychologist*
Mayuri Jagirdar, *Internal Med*
EMP: 151
SALES (corp-wide): 69.3MM **Privately Held**
WEB: www.gardnerfamilyhealth.com
SIC: 8011 Clinic, operated by physicians
PA: Gardner Family Health Network, Inc.
160 E Virginia St Ste 100
San Jose CA 95112
408 457-7100

(P-15411)
GARDNER FAMILY HLTH NETWRK INC (PA)
Also Called: GARDNER HEALTH SERVICES
160 E Virginia St Ste 100, San Jose (95112-5865)
PHONE....................408 457-7100
Reymundo C Espinoza, *CEO*
Jennifer De La Cruz, *Executive Asst*
Rose Rivera, *Executive Asst*
Alyssa Roy, *Quality Imp Dir*
Maribel Montanez, *Director*
EMP: 50 **EST:** 1968
SALES: 69.3MM **Privately Held**
WEB: www.gardnerfamilyhealth.com
SIC: 8011 Clinic, operated by physicians

(P-15412)
GARDNER FAMILY HLTH NETWRK INC
Also Called: Alviso Health Center
1621 Gold St, Alviso (95002-3530)
PHONE....................408 457-7100
EMP: 151
SALES (corp-wide): 69.3MM **Privately Held**
WEB: www.gardnerfamilyhealth.com
SIC: 8011 Clinic, operated by physicians
PA: Gardner Family Health Network, Inc.
160 E Virginia St Ste 100
San Jose CA 95112
408 457-7100

(P-15413)
GARY M ALEGRE MD
Also Called: Alpine Orthopedic Med Group
2488 N California St, Stockton (95204-5508)
PHONE....................209 946-7162
Gary M Alegre MD, *Principal*
Richard Barnes, *CIO*
Michael Lin, *Surgeon*
Rosie McCune, *Surgeon*
Jaspreet Sidhu, *Surgeon*
EMP: 50 **EST:** 2007
SALES (est): 11.9MM **Privately Held**
WEB: www.alpineorthopaedic.com
SIC: 8011 Orthopedic physician

(P-15414)
GASTROENTEROLOGY DIVISION
Also Called: San Francisco General Hospital
1001 Potrero Ave Ste 1e21, San Francisco (94110-3518)
PHONE....................415 206-8823
Amy Akbarian, *Administration*
Julie Russell, *Supervisor*
EMP: 98 **EST:** 1998
SALES (est): 19.8MM **Privately Held**
SIC: 8011 Gastronomist

(P-15415)
GILBERT SMOLIN MD INC
Also Called: Peninsula Ophthalmology Group
1720 El Camino Real, Burlingame (94010-3224)
PHONE....................650 697-3200
Gilbert Smolin MD, *President*
Kenneth Chern, *Partner*
Edward Koo, *Principal*
EMP: 41 **EST:** 1967
SQ FT: 1,500
SALES (est): 2.8MM **Privately Held**
WEB: www.pogeyes.com
SIC: 8011 Ophthalmologist; surgeon

(P-15416)
GOLDEN GATE UROLOGY INC (PA)
1661 Mission St, San Francisco (94103-2413)
PHONE....................415 543-2830
Lawrence Werboff, *CEO*
Andrew Piekny, *President*
Raul Hernandez MD, *Admin Sec*
James Honen, *Opers Mgr*
Nisa Jackson, *Surgeon*
EMP: 60 **EST:** 2009
SALES (est): 27.6MM **Privately Held**
WEB: www.goldengateurology.com
SIC: 8011 Urologist

(P-15417)
GOLDEN VALLEY HEALTH CENTERS (PA)
737 W Childs Ave, Merced (95341-6805)
PHONE....................209 383-1848
Tony Weber, *CEO*
Rebecca Cabrera-Reyes, *President*
Lue Thao, *CFO*
Lue Thao MBA, *CFO*
Tim Adam, *Bd of Directors*
EMP: 250 **EST:** 1972
SQ FT: 23,000
SALES: 107.4MM **Privately Held**
WEB: www.gvhc.org
SIC: 8011 Clinic, operated by physicians

(P-15418)
GRASS VALLEY SURGERY CTR LLC
408 Sierra College Dr, Grass Valley (95945-5089)
PHONE....................530 271-2282
Mary Whitmore, *Mng Member*
EMP: 59 **EST:** 2004
SALES (est): 3.9MM **Privately Held**
WEB: www.grassvalleysurgery.com
SIC: 8011 8093 Surgeon; ambulatory surgical center; specialty outpatient clinics

(P-15419)
GREATER MDSTO MED SRGCAL ASSOC (HQ)
1541 Florida Ave, Modesto (95350-4429)
PHONE....................209 577-3388
Uzay Yasar, *Principal*
EMP: 50 **EST:** 2009
SALES (est): 7.2MM
SALES (corp-wide): 17.6B **Publicly Held**
WEB: www.fcppcentralvalley.com
SIC: 8011 General & family practice, physician/surgeon
PA: Tenet Healthcare Corporation
14201 Dallas Pkwy
Dallas TX 75254
469 893-2200

(P-15420)
GREATER SECREMENT PEDIATRICS (PA)
6555 Coyle Ave Ste 310, Carmichael (95608-0303)
PHONE....................916 965-4612
Mehdi K Arab MD, *Owner*
EMP: 40 **EST:** 1986
SALES (est): 5.2MM **Privately Held**
SIC: 8011 Pediatrician

(P-15421)
GRUTZMACHER & LEWIS MED CORP
1515 River Park Dr # 100, Sacramento (95815-4605)
PHONE....................916 649-1515
R Grutzmacher MD, *President*
Richard Lewis MD, *Partner*
Richard Grutzmacher MD, *President*
EMP: 37 **EST:** 1987
SQ FT: 1,200
SALES (est): 5.9MM **Privately Held**
WEB: www.sacramentoeyeconsultants.com
SIC: 8011 Ophthalmologist

(P-15422)
HACIENDA SURGERY CENTER LLC (PA)
4626 Willow Rd Ste 100, Pleasanton (94588-8555)
PHONE....................925 734-6744
Phillip A Wolfe, *Mng Member*
Roger D Dainer,
Gregory Horner,
EMP: 127 **EST:** 2007
SALES (est): 8MM **Privately Held**
WEB: www.haciendasurgery.com
SIC: 8011

(P-15423)
HAMILTON AVENUE MED GROUP INC
Also Called: Hamilton Medical Group
295 Oconnor Dr, San Jose (95128-1624)
PHONE....................408 279-0548
John Luong, *President*
Jean Luong, *President*
Dr Michael Cahn, *Vice Pres*
Masha M Nakelchik, *Internal Med*
EMP: 80 **EST:** 1970
SQ FT: 4,100
SALES (est): 5.2MM **Privately Held**
SIC: 8011 Physicians' office, including specialists

(P-15424)
HAND SURGERY ASSOCIATES
Also Called: Wiedeman, Geoffrey Jr MD
1201 Alhambra Blvd # 410, Sacramento (95816-5243)
PHONE....................916 457-4263
M R Goldberg MD, *President*
James Lilla MD, *President*
Scott R Lipson, *Surgeon*
▲ **EMP:** 50 **EST:** 1978
SQ FT: 2,400
SALES (est): 6.7MM **Privately Held**
SIC: 8011 Surgeon; orthopedic physician

(P-15425)
HASEEB AL-MUFTI MD INC (PA)
660 4th St Unit 349, San Francisco (94107-1618)
PHONE....................510 604-6012
Haseeb I Al-Mufti, *Principal*
EMP: 38 **EST:** 2010
SALES (est): 567.9K **Privately Held**
SIC: 8011 Offices & clinics of medical doctors

(P-15426)
HAZEL HAWKINS MEMORIAL HOSP
Also Called: Hasel Hawkins Clinic
930 Sunset Dr Ste 3, Hollister (95023-5620)
PHONE....................831 636-2664
Diana Sugno, *Superintendent*
Mishel Thomas, *Nurse*
EMP: 47
SALES (corp-wide): 115.1MM **Privately Held**
SIC: 8011 8049 Clinic, operated by physicians; nutrition specialist
PA: Hawkins Hazel Memorial Hospital
911 Sunset Dr Ste A
Hollister CA 95023
831 637-5711

(P-15427)
HEALDSBURG PRIMARY CARE INC
1312 Prentice Dr, Healdsburg (95448-3381)
PHONE....................707 433-3383
Jean Killian, *Manager*
Doug Pile, *Vice Pres*
Locke Wilson, *Admin Sec*
EMP: 35 **EST:** 1995
SQ FT: 8,000
SALES (est): 3.1MM **Privately Held**
WEB: www.healdsburgdistricthospital.org
SIC: 8011 Clinic, operated by physicians

(P-15428)
HEALTHTAP INC
Also Called: Docphin
2465 Latham St Fl 3, Mountain View (94040-4792)
PHONE....................650 268-9806
Bill Gossman, *CEO*
Kurt Blasena, *Officer*
Michael Nichols, *Officer*
Jay Wohlgemuth, *Officer*
Kathleen Donahue, *Vice Pres*
EMP: 66 **EST:** 2010
SQ FT: 16,000
SALES (est): 1.6MM **Privately Held**
WEB: www.healthtap.com
SIC: 8011 7372 Group health association; application computer software; business oriented computer software

(P-15429)
HERNDON INVESTORS
Also Called: Internal Medicine
1515 E Alluvial Ave 101, Fresno (93720-3832)
PHONE....................559 435-2630
A Paul Mello, *Partner*
D J Cavagnaro MD, *Co-Venturer*
S H Chooljian MD, *Co-Venturer*
Thomas Griffin, *Co-Venturer*
Dr R L Bennett, *Partner*
EMP: 62 **EST:** 1978
SALES (est): 2MM **Privately Held**
WEB: www.samc.com
SIC: 8011 Physicians' office, including specialists

(P-15430)
HERNDON SURGERY CENTER INC
Also Called: Amsurg
1843 E Fir Ave Ste 104, Fresno (93720-3863)
PHONE....................559 323-6611
Eric Poulsen, *President*
Michelle Bay, *Administration*
EMP: 87 **EST:** 2006
SALES (est): 5.5MM **Privately Held**
WEB: www.amsurg.com
SIC: 8011 Surgeon

(P-15431)
HILL COUNTRY COMMUNITY CLINIC
29632 E Highway 299, Round Mountain (96084-8000)
P.O. Box 228 (96084-0228)
PHONE....................530 337-6243
Lynn Dorroh, *Exec Dir*
Richard B Hardie III, *Bd of Directors*
Shayna Williams, *Hum Res Coord*
Donna Holscher, *Gnrl Med Prac*
Mirtha Balcazar, *Internal Med*
EMP: 38 **EST:** 1982
SALES (est): 13.6MM **Privately Held**
WEB: www.hillcountryclinic.org
SIC: 8011 General & family practice, physician/surgeon

(P-15432)
HILL PHYSICIANS MED GROUP INC (PA)
2409 Camino Ramon, San Ramon (94583-4285)
P.O. Box 5080 (94583-0980)
PHONE....................800 445-5747
David Joyner, *CEO*
Rick Messman, *CFO*
Mitra Javidi, *Vice Pres*
Dawn Bell, *Executive*
Matthew Bronaugh, *Program Mgr*
EMP: 412 **EST:** 1984
SQ FT: 36,000
SALES (est): 2MM **Privately Held**
WEB: www.hillphysicians.com
SIC: 8011 8031 General & family practice, physician/surgeon; offices & clinics of osteopathic physicians

(P-15433)
INDIAN HLTH CTR SNTA CLARA VLY
1333 Meridian Ave, San Jose (95125-5212)
PHONE....................408 445-3400
Sonya M Tetnowski, *CEO*
Barbara Miao, *CFO*
EMP: 200 **EST:** 1977
SQ FT: 10,000
SALES: 34.8MM **Privately Held**
WEB: www.indianhealthcenter.org
SIC: 8011 8322 Clinic, operated by physicians; individual & family services

8011 - Offices & Clinics Of Doctors Of Medicine County (P-15434)

(P-15434)
INSITE DIGESTIVE HEALTH CARE
200 Jose Figueres Ave, San Jose (95116-1500)
PHONE..................408 471-2222
Margarita Joaquin, *Branch Mgr*
EMP: 84
SALES (corp-wide): 25.1MM **Privately Held**
WEB: www.insitedigestive.com
SIC: 8011 Gastronomist
PA: Insite Digestive Health Care
    5525 Etiwanda Ave Ste 110
    Tarzana CA 91356
    818 437-8105

(P-15435)
INTEGRATED PAIN MANAGEMENT
450 N Wiget Ln, Walnut Creek (94598-2408)
PHONE..................925 691-9806
Jacob Rosenberg, *President*
Lawrence Weil, *Principal*
Hasina Mojadidi, *Physician Asst*
Douglas Grant, *Manager*
Kenneth Kim, *Manager*
EMP: 78 EST: 2001
SALES (est): 14.5MM **Privately Held**
WEB: www.ipmdoctors.com
SIC: 8011 General & family practice, physician/surgeon

(P-15436)
INTERIOR UNITED STATES DEPT
1 Shields Ave, Davis (95616-5270)
PHONE..................530 752-6745
EMP: 67 **Publicly Held**
WEB: www.doi.gov
SIC: 8011 Pathologist
HQ: United States Department Of Interior
    1849 C St Nw
    Washington DC 20240
    202 208-7351

(P-15437)
INTERNAL REVENUE SERVICE
2469 Arf Ave, Hayward (94545-4107)
PHONE..................510 576-7589
EMP: 169 **Publicly Held**
WEB: www.irs.gov
SIC: 8011 Internal medicine, physician/surgeon
HQ: Internal Revenue Service
    1973 N Rulon White Blvd
    Ogden UT 84404
    202 803-9000

(P-15438)
INTERNAL REVENUE SERVICE
9006 Morganfield Pl, Elk Grove (95624-3608)
PHONE..................916 974-5678
EMP: 169 **Publicly Held**
WEB: www.irs.gov
SIC: 8011 Internal medicine, physician/surgeon
HQ: Internal Revenue Service
    1973 N Rulon White Blvd
    Ogden UT 84404
    202 803-9000

(P-15439)
ISRS/AAO
655 Beach St, San Francisco (94109-1342)
PHONE..................415 447-0369
Jorge Alio, *Principal*
Kathi Renk, *Executive Asst*
Brian Waechter, *Info Tech Dir*
Hans Huang, *IT/INT Sup*
Ryan Bucsi, *Analyst*
EMP: 35 EST: 2008
SALES (est): 3.6MM **Privately Held**
WEB: www.aao.org
SIC: 8011 Surgeon

(P-15440)
JENNIFER LEE MD INC (PA)
700 W Parr Ave Ste A, Los Gatos (95032-1416)
PHONE..................408 866-1135
Jennifer Lee, *Principal*
EMP: 57 EST: 2009
SALES (est): 265.3K **Privately Held**
SIC: 8011 General & family practice, physician/surgeon

(P-15441)
JOHN MUIR PHYSICIAN NETWORK
1914 Tice Valley Blvd, Walnut Creek (94595-2203)
PHONE..................925 988-7580
Michelle Mason, *Branch Mgr*
Paul McWhirter, *Med Doctor*
EMP: 40
SALES (corp-wide): 376.6MM **Privately Held**
WEB: www.johnmuirhealth.com
SIC: 8011 General & family practice, physician/surgeon
PA: John Muir Physician Network
    1450 Treat Blvd
    Walnut Creek CA 94597
    925 296-9700

(P-15442)
JOSEPH B HAWKINS JR MD INC
Also Called: Sierra Endcrine Assoc Med Grou
7230 N Millbrook Ave, Fresno (93720-3340)
PHONE..................559 431-6197
Joseph B Hawkins MD, *President*
EMP: 38 EST: 1989
SQ FT: 8,500
SALES (est): 3.8MM **Privately Held**
WEB: www.endocrineanswers.com
SIC: 8011 Endocrinologist

(P-15443)
JOSEPH R MARTEL MD INC
Also Called: Martel Eye Medical Group
11216 Trinity River Dr, Rancho Cordova (95670-2968)
PHONE..................916 635-6161
Joseph R Martel, *President*
EMP: 47 EST: 1986
SALES (est): 4.8MM **Privately Held**
WEB: www.martelmd.com
SIC: 8011 Ophthalmologist

(P-15444)
KAISER FOUNDATION HOSPITALS
Also Called: Roseville Med Cntr-Rdtion Onclo
504 Gibson Dr, Roseville (95678-5799)
PHONE..................916 771-2871
Judy Roth, *Office Mgr*
EMP: 235
SALES (corp-wide): 30.5B **Privately Held**
WEB: www.kaisercenter.com
SIC: 8011 Oncologist
HQ: Kaiser Foundation Hospitals Inc
    1 Kaiser Plz
    Oakland CA 94612
    510 271-6611

(P-15445)
KAISER FOUNDATION HOSPITALS
Also Called: Kaiser Prmnnte Snta Rosa Med C
401 Bicentennial Way, Santa Rosa (95403-2149)
PHONE..................707 393-4000
Susan Janvirin, *Branch Mgr*
Karen Tejcka, *Officer*
Blake Main, *Vice Pres*
Stacy Young, *Vice Pres*
Columba Mancha, *General Mgr*
EMP: 235
SALES (corp-wide): 30.5B **Privately Held**
WEB: www.kaisercenter.com
SIC: 8011 Medical centers
HQ: Kaiser Foundation Hospitals Inc
    1 Kaiser Plz
    Oakland CA 94612
    510 271-6611

(P-15446)
KAISER FOUNDATION HOSPITALS
Also Called: Kaiser Prmnnte Antioch Med Ctr
4501 Sand Creek Rd, Antioch (94531-8687)
PHONE..................925 813-6500
Albert L Carver, *Branch Mgr*
EMP: 235
SALES (corp-wide): 30.5B **Privately Held**
WEB: www.kaisercenter.com
SIC: 8011 Internal medicine practitioners
HQ: Kaiser Foundation Hospitals Inc
    1 Kaiser Plz
    Oakland CA 94612
    510 271-6611

(P-15447)
KAISER FOUNDATION HOSPITALS
Also Called: Kaiser Foundation Health Plan
2350 Geary Blvd Fl 2, San Francisco (94115-3305)
PHONE..................415 833-2616
Becky Groebler, *Info Tech Mgr*
Chanel Hong, *Project Mgr*
Lyle Shlager, *Gastroenterlgy*
Matthew Chang, *Internal Med*
Mary Donati, *Internal Med*
EMP: 235
SALES (corp-wide): 30.5B **Privately Held**
WEB: www.kaisercenter.com
SIC: 8011 Medical centers
HQ: Kaiser Foundation Hospitals Inc
    1 Kaiser Plz
    Oakland CA 94612
    510 271-6611

(P-15448)
KAISER FOUNDATION HOSPITALS
Also Called: Kaiser Permanente
710 S Broadway, Walnut Creek (94596-5294)
PHONE..................925 295-4145
Vikki Antonelli, *Manager*
Ryan E Kolakoski, *Psychologist*
Wendy Paik, *Psychologist*
Asma Asyyed, *Internal Med*
Walter Keller, *Pediatrics*
EMP: 235
SALES (corp-wide): 30.5B **Privately Held**
WEB: www.kaisercenter.com
SIC: 8011 Medical centers
HQ: Kaiser Foundation Hospitals Inc
    1 Kaiser Plz
    Oakland CA 94612
    510 271-6611

(P-15449)
KAISER FOUNDATION HOSPITALS
1721 Technology Dr, San Jose (95110-1305)
PHONE..................408 439-6808
EMP: 235
SALES (corp-wide): 30.5B **Privately Held**
WEB: www.kaisercenter.com
SIC: 8011 Offices & clinics of medical doctors
HQ: Kaiser Foundation Hospitals Inc
    1 Kaiser Plz
    Oakland CA 94612
    510 271-6611

(P-15450)
KAISER FOUNDATION HOSPITALS
Also Called: Oakland Medical Center
3600 Broadway, Oakland (94611-5730)
P.O. Box 12929 (94604-3010)
PHONE..................510 752-1000
David J Artenburn, *Manager*
Rajesh Singh, *Vice Pres*
Patrick Buell, *Surgery Dir*
Edie Augustine, *Admin Asst*
Warren King, *Administration*
EMP: 2200
SALES (corp-wide): 30.5B **Privately Held**
WEB: www.kaisercenter.com
SIC: 8011 8062 Medical centers; general medical & surgical hospitals
HQ: Kaiser Foundation Hospitals Inc
    1 Kaiser Plz
    Oakland CA 94612
    510 271-6611

(P-15451)
KAISER FOUNDATION HOSPITALS
Also Called: Kaiser Permanente San
2425 Geary Blvd, San Francisco (94115-3358)
PHONE..................415 833-2000
Harry Chima, *Branch Mgr*
Cristine Robisch, *Vice Pres*
David N Rubin, *Principal*
Sandra Choe, *Administration*
Marcie Roble, *Network Enginr*
EMP: 750
SALES (corp-wide): 30.5B **Privately Held**
WEB: www.kaisercenter.com
SIC: 8011 8062 Medical centers; general medical & surgical hospitals
HQ: Kaiser Foundation Hospitals Inc
    1 Kaiser Plz
    Oakland CA 94612
    510 271-6611

(P-15452)
KAISER FOUNDATION HOSPITALS
Also Called: Unknown
1650 Los Gamos Dr, San Rafael (94903-1850)
PHONE..................415 491-1164
EMP: 235
SALES (corp-wide): 30.5B **Privately Held**
WEB: www.kaisercenter.com
SIC: 8011 8062 Offices & clinics of medical doctors; general medical & surgical hospitals
HQ: Kaiser Foundation Hospitals Inc
    1 Kaiser Plz
    Oakland CA 94612
    510 271-6611

(P-15453)
KAISER FOUNDATION HOSPITALS
Also Called: Kaiser Permanente
99 Montecillo Rd, San Rafael (94903-3308)
PHONE..................415 444-2000
Patricia Kendall, *Administration*
Diane Hernandez, *Officer*
Bill Wehrle, *Vice Pres*
Jerry Iroz, *Executive*
William McCarthy, *Exec Dir*
EMP: 1500
SALES (corp-wide): 30.5B **Privately Held**
WEB: www.kaisercenter.com
SIC: 8011 8062 Medical centers; general medical & surgical hospitals
HQ: Kaiser Foundation Hospitals Inc
    1 Kaiser Plz
    Oakland CA 94612
    510 271-6611

(P-15454)
KAISER FOUNDATION HOSPITALS
Also Called: Kaiser Permanente
901 Nevin Ave, Richmond (94801-3143)
PHONE..................510 307-1500
Debbie Vachau, *Manager*
Kwame Denianke, *Officer*
Michelle Williams, *Admin Sec*
Ryona Durham, *Administration*
Eric Miller, *Info Tech Dir*
EMP: 235
SALES (corp-wide): 30.5B **Privately Held**
WEB: www.kaisercenter.com
SIC: 8011 8062 Medical centers; general medical & surgical hospitals
HQ: Kaiser Foundation Hospitals Inc
    1 Kaiser Plz
    Oakland CA 94612
    510 271-6611

(P-15455)
KAISER FOUNDATION HOSPITALS
Also Called: Vacaville Medical Center
1 Quality Dr, Vacaville (95688-9494)
PHONE..................707 624-4000
EMP: 235
SALES (corp-wide): 30.5B **Privately Held**
WEB: www.kaisercenter.com
SIC: 8011 Medical centers
HQ: Kaiser Foundation Hospitals Inc
    1 Kaiser Plz
    Oakland CA 94612
    510 271-6611

8011 - Offices & Clinics Of Doctors Of Medicine County (P-15476)

(P-15456)
KAISER FOUNDATION HOSPITALS
Also Called: Tracy Medical Offices
2185 W Grant Line Rd, Tracy (95377-7309)
PHONE..................209 839-3200
Anale Cunningham, *Branch Mgr*
Gurneet Kaur, *Med Doctor*
EMP: 235
SALES (corp-wide): 30.5B **Privately Held**
WEB: www.kaisercenter.com
SIC: 8011 Medical centers
HQ: Kaiser Foundation Hospitals Inc
 1 Kaiser Plz
 Oakland CA 94612
 510 271-6611

(P-15457)
KAISER FOUNDATION HOSPITALS
Also Called: Union City Medical Offices
3555 Whipple Rd, Union City (94587-1507)
PHONE..................510 675-4010
Andrea Wilcox, *President*
Ofelia Agbayani, *Assistant*
EMP: 235
SALES (corp-wide): 30.5B **Privately Held**
WEB: www.kaisercenter.com
SIC: 8011 Medical centers
HQ: Kaiser Foundation Hospitals Inc
 1 Kaiser Plz
 Oakland CA 94612
 510 271-6611

(P-15458)
KAISER FOUNDATION HOSPITALS
Also Called: Fairfield Medical Offices
1550 Gateway Blvd, Fairfield (94533-6901)
PHONE..................707 427-4000
Gregory A Adams, *CEO*
EMP: 235
SALES (corp-wide): 30.5B **Privately Held**
WEB: www.kaisercenter.com
SIC: 8011 Medical centers
HQ: Kaiser Foundation Hospitals Inc
 1 Kaiser Plz
 Oakland CA 94612
 510 271-6611

(P-15459)
KAISER FOUNDATION HOSPITALS
Also Called: Folsom Ambulatory Surgery Ctr
285 Palladio Pkwy, Folsom (95630-8741)
PHONE..................916 986-4178
EMP: 235
SALES (corp-wide): 30.5B **Privately Held**
WEB: www.kaisercenter.com
SIC: 8011 Ambulatory surgical center
HQ: Kaiser Foundation Hospitals Inc
 1 Kaiser Plz
 Oakland CA 94612
 510 271-6611

(P-15460)
KAISER FOUNDATION HOSPITALS
Also Called: Lincoln Medical Offices
1900 Dresden Dr, Lincoln (95648-8803)
PHONE..................916 543-5153
EMP: 235
SALES (corp-wide): 30.5B **Privately Held**
WEB: www.kaisercenter.com
SIC: 8011 Medical centers
HQ: Kaiser Foundation Hospitals Inc
 1 Kaiser Plz
 Oakland CA 94612
 510 271-6611

(P-15461)
KAISER FOUNDATION HOSPITALS
Also Called: Modesto Medical Offices
4601 Dale Rd, Modesto (95356-9718)
PHONE..................209 735-5000
EMP: 235
SALES (corp-wide): 30.5B **Privately Held**
WEB: www.kaisercenter.com
SIC: 8011 Medical centers
HQ: Kaiser Foundation Hospitals Inc
 1 Kaiser Plz
 Oakland CA 94612
 510 271-6611

(P-15462)
KAISER FOUNDATION HOSPITALS
Also Called: Bangs Avenue Medical Offices
4125 Bangs Ave, Modesto (95356-8713)
PHONE..................209 735-5000
EMP: 235
SALES (corp-wide): 30.5B **Privately Held**
WEB: www.kaisercenter.com
SIC: 8011 Medical centers
HQ: Kaiser Foundation Hospitals Inc
 1 Kaiser Plz
 Oakland CA 94612
 510 271-6611

(P-15463)
KAISER FOUNDATION HOSPITALS
Also Called: Pinole Medical Offices
1301 Pinole Valley Rd, Pinole (94564-1384)
PHONE..................510 243-4000
EMP: 235
SALES (corp-wide): 30.5B **Privately Held**
WEB: www.kaisercenter.com
SIC: 8011 Offices & clinics of medical doctors
HQ: Kaiser Foundation Hospitals Inc
 1 Kaiser Plz
 Oakland CA 94612
 510 271-6611

(P-15464)
KAISER FOUNDATION HOSPITALS
Also Called: Kaiser Prmnnte San Mteo Med Ct
1000 Franklin Pkwy, San Mateo (94403-1922)
PHONE..................650 358-7000
David Kvancz, *Vice Pres*
EMP: 235
SALES (corp-wide): 30.5B **Privately Held**
WEB: www.kaisercenter.com
SIC: 8011 Medical centers
HQ: Kaiser Foundation Hospitals Inc
 1 Kaiser Plz
 Oakland CA 94612
 510 271-6611

(P-15465)
KAISER FOUNDATION HOSPITALS
Also Called: Kaiser Prmnnte San Lndro Med C
2500 Merced St, San Leandro (94577-4201)
PHONE..................510 454-1000
Thomas S Hanenburg, *Senior VP*
Hasina Nasir, *Family Practiti*
Xiangping Lu, *Pathologist*
Kian Mostafavi, *Surgeon*
James Waterhouse, *Internal Med*
EMP: 235
SALES (corp-wide): 30.5B **Privately Held**
WEB: www.kaisercenter.com
SIC: 8011 8062 Medical centers; general medical & surgical hospitals
HQ: Kaiser Foundation Hospitals Inc
 1 Kaiser Plz
 Oakland CA 94612
 510 271-6611

(P-15466)
KAISER FOUNDATION HOSPITALS
Also Called: Santa Clara Arques Med Offs
1263 E Arques Ave, Sunnyvale (94085-4701)
PHONE..................408 851-1000
EMP: 235
SALES (corp-wide): 30.5B **Privately Held**
WEB: www.kaisercenter.com
SIC: 8011 Medical centers
HQ: Kaiser Foundation Hospitals Inc
 1 Kaiser Plz
 Oakland CA 94612
 510 271-6611

(P-15467)
KAISER FOUNDATION HOSPITALS
Also Called: Kaiser Prmnnte Oakland Med Ctr
280 W Macarthur Blvd, Oakland (94611-5642)
PHONE..................510 752-1000
Barbara Stumpf, *Director*
Patrick Chen, *Family Practiti*
Timothy Brown, *Psychologist*
Jonathan Svahn, *Surgeon*
Barbara Jung, *Obstetrician*
EMP: 235
SALES (corp-wide): 30.5B **Privately Held**
WEB: www.kaisercenter.com
SIC: 8011 Medical centers
HQ: Kaiser Foundation Hospitals Inc
 1 Kaiser Plz
 Oakland CA 94612
 510 271-6611

(P-15468)
KAISER FOUNDATION HOSPITALS
Also Called: Kaiser Permanente
250 Hospital Pkwy, San Jose (95119-1103)
PHONE..................408 972-7000
Joann Zimmerman, *Branch Mgr*
Michael Rowe, *Senior VP*
Karen Counts, *Admin Asst*
Jessica Brawley, *Administration*
Jean-Philippe Fournier, *Administration*
EMP: 235
SALES (corp-wide): 30.5B **Privately Held**
WEB: www.kaisercenter.com
SIC: 8011 Medical centers
HQ: Kaiser Foundation Hospitals Inc
 1 Kaiser Plz
 Oakland CA 94612
 510 271-6611

(P-15469)
KAISER FOUNDATION HOSPITALS
2238 Geary Blvd Fl 3, San Francisco (94115-3416)
PHONE..................415 216-5853
EMP: 235
SALES (corp-wide): 30.5B **Privately Held**
WEB: www.kaisercenter.com
SIC: 8011 Offices & clinics of medical doctors
HQ: Kaiser Foundation Hospitals Inc
 1 Kaiser Plz
 Oakland CA 94612
 510 271-6611

(P-15470)
KAISER FOUNDATION HOSPITALS
Also Called: Kaiser Permanente
1100 Veterans Blvd, Redwood City (94063-2037)
PHONE..................650 299-2000
Eric Rasmussen, *Manager*
Kenny Lai, *Ch Radiology*
Reza Adineh, *Security Dir*
Kunjan Mawar, *Finance Mgr*
Margaret Chung, *Human Res Dir*
EMP: 235
SALES (corp-wide): 30.5B **Privately Held**
WEB: www.kaisercenter.com
SIC: 8011 8062 Medical centers; general medical & surgical hospitals
HQ: Kaiser Foundation Hospitals Inc
 1 Kaiser Plz
 Oakland CA 94612
 510 271-6611

(P-15471)
KAISER FOUNDATION HOSPITALS
Also Called: Kaiser Permanente
1425 S Main St, Walnut Creek (94596-5318)
PHONE..................925 295-4000
Michael Tully-Cintron, *Branch Mgr*
Fausan S Tsai, *Principal*
Norma Rutherford, *Project Mgr*
Jessica Arroyo-Bansraj, *Technology*
Erin Heinrich, *Recruiter*
EMP: 235
SQ FT: 11,840
SALES (corp-wide): 30.5B **Privately Held**
WEB: www.kaisercenter.com
SIC: 8011 Medical centers
HQ: Kaiser Foundation Hospitals Inc
 1 Kaiser Plz
 Oakland CA 94612
 510 271-6611

(P-15472)
KAISER FOUNDATION HOSPITALS
Also Called: Unknown
1001 Riverside Ave, Roseville (95678-5134)
PHONE..................916 614-4350
Ronald Duran, *President*
EMP: 235
SALES (corp-wide): 30.5B **Privately Held**
WEB: www.kaisercenter.com
SIC: 8011 Medical centers
HQ: Kaiser Foundation Hospitals Inc
 1 Kaiser Plz
 Oakland CA 94612
 510 271-6611

(P-15473)
KAISER FOUNDATION HOSPITALS
Also Called: Kaiser Prmnnte San Frncsco Med
601 Van Ness Ave Ste 2008, San Francisco (94102-6310)
PHONE..................415 833-9688
EMP: 235
SALES (corp-wide): 30.5B **Privately Held**
WEB: www.kaisercenter.com
SIC: 8011 Medical centers
HQ: Kaiser Foundation Hospitals Inc
 1 Kaiser Plz
 Oakland CA 94612
 510 271-6611

(P-15474)
KAISER FOUNDATION HOSPITALS
5615 Scotts Valley Dr, Scotts Valley (95066-3492)
PHONE..................831 430-2700
EMP: 235
SALES (corp-wide): 30.5B **Privately Held**
WEB: www.kaisercenter.com
SIC: 8011 Offices & clinics of medical doctors
HQ: Kaiser Foundation Hospitals Inc
 1 Kaiser Plz
 Oakland CA 94612
 510 271-6611

(P-15475)
KAISER FOUNDATION HOSPITALS
Also Called: Milpitas Medical Offices
770 E Calaveras Blvd, Milpitas (95035-5491)
PHONE..................408 945-2900
Ellen Sinclair, *Manager*
Danna Doering, *Obstetrician*
Sandhya Yadav, *Dermatology*
Giao Tran, *Internal Med*
Quang D Dao, *Pediatrics*
EMP: 235
SALES (corp-wide): 30.5B **Privately Held**
WEB: www.kaisercenter.com
SIC: 8011 8062 Medical centers; general medical & surgical hospitals
HQ: Kaiser Foundation Hospitals Inc
 1 Kaiser Plz
 Oakland CA 94612
 510 271-6611

(P-15476)
KAISER FOUNDATION HOSPITALS
Kaiser Permanente
1950 Franklin St, Oakland (94612-5190)
PHONE..................510 987-1000
Maryanne Williams, *Manager*
Carol Smith, *Vice Pres*
Qusai Shikari, *Area Mgr*
Katy Hoxworth, *Office Admin*
Sameer V Awsare, *Admin Sec*
EMP: 793

8011 - Offices & Clinics Of Doctors Of Medicine County (P-15477)

PRODUCTS & SERVICES SECTION

SALES (corp-wide): 30.5B Privately Held
WEB: www.kaisercenter.com
SIC: 8011 Health maintenance organization
HQ: Kaiser Foundation Hospitals Inc
   1 Kaiser Plz
   Oakland CA 94612
   510 271-6611

(P-15477)
KAISER FOUNDATION HOSPITALS
Also Called: Davis Medical Offices
1955 Cowell Blvd, Davis (95618-6325)
PHONE..................................530 757-7100
Robert Talkington, *Manager*
Cathy Jang, *Obstetrician*
David Honeychurch, *Pediatrics*
Corrinna Tiongson, *Pediatrics*
Sydney Taylor,
EMP: 235
SALES (corp-wide): 30.5B Privately Held
WEB: www.kaisercenter.com
SIC: 8011 Medical centers
HQ: Kaiser Foundation Hospitals Inc
   1 Kaiser Plz
   Oakland CA 94612
   510 271-6611

(P-15478)
KAISER FOUNDATION HOSPITALS
Also Called: Petaluma Medical Offices
3900 Lakeville Hwy, Petaluma (94954-5698)
PHONE..................................707 765-3900
Claudia Renate Viazzoli, *Principal*
Susan Gross, *Family Practiti*
Amos Yew, *Psychologist*
Karen Bloom, *Internal Med*
Roberto Gonzalez, *Internal Med*
EMP: 235
SQ FT: 39,000
SALES (corp-wide): 30.5B Privately Held
WEB: www.kaisercenter.com
SIC: 8011 Medical centers
HQ: Kaiser Foundation Hospitals Inc
   1 Kaiser Plz
   Oakland CA 94612
   510 271-6611

(P-15479)
KAISER FOUNDATION HOSPITALS
Also Called: Novato Medical Offices
97 San Marin Dr, Novato (94945-1100)
PHONE..................................415 899-7400
Margaret R Hill, *Principal*
Sharina Belani, *Internal Med*
EMP: 235
SALES (corp-wide): 30.5B Privately Held
WEB: www.kaisercenter.com
SIC: 8011 Medical centers
HQ: Kaiser Foundation Hospitals Inc
   1 Kaiser Plz
   Oakland CA 94612
   510 271-6611

(P-15480)
KAISER FOUNDATION HOSPITALS
Also Called: Kaiser Prmnnte Hayward Med Ctr
27400 Hesperian Blvd, Hayward (94545-4235)
PHONE..................................510 678-4000
Cynthia Seay, *Manager*
Barbara Smith-Walker, *Admin Asst*
Arcadio Mariano, *Administration*
Roger Mennis, *Administration*
Chester Boltwood, *Cardiology*
EMP: 235
SALES (corp-wide): 30.5B Privately Held
WEB: www.kaisercenter.com
SIC: 8011 Medical centers
HQ: Kaiser Foundation Hospitals Inc
   1 Kaiser Plz
   Oakland CA 94612
   510 271-6611

(P-15481)
KAISER FOUNDATION HOSPITALS
Also Called: Permanentee Medical Group
1001 Riverside Ave, Roseville (95678-5134)
PHONE..................................916 784-4000
Deb Royer, *Manager*
Dove Cai, *Family Practiti*
Wenny Jean, *Family Practiti*
Jasvinder Johal, *Family Practiti*
Cindy Loh, *Family Practiti*
EMP: 235
SALES (corp-wide): 30.5B Privately Held
WEB: www.kaisercenter.com
SIC: 8011 Medical centers
HQ: Kaiser Foundation Hospitals Inc
   1 Kaiser Plz
   Oakland CA 94612
   510 271-6611

(P-15482)
KAISER FOUNDATION HOSPITALS
Also Called: Kaiser Permanente
2241 Geary Blvd Ste 118, San Francisco (94115-3415)
PHONE..................................415 833-3450
Lee Hemmingway, *Manager*
Nancy Dang, *Accountant*
Dilenna Harris, *Manager*
Manasi Kulkarni, *Consultant*
EMP: 235
SALES (corp-wide): 30.5B Privately Held
WEB: www.kaisercenter.com
SIC: 8011 Medical centers
HQ: Kaiser Foundation Hospitals Inc
   1 Kaiser Plz
   Oakland CA 94612
   510 271-6611

(P-15483)
KAISER FOUNDATION HOSPITALS
Also Called: Kaiser Perminente
2155 Iron Point Rd, Folsom (95630-8707)
PHONE..................................916 817-5200
Larry Marini, *Manager*
Ryan Pearson, *Family Practiti*
Hamid R Kazerouni Zadeh, *Internal Med*
Darryl Hunter, *Oncology*
Jonathan Najman, *Emerg Med Spec*
EMP: 235
SALES (corp-wide): 30.5B Privately Held
WEB: www.kaisercenter.com
SIC: 8011 Health maintenance organization
HQ: Kaiser Foundation Hospitals Inc
   1 Kaiser Plz
   Oakland CA 94612
   510 271-6611

(P-15484)
KAISER FOUNDATION HOSPITALS
Also Called: Kaiser Permanente
1200 El Camino Real, South San Francisco (94080-3208)
PHONE..................................650 742-2000
Evelyn Chan, *Branch Mgr*
Rick Tenerowicz, *Records Dir*
Edmond Schmulbach, *Executive*
Ryan Wong, *Associate Dir*
Terrill Tang, *Business Dir*
EMP: 235
SALES (corp-wide): 30.5B Privately Held
WEB: www.kaisercenter.com
SIC: 8011 8062 Medical centers; general medical & surgical hospitals
HQ: Kaiser Foundation Hospitals Inc
   1 Kaiser Plz
   Oakland CA 94612
   510 271-6611

(P-15485)
KAISER FOUNDATION HOSPITALS
Also Called: Kaiser Prmnnte S Scrmnto Med C
6600 Bruceville Rd, Sacramento (95823-4671)
PHONE..................................916 688-2000
Sarah Krevans, *Branch Mgr*
Joel Weber,
Patricia Pon, *Program Mgr*
Ruby Acojedo, *Department Mgr*
Jennifer Heffernan, *Admin Asst*
EMP: 3600
SALES (corp-wide): 30.5B Privately Held
WEB: www.kaisercenter.com
SIC: 8011 Medical centers
HQ: Kaiser Foundation Hospitals Inc
   1 Kaiser Plz
   Oakland CA 94612
   510 271-6611

(P-15486)
KAISER FOUNDATION HOSPITALS
Also Called: Kaiser Permanente
39400 Paseo Padre Pkwy, Fremont (94538-2310)
PHONE..................................510 248-3000
Calvin Wheeler, *Manager*
Peter H D, *IT/INT Sup*
Phil Wald, *Controller*
Linda Twilling, *Psychologist*
Vinh Bui, *Surgeon*
EMP: 235
SQ FT: 86,710
SALES (corp-wide): 30.5B Privately Held
WEB: www.kaisercenter.com
SIC: 8011 8062 Medical centers; general medical & surgical hospitals
HQ: Kaiser Foundation Hospitals Inc
   1 Kaiser Plz
   Oakland CA 94612
   510 271-6611

(P-15487)
KAISER FOUNDATION HOSPITALS
Also Called: Kaiser Foundation Health Plan
2417 Central Ave, Alameda (94501-4515)
PHONE..................................510 752-1190
Michael Gorin, *Branch Mgr*
EMP: 235
SALES (corp-wide): 30.5B Privately Held
WEB: www.kaisercenter.com
SIC: 8011 Medical centers
HQ: Kaiser Foundation Hospitals Inc
   1 Kaiser Plz
   Oakland CA 94612
   510 271-6611

(P-15488)
KAISER FOUNDATION HOSPITALS
Also Called: Kaiser Prmnnte San Jose Med Ct
250 Hospital Pkwy Bldg D, San Jose (95119-1103)
PHONE..................................408 972-3000
Thomas Hau, *Branch Mgr*
Francis Abueg, *Psychologist*
Faezeh Ghaffari, *Obstetrician*
Wesley Leong, *Obstetrician*
Shenee Slade, *Obstetrician*
EMP: 235
SQ FT: 5,976
SALES (corp-wide): 30.5B Privately Held
WEB: www.kaisercenter.com
SIC: 8011 8062 General & family practice, physician/surgeon; general medical & surgical hospitals
HQ: Kaiser Foundation Hospitals Inc
   1 Kaiser Plz
   Oakland CA 94612
   510 271-6611

(P-15489)
KAISER FOUNDATION HOSPITALS
Also Called: Kaiser Permanente
2425 Geary Blvd, San Francisco (94115-3358)
PHONE..................................415 833-2000
Mike Alexander, *Senior VP*
Pharm Sharma, *Analyst*
Karen Lai, *Pharmacist*
Nenita Egar, *Assistant*
Marc Beezy, *Consultant*
EMP: 720
SALES (corp-wide): 30.5B Privately Held
WEB: www.kaisercenter.com
SIC: 8011 Medical centers
HQ: Kaiser Foundation Hospitals Inc
   1 Kaiser Plz
   Oakland CA 94612
   510 271-6611

(P-15490)
KAISER FOUNDATION HOSPITALS
Also Called: Kaiser Prmnnte Lvrmore Med Ctr
3000 Las Positas Rd, Livermore (94551-9627)
PHONE..................................925 432-6000
Ian Bartos, *Pediatrics*
William Ong, *Pediatrics*
EMP: 235
SALES (corp-wide): 30.5B Privately Held
WEB: www.kaisercenter.com
SIC: 8011 8062 Medical centers; general medical & surgical hospitals
HQ: Kaiser Foundation Hospitals Inc
   1 Kaiser Plz
   Oakland CA 94612
   510 271-6611

(P-15491)
KAISER FOUNDATION HOSPITALS
Also Called: Department of Allergy
1635 Divisadero St Fl 1, San Francisco (94115-3036)
PHONE..................................415 833-3780
Jodi Thirtyarte, *Director*
David Delaney, *Vice Pres*
Mallen Fajardo, *Administration*
Xiaoyan Zhang, *Psychiatry*
EMP: 235
SALES (corp-wide): 30.5B Privately Held
WEB: www.kaisercenter.com
SIC: 8011 Allergist
HQ: Kaiser Foundation Hospitals Inc
   1 Kaiser Plz
   Oakland CA 94612
   510 271-6611

(P-15492)
KAISER FOUNDATION HOSPITALS
Also Called: Kaiser Permanente
7300 N Fresno St, Fresno (93720-2941)
PHONE..................................559 448-4500
Susan Ryan, *Senior VP*
EMP: 235
SALES (corp-wide): 30.5B Privately Held
WEB: www.kaisercenter.com
SIC: 8011 Medical centers
HQ: Kaiser Foundation Hospitals Inc
   1 Kaiser Plz
   Oakland CA 94612
   510 271-6611

(P-15493)
KAISER FUNDATION HLTH PLAN INC (PA)
1 Kaiser Plz, Oakland (94612-3610)
PHONE..................................510 271-5800
Greg Adams, *Ch of Bd*
Gregory A Adams, *President*
Carrie Owen Plietz, *President*
Dave Underriner, *President*
Laura Gallardo, *COO*
EMP: 450 EST: 1955
SQ FT: 90,000
SALES (est): 30.5B Privately Held
WEB: www.healthy.kaiserpermanente.org
SIC: 8011 Health maintenance organization

(P-15494)
KARTHIKEYA DEVIREDDY MD INC
311 W I St, Los Banos (93635-3479)
PHONE..................................209 826-2222
EMP: 85
SALES (est): 8MM Privately Held
SIC: 8011 Offices & clinics of medical doctors

(P-15495)
LA CLINICA DE LA RAZA INC
1515 Fruitvale Ave, Oakland (94601-2355)
PHONE..................................510 535-6300
Jim Eitel, *Partner*
Maria Hernandez, *COO*
Nancy Lewis, *Web Dvlpr*
Vicky Cuevas, *MIS Staff*
Wendy Jeter, *Site Mgr*
EMP: 199

PRODUCTS & SERVICES SECTION
8011 - Offices & Clinics Of Doctors Of Medicine County (P-15517)

SALES (corp-wide): 115.6MM **Privately Held**
WEB: www.laclinica.org
SIC: 8011 8699 Clinic, operated by physicians; charitable organization
PA: La Clinica De La Raza, Inc.
  1450 Fruitvale Ave Fl 3
  Oakland CA 94601
  510 535-4000

(P-15496)
LA CLINICA DE LA RAZA INC
243 Georgia St, Vallejo (94590-5905)
PHONE.................................707 556-8100
Jane Garcia, *Branch Mgr*
Mila Hernandez, *Admin Asst*
Wasfa Jahangiri, *Family Practiti*
EMP: 199
SALES (corp-wide): 115.6MM **Privately Held**
WEB: www.laclinica.org
SIC: 8011 Clinic, operated by physicians
PA: La Clinica De La Raza, Inc.
  1450 Fruitvale Ave Fl 3
  Oakland CA 94601
  510 535-4000

(P-15497)
LA CLINICA DE LA RAZA INC
Also Called: Wic
1450 Fruitvale Ave B, Oakland (94601-2313)
PHONE.................................510 535-4110
Ana Dorman, *Branch Mgr*
Dolly Davar, *Business Dir*
Jennifer Ogg, *Executive Asst*
Kim Sloan, *Info Tech Mgr*
Katie Riemer, *Comp Tech*
EMP: 199
SALES (corp-wide): 115.6MM **Privately Held**
WEB: www.laclinica.org
SIC: 8011 Clinic, operated by physicians
PA: La Clinica De La Raza, Inc.
  1450 Fruitvale Ave Fl 3
  Oakland CA 94601
  510 535-4000

(P-15498)
LA CLINICA DE LA RAZA INC (PA)
1450 Fruitvale Ave Fl 3, Oakland (94601-2313)
P.O. Box 22210 (94623-2210)
PHONE.................................510 535-4000
Jane Garcia, *CEO*
Patricia Aguilera, *CFO*
Fernando Cortez, *Officer*
Kelly Hernandez, *Office Mgr*
Juan Salinas, *Office Mgr*
EMP: 40 **EST:** 1971
SQ FT: 2,500
SALES: 115.6MM **Privately Held**
WEB: www.laclinica.org
SIC: 8011 Clinic, operated by physicians

(P-15499)
LA CLINICA DE LA RAZA INC
3050 E 16th St, Oakland (94601-2319)
PHONE.................................510 535-4700
Magnolia Rios, *Office Mgr*
Edward Rothman, *Med Doctor*
Ariane Terlet, *Director*
EMP: 199
SQ FT: 5,208
SALES (corp-wide): 115.6MM **Privately Held**
WEB: www.laclinica.org
SIC: 8011 Clinic, operated by physicians
PA: La Clinica De La Raza, Inc.
  1450 Fruitvale Ave Fl 3
  Oakland CA 94601
  510 535-4000

(P-15500)
LA CLINICA DE LA RAZA INC
Also Called: Mental Health Department
1601 Fruitvale Ave, Oakland (94601-2418)
PHONE.................................510 535-6200
Jane Garcia, *CEO*
Scott Taylor, *Surgeon*
Susanna Moore, *Psychiatry*
Julie Kuri, *Supervisor*
EMP: 199

SALES (corp-wide): 115.6MM **Privately Held**
WEB: www.laclinica.org
SIC: 8011 Clinic, operated by physicians
PA: La Clinica De La Raza, Inc.
  1450 Fruitvale Ave Fl 3
  Oakland CA 94601
  510 535-4000

(P-15501)
LA CLINICA DE LA RAZA INC
Also Called: Laclinica
337 E Leland Rd, Pittsburg (94565-4911)
PHONE.................................925 431-1250
Viola Lujan, *Branch Mgr*
Keri Zug, *Admin Sec*
Sunshine Monastirial, *Planning*
Cynthia Morford, *Fmly & Gen Dent*
Karen Nguyen, *Assistant*
EMP: 199
SALES (corp-wide): 115.6MM **Privately Held**
WEB: www.laclinica.org
SIC: 8011 Clinic, operated by physicians
PA: La Clinica De La Raza, Inc.
  1450 Fruitvale Ave Fl 3
  Oakland CA 94601
  510 535-4000

(P-15502)
LASER SKIN SRGERY MED GROUP IN
Also Called: Laser Skin Srgery Ctr Nthrn Ca
3835 J St, Sacramento (95816-5520)
PHONE.................................916 456-0400
Suzanne L Kilmer MD, *President*
Julie Olin Caselli, *Administration*
EMP: 44 **EST:** 1997
SALES (est): 5.9MM **Privately Held**
WEB: www.skinlasers.com
SIC: 8011 7231 Plastic surgeon; dermatologist; depilatory salon, electrolysis

(P-15503)
LASSEN MEDICAL GROUP INC (PA)
Also Called: Mercy Medical
2450 Sster Mary Clumba Dr, Red Bluff (96080-4356)
PHONE.................................530 527-0414
Kimberli R Frantz, *President*
Angie Dudley, *CFO*
Dan Mc Daniel MD, *Treasurer*
Richard Wickenheiser, *Principal*
Kelley Ottman, *Office Mgr*
EMP: 41 **EST:** 1954
SALES (est): 10.9MM **Privately Held**
WEB: www.dignityhealth.org
SIC: 8011 8099 Physicians' office, including specialists; blood related health services

(P-15504)
LEWIS S BLISS MD
Also Called: Bliss Eye Associates
5773 Greenback Ln, Sacramento (95841-2013)
PHONE.................................916 863-3143
Lewis S Bliss MD, *Owner*
Keith Yamanishi
EMP: 40 **EST:** 1997
SALES (est): 6.6MM **Privately Held**
WEB: www.blisseye.com
SIC: 8011 8042 Ophthalmologist; offices & clinics of optometrists

(P-15505)
LIFELONG MEDICAL CARE (PA)
Also Called: OVER 60 HEALTH CENTER
2344 6th St, Berkeley (94710-2412)
P.O. Box 11247 (94712-2247)
PHONE.................................510 704-6010
Marty A Lynch, *CEO*
Brenda Shipp, *COO*
Rick Clark, *CFO*
Kimberly Ceci, *Associate Dir*
Sasha Gayle-Schneider, *Executive Asst*
EMP: 50 **EST:** 1976
SQ FT: 4,200
SALES: 96MM **Privately Held**
WEB: www.lifelongmedical.org
SIC: 8011 Clinic, operated by physicians

(P-15506)
LIVERMORE PEDIATRICS
Also Called: Flanzbaum, Jonathan M MD
1171 Murrieta Blvd, Livermore (94550-4143)
PHONE.................................925 455-5050
Bruce Gach MD, *Owner*
Anthony V Chiong, *Pediatrics*
Vicente Chiong, *Pediatrics*
EMP: 36 **EST:** 1997
SALES (est): 2.4MM **Privately Held**
WEB: www.stanfordchildrens.org
SIC: 8011 Pediatrician

(P-15507)
LIVINGSTON COMMUNITY HEALTH (PA)
Also Called: LIVINGSTON HEALTH CENTER
600 B St Bldg A, Livingston (95334-9593)
PHONE.................................209 394-7913
Leslie McGowan, *CEO*
Selina Montoya, *CFO*
Rosa Camacho, *Manager*
Charlene Vest, *Clerk*
EMP: 98 **EST:** 1970
SALES (est): 18.9MM **Privately Held**
WEB: www.visitlch.org
SIC: 8011 Primary care medical clinic

(P-15508)
LODI MEMORIAL HOSP ASSN INC
Also Called: Rehabilitation Center
800 S Lower Sacramento Rd, Lodi (95242-3635)
PHONE.................................209 333-3100
Linda Escobar, *Director*
EMP: 35
SALES (corp-wide): 4.5B **Privately Held**
WEB: www.lodihealth.org
SIC: 8011 8069 Specialized medical practitioners, except internal; specialty hospitals, except psychiatric
HQ: Lodi Memorial Hospital Association, Inc.
  975 S Fairmont Ave
  Lodi CA 95240
  209 334-3411

(P-15509)
LONG VALLEY HEALTH CENTER
50 Branscomb Rd, Laytonville (95454)
P.O. Box 870 (95454-0870)
PHONE.................................707 984-6131
Laura Chenet-Leonard, *Exec Dir*
Jane A Keeley, *Nurse Practr*
EMP: 45 **EST:** 1978
SQ FT: 3,000
SALES: 4.2MM **Privately Held**
WEB: www.longvalley.org
SIC: 8011 Clinic, operated by physicians

(P-15510)
LOS GATOS IMAGING CENTER LTD
800 Pollard Rd Ste B101, Los Gatos (95032-1445)
PHONE.................................408 374-8897
Gatos Los, *Branch Mgr*
EMP: 79
SALES (corp-wide): 278.8K **Privately Held**
WEB: www.mammo.net
SIC: 8011 Radiologist
PA: Los Gatos Imaging Center, Ltd.
  26250 Entp Ct Ste 100
  Lake Forest CA
  949 282-6200

(P-15511)
LOS OLIVOS WNS MED GROUP INC (PA)
15151 National Ave Ste 1, Los Gatos (95032-2627)
PHONE.................................408 356-0431
Martin Silvermen MD, *President*
Maureen Wong, *COO*
Karen Kunzel MD, *Admin Sec*
Debbie L Sanders, *Business Mgr*
Eve Ladwig-Scott, *Obstetrician*
EMP: 49 **EST:** 1958
SQ FT: 13,194

SALES (est): 5.9MM **Privately Held**
WEB: www.losolivos-obgyn.com
SIC: 8011 Obstetrician; gynecologist; fertility specialist, physician

(P-15512)
LRIMG INC
Also Called: Los Robles Proffessional Group
15215 National Ave # 200, Los Gatos (95032-2425)
PHONE.................................408 358-2479
Dennis Penner MD, *President*
Richard A Bobis MD, *Principal*
Donald Posthumus MD, *Principal*
S J Salsen MD, *Principal*
Stacey Hein, *Med Doctor*
EMP: 67 **EST:** 1974
SQ FT: 6,000
SALES (est): 2.6MM **Privately Held**
SIC: 8011 Internal medicine practitioners

(P-15513)
LYON-MARTIN WNS HLTH SVCS INC
1735 Mission St, San Francisco (94103-2417)
PHONE.................................415 565-7667
Gloria Nieto, *Exec Dir*
EMP: 35 **EST:** 1979
SALES (est): 2.2MM **Privately Held**
WEB: www.healthright360.org
SIC: 8011 Clinic, operated by physicians; gynecologist

(P-15514)
LYRA HEALTH INC
287 Lorton Ave 2, Burlingame (94010-4203)
PHONE.................................650 477-2991
David Ebersman, *CEO*
Sean McBride, *Partner*
Jenny Gonsalves, *Vice Pres*
Hang Cheng, *Sr Software Eng*
Alex Macy, *Engineer*
EMP: 145 **EST:** 2015
SALES (est): 26.3MM **Privately Held**
WEB: www.lyrahealth.com
SIC: 8011 Clinic, operated by physicians

(P-15515)
MADERA FAMILY MED GROUP INC
Also Called: Madera Industrial Med Group
1111 W 4th St, Madera (93637-4474)
PHONE.................................559 673-3000
Aftab Naz, *President*
EMP: 52 **EST:** 1995
SALES (est): 13.4MM **Privately Held**
WEB: www.mfmg.net
SIC: 8011 General & family practice, physician/surgeon

(P-15516)
MANGROVE MEDICAL GROUP
Also Called: Mangrove Lab & X-Ray
1040 Mangrove Ave, Chico (95926-3509)
PHONE.................................530 345-0064
Dewayne E Caviness MD, *Principal*
Randall E Caviness MD, *Principal*
Kurt E Johnson MD, *Principal*
Dean P Smith MD, *Principal*
Randall S Williams MD, *Principal*
EMP: 50 **EST:** 1962
SQ FT: 12,000
SALES (est): 9.8MM **Privately Held**
WEB: www.mangrovemedicalclinic.com
SIC: 8011 General & family practice, physician/surgeon

(P-15517)
MARIN CANCER CARE INC
Also Called: Oncology Group Practice
1350 S Eliseo Dr Ste 200, Greenbrae (94904-2018)
PHONE.................................415 925-5000
Jaime Chang, *Principal*
Peter Eisenberg, *Principal*
Leesa Helmlinger,
EMP: 38 **EST:** 2010
SALES (est): 3.1MM **Privately Held**
WEB: www.marincancercare.com
SIC: 8011 Oncologist

8011 - Offices & Clinics Of Doctors Of Medicine County (P-15518)

(P-15518)
MARIN COMMUNITY CLINIC
Also Called: MARIN COMMUNITY CLINICS
9 Commercial Blvd Ste 100, Novato (94949-6137)
PHONE 415 448-1500
Linda Tavaszi, *CEO*
Peggy Dracker, *COO*
David Klinetobe, *CFO*
Connie Kadera, *Officer*
John Shen, *Exec Dir*
EMP: 99 **EST:** 1974
SQ FT: 9,000
SALES (est): 58MM **Privately Held**
WEB: www.marinclinic.org
SIC: 8011 Clinic, operated by physicians

(P-15519)
MARIN OPHTHLMIC CONS A MED COR
Also Called: Marin Eyes
901 E St Ste 285, San Rafael (94901-2850)
PHONE 415 454-5565
John R Campbell MD, *President*
John C Shin, *Admin Sec*
Kristine Adams, *Technical Staff*
John Shin, *Med Doctor*
Patricia Tang, *Med Doctor*
EMP: 84 **EST:** 1980
SALES (est): 12.5MM **Privately Held**
WEB: www.marineyes.com
SIC: 8011 Ophthalmologist

(P-15520)
MARK E JACOBSON M D
1260 N Dutton Ave Ste 230, Santa Rosa (95401-7161)
PHONE 707 571-4022
EMP: 60
SALES (est): 658.3K **Privately Held**
SIC: 8011 Offices And Clinics Medical Doctors,Nsk

(P-15521)
MARK H NISHIKI MD
Also Called: David P Enfield MD
1800 N California St, Stockton (95204-6019)
PHONE 209 465-6221
Mark H Nishiki MD, *Partner*
EMP: 58 **EST:** 1967
SALES (est): 208.3K **Privately Held**
SIC: 8011 Pathologist

(P-15522)
MAYVIEW COMMUNITY HLTH CTR INC (PA)
270 Grant Ave Ste 102, Palo Alto (94306-1908)
PHONE 650 327-8717
Shamima Hasan, *CEO*
Louise Baker, *Chairman*
Shannon Wu, *Executive Asst*
Joseph Awender, *Chiropractor*
Aarthi Anand, *Med Doctor*
▼ **EMP:** 35 **EST:** 1972
SALES (est): 7.3MM **Privately Held**
WEB: www.ravenswoodfhn.org
SIC: 8011 Clinic, operated by physicians

(P-15523)
MCHENRY MEDICAL GROUP INC
1541 Florida Ave Ste 200, Modesto (95350-4438)
PHONE 209 577-3388
John Porteous, *President*
Harris M Goodman, *Treasurer*
EMP: 91 **EST:** 1969
SQ FT: 22,000
SALES (est): 8.5MM **Privately Held**
WEB: www.fcppcentralvalley.com
SIC: 8011 Internal medicine, physician/surgeon

(P-15524)
MD IMAGING INC A PROF MED CORP
Also Called: Women's Imaging Center
2020 Court St, Redding (96001-1822)
PHONE 530 243-1249
Michael G Davis, *CEO*
Richard J Slepicka, *CFO*
Mike Wheeler, *Exec Dir*
Cheryl Cutchin, *Office Mgr*
Melody Christenson, *Marketing Mgr*
EMP: 100 **EST:** 1994
SALES (est): 26MM **Privately Held**
WEB: www.mdimaging.net
SIC: 8011 Radiologist

(P-15525)
MEDAMERICA INC
Also Called: Samaritan Medical Care
554 Blossom Hill Rd, San Jose (95123-3212)
PHONE 408 281-2772
Colleen Nobil, *Branch Mgr*
Brent Phung, *Vice Pres*
Jack Lyle, *VP Bus Dvlpt*
Vickie Hanson, *Regional Mgr*
Julie Chapple, *Executive Asst*
EMP: 39
SALES (corp-wide): 500MM **Privately Held**
WEB: www.medamerica.com
SIC: 8011 Physicians' office, including specialists
HQ: Medamerica, Inc.
2100 Powell St Ste 900
Emeryville CA 94608
510 350-2600

(P-15526)
MEDICAL ANESTHESIA CONS LLC
100 N Wiget Ln Ste 160, Walnut Creek (94598-5917)
PHONE 925 287-1505
David Fitzgerald, *Branch Mgr*
Raymond Cheung, *Assistant*
EMP: 138 **Publicly Held**
WEB: www.macmgi.com
SIC: 8011 Anesthesiologist
HQ: Medical Anesthesia Consultants Llc
2175 N Calif Blvd Ste 425
Walnut Creek CA 94596
925 543-0140

(P-15527)
MEDICAL ANESTHESIA CONS LLC (DH)
2175 N Calif Blvd Ste 425, Walnut Creek (94596-7164)
PHONE 925 543-0140
David C Fitzgerald MD, *President*
Jie Lan, *Shareholder*
Barbara Atherwood, *Technology*
Diane Chamberlin, *Controller*
Gavin Westberg, *Opers Staff*
EMP: 50 **EST:** 2013
SALES (est): 20.3MM **Publicly Held**
WEB: www.macmgi.com
SIC: 8011 Anesthesiologist

(P-15528)
MEDICAL VISION TECHNOLOGY INC (PA)
1700 Alhambra Blvd # 202, Sacramento (95816-7050)
PHONE 916 731-8040
Robert R Peabody Jr, *President*
Robert B Miller MD, *Shareholder*
Robert Miller, *Shareholder*
Willis W Pickel MD, *Shareholder*
Bruce A Winters MD, *Shareholder*
EMP: 40 **EST:** 1987
SQ FT: 4,500
SALES (est): 15.7MM **Privately Held**
WEB: www.medvistech.com
SIC: 8011 Ophthalmologist

(P-15529)
MENDOCINO CMNTY HLTH CLNIC INC (PA)
Also Called: MCHC
333 Laws Ave, Ukiah (95482-6540)
PHONE 707 468-1010
John Pavoni, *CEO*
Karen Oslund, *Vice Chairman*
Kathleen Stone, *Officer*
Diane Behne, *Technician*
Cindy Peterson, *Opers Staff*
EMP: 130 **EST:** 1992
SQ FT: 24,000
SALES: 39.2MM **Privately Held**
WEB: www.mchcinc.org
SIC: 8011 Primary care medical clinic

(P-15530)
MENDOCINO CMNTY HLTH CLNIC INC
45 Hazel St, Willits (95490-4222)
PHONE 707 456-9600
Deborah Frank, *Manager*
Navneet Mansukhani, *Director*
EMP: 105
SALES (corp-wide): 39.2MM **Privately Held**
WEB: www.mchcinc.org
SIC: 8011 Primary care medical clinic
PA: Mendocino Community Health Clinic, Inc.
333 Laws Ave
Ukiah CA 95482
707 468-1010

(P-15531)
MERCED FACULTY ASSOCIATES (PA)
220 E 13th St Ste B, Merced (95341-6251)
P.O. Box 3768 (95344-3768)
PHONE 209 723-3704
Timothy Johnston, *CEO*
Becky Shaw, *CEO*
Susan Harris, *COO*
J E Hughell MD, *Treasurer*
Kimm Pollock, *Office Mgr*
EMP: 39 **EST:** 1989
SALES (est): 10.1MM **Privately Held**
WEB: www.mfamg.com
SIC: 8011 Pediatrician

(P-15532)
MERCED MEDICAL CLINIC INC
650 W Olive Ave, Merced (95348-2400)
PHONE 209 722-8047
Satnam S Uppal MD, *President*
Maciej G Ossowski MD, *Vice Pres*
John Anglin MD, *Principal*
EMP: 37 **EST:** 1936
SQ FT: 7,000
SALES (est): 1MM **Privately Held**
SIC: 8011 Clinic, operated by physicians; surgeon

(P-15533)
MERCED ORTHOPEDIC MED GROUP
Also Called: Cooman, Lynn W Jr
123 W North Bear Creek Dr, Merced (95348-3420)
P.O. Box 2306 (95344-0306)
PHONE 209 722-8161
Lynn Cooman, *President*
Mark Via, *Corp Secy*
Samuel Tacke, *Vice Pres*
EMP: 52 **EST:** 1969
SQ FT: 5,200
SALES (est): 2.7MM **Privately Held**
WEB: www.mercedorthopaedicgroup.com
SIC: 8011 Orthopedic physician

(P-15534)
MERCED UROLOGY MED GROUP INC
2517 Canal St Ste 1, Merced (95340-2829)
P.O. Box 2510 (95344-0510)
PHONE 209 723-2122
Dennis Ceasar, *President*
Roderick Harris MD, *Vice Pres*
Susana Ramirez, *Assoc Prof*
EMP: 48 **EST:** 1976
SQ FT: 3,000
SALES (est): 3.1MM **Privately Held**
WEB: www.ucmerced.edu
SIC: 8011 Urologist

(P-15535)
MERCY DOCTORS MED GROUP INC
Also Called: Hilbert, Diana L MD
1 Shrader St Ste 640, San Francisco (94117-1018)
PHONE 415 752-0100
Albert Frietzsche MD, *Partner*
Hilbert D L MD, *Partner*
Wil Castaneda, *Administration*
EMP: 45 **EST:** 1968
SALES (est): 3MM **Privately Held**
WEB: www.mercydoctorsmedicalgroup.com
SIC: 8011 General & family practice, physician/surgeon; physicians' office, including specialists

(P-15536)
METROPLTAN PAIN MGT CONS INC A
Also Called: Metropolitan Pain Mgmt Cons
2288 Auburn Blvd Ste 106, Sacramento (95821-1619)
PHONE 916 568-8338
Lee T Snook MD, *President*
EMP: 35 **EST:** 1986
SALES (est): 6.2MM **Privately Held**
WEB: www.pain-mpmc.com
SIC: 8011 Orthopedic physician

(P-15537)
MINIMLLY INVSIVE SRGCAL SLTONS
Also Called: Minimlly Invsive Srgcal Sltons
105 N Bascom Ave Ste 104, San Jose (95128-1811)
PHONE 408 750-4658
Reza Malek, *CEO*
Arash M Padidar, *Med Doctor*
EMP: 40 **EST:** 2003
SALES (est): 7.7MM **Privately Held**
WEB: www.endovascularsurgery.com
SIC: 8011 Surgeon

(P-15538)
MISSION NEIGHBORHOOD HLTH CTR (PA)
Also Called: Mission Neighborhood Hlth Ctr
240 Shotwell St, San Francisco (94110-1323)
PHONE 415 552-3870
Brenda Storey, *CEO*
Amelia Martinez, *President*
Charles Moser, *Trustee*
Luisa Eztouerro, *Vice Pres*
Yrama Laria-Jensen, *Pharmacy Dir*
EMP: 110 **EST:** 1968
SQ FT: 21,000
SALES (est): 22.4MM **Privately Held**
WEB: www.mnhc.org
SIC: 8011 Primary care medical clinic

(P-15539)
MISSION PEAK ORTHOPEDICS
5924 Stoneridge Dr # 200, Pleasanton (94588-2887)
PHONE 510 797-3933
Co V Banh, *Principal*
EMP: 65 **EST:** 2010
SALES (est): 2.5MM **Privately Held**
WEB: www.mportho.com
SIC: 8011 Orthopedic physician

(P-15540)
MODESTO IMAGING CENTER
157 E Coolidge Ave, Modesto (95350-4565)
PHONE 209 524-6800
James Carlson MD, *Partner*
Rodney Cornelson MD, *Partner*
Steven Endsley MD, *Partner*
Tom Gray MD, *Partner*
Mat Harris MD, *Partner*
EMP: 89 **EST:** 1990
SQ FT: 17,000
SALES (est): 1.7MM **Privately Held**
WEB: www.radnet.com
SIC: 8011 Radiologist

(P-15541)
MUIR DBLO OCCPTNAL MDCINE MED
2231 Galaxy Ct, Concord (94520-4933)
PHONE 925 685-7744
John Gunderson, *CEO*
Ken Anderson, *CEO*
Mindy Burchfiel, *Office Mgr*
Pat Brock, *Financial Exec*
Gary Hamilton, *Med Doctor*
EMP: 35 **EST:** 1992
SALES (est): 3.1MM **Privately Held**
SIC: 8011 Occupational & industrial specialist, physician/surgeon

(P-15542)
MUIR ORTHOPEDIC SPECIALISTS
2405 Shadelands Dr # 210, Walnut Creek (94598-5905)
PHONE 925 939-8585
K C Campion, *CEO*

PRODUCTS & SERVICES SECTION

8011 - Offices & Clinics Of Doctors Of Medicine County (P-15567)

Ramiro Miranda MD, *President*
Annie Jarrett, *Officer*
Katie Smith, *Department Mgr*
Monica Begor, *Opers Staff*
EMP: 177 **EST:** 1982
SALES (est): 20MM **Privately Held**
WEB: www.muirortho.com
SIC: 8011 Orthopedic physician

(P-15543)
MUIR ORTHOPEDICS INC
Also Called: Mc Ivor, William MD
2405 Shadelands Dr # 210, Walnut Creek (94598-5905)
P.O. Box 31396 (94598-8396)
PHONE 925 939-8585
William Mc Ivor, *President*
EMP: 67 **EST:** 1980
SALES (est): 10.6MM **Privately Held**
WEB: www.muirortho.com
SIC: 8011 Orthopedic physician

(P-15544)
NAPA VLY ORTHPDIC MED GROUP IN
3273 Claremont Way # 100, NAPA (94558-3306)
P.O. Box 2059 (94558-0502)
PHONE 707 254-7117
John N Diana, *President*
Michael Shifflett, *Partner*
Daneil P Birkbeck, *Vice Pres*
Adam M Freedhand, *Vice Pres*
Jason T Huffman, *Vice Pres*
EMP: 46 **EST:** 2004
SQ FT: 5,000
SALES (est): 11.5MM **Privately Held**
WEB: www.napavalleyortho.com
SIC: 8011 Orthopedic physician

(P-15545)
NATIVE AMERICAN HEALTH CTR INC (PA)
2950 International Blvd, Oakland (94601-2228)
PHONE 510 535-4400
Martin Waukazoo, *CEO*
Ana M Oconnor, *COO*
Alan Wong, *CFO*
Dr Joseph Marquis, *Chief Mktg Ofcr*
Karen Harrison, *Office Mgr*
EMP: 80 **EST:** 1971
SQ FT: 16,000
SALES: 29.1MM **Privately Held**
WEB: www.nativehealth.org
SIC: 8011 8021 8093 Clinic, operated by physicians; dentists' office; mental health clinic, outpatient

(P-15546)
NCSRA MEDICAL CORPORATION
2801 K St Ste 410, Sacramento (95816-5119)
PHONE 916 389-7100
Mark F Hambly, *President*
EMP: 45 **EST:** 2001
SALES (est): 2.2MM **Privately Held**
WEB: www.ncsramedical.com
SIC: 8011 Medical centers; physical medicine, physician/surgeon

(P-15547)
NEPHROLOGY GROUP INC (PA)
568 E Herndon Ave, Fresno (93720-2989)
PHONE 559 228-6600
Hemant Bhingra, *President*
Sukhvir Atwal, *Treasurer*
Harpreet S Dhindsa, *Exec VP*
Joseph C Duflot, *Vice Pres*
Yangming Cao, *Admin Sec*
EMP: 52 **EST:** 1979
SALES (est): 10.8MM **Privately Held**
WEB: www.thenephrologygroupinc.com
SIC: 8011 Nephrologist

(P-15548)
NES HEALTH CARE GROUP
39 Main St, Belvedere Tiburon (94920-2507)
P.O. Box 156 (94920-0156)
PHONE 415 435-4591
Thomas Zguris, *Branch Mgr*
Brian Mummert, *President*
Randy Wellman, *Info Tech Dir*
Lisa Mennucci, *Finance*
Leslie Miller, *Recruiter*
EMP: 40 **Privately Held**
WEB: www.neshealth-care.com
SIC: 8011 Offices & clinics of medical doctors
HQ: Nes Health Care Group
4250 Veterans Memorial
Holbrook NY 11741

(P-15549)
NEUROSRGCAL ASSOC MED GROUP IN
7130 N Sharon Ave Ste 100, Fresno (93720-3386)
PHONE 559 449-1100
Dr Brian H Clague, *Principal*
Dr Adam Brant, *Principal*
Dr Ali Najafi, *Principal*
EMP: 74 **EST:** 1976
SQ FT: 6,880
SALES (est): 3.3MM **Privately Held**
SIC: 8011 Neurosurgeon

(P-15550)
NORTH CAST SRGICAL SPECIALISTS
2321 Harrison Ave, Eureka (95501-3216)
PHONE 707 443-2248
John V Speybroeck, *Owner*
▲ **EMP:** 47 **EST:** 1959
SALES (est): 7MM **Privately Held**
SIC: 8011 Surgeon

(P-15551)
NORTH COAST CLINICS NETWORK (PA)
770 10th St, Arcata (95521-6210)
PHONE 707 826-8610
Herman Stettzler, *Director*
EMP: 36 **EST:** 1977
SALES (est): 764.2K **Privately Held**
WEB: www.northcoastclinics.org
SIC: 8011 Clinic, operated by physicians

(P-15552)
NORTH STATE RADIOLOGY
Also Called: North State Imaging
1702 Esplanade, Chico (95926-3315)
PHONE 530 898-0504
Scot Woolley, *CEO*
Don Hubbard, *CFO*
Chris Jones, *Info Tech Mgr*
Lara Bussey, *Radiology*
EMP: 50 **EST:** 1970
SALES (est): 13.6MM **Privately Held**
WEB: www.nsradiology.com
SIC: 8011 Radiologist

(P-15553)
NORTH VALLEY DERMATOLOGY
Also Called: O Jay On PA
251 Cohasset Rd Ste 240, Chico (95926-2235)
PHONE 530 809-2127
Donald Richey MD, *Principal*
Mary Fredenberg, *Dermatology*
Craig Heiner, *Dermatology*
Kafele Hodari, *Dermatology*
Adam Sorensen, *Dermatology*
EMP: 36 **EST:** 1992
SALES (est): 5.7MM **Privately Held**
SIC: 8011 Dermatologist

(P-15554)
NORTHCOUNTRY CLINIC
Also Called: Dickinson, Diane MD
785 18th St, Arcata (95521-5683)
PHONE 707 822-2481
Herrmann Spetzler, *Administration*
Rick Davis, *Info Tech Mgr*
Judy Burns, *Med Doctor*
Sheyenne Spetzler, *Director*
EMP: 43 **EST:** 1976
SQ FT: 10,000
SALES (est): 1.9MM **Privately Held**
WEB: www.northcoastclinics.org
SIC: 8011 Clinic, operated by physicians

(P-15555)
NORTHEASTERN RUR HLTH CLINICS (PA)
Also Called: WESTWOOD FAMILY PRACTICE
1850 Spring Ridge Dr, Susanville (96130-6100)
PHONE 530 251-5000
Phil Nowak, *CEO*
Lacey Lively, *CFO*
Richard Hrezo, *Treasurer*
Pamela Robbins, *Admin Sec*
Nicole Berry, *Human Res Mgr*
EMP: 65 **EST:** 1977
SQ FT: 27,000
SALES: 11.5MM **Privately Held**
WEB: www.northeasternhealth.org
SIC: 8011 Clinic, operated by physicians

(P-15556)
NORTHERN CAL MED ASSOC INC (PA)
3536 Mendocino Ave # 200, Santa Rosa (95403-3634)
PHONE 707 573-6925
Thomas Dunlap, *President*
George L Smith, *President*
Greg Hopkins MD, *Treasurer*
Charles Nydegger, *Vice Pres*
Michael Avedissian, *Admin Sec*
EMP: 45 **EST:** 1975
SQ FT: 7,000
SALES (est): 26.1MM **Privately Held**
SIC: 8011 Cardiologist & cardio-vascular specialist

(P-15557)
NORTHSTATE CARDIOLOGY CONS
198 Cohasset Rd, Chico (95926-2202)
PHONE 530 342-0123
Stephen A Schwartz, *President*
Allie Smith, *Manager*
EMP: 50 **EST:** 1983
SALES (est): 7.9MM **Privately Held**
SIC: 8011 Cardiologist & cardio-vascular specialist

(P-15558)
NORTHWEST MEDICAL GROUP INC
Also Called: Good Neighbor Pharmacy
7355 N Palm Ave Ste 100, Fresno (93711-5770)
PHONE 559 271-6302
Cecil Bullard, *President*
Diane Hubbard, *Shareholder*
Vivian Hernandez MD, *Admin Sec*
Lisa Jelinek, *Administration*
Roman Malley, *Internal Med*
EMP: 43 **EST:** 1958
SQ FT: 5,000
SALES (est): 7.9MM **Privately Held**
WEB: www.northwestmed.net
SIC: 8011 5912 Pediatrician; drug stores

(P-15559)
NORTHWEST PHYSCANS MED GROUP I (PA)
7355 N Palm Ave Ste 100, Fresno (93711-5770)
PHONE 559 271-6300
John Lattin, *President*
EMP: 85 **EST:** 1988
SALES (est): 6.4MM **Privately Held**
SIC: 8011 Internal medicine, physician/surgeon

(P-15560)
NVISION LASER EYE CENTERS INC
711 Van Ness Ave Ste 320, San Francisco (94102-3285)
PHONE 415 421-8667
George Lalousis, *Vice Pres*
EMP: 52
SALES (corp-wide): 40.5MM **Privately Held**
WEB: www.nvisioncenters.com
SIC: 8011 Ophthalmologist
PA: Nvision Laser Eye Centers Inc.
75 Enterprise Ste 200
Aliso Viejo CA 92656
877 455-9942

(P-15561)
OAKLAND MEDICAL GROUP INC
3300 Webster St Ste 1000, Oakland (94609-3125)
PHONE 510 452-4824
J Gordon Frierson, *President*
James R Saunders Jr, *Treasurer*
Anthony S Ravnik, *Admin Sec*
Hiroshi Terashima, *Asst Sec*
EMP: 43 **EST:** 1970
SQ FT: 3,444
SALES (est): 2.8MM **Privately Held**
WEB: www.affiliatesindermatology.com
SIC: 8011 Dermatologist

(P-15562)
OB/GYN PRTNERS FOR HLTH MED GR
365 Hawthorne Ave Ste 301, Oakland (94609-3113)
PHONE 510 893-1700
Madgy Girgis, *CEO*
Thomas Hambrick, *Shareholder*
Karen Kashkin, *Shareholder*
Goldee Gross, *Vice Pres*
Hong Fong, *Admin Sec*
EMP: 37 **EST:** 1997
SALES (est): 809.8K **Privately Held**
SIC: 8011 Obstetrician; gynecologist

(P-15563)
OBSTETRIX MED GROUP CAL A PROF (HQ)
900 E Hamilton Ave # 220, Campbell (95008-0664)
PHONE 800 463-6628
M D Cunningham MD, *Principal*
EMP: 50 **EST:** 1998
SALES (est): 12.9MM **Publicly Held**
WEB: www.mednax.com
SIC: 8011 Pediatrician

(P-15564)
OCONNOR HOSPITAL
Also Called: O'Conner Wound Care Clinic
2105 Forest Ave, San Jose (95128-1471)
PHONE 408 947-2804
Jena Eibschun, *Business Mgr*
EMP: 92 **Privately Held**
WEB: www.och.sccgov.org
SIC: 8011 Medical centers
HQ: O'connor Hospital
2105 Forest Ave
San Jose CA 95128
408 947-2500

(P-15565)
OLE HEALTH
1141 Pear Tree Ln Ste 100, NAPA (94558-6485)
PHONE 707 254-1770
Alicia Hardy, *CEO*
Molly Nelson, *CFO*
Vincent Filanova, *CIO*
Victor Rodriguez, *Finance Asst*
Georgina Vega, *Recruiter*
EMP: 99 **EST:** 1972
SALES: 2.4MM **Privately Held**
WEB: www.olehealth.org
SIC: 8011 General & family practice, physician/surgeon

(P-15566)
OMNI WOMENS HLTH MED GROUP INC (PA)
3812 N 1st St, Fresno (93726-4301)
PHONE 559 495-3120
Harold Felix Grooms, *President*
Robert Frediani, *Principal*
Yong Lee, *Administration*
Joanne Hurado, *VP Opers*
Christina Soriano, *Manager*
EMP: 67 **EST:** 1997
SALES (est): 11.8MM **Privately Held**
WEB: www.omniwomenshealth.com
SIC: 8011 Gynecologist

(P-15567)
ON LOK INC
1333 Bush St, San Francisco (94109-5691)
PHONE 415 292-8888
Grace LI, *CEO*
Kelly Walsh, *CFO*
Kelvin Quan, *Officer*

(PA)=Parent Co (HQ)=Headquarters (DH)=Div Headquarters
✿ = New Business established in last 2 years

8011 - Offices & Clinics Of Doctors Of Medicine County (P-15568)

EMP: 99 **EST:** 1989
SALES: 14.9MM *Privately Held*
WEB: www.onlok.org
SIC: 8011 Offices & clinics of medical doctors

(P-15568)
OPEN DOOR COMMUNITY HLTH CTRS
3800 Janes Rd, Arcata (95521-4742)
PHONE..................707 822-1385
Cheyenne Spetzler, *COO*
Paula-Marie Schneider, *Nurse*
Debra Webb,
Briana Dominguez, *Receptionist*
Desiree Martin, *Receptionist*
EMP: 35 *Privately Held*
WEB: www.opendoorhealth.com
SIC: 8011 Primary care medical clinic
PA: Open Door Community Health Centers
670 9th St Ste 203cfo
Arcata CA 95521

(P-15569)
OPEN DOOR COMMUNITY HLTH CTRS
685 11th St, Arcata (95521-5802)
PHONE..................707 826-8636
EMP: 35 *Privately Held*
WEB: www.opendoorhealth.com
SIC: 8011 Clinic, operated by physicians
PA: Open Door Community Health Centers
670 9th St Ste 203cfo
Arcata CA 95521

(P-15570)
ORANGEBURG MEDICAL GROUP
Also Called: Banuelos, Jose L Jr MD
1448 Florida Ave, Modesto (95350-4443)
PHONE..................209 343-8126
Donald V Howe MD, *Partner*
Jose L Banuelos MD, *Partner*
Robert E Caton MD, *Partner*
L R Cimino MD, *Partner*
Antonio K Coirin MD, *Partner*
EMP: 80 **EST:** 1949
SQ FT: 10,000
SALES (est): 6.7MM *Privately Held*
WEB: www.orangeburgmedicalgroup.com
SIC: 8011 General & family practice, physician/surgeon

(P-15571)
OROHEALTH CORPORATION
Also Called: Oroville Hospital
900 Oro Dam Blvd E, Oroville (95965-5832)
PHONE..................530 534-9183
Mark Heinrich, *Director*
EMP: 1127
SALES (corp-wide): 4.2MM *Privately Held*
SIC: 8011 8062 Internal medicine, physician/surgeon; general medical & surgical hospitals
PA: Orohealth Corporation A Nonprofit Healthcare System
2767 Olive Hwy
Oroville CA 95966
530 533-8500

(P-15572)
OROVILLE INTRNAL MDCINE MED GR
Also Called: Roy C Shannon MD
2721 Olive Hwy Ste 12, Oroville (95966-6115)
PHONE..................530 538-3171
Roy Shannon, *President*
EMP: 47 **EST:** 1975
SQ FT: 3,600
SALES (est): 5.6MM *Privately Held*
WEB: www.orovillehospital.com
SIC: 8011 Internal medicine, physician/surgeon; physicians' office, including specialists

(P-15573)
ORTHONORCAL INC ◆
340 Dardanelli Ln Ste 10, Los Gatos (95032-1418)
PHONE..................408 356-0464
Nathaniel P Cohen, *Principal*
Marisa Arzate, *Comp Spec*
Jessie Bettencourt, *Opers Staff*
Carey Kouretas, *Surgeon*
Scott McFarland, *Physician Asst*
EMP: 35 **EST:** 2021
SALES (est): 13MM *Privately Held*
WEB: www.orthonorcal.com
SIC: 8011 Orthopedic physician

(P-15574)
ORTHOPEDIC ASSOC NTHRN CAL
Also Called: Orthopedic Assoc Nthrn Califo
131 Raley Blvd, Chico (95928-8347)
PHONE..................530 897-4500
Francine Marquis, *Administration*
Moody Cameron, *Technology*
Leonard Brazil, *Surgeon*
Taylor Konkin, *Surgeon*
Bill Watson, *Surgeon*
EMP: 36 **EST:** 1998
SALES (est): 6MM *Privately Held*
WEB: www.oanc.org
SIC: 8011 Orthopedic physician

(P-15575)
PACIFIC EYE ASSOCIATED INC
2100 Webster St Ste 214, San Francisco (94115-2375)
PHONE..................415 923-3007
Wayne E Fung MD, *President*
Arthur W Allen Jr, *Vice Pres*
Scott Neilson, *Exec Dir*
Jennifer U Sung, *Med Doctor*
EMP: 130 **EST:** 1970
SQ FT: 8,000
SALES (est): 22.3MM *Privately Held*
WEB: www.pacificeye.com
SIC: 8011 Ophthalmologist

(P-15576)
PACIFIC HART VSCULAR MED GROUP
1801 E March Ln Ste D400, Stockton (95210-6675)
PHONE..................209 464-3615
Dr Lee Stenzler, *Partner*
Daren Primack, *Partner*
Dr Lee Stenzler, *Partner*
Daren S Primack, *Cardiology*
Manreet Basra, *Internal Med*
EMP: 39 **EST:** 2006
SALES (est): 11.3MM *Privately Held*
SIC: 8011 Cardiologist & cardio-vascular specialist

(P-15577)
PACIFIC HMTLOGY ONCOLOGY ASSOC
2100 Webster St Ste 225, San Francisco (94115-2376)
PHONE..................415 923-3012
Kathleen Grant, *Owner*
Dr ARI Baron, *Partner*
Dr Bertrand Y Tuan, *Partner*
Aida Moss, *Hematology*
Steven Eisenberg, *Med Doctor*
EMP: 95 **EST:** 1979
SQ FT: 1,856
SALES (est): 14.2MM *Privately Held*
WEB: www.phoamd.com
SIC: 8011 Hematologist

(P-15578)
PACIFIC INPTIENT MED GROUP INC
9 Jeffrey Ct, Novato (94945-1739)
P.O. Box 1606 (94948-1606)
PHONE..................415 485-8824
Fabiola Cobarrubias, *President*
Christopher M Valentino, *COO*
EMP: 45 **EST:** 2007
SALES (est): 2.4MM *Privately Held*
WEB: www.pimgsf.com
SIC: 8011 Offices & clinics of medical doctors

(P-15579)
PACIFIC INTRNAL MEDICINE ASSOC
2100 Webster St Ste 423, San Francisco (94115-2380)
PHONE..................415 923-3050
Martin Brotman, *Partner*
Damian Augustyn, *Partner*
Lloyd Gross, *Partner*
Joel Klompus, *Partner*
Jane Milnick, *Partner*
EMP: 66 **EST:** 1969
SALES (est): 8.6MM *Privately Held*
WEB: www.pima.yourmd.com
SIC: 8011 Internal medicine, physician/surgeon

(P-15580)
PACIFIC REDWOOD MEDICAL GROUP
275 Hospital Dr, Ukiah (95482-4531)
P.O. Box 2800 (95482-2800)
PHONE..................707 462-7900
Mark H Luoto, *Principal*
Gary Fausone, *President*
Charles Evans, *CEO*
EMP: 54 **EST:** 2005
SALES (est): 7.6MM *Privately Held*
WEB: www.pacificredwoodmedicalgroup.com
SIC: 8011 Freestanding emergency medical center

(P-15581)
PACKARD CHILDRENS HLTH ALIANCE
Also Called: Pcha
725 Welch Rd, Palo Alto (94304-1601)
PHONE..................650 497-8000
Kim Robert, *CEO*
Lisa Holbrook, *COO*
Andrew Kronemyer, *IT/INT Sup*
James Dunn, *Med Doctor*
Anh-Thu Lewis, *Nurse Practr*
EMP: 100 **EST:** 2012
SALES: 107.3MM
SALES (corp-wide): 12.4B *Privately Held*
WEB: www.stanfordchildrens.org
SIC: 8011 Pediatrician
HQ: Lucile Salter Packard Children's Hospital At Stanford
725 Welch Rd
Palo Alto CA 94304
650 497-8000

(P-15582)
PAIN DIAGNSTC & TRTMNT CTR LLP
2805 J St Ste 200, Sacramento (95816-4307)
PHONE..................916 231-8755
L Pucher-Petersen, *Principal*
Lorraine Pucher-Petersen, *Principal*
Sandy Atkins, *Manager*
EMP: 43 **EST:** 2000
SALES (est): 9.5MM *Privately Held*
WEB: www.paindiagnostic.com
SIC: 8011 Ambulatory surgical center

(P-15583)
PARADISE MEDICAL GROUP INC
6470 Pentz Rd Ste A, Paradise (95969-3674)
PHONE..................530 877-3951
Richard Thorp, *President*
Jane Ahlswede, *Office Mgr*
Kenneth Gillen, *Internal Med*
EMP: 44 **EST:** 2001
SALES (est): 5.1MM *Privately Held*
WEB: www.paradisemedicalgroup.com
SIC: 8011 General & family practice, physician/surgeon

(P-15584)
PASSPORT HEALTH LLC
Also Called: Passport Hlth Plsant Hl Trvl C
3478 Buskirk Ave Ste 1000, Pleasant Hill (94523-4378)
PHONE..................925 239-8794
Terri Cluff, *Director*
EMP: 35
SALES (corp-wide): 913.5MM *Privately Held*
WEB: www.passporthealthglobal.com
SIC: 8011 Clinic, operated by physicians
HQ: Passport Health, Llc
8324 E Hartford Dr # 200
Scottsdale AZ 85255
480 345-6800

(P-15585)
PATEL PLLIAM HBLI A PROF MED C
Also Called: Tracy Occupational Medical Ctr
644 W 12th St, Tracy (95376-3437)
PHONE..................209 832-8984
Jagdish Patel, *President*
Dr Ian Pulliam, *Vice Pres*
EMP: 38 **EST:** 1991
SALES (est): 2.9MM *Privately Held*
WEB: www.pph644.com
SIC: 8011 General & family practice, physician/surgeon; occupational & industrial specialist, physician/surgeon

(P-15586)
PATHGROUP SAN FRANCISCO LLC (HQ)
Also Called: Marin Medical Laboratories
1615 Hill Rd Ste B, Novato (94947-4338)
PHONE..................415 898-7649
Paul Wasserstein, *Partner*
EMP: 43 **EST:** 1981
SQ FT: 2,000
SALES (est): 9.8MM
SALES (corp-wide): 229.1MM *Privately Held*
WEB: www.pathgroup.com
SIC: 8011 8071 Pathologist; pathological laboratory
PA: Associated Pathologists, Llc
5301 Virginia Way Ste 300
Brentwood TN 37027
615 221-4455

(P-15587)
PAUL D ABRAMSON MD INC (PA) ◆
Also Called: My Doctor Medical Group
450 Sutter St Rm 840, San Francisco (94108-3915)
PHONE..................415 963-4431
Paul Abramson, *CEO*
Justin Davis, *Physician Asst*
Jennifer Banta, *Director*
EMP: 38 **EST:** 2021
SALES (est): 5.6MM *Privately Held*
WEB: www.mydoctorsf.com
SIC: 8011 General & family practice, physician/surgeon

(P-15588)
PEACH TREE HEALTHCARE
5730 Packard Ave Ste 500, Marysville (95901-7119)
PHONE..................530 749-3242
Thomas Walther, *President*
Maria Abordo, *Pediatrics*
Joe Lobaccaro, *Nurse Practr*
Sheila Petree, *Manager*
EMP: 97 **EST:** 2000
SALES (est): 28.2MM *Privately Held*
WEB: www.pickpeach.org
SIC: 8011 Clinic, operated by physicians

(P-15589)
PEACHWOOD MED GROUP CLOVIS INC
275 W Herndon Ave, Clovis (93612-0204)
PHONE..................559 324-6200
Lee Copeland MD, *President*
Jeffrey Hubbard, *Vice Pres*
Sue Marino, *Administration*
Jennifer Nay, *Physician Asst*
Jennifer K Nay, *Med Doctor*
EMP: 70 **EST:** 1995
SQ FT: 33,595
SALES (est): 23MM *Privately Held*
WEB: www.peachwoodmedicalgroup.com
SIC: 8011 General & family practice, physician/surgeon

(P-15590)
PENINSULA HLTHCARE CNNCTION IN (PA)
33 Encina Ave Ste 103, Palo Alto (94301-2343)
PHONE..................650 853-0321
Eileen Richardson, *CEO*
Lien Huynh, *Accountant*
Teresa Garcia, *Assistant*
EMP: 50 **EST:** 2010

PRODUCTS & SERVICES SECTION
8011 - Offices & Clinics Of Doctors Of Medicine County (P-15611)

SALES (est): 3.4MM Privately Held
WEB: www.peninsulahcc.org
SIC: 8011 Offices & clinics of medical doctors

(P-15591)
PERMANENTE MEDICAL GROUP INC
395 Hickey Blvd Fl 2, Daly City (94015-2770)
PHONE.................650 301-5800
Jessica Freilich, *Admin Asst*
Jennifer Normoyle, *Obstetrician*
John Skerry, *Ophthalmology*
Jaime Ocampo MD, *Med Doctor*
Dennis Tom, *Med Doctor*
EMP: 628
SALES (corp-wide): 30.5B Privately Held
WEB: www.permanente.org
SIC: 8011 Medical centers
HQ: The Permanente Medical Group Inc
    1950 Franklin St Fl 18th
    Oakland CA 94612
    866 858-2226

(P-15592)
PERMANENTE MEDICAL GROUP INC
1617 Broadway St, Vallejo (94590-2406)
PHONE.................707 765-3930
Robin E Bjorger, *Branch Mgr*
Christian Lopez Reyes, *Internal Med*
Matthew Smith, *Physician Asst*
Michael Cheng, *Med Doctor*
Gray Williams, *Director*
EMP: 628
SALES (corp-wide): 30.5B Privately Held
WEB: www.permanente.org
SIC: 8011 Medical centers
HQ: The Permanente Medical Group Inc
    1950 Franklin St Fl 18th
    Oakland CA 94612
    866 858-2226

(P-15593)
PERMANENTE MEDICAL GROUP INC
1800 Harrison St Fl 7th, Oakland (94612-3467)
PHONE.................510 625-6262
Connie Wilson, *Branch Mgr*
Preeti Sharma, *Internal Med*
Johanna Reneke, *Med Doctor*
Irene Lee, *Manager*
Glenda Wilkins, *Manager*
EMP: 628
SALES (corp-wide): 30.5B Privately Held
WEB: www.permanente.org
SIC: 8011 Medical centers
HQ: The Permanente Medical Group Inc
    1950 Franklin St Fl 18th
    Oakland CA 94612
    866 858-2226

(P-15594)
PERMANENTE MEDICAL GROUP INC
7300 N Fresno St, Fresno (93720-2941)
PHONE.................559 448-4500
Irene A Heetebry, *Principal*
Ken Ellzey, *Med Doctor*
EMP: 628
SALES (corp-wide): 30.5B Privately Held
WEB: www.permanente.org
SIC: 8011 Medical centers
HQ: The Permanente Medical Group Inc
    1950 Franklin St Fl 18th
    Oakland CA 94612
    866 858-2226

(P-15595)
PERMANENTE MEDICAL GROUP INC
6600 Bruceville Rd, Sacramento (95823-4671)
PHONE.................916 688-2055
Kevin L Smith, *Branch Mgr*
Russell Vaughan, *Med Doctor*
EMP: 628
SALES (corp-wide): 30.5B Privately Held
WEB: www.permanente.org
SIC: 8011 Gynecologist

(P-15596)
PERMANENTE MEDICAL GROUP INC
901 El Camino Real, San Bruno (94066-3009)
PHONE.................650 742-2100
Cheryl Halcovich, *Manager*
EMP: 628
SALES (corp-wide): 30.5B Privately Held
WEB: www.permanente.org
SIC: 8011 Medical centers
HQ: The Permanente Medical Group Inc
    1950 Franklin St Fl 18th
    Oakland CA 94612
    866 858-2226

(P-15597)
PERMANENTE MEDICAL GROUP INC
3558 Round Barn Blvd, Santa Rosa (95403-1780)
PHONE.................707 393-4000
Pat Henson, *Principal*
Jean Lim, *Dermatology*
Christine Kaiser, *Internal Med*
Cheryl L McBride, *Emerg Med Spec*
EMP: 628
SALES (corp-wide): 30.5B Privately Held
WEB: www.permanente.org
SIC: 8011 Medical centers
HQ: The Permanente Medical Group Inc
    1950 Franklin St Fl 18th
    Oakland CA 94612
    866 858-2226

(P-15598)
PERMANENTE MEDICAL GROUP INC
Also Called: Labratory
2425 Geary Blvd, San Francisco (94115-3358)
PHONE.................415 833-2000
Harry Chima, *Manager*
Christina Armatas, *Med Doctor*
Kristina Casadei, *Med Doctor*
EMP: 628
SALES (corp-wide): 30.5B Privately Held
WEB: www.permanente.org
SIC: 8011 Medical centers
HQ: The Permanente Medical Group Inc
    1950 Franklin St Fl 18th
    Oakland CA 94612
    866 858-2226

(P-15599)
PERMANENTE MEDICAL GROUP INC
275 Hospital Pkwy Ste 470, San Jose (95119-1138)
PHONE.................408 972-6883
Maurice Alfaro, *Director*
EMP: 628
SALES (corp-wide): 30.5B Privately Held
WEB: www.permanente.org
SIC: 8011 Medical centers
HQ: The Permanente Medical Group Inc
    1950 Franklin St Fl 18th
    Oakland CA 94612
    866 858-2226

(P-15600)
PERMANENTE MEDICAL GROUP INC
200 Muir Rd, Martinez (94553-4614)
PHONE.................925 372-1000
Babak Rashidi, *Gnrl Med Prac*
EMP: 628
SALES (corp-wide): 30.5B Privately Held
WEB: www.permanente.org
SIC: 8011 Medical centers
HQ: The Permanente Medical Group Inc
    1950 Franklin St Fl 18th
    Oakland CA 94612
    866 858-2226

(P-15601)
PERMANENTE MEDICAL GROUP INC
3779 Piedmont Ave, Oakland (94611-5347)
PHONE.................510 752-1000
Ellen P Brennan, *Branch Mgr*
Anastasia B Cua, *Med Doctor*
EMP: 628
SALES (corp-wide): 30.5B Privately Held
WEB: www.permanente.org
SIC: 8011 Medical centers
HQ: The Permanente Medical Group Inc
    1950 Franklin St Fl 18th
    Oakland CA 94612
    866 858-2226

(P-15602)
PERMANENTE MEDICAL GROUP INC
39400 Paseo Padre Pkwy, Fremont (94538-2310)
PHONE.................510 248-3000
EMP: 628
SALES (corp-wide): 30.5B Privately Held
WEB: www.permanente.org
SIC: 8011 Medical centers
HQ: The Permanente Medical Group Inc
    1950 Franklin St Fl 18th
    Oakland CA 94612
    866 858-2226

(P-15603)
PERMANENTE MEDICAL GROUP INC
235 W Macarthur Blvd, Oakland (94611-5641)
PHONE.................510 752-1190
Marta Perl, *Branch Mgr*
Trin To, *Administration*
Shanti Kondepudi, *Business Anlyst*
EMP: 628
SALES (corp-wide): 30.5B Privately Held
WEB: www.permanente.org
SIC: 8011 Medical centers
HQ: The Permanente Medical Group Inc
    1950 Franklin St Fl 18th
    Oakland CA 94612
    866 858-2226

(P-15604)
PERMANENTE MEDICAL GROUP INC
770 E Calaveras Blvd, Milpitas (95035-5491)
PHONE.................408 945-2900
Bindu Israni, *Branch Mgr*
EMP: 628
SALES (corp-wide): 30.5B Privately Held
WEB: www.permanente.org
SIC: 8011 Medical centers
HQ: The Permanente Medical Group Inc
    1950 Franklin St Fl 18th
    Oakland CA 94612
    866 858-2226

(P-15605)
PERMANENTE MEDICAL GROUP INC
4501 Sand Creek Rd, Antioch (94531-8687)
PHONE.................925 813-6149
Kim Daily, *Branch Mgr*
Jared Cozen, *Psychologist*
Christine Lim, *Psychiatry*
EMP: 628
SALES (corp-wide): 30.5B Privately Held
WEB: www.permanente.org
SIC: 8011 Medical centers
HQ: The Permanente Medical Group Inc
    1950 Franklin St Fl 18th
    Oakland CA 94612
    866 858-2226

(P-15606)
PERMANENTE MEDICAL GROUP INC
1150 Veterans Blvd, Redwood City (94063-2037)
PHONE.................650 299-2000
Arlene McCarthy, *Principal*
Anna Phothisane, *Administration*
Tony Ou, *Analyst*
Malika N Kheraj, *Infectious Dis*
David Bradley, *Surgeon*
EMP: 628
SALES (corp-wide): 30.5B Privately Held
WEB: www.permanente.org
SIC: 8011 Medical centers

(P-15607)
PERMANENTE MEDICAL GROUP INC
910 Marshall St, Redwood City (94063-2033)
PHONE.................650 299-2015
Christina Apostolakos, *Director*
Dennis Hou, *Obstetrician*
Kristine Hendrickson, *Med Doctor*
Allison Glubiak, *Nurse*
Sylvia Nunez, *Manager*
EMP: 628
SALES (corp-wide): 30.5B Privately Held
WEB: www.permanente.org
SIC: 8011 Medical centers
HQ: The Permanente Medical Group Inc
    1950 Franklin St Fl 18th
    Oakland CA 94612
    866 858-2226

(P-15608)
PERMANENTE MEDICAL GROUP INC
914 Marina Way S, Richmond (94804-3739)
PHONE.................510 231-5406
C J Bhalla, *Vice Pres*
Tasha Morales, *Director*
EMP: 628
SALES (corp-wide): 30.5B Privately Held
WEB: www.permanente.org
SIC: 8011 Medical centers
HQ: The Permanente Medical Group Inc
    1950 Franklin St Fl 18th
    Oakland CA 94612
    866 858-2226

(P-15609)
PERMANENTE MEDICAL GROUP INC
3184 Arden Way, Sacramento (95825-3701)
PHONE.................916 486-5686
Greg Chappel, *Branch Mgr*
EMP: 628
SALES (corp-wide): 30.5B Privately Held
WEB: www.permanente.org
SIC: 8011 Medical centers
HQ: The Permanente Medical Group Inc
    1950 Franklin St Fl 18th
    Oakland CA 94612
    866 858-2226

(P-15610)
PERMANENTE MEDICAL GROUP INC
2500 Merced St, San Leandro (94577-4201)
PHONE.................510 454-1000
Shurea Wilson, *Anesthesiology*
Harry J Duh, *Pediatrics*
Aruna Koduri, *Pediatrics*
Elizabeth J Rosen, *Otolaryngology*
Shabnam Kapur, *Emerg Med Spec*
EMP: 628
SALES (corp-wide): 30.5B Privately Held
WEB: www.permanente.org
SIC: 8011 Medical centers
HQ: The Permanente Medical Group Inc
    1950 Franklin St Fl 18th
    Oakland CA 94612
    866 858-2226

(P-15611)
PERMANENTE MEDICAL GROUP INC
99 Montecillo Rd, San Rafael (94903-3308)
PHONE.................415 444-2000
Elizaveta Shostakovich, *Med Doctor*
EMP: 628
SALES (corp-wide): 30.5B Privately Held
WEB: www.permanente.org
SIC: 8011 Medical centers
HQ: The Permanente Medical Group Inc
    1950 Franklin St Fl 18th
    Oakland CA 94612
    866 858-2226

8011 - Offices & Clinics Of Doctors Of Medicine County (P-15612)

(P-15612)
PERMANENTE MEDICAL GROUP INC
320 Lennon Ln, Walnut Creek (94598-2419)
PHONE..................925 906-2000
David Peterson, *IT/INT Sup*
Lynn Arsenault, *Med Doctor*
Thomas Connolly, *Med Doctor*
Rochelle Benning, *Director*
EMP: 628
SALES (corp-wide): 30.5B **Privately Held**
WEB: www.permanente.org
SIC: 8011 Medical centers
HQ: The Permanente Medical Group Inc
1950 Franklin St Fl 18th
Oakland CA 94612
866 858-2226

(P-15613)
PERMANENTE MEDICAL GROUP INC
100 Rowland Way Ste 125, Novato (94945-5012)
PHONE..................415 209-2444
Kim Ogieglo, *Administration*
EMP: 628
SALES (corp-wide): 30.5B **Privately Held**
WEB: www.permanente.org
SIC: 8011 Medical centers
HQ: The Permanente Medical Group Inc
1950 Franklin St Fl 18th
Oakland CA 94612
866 858-2226

(P-15614)
PERMANENTE MEDICAL GROUP INC
97 San Marin Dr, Novato (94945-1100)
PHONE..................415 899-7400
Willa Jefferson-Stokes, *Manager*
Shawn M Donald, *Internal Med*
EMP: 628
SALES (corp-wide): 30.5B **Privately Held**
WEB: www.permanente.org
SIC: 8011 Internal medicine practitioners
HQ: The Permanente Medical Group Inc
1950 Franklin St Fl 18th
Oakland CA 94612
866 858-2226

(P-15615)
PERMANENTE MEDICAL GROUP INC
1600 Eureka Rd, Roseville (95661-3027)
PHONE..................916 784-4000
Craig Green MD, *Director*
EMP: 628
SALES (corp-wide): 30.5B **Privately Held**
WEB: www.permanente.org
SIC: 8011 Medical centers
HQ: The Permanente Medical Group Inc
1950 Franklin St Fl 18th
Oakland CA 94612
866 858-2226

(P-15616)
PERMANENTE MEDICAL GROUP INC
7373 West Ln, Stockton (95210-3377)
PHONE..................209 476-3737
Michael Coleman, *Principal*
Suhail Khan, *Gnrl Med Prac*
EMP: 628
SALES (corp-wide): 30.5B **Privately Held**
WEB: www.permanente.org
SIC: 8011 Medical centers
HQ: The Permanente Medical Group Inc
1950 Franklin St Fl 18th
Oakland CA 94612
866 858-2226

(P-15617)
PERMANENTE MEDICAL GROUP INC
2238 Geary Blvd, San Francisco (94115-3416)
PHONE..................415 833-2000
Philip R Madvig MD Physn, *Principal*
Gregory V Mandrussow, *Emerg Med Spec*
Leah Klinger, *Med Doctor*
Nellya Vayngortin, *Med Doctor*
Dee Marie Munoz, *Pharmacist*
EMP: 628
SALES (corp-wide): 30.5B **Privately Held**
WEB: www.permanente.org
SIC: 8011 Medical centers
HQ: The Permanente Medical Group Inc
1950 Franklin St Fl 18th
Oakland CA 94612
866 858-2226

(P-15618)
PERMANENTE MEDICAL GROUP INC
1750 2nd St, Berkeley (94710-1705)
PHONE..................510 559-5338
Dianne Easterwood, *General Mgr*
EMP: 628
SALES (corp-wide): 30.5B **Privately Held**
WEB: www.permanente.org
SIC: 8011 Medical centers
HQ: The Permanente Medical Group Inc
1950 Franklin St Fl 18th
Oakland CA 94612
866 858-2226

(P-15619)
PERMANENTE MEDICAL GROUP INC
3900 Lakeville Hwy, Petaluma (94954-5698)
PHONE..................707 765-3900
Willa Jefferson-Stokes, *Manager*
Laurie Dibble, *Obstetrician*
Roberto Z Gonzalez, *Internal Med*
Maurice Kinsolving, *Med Doctor*
EMP: 628
SALES (corp-wide): 30.5B **Privately Held**
WEB: www.permanente.org
SIC: 8011 Clinic, operated by physicians
HQ: The Permanente Medical Group Inc
1950 Franklin St Fl 18th
Oakland CA 94612
866 858-2226

(P-15620)
PERMANENTE MEDICAL GROUP INC
1305 Tommydon St, Stockton (95210-3364)
PHONE..................209 476-2000
Jack Gillimand, *Branch Mgr*
Lin Jiang, *Med Doctor*
EMP: 628
SALES (corp-wide): 30.5B **Privately Held**
WEB: www.permanente.org
SIC: 8011 Medical centers
HQ: The Permanente Medical Group Inc
1950 Franklin St Fl 18th
Oakland CA 94612
866 858-2226

(P-15621)
PERMANENTE MEDICAL GROUP INC
3000 Las Positas Rd, Livermore (94551-9627)
PHONE..................925 243-2600
Stan Combs, *Manager*
EMP: 628
SALES (corp-wide): 30.5B **Privately Held**
WEB: www.permanente.org
SIC: 8011 Medical centers
HQ: The Permanente Medical Group Inc
1950 Franklin St Fl 18th
Oakland CA 94612
866 858-2226

(P-15622)
PERMANENTE MEDICAL GROUP INC
10725 International Dr, Rancho Cordova (95670-7967)
PHONE..................916 631-3000
Donald Forrester, *Branch Mgr*
EMP: 628
SALES (corp-wide): 30.5B **Privately Held**
WEB: www.permanente.org
SIC: 8011 Clinic, operated by physicians
HQ: The Permanente Medical Group Inc
1950 Franklin St Fl 18th
Oakland CA 94612
866 858-2226

(P-15623)
PERMANENTE MEDICAL GROUP INC
395 Hickey Blvd Fl 1, Daly City (94015-2770)
PHONE..................650 301-5860
Jennifer Normoyle, *Branch Mgr*
Betty Lee, *Obstetrician*
Yvonne Ong, *Pediatrics*
Laura Prager, *Pediatrics*
Bertha Saucedo, *Pediatrics*
EMP: 628
SALES (corp-wide): 30.5B **Privately Held**
WEB: www.permanente.org
SIC: 8011 Medical centers
HQ: The Permanente Medical Group Inc
1950 Franklin St Fl 18th
Oakland CA 94612
866 858-2226

(P-15624)
PERMANENTE MEDICAL GROUP INC
1000 Franklin Pkwy, San Mateo (94403-1922)
PHONE..................650 358-7000
Diane Oliver, *Med Doctor*
EMP: 628
SALES (corp-wide): 30.5B **Privately Held**
WEB: www.permanente.org
SIC: 8011 Medical centers
HQ: The Permanente Medical Group Inc
1950 Franklin St Fl 18th
Oakland CA 94612
866 858-2226

(P-15625)
PERMANENTE MEDICAL GROUP INC
Also Called: Kaiser Prmnnte Modesto Med Ctr
4601 Dale Rd, Modesto (95356-9718)
PHONE..................209 735-5000
Jennifer A Beard, *Principal*
Jennifer Beard, *Officer*
Ernesto Jacobo, *IT/INT Sup*
Naresh A Patel, *Hematology*
Megumi Tomita, *Internal Med*
EMP: 628
SALES (corp-wide): 30.5B **Privately Held**
WEB: www.permanente.org
SIC: 8011 Offices & clinics of medical doctors
HQ: The Permanente Medical Group Inc
1950 Franklin St Fl 18th
Oakland CA 94612
866 858-2226

(P-15626)
PETALUMA HEALTH CENTER INC
1179 N Mcdowell Blvd A, Petaluma (94954-1171)
PHONE..................707 559-7500
Kathryn Powell, *CEO*
Daymon Doss, *COO*
Jane Read, *COO*
Brian Burns, *CFO*
Carlin CHI, *Associate Dir*
EMP: 325 EST: 1999
SALES (est): 43.4MM **Privately Held**
WEB: www.phealthcenter.atsondemand.com
SIC: 8011 Clinic, operated by physicians

(P-15627)
PETER CASTILLO MD PA
Also Called: Kaiser Permanente Santa Clara
700 Lawrence Expy, Santa Clara (95051-5173)
PHONE..................408 236-6400
Peter Castillo, *Owner*
Preeti Shah, *Partner*
Terri Pillow-Noriega, *Officer*
Kurt Lieber, *Exec Dir*
Linda Frankenberger, *Managing Dir*
EMP: 130 EST: 2007
SALES (est): 12.2MM **Privately Held**
SIC: 8011 General & family practice, physician/surgeon

(P-15628)
PETS CHOICE INC
8732 La Riviera Dr, Sacramento (95826-1808)
PHONE..................916 229-9587
Karen Pazzi, *Branch Mgr*
EMP: 50
SALES (corp-wide): 42.8B **Privately Held**
SIC: 8011 Medical centers
HQ: Pet's Choice, Inc
305 108th Ave Ne Ste 102
Bellevue WA 98004

(P-15629)
PIT RIVER TRIBAL COUNCIL
Also Called: Pit River Health Services
36977 Park Ave, Burney (96013-4067)
PHONE..................530 335-3651
Keith Ratcliff, *Manager*
EMP: 52
SALES (corp-wide): 12.2MM **Privately Held**
WEB: www.pitrivertribe.org
SIC: 8011 8021 Offices & clinics of medical doctors; offices & clinics of dentists
PA: Pit River Tribal Council
37960 Park Ave
Burney CA 96013
530 335-5487

(P-15630)
PLACER DRMTLOGY SKIN CARE CTR (PA)
9285 Sierra College Blvd, Roseville (95661-5919)
PHONE..................916 784-3376
Artur Z Henke, *President*
EMP: 48 EST: 2007
SALES (est): 3.7MM **Privately Held**
WEB: www.placerdermatology.com
SIC: 8011 Dermatologist

(P-15631)
PLUSHCARE INC
650 5th St Ste 405, San Francisco (94107-1541)
PHONE..................415 231-5333
Ryan McQuaid, *Principal*
James Wantuck, *Principal*
EMP: 100 EST: 2013
SALES (est): 8.5MM **Publicly Held**
WEB: www.accolade.com
SIC: 8011 Offices & clinics of medical doctors
PA: Accolade, Inc.
1201 3rd Ave Ste 1700
Seattle WA 98101

(P-15632)
PRECISION MEDICAL PRODUCTS INC
2217 Plaza Dr, Rocklin (95765-4421)
PHONE..................573 474-9302
EMP: 99
SALES (est): 835K **Privately Held**
SIC: 8011 Medical Doctor's Office

(P-15633)
PREDICINE INC
3555 Arden Rd, Hayward (94545-3922)
PHONE..................650 300-2188
Shidong Jia, *CEO*
Leslie Leiva, *Research*
EMP: 50 EST: 2015
SALES (est): 10.5MM **Privately Held**
WEB: www.predicine.com
SIC: 8011 Health maintenance organization

(P-15634)
PREMIER EYECARE SAN FRANCISCO
Also Called: Andrew F Calman, Md, PHD
2480 Mission St Ste 212, San Francisco (94110-2480)
PHONE..................415 648-3600
Andrew Calman, *Owner*
Jeanette Montesclaros, *Technician*
Elizabeth Peckham, *Neurology*
Terry Peery, *Neurology*
Robert F Stegura, *Med Doctor*
EMP: 39 EST: 1993
SQ FT: 3,200

PRODUCTS & SERVICES SECTION

8011 - Offices & Clinics Of Doctors Of Medicine County (P-15658)

SALES (est): 4.7MM **Privately Held**
WEB: www.premier-eyecare.com
SIC: **8011** Ophthalmologist

(P-15635)
PREMIER SURGERY CENTER LP
2222 East St Ste 200, Concord (94520-2065)
PHONE 925 691-5000
Kevin Degnan, *General Ptnr*
Victoria Hernandez-Marti, *Surgeon*
EMP: 43 EST: 2004
SALES (est): 6.4MM **Privately Held**
WEB: www.premiersurgery.us
SIC: **8011** Surgeon

(P-15636)
QUALIUM CORP (PA)
Also Called: Bay Sleep Clinic
14981 National Ave Ste 1, Los Gatos (95032-2600)
PHONE 408 402-3697
Kin M Yuen, *Principal*
Anooshiravan Mostowfipour, *Principal*
Tara Nader, *Principal*
EMP: 81 EST: 2008
SALES (est): 9.8MM **Privately Held**
WEB: www.baysleepclinic.com
SIC: **8011** Specialized medical practitioners, except internal

(P-15637)
QUANTUM HLTHCARE MED ASSOC INC (PA)
Also Called: Emergency Physicians
5000 Hopyard Rd Ste 100, Pleasanton (94588-3146)
P.O. Box 788 (94566-0078)
PHONE 925 924-1600
Richard Cravolth, *President*
EMP: 35 EST: 1965
SQ FT: 14,000
SALES (est): 9.2MM **Privately Held**
SIC: **8011** Offices & clinics of medical doctors

(P-15638)
R SCOTT FOSTER MD
Also Called: Central Valley Eye
36 W Yokuts Ave Ste 1, Stockton (95207-5713)
PHONE 209 952-3700
R S Foster MD, *Owner*
Stevens Y Kim, *CFO*
Foster R Scott, *Principal*
Carol Ritchie, *Office Mgr*
EMP: 48 EST: 1974
SALES (est): 3.9MM **Privately Held**
WEB: www.cvemg.com
SIC: **8011** **8042** Ophthalmologist; physicians' office, including specialists; offices & clinics of optometrists

(P-15639)
REDDING DRMTLOGY MED GROUP INC
2107 Airpark Dr, Redding (96001-2433)
PHONE 530 241-1111
Craig A Kraffert MD, *President*
Craig Kraffert, *Dermatology*
EMP: 49 EST: 1989
SALES (est): 8.2MM **Privately Held**
WEB: www.reddingderm.com
SIC: **8011** Dermatologist

(P-15640)
REDDING PATHOLOGISTS LAB (PA)
1725 Gold St, Redding (96001-1820)
PHONE 530 225-8000
Richard Severance MD, *Partner*
Tikoes Blankenberg MD, *Partner*
Richard O Boyd MD, *Partner*
John P Greaves Jr, *Partner*
William Reuss MD, *Partner*
EMP: 115 EST: 1954
SQ FT: 8,000
SALES (est): 10.4MM **Privately Held**
WEB: www.shastapathologyassociates.com
SIC: **8011** **8071** Pathologist; medical laboratories

(P-15641)
REDWOOD COAST MEDICAL SVCS INC (PA)
46900 Ocean Dr, Gualala (95445)
P.O. Box 1100 (95445-1100)
PHONE 707 884-1721
Dianne Agee, *Director*
Thomas A Bertolli, *Exec Dir*
Alysia Olson,
Casey Swingle, *Manager*
Harm Wilkinson, *Coordinator*
EMP: 43 EST: 1977
SQ FT: 5,000
SALES: 9.3MM **Privately Held**
WEB: www.rcms-healthcare.org
SIC: **8011** Clinic, operated by physicians

(P-15642)
REDWOOD FMLY DRMTLOGY MED ASSO
2725 Mendocino Ave, Santa Rosa (95403-2805)
PHONE 707 545-4537
Jeff Sugarman, *Principal*
Dr Judith Hong, *Principal*
Dr Ligaya Park, *Principal*
Dralbert Peng, *Principal*
Heather N Lowe, *Physician Asst*
EMP: 45 EST: 2006
SQ FT: 8,204
SALES (est): 11.9MM **Privately Held**
WEB: www.redwoodfamilydermatology.com
SIC: **8011** Dermatologist

(P-15643)
REDWOOD ORTHPDIC SURGERY ASSOC
208 Concourse Blvd Ste 1, Santa Rosa (95403-8210)
PHONE 707 544-3400
Jeffrey Tompkins, *President*
Kent Yinger, *Surgeon*
Samantha Gentile, *Assistant*
EMP: 47 EST: 1975
SALES (est): 8.4MM **Privately Held**
WEB: www.redwoodorthopaedic.com
SIC: **8011** Orthopedic physician

(P-15644)
REDWOOD REGIONAL HEMATOLOGY
3555 Round Barn Cir 100, Santa Rosa (95403-1757)
PHONE 707 528-1050
Leroy Wayne Keiser, *Partner*
EMP: 50 EST: 1990
SALES (est): 4.8MM **Privately Held**
WEB: www.psjhmedgroups.org
SIC: **8011** Hematologist; oncologist

(P-15645)
REDWOOD REGIONAL MEDICAL GROUP
1165 S Dora St Bldg H, Ukiah (95482-8325)
PHONE 707 463-3636
Jay Joseph, *Branch Mgr*
EMP: 41
SALES (corp-wide): 11.1MM **Privately Held**
SIC: **8011** General & family practice, physician/surgeon
PA: Redwood Regional Medical Group Drug Company, Llc
990 Sonoma Ave Ste 15
Santa Rosa CA 95404
707 525-4080

(P-15646)
REDWOOD RGNAL MED GROUP DRG LL
Also Called: Mirda, Daniel P MD
1100 Trancas St Ste 256, NAPA (94558-2921)
PHONE 707 253-7161
Paul J Dugan, *Director*
EMP: 41
SALES (corp-wide): 11.1MM **Privately Held**
SIC: **8011** Hematologist
PA: Redwood Regional Medical Group Drug Company, Llc
990 Sonoma Ave Ste 15
Santa Rosa CA 95404
707 525-4080

(P-15647)
REDWOODS RURAL HEALTH CTR INC
101 Westcoast Rd, Redway (95560)
P.O. Box 769 (95560-0769)
PHONE 707 923-2783
Tina Tvedt, *Exec Dir*
Taylor Barb, *Opers Staff*
Mandy Battles, *Physician Asst*
EMP: 38 EST: 1976
SQ FT: 6,000
SALES (est): 6.2MM **Privately Held**
WEB: www.rrhc.org
SIC: **8011** **8093** **8021** Primary care medical clinic; mental health clinic, outpatient; dental clinics & offices

(P-15648)
REGIONAL CARDIOLOGY ASSOCIATE (PA)
8120 Timberlake Way # 108, Sacramento (95823-5412)
PHONE 916 564-3040
Michael Changa, *Partner*
John Chin, *Partner*
Nick Magitich, *Partner*
Marijo Classen, *Supervisor*
EMP: 38 EST: 1986
SALES (est): 12.6MM **Privately Held**
SIC: **8011** Cardiologist & cardio-vascular specialist

(P-15649)
REPRODUCTIVE SCIENCE CENTER
Also Called: Reproductive Science Ctr Bay
100 Park Pl Ste 200, San Ramon (94583-4416)
PHONE 925 867-1800
Susan Willman, *CEO*
Donald I Galen, *Vice Pres*
Louis Weckstein, *Vice Pres*
Sheldon Josephs, *Exec Dir*
Larissa Latorre, *Admin Asst*
EMP: 75 EST: 1985
SALES (est): 17.1MM **Privately Held**
WEB: www.rscbayarea.com
SIC: **8011** Physicians' office, including specialists

(P-15650)
RETINA-VITREOUS ASSOC INC
Also Called: Northern Cal Rtina Vtrous Asso
2512 Samaritan Ct Ste A, San Jose (95124-4002)
PHONE 408 402-3239
Sterling J Haidt MD, *President*
Sharon Kutis, *Officer*
Sharon De Paz, *Research*
Christina Herlitz, *Ophthalmic Tech*
EMP: 38 EST: 1982
SALES (est): 5.3MM **Privately Held**
WEB: www.ncrva.com
SIC: **8011** Surgeon; ophthalmologist

(P-15651)
RETINAL CONSULTANTS INC (PA)
3939 J St Ste 106, Sacramento (95819-3631)
PHONE 916 454-4861
Neil E Kelly MD, *President*
Arun C Patel, *Shareholder*
Robert T Wendel, *Shareholder*
James W Wells Jr, *Vice Pres*
Thomas C Salzano MD, *Admin Sec*
EMP: 65 EST: 1975
SALES (est): 14.5MM **Privately Held**
WEB: www.retinalmd.com
SIC: **8011** Ophthalmologist

(P-15652)
RICHARD C SHEBELUT INC
6215 N Fresno St Ste 108, Fresno (93710-5267)
PHONE 559 439-1835
Richard Shebelut, *President*
EMP: 36 EST: 1984

SALES (est): 1MM **Privately Held**
SIC: **8011** Gynecologist

(P-15653)
ROUND VLY INDIAN HLTH CTR INC
Hwy 162 Biggar Ln, Covelo (95428)
P.O. Box 247 (95428-0247)
PHONE 707 983-6182
James Russ, *Exec Dir*
Ramona Waldman, *Nurse*
Kianna Zielesh, *Director*
EMP: 81 EST: 1968
SALES (est): 11.4MM **Privately Held**
WEB: www.roundvalleyindianhealthcenter.com
SIC: **8011** **8021** Clinic, operated by physicians; dental clinic

(P-15654)
SACRAMENTO EAR NOSE & THROAT (PA)
1111 Expo Blvd Bldg 700, Sacramento (95815-4314)
PHONE 916 736-3399
Ernest E Johnson MD, *President*
Kevin Mc Kennan MD, *Treasurer*
Richard G Areen MD, *Admin Sec*
Richard Areen, *Otolaryngology*
Kristin Bennett, *Otolaryngology*
EMP: 55 EST: 1954
SQ FT: 12,000
SALES (est): 9.7MM **Privately Held**
WEB: www.sacent.com
SIC: **8011** Ears, nose & throat specialist: physician/surgeon

(P-15655)
SACRAMENTO HEART AND CARDIOVAS (PA)
500 University Ave # 100, Sacramento (95825-6527)
PHONE 916 830-2000
Phillip Bach, *Partner*
Drraye L Bellinger, *Partner*
Javed Nasir, *Internal Med*
Kyle Michaelis, *Director*
EMP: 41 EST: 1976
SQ FT: 45,000
SALES (est): 10.4MM **Privately Held**
WEB: www.sacheart.com
SIC: **8011** Cardiologist & cardio-vascular specialist

(P-15656)
SACRAMNTO GSTRNTRLOGY MED GROU
3941 J St Ste 450, Sacramento (95819-3633)
P.O. Box 19335 (95819-0335)
PHONE 916 454-0655
Ralph E Koldinger MD, *President*
Tommy J Poirier MD, *Treasurer*
David Arenson MD, *Vice Pres*
Gautam Gandhi MD, *Vice Pres*
Jefferey Goldstein MD, *Admin Sec*
EMP: 75 EST: 1972
SALES (est): 5.1MM **Privately Held**
SIC: **8011** Gastronomist; physicians' office, including specialists

(P-15657)
SACRAMNTO NTIV AMERCN HLTH CTR
2020 J St, Sacramento (95811-3120)
PHONE 916 341-0575
Britta Guerrero, *Exec Dir*
Ricardo Torres, *Ch of Bd*
Vanessa Cuevas-Romero, *Officer*
Britta Guerrero, *Exec Dir*
Mark Inghram, *Info Tech Mgr*
EMP: 119 EST: 2005
SQ FT: 39,573
SALES: 20.1MM **Privately Held**
WEB: www.snahc.org
SIC: **8011** Clinic, operated by physicians

(P-15658)
SACRAMNTO PLSTIC RCNSTRCTIVE S
Also Called: Plastic Surgery Center, The
95 Scripps Dr, Sacramento (95825-6320)
PHONE 916 929-1833
Wayne I Yamahata, *President*
Dr Donald R Jasper, *Vice Pres*

8011 - Offices & Clinics Of Doctors Of Medicine County (P-15659)

Dr Debra Johnson, *Vice Pres*
Wayne Yamahata, *Plastic Surgeon*
EMP: 51 **EST:** 1968
SQ FT: 12,100
SALES (est): 6.3MM **Privately Held**
WEB: www.sacplasticsurgery.com
SIC: 8011 Plastic surgeon

(P-15659)
SALUD PARA LA GENTE
Also Called: Salud Para La Gnte Hlth Clinic
195 Aviation Way Ste 200, Watsonville (95076-2059)
PHONE 831 728-0222
Dori Rose Inda, *CEO*
Tony Balistreri, *CFO*
Maritza Lara, *Program Mgr*
Obdulia Landaverry, *Finance Asst*
Guillermina Porraz, *Human Res Dir*
EMP: 125 **EST:** 1980
SALES (est): 40.6MM **Privately Held**
WEB: www.splg.org
SIC: 8011 Clinic, operated by physicians

(P-15660)
SAMARITAN FAMILY PRACTICE
15425 Los Gatos Blvd # 120, Los Gatos (95032-2577)
PHONE 408 358-1911
Norman Woods, *Director*
EMP: 43 **EST:** 1968
SALES (est): 3.8MM **Privately Held**
SIC: 8011 General & family practice, physician/surgeon

(P-15661)
SAN BENITO HEALTH FOUNDATION
351 Felice Dr, Hollister (95023-3361)
PHONE 831 637-6871
Vivian Fernadez, *Administration*
Ken Williams, *Accountant*
Christina Fernandez, *Supervisor*
EMP: 42 **EST:** 1975
SQ FT: 7,220
SALES (est): 5.4MM **Privately Held**
WEB: www.sanbenitohealth.org
SIC: 8011 Clinic, operated by physicians

(P-15662)
SAN FRANCISCO CRITICAL CARE
2351 Clay St Ste 501, San Francisco (94115-1931)
PHONE 415 923-3421
James Hershon MD, *Principal*
Christopher Brown, *Principal*
Veronica Shi, *Dermatology*
Xin Lao, *Internal Med*
Kelly Lo, *Internal Med*
EMP: 64 **EST:** 2000
SALES (est): 6.7MM **Privately Held**
WEB: www.sflung.com
SIC: 8011 Pulmonary specialist, physician/surgeon

(P-15663)
SAN FRANCISCO SURGERY CTR LP
450 Sutter St Rm 500, San Francisco (94108-3907)
PHONE 415 393-9600
Ayse McDow, *Partner*
EMP: 54 **EST:** 2005
SALES (est): 16.7MM **Privately Held**
WEB: www.sf-sc.com
SIC: 8011 Ambulatory surgical center

(P-15664)
SAN LEANDRO IMAGING CTR A CAL
Also Called: Pacific Imaging Consultants
2450 Washington Ave # 120, San Leandro (94577-5996)
PHONE 510 351-7734
Richard M Colbert, *Partner*
Richard J Keen MD, *Partner*
EMP: 41 **EST:** 1985
SALES (est): 538.8K **Privately Held**
SIC: 8011 Radiologist

(P-15665)
SAN LNDRO SRGERY CTR LTD A CAL
15035 E 14th St, San Leandro (94578-1901)
PHONE 510 276-2800
Sheila Cook, *Partner*
EMP: 72 **EST:** 1994
SQ FT: 33,000
SALES (est): 9.2MM **Privately Held**
SIC: 8011 Surgeon

(P-15666)
SANTA CLARA COUNTY OF
751 S Bascom Ave, San Jose (95128-2604)
PHONE 408 885-5000
Jeffrey Smith, *CEO*
Sean Rooney, *Division Mgr*
Rocky Gupta, *Technology*
Ingrid Bossen, *Obstetrician*
Lily K Nguyen, *Obstetrician*
EMP: 61 **Privately Held**
WEB: www.sccgov.org
SIC: 8011 Internal medicine, physician/surgeon
PA: County Of Santa Clara
70 W Hedding St 2wing
San Jose CA 95110
408 299-5200

(P-15667)
SANTA CLARA COUNTY OF
751 S Bascom Ave Fl 4, San Jose (95128-2604)
PHONE 408 885-6666
EMP: 61 **Privately Held**
WEB: www.sccgov.org
SIC: 8011 Medical centers
PA: County Of Santa Clara
70 W Hedding St 2wing
San Jose CA 95110
408 299-5200

(P-15668)
SANTA CLARA VALLEY MEDICAL CTR
2400 Moorpark Ave, San Jose (95128-2631)
PHONE 408 885-6300
Albert Chiang, *Anesthesiology*
Ben Wong, *Internal Med*
John Sum, *Neurology*
Anne Trull, *Nurse*
Yuhee OH,
EMP: 44 **Privately Held**
WEB: www.scvmc.org
SIC: 8011 Medical centers
PA: Santa Clara Valley Medical Center
751 S Bascom Ave
San Jose CA 95128

(P-15669)
SANTA CLARA VALLEY MEDICAL CTR
976 Lenzen Ave, San Jose (95126-2737)
PHONE 408 792-5586
Quelan To, *Pharmacist*
EMP: 44 **Privately Held**
WEB: www.scvmc.org
SIC: 8011 Clinic, operated by physicians
PA: Santa Clara Valley Medical Center
751 S Bascom Ave
San Jose CA 95128

(P-15670)
SANTA CRUZ MEDICAL FOUNDATION (HQ)
2025 Soquel Ave, Santa Cruz (95062-1323)
PHONE 831 458-5537
Larry De Ghetaldi, *Director*
Shawna Riddle, *Family Practiti*
William R Raffo, *Nephrology*
Sarah Maufe, *Pediatrics*
Scott S Merlo, *Physician Asst*
EMP: 50 **EST:** 1953
SQ FT: 60,000
SALES (est): 31.6MM
SALES (corp-wide): 13.2B **Privately Held**
WEB: www.santacruzmedical.org
SIC: 8011 General & family practice, physician/surgeon

PA: Sutter Health
2200 River Plaza Dr
Sacramento CA 95833
916 733-8800

(P-15671)
SANTA CRUZ MEDICAL FOUNDATION
2915 Chanticleer Ave, Santa Cruz (95065-1815)
PHONE 831 477-2375
Steven Roberts, *Manager*
Kathleen Halat, *Podiatrist*
EMP: 1350
SALES (corp-wide): 13.2B **Privately Held**
WEB: www.santacruzmedical.org
SIC: 8011 General & family practice, physician/surgeon
HQ: Santa Cruz Medical Foundation
2025 Soquel Ave
Santa Cruz CA 95062
831 458-5537

(P-15672)
SANTA CRUZ MEDICAL FOUNDATION
2900 Chanticleer Ave, Santa Cruz (95065-1816)
PHONE 831 477-2325
Vicki Wilson, *Branch Mgr*
EMP: 1350
SALES (corp-wide): 13.2B **Privately Held**
WEB: www.santacruzmedical.org
SIC: 8011 General & family practice, physician/surgeon
HQ: Santa Cruz Medical Foundation
2025 Soquel Ave
Santa Cruz CA 95062
831 458-5537

(P-15673)
SANTA CRUZ SURGERY
3003 Paul Sweet Rd, Santa Cruz (95065-1503)
PHONE 831 462-5512
Patrick Haley, *Principal*
Melissa Sullivan, *CIO*
Christine Werra, *Manager*
EMP: 38 **EST:** 1988
SQ FT: 7,500
SALES (est): 5MM **Privately Held**
WEB: www.santacruzsurgery.com
SIC: 8011 Surgeon

(P-15674)
SANTA ROSA COMMUNITY HLTH CTRS (PA)
3569 Round Barn Cir, Santa Rosa (95403-5781)
PHONE 707 547-2222
Naomi Fuchs, *CEO*
Gabriela Bernal, *COO*
Harold Brockman, *CFO*
Marla Pfohl, *Program Mgr*
Elaine Brown, *Executive Asst*
EMP: 107 **EST:** 1996
SALES (est): 74.5MM **Privately Held**
WEB: www.srhealth.org
SIC: 8011 Clinic, operated by physicians

(P-15675)
SANTA ROSA ORTHPDICS MED GROUP
Also Called: Schakel, Mark E II MD
1405 Montgomery Dr, Santa Rosa (95405-4557)
PHONE 707 546-1922
Gary Stein, *President*
Mark Schakel MD, *Treasurer*
Thomas C Degenhardt MD, *Vice Pres*
Michael Star MD, *Admin Sec*
EMP: 105 **EST:** 1966
SQ FT: 2,000
SALES (est): 9.4MM **Privately Held**
WEB: www.srortho.com
SIC: 8011 Orthopedic physician; physicians' office, including specialists; surgeon

(P-15676)
SCENIC FACULTY MED GROUP INC
Also Called: Pmp Family
830 Scenic Dr, Modesto (95350-6131)
PHONE 209 558-7248

George Kilian, *Administration*
Kathy Spanel, *Finance*
Sunita Saini, *Med Doctor*
Thomas Wenstrup, *Med Doctor*
EMP: 39 **EST:** 1992
SALES (est): 5.8MM **Privately Held**
WEB: www.scenicfacultymedgrp.com
SIC: 8011 General & family practice, physician/surgeon

(P-15677)
SEQUOIA MEDICAL CLINIC (PA)
Also Called: Sequoia Medical Associates
2900 Whipple Ave Ste 130, Redwood City (94062-2844)
PHONE 650 261-2300
George Block MD, *President*
Wayne Silveria, *Accountant*
EMP: 71 **EST:** 1995
SALES (est): 737.4K **Privately Held**
WEB: www.obgynredwoodcity.com
SIC: 8011 Primary care medical clinic

(P-15678)
SHASTA EYE MEDICAL GROUP INC (PA)
3190 Churn Creek Rd, Redding (96002-2122)
PHONE 530 226-5966
Bryan Crum, *Partner*
Christopher Lin, *Partner*
Bruce Silverstein, *Partner*
Robert Trent, *Partner*
Erin Pillsbury, *Manager*
EMP: 54 **EST:** 1987
SALES (est): 7.9MM **Privately Held**
WEB: www.shastaeye.com
SIC: 8011 General & family practice, physician/surgeon; ophthalmologist

(P-15679)
SHASTA ORTHPEDICS SPT MEDICINE
1255 Liberty St, Redding (96001-0814)
PHONE 530 246-2467
Paul Schwartz, *President*
Sherrie Hamilton, *Office Mgr*
Tony Chang, *Med Doctor*
EMP: 49 **EST:** 1959
SQ FT: 4,000
SALES (est): 5.6MM **Privately Held**
WEB: www.shastaortho.com
SIC: 8011 Orthopedic physician

(P-15680)
SHIFAMED LLC
590 Division St, Campbell (95008-6906)
PHONE 408 560-2500
AMR Salahieh,
David Voris, *CFO*
Brian Brandt, *Research*
Daniel Hildebrand, *Research*
Matt Munoz, *Research*
EMP: 42 **EST:** 2007
SALES (est): 12.3MM **Privately Held**
WEB: www.shifamed.com
SIC: 8011 Offices & clinics of medical doctors

(P-15681)
SIEMENS MED SOLUTIONS USA INC
Ultra Sound Division
685 E Middlefield Rd, Mountain View (94043-4045)
P.O. Box 7393 (94039-7393)
PHONE 650 694-5747
Franz Wiehler, *CFO*
Gayatri James, *Admin Asst*
Henry Lai, *Planning*
Benjamin Beaver, *Regl Sales Mgr*
Manuel Noda, *Director*
EMP: 300
SQ FT: 373,000
SALES (corp-wide): 67.4B **Privately Held**
WEB: www.siemens.com
SIC: 8011 Medical centers
HQ: Siemens Medical Solutions Usa, Inc.
40 Liberty Blvd
Malvern PA 19355
888 826-9702

PRODUCTS & SERVICES SECTION
8011 - Offices & Clinics Of Doctors Of Medicine County (P-15705)

(P-15682)
SIERRA FAMILY MED CLINIC INC (PA)
15301 Tyler Foote Rd, Nevada City (95959-9318)
P.O. Box 995, Grass Valley (95945-0995)
PHONE.................................530 292-3478
Steve Weber, *CEO*
Naidhruva Rush, *President*
Terry Strom, *COO*
Gary Graeber, *CFO*
Robert Shapiro, *Treasurer*
EMP: 43 EST: 1982
SALES (est): 3.5MM **Privately Held**
WEB: www.sierraclinic.org
SIC: 8011 Clinic, operated by physicians

(P-15683)
SIERRA IMGING ASSOC MED GROUP
231 W Fir Ave, Clovis (93611-0220)
PHONE.................................559 297-0300
Clay Stevens, *Director*
Sadri M Akin, *Shareholder*
Mark D Alson, *Shareholder*
Leyla M Azmoun, *Shareholder*
Glenn I Hananouchi, *Shareholder*
EMP: 103 EST: 2004
SQ FT: 10,550
SALES (est): 5.5MM **Privately Held**
WEB: www.radnet.com
SIC: 8011 Radiologist

(P-15684)
SIERRA INTRNAL MDCINE MED GROU
680 Guzzi Ln Ste 201, Sonora (95370-5288)
PHONE.................................209 536-3738
James D Mosson, *President*
Terrel Spitze, *President*
Terril Spitze, *Treasurer*
Henry KAO, *Vice Pres*
Lynn Austin, *Admin Sec*
EMP: 163 EST: 1985
SALES (est): 6.1MM
SALES (corp-wide): 4.5B **Privately Held**
WEB: www.adventhealth.org
SIC: 8011 Internal medicine, physician/surgeon
PA: Adventist Health System/West, Corporation
 1 Adventist Health Way
 Roseville CA 95661
 844 574-5686

(P-15685)
SIERRA PACIFIC SURGERY CTR LLC
Also Called: Summit Surgical
1630 E Herndon Ave # 100, Fresno (93720-3391)
PHONE.................................559 256-5200
Christopher Holden,
Paramjeet Gill, *Officer*
Clare Peoples, *Office Mgr*
Kim Brinker, *Materials Mgr*
Jeremy Ealand, *Opers Staff*
EMP: 40 EST: 2000
SALES (est): 7.1MM **Privately Held**
WEB: www.spoc-ortho.com
SIC: 8011 Ambulatory surgical center; orthopedic physician

(P-15686)
SIERRA PCF ORTHPDIC CTR MED GR
1630 E Herndon Ave, Fresno (93720-3391)
PHONE.................................559 256-5200
Joe Clark, *CEO*
Eric C Hanson, *President*
Annette Hopkins, *Office Mgr*
Jerome Dunklin, *Surgeon*
Francis E Glaser, *Surgeon*
EMP: 200 EST: 2000
SALES (est): 20.4MM **Privately Held**
WEB: www.spoc-ortho.com
SIC: 8011 Orthopedic physician

(P-15687)
SIERRA VIEW MEDICAL EYE INC
Also Called: Medical Eye Group
400 Sierra College Dr A, Grass Valley (95945-5093)
PHONE.................................530 272-3411
A James Hagele Jr, *Principal*
Andrew J Hagele Jr, *President*
EMP: 57 EST: 1962
SQ FT: 3,000
SALES (est): 6MM **Privately Held**
WEB: www.svme2020.com
SIC: 8011 Ophthalmologist

(P-15688)
SISKIYOU HOSPITAL INC
Also Called: Fairchild Medical Center
475 Bruce St Ste 200, Yreka (96097-3463)
PHONE.................................530 841-6211
Larry Mulloy, *CEO*
Kathy Shelvock, *Bd of Directors*
Jody Gretzke, *Office Mgr*
Mike Madden, *Asst Admin*
Joann Sarmento, *Human Res Mgr*
EMP: 56 EST: 1962
SQ FT: 4,300
SALES (est): 2.2MM **Privately Held**
WEB: www.fairchildmed.org
SIC: 8011 Clinic, operated by physicians

(P-15689)
SLEEPMED INCORPORATED
4735 Mangels Blvd, Fairfield (94534-4175)
PHONE.................................707 864-1869
EMP: 40
SALES (corp-wide): 7.7MM **Privately Held**
WEB: www.sleepmedinc.com
SIC: 8011 Specialized medical practitioners, except internal
HQ: Sleepmed Incorporated
 3330 Cumberland Blvd Se # 800
 Atlanta GA 30339

(P-15690)
SMALL TALK PEDIATRIC SVCS INC (PA)
2526 Goodwater Ave Ste A, Redding (96002-1572)
PHONE.................................530 226-8255
H Hartigan, *Principal*
EMP: 44 EST: 2010
SALES (est): 1.2MM **Privately Held**
WEB: www.smalltalkpeds.com
SIC: 8011 Physical medicine, physician/surgeon

(P-15691)
SOLANO HEMATOLOGY/ONCOLOGY LLC
100 Hospital Dr Ste 110, Vallejo (94589-2577)
PHONE.................................707 551-3300
Chainarong Limvarapuss, *Mng Member*
EMP: 42 EST: 2004
SALES (est): 7.7MM **Privately Held**
WEB: www.solanohemonc.com
SIC: 8011 Oncologist

(P-15692)
SOLIMAN HISHAM M D INC
Also Called: Folsom Psychiatry Associates
510 Plaza Dr Ste 170, Folsom (95630-4790)
PHONE.................................916 351-9400
Larry Poore, *Principal*
Randa Barajas, *Office Mgr*
EMP: 45 EST: 2010
SALES (est): 5.8MM **Privately Held**
SIC: 8011 Internal medicine, physician/surgeon; psychiatrist

(P-15693)
SONOMA CNTY INDIAN HLTH PRJ IN (PA)
Also Called: SCIHP
144 Stony Point Rd, Santa Rosa (95401-4122)
PHONE.................................707 521-4545
Betty Arterverry, *CEO*
Molin T Malicay, *CEO*
Lori Houston, *Planning*
Kellie Kozel, *Nurse*
Katherine Duncan, *Pharmacist*
EMP: 150 EST: 1971
SQ FT: 70,000
SALES (est): 26.6MM **Privately Held**
WEB: www.scihp.org
SIC: 8011 Clinic, operated by physicians

(P-15694)
SONOMA VALLEY CMNTY HLTH CTR
19270 Highway 12, Sonoma (95476-5414)
PHONE.................................707 939-6070
Cheryl Johnson, *CEO*
Susan Torres, *CFO*
Patricia Talbot, *Exec Dir*
Mark Manzon, *Nurse*
Susan Drake, *Director*
EMP: 36 EST: 1992
SALES (est): 13.2MM **Privately Held**
WEB: www.svchc.org
SIC: 8011 Primary care medical clinic

(P-15695)
SONORA COMMUNITY HOSPITAL
1000 Greenley Rd, Sonora (95370-5200)
PHONE.................................209 536-5012
David L Larsen, *Principal*
EMP: 213 EST: 1958
SALES (est): 258.4MM **Privately Held**
WEB: www.adventisthealth.org
SIC: 8011 General & family practice, physician/surgeon

(P-15696)
SOUTH CNTY CMNTY HLTH CTR INC (PA)
Also Called: RAVENSWOOD FAMILY HEALTH CENTE
1885 Bay Rd, East Palo Alto (94303-1312)
PHONE.................................650 330-7407
Wayne Yost, *CFO*
Laila Gulzar, *Officer*
Luisa Buada, *Exec Dir*
Wilma Balmonte, *Accounting Mgr*
Marina Yu, *Contract Mgr*
EMP: 70 EST: 2001
SALES (est): 31.9MM **Privately Held**
WEB: www.ravenswoodfhn.org
SIC: 8011 Clinic, operated by physicians

(P-15697)
SOUTH E BAY PDTRIC MED GROUP I
Also Called: Dorsey, D J MD
2191 Mowry Ave Ste 600c, Fremont (94538-1702)
PHONE.................................510 792-4373
Steven Fridekin, *President*
Dr Patrick Burke, *Principal*
Sahara Dobbs, *Principal*
Susan Dugoni MD, *Principal*
Steven Friedken MD, *Principal*
EMP: 40 EST: 1972
SALES (est): 7.5MM **Privately Held**
WEB: www.sebpmg.com
SIC: 8011 Pediatrician

(P-15698)
SPINECARE MED GROUP INC A PROF
455 Hickey Blvd Ste 310, Daly City (94015-2630)
PHONE.................................650 985-7500
Arthur H White MD, *Ch of Bd*
James B Reynolds MD, *President*
Noel D Goldthwaite MD, *Treasurer*
Richard Derby MD, *Vice Pres*
Garrett Kine MD, *Vice Pres*
EMP: 61 EST: 1987
SQ FT: 82,000
SALES (est): 3.2MM **Privately Held**
SIC: 8011 Clinic, operated by physicians; surgeon

(P-15699)
SPORTS MEDICINE
Also Called: Sub St Francis Mem Hosp
1777 Botelho Dr Ste 110, Walnut Creek (94596-5083)
PHONE.................................925 934-3536
Sheryl Palmer, *Managing Prtnr*
EMP: 82 EST: 1993

SALES (est): 5.9MM **Privately Held**
WEB: www.kidbones.net
SIC: 8011 8043 8049 7991 Clinic, operated by physicians; offices & clinics of podiatrists; physical therapist; aerobic dance & exercise classes
HQ: Dignity Health
 185 Berry St Ste 200
 San Francisco CA 94107
 415 438-5500

(P-15700)
ST JOSEPHS SURGERY CENTER LP
1800 N California St # 1, Stockton (95204-6019)
PHONE.................................209 467-6316
Don Wiley, *President*
EMP: 75 EST: 2004
SALES (est): 10.7MM
SALES (corp-wide): 17.6B **Publicly Held**
WEB: www.stjosephs-sc.com
SIC: 8011 Surgeon
PA: Tenet Healthcare Corporation
 14201 Dallas Pkwy
 Dallas TX 75254
 469 893-2200

(P-15701)
STANFORD BLOOD CENTER LLC (PA)
3373 Hillview Ave, Palo Alto (94304-1274)
PHONE.................................650 723-7994
Shirley Weber,
Harpreet Sandhu, *CEO*
Alpa Vyas, *Vice Pres*
Jenn Wagner, *Comms Mgr*
Jennifer Alexander, *Admin Asst*
EMP: 182 EST: 2015
SALES (est): 69.2MM **Privately Held**
WEB: www.stanfordbloodcenter.org
SIC: 8011 Physicians' office, including specialists

(P-15702)
STANIFLAUS CARDIOLOGY
3621 Forest Glenn Dr, Modesto (95355-1339)
PHONE.................................209 521-9661
Samuel S Baker Jr, *Partner*
Samuel Baker Jr, *Partner*
Hassan Hussain MD, *Partner*
Tsuji Jack MD, *Partner*
Kent Wong MD, *Partner*
EMP: 38 EST: 1984
SQ FT: 1,344
SALES (est): 3.3MM **Privately Held**
SIC: 8011 Cardiologist & cardio-vascular specialist

(P-15703)
STANISLAUS COUNTY HSA
830 Scenic Dr A, Modesto (95350-6131)
P.O. Box 492 (95353-0492)
PHONE.................................209 558-7094
SA Vang, *Principal*
EMP: 43 EST: 2007
SALES (est): 6.3MM **Privately Held**
WEB: www.schsa.org
SIC: 8011 Physicians' office, including specialists

(P-15704)
STEVEN P ABELOW MD
2311 Lake Tahoe Blvd, South Lake Tahoe (96150-7129)
PHONE.................................530 544-8033
Steven Abelow MD, *Owner*
EMP: 100 EST: 1982
SALES (est): 2.9MM **Privately Held**
SIC: 8011 Orthopedic physician; general & family practice, physician/surgeon

(P-15705)
STOCKTON AMBLTORY SRGERY CTR L
Also Called: Ambulatory Surgery Ctr Stockton
2388 N California St, Stockton (95204-5506)
PHONE.................................209 944-9100
Brooke Rohrer, *Exec Dir*
EMP: 71 EST: 2000
SALES (est): 11.7MM **Privately Held**
WEB: www.ascstockton.com
SIC: 8011 Ambulatory surgical center

8011 - Offices & Clinics Of Doctors Of Medicine County (P-15706)

(P-15706)
STOCKTON CRDLGY MED GROUP CMPL (PA)
415 E Harding Way Ste D, Stockton (95204-6118)
PHONE..................................209 994-5750
Rajiv Punjya, *President*
Tuan A Pham, *Treasurer*
John A Bouteller, *Vice Pres*
EMP: 50 **EST:** 1976
SQ FT: 6,500
SALES: 12.6MM **Privately Held**
WEB: www.stocktoncardiology.com
SIC: 8011 Cardiologist & cardio-vascular specialist

(P-15707)
SULLIVAN CTR FOR CHLDREN A PSY
3443 W Shaw Ave, Fresno (93711-3249)
PHONE..................................559 271-1186
Kathy Sullivan, *President*
David Fox, *Director*
EMP: 83 **EST:** 1989
SQ FT: 5,200
SALES (est): 17.1MM **Privately Held**
WEB: www.sullivancenterforchildren.com
SIC: 8011 Offices & clinics of medical doctors

(P-15708)
SUTTER BAY HOSPITALS
3698 California St, San Francisco (94118-1702)
P.O. Box 7999 (94120-7999)
PHONE..................................415 600-2632
EMP: 39
SALES (corp-wide): 13.2B **Privately Held**
WEB: www.cpmc.org
SIC: 8011 8093 8062 General & family practice, physician/surgeon; rehabilitation center, outpatient treatment; general medical & surgical hospitals
HQ: Sutter Bay Hospitals
475 Brannan St Ste 130
San Francisco CA 94107
415 600-6000

(P-15709)
SUTTER BAY MEDICAL FOUNDATION (HQ)
Also Called: Palo Alto Med Fndtion For Hlth
795 El Camino Real, Palo Alto (94301-2302)
P.O. Box 254738, Sacramento (95865-4738)
PHONE..................................650 321-4121
David Drucker, *President*
Jeff Gerard, *CEO*
Null M Null Akhtar, *Officer*
Madeleine Viden, *Officer*
Mara Hook, *Vice Pres*
EMP: 700 **EST:** 1948
SQ FT: 200,000
SALES (est): 411.2MM
SALES (corp-wide): 13.2B **Privately Held**
WEB: www.mycaminomedical.org
SIC: 8011 General & family practice, physician/surgeon
PA: Sutter Health
2200 River Plaza Dr
Sacramento CA 95833
916 733-8800

(P-15710)
SUTTER BAY MEDICAL FOUNDATION
Also Called: Pamf - PA Division
2951 Gordon Ave, Santa Clara (95051-0709)
PHONE..................................650 812-3751
Jessica Memosano, *Manager*
EMP: 62
SALES (corp-wide): 13.2B **Privately Held**
WEB: www.mycaminomedical.org
SIC: 8011 Clinic, operated by physicians
HQ: Sutter Bay Medical Foundation
795 El Camino Real
Palo Alto CA 94301
650 321-4121

(P-15711)
SUTTER BAY MEDICAL FOUNDATION
Also Called: Patient Accounting
535 Oakmead Pkwy, Sunnyvale (94085-4023)
PHONE..................................408 730-4321
Lynn Murray, *Principal*
Reyne Rafoth, *Analyst*
Claudia Sotelo, *Analyst*
Dana Behnke, *Buyer*
Kristin Welter, *Med Doctor*
EMP: 120
SALES (corp-wide): 13.2B **Privately Held**
WEB: www.mycaminomedical.org
SIC: 8011 Medical centers
HQ: Sutter Bay Medical Foundation
795 El Camino Real
Palo Alto CA 94301
650 321-4121

(P-15712)
SUTTER BAY MEDICAL FOUNDATION
877 W Fremont Ave Ste N, Sunnyvale (94087-2332)
PHONE..................................650 934-7956
Richard Slavin, *Principal*
Karen Siesnizk, *Nurse Practr*
EMP: 62
SALES (corp-wide): 13.2B **Privately Held**
WEB: www.mycaminomedical.org
SIC: 8011 Clinic, operated by physicians
HQ: Sutter Bay Medical Foundation
795 El Camino Real
Palo Alto CA 94301
650 321-4121

(P-15713)
SUTTER GOULD MED FOUNDATION (PA)
600 Coffee Rd, Modesto (95355-4201)
PHONE..................................209 948-5940
David Bradley, *CEO*
E Lewis Cobb, *Obstetrician*
Adam Dodd, *Obstetrician*
Brigida Andaya, *Anesthesiology*
Pratap S Kurra, *Anesthesiology*
EMP: 50 **EST:** 1993
SALES (est): 69.4MM **Privately Held**
WEB: www.suttergould.org
SIC: 8011 Physicians' office, including specialists

(P-15714)
SUTTER HEALTH
795 El Camino Real, Palo Alto (94301-2302)
PHONE..................................650 853-2975
Kelvin Chang, *Regional Mgr*
Jack Byrd, *Engineer*
Brian Dula, *Anesthesiology*
Kyaw Lwin, *Anesthesiology*
Susan Butler, *Dermatology*
EMP: 76
SALES (corp-wide): 13.2B **Privately Held**
WEB: www.suttermedicalcenter.org
SIC: 8011 General & family practice, physician/surgeon
PA: Sutter Health
2200 River Plaza Dr
Sacramento CA 95833
916 733-8800

(P-15715)
SUTTER HEALTH
5196 Hill Rd E Ste 300, Lakeport (95453-6374)
PHONE..................................707 263-6885
Harneet Bath, *Branch Mgr*
Lisa Mazor, *Property Mgr*
EMP: 76
SALES (corp-wide): 13.2B **Privately Held**
WEB: www.suttermedicalcenter.org
SIC: 8011 Offices & clinics of medical doctors
PA: Sutter Health
2200 River Plaza Dr
Sacramento CA 95833
916 733-8800

(P-15716)
SUTTER HEALTH
Also Called: Vascular and Varicose Vein Ctr
1680 E Rsvlle Pkwy Ste 10, Roseville (95661)
PHONE..................................916 783-8114
EMP: 76
SALES (corp-wide): 13.2B **Privately Held**
WEB: www.suttermedicalcenter.org
SIC: 8011 8071 Offices & clinics of medical doctors; medical laboratories
PA: Sutter Health
2200 River Plaza Dr
Sacramento CA 95833
916 733-8800

(P-15717)
SUTTER HEALTH
1500 Expo Pkwy, Sacramento (95815-4227)
PHONE..................................916 646-8300
EMP: 1000
SALES (corp-wide): 11B **Privately Held**
SIC: 8011 8071 Medical Doctor's Office Medical Laboratory
PA: Sutter Health
2200 River Plaza Dr
Sacramento CA 95833
916 286-6670

(P-15718)
SUTTER HEALTH
Also Called: South Imaging Center
8118 Timberlake Way # 110, Sacramento (95823-5400)
PHONE..................................916 681-8852
Fred Gaschen, *Principal*
Marja Meadows, *Supervisor*
EMP: 76
SALES (corp-wide): 13.2B **Privately Held**
WEB: www.suttermedicalcenter.org
SIC: 8011 8071 Offices & clinics of medical doctors; medical laboratories
PA: Sutter Health
2200 River Plaza Dr
Sacramento CA 95833
916 733-8800

(P-15719)
SUTTER HEALTH
3 Medical Plaza Dr # 100, Roseville (95661-3088)
PHONE..................................530 406-5600
Judi Monday, *Director*
EMP: 76
SALES (corp-wide): 13.2B **Privately Held**
WEB: www.suttermedicalcenter.org
SIC: 8011 Offices & clinics of medical doctors
PA: Sutter Health
2200 River Plaza Dr
Sacramento CA 95833
916 733-8800

(P-15720)
SUTTER HEALTH
Also Called: Sutter Pacific Med Foundation
5196 Hill Rd E Ste 300, Lakeport (95453-6374)
PHONE..................................707 263-6885
EMP: 121
SALES (corp-wide): 11B **Privately Held**
SIC: 8011 Offices And Clinics Of Medical Doctors, N
PA: Sutter Health
2200 River Plaza Dr
Sacramento CA 95833
916 733-8800

(P-15721)
SUTTER HEALTH
Also Called: Breast Imaging Center
3161 L St, Sacramento (95816-5234)
PHONE..................................916 451-3344
Jerry Fosselman, *Branch Mgr*
EMP: 76
SALES (corp-wide): 13.2B **Privately Held**
WEB: www.suttermedicalcenter.org
SIC: 8011 8071 Offices & clinics of medical doctors; medical laboratories
PA: Sutter Health
2200 River Plaza Dr
Sacramento CA 95833
916 733-8800

(P-15722)
SUTTER HEALTH
Also Called: Mercy Gen Radiation Oncology
2800 L St, Sacramento (95816-5616)
PHONE..................................916 453-4528
Nancy Mathai, *Branch Mgr*
Andrew Juris, *Cardiology*
Yinka Davies, *Gastroenterlgy*
EMP: 76
SALES (corp-wide): 13.2B **Privately Held**
WEB: www.suttermedicalcenter.org
SIC: 8011 8071 Offices & clinics of medical doctors; medical laboratories
PA: Sutter Health
2200 River Plaza Dr
Sacramento CA 95833
916 733-8800

(P-15723)
SUTTER HEALTH
Also Called: Campus Commons Imaging
2 Scripps Dr Ste 110, Sacramento (95825-6207)
PHONE..................................916 929-3393
Jan Curry, *Branch Mgr*
Roland D Marco, *Radiology*
EMP: 76
SALES (corp-wide): 13.2B **Privately Held**
WEB: www.suttermedicalcenter.org
SIC: 8011 8071 General & family practice, physician/surgeon; medical laboratories
PA: Sutter Health
2200 River Plaza Dr
Sacramento CA 95833
916 733-8800

(P-15724)
SUTTER HEALTH
Also Called: Fort Sutter Diagnostic Imaging
2801 K St Ste 110, Sacramento (95816-5118)
PHONE..................................916 733-5051
Dawn Gonzales, *Branch Mgr*
Melissa Taylor, *Librarian*
Arzou Ahsan, *Obstetrician*
Huu-Ninh V Dao, *Diag Radio*
A Brandt Schraner, *Diag Radio*
EMP: 76
SALES (corp-wide): 13.2B **Privately Held**
WEB: www.suttermedicalcenter.org
SIC: 8011 8071 Offices & clinics of medical doctors; medical laboratories
PA: Sutter Health
2200 River Plaza Dr
Sacramento CA 95833
916 733-8800

(P-15725)
SUTTER HEALTH
2725 Capitol Ave Dept 404, Sacramento (95816-6032)
PHONE..................................916 262-9456
EMP: 76
SALES (corp-wide): 13.2B **Privately Held**
WEB: www.suttermedicalcenter.org
SIC: 8011 Medical centers
PA: Sutter Health
2200 River Plaza Dr
Sacramento CA 95833
916 733-8800

(P-15726)
SUTTER HEALTH AT WORK
Also Called: Sutter Hlth At Work - Natomas
1014 N Market Blvd Ste 20, Sacramento (95834-1986)
PHONE..................................916 565-8607
Judi Monday, *President*
EMP: 37 **EST:** 1981
SALES (est): 570.1K **Privately Held**
WEB: www.sutterhealth.org
SIC: 8011 General & family practice, physician/surgeon

(P-15727)
SUTTER HLTH SCRMNTO SIERRA REG
Also Called: Sutter Counseling Center
7700 Folsom Blvd, Sacramento (95826-2608)
PHONE..................................916 386-3000
Diane Stewart, *Branch Mgr*
Nora Jimenez, *Sr Corp Ofcr*
Gregory Gisla, *Psychologist*
Ryan Courdy, *Psychiatry*
EMP: 162

PRODUCTS & SERVICES SECTION **8011 - Offices & Clinics Of Doctors Of Medicine County (P-15750)**

SALES (corp-wide): 13.2B **Privately Held**
WEB: www.sutterhealth.org
SIC: **8011** 8621 Psychiatrist; professional membership organizations
HQ: Sutter Health Sacramento Sierra Region
2200 River Plaza Dr
Sacramento CA 95833
916 733-8800

(P-15728)
SUTTER INC
Also Called: Joshua H Hoffman MD
1020 29th St Ste 480, Sacramento (95816-5173)
PHONE..................916 733-5097
Joshua H Hoffman, *President*
Vernon Giang, *CEO*
Amoolya Garg, *Executive*
Miriam Gonzalez, *Business Anlyst*
Kyndra Adams, *Accounting Mgr*
EMP: 50 EST: 1985
SALES (est): 1.3MM **Privately Held**
WEB: www.sutterhealth.org
SIC: **8011** Internal medicine, physician/surgeon

(P-15729)
SUTTER MED GROUP OF REDWOODS
3883 Airway Dr Ste 202, Santa Rosa (95403-1671)
PHONE..................707 546-2788
John Dervin MD, *President*
Steven Levenberg, *President*
Sean Gaskie MD, *Treasurer*
Romayne Farrell Fnp, *Admin Sec*
Jesse Rael, *Diag Radio*
EMP: 120 EST: 1992
SALES (est): 22.5MM
SALES (corp-wide): 13.2B **Privately Held**
WEB: www.suttersantarosa.org
SIC: **8011** General & family practice, physician/surgeon
HQ: Sutter Santa Rosa Regional Hospital
30 Mark West Springs Rd
Santa Rosa CA 95403
707 576-4000

(P-15730)
SUTTER NORTH MED FOUNDATION (PA)
Also Called: Multi Specialty Group Practice
969 Plumas St, Yuba City (95991-4011)
PHONE..................530 741-1300
Bruce Tigner, *CEO*
Tom Walther, *COO*
Kelly Danna, *CFO*
Emilio Bethencourt, *Business Dir*
Julie Eckardt, *Marketing Mgr*
EMP: 160 EST: 1947
SALES (est): 21.9MM **Privately Held**
WEB: www.sutternorth.com
SIC: **8011** General & family practice, physician/surgeon; clinic, operated by physicians

(P-15731)
SUTTER REGIONAL MED FOUNDATION
2720 Low Ct, Fairfield (94534-9771)
PHONE..................707 631-9423
Carolyn Appenzeller, *Principal*
Ella Gupta, *Internal Med*
EMP: 71
SALES (corp-wide): 58.3MM **Privately Held**
SIC: **8011** Physicians' office, including specialists
PA: Sutter Regional Medical Foundation Inc
2702 Low Ct
Fairfield CA 94534
707 427-4900

(P-15732)
SUTTER REGIONAL MED FOUNDATION (PA)
Also Called: Dr. Yelena L Krijanovski
2702 Low Ct, Fairfield (94534-9771)
PHONE..................707 427-4900
John Ray, *CEO*
Kevin Engle, *Opers Staff*
Douglas Dennis, *Surgeon*
Marlene Freeman, *Obstetrician*
Richard Gould, *Gastroenterlgy*
EMP: 426 EST: 2003
SQ FT: 28,571
SALES (est): 58.3MM **Privately Held**
SIC: **8011** Physicians' office, including specialists

(P-15733)
SUTTER REGIONAL MED FOUNDATION
770 Mason St, Vacaville (95688-4646)
PHONE..................707 454-5800
EMP: 71
SALES (corp-wide): 58.3MM **Privately Held**
WEB: www.suttermedicalfoundation.org
SIC: **8011** Physicians' office, including specialists
PA: Sutter Regional Medical Foundation Inc
2702 Low Ct
Fairfield CA 94534
707 427-4900

(P-15734)
SUTTER VALLEY MED FOUNDATION
Also Called: Sutter Medical Plaza Roseville
3100 Douglas Blvd, Roseville (95661-3866)
PHONE..................916 865-1140
Craig Ruggles, *Treasurer*
EMP: 121 **Privately Held**
WEB: www.suttermedicalfoundation.org
SIC: **8011** Physicians' office, including specialists
PA: Sutter Valley Medical Foundation
2700 Gateway Oaks Dr
Sacramento CA 95833

(P-15735)
SUTTER/YUBA B-CNTY MNTAL HLTH
Also Called: Inpatient Psychiatric Services
1965 Live Oak Blvd, Yuba City (95991-8850)
PHONE..................530 822-7200
Joan Hoss, *Director*
Chunlin Yang, *Med Doctor*
EMP: 38 EST: 1987
SALES (est): 1.2MM **Privately Held**
WEB: www.suttercounty.org
SIC: **8011** Psychiatric clinic

(P-15736)
TAHOE FOREST HOSPITAL DISTRICT
10710 Donner Pass Rd, Truckee (96161-4812)
PHONE..................530 582-7488
Nina Winans, *Branch Mgr*
Peter Stokich, *Director*
EMP: 40
SALES (corp-wide): 218.4MM **Privately Held**
WEB: www.tfhd.com
SIC: **8011** General & family practice, physician/surgeon
PA: Tahoe Forest Hospital District
10121 Pine Ave
Truckee CA 96161
530 587-6011

(P-15737)
TAHOE FOREST WOMENS CENTER
10175 Levone Ave, Truckee (96161-4821)
PHONE..................530 587-1041
Steve Thompson, *Partner*
Peter Taylor, *Partner*
EMP: 39 EST: 1990
SQ FT: 2,500
SALES (est): 1.6MM **Privately Held**
WEB: www.tfhd.com
SIC: **8011** Gynecologist; obstetrician

(P-15738)
TELEHEALTH SERVICES USA
Also Called: Hazel Health Services
10775 Pioneer Trl Ste 215, Truckee (96161-0234)
PHONE..................415 424-4266
Kami Salopek, *President*
Robert Darzynkiewicz, *Principal*
Vivek Maheshwari, *Principal*
EMP: 53 EST: 2017

SALES (est): 2.2MM **Privately Held**
WEB: www.hazel.co
SIC: **8011** Freestanding emergency medical center

(P-15739)
TENET HEALTHSYSTEM MEDICAL INC
414 Cliffside Dr, Danville (94526-4810)
PHONE..................925 275-8303
Phillip Gustafson, *Director*
EMP: 57
SALES (corp-wide): 17.6B **Publicly Held**
WEB: www.tenethealth.com
SIC: **8011** Offices & clinics of medical doctors
HQ: Tenet Healthsystem Medical, Inc.
14201 Dallas Pkwy
Dallas TX 75254
469 893-2000

(P-15740)
THEODORE E STAAHL MD INC (PA)
1329 Spanos Ct Ste A1, Modesto (95355-2818)
PHONE..................209 577-5700
Theodore E Staahl, *President*
Nancy Staahl, *Administration*
EMP: 47 EST: 1995
SALES (est): 1.4MM **Privately Held**
WEB: www.drstaahl.com
SIC: **8011** Plastic surgeon

(P-15741)
TIBURCIO VASQUEZ HLTH CTR INC (PA)
22211 Foothill Blvd, Hayward (94541-2712)
PHONE..................510 471-5880
David B Vliet, *CEO*
Luis Arenas, *Partner*
Yolanda Triana, *President*
Brent Copen, *CFO*
Malou Martinez, *CFO*
EMP: 50 EST: 1971
SALES (est): 45.6MM **Privately Held**
WEB: www.tvhc.org
SIC: **8011** Primary care medical clinic

(P-15742)
TUOLUMNE M-WUK INDIAN HLTH CTR
Also Called: TUOLUMNE MEWUK INDIAN HEALTH
18880 Cherry Valley Blvd, Tuolumne (95379-9506)
PHONE..................209 928-5400
Frank Isele, *Officer*
Darla Merlin, *Ch of Bd*
Christopher Gorsky, *Principal*
Tammy Barker, *Finance Dir*
EMP: 90 EST: 2003
SQ FT: 11,000
SALES (est): 15.7MM **Privately Held**
WEB: www.tmwihc.org
SIC: **8011** 8021 Offices & clinics of medical doctors; dental clinics & offices

(P-15743)
TURNING POINT CENTRAL CAL INC
1311 11th St, Reedley (93654-2926)
PHONE..................559 638-8588
Walt Lunsford, *Principal*
EMP: 40
SALES (corp-wide): 54.6MM **Privately Held**
WEB: www.tpocc.org
SIC: **8011** Offices & clinics of medical doctors
PA: Turning Point Of Central California, Inc.
615 S Atwood St
Visalia CA 93277
559 732-8086

(P-15744)
TURNURE MEDICAL GROUP INC
6805 Five Star Blvd Ste 1, Rocklin (95677-4135)
PHONE..................916 300-1188
Raymond Turnure MD, *President*
Pang Her, *Nurse Practr*
Kathy Goodrich, *Manager*

EMP: 41 EST: 2000
SQ FT: 4,315
SALES (est): 6.6MM **Privately Held**
WEB: www.turnuremedicalgroup.net
SIC: **8011** General & family practice, physician/surgeon

(P-15745)
U C SAN FRANCISCO GYNECOLOGY
2356 Sutter St, San Francisco (94115-3006)
PHONE..................415 885-7788
Kimberly Calvail, *Manager*
Josh Adler MD, *Exec VP*
Sheila Antrum, *Vice Pres*
Shelby Decosta, *Vice Pres*
Brian Newman, *Vice Pres*
EMP: 57 EST: 2011
SALES (est): 22.2MM
SALES (corp-wide): 59MM **Privately Held**
WEB: www.ucop.edu
SIC: **8011** Physicians' office, including specialists
PA: Uc San Francisco
1111 Franklin St Fl 12
Oakland CA 94607
858 534-7323

(P-15746)
UC DAVIS HLTH SYS FCLTIES DSIG
Also Called: Uc Davis Medical Center
4800 2nd Ave Ste 3010, Sacramento (95817-2216)
PHONE..................916 734-7024
Eugene Labrie, *Manager*
Michael Condrin, *Exec Dir*
David Lubarsky, *Vice Chancellor*
Annie Wong, *Director*
EMP: 49 EST: 2008
SALES (est): 27.3MM **Privately Held**
WEB: www.ucdavis.edu
SIC: **8011** Medical centers

(P-15747)
UCD NCADC
Also Called: Uc Davis Alzhimers Disease Ctr
150 Muir Rd Ste 127a, Martinez (94553-4668)
PHONE..................925 372-2485
William Jagust, *Director*
Javier Nazario-Santiag, *Project Mgr*
EMP: 62 EST: 1985
SALES (est): 314K **Privately Held**
SIC: **8011** Psychiatric clinic

(P-15748)
UCSF CARDIOVASCULAR CARE
535 Mission Bay Blvd S, San Francisco (94143-2156)
PHONE..................415 353-2873
Ucsf RAO, *Cardiology*
Damaris Cruz, *Ophthalmology*
Michael Blum, *Cardiovascular*
Chris Moffet, *Manager*
EMP: 60 **Privately Held**
WEB: www.ucsfmedicalcenter.org
SIC: **8011** Medical centers
PA: Ucsf Cardiovascular Care
400 Parnassus Ave
San Francisco CA 94143

(P-15749)
UCSF FERTILITY GROUP
Also Called: U C S F Frtlity Ctr For Rprdct
2356 Sutter St, San Francisco (94115-3006)
PHONE..................415 353-2667
Mark Laret, *CEO*
EMP: 42 EST: 1983
SALES (est): 3.5MM **Privately Held**
WEB: www.ucsf.edu
SIC: **8011** Specialized medical practitioners, except internal

(P-15750)
UNITED HLTH CTRS OF SAN JQUIN (PA)
3875 W Beechwood Ave, Fresno (93711-0795)
P.O. Box 790, Parlier (93648-0790)
PHONE..................559 646-6618

(PA)=Parent Co (HQ)=Headquarters (DH)=Div Headquarters
✪ = New Business established in last 2 years

2022 Northern California Business Directory and Buyers Guide

699

8011 - Offices & Clinics Of Doctors Of Medicine County (P-15751)

Colleen Curtis, *CEO*
Justin Preas, *COO*
Robert Shankerman, *Principal*
Sonia Relingo, *Director*
EMP: 70 **EST:** 1971
SQ FT: 7,500
SALES (est): 108.1MM **Privately Held**
WEB: www.unitedhealthcenters.org
SIC: 8011 Clinic, operated by physicians

(P-15751)
UNITED INDIAN HEALTH SVCS INC (PA)
Also Called: Potawot Health Clinic
1600 Weeot Way, Arcata (95521-4734)
PHONE..................707 825-5000
David Rosen, *CFO*
Terry Raymer, *Program Mgr*
Sandra Jones, *Nursing Mgr*
Amy Brom, *Psychologist*
Theressa Green, *Nurse*
EMP: 150
SQ FT: 46,304
SALES (est): 26.7MM **Privately Held**
WEB: www.unitedindianhealthservices.org
SIC: 8011 8021 8031 5912 Clinic, operated by physicians; primary care medical clinic; dental clinics & offices; offices & clinics of osteopathic physicians; drug stores; mental health clinic, outpatient; community center

(P-15752)
UNIVERSITY CAL SAN FRANCISCO
1545 Divisadero St, San Francisco (94143-3400)
PHONE..................415 353-7900
Vera Nelson, *Vice Pres*
Thompson Julee, *Admin Sec*
Deguzman Frances, *Admin Asst*
Crisologo Allan, *Technician*
Garde Erwin, *Engineer*
EMP: 116 **Privately Held**
WEB: www.ucsf.edu
SIC: 8011 8221 9411 Medical centers; university; administration of educational programs;
HQ: University Cal San Francisco
513 Parnassus Ave 115f
San Francisco CA 94143

(P-15753)
UNIVERSITY CAL SAN FRANCISCO
Also Called: Ucsf Orthpdic Srgery Fclty Prc
1500 Owens St, San Francisco (94158-2334)
PHONE..................415 353-1915
Piere Leavell, *Principal*
Wendy Katzman, *Professor*
Igor Immerman, *Surgeon*
Michelle Albert, *Cardiology*
Nicholas Fleming, *Internal Med*
EMP: 116 **Privately Held**
WEB: www.ucsf.edu
SIC: 8011 8221 9411 Medical centers; university; administration of educational programs;
HQ: University Cal San Francisco
513 Parnassus Ave 115f
San Francisco CA 94143

(P-15754)
UNIVERSITY CAL SAN FRANCISCO
Also Called: Ucsf Otlrynglogy - Head Neck S
2380 Sutter St Fl 3, San Francisco (94115-3006)
PHONE..................415 353-2757
Steven Cheung, *Otolaryngology*
EMP: 103 **Privately Held**
WEB: www.ucsf.edu
SIC: 8221 9411 8011 University; administration of educational programs; ; medical centers
HQ: University Cal San Francisco
513 Parnassus Ave 115f
San Francisco CA 94143

(P-15755)
UNIVERSITY CAL SAN FRANCISCO
311 California St Ste 410, San Francisco (94104-2616)
PHONE..................415 989-5339
Susan C Lambe, *Med Doctor*
Trinh Tang, *Med Doctor*
EMP: 116 **Privately Held**
WEB: www.ucsf.edu
SIC: 8011 Offices & clinics of medical doctors
HQ: University Cal San Francisco
513 Parnassus Ave 115f
San Francisco CA 94143

(P-15756)
UNIVERSITY CAL SAN FRANCISCO
Also Called: Ucsf Design Construction
3333 California St # 115, San Francisco (94118-1981)
PHONE..................415 885-7257
Tim Mahaney, *Director*
EMP: 103 **Privately Held**
WEB: www.ucsf.edu
SIC: 8221 9411 8011 University; administration of educational programs; ; medical centers
HQ: University Cal San Francisco
513 Parnassus Ave 115f
San Francisco CA 94143

(P-15757)
UNIVERSITY CAL SAN FRANCISCO
400 Parnassus Ave, San Francisco (94143-2202)
PHONE..................415 353-2383
Michael Prados, *Branch Mgr*
EMP: 116 **Privately Held**
WEB: www.ucsf.edu
SIC: 8011 8221 9411 Internal medicine practitioners; university; administration of educational programs;
HQ: University Cal San Francisco
513 Parnassus Ave 115f
San Francisco CA 94143

(P-15758)
UNIVERSITY CAL SAN FRANCISCO
Also Called: Ucsf Sports Medicine Center
1701 Divisadero St # 240, San Francisco (94115-3011)
PHONE..................415 353-7576
Bill Durmey, *Branch Mgr*
EMP: 116 **Privately Held**
WEB: www.ucsf.edu
SIC: 8011 8221 9411 Medical centers; university; administration of educational programs;
HQ: University Cal San Francisco
513 Parnassus Ave 115f
San Francisco CA 94143

(P-15759)
UNIVERSITY CAL SAN FRANCISCO
Also Called: Ucsf Pdiatric Pulmonary Clinic
5565 W Las Psts Blvd, Pleasanton (94588-4001)
PHONE..................925 598-3500
Margaret Craig, *Branch Mgr*
EMP: 116 **Privately Held**
WEB: www.ucsf.edu
SIC: 8011 8221 9411 Medical centers; university; administration of educational programs;
HQ: University Cal San Francisco
513 Parnassus Ave 115f
San Francisco CA 94143

(P-15760)
UNIVERSITY CAL SAN FRANCISCO
Also Called: Osher Ctr For Intgrtive Mdcine
1545 Divisadero St Fl 4, San Francisco (94143-3400)
P.O. Box 1726 (94143)
PHONE..................415 353-7700
Margareth Chesney, *Director*
EMP: 103 **Privately Held**
WEB: www.ucsf.edu
SIC: 8221 9411 8011 University; administration of educational programs; medical centers
HQ: University Cal San Francisco
513 Parnassus Ave 115f
San Francisco CA 94143

(P-15761)
UNIVERSITY CAL SAN FRANCISCO
Also Called: General Internal Medicine
1701 Divisadero St, San Francisco (94115-3011)
PHONE..................415 353-7300
Margareth Chesney, *Director*
EMP: 103 **Privately Held**
WEB: www.ucsf.edu
SIC: 8221 9411 8011 University; administration of educational programs; ; medical centers
HQ: University Cal San Francisco
513 Parnassus Ave 115f
San Francisco CA 94143

(P-15762)
UNIVERSITY CAL SAN FRANCISCO
Also Called: Ucsf/Div Behv & Dev Pediatrics
400 Parnassus Ave Fl 2, San Francisco (94143-2202)
PHONE..................415 476-4575
W Thomas Voice, *Branch Mgr*
EMP: 116 **Privately Held**
WEB: www.ucsf.edu
SIC: 8011 8221 9411 Medical centers; university; administration of educational programs;
HQ: University Cal San Francisco
513 Parnassus Ave 115f
San Francisco CA 94143

(P-15763)
UNIVERSITY CAL SAN FRANCISCO
Also Called: Ucsf Mmory Clnic Alzhimers Ctr
1500 Owens St Ste 320, San Francisco (94158-2335)
PHONE..................415 885-3668
Bruce Miller, *Director*
Mackenzie Hepker, *Research*
David Soleimani-Meigo, *Neurology*
Joey D English, *Med Doctor*
Vineeta Singh, *Med Doctor*
EMP: 103 **Privately Held**
WEB: www.ucsf.edu
SIC: 8221 9411 8011 University; administration of educational programs; ; medical centers
HQ: University Cal San Francisco
513 Parnassus Ave 115f
San Francisco CA 94143

(P-15764)
UNIVERSITY CAL SAN FRANCISCO
Also Called: Ucsf/Mz Neurosurgery Abic
2233 Post St Ste 303, San Francisco (94115-3471)
PHONE..................415 885-7495
Charles Intyre, *Branch Mgr*
EMP: 103 **Privately Held**
WEB: www.ucsf.edu
SIC: 8221 9411 8011 University; administration of educational programs; ; medical centers
HQ: University Cal San Francisco
513 Parnassus Ave 115f
San Francisco CA 94143

(P-15765)
UNIVERSITY CAL SAN FRANCISCO
Also Called: Ucsf/Obgyn Oncology
2356 Sutter St Fl 3, San Francisco (94115-3006)
PHONE..................415 885-3610
Wendy Miner, *Branch Mgr*
EMP: 103 **Privately Held**
WEB: www.ucsf.edu
SIC: 8221 9411 8011 University; administration of educational programs; ; medical centers
HQ: University Cal San Francisco
513 Parnassus Ave 115f
San Francisco CA 94143

(P-15766)
UNIVERSITY CAL SAN FRANCISCO
Also Called: Ucsf Plstic Rcnstrctive Srgery
350 Parnassus Ave Ste 509, San Francisco (94117-3608)
PHONE..................415 476-3061
Rob Ducca, *Branch Mgr*
EMP: 103 **Privately Held**
WEB: www.ucsf.edu
SIC: 8221 9411 8011 University; administration of educational programs; ; medical centers
HQ: University Cal San Francisco
513 Parnassus Ave 115f
San Francisco CA 94143

(P-15767)
UNIVERSITY CAL SAN FRANCISCO
Also Called: Pulmonary Prctice At Parnassus
400 Parnassus Ave Fl 5, San Francisco (94143-2202)
PHONE..................415 353-2961
Clarice Estrada, *Division Mgr*
Sophie Ou, *Research*
Matthew Lau, *Analyst*
Linda Yee, *Personnel*
Nirav Bhakta, *Med Doctor*
EMP: 103 **Privately Held**
WEB: www.ucsf.edu
SIC: 8221 9411 8011 University; administration of educational programs; ; medical centers
HQ: University Cal San Francisco
513 Parnassus Ave 115f
San Francisco CA 94143

(P-15768)
UNIVERSITY CAL SAN FRANCISCO
Also Called: Ucsf Mount Zion Cancer Center
2356 Sutter St, San Francisco (94115-3006)
PHONE..................415 885-7478
Debasish MD Tripathy, *Principal*
EMP: 103 **Privately Held**
WEB: www.ucsf.edu
SIC: 8221 9411 8011 University; administration of educational programs; ; medical centers
HQ: University Cal San Francisco
513 Parnassus Ave 115f
San Francisco CA 94143

(P-15769)
UNIVERSITY CALIFORNIA DAVIS
4150 V St, Sacramento (95817-1460)
PHONE..................916 734-8514
Dua Anderson, *Branch Mgr*
Aman Parikh, *Med Doctor*
EMP: 83 **Privately Held**
WEB: www.ucdavis.edu
SIC: 8011 8221 9411 Medical centers; university; administration of educational programs;
HQ: University Of California, Davis
1 Shields Ave
Davis CA 95616

PRODUCTS & SERVICES SECTION
8011 - Offices & Clinics Of Doctors Of Medicine County (P-15790)

(P-15770)
UNIVERSITY CALIFORNIA DAVIS
550 W Ranch View Dr # 20, Rocklin (95765-5396)
PHONE 916 295-5700
EMP: 83 **Privately Held**
WEB: www.ucdavis.edu
SIC: 8011 8221 9411 General & family practice, physician/surgeon; university; administration of educational programs;
HQ: University Of California, Davis
1 Shields Ave
Davis CA 95616

(P-15771)
UNIVERSITY CALIFORNIA DAVIS
Also Called: Khamishon, Ilya MD
251 Turn Pike Dr, Folsom (95630-8129)
PHONE 916 985-9300
Mary Simpson, *Branch Mgr*
Mary Ann Simpson, *Nurse Practr*
Stephanie Esparza, *Nurse*
EMP: 83 **Privately Held**
WEB: www.ucdavis.edu
SIC: 8011 8221 9411 Offices & clinics of medical doctors; university; administration of educational programs;
HQ: University Of California, Davis
1 Shields Ave
Davis CA 95616

(P-15772)
UNIVERSITY CALIFORNIA DAVIS
Also Called: Specialty Clinic
2660 W Covell Blvd, Davis (95616-5645)
PHONE 530 747-3000
Lily Yen, *Principal*
Vinita Anantavat, *Analyst*
Marci Snodgrass, *Family Practiti*
Paul Riggle, *Gnrl Med Prac*
Susan Perry, *OB/GYN*
EMP: 83 **Privately Held**
WEB: www.ucdavis.edu
SIC: 8011 8221 9411 Offices & clinics of medical doctors; university; administration of educational programs;
HQ: University Of California, Davis
1 Shields Ave
Davis CA 95616

(P-15773)
UNIVERSITY CALIFORNIA DAVIS
4430 V St, Sacramento (95817-1466)
PHONE 916 734-3574
Elena F Swartz, *Director*
EMP: 83 **Privately Held**
WEB: www.ucdavis.edu
SIC: 8011 8221 9411 Psychiatrist; university; administration of educational programs;
HQ: University Of California, Davis
1 Shields Ave
Davis CA 95616

(P-15774)
UNIVERSITY CALIFORNIA DAVIS
Also Called: Uc Davis Children's Hospital
2315 Stockton Blvd # 6309, Sacramento (95817-2201)
PHONE 916 734-2846
Valerie Adame, *Branch Mgr*
Jeremiah Maher, *Associate Dir*
Aaron Baker, *Principal*
Diana Sundberg, *Analyst*
Bahareh Nejad, *Obstetrician*
EMP: 83 **Privately Held**
WEB: www.ucdavis.edu
SIC: 8011 8221 9411 Surgeon; university; administration of educational programs;
HQ: University Of California, Davis
1 Shields Ave
Davis CA 95616

(P-15775)
UNIVERSITY CALIFORNIA DAVIS
Also Called: Davis Medical Group
4860 Y St, Sacramento (95817-2307)
PHONE 916 734-3588
Valerie Adame, *Branch Mgr*
W Suzanne Eidson-Ton, *Obstetrician*
Catherine Le, *Neurology*
EMP: 83 **Privately Held**
WEB: www.ucdavis.edu
SIC: 8011 8221 9411 Primary care medical clinic; university; administration of educational programs;
HQ: University Of California, Davis
1 Shields Ave
Davis CA 95616

(P-15776)
UNIVERSITY CALIFORNIA DAVIS
3200 Bell Rd, Auburn (95603-9244)
PHONE 530 885-5618
Lupe Avila, *Principal*
Dan Merck, *Internal Med*
Tennyson Lee, *Med Doctor*
Richard Roehrkasse, *Med Doctor*
EMP: 83 **Privately Held**
WEB: www.ucdavis.edu
SIC: 8011 8221 9411 Offices & clinics of medical doctors; university; administration of educational programs;
HQ: University Of California, Davis
1 Shields Ave
Davis CA 95616

(P-15777)
UNIVERSITY CALIFORNIA DAVIS
2521 Stockton Blvd, Sacramento (95817-2207)
PHONE 916 734-2105
Dr Caroline Chantry, *Principal*
EMP: 83 **Privately Held**
WEB: www.ucdavis.edu
SIC: 8011 8221 9411 Offices & clinics of medical doctors; university; administration of educational programs;
HQ: University Of California, Davis
1 Shields Ave
Davis CA 95616

(P-15778)
UNIVERSITY CALIFORNIA DAVIS
Also Called: Wildlife Health Center
Rm Tb 128 Old Davis Rd, Davis (95616)
PHONE 530 752-4167
Jonna Mazet, *Director*
EMP: 83 **Privately Held**
WEB: www.ucdavis.edu
SIC: 8011 8221 9411 Medical centers; university; administration of educational programs;
HQ: University Of California, Davis
1 Shields Ave
Davis CA 95616

(P-15779)
UNIVERSITY CALIFORNIA DAVIS
Also Called: Cowell Student Health Center
Student Hse Ctr Univ Of C, Davis (95616)
PHONE 530 752-2300
Dr Michelle Famula, *Director*
EMP: 83 **Privately Held**
WEB: www.ucdavis.edu
SIC: 8011 8221 9411 Medical centers; university; administration of educational programs;
HQ: University Of California, Davis
1 Shields Ave
Davis CA 95616

(P-15780)
UNIVERSITY CALIFORNIA DAVIS
Also Called: Department of Neurology
4860 Y St Ste 3700, Sacramento (95817-2307)
PHONE 916 734-6280
Agius Mark, *Manager*
EMP: 83 **Privately Held**
WEB: www.ucdavis.edu
SIC: 8011 8221 9411 Neurologist; university; administration of educational programs;
HQ: University Of California, Davis
1 Shields Ave
Davis CA 95616

(P-15781)
UNIVERSITY CALIFORNIA DAVIS
Also Called: Zacharias, Don M MD
500 University Ave # 220, Sacramento (95825-6504)
PHONE 916 442-1011
EMP: 83 **Privately Held**
WEB: www.ucdavis.edu
SIC: 8011 8221 9411 General & family practice, physician/surgeon; university; administration of educational programs;
HQ: University Of California, Davis
1 Shields Ave
Davis CA 95616

(P-15782)
UNIVERSITY CALIFORNIA DAVIS
Also Called: Employee Health Services
501 Oak Ave, Davis (95616-3624)
PHONE 530 752-2330
Dr Micheal J Malley, *Director*
EMP: 83 **Privately Held**
WEB: www.ucdavis.edu
SIC: 8011 8221 9411 Dispensery, operated by physicians; university; administration of educational programs;
HQ: University Of California, Davis
1 Shields Ave
Davis CA 95616

(P-15783)
UROLOGY ASSOCIATES CENTRAL CAL
7014 N Whitney Ave Ste A, Fresno (93720-0155)
PHONE 559 321-2800
Gilbert Dale MD, *President*
Artin Jibilian MD, *Treasurer*
Irwin S Barg MD, *Vice Pres*
Yuk-Yuen Leung, *Managing Dir*
William Schiff MD, *Admin Sec*
EMP: 90 **EST:** 1997
SQ FT: 28,074
SALES (est): 10.4MM **Privately Held**
WEB: www.urologyassociates.net
SIC: 8011 Urologist

(P-15784)
VALLEY CHLD HLTHCARE FUNDATION
9300 Valley Childrens Pl, Madera (93636-8761)
PHONE 559 353-3000
Todd Suntrapak, *CEO*
Shaghig Kouyoumjan,
Swati Banerjee, *Vice Chairman*
Bill Smittcamp, *Vice Chairman*
Danielle Barry, *Vice Pres*
EMP: 2800 **EST:** 2013
SALES: 793.8MM **Privately Held**
WEB: www.valleychildrens.org
SIC: 8011 8069 Physical medicine, physician/surgeon; physicians' office, including specialists; children's hospital

(P-15785)
VALLEY VASCULAR SURGERY ASSOC
1247 E Alluvial Ave # 101, Fresno (93720-2686)
PHONE 559 431-6226
Meila Williams MD, *Principal*

EMP: 35 **EST:** 2001
SQ FT: 10,177
SALES (est): 1.1MM **Privately Held**
SIC: 8011 Physicians' office, including specialists

(P-15786)
VEP HEALTHCARE INC
1001 Galaxy Way Ste 400, Concord (94520-5725)
PHONE 925 482-2839
Steve Maron, *President*
Kelly Danna, *CFO*
Harneet Singh Bath, *Vice Pres*
Robert Wyman, *Vice Pres*
Zafia Anklesaria, *Associate Dir*
EMP: 200 **EST:** 2015
SALES (est): 27.1MM **Privately Held**
WEB: www.usacs.com
SIC: 8011 Specialized medical practitioners, except internal; physicians' office, including specialists

(P-15787)
VETERANS HEALTH ADMINISTRATION
Also Called: Mare Island Outpatient Clinic
Walnut Ave Bldg 201, Vallejo (94589)
PHONE 707 562-8200
Debra Nathanson, *Manager*
EMP: 111 **Publicly Held**
WEB: www.va.gov
SIC: 8011 9451 Clinic, operated by physicians; psychiatric clinic;
HQ: Veterans Health Administration
810 Vermont Ave Nw
Washington DC 20420

(P-15788)
VETERANS HEALTH ADMINISTRATION
Also Called: Sacramento Mental Hlth Clinic
10535 Hospital Way, Mather (95655-4200)
PHONE 916 366-5427
Charles Barnett, *Manager*
EMP: 111 **Publicly Held**
WEB: www.va.gov
SIC: 8011 9451 Clinic, operated by physicians;
HQ: Veterans Health Administration
810 Vermont Ave Nw
Washington DC 20420

(P-15789)
VETERANS HEALTH ADMINISTRATION
Also Called: VA Fremont Clinic
39199 Liberty St, Fremont (94538-1501)
PHONE 510 791-4000
EMP: 111 **Publicly Held**
WEB: www.va.gov
SIC: 8011 9451 Clinic, operated by physicians;
HQ: Veterans Health Administration
810 Vermont Ave Nw
Washington DC 20420

(P-15790)
VETERANS HEALTH ADMINISTRATION
Also Called: Central Cal Healthcare Sys
2615 E Clinton Ave, Fresno (93703-2223)
PHONE 559 225-6100
Al Perry, *Branch Mgr*
Arnold Friedman, *Ch Radiology*
James Weyant, *Security Dir*
Kelli Johnston, *Director*
Peter Leong, *Director*
EMP: 111 **Publicly Held**
WEB: www.benefits.va.gov
SIC: 8011 9451 Medical centers; administration of veterans' affairs;
HQ: Veterans Health Administration
810 Vermont Ave Nw
Washington DC 20420

8011 - Offices & Clinics Of Doctors Of Medicine County (P-15791)   PRODUCTS & SERVICES SECTION

(P-15791)
VETERANS HEALTH ADMINISTRATION
Also Called: Redding V A Outpatient Clinic
351 Hartnell Ave, Redding (96002-1845)
PHONE..................530 226-7555
Anthony Pineda, *Branch Mgr*
Corsini Templado, *Internal Med*
EMP: 111 **Publicly Held**
WEB: www.benefits.va.gov
SIC: 8011 9451 Clinic, operated by physicians; psychiatric clinic;
HQ: Veterans Health Administration
810 Vermont Ave Nw
Washington DC 20420

(P-15792)
VETERANS HEALTH ADMINISTRATION
Also Called: Palo Alto VA Medical Center
3801 Miranda Ave Bldg 101, Palo Alto (94304-1207)
PHONE..................650 493-5000
Elizabeth Freeman, *Director*
Edward Bertaccini, *Med Doctor*
Mike Hosseini, *Supervisor*
EMP: 111 **Publicly Held**
WEB: www.benefits.va.gov
SIC: 8011 9451 Medical centers;
HQ: Veterans Health Administration
810 Vermont Ave Nw
Washington DC 20420

(P-15793)
VETERANS HEALTH ADMINISTRATION
Also Called: Sierra Fthlls Otpatient Clinic
3123 Professional Dr, Auburn (95603-2462)
PHONE..................530 889-0872
Loretta Clukey, *Manager*
EMP: 111 **Publicly Held**
WEB: www.va.gov
SIC: 8011 9451 Clinic, operated by physicians; administration of veterans' affairs
HQ: Veterans Health Administration
810 Vermont Ave Nw
Washington DC 20420

(P-15794)
VETERANS HEALTH ADMINISTRATION
Also Called: Oakland V A Outpatient Clinic
2221 Mrtin Lther King Jr, Oakland (94612-1318)
PHONE..................510 267-7820
Dr Elmer Anderson, *Principal*
EMP: 111 **Publicly Held**
WEB: www.va.gov
SIC: 8011 9451 Clinic, operated by physicians;
HQ: Veterans Health Administration
810 Vermont Ave Nw
Washington DC 20420

(P-15795)
VETERANS HEALTH ADMINISTRATION
Also Called: San Francisco Vamc
4150 Clement St Bldg 6, San Francisco (94121-1563)
PHONE..................415 750-2009
Brian J Kelly, *Manager*
Bonnie Graham, *Officer*
Ellen Peterson, *Nursing Mgr*
Hussam Alkhadra, *Safety Dir*
Reginald Tims, *Maintence Staff*
EMP: 111 **Publicly Held**
WEB: www.benefits.va.gov
SIC: 8011 9451 Medical centers;
HQ: Veterans Health Administration
810 Vermont Ave Nw
Washington DC 20420

(P-15796)
VETERANS HEALTH ADMINISTRATION
Also Called: Martinez Outpatient Clinic
150 Muir Rd, Martinez (94553-4668)
PHONE..................925 372-2000
Dina Moore, *Director*
Joan Kotun, *Psychiatry*
Rick Ross, *Nurse*
EMP: 111 **Publicly Held**
WEB: www.benefits.va.gov
SIC: 8011 9451 Clinic, operated by physicians;
HQ: Veterans Health Administration
810 Vermont Ave Nw
Washington DC 20420

(P-15797)
VETERANS HEALTH ADMINISTRATION
Also Called: Chico V A Outpatient Clinic
280 Cohasset Rd, Chico (95926-2210)
PHONE..................530 879-5000
Sonny Morgan, *Manager*
EMP: 111 **Publicly Held**
WEB: www.benefits.va.gov
SIC: 8011 9451 Clinic, operated by physicians;
HQ: Veterans Health Administration
810 Vermont Ave Nw
Washington DC 20420

(P-15798)
VETERANS HEALTH ADMINISTRATION
Also Called: Fairfield V A Outpatient Clinic
103 Bodin Cir, Fairfield (94535-1801)
PHONE..................707 437-1800
Hannelore Catania, *Manager*
EMP: 111 **Publicly Held**
WEB: www.va.gov
SIC: 8011 9451 Clinic, operated by physicians;
HQ: Veterans Health Administration
810 Vermont Ave Nw
Washington DC 20420

(P-15799)
VETERANS HEALTH ADMINISTRATION
Also Called: Santa Rosa Clinic
3315 Chanate Rd, Santa Rosa (95404-1736)
PHONE..................707 570-3800
Donald B Dean, *Manager*
EMP: 111 **Publicly Held**
WEB: www.benefits.va.gov
SIC: 8011 9451 Clinic, operated by physicians;
HQ: Veterans Health Administration
810 Vermont Ave Nw
Washington DC 20420

(P-15800)
VETERANS HEALTH ADMINISTRATION
40597 Westlake Dr, Oakhurst (93644-9024)
PHONE..................702 341-3020
Erin Potter, *Branch Mgr*
EMP: 111 **Publicly Held**
WEB: www.va.gov
SIC: 8011 9451 Medical centers;
HQ: Veterans Health Administration
810 Vermont Ave Nw
Washington DC 20420

(P-15801)
VETERANS HEALTH ADMINISTRATION
Also Called: Ukiah V A Outpatient Clinic
630 Kings Ct, Ukiah (95482-5003)
PHONE..................707 468-7700
Linda Muligan, *Director*
Pamela Polk, *Manager*
EMP: 111 **Publicly Held**
WEB: www.va.gov
SIC: 8011 9451 Clinic, operated by physicians;

HQ: Veterans Health Administration
810 Vermont Ave Nw
Washington DC 20420

(P-15802)
VETERANS HEALTH ADMINISTRATION
Also Called: Sacramento V A Medical Center
10535 Hospital Way, Mather (95655-4200)
PHONE..................916 843-7000
Lawrence Sandlers, *Director*
Kevin Nugent,
Charles Barnett, *Ch Radiology*
Elizabeth Blohm, *Records Dir*
Ivan Meadows, *Lab Dir*
EMP: 111 **Publicly Held**
WEB: www.va.gov
SIC: 8011 9451 Medical centers; administration of veterans' affairs;
HQ: Veterans Health Administration
810 Vermont Ave Nw
Washington DC 20420

(P-15803)
VETERANS HEALTH ADMINISTRATION
Also Called: Livermore VA Medical Center
4951 Arroyo Rd, Livermore (94550-9650)
PHONE..................925 447-2560
C H Nixon, *Director*
EMP: 111 **Publicly Held**
WEB: www.benefits.va.gov
SIC: 8011 9451 Medical centers;
HQ: Veterans Health Administration
810 Vermont Ave Nw
Washington DC 20420

(P-15804)
VETERANS HEALTH ADMINISTRATION
Also Called: Menlo Park VA Medical Center
795 Willow Rd, Menlo Park (94025-2539)
PHONE..................650 614-9997
Lisa Freeman, *Director*
EMP: 111 **Publicly Held**
WEB: www.va.gov
SIC: 8011 9451 Medical centers; psychiatric clinic;
HQ: Veterans Health Administration
810 Vermont Ave Nw
Washington DC 20420

(P-15805)
VETERANS HEALTH ADMINISTRATION
Also Called: Concord Vet Center
1333 Willow Pass Rd # 10, Concord (94520-7930)
PHONE..................925 680-4526
Al Perstposa, *Manager*
EMP: 111 **Publicly Held**
WEB: www.va.gov
SIC: 8011 9451 Medical centers;
HQ: Veterans Health Administration
810 Vermont Ave Nw
Washington DC 20420

(P-15806)
VETERANS HEALTH ADMINISTRATION
Also Called: Martinez Center For Rehab
150 Muir Rd 90c, Martinez (94553-4668)
PHONE..................925 372-2076
Ralph Swain, *Manager*
EMP: 111 **Publicly Held**
WEB: www.benefits.va.gov
SIC: 8011 9451 Medical centers; administration of veterans' affairs
HQ: Veterans Health Administration
810 Vermont Ave Nw
Washington DC 20420

(P-15807)
VETERINARY SURGICAL ASSOCIATES
251 N Amphlett Blvd, San Mateo (94401-1805)
PHONE..................650 696-8196
Sharon Ullman, *Manager*

EMP: 74
SALES (corp-wide): 14.5MM **Privately Held**
WEB: www.sagecenters.com
SIC: 8011 0742 Freestanding emergency medical center; surgeon; veterinarian, animal specialties
PA: Veterinary Surgical Associates
1410 Monu Blvd Ste 100
Concord CA 94520
925 827-1777

(P-15808)
VISION CARE CTR A MED GROUP IN (PA)
Also Called: Vision Care Center Central Cal
7075 N Sharon Ave, Fresno (93720-3329)
PHONE..................559 486-2000
Julie Cleeland, *CEO*
Ralph Hadley Od, *President*
Michael Herman, *CFO*
EMP: 82 **EST:** 1963
SQ FT: 18,000
SALES (est): 14.2MM **Privately Held**
WEB: www.eyeqvc.com
SIC: 8011 8042 Ophthalmologist; offices & clinics of optometrists

(P-15809)
VISTA CMPLETE CARE INC A PROF
13555 Bowman Rd Ste 100, Auburn (95603-3197)
PHONE..................530 885-3951
Daniel Sewell, *President*
EMP: 38 **EST:** 2010
SALES (est): 3MM **Privately Held**
WEB: www.vistacompletecare.com
SIC: 8011 General & family practice, physician/surgeon

(P-15810)
VOLPE CHIU ABEL STERNBERG
Also Called: Abel, Michael E MD
3838 California St Rm 616, San Francisco (94118-1508)
PHONE..................415 668-0411
Peter A Volpe, *Partner*
Michael E Abel, *Partner*
Yanek Chiu, *Partner*
Thomas R Russell, *Partner*
Jeffrey Sternberg, *Partner*
EMP: 50 **EST:** 1949
SALES (est): 5MM **Privately Held**
SIC: 8011 Surgeon

(P-15811)
WAVERLEY SURGERY CENTER LP (PA)
400 Forest Ave, Palo Alto (94301-2608)
PHONE..................650 324-0600
Steven Kanter, *Partner*
Carlokim Chace, *Office Mgr*
Carlos Reyes, *Office Mgr*
Christabelle Dagun, *CIO*
Julia Delao,
▲ **EMP:** 58 **EST:** 2002
SQ FT: 9,600
SALES (est): 7MM **Privately Held**
WEB: www.waverleysurgery.com
SIC: 8011 Ambulatory surgical center

(P-15812)
WEBSTER ORTHPDC MED GRP A PROF
200 Porter Dr Ste 101, San Ramon (94583-1524)
PHONE..................925 362-2116
Sheila Cayzer, *Manager*
Jodie Herr, *Finance*
Omega Viola-King, *Opers Staff*
Hany Elrashidy, *Sports Medicine*
Stephen Powers, *Physician Asst*
EMP: 40
SALES (corp-wide): 13.6MM **Privately Held**
WEB: www.websterorthopedics.com
SIC: 8011 Orthopedic physician
PA: Webster Orthopaedic Medical Group A Professional Corp
3315 Broadway
Oakland CA 94611
510 238-1200

PRODUCTS & SERVICES SECTION

8021 - Offices & Clinics Of Dentists County (P-15836)

(P-15813)
WEBSTER SURGERY CENTER LP (PA)
80 Grand Ave Ste 250, Oakland (94612-3743)
PHONE.....................510 451-0957
Glen K Lau MD, *Medical Dir*
EMP: 51 **EST:** 2000
SQ FT: 6,000
SALES (est): 6.9MM **Privately Held**
WEB: www.webstersurgerycenter.com
SIC: 8011 Surgeon

(P-15814)
WEST CAST RETINA MED GROUP INC
1445 Bush St, San Francisco (94109-5520)
PHONE.....................415 972-4600
Benjamin Higginbotham, *CEO*
Robert Johnson MD, *Treasurer*
H R McDonald MD, *Admin Sec*
EMP: 47 **EST:** 1974
SQ FT: 1,500
SALES (est): 6.6MM **Privately Held**
WEB: www.westcoastretina.com
SIC: 8011 Ophthalmologist; general & family practice, physician/surgeon

(P-15815)
WEST COUNTY HEALTH CENTERS INC (PA)
16312 3rd St, Guerneville (95446)
P.O. Box 1449 (95446-1449)
PHONE.....................707 869-1594
Mary Szecsey, *Exec Dir*
John Kornfeld, *President*
Dwight Cary, *Treasurer*
Susan Cousineau, *Officer*
Debra Johnson, *Vice Pres*
EMP: 75 **EST:** 1974
SALES (est): 12.3MM **Privately Held**
WEB: www.wchealth.org
SIC: 8011 Primary care medical clinic; clinic, operated by physicians

(P-15816)
WILLOW SPRINGS LLC
Also Called: Sierra Vista Hospital
8001 Bruceville Rd, Sacramento (95823-2329)
PHONE.....................916 288-0300
Mike Zauner, *CEO*
Tameka Primm, *Human Res Dir*
Brenda Gaffney, *Director*
Amanda Shedd, *Director*
EMP: 55
SALES (corp-wide): 11.5B **Publicly Held**
WEB: www.uhs.com
SIC: 8011 8063 Psychiatric clinic; psychiatric hospitals
HQ: Willow Springs, Llc
6640 Carothers Pkwy # 400
Franklin TN 37067
615 312-5700

(P-15817)
WILLOW SPRINGS LLC
Fremont Hospital
39001 Sundale Dr, Fremont (94538-2005)
PHONE.....................510 796-1100
Toll Free:.....................888
Joan Bettencourt Newman, *Principal*
Zubin Kachhi, *Business Dir*
Mini Dhiman, *Nursing Dir*
Jessica Cedillo,
Satwinder Mahabir, *Director*
EMP: 55
SALES (corp-wide): 11.5B **Publicly Held**
WEB: www.uhs.com
SIC: 8011 8093 8361 8069 Psychiatric clinic; specialty outpatient clinics; residential care; specialty hospitals, except psychiatric; psychiatric hospitals
HQ: Willow Springs, Llc
6640 Carothers Pkwy # 400
Franklin TN 37067
615 312-5700

(P-15818)
WOMENS HEALTH SPECIALISTS
2299 Mowry Ave Ste 3c, Fremont (94538-1621)
PHONE.....................510 248-1470
Gary Charland, *Office Mgr*
EMP: 69 **EST:** 1987
SQ FT: 5,300
SALES (est): 5MM **Privately Held**
WEB: www.mywtmf.com
SIC: 8011 Obstetrician; gynecologist

(P-15819)
ZEITER EYE MEDICAL GROUP INC (PA)
255 E Weber Ave, Stockton (95202-2706)
PHONE.....................209 366-0446
John H Zeiter MD, *President*
Joseph Zeiter MD, *CFO*
Henry J Zeiter MD, *Vice Pres*
Henry Zeiter, *Vice Pres*
Gabriela Magdaleno, *Office Mgr*
EMP: 65 **EST:** 1962
SQ FT: 11,500
SALES (est): 10.6MM **Privately Held**
WEB: www.zeitereye.com
SIC: 8011 Ophthalmologist

8021 Offices & Clinics Of Dentists

(P-15820)
ALAN J VALLARINE DDS INC
1840 N Olive Ave Ste 4, Turlock (95382-2502)
PHONE.....................209 669-8120
Alan J Vallarine DDS, *President*
Alan J Vallarine, *President*
Alan Vallarine, *Fmly & Gen Dent*
EMP: 37 **EST:** 1983
SALES (est): 997.8K **Privately Held**
SIC: 8021 Dentists' office

(P-15821)
AMPLA HEALTH (PA)
935 Market St, Yuba City (95991-4217)
PHONE.....................530 674-4261
Benjamin Flores, *CEO*
Hilton Perez, *COO*
Dale Johnson, *CFO*
Harjit Jhikka, *Officer*
Carlos Peralta, *Officer*
EMP: 245 **EST:** 1964
SQ FT: 10,200
SALES: 70.3MM **Privately Held**
WEB: www.amplahealth.org
SIC: 8021 8011 Dental clinic; health maintenance organization; primary care medical clinic; pediatrician

(P-15822)
ASHEN COMPANY LTD (PA)
3901 Marconi Ave, Sacramento (95821-3902)
PHONE.....................916 487-0117
Charles Ashen, *President*
Michael Ahen, *Manager*
EMP: 53 **EST:** 1980
SQ FT: 7,500
SALES (est): 7.1MM **Privately Held**
WEB: www.californiadental.com
SIC: 8021 Group & corporate practice dentists

(P-15823)
ASHOK N VEERANKI DDS A PRO (PA)
620 W Eaton Ave, Tracy (95376-3361)
PHONE.....................209 836-3870
Joseph Giuliani, *Principal*
EMP: 56 **EST:** 2007
SALES (est): 1MM **Privately Held**
WEB: www.drveeranki.com
SIC: 8021 Dental surgeon

(P-15824)
BARRERA ADOLFO DDS (PA)
40 Jeffers Way, Campbell (95008-2891)
PHONE.....................408 871-2885
Adolfo Barrera, *Principal*
EMP: 41 **EST:** 2009
SALES (est): 989.2K **Privately Held**
WEB: www.barreradds.com
SIC: 8021 Dental clinic

(P-15825)
BLUE OAK DENTAL GROUP
Also Called: Blue Oak Dental Group
15 Sierra Gate Plz, Roseville (95678-6602)
PHONE.....................916 786-6777
Dr Michael Gade DDS, *Partner*
Dr Mark Arena DDS, *Partner*
Dr A R Wilkes DDS, *Partner*
Kari McKinley, *Office Mgr*
EMP: 36 **EST:** 1977
SQ FT: 6,000
SALES (est): 2MM **Privately Held**
WEB: www.blueoakdentalgroup.com
SIC: 8021 Dentists' office

(P-15826)
CASTLE DENTAL SURGERY CENTRE
Also Called: Central Cal Dntl Surgicenter
3605 Hospital Rd Ste H, Atwater (95301-5173)
PHONE.....................209 381-2047
Lawrence Church, *General Ptnr*
EMP: 37 **EST:** 1999
SQ FT: 6,000
SALES (est): 722K **Privately Held**
SIC: 8021 Dental surgeon

(P-15827)
CHAI DDS INC
3514 Verona Ter, Davis (95618-6755)
PHONE.....................909 810-7287
EMP: 108
SALES (corp-wide): 372.6K **Privately Held**
SIC: 8021 Offices & clinics of dentists
PA: Chai Dds, Inc.
508 2nd St Ste 107b
Davis CA

(P-15828)
CHAPA-DE INDIAN HLTH PRGRAM IN
1350 E Main St, Grass Valley (95945-5208)
PHONE.....................530 477-8545
Pamela Padilla, *Branch Mgr*
Cathy Murchisona, *Administration*
EMP: 60
SALES (corp-wide): 60.9MM **Privately Held**
WEB: www.chapa-de.org
SIC: 8021 8011 8322 Dentists' office; clinic, operated by physicians; outreach program; multi-service center
PA: Chapa-De Indian Health Program, Inc.
11670 Atwood Rd
Auburn CA 95603
530 887-2800

(P-15829)
CREATIVE DMNSIONS IN DENTISTRY (PA)
Also Called: Creative Dmnsions In Dentistry
20265 Lake Chabot Rd, Castro Valley (94546-5307)
PHONE.....................510 881-8010
Ugene Santuecci, *President*
Michael Erickson, *CFO*
Robert M Maass, *Admin Sec*
Mundeep Chhina, *Fmly & Gen Dent*
EMP: 49 **EST:** 1965
SQ FT: 8,400
SALES (est): 2.9MM **Privately Held**
WEB: www.cddentists.com
SIC: 8021 Dentists' office

(P-15830)
CUPERTINO DENTAL GROUP
Also Called: Frangadakis, Kenneth DDS
10383 Torre Ave Ste I, Cupertino (95014-3297)
PHONE.....................408 257-3031
Ken Frangadakis, *Partner*
Gary E Pagonis, *Partner*
Milton J Pagonis, *Partner*
EMP: 60 **EST:** 1978
SQ FT: 4,000
SALES (est): 8.9MM **Privately Held**
WEB: www.cupertinodentalgroup.com
SIC: 8021 Dentists' office

(P-15831)
DEL ROSARIO RENE DMD (PA)
Also Called: Union Landing Dental Center
32364 Dyer St, Union City (94587-1720)
PHONE.....................510 324-2000
Rene Del Rosario DMD, *President*
EMP: 45 **EST:** 2000
SQ FT: 13,674
SALES (est): 3.1MM **Privately Held**
WEB: www.delrosariodental.com
SIC: 8021 Dentists' office

(P-15832)
DENTAL BNEFT PROVIDERS CAL INC
425 Market St Fl 12, San Francisco (94105-2532)
PHONE.....................415 778-3800
Irma CHI Kato, *CEO*
EMP: 42 **EST:** 1985
SALES (est): 1.5MM
SALES (corp-wide): 257.1B **Publicly Held**
WEB: www.unitedhealthgroup.com
SIC: 8021 Dental insurance plan
PA: Unitedhealth Group Incorporated
9900 Bren Rd E Ste 300w
Minnetonka MN 55343
952 936-1300

(P-15833)
ENDODONTICS ASSOCIATES
2000 Forest Ave Ste D, San Jose (95128-4831)
PHONE.....................408 294-4149
Allen D Hiura, *Partner*
Michael Fukawa, *Partner*
Michael McKee, *Partner*
EMP: 47 **EST:** 1971
SQ FT: 1,000
SALES (est): 6.1MM **Privately Held**
SIC: 8021 Periodontist

(P-15834)
FRESNO ORAL MXLLFCIAL SRGERY D
1903 E Fir Ave Ste 101, Fresno (93720-3862)
PHONE.....................559 226-2722
Howell Wiggins Jr, *Partner*
Gerald Alexander DDS, *Partner*
Brian Huh, *Surgeon*
Shannon Barnhart, *Fmly & Gen Dent*
EMP: 42 **EST:** 1975
SALES (est): 2.9MM **Privately Held**
WEB: www.fresnooralsurgery.com
SIC: 8021 Maxillofacial specialist; oral pathologist

(P-15835)
GENTLE DENTAL
853 Middlefield Rd Ste 1, Palo Alto (94301-2900)
PHONE.....................650 341-8008
Robert Rideau,
EMP: 826 **EST:** 1990
SQ FT: 2,200
SALES (est): 5.6MM
SALES (corp-wide): 119.8MM **Privately Held**
WEB: www.interdent.com
SIC: 8021 Dental clinic
HQ: Interdent Service Corporation
9800 S La Cnga Blvd # 800
Inglewood CA 90301

(P-15836)
HOLM MCHAEL B DDS JOHN C RACH
Also Called: American River Dental Center
10350 Coloma Rd, Rancho Cordova (95670-2106)
PHONE.....................916 362-9247
Michael B Holm DDS, *Partner*
Guy Acheson DDS, *Partner*
Dr John Riach, *Partner*
Mike Gaide, *Business Mgr*
Mike Holm, *Fmly & Gen Dent*
EMP: 43 **EST:** 1981
SQ FT: 3,000
SALES (est): 2.9MM **Privately Held**
WEB: www.americanriverdental.com
SIC: 8021 Dentists' office

8021 - Offices & Clinics Of Dentists County (P-15837)

(P-15837)
IFEATU NNEBE DDS INC (PA)
2700 E Bidwell St Ste 300, Folsom (95630-6434)
PHONE.....................................916 299-9487
EMP: 44 EST: 2019
SALES (est): 394.9K Privately Held
SIC: 8021 Offices & clinics of dentists

(P-15838)
INTERDENT SERVICE CORPORATION
Also Called: Martin, Steve DDS
1421 Guerneville Rd # 102, Santa Rosa (95403-7220)
PHONE.....................................707 528-7000
R Pranin, Branch Mgr
Peggy Porter, CIO
Paul Anderson, Surgeon
Ashley Moler, Chiropractor
Mairin Bryan, Fmly & Gen Dent
EMP: 105
SALES (corp-wide): 119.8MM Privately Held
WEB: www.interdent.com
SIC: 8021 Dental clinic
HQ: Interdent Service Corporation
9800 S La Cnga Blvd # 800
Inglewood CA 90301

(P-15839)
JACKSON CREEK DENTAL GROUP
100 French Bar Rd Ste 101, Jackson (95642-2557)
PHONE.....................................209 223-2712
Ron M Ask, President
Ron Ask, President
Jeri Michelson, Office Mgr
Dwight Simpson, Fmly & Gen Dent
EMP: 36 EST: 1978
SQ FT: 1,232
SALES (est): 3.3MM Privately Held
WEB: www.jacksoncreekdental.com
SIC: 8021 Dentists' office

(P-15840)
JARED G DNIELSON DDS DNTL CORP (PA)
3628 Walker Park Dr, El Dorado Hills (95762-7609)
PHONE.....................................916 230-8837
Jared G Danielson, CEO
EMP: 55 EST: 2012
SALES (est): 567.6K Privately Held
SIC: 8021 Offices & clinics of dentists

(P-15841)
JEFFREY HUNG-YIP LEE DDS INC (PA)
615 Arcadia Ter Unit 304, Sunnyvale (94085-2355)
PHONE.....................................650 325-2496
Jeffrey Hung-Yip Lee, CEO
EMP: 46 EST: 2017
SALES (est): 313.2K Privately Held
SIC: 8021 Offices & clinics of dentists

(P-15842)
JOHN A HUGHES DDS INCORPORATED
Also Called: Hughes Dental Group
1580 Winchester Blvd # 30, Campbell (95008-0519)
PHONE.....................................408 378-3489
James A Carter DDS, President
Thomas A Hughes DDS, Vice Pres
Clifford O Marks DDS, Admin Sec
Sharon Mc Intosh, Finance
Nannette J Benedict DDS, Director
EMP: 60 EST: 1954
SQ FT: 4,650
SALES (est): 8MM Privately Held
WEB: www.hughesdental.com
SIC: 8021 Dentists' office

(P-15843)
JOHN VELLEQUETTE DDS
877 W Fremont Ave Ste L3, Sunnyvale (94087-2319)
PHONE.....................................408 245-7500
John Vellequette, Owner
EMP: 35 EST: 1983

SALES (est): 1MM Privately Held
WEB: www.drjohn.net
SIC: 8021 Dentists' office

(P-15844)
JOSEPH BUI DMD INC (PA)
1110 W Kettleman Ln # 47, Lodi (95240-6031)
PHONE.....................................209 224-8104
Joseph Bui, Principal
EMP: 42 EST: 2015
SALES (est): 90K Privately Held
SIC: 8021 Offices & clinics of dentists

(P-15845)
LAKE CNTY TRBAL HLTH CNSRTIUM
925 Bevins Ct, Lakeport (95453-9754)
P.O. Box 1950 (95453-1950)
PHONE.....................................707 263-8382
Mike Icay, President
Crista Ray, Ch of Bd
Tanya Michel, CFO
Tina Ramos, Chairman
Bret Woods, Executive
EMP: 80 EST: 1983
SQ FT: 10,832
SALES: 26MM Privately Held
WEB: www.lcthc.com
SIC: 8021 Dental clinic

(P-15846)
LORA H COSTA DDS INC (PA)
1286 Kifer Rd Ste 110, Sunnyvale (94086-5326)
PHONE.....................................408 774-1200
Lora Costa, Principal
EMP: 40 EST: 2008
SALES (est): 672.5K Privately Held
WEB: www.lorahuynhdentist.com
SIC: 8021 Dentists' office

(P-15847)
MALIK DENTAL CORP (PA)
15051 Hesperian Blvd, San Leandro (94578-3536)
PHONE.....................................925 692-2010
Jay A Goble, Owner
EMP: 35 EST: 2010
SALES (est): 1.5MM Privately Held
SIC: 8021 Dental clinic

(P-15848)
MC DONALD SLOAN M DDS RBRTO J
5201 Deer Valley Rd 2b, Antioch (94531-7429)
PHONE.....................................925 778-2100
Sloan M Mc Donald DDS, Partner
Roberto J Deloso, Partner
Sloan Mc Donald, Partner
Sloan McDonald, Director
EMP: 35 EST: 1988
SALES (est): 2MM Privately Held
WEB: www.eastcountyoralsurgery.com
SIC: 8021 Dentists' office

(P-15849)
MOORE WILLIAM AND KAY MARK DDS
1396 Solano Ave, Albany (94706-1832)
PHONE.....................................510 525-5510
Mark B Kay DDS, Partner
Mark Kay, Partner
William Moore DDS, Partner
EMP: 40 EST: 1972
SQ FT: 384
SALES (est): 927.8K Privately Held
SIC: 8021 Dentists' office

(P-15850)
NORTHERN VLY INDIAN HLTH INC
845 W East Ave, Chico (95926-2002)
PHONE.....................................530 896-9400
Maureen Self, Manager
Regina Dock, Admin Sec
Deborah Harrington, Technician
Alexis Rocha, Purchasing
Rita Jenkins, Purch Agent
EMP: 42

SALES (corp-wide): 47.1MM Privately Held
WEB: www.nvih.org
SIC: 8021 8011 Dental clinic; primary care medical clinic
PA: Northern Valley Indian Health, Inc.
207 N Butte St
Willows CA
530 934-9293

(P-15851)
NORTHERN VLY INDIAN HLTH INC
2500 Main St, Red Bluff (96080-2336)
PHONE.....................................530 529-2567
Robin Brownfield, Manager
Tim Pigmon, Marketing Staff
Larissa Tamble, Director
EMP: 42
SALES (corp-wide): 47.1MM Privately Held
WEB: www.nvih.org
SIC: 8021 Offices & clinics of dentists
PA: Northern Valley Indian Health, Inc.
207 N Butte St
Willows CA
530 934-9293

(P-15852)
ORCHARD DENTAL GROUP
11121 Fair Oaks Blvd, Fair Oaks (95628-5199)
PHONE.....................................916 961-6810
Roger J Taylor, Partner
James C Wallace, Partner
EMP: 39 EST: 1975
SQ FT: 10,000
SALES (est): 5.1MM Privately Held
WEB: www.orcharddentalgroup.net
SIC: 8021 Dentists' office

(P-15853)
PARK DDS MPH INC (PA)
1067 C St Ste 125, Galt (95632-1759)
PHONE.....................................209 744-0463
David S Park, Owner
EMP: 44 EST: 2014
SALES (est): 543.9K Privately Held
SIC: 8021 Dental clinic

(P-15854)
PATRICK L ROETZER DDS INC
Also Called: Carquinez Dental Group
142 E D St, Benicia (94510-3223)
PHONE.....................................707 745-8002
Patrick L Roetzer DDS, President
Nancy Roetzer, Vice Pres
EMP: 41 EST: 1977
SQ FT: 1,682
SALES (est): 2MM Privately Held
SIC: 8021 Dentists' office

(P-15855)
RAEL BERNSTEIN DDS A PROF CORP (PA)
Also Called: Bernstein Orthodontics
2180 Northpoint Pkwy, Santa Rosa (95407-7395)
PHONE.....................................707 575-0600
Rael Bernstein, President
Anne-Marie Miklos, Administration
EMP: 36 EST: 2007
SALES (est): 2.9MM Privately Held
WEB: www.bernsteinbraces.com
SIC: 8021 Orthodontist

(P-15856)
RICKEY & WONG DDS INC
Also Called: Quality Dentistry
3608 Dale Rd, Modesto (95356-0500)
PHONE.....................................209 577-0777
Annette Rold, Exec Dir
Janis Chapman, Principal
Jim Muncy, CIO
Sean Kennedy, Software Engr
EMP: 49 EST: 2012
SALES (est): 3MM Privately Held
WEB: www.qualitydentists.com
SIC: 8021 Dentists' office

(P-15857)
SANTA ROSA DENTAL GROUP
80 Doctors Park Dr, Santa Rosa (95405)
PHONE.....................................707 545-0944
Allen Barbieri, Partner
Perry Bingham, Partner

Richard L Blechel, Partner
James J Bridges, Partner
Ted Degolia, Partner
EMP: 50 EST: 1969
SQ FT: 8,000
SALES (est): 1.6MM Privately Held
WEB: www.santarosadental.com
SIC: 8021 Dentists' office

(P-15858)
STEVEN K OLSEN DDS PROF CORP
2 Embarcadero Ctr, San Francisco (94111-3823)
PHONE.....................................415 398-4400
Steven K Olsen DDS, President
EMP: 44 EST: 1974
SQ FT: 3,000
SALES (est): 1.7MM Privately Held
WEB: www.embarcaderodentistry.com
SIC: 8021 Dentists' office

(P-15859)
STORY DENTAL HEALTH CENTER
2454 Story Rd, San Jose (95122-1058)
PHONE.....................................408 272-0888
Deepika Jain DDS, President
EMP: 42 EST: 1977
SALES (est): 2.5MM Privately Held
SIC: 8021 Dental clinic

(P-15860)
ULAB SYSTEMS INC (PA)
1820 Gateway Dr Ste 300, San Mateo (94404-4024)
PHONE.....................................866 900-8522
Amir Abolfathi, CEO
Nicola Downes, CFO
Joe Breeland, Exec VP
Charlie Wen, CTO
Donald Steckey, Technical Staff
EMP: 41 EST: 2015
SALES (est): 5.3MM Privately Held
WEB: www.ulabsystems.com
SIC: 8021 Dental clinics & offices

(P-15861)
UNIVERSITY CAL SAN FRANCISCO
Also Called: Ucsf Dental Center-Buchanan
100 Buchanan St, San Francisco (94102-6147)
PHONE.....................................415 476-5608
Mark Kirkland DDS, Administration
Andrew Hom, Professor
Arnold Kahn, Professor
Chui Chan, Med Doctor
Jyoti S Singh, Med Doctor
EMP: 77 Privately Held
WEB: www.ucsf.edu
SIC: 8021 Dental clinics & offices; maxillofacial specialist
HQ: University Cal San Francisco
513 Parnassus Ave 115f
San Francisco CA 94143

(P-15862)
VALLEY OAK DENTAL GROUP
1507 W Yosemite Ave, Manteca (95337-5182)
PHONE.....................................209 823-9341
Marvin Bledsoe, President
Bonnie Morehead DDS, Corp Secy
Rudy R Ciccarelli DDS, Vice Pres
Mark Hochhalter DDS, Vice Pres
Mohammad E Farra, Surgeon
EMP: 36 EST: 1975
SALES (est): 8.3MM Privately Held
WEB: www.valleyoakdentalgroup.com
SIC: 8021 Dentists' office

(P-15863)
YELLICH STEEL & KLEIN
1663 Dominican Way # 112, Santa Cruz (95065-1527)
PHONE.....................................831 475-0221
George M Yellich DDS, Partner
Corrine A Cline-Fortunato DDS, Partner
EMP: 51 EST: 1982
SQ FT: 3,000
SALES (est): 1.3MM Privately Held
SIC: 8021 Dental surgeon

PRODUCTS & SERVICES SECTION

8049 - Offices & Clinics Of Health Practitioners, NEC County (P-15886)

8041 Offices & Clinics Of Chiropractors

(P-15864)
CONNEALY CHIROPRACTIC INC (PA)
930 Detroit Ave Ste A, Concord (94518-2539)
PHONE...................913 669-8023
Alan Connealy, *Principal*
EMP: 35 EST: 2014
SALES (est): 185.5K **Privately Held**
WEB: www.connealychiro.com
SIC: 8041 Offices & clinics of chiropractors

(P-15865)
LANDMARK HEALTHCARE SVCS INC (DH)
1610 Arden Way Ste 280, Sacramento (95815-4050)
PHONE....................800 638-4557
Adam Boehler, *CEO*
Christopher Goldsmith, *President*
Carol Devol, *CFO*
EMP: 120 EST: 1986
SQ FT: 330,215
SALES (est): 28.8MM
SALES (corp-wide): 160.4B **Publicly Held**
WEB: www.landmarkhealthcare.com
SIC: 8041 8049 Offices & clinics of chiropractors; acupuncturist
HQ: Carecore National, Llc
400 Buckwalter Place Blvd
Bluffton SC 29910
800 918-8924

(P-15866)
LATCH SO CHROPRACTIC PROF CORP
1237 Van Ness Ave Ste 300, San Francisco (94109-5506)
PHONE....................415 775-4204
Kenneth So, *Co-Owner*
Daniel Latch, *Co-Owner*
Rebecca Wu, *CIO*
David Latch, *Chiropractor*
EMP: 37 EST: 1959
SALES (est): 3.3MM **Privately Held**
WEB: www.latchandsochiropractic.com
SIC: 8041 Offices & clinics of chiropractors

8042 Offices & Clinics Of Optometrists

(P-15867)
BROOKSIDE OPTOMETRIC GROUP
3133 W March Ln Ste 2020, Stockton (95219-2361)
PHONE....................209 951-0820
Craig K Hisaka Od, *Partner*
John Demshear, *Partner*
Robert Melrose Od, *Partner*
Rosemary Melrose Od, *Partner*
Richard Vanover, *Partner*
EMP: 40 EST: 1974
SQ FT: 3,000
SALES (est): 4.8MM **Privately Held**
WEB: www.brooksideoptometric.com
SIC: 8042 Specialized optometrists

(P-15868)
FAMILY EYE CARE OPTOMETRY CORP
Also Called: Dr Ross, Wan & Taylor
338 E Hamilton Ave, Campbell (95008-0207)
PHONE....................408 379-2020
Peter Ross, *President*
Peter H Taylor, *Treasurer*
Larry R Wan, *Vice Pres*
EMP: 57 EST: 1970
SQ FT: 4,000
SALES (est): 5.3MM **Privately Held**
WEB: www.familyeyecare.com
SIC: 8042 8011 Specialized optometrists; offices & clinics of medical doctors

(P-15869)
GOLDEN OPTICAL CORPORATION
2855 Stevens Creek Blvd, Santa Clara (95050-6709)
PHONE....................408 246-4500
EMP: 84
SALES (corp-wide): 91.7MM **Privately Held**
SIC: 8042 Offices & clinics of optometrists
PA: Golden Optical Corporation
19800 W 8 Mile Rd
Southfield MI 48075
248 354-7100

(P-15870)
JAMES HAZLEHURST
Also Called: Chico Eye Center
605 W East Ave, Chico (95926-7201)
PHONE....................530 895-1727
James A Hazlehurst, *Partner*
Pablo M Arregui, *Partner*
EMP: 39 EST: 1990
SQ FT: 9,500
SALES (est): 2.5MM **Privately Held**
WEB: www.chicoeye.com
SIC: 8042 Specialized optometrists

(P-15871)
MILPITAS OPTOMETRIC GROUP INC
1301 E Calaveras Blvd, Milpitas (95035-5543)
PHONE....................408 263-2040
Gary R Stocker, *Partner*
Susan Gordon, *Partner*
Cris Kavanaugh, *Partner*
EMP: 40 EST: 1982
SQ FT: 1,550
SALES (est): 5.5MM **Privately Held**
WEB: www.milpitasoptometric.com
SIC: 8042 Specialized optometrists

(P-15872)
SANTEN INCORPORATED
6401 Hollis St Ste 125, Emeryville (94608-1462)
PHONE....................415 268-9100
Tatsuya Kaihara, *Officer*
Xavier Avat, *President*
Reza M Haque, *Senior VP*
Mika Masunari, *Vice Pres*
Kathy Kenyon, *Surgery Dir*
EMP: 100 EST: 1993
SQ FT: 46,000
SALES (est): 40.9MM **Privately Held**
WEB: www.santenusa.com
SIC: 8042 Specialized optometrists
PA: Santen Pharmaceutical Co., Ltd.
4-20, Ofukacho, Kita-Ku
Osaka OSK 530-0

(P-15873)
SILICON VLY EYE CARE OPTMTRY C
770 Scott Blvd, Santa Clara (95050-6927)
PHONE....................408 296-0511
Wayne W Zimmerman Od, *Partner*
Louann Alexander, *Partner*
Jeffrey Calmere, *Partner*
Debra McBride, *Partner*
Wayne W Zimmerman, *Partner*
EMP: 37 EST: 1990
SQ FT: 2,000
SALES (est): 3.3MM **Privately Held**
WEB: www.sve.com
SIC: 8042 Specialized optometrists

(P-15874)
THOMAS H MURPHY OD
Also Called: Eye Design Optometry
1689 Arden Way Ste 1091, Sacramento (95815-4096)
PHONE....................916 929-1169
Thomas Murphy, *Owner*
Heidi Qt Pham,
EMP: 35 EST: 1978
SALES (est): 4MM **Privately Held**
SIC: 8042 Contact lense specialist optometrist

(P-15875)
VALLEY OPTOMETRIC CENTER
Also Called: Valley Health Team
449 S Madera Ave, Kerman (93630-1537)
PHONE....................559 846-5252
EMP: 48
SALES (est): 1.1MM **Privately Held**
SIC: 8042 5999 5995 Optometrist's Office Ret Misc Merchandise Ret Optical Goods

(P-15876)
VSP VNTRES OPTMTRIC SLTONS LLC (HQ)
3333 Quality Dr, Rancho Cordova (95670-7985)
PHONE....................916 858-5656
Steve Baker, *President*
EMP: 50 EST: 2019
SALES (est): 5.5MM
SALES (corp-wide): 1.8B **Privately Held**
WEB: www.vspglobal.com
SIC: 8042 Offices & clinics of optometrists
PA: Vision Service Plan, Inc.
3333 Quality Dr
Rancho Cordova CA 95670
916 851-5000

8049 Offices & Clinics Of Health Practitioners, NEC

(P-15877)
A IS FOR APPLE INC
1485 Saratoga Ave Ste 200, San Jose (95129-4965)
PHONE....................877 991-0009
Marilyn Freeman, *President*
John Freeman, *Vice Pres*
EMP: 52 EST: 1999
SALES (est): 2.2MM **Privately Held**
WEB: www.aisforapple.com
SIC: 8049 Speech pathologist

(P-15878)
ADDUS HEALTHCARE INC
2851 Park Marina Dr # 150, Redding (96001-2824)
PHONE....................530 247-0858
Michele Dugar, *Branch Mgr*
EMP: 45 **Publicly Held**
WEB: www.addus.com
SIC: 8049 8011 Nurses & other medical assistants; clinic, operated by physicians
HQ: Addus Healthcare, Inc.
2300 Warrenville Rd # 100
Downers Grove IL 60515
630 296-3400

(P-15879)
ADRENAS THERAPEUTICS INC
421 Kipling St, Palo Alto (94301-1530)
PHONE....................408 899-9018
Eric David, *CEO*
Rafael Escandon, *Vice Pres*
Fred Porter, *Vice Pres*
Kaye Spratt, *Vice Pres*
EMP: 50 EST: 2018
SALES (est): 1MM
SALES (corp-wide): 8.2MM **Publicly Held**
WEB: www.bridgebio.com
SIC: 8049 Occupational therapist
PA: Bridgebio Pharma, Inc.
421 Kipling St
Palo Alto CA 94301
650 391-9740

(P-15880)
ADVENTIST HEALTH SYSTEM/WEST
Also Called: Unknown
1150 E Washington Ave, Reedley (93654-4239)
PHONE....................559 638-2154
EMP: 47
SALES (corp-wide): 4.1B **Privately Held**
SIC: 8049 Health Practitioner's Office
PA: Adventist Health System/West
2100 Douglas Blvd
Roseville CA 95661
916 781-2000

(P-15881)
ANBERRY PHYSCL RHBLTTION CTR I
1685 Shaffer Rd, Atwater (95301-4456)
PHONE....................209 357-5121
Michael Ramstead, *Administration*
EMP: 59 EST: 2001
SALES (est): 662.5K **Privately Held**
SIC: 8049 8051 Physical therapist; convalescent home with continuous nursing care

(P-15882)
ANDERSON PHYSICAL THERAPY
202 Prvdnce Mine Rd # 206, Nevada City (95959-2946)
PHONE....................530 265-8100
Joni Anderson, *Vice Pres*
EMP: 39 EST: 2008
SALES (est): 1MM
SALES (corp-wide): 73.6MM **Privately Held**
WEB: www.andersonptandsportsmedicine.com
SIC: 8049 Physiotherapist
PA: Therapeutic Associates, Inc.
20829 72nd Ave S Ste 710
Kent WA 98032
253 872-6028

(P-15883)
BERKELEY THERAPY INSTITUTE
1749 Mrtin Lther King Jr, Berkeley (94709-2139)
PHONE....................510 841-8484
Sharon Friedman, *Director*
Naomi Hartwig, *President*
Sharon Freedman MA, *Exec Dir*
Joseph Chernick, *Exec Dir*
Claramarie Collins, *Psychologist*
EMP: 55 EST: 1971
SQ FT: 4,400
SALES (est): 5MM **Privately Held**
WEB: www.bti.org
SIC: 8049 8322 Psychiatric social worker; clinical psychologist; family (marriage) counseling

(P-15884)
BRIGHT PATH THERAPISTS INC
49 Bennit Ave, San Anselmo (94960-1540)
PHONE....................415 689-1700
Seth Zimring, *CFO*
Rya Chang,
Julia Evans, *Supervisor*
EMP: 45 EST: 2017
SALES (est): 2.8MM **Privately Held**
WEB: www.spgtherapy.com
SIC: 8049 Physical therapist

(P-15885)
BURGER PHYSCL THERAPY SVCS INC (HQ)
Also Called: Burger Physcl Thrapy Rhblttion
1301 E Bidwell St Ste 201, Folsom (95630-3565)
PHONE....................916 983-5900
Carol Burger, *President*
Elizabeth Johnson, *Human Res Dir*
Lauren Bahr,
Felicia Krieger, *Manager*
EMP: 140 EST: 1985
SALES (est): 20.8MM **Privately Held**
WEB: www.burgerrehab.com
SIC: 8049 Physical therapist

(P-15886)
BURGER PHYSCL THERAPY SVCS INC
Also Called: Placerville Physical Therapy
4250 Fowler Ln Ste 101, Diamond Springs (95619-9782)
PHONE....................530 626-4734
Jerusha McRoberts, *Manager*
EMP: 39 **Privately Held**
WEB: www.burgerrehab.com
SIC: 8049 Physical therapist
HQ: Burger Physical Therapy Services, Inc.
1301 E Bidwell St Ste 201
Folsom CA 95630
916 983-5900

8049 - Offices & Clinics Of Health Practitioners, NEC County (P-15887)

(P-15887)
BURGER PHYSCL THERAPY SVCS INC
11990 Heritage Oak Pl # 8, Auburn (95603-2455)
PHONE....................530 823-6835
Carol Burger, *Owner*
EMP: 39 **Privately Held**
WEB: www.burgerrehab.com
SIC: 8049 Physical therapist; occupational therapist
HQ: Burger Physical Therapy Services, Inc.
1301 E Bidwell St Ste 201
Folsom CA 95630
916 983-5900

(P-15888)
BURGER RHBLITATION SYSTEMS INC (PA)
1301 E Bidwell St Ste 201, Folsom (95630-3565)
PHONE....................800 900-8491
Carol K Burger, *President*
Jay Rich, *IT/INT Sup*
Renee Robinson, *Technician*
Carol Burger, *Data Proc Staff*
Kathy Pugh, *Controller*
EMP: 200 **EST:** 1978
SQ FT: 5,000
SALES (est): 21.5MM **Privately Held**
WEB: www.burgerrehab.com
SIC: 8049 Occupational therapist; speech specialist; physical therapist

(P-15889)
COUNTY OF SONOMA
3333 Skaggs Springs Rd, Geyserville (95441-9465)
PHONE....................707 433-0728
Jim Piccini, *Manager*
EMP: 47
SALES (corp-wide): 1B **Privately Held**
WEB: www.sonomacounty.ca.gov
SIC: 9221 9199 8049 Sheriffs' offices; ;
PA: County Of Sonoma
585 Fiscal Dr 100
Santa Rosa CA 95403
707 565-2431

(P-15890)
ENLOE MEDICAL CENTER
Also Called: Enloe Rehabilitation Center
340 W East Ave, Chico (95926-7238)
PHONE....................530 332-6138
Diane Jones, *Administration*
Marcia Nelson, *Vice Pres*
Mandy Robins, *Vice Pres*
Christopher Marking, *Pharmacy Dir*
Linda Irvine, *Human Res Dir*
EMP: 71
SQ FT: 61,571
SALES (corp-wide): 675.2MM **Privately Held**
WEB: www.enloe.org
SIC: 8049 Physical therapist
PA: Enloe Medical Center
1531 Esplanade
Chico CA 95926
530 332-7300

(P-15891)
KAISER FOUNDATION HOSPITALS
Also Called: Novato Hearing Center
100 Rowland Way Ste 125, Novato (94945-5012)
PHONE....................415 209-2444
EMP: 157
SALES (corp-wide): 30.5B **Privately Held**
WEB: www.kaisercenter.com
SIC: 8049 Audiologist
HQ: Kaiser Foundation Hospitals Inc
1 Kaiser Plz
Oakland CA 94612
510 271-6611

(P-15892)
MONARCH DENTAL CORP
5867 Lone Tree Way, Antioch (94531-8622)
PHONE....................925 732-4648
EMP: 36

SALES (corp-wide): 335MM **Privately Held**
WEB: www.monarchdental.com
SIC: 8049 8021 Dental hygienist; specialized dental practitioners
HQ: Monarch Dental Corp
7989 Belt Line Rd Ste 90
Dallas TX 75248

(P-15893)
OROVILLE HOSPITAL
Also Called: Golden Vly Occpational Therapy
2353 Myers St Ste B, Oroville (95966-5334)
PHONE....................530 538-8700
Trish Hopps, *Branch Mgr*
EMP: 144
SALES (corp-wide): 353.1MM **Privately Held**
WEB: www.orovillehospital.com
SIC: 8049 Physical therapist
PA: Oroville Hospital
2767 Olive Hwy
Oroville CA 95966
530 533-8500

(P-15894)
PHYSICAL REHABILITATION NETWRK
2833 Junction Ave Ste 206, San Jose (95134-1920)
P.O. Box 612260 (95161-2260)
PHONE....................408 570-0510
Fax: 408 570-0516
EMP: 50 **Privately Held**
SIC: 8049 8742 Health Practitioner's Office Management Consulting Services
PA: Physical Rehabilitation Network
5962 La Place Ct Ste 170
Carlsbad CA 92011

(P-15895)
ROCKLIN PHYSICAL THERAPY PC
2217 Sunset Blvd Ste 711, Rocklin (95765-4783)
PHONE....................916 435-3500
John Zieour, *President*
Robyn Heslop, *Office Mgr*
EMP: 125 **EST:** 1991
SALES (est): 2.8MM **Privately Held**
WEB: www.rocklinpt.com
SIC: 8049 Physiotherapist; physical therapist
PA: Physical Rehabilitation Network, Llc
2035 Corte Del Nogal # 20
Carlsbad CA 92011

(P-15896)
SAN FRNCSCO SPORT SPINE PHYSCL (PA)
100 Bush St Ste 800, San Francisco (94104-3911)
PHONE....................415 593-2532
Sturdy McKee, *CEO*
Jerry Durham, *Admin Sec*
Heather Stone,
Dwayne Moore, *Director*
Liesl Nelson, *Assistant*
EMP: 78 **EST:** 2001
SALES (est): 2.2MM **Privately Held**
WEB: www.sfphysicaltherapy.com
SIC: 8049 Physical therapist

(P-15897)
SAN JQUIN VLY RHBLTTION HOSP A
40232 Junction Dr, Oakhurst (93644-8719)
PHONE....................559 658-6490
Susan Jackson, *Branch Mgr*
Ashley Williams, *Admin Asst*
Karen Hall, *Director*
EMP: 150
SALES (corp-wide): 759.7MM **Privately Held**
WEB: www.vibrahealthcare.com
SIC: 8049 Physical therapist
HQ: San Joaquin Valley Rehabilitation Hospital, A Delaware Limited Partnership
7173 N Sharon Ave
Fresno CA 93720
559 436-3600

(P-15898)
SILVER CREEK FTNES PHYSCL THRA
4205 San Felipe Rd # 100, San Jose (95135-1503)
PHONE....................408 238-1552
Randy Waltz, *CEO*
Ryan Rausch, *Partner*
Todd Jones, *President*
Brenda Sanchez, *Human Resources*
EMP: 36 **EST:** 2001
SQ FT: 4,200
SALES (est): 3.1MM **Privately Held**
WEB: www.gbtherapypartners.com
SIC: 8049 Physical therapist

(P-15899)
SUTTER VALLEY MED FOUNDATION
1625 Stockton Blvd # 110, Sacramento (95816-7097)
PHONE....................916 924-7764
Judi Monday, *Branch Mgr*
Jesily Avila, *Accountant*
Teresa Montoya, *Manager*
EMP: 81 **Privately Held**
WEB: www.sutterhealth.org
SIC: 8049 8011 Physical therapist; offices & clinics of medical doctors
PA: Sutter Valley Medical Foundation
2700 Gateway Oaks Dr
Sacramento CA 95833

(P-15900)
THERAPUTIC SOLUTIONS PROF CORP
3255 Esplanade, Chico (95973-0255)
PHONE....................530 899-3150
Aahmed Aboubsh, *President*
Carrie Henderson, *Principal*
Karim Mohammed, *Psychiatry*
Samantha Luger, *Director*
Aimee Sagli, *Supervisor*
EMP: 42 **EST:** 2008
SALES (est): 6.2MM **Privately Held**
WEB: www.therapeutic-solutions.com
SIC: 8049 7299 Physical therapist; massage parlor

(P-15901)
THERAPYDIA INC
18 E Blithedale Ave # 21, Mill Valley (94941-1946)
PHONE....................802 772-7801
Leah Nottingham, *Principal*
Dena Goldberg,
Darci Whitehorne, *Director*
EMP: 46 **EST:** 2013
SALES (est): 5.7MM **Privately Held**
WEB: www.therapydia.com
SIC: 8049 Physical therapist

(P-15902)
WRIGHT INSTITUTE
2728 Durant Ave, Berkeley (94704-1796)
PHONE....................510 841-9230
Peter Dybwad, *President*
Gilbert Newman, *Vice Pres*
Tricia O 'reilly, *Executive*
Hanna Mae Levenson, *Principal*
Luli Emmons, *Exec Dir*
EMP: 78 **EST:** 1968
SQ FT: 20,000
SALES: 15.8MM **Privately Held**
WEB: www.wi.edu
SIC: 8049 Clinical psychologist

8051 Skilled Nursing Facilities

(P-15903)
1000 EXECUTIVE PARKWAY LLC
Also Called: Oroville Hosp Post Acute Ctr
1000 Executive Pkwy, Oroville (95966-5100)
PHONE....................530 533-7335
Tina Nickolas, *Administration*
EMP: 161 **EST:** 2013

SALES: 14.2MM
SALES (corp-wide): 353.1MM **Privately Held**
WEB: www.orovillepostacute.com
SIC: 8051 Mental retardation hospital
PA: Oroville Hospital
2767 Olive Hwy
Oroville CA 95966
530 533-8500

(P-15904)
150 THE TUNNEL CENTER FOR REHA
1359 Pine St, San Francisco (94109-4807)
PHONE....................415 673-8405
Paul Diaz, *Principal*
EMP: 48 **EST:** 2010
SALES (est): 26.4MM **Privately Held**
SIC: 8051 Convalescent home with continuous nursing care

(P-15905)
A B C D ASSOCIATES
Also Called: Casa Coloma Health Care Center
10410 Coloma Rd, Rancho Cordova (95670-2108)
PHONE....................916 363-4843
Deborah Portela, *Partner*
Arden Millermon, *Partner*
Betty Millermon, *Partner*
EMP: 106 **EST:** 1975
SQ FT: 37,000
SALES (est): 15.3MM **Privately Held**
SIC: 8051 8052 Convalescent home with continuous nursing care; intermediate care facilities

(P-15906)
AGEMARK CORPORATION (PA)
25 Avenida De Orinda, Orinda (94563-2305)
PHONE....................925 257-4671
Richard J Westin, *Ch of Bd*
Jesse A Pittore, *CEO*
James P Tolley, *CFO*
Linda Larkin, *Vice Pres*
Terri Jo, *Exec Dir*
EMP: 133 **EST:** 1989
SQ FT: 2,100
SALES (est): 10.8MM **Privately Held**
WEB: www.agemark.com
SIC: 8051 Convalescent home with continuous nursing care

(P-15907)
ALAMEDA HLTHCARE & WELLNSS CTR
Also Called: Alameda Halthcare Wellness Ctr
430 Willow St, Alameda (94501-6130)
PHONE....................510 523-8857
Sharrod Brooks,
Sol Healthcare LLC,
Sol Majer,
Abby MA, *Director*
Jasmin Gorostiza, *Manager*
EMP: 99 **EST:** 2010
SALES (est): 11.9MM **Privately Held**
WEB: www.alamedahc.com
SIC: 8051 Convalescent home with continuous nursing care

(P-15908)
ALL SAINTSIDENCE OPCO LLC
Also Called: All Snts Sbcute Trnstonal Care
1652 Mono Ave, San Leandro (94578-2020)
PHONE....................510 481-3200
Jason Murray, *President*
EMP: 41 **EST:** 2015
SALES (est): 33.6MM **Privately Held**
WEB: www.allsaintshc.com
SIC: 8051 Convalescent home with continuous nursing care

(P-15909)
APPLE VLY CNVALESCENT HOSP INC
Also Called: Apple Valley Care & Rehab
1035 Gravenstein Hwy N, Sebastopol (95472-2811)
PHONE....................707 823-7675
Jeff Barbieri, *Administration*
Nathan Noe, *Administration*
Barbie Robles, *Chf Purch Ofc*

Robert Reyes, *Director*
Sara Reyes, *Manager*
EMP: 72 **EST:** 1966
SQ FT: 20,000
SALES (est): 14.9MM **Privately Held**
WEB: www.applevalleyrehab.com
SIC: 8051 8322 Convalescent home with continuous nursing care; rehabilitation services

(P-15910)
AQUINAS CORPORATION
Also Called: San Tomas Convalescent Hosp
3580 Payne Ave, San Jose (95117-2925)
PHONE......................408 248-7100
Ken Dunton, *Ch of Bd*
Julita Javier, *President*
EMP: 135 **EST:** 1974
SQ FT: 15,000
SALES (est): 10.4MM **Privately Held**
WEB: www.stchospital.com
SIC: 8051 8059 Convalescent home with continuous nursing care; convalescent home

(P-15911)
ASIAN COMMUNITY CENTER OF SAC
7801 Rush River Dr, Sacramento (95831-4602)
PHONE......................916 393-9020
Darren Trisel, *Branch Mgr*
Amy Voong, *Admin Asst*
Tamara Kario, *Administration*
Mark Williams, *Opers Staff*
Marissa Belmes, *Manager*
EMP: 48
SALES (corp-wide): 26.8MM **Privately Held**
WEB: www.accsv.org
SIC: 8051 Skilled nursing care facilities
PA: Asian Community Center Of Sacramento Valley, Inc.
7334 Park City Dr
Sacramento CA 95831
916 394-6399

(P-15912)
AUBURN OAKS CARE CENTER
3400 Bell Rd, Auburn (95603-9241)
PHONE......................650 949-7777
Ellen Kuykendall, *President*
Kevin Hadfield, *Administration*
EMP: 99 **EST:** 2011
SALES (est): 12.8MM **Privately Held**
WEB: www.auburnoakscarecenter.com
SIC: 8051 Convalescent home with continuous nursing care

(P-15913)
AVALON CARE CEN
Also Called: Hy-Lond Hlth Care Cnter-Merced
3170 M St, Merced (95348-2403)
PHONE......................209 723-1056
Charles R Kirton,
Sue Wilburn, *Manager*
EMP: 39 **EST:** 2003
SALES (est): 17.8MM
SALES (corp-wide): 1.1B **Privately Held**
WEB: www.avalonhealthcare.com
SIC: 8051 Skilled nursing care facilities
PA: Avalon Health Care, Inc.
206 N 2100 W Ste 300
Salt Lake City UT 84116
801 596-8844

(P-15914)
AVALON CARE CENTER - MODESTO
Also Called: Hy-Lond Hlth Care Cntr-Modesto
1900 Coffee Rd, Modesto (95355-2703)
PHONE......................209 526-1775
Randy Kirton, *CEO*
Sheree Clarke, *Executive*
Gabriel Okere, *Administration*
Becky Singleton, *Administration*
Ashourena Ortega, *Director*
EMP: 134 **EST:** 2003
SALES (est): 55.9MM
SALES (corp-wide): 1.1B **Privately Held**
WEB: www.avalonhealthcare.com
SIC: 8051 Convalescent home with continuous nursing care

PA: Avalon Health Care, Inc.
206 N 2100 W Ste 300
Salt Lake City UT 84116
801 596-8844

(P-15915)
AVALON CARE CTR - CHWCHLLA LLC
Also Called: Chowchilla Conv. Center
1010 Ventura Ave, Chowchilla (93610-2368)
PHONE......................559 665-4826
EMP: 65 **EST:** 2003
SALES (est): 42.4MM
SALES (corp-wide): 1.1B **Privately Held**
WEB: www.avalonhealthcare.com
SIC: 8051 Skilled nursing care facilities
PA: Avalon Health Care, Inc.
206 N 2100 W Ste 300
Salt Lake City UT 84116
801 596-8844

(P-15916)
AVALON CARE CTR - MODESTO LLC
515 E Orangeburg Ave, Modesto (95350-5510)
PHONE......................209 529-0516
Darla Lorenzen, *Exec Dir*
Mark Fairbanks, *Maintence Staff*
EMP: 70
SALES (est): 15MM
SALES (corp-wide): 1.1B **Privately Held**
WEB: www.avalonhealthcare.com
SIC: 8051 Skilled nursing care facilities
PA: Avalon Health Care, Inc.
206 N 2100 W Ste 300
Salt Lake City UT 84116
801 596-8844

(P-15917)
AVALON CARE CTR - MRCED FRNCSC
Also Called: Franciscan Conv. Hospital
3169 M St, Merced (95348-2404)
PHONE......................209 722-6231
Larry Imperial, *Administration*
EMP: 76 **EST:** 2003
SALES (est): 17.8MM
SALES (corp-wide): 1.1B **Privately Held**
WEB: www.avalonhealthcare.com
SIC: 8051 Skilled nursing care facilities
PA: Avalon Health Care, Inc.
206 N 2100 W Ste 300
Salt Lake City UT 84116
801 596-8844

(P-15918)
AVALON CARE CTR - NEWMAN LLC
Also Called: San Luis Care Center
709 N St, Newman (95360-1162)
PHONE......................209 862-2862
David Robinson,
Rose Sadje, *Nursing Dir*
Christina Corella, *Hlthcr Dir*
EMP: 90 **EST:** 2003
SALES (est): 6.8MM
SALES (corp-wide): 1.1B **Privately Held**
WEB: www.avalonhealthcare.com
SIC: 8051 Convalescent home with continuous nursing care
PA: Avalon Health Care, Inc.
206 N 2100 W Ste 300
Salt Lake City UT 84116
801 596-8844

(P-15919)
AVALON CARE CTR - SAN ANDREAS
Also Called: Mark Twain Conv. Hospital
900 Mountain Ranch Rd, San Andreas (95249-9713)
PHONE......................209 754-3823
Larry Washington, *Admin Mgr*
EMP: 113 **EST:** 2003
SALES (est): 36.3MM
SALES (corp-wide): 1.1B **Privately Held**
WEB: www.avalonhealthcare.com
SIC: 8051 Convalescent home with continuous nursing care
PA: Avalon Health Care, Inc.
206 N 2100 W Ste 300
Salt Lake City UT 84116
801 596-8844

(P-15920)
AVALON CARE CTR - SONORA LLC
Also Called: AVALON HEALTH CARE GROUP
19929 Greenley Rd, Sonora (95370-5996)
PHONE......................209 533-2500
Faye Lincoln, *Vice Pres*
Randall Ceja, *Opers Staff*
EMP: 106 **EST:** 2003
SALES (est): 19.5MM
SALES (corp-wide): 1.1B **Privately Held**
WEB: www.avalonhealthcare.com
SIC: 8051 Convalescent home with continuous nursing care
PA: Avalon Health Care, Inc.
206 N 2100 W Ste 300
Salt Lake City UT 84116
801 596-8844

(P-15921)
AZALEA HOLDINGS LLC
Also Called: McKinley Park Care Center
3700 H St, Sacramento (95816-4611)
PHONE......................916 452-3592
Radio Shey, *Administration*
Jared Bake, *Principal*
Maria Lopez, *Office Mgr*
Gary Weemers, *Administration*
Christina Lallian, *Sales Staff*
EMP: 88 **EST:** 2001
SALES (est): 29.5MM **Privately Held**
WEB: www.mckinleyparkcarecenter.com
SIC: 8051 Convalescent home with continuous nursing care

(P-15922)
BALBOA ENTERPRISES INC
Also Called: Mountain View Healthcare Ctr
2530 Solace Pl, Mountain View (94040-4309)
PHONE......................650 961-6161
Karl Vitt, *President*
Magdalena Flores, *Office Mgr*
Rick Gagarin, *Marketing Staff*
Lala Mammedova, *Nursing Dir*
Aj Bowline, *Director*
EMP: 110 **EST:** 1964
SQ FT: 30,000
SALES (est): 17.2MM **Privately Held**
SIC: 8051 Convalescent home with continuous nursing care

(P-15923)
BAY VIEW RHBILITATION HOSP LLC
516 Willow St, Alameda (94501-6132)
PHONE......................510 521-5600
Thomas Chambers, *Mng Member*
Adrian Manesh, *CFO*
Brooke Saunders, *Officer*
Earl Nicholson, *Vice Pres*
EMP: 99 **EST:** 2012
SALES (est): 19.2MM **Privately Held**
WEB: www.bayviewnursing.com
SIC: 8051 8062 8361 Convalescent home with continuous nursing care; general medical & surgical hospitals; rehabilitation center, residential: health care incidental

(P-15924)
BAYBERRY INC
15120 Lakeshore Dr C, Clearlake (95422-8106)
PHONE......................707 995-1643
Lora Heise, *Branch Mgr*
EMP: 71
SALES (corp-wide): 6.8MM **Privately Held**
WEB: www.bayberry.biz
SIC: 5999 8051 Medical apparatus & supplies; mental retardation hospital
PA: Bayberry, Inc.
1700 2nd St Ste 350
Napa CA 94559
707 252-5587

(P-15925)
BEAVER DAM HEALTH CARE CENTER
Also Called: Beverly
1306 E Sumner Ave, Fowler (93625-2627)
PHONE......................559 834-2542
Christine Clark, *Branch Mgr*
EMP: 40
SALES (corp-wide): 1B **Privately Held**
WEB: www.beaverdamhcc.com
SIC: 8051 8082 Skilled nursing care facilities; home health care services
PA: Beaver Dam Health Care Center
5220 Tennyson Pkwy # 400
Plano TX 75024
972 372-6300

(P-15926)
BEAVER DAM HEALTH CARE CENTER
Also Called: Golden Living Center - Chateau
1221 Rosemarie Ln, Stockton (95207-6703)
PHONE......................707 546-0471
Susan Morgan, *Manager*
EMP: 40
SALES (corp-wide): 1B **Privately Held**
WEB: www.beaverdamhcc.com
SIC: 8051 Convalescent home with continuous nursing care
PA: Beaver Dam Health Care Center
5220 Tennyson Pkwy # 400
Plano TX 75024
972 372-6300

(P-15927)
BEAVER DAM HEALTH CARE CENTER
Also Called: Golden Lvngcnter - Cntry View
925 N Cornelia Ave, Fresno (93706-1031)
PHONE......................559 275-4785
Deann Walters, *Manager*
EMP: 40
SALES (corp-wide): 1B **Privately Held**
WEB: www.beaverdamhcc.com
SIC: 8051 8059 Skilled nursing care facilities; convalescent home
PA: Beaver Dam Health Care Center
5220 Tennyson Pkwy # 400
Plano TX 75024
972 372-6300

(P-15928)
BEAVER DAM HEALTH CARE CENTER
Also Called: Beverly Healthcare
14966 Terreno De Flores, Los Gatos (95032-2023)
PHONE......................408 356-8136
Richard Gotmaster, *Branch Mgr*
EMP: 40
SALES (corp-wide): 1B **Privately Held**
WEB: www.beaverdamhcc.com
SIC: 8051 Skilled nursing care facilities
PA: Beaver Dam Health Care Center
5220 Tennyson Pkwy # 400
Plano TX 75024
972 372-6300

(P-15929)
BEAVER DAM HEALTH CARE CENTER
Also Called: Beverly
2984 N Maroa Ave, Fresno (93704-5607)
PHONE......................559 226-9401
Linda Neelen, *Branch Mgr*
EMP: 40
SALES (corp-wide): 1B **Privately Held**
WEB: www.beaverdamhcc.com
SIC: 8051 Skilled nursing care facilities
PA: Beaver Dam Health Care Center
5220 Tennyson Pkwy # 400
Plano TX 75024
972 372-6300

(P-15930)
BEAVER DAM HEALTH CARE CENTER
Also Called: Beverly Healthcare
950 S Fairmont Ave, Lodi (95240-5131)
PHONE......................209 368-0693
Beverly Mannon, *Principal*
EMP: 40
SALES (corp-wide): 1B **Privately Held**
WEB: www.beaverdamhcc.com
SIC: 8051 Convalescent home with continuous nursing care
PA: Beaver Dam Health Care Center
5220 Tennyson Pkwy # 400
Plano TX 75024
972 372-6300

8051 - Skilled Nursing Facilities County (P-15931)

(P-15931)
BEAVER DAM HEALTH CARE CENTER
Also Called: Golden Lvngcenter - Santa Rosa
4650 Hoen Ave, Santa Rosa (95405-9407)
PHONE 707 546-0471
Georgia Otterson, *Exec Dir*
Constance Smith, *Director*
EMP: 40
SALES (corp-wide): 1B **Privately Held**
WEB: www.beaverdamhcc.com
SIC: 8051 8069 Skilled nursing care facilities; specialty hospitals, except psychiatric
PA: Beaver Dam Health Care Center
    5220 Tennyson Pkwy # 400
    Plano TX 75024
    972 372-6300

(P-15932)
BEAVER DAM HEALTH CARE CENTER
Also Called: Beverly
5425 Mayme Ave, San Jose (95129-4833)
PHONE 408 366-6510
Ronald Anderson, *Manager*
EMP: 40
SALES (corp-wide): 1B **Privately Held**
WEB: www.beaverdamhcc.com
SIC: 8051 Skilled nursing care facilities
PA: Beaver Dam Health Care Center
    5220 Tennyson Pkwy # 400
    Plano TX 75024
    972 372-6300

(P-15933)
BEAVER DAM HEALTH CARE CENTER
Also Called: Golden Livingcenter - Petaluma
217 Lakeville St Apt 3, Petaluma (94952-3166)
PHONE 707 763-4109
Monica Choperena, *General Mgr*
EMP: 40
SALES (corp-wide): 1B **Privately Held**
WEB: www.beaverdamhcc.com
SIC: 8051 Skilled nursing care facilities
PA: Beaver Dam Health Care Center
    5220 Tennyson Pkwy # 400
    Plano TX 75024
    972 372-6300

(P-15934)
BEAVER DAM HEALTH CARE CENTER
Also Called: Beverly Healthcare
1700 Howard Rd, Madera (93637-5131)
PHONE 559 673-9278
Ken Evans, *Principal*
EMP: 40
SALES (corp-wide): 1B **Privately Held**
WEB: www.beaverdamhcc.com
SIC: 8051 Skilled nursing care facilities
PA: Beaver Dam Health Care Center
    5220 Tennyson Pkwy # 400
    Plano TX 75024
    972 372-6300

(P-15935)
BEAVER DAM HEALTH CARE CENTER
Also Called: Golden Livingcenter - San Jose
401 Ridge Vista Ave, San Jose (95121-1501)
PHONE 408 923-7232
Almaroos Apapira, *Exec Dir*
EMP: 40
SALES (corp-wide): 1B **Privately Held**
WEB: www.beaverdamhcc.com
SIC: 8051 Skilled nursing care facilities
PA: Beaver Dam Health Care Center
    5220 Tennyson Pkwy # 400
    Plano TX 75024
    972 372-6300

(P-15936)
BEAVER DAM HEALTH CARE CENTER
3510 E Shields Ave, Fresno (93726-6909)
PHONE 559 222-4807
Kara Pappanduros, *Manager*
EMP: 40
SALES (corp-wide): 1B **Privately Held**
WEB: www.beaverdamhcc.com
SIC: 8051 Skilled nursing care facilities
PA: Beaver Dam Health Care Center
    5220 Tennyson Pkwy # 400
    Plano TX 75024
    972 372-6300

(P-15937)
BEAVER DAM HEALTH CARE CENTER
Also Called: Golden Livingcenter - Clovis
111 Barstow Ave, Clovis (93612-2225)
PHONE 559 299-2591
Michelle Tathem, *Manager*
EMP: 40
SALES (corp-wide): 1B **Privately Held**
WEB: www.beaverdamhcc.com
SIC: 8051 Convalescent home with continuous nursing care
PA: Beaver Dam Health Care Center
    5220 Tennyson Pkwy # 400
    Plano TX 75024
    972 372-6300

(P-15938)
BEAVER DAM HEALTH CARE CENTER
Also Called: Beverly Healthcare
3672 N 1st St, Fresno (93726-6810)
PHONE 559 227-5383
Kristine Clark, *Manager*
EMP: 40
SALES (corp-wide): 1B **Privately Held**
WEB: www.beaverdamhcc.com
SIC: 8051 Skilled nursing care facilities
PA: Beaver Dam Health Care Center
    5220 Tennyson Pkwy # 400
    Plano TX 75024
    972 372-6300

(P-15939)
BEAVER DAM HEALTH CARE CENTER
Also Called: Golden Livingcenter - Reedley
1090 E Dinuba Ave, Reedley (93654-3577)
PHONE 559 638-3577
Julie Whiteside, *Manager*
EMP: 40
SALES (corp-wide): 1B **Privately Held**
WEB: www.beaverdamhcc.com
SIC: 8051 8082 Skilled nursing care facilities; home health care services
PA: Beaver Dam Health Care Center
    5220 Tennyson Pkwy # 400
    Plano TX 75024
    972 372-6300

(P-15940)
BEAVER DAM HEALTH CARE CENTER
Also Called: Beverly Healthcare
1900 Coffee Rd, Modesto (95355-2703)
PHONE 209 548-0318
Belinda Guzman, *CEO*
Kim Damale, *Vice Pres*
EMP: 40
SALES (corp-wide): 1B **Privately Held**
WEB: www.beaverdamhcc.com
SIC: 8051 Skilled nursing care facilities
PA: Beaver Dam Health Care Center
    5220 Tennyson Pkwy # 400
    Plano TX 75024
    972 372-6300

(P-15941)
BEAVER DAM HEALTH CARE CENTER
Also Called: Beverly Healthcare
350 De Soto Dr, Los Gatos (95032-2402)
PHONE 408 356-9151
Julie Okada, *Exec Dir*
EMP: 40
SALES (corp-wide): 1B **Privately Held**
WEB: www.beaverdamhcc.com
SIC: 8051 Convalescent home with continuous nursing care
PA: Beaver Dam Health Care Center
    5220 Tennyson Pkwy # 400
    Plano TX 75024
    972 372-6300

(P-15942)
BEAVER DAM HEALTH CARE CENTER
Also Called: Golden Livingcenter - Portside
2740 N California St, Stockton (95204-5529)
PHONE 209 466-3522
Judy Thornhill, *Director*
EMP: 40
SALES (corp-wide): 1B **Privately Held**
WEB: www.beaverdamhcc.com
SIC: 8051 Convalescent home with continuous nursing care
PA: Beaver Dam Health Care Center
    5220 Tennyson Pkwy # 400
    Plano TX 75024
    972 372-6300

(P-15943)
BEAVER DAM HEALTH CARE CENTER
Also Called: Golden Lvngcnter - Lndon Hse S
678 2nd St W, Sonoma (95476-6901)
PHONE 707 938-1096
Keith Gold, *Administration*
EMP: 40
SALES (corp-wide): 1B **Privately Held**
WEB: www.beaverdamhcc.com
SIC: 8051 Skilled nursing care facilities
PA: Beaver Dam Health Care Center
    5220 Tennyson Pkwy # 400
    Plano TX 75024
    972 372-6300

(P-15944)
BEAVER DAM HEALTH CARE CENTER
Also Called: Beverly Healthcare
188 Cohasset Ln, Chico (95926-2206)
PHONE 530 343-6084
John Crowley, *Administration*
Barbara Juede Santos, *Director*
EMP: 40
SALES (corp-wide): 1B **Privately Held**
WEB: www.beaverdamhcc.com
SIC: 8051 Extended care facility
PA: Beaver Dam Health Care Center
    5220 Tennyson Pkwy # 400
    Plano TX 75024
    972 372-6300

(P-15945)
BEAVER DAM HEALTH CARE CENTER
Also Called: Beverly Healthcare
709 N St, Newman (95360-1162)
PHONE 209 862-2862
Darla Larinda, *Exec Dir*
EMP: 40
SALES (corp-wide): 1B **Privately Held**
WEB: www.beaverdamhcc.com
SIC: 8051 Convalescent home with continuous nursing care
PA: Beaver Dam Health Care Center
    5220 Tennyson Pkwy # 400
    Plano TX 75024
    972 372-6300

(P-15946)
BERRYMAN HEALTH INC
Also Called: Ukiah Convalescent Hospital
1349 S Dora St, Ukiah (95482-6512)
PHONE 707 462-8864
Barbara Jimenez, *Principal*
EMP: 47
SALES (corp-wide): 3.5MM **Privately Held**
SIC: 8051 Convalescent home with continuous nursing care
PA: Berryman Health Inc
    615 E Chapman Ave Ste 3
    Orange CA 92866
    714 921-1919

(P-15947)
BETHANY HM SOC SAN JQUIN CNTY
Also Called: Bethany Adult Day Care
368 S Wilma Ave, Ripon (95366-2356)
PHONE 209 599-7670
Ken Iremonger, *Manager*
EMP: 70
SALES (corp-wide): 15.7MM **Privately Held**
WEB: www.bethanyripon.org
SIC: 8051 8361 Convalescent home with continuous nursing care; residential care
PA: Bethany Home Society Of San Joaquin County, Inc.
    930 W Main St
    Ripon CA
    209 599-4221

(P-15948)
C J HEALTH SERVICES INC
Also Called: Marina Convalescent Center
38650 Mission Blvd, Fremont (94536-4391)
PHONE 510 793-3000
Catherine Joseph, *President*
Bernice Zimmerman, *Exec Dir*
EMP: 87 EST: 1958
SQ FT: 5,000
SALES (est): 6.3MM **Privately Held**
SIC: 8051 Convalescent home with continuous nursing care

(P-15949)
CALIFORNIA PARK REHAB HOS
2850 Sierra Sunrise Ter, Chico (95928-8401)
PHONE 530 894-1010
Shannon J Campbell, *Principal*
Erica Vonbargen, *Records Dir*
Terri Wilson, *Office Mgr*
Pete Becker, *Director*
Carla Bennett, *Director*
EMP: 37 EST: 2008
SALES (est): 9.8MM **Privately Held**
WEB: www.calparkrehab.com
SIC: 8051 Skilled nursing care facilities

(P-15950)
CANYON SPRINGS POST-ACUTE
180 N Jackson Ave, San Jose (95116-1907)
PHONE 408 259-8700
Toby Tilford, *CEO*
EMP: 38 EST: 2015
SALES (est): 18.4MM **Privately Held**
WEB: www.canyonspringspostacute.com
SIC: 8051 Convalescent home with continuous nursing care

(P-15951)
CAREAGE INC
Also Called: Mission De La Casa
2501 Alvin Ave, San Jose (95121-1660)
PHONE 408 238-9751
Kim Nguyen, *Branch Mgr*
Tiffany Nguyen, *Social Dir*
Huynh Vo, *Admin Asst*
Josh Hedger, *Administration*
Brian Gilligan, *Supervisor*
EMP: 50
SALES (corp-wide): 25.5MM **Privately Held**
WEB: www.careage.com
SIC: 8051 Convalescent home with continuous nursing care
PA: Careage Construction, Inc.
    4411 Point Fosdick Dr
    Gig Harbor WA 98335
    253 853-4457

(P-15952)
CARMICHAEL CARE INC
Also Called: Rosewood Rehabilitation
6041 Fair Oaks Blvd, Carmichael (95608-4816)
PHONE 916 483-8103
John L Sorensen, *President*
Donald Laws, *Shareholder*
David Sorensen, *Shareholder*
EMP: 48 EST: 2001
SALES (est): 9.8MM **Privately Held**
SIC: 8051 Convalescent home with continuous nursing care

(P-15953)
CASAVINA FOUNDATION CORP
2501 Alvin Ave, San Jose (95121-1660)
PHONE 408 238-9751
Ngai Nguyen, *President*
CHI Nguyen, *Admin Sec*
EMP: 101 EST: 2004

PRODUCTS & SERVICES SECTION **8051 - Skilled Nursing Facilities County (P-15975)**

SALES (est): 6.7MM Privately Held
WEB: www.missiondelacasa.com
SIC: 8051 Convalescent home with continuous nursing care

(P-15954)
CATHEDRAL PIONEER CHURCH HOMES (PA)
Also Called: Pioneer House
415 P St Ofc, Sacramento (95814-5300)
PHONE..................916 442-4906
Calvin Hara, *Administration*
Stephanie Butler, *Human Res Dir*
Robert Godfrey, *Director*
EMP: 96 EST: 1963
SQ FT: 52,000
SALES (est): 3.9K Privately Held
WEB: www.pioneerhouseretirement.org
SIC: 8051 8699 Skilled nursing care facilities; charitable organization

(P-15955)
CEP AMERICA - ILLINOIS SNF LLP
2100 Powell St Ste 400, Emeryville (94608-1826)
PHONE..................510 350-2777
Phillip Piccinini, *Partner*
EMP: 50 EST: 2020
SALES (est): 4.4MM Privately Held
WEB: www.cepamerica.com
SIC: 8051 Skilled nursing care facilities

(P-15956)
CF MERCED LA SIERRA LLC
Also Called: La Sierra Care Center
2424 M St, Merced (95340-2808)
PHONE..................209 723-4224
Carson Day, *President*
Bryan Tanner, *COO*
EMP: 82 EST: 1966
SQ FT: 15,000
SALES (est): 6.6MM
SALES (corp-wide): 78.2MM Privately Held
SIC: 8051 Skilled nursing care facilities
PA: Country Villa Service Corp.
    2400 E Katella Ave # 800
    Anaheim CA 92806
    310 574-3733

(P-15957)
CF SUSANVILLE LLC
Also Called: Country Vlla Rvrview Rhab Hlth
2005 River St, Susanville (96130-4524)
PHONE..................530 257-5341
Rick Denning,
Judy Smith, *Records Dir*
Antoine Goodie, *Administration*
Cheryl Randoff, *Administration*
Mercedes Frias, *Food Svc Dir*
EMP: 60 EST: 2004
SALES (est): 5.2MM Privately Held
SIC: 8051 Skilled nursing care facilities

(P-15958)
CHANCELLOR HLTH CARE OF CAL IV
Also Called: Chancellor Place of Lodi
2220 W Kettleman Ln Ofc, Lodi (95242-4348)
PHONE..................209 367-8870
Keith Payne, *Director*
Edmond Peters, *Vice Ch Bd*
Roger Vitrano, *VP Finance*
Arline Delacruz, *Director*
EMP: 263 EST: 1998
SALES (est): 5.5MM Privately Held
WEB: www.chancellorhealthcare.com
SIC: 8051 Convalescent home with continuous nursing care
PA: Chancellor Health Care, Inc.
    115 Johnson St
    Windsor CA

(P-15959)
CHAPARRAL FOUNDATION
Also Called: Chaparral House
1309 Allston Way, Berkeley (94702-1920)
PHONE..................510 848-8774
K J Paige, *Administration*
Charles Perry, *Records Dir*
Brigitte Aka, *Nurse*
EMP: 90 EST: 1978
SQ FT: 21,000
SALES (est): 6.1MM Privately Held
WEB: www.chaparralhouse.org
SIC: 8051 Convalescent home with continuous nursing care

(P-15960)
CHOWCHILLA MEM HLTH CARE DST (PA)
1104 Ventura Ave, Chowchilla (93610-2244)
PHONE..................559 665-3781
Cathy Flores, *Administration*
Leland Decker, *Principal*
EMP: 55 EST: 1956
SQ FT: 23,000
SALES (est): 1.9MM Privately Held
WEB: www.chowchillahealth.specialdistrict.org
SIC: 8051 Skilled nursing care facilities

(P-15961)
COALINGA DSTNGISHED CMNTY CARE
834 Maple Rd, Coalinga (93210-1348)
PHONE..................559 935-5939
EMP: 67
SQ FT: 52,000
SALES (est): 1.1MM Privately Held
SIC: 8051 Skilled Nursing Care Facility

(P-15962)
COUNTY OF SACRAMENTO
Also Called: Public Health Nursing Service
9616 Micron Ave Ste 750, Sacramento (95827-2604)
PHONE..................916 875-0900
Jan Peters, *Director*
EMP: 109
SALES (corp-wide): 3.1B Privately Held
WEB: www.saccounty.net
SIC: 8051 9431 Skilled nursing care facilities; administration of public health programs;
PA: County Of Sacramento
    700 H St Ste 7650
    Sacramento CA 95814
    916 874-8515

(P-15963)
COVENANT CARE LLC
Also Called: Pacific Coast Manor
1935 Wharf Rd, Capitola (95010-2606)
PHONE..................831 476-0770
Christine Sims, *Manager*
Eliza Hurst, *Social Dir*
Mickey Paioni, *Office Mgr*
Jenny Davis, *Education*
Molini Guttenbeil, *Education*
EMP: 94 EST: 2006
SALES (est): 34.1MM Privately Held
WEB: www.covenantcare.com
SIC: 8051 Convalescent home with continuous nursing care
HQ: Covenant Care California, Llc
    120 Vantis Dr Ste 200
    Aliso Viejo CA 92656

(P-15964)
COVENANT CARE CALIFORNIA LLC
Also Called: Wagner Hts Nrsing Rhbltton Ct
9289 Branstetter Pl, Stockton (95209-1700)
PHONE..................209 477-5252
Janey Hargreaves, *Branch Mgr*
Jennifer Hasten, *Records Dir*
Ruby Maes, *Human Res Dir*
Frank Cervantes, *Director*
EMP: 55 Privately Held
WEB: www.covenantcare.com
SIC: 8051 Convalescent home with continuous nursing care
HQ: Covenant Care California, Llc
    120 Vantis Dr Ste 200
    Aliso Viejo CA 92656

(P-15965)
COVENANT CARE CALIFORNIA LLC
Also Called: Palo Alto Nursing Center
911 Bryant St, Palo Alto (94301-2711)
PHONE..................415 327-0511
Roland Gandy, *Branch Mgr*
Juana Castaneda, *Human Res Dir*
Susan Aguinaldo, *Food Svc Dir*
Marina Safro, *Hlthcr Dir*
EMP: 55 Privately Held
WEB: www.covenantcare.com
SIC: 8051 8059 Convalescent home with continuous nursing care; personal care home, with health care
HQ: Covenant Care California, Llc
    120 Vantis Dr Ste 200
    Aliso Viejo CA 92656

(P-15966)
COVENANT CARE CALIFORNIA LLC
Also Called: Mission Skilled Nursing Home
410 N Winchester Blvd, Santa Clara (95050-6325)
PHONE..................408 248-3736
Kathleen Glass, *Manager*
Myra Prenger, *Human Res Dir*
Mary Bautista, *Education*
EMP: 55 Privately Held
WEB: www.covenantcare.com
SIC: 8051 Convalescent home with continuous nursing care
HQ: Covenant Care California, Llc
    120 Vantis Dr Ste 200
    Aliso Viejo CA 92656

(P-15967)
COVENANT CARE CALIFORNIA LLC
Also Called: Willow Tree Nursing Center
2124 57th Ave, Oakland (94621-4322)
PHONE..................510 261-2628
Tony Moya, *Manager*
EMP: 55 Privately Held
WEB: www.covenantcare.com
SIC: 8051 Convalescent home with continuous nursing care
HQ: Covenant Care California, Llc
    120 Vantis Dr Ste 200
    Aliso Viejo CA 92656

(P-15968)
COVENANT CARE CALIFORNIA LLC
Also Called: Pacific Gardens Hlth Care Ctr
577 S Peach Ave, Fresno (93727-3952)
PHONE..................559 251-8463
Bart Vanderwal, *Branch Mgr*
Melissa Tapia, *Director*
EMP: 55
SQ FT: 40,000 Privately Held
WEB: www.covenantcare.com
SIC: 8051 Convalescent home with continuous nursing care
HQ: Covenant Care California, Llc
    120 Vantis Dr Ste 200
    Aliso Viejo CA 92656

(P-15969)
COVENANT CARE CALIFORNIA LLC
Also Called: Capital Transitional Care
6821 24th St, Sacramento (95822-4037)
PHONE..................916 391-6011
Richard Thorp, *Branch Mgr*
Remedios Ubaldo, *Records Dir*
Michelle Carter, *Social Dir*
Vicky Mosebey, *Chf Purch Ofc*
Cynthia Miller, *Director*
EMP: 55 Privately Held
WEB: www.covenantcare.com
SIC: 8051 Skilled nursing care facilities
HQ: Covenant Care California, Llc
    120 Vantis Dr Ste 200
    Aliso Viejo CA 92656

(P-15970)
COVENANT CARE CALIFORNIA LLC
Also Called: Turlock Nrsing Rhabilation Ctr
1111 E Tuolumne Rd, Turlock (95382-1541)
PHONE..................209 632-3821
Loris Gielczyk, *Principal*
Theresa Howard, *Records Dir*
Kelly Eusey, *Social Dir*
Gloria Resuerzo, *Education*
Macey Graham, *Hlthcr Dir*
EMP: 55 Privately Held
WEB: www.covenantcare.com
SIC: 8051 Convalescent home with continuous nursing care
HQ: Covenant Care California, Llc
    120 Vantis Dr Ste 200
    Aliso Viejo CA 92656

(P-15971)
COVENANT CARE CALIFORNIA LLC
Also Called: Gilroy Health Care
8170 Murray Ave, Gilroy (95020-4605)
PHONE..................408 842-9311
Doreen McGary, *Director*
Suzanne Varnum, *Records Dir*
Donna Gamez, *Med Doctor*
EMP: 55 Privately Held
WEB: www.covenantcare.com
SIC: 8051 Convalescent home with continuous nursing care
HQ: Covenant Care California, Llc
    120 Vantis Dr Ste 200
    Aliso Viejo CA 92656

(P-15972)
COVENANT CARE CALIFORNIA LLC
Also Called: Los Altos Sb-Cute Rhbltttion Ct
809 Fremont Ave, Los Altos (94024-5617)
PHONE..................650 941-5255
Annie Buerhaus, *Exec Dir*
Maria Deveraturda, *Nursing Dir*
Eunice Pino, *Nursing Dir*
EMP: 55 Privately Held
WEB: www.covenantcare.com
SIC: 8051 8093 Convalescent home with continuous nursing care; rehabilitation center, outpatient treatment
HQ: Covenant Care California, Llc
    120 Vantis Dr Ste 200
    Aliso Viejo CA 92656

(P-15973)
COVENANT CARE COURTYARD LLC
Also Called: Courtyard Healthcare
1850 E 8th St, Davis (95616-2502)
PHONE..................530 756-1800
Robert Levin, *CEO*
Terri Chisholm, *Case Mgmt Dir*
George Thaxton, *Maintence Staff*
Kathryn Hempel, *Nurse*
Stephanie Vasher,
EMP: 113 EST: 2011
SALES (est): 38.3MM Privately Held
WEB: www.covenantcare.com
SIC: 8051 Convalescent home with continuous nursing care
HQ: Covenant Care California, Llc
    120 Vantis Dr Ste 200
    Aliso Viejo CA 92656

(P-15974)
CREEKSIDE CNVALESCENT HOSP INC
850 Sonoma Ave, Santa Rosa (95404-4715)
PHONE..................707 544-7750
Robert Bates, *Administration*
Lawrence R De Beni, *President*
EMP: 44 EST: 1984
SQ FT: 44,000
SALES (est): 862.1K Privately Held
SIC: 8051 Convalescent home with continuous nursing care

(P-15975)
CREEKSIDE HEALTHCARE CTR
1900 Church Ln, San Pablo (94806-3708)
PHONE..................510 235-5514
Dianna Haines, *Administration*
EMP: 50 EST: 2009
SALES (est): 5MM Privately Held
SIC: 8051 Extended care facility

8051 - Skilled Nursing Facilities County (P-15976)

(P-15976)
CRESTWOOD BEHAVIORAL HLTH INC
Also Called: 1143 Pleasant Hill Bridge
550 Blvd, Pleasant Hill (94523)
PHONE..................925 938-8050
Travis Curran, *Mng Member*
EMP: 44
SALES (corp-wide): 238MM **Privately Held**
SIC: 8051 Skilled nursing care facilities
PA: Crestwood Behavioral Health, Inc.
520 Capitol Mall Ste 800
Sacramento CA 95814
510 651-1244

(P-15977)
CROCUS HOLDINGS LLC
Also Called: Roseville Care Center
1161 Cirby Way, Roseville (95661-4421)
PHONE..................916 782-1238
James Huish,
Myrna De Guzman, *Controller*
Jessica Abney, *Food Svc Dir*
EMP: 99 EST: 2011 **Privately Held**
WEB: www.capitalrehabcampus.com
SIC: 8051 Convalescent home with continuous nursing care

(P-15978)
CUPERTINO HEALTHCARE
Also Called: Cupertino Hlthcare Wllness Ctr
22590 Voss Ave, Cupertino (95014-2627)
PHONE..................408 253-9034
Aaron Robin, *Mng Member*
Bradley Burgoyne, *Director*
EMP: 99 EST: 2010 **Privately Held**
WEB: www.cupertinohc.com
SIC: 8051 Convalescent home with continuous nursing care

(P-15979)
DANVILLE LONG-TERM CARE INC
Also Called: Danville Post Acute Rehab
336 Diablo Rd, Danville (94526-3417)
PHONE..................925 837-4566
John L Sorensen, *President*
Tim Paulsen, *Vice Pres*
Brittanie Saechao, *Office Mgr*
Taylor Ellis, *Administration*
Latoya Lewis, *Marketing Staff*
EMP: 57 EST: 1997
SALES (est): 24.4MM **Privately Held**
WEB: www.danvillerehab.com
SIC: 8051 Convalescent home with continuous nursing care

(P-15980)
EASTERN PLUMAS HEALTH CARE
700 3rd St, Loyalton (96118)
PHONE..................530 993-1225
G Koortbojian, *Administration*
Susan Horstmeyer, *Admin Asst*
Camille Coverdell, *Analyst*
Mandy Rivas, *Assistant*
EMP: 52 EST: 1951
SQ FT: 20,000
SALES (est): 27.4MM **Privately Held**
WEB: www.ephc.org
SIC: 8051 Skilled nursing care facilities

(P-15981)
ELDER CARE ALLIANCE SAN MATEO
Also Called: Villa At San Mateo
4000 S El Camino Real, San Mateo (94403-4566)
PHONE..................650 212-4400
EMP: 56
SALES (corp-wide): 4.1MM **Privately Held**
WEB: www.eldercarealliance.org
SIC: 8051 Skilled nursing care facilities
HQ: Elder Care Alliance Of San Mateo
1301 Marina Vil Pkwy 21 # 210
Alameda CA 94501
510 769-2700

(P-15982)
ELDER CARE ALLIANCE SAN RAFAEL
1301 Marina Village Pkwy # 2, Alameda (94501-1082)
PHONE..................510 769-2700
Jesse Janteen, *President*
EMP: 37 EST: 2003
SALES: 11MM **Privately Held**
WEB: www.eldercarealliance.org
SIC: 8051 Convalescent home with continuous nursing care

(P-15983)
ELDER CARE ALNCE SAN FRANCISCO
Also Called: Almavia of San Francisco
1 Thomas More Way, San Francisco (94132-2914)
PHONE..................415 337-1339
Janeane Randolph, *Principal*
Christine Mills, *Assistant*
EMP: 62 EST: 1999
SALES (est): 26MM **Privately Held**
WEB: www.eldercarealliance.org
SIC: 8051 Skilled nursing care facilities

(P-15984)
EMERITUS CORPORATION
38035 Martha Ave, Fremont (94536-3808)
PHONE..................510 797-4011
Trish Rosner, *Branch Mgr*
EMP: 155
SALES (corp-wide): 3.5B **Publicly Held**
WEB: www.brookdale.com
SIC: 8051 Skilled nursing care facilities
HQ: Emeritus Corporation
6737 W Wa St Ste 2300
Milwaukee WI 53214

(P-15985)
EMERITUS CORPORATION
2261 Tuolumne St, Vallejo (94589-2560)
PHONE..................707 552-3336
EMP: 155
SALES (corp-wide): 3.5B **Publicly Held**
WEB: www.brookdale.com
SIC: 8051 Skilled nursing care facilities
HQ: Emeritus Corporation
6737 W Wa St Ste 2300
Milwaukee WI 53214

(P-15986)
EMPRES FINANCIAL SERVICES LLC
Also Called: Living Centers
1527 Springs Rd, Vallejo (94591-5448)
PHONE..................707 643-2793
David Hicks, *Manager*
EMP: 886
SALES (corp-wide): 5MM **Privately Held**
WEB: www.empres.com
SIC: 8051 Skilled nursing care facilities
HQ: Empres Financial Services, Llc
4601 Ne 77th Ave Ste 300
Vancouver WA 98662
360 892-6628

(P-15987)
EMPRESS CARE CENTER LLC
1299 S Bascom Ave, San Jose (95128-3514)
PHONE..................408 287-0616
Ben Laub, *Director*
Kin Mohamed, *Director*
EMP: 50 EST: 1968
SALES (est): 21.8MM **Privately Held**
WEB: www.empresscare.com
SIC: 8051 Convalescent home with continuous nursing care

(P-15988)
ENGLISH OAKS CONVALESCENT
Also Called: English Oaks Cnvlscent Rhbltti
2633 W Rumble Rd, Modesto (95350-0154)
PHONE..................209 577-1001
Terry L Mundy, *President*
Pamela Mundy, *Admin Sec*
EMP: 66 EST: 1985
SQ FT: 57,000
SALES (est): 11.9MM **Privately Held**
WEB: www.lifegen.net
SIC: 8051 Convalescent home with continuous nursing care

(P-15989)
ENSIGN CLOVERDALE LLC
Also Called: Cloverdale Healthcare Center
300 Cherry Creek Rd, Cloverdale (95425-3811)
PHONE..................707 894-5201
Soon Burnam, *Administration*
Misty Robinson, *Social Dir*
Adam Willits, *Administration*
Trang Davis, *Human Res Dir*
Myra Granados, *Hlthcr Dir*
EMP: 201 EST: 2004
SALES (est): 15.1MM
SALES (corp-wide): 2.4B **Publicly Held**
WEB: www.cloverdalehealthcare.com
SIC: 8051 Convalescent home with continuous nursing care
HQ: Northern Pioneer Healthcare, Inc.
27101 Puerta Real
Mission Viejo CA 92691
949 487-9500

(P-15990)
ENSIGN GROUP INC
Also Called: Park View Gardens
3751 Montgomery Dr, Santa Rosa (95405-5214)
PHONE..................707 525-1250
Eric Moessing, *Director*
Susan Rankin, *Executive*
EMP: 80
SALES (corp-wide): 2.4B **Publicly Held**
WEB: www.ensigngroup.net
SIC: 8051 Convalescent home with continuous nursing care
PA: The Ensign Group Inc
29222 Rncho Vejo Rd Ste 1
San Juan Capistrano CA 92675
949 487-9500

(P-15991)
ENSIGN PLEASANTON LLC
Also Called: Ukiah Post Acute
1349 S Dora St, Ukiah (95482-6512)
PHONE..................707 462-8864
Lowell Smith, *CEO*
Soon Burnam, *Treasurer*
Ferdinand Buot, *Exec Dir*
EMP: 144 EST: 2001
SALES (est): 13.1MM
SALES (corp-wide): 2.4B **Publicly Held**
WEB: www.ukiahpostacute.com
SIC: 8051 Convalescent home with continuous nursing care
PA: The Ensign Group Inc
29222 Rncho Vejo Rd Ste 1
San Juan Capistrano CA 92675
949 487-9500

(P-15992)
ENSIGN SONOMA LLC
Also Called: Broadway Villa Post Acute
1250 Broadway, Sonoma (95476-7500)
PHONE..................707 938-8406
Michael Empey, *Exec Dir*
EMP: 179 EST: 2001
SALES (est): 17.8MM
SALES (corp-wide): 2.4B **Publicly Held**
WEB: www.broadwayvillapostacute.com
SIC: 8051 Convalescent home with continuous nursing care
HQ: Northern Pioneer Healthcare, Inc.
27101 Puerta Real
Mission Viejo CA 92691
949 487-9500

(P-15993)
ENSIGN WILLITS LLC
Also Called: Northbrook Healthcare Center
64 Northbrook Way, Willits (95490-3019)
PHONE..................707 459-5592
Shawndee Gamble, *Exec Dir*
EMP: 244 EST: 2001
SALES (est): 22.2MM
SALES (corp-wide): 2.4B **Publicly Held**
WEB: www.northbrooknursing.com
SIC: 8051 Convalescent home with continuous nursing care
PA: The Ensign Group Inc
29222 Rncho Vejo Rd Ste 1
San Juan Capistrano CA 92675
949 487-9500

(P-15994)
ESKATON PROPERTIES INC
Also Called: Eskaton Village Care Center
3847 Walnut Ave, Carmichael (95608-2148)
PHONE..................916 974-2060
Larry Bahr, *Manager*
John Mueggenburg, *Manager*
EMP: 372 **Privately Held**
WEB: www.eskaton.org
SIC: 8051 Skilled nursing care facilities
PA: Eskaton Properties Incorporated
5105 Manzanita Ave Ste A
Carmichael CA 95608

(P-15995)
EUREKA REHAB & WELLNESS CENTER
2353 23rd St, Eureka (95501-3201)
PHONE..................707 445-3261
Sharrod Brooks, *Partner*
Shlomo Rechnitz, *Partner*
EMP: 98 EST: 2011
SALES (est): 8.1MM **Privately Held**
WEB: www.eurekarehabwc.com
SIC: 8051 Skilled nursing care facilities

(P-15996)
EVERGREEN AT CHICO LLC
Also Called: Twin Oaks Nrsing Rhblttion Ctr
1200 Springfield Dr, Chico (95928-6340)
PHONE..................530 342-4885
Barbara Addington, *Manager*
Charles Garretson, *Director*
EMP: 143
SALES (corp-wide): 5MM **Privately Held**
SIC: 8051 8069 Convalescent home with continuous nursing care; specialty hospitals, except psychiatric
HQ: Evergreen At Chico, L.L.C.
4601 Ne 77th Ave Ste 300
Vancouver WA 98662
530 342-4885

(P-15997)
EVERGREEN AT HEARTWOOD AVE LLC
1044 Heartwood Ave, Vallejo (94591-5637)
PHONE..................707 643-2267
Judy Stevens, *Office Mgr*
Cherry James, *Human Res Dir*
Ruth Gildea, *Chf Purch Ofc*
Cat Lacuata-Remorin, *Corp Comm Staff*
Catherine Johnson, *Food Svc Dir*
EMP: 48 EST: 1998
SALES (est): 3.7MM **Privately Held**
SIC: 8051 Skilled nursing care facilities

(P-15998)
EVERGREEN AT LAKEPORT LLC (PA)
Also Called: Evergreen Lkport Hlthcare Ctr
1291 Craig Ave, Lakeport (95453-5704)
PHONE..................707 263-6382
Steve Hendrickson, *Administration*
Rhonda Daughtery, *Executive*
Bob Harrington, *Sales Staff*
Jason Brey, *Director*
EMP: 100 EST: 1986
SQ FT: 36,240
SALES (est): 8.1B **Privately Held**
SIC: 8051 Convalescent home with continuous nursing care

(P-15999)
EVERGREEN AT PETALUMA LLC
Also Called: Empres Post Acute Rhbilitation
300 Douglas St, Petaluma (94952-2503)
PHONE..................707 763-6887
Connie Smith, *Exec Dir*
Curtis Bonner, *Office Mgr*
Bobby Singh, *Food Svc Dir*
Ahmed El-Ghoneimy, *Director*
EMP: 100 EST: 1969
SQ FT: 21,965
SALES (est): 38.7MM **Privately Held**
WEB: www.empres.com
SIC: 8051 Skilled nursing care facilities

PRODUCTS & SERVICES SECTION
8051 - Skilled Nursing Facilities County (P-16022)

PA: Empres California Healthcare, Llc
4601 Ne 77th Ave Ste 300
Vancouver WA 98662
360 892-6628

(P-16000)
EVERGREEN AT SPRINGS ROAD LLC
Also Called: Springs Road Healthcare
1527 Springs Rd, Vallejo (94591-5448)
PHONE.................360 892-6628
Brent Well,
EMP: 74
SALES (est): 6.1MM Privately Held
WEB: www.empres.com
SIC: 8051 Convalescent home with continuous nursing care

(P-16001)
FAIRFIELD HEALTH CARE INC
Also Called: Fairfield Post-Acute Rehab
1255 Travis Blvd, Fairfield (94533-4801)
PHONE.................707 425-0623
Steve Hendrickson, Administration
Joanne Lane, General Mgr
Joan Wandyke, Administration
Patti Turner, Info Tech Mgr
Meleah Lugtu,
EMP: 130 EST: 1971
SALES (est): 25.5MM Privately Held
WEB: www.fairfieldrehab.net
SIC: 8051 Convalescent home with continuous nursing care

(P-16002)
FERN LODGE INC
Also Called: Fern Ldge Chrstn Scnce Nursing
18457 Madison Ave, Castro Valley (94546-1699)
PHONE.................510 886-2448
George Strong, Administration
Sharon Strong, Director
Rozanne Zwick, Director
EMP: 43 EST: 1971
SQ FT: 15,000
SALES: 1.7MM Privately Held
WEB: www.fernlodge.org
SIC: 8051 Convalescent home with continuous nursing care

(P-16003)
FIG HOLDINGS LLC
Also Called: GARDEN CITY HEALTHCARE CENTER
1310 W Granger Ave, Modesto (95350-3911)
PHONE.................209 524-4817
Gary Collins,
Trina Butler, Records Dir
Vikashni Sharma, Records Dir
Renee Pugh, Treasurer
Richelle Ballesteros, Office Mgr
EMP: 100 EST: 2002
SQ FT: 23,000
SALES (est): 15.8MM
SALES (corp-wide): 66MM Privately Held
WEB: www.plumhealthcaregroup.com
SIC: 8051 Convalescent home with continuous nursing care
PA: Plum Healthcare Group, Llc
100 E San Marcos Blvd # 200
San Marcos CA 92069
760 471-0388

(P-16004)
FIVE STAR QUALITY CARE INC
Also Called: Somerford Place Fresno
6075 N Marks Ave, Fresno (93711-1600)
PHONE.................559 446-6262
EMP: 46 Publicly Held
WEB: www.fivestarseniorliving.com
SIC: 8051 Skilled nursing care facilities
PA: Five Star Senior Living Inc.
400 Centre St Ste 100
Newton MA 02458

(P-16005)
FIVE STAR QULTY CARE-CA II LLC
Also Called: Lasaltte Hlth Rhbilitation Ctr
537 E Fulton St, Stockton (95204-2227)
PHONE.................209 466-2066
Gus Ropalidis, Administration
Manjit Kaur, Nurse
EMP: 105 Publicly Held
SIC: 8051 Skilled nursing care facilities
HQ: Five Star Quality Care-Ca Ii, Llc
93 W Avnida De Los Arbles
Thousand Oaks CA 91360
805 492-2444

(P-16006)
FOOTHILL OAKS CARE CENTER INC
3400 Bell Rd, Auburn (95603-9241)
PHONE.................530 888-6257
Art Whitney, CEO
Ellen Kuykendall, President
Jorin Larsen, Director
EMP: 47 EST: 1985
SALES (est): 17.9MM Privately Held
WEB: www.auburnoakscarecenter.com
SIC: 8051 8093 8062 Convalescent home with continuous nursing care; rehabilitation center, outpatient treatment; general medical & surgical hospitals
HQ: Horizon West Healthcare, Inc.
4020 Sierra College Blvd # 190
Rocklin CA 95677
916 624-6230

(P-16007)
FORTUNA RHBLTTION WLLNESS CTR
Also Called: Fortuna Rhbltion Wellness Ctr
2321 Newburg Rd, Fortuna (95540-2815)
PHONE.................707 725-4467
Brad Gibson, CEO
EMP: 43
SALES (est): 6.9MM Privately Held
WEB: www.fortunarwc.wpengine.com
SIC: 8051 Convalescent home with continuous nursing care

(P-16008)
FORUM HEALTHCARE CENTER
23600 Via Esplendor, Cupertino (95014-6571)
PHONE.................650 944-0200
Lynda Kaser, Administration
EMP: 59 EST: 1998
SALES (est): 9.3MM Privately Held
WEB: www.theforum-seniorliving.com
SIC: 8051 8052 Convalescent home with continuous nursing care; intermediate care facilities

(P-16009)
FRESNO SKILLED NURSING
Also Called: Healthcare Centre of Fresno
1665 M St, Fresno (93721-1121)
PHONE.................559 268-5361
Sharrod Brooks,
EMP: 99 EST: 2009
SALES (est): 10.2MM Privately Held
WEB: www.hcfresno.com
SIC: 8051 Mental retardation hospital

(P-16010)
FSQ RIO LAS PALMAS BUSINESS TR
877 E March Ln Apt 378, Stockton (95207-5880)
PHONE.................209 957-4711
Sam Ogden, Partner
EMP: 101 EST: 1998
SALES (est): 20.7MM Publicly Held
WEB: www.riolaspalmasretirement.com
SIC: 8051 Skilled nursing care facilities
PA: Five Star Senior Living Inc.
400 Centre St Ste 100
Newton MA 02458

(P-16011)
GARFIELD NURSING HOME INC
Also Called: Morton Bakar Center
1100 Marina Village Pkwy # 100, Alameda (94501-6461)
PHONE.................510 582-7676
Ann Bakar, CEO
Robert H Guttman, President
Marshall D Langfeld, CFO
Ross C Peterson, Vice Pres
EMP: 111 EST: 1980
SALES (est): 10.8MM
SALES (corp-wide): 140.9MM Privately Held
WEB: www.telecarecorp.com
SIC: 8051 Convalescent home with continuous nursing care
PA: Telecare Corporation
1080 Marina Village Pkwy # 100
Alameda CA 94501
510 337-7950

(P-16012)
GENESIS HEALTHCARE LLC
Also Called: Creekside Center
9107 Davis Rd, Stockton (95209-1807)
PHONE.................209 478-6488
Judy Treloar, Administration
Stephanie Godfrey, Human Res Dir
Christine McGahey, Education
Andrea Britto, Director
Thomas Williams, Director
EMP: 211 Privately Held
WEB: www.genesishcc.com
SIC: 8051 Convalescent home with continuous nursing care
HQ: Genesis Healthcare Llc
101 E State St
Kennett Square PA 19348

(P-16013)
GLADIOLUS HOLDINGS LLC
Also Called: Pines At Plcrvlle Hlthcare Ctr
1040 Marshall Way, Placerville (95667-5706)
PHONE.................530 622-3400
Nick Anderson, President
Victoria Rapoza, Records Dir
Kristina Brown, Social Dir
Kristi Demasters, Chf Purch Ofc
Deborah Herman, Director
EMP: 41 EST: 2011 Privately Held
WEB: www.pinesatplacerville.com
SIC: 8051 Convalescent home with continuous nursing care

(P-16014)
GOLD COUNTRY HEALTH CENTER INC (PA)
4301 Golden Center Dr, Placerville (95667-6260)
PHONE.................530 621-1100
Suzanne Valoppi, Administration
Sandra Haskins, Exec Dir
Rachel Priolo, Education
Vicky Hume Estrada, Hlthcr Dir
Mary Fatooh, Director
EMP: 130 EST: 1984
SQ FT: 57,000
SALES (est): 13.5MM Privately Held
WEB: www.goldcountryretirement.org
SIC: 8051 Skilled nursing care facilities

(P-16015)
GRIDLEY HLTHCARE & WELLNSS CEN
246 Spruce St, Gridley (95948-2216)
PHONE.................530 846-6266
Sharrod Brooks,
EMP: 99 EST: 2010
SALES (est): 6.8MM Privately Held
WEB: www.windsorartesia.com
SIC: 8051 Mental retardation hospital

(P-16016)
H C C S INC
Also Called: Sherwood Healthcare Center
4700 Elvas Ave, Sacramento (95819-2250)
PHONE.................916 454-5752
David Hilburn, Director
John Lund, Director
EMP: 60 EST: 1998
SALES (est): 13.5MM Privately Held
WEB: www.sherwoodhealthcarecenter.com
SIC: 8051 Convalescent home with continuous nursing care

(P-16017)
HAYES CONVALESCENT HOSPITAL
Also Called: John Chailch
1250 Hayes St, San Francisco (94117-1597)
PHONE.................415 931-8806
John Chalich,
Tana Chalich,
EMP: 50 EST: 1996
SQ FT: 10,000
SALES (est): 13MM Privately Held
WEB: www.hayesconvalescent.com
SIC: 8051 8322 Convalescent home with continuous nursing care; rehabilitation services

(P-16018)
HCR MANORCARE INC
2005 De La Cruz Blvd, Santa Clara (95050-3013)
PHONE.................408 450-7850
Jenifer Crane, Purchasing
Emili Jayne,
Regina Roberts, Assistant
EMP: 60
SALES (corp-wide): 6.1B Privately Held
WEB: www.promedicaseniorcare.org
SIC: 8051 Convalescent home with continuous nursing care
HQ: Hcr Manorcare, Inc.
333 N Summit St
Toledo OH 43604
419 252-5743

(P-16019)
HCR MANORCARE INC
Also Called: In Home Health
1575 Bayshore Hwy Ste 200, Burlingame (94010-1616)
PHONE.................419 252-5743
Thomas R Kile, Treasurer
Kandice Pope, Nursing Mgr
Linda De Perez, Sales Staff
Kathryn Mestanza, Nurse
Anisha Monis, Nurse
EMP: 55
SALES (corp-wide): 6.1B Privately Held
WEB: www.promedicaseniorcare.org
SIC: 8051 Convalescent home with continuous nursing care
HQ: Hcr Manorcare, Inc.
333 N Summit St
Toledo OH 43604
419 252-5743

(P-16020)
HEBREW HOME FOR AGED DISABLED
Also Called: JEWISH HOME FOR THE AGED
302 Silver Ave, San Francisco (94112-1510)
PHONE.................415 334-2500
Daniel Ruth, President
Kevin T Potter, CFO
Ilana Glaun, Officer
Christine R Soares, Social Dir
Jan Reicher, Exec Dir
EMP: 600 EST: 1889
SALES: 78.2MM Privately Held
WEB: www.sfcjl.org
SIC: 8051 Skilled nursing care facilities

(P-16021)
HELIOS HEALTHCARE LLC
Also Called: El Camino Care Center
2540 Carmichael Way, Carmichael (95608-5314)
PHONE.................916 482-0465
Evelyn McGraff, Administration
Roxanne L Henry, Social Dir
EMP: 62
SALES (corp-wide): 27.5MM Privately Held
WEB: www.windsorelcamino.com
SIC: 8051 Skilled nursing care facilities
PA: Helios Healthcare, Llc
520 Capitol Mall Ste 800
Sacramento CA 95814
916 471-2241

(P-16022)
HELIOS HEALTHCARE LLC
Also Called: Chico Creek Care Rhabilitation
587 Rio Lindo Ave, Chico (95926-1816)
PHONE.................530 345-1306
Carl Lewis, Manager
EMP: 62
SQ FT: 51,457
SALES (corp-wide): 27.5MM Privately Held
SIC: 8051 Skilled nursing care facilities

8051 - Skilled Nursing Facilities County (P-16023)

PA: Helios Healthcare, Llc
520 Capitol Mall Ste 800
Sacramento CA 95814
916 471-2241

(P-16023)
HERMAN SANITARIUM
Also Called: Herman Health Care Center
2295 Plummer Ave, San Jose
(95125-4767)
PHONE 408 269-0701
Mandy S Sollis, *President*
Steve Marcus, *Administration*
Mandy Sollis, *Mktg Dir*
Mike Bottarini, *Food Svc Dir*
Sandra Stumps, *Director*
EMP: 80 **EST:** 1944
SQ FT: 4,500
SALES (est): 11.5MM **Privately Held**
SIC: 8051 Convalescent home with continuous nursing care

(P-16024)
HILLVIEW CONVALESCENT HOSPITAL
530 W Dunne Ave, Morgan Hill
(95037-4823)
PHONE 408 779-3633
James Ross, *Owner*
Richard Ross, *Co-Owner*
Steve Ross, *Administration*
EMP: 35 **EST:** 1968
SQ FT: 10,000
SALES (est): 9MM **Privately Held**
WEB: www.hillviewconvalescenthospital.com
SIC: 8051 Convalescent home with continuous nursing care

(P-16025)
HORIZON WEST INC
Also Called: Walnut Whtney Convalecent Hosp
3529 Walnut Ave, Carmichael
(95608-3049)
PHONE 916 488-8601
Kathy Spake, *Branch Mgr*
EMP: 39 **Privately Held**
SIC: 8051 Convalescent home with continuous nursing care
PA: Horizon West, Inc.
4020 Sierra College Blvd
Rocklin CA 95677

(P-16026)
HORIZON WEST INC
Also Called: Heritage Conalescent Hospital
5255 Hemlock St, Sacramento
(95841-3017)
PHONE 916 331-4590
Randy Balecha, *Manager*
EMP: 39 **Privately Held**
SIC: 8051 8361 8059 Skilled nursing care facilities; residential care; convalescent home
PA: Horizon West, Inc.
4020 Sierra College Blvd
Rocklin CA 95677

(P-16027)
HORIZON WEST INC (PA)
4020 Sierra College Blvd, Rocklin
(95677-3906)
PHONE 916 624-6230
Ken McGuire, *President*
Alan MA, *CFO*
Linda Lutz, *Admin Sec*
EMP: 35 **EST:** 1987
SALES (est): 381MM **Privately Held**
SIC: 8051 Skilled nursing care facilities

(P-16028)
HORIZON WEST HEALTHCARE INC (HQ)
4020 Sierra College Blvd # 190, Rocklin
(95677-3906)
PHONE 916 624-6230
Martine D Harmon, *CEO*
Dennis Roccaforte, *Corp Secy*
Bernice Schrabeck, *Vice Pres*
EMP: 40 **EST:** 1973
SQ FT: 6,000
SALES (est): 184.2MM **Privately Held**
SIC: 8051 Convalescent home with continuous nursing care

(P-16029)
HOSPICE OF SAN JOAQUIN
3888 Pacific Ave, Stockton (95204-1953)
PHONE 209 957-3888
Stephen L Guasco, *CEO*
Kerrie Biddle, *CFO*
Heather Stout, *CFO*
Melanie Payne, *Officer*
Sandra Smith, *Officer*
EMP: 90 **EST:** 1980
SQ FT: 5,000
SALES (est): 21.3MM **Privately Held**
WEB: www.hospicesj.org
SIC: 8051 8641 Skilled nursing care facilities; social associations

(P-16030)
KARMA INC
Also Called: Manteca Care Rhabilitation Ctr
410 Eastwood Ave, Manteca (95336-3167)
PHONE 209 239-1222
Antony Thekkek, *President*
Prema Thekkek, *Vice Pres*
EMP: 156 **EST:** 2003
SQ FT: 29,700
SALES (est): 29.2MM **Privately Held**
SIC: 8051 Convalescent home with continuous nursing care
PA: Paksn, Inc.
540 W Monte Vista Ave
Vacaville CA 95688
707 449-3400

(P-16031)
KIRKWOOD ASSSTED LVING RSDENCE
395 Hilltop Dr, Redding (96003-3710)
PHONE 530 241-2900
Michael Sawyer, *Administration*
Carma Hunter, *Director*
Stacey McGarvin, *Director*
Cara Morehouse, *Clerk*
EMP: 36 **EST:** 2001
SALES (est): 8MM **Privately Held**
WEB: www.compass-living.com
SIC: 8051 Skilled nursing care facilities

(P-16032)
KISSITO HEALTHCARE INC
Also Called: Arbor Vly Nrsing Rhblttion Ctr
1310 W Granger Ave, Modesto
(95350-3911)
PHONE 209 524-4817
Al Johnson, *Branch Mgr*
EMP: 39 **Privately Held**
WEB: www.kissito.org
SIC: 8051 8361 Convalescent home with continuous nursing care; rehabilitation center, residential: health care incidental
PA: Kissito Healthcare, Inc.
7500 Shadwell Dr
Roanoke VA 24019

(P-16033)
KIT CARSON NURSING & REHAB
811 Court St, Jackson (95642-2131)
PHONE 209 223-2231
EMP: 38
SALES (est): 4.3MM **Privately Held**
SIC: 8051 Skilled Nursing Care Facilities, Nsk

(P-16034)
KU KYOUNG
Also Called: Eden Villa
Unknown, Redding (96003)
P.O. Box 590428
PHONE 510 582-2765
Kyoung Ku, *Owner*
EMP: 170 **EST:** 1986
SQ FT: 37,157
SALES (est): 10.6MM **Privately Held**
SIC: 8051 1522 Convalescent home with continuous nursing care; residential construction

(P-16035)
LEGACY AND NURSING REHAB
1790 Muir Rd, Martinez (94553-4718)
PHONE 925 228-8383
Dipa Gupta, *Owner*
Thomas Joseph, *Principal*
Burnadett Joseph, *Admin Asst*
Sherry Jansen, *Director*
EMP: 90 **EST:** 1998
SALES (est): 7.7MM **Privately Held**
SIC: 8051 Convalescent home with continuous nursing care

(P-16036)
LIFE GNERATIONS HEALTHCARE LLC
Also Called: Walnut Creek Sklled Nrsing Rhb
1224 Rossmoor Pkwy, Walnut Creek
(94595-2501)
PHONE 925 937-7450
EMP: 47
SALES (corp-wide): 112.7MM **Privately Held**
SIC: 8051 Convalescent home with continuous nursing care
PA: Life Generations Healthcare Llc
6 Hutton Cntre Dr Ste 400
Santa Ana CA 92707
714 241-5600

(P-16037)
LILY HOLDINGS LLC
Also Called: Oakwood Gardens Care Center
3510 E Shields Ave, Fresno (93726-6909)
PHONE 559 222-4807
Ashley Specht,
Lisa Perez, *Office Mgr*
Leslie Cotham, *Administration*
Richard Martin,
EMP: 41 **EST:** 2011
SALES (est): 14.7MM **Privately Held**
WEB: www.oakwoodgardenscarecenter.com
SIC: 8051 Convalescent home with continuous nursing care

(P-16038)
LONE TREE CNVALESCENT HOSP INC
4001 Lone Tree Way, Antioch
(94509-6232)
PHONE 925 754-0470
Lowell Callaway, *President*
Mark Callaway, *Corp Secy*
Velda C Pierce, *Vice Pres*
EMP: 135 **EST:** 1968
SQ FT: 10,000
SALES (est): 17MM **Privately Held**
SIC: 8051 Convalescent home with continuous nursing care

(P-16039)
MADERA CONVALESCENT HOSP INC (PA)
517 S A St, Madera (93638-3896)
PHONE 559 673-9228
Arden Bennett, *CEO*
Dennis Albers, *Ch of Bd*
Mathilde Albers, *Corp Secy*
Emile Damia, *Vice Pres*
EMP: 160 **EST:** 1965
SQ FT: 1,500
SALES (est): 8.5MM **Privately Held**
WEB: www.maderarehab.com
SIC: 8051 Convalescent home with continuous nursing care

(P-16040)
MANNING GARDENS CARE CTR INC
2113 E Manning Ave, Fresno (93725-9681)
PHONE 559 834-2586
Ronald Kinnersley, *President*
EMP: 82 **EST:** 2011
SALES (est): 7.7MM **Privately Held**
WEB: www.manninggardensnr.com
SIC: 8051 Skilled nursing care facilities

(P-16041)
MANOR CARE SUNNYVALE CA LLC
Also Called: Manorcare Hlth Svcs Sunnyvale
1150 Tilton Dr, Sunnyvale (94087-2440)
PHONE 408 735-7200
Jorge Rojo, *Food Svc Dir*
Walter Long, *Director*
EMP: 232 **EST:** 2016
SALES (est): 27.3MM
SALES (corp-wide): 6.1B **Privately Held**
WEB: www.promedicaseniorcare.com
SIC: 8051 Convalescent home with continuous nursing care
HQ: Hcr Manorcare, Inc.
333 N Summit St
Toledo OH 43604
419 252-5743

(P-16042)
MARIN CNVLSCENT RHBLTTION HOSP
30 Hacienda Dr, Belvedere Tiburon
(94920-1127)
PHONE 415 435-4554
Mary Wollam, *President*
Debbie Litchfield,
EMP: 76 **EST:** 1950
SQ FT: 5,000
SALES (est): 12.5MM **Privately Held**
WEB: www.marinconvalescent.com
SIC: 8051 Convalescent home with continuous nursing care

(P-16043)
MARINA GARDEN NURSING CTR INC
3201 Fernside Blvd, Alameda
(94501-1797)
PHONE 510 523-2363
Belinda Leung, *President*
EMP: 36 **EST:** 2004
SALES (est): 10.7MM **Privately Held**
WEB: www.marinanursing.com
SIC: 8051 Convalescent home with continuous nursing care

(P-16044)
MARINER HEALTH CARE INC
Also Called: Arden Health & Rehab Ctr
3400 Alta Arden Expy, Sacramento
(95825-2103)
PHONE 916 481-5500
John Pritchard, *Manager*
EMP: 36
SALES (corp-wide): 1B **Privately Held**
WEB: www.marinerhealthcare.com
SIC: 8051 8069 Extended care facility; specialty hospitals, except psychiatric
HQ: Mariner Health Care, Inc.
3060 Mercer University Dr # 200
Atlanta GA 30341
678 443-7000

(P-16045)
MARINER HEALTH CARE INC
Also Called: Freemont Health Care Center
39022 Presidio Way, Fremont
(94538-1221)
PHONE 510 792-3743
Carinagayle Gorospe, *Administration*
Mary Grace Abuan, *Chf Purch Ofc*
Ric Dee, *Director*
EMP: 36
SALES (corp-wide): 1B **Privately Held**
WEB: www.marinerhealthcare.com
SIC: 8051 Extended care facility
HQ: Mariner Health Care, Inc.
3060 Mercer University Dr # 200
Atlanta GA 30341
678 443-7000

(P-16046)
MARINER HEALTH CARE INC
Also Called: Gilroy Health & Rehab Ctr
8170 Murray Ave, Gilroy (95020-4605)
PHONE 408 842-9311
Gerald Hunter, *Administration*
Molini Guttenbeil, *Education*
EMP: 36
SALES (corp-wide): 1B **Privately Held**
WEB: www.marinerhealthcare.com
SIC: 8051 Extended care facility
HQ: Mariner Health Care, Inc.
3060 Mercer University Dr # 200
Atlanta GA 30341
678 443-7000

(P-16047)
MARINER HEALTH CARE INC
Also Called: Skyline Health Care Center
2065 Forest Ave, San Jose (95128-4807)
PHONE 408 298-3950
Richard Park, *Administration*
EMP: 36

PRODUCTS & SERVICES SECTION
8051 - Skilled Nursing Facilities County (P-16072)

SALES (corp-wide): 1B Privately Held
WEB: www.marinerhealthcare.com
SIC: 8051 Extended care facility
HQ: Mariner Health Care, Inc.
3060 Mercer University Dr # 200
Atlanta GA 30341
678 443-7000

(P-16048)
MARINER HEALTH CARE INC
7400 24th St, Sacramento (95822-5350)
PHONE.................................916 422-4825
Robert Lorenzo, Manager
EMP: 36
SALES (corp-wide): 1B Privately Held
WEB: www.marinerhealthcare.com
SIC: 8051 Extended care facility
HQ: Mariner Health Care, Inc.
3060 Mercer University Dr # 200
Atlanta GA 30341
678 443-7000

(P-16049)
MARINER HEALTH CARE INC
Also Called: Parkview Healthcare Center
27350 Tampa Ave, Hayward (94544-4429)
PHONE.................................510 783-8150
Ada Lukban, Manager
Lisa Long, Executive
EMP: 36
SALES (corp-wide): 1B Privately Held
WEB: www.marinerhealthcare.com
SIC: 8051 Extended care facility
HQ: Mariner Health Care, Inc.
3060 Mercer University Dr # 200
Atlanta GA 30341
678 443-7000

(P-16050)
MARINER HEALTH CARE INC
Also Called: Vale Healthcare Center
13484 San Pablo Ave, San Pablo (94806-3904)
PHONE.................................510 232-5945
Remy Dise, Director
Christine D 'souza, Nursing Dir
David Groch-Tochman, Director
EMP: 36
SALES (corp-wide): 1B Privately Held
WEB: www.marinerhealthcare.com
SIC: 8051 Extended care facility
HQ: Mariner Health Care, Inc.
3060 Mercer University Dr # 200
Atlanta GA 30341
678 443-7000

(P-16051)
MARINER HEALTH CARE INC
Also Called: Driftwood Convalescent Hosp
1850 E 8th St, Davis (95616-2502)
PHONE.................................530 756-1800
David Ormiston, Principal
EMP: 36
SALES (corp-wide): 1B Privately Held
WEB: www.marinerhealthcare.com
SIC: 8051 Extended care facility
HQ: Mariner Health Care, Inc.
3060 Mercer University Dr # 200
Atlanta GA 30341
678 443-7000

(P-16052)
MARINER HEALTH CARE INC
675 24th Ave, Santa Cruz (95062-4205)
PHONE.................................831 475-6323
EMP: 36
SALES (corp-wide): 1B Privately Held
WEB: www.marinerhealthcare.com
SIC: 8051 Extended care facility
HQ: Mariner Health Care, Inc.
3060 Mercer University Dr # 200
Atlanta GA 30341
678 443-7000

(P-16053)
MARINER HEALTH CARE INC
Also Called: Hayward Hills Health Care Ctr
1768 B St, Hayward (94541-3102)
PHONE.................................510 538-4424
Annamarie Magna, Branch Mgr
EMP: 36
SALES (corp-wide): 1B Privately Held
WEB: www.marinerhealthcare.com
SIC: 8051 Extended care facility

HQ: Mariner Health Care, Inc.
3060 Mercer University Dr # 200
Atlanta GA 30341
678 443-7000

(P-16054)
MARINER HEALTH CARE INC
Also Called: Driftwood Healthcare Center
19700 Hesperian Blvd, Hayward (94541-4704)
PHONE.................................510 785-2880
Ellen Renner, Administration
EMP: 36
SALES (corp-wide): 1B Privately Held
WEB: www.marinerhealthcare.com
SIC: 8051 Extended care facility
HQ: Mariner Health Care, Inc.
3060 Mercer University Dr # 200
Atlanta GA 30341
678 443-7000

(P-16055)
MARINER HEALTH CARE INC
Also Called: Pinedridge Care Ctr
45 Professional Ctr Pkwy, San Rafael (94903-2702)
PHONE.................................415 479-3610
Louise Kalchek, Director
Conrad Bustamante, Facilities Dir
EMP: 36
SALES (corp-wide): 1B Privately Held
WEB: www.marinerhealthcare.com
SIC: 8051 Extended care facility
HQ: Mariner Health Care, Inc.
3060 Mercer University Dr # 200
Atlanta GA 30341
678 443-7000

(P-16056)
MARINER HEALTH CARE INC
Also Called: Almaden Health & Rehab Ctr
2065 Los Gatos Almaden Rd, San Jose (95124-5417)
PHONE.................................408 377-9275
Yvette Bonnet, Branch Mgr
Melissa Hoover, Recruiter
EMP: 36
SALES (corp-wide): 1B Privately Held
WEB: www.marinerhealthcare.com
SIC: 8051 Extended care facility
HQ: Mariner Health Care, Inc.
3060 Mercer University Dr # 200
Atlanta GA 30341
678 443-7000

(P-16057)
MARINER HEALTH CARE INC
Also Called: Excell Care Ctr
3025 High St, Oakland (94619-1807)
PHONE.................................510 261-5200
Elma Conway, Administration
EMP: 36
SALES (corp-wide): 1B Privately Held
WEB: www.marinerhealthcare.com
SIC: 8051 Extended care facility
HQ: Mariner Health Care, Inc.
3060 Mercer University Dr # 200
Atlanta GA 30341
678 443-7000

(P-16058)
MARINER HEALTH CARE INC
Also Called: La Salette Rehab Convlesc Hos
537 E Fulton St, Stockton (95204-2227)
PHONE.................................209 466-2066
Karol Ford, Manager
EMP: 36
SALES (corp-wide): 1B Privately Held
WEB: www.marinerhealthcare.com
SIC: 8051 Extended care facility
HQ: Mariner Health Care, Inc.
3060 Mercer University Dr # 200
Atlanta GA 30341
678 443-7000

(P-16059)
MARQUIS COMPANIES I INC
Also Called: Marquis Care At Shasta
3550 Churn Creek Rd, Redding (96002-2718)
PHONE.................................530 222-3630
Phil Fogg, Branch Mgr
Shellie Anderson, Mfg Staff
Jennifer Conrad, Director
EMP: 40 Privately Held
WEB: www.marquiscompanies.com

SIC: 8051 Skilled nursing care facilities
PA: Marquis Companies I, Inc.
725 Se 202nd Ave
Portland OR 97233

(P-16060)
MEADOWOOD HLTH REHABILITATION
Also Called: Meadowood Care Center
3110 Wagner Heights Rd, Stockton (95209-4848)
PHONE.................................209 956-3444
Keith Berry, President
Chard Hardcastle, President
Michelle Smith, Administration
Gail Gamez, Food Svc Dir
Lisa Cox, Hlthcr Dir
EMP: 39 EST: 1997
SQ FT: 43,800
SALES (est): 7.9MM Privately Held
WEB: www.meadowood.com
SIC: 8051 Skilled nursing care facilities

(P-16061)
MEDICAL CARE PROFESSIONALS INC
363 El Cmino Real Ste 215, South San Francisco (94080)
PHONE.................................650 583-9898
Sharon Youngberg, President
EMP: 46 EST: 1987
SQ FT: 550
SALES (est): 13.6MM Privately Held
WEB: www.medicalcareprofessionals.com
SIC: 8051 8082 Skilled nursing care facilities; home health care services

(P-16062)
MEK NORWOOD PINES LLC
500 Jessie Ave, Sacramento (95838-2609)
PHONE.................................916 922-7177
Bobby Federico, Manager
Marilyn Johnson-Towns, Admin Asst
Fernan Pedraja, Controller
EMP: 52 EST: 2007
SALES (est): 11.8MM Privately Held
WEB: www.norwoodpinesalz.com
SIC: 8051 Convalescent home with continuous nursing care

(P-16063)
MELON HOLDINGS LLC
Also Called: Marysville Post-Acute
1617 Ramirez St, Marysville (95901-4334)
PHONE.................................530 742-7311
Joseph Cunliffe, Administration
Nicklas Anderson, President
Matt Jackson, President
Godwin Aka, Administration
EMP: 99 EST: 2016
SALES (est): 7.8MM Privately Held
WEB: www.marysvillepostacute.com
SIC: 8051 Convalescent home with continuous nursing care

(P-16064)
NADHAN INC
Also Called: Creekside Convalescent Hosp
850 Sonoma Ave, Santa Rosa (95404-4715)
PHONE.................................707 544-7750
Antony P Thekkek, Principal
EMP: 53 EST: 2001
SALES (est): 5.3MM Privately Held
SIC: 8051 Convalescent home with continuous nursing care

(P-16065)
NAPA NURSING CENTER INC
3275 Villa Ln, NAPA (94558-3094)
PHONE.................................707 257-0931
Martine D Harmon, CEO
Tim Motooka, President
Georgia Otterson, Administration
Lupe Hermosillo, Human Res Dir
EMP: 49 EST: 1983
SQ FT: 48,000
SALES (est): 57.4MM Privately Held
WEB: www.napavalleycarecenter.com
SIC: 8051 Convalescent home with continuous nursing care
HQ: Horizon West Healthcare, Inc.
4020 Sierra College Blvd # 190
Rocklin CA 95677
916 624-6230

(P-16066)
NAPAIDENCE OPCO LLC
Also Called: NAPA Post Acute
705 Trancas St, NAPA (94558-3014)
PHONE.................................707 255-6060
Jason Murray, Principal
Mark Hancock, Principal
EMP: 130 EST: 2016
SALES (est): 12MM Privately Held
SIC: 8051 Skilled nursing care facilities

(P-16067)
NEDILJKA COLMA INC (PA)
Also Called: Home Sweet Home
1560 Bryant St, Daly City (94015-1926)
PHONE.................................650 992-2727
Irena Nedilijka, President
EMP: 35 EST: 1987
SQ FT: 14,300
SALES (est): 5.3MM Privately Held
WEB: www.hshseniorcare.com
SIC: 8051 Skilled nursing care facilities

(P-16068)
NIA HEALTHCARE SERVICES INC (PA)
Also Called: Alice Manner
8448 E Adams Ave, Fowler (93625-9773)
P.O. Box 28 (93625-0028)
PHONE.................................559 834-2519
Gary L Williamsm Jr, President
EMP: 44 EST: 1993
SQ FT: 4,500
SALES (est): 10.7MM Privately Held
SIC: 8051 Convalescent home with continuous nursing care

(P-16069)
NIA HEALTHCARE SERVICES INC
Also Called: Selma Convalescent Hospital
2108 Stillman St, Selma (93662-3026)
PHONE.................................559 896-4990
Kris Clark, Administration
EMP: 40
SALES (corp-wide): 10.7MM Privately Held
SIC: 8051 8361 Convalescent home with continuous nursing care; rehabilitation center, residential: health care incidental
PA: Nia Healthcare Services, Inc.
8448 E Adams Ave
Fowler CA 93625
559 834-2519

(P-16070)
NIA HEALTHCARE SERVICES INC
Also Called: Alice Manor
8448 E Adams Ave, Fowler (93625-9773)
PHONE.................................559 834-2519
Jewell Williams, Manager
EMP: 52
SALES (corp-wide): 10.7MM Privately Held
SIC: 8051 Convalescent home with continuous nursing care
PA: Nia Healthcare Services, Inc.
8448 E Adams Ave
Fowler CA 93625
559 834-2519

(P-16071)
NIGHTSHADE HOLDINGS LLC
Also Called: Redwood Cove Healthcare Center
1162 S Dora St, Ukiah (95482-6340)
PHONE.................................707 462-1436
Toby Tilford, Principal
Kenneth Chambers, Office Mgr
Gabriel Barraza, Asst Admin
Leticia Briseno, Human Res Dir
Brenda Gallegos, Education
EMP: 43 EST: 2015
SALES (est): 18.2MM Privately Held
WEB: www.redwoodcove.com
SIC: 8051 Skilled nursing care facilities

(P-16072)
NORCAL CARE CENTERS INC
Also Called: Antioch Convalescent Hospital
1210 A St, Antioch (94509-2327)
PHONE.................................925 757-8787
Thaylene Sunga, Manager
EMP: 80

8051 - Skilled Nursing Facilities County (P-16073)

SALES (corp-wide): 9.1MM **Privately Held**
WEB: www.tranquilityinconline.com
SIC: 8051 Convalescent home with continuous nursing care
PA: Norcal Care Centers, Inc.
3788 Fairway Dr
Cameron Park CA
530 677-9477

(P-16073)
NORTH BAY POST ACUTE LLC
300 Douglas St, Petaluma (94952-2503)
PHONE.................................707 763-6887
Jacob Unger,
EMP: 40 EST: 2020
SALES (est): 1.3MM **Privately Held**
SIC: 8051 Skilled nursing care facilities

(P-16074)
NORTH PT HLTH WELLNESS CTR LLC
Also Called: Northpointe Healthcare Centre
668 E Bullard Ave, Fresno (93710-5401)
PHONE.................................559 320-2200
Stephen Reissman,
Janet Bamper,
Cheryl Petterson,
Deseray Martinez, *Director*
EMP: 99 EST: 2011
SALES (est): 13MM **Privately Held**
WEB: www.northpointhc.com
SIC: 8051 Convalescent home with continuous nursing care

(P-16075)
NORTH SHORE INVESTMENT INC
Also Called: Crescent Cy Convalescent Hosp
1280 Marshall St, Crescent City (95531-2217)
PHONE.................................707 464-6151
Jeffery Davis, *President*
EMP: 100
SQ FT: 35,000
SALES (est): 5.4MM **Privately Held**
SIC: 8051 Convalescent home with continuous nursing care

(P-16076)
NORTHERN CALIFORNIA PRESBYTERI
Also Called: Sequos-San Frncsco Residential
1400 Geary Blvd, San Francisco (94109-6561)
PHONE.................................415 922-9700
Michael Daugherty, *Branch Mgr*
EMP: 145
SALES (corp-wide): 85.5MM **Privately Held**
WEB: www.sequoialiving.org
SIC: 8051 Convalescent home with continuous nursing care
PA: Sequoia Living, Inc.
1525 Post St
San Francisco CA 94109
415 202-7808

(P-16077)
NOVATO HEALTHCARE CENTER LLC
1565 Hill Rd, Novato (94947-4063)
PHONE.................................415 897-6161
Michael J Torgan,
Sharrod Brooks,
EMP: 200 EST: 2007
SALES: 19.9MM **Privately Held**
WEB: www.novatohealthcare.com
SIC: 8051 Convalescent home with continuous nursing care

(P-16078)
OAK KNOLL CONVALESCENT CTR INC
Also Called: Oaks, The
450 Hayes Ln, Petaluma (94952-4010)
PHONE.................................707 778-8686
Ann Abbott, *President*
Tony Meyers, *CEO*
EMP: 57 EST: 1980
SQ FT: 36,000
SALES (est): 7.2MM **Privately Held**
SIC: 8051 Convalescent home with continuous nursing care

(P-16079)
OAK RIVER REHABILITATION
3300 Franklin St, Anderson (96007-3279)
PHONE.................................530 365-0025
Andy Tanner, *Manager*
Krista Brown, *Executive*
Dan Funk, *Administration*
Rick King, *Maintence Staff*
Matt Flake, *Director*
EMP: 150 EST: 2007
SQ FT: 3,000
SALES: 19.6MM **Privately Held**
WEB: www.oakriver-rehab.com
SIC: 8051 Convalescent home with continuous nursing care

(P-16080)
OAKHURST SKLLED NRSING WLLNESS
Also Called: Oakhurst Hlthcare Wllness Cntr
40131 Highway 49, Oakhurst (93644-9560)
PHONE.................................559 683-2244
Stepan Sarmazian, *Administration*
EMP: 99 EST: 2009
SALES: 5.6MM **Privately Held**
SIC: 8051 Convalescent home with continuous nursing care

(P-16081)
OCADIAN CARE CENTERS LLC
Also Called: Northern Cal Rehabilitation
2801 Eureka Way, Redding (96001-0222)
PHONE.................................530 246-9000
Chris Jones, *Exec Dir*
Jody Carter, *Radiology Dir*
Kevin Rainsford, *Director*
Debbie Wiechman, *Director*
EMP: 448
SALES (corp-wide): 72.6MM **Privately Held**
WEB: www.vibrahealthcare.com
SIC: 8051 5912 8069 Convalescent home with continuous nursing care; drug stores & proprietary stores; specialty hospitals, except psychiatric
PA: Ocadian Care Centers, Llc
104 Main St
Belvedere Tiburon CA 94920
415 789-5427

(P-16082)
OCADIAN CARE CENTERS LLC
Also Called: Medical Hill Rehabilitation
475 29th St, Oakland (94609-3510)
PHONE.................................510 832-3222
Robert G Peirce, *President*
EMP: 448
SALES (corp-wide): 72.6MM **Privately Held**
SIC: 8051 Convalescent home with continuous nursing care
PA: Ocadian Care Centers, Llc
104 Main St
Belvedere Tiburon CA 94920
415 789-5427

(P-16083)
OCADIAN CARE CENTERS LLC
Also Called: Alta Bates Medical Center
2450 Ashby Ave, Berkeley (94705-2067)
PHONE.................................510 204-5801
Cindy Cirdz, *Branch Mgr*
EMP: 448
SALES (corp-wide): 72.6MM **Privately Held**
SIC: 8051 Skilled nursing care facilities
PA: Ocadian Care Centers, Llc
104 Main St
Belvedere Tiburon CA 94920
415 789-5427

(P-16084)
OCADIAN CARE CENTERS LLC
Also Called: Greenbrea Care Center
1220 S Eliseo Dr, Greenbrae (94904-2006)
PHONE.................................415 461-9700
Susan Weaver, *Manager*
EMP: 448
SALES (corp-wide): 72.6MM **Privately Held**
SIC: 8051 8069 8052 Skilled nursing care facilities; specialty hospitals, except psychiatric; intermediate care facilities

PA: Ocadian Care Centers, Llc
104 Main St
Belvedere Tiburon CA 94920
415 789-5427

(P-16085)
OCADIAN CARE CENTERS LLC
1550 Silveira Pkwy, San Rafael (94903-4879)
PHONE.................................415 499-1000
Linda Creekmoore, *Manager*
EMP: 448
SALES (corp-wide): 72.6MM **Privately Held**
SIC: 8051 8361 Convalescent home with continuous nursing care; residential care
PA: Ocadian Care Centers, Llc
104 Main St
Belvedere Tiburon CA 94920
415 789-5427

(P-16086)
OCADIAN CARE CENTERS LLC
Also Called: Homewood Care Center
75 N 13th St, San Jose (95112-3439)
PHONE.................................408 295-2665
David Martinez, *Administration*
EMP: 448
SALES (corp-wide): 72.6MM **Privately Held**
SIC: 8051 Convalescent home with continuous nursing care
PA: Ocadian Care Centers, Llc
104 Main St
Belvedere Tiburon CA 94920
415 789-5427

(P-16087)
OLEANDER HOLDINGS LLC
Also Called: Sacramento Post-Acute
5255 Hemlock St, Sacramento (95841-3017)
PHONE.................................916 331-4590
James Huish,
Jessica Fulkerson, *Office Mgr*
David Terry, *Administration*
Myrna De Guzman, *Controller*
Nick Anderson,
EMP: 99 EST: 2011
SALES (est): 12.3MM **Privately Held**
WEB: www.sacpostacute.com
SIC: 8051 Convalescent home with continuous nursing care

(P-16088)
OUR LADY FATIMA VILLA INC
20400 Srtoga Los Gatos Rd, Saratoga (95070-5997)
PHONE.................................408 741-2950
Bella Mahoney, *Administration*
EMP: 90 EST: 1945
SQ FT: 45,123
SALES (est): 9.4MM **Privately Held**
WEB: www.fatimavilla.org
SIC: 8051 Skilled nursing care facilities

(P-16089)
PACIFICA CARE CENTER
Also Called: Pacifica Nursing & Rehab Ctr
385 Esplanade Ave, Pacifica (94044-1882)
PHONE.................................650 355-5622
Jacob Beaman, *Administration*
Elizabeth De Guzman, *Records Dir*
Filipina Atienza, *Director*
EMP: 93 EST: 1996
SALES (est): 11.6MM **Privately Held**
WEB: www.pacificarehab.com
SIC: 8051 Convalescent home with continuous nursing care

(P-16090)
PACIFICA LINDA MAR INC
Also Called: Linda Mar Care Center
751 San Pedro Terrace Rd, Pacifica (94044-4101)
PHONE.................................650 359-4800
David Mahrt, *Administration*
Geoff Gerding, *Administration*
Richard Barnes, *CIO*
Alicia McDaniel, *Nursing Dir*
EMP: 93 EST: 1964
SQ FT: 10,000
SALES (est): 13.3MM **Privately Held**
WEB: www.lindamarrehab.com
SIC: 8051 Convalescent home with continuous nursing care

(P-16091)
PALM HAVEN NURSING & REHAB LLC
Also Called: Palm Haven Care Center
469 E North St, Manteca (95336-4710)
PHONE.................................209 823-1788
Joseph Pallivathicla,
EMP: 104 EST: 1962
SQ FT: 24,000
SALES (est): 5.8MM **Privately Held**
SIC: 8051 Convalescent home with continuous nursing care

(P-16092)
PARA & PALLI INC
Also Called: Los Banos Nursing and Rehab
931 Idaho Ave, Los Banos (93635-3405)
PHONE.................................209 826-0790
Joseph Palli, *President*
▲ EMP: 97 EST: 1964
SQ FT: 1,000
SALES (est): 10.8MM **Privately Held**
WEB: www.losbanosnursingrehab.com
SIC: 8051 Convalescent home with continuous nursing care

(P-16093)
PARK CNTL CARE RHBLITATION CTR
2100 Parkside Dr, Fremont (94536-5326)
PHONE.................................510 797-5300
Anthony P Thekkek, *President*
Prema Thekkek, *Vice Pres*
EMP: 40 EST: 2003
SALES (est): 17.4MM **Privately Held**
SIC: 8051 Convalescent home with continuous nursing care

(P-16094)
PARK MERCED LLC (PA)
3144 G St, Merced (95340-1300)
PHONE.................................209 722-3944
Elina Moilanen, *Records Dir*
EMP: 37 EST: 2017
SALES (est): 1.4MM **Privately Held**
WEB: www.parkmerced.com
SIC: 8051 Skilled nursing care facilities

(P-16095)
PETALUMA POST-ACUTE REHAB
Also Called: Petaluma Care
1115 B St, Petaluma (94952-4028)
PHONE.................................707 765-3030
John L Sorensen, *Chairman*
Ema Hernandez, *Food Svc Dir*
Shirley Kraft, *Nursing Dir*
Veronica Diaz, *Hlthcr Dir*
Nicholas Forester, *Hlthcr Dir*
EMP: 38 EST: 2015
SALES (est): 11.6MM **Privately Held**
WEB: www.petalumapostacute.com
SIC: 8051 Convalescent home with continuous nursing care

(P-16096)
PINERS NURSING HOME INC
Also Called: Piner's Medical Supply
1800 Pueblo Ave, NAPA (94558-4751)
PHONE.................................707 224-7925
Gary Piner, *President*
Starr Piner, *Treasurer*
Malinda Meeker, *Office Mgr*
Wendy Taylor, *Graphic Designe*
Jeremy Piner, *Opers Mgr*
EMP: 65 EST: 1944
SQ FT: 20,000
SALES (est): 8.4MM **Privately Held**
WEB: www.pinersnursinghome.com
SIC: 8051 4119 5999 Convalescent home with continuous nursing care; ambulance service; medical apparatus & supplies

(P-16097)
PITTSBURG CARE CENTER INC
Also Called: Pittsburg Skilled Nursing Ctr
535 School St, Pittsburg (94565-3937)
PHONE.................................925 432-3831
Abby Tiller, *Principal*
EMP: 70 EST: 2002
SQ FT: 20,000
SALES (est): 12.4MM **Privately Held**
WEB: www.cchealth.org
SIC: 8051 Extended care facility

PRODUCTS & SERVICES SECTION
8051 - Skilled Nursing Facilities County (P-16122)

(P-16098)
R FELLEN INC
Also Called: Sunnyside Convalescent Hosp
2939 S Peach Ave, Fresno (93725-9302)
PHONE..................................559 233-6248
Michael Fellen, *President*
Steven Fellen, *Vice Pres*
EMP: 95 **EST:** 1970
SQ FT: 10,000
SALES (est): 9.4MM **Privately Held**
SIC: 8051 Convalescent home with continuous nursing care

(P-16099)
RAISER SENIOR SERVICES LLC
Also Called: Stratford
601 Laurel Ave Apt 903, San Mateo (94401-4164)
PHONE..................................650 342-4106
Jennifer Raiser, *President*
Phillip Raiser, *Vice Pres*
EMP: 73 **EST:** 1992
SQ FT: 184,000
SALES (est): 5.2MM **Privately Held**
WEB: www.sunriseseniorliving.com
SIC: 8051 Skilled nursing care facilities

(P-16100)
RIVER BEND HOLDINGS LLC
Also Called: River Bend Nursing Center
2215 Oakmont Way, West Sacramento (95691-3022)
PHONE..................................916 371-1890
Nell Stamm,
Bryan Boeher,
Richard Martin,
EMP: 153 **EST:** 1968
SQ FT: 34,000
SALES (est): 10.1MM **Privately Held**
WEB: www.riverbendnursingcenter.com
SIC: 8051 Convalescent home with continuous nursing care

(P-16101)
RIVER VALLEY CARE CENTER
9000 Larkin Rd, Live Oak (95953-9599)
PHONE..................................530 695-8020
Randy Balecha, *Administration*
Rose Holeman, *Office Mgr*
Rebecca May, *Office Mgr*
Nicole Rosario, *Administration*
Ruby Foster, *Food Svc Dir*
EMP: 68 **EST:** 2011
SALES (est): 17.6MM **Privately Held**
WEB: www.rivervalleycarecenter.com
SIC: 8051 Convalescent home with continuous nursing care

(P-16102)
S&F MANAGEMENT COMPANY INC
2030 Evergreen Ave, Modesto (95350-3785)
PHONE..................................209 846-9744
EMP: 518 **Privately Held**
SIC: 8051 Convalescent home with continuous nursing care
PA: S&F Management Company, Llc
9200 W Sunset Blvd # 700
West Hollywood CA 90069

(P-16103)
S&F MANAGEMENT COMPANY LLC
Also Called: Windsor Sacramento Estates
501 Jessie Ave, Sacramento (95838-2608)
PHONE..................................916 922-8855
EMP: 518 **Privately Held**
WEB: www.windsorsacramento.com
SIC: 8051 Convalescent home with continuous nursing care
PA: S&F Management Company, Llc
9200 W Sunset Blvd # 700
West Hollywood CA 90069

(P-16104)
S&F MANAGEMENT COMPANY LLC
Windsor Hampton Care Center
442 E Hampton St, Stockton (95204-5519)
PHONE..................................209 466-0456
Angela Riungu, *Social Dir*
Armand Holland, *Administration*
Kristen Merin, *Director*
EMP: 518 **Privately Held**
SIC: 8051 Convalescent home with continuous nursing care
PA: S&F Management Company, Llc
9200 W Sunset Blvd # 700
West Hollywood CA 90069

(P-16105)
SACRAMENTO OPERATING CO LP
Also Called: Double Tree Past Acute
7400 24th St, Sacramento (95822-5350)
PHONE..................................916 422-4825
Kenneth Tabler, *Partner*
Cynthia Mitchell,
Rodel Cabaloza, *Director*
EMP: 120 **EST:** 2006
SALES (est): 14.8MM **Privately Held**
SIC: 8051 Extended care facility

(P-16106)
SAINT CLAIRES NURSING CTR LLC
6248 66th Ave, Sacramento (95823-2733)
PHONE..................................916 392-4440
Kathryn J Hill, *President*
Michael Maderas, *Administration*
EMP: 124 **EST:** 1983
SALES (est): 6.5MM **Privately Held**
SIC: 8051 Skilled nursing care facilities

(P-16107)
SAINT JOHN KRNSTADT HM FOR AGE
Also Called: Saint John Krnstadt Cnvlscent
4432 James Ave, Castro Valley (94546-3533)
PHONE..................................510 889-7000
Felix Barrese, *Administration*
EMP: 49 **EST:** 1971
SQ FT: 20,000
SALES (est): 5.2MM **Privately Held**
WEB: www.stjohnkronstadt.com
SIC: 8051 Convalescent home with continuous nursing care

(P-16108)
SAN JOSE HLTHCARE WLLNESS CTR
Also Called: San Jose Hlthcare Wellness Ctr
75 N 13th St, San Jose (95112-3439)
PHONE..................................408 295-2665
Sole Majer, *Mng Member*
Aaron Robins,
Shawna Martinez, *Director*
EMP: 87 **EST:** 2004
SALES (est): 14.9MM **Privately Held**
WEB: www.sanjosehc.com
SIC: 8051 Convalescent home with continuous nursing care

(P-16109)
SAN LEANDRO HEALTHCARE CENTER
368 Juana Ave, San Leandro (94577-4811)
PHONE..................................510 357-4015
Pat Poddatoori, *President*
Laslo Hites, *Director*
EMP: 70 **EST:** 2003
SALES (est): 8.5MM **Privately Held**
WEB: www.sanleandro.org
SIC: 8051 Convalescent home with continuous nursing care

(P-16110)
SAN RFAEL HLTHCARE WLLNESS CTR
1601 5th Ave, San Rafael (94901-1808)
PHONE..................................415 456-7170
Blanca Cuano, *Director*
Al Nato, *Education*
EMP: 35 **EST:** 2012
SALES (est): 21.3MM **Privately Held**
WEB: www.sanrafaelhc.com
SIC: 8051 8059 Convalescent home with continuous nursing care; personal care home, with health care

(P-16111)
SANHYD INC
Also Called: Kyakamena Sklled Nrsing Fcilty
2131 Carleton St, Berkeley (94704-3213)
PHONE..................................510 843-2131
Pat Poddatoori, *President*
EMP: 52 **EST:** 1965
SQ FT: 15,000
SALES (est): 4.8MM **Privately Held**
SIC: 8051 Convalescent home with continuous nursing care

(P-16112)
SANTA ROSAIDENCE OPCO LLC
Also Called: Santa Rosa Post Acute
4650 Hoen Ave, Santa Rosa (95405-9407)
PHONE..................................707 546-0471
Jason Murray, *Principal*
Mark Hancock, *Principal*
EMP: 135 **EST:** 2016
SALES (est): 17.6MM **Privately Held**
WEB: www.santarosapostacute.com
SIC: 8051 Skilled nursing care facilities

(P-16113)
SCOTT ST SNIOR HSING CMPLEX IN
Also Called: RHODA GOLDMAN PLAZA
2180 Post St, San Francisco (94115-6013)
PHONE..................................415 345-5083
Marrianne Nannesthad, *Director*
Eric Luu, *CFO*
Ira Kurtz, *Exec Dir*
Van Ly, *Office Mgr*
Melanie Miguel, *Administration*
EMP: 105 **EST:** 2000
SQ FT: 195,000
SALES (est): 16MM **Privately Held**
WEB: www.rgplaza.org
SIC: 8051 Skilled nursing care facilities

(P-16114)
SHATTUCK HEALTH CARE INC
Also Called: Elmwood Care Center
2829 Shattuck Ave, Berkeley (94705-1037)
PHONE..................................510 665-2800
Pat Podatorri, *President*
Terry McGregor, *CFO*
Sherry Brockmeier, *Administration*
Judy Deering, *Administration*
Lori Campisi, *Human Res Mgr*
EMP: 97 **EST:** 2005
SQ FT: 34,404
SALES (est): 9.1MM **Privately Held**
WEB: www.elmwoodnursingrehab.com
SIC: 8051 Convalescent home with continuous nursing care

(P-16115)
SHERWOOD OAKS ENTERPRISES INC
Also Called: Sherwood Oaks Health Center
130 Dana St, Fort Bragg (95437-4506)
PHONE..................................707 964-6333
Melanie Reding, *President*
Joe Reding, *Corp Secy*
EMP: 90 **EST:** 1975
SQ FT: 19,000
SALES (est): 9.7MM **Privately Held**
WEB: www.sherwoodoakshealthcenter.com
SIC: 8051 Convalescent home with continuous nursing care

(P-16116)
SHIELDS NURSING CENTERS INC (PA)
606 Alfred Nobel Dr, Hercules (94547-1834)
PHONE..................................510 724-9911
William Shields Jr, *CEO*
EMP: 150 **EST:** 1978
SQ FT: 6,100
SALES (est): 12.7MM **Privately Held**
WEB: www.shieldsnursingcenters.com
SIC: 8051 Convalescent home with continuous nursing care

(P-16117)
SIERRA HILLS CARE CENTER INC
1139 Cirby Way, Roseville (95661-4421)
PHONE..................................916 782-7007
Ellen L Kuykendall, *President*
Brad Wilcox, *Treasurer*
Amy Griffis, *Nursing Dir*
EMP: 64 **EST:** 1986
SQ FT: 30,000
SALES (est): 10.6MM **Privately Held**
WEB: www.pinecreekcarecenter.com
SIC: 8051 Convalescent home with continuous nursing care
HQ: Horizon West Healthcare, Inc.
4020 Sierra College Blvd # 190
Rocklin CA 95677
916 624-6230

(P-16118)
SIERRA VIEW HOMES
Also Called: SIERRA VIEW HOMES RESIDENTIAL
1155 E Springfield Ave, Reedley (93654-3225)
PHONE..................................559 637-2256
Vito Genna, *Exec Dir*
Kecia Friesen, *Admin Asst*
Arlee Johnson, *Pastor*
Barbara Alatorre, *Nursing Dir*
Jodi Botello, *Director*
EMP: 140 **EST:** 1960
SQ FT: 63,600
SALES (est): 9.8MM **Privately Held**
WEB: www.sierraview.org
SIC: 8051 8059 6513 Skilled nursing care facilities; personal care home, with health care; apartment hotel operation

(P-16119)
SILVER OAK HEALTH SERVICES
Also Called: Silver Oak Manor
788 Holmes St, Livermore (94550-4229)
PHONE..................................925 447-2280
Anelli Stamm, *President*
Fred Stamm, *Vice Pres*
Sylvia Chaney, *Administration*
EMP: 38 **EST:** 1983
SQ FT: 5,000
SALES (est): 6.1MM **Privately Held**
SIC: 8051 Skilled nursing care facilities

(P-16120)
SILVERADO SENIOR LIVING INC
Also Called: Bay Area At Home
1301 Ralston Ave Ste A, Belmont (94002-1961)
PHONE..................................650 226-8017
Nathan Levoit, *Senior VP*
Rachele Demaster, *Exec Dir*
Melinda Axel, *Executive Asst*
Chae Ianni, *Executive Asst*
Laura Printy, *Administration*
EMP: 59
SALES (corp-wide): 173.8MM **Privately Held**
WEB: www.silverado.com
SIC: 8051 Skilled nursing care facilities
PA: Senior Silverado Living Inc
6400 Oak Cyn Ste 200
Irvine CA 92618
949 240-7200

(P-16121)
SILVERADO SENIOR LIVING INC
Also Called: Belmont Hlls Memory Care Cmnty
1301 Ralston Ave Ste A, Belmont (94002-1961)
PHONE..................................650 264-9020
EMP: 59
SALES (corp-wide): 173.8MM **Privately Held**
WEB: www.silverado.com
SIC: 8051 Skilled nursing care facilities
PA: Senior Silverado Living Inc
6400 Oak Cyn Ste 200
Irvine CA 92618
949 240-7200

(P-16122)
SKILL NURSE
13435 Peach Ave, Livingston (95334-9312)
PHONE..................................209 394-2440
Robert Isaac, *Administration*
EMP: 38 **EST:** 1959
SQ FT: 11,000
SALES (est): 2.3MM **Privately Held**
SIC: 8051 Convalescent home with continuous nursing care

8051 - Skilled Nursing Facilities County (P-16123)

(P-16123)
SLHCC INC
Also Called: Saylor Lane Healthcare Center
3500 Folsom Blvd, Sacramento
(95816-6615)
PHONE..................916 457-6521
Dave Hilburn, *President*
EMP: 48 **EST:** 2001
SALES (est): 9.5MM **Privately Held**
WEB: www.saylorlanehealthcare.com
SIC: 8051 Convalescent home with continuous nursing care

(P-16124)
SONOMA ACRES CONVALESCENT INC
765 Donald St, Sonoma (95476-4604)
PHONE..................707 996-2161
John H Collister, *Administration*
C David Benfield, *Owner*
EMP: 35 **EST:** 1987
SQ FT: 10,801
SALES (est): 1.4MM **Privately Held**
WEB: www.sonomaacres.net
SIC: 8051 Convalescent home with continuous nursing care

(P-16125)
SPRING HL MNOR CNVLSCENT RHBLT
Also Called: Spring Hl Mnor Cnvlescent Hosp
355 Joerschke Dr, Grass Valley (95945-5288)
PHONE..................530 273-7247
Brian Collier, *Principal*
Patricia Vixie, *Treasurer*
Gregory Vixie, *Vice Pres*
EMP: 50 **EST:** 1966
SQ FT: 14,000
SALES (est): 8.5MM **Privately Held**
WEB: www.case-5-19-cv-07071-svk.info
SIC: 8051 Skilled nursing care facilities

(P-16126)
SSC CARMICHAEL OPERATING CO LP
Also Called: Mission Crmchael Halthcare Ctr
3630 Mission Ave, Carmichael (95608-2933)
PHONE..................916 485-4793
Anne Gilles, *Administration*
Wayne M Sanner, *Partner*
Angela Hoy, *Director*
EMP: 211 **EST:** 2004
SALES (est): 72.5MM
SALES (corp-wide): 1.3B **Privately Held**
WEB: www.carmichaeltimes.com
SIC: 8051 Skilled nursing care facilities
HQ: Savaseniorcare, Llc
8601 Dunwoody Pl
Atlanta GA 30250
770 829-5100

(P-16127)
SSC SAN JOSE OPERATING CO LP
Also Called: Courtyard Care Center
340 Northlake Dr, San Jose (95117-1251)
PHONE..................408 249-0344
Wayne M Sanner,
Lee Lopez, *Director*
Remedios B Tibayan, *Director*
EMP: 331 **EST:** 2005
SALES (est): 36.8MM
SALES (corp-wide): 1.3B **Privately Held**
WEB: www.savaseniorcare.com
SIC: 8051 Convalescent home with continuous nursing care
HQ: Savaseniorcare, Llc
8601 Dunwoody Pl
Atlanta GA 30250
770 829-5100

(P-16128)
ST ANTHONY CARE CENTER INC
553 Smalley Ave, Hayward (94541-4919)
PHONE..................510 733-3877
Melanie Rapp, *President*
EMP: 38 **EST:** 1974
SQ FT: 9,000
SALES (est): 9.6MM **Privately Held**
SIC: 8051 Convalescent home with continuous nursing care

(P-16129)
ST CHRSTPHER CNVLSCENT HOSP I
22822 Myrtle St, Hayward (94541-6321)
PHONE..................510 537-4844
Lucy Xie, *President*
Melanie Rapp, *President*
EMP: 35 **EST:** 1964
SQ FT: 18,000
SALES (est): 2.5MM **Privately Held**
SIC: 8051 Skilled nursing care facilities

(P-16130)
STONEBROOK CONVALESCENT CENTER
Also Called: Stonebrook Health Care Center
4367 Concord Blvd, Concord (94521-1100)
PHONE..................925 689-7457
James D Hightower, *President*
Shirley Jackson, *Social Dir*
Alita Wills, *Office Mgr*
Lori Cooper, *Administration*
Yvette Ortega, *Administration*
EMP: 117 **EST:** 1990
SQ FT: 44,000
SALES (est): 53MM **Privately Held**
WEB: www.stonebrookhc.com
SIC: 8051 Convalescent home with continuous nursing care
PA: Healthmark Services Inc
217 Lakewood Rd
Van Buren AR 72956

(P-16131)
SUMMERVILLE AT HAZEL CREEK LLC
Also Called: Hazel Creek Assisted Living
6125 Hazel Ave, Orangevale (95662-4558)
PHONE..................916 988-7901
Lonnie Irvine, *President*
EMP: 303 **EST:** 2006
SALES (est): 6.9MM
SALES (corp-wide): 3.5B **Publicly Held**
WEB: www.brookdale.com
SIC: 8051 Skilled nursing care facilities
HQ: Emeritus Corporation
6737 W Wa St Ste 2300
Milwaukee WI 53214

(P-16132)
SUMMERVILLE SENIOR LIVING INC
Also Called: Creekside Healthcare Center
1900 Church Ln, San Pablo (94806-3708)
PHONE..................510 235-5514
Mary Hart, *Manager*
EMP: 42
SALES (corp-wide): 3.5B **Publicly Held**
SIC: 8051 Skilled nursing care facilities
HQ: Summerville Senior Living, Inc.
3131 Elliott Ave Ste 500
Seattle WA 98121
206 298-2909

(P-16133)
SUMMERVILLE SENIOR LIVING INC
Also Called: El Cerrito Ryale Retirement HM
6510 Gladys Ave, El Cerrito (94530-2210)
PHONE..................510 234-5200
Sonja Givens, *Branch Mgr*
EMP: 42
SALES (corp-wide): 3.5B **Publicly Held**
SIC: 8051 Skilled nursing care facilities
HQ: Summerville Senior Living, Inc.
3131 Elliott Ave Ste 500
Seattle WA 98121
206 298-2909

(P-16134)
SUNBRDGE BRTTANY RHBLTTION CTR
Also Called: American Rver Care Rhblttion C
3900 Garfield Ave, Carmichael (95608-6647)
PHONE..................916 484-1393
Andrew Turner, *President*
Carly Migdal, *Social Dir*
Anne Butler, *Administration*
Anju Krishna, *Human Res Dir*
James Haughton, *Director*
EMP: 1651 **EST:** 1986
SALES (est): 26.8MM **Privately Held**
SIC: 8051 8069 Skilled nursing care facilities; specialty hospitals, except psychiatric
HQ: Regency Health Services, Inc.
5100 Sun Ave Ne
Albuquerque NM 87109
505 821-3355

(P-16135)
SUNBRDGE PRDISE RHBLTTION CTR
Also Called: Pine View Center
8777 Skyway, Paradise (95969-2110)
PHONE..................530 872-3200
Annie Buerhaus, *Branch Mgr*
EMP: 5201 **Privately Held**
SIC: 8051 8049 Convalescent home with continuous nursing care; speech therapist
HQ: Sunbridge Paradise Rehabilitation Center, Llc
101 Sun Ave Ne
Albuquerque NM 87109
530 872-3200

(P-16136)
SUNBRIDGE CARE ENTPS W LLC
Also Called: Kingsburg Center
1101 Stroud Ave, Kingsburg (93631-1016)
PHONE..................559 897-5881
EMP: 1938
SALES: 7.6MM **Privately Held**
WEB: www.kingsburgsmilecenter.com
SIC: 8051 Skilled Nursing Care Facility
HQ: Genesis Healthcare Llc
101 E State St
Kennett Square PA 19348

(P-16137)
SUNBRIDGE CARE ENTPS W LLC
Also Called: Kingsburg Center
1101 Stroud Ave, Kingsburg (93631-1016)
PHONE..................559 897-5881
Ron Kennersly, *Manager*
J Richard Edwards, *Treasurer*
EMP: 160 **Privately Held**
SIC: 8051 Convalescent home with continuous nursing care
HQ: Sunbridge Care Enterprises West, Llc
101 Sun Ave Ne
Albuquerque NM 87109
530 938-4429

(P-16138)
SUNNYVALE HEALTHCARE CENTER
Also Called: Sunnyvale Health Care
1291 S Bernardo Ave, Sunnyvale (94087-2060)
PHONE..................408 245-8070
Hermina Chavez, *CEO*
Maricel De Guzman, *Records Dir*
Vanessa Chavez, *Treasurer*
Mario Chavez, *Vice Pres*
John Chavez, *Admin Sec*
EMP: 108 **EST:** 1969
SQ FT: 26,679
SALES (est): 15.3MM **Privately Held**
WEB: www.sunnyvalepostacute.com
SIC: 8051 Convalescent home with continuous nursing care

(P-16139)
SUNRISE OF PETALUMA
815 Wood Sorrel Dr, Petaluma (94954-6857)
PHONE..................707 776-2885
Erin Carlson, *Director*
Belvia Robbins, *Principal*
Rob Graves, *Maintence Staff*
EMP: 45 **EST:** 1996
SALES (est): 5.5MM **Privately Held**
WEB: www.sunriseseniorliving.com
SIC: 8051 Skilled nursing care facilities

(P-16140)
SUTTER HEALTH
3707 Schriever Ave, Mather (95655-4202)
PHONE..................916 454-8200
Sheila Black, *Branch Mgr*
Edwin Bean, *Program Mgr*
Morton Anderson, *Network Enginr*
Philip Miller, *Project Mgr*
Teresa Soto, *Project Mgr*
EMP: 60
SALES (corp-wide): 13.2B **Privately Held**
WEB: www.suttermedicalcenter.org
SIC: 8051 8062 Skilled nursing care facilities; general medical & surgical hospitals
PA: Sutter Health
2200 River Plaza Dr
Sacramento CA 95833
916 733-8800

(P-16141)
SUTTER VSTING NRSE ASSN HSPICE
1651 Alvarado St, San Leandro (94577-2636)
PHONE..................510 618-5277
Rosemarie Avery, *Manager*
EMP: 228
SALES (corp-wide): 13.2B **Privately Held**
WEB: www.suttercareathome.org
SIC: 8051 8082 Skilled nursing care facilities; home health care services
HQ: Sutter Visiting Nurse Association & Hospice
1900 Powell St Ste 300
Emeryville CA 94608
866 652-9178

(P-16142)
TDC CONVALESCENT INC
Also Called: Horizon Health & Subacute Ctr
3034 E Herndon Ave, Fresno (93720-0300)
PHONE..................559 321-0883
Thomas D Clark, *President*
Kimberly Santos, *Office Mgr*
Teresa Ewing, *Administration*
EMP: 118 **EST:** 1985
SQ FT: 60,000
SALES (est): 22.2MM **Privately Held**
WEB: www.horizonhealthfresno.com
SIC: 8051 Convalescent home with continuous nursing care

(P-16143)
TLC OF BAY AREA INC
Also Called: Valley House Care Center
991 Clyde Ave, Santa Clara (95054-1905)
P.O. Box 607, Indiana PA (15701-0607)
PHONE..................408 988-7667
Marcy Colkitt, *President*
Merlin Davey, *Exec Dir*
Michael Montgomery, *Info Tech Dir*
Lorna Santillan, *Marketing Staff*
Preet Sohi, *Director*
EMP: 80 **EST:** 1994
SALES (est): 20.8MM **Privately Held**
WEB: www.valleyhouserehab.com
SIC: 8051 Convalescent home with continuous nursing care

(P-16144)
TRI VALLEY HOME HEALTH CARE
1231 W Robinhood Dr D5, Stockton (95207-5506)
PHONE..................209 957-0708
Necita Triguero, *Owner*
EMP: 61 **EST:** 1999
SALES (est): 3.6MM **Privately Held**
SIC: 8051 8322 8082 8049 Skilled nursing care facilities; individual & family services; home health care services; physical therapist

(P-16145)
TWILIGHT HAVEN
1717 S Winery Ave, Fresno (93727-5011)
PHONE..................559 251-8417
David Viancourt, *Administration*
Liberty Oie, *Records Dir*
Kenneth Karle, *President*
Robert Herman, *Vice Pres*
Kathy Valley, *Social Dir*
EMP: 95 **EST:** 1957
SQ FT: 70,000
SALES (est): 6MM **Privately Held**
WEB: www.twilighthaven.com
SIC: 8051 8052 8361 Convalescent home with continuous nursing care; personal care facility; rest home, with health care incidental

PRODUCTS & SERVICES SECTION

8052 - Intermediate Care Facilities County (P-16169)

(P-16146)
UCSF BTTY IRENE MOORE WNS HOSP (HQ)
Also Called: Ucsf Medical Center
1855 4th St, San Francisco (94143-2350)
PHONE..............................415 476-1000
Aquila Yeargin, *COO*
Karen Gee, *Office Mgr*
Crisologo Allan, *Technician*
My Nguy, *Technology*
Saba Mirza, *Human Resources*
EMP: 40 **EST:** 2015
SALES (est): 286.7MM **Privately Held**
WEB: www.ucsfhealth.org
SIC: 8051 Skilled nursing care facilities
PA: State Of California
State Capital
Sacramento CA 95814
916 445-2864

(P-16147)
UNITED COM SERVE
Also Called: Fountains, The
1260 Williams Way, Yuba City (95991-2400)
PHONE..............................530 790-3000
Ryan Dickerson, *President*
Chris Parker, *Administration*
EMP: 231 **EST:** 1990
SQ FT: 40,000
SALES: 25.2MM
SALES (corp-wide): 26.9MM **Privately Held**
WEB: www.adventisthealth.org
SIC: 8051 Skilled nursing care facilities
PA: Freemont Rideout Health Group
989 Plumas St
Yuba City CA 95991
530 751-4010

(P-16148)
UNITED HEALTH SYSTEMS INC
Also Called: Alderson Convalescent Hospital
124 Walnut St, Woodland (95695-3137)
PHONE..............................530 662-9161
Santiago M S Miguel, *CEO*
Lisa Miguel, *Records Dir*
Thomas E Mullen, *President*
Andrew Gamboa, *Social Dir*
Lynn Mullen, *Admin Sec*
EMP: 154
SQ FT: 40,000
SALES: 10.9MM **Privately Held**
WEB: www.achwoodland.com
SIC: 8051 Convalescent home with continuous nursing care

(P-16149)
VALE OPERATING COMPANY LP
Also Called: Vale Healthcare Center
13484 San Pablo Ave, San Pablo (94806-3904)
PHONE..............................510 232-5945
Tim Neal, *Principal*
Remy Rhodes, *President*
Kenneth Tabler, *President*
EMP: 5020
SALES (corp-wide): 1B **Privately Held**
SIC: 8051 Skilled nursing care facilities
HQ: Vale Operating Company, Lp
1 Ravinia Dr Ste 1400
Atlanta GA 30346

(P-16150)
VALLEY HEALTHCARE CENTER LLC
4840 E Tulare Ave, Fresno (93727-3062)
PHONE..............................559 251-7161
George V Hagaer Jr, *CEO*
EMP: 100 **EST:** 2003
SALES (est): 27.5MM **Privately Held**
WEB: www.genesishcc.com
SIC: 8051 Convalescent home with continuous nursing care
HQ: Genesis Healthcare Llc
101 E State St
Kennett Square PA 19348

(P-16151)
VALLEY WEST HEALTH CARE INC
Also Called: Valley View Care Center
2649 Topeka St, Riverbank (95367-2248)
PHONE..............................209 869-2569
Terry Bane, *Principal*
EMP: 43
SALES (corp-wide): 6.3MM **Privately Held**
SIC: 8051 8062 Convalescent home with continuous nursing care; general medical & surgical hospitals
PA: Valley West Health Care Inc
1224 E St
Williams CA 95987
530 473-5321

(P-16152)
VIENNA CONVALESCENT HOSP INC
800 S Ham Ln, Lodi (95242-3543)
PHONE..............................209 368-7141
Kenneth Heffel, *President*
Diana Heffel, *Admin Sec*
Ida Ventura, *Director*
Alfred Loza, *Supervisor*
EMP: 131
SQ FT: 25,000
SALES (est): 827MM **Privately Held**
WEB: www.viennanursingrehab.com
SIC: 8051 Convalescent home with continuous nursing care

(P-16153)
VILLA DEL REY
3255 Villa Ln, NAPA (94558-3048)
PHONE..............................707 252-3333
Becky Gibons, *Exec Dir*
EMP: 77 **EST:** 1975
SALES (est): 2MM
SALES (corp-wide): 3.5B **Publicly Held**
SIC: 8051 Skilled nursing care facilities
HQ: Summerville Senior Living, Inc.
3131 Elliott Ave Ste 500
Seattle WA 98121
206 298-2909

(P-16154)
VINDRA INC
Also Called: Meadowood Nursing Center
3805 Dexter Ln, Clearlake (95422-8850)
PHONE..............................707 994-7738
Calvin Baker Jr, *President*
Gloria Ghiringhelli, *Office Mgr*
EMP: 100 **EST:** 1984
SQ FT: 30,250
SALES (est): 12.4MM **Privately Held**
SIC: 8051 8069 Convalescent home with continuous nursing care; specialty hospitals, except psychiatric

(P-16155)
WATERS EDGE INC
Also Called: Waters Edge Nursing Home
2401 Blanding Ave, Alameda (94501-1503)
PHONE..............................510 748-4300
Christian Zimmerman, *President*
John C Zimmerman, *President*
Virginia Zimmerman, *Corp Secy*
Sandra Davis, *VP Finance*
EMP: 41 **EST:** 1972
SQ FT: 24,000
SALES (est): 5.4MM **Privately Held**
SIC: 8051 Convalescent home with continuous nursing care

(P-16156)
WEST COAST HOSPITALS INC
Also Called: Valley Convalescent Hospital
919 Freedom Blvd, Watsonville (95076-3804)
P.O. Box 1242 (95077-1242)
PHONE..............................831 722-3581
Richard Murphy, *Principal*
Debra Serrano, *Records Dir*
Leslie Nunes, *Office Mgr*
Nicole Beckwith, *Human Res Dir*
Laura Terrazaz, *Food Svc Dir*
EMP: 40 **EST:** 1962
SQ FT: 20,000
SALES (est): 6.5MM **Privately Held**
SIC: 8051 Skilled nursing care facilities

(P-16157)
WESTERN SLOPE HEALTH CENTER
Also Called: Western Slope Health Care
3280 Washington St, Placerville (95667-5838)
PHONE..............................530 622-6842
Jeff Maggard, *Owner*
Doug Hawkings, *Administration*
EMP: 111 **EST:** 1983
SALES: 12.6MM **Privately Held**
WEB: www.westernslopehealthcenter.com
SIC: 8051 Convalescent home with continuous nursing care

(P-16158)
WESTGATE RHAB SPCALTY CARE CRT
1601 Petersen Ave, San Jose (95129-4844)
PHONE..............................408 253-7502
Stephen Hooker, *President*
EMP: 39 **EST:** 2005
SALES (est): 626.1K **Privately Held**
WEB: www.amberwoodgardens.com
SIC: 8051 Convalescent home with continuous nursing care

(P-16159)
WHITNEY OAKS CARE CENTER
3529 Walnut Ave, Carmichael (95608-3049)
PHONE..............................916 488-8601
Kyle Dahl, *Principal*
EMP: 53 **EST:** 2011
SALES (est): 15.9MM **Privately Held**
WEB: www.whitneyoakscarecenter.com
SIC: 8051 Convalescent home with continuous nursing care

(P-16160)
WILD KARMA INC
Also Called: Divine Home Care
5275 Broadway, Oakland (94618-1425)
PHONE..............................510 639-9088
Robbin R Beebe, *CEO*
Robin Beebe, *CEO*
Monica Stidham, *Office Mgr*
EMP: 270 **EST:** 2007
SALES (est): 31.9MM **Privately Held**
WEB: www.homecareassistance.com
SIC: 8051 8059 Convalescent home with continuous nursing care; personal care home, with health care

(P-16161)
WILLIAMS-FOSTER GROUP LLC
Also Called: Dycora Trnsitional Hlth Living
7475 N Palm Ave Ste 106, Fresno (93711-5763)
PHONE..............................317 786-3230
Julianne Williams, *Mng Member*
EMP: 50 **EST:** 2018
SALES (est): 4.7MM **Privately Held**
SIC: 8051 Skilled nursing care facilities

(P-16162)
WILLOW CREEK HALTHCARE CTR LLC
650 W Alluvial Ave, Clovis (93611-6716)
PHONE..............................559 323-6200
George V Hager Jr, *CEO*
EMP: 200
SALES (est): 10.8MM **Privately Held**
WEB: www.genesishcc.com
SIC: 8051 Convalescent home with continuous nursing care
HQ: Genesis Healthcare Llc
101 E State St
Kennett Square PA 19348

(P-16163)
WINDSOR CARE CTR PETALUMA LLC
Also Called: Windsor Care Center Petaluma
523 Hayes Ln, Petaluma (94952-4011)
PHONE..............................707 763-2457
Ash Chawla, *Principal*
Donny Feldman,
EMP: 43 **EST:** 2011
SALES (est): 11.1MM **Privately Held**
WEB: www.windsorpetaluma.com
SIC: 8051 Skilled nursing care facilities

(P-16164)
WINDSOR CNVLSCENT RHBLTTION CT
Also Called: Windsor Mnor Rhabilitation Ctr
3806 Clayton Rd, Concord (94521-2516)
PHONE..............................925 689-2266
Lee Samson, *Mng Member*
EMP: 207 **EST:** 1950
SALES (est): 21.4MM **Privately Held**
WEB: www.windsorconcord.com
SIC: 8051 Convalescent home with continuous nursing care
PA: Lexington Group International, Inc
9200 W Sunset Blvd # 600
West Hollywood CA 90069

(P-16165)
WINDSOR CNVLSCENT RHBLTTION CT
Also Called: Windsor Park Care Ctr Fremont
2400 Parkside Dr, Fremont (94536-5332)
PHONE..............................510 793-7222
Lee Samson, *Mng Member*
Kim Cobbs, *Social Dir*
Alvin Aplaon, *Maintenance Dir*
EMP: 76 **EST:** 2005
SALES (est): 38.6MM **Privately Held**
WEB: www.windsorparkcare.com
SIC: 8051 Convalescent home with continuous nursing care
PA: Lexington Group International, Inc
9200 W Sunset Blvd # 600
West Hollywood CA 90069

(P-16166)
WINDSOR REDDING CARE CTR LLC
2490 Court St, Redding (96001-2540)
PHONE..............................530 246-0600
Lawrence E Feigen,
Susan Metcalfe, *CIO*
Lee C Samson,
EMP: 99 **EST:** 2007
SALES (est): 13.8MM **Privately Held**
WEB: www.windsorreddingcc.com
SIC: 8051 Convalescent home with continuous nursing care

(P-16167)
WINE COUNTRY CARE CENTER
321 W Turner Rd, Lodi (95240-0517)
PHONE..............................209 334-3760
Paul Gross, *Administration*
Robin Kuehne, *Director*
EMP: 35 **EST:** 2006
SALES: 6.4MM **Privately Held**
WEB: www.winecountrycarecenter.com
SIC: 8051 8062 Convalescent home with continuous nursing care; general medical & surgical hospitals

(P-16168)
YUBA CITY NURSING & REHAB LLC
1220 Plumas St, Yuba City (95991-3411)
PHONE..............................530 671-0550
Joseph Pallivathucal,
Babu Parayil,
James Paul,
Chris McConnell, *Director*
EMP: 59 **EST:** 2003
SALES (est): 4.9MM **Privately Held**
WEB: www.yubacitypostacute.com
SIC: 8051 Convalescent home with continuous nursing care

8052 Intermediate Care Facilities

(P-16169)
AMERICAN RIVER HOSPICE SVCS
1451 River Park Dr # 241, Sacramento (95815-4507)
PHONE..............................229 255-4609
EMP: 50 **EST:** 2018
SALES (est): 2.2MM **Privately Held**
WEB: www.arhssac.com
SIC: 8052 Personal care facility

(PA)=Parent Co (HQ)=Headquarters (DH)=Div Headquarters
✪ = New Business established in last 2 years

2022 Northern California Business Directory and Buyers Guide

8052 - Intermediate Care Facilities County (P-16170)

(P-16170)
BIG HEALTH INC
Also Called: Sleepio
461 Bush St Ste 200, San Francisco (94108-3716)
PHONE..................................415 867-3473
Peter Andrew, *CEO*
Berenice Franco, *Officer*
Henrietta Haizel, *Officer*
Dickon Waterfield, *Officer*
Richard Barnes, *Vice Pres*
EMP: 51 **EST:** 2015
SALES (est): 5.9MM **Privately Held**
WEB: www.sleepio.com
SIC: 8052 Home for the mentally retarded, with health care

(P-16171)
BRISTOL HOSPICE FOUNDATION CAL
4568 Feather River Dr, Stockton (95219-6508)
P.O. Box None (95219)
PHONE..................................661 670-8000
Eric Escobedo, *Branch Mgr*
Karol Ford, *Administration*
EMP: 68
SALES (corp-wide): 170.2K **Privately Held**
WEB: www.bristolhospicefoundationca.org
SIC: 8052 Personal care facility
PA: Bristol Hospice Foundation Of California
1227 Chester Ave Ste A
Bakersfield CA 93301
661 410-3000

(P-16172)
BRISTOL HOSPICE FOUNDATION CAL
1101 Sylvan Ave Ste B10, Modesto (95350-1679)
PHONE..................................209 338-3000
Ann Smart, *Branch Mgr*
EMP: 68
SALES (corp-wide): 170.2K **Privately Held**
WEB: www.bristolhospicefoundationca.org
SIC: 8052 Personal care facility
PA: Bristol Hospice Foundation Of California
1227 Chester Ave Ste A
Bakersfield CA 93301
661 410-3000

(P-16173)
BRISTOL HSPICE - SCRAMENTO LLC
2140 Prof Dr Ste 210, Roseville (95661)
PHONE..................................916 782-5511
Erin Starr, *Exec Dir*
Brandi Bratsafolis, *Vice Pres*
Jeanette Dove, *Vice Pres*
James Escobedo, *Office Mgr*
Rebecca Conrad, *Administration*
EMP: 63 **EST:** 2007
SALES: 8.9MM
SALES (corp-wide): 1.1B **Privately Held**
WEB: www.bristolhospice-sacramento.com
SIC: 8052 Personal care facility
PA: Avalon Health Care, Inc.
206 N 2100 W Ste 300
Salt Lake City UT 84116
801 596-8844

(P-16174)
CAREONE HM HLTH & HOSPICE INC
2813 Coffee Rd Ste C1, Modesto (95355-1755)
PHONE..................................209 632-8888
Balbir Dhillon, *CEO*
Linda Singer, *Human Res Dir*
Sat Dhillon, *Opers Mgr*
Darrell Mulligan, *Marketing Staff*
Dani H Gilbreath, *Accounts Exec*
EMP: 46 **EST:** 2010
SALES (est): 8MM **Privately Held**
WEB: www.careonehomehealth.net
SIC: 8052 Personal care facility

(P-16175)
CC-PALO ALTO INC
Also Called: VI At Palo Alto
620 Sand Hill Rd, Palo Alto (94304-2002)
PHONE..................................650 853-5000
Penny Pritzker, *President*
Rodrey Degracia, *Director*
Jessica Lyngaas, *Director*
EMP: 64 **EST:** 2004
SALES (est): 32.1MM **Privately Held**
WEB: www.paloaltou.edu
SIC: 8052 8322 8361 Personal care facility; adult day care center; rehabilitation center, residential: health care incidental

(P-16176)
CEDARS OF MARIN (PA)
115 Upper Rd, Ross (94957-9686)
P.O. Box 947 (94957-0947)
PHONE..................................415 454-5310
Brenda McIvor, *Exec Dir*
Chuck Greene, *Exec Dir*
Sue Sherer, *Controller*
Eric Andrus, *Maint Spvr*
Natasha Annenkova, *Program Dir*
EMP: 94 **EST:** 1919
SQ FT: 35,000
SALES (est): 18.7MM **Privately Held**
WEB: www.cedarslife.org
SIC: 8211 8052 School for the retarded; boarding school; intermediate care facilities

(P-16177)
COMMUNITY HOME PARTNERS LLC
Also Called: Pacific Gardens
2384 Pacific Dr, Santa Clara (95051-1458)
PHONE..................................408 985-5252
Maxine Brookner, *Founder*
EMP: 85 **EST:** 1998
SQ FT: 56,300
SALES (est): 4MM **Privately Held**
WEB: www.pacificgardens.org
SIC: 8052 Intermediate care facilities

(P-16178)
COMMUNITY HOSPICE INC (PA)
Also Called: C H I
4368 Spyres Way, Modesto (95356-9259)
PHONE..................................209 578-6300
Charlotte McLeod, *CEO*
Rick Dahlseid, *CFO*
Laurie Miller, *Officer*
Monica Ojcius, *Exec Dir*
Karen Aiello, *Admin Asst*
EMP: 125 **EST:** 1979
SQ FT: 24,000
SALES (est): 25.8MM **Privately Held**
WEB: www.hospiceheart.org
SIC: 8052 8069 Personal care facility; specialty hospitals, except psychiatric

(P-16179)
COUNTY OF SOLANO
Also Called: Adult Mddlhlth Otptient Clinic
2101 Courage Dr, Fairfield (94533-6717)
PHONE..................................707 784-2080
Rod Kennedy, *Manager*
EMP: 85
SALES (corp-wide): 740.7MM **Privately Held**
WEB: www.solanocounty.com
SIC: 8052 5719 Intermediate care facilities; linens
PA: County Of Solano
675 Texas St Ste 2600
Fairfield CA 94533
707 784-6706

(P-16180)
COVENANT CARE CALIFORNIA LLC
Also Called: Turlock Rsidential Care Fcilty
1101 E Tuolumne Rd, Turlock (95382-1541)
PHONE..................................209 667-8409
Melina Nunez, *Exec Dir*
Sandra Petersen, *Office Mgr*
EMP: 52 **Privately Held**
WEB: www.covenantcare.com
SIC: 8052 8361 Personal care facility; residential care
HQ: Covenant Care California, Llc
120 Vantis Dr Ste 200
Aliso Viejo CA 92656

(P-16181)
EMERITUS CORPORATION
Also Called: Emerald Hlls Asssted Lving Fcl
11550 Education St # 212, Auburn (95602-2463)
PHONE..................................530 653-1974
Lisa Huntzinger, *Manager*
Nicole Wirth, *Assistant*
EMP: 148
SALES (corp-wide): 3.5B **Publicly Held**
WEB: www.brookdale.com
SIC: 8052 8051 Personal care facility; skilled nursing care facilities
HQ: Emeritus Corporation
6737 W Wa St Ste 2300
Milwaukee WI 53214

(P-16182)
EMERITUS CORPORATION
800 Oregon St, Sonoma (95476-6445)
PHONE..................................707 996-7101
EMP: 148
SALES (corp-wide): 3.5B **Publicly Held**
WEB: www.brookdale.com
SIC: 8052 8361 Personal care facility; geriatric residential care
HQ: Emeritus Corporation
6737 W Wa St Ste 2300
Milwaukee WI 53214

(P-16183)
EMERITUS CORPORATION
300 Fountaingrove Pkwy, Santa Rosa (95403-5720)
PHONE..................................707 324-7087
Scott Bissey, *Branch Mgr*
EMP: 148
SALES (corp-wide): 3.5B **Publicly Held**
WEB: www.brookdale.com
SIC: 8052 6513 Personal care facility; retirement hotel operation
HQ: Emeritus Corporation
6737 W Wa St Ste 2300
Milwaukee WI 53214

(P-16184)
GOLDEN GATEIDENCE OPCO LLC
Also Called: Victorian Post Acute
2121 Pine St, San Francisco (94115-2829)
PHONE..................................415 922-5085
EMP: 122 **EST:** 2017
SALES (est): 2.5MM **Privately Held**
SIC: 8052 8051 Intermediate care facilities; skilled nursing care facilities

(P-16185)
HINDS HOSPICE (PA)
2490 W Shaw Ave Ste 100a, Fresno (93711-3305)
P.O. Box 1325, Madera (93639-1325)
PHONE..................................559 674-0407
Nancy Hinds, *Exec Dir*
Michael Kosareff, *CFO*
Kathy Cromwell, *Exec Dir*
Lynne Pietz, *Exec Dir*
Lusy Viloria, *Office Mgr*
EMP: 170
SALES (est): 17.9MM **Privately Held**
WEB: www.hindshospice.org
SIC: 8052 Personal care facility

(P-16186)
HOSPICE AND PALLIATIVE CARE
Also Called: Hospice of The East Bay
2849 Miranda Ave, Alamo (94507-1443)
PHONE..................................925 945-8924
Laura Pakar, *Branch Mgr*
EMP: 75 **Privately Held**
WEB: www.hospiceeastbay.org
SIC: 8052 Personal care facility
PA: Hospice And Palliative Care
3470 Buskirk Ave
Concord CA 94523

(P-16187)
HOSPICE SERVICES LAKE COUNTY
1862 Parallel Dr, Lakeport (95453-9388)
PHONE..................................707 263-6222
C Gommenginger, *Exec Dir*
Corrigan Gommenginger, *Exec Dir*
Darnette Daniels, *Marketing Staff*
Ruth Lincoln, *Director*
EMP: 35 **EST:** 1989
SQ FT: 10,400
SALES (est): 3.5MM **Privately Held**
WEB: www.lakecountyhospice.org
SIC: 8052 Personal care facility

(P-16188)
LAKEPORT POST ACUTE LLC
1291 Craig Ave, Lakeport (95453-5704)
PHONE..................................707 263-6382
Mark Hancock, *Mng Member*
Kimberlee Armstrong, *Office Mgr*
EMP: 81 **EST:** 2018
SALES (est): 7.7MM **Privately Held**
WEB: www.lakeportpa.com
SIC: 8052 Intermediate care facilities

(P-16189)
MADRONE HOSPICE INC (PA)
255 Collier Cir, Yreka (96097-2276)
PHONE..................................530 842-3160
Tana Gliatto, *President*
Dawna Cozzalio, *Treasurer*
Terry Beresten, *Exec Dir*
Lauri Hunner, *Exec Dir*
Doug Langford, *Finance*
EMP: 39 **EST:** 2000
SALES (est): 2.2MM **Privately Held**
WEB: www.madronehospice.org
SIC: 8052 Personal care facility

(P-16190)
MARYMOUNT VILLA LLC
345 Davis St Ofc, San Leandro (94577-2795)
PHONE..................................510 895-5007
Jasbir Walia, *Mng Member*
Arjun Bhagat, *Mng Member*
EMP: 65 **EST:** 2004
SALES (est): 6.5MM **Privately Held**
WEB: www.marymountvilla.com
SIC: 8052 8059 Personal care facility; convalescent home

(P-16191)
MILESTONES DEVELOPMENT INC
1 Florida St, Vallejo (94590-5000)
PHONE..................................707 644-0496
Cynthia Mack, *Purch Dir*
Joan Yates, *Ch of Bd*
Faith Ohara, *Admin Sec*
EMP: 36 **EST:** 1977
SQ FT: 7,564
SALES (est): 5.1MM **Privately Held**
WEB: www.milestonesofdevelopment.org
SIC: 8052 Home for the mentally retarded, with health care

(P-16192)
MISSION HOSPICE & HM CARE INC
66 Bovet Rd Ste 100, San Mateo (94402-3126)
PHONE..................................650 554-1000
Dwight Wilson, *Executive*
Brandy Waldrop, *Volunteer Dir*
Frances Blackburn, *Comms Dir*
Craig Schroeder, *Managing Dir*
Constance Sweeney, *Info Tech Dir*
EMP: 200 **EST:** 1979
SALES: 20MM **Privately Held**
WEB: www.missionhospice.org
SIC: 8052 Personal care facility

(P-16193)
MOUNTAIN VLY CHILD FMLY SVCS I
24077 State Highway 49, Nevada City (95959-8519)
PHONE..................................530 265-9057
Daniel Petrie, *CEO*
Richard Milhous, *CFO*
Janet Milhous, *Business Mgr*
Teresa Petrie, *Food Svc Dir*
Jillian Murphy, *Manager*

PRODUCTS & SERVICES SECTION
8059 - Nursing & Personal Care Facilities, NEC County (P-16218)

EMP: 220 **EST:** 1972
SQ FT: 22,000
SALES: 12.3MM **Privately Held**
WEB: www.mountainvalleyfamilyservices.net
SIC: 8052 8361 Intermediate care facilities; residential care

(P-16194)
OAKHURST HEALTHCARE CENTER LLC
Also Called: Skilled Nursing Facility
40131 Highway 49, Oakhurst (93644-9560)
PHONE.................................559 683-2244
John Harshman III, *Principal*
EMP: 93 **EST:** 2018
SALES (est): 3.6MM **Privately Held**
WEB: www.oakhursthc.com
SIC: 8052 Intermediate care facilities

(P-16195)
OAKLANDIDENCE OPCO LLC
Also Called: Medical Hill Healthcare Center
475 29th St, Oakland (94609-3510)
PHONE.................................510 832-3222
Jason Murray, *Principal*
Debra Gogerty, *Principal*
EMP: 99 **EST:** 2017
SALES (est): 2.6MM **Privately Held**
SIC: 8052 Intermediate care facilities

(P-16196)
PRAIRIE CITY COMMONS LLC
Also Called: Prairie City Landing
645 Willard Dr, Folsom (95630-4048)
PHONE.................................916 458-0303
Eric Hostetter, *Mng Member*
Tina Mora, *Office Mgr*
Mary Campbell, *Director*
Marcia McCuen, *Receptionist*
EMP: 85 **EST:** 2016
SALES (est): 8.9MM **Privately Held**
WEB: www.prairiecitylanding.com
SIC: 8052 Intermediate care facilities

(P-16197)
RES-CARE INC
5250 Claremont Ave, Stockton (95207-5700)
PHONE.................................209 473-1202
Gregory Kessinger, *CFO*
EMP: 82
SALES (corp-wide): 2B **Privately Held**
WEB: www.rescare.com
SIC: 8052 Home for the mentally retarded, with health care
HQ: Res-Care, Inc.
805 N Whittington Pkwy
Louisville KY 40222
502 394-2100

(P-16198)
RES-CARE INC
1485 Response Rd, Sacramento (95815-4847)
PHONE.................................916 567-1244
Brenda Collins, *Branch Mgr*
EMP: 82
SALES (corp-wide): 2B **Privately Held**
WEB: www.rescare.com
SIC: 8052 Home for the mentally retarded, with health care
HQ: Res-Care, Inc.
805 N Whittington Pkwy
Louisville KY 40222
502 394-2100

(P-16199)
RES-CARE INC
Also Called: Rcca Dutra Place
545 Dutra Pl, Manteca (95337-6669)
PHONE.................................800 866-0860
Deena Ombres, *Manager*
EMP: 82
SALES (corp-wide): 2B **Privately Held**
WEB: www.rescare.com
SIC: 8052 Home for the mentally retarded, with health care
HQ: Res-Care, Inc.
805 N Whittington Pkwy
Louisville KY 40222
502 394-2100

(P-16200)
RES-CARE INC
618 Court St Ste D, Woodland (95695-3463)
PHONE.................................530 406-8603
Bill Rutgers, *Manager*
EMP: 82
SALES (corp-wide): 2B **Privately Held**
WEB: www.rescare.com
SIC: 8052 Home for the mentally retarded, with health care
HQ: Res-Care, Inc.
805 N Whittington Pkwy
Louisville KY 40222
502 394-2100

(P-16201)
RONALD VANDERBEEK
6101 Fair Oaks Blvd, Carmichael (95608-4818)
PHONE.................................916 488-7211
Stuart Drake, *Manager*
EMP: 42
SALES (corp-wide): 4.3MM **Privately Held**
SIC: 8052 8059 Intermediate care facilities; nursing home, except skilled & intermediate care facility
PA: Ronald Vanderbeek
2100 Butano Dr
Sacramento CA 95825
916 481-9240

(P-16202)
SENIOR LIVING SOLUTIONS LLC
1725 S Bascom Ave Apt 105, Campbell (95008-0676)
PHONE.................................408 385-1835
EMP: 120
SALES (est): 1.9MM **Privately Held**
SIC: 8052 Intermediate Care Facilities

(P-16203)
SILVERADO SENIOR LIVING INC
Also Called: Bay Area Hospice
1000 Marina Blvd Ste 200, Brisbane (94005-1841)
PHONE.................................650 226-4152
EMP: 56
SALES (corp-wide): 173.8MM **Privately Held**
WEB: www.silverado.com
SIC: 8052 Personal care facility
PA: Senior Silverado Living Inc
6400 Oak Cyn Ste 200
Irvine CA 92618
949 240-7200

(P-16204)
SNOWLINE HSPICE EL DORADO CNTY
6520 Pleasant Valley Rd, Diamond Springs (95619-9512)
PHONE.................................530 621-7820
Michael Sehmidt, *Exec Dir*
Richard B Esposito, *President*
William Fisher, *Treasurer*
Jon Lehrman, *Vice Pres*
Leah Hall, *Admin Sec*
EMP: 140 **EST:** 2003
SQ FT: 8,900
SALES: 15.9MM **Privately Held**
WEB: www.snowlinehospice.org
SIC: 8052 Personal care facility

(P-16205)
SNOWLINE HSPICE OF EL DRADO CN
6520 Pleasant Valley Rd, Diamond Springs (95619-9512)
PHONE.................................916 817-2338
Tom Heflin, *President*
William Fisher, *Treasurer*
Mary Newton, *Exec Dir*
Michael Schmidt, *Exec Dir*
Leah Hall, *Admin Sec*
EMP: 104 **EST:** 1980
SQ FT: 8,900
SALES (est): 28.2MM **Privately Held**
WEB: www.snowlinehospice.org
SIC: 8052 Personal care facility

(P-16206)
SONOMAIDENCE OPCO LLC
Also Called: Sonoma Post Acute
678 2nd St W, Sonoma (95476-6901)
PHONE.................................707 938-1096
Jason Murray, *Principal*
Mark Hancock, *Principal*
EMP: 86 **EST:** 2016
SALES (est): 5.3MM **Privately Held**
WEB: www.sonomapostacute.com
SIC: 8052 8051 Intermediate care facilities; skilled nursing care facilities

(P-16207)
STRATGIES TO EMPWER PEOPLE INC (PA)
Also Called: Step
2330 Glendale Ln, Sacramento (95825-2455)
PHONE.................................916 679-1527
Jacquine Difoss, *President*
Rebecca Laboriel, *Vice Pres*
William Marks, *Office Mgr*
Claudia Loveless, *Controller*
Lydia Edinborough, *Human Res Mgr*
EMP: 316 **EST:** 1994
SALES (est): 15.3MM **Privately Held**
WEB: www.stepagency.com
SIC: 8052 Personal care facility

(P-16208)
SUTTER HEALTH
1651 Alvarado St, San Leandro (94577-2636)
PHONE.................................510 618-5200
Phyllis Weis, *Human Res Dir*
EMP: 161
SALES (corp-wide): 13.2B **Privately Held**
WEB: www.suttermedicalcenter.org
SIC: 8052 Personal care facility
PA: Sutter Health
2200 River Plaza Dr
Sacramento CA 95833
916 733-8800

(P-16209)
VITAS HEALTHCARE CORP CAL
Also Called: Vitas Innovative Hospice Care
670 N Mccarthy Blvd # 22, Milpitas (95035-5119)
PHONE.................................408 964-6800
Roslyn Stenson, *Branch Mgr*
Jenelyn Lim, *Director*
EMP: 35
SALES (corp-wide): 2B **Publicly Held**
WEB: www.vitas.com
SIC: 8052 Personal care facility
HQ: Vitas Healthcare Corporation Of California
7888 Mission Grove Pkwy S
Riverside CA 92508
305 374-4143

(P-16210)
VITAS HEALTHCARE CORP CAL
355 Lennon Ln Ste 150, Walnut Creek (94598-2475)
PHONE.................................925 930-9373
Shirley Blethen, *Branch Mgr*
Katie Roberts Kremer, *General Mgr*
EMP: 35
SALES (corp-wide): 2B **Publicly Held**
SIC: 8052 Personal care facility
HQ: Vitas Healthcare Corporation Of California
7888 Mission Grove Pkwy S
Riverside CA 92508
305 374-4143

(P-16211)
VITAS HEALTHCARE CORPORATION
1388 Sutter St Ste 700, San Francisco (94109-5453)
PHONE.................................415 874-4400
EMP: 78
SALES (corp-wide): 2B **Publicly Held**
WEB: www.vitas.com
SIC: 8052 Personal care facility
HQ: Vitas Healthcare Corporation
201 S Biscayne Blvd # 400
Miami FL 33131
305 374-4143

8059 Nursing & Personal Care Facilities, NEC

(P-16212)
14766 WASH AVE OPERATIONS LLC
14766 Washington Ave, San Leandro (94578-4220)
PHONE.................................510 352-2211
EMP: 90
SALES (est): 5.7MM **Privately Held**
WEB: www.washingtoncenter.com
SIC: 8059 Nursing home, except skilled & intermediate care facility
HQ: Sun Healthcare Group, Inc.
27442 Portola Pkwy # 200
Foothill Ranch CA 92610

(P-16213)
A T ASSOCIATES INC
Also Called: Berkeley Pines Care Center
2223 Ashby Ave, Berkeley (94705-1907)
PHONE.................................510 649-6670
EMP: 50 **Privately Held**
SIC: 8059 Nursing And Personal Care, Nec, Nsk
PA: A T Associates, Inc
535 School St
Pittsburg CA 94565

(P-16214)
A T ASSOCIATES INC
Also Called: Oakridge Care Center
2919 Fruitvale Ave, Oakland (94602-2108)
PHONE.................................510 261-8564
EMP: 100 **Privately Held**
SIC: 8059 8051 Nursing And Personal Care, Nec, Nsk
PA: A T Associates, Inc
535 School St
Pittsburg CA 94565

(P-16215)
A T ASSOCIATES INC (PA)
535 School St, Pittsburg (94565-3937)
PHONE.................................925 808-6540
EMP: 75 **Privately Held**
WEB: www.atassociatesinc.com
SIC: 8059 8011 Nursing And Personal Care, Nec, Nsk

(P-16216)
ASBURY PK NRSING RHBLTTION CTR
2257 Fair Oaks Blvd, Sacramento (95825-5501)
PHONE.................................916 649-2000
John Lund, *President*
Aisha Aslam, *Manager*
EMP: 130 **EST:** 1997
SQ FT: 30,000
SALES (est): 10.9MM **Privately Held**
WEB: www.asburyparknursing.com
SIC: 8059 Nursing home, except skilled & intermediate care facility

(P-16217)
BASSARD CNVALESCENT MED HM INC (PA)
Also Called: Bassard Convalscent Home
3269 D St, Hayward (94541-4585)
PHONE.................................510 537-6700
Prema Thekkek, *President*
Bobby Singh, *Administration*
Heather Vance, *Accountant*
EMP: 65 **EST:** 1963
SQ FT: 25,000
SALES (est): 3MM **Privately Held**
SIC: 8059 Convalescent home

(P-16218)
BETHEL LUTHERAN HOME INC
2280 Dockery Ave, Selma (93662-3898)
PHONE.................................559 896-4900
C Kaylene Steele, *Administration*
Kathi Mehrten, *Assistant*
EMP: 100 **EST:** 1928
SQ FT: 33,000

8059 - Nursing & Personal Care Facilities, NEC County (P-16219)

SALES (est): 10.4MM **Privately Held**
WEB: www.bethellutheranhome.org
SIC: 8059 8051 Domiciliary care; extended care facility

(P-16219)
BETHEL RTRMENT CMNTY A CAL LTD
2345 Scenic Dr Ofc C, Modesto (95355-4575)
PHONE 209 577-1901
Tony Musolino, *General Ptnr*
Kenneth Lemmings DDS, *Partner*
Robert Pirtle, *Partner*
Stephen P Thomas, *Partner*
Kim Viviano, *Exec Dir*
EMP: 39 **EST:** 1988
SALES (est): 10.8MM **Privately Held**
WEB: www.bethelretirement.com
SIC: 8059 8361 Nursing home, except skilled & intermediate care facility; home for the aged

(P-16220)
BOUNDLESS CARE INC
5988 Silver Creek Valley, San Jose (95138-1077)
PHONE 408 363-8900
Mary Vivian M Aranda, *President*
Arlene Horvatic, *CEO*
W Cary Selden, *Info Tech Mgr*
EMP: 37 **EST:** 2006
SALES (est): 2MM **Privately Held**
WEB: www.boundlesscare.org
SIC: 8059 4789 8742 7371 Personal care home, with health care; cargo loading & unloading services; hospital & health services consultant; computer software development & applications

(P-16221)
BRENTWOOD SKLLED NRSING RHBLTT
Also Called: Brentwood Sklled Nrsing Rhbltt
1795 Walnut St, Red Bluff (96080-3645)
PHONE 530 527-2046
Phil Sullivan, *Administration*
Daniel McNeal, *Maint Spvr*
Terri Sullivan, *Nursing Dir*
Stephen Datu, *Director*
Becky Taroli, *Receptionist*
EMP: 56 **EST:** 1975
SQ FT: 1,600
SALES (est): 7.4MM **Privately Held**
SIC: 8059 Convalescent home

(P-16222)
CALIFORNIA HM FOR THE AGED INC
Also Called: CALIFORNIA ARMENIAN HOME
6720 E Kings Canyon Rd, Fresno (93727-3603)
PHONE 559 251-8414
Ray Wark, *Administration*
EMP: 165 **EST:** 1950
SQ FT: 39,000
SALES: 24MM **Privately Held**
WEB: www.lifeatthevineyards.org
SIC: 8059 Convalescent home

(P-16223)
CALIFORNIA VOCATIONS INC
Also Called: Arthur Schawlow Center
564 Rio Lindo Ave Ste 204, Chico (95926-1852)
P.O. Box 538, Paradise (95967-0538)
PHONE 530 877-0937
Bob Irvine, *Exec Dir*
Richard Welsh, *President*
George Dailey, *Treasurer*
Lisa Nixon, *Officer*
Paul Johnson, *Admin Sec*
EMP: 195 **EST:** 1984
SQ FT: 5,700
SALES (est): 7.4MM **Privately Held**
WEB: www.calvoc.org
SIC: 8059 Home for the mentally retarded, exc. skilled or intermediate

(P-16224)
CALIFRNIA-NEVADA METHDST HOMES
Also Called: Lake Park Retirment Residence
1850 Alice St Ofc, Oakland (94612-4169)
PHONE 510 835-5511
Steve Jacobson, *Branch Mgr*
Isabel Banuelos, *Human Res Mgr*
Tesfai Haile, *Director*
EMP: 197
SALES (corp-wide): 22.9MM **Privately Held**
WEB: www.cnmh.org
SIC: 8059 Rest home, with health care
PA: California-Nevada Methodist Homes
  201 19th St Ste 100
  Oakland CA 94612
  510 893-8989

(P-16225)
CARE AT HOME
5555 Montgomery Dr, Santa Rosa (95409-8846)
PHONE 707 579-6822
EMP: 35 **EST:** 2007
SALES (est): 272.8K **Privately Held**
SIC: 8059 Nursing/Personal Care

(P-16226)
CARLMONT GARDENS LLC
2140 Carlmont Dr, Belmont (94002-3417)
PHONE 650 591-9601
Bonne Bertetta,
Brian Coley, *Maintence Staff*
EMP: 60 **EST:** 1962
SALES (est): 21.2MM **Privately Held**
WEB: www.carlmontgardens.com
SIC: 8059 Nursing home, except skilled & intermediate care facility

(P-16227)
CHANNING HOUSE
850 Webster St Ofc, Palo Alto (94301-2859)
PHONE 650 327-0950
Melvin Matsumoto, *CEO*
Honey Faustino, *Records Dir*
Dr Thomas Fiene, *Trustee*
Carl Braginsky, *Exec Dir*
Mel Matsumoto, *Exec Dir*
EMP: 100 **EST:** 1960
SQ FT: 300,000
SALES: 20.3MM **Privately Held**
WEB: www.channinghouse.org
SIC: 8059 Rest home, with health care

(P-16228)
COVENANT CARE CALIFORNIA LLC
Also Called: Vintage Fire Nrsing Rhbltion C
3620 Dale Rd Ste B, Modesto (95356-0598)
PHONE 209 521-2094
Julie Abram, *Administration*
Emelyn Lawler, *Exec Dir*
Nancy Borges, *Human Res Dir*
Maria Rangel, *Food Svc Dir*
Prithika Singh, *Director*
EMP: 41 **Privately Held**
WEB: www.covenantcare.com
SIC: 8059 8051 Convalescent home; skilled nursing care facilities
HQ: Covenant Care California, Llc
  120 Vantis Dr Ste 200
  Aliso Viejo CA 92656

(P-16229)
CRESTWOOD BEHAVIORAL HLTH INC
Also Called: 1140 Kingsburg Mhrc
1200 Smith St, Kingsburg (93631-2216)
PHONE 559 238-6981
Martha Crawford, *Administration*
EMP: 65
SALES (corp-wide): 238MM **Privately Held**
WEB: www.crestwoodbehavioralhealth.com
SIC: 8059 Domiciliary care
PA: Crestwood Behavioral Health, Inc.
  520 Capitol Mall Ste 800
  Sacramento CA 95814
  510 651-1244

(P-16230)
CRESTWOOD BEHAVIORAL HLTH INC
Also Called: 1110 Eureka Mhrc
2370 Buhne St, Eureka (95501-3237)
PHONE 707 442-5721
Nicole Paiste, *Administration*
Michael Floyd, *Director*
Willard Hunter, *Director*
EMP: 48
SALES (corp-wide): 238MM **Privately Held**
WEB: www.crestwoodbehavioralhealth.com
SIC: 8059 Domiciliary care
PA: Crestwood Behavioral Health, Inc.
  520 Capitol Mall Ste 800
  Sacramento CA 95814
  510 651-1244

(P-16231)
CRESTWOOD BEHAVIORAL HLTH INC
Also Called: 1166 San Francisco Mhrc
450 Stanyan St Fl 5, San Francisco (94117-1019)
PHONE 415 213-7993
Joel Mensonides, *Administration*
EMP: 58
SALES (corp-wide): 238MM **Privately Held**
WEB: www.crestwoodbehavioralhealth.com
SIC: 8059 Domiciliary care
PA: Crestwood Behavioral Health, Inc.
  520 Capitol Mall Ste 800
  Sacramento CA 95814
  510 651-1244

(P-16232)
ESCUETA CARE HOME 3 INC (PA)
23571 Ronald Ln, Hayward (94541-7555)
PHONE 510 785-0203
Milanette Escueta, *Principal*
EMP: 69 **EST:** 2008
SALES (est): 534.9K **Privately Held**
SIC: 8059 Nursing & personal care

(P-16233)
FRONT ST INC
Also Called: Front St Residential Care
2115 7th Ave, Santa Cruz (95062-1663)
PHONE 831 420-0120
Anne Butler, *President*
Peggy Butler, *Vice Pres*
Patrice Sovyak, *Exec Dir*
EMP: 120 **EST:** 1989
SALES (est): 17.7MM **Privately Held**
WEB: www.frontst.com
SIC: 8059 Personal care home, with health care

(P-16234)
GAFFAR ENTERPRISE INC
Also Called: Lake Shore Convalescent Hosp
1901 3rd Ave, Oakland (94606-1853)
PHONE 510 834-9880
Gaffar Syed, *President*
Jack W Neumann, *Accountant*
EMP: 50 **EST:** 1946
SQ FT: 10,000
SALES (est): 3MM **Privately Held**
SIC: 8059 Convalescent home

(P-16235)
GHC OF SUNNYVALE LLC
Also Called: Cedar Crest Nrsing Rhbltion C
797 E Fremont Ave, Sunnyvale (94087-2805)
PHONE 408 738-4880
Thomas Olds Jr,
Judie Williams, *Human Res Dir*
Jose Contreras, *Director*
Nelia Montojo, *Director*
Scott Morley, *Manager*
EMP: 150 **EST:** 2000
SALES (est): 35.5MM
SALES (corp-wide): 112.7MM **Privately Held**
SIC: 8059 8051 Nursing home, except skilled & intermediate care facility; skilled nursing care facilities
PA: Life Generations Healthcare Llc
  6 Hutton Cntre Dr Ste 400
  Santa Ana CA 92707
  714 241-5600

(P-16236)
GOLDEN AGE CNVLESCENT HOSP INC
523 Burlingame Ave, Capitola (95010-3307)
P.O. Box H, Santa Clara (95055-3729)
PHONE 831 475-0722
EMP: 35
SQ FT: 11,000
SALES (est): 1MM **Privately Held**
SIC: 8059 8051 7363 Nursing/Personal Care Skilled Nursing Care Facility Help Supply Services

(P-16237)
HANK FISHER PROPERTIES INC
Also Called: Chateau At River's Edge
641 Feature Dr Apt 233, Sacramento (95825-8331)
PHONE 916 921-1970
Jeff Hertzig, *Director*
EMP: 172 **EST:** 1988
SALES (est): 5MM
SALES (corp-wide): 15.8MM **Privately Held**
WEB: www.hankfisherproperties.com
SIC: 8059 8052 Convalescent home; intermediate care facilities
PA: Hank Fisher Properties, Inc.
  641 Fulton Ave Ste 200
  Sacramento CA 95825
  916 485-1441

(P-16238)
HELIOS HEALTHCARE LLC
Also Called: Windsor Vallejo Care Center
2200 Tuolumne St, Vallejo (94589-2523)
PHONE 707 644-7401
Laura Curly, *Manager*
EMP: 46
SALES (corp-wide): 27.5MM **Privately Held**
SIC: 8059 8051 Convalescent home; skilled nursing care facilities
PA: Helios Healthcare, Llc
  520 Capitol Mall Ste 800
  Sacramento CA 95814
  916 471-2241

(P-16239)
HILLSDALE GROUP LP
Also Called: Green Hills Retirement Center
1201 Broadway Ofc, Millbrae (94030-1976)
PHONE 650 742-9150
Pooja Sadarangani, *Manager*
EMP: 147
SALES (corp-wide): 20.1MM **Privately Held**
SIC: 8059 8051 Nursing home, except skilled & intermediate care facility; skilled nursing care facilities
PA: The Hillsdale Group L P
  1199 Howard Ave Ste 200
  Burlingame CA

(P-16240)
HILLSDALE GROUP LP
Also Called: Hayward Convalescent Hospital
1832 B St, Hayward (94541-3140)
PHONE 510 538-3866
Mark Bornta, *Manager*
EMP: 147
SALES (corp-wide): 20.1MM **Privately Held**
SIC: 8059 8051 Nursing home, except skilled & intermediate care facility; convalescent home with continuous nursing care
PA: The Hillsdale Group L P
  1199 Howard Ave Ste 200
  Burlingame CA

(P-16241)
HUMANGOOD (PA)
Also Called: TERRACES AT SQUAW PEAK
6120 Stoneridge Mall Rd, Pleasanton (94588-3296)
PHONE 602 906-4024
John Cochran, *CEO*
Bill Canteen, *Vice Pres*
Andrew McDonald, *Vice Pres*
Declan Brown, *Admin Asst*
Eileen Haller, *Administration*
EMP: 262 **EST:** 1959

PRODUCTS & SERVICES SECTION
8059 - Nursing & Personal Care Facilities, NEC County (P-16266)

SQ FT: 161,000
SALES: 25.9MM **Privately Held**
WEB: www.humangood.org
SIC: **8059** 8051 8322 Rest home, with health care; skilled nursing care facilities; old age assistance

(P-16242)
HUMANGOOD NORCAL
Also Called: Pilgrim Haven Retirement Home
373 Pine Ln, Los Altos (94022-1694)
PHONE.................................650 948-8291
Rae Holt, *Manager*
EMP: 77
SQ FT: 95,130
SALES (corp-wide): 25.9MM **Privately Held**
WEB: www.humangood.org
SIC: **8059** 8052 8051 Convalescent home; intermediate care facilities; skilled nursing care facilities
HQ: Humangood Norcal
6120 Stnrdge Mall Rd Ste
Pleasanton CA 94588
925 924-7100

(P-16243)
HUMANGOOD NORCAL
Also Called: Terraces of Los Gatos Agei
800 Blossom Hill Rd Ofc, Los Gatos (95032-3563)
PHONE.................................408 357-1100
A Candalla, *Exec Dir*
Patty Lopez, *Food Svc Dir*
EMP: 77
SALES (corp-wide): 25.9MM **Privately Held**
WEB: www.humangood.org
SIC: **8059** 8052 8051 6513 Rest home, with health care; intermediate care facilities; skilled nursing care facilities; apartment building operators
HQ: Humangood Norcal
6120 Stnrdge Mall Rd Ste
Pleasanton CA 94588
925 924-7100

(P-16244)
INDEPENDENT QUALITY CARE INC (PA)
Also Called: Woodland Lfytte Cnvlscent Hosp
3 Crow Canyon Ct, San Ramon (94583-1619)
PHONE.................................925 855-0881
▲ EMP: 75
SALES (est): 12.8MM **Privately Held**
SIC: **8059** Nursing And Personal Care, Nec, Nsk

(P-16245)
INDEPENDENT QUALITY CARE INC
Also Called: Northgate Convalescent Hosp
40 Professional Ctr Pkwy, San Rafael (94903-2703)
PHONE.................................415 479-1230
EMP: 75
SALES (corp-wide): 12.8MM **Privately Held**
SIC: **8059** Nursing And Personal Care, Nec, Nsk
PA: Independent Quality Care, Inc.
3 Crow Canyon Ct
San Ramon CA 94583
925 855-0881

(P-16246)
INDEPENDENT QUALITY CARE INC
Also Called: San Bruno Skilled Nursing Hosp
890 El Camino Real, San Bruno (94066-3137)
PHONE.................................650 583-7768
EMP: 40
SALES (corp-wide): 12.8MM **Privately Held**
SIC: **8059** 8051 Nursing And Personal Care, Nec, Nsk
PA: Independent Quality Care, Inc.
3 Crow Canyon Ct
San Ramon CA 94583
925 855-0881

(P-16247)
INDEPENDENT QUALITY CARE INC
Also Called: McClure Convalescent Hospital
2910 Mcclure St, Oakland (94609-3505)
PHONE.................................510 836-3677
EMP: 55
SQ FT: 5,000
SALES (corp-wide): 12.8MM **Privately Held**
WEB: www.mcclurehc.com
SIC: **8059** Nursing And Personal Care, Nec, Nsk
PA: Independent Quality Care, Inc.
3 Crow Canyon Ct
San Ramon CA 94583
925 855-0881

(P-16248)
INDEPENDENT QUALITY CARE INC
Also Called: Woodland Lfyett Sklled Nursing
3721 Mt Diablo Blvd, Lafayette (94549-3538)
PHONE.................................925 284-5544
EMP: 75
SALES (corp-wide): 12.8MM **Privately Held**
SIC: **8059** Nursing And Personal Care, Nec, Nsk
PA: Independent Quality Care, Inc.
3 Crow Canyon Ct
San Ramon CA 94583
925 855-0881

(P-16249)
INSTITUTE ON AGING
2880 Zanker Rd, San Jose (95134-2117)
PHONE.................................510 536-3377
Christina Strine, *Manager*
EMP: 179 **Privately Held**
WEB: www.ioaging.org
SIC: **8059** Convalescent home
PA: Institute On Aging
3575 Geary Blvd
San Francisco CA 94118

(P-16250)
MARK ONE CORPORATION
Also Called: Hale Aloha Convalescent
812 W Main St, Turlock (95380-4645)
P.O. Box 1129 (95381-1129)
PHONE.................................209 667-2484
John C Sims, *CEO*
Dee Pursely, *Human Res Dir*
EMP: 190 EST: 1962
SQ FT: 33,000
SALES (est): 10.6MM **Privately Held**
SIC: **8059** 8051 Nursing home, except skilled & intermediate care facility; skilled nursing care facilities

(P-16251)
MARK ONE CORPORATION
Also Called: Ha-Le Aloha Convalescent Hosp
1711 Richland Ave, Ceres (95307-4509)
PHONE.................................209 537-4581
Fax: 209 537-0035
EMP: 50
SALES (corp-wide): 12.7MM **Privately Held**
SIC: **8059** Nursing And Personal Care, Nec, Nsk
PA: Mark One Corporation
812 W Main St
Turlock CA 95380
209 667-2484

(P-16252)
MCWEALTH CARE INC
1616 W Shaw Ave Ste B4, Fresno (93711-3513)
PHONE.................................559 293-3174
Joshua McWealth, *President*
EMP: 45 EST: 2014
SALES (est): 3.2MM **Privately Held**
SIC: **8059** Nursing & personal care

(P-16253)
MILLBRAE SERRA SANITARIUM
Also Called: Millbrae Srra Cnvalescent Hosp
150 Serra Ave, Millbrae (94030-2629)
P.O. Box 789 (94030-0789)
PHONE.................................650 697-8386
Fax: 650 697-3058
EMP: 125
SQ FT: 10,000
SALES: 4.6MM **Privately Held**
SIC: **8059** 8051 Skilled Nursing Care Facility

(P-16254)
MONTVALE INC
Also Called: Sunnyside Gardens
21060 Homestead Rd # 120, Cupertino (95014-0204)
PHONE.................................408 739-5446
Jason Chartier, *President*
Stan Howard, *CFO*
Keith Kolker, *Vice Pres*
EMP: 39 EST: 1988
SQ FT: 8,000
SALES (est): 1MM **Privately Held**
SIC: **8059** Domiciliary care

(P-16255)
NORTHGATE CARE CENTER INC
40 Professional Ctr Pkwy, San Rafael (94903-2703)
PHONE.................................415 479-1230
EMP: 52
SQ FT: 11,000
SALES (est): 3MM
SALES (corp-wide): 12.8MM **Privately Held**
WEB: www.northgatecares.com
SIC: **8059** Nursing And Personal Care, Nec, Nsk
PA: Independent Quality Care, Inc.
3 Crow Canyon Ct
San Ramon CA 94583
925 855-0881

(P-16256)
OUR HUSE RSDNTIAL CARE CTR INC
109 E Central Ave, Madera (93638-3109)
PHONE.................................559 674-8670
Carolyn Pipes, *President*
EMP: 48 EST: 1996
SALES (est): 5.6MM **Privately Held**
SIC: **8059** Rest home, with health care

(P-16257)
PENNYS GUEST HOME LLC (PA)
Also Called: Residntial Care Fclty For Eldr
990 Rosehedge Ct, Concord (94521-5453)
PHONE.................................925 286-0424
Josefina Gardner, *Manager*
Penny Gardner,
EMP: 46 EST: 2002
SALES (est): 1.1MM **Privately Held**
WEB: www.pennysguesthome.com
SIC: **8059** Rest home, with health care

(P-16258)
PLACERVLLE PNES CNVLSCENT HOSP
1040 Marshall Way, Placerville (95667-5706)
PHONE.................................530 622-3400
Jared Edmunds, *Administration*
Kristina Brown, *QC Dir*
EMP: 41 EST: 1963
SQ FT: 40,000
SALES (est): 37.9MM **Privately Held**
WEB: www.pinesatplacerville.com
SIC: **8059** 8051 Convalescent home; skilled nursing care facilities
HQ: Horizon West Healthcare, Inc.
4020 Sierra College Blvd # 190
Rocklin CA 95677
916 624-6230

(P-16259)
RAFAEL CONVALESCENT HOSPITAL
234 N San Pedro Rd, San Rafael (94903-2858)
PHONE.................................415 479-3450
Timothy J Egan, *President*
Michael Egan, *Admin Sec*
EMP: 87 EST: 1958
SQ FT: 9,000
SALES (est): 14MM **Privately Held**
WEB: www.rafaelconvalescent.com
SIC: **8059** 8051 Convalescent home; skilled nursing care facilities

(P-16260)
REDWOOD CONVALESCENT HOSPITAL
22103 Redwood Rd, Castro Valley (94546-7173)
PHONE.................................510 537-8848
Frank V Kreske MD, *President*
Elizabeth Kreske, *Vice Pres*
EMP: 40 EST: 1966
SQ FT: 10,000
SALES (est): 13.7MM **Privately Held**
SIC: **8059** Convalescent home

(P-16261)
RIVER OAK CENTER FOR CHILDREN
5445 Laurel Hills Dr, Sacramento (95841-3105)
PHONE.................................916 550-5600
EMP: 94
SALES (corp-wide): 13.5MM **Privately Held**
SIC: **8059** 8063 Nursing/Personal Care Psychiatric Hospital
PA: River Oak Center For Children
5445 Laurel Hills Dr
Sacramento CA 95841
916 609-5100

(P-16262)
RIVERSIDE CNVALESCENT HOSP INC
375 Cohasset Rd, Chico (95926-2211)
PHONE.................................530 343-5595
Gladys Jennings, *President*
Rod Willis, *Assistant*
EMP: 72 EST: 1963
SQ FT: 50,000
SALES (est): 6.1MM **Privately Held**
WEB: www.riversideconvalescent.com
SIC: **8059** Convalescent home

(P-16263)
RIVERSIDE HEALTH CARE CORP (PA)
1469 Humboldt Rd Ste 175, Chico (95928-9204)
PHONE.................................530 897-5100
Sharon Jennings Kearns, *CEO*
EMP: 60 EST: 1985
SQ FT: 9,000
SALES (est): 44.6MM **Privately Held**
WEB: www.riversidehealthca.com
SIC: **8059** Convalescent home

(P-16264)
RONALD VANDERBEEK (PA)
Also Called: Mountain Manor
2100 Butano Dr, Sacramento (95825-0448)
PHONE.................................916 481-9240
Ronald T Vanderbeek, *Owner*
Stuart Drake, *Administration*
EMP: 40 EST: 1977
SQ FT: 40,000
SALES (est): 4.3MM **Privately Held**
SIC: **8059** 6513 8052 Rest home, with health care; retirement hotel operation; intermediate care facilities

(P-16265)
SAN FRANCISCOIDENCE OPCO LLC
Also Called: San Francisco Post Acute
5767 Mission St, San Francisco (94112-4208)
PHONE.................................415 584-3294
Jason Murray, *President*
Mark Hancock, *CFO*
EMP: 95 EST: 2014
SALES (est): 5.6MM **Privately Held**
SIC: **8059** Nursing & personal care

(P-16266)
SANHYD INC
Also Called: Jones Rest HM Cnvalescent Hosp
524 Callan Ave, San Leandro (94577-4610)
PHONE.................................510 483-6200
Pratap Poddatoori, *President*

8059 - Nursing & Personal Care Facilities, NEC County (P-16267)

Lucy Lopez, *Human Res Dir*
Sergio Flores, *Director*
EMP: 64 **EST:** 1948
SQ FT: 25,000
SALES (est): 7.1MM **Privately Held**
WEB: www.sanleandrobytes.com
SIC: 8059 Convalescent home; rest home, with health care

(P-16267)
SEQUOIA LIVING INC
Also Called: Sequoia Living Health Services
1400 Geary Blvd, San Francisco (94109-6561)
PHONE 415 351-7956
EMP: 109
SALES (corp-wide): 85.5MM **Privately Held**
WEB: www.sequoialiving.org
SIC: 8059 8361 8051 Convalescent home; home for the aged; convalescent home with continuous nursing care
PA: Sequoia Living, Inc.
   1525 Post St
   San Francisco CA 94109
   415 202-7808

(P-16268)
SEQUOIA LIVING INC
Also Called: Tamal Pais
501 Via Casitas Ofc, Greenbrae (94904-1958)
PHONE 415 464-1767
Nan Boyd, *CFO*
David Latina, *Officer*
Wesley Bard, *Exec Dir*
Michael Cataldo, *Exec Dir*
Glen Goddard, *Exec Dir*
EMP: 109
SALES (corp-wide): 85.5MM **Privately Held**
WEB: www.sequoialiving.org
SIC: 8059 8062 8051 8052 Rest home, with health care; general medical & surgical hospitals; skilled nursing care facilities; intermediate care facilities
PA: Sequoia Living, Inc.
   1525 Post St
   San Francisco CA 94109
   415 202-7808

(P-16269)
SISTERS OF NAZARETH
Also Called: Nazareth House
245 Nova Albion Way, San Rafael (94903-3539)
P.O. Box 165, Fairfield (94533-0165)
PHONE 415 479-8282
Sister Rose Hoye, *Principal*
Sister John Berchmans, *Administration*
EMP: 56 **EST:** 1962
SALES (est): 15.3MM **Privately Held**
WEB: www.sistersofnazareth.com
SIC: 8059 8051 Rest home, with health care; skilled nursing care facilities

(P-16270)
SSC OAKLAND FRUITVALE OPER LP
Also Called: Fruitvale Healthcare Center
3020 E 15th St, Oakland (94601-2305)
PHONE 510 261-5613
Remy Tibayan, *Principal*
Dan Medine, *Executive*
EMP: 99 **EST:** 2000
SALES (est): 6.3MM **Privately Held**
SIC: 8059 8051 Convalescent home; skilled nursing care facilities

(P-16271)
SSC PITTSBURG OPERATING CO LP
Also Called: Diamond Ridge Healthcare Ctr
2351 Loveridge Rd, Pittsburg (94565-5117)
PHONE 925 427-4444
Gisselle Jimenez, *Human Res Dir*
Aman Dhaliwal, *Hlthcr Dir*
Wayne M Sanner,
Mandy Garcia, *Director*
EMP: 166 **EST:** 2011
SALES (est): 13.4MM
SALES (corp-wide): 1.3B **Privately Held**
WEB: www.savaseniorcare.com
SIC: 8059 Nursing home, except skilled & intermediate care facility

HQ: Savaseniorcare, Llc
   8601 Dunwoody Pl
   Atlanta GA 30350
   770 829-5100

(P-16272)
ST FRANCIS EXTENDED CARE INC
718 Bartlett Ave, Hayward (94541-3698)
PHONE 510 785-3630
Sally Rapp, *President*
Roland Rapp, *Vice Pres*
EMP: 50 **EST:** 1965
SQ FT: 13,120
SALES (est): 10.3MM **Privately Held**
SIC: 8059 Convalescent home

(P-16273)
ST FRANCIS HTS CONVALESCENT
35 Escuela Dr, Daly City (94015-4003)
PHONE 650 755-9515
Kordel Erickson, *Administration*
Evelyn Goddard, *Principal*
Kathleen Lovato, *Administration*
Glen Gotter, *Director*
EMP: 72 **EST:** 1967
SQ FT: 12,000
SALES (est): 10.8MM **Privately Held**
WEB: www.lifegen.net
SIC: 8059 8051 Convalescent home; skilled nursing care facilities

(P-16274)
ST JOHNS RETIREMENT VILLAGE
Also Called: Stollwood Convalescent Hosp
135 Woodland Ave, Woodland (95695-2701)
PHONE 530 662-9674
John Prichard, *Administration*
Barbara Fleck, *Manager*
EMP: 142 **EST:** 1964
SALES: 10.8MM **Privately Held**
WEB: www.sjrv.org
SIC: 8059 8051 8361 Convalescent home; convalescent home with continuous nursing care; geriatric residential care

(P-16275)
STOCKTON EDSON HEALTHCARE CORP
Also Called: GOOD SAMARITAN REHAB AND CARE
1630 N Edison St, Stockton (95204-5633)
PHONE 209 948-8762
Emanuel Bernabe, *President*
Gilda Dizon, *Corp Secy*
Sedy Demesa, *Exec VP*
EMP: 100 **EST:** 1988
SQ FT: 4,000
SALES: 9MM **Privately Held**
SIC: 8059 8051 Nursing home, except skilled & intermediate care facility; skilled nursing care facilities

(P-16276)
SUNNY RETIREMENT HOME
22445 Cupertino Rd, Cupertino (95014-1052)
PHONE 408 454-5600
Sally Plank, *Exec Dir*
EMP: 75 **EST:** 1964
SQ FT: 112,000
SALES (est): 16.7MM **Privately Held**
WEB: www.sunny-view.org
SIC: 8059 Rest home, with health care

(P-16277)
THRIVING SENIORS LLC
Also Called: Always Best Care Senior Svcs
479 Mason St Ste 109, Vacaville (95688-4541)
PHONE 707 317-1740
Rebecca Smith, *President*
EMP: 67 **EST:** 2016
SALES (est): 4.2MM **Privately Held**
WEB: www.alwaysbestcare.com
SIC: 8059 Nursing & personal care

(P-16278)
TIMBERLAKE-FORREST INC (PA)
Also Called: California Convalescent Hosp
1133 S Van Ness Ave, San Francisco (94110-3214)
PHONE 415 647-3117
Mary Ellen Forrest, *President*
EMP: 40 **EST:** 1962
SALES (est): 4MM **Privately Held**
SIC: 8059 Convalescent home

(P-16279)
TJD LLC
Also Called: Anberry Rehabilitation Hosp
1685 Shaffer Rd, Atwater (95301-4456)
PHONE 209 357-3420
Donald W Gormly Jr,
Joshua Ooka, *Office Mgr*
Jerry Holloway,
Kathy Brown, *Director*
EMP: 140 **EST:** 2000
SQ FT: 40,000
SALES (est): 11.9MM **Privately Held**
WEB: www.anberryhospital.com
SIC: 8059 8051 8093 Nursing home, except skilled & intermediate care facility; convalescent home with continuous nursing care; rehabilitation center, outpatient treatment

(P-16280)
TRANQUILITY INCORPORATED
Also Called: San Miguel Villa
1050 San Miguel Rd, Concord (94518-2094)
PHONE 925 825-4280
Velda Pierce, *CEO*
EMP: 180 **EST:** 1976
SQ FT: 20,000
SALES (est): 17.3MM **Privately Held**
SIC: 8059 8051 Convalescent home; skilled nursing care facilities

(P-16281)
VACAVLLE CNVALESCENT REHAB CTR
585 Nut Tree Ct, Vacaville (95687-3353)
PHONE 707 449-8000
Joe Nicolli, *President*
EMP: 83 **EST:** 1994
SQ FT: 38,000
SALES (est): 14MM **Privately Held**
SIC: 8059 Convalescent home

(P-16282)
VALLEY WEST HEALTH CARE INC (PA)
Also Called: Valley West Care Center
1224 E St, Williams (95987-5187)
P.O. Box 1059 (95987-1059)
PHONE 530 473-5321
Sharon Jennings, *President*
Gladys Jennings, *CFO*
Grace Oculam,
EMP: 52 **EST:** 1965
SQ FT: 32,000
SALES (est): 6.3MM **Privately Held**
SIC: 8059 Convalescent home

(P-16283)
WESTLAKE DEVELOPMENT GROUP LLC
Also Called: Leisure Gardens Retirement HM
799 Yellowstone Dr Ofc, Vacaville (95687-3470)
PHONE 707 447-7496
EMP: 176
SALES (corp-wide): 17.8MM **Privately Held**
WEB: www.westlake-realty.com
SIC: 8059 Convalescent home
PA: Westlake Development Group, Llc
   520 S El Camino Real # 900
   San Mateo CA 94402
   650 579-1010

(P-16284)
WINDSOR GARDENS HEALTHCARE C
1628 B St, Hayward (94541-3020)
PHONE 510 582-4636
Lee Samson, *CEO*
EMP: 133 **EST:** 1968
SQ FT: 5,000
SALES (est): 8.8MM **Privately Held**
WEB: www.windsorgardenshayward.com
SIC: 8059 Convalescent home
PA: Lexington Group International, Inc
   9200 W Sunset Blvd # 600
   West Hollywood CA 90069

8062 General Medical & Surgical Hospitals

(P-16285)
1125 SIR FRNCIS DRAKE BLVD OPE
Also Called: Kentfield Rehabilitation Hosp
1125 Sir Frncis Drake Blv, Kentfield (94904-1418)
PHONE 415 456-9680
Brad Hollinger,
Denise Mace, *Radiology Dir*
Chris Yarnovich, *Office Mgr*
Robert Lasser, *Psychologist*
Anucheat Chea, *Infectious Dis*
EMP: 250 **EST:** 2003
SALES (est): 35MM
SALES (corp-wide): 759.7MM **Privately Held**
WEB: www.kentfieldhospital.com
SIC: 8062 General medical & surgical hospitals
PA: Vibra Healthcare, Llc
   4600 Lena Dr Ste 100
   Mechanicsburg PA 17055
   717 591-5700

(P-16286)
ADVENTIST HEALTH SELMA
Also Called: Urgent Care-Selma Dst Hosp
1141 Rose Ave, Selma (93662-3241)
PHONE 559 891-1000
Wayne Ferch, *President*
Lena Madrigal, *Executive*
Michael Aubry, *CIO*
Christine Pickering, *Pub Rel Dir*
James C Forsythe, *Radiology*
EMP: 339 **EST:** 1962
SQ FT: 67,000
SALES (est): 33.1MM **Privately Held**
WEB: www.adventisthealth.org
SIC: 8062 8051 General medical & surgical hospitals; skilled nursing care facilities

(P-16287)
ADVENTIST HEALTH SONORA
179 Fairview Ln, Sonora (95370-4809)
PHONE 209 536-5000
Gideon P Naude, *Surgeon*
EMP: 37
SALES (corp-wide): 4.5B **Privately Held**
WEB: www.adventisthealth.org
SIC: 8062 General medical & surgical hospitals
HQ: Adventist Health Sonora
   1000 Greenley Rd
   Sonora CA 95370
   209 532-5000

(P-16288)
ADVENTIST HEALTH SONORA
690 Guzzi Ln Ste A, Sonora (95370-5292)
PHONE 209 536-5070
EMP: 37
SALES (corp-wide): 4.5B **Privately Held**
WEB: www.adventisthealth.org
SIC: 8062 General medical & surgical hospitals
HQ: Adventist Health Sonora
   1000 Greenley Rd
   Sonora CA 95370
   209 532-5000

(P-16289)
ADVENTIST HEALTH SONORA
680 Guzzi Ln, Sonora (95370-5288)
PHONE 209 532-0126
EMP: 37
SALES (corp-wide): 4.5B **Privately Held**
WEB: www.adventisthealth.org
SIC: 8062 General medical & surgical hospitals

PRODUCTS & SERVICES SECTION **8062 - General Medical & Surgical Hospitals County (P-16310)**

HQ: Adventist Health Sonora
1000 Greenley Rd
Sonora CA 95370
209 532-5000

(P-16290)
ADVENTIST HEALTH SONORA
14540 Mono Way, Sonora (95370-8858)
PHONE..................209 532-3167
David Larsen, *Vice Pres*
Robert W Lyons, *Med Doctor*
EMP: 37
SALES (corp-wide): 4.5B Privately Held
WEB: www.adventisthealth.org
SIC: 8062 General medical & surgical hospitals
HQ: Adventist Health Sonora
1000 Greenley Rd
Sonora CA 95370
209 532-5000

(P-16291)
ADVENTIST HEALTH SONORA
Also Called: Arnold Family Medical Center
2037 Hwy 4, Arnold (95223-9420)
P.O. Box 67 (95223-0067)
PHONE..................209 795-1270
EMP: 37
SALES (corp-wide): 4.5B Privately Held
WEB: www.adventisthealth.org
SIC: 8062 General medical & surgical hospitals
HQ: Adventist Health Sonora
1000 Greenley Rd
Sonora CA 95370
209 532-5000

(P-16292)
ADVENTIST HEALTH SONORA (HQ)
1000 Greenley Rd, Sonora (95370-5200)
PHONE..................209 532-5000
Michelle Fuentes, *President*
David Larsen, *CFO*
Greg McCulloch, *CFO*
Julie Kline, *Vice Pres*
Lynn Bradshaw, *Administration*
EMP: 712 EST: 1957
SQ FT: 60,000
SALES: 267MM
SALES (corp-wide): 4.5B Privately Held
WEB: www.adventisthealth.org
SIC: 8062 8051 General medical & surgical hospitals; skilled nursing care facilities
PA: Adventist Health System/West, Corporation
1 Adventist Health Way
Roseville CA 95661
844 574-5686

(P-16293)
ADVENTIST HEALTH SONORA
680 Guzzi Ln Ste 101, Sonora (95370-5288)
PHONE..................209 536-5770
EMP: 37
SALES (corp-wide): 4.5B Privately Held
WEB: www.adventisthealth.org
SIC: 8062 General medical & surgical hospitals
HQ: Adventist Health Sonora
1000 Greenley Rd
Sonora CA 95370
209 532-5000

(P-16294)
ADVENTIST HEALTH SONORA
14542 Lolly Ln, Sonora (95370-9226)
PHONE..................209 536-3900
Arturo Rivera, *Facilities Dir*
EMP: 37
SALES (corp-wide): 4.5B Privately Held
WEB: www.adventisthealth.org
SIC: 8062 General medical & surgical hospitals
HQ: Adventist Health Sonora
1000 Greenley Rd
Sonora CA 95370
209 532-5000

(P-16295)
ADVENTIST HEALTH SONORA
Also Called: Hillside Internal Medicine
690 Guzzi Ln Ste B, Sonora (95370-5292)
PHONE..................209 536-5060
EMP: 37

SALES (corp-wide): 4.5B Privately Held
WEB: www.adventisthealth.org
SIC: 8062 General medical & surgical hospitals
HQ: Adventist Health Sonora
1000 Greenley Rd
Sonora CA 95370
209 532-5000

(P-16296)
ADVENTIST HEALTH SONORA
Also Called: Greenley Primary Care Center
1000 Greenley Rd, Sonora (95370-5200)
PHONE..................209 536-2665
Byron Palmer MD, *Principal*
Tim Colwell, *Controller*
Kathrina McRee, *Recruiter*
Bruce Kennedy, *Education*
EMP: 37
SALES (corp-wide): 4.5B Privately Held
WEB: www.adventisthealth.org
SIC: 8062 8011 General medical & surgical hospitals; general & family practice, physician/surgeon
HQ: Adventist Health Sonora
1000 Greenley Rd
Sonora CA 95370
209 532-5000

(P-16297)
ADVENTIST HEALTH SYSTEM/WEST
111 Raley Blvd, Chico (95928-8351)
PHONE..................530 342-4576
EMP: 61
SALES (corp-wide): 4.5B Privately Held
WEB: www.adventisthealth.org
SIC: 8062 General medical & surgical hospitals
PA: Adventist Health System/West, Corporation
1 Adventist Health Way
Roseville CA 95661
844 574-5686

(P-16298)
ADVENTIST HEALTH SYSTEM/WEST
18990 Coyote Valley Rd # 11, Hidden Valley Lake (95467-8337)
PHONE..................707 987-8344
EMP: 61
SALES (corp-wide): 4.5B Privately Held
WEB: www.adventisthealth.org
SIC: 8062 General medical & surgical hospitals
PA: Adventist Health System/West, Corporation
1 Adventist Health Way
Roseville CA 95661
844 574-5686

(P-16299)
ADVENTIST HEALTH SYSTEM/WEST
Also Called: Adventst Hlth Cmmnty Cre-or
1455 Park Blvd, Orange Cove (93646-9322)
PHONE..................559 626-0882
Wayne Ferch, *CEO*
EMP: 61
SALES (corp-wide): 4.5B Privately Held
WEB: www.adventisthealth.org
SIC: 8062 General medical & surgical hospitals
PA: Adventist Health System/West, Corporation
1 Adventist Health Way
Roseville CA 95661
844 574-5686

(P-16300)
ADVENTIST HEALTH SYSTEM/WEST
Also Called: Rehabilitation Services
1000 Greenley Rd, Sonora (95370-5200)
PHONE..................209 532-3161
EMP: 61
SALES (corp-wide): 4.5B Privately Held
WEB: www.adventisthealth.org
SIC: 8062 General medical & surgical hospitals

PA: Adventist Health System/West, Corporation
1 Adventist Health Way
Roseville CA 95661
844 574-5686

(P-16301)
ADVENTIST HEALTH SYSTEM/WEST
501 E St Ste B, Williams (95987-5810)
PHONE..................530 473-5641
Kirby McKague, *Branch Mgr*
EMP: 61
SALES (corp-wide): 4.5B Privately Held
WEB: www.adventisthealth.org
SIC: 8062 General medical & surgical hospitals
PA: Adventist Health System/West, Corporation
1 Adventist Health Way
Roseville CA 95661
844 574-5686

(P-16302)
ADVENTIST HEALTH SYSTEM/WEST
13808 Mono Way, Sonora (95370-8864)
PHONE..................209 536-5043
EMP: 61
SALES (corp-wide): 4.5B Privately Held
WEB: www.adventisthealth.org
SIC: 8062 General medical & surgical hospitals
PA: Adventist Health System/West, Corporation
1 Adventist Health Way
Roseville CA 95661
844 574-5686

(P-16303)
ADVENTIST HLTH CLRLAKE HOSP IN (HQ)
Also Called: Saint Helena Hosp Clearlake
15630 18th Ave, Clearlake (95422-9336)
PHONE..................707 994-6486
David Santos, *CEO*
Carlton Jacobson, *CFO*
Meredith Jobe, *Admin Sec*
Vlad Toca, *Opers Mgr*
Michael Shepherd, *Obstetrician*
EMP: 287 EST: 1968
SQ FT: 41,750
SALES (est): 101MM
SALES (corp-wide): 4.5B Privately Held
WEB: www.adventisthealth.org
SIC: 8062 8011 Hospital, affiliated with AMA residency; medical centers
PA: Adventist Health System/West, Corporation
1 Adventist Health Way
Roseville CA 95661
844 574-5686

(P-16304)
ADVENTIST HLTH CLRLAKE HOSP IN
15140 Lakeshore Dr, Clearlake (95422-8106)
PHONE..................707 994-6486
Nancy Bailey, *Manager*
EMP: 199
SALES (corp-wide): 4.5B Privately Held
WEB: www.adventisthealth.org
SIC: 8062 8071 General medical & surgical hospitals; medical laboratories
HQ: Adventist Health Clearlake Hospital, Inc.
15630 18th Ave
Clearlake CA 95422
707 994-6486

(P-16305)
ADVENTIST HLTH SYSTM/WEST CORP
Also Called: Central Vly Fmly Hlth-Slma Cnt
2141 High St Ste E, Selma (93662-3065)
PHONE..................559 856-6110
Kirby McKague, *Branch Mgr*
EMP: 61
SALES (corp-wide): 4.5B Privately Held
WEB: www.adventisthealth.org
SIC: 8062 General medical & surgical hospitals

PA: Adventist Health System/West, Corporation
1 Adventist Health Way
Roseville CA 95661
844 574-5686

(P-16306)
ADVENTIST HLTH SYSTM/WEST CORP
Also Called: Adventist Hlth Cmnty Cr-Prlier
155 S Newmark Ave, Parlier (93648-2531)
PHONE..................559 646-1200
EMP: 61
SALES (corp-wide): 4.5B Privately Held
WEB: www.adventisthealth.org
SIC: 8062 General medical & surgical hospitals
PA: Adventist Health System/West, Corporation
1 Adventist Health Way
Roseville CA 95661
844 574-5686

(P-16307)
ADVENTIST HLTH SYSTM/WEST CORP
11976 Road 37, Madera (93636-8612)
PHONE..................559 645-4191
EMP: 61
SALES (corp-wide): 4.5B Privately Held
WEB: www.adventisthealth.org
SIC: 8062 General medical & surgical hospitals
PA: Adventist Health System/West, Corporation
1 Adventist Health Way
Roseville CA 95661
844 574-5686

(P-16308)
ADVENTIST HLTH SYSTM/WEST CORP
300 S Leon S. Peters Blvd, Fowler (93625-2538)
PHONE..................559 834-1614
Irma Carbajal, *Branch Mgr*
EMP: 61
SALES (corp-wide): 4.5B Privately Held
WEB: www.adventisthealth.org
SIC: 8062 General medical & surgical hospitals
PA: Adventist Health System/West, Corporation
1 Adventist Health Way
Roseville CA 95661
844 574-5686

(P-16309)
ADVENTIST HLTH SYSTM/WEST CORP
14880 Olympic Dr, Clearlake (95422-9521)
P.O. Box 6710 (95422-6710)
PHONE..................707 995-4888
Patricia Van Horn, *Manager*
Ferdinand Buot, *Exec Dir*
Ron Ryskalczyk, *Sales Staff*
Allyne Brown, *Director*
EMP: 61
SALES (corp-wide): 4.5B Privately Held
WEB: www.adventisthealth.org
SIC: 8062 General medical & surgical hospitals
PA: Adventist Health System/West, Corporation
1 Adventist Health Way
Roseville CA 95661
844 574-5686

(P-16310)
ADVENTIST HLTH SYSTM/WEST CORP (PA)
1 Adventist Health Way, Roseville (95661-3266)
P.O. Box 619002 (95661-9002)
PHONE..................844 574-5686
Kerry Heinrich, *CEO*
Carrie Bannister, *President*
Roland Fargo, *President*
Michelle Fuentes, *President*
Andrew Jahn, *President*
EMP: 350 EST: 1973
SQ FT: 55,000

8062 - General Medical & Surgical Hospitals County (P-16311)

SALES (est): 4.5B **Privately Held**
WEB: www.adventisthealth.org
SIC: **8062** General medical & surgical hospitals

(P-16311)
ADVENTIST HLTH SYSTM/WEST CORP
Also Called: Central Vly Fmly Hlth-Cruthers
2440 W Tahoe Ave, Caruthers (93609-9476)
PHONE.................................559 864-3212
EMP: 61
SALES (corp-wide): 4.5B **Privately Held**
WEB: www.adventisthealth.org
SIC: **8062** General medical & surgical hospitals
PA: Adventist Health System/West, Corporation
1 Adventist Health Way
Roseville CA 95661
844 574-5686

(P-16312)
ADVENTIST HLTH SYSTM/WEST CORP
Also Called: Clearlake Family Health Center
15230 Lakeshore Dr, Clearlake (95422-8107)
PHONE.................................707 995-4500
Ilona Horton, *Director*
Luis Diaz, *Pediatrics*
Alyssa Hempel, *Manager*
EMP: 61
SALES (corp-wide): 4.5B **Privately Held**
WEB: www.adventisthealth.org
SIC: **8062** General medical & surgical hospitals
PA: Adventist Health System/West, Corporation
1 Adventist Health Way
Roseville CA 95661
844 574-5686

(P-16313)
ADVENTIST HLTH SYSTM/WEST CORP
Also Called: Central Vly Fmly Health-Kerman
1000 S Madera Ave, Kerman (93630-1750)
PHONE.................................559 846-9370
Anna Marie Gonzalez, *Branch Mgr*
EMP: 61
SALES (corp-wide): 4.5B **Privately Held**
WEB: www.adventisthealth.org
SIC: **8062** General medical & surgical hospitals
PA: Adventist Health System/West, Corporation
1 Adventist Health Way
Roseville CA 95661
844 574-5686

(P-16314)
ADVENTIST HLTH SYSTM/WEST CORP
Also Called: Central Vly Fmly Health-Sanger
1939 Academy Ave, Sanger (93657-3737)
PHONE.................................559 875-6900
Rosemary Rusca, *Manager*
Darla Seher, *Supervisor*
EMP: 61
SALES (corp-wide): 4.5B **Privately Held**
WEB: www.adventisthealth.org
SIC: **8062** General medical & surgical hospitals
PA: Adventist Health System/West, Corporation
1 Adventist Health Way
Roseville CA 95661
844 574-5686

(P-16315)
ADVENTIST HLTH SYSTM/WEST CORP
Also Called: Central Vly Fmly Health-Selma
1041 Rose Ave, Selma (93662-3240)
PHONE.................................559 856-6090
Diane Smith, *Branch Mgr*
Ye Min, *Family Practiti*
Joe McCracken, *Supervisor*
EMP: 61
SALES (corp-wide): 4.5B **Privately Held**
WEB: www.adventisthealth.org
SIC: **8062** General medical & surgical hospitals
PA: Adventist Health System/West, Corporation
1 Adventist Health Way
Roseville CA 95661
844 574-5686

(P-16316)
ADVENTIST HLTH SYSTM/WEST CORP
Also Called: St Helena Hospital Clearlake
18th Ave Hwy 53, Clearlake (95422)
PHONE.................................707 994-6486
Kendall Fults, *CEO*
Colleen Assavapisitkul, *Officer*
Wendi Fox, *Marketing Staff*
Patricia Rutherford, *Director*
EMP: 61
SALES (corp-wide): 4.5B **Privately Held**
WEB: www.adventisthealth.org
SIC: **8062** General medical & surgical hospitals
PA: Adventist Health System/West, Corporation
1 Adventist Health Way
Roseville CA 95661
844 574-5686

(P-16317)
ADVENTIST HLTH SYSTM/WEST CORP
20100 Cedar Rd N, Sonora (95370-5925)
PHONE.................................209 536-5700
EMP: 61
SALES (corp-wide): 4.5B **Privately Held**
WEB: www.adventisthealth.org
SIC: **8062** General medical & surgical hospitals
PA: Adventist Health System/West, Corporation
1 Adventist Health Way
Roseville CA 95661
844 574-5686

(P-16318)
ADVINTIST HLTH CLEARLAKE HOSP
Also Called: St Helana Hospital Clearlake
18th Ave & Hwy 53, Clearlake (95422)
PHONE.................................707 994-6486
Terry Newmeyer, *CEO*
Jeniffer Swenson, *Vice Pres*
EMP: 85 EST: 1975
SQ FT: 62,000
SALES (est): 3.4MM **Privately Held**
WEB: www.adventisthealth.org
SIC: **8062** General medical & surgical hospitals

(P-16319)
AMADOR VLY MED GROUP LTD A CA
Also Called: Amador Valley Medical Clinic
3253 Patina Ct, Tracy (95377-6664)
PHONE.................................925 828-9211
Edmund Kemprud MD, *Partner*
EMP: 55 EST: 1983
SALES (est): 2.6MM **Privately Held**
SIC: **8062** General medical & surgical hospitals

(P-16320)
AMERICAN HOSPITAL MGT CORP (PA)
Also Called: Mad River Community Hospital
3800 Janes Rd, Arcata (95521-4742)
P.O. Box 1115 (95518-1115)
PHONE.................................707 822-3621
Allen E Shaw, *President*
Michael Young, *CFO*
Doug A Shaw, *Vice Pres*
Charles F Forbes, *Admin Sec*
Pamela Floyd, *QA Dir*
EMP: 500 EST: 1955
SQ FT: 60,000
SALES (est): 87.3MM **Privately Held**
WEB: www.madriverhospital.com
SIC: **8062** General medical & surgical hospitals

(P-16321)
AMERICAN HOSPITAL MGT CORP
4605 Valley West Blvd, Arcata (95521-4635)
PHONE.................................707 826-8420
EMP: 45
SALES (corp-wide): 59.4MM **Privately Held**
SIC: **8062** 8322 General Hospital Individual/Family Services
PA: American Hospital Management Corporation
3800 Janes Rd.
Arcata CA 95521
707 822-3621

(P-16322)
AUBURN OTPTENT SRGERY DGNSTC C
Also Called: Auburn Surgery Center
3123 Prfcional Dr Ste 100, Auburn (95603)
PHONE.................................530 888-8899
Richard Lewis, *Manager*
EMP: 70 EST: 1989
SQ FT: 16,000
SALES (est): 6.3MM **Privately Held**
SIC: **8062** General medical & surgical hospitals

(P-16323)
BANNER HEALTH
1800 Spring Ridge Dr, Susanville (96130-6100)
PHONE.................................530 251-3147
Molly Jones, *Technician*
Paul Holmes, *Gnrl Med Prac*
Sharon Almeida,
Karen Gardella,
Lindsey Larson,
EMP: 124
SALES (corp-wide): 10.4B **Privately Held**
WEB: www.bannerhealth.com
SIC: **8062** General medical & surgical hospitals
PA: Banner Health
7251 W 4th St
Greeley CO 80634
602 747-4000

(P-16324)
BANNER LSSEN MED CTR FNDTION I
1800 Spring Ridge Dr, Susanville (96130-6100)
PHONE.................................530 252-2000
Bob Edwards, *CEO*
Kearstin Anderson, *Records Dir*
Michele Harrison, *Ch of Bd*
Shelby Diede, *CFO*
Phyllis Doulaveris, *Ch Nursing Ofcr*
EMP: 200 EST: 1996
SALES (est): 15.6MM **Privately Held**
WEB: www.bannerhealth.com
SIC: **8062** 8051 General medical & surgical hospitals; skilled nursing care facilities

(P-16325)
BARTON MEMORIAL HOSPITAL (HQ)
2170 South Ave, South Lake Tahoe (96150-7008)
P.O. Box 9578 (96158-9578)
PHONE.................................530 541-3420
Clint Purvance, *President*
Dick Derby, *CFO*
Rhonda Sneeringer, *Chief Mktg Ofcr*
Julie Clayton, *Officer*
Sue Fairley, *Vice Pres*
EMP: 535 EST: 1980
SALES: 117.9MM
SALES (corp-wide): 179.5MM **Privately Held**
WEB: www.bartonhealth.org
SIC: **8062** 8051 General medical & surgical hospitals; skilled nursing care facilities
PA: Barton Healthcare System
2170 South Ave
South Lake Tahoe CA 96150
530 541-3420

(P-16326)
CARDIVSCLAR MDCINE CRNARY INTR
2900 Whipple Ave Ste 230, Redwood City (94062-2852)
PHONE.................................650 306-2300
John B Simpson MD, *Director*
Tomoaki Hinohara, *President*
Bruce J McAuley MD, *CFO*
Gloria Villarreal, *Administration*
Mary Larson, *Cardiovascular*
EMP: 104 EST: 1991
SALES (est): 8.7MM **Privately Held**
WEB: www.dignityhealth.org
SIC: **8062** General medical & surgical hospitals

(P-16327)
CAREMORE HEALTH PLAN
4855 Atherton Ave, San Jose (95130-1026)
PHONE.................................408 963-2400
EMP: 35
SALES (corp-wide): 121.8B **Publicly Held**
WEB: www.caremore.com
SIC: **8062** General medical & surgical hospitals
HQ: Caremore Health Plan
12900 Park Plaza Dr # 150
Cerritos CA 90703
562 622-2950

(P-16328)
CENTRAL VLY SPECIALTY HOSP INC
730 17th St, Modesto (95354-1209)
PHONE.................................209 248-7700
Gia Smith, *CEO*
Kim Cuevas, *Records Dir*
Helen Noh, *Pharmacy Dir*
Prashil Prasad, *Security Dir*
Reyle Hutchins, *Analyst*
EMP: 123 EST: 2012
SALES (est): 53.7MM **Privately Held**
WEB: www.centralvalleyspecialty.com
SIC: **8062** General medical & surgical hospitals

(P-16329)
CHILDRENS HOSP RES CTR AT OKLA (PA)
Also Called: UCSF BENIOFF CHILDREN'S HOSPITAL
747 52nd St, Oakland (94609-1809)
PHONE.................................510 428-3000
Matthew Cook, *President*
Harold Davis, *Ch of Bd*
Kathleen Cain, *CFO*
Rina Smith, *CFO*
Betsy Biern, *Senior VP*
EMP: 1900 EST: 1912
SQ FT: 160,000
SALES: 661.6MM **Privately Held**
WEB: www.childrenshospitaloakland.org
SIC: **8062** Hospital, AMA approved residency

(P-16330)
CHINESE HOSPITAL ASSOCIATION (PA)
845 Jackson St, San Francisco (94133-4899)
PHONE.................................415 982-2400
Brenda Yee, *CEO*
Irwin Chow,
Roger Eng, *Ch Radiology*
Linda Schumacher, *COO*
Thomas Bolger, *CFO*
EMP: 279 EST: 1923
SQ FT: 54,000
SALES: 207.6B **Privately Held**
WEB: www.chinesehospital.com
SIC: **8062** General medical & surgical hospitals

(P-16331)
CHW MRCY MRCED CMNTY HOSP KIDS
Also Called: Kids Care
1260 D St, Merced (95341-6248)
PHONE.................................209 564-4500
Alicia Bolke, *Manager*
EMP: 38 EST: 2006
SALES (est): 4.7MM **Privately Held**
WEB: www.dignityhealth.org
SIC: **8062** General medical & surgical hospitals
HQ: Dignity Health
185 Berry St Ste 200
San Francisco CA 94107
415 438-5500

PRODUCTS & SERVICES SECTION

8062 - General Medical & Surgical Hospitals County (P-16351)

(P-16332)
CITY & COUNTY OF SAN FRANCISCO
Also Called: San Francisco General Hospital
1001 Potrero Ave, San Francisco (94110-3518)
PHONE 415 206-8000
Susan Currin, *Principal*
Mark Wilson, *Ch Radiology*
Sarah Haynes, *Principal*
Jean O'Connel, *Principal*
Basil Price, *Security Dir*
EMP: 8000
SALES (corp-wide): 7.1B **Privately Held**
WEB: www.sf.gov
SIC: **8062** General medical & surgical hospitals
PA: City & County Of San Francisco
   1 Dr Carlton B Goodlett P
   San Francisco CA 94102
   415 554-7500

(P-16333)
CITY ALAMEDA HEALTH CARE CORP
Also Called: Alameda Hospital
2070 Clinton Ave, Alameda (94501-4399)
PHONE 510 522-3700
Deborah E Stebbins, *CEO*
Laura Condon, *Records Dir*
Luis Fonseca, *COO*
Kimberly Miranda, *CFO*
Ghassan Jamaleddine, *Chief Mktg Ofcr*
EMP: 520 EST: 1894
SQ FT: 150,000
SALES (est): 112.9MM **Privately Held**
WEB: www.alamedahealthsystem.org
SIC: **8062** 8051 General medical & surgical hospitals; skilled nursing care facilities

(P-16334)
COALINGA REGIONAL MED CTR AUX
Also Called: Crmc
1191 Phelps Ave, Coalinga (93210-9609)
PHONE 559 935-6400
Sharon A Spurgen, *CEO*
Sandy Beach, *President*
Sandra Earls, *CFO*
Mark Gritton, *Vice Pres*
Catherine Underwood, *Vice Pres*
EMP: 230 EST: 1947
SQ FT: 60,000
SALES: 20.1MM
SALES (corp-wide): 4.5B **Privately Held**
WEB: www.coalingamedicalcenter.com
SIC: **8062** 8051 Hospital, affiliated with AMA residency; skilled nursing care facilities
PA: Adventist Health System/West, Corporation
   1 Adventist Health Way
   Roseville CA 95661
   844 574-5686

(P-16335)
COMMUNITY HOSPITALS CENTL CAL (PA)
Also Called: COMMUNITY HEALTH SYSTEM
2823 Fresno St, Fresno (93721-1324)
P.O. Box 1232 (93715-1232)
PHONE 559 459-6000
Tim A Joslin, *CEO*
Gordon Webster Jr, *Vice Chairman*
Phyllis Baltz, *COO*
Craig S Castro, *COO*
Tracy Kiritani, *CFO*
EMP: 3400 EST: 1945
SQ FT: 200,000
SALES: 1.8B **Privately Held**
WEB: www.communitymedical.org
SIC: **8062** 8011 8051 General medical & surgical hospitals; ambulatory surgical center; extended care facility

(P-16336)
COMMUNITY HOSPITALS CENTL CAL
Also Called: Community Regional Medical Ctr
2823 Fresno St, Fresno (93721-1324)
PHONE 559 459-6000
Tim Joslin, *President*
Matt Joslin, *Vice Pres*
Jonathan Miller, *Vice Pres*
Ed Hughes, *Administration*
Michael Bailey, *Planning*
EMP: 1000 EST: 1982
SALES: 1.5B **Privately Held**
WEB: www.communitymedical.org
SIC: **8062** General medical & surgical hospitals

(P-16337)
COMMUNITY MEDICAL CENTER
Also Called: Clovis Community Living
3003 N Mariposa St, Fresno (93703-1127)
PHONE 559 222-7416
EMP: 150
SALES (corp-wide): 1.6B **Privately Held**
SIC: **8062** 8051 Hospital Skilled Nursing Care Facility
PA: Community Hospitals Of Central California
   2823 Fresno St
   Fresno CA 93721
   559 459-6000

(P-16338)
COUNTY OF ALAMEDA
Also Called: Fairmont Hospital-Regist
15400 Foothill Blvd, San Leandro (94578-1009)
PHONE 510 895-4200
Michael Wall, *President*
Paul Schwarz,
Leeann Schierburg, *Records Dir*
David Cox, *CFO*
Feuy S Saechao, *Lab Dir*
EMP: 58 **Privately Held**
WEB: www.acgov.org
SIC: **8062** 9431 General medical & surgical hospitals; administration of public health programs;
PA: County Of Alameda
   1221 Oak St Ste 555
   Oakland CA 94612
   510 272-6691

(P-16339)
COUNTY OF CONTRA COSTA
Also Called: Department of Health Services
2500 Alhambra Ave, Martinez (94553-3156)
PHONE 925 370-5000
Jeff Smith, *CEO*
Robert Liebig, *Ch Radiology*
Donna Page, *Records Dir*
Anna Roth, *Officer*
Xiaohui Xiong, *Lab Dir*
EMP: 200
SALES (corp-wide): 2.5B **Privately Held**
WEB: www.cc-courts.org
SIC: **8062** 9431 General medical & surgical hospitals; administration of public health programs;
PA: County Of Contra Costa
   625 Court St Ste 100
   Martinez CA 94553
   925 957-5280

(P-16340)
COUNTY OF SONOMA
Also Called: Palm Drive Healthcare District
501 Petaluma Ave, Sebastopol (95472-4215)
PHONE 707 823-8511
Shawndra Nimtz, *CEO*
EMP: 200
SQ FT: 3,684
SALES (corp-wide): 1B **Privately Held**
WEB: www.sonomacounty.ca.gov
SIC: **8062** 8051 General medical & surgical hospitals; skilled nursing care facilities
PA: County Of Sonoma
   585 Fiscal Dr 100
   Santa Rosa CA 95403
   707 565-2431

(P-16341)
COUNTY OF STANISLAUS
Also Called: Stanislaus Medical Center
830 Scenic Dr, Modesto (95350-6131)
P.O. Box 3271 (95353-3271)
PHONE 209 525-7000
Beverly M Finley, *Manager*
Marcia Cunningham, *Info Tech Dir*
Marty Rojas, *Accountant*
Baris Kourdou, *Teacher*
Nancy Brown, *Pediatrics*
EMP: 164
SQ FT: 1,866
SALES (corp-wide): 1.2B **Privately Held**
WEB: www.stancounty.com
SIC: **8062** General medical & surgical hospitals
PA: County Of Stanislaus
   1010 10th St Ste 5100
   Modesto CA 95354
   209 525-6398

(P-16342)
COVENANT CARE CALIFORNIA LLC
Also Called: Grant-Cuesta Nursing Center
1949 Grant Rd, Mountain View (94040-3217)
PHONE 650 964-0543
Cheryl Cartney, *Branch Mgr*
April Linaac, *Records Dir*
Katya Kim, *Manager*
EMP: 55 **Privately Held**
WEB: www.covenantcare.com
SIC: **8062** 8051 8069 General medical & surgical hospitals; skilled nursing care facilities; specialty hospitals, except psychiatric
HQ: Covenant Care California, Llc
   120 Vantis Dr Ste 200
   Aliso Viejo CA 92656

(P-16343)
COVENANT LIVING WEST
Also Called: Brandel Manor
1801 N Olive Ave, Turlock (95382-2568)
PHONE 209 667-5600
Dawn Sughruel, *Director*
Jennifer Ribeiro, *Technology*
Jana Mitchell, *Director*
Julia Bava, *Manager*
EMP: 100
SQ FT: 58,282 **Privately Held**
WEB: www.covliving.org
SIC: **8062** 8051 General medical & surgical hospitals; convalescent home with continuous nursing care
HQ: Covenant Living West
   5700 Old Orchard Rd # 10
   Skokie IL 60077

(P-16344)
DAMERON HOSPITAL ASSOCIATION (HQ)
525 W Acacia St, Stockton (95203-2484)
PHONE 209 944-5550
Daniel Wolcott, *President*
Melanie Parker,
Michael Glasberg, *COO*
Susan Engelke, *CFO*
Elizabeth Propp, *CFO*
EMP: 987 EST: 1943
SQ FT: 136,061
SALES (est): 187.5MM
SALES (corp-wide): 4.5B **Privately Held**
WEB: www.dameronhospital.org
SIC: **8062** General medical & surgical hospitals
PA: Adventist Health System/West, Corporation
   1 Adventist Health Way
   Roseville CA 95661
   844 574-5686

(P-16345)
DAVIS UC MEDICAL CENTER
Also Called: Care Management Services
4800 2nd Ave 3010, Sacramento (95817-2216)
PHONE 916 734-2011
Janet Heath, *President*
Shinjiro Hirose, *Vice Chairman*
Janice Bramson, *Program Mgr*
Stacy Hevener, *Nursing Mgr*
Mary Cardiff, *Admin Asst*
EMP: 274 EST: 2012
SALES (est): 269.5MM **Privately Held**
WEB: www.ucdavis.edu
SIC: **8062** General medical & surgical hospitals

(P-16346)
DIGNITY COMMUNITY CARE (PA)
185 Berry St Ste 300, San Francisco (94107-1773)
PHONE 415 438-5500
Lloyd H Dean, *CEO*
Marvin Oquinn, *President*
Kevin E Lofton, *CEO*
Daniel Morissette, *CFO*
Elizabeth Shih, *Executive*
EMP: 40 EST: 2017
SALES (est): 22.1MM **Privately Held**
WEB: www.dignityhealth.org
SIC: **8062** General medical & surgical hospitals

(P-16347)
DIGNITY HEALTH (HQ)
185 Berry St Ste 200, San Francisco (94101-1777)
PHONE 415 438-5500
Lloyd Dean, *President*
Marvin O'Quinn, *COO*
Michael Blaszyk, *CFO*
Lisa Zuckerman, *Treasurer*
Kevin E Lofton, *Co-CEO*
▲ EMP: 120 EST: 1954
SALES: 9.9B **Privately Held**
WEB: www.dignityhealth.org
SIC: **8062** General medical & surgical hospitals

(P-16348)
DIGNITY HEALTH
Also Called: Mercy San Juan Medical Center
6501 Coyle Ave, Carmichael (95608-0306)
PHONE 916 537-5000
Rian Ivie, *Director*
Cecilia Sandoval, *Human Res Dir*
Lucinda Wiseman, *Oncology*
Jacob A Bair, *Emerg Med Spec*
Natalie Hoover, *Emerg Med Spec*
EMP: 1500 **Privately Held**
WEB: www.dignityhealth.org
SIC: **8062** 8011 General medical & surgical hospitals; offices & clinics of medical doctors
HQ: Dignity Health
   185 Berry St Ste 200
   San Francisco CA 94107
   415 438-5500

(P-16349)
DIGNITY HEALTH
Also Called: Methodist Hospital Sacramento
7500 Hospital Dr, Sacramento (95823-5403)
PHONE 916 423-5940
William J Hunt, *Principal*
Kip Virts,
Charlene Almocera, *Records Dir*
Jennifer Velez, *Officer*
Chris Champlin, *Vice Pres*
EMP: 193 **Privately Held**
WEB: www.dignityhealth.org
SIC: **8062** General medical & surgical hospitals
HQ: Dignity Health
   185 Berry St Ste 200
   San Francisco CA 94107
   415 438-5500

(P-16350)
DIGNITY HEALTH
Also Called: St. Mary's Medical Center
450 Stanyan St, San Francisco (94117-1019)
PHONE 415 668-1000
John Allen, *President*
Quezada Amber, *Executive Asst*
Christine Gonzalez, *Executive Asst*
Jennean Rogers, *Administration*
Mike Waltman, *Info Tech Mgr*
EMP: 1100 **Privately Held**
WEB: www.dignityhealth.org
SIC: **8062** 8322 General medical & surgical hospitals; adult day care center
HQ: Dignity Health
   185 Berry St Ste 200
   San Francisco CA 94107
   415 438-5500

(P-16351)
DIGNITY HEALTH MED FOUNDATION
Also Called: Dignity Hlth Med Group - Dmnca
1667 Dominican Way # 134, Santa Cruz (95065-1518)
PHONE 831 475-8834
George Lenzi, *CFO*
EMP: 74 **Privately Held**
WEB: www.dignityhealth.org

8062 - General Medical & Surgical Hospitals County (P-16352)

SIC: 8062 General medical & surgical hospitals
HQ: Dignity Health Medical Foundation
3400 Data Dr
Rancho Cordova CA 95670

(P-16352)
DIGNITY HEALTH MED FOUNDATION
Also Called: Dignity Hlth Med Grp-Dominican
3400 Data Dr, Rancho Cordova (95670-7956)
PHONE.................................916 379-2840
Laurie Schwarctz, *President*
EMP: 74
SQ FT: 45,000 **Privately Held**
WEB: www.dignityhealth.org
SIC: 8062 General medical & surgical hospitals
HQ: Dignity Health Medical Foundation
3400 Data Dr
Rancho Cordova CA 95670

(P-16353)
DIGNITY HEALTH MED FOUNDATION
9837 Folsom Blvd Ste F, Sacramento (95827-1356)
PHONE.................................916 450-2600
EMP: 74 **Privately Held**
WEB: www.dignityhealth.org
SIC: 8062 General medical & surgical hospitals
HQ: Dignity Health Medical Foundation
3400 Data Dr
Rancho Cordova CA 95670

(P-16354)
DIGNITY HEALTH MED FOUNDATION (DH)
Also Called: Dignity Hlth Med Grp-Dominican
3400 Data Dr, Rancho Cordova (95670-7956)
PHONE.................................916 379-2840
Laurie Schwarctz, *President*
Theresa Hylen, *CFO*
Sherry Penlesky, *Admin Asst*
Erik Eklund, *Technology*
Sonja Greene, *Financial Analy*
EMP: 200
SQ FT: 45,000
SALES: 570.1MM **Privately Held**
WEB: www.dignityhealth.org
SIC: 8062 General medical & surgical hospitals
HQ: Dignity Health
185 Berry St Ste 300
San Francisco CA 94107
415 438-5500

(P-16355)
DIGNITY HEALTH MED FOUNDATION
Also Called: Dominican Medical Foundation
1595 Soquel Dr Ste 140, Santa Cruz (95065-1717)
PHONE.................................831 475-1111
Michael Walsh, *Branch Mgr*
EMP: 74 **Privately Held**
WEB: www.dignityhealth.org
SIC: 8062 General medical & surgical hospitals
HQ: Dignity Health Medical Foundation
3400 Data Dr
Rancho Cordova CA 95670

(P-16356)
DOCTORS HOSPITAL MANTECA INC
1205 E North St, Manteca (95336-4900)
PHONE.................................209 823-3111
Nicholas Tejeda, *CEO*
Mark Lisa, *President*
Katherine Medeiros, *President*
Gregg Garrison, *CFO*
Tracy Roman, *CFO*
EMP: 400 **EST:** 2001
SALES (est): 57.1MM
SALES (corp-wide): 17.6B **Publicly Held**
WEB: www.doctorsmanteca.com
SIC: 8062 General medical & surgical hospitals
PA: Tenet Healthcare Corporation
14201 Dallas Pkwy
Dallas TX 75254
469 893-2200

(P-16357)
DOMINICAN HOSPITAL FOUNDATION (DH)
1555 Soquel Dr, Santa Cruz (95065-1794)
PHONE.................................831 462-7700
Beverly Grova, *CEO*
Chuck Maffia, *President*
Jon Sisk, *President*
Sam Leask, *CEO*
Ted Burke, *Vice Pres*
EMP: 207 **EST:** 1966
SQ FT: 110,000
SALES: 6.8MM **Privately Held**
WEB: www.supportdominican.org
SIC: 8062 8051 General medical & surgical hospitals; skilled nursing care facilities
HQ: Dignity Health
185 Berry St Ste 200
San Francisco CA 94107
415 438-5500

(P-16358)
EAST BAY ENDOSCOPY CENTER LP
5858 Horton St Ste 100, Emeryville (94608-2007)
PHONE.................................510 654-4554
Mark Kogan,
EMP: 73 **EST:** 1999
SALES (est): 13.1MM
SALES (corp-wide): 257.1B **Publicly Held**
SIC: 8062 General medical & surgical hospitals
PA: Unitedhealth Group Incorporated
9900 Bren Rd E Ste 300w
Minnetonka MN 55343
952 936-1300

(P-16359)
EAST BAY FMLY PRCTICE MED GROU
3100 Telg Ave Ste 2109, Oakland (94609)
PHONE.................................510 645-9900
Polly T Young, *President*
EMP: 40 **EST:** 1994
SALES (est): 7.9MM **Privately Held**
SIC: 8062 General medical & surgical hospitals

(P-16360)
EDEN LABS MED GROUP INC
20103 Lake Chabot Rd, Castro Valley (94546-5305)
PHONE.................................510 537-1234
John Carney, *President*
Katherine Thomas, *Admin Sec*
EMP: 128 **EST:** 1971
SQ FT: 9,000
SALES (est): 15.5MM **Privately Held**
WEB: www.edenmedicalcenter.org
SIC: 8062 General medical & surgical hospitals

(P-16361)
EL CAMINO SURGERY CENTER LLC
15046 Karl Ave, Monte Sereno (95030-2211)
PHONE.................................650 961-1200
Lisa Cooper, *Mng Member*
Judy Twitchell, *Info Tech Mgr*
Marla Marlow, *Mng Member*
EMP: 70 **EST:** 1987
SALES: 15K **Privately Held**
SIC: 8062 General medical & surgical hospitals

(P-16362)
EMANUEL MEDICAL CENTER INC (DH)
825 Delbon Ave, Turlock (95382-2016)
PHONE.................................209 667-4200
Susan Micheletti, *CEO*
Huy Dao,
Ronald Arakelian MD,
Joseph L Higgins, *Ch Radiology*
Julie Riddick, *President*
EMP: 850 **EST:** 1974
SQ FT: 200,000
SALES: 209.5MM
SALES (corp-wide): 17.6B **Publicly Held**
WEB: www.emanuelmedicalcenter.org
SIC: 8062 General medical & surgical hospitals
HQ: Doctors Medical Center Of Modesto, Inc.
14201 Dallas Pkwy
Dallas TX 75254
209 578-1211

(P-16363)
ENLOE HOSPT-PHYS THRPY (PA)
1600 Esplanade, Chico (95926-3369)
PHONE.................................530 891-7300
Brenda Logan, *Director*
EMP: 255 **EST:** 1970
SALES (est): 10.1MM **Privately Held**
WEB: www.enloe.org
SIC: 8062 General medical & surgical hospitals

(P-16364)
ENLOE HOSPT-PHYS THRPY
1444 Magnolia Ave, Chico (95926-3227)
PHONE.................................530 891-7300
Brenda Logan, *Director*
EMP: 142
SALES (corp-wide): 10.1MM **Privately Held**
WEB: www.enloe.org
SIC: 8062 General medical & surgical hospitals
PA: Enloe Hospital - Physical Therapy Dept
1600 Esplanade
Chico CA 95926
530 891-7300

(P-16365)
ENLOE MEDICAL CENTER
Also Called: E E G and E P
560 Cohasset Rd, Chico (95926-2281)
PHONE.................................530 332-4111
Joan Lilly, *Principal*
Sandra Bernstein, *Nursing Mgr*
Analy Nava, *Technician*
Rupesh Kanji, *Pharmacist*
Gary Lautt, *Pharmacist*
EMP: 236
SALES (corp-wide): 675.2MM **Privately Held**
WEB: www.enloe.org
SIC: 8062 General medical & surgical hospitals
PA: Enloe Medical Center
1531 Esplanade
Chico CA 95926
530 332-7300

(P-16366)
ENLOE MEDICAL CENTER
Also Called: Payroll Dept.
175 W 5th Ave, Chico (95926)
PHONE.................................530 332-7522
Linda Irvine, *Branch Mgr*
EMP: 236
SALES (corp-wide): 675.2MM **Privately Held**
WEB: www.enloe.org
SIC: 8062 General medical & surgical hospitals
PA: Enloe Medical Center
1531 Esplanade
Chico CA 95926
530 332-7300

(P-16367)
ENLOE MEDICAL CENTER
Also Called: Enloe Hospice Program
1536 Arcadian Ave, Chico (95926-3217)
PHONE.................................530 332-5520
Janet Miller, *Manager*
EMP: 236
SQ FT: 1,283
SALES (corp-wide): 675.2MM **Privately Held**
WEB: www.enloe.org
SIC: 8062 General medical & surgical hospitals
PA: Enloe Medical Center
1531 Esplanade
Chico CA 95926
530 332-7300

(P-16368)
ENLOE MEDICAL CENTER
Also Called: Enloe Outpatient Center
888 Lakeside Vlg Cmns, Chico (95928-3979)
PHONE.................................530 332-6400
Joleen Nixon, *Director*
Kathy Buck, *Director*
EMP: 236
SQ FT: 44,171
SALES (corp-wide): 675.2MM **Privately Held**
WEB: www.enloe.org
SIC: 8062 8093 General medical & surgical hospitals; specialty outpatient clinics
PA: Enloe Medical Center
1531 Esplanade
Chico CA 95926
530 332-7300

(P-16369)
ENLOE MEDICAL CENTER
Also Called: Children's Health Center
1515 Sprngfeld Dr Ste 175, Chico (95928)
PHONE.................................530 332-6000
Dorothy Chinnock, *Branch Mgr*
Prathima Prodduturi, *Hematology*
EMP: 236
SALES (corp-wide): 675.2MM **Privately Held**
WEB: www.enloe.org
SIC: 8062 General medical & surgical hospitals
PA: Enloe Medical Center
1531 Esplanade
Chico CA 95926
530 332-7300

(P-16370)
FREE FLOW MEDICAL INC (PA)
44380 S Grimmer Blvd, Fremont (94538-6385)
PHONE.................................717 669-2566
EMP: 95 **EST:** 2018
SALES (est): 2.7MM **Privately Held**
WEB: www.freeflowmed.com
SIC: 8062 General medical & surgical hospitals

(P-16371)
FREEMONT RIDEOUT HEALTH GROUP
Also Called: Fremont-Rideout Health Group
726 4th St, Marysville (95901-5656)
PHONE.................................530 751-4270
Gloria Lees, *Branch Mgr*
Anabel Duenas, *Records Dir*
Rick Rawson, *Officer*
April Hayes, *Office Mgr*
Tejveer Dhillon, *Administration*
EMP: 75
SALES (corp-wide): 26.9MM **Privately Held**
WEB: www.adventisthealth.org
SIC: 8062 8741 General medical & surgical hospitals; management services
PA: Freemont Rideout Health Group
989 Plumas St
Yuba City CA 95991
530 751-4010

(P-16372)
FREEMONT RIDEOUT HEALTH GROUP
481 Plumas Blvd Ste 105, Yuba City (95991-5075)
PHONE.................................530 671-2883
Karanbir Grewal, *Branch Mgr*
Debbie Mireles, *COO*
EMP: 75
SALES (corp-wide): 26.9MM **Privately Held**
WEB: www.adventisthealth.org
SIC: 8062 General medical & surgical hospitals
PA: Freemont Rideout Health Group
989 Plumas St
Yuba City CA 95991
530 751-4010

PRODUCTS & SERVICES SECTION
8062 - General Medical & Surgical Hospitals County (P-16392)

(P-16373)
FREMONT HOSPITAL
Also Called: Fremont Medical Center
620 J St, Marysville (95901-5413)
PHONE 530 751-4000
Thomas P Hayes, *CEO*
Jeanne Martin, *Admin Sec*
EMP: 194 **EST:** 1985
SQ FT: 121,000
SALES (est): 186.4K
SALES (corp-wide): 26.9MM **Privately Held**
WEB: www.adventisthealth.org
SIC: 8062 General medical & surgical hospitals
PA: Fremont Rideout Health Group
989 Plumas St
Yuba City CA 95991
530 751-4010

(P-16374)
FREMONT RIDEOUT COMP CLINIC
Also Called: Fremont-Rdout Occpational Hlth
1531 Plumas Ct, Yuba City (95991-2966)
PHONE 530 749-4411
Lynn Taylor, *Director*
Lisabeth Cummings-Gilbert, *Principal*
EMP: 97 **EST:** 1997
SALES (est): 93.2K
SALES (corp-wide): 26.9MM **Privately Held**
WEB: www.adventisthealth.org
SIC: 8062 General medical & surgical hospitals
PA: Fremont Rideout Health Group
989 Plumas St
Yuba City CA 95991
530 751-4010

(P-16375)
FRESNO CMNTY HOSP & MED CTR
Also Called: Clovis Community Medical Ctr
2755 Herndon Ave, Clovis (93611-6800)
PHONE 559 324-4000
Phyllis Baltz, *Manager*
Jonathan Miller, *Vice Pres*
Khalil Sheibani, *Vice Pres*
John R Strubert, *Vice Pres*
Jim Thomas, *Vice Pres*
EMP: 95
SQ FT: 36,000
SALES (corp-wide): 1.8B **Privately Held**
WEB: www.communitymedical.org
SIC: 8062 General medical & surgical hospitals
HQ: Fresno Community Hospital And Medical Center
2823 Fresno St
Fresno CA 93721

(P-16376)
FRESNO CMNTY HOSP & MED CTR (HQ)
2823 Fresno St, Fresno (93721-1324)
P.O. Box 1232 (93715-1232)
PHONE 559 459-3948
Phillip Hinton, *President*
Tim A Joslin, *CEO*
William Grigg, *CFO*
Roger Fretwell, *Treasurer*
Mike Kingbury, *Senior VP*
EMP: 3000 **EST:** 1945
SQ FT: 2,469
SALES (est): 535.5MM
SALES (corp-wide): 1.8B **Privately Held**
WEB: www.communitymedical.org
SIC: 8062 General medical & surgical hospitals
PA: Community Hospitals Of Central California
2823 Fresno St
Fresno CA 93721
559 459-6000

(P-16377)
FRESNO HEART HOSPITAL LLC
15 E Audubon Dr, Fresno (93720-1542)
PHONE 559 433-8000
Wanda Holderman, *Mng Member*
Tim A Joslin, *CEO*
Patrick Rafferty, *Exec VP*
Peg Breen, *Senior VP*
Jonathon Anderson, *Telecomm Dir*
EMP: 330 **EST:** 1999
SQ FT: 140,000
SALES (est): 48.1MM
SALES (corp-wide): 1.8B **Privately Held**
WEB: www.communitymedical.org
SIC: 8062 General medical & surgical hospitals
PA: Community Hospitals Of Central California
2823 Fresno St
Fresno CA 93721
559 459-6000

(P-16378)
FRESNO SURGERY CENTER LP (PA)
Also Called: Fresno Surgical Hospital
6125 N Fresno St, Fresno (93710-5207)
PHONE 559 431-8000
Kristine Kassahn, *CEO*
Bruce Cecil, *CFO*
Paramjeet Gill, *Chairman*
Julie Gresham, *Officer*
Sandra Kneefel, *Business Dir*
EMP: 212 **EST:** 1987
SQ FT: 32,000
SALES (est): 74MM **Privately Held**
WEB: www.fresnosurgicalhospital.com
SIC: 8062 8011 General medical & surgical hospitals; orthopedic physician

(P-16379)
GLENN MEDICAL CENTER INC
1133 W Sycamore St, Willows (95988-2601)
PHONE 530 934-4681
William Casey, *CEO*
Gary Pea, *CFO*
Mike Cammarano, *Radiology Dir*
Dawna Keolanui, *Radiology Dir*
Amber Avila, *Human Res Dir*
EMP: 99 **EST:** 1898
SQ FT: 62,000
SALES (est): 17.6MM **Privately Held**
WEB: www.gmcmed.org
SIC: 8062 General medical & surgical hospitals

(P-16380)
GOLDEN EMPIRE CONVALESCENT HOS
121 Dorsey Dr, Grass Valley (95945-5201)
PHONE 530 273-1316
Vicki Young, *Partner*
Chan Sinsaeng, *Social Dir*
Pat Ivey, *QC Dir*
Liz Marker, *Sales Staff*
Debbie Hughes, *Food Svc Dir*
EMP: 180 **EST:** 1996
SALES (est): 12.9MM **Privately Held**
WEB: www.goldenempiresnf.com
SIC: 8062 General medical & surgical hospitals

(P-16381)
GOOD SAMARITAN HOSPITAL LP (DH)
2425 Samaritan Dr, San Jose (95124-3985)
P.O. Box 240002 (95154-2402)
PHONE 408 559-2011
William Ennen,
Kenneth Ong, *Ch Radiology*
Paul Beaupre, *COO*
Jordan Herget, *COO*
Lana Arad, *CFO*
EMP: 1200 **EST:** 1983
SALES (est): 618.4MM **Publicly Held**
WEB: www.goodsamsanjose.com
SIC: 8062 General medical & surgical hospitals
HQ: Hca Inc.
1 Park Plz
Nashville TN 37203
615 344-9551

(P-16382)
GOOD SAMARITAN HOSPITAL LP
Also Called: Good Samaritan Breastcare Ctr
15400 National Ave # 200, Los Gatos (95032-2433)
PHONE 408 358-8414
Tricia Baker, *Manager*
EMP: 182 **Publicly Held**
WEB: www.goodsamsanjose.com
SIC: 8062 8099 General medical & surgical hospitals; health screening service
HQ: Good Samaritan Hospital, L.P.
2425 Samaritan Dr
San Jose CA 95124
408 559-2011

(P-16383)
GOOD SAMARITAN HOSPITAL LP
Also Called: Mission Oaks Hospital
15891 Los Gtos Almaden Rd, Los Gatos (95032-3742)
PHONE 408 356-4111
Brian Knecht, *COO*
Ron Terras, *Director*
EMP: 182 **Publicly Held**
WEB: www.goodsamsanjose.com
SIC: 8062 General medical & surgical hospitals
HQ: Good Samaritan Hospital, L.P.
2425 Samaritan Dr
San Jose CA 95124
408 559-2011

(P-16384)
HALSEN HEALTHCARE LLC
Also Called: Watsonville Community Hospital
75 Nielson St, Watsonville (95076-2468)
PHONE 831 724-4741
Sean Fowler, *CEO*
EMP: 820
SALES (corp-wide): 69.2MM **Privately Held**
WEB: www.watsonvillehospital.com
SIC: 8062 General medical & surgical hospitals
PA: Halsen Healthcare, Llc
1872 Sharon Ln
Santa Ana CA 92705
714 726-6189

(P-16385)
HAYWARD SISTERS HOSPITAL (HQ)
Also Called: St Rose Hospital
27200 Calaroga Ave, Hayward (94545-4339)
PHONE 510 264-4000
Michael Mahoney, *President*
Leeann Schierburg, *Records Dir*
Laura Stephens, *Business Dir*
Sylvia Ventura, *Ch Nursing Ofcr*
Michael Cobb, *Exec Dir*
EMP: 842
SQ FT: 173,000
SALES: 136.6MM **Privately Held**
WEB: www.strosehospital.org
SIC: 8062 Hospital, affiliated with AMA residency

(P-16386)
HAZEL HAWKINS MEMORIAL HOSP (PA)
Also Called: Hazel Hawkins Memorial Hosp
911 Sunset Dr Ste A, Hollister (95023-5608)
PHONE 831 637-5711
Jordan Wright, *CEO*
Amitabh Mathur,
Beth Ivy, *President*
Mark Robinson, *CFO*
Tisi Stewart, *Trustee*
▲ **EMP:** 270 **EST:** 1907
SQ FT: 42,000
SALES: 115.1MM **Privately Held**
SIC: 8062 8051 8059 General medical & surgical hospitals; skilled nursing care facilities; convalescent home

(P-16387)
HEALTHCARE BARTON SYSTEM (PA)
2170 South Ave, South Lake Tahoe (96150-7026)
P.O. Box 9578 (96158-9578)
PHONE 530 541-3420
Clint Purvance, *CEO*
Kelly Neiger, *CFO*
Kathryn Biasotti, *Risk Mgmt Dir*
Sue Fairley, *Ch Nursing Ofcr*
Rich Belli, *Administration*
EMP: 554
SQ FT: 112,190
SALES: 179.5MM **Privately Held**
WEB: www.bartonhealth.org
SIC: 8062 General medical & surgical hospitals

(P-16388)
INDIAN VALLEY HEALTH CARE DIST
Also Called: Indian Valley Hospital
184 Hot Springs Rd, Greenville (95947-9747)
PHONE 530 284-7191
Sue Neer, *CEO*
Wick Viswell, *Administration*
EMP: 45 **EST:** 1956
SQ FT: 20,000
SALES (est): 6.1MM **Privately Held**
WEB: www.indianvalleyhospital.com
SIC: 8062 General medical & surgical hospitals

(P-16389)
JOHN C FREMONT HEALTHCARE DST
Also Called: Fremont Hospital
5189 Hospital Rd, Mariposa (95338-9524)
P.O. Box 216 (95338-0216)
PHONE 209 966-3631
Matthew Matthiessen, *CEO*
Dana Oster, *Bd of Directors*
Kathy Blalock, *Pharmacy Dir*
Laura Donahue, *Quality Imp Dir*
Rebecca Swisher, *Opers Staff*
EMP: 265 **EST:** 1951
SQ FT: 59,112
SALES: 26.2MM **Privately Held**
WEB: www.jcf-hospital.com
SIC: 8062 General medical & surgical hospitals

(P-16390)
JOHN C FREMONT HOSP FOUNDATION
5189 Hospital Rd, Mariposa (95338-9524)
P.O. Box 1093 (95338-1093)
PHONE 209 966-0850
Dana Oster, *President*
Matthew Matthiessen, *Officer*
Steve Hoppe, *Director*
EMP: 50 **EST:** 1980
SALES (est): 38.7K **Privately Held**
WEB: www.jcf-hospital.com
SIC: 8062 General medical & surgical hospitals

(P-16391)
JOHN MUIR DIABETES CNTR WALNUT
175 La Casa Via, Walnut Creek (94598-3010)
PHONE 925 952-2944
Calvin Knight, *CEO*
EMP: 40 **EST:** 2010
SALES (est): 1.5MM **Privately Held**
WEB: www.johnmuirhealth.com
SIC: 8062 General medical & surgical hospitals

(P-16392)
JOHN MUIR HEALTH (HQ)
1601 Ygnacio Valley Rd, Walnut Creek (94598-3122)
P.O. Box 9023 (94596-9023)
PHONE 925 947-4449
Calvin Knight, *CEO*
Sally L Davis, *Vice Chairman*
Michael S Thomas, *President*
Jane A Willemsen, *President*
Elizabeth Stallings, *COO*
EMP: 1600
SQ FT: 5,500
SALES: 1.8B
SALES (corp-wide): 373.2MM **Privately Held**
WEB: www.johnmuirhealth.com
SIC: 8062 General medical & surgical hospitals
PA: John Muir Physician Network
1450 Treat Blvd
Walnut Creek CA 94597
925 296-9700

8062 - General Medical & Surgical Hospitals County (P-16393)   PRODUCTS & SERVICES SECTION

(P-16393)
JOHN MUIR HEALTH
Also Called: John Muir Medical Center
1601 Ygnacio Valley Rd, Walnut Creek
(94598-3122)
PHONE...................................925 939-3000
Vicki C Lee, *Administration*
Craig Devinney, *Officer*
Michael Moody, *Senior VP*
Laura Kazaglis, *Vice Pres*
Michael Kern, *Vice Pres*
EMP: 775
SALES (corp-wide): 376.6MM **Privately Held**
WEB: www.johnmuirhealth.com
SIC: 8062 General medical & surgical hospitals
HQ: John Muir Health
 1601 Ygnacio Valley Rd
 Walnut Creek CA 94598
 925 947-4449

(P-16394)
JOHN MUIR PHYSICIAN NETWORK (PA)
Also Called: JOHN MUIR MEDICAL CENTER
1450 Treat Blvd, Walnut Creek
(94597-2168)
PHONE...................................925 296-9700
Cal Knight, *Principal*
Tom G Rundall, *Bd of Directors*
Anna Pascua, *Chief Mktg Ofcr*
George Sauter, *Officer*
Hetal Vellanki, *Research*
EMP: 1601 **EST:** 1997
SQ FT: 83,579
SALES: 376.6MM **Privately Held**
WEB: www.johnmuirhealth.com
SIC: 8062 8069 8093 7363 General medical & surgical hospitals; substance abuse hospitals; substance abuse clinics (outpatient); medical help service

(P-16395)
KAISER FOUNDATION HOSPITALS
Also Called: Santa Rosa Chrnic Pain Endcrnl
3559 Round Barn Blvd, Santa Rosa
(95403-1763)
PHONE...................................707 393-4633
Judy Coffey, *Branch Mgr*
EMP: 522
SALES (corp-wide): 30.5B **Privately Held**
WEB: www.kaisercenter.com
SIC: 8062 General medical & surgical hospitals
HQ: Kaiser Foundation Hospitals Inc
 1 Kaiser Plz
 Oakland CA 94612
 510 271-6611

(P-16396)
KAISER FOUNDATION HOSPITALS
Also Called: Kaiser Foundation Health Plan
1 Quality Dr Fl A1, Vacaville (95688-9494)
PHONE...................................707 624-4000
Kim Trumbull, *Branch Mgr*
Dana Vierra, *CIO*
Paul Luttrell, *Chief Engr*
Gina Romoriez, *Safety Dir*
Azim Ahmady, *Family Practiti*
EMP: 522
SALES (corp-wide): 30.5B **Privately Held**
WEB: www.kaisercenter.com
SIC: 8062 General medical & surgical hospitals
HQ: Kaiser Foundation Hospitals Inc
 1 Kaiser Plz
 Oakland CA 94612
 510 271-6611

(P-16397)
KAISER FOUNDATION HOSPITALS
Also Called: Kaiser Prmnnte Eye Svcs - Optm
1680 E Roseville Pkwy, Roseville
(95661-3988)
PHONE...................................916 746-3937
Daniel Rule, *Branch Mgr*
Tavares Anderson, *Nurse*
Kathy Gibbs, *Director*
EMP: 522
SALES (corp-wide): 30.5B **Privately Held**
WEB: www.kaisercenter.com
SIC: 8062 General medical & surgical hospitals
HQ: Kaiser Foundation Hospitals Inc
 1 Kaiser Plz
 Oakland CA 94612
 510 271-6611

(P-16398)
KAISER FOUNDATION HOSPITALS
Also Called: Park Shadelands Medical Offs
320 Lennon Ln, Walnut Creek
(94598-2419)
PHONE...................................925 906-2380
David Nievr, *President*
Charu Gupta, *Family Practiti*
Susan Chuang, *Internal Med*
Jaya Francis, *Internal Med*
Zahra Promes, *Internal Med*
EMP: 522
SALES (corp-wide): 30.5B **Privately Held**
WEB: www.kaisercenter.com
SIC: 8062 8011 General medical & surgical hospitals; general & family practice, physician/surgeon
HQ: Kaiser Foundation Hospitals Inc
 1 Kaiser Plz
 Oakland CA 94612
 510 271-6611

(P-16399)
KAISER FOUNDATION HOSPITALS
901 Marshall St, Redwood City
(94063-2026)
PHONE...................................650 299-2234
Linh Nguyen, *Software Dev*
EMP: 522
SALES (corp-wide): 30.5B **Privately Held**
WEB: www.kaisercenter.com
SIC: 8062 General medical & surgical hospitals
HQ: Kaiser Foundation Hospitals Inc
 1 Kaiser Plz
 Oakland CA 94612
 510 271-6611

(P-16400)
KAISER FOUNDATION HOSPITALS (HQ)
Also Called: Kaiser Permanente
1 Kaiser Plz, Oakland (94612-3610)
P.O. Box 12929 (94604-3010)
PHONE...................................510 271-6611
Gregory A Adams, *CEO*
Janet Liang, *President*
Kathy Lancaster, *CFO*
Catherine Hernandez, *Ch Credit Ofcr*
Anthony Barreta, *Senior VP*
▲ **EMP:** 250 **EST:** 1948
SQ FT: 90,000
SALES (est): 24.9B
SALES (corp-wide): 30.5B **Privately Held**
WEB: www.kaisercenter.com
SIC: 8062 8011 General medical & surgical hospitals; medical centers
PA: Kaiser Foundation Health Plan, Inc.
 1 Kaiser Plz
 Oakland CA 94612
 510 271-5800

(P-16401)
KAISER FOUNDATION HOSPITALS
Also Called: Kaiser Permanente
2200 Ofarrell St, San Francisco
(94115-3357)
PHONE...................................415 833-2200
Dee M Munoz, *Principal*
James Marcotte, *Exec Dir*
Preeti Joshi, *Program Mgr*
Jeannie Hagler, *Admin Sec*
Julie Velez, *Administration*
EMP: 522
SQ FT: 14,712
SALES (corp-wide): 30.5B **Privately Held**
WEB: www.kaisercenter.com
SIC: 8062 General medical & surgical hospitals
HQ: Kaiser Foundation Hospitals Inc
 1 Kaiser Plz
 Oakland CA 94612
 510 271-6611

(P-16402)
KAISER FOUNDATION HOSPITALS
Also Called: Kaiser Permanente
280 W Macarthur Blvd, Oakland
(94611-5642)
PHONE...................................510 752-1000
Bettie Coles, *Manager*
Shakeya McDow, *Vice Pres*
Brian Helberg, *Exec Dir*
Brendan Simon, *Program Mgr*
Natasha Robinson, *Nursing Mgr*
EMP: 522
SALES (corp-wide): 30.5B **Privately Held**
WEB: www.kaisercenter.com
SIC: 8062 General medical & surgical hospitals
HQ: Kaiser Foundation Hospitals Inc
 1 Kaiser Plz
 Oakland CA 94612
 510 271-6611

(P-16403)
KAISER FOUNDATION HOSPITALS
Also Called: Kaiser Permanente
501 J St, Sacramento (95814-2325)
PHONE...................................916 558-6520
Valentina Salinas, *Technician*
Michael Tianco, *Project Mgr*
Steve Diaz, *Director*
Barry Koob, *Ophthalmic Tech*
Phillip Askew, *Consultant*
EMP: 522
SALES (corp-wide): 30.5B **Privately Held**
WEB: www.kaisercenter.com
SIC: 8062 8011 General medical & surgical hospitals; medical centers
HQ: Kaiser Foundation Hospitals Inc
 1 Kaiser Plz
 Oakland CA 94612
 510 271-6611

(P-16404)
KAISER FOUNDATION HOSPITALS
280 Hospital Pkwy, San Jose (95119-1103)
PHONE...................................408 972-6010
Rajan Bhandari, *Branch Mgr*
Fauzia Basit, *Family Practiti*
Silvia Shin, *Family Practiti*
Sandra Torres, *Family Practiti*
Francis Abueg, *Psychologist*
EMP: 522
SALES (corp-wide): 30.5B **Privately Held**
WEB: www.kaisercenter.com
SIC: 8062 General medical & surgical hospitals
HQ: Kaiser Foundation Hospitals Inc
 1 Kaiser Plz
 Oakland CA 94612
 510 271-6611

(P-16405)
KAISER FOUNDATION HOSPITALS
Also Called: Kaiser Prmanente Internet Svcs
5820 Owens Dr Bldg E-2, Pleasanton
(94588-3900)
PHONE...................................925 598-2799
Timothy Beresford-Howe, *Manager*
EMP: 522
SALES (corp-wide): 30.5B **Privately Held**
WEB: www.kaisercenter.com
SIC: 8062 General medical & surgical hospitals
HQ: Kaiser Foundation Hospitals Inc
 1 Kaiser Plz
 Oakland CA 94612
 510 271-6611

(P-16406)
KAISER FOUNDATION HOSPITALS
Also Called: Kaiser Permanente
3900 Freedom Cir Ste 201, Santa Clara
(95054-1222)
PHONE...................................408 235-4005
Akash Chaudhari, *Software Engr*
Benjamin Fisch, *Oncology*
Brian Missett, *Oncology*
EMP: 522

(P-16407)
KAISER FOUNDATION HOSPITALS
Also Called: Kaiser Permanente - Hr Svc Ctr
1451 Harbor Bay Pkwy, Alameda
(94502-7070)
PHONE...................................510 749-3021
EMP: 522
SALES (corp-wide): 30.5B **Privately Held**
WEB: www.kaisercenter.com
SIC: 8062 General medical & surgical hospitals
HQ: Kaiser Foundation Hospitals Inc
 1 Kaiser Plz
 Oakland CA 94612
 510 271-6611

(P-16408)
KAISER FOUNDATION HOSPITALS
Also Called: Kaiser Permanente
1650 Response Rd, Sacramento
(95815-4807)
PHONE...................................916 973-5000
Sandra Lee Panora, *Branch Mgr*
Kirk Whelan, *Vice Pres*
Connor Deck, *Sales Associate*
Kristen Carbone, *Marketing Staff*
Parul Patel, *Family Practiti*
EMP: 522
SALES (corp-wide): 30.5B **Privately Held**
WEB: www.kaisercenter.com
SIC: 8062 General medical & surgical hospitals
HQ: Kaiser Foundation Hospitals Inc
 1 Kaiser Plz
 Oakland CA 94612
 510 271-6611

(P-16409)
KAISER FOUNDATION HOSPITALS
Also Called: Rancho Cordova Medical Offices
10725 International Dr, Rancho Cordova
(95670-7967)
PHONE...................................916 631-3088
David Haddad, *Principal*
Doria Easter, *Family Practiti*
Karl Buddenhagen, *Psychologist*
Robert Burns, *Dermatology*
Maureen Lloy, *Gnrl Med Prac*
EMP: 522
SALES (corp-wide): 30.5B **Privately Held**
WEB: www.kaisercenter.com
SIC: 8062 General medical & surgical hospitals
HQ: Kaiser Foundation Hospitals Inc
 1 Kaiser Plz
 Oakland CA 94612
 510 271-6611

(P-16410)
KAISER FOUNDATION HOSPITALS
Also Called: Permanente Medical Group
555 Castro St Fl 3, Mountain View
(94041-2009)
PHONE...................................650 903-3000
Patricia Carpenter, *Director*
Andrea Aslan, *Obstetrician*
Cheryl Branson, *Obstetrician*
Andrea Forgy, *Med Doctor*
Wakako Nomura, *Med Doctor*
EMP: 522
SALES (corp-wide): 30.5B **Privately Held**
WEB: www.kaisercenter.com
SIC: 8062 Hospital, affiliated with AMA residency
HQ: Kaiser Foundation Hospitals Inc
 1 Kaiser Plz
 Oakland CA 94612
 510 271-6611

PRODUCTS & SERVICES SECTION
8062 - General Medical & Surgical Hospitals County (P-16429)

(P-16411)
KAISER FOUNDATION HOSPITALS
Also Called: Kaiser Permanente
501 Lennon Ln, Walnut Creek (94598-2414)
PHONE 925 906-2000
Christina Robinson, Principal
Fran Lager, Project Mgr
Jeanette Cable, Technology
Zahra Promes, Internal Med
Brad Lewis, Pediatrics
EMP: 522
SALES (corp-wide): 30.5B Privately Held
WEB: www.kaisercenter.com
SIC: 8062 General medical & surgical hospitals
HQ: Kaiser Foundation Hospitals Inc
1 Kaiser Plz
Oakland CA 94612
510 271-6611

(P-16412)
KAISER FOUNDATION HOSPITALS
Also Called: Kaiser Permanente
7601 Stoneridge Dr, Pleasanton (94588-4501)
PHONE 925 847-5000
Linsey Dicks, Admin Director
Leyla Gahrahmat, Family Practiti
Sheila Beth Pearlman, Psychologist
Janet Stavosky, Psychologist
Jerome Deck Jr, Internal Med
EMP: 522
SALES (corp-wide): 30.5B Privately Held
WEB: www.kaisercenter.com
SIC: 8062 General medical & surgical hospitals
HQ: Kaiser Foundation Hospitals Inc
1 Kaiser Plz
Oakland CA 94612
510 271-6611

(P-16413)
KAISER FOUNDATION HOSPITALS
Also Called: Kaiser Permanente
1800 Harrison St Fl 16, Oakland (94612-3466)
PHONE 510 625-3431
Stanley Watson, Vice Pres
Carol Davis-Smith, Vice Pres
Rame Hemstreet, Vice Pres
Miesha Hinds, Vice Pres
Peter Hohl, Vice Pres
EMP: 40
SALES (corp-wide): 30.5B Privately Held
WEB: www.kaisercenter.com
SIC: 8062 General medical & surgical hospitals
HQ: Kaiser Foundation Hospitals Inc
1 Kaiser Plz
Oakland CA 94612
510 271-6611

(P-16414)
KAISER FOUNDATION HOSPITALS
Also Called: Kaiser Prmnnte Vallejo Med Ctr
975 Sereno Dr, Vallejo (94589-2441)
PHONE 707 651-1000
Katie Rickleff, Principal
Gwendolyn Isaacs, Managing Dir
Bonnie Childs, Admin Asst
Jaime Wong, Admin Asst
Kenya Collier, Administration
EMP: 522
SALES (corp-wide): 30.5B Privately Held
WEB: www.kaisercenter.com
SIC: 8062 General medical & surgical hospitals
HQ: Kaiser Foundation Hospitals Inc
1 Kaiser Plz
Oakland CA 94612
510 271-6611

(P-16415)
KAISER FOUNDATION HOSPITALS
Also Called: Kaiser Prmnnte San Jose Med Ct
275 Hospital Pkwy 765a, San Jose (95119-1106)
PHONE 408 972-6700
Diana Ochoa, Branch Mgr
Kelan Dennis, Engineer
Roland Green, Psychologist
Marcus Chow, Internal Med
Karen Wallace, Diag Radio
EMP: 522
SALES (corp-wide): 30.5B Privately Held
WEB: www.kaisercenter.com
SIC: 8062 8021 General medical & surgical hospitals; offices & clinics of dentists
HQ: Kaiser Foundation Hospitals Inc
1 Kaiser Plz
Oakland CA 94612
510 271-6611

(P-16416)
KAISER FOUNDATION HOSPITALS
5800 Coliseum Way, Oakland (94621-4043)
PHONE 510 434-5835
Todd Scott, Branch Mgr
EMP: 522
SALES (corp-wide): 30.5B Privately Held
WEB: www.kaisercenter.com
SIC: 8062 General medical & surgical hospitals
HQ: Kaiser Foundation Hospitals Inc
1 Kaiser Plz
Oakland CA 94612
510 271-6611

(P-16417)
KAISER FOUNDATION HOSPITALS
Also Called: Kaiser Permanente
1600 Eureka Rd, Roseville (95661-3027)
PHONE 916 784-4000
Douglas Freeman, Branch Mgr
Zuhra Dugumovic, Administration
Karen Martins, Human Res Dir
Jeffrey Asselin, Chief
Cheryl Kenner, Education
EMP: 2300
SALES (corp-wide): 30.5B Privately Held
WEB: www.kaisercenter.com
SIC: 8062 General medical & surgical hospitals
HQ: Kaiser Foundation Hospitals Inc
1 Kaiser Plz
Oakland CA 94612
510 271-6611

(P-16418)
KAISER FOUNDATION HOSPITALS
Also Called: Kaiser Prmnnte Advice Ctr - Al
7300 Wyndham Dr, Sacramento (95823-4913)
PHONE 916 525-6300
Tony Le, Manager
May Kim, Psychologist
Craig Snider, Ophthalmology
Humberto Temporini, Psychiatry
Brian Rankin,
EMP: 522
SALES (corp-wide): 30.5B Privately Held
WEB: www.kaisercenter.com
SIC: 8062 General medical & surgical hospitals
HQ: Kaiser Foundation Hospitals Inc
1 Kaiser Plz
Oakland CA 94612
510 271-6611

(P-16419)
KAISER FOUNDATION HOSPITALS
Also Called: Kaiser Permanente
7373 West Ln, Stockton (95210-3377)
PHONE 209 476-3101
Gene Long, Branch Mgr
David Catanzarite, Engineer
Maria Bugay, Family Practiti
Amrit Dhanota, Family Practiti
Theresa Ordona, Family Practiti
EMP: 522
SALES (corp-wide): 30.5B Privately Held
WEB: www.kaisercenter.com
SIC: 8062 General medical & surgical hospitals
HQ: Kaiser Foundation Hospitals Inc
1 Kaiser Plz
Oakland CA 94612
510 271-6611

(P-16420)
KAISER FOUNDATION HOSPITALS
Also Called: Kaiser Prmnnte Snta Clara Med
710 Lawrence Expy, Santa Clara (95051-5173)
PHONE 408 851-1000
Ana Herdocia, Executive Asst
Nancy Maenner, Vice Pres
Diane Yee, Exec Dir
Kathy Cox, Program Mgr
Darlene Forrest, Program Mgr
EMP: 522
SALES (corp-wide): 30.5B Privately Held
WEB: www.kaisercenter.com
SIC: 8062 General medical & surgical hospitals
HQ: Kaiser Foundation Hospitals Inc
1 Kaiser Plz
Oakland CA 94612
510 271-6611

(P-16421)
KAISER PERMANENTE
3505 Broadway, Oakland (94611-5798)
PHONE 510 450-2109
T Raine Bennett, Med Doctor
Rich E Smith, Vice Pres
Gregory A Hughes, Executive
Jeff Collins, Regional Pres
Haley Donaldson, Administration
EMP: 47 EST: 2015
SALES (est): 42.6MM Privately Held
WEB: www.kaiserpermanentelocations.com
SIC: 8062 General medical & surgical hospitals

(P-16422)
KINDRED HEALTHCARE LLC
10100 Trinity Pkwy, Stockton (95219-7238)
PHONE 209 474-7884
EMP: 142
SALES (corp-wide): 6B Privately Held
WEB: www.kindredhealthcare.com
SIC: 8062 8099 8082 General medical & surgical hospitals; blood related health services; home health care services
HQ: Kindred Healthcare, Llc
680 S 4th St
Louisville KY 40202
502 596-7300

(P-16423)
KINDRED HEALTHCARE LLC
4030 Moorpark Ave Ste 251, San Jose (95117-1807)
PHONE 408 261-6943
Dave Lokey, Marketing Staff
Carol Hancock, Education
Lauren Caswell, Nurse
Ian Middleton, Manager
EMP: 142
SALES (corp-wide): 6B Privately Held
WEB: www.kindredhealthcare.com
SIC: 8062 8082 General medical & surgical hospitals; home health care services
HQ: Kindred Healthcare, Llc
680 S 4th St
Louisville KY 40202
502 596-7300

(P-16424)
KINDRED HEALTHCARE OPER LLC
Also Called: Kindred Hospital
2800 Benedict Dr, San Leandro (94577-6840)
PHONE 510 357-8300
Wendy Mamoon, CEO
Katrina Webb, Purch Dir
Aamir Faruqui, Director
EMP: 450
SALES (corp-wide): 6B Privately Held
WEB: www.kindredhealthcare.com
SIC: 8062 General medical & surgical hospitals
HQ: Kindred Healthcare Operating, Llc
680 S 4th St
Louisville KY 40202
502 596-7300

(P-16425)
LAST FRONTIER HEALTHCARE DST
Also Called: Modoc Medical Center
1111 N Nagle St, Alturas (96101-3840)
P.O. Box 190 (96101-0190)
PHONE 530 708-8800
Kevin Kramer, CEO
Jo Knoch, CFO
Jennifer Cipro, Controller
Diane Hagelthorne, Human Resources
Marty Shaffer, Opers Staff
EMP: 190 EST: 2012
SQ FT: 56,094
SALES (est): 18.5MM Privately Held
WEB: www.modocmedicalcenter.org
SIC: 8062 General medical & surgical hospitals

(P-16426)
LODI MEMORIAL HOSP ASSN INC
Also Called: Loda Mem Hosp Occpational Hlth
975 S Fairmont Ave Ste 8, Lodi (95240-5118)
PHONE 209 339-7441
EMP: 78
SALES (corp-wide): 4.5B Privately Held
WEB: www.lodihealth.org
SIC: 8062 General medical & surgical hospitals
HQ: Lodi Memorial Hospital Association, Inc.
975 S Fairmont Ave
Lodi CA 95240
209 334-3411

(P-16427)
LODI MEMORIAL HOSP ASSN INC (HQ)
Also Called: Adventist Health Lodi Memorial
975 S Fairmont Ave, Lodi (95240-5118)
P.O. Box 3004 (95241-1908)
PHONE 209 334-3411
Daniel Wolcott, CEO
Roland Simeon,
Nagui N Sorour,
Todd Primack,
Joseph P Harrington, President
EMP: 700 EST: 1945
SQ FT: 97,057
SALES: 246.1MM
SALES (corp-wide): 4.5B Privately Held
WEB: www.lodihealth.org
SIC: 8062 Hospital, affiliated with AMA residency
PA: Adventist Health System/West, Corporation
1 Adventist Health Way
Roseville CA 95661
844 574-5686

(P-16428)
LODI MEMORIAL HOSP ASSN INC
Also Called: Conrad Lab, The
1200 W Vine St, Lodi (95240-5136)
PHONE 209 339-7583
Dave Mack, Director
Sue Anderson, Admin Sec
EMP: 78
SALES (corp-wide): 4.5B Privately Held
WEB: www.lodihealth.org
SIC: 8062 General medical & surgical hospitals
HQ: Lodi Memorial Hospital Association, Inc.
975 S Fairmont Ave
Lodi CA 95240
209 334-3411

(P-16429)
LODI MEMORIAL HOSP ASSN INC
Also Called: Ione Primemed Clinic
395 Preston Ave, Ione (95640-9158)
P.O. Box 1580 (95640-1580)
PHONE 209 274-2183
Pam Schneider, Director
EMP: 78
SALES (corp-wide): 4.5B Privately Held
WEB: www.lodihealth.org
SIC: 8062 General medical & surgical hospitals

8062 - General Medical & Surgical Hospitals County (P-16430)

HQ: Lodi Memorial Hospital Association, Inc.
975 S Fairmont Ave
Lodi CA 95240
209 334-3411

(P-16430)
LODI REGIONAL HLTH SYSTEMS INC (PA)
975 S Fairmont Ave, Lodi (95240-5118)
P.O. Box 3004 (95241-1908)
PHONE 800 323-3360
Daniel Wolcott, *CEO*
EMP: 92 **EST:** 2001
SALES (est): 2.5MM **Privately Held**
WEB: www.adventisthealth.org
SIC: 8062 General medical & surgical hospitals

(P-16431)
LODI REGIONAL HLTH SYSTEMS INC
10200 Trinity Pkwy # 102, Stockton (95219-7286)
PHONE 209 948-0808
Dena Romero, *Technician*
EMP: 107
SALES (corp-wide): 2.5MM **Privately Held**
WEB: www.adventisthealth.org
SIC: 8062 General medical & surgical hospitals
PA: Lodi Regional Health Systems, Inc.
975 S Fairmont Ave
Lodi CA 95240
800 323-3360

(P-16432)
LUCILE PACKARD CHILDRENS HOSP
730 Welch Rd Ste B, Palo Alto (94304-1504)
PHONE 650 321-2545
Christophe Dawes, *CEO*
Patrick Idemoto, *Officer*
Cynthia Samson, *Lab Dir*
Garima Srivastava, *Business Dir*
Anthony Alabastro, *Security Dir*
EMP: 57 **EST:** 2013
SALES (est): 134MM **Privately Held**
SIC: 8062 General medical & surgical hospitals

(P-16433)
MADERA CMNTY HOSP FOUNDATION
1250 E Almond Ave, Madera (93637-5606)
P.O. Box 1328 (93639-1328)
PHONE 559 673-5101
Ray Gomes, *Exec Dir*
EMP: 84 **EST:** 1978
SQ FT: 225
SALES: 137.4K **Privately Held**
WEB: www.maderahospital.org
SIC: 8062 General medical & surgical hospitals

(P-16434)
MADERA COMMUNITY HOSPITAL
Also Called: Family Health Services Clinic
1210 E Almond Ave Ste A, Madera (93637-5606)
PHONE 559 675-5530
Robert Kelly, *CEO*
EMP: 49
SALES (corp-wide): 90.2MM **Privately Held**
WEB: www.maderahospital.org
SIC: 8062 General medical & surgical hospitals
PA: Madera Community Hospital
1250 E Almond Ave
Madera CA 93637
559 675-5555

(P-16435)
MADERA COMMUNITY HOSPITAL
Also Called: Chowchilla Medical Center
285 Hospital Dr, Chowchilla (93610-2041)
PHONE 559 665-3768
Karen Paolinelli, *CEO*
EMP: 49

SALES (corp-wide): 90.2MM **Privately Held**
WEB: www.maderahospital.org
SIC: 8062 General medical & surgical hospitals
PA: Madera Community Hospital
1250 E Almond Ave
Madera CA 93637
559 675-5555

(P-16436)
MADERA COMMUNITY HOSPITAL (PA)
Also Called: MCH
1250 E Almond Ave, Madera (93637-5696)
P.O. Box 1328 (93639-1328)
PHONE 559 675-5555
Karen Paolinelli, *CEO*
Bruce Norton, *Bd of Directors*
Connie Wise, *Officer*
Dale Costantino, *Business Dir*
Mike Brink, *Principal*
EMP: 703 **EST:** 1975
SQ FT: 66,300
SALES: 90.2MM **Privately Held**
WEB: www.maderahospital.org
SIC: 8062 General medical & surgical hospitals

(P-16437)
MARIN GENERAL HOSPITAL
250 Bon Air Rd, Kentfield (94904-1784)
PHONE 415 925-7000
Lee Domanico, *CEO*
Heather Carlberg, *Ch of Bd*
David Bradley, *CEO*
Theresa Daughton, *CFO*
Joel Sklar, *Sr Corp Ofcr*
EMP: 1100 **EST:** 1947
SQ FT: 125,000
SALES (est): 530.6K
SALES (corp-wide): 531.1K **Privately Held**
WEB: www.mymarinhealth.org
SIC: 8062 8011 General medical & surgical hospitals; offices & clinics of medical doctors
PA: Marin Healthcare District
100 Drakes Landing Rd B
Greenbrae CA 94904
415 464-2090

(P-16438)
MARIN HEALTHCARE DISTRICT (PA)
100 Drakes Landing Rd B, Greenbrae (94904-2404)
PHONE 415 464-2090
Barry Woerman, *Director*
Kristine Schaefer, *Manager*
EMP: 72 **EST:** 2000
SALES (est): 531.1K **Privately Held**
WEB: www.marinhealthcare.org
SIC: 8062 General medical & surgical hospitals

(P-16439)
MARK TWAIN MEDICAL CENTER
Also Called: Arnold Medical Clinic
2182 Hwy 4 Ste A100, Arnold (95223-9420)
P.O. Box 660 (95223-0660)
PHONE 209 795-4193
Benny Estoesta, *Director*
EMP: 43 **Privately Held**
WEB: www.dignityhealth.org
SIC: 8062 General medical & surgical hospitals
HQ: Mark Twain Medical Center
768 Mountain Ranch Rd
San Andreas CA 95249

(P-16440)
MARK TWAIN MEDICAL CENTER (DH)
Also Called: MARK TWAIN ST JOSEPH'S HOSPITAL
768 Mountain Ranch Rd, San Andreas (95249-9707)
PHONE 209 754-3521
Craig J Marks, *CEO*
Greg Jordan, *President*
Jacob Lews, *CFO*
Linda Lewis, *Treasurer*
Anita Paque, *Vice Pres*

EMP: 225 **EST:** 1984
SQ FT: 40,000
SALES: 72.5MM **Privately Held**
WEB: www.dignityhealth.org
SIC: 8062 General medical & surgical hospitals
HQ: Dignity Health
185 Berry St Ste 200
San Francisco CA 94107
415 438-5500

(P-16441)
MARK TWAIN MEDICAL CENTER
Also Called: Silver Service
768 Mountain Ranch Rd, San Andreas (95249-9707)
PHONE 209 754-1487
Mike Lawson, *President*
EMP: 43 **Privately Held**
WEB: www.dignityhealth.org
SIC: 8062 8322 General medical & surgical hospitals; geriatric social service
HQ: Mark Twain Medical Center
768 Mountain Ranch Rd
San Andreas CA 95249

(P-16442)
MARSHALL MEDICAL CENTER
941 Spring St Ste A, Placerville (95667-4546)
PHONE 530 626-3682
Dana Hoehenberger, *Manager*
EMP: 43
SALES (corp-wide): 290.9MM **Privately Held**
WEB: www.marshallmedical.org
SIC: 8062 General medical & surgical hospitals
PA: Marshall Medical Center
1100 Marshall Way
Placerville CA 95667
530 622-1441

(P-16443)
MARSHALL MEDICAL CENTER
5137 Golden Foothill Pkwy # 120, El Dorado Hills (95762-9671)
PHONE 530 344-5400
Shannon Truesdell, *COO*
Tarandeep Kaur, *Family Practiti*
Steven Mills, *Family Practiti*
Mary Taylor, *Assistant*
EMP: 43
SALES (corp-wide): 290.9MM **Privately Held**
WEB: www.marshallmedical.org
SIC: 8062 General medical & surgical hospitals
PA: Marshall Medical Center
1100 Marshall Way
Placerville CA 95667
530 622-1441

(P-16444)
MARSHALL MEDICAL CENTER
Also Called: Marshall Hospital Home Care
681 Main St Ste 206, Placerville (95667-5747)
PHONE 530 626-2900
Martha Pike, *Branch Mgr*
Mary Abel, *Technology*
EMP: 43
SALES (corp-wide): 290.9MM **Privately Held**
WEB: www.marshallmedical.org
SIC: 8062 8082 General medical & surgical hospitals; home health care services
PA: Marshall Medical Center
1100 Marshall Way
Placerville CA 95667
530 622-1441

(P-16445)
MARSHALL MEDICAL CENTER
Also Called: Medical Surgery Unit
Marshall Way, Placerville (95667)
P.O. Box 872 (95667-0872)
PHONE 530 626-2616
Patty Garcia, *Principal*
Gary Gremel, *Analyst*
EMP: 43

SALES (corp-wide): 290.9MM **Privately Held**
WEB: www.marshallmedical.org
SIC: 8062 General medical & surgical hospitals
PA: Marshall Medical Center
1100 Marshall Way
Placerville CA 95667
530 622-1441

(P-16446)
MARSHALL MEDICAL CENTER
Also Called: Marshall Ob/Gyn
1095 Marshall Way Fl 2, Placerville (95667-5722)
PHONE 530 344-5470
Kim Cramer, *Financial Analy*
Kathleen Hertzer, *Surgeon*
Evgenia Polosina, *Obstetrician*
Maria Rosen, *Nurse Practr*
EMP: 43
SALES (corp-wide): 290.9MM **Privately Held**
WEB: www.marshallmedical.org
SIC: 8062 General medical & surgical hospitals
PA: Marshall Medical Center
1100 Marshall Way
Placerville CA 95667
530 622-1441

(P-16447)
MARSHALL MEDICAL CENTER
3501 Palmer Dr, Cameron Park (95682-8276)
PHONE 530 672-7040
Roy Marsh, *Branch Mgr*
EMP: 43
SALES (corp-wide): 290.9MM **Privately Held**
WEB: www.marshallmedical.org
SIC: 8062 General medical & surgical hospitals
PA: Marshall Medical Center
1100 Marshall Way
Placerville CA 95667
530 622-1441

(P-16448)
MARSHALL MEDICAL CENTER
4341b Golden Center Dr, Placerville (95667-6260)
PHONE 530 621-3600
EMP: 43
SALES (corp-wide): 290.9MM **Privately Held**
WEB: www.marshallmedical.org
SIC: 8062 General medical & surgical hospitals
PA: Marshall Medical Center
1100 Marshall Way
Placerville CA 95667
530 622-1441

(P-16449)
MARSHALL MEDICAL CENTER
1100 Marshall Way, El Dorado Hills (95762)
PHONE 916 933-2273
EMP: 43
SALES (corp-wide): 290.9MM **Privately Held**
WEB: www.marshallmedical.org
SIC: 8062 General medical & surgical hospitals
PA: Marshall Medical Center
1100 Marshall Way
Placerville CA 95667
530 622-1441

(P-16450)
MARSHALL MEDICAL CENTER
Also Called: Family Intrnal Mdcn-Plcerville
1095 Marshall Way, Placerville (95667-5722)
PHONE 530 626-2920
Maria Rosen, *Nurse Practr*
EMP: 43
SALES (corp-wide): 290.9MM **Privately Held**
WEB: www.marshallmedical.org
SIC: 8062 General medical & surgical hospitals

PRODUCTS & SERVICES SECTION
8062 - General Medical & Surgical Hospitals County (P-16470)

PA: Marshall Medical Center
1100 Marshall Way
Placerville CA 95667
530 622-1441

(P-16451)
MARSHALL MEDICAL CENTER (PA)
Also Called: Marshall Hospital
1100 Marshall Way, Placerville (95667-6533)
P.O. Box 872 (95667-0872)
PHONE..................530 622-1441
James Whipple, CEO
Shannon Truesdell, COO
Laurie Eldridge, CFO
Michelle Norriseven, Exec Dir
Marlene Markowich, General Mgr
EMP: 1000 EST: 1959
SQ FT: 124,000
SALES (est): 290.9MM Privately Held
WEB: www.marshallmedical.org
SIC: 8062 8071 8082 General medical & surgical hospitals; medical laboratories; X-ray laboratory, including dental; home health care services

(P-16452)
MARSHALL MEDICAL CENTER
Also Called: Cancer Resource Center
3581 Palmer Dr Ste 202, Cameron Park (95682-8237)
PHONE..................530 672-7050
Frank Nachtman, Manager
Swetha Mudunuri, Internal Med
Jeremy Ernst, Psychiatry
Alice Phillips, Nurse
Sherry Geurin,
EMP: 43
SQ FT: 31,030
SALES (corp-wide): 290.9MM Privately Held
WEB: www.marshallmedical.org
SIC: 8062 8071 General medical & surgical hospitals; X-ray laboratory, including dental
PA: Marshall Medical Center
1100 Marshall Way
Placerville CA 95667
530 622-1441

(P-16453)
MATER MISERICORDIAE HOSPITAL (PA)
Also Called: MERCY MEDICAL CENTER MERCED
333 Mercy Ave, Merced (95340-8319)
PHONE..................209 564-5000
David Dunham, CEO
Mika Grisham, Risk Mgmt Dir
Sandra Barker, Food Svc Dir
Jason Antunez, Emerg Med Spec
Roseli Oestreicher, Director
EMP: 668 EST: 1948
SQ FT: 60,000
SALES (est): 298.8MM Privately Held
SIC: 8062 General medical & surgical hospitals

(P-16454)
MATERNAL CNNCTONS EL CMINO HOS
2110 Forest Ave Ste B, San Jose (95128-1469)
PHONE..................650 988-8287
Richard Warren, CEO
Lee Domonico, CEO
EMP: 45 EST: 1961
SALES (est): 10.1MM Privately Held
WEB: www.elcaminohealth.org
SIC: 8062 General medical & surgical hospitals

(P-16455)
MENDOCINO COAST DISTRICT HOSP (PA)
700 River Dr, Fort Bragg (95437-5403)
PHONE..................707 961-1234
Jonathan Baker, CEO
Mark Smith, CFO
Patricia Jauregui Darland, Chairman
Tom Birdsell, Treasurer
Camille Ranker, Treasurer
▲ EMP: 300 EST: 1971
SQ FT: 71,500
SALES: 59MM Privately Held
WEB: www.mcdh.org
SIC: 8062 General medical & surgical hospitals

(P-16456)
MERCY HM SVCS A CAL LTD PARTNR (DH)
Also Called: Mercy Medical Center - Redding
2175 Rosaline Ave Ste A, Redding (96001-2549)
P.O. Box 496009 (96049-6009)
PHONE..................530 225-6000
George A Govier, CEO
Brian Moon,
Peggy Podliska, Buyer
Hojin Wang, Anesthesiology
Michael Neal, Internal Med
EMP: 700 EST: 1987
SQ FT: 250,000
SALES (est): 385.6MM Privately Held
WEB: www.dignityhealth.org
SIC: 8062 Hospital, affiliated with AMA residency
HQ: Dignity Health
185 Berry St Ste 200
San Francisco CA 94107
415 438-5500

(P-16457)
MERCY SURGERY CENTER LP
2175 Rosaline Ave Ste A, Redding (96001-2510)
PHONE..................530 225-7400
Catholic Healthcare, Partner
Kristi Manutai, Administration
EMP: 52 EST: 2003
SALES (est): 13.8MM Privately Held
WEB: www.mercy-sc.com
SIC: 8062 General medical & surgical hospitals

(P-16458)
MOFFITT H C HOSPITAL
505 Parnassus Ave, San Francisco (94143-2204)
PHONE..................415 476-1000
EMP: 148 EST: 2008
SALES (est): 283.3K
SALES (corp-wide): 9.5B Privately Held
SIC: 8062 General Hospital
HQ: University Of California, San Francisco
505 Parnassus Ave
San Francisco CA 94143
415 476-9000

(P-16459)
MOUNTAIN CMMNTIES HLTH CARE DS (PA)
Also Called: Trinity Hospital
60 Easter Ave, Weaverville (96093-8054)
P.O. Box 1229 (96093-1229)
PHONE..................530 623-5541
Aaron Rogers, CEO
Julie Roselli-Raya,
Jessie Thorpe, Records Dir
Victoria Williams, Lab Dir
Wade Nakatani, Radiology Dir
EMP: 139 EST: 2006
SALES: 15.2MM Privately Held
WEB: www.mcmedical.org
SIC: 8062 General medical & surgical hospitals

(P-16460)
MT DIABLO SURGERY CENTER
2540 East St Fl A22, Concord (94520-1906)
PHONE..................925 674-4740
Debbie Mack, President
EMP: 47 EST: 2005
SALES (est): 12.6MM
SALES (corp-wide): 1.9B Publicly Held
WEB: www.johnmuirhealth.com
SIC: 8062 General medical & surgical hospitals
HQ: National Surgical Hospitals, Inc.
250 S Wacker Dr Ste 500
Chicago IL 60606
312 627-8400

(P-16461)
MUIR JOHN MGNTIC IMGING CTR L
Also Called: John Muir Inptient Therapy Ctr
1601 Ygnacio Valley Rd, Walnut Creek (94598-3122)
PHONE..................925 296-7156
Edward Miller, Director
EMP: 72 EST: 1991
SQ FT: 5,000
SALES (est): 2.8MM Privately Held
WEB: www.johnmuirhealth.com
SIC: 8062 General medical & surgical hospitals

(P-16462)
MUIR LABS
Also Called: Muirlab
1601 Ygnacio Valley Rd, Walnut Creek (94598-3122)
PHONE..................925 947-3335
Pat Morgan, Director
EMP: 35 EST: 1960
SALES (est): 1.3MM Privately Held
WEB: www.johnmuirhealth.com
SIC: 8062 General medical & surgical hospitals

(P-16463)
NORTH SONOMA COUNTY HOSP DST
Also Called: Healdsburg District Hospital
1375 University St, Healdsburg (95448-3382)
PHONE..................707 431-6500
Evan J Rayner, CEO
Chung LI, Records Dir
Dan Hull, CFO
Shahriar Taj, CFO
Johnny Hargrove, Vice Pres
EMP: 171 EST: 2001
SALES (est): 41.3MM Privately Held
WEB: www.healdsburgdistricthospital.org
SIC: 8062 General medical & surgical hospitals

(P-16464)
NORTH VLY ORTHPD HAND SRGERY A
Also Called: Burky, Robert E Jr MD
470 Plumas Blvd Ste 201, Yuba City (95991-5077)
PHONE..................530 671-2650
Susan Wilkins, Manager
Linda Southard, Principal
EMP: 52 EST: 1972
SQ FT: 9,000
SALES (est): 3.3MM Privately Held
SIC: 8062 General medical & surgical hospitals

(P-16465)
NORTHBAY HEALTHCARE CORP (PA)
Also Called: Northbay Healthcare System
1200 B Gale Wilson Blvd, Fairfield (94533-3552)
PHONE..................707 646-5000
Gary J Passama, President
Dante Tolbert, President
Nicole Brocato, Officer
Justine Zilliken, Assoc VP
Elizabeth Gladney, Program Mgr
EMP: 114 EST: 1987
SQ FT: 24,000
SALES (est): 530.8MM Privately Held
WEB: www.northbay.org
SIC: 8062 8011 General medical & surgical hospitals; offices & clinics of medical doctors

(P-16466)
NORTHBAY HEALTHCARE GROUP (HQ)
Also Called: Northbay Medical Center
1200 B Gale Wilson Blvd, Fairfield (94533-3552)
PHONE..................707 646-5000
Toll Free:..................888 -
Deborah Sugiyama, CEO
Jim Andersen, Vice Pres
Nicole Brocato, Vice Pres
Katie Lydon, Admin Sec
Aaron Perez, IT/INT Sup
EMP: 900 EST: 1954
SQ FT: 125,000
SALES: 530.8MM Privately Held
WEB: www.northbay.org
SIC: 8062 General medical & surgical hospitals
PA: Northbay Healthcare Corporation
1200 B Gale Wilson Blvd
Fairfield CA 94533
707 646-5000

(P-16467)
NORTHBAY HEALTHCARE GROUP
Also Called: Vaca Valley Hospital
1000 Nut Tree Rd, Vacaville (95687-4100)
PHONE..................707 446-4000
Debra Sugijama, President
Elnora Cameron, Vice Pres
Lorie Jarvis, Personnel Assit
Angeli Rivero, Nurse
Kimberly McQueen,
EMP: 300
SQ FT: 59,000
SALES (corp-wide): 530.8MM Privately Held
WEB: www.northbay.org
SIC: 8062 General medical & surgical hospitals
HQ: Northbay Healthcare Group
1200 B Gale Wilson Blvd
Fairfield CA 94533
707 646-5000

(P-16468)
NORTHERN CAL RHBLTTION HOSP LL
2801 Eureka Way, Redding (96001-0222)
PHONE..................530 246-9000
Brad Hollinger, Mng Member
Lisa Stevens, Officer
Stephen Marcus,
EMP: 117 EST: 2005
SALES (est): 10.7MM
SALES (corp-wide): 759.7MM Privately Held
WEB: www.vibrahealthcare.com
SIC: 8062 General medical & surgical hospitals
PA: Vibra Healthcare, Llc
4600 Lena Dr Ste 100
Mechanicsburg PA 17055
717 591-5700

(P-16469)
OAK VALLEY HOSPITAL DISTRICT
Also Called: Riverbank Health Center
2603 Patterson Rd Ste 3, Riverbank (95367-3407)
PHONE..................209 869-8102
Andres Mariano, Director
EMP: 74
SALES (corp-wide): 72.2MM Privately Held
WEB: www.oakvalleyhospital.com
SIC: 8062 9431 General medical & surgical hospitals; public health agency administration, government
PA: Oak Valley Hospital District
350 S Oak Ave
Oakdale CA 95361
209 847-3011

(P-16470)
OAK VALLEY HOSPITAL DISTRICT (PA)
350 S Oak Ave, Oakdale (95361-3519)
PHONE..................209 847-3011
John McCormick, CEO
Bob Wikoff, Ch of Bd
Gail Sward, Vice Ch Bd
Chrissy Schoonover, Lab Dir
James Trevina, Radiology Dir
EMP: 325 EST: 1971
SQ FT: 55,000
SALES: 72.2MM Privately Held
WEB: www.oakvalleyhospital.com
SIC: 8062 8051 General medical & surgical hospitals; skilled nursing care facilities

8062 - General Medical & Surgical Hospitals County (P-16471)

(P-16471)
OCONNOR HOSPITAL
Also Called: O'Connor Hosp Pdtric Ctr For L
2039 Forest Ave, San Jose (95128-4817)
P.O. Box 1387, San Carlos (94070-7387)
PHONE..............................408 947-2929
James F Dover, *President*
EMP: 204 **Privately Held**
WEB: www.och.sccgov.org
SIC: 8062 General medical & surgical hospitals
HQ: O'connor Hospital
2105 Forest Ave
San Jose CA 95128
408 947-2500

(P-16472)
OCONNOR HOSPITAL (HQ)
Also Called: O'Connor Wound Care Clinic
2105 Forest Ave, San Jose (95128-1471)
PHONE..............................408 947-2500
Richard Adcock, *CEO*
James F Dover, *CEO*
David W Carroll, *Senior VP*
Craig Rucker, *Vice Pres*
Ilinka Golomeic, *Hum Res Coord*
EMP: 1000 **EST:** 1889
SQ FT: 750,000
SALES (est): 201.4MM **Privately Held**
WEB: www.och.sccgov.org
SIC: 8062 General medical & surgical hospitals
PA: County Of Santa Clara
70 W Hedding St 2wing
San Jose CA 95110
408 299-5200

(P-16473)
ORCHARD HOSPITAL
240 Spruce St, Gridley (95948-2216)
P.O. Box 97 (95948-0097)
PHONE..............................530 846-9000
Steve Stark, *CEO*
Kristina Sanke, *CFO*
Art Cota, *Bd of Directors*
Jatinder S Kullar, *Bd of Directors*
Lutch Perumal, *Human Res Dir*
EMP: 235 **EST:** 1946
SQ FT: 12,000
SALES: 34.4MM **Privately Held**
WEB: www.orchardhospital.com
SIC: 8062 General medical & surgical hospitals

(P-16474)
OROVILLE HOSPITAL (PA)
2767 Olive Hwy, Oroville (95966-6118)
PHONE..............................530 533-8500
Robert J Wentz, *CEO*
Scott Chapple, *COO*
Ashok Khanchandani, *CFO*
Sultan Chopan, *Trustee*
Matthew Fine, *Chief Mktg Ofcr*
EMP: 732 **EST:** 1966
SQ FT: 68,133
SALES: 353.1MM **Privately Held**
WEB: www.orovillehospital.com
SIC: 8062 General medical & surgical hospitals

(P-16475)
OROVILLE HOSPITAL
Also Called: Attic
2170 Bird St, Oroville (95965-4915)
PHONE..............................530 532-8697
Kim Nixon, *Director*
EMP: 479
SALES (corp-wide): 353.1MM **Privately Held**
WEB: www.orovillehospital.com
SIC: 8062 General medical & surgical hospitals
PA: Oroville Hospital
2767 Olive Hwy
Oroville CA 95966
530 533-8500

(P-16476)
PACIFIC CAST CRDIAC VSCLAR SRG
2900 Whipple Ave Ste 225, Redwood City (94062-2851)
PHONE..............................650 366-0225
Vincent A Gaudiani MD, *President*
Perry M Shoor MD, *Treasurer*
Paul R Cipriano MD, *Vice Pres*
James Zimmerman MD, *Vice Pres*
Joann Roser, *Financial Exec*
EMP: 44 **EST:** 1971
SQ FT: 4,000
SALES (est): 8.1MM **Privately Held**
SIC: 8062 General medical & surgical hospitals

(P-16477)
PATIENTS HOSPITAL
2900 Eureka Way, Redding (96001-0220)
PHONE..............................530 225-8700
James D Tate MD, *President*
Shari Lejsek, *Administration*
Richard Barnes, *CIO*
Ezra Hemping, *Engineer*
Brenda Meline, *Human Res Mgr*
EMP: 94 **EST:** 1993
SALES: 6.8MM **Privately Held**
WEB: www.patientshospital.com
SIC: 8062 General medical & surgical hospitals

(P-16478)
PEDIATRIC ANESTHESIA ASSOC MED
Also Called: Community Medical Centers
6235 N Fresno St Ste 103, Fresno (93710-5269)
PHONE..............................559 449-4350
Newton Seiden, *President*
Shirley Flanagan, *Office Mgr*
T Greades, *Admin Sec*
Bruce J Witmer, *Orthopedist*
Patrick Ginn, *Med Doctor*
EMP: 86 **EST:** 1971
SQ FT: 1,200
SALES (est): 24.3MM **Privately Held**
WEB: www.paamg.info
SIC: 8062 General medical & surgical hospitals

(P-16479)
PERMANENTE MEDICAL GROUP INC
1550 Gateway Blvd, Fairfield (94533-6901)
PHONE..............................707 427-4000
Laura Coffman, *Branch Mgr*
Sheena Thomas, *Internal Med*
Pat Van Nordstrom, *Manager*
EMP: 1396
SALES (corp-wide): 30.5B **Privately Held**
WEB: www.permanente.org
SIC: 8062 General medical & surgical hospitals
HQ: The Permanente Medical Group Inc
1950 Franklin St Fl 18th
Oakland CA 94612
866 858-2226

(P-16480)
PETALUMA VALLEY HOSPITAL AUX
400 N Mcdowell Blvd, Petaluma (94954-2369)
P.O. Box 2732 (94953-2732)
PHONE..............................707 778-1111
Kathleen Sartori, *President*
EMP: 69 **EST:** 1962
SQ FT: 500
SALES (est): 4.7MM **Privately Held**
SIC: 8062 General medical & surgical hospitals

(P-16481)
PLUMAS HOSPITAL DISTRICT (PA)
1065 Bucks Lake Rd, Quincy (95971-9507)
PHONE..............................530 283-2121
Jodee Read, *CEO*
Doug Lafferty, *President*
Greg Perkins, *Internal Med*
Jeffrey Kepple, *Med Doctor*
Susan Brown, *Nurse*
▲ **EMP:** 180 **EST:** 1959
SQ FT: 30,000
SALES (est): 29.9MM **Privately Held**
WEB: www.pdh.org
SIC: 8062 Hospital, affiliated with AMA residency

(P-16482)
PRESIDIO SURGERY CENTER LLC
1635 Divisadero St # 200, San Francisco (94115-3043)
PHONE..............................415 346-1218
Cynthia Cleveland, *Principal*
Debbie Symes, *Office Mgr*
EMP: 36 **EST:** 2007
SALES (est): 35.5MM
SALES (corp-wide): 257.1B **Publicly Held**
WEB: www.presidiosurgery.com
SIC: 8062 8011 General medical & surgical hospitals; clinic, operated by physicians
PA: Unitedhealth Group Incorporated
9900 Bren Rd E Ste 300w
Minnetonka MN 55343
952 936-1300

(P-16483)
PRIME HLTHCARE SVCS - SHSTA LL
Also Called: Shasta Regional Med Ctr Srmc
1100 Butte St, Redding (96001-0852)
P.O. Box 491810 (96049-1810)
PHONE..............................530 244-5400
Cyndy Gordon, *CEO*
Linda Leaell, *COO*
Roger Moore, *Bd of Directors*
Laura Van Winkle, *Human Resources*
EMP: 850 **EST:** 2004
SALES (est): 152.3MM
SALES (corp-wide): 1B **Privately Held**
WEB: www.shastaregional.com
SIC: 8062 8011 General medical & surgical hospitals; offices & clinics of medical doctors
HQ: Prime Healthcare Services Inc
3480 E Guasti Rd
Ontario CA 91761

(P-16484)
PROGRESSIVE SUB-ACUTE CARE
Also Called: Sub-Acute Saratoga Hospital
13425 Sousa Ln, Saratoga (95070-4637)
PHONE..............................408 378-8875
Michael Zarcone, *President*
Josie Guzman, *Records Dir*
Gary Landi, *Business Dir*
Diana Zussman, *Human Res Dir*
Tara Rokouei, *Education*
EMP: 73 **EST:** 1987
SQ FT: 10,000
SALES (est): 19.1MM **Privately Held**
SIC: 8062 General medical & surgical hospitals

(P-16485)
PROVIDENCE HEALTH & SVCS - ORE
540 23rd St, Oakland (94612-1724)
PHONE..............................510 444-0839
Tim Zaricznyj, *Director*
EMP: 117
SALES (corp-wide): 32.7MM **Privately Held**
WEB: www.providence.org
SIC: 8062 General medical & surgical hospitals
HQ: Providence Health & Services - Oregon
1801 Lind Ave Sw
Renton WA 98057
425 525-3355

(P-16486)
QUEEN OF VLY MED CTR FUNDATION (DH)
1000 Trancas St, NAPA (94558-2906)
PHONE..............................707 252-4411
Lawrence Michael Coomes, *President*
Vincent Morgese, *COO*
Bob Diehl, *CFO*
Don Miller, *CFO*
Mich Riccioni, *CFO*
EMP: 653 **EST:** 1953
SQ FT: 278,500
SALES (est): 268.1MM
SALES (corp-wide): 32.7MM **Privately Held**
WEB: www.thequeen.org
SIC: 8062 General medical & surgical hospitals
HQ: St. Joseph Health System
3345 Michelson Dr Ste 100
Irvine CA 92612
949 381-4000

(P-16487)
QUEEN OF VLY MED CTR FUNDATION
Also Called: Care Network
3448 Villa Ln Ste 102, NAPA (94558-6471)
PHONE..............................707 251-2000
Cris Galleger, *Manager*
Dana Codron, *Manager*
EMP: 293
SALES (corp-wide): 32.7MM **Privately Held**
WEB: www.thequeen.org
SIC: 8062 General medical & surgical hospitals
HQ: Queen Of The Valley Medical Center Foundation
1000 Trancas St
Napa CA 94558
707 252-4411

(P-16488)
REDWOOD MEMORIAL HOSP FORTUNA (PA)
3300 Renner Dr, Fortuna (95540-3120)
PHONE..............................707 725-7327
Thomas McConnell, *CEO*
Bob Branigan, *COO*
Kevin Clouder, *CFO*
Neil Palmer, *Business Dir*
EMP: 150 **EST:** 1954
SQ FT: 65,000
SALES (est): 26.8MM **Privately Held**
SIC: 8062 Hospital, affiliated with AMA residency

(P-16489)
REEDLEY COMMUNITY HOSPITAL
Also Called: Adventist Med Center-Reedley
372 W Cypress Ave, Reedley (93654-2113)
PHONE..............................559 638-8155
Wayne Ferch, *President*
EMP: 80 **EST:** 2011
SALES: 178MM **Privately Held**
WEB: www.adventisthealth.org
SIC: 8062 General medical & surgical hospitals

(P-16490)
RIDEOUT MEMORIAL HOSPITAL (HQ)
726 4th St, Marysville (95901-5656)
P.O. Box 2128 (95901-0075)
PHONE..............................530 749-4416
Ronald M Sweeney, *Chairman*
Theresa Hamilton, *CEO*
John Cary, *Treasurer*
Lisa Del Pero, *Admin Sec*
Alison Barrow, *Emerg Med Spec*
EMP: 700 **EST:** 1907
SQ FT: 100,000
SALES (est): 744.9K
SALES (corp-wide): 26.9MM **Privately Held**
WEB: www.adventisthealth.org
SIC: 8062 8082 General medical & surgical hospitals; home health care services
PA: Freemont Rideout Health Group
989 Plumas St
Yuba City CA 95991
530 751-4010

(P-16491)
SAINT AGNES MED PROVIDERS INC
1379 E Herndon Ave, Fresno (93720-3309)
PHONE..............................559 435-2630
David J Cavagnaro MD, *Partner*
EMP: 58
SALES (corp-wide): 54.2MM **Privately Held**
WEB: www.samc.com
SIC: 8062 General medical & surgical hospitals

▲ = Import ▼=Export
◆ =Import/Export

PRODUCTS & SERVICES SECTION
8062 - General Medical & Surgical Hospitals County (P-16512)

PA: Saint Agnes Medical Providers, Inc.
1510 E Herndon Ave # 210
Fresno CA 93720
559 450-7200

(P-16492)
SAINT AGNES MED PROVIDERS INC
Also Called: Saint Agnes Med Prviders Obgyn
6121 N Thesta St Ste 303, Fresno (93710-5294)
PHONE 559 450-2300
Beckie Villanueva, *Branch Mgr*
EMP: 58
SALES (corp-wide): 54.2MM **Privately Held**
WEB: www.samc.com
SIC: 8062 General medical & surgical hospitals
PA: Saint Agnes Medical Providers, Inc.
1510 E Herndon Ave # 210
Fresno CA 93720
559 450-7200

(P-16493)
SAINT AGNES MEDICAL CENTER (HQ)
1303 E Herndon Ave, Fresno (93720-3309)
PHONE 559 450-3000
Nancy R Hollingsworth, *CEO*
Tom Anderson,
Teresa Gresko, *CFO*
Andrea Lanier, *Treasurer*
Thomas Brown, *Bd of Directors*
EMP: 1688 **EST:** 1929
SQ FT: 200,000
SALES: 530.9MM
SALES (corp-wide): 18.8B **Privately Held**
WEB: www.samc.com
SIC: 8062 General medical & surgical hospitals
PA: Trinity Health Corporation
20555 Victor Pkwy
Livonia MI 48152
734 343-1000

(P-16494)
SAINT FRANCIS MEMORIAL HOSP (DH)
900 Hyde St, San Francisco (94109-4806)
PHONE 415 353-6000
Thomas G Hennessy, *CEO*
John G Williams, *President*
Tiffany Caster, *COO*
Cheryl A Fama Rn, *COO*
Markham Miller, *Vice Pres*
EMP: 800 **EST:** 1905
SQ FT: 300,000
SALES: 174.1K **Privately Held**
WEB: www.dignityhealth.org
SIC: 8062 General medical & surgical hospitals
HQ: Dignity Health
185 Berry St Ste 200
San Francisco CA 94107
415 438-5500

(P-16495)
SAINT FRANCIS MEMORIAL HOSP
Also Called: Womankind
900 Hide St, San Francisco (94120)
P.O. Box 7590 (94120-7590)
PHONE 415 353-6000
Jeff Niuatoa, *Branch Mgr*
EMP: 40 **Privately Held**
WEB: www.dignityhealth.org
SIC: 8062 General medical & surgical hospitals
HQ: Francis Saint Memorial Hospital
900 Hyde St
San Francisco CA 94109
415 353-6000

(P-16496)
SAINT FRANCIS MEMORIAL HOSP
900 High St Ste 1201, San Francisco (94109)
PHONE 415 353-6000
John Williams, *Principal*
EMP: 40 **Privately Held**
WEB: www.dignityhealth.org
SIC: 8062 General medical & surgical hospitals

HQ: Francis Saint Memorial Hospital
900 Hyde St
San Francisco CA 94109
415 353-6000

(P-16497)
SAINT FRANCIS MEMORIAL HOSP
Also Called: Catholic Health Care West
909 Hyde St, San Francisco (94109-4822)
PHONE 415 673-1317
Thomas Hennesey, *President*
EMP: 40 **Privately Held**
WEB: www.dignityhealth.org
SIC: 8062 General medical & surgical hospitals
HQ: Francis Saint Memorial Hospital
900 Hyde St
San Francisco CA 94109
415 353-6000

(P-16498)
SAINT FRANCIS MEMORIAL HOSP
900 Hyde St, San Francisco (94109-4806)
PHONE 415 353-6600
Dr David Klein, *President*
EMP: 40 **Privately Held**
WEB: www.dignityhealth.org
SIC: 8062 General medical & surgical hospitals
HQ: Francis Saint Memorial Hospital
900 Hyde St
San Francisco CA 94109
415 353-6000

(P-16499)
SAINT FRANCIS MEMORIAL HOSP
Also Called: St Francis Memorial Hospital
900 Hyde St, San Francisco (94109-4806)
PHONE 415 353-6420
John L Meyer MD, *Director*
John Meyer, *Med Doctor*
EMP: 40 **Privately Held**
WEB: www.dignityhealth.org
SIC: 8062 General medical & surgical hospitals
HQ: Francis Saint Memorial Hospital
900 Hyde St
San Francisco CA 94109
415 353-6000

(P-16500)
SAINT FRANCIS MEMORIAL HOSP
San Francisco Spine Clinic
1199 Bush St Ste 300, San Francisco (94109-5974)
PHONE 415 353-6464
Carla Helmbrecht, *Manager*
EMP: 40 **Privately Held**
WEB: www.dignityhealth.org
SIC: 8062 General medical & surgical hospitals
HQ: Francis Saint Memorial Hospital
900 Hyde St
San Francisco CA 94109
415 353-6000

(P-16501)
SAINT LOUISE HOSPITAL
9400 N Name Uno, Gilroy (95020-3528)
PHONE 408 848-2000
Jim Dober, *CEO*
Terry Curley, *Vice Pres*
Joanne Allan, *Principal*
EMP: 500 **EST:** 2005
SALES (est): 90.6MM **Privately Held**
WEB: www.slrh.sccgov.org
SIC: 8062 General medical & surgical hospitals

(P-16502)
SAMARTAN INTRNAL MDCINE MED GR
2410 Samaritan Dr Ste 201, San Jose (95124-3909)
PHONE 408 371-9010
Randall Spencer MD, *Partner*
Jane Chien MD, *Partner*
Joe L Morgensen MD, *Partner*
Cameron Oba MD, *Partner*
Shawn J Foley, *Family Practiti*
EMP: 44 **EST:** 1997

SQ FT: 5,000
SALES (est): 12.4MM **Privately Held**
SIC: 8062 General medical & surgical hospitals

(P-16503)
SAN JOAQUIN GENERAL HOSPITAL (PA)
500 W Hospital Rd, French Camp (95231-9693)
P.O. Box 1020, Stockton (95201-3120)
PHONE 209 468-6000
David Cullberson, *CEO*
Deborah Kolhede, *COO*
Chris Roberts, *CFO*
Sheila Kapre, *Chief Mktg Ofcr*
Linda Juarez, *Vice Pres*
EMP: 1312 **EST:** 2000
SALES (est): 152.2MM **Privately Held**
WEB: www.sanjoaquingeneral.org
SIC: 8062 General medical & surgical hospitals

(P-16504)
SAN JOSE HEALTHCARE SYSTEM LP
Also Called: Regional Medical Ctr San Jose
225 N Jackson Ave, San Jose (95116-1603)
PHONE 408 259-5000
Kenneth West, *President*
Veeral Shah, *Officer*
David Hutto, *Op Rm Dir*
Darrel Odell, *MIS Dir*
Cheryl Mosses, *Opers Staff*
EMP: 1200 **EST:** 1984
SQ FT: 203,685
SALES (est): 103.8MM **Publicly Held**
WEB: www.regionalmedicalsanjose.com
SIC: 8062 General medical & surgical hospitals
HQ: Hca Inc.
1 Park Plz
Nashville TN 37203
615 344-9551

(P-16505)
SAN JQUIN GEN HOSP FNDTION A C
Also Called: Healthcare Services
500 W Hospital Rd, French Camp (95231-9693)
PHONE 209 468-6000
David Colberson, *CEO*
Ronald Kruetner, *CFO*
Betty Riendel, *Department Mgr*
EMP: 1300 **EST:** 2001
SALES (est): 313MM **Privately Held**
WEB: www.sjcclinics.com
SIC: 8062 General medical & surgical hospitals

(P-16506)
SAN LEANDRO HOSPITAL LP
13855 E 14th St, San Leandro (94578-2600)
PHONE 510 357-6500
Ronnie Bayduza, *CEO*
Janay Defer, *Administration*
Sue Magidson, *Pastor Care Dir*
EMP: 475 **EST:** 1994
SALES (est): 73.6MM **Privately Held**
WEB: www.alamedahealthsystem.org
SIC: 8062 8361 General medical & surgical hospitals; residential care
PA: Alameda Health System
1411 E 31st St
Oakland CA 94602

(P-16507)
SAN RAMON ENDOSCOPY CENTER INC
5801 Norris Canyon Rd # 100, San Ramon (94583-5440)
PHONE 925 275-9910
David Wong, *President*
EMP: 41 **EST:** 2004
SQ FT: 34,703
SALES (est): 9.9MM **Privately Held**
SIC: 8062 General medical & surgical hospitals

(P-16508)
SAN RAMON REGIONAL MED CTR LLC
6001 Norris Canyon Rd, San Ramon (94583-5400)
PHONE 925 275-9200
Shawn Dewers,
Emma Haag, *Social Dir*
Caryn Thornburg, *Engineer*
Kevin Littrell, *Purch Dir*
Rosemary Sandoval, *Pathologist*
EMP: 600 **EST:** 1983
SALES (est): 85.7MM
SALES (corp-wide): 17.6B **Publicly Held**
WEB: www.sanramonmedctr.com
SIC: 8062 8093 General medical & surgical hospitals; rehabilitation center, outpatient treatment
PA: Tenet Healthcare Corporation
14201 Dallas Pkwy
Dallas TX 75254
469 893-2200

(P-16509)
SANTA CLARA COUNTY OF
Also Called: Santa Clara Vlly Hlth & Hsptl
2325 Enborg Ln 2h260, San Jose (95128-2659)
PHONE 408 885-7470
Katelyn Hart, *Admin Asst*
EMP: 135 **Privately Held**
WEB: www.sccgov.org
SIC: 8062 General medical & surgical hospitals
PA: County Of Santa Clara
70 W Hedding St 2wing
San Jose CA 95110
408 299-5200

(P-16510)
SANTA CLARA COUNTY OF
Also Called: Santa Clara Vly Hlth Hosp Sys
2325 Enborg Ln Fl 4, San Jose (95128-2649)
PHONE 408 885-5451
James Murphy, *Director*
EMP: 135 **Privately Held**
WEB: www.sccgov.org
SIC: 8062 9431 General medical & surgical hospitals; administration of public health programs
PA: County Of Santa Clara
70 W Hedding St 2wing
San Jose CA 95110
408 299-5200

(P-16511)
SANTA CLARA COUNTY OF
Also Called: St. Louise Regional Hospital
9400 N Name Uno, Gilroy (95020-3528)
PHONE 408 848-2000
Dub Drees, *Vice Pres*
Lisa Turallo, *Executive Asst*
Laura Reyes, *Admin Asst*
Patrick Ycaro, *Analyst*
Brian Saavedra, *Med Doctor*
EMP: 135 **Privately Held**
WEB: www.sccgov.org
SIC: 8062 General medical & surgical hospitals
PA: County Of Santa Clara
70 W Hedding St 2wing
San Jose CA 95110
408 299-5200

(P-16512)
SANTA CLARA COUNTY OF
Also Called: Santa Clara Valley Health & Ho
2325 Enborg Ln Ste 380, San Jose (95128-2649)
PHONE 408 885-6818
Kim Roberts, *Finance*
EMP: 50 **Privately Held**
WEB: www.sccgov.org
SIC: 8062 9431 9311 Hospital, medical school affiliated with nursing & residency; administration of public health programs; ; finance, taxation & monetary policy;
PA: County Of Santa Clara
70 W Hedding St 2wing
San Jose CA 95110
408 299-5200

8062 - General Medical & Surgical Hospitals County (P-16513)

(P-16513)
SANTA CLARA VALLEY MEDICAL CTR (PA)
Also Called: Scvmc
751 S Bascom Ave, San Jose (95128-2699)
PHONE......................408 885-5000
Paul E Lorenz, *CEO*
Chitra Venketesh, *Records Dir*
Dianne Tiernan, *Radiology Dir*
Teresa Goodman, *Office Mgr*
Sylvia Ramirez, *Executive Asst*
EMP: 475 **EST:** 2010
SALES (est): 490.9MM **Privately Held**
WEB: www.scvmc.org
SIC: 8062 6324 General medical & surgical hospitals; hospital & medical service plans

(P-16514)
SANTA ROSA MEMORIAL HOSPITAL
Also Called: St. Joseph Dental
751 Lombardi Ct, Santa Rosa (95407-6798)
PHONE......................707 547-2221
Kathy Ficco, *Manager*
Stacey Stirling, *Manager*
EMP: 100
SALES (corp-wide): 32.7MM **Privately Held**
WEB: www.stjoesonoma.org
SIC: 8062 General medical & surgical hospitals
HQ: St. Joseph Health Northern California, Llc
1165 Montgomery Dr
Santa Rosa CA 95405
707 546-3210

(P-16515)
SANTA ROSA MEMORIAL HOSPITAL
Also Called: Montgomery Center
1170 Montgomery Dr, Santa Rosa (95405-4802)
PHONE......................707 542-4704
Linda Baku, *Nurse*
EMP: 100
SALES (corp-wide): 32.7MM **Privately Held**
WEB: www.stjoesonoma.org
SIC: 8062 General medical & surgical hospitals
HQ: St. Joseph Health Northern California, Llc
1165 Montgomery Dr
Santa Rosa CA 95405
707 546-3210

(P-16516)
SANTA ROSA MEMORIAL HOSPITAL
2700 Dolbeer St, Eureka (95501-4736)
PHONE......................707 525-5300
Tory Starr, *Branch Mgr*
Laurie Watsonstone, *Mktg Dir*
Kristy Nickols, *Sales Staff*
Janet Hildebrand, *Media Spec*
EMP: 100
SALES (corp-wide): 32.7MM **Privately Held**
WEB: www.stjoesonoma.org
SIC: 8062 General medical & surgical hospitals
HQ: St. Joseph Health Northern California, Llc
1165 Montgomery Dr
Santa Rosa CA 95405
707 546-3210

(P-16517)
SANTA ROSA SURGERY CENTER LP
Also Called: Sutter Health
1111 Sonoma Ave Ste 214, Santa Rosa (95405-4833)
PHONE......................707 575-5831
Dan Peterson, *Administration*
Jiries Mogannam, *Principal*
EMP: 46 **EST:** 1983
SQ FT: 8,000
SALES (est): 19.8MM **Privately Held**
SIC: 8062 General medical & surgical hospitals

(P-16518)
SCOTTS VALLEY MEDICAL CLINIC
2890 El Rancho Dr, Santa Cruz (95060-1104)
PHONE......................831 438-1430
Dawn Motyka, *Partner*
Anne-Marie McDaniel, *Family Practiti*
Michael J Coulson, *Med Doctor*
EMP: 35 **EST:** 1985
SALES (est): 1.9MM **Privately Held**
SIC: 8062 General medical & surgical hospitals

(P-16519)
SENECA HEALTHCARE DISTRICT (PA)
Also Called: SHD
130 Brentwood Dr, Chester (96020)
P.O. Box 737 (96020-0737)
PHONE......................530 258-2151
Linda Wagner, *CEO*
David Slusher Jr, *President*
Steve Boline, *CFO*
Cheryl Darnell, *CFO*
William Howe, *Treasurer*
EMP: 105 **EST:** 1952
SQ FT: 12,417
SALES (est): 26.3MM **Privately Held**
WEB: www.senecahospital.org
SIC: 8062 General medical & surgical hospitals

(P-16520)
SEQUOIA HEALTH SERVICES (DH)
Also Called: Sequoia Hospital
170 Alameda De Las Pulgas, Redwood City (94062-2751)
PHONE......................650 369-5811
Glenna Vaskellas, *Administration*
Michael Hollett, *Ch Radiology*
Melissa Sims, *Ch Radiology*
Krissy Mangiola, *Administration*
Lisa Boohar, *Oncology*
EMP: 1143 **EST:** 1947
SQ FT: 350,000
SALES: 159.1K **Privately Held**
WEB: www.dignityhealth.org
SIC: 8062 General medical & surgical hospitals
HQ: Dignity Health
185 Berry St Ste 200
San Francisco CA 94107
415 438-5500

(P-16521)
SEQUOIA SURGICAL CENTER LP
Also Called: Sequoia Surgical Pavilion
2405 Shadelands Dr # 200, Walnut Creek (94598-5916)
PHONE......................925 935-6700
Debbie Mack, *General Ptnr*
Angie Blankinship, *Administration*
Christina Barroso, *Analyst*
Julie Habiger, *Opers Staff*
Dana Cooper, *Nurse*
EMP: 50 **EST:** 2000
SQ FT: 14,750
SALES (est): 10MM
SALES (corp-wide): 1.9B **Publicly Held**
WEB: www.sequoiasurgery.org
SIC: 8062 General medical & surgical hospitals
HQ: National Surgical Hospitals, Inc.
250 S Wacker Dr Ste 500
Chicago IL 60606
312 627-8400

(P-16522)
SETON MEDICAL CENTER (HQ)
1900 Sullivan Ave, Daly City (94015-2229)
PHONE......................650 992-4000
Mark S Fratzke, *President*
Mark Fratzke, *Officer*
Suzy Beeler, *Director*
Terrie L Hairston, *Manager*
EMP: 1099
SQ FT: 400,000
SALES (est): 163.6MM
SALES (corp-wide): 596.3MM **Privately Held**
WEB: www.seton.verity.org
SIC: 8062 8051 General medical & surgical hospitals; skilled nursing care facilities
PA: Verity Health System Of California, Inc.
1500 Suthgate Ave Ste 102
Daly City CA 91367
650 551-6650

(P-16523)
SETON MEDICAL CENTER
Also Called: Seton Medical Center Coastside
600 Marine Blvd, Moss Beach (94038-9641)
PHONE......................650 563-7100
Judy Cook, *Branch Mgr*
Sue Desoto, *Radiology Dir*
Robert Telfer MD, *Med Doctor*
EMP: 130
SALES (corp-wide): 163.6MM **Privately Held**
WEB: www.seton.verity.org
SIC: 8062 5812 8051 General medical & surgical hospitals; eating places; skilled nursing care facilities
PA: Seton Medical Center
1900 Sullivan Ave
Daly City CA 94015
650 992-4000

(P-16524)
SETON MEDICAL CENTER
West Bay HM Hlth & Cmnty Svcs
1784 Sullivan Ave Ste 200, Daly City (94015-2067)
PHONE......................650 992-4000
Fax: 650 991-4146
EMP: 60
SALES (corp-wide): 225.4MM **Privately Held**
SIC: 8062 7361 8082 General Hospital Employment Agency Home Health Care Services
HQ: Seton Medical Center
1900 Sullivan Ave
Daly City CA 94015
650 992-4000

(P-16525)
SHRINERS HSPITALS FOR CHILDREN
2425 Stockton Blvd, Sacramento (95817-2215)
PHONE......................916 453-2050
Margaret Bryan, *Administration*
Lin Kassouni, *Lab Dir*
John Bevel, *Info Tech Mgr*
Butters David, *Technology*
Tommy Deorosan, *Opers Staff*
EMP: 500 **Privately Held**
WEB: www.shrinerschildrens.org
SIC: 8062 General medical & surgical hospitals
HQ: Shriners Hospitals For Children
12502 Usf Pine Dr
Tampa FL 33612
813 972-2250

(P-16526)
SIERRA NEV MMORIAL-MINERS HOSP (DH)
Also Called: Sierra Nevada Memorial Hosp
155 Glasson Way, Grass Valley (95945-5723)
PHONE......................530 274-6000
Katherine A Medeiros, *President*
Don Coots, *Ch of Bd*
Brian Evans, *Officer*
Rhonda Horne, *Lab Dir*
Jerry Angove, *Admin Sec*
EMP: 49 **EST:** 1934
SQ FT: 104,000
SALES (est): 155.7MM **Privately Held**
WEB: www.snmh.org
SIC: 8062 General medical & surgical hospitals
HQ: Dignity Health
185 Berry St Ste 200
San Francisco CA 94107
415 438-5500

(P-16527)
SISKIYOU HOSPITAL INC
Also Called: Fairchild Medical Center
444 Bruce St, Yreka (96097-3450)
PHONE......................530 842-4121
Dwayne Jones, *CEO*
Steven Nelson,
Marcus Issoglio, *President*
Jonathon C Andrus, *CEO*
Arvid Magnuson, *Lab Dir*
EMP: 450 **EST:** 1969
SALES (est): 77.3MM **Privately Held**
WEB: www.fairchildmed.org
SIC: 8062 General medical & surgical hospitals

(P-16528)
SISTERS OF ST JOSEPH ORANGE
205 East St, Healdsburg (95448-4434)
PHONE......................707 431-1135
EMP: 5020
SALES (corp-wide): 32.7MM **Privately Held**
WEB: www.csjorange.org
SIC: 8062 General medical & surgical hospitals
HQ: Sisters Of St. Joseph Of Orange
480 S Batavia St
Orange CA 92868
714 633-8121

(P-16529)
SONOMA VALLEY HEALTH CARE DST (PA)
Also Called: Sonoma Valley Hospital
347 Andrieux St, Sonoma (95476-6811)
PHONE......................707 935-5000
Carl Gerlach, *CEO*
Timothy Noakes, *CFO*
Pauline Headley, *Bd of Directors*
Michelle Donaldson, *Officer*
Richard Barnes, *CIO*
EMP: 445
SQ FT: 115,000
SALES: 58.3MM **Privately Held**
WEB: www.svh.com
SIC: 8062 General medical & surgical hospitals

(P-16530)
SOUTH COAST MEDICAL CENTER (PA)
2100 Douglas Blvd, Roseville (95661-3804)
PHONE......................916 781-2000
Bruce Christian, *President*
EMP: 690 **EST:** 1954
SQ FT: 220,000
SALES (est): 30.4MM **Privately Held**
SIC: 8062 General medical & surgical hospitals

(P-16531)
SOUTHERN HMBLDT CMNTY DST HOSP
Also Called: Southern Humboldt Cmnty Clinic
733 Cedar St, Garberville (95542-3201)
PHONE......................707 923-3921
Deborah Scaife, *President*
Jason Dockins, *Manager*
EMP: 93 **EST:** 1980
SQ FT: 17,000
SALES (est): 11.5MM **Privately Held**
WEB: www.sohumhealth.org
SIC: 8062 General medical & surgical hospitals

(P-16532)
SOUTHERN HMBLDT CMNTY HLTH CAR
733 Cedar St, Garberville (95542-3201)
PHONE......................707 923-3921
Matt Rees, *CEO*
Kent Sown, *COO*
Pepe Olano, *Lab Dir*
Judy Gallagher, *Ch Nursing Ofcr*
Susan Gardner, *Admin Asst*
EMP: 85 **EST:** 2001
SALES (est): 9.7MM **Privately Held**
WEB: www.sohumhealth.org
SIC: 8062 General medical & surgical hospitals

PRODUCTS & SERVICES SECTION

8062 - General Medical & Surgical Hospitals County (P-16551)

(P-16533)
SOUTHERN MONO HEALTHCARE DST
Also Called: MAMMOTH HOSPITAL
85 Sierra Park Rd, Mammoth Lakes (93546-2073)
P.O. Box 660 (93546-0660)
PHONE 760 934-3311
Helen Shepherd, *Chairman*
Gary Myers, *CEO*
Stephen Swisher M D, *Treasurer*
Christy Mc Millan, *Director*
EMP: 350 **EST:** 1978
SQ FT: 20,000
SALES: 80.5MM **Privately Held**
WEB: www.mammothhospital.org
SIC: 8062 General medical & surgical hospitals

(P-16534)
SRM ALLIANCE HOSPITAL SERVICES (PA)
Also Called: Petaluma Valley Hospital
400 N Mcdowell Blvd, Petaluma (94954-2339)
PHONE 707 778-1111
Deborah A Proctor, *President*
Jane Reed, *Vice Pres*
Kathleen Sartori, *Facilities Mgr*
Henry L Fong, *Med Doctor*
EMP: 400 **EST:** 1996
SQ FT: 50,000
SALES: 89.2MM **Privately Held**
SIC: 8062 General medical & surgical hospitals

(P-16535)
ST ELIZABETH COMMUNITY HOSP (DH)
2550 Sster Mary Clumba Dr, Red Bluff (96080-4327)
PHONE 530 529-7760
Todd Smith, *CEO*
Charlene Almocera, *Records Dir*
John Halfhide, *President*
Kristine Kuebli, *Director*
Patricia Manoli, *Director*
EMP: 441 **EST:** 1901
SQ FT: 98,000
SALES (est): 88.3MM **Privately Held**
WEB: www.dignityhealth.org
SIC: 8062 6513 General medical & surgical hospitals; retirement hotel operation
HQ: Dignity Health
185 Berry St Ste 200
San Francisco CA 94107
415 438-5500

(P-16536)
ST HELENA HOSPITAL (HQ)
Also Called: Deer Park Pharmacy
10 Woodland Rd, Saint Helena (94574-9554)
PHONE 707 963-3611
Steven Herber, *CEO*
Whie OH,
Timothy J Kares, *CFO*
Ileana Douglas, *Vice Pres*
Wendell Bobst, *Info Tech Dir*
EMP: 750 **EST:** 1878
SQ FT: 200,000
SALES: 239.5MM
SALES (corp-wide): 4.5B **Privately Held**
WEB: www.adventisthealth.org
SIC: 8062 8063 General medical & surgical hospitals; psychiatric hospitals
PA: Adventist Health System/West, Corporation
1 Adventist Health Way
Roseville CA 95661
844 574-5686

(P-16537)
ST JOSEPH HLTH NTHRN CAL LLC (DH)
Also Called: Santa Rosa Memorial Hospital
1165 Montgomery Dr, Santa Rosa (95405-4801)
P.O. Box 522 (95402-0522)
PHONE 707 546-3210
Todd Salnas, *CEO*
Mich Riccioni, *CFO*
Gary Greensweig, *Vice Pres*
Larry Munkelt, *Pharmacy Dir*
Kathrine Hardin, *Ch Nursing Ofcr*
EMP: 1500 **EST:** 1948
SQ FT: 163,692
SALES (est): 518MM
SALES (corp-wide): 32.7MM **Privately Held**
WEB: www.stjoesonoma.org
SIC: 8062 General medical & surgical hospitals
HQ: St. Joseph Health System
3345 Michelson Dr Ste 100
Irvine CA 92612
949 381-4000

(P-16538)
ST JOSEPH HOSPITAL (PA)
2700 Dolbeer St, Eureka (95501-4799)
PHONE 707 445-8121
Toll Free: .... 888 -
Joseph Mark, *CEO*
Don Wheeler, *Ch Radiology*
David O'Brien, *President*
Andrew Rybolt, *CFO*
William Parks MD, *Chief Mktg Ofcr*
▲ **EMP:** 707 **EST:** 1920
SQ FT: 125,000
SALES (est): 104MM **Privately Held**
WEB: www.stjoehumboldt.org
SIC: 8062 General medical & surgical hospitals

(P-16539)
ST JOSEPH HOSPITAL
Humboldt Central Laboratory
2700 Dolbeer St, Eureka (95501-4799)
PHONE 707 445-8121
Sandeep Talwar, *Owner*
EMP: 35
SQ FT: 6,000
SALES (corp-wide): 104MM **Privately Held**
WEB: www.stjoehumboldt.org
SIC: 8062 8071 General medical & surgical hospitals; pathological laboratory
PA: St. Joseph Hospital
2700 Dolbeer St
Eureka CA 95501
707 445-8121

(P-16540)
ST JOSEPH HOSPITAL
Radiation Oncology Department
2700 Dolbeer St, Eureka (95501-4799)
PHONE 707 445-8121
Dr John W Harris, *Director*
EMP: 35
SALES (corp-wide): 104MM **Privately Held**
WEB: www.stjoehumboldt.org
SIC: 8062 8011 General medical & surgical hospitals; oncologist
PA: St. Joseph Hospital
2700 Dolbeer St
Eureka CA 95501
707 445-8121

(P-16541)
ST JOSEPH HOSPITAL
Also Called: Neurosurgery
2752 Harrison Ave Ste A, Eureka (95501-4738)
PHONE 707 268-0190
Maureen Lawlor, *Manager*
EMP: 35
SALES (corp-wide): 104MM **Privately Held**
WEB: www.stjoehumboldt.org
SIC: 8062 General medical & surgical hospitals
PA: St. Joseph Hospital
2700 Dolbeer St
Eureka CA 95501
707 445-8121

(P-16542)
ST JOSEPH HOSPITAL
Also Called: Center For Women's Health Care
3645 E St, Eureka (95503-5330)
PHONE 707 445-8121
Maggie Selenski, *Director*
EMP: 35
SALES (corp-wide): 104MM **Privately Held**
WEB: www.stjoehumboldt.org
SIC: 8062 8011 General medical & surgical hospitals; surgeon
PA: St. Joseph Hospital
2700 Dolbeer St
Eureka CA 95501
707 445-8121

(P-16543)
ST JOSEPH HOSPITAL OF EUREKA
2700 Dolbeer St, Eureka (95501-4736)
P.O. Box 5600, Orange (92863-5600)
PHONE 707 445-8121
Sherie Henderson-Bialo, *Engineer*
Laurie Stone, *Marketing Staff*
Frederick Hanf, *Pathologist*
Omar Salam, *Obstetrician*
Dennis Knoernschild, *Anesthesiology*
EMP: 306 **EST:** 2011
SALES: 292.2MM
SALES (corp-wide): 32.7MM **Privately Held**
WEB: www.stjoehumboldt.org
SIC: 8062 General medical & surgical hospitals
HQ: St. Joseph Hospital Of Orange
1100 W Stewart Dr
Orange CA 92868
714 633-9111

(P-16544)
ST JOSEPHS BEHAVIORAL HLTH CTR (DH)
2510 N California St, Stockton (95204-5502)
PHONE 209 462-2826
Paul Rains, *Officer*
Nikhil Meswani, *Controller*
Lisa Helton, *Manager*
EMP: 85 **EST:** 1984
SALES (est): 39.5MM **Privately Held**
WEB: www.dignityhealth.org
SIC: 8062 General medical & surgical hospitals
HQ: Dignity Health
185 Berry St Ste 200
San Francisco CA 94107
415 438-5500

(P-16545)
ST JOSEPHS MED CTR STOCKTON
1800 N California St, Stockton (95204-6019)
P.O. Box 213008 (95213-9008)
PHONE 209 943-2000
Donald J Wiley, *President*
Lindsay Bureaux, *Officer*
Christine Hankins, *Planning*
EMP: 2366 **EST:** 1899
SALES (est): 230.1MM **Privately Held**
WEB: www.dignityhealth.org
SIC: 8062 General medical & surgical hospitals
HQ: Dignity Health
185 Berry St Ste 200
San Francisco CA 94107
415 438-5500

(P-16546)
ST JOSEPHS MEDICAL CENTER INC
1800 N California St, Stockton (95204-6019)
P.O. Box 213008 (95213-9008)
PHONE 209 943-2000
Donald J Wiley, *President*
Dr Susan McDonald, *Vice Pres*
Terry Spring, *Vice Pres*
Kathy Tohrnan, *Vice Pres*
Rae Charos, *Executive*
EMP: 150 **EST:** 1995
SQ FT: 18,000
SALES (est): 67.9MM **Privately Held**
WEB: www.dignityhealth.org
SIC: 8062 General medical & surgical hospitals
HQ: Dignity Health
185 Berry St Ste 200
San Francisco CA 94107
415 438-5500

(P-16547)
ST LUKES HEALTH CARE CENTER
Also Called: St Lukes Neighborhood Clinic
1580 Valencia St Ste 506, San Francisco (94110-4418)
PHONE 415 647-8600
Judy LI, *Administration*
Kristie Fox, *Accountant*
EMP: 82 **EST:** 1977
SALES (est): 8.9MM **Privately Held**
SIC: 8062 General medical & surgical hospitals

(P-16548)
ST MARYS MED CTR FOUNDATION
450 Stanyan St, San Francisco (94117-1019)
PHONE 415 668-1000
Ken Steele, *President*
James Wentz, *CFO*
Dee Mostofi, *Marketing Staff*
Natalia Petrosova, *Anesthesiology*
EMP: 186 **EST:** 1983
SALES: 3.8MM **Privately Held**
WEB: www.supportstmaryssf.org
SIC: 8062 Hospital, professional nursing school
HQ: Dignity Health
185 Berry St Ste 200
San Francisco CA 94107
415 438-5500

(P-16549)
ST MARYS MEDICAL CENTER INC
Also Called: Surgery Department
450 Stanyan St, San Francisco (94117-1019)
PHONE 415 668-1000
Ken Steele, *President*
Matthew Jeong, *Internal Med*
EMP: 5020
SALES (corp-wide): 17.6B **Publicly Held**
WEB: www.stmarysmc.com
SIC: 8062 Hospital, affiliated with AMA residency
HQ: St. Mary's Medical Center, Inc.
901 45th St
Mangonia Park FL 33407
561 844-6300

(P-16550)
STANFORD HEALTH CARE
Also Called: Stanford Schl Mdcine Jay McHae
1000 Welch Rd Ste 300, Palo Alto (94304-1812)
PHONE 650 723-5171
Bert Hurlbut, *Vice Pres*
Gary May, *Vice Pres*
Olga Grujic, *QC Mgr*
Ryan Berroya, *Opers Staff*
Jessica Jang, *Neurology*
EMP: 45
SALES (corp-wide): 12.4B **Privately Held**
WEB: www.stanfordhealthcare.org
SIC: 8062 General medical & surgical hospitals
HQ: Stanford Health Care
300 Pasteur Dr
Stanford CA 94305
650 723-4000

(P-16551)
STANFORD HEALTH CARE
1510 Page Mill Rd Ste 2, Palo Alto (94304-1133)
PHONE 650 213-8360
Martha Marsh, *President*
Katie Lipovsky, *Corp Comm Staff*
Vivianne Tawfik, *Anesthesiology*
Lisa Levin, *Nurse*
Yvonne Rodrigues,
EMP: 45
SALES (corp-wide): 12.4B **Privately Held**
WEB: www.stanfordhealthcare.org
SIC: 8062 Hospital, medical school affiliated with residency
HQ: Stanford Health Care
300 Pasteur Dr
Stanford CA 94305
650 723-4000

8062 - General Medical & Surgical Hospitals County (P-16552)

(P-16552)
STANFORD HEALTH CARE
300 Pasteur Dr, Stanford (94305-2200)
PHONE 650 736-6661
David Haray, *Vice Pres*
Diane Meyer, *Vice Pres*
Whitney Greene, *Exec Dir*
Anne Gordon, *Administration*
Sashi Ram, *Administration*
EMP: 45
SALES (corp-wide): 12.4B **Privately Held**
WEB: www.stanfordhealthcare.org
SIC: 8062 General medical & surgical hospitals
HQ: Stanford Health Care
300 Pasteur Dr
Stanford CA 94305
650 723-4000

(P-16553)
STANFORD HEALTH CARE
725 Welch Rd, Palo Alto (94304-1601)
PHONE 650 497-8953
Josie Guzman, *Records Dir*
Nicole Prinz, *Treasurer*
Jake McCarty, *Officer*
Will Gibbs, *Vice Pres*
Gary Landi, *Business Dir*
EMP: 45
SALES (corp-wide): 12.4B **Privately Held**
WEB: www.stanfordhealthcare.org
SIC: 8062 General medical & surgical hospitals
HQ: Stanford Health Care
300 Pasteur Dr
Stanford CA 94305
650 723-4000

(P-16554)
STANFORD HEALTH CARE
Also Called: Quality Management
300 Pasteur Dr, Stanford (94305-2200)
PHONE 650 723-4000
Merisa Kline, *President*
Jerry Harris, *COO*
Nancy Szaflarski, *Treasurer*
Bert Hurlbut, *Vice Pres*
James Martin, *Vice Pres*
EMP: 2523
SALES (corp-wide): 12.4B **Privately Held**
WEB: www.stanfordhealthcare.org
SIC: 8062 8099 Hospital, medical school affiliated with residency; childbirth preparation clinic
HQ: Stanford Health Care
300 Pasteur Dr
Stanford CA 94305
650 723-4000*

(P-16555)
STANFORD HEALTH CARE
Also Called: Stanford Cancer Center S Bay
2589 Samaritan Dr, San Jose (95124-4102)
PHONE 408 426-4900
Patrick Swift, *Med Doctor*
Robin Cisco, *Surgeon*
Ling Chen, *Nurse*
CHI Hoang, *Nurse*
Christine Henley,
EMP: 45
SALES (corp-wide): 12.4B **Privately Held**
WEB: www.stanfordhealthcare.org
SIC: 8062 Hospital, medical school affiliated with residency
HQ: Stanford Health Care
300 Pasteur Dr
Stanford CA 94305
650 723-4000

(P-16556)
STANFORD HEALTH CARE
Valleycare Medical Center
5555 W Las Positas Blvd, Pleasanton (94588-4000)
PHONE 925 847-3000
David Entwistle, *CEO*
Gina Teeples, *Ch Nursing Ofcr*
Jennifer Berg, *Exec Dir*
Soumya Mamidala, *Data Admn*
Scott Conway, *Engineer*
EMP: 45
SALES (corp-wide): 12.4B **Privately Held**
WEB: www.stanfordhealthcare.org
SIC: 8062 Hospital, medical school affiliated with residency

HQ: Stanford Health Care
300 Pasteur Dr
Stanford CA 94305
650 723-4000

(P-16557)
STANFORD HEALTH CARE (HQ)
Also Called: Stanford Medical Center
300 Pasteur Dr, Stanford (94305-2200)
PHONE 650 723-4000
David Entwistle, *CEO*
Barbara Clemons, *President*
Quinn McKenna, *COO*
Quinn L McKenna, *COO*
Lynda Hoff, *CFO*
▲ **EMP:** 9020 **EST:** 1957
SALES: 5.5B
SALES (corp-wide): 12.4B **Privately Held**
WEB: www.stanfordhealthcare.org
SIC: 8062 Hospital, medical school affiliated with residency
PA: Leland Stanford Junior University
450 Jane Stanford Way
Stanford CA 94305
650 723-2300

(P-16558)
STANFORD HEALTH CARE
Also Called: Shc Reference Laboratory
3375 Hillview Ave, Palo Alto (94304-1204)
PHONE 650 736-7844
Jerry Maki, *Vice Pres*
Sharon Bird, *Opers Staff*
Erica Trejo, *Opers Staff*
Justin Odegaard, *Pathologist*
Jill Yano,
EMP: 45
SALES (corp-wide): 12.4B **Privately Held**
WEB: www.stanfordhealthcare.org
SIC: 8062 General medical & surgical hospitals
HQ: Stanford Health Care
300 Pasteur Dr
Stanford CA 94305
650 723-4000

(P-16559)
STANFORD HEALTH CARE ADVANTAGE
300 Pasteur Dr, Stanford (94305-2200)
PHONE 650 723-4000
David Entwistle, *President*
Catherine Krna, *President*
Richard Shumway, *President*
Quinn McKenna, *COO*
Linda Hoff, *CFO*
EMP: 13810 **EST:** 2013
SALES: 50.1MM **Privately Held**
WEB: www.stanfordhealthcare.org
SIC: 8062 General medical & surgical hospitals
HQ: Essence Healthcare, Inc.
13900 Riverport Dr
Maryland Heights MO 63043

(P-16560)
STANISLAUS SURGICAL HOSP LLC (PA)
Also Called: STANISLAUS SURGICAL CENTER
1421 Oakdale Rd, Modesto (95355-3356)
PHONE 209 572-2700
Douglas V Johnson, *CEO*
Tony Gomez, *CFO*
Leslie Konkin,
Timothy J Noakes, *Mng Member*
EMP: 140 **EST:** 1985
SQ FT: 50,000
SALES: 29MM **Privately Held**
WEB: www.stanislaussurgical.com
SIC: 8062 General medical & surgical hospitals

(P-16561)
STOCKTON ORTHPD MED GROUP INC
Also Called: Crooks, Jerry C MD
2545 W Hammer Ln, Stockton (95209-2839)
PHONE 209 948-1641
Kevin Mikaelian, *Principal*
Scott Bethune, *Treasurer*
Miklein Kevin MD, *Vice Pres*
Dean Sloan, *Surgeon*
Khin MA, *Endocrinology*

EMP: 56 **EST:** 1970
SALES (est): 1.5MM **Privately Held**
SIC: 8062 General medical & surgical hospitals; hospital, professional nursing school

(P-16562)
SUMMIT MEDICAL CENTER
Also Called: Skilled Nursing Facility
3100 Summit St, Oakland (94609-3412)
PHONE 510 869-6758
Kathy Delaney, *President*
EMP: 200
SQ FT: 600
SALES (corp-wide): 13.2B **Privately Held**
WEB: www.sutterhealth.org
SIC: 8062 General medical & surgical hospitals
HQ: Summit Medical Center
350 Hawthorne Ave
Oakland CA 94609
510 655-4000

(P-16563)
SURGERY CENTER OF MARIN
250 Bon Air Rd, Greenbrae (94904-1702)
PHONE 415 925-7266
Beverly Munson, *Principal*
Linda Lang, *Officer*
David Hill, *Executive*
Futter Health, *Principal*
Ellen Akre, *Exec Dir*
▲ **EMP:** 49 **EST:** 2002
SALES (est): 9.3MM **Privately Held**
WEB: www.mymarinhealth.org
SIC: 8062 General medical & surgical hospitals

(P-16564)
SURGERY CTR OF ALTA BTES SMMIT (HQ)
Also Called: Alta Bates Summit Medical Ctr
2450 Ashby Ave, Berkeley (94705-2067)
PHONE 510 204-4444
Warren Kirk, *President*
Robert Petrina, *CFO*
Vanessa Kerr, *Admin Asst*
Maureen Reed, *Finance Mgr*
Elizabeth Smith, *Safety Dir*
EMP: 653 **EST:** 1936
SQ FT: 749,000
SALES (est): 732.4MM
SALES (corp-wide): 13.2B **Privately Held**
WEB: www.altabatessummit.org
SIC: 8062 General medical & surgical hospitals
PA: Sutter Health
2200 River Plaza Dr
Sacramento CA 95833
916 733-8800

(P-16565)
SURGERY CTR OF ALTA BTES SMMIT
5730 Telegraph Ave, Oakland (94609-1710)
PHONE 510 204-1880
Kathy Sloan, *Branch Mgr*
Belinda Krstic, *Manager*
EMP: 50
SALES (corp-wide): 13.2B **Privately Held**
WEB: www.altabatessummit.org
SIC: 8062 General medical & surgical hospitals
HQ: The Surgery Center Of Alta Bates Summit Medical Center Llc
2450 Ashby Ave
Berkeley CA 94705
510 204-4444

(P-16566)
SURGERY CTR OF ALTA BTES SMMIT
Also Called: Alta Btes Cmprhnsive Cncer Ctr
2001 Dwight Way, Berkeley (94704-2608)
PHONE 510 204-1591
Peter H Jessup, *CEO*
Oliver Delarosa, *Security Dir*
Oliver De La Rosa, *Security Dir*
Jessica Johnson, *Manager*
EMP: 50
SALES (corp-wide): 13.2B **Privately Held**
WEB: www.altabatessummit.org
SIC: 8062 General medical & surgical hospitals

HQ: The Surgery Center Of Alta Bates Summit Medical Center Llc
2450 Ashby Ave
Berkeley CA 94705
510 204-4444

(P-16567)
SURPRISE VALLEY HLTH CARE DST
741 Main St, Cedarville (96104-1038)
P.O. Box 246 (96104-0246)
PHONE 530 279-6111
Wanda Grove, *CEO*
Jason Diven, *President*
Megan Grove, *CFO*
Cindy Linker, *Treasurer*
Carl Quigley, *Vice Pres*
EMP: 72 **EST:** 1984
SQ FT: 13,330
SALES: 7MM **Privately Held**
WEB: www.surprisevalleychamber.com
SIC: 8062 General medical & surgical hospitals

(P-16568)
SUTTER BAY HOSPITALS (HQ)
Also Called: Califrnia PCF Med Ctr RES Inst
475 Brannan St Ste 130, San Francisco (94107-5419)
P.O. Box 7999 (94120-7999)
PHONE 415 600-6000
Jeff Gerard, *CEO*
Martin Brotman, *President*
Jamey Schmidt, *Administration*
Jeffrey Ziarno, *Analyst*
Conrad M Vial, *Surgeon*
EMP: 2578 **EST:** 1885
SALES: 4.5B
SALES (corp-wide): 13.2B **Privately Held**
WEB: www.cpmcri.org
SIC: 8062 General medical & surgical hospitals
PA: Sutter Health
2200 River Plaza Dr
Sacramento CA 95833
916 733-8800

(P-16569)
SUTTER BAY HOSPITALS
Also Called: Alta Bates Summit Medical Ctr
2420 Ashby Ave, Berkeley (94705-2002)
PHONE 510 869-6199
Sarah Love, *Principal*
Wilson Serene, *Program Mgr*
Thomas Reichert, *Project Mgr*
Andrew K Moon, *Anesthesiology*
Charu Puri, *Internal Med*
EMP: 86
SALES (corp-wide): 13.2B **Privately Held**
WEB: www.cpmcri.org
SIC: 8062 General medical & surgical hospitals
HQ: Sutter Bay Hospitals
475 Brannan St Ste 130
San Francisco CA 94107
415 600-6000

(P-16570)
SUTTER BAY HOSPITALS
Califrnia PCF Stnley Hlth Cntr
3801 Sacramento St Ste 61, San Francisco (94118-1625)
PHONE 415 600-2403
Joyce Hansen, *Director*
Ron Frianeza, *Research*
Sally V Krueger, *Anesthesiology*
Xin Lao, *Internal Med*
Christine Lee, *Internal Med*
EMP: 86
SALES (corp-wide): 13.2B **Privately Held**
WEB: www.cpmc.org
SIC: 8062 General medical & surgical hospitals
HQ: Sutter Bay Hospitals
475 Brannan St Ste 130
San Francisco CA 94107
415 600-6000

(P-16571)
SUTTER BAY HOSPITALS
Also Called: Alta Bates Summit Medical Ctr
350 Hawthorne Ave, Oakland (94609-3108)
PHONE 510 655-4000
Annette Shaieb, *Ch Pathology*
Denise Navellier,

PRODUCTS & SERVICES SECTION 8062 - General Medical & Surgical Hospitals County (P-16591)

Goldee Gross, *Ch OB/GYN*
Linda Gordon, *Ch Radiology*
Wendy Brandon, *COO*
EMP: 86
SALES (corp-wide): 13.2B **Privately Held**
WEB: www.cpmcri.org
SIC: 8062 General medical & surgical hospitals
HQ: Sutter Bay Hospitals
475 Brannan St Ste 130
San Francisco CA 94107
415 600-6000

(P-16572)
SUTTER BAY HOSPITALS
Also Called: Sutter Maternity & Surgery
2025 Soquel Ave, Santa Cruz (95062-1323)
PHONE...................831 423-4111
Jim Macksood, *Vice Pres*
Jenifer Turnbull, *Vice Pres*
William R Raffo, *Nephrology*
Darien Heron, *Med Doctor*
EMP: 86
SALES (corp-wide): 13.2B **Privately Held**
WEB: www.cpmcri.org
SIC: 8062 General medical & surgical hospitals
HQ: Sutter Bay Hospitals
475 Brannan St Ste 130
San Francisco CA 94107
415 600-6000

(P-16573)
SUTTER BAY HOSPITALS
3100 Summit St, Oakland (94609-3412)
PHONE...................510 869-8377
George Derbedrosian, *Branch Mgr*
Elizabeth Silva, *Project Mgr*
Tamara Jurson, *Anesthesiology*
EMP: 86
SALES (corp-wide): 13.2B **Privately Held**
WEB: www.cpmcri.org
SIC: 8062 General medical & surgical hospitals
HQ: Sutter Bay Hospitals
475 Brannan St Ste 130
San Francisco CA 94107
415 600-6000

(P-16574)
SUTTER BAY HOSPITALS
Also Called: Alta Bates Summit Medical Ctr
2450 Ashby Ave, Berkeley (94705-2067)
PHONE...................510 204-4444
Chuck Prosper, *CEO*
Julie Bertini, *Officer*
Alta Bates, *Executive*
Hester Perez, *Nursing Mgr*
Angel Borja, *Chief Engr*
EMP: 86
SALES (corp-wide): 13.2B **Privately Held**
WEB: www.cpmcri.org
SIC: 8062 General medical & surgical hospitals
HQ: Sutter Bay Hospitals
475 Brannan St Ste 130
San Francisco CA 94107
415 600-6000

(P-16575)
SUTTER CENTRAL VLY HOSPITALS
Also Called: Memorial Medical Center
1200 Scenic Dr Ste 200, Modesto (95350-6167)
PHONE...................209 572-5900
EMP: 957
SALES (corp-wide): 13.2B **Privately Held**
WEB: www.sutterhealth.org
SIC: 8062 General medical & surgical hospitals
HQ: Sutter Central Valley Hospitals
1700 Coffee Rd
Modesto CA 95355
209 526-4500

(P-16576)
SUTTER CENTRAL VLY HOSPITALS (HQ)
Also Called: Memorial Medical Center
1700 Coffee Rd, Modesto (95355-2803)
P.O. Box 942 (95353-0942)
PHONE...................209 526-4500
James Conforti, *CEO*
Todd Smith, *Ch of Bd*

David P Benn, *CEO*
Sutter Pat Fry, *CEO*
Steve Mitchell, *COO*
EMP: 112 **EST:** 1947
SQ FT: 180,000
SALES: 772MM
SALES (corp-wide): 13.2B **Privately Held**
WEB: www.sutterhealth.org
SIC: 8062 General medical & surgical hospitals
PA: Sutter Health
2200 River Plaza Dr
Sacramento CA 95833
916 733-8800

(P-16577)
SUTTER CENTRAL VLY HOSPITALS
1800 Coffee Rd Ste 30, Modesto (95355-2700)
P.O. Box 942 (95353-0942)
PHONE...................209 569-7544
David P Benn, *Branch Mgr*
Lisa Sheppard, *Partner*
George Y Chao, *Endocrinology*
Jill Ayres, *Director*
Tiffany McElvy, *Director*
EMP: 957
SQ FT: 65,294
SALES (corp-wide): 13.2B **Privately Held**
WEB: www.sutterhealth.org
SIC: 8062 Hospital, AMA approved residency
HQ: Sutter Central Valley Hospitals
1700 Coffee Rd
Modesto CA 95355
209 526-4500

(P-16578)
SUTTER CENTRAL VLY HOSPITALS
Also Called: Medi-Flight Northern Cal
1700 Coffee Rd, Modesto (95355-2803)
PHONE...................209 526-4500
Terry Sweeney, *Director*
EMP: 957
SALES (corp-wide): 13.2B **Privately Held**
WEB: www.sutterhealth.org
SIC: 8062 General medical & surgical hospitals
HQ: Sutter Central Valley Hospitals
1700 Coffee Rd
Modesto CA 95355
209 526-4500

(P-16579)
SUTTER CENTRAL VLY HOSPITALS
1316 Celeste Dr Ste 104, Modesto (95355-2437)
PHONE...................209 572-8270
David Benn, *CEO*
EMP: 957
SALES (corp-wide): 13.2B **Privately Held**
WEB: www.sutterhealth.org
SIC: 8062 General medical & surgical hospitals
HQ: Sutter Central Valley Hospitals
1700 Coffee Rd
Modesto CA 95355
209 526-4500

(P-16580)
SUTTER COAST HOSPITAL (HQ)
800 E Washington Blvd, Crescent City (95531-8359)
PHONE...................707 464-8511
Eugene Suksi, *President*
Jim Strong, *CFO*
Karen Degler, *Administration*
Candi Owens, *Planning*
Debra Faulk, *Systems Mgr*
▲ **EMP:** 250 **EST:** 1985
SQ FT: 70,000
SALES (est): 101MM
SALES (corp-wide): 13.2B **Privately Held**
WEB: www.suttercoast.org
SIC: 8062 General medical & surgical hospitals
PA: Sutter Health
2200 River Plaza Dr
Sacramento CA 95833
916 733-8800

(P-16581)
SUTTER DELTA MEDICAL CENTER
3901 Lone Tree Way, Antioch (94509-6200)
P.O. Box 3225 (94531-3225)
PHONE...................925 779-7200
Linda Lee Rovai, *President*
Ravikesh Chandra, *Records Dir*
Wendy Kitt, *Admin Asst*
Linda Horn, *Administration*
Linda Lawson, *CIO*
EMP: 136 **EST:** 1927
SQ FT: 150,000
SALES (est): 32.2MM **Privately Held**
WEB: www.sutterdelta.org
SIC: 8062 8082 8093 8069 General medical & surgical hospitals; home health care services; specialty outpatient clinics; orthopedic hospital

(P-16582)
SUTTER HEALTH
2068 John Jones Rd # 100, Davis (95616-9711)
PHONE...................530 747-0389
EMP: 169
SALES (corp-wide): 13.2B **Privately Held**
WEB: www.suttermedicalcenter.org
SIC: 8062 General medical & surgical hospitals
PA: Sutter Health
2200 River Plaza Dr
Sacramento CA 95833
916 733-8800

(P-16583)
SUTTER HEALTH
1625 Stockton Blvd # 207, Sacramento (95816-7097)
PHONE...................916 733-1025
Katie Scott, *Human Resources*
Christy Shaw, *Psychologist*
Garrett Sheng, *Pediatrics*
EMP: 169
SALES (corp-wide): 13.2B **Privately Held**
WEB: www.suttermedicalcenter.org
SIC: 8062 General medical & surgical hospitals
PA: Sutter Health
2200 River Plaza Dr
Sacramento CA 95833
916 733-8800

(P-16584)
SUTTER HEALTH
Also Called: Mamone James M
2 Medical Plaza Dr, Roseville (95661-3043)
PHONE...................916 797-4725
Martin Neft, *Med Doctor*
Karen Nishimura, *Med Doctor*
Mark Ross, *Director*
EMP: 169
SALES (corp-wide): 13.2B **Privately Held**
WEB: www.suttermedicalcenter.org
SIC: 8062 General medical & surgical hospitals
PA: Sutter Health
2200 River Plaza Dr
Sacramento CA 95833
916 733-8800

(P-16585)
SUTTER HEALTH
Also Called: Cpmc
2395 Sacramento St, San Francisco (94115-2328)
P.O. Box 7999 (94120-7999)
PHONE...................415 600-7034
Jennifer Boyich, *Physician Asst*
Suzann Samet, *Supervisor*
EMP: 169
SALES (corp-wide): 13.2B **Privately Held**
WEB: www.suttermedicalcenter.org
SIC: 8062 8051 8011 6513 General medical & surgical hospitals; skilled nursing care facilities; offices & clinics of medical doctors; retirement hotel operation
PA: Sutter Health
2200 River Plaza Dr
Sacramento CA 95833
916 733-8800

(P-16586)
SUTTER HEALTH
1020 29th St Ste 600, Sacramento (95816-5126)
PHONE...................916 733-9588
Sylvia Hailes, *Admin Sec*
Ronda Willis, *Admin Asst*
Adriana Edeza, *Accountant*
Ramandeep Bains, *Internal Med*
Linh Nguyen, *Nurse*
EMP: 169
SALES (corp-wide): 13.2B **Privately Held**
WEB: www.suttermedicalcenter.org
SIC: 8062 General medical & surgical hospitals
PA: Sutter Health
2200 River Plaza Dr
Sacramento CA 95833
916 733-8800

(P-16587)
SUTTER HEALTH
2734 El Camino Real, Santa Clara (95051-3007)
PHONE...................408 524-5952
Hossein Azimi, *Analyst*
Catherine Wang,
EMP: 169
SALES (corp-wide): 13.2B **Privately Held**
WEB: www.suttermedicalcenter.org
SIC: 8062 General medical & surgical hospitals
PA: Sutter Health
2200 River Plaza Dr
Sacramento CA 95833
916 733-8800

(P-16588)
SUTTER HEALTH
3901 Lone Tree Way, Antioch (94509-6200)
PHONE...................925 779-7273
Susan Bumatay, *Asst Admin*
Alfort Santos, *Family Practiti*
Scott Wada, *Obstetrician*
Kyla Yee, *Obstetrician*
Grant E Hasson, *Anesthesiology*
EMP: 169
SALES (corp-wide): 13.2B **Privately Held**
WEB: www.suttermedicalcenter.org
SIC: 8062 General medical & surgical hospitals
PA: Sutter Health
2200 River Plaza Dr
Sacramento CA 95833
916 733-8800

(P-16589)
SUTTER HEALTH
3468 California St, San Francisco (94118-1837)
PHONE...................415 345-0100
Leslie Santiago, *Nursing Mgr*
Pamela Fotu, *Executive Asst*
John Meyer, *Business Anlyst*
Kathryn Simpson, *Project Mgr*
Virginia Fong, *Technology*
EMP: 169
SALES (corp-wide): 13.2B **Privately Held**
WEB: www.suttermedicalcenter.org
SIC: 8062 General medical & surgical hospitals
PA: Sutter Health
2200 River Plaza Dr
Sacramento CA 95833
916 733-8800

(P-16590)
SUTTER HEALTH
1335 S Fairmont Ave, Lodi (95240-5520)
PHONE...................209 366-2007
EMP: 169
SALES (corp-wide): 13.2B **Privately Held**
WEB: www.suttermedicalcenter.org
SIC: 8062 General medical & surgical hospitals
PA: Sutter Health
2200 River Plaza Dr
Sacramento CA 95833
916 733-8800

(P-16591)
SUTTER HEALTH
100 Mission Blvd, Jackson (95642-2536)
PHONE...................209 223-5445
Melody Eurbe, *Officer*

(PA)=Parent Co (HQ)=Headquarters (DH)=Div Headquarters
✿ = New Business established in last 2 years

8062 - General Medical & Surgical Hospitals County (P-16592)

PRODUCTS & SERVICES SECTION

Mindy Epperson, *Office Mgr*
EMP: 169
SALES (corp-wide): 13.2B **Privately Held**
WEB: www.suttermedicalcenter.org
SIC: 8062 General medical & surgical hospitals
PA: Sutter Health
2200 River Plaza Dr
Sacramento CA 95833
916 733-8800

(P-16592) SUTTER HEALTH
595 Buckingham Way # 515, San Francisco (94132-1909)
P.O. Box 320427 (94132-0427)
PHONE 415 731-6300
Diane Watkins, *Comp Tech*
Lauron Racquel,
EMP: 169
SALES (corp-wide): 13.2B **Privately Held**
WEB: www.suttermedicalcenter.org
SIC: 8062 General medical & surgical hospitals
PA: Sutter Health
2200 River Plaza Dr
Sacramento CA 95833
916 733-8800

(P-16593) SUTTER HEALTH
Also Called: Sutter Pacific Med Foundation
1375 Sutter St Ste 406, San Francisco (94109-5467)
PHONE 415 600-0110
Jessie Perez, *Assistant*
EMP: 169
SALES (corp-wide): 13.2B **Privately Held**
WEB: www.suttermedicalcenter.org
SIC: 8062 General medical & surgical hospitals
PA: Sutter Health
2200 River Plaza Dr
Sacramento CA 95833
916 733-8800

(P-16594) SUTTER HEALTH
1301 Mission St, Santa Cruz (95060-3530)
PHONE 831 458-6310
Roger A Larsen, *President*
Anna R Matelski, *Executive Asst*
Sandra Martinez, *Administration*
Brad Dowd, *Technician*
Javier Mendoza, *Technical Staff*
EMP: 169
SALES (corp-wide): 13.2B **Privately Held**
WEB: www.suttermedicalcenter.org
SIC: 8062 General medical & surgical hospitals
PA: Sutter Health
2200 River Plaza Dr
Sacramento CA 95833
916 733-8800

(P-16595) SUTTER HEALTH
3 Medical Plaza Dr # 100, Roseville (95661-3088)
PHONE 916 797-4715
Kooyer Sharyl, *Administration*
Karen Nishimura, *Med Doctor*
Carla Ellis,
Mark Ross, *Director*
Heather Wilson, *Supervisor*
EMP: 169
SALES (corp-wide): 13.2B **Privately Held**
WEB: www.suttermedicalcenter.org
SIC: 8062 General medical & surgical hospitals
PA: Sutter Health
2200 River Plaza Dr
Sacramento CA 95833
916 733-8800

(P-16596) SUTTER HEALTH
2030 Sutter Pl Ste 1000, Davis (95616-6215)
PHONE 530 750-5904
Lydia Lindsay, *Branch Mgr*
Harris Levin, *Otolaryngology*
EMP: 169
SALES (corp-wide): 13.2B **Privately Held**
WEB: www.suttermedicalcenter.org
SIC: 8062 General medical & surgical hospitals
PA: Sutter Health
2200 River Plaza Dr
Sacramento CA 95833
916 733-8800

(P-16597) SUTTER HEALTH
8170 Laguna Blvd Ste 210, Elk Grove (95758-7902)
PHONE 916 691-5900
Solomon Yeung, *President*
Christiana Kopf, *Obstetrician*
EMP: 169
SALES (corp-wide): 13.2B **Privately Held**
WEB: www.suttermedicalcenter.org
SIC: 8062 General medical & surgical hospitals
PA: Sutter Health
2200 River Plaza Dr
Sacramento CA 95833
916 733-8800

(P-16598) SUTTER HEALTH
110 Stony Point Rd # 200, Santa Rosa (95401-4189)
PHONE 707 535-5600
Pam Carroll, *Manager*
EMP: 169
SALES (corp-wide): 13.2B **Privately Held**
WEB: www.suttermedicalcenter.org
SIC: 8062 General medical & surgical hospitals
PA: Sutter Health
2200 River Plaza Dr
Sacramento CA 95833
916 733-8800

(P-16599) SUTTER HEALTH
Also Called: Sutter Alhambra Surgery Center
8170 Laguna Blvd Ste 103, Elk Grove (95758-7902)
PHONE 916 455-8137
Debbie Johnson, *Partner*
Elena Wheeler, *Executive Asst*
Julia Earl, *Admin Sec*
Amanda Scott, *Admin Sec*
Alyssa Atc, *Technician*
EMP: 169
SALES (corp-wide): 13.2B **Privately Held**
WEB: www.suttermedicalcenter.org
SIC: 8062 General medical & surgical hospitals
PA: Sutter Health
2200 River Plaza Dr
Sacramento CA 95833
916 733-8800

(P-16600) SUTTER HEALTH
2340 Clay St Rm 121, San Francisco (94115-1932)
P.O. Box 7999 (94120-7999)
PHONE 415 600-1020
Matt Field, *Partner*
Karrie Abe, *General Mgr*
Chris Riley, *Sr Ntwrk Engine*
John Meyer, *Business Anlyst*
Asaad Abdelmalek, *Opers Staff*
EMP: 169
SALES (corp-wide): 13.2B **Privately Held**
WEB: www.suttermedicalcenter.org
SIC: 8062 General medical & surgical hospitals
PA: Sutter Health
2200 River Plaza Dr
Sacramento CA 95833
916 733-8800

(P-16601) SUTTER HEALTH
2725 Capitol Ave, Sacramento (95816-6004)
PHONE 916 262-9400
Garrett P Ryle, *Principal*
Eric London, *Surgeon*
Serag Dredar, *Gastroenterlgy*
Damon Namvar, *Podiatrist*
Sheri Burns, *Nursing Dir*
EMP: 169
SALES (corp-wide): 13.2B **Privately Held**
WEB: www.suttermedicalcenter.org
SIC: 8062 General medical & surgical hospitals
PA: Sutter Health
2200 River Plaza Dr
Sacramento CA 95833
916 733-8800

(P-16602) SUTTER HEALTH
2880 Gateway Oaks Dr # 200, Sacramento (95833-4338)
PHONE 916 566-4819
Vicki Flemming, *Branch Mgr*
Mike Bray, *Program Mgr*
Scott Dasko, *Director*
Troy Franklin, *Manager*
Robert Stephens, *Manager*
EMP: 169
SALES (corp-wide): 13.2B **Privately Held**
WEB: www.suttermedicalcenter.org
SIC: 8062 General medical & surgical hospitals
PA: Sutter Health
2200 River Plaza Dr
Sacramento CA 95833
916 733-8800

(P-16603) SUTTER HEALTH
2950 Research Park Dr, Soquel (95073-2000)
PHONE 831 458-6272
James Ferrara, *Bd of Directors*
EMP: 169
SALES (corp-wide): 13.2B **Privately Held**
WEB: www.suttermedicalcenter.org
SIC: 8062 General medical & surgical hospitals
PA: Sutter Health
2200 River Plaza Dr
Sacramento CA 95833
916 733-8800

(P-16604) SUTTER HEALTH
Also Called: Sutter Elk Grove Surgery Ctr
8200 Laguna Blvd, Elk Grove (95758-7956)
PHONE 916 544-5423
EMP: 169
SALES (corp-wide): 13.2B **Privately Held**
WEB: www.suttermedicalcenter.org
SIC: 8062 General medical & surgical hospitals
PA: Sutter Health
2200 River Plaza Dr
Sacramento CA 95833
916 733-8800

(P-16605) SUTTER HEALTH
520 W I St, Los Banos (93635-3419)
PHONE 209 827-4866
Lena Reza, *Office Mgr*
EMP: 169
SALES (corp-wide): 13.2B **Privately Held**
WEB: www.suttermedicalcenter.org
SIC: 8062 General medical & surgical hospitals
PA: Sutter Health
2200 River Plaza Dr
Sacramento CA 95833
916 733-8800

(P-16606) SUTTER HEALTH
1375 Sutter St Ste 208, San Francisco (94109-5465)
PHONE 415 600-0140
Tanya Watts, *Administration*
Sophia Katuta, *Manager*
EMP: 169
SALES (corp-wide): 13.2B **Privately Held**
WEB: www.suttermedicalcenter.org
SIC: 8062 General medical & surgical hospitals
PA: Sutter Health
2200 River Plaza Dr
Sacramento CA 95833
916 733-8800

(P-16607) SUTTER HEALTH
2015 Steiner St Fl 1, San Francisco (94115-2627)
PHONE 415 600-4280
Dorothy Coleman-Riese MD, *President*
Elizabeth Peralta, *Surgeon*
William Black, *Internal Med*
EMP: 169
SALES (corp-wide): 13.2B **Privately Held**
WEB: www.suttermedicalcenter.org
SIC: 8062 General medical & surgical hospitals
PA: Sutter Health
2200 River Plaza Dr
Sacramento CA 95833
916 733-8800

(P-16608) SUTTER HEALTH
Also Called: Eden Medical Center
20103 Lake Chabot Rd, Castro Valley (94546-5305)
PHONE 510 537-1234
Patricia Ryan, *CEO*
Toni McKnight, *Analyst*
Charles Ruhlin, *Med Doctor*
Jody Gilman, *Director*
Alex Tong, *Manager*
EMP: 169
SALES (corp-wide): 13.2B **Privately Held**
WEB: www.edenmedicalcenter.org
SIC: 8062 General medical & surgical hospitals
PA: Sutter Health
2200 River Plaza Dr
Sacramento CA 95833
916 733-8800

(P-16609) SUTTER HEALTH
100 Rowland Way Ste 210, Novato (94945-5041)
PHONE 415 897-8495
Vicki Del, *Branch Mgr*
EMP: 169
SALES (corp-wide): 13.2B **Privately Held**
WEB: www.suttermedicalcenter.org
SIC: 8062 General medical & surgical hospitals
PA: Sutter Health
2200 River Plaza Dr
Sacramento CA 95833
916 733-8800

(P-16610) SUTTER HEALTH
4830 Bus Center Dr # 200, Fairfield (94534-1797)
PHONE 707 864-4660
Marcia Reissig, *Branch Mgr*
Sharon Holbert, *Executive Asst*
EMP: 169
SALES (corp-wide): 13.2B **Privately Held**
WEB: www.suttermedicalcenter.org
SIC: 8062 General medical & surgical hospitals
PA: Sutter Health
2200 River Plaza Dr
Sacramento CA 95833
916 733-8800

(P-16611) SUTTER HEALTH
2725 Capitol Ave Dept 304, Sacramento (95816-6006)
PHONE 916 262-9414
EMP: 169
SALES (corp-wide): 13.2B **Privately Held**
WEB: www.suttermedicalcenter.org
SIC: 8062 General medical & surgical hospitals
PA: Sutter Health
2200 River Plaza Dr
Sacramento CA 95833
916 733-8800

(P-16612) SUTTER HEALTH
Also Called: Clay, Kenneth MD
2030 Sutter Pl Ste 2000, Davis (95616-6216)
PHONE 530 750-5800
Courtney Tibble, *Endocrinology*
EMP: 169

PRODUCTS & SERVICES SECTION

8062 - General Medical & Surgical Hospitals County (P-16633)

SALES (corp-wide): 13.2B **Privately Held**
WEB: www.suttermedicalcenter.org
SIC: **8062** General medical & surgical hospitals
PA: Sutter Health
    2200 River Plaza Dr
    Sacramento CA 95833
    916 733-8800

(P-16613)
SUTTER HEALTH
3875 Telegraph Ave, Oakland (94609-2428)
PHONE..........................510 547-2244
Aaron Adams, *Branch Mgr*
Kim Dambrosia, *Administration*
Powell Jose, *Cardiovascular*
EMP: 169
SALES (corp-wide): 13.2B **Privately Held**
WEB: www.suttermedicalcenter.org
SIC: **8062** General medical & surgical hospitals
PA: Sutter Health
    2200 River Plaza Dr
    Sacramento CA 95833
    916 733-8800

(P-16614)
SUTTER HEALTH
3000 Telegraph Ave, Oakland (94609-3218)
PHONE..........................510 869-8777
Stefan Arnold, *Branch Mgr*
Kim Andrews, *Manager*
Rick Beach, *Manager*
Jessica Romo, *Assistant*
EMP: 169
SALES (corp-wide): 13.2B **Privately Held**
WEB: www.suttermedicalcenter.org
SIC: **8062** General medical & surgical hospitals
PA: Sutter Health
    2200 River Plaza Dr
    Sacramento CA 95833
    916 733-8800

(P-16615)
SUTTER HEALTH
6 Medical Plaza Dr, Roseville (95661-3037)
PHONE..........................916 878-2588
EMP: 169
SALES (corp-wide): 13.2B **Privately Held**
WEB: www.suttermedicalcenter.org
SIC: **8062** General medical & surgical hospitals
PA: Sutter Health
    2200 River Plaza Dr
    Sacramento CA 95833
    916 733-8800

(P-16616)
SUTTER HEALTH
Also Called: Cpmc Van Ness Campus
1101 Van Ness Ave, San Francisco (94109-6919)
PHONE..........................415 600-6000
Robert Ray, *Engineer*
Delynn Peltz, *Director*
Jeana Schupp, *Manager*
EMP: 169
SALES (corp-wide): 13.2B **Privately Held**
WEB: www.suttermedicalcenter.org
SIC: **8062** General medical & surgical hospitals
PA: Sutter Health
    2200 River Plaza Dr
    Sacramento CA 95833
    916 733-8800

(P-16617)
SUTTER HEALTH (PA)
Also Called: Sutter Health Sacsierra Region
2200 River Plaza Dr, Sacramento (95833-4134)
PHONE..........................916 733-8800
Patrick Fry, *President*
Diane Broderick, *Records Dir*
Jim Gray, *Ch of Bd*
Tom Jackson, *Vice Chairman*
Robert D Reed, *CFO*
EMP: 900 EST: 1981

SALES (est): 13.2B **Privately Held**
WEB: www.suttermedicalcenter.org
SIC: **8062** 8051 8011 6513 General medical & surgical hospitals; skilled nursing care facilities; offices & clinics of medical doctors; retirement hotel operation

(P-16618)
SUTTER HEALTH
475 Pioneer Ave Ste 400, Woodland (95776-4905)
PHONE..........................530 406-5600
Manuel Diaz, *President*
Randall H Leefeldt, *Med Doctor*
EMP: 169
SALES (corp-wide): 13.2B **Privately Held**
WEB: www.suttermedicalcenter.org
SIC: **8062** General medical & surgical hospitals
PA: Sutter Health
    2200 River Plaza Dr
    Sacramento CA 95833
    916 733-8800

(P-16619)
SUTTER HEALTH
75 Encina Ave, Palo Alto (94301-2322)
PHONE..........................916 297-9923
EMP: 169
SALES (corp-wide): 13.2B **Privately Held**
WEB: www.suttermedicalcenter.org
SIC: **8062** General medical & surgical hospitals
PA: Sutter Health
    2200 River Plaza Dr
    Sacramento CA 95833
    916 733-8800

(P-16620)
SUTTER HEALTH
Also Called: Radiation Oncology Center
2 Medical Plaza Dr # 180, Roseville (95661-3043)
PHONE..........................916 781-1225
Nancy Mathai, *Branch Mgr*
Seth Rosenthal, *Oncology*
Carole Adell, *Consultant*
EMP: 169
SALES (corp-wide): 13.2B **Privately Held**
WEB: www.suttermedicalcenter.org
SIC: **8062** General medical & surgical hospitals
PA: Sutter Health
    2200 River Plaza Dr
    Sacramento CA 95833
    916 733-8800

(P-16621)
SUTTER HEALTH
2516 E Whitmore Ave, Ceres (95307-2645)
PHONE..........................209 538-1733
Ray Thorpe, *Regional Mgr*
Leslie Warren,
Lai Chan,
Karin Gong,
Lisa Ohman, *Assistant*
EMP: 169
SALES (corp-wide): 13.2B **Privately Held**
WEB: www.suttermedicalcenter.org
SIC: **8062** General medical & surgical hospitals
PA: Sutter Health
    2200 River Plaza Dr
    Sacramento CA 95833
    916 733-8800

(P-16622)
SUTTER HEALTH
3612 Dale Rd, Modesto (95356-0500)
PHONE..........................209 522-0146
Yanyan Hong, *Technical Staff*
Kristina Saich, *Personnel Assit*
Audelia Santana, *Corp Comm Staff*
Young Kwon, *Nurse*
Netta Berry,
EMP: 169
SALES (corp-wide): 13.2B **Privately Held**
WEB: www.suttermedicalcenter.org
SIC: **8062** General medical & surgical hospitals
PA: Sutter Health
    2200 River Plaza Dr
    Sacramento CA 95833
    916 733-8800

(P-16623)
SUTTER HEALTH
8170 Laguna Blvd Ste 220, Elk Grove (95758-7902)
PHONE..........................916 691-5900
EMP: 169
SALES (corp-wide): 13.2B **Privately Held**
WEB: www.suttermedicalcenter.org
SIC: **8062** General medical & surgical hospitals
PA: Sutter Health
    2200 River Plaza Dr
    Sacramento CA 95833
    916 733-8800

(P-16624)
SUTTER HEALTH
50 S San Mateo Dr Ste 470, San Mateo (94401-3833)
PHONE..........................650 262-4262
Roger Larsen, *President*
Jenny Breen, *Administration*
Cheryl Cummings, *Physician Asst*
Harvey Matlof, *Med Doctor*
Alicia Benningfield,
EMP: 169
SALES (corp-wide): 13.2B **Privately Held**
WEB: www.suttermedicalcenter.org
SIC: **8062** General medical & surgical hospitals
PA: Sutter Health
    2200 River Plaza Dr
    Sacramento CA 95833
    916 733-8800

(P-16625)
SUTTER HEALTH
2880 Soquel Ave Ste 10, Santa Cruz (95062-1423)
PHONE..........................831 477-3600
Kathleen McNupp, *Manager*
Jeanne Wilkins,
Betsy Stone, *Director*
EMP: 169
SALES (corp-wide): 13.2B **Privately Held**
WEB: www.suttermedicalcenter.org
SIC: **8062** General medical & surgical hospitals
PA: Sutter Health
    2200 River Plaza Dr
    Sacramento CA 95833
    916 733-8800

(P-16626)
SUTTER HEALTH
999 S Fairmont Ave # 200, Lodi (95240-5100)
PHONE..........................209 334-3333
Carol Nakashima, *Med Doctor*
EMP: 169
SALES (corp-wide): 13.2B **Privately Held**
WEB: www.suttermedicalcenter.org
SIC: **8062** General medical & surgical hospitals
PA: Sutter Health
    2200 River Plaza Dr
    Sacramento CA 95833
    916 733-8800

(P-16627)
SUTTER HEALTH
Also Called: Nguyen, Myhanh MD
325 N Mathilda Ave, Sunnyvale (94085-4207)
PHONE..........................408 733-4380
Connie Conover, *Branch Mgr*
Melissa Guerrero, *Program Mgr*
Michael Fain,
April Espaniola, *Supervisor*
EMP: 169
SALES (corp-wide): 13.2B **Privately Held**
WEB: www.suttermedicalcenter.org
SIC: **8062** General medical & surgical hospitals
PA: Sutter Health
    2200 River Plaza Dr
    Sacramento CA 95833
    916 733-8800

(P-16628)
SUTTER HEALTH
Also Called: Sutter Pacific Med Foundation
4702 Hoen Ave, Santa Rosa (95405-7824)
PHONE..........................707 545-2255
Rodger Simmons, *Software Engr*
Cheri Kai, *Nurse*

Korrin Jensen,
Suzanne Zolfo, *Director*
Garrett Walker, *Receptionist*
EMP: 169
SALES (corp-wide): 13.2B **Privately Held**
WEB: www.suttermedicalcenter.org
SIC: **8062** General medical & surgical hospitals
PA: Sutter Health
    2200 River Plaza Dr
    Sacramento CA 95833
    916 733-8800

(P-16629)
SUTTER HEALTH
Also Called: Palo Alpo Medical Foudation
795 El Camino Real, Palo Alto (94301-2302)
PHONE..........................650 853-2904
Nan A Link, *Branch Mgr*
EMP: 169
SALES (corp-wide): 13.2B **Privately Held**
WEB: www.suttermedicalcenter.org
SIC: **8062** General medical & surgical hospitals
PA: Sutter Health
    2200 River Plaza Dr
    Sacramento CA 95833
    916 733-8800

(P-16630)
SUTTER HEALTH
1020 29th St Ste 570b, Sacramento (95816-5173)
PHONE..........................916 453-5955
Kristi Fink, *Assistant*
EMP: 169
SALES (corp-wide): 13.2B **Privately Held**
WEB: www.suttermedicalcenter.org
SIC: **8062** General medical & surgical hospitals
PA: Sutter Health
    2200 River Plaza Dr
    Sacramento CA 95833
    916 733-8800

(P-16631)
SUTTER HEALTH
1900 Powell St Ste 140, Emeryville (94608-1756)
PHONE..........................510 450-8900
EMP: 169
SALES (corp-wide): 13.2B **Privately Held**
WEB: www.suttermedicalcenter.org
SIC: **8062** General medical & surgical hospitals
PA: Sutter Health
    2200 River Plaza Dr
    Sacramento CA 95833
    916 733-8800

(P-16632)
SUTTER HEALTH
Also Called: Cpmc Mission Bernal Campus
1580 Valencia St Ste 237, San Francisco (94110-4430)
PHONE..........................415 600-6000
Warren Browner MD, *CEO*
Vic Reynov, *Technician*
Adrian Gutierrez, *Opers Mgr*
Yolanda Ornelas, *Social Worker*
Sharon Patrick, *Manager*
EMP: 169
SALES (corp-wide): 13.2B **Privately Held**
WEB: www.suttermedicalcenter.org
SIC: **8062** General medical & surgical hospitals
PA: Sutter Health
    2200 River Plaza Dr
    Sacramento CA 95833
    916 733-8800

(P-16633)
SUTTER HEALTH
5176 Hill Rd E, Lakeport (95453-6300)
PHONE..........................707 262-5000
Frank Ignacio, *Branch Mgr*
Jill Minudri, *Pharmacist*
Mike Wilkinson, *Manager*
Nicole Lamm, *Coordinator*
EMP: 169
SALES (corp-wide): 13.2B **Privately Held**
WEB: www.suttermedicalcenter.org
SIC: **8062** General medical & surgical hospitals

8062 - General Medical & Surgical Hospitals County (P-16634)

PA: Sutter Health
2200 River Plaza Dr
Sacramento CA 95833
916 733-8800

(P-16634)
SUTTER HEALTH
2300 California St, San Francisco (94115-2753)
PHONE 415 600-4325
EMP: 169
SALES (corp-wide): 13.2B Privately Held
WEB: www.suttermedicalcenter.org
SIC: 8062 General medical & surgical hospitals
PA: Sutter Health
2200 River Plaza Dr
Sacramento CA 95833
916 733-8800

(P-16635)
SUTTER HEALTH
440 Plumas Blvd, Yuba City (95991-5071)
PHONE 530 741-1300
Christopher Boylan, *Branch Mgr*
Martha Duenas, *Regional Mgr*
Sharmila Amolik, *Internal Med*
Dung Tran, *Internal Med*
Minh Bui, *Cardiovascular*
EMP: 169
SALES (corp-wide): 13.2B Privately Held
WEB: www.suttermedicalcenter.org
SIC: 8062 General medical & surgical hospitals
PA: Sutter Health
2200 River Plaza Dr
Sacramento CA 95833
916 733-8800

(P-16636)
SUTTER HEALTH
7700 Folsom Blvd, Sacramento (95826-2608)
PHONE 916 386-3000
Stephen Heath, *Manager*
Tezza Manuel, *Purch Mgr*
EMP: 169
SALES (corp-wide): 13.2B Privately Held
WEB: www.suttermedicalcenter.org
SIC: 8062 General medical & surgical hospitals
PA: Sutter Health
2200 River Plaza Dr
Sacramento CA 95833
916 733-8800

(P-16637)
SUTTER HEALTH
2200 Webster St, San Francisco (94115-1821)
PHONE 415 600-1400
Adrian Wadley, *Manager*
June Jalbuena, *Info Tech Mgr*
Milena Ferreira, *Research*
Erin Hsu, *Infectious Dis*
Benjamin Romick, *Cardiology*
EMP: 169
SALES (corp-wide): 13.2B Privately Held
WEB: www.suttermedicalcenter.org
SIC: 8062 General medical & surgical hospitals
PA: Sutter Health
2200 River Plaza Dr
Sacramento CA 95833
916 733-8800

(P-16638)
SUTTER HEALTH
20130 Lake Chabot Rd # 201, Castro Valley (94546-5340)
PHONE 510 537-1234
Bob De Mann, *Principal*
Simon Dunn, *Lab Dir*
Debora Hendrickson, *Exec Dir*
Alexander Ang-Angco, *Admin Sec*
Toni McKnight, *Analyst*
EMP: 169
SALES (corp-wide): 13.2B Privately Held
WEB: www.suttermedicalcenter.org
SIC: 8062 General medical & surgical hospitals
PA: Sutter Health
2200 River Plaza Dr
Sacramento CA 95833
916 733-8800

(P-16639)
SUTTER HEALTH
100 Hospital Dr, Vallejo (94589-2580)
PHONE 707 551-3400
Carolyn Appenzeller, *Principal*
EMP: 169
SALES (corp-wide): 13.2B Privately Held
WEB: www.suttermedicalcenter.org
SIC: 8062 General medical & surgical hospitals
PA: Sutter Health
2200 River Plaza Dr
Sacramento CA 95833
916 733-8800

(P-16640)
SUTTER HEALTH
969 Plumas St Ste 103116, Yuba City (95991-4011)
PHONE 530 749-3585
Aparna Kareti, *Branch Mgr*
Kate Helm, *Director*
EMP: 169
SALES (corp-wide): 13.2B Privately Held
WEB: www.suttermedicalcenter.org
SIC: 8062 General medical & surgical hospitals
PA: Sutter Health
2200 River Plaza Dr
Sacramento CA 95833
916 733-8800

(P-16641)
SUTTER HEALTH
2333 Buchanan St, San Francisco (94115-1925)
PHONE 415 600-6000
Michael P Holdsworth, *Manager*
Anabelle Alviar, *Technician*
Alex Gonzalez, *Project Mgr*
Peter Gasper, *Research*
Sue Lesage, *Technology*
EMP: 169
SALES (corp-wide): 13.2B Privately Held
WEB: www.suttermedicalcenter.org
SIC: 8062 General medical & surgical hospitals
PA: Sutter Health
2200 River Plaza Dr
Sacramento CA 95833
916 733-8800

(P-16642)
SUTTER HEALTH
1700 California St # 530, San Francisco (94109-4586)
PHONE 415 600-4280
Adair K Look, *Director*
EMP: 169
SALES (corp-wide): 13.2B Privately Held
WEB: www.suttermedicalcenter.org
SIC: 8062 General medical & surgical hospitals
PA: Sutter Health
2200 River Plaza Dr
Sacramento CA 95833
916 733-8800

(P-16643)
SUTTER HEALTH
2340 Clay St Fl 4, San Francisco (94115-1932)
PHONE 415 600-1000
Robert Gish, *Branch Mgr*
Christina Chou, *Internal Med*
Suzanne Much, *Oncology*
Samuel Choi, *Cardiovascular*
Sung Choi, *Cardiovascular*
EMP: 169
SALES (corp-wide): 13.2B Privately Held
WEB: www.suttermedicalcenter.org
SIC: 8062 General medical & surgical hospitals
PA: Sutter Health
2200 River Plaza Dr
Sacramento CA 95833
916 733-8800

(P-16644)
SUTTER HEALTH
1720 Carmelita Ave Ste 22, Burlingame (94010-4905)
PHONE 650 696-5838
Michael Cowan, *Branch Mgr*
Michelle Shimamoto, *Pathologist*
Karin Wertz, *Pediatrics*
Manjula Amarnath, *Director*
Nancy Keegan, *Director*
EMP: 169
SALES (corp-wide): 13.2B Privately Held
WEB: www.suttermedicalcenter.org
SIC: 8062 General medical & surgical hospitals
PA: Sutter Health
2200 River Plaza Dr
Sacramento CA 95833
916 733-8800

(P-16645)
SUTTER HEALTH
2700 Low Ct, Fairfield (94534-9715)
PHONE 707 432-2500
Franklyn Seabrooks, *Branch Mgr*
EMP: 169
SALES (corp-wide): 13.2B Privately Held
WEB: www.suttermedicalcenter.org
SIC: 8062 General medical & surgical hospitals
PA: Sutter Health
2200 River Plaza Dr
Sacramento CA 95833
916 733-8800

(P-16646)
SUTTER HEALTH
2000 Powell St, Emeryville (94608-1804)
PHONE 510 204-6600
James Mitchell, *Branch Mgr*
Trina White, *Vice Pres*
Alicia Johnson, *Project Mgr*
Daniel Baer, *Director*
Jackie Rayford, *Manager*
EMP: 169
SALES (corp-wide): 13.2B Privately Held
WEB: www.suttermedicalcenter.org
SIC: 8062 General medical & surgical hospitals
PA: Sutter Health
2200 River Plaza Dr
Sacramento CA 95833
916 733-8800

(P-16647)
SUTTER HEALTH
701 E El Camino Real, Mountain View (94040-2833)
PHONE 650 934-7000
Ronald Hess, *Branch Mgr*
Sirrie Auzenne, *Executive Asst*
Kathy Wilhelms, *Executive Asst*
Robela Cruz, *Project Mgr*
David Cruz, *Graphic Designe*
EMP: 169
SALES (corp-wide): 13.2B Privately Held
WEB: www.suttermedicalcenter.org
SIC: 8062 General medical & surgical hospitals
PA: Sutter Health
2200 River Plaza Dr
Sacramento CA 95833
916 733-8800

(P-16648)
SUTTER HEALTH
Also Called: All Bates Summit Medical Ctr
3030 Telegraph Ave, Berkeley (94705-2037)
PHONE 510 204-1554
Peral Abeleda, *Branch Mgr*
EMP: 169
SALES (corp-wide): 13.2B Privately Held
WEB: www.suttermedicalcenter.org
SIC: 8062 General medical & surgical hospitals
PA: Sutter Health
2200 River Plaza Dr
Sacramento CA 95833
916 733-8800

(P-16649)
SUTTER HEALTH
Also Called: California PCF Med Ctr Depts
115 Diamond St, San Francisco (94114-2413)
PHONE 415 861-1110
Richard Nasca, *Manager*
Rich Nasca, *Director*
EMP: 169
SALES (corp-wide): 13.2B Privately Held
WEB: www.suttermedicalcenter.org
SIC: 8062 General medical & surgical hospitals
PA: Sutter Health
2200 River Plaza Dr
Sacramento CA 95833
916 733-8800

(P-16650)
SUTTER HEALTH
Also Called: Eden Medical Center
P.O. Box 160100 (95816-0100)
PHONE 916 731-5672
Laura Hastie, *Director*
EMP: 169
SALES (corp-wide): 13.2B Privately Held
WEB: www.suttermedicalcenter.org
SIC: 8062 General medical & surgical hospitals
PA: Sutter Health
2200 River Plaza Dr
Sacramento CA 95833
916 733-8800

(P-16651)
SUTTER HEALTH
1020 29th St Ste 120, Sacramento (95816-5173)
PHONE 916 453-9999
Jonathan Breslau, *President*
Kiumars Hekmat, *Urology*
EMP: 169
SALES (corp-wide): 13.2B Privately Held
WEB: www.suttermedicalcenter.org
SIC: 8062 General medical & surgical hospitals
PA: Sutter Health
2200 River Plaza Dr
Sacramento CA 95833
916 733-8800

(P-16652)
SUTTER HEALTH
Also Called: Carmichael Imaging
6620 Coyle Ave Ste 110, Carmichael (95608-6336)
PHONE 916 961-4910
EMP: 169
SALES (corp-wide): 13.2B Privately Held
WEB: www.sutterhealth.org
SIC: 8062 General medical & surgical hospitals
PA: Sutter Health
2200 River Plaza Dr
Sacramento CA 95833
916 733-8800

(P-16653)
SUTTER HEALTH
Also Called: Sutter Occupational Hlth Svcs
3 Medical Plaza Dr # 100, Roseville (95661-3088)
PHONE 916 797-4700
Dave Gladden, *Branch Mgr*
John Hodge, *Officer*
Fiona Yang, *Nurse*
Sarah Alani,
Desirae Alfaro, *Assistant*
EMP: 169
SALES (corp-wide): 13.2B Privately Held
WEB: www.suttermedicalcenter.org
SIC: 8062 General medical & surgical hospitals
PA: Sutter Health
2200 River Plaza Dr
Sacramento CA 95833
916 733-8800

(P-16654)
SUTTER HEALTH
Also Called: Sutter Center For Rehab
8170 Laguna Blvd Ste 103, Elk Grove (95758-7902)
PHONE 916 731-7900
Sue Duckworth, *Manager*
EMP: 169
SALES (corp-wide): 13.2B Privately Held
WEB: www.suttermedicalcenter.org
SIC: 8062 General medical & surgical hospitals
PA: Sutter Health
2200 River Plaza Dr
Sacramento CA 95833
916 733-8800

PRODUCTS & SERVICES SECTION
8062 - General Medical & Surgical Hospitals County (P-16674)

(P-16655)
SUTTER HEALTH
2449 Summerfield Rd, Santa Rosa (95405-7815)
PHONE.................................707 523-7253
Lisa Amador, *Marketing Mgr*
EMP: 169
SALES (corp-wide): 13.2B **Privately Held**
WEB: www.suttermedicalcenter.org
SIC: 8062 General medical & surgical hospitals
PA: Sutter Health
 2200 River Plaza Dr
 Sacramento CA 95833
 916 733-8800

(P-16656)
SUTTER HEALTH
633 Folsom St Fl 7, San Francisco (94107-3618)
PHONE.................................916 286-8267
Linda Johnson, *Manager*
Albert Lee, *Manager*
EMP: 169
SALES (corp-wide): 13.2B **Privately Held**
WEB: www.suttermedicalcenter.org
SIC: 8062 8051 8011 General medical & surgical hospitals; skilled nursing care facilities; offices & clinics of medical doctors
PA: Sutter Health
 2200 River Plaza Dr
 Sacramento CA 95833
 916 733-8800

(P-16657)
SUTTER HEALTH
Also Called: Shuler, Kurt MD
2030 Sutter Pl Ste 1300, Davis (95616-6215)
PHONE.................................530 750-5888
EMP: 169
SALES (corp-wide): 13.2B **Privately Held**
WEB: www.suttermedicalcenter.org
SIC: 8062 General medical & surgical hospitals
PA: Sutter Health
 2200 River Plaza Dr
 Sacramento CA 95833
 916 733-8800

(P-16658)
SUTTER HEALTH
100 Rowland Way, Novato (94945-5011)
PHONE.................................415 602-5380
Bill Davis, *CEO*
John Jolley, *Gastroenterlgy*
EMP: 169
SALES (corp-wide): 13.2B **Privately Held**
WEB: www.suttermedicalcenter.org
SIC: 8062 General medical & surgical hospitals
PA: Sutter Health
 2200 River Plaza Dr
 Sacramento CA 95833
 916 733-8800

(P-16659)
SUTTER HLTH RHABILITATION SVCS
Also Called: Sutter Medical Ctr Sacramento
2801 L St Fl 3, Sacramento (95816-5615)
P.O. Box 160727 (95816-0727)
PHONE.................................916 733-3040
Lisa Drewslucero, *Manager*
Lori Rose, *Human Res Dir*
Yuhwan Hong, *Surg-Orthopdc*
Amanda Dewey, *Med Doctor*
EMP: 70 **EST:** 1980
SALES (est): 5.5MM **Privately Held**
WEB: www.sutterhealth.org
SIC: 8062 General medical & surgical hospitals

(P-16660)
SUTTER HLTH SCRMNTO SIERRA REG
Also Called: Sutter West Foundation
2030 Sutter Pl Ste 2000, Davis (95616-6216)
PHONE.................................530 747-5010
Jo Lisa Miller, *Radiology*
EMP: 359
SALES (corp-wide): 13.2B **Privately Held**
WEB: www.sutterhealth.org
SIC: 8062 General medical & surgical hospitals
HQ: Sutter Health Sacramento Sierra Region
 2200 River Plaza Dr
 Sacramento CA 95833
 916 733-8800

(P-16661)
SUTTER HLTH SCRMNTO SIERRA REG
Also Called: Sutter Amador Hospital Lab
100 Mission Blvd, Jackson (95642-2536)
PHONE.................................209 223-7540
Margie Souza, *Branch Mgr*
David Beffa, *Surgeon*
Melody Montgomery, *Surgeon*
EMP: 359
SALES (corp-wide): 13.2B **Privately Held**
WEB: www.sutterhealth.org
SIC: 8062 General medical & surgical hospitals
HQ: Sutter Health Sacramento Sierra Region
 2200 River Plaza Dr
 Sacramento CA 95833
 916 733-8800

(P-16662)
SUTTER HLTH SCRMNTO SIERRA REG (HQ)
Also Called: Sutter Memorial Hospital
2200 River Plaza Dr, Sacramento (95833-4134)
P.O. Box 160727 (95816-0727)
PHONE.................................916 733-8800
Patrick E Fry, *CEO*
Darling Lones, *President*
Scott Foster, *Radiology*
David Gover, *Radiology*
Linda Mar, *Radiology*
▲ **EMP:** 300 **EST:** 1935
SQ FT: 20,000
SALES (est): 462.9MM
SALES (corp-wide): 13.2B **Privately Held**
WEB: www.sutterhealth.org
SIC: 8062 8063 8052 General medical & surgical hospitals; psychiatric hospitals; intermediate care facilities
PA: Sutter Health
 2200 River Plaza Dr
 Sacramento CA 95833
 916 733-8800

(P-16663)
SUTTER HLTH SCRMNTO SIERRA REG
Also Called: Sutter Material Management
1600 Cebrian St, West Sacramento (95691-3802)
PHONE.................................916 373-3400
Dan Javor, *Principal*
EMP: 359
SALES (corp-wide): 13.2B **Privately Held**
WEB: www.sutterhealth.org
SIC: 8062 General medical & surgical hospitals
HQ: Sutter Health Sacramento Sierra Region
 2200 River Plaza Dr
 Sacramento CA 95833
 916 733-8800

(P-16664)
SUTTER HLTH SCRMNTO SIERRA REG
Also Called: Sutter Memorial Hospital
5151 F St, Sacramento (95819-3223)
P.O. Box 160727 (95816-0727)
PHONE.................................916 454-2222
Richard Foohoo, *Administration*
John Culver, *QA Dir*
Margo Gochangco, *Software Dev*
Ryan Kimbrel, *Technology*
Kermit Forrest, *Engineer*
EMP: 359
SALES (corp-wide): 13.2B **Privately Held**
WEB: www.sutterhealth.org
SIC: 8062 8011 General medical & surgical hospitals; offices & clinics of medical doctors

(P-16665)
SUTTER HLTH SCRMNTO SIERRA REG
Also Called: Sutter Senior Care
1234 U St, Sacramento (95818-1433)
PHONE.................................916 446-3100
Janet Tedesco, *Branch Mgr*
EMP: 359
SALES (corp-wide): 13.2B **Privately Held**
WEB: www.sutterhealth.org
SIC: 8062 General medical & surgical hospitals
HQ: Sutter Health Sacramento Sierra Region
 2200 River Plaza Dr
 Sacramento CA 95833
 916 733-8800

(P-16666)
SUTTER HLTH SCRMNTO SIERRA REG
Also Called: Recruitment Service
2700 Gateway Oaks Dr, Sacramento (95833-4337)
PHONE.................................916 924-7666
Debbie Mareno, *Manager*
EMP: 359
SALES (corp-wide): 13.2B **Privately Held**
WEB: www.sutterhealth.org
SIC: 8062 General medical & surgical hospitals
HQ: Sutter Health Sacramento Sierra Region
 2200 River Plaza Dr
 Sacramento CA 95833
 916 733-8800

(P-16667)
SUTTER HLTH SCRMNTO SIERRA REG
300 Hospital Dr, Vallejo (94589-2574)
PHONE.................................707 554-4444
Phillip Riddle,
Justin Paulk, *Comp Spec*
Mike Boyce, *Engineer*
Tracy Falck, *Safety Dir*
Ilene Gregorio, *Pharmacist*
EMP: 359
SALES (corp-wide): 13.2B **Privately Held**
WEB: www.sutterhealth.org
SIC: 8062 General medical & surgical hospitals
HQ: Sutter Health Sacramento Sierra Region
 2200 River Plaza Dr
 Sacramento CA 95833
 916 733-8800

(P-16668)
SUTTER HLTH SCRMNTO SIERRA REG
Also Called: Sutter Medical Center
2800 L St, Sacramento (95816-5616)
P.O. Box 160727 (95816-0727)
PHONE.................................916 733-3095
Sarah Krevans, *Branch Mgr*
EMP: 359
SALES (corp-wide): 13.2B **Privately Held**
WEB: www.sutterhealth.org
SIC: 8062 General medical & surgical hospitals
HQ: Sutter Health Sacramento Sierra Region
 2200 River Plaza Dr
 Sacramento CA 95833
 916 733-8800

(P-16669)
SUTTER HLTH SCRMNTO SIERRA REG
Also Called: Sutter Medical Center
475 Pioneer Ave Ste 100, Woodland (95776-4905)
PHONE.................................530 406-5616
Leefeldt Randall, *Branch Mgr*
EMP: 359
SALES (corp-wide): 13.2B **Privately Held**
WEB: www.sutterhealth.org
SIC: 8062 General medical & surgical hospitals
HQ: Sutter Health Sacramento Sierra Region
 2200 River Plaza Dr
 Sacramento CA 95833
 916 733-8800

(P-16670)
SUTTER MEDICAL GROUP INC (PA)
Also Called: Sutter Health
1201 Alhambra Blvd # 330, Sacramento (95816-5242)
PHONE.................................916 733-5090
Christine Griger, *President*
David Olson MD, *Treasurer*
Albert Chan, *Vice Pres*
Nancy Wilbur, *Office Mgr*
Jay Owens MD, *Admin Sec*
EMP: 40 **EST:** 1984
SALES (est): 28MM **Privately Held**
WEB: www.sutterhealth.org
SIC: 8062 General medical & surgical hospitals

(P-16671)
SUTTER MTRNTY/SRGRY CTR-SNT CR
2900 Chanticleer Ave, Santa Cruz (95065-1816)
PHONE.................................831 477-2200
Larry De Ghetaldi, *CEO*
Monica Harish, *Ch Radiology*
Cathy Novak, *Lab Dir*
Richard Nichols, *Administration*
Mark Riley, *Mktg Dir*
EMP: 92 **EST:** 1992
SALES (est): 15.7MM **Privately Held**
WEB: www.suttersantacruz.org
SIC: 8062 General medical & surgical hospitals

(P-16672)
SUTTER N MED GROUP A PROF CORP (PA)
969 Plumas St Ste 205, Yuba City (95991-4011)
PHONE.................................530 749-3661
Robert H Wright Jr, *President*
EMP: 82 **EST:** 1992
SQ FT: 30,096
SALES (est): 5.7MM **Privately Held**
SIC: 8062 General medical & surgical hospitals

(P-16673)
SUTTER ROSEVILLE MEDICAL CTR
1 Medical Plaza Dr, Roseville (95661-3037)
PHONE.................................916 781-1000
Patrick Brady, *CEO*
Rebecca Thompson, *Sr Corp Ofcr*
Marthea Johnson, *Analyst*
Julie Fralick, *Human Res Mgr*
Manny Peralta, *Opers Spvr*
EMP: 1700 **EST:** 1950
SALES: 669.3MM **Privately Held**
WEB: www.sutterroseville.org
SIC: 8062 General medical & surgical hospitals

(P-16674)
SUTTER RSVLLE MED CTR FNDATION
1 Medical Plaza Dr, Roseville (95661-3037)
PHONE.................................916 781-1000
Patricia Marquez, *President*
Lee Wong, *Med Doctor*
Mitch Davenport, *Manager*
John Hailes, *Supervisor*
EMP: 94 **EST:** 1950
SALES (est): 15.8MM **Privately Held**
WEB: www.sutterroseville.org
SIC: 8062 General medical & surgical hospitals

8062 - General Medical & Surgical Hospitals County (P-16675)

(P-16675)
SUTTER SOLANO MEDICAL CENTER
Also Called: SSMC
300 Hospital Dr, Vallejo (94589-2594)
PHONE 707 554-4444
Mary A Hayes, *Principal*
Brett Moore, *CFO*
Abhishek Dosi, *Officer*
Robert Butler, *Project Mgr*
Ilene Gregorio, *Pharmacist*
EMP: 560 **EST:** 1920
SQ FT: 94,000
SALES (est): 91.2MM
SALES (corp-wide): 13.2B **Privately Held**
WEB: www.suttermedicalcenter.org
SIC: 8062 General medical & surgical hospitals
PA: Sutter Health
2200 River Plaza Dr
Sacramento CA 95833
916 733-8800

(P-16676)
SUTTER SURGICAL HOSPITAL N VLY
455 Plumas Blvd, Yuba City (95991-5074)
PHONE 530 749-5700
Toni Morris, *Principal*
EMP: 117 **EST:** 2010
SALES (est): 39.3MM
SALES (corp-wide): 1.9B **Publicly Held**
WEB: www.sshnv.org
SIC: 8062 General medical & surgical hospitals
HQ: National Surgical Hospitals, Inc.
250 S Wacker Dr Ste 500
Chicago IL 60606
312 627-8400

(P-16677)
SUTTER VALLEY HOSPITALS (HQ)
Also Called: SUTTER C H S
2200 River Plaza Dr, Sacramento (95833-4134)
PHONE 916 733-8800
Anne Platt, *CEO*
Raychiel Craven, *Technical Staff*
Lena La Point, *Accounting Mgr*
Beverly Revels, *Human Res Mgr*
Keri Steele, *Sales Associate*
EMP: 385 **EST:** 1993
SALES (est): 3.7B
SALES (corp-wide): 13.2B **Privately Held**
WEB: www.suttermedicalcenter.org
SIC: 8062 General medical & surgical hospitals
PA: Sutter Health
2200 River Plaza Dr
Sacramento CA 95833
916 733-8800

(P-16678)
SUTTER VALLEY HOSPITALS
Also Called: Sutter Amador Hospital
200 Mission Blvd, Jackson (95642-2564)
PHONE 209 223-7514
EMP: 385
SALES (corp-wide): 13.2B **Privately Held**
WEB: www.sutteramador.org
SIC: 8062 General medical & surgical hospitals
HQ: Sutter Valley Hospitals
2200 River Plaza Dr
Sacramento CA 95833

(P-16679)
SUTTER VALLEY MED FOUNDATION
Also Called: Sutter Gould Med Foundation
600 Coffee Rd, Modesto (95355-4201)
PHONE 209 524-1211
Laurie Scott, *Principal*
Macedo Shannon, *Partner*
John Sablan, *Officer*
Joyce Garcia, *Buyer*
Tammie Waddle, *Safety Mgr*
EMP: 269 **Privately Held**
WEB: www.sutterhealth.org
SIC: 8062 General medical & surgical hospitals

PA: Sutter Valley Medical Foundation
2700 Gateway Oaks Dr
Sacramento CA 95833

(P-16680)
SUTTER WEST BAY HOSPITALS
100 Rowland Way Ste 310, Novato (94945-5041)
P.O. Box 8010, San Rafael (94912-8010)
PHONE 415 492-4800
Rojanne Sutsos, *Branch Mgr*
Richard Bodony, *Emerg Med Spec*
EMP: 101
SALES (corp-wide): 13.2B **Privately Held**
WEB: www.novatocommunity.org
SIC: 8062 General medical & surgical hospitals
HQ: Sutter West Bay Hospitals
180 Rowland Way
Novato CA 94945
415 209-1300

(P-16681)
SUTTER WEST BAY HOSPITALS (HQ)
Also Called: Novato Community Hospital
180 Rowland Way, Novato (94945-5009)
P.O. Box 1108 (94948-1108)
PHONE 415 209-1300
Brian Alexander, *CEO*
David Bradley, *President*
Sherie Hickman, *Administration*
Tara Barth, *Opers Staff*
Jonathan Hsiao, *Anesthesiology*
▲ **EMP:** 329 **EST:** 1952
SQ FT: 50,000
SALES: 68MM
SALES (corp-wide): 13.2B **Privately Held**
WEB: www.novatocommunity.org
SIC: 8062 General medical & surgical hospitals
PA: Sutter Health
2200 River Plaza Dr
Sacramento CA 95833
916 733-8800

(P-16682)
SUTTER WEST BAY HOSPITALS
Also Called: Sutter Lakeside Hospital
5176 Hill Rd E, Lakeport (95453-6300)
PHONE 707 262-5000
Daniel Peterson, *Officer*
Rachel Walsh, *Hlthcr Dir*
EMP: 340
SALES (corp-wide): 13.2B **Privately Held**
WEB: www.novatocommunity.org
SIC: 8062 General medical & surgical hospitals
HQ: Sutter West Bay Hospitals
180 Rowland Way
Novato CA 94945
415 209-1300

(P-16683)
SUTTERCARE CORPORATION
Also Called: Menlo Park Surgical Hospital
1501 Trousdale Dr, Burlingame (94010-4506)
PHONE 650 853-8500
EMP: 1529
SALES (corp-wide): 13.2B **Privately Held**
SIC: 8062 General medical & surgical hospitals
HQ: Suttercare Corporation
2200 River Plaza Dr
Sacramento CA 95833
916 733-8800

(P-16684)
TAHOE FOREST HOSPITAL DISTRICT
Also Called: Tahoe Workx
10956 Dnner Paca Rd Ste 2, Truckee (96161)
PHONE 530 582-3277
Ricardo Fergazo, *Director*
Celia Sutton-Pado, *Family Practiti*
Kevin Cahill, *Gnrl Med Prac*
Else Uglum, *Pediatrics*
Mark Wainstein, *Urology*
EMP: 89

SALES (corp-wide): 218.4MM **Privately Held**
WEB: www.tfhd.com
SIC: 8062 8071 General medical & surgical hospitals; X-ray laboratory, including dental
PA: Tahoe Forest Hospital District
10121 Pine Ave
Truckee CA 96161
530 587-6011

(P-16685)
TAHOE FOREST HOSPITAL DISTRICT (PA)
10121 Pine Ave, Truckee (96161-4856)
PHONE 530 587-6011
Robert Schapper, *CEO*
David Kitts,
Crystal Betts, *CFO*
Alex Maclennan, *Officer*
Rick McConn, *Officer*
EMP: 302 **EST:** 1952
SQ FT: 120,000
SALES: 218.4MM **Privately Held**
WEB: www.tfhd.com
SIC: 8062 General medical & surgical hospitals

(P-16686)
TENET HEALTHSYSTEM MEDICAL INC
Also Called: Tenet Health System Hospital
1205 E North St, Manteca (95336-4932)
PHONE 209 823-3111
Brenden Panzarello, *Branch Mgr*
Barbara Cummins,
EMP: 127
SALES (corp-wide): 17.6B **Publicly Held**
WEB: www.tenethealth.com
SIC: 8062 General medical & surgical hospitals
HQ: Tenet Healthsystem Medical, Inc.
14201 Dallas Pkwy
Dallas TX 75254
469 893-2000

(P-16687)
TENET HEALTHSYSTEM MEDICAL INC
Cnty HSP/Rhb Ctr/Ls GTS-Srtg
815 Pollard Rd, Los Gatos (95032-1438)
PHONE 408 378-6131
Toll Free: ....888 -
Gary Honts, *CEO*
EMP: 127
SALES (corp-wide): 17.6B **Publicly Held**
WEB: www.tenethealth.com
SIC: 8062 8011 General medical & surgical hospitals; offices & clinics of medical doctors
HQ: Tenet Healthsystem Medical, Inc.
14201 Dallas Pkwy
Dallas TX 75254
469 893-2000

(P-16688)
TRACY SUTTER COMMUNITY HOSP
1420 N Tracy Blvd, Tracy (95376-3451)
PHONE 209 835-1500
David Thompson, *President*
Q Laura Zhang, *Pharmacy Dir*
Scott Knight, *Asst Admin*
Eric Dalton, *Administration*
George V Dous, *Cardiology*
▲ **EMP:** 400 **EST:** 1945
SQ FT: 80,000
SALES (est): 54.9MM
SALES (corp-wide): 13.2B **Privately Held**
WEB: www.sutterhealth.org
SIC: 8062 8051 8011 General medical & surgical hospitals; skilled nursing care facilities; offices & clinics of medical doctors
PA: Sutter Health
2200 River Plaza Dr
Sacramento CA 95833
916 733-8800

(P-16689)
UAS MANAGEMENT INC
Also Called: University Srgcal Diagnstc Ctr
1390 E Yosemite Ave Ste B, Merced (95340-8221)
PHONE 209 580-3400
Sam Tacke, *CEO*

EMP: 95 **EST:** 1999
SALES (est): 27.8MM **Privately Held**
SIC: 8062 General medical & surgical hospitals

(P-16690)
UCSF EAST BAY SURGERY PROGRAM (PA)
Also Called: Highland Hospital
1411 E 31st St, Oakland (94602-1018)
PHONE 510 437-4800
Alden Harken, *Principal*
David Cox, *CFO*
Iesha Brandon, *Executive Asst*
Diana Thamrin, *Opers Staff*
Maryann Mbaka, *Surgeon*
EMP: 40 **EST:** 2000
SALES (est): 22MM **Privately Held**
WEB: www.alamedahealthsystem.org
SIC: 8062 8221 General medical & surgical hospitals; colleges universities & professional schools

(P-16691)
UKIAH ADVENTIST HOSPITAL
1165 S Dora St Ste C2, Ukiah (95482-6353)
PHONE 707 462-8855
Hubert R Fernande, *CFO*
EMP: 51
SALES (corp-wide): 4.5B **Privately Held**
WEB: www.adventisthealth.org
SIC: 8062 General medical & surgical hospitals
HQ: Ukiah Adventist Hospital
275 Hospital Dr
Ukiah CA 95482
707 462-3111

(P-16692)
UKIAH ADVENTIST HOSPITAL (HQ)
Also Called: Ukiah Valley Medical Center
275 Hospital Dr, Ukiah (95482-4531)
PHONE 707 462-3111
Terry Burns, *President*
Jeremy Mann, *Bd of Directors*
Janette Wilson, *Admin Sec*
Heather Housen, *Quality Imp Dir*
Debra McEntee, *Network Enginr*
EMP: 500 **EST:** 1967
SQ FT: 50,000
SALES: 200.7MM
SALES (corp-wide): 4.5B **Privately Held**
WEB: www.uvmcphilanthropy.org
SIC: 8062 General medical & surgical hospitals
PA: Adventist Health System/West, Corporation
1 Adventist Health Way
Roseville CA 95661
844 574-5686

(P-16693)
UKIAH ADVENTIST HOSPITAL
245 Hospital Dr, Ukiah (95482-4531)
PHONE 707 463-7587
EMP: 51
SALES (corp-wide): 4.5B **Privately Held**
WEB: www.adventisthealth.org
SIC: 8062 General medical & surgical hospitals
HQ: Ukiah Adventist Hospital
275 Hospital Dr
Ukiah CA 95482
707 462-3111

(P-16694)
UKIAH ADVENTIST HOSPITAL
1120 S Dora St, Ukiah (95482-6340)
PHONE 707 462-3111
Val Gene Devitt, *Branch Mgr*
EMP: 51
SQ FT: 43,500
SALES (corp-wide): 4.5B **Privately Held**
WEB: www.adventisthealth.org
SIC: 8062 General medical & surgical hospitals
HQ: Ukiah Adventist Hospital
275 Hospital Dr
Ukiah CA 95482
707 462-3111

PRODUCTS & SERVICES SECTION
8062 - General Medical & Surgical Hospitals County (P-16714)

(P-16695)
UNIVERSITY CAL SAN FRANCISCO
Ucsf Lngley Prter Psychtric In
401 Parnassus Ave, San Francisco (94143-2211)
PHONE.................................415 476-7000
Craig Van Dyke, *Manager*
Stephen Hinshaw, *Vice Chairman*
Anna Lisa Des Prez, *Administration*
Sarah Pennisten, *Project Mgr*
Karen Hauer, *Assoc Prof*
EMP: 257 **Privately Held**
WEB: www.ucsf.edu
SIC: 8062 8221 9411 General medical & surgical hospitals; university; administration of educational programs;
HQ: University Cal San Francisco
513 Parnassus Ave 115f
San Francisco CA 94143

(P-16696)
UNIVERSITY CAL SAN FRANCISCO
Also Called: Department of Urology
400 Parnassus Ave A633, San Francisco (94143-2202)
P.O. Box 738 (94104-0738)
PHONE.................................415 476-1611
Christine McDevitt, *Manager*
Manuel Eisenberg, *Urology*
EMP: 257 **Privately Held**
WEB: www.ucsf.edu
SIC: 8062 8221 9411 General medical & surgical hospitals; university; administration of educational programs
HQ: University Cal San Francisco
513 Parnassus Ave 115f
San Francisco CA 94143

(P-16697)
UNIVERSITY CAL SAN FRANCISCO
Also Called: Clinical Pharmacy
521 Parnassus Ave Rm C152, San Francisco (94143-2206)
P.O. Box 622 (94104-0622)
PHONE.................................415 476-3016
Debra Petrie, *Manager*
Katy Rau, *Office Mgr*
Michele Keller, *Marketing Staff*
Lawrence Litt, *Professor*
Michael Pogrel, *Fmly & Gen Dent*
EMP: 103 **Privately Held**
WEB: www.ucsf.edu
SIC: 8221 9411 8062 University; administration of educational programs; ; general medical & surgical hospitals
HQ: University Cal San Francisco
513 Parnassus Ave 115f
San Francisco CA 94143

(P-16698)
UNIVERSITY CAL SAN FRANCISCO
Also Called: Ucsf Medical Center At Mt Zion
1600 Divisadero St, San Francisco (94143-3010)
PHONE.................................415 567-6600
Mark Laret, *Manager*
Edmon Obiniana, *Office Mgr*
Ed Torrento, *Purch Mgr*
Calvin Tang, *Opers Spvr*
Thomas Vail, *Surgeon*
EMP: 257 **Privately Held**
WEB: www.ucsf.edu
SIC: 8062 8221 9411 General medical & surgical hospitals; university;
HQ: University Cal San Francisco
513 Parnassus Ave 115f
San Francisco CA 94143

(P-16699)
UNIVERSITY CAL SAN FRANCISCO
Also Called: Occupational Health Clinic
2550 23rd St Rm 10, San Francisco (94110-3504)
PHONE.................................415 206-8812
Mary Spangler, *Branch Mgr*
Mauricio Guerrero, *Executive Asst*
Ashani Chand, *Research*
R Trigg McClellann, *Surgeon*
EMP: 257 **Privately Held**
WEB: www.ucsf.edu
SIC: 8062 8221 9411 General medical & surgical hospitals; university; administration of educational programs
HQ: University Cal San Francisco
513 Parnassus Ave 115f
San Francisco CA 94143

(P-16700)
UNIVERSITY CALIFORNIA DAVIS
Also Called: School of Veterinary Medicine
4112a Tupper Hl, Davis (95616)
PHONE.................................530 752-1653
R H Bondurant, *Chairman*
EMP: 74 **Privately Held**
WEB: www.ucdavis.edu
SIC: 8221 9411 8062 University; administration of educational programs; ; general medical & surgical hospitals
HQ: University Of California, Davis
1 Shields Ave
Davis CA 95616

(P-16701)
UNIVERSITY CALIFORNIA DAVIS
Also Called: Medical Centre
4400 V St, Sacramento (95817-1445)
PHONE.................................916 734-3141
Dr William Ellis, *Principal*
Christine Yee, *Family Practiti*
EMP: 185 **Privately Held**
WEB: www.ucdavis.edu
SIC: 8062 8221 9411 General medical & surgical hospitals; university; administration of educational programs
HQ: University Of California, Davis
1 Shields Ave
Davis CA 95616

(P-16702)
UNIVERSITY CALIFORNIA DAVIS
Also Called: Uc Davis Medical Center
2315 Stockton Blvd, Sacramento (95817-2201)
PHONE.................................916 734-2011
Mauda Butte, *Principal*
Praveen Kumar, *Prgrmr*
Roger K Low, *Urology*
EMP: 185 **Privately Held**
WEB: www.ucdavis.edu
SIC: 8062 8221 9411 General medical & surgical hospitals; university; administration of educational programs;
HQ: University Of California, Davis
1 Shields Ave
Davis CA 95616

(P-16703)
UNIVERSITY CALIFORNIA DAVIS
Also Called: Department Ansthslogy Pain Mdc
4150 V St Ste 1200, Sacramento (95817-1460)
PHONE.................................916 734-5113
Karen Anderson, *Manager*
Pia Anette Hof, *Anesthesiology*
EMP: 185 **Privately Held**
WEB: www.ucdavis.edu
SIC: 8062 8221 9411 General medical & surgical hospitals; university; administration of educational programs
HQ: University Of California, Davis
1 Shields Ave
Davis CA 95616

(P-16704)
VALLEY CHILDRENS HOSPITAL
Also Called: Charlie Mitchell Chld Clinic
9300 Valley Childrens Pl, Madera (93636-8762)
PHONE.................................559 353-6425
Annette Humphrys, *Manager*
Carl Owada, *Vice Chairman*
Beverly Hayden-Pugh, *Officer*
Brian Smullin, *Vice Pres*
Stephanie Vance, *Vice Pres*
EMP: 114
SALES (corp-wide): 771.1MM **Privately Held**
WEB: www.valleychildrens.org
SIC: 8062 General medical & surgical hospitals
PA: Valley Children's Hospital
9300 Valley Childrens Pl
Madera CA 93636
559 353-3000

(P-16705)
VALLEY CHILDRENS HOSPITAL (PA)
9300 Valley Childrens Pl, Madera (93636-8762)
PHONE.................................559 353-3000
Todd Sunterapak, *President*
Jessie Hudgins, *COO*
Michele Waldrin, *CFO*
David Krause, *Bd of Directors*
Jeff Mayer, *Bd of Directors*
EMP: 1500 **EST:** 1949
SQ FT: 300,000
SALES: 771.1MM **Privately Held**
WEB: www.valleychildrens.org
SIC: 8062 General medical & surgical hospitals

(P-16706)
VALLEY CHILDRENS HOSPITAL
Also Called: Children's Home Care
5085 E Mckinley Ave, Fresno (93727-1964)
PHONE.................................559 353-7442
Harry Tozlian, *Manager*
Jose Elgorriaga, *Vice Chairman*
Jane Willson, *Vice Pres*
Stephen Kassel, *Lab Dir*
Rosemarie Huggins, *Admin Sec*
EMP: 114
SALES (corp-wide): 771.1MM **Privately Held**
WEB: www.valleychildrens.org
SIC: 8062 General medical & surgical hospitals
PA: Valley Children's Hospital
9300 Valley Childrens Pl
Madera CA 93636
559 353-3000

(P-16707)
VALLEY SURGICAL CENTER
5555 W Las Positas Blvd, Pleasanton (94588-4000)
PHONE.................................925 734-3360
Janice Bickert, *Director*
EMP: 41 **EST:** 1987
SQ FT: 11,000
SALES (est): 1.2MM **Privately Held**
WEB: www.valleycare.com
SIC: 8062 General medical & surgical hospitals

(P-16708)
VALLEYCARE HOSPITAL CORP
1119 E Stanley Blvd, Livermore (94550-4115)
PHONE.................................925 447-7000
Marcy Feit, *Branch Mgr*
Joe Carlucci, *Exec Dir*
EMP: 210
SALES (corp-wide): 12.4B **Privately Held**
WEB: www.valleycare.com
SIC: 8062 7999 General medical & surgical hospitals; gymnastic instruction, non-membership
HQ: Valleycare Hospital Corporation
1111 E Stanley Blvd
Livermore CA 94550

(P-16709)
VALLEYCARE HOSPITAL CORP (DH)
Also Called: Valleycare Health
1111 E Stanley Blvd, Livermore (94550-4115)
PHONE.................................925 447-7000
Marcelina L Feit, *President*
Tracy McClain, *CFO*
Felicia Ziomek, *Officer*
Richard Hayashi, *Executive Asst*
Kurt Johnson, *Info Tech Mgr*
EMP: 648 **EST:** 1988
SALES (est): 39.1MM
SALES (corp-wide): 12.4B **Privately Held**
WEB: www.valleycare.com
SIC: 8062 General medical & surgical hospitals
HQ: The Hospital Committee For The Livermore-Pleasanton Areas
5555 W Las Positas Blvd
Pleasanton CA 94588
925 847-3000

(P-16710)
VERITY HEALTH SYSTEM CAL INC
Also Called: St Francis Medical Center
203 Redwood Shores Pkwy, Redwood City (94065-1198)
PHONE.................................310 900-8900
Fax: 626 744-3686
EMP: 300
SALES (corp-wide): 225.4MM **Privately Held**
SIC: 8062 General Hospital
PA: Verity Health System Of California, Inc.
2040 E Mariposa Ave
El Segundo CA 91367
650 551-6650

(P-16711)
VERITY HEALTH SYSTEM CAL INC
Also Called: O'Connor Hospital
2105 Forest Ave, San Jose (95128-1425)
PHONE.................................408 947-2500
Robert Curry, *CEO*
Derek Drake, *Ch Nursing Ofcr*
Aaron Salazar, *Security Dir*
Sheryl Addotta, *Executive Asst*
Roberto Dino, *Manager*
EMP: 5983
SALES (corp-wide): 238.8MM **Privately Held**
WEB: www.verity.org
SIC: 8062 General medical & surgical hospitals
PA: Verity Health System Of California, Inc.
6300 Canoga Ave Ste 1500
Woodland Hills CA 91367

(P-16712)
VERITY HEALTH SYSTEM CAL INC
Also Called: Paryroll Department
203 Redwood Shores Pkwy # 700, Redwood City (94065-1198)
PHONE.................................650 551-6507
EMP: 200
SALES (corp-wide): 225.4MM **Privately Held**
SIC: 8062 8721 General Hospital Accounting/Auditing/Bookkeeping
PA: Verity Health System Of California, Inc.
2040 E Mariposa Ave
El Segundo CA 91367
650 551-6650

(P-16713)
VETERANS HEALTH ADMINISTRATION
Also Called: VA Hospital
2615 E Clinton Ave, Fresno (93703-2223)
PHONE.................................559 225-6100
Rhonda Aday, *CFO*
Michael Gatley,
Vishnu Bobba, *Chief*
James Apok, *Supervisor*
EMP: 247 **Publicly Held**
WEB: www.benefits.va.gov
SIC: 8062 9451 General medical & surgical hospitals;
HQ: Veterans Health Administration
810 Vermont Ave Nw
Washington DC 20420

(P-16714)
VIBRA HEALTHCARE LLC
1315 Shaw Ave Ste 102, Clovis (93612-3963)
PHONE.................................559 325-5601
Scott Mooneyham, *Branch Mgr*
Randi Miller-Laird, *Manager*
EMP: 47

8062 - General Medical & Surgical Hospitals

SALES (corp-wide): 759.7MM **Privately Held**
WEB: www.vibrahealthcare.com
SIC: **8062** General medical & surgical hospitals
PA: Vibra Healthcare, Llc
4600 Lena Dr Ste 100
Mechanicsburg PA 17055
717 591-5700

(P-16715)
VIBRA HEALTHCARE LLC
Also Called: Vibra Hospital Northern Cal
2801 Eureka Way, Redding (96001-0222)
PHONE 530 246-9000
Penny Booth, *Records Dir*
Kristi Rupp, *Social Dir*
Rich Schubert, *Food Svc Dir*
Thiruvoipati Nandakumar, *Med Doctor*
Dayna Patania, *Cert Phar Tech*
EMP: 47
SALES (corp-wide): 759.7MM **Privately Held**
WEB: www.vibrahealthcare.com
SIC: **8062** General medical & surgical hospitals
PA: Vibra Healthcare, Llc
4600 Lena Dr Ste 100
Mechanicsburg PA 17055
717 591-5700

(P-16716)
VIBRA HEALTHCARE LLC
7173 N Sharon Ave, Fresno (93720-3329)
PHONE 559 436-3600
Mary Jacobson, *Principal*
EMP: 47
SALES (corp-wide): 759.7MM **Privately Held**
WEB: www.vibrahealthcare.com
SIC: **8062** General medical & surgical hospitals
PA: Vibra Healthcare, Llc
4600 Lena Dr Ste 100
Mechanicsburg PA 17055
717 591-5700

(P-16717)
VIBRA HEALTHCARE LLC
Also Called: Kentfield Hospital
1125 Sir Frncis Drake Blv, Kentfield (94904-1418)
PHONE 415 853-9499
EMP: 71
SALES (corp-wide): 224.1MM **Privately Held**
WEB: www.vibrahealthcare.com
SIC: **8062** General Hospital
PA: Vibra Healthcare, Llc
4600 Lena Dr Ste 100
Mechanicsburg PA 17055
717 591-5700

(P-16718)
VIBRA HEALTHCARE LLC
7033 N Fresno St 101, Fresno (93720-2976)
PHONE 559 431-2635
Dan Beckstead, *Branch Mgr*
EMP: 47
SALES (corp-wide): 759.7MM **Privately Held**
WEB: www.vibrahealthcare.com
SIC: **8062** General medical & surgical hospitals
PA: Vibra Healthcare, Llc
4600 Lena Dr Ste 100
Mechanicsburg PA 17055
717 591-5700

(P-16719)
VIBRA HOSPITAL SACRAMENTO LLC
330 Montrose Dr, Folsom (95630-2720)
PHONE 916 351-9151
Janet Biedrone, *CEO*
Kimberly Horton, *Officer*
Varun Chauhan,
Tammy Silvey, *Hlthcr Dir*
Brad E Hollinger, *Mng Member*
EMP: 246 EST: 2013
SQ FT: 22,000

SALES (est): 42.1MM
SALES (corp-wide): 759.7MM **Privately Held**
WEB: www.vibrahealthcare.com
SIC: **8062** General medical & surgical hospitals
PA: Vibra Healthcare, Llc
4600 Lena Dr Ste 100
Mechanicsburg PA 17055
717 591-5700

(P-16720)
WASHINGTON CENTER
14766 Washington Ave, San Leandro (94578-4220)
PHONE 510 352-2211
Diana Hoskins, *Records Dir*
Aileen Agcaoili, *Office Mgr*
Georgina Simpson, *Chf Purch Ofc*
Susan Bonilla, *Marketing Staff*
EMP: 100 EST: 2019
SALES (est): 6.2MM **Privately Held**
WEB: www.washingtoncenter.com
SIC: **8062** General medical & surgical hospitals

(P-16721)
WASHINGTON HOSP HEALTHCARE SYS
2000 Mowry Ave, Fremont (94538-1716)
PHONE 510 797-3342
Nancy Farber, *CEO*
Chris Henry, *CFO*
Cathy Messman, *Treasurer*
Young Kang, *Officer*
Colleen Allison, *Vice Pres*
EMP: 1600 EST: 1948
SQ FT: 250,000
SALES: 512.9MM **Privately Held**
WEB: www.whhs.com
SIC: **8062** General medical & surgical hospitals

(P-16722)
WASHINGTON OTPTENT SRGERY CTR
Also Called: Washington Otptent Surgery Ctr
2299 Mowry Ave Fl 1, Fremont (94538-1621)
PHONE 510 791-5374
Gary Charland, *Partner*
Trevin Hunt, *Administration*
Martha Garcia, *Accounting Mgr*
Stacey Barrie, *Obstetrician*
Pat Lum,
EMP: 97 EST: 1986
SQ FT: 18,000
SALES (est): 22.8MM
SALES (corp-wide): 33.4MM **Privately Held**
WEB: www.washosc.com
SIC: **8062** General medical & surgical hospitals
PA: Washington Township Hospital Development Corporation
2000 Mowry Ave
Fremont CA 94538
510 797-1111

(P-16723)
WASHINGTON RDOLOGIST MED GROUP
Also Called: Johnson, David L MD
2000 Mowry Ave, Fremont (94538-1716)
PHONE 510 797-1111
Bruce Nixon MD, *President*
EMP: 43 EST: 1971
SQ FT: 3,000
SALES (est): 3MM **Privately Held**
WEB: www.whhs.com
SIC: **8062** General medical & surgical hospitals

(P-16724)
WILLITS HOSPITAL INC
Also Called: Howard Frank R Memorial Hosp
1 Marcela Dr, Willits (95490-5769)
PHONE 707 459-6801
Rich Bockmann, *CEO*
Carlton Jacobsen, *CFO*
Karen Scott Vpres, *Vice Pres*
Denice Brown, *Executive Asst*
Tedd Dawson, *Med Doctor*
EMP: 283 EST: 1928
SQ FT: 27,000

SALES (est): 66MM
SALES (corp-wide): 4.5B **Privately Held**
WEB: www.willitsanimalhospital.com
SIC: **8062** General medical & surgical hospitals
PA: Adventist Health System/West, Corporation
1 Adventist Health Way
Roseville CA 95661
844 574-5686

(P-16725)
WILLOW SPRINGS LLC
Heritage Oaks Hospital
4250 Auburn Blvd, Sacramento (95841-4100)
PHONE 916 489-3336
Shawn Silva, *CEO*
Rosemarie Hamer, *Records Dir*
EMP: 123
SALES (corp-wide): 11.5B **Publicly Held**
WEB: www.uhs.com
SIC: **8062** General medical & surgical hospitals
HQ: Willow Springs, Llc
6640 Carothers Pkwy # 400
Franklin TN 37067
615 312-5700

(P-16726)
WOODLAND HEALTHCARE
Also Called: Woodland Healthcare Home Hlth
261 California St, Woodland (95695-2910)
PHONE 530 669-5680
Claudia Owens, *Manager*
EMP: 177 **Privately Held**
WEB: www.dignityhealth.org
SIC: **8062 8082** General medical & surgical hospitals; home health care services
HQ: Woodland Healthcare
1325 Cottonwood St
Woodland CA 95695
530 662-3961

(P-16727)
WOODLAND HEALTHCARE
2660 W Covell Blvd, Davis (95616-5645)
PHONE 530 756-2364
Kevin Mould, *Branch Mgr*
Philip M Laughlin MD, *Med Doctor*
Kevin S Mould MD, *Med Doctor*
EMP: 177 **Privately Held**
WEB: www.dignityhealth.org
SIC: **8062 8011** General medical & surgical hospitals; offices & clinics of medical doctors
HQ: Woodland Healthcare
1325 Cottonwood St
Woodland CA 95695
530 662-3961

(P-16728)
WOODLAND HEALTHCARE
1207 Fairchild Ct, Woodland (95695-4321)
PHONE 530 668-2600
Bill Hunt, *Principal*
EMP: 177 **Privately Held**
WEB: www.dignityhealth.org
SIC: **8062 8011** General medical & surgical hospitals; offices & clinics of medical doctors
HQ: Woodland Healthcare
1325 Cottonwood St
Woodland CA 95695
530 662-3961

(P-16729)
WOODLAND MEMORIAL HOSPITAL (PA)
1325 Cottonwood St, Woodland (95695-5131)
PHONE 530 669-5323
Gena Bravo, *CEO*
James Allen,
Denise Foreman, *Business Dir*
George Garcia, *Security Dir*
EMP: 196 EST: 2004
SALES (est): 911.5K **Privately Held**
WEB: www.woodlandchamber.org
SIC: **8062** General medical & surgical hospitals

(P-16730)
WOODLAND MEMORIAL HOSPITAL
Also Called: Woodland Healthcare
1321 Cottonwood St, Woodland (95695-5131)
PHONE 530 669-5600
Bill Gilligan, *Director*
Susan Barajas, *Principal*
Matthew Zavod, *Otolaryngology*
EMP: 42 EST: 1989
SQ FT: 15,000
SALES: 1.2MM **Privately Held**
WEB: www.supportwoodlandhealthcare.org
SIC: **8062** General medical & surgical hospitals

8063 Psychiatric Hospitals

(P-16731)
7TH AVENUE CENTER LLC
1171 7th Ave, Santa Cruz (95062-2714)
PHONE 831 476-1700
Ann Butler,
Tami Toop, *Office Mgr*
Diana Cornell, *Bookkeeper*
EMP: 42 EST: 2000
SALES (est): 19.9MM **Privately Held**
WEB: www.7thavecenter.com
SIC: **8063 8361 8011** Psychiatric hospitals; residential care; offices & clinics of medical doctors

(P-16732)
COUNTY OF ALAMEDA
Also Called: John George Psychiatric
2060 Fairmont Dr, San Leandro (94578-1001)
PHONE 510 346-1300
Ken Cohen, *CEO*
Karyn Tribble, *Officer*
Jason Terry, *Food Svc Dir*
Craig Beaty, *Psychiatry*
Varendra Gosein, *Psychiatry*
EMP: 43 **Privately Held**
WEB: www.acgov.org
SIC: **8063 9431** Psychiatric hospitals; administration of public health programs
PA: County Of Alameda
1221 Oak St Ste 555
Oakland CA 94612
510 272-6691

(P-16733)
COUNTY OF SONOMA
Department Mental Health Svcs
2227 Capricorn Way # 207, Santa Rosa (95407-5478)
PHONE 707 565-4850
Marcus Crosdowny, *Director*
Terina Tracy, *Opers Staff*
Mark Davidow, *Psychiatry*
EMP: 71
SALES (corp-wide): 1B **Privately Held**
WEB: www.sonomacounty.ca.gov
SIC: **8063** Hospital for the mentally ill
PA: County Of Sonoma
585 Fiscal Dr 100
Santa Rosa CA 95403
707 565-2431

(P-16734)
CRESTWOOD BEHAVIORAL HLTH INC
Also Called: 1112 Modesto Snf/STP
1400 Celeste Dr, Modesto (95355-5041)
PHONE 209 526-8050
Lauri Blaufus, *Branch Mgr*
EMP: 343
SQ FT: 56,538
SALES (corp-wide): 238MM **Privately Held**
WEB: www.crestwoodbehavioralhealth.com
SIC: **8063** Psychiatric hospitals
PA: Crestwood Behavioral Health, Inc.
520 Capitol Mall Ste 800
Sacramento CA 95814
510 651-1244

8069 - Specialty Hospitals, Except Psychiatric

(P-16735)
CRESTWOOD BEHAVIORAL HLTH INC (PA)
Also Called: 1101 Corporate-Sacramento
520 Capitol Mall Ste 800, Sacramento (95814-4716)
PHONE..................510 651-1244
Robyn Ramsey, *CEO*
Patricia Blum, *Vice Pres*
Lori Blackburn,
EMP: 52 EST: 1997
SALES (est): 238MM **Privately Held**
WEB: www.crestwoodbehavioralhealth.com
SIC: **8063** Psychiatric hospitals

(P-16736)
CRESTWOOD BEHAVIORAL HLTH INC
Also Called: 1106 Sacramento Mhrc
2600 Stockton Blvd, Sacramento (95817-2210)
PHONE..................916 452-1431
Adrain Smith, *CEO*
EMP: 66
SALES (corp-wide): 238MM **Privately Held**
WEB: www.crestwoodbehavioralhealth.com
SIC: **8063** 8361 Hospital for the mentally ill; residential care
PA: Crestwood Behavioral Health, Inc.
520 Capitol Mall Ste 800
Sacramento CA 95814
510 651-1244

(P-16737)
CRESTWOOD BEHAVIORAL HLTH INC
Also Called: 1156 Sacramento PHF
2600 Stockton Blvd, Sacramento (95817-2210)
PHONE..................916 452-1431
Adrain Smith, *Administration*
EMP: 59
SALES (corp-wide): 238MM **Privately Held**
WEB: www.crestwoodbehavioralhealth.com
SIC: **8063** Psychiatric hospitals
PA: Crestwood Behavioral Health, Inc.
520 Capitol Mall Ste 800
Sacramento CA 95814
510 651-1244

(P-16738)
CRESTWOOD BEHAVIORAL HLTH INC
Also Called: 1157 San Jose PHF
1425 Fruitdale Ave, San Jose (95128-3234)
PHONE..................408 275-1067
Gail McDonald, *Administration*
EMP: 42
SALES (corp-wide): 238MM **Privately Held**
WEB: www.crestwoodbehavioralhealth.com
SIC: **8063** Psychiatric hospitals
PA: Crestwood Behavioral Health, Inc.
520 Capitol Mall Ste 800
Sacramento CA 95814
510 651-1244

(P-16739)
CRESTWOOD BEHAVIORAL HLTH INC
Also Called: 1159 Solano PHF
2201 Tuolumne St, Vallejo (94589-2524)
PHONE..................707 234-2222
Helen Okeigwe, *Administration*
EMP: 52
SALES (corp-wide): 238MM **Privately Held**
WEB: www.crestwoodbehavioralhealth.com
SIC: **8063** Psychiatric hospitals
PA: Crestwood Behavioral Health, Inc.
520 Capitol Mall Ste 800
Sacramento CA 95814
510 651-1244

(P-16740)
CRESTWOOD BEHAVIORAL HLTH INC
Also Called: 1101 Stockton Accounting Off
7590 Shoreline Dr, Stockton (95219-5455)
PHONE..................209 478-5291
Margarita Rosero, *Administration*
EMP: 89
SALES (corp-wide): 238MM **Privately Held**
WEB: www.crestwoodbehavioralhealth.com
SIC: **8063** Psychiatric hospitals
PA: Crestwood Behavioral Health, Inc.
520 Capitol Mall Ste 800
Sacramento CA 95814
510 651-1244

(P-16741)
CRESTWOOD BEHAVIORAL HLTH INC
Also Called: 1153 American River PHF
4741 Engle Rd, Carmichael (95608-2223)
PHONE..................916 977-0949
Shawna Valverde, *Administration*
EMP: 48
SALES (corp-wide): 238MM **Privately Held**
WEB: www.crestwoodbehavioralhealth.com
SIC: **8063** Psychiatric hospitals
PA: Crestwood Behavioral Health, Inc.
520 Capitol Mall Ste 800
Sacramento CA 95814
510 651-1244

(P-16742)
JOHN MUIR BEHAVIORAL HLTH CTR
2740 Grant St, Concord (94520-2265)
PHONE..................925 674-4100
Elizabeth Stallings, *COO*
Susan Ingebresten, *Records Dir*
Harold Huskins, *Officer*
Joanna Peterson, *Social Dir*
Kevin Lane, *Business Dir*
EMP: 62 EST: 1991
SQ FT: 40,000
SALES (est): 10.6MM **Privately Held**
WEB: www.johnmuirhealth.com
SIC: **8063** 8051 Psychiatric hospitals; skilled nursing care facilities

(P-16743)
MARIN COUNTY SART PROGRAM
Also Called: Canyon Mnor Rsdntial Trtmnt Ct
655 Canyon Rd, Novato (94947-4331)
P.O. Box 865 (94948-0865)
PHONE..................415 892-1628
Donald Harris, *President*
Ben Lan, *Corp Secy*
EMP: 38 EST: 1976
SQ FT: 15,000
SALES (est): 2.4MM **Privately Held**
WEB: www.canyonmanor.com
SIC: **8063** 8361 8069 Hospital for the mentally ill; residential care; specialty hospitals, except psychiatric

(P-16744)
NORTHERN VLY INDIAN HLTH INC
175 W Court St, Woodland (95695-2913)
PHONE..................530 661-4400
EMP: 104
SALES (corp-wide): 47.1MM **Privately Held**
WEB: www.nvih.org
SIC: **8063** Psychiatric hospitals
PA: Northern Valley Indian Health, Inc.
207 N Butte St
Willows CA
530 934-9293

(P-16745)
STATE HOSPITALS CAL DEPT
Also Called: Coalinga State Hospital
24511 W Jayne Ave, Coalinga (93210-9503)
P.O. Box 5000 (93210-5000)
PHONE..................559 935-4300
Tom Voss, *Director*
Lori Clark, *Director*
EMP: 456 **Privately Held**
WEB: www.ca.gov
SIC: **8063** 9431 Psychiatric hospitals; mental health agency administration, government;
HQ: California Department Of State Hospitals
1600 9th St Ste 350
Sacramento CA 95814

(P-16746)
STATE HOSPITALS CAL DEPT
Also Called: NAPA State Hospital
2100 Napa Vallejo Hwy, NAPA (94558-6234)
PHONE..................707 253-5000
Sidney Herndon, *Branch Mgr*
Carol A Kuchmak, *Med Doctor*
Beverly De Chavez,
Margie Van Dam,
EMP: 456 **Privately Held**
WEB: www.ca.gov
SIC: **8063** 9431 8361 Hospital for the mentally ill; mental health agency administration, government; ; residential care
HQ: California Department Of State Hospitals
1600 9th St Ste 350
Sacramento CA 95814

(P-16747)
STATE HOSPITALS CAL DEPT
Also Called: Vacaville Psychiatric Program
1600 California Dr, Vacaville (95696)
P.O. Box 2297 (95696-8297)
PHONE..................707 449-6504
Victor Brewer, *Director*
EMP: 456 **Privately Held**
WEB: www.ca.gov
SIC: **8063** 9431 Hospital for the mentally ill; mental health agency administration, government;
HQ: California Department Of State Hospitals
1600 9th St Ste 350
Sacramento CA 95814

(P-16748)
TELECARE CORPORATION (PA)
1080 Marina Village Pkwy # 100, Alameda (94501-1078)
PHONE..................510 337-7950
Anne L Bakar, *President*
Rachel Cook, *Records Dir*
Marshall Langfeld, *CFO*
David J Kears, *Bd of Directors*
James K Newman, *Bd of Directors*
EMP: 719 EST: 1965
SQ FT: 15,000
SALES (est): 140.9MM **Privately Held**
WEB: www.telecarecorp.com
SIC: **8063** 8011 Psychiatric hospitals; health maintenance organization

(P-16749)
UNIVERSITY CAL SAN FRANCISCO
Also Called: San Francisco General Hospital
1001 Potrero Ave Ste 7m, San Francisco (94110-3518)
PHONE..................415 206-8430
Dan Karasic, *Branch Mgr*
EMP: 193 **Privately Held**
WEB: www.ucsf.edu
SIC: **8063** 8221 9411 Psychiatric hospitals; university; administration of educational programs
HQ: University Cal San Francisco
513 Parnassus Ave 115f
San Francisco CA 94143

(P-16750)
YUBA CITY COMMUNITY HOSP INC
39001 Sundale Dr, Fremont (94538-2005)
PHONE..................510 796-1100
Jay Kellison, *CEO*
John Cooper, *CEO*
EMP: 42 EST: 1993
SALES (est): 810.1K **Privately Held**
SIC: **8063** Psychiatric hospitals

8069 Specialty Hospitals, Except Psychiatric

(P-16751)
ASIAN AMERCN RECOVERY SVCS INC
Also Called: Place Asian Amrcn Rcovery Svcs
1340 Tully Rd Ste 304, San Jose (95122-3055)
PHONE..................408 271-3900
Jeff Mori, *Exec Dir*
EMP: 125 **Privately Held**
SIC: **8069** Drug addiction rehabilitation hospital
PA: Asian American Recovery Services, Inc.
1115 Mission Rd 2
South San Francisco CA 94080

(P-16752)
BURN UNIT UCD MEDICAL CENTER
Also Called: Regional Burn Center
2315 Stockton Blvd, Sacramento (95817-2201)
PHONE..................916 734-3637
Linda Moore, *Manager*
EMP: 41 EST: 2005
SALES (est): 5.2MM **Privately Held**
SIC: **8069** Specialty hospitals, except psychiatric

(P-16753)
CHILDRENS RECOVERY CTR 1 LLC
Also Called: Childrens Rcvery Ctr Nthrn Cal
3777 S Bascom Ave, Campbell (95008-7320)
PHONE..................408 558-3640
Ken McGuire, *CEO*
Christy Bracco, *Records Dir*
Damoun Alizadeh, *CIO*
EMP: 83 EST: 1997
SQ FT: 17,000
SALES (est): 25.9MM **Privately Held**
SIC: **8069** Children's hospital

(P-16754)
CRC HEALTH LLC (DH)
20400 Stevns Crk Blvd # 600, Cupertino (95014-2217)
PHONE..................877 272-8668
R Andrew Eckert, *Ch of Bd*
Jerome E Rhodes, *CEO*
Leanne M Stewart, *CFO*
Mary A Detmer, *Treasurer*
Philip L Herschman, *Officer*
EMP: 80 EST: 2002
SALES (est): 505.2MM **Publicly Held**
WEB: www.legalrecruiterdirectory.org
SIC: **8069** 8099 8322 8093 Drug addiction rehabilitation hospital; medical services organization; general counseling services; substance abuse clinics (outpatient)

(P-16755)
DAVIS COMMUNITY CLINIC
Also Called: John H Jones Community Clinic
500 Jefferson Blvd B195, West Sacramento (95605-2350)
PHONE..................916 403-2970
Randy Tryon, *Exec Dir*
EMP: 50
SALES (corp-wide): 9.9MM **Privately Held**
WEB: www.communicarehc.org
SIC: **8069** Drug addiction rehabilitation hospital
PA: Davis Community Clinic
2040 Sutter Pl
Davis CA 95616
530 758-2060

(P-16756)
DEVELOPMENTAL SVCS CAL DEPT
Also Called: Sonoma Development Center
15000 Arnold Dr, Eldridge (95431-8900)
P.O. Box 1493 (95431-1493)
PHONE..................707 938-6000
Douglas Rice, *Director*

8069 - Specialty Hospitals, Except Psychiatric County (P-16757)

EMP: 667 **Privately Held**
WEB: www.ca.gov
SIC: 8069 9431 Specialty hospitals, except psychiatric; categorical health program administration, government
HQ: California Department Of Developmental Services
1215 O St
Sacramento CA 95814

(P-16757)
ENCOMPASS COMMUNITY SERVICES
Also Called: Tyler House
2716 Freedom Blvd, Watsonville (95076-1027)
PHONE.....................831 688-6293
Adriann Jackson, *Manager*
EMP: 63
SALES (corp-wide): 31MM **Privately Held**
WEB: www.encompasscs.org
SIC: 8069 Alcoholism rehabilitation hospital
PA: Encompass Community Services
380 Encinal St Ste 200
Santa Cruz CA 95060
831 427-9670

(P-16758)
ENLIGHTICARE INC
Also Called: Elevate Addiction Services
138 Victoria Ln, Aptos (95003-3027)
P.O. Box 1690 (95001-1690)
PHONE.....................831 750-3546
Daniel Manson, *President*
EMP: 90 **EST:** 2017
SALES (est): 5.5MM **Privately Held**
SIC: 8069 Substance abuse hospitals

(P-16759)
GUAVA HOLDINGS LLC
Also Called: Yuba City Post-Acute
1220 Plumas St, Yuba City (95991-3411)
PHONE.....................530 671-0550
Toby Tilford, *President*
Dustin Murray, *Administration*
Nicklas Anderson, *Manager*
Naveed Hakim, *Manager*
EMP: 50 **EST:** 2017
SALES (est): 5.7MM **Privately Held**
WEB: www.yubacitypostacute.com
SIC: 8069 Geriatric hospital

(P-16760)
HEALTHCARE CENTRE OF FRESNO
1665 M St, Fresno (93721-1121)
PHONE.....................559 268-5361
Lucille Epperson, *Administration*
Charles J Enoch, *Partner*
Joyce S Lopez, *Partner*
Laverne E Masten, *Partner*
Barbara H Rose, *Partner*
EMP: 175 **EST:** 1957
SQ FT: 87,000
SALES (est): 18.7MM **Privately Held**
WEB: www.hcfresno.com
SIC: 8069 8051 Specialty hospitals, except psychiatric; convalescent home with continuous nursing care

(P-16761)
JANUS OF SANTA CRUZ
200 7th Ave Ste 150, Santa Cruz (95062-4669)
PHONE.....................831 462-1060
Rod Libbey, *Exec Dir*
Morgan Sandoval, *Office Mgr*
Jesse Gifford, *Info Tech Mgr*
Calli Morrow, *Technician*
Erin Carlson-Jones, *Director*
EMP: 100 **EST:** 1976
SALES (est): 11MM **Privately Held**
WEB: www.janussc.org
SIC: 8069 Drug addiction rehabilitation hospital

(P-16762)
KINGS VIEW
49269 Golden Oak Dr 204b, Oakhurst (93644-9477)
PHONE.....................559 641-2805
EMP: 36
SALES (corp-wide): 26.8MM **Privately Held**
WEB: www.kingsview.org
SIC: 8069 8093 8322 Alcoholism rehabilitation hospital; alcohol clinic, outpatient; social service center
PA: Kings View
7170 N Fincl Dr Ste 110
Fresno CA 93720
559 256-0100

(P-16763)
LELAND STANFORD JUNIOR UNIV (PA)
Also Called: Stanford University
450 Jane Stanford Way, Stanford (94305-2004)
P.O. Box 20410, Palo Alto (94309-0410)
PHONE.....................650 723-2300
Tessier Lavigne, *President*
Marc Tessier-Lavigne, *President*
Randall S Livingston, *CFO*
Debra Zumwalt, *Vice Pres*
Maria Maravilla, *Executive*
▲ **EMP:** 200 **EST:** 1891
SALES (est): 12.4B **Privately Held**
WEB: www.stanford.edu
SIC: 8221 8069 8062 University; children's hospital; general medical & surgical hospitals

(P-16764)
LELAND STANFORD JUNIOR UNIV
Also Called: Stanford University - Et
505 Broadway St Fl 4, Redwood City (94063-3122)
PHONE.....................650 935-5365
Marc Tessier-Lavigne, *President*
EMP: 1000
SALES (corp-wide): 12.4B **Privately Held**
WEB: www.stanford.edu
SIC: 8221 8069 8062 University; children's hospital; general medical & surgical hospitals
PA: Leland Stanford Junior University
450 Jane Stanford Way
Stanford CA 94305
650 723-2300

(P-16765)
LIVONGO HEALTH INC (HQ)
150 W Evelyn Ave Ste 150 # 150, Mountain View (94041-1556)
PHONE.....................866 435-5643
Zane Burke, *CEO*
Glen E Tullman, *Ch of Bd*
Jennifer Schneider, *President*
Lee Shapiro, *CFO*
James Pursley, *Officer*
▲ **EMP:** 50
SQ FT: 30,019
SALES: 68.4MM **Publicly Held**
WEB: www.livongo.com
SIC: 8069 Chronic disease hospital

(P-16766)
LUCILE SLTER PCKARD CHLD HOSP (HQ)
Also Called: Lucile Packard Childrens Hosp
725 Welch Rd, Palo Alto (94304-1601)
PHONE.....................650 497-8000
Christopher Dawes, *President*
Timothy W Carmack, *CFO*
Greg Souza, *Officer*
Bernadine Fong, *Vice Pres*
Alvaro Jimenez, *Vice Pres*
▲ **EMP:** 859 **EST:** 1919
SALES: 2B
SALES (corp-wide): 12.4B **Privately Held**
WEB: www.stanfordchildrens.org
SIC: 8069 8082 5912 Children's hospital; home health care services; drug stores & proprietary stores
PA: Leland Stanford Junior University
450 Jane Stanford Way
Stanford CA 94305
650 723-2300

(P-16767)
MAITRI COMPASSIONATE CARE
401 Duboce Ave, San Francisco (94117-3551)
PHONE.....................415 558-3000
Tim Patriarca, *Exec Dir*
Anne Gimbel, *Exec Dir*
Michael Sorensen, *Exec Dir*
Barbara Smith, *Office Mgr*
Yana Mikheleva, *Nursing Mgr*
EMP: 46 **EST:** 1987
SQ FT: 20,000
SALES (est): 3MM **Privately Held**
WEB: www.maitrisf.org
SIC: 8069 8322 Specialty hospitals, except psychiatric; individual & family services

(P-16768)
NEW START RCVERY SOLUTIONS INC
2167 Montgomery St Ste A, Oroville (95965-4945)
P.O. Box 2456 (95965-2456)
PHONE.....................530 854-4119
Joseph Henderson, *CEO*
EMP: 80
SALES (est): 30MM **Privately Held**
WEB: www.newstartrecoverysolutions.com
SIC: 8069 Drug addiction rehabilitation hospital

(P-16769)
PATHOLOGY ASSOCIATES
305 Park Creek Dr, Clovis (93611-4426)
PHONE.....................559 326-2800
Katherine A Huber, *Principal*
Steve Frediani, *COO*
Melissa Matthes, *Human Resources*
Andy Batson, *Accounts Exec*
EMP: 136 **EST:** 2009
SALES (est): 57.4MM **Privately Held**
WEB: www.pathology-associates.com
SIC: 8069 Specialty hospitals, except psychiatric

(P-16770)
SUCCESSFUL ALTRNTVES FOR ADDCT (HQ)
1628 Broadway St, Vallejo (94590-2405)
PHONE.....................707 649-8300
Raymond Mc Murray, *Principal*
EMP: 50 **EST:** 2004
SALES (est): 1.6MM
SALES (corp-wide): 50.2MM **Privately Held**
WEB: www.medmark.com
SIC: 8069 Drug addiction rehabilitation hospital
PA: Medmark Services, Inc.
1720 Lakepointe Dr # 117
Lewisville TX 75057
214 379-3300

(P-16771)
VALLEY CHILDRENS MEDICAL GROUP
9300 Valley Childrens Pl Sc61, Madera (93636-8761)
PHONE.....................559 353-6241
Michael Goldring, *President*
Trish Panedo, *President*
David Singh, *COO*
Linda Fraley, *Admin Sec*
EMP: 53 **EST:** 2013
SALES (est): 129.3MM **Privately Held**
WEB: www.valleychildrenspediatrics.org
SIC: 8069 Children's hospital

8071 Medical Laboratories

(P-16772)
ASCEND CLINICAL LLC (PA)
1400 Industrial Way, Redwood City (94063-1101)
PHONE.....................800 800-5655
Paul F Beyer, *CEO*
Jeffrey Vizethann, *President*
Patricia Hunsader, *COO*
Olivier Gindraux, *CFO*
Martin Blair, *Vice Pres*
▲ **EMP:** 65 **EST:** 2000
SALES (est): 31.7MM **Privately Held**
WEB: www.clinical.aclab.com
SIC: 8071 Blood analysis laboratory

(P-16773)
ASSOCIATED PATHOLOGY MED GROUP
459 Monterey Ave, Los Gatos (95030-5302)
P.O. Box 665 (95031-0665)
PHONE.....................408 399-5010
Robert Rinehart MD, *President*
Julia Chan MD, *Treasurer*
Carlene A Hawksley, *Vice Pres*
Paula S Quinn, *Principal*
Warner Stamm, *Principal*
EMP: 67 **EST:** 1962
SQ FT: 3,000
SALES (est): 3.1MM **Privately Held**
WEB: www.apmglab.com
SIC: 8071 Pathological laboratory

(P-16774)
BILLIONTOONE INC
1035 Obrien Dr, Menlo Park (94025-1408)
PHONE.....................650 666-6443
Oguzhan Atay, *CEO*
Nipun Soni, *CFO*
Shan Riku, *Vice Pres*
David Tsao, *CTO*
EMP: 95 **EST:** 2016
SALES (est): 5.9MM **Privately Held**
WEB: www.billiontoone.com
SIC: 8071 8731 Medical laboratories; commercial physical research

(P-16775)
BRIGHTSEED BIO ✪
201 Haskins Way Ste 310, South San Francisco (94080-6215)
PHONE.....................415 965-7778
James Flatt, *CEO*
EMP: 45 **EST:** 2021
SALES (est): 196.7K **Privately Held**
SIC: 8071 Biological laboratory

(P-16776)
CAREDX INC (PA)
1 Tower Pl Fl 9, South San Francisco (94080-1828)
PHONE.....................415 287-2300
Reginald Seeto, *President*
Peter Maag, *Ch of Bd*
Ankur Dhingra, *CFO*
Sasha King, *Officer*
Paul Ciccolella, *Vice Pres*
EMP: 308 **EST:** 1998
SQ FT: 28,968
SALES (est): 192.1MM **Publicly Held**
WEB: www.caredx.com
SIC: 8071 8733 Medical laboratories; non-commercial research organizations

(P-16777)
COUNTY OF SAN JOAQUIN
1601 E Hazelton Ave, Stockton (95205-6229)
PHONE.....................209 468-3460
Bill Mitchell, *Principal*
EMP: 48
SALES (corp-wide): 1.2B **Privately Held**
WEB: www.sjgov.org
SIC: 8071 Medical laboratories
PA: County Of San Joaquin
44 N San Joaquin St # 640
Stockton CA 95202
209 468-3203

(P-16778)
COUNTY OF SOLANO
Also Called: Public Health Laboratory, The
355 Tuolumne St, Vallejo (94590-5700)
PHONE.....................707 553-5029
Al Shabndi, *Director*
Victor Hernandez, *Education*
Mark Maus, *Family Practiti*
EMP: 40
SQ FT: 1,368
SALES (corp-wide): 740.7MM **Privately Held**
WEB: www.solanocounty.com
SIC: 8071 Medical laboratories
PA: County Of Solano
675 Texas St Ste 2600
Fairfield CA 94533
707 784-6706

▲ = Import ▼ = Export
◆ = Import/Export

PRODUCTS & SERVICES SECTION

8071 - Medical Laboratories County (P-16801)

(P-16779)
DAVE DRUNKER
Also Called: Research Institute
795 El Camino Real, Palo Alto (94301-2302)
PHONE..................650 853-4827
David Druker, *Principal*
Mark McLaughlin, *Principal*
EMP: 40
SALES (est): 950K **Privately Held**
SIC: 8071 Medical laboratories

(P-16780)
EBREASTIMAGING LLC (PA)
15195 National Ave # 201, Los Gatos (95032-2631)
PHONE..................408 800-5247
Dipa H Patel, *Principal*
EMP: 42 **EST:** 2016
SALES (est): 276.5K **Privately Held**
WEB: www.ebreastimaging.com
SIC: 8071 Ultrasound laboratory

(P-16781)
GENOMIC HEALTH INC (HQ)
301 Penobscot Dr, Redwood City (94063-4700)
PHONE..................650 556-9300
Kevin T Conroy, *President*
Jeffrey T Elliott, *CFO*
Felix Baker, *Bd of Directors*
Jason Radford, *Officer*
James Vaughn, *Officer*
EMP: 661 **EST:** 2000
SQ FT: 180,700
SALES: 394.1MM
SALES (corp-wide): 1.4B **Publicly Held**
WEB: www.exactsciences.com
SIC: 8071 8731 Medical laboratories; biotechnical research, commercial
PA: Exact Sciences Corporation
5505 Endeavor Ln
Madison WI 53719
608 284-5700

(P-16782)
GUARDANT HEALTH INC (PA)
505 Penobscot Dr, Redwood City (94063-4737)
PHONE..................855 698-8887
Helmy Eltoukhy, *CEO*
Amirali Talasaz, *Ch of Bd*
Derek Bertocci, *CFO*
Stan Meresman, *Bd of Directors*
Richard Lanman, *Chief Mktg Ofcr*
EMP: 275 **EST:** 2011
SQ FT: 114,000
SALES (est): 286.7MM **Publicly Held**
WEB: www.guardanthealth.com
SIC: 8071 Medical laboratories

(P-16783)
HEALTH VENTURES INC (DH)
Also Called: Medical Center Mgntic Imaging
350 Hawthorne Ave, Oakland (94609-3108)
PHONE..................510 869-6703
Victor Meinke, *President*
EMP: 50 **EST:** 1983
SQ FT: 3,000
SALES (est): 4.3MM
SALES (corp-wide): 13.2B **Privately Held**
WEB: www.altabatessummit.org
SIC: 8071 Medical laboratories
HQ: The Surgery Center Of Alta Bates Summit Medical Center Llc
2450 Ashby Ave
Berkeley CA 94705
510 204-4444

(P-16784)
HEALTHCARE CLINICAL LABS (PA)
1800 N California St, Stockton (95204-6019)
PHONE..................209 467-6330
Denise Facaros, *Manager*
EMP: 62 **EST:** 1984
SALES (est): 3.1MM **Privately Held**
WEB: www.hccl.com
SIC: 8071 Testing laboratories

(P-16785)
IGENEX INC
Also Called: Igenex Reference Laboratory
556 Gibraltar Dr, Milpitas (95035-6315)
PHONE..................650 424-1191
Jyotsna Shah, *CEO*
Joe Sullivan, *Marketing Staff*
Johan Gumaelius, *Sales Staff*
Monique TSO, *Assistant*
EMP: 50 **EST:** 1991
SALES (est): 14.2MM **Privately Held**
WEB: www.igenex.com
SIC: 8071 Testing laboratories

(P-16786)
INVITAE CORPORATION (PA)
1400 16th St, San Francisco (94103-5110)
PHONE..................415 374-7782
Randal W Scott, *Ch of Bd*
Sean George, *CEO*
Roxi Wen, *CFO*
Robert L Nussbaum, *Chief Mktg Ofcr*
Patty Dumond, *Officer*
EMP: 90 **EST:** 2010
SQ FT: 7,795
SALES (est): 279.6MM **Publicly Held**
WEB: www.invitae.com
SIC: 8071 Testing laboratories

(P-16787)
KAISER FOUNDATION HOSPITALS
Also Called: Kaiser Permanente
2155 Iron Point Rd, Folsom (95630-8707)
PHONE..................916 817-5651
John Vogelsang, *Obstetrician*
Sudha Chappidi, *Internal Med*
Anthony Retodo, *Internal Med*
James Siy, *Internal Med*
Abraham Thomas Jr, *Internal Med*
EMP: 235
SALES (corp-wide): 30.5B **Privately Held**
WEB: www.kaisercenter.com
SIC: 8071 8099 Medical laboratories; medical services organization
HQ: Kaiser Foundation Hospitals Inc
1 Kaiser Plz
Oakland CA 94612
510 271-6611

(P-16788)
MAGNETIC IMAGING AFFILATES
5730 Telegraph Ave, Oakland (94609-1710)
PHONE..................510 204-1820
Stefan Arnold, *Director*
EMP: 40 **EST:** 1985
SQ FT: 3,500
SALES (est): 6.2MM **Privately Held**
WEB: www.altabatessummit.org
SIC: 8071 Medical laboratories

(P-16789)
MYOME INC (PA)
201 Industrial Rd Ste 410, San Carlos (94070-2396)
PHONE..................541 826-6778
Premal Shah PHD, *CEO*
EMP: 49 **EST:** 2019
SALES (est): 507.6K **Privately Held**
WEB: www.myome.com
SIC: 8071 Biological laboratory

(P-16790)
MYRIAD WOMENS HEALTH INC
180 Kimball Way, South San Francisco (94080-6218)
PHONE..................888 268-6795
Ramji Srinivasan, *CEO*
Joel Jung, *CFO*
Noah Nasser, *Ch Credit Ofcr*
Eric A Evans, *Officer*
Eric Evans, *Officer*
EMP: 281 **EST:** 2007
SALES (est): 70MM **Publicly Held**
WEB: www.myriadwomenshealth.com
SIC: 8071 Medical laboratories
PA: Myriad Genetics, Inc.
320 S Wakara Way
Salt Lake City UT 84108

(P-16791)
NORTH COAST LABORATORIES LTD
5680 West End Rd, Arcata (95521-9202)
PHONE..................707 822-4649
Jesse G Chaney, *President*
Jeff Schindler, *Officer*
Jane Paige Noon, *Vice Pres*
Suzanne Ross, *Admin Asst*
Roxanne Golich Moore, *Opers Staff*
EMP: 39 **EST:** 1980
SQ FT: 9,300
SALES (est): 4.5MM **Privately Held**
WEB: www.northcoastlabs.com
SIC: 8071 8734 Testing laboratories; soil analysis

(P-16792)
PENNISULA PTHLOGISTS MED GROUP
Also Called: Peninsula Pathology Associates
393 E Grand Ave Ste I, South San Francisco (94080-6233)
PHONE..................650 616-2940
Leonard A Valentino MD, *President*
Judy Alonzo, *President*
Carolyn Katzen MD, *Treasurer*
Jay A Guichard MD, *Vice Pres*
Martha S Hales, *Admin Sec*
EMP: 114 **EST:** 1971
SALES (est): 13.5MM **Privately Held**
WEB: www.ppmgpath.com
SIC: 8071 Pathological laboratory

(P-16793)
PERSONALIS INC (PA)
1330 Obrien Dr, Menlo Park (94025-1436)
PHONE..................650 752-1300
John West, *President*
Jonathan Macquitty, *Ch of Bd*
Aaron Tachibana, *CFO*
Richard Chen, *Officer*
Clinton Musil, *Officer*
EMP: 135 **EST:** 2011
SQ FT: 31,280
SALES (est): 78.6MM **Publicly Held**
WEB: www.personalis.com
SIC: 8071 Biological laboratory

(P-16794)
PRECLNCAL MDVICE INNVTIONS LLC
Also Called: PMI
1031 Bing St, San Carlos (94070-5320)
PHONE..................510 704-0140
J T Purban, *Mng Member*
Brian Diehorne, *COO*
Michael Doland, *CFO*
Susannah McCreery, *Project Mgr*
EMP: 37 **EST:** 2007
SQ FT: 20,800
SALES (est): 10.2MM **Privately Held**
WEB: www.medtech.labcorp.com
SIC: 8071 Medical laboratories

(P-16795)
PTS DIAGNOSTICS CALIFORNIA INC
510 Oakmead Pkwy, Sunnyvale (94085-4022)
PHONE..................877 870-5610
Robert Huffstodt, *CEO*
Stephen Riendeau, *Officer*
Ferida Turnadzic, *Prdtn Mgr*
Chad Southard, *Sales Staff*
Bridget Melland, *Director*
EMP: 200 **EST:** 2016
SALES (est): 7.4MM **Privately Held**
WEB: www.ptsdiagnostics.com
SIC: 8071 Medical laboratories

(P-16796)
QUEST DGNSTICS CLNCAL LABS INC
2369 Bering Dr, San Jose (95131-1125)
PHONE..................408 975-1015
Dennis Hogle, *Manager*
Richard Sutt, *Supervisor*
EMP: 62
SALES (corp-wide): 9.4B **Publicly Held**
WEB: www.questdiagnostics.com
SIC: 8071 Testing laboratories
HQ: Quest Diagnostics Clinical Laboratories, Inc.
1201 S Collegeville Rd
Collegeville PA 19426
610 454-6000

(P-16797)
QUEST DGNSTICS CLNCAL LABS INC
7075 N Maple Ave Ste 104, Fresno (93720-8014)
PHONE..................559 299-5074
EMP: 62
SALES (corp-wide): 9.4B **Publicly Held**
WEB: www.questdiagnostics.com
SIC: 8071 Medical laboratories
HQ: Quest Diagnostics Clinical Laboratories, Inc.
1201 S Collegeville Rd
Collegeville PA 19426
610 454-6000

(P-16798)
QUEST DGNSTICS CLNCAL LABS INC
2291 W March Ln Ste F145, Stockton (95207-6664)
PHONE..................209 951-5831
Jeff Owens, *Branch Mgr*
EMP: 62
SALES (corp-wide): 9.4B **Publicly Held**
WEB: www.questdiagnostics.com
SIC: 8071 Testing laboratories
HQ: Quest Diagnostics Clinical Laboratories, Inc.
1201 S Collegeville Rd
Collegeville PA 19426
610 454-6000

(P-16799)
QUEST DGNSTICS CLNCAL LABS INC
155 N Jackson Ave Ste 102, San Jose (95116-1925)
PHONE..................408 259-6806
Talaya Johnson, *Manager*
EMP: 62
SALES (corp-wide): 9.4B **Publicly Held**
WEB: www.questdiagnostics.com
SIC: 8071 Medical laboratories
HQ: Quest Diagnostics Clinical Laboratories, Inc.
1201 S Collegeville Rd
Collegeville PA 19426
610 454-6000

(P-16800)
READCOOR INC
6230 Stoneridge Mall Rd, Pleasanton (94588-3260)
PHONE..................617 453-2660
Serge Saxonov, *CEO*
Jermaine Reid, *Vice Pres*
Jeff Peck, *CIO*
Keaton Armentrout, *Software Engr*
David Barclay, *Research*
EMP: 53 **EST:** 2016
SALES (est): 9.4MM
SALES (corp-wide): 298.8MM **Publicly Held**
WEB: www.10xgenomics.com
SIC: 8071 Biological laboratory
PA: 10x Genomics, Inc.
6230 Stoneridge Mall Rd
Pleasanton CA 94588
925 401-7300

(P-16801)
REDDING PATHOLOGISTS LAB
2036 Railroad Ave, Redding (96001-1801)
PHONE..................530 225-8050
EMP: 55
SALES (corp-wide): 11.6MM **Privately Held**
SIC: 8071 Pathological Laboratory
PA: Redding Pathologists Laboratory
1725 Gold St
Redding CA 96001
530 225-8050

8071 - Medical Laboratories

(P-16802)
REDWOOD REGIONAL MEDICAL GROUP (PA)
Also Called: Redwood Regional Oncology Ctr
990 Sonoma Ave Ste 15, Santa Rosa (95404-4813)
PHONE....................707 525-4080
Mike Smith, CFO
Allan P Fishbein,
David A Keefer,
EMP: 70 EST: 1996
SQ FT: 20,000
SALES (est): 11.1MM Privately Held
SIC: 8071 8011 X-ray laboratory, including dental; radiologist

(P-16803)
REDWOOD RGNAL MED GROUP DRG LL
5150 Hill Rd E Ste F, Lakeport (95453-5100)
PHONE....................707 262-3060
Marysol Rodriguez, Manager
EMP: 41
SALES (corp-wide): 11.1MM Privately Held
SIC: 8071 8011 X-ray laboratory, including dental; offices & clinics of medical doctors
PA: Redwood Regional Medical Group Drug Company, Llc
990 Sonoma Ave Ste 15
Santa Rosa CA 95404
707 525-4080

(P-16804)
REDWOOD TOXICOLOGY LAB INC
3650 Westwind Blvd, Santa Rosa (95403-1066)
P.O. Box 5680 (95402-5680)
PHONE....................707 577-7958
Albert Berger, CEO
Wayne Ross, Shareholder
Alber Berger, CEO
Barry Chapman, CFO
Jennifer Camp, Sales Associate
▲ EMP: 120 EST: 1994
SQ FT: 23,000
SALES (est): 35.4MM
SALES (corp-wide): 34.6B Publicly Held
WEB: www.redwoodtoxicology.com
SIC: 8071 8734 Testing laboratories; testing laboratories
HQ: Alere Inc.
51 Sawyer Rd Ste 200
Waltham MA 02453
781 647-3900

(P-16805)
SANTA ROSA RADIOLOGY MED GROUP (PA)
121 Sotoyome St, Santa Rosa (95405-4871)
PHONE....................707 546-4062
Kim Miranda, CFO
Lesley Morgan, Human Resources
EMP: 50 EST: 1976
SQ FT: 20,000
SALES (est): 8.9MM Privately Held
WEB: www.psjhmedgroups.org
SIC: 8071 8011 X-ray laboratory, including dental; radiologist

(P-16806)
SPRUCE MULTI SPECIALTY GROUP
1275 W Spruce Ave, Fresno (93650-1086)
PHONE....................559 229-2786
Alan M Birnbaum MD,
EMP: 41 EST: 2009
SALES (est): 2.6MM Privately Held
WEB: www.sprucemed.com
SIC: 8071 Medical laboratories

(P-16807)
SUTTER HEALTH
Also Called: Sutter Cancer Ctr
2800 L St Ste 10, Sacramento (95816-5616)
PHONE....................916 454-6600
Nancy Mathai, Branch Mgr
Daniel Ichel, Diag Radio
EMP: 76

SALES (corp-wide): 13.2B Privately Held
WEB: www.suttermedicalcenter.org
SIC: 8071 8011 Medical laboratories; offices & clinics of medical doctors
PA: Sutter Health
2200 River Plaza Dr
Sacramento CA 95833
916 733-8800

(P-16808)
SUTTER HEALTH
Also Called: Roseville Imaging
1640 E Rsvlle Pkwy Ste 10, Roseville (95661)
PHONE....................916 784-2277
Jerry Fosselman, Manager
EMP: 76
SALES (corp-wide): 13.2B Privately Held
WEB: www.suttermedicalcenter.org
SIC: 8071 8011 Medical laboratories; specialized medical practitioners, except internal
PA: Sutter Health
2200 River Plaza Dr
Sacramento CA 95833
916 733-8800

(P-16809)
SUTTER HEALTH
1655 Creekside Dr, Folsom (95630-3489)
PHONE....................916 984-0739
Jerry Fosselman, Branch Mgr
Glenn Hofer, Radiology
Huu Ninh V Dao, Diag Radio
L Todd Dudley, Diag Radio
A Brandt Schraner, Diag Radio
EMP: 76
SALES (corp-wide): 13.2B Privately Held
WEB: www.suttermedicalcenter.org
SIC: 8071 8011 Medical laboratories; offices & clinics of medical doctors
PA: Sutter Health
2200 River Plaza Dr
Sacramento CA 95833
916 733-8800

(P-16810)
TPMG LABORATORY STOCKTON
Also Called: Kaiser Permanente
7373 West Ln, Stockton (95210-3377)
PHONE....................209 476-3646
Jennifer Jose-Banana, Branch Mgr
Issa Fakhouri, Officer
Susan Velasquez, Area Mgr
Carlo Castaneda, IT/INT Sup
Gudalupe Vega, Sales Staff
EMP: 55 EST: 2010
SALES (est): 24.1MM Privately Held
SIC: 8071 Medical laboratories

(P-16811)
UNCHAINED LABS (PA)
Also Called: Optim
6870 Koll Center Pkwy, Pleasanton (94566-3176)
PHONE....................925 587-9800
Tim Harness, CEO
Jason Novi, COO
Terry Salyer, Ch Credit Ofcr
Shelly Morales, Officer
Taegen Clary, Vice Pres
EMP: 140 EST: 2014
SALES (est): 122.7MM Privately Held
WEB: www.unchainedlabs.com
SIC: 8071 3826 Medical laboratories; analytical instruments

(P-16812)
UNILAB CORPORATION
3714 Northgate Blvd, Sacramento (95834-1617)
PHONE....................916 927-9900
Surya Mohapatra, CEO
Trish Rubel, Info Tech Dir
EMP: 948
SALES (corp-wide): 9.4B Publicly Held
WEB: www.questdiagnostics.com
SIC: 8071 Testing laboratories
HQ: Unilab Corporation
8401 Fallbrook Ave
West Hills CA 91304
818 737-6000

(P-16813)
UNILAB CORPORATION
Also Called: Quest Diagnostics
51 N Sunrise Ave Ste 515, Roseville (95661)
PHONE....................916 781-3031
Susan Spivey, Branch Mgr
EMP: 948
SALES (corp-wide): 9.4B Publicly Held
WEB: www.questdiagnostics.com
SIC: 8071 Testing laboratories
HQ: Unilab Corporation
8401 Fallbrook Ave
West Hills CA 91304
818 737-6000

(P-16814)
UNILAB CORPORATION
470 27th St, Oakland (94612-2413)
PHONE....................510 444-5213
EMP: 948
SALES (corp-wide): 9.4B Publicly Held
WEB: www.questdiagnostics.com
SIC: 8071 Medical laboratories
HQ: Unilab Corporation
8401 Fallbrook Ave
West Hills CA 91304
818 737-6000

(P-16815)
UNILAB CORPORATION
6475 Camden Ave Ste 104, San Jose (95120-2847)
PHONE....................408 927-8331
Ian Brotchie, President
EMP: 948
SALES (corp-wide): 9.4B Publicly Held
WEB: www.questdiagnostics.com
SIC: 8071 Testing laboratories
HQ: Unilab Corporation
8401 Fallbrook Ave
West Hills CA 91304
818 737-6000

(P-16816)
UNILAB CORPORATION
Also Called: Physicians Clinical Lab
3160 Folsom Blvd, Sacramento (95816-5202)
PHONE....................916 733-3330
Taylor McKeyman, Branch Mgr
EMP: 948
SALES (corp-wide): 9.4B Publicly Held
WEB: www.questdiagnostics.com
SIC: 8071 Medical laboratories
HQ: Unilab Corporation
8401 Fallbrook Ave
West Hills CA 91304
818 737-6000

(P-16817)
UNILAB CORPORATION
5325 N Fresno St Ste 106, Fresno (93710-6849)
PHONE....................559 225-5076
Ramona Franco, Branch Mgr
EMP: 948
SALES (corp-wide): 9.4B Publicly Held
WEB: www.questdiagnostics.com
SIC: 8071 Medical laboratories
HQ: Unilab Corporation
8401 Fallbrook Ave
West Hills CA 91304
818 737-6000

(P-16818)
UNIVERSITY CALIFORNIA DAVIS
Also Called: Veterinary Genetics Laboratory
980 Old Davis Rd, Davis (95616)
PHONE....................530 752-2314
Linda P B Katehi, Branch Mgr
EMP: 83 Privately Held
WEB: www.ucdavis.edu
SIC: 8071 8221 9411 Testing laboratories; university; administration of educational programs;
HQ: University Of California, Davis
1 Shields Ave
Davis CA 95616

(P-16819)
VALLEY TOXICOLOGY SERVICE INC
Also Called: Valtox Laboratories
2401 Port St, West Sacramento (95691-3501)
P.O. Box 427 (95691-0427)
PHONE....................916 371-5440
Jon Knapp, President
Carol Knapp, Admin Sec
Doreen Kumer, Manager
EMP: 36 EST: 1970
SQ FT: 7,000
SALES (est): 2.1MM Privately Held
SIC: 8071 Bacteriological laboratory

(P-16820)
VERACYTE INC (PA)
6000 Shoreline Ct Ste 300, South San Francisco (94080-7606)
PHONE....................650 243-6300
Marc Stapley, CEO
Bonnie H Anderson, Ch of Bd
Beverly Jane Alley, CFO
Rebecca Chambers, CFO
Giulia C Kennedy, Chief Mktg Ofcr
EMP: 244 EST: 2006
SQ FT: 59,000
SALES (est): 117.4MM Publicly Held
WEB: www.veracyte.com
SIC: 8071 8733 2835 Medical laboratories; medical research; cytology & histology diagnostic agents

(P-16821)
WEST COAST PATHOLOGY LAB
Also Called: Medical Billing Services
712 Alfred Nobel Dr, Hercules (94547-1805)
P.O. Box 624, Pinole (94564-0624)
PHONE....................510 662-5200
John Compagno, Owner
Bikash Panda, Info Tech Dir
Mary Essa, Manager
Danielle Hill, Representative
Alana Wilkins, Accounts Exec
EMP: 59 EST: 1996
SALES (est): 10.9MM Privately Held
SIC: 8071 Pathological laboratory

(P-16822)
YOSEMITE PTHLOGY MED GROUP INC (PA)
4301 N Star Way, Modesto (95356-9262)
P.O. Box 4140 (95352-4140)
PHONE....................209 577-1200
William Knapp MD, President
Robert Colletti, COO
Brian Cummings, Administration
Mike Murray, Information Mgr
Tom Vongphakdy, Research
EMP: 35 EST: 1979
SQ FT: 5,000
SALES (est): 12.1MM Privately Held
WEB: www.ypmg.com
SIC: 8071 8011 Pathological laboratory; offices & clinics of medical doctors

8072 Dental Laboratories

(P-16823)
CALIFORNIA DENTAL ARTS LLC
20421 Pacifica Dr, Cupertino (95014-3013)
PHONE....................408 255-1020
Leon Frangadakis, Mng Member
Matt Froess, COO
Jan Martz, CIO
Janice Vien, Technician
Jan Koshi, VP Human Res
EMP: 58 EST: 1992
SQ FT: 4,000
SALES (est): 9.7MM Privately Held
WEB: www.caldentalarts.com
SIC: 8072 Crown & bridge production

(P-16824)
DURA-METRICS INC (PA)
2628 El Camino Ave Ste B1, Sacramento (95821-5980)
P.O. Box 873, Santa Rosa (95402-0873)
PHONE....................707 546-5138
Michael Kulwiec, President
EMP: 68 EST: 1968

PRODUCTS & SERVICES SECTION

8082 - Home Health Care Svcs County (P-16848)

SALES (est): 5.3MM **Privately Held**
WEB: www.dura-metrics.com
SIC: **8072** Dental laboratories

8082 Home Health Care Svcs

(P-16825)
1ST CHICE HM HALTHCARE HOSPICE
1291 E Hillsdale Blvd, Foster City (94404-1220)
PHONE..................................650 393-5936
Mohammed Hayat, *President*
EMP: 45 EST: 2016
SALES (est): 2.5MM **Privately Held**
WEB: www.firstchoice-hha.com
SIC: **8082** Home health care services

(P-16826)
24HR HOMECARE LLC
228 Hamilton Ave Ste 300, Palo Alto (94301-2583)
PHONE..................................650 209-3295
EMP: 53
SALES (corp-wide): 70.7MM **Privately Held**
WEB: www.24hrcares.com
SIC: **8082** Home health care services
PA: 24hr Homecare L.L.C.
    300 N Pacific Coast Hwy # 1065
    El Segundo CA 90245
    310 906-3683

(P-16827)
24HR HOMECARE LLC
951 Mariners Island Blvd, San Mateo (94404-1558)
PHONE..................................650 209-3248
EMP: 53
SALES (corp-wide): 70.7MM **Privately Held**
WEB: www.24hrcares.com
SIC: **8082** Home health care services
PA: 24hr Homecare L.L.C.
    300 N Pacific Coast Hwy # 1065
    El Segundo CA 90245
    310 906-3683

(P-16828)
24HR HOMECARE LLC
4675 Stevens Creek Blvd # 121, Santa Clara (95051-6759)
PHONE..................................408 550-8295
EMP: 53
SALES (corp-wide): 70.7MM **Privately Held**
WEB: www.24hrcares.com
SIC: **8082** Home health care services
PA: 24hr Homecare L.L.C.
    300 N Pacific Coast Hwy # 1065
    El Segundo CA 90245
    310 906-3683

(P-16829)
24HR HOMECARE LLC
1399 Ygnacio Valley Rd # 35, Walnut Creek (94598-2884)
PHONE..................................925 322-8627
EMP: 53
SALES (corp-wide): 70.7MM **Privately Held**
WEB: www.24hrcares.com
SIC: **8082** Home health care services
PA: 24hr Homecare L.L.C.
    300 N Pacific Coast Hwy # 1065
    El Segundo CA 90245
    310 906-3683

(P-16830)
ABCSP LLC
Also Called: Always Best Care Senior Svcs
1406 Blue Oaks Blvd Ste 1, Roseville (95747-5199)
PHONE..................................855 470-2273
Michael Newman, *Ch of Bd*
Jake Brown, *President*
Pat O`kane, *CFO*
Sheila Davis, *Senior VP*
David J Caesar, *Vice Pres*
EMP: 121 EST: 1996
SQ FT: 3,000
SALES (est): 17.6MM **Privately Held**
WEB: www.alwaysbestcare.com
SIC: **8082** Home health care services

(P-16831)
ACCENTCARE HM HLTH SCRMNTO INC
2880 Sunrise Blvd Ste 218, Rancho Cordova (95742-6101)
PHONE..................................916 852-5888
Karin Stark, *President*
Rochelle Ward, *Vice Pres*
EMP: 777 EST: 1993
SQ FT: 10,000
SALES (est): 13.6MM
SALES (corp-wide): 1.3B **Privately Held**
SIC: **8082** Visiting nurse service
HQ: Accentcare Home Health, Inc.
    135 Technology Dr Ste 150
    Irvine CA 92618

(P-16832)
ADDUS HEALTHCARE INC
817 Coffee Rd Ste B1, Modesto (95355-4241)
PHONE..................................209 526-8451
Linda Stinson, *Branch Mgr*
EMP: 74 **Publicly Held**
WEB: www.addus.com
SIC: **8082** Home health care services
HQ: Addus Healthcare, Inc.
    2300 Warrenville Rd # 100
    Downers Grove IL 60515
    630 296-3400

(P-16833)
ADDUS HEALTHCARE INC
196 Cohasset Rd Ste 200, Chico (95926-2287)
PHONE..................................530 566-0405
Mary Gorman, *Manager*
EMP: 74 **Publicly Held**
WEB: www.addus.com
SIC: **8082** Home health care services
HQ: Addus Healthcare, Inc.
    2300 Warrenville Rd # 100
    Downers Grove IL 60515
    630 296-3400

(P-16834)
ADDUS HEALTHCARE INC
1730 S Amphlett Blvd, San Mateo (94402-2707)
PHONE..................................650 638-7943
Nancy Kline, *Manager*
EMP: 74 **Publicly Held**
WEB: www.addus.com
SIC: **8082** Home health care services
HQ: Addus Healthcare, Inc.
    2300 Warrenville Rd # 100
    Downers Grove IL 60515
    630 296-3400

(P-16835)
ADDUS HOMECARE CORPORATION (HQ)
Also Called: Addus Healthcare
817 Coffee Rd Ste B, Modesto (95355-4241)
PHONE..................................209 526-8451
Kristin Akins, *Director*
Annette Distasi, *Manager*
EMP: 50 EST: 2013
SALES (est): 2MM
SALES (corp-wide): 2B **Publicly Held**
WEB: www.addus.com
SIC: **8082** Home health care services
PA: Lhc Group, Inc.
    901 Hugh Wallis Rd S
    Lafayette LA 70508
    866 542-4768

(P-16836)
ADVANCED HOME HEALTH INC
4354 Auburn Blvd, Sacramento (95841-4107)
PHONE..................................916 978-0744
Angela Sehr, *President*
Angie Macadangdang, *Principal*
Kathleen Boesch, *Info Tech Dir*
EMP: 75 EST: 1982
SQ FT: 4,000
SALES (est): 15.7MM **Privately Held**
WEB: www.excelin.com
SIC: **8621** Visiting nurse service; nursing association

(P-16837)
ADVOLIFE INC (HQ)
828 S Bascom Ave Ste 280, San Jose (95128-2653)
PHONE..................................408 879-1835
Paul Mastrata, *CEO*
Joel Theisen, *President*
EMP: 62 EST: 1998
SALES (est): 2.8MM
SALES (corp-wide): 75.7MM **Privately Held**
WEB: www.arosacare.com
SIC: **8082** Home health care services
PA: Livhome, Inc.
    5670 Wilshire Blvd # 500
    Los Angeles CA 90036
    800 807-5854

(P-16838)
AEGIS SENIOR COMMUNITIES LLC
Also Called: Aegis Gardens
36281 Fremont Blvd, Fremont (94536-3509)
PHONE..................................510 739-0909
Emily Poon, *Manager*
Lucy Lou, *Marketing Staff*
Kenny Liu, *Food Svc Dir*
EMP: 106
SALES (corp-wide): 137.2MM **Privately Held**
SIC: **8082 8051** Home health care services; skilled nursing care facilities
PA: Senior Aegis Communities Llc
    415 118th Ave Se
    Bellevue WA 98005
    866 688-5829

(P-16839)
AEGIS SENIOR COMMUNITIES LLC
Also Called: Aegis Living
1660 Oak Park Blvd, Pleasant Hill (94523-4422)
PHONE..................................925 588-7030
Fax: 925 939-2785
EMP: 70
SALES (corp-wide): 138.5MM **Privately Held**
SIC: **8082 8051** Home Health Care Services Skilled Nursing Care Facility
PA: Senior Aegis Communities Llc
    415 118th Ave Se
    Bellevue WA 98005
    866 688-5829

(P-16840)
AEGIS SENIOR COMMUNITIES LLC
Also Called: Aegis Assisted Living
125 Heather Ter, Aptos (95003-3825)
PHONE..................................831 684-2700
Janice Ibaio, *Manager*
Derrick Skinner, *Vice Pres*
Delila Garcia, *Office Mgr*
Heather Reynolds, *Office Mgr*
Deidre Schaaf, *Accountant*
EMP: 106
SALES (corp-wide): 137.2MM **Privately Held**
WEB: www.aegisliving.com
SIC: **8082 8051** Home health care services; skilled nursing care facilities
PA: Senior Aegis Communities Llc
    415 118th Ave Se
    Bellevue WA 98005
    866 688-5829

(P-16841)
AEGIS SENIOR COMMUNITIES LLC
Also Called: Aegis of South San Francisco
2280 Gellert Blvd, South San Francisco (94080-5411)
PHONE..................................650 952-6100
Charles Stevenson, *Exec Dir*
EMP: 106
SALES (corp-wide): 137.2MM **Privately Held**
WEB: www.aegisliving.com
SIC: **8082 8051** Home health care services; skilled nursing care facilities
PA: Senior Aegis Communities Llc
    415 118th Ave Se
    Bellevue WA 98005
    866 688-5829

(P-16842)
ALLIANCE HOSPITAL SERVICES
Also Called: Mills-Peninsula Health HM Care
100 S San Mateo Dr, San Mateo (94401-3805)
PHONE..................................650 697-6900
Sheila Schubert, *Branch Mgr*
Helen C Galligan, *Vice Chairman*
Francine Serafin-Dickson, *Exec Dir*
EMP: 330 **Privately Held**
SIC: **8082** Home health care services
PA: Alliance Hospital Services, Inc
    309 Lennon Ln Ste 200
    Walnut Creek CA 94598

(P-16843)
ALTUS HEALTH INC
Also Called: Brightstar Healthcare
151 N Sunrise Ave # 1011, Roseville (95661-2930)
PHONE..................................916 781-6500
Ignacio Cespedes, *CEO*
EMP: 150 EST: 2008
SALES (est): 6.8MM **Privately Held**
WEB: www.brightstarcare.com
SIC: **8082** Home health care services

(P-16844)
ALWAYS HOME NURSING SVC INC
7777 Greenback Ln Ste 208, Citrus Heights (95610-5800)
PHONE..................................916 989-6420
Nancy Giachino, *President*
EMP: 200 EST: 1994
SALES (est): 6.8MM **Privately Held**
WEB: www.alwayshomenursing.com
SIC: **8082** Visiting nurse service

(P-16845)
AMADOR HOME CARE SERVICE
Also Called: Rocky Mountain Home Care
245 New York Ranch Rd A, Jackson (95642-2172)
P.O. Box 640 (95642-0640)
PHONE..................................209 223-3866
Stacey Mathis, *Administration*
Deborah Long, *Office Mgr*
EMP: 36 EST: 1999
SALES (est): 2MM **Privately Held**
SIC: **8082** Home health care services

(P-16846)
AMERICAN CAREQUEST INC (PA)
819 Cowan Rd Ste C, Burlingame (94010-1220)
PHONE..................................415 885-9100
Margarita Riskin, *President*
Marsha Rudakov, *CFO*
Eric Levsky, *Admin Sec*
EMP: 49 EST: 2002
SQ FT: 1,100
SALES (est): 5.4MM **Privately Held**
WEB: www.americancarequest.com
SIC: **8082 5047 8742** Home health care services; medical & hospital equipment; management consulting services

(P-16847)
AMITY HOME HEALTH CARE INC
27001 Calaroga Ave, Hayward (94545-4345)
PHONE..................................510 785-9088
Sanjiv Gupta, *Principal*
Hilda Tacorda, *Marketing Staff*
EMP: 35 EST: 2011
SALES (est): 11.8MM **Privately Held**
WEB: www.amityhhc.com
SIC: **8082** Home health care services

(P-16848)
APEX HEALTHCARE SERVICES LLC
2120 Rosswood Dr, San Jose (95124-5427)
PHONE..................................925 922-3525
Sonal Dubey, *Principal*
EMP: 52 EST: 2015

8082 - Home Health Care Svcs County (P-16849)

PRODUCTS & SERVICES SECTION

SALES (est): 3MM **Privately Held**
WEB: www.apexhealth.org
SIC: **8082** Home health care services

(P-16849)
APEXCARE INC (PA)
1418 Howe Ave Ste B, Sacramento (95825-3230)
PHONE.................................916 924-9111
Kenneth Wang, *President*
Kathryn Fabiani, *Manager*
Kierstin McFee, *Manager*
EMP: 1655 EST: 2005
SALES (est): 25.4MM **Privately Held**
WEB: www.apexcare.com
SIC: **8082** Home health care services

(P-16850)
ASIA NETWORK PACIFIC HOME CARE (PA)
212 9th St Ste 205, Oakland (94607-4478)
PHONE.................................510 268-1118
Nancy Chang, *President*
Ivy Kwong, *CFO*
Tracy WEI,
Keith L Wong, *Director*
▲ EMP: 43 EST: 1991
SQ FT: 609
SALES: 3.7MM **Privately Held**
WEB: www.asiannetwork.com
SIC: **8082** Home health care services

(P-16851)
ASPIRANET
Also Called: Aspira Wellness
440 E Canal Dr, Turlock (95380-3936)
PHONE.................................209 669-2583
Vernon Brown, *Branch Mgr*
EMP: 44
SALES (corp-wide): 80.8MM **Privately Held**
WEB: www.aspiranet.org
SIC: **8082** Home health care services
PA: Aspiranet
400 Oyster Point Blvd
South San Francisco CA 94080
650 866-4080

(P-16852)
BANA SOLOMON LLC
Also Called: Home Helpers of Santa Rosa
703 2nd St Ste 306, Santa Rosa (95404-6536)
PHONE.................................707 867-1770
Bana Solomon,
EMP: 45 EST: 2016
SALES (est): 1.3MM **Privately Held**
WEB: www.homehelpershomecare.com
SIC: **8082** Home health care services

(P-16853)
BARBEE ELC
1406 Blue Oaks Blvd Ste 1, Roseville (95747-5199)
PHONE.................................916 884-1983
Daniel Barbee, *President*
EMP: 99 EST: 2017
SALES (est): 2.9MM **Privately Held**
SIC: **8082** Home health care services

(P-16854)
BAYWOOD COURT (PA)
Also Called: Baywood Court Retirement Ctr
21966 Dolores St Apt 143, Castro Valley (94546-6961)
PHONE.................................510 733-2102
Kelly Wiest, *Exec Dir*
Lisa Ray, *Controller*
Jody Holdsworth, *Marketing Staff*
Keshwar Singh, *Education*
Nathaniel Tuazon, *Food Svc Dir*
EMP: 145 EST: 1984
SALES (est): 19.3MM **Privately Held**
WEB: www.baywoodcourt.com
SIC: **8082** 8051 6513 Home health care services; skilled nursing care facilities; retirement hotel operation

(P-16855)
BBT HEALTH LLC
5105 E Dakota Ave, Fresno (93727-7443)
PHONE.................................559 248-0131
Christopher Dery, *CEO*
EMP: 52 EST: 2016
SALES (est): 2.7MM **Privately Held**
SIC: **8082** Home health care services

(P-16856)
BEAR FLAG MARKETING CORP
Also Called: At Home Caregivers
7599 Redwood Blvd Ste 200, Novato (94945-7706)
PHONE.................................415 899-8466
Peter L Rubens, *CEO*
EMP: 117 EST: 2000
SQ FT: 1,200
SALES (est): 5.2MM **Privately Held**
WEB: www.bearflagmarketing.com
SIC: **8082** Home health care services

(P-16857)
BERK STREET ENTERPRISES INC
Also Called: Bravo Personal Care Services
2377 Gold Meadow Way # 100, Gold River (95670-4444)
PHONE.................................916 370-6179
Janet Phillips, *Administration*
EMP: 53 EST: 2016
SALES (est): 9MM **Privately Held**
SIC: **8082** Home health care services

(P-16858)
BERKELEY COMMUNITY HEALTH PRJ
Also Called: BERKELEY FREE CLINIC
2339 Durant Ave, Berkeley (94704-1606)
PHONE.................................510 548-2570
John Day, *President*
Scott Carroll, *Director*
Sally Jeon, *Director*
Eva Stevenson, *Director*
EMP: 35 EST: 1970
SALES (est): 462.4K **Privately Held**
WEB: www.berkeleyfreeclinic.org
SIC: **8082** 8322 Home health care services; individual & family services

(P-16859)
BESTLIVING CARE LLC
2401 Merced St Ste 300, San Leandro (94577-4200)
PHONE.................................510 862-3508
EMP: 60 EST: 2018
SALES (est): 3.3MM **Privately Held**
WEB: www.bestlivingcare.com
SIC: **8082** Home health care services

(P-16860)
BLIZE HEALTHCARE CAL INC
750 Alfred Nobel Dr # 202, Hercules (94547-1836)
PHONE.................................800 343-2549
Ukeje Elendu, *President*
Blessing Elendu, *COO*
EMP: 100 EST: 2010
SQ FT: 3,700
SALES (est): 8.4MM **Privately Held**
WEB: www.blizecare.com
SIC: **8082** Home health care services

(P-16861)
BRISTOL HOSPICE FOUNDATION CAL
Also Called: Optimal Hospice Care
3375 Scott Blvd Ste 410, Santa Clara (95054-3114)
PHONE.................................408 207-9222
Doug Clary, *CEO*
EMP: 36
SALES (corp-wide): 170.2K **Privately Held**
WEB: www.bristolhospicefoundationca.org
SIC: **8082** Home health care services
PA: Bristol Hospice Foundation Of California
1227 Chester Ave Ste A
Bakersfield CA 93301
661 410-3000

(P-16862)
BUTTE HOME HEALTH INC
Also Called: Butte Home Health & Hospice
10 Constitution Dr, Chico (95973-4903)
P.O. Box 5171 (95927-5171)
PHONE.................................530 895-0462
Brooke Quilici, *President*
Mike Quilici, *Vice Pres*
Robert Love, *Exec Dir*
Traci Butcher, *Admin Asst*
EMP: 80 EST: 1984
SQ FT: 7,100
SALES: 7.2MM **Privately Held**
WEB: www.buttehomehealth.com
SIC: **8082** Visiting nurse service

(P-16863)
BY THE BAY HEALTH (PA)
Also Called: HOSPICE OF MARIN
17 E Sir Francis Drake Bl, Larkspur (94939-1708)
PHONE.................................415 927-2273
Kitty Whitaker, *CEO*
Mary Taverna, *President*
Denis Viscek, *CFO*
Dennis A Gilardi, *Chairman*
Michael R Dailey, *Treasurer*
EMP: 220 EST: 1975
SQ FT: 8,000
SALES: 64.6MM **Privately Held**
WEB: www.bythebayhealth.org
SIC: **8082** Home health care services

(P-16864)
BY THE BAY HEALTH
1540 Market St Ste 350, San Francisco (94102-6069)
PHONE.................................415 626-5900
Sandra Lew, *CEO*
Connie Borden, *Exec Dir*
Donald Bensen, *Technology*
Julie Smith, *Technology*
Lisa Burleson, *Accountant*
EMP: 42
SALES (corp-wide): 64.6MM **Privately Held**
WEB: www.bythebayhealth.org
SIC: **8082** Home health care services
PA: By The Bay Health
17 E Sir Francis Drake Bl
Larkspur CA 94939
415 927-2273

(P-16865)
CALIFRNIA PRSON HLTHCARE RCVRS
501 J St Ste 100, Sacramento (95814-2325)
P.O. Box 588500, Elk Grove (95758-8500)
PHONE.................................916 691-6721
J Clark Kelso, *President*
Glenn Welker, *Associate Dir*
EMP: 63 EST: 2006
SALES: 2.6MM **Privately Held**
WEB: www.cphcs.ca.gov
SIC: **8082** Home health care services

(P-16866)
CARE AT HOME INC
1333 Bush St, San Francisco (94109-5611)
PHONE.................................408 379-3990
Denise Altomere, *CEO*
Michael Ascunsion, *Owner*
Eddie Norris, *Managing Prtnr*
Stephanie Davies, *Human Res Dir*
Michelle Grozier, *Human Res Dir*
EMP: 37 EST: 2000
SALES (est): 4.9MM **Privately Held**
WEB: www.careathomehealth.com
SIC: **8082** Home health care services

(P-16867)
CARE INDEED INC (PA)
890 Santa Cruz Ave Ste A, Menlo Park (94025-4673)
PHONE.................................650 800-7645
Dee Bustos, *Office Mgr*
Vanessa Valerio, *COO*
Divine Grubbs, *Executive*
William Quigley, *Managing Dir*
Chris Lyons, *Persnl Dir*
EMP: 81 EST: 2010
SALES (est): 38.8MM **Privately Held**
WEB: www.careindeed.com
SIC: **8082** Home health care services

(P-16868)
CARE OPTONS MGT PLANS SPPRTIVE (PA)
Also Called: C.O.M.P.A.S.S.
1020 Market St, Redding (96001-0512)
P.O. Box 993753 (96099-3753)
PHONE.................................530 242-8580
Sadie Hess, *Mng Member*
Eric Hess, *CFO*
Lois Planco, *Broker*
Valerie Legg, *Human Res Mgr*
Melanie Anderson, *Train & Dev Mgr*
▲ EMP: 134 EST: 1996
SALES (est): 24.7MM **Privately Held**
WEB: www.optioncarehealth.com
SIC: **8082** Home health care services

(P-16869)
CASTRO VALLEY HEALTH INC
Also Called: Cvh Home Health Services
39 Beta Ct, San Ramon (94583-1201)
PHONE.................................510 690-1930
Mark R Parinas, *CEO*
Isobel Parinas, *CFO*
Marc Pineda, *Chief Mktg Ofcr*
Chan Zeb, *Accountant*
Priyanka Khole, *Consultant*
EMP: 200 EST: 2005
SALES (est): 17.7MM **Privately Held**
SIC: **8082** Visiting nurse service

(P-16870)
CHAROLAIS CARE V INC
Also Called: San Frncsco Bay Cmpssnate Cmnt
1426 Fillmore St Ste 207, San Francisco (94115-4164)
PHONE.................................415 921-5038
Jim Everton, *CEO*
EMP: 41 EST: 2008
SALES (est): 3.2MM
SALES (corp-wide): 33.3MM **Privately Held**
WEB: www.brphealth.com
SIC: **8082** Home health care services
PA: B.R.P. Health Management Systems, Inc.
275 S 5th Ave Lowr Level
Pocatello ID 83201
208 233-4673

(P-16871)
COLLABRIA CARE
414 S Jefferson St, NAPA (94559-4515)
PHONE.................................707 258-9080
Linda Gibson, *President*
Veronna Ladd, *Program Mgr*
Jackie Savoy, *Executive Asst*
Cathy Poliak, *Human Res Dir*
Caroline Wynne, *Human Res Dir*
EMP: 90
SALES: 12.1MM **Privately Held**
WEB: www.collabriacare.org
SIC: **8082** Home health care services

(P-16872)
CORAM HALTHCARE CORP NTHRN CAL
3160 Corporate Pl, Hayward (94545-3916)
PHONE.................................415 292-6811
Patricia Igarashi, *Manager*
Jim Sepeda, *Mktg Dir*
EMP: 667
SALES (corp-wide): 268.7B **Publicly Held**
WEB: www.coramhc.com
SIC: **8082** Home health care services
HQ: Coram Healthcare Corporation Of Northern California
2211 Sanders Rd
Northbrook IL 60062

(P-16873)
COUNTY OF ALAMEDA
Also Called: Health Care Fund
1411 E 31st St, Oakland (94602-1018)
PHONE.................................510 437-4190
Carl N Lester, *Principal*
Anna Domingo, *Executive Asst*
Kelley Bullard, *Med Doctor*
Priya Patel, *Manager*
EMP: 55 EST: 2009
SALES (est): 19.1MM **Privately Held**
WEB: www.acgov.org
SIC: **8082** Home health care services
PA: County Of Alameda
1221 Oak St Ste 555
Oakland CA 94612
510 272-6691

(P-16874)
COUNTY OF SONOMA
Also Called: Dmh - Frnsic Assrtive Cmmnty T
2350 Professional Dr, Santa Rosa (95403-3018)
PHONE.................................707 565-4963
EMP: 47

▲ = Import ▼ = Export
◆ = Import/Export

PRODUCTS & SERVICES SECTION
8082 - Home Health Care Svcs County (P-16899)

SALES (corp-wide): 1B Privately Held
WEB: www.sonomacounty.ca.gov
SIC: 8082 Home health care services
PA: County Of Sonoma
585 Fiscal Dr 100
Santa Rosa CA 95403
707 565-2431

(P-16875)
CRESCENT HEALTHCARE INC
25901 Industrial Blvd, Hayward (94545-2995)
PHONE.................510 264-5454
Eileen Callaghan, Director
EMP: 53
SALES (corp-wide): 132.5B Publicly Held
WEB: www.crescenthealthcare.com
SIC: 8082 Home health care services
HQ: Crescent Healthcare, Inc.
11980 Telg Rd Ste 100
Santa Fe Springs CA 90670

(P-16876)
CRESCENT HEALTHCARE INC
131 Stony Cir Ste 200, Santa Rosa (95401-9593)
PHONE.................707 543-5822
Robert Funari, Manager
EMP: 53
SALES (corp-wide): 132.5B Publicly Held
WEB: www.crescenthealthcare.com
SIC: 8082 Home health care services
HQ: Crescent Healthcare, Inc.
11980 Telg Rd Ste 100
Santa Fe Springs CA 90670

(P-16877)
CVH CARE
39 Beta Ct, San Ramon (94583-1201)
PHONE.................650 393-5657
Kristen Hunter, Officer
Richard Swartzbaugh, Officer
Frances Marzano, Executive Asst
Cynthia Fountaine, Technology
Princess Frijas, Nursing Dir
EMP: 46 EST: 2015
SALES (est): 20.9MM Privately Held
WEB: www.cvhcare.com
SIC: 8082 Home health care services

(P-16878)
DIGNITY HEALTH
Home Health Dept of St Joseph
2333 W March Ln Ste B, Stockton (95207-5272)
PHONE.................209 943-4663
EMP: 50
SALES (corp-wide): 10.4B Privately Held
SIC: 8082 Home Health Care Services
PA: Dignity Health
185 Berry St Ste 300
San Francisco CA 94107
415 438-5500

(P-16879)
DNT IN HOME CARE INC
Also Called: Senior Helpers
3440 Palmer Dr Ste 8h, Cameron Park (95682-8234)
PHONE.................530 556-4030
Desiree Trunzo, Principal
Nicholas Trunzo, Principal
EMP: 50 EST: 2018
SALES (est): 1MM Privately Held
WEB: www.seniorhelpers.com
SIC: 8082 Home health care services

(P-16880)
EL CAMINO HOSPITAL AUXILIARY
2500 Grant Rd, Mountain View (94040-4378)
P.O. Box 7025 (94039-7025)
PHONE.................650 940-7214
Linda Heider, President
EMP: 600 EST: 1958
SQ FT: 2,000
SALES (est): 41K
SALES (corp-wide): 1.1B Privately Held
WEB: www.elcaminohealth.org
SIC: 8082 Home health care services
PA: El Camino Hospital
2500 Grant Rd
Mountain View CA 94040
650 940-7000

(P-16881)
ENLOE MEDICAL CENTER
Also Called: Enloe Homecare Services
1390 E Lassen Ave, Chico (95973-7823)
PHONE.................530 332-6050
Leslie Gunghl, Director
Kathaleen Chaney, Supervisor
EMP: 118
SALES (corp-wide): 675.2MM Privately Held
WEB: www.enloe.org
SIC: 8082 Home health care services
PA: Enloe Medical Center
1531 Esplanade
Chico CA 95926
530 332-7300

(P-16882)
ESKATON
9722 Fair Oaks Blvd Ste A, Fair Oaks (95628-7039)
PHONE.................916 536-3750
Marilyn Swick, Branch Mgr
EMP: 342
SALES (corp-wide): 148.8MM Privately Held
WEB: www.eskaton.org
SIC: 8082 Home health care services
PA: Eskaton
5105 Manzanita Ave Ste D
Carmichael CA 95608
916 334-0296

(P-16883)
FAMILIAR SRRNDINGS HM CARE LLC
1568 Meridian Ave, San Jose (95125-5319)
PHONE.................408 979-9990
Laura Wentling, Principal
Denise Huber, Admin Asst
Steve Lane, Sales Staff
EMP: 36 EST: 2010
SALES (est): 15.1MM Privately Held
WEB: www.fshomecare.com
SIC: 8082 Home health care services

(P-16884)
FORTUNE SENIOR ENTERPRISES
Also Called: Comfort Keepers
6060 Sunrise Vista Dr # 1180, Citrus Heights (95610-7061)
PHONE.................916 560-9100
Vince Maffeo, CEO
EMP: 214 EST: 2002
SQ FT: 2,500
SALES (est): 1.5MM Privately Held
WEB: www.comfortkeepers.com
SIC: 8082 Home health care services

(P-16885)
GENTIVA HEALTH SERVICES INC
1260 N Dutton Ave Ste 150, Santa Rosa (95401-4680)
PHONE.................707 545-7114
Linda Ecker, Manager
EMP: 77
SALES (corp-wide): 1.1B Privately Held
WEB: www.kindredathome.com
SIC: 8082 Home health care services
PA: Gentiva Health Services, Inc.
3350 Rvrwood Pkwy Se # 140
Atlanta GA 30339
770 951-6450

(P-16886)
GLOBAL HEALTHCARE SERVICES LLC
400 12th St Ste 25, Modesto (95354-2415)
PHONE.................209 549-9875
Grace Janolino Flores,
Flor Ungab, Office Mgr
Grace Flores, Administration
Madel Maniwan, Administration
EMP: 54
SALES: 3.3MM Privately Held
WEB: www.globalhealthcareservices.net
SIC: 8082 Home health care services

(P-16887)
HEART HUMANITY HEALTH SVCS INC (PA)
1400 Grant Ave Ste 203, Novato (94945-3156)
PHONE.................415 898-4278
Verlinda Montoya, President
Jaqueline Gallmon, Opers Staff
EMP: 62 EST: 1997
SALES (est): 6.2MM Privately Held
WEB: www.heartofhumanity.com
SIC: 8082 Visiting nurse service

(P-16888)
HELP & CARE LLC (PA)
14417 Big Basin Way Ste B, Saratoga (95070-6181)
PHONE.................408 384-4412
Markus Breitbach, CEO
Christine Cendana, Manager
EMP: 89 EST: 2014
SALES (est): 2.5MM Privately Held
WEB: www.helpandcare.com
SIC: 8082 Home health care services

(P-16889)
HELPING HEARTS FOUNDATION INC
3050 Fite Cir Ste 108, Sacramento (95827-1808)
PHONE.................916 368-7200
James Borgmeyer, President
Mala Prasad, Officer
Stephanie Garcia, Vice Pres
Marsha Vacca, Manager
Hayley Pederson, Supervisor
EMP: 55 EST: 2011
SALES (est): 1.2MM Privately Held
WEB: www.helping-hearts.org
SIC: 8082 Home health care services

(P-16890)
HIRED HANDS INC (PA)
Also Called: Hired Hands Home Care
1744 Novato Blvd Ste 200, Novato (94947-3092)
PHONE.................415 884-4343
Lynn Winter, CEO
Mark Winter, President
Erick Larson, Director
EMP: 96 EST: 1994
SQ FT: 2,000 Privately Held
WEB: www.hiredhandshomecare.com
SIC: 8082 Home health care services

(P-16891)
HOME CARE ASSISTANCE LLC (PA)
1808 Tice Valley Blvd, Walnut Creek (94595-2224)
PHONE.................650 462-9501
Dr Kathy Johnson, CEO
Ty Shay, President
Michael Schantz, CFO
Mitch Bowling, Bd of Directors
Amanda Butas, Officer
EMP: 627 EST: 2010
SALES (est): 84.5MM Privately Held
WEB: www.homecareassistance.com
SIC: 8082 Home health care services

(P-16892)
HOME HEALTH CARE MGT INC
1398 Ridgewood Dr, Chico (95973-7801)
PHONE.................530 343-0727
Barbara Hanna, President
Terry Gordon, Vice Pres
Julie Lehmann, General Mgr
Samantha Luger, Human Res Dir
Mary Bonney, Human Res Mgr
EMP: 100 EST: 1985
SQ FT: 27,007
SALES (est): 3.5MM Privately Held
WEB: www.homeandhealthcaremanagement.com
SIC: 8082 8322 Visiting nurse service; general counseling services

(P-16893)
HORIZON HOME CARE LLC
255 W Fllbrook Ave Ste, Fresno (93711)
PHONE.................559 840-1559
Geoffrey Montoya,
EMP: 44
SALES: 2.6MM Privately Held
WEB: www.horizonhome.care
SIC: 8082 Home health care services

(P-16894)
HOSPICE & HOME HEALTH OF E BAY
Also Called: Pathways
333 Hegenberger Rd # 700, Oakland (94621-1420)
PHONE.................510 632-4390
Barbara Burgess, President
Donna Lopez, Vice Pres
EMP: 50 EST: 1995
SQ FT: 10,000
SALES (est): 371K Privately Held
SIC: 8082 Home health care services

(P-16895)
HOSPICE OF FOOTHILLS (PA)
11270 Rough And Ready Hwy, Grass Valley (95945-8530)
PHONE.................530 272-5739
Vanessa Bengston, Director
Brian Lafreniere, IT/INT Sup
Mary Davis, Marketing Staff
Janet Sisson, Social Worker
Rene Kronland, Director
EMP: 85 EST: 1979
SQ FT: 5,000
SALES: 7.9MM Privately Held
WEB: www.hospiceofthefoothills.org
SIC: 8082 Visiting nurse service

(P-16896)
HOSPICE OF SANTA CRUZ COUNTY (PA)
Also Called: HOSPICE CARING PROJECT
940 Disc Dr, Scotts Valley (95066-4544)
PHONE.................831 430-3000
Michael Milward, CEO
Kuntal Thaker, Bd of Directors
Kieran Shah, Officer
Rachelle France, Executive Asst
Alethea Flickinger, Accountant
EMP: 110 EST: 1978
SQ FT: 2,300
SALES (est): 22.1MM Privately Held
WEB: www.hospicesantacruz.org
SIC: 8082 Home health care services

(P-16897)
HOSPICE OF SANTA CRUZ COUNTY
Also Called: Hospice Caring Project
65 Nielson St Ste 121, Watsonville (95076-2491)
PHONE.................831 430-3000
Michael Milward, CEO
Gloria Reed, Officer
Diane Syrcle, Officer
Jennifer Drummond, Associate Dir
Katie Mekis, Accounting Mgr
EMP: 60 Privately Held
WEB: www.hospicesantacruz.org
SIC: 8082 Home health care services
PA: Hospice Of Santa Cruz County
940 Disc Dr
Scotts Valley CA 95066

(P-16898)
HOSPICE OF VALLEY (PA)
4850 Union Ave, San Jose (95124-5156)
PHONE.................408 947-1233
Sally Adelus, Director
Neal E Slatkin, Chief Mktg Ofcr
Gary Montrezzo, Principal
Gary Bertuccelli, Social Worker
Terry Rabinowitz, Director
EMP: 47 EST: 1979
SALES (est): 2.4MM Privately Held
WEB: www.hospicevalley.org
SIC: 8082 8322 Home health care services; individual & family services

(P-16899)
IN HOME SERVICES LLC ○
Also Called: Comfort Keepers
1673 Lewis St, Kingsburg (93631-1923)
P.O. Box 510 (93631-0510)
PHONE.................559 897-5161
Stephen Simmons, Mng Member
Sarah Quintana, Mng Member
EMP: 40 EST: 2021

8082 - Home Health Care Svcs County (P-16900)

SALES (est): 878.4K **Privately Held**
WEB: www.comfortkeepers.com
SIC: **8082** 7389 Home health care services; business services

(P-16900)
INTERIM ASSSTED CARE E BAY INC
91 Gregory Ln Ste 7, Pleasant Hill (94523-4914)
PHONE.................................925 944-5779
Joseph Bettencourt, *President*
Charles B Baker, *CFO*
EMP: 40 EST: 2004
SALES (est): 2.7MM **Privately Held**
WEB: www.interimhealthcare.com
SIC: **8082** Home health care services

(P-16901)
K&B PICHETTE ENTERPRISES INC
Also Called: Interim Healthcare of Jackson
11992 State Highway 88 # 20, Jackson (95642-9404)
PHONE.................................209 452-5999
Brenden Pichette, *President*
Katherine Pichette, *Vice Pres*
EMP: 70 EST: 2017
SALES (est): 769K **Privately Held**
SIC: **8082** Home health care services

(P-16902)
KAISER FOUNDATION HOSPITALS
Also Called: Kaiser Permanente
50 Great Oaks Blvd, San Jose (95119-1381)
PHONE.................................408 361-2100
EMP: 261
SALES (corp-wide): 30.5B **Privately Held**
WEB: www.kaisercenter.com
SIC: **8082** 8011 Home health care services; health maintenance organization
HQ: Kaiser Foundation Hospitals Inc
1 Kaiser Plz
Oakland CA 94612
510 271-6611

(P-16903)
KIDS OVERCOMING LLC
40029 St Ste 204, Oakland (94609)
PHONE.................................415 748-8052
Anne Swinney, *CFO*
Matt McAlear,
EMP: 75 EST: 2013
SALES (est): 3MM **Privately Held**
WEB: www.kadiant.com
SIC: **8082** Home health care services

(P-16904)
KIND HOMECARE INC
3705 Haven Ave Ste 104, Menlo Park (94025-1011)
P.O. Box 1914, Mountain View (94042-1914)
PHONE.................................888 885-5463
Aida Bruun, *CEO*
EMP: 99 EST: 2016
SALES (est): 1.1MM **Privately Held**
WEB: www.kindhc.com
SIC: **8082** 7389 Home health care services;

(P-16905)
KINDRED HEALTHCARE LLC
Also Called: Professional Healthcare At HM
901 Campisi Way Ste 205, Campbell (95008-2348)
PHONE.................................408 871-9860
EMP: 71
SALES (corp-wide): 6B **Privately Held**
WEB: www.kindredhealthcare.com
SIC: **8082** Home health care services
HQ: Kindred Healthcare, Llc
680 S 4th St
Louisville KY 40202
502 596-7300

(P-16906)
KINDRED HEALTHCARE LLC
4820 Bus Center Dr # 105, Fairfield (94534-1696)
PHONE.................................707 639-4155
EMP: 71

SALES (corp-wide): 6B **Privately Held**
WEB: www.kindredhealthcare.com
SIC: **8082** Home health care services
HQ: Kindred Healthcare, Llc
680 S 4th St
Louisville KY 40202
502 596-7300

(P-16907)
KINSA INC
535 Mission St Fl 18, San Francisco (94105-3256)
PHONE.................................347 405-4315
Anna Aronowitz, *Program Mgr*
Jason Yow, *Engineer*
Mark Jenkins, *Director*
Nita Nehru, *Manager*
Eliana Ward-Lev, *Manager*
EMP: 52 EST: 2012
SALES (est): 16.1MM **Privately Held**
WEB: www.kinsahealth.co
SIC: **8082** Home health care services

(P-16908)
KISSITO HEALTH CASE INC
Also Called: Willow Pass Healthcare Center
3318 Willow Pass Rd, Concord (94519-2316)
PHONE.................................925 689-9222
Fax: 925 689-3412
EMP: 100
SALES (corp-wide): 62.4MM **Privately Held**
SIC: **8082** 8051 Home Health Care Services Skilled Nursing Care Facility
PA: Kissito Health Care, Inc.
5228 Valleypointe Pkwy
Roanoke VA 24019
540 265-0322

(P-16909)
LINCARE INC
7545 N Del Mar Ave # 102, Fresno (93711-6871)
PHONE.................................559 435-6379
Robert Clegg, *Branch Mgr*
EMP: 52 **Privately Held**
WEB: www.lincare.com
SIC: **8082** Home health care services
HQ: Lincare Inc.
19387 Us Highway 19 N
Clearwater FL 33764
727 530-7700

(P-16910)
LITA & AVA INC
Also Called: A Grace Sub Acute Skilled Care
1250 S Winchester Blvd, San Jose (95128-3906)
PHONE.................................408 241-3844
Julita A Javier, *CEO*
EMP: 40 EST: 2008
SALES (est): 9.3MM **Privately Held**
WEB: www.agracesubacute.com
SIC: **8082** Home health care services

(P-16911)
MAXIM HEALTHCARE SERVICES INC
631 River Oaks Pkwy, San Jose (95134-1907)
PHONE.................................408 914-7478
Michelle Mar,
EMP: 184 **Privately Held**
WEB: www.maximhealthcare.com
SIC: **8082** Home health care services
PA: Maxim Healthcare Services, Inc.
7227 Lee Deforest Dr
Columbia MD 21046

(P-16912)
MAXIM HEALTHCARE SERVICES INC
Also Called: Fresno Respite Companion Svcs
6051 N Fresno St Ste 102, Fresno (93710-5280)
PHONE.................................559 227-2250
Melissa Cantu, *Manager*
EMP: 184 **Privately Held**
WEB: www.maximhealthcare.com
SIC: **8082** Home health care services
PA: Maxim Healthcare Services, Inc.
7227 Lee Deforest Dr
Columbia MD 21046

(P-16913)
MEDICAL HOME SPECIALISTS INC
Also Called: Medical HM Care Professionals
2115 Churn Creek Rd, Redding (96002-0732)
PHONE.................................530 226-5577
Kathy A McKillop, *CEO*
Elaine Flores, *COO*
Carol Right, *Executive*
Gayle Ashton, *Admin Sec*
Dylia Voorhies,
EMP: 80 EST: 1987
SQ FT: 1,600
SALES (est): 5.2MM **Privately Held**
WEB: www.medicalhomecarepros.com
SIC: **8082** Home health care services

(P-16914)
NATIONAL HOME HEALTH SVCS INC
2880 Zanker Rd Ste 101, San Jose (95134-2121)
PHONE.................................408 786-1035
Alex Rudakov, *CEO*
Danica Espinoza,
EMP: 45 EST: 2009
SALES (est): 23.1MM **Privately Held**
WEB: www.nationalhha.com
SIC: **8082** Home health care services

(P-16915)
NEW HAVEN HOME HEALTH SVCS INC
333 Gellert Blvd Ste 249a, Daly City (94015-2622)
PHONE.................................650 301-1660
Euncie Bejar-Lee, *President*
EMP: 40 EST: 2001
SALES (est): 3MM **Privately Held**
SIC: **8082** 8049 8322 8059 Visiting nurse service; physical therapist; social worker; personal care home, with health care

(P-16916)
NORTH VLY DVLOPMENTAL SVCS INC
Also Called: Nova
2970 Innsbruck Dr Ste C, Redding (96003-9357)
PHONE.................................530 222-5633
Cindy Green, *President*
Gary Green, *Principal*
Barbara Dewitt, *Administration*
EMP: 53 EST: 2003
SALES (est): 13.2MM **Privately Held**
SIC: **8082** Home health care services

(P-16917)
NOVA CARE HOME HEALTH SERVICES
181 Sand Creek Rd Ste B, Brentwood (94513-2209)
PHONE.................................925 240-2334
Dolly Thomas, *CEO*
EMP: 40 EST: 2011
SALES (est): 2.9MM **Privately Held**
WEB: www.novahealthathome.com
SIC: **8082** Home health care services

(P-16918)
NUEVACARE LLC (PA)
1900 S Norfolk St Ste 350, San Mateo (94403-1171)
PHONE.................................650 539-2000
Kamran Nasser, *CEO*
EMP: 74 EST: 2012
SALES (est): 3.6MM **Privately Held**
WEB: www.homecareassistance.com
SIC: **8082** Home health care services

(P-16919)
OAK HILL CAPITAL PARTNERS LP
2775 Sand Hill Rd Ste 220, Menlo Park (94025-7085)
PHONE.................................650 234-0500
Steven B Gruber, *President*
Karen Capparelli, *Executive Asst*
Ann Daniel, *Executive Asst*
Jim Tarnok, *Controller*
EMP: 913

SALES (corp-wide): 395.4MM **Privately Held**
WEB: www.oakhill.com
SIC: **8082** Home health care services
PA: Oak Hill Capital Partners, L.P.
65 E 55th St Fl 32
New York NY 10022
212 527-8400

(P-16920)
OMADA HEALTH INC
500 Sansome St Ste 200, San Francisco (94111-3215)
PHONE.................................888 987-8337
Sean Duffy, *CEO*
Michelle Crank, *Vice Pres*
Justin Kowaleski, *Vice Pres*
Pamela Nordin, *Vice Pres*
Maria Latushkin, *CTO*
EMP: 260 EST: 2011
SALES (est): 37.2MM **Privately Held**
WEB: www.omadahealth.com
SIC: **8082** Home health care services

(P-16921)
ONMYCARE LLC
Also Called: Onmycare Home Health
39159 Pseo Ptre Prkwy Ste, Fremont (94538)
PHONE.................................510 858-2273
Hansjeet Gill, *Mng Member*
Emma Chaplin,
Kirk Langer, *Supervisor*
EMP: 56 EST: 2015
SALES (est): 1.1MM **Privately Held**
WEB: www.onmycare.com
SIC: **8082** Visiting nurse service

(P-16922)
PACIFIC COAST SERVICES INC
Also Called: Pacific Homecare Services
3202 W March Ln Ste D, Stockton (95219-2351)
PHONE.................................209 956-2532
Leticia Robles, *President*
Damian Gutierrez, *Vice Pres*
Jorge Robles, *Vice Pres*
Eva Avila, *Manager*
Ashley Romero, *Assistant*
EMP: 3043 EST: 2007
SQ FT: 2,000
SALES (est): 59.2MM **Privately Held**
WEB: www.pacifichomecare.com
SIC: **8082** Visiting nurse service

(P-16923)
PATIENT HOME MONITORING INC (DH)
550 Kearny St Ste 300, San Francisco (94108-2597)
PHONE.................................415 693-9690
David Hayes, *CEO*
Michael Dalsin, *Ch of Bd*
Andrew Folmer, *President*
Greg Crawford, *COO*
Jess Cuthbert, *COO*
EMP: 85 EST: 2010
SALES (est): 17.7MM
SALES (corp-wide): 97.7MM **Publicly Held**
WEB: www.quipthomemedical.com
SIC: **8082** Visiting nurse service
HQ: P H M Corp.
1019 Town Dr
Highland Heights KY 41076
859 340-3114

(P-16924)
POLARIS HOME CARE LLC
830 Stewart Dr Ste 211, Sunnyvale (94085-4513)
PHONE.................................408 400-7020
Gregory Kemper, *Principal*
EMP: 55 EST: 2017
SALES (est): 2.5MM **Privately Held**
WEB: www.polarishomecare.com
SIC: **8082** Home health care services

(P-16925)
PROFESSIONAL HEALTHCARE AT HM
185 N Redwood Dr Ste 150, San Rafael (94903-1965)
PHONE.................................415 492-8400
EMP: 37

PRODUCTS & SERVICES SECTION

8082 - Home Health Care Svcs County (P-16949)

SALES (corp-wide): 6MM Privately Held
WEB: www.kindredhealthcare.com
SIC: 8082 Home Health Care Services
PA: Professional Healthcare At Home, Llc
395 Taylor Blvd Ste 118
Pleasant Hill CA 94523
925 849-1160

(P-16926)
PROFESSNAL HALTHCARE AT HM LLC
395 Taylor Blvd Ste 118, Pleasant Hill (94523-2276)
PHONE 510 450-0422
Joseph L Landenwich, *Mng Member*
Kimberly Webb,
EMP: 57 **EST:** 2007
SALES (est): 862.3K Privately Held
SIC: 8082 Home health care services

(P-16927)
PROFESSNAL HALTHCARE AT HM LLC (PA)
395 Taylor Blvd Ste 118, Pleasant Hill (94523-2276)
PHONE 925 849-1160
Karen Caine, *CEO*
James Sullivan, *CFO*
Laura Pescetti,
Terri Lane, *Case Mgr*
EMP: 90 **EST:** 1999
SQ FT: 2,500
SALES (est): 12MM Privately Held
SIC: 8082 Home health care services

(P-16928)
PROVIDENT CARE INC
1025 14th St, Modesto (95354-1001)
P.O. Box 3558 (95352-3558)
PHONE 209 578-1210
Robin Conley, *President*
▲ **EMP:** 167 **EST:** 2001
SQ FT: 4,571
SALES (est): 9.6MM Privately Held
WEB: www.providentcare.com
SIC: 8082 Home health care services

(P-16929)
RES-CARE INC
3315 Green Park Ln, Carmichael (95608-3712)
PHONE 916 487-7497
Odelia Johns, *Principal*
EMP: 43
SALES (corp-wide): 2B Privately Held
WEB: www.rescare.com
SIC: 8082 Home health care services
HQ: Res-Care, Inc.
805 N Whittington Pkwy
Louisville KY 40222
502 394-2100

(P-16930)
RES-CARE INC
Also Called: Nightingale Nursing
101 Callan Ave Ste 208, San Leandro (94577-4558)
PHONE 510 357-4222
John Chin, *Branch Mgr*
EMP: 43
SALES (corp-wide): 2B Privately Held
WEB: www.rescare.com
SIC: 8082 Home health care services
HQ: Res-Care, Inc.
805 N Whittington Pkwy
Louisville KY 40222
502 394-2100

(P-16931)
RES-CARE INC
5346 Madison Ave Ste E, Sacramento (95841-3168)
PHONE 916 307-3737
Cassiana Bush, *Branch Mgr*
EMP: 43
SALES (corp-wide): 2B Privately Held
WEB: www.rescare.com
SIC: 8082 Home health care services
HQ: Res-Care, Inc.
805 N Whittington Pkwy
Louisville KY 40222
502 394-2100

(P-16932)
RES-CARE INC
4090 Truxel Rd Ste 250, Sacramento (95834-3776)
PHONE 530 823-6475
EMP: 43
SALES (corp-wide): 2B Privately Held
WEB: www.rescare.com
SIC: 8082 Home health care services
HQ: Res-Care, Inc.
805 N Whittington Pkwy
Louisville KY 40222
502 394-2100

(P-16933)
RES-CARE INC
1775 Augusta Ln, Yuba City (95993-8241)
PHONE 530 755-3027
EMP: 43
SALES (corp-wide): 2B Privately Held
WEB: www.rescare.com
SIC: 8082 Home health care services
HQ: Res-Care, Inc.
805 N Whittington Pkwy
Louisville KY 40222
502 394-2100

(P-16934)
RES-CARE INC
55 S Highway 26 Ste 3, Valley Springs (95252-8422)
PHONE 209 227-4568
EMP: 43
SALES (corp-wide): 2B Privately Held
WEB: www.rescare.com
SIC: 8082 Home health care services
HQ: Res-Care, Inc.
805 N Whittington Pkwy
Louisville KY 40222
502 394-2100

(P-16935)
RES-CARE INC
18540 Gateway Blvd 280, Concord (94521)
PHONE 925 283-5076
EMP: 43
SALES (corp-wide): 2B Privately Held
WEB: www.rescare.com
SIC: 8082 Home health care services
HQ: Res-Care, Inc.
805 N Whittington Pkwy
Louisville KY 40222
502 394-2100

(P-16936)
RES-CARE INC
Also Called: Community Access Program
11960 Heritage Oak Pl # 10, Auburn (95603-2401)
PHONE 530 888-6580
Shannon Granados, *Manager*
EMP: 43
SALES (corp-wide): 2B Privately Held
WEB: www.rescare.com
SIC: 8082 Home health care services
HQ: Res-Care, Inc.
805 N Whittington Pkwy
Louisville KY 40222
502 394-2100

(P-16937)
RES-CARE INC
3732 Mt Diablo Blvd # 286, Lafayette (94549-3632)
PHONE 925 283-5076
Barbara Schuh, *Branch Mgr*
EMP: 43
SALES (corp-wide): 2B Privately Held
WEB: www.rescare.com
SIC: 8082 Home health care services
HQ: Res-Care, Inc.
805 N Whittington Pkwy
Louisville KY 40222
502 394-2100

(P-16938)
RES-CARE INC
1101 Sylvan Ave, Modesto (95350-1607)
PHONE 209 523-9130
Regan Kisinger, *Branch Mgr*
EMP: 43
SALES (corp-wide): 2B Privately Held
WEB: www.rescare.com
SIC: 8082 Home health care services
HQ: Res-Care, Inc.
805 N Whittington Pkwy
Louisville KY 40222
502 394-2100

(P-16939)
RIDI HOME CARE INC
Also Called: Right At Home Modesto
611 Scenic Dr Ste A, Modesto (95350-6156)
P.O. Box 579760 (95357-9760)
PHONE 209 579-9445
Richard Carson, *CEO*
Rick Carson, *President*
Morgan Carson, *Accounting Mgr*
Diane Carson, *Manager*
EMP: 40 **EST:** 2009
SALES (est): 1.5MM Privately Held
WEB: www.rightathome.net
SIC: 8082 Home health care services

(P-16940)
SCOTT SHAW ENTRPRISES INC
Also Called: Home Instead Senior Care
11160 Sun Center Dr, Rancho Cordova (95670-6121)
PHONE 916 920-2273
Scott Shaw, *President*
Marie Bennett, *Opers Staff*
Symphony Krueger, *Director*
Lori French, *Consultant*
Jill Painter, *Consultant*
EMP: 85 **EST:** 1997
SALES (est): 12.7MM Privately Held
WEB: www.homeinstead.com
SIC: 8082 Home health care services

(P-16941)
SENIOR COMPANIONS AT HOME LLC
650 El Camino Real Ste E, Redwood City (94063-1345)
P.O. Box 5715 (94063-0715)
PHONE 650 364-1265
EMP: 50
SALES (est): 1.2MM Privately Held
WEB: www.bestseniorcompanions.com
SIC: 8082 Home Health Care Services

(P-16942)
SEQUOIA SENIOR SOLUTIONS INC
825 S Main St, Lakeport (95453-5510)
PHONE 707 263-3070
EMP: 98
SALES (corp-wide): 8.9MM Privately Held
WEB: www.sequoiaseniorsolutions.com
SIC: 8082 Home Health Care Services
PA: Sequoia Senior Solutions, Inc.
1372 N Mcdowell Blvd S
Petaluma CA 94954
707 763-6600

(P-16943)
SEQUOIA SENIOR SOLUTIONS INC (PA)
1372 N Mcdowell Blvd S, Petaluma (94954-1179)
PHONE 707 763-6600
Gabriella Ambrosi, *CEO*
Stanton Lawson, *CFO*
Gwen Bassett, *Area Mgr*
Jamie Mendonca, *Office Mgr*
Naudia Ibanez, *Human Res Dir*
EMP: 170 **EST:** 2004
SALES (est): 8MM Privately Held
WEB: www.sequoiaseniorsolutions.com
SIC: 8082 Home health care services

(P-16944)
SIERRA NEVADA MEM HM CARE INC
Also Called: Sierra Nevada Home Care
1020 Mccourtney Rd Ste A, Grass Valley (95949-7453)
P.O. Box 1029 (95945-1029)
PHONE 530 274-6350
Sharon Turner, *Director*
EMP: 248 **EST:** 1986
SQ FT: 6,200
SALES (est): 21.9MM Privately Held
WEB: www.dignityhealth.org
SIC: 8082 7361 Home health care services; nurses' registry
HQ: Dignity Health
185 Berry St Ste 200
San Francisco CA 94107
415 438-5500

(P-16945)
SIRONA MEDICAL INC
703 Market St Ste 1900, San Francisco (94103-2148)
PHONE 415 729-7301
Cameron Andrews, *CEO*
Ankit Goyal, *Principal*
EMP: 40 **EST:** 2018
SALES (est): 2.7MM Privately Held
WEB: www.sironamedical.com
SIC: 8082 7371 Home health care services; computer software development & applications

(P-16946)
SISTERS OF ST JOSEPH ORANGE
111 Sonoma Ave Ste 308, Santa Rosa (95405)
PHONE 747 206-9124
EMP: 3526
SALES (corp-wide): 32.7MM Privately Held
WEB: www.thecsd.org
SIC: 8082 Home health care services
HQ: Sisters Of St. Joseph Of Orange
480 S Batavia St
Orange CA 92868
714 633-8121

(P-16947)
SISTERS OF ST JOSEPH ORANGE
2127 Harrison Ave Ste 3, Eureka (95501-3241)
PHONE 707 443-9332
Kristy Nickols, *Executive*
Suzanne Moore, *Admin Asst*
Erika Salmeron, *Admin Asst*
Phil St John, *IT/INT Sup*
Maureen Welker, *Nurse Practr*
EMP: 3526
SALES (corp-wide): 32.7MM Privately Held
WEB: www.thecsd.org
SIC: 8082 Visiting nurse service
HQ: Sisters Of St. Joseph Of Orange
480 S Batavia St
Orange CA 92868
714 633-8121

(P-16948)
SPOTLIGHT THERAPY INC
600 Pnnsylvania Ave Unit 3, Los Gatos (95030)
PHONE 408 649-7349
Michael Brando, *CEO*
Adam Brando, *Vice Pres*
EMP: 48 **EST:** 2016
SALES (est): 2.8MM Privately Held
WEB: www.spotlighttherapy.com
SIC: 8082 8093 Home health care services; mental health clinic, outpatient

(P-16949)
ST JOSEPH HOME HEALTH NETWORK (DH)
441 College Ave, Santa Rosa (95401-5141)
PHONE 714 712-9500
Linda Glomp, *Director*
Vincent Castaldo, *CFO*
Liz Wessel, *Director*
EMP: 84 **EST:** 1982
SQ FT: 25,000
SALES (est): 27.7MM
SALES (corp-wide): 32.7MM Privately Held
WEB: www.stjosephhomehealth.org
SIC: 8082 Home health care services
HQ: St. Joseph Health System
3345 Michelson Dr Ste 100
Irvine CA 92612
949 381-4000

(PA)=Parent Co (HQ)=Headquarters (DH)=Div Headquarters
✿ = New Business established in last 2 years

8082 - Home Health Care Svcs County (P-16950)
PRODUCTS & SERVICES SECTION

(P-16950)
SUPPORT STAFF SERVICES INC
Also Called: Pacific Home Health
175 N Jackson Ave 103a, San Jose (95116-1909)
PHONE..............................408 258-5803
Lemuel Ignacio Jr, *President*
Gena Ignacio, *Corp Secy*
Anne Davis, *Social Worker*
Cortney Gatch, *Manager*
Reyna Espinoza, *Accounts Exec*
EMP: 36 **EST:** 1989
SQ FT: 4,000
SALES (est): 2.8MM **Privately Held**
SIC: 8082 Home health care services

(P-16951)
SUTTER BAY HOSPITALS
Also Called: Sutter Lakeside Home Med Svcs
843 Parallel Dr, Lakeport (95453-5707)
PHONE..............................707 263-7400
Debra Lozaro, *Branch Mgr*
EMP: 43
SALES (corp-wide): 13.2B **Privately Held**
WEB: www.sutterlakeside.org
SIC: 8082 Home health care services
HQ: Sutter Bay Hospitals
475 Brannan St Ste 130
San Francisco CA 94107
415 600-6000

(P-16952)
SUTTER CARE & HOME
700 S Claremont St # 220, San Mateo (94402-1452)
PHONE..............................650 685-2800
Pat Murphy, *Director*
Maureen Gaynor, *Administration*
Cindy Weber, *Administration*
Annie St John, *Nurse*
Lei-Lani Thomas, *Nurse*
EMP: 67 **EST:** 2000
SALES (est): 3MM **Privately Held**
WEB: www.sutterhealth.org
SIC: 8082 Visiting nurse service

(P-16953)
SUTTER COAST HOSPITAL
983 3rd St Ste D, Crescent City (95531-4331)
PHONE..............................707 464-8741
Chris Vancamp, *Branch Mgr*
EMP: 275
SALES (corp-wide): 13.2B **Privately Held**
WEB: www.suttercoast.org
SIC: 8082 Home health care services
HQ: Sutter Coast Hospital
800 E Washington Blvd
Crescent City CA 95531

(P-16954)
SUTTER VSTING NRSE ASSN HSPICE
1625 Van Ness Ave, San Francisco (94109-3370)
PHONE..............................415 600-6200
Cindy Brown, *Manager*
EMP: 114
SALES (corp-wide): 13.2B **Privately Held**
WEB: www.suttercareathome.org
SIC: 8082 8049 7361 Visiting nurse service; nurses & other medical assistants; nurses' registry
HQ: Sutter Visiting Nurse Association & Hospice
1900 Powell St Ste 300
Emeryville CA 94608
866 652-9178

(P-16955)
SUTTER VSTING NRSE ASSN HSPICE
Respiratory Care & HM Med Eqp
2953 Teagarden St, San Leandro (94577-5718)
PHONE..............................510 895-4403
EMP: 114
SALES (corp-wide): 13.2B **Privately Held**
WEB: www.suttercareathome.org
SIC: 8082 Visiting nurse service
HQ: Sutter Visiting Nurse Association & Hospice
1900 Powell St Ste 300
Emeryville CA 94608
866 652-9178

(P-16956)
SUTTER VSTING NRSE ASSN HSPICE (HQ)
Also Called: SUTTER C H S
1900 Powell St Ste 300, Emeryville (94608-1815)
P.O. Box 22250, Salt Lake City UT (84122-0250)
PHONE..............................866 652-9178
Marcia Reissig, *CEO*
Maryellen Rota, *COO*
Gregg Davis, *CFO*
Annette Pabilona, *Administration*
Douglas Gilbert, *Facilities Mgr*
EMP: 50 **EST:** 1906
SQ FT: 24,000
SALES (est): 453MM
SALES (corp-wide): 13.2B **Privately Held**
WEB: www.suttermedicalcenter.org
SIC: 8082 Visiting nurse service
PA: Sutter Health
2200 River Plaza Dr
Sacramento CA 95833
916 733-8800

(P-16957)
SUTTER VSTING NRSE ASSN HSPICE
1316 Celeste Dr Ste 140, Modesto (95355-2437)
PHONE..............................209 342-4048
Shannon Agulay, *Branch Mgr*
EMP: 114
SALES (corp-wide): 13.2B **Privately Held**
SIC: 8082 Visiting nurse service
HQ: Sutter Visiting Nurse Association & Hospice
1900 Powell St Ste 300
Emeryville CA 94608
866 652-9178

(P-16958)
SUTTER VSTING NRSE ASSN HSPICE
Also Called: Sutter Vsiting Nurse Assn Hosp
5099 Coml Cir Ste 2059452, Concord (94520)
PHONE..............................925 677-4250
Windi Heaton, *Manager*
EMP: 114
SALES (corp-wide): 13.2B **Privately Held**
SIC: 8082 Visiting nurse service
HQ: Sutter Visiting Nurse Association & Hospice
1900 Powell St Ste 300
Emeryville CA 94608
866 652-9178

(P-16959)
TENDER ROSE HOME CARE LLC
2001 Junipero Serra Blvd # 520, Daly City (94014-3888)
PHONE..............................415 340-3990
Jim Kimzey, *COO*
Paula Marks, *Vice Pres*
Stephanie Simon, *Vice Pres*
Sadaf Shafer, *Human Res Dir*
Amanda Denny, *Marketing Staff*
EMP: 37 **EST:** 2009
SALES (est): 3.1MM **Privately Held**
WEB: www.tenderrose.com
SIC: 8082 Home health care services

(P-16960)
TENET HEALTHSYSTEM MEDICAL INC
Also Called: Redding Medical Home Care
475 Knollcrest Dr, Redding (96002-0101)
P.O. Box 494130 (96049-4130)
PHONE..............................530 222-1992
Judith Moroney, *Manager*
EMP: 63
SALES (corp-wide): 17.6B **Publicly Held**
WEB: www.tenethealth.com
SIC: 8082 Home health care services
HQ: Tenet Healthsystem Medical, Inc.
14201 Dallas Pkwy
Dallas TX 75254
469 893-2000

(P-16961)
THERAEX REHAB SERVICES INC (PA)
Also Called: Theraex Staffing Services
211 Apollo Apt 6, Hercules (94547-1905)
PHONE..............................510 239-9614
Rey David Rivera, *President*
Cecilia Bayan, *Recruiter*
Vanessa Cueva, *Manager*
Crystal White, *Manager*
EMP: 165 **EST:** 2009
SQ FT: 1,000
SALES (est): 12MM **Privately Held**
WEB: www.theraexstaffing.com
SIC: 8082 8049 8062 8051 Home health care services; physical therapist; general medical & surgical hospitals; skilled nursing care facilities

(P-16962)
UNIVERSITY HEALTHCARE ALLIANCE
Also Called: STANFORD MEDICAL CENTER
7999 Gateway Blvd Ste 200, Newark (94560-1197)
PHONE..............................510 974-8281
Bruce Harrison, *CEO*
Brian Bohman, *President*
David Overton, *Executive*
Dena Hall-Nelson, *Opers Staff*
Judith Stanton, *Director*
EMP: 846 **EST:** 2010
SALES: 355.1MM
SALES (corp-wide): 12.4B **Privately Held**
WEB: www.universityhealthcarealliance.org
SIC: 8082 Home health care services
HQ: Stanford Health Care
300 Pasteur Dr
Stanford CA 94305
650 723-4000

(P-16963)
US CARENET SERVICES LLC
901 Campisi Way Ste 205, Campbell (95008-2348)
PHONE..............................408 871-9860
Kelly Tripps, *Principal*
EMP: 106
SALES (corp-wide): 98.3MM **Privately Held**
WEB: www.navcare.com
SIC: 8082 Home health care services
HQ: Us Carenet Services, Llc
699 Broad St Ste 1001
Augusta GA 30901

(P-16964)
US CARENET SERVICES LLC
815 Pollard Rd, Los Gatos (95032-1438)
PHONE..............................408 378-6131
Carol Parker, *Branch Mgr*
EMP: 106
SALES (corp-wide): 98.3MM **Privately Held**
WEB: www.navcare.com
SIC: 8082 Home health care services
HQ: Us Carenet Services, Llc
699 Broad St Ste 1001
Augusta GA 30901

(P-16965)
VISITING NRSE ASSN OF SNTA CRU (DH)
Also Called: Palo Alto Med Fndtion For Hlth
2880 Soquel Ave Ste 10, Santa Cruz (95062-1423)
PHONE..............................831 477-2600
Bella Hughes, *Exec Dir*
EMP: 100 **EST:** 1946
SQ FT: 19,000
SALES (est): 13.3MM
SALES (corp-wide): 13.2B **Privately Held**
WEB: www.santacruzvna.org
SIC: 8082 Visiting nurse service
HQ: Sutter Bay Medical Foundation
795 El Camino Real
Palo Alto CA 94301
650 321-4121

(P-16966)
VONHOF ENTERPRISES INC
Also Called: Visiting Angels
3050 Victor Ave Ste B, Redding (96002-1456)
PHONE..............................530 223-2400
Robert Vonhof, *CEO*
Jacob Buffington, *Exec Dir*
Kimberly McCain, *Admin Sec*
Karen Vonhof, *Admin Sec*
EMP: 42 **EST:** 2008
SALES (est): 5.7MM **Privately Held**
WEB: www.visitingangels.com
SIC: 8082 Home health care services

(P-16967)
WCHS INC
20400 Stevens Creek Blvd, Cupertino (95014-2217)
PHONE..............................877 706-0510
Jerome Rhodes, *Principal*
EMP: 40 **EST:** 2008
SALES (est): 1.9MM **Publicly Held**
WEB: www.acadiahealthcare.com
SIC: 8082 Home health care services
PA: Acadia Healthcare Company, Inc.
6100 Tower Cir Ste 1000
Franklin TN 37067

(P-16968)
WELBE HEALTH LLC (PA)
934 Santa Cruz Ave Ste B, Menlo Park (94025-4634)
PHONE..............................650 862-6371
Si France, *CEO*
Ethan Epstein, *CFO*
Richard Gurley, *Exec VP*
Jillian Simon, *Exec Dir*
Nigel Guyot, *Senior Mgr*
EMP: 83 **EST:** 2017
SALES (est): 16.2MM **Privately Held**
WEB: www.welbehealth.com
SIC: 8082 Home health care services

(P-16969)
WELL BEING SENIOR SOLUTIONS
Also Called: Holistic Homecare
55 Shaw Ave Ste 220, Clovis (93612-3819)
PHONE..............................559 321-8295
Rachelle Dyson, *President*
Marc Dyson, *CFO*
Janette Becerra, *Opers Mgr*
EMP: 80 **EST:** 2011
SALES (est): 2.5MM **Privately Held**
SIC: 8082 Home health care services

(P-16970)
WILLOW PASS HLTH CARE CTR INC
3318 Willow Pass Rd, Concord (94519-2316)
PHONE..............................925 689-9222
Pratap Poddatoori, *CEO*
Susan Sotto, *Nurse*
Mark Pagaduan, *Director*
EMP: 100 **EST:** 2003
SALES (est): 13.7MM **Privately Held**
WEB: www.willowpasshc.net
SIC: 8082 8051 Home health care services; skilled nursing care facilities
PA: Hycare, Inc.
524 Callan Ave
San Leandro CA 94577

(P-16971)
YOLO HOSPICE INC (PA)
1909 Galileo Ct Ste A, Davis (95618-4890)
P.O. Box 1014 (95617-1014)
PHONE..............................530 758-5566
Doug Jena, *Exec Dir*
Lori Delappe-Grondin, *Marketing Staff*
Jan McMahon, *Nurse*
Cher Pearson,
Liz Romero, *Manager*
EMP: 59 **EST:** 1979
SALES (est): 9.5MM **Privately Held**
WEB: www.yolohospice.org
SIC: 8082 8322 Home health care services; individual & family services

PRODUCTS & SERVICES SECTION

8093 - Specialty Outpatient Facilities, NEC County (P-16992)

8092 Kidney Dialysis Centers

(P-16972)
DAVITA INC
Also Called: Davita Health Care
14020 San Pablo Ave Ste B, San Pablo (94806-3619)
PHONE.....................510 234-0835
Vijendra Vareed, *Technician*
Caroline Chinn, *Director*
EMP: 35 **Publicly Held**
WEB: www.davita.com
SIC: 8092 Kidney dialysis centers
PA: Davita Inc.
  2000 16th St
  Denver CO 80202

(P-16973)
FRESENIUS MED CARE CLOVIS LLC
Also Called: Fresenius Kidney Care Clovis
2585 Alluvial Ave, Clovis (93611-9505)
PHONE.....................559 324-8023
Josh Howard,
EMP: 637 **EST:** 2013
SALES (est): 1MM
SALES (corp-wide): 21.1B **Privately Held**
WEB: www.fmcna.com
SIC: 8092 Kidney dialysis centers
HQ: Fresenius Medical Care North America Holdings Limited Partnership
  920 Winter St
  Waltham MA 02451

(P-16974)
FRESENIUS MED CARE SLANO CNTY
Also Called: Fresenius Med Care Solano Cnty
125 N Lincoln St Ste B, Dixon (95620-3259)
PHONE.....................707 678-6433
Susan Lajoie, *Admin Asst*
Ron Kuerbitz, *CEO*
Jeff Norton, *Manager*
EMP: 94
SALES (corp-wide): 3.3MM **Privately Held**
SIC: 8092 Kidney dialysis centers
PA: Fresenius Medical Care Solano County Llc
  920 Winter St Ste A
  Waltham MA 02451
  800 662-1237

(P-16975)
FRESENIUS MED CARE WDLND CAL L
Also Called: Fresenius Medical Care Wdlnd Cal L
35 W Main St, Woodland (95695-3015)
PHONE.....................530 668-4503
Susan Lajoie, *Admin Asst*
Ron Kuerbitz, *President*
EMP: 94
SALES (corp-wide): 5.9MM **Privately Held**
WEB: www.freseniuskidneycare.com
SIC: 8092 Kidney dialysis centers
PA: Fresenius Medical Care Woodland (California), Llc
  920 Winter St Ste A
  Waltham MA 02451
  800 622-1237

(P-16976)
RAI CARE CTRS NTHRN CAL I LLC
Rai N California Stockton
2350 N California St, Stockton (95204-5506)
PHONE.....................209 943-0854
Nichole Berg, *Branch Mgr*
EMP: 113
SALES (corp-wide): 21.1B **Privately Held**
WEB: www.fmcna.com
SIC: 8092 Kidney dialysis centers
HQ: Rai Care Centers Of Northern California I, Llc
  920 Winter St
  Waltham MA 02451
  781 699-9000

(P-16977)
RAI CARE CTRS NTHRN CAL I LLC
Also Called: Rai-Chadbourne-Fairfield
490 Chadbourne Rd Ste D, Fairfield (94534-9613)
PHONE.....................707 434-9088
Josh Howard, *Branch Mgr*
Rebecca Scorse, *Senior Mgr*
EMP: 113
SALES (corp-wide): 21.1B **Privately Held**
WEB: www.fmcna.com
SIC: 8092 Kidney dialysis centers
HQ: Rai Care Centers Of Northern California I, Llc
  920 Winter St
  Waltham MA 02451
  781 699-9000

(P-16978)
RAI CARE CTRS NTHRN CAL II LLC
Rai Ocean Ave San Francisco
1738 Ocean Ave, San Francisco (94112-1737)
PHONE.....................415 406-1090
Monique Hartell, *Branch Mgr*
EMP: 40
SALES (corp-wide): 21.1B **Privately Held**
WEB: www.freseniuskidneycare.com
SIC: 8092 Kidney dialysis centers
HQ: Rai Care Centers Of Northern California Ii, Llc
  920 Winter St
  Waltham MA 02451
  781 699-9000

(P-16979)
SATELLITE HEALTHCARE INC (PA)
Also Called: SATELLITE DIALYSIS CENTERS
300 Santana Row Ste 300 # 300, San Jose (95128-2424)
PHONE.....................650 404-3600
Jeffrey Goffman, *CEO*
Norman S Coplon, *Ch of Bd*
Rick J Barnett, *President*
Bernadette Vincent, *President*
Dave Carter, *COO*
EMP: 75 **EST:** 1973
SQ FT: 12,000
SALES: 268.6MM **Privately Held**
WEB: www.satellitehealthcare.com
SIC: 8092 Kidney dialysis centers

(P-16980)
SATELLITE HEALTHCARE INC
927 Hamilton Ave, Menlo Park (94025-1431)
PHONE.....................650 566-0180
EMP: 35
SALES (corp-wide): 188.9MM **Privately Held**
SIC: 8092 Kidney Dialysis Centers
PA: Satellite Healthcare, Inc.
  300 Santana Row Ste 300
  San Jose CA 95128
  650 404-3600

(P-16981)
SATELLITE HEALTHCARE INC
Also Called: Satellite Dialysis
205 Kenwood Way, South San Francisco (94080-5737)
PHONE.....................650 377-0888
EMP: 40
SALES (corp-wide): 188.9MM **Privately Held**
SIC: 8092 Kidney Dialysis Centers
PA: Satellite Healthcare, Inc.
  300 Santana Row Ste 300
  San Jose CA 95128
  650 404-3600

8093 Specialty Outpatient Facilities, NEC

(P-16982)
21ST CENTURY HEALTH CLUB (PA)
680a E Cotati Ave, Cotati (94931-4092)
PHONE.....................707 795-0400
John Ford, *President*
Dr Robert Gardner, *Treasurer*
Frank Ford, *Vice Pres*
Elizabeth Gardner, *Admin Sec*
David Chasin, *Manager*
▲ **EMP:** 70 **EST:** 1988
SQ FT: 20,000
SALES (est): 5.2MM **Privately Held**
WEB: www.21stcenturyhealthclub.com
SIC: 8093 7991 Rehabilitation center, outpatient treatment; health club

(P-16983)
AL TABASE SUMMIT HOSPITAL
350 Hawthorne Ave, Oakland (94609-3108)
PHONE.....................510 869-6600
Annette Burder, *Director*
EMP: 69 **EST:** 2002
SALES (est): 5.3MM **Privately Held**
WEB: www.altabatessummit.org
SIC: 8093 8062 Specialty outpatient clinics; general medical & surgical hospitals

(P-16984)
ALAMEDA CNTY MENTAL HLTH ASSN
Also Called: MENTAL HEALTH ASSOCIATION OF A
954 60th St Ste 10, Oakland (94608-2369)
PHONE.....................510 835-5010
Stephen Bischoff, *Director*
Eva McRae, *Officer*
Stephen Bischoff, *Exec Dir*
Stephen J Bischoff, *Exec Dir*
Janellen O'Hara, *Exec Dir*
EMP: 51 **EST:** 1998
SALES (est): 3.5MM **Privately Held**
WEB: www.mhaac.org
SIC: 8093 Mental health clinic, outpatient

(P-16985)
ALLIANT INTERNATIONAL UNIV INC
5130 E Clinton Way, Fresno (93727-2014)
PHONE.....................559 456-2777
Jennifer Wilson, *Branch Mgr*
EMP: 54
SALES (corp-wide): 147.7MM **Privately Held**
WEB: www.alliant.edu
SIC: 8093 8221 Mental health clinic, outpatient; university
HQ: Alliant International University, Inc.
  10455 Pomerado Rd
  San Diego CA 92131
  415 955-2000

(P-16986)
AMBERWOOD GARDENS
1601 Petersen Ave, San Jose (95129-4844)
PHONE.....................408 253-7502
Ed Basa, *Principal*
Beth Baisas, *Executive*
Maricris Gatip, *Office Mgr*
Kenneth Vicente, *Info Tech Mgr*
Gennisa Colar, *Mktg Dir*
EMP: 54 **EST:** 2006
SALES (est): 12.2MM **Privately Held**
WEB: www.amberwoodgardens.com
SIC: 8093 8361 8082 Rehabilitation center, outpatient treatment; home for the aged; home health care services

(P-16987)
AMERICAN CLG TRDTNL CHNSE MDCN (PA)
Also Called: Actcm
455 Arkansas St, San Francisco (94107-2813)
PHONE.....................415 282-0316
Lixin Huang, *President*
Gail Bergunde, *Vice Pres*
Elizabeth Goldblatt, *Vice Pres*
Felipe Restrepo, *Program Mgr*
Heather Scheuring, *Technician*
EMP: 90 **EST:** 1980
SQ FT: 7,000
SALES: 3.7MM **Privately Held**
WEB: www.actcm.edu
SIC: 8221 8093 University; mental health clinic, outpatient

(P-16988)
ASIAN COMMUNITY MENTAL HLTH BD
Also Called: Asian Cmnty Mental Hlth Svcs
310 8th St Ste 303, Oakland (94607-4253)
P.O. Box 10750 (94610-0750)
PHONE.....................510 869-6003
Lawrence Fong, *President*
John Fong, *Treasurer*
Betty Hong, *Vice Pres*
Sharon Sue, *Admin Sec*
Albert Gaw, *Psychiatry*
EMP: 95 **EST:** 1974
SALES (est): 963K **Privately Held**
WEB: www.acmhs.org
SIC: 8093 Mental health clinic, outpatient

(P-16989)
AURORA BHVRAL HLTHCARE - STA R
1287 Fulton Rd, Santa Rosa (95401-4923)
PHONE.....................707 800-7700
Susan Rose, *CEO*
Al Jennings, *Human Res Dir*
David Walker, *Opers Staff*
Robert Isaacs, *Family Practiti*
Amit Bhakhri, *Psychiatry*
EMP: 75 **EST:** 2000
SQ FT: 50,000
SALES (est): 20.2MM
SALES (corp-wide): 4.5B **Publicly Held**
WEB: www.aurorasantarosa.com
SIC: 8093 Mental health clinic, outpatient
HQ: Aurora Behavioral Healthcare Llc
  4238 Green River Rd
  Corona CA 92878
  951 549-8032

(P-16990)
AXIS COMMUNITY HEALTH INC
4361 Railroad Ave, Pleasanton (94566-6611)
PHONE.....................925 462-1755
Sue Compton, *CEO*
Christina McFadden, *COO*
Joe Flarity, *CFO*
Lucien Freeman, *CFO*
Kanwar Singh, *CFO*
EMP: 99 **EST:** 1972
SALES: 20.9MM **Privately Held**
WEB: www.axishealth.org
SIC: 8093 Mental health clinic, outpatient

(P-16991)
BAART BEHAVIORAL HLTH SVCS INC (HQ)
Also Called: Bbhs
1145 Market St Fl 10, San Francisco (94103-1566)
PHONE.....................415 552-7914
Jason Kletter, *President*
Evan Kletter, *CFO*
Stephen Rosen, *Vice Pres*
Cyndi Bauer, *Principal*
Collin Schour, *Engineer*
EMP: 50 **EST:** 1981
SALES (est): 13.3MM
SALES (corp-wide): 84.5MM **Privately Held**
WEB: www.baymark.com
SIC: 8093 Substance abuse clinics (outpatient)
PA: Baymark Health Services, Inc.
  1720 Lakepointe Dr # 117
  Lewisville TX 75057
  214 379-3300

(P-16992)
BAKER PLACES INC
101 Gough St, San Francisco (94102-5903)
PHONE.....................415 503-3137
EMP: 84
SALES (corp-wide): 19.9MM **Privately Held**
WEB: www.prcsf.org
SIC: 8093 Substance abuse clinics (outpatient)
PA: Baker Places, Inc.
  170 9th St
  San Francisco CA 94103
  415 864-4655

8093 - Specialty Outpatient Facilities, NEC County (P-16993)

(P-16993)
BASQUEZ TIBURCIO HEALTH CENTER
33255 9th St, Union City (94587-2137)
PHONE...............................510 471-5907
Jose J Garcia, *CEO*
EMP: 36 EST: 1971
SALES (est): 756.7K **Privately Held**
SIC: 8093 Specialty outpatient clinics

(P-16994)
BAYVIEW HNTERS PT FNDTION FOR
Also Called: Bay View Hnters Pt Sbstnce Abu
1625 Carroll Ave, San Francisco (94124-3219)
PHONE...............................415 822-8200
Alfreda Nesbitt, *Director*
Kimberly Yano, *Manager*
EMP: 37
SALES (corp-wide): 5.6MM **Privately Held**
WEB: www.bayviewci.org
SIC: 8093 Drug clinic, outpatient
PA: Bayview Hunters Point Foundation For Community Improvement
150 Executive Park Blvd
San Francisco CA 94134
415 468-5100

(P-16995)
BEHAVIOR FRONTIERS LLC
4030 Moorpark Ave Ste 105, San Jose (95117-1848)
PHONE...............................310 856-0800
Helen Mader, *Principal*
Claire Johnston, *Technician*
Jamie Bowling, *Instructor*
EMP: 41 EST: 2012
SALES (est): 15MM **Privately Held**
WEB: www.behaviorfrontiers.com
SIC: 8093 Rehabilitation center, outpatient treatment

(P-16996)
BUCKELEW PROGRAMS (PA)
201 Alameda Del Prado # 103, Novato (94949-6698)
PHONE...............................415 457-6964
Chris Kughn, *CEO*
Keith Edwards, *CFO*
Mary McDevitt, *Bd of Directors*
Cyrus Mehra, *Info Tech Mgr*
Sarah Chapman, *Program Dir*
EMP: 134 EST: 1970
SALES (est): 13.9MM **Privately Held**
WEB: www.buckelew.org
SIC: 8093 Substance abuse clinics (outpatient)

(P-16997)
CAMINAR
Also Called: Jobs Plus
376 Rio Lindo Ave, Chico (95926-1914)
PHONE...............................530 343-4421
Tracy Watkins, *Branch Mgr*
Charles Huggins, *CEO*
EMP: 41
SALES (corp-wide): 18.6MM **Privately Held**
WEB: www.caminar.org
SIC: 8093 Mental health clinic, outpatient
PA: Caminar
2600 S El Cmino Real Ste
San Mateo CA 94403
650 372-4080

(P-16998)
CAMINAR
902 Tuolumne St, Vallejo (94590-4641)
PHONE...............................707 648-8121
James Wagner, *Branch Mgr*
Charles Huggins, *CEO*
Richard Van Doren Jr, *Director*
EMP: 41
SALES (corp-wide): 18.6MM **Privately Held**
WEB: www.caminar.org
SIC: 8093 Mental health clinic, outpatient
PA: Caminar
2600 S El Cmino Real Ste
San Mateo CA 94403
650 372-4080

(P-16999)
CHOICE IN AGING (PA)
Also Called: MT DIABLO CENTER ADULT DAY HEA
490 Golf Club Rd, Pleasant Hill (94523-1553)
PHONE...............................925 682-6330
Debbie Toth, *CEO*
Lisa Duncan, *Admin Asst*
Tonya Huddleston, *CIO*
Jeaneen McPherson, *Finance*
Joanne McClellan, *Accountant*
EMP: 79 EST: 1949
SQ FT: 24,335
SALES (est): 5.8MM **Privately Held**
WEB: www.choiceinaging.org
SIC: 8093 8331 Rehabilitation center, outpatient treatment; vocational rehabilitation agency

(P-17000)
CIELO HOUSE INC (HQ)
750 El Camino Real, Burlingame (94010-5005)
PHONE...............................650 292-0253
Matthew Keck, *President*
Sofia Keck, *Chief Mktg Ofcr*
Matthew J Keck, *Director*
EMP: 50 EST: 2009
SALES (est): 20.1MM
SALES (corp-wide): 27MM **Privately Held**
WEB: www.cielohouse.com
SIC: 8093 Mental health clinic, outpatient
PA: Refresh Mental Health, Inc.
320 1st St N Ste 712
Jacksonville Beach FL 32250
904 746-3396

(P-17001)
COMMUNITY ACTION MARIN
Also Called: Community Action Marine
1108 Tamalpais Ave, San Rafael (94901-3247)
PHONE...............................415 459-6330
Michael Payne, *President*
EMP: 135
SALES (corp-wide): 19.9MM **Privately Held**
WEB: www.camarin.org
SIC: 8093 Mental health clinic, outpatient
PA: Community Action Marin
555 Northgate Dr Ste 201
San Rafael CA 94903
415 485-1489

(P-17002)
COMMUNITY HLTH FOR ASIAN AMRCA
1141 Harbor Bay Pkwy # 103, Alameda (94502-2219)
PHONE...............................925 778-1667
Ji Won Chung, *Exec Dir*
John Chung, *Exec Dir*
Todd Borgie,
Kenneth Kim, *Director*
Sean Kirkpatrick, *Director*
EMP: 40 EST: 1996
SALES (est): 2.8MM **Privately Held**
WEB: www.chaaweb.org
SIC: 8093 Mental health clinic, outpatient

(P-17003)
COMMUNITY MEDICAL CENTERS INC (PA)
7210 Murray Dr, Stockton (95210-3339)
PHONE...............................209 373-2800
Kathleen Marshall, *CEO*
Sue Hopwood, *Partner*
Art Feagles, *CFO*
Maria Flores, *Executive*
Michael Kirkpatrick, *General Mgr*
EMP: 90 EST: 1978
SQ FT: 14,000
SALES: 87.1MM **Privately Held**
WEB: www.communitymedicalcenters.org
SIC: 8093 8011 Specialty outpatient clinics; offices & clinics of medical doctors

(P-17004)
CONSOLDTED TRIBAL HLTH PRJ INC
6991 N State St, Redwood Valley (95470-9629)
P.O. Box 387, Calpella (95418-0387)
PHONE...............................707 485-5115
Michael Knight, *Chairman*
George Provencher, *Treasurer*
Debra Ramirez, *Principal*
Donna Schuler, *Admin Sec*
Amy Redmer, *Family Practiti*
EMP: 65 EST: 1984
SALES (est): 10.7MM **Privately Held**
WEB: www.cthp.org
SIC: 8093 Mental health clinic, outpatient

(P-17005)
CORE MEDICAL CLINIC INC
3990 Industrial Blvd, West Sacramento (95691-3430)
PHONE...............................916 796-0020
Randall Stenson, *Branch Mgr*
EMP: 40
SALES (corp-wide): 9.6MM **Privately Held**
WEB: www.coremedicalclinic.com
SIC: 8093 Substance abuse clinics (outpatient)
PA: Core Medical Clinic, Inc
2100 Capitol Ave
Sacramento CA 95816
916 442-4985

(P-17006)
COUNTY OF MENDOCINO
Also Called: County of Medocina Dept of Mnt
860a N Bush St, Ukiah (95482-3919)
PHONE...............................707 463-4396
EMP: 200 **Privately Held**
SIC: 8093 9111 Specialty Outpatient Clinic Executive Office
PA: County Of Mendocino
501 Low Gap Rd Rm 1010
Ukiah CA 95482
707 463-4441

(P-17007)
COUNTY OF SAN JOAQUIN
Also Called: Rehabltion Ctr At San Jquin G
500 W Hospital Rd, French Camp (95231-9693)
PHONE...............................209 468-6280
Rachel Torres, *Branch Mgr*
Carla Bomben, *Risk Mgmt Dir*
EMP: 43
SALES (corp-wide): 1.2B **Privately Held**
WEB: www.sjgov.org
SIC: 8093 9431 Rehabilitation center, outpatient treatment; communicable disease program administration, government
PA: County Of San Joaquin
44 N San Joaquin St # 640
Stockton CA 95202
209 468-3203

(P-17008)
COUNTY OF SAN JOAQUIN
Also Called: Mental Health Services
1212 N California St, Stockton (95202-1552)
PHONE...............................209 468-8750
Bruce Hopperstead, *Principal*
EMP: 43
SALES (corp-wide): 1.2B **Privately Held**
WEB: www.sjgov.org
SIC: 8093 9111 8361 Mental health clinic, outpatient; county supervisors' & executives' offices; residential care
PA: County Of San Joaquin
44 N San Joaquin St # 640
Stockton CA 95202
209 468-3203

(P-17009)
COUNTY OF SAN JOAQUIN
Also Called: Bureau of Narcotic Enforcement
P.O. Box 7838 (95267-0838)
PHONE...............................209 948-3612
Jess Dubois, *Branch Mgr*
EMP: 53
SALES (corp-wide): 1.2B **Privately Held**
WEB: www.sjgov.org
SIC: 9221 8093 Bureau of criminal investigation, government; ; drug clinic, outpatient
PA: County Of San Joaquin
44 N San Joaquin St # 640
Stockton CA 95202
209 468-3203

(P-17010)
COUNTY OF STANISLAUS
Also Called: Stanisluas County Mental Hlth
800 Scenic Dr Bldg B, Modesto (95350-6131)
PHONE...............................209 525-7423
Dennise Han, *Director*
EMP: 66
SALES (corp-wide): 1.2B **Privately Held**
WEB: www.stancounty.com
SIC: 8093 Specialty outpatient clinics
PA: County Of Stanislaus
1010 10th St Ste 5100
Modesto CA 95354
209 525-6398

(P-17011)
COUNTY OF STANISLAUS
Also Called: Department of Mental Health
2101 Geer Rd Ste 120, Turlock (95382-2456)
PHONE...............................209 664-8044
Adrian Carroll, *Director*
EMP: 66
SALES (corp-wide): 1.2B **Privately Held**
WEB: www.stancounty.com
SIC: 8093 9431 Mental health clinic, outpatient; administration of public health programs;
PA: County Of Stanislaus
1010 10th St Ste 5100
Modesto CA 95354
209 525-6398

(P-17012)
CRC HEALTH CORPORATE (DH)
Also Called: Willamette Valley Trtmnt Ctr
20400 Stevns Crk Blvd, Cupertino (95014-2217)
PHONE...............................408 367-0044
R Andrew Eckert, *CEO*
Kevin Hogge, *CFO*
Gary Fisher, *Chief Mktg Ofcr*
Pamela B Burke, *Vice Pres*
James Hudak, *Vice Pres*
EMP: 60 EST: 2002
SALES (est): 100MM **Publicly Held**
WEB: www.legalrecruiterdirectory.org
SIC: 8093 Substance abuse clinics (outpatient)
HQ: Crc Health Llc
20400 Stevns Crk Blvd # 600
Cupertino CA 95014
877 272-8668

(P-17013)
CRC HEALTH GROUP INC
256 E Hamilton Ave Ste I, Campbell (95008-0237)
PHONE...............................408 866-8167
EMP: 75 **Publicly Held**
SIC: 8093 Substance abuse clinics (outpatient)
HQ: Crc Health Group, Inc.
6100 Tower Cir Ste 1000
Franklin TN 37067

(P-17014)
CREEKSIDE RHBLTTION BHVRAL HLT
850 Sonoma Ave, Santa Rosa (95404-4715)
PHONE...............................707 524-7030
Paul Duranczsk, *Administration*
Prema Thekkek, *President*
Laura O 'leary, *Vice Pres*
EMP: 66 EST: 2000
SALES (est): 1.1MM **Privately Held**
WEB: www.creeksiderehab.net
SIC: 8093 Mental health clinic, outpatient

(P-17015)
DRUG ABUSE ALTERNATIVES CENTER
Also Called: Redwood Empire Addctons Prgram
2403 Prof Dr Ste 103, Santa Rosa (95403)
PHONE...............................707 571-2233
Sushana Taylor, *President*
EMP: 101

PRODUCTS & SERVICES SECTION
8093 - Specialty Outpatient Facilities, NEC County (P-17038)

SALES (corp-wide): 5MM **Privately Held**
WEB: www.daacinfo.org
SIC: 8093 Drug clinic, outpatient
PA: Drug Abuse Alternatives Center
2403 Prof Dr Ste 102
Santa Rosa CA 95403
707 544-3295

(P-17016)
DUFFYS MYRTLEDALE
3076 Myrtledale Rd, Calistoga (94515-1052)
P.O. Box 737 (94515-0737)
PHONE.....................707 942-6888
Gene Duffy Jr, *President*
Mick Duffy, *Exec VP*
Mike Duffy, *Vice Pres*
Steven Duffy, *Vice Pres*
EMP: 52 EST: 1967
SALES (est): 6.2MM **Privately Held**
WEB: www.duffysrehab.com
SIC: 8093 Substance abuse clinics (outpatient)

(P-17017)
DUNAMIS CENTER INC
Also Called: Dunamis Ctr Cunseling Wellness
1465 Victor Ave Ste B, Redding (96003-4856)
PHONE.....................530 338-0087
Jill Clark, *CEO*
Jill Clarke, *CEO*
EMP: 90 EST: 2017
SQ FT: 4,000
SALES (est): 8MM **Privately Held**
WEB: www.dunamiscenter.com
SIC: 8093 8322 8041 8049 Mental health clinic, outpatient; rehabilitation services; family (marriage) counseling; general counseling services; offices & clinics of chiropractors; clinical psychologist

(P-17018)
ED SUPPORTS LLC
Also Called: Juvo Atism Bhavioral Hlth Svcs
1045 Willow St, San Jose (95125-2346)
PHONE.....................201 478-8711
Adam Schreiber, *Branch Mgr*
EMP: 60
SALES (corp-wide): 33.1MM **Privately Held**
SIC: 8093 Mental health clinic, outpatient
HQ: Ed Supports Llc
1200 Concord Ave Ste 100
Concord CA 94520
510 832-4383

(P-17019)
ED SUPPORTS LLC
Also Called: Juvo Atism Bhavioral Hlth Svcs
6001 Telegraph Ave, Oakland (94609-1310)
PHONE.....................201 478-8711
Adam Schreiber, *Branch Mgr*
EMP: 80
SALES (corp-wide): 33.1MM **Privately Held**
SIC: 8093 Mental health clinic, outpatient
HQ: Ed Supports Llc
1200 Concord Ave Ste 100
Concord CA 94520
510 832-4383

(P-17020)
GRANITE WELLNESS CENTERS
Also Called: Corr
180 Sierra College Dr, Grass Valley (95945-5768)
PHONE.....................530 878-5166
Warren Daniels, *Exec Dir*
Christine Findley, *Program Dir*
EMP: 101 EST: 1974
SALES (est): 30.2MM **Privately Held**
WEB: www.granitewellness.org
SIC: 8093 Substance abuse clinics (outpatient)

(P-17021)
GREATER SACRAMENTO SUR
Also Called: Greater Sacramento Surgery Ctr
2288 Auburn Blvd Ste 201, Sacramento (95821-1620)
PHONE.....................916 929-7229
Marvin Kamras, *Partner*
EMP: 60 EST: 1983
SQ FT: 15,000
SALES (est): 8.8MM **Privately Held**
WEB: www.gssc-asc.com
SIC: 8093 8011 Specialty outpatient clinics; ambulatory surgical center

(P-17022)
HERNDON RECOVERY CENTER LLC (PA)
7361 N Sierra Vista Ave, Fresno (93720-0157)
PHONE.....................559 472-3669
Satnam Atwal, *Principal*
EMP: 46 EST: 2008
SALES (est): 187K **Privately Held**
WEB: www.herndonrecovery.org
SIC: 8093 Substance abuse clinics (outpatient)

(P-17023)
HOSPICE OF HUMBOLDT INC (PA)
3327 Timber Fall Ct, Eureka (95503-4894)
PHONE.....................707 445-8443
Marylee Bytheriver, *Director*
Gay Miller, *President*
Neal Ewald, *Treasurer*
Peter Lavallee, *Bd of Directors*
Mary Gearheart, *Vice Pres*
EMP: 41 EST: 1978
SQ FT: 1,000
SALES (est): 9.3MM **Privately Held**
WEB: www.hospiceofhumboldt.org
SIC: 8093 8082 Specialty outpatient clinics; home health care services

(P-17024)
HUMAN RESOURCE CONSULTANTS
3727 Marconi Ave, Sacramento (95821-5303)
PHONE.....................916 485-6500
Lynn Place, *Exec Dir*
Jacki Richardson, *Opers Staff*
Timothy L Nobbe,
Thomas Hushen, *Assistant*
EMP: 44 EST: 1979
SALES (est): 5.2MM **Privately Held**
WEB: www.hopecoop.org
SIC: 8093 Mental health clinic, outpatient

(P-17025)
HUMANSTIC ALTRNTVES TO ADDCTIO
Also Called: Haart
10850 Macarthur Blvd # 20, Oakland (94605-5266)
PHONE.....................510 875-2300
Michelle Burch, *Exec Dir*
Anne Branch, *Exec Dir*
Michael Martinez, *Director*
EMP: 47 EST: 1979
SQ FT: 6,000
SALES (est): 5.5MM **Privately Held**
WEB: www.haartoakland.org
SIC: 8093 Drug clinic, outpatient

(P-17026)
INNOVATIVE PATHWAYS INC
14895 E 14th St, San Leandro (94578-2922)
PHONE.....................510 346-7100
Bahrig Mikaelian, *Branch Mgr*
Laura Smith, *Program Mgr*
Wendy Rodas, *Manager*
Erika Suarez, *Manager*
EMP: 62
SALES (corp-wide): 1.2MM **Privately Held**
WEB: www.innovativepathwaysinc.com
SIC: 8093 Mental health clinic, outpatient
PA: Innovative Pathways Inc.
1534 Plaza Ln Ste 358
Burlingame CA 94010
650 259-0330

(P-17027)
KAISER FOUNDATION HOSPITALS
Chemical Dpndncy Rcvery Prgram
2829 Watt Ave Ste 150, Sacramento (95821-6245)
PHONE.....................916 482-1132
Terry Obrien, *Branch Mgr*
EMP: 209
SALES (corp-wide): 30.5B **Privately Held**
WEB: www.kaisercenter.com
SIC: 8093 Detoxification center, outpatient; substance abuse clinics (outpatient)
HQ: Kaiser Foundation Hospitals Inc
1 Kaiser Plz
Oakland CA 94612
510 271-6611

(P-17028)
KAISER FOUNDATION HOSPITALS
Also Called: Kaiser Permanente Chemical Dep
3551 Whipple Rd Bldg C, Union City (94587-1507)
PHONE.....................510 675-2377
Harriet Smith, *Radiology*
Dien Nguyen,
EMP: 209
SALES (corp-wide): 30.5B **Privately Held**
WEB: www.kaisercenter.com
SIC: 8093 Substance abuse clinics (outpatient)
HQ: Kaiser Foundation Hospitals Inc
1 Kaiser Plz
Oakland CA 94612
510 271-6611

(P-17029)
KAISER FOUNDATION HOSPITALS
Also Called: Kaiser Permanente Med Ctr S
8247 E Stockton Blvd, Sacramento (95828-8200)
PHONE.....................916 525-6790
EMP: 209
SALES (corp-wide): 30.5B **Privately Held**
WEB: www.kaisercenter.com
SIC: 8093 Substance abuse clinics (outpatient)
HQ: Kaiser Foundation Hospitals Inc
1 Kaiser Plz
Oakland CA 94612
510 271-6611

(P-17030)
KAISER FOUNDATION HOSPITALS
Also Called: Kaiser Permanente
3400 Delta Fair Blvd, Antioch (94509-4004)
PHONE.....................925 779-5000
Dan Sonnier, *Manager*
Marlane Fretz, *Internal Med*
Samina Rashid, *Internal Med*
Alice Truscott, *Pediatrics*
Alison Jacobi, *Med Doctor*
EMP: 209
SQ FT: 47,307
SALES (corp-wide): 30.5B **Privately Held**
WEB: www.kaisercenter.com
SIC: 8093 8011 8062 Specialty outpatient clinics; general & family practice, physician/surgeon; general medical & surgical hospitals
HQ: Kaiser Foundation Hospitals Inc
1 Kaiser Plz
Oakland CA 94612
510 271-6611

(P-17031)
KIMA W MEDICAL CENTER
535 Airport Rd, Hoopa (95546-9615)
P.O. Box 1288 (95546-1288)
PHONE.....................530 625-4114
Emmit Chase, *CEO*
Dennis Jones, *COO*
EMP: 80 EST: 1998
SQ FT: 11,000
SALES (est): 13.2MM **Privately Held**
WEB: www.kimaw.org
SIC: 8093 8399 Specialty outpatient clinics; health systems agency

(P-17032)
KINGSVIEW CORP
Also Called: Tuolomne Cnty Bhvral Hlth Rcve
2 S Green St, Sonora (95370-4618)
PHONE.....................209 533-6245
Jack Tanebaum, *Exec Dir*
EMP: 40 EST: 2002
SALES (est): 1.1MM **Privately Held**
WEB: www.kingsview.com
SIC: 8093 Mental health clinic, outpatient

(P-17033)
LATINO COMM ON ALCHOL DRG ABUS (PA)
1001 Sneath Ln Ste 307, San Bruno (94066-2349)
PHONE.....................650 244-1444
Debra Camarillo, *Principal*
Rosario Zatarain, *Opers Staff*
Maria Newson, *Director*
EMP: 42 EST: 2000
SALES: 2.6MM **Privately Held**
WEB: www.thelatinocommission.org
SIC: 8093 8361 Mental health clinic, outpatient; home for the mentally retarded

(P-17034)
LEARNING SERVICES CORPORATION
Also Called: Learning Services Northern Cal
10855 De Bruin Way, Gilroy (95020-9315)
PHONE.....................408 848-4379
Kayree Fhreeve, *Director*
Vince Shoeck, *COO*
Chris Pigula, *Engineer*
Kayree Shreeve, *Program Dir*
EMP: 43
SALES (corp-wide): 36.5MM **Privately Held**
WEB: www.collagerehab.com
SIC: 8093 Rehabilitation center, outpatient treatment
HQ: Learning Services Corporation
131 Langley Dr Ste B
Lawrenceville GA 30046
470 235-4700

(P-17035)
LINCOLN (PA)
1266 14th St, Oakland (94607-2247)
PHONE.....................510 273-4700
Nancy L Oakley, *COO*
Enrico Hernandez, *CFO*
Allison Becwar, *Principal*
Hazel Zetino, *Program Mgr*
Nathan Yuen, *IT/INT Sup*
EMP: 190 EST: 1883
SQ FT: 40,000
SALES: 23.1MM **Privately Held**
WEB: www.lincolnfamilies.org
SIC: 8093 8361 8049 Mental health clinic, outpatient; orphanage; psychiatric social worker

(P-17036)
LYRIC RECOVERY SERVICES INC
1210 S Bascom Ave Ste 205, San Jose (95128-3535)
PHONE.....................408 219-4681
EMP: 35 EST: 2015
SALES (est): 1.3MM **Privately Held**
WEB: www.lyricrecoveryservices.com
SIC: 8093 Substance abuse clinics (outpatient)

(P-17037)
MARIN TREATMENT CENTER
1466 Lincoln Ave, San Rafael (94901-2021)
PHONE.....................415 457-3755
Brian Slattery, *CEO*
Jonathan Fong, *Officer*
▲ EMP: 54 EST: 1976
SQ FT: 4,265
SALES (est): 3.6MM **Privately Held**
WEB: www.marintreatmentcenter.org
SIC: 8093 Drug clinic, outpatient

(P-17038)
MEDMARK TRTMNT CTRS - SCRMNTO
7240 E Southgate Dr Ste G, Sacramento (95823-2627)
PHONE.....................916 391-4293
David K White, *CEO*
Frank Baumann, *COO*
Daniel Gutschenritter, *CFO*
Grace Diaz, *Program Dir*
EMP: 35 EST: 2006
SALES (est): 1.6MM
SALES (corp-wide): 50.2MM **Privately Held**
WEB: www.medmark.com
SIC: 8093 Substance abuse clinics (outpatient)

8093 - Specialty Outpatient Facilities, NEC County (P-17039)

PA: Medmark Services, Inc.
1720 Lakepointe Dr # 117
Lewisville TX 75057
214 379-3300

(P-17039)
MENDOCINO COAST CLINICS INC
205 South St, Fort Bragg (95437-5540)
PHONE.................707 964-1251
Paula Cohen, *Exec Dir*
Jeff Warner, *Chairman*
Richard Moon, *Treasurer*
Claudia Boudreau, *Admin Sec*
Meryl Schlingheyde, *Opers Dir*
▲ **EMP:** 93 **EST:** 1992
SQ FT: 5,000
SALES: 13.2MM **Privately Held**
WEB: www.mendocinocoastclinics.org
SIC: 8093 Family planning & birth control clinics

(P-17040)
MENTAL HLTH ASSN SAN FRANCISCO
870 Market St Ste 928, San Francisco (94102-2923)
PHONE.................415 421-2926
Quintin Mecke, *President*
Mason Turner, *President*
Jennifer Simon, *Vice Pres*
Belinda Lyons, *Exec Dir*
Eduardo Vega, *Exec Dir*
EMP: 37 **EST:** 1946
SQ FT: 2,600
SALES (est): 3.2MM **Privately Held**
WEB: www.mentalhealthsf.org
SIC: 8093 Mental health clinic, outpatient

(P-17041)
MERU HEALTH HOLDING INC
19 S B St, San Mateo (94401-3994)
PHONE.................760 841-8040
Kristian Ranta, *CEO*
Riku Lindholm, *COO*
Brett Shrewsbury, *Officer*
EMP: 35 **EST:** 2015
SALES (est): 10.9MM **Privately Held**
WEB: www.meruhealth.com
SIC: 8093 Mental health clinic, outpatient

(P-17042)
MHM SERVICES INC
155 Glen Cove Marina Rd E, Vallejo (94591-7284)
PHONE.................707 652-2688
EMP: 148 **Publicly Held**
WEB: www.mhm-services.com
SIC: 8093 Mental health clinic, outpatient
HQ: Mhm Services, Inc.
1593 Spring Hill Rd # 600
Vienna VA 22182
703 749-4600

(P-17043)
MHM SERVICES INC
6041 N 1st St, Fresno (93710-5444)
PHONE.................559 412-8121
EMP: 148 **Publicly Held**
WEB: www.mhm-services.com
SIC: 8093 Mental health clinic, outpatient
HQ: Mhm Services, Inc.
1593 Spring Hill Rd # 600
Vienna VA 22182
703 749-4600

(P-17044)
MHM SERVICES INC
2380 Professional Dr, Santa Rosa (95403-3016)
PHONE.................707 623-9080
EMP: 148 **Publicly Held**
WEB: www.mhm-services.com
SIC: 8093 Mental health clinic, outpatient
HQ: Mhm Services, Inc.
1593 Spring Hill Rd # 600
Vienna VA 22182
703 749-4600

(P-17045)
MHM SERVICES INC
350 Brannan St, San Francisco (94102-1879)
PHONE.................415 416-6992
EMP: 148 **Publicly Held**
WEB: www.mhm-services.com
SIC: 8093 Mental health clinic, outpatient
HQ: Mhm Services, Inc.
1593 Spring Hill Rd # 600
Vienna VA 22182
703 749-4600

(P-17046)
MIDVALLEY RECOVERY FACILITIES
Also Called: PATHWAYS
430 Teegarden Ave, Yuba City (95991-4541)
PHONE.................530 742-6670
Edward Anderson, *President*
Peggy Smith, *Opers Staff*
EMP: 37 **EST:** 1974
SQ FT: 3,800
SALES (est): 1.5MM **Privately Held**
WEB: www.yspathways.net
SIC: 8093 Substance abuse clinics (outpatient)

(P-17047)
MODERN LIFE INC (PA)
Also Called: Modern Health
450 Sansome St Fl 12, San Francisco (94111-3306)
PHONE.................617 980-9633
Alyson Watson, *CEO*
EMP: 80 **EST:** 2017
SALES (est): 10.6MM **Privately Held**
SIC: 8093 Mental health clinic, outpatient

(P-17048)
MOMENTUM FOR HEALTH (PA)
1922 The Alameda, San Jose (95126-1457)
PHONE.................408 254-6828
David Mineta, *CEO*
Nancy Flannigan, *Ch of Bd*
Mary Williams, *President*
Melinda Golden, *CFO*
Jack Smelser, *CFO*
EMP: 35 **EST:** 1997
SALES (est): 52.7MM **Privately Held**
WEB: www.momentumforhealth.org
SIC: 8093 Mental health clinic, outpatient

(P-17049)
NEW BRIDGE FOUNDATION INC
2323 Hearst Ave, Berkeley (94709-1319)
PHONE.................510 548-7270
Kosta Markakis, *CEO*
Jenny Knowles, *CFO*
Aisha Ware, *Opers Staff*
Veronica Chinsoon, *Director*
EMP: 65 **EST:** 1971
SALES (est): 5.6MM **Privately Held**
WEB: www.newbridgefoundation.org
SIC: 8093 Substance abuse clinics (outpatient)

(P-17050)
OCTAVE HEALTH GROUP INC
575 Market St Ste 600, San Francisco (94105-5811)
PHONE.................415 360-3833
Sandeep Acharya, *CEO*
EMP: 60 **EST:** 2017
SALES (est): 1.4MM **Privately Held**
SIC: 8093 Mental health clinic, outpatient

(P-17051)
OPEN DOOR COMMUNITY HLTH CTRS (PA)
670 9th St Ste 203cfo, Arcata (95521-6248)
PHONE.................707 826-8642
Sydney Fisher Larsen, *CEO*
Jarrett Nicholson, *Office Mgr*
Teresa Sawatzky, *Office Mgr*
Christina Boone, *Admin Asst*
Breanna Mueller, *Administration*
EMP: 70 **EST:** 1971
SQ FT: 18,000
SALES (est): 196.1K **Privately Held**
WEB: www.opendoorhealth.com
SIC: 8093 Smoking clinic

(P-17052)
OPYA INC
1720 S Amphlett Blvd # 110, San Mateo (94402-2702)
PHONE.................650 931-6300
Jonathan Wright, *CEO*
Keiko Ikeda, *COO*
Suchi Deshpande, *Vice Pres*
Daniel Kuschel, *Opers Mgr*
Elizabeth Porter, *Speech Therapis*
EMP: 55 **EST:** 2017
SALES (est): 5.8MM **Privately Held**
WEB: www.opyacare.com
SIC: 8093 8049 7371 Specialty outpatient clinics; speech therapist; computer software development & applications

(P-17053)
PARAGON HEALTH & REHAB CT
1090 E Dinuba Ave, Reedley (93654-3577)
PHONE.................559 638-3578
EMP: 50 **EST:** 2005
SALES (est): 2.3MM **Privately Held**
SIC: 8093 Specialty Outpatient Clinic

(P-17054)
PLANNED PRNTHOD SHST-DBLO INC (PA)
Also Called: PLANNED PARENTHOOD NORTHERN CA
2185 Pacheco St, Concord (94520-2309)
PHONE.................925 676-0300
Heather Estes, *CEO*
Laura Skaggs, *Partner*
Cecile Richards, *President*
Tia Baratelle, *Officer*
Fred Engineer, *Officer*
EMP: 50 **EST:** 1962
SQ FT: 5,500
SALES: 60MM **Privately Held**
WEB: www.plannedparenthood.org
SIC: 8093 Family planning clinic

(P-17055)
PLANNED PRNTHOD SHST-DBLO INC
Also Called: Planned Parenthood Nthrn Cal
1522 Bush St, San Francisco (94109-5420)
PHONE.................415 821-1282
Gilda Gonzales, *CEO*
EMP: 35
SALES (corp-wide): 60MM **Privately Held**
WEB: www.plannedparenthood.org
SIC: 8093 Family planning clinic
PA: Planned Parenthood Shasta-Diablo, Inc.
2185 Pacheco St
Concord CA 94520
925 676-0300

(P-17056)
PLANNED PRNTHOOD MAR MONTE INC (PA)
1691 The Alameda, San Jose (95126-2203)
PHONE.................408 287-7532
Linda T Williams, *President*
John Giambruno, *CFO*
Jeanne Ewy, *Vice Pres*
Alison Gaulden, *Vice Pres*
Rosemary Kamei, *Vice Pres*
EMP: 58
SQ FT: 41,000
SALES: 120.5MM **Privately Held**
WEB: www.plannedparenthood.org
SIC: 8093 Family planning clinic

(P-17057)
PLANNED PRNTHOOD OF SANTA CRUZ (PA)
1119 Pacific Ave Ste 210, Santa Cruz (95060-4464)
PHONE.................831 426-5550
Linda Williams, *CEO*
EMP: 40 **EST:** 1971
SALES (est): 2.8MM **Privately Held**
WEB: www.santacruz.com
SIC: 8093 8322 Family planning clinic; birth control clinic; individual & family services

(P-17058)
PLASTIC SURGERY CENTER LLC
1515 El Camino Real Ste A, Palo Alto (94306-1000)
PHONE.................650 322-6291
Michael Papalian, *Director*
George Commons MD, *Partner*
Ernest Kaplan MD, *Partner*
Donald Laub MD, *Partner*
Angeline Lim, *Plastic Surgeon*
EMP: 49 **EST:** 1990
SALES (est): 14.4MM **Privately Held**
WEB: www.duetplasticsurgery.com
SIC: 8093 8011 Specialty outpatient clinics; offices & clinics of medical doctors

(P-17059)
PYRAMID ALTERNATIVES INC (PA)
480 Manor Pl, Pacifica (94044)
PHONE.................650 355-8787
Linda Malone, *Exec Dir*
Alison Rodrigues, *Assistant*
EMP: 45 **EST:** 1974
SQ FT: 5,000
SALES (est): 1.4MM **Privately Held**
WEB: www.pyramid.i-tul.com
SIC: 8093 8322 Mental health clinic, outpatient; individual & family services

(P-17060)
RICHMOND AREA MLT-SERVICES INC
1282 Market St, San Francisco (94102-4801)
PHONE.................415 579-3021
Kenneth Choi, *CFO*
EMP: 61
SALES (corp-wide): 19.7MM **Privately Held**
WEB: www.ramsinc.org
SIC: 8093 Mental health clinic, outpatient
PA: Richmond Area Multi-Services, Inc.
4355 Geary Blvd
San Francisco CA 94118
415 800-0699

(P-17061)
RICHMOND AREA MLT-SERVICES INC (PA)
4355 Geary Blvd, San Francisco (94118-3003)
PHONE.................415 800-0699
Kavoos Bassiri, *CEO*
Lenore Williams, *CFO*
Eddie Chiu, *Officer*
Natalie Quan, *Admin Asst*
David Alexander, *Opers Staff*
EMP: 76 **EST:** 1974
SQ FT: 8,400
SALES: 19.7MM **Privately Held**
WEB: www.ramsinc.org
SIC: 8093 Mental health clinic, outpatient

(P-17062)
RIVER OAK CENTER FOR CHILDREN (PA)
5445 Laurel Hills Dr, Sacramento (95841-3105)
PHONE.................916 609-5100
Laurie Clothier, *CEO*
Roland Udy, *Officer*
Kylie Swaleh, *Program Mgr*
Steve Benitez, *Technician*
Megan Dye, *Psychiatry*
EMP: 140 **EST:** 1966
SQ FT: 26,000
SALES: 14.2MM **Privately Held**
WEB: www.riveroak.org
SIC: 8093 8699 Mental health clinic, outpatient; charitable organization

(P-17063)
SACRAMNTO MDTOWN ENDOSCOPY CTR
3941 J St Ste 460, Sacramento (95819-3633)
PHONE.................916 733-6940
Tom Poirier, *Medical Dir*
Mercy General Hospital,
EMP: 54 **EST:** 1987
SQ FT: 3,200
SALES (est): 4.8MM **Privately Held**
WEB: www.sacramentomidtownendoscopy.com
SIC: 8093 8062 Specialty outpatient clinics; general medical & surgical hospitals

(P-17064)
SAN JOAQUIN VALLEY REHABILI (HQ)
7173 N Sharon Ave, Fresno (93720-3329)
PHONE.................559 436-3600

8093 - Specialty Outpatient Facilities, NEC County (P-17085)

Edward C Palacios, *Partner*
Ralph Renteria, *Records Dir*
Diane Kisling, *Accountant*
Paul Herrera, *Human Res Dir*
Mark Rakis, *Opers Mgr*
EMP: 275 **EST:** 2000
SALES (est): 35MM
SALES (corp-wide): 759.7MM **Privately Held**
WEB: www.vibrahealthcare.com
SIC: 8093 Rehabilitation center, outpatient treatment
PA: Vibra Healthcare, Llc
4600 Lena Dr Ste 100
Mechanicsburg PA 17055
717 591-5700

(P-17065)
SANTA CLARA COUNTY OF
Also Called: Public Health Dept
976 Lenzen Ave Ste 1800, San Jose (95126-2737)
PHONE.................408 792-5020
Guadalupe Olivas, *Director*
Grace Meregillano, *Manager*
EMP: 54 **Privately Held**
WEB: www.sccgov.org
SIC: 8093 9431 Rehabilitation center, outpatient treatment; administration of public health programs;
PA: County Of Santa Clara
70 W Hedding St 2wing
San Jose CA 95110
408 299-5200

(P-17066)
SANTA CLARA COUNTY OF
Also Called: Mental Hlth Dpt-Administration
828 S Bascom Ave Ste 100, San Jose (95128-2652)
PHONE.................408 885-5770
Nancy Pena, *Branch Mgr*
EMP: 54 **Privately Held**
WEB: www.sccgov.org
SIC: 8093 9431 Mental health clinic, outpatient; mental health agency administration, government;
PA: County Of Santa Clara
70 W Hedding St 2wing
San Jose CA 95110
408 299-5200

(P-17067)
SANTA CLARA COUNTY OF
Also Called: Alcohol & Drug Svcs Dept
231 Grant Ave, Palo Alto (94306-1907)
PHONE.................408 918-7755
Jolene Wing, *Branch Mgr*
EMP: 54 **Privately Held**
WEB: www.sccgov.org
SIC: 8093 9431 Alcohol clinic, outpatient; mental health agency administration, government;
PA: County Of Santa Clara
70 W Hedding St 2wing
San Jose CA 95110
408 299-5200

(P-17068)
SANTA CLARA COUNTY OF
Also Called: Mental Health Services
614 Tully Rd Ste A, San Jose (95111-1048)
PHONE.................408 494-1561
Rhonda Brown, *Branch Mgr*
EMP: 54 **Privately Held**
WEB: www.sccgov.org
SIC: 8093 9431 Mental health clinic, outpatient; mental health agency administration, government;
PA: County Of Santa Clara
70 W Hedding St 2wing
San Jose CA 95110
408 299-5200

(P-17069)
SANTA CLARA COUNTY OF
Also Called: Santa Clara Medical Center
2400 Moorpark Ave Ste 118, San Jose (95128-2623)
PHONE.................408 885-5920
Jennifer Howard, *Branch Mgr*
EMP: 54 **Privately Held**
WEB: www.sccgov.org
SIC: 8093 9431 Rehabilitation center, outpatient treatment; administration of public health programs;

PA: County Of Santa Clara
70 W Hedding St 2wing
San Jose CA 95110
408 299-5200

(P-17070)
SANTA ROSA MEMORIAL HOSPITAL
Also Called: Centerism Memorial Hospital
1450 Medical Center Dr # 1, Rohnert Park (94928-2924)
PHONE.................707 584-0672
Mauree Rogers, *Director*
EMP: 40
SQ FT: 14,560
SALES (corp-wide): 32.7MM **Privately Held**
WEB: www.stjoesonoma.org
SIC: 8093 8011 Specialty outpatient clinics; offices & clinics of medical doctors;
HQ: St. Joseph Health Northern California, Llc
1165 Montgomery Dr
Santa Rosa CA 95405
707 546-3210

(P-17071)
SEEDS OF AWARENESS INC
2501 Harrison St, Oakland (94612-3811)
PHONE.................510 788-0876
EMP: 44
SALES (est): 598K **Privately Held**
WEB: www.seeds-of-awareness.org
SIC: 8093 Specialty outpatient clinics

(P-17072)
SERENITY KNOLLS
145 Tamal Rd, Forest Knolls (94933)
P.O. Box 640 (94933-0640)
PHONE.................415 488-0400
Micheal Neustadt, *President*
Andrew Schaeffer, *CFO*
John Healy, *Vice Pres*
Louise Neustadt, *Admin Sec*
Mila Sardelli, *Marketing Staff*
EMP: 67 **EST:** 1990
SALES (est): 3.1MM **Publicly Held**
WEB: www.serenityknolls.com
SIC: 8093 Substance abuse clinics (outpatient)
PA: Acadia Healthcare Company, Inc.
6100 Tower Cir Ste 1000
Franklin TN 37067

(P-17073)
SIERRA HLTH WELLNESS GROUP LLC
Also Called: New Start Recovery Solutions
2167 Montgomery St Ste A, Oroville (95965-4945)
PHONE.................530 854-4119
Joe Henderson, *Mng Member*
Shawn Vang, *Principal*
John Dolores, *Mng Member*
EMP: 150 **EST:** 2019
SALES (est): 200K **Privately Held**
WEB: www.sierrahealthwellnesscenters.com
SIC: 8093 Mental health clinic, outpatient

(P-17074)
SOCIAL VOCATIONAL SERVICES INC
37400 Cedar Blvd Ste A, Newark (94560-4163)
PHONE.................510 797-1916
Kathy Damario, *Director*
EMP: 37
SALES (corp-wide): 118MM **Privately Held**
WEB: www.socialvocationalservices.org
SIC: 8093 Rehabilitation center, outpatient treatment
PA: Social Vocational Services, Inc.
3555 Torrance Blvd
Torrance CA 90503
310 944-3303

(P-17075)
STATE HOSPITALS CAL DEPT
Also Called: Community Behavioral Health
1380 Howard St Fl 5, San Francisco (94103-2652)
PHONE.................415 255-3400

Marcelina Ogbu, *Director*
EMP: 152 **Privately Held**
WEB: www.ca.gov
SIC: 9199 8093 ; mental health clinic, outpatient
HQ: California Department Of State Hospitals
1600 9th St Ste 350
Sacramento CA 95814

(P-17076)
SUBACUTE TRTMNT ADOLESCNT REHA (PA)
Also Called: Stars
545 Estudillo Ave, San Leandro (94577-4611)
PHONE.................510 352-9200
Peter Zucker, *President*
John Weller, *CFO*
Kent Dunlap, *Senior VP*
Karly Abner, *Administration*
Stephen Albrecht, *Administration*
EMP: 76 **EST:** 1996
SQ FT: 7,442
SALES (est): 11.2MM **Privately Held**
WEB: www.starsinc.com
SIC: 8093 8051 Mental health clinic, outpatient; mental retardation hospital

(P-17077)
SUCCESSFUL ALTRNTVES FOR ADDCT
795 Fletcher Ln, Hayward (94544-1008)
PHONE.................510 247-8300
David K White, *CEO*
Frank Baumann, *COO*
Daniel Gutschenritter, *CFO*
EMP: 54 **EST:** 1994
SQ FT: 1,700
SALES (est): 2.3MM
SALES (corp-wide): 50.2MM **Privately Held**
WEB: www.medmark.com
SIC: 8093 Substance abuse clinics (outpatient)
PA: Medmark Services, Inc.
1720 Lakepointe Dr # 117
Lewisville TX 75057
214 379-3300

(P-17078)
SUSANVILLE INDIAN RANCHERIA (PA)
745 Joaquin St, Susanville (96130-3628)
PHONE.................530 257-6264
Stacy Dixon, *Chairman*
Devon Joseph, *Corp Secy*
Tonya Smith, *Admin Asst*
Amy Langslet, *Director*
Roselynn Lwenya, *Director*
EMP: 40 **EST:** 1986
SQ FT: 5,000
SALES (est): 17.9MM **Privately Held**
WEB: www.sir-nsn.gov
SIC: 8093 Substance abuse clinics (outpatient); mental health clinic, outpatient

(P-17079)
SUTTER HEALTH
Sutter Health At Work
1201 Alhambra Blvd # 210, Sacramento (95816-5238)
PHONE.................916 220-1927
Colleen Cooke, *Manager*
Nicholas So, *Officer*
Karen Hall, *Vice Pres*
Bryanne Taylor, *Associate Dir*
Karen Becraft, *Admin Mgr*
EMP: 68
SALES (corp-wide): 13.2B **Privately Held**
WEB: www.suttermedicalcenter.org
SIC: 8093 8011 Specialty outpatient clinics; offices & clinics of medical doctors; occupational & industrial specialist, physician/surgeon
PA: Sutter Health
2200 River Plaza Dr
Sacramento CA 95833
916 733-8800

(P-17080)
SUTTERCARE CORPORATION
1601 Trousdale Dr, Burlingame (94010-4520)
PHONE.................650 696-5363

Janet Wagner, *Manager*
EMP: 612
SALES (corp-wide): 13.2B **Privately Held**
SIC: 8093 Substance abuse clinics (outpatient)
HQ: Suttercare Corporation
2200 River Plaza Dr
Sacramento CA 95833
916 733-8800

(P-17081)
TOMOTHERAPY INC
1310 Chesapeake Ter, Sunnyvale (94089-1100)
PHONE.................408 716-4600
Elizabeth Davila, *COO*
Susan Savich, *Vice Pres*
Tom Snarsky, *Vice Pres*
Josh King, *Regional Mgr*
Nicolay Postarnakevich, *Software Engr*
EMP: 35 **EST:** 2019
SALES (est): 16.5MM **Privately Held**
WEB: www.radixact.com
SIC: 8093 Rehabilitation center, outpatient treatment

(P-17082)
TURN BEHAVIORAL HLTH SVCS INC
Also Called: MHS
2550 W Clinton Ave, Fresno (93705-4206)
PHONE.................559 264-7521
Kimberly R Bond, *President*
EMP: 35
SALES (corp-wide): 91.4MM **Privately Held**
WEB: www.mhsinc.org
SIC: 8093 8011 Mental health clinic, outpatient; medical centers
PA: Mental Health Systems, Inc.
9465 Farnham St
San Diego CA 92123
858 573-2600

(P-17083)
TURNING POINT CMNTY PROGRAMS (PA)
10850 Gold Center Dr # 325, Rancho Cordova (95670-6177)
PHONE.................916 364-8395
Al Rowlett, *CEO*
Diana White, *COO*
Bruce Jefferson, *CFO*
Karen M Leland-Dolce, *CFO*
Peter Daniels, *Treasurer*
EMP: 65 **EST:** 1976
SQ FT: 6,000
SALES: 61.6MM **Privately Held**
WEB: www.tpcp.org
SIC: 8093 8322 Mental health clinic, outpatient; community center

(P-17084)
UNITED BEHAVIORAL HEALTH
Also Called: Pacificare
8880 Cal Center Dr # 300, Sacramento (95826-3222)
PHONE.................916 927-0606
EMP: 37
SALES (corp-wide): 257.1B **Publicly Held**
WEB: www.liveandworkwell.com
SIC: 8093 Specialty Outpatient Clinic
HQ: United Behavioral Health
425 Market St Fl 18
San Francisco CA 94105
415 547-1403

(P-17085)
UNIVERSITY CAL SAN FRANCISCO
982 Mission St, San Francisco (94103-2911)
PHONE.................415 597-8047
David Fariello, *Principal*
Virginia Mommsen, *Psychiatry*
EMP: 103 **Privately Held**
WEB: www.ucsf.edu
SIC: 8093 8221 9411 Specialty outpatient clinics; university; administration of educational programs;
HQ: University Cal San Francisco
513 Parnassus Ave 115f
San Francisco CA 94143

8093 - Specialty Outpatient Facilities, NEC County

(P-17086)
VIBRANTCARE OUTPATIENT REHAB (PA)
2270 Douglas Blvd Ste 216, Roseville (95661-4239)
PHONE..................916 782-1212
David Smith, *President*
Gary Trubell, *Vice Pres*
Roberto Saavedra, *Administration*
Heather Conway, *Opers Staff*
Anusha Singh, *Assistant*
EMP: 84 EST: 1997
SALES (est): 28.5MM **Privately Held**
WEB: www.vibrantcare.com
SIC: **8093** Rehabilitation center, outpatient treatment

(P-17087)
VICTOR CMNTY SUPPORT SVCS INC
900 E Main St Ste 201, Grass Valley (95945-5853)
PHONE..................530 273-2244
Rachel Pena, *Exec Dir*
EMP: 137
SALES (corp-wide): 62.2MM **Privately Held**
WEB: www.victor.org
SIC: **8093** Mental health clinic, outpatient
PA: Victor Community Support Services, Inc.
1360 E Lassen Ave
Chico CA 95973
530 893-0758

(P-17088)
VICTOR CMNTY SUPPORT SVCS INC
Also Called: Stockton Fics
2495 W March Ln Ste 125, Stockton (95207-8224)
PHONE..................209 465-1080
Debi Scott, *Branch Mgr*
Tracy Cutino, *Supervisor*
Marla Long, *Supervisor*
EMP: 137
SALES (corp-wide): 62.2MM **Privately Held**
WEB: www.victor.org
SIC: **8093** Mental health clinic, outpatient
PA: Victor Community Support Services, Inc.
1360 E Lassen Ave
Chico CA 95973
530 893-0758

(P-17089)
VICTOR CMNTY SUPPORT SVCS INC
Also Called: Butte Fics
1360 E Lassen Ave, Chico (95973-7823)
PHONE..................530 267-1710
Trudi Engelhardt, *Branch Mgr*
EMP: 137
SALES (corp-wide): 62.2MM **Privately Held**
WEB: www.victor.org
SIC: **8093** Mental health clinic, outpatient
PA: Victor Community Support Services, Inc.
1360 E Lassen Ave
Chico CA 95973
530 893-0758

(P-17090)
VISIONS UNLIMITED (PA)
6833 Stockton Blvd # 485, Sacramento (95823-2376)
PHONE..................916 394-0800
Roleda Bates, *CEO*
EMP: 82 EST: 1978
SQ FT: 20,000
SALES: 4.1MM **Privately Held**
WEB: www.vuinc.org
SIC: **8093** Mental health clinic, outpatient

(P-17091)
WELLSPACE HEALTH (PA)
Also Called: Effort, The
1820 J St, Sacramento (95811-3010)
PHONE..................916 325-5556
Robert Caulk, *CEO*
Jonathan Porteus, *President*
Sherlynn Clifford, *CEO*
Karen Dubois, *Officer*
Cathy Frey, *Regional Mgr*
EMP: 56 EST: 1970
SQ FT: 12,500
SALES (est): 29MM **Privately Held**
WEB: www.wellspacehealth.org
SIC: **8093** Mental health clinic, outpatient; alcohol clinic, outpatient; rehabilitation center, outpatient treatment

(P-17092)
WEST OAKLAND HEALTH COUNCIL (PA)
Also Called: WEST OAKLAND HEALTH CENTER
700 Adeline St, Oakland (94607-2608)
PHONE..................510 835-9610
Benjamin Pettus, *CEO*
Lewis Woods, *Pediatrics*
Carol McKinney, *Manager*
EMP: 151 EST: 1968
SQ FT: 26,000
SALES: 22.6MM **Privately Held**
WEB: www.westoaklandhealth.org
SIC: **8093** 8021 8011 Mental health clinic, outpatient; dental clinic; offices & clinics of medical doctors

(P-17093)
WESTCOAST CHILDRENS CLINIC
3301 E 12th St Ste 259, Oakland (94601-2940)
PHONE..................510 269-9030
Stacy Anne Katz, *Exec Dir*
Eric Kelly, *COO*
Edwin Calles, *Admin Asst*
Diane Ramirez, *Project Mgr*
Danna Basson, *Research*
EMP: 140 EST: 1979
SALES (est): 16.5MM **Privately Held**
WEB: www.westcoastcc.org
SIC: **8093** Mental health clinic, outpatient

(P-17094)
WESTSIDE CMNTY MENTAL HLTH CTR
Also Called: Methadone Treatment Center
1301 Pierce St, San Francisco (94115-4005)
PHONE..................415 563-8200
Terry Mitchell, *Director*
EMP: 44
SALES (corp-wide): 8.9MM **Privately Held**
WEB: www.westside-health.org
SIC: **8093** 8069 8322 Mental health clinic, outpatient; drug addiction rehabilitation hospital; individual & family services
PA: Westside Community Mental Health Center
1153 Oak St
San Francisco CA 94117
415 431-9000

(P-17095)
WESTSIDE CMNTY MENTAL HLTH CTR
Also Called: Westside Community Crisis Ctr
888 Turk St, San Francisco (94102-3118)
PHONE..................415 355-0311
Ruth Bertrand, *Manager*
Vanessa Garcia, *Med Doctor*
EMP: 44
SALES (corp-wide): 8.9MM **Privately Held**
WEB: www.westside-health.org
SIC: **8093** Mental health clinic, outpatient
PA: Westside Community Mental Health Center
1153 Oak St
San Francisco CA 94117
415 431-9000

(P-17096)
WOMEN HEALTH CENTER
Also Called: Women's Heath Specialist
1442 Ethan Way Ste 200, Sacramento (95825-2232)
PHONE..................707 537-1171
Penny Bertch, *Superintendent*
EMP: 45
SALES (corp-wide): 6.2MM **Privately Held**
WEB: www.womenshealthspecialists.org
SIC: **8093** Specialty outpatient clinics
PA: Women Health Center
1469 Humboldt Rd Ste 200
Chico CA 95928
530 891-1917

(P-17097)
WOMENS COMMUNITY CLINIC
1735 Mission St, San Francisco (94103-2417)
PHONE..................415 379-7800
Carlina Hanson, *Director*
Tarah Huntley, *Accountant*
Carleena Hanson, *Director*
EMP: 52 EST: 1999
SALES (est): 2.1MM **Privately Held**
WEB: www.healthright360.org
SIC: **8093** 8011 Family planning & birth control clinics; offices & clinics of medical doctors

---

8099 Health & Allied Svcs, NEC

(P-17098)
AESYNTIX HEALTH INC (HQ)
3300 Douglas Blvd Ste 100, Roseville (95661-4287)
PHONE..................916 791-9500
Clark P Avery, *President*
EMP: 60 EST: 2008
SALES (est): 3.8MM
SALES (corp-wide): 118.4MM **Privately Held**
WEB: www.modmed.com
SIC: **8099** Medical services organization
PA: Modernizing Medicine, Inc.
4850 Network Way Ste 200
Boca Raton FL 33431
561 880-2998

(P-17099)
AMEN CLINICS INC A MED CORP
350 N Wiget Ln Ste 105, Walnut Creek (94598-5960)
PHONE..................650 416-7830
Daniel G Amen MD, *Branch Mgr*
EMP: 50
SALES (corp-wide): 27.4MM **Privately Held**
WEB: www.amenclinics.com
SIC: **8099** Blood related health services
PA: Amen Clinics, Inc., A Medical Corporation
3150 Bristol St Ste 400
Costa Mesa CA 92626
888 564-2700

(P-17100)
AMERICAN HLTHCARE ADM SVCS INC
Also Called: American Health Care
3850 Atherton Rd, Rocklin (95765-3700)
PHONE..................916 773-7227
Lance Aizen, *CEO*
Christine Lee, *Ch Credit Ofcr*
Lukasz Karbownik, *Engineer*
Rebecca Gaffey, *Business Mgr*
Kelly Jackson, *Manager*
EMP: 490 EST: 1987
SQ FT: 8,000
SALES (est): 45.8MM **Privately Held**
WEB: www.americanhealthcare.com
SIC: **8099** Medical services organization

(P-17101)
ASSURED CARE ENTERPRISES INC
1361 S Wnchester Blvd, San Jose (95128-4328)
PHONE..................408 379-7000
Runa Chatterjee, *Mng Member*
EMP: 40 EST: 2013
SALES (est): 1.2MM **Privately Held**
SIC: **8099** Health & allied services

(P-17102)
ATLAS LIFT TECH INC
210 Porter Dr Ste 300, San Ramon (94583-1525)
PHONE..................415 283-1804
Eric Race, *President*
Robert Zuckswert, *COO*
Wendy McCollom, *CFO*
Ken Meehan, *Officer*
Gregory Beamer, *Vice Pres*
EMP: 150 EST: 2012
SALES (est): 30.7MM **Privately Held**
WEB: www.atlaslifttech.com
SIC: **8099** Health screening service

(P-17103)
BAY AREA HEALTHCARE CENTER
1833 10th Ave, Oakland (94606-3023)
PHONE..................510 536-6512
Shirley MA, *CEO*
Michael Chau, *Director*
EMP: 48 EST: 2008
SALES (est): 12.6MM **Privately Held**
WEB: www.bayareahc.com
SIC: **8099** Medical services organization

(P-17104)
BERKELEY EMRGNCY MED GROUP INC
2000 Crow Canyon Pl, San Ramon (94583-4633)
PHONE..................925 962-1067
Teven Mark Sornsin, *CEO*
Brad Wiley, *Administration*
EMP: 80 EST: 1995
SQ FT: 3,000
SALES (est): 12MM **Privately Held**
WEB: www.bemg.org
SIC: **8099** Blood related health services

(P-17105)
BLOOD BANK OF REDWOODS (PA)
Also Called: Blood Center of The Pacific
3505 Industrial Dr, Santa Rosa (95403-2064)
PHONE..................707 545-1222
Cathy Bryan, *Administration*
EMP: 107 EST: 1948
SQ FT: 13,540
SALES (est): 8.4MM **Privately Held**
SIC: **8099** Blood bank

(P-17106)
BLOODSOURCE INC (PA)
10536 Peter A Mccuen Blvd, Mather (95655-4128)
PHONE..................916 456-1500
Michael J Fuller, *CEO*
Jim Eldridge, *CFO*
Dirk Johnson, *Vice Pres*
Sinclair Duong, *Prgrmr*
Erin Frye, *Director*
EMP: 325
SQ FT: 105,000
SALES: 85MM **Privately Held**
WEB: www.vitalant.org
SIC: **8099** Blood bank

(P-17107)
BLOODSOURCE INC
382 E Yosemite Ave, Merced (95340-9100)
PHONE..................209 724-0428
Jaime Suarez, *Manager*
EMP: 47
SALES (corp-wide): 85MM **Privately Held**
WEB: www.vitalant.org
SIC: **8099** Blood bank
PA: Bloodsource, Inc.
10536 Peter A Mccuen Blvd
Mather CA 95655
916 456-1500

(P-17108)
BLOODSOURCE INC
3099 Fair Oaks Blvd, Sacramento (95864-5613)
PHONE..................916 488-1701
Whitney Karen, *Branch Mgr*
EMP: 47
SALES (corp-wide): 85MM **Privately Held**
WEB: www.vitalant.org
SIC: **8099** Blood bank
PA: Bloodsource, Inc.
10536 Peter A Mccuen Blvd
Mather CA 95655
916 456-1500

PRODUCTS & SERVICES SECTION
8099 - Health & Allied Svcs, NEC County (P-17133)

(P-17109)
BLOODSOURCE INC
Also Called: Bloodsource North Valley
555 Rio Lindo Ave, Chico (95926-1816)
PHONE..................530 893-5433
Bettina Baur, *Manager*
EMP: 47
SALES (corp-wide): 85MM **Privately Held**
WEB: www.vitalant.org
SIC: 8099 Blood bank
PA: Bloodsource, Inc.
   10536 Peter A Mccuen Blvd
   Mather CA 95655
   916 456-1500

(P-17110)
BRIGHTSIDE HEALTH INC
2471 Peralta St Unit A, Oakland (94607-1703)
PHONE..................415 662-8618
Brad Kittredge, *CEO*
Mimi Winsberg, *Chief Mktg Ofcr*
Jeremy Barth, *CTO*
EMP: 44 EST: 2018
SALES (est): 5.9MM **Privately Held**
WEB: www.brightside.com
SIC: 8099 Health & allied services

(P-17111)
BROOKS HOME HEALTH CARE
5070 N 6th St Ste 169, Fresno (93710-7508)
PHONE..................559 221-4800
Kelly Brooks, *Principal*
EMP: 41 EST: 2010
SALES (est): 1.1MM **Privately Held**
WEB: www.brooksinfusion.com
SIC: 8099 Blood related health services

(P-17112)
CALIFORNIA ADVNCD IMAGING MED
504 Redwood Blvd Ste 300, Novato (94947-6925)
PHONE..................415 884-3413
Jay Kaiser, *Principal*
Diana B Baker, *Radiology*
Russell C Fritz, *Radiology*
Jean-Pierre Phancao, *Radiology*
EMP: 40 EST: 2008
SALES (est): 13.9MM **Privately Held**
SIC: 8099 Health & allied services

(P-17113)
CALIFORNIA CRYOBANK INC
Also Called: Califrnia Cryobank Lf Sciences
611 Gateway Blvd Ste 820, South San Francisco (94080-7029)
PHONE..................650 635-1420
EMP: 300
SALES (corp-wide): 59.9MM **Privately Held**
WEB: www.cryobank.com
SIC: 8099 Blood bank
PA: California Cryobank Llc
   11915 La Grange Ave
   Los Angeles CA 90025
   310 496-5691

(P-17114)
CALIFRNIA FRNSIC MED GROUP INC
Also Called: Cfmg
300 Forni Rd, Kelsey (95667-5400)
PHONE..................530 573-3035
Elaine Huestand, *Manager*
EMP: 98
SALES (corp-wide): 33.7MM **Privately Held**
SIC: 8099 Medical services organization
PA: California Forensic Medical Group, Incorporated
   1283 Murfreesboro Pike # 500
   Nashville TN 37217
   831 649-8994

(P-17115)
CAPSTONE HEALTH INC (PA)
5424 Sunol Blvd, Pleasanton (94566-7705)
PHONE..................408 667-6004
Nicholas Dugbartey, *Owner*
EMP: 59 EST: 2018
SALES (est): 269.5K **Privately Held**
WEB: www.capstonehealth.org
SIC: 8099 Health & allied services

(P-17116)
CENPATICO BEHAVIORAL HLTH LLC
1740 Creekside Oaks Dr, Sacramento (95833-3639)
PHONE..................877 858-3855
Jason Harrold, *Manager*
EMP: 139 EST: 2018
SALES (est): 1.7MM **Publicly Held**
WEB: www.centene.com
SIC: 8099 Health & allied services
PA: Centene Corporation
   7700 Forsyth Blvd Ste 800
   Saint Louis MO 63105

(P-17117)
CENTER FOR YOUTH WELLNESS
3450 3rd St Ste 201, San Francisco (94124-1400)
PHONE..................415 684-9520
Nadine Burke Harris, *CEO*
Robert Benavidez, *Vice Pres*
Latanya Hilton, *Vice Pres*
Alisa Tantraphol, *Vice Pres*
Shirmila Cooray, *Associate Dir*
EMP: 37 EST: 2015
SALES (est): 7.6MM **Privately Held**
WEB: www.centerforyouthwellness.org
SIC: 8099 Blood related health services

(P-17118)
CENTER TO PRMOTE HLTHCARE ACCE
Also Called: Social Interest Solutions
1 Capitol Mall Ste 300, Sacramento (95814-3296)
PHONE..................916 563-4004
John Caterham, *President*
Stacy Dean, *Bd of Directors*
Robert Groth, *Vice Pres*
Cortnie Childers, *Executive*
Melissa Lucas, *Comms Mgr*
EMP: 59 **Privately Held**
WEB: www.alluma.org
SIC: 8099 Medical services organization
PA: The Center To Promote Healthcare Access Inc
   1951 Webster St Fl 2
   Oakland CA 94612

(P-17119)
CENTER TO PRMOTE HLTHCARE ACCE (PA)
Also Called: SOCIAL INTEREST SOLUTIONS
1951 Webster St Fl 2, Oakland (94612-2909)
PHONE..................510 273-4651
John Caterham, *CEO*
Robert Phillips, *President*
Steve Spiker, *Officer*
Duarte Furtado, *Administration*
Avinash Peechari, *Sr Software Eng*
EMP: 61 EST: 2006
SQ FT: 6,000
SALES (est): 33.1MM **Privately Held**
WEB: www.alluma.org
SIC: 8099 7373 Medical services organization; systems software development services

(P-17120)
CENTRAL CALIFORNIA BLOOD CTR
Also Called: Ccbc Reference Lab
4343 W Herndon Ave, Fresno (93722-3794)
PHONE..................559 389-5433
EMP: 98
SALES (corp-wide): 21.6MM **Privately Held**
SIC: 8099 8071 Health/Allied Services Medical Laboratory
PA: Central California Blood Center
   4343 W Herndon Ave
   Fresno CA 93722
   559 389-5433

(P-17121)
CENTRAL CALIFORNIA BLOOD CTR (PA)
4343 W Herndon Ave, Fresno (93722-3794)
PHONE..................559 389-5433
Christopher Staub, *President*
Janet Ripley, *CFO*
Monica Rivera, *General Mgr*
Lori Orosco, *Technical Staff*
Doane Stewart, *Opers Staff*
EMP: 180 EST: 1954
SQ FT: 53,000
SALES: 21.8MM **Privately Held**
WEB: www.donateblood.org
SIC: 8099 Blood bank

(P-17122)
CENTRAL CALIFORNIA FACULTY MED
1085 W Minnesota Ave, Turlock (95382-0827)
PHONE..................209 620-6937
Jason Elliot, *Principal*
EMP: 60
SALES (corp-wide): 54.7MM **Privately Held**
WEB: www.universitymds.com
SIC: 8099 Blood related health services
PA: Central California Faculty Medical Group, Inc.
   2625 E Divisadero St
   Fresno CA 93721
   559 453-5200

(P-17123)
CHILD FAMILY HEALTH INTER (PA)
400 29th St Ste 508, Oakland (94609-3550)
P.O. Box 929, El Cerrito (94530-0929)
PHONE..................415 957-9000
Evaleen Jones, *President*
EMP: 52 EST: 2014
SALES (est): 2.9MM **Privately Held**
WEB: www.cfhi.org
SIC: 8099 Health & allied services

(P-17124)
CLOVER HEALTH LABS LLC
22 4th St Fl 6, San Francisco (94103-3174)
PHONE..................415 548-6456
Ashley Stevens, *Records Dir*
Marcel Van Der Brug, *Officer*
Matt Wallaert, *Officer*
Melody Pereira, *Vice Pres*
Michael Pica, *Vice Pres*
EMP: 42 EST: 2014
SALES (est): 19MM **Privately Held**
WEB: www.cloverhealth.com
SIC: 8099 Childbirth preparation clinic

(P-17125)
COMMUNITY HEALTH PARTNR INC
408 N Capitol Ave, San Jose (95133-1938)
PHONE..................408 556-6605
Rhonda McClinton Brown, *Exec Dir*
Diana Dunckelmann, *CFO*
MAI MAI Cantos, *Vice Pres*
Danielle Malone, *Project Mgr*
Jesse Tarango, *Deputy Dir*
EMP: 46 EST: 1993
SALES (est): 2.9MM **Privately Held**
WEB: www.chpscc.org
SIC: 8099 Medical services organization

(P-17126)
COMPASSIONATE HEALTH OPTIONS (PA)
755 29th Ave, San Francisco (94121-3515)
PHONE..................415 255-1200
Hanya Barth, *Principal*
EMP: 70 EST: 2009
SALES (est): 6.6MM **Privately Held**
WEB: www.hanyabarthmd.com
SIC: 8099 Childbirth preparation clinic

(P-17127)
COUNTY OF CONTRA COSTA
50 Douglas Dr, Martinez (94553-4098)
PHONE..................510 463-7325
Ehukai Sako, *Officer*
Ed Randle, *Manager*
Kimberly Thai, *Manager*
Colleen Samsing, *Supervisor*
EMP: 42 EST: 2011
SALES (est): 15.5MM **Privately Held**
WEB: www.contracosta.ca.gov
SIC: 8099 Health & allied services

(P-17128)
COUNTY OF SACRAMENTO
2921 Stockton Blvd, Sacramento (95817-2305)
PHONE..................916 874-9670
David Earwicker, *Branch Mgr*
EMP: 44
SALES (corp-wide): 3.1B **Privately Held**
WEB: www.saccounty.net
SIC: 8099 Blood related health services
PA: County Of Sacramento
   700 H St Ste 7650
   Sacramento CA 95814
   916 874-8515

(P-17129)
COUNTY OF STANISLAUS
Also Called: W I C Program
108 Campus Way, Modesto (95350-5803)
PHONE..................209 558-7377
Deborah Bogg, *Branch Mgr*
EMP: 66
SALES (corp-wide): 1.2B **Privately Held**
WEB: www.stancounty.com
SIC: 8099 Nutrition services
PA: County Of Stanislaus
   1010 10th St Ste 5100
   Modesto CA 95354
   209 525-6398

(P-17130)
CUROLOGY INC (PA)
Also Called: Curology Medical Group
353 Sacramento St # 2000, San Francisco (94111-3675)
PHONE..................858 859-1188
David Nicholas Lortscher, *Administration*
Carrie Welch, *COO*
Julia Liu, *Senior VP*
Aj Brustein, *Vice Pres*
Victoria Sun, *Vice Pres*
EMP: 428 EST: 2017
SALES (est): 50.6MM **Privately Held**
WEB: www.curology.com
SIC: 8099 Plasmapherous center

(P-17131)
CVS HEALTH CORPORATION
995 Market St, San Francisco (94103-1702)
PHONE..................415 348-1814
EMP: 447
SALES (corp-wide): 268.7B **Publicly Held**
WEB: www.cvshealth.com
SIC: 5912 5961 8099 Pharmacy Health Care Services
PA: Cvs Health Corporation
   1 Cvs Dr
   Woonsocket RI 02895
   401 765-1500

(P-17132)
DCI DONOR SERVICES INC
Also Called: Sierra Eye Tissue Donor
3940 Industrial Blvd, West Sacramento (95691-6505)
PHONE..................877 401-2546
Keith Johnson, *President*
Teresa Thompson, *CFO*
Chris Cowan, *Surgery Dir*
Donna Smith, *Surgery Dir*
Sam Ramos, *Exec Dir*
EMP: 95 **Privately Held**
WEB: www.dcids.org
SIC: 8099 Organ bank
PA: Dci Donor Services, Inc.
   566 Mainstream Dr Ste 300
   Nashville TN 37228

(P-17133)
DCI DONOR SERVICES INC
Also Called: Golden State Donor Services
3940 Industrial Blvd # 100, West Sacramento (95691-6505)
PHONE..................916 567-1600
Helen Nels, *Manager*
EMP: 95 **Privately Held**

8099 - Health & Allied Svcs, NEC County (P-17134)

PRODUCTS & SERVICES SECTION

WEB: www.dcids.org
SIC: 8099 Organ bank
PA: Dci Donor Services, Inc.
566 Mainstream Dr Ste 300
Nashville TN 37228

(P-17134)
DELTA BLOOD BANK LLC (HQ)
Also Called: American Nat Red Cross - Blood
65 N Commerce St, Stockton (95202-2318)
P.O. Box 800 (95201-0800)
PHONE..............................800 244-6794
Benjamin Spindler, CEO
Robert Lawrence, Ch of Bd
Alfonso Figueroa, CFO
◆ EMP: 85 EST: 1954
SQ FT: 30,000
SALES (est): 17MM
SALES (corp-wide): 2.8B Privately Held
WEB: www.deltabloodbank.org
SIC: 8099 Blood bank
PA: The American National Red Cross
431 18th St Nw
Washington DC 20006
202 737-8300

(P-17135)
DONOR NETWORK WEST
6721 N Willow Ave Ste 104, Fresno (93710-5950)
PHONE..............................510 418-0336
Denise Kinder, Manager
Ahmad Salehi, Research
Waldo Concepcion, Senior Mgr
Susan Hall, Director
Linda Saypalia, Regional
EMP: 50
SALES (corp-wide): 99MM Privately Held
WEB: www.donornetworkwest.org
SIC: 8099 Medical services organization
PA: Donor Network West
12667 Alcosta Blvd # 500
San Ramon CA 94583
925 480-3100

(P-17136)
DONOR NETWORK WEST (PA)
12667 Alcosta Blvd # 500, San Ramon (94583-5272)
PHONE..............................925 480-3100
Cynthia D Siljestrom, CEO
Jackie Manzanedo, Partner
Jeremy Gimbel, CFO
Sandra Mejia, CFO
Nikole Neidlinger, Bd of Directors
EMP: 121 EST: 1987
SQ FT: 41,039
SALES (est): 99MM Privately Held
WEB: www.donornetworkwest.org
SIC: 8099 Medical services organization

(P-17137)
DONOR NETWORK WEST
Also Called: Ctdn - Redding
5800 Airport Rd Ste B, Redding (96002-9359)
PHONE..............................510 418-0336
EMP: 50
SALES (corp-wide): 99MM Privately Held
WEB: www.donornetworkwest.org
SIC: 8099 Medical services organization
PA: Donor Network West
12667 Alcosta Blvd # 500
San Ramon CA 94583
925 480-3100

(P-17138)
DOULAS BY BAY LLC
1201 Liberty St, El Cerrito (94530-2359)
PHONE..............................415 510-9736
Shakila Marando, Mng Member
EMP: 85 EST: 2014
SALES (est): 2.8MM Privately Held
WEB: www.doulasbythebay.com
SIC: 8099 Childbirth preparation clinic

(P-17139)
EASTER SEAL SOC SUPERIOR CAL (PA)
Also Called: Easter Seals Main Office
3205 Hurley Way, Sacramento (95864-3853)
P.O. Box 254867 (95865-4867)
PHONE..............................916 485-6711
Gary T Kasai, President
Don Nguyen, CFO
Sue Harris, General Mgr
Kathie Wright, Director
EMP: 100 EST: 1934
SQ FT: 28,500
SALES (est): 12.1MM Privately Held
WEB: www.easterseals.com
SIC: 8099 8093 Medical services organization; rehabilitation center, outpatient treatment

(P-17140)
EASTERN PLMAS HLTH CARE FNDTIO (PA)
Also Called: EASTERN PLUMAS HOSPITAL
500 1st Ave, Portola (96122-9406)
PHONE..............................530 832-4277
Tom Hayes, CEO
Virginia Luhring, President
Jeri Nelson, CFO
Bill Carlson, Lab Dir
Michele Dillon, Radiology Dir
EMP: 161 EST: 1992
SQ FT: 18,500
SALES: 63.6K Privately Held
WEB: www.ephc.org
SIC: 8099 8011 8322 Medical services organization; primary care medical clinic; rehabilitation services

(P-17141)
EDEN HOME HEALTH ELK GROVE LLC
9299 E Stockton Blvd # 10, Elk Grove (95624-4097)
PHONE..............................916 681-4949
Tina Nickolas, Principal
EMP: 44 EST: 2016
SALES (est): 1.1MM Privately Held
SIC: 8099 Blood related health services

(P-17142)
EHEALTHWIRECOM INC
2450 Venture Oaks Way # 100, Sacramento (95833-3292)
PHONE..............................916 924-8092
Yousry Mekhamer, Chairman
Sue Barnes, Executive
Kwabena Nantwi, IT/INT Sup
EMP: 250 EST: 1999
SQ FT: 17,000
SALES (est): 13.7MM Privately Held
SIC: 8099 Health screening service

(P-17143)
EPOCRATES INC (DH)
50 Hawthorne St, San Francisco (94105-3902)
PHONE..............................650 227-1700
Rob Cosinuke, President
Meredith Aucker, President
Murat Erdem, President
Patti Paczkowski, President
Howard Schargel, President
EMP: 343 EST: 2005
SQ FT: 59,000
SALES (est): 54.9MM
SALES (corp-wide): 1.2B Privately Held
WEB: www.epocrates.com
SIC: 8099 Health screening service
HQ: Athenahealth, Inc.
311 Arsenal St Ste 14
Watertown MA 02472
617 402-1000

(P-17144)
EVIDATION HEALTH INC (PA)
63 Bovet Rd 146, San Mateo (94402-3104)
PHONE..............................833 234-7048
EMP: 129 EST: 2018
SALES (est): 15.8MM Privately Held
WEB: www.evidation.com
SIC: 8099 Health & allied services

(P-17145)
EVOLENT HEALTH INC
1 Kearny St Ste 300, San Francisco (94108-5549)
PHONE..............................571 389-6000
Ken Wood, Vice Pres
EMP: 400
SALES (corp-wide): 1B Publicly Held
WEB: www.evolenthealth.com
SIC: 8099 Medical services organization
PA: Evolent Health, Inc.
800 N Glebe Rd Ste 500
Arlington VA 22203
571 389-6000

(P-17146)
FAIRCHILD MED CTR FNDATION INC
444 Bruce St, Yreka (96097-3450)
PHONE..............................530 842-4121
John Pomeroy, CEO
Susan Iken Berry, Director
EMP: 61 EST: 2002
SALES (est): 107.1K Privately Held
WEB: www.fairchildmed.org
SIC: 8099 Medical services organization

(P-17147)
FALCON CRITICAL CARE TRANS A
3508 San Pablo Dam Rd, El Sobrante (94803-2728)
PHONE..............................510 223-1171
Carin Johnson, President
Brian Johnson, Vice Pres
Tammy Collins, Office Mgr
Curtis Tuggle, Director
EMP: 40 EST: 1998
SALES (est): 7.8MM Privately Held
WEB: www.falconambulance.com
SIC: 8099 8082 Childbirth preparation clinic; home health care services

(P-17148)
FOLSOM CARE CENTER
Also Called: Skilled Nursing
510 Mill St, Folsom (95630-2607)
PHONE..............................916 985-3641
Calvin Callaway, President
Julia Trujillo, Office Mgr
Brett Elmont, Controller
Penny Rodgers, Education
EMP: 44 EST: 1965
SALES (est): 689.2K Privately Held
WEB: www.folsomcarecenter.com
SIC: 8099 Health & allied services

(P-17149)
GLOBAL MEDDATA INC (PA)
3705 Haven Ave 124, Menlo Park (94025-1011)
PHONE..............................650 369-9734
Raj Patel, CEO
Naina Khatri, Director
EMP: 61 EST: 2000
SALES (est): 3.3MM Privately Held
SIC: 8099 7374 Medical services organization; data processing & preparation

(P-17150)
GRAND ROUNDS INC (PA)
1 California St Ste 2300, San Francisco (94111-5424)
PHONE..............................800 929-0926
Owen Tripp, CEO
Heather Conroy, Records Dir
Mike Matteo, President
Gabe Cortes, CFO
Deborah Conrad, Chief Mktg Ofcr
EMP: 156 EST: 2011
SALES (est): 48.9MM Privately Held
WEB: www.grandrounds.com
SIC: 8099 Physical examination & testing services

(P-17151)
HEALTH IQ
2513 Charleston Rd # 102, Mountain View (94043-1634)
PHONE..............................917 770-2190
Tanmay Kar, Vice Pres
Julie Magnuson, Exec VP
Stephen Sprague, Department Mgr
Sebastian Bierman-Lytle, Software Engr
David Trevino, Training Spec
EMP: 61 EST: 2016
SALES (est): 14.2MM Privately Held
WEB: www.healthiq.com
SIC: 8099 Health & allied services

(P-17152)
HEALTH LF ORGNIZATION INC HALO
Also Called: Sacramento Community Clinic
3030 Explorer Dr, Sacramento (95827-2728)
PHONE..............................916 428-3788
Bilatout Jerry, CEO
EMP: 80 EST: 2015
SALES (est): 1.7MM Privately Held
WEB: www.halocares.org
SIC: 8099 Medical services organization

(P-17153)
HINGE HEALTH INC (PA)
455 Market St Fl 7, San Francisco (94105-2437)
PHONE..............................855 902-7777
Daniel Perez, CEO
Ron Will, CFO
Gabriel Mecklenburg, Officer
Ryan Russell, Senior VP
Margaret Dowling, Vice Pres
EMP: 771 EST: 2015
SALES (est): 56.1MM Privately Held
WEB: www.hingehealth.com
SIC: 8099 Physical examination & testing services

(P-17154)
HUMBOLDT BAY FIRE JINT PWERS A
533 C St, Eureka (95501-0340)
PHONE..............................707 441-4000
Kenneth Woods,
Melinda Ciarabellini,
Joann Gath,
Bill Gillespie, Manager
EMP: 60 EST: 2012
SQ FT: 18,700 Privately Held
WEB: www.hbfire.org
SIC: 9224 8099 ; medical services organization

(P-17155)
INNOVATIVE INTEGRATED HLTH INC
2042 Kern St, Fresno (93721-2008)
PHONE..............................949 228-5577
Ibrahim Marouf, Principal
Phillip Tsunoda, Vice Pres
EMP: 150 EST: 2016
SALES (est): 8.2MM Privately Held
WEB: www.innovativeih.com
SIC: 8099 Health & allied services

(P-17156)
INSTITUTO FAMILIAR DE LA RAZA
2919 Mission St, San Francisco (94110-3917)
PHONE..............................415 229-0500
Juanita Quintero, Manager
EMP: 50
SALES (corp-wide): 12.4MM Privately Held
WEB: www.ifrsf.org
SIC: 8099 8322 8999 Blood related health services; health screening service; general counseling services; referral service for personal & social problems; family counseling services; psychological consultant
PA: Instituto Familiar De La Raza Inc
2919 Mission St
San Francisco CA 94110
415 647-4033

(P-17157)
KIMCO STAFFING SERVICES INC
1801 Oakland Blvd Ste 220, Walnut Creek (94596-7033)
PHONE..............................925 945-1444
EMP: 1113
SALES (corp-wide): 89.9MM Privately Held
WEB: www.kimco.com
SIC: 8099 Medical services organization

▲ = Import ▼ = Export
◆ = Import/Export

PRODUCTS & SERVICES SECTION

8099 - Health & Allied Svcs, NEC County (P-17182)

PA: Kimco Staffing Services, Inc.
17872 Cowan
Irvine CA 92614
949 331-1199

(P-17158)
LA CLINICA DE LA RAZA INC
Also Called: Billing & Registration
3451 E 12th St, Oakland (94601-3463)
PHONE.................510 535-3500
Jean Garcia, *CEO*
Rosa Villalobos, *Executive*
Benjamin Durant, *Family Practiti*
Rebecca McEntee, *Family Practiti*
Sara Johnson, *Obstetrician*
EMP: 177
SQ FT: 38,780
SALES (corp-wide): 115.6MM **Privately Held**
WEB: www.laclinica.org
SIC: 8099 8011 Medical services organization; medical centers
PA: La Clinica De La Raza, Inc.
1450 Fruitvale Ave Fl 3
Oakland CA 94601
510 535-4000

(P-17159)
LA CLINICA DE LA RAZA INC
Also Called: Health Education
1537 Fruitvale Ave, Oakland (94601-2322)
PHONE.................510 535-4130
Berta Hernandez, *Manager*
Leticia Cazares, *Regional Mgr*
Jennifer Ogg, *Executive Asst*
Rochelle Ramirez, *Administration*
Maria Alvarez, *MIS Mgr*
EMP: 177
SALES (corp-wide): 115.6MM **Privately Held**
WEB: www.laclinica.org
SIC: 8099 8011 Medical services organization; medical centers
PA: La Clinica De La Raza, Inc.
1450 Fruitvale Ave Fl 3
Oakland CA 94601
510 535-4000

(P-17160)
MDUSD
1936 Carlotta Dr, Concord (94519-1358)
PHONE.................925 682-8000
Richard Nicoll, *Principal*
Bob Bailey, *Teacher*
Sherri Gardner, *Assistant*
EMP: 40 **EST:** 2010
SALES (est): 11.7MM **Privately Held**
WEB: www.mdusd.org
SIC: 8099 Nutrition services

(P-17161)
MES SOLUTIONS
11010 White Rock Rd # 160, Rancho Cordova (95670-6083)
PHONE.................916 920-1222
Greg Durio, *Branch Mgr*
Lisa Spellman, *Analyst*
EMP: 37 **Privately Held**
WEB: www.messolutions.com
SIC: 8099 Childbirth preparation clinic
HQ: Mes Group, Llc
150 Presidential Way # 110
Woburn MA 01801
781 933-1782

(P-17162)
MORRISON MGT SPECIALISTS INC
Also Called: Morrison MGT Specialists
2823 Fresno St, Fresno (93721-1324)
PHONE.................559 459-6449
EMP: 200
SALES (corp-wide): 27.3B **Privately Held**
SIC: 8099 Health/Allied Services
HQ: Morrison Management Specialists, Inc.
5801 Pachtree Dunwoody Rd
Atlanta GA 30350

(P-17163)
MUIR WOOD LLC
Also Called: Muir WD Adolescent & Fmly Svcs
55 Shaver St Ste 200, San Rafael (94901-2784)
PHONE.................310 903-1155

Scott Sowle, *Exec Dir*
Delilah Holmes, *Psychologist*
Nicholas P Reeves, *Psychiatry*
Mark Schiller, *Psychiatry*
Rosa Larsen, *Director*
EMP: 37 **EST:** 2013
SALES (est): 16.1MM **Privately Held**
WEB: www.muirwoodteen.com
SIC: 8099 Childbirth preparation clinic

(P-17164)
ONCOLOGY SVCS MED GROUP INC
1445 Livorna Rd, Alamo (94507-1103)
P.O. Box 756, Danville (94526-0756)
PHONE.................925 952-8700
Tim Scott MD, *CEO*
W Brian Fuery, *Principal*
EMP: 45 **EST:** 2005
SALES (est): 1.4MM **Privately Held**
SIC: 8099 Health & allied services

(P-17165)
ONSITE HEALTH INC
6610 Goodyear Rd, Benicia (94510-1250)
PHONE.................888 411-2290
Laura Dutch, *Manager*
EMP: 82 **Privately Held**
SIC: 8099 Medical services organization
PA: Onsite Health, Inc.
85 Argonaut Ste 220
Aliso Viejo CA 92656

(P-17166)
PATHWAYS HOME HEALTH
395 Oyster Point Blvd # 12, South San Francisco (94080-1928)
PHONE.................650 634-0133
Mary Dias, *Manager*
Medha Bansode, *Director*
Susan Hughes, *Assistant*
EMP: 41 **EST:** 1998
SALES (est): 425K **Privately Held**
SIC: 8099 Health & allied services

(P-17167)
PERMANENTE MEDICAL GROUP INC (DH)
1950 Franklin St Fl 18th, Oakland (94612-5118)
PHONE.................866 858-2226
Robert M Pearl, *CEO*
Gerard C Bajada, *CFO*
Pat Conolly, *Exec Dir*
Sue Schepers, *Administration*
Thomas Burns, *Med Doctor*
EMP: 500 **EST:** 1945
SQ FT: 10,000
SALES (est): 748.7MM
SALES (corp-wide): 30.5B **Privately Held**
WEB: www.permanente.org
SIC: 8099 Medical services organization
HQ: Kaiser Foundation Hospitals Inc
1 Kaiser Plz
Oakland CA 94612
510 271-6611

(P-17168)
PIT RIVER HEALTH SERVICE INC (PA)
36977 Park Ave, Burney (96013-4067)
PHONE.................530 335-3651
Glenna Moore, *Exec Dir*
Inder Wadhwa, *Administration*
EMP: 51 **EST:** 1979
SALES (est): 6.9MM **Privately Held**
WEB: www.pitriverhealthservice.org
SIC: 8099 Medical services organization

(P-17169)
PUBLIC HEALTH INSTITUTE
1825 Bell St Ste 203, Sacramento (95825-1020)
PHONE.................916 285-1231
Arti Parikhpatel, *Branch Mgr*
EMP: 106
SALES (corp-wide): 112.1MM **Privately Held**
WEB: www.phi.org
SIC: 8099 Blood related health services
PA: Public Health Institute
555 12th St Ste 290
Oakland CA 94607
510 285-5500

(P-17170)
RALLY HEALTH INC
665 3rd St Ste 200, San Francisco (94107-1985)
PHONE.................408 821-5414
Jonathan West, *Sr Software Eng*
Eric Mann, *VP Mktg*
Sameer Jain, *Manager*
EMP: 39
SALES (corp-wide): 257.1B **Publicly Held**
WEB: www.rallyhealth.com
SIC: 8099 Physical examination & testing services
HQ: Rally Health, Inc.
3000 K St Nw Ste 350
Washington DC 20007
202 469-7728

(P-17171)
RECRUITMENT ALLEY LLC
Also Called: Healthcare Staffing
2505 W Shaw Ave Ste 150, Fresno (93711-3334)
PHONE.................559 614-5024
Lee Her, *CEO*
EMP: 50 **EST:** 2019
SALES (est): 2.2MM **Privately Held**
WEB: www.recruitmentalley.net
SIC: 8099 7361 Health & allied services; employment agencies; executive placement

(P-17172)
RICHMOND POST ACUTE CARE LLC
955 23rd St, Richmond (94804-1250)
PHONE.................510 237-5182
James Jordan, *Principal*
EMP: 55 **EST:** 2019
SALES (est): 4.6MM **Privately Held**
WEB: www.richmondpostacute.com
SIC: 8099 Health & allied services

(P-17173)
S&F MANAGEMENT COMPANY LLC
Also Called: Windsor Post Acute Care Center
25919 Gading Rd, Hayward (94544-2725)
PHONE.................310 385-1088
Lee C Samson, *President*
EMP: 207 **Privately Held**
WEB: www.windsorpostacutehayward.com
SIC: 8099 Childbirth preparation clinic
PA: S&F Management Company, Llc
9200 W Sunset Blvd # 700
West Hollywood CA 90069

(P-17174)
SAN MATEO HEALTH COMMISSION
Also Called: Health Plan of San Mateo
801 Gateway Blvd Ste 100, South San Francisco (94080-7408)
PHONE.................650 616-0050
Maya Altman, *CEO*
Ron Robinson, *CFO*
Corinne Burgess, *Executive Asst*
Shawnesha Guillory, *Admin Asst*
Darren Kattenhorn, *Chief Engr*
EMP: 211 **EST:** 1986
SQ FT: 58,758
SALES (est): 42.9MM **Privately Held**
WEB: www.hpsm.org
SIC: 8099 Physical examination service, insurance

(P-17175)
SANTA CLARA COUNTY OF
Also Called: Santa Clara Family Health
6201 San Ignacio Ave, San Jose (95119-1325)
PHONE.................408 362-9817
EMP: 54 **Privately Held**
WEB: www.scfhp.com
SIC: 8099 Medical services organization
PA: County Of Santa Clara
70 W Hedding St 2wing
San Jose CA 95110
408 299-5200

(P-17176)
SANTA CLARA VALLEY MEDICA
P.O. Box 5460 (95150-5460)
PHONE.................408 885-6839
EMP: 58 **EST:** 2009
SALES (est): 3.9MM **Privately Held**
WEB: www.scvmc.org
SIC: 8099 Health & allied services

(P-17177)
SANTA CLARA VALLEY MEDICAL CTR
2220 Moorpark Ave, San Jose (95128-2613)
PHONE.................408 885-5730
EMP: 39 **Privately Held**
WEB: www.scvmc.org
SIC: 8099 Childbirth preparation clinic
PA: Santa Clara Valley Medical Center
751 S Bascom Ave
San Jose CA 95128

(P-17178)
SENDER INC
Also Called: Sendoso
447 Battery St Ste 200, San Francisco (94111-3235)
PHONE.................888 717-3287
Michelle Palleschi, *COO*
Sam East, *Officer*
Rizwan Ansary, *Vice Pres*
Hetal Giaimo, *Vice Pres*
Danielle Middlebrook, *Vice Pres*
EMP: 91 **EST:** 2017
SALES (est): 11.7MM **Privately Held**
WEB: www.sendoso.com
SIC: 8099 Health & allied services

(P-17179)
SEVA FOUNDATION
1786 5th St, Berkeley (94710-1716)
PHONE.................510 845-7382
Jack Blanks, *Exec Dir*
Deborah Moses, *CFO*
Mark Lancaster, *Exec Dir*
Leslie Louie, *Exec Dir*
Kate Moynihan, *Exec Dir*
EMP: 54 **EST:** 1978
SQ FT: 2,000
SALES (est): 7.3MM **Privately Held**
WEB: www.seva.org
SIC: 8099 Blood related health services

(P-17180)
SIERRA HLTH WELLNESS CTRS LLC
2167 Montgomery St Ste A, Oroville (95965-4945)
P.O. Box 2456 (95965-2456)
PHONE.................530 854-4119
Joseph Henderson, *Mng Member*
Shawn Vang, *Mng Member*
EMP: 80 **EST:** 2019
SALES (est): 6.1MM **Privately Held**
WEB: www.sierrahealthwellnesscenters.com
SIC: 8099 8322 Blood related health services; rehabilitation services

(P-17181)
SONIA CORINA INC
Also Called: Bay Respite Care
1100 Rose Dr Ste 140, Benicia (94510-3623)
PHONE.................707 644-4491
Jodi Johnson, *CEO*
EMP: 38 **EST:** 2002
SALES (est): 8.5MM **Privately Held**
WEB: www.soniacorina.org
SIC: 8099 Childbirth preparation clinic

(P-17182)
STANFORD HEALTH CARE
Also Called: Stanford Cancer Center
900 Blake Wilbur Dr, Palo Alto (94304-2201)
PHONE.................650 723-8561
Ana Herrera, *Officer*
Joni Schott, *Admin Dir*
Kimberly Nguyen, *Program Mgr*
Jason Williams, *Technician*
Gary Goldstein, *Business Mgr*
EMP: 43 **EST:** 2018

(PA)=Parent Co (HQ)=Headquarters (DH)=Div Headquarters
✿ = New Business established in last 2 years

8099 - Health & Allied Svcs, NEC County (P-17183)

SALES (est): 8.5MM **Privately Held**
WEB: www.careers.stanfordhealthcare.org
SIC: **8099** Health & allied services

(P-17183)
SUTTER HEALTH
2950 Collier Canyon Rd, Livermore (94551-9224)
PHONE......................925 371-3800
Ronald D Workman, *Branch Mgr*
Rita Ranger, *Case Mgr*
EMP: 68
SALES (corp-wide): 13.2B **Privately Held**
WEB: www.suttermedicalcenter.org
SIC: **8099** Blood related health services
PA: Sutter Health
2200 River Plaza Dr
Sacramento CA 95833
916 733-8800

(P-17184)
SUTTER HLTH SCRMNTO SIERRA REG
701 Howe Ave Ste F20, Sacramento (95825-4681)
PHONE......................916 733-7080
Mary Ashuckian, *Branch Mgr*
Barbara Berry, *Manager*
EMP: 144
SALES (corp-wide): 13.2B **Privately Held**
WEB: www.sutterhealth.org
SIC: **8099** Blood related health services
HQ: Sutter Health Sacramento Sierra Region
2200 River Plaza Dr
Sacramento CA 95833
916 733-8800

(P-17185)
SYNCHR INC
2201 Broadway Ste 701, Oakland (94612-3024)
PHONE......................720 893-2000
Jeffrey M Closs, *President*
Michael Sirkin, *Partner*
Alan R Hoops, *Ch of Bd*
Brad Pearse, *President*
Sanjiv Luthra, *COO*
EMP: 60 EST: 2000
SALES (est): 2.3MM **Privately Held**
WEB: www.synchr.com
SIC: **8099** Health screening service

(P-17186)
SYNERGY HEALTH COMPANIES INC
1521 N Carptr Rd Ste D1, Modesto (95351)
PHONE......................209 577-4625
Ronald Murphy, *CEO*
Anita Murphy, *CEO*
Ronald Edward Murphy, *CEO*
EMP: 95 EST: 2013
SALES: 5.4MM **Privately Held**
SIC: **8099** Health & allied services

(P-17187)
VIRTA HEALTH CORP
501 Folsom St Fl 1, San Francisco (94105-3175)
PHONE......................844 847-8216
Sami Inkinen, *CEO*
Alok Bhushan, *CFO*
Robert Ratner, *Officer*
Meredith Loring, *Vice Pres*
Trent Myers, *Vice Pres*
EMP: 70 EST: 2014
SALES (est): 10.6MM **Privately Held**
WEB: www.virtahealth.com
SIC: **8099** Blood related health services

(P-17188)
VITALANT RESEARCH INSTITUTE
Also Called: Peninsula South Bay
111 Rollins Rd, Millbrae (94030-3114)
PHONE......................650 697-4034
Tatiana Bobrova, *Director*
EMP: 49
SALES (corp-wide): 59.7MM **Privately Held**
WEB: www.research.vitalant.org
SIC: **8099** 8071 Blood bank; medical laboratories

PA: Vitalant Research Institute
270 Masonic Ave
San Francisco CA 94118
415 567-6400

(P-17189)
VITALANT RESEARCH INSTITUTE (PA)
Also Called: Shasta Blood Center
270 Masonic Ave, San Francisco (94118-4417)
PHONE......................415 567-6400
Nora Hirschler, *President*
Lage Anderson, *Treasurer*
Angelina Lee, *Officer*
Maria Piccone, *Officer*
Maureen O'Dea, *Admin Asst*
EMP: 120 EST: 1941
SQ FT: 67,000
SALES (est): 59.7MM **Privately Held**
WEB: www.research.vitalant.org
SIC: **8099** Blood bank

(P-17190)
VITALANT RESEARCH INSTITUTE
Also Called: NAPA Solano Cmnty Blood Ctr
1325 Gateway Blvd Ste C1, Fairfield (94553-6919)
PHONE......................707 428-6001
Lana Dyson, *Manager*
EMP: 49
SALES (corp-wide): 59.7MM **Privately Held**
WEB: www.research.vitalant.org
SIC: **8099** Blood bank
PA: Vitalant Research Institute
270 Masonic Ave
San Francisco CA 94118
415 567-6400

(P-17191)
VITALANT RESEARCH INSTITUTE
2680 Larkspur Ln, Redding (96002-1016)
PHONE......................530 221-0600
Ellie Delgado, *Branch Mgr*
EMP: 49
SALES (corp-wide): 59.7MM **Privately Held**
WEB: www.research.vitalant.org
SIC: **8099** Blood bank
PA: Vitalant Research Institute
270 Masonic Ave
San Francisco CA 94118
415 567-6400

(P-17192)
VITALANT RESEARCH INSTITUTE
570 Price Ave Ste 100, San Rafael (94901)
PHONE......................415 454-2700
Nore Hurslen, *President*
EMP: 49
SALES (corp-wide): 59.7MM **Privately Held**
WEB: www.research.vitalant.org
SIC: **8099** Blood bank
PA: Vitalant Research Institute
270 Masonic Ave
San Francisco CA 94118
415 567-6400

(P-17193)
WARBRITTON & ASSOC IMPAIRMENT (PA)
300 Frank H Ogawa Plz, Oakland (94612-2037)
PHONE......................510 251-8851
John D Warbritton III, *Principal*
EMP: 57 EST: 2008
SALES (est): 3MM **Privately Held**
SIC: **8099** Childbirth preparation clinic

(P-17194)
WEST SIDE CMNTY HEALTHCARE DST
990 Tulare St Ste C, Newman (95360-1350)
PHONE......................209 862-2951
Michael Courtney, *COO*
Dennis Brazil,
Roberta Casteel,
EMP: 35 EST: 1957

SALES (est): 2.6MM **Privately Held**
WEB: www.westsideambulance.com
SIC: **8099** Health & allied services

(P-17195)
WINTERS HLTHCARE FUNDATION INC
172 E Grant Ave, Winters (95694-1780)
PHONE......................530 795-4377
Chris Kelsch, *CEO*
Jeff Uppington, *President*
Penny Herbert, *Treasurer*
Erik Brunkel, *Vice Pres*
Joel Weismann, *Admin Sec*
EMP: 38 EST: 2001
SALES (est): 5.4MM **Privately Held**
WEB: www.wintershealth.org
SIC: **8099** 8021 Medical services organization; dental clinics & offices

8111 Legal Svcs

(P-17196)
AARON DOWLING INCORPORATED
8080 N Palm Ave Ste 300, Fresno (93711-5797)
P.O. Box 28902 (93729-8902)
PHONE......................559 432-4500
Larry B Lindenau, *CEO*
Mark Kruthers, *Shareholder*
Tim Larson, *Shareholder*
William Littlewood, *Shareholder*
Anthony Oceguera, *Shareholder*
EMP: 80 EST: 1977
SQ FT: 16,000
SALES (est): 12.3MM **Privately Held**
WEB: www.fennemorelaw.com
SIC: **8111** General practice attorney, lawyer

(P-17197)
ABBEY WTZNBERG WRREN EMERY A P
Also Called: Warren, Lewis R
100 Stony Point Rd # 200, Santa Rosa (95401-4117)
P.O. Box 1566 (95402-1566)
PHONE......................415 986-3103
Patrick Emery, *President*
Lewis Warren, *Shareholder*
Richard W Abbey, *Principal*
David W Berry, *Principal*
Mitchell Greenberg, *Principal*
EMP: 35 EST: 1925
SALES (est): 3.1MM **Privately Held**
WEB: www.abbeylaw.com
SIC: **8111** General practice attorney, lawyer

(P-17198)
ADLER & COLVIN A LAW CORP
135 Main St Ste 2000, San Francisco (94105-1854)
PHONE......................415 421-7555
Robert Wexler, *President*
Jordan Brown, *President*
Michelle Leung, *President*
Gregory L Colvin, *Treasurer*
Betsy Buchalter Adler, *Vice Pres*
EMP: 35 EST: 1971
SALES (est): 4.5MM **Privately Held**
WEB: www.adlercolvin.com
SIC: **8111** General practice attorney, lawyer

(P-17199)
ALSTON & BIRD LLP
560 Mission St, San Francisco (94105-2907)
PHONE......................415 243-3440
EMP: 65
SALES (corp-wide): 216.9MM **Privately Held**
WEB: www.alston.com
SIC: **8111** General practice attorney, lawyer
PA: Alston & Bird Llp
1201 W Peachtree St Nw # 4000
Atlanta GA 30309
404 881-7000

(P-17200)
ALSTON & BIRD LLP
1950 University Ave # 500, East Palo Alto (94303-2282)
P.O. Box 51058, Palo Alto (94303-0684)
PHONE......................650 838-2000
Ted Hollifield, *Branch Mgr*
EMP: 65
SALES (corp-wide): 216.9MM **Privately Held**
WEB: www.alston.com
SIC: **8111** General practice attorney, lawyer
PA: Alston & Bird Llp
1201 W Peachtree St Nw # 4000
Atlanta GA 30309
404 881-7000

(P-17201)
ANDERSON ZEIGLER DISHAROON (PA)
50 Old Courthouse Sq # 500, Santa Rosa (95404-4925)
P.O. Box 1498 (95402-1498)
PHONE......................707 545-4910
Edwin C Anderson, *President*
Dan E Post, *Partner*
Donald Black, *Shareholder*
Robdebi Hutchinson, *President*
Catherine J Banti, *Bd of Directors*
EMP: 40 EST: 1982
SQ FT: 11,000
SALES (est): 5.3MM **Privately Held**
WEB: www.andersonzeigler.com
SIC: **8111** General practice law office

(P-17202)
ANGELO KILDAY & KILDUFF
601 University Ave # 150, Sacramento (95825-6706)
PHONE......................916 564-6100
Bruce Kilday, *Partner*
Lawrence Angelo, *Partner*
Carolee Kilduff, *Partner*
Melanie Fitzpatrick, *Admin Asst*
Jandy Jorgensen, *Legal Staff*
EMP: 87 EST: 1997
SALES (est): 10.1MM **Privately Held**
WEB: www.akk-law.com
SIC: **8111** General practice law office

(P-17203)
ARNOLD & PORTER PC
3 Embarcadero Ctr Fl 7, San Francisco (94111-4003)
PHONE......................415 434-1600
Lawrence Rabkin, *Ch of Bd*
Stuart Lipton, *Partner*
Alina Austin, *President*
Judy Lord, *President*
Howard N Rice, *Principal*
▲ EMP: 350 EST: 1957
SQ FT: 70,000
SALES (est): 27.3MM **Privately Held**
SIC: **8111** Corporate, partnership & business law

(P-17204)
BAKER & MCKENZIE LLP
2 Embarcadero Ctr # 1100, San Francisco (94111-3911)
PHONE......................415 576-3000
Peter Engstrom, *Manager*
Bartley Baer, *Partner*
Robin Chesler, *Partner*
Peter Denwood, *Partner*
Tyrrell Prosser, *Partner*
EMP: 120
SALES (corp-wide): 782.2MM **Privately Held**
WEB: www.bakermckenzie.com
SIC: **8111** Administrative & government law; corporate, partnership & business law
PA: Baker & Mckenzie Llp
300 E Randolph St # 5000
Chicago IL 60601
312 861-8000

(P-17205)
BAKER & MCKENZIE LLP
660 Hansen Way Ste 1, Palo Alto (94304-1045)
PHONE......................650 856-2400
Peter Engstrom, *Branch Mgr*
Jon Appleton, *Partner*

PRODUCTS & SERVICES SECTION

8111 - Legal Svcs County (P-17227)

Bartley Baer, *Partner*
Michael Bumbaca, *Partner*
Robin Chesler, *Partner*
EMP: 60
SALES (corp-wide): 782.2MM **Privately Held**
WEB: www.bakermckenzie.com
SIC: 8111 8011 General practice law office; medical centers
PA: Baker & Mckenzie Llp
300 E Randolph St # 5000
Chicago IL 60601
312 861-8000

(P-17206)
BAKER MANOCK & JENSEN PC
Also Called: Baker Mnock Jnsen Attys At Law
5260 N Palm Ave Ste 201, Fresno
(93704-2217)
PHONE...........................559 432-5400
Bob Smittcamp, *CEO*
Donald P Fishbach, *Senior Partner*
Douglas B Jensen, *Senior Partner*
Kendall Manock, *Senior Partner*
David Camenson, *Vice Pres*
EMP: 82 **EST:** 1904
SALES (est): 5.6MM **Privately Held**
WEB: www.bakermanock.com
SIC: 8111 General practice law office

(P-17207)
BARRY BISHOP
6001 Shellmound St # 875, Emeryville
(94608-1957)
PHONE...........................510 596-0888
Nelson C Barry Sr, *President*
Carol Healey, *Shareholder*
Nelson C Barry III, *Vice Pres*
Jeffrey N Haney, *Vice Pres*
Fredric W Trester, *Vice Pres*
EMP: 60 **EST:** 1917
SQ FT: 14,000
SALES (est): 7MM **Privately Held**
WEB: www.bishop-barry.com
SIC: 8111 General practice law office

(P-17208)
BARTKO ZANKEL TARRANT & MIL
1 Embarcadero Ctr Ste 800, San Francisco
(94111-3629)
PHONE...........................415 956-1900
Richard T Tarrant, *President*
Martin I Zankel, *Chairman*
Charles Miller, *Vice Pres*
May Tolentino, *Executive*
John Bartko, *Principal*
EMP: 80 **EST:** 1975
SQ FT: 18,000
SALES (est): 9.7MM **Privately Held**
WEB: www.bzbm.com
SIC: 8111 Corporate, partnership & business law

(P-17209)
BAY AREA LEGAL AID (PA)
1735 Telegraph Ave, Oakland
(94612-2107)
PHONE...........................510 663-4755
Rob Goodin, *Ch of Bd*
Ramon Arias, *President*
Mohammad Sheikh, *CFO*
Elgina Haymon, *Office Mgr*
Athena Chavira, *Technology*
EMP: 40 **EST:** 1966
SQ FT: 15,000
SALES (est): 20MM **Privately Held**
WEB: www.baylegal.org
SIC: 8111 Legal aid service

(P-17210)
BERDING & WEIL LLP (PA)
2175 N Calif Blvd Ste 500, Walnut Creek
(94596-7336)
PHONE...........................925 838-2090
Tyler Berding, *Partner*
Terri Nocco, *President*
Ivanna Arceo, *Analyst*
Lisa Bertorello, *Analyst*
Laurie Schremp, *Analyst*
EMP: 75
SQ FT: 20,000
SALES (est): 16MM **Privately Held**
WEB: www.berding-weil.com
SIC: 8111 General practice attorney, lawyer

(P-17211)
BERG WLLIAM L ATTORNEY AT LAW (PA)
Also Called: Berg Injury Lawyers
2440 Santa Clara Ave, Alameda
(94501-4537)
PHONE...........................510 523-3200
William L Berg, *Owner*
Linda Thomas, *General Mgr*
Carla Williams, *Personnel*
Bernadette Siona, *Opers Staff*
William Ginsburg, *Litigation*
EMP: 50 **EST:** 1980
SALES (est): 5MM **Privately Held**
WEB: www.berginjurylawyers.com
SIC: 8111 Criminal law; specialized law offices, attorneys

(P-17212)
BERLINER COHEN LLP
2844 Park Ave, Merced (95348-3375)
PHONE...........................209 385-0700
Kevin Kelly, *Partner*
Sanford A Berliner, *Partner*
Linda A Callon, *Partner*
Steven J Casad, *Partner*
James P Cashman, *Partner*
EMP: 35
SALES (corp-wide): 16.4MM **Privately Held**
WEB: www.berliner.com
SIC: 8111 General practice law office
PA: Berliner Cohen Llp
10 Almaden Blvd Fl 11
San Jose CA 95113
408 286-5800

(P-17213)
BERLINER COHEN LLP
1601 I St Ste 150, Modesto (95354-1128)
PHONE...........................209 576-1197
Alan J Pinner, *Branch Mgr*
David A Bellumori, *Associate*
EMP: 35
SALES (corp-wide): 16.4MM **Privately Held**
WEB: www.berliner.com
SIC: 8111 General practice law office
PA: Berliner Cohen Llp
10 Almaden Blvd Fl 11
San Jose CA 95113
408 286-5800

(P-17214)
BHATNAGAR LAW OFFICE
84 W Santa Clara St # 560, San Jose
(95113-1812)
PHONE...........................408 564-8051
Nikhil Bhatnagar, *Owner*
EMP: 50 **EST:** 2014
SALES (est): 1.4MM **Privately Held**
SIC: 8111 General practice law office

(P-17215)
BLEDSOE CTHCART DSTEL PETERSON
601 California St Fl 16, San Francisco
(94108-2821)
PHONE...........................415 981-5411
James Treppa, *Partner*
Richard S Deistel, *Partner*
Holly Graves, *Associate*
Jeffrey Hughes, *Associate*
Brie Hutton, *Associate*
EMP: 47 **EST:** 1947
SQ FT: 10,000
SALES (est): 3.4MM **Privately Held**
WEB: www.bledsoelaw.com
SIC: 8111 General practice law office

(P-17216)
BOHM LAW GROUP INC (PA)
4600 Northgate Blvd # 210, Sacramento
(95834-1133)
PHONE...........................916 927-5574
Lawrance Bohm, *CEO*
Zane Hilton,
Bradley Mancuso,
Andrew Kim, *Sr Associate*
Brenda Barragan, *Case Mgr*
EMP: 50 **EST:** 2007
SALES (est): 6.9MM **Privately Held**
WEB: www.bohmlaw.com
SIC: 8111 General practice law office

(P-17217)
BOWLES & VERNA
2121 N Calif Blvd Ste 875, Walnut Creek
(94596-7335)
PHONE...........................925 935-3300
Richard Bowles, *Partner*
Richard Ergo, *Partner*
Kp Dean Harper, *Partner*
Mary Sullivan, *Partner*
Michael Verna, *Partner*
EMP: 50 **EST:** 1985
SQ FT: 15,000
SALES (est): 7.4MM **Privately Held**
WEB: www.bowlesverna.com
SIC: 8111 General practice attorney, lawyer

(P-17218)
BRADFORD & BARTHEL LLP (PA)
2518 River Plaza Dr, Sacramento
(95833-3673)
PHONE...........................916 569-0790
Donald R Barthel, *Partner*
Tom Bradford, *Partner*
Tahmeena Ahmed, *Managing Prtnr*
Fritzie Gumalo, *President*
Arna Hines, *President*
EMP: 50
SALES (est): 37MM **Privately Held**
WEB: www.bradfordbarthel.com
SIC: 8111 General practice law office

(P-17219)
BRAUNHAGEY & BORDEN LLP
351 California St Fl 10, San Francisco
(94104-2411)
PHONE...........................415 599-0210
Noah Hagey, *Partner*
Matt Borden, *Partner*
Sierra Talavera-Baca, *Opers Mgr*
Alexis Smith, *Opers Staff*
Katie Kushnir, *Legal Staff*
EMP: 35 **EST:** 2010
SALES (est): 6.3MM **Privately Held**
WEB: www.braunhagey.com
SIC: 8111 Corporate, partnership & business law

(P-17220)
BRAYTON PURCELL
222 Rush Landing Rd, Novato
(94945-2469)
PHONE...........................801 521-1712
David R Donadio, *Partner*
Kim Beary, *CFO*
Shawna Mahoney, *Admin Sec*
Kelly Rivera, *Admin Asst*
Mike Molakides, *Administration*
EMP: 43 **EST:** 2018
SALES (est): 3.3MM **Privately Held**
WEB: www.braytonlaw.com
SIC: 8111 General practice attorney, lawyer

(P-17221)
BRAYTON PURCELL APC (PA)
222 Rush Landing Rd, Novato
(94945-2469)
P.O. Box 6169 (94948-6169)
PHONE...........................415 898-1555
Alan Richard Brayton, *CEO*
Tom Gremmels, *CFO*
Brandy McCamish, *Executive*
Diane Jacob, *Recruiter*
Jacob Darby, *Facilities Asst*
EMP: 182 **EST:** 1982
SQ FT: 40,000
SALES (est): 25.3MM **Privately Held**
WEB: www.braytonlaw.com
SIC: 8111 General practice attorney, lawyer

(P-17222)
BURNHAM BROWN A PROF CORP
Also Called: Burnham & Brown
1901 Harrison St Ste 1100, Oakland
(94612-3648)
P.O. Box 119 (94604-0119)
PHONE...........................510 444-6800
Gregory D Brown, *President*
Thomas Downey, *Partner*
Michael Johnson, *Partner*
John Verber, *Managing Prtnr*
Linda Andrew-Marshall, *President*
EMP: 120 **EST:** 1899
SQ FT: 50,000
SALES (est): 19.3MM **Privately Held**
WEB: www.burnhambrown.com
SIC: 8111 General practice law office

(P-17223)
CALIFORNIA APPELLATE PROJECT (PA)
345 California St # 1400, San Francisco
(94104-2653)
PHONE...........................415 495-0500
Michael Millman, *Exec Dir*
Mark Garavaglia, *Officer*
Mansi Thakkar, *Counsel*
James McPherson, *Director*
Katrina Hinojosa, *Manager*
EMP: 39 **EST:** 1983
SALES (est): 11.1MM **Privately Held**
WEB: www.capsf.org
SIC: 8111 Administrative & government law

(P-17224)
CANAL ALLIANCE
91 Larkspur St, San Rafael (94901-4820)
PHONE...........................415 485-3074
Gary Phillips, *Principal*
Monica Bonny, *CFO*
Thomas Vogl, *Accountant*
Luat Tran, *Hum Res Coord*
Barbara Smith, *Human Resources*
EMP: 52 **EST:** 2010
SALES (est): 10.2MM **Privately Held**
WEB: www.canalalliance.org
SIC: 8111 Administrative & government law

(P-17225)
CARR & FERRELL LLP (PA)
120 Constitution Dr, Menlo Park
(94025-1107)
PHONE...........................650 812-3400
Barry Carr, *Partner*
John S Ferrell, *General Ptnr*
Stuart Clark, *Partner*
Jill E Fishbein, *Partner*
Jefferson F Scher, *Partner*
EMP: 67 **EST:** 1988
SALES (est): 9.5MM **Privately Held**
WEB: www.carrferrell.com
SIC: 8111 General practice attorney, lawyer; corporate, partnership & business law; patent, trademark & copyright law; labor & employment law

(P-17226)
CARR MC CLELLAN INGERSOLL THOM (PA)
Also Called: Carr, McClellan
216 Park Rd, Burlingame (94010-4200)
P.O. Box 513 (94011-0513)
PHONE...........................650 342-9600
Mark A Cassanego, *President*
Tracy Francis, *President*
Vanessa Hodam, *President*
Steven D Anderson, *CFO*
Krista Mencarelli, *Exec Dir*
EMP: 64 **EST:** 1946
SQ FT: 19,000
SALES (est): 14.2MM **Privately Held**
WEB: www.carr-mcclellan.com
SIC: 8111 General practice attorney, lawyer

(P-17227)
CARROLL BURDICK MC DONOUGH LLP (PA)
275 Battery St Ste 2600, San Francisco
(94111-3358)
PHONE...........................415 989-5900
Angela Bradstreet, *Partner*
Marcelino Nogueiro, *Analyst*
Kelly Sanderson, *Legal Staff*
Carmen Tapia, *Legal Staff*
G David Godwin,
EMP: 142 **EST:** 1948
SQ FT: 50,000
SALES (est): 25.9MM **Privately Held**
WEB: www.squirepattonboggs.com
SIC: 8111 General practice attorney, lawyer

8111 - Legal Svcs County (P-17228)

(P-17228)
CENTRAL VALLEY INJURED (PA)
3101 Mchenry Ave, Modesto (95350-1439)
P.O. Box 3247 (95353-3247)
PHONE 209 522-2777
John R Gonzalez, *President*
EMP: 68 **EST:** 1998
SALES (est): 675.6K **Privately Held**
WEB: www.centralvalleyinjuredworker.com
SIC: 8111 Labor & employment law

(P-17229)
CITY OF VALLEJO
Also Called: Vallejo Plice Dept Plg RES Uni
111 Amador St, Vallejo (94590-6301)
P.O. Box 1031 (94590-0634)
PHONE 707 648-4361
Robert Nichelini, *Chief*
Darrell Handy, *Manager*
EMP: 40
SALES (corp-wide): 166.6MM **Privately Held**
WEB: www.ci.vallejo.ca.us
SIC: 9221 8111 ; legal services
PA: City Of Vallejo
555 Santa Clara St
Vallejo CA 94590
707 648-4575

(P-17230)
CLAPP MORONEY (PA)
5860 Owens Dr Ste 410, Pleasanton
(94588-3980)
PHONE 925 734-0990
L Theodore Scheley III, *President*
Christopher Beeman, *Senior VP*
Robert Bellagamba, *Admin Sec*
Ashley Meyers, *Nurse*
Paula Billanes, *Legal Staff*
EMP: 40
SQ FT: 12,571
SALES (est): 8.8MM **Privately Held**
WEB: www.clappmoroney.com
SIC: 8111 General practice law office

(P-17231)
COBLENTZ PATCH DUFFY BASS LLP
1 Montgomery St Ste 3000, San Francisco
(94104-5500)
PHONE 510 655-4598
Michael Meyers, *Partner*
Coblentz William, *Senior Partner*
Paul Escobosa, *Partner*
Sara Finigan, *Partner*
Susan Jamison, *Partner*
EMP: 100 **EST:** 1997
SQ FT: 30,000
SALES (est): 25.6MM **Privately Held*
WEB: www.coblentzlaw.com
SIC: 8111 General practice attorney, lawyer

(P-17232)
CODDINGTON HCKS DNFRTH A PROF
555 Twin Dolphin Dr # 30, Redwood City
(94065-2129)
PHONE 650 592-5400
Lee J Danforth, *President*
Hyon M Kientzy, *Shareholder*
R Loveland, *Shareholder*
Min Kang, *Practice Mgr*
Richard Grotch, *Admin Sec*
EMP: 44 **EST:** 1981
SQ FT: 8,000
SALES (est): 8.3MM **Privately Held**
WEB: www.chdlawyers.com
SIC: 8111 General practice law office

(P-17233)
COLEMAN CHAVEZ & ASSOC LLP
1731 E Rsvlle Pkwy Ste 20, Roseville
(95661)
PHONE 916 787-2310
Chad Coleman, *Partner*
Anne Brownell, *Partner*
William Hong, *Partner*
Noelle Sage, *Partner*
Thomas Trutanich, *Partner*
EMP: 75 **EST:** 2018
SALES (est): 3.5MM **Privately Held**
WEB: www.cca-law.com
SIC: 8111 General practice law office

(P-17234)
COOLEY LLP
Also Called: Cooley Godward Kronish
3 Embarcadero Ctr Fl 20, San Francisco
(94111-4004)
PHONE 415 693-2000
Lee Benton, *Partner*
Mike Klisch, *Partner*
Edwin Lansang, *Partner*
Phillip Morton, *Partner*
Andrea Perryman, *Partner*
EMP: 100
SALES (corp-wide): 169MM **Privately Held**
WEB: www.cooley.com
SIC: 8111 Specialized law offices, attorneys
PA: Cooley Llp
3175 Hanover St
Palo Alto CA 94304
650 843-5000

(P-17235)
COOLEY LLP (PA)
3175 Hanover St, Palo Alto (94304-1130)
PHONE 650 843-5000
Joe Conroy, *Managing Prtnr*
Tom Reicher -, *Partner*
Kenneth J Adelson, *Partner*
Mike Attanasio, *Partner*
Andrew Basile, *Partner*
EMP: 300 **EST:** 1935
SALES (est): 169MM **Privately Held**
WEB: www.cooley.com
SIC: 8111 General practice attorney, lawyer

(P-17236)
COOPER WHITE & COOPER LLP (PA)
201 California St Fl 17, San Francisco
(94111-5002)
PHONE 415 433-1900
Mark P Schreiber, *Partner*
Walter Hansell, *Partner*
Keith Howard, *Partner*
Peter Sibley, *Partner*
Jed Solomon, *Partner*
EMP: 120
SQ FT: 44,000
SALES (est): 13.8MM **Privately Held**
WEB: www.cwclaw.com
SIC: 8111 General practice attorney, lawyer

(P-17237)
COTCHETT PITRE & MCCARTHY LLP
840 Malcolm Rd Ste 200, Burlingame
(94010-1413)
PHONE 650 697-6000
Frank M Pitre, *Partner*
Joseph W Cotchett, *Partner*
Niall Mccarthy, *Partner*
Victor Luscap, *Chief Mktg Ofcr*
Phyllis Lee, *Executive*
EMP: 40 **EST:** 1967
SALES (est): 10MM **Privately Held**
WEB: www.cpmlegal.com
SIC: 8111 Specialized law offices, attorneys

(P-17238)
COUNTY OF ALAMEDA
Also Called: District Attorney
1401 Lakeside Dr Ste 802, Oakland
(94612-4305)
PHONE 510 272-6222
Dave Vudde, *Director*
EMP: 58 **Privately Held**
WEB: www.acgov.org
SIC: 9222 8111 District Attorneys' offices; ; specialized legal services
PA: County Of Alameda
1221 Oak St Ste 555
Oakland CA 94612
510 272-6691

(P-17239)
COUNTY OF SACRAMENTO
Also Called: Sheriff's Dept
1000 River Walk Way, Carmichael
(95608-6134)
PHONE 916 874-1953
Don Devlin, *Branch Mgr*
EMP: 55
SALES (est): 3.1B **Privately Held**
WEB: www.saccounty.net
SIC: 9221 8111 Sheriffs' offices; ; legal services
PA: County Of Sacramento
700 H St Ste 7650
Sacramento CA 95814
916 874-8515

(P-17240)
COUNTY OF YUBA
Also Called: Office of District Attorney
215 5th St Ste 152, Marysville
(95901-5737)
PHONE 530 749-7770
Tonya English, *Supervisor*
EMP: 55
SALES (corp-wide): 212MM **Privately Held**
WEB: www.co.yuba.ca.us
SIC: 8111 9199 Legal services;
PA: County Of Yuba
915 8th St Ste 109
Marysville CA 95901
530 749-7575

(P-17241)
COX WTTON GRFFIN HNSEN PLOS LL
900 Front St, San Francisco (94111-1427)
PHONE 415 438-4600
Terence Cox, *Partner*
Mitchell Griffin, *Partner*
Rupert Hansen, *Partner*
Gregory Poulous, *Partner*
Richard Wootton, *Partner*
▲ **EMP:** 56 **EST:** 1996
SALES (est): 5.9MM **Privately Held**
WEB: www.cwlfirm.com
SIC: 8111 Corporate, partnership & business law

(P-17242)
CUNEO BLACK WARD MISSLER A LAW
Also Called: Cuneo, Black, Ward & Missler
700 University Ave # 110, Sacramento
(95825-6722)
P.O. Box 276650 (95827-6650)
PHONE 916 363-8822
John Black, *President*
Jim Cuneo, *Partner*
Jim Missler, *Partner*
James Missler, *Shareholder*
Alan Jong, *CFO*
EMP: 50 **EST:** 1990
SQ FT: 13,000
SALES (est): 5.4MM **Privately Held**
WEB: www.cbwmlaw.com
SIC: 8111 General practice attorney, lawyer

(P-17243)
CURTIS LGAL GROUP A PROF LAW C
1300 K St Fl 2, Modesto (95354-0928)
P.O. Box 3030 (95353-3030)
PHONE 209 521-1800
Ralph S Curtis, *Partner*
Carol Gilbert, *Legal Staff*
EMP: 50 **EST:** 1953
SQ FT: 18,000
SALES (est): 6.6MM **Privately Held**
WEB: www.curtislegalgroup.com
SIC: 8111 General practice law office

(P-17244)
DAMRELL NELSON SCHRIMP PALL (PA)
1601 I St Ste 500, Modesto (95354-1134)
PHONE 209 526-3500
Duane Nelson, *President*
Frank C Damrell Jr, *President*
Michelle Kenzie, *CFO*
Kirin Virk, *Officer*
Duane L Nelson, *Vice Pres*
EMP: 46 **EST:** 1970
SALES (est): 5.4MM **Privately Held**
WEB: www.modestolawyers.com
SIC: 8111 General practice law office

(P-17245)
DANNIS WLVER KLLEY A PROF CORP (PA)
275 Battery St Ste 1150, San Francisco
(94111-3333)
PHONE 415 543-4111
Gregory Dannis, *President*
Candace Bandoian, *Shareholder*
Mark Kelley, *Shareholder*
Jonathan Pearl, *Shareholder*
Sarah Sutherland, *Shareholder*
EMP: 70 **EST:** 1976
SQ FT: 14,000
SALES (est): 10.4MM **Privately Held**
WEB: www.dwkesq.com
SIC: 8111 General practice attorney, lawyer

(P-17246)
DAVID ALLEN & ASSOCIATES (PA)
Also Called: Allen David & Assoc Lm 724
5230 Folsom Blvd, Sacramento
(95819-4537)
PHONE 916 455-4800
David Allen, *President*
Bill Allen, *Exec Dir*
Louisa Rendon, *Office Mgr*
Daniel Garcia, *IT/INT Sup*
Clark Betscharт, *Controller*
EMP: 36 **EST:** 1985
SQ FT: 4,000
SALES (est): 7.2MM **Privately Held**
WEB: www.davidallenlaw.com
SIC: 8111 General practice attorney, lawyer

(P-17247)
DAVID DARROCH
300 Lakeside Dr Fl 24, Oakland
(94612-3534)
PHONE 510 835-9100
H James Wulfsberg, *Ch of Bd*
Charles W Reese, *President*
Wulfsberg Colvig, *Producer*
EMP: 42 **EST:** 1969
SQ FT: 34,000
SALES (est): 868.4K **Privately Held**
SIC: 8111 General practice attorney, lawyer

(P-17248)
DAVIS POLK & WARDWELL LLP
1600 El Camino Real # 100, Menlo Park
(94025-4121)
PHONE 650 752-2000
Carol Icasiano, *Admin Mgr*
Pascale Voillot, *Office Mgr*
Rhonda Hart, *Admin Asst*
Debra Schlesinger, *Admin Asst*
Rachel Kleinberg, *Administration*
EMP: 92
SALES (corp-wide): 375.3MM **Privately Held**
WEB: www.davispolk.com
SIC: 8111 General practice attorney, lawyer
PA: Davis Polk & Wardwell Llp
450 Lexington Ave Fl 10
New York NY 10017
212 450-4000

(P-17249)
DAVIS WRIGHT TREMAINE LLP
505 Montgomery St Ste 800, San Francisco
(94111-6533)
PHONE 415 276-6500
Jeff Gray, *Partner*
Gerald Hinkley, *Partner*
Michael Labianca, *Partner*
Paul Leboffe, *Partner*
Gregory Miller, *Partner*
EMP: 91
SALES (corp-wide): 238.7MM **Privately Held**
WEB: www.dwtholiday.com
SIC: 8111 General practice attorney, lawyer
PA: Davis Wright Tremaine Llp
920 5th Ave Ste 3300
Seattle WA 98104
206 622-3150

▲ = Import ▼ = Export
♦ = Import/Export

PRODUCTS & SERVICES SECTION

8111 - Legal Svcs County (P-17272)

(P-17250)
DICKENSON PTMAN FGRTY INC A PR (PA)
1455 1st St Ste 301, NAPA (94559-2822)
PHONE..................707 252-7122
Rodeo Ocampo, *Office Mgr*
Scott Gerien, *Partner*
Elizabeth Mayhew, *Trust Officer*
Charles Dickenson, *Info Tech Mgr*
Melvin Cheah, *Network Mgr*
EMP: 44 **EST:** 1966
SQ FT: 3,000
SALES (est): 7.1MM **Privately Held**
WEB: www.dpf-law.com
SIC: 8111 General practice attorney, lawyer; general practice law office

(P-17251)
DIEPENBROCK ELKIN LLP
555 University Ave # 200, Sacramento (95825-6585)
PHONE..................916 492-5000
Bradley Elkin, *President*
Michael V Brady, *Shareholder*
Karen Diepenbrock, *Shareholder*
Michael Brady, *Chairman*
Mark Harrison, *Vice Pres*
EMP: 35 **EST:** 1994
SQ FT: 20,000
SALES (est): 4.7MM **Privately Held**
WEB: www.diepenbrock.com
SIC: 8111 General practice attorney, lawyer

(P-17252)
DILLINGHAM & MURPHY LLP (PA)
353 Sacramento St # 2000, San Francisco (94111-3675)
PHONE..................415 397-2700
William Dillingham, *Partner*
Lucy Bettis, *Partner*
John N Dahlberg, *Partner*
Albert A Foster, *Partner*
William Gaus, *Partner*
EMP: 42 **EST:** 1982
SQ FT: 4,600
SALES (est): 5.8MM **Privately Held**
WEB: www.dillinghammurphy.com
SIC: 8111 General practice attorney, lawyer

(P-17253)
DISABILITY RIGHTS CALIFORNIA (PA)
Also Called: D R C
1831 K St, Sacramento (95811-4114)
PHONE..................916 488-9950
Izetta Jackson, *President*
Herb Anderson, *CFO*
Diana Lynn Nelson, *CFO*
Melody Pomraning, *Comms Dir*
Catherine Blakemore, *Exec Dir*
EMP: 55 **EST:** 1978
SQ FT: 8,500
SALES (est): 36MM **Privately Held**
WEB: www.disabilityrightsca.org
SIC: 8111 Legal services

(P-17254)
DONAHUE & DAVIES LLP
1 Natoma St, Folsom (95630-2637)
P.O. Box 277010, Sacramento (95827-7010)
PHONE..................916 817-2900
Jim Donahue, *Partner*
Richard Caulfield, *Partner*
Robert Davies, *Partner*
James Donahue, *Partner*
Marcella Schafer, *Admin Sec*
EMP: 37 **EST:** 1984
SQ FT: 10,267
SALES (est): 5.1MM **Privately Held**
WEB: www.donahuedavies.com
SIC: 8111 General practice attorney, lawyer

(P-17255)
DONAHUE FITZGERALD LLP
1999 Harrison St Ste 2600, Oakland (94612-4702)
PHONE..................510 451-3300
Michael J Dalton, *Partner*
EMP: 36 **EST:** 2014
SALES (est): 10.7MM **Privately Held**
WEB: www.donahue.com
SIC: 8111 General practice law office

(P-17256)
DONAHUE GALLAGER WOODS LLP (PA)
1999 Harrison St Ste 2500, Oakland (94612-4705)
PHONE..................415 381-4161
Lawrence K Rockwell, *Partner*
George J Barron, *Partner*
John J Coppinger, *Partner*
Michael J Dalton, *Partner*
Eric W Doney, *Partner*
EMP: 75 **EST:** 1918
SQ FT: 20,827
SALES (est): 7MM **Privately Held**
WEB: www.donahue.com
SIC: 8111 General practice attorney, lawyer

(P-17257)
DOWNEY BRAND LLP (PA)
621 Capitol Mall Fl 18, Sacramento (95814-4731)
PHONE..................916 444-1000
Dale A Stern, *Managing Prtnr*
David R E Aladjem, *Partner*
Rhonda Cate Canby, *Partner*
Julie A Carter, *Partner*
Thomas N Cooper, *Partner*
EMP: 207 **EST:** 1926
SALES (est): 30MM **Privately Held**
WEB: www.downeybrand.com
SIC: 8111 General practice attorney, lawyer

(P-17258)
DREYER BBICH BCCOLA CLLHAM LLP
20 Bicentennial Cir, Sacramento (95826-2802)
PHONE..................916 379-3500
Roger A Dreyer, *Managing Prtnr*
Joseph J Babich, *Partner*
Robert A Buccola, *Partner*
William Callaham, *Partner*
Kristina Bickford, *Admin Sec*
EMP: 53 **EST:** 1984
SQ FT: 5,000
SALES (est): 6.2MM **Privately Held**
WEB: www.dbbwc.com
SIC: 8111 General practice attorney, lawyer

(P-17259)
DREYER BBICH BCCOLA WD CMPORA (PA)
20 Bicentennial Cir, Sacramento (95826-2802)
PHONE..................916 379-3500
Roger Dreyer, *Principal*
Nathaniel Smith, *Partner*
Noemi Esparza, *Bd of Directors*
Joseph Babich, *Principal*
Robert Buccola, *Principal*
EMP: 96 **EST:** 2012
SALES (est): 10.1MM **Privately Held**
WEB: www.dbbwc.com
SIC: 8111 General practice attorney, lawyer

(P-17260)
DURIE TANGRI LLP
217 Leidesdorff St, San Francisco (94111-3007)
PHONE..................415 362-6666
Johanna Calabria, *Partner*
Daralyn Durie, *Partner*
Andrea Dupree, *Admin Sec*
Sarka Trenciansky, *Admin Sec*
Christi Vaughn, *Bookkeeper*
EMP: 35 **EST:** 2010
SALES (est): 7MM **Privately Held**
WEB: www.durietangri.com
SIC: 8111 Specialized legal services

(P-17261)
EILEEN NOTTOLI
Also Called: Allen Matkins
3 Embarcadero Ctr # 1200, San Francisco (94111-4003)
PHONE..................415 837-1515
EMP: 75 **EST:** 2013
SALES (est): 1.7MM **Privately Held**
SIC: 8111 Legal Services Office

(P-17262)
EPSTEIN BECKER & GREEN PC
655 Montgomery St # 1150, San Francisco (94111-2635)
PHONE..................415 398-3500
Bill Helvestine, *Managing Prtnr*
Rheonna Winston, *Office Mgr*
Nathaniel M Glasser,
EMP: 81
SALES (corp-wide): 117MM **Privately Held**
WEB: www.ebglaw.com
SIC: 8111 General practice attorney, lawyer
PA: Epstein Becker & Green, P.C.
875 3rd Ave Fl 19
New York NY 10022
212 351-4500

(P-17263)
EQUAL RIGHTS ADVOCATES INC
611 Mission St Fl 4, San Francisco (94105-3535)
PHONE..................415 621-0672
Irma D Herrera, *Exec Dir*
Francesca Bitton, *COO*
Maria Alvarez, *Finance*
Jess Eagle, *Corp Comm Staff*
Kathy Mayer, *Deputy Dir*
EMP: 48 **EST:** 1972
SALES (est): 2.8MM **Privately Held**
WEB: www.equalrights.org
SIC: 8111 General practice attorney, lawyer; general practice law office

(P-17264)
FENWICK & WEST LLP (PA)
801 California St, Mountain View (94041-1990)
PHONE..................650 988-8500
Gordon K Davidson, *General Ptnr*
Michael R Blum, *Partner*
Darren E Donnelly, *Partner*
Dan Dorosin, *Partner*
Joshua Geffon, *Partner*
EMP: 375 **EST:** 1971
SALES (est): 139.3MM **Privately Held**
WEB: www.fenwick.com
SIC: 8111 General practice attorney, lawyer

(P-17265)
FENWICK & WEST LLP
555 California St # 1200, San Francisco (94104-1503)
PHONE..................415 875-2300
Kacey Leonis, *Office Mgr*
Sam Angus, *Partner*
Madison Kaiser, *President*
Linda Kinard, *Admin Sec*
Phyllis O 'sullivan, *Admin Sec*
EMP: 120
SALES (corp-wide): 139.3MM **Privately Held**
WEB: www.fenwick.com
SIC: 8111 General practice attorney, lawyer; patent, trademark & copyright law; taxation law
PA: Fenwick & West Llp
801 California St
Mountain View CA 94041
650 988-8500

(P-17266)
FITZGRALD ABBOTT BEARDSLEY LLP
1221 Broadway Fl 21, Oakland (94612-1837)
P.O. Box 12867 (94604-2867)
PHONE..................510 451-3300
Michael S Word, *Managing Prtnr*
Susan Von,
EMP: 37 **EST:** 1884
SQ FT: 20,000
SALES (est): 1.9MM **Privately Held**
SIC: 8111 General practice law office

(P-17267)
FITZGRALD ALVREZ CMMO A PROF L
Also Called: Madera Public Defender Office
221 N I St, Madera (93637-4491)
PHONE..................559 674-4696
Mike Fitzgerald, *Branch Mgr*
EMP: 41
SALES (corp-wide): 4.8MM **Privately Held**
WEB: www.ciummolaw.com
SIC: 8111 General practice attorney, lawyer
PA: Fitzgerald, Alvarez & Ciummo, A Professional Law Corporation
123 E 4th St
Madera CA 93638
559 673-7227

(P-17268)
FOX ROTHSCHILD LLP
1 Sansome St Ste 2850, San Francisco (94104-4426)
PHONE..................415 539-3336
Raquel L Sefton, *Branch Mgr*
EMP: 70
SALES (corp-wide): 113.3MM **Privately Held**
WEB: www.foxrothschild.com
SIC: 8111 Divorce & family law
PA: Fox Rothschild Llp
2000 Market St Fl 20
Philadelphia PA 19103
215 299-2000

(P-17269)
FREEMAN D AIUTO PROF LAW CORP
Also Called: Freeman Brown Sperry & D Aiuto
1818 Grand Canal Blvd # 4, Stockton (95207-8109)
PHONE..................209 474-1818
Maxwell Freeman, *Principal*
Dolores Montion, *Office Mgr*
EMP: 66 **EST:** 1965
SQ FT: 2,000
SALES (est): 3.3MM **Privately Held**
WEB: www.freemanfirm.com
SIC: 8111 General practice attorney, lawyer; general practice law office

(P-17270)
GALLOWAY LUCCHESE EVERSON
2300 Contra Costa Blvd, Walnut Creek (94596)
PHONE..................925 930-9090
G Patrick Galloway, *President*
David Lucchese, *Senior Partner*
David R Lucchese, *Vice Pres*
Julie Shivji, *Accounting Mgr*
Carrie Hughes, *Legal Staff*
EMP: 50 **EST:** 1975
SQ FT: 13,700
SALES (est): 5.5MM **Privately Held**
WEB: www.glattys.com
SIC: 8111 General practice law office

(P-17271)
GAW VAN MALE SMITH MYERS
1411 Oliver Rd Ste 300, Fairfield (94534-3433)
PHONE..................707 425-1250
EMP: 62
SALES (corp-wide): 9.4MM **Privately Held**
WEB: www.gvmlaw.com
SIC: 8111 Attorneys
PA: Gaw, Van Male, Smith, Myers & Miroglio A Professional Corp
1000 Main St Ste 300
Napa CA 94559
707 469-7100

(P-17272)
GCA LAW PARTNERS LLP
2570 W El Cmino Real Ste, Mountain View (94040)
PHONE..................650 428-3900
John W Hollingsworth, *Partner*
Deborah Aikins, *Partner*
Betsy Bayha, *Partner*
William Connell, *Partner*
Kimberly Donovan, *Partner*

(PA)=Parent Co (HQ)=Headquarters (DH)=Div Headquarters
✪ = New Business established in last 2 years

8111 - Legal Svcs County (P-17273)

EMP: 45 EST: 1988
SQ FT: 10,000
SALES (est): 7MM Privately Held
WEB: www.gcalaw.com
SIC: 8111 General practice law office

(P-17273)
GIANELLI & ASSOCIATES
1014 16th St, Modesto (95354-1106)
PHONE 209 521-6260
Michael L Gianelli, *CEO*
Rachelle V Pol, *Bd of Directors*
David Gianelli, *Vice Pres*
Judi Acevedo, *Legal Staff*
Lynette Miller, *Legal Staff*
EMP: 41 EST: 1974
SQ FT: 7,000
SALES (est): 4.1MM Privately Held
WEB: www.gianelli-law.com
SIC: 8111 General practice law office

(P-17274)
GLASPY & GLASPY A PROF CORP
100 Pringle Ave Ste 750, Walnut Creek (94596-7330)
P.O. Box 8104 (94596-8104)
PHONE 408 279-8844
David M Glaspy, *President*
Thomas C Glaspy, *Vice Pres*
▲ EMP: 50 EST: 1978
SALES (est): 3.7MM Privately Held
WEB: www.mgmlaw.com
SIC: 8111 General practice law office

(P-17275)
GOLDFARB & LIPMAN LLP (PA)
1300 Clay St Fl 11th, Oakland (94612-1429)
PHONE 510 836-6336
Thomas Webber, *Managing Prtnr*
M David Kroot, *Managing Prtnr*
M Kroot, *Managing Prtnr*
Karen Tiedemann, *Managing Prtnr*
Carolyn Harper, *Executive*
EMP: 40 EST: 1969
SQ FT: 12,000
SALES (est): 5.8MM Privately Held
WEB: www.goldfarblipman.com
SIC: 8111 General practice law office

(P-17276)
GOLDSTEIN DMCHAK BLLER BRGEN D
300 Lakeside Dr Ste 1000, Oakland (94612-3536)
PHONE 510 763-9800
Teresa Demchak, *President*
Morris Baller, *Principal*
David Borgen, *Principal*
Linda Dardarian, *Principal*
Theresa Denchak, *Principal*
EMP: 42 EST: 1981
SALES (est): 4.3MM Privately Held
WEB: www.gbdhlegal.com
SIC: 8111 General practice law office

(P-17277)
GORDON REES SCULLY MANSUKHANI
655 University Ave # 200, Sacramento (95825-6707)
PHONE 916 830-6900
Kathleen M Rhoads, *Managing Prtnr*
Veronica Whitaker, *Admin Sec*
Cindy Wallin, *Legal Staff*
Kristin Blocher, *Counsel*
Kara Keister, *Counsel*
EMP: 35
SALES (corp-wide): 271.7MM Privately Held
WEB: www.grsm.com
SIC: 8111 Specialized law offices, attorneys
PA: Gordon Rees Scully Mansukhani, Llp.
275 Battery St Ste 2000
San Francisco CA 94111
415 986-5900

(P-17278)
GORDON REES SCULLY MANSUKHANI
Also Called: Gordon & Rees
1111 Broadway Ste 1700, Oakland (94607-4023)
PHONE 510 463-8600
Dion N Cominos, *Principal*
Frank Gonzalez, *Executive Asst*
Frances Perez, *Admin Sec*
Kristine Blanco, *Administration*
Jovencio Chan, *Technology*
EMP: 35
SALES (corp-wide): 271.7MM Privately Held
WEB: www.grsm.com
SIC: 8111 Specialized law offices, attorneys
PA: Gordon Rees Scully Mansukhani, Llp.
275 Battery St Ste 2000
San Francisco CA 94111
415 986-5900

(P-17279)
GORDON REES SCULLY MANSUKHANI (PA)
275 Battery St Ste 2000, San Francisco (94111-3361)
PHONE 415 986-5900
Dion N Cominos, *Partner*
Jorge J Perez, *Partner*
Hayes J Ryan, *Partner*
Kenneth Strong, *Partner*
David C Capell, *Managing Prtnr*
EMP: 325 EST: 1974
SQ FT: 57,500
SALES (est): 271.7MM Privately Held
WEB: www.grsm.com
SIC: 8111 Corporate, partnership & business law

(P-17280)
GRAHAM & JAMES LLP
Also Called: Squires, Sanders and Dempsey
1 Maritime Plz Fl 3, San Francisco (94111-3406)
PHONE 415 954-0200
Tom Wobster, *Manager*
Alexander D Calhoun, *Counsel*
Patrick J Fields, *Counsel*
David M Lofholm, *Counsel*
Bernard F Rose, *Counsel*
EMP: 700 EST: 1925
SQ FT: 60,000
SALES (est): 26.8MM Privately Held
SIC: 8111 General practice law office

(P-17281)
GREENAN PFFER SLLNDER LLLY LLP
6111 Bollinger Canyon Rd # 500, San Ramon (94583-5186)
P.O. Box 10 (94583-0010)
PHONE 925 866-1000
H R Peffer, *Principal*
Nelson Hsieh, *Partner*
Jim Greenan, *Tech/Comp Coord*
Helen Chen, *Counsel*
Cheryl Calone, *Manager*
EMP: 40 EST: 2001
SALES (est): 6.2MM Privately Held
WEB: www.gpsllp.com
SIC: 8111 8011 General practice attorney, lawyer; medical centers

(P-17282)
GREENBERG TRAURIG LLP
1900 University Ave Fl 5, East Palo Alto (94303-2283)
PHONE 650 328-8500
Lance Joseph, *Branch Mgr*
Jeff Henderson, *Shareholder*
Ross Kaufman, *Shareholder*
Mike Robson, *Shareholder*
Rhonda Taylor, *Admin Asst*
EMP: 73
SALES (corp-wide): 1.1B Privately Held
WEB: www.eb5insights.com
SIC: 8111 General practice attorney, lawyer
HQ: Greenberg Traurig, Llp
1 Intl Pl Ste 2000
Boston MA 02110

(P-17283)
GREENE RDVSKY MALONEY SHARE LP
4 Embarcadero Ctr # 4000, San Francisco (94111-4100)
PHONE 415 981-1400
Mark Hennigh, *Managing Prtnr*
Richard Green, *Senior Partner*
James Abrams, *Partner*
Thomas Feldstein, *Partner*
James Fotenos, *Partner*
EMP: 69 EST: 1984
SQ FT: 18,800
SALES (est): 11.7MM Privately Held
WEB: www.greeneradovsky.com
SIC: 8111 Specialized law offices, attorneys; corporate, partnership & business law; real estate law; taxation law

(P-17284)
GRUNSKY EBEY FARRAR & HOWEL
240 Westgate Dr Ste 100, Watsonville (95076-2462)
PHONE 831 688-1180
Frederick H Ebey, *President*
Bob Wall, *Shareholder*
Alan J Smith, *CFO*
James S Farrar, *Vice Pres*
Kathleen A Franke, *Vice Pres*
EMP: 41 EST: 1945
SQ FT: 16,000
SALES (est): 4.2MM Privately Held
WEB: www.grunskylaw.com
SIC: 8111 Real estate law; general practice law office

(P-17285)
GUNDERSON DETTMER STOUGH VILLE (PA)
550 Allerton St, Redwood City (94063-1524)
PHONE 650 321-2400
Robert Gunderson, *Partner*
Darrin Brown, *Partner*
Colin Chapman, *Partner*
Dan O Connor, *Partner*
Joshua Cook, *Partner*
EMP: 125
SALES (est): 28.1MM Privately Held
WEB: www.gunder.com
SIC: 8111 General practice law office

(P-17286)
HANNA BRPHY MCLEAN MCLEER JNSE (PA)
1956 Webster St Ste 450, Oakland (94612-2930)
PHONE 510 839-1180
Michael White, *Managing Prtnr*
Joseph Nisim, *Partner*
Barbara Wood, *Partner*
Leslie Tuxhorn, *Managing Prtnr*
Wendy Harnett, *Admin Mgr*
EMP: 50 EST: 1943
SQ FT: 10,000
SALES (est): 31.9MM Privately Held
WEB: www.hannabrophy.com
SIC: 8111 General practice law office

(P-17287)
HANSON BRIDGETT LLP (PA)
425 Market St Fl 26, San Francisco (94105-5401)
PHONE 415 543-2055
Andrew G Giacomini, *Partner*
Lawrence Cirelli, *Partner*
John T CU, *Partner*
Batya Forsyth, *Partner*
Bradfordr Hise, *Partner*
EMP: 263 EST: 1958
SQ FT: 79,120
SALES (est): 37.2MM Privately Held
WEB: www.hansonbridgett.com
SIC: 8111 General practice attorney, lawyer

(P-17288)
HASSARD BONNINGTON LLP (PA)
Also Called: HB
275 Battery St Ste 1600, San Francisco (94111-3993)
PHONE 415 288-9800
James M Goodman, *General Prtnr*
Phillip F Ward, *Partner*
Graham Gillies, *Info Tech Mgr*
Eliza Busch, *Legal Staff*
Renee Richards, *Counsel*
EMP: 77 EST: 1945
SALES (est): 10.8MM Privately Held
WEB: www.hassard.com
SIC: 8111 General practice attorney, lawyer

(P-17289)
HAYES SCOTT BNINO ELLNGSON MCL
999 Skyway Rd Ste 310, San Carlos (94070-2722)
PHONE 650 551-8929
Matthew A Bisbee, *Partner*
Mark G Bonino, *Partner*
Daniel S Clark Jr, *Partner*
George E Clause, *Partner*
Vivian V Countryman, *Partner*
EMP: 37 EST: 2010
SALES (est): 7.6MM Privately Held
WEB: www.hayesscott.com
SIC: 8111 General practice law office

(P-17290)
HICKMAN PLRMO TRONG BECKER LLP
1 Almaden Blvd 12, San Jose (95113-2211)
PHONE 408 414-1080
Edward Becker, *Managing Prtnr*
Edward A Becker, *Managing Prtnr*
Darci Sakamoto, *Admin Sec*
Teresa Austin, *Administration*
Sarah Bassett, *Counsel*
EMP: 45 EST: 2000
SQ FT: 17,500
SALES (est): 6.4MM Privately Held
WEB: www.hickmanbecker.com
SIC: 8111 General practice attorney, lawyer

(P-17291)
HOGAN LOVELLS US LLP
3 Embarcadero Ctr # 1500, San Francisco (94111-4038)
PHONE 415 374-2300
Richard Barnes, *CIO*
Christine Gateau, *Counsel*
Anna Glinke, *Sr Associate*
Michael Roberts, *Sr Associate*
Karen Snell, *Manager*
EMP: 63
SALES (corp-wide): 473.1MM Privately Held
WEB: www.hlregulation.com
SIC: 8111 Corporate, partnership & business law
PA: Hogan Lovells Us Llp
555 13th St Nw
Washington DC 20004
202 637-5600

(P-17292)
HOGAN LOVELLS US LLP
4085 Campbell Ave, Menlo Park (94025-1939)
PHONE 650 463-4000
Joanna Nicholson, *Business Mgr*
Marianne Johnson, *Human Resources*
Alali Dagogo-Jack, *Sr Associate*
EMP: 63
SALES (corp-wide): 473.1MM Privately Held
WEB: www.hlregulation.com
SIC: 8111 Corporate, partnership & business law
PA: Hogan Lovells Us Llp
555 13th St Nw
Washington DC 20004
202 637-5600

(P-17293)
HOPKINS & CARLEY A LAW CORP (PA)
70 S 1st St, San Jose (95113-2406)
P.O. Box 1469 (95109-1469)
PHONE 408 286-9800
William S Klein, *Principal*
Karin M Cogbill, *Shareholder*
Steven A Ellenberg, *Shareholder*
Ernie Malaspina, *Shareholder*
John F Hopkins, *President*
EMP: 80 EST: 1968
SQ FT: 33,000

▲ = Import ▼ = Export
◆ = Import/Export

PRODUCTS & SERVICES SECTION

8111 - Legal Svcs County (P-17316)

SALES (est): 29.8MM **Privately Held**
WEB: www.hopkinscarley.com
SIC: 8111 Corporate, partnership & business law; divorce & family law; environmental law; real estate law

(P-17294)
IMT ASSOCIATES
1850 San Leandro Blvd, San Leandro (94577-3547)
PHONE.....................510 352-6000
Sharon Toth, *Owner*
Connie Muir, *Office Mgr*
Tina Chancellor, *Bookkeeper*
Rik Van Antwerpen, *Case Mgr*
Elyssa Eldridge, *Manager*
EMP: 35 **EST:** 1985
SQ FT: 7,000
SALES (est): 2.6MM **Privately Held**
WEB: www.imtassociates.com
SIC: 8111 6733 Legal services; administrator of private estates, non-operating

(P-17295)
JACKSON & HERTOGS LLP
909 Montgomery St Ste 200, San Francisco (94133-4650)
PHONE.....................415 986-4559
Ilana Drummond, *Partner*
Norman C Plotkin, *Partner*
Brooks Paine, *Office Mgr*
Thomas Kocon, *Info Tech Mgr*
Lisa Gelardi, *Human Res Mgr*
EMP: 40 **EST:** 1947
SALES (est): 5.7MM **Privately Held**
WEB: www.jackson-hertogs.com
SIC: 8111 General practice law office

(P-17296)
JAMES CUNNINGHAM
Also Called: Cunningham Legal
200 Auburn Folsom Rd # 106, Auburn (95603-5028)
PHONE.....................530 269-1515
James Cunningham, *Owner*
April Shemtov, *Planning*
Terri Rose, *Controller*
Laura Gleason, *Director*
EMP: 43 **EST:** 2014
SALES (est): 5.8MM **Privately Held**
WEB: www.cunninghamlegal.com
SIC: 8111 General practice attorney, lawyer

(P-17297)
JOHNSON SCHCHTER LWIS A PROF L
2180 Harvard St Ste 560, Sacramento (95815-3320)
PHONE.....................916 921-5800
Robert H Johnson, *Chairman*
Luther Lewis, *Treasurer*
Alesa Schachter, *Vice Pres*
George Holt, *Director*
Kellie M Murphy, *Director*
EMP: 42 **EST:** 1981
SQ FT: 8,500
SALES (est): 3.5MM **Privately Held**
WEB: www.jsl-law.com
SIC: 8111 General practice law office

(P-17298)
JONES HALL A PROF LAW CORP
475 Sansome St Ste 1700, San Francisco (94111-3147)
PHONE.....................415 391-5780
William H Madison, *President*
James A Wawrzyniak, *Shareholder*
Michael Castelli, *Vice Pres*
Thomas Downey, *Vice Pres*
Greg Harrington, *Vice Pres*
EMP: 35 **EST:** 1978
SALES (est): 6.8MM **Privately Held**
WEB: www.joneshall.com
SIC: 8111 Specialized law offices, attorneys

(P-17299)
JORGENSEN SGEL MC CLURE FLGEL
1100 Alma St Ste 210, Menlo Park (94025-3344)
PHONE.....................650 324-9300
John L Flegel, *Partner*
Diane Greenburg, *Partner*
John Jorgensen, *Partner*
William L Mc Clure, *Partner*
Mavin S Siegel, *Partner*
EMP: 47 **EST:** 1960
SALES (est): 5.3MM **Privately Held**
WEB: www.jsmf.com
SIC: 8111 General practice attorney, lawyer

(P-17300)
JULIE PEARL A PROF CORP
Also Called: Pearl Law Group
560 Miramonte Ave, Palo Alto (94306-1036)
PHONE.....................415 771-7500
Julie Pearl, *CEO*
Patti Paul, *CFO*
Elke Osadnik, *Vice Pres*
Evan Green, *Principal*
Kenneth Kc Ing, *Principal*
EMP: 92 **EST:** 1993
SALES (est): 6.4MM **Privately Held**
SIC: 8111 General practice law office

(P-17301)
JUSTICE DVRSITY CTR OF THE BAR
1360 Mission St, San Francisco (94103-2626)
PHONE.....................415 575-3130
Teresa Friend, *Branch Mgr*
EMP: 71 **Privately Held**
WEB: www.sfbar.org
SIC: 8111 Legal aid service
HQ: The Justice And Diversity Center Of The Bar Association Of San Francisco
201 Mission St Ste 400
San Francisco CA 94105
415 982-1600

(P-17302)
KAZAN MCCLAIN STTRLEY GRNWOOD
55 Harrison St Ste 400, Oakland (94607-3858)
PHONE.....................877 995-6372
Steven Kazan, *Partner*
Denise Abrams, *Partner*
Justin Bosl, *Partner*
Denyse Clancy, *Partner*
Gordon Greenwood, *Partner*
EMP: 108 **EST:** 1975
SALES (est): 1.5MM **Privately Held**
WEB: www.kazanlaw.com
SIC: 8111 General practice law office

(P-17303)
KEKER VAN NEST & PETERS LLP
633 Battery St Bsmt 91, San Francisco (94111-1899)
PHONE.....................415 391-5400
John W Keker,
Steven Taylor, *Managing Prtnr*
DOT D Fox, *President*
Patty Lemos, *President*
Laure Mandin, *President*
EMP: 100 **EST:** 1978
SQ FT: 70,000
SALES (est): 21MM **Privately Held**
WEB: www.keker.com
SIC: 8111 Criminal law; specialized law offices, attorneys

(P-17304)
KIRKLAND & ELLIS LLP
555 California St # 2700, San Francisco (94104-1503)
PHONE.....................415 439-1400
Caroline Recht, *Manager*
Bao Nguyen, *Executive*
Samantha Benson, *Admin Sec*
Jodie Powell, *Admin Sec*
Mark Wilson, *Admin Sec*
EMP: 200
SALES (corp-wide): 732.6MM **Privately Held**
WEB: www.kirkland.com
SIC: 8111 General practice attorney, lawyer
PA: Kirkland & Ellis Llp
300 N La Salle Dr # 2400
Chicago IL 60654
312 862-2000

(P-17305)
KNOBBE MARTENS OLSON BEAR LLP
333 Bush St Fl 21, San Francisco (94104-2806)
PHONE.....................415 954-4114
James B Bear, *Branch Mgr*
David Trossen, *Assistant*
EMP: 39
SALES (corp-wide): 66.7MM **Privately Held**
WEB: www.knobbe.com
SIC: 8111 General practice law office
PA: Knobbe Martens Olson & Bear, Llp
2040 Main St Fl 14
Irvine CA 92614
949 760-0404

(P-17306)
KRONICK MSKVITZ TDMANN GRARD A (PA)
1331 Garden Hwy Ste 350, Sacramento (95833-9774)
PHONE.....................916 321-4500
Robert Murphy, *Chairman*
Michael A Grob, *President*
Bruce A Scheidt, *CEO*
Rick Fowler, *COO*
Kren A Sluiter, *CFO*
EMP: 116 **EST:** 1959
SALES (est): 20.8MM **Privately Held**
SIC: 8111 General practice law office

(P-17307)
LA RAZA CENTRO LEGAL SF
474 Valencia St Ste 295, San Francisco (94103-5927)
PHONE.....................415 575-3500
Annanaria Loya, *Director*
Julio Loyola, *President*
Alejandro Garcia, *Legal Staff*
Genevie Gallegos, *Director*
Annamaria Loya, *Director*
◆ **EMP:** 38 **EST:** 1974
SALES (est): 1.3MM **Privately Held**
WEB: www.lrcl.org
SIC: 8111 Immigration & naturalization law

(P-17308)
LANG RICHERT & PATCH
Also Called: Attorneys At Law
5200 N Palm Ave Ste 401, Fresno (93704-2227)
P.O. Box 14179 (93650-4179)
PHONE.....................559 228-6700
Val W Saldana, *President*
Robert Patch, *President*
Douglas Griffin, *CFO*
Rene La Streto II, *Vice Pres*
Victoria Salisch, *Admin Sec*
EMP: 50 **EST:** 1962
SQ FT: 17,500
SALES (est): 6.9MM **Privately Held**
WEB: www.lrplaw.net
SIC: 8111 General practice law office

(P-17309)
LAUGHLIN FALBO LEVY MORESI LLP (PA)
1001 Galaxy Way Ste 200, Concord (94520-5735)
PHONE.....................510 628-0496
John Geyer, *Partner*
John Bennett Jr, *Partner*
Robert A Guttman, *Partner*
Phillip J Klein, *Partner*
James Wesolowski, *Partner*
EMP: 76 **EST:** 1985
SALES (est): 38.5MM **Privately Held**
WEB: www.lflm.com
SIC: 8111 General practice law office

(P-17310)
LAW FOUNDATION SILICON VALLEY
4 N 2nd St Ste 1350, San Jose (95113-1330)
PHONE.....................408 293-4790
Alison Brunner, *CEO*
Carrie Chung, *Admin Asst*
Kyra Kazantzis, *Info Tech Mgr*
Eva Fong, *Analyst*
Victoria Vargas, *Opers Mgr*
EMP: 39 **EST:** 1974
SALES (est): 11.2MM **Privately Held**
WEB: www.lawfoundation.org
SIC: 8111 Legal aid service

(P-17311)
LAW OFFCES RUDY EXLROD ZEFF LL
Also Called: Rudy, Exelrod, Zieff, & True
351 California St Ste 700, San Francisco (94104-2408)
PHONE.....................415 434-9800
Alan B Exelrod, *Managing Prtnr*
Allan Exelrod, *Managing Prtnr*
David Lowe, *Managing Prtnr*
Mark Rudy, *Managing Prtnr*
Steve Zieff, *Managing Prtnr*
EMP: 39 **EST:** 1995
SALES (est): 4MM **Privately Held**
WEB: www.rezlaw.com
SIC: 8111 General practice attorney, lawyer

(P-17312)
LAW OFFICE ROBERT B JOBE PC
100 Bush St Ste 1250, San Francisco (94104-3938)
PHONE.....................415 956-5513
Robert B Jobe, *CEO*
Nikkol Kinoshita, *Admin Asst*
Sergio Velarde, *Associate*
EMP: 62 **EST:** 1991
SALES (est): 5.6MM **Privately Held**
WEB: www.jobelaw.com
SIC: 8111 Immigration & naturalization law

(P-17313)
LEGAL SERVICES NORTHERN CAL (PA)
517 12th St, Sacramento (95814-1418)
PHONE.....................916 551-2150
Gary F Smith, *Exec Dir*
Alan Stott, *Executive*
Gary Smith, *Exec Dir*
Liz Ramirez, *Office Mgr*
Barbara Walters, *Office Mgr*
EMP: 44 **EST:** 1956
SQ FT: 6,000
SALES (est): 11.1MM **Privately Held**
WEB: www.lsnc.net
SIC: 8111 Legal aid service

(P-17314)
LEGALMATCHCOM (PA)
395 Oyster Point Blvd # 55, South San Francisco (94080-1928)
P.O. Box 27472, San Francisco (94127-0472)
PHONE.....................415 946-0800
Randy Wells, *CEO*
Eric Briese, *CFO*
Robert Proden, *Associate Dir*
Matt Griffith, *General Mgr*
Neil Fradkin, *CTO*
EMP: 50 **EST:** 1999
SQ FT: 25,000
SALES (est): 11.9MM **Privately Held**
WEB: www.legalmatch.com
SIC: 8111 General practice attorney, lawyer

(P-17315)
LELAND PRCHINI STNBERG MTZGER
199 Fremont St Fl 21, San Francisco (94105-6640)
PHONE.....................415 957-1800
Lissa Rapoport, *Managing Prtnr*
James M Allen, *Managing Prtnr*
Christopher Donnelly, *Managing Prtnr*
Harvey Gould, *Managing Prtnr*
Nina Kwan, *Managing Prtnr*
EMP: 44 **EST:** 1930
SQ FT: 12,000
SALES (est): 7MM **Privately Held**
WEB: www.lpslaw.com
SIC: 8111 General practice attorney, lawyer; general practice law office

(P-17316)
LEWIS BRSBOIS BSGARD SMITH LLP
333 Bush St, San Francisco (94104-2806)
PHONE.....................415 362-2580
Cindy Aiello, *Manager*

(PA)=Parent Co (HQ)=Headquarters (DH)=Div Headquarters
✪ = New Business established in last 2 years

2022 Northern California Business Directory and Buyers Guide

Kathryn L Anderson, *Partner*
Jeffrey Bairey, *Partner*
Donald E Brier, *Partner*
Peter Dixon, *Partner*
EMP: 81
SALES (corp-wide): 284.9MM **Privately Held**
WEB: www.lewisbrisbois.com
SIC: 8111 General practice law office
PA: Lewis Brisbois Bisgaard & Smith Llp
　633 W 5th St Ste 4000
　Los Angeles CA 90071
　213 250-1800

(P-17317)
LIEFF CBRSER HMANN BRNSTEIN LL (PA)
275 Battery St Fl 29, San Francisco (94111-3305)
PHONE.....................................415 788-0245
Robert L Lieff, *Partner*
Katherine Lub Benson, *Partner*
William Bernstein, *Partner*
Kenneth S Byrd, *Partner*
Elizabeth J Cabraser, *Partner*
◆ **EMP:** 120 **EST:** 1972
SQ FT: 42,592
SALES (est): 42.8MM **Privately Held**
WEB: www.lieffcabraser.com
SIC: 8111 Antitrust & trade regulation law; environmental law; labor & employment law; securities law

(P-17318)
LITTLER MENDELSON PC (PA)
333 Bush St Fl 34, San Francisco (94104-2874)
P.O. Box 45547 (94145-0547)
PHONE.....................................415 433-1940
Thomas Bender, *CEO*
Craig Borowski, *Shareholder*
Bradford Hammock, *Shareholder*
Ryan Morley, *Shareholder*
Amy Todd-Gher, *Shareholder*
EMP: 500 **EST:** 1942
SQ FT: 85,000
SALES (est): 682.4MM **Privately Held**
WEB: www.littler.com
SIC: 8111 General practice law office

(P-17319)
LOMBARDI LOPER & CONANT LLP
2030 Franklin St Fl 7th, Oakland (94612-2914)
PHONE.....................................510 433-2600
Ralph A Lombardi, *General Ptnr*
Matthew S Conant, *General Ptnr*
Peter O Glassier, *General Ptnr*
Chris P Lavdiotis, *General Ptnr*
Bruce P Loper, *General Ptnr*
EMP: 35 **EST:** 1999
SALES (est): 3.6MM **Privately Held**
WEB: www.lombardiloper.com
SIC: 8111 General practice attorney, lawyer

(P-17320)
LONG & LEVIT LLP
465 California St Ste 500, San Francisco (94104-1814)
PHONE.....................................415 397-2222
Joseph McMonigle, *Managing Prtnr*
Laurie Myers, *Executive Asst*
Jan Bowe, *Admin Sec*
Kate Kimberlin, *Counsel*
Benjamin Mains, *Counsel*
EMP: 57 **EST:** 1927
SQ FT: 48,500
SALES (est): 9.9MM **Privately Held**
WEB: www.longlevit.com
SIC: 8111 General practice attorney, lawyer; taxation law; environmental law

(P-17321)
LOW BALL & LYNCH A PROF CORP (PA)
505 Montgomery St Fl 7, San Francisco (94111-2584)
P.O. Box 2327 (94126-2327)
PHONE.....................................415 981-6630
Steven D Werth, *President*
Sonja Blomquist, *Partner*
Laura Flynn, *Shareholder*
Christine Reed, *Shareholder*
Mark Hazelwood, *Treasurer*
EMP: 72 **EST:** 1943
SQ FT: 20,000
SALES (est): 9.2MM **Privately Held**
SIC: 8111 General practice law office

(P-17322)
LOZANO SMITH LLP
7404 N Spalding Ave, Fresno (93720-3370)
PHONE.....................................559 431-5600
Shaun Ardemagni, *Admin Sec*
Mariela Cantoriano, *Admin Sec*
Melissa Gonzales, *Admin Sec*
Kip Pinette, *Admin Sec*
Carlita Romero-Begley, *Human Res Mgr*
EMP: 167 **EST:** 1988
SALES (est): 30K **Privately Held**
WEB: www.lozanosmith.com
SIC: 8111 Specialized law offices, attorneys

(P-17323)
LOZANO SMITH A PROF CORP (PA)
7404 N Spalding Ave, Fresno (93720-3370)
PHONE.....................................559 431-5600
Gregory A Wedner, *CEO*
Jerry Behrens, *Shareholder*
Tina Cobabe, *President*
Lou Lozano, *President*
Krista Steiner, *President*
EMP: 54
SALES (est): 19.1MM **Privately Held**
WEB: www.lozanosmith.com
SIC: 8111 Corporate, partnership & business law

(P-17324)
LYNCH GILARDI & GRUMMER LLP
170 Columbus Ave Fl 5, San Francisco (94133-5128)
P.O. Box 143 (94104-0143)
PHONE.....................................415 397-2800
Robert Lynch, *Managing Prtnr*
Dwane Grummer, *Managing Prtnr*
William A Bogdan,
James E Sell,
Kenneth F Vierra Jr,
EMP: 39 **EST:** 1978
SQ FT: 4,000
SALES (est): 3.2MM **Privately Held**
SIC: 8111 Malpractice & negligence law; product liability law; corporate, partnership & business law

(P-17325)
MARKMONITOR (ALL-D) INC
425 Market St Ste 500, San Francisco (94105-2464)
PHONE.....................................415 278-8400
Irfan Salim, *President*
Chuck Drake, *Chief Mktg Ofcr*
Ted Sergott, *Engineer*
EMP: 52 **EST:** 1998
SALES (est): 1.8MM **Privately Held**
WEB: www.markmonitor.com
SIC: 8111 7379 Legal services; computer related maintenance services

(P-17326)
MATHENY SARS LINKERT JAIME LLP
3638 American River Dr, Sacramento (95864-5901)
PHONE.....................................916 978-3434
Richard S Linkert, *Partner*
Doug A Sears, *Senior Partner*
Matthew C Jamie, *Partner*
Douglas A Sears, *Partner*
Matthew C Jaime, *Managing Prtnr*
EMP: 61 **EST:** 1974
SQ FT: 12,000
SALES (est): 4.3MM **Privately Held**
WEB: www.mathenysears.com
SIC: 8111 General practice law office

(P-17327)
MAYALL HRLEY KNTSEN SMITH GREE
2453 Grand Canal Blvd # 2, Stockton (95207-8259)
PHONE.....................................209 465-8733
J Anthony Abbott, *CEO*
William W Hale, *CFO*
Mark S Adams, *Admin Sec*
EMP: 36 **EST:** 1935
SQ FT: 15,000
SALES (est): 1.9MM **Privately Held**
SIC: 8111 General practice attorney, lawyer

(P-17328)
MC NAMARA DODGE NEY BEATT (PA)
3480 Buskirk Ave Ste 250, Pleasant Hill (94523-7310)
PHONE.....................................925 939-5330
Richard Dodge, *General Ptnr*
Thomas G Beatty, *Partner*
Guy Borges, *Partner*
Roger Brothers, *Partner*
Robert Hodges, *Partner*
EMP: 70 **EST:** 1965
SQ FT: 9,500
SALES (est): 12.2MM **Privately Held**
WEB: www.mcnamaralaw.com
SIC: 8111 Specialized law offices, attorneys; malpractice & negligence law

(P-17329)
MCCORMICK BRSTOW SHPPARD WYTE (PA)
Also Called: McCormick Barstow
7647 N Fresno St, Fresno (93720-2578)
P.O. Box 28912 (93729-8912)
PHONE.....................................559 433-1300
Jeffrey M Reid, *Managing Prtnr*
Kenneth A Baldwin, *Partner*
Michael F Ball, *Partner*
Todd W Baxter, *Partner*
Mario L Beltramo Jr, *Partner*
EMP: 198 **EST:** 1951
SQ FT: 67,000
SALES (est): 31.5MM **Privately Held**
WEB: www.mccormickbarstow.com
SIC: 8111 Antitrust & trade regulation law

(P-17330)
MCINERNEY & DILLON PC
180 Grand Ave Ste 1390, Oakland (94612-3750)
PHONE.....................................510 465-7100
William H McInerny Sr, *President*
William H Mc Inerney Sr, *President*
Robert Leslie, *Treasurer*
William M Inerney, *Vice Pres*
William Mc Inerney Jr, *Vice Pres*
EMP: 43 **EST:** 1953
SALES (est): 2.9MM **Privately Held**
WEB: www.mcinerney-dillon.com
SIC: 8111 General practice law office

(P-17331)
MCMANIS FAULKNER A PROF CORP
50 W San Fernando St # 1000, San Jose (95113-2415)
PHONE.....................................408 279-8700
James McManis, *President*
Sharon Kirsch, *President*
Carlos Nunez, *President*
William Faulkner, *Admin Sec*
Amy Sines, *Admin Asst*
EMP: 50 **EST:** 1971
SALES (est): 6.6MM **Privately Held**
WEB: www.mcmanislaw.com
SIC: 8111 General practice law office

(P-17332)
MEYERS NAVE A PROF CORP (PA)
1999 Harrison St Ste 900, Oakland (94612-3578)
PHONE.....................................510 351-4300
David W Skinner, *CEO*
Jo Barrington, *President*
Terry Bremer, *President*
Sandra Chao, *President*
Anabelle Cotapos, *President*
EMP: 100 **EST:** 1986
SALES (est): 26.1MM **Privately Held**
WEB: www.meyersnave.com
SIC: 8111 Specialized law offices, attorneys

(P-17333)
MILES SEARS EANNI A PROF CORP
2844 Fresno St, Fresno (93721-1306)
P.O. Box 1432 (93716-1432)
PHONE.....................................559 486-5200
Richard Watters, *President*
Carmen Eanni, *Corp Secy*
Douglas L Gordon,
Christopher C Watters,
EMP: 38 **EST:** 1954
SQ FT: 9,000
SALES (est): 1.3MM **Privately Held**
WEB: www.mse-law.com
SIC: 8111 General practice attorney, lawyer; specialized law offices, attorneys

(P-17334)
MILLER LAW GROUP A PROF CORP
101 Montgomery St # 1400, San Francisco (94104-4128)
PHONE.....................................415 464-4300
Michele Miller, *President*
Elena Hillman, *Counsel*
Ethan Chernin, *Associate*
Kathryn Conard, *Associate*
EMP: 40 **EST:** 1998
SALES (est): 5.2MM **Privately Held**
WEB: www.cozen.com
SIC: 8111 General practice attorney, lawyer

(P-17335)
MILLER STARR RGLIA A PROF LAW (PA)
1331 N Calif Blvd Fl 5, Walnut Creek (94596-4537)
P.O. Box 8177 (94596-8177)
PHONE.....................................925 935-9400
Anthony M Leones, *CEO*
Lance Anderson, *Shareholder*
Mike Digeronimo, *Shareholder*
Arielle O Harris, *Shareholder*
Sean Marciniak, *Shareholder*
EMP: 90
SQ FT: 30,000
SALES (est): 11.9MM **Privately Held**
WEB: www.msrlegal.com
SIC: 8111 General practice law office

(P-17336)
MINAMI TAMAKI LLP
360 Post St Fl 8, San Francisco (94108-4911)
PHONE.....................................415 788-9000
Dale Minami, *Co-Owner*
Minette Kwok, *Partner*
Jack Lee, *Partner*
Donald K Tamaki, *Partner*
Brad Yamauchi, *Partner*
EMP: 50 **EST:** 1975
SQ FT: 4,500 **Privately Held**
WEB: www.minamitamaki.com
SIC: 8111 General practice attorney, lawyer

(P-17337)
MORGAN LEWIS & BOCKIUS LLP (HQ)
1 Market Spear St Tower, San Francisco (94105)
PHONE.....................................415 442-1000
Brian C Rocca, *Managing Prtnr*
Dale Barnes, *Partner*
Michael Begert, *Partner*
Charles Crompton, *Partner*
Anne Deibert, *Partner*
EMP: 271 **EST:** 1880
SALES (est): 83MM
SALES (corp-wide): 470.5MM **Privately Held**
WEB: www.morganlewisandbockius.com
SIC: 8111 General practice law office
PA: Morgan, Lewis & Bockius Llp
　1701 Market St Ste Con
　Philadelphia PA 19103
　215 963-5000

PRODUCTS & SERVICES SECTION
8111 - Legal Svcs County (P-17358)

(P-17338)
MORRISON & FOERSTER LLP (PA)
Also Called: Mofo
425 Market St Fl 32, San Francisco (94105-2467)
PHONE..............................415 268-7000
Larren Nashelsky, *Managing Prtnr*
Jay Baris, *Partner*
Tien-Yo Chao, *Partner*
Penelope Preovolos, *Partner*
Darryl Rains, *Partner*
EMP: 400 **EST:** 2000
SALES (est): 392.2MM **Privately Held**
WEB: www.mofo.com
SIC: 8111 General practice attorney, lawyer

(P-17339)
MOTSCHDLER MCHLIDES WISHON LLP
1690 W Shaw Ave Ste 200, Fresno (93711-3519)
PHONE..............................559 439-4000
J Carl Motschiedler, *Partner*
C William Brewer, *Partner*
David R Jenkins, *Partner*
James A McKelvey, *Partner*
Philip Michaelides, *Partner*
▲ **EMP:** 52 **EST:** 1977
SQ FT: 6,000
SALES (est): 5.3MM **Privately Held**
WEB: www.mmwbr.com
SIC: 8111 Labor & employment law; real estate law

(P-17340)
MUNGER TOLLES OLSON FOUNDATION
560 Mission St Fl 27, San Francisco (94105-3089)
PHONE..............................415 512-4000
Kim Coates, *Branch Mgr*
EMP: 47
SALES (corp-wide): 1.2MM **Privately Held**
SIC: 8111 General practice attorney, lawyer
PA: Munger Tolles & Olson Foundation
350 S Grand Ave Fl 50
Los Angeles CA 90071
213 683-9100

(P-17341)
MURPHY ASTIN ADAMS SCHNFELD LL
555 Capitol Mall Ste 800, Sacramento (95814-4512)
P.O. Box 1319 (95812-1319)
PHONE..............................916 446-2300
Cary M Adams, *Partner*
Russell J Austin, *Partner*
Donald E Brodeur, *Partner*
Raymond M Cadei, *Partner*
Jeffrey W Curcio, *Partner*
EMP: 39 **EST:** 1999
SQ FT: 16,500
SALES (est): 6.4MM **Privately Held**
WEB: www.murphyaustin.com
SIC: 8111 Corporate, partnership & business law; general practice law office; labor & employment law; real estate law

(P-17342)
MURPHY PRSON BRDLEY FNEY INC A (PA)
580 California St # 1100, San Francisco (94104-1000)
PHONE..............................415 788-1900
Michael P Bradley, *President*
Jeff Hsu, *Managing Prtnr*
Arthur Pearson, *Shareholder*
Harlan Watkins, *Shareholder*
Gena James, *President*
EMP: 53 **EST:** 1978
SALES (est): 18.4MM **Privately Held**
WEB: www.mpbf.com
SIC: 8111 General practice law office

(P-17343)
NATIONAL CTR FOR LSBIAN RIGHTS
870 Market St Ste 370, San Francisco (94102-3009)
PHONE..............................415 392-6257
Kate Kendell, *Exec Dir*
Christopher R Vasquez, *Comms Dir*
Cindy Myers, *Exec Dir*
Shannon Minter, *Legal Staff*
Noemi Calonje, *Director*
EMP: 36 **EST:** 1977
SALES (est): 1.2MM **Privately Held**
WEB: www.nclrights.org
SIC: 8111 Legal services

(P-17344)
NELSON & KENNARD LAW OFFICES
Also Called: Sipes, Mike K
5011 Dudlley Blvd Bldg 25, Newcastle (95658)
P.O. Box 13807, Sacramento (95853-3807)
PHONE..............................916 920-2295
Donald G Nelson, *Partner*
Robert Scot Kennard, *Partner*
Scott Kennard, *Managing Prtnr*
Shirley Smith, *Office Mgr*
Sam Chang, *Info Tech Mgr*
EMP: 40 **EST:** 1977
SQ FT: 3,200
SALES (est): 5.7MM **Privately Held**
WEB: www.nelson-kennard.com
SIC: 8111 General practice law office

(P-17345)
NEUMILLER BARDSLEE A PROF CORP
3121 W March Ln Ste 100, Stockton (95219-2367)
P.O. Box 20 (95201-3020)
PHONE..............................209 948-8200
Duncan R McPherson, *Vice Pres*
James Nuss, *Shareholder*
Duncan R Mc Pherson, *Vice Pres*
Robert C Morrison,
Diane Dias, *Legal Staff*
EMP: 65 **EST:** 1903
SALES (est): 4.8MM **Privately Held**
WEB: www.neumiller.com
SIC: 8111 General practice law office

(P-17346)
NOSSAMAN LLP
Also Called: Bagley, William T
50 California St Ste 3400, San Francisco (94111-4799)
PHONE..............................415 398-3600
Susan Eres, *Manager*
Nancy Neptune, *Admin Asst*
Barney Allison,
Martin A Mattes,
EMP: 51
SALES (corp-wide): 43.4MM **Privately Held**
WEB: www.nossaman.com
SIC: 8111 General practice attorney, lawyer
PA: Nossaman Llp
777 S Figueroa St # 3400
Los Angeles CA 90017
213 612-7800

(P-17347)
NOSSAMAN LLP
915 L St Ste 1000, Sacramento (95814-3705)
PHONE..............................916 442-8888
Kevin Adams, *Manager*
Mary Powers Antoine, *Partner*
Thomas W Eres, *Partner*
Frank A Iwama, *Partner*
Jeffrey Starsky, *Partner*
EMP: 51
SALES (corp-wide): 43.4MM **Privately Held**
WEB: www.nossaman.com
SIC: 8111 8743 General practice attorney, lawyer; lobbyist
PA: Nossaman Llp
777 S Figueroa St # 3400
Los Angeles CA 90017
213 612-7800

(P-17348)
OBRIEN WATTERS & DAVIS LLP
3510 Unocal Pl Ste 200, Santa Rosa (95403-0969)
P.O. Box 3759 (95402-3759)
PHONE..............................707 545-7010
John R O'Brien, *Partner*
Daniel Davis, *Partner*
Gary Nelson, *Associate*
EMP: 39 **EST:** 1981
SQ FT: 10,000
SALES (est): 3.1MM **Privately Held**
WEB: www.obrienlaw.com
SIC: 8111 General practice attorney, lawyer

(P-17349)
OLSON HAGEL FISHBURN LLC
555 Capitol Mall Ste 400, Sacramento (95814-4503)
PHONE..............................916 442-2952
Lance Olson, *Partner*
Diane Fishburn, *Partner*
Elizabeth Gade, *Partner*
Bruce Hagel, *Partner*
Chuck Donovan, *Vice Pres*
EMP: 48 **EST:** 1978
SQ FT: 11,000
SALES (est): 6.7MM **Privately Held**
WEB: www.olsonhagel.com
SIC: 8111 General practice law office

(P-17350)
ORRICK HRRINGTN SUT FOUNDTN
400 Capitol Mall Ste 3000, Sacramento (95814-4497)
PHONE..............................916 329-7928
Ralph Baxter, *CEO*
Jonathan Ocker, *Partner*
Alan Talkington, *Partner*
Laura Saklad, *Marketing Staff*
Jeanette Ponce, *Litigation*
EMP: 37 **EST:** 1999
SALES (est): 1.3MM **Privately Held**
WEB: www.orrick.com
SIC: 8111 General practice attorney, lawyer

(P-17351)
ORRICK HRRINGTON SUTCLIFFE LLP (PA)
405 Howard St, San Francisco (94105-2625)
PHONE..............................415 773-5700
Ralph H Baxter Jr, *CEO*
Martin Bartlam, *Partner*
Peter A Bicks, *Partner*
Benedikt Burger, *Partner*
Neel Chatterjee, *Partner*
EMP: 699 **EST:** 1863
SQ FT: 146,000
SALES (est): 490.6MM **Privately Held**
WEB: www.orrick.com
SIC: 8111 General practice attorney, lawyer

(P-17352)
ORRICK HRRINGTON SUTCLIFFE LLP
1000 Marsh Rd, Menlo Park (94025-1015)
PHONE..............................650 614-7400
Don Keller, *Branch Mgr*
Jessica R Perry, *Partner*
Barbara Whiteley, *Office Mgr*
Lynne C Hermle,
Akasha Perez, *Associate*
EMP: 160
SALES (corp-wide): 490.6MM **Privately Held**
WEB: www.orrick.com
SIC: 8111 General practice attorney, lawyer
PA: Orrick, Herrington & Sutcliffe, Llp
405 Howard St
San Francisco CA 94105
415 773-5700

(P-17353)
PACIFIC LEGAL FOUNDATION (PA)
930 G St, Sacramento (95814-1802)
PHONE..............................916 419-7111
Robert K Best, *President*
John C Harris, *Ch of Bd*
Robin L Rivett, *President*
Chad Wilcox, *COO*
James Katzinski, *Officer*
EMP: 50 **EST:** 1973
SQ FT: 14,000
SALES (est): 16.5MM **Privately Held**
WEB: www.pacificlegal.org
SIC: 8111 General practice law office

(P-17354)
PARACORP INCORPORATED (PA)
Also Called: Parasec
2804 Gateway Oaks Dr # 100, Sacramento (95833-4345)
P.O. Box 160568 (95816-0568)
PHONE..............................916 576-7000
Matthew Marzucco, *President*
Barbara Geiger, *Vice Pres*
Jocelyn Heredia, *Executive*
Abigale Peterson, *Technician*
Jessica Sierras, *Opers Mgr*
▲ **EMP:** 53 **EST:** 1977
SALES (est): 14.8MM **Privately Held**
WEB: www.parasec.com
SIC: 8111 Specialized legal services

(P-17355)
PARKER KERN NARD WNZEL PROF CO
7112 N Fresno St Ste 300, Fresno (93720-2947)
PHONE..............................559 449-2558
Dennis G Nard, *CEO*
Eric Wenzel, *Senior Partner*
David Parker, *Shareholder*
Michele Polanco, *President*
Barry Katz, *Administration*
EMP: 58 **EST:** 1992
SALES (est): 5.5MM **Privately Held**
WEB: www.pknwlaw.com
SIC: 8111 Specialized law offices, attorneys

(P-17356)
PILLSBURY WINTHROP SHAW
4 Embarcadero Ctr Fl 22, San Francisco (94111-5998)
PHONE..............................415 983-1000
Jeffrey M Vesely, *General Ptnr*
Terri Chytrowski, *Comms Dir*
Jessica Slater, *Business Dir*
Linda Magyar, *Office Mgr*
David Kramlick, *Admin Sec*
EMP: 194
SALES (corp-wide): 192.2MM **Privately Held**
WEB: www.pillsburylaw.com
SIC: 8111 General practice law office
PA: Pillsbury Winthrop Shaw Pittman Llp
31 W 52nd St Fl 29
New York NY 10019
212 858-1000

(P-17357)
PILLSBURY WINTHROP SHAW
50 Fremont St Ste 522, San Francisco (94105-2232)
P.O. Box 7880 (94120-7880)
PHONE..............................415 983-1075
Jeffrey M Vesely, *Partner*
Christopher Patay, *Partner*
Amanda G Halter, *Managing Prtnr*
Catherine Schmitz, *President*
Sean P Whelan, *COO*
EMP: 300
SALES (corp-wide): 192.2MM **Privately Held**
WEB: www.pillsburylaw.com
SIC: 8111 General practice law office
PA: Pillsbury Winthrop Shaw Pittman Llp
31 W 52nd St Fl 29
New York NY 10019
212 858-1000

(P-17358)
POLSINELLI PC
Also Called: Polsinelli LLP
1661 Page Mill Rd Ste A, Palo Alto (94304-1209)
PHONE..............................650 461-7700
Fabio E Marino, *Office Mgr*
Joseph Greenslade, *Counsel*
EMP: 45

8111 - Legal Svcs County (P-17359)

SALES (corp-wide): 227.6MM **Privately Held**
SIC: 8111 Corporate, partnership & business law
PA: Polsinelli Pc
900 W 48th Pl Ste 900 # 900
Kansas City MO 64112
816 753-1000

(P-17359)
QUEST DISCOVERY SERVICES INC (PA)
Also Called: Ontellus
981 Ridder Park Dr, San Jose (95131-2305)
PHONE.................408 441-7000
Elizabeth Whitmore, CEO
Ken Croney, Admin Sec
Greg Johnson, Director
Linda Hoeser, Manager
Kali Trombley, Manager
EMP: 132 EST: 1996
SQ FT: 16,000
SALES (est): 11.9MM **Privately Held**
WEB: www.ontellus.com
SIC: 8111 Specialized legal services; specialized law offices, attorneys

(P-17360)
REED SMITH LLP
101 2nd St Ste 1800, San Francisco (94105-3659)
PHONE.................415 543-8700
Bettie B Epstein, Partner
Sandi Brooks, Admin Sec
Jessica Delgadillo, Admin Sec
James Schad, Analyst
Jenny Cooper, Opers Staff
EMP: 158
SALES (corp-wide): 632.8MM **Privately Held**
WEB: www.adlawbyrequest.com
SIC: 8111 General practice attorney, lawyer
PA: Reed Smith Llp
225 5th Ave Ste 1200
Pittsburgh PA 15222
412 288-3131

(P-17361)
RENNE SLOAN HOLTZMAN SAKAI LLP (PA)
555 Capitol Mall Ste 600, Sacramento (95814-4581)
PHONE.................415 678-3800
Steve Cikes, Principal
Ivan Delventhal, Partner
Scott Dickey, Partner
Nikki Hall, Partner
Art Hartinger, Partner
EMP: 46 EST: 2004
SQ FT: 7,000
SALES (est): 11.1MM **Privately Held**
WEB: www.caperb.com
SIC: 8111 General practice attorney, lawyer

(P-17362)
REUBEN JUNIUS & ROSE LLP
1 Bush St Ste 600, San Francisco (94104-4411)
PHONE.................415 567-9000
James A Reuben, Partner
John McInerney, Counsel
Andrew J Junius,
Shelly Sparks, Manager
Chloe Angelis, Associate
EMP: 40 EST: 2006
SALES (est): 3.5MM **Privately Held**
WEB: www.reubenlaw.com
SIC: 8111 General practice attorney, lawyer

(P-17363)
ROGERS JOSEPH ODONNELL A PRO (PA)
311 California St Fl 10, San Francisco (94104-2695)
PHONE.................415 956-2828
Neil H O' Donnell, President
Merri A Baldwin, Shareholder
Lauren Kramer, Shareholder
Patricia Meagher, Shareholder
Allan J Joseph, Corp Secy
EMP: 66 EST: 1981
SQ FT: 22,000

SALES (est): 8.6MM **Privately Held**
WEB: www.rjo.com
SIC: 8111 General practice attorney, lawyer

(P-17364)
ROPERS MAJESKI A PROF CORP (PA)
1001 Marshall St Fl 5, Redwood City (94063-2052)
PHONE.................650 364-8200
Jesshill E Love, CEO
Anthony CHI-Hung, Partner
Anthony Grande, Partner
Geoffrey Heineman, Partner
Eugene J Majeski, Partner
EMP: 81 EST: 1950
SQ FT: 69,000
SALES (est): 5.2MM **Privately Held**
WEB: www.ropers.com
SIC: 8111 General practice law office

(P-17365)
ROSEN BIEN GALVAN GRUNFELD LLP
101 Mission St Ste 600, San Francisco (94105-1738)
PHONE.................415 433-6830
Gay Grunfeld, Managing Prtnr
Michael Bien, Partner
Jeffrey Bornstein, Partner
Lisa Ells, Partner
Ernest Galvan, Partner
EMP: 44 EST: 1991
SALES (est): 1.8MM **Privately Held**
WEB: www.rbgg.com
SIC: 8111 Legal services

(P-17366)
SCHUERING ZIMMERMAN & SCULLY
400 University Ave, Sacramento (95825-6502)
PHONE.................916 567-0400
Leo Schuering, Partner
Keith Chidlaw, Partner
Thomas Doyle, Partner
Lawrence Giardina, Partner
Anthony D Lauria, Partner
EMP: 40 EST: 1989
SALES (est): 5.8MM **Privately Held**
WEB: www.szs.com
SIC: 8111 General practice attorney, lawyer

(P-17367)
SCOTT A PORTER PROF CORP
350 University Ave # 200, Sacramento (95825-6581)
PHONE.................916 929-1481
Sherrie Cork, Office Mgr
Tom Bailey, Partner
Tim Blaine, Partner
Craig Caldwell, Partner
Carl Calnero, Partner
EMP: 85 EST: 1976
SALES (est): 24.6MM **Privately Held**
WEB: www.porterscott.com
SIC: 8111 General practice attorney, lawyer; general practice law office

(P-17368)
SEVERSON & WERSON A PROF CORP
1 Embarcadero Ctr Ste 260, San Francisco (94111-3628)
PHONE.................415 398-3344
Mary Kate Sullivan, CEO
James B Werson, Ch of Bd
Sylvia Coleman, President
Emily Rhea, President
Robert L Lofts, CFO
EMP: 132 EST: 1945
SQ FT: 40,000
SALES (est): 24.1MM **Privately Held**
WEB: www.severson.com
SIC: 8111 Labor & employment law; corporate, partnership & business law

(P-17369)
SEYFARTH SHAW LLP
560 Mission St Fl 31, San Francisco (94105-2930)
PHONE.................415 397-2823
William Dritsas, Principal

Janine McDermott, Admin Sec
Karen Shepardson, Admin Sec
Lauren Abria, Admin Asst
Constance Hughes, Admin Asst
EMP: 100
SALES (corp-wide): 330MM **Privately Held**
WEB: www.seyfarth.com
SIC: 8111 General practice law office
PA: Seyfarth Shaw Llp
233 S Wacker Dr Ste 8000
Chicago IL 60606
312 460-5000

(P-17370)
SEYFARTH SHAW LLP
400 Capitol Mall Ste 2350, Sacramento (95814-4428)
PHONE.................916 448-0159
Rachel Miller, Branch Mgr
Gertel Paul-Overall, President
Shelley Gordon, Admin Sec
Lillian Moore, Admin Sec
Amie Aldana, Nurse
EMP: 141
SALES (corp-wide): 330MM **Privately Held**
WEB: www.seyfarth.com
SIC: 8111 General practice attorney, lawyer
PA: Seyfarth Shaw Llp
233 S Wacker Dr Ste 8000
Chicago IL 60606
312 460-5000

(P-17371)
SHARTSIS FRIESE LLP
1 Maritime Plz Fl 18, San Francisco (94111-3508)
PHONE.................415 421-6500
Arthur J Shartsis, Partner
Derek Boswell, Partner
John P Broadhurst, Partner
Zesara Chan, Partner
Frank Cialone, Partner
EMP: 120 EST: 1975
SQ FT: 47,709
SALES (est): 18.9MM **Privately Held**
WEB: www.sflaw.com
SIC: 8111 Patent, trademark & copyright law

(P-17372)
SHEPPARD MLLIN RCHTER HMPTON L
4 Embarcadero Ctr # 1700, San Francisco (94111-4106)
PHONE.................415 434-9100
Aline Pearl, Office Admin
Phipp Atkins-Pattensen, Partner
Julie Ebert, Partner
Douglas R Hart, Partner
Betsey McDaniel, Partner
EMP: 62
SALES (corp-wide): 956.5K **Privately Held**
WEB: www.sheppardmullin.com
SIC: 8111 General practice law office
PA: Sheppard, Mullin, Richter & Hampton, Llp
333 S Hope St Fl 43
Los Angeles CA 90071
213 620-1780

(P-17373)
SHOOK HARDY & BACON LLP
1 Montgomery St Ste 2700, San Francisco (94104-5527)
PHONE.................415 544-1900
Shannon Spangler, Managing Prtnr
Sharon Teater, Admin Sec
Lolly Cerda, Analyst
Michael Scheller, Patent Law
Susan Wiens,
EMP: 239
SALES (corp-wide): 147.9MM **Privately Held**
WEB: www.shb.com
SIC: 8111 General practice law office
PA: Shook, Hardy & Bacon L.L.P.
2555 Grand Blvd
Kansas City MO 64108
816 474-6550

(P-17374)
SHUTE MIHALY & WEINBERGER
396 Hayes St, San Francisco (94102-4421)
PHONE.................415 552-7272
Richard Taylor, Managing Prtnr
Rachael B Hooper, Partner
Fran M Layton, Partner
Mark I Weinberger, Partner
Marc B Mihaly, Partner
EMP: 40 EST: 1980
SALES (est): 5.6MM **Privately Held**
WEB: www.smwlaw.com
SIC: 8111 General practice law office

(P-17375)
SIDEMAN & BANCROFT LLP
1 Embarcadero Ctr Fl 22, San Francisco (94111-3711)
PHONE.................415 392-1960
Jeffrey Hallam, General Ptnr
Kelly P McCarthy, Partner
Hilary Pierce, Partner
Mary Eslava, President
Janice Graves, President
EMP: 95
SALES (est): 16.2MM **Privately Held**
WEB: www.sideman.com
SIC: 8111 General practice law office

(P-17376)
SILICON VLY LAW GROUP A LAW CO
1 N Market St 200, San Jose (95113-1207)
PHONE.................408 573-5700
Myron Brody, President
James Chapman, Vice Pres
F M Small Jr, Vice Pres
David Duperraul, Asst Sec
EMP: 40 EST: 1994
SALES (est): 8.9MM **Privately Held**
WEB: www.svlg.com
SIC: 8111 General practice law office

(P-17377)
STEELE CIS LLC
1 Sansome St Ste 3500, San Francisco (94104-4436)
PHONE.................415 692-5000
Ken Kurtz, President
Andrew Glikman, Manager
EMP: 350 EST: 2011
SALES (est): 28.6MM **Privately Held**
SIC: 8111 Legal services

(P-17378)
STEIN & LUBIN LLP
600 Montgomery St 14, San Francisco (94111-2716)
PHONE.................415 981-0550
Mark Lubin, Partner
Robert S Stein, Partner
Eyleen Nadolny, President
Jennifer Dominik, Admin Sec
Catherine Montoya, Admin Sec
EMP: 36 EST: 2007
SALES (est): 3.2MM **Privately Held**
WEB: www.lubinolson.com
SIC: 8111 General practice law office

(P-17379)
STOEL RIVES LLP (PA)
500 Capitol Mall Ste 1600, Sacramento (95814-4740)
PHONE.................916 447-0700
Sean E McCarthy, Principal
Thomas A Woods, Counsel
Carolyn Aschenbrener, Assistant
Parissa Ebrahimzadeh, Associate
Bryan L Hawkins, Associate
EMP: 69 EST: 2007
SALES (est): 5.3MM **Privately Held**
WEB: www.stoel.com
SIC: 8111 General practice attorney, lawyer

(P-17380)
THOITS LOVE HERSCHBERGER & MCL (PA)
285 Hamilton Ave Ste 300, Palo Alto (94301-2539)
PHONE.................650 330-7321
Terrence Conner, CEO
Stephen A Dennis, CFO
Michael Curtis, Vice Pres

PRODUCTS & SERVICES SECTION

8111 - Legal Svcs County (P-17401)

Thomas B Jacob, *Admin Sec*
EMP: 35 **EST:** 1944
SQ FT: 16,000
SALES (est): 5.1MM **Privately Held**
WEB: www.thoits.com
SIC: 8111 General practice law office

(P-17381)
THOITS LOVE HERSCHBERGER & MCL
400 Main St Ste 250, Los Altos (94022-2842)
PHONE...........................650 327-4200
Steve Dennis, *CFO*
EMP: 37
SALES (corp-wide): 5.1MM **Privately Held**
WEB: www.thoits.com
SIC: 8111 General practice law office
PA: Thoits, Love, Hershberger & Mclean, A Professional Law Corporation
285 Hamilton Ave Ste 300
Palo Alto CA 94301
650 330-7321

(P-17382)
TOWN OF PARADISE
Also Called: Paradise Police Dept
5595 Black Olive Dr, Paradise (95969-4606)
PHONE...........................530 872-6241
Gabriela Tazzari-Dineen, *Chief*
EMP: 40
SALES (corp-wide): 25MM **Privately Held**
WEB: www.townofparadise.com
SIC: 9221 8111 ; legal services
PA: Town Of Paradise
5555 Skyway
Paradise CA 95969
530 872-6291

(P-17383)
TRAINOR FAIRBROOK A PROF CORP
980 Fulton Ave, Sacramento (95825-4558)
P.O. Box 255824 (95865-5824)
PHONE...........................916 929-7000
Charles W Trainor, *President*
Candy Harper, *Shareholder*
Candace B Harper, *CFO*
Colby Campbell, *Chairman*
Anthony A Arostegui, *Vice Pres*
EMP: 40 **EST:** 1978
SQ FT: 17,505
SALES (est): 7.3MM **Privately Held**
WEB: www.trainorfairbrook.com
SIC: 8111 General practice attorney, lawyer

(P-17384)
TRUCKER HUSS A PROFESSIONAL
1 Embarcadero Ctr Fl 12, San Francisco (94111-3617)
PHONE...........................415 788-3111
Lee Trucker, *President*
R Bradford Huss, *Treasurer*
Julie Burbank-Colema, *Vice Pres*
Deborah Wiener, *Vice Pres*
Barbara Creed, *Admin Sec*
EMP: 42 **EST:** 1986
SQ FT: 11,000
SALES (est): 7.5MM **Privately Held**
WEB: www.truckerhuss.com
SIC: 8111 General practice law office

(P-17385)
VAN DE POEL LEVY & ALLEN LLP
1600 S Main St Ste 325, Walnut Creek (94596-8812)
PHONE...........................925 274-7650
David Levy, *Partner*
Jay Van Depoel, *Partner*
Darla Smith, *Exec Dir*
Jenny Balestrieri, *Administration*
Richard Barnes, *CIO*
EMP: 40 **EST:** 2001
SALES (est): 6MM **Privately Held**
WEB: www.vanlevylaw.com
SIC: 8111 General practice law office

(P-17386)
VAN DER HOUT BRGGLANO NGHTNGAL
180 Sutter St Fl 5, San Francisco (94104-4010)
PHONE...........................415 981-3000
Marc Van Der Hout, *Partner*
Christine Brigagliano, *Partner*
Fatima Guadamuz, *Opers Staff*
Stefanie Lino, *Instructor*
EMP: 36 **EST:** 1980
SALES (est): 5.9MM **Privately Held**
WEB: www.vblaw.com
SIC: 8111 Divorce & family law; immigration & naturalization law

(P-17387)
VENABLE LLP
101 California St # 3800, San Francisco (94111-5802)
PHONE...........................415 653-3750
John Porter, *Office Admin*
Benjamin Pelletier, *Counsel*
Cathleen Madlansacay, *Assistant*
Gregory Berlin, *Associate*
EMP: 35
SALES (corp-wide): 108.3MM **Privately Held**
SIC: 8111 General practice attorney, lawyer
PA: Venable Llp
600 Massachusetts Ave Nw # 9
Washington DC 20001
202 344-4000

(P-17388)
WAGNER KRKMN BLNE KLMP & YMNS (PA)
Also Called: WKBk&y
10640 Mather Blvd Ste 200, Mather (95655-4189)
PHONE...........................916 920-5286
Carl P Blaine, *Partner*
Douglas E Kirkman, *Partner*
Belan Kirk Wagner, *Partner*
Tricia Milburn, *Admin Sec*
Amber Seals, *Admin Sec*
EMP: 38 **EST:** 1982
SQ FT: 17,000
SALES (est): 6.6MM **Privately Held**
WEB: www.wkblaw.com
SIC: 8111 General practice attorney, lawyer

(P-17389)
WALKUP MLDIA KLLY SCHNBRGER A
Also Called: Walkup Law Office
650 California St Fl 26, San Francisco (94108-2615)
PHONE...........................415 981-7210
Paul W Melodia, *President*
Kevin Domecus, *Treasurer*
Jefferey Holl, *Vice Pres*
Michael Kelly, *Vice Pres*
Richard Schoenberger, *Vice Pres*
EMP: 50 **EST:** 1953
SQ FT: 30,000
SALES (est): 7.8MM **Privately Held**
WEB: www.walkuplawoffice.com
SIC: 8111 Labor & employment law; malpractice & negligence law

(P-17390)
WANGER JONES HELSLEY PC
265 E Rver Pk Cir Ste 310, Fresno (93720)
P.O. Box 28340 (93729-8340)
PHONE...........................559 233-4800
Timothy Jones, *President*
Toni Scarborough, *President*
Michael S Helsley, *Vice Pres*
Lynn Hoffman, *Administration*
EMP: 47 **EST:** 1994
SQ FT: 23,000
SALES (est): 3MM **Privately Held**
WEB: www.wjhattorneys.com
SIC: 8111 General practice attorney, lawyer

(P-17391)
WEAVER SCHLENGER AND MAZEL
550 Montgomery St Ste 650, San Francisco (94111-6509)
PHONE...........................415 395-9331
Kirsten Schlenger, *Managing Prtnr*
Laura Mazel, *Partner*
Mary Jane Weaver, *Partner*
Emily Fotiadi, *Opers Mgr*
Katy Chase, *Associate*
EMP: 36 **EST:** 1997
SALES (est): 4.9MM **Privately Held**
WEB: www.wsmimmigration.com
SIC: 8111 General practice law office

(P-17392)
WEIL GOTSHAL & MANGES LLP
201 Rdwood Shres Pkwy Ste, Redwood City (94065)
PHONE...........................650 802-3000
Craig Adas, *Managing Prtnr*
Rod J Howard, *Partner*
Kyle C Krpata, *Partner*
Curtis L MO, *Partner*
Edward R Reines, *Partner*
EMP: 180
SALES (corp-wide): 290.5MM **Privately Held**
WEB: www.weil.com
SIC: 8111 General practice law office
PA: Weil, Gotshal & Manges Llp
767 5th Ave Fl Conc1
New York NY 10153
212 310-8000

(P-17393)
WEINBERG ROGER & RESENFELD (PA)
1001 Marina Village Pkwy # 200, Alameda (94501-6430)
PHONE...........................510 337-1001
Stewart Weinberg, *President*
Conchita Lozano-Batista, *Shareholder*
Emily Rich, *Shareholder*
David Rosenfeld, *Shareholder*
Lara Hull, *President*
EMP: 69 **EST:** 1964
SQ FT: 12,000
SALES (est): 10.6MM **Privately Held**
WEB: www.unioncounsel.net
SIC: 8111 General practice law office

(P-17394)
WEINTRAUB TOBIN CHEDIAK (PA)
400 Capitol Mall Fl 11, Sacramento (95814-4434)
PHONE...........................916 558-6000
Michael Kvarme, *CEO*
Thadd A Blizzard, *Partner*
Karen L Boon, *Partner*
Kelly L Borelli, *Partner*
Geoffrey Burroughs, *Partner*
EMP: 50 **EST:** 1991
SQ FT: 44,900
SALES (est): 27.3MM **Privately Held**
WEB: www.weintraub.com
SIC: 8111 General practice law office

(P-17395)
WENDEL ROSEN LLP (PA)
1111 Broadway Ste 2400, Oakland (94607-4053)
PHONE...........................510 834-6600
Howard Lance, *Managing Prtnr*
C Gregg Ankenman, *Partner*
Mark S Bostic, *Partner*
Elizabeth Burke-Dreyfuss, *Partner*
Joan M Cambray, *Partner*
EMP: 107 **EST:** 1909
SQ FT: 40,000
SALES (est): 14.5MM **Privately Held**
WEB: www.wendel.com
SIC: 8111 General practice attorney, lawyer

(P-17396)
WHITING FALLON & ROSS
Also Called: Abel, Gregory C
101 Ygnacio Valley Rd # 250, Walnut Creek (94596-4087)
PHONE...........................925 296-6000
William Whiting, *Partner*
Gregory C Abel, *Partner*
R N Fallon, *Partner*
Andrew Ross, *Partner*
Debbie Chase, *Legal Staff*
EMP: 42 **EST:** 1987
SALES (est): 4.5MM **Privately Held**
WEB: www.disso.com
SIC: 8111 General practice attorney, lawyer

(P-17397)
WILD CRTER TIPTON A PROF CORP
246 W Shaw Ave, Fresno (93704-2644)
PHONE...........................559 224-2131
G Dana French, *President*
Bruce M Brown, *District Mgr*
Amber Scott, *Legal Staff*
Russell Vanrozeboom, *Counsel*
David A Yengoyan, *Associate*
EMP: 49 **EST:** 1893
SQ FT: 19,000
SALES (est): 6.6MM **Privately Held**
WEB: www.wctlaw.com
SIC: 8111 General practice law office; criminal law; corporate, partnership & business law; taxation law

(P-17398)
WILKINS DRLSHGEN CZSHINSKI LLP
6785 N Willow Ave, Fresno (93710-5900)
PHONE...........................559 438-2390
James Wilkins, *Partner*
Michael Czeshinski, *Partner*
John Drolshagen, *Partner*
Hilda R Lopez, *Office Admin*
Matthew Wilkins, *Associate*
EMP: 37 **EST:** 1997
SALES (est): 4.2MM **Privately Held**
WEB: www.wdcllp.com
SIC: 8111 Corporate, partnership & business law; bankruptcy law

(P-17399)
WILSON ELSER MSKWITZ EDLMAN DC
525 Market St Fl 17, San Francisco (94105-2708)
PHONE...........................202 626-7660
Ed Ash, *Manager*
Ralph Robinson, *Partner*
Gladys Campbell, *Office Admin*
Marilee Barlow, *Admin Sec*
Kimberly Denton, *Admin Sec*
EMP: 36
SQ FT: 1,000
SALES (corp-wide): 307MM **Privately Held**
WEB: www.wilsonelser.com
SIC: 8111 General practice law office
PA: Wilson, Elser, Moskowitz, Edelman & Dicker Llp
150 E 42nd St Fl 23
New York NY 10017
212 490-3000

(P-17400)
WILSON SNSINI GDRICH RSATI PRO (PA)
650 Page Mill Rd, Palo Alto (94304-1001)
PHONE...........................650 493-9300
Steven E Bochner, *CEO*
Bradford Obrien, *General Ptnr*
James Jensen, *Partner*
Jack Sheridan, *Partner*
Effie Toshav, *Partner*
EMP: 1100 **EST:** 1961
SQ FT: 184,000
SALES (est): 140.8MM **Privately Held**
WEB: www.wsgr.com
SIC: 8111 Corporate, partnership & business law

(P-17401)
WINSTON & STRAWN LLP
101 California St # 3500, San Francisco (94111-5894)
PHONE...........................415 591-1000
James Schwarz, *Administration*
Raquel M Hagan, *Associate*
Scotia Hicks, *Associate*
Thomas Kearney, *Associate*
Ian Papendick, *Associate*
EMP: 60
SALES (corp-wide): 25.4K **Privately Held**
WEB: www.winston.com
SIC: 8111 Legal services

8111 - Legal Svcs County

PA: Winston & Strawn Llp
35 W Wacker Dr Ste 4200
Chicago IL 60601
312 558-5600

(P-17402)
YOUNG MINNEY & CORR LLP
655 University Ave # 150, Sacramento (95825-6707)
PHONE 916 646-1400
Paul C Minney, *Partner*
Lisa A Corr, *Partner*
Sarah J Kollman, *Partner*
Megan M Moore, *Partner*
Chastin H Pierman, *Partner*
EMP: 44 **EST:** 2012
SALES (est): 5.4MM **Privately Held**
WEB: www.mycharterlaw.com
SIC: 8111 Specialized law offices, attorneys

(P-17403)
ZWICKER & ASSOCIATES PC
1320 Willow Paca Rd Ste 73, Concord (94520)
PHONE 925 689-7070
Jonathan Espinola, *Vice Pres*
EMP: 58 **Privately Held**
WEB: www.zwickerpc.com
SIC: 8111 General practice attorney, lawyer
PA: Zwicker & Associates, P.C.
80 Minuteman Rd
Andover MA 01810

8322 Individual & Family Social Svcs

(P-17404)
ABILITYPATH
Also Called: Impact Business Service
350 Twin Dolphin Dr # 12, Redwood City (94065-1457)
PHONE 650 259-8500
Sheryl Young, *CEO*
Linda Leao, *Vice Chairman*
Ken Barker, *Officer*
Tracey Fecher, *Vice Pres*
Kim Malhotra, *Vice Pres*
EMP: 120 **EST:** 1920
SQ FT: 25,000
SALES (est): 13.6MM **Privately Held**
WEB: www.gatepath.org
SIC: 8322 Social services for the handicapped

(P-17405)
ABILITYPATH HOUSING (PA)
Also Called: Abilities United
350 Twin Dolphin Dr # 12, Redwood City (94065-1457)
PHONE 650 494-0550
Charlie Weidanz, *CEO*
Jane Machin, *CFO*
Soheila Razban, *Vice Pres*
Misty Accristo, *Program Mgr*
Greg Gonzalez, *Admin Sec*
EMP: 85 **EST:** 1954
SALES (est): 5.2MM **Privately Held**
WEB: www.abilitypath.org
SIC: 8322 8361 Multi-service center; residential care

(P-17406)
ABODE SERVICES (PA)
40849 Fremont Blvd, Fremont (94538-4306)
PHONE 510 657-7409
Louis Chicoine, *Exec Dir*
Kara Carnahan, *Vice Pres*
Sophora Acheson, *Social Dir*
Janine Evans, *Social Dir*
Suphia Mahmood, *Planning*
EMP: 57 **EST:** 1988
SALES: 68.6MM **Privately Held**
WEB: www.abodeservices.org
SIC: 8322 Social service center

(P-17407)
ADOPTION CLINICAL SERVICES LLC
510 3rd St Ste 9, Eureka (95501-0466)
PHONE 405 476-1983
Bryan Post,
EMP: 46 **EST:** 2019
SALES (est): 547.7K **Privately Held**
SIC: 8322 Adoption services

(P-17408)
AEGIS TREATMENT CENTERS
1947 N California St, Stockton (95204-6029)
PHONE 209 565-5982
EMP: 41 **EST:** 2017
SALES (est): 42.4K **Privately Held**
WEB: www.pinnacletreatment.com
SIC: 8322 8099 8093 Substance abuse counseling; health & allied services; substance abuse clinics (outpatient)

(P-17409)
AGING CALIFORNIA DEPARTMENT
Also Called: Passages Adult Research Center
2491 Carmichael Dr, Chico (95928-7190)
PHONE 530 898-5923
Vicky Paxton, *Director*
EMP: 42 **Privately Held**
WEB: www.aging.ca.gov
SIC: 8322 9441 Senior citizens' center or association; administration of social & manpower programs;
HQ: California Department Of Aging
2880 Gateway Oaks Dr # 200
Sacramento CA 95833

(P-17410)
AIM HIGHER INCORPORATED (PA)
1132 Smith Ln, Roseville (95661-4104)
P.O. Box 815 (95661-0815)
PHONE 916 786-0351
Edgar David, *President*
Simona Samson, *Officer*
Max Woodford, *Exec Dir*
David Lopez, *Program Dir*
Marina David, *Client Mgr*
EMP: 64 **EST:** 2005
SALES (est): 8.8MM **Privately Held**
WEB: www.aimhigherinc.com
SIC: 8322 Adult day care center

(P-17411)
ALAMEDA CNTY CMNTY FD BNK INC
7900 Edgewater Dr, Oakland (94621-2004)
P.O. Box 2599 (94614-0599)
PHONE 510 635-3663
Suzan Bateson, *President*
Demetri Price, *Admin Asst*
Kate Cheyne, *Research*
Martha Orozco, *Research*
Marie-Edith Aubry, *Finance*
EMP: 70 **EST:** 1985
SQ FT: 118,000
SALES: 101.7MM **Privately Held**
WEB: www.accfb.org
SIC: 8322 Social service center

(P-17412)
ALCOHOL DRG AWARENESS PROGRAM
1981 Cherokee Rd, Stockton (95205-2720)
P.O. Box 5070 (95205-0070)
PHONE 209 870-6500
Dale Benner, *Exec Dir*
Steve Jazulin, *Program Dir*
EMP: 35 **EST:** 1993
SALES (est): 2.6MM **Privately Held**
WEB: www.newdirectionsstockton.org
SIC: 8322 General counseling services

(P-17413)
ALDEA INC
470 Chadbourne Rd Ste F, Fairfield (94534-9620)
PHONE 925 577-3102
EMP: 40
SALES (corp-wide): 8.4MM **Privately Held**
WEB: www.aldeainc.org
SIC: 8322 Family counseling services
PA: Aldea, Inc.
2310 1st St
Napa CA 94559
707 224-8266

(P-17414)
ALMADEN VLY COUNSELING SVC INC
6529 Crown Blvd Ste D, San Jose (95120-2905)
PHONE 408 997-0200
Karen Sumi, *Exec Dir*
Pat Treadway, *Manager*
EMP: 41 **EST:** 1980
SQ FT: 1,500
SALES (est): 4.6MM **Privately Held**
WEB: www.avcounseling.org
SIC: 8322 Family counseling services

(P-17415)
ALTA CAL REGIONAL CTR INC
283 W Court St, Woodland (95695-2900)
PHONE 530 666-3391
Mechelle Johnson, *Branch Mgr*
EMP: 147
SALES (corp-wide): 515.1MM **Privately Held**
WEB: www.altaregional.org
SIC: 8322 8082 Social service center; home health care services
PA: Alta California Regional Center, Inc.
2241 Harvard St Ste 100
Sacramento CA 95815
916 978-6400

(P-17416)
ALTA CAL REGIONAL CTR INC
Also Called: Alta California Regional Ctr
807 Douglas Blvd, Roseville (95678-2762)
PHONE 916 786-8110
Jean Onesi, *Manager*
EMP: 147
SALES (corp-wide): 515.1MM **Privately Held**
WEB: www.altaregional.org
SIC: 8322 7389 Social service center; fund raising organizations
PA: Alta California Regional Center, Inc.
2241 Harvard St Ste 100
Sacramento CA 95815
916 978-6400

(P-17417)
ALTA CAL REGIONAL CTR INC
950 Tharp Rd, Yuba City (95993-8344)
PHONE 530 674-3070
Terry Rhoades, *Manager*
EMP: 147
SALES (corp-wide): 515.1MM **Privately Held**
WEB: www.altaregional.org
SIC: 8322 8699 General counseling services; charitable organization
PA: Alta California Regional Center, Inc.
2241 Harvard St Ste 100
Sacramento CA 95815
916 978-6400

(P-17418)
ALTAMEDIX CORPORATION
4234 N Freeway Blvd # 500, Sacramento (95834-1294)
PHONE 916 648-3999
Yana Balyasny, *President*
Natalia Romachova, *Vice Pres*
Aleriy Barash, *Admin Sec*
EMP: 64 **EST:** 1998
SQ FT: 10,000
SALES (est): 1MM **Privately Held**
WEB: www.altamedix.com
SIC: 8322 Adult day care center

(P-17419)
ALUM ROCK COUNSELING CTR INC (PA)
777 N 1st St Ste 444, San Jose (95112-6339)
PHONE 408 240-0070
Patricia Chiapellone, *Exec Dir*
Norma Sanchez, *CFO*
Victoria Konopka, *Office Mgr*
Melissa Sanchez, *Executive Asst*
Jasmine Velazquez, *Administration*
EMP: 39 **EST:** 1973
SALES: 7MM **Privately Held**
WEB: www.alumrockcc.org
SIC: 8322 Family (marriage) counseling; crisis intervention center; settlement house

(P-17420)
ALZHEIMERS SVCS OF EAST BAY (PA)
Also Called: ALZHEIMER'S SERVICES OF THE EA
2320 Channing Way, Berkeley (94704-2202)
PHONE 510 644-3181
Michelle Pope, *CEO*
Kelly Anderson, *Administration*
Frederic Walker, *Human Resources*
EMP: 36 **EST:** 1988
SQ FT: 8,000
SALES (est): 1.8MM **Privately Held**
WEB: www.aseb.org
SIC: 8322 Adult day care center

(P-17421)
AMERICAN NATIONAL RED CROSS
Also Called: American Nat Red Cross - Blood
140 Gregory Ln Ste 120, Pleasant Hill (94523-3395)
PHONE 925 602-1460
EMP: 48
SALES (corp-wide): 2.8B **Privately Held**
WEB: www.redcross.org
SIC: 8322 Social service center
PA: The American National Red Cross
431 18th St Nw
Washington DC 20006
202 737-8300

(P-17422)
AMERICAN NATIONAL RED CROSS
Also Called: American Nat Red Cross - Blood
6230 Claremont Ave, Oakland (94618-1324)
PHONE 510 594-5100
Jay Winkenbach, *CEO*
Sylvia Preciado, *Manager*
EMP: 48
SQ FT: 42,714
SALES (corp-wide): 2.8B **Privately Held**
WEB: www.redcross.org
SIC: 8322 Social service center
PA: The American National Red Cross
431 18th St Nw
Washington DC 20006
202 737-8300

(P-17423)
AMERICAN NATIONAL RED CROSS
6230 Claremont Ave, Oakland (94618-1324)
PHONE 510 595-4400
Charles Telehila, *Office Mgr*
EMP: 48
SALES (corp-wide): 2.8B **Privately Held**
WEB: www.redcross.org
SIC: 8322 Social service center
PA: The American National Red Cross
431 18th St Nw
Washington DC 20006
202 737-8300

(P-17424)
AMERICAN NATIONAL RED CROSS
Also Called: American Red Cross
850 Sanguinetti Rd, Sonora (95370-5280)
PHONE 209 533-1513
Victoria Raleigh, *Exec Dir*
Vincent Valenzuela, *Program Mgr*
Brittany Seidt, *Executive Asst*
Katrina Couch, *IT/INT Sup*
Archila Alma, *Technician*
EMP: 48
SALES (corp-wide): 2.8B **Privately Held**
WEB: www.redcross.org
SIC: 8322 Social service center
PA: The American National Red Cross
431 18th St Nw
Washington DC 20006
202 737-8300

PRODUCTS & SERVICES SECTION
8322 - Individual & Family Social Svcs County (P-17446)

(P-17425)
AMERICAN NATIONAL RED CROSS
Also Called: American Red Cross
569 Terry A Francois Blvd, San Francisco (94158-2207)
PHONE..................................415 371-1740
EMP: 48
SALES (corp-wide): 2.8B **Privately Held**
WEB: www.redcross.org
SIC: 8322 Social service center
PA: The American National Red Cross
   431 18th St Nw
   Washington DC 20006
   202 737-8300

(P-17426)
AMERICAN NATIONAL RED CROSS
Also Called: American Red Cross
5880 W Las Psts Blvd # 34, Pleasanton (94588-8552)
PHONE..................................800 733-2767
Christy Woods, *Director*
EMP: 48
SALES (corp-wide): 2.8B **Privately Held**
WEB: www.redcross.org
SIC: 8322 Social service center
PA: The American National Red Cross
   431 18th St Nw
   Washington DC 20006
   202 737-8300

(P-17427)
AMERICAN NATIONAL RED CROSS
Also Called: American Red Cross
5665 Power Inn Rd, Sacramento (95824-2333)
PHONE..................................800 733-2767
EMP: 48
SALES (corp-wide): 2.8B **Privately Held**
WEB: www.redcross.org
SIC: 8322 Social service center
PA: The American National Red Cross
   431 18th St Nw
   Washington DC 20006
   202 737-8300

(P-17428)
AMERICAN NATIONAL RED CROSS
Also Called: American Red Cross
1300 Alberta Way, Concord (94521-3705)
PHONE..................................925 603-7400
Harold Brooks, *Principal*
EMP: 48
SQ FT: 4,765
SALES (corp-wide): 2.8B **Privately Held**
WEB: www.redcross.org
SIC: 8322 Social service center
PA: The American National Red Cross
   431 18th St Nw
   Washington DC 20006
   202 737-8300

(P-17429)
APA FAMILY SUPPORT SERVICES
10 Nottingham Pl, San Francisco (94133-4523)
PHONE..................................415 617-0061
Rick Yuen, *Exec Dir*
Amor Santiago, *Exec Dir*
Jack Siu, *Program Mgr*
Rosetta Lau, *Office Mgr*
Silva Luna, *Opers Mgr*
EMP: 44 EST: 2008
SALES (est): 2.7MM **Privately Held**
WEB: www.apafss.org
SIC: 8322 Social service center

(P-17430)
ARC OF BUTTE COUNTY (PA)
2030 Park Ave, Chico (95928-6701)
P.O. Box 3697 (95927-3697)
PHONE..................................530 891-5865
Courtney Casey, *CEO*
Michael McGinnis, *CEO*
Jean Campbell, *Treasurer*
Nelson Corwin, *Associate Dir*
Jennifer White, *Office Admin*
EMP: 200 EST: 1962
SQ FT: 12,268
SALES: 9.2MM **Privately Held**
WEB: www.arcbutte.org
SIC: 8322 Individual & family services

(P-17431)
ARC OF THE EAST BAY (PA)
1101 Walpert St, Hayward (94541-6705)
PHONE..................................510 357-3569
Ron Luter, *Exec Dir*
Frank Alvarado, *President*
Francis Zamora, *Production*
Mary Foster, *Program Dir*
Cecilia Connolly, *Director*
▲ EMP: 35 EST: 1969
SALES (est): 3.1MM **Privately Held**
WEB: www.arceastbay.org
SIC: 8322 Association for the handicapped

(P-17432)
ARGONAUT KENSINGTON ASSOCIATES
Also Called: Kensington Place
1580 Geary Rd Ofc, Walnut Creek (94597-2786)
PHONE..................................925 943-1121
Richard Fordiani, *Partner*
James Houston, *Partner*
EMP: 41 EST: 1988
SALES (est): 5.2MM **Privately Held**
SIC: 8322 Senior citizens' center or association

(P-17433)
ASIAN PCF ISLNDER WLLNESS CTR
Also Called: San Francisco Cmnty Hlth Ctr
730 Polk St Fl 4, San Francisco (94109-7813)
PHONE..................................415 292-3400
Lance Toma, *Exec Dir*
Ming M Kwan, *COO*
Michael Rabanal, *Bd of Directors*
Alisson Sombredero, *Chief Mktg Ofcr*
Sarah Pierce, *Associate Dir*
▲ EMP: 36
SQ FT: 1,900
SALES: 5.6MM **Privately Held**
WEB: www.sfcommunityhealth.org
SIC: 8322 Social service center

(P-17434)
AVENIDAS (PA)
Also Called: AVENIDAS SENIOR HEALTH DAY HEA
4000 Middlefield Rd Ste I, Palo Alto (94303-4761)
PHONE..................................650 289-5400
Lisa Hendrickson, *President*
Sue Campbell, *Treasurer*
Maureen Breen, *Vice Pres*
Morien Breen, *Vice Pres*
Mary Hohensee, *Vice Pres*
EMP: 36 EST: 1961
SQ FT: 25,000
SALES: 8.1MM **Privately Held**
WEB: www.avenidas.org
SIC: 8322 Senior citizens' center or association

(P-17435)
BAKER PLACES INC
Also Called: Grove Street
2157 Grove St, San Francisco (94117-1008)
PHONE..................................415 387-2275
Silvia Dunning, *Director*
EMP: 63
SALES (corp-wide): 19.9MM **Privately Held**
WEB: www.prcsf.org
SIC: 8322 Social service center
PA: Baker Places, Inc.
   170 9th St
   San Francisco CA 94103
   415 864-4655

(P-17436)
BAY AREA CMNTY RESOURCES INC
11175 San Pablo Ave, El Cerrito (94530-2157)
PHONE..................................510 559-3000
Martin Weinstein, *Principal*
Ana Martinez, *Exec Dir*
Eric Rego, *Program Mgr*
Rebecca Wong, *Program Mgr*
Maria Vega, *Office Mgr*
EMP: 36
SALES (corp-wide): 49MM **Privately Held**
WEB: www.bacr.org
SIC: 8322 8093 Alcoholism counseling, nontreatment; drug clinic, outpatient
PA: Bay Area Community Resources, Inc.
   171 Carlos Dr
   San Rafael CA 94903
   415 444-5580

(P-17437)
BAY AREA COMMUNITY SVCS INC
40963 Grimmer Blvd, Fremont (94538-2846)
PHONE..................................510 656-7742
Priscilla Mathews, *Branch Mgr*
Chika Williams, *Med Doctor*
Kelly Miller, *Hlthcr Dir*
Aimee Armata, *Senior Mgr*
Patricia Sanchez, *Manager*
EMP: 95
SALES (corp-wide): 57.7MM **Privately Held**
WEB: www.bayareacs.org
SIC: 8322 Social service center
PA: Bay Area Community Services, Inc.
   390 40th St
   Oakland CA 94609
   510 613-0330

(P-17438)
BAY AREA COMMUNITY SVCS INC (PA)
Also Called: EAST BAY TRANSITIONAL HOMES
390 40th St, Oakland (94609-2633)
PHONE..................................510 613-0330
Jamie Almanza, *CEO*
David Stoloff, *Chairman*
Shanice Kelley, *Associate Dir*
Adam Hudson, *Program Mgr*
Jennifer Rodway, *Program Mgr*
EMP: 50 EST: 1953
SQ FT: 1,000
SALES (est): 57.7MM **Privately Held**
WEB: www.bayareacs.org
SIC: 8322 8093 Social service center; mental health clinic, outpatient

(P-17439)
BAY AREA COMMUNITY SVCS INC
Also Called: Bacs Adult Day Care
5714 Mrtin Lther King Jr, Oakland (94609-1673)
PHONE..................................510 601-1074
Rita Stuckey, *Branch Mgr*
EMP: 95
SALES (corp-wide): 57.7MM **Privately Held**
WEB: www.bayareacs.org
SIC: 8322 8399 Adult day care center; advocacy group
PA: Bay Area Community Services, Inc.
   390 40th St
   Oakland CA 94609
   510 613-0330

(P-17440)
BAY AREA RESCUE MISSION (PA)
2114 Macdonald Ave, Richmond (94801-3311)
P.O. Box 1112 (94802-0112)
PHONE..................................510 215-4555
John M Anderson, *President*
Debra Anderson, *Vice Pres*
Tim Hammack, *Vice Pres*
Jonathan Russell, *Vice Pres*
Woody Tausend, *Vice Pres*
EMP: 51 EST: 1965
SQ FT: 80,000
SALES (est): 10.3MM **Privately Held**
WEB: www.bayarearescue.org
SIC: 8322 Emergency shelters

(P-17441)
BAY AREA SENIOR SERVICES INC
Also Called: Peninsula Regent, The
1 Baldwin Ave Ofc, San Mateo (94401-3837)
PHONE..................................650 579-5500
M Mannstab, *Exec Dir*
Gail Hunter, *Director*
Melissa Shefer, *Manager*
EMP: 151
SALES (corp-wide): 30.6MM **Privately Held**
WEB: www.retirement.org
SIC: 8322 Senior citizens' center or association
HQ: Bay Area Senior Services Inc
   1 Hawthorne St Ste 400
   San Francisco CA 94105
   415 989-1111

(P-17442)
BERKELEY YOUTH ALTERNATIVES (PA)
1255 Allston Way, Berkeley (94702-1833)
PHONE..................................510 845-9010
Nicci Williams, *Exec Dir*
Robert L Walker, *Treasurer*
Mieka Claridy, *Program Mgr*
Randall C Ferguson,
Alex Williams, *Program Dir*
EMP: 56 EST: 1969
SQ FT: 22,000
SALES: 1.8MM **Privately Held**
WEB: www.byaonline.org
SIC: 8322 Social service center

(P-17443)
BERNARD OSHER MRIN JWISH CMNTY
Also Called: J C C
200 N San Pedro Rd, San Rafael (94903-4213)
PHONE..................................415 444-8000
Marty Friedman, *President*
Diana McKim, *CEO*
Michael Baumstein, *COO*
Tom Esperance, *CFO*
George Mann, *CFO*
EMP: 200 EST: 1995
SQ FT: 90,000
SALES (est): 11.2MM **Privately Held**
WEB: www.marinjcc.org
SIC: 8322 Community center

(P-17444)
BETTER WAY FSTER FMLY ADPTION
3200 Adeline St, Berkeley (94703-2407)
PHONE..................................510 601-0203
Shahnaz Mazandarni, *Exec Dir*
Mark Pasley, *Executive Asst*
Kimberly Murphy, *Supervisor*
EMP: 35 EST: 1996
SQ FT: 11,592
SALES (est): 858.7K **Privately Held**
WEB: www.abetterwayinc.net
SIC: 8322 Individual & family services

(P-17445)
BILL WILSON CENTER (PA)
3490 The Alameda, Santa Clara (95050-4333)
PHONE..................................408 243-0222
Sparky Harlan, *CEO*
John Anyosa, *Program Mgr*
Kirsten Mc Keraghan, *Program Mgr*
Priscilla Wong, *Accountant*
Judy Whittier, *Commissioner*
EMP: 88 EST: 1973
SQ FT: 19,000
SALES: 25.9MM **Privately Held**
WEB: www.billwilsoncenter.org
SIC: 8322 Social service center

(P-17446)
BONITA HOUSE INC
6333 Telg Ave Ste 102, Oakland (94609)
PHONE..................................510 923-0180
Rick Crispino, *Exec Dir*
Lorna Jones, *Exec Dir*
Lori Magistrado, *General Mgr*
Gangaa Sandagsuren, *Admin Asst*
Amanda Ollis, *Program Dir*
EMP: 76 EST: 1971

8322 - Individual & Family Social Svcs County (P-17447)

SQ FT: 4,000
SALES: 8MM **Privately Held**
WEB: www.bonitahouse.org
SIC: 8322 Association for the handicapped

(P-17447)
BREAKTHROUGH BEHAVIORAL INC
702 Marshall St Ste 340, Redwood City (94063-1825)
PHONE..................888 282-2522
Julian Cohen, *President*
EMP: 134 EST: 2011
SALES (est): 1.2MM
SALES (corp-wide): 160.4B **Publicly Held**
WEB: www.mdlive.com
SIC: 8322 General counseling services
HQ: Mdlive, Inc.
3350 Sw 148th Ave Ste 300
Miramar FL 33027

(P-17448)
BRIGHTER BEGINNINGS (PA)
2727 Macdonald Ave, Richmond (94804-3006)
PHONE..................510 903-7503
Barbara B McCullough, *CEO*
Diana Gamino, *Program Mgr*
Wendy Escamilla, *Administration*
Erica Lipschultz, *Nurse*
Liz Nickels, *Director*
EMP: 50 EST: 1983
SALES (est): 5.6MM **Privately Held**
WEB: www.brighter-beginnings.org
SIC: 8322 8011 8093 Individual & family services; primary care medical clinic; mental health clinic, outpatient

(P-17449)
BUREAU OF RECLAMATION
2420 W Brannan Island Rd, Isleton (95641-9716)
PHONE..................916 777-6992
EMP: 39 **Publicly Held**
WEB: www.usbr.gov
SIC: 8322 Community center
HQ: Bureau of Reclamation
1849 C St Nw
Washington DC 20240

(P-17450)
CALIFORNIA AUTISM CENTER
1630 E Shaw Ave Ste 190, Fresno (93710-8114)
PHONE..................559 475-7860
Amanda Nicholson Adams, *CEO*
William Forath, *Administration*
Nicholas De La Torre, *Human Res Dir*
Cristina Cendejas, *Personnel Assit*
Candra Donaldson, *QC Mgr*
EMP: 55 EST: 2013
SALES (est): 7.5MM **Privately Held**
WEB: www.calautismcenter.org
SIC: 8322 6321 Individual & family services; health insurance carriers

(P-17451)
CALIFORNIA TRIBAL TANF PARTNR (PA)
Also Called: Cttp
991 Parallel Dr Ste B, Lakeport (95453-5717)
PHONE..................707 262-4404
Jeff Schueller, *Exec Dir*
Lisa Pendleton, *Administration*
Karli Barger, *Site Mgr*
Cenza Mehr, *Site Mgr*
Kelly Partridge, *Manager*
EMP: 51 EST: 2009
SALES (est): 10.4MM **Privately Held**
WEB: www.cttp.net
SIC: 8322 Social service center

(P-17452)
CALIFRNIA CHILD CARE RSRCE RFR
Also Called: Infant/Toddler Consort
5232 Claremont Ave, Oakland (94618-1033)
PHONE..................510 658-0381
Betty Cohen, *Exec Dir*
EMP: 40

SALES (corp-wide): 3.7MM **Privately Held**
WEB: www.rrnetwork.org
SIC: 8322 Referral service for personal & social problems
PA: California Child Care Resource And Referral Network
1 Polk St Unit 201
San Francisco CA 94102
415 882-0234

(P-17453)
CALVARY CROSS CH OF HIGHLANDS (PA)
1900 Monterey Dr, San Bruno (94066-2571)
PHONE..................650 873-4095
Leighton Sheley, *Pastor*
EMP: 101 EST: 1972
SQ FT: 50,000
SALES (est): 12.2MM **Privately Held**
WEB: www.highlands.us
SIC: 8661 8322 8299 Community church; general counseling services; religious school

(P-17454)
CAMP WELLSPRING LLC (DH)
Also Called: Wellspring Family Camp
42675 Road 44, Reedley (93654-9146)
PHONE..................559 638-5374
Ryan Craig, *President*
EMP: 35 EST: 2004
SALES (est): 1.2MM **Publicly Held**
WEB: www.wellspringcamps.com
SIC: 8322 General counseling services
HQ: Aspen Education Group, Inc.
17777 Center Court Dr N # 300
Cerritos CA 90703
562 467-5500

(P-17455)
CASA ALLEGRA COMMUNITY SVCS
35 Mitchell Blvd Ste 8, San Rafael (94903-2012)
PHONE..................415 499-1116
Jeanne Santangelo, *Director*
Mia Brown, *Bd of Directors*
Kimberlyn Leon, *Manager*
Javier Miranda, *Manager*
EMP: 70 EST: 2011
SALES: 5.8MM **Privately Held**
WEB: www.casaallegra.org
SIC: 8322 Social service center

(P-17456)
CATHOLIC CHRTIES CYO OF THE AR
810 Avenue D, San Francisco (94130-2002)
PHONE..................415 743-0017
Nella Goncalves, *Principal*
EMP: 38
SALES (corp-wide): 63.3MM **Privately Held**
WEB: www.catholiccharitiessf.org
SIC: 8322 Social service center
PA: Catholic Charities Cyo Of The Archdiocese Of San Francisco
1 Saint Vincents Dr
San Rafael CA 94903
415 972-1200

(P-17457)
CATHOLIC CHRTIES CYO OF THE AR
Also Called: Leland House
141 Leland Ave, San Francisco (94134-2847)
PHONE..................415 405-2000
Jeff Bialik, *Exec Dir*
Jose Cartagena, *Program Mgr*
Steve Grant, *Director*
EMP: 38
SALES (corp-wide): 63.3MM **Privately Held**
WEB: www.catholiccharitiessf.org
SIC: 8322 Social service center
PA: Catholic Charities Cyo Of The Archdiocese Of San Francisco
1 Saint Vincents Dr
San Rafael CA 94903
415 972-1200

(P-17458)
CATHOLIC CHRTIES CYO OF THE AR
1390 Mission St, San Francisco (94103-2668)
PHONE..................415 863-1141
John Heenan, *Maintence Staff*
EMP: 38
SALES (corp-wide): 63.3MM **Privately Held**
WEB: www.catholiccharitiessf.org
SIC: 8322 Social service center
PA: Catholic Charities Cyo Of The Archdiocese Of San Francisco
1 Saint Vincents Dr
San Rafael CA 94903
415 972-1200

(P-17459)
CATHOLIC CHRTIES CYO OF THE AR
1111 Junipero Serra Blvd, San Francisco (94132-2653)
PHONE..................415 334-5550
Jeffrey Bialik V, *Principal*
Colleen McCarthy, *Contract Mgr*
Steve Jacob, *Opers Mgr*
Ernest Brown, *Director*
Deanna Crespo, *Case Mgr*
EMP: 38
SALES (corp-wide): 63.3MM **Privately Held**
WEB: www.catholiccharitiessf.org
SIC: 8322 Social service center
PA: Catholic Charities Cyo Of The Archdiocese Of San Francisco
1 Saint Vincents Dr
San Rafael CA 94903
415 972-1200

(P-17460)
CATHOLIC CHRTIES CYO OF THE AR
Also Called: Derek Silva Community
20 Franklin St, San Francisco (94102-6000)
PHONE..................415 553-8700
Theresa Flores, *Principal*
Erwin Barrios, *Case Mgr*
EMP: 38
SALES (corp-wide): 63.3MM **Privately Held**
WEB: www.catholiccharitiessf.org
SIC: 8322 Social service center
PA: Catholic Charities Cyo Of The Archdiocese Of San Francisco
1 Saint Vincents Dr
San Rafael CA 94903
415 972-1200

(P-17461)
CATHOLIC CHRTIES CYO OF THE AR (PA)
1 Saint Vincents Dr, San Rafael (94903-1504)
PHONE..................415 972-1200
Jeffrey V Bialik, *CEO*
Chas J Lopez, *COO*
Keith Spindle, *CFO*
Charlene Naughton, *Officer*
Jeff Bialik, *Exec Dir*
EMP: 56 EST: 1907
SALES (est): 63.3MM **Privately Held**
WEB: www.catholiccharitiessf.org
SIC: 8322 Social service center

(P-17462)
CATHOLIC CHRTIES CYO OF THE AR
1 Saint Vincents Dr, San Rafael (94903-1504)
PHONE..................415 507-2000
Chuck Fernandez, *Branch Mgr*
Matthew Carter, *Director*
EMP: 38
SALES (corp-wide): 63.3MM **Privately Held**
WEB: www.catholiccharitiessf.org
SIC: 8322 8641 Child related social services; civic social & fraternal associations
PA: Catholic Charities Cyo Of The Archdiocese Of San Francisco
1 Saint Vincents Dr
San Rafael CA 94903
415 972-1200

(P-17463)
CATHOLIC CHRTIES CYO OF THE AR
Also Called: San Franciso Adult Day Svcs
50 Broad St, San Francisco (94112-3002)
PHONE..................415 452-3500
Patty Clement-Cihak, *Branch Mgr*
EMP: 38
SALES (corp-wide): 63.3MM **Privately Held**
WEB: www.catholiccharitiessf.org
SIC: 8322 Social service center
PA: Catholic Charities Cyo Of The Archdiocese Of San Francisco
1 Saint Vincents Dr
San Rafael CA 94903
415 972-1200

(P-17464)
CATHOLIC CHRTIES CYO OF THE AR
Also Called: Boys and Girls Homes Shelter
750 33rd Ave, San Francisco (94121-3428)
PHONE..................415 668-9543
Dan Gallagher, *Branch Mgr*
EMP: 38
SALES (corp-wide): 63.3MM **Privately Held**
WEB: www.catholiccharitiessf.org
SIC: 8322 Social service center
PA: Catholic Charities Cyo Of The Archdiocese Of San Francisco
1 Saint Vincents Dr
San Rafael CA 94903
415 972-1200

(P-17465)
CATHOLIC CHRTIES CYO OF THE AR
Also Called: St. Joseph's Family Center
899 Guerrero St, San Francisco (94110-2222)
PHONE..................415 206-1467
Tere Brown, *Opers Staff*
Bruce Blagsvedt, *Facilities Mgr*
Jane Ferguson Flout, *Director*
Steve Farbstein, *Manager*
EMP: 38
SALES (corp-wide): 63.3MM **Privately Held**
WEB: www.catholiccharitiessf.org
SIC: 8322 Social service center
PA: Catholic Charities Cyo Of The Archdiocese Of San Francisco
1 Saint Vincents Dr
San Rafael CA 94903
415 972-1200

(P-17466)
CATHOLIC CHRTIES OF THE DCESE
Also Called: Ombudsman Patients Advocate
2351 Tenaya Dr D, Modesto (95354-3925)
PHONE..................209 529-3784
Monica Raymos, *Manager*
Ana Guzman, *Program Mgr*
Yolanda Ochoa, *Human Resources*
Joanna Galindo, *Program Dir*
Amber Butler, *Director*
EMP: 73
SALES (corp-wide): 6.3MM **Privately Held**
WEB: www.ccstockton.org
SIC: 8322 Social service center
PA: Catholic Charities Of The Diocese Of Stockton
1106 N El Dorado St
Stockton CA 95202
209 444-5900

(P-17467)
CATHOLIC CHRTIES OF THE DCESE (PA)
Also Called: CATHOLIC CHARITIES OF EAST BAY
433 Jefferson St, Oakland (94607-3539)
P.O. Box 23245 (94623-0245)
PHONE..................510 768-3100
Chuck Fernandez, *Exec Dir*
Christopher Martinez, *Officer*
Diana Pascual, *Officer*
Maciel Jacques, *Executive*
Solomon Belette, *Exec Dir*
EMP: 83 EST: 1935
SQ FT: 10,376

PRODUCTS & SERVICES SECTION
8322 - Individual & Family Social Svcs County (P-17492)

SALES (est): 24.1MM Privately Held
WEB: www.cceb.org
SIC: 8322 8661 Social service center; religious organizations

(P-17468)
CATHOLIC CHRTIES SNTA CLARA CN
Also Called: John Xxiii Snior Ntrtn Site Ct
195 E San Fernando St, San Jose (95112-3503)
PHONE.................................408 282-8600
Tatiana Colon, *Director*
EMP: 88
SALES (corp-wide): 36.6MM Privately Held
WEB: www.catholiccharitiesscc.org
SIC: 8322 Social service center
PA: Catholic Charities Of Santa Clara County
    2625 Zanker Rd Ste 200
    San Jose CA 95134
    408 468-0100

(P-17469)
CATHOLIC CHRTIES SNTA CLARA CN (PA)
2625 Zanker Rd Ste 200, San Jose (95134-2130)
PHONE.................................408 468-0100
Gregory Kepferle, *CEO*
Susan L Taylor, *Officer*
Linda Franks, *Business Dir*
Wanda Hale, *Program Mgr*
SOO Poumele, *Program Mgr*
EMP: 200 EST: 1981
SQ FT: 50,000
SALES: 36.6MM Privately Held
WEB: www.catholiccharitiesscc.org
SIC: 8322 Social service center

(P-17470)
CBEM LLC CORPORATE OFFICE (PA)
270 Lafayette Cir, Lafayette (94549-4379)
PHONE.................................925 283-9000
Steve Westemeier, *CEO*
Karre Williams, *COO*
Gene Ho, *CFO*
Weihe Huang, *Vice Pres*
Ferial Trammell, *Admin Asst*
EMP: 71 EST: 2012
SALES (est): 16.1MM Privately Held
WEB: www.cbemllc.com
SIC: 8322 Crisis intervention center

(P-17471)
CENTER FOR DOMESTIC PEACE
Also Called: MARIN ABUSED WOMEN'S SERVICES
734 A St, San Rafael (94901-3923)
PHONE.................................415 457-2464
Donna Garske, *Exec Dir*
Kate Kain, *Exec Dir*
Keith Kane, *Exec Dir*
Emily Wilson, *Finance*
Shihuan Luo, *Accountant*
EMP: 50 EST: 1977
SALES (est): 4.6MM Privately Held
WEB: www.centerfordomesticpeace.org
SIC: 8322 Social service center

(P-17472)
CENTER FOR FATHERS & FAMILIES
920 Del Paso Blvd, Sacramento (95815-3513)
PHONE.................................916 568-3237
Rick Jennings, *Exec Dir*
Julius Austin, *Director*
Rashid Sidqe, *Director*
EMP: 36 EST: 1993
SALES (est): 1.5MM Privately Held
WEB: www.cffsacramento.org
SIC: 8322 Family service agency

(P-17473)
CENTER FOR HUMAN SERVICES (PA)
2000 W Briggsmore Ave I, Modesto (95350-3839)
PHONE.................................209 526-1476
Linda Kovacs, *Exec Dir*
Cindy Duenas, *Exec Dir*
David Collins, *Program Mgr*

Jody Schloderer, *Administration*
Carmen Wilson, *Opers Staff*
EMP: 146 EST: 1970
SQ FT: 8,000
SALES: 15.6MM Privately Held
WEB: www.centerforhumanservices.org
SIC: 8322 8331 Child guidance agency; job training services

(P-17474)
CENTER FOR LRNG ATISM SPPORT S
Also Called: Class
424 Peninsula Ave, San Mateo (94401-1653)
PHONE.................................800 538-8365
Denise Pollard, *CEO*
Ross Berman, *Vice Pres*
Natalia Villalba, *Human Res Mgr*
Pooja Singh, *Recruiter*
Angela Case, *Director*
EMP: 400 EST: 2016
SALES (est): 29.2MM Privately Held
WEB: www.classaba.com
SIC: 8322 Family counseling services

(P-17475)
CENTER FOR SOCIAL DYNAMICS LLC (PA)
Also Called: Csd Autism Services
1025 Atlantic Ave Ste 101, Alameda (94501-1188)
PHONE.................................510 268-8120
Pedro Torres, *CEO*
Brad Kerstetter, *CFO*
EMP: 394 EST: 2017
SALES (est): 26.8MM Privately Held
WEB: www.csdautismservices.com
SIC: 8322 General counseling services

(P-17476)
CENTER POINT INC (PA)
135 Paul Dr, San Rafael (94903-2023)
PHONE.................................415 492-4444
Sushma D Taylor PHD, *Exec Dir*
Terrell Anderson, *Treasurer*
Marc Hering, *Vice Pres*
Richard Jimenez, *Vice Pres*
Dennis McCray, *Vice Pres*
EMP: 136 EST: 1971
SQ FT: 7,750
SALES: 29.9MM Privately Held
WEB: www.cpinc.org
SIC: 8322 Social service center

(P-17477)
CENTRAL CITY HOSPITALITY HOUSE
290 Turk St, San Francisco (94102-3808)
PHONE.................................415 749-2100
Jackie Jenks, *Exec Dir*
Howard Maull, *CFO*
David McKinley, *Program Mgr*
Paul Sedita, *Admin Asst*
Mara Raider, *Finance*
EMP: 43 EST: 1967
SQ FT: 4,000
SALES (est): 6.2MM Privately Held
WEB: www.hospitalityhouse.org
SIC: 8322 Community center

(P-17478)
CENTRAL VLY CHLD SVCS NETWRK
1911 N Helm Ave, Fresno (93727-1614)
PHONE.................................559 456-1100
Jane Martin, *Exec Dir*
Irene Alvarado, *Admin Asst*
Janie Chvez, *Admin Asst*
Voni Maldonado, *Teacher*
Gayle Duffy, *Director*
EMP: 73 EST: 1984
SQ FT: 15,000
SALES (est): 18.7MM Privately Held
WEB: www.cvcsn.org
SIC: 8322 Social service center

(P-17479)
CENTRO LA FAMILIA ADVACASY SVC
Also Called: CENTRO LA FAMILIA ADVOCACY
302 Fresno St Ste 102, Fresno (93706-3641)
PHONE.................................559 237-2961

Margarita Rocha, *Director*
Edgar Olivera, *Executive*
Mario Gonzalez, *Deputy Dir*
EMP: 42 EST: 1976
SALES (est): 5.2MM Privately Held
WEB: www.centrolafamilia.org
SIC: 8322 Social service center

(P-17480)
CHANCE 4 CHANGE INC (PA)
525 2nd St Ste 213, Eureka (95501-0488)
PHONE.................................707 443-8601
Jill A Powell, *President*
Ericka Everhart, *Director*
EMP: 44 EST: 2009
SALES (est): 1.5MM Privately Held
WEB: www.chance4change.net
SIC: 8322 Adult day care center

(P-17481)
CHARIS YOUTH CENTER
714 W Main St, Grass Valley (95945-6410)
PHONE.................................530 477-9800
Carol Powell, *Exec Dir*
Deb Miller, *Administration*
EMP: 39 EST: 1984
SQ FT: 4,500
SALES (est): 4.5MM Privately Held
WEB: www.charisyouthcenter.org
SIC: 8322 Youth center

(P-17482)
CHILD ABUSE PRVNTION CNCIL SCR
4700 Roseville Rd Ste 102, North Highlands (95660-5100)
PHONE.................................916 244-1900
Sheila Anderson, *President*
Jessica Trudeau, *Exec Dir*
Kelly Barton, *Executive Asst*
Clay Merrill, *Director*
EMP: 44 EST: 1982
SALES (est): 8.3MM Privately Held
WEB: www.thecapcenter.org
SIC: 8322 Child related social services

(P-17483)
CHILD SUPPORT SVCS CAL DEPT (DH)
11150 International Dr, Rancho Cordova (95670-6072)
P.O. Box 419064 (95741-9064)
PHONE.................................916 464-5000
Jan Sturla, *Director*
EMP: 453 EST: 1999
SALES (est): 80MM Privately Held
WEB: www.childsup.ca.gov
SIC: 8322 9441 Family counseling services; administration of social & manpower programs

(P-17484)
CHILDRENS CRSIS CTR STNSLAUS C
1244 Fiori Ave, Modesto (95350-5503)
P.O. Box 1062 (95353-1062)
PHONE.................................209 577-4413
Colleen Garcia, *Director*
Kimberlee Speidel, *Human Res Mgr*
EMP: 37 EST: 1980
SALES: 4.4MM Privately Held
WEB: www.childrenscrisiscenter.com
SIC: 8322 Social service center

(P-17485)
CHILDRENS CUNCIL SAN FRANCISCO (PA)
445 Church St, San Francisco (94114-1720)
PHONE.................................415 343-3378
Sandee Blechman, *Exec Dir*
Fran Maier, *Bd of Directors*
Jennifer Brooks, *Officer*
Kim Kruckel, *Exec Dir*
Robert Wiseman, *Admin Mgr*
EMP: 85 EST: 1973
SALES (est): 109.8MM Privately Held
WEB: www.childrenscouncil.org
SIC: 8322 8351 Youth center; child day care services

(P-17486)
CHILDRENS HLTH CNCIL OF THE MD
650 Clark Way, Palo Alto (94304-2300)
PHONE.................................650 326-5530
Stephen Joffe, *Director*
Catherine Harvey, *Vice Chairman*
Elizabeth Sun, *Office Mgr*
Charles Caulfield, *Administration*
Francesca Carabio, *CIO*
EMP: 168 EST: 1954
SQ FT: 56,000
SALES (est): 29.9MM Privately Held
WEB: www.chconline.org
SIC: 8211 8322 Private special education school; child related social services

(P-17487)
CHILDRENS PROTECTIVE SERVICES
5730 Packard Ave, Marysville (95901-7118)
P.O. Box 2320 (95901-0082)
PHONE.................................530 749-6311
EMP: 60
SALES (est): 492.9K Privately Held
WEB: www.childrensprotectiveservices.com
SIC: 8322 Individual/Family Services

(P-17488)
CHILDRENS RECVG HM SACRAMENTO
3555 Auburn Blvd, Sacramento (95821-2071)
PHONE.................................916 482-2370
David Ballard, *CEO*
Rich Bryan, *CFO*
EMP: 160 EST: 1944
SQ FT: 26,000
SALES: 7.8MM Privately Held
WEB: www.crhkids.org
SIC: 8322 Social service center

(P-17489)
CHILDRENS VLG OF SONOMA CNTY
1321 Lia Ln, Santa Rosa (95404-8087)
P.O. Box 2025 (95405-0025)
PHONE.................................707 566-7044
EMP: 50
SALES: 111K Privately Held
WEB: www.tlc4kids.org
SIC: 8322 Individual/Family Services

(P-17490)
CITY AND COUNTY OF SAN FRANCIS
170 Otis St, San Francisco (94103-1221)
PHONE.................................415 557-5000
Trent Rhorer, *Owner*
Chandra Johnson, *Comms Dir*
Elizabeth Labarre, *Exec Dir*
Nikki Iroko, *Admin Mgr*
Sandra Yan, *Admin Sec*
EMP: 35 EST: 2014
SALES (est): 2.8MM Privately Held
WEB: www.sfhsa.org
SIC: 8322 Family service agency

(P-17491)
COMMITTEE ON SHELTERLESS
Also Called: COTS
900 Hopper St, Petaluma (94952-3388)
P.O. Box 2744 (94953-2744)
PHONE.................................707 765-6530
John Records, *Director*
Jamieson Bunn, *Director*
Jules Pelican, *Director*
Kiera Stewart, *Director*
Rachell Salyer, *Case Mgr*
EMP: 40 EST: 1988
SALES (est): 5.6MM Privately Held
WEB: www.cots.org
SIC: 8322 Emergency shelters

(P-17492)
COMMONWEAL
451 Mesa Rd, Bolinas (94924)
P.O. Box 316 (94924-0316)
PHONE.................................415 868-0970
Michael Lerner, *President*
Michael Lerner PHD, *President*
Tracy Cathcart, *Opers Staff*

8322 - Individual & Family Social Svcs County (P-17493)

Susan Braun, *Director*
James Quay, *Director*
EMP: 58 **EST:** 1976
SQ FT: 10,800
SALES: 5.2MM **Privately Held**
WEB: www.commonweal.org
SIC: 8322 Social service center; refugee service

(P-17493)
COMMUNITY BRIDGES (PA)
Also Called: CHILD CARE FOOD PROGRAM
519 Main St, Watsonville (95076-4356)
PHONE....................831 688-8840
Sam Story, *CEO*
Cathy Benson, *CFO*
Denise Andrews, *Bd of Directors*
Seth McGibben, *Officer*
Kyle Morse, *Vice Pres*
EMP: 40 **EST:** 1977
SQ FT: 3,500
SALES: 17.5MM **Privately Held**
WEB: www.communitybridges.org
SIC: 8322 Social service center

(P-17494)
COMMUNITY BRIDGES
Also Called: Golden Age Nutrition Program
114 E 5th St, Watsonville (95076-4309)
PHONE....................831 724-2024
Valerie Rivera, *Principal*
EMP: 77
SALES (corp-wide): 17.5MM **Privately Held**
WEB: www.communitybridges.org
SIC: 8322 Senior citizens' center or association
PA: Community Bridges
519 Main St
Watsonville CA 95076
831 688-8840

(P-17495)
COMMUNITY FORWARD SF INC (PA)
1171 Mission St Fl 2, San Francisco (94103-1519)
PHONE....................415 241-1199
Janet Goy, *Exec Dir*
John Uselman, *CFO*
EMP: 95 **EST:** 1978
SQ FT: 1,600
SALES (est): 10.6MM **Privately Held**
WEB: www.communityforwardsf.org
SIC: 8322 8069 Substance abuse counseling; drug addiction rehabilitation hospital

(P-17496)
COMMUNITY HLTH AWRNESS COUNCIL
Also Called: CHAC
590 W El Camino Real, Mountain View (94040-2612)
PHONE....................650 965-2020
Monique Kane, *Director*
Betty Mackey, *Executive*
John Lents, *Principal*
Marsha Deslauriers, *Exec Dir*
Paul Schutz, *Exec Dir*
EMP: 48 **EST:** 1972
SALES (est): 3.1MM **Privately Held**
WEB: www.chacmv.org
SIC: 8322 Social service center

(P-17497)
COMMUNITY INTGRTED WORK PRGRAM
Also Called: Ciwp
1735 Ashby Rd Ste D, Merced (95348-4309)
PHONE....................209 723-4025
Amy Weber, *Director*
EMP: 43
SALES (corp-wide): 17.3MM **Privately Held**
WEB: www.ciwp.org
SIC: 8322 Individual & family services
PA: Community Integrated Work Program, Inc.
3701 Stocker St Ste 203
View Park CA 90008
925 776-1040

(P-17498)
COMMUNITY INTGRTED WORK PRGRAM
Also Called: Cwip
4623 W Jacquelyn Ave, Fresno (93722-6413)
PHONE....................559 276-8564
Louis Leon, *Director*
Luis Leon, *Exec Dir*
EMP: 43
SALES (corp-wide): 17.3MM **Privately Held**
WEB: www.ciwp.org
SIC: 8322 Individual & family services
PA: Community Integrated Work Program, Inc.
3701 Stocker St Ste 203
View Park CA 90008
925 776-1040

(P-17499)
COMMUNITY SLTONS FOR CHLDREN F (PA)
9015 Murray Ave Ste 100, Gilroy (95020-3675)
P.O. Box 546, Morgan Hill (95038-0546)
PHONE....................408 842-7138
Erin O'Brien, *CEO*
Joann Davis, *CFO*
Melody Boykins, *Program Mgr*
Jason Deitz, *Program Mgr*
Erica Elliott, *Program Mgr*
EMP: 120 **EST:** 1973
SALES: 36.2MM **Privately Held**
WEB: www.communitysolutions.org
SIC: 8322 Social service center; family counseling services

(P-17500)
COMMUNITY SVCS AGCY MTN VIEW L
204 Stierlin Rd, Mountain View (94043-4618)
PHONE....................650 968-0836
Karol Olson, *President*
Paul Davis, *Vice Pres*
Tom Myers, *Exec Dir*
Marvin Sabarto, *Finance Mgr*
Marvin Sabado, *Finance*
EMP: 120 **EST:** 1957
SQ FT: 8,600
SALES (est): 8.6MM **Privately Held**
SIC: 8322 Social service center

(P-17501)
COMMUNITY VOCATIONAL SVCS LLC
3419 W Shaw Ave, Fresno (93711-3204)
P.O. Box 25192 (93729-5192)
PHONE....................559 227-8287
Cindy Pishione, *Principal*
EMP: 35 **EST:** 2010
SALES: 2.2MM **Privately Held**
SIC: 8322 General counseling services

(P-17502)
COMPASS FAMILY SERVICES (PA)
37 Grove St, San Francisco (94102-4702)
PHONE....................415 644-0504
Eirca Kisch, *Director*
Carrie Hook, *CFO*
Anna Cain, *Associate Dir*
Antonio Zamora, *Technician*
Marisa Chow, *Human Res Dir*
EMP: 42 **EST:** 1914
SALES: 17.6MM **Privately Held**
WEB: www.compass-sf.org
SIC: 8322 8351 General counseling services; child day care services

(P-17503)
COMPASS FAMILY SERVICES
Also Called: Compass Family Shelter
626 Polk St, San Francisco (94102-3328)
PHONE....................415 644-0504
Erica Kisch, *Exec Dir*
EMP: 80
SALES (corp-wide): 17.6MM **Privately Held**
WEB: www.compass-sf.org
SIC: 8322 Family (marriage) counseling
PA: Compass Family Services
37 Grove St
San Francisco CA 94102
415 644-0504

(P-17504)
COMPASS FAMILY SERVICES
Also Called: Compass Clara House
111 Page St, San Francisco (94102-5892)
PHONE....................415 644-0504
Erica Kisch, *Exec Dir*
EMP: 80
SALES (corp-wide): 17.6MM **Privately Held**
WEB: www.compass-sf.org
SIC: 8322 Individual & family services
PA: Compass Family Services
37 Grove St
San Francisco CA 94102
415 644-0504

(P-17505)
COMPRHNSIVE YUTH SVCS FRSNO IN
Also Called: C Y S
4545 N West Ave Ste 101, Fresno (93705-0946)
PHONE....................559 229-3561
Captain Mike Reid, *President*
Sylvia Kim, *Treasurer*
Kevin Torosian, *Vice Pres*
Jacqueline Smith, *Exec Dir*
Lisa Brott, *Program Mgr*
EMP: 53 **EST:** 1973
SQ FT: 9,000
SALES (est): 6.6MM **Privately Held**
WEB: www.cysfresno.org
SIC: 8322 Child related social services

(P-17506)
CONSULTNTS IN EDCTL PER SKILLS (PA)
Also Called: Ceps
5825 Auburn Blvd Ste 1, Sacramento (95841-2977)
P.O. Box 417010 (95841-7010)
PHONE....................916 348-1890
Patricia Vollenweider, *Exec Dir*
Robin Burris, *Accounts Mgr*
EMP: 51 **EST:** 1995
SALES (est): 1.4MM **Privately Held**
WEB: www.cepsonline.org
SIC: 8322 General counseling services

(P-17507)
CORA CMNTY OVRCMING RLTNSHIP A
Also Called: C O R A
2211 Palm Ave, San Mateo (94403-1814)
P.O. Box 5090 (94402-0090)
PHONE....................650 652-0800
Melissa Lukin, *Director*
Charles Cavallino, *Managing Dir*
Cheryle Matteo, *Finance Dir*
Mariluisa Diaz, *Education*
Lynn Engel, *Director*
EMP: 42 **EST:** 1977
SQ FT: 14,400
SALES: 5.6MM **Privately Held**
WEB: www.corasupport.org
SIC: 8322 Social service center

(P-17508)
COUNTRY VILLA SERVICE CORP
Also Called: Cntry Vlla Merced Hlthcre Cntr
510 W 26th St, Merced (95340-2804)
PHONE....................209 723-2911
Joel Saltzburg, *CEO*
Selena Lucero, *Chf Purch Ofc*
Jessica Arenivas, *Director*
EMP: 62
SALES (corp-wide): 78.2MM **Privately Held**
SIC: 8322 8051 Rehabilitation services; skilled nursing care facilities
PA: Country Villa Service Corp.
2400 E Katella Ave # 800
Anaheim CA 92806
310 574-3733

(P-17509)
COUNTY OF LOS ANGELES
Also Called: Madera County Probation Dept
209 W Yosemite Ave, Madera (93637-3534)
PHONE....................559 675-7739
Linda Nash, *Manager*
EMP: 38
SALES (corp-wide): 25.2B **Privately Held**
WEB: www.lacounty.gov
SIC: 8322 Individual & family services
PA: County Of Los Angeles
500 W Temple St Ste 437
Los Angeles CA 90012
213 974-1101

(P-17510)
COUNTY OF PLACER
Also Called: South Plcer Fire Prtection Dst
6900 Eureka Rd, Granite Bay (95746-6531)
PHONE....................916 791-7059
Eric Walter, *Chief*
Melody Glaspey, *CFO*
Eric Walder, *Officer*
Kathy Medeiros, *Finance*
Darren McMillin, *Chief*
EMP: 86
SQ FT: 2,908
SALES (corp-wide): 700.7MM **Privately Held**
WEB: www.placer.ca.gov
SIC: 9224 8322 Fire department, not including volunteer; ; first aid service
PA: County Of Placer
2986 Richardson Dr
Auburn CA 95603
530 889-4200

(P-17511)
COUNTY OF SAN JOAQUIN
Also Called: San Jquin Cnty Off Sbstnce Abu
1201 N El Dorado St, Stockton (95202-1306)
PHONE....................209 468-3720
Jarrett Spurgeon, *Analyst*
EMP: 64
SALES (corp-wide): 1.2B **Privately Held**
WEB: www.sjgov.org
SIC: 9111 8322 County supervisors' & executives' offices; substance abuse counseling
PA: County Of San Joaquin
44 N San Joaquin St # 640
Stockton CA 95202
209 468-3203

(P-17512)
COUNTY OF SOLANO
Also Called: Solano Juvenile Institution
740 Beck Ave, Fairfield (94533-4440)
PHONE....................707 784-6570
EMP: 89
SALES (corp-wide): 740.7MM **Privately Held**
WEB: www.solanocounty.com
SIC: 9223 8322 8211 Detention center, government; probation office; high school, junior or senior
PA: County Of Solano
675 Texas St Ste 2600
Fairfield CA 94533
707 784-6706

(P-17513)
COUNTY OF SONOMA
1450 Neotomas Ave Ste 200, Santa Rosa (95405-7574)
PHONE....................707 565-4711
Jill Rothberg, *Psychiatry*
Susie Shin-Calandrell, *Psychiatry*
EMP: 58
SALES (est): 31.4MM **Privately Held**
WEB: www.sonomasheriff.org
SIC: 8322 Individual & family services

(P-17514)
COUNTY OF STANISLAUS
Also Called: Community Services
830 Scenic Dr, Modesto (95350-6131)
PHONE....................209 558-8828
Nancy Fisher, *Superintendent*
EMP: 49
SALES (corp-wide): 1.2B **Privately Held**
WEB: www.stancounty.com
SIC: 8322 Youth self-help agency

PRODUCTS & SERVICES SECTION

8322 - Individual & Family Social Svcs County (P-17539)

PA: County Of Stanislaus
1010 10th St Ste 5100
Modesto CA 95354
209 525-6398

(P-17515)
COUNTY OF STANISLAUS
Also Called: Probation Dept
801 11th St, Modesto (95354-2348)
PHONE.................................209 567-4120
Mike Hamasaki, *Branch Mgr*
EMP: 49
SALES (corp-wide): 1.2B **Privately Held**
WEB: www.stancounty.com
SIC: 8322 Probation office
PA: County Of Stanislaus
1010 10th St Ste 5100
Modesto CA 95354
209 525-6398

(P-17516)
COUNTY OF STANISLAUS
108 Campus Way, Modesto (95350-5803)
PHONE.................................209 558-7377
Elaine Emory, *Manager*
EMP: 49
SALES (corp-wide): 1.2B **Privately Held**
WEB: www.stancounty.com
SIC: 8322 Individual & family services
PA: County Of Stanislaus
1010 10th St Ste 5100
Modesto CA 95354
209 525-6398

(P-17517)
COUNTY OF STANISLAUS
Also Called: Dcss
251 E Hackett Rd, Modesto (95358-9800)
P.O. Box 4189 (95352-4189)
PHONE.................................209 558-9675
Tamara Thomas, *Branch Mgr*
EMP: 49
SALES (corp-wide): 1.2B **Privately Held**
WEB: www.stancounty.com
SIC: 8322 Family counseling services
PA: County Of Stanislaus
1010 10th St Ste 5100
Modesto CA 95354
209 525-6398

(P-17518)
COUNTY OF STANISLAUS
Also Called: Family Support Division
108 Campus Way, Modesto (95350-5803)
P.O. Box 4189 (95352-4189)
PHONE.................................209 558-2500
Joan Kingman, *Branch Mgr*
EMP: 49
SALES (corp-wide): 1.2B **Privately Held**
WEB: www.stancounty.com
SIC: 8322 Child related social services
PA: County Of Stanislaus
1010 10th St Ste 5100
Modesto CA 95354
209 525-6398

(P-17519)
COUNTY OF YUBA
Also Called: Yuba Cnty Prbtion Chldren Fmli
209 6th St, Marysville (95901-5570)
PHONE.................................530 741-6275
Jason Roper, *Program Mgr*
EMP: 66
SALES (corp-wide): 212MM **Privately Held**
WEB: www.co.yuba.ca.us
SIC: 8322 9199 Probation office;
PA: County Of Yuba
915 8th St Ste 109
Marysville CA 95901
530 749-7575

(P-17520)
COUNTY OF YUBA
Also Called: Adult Services Division
5730 Packard Ave Ste 100, Marysville (95901-7117)
P.O. Box 2320 (95901-0082)
PHONE.................................530 749-6471
Jennifer Vasquez, *Manager*
EMP: 66
SALES (corp-wide): 212MM **Privately Held**
WEB: www.co.yuba.ca.us
SIC: 8322 9441 Public welfare center;

PA: County Of Yuba
915 8th St Ste 109
Marysville CA 95901
530 749-7575

(P-17521)
COUNTY OF YUBA
Also Called: Yuba County Probation Dept
215 5th St Ste 154, Marysville (95901-5737)
PHONE.................................530 749-7550
Jim Arnold, *Director*
EMP: 66
SALES (corp-wide): 212MM **Privately Held**
WEB: www.co.yuba.ca.us
SIC: 8322 9199 Probation office;
PA: County Of Yuba
915 8th St Ste 109
Marysville CA 95901
530 749-7575

(P-17522)
COVIA AFFORDABLE COMMUNITIES
2185 N Calif Blvd Ste 215, Walnut Creek (94596-3566)
PHONE.................................925 956-7400
Kevin Gerber, *CEO*
Jonathan Casey, *CFO*
EMP: 180
SALES: 5.6MM **Privately Held**
WEB: www.covia.org
SIC: 8322 6513 Individual & family services; apartment building operators

(P-17523)
CREEKSIDE COUNSELING CTR INC
1170 Industrial St, Redding (96002-0734)
P.O. Box 491750 (96049-1750)
PHONE.................................530 722-9957
Keith Manner, *Ch of Bd*
Kristin G Kirk, *Admin Sec*
EMP: 37 **EST:** 1998
SQ FT: 5,200
SALES (est): 1.6MM **Privately Held**
WEB: www.creeksidecounseling.org
SIC: 8322 Family (marriage) counseling; general counseling services

(P-17524)
CRESTWOOD BEHAVIORAL HLTH INC
Also Called: 1172 Solano Csu
2101 Courage Dr, Fairfield (94533-6717)
PHONE.................................707 428-1131
Shalon Dean, *Administration*
EMP: 47
SALES (corp-wide): 238MM **Privately Held**
WEB: www.crestwoodbehavioralhealth.com
SIC: 8322 Individual & family services
PA: Crestwood Behavioral Health, Inc.
520 Capitol Mall Ste 800
Sacramento CA 95814
510 651-1244

(P-17525)
CRUCIBLE
1260 7th St, Oakland (94607-2150)
PHONE.................................510 444-0919
Susan Mernit, *Exec Dir*
Michael Sturtz, *Exec Dir*
Steven Young, *Exec Dir*
EMP: 215 **EST:** 1997
SQ FT: 46,980
SALES (est): 2.9MM **Privately Held**
WEB: www.thecrucible.org
SIC: 8322 8331 Outreach program; skill training center

(P-17526)
CURRY SENIOR CENTER (PA)
Also Called: CURRY SENIOR CENTER
333 Turk St, San Francisco (94102-3703)
PHONE.................................415 885-2274
David Knego, *Exec Dir*
Rick Crane, *Officer*
Angela Di Martino, *Admin Sec*
Toby Shorts, *Admin Sec*
Faiza Saeed, *Administration*
EMP: 46 **EST:** 1972
SQ FT: 10,000

SALES: 4.9MM **Privately Held**
WEB: www.curryseniorcenter.org
SIC: 8322 Senior citizens' center or association

(P-17527)
CV STARR COMMUNITY CENTER
300 S Lincoln St, Fort Bragg (95437-4416)
PHONE.................................707 964-9446
Dan Keyes, *Administration*
EMP: 99 **EST:** 2012
SALES (est): 2.2MM **Privately Held**
WEB: www.mendocoastrec.org
SIC: 8322 Community center

(P-17528)
DAVIS COMMUNITY MEALS INC
202 F St, Davis (95616-4515)
P.O. Box 72463 (95617-2463)
PHONE.................................530 756-4008
Bill Pride, *Exec Dir*
William D Pride, *Exec Dir*
EMP: 60 **EST:** 1992
SALES (est): 4MM **Privately Held**
WEB: www.daviscommunitymeals.org
SIC: 8322 Social service center

(P-17529)
DAVIS STREET COMMUNITY CENTER (PA)
Also Called: DAVIS STREET FAMILY RESOURCE C
3081 Teagarden St, San Leandro (94577-5720)
PHONE.................................510 347-4620
Rose Johnson, *Exec Dir*
Adrian Williams, *Executive Asst*
Jessica Ho, *Opers Staff*
Laura Jarvis, *Psychologist*
Michelle Hiscox, *Med Doctor*
EMP: 73 **EST:** 1971
SQ FT: 22,450
SALES: 16.6MM **Privately Held**
WEB: www.davisstreet.org
SIC: 8322 8021 8011 8093 Community center; dental clinic; primary care medical clinic; mental health clinic, outpatient

(P-17530)
DEVELOP DISABILITIES SVC ORG
Also Called: Community Integration Program
2331 Saint Marks Way G1, Sacramento (95864-0626)
PHONE.................................916 973-1951
EMP: 75
SALES (est): 897K **Privately Held**
SIC: 8322 Individual And Family Services, Nsk

(P-17531)
DEVELPMNTAL DSBLTIES SVC ORGNZ (PA)
Also Called: DDSO
5051 47th Ave, Sacramento (95824-4036)
PHONE.................................916 456-5166
Yvonne Soto, *Acting CEO*
Jon Hutchison, *Ch of Bd*
Ann Larson, *Ch of Bd*
Jennifer Bonacorso, *CFO*
Darlene Demott, *Broker*
EMP: 63 **EST:** 1975
SQ FT: 36,000
SALES: 4.3MM **Privately Held**
WEB: www.ddso.org
SIC: 8322 Community center

(P-17532)
DIAMOND LEARNING CENTER INC
1620 W Fairmont Ave, Fresno (93705-0323)
PHONE.................................559 241-0580
Jamie Delacerda, *President*
Daniel F Delacerda, *Vice Pres*
Cheryl Martinez, *Associate Dir*
Kelly Pesenti, *Associate Dir*
Daniel De, *Director*
EMP: 53 **EST:** 2004
SALES (est): 910.1K **Privately Held**
WEB: www.dlclife.org
SIC: 8322 Adult day care center

(P-17533)
DISCOVERY CNSLING CTR OF SAN R
115 Town And Country Dr A, Danville (94526-3960)
PHONE.................................925 837-0505
Kathy Shiverton, *Director*
Alex Hays, *Office Mgr*
Danielle Hernandez, *Admin Asst*
Kathy Kane, *Training Dir*
EMP: 58 **EST:** 1969
SQ FT: 1,400
SALES: 1.9MM **Privately Held**
WEB: www.discoveryctr.net
SIC: 8322 General counseling services

(P-17534)
DONATIONS WITH CARE
6220 Winding Way, Carmichael (95608-1135)
PHONE.................................916 544-3080
Serge Borodulin, *Principal*
James Mitchell, *Principal*
Kay Ralston, *Principal*
Elle Rubinger, *Principal*
EMP: 73 **EST:** 2020
SALES (est): 449K **Privately Held**
SIC: 8322 Individual & family services

(P-17535)
EAST BAY ASIAN YOUTH CENTER (PA)
Also Called: Ebayc
2025 E 12th St, Oakland (94606-4925)
PHONE.................................510 533-1092
David Kakishiba, *Director*
Suman Murthy, *Comms Dir*
Rany Ath, *Managing Dir*
Amy Shiu, *Administration*
Juan Campos, *Program Dir*
▲ **EMP:** 40 **EST:** 1976
SALES (est): 5.1MM **Privately Held**
WEB: www.ebayc.org
SIC: 8322 Youth center

(P-17536)
EAST BAY ASIAN YOUTH CENTER
2025 E 12th St, Oakland (94606-4925)
PHONE.................................510 533-1092
Gianna Tran, *President*
EMP: 90
SALES (corp-wide): 5.1MM **Privately Held**
WEB: www.ebayc.org
SIC: 8322 Youth center
PA: East Bay Asian Youth Center
2025 E 12th St
Oakland CA 94606
510 533-1092

(P-17537)
EASTER SEALS CENTRAL CAL
9010 Soquel Dr, Aptos (95003-4082)
PHONE.................................831 684-2166
Bruce Hinman, *President*
Anne Bourdeau, *Technology*
Larry Doan, *Director*
EMP: 62 **EST:** 1949
SALES (est): 2.1MM **Privately Held**
WEB: www.easterseals.com
SIC: 8322 Social service center

(P-17538)
ED SUPPORTS LLC
Also Called: Juvo Atism Bhavioral Hlth Svcs
3240 Lone Tree Way Ste 10, Antioch (94509-5559)
PHONE.................................201 478-8711
Adam Schreiber, *Branch Mgr*
EMP: 75
SALES (corp-wide): 33.1MM **Privately Held**
SIC: 8322 Child related social services
HQ: Ed Supports Llc
1200 Concord Ave Ste 100
Concord CA 94520
510 832-4383

(P-17539)
ED SUPPORTS LLC
Also Called: Juvo Atism Bhavioral Hlth Svcs
1710 Pririe Cy Rd Ste 100, Folsom (95630)
PHONE.................................201 478-8711
Kaye Wagner, *Contract Mgr*

8322 - Individual & Family Social Svcs County (P-17540)

Tanya Scott, *Senior Mgr*
Rachel Finegan, *Director*
EMP: 60
SALES (corp-wide): 33.1MM **Privately Held**
SIC: 8322 Individual & family services
HQ: Ed Supports Llc
1200 Concord Ave Ste 100
Concord CA 94520
510 832-4383

(P-17540)
EL CONCILIO CALIFORNIA (PA)
445 N San Joaquin St A, Stockton (95202-2026)
PHONE 209 644-2600
Jose Rodriguez, *CEO*
Mark Apostolon, *Officer*
Francisco Carlos, *Officer*
EMP: 156 **EST:** 1968
SQ FT: 8,000
SALES (est): 14.9MM **Privately Held**
WEB: www.elconcilio.org
SIC: 8322 Social service center

(P-17541)
ELDER OPTIONS (PA)
82 Main St, Placerville (95667-5506)
P.O. Box 2113 (95667-2113)
PHONE 530 626-6939
Carol Heape, *Owner*
Simone Devane, *Accountant*
Lori Wittlin, *Manager*
EMP: 44 **EST:** 1988
SALES (est): 2.5MM **Privately Held**
WEB: www.elderoptionsca.com
SIC: 8322 Senior citizens' center or association; geriatric social service

(P-17542)
ELIJAH HOUSE SLE
1980 Arnold Ave, Oroville (95966-6903)
PHONE 530 370-8386
Joseph Henderson, *CEO*
Shawn Vang, *Manager*
EMP: 45 **EST:** 2016
SALES (est): 978.7K **Privately Held**
SIC: 8322 Rehabilitation services

(P-17543)
EMPOWER YOLO INC
175 Walnut St, Woodland (95695-3154)
PHONE 530 662-1133
Lynnette Irlmeier, *Exec Dir*
Anne Marie Flynn, *President*
Celine Alvarez, *Associate Dir*
Tracie Polkinghorne, *Finance Dir*
EMP: 50 **EST:** 1977
SQ FT: 3,300
SALES (est): 4.3MM **Privately Held**
WEB: www.empoweryolo.org
SIC: 8322 Social service center

(P-17544)
EMQ FAMILIES FIRST (PA)
251 Llewellyn Ave, Campbell (95008-1940)
PHONE 408 379-3790
Darrell Evora, *CEO*
Lyn Farr, *COO*
Jason Gurahoo, *CFO*
Abram Rosenblatt, *Vice Pres*
Marilyn Bamford, *Principal*
EMP: 97 **EST:** 2011
SALES (est): 7.3MM **Privately Held**
WEB: www.upliftfs.org
SIC: 8322 Family counseling services

(P-17545)
EMQ FAMILIESFIRST
499 Loma Alta Ave, Los Gatos (95030-6227)
PHONE 408 354-0149
Darrell Evora, *President*
Julie Deakins, *Business Anlyst*
Wineta Brandt, *Purch Mgr*
Aj Anderson, *Director*
Susie Davis, *Manager*
EMP: 42 **EST:** 2009
SALES (est): 10.3MM **Privately Held**
WEB: www.upliftfs.org
SIC: 8322 Social service center

(P-17546)
ENCOMPASS COMMUNITY SERVICES
Also Called: El Dorado Center
941 El Dorado Ave, Santa Cruz (95062-2863)
PHONE 831 479-9494
David Campbell, *Manager*
Kate Welty, *Officer*
EMP: 42
SQ FT: 45,607
SALES (corp-wide): 31MM **Privately Held**
WEB: www.encompasscs.org
SIC: 8322 Crisis center
PA: Encompass Community Services
380 Encinal St Ste 200
Santa Cruz CA 95060
831 427-9670

(P-17547)
ENCOMPASS COMMUNITY SERVICES
Also Called: Alto Counseling Center
716 Ocean St Ste 230, Santa Cruz (95060-4034)
PHONE 831 423-2003
Tim Mayo, *Branch Mgr*
Jennifer Detoy, *Human Res Dir*
Sara Anderson, *Director*
EMP: 42
SALES (corp-wide): 31MM **Privately Held**
WEB: www.encompasscs.org
SIC: 8322 Individual & family services; county supervisors' & executives' offices
PA: Encompass Community Services
380 Encinal St Ste 200
Santa Cruz CA 95060
831 427-9670

(P-17548)
ENCOMPASS COMMUNITY SERVICES
Also Called: STA Cruz Residential Care Svc
125 Rigg St, Santa Cruz (95060-4203)
PHONE 831 423-3890
Jorge Sanchez, *Office Mgr*
EMP: 42
SALES (corp-wide): 31MM **Privately Held**
WEB: www.encompasscs.org
SIC: 8322 Social service center
PA: Encompass Community Services
380 Encinal St Ste 200
Santa Cruz CA 95060
831 427-9670

(P-17549)
ENCOMPASS COMMUNITY SERVICES
Also Called: Youth Services North
380 Encinal St Ste 200, Santa Cruz (95060-2178)
PHONE 831 425-0771
Bill McCabe, *Director*
Eve Andrews, *Representative*
EMP: 42
SALES (corp-wide): 31MM **Privately Held**
WEB: www.encompasscs.org
SIC: 8322 9111 Social service center; county supervisors' & executives' offices
PA: Encompass Community Services
380 Encinal St Ste 200
Santa Cruz CA 95060
831 427-9670

(P-17550)
ENCOMPASS COMMUNITY SERVICES
Also Called: Youth Services
241 E Lake Ave, Watsonville (95076-4717)
PHONE 831 728-2226
Clare Wesley, *Director*
EMP: 42
SALES (corp-wide): 31MM **Privately Held**
WEB: www.encompasscs.org
SIC: 8322 9111 Community center; county supervisors' & executives' offices
PA: Encompass Community Services
380 Encinal St Ste 200
Santa Cruz CA 95060
831 427-9670

(P-17551)
ENCOMPASS COMMUNITY SERVICES
Also Called: Headstart
225 Westridge Dr, Watsonville (95076-4168)
P.O. Box 927 (95077-0927)
PHONE 831 724-3885
Gloria Martinez, *Branch Mgr*
Corey Vestal, *Manager*
EMP: 42
SALES (corp-wide): 31MM **Privately Held**
WEB: www.encompasscs.org
SIC: 8322 8351 Social service center; head start center, except in conjunction with school
PA: Encompass Community Services
380 Encinal St Ste 200
Santa Cruz CA 95060
831 427-9670

(P-17552)
ENCOMPASS COMMUNITY SERVICES
Also Called: Community Support Services
716 Ocean St Ste 200, Santa Cruz (95060-4034)
PHONE 831 459-6644
Betsy Clark, *Manager*
Armando Alcaraz, *Manager*
Meg Clark, *Manager*
Randa Johnson, *Supervisor*
Shanowa Simington, *Supervisor*
EMP: 42
SALES (corp-wide): 31MM **Privately Held**
WEB: www.encompasscs.org
SIC: 8322 Social service center
PA: Encompass Community Services
380 Encinal St Ste 200
Santa Cruz CA 95060
831 427-9670

(P-17553)
EPISCPAL CMNTY SVCS SAN FRNCSC (PA)
Also Called: ECS
165 8th St Fl 3, San Francisco (94103-2726)
PHONE 415 487-3300
Kenneth J Reggio, *Exec Dir*
Sedge Dienst, *President*
Peter Mc Coy, *CEO*
Jan-Marie Bannon, *CFO*
Eric Larra, *CFO*
EMP: 36 **EST:** 1982
SQ FT: 12,000
SALES: 45.2MM **Privately Held**
WEB: www.ecs-sf.org
SIC: 8322 Social service center

(P-17554)
ESKATON PROPERTIES INC
Also Called: Carmichael Adult Day Hlth Ctr
5105 Manzanita Ave Ste D, Carmichael (95608-0523)
PHONE 916 334-0296
Jill Youngling, *Director*
EMP: 112 **Privately Held**
WEB: www.eskaton.org
SIC: 8322 Adult day care center
PA: Eskaton Properties Incorporated
5105 Manzanita Ave Ste A
Carmichael CA 95608

(P-17555)
ETR ASSOCIATES INC
100 Enterprise Way, Scotts Valley (95066-3248)
PHONE 831 438-4060
Vincent Lafronza, *President*
Kim Wiese, *Vice Pres*
EMP: 51 **EST:** 1980
SALES (est): 14.2MM **Privately Held**
WEB: www.etr.org
SIC: 8322 Social service center

(P-17556)
EXCEPTNAL PRENTS UNLIMITED INC
Also Called: E P U
4440 N 1st St, Fresno (93726-2304)
PHONE 559 229-2000
Lowell Ens, *CEO*
Suzanne Ellis, *CFO*
Melisa Santacruz, *Admin Sec*
Kim Majors, *Human Res Dir*
Krista Rose, *Education*
EMP: 115 **EST:** 1976
SQ FT: 24,000
SALES: 8.1MM **Privately Held**
WEB: www.epuchildren.org
SIC: 8322 Family counseling services

(P-17557)
FACES SF FMLY CHILD EMPWRMENT
1101 Masonic Ave, San Francisco (94117-2914)
PHONE 415 567-2357
Lawland Long, *CEO*
Maggie Ni, *Finance Dir*
Zhen Ni, *Accountant*
Lindsay Nieri, *Human Res Dir*
Kim Wong, *Program Dir*
EMP: 37 **EST:** 2012
SALES (est): 12.7MM **Privately Held**
WEB: www.facessf.org
SIC: 8322 Individual & family services

(P-17558)
FAMILY & CHILDREN SERVICES
375 Cambridge Ave, Palo Alto (94306-1613)
PHONE 650 326-6576
Jim Welsh, *President*
Lauren Grey, *Exec Dir*
Fish Williams, *Finance Dir*
Jill H Maher, *Director*
Elnora Newkirk, *Receptionist*
EMP: 53 **EST:** 1948
SQ FT: 6,000
SALES (est): 2.8MM **Privately Held**
WEB: www.fcservices.org
SIC: 8322 Child related social services

(P-17559)
FAMILY BRIDGES INC
168 11th St, Oakland (94607-4841)
PHONE 510 839-2270
Corinne Jan, *Exec Dir*
Monica Lau, *COO*
Susanna Ng-Lee, *Vice Pres*
Mary Marshall, *Admin Sec*
Denver Yu, *Human Res Dir*
EMP: 126 **EST:** 1968
SQ FT: 5,000
SALES: 8.2MM **Privately Held**
WEB: www.familybridges.org
SIC: 8322 8641 Social service center; civic social & fraternal associations

(P-17560)
FAMILY CAREGIVER ALLIANCE
101 Montgomery St # 2150, San Francisco (94104-4157)
PHONE 415 434-3388
Kathleen Kelly, *Exec Dir*
Albert Martinez, *Comms Dir*
Sima Schoen, *Exec Dir*
Annie Roche, *Director*
Cassandra Castillo, *Assistant*
EMP: 38 **EST:** 1976
SQ FT: 5,000
SALES (est): 3.7MM **Privately Held**
WEB: www.caregiver.org
SIC: 8322 Social service center

(P-17561)
FAMILY HOUSE INC (PA)
540 Mission Bay Blvd N, San Francisco (94158-2382)
PHONE 415 476-8321
Jessica Creager, *CFO*
John Foote, *President*
Jeanine Homich, *Office Mgr*
Joe Blodgett, *Info Tech Mgr*
Araceli Bermudez, *Engineer*
EMP: 36 **EST:** 1981
SQ FT: 9,157

PRODUCTS & SERVICES SECTION **8322 - Individual & Family Social Svcs County (P-17583)**

SALES: 6.9MM Privately Held
WEB: www.familyhouseinc.org
SIC: 8322 8699 8361 Aid to families with dependent children (AFDC); charitable organization; residential care for children

(P-17562)
FAMILY PATHS INC
22320 Fthill Blvd Ste 400, Hayward (94541)
PHONE..................................510 582-0148
Marcella Revees, *Exec Dir*
Martha Winnacker, *Exec Dir*
Rene Dvalery, *Program Mgr*
Kathy Davis, *Controller*
Melanie Hunter, *Opers Staff*
EMP: 40
SALES (corp-wide): 4.6MM Privately Held
WEB: www.familypaths.org
SIC: 8322 Family counseling services
PA: Family Paths, Inc.
1727 Mrtin Lther King Jr
Oakland CA 94612
510 893-9230

(P-17563)
FAMILY RESOURCE & REFERRAL CTR
509 W Weber Ave Ste 101, Stockton (95203-3107)
PHONE..................................209 948-1553
Fax: 209 948-3554
EMP: 100
SALES (est): 28.6MM Privately Held
SIC: 8322 Individual/Family Services

(P-17564)
FAMILY SUPPORT SERVICES (PA)
303 Hegenberger Rd # 400, Oakland (94621-1419)
PHONE..................................510 834-2443
Lou Fox, *Exec Dir*
Janette E Drew, *Treasurer*
Elizabeth Adeyi, *Officer*
Aster Mitiku, *Administration*
Joseph Lannutti, *Financial Analy*
EMP: 41 EST: 1989
SALES: 5MM Privately Held
WEB: www.fssba.org
SIC: 8322 Social service center

(P-17565)
FAMILY SVC AGCY OF CENTL COAST
104 Walnut Ave Ste 208, Santa Cruz (95060-3929)
PHONE..................................831 423-9444
David Bianchi, *Exec Dir*
Rita Flores, *Principal*
Dolores Ledesma, *Counsel*
Nancy Cleveland, *Director*
Megan Williams, *Associate*
EMP: 51 EST: 1957
SALES (est): 2MM Privately Held
WEB: www.fsa-cc.org
SIC: 8322 Social service center

(P-17566)
FAMILY SVCS AGCY MARIN CNTY (PA)
Also Called: Family Service Agency
555 Northgate Dr, San Rafael (94903-3680)
PHONE..................................415 491-5700
Margret Hallett, *Director*
Kelly Hinde, *Human Res Dir*
Alex Tolkach, *Opers Staff*
Amber Kennedy, *Governor*
Teresa Bowman, *Director*
EMP: 82 EST: 1952
SALES (est): 3.8MM Privately Held
WEB: www.fsamarin.org
SIC: 8322 Family (marriage) counseling

(P-17567)
FAR NRTHERN CRDNTING CNCIL ON
Also Called: Regional Center
1377 E Lassen Ave, Chico (95973-7824)
PHONE..................................530 895-8633
Laura Larson, *Info Tech Mgr*
Cindy Presidio, *COO*
Melissa Gruhler, *Exec Dir*

Sharon Rhodes, *Office Spvr*
Ivor Thomas, *Analyst*
EMP: 77
SALES (corp-wide): 186.6MM Privately Held
WEB: www.farnothernrc.org
SIC: 8322 8399 Social services for the handicapped; health & welfare council
PA: Far Northern Coordinating Council On Developmental Disabilities
1900 Churn Creek Rd # 114
Redding CA 96002
530 222-4791

(P-17568)
FAR NRTHERN CRDNTING CNCIL ON (PA)
Also Called: FAR NORTHERN REGIONAL CENTER
1900 Churn Creek Rd # 114, Redding (96002-0292)
P.O. Box 492418 (96049-2418)
PHONE..................................530 222-4791
Laura L Larson, *Exec Dir*
Michael J Mintline, *CFO*
Kathy Jennings, *Human Resources*
Denis Villanueva, *Manager*
EMP: 100 EST: 1967
SALES: 186.6MM Privately Held
WEB: www.farnothernrc.org
SIC: 8322 Association for the handicapped; social services for the handicapped

(P-17569)
FIRST 5 ALAMEDA COUNTY
1115 Atlantic Ave, Alameda (94501-1145)
PHONE..................................510 227-6900
Janis Burger, *CEO*
Amalia Alcala, *COO*
Christine Hom, *Officer*
Sujata Bansal, *Administration*
Maria Canteros, *Administration*
EMP: 60 EST: 2014 Privately Held
WEB: www.first5alameda.org
SIC: 9441 8322 Administration of social & manpower programs; family service agency

(P-17570)
FIRST 5 SANTA CLARA COUNTY
Also Called: Children & Families First Comm
4000 Moorpark Ave Ste 200, San Jose (95117-1839)
PHONE..................................408 260-3700
Jolene Smith, *Director*
David Brody, *Exec Dir*
Jodi Lindenthal, *Executive Asst*
Patience Davidson-Lutz, *Human Resources*
Evelyn Omarah, *Corp Comm Staff*
EMP: 45 EST: 1999
SQ FT: 24,157
SALES (est): 12.1MM Privately Held
WEB: www.first5kids.org
SIC: 8322 Social service center

(P-17571)
FIRST PLACE FOR YOUTH (PA)
426 17th St Ste 100, Oakland (94612-2814)
PHONE..................................510 272-0979
Sam Cobbs, *Exec Dir*
EMP: 39 EST: 1999
SALES (est): 18.6MM Privately Held
WEB: www.firstplaceforyouth.org
SIC: 8322 Youth center

(P-17572)
FIVE KEYS SCHOOLS AND PROGRAMS
70 Oak Grove St, San Francisco (94107-1019)
PHONE..................................415 734-3310
Steve Good, *Exec Dir*
Leslie Guardado, *Analyst*
Kara Cooperrider, *Teacher*
Gale Eed, *Teacher*
Angel Giron, *Teacher*
EMP: 48 EST: 2003
SALES (est): 9MM Privately Held
WEB: www.fivekeyscharter.org
SIC: 8211 8322 ; substance abuse counseling

(P-17573)
FOOD FOR PEOPLE INC
Also Called: Food Bank For Humboldt County
307 W 14th St, Eureka (95501-2267)
P.O. Box 4922 (95502-4922)
PHONE..................................707 445-3166
Anne Holcomb, *Exec Dir*
Peggy Leviton, *General Mgr*
Corey Tipton, *Bookkeeper*
Tim Crosby, *Opers Staff*
Kayla Watkins, *Education*
EMP: 73 EST: 1980
SQ FT: 3,000
SALES: 5.3MM Privately Held
WEB: www.foodforpeople.org
SIC: 8322 Social service center

(P-17574)
FRESNO CNTY ECNMIC OPPRTNTIES
3120 W Neilson, Fresno (93706-1139)
PHONE..................................559 486-6587
George Egawa, *Branch Mgr*
EMP: 46
SALES (corp-wide): 108MM Privately Held
WEB: www.fresnoeoc.org
SIC: 8322 Social service center
PA: Fresno County Economic Opportunities Commission
1920 Mariposa Mall # 300
Fresno CA 93721
559 263-1010

(P-17575)
FRESNO CNTY ECNMIC OPPRTNTIES
311 Coalinga Plz, Coalinga (93210-1703)
PHONE..................................559 935-2058
Alfonso Dominguez, *Manager*
EMP: 46
SALES (corp-wide): 108MM Privately Held
WEB: www.fresnoeoc.org
SIC: 8322 Social service center
PA: Fresno County Economic Opportunities Commission
1920 Mariposa Mall # 300
Fresno CA 93721
559 263-1010

(P-17576)
FRESNO CNTY ECNMIC OPPRTNTIES
Also Called: Fresno Eoc
1900 Mariposa Mall # 300, Fresno (93721-2514)
PHONE..................................559 263-1000
Bryan Angus, *CEO*
Barigye McCoy, *Bd of Directors*
Arthur Montejano, *Finance*
Maria Agilar, *Supervisor*
EMP: 46
SALES (corp-wide): 108MM Privately Held
WEB: www.fresnoeoc.org
SIC: 8322 Social service center
PA: Fresno County Economic Opportunities Commission
1920 Mariposa Mall # 300
Fresno CA 93721
559 263-1010

(P-17577)
FRESNO CNTY ECNMIC OPPRTNTIES (PA)
Also Called: FRESNO EOC
1920 Mariposa Mall # 300, Fresno (93721-2504)
PHONE..................................559 263-1010
Brian Angus, *CEO*
Vongsavanh Mouanoutoua, *President*
Salam Nalia, *CFO*
Marina Magdaleno, *Treasurer*
Leroy Candler, *Bd of Directors*
EMP: 600 EST: 1965
SQ FT: 115,312
SALES: 108MM Privately Held
WEB: www.fresnoeoc.org
SIC: 8322 8399 Social service center; community development groups

(P-17578)
FRESNO CNTY ECNMIC OPPRTNTIES
Also Called: Jefferson Head Start
1240 E Washington Ave, Reedley (93654-3595)
PHONE..................................559 637-0025
Kathleen Shivaprasad, *Director*
EMP: 46
SALES (corp-wide): 108MM Privately Held
WEB: www.fresnoeoc.org
SIC: 8322 Social service center
PA: Fresno County Economic Opportunities Commission
1920 Mariposa Mall # 300
Fresno CA 93721
559 263-1010

(P-17579)
FRESNO CNTY ECNMIC OPPRTNTIES
1325 Stillman St, Selma (93662-3221)
PHONE..................................559 896-0142
EMP: 46
SALES (corp-wide): 108MM Privately Held
WEB: www.fresnoeoc.org
SIC: 8322 Social service center
PA: Fresno County Economic Opportunities Commission
1920 Mariposa Mall # 300
Fresno CA 93721
559 263-1010

(P-17580)
FRESNO CNTY ECNMIC OPPRTNTIES
3120 W Nielsen Ave, Fresno (93706-1139)
PHONE..................................559 485-3733
EMP: 46
SQ FT: 14,184
SALES (corp-wide): 108MM Privately Held
WEB: www.fresnoeoc.org
SIC: 8322 Social service center
PA: Fresno County Economic Opportunities Commission
1920 Mariposa Mall # 300
Fresno CA 93721
559 263-1010

(P-17581)
FRESNO CNTY ECNMIC OPPRTNTIES
Also Called: Eoc Resource Development
1920 Mariposa Mall, Fresno (93721-2504)
PHONE..................................559 263-1013
Roger Palomino, *Manager*
EMP: 46
SALES (corp-wide): 108MM Privately Held
WEB: www.fresnoeoc.org
SIC: 8322 Social service center
PA: Fresno County Economic Opportunities Commission
1920 Mariposa Mall # 300
Fresno CA 93721
559 263-1010

(P-17582)
FRESNO CNTY ECNMIC OPPRTNTIES
3120 W Nielsen Ave # 102, Fresno (93706-1139)
PHONE..................................559 485-3733
George Egawa, *Manager*
EMP: 46
SALES (corp-wide): 108MM Privately Held
WEB: www.fresnoeoc.org
SIC: 8322 Social service center
PA: Fresno County Economic Opportunities Commission
1920 Mariposa Mall # 300
Fresno CA 93721
559 263-1010

(P-17583)
FRESNO CNTY ECNMIC OPPRTNTIES
Also Called: Food Services Division
3100 W Nielsen Ave, Fresno (93706-1139)
PHONE..................................559 266-3663

8322 - Individual & Family Social Svcs County (P-17584)

Gary Joseph, *Manager*
EMP: 46
SALES (corp-wide): 108MM **Privately Held**
WEB: www.fresnoeoc.org
SIC: 8322 Social service center
PA: Fresno County Economic Opportunities Commission
1920 Mariposa Mall # 300
Fresno CA 93721
559 263-1010

(P-17584)
FRESNO RESCUE MISSION INC (PA)
263 G St, Fresno (93706-3452)
P.O. Box 470, West Yellowstone MT (59758-0470)
PHONE..........................559 268-0839
Larry Arce, *CEO*
Rob Cravy, *COO*
Angela Gonzales, *Executive Asst*
Jay Carroll, *Pastor*
Karen Gutilla, *Director*
EMP: 48 EST: 1949
SQ FT: 29,000
SALES: 28MM **Privately Held**
WEB: www.fresnomission.org
SIC: 8322 Emergency shelters; child related social services

(P-17585)
FRIENDS OUTSIDE
1148 W Fremont St, Stockton (95203-2622)
P.O. Box 4085 (95204-0085)
PHONE..........................209 955-0701
Gretchen Newby, *Exec Dir*
EMP: 57 EST: 1963
SALES (est): 3.4MM **Privately Held**
WEB: www.friendsoutside.org
SIC: 8322 Social service center

(P-17586)
FUTURES EXPLORED
2150 John Glenn Dr Ste 30, Concord (94520-5671)
P.O. Box 418 (94522-0418)
PHONE..........................925 332-7183
Karen Smith, *Exec Dir*
Lindsey Dyba, *Associate Dir*
Angelique Goldberg, *Principal*
Jenny McKeon, *Principal*
Eric Vale, *Principal*
EMP: 125 EST: 1964
SQ FT: 1,740
SALES (est): 11.2MM **Privately Held**
WEB: www.futures-explored.org
SIC: 8322 Association for the handicapped

(P-17587)
G&R ALMEDA HEALTHCARE SVCS LLC
Also Called: Crown Bay Nrsing Rhbltion Ctr
508 Westline Dr, Alameda (94501-5847)
PHONE..........................510 521-5765
Tony Agoncillo, *Mng Member*
Emily Pantaleo, *Office Mgr*
EMP: 73 EST: 2007
SALES (est): 5.4MM **Privately Held**
WEB: www.cbnrc.com
SIC: 8322 8051 Rehabilitation services; convalescent home with continuous nursing care

(P-17588)
GATEWAY RESIDENTIAL PROGRAMS
1780 Vernon St Ste 1&5, Roseville (95678-6311)
P.O. Box 2258, Fair Oaks (95628-2258)
PHONE..........................916 782-1111
Lee Hiatt, *Exec Dir*
EMP: 35 EST: 1991
SQ FT: 5,000
SALES: 5.1MM **Privately Held**
WEB:
SIC: 8322 Social service center

(P-17589)
GOLDEN GATE REGIONAL CTR INC (PA)
1355 Market St Ste 220, San Francisco (94103-1314)
PHONE..........................415 546-9222
Ron Fell, *CEO*

David Koeppel, *Partner*
Tracey Bullock, *Treasurer*
Davin Camara, *Bd of Directors*
Eric Zigman, *Bd of Directors*
EMP: 120 EST: 1966
SQ FT: 16,901
SALES: 330.3MM **Privately Held**
WEB: www.ggrc.org
SIC: 8322 Referral service for personal & social problems; outreach program

(P-17590)
GOLDEN GATE REGIONAL CTR INC
3130 La Selva St Ste 202, San Mateo (94403-2191)
PHONE..........................650 574-9232
David Beuerman, *General Mgr*
Lisa Ashley, *Social Worker*
Melanie Tucker, *Case Mgr*
EMP: 45
SALES (corp-wide): 330.3MM **Privately Held**
WEB: www.ggrc.org
SIC: 8322 Social services for the handicapped
PA: Golden Gate Regional Center, Inc.
1355 Market St Ste 220
San Francisco CA 94103
415 546-9222

(P-17591)
GOLDEN GATE REGIONAL CTR INC
Also Called: Ggrc
4000 Civic Center Dr # 310, San Rafael (94903-4171)
PHONE..........................415 446-3000
Patricia Wall, *Manager*
EMP: 45
SALES (corp-wide): 330.3MM **Privately Held**
WEB: www.ggrc.org
SIC: 8322 Referral service for personal & social problems; outreach program
PA: Golden Gate Regional Center, Inc.
1355 Market St Ste 220
San Francisco CA 94103
415 546-9222

(P-17592)
GOOD SMRITAN FMLY RESOURCE CTR
1294 Potrero Ave Unit 1, San Francisco (94110-3571)
PHONE..........................415 401-4253
Frank Degrosa, *President*
Frank De-Grosa, *President*
Kian Alavi, *Deputy Dir*
Maria Villegas, *Teacher*
Jacquie Beja, *Director*
EMP: 47 EST: 1894
SALES (est): 6MM **Privately Held**
WEB: www.goodsamfrc.org
SIC: 8322 Social service center

(P-17593)
GOODWILL CNTL SOUTHERN IND INC
Also Called: Goodwill Industries
566 Center St, Moraga (94556-2207)
PHONE..........................925 631-0148
Greg Curtin, *Branch Mgr*
EMP: 42
SALES (corp-wide): 118MM **Privately Held**
WEB: www.goodwillindy.org
SIC: 8322 5932 Individual & family services; used merchandise stores
PA: Goodwill Of Central And Southern Indiana, Inc
1635 W Michigan St
Indianapolis IN 46222
317 564-4313

(P-17594)
GOODWILL INDS OF RDWOOD EMPIRE
Also Called: Interlink Self-Help Center
1033 4th St, Santa Rosa (95404-4329)
PHONE..........................707 546-4481
Sean Wilson, *Director*
EMP: 43

SALES (corp-wide): 14.1MM **Privately Held**
WEB: www.gire.org
SIC: 8322 Social services for the handicapped
PA: Goodwill Industries Of The Redwood Empire
651 Yolanda Ave
Santa Rosa CA 95404
707 523-0550

(P-17595)
GOODWILL INDS SAN JQUIN VLY FN (PA)
129 S Grant St, Stockton (95202-3103)
PHONE..........................209 466-2311
David L Miller, *President*
Linda Huntley, *Vice Pres*
Joe Dittmann, *Admin Sec*
Ellen McDuffie, *Human Resources*
Steve Celaya, *Director*
EMP: 100
SQ FT: 50,000
SALES: 19.7MM **Privately Held**
WEB: www.goodwill-sjv.org
SIC: 5932 8322 Clothing, secondhand; helping hand service (Big Brother, etc.)

(P-17596)
GOSPEL CTR RESCUE MISSION INC
Also Called: Gospel Center Rescue Mission I
343 S San Joaquin St # 111, Stockton (95203-3535)
P.O. Box 816 (95201-0816)
PHONE..........................209 466-2138
William Brown, *Exec Dir*
G Richardson, *Vice Pres*
Monica Kimball, *Asst Director*
Dianna Clay, *Director*
Viola Dinkins, *Director*
EMP: 38 EST: 2019
SALES (est): 11.2MM **Privately Held**
WEB: www.gcrms.org
SIC: 8322 Social service center

(P-17597)
HAMILTON FAMILIES
1631 Hayes St, San Francisco (94117-1326)
PHONE..........................415 409-2100
Rosa Caspaneda, *Director*
Brian Stanley, *COO*
Monica Harlow, *Officer*
Elizabeth Stokes, *Exec Dir*
Allison Deck-Shipley, *Admin Sec*
EMP: 65 EST: 1987
SALES: 18MM **Privately Held**
WEB: www.hamiltonfamilies.org
SIC: 8322 Social service center

(P-17598)
HAVEN WNS CTR STANISLAUS CNTY
Also Called: Haven Womens Center Stanislaus
618 13th St, Modesto (95354-2436)
P.O. Box 580765 (95358-0014)
PHONE..........................209 524-4331
Leah Silvestre, *Director*
Jane Jackson, *Bd of Directors*
Holly Currie, *Associate Dir*
Belinda Rolicheck, *Exec Dir*
Victoria Carrera, *Program Mgr*
EMP: 50 EST: 1977
SALES: 2.9MM **Privately Held**
WEB: www.havenwcs.org
SIC: 8322 Emergency social services

(P-17599)
HEALTH TRUST
Also Called: Meals On Wheels
3180 Newberry Dr Ste 200, San Jose (95118-1566)
PHONE..........................408 513-8700
Michele Lew, *CEO*
EMP: 100
SALES (corp-wide): 25.5MM **Privately Held**
WEB: www.healthtrust.org
SIC: 8322 Meal delivery program
PA: The Health Trust
3180 Newberry Dr Ste 200
San Jose CA 95118
408 513-8700

(P-17600)
HEARTLAND CHILD & FAMILY SVCS
Also Called: North Area Cmnty Mntal Hlth Ct
811 Grand Ave Ste D, Sacramento (95838-3466)
PHONE..........................916 922-9868
Sarah Bailey, *CFO*
William Moss, *President*
William Benda, *Director*
Todd Palumbo, *Director*
EMP: 70 EST: 1980
SALES (est): 7.5MM **Privately Held**
WEB: www.doingwhateverittakes.org
SIC: 8322 General counseling services

(P-17601)
HOME FIRST
507 Valley Way, Milpitas (95035-4105)
PHONE..........................408 539-2125
Lindahazel Valencia, *Case Mgr*
EMP: 46 EST: 2016
SALES (est): 687.5K **Privately Held**
WEB: www.homefirstscc.org
SIC: 8322 Social service center

(P-17602)
HOMEBRIDGE INC
Also Called: IHSS CONSORTIUM, THE
1035 Market St Ste L1, San Francisco (94103-1666)
PHONE..........................415 255-2079
Gay Kaplan, *CEO*
Simon Pitchford, *COO*
Nenita Sayson, *Executive*
Margaret Baran, *Principal*
Mark Burns, *Principal*
EMP: 500 EST: 1994
SALES (est): 28.6MM **Privately Held**
WEB: www.homebridgeca.org
SIC: 8322 Homemakers' service

(P-17603)
HOMEFRST SVCS SANTA CLARA CNTY
Also Called: EHC LIFEBUILDERS
507 Valley Way, Milpitas (95035-4105)
PHONE..........................408 539-2100
Jennifer Niklaus, *CEO*
Rene D Ramirez, *COO*
Mary Zavala, *Officer*
Erica Andrade, *Executive Asst*
Charu Malpani, *Intrm Mgr*
EMP: 115 EST: 1980
SALES: 25.1MM **Privately Held**
WEB: www.homefirstscc.org
SIC: 8322 Social service center

(P-17604)
HOMELESS PRENATAL PROGRAM
33 Middle Point Rd, San Francisco (94124-4439)
PHONE..........................415 546-6756
Martha Ryan, *Director*
Carol Brennan, *Office Mgr*
Carrie Hamilton, *Technology*
Beverly Ashworth, *Finance Dir*
Aisianti Darmawan, *Accountant*
EMP: 50 EST: 1991
SALES (est): 8MM **Privately Held**
WEB: www.homelessprenatal.org
SIC: 8322 Social service center

(P-17605)
HORIZONS UNLMTED SAN FRNCSCO I
440 Potrero Ave, San Francisco (94110-1430)
PHONE..........................415 487-6700
Salina Lucero, *Exec Dir*
Celina Lucero, *Bd of Directors*
Shirley Maciel, *Program Dir*
EMP: 66 EST: 1965
SQ FT: 10,000
SALES: 3MM **Privately Held**
WEB: www.horizons-sf.org
SIC: 8322 Youth center

(P-17606)
HOUSING MATTERS
115b Coral St, Santa Cruz (95060-2143)
PHONE..........................831 458-6020
Monica Martinez, *Director*
Marsa Greenspan, *Associate Dir*

PRODUCTS & SERVICES SECTION
8322 - Individual & Family Social Svcs County (P-17627)

Evyn Simpson, *Program Mgr*
Jordan Boyer, *Manager*
Sarah Michels, *Manager*
EMP: 75 **EST:** 1986
SALES (est): 6.1MM **Privately Held**
WEB: www.housingmattersc.org
SIC: 8322 Social service center

(P-17607)
HR-OAKMONT F/C 5212
2801 Cohasset Rd, Chico (95973-0979)
PHONE.................530 895-0123
Fred Blue, *General Mgr*
EMP: 40 **EST:** 2011
SALES (est): 997.5K **Privately Held**
SIC: 8322 Senior citizens' center or association

(P-17608)
HUMBOLDT CMNTY ACCESS RSRCE CT
Also Called: Bay Center
1001 Searles St, Eureka (95501-1236)
PHONE.................707 441-8625
Joanne Diaz, *Manager*
EMP: 66
SALES (corp-wide): 4.2MM **Privately Held**
WEB: www.211humboldt.org
SIC: 8322 8052 Social service center; home for the mentally retarded, with health care
PA: Humboldt Community Access And Resource Center
1707 E St Ste 2
Eureka CA 95501
707 443-7077

(P-17609)
HUMBOLDT CMNTY ACCESS RSRCE CT
Also Called: Baybridge Employment Services
1707 E St Ste 2, Eureka (95501-7621)
PHONE.................707 443-7077
Ross Jantz, *Principal*
EMP: 66
SALES (corp-wide): 4.2MM **Privately Held**
WEB: www.211humboldt.org
SIC: 8322 Referral service for personal & social problems
PA: Humboldt Community Access And Resource Center
1707 E St Ste 2
Eureka CA 95501
707 443-7077

(P-17610)
HUMBOLDT COMMNTY ACCSS RESRC (PA)
1707 E St Ste 2, Eureka (95501-7621)
PHONE.................707 443-7077
Donna Shipley, *Exec Dir*
Ross Jantz, *Opers Mgr*
EMP: 105 **EST:** 1955
SQ FT: 3,800
SALES (est): 4.2MM **Privately Held**
WEB: www.hcar.us
SIC: 8322 Individual & family services

(P-17611)
HUMBOLDT SENIOR RESOURCE CTR (PA)
1910 California St, Eureka (95501-2899)
PHONE.................707 443-9747
Joyce Hayes, *Exec Dir*
Claudia Padilla, *Information Mgr*
Rene Arche, *Corp Comm Staff*
Barbara Walser, *Nutritionist*
Tony De Laurentis, *Manager*
EMP: 60 **EST:** 1974
SQ FT: 14,000
SALES (est): 25.1MM **Privately Held**
WEB: www.humsenior.org
SIC: 8322 8741 Senior citizens' center or association; management services

(P-17612)
IMMIGRATION INST OF BAY AREA (PA)
Also Called: International Inst of Bay Area
1111 Market St Fl 4, San Francisco (94103-1510)
P.O. Box 88 (94104-0088)
PHONE.................415 538-8100
Ellen Dumesnil, *Exec Dir*
Dekri Vonan, *Finance*
Soojin Tae, *Internal Med*
Valerie Tensfeldt, *Senior Mgr*
EMP: 41 **EST:** 1946
SALES (est): 6.2MM **Privately Held**
WEB: www.iibayarea.org
SIC: 8322 Social service center

(P-17613)
INDIVIDUALS NOW
Also Called: Social Advocates For Youth
2447 Summerfield Rd, Santa Rosa (95405-7815)
PHONE.................707 544-3299
Matt Martin, *CEO*
Katrina Thurman, *COO*
Dave Koressel, *CFO*
Brett Bradford, *Bd of Directors*
Cat Cvengros, *Officer*
EMP: 55 **EST:** 1970
SALES (est): 5.5MM **Privately Held**
WEB: www.saysc.org
SIC: 8322 Child guidance agency; youth center

(P-17614)
INNVISION WAY HOME
Also Called: Inn Vision Homeless Shelter
358 N Montgomery St, San Jose (95110-2325)
PHONE.................408 271-5160
Jim Githens, *Branch Mgr*
EMP: 95
SALES (corp-wide): 36.1K **Privately Held**
WEB: www.lifemoves.org
SIC: 8322 Social service center
PA: Innvision The Way Home
181 Constitution Dr
Menlo Park CA 94025
408 292-4286

(P-17615)
INSTITUTE ON AGING
Also Called: Irene Swndlls Adult Day Care P
3698 California St, San Francisco (94118-1702)
PHONE.................415 600-2690
Cindy Kauffman, *Administration*
Mary Griffin, *Vice Pres*
Aaron McPherson, *Vice Pres*
Austin Ord, *Vice Pres*
Marlene Litvak, *Admin Sec*
EMP: 71 **Privately Held**
WEB: www.ioaging.org
SIC: 8322 Senior citizens' center or association
PA: Institute On Aging
3575 Geary Blvd
San Francisco CA 94118

(P-17616)
INSTITUTE ON AGING (PA)
Also Called: Mssp
3575 Geary Blvd, San Francisco (94118-3212)
PHONE.................415 750-4101
J Thomas Briody, *President*
Anne Hinton, *Vice Chairman*
Cindy Kaufmann, *COO*
Roxana Tsougarakis, *CFO*
David Lowenkopf, *Treasurer*
EMP: 100 **EST:** 1985
SQ FT: 10,000
SALES (est): 38.9MM **Privately Held**
WEB: www.ioaging.org
SIC: 8322 Senior citizens' center or association

(P-17617)
INTEGRATED COMMUNITY SERVICES
Also Called: I C S
3020 Kerner Blvd Ste A, San Rafael (94901-5444)
PHONE.................415 455-8481
Donna Lemmon, *Exec Dir*
Lisa Newmark, *Director*
Michael Pinkerton, *Director*
Kathy Moreno, *Manager*
EMP: 61 **EST:** 1994
SALES (est): 3.6MM **Privately Held**
WEB: www.connectics.org
SIC: 8322 8699 Social services for the handicapped; charitable organization

(P-17618)
INTER-TRIBAL COUNCIL CAL INC (PA)
3400 Douglas Blvd Ste 230, Roseville (95661-4283)
PHONE.................916 973-9581
Connie Solas, *Exec Dir*
Stanley Brown, *CFO*
Michael Moreno, *Admin Asst*
Manuel Frasto, *Deputy Dir*
Hason Johnson, *Manager*
EMP: 38 **EST:** 1968
SALES (est): 1.5MM **Privately Held**
WEB: www.itccinc.org
SIC: 8322 Social service center

(P-17619)
JAY NOLAN COMMUNITY SVCS INC
1190 S Bascom Ste 240, Campbell (95008)
PHONE.................408 293-5002
Jennifer Lengyel, *Branch Mgr*
EMP: 114
SALES (corp-wide): 21.6MM **Privately Held**
WEB: www.jaynolan.org
SIC: 8322 Association for the handicapped
PA: Jay Nolan Community Services, Inc.
15501 San Fernando Missio
Mission Hills CA 91345
818 361-6400

(P-17620)
JAY NOLAN COMMUNITY SVCS INC
1190 S Bastom, San Jose (95128)
PHONE.................408 293-5002
EMP: 114
SALES (corp-wide): 21.6MM **Privately Held**
WEB: www.jaynolan.org
SIC: 8322 8331 8361 Social services for the handicapped; job training & vocational rehabilitation services; residential care
PA: Jay Nolan Community Services, Inc.
15501 San Fernando Missio
Mission Hills CA 91345
818 361-6400

(P-17621)
JEWISH CMNTY FDRTION OF GRTER (PA)
Also Called: Jewish Cmnty Relations Council
300 Grand Ave, Oakland (94610-4826)
P.O. Box 370, Berkeley (94701-0370)
PHONE.................510 839-2900
AMI Nahshon, *Exec VP*
Liora Brosbe, *Officer*
Andrew Kastner, *Executive*
Lisa Tabak, *Exec Dir*
Allan Lavigne, *Security Dir*
EMP: 35 **EST:** 1910
SQ FT: 10,000
SALES (est): 3.5MM **Privately Held**
WEB: www.jewishfed.org
SIC: 8322 Social service center

(P-17622)
JEWISH CMNTY FDRTION OF GRTER
Also Called: Berkely/Rchmond Jwish Cmnty Ct
1414 Walnut St, Berkeley (94709-1405)
PHONE.................510 848-0237
Ruth Shorer, *Director*
Margot Sands, *Asst Director*
Ave Long, *Director*
Rachel Barron, *Manager*
EMP: 78
SALES (corp-wide): 3.5MM **Privately Held**
WEB: www.jewishfed.org
SIC: 8322 8661 Community center; religious organizations
PA: Jewish Community Federation Of The Greater East Bay
300 Grand Ave
Oakland CA 94610
510 839-2900

(P-17623)
JEWISH COMMUNITY CTR OF E BAY
Also Called: JCCEB
1414 Walnut St, Berkeley (94709-1405)
PHONE.................510 848-0237
Sally Slinchvaugh, *Director*
Josh Langenthal, *President*
Samantha Kelman, *COO*
Isabel Balee, *Executive Asst*
Barbara Sutherland, *Info Tech Mgr*
EMP: 48 **EST:** 2008
SQ FT: 21,502
SALES (est): 5.7MM **Privately Held**
WEB: www.jcceastbay.org
SIC: 8322 Community center

(P-17624)
JEWISH FAMILY AND CHLD SVCS
Also Called: Seniors At Home
200 Channing Ave, Palo Alto (94301-2720)
PHONE.................650 931-1860
Cheryl Magid, *Administration*
Karen Friedland, *Webmaster*
Nancy Masters, *Director*
EMP: 119
SALES (corp-wide): 40.4MM **Privately Held**
WEB: www.jfcs.org
SIC: 8322 Social service center
PA: Jewish Family And Children's Services
2150 Post St
San Francisco CA 94115
415 449-1200

(P-17625)
JEWISH FAMILY AND CHLD SVCS (PA)
Also Called: CLEANERIFIC
2150 Post St, San Francisco (94115-3508)
P.O. Box 159004 (94115-9004)
PHONE.................415 449-1200
Anita Friedman, *Exec Dir*
Michael R Zent, *CEO*
Marga Dusedau, *CFO*
Javier Favela, *CFO*
Laura Jamieson, *CFO*
EMP: 80 **EST:** 1850
SALES: 40.4MM **Privately Held**
WEB: www.jfcs.org
SIC: 8322 Social service center

(P-17626)
JEWISH FAMILY AND CHLD SVCS
Also Called: Parents Place
200 Channing Ave, Palo Alto (94301-2720)
PHONE.................650 688-3030
Diane Wasson, *Branch Mgr*
Claire H O'Neill, *Manager*
EMP: 119
SALES (corp-wide): 40.4MM **Privately Held**
WEB: www.jfcs.org
SIC: 8322 Social service center
PA: Jewish Family And Children's Services
2150 Post St
San Francisco CA 94115
415 449-1200

(P-17627)
JEWISH FAMILY AND CHLD SVCS
Also Called: Parentals Place Parent Educatn
600 5th Ave, San Rafael (94901-3348)
PHONE.................415 449-3862
Gayle Zahler, *Director*
Nan Toder, *Partner*
Robert Nguyen, *Vice Pres*
Albert Schattner, *Exec Dir*
Curtis Ardourel, *Admin Asst*
EMP: 119
SALES (corp-wide): 40.4MM **Privately Held**
WEB: www.jfcs.org
SIC: 8322 Social service center
PA: Jewish Family And Children's Services
2150 Post St
San Francisco CA 94115
415 449-1200

8322 - Individual & Family Social Svcs County (P-17628)

(P-17628)
JEWISH FMLY & CMNTY SVCS E BAY (PA)
Also Called: JFCS/EAST BAY
2484 Shattuck Ave Ste 210, Berkeley (94704-2076)
PHONE....................510 704-7475
AVI Rose, *Exec Dir*
EMP: 40 **EST:** 1996
SALES (est): 9.5MM **Privately Held**
WEB: www.jfcs-eastbay.org
SIC: 8322 8049 Senior citizens' center or association; psychologist, psychotherapist & hypnotist

(P-17629)
JON K TAKATA CORPORATION (PA)
Also Called: Restoration Management Company
4142 Point Eden Way, Hayward (94545-3703)
PHONE....................510 315-5400
Jon Takata, *President*
Diane Viodes, *Treasurer*
Dave Masters, *Officer*
Bob Aitken, *Branch Mgr*
Mark Burke, *Branch Mgr*
EMP: 70 **EST:** 1985
SQ FT: 100,000
SALES (est): 54.4MM **Privately Held**
WEB: www.rmc.com
SIC: 8322 1799 4959 Disaster service; asbestos removal & encapsulation; environmental cleanup services

(P-17630)
KAINOS HM TRNING CTR FOR DVLPM
Also Called: Kainos Work Activity Ctr
2761 Fair Oaks Ave Ste A, Redwood City (94063-3540)
PHONE....................650 361-1355
Christen Rodgers, *Manager*
Andy Frisch, *Exec Dir*
Andrea Stilleson, *Program Dir*
Ria Agramon, *Senior Mgr*
Kristen Uthman, *Director*
EMP: 68
SALES (corp-wide): 7.3MM **Privately Held**
WEB: www.kainosusa.org
SIC: 8322 Social services for the handicapped
PA: Kainos Home & Training Center For Developmentally Disabled Adults
3631 Jefferson Ave
Redwood City CA
650 363-2423

(P-17631)
LA CASA DE LAS MADRES
1269 Howard St, San Francisco (94103-2711)
PHONE....................415 503-0500
Kathy Black, *Exec Dir*
Jordan Sharpe, *Case Mgr*
EMP: 35 **EST:** 1976
SALES: 5.3MM **Privately Held**
WEB: www.lacasa.org
SIC: 8322 Social service center; emergency shelters

(P-17632)
LA FAMILIA COUNSELING CTR INC
5523 34th St, Sacramento (95820-4725)
PHONE....................916 452-3601
Rachell R Rios, *Exec Dir*
Rachel R Rios, *Director*
EMP: 71 **EST:** 1975
SALES (est): 6MM **Privately Held**
WEB: www.lafcc.org
SIC: 8322 Social service center

(P-17633)
LAKE CNTY FIRE PROTECTION DST
Also Called: Lakeshore Fire Dept
14815 Olympic Dr, Clearlake (95422-9522)
PHONE....................707 994-2170
Richard More, *President*
Mike Dean, *Vice Chairman*
Darrell Jarrett, *Treasurer*
John Spriet, *Vice Pres*
Deborah Douglas, *General Mgr*
EMP: 70 **EST:** 1946
SQ FT: 18,000 **Privately Held**
WEB: www.lakecountyfire.com
SIC: 9224 8322 Fire department, volunteer; first aid service

(P-17634)
LARKIN STREET YOUTH SERVICES
Also Called: Diamond Youth Shelter
6324 Geary Blvd, San Francisco (94121-1824)
PHONE....................415 567-1020
Stanley Joseph, *Manager*
EMP: 60
SQ FT: 2,650
SALES (corp-wide): 31.2MM **Privately Held**
WEB: www.larkinstreetyouth.org
SIC: 8322 Youth center; emergency social services
PA: Larkin Street Youth Services
134 Golden Gate Ave
San Francisco CA 94102
415 673-0911

(P-17635)
LIFEHOUSE INC (PA)
18 Prfssnal Ctr Pkwy Fl 2, San Rafael (94903-2753)
PHONE....................415 472-2373
Nancy Dow Moody, *CEO*
Trice Padecky, *Administration*
Christine Rohmer, *Administration*
Viola Morris, *Finance*
Liza Padua, *Controller*
EMP: 335 **EST:** 1957
SALES (est): 19.7MM **Privately Held**
WEB: www.lifehouseagency.org
SIC: 8322 8361 Social services for the handicapped; general counseling services; self-help organization; residential care for the handicapped

(P-17636)
LIGHTHUSE FOR BLIND VSLLY IMPR (PA)
1155 Market St Fl 10, San Francisco (94103-1540)
PHONE....................415 431-1481
Joshua A Miele, *President*
Tony Lau, *CFO*
Joseph Chan, *Treasurer*
Ed Zaik, *Vice Pres*
Will Butler, *Comms Dir*
EMP: 42
SQ FT: 12,360
SALES: 18.1MM **Privately Held**
WEB: www.lighthouse-sf.org
SIC: 8322 Association for the handicapped; social services for the handicapped

(P-17637)
LIVE OAK ADULT DAY SERVICES
1147 Minnesota Ave, San Jose (95125-3324)
PHONE....................408 971-9363
Collen Hudgen, *Exec Dir*
Toni A Ensunsa, *CFO*
Leta Friedlander, *Exec Dir*
EMP: 38 **EST:** 1981
SQ FT: 2,800
SALES (est): 1.9MM **Privately Held**
WEB: www.liveoakadultdaycare.org
SIC: 8322 Senior citizens' center or association; adult day care center

(P-17638)
LUCILE PCKARD FNDTION FOR CHLD (PA)
400 Hamilton Ave Ste 240, Palo Alto (94301-1834)
PHONE....................650 497-8365
Steven Peets, *President*
Kathy Coulbourn, *CFO*
Margaret Cruz, *Officer*
Jodi Mouratis, *Officer*
Robin Nelson, *Officer*
EMP: 43 **EST:** 1998
SQ FT: 9,000
SALES: 19.5MM **Privately Held**
WEB: www.lpfch.org
SIC: 8322 Child related social services

(P-17639)
LYDIA C GONZALEZ
1400 Veterans Blvd, Redwood City (94063-2612)
PHONE....................650 299-4707
EMP: 50
SALES (est): 1.9MM **Privately Held**
SIC: 8322 Individual/Family Services

(P-17640)
MANCHESTER BAND POMO INDIANS
Also Called: Manchster Pt Arena Band Pomo I
24 Mamie Laiwa Dr, Point Arena (95468)
P.O. Box 623 (95468-0623)
PHONE....................707 882-2788
Christina Dukatz, *CEO*
Nelson Pinola, *Chairman*
EMP: 61 **EST:** 1928
SALES (est): 3.1MM **Privately Held**
SIC: 8322 Individual & family services

(P-17641)
MARIN COMMUNITY FOOD BANK
2550 Kerner Blvd, San Rafael (94901-2505)
PHONE....................415 883-1302
Anne Rogers, *Exec Dir*
Matt Taddei, *Chairman*
EMP: 39 **EST:** 1981
SQ FT: 4,700
SALES (est): 3.7MM **Privately Held**
WEB: www.sfmfoodbank.org
SIC: 8322 Social service center

(P-17642)
MARTIS CAMP CLUB
7951 Fleur Du Lac Ct, Truckee (96161-4261)
PHONE....................530 550-6000
Mark Johnson, *President*
Carla Yeager, *Treasurer*
Ron Parr, *Vice Pres*
Jonas Mikals, *Sales Executive*
Jayce Coziar, *Corp Comm Staff*
EMP: 300 **EST:** 2011
SQ FT: 80,000
SALES (est): 17MM **Privately Held**
WEB: www.martiscamp.com
SIC: 8322 Community center

(P-17643)
MEALS ON WHEELS BY ACC
7375 Park City Dr, Sacramento (95831-3866)
PHONE....................916 444-9533
Winston Ashizawa, *President*
Raymond Gee, *Controller*
EMP: 37 **EST:** 2010
SALES (est): 6.4MM **Privately Held**
WEB: www.mowsac.org
SIC: 8322 Meal delivery program

(P-17644)
MEALS ON WHEELS DIABLO REGION (PA)
1300 Civic Dr Fl 1, Walnut Creek (94596-4398)
PHONE....................925 937-8311
Elaine Clark, *Director*
Susannah Meyer, *Officer*
Nancy Sorensen, *Finance*
Connie Ekren, *Accountant*
Rosa Loya, *Director*
EMP: 42 **EST:** 1984
SQ FT: 5,500
SALES: 3.3MM **Privately Held**
WEB: www.mowdiabloregion.org
SIC: 8322 Meal delivery program; family counseling services; geriatric social service; social services for the handicapped

(P-17645)
MEALS ON WHELS SAN FRNCSCO INC
1375 Fairfax Ave, San Francisco (94124-1735)
PHONE....................415 920-1111
Ashley McCumber, *Exec Dir*
Anne Quaintance, *Principal*
Michele Furlong, *Executive Asst*
Frank Landin, *Human Res Dir*
Marie Nedich, *Marketing Staff*
EMP: 50 **EST:** 1970
SQ FT: 19,330
SALES (est): 24.1MM **Privately Held**
WEB: www.mowsf.org
SIC: 8322 Meal delivery program

(P-17646)
MEALS ON WHELS SOLANO CNTY INC
95 Marina Ctr, Suisun City (94585-2522)
PHONE....................707 426-3079
Cathy Hall, *Exec Dir*
Laurie Hartmann, *Exec Dir*
Keith Davis, *Case Mgr*
Erick Florendo, *Case Mgr*
Megan Houle, *Case Mgr*
EMP: 77 **EST:** 1978
SALES (est): 3.2MM **Privately Held**
WEB: www.mealsonwheelssolano.org
SIC: 8322 Senior citizens' center or association

(P-17647)
MENTIS
709 Franklin St, NAPA (94559-2920)
PHONE....................707 255-0966
Rob Weiss, *Exec Dir*
EMP: 35 **EST:** 1950
SQ FT: 1,638
SALES (est): 2.6MM **Privately Held**
WEB: www.mentisnapa.org
SIC: 8322 Family (marriage) counseling

(P-17648)
MERCY SERVICES CORPORATION
Also Called: Oceana Terrace Senior Housing
903 Oceana Blvd Ofc, Pacifica (94044-2396)
PHONE....................650 359-6161
Judy Cannon, *Manager*
Heather Heyd, *Director*
EMP: 41
SALES (corp-wide): 334.5K **Privately Held**
SIC: 8322 Senior citizens' center or association
PA: Mercy Services Corporation
3120 Freeboard Dr Ste 202
West Sacramento CA
916 414-4400

(P-17649)
MHN GOVERNMENT SERVICES LLC
2370 Kerner Blvd, San Rafael (94901-5613)
PHONE....................916 294-4941
Billy Maynard, *President*
Lisa Ostergren, *Info Tech Mgr*
EMP: 2268 **EST:** 2005
SQ FT: 67,000
SALES (est): 35.9MM **Publicly Held**
WEB: www.healthnet.com
SIC: 8322 Individual & family services
HQ: Health Net, Llc
21650 Oxnard St Fl 25
Woodland Hills CA 91367
818 676-6000

(P-17650)
MISSION CNCIL ALCHOL ABUSE SPN
Also Called: Latino Family Center
154a Capp St, San Francisco (94110-1210)
PHONE....................415 826-6767
Jose Luis Aguirre, *Director*
Omar Chicas, *Officer*
Crystal Wallstrom, *Consultant*
EMP: 37 **EST:** 1979
SALES: 785K **Privately Held**
WEB: www.missioncouncil.org
SIC: 8322 8093 Rehabilitation services; substance abuse clinics (outpatient)

PRODUCTS & SERVICES SECTION
8322 - Individual & Family Social Svcs County (P-17674)

(P-17651)
MT DIABLO UNIFIED SCHOOL DST
Also Called: Mt Diablo Adult Education
1266 San Carlos Ave, Concord (94518-1102)
PHONE.....................925 685-7340
Vittore Abbate, *Principal*
EMP: 57
SALES (corp-wide): 431.8MM **Privately Held**
WEB: www.mdusd.org
SIC: 8211 8322 Public elementary & secondary schools; adult day care center
PA: Mt. Diablo Unified School District
1936 Carlotta Dr
Concord CA 94519
925 682-8000

(P-17652)
MUTUAL ASSSTNCE NTWRK OF DEL P (PA)
811 Grand Ave Ste A, Sacramento (95838-3466)
PHONE.....................916 927-7694
Richard Dana, *Exec Dir*
EMP: 41 EST: 1992
SALES: 3.1MM **Privately Held**
WEB: www.mutualassistance.org
SIC: 8322 Disaster service

(P-17653)
NATALIE DSTINY ENTPS LTD LBLTY
Also Called: California Seniors Care
42 W Campbell Ave Ste 101, Campbell (95008-1042)
PHONE.....................408 429-8665
Jason Broberg, *Vice Pres*
EMP: 48 EST: 2008
SALES (est): 693.1K **Privately Held**
WEB: www.cschomecare.com
SIC: 8322 8082 Geriatric social service; home health care services

(P-17654)
NEW MRNING YOUTH FMLY SVCS INC
Also Called: NEW MORNING YOUTH & FAMILY COU
6767 Green Valley Rd F, Placerville (95667-8984)
PHONE.....................530 622-5551
David Ashby, *Exec Dir*
Marsha Repschlaeger, *Manager*
EMP: 35 EST: 1971
SQ FT: 2,000
SALES (est): 2.9MM **Privately Held**
WEB: www.newmorningyfs.org
SIC: 8322 Family service agency

(P-17655)
NIC USA INC
Also Called: Happy Valley I.C.F.
2478 Warren Ln B, Walnut Creek (94597-3036)
PHONE.....................925 944-1222
Costin Niculescu, *President*
Angela Niculescu, *Admin Sec*
EMP: 40 EST: 1997
SQ FT: 4,000
SALES (est): 3MM **Privately Held**
SIC: 8322 Emergency social services

(P-17656)
NORCAL VOCATIONAL INC (PA)
77 Mark Dr Ste 20, San Rafael (94903-2267)
P.O. Box 10387 (94912-0387)
PHONE.....................415 206-9766
Susan Savage, *President*
Patricia Terranova, *CFO*
EMP: 73 EST: 1991
SQ FT: 1,500 **Privately Held**
WEB: www.norcalvocational.org
SIC: 8322 Social services for the handicapped

(P-17657)
NORTH MARIN COMMUNITY SERVICES (PA)
680 Wilson Ave, Novato (94947-3825)
PHONE.....................415 892-1643
Cheryl Paddack, *Exec Dir*
Richard Barnes, *CIO*
Brianna Turner, *Teacher*
Liliana Palu, *Case Mgr*
Isaura Resendiz, *Case Mgr*
EMP: 47 EST: 1966
SQ FT: 26,000
SALES: 4.8MM **Privately Held**
WEB: www.northmarincs.org
SIC: 8322 5932 Youth center; used merchandise stores

(P-17658)
NORTHERN CAL CHILD DEV INC
Also Called: Corning Head Start Center
617 Fig Ln, Corning (96021-3300)
P.O. Box 193 (96021-0193)
PHONE.....................530 838-1034
Brian Heese, *Director*
Tori Prest, *Director*
Jennifer Torres, *Manager*
EMP: 56
SALES (corp-wide): 5.4MM **Privately Held**
WEB: www.nccdi.com
SIC: 8322 8351 Family service agency; head start center, except in conjunction with school
PA: Northern California Child Development, Inc.
220 Sycamore St Ste 200
Red Bluff CA 96080
530 529-1500

(P-17659)
NORTHERN CALIFORNIA INALLIANCE
411 4th St, Wheatland (95692-9467)
PHONE.....................530 633-9695
Andrea Croom, *Exec Dir*
EMP: 75
SALES (corp-wide): 20.6MM **Privately Held**
WEB: www.inallianceinc.com
SIC: 8322 Social service center
PA: Northern California Inalliance
6950 21st Ave
Sacramento CA 95820
916 381-1300

(P-17660)
NORTHERN CALIFORNIA INALLIANCE (PA)
6950 21st Ave, Sacramento (95820-5948)
PHONE.....................916 381-1300
Richard Royse, *Exec Dir*
Andrea Croom, *Exec Dir*
Diana Derodeff, *Exec Dir*
Charlene Modica, *Admin Asst*
Fatima Weish, *Personnel Assit*
EMP: 190 EST: 1968
SQ FT: 20,000
SALES: 20.6MM **Privately Held**
WEB: www.inallianceinc.com
SIC: 8322 Social service center

(P-17661)
NORTHERN CALIFORNIA INALLIANCE
660 Main St, Placerville (95667-5704)
PHONE.....................530 344-1244
Van Traker, *Manager*
Ben Praker, *Manager*
EMP: 75
SQ FT: 28,324
SALES (corp-wide): 20.6MM **Privately Held**
WEB: www.inallianceinc.com
SIC: 8322 Social service center
PA: Northern California Inalliance
6950 21st Ave
Sacramento CA 95820
916 381-1300

(P-17662)
NORTHERN VLY CTHLIC SCIAL SVC
2400 Washington Ave, Redding (96001-2802)
PHONE.....................530 241-0552
Jan Maurer Watkins, *CEO*
Don C Chapman, *CEO*
Heather Yohn, *Manager*
EMP: 151 EST: 2004
SALES (est): 15MM **Privately Held**
WEB: www.nvcss.org
SIC: 8322 Outreach program

(P-17663)
OLDER ADULTS CARE MGT INC (PA)
881 Fremont Ave Ste A2, Los Altos (94024-5637)
PHONE.....................650 329-1411
Cherry Jackson, *Director*
Jim Wilde, *Supervisor*
EMP: 180 EST: 1982
SQ FT: 2,000
SALES (est): 3.6MM **Privately Held**
SIC: 8322 8741 8082 Geriatric social service; general counseling services; management services; home health care services

(P-17664)
OPERATION DIGNITY INC
3850 San Pablo Ave # 102, Emeryville (94608-3807)
PHONE.....................510 287-8465
Alex McElree, *Exec Dir*
Margarie Wolf, *President*
Marguerite Bachand, *Exec Dir*
Morgan Clyde, *CIO*
Gretel Tortolani, *VP Finance*
EMP: 43 EST: 1993
SALES (est): 4.8MM **Privately Held**
WEB: www.operationdignity.org
SIC: 8322 Social service center

(P-17665)
OPPORTNTY FOR INDPENDENCE INC
20 H St, San Rafael (94901-1779)
PHONE.....................415 721-7772
Eric Vanderville, *Exec Dir*
Eric Van Derville, *Director*
EMP: 51 EST: 1991
SQ FT: 7,000
SALES: 2.2MM **Privately Held**
WEB: www.ofiinc.org
SIC: 8322 8331 Social service center; vocational training agency

(P-17666)
OSHMAN FAMILY JEWISH CMNTY CTR
3921 Fabian Way, Palo Alto (94303-4640)
PHONE.....................650 223-8700
Alan Sataloff, *Exec Dir*
Haim Hovav, *CFO*
Olivia Cote, *Admin Asst*
Paul Raczynski, *Info Tech Dir*
Joe Kelso, *Human Resources*
EMP: 200 EST: 1988
SALES: 31.7MM **Privately Held**
SIC: 8322 Community center

(P-17667)
OUTREACH & ESCORT INC (PA)
2221 Oakland Rd Ste 200, San Jose (95131-1415)
P.O. Box 640910 (95164-0910)
PHONE.....................408 678-8585
Katheryn H Heatley, *President*
William Chawarz, *Vice Pres*
EMP: 76 EST: 1979
SQ FT: 20,000
SALES: 1.5MM **Privately Held**
WEB: www.outreach1.org
SIC: 8322 Individual & family services

(P-17668)
PAJARO VLY PRVNTION STDNT ASSS
335 E Lake Ave, Watsonville (95076-4826)
PHONE.....................831 728-6445
Erica Padilla-Chavez, *CEO*
Adriana Mata, *Administration*
EMP: 61 EST: 1984
SALES (est): 5.1MM **Privately Held**
WEB: www.pvpsa.org
SIC: 8322 Alcoholism counseling, nontreatment; drug abuse counselor, nontreatment

(P-17669)
PARTNERS ADVCTES FOR RMRKBLE C
Also Called: Parca
800 Airport Blvd Ste 320, Burlingame (94010-1919)
PHONE.....................650 312-0730
Diana Conti, *Exec Dir*
Kendra Vera, *Controller*
Joseph Fenerty, *Anesthesiology*
Joel Bouza, *Director*
Lori Milburn, *Director*
EMP: 71 EST: 1952
SALES (est): 12.2MM **Privately Held**
WEB: www.parca.org
SIC: 8322 Association for the handicapped

(P-17670)
PATHWAY TO CHOICES INC
751 Belmont Way, Pinole (94564-2661)
PHONE.....................510 724-9044
Juan Velasquez, *President*
Maria Velasquez, *Human Resources*
EMP: 36 EST: 2002
SALES (est): 1.8MM **Privately Held**
WEB: www.pathwaytochoices.net
SIC: 8322 Social service center

(P-17671)
PENINSULA FAMILY SERVICE
Also Called: Leo J Ryan Child Care Ctr
1200 Miller Ave, South San Francisco (94080-1221)
PHONE.....................650 952-6848
Liliya Sergiyemko, *Branch Mgr*
Diana Alcazar-Lopez, *Exec Dir*
EMP: 64
SALES (corp-wide): 14MM **Privately Held**
WEB: www.peninsulafamilyservice.org
SIC: 8322 8351 Family (marriage) counseling; child day care services
PA: Peninsula Family Service
24 2nd Ave
San Mateo CA 94401
650 403-4300

(P-17672)
PENINSULA JEWISH COMMUNITY CTR
800 Foster City Blvd, Foster City (94404-2228)
PHONE.....................650 212-7522
Paul Gedulig, *CEO*
Fred Weiner, *CFO*
Seth Hazen, *Officer*
Ginger Watts, *General Mgr*
Renee Keller, *Office Admin*
EMP: 82 EST: 1995
SALES (est): 15.4MM **Privately Held**
WEB: www.pjcc.org
SIC: 8322 Community center

(P-17673)
PIT RIVER TRIBAL COUNCIL
Also Called: Pit Rivr Indian Trib Chld Welf
36970 Park Ave, Burney (96013-4072)
P.O. Box 724 (96013-0724)
PHONE.....................530 335-5421
Greg Thompson, *Manager*
EMP: 35
SALES (corp-wide): 12.2MM **Privately Held**
WEB: www.pitrivertribe.org
SIC: 8322 Social service center
PA: Pit River Tribal Council
37960 Park Ave
Burney CA 96013
530 335-5487

(P-17674)
PLUMAS RURAL SERVICES
711 E Main St, Quincy (95971-9722)
PHONE.....................530 283-2725
Michele Pillar, *Exec Dir*
EMP: 35 EST: 2011
SQ FT: 6,000
SALES (est): 5.5MM **Privately Held**
WEB: www.plumasrualservices.org
SIC: 8322 Drug abuse counselor, nontreatment

8322 - Individual & Family Social Svcs County (P-17675)

(P-17675)
POMEROY RCRTION RHBLTATION CTR (PA)
Also Called: R C H
207 Skyline Blvd, San Francisco (94132-1025)
PHONE..............................415 665-4100
John McCue, *Exec Dir*
Henry Woo, *Exec Dir*
Ryan Downey, *Administration*
Lesley Steele, *Administration*
Catrina Johnson, *Prgrmr*
EMP: 178 **EST:** 1954
SQ FT: 22,000
SALES (est): 11.7MM **Privately Held**
WEB: www.prrcsf.org
SIC: 8322 Social services for the handicapped

(P-17676)
POSITIVE OPTION FAMILY SERVICE (PA)
Also Called: Wellspring
2400 Glendale Ln Ste H, Sacramento (95825-2431)
P.O. Box 202, Citrus Heights (95611-0202)
PHONE..............................916 973-2838
Joseph B Kovill, *CEO*
EMP: 45
SALES: 1.3MM **Privately Held**
WEB: www.positiveoption.org
SIC: 8322 8211 Adoption services; elementary & secondary schools

(P-17677)
PRECISION HOME CARE LLC
2365 Iron Point Rd # 270, Folsom (95630-8712)
PHONE..............................916 749-4051
John Alves, *Mng Member*
Jonathan Bliss, *Mng Member*
Chris Simmons, *Mng Member*
EMP: 56 **EST:** 2016
SALES (est): 2.7MM **Privately Held**
SIC: 8322 8361 Old age assistance; residential care

(P-17678)
PROJECT OPEN HAND (PA)
730 Polk St Fl 3, San Francisco (94109-7813)
PHONE..............................415 292-3400
Paul Hepfer, *CEO*
Christine Lias, *Officer*
Teresa Ballete, *Controller*
Keith Rozek, *Director*
Serena Ngo, *Manager*
EMP: 96 **EST:** 1986
SQ FT: 50,000
SALES: 14.9MM **Privately Held**
WEB: www.openhand.org
SIC: 8322 Social service center

(P-17679)
RAPHAEL HSE SAN FRANCISCO INC
1065 Sutter St, San Francisco (94109-5891)
PHONE..............................415 345-7200
Kate Smith, *President*
Karol K Denniston, *Partner*
Judy Davies, *Vice Pres*
Father David Lowell, *Exec Dir*
Ralph Payton, *Exec Dir*
EMP: 122 **EST:** 1977
SQ FT: 10,000
SALES: 2.5MM **Privately Held**
WEB: www.raphaelhouse.org
SIC: 8322 8661 Emergency shelters; non-church religious organizations

(P-17680)
RAY STONE INCORPORATED
Ray Stone Senior Communities
6017 Winding Way, Carmichael (95608-1434)
PHONE..............................916 482-2363
EMP: 50
SALES (corp-wide): 49MM **Privately Held**
WEB: www.raystoneinc.com
SIC: 8322 Community center
PA: Ray Stone Incorporated
550 Howe Ave Ste 200
Sacramento CA 95825
916 649-7500

(P-17681)
RAY STONE INCORPORATED
Also Called: Hilltop Commons Senior Living
131 Eureka St, Grass Valley (95945-6355)
PHONE..............................530 272-5274
Dave Thomas, *Administration*
EMP: 50
SALES (corp-wide): 49MM **Privately Held**
WEB: www.raystoneinc.com
SIC: 8322 Senior citizens' center or association
PA: Ray Stone Incorporated
550 Howe Ave Ste 200
Sacramento CA 95825
916 649-7500

(P-17682)
REDF
2526 Piedmont Ave, Berkeley (94704-3120)
PHONE..............................415 561-6677
Carla Javits, *CEO*
Carrie McKellogg, *Officer*
Jo Greer, *Vice Pres*
Sean Tennerson, *Program Mgr*
Vanessa Collins, *Admin Mgr*
EMP: 47 **EST:** 2003
SALES (est): 11.6MM **Privately Held**
WEB: www.redf.org
SIC: 8322 Social service center

(P-17683)
REDWOOD CITY SCHOOL DISTRICT
Also Called: Child Dev Enrollment Off
3600 Middlefield Rd, Menlo Park (94025-3010)
PHONE..............................650 568-3820
Merrily Fris, *Manager*
EMP: 36
SALES (corp-wide): 211.9MM **Privately Held**
WEB: www.rcsdk8.net
SIC: 8211 8322 Public elementary & secondary schools; child related social services
PA: Redwood City School District
750 Bradford St
Redwood City CA 94063
650 423-2200

(P-17684)
REDWOOD COAST SENIORS INC
Also Called: Senior Nutrition
490 N Harold St, Fort Bragg (95437-3331)
PHONE..............................707 964-0443
Joseph Curren, *Exec Dir*
EMP: 37 **EST:** 1976
SALES (est): 1.7MM **Privately Held**
WEB: www.rcscenter.org
SIC: 8322 Senior citizens' center or association

(P-17685)
REDWOOD COMMUNITY SERVICES INC
Also Called: Childrens Therapeutic Services
350 E Gobbi St, Ukiah (95482-5511)
PHONE..............................707 472-2922
Dan Anderson, *Office Mgr*
Pamela Lucas, *Supervisor*
EMP: 66 **Privately Held**
WEB: www.redwoodcommunityservices.org
SIC: 8322 8059 Family service agency; personal care home, with health care
PA: Redwood Community Services, Inc.
631 S Orchard Ave
Ukiah CA 95482

(P-17686)
REDWOOD EMPIRE FOOD BANK
3990 Brickway Blvd, Santa Rosa (95403-1070)
PHONE..............................707 523-7900
David Goodman, *CEO*
David Guhin, *President*
Suzy Marzalek, *President*
Jean Larson, *COO*
Howard Daulton, *Treasurer*
EMP: 40 **EST:** 1987
SQ FT: 20,160
SALES (est): 57.6MM **Privately Held**
WEB: www.refb.org
SIC: 8322 Social service center

(P-17687)
REGIONAL CENTER OF E BAY INC (PA)
Also Called: RCEB
500 Davis St Ste 100, San Leandro (94577-2758)
PHONE..............................510 618-6100
Kathy Hebert, *CEO*
Tasia Christon, *Admin Sec*
MAI Hong, *Admin Sec*
Ravneet Kaur, *Analyst*
Terri Jones, *Human Res Dir*
EMP: 150 **EST:** 1975
SQ FT: 26,000
SALES (est): 547MM **Privately Held**
WEB: www.rceb.org
SIC: 8322 Social services for the handicapped

(P-17688)
REGIONAL CENTER OF E BAY INC
Also Called: Rceb
1320 Willow Pass Rd # 300, Concord (94520-5232)
PHONE..............................925 691-2300
EMP: 100
SALES (corp-wide): 547MM **Privately Held**
WEB: www.rceb.org
SIC: 8322 Social services for the handicapped
PA: Regional Center Of The East Bay, Inc.
500 Davis St Ste 100
San Leandro CA 94577
510 618-6100

(P-17689)
RELATIONSHIP SKILLS CENTER
9719 Lincoln, Sacramento (95827)
PHONE..............................916 362-1900
Fax: 916 362-1300
EMP: 45
SALES: 894.3K **Privately Held**
WEB: www.sacramentohealthymarriage.org
SIC: 8322 Individual/Family Services

(P-17690)
RESCUE CHILDREN INC
Also Called: CRAYCROFT YOUTH CENTER
335 G St, Fresno (93706-3422)
P.O. Box 1422 (93716-1422)
PHONE..............................559 268-1123
Fax: 559 268-3465
EMP: 50
SALES: 1.3MM **Privately Held**
SIC: 8322 Individual/Family Services

(P-17691)
RESOURCE CNNCTION OF AMDOR CLV (PA)
Also Called: RESOURCE CONNECTION, THE
444 E Saint Charles St, San Andreas (95249-9658)
P.O. Box 919 (95249-0919)
PHONE..............................209 754-3114
Linda Foster, *Ch of Bd*
Amber Shelton, *Principal*
Kelli Fraguero, *Admin Dir*
Susan Lang, *Admin Asst*
Beverly Stewart, *Human Res Dir*
EMP: 106 **EST:** 1980
SALES (est): 10.5MM **Privately Held**
WEB: www.trcac.org
SIC: 8322 Social service center

(P-17692)
RESOURCES FOR IND LIVING INC
Also Called: Ril
420 I St Ste 3, Sacramento (95814-2319)
PHONE..............................916 446-3074
Frances Gracechild, *Director*
Sean Rogers, *Accounting Mgr*
EMP: 52 **EST:** 1976
SALES: 679.6K **Privately Held**
WEB: www.ril-sacramento.org
SIC: 8322 Social service center

(P-17693)
REUTLINGER COMMUNITY
Also Called: REUTLINGER COMMUNITY FOR JEWIS
4000 Camino Tassajara, Danville (94506-4711)
PHONE..............................925 964-2062
Jay Zimmer, *CEO*
EMP: 160 **EST:** 1972
SALES: 19.6MM **Privately Held**
WEB: www.rcjl.org
SIC: 8322 Individual & family services

(P-17694)
RICHMOND DST NEIGHBORHOOD CTR (PA)
741 30th Ave, San Francisco (94121-3519)
PHONE..............................415 751-6600
Michelle Cusano, *Exec Dir*
Michael T Riordan, *Treasurer*
Will Shenton, *Comms Mgr*
Nick Colella, *Program Mgr*
Linda Iles, *Program Mgr*
EMP: 75 **EST:** 1983
SALES: 5.6MM **Privately Held**
WEB: www.richmondsf.org
SIC: 8322 Community center; outreach program

(P-17695)
ROMAN CATHLIC BISHP SACRAMENTO
Also Called: Catholic Social Service
125 Corporate Pl, Vallejo (94590-6285)
PHONE..............................707 556-9317
Kurt Chifmark, *Director*
EMP: 88
SALES (corp-wide): 33.6MM **Privately Held**
WEB: www.scd.org
SIC: 8661 8322 8111 Catholic Church; senior citizens' center or association; immigration & naturalization law
PA: Roman Catholic Bishop Of Sacramento
2110 Broadway
Sacramento CA 95818
916 733-0100

(P-17696)
RURAL CMNTY ASSISTANCE CORP (PA)
Also Called: Rcac
3120 Freeboard Dr Ste 201, West Sacramento (95691-5039)
PHONE..............................916 447-2854
Stan Keasling, *CEO*
Kevin McCumber, *CFO*
Stephanie Villegas, *Program Mgr*
Rachel Smith, *Executive Asst*
Savanna Bales, *Prgrmr*
EMP: 60
SALES: 24.3MM **Privately Held**
WEB: www.rcac.org
SIC: 8322 6111 Individual & family services; federal & federally sponsored credit agencies

(P-17697)
RURAL HUMAN SERVICES (PA)
Also Called: DEL NORTE WORKFORCE CENTER
286 M St Ste A, Crescent City (95531-4115)
PHONE..............................707 464-7441
Teri E McCune-Oostra, *Director*
Stephanie Bruce, *Executive Asst*
Donald Youtsey, *Director*
EMP: 42 **EST:** 1981
SQ FT: 17,267
SALES: 1.8MM **Privately Held**
WEB: www.ruralhumanservices.org
SIC: 8322 Emergency social services

(P-17698)
SACRAMENTO AREA EMERG HOUSING
Also Called: Emergency Housing Chld Program
4516 Parker Ave, Sacramento (95820-4029)
PHONE..............................916 455-2160
Bonnie Hager, *Director*
Lor Pimm, *Program Mgr*
EMP: 66 **Privately Held**
WEB: www.nextmovesacramento.org

PRODUCTS & SERVICES SECTION

8322 - Individual & Family Social Svcs County (P-17721)

SIC: 8322 6513 Social service center; apartment building operators
PA: Next Move Homeless Services
8001 Folsom Blvd
Sacramento CA 95826

(P-17699)
SACRAMENTO LOAVES & FISHES (PA)
1351 N C St Ste 22, Sacramento (95811-0608)
P.O. Box 2161 (95812-2161)
PHONE.................................916 446-0874
Libby Hernandez, Director
Noel Kammermann, Exec Dir
Lucia Vega, Office Mgr
Garren Bratcher, Director
Shannon Dominguez-Steve, Director
EMP: 55 EST: 1983
SALES (est): 5.9MM Privately Held
WEB: www.sacloaves.org
SIC: 8322 Social service center

(P-17700)
SACRAMNTO CHNESE CMNTY SVCS CT
420 I St Ste 5, Sacramento (95814-2319)
PHONE.................................916 442-4228
Henry Kloczkowski, Director
Choua Yang, Associate Dir
Oscar Bermudez, Program Mgr
David Constancio, Program Mgr
Andrea Cunningham, Program Mgr
EMP: 200 EST: 1978
SQ FT: 2,000
SALES: 9.1MM Privately Held
WEB: www.sccsc.org
SIC: 8322 8699 8611 Social service center; charitable organization; community affairs & services

(P-17701)
SACRED HEART COMMUNITY SERVICE
1381 S 1st St, San Jose (95110-3431)
PHONE.................................408 278-2160
Poncho Guevara, CEO
Felicia Madsen, President
Lydia Bustamante, Associate Dir
Richard Barnes, Exec Dir
Rachel Wright, Research
EMP: 38 EST: 1964
SQ FT: 6,500
SALES: 43.4MM Privately Held
WEB: www.sacredheartcs.org
SIC: 8322 Individual & family services

(P-17702)
SAFE & SOUND
1757 Waller St, San Francisco (94117-2727)
PHONE.................................415 668-0494
Katie Albright, Director
Deborah Shen, CFO
Kate Frankfurt, Officer
Pamela Candelaria, Controller
Hilario Landin, Human Res Mgr
EMP: 40 EST: 1976
SQ FT: 2,500
SALES (est): 7.4MM Privately Held
WEB: www.safeandsound.org
SIC: 8322 Family service agency

(P-17703)
SAGE PROJECT INC
68 12th St, San Francisco (94103-1297)
PHONE.................................415 905-5050
Ellyn Green, Exec Dir
Paul Burrin, Vice Pres
Monique Henningfield, Engineer
Gail Rickabaugh, Analyst
Francine Braae, Director
EMP: 51 EST: 1995
SQ FT: 5,830
SALES (est): 1.5MM Privately Held
WEB: www.sagesf.org
SIC: 8322 8069 Alcoholism counseling, nontreatment; drug addiction rehabilitation hospital

(P-17704)
SALESFORCECOM/FOUNDATION
The Landmark One St The Landma, San Francisco (94105)
PHONE.................................800 667-6389
Marc Benioff, CEO
Keith Block, President
Suzanne Dibianca, President
Rob Acker, COO
Kurt Hagen, CFO
EMP: 150 EST: 1999
SALES (est): 26.1MM Privately Held
SIC: 8322 Disaster service; temporary relief service

(P-17705)
SALVATION ARMY GLDEN STATE DIV (PA)
832 Folsom St Fl 6, San Francisco (94107-1142)
PHONE.................................415 553-3500
Steve Smith, Principal
Tammy Ray, Officer
Julio Perez, Business Dir
Darren Trimmer, Admin Sec
Eric Hansen, Human Res Dir
EMP: 61 EST: 2010
SALES: 10.8MM Privately Held
WEB: www.goldenstate.salvationarmy.org
SIC: 8322 8741 Social service center; administrative management

(P-17706)
SAMARITAN VILLAGE INC
7700 Fox Rd, Hughson (95326-9100)
P.O. Box 444, Yuba City (95992-0444)
PHONE.................................209 883-3212
Daniel Aguilar, CEO
Victor Savage, CEO
EMP: 115 EST: 2002
SALES: 60K Privately Held
WEB: www.svliving.org
SIC: 8322 Adult day care center

(P-17707)
SAN ANDREAS REGIONAL CENTER (PA)
6203 San Ignacio Ave # 200, San Jose (95119-1371)
P.O. Box 50002 (95150-0002)
PHONE.................................408 374-9960
Mary Lu Gonzalez, CEO
Yoshiharu Kuroiwa, CFO
Lisa Lopez, Vice Pres
Javier Zaldivar, Exec Dir
Mia Garza, District Mgr
EMP: 174 EST: 1969
SQ FT: 29,000
SALES: 481MM Privately Held
WEB: www.sarc.org
SIC: 8322 Association for the handicapped

(P-17708)
SAN FRANCISCO AIDS FOUNDATION (PA)
1035 Market St Ste 400, San Francisco (94103-1665)
PHONE.................................415 487-3000
Joe Hollendoner, CEO
Jody Schaffer, Volunteer Dir
Rick Andrews, Owner
Elizabeth Pesch, CFO
Robert Grant, Chief Mktg Ofcr
EMP: 100 EST: 1982
SQ FT: 45,000
SALES: 51.3MM Privately Held
WEB: www.sfaf.org
SIC: 8322 Social service center

(P-17709)
SAN FRANCISCO AIDS FOUNDATION
Also Called: Aids Lifecycle
1035 Market St Ste 400, San Francisco (94103-1665)
PHONE.................................415 581-7077
Susan Parish, Associate Dir
Brian Bostwick, Prdtn Mgr
Samantha Alvarez, Production
Kathleen Jaffe, Production
Nick Moore, Marketing Staff
EMP: 40
SALES (corp-wide): 51.3MM Privately Held
WEB: www.aidslifecycle.org
SIC: 8322 Social service center
PA: The San Francisco Aids Foundation
1035 Market St Ste 400
San Francisco CA 94103
415 487-3000

(P-17710)
SAN FRANCISCO FOOD BANK
Also Called: SF-MARIN FOOD BANK
900 Pennsylvania Ave, San Francisco (94107-3498)
PHONE.................................415 282-1900
Paul Ash, Exec Dir
Leslie Bacho, COO
Michael Braude, CFO
Sean Brooks, Officer
Barbara Abbott, Vice Pres
EMP: 80 EST: 1987
SQ FT: 55,000
SALES: 152.3MM Privately Held
WEB: www.sfmfoodbank.org
SIC: 8322 Social service center

(P-17711)
SAN FRNCSCO LSBIAN GAY BSXUAL
Also Called: SAN FRANCISCO LGBT COMMUNITY C
1800 Market St, San Francisco (94102-6227)
PHONE.................................415 865-5649
Rebecca Rolfe, Exec Dir
Matthew Rizzie, Associate Dir
Emilia Quinones, Opers Staff
Wayne Rafus, Director
Corey Bigoni, Manager
EMP: 40 EST: 1998
SQ FT: 35,000
SALES: 4.4MM Privately Held
WEB: www.sfcenter.org
SIC: 8322 Community center

(P-17712)
SAN FRNCSCO PRTCLAR CNCIL OF T
525 5th St, San Francisco (94107-1012)
PHONE.................................415 255-3525
Lisa Handley, Director
EMP: 63
SALES (corp-wide): 9.5MM Privately Held
WEB: www.svdp-sf.org
SIC: 8322 Social service center
PA: The San Francisco Particular Council Of The Society Of St Vincent De Paul
1175 Howard St
San Francisco CA 94103
415 552-2943

(P-17713)
SAN FRNCSCO SCIDE PRVNTION INC
230 8th St, San Francisco (94103-3923)
P.O. Box 191350 (94119-1350)
PHONE.................................415 984-1900
Eve Meyer, Exec Dir
EMP: 46 EST: 1962
SQ FT: 2,800
SALES (est): 1MM Privately Held
WEB: www.sfsuicide.org
SIC: 8322 Crisis intervention center

(P-17714)
SAN JOAQUIN CNTY AGING & COMMU
102 S San Joaquin St, Stockton (95202-3213)
P.O. Box 201056 (95201-3006)
PHONE.................................209 468-9455
Michael Miller, Director
Kirsten Yeh, Analyst
EMP: 120 EST: 2010
SALES (est): 10MM Privately Held
WEB: www.sjchsa.org
SIC: 8322 Senior citizens' center or association

(P-17715)
SANCTUARY
Also Called: Club Sanctuary Video Prod
2336 Calaveras St, Fresno (93721-1104)
PHONE.................................559 498-8543
Stacie Hines, Director
Mark Wilson, Director
EMP: 41 EST: 1996
SALES (est): 1MM Privately Held
WEB: www.fresnoeoc.org
SIC: 8322 Social service center

(P-17716)
SANTA CLARA COUNTY OF
Also Called: Adult Probation Department
2600 N 1st St, San Jose (95134-2014)
PHONE.................................408 435-2000
Karen Fletcher, Chief
EMP: 41 Privately Held
WEB: www.sccgov.org
SIC: 8322 Probation office
PA: County of Santa Clara
70 W Hedding St 2wing
San Jose CA 95110
408 299-5200

(P-17717)
SANTA CLARA COUNTY OF
Also Called: Social Service Agency
333 W Julian St Ste 100, San Jose (95110-2314)
PHONE.................................408 299-5437
Norma Sparks, Director
Peter Jensen, Administration
John Scavio, Info Tech Mgr
Gloria Maturino, Project Dir
Brian Chan, Manager
EMP: 41 Privately Held
WEB: www.sccgov.org
SIC: 8322 Child related social services
PA: County Of Santa Clara
70 W Hedding St 2wing
San Jose CA 95110
408 299-5200

(P-17718)
SANTA CLARA COUNTY OF
Also Called: Social Service Agency
90 Highland Ave, San Martin (95046-9504)
PHONE.................................408 686-3800
Connie Vega, Manager
EMP: 41 Privately Held
WEB: www.sccgov.org
SIC: 8322 9441 Individual & family services; administration of social & manpower programs;
PA: County Of Santa Clara
70 W Hedding St 2wing
San Jose CA 95110
408 299-5200

(P-17719)
SANTA CLARA COUNTY OF
Also Called: Social Services Agency
90 Highland Ave, San Martin (95046-9504)
PHONE.................................408 846-5000
Mary Grimm, Director
EMP: 41
SQ FT: 4,800 Privately Held
WEB: www.sccgov.org
SIC: 8322 9441 Social service center; administration of social & manpower programs;
PA: County Of Santa Clara
70 W Hedding St 2wing
San Jose CA 95110
408 299-5200

(P-17720)
SANTA CLARA COUNTY OF
Also Called: Social Service Agency
1879 Senter Rd, San Jose (95112-2527)
PHONE.................................408 758-3500
EMP: 41 Privately Held
WEB: www.sccgov.org
SIC: 8322 9441 Individual & family services; administration of social & manpower programs;
PA: County Of Santa Clara
70 W Hedding St 2wing
San Jose CA 95110
408 299-5200

(P-17721)
SANTA CLARA COUNTY OF
Also Called: Probation Dept
270 Grant Ave Ste 303, Palo Alto (94306-1910)
PHONE.................................650 324-6500
Carol Siddall, Superintendent
EMP: 41 Privately Held

8322 - Individual & Family Social Svcs County (P-17722) — PRODUCTS & SERVICES SECTION

WEB: www.sccgov.org
SIC: 8322 9223 Probation office; parole office; correctional institutions
PA: County Of Santa Clara
70 W Hedding St 2wing
San Jose CA 95110
408 299-5200

(P-17722)
SANTA CLARA COUNTY OF
Also Called: Health & Human Care
976 Lenzen Ave Ste 1800, San Jose (95126-2737)
PHONE..............................408 792-5050
Jim McPherson, *Director*
EMP: 41 Privately Held
WEB: www.sccgov.org
SIC: 8322 9431 Multi-service center; administration of public health programs;
PA: County Of Santa Clara
70 W Hedding St 2wing
San Jose CA 95110
408 299-5200

(P-17723)
SECOND CHANCE INC (PA)
Also Called: NEWARK CRISIS CENTER
6330 Thornton Ave Ste B, Newark (94560-3734)
P.O. Box 643 (94560-0643)
PHONE..............................510 792-4357
Jimmy Rogers, *Managing Dir*
Mark Conville, *Exec Dir*
Mark McConville, *Exec Dir*
John Balentine, *Office Mgr*
Ron Erlantson, *CTO*
EMP: 40 EST: 1971
SQ FT: 10,000
SALES: 3.9MM Privately Held
SIC: 8322 Crisis intervention center

(P-17724)
SECOND HARVEST SILICON VALLEY (PA)
750 Curtner Ave, San Jose (95125-2113)
PHONE..............................408 266-8866
Kathryn Jackson, *CEO*
EMP: 50 EST: 1974
SQ FT: 65,000
SALES: 214.4MM Privately Held
WEB: www.shfb.org
SIC: 8322 Social service center

(P-17725)
SECOND HRVEST FD BNK SRVING SN
800 Ohlone Pkwy, Watsonville (95076-7005)
PHONE..............................831 722-7110
Willy Elliott-Mccrea, *Exec Dir*
Misty Koger - Ojure, *Contract Mgr*
Josue Barajas, *Nutritionist*
Jan Kamman, *Director*
Jennifer Welling, *Director*
EMP: 42 EST: 1986
SALES: 27MM Privately Held
WEB: www.thefoodbank.org
SIC: 8322 Social service center

(P-17726)
SELF-DSCVERY THRPTIC EXPRNCE P
14976 Swenson St, San Leandro (94579-1744)
PHONE..............................650 303-7365
Camille Mariategue, *CEO*
EMP: 40
SALES (est): 216K Privately Held
SIC: 8322 General counseling services

(P-17727)
SELF-HELP FOR ELDERLY
777 Stockton St Ste 110, San Francisco (94108-2372)
PHONE..............................415 391-3843
EMP: 86
SALES (corp-wide): 27.9MM Privately Held
WEB: www.selfhelpelderly.org
SIC: 8322 Senior citizens' center or association
PA: Self-Help For The Elderly
731 Sansome St Ste 100
San Francisco CA 94111
415 677-7600

(P-17728)
SELF-HELP FOR ELDERLY (PA)
Also Called: SAN FRANCISCO RESIDENTIAL CARE
731 Sansome St Ste 100, San Francisco (94111-1735)
PHONE..............................415 677-7600
Anni Chung, *President*
Janie Kaung, *Vice Chairman*
William Schulte, *Chairman*
Gerald Lee, *Treasurer*
Linda Wang, *Admin Sec*
EMP: 145 EST: 1980
SALES: 27.9MM Privately Held
WEB: www.selfhelpelderly.org
SIC: 8322 8361 8082 Senior citizens' center or association; residential care; home health care services

(P-17729)
SENECA FAMILY OF AGENCIES
Also Called: Seneca Center
8945 Golf Links Rd, Oakland (94605-4124)
PHONE..............................510 317-1444
Ken Berrick, *CEO*
EMP: 286
SALES (corp-wide): 138.9MM Privately Held
WEB: www.senecafoa.org
SIC: 8322 8361 Social service center; residential care for children
PA: Seneca Family Of Agencies
8945 Golf Links Rd
Oakland CA 94605
510 317-1444

(P-17730)
SENECA FAMILY OF AGENCIES (PA)
Also Called: SENECA CENTER
8945 Golf Links Rd, Oakland (94605-4124)
PHONE..............................510 317-1444
Ken Berrick, *CEO*
Kanwar Singh, *CFO*
Catherine West, *Exec Dir*
Michelle Scavarda, *Administration*
John Zak, *Software Dev*
EMP: 35 EST: 1985
SALES: 138.9MM Privately Held
WEB: www.senecafoa.org
SIC: 8322 8299 8082 Social service center; educational services; home health care services

(P-17731)
SENECA FAMILY OF AGENCIES
1234 Empire St, Fairfield (94533-5711)
PHONE..............................707 429-4440
Ken Berrick, *Branch Mgr*
Caleb Hervey, *Program Dir*
EMP: 286
SALES (corp-wide): 138.9MM Privately Held
WEB: www.senecafoa.org
SIC: 8322 Social service center
PA: Seneca Family Of Agencies
8945 Golf Links Rd
Oakland CA 94605
510 317-1444

(P-17732)
SENECA FAMILY OF AGENCIES
Also Called: Building Blocks
3695 High St, Oakland (94619-2105)
PHONE..............................510 434-7990
Andrew Boring, *Director*
EMP: 286
SALES (corp-wide): 138.9MM Privately Held
WEB: www.senecafoa.org
SIC: 8322 8351 Social service center; child day care services
PA: Seneca Family Of Agencies
8945 Golf Links Rd
Oakland CA 94605
510 317-1444

(P-17733)
SER-JOBS FOR PRGRESS INC - SAN (PA)
255 N Fulton St Ste 106, Fresno (93701-1600)
PHONE..............................559 452-0881
Rebecca Mendibles, *Exec Dir*
Michael Jimenez, *President*
Ofelia Gamez, *Chairman*
EMP: 66 EST: 1973
SQ FT: 1,500
SALES: 7.4MM Privately Held
WEB: www.sercalifornia.org
SIC: 8322 Social service center

(P-17734)
SERENITY SPPRTED LVING SVC LLC (PA)
813 Harbor Blvd, West Sacramento (95691-2201)
PHONE..............................650 773-2762
Mona Joanne Toloumu, *Principal*
EMP: 46 EST: 2017
SALES (est): 457.1K Privately Held
SIC: 8322 Individual & family services

(P-17735)
SERVICE LEAGUE SAN MATEO CNTY
Also Called: HOPE HOUSE
727 Middlefield Rd, Redwood City (94063-1626)
PHONE..............................650 364-4664
Mike Nevin, *Exec Dir*
Walz Gretchen, *Office Mgr*
EMP: 43 EST: 1960
SQ FT: 4,000
SALES (est): 2.5MM Privately Held
WEB: www.serviceleague.org
SIC: 8322 Social service center

(P-17736)
SERVICE OPPRTUNITY FOR SENIORS
Also Called: MEALS ON WHEELS
2235 Polvorosa Ave # 260, San Leandro (94577-2249)
PHONE..............................510 582-1263
Connie Mc Cabe, *Exec Dir*
Connie McCabe, *Exec Dir*
Rosemary Borja, *Finance Dir*
EMP: 40 EST: 1968
SALES: 5.9MM Privately Held
WEB: www.sosmow.org
SIC: 8322 Senior citizens' center or association

(P-17737)
SHASCADE COMMUNITY SVCS INC
Also Called: Lorin Robinson Center
900 Twin View Blvd, Redding (96003-2006)
PHONE..............................530 247-8324
Ramone Valarde, *Exec Dir*
EMP: 91
SALES (corp-wide): 5.9MM Privately Held
WEB: www.shascade.org
SIC: 8322 Social service center
PA: Shascade Community Services, Inc.
900 Twin View Blvd
Redding CA 96003
530 243-1651

(P-17738)
SHASCADE COMMUNITY SVCS INC
1319 Sacramento St, Redding (96001-1916)
PHONE..............................530 243-1653
Ramon Velade, *Manager*
EMP: 91
SALES (corp-wide): 5.9MM Privately Held
WEB: www.shascade.org
SIC: 8322 Social services for the handicapped
PA: Shascade Community Services, Inc.
900 Twin View Blvd
Redding CA 96003
530 243-1651

(P-17739)
SHASTA COUNTY WOMEN S REFUGE
Also Called: WOMEN'S REFUGE
2280 Benton Dr Ste A, Redding (96003-5362)
PHONE..............................530 244-0117
Fax: 530 244-2653
EMP: 39

SALES: 2.8MM Privately Held
WEB: www.shastacapc.org
SIC: 8322 Individual & Family Social Services

(P-17740)
SHASTA SENIOR NTRTN PROGRAM (DH)
Also Called: Ssnp
200 Mercy Oaks Dr, Redding (96003-8641)
PHONE..............................530 226-3059
Virginia Webster, *Exec Dir*
Jennifer Powell, *Asst Director*
Janice Holbrook, *Supervisor*
EMP: 35 EST: 1979
SQ FT: 3,000
SALES (est): 3.7MM Privately Held
WEB: www.ssnpweb.org
SIC: 8322 Senior citizens' center or association
HQ: Dignity Health
185 Berry St Ste 200
San Francisco CA 94107
415 438-5500

(P-17741)
SHELTER INC (PA)
1333 Willow Pass Rd # 206, Concord (94520-7931)
P.O. Box 5368 (94524-0368)
PHONE..............................925 335-0698
John Eckstrom, *CEO*
Karri Edgers, *COO*
Barbara Simpson, *Program Mgr*
Teresa Schow, *Admin Sec*
Carmen Salais, *Project Mgr*
EMP: 56 EST: 1986
SQ FT: 7,000
SALES (est): 14.3MM Privately Held
WEB: www.shelterinc.org
SIC: 8322 Emergency social services

(P-17742)
SHELTER SOLANO INC
1333 Willow Pass Rd # 20, Concord (94520-7930)
PHONE..............................925 957-7576
John Eckstrom, *CEO*
EMP: 99 EST: 2018
SALES (est): 565.4K Privately Held
WEB: www.shelterinc.org
SIC: 8322 Social service center

(P-17743)
SHINE A LGHT CUNSELING CTR INC
809 N Branciforte Ave, Santa Cruz (95062-1027)
PHONE..............................530 748-8098
Dennis M Gardner, *Principal*
Penelope Sargent,
EMP: 48 EST: 2016
SALES (est): 598K Privately Held
WEB: www.shinealight.info
SIC: 8322 General counseling services

(P-17744)
SIERRA FOREVER FAMILIES
Also Called: Sff
8912 Volunteer Ln, Sacramento (95826-3221)
PHONE..............................916 368-5114
Bob Herne, *Exec Dir*
Jordyn Dollarhide, *Marketing Staff*
Deonia Young, *Social Worker*
Marilyn Edling, *Consultant*
Kitty Hoffman, *Associate*
EMP: 39 EST: 1982
SALES: 4.9MM Privately Held
WEB: www.ssyaf.org
SIC: 8322 Adoption services

(P-17745)
SIERRA MOUNTAIN CNSTR INC
13919 Mono Way, Sonora (95370-2807)
PHONE..............................209 928-1900
Douglas J Benton, *President*
David Lomeli, *Project Mgr*
Ty Odom, *Project Engr*
Dustin Hemphill, *Superintendent*
EMP: 75 EST: 2003
SALES (est): 24.5MM Privately Held
WEB: www.sierramtn.net
SIC: 8322 1389 Disaster service; construction, repair & dismantling services

PRODUCTS & SERVICES SECTION
8322 - Individual & Family Social Svcs County (P-17769)

(P-17746)
SOCIAL SERVICES CAL DEPT
Also Called: Adoptions
1330 E Shaw Ave, Fresno (93710-7924)
PHONE.................................559 248-8400
Rosalie Gutierrez, *Principal*
EMP: 55 **Privately Held**
WEB: www.ca.gov
SIC: 8322 9441 Adoption services; administration of social & manpower programs;
HQ: California Dept Of Social Services
   744 P St
   Sacramento CA 95814

(P-17747)
SOCIAL SERVICES CAL DEPT
Also Called: Food Stamp Office
11519 B Ave, Auburn (95603-2604)
PHONE.................................530 889-7610
Brenda Greene, *Branch Mgr*
EMP: 55 **Privately Held**
WEB: www.ca.gov
SIC: 8322 Social service center
HQ: California Dept Of Social Services
   744 P St
   Sacramento CA 95814

(P-17748)
SOCIAL SERVICES CAL DEPT
Also Called: Community Care Licensing Div
744 P St, Sacramento (95814-6400)
PHONE.................................916 657-2346
Rita Saenz, *Manager*
EMP: 55 **Privately Held**
WEB: www.ca.gov
SIC: 8322 9441 Individual & family services; administration of social & manpower programs;
HQ: California Dept Of Social Services
   744 P St
   Sacramento CA 95814

(P-17749)
SOCIETY OF ST VNCENT DE PAUL D
822 B St, San Rafael (94901-3014)
P.O. Box 150527 (94915-0527)
PHONE.................................415 454-3303
Susan Board, *President*
John Zeiter, *Treasurer*
Richard Gallagher, *Vice Pres*
Phil Garcia, *Admin Sec*
Katrina Redahan, *Corp Comm Staff*
EMP: 50 **EST:** 1967
SQ FT: 16,000
SALES: 5.2MM **Privately Held**
WEB: www.vinnies.org
SIC: 8322 Emergency social services

(P-17750)
SOURCEWISE
3100 De La Cruz Blvd # 310, Santa Clara (95054-2452)
PHONE.................................408 350-3200
Stephen M Schmoll, *Director*
Altamirano Manuel, *COO*
Kimberly Marlar, *CFO*
Mary Cyrus, *Prgrmr*
Judy Nguyen, *Finance*
EMP: 100 **EST:** 1974
SALES (est): 13.9MM **Privately Held**
WEB: www.mysourcewise.com
SIC: 8322 Senior citizens' center or association; old age assistance

(P-17751)
SPANISH SPKING UNITY CNCIL ALM (PA)
1900 Fruitvale Ave Ste 2a, Oakland (94601-2468)
PHONE.................................510 535-6900
Gilda Gonzales, *CEO*
Chris Iglesias, *Principal*
Arabella Martinez, *Exec Dir*
Bianca Diaz, *Admin Mgr*
Artie Rodriguez, *Executive Asst*
EMP: 40 **EST:** 1964
SQ FT: 15,000
SALES: 36.4MM **Privately Held**
WEB: www.unitycouncil.org
SIC: 8322 Community center

(P-17752)
ST ANTHONY FOUNDATION (PA)
150 Golden Gate Ave, San Francisco (94102-3810)
PHONE.................................415 241-2600
John Hardin, *Exec Dir*
Tere Brown, *Exec Dir*
Barry J Stenger, *Exec Dir*
Bryan Young, *Human Res Dir*
Ruth Selby, *Production*
EMP: 50 **EST:** 1950
SQ FT: 45,000
SALES (est): 36.1MM **Privately Held**
WEB: www.stanthonysf.org
SIC: 8322 Social service center

(P-17753)
ST MARYS CENTER
925 Brockhurst St, Oakland (94608-4222)
PHONE.................................510 923-9600
Carol Johnson, *Exec Dir*
Alicia Alexander, *Office Mgr*
Janny Castillo, *Director*
Jameisha Hood, *Manager*
EMP: 45 **EST:** 1992
SALES (est): 4.3MM **Privately Held**
WEB: www.stmaryscenter.org
SIC: 8322 Community center

(P-17754)
ST MARYS DINING ROOM
545 W Sonora St, Stockton (95203-3329)
P.O. Box 133 (95201-0133)
PHONE.................................209 467-0703
Edward Figueroa, *CEO*
Mercedes Moreno, *Social Dir*
Lorrie Herrera, *Administration*
Daniel Castillo, *Director*
Rebecca Glissman, *Director*
EMP: 66 **EST:** 1955
SALES (est): 10.3MM **Privately Held**
WEB: www.stmarysdiningroom.org
SIC: 8322 Social service center

(P-17755)
ST VNCENT DE PAUL BLTMORE INC
3100 Norris Ave, Sacramento (95821-4023)
PHONE.................................916 485-3482
EMP: 64
SALES (corp-wide): 30.6MM **Privately Held**
WEB: www.vincentbaltimore.org
SIC: 8322 Social service center
PA: St. Vincent De Paul Of Baltimore, Inc.
   2305 N Charles St Ste 300
   Baltimore MD 21218
   410 662-0500

(P-17756)
STAND FOR FMLIES FREE VOLENCE
3220 Blume Dr, San Pablo (94806-1767)
PHONE.................................510 964-7109
Julia Pattinson, *Human Res Dir*
EMP: 61 **Privately Held**
WEB: www.standffov.org
SIC: 8322 Crisis intervention center
PA: Stand For Families Free Of Violence
   1410 Danzig Plz Fl 2
   Concord CA 94520

(P-17757)
STANFORD SETTLEMENT INC
450 W El Camino Ave, Sacramento (95833-2299)
PHONE.................................916 927-1303
Sister Jeanne Felion, *Director*
Mary Doll,
EMP: 45 **EST:** 1936
SQ FT: 48,840
SALES (est): 808K **Privately Held**
WEB: www.stanfordsettlement.org
SIC: 8322 Social service center; neighborhood center; child related social services

(P-17758)
STANFORD UNIV MED CTR AUX
300 Pasteur Dr, Stanford (94305-2200)
PHONE.................................650 723-6636
Mary Dahlquist, *CEO*
Sarah Clark, *President*
M Allen, *Associate Dir*
P Joanne Cornbleet, *Pathologist*
Robert V Rouse, *Pathologist*
EMP: 291 **EST:** 1959
SALES (est): 30.1MM
SALES (corp-wide): 12.4B **Privately Held**
WEB: www.stanfordhealthcare.org
SIC: 8322 Adult day care center
PA: Leland Stanford Junior University
   450 Jane Stanford Way
   Stanford CA 94305
   650 723-2300

(P-17759)
STANFORD YOUTH SOLUTIONS (PA)
Also Called: Stanford Lthrop Mem HM For Frn
8912 Volunteer Ln, Sacramento (95826-3221)
PHONE.................................916 344-0199
Jovina Neves, *CFO*
Laura Heintz, *Principal*
Deborah Bennett, *Director*
Susan Davini, *Manager*
Laura Stainforth, *Associate*
EMP: 84 **EST:** 1900
SQ FT: 30,000
SALES: 12.8MM **Privately Held**
WEB: www.ssyaf.org
SIC: 8322 Social service center

(P-17760)
STARVISTA
610 Elm St Ste 212, San Carlos (94070-3070)
PHONE.................................650 591-9623
Michael GRB, *CEO*
Michelle Blakely, *Bd of Directors*
Janel Guinane, *Program Mgr*
Islam Hassanein, *Program Mgr*
Merle Saber, *Program Mgr*
EMP: 118 **EST:** 1989
SQ FT: 7,200
SALES (est): 15.7MM **Privately Held**
WEB: www.star-vista.org
SIC: 8322 Substance abuse counseling

(P-17761)
SUMMITVIEW CHILD & FAMILY SVCS
670 Placerville Dr Ste 2, Placerville (95667-4200)
PHONE.................................530 644-2412
Carla Well, *Principal*
Carla Wills, *Exec Dir*
Amanda Henderson, *Admin Asst*
Jessica Prescott, *Human Resources*
Chris Stedeford, *Director*
EMP: 80 **EST:** 2006
SALES (est): 12.2MM **Privately Held**
WEB: www.summitviewcf.org
SIC: 8322 8093 Family counseling services; mental health clinic, outpatient

(P-17762)
SUPPORT FOR FAMILY LLC
Also Called: Apexcare
1333 Howe Ave Ste 206, Sacramento (95825-3362)
PHONE.................................877 916-9111
Jason Wu,
EMP: 59 **EST:** 2015
SALES (est): 2.5MM **Privately Held**
WEB: www.apexcare.com
SIC: 8322 Individual & family services

(P-17763)
SUPPORT FOR FMLIES CHLDREN WIT
1663 Mission St Ste 700, San Francisco (94103-2489)
PHONE.................................415 920-5040
Juno Duenas, *Exec Dir*
Joanna Van Brusselen, *Education*
Sarah Bennett, *Social Worker*
Tim Carter, *Manager*
Christina Share, *Manager*
EMP: 43 **EST:** 1982
SALES (est): 4.4MM **Privately Held**
WEB: www.supportforfamilies.org
SIC: 8322 5999 Social service center; technical aids for the handicapped

(P-17764)
SUSTAINABLE SAN MATEO COUNTY
848 Kearny St, San Francisco (94108-1743)
PHONE.................................415 398-3250
EMP: 40
SALES (corp-wide): 123.1K **Privately Held**
WEB: www.selfhelpelderly.org
SIC: 8322 Senior citizens' center or association
PA: Sustainable San Mateo County
   731 Sansome St Ste 100
   San Francisco CA 94111
   415 677-7600

(P-17765)
TEACH INC
112 E 2nd St, Alturas (96101-4008)
PHONE.................................530 233-3111
Corrol Callaghan, *Exec Dir*
EMP: 67 **EST:** 1978
SQ FT: 6,000
SALES (est): 1.4MM **Privately Held**
WEB: www.teachinc.org
SIC: 8322 8351 Social service center; child day care services

(P-17766)
TEEN CHALLENGE NORWESTCAL NEV
Also Called: Southbay Teen Challenge
390 Mathew St, Santa Clara (95050-3114)
P.O. Box 24309, San Jose (95154-4309)
PHONE.................................408 703-2001
Dana Rowe, *Director*
EMP: 46 **EST:** 1971
SALES (est): 4MM **Privately Held**
WEB: www.teenchallenge.net
SIC: 8322 Social service center

(P-17767)
TELEGRAPH HL NEIGHBORHOOD CTR
Also Called: Telegraph Hill Nursery
660 Lombard St, San Francisco (94133-2315)
PHONE.................................415 421-6443
Tim Daniels, *Exec Dir*
Nestor L Fernandez, *Exec Dir*
Nestor Fernandez, *Exec Dir*
Melody Wong, *Program Dir*
EMP: 35 **EST:** 1909
SALES: 4.2MM **Privately Held**
WEB: www.telhi.org
SIC: 8322 8351 Social service center; nursery school

(P-17768)
TERRA NOVA COUNSELING (PA)
5750 Sunrise Blvd Ste 100, Citrus Heights (95610-7639)
PHONE.................................916 344-0249
Mary Stroube, *Exec Dir*
Bonnie Hinojos, *Manager*
EMP: 80
SQ FT: 4,789
SALES: 3.3MM **Privately Held**
WEB: www.terranovacounseling.org
SIC: 8322 General counseling services; drug abuse counselor, nontreatment; family (marriage) counseling; family counseling services

(P-17769)
TLCS INC
Also Called: HOPE COOPERATIVE
650 Howe Ave Ste 400-A, Sacramento (95825-4731)
PHONE.................................916 441-0123
Erin Johansen, *CEO*
Fatima Hessabi, *CFO*
Paul Powell, *Associate Dir*
Kim Gilbert, *Admin Dir*
Michael Lazar, *Exec Dir*
EMP: 250 **EST:** 1981
SQ FT: 1,868
SALES (est): 19.4MM **Privately Held**
WEB: www.hopecoop.org
SIC: 8322 Social service center

8322 - Individual & Family Social Svcs County (P-17770)

(P-17770)
TOOLWORKS INC
3075 Adeline St Ste 230, Berkeley (94703-2578)
PHONE....................510 649-1322
Steve Crabiel, *Branch Mgr*
Young Lee, *Admin Sec*
David Green, *IT/INT Sup*
Terry Goodwin, *Director*
Mark Melanson, *Director*
EMP: 48
SALES (corp-wide): 16MM **Privately Held**
WEB: www.toolworks.org
SIC: 8322 Social service center
PA: Toolworks Inc
    25 Kearny St Ste 400
    San Francisco CA 94108
    415 733-0990

(P-17771)
TRAINING TOWARD SELF RELIANCE
Also Called: Ttsr
1007 7th St Fl 4, Sacramento (95814-3407)
PHONE....................916 442-8877
Nancy Chance, *Director*
Angela Vela, *CIO*
Rabekah Amey, *Instructor*
Ttsr Employee, *Manager*
EMP: 50 EST: 1982
SALES (est): 1.2MM **Privately Held**
WEB: www.ttsr.org
SIC: 8322 Social services for the handicapped

(P-17772)
TRUE NORTH HOUSING ALIANCE INC
Also Called: Torres Community Shelter
101 Silver Dollar Way, Chico (95928-4402)
PHONE....................530 891-9048
Joy Amaro, *Exec Dir*
EMP: 35 EST: 2000
SALES: 1.5MM **Privately Held**
WEB: www.torresshelter.org
SIC: 8322 Emergency shelters

(P-17773)
TUPAZ DAY CARE SERVICES INC
3015 Union Ave, San Jose (95124-2006)
PHONE....................408 377-1622
Rosario Tupaz, *President*
Beebe Tupaz, *Vice Pres*
EMP: 75 EST: 2000
SALES (est): 2.9MM **Privately Held**
SIC: 8322 Adult day care center

(P-17774)
UNITED WAY CAL CAPITL REG
10389 Old Placerville Rd, Sacramento (95827-2506)
PHONE....................916 368-3000
Stephen Heath, *President*
Kristina Schuett Ricci, *Officer*
Amy Williamson, *Officer*
Thomas Bennett, *Senior VP*
Tom Bennett, *Vice Pres*
EMP: 35 EST: 1924
SQ FT: 57,000
SALES: 11.7MM **Privately Held**
WEB: www.yourlocalunitedway.org
SIC: 8322 Social service center

(P-17775)
UNITED WAY OF BAY AREA (PA)
Also Called: UNITED WAY, THE
550 Kearny St Ste 1000, San Francisco (94108-2524)
PHONE....................415 808-4300
Anne Wilson, *CEO*
Michael Scanlon, *Chairman*
Moses Awe, *Treasurer*
Susan Sutherland, *Vice Pres*
Norman Cheng, *Analyst*
EMP: 77 EST: 1923
SQ FT: 40,000
SALES: 34.4MM **Privately Held**
WEB: www.uwba.org
SIC: 8322 8399 Social service center; fund raising organization, non-fee basis

(P-17776)
UNITED WAY SILICON VALLEY
1400 Parkmoor Ave Ste 250, San Jose (95126-3735)
PHONE....................408 260-3915
Anne Wilson, *CEO*
Carole Leigh Hutton, *President*
Mark Walker, *President*
Eric McDonnell, *COO*
Joan Catherine Braun, *CFO*
EMP: 42 EST: 1959
SQ FT: 44,000
SALES (est): 2MM **Privately Held**
WEB: www.unitedway.org
SIC: 8322 Social service center

(P-17777)
UNITY CARE GROUP
1400 Parkmoor Ave Ste 115, San Jose (95126-3797)
P.O. Box 730276 (95173-0276)
PHONE....................408 971-9822
Andre Chapman, *CEO*
Gary Rummelhoff, *CFO*
Linda Phillips, *Principal*
Jeffrey Jefferson, *Program Mgr*
Yvette Madrigal, *Executive Asst*
EMP: 70 EST: 1992
SALES (est): 6.1MM **Privately Held**
WEB: www.unitycare.org
SIC: 8322 Child related social services

(P-17778)
UPLIFT FAMILY SERVICES (PA)
Also Called: EMQ FAMILIESFIRST
251 Llewellyn Ave, Campbell (95008-1940)
PHONE....................408 379-3790
Darrell Evora, *CEO*
Rosie Garcia, *Partner*
Veronica Guzman, *Partner*
Julie Martinez, *Partner*
Kathryn McCarthy, *COO*
EMP: 60 EST: 1973
SQ FT: 65,000
SALES: 105.5MM **Privately Held**
WEB: www.upliftfs.org
SIC: 8322 Individual & family services

(P-17779)
VALLEY-MNTAIN REGIONAL CTR INC (PA)
702 N Aurora St, Stockton (95202-2200)
P.O. Box 692290 (95269-2290)
PHONE....................209 473-0951
Paul Billodeau, *CEO*
Debra Roth, *CFO*
Tony Anderson, *Exec Dir*
Cindy Mix, *Program Mgr*
Jirii Sakata, *Program Mgr*
EMP: 160 EST: 1974
SQ FT: 63,000
SALES: 257.2MM **Privately Held**
WEB: www.vmrc.net
SIC: 8322 Multi-service center

(P-17780)
VALLEY-MNTAIN REGIONAL CTR INC
Cummins Dr, MODESTO (95350)
P.O. Box 692290, Stockton (95269-2290)
PHONE....................209 955-3207
Anthony Hill, *Program Mgr*
Mary Svendsen, *Personnel Assit*
Mary Sheehan, *Manager*
EMP: 80
SALES (corp-wide): 257.2MM **Privately Held**
WEB: www.vmrc.net
SIC: 8322 Multi-service center
PA: Valley-Mountain Regional Center, Inc.
    702 N Aurora St
    Stockton CA 95202
    209 473-0951

(P-17781)
VIVALON
Also Called: Whistlestop
930 Tamalpais Ave, San Rafael (94901-3325)
PHONE....................415 454-0964
Joe O'Hehir, *CEO*
Linda Compton, *CEO*
Nancy Geisse, *COO*
Jeff Wands, *CFO*
Ashley Baker, *Officer*
EMP: 94 EST: 1954
SQ FT: 12,000
SALES (est): 17.1MM **Privately Held**
WEB: www.vivalon.org
SIC: 8322 Senior citizens' center or association

(P-17782)
VOLUNTEER CENTER SONOMA COUNTY (PA)
Also Called: Volunteer Referral Service
153 Stony Cir Ste 100, Santa Rosa (95401-9516)
PHONE....................707 573-3399
Eunice Valentine, *Director*
Martin Grove, *President*
Priscilla C Essert, *Officer*
Cami Kahl, *Exec Dir*
Denise Silva, *Executive Asst*
EMP: 39 EST: 1971
SALES (est): 2.3MM **Privately Held**
WEB: www.volunteernow.org
SIC: 8322 Social service center

(P-17783)
VOLUNTERS AMER NTHRN CAL NTHRN (PA)
3434 Marconi Ave, Sacramento (95821-6242)
PHONE....................916 265-3400
Leo McFarland, *CEO*
Amani Sawires, *COO*
Joel Rusco, *CFO*
Rachele Burton, *Officer*
Jill Fox, *QA Dir*
EMP: 283 EST: 1985
SALES (est): 34.9MM **Privately Held**
WEB: www.voa-ncnn.org
SIC: 8322 Social service center

(P-17784)
WATCH RESOURCES INC (PA)
Also Called: T.C.A.H
12801 Cabezut Rd, Sonora (95370-5294)
PHONE....................209 533-0510
Christine Daily, *Exec Dir*
Jeff Rains, *President*
Eric Carlson, *Treasurer*
Jason Land, *Vice Pres*
Christine Daly, *Exec Dir*
EMP: 50 EST: 1972
SQ FT: 7,200
SALES: 2.9MM **Privately Held**
WEB: www.watchresources.org
SIC: 8322 0782 7349 4783 Association for the handicapped; landscape contractors; janitorial service, contract basis; packing & crating; mailing & messenger services

(P-17785)
WIND YOUTH SERVICES INC
815 S St Fl 1, Sacramento (95811-7065)
PHONE....................916 532-5185
Chris Russell, *President*
Peter His, *Associate Dir*
Suzi Dotson, *Exec Dir*
Alex Berg, *Finance*
Emily Martin, *Director*
EMP: 40 EST: 1968
SALES (est): 4.3MM **Privately Held**
WEB: www.windyouth.org
SIC: 8322 Social service center; emergency shelters

(P-17786)
WOMENS CENTER-YOUTH FMLY SVCS (PA)
620 N San Joaquin St, Stockton (95202-2030)
PHONE....................209 941-2611
Joelle Gomez, *CEO*
Elizabeth Bifhay, *Principal*
Kimberly Miller, *Administration*
EMP: 82 EST: 1978
SALES: 3.8MM **Privately Held**
WEB: www.womenscenteryfs.org
SIC: 8322 Child related social services

(P-17787)
WORLD RLIEF CORP OF NAT ASSN E
4616 Roseville Rd Ste 107, North Highlands (95660-5161)
PHONE....................916 978-2650
Betty Eastman, *Director*
Heather Burton, *Administration*
Alla Slabosnitsky, *Comp Spec*
Roza Rudeychuk, *Director*
Becca Brown, *Manager*
EMP: 79
SALES (corp-wide): 46MM **Privately Held**
WEB: www.worldrelief.org
SIC: 8322 Emergency social services
HQ: World Relief Corporation Of National Association Of Evangelicals
    7 E Baltimore St
    Baltimore MD 21202
    443 451-1900

(P-17788)
YOSEMITE CHURCH
2230 E Yosemite Ave, Merced (95340-9666)
PHONE....................209 383-5038
Jeffrey Leis, *Pastor*
Della Chambers, *Admin Asst*
Leis Jeffrey, *Relg Ldr*
Angel Barragan, *Pastor*
Marifel Herland, *Director*
EMP: 35 EST: 1975
SQ FT: 10,000
SALES (est): 3.2MM **Privately Held**
WEB: www.yc.church
SIC: 8661 8322 Non-denominational church; miscellaneous denomination church; outreach program

(P-17789)
YOUNG COMMUNITY DEVELOPERS
1715 Yosemite Ave, San Francisco (94124-2621)
PHONE....................415 822-3491
Al Williams, *Principal*
Anthony Peters, *IT/INT Sup*
Jenny Yoo, *Controller*
Chadid Conley, *Education*
Diane Gray, *Program Dir*
EMP: 40 EST: 1972
SALES (est): 6.2MM **Privately Held**
WEB: www.ycdjobs.org
SIC: 8322 8331 Youth center; community service employment training program

(P-17790)
YOUNG MNS CHRSTN ASSN SAN FRNC
Also Called: YMCA
1486 Huntington Ave # 100, South San Francisco (94080-5970)
PHONE....................650 877-8642
Carrie Herrera, *Exec Dir*
EMP: 73
SALES (corp-wide): 95MM **Privately Held**
WEB: www.ymcasf.org
SIC: 8322 Individual & family services
PA: Young Men's Christian Association Of San Francisco
    50 California St Ste 650
    San Francisco CA 94111
    415 777-9622

(P-17791)
YOUTH FOR CHANGE (PA)
Also Called: PARADISE RIDGE FAMILY RESOURCE
5538 Skyway, Paradise (95969-4932)
P.O. Box 1476 (95967-1476)
PHONE....................530 877-8187
Dennis Cargile, *Principal*
Janet Goodson, *Partner*
Andy Martinez, *CFO*
Michele Peterson, *Chairman*
Alan White, *Chairman*
EMP: 115 EST: 1990
SQ FT: 5,000
SALES (est): 14.9MM **Privately Held**
WEB: www.youth4change.org
SIC: 8322 Youth center

(P-17792)
YWCA CONTRA COSTA/SACRAMENTO (PA)
1320 Arnold Dr Ste 170, Martinez (94553-6537)
PHONE....................925 372-4213
Nancy Atkinson, *CEO*
Annette Hee Jimenez, *Director*

PRODUCTS & SERVICES SECTION 8331 - Job Training & Vocational Rehabilitation Svcs County (P-17813)

EMP: 60 EST: 1945
SQ FT: 8,000
SALES: 3.6MM Privately Held
WEB: www.ywcaccc.org
SIC: 8322 8641 8351 Individual & family services; community membership club; child day care services

8331 Job Training & Vocational Rehabilitation Svcs

(P-17793)
ARC FRESNO/MADERA COUNTIES (PA)
4490 E Ashlan Ave, Fresno (93726-2647)
PHONE 559 226-6268
Lori Rmirez, CEO
Carolyn Wallace, President
Mike Takechi, Treasurer
Peter Mersino, Vice Pres
Lori Ramirez, Executive
EMP: 140 EST: 1953
SALES: 11.2MM Privately Held
WEB: www.arcfresno.org
SIC: 8331 Job training services

(P-17794)
ARC SAN FRANCISCO (PA)
1500 Howard St, San Francisco (94103-2525)
PHONE 415 255-7200
Timothy Hornbecker, Exec Dir
Gloria Louie, Vice Chairman
Kirsten Mellor, CEO
Brian Wagman, CFO
Ann Relling, Officer
EMP: 153 EST: 1951
SQ FT: 30,000
SALES: 10.2MM Privately Held
WEB: www.thearcsf.org
SIC: 8331 8361 7361 Job training services; home for the mentally handicapped; employment agencies

(P-17795)
ARRIBA JUNTOS (PA)
1850 Mission St, San Francisco (94103-3502)
PHONE 415 487-3240
Dalila Ohumada, Director
Nenette Tabernilla, Finance
Chris Castle, Instructor
Reyna Tiscareno, Manager
EMP: 35 EST: 1965
SQ FT: 10,000
SALES (est): 7.2MM Privately Held
WEB: www.arribajuntos.org
SIC: 8331 Community service employment training program

(P-17796)
CALIDAD INDUSTRIES INC
1301 30th Ave, Oakland (94601-2208)
PHONE 510 698-7200
Robert Taylor, CEO
James Caponigro, CEO
Patrick Schmalz, CFO
EMP: 356 EST: 1989
SQ FT: 35,000
SALES (est): 1MM
SALES (corp-wide): 23.9MM Privately Held
WEB: www.eastbaygoodwill.org
SIC: 8331 Vocational training agency
PA: Goodwill Industries Of The Greater East Bay, Inc.
1301 30th Ave
Oakland CA 94601
510 698-7200

(P-17797)
CALIFORNIA FIRE FGHTRS APPRENT
Also Called: Califrnia Fire Fghtr Joint App
1780 Creekside Oaks Dr, Sacramento (95833-3633)
PHONE 916 648-1717
Yvonne Delapena, Director
Deborah Jackson-Lee, Manager
EMP: 40 EST: 1985

SALES (est): 5.8MM Privately Held
WEB: www.cpf.org
SIC: 8331 Job training services

(P-17798)
CALIFORNIA HUMAN DEV CORP (PA)
Also Called: ANTHONY SOTO EMPLOYMENT TRAINI
3315 Airway Dr, Santa Rosa (95403-2005)
PHONE 707 523-1155
Miguel Mejia, Chairman
Christopher Paige, CEO
Doris Unsod, Treasurer
Kathy Differding, Program Mgr
Narci Bravo, Regional Mgr
EMP: 140 EST: 1967
SQ FT: 15,000
SALES: 14.4MM Privately Held
WEB: www.californiahumandevelopment.org
SIC: 8331 7361 8399 7374 Job training services; placement agencies; community development groups; calculating service (computer)

(P-17799)
CALIFRNIA FIRE RSCUE TRNING AU
3121 Gold Canal Dr, Rancho Cordova (95670-6111)
PHONE 916 475-1660
Joe Gear, Exec Dir
Sherri Martucci, Finance
Matt Kelly, Council Mbr
Lloyd Ogan, Council Mbr
EMP: 105 EST: 2011
SQ FT: 3,000
SALES (est): 5.1MM Privately Held
WEB: www.fireandrescuetraining.ca.gov
SIC: 8331 Job training & vocational rehabilitation services

(P-17800)
CALIFRNIA INDIAN MNPWER CNSRTI (PA)
Also Called: Cimc
738 N Market Blvd, Sacramento (95834-1206)
PHONE 916 920-0285
Lorenda T Sanchez, Exec Dir
Benjamin Charley, Chairman
Arlene Craft, Chairman
Robert H Smith, Treasurer
EMP: 35 EST: 1978
SQ FT: 16,000
SALES (est): 14.7MM Privately Held
WEB: www.cimcinc.org
SIC: 8331 Job training services

(P-17801)
CENTER FOR EMPLOYMENT TRAINING (PA)
Also Called: C E T
701 Vine St, San Jose (95110-2940)
PHONE 408 287-7924
Hermelinda Sapien, CEO
Asbjorn Osland, Vice Chairman
Mohammad Aryanpour, CFO
Daniel Ezquerro, Treasurer
Greg Adams, Bd of Directors
EMP: 70 EST: 1967
SQ FT: 120,000
SALES: 29.3MM Privately Held
WEB: www.cetweb.edu
SIC: 8331 9721 Vocational training agency; immigration services, government

(P-17802)
CENTRAL VALLEY OPRTNTY CTR INC (PA)
Also Called: Cvoc
6838 Bridget Ct, Winton (95388)
P.O. Box 1389 (95388-1389)
PHONE 209 357-0062
Ernie Flores, Exec Dir
John Jepson, Planning
Maria Romero, Software Dev
Ofelia Reynoso, Persnl Dir
Don Curiel-Ruth, Manager
EMP: 63 EST: 1979
SQ FT: 27,000

SALES: 10.4MM Privately Held
WEB: www.cvoc.org
SIC: 8331 Vocational training agency

(P-17803)
CITY OF YUBA CITY
Also Called: Community Facilities District
1201 Civic Center Blvd, Yuba City (95993-3005)
PHONE 530 822-4601
Steve Zoet, Manager
Kevin Cooper, Officer
Eric Southward, Officer
Judy Sanchez, Executive Asst
Samantha Benzel, Admin Asst
EMP: 65 EST: 2010
SALES (est): 15.8MM
SALES (corp-wide): 72.9MM Privately Held
WEB: www.yubacity.net
SIC: 8331 Community service employment training program
PA: City Of Yuba City
1201 Civic Center Blvd
Yuba City CA 95993
530 822-4622

(P-17804)
CITYTEAM MINISTRIES (PA)
Also Called: NEW GENERATIONS INTERNATIONAL
2304 Zanker Rd, San Jose (95131-1115)
P.O. Box 18113 (95158-8113)
PHONE 408 885-8080
Patrick J Robertson, President
Thoma Bravo, Partner
Joan Braddi, Vice Chairman
Jeff Cherniss, CFO
Bruce Gregory, Treasurer
EMP: 45 EST: 1957
SQ FT: 34,000
SALES: 6.1MM Privately Held
WEB: www.cityteam.org
SIC: 8331 8322 Job training services; emergency social services

(P-17805)
COGNIFIT INC
600 California St Fl 11, San Francisco (94108-2727)
PHONE 646 340-1740
Nathanael Eisenberg, Chairman
Tommy Sagcoun, President
Michal Frenkiel, Vice Pres
EMP: 51 EST: 2000
SALES (est): 2MM Privately Held
WEB: www.cognifit.com
SIC: 8331 7371 Skill training center; computer software development & applications

(P-17806)
COMMUNITY INTGRTED WORK PRGRAM
651 Division St, Campbell (95008-6828)
PHONE 408 871-9680
Angela White, Director
EMP: 43
SALES (corp-wide): 17.3MM Privately Held
WEB: www.ciwp.org
SIC: 8331 7361 Vocational training agency; employment agencies
PA: Community Integrated Work Program, Inc.
3701 Stocker St Ste 203
View Park CA 90008
925 776-1040

(P-17807)
COMMUNITY INTGRTED WORK PRGRAM
Also Called: Community Intgrted Work Prgram
980 Emily Way Ste A, Madera (93637-5647)
PHONE 559 673-5174
Michael Bodily, Manager
Amy Webber, Director
EMP: 43
SALES (corp-wide): 17.3MM Privately Held
WEB: www.ciwp.org
SIC: 8331 Job training & vocational rehabilitation services

PA: Community Integrated Work Program, Inc.
3701 Stocker St Ste 203
View Park CA 90008
925 776-1040

(P-17808)
CONSERVATION CORPS N BAY INC
11 Pimentel Ct, Novato (94949-5661)
PHONE 415 454-4554
Angel Minor, Exec Dir
Marilee Eckert, Exec Dir
Brandy Faulkner, Controller
Eileen Callahan, Human Res Dir
Kari Larsen, Human Res Mgr
EMP: 45 EST: 1982
SALES (est): 6.6MM Privately Held
WEB: www.ccnorthbay.org
SIC: 8331 8641 Job training services; civic social & fraternal associations

(P-17809)
COUNTY OF SAN JOAQUIN
San Joaquin County
56 S Lincoln St, Stockton (95203-3100)
PHONE 209 468-3500
EMP: 200 Privately Held
SIC: 8331 9111 Job training/Related Services Executive Office
PA: County Of San Joaquin
44 N San Joaquin St # 640
Stockton CA 95202
209 468-3203

(P-17810)
COUNTY OF STANISLAUS
Also Called: Department Workforce Dev
251 E Hackett Rd Ste 2, Modesto (95358-9800)
P.O. Box 3389 (95353-3389)
PHONE 209 558-2100
Doris Foster, Director
EMP: 49
SALES (corp-wide): 1.2B Privately Held
WEB: www.stancounty.com
SIC: 8331 Job training & vocational rehabilitation services
PA: County Of Stanislaus
1010 10th St Ste 5100
Modesto CA 95354
209 525-6398

(P-17811)
DEL NORTE ASSOC FOR DVLPMNTL S
Also Called: COASTLINE ENTERPRISES
838 4th St, Crescent City (95531-4011)
P.O. Box 1025 (95531-1025)
PHONE 707 464-8338
Nancy Borge, Exec Dir
Jackie Peel, Exec Dir
Cathy Walker, Director
EMP: 36 EST: 1974
SQ FT: 7,000
SALES (est): 730K Privately Held
SIC: 8331 Vocational rehabilitation agency

(P-17812)
EDEN AREA RGNAL OCCPTNAL PRGRA
Also Called: Eden Area Rop School
26316 Hesperian Blvd, Hayward (94545-2458)
PHONE 510 293-2900
Cyril Bonanno, Exec Dir
Robert Remley, Tech/Comp Coord
Lance Bohn, Teacher
EMP: 62 EST: 1979
SQ FT: 74,000
SALES (est): 13.5MM Privately Held
WEB: www.edenrop.org
SIC: 8331 8249 Vocational training agency; skill training center; vocational schools

(P-17813)
GOODWILL INDS OF GRTER E BAY I (PA)
1301 30th Ave, Oakland (94601-2208)
PHONE 510 698-7200
John Latchford, President
John B Latchford, President
Virginia Robbins, COO
Michael Conlon, CFO

8331 - Job Training & Vocational Rehabilitation Svcs County (P-17814)

Patrick Schmalz, *CFO*
EMP: 100 **EST:** 1919
SQ FT: 47,000
SALES: 23.9MM **Privately Held**
WEB: www.eastbaygoodwill.org
SIC: 5932 8331 Clothing, secondhand; job training & vocational rehabilitation services

(P-17814)
GOODWILL INDS OF RDWOOD EMPIRE (PA)
651 Yolanda Ave, Santa Rosa (95404-6324)
PHONE 707 523-0550
Mark Ihde, *President*
Heather Wilson, *Regional Mgr*
Lee Johnson, *Controller*
Joann Moser, *Opers Staff*
Regine Dunn, *Director*
▲ **EMP:** 100 **EST:** 1974
SQ FT: 14,000
SALES (est): 14.1MM **Privately Held**
WEB: www.gire.org
SIC: 5932 8331 Clothing, secondhand; furniture, secondhand; household appliances, used; vocational rehabilitation agency

(P-17815)
GOODWILL INDS SAN FRNCSCO SAN (PA)
750 Post St, San Francisco (94109-6106)
PHONE 415 575-2101
Maureen Sedonaen, *President*
JP M Elmaraslami, *Vice Chairman*
Terry Fitzpatrick, *CFO*
Val Culliver, *Vice Pres*
Kristin Keller, *Program Mgr*
▲ **EMP:** 350 **EST:** 1916
SALES: 36.8MM **Privately Held**
WEB: www.sfgoodwill.org
SIC: 5932 8331 8641 Clothing, secondhand; skill training center; civic social & fraternal associations

(P-17816)
HOPE SERVICES (PA)
30 Las Colinas Ln, San Jose (95119-1212)
PHONE 408 284-2849
Charles Huggins, *CEO*
Daniel Burns, *Senior Partner*
Clayton Ng, *CFO*
Tara Beckman, *Officer*
Paul Shea, *Vice Pres*
EMP: 50 **EST:** 1952
SQ FT: 29,400
SALES (est): 46MM **Privately Held**
WEB: www.hopeservices.org
SIC: 8331 Vocational rehabilitation agency

(P-17817)
HOWARD PREP (PA)
1424 Stonum Rd, Modesto (95351-5147)
PHONE 209 538-2431
Claudia K Miller, *Exec Dir*
Angelina Melgoza, *Human Res Mgr*
Leonard Hansen, *Opers Staff*
Reggie Hager, *Maintence Staff*
Lisa Ramsey, *Manager*
EMP: 50 **EST:** 1953
SQ FT: 10,000
SALES (est): 6.3MM **Privately Held**
WEB: www.howardprep.org
SIC: 8331 Skill training center

(P-17818)
HOWARD PREP
4801 Stratos Way Ste A, Modesto (95356-9043)
PHONE 209 521-9877
Claudia Miller, *Manager*
Dennis Pinaire, *Manager*
EMP: 41
SALES (corp-wide): 6.3MM **Privately Held**
WEB: www.howardprep.org
SIC: 8331 8244 Skill training center; business & secretarial schools
PA: Howard Prep
  1424 Stonum Rd
  Modesto CA 95351
  209 538-2431

(P-17819)
JEWISH VCTNAL CREER CNSLING SV
5106 Camden St, Oakland (94619-3460)
PHONE 415 391-3600
Lisa Countryman-Quiroz, *CEO*
Sadie Robertson, *Partner*
Nicoll Mischel, *COO*
Kathryn Beeley, *CFO*
Jamie Austin, *Vice Pres*
EMP: 70 **EST:** 1974
SQ FT: 8,000
SALES (est): 10.8MM **Privately Held**
WEB: www.jvs.org
SIC: 8331 Job counseling; job training services

(P-17820)
JOBTRAIN INC
1200 Obrien Dr, Menlo Park (94025-1413)
PHONE 650 330-6429
Sharon Williams, *Exec Dir*
Nora Sobolov, *Exec Dir*
Nancy-Sonja Jacobs, *Administration*
Anabel Osuna, *IT/INT Sup*
Tzlil Shefer, *IT/INT Sup*
EMP: 49 **EST:** 1965
SQ FT: 31,000
SALES (est): 6.2MM **Privately Held**
WEB: www.jobtrainworks.org
SIC: 8331 8249 8351 Job training services; restaurant operation school; child day care services

(P-17821)
MARIN COUNTY OFFICE EDUCATION (PA)
1111 Las Gallinas Ave, San Rafael (94903-1843)
P.O. Box 4925 (94913-4925)
PHONE 415 472-4110
Mary Jane Burke, *Supervisor*
Cindy Kerr-Friberg, *Program Mgr*
Terry Sullivan, *Program Mgr*
Gonzalez Laura, *Admin Sec*
Godinez Saul, *Admin Sec*
EMP: 260 **EST:** 1854
SQ FT: 36,000
SALES (est): 55.2MM **Privately Held**
WEB: www.marinschools.org
SIC: 8211 8331 Public elementary & secondary schools; specialty education; job training & vocational rehabilitation services

(P-17822)
METROPOLITAN EDUCATION DST (PA)
760 Hillsdale Ave Bldg 6, San Jose (95136-1106)
PHONE 408 723-6464
Alyssa Lynch, *Superintendent*
Scott Hall, *Facilities Mgr*
Kathy Jasper, *Teacher*
Norma Martinez, *Education*
EMP: 492 **EST:** 1982
SQ FT: 240,000
SALES (est): 30MM **Privately Held**
WEB: www.metroed.net
SIC: 8249 8331 Vocational schools; job training & vocational rehabilitation services

(P-17823)
MIDDLE WAY
Also Called: Middle Way Landscaping Svcs
1425 Corporate Cntr Pkwy, Santa Rosa (95407-5434)
PHONE 707 823-8755
EMP: 45 **EST:** 1979
SALES (est): 2.1MM **Privately Held**
WEB: www.middleway.org
SIC: 8331 Non Profit Rehabilitation Center

(P-17824)
MOTHER LODE JOB TRAINING
197 Mono Way Ste B, Sonora (95370-5209)
PHONE 209 533-8211
Woody Smallwood, *Exec Dir*
Kelly Smith, *Admin Asst*
EMP: 45 **EST:** 1982
SALES (est): 4.4MM **Privately Held**
WEB: www.mljt.org
SIC: 8331 Job training services

(P-17825)
NAPA VALLEY PSI INC
651 Trabajo Ln, NAPA (94559-4258)
P.O. Box 600 (94559-0600)
PHONE 707 255-0177
Jeanne Fauquet, *President*
Rick Wood, *General Mgr*
EMP: 80 **EST:** 1972
SQ FT: 43,800
SALES (est): 848.8K **Privately Held**
WEB: www.napavalleypsi.org
SIC: 8331 2521 2511 Vocational rehabitation agency; filing cabinets (boxes), office: wood; wood household furniture

(P-17826)
NORTH BAY DVLPMNTAL DSBLTIES S (PA)
Also Called: NORTH BAY REGIONAL CENTER
10 Executive Ct Ste A, NAPA (94558-6331)
P.O. Box 3360 (94558-0295)
PHONE 707 256-1224
Toll Free: .... 888 -
Nancy Gardner, *Exec Dir*
Gabriel Rogin, *Exec Dir*
Christina Comic, *Director*
EMP: 100 **EST:** 1972
SALES: 315.1MM **Privately Held**
WEB: www.nbrc.net
SIC: 8331 8322 Job training services; individual & family services

(P-17827)
NORTHERN CALIFORNIA SVC LEAG (PA)
40 Boardman Pl, San Francisco (94103-4729)
PHONE 415 621-5661
Shirley Melnicoe, *Exec Dir*
Isam Iddeen, *Exec Dir*
Barbara Grossi, *Administration*
Stephanie Hall, *Program Dir*
EMP: 35 **EST:** 1948
SALES (est): 410.3K **Privately Held**
WEB: www.cjcj.org
SIC: 8249 8331 Vocational schools; community service employment training program

(P-17828)
NTSI CORPORATION
Also Called: National Traffic Safety Inst
275 N 4th St Fl 2, San Jose (95112-5559)
PHONE 408 297-7200
Rodney Stark, *Branch Mgr*
Jacob Zamora, *Regional Mgr*
Roger Adams, *Administration*
Teresa Colasurdo, *Regional*
EMP: 45
SQ FT: 5,000
SALES (corp-wide): 6MM **Privately Held**
WEB: www.ntsi.com
SIC: 8331 8748 8741 Job training & vocational rehabilitation services; business consulting; administrative management
PA: Ntsi Corporation
  15 1st Ave Nw
  Issaquah WA 98027
  425 391-1884

(P-17829)
OAKLAND PRVATE INDUST CNCIL IN
268 Grand Ave, Oakland (94610-4724)
PHONE 510 768-4400
Gay Plair Cobb, *President*
EMP: 40 **EST:** 1980
SALES (est): 3.9MM **Privately Held**
WEB: www.oaklandpic.org
SIC: 8331 Community service employment training program; job training services

(P-17830)
OPERATING ENGINEERS JAC
Also Called: Rmtc Training Center
14738 Cantova Way, Rancho Murieta (95683-9740)
PHONE 916 354-2029
Tammy Castillo, *Director*
Nate Tucker, *Treasurer*
Cynthia Holloway,
EMP: 67 **EST:** 1971
SALES (est): 8MM **Privately Held**
WEB: www.oe3.org
SIC: 8331 Skill training center

(P-17831)
PACE SOLANO
1955 W Texas St, Fairfield (94533-4462)
PHONE 707 426-6932
Kimberly Yarbor, *Branch Mgr*
EMP: 71
SALES (corp-wide): 8.7MM **Privately Held**
WEB: www.pacesolano.org
SIC: 8331 8361 Job training services; home for the mentally handicapped
PA: Pace Solano
  419 Mason St Ste 118
  Vacaville CA 95688
  707 448-2283

(P-17832)
PLUMBING INDUST APPRENTICESHIP
Also Called: Pipe Trades J A T C
780 Commercial St, San Jose (95112-1408)
PHONE 408 453-6330
Carl Cimino, *Director*
EMP: 51 **EST:** 1941
SQ FT: 100,000
SALES: 5.8MM **Privately Held**
WEB: www.pttc.edu
SIC: 8331 Job training services

(P-17833)
PROGRSSIVE EMPLOYMENT CONCEPTS (PA)
6060 Sunrise Vista Dr # 1, Citrus Heights (95610-7053)
PHONE 916 723-3112
Carole Watilo, *President*
Robert Black, *Treasurer*
Debbie Bates, *Bd of Directors*
Mark Savickas, *Bd of Directors*
Joann Pingree, *Admin Sec*
EMP: 46 **EST:** 1995
SQ FT: 1,500
SALES (est): 2.9MM **Privately Held**
WEB: www.progressiveemployment.org
SIC: 8331 Job training & vocational rehabilitation services

(P-17834)
SACRAMENTO EMPLOYEMENT & TRAIN (PA)
Also Called: Seta
925 Del Paso Blvd Ste 100, Sacramento (95815-3568)
PHONE 916 263-3800
Kathy Kossick, *Exec Dir*
Elizabeth Ponce, *Officer*
Stephany Murphy, *Executive Asst*
Earl Sullaway, *Network Enginr*
Mary Bonanno, *Accountant*
EMP: 250 **EST:** 1978
SQ FT: 30,000
SALES (est): 37.5MM **Privately Held**
WEB: www.seta.net
SIC: 8331 7361 8351 Job training services; employment agencies; child day care services

(P-17835)
SACRAMENTO JOB CORP
3100 Meadowview Rd, Sacramento (95832-1498)
PHONE 916 391-1016
Tom Zender, *Exec Dir*
EMP: 38 **EST:** 2013
SALES (est): 9.2MM **Privately Held**
WEB: www.jobcorps.gov
SIC: 8331 Job training & vocational rehabilitation services

(P-17836)
SACRAMNTO EMPLYMENT TRNING AGC
Also Called: Set A Head Start Westside
925 Del Paso Blvd Ste 100, Sacramento (95815-3568)
PHONE 916 263-3800
Kathy Kossick, *Exec Dir*
EMP: 175 **Privately Held**
WEB: www.seta.net

▲ = Import ▼ = Export
◆ = Import/Export

PRODUCTS & SERVICES SECTION
8351 - Child Day Care Svcs County (P-17860)

SIC: **8331** 8351 Job training services; head start center, except in conjunction with school
PA: Sacramento Employment & Training Agency
925 Del Paso Blvd Ste 100
Sacramento CA 95815

(P-17837)
SAN JOSE CONSERVATION CORPS
2650 Senter Rd, San Jose (95111-1121)
PHONE.................................408 283-7171
Bob Hennessy, *CEO*
Dorsey Moore, *CEO*
Art Ruiz, *CFO*
Mary Bravo, *Program Mgr*
Tanisha Glenn, *Admin Sec*
EMP: **86** EST: 1987
SQ FT: 1,800
SALES (est): 14MM **Privately Held**
WEB: www.sjccs.org
SIC: **8331** Community service employment training program; job counseling

(P-17838)
SISKIYOU OPPORTUNITY CENTER (PA)
1516 S Mount Shasta Blvd, Mount Shasta (96067-2700)
P.O. Box 304 (96067-0304)
PHONE.................................530 926-4698
Daniel Chianello, *Director*
Laurinda Palmer, *Admin Asst*
Tena Rulofson, *Admin Asst*
Danielle Smothers, *Admin Asst*
EMP: **60** EST: 1970
SQ FT: 4,820
SALES: 2.6MM **Privately Held**
WEB: www.siskiyouoc.org
SIC: **8331** Job counseling

(P-17839)
SMART BUSINESS RESOURCE CENTER
1201 Placer St, Redding (96001-1016)
PHONE.................................530 246-7911
Anna Brassart, *CEO*
Hiram Oilar, *President*
Marie Granberry, *Controller*
Inez Bays, *Advisor*
EMP: **35** EST: 1979
SQ FT: 20,000
SALES (est): 3.3MM **Privately Held**
WEB: www.thesmartcenter.biz
SIC: **8331** Community service employment training program

(P-17840)
SOUTH BAY REGL PUBLIC SAFETY T
Also Called: Sbrpstc
560 Bailey Ave, San Jose (95141-1004)
PHONE.................................408 270-6494
Steve Cushing, *President*
Gregg Giusiana, *Vice Pres*
Al J Padron, *Opers Staff*
Russ Balushian, *Teacher*
Laurie Hogue, *Assistant*
EMP: **50** EST: 1994
SALES (est): 5.3MM **Privately Held**
WEB: www.theacademy.ca.gov
SIC: **8331** Job training services

(P-17841)
SOUTHERN OREGON GOODWILL INDS
1202 S Main St, Yreka (96097-3411)
PHONE.................................530 842-6627
Shae Johns, *Branch Mgr*
Dave Robison, *COO*
EMP: **63**
SALES (corp-wide): 19.1MM **Privately Held**
WEB: www.sogoodwill.com
SIC: **8331** Job training services
PA: Southern Oregon Goodwill Industries Inc
11 W Jackson St
Medford OR 97501
541 772-3300

(P-17842)
TOOLWORKS INC (PA)
25 Kearny St Ste 400, San Francisco (94108-5518)
PHONE.................................415 733-0990
Steve Crabiel, *Exec Dir*
Jan Behr, *COO*
Jonathan McAdams, *Info Tech Mgr*
Nancy Kwok, *Finance*
Stefan Lazar, *Human Res Dir*
EMP: **422** EST: 1975
SQ FT: 3,500
SALES: 16MM **Privately Held**
WEB: www.toolworks.org
SIC: **8331** Vocational rehabilitation agency

(P-17843)
VALLEY RGNAL OCCPTNAL PROGRAMS
1305 Q St, Sanger (93657-3466)
PHONE.................................559 876-2122
Fabrizio Lofaro, *Superintendent*
Terry Hofer, *Technology*
Breanna Wilson, *Technology*
Joelle Bruce, *Teacher*
Brian Donovan, *Teacher*
EMP: **67** EST: 1971
SQ FT: 933
SALES (est): 12.8MM **Privately Held**
WEB: www.valleyrop.net
SIC: **8331** Vocational training agency

(P-17844)
VOCATION PLUS INC
3985 N Fresno St Ste 106, Fresno (93726-4000)
PHONE.................................559 221-8019
Judy Rogers, *President*
Wayne Richardson, *Vice Pres*
EMP: **125** EST: 1991
SQ FT: 5,000
SALES (est): 3.5MM **Privately Held**
WEB: www.vocationplusconnections.com
SIC: **8331** Vocational rehabilitation agency; job counseling; job training services

(P-17845)
WORK2FUTURE FOUNDATION (PA)
38 N Almaden Blvd # 306, San Jose (95110-2724)
PHONE.................................408 794-1100
David Mirrione, *CEO*
Sean Guess, *Program Mgr*
Dianamarie Mungaray, *Office Spvr*
Rafael Cebrero, *Site Mgr*
Codyrae Arechiga, *Case Mgr*
EMP: **435** EST: 2010
SALES (est): 5.1MM **Privately Held**
WEB: www.work2futurefoundation.org
SIC: **8331** Job training services; skill training center

(P-17846)
WORK2FUTURE FOUNDATION
Also Called: Work2fture - Yuth Training Ctr
2072 Lucretia Ave, San Jose (95122-3305)
PHONE.................................408 794-1234
EMP: **40**
SALES (corp-wide): 5.1MM **Privately Held**
WEB: www.work2futurefoundation.org
SIC: **8331** Skill training center
PA: Work2future Foundation
38 N Almaden Blvd # 306
San Jose CA 95110
408 794-1100

(P-17847)
WORK2FUTURE FOUNDATION
Also Called: North San Jose Job Center
1901 Zanker Rd, San Jose (95112-4217)
PHONE.................................408 216-6202
EMP: **40**
SALES (corp-wide): 5.1MM **Privately Held**
WEB: www.work2futurefoundation.org
SIC: **8331** Job training services
PA: Work2future Foundation
38 N Almaden Blvd # 306
San Jose CA 95110
408 794-1100

(P-17848)
WORK2FUTURE FOUNDATION
Also Called: Work2future - Gilroy Job Ctr
379 Tomkins Ct, Gilroy (95020-3631)
PHONE.................................408 758-3477
EMP: **40**
SALES (corp-wide): 5.1MM **Privately Held**
WEB: www.work2futurefoundation.org
SIC: **8331** Skill training center
PA: Work2future Foundation
38 N Almaden Blvd # 306
San Jose CA 95110
408 794-1100

(P-17849)
YOLO EMPLOYMENT SERVICES
660 6th St, Woodland (95695-4162)
PHONE.................................530 662-8616
Alice Tapley, *Director*
EMP: **45** EST: 1968
SQ FT: 11,000
SALES (est): 1.7MM **Privately Held**
WEB: www.yoloes.org
SIC: **8331** Vocational training agency

(P-17850)
YOUTH EMPLOYMENT PARTNR INC
Also Called: Alameda Office Edction Opprtni
2300 International Blvd, Oakland (94601-1019)
PHONE.................................510 533-3447
Michelle Clark-Clough, *Exec Dir*
Michele Clark, *Executive*
Michelle Clough, *Exec Dir*
Dennis Smith, *General Mgr*
Alex Colt, *Train & Dev Mgr*
EMP: **71** EST: 1984
SQ FT: 26,000
SALES: 3.5MM **Privately Held**
WEB: www.yep.org
SIC: **8331** Job training services

8351 Child Day Care Svcs

(P-17851)
A CCESS (PA)
1850 Wardrobe Ave, Merced (95341-6407)
PHONE.................................209 383-7147
Valerie Anthony, *Principal*
EMP: **72** EST: 2010
SALES (est): 140.8K **Privately Held**
WEB: www.mcoe.org
SIC: **8351** Child day care services

(P-17852)
ADVANCE DAY CARE CENTER INC
2236 International Blvd, Oakland (94606-5004)
PHONE.................................510 434-9288
Molly Chan, *President*
Jacky LI, *President*
Kitti LI, *Vice Pres*
EMP: **36** EST: 1999
SALES (est): 484.9K **Privately Held**
SIC: **8351** Child day care services

(P-17853)
ALA CSTA CTR PRGRAM FOR THE DV (PA)
1300 Rose St, Berkeley (94702-1108)
PHONE.................................510 527-2550
Michael Pereira, *Exec Dir*
Ron Halog, *Exec Dir*
EMP: **41** EST: 1973
SALES: 1.6MM **Privately Held**
WEB: www.alacostacenters.org
SIC: **8351** Child day care services

(P-17854)
ALAMEDA FAMILY SERVICES
2325 Clement Ave, Alameda (94501-7063)
PHONE.................................510 629-6300
Irene Kudarauskas, *Exec Dir*
Marianne Boudreau, *Executive*
Katherine Schwartz, *Exec Dir*
Bruce Kariya, *VP Finance*
Tom Gallagher, *Finance*
EMP: **110** EST: 1970
SALES (est): 6.2MM **Privately Held**
WEB: www.alamedafs.org
SIC: **8351** 8322 Head start center, except in conjunction with school; youth self-help organization; offender rehabilitation agency; child guidance agency; general counseling services

(P-17855)
ALTO INTERNATIONAL SCHOOL
475 Pope St, Menlo Park (94025-2826)
PHONE.................................650 324-8617
Michael Chapman, *Principal*
Hanspeter Metzger, *Principal*
Susi Lindley, *Business Mgr*
Evelyn Lassman, *Bookkeeper*
Michaela Coan, *Teacher*
EMP: **47** EST: 1989
SALES (est): 7.5MM **Privately Held**
WEB: www.siliconvalleyinternational.org
SIC: **8351** Preschool center

(P-17856)
ALWAYS BE LEARNING INC
156 2nd St Ste 100, San Francisco (94105-3725)
PHONE.................................650 450-2603
Adam Pisoni, *CEO*
Nikki Champagne, *Technical Staff*
EMP: **40** EST: 2016
SALES (est): 2.8MM **Privately Held**
SIC: **8351** Child day care services

(P-17857)
BAY AREA HSPANO INST FOR ADVNC
Also Called: CENTRO VIDA
1000 Camelia St, Berkeley (94710-1514)
PHONE.................................510 525-1463
Beatriz Leyva Cutler, *Director*
Beatriz Leyva, *Exec Dir*
Virginia Turner, *Supervisor*
EMP: **66** EST: 1975
SQ FT: 1,200
SALES (est): 1.8MM **Privately Held**
WEB: www.bahiainc.org
SIC: **8351** 8299 Group day care center; preschool center; educational services

(P-17858)
BELMONT OAKS ACADEMY
2200 Carlmont Dr, Belmont (94002-3310)
PHONE.................................650 593-6175
Pamela Clarke, *President*
Brandi Aceves, *Teacher*
Danielle Casini, *Teacher*
Airon Green-Brittany, *Teacher*
Heather Jones, *Teacher*
EMP: **63** EST: 1946
SALES (est): 4MM **Privately Held**
WEB: www.mmboa.org
SIC: **8351** 8211 Preschool center; private elementary school

(P-17859)
BERKELEY MONTESSORI SCHOOL INC
2030 Francisco St, Berkeley (94709-2198)
PHONE.................................510 843-9374
Mary Jean Rioux, *President*
Bruce D'Ambrosio, *Treasurer*
Pat Bergman, *Vice Pres*
Alice Jordan, *Admin Sec*
Denise Fleig, *Administration*
EMP: **53** EST: 1963
SQ FT: 1,408
SALES (est): 1.7MM **Privately Held**
WEB: www.theberkeleyschool.org
SIC: **8351** 8211 Montessori child development center; private elementary school

(P-17860)
BERKWOOD HEDGE SCHOOL
1809 Bancroft Way, Berkeley (94703-1711)
PHONE.................................510 883-6990
Jane Friedman, *Director*
Walker Brents, *Teacher*
Paolo Diaz, *Teacher*
Elisa Edwards, *Teacher*
Harry Gray, *Teacher*
EMP: **53** EST: 1951
SALES (est): 2.6MM **Privately Held**
WEB: www.berkwood.org
SIC: **8211** 8351 Elementary & secondary schools; child day care services

8351 - Child Day Care Svcs County (P-17861)

(P-17861)
BETHEL CHURCH OF SAN JOSE
Also Called: Bethel Pre School
1201 S Winchester Blvd, San Jose (95128-3912)
PHONE..................................408 246-6790
Bret Allen, *Pastor*
Tiffany Okoye, *Admin Asst*
Jason Meleen, *Facilities Mgr*
EMP: 53 **EST:** 1948
SQ FT: 150,000
SALES (est): 6.6MM **Privately Held**
WEB: www.bethel.org
SIC: 8661 8351 Assembly of God Church; child day care services

(P-17862)
BIG VALLEY GRACE CMNTY CH INC (PA)
Also Called: Big Valley Christian School
4040 Tully Rd Ste D, Modesto (95356-8835)
PHONE..................................209 577-1604
Rick Countryman, *Pastor*
Brandon Gallasso, *Officer*
Erin Countryman, *Associate Dir*
Julie Lunsford, *Comms Dir*
Bob Yovino, *Principal*
EMP: 110 **EST:** 1966
SALES (est): 15.6MM **Privately Held**
WEB: www.bigvalleygrace.org
SIC: 8661 8211 8351 Non-denominational church; private elementary school; preschool center

(P-17863)
BJ JRDAN CHILD CARE PRGRAMS (PA)
Also Called: BEANSTALK
1771 Tribute Rd Ste A, Sacramento (95815-4408)
PHONE..................................916 344-6259
Farooq Azhar, *CFO*
John Brokenshire, *Maintence Staff*
Qari Aurangzeb, *Director*
EMP: 40 **EST:** 1973
SQ FT: 9,750
SALES: 11.4MM **Privately Held**
WEB: www.beanstalk.ws
SIC: 8351 Preschool center

(P-17864)
BLUE SKIES FOR CHILDREN
3021 Brookdale Ave, Oakland (94602-2715)
PHONE..................................510 261-1076
Claire Bainer, *Exec Dir*
Christa Edwards, *Teacher*
Ameena Muhammed, *Program Dir*
Liisa C Hail, *Co-Director*
EMP: 45 **EST:** 1983
SQ FT: 11,480
SALES: 2.5MM **Privately Held**
WEB: www.blueskies4children.org
SIC: 8351 Preschool center

(P-17865)
BOOKHEADED LEARNING LLC
610 Daniel Young Dr, Sonoma (95476-7278)
PHONE..................................707 996-3427
Robert Romano, *Principal*
Bradley McCord, *CFO*
Leah Osterman, *Vice Pres*
Cyndi Smith, *Vice Pres*
Joshua Luther, *Prdtn Dir*
EMP: 94 **EST:** 2010
SALES (est): 3.2MM **Privately Held**
WEB: www.studysync.com
SIC: 8351 Group day care center

(P-17866)
BRIGHTEN ACADEMY PRESCHOOL INC
1825 Austin Ave, Clovis (93611-5388)
PHONE..................................559 299-8100
Graham Peterson, *President*
Kristin Peterson, *Treasurer*
EMP: 41 **EST:** 2008
SQ FT: 4,700
SALES (est): 5.8MM **Privately Held**
WEB: www.brightenacademypreschool.com
SIC: 8351 Preschool center

(P-17867)
C 5 CHILDREN SCHOOL
525 Golden Gate Ave, San Francisco (94102-3220)
PHONE..................................415 626-4880
Beverly Melugin, *Exec Dir*
EMP: 46 **EST:** 1986
SQ FT: 2,600
SALES (est): 2.4MM **Privately Held**
WEB: www.c5children.org
SIC: 8351 Preschool center

(P-17868)
C 5 CHILDRENS SCHOOL
455 Golden Gate Ave # 2400, San Francisco (94102-3668)
PHONE..................................415 703-1277
Beverly Melugin, *Exec Dir*
Selene Mendoza, *Teacher*
Joe Wiseman, *Director*
Joseph Wiseman, *Director*
EMP: 56 **EST:** 1999
SALES (est): 2.7MM **Privately Held**
WEB: www.c5children.org
SIC: 8351 Preschool center

(P-17869)
CABRILLO COLLEGE CHILDREN CTR
6500 Soquel Dr, Aptos (95003-3198)
PHONE..................................831 479-6352
Erick Hoffman, *Director*
EMP: 37 **EST:** 1972
SALES (est): 318K **Privately Held**
WEB: www.cabrillo.edu
SIC: 8351 8221 Child day care services; colleges universities & professional schools

(P-17870)
CALIFORNIA PARENTING INSTITUTE
Also Called: CHILD PARENT INSTITUTE
3650 Standish Ave, Santa Rosa (95407-8113)
PHONE..................................707 585-6108
Robin Bowen, *Director*
Kathy Kever, *Executive*
Casandra McGee, *CIO*
Jessica Headington, *Human Res Mgr*
Katie Luciani, *Director*
EMP: 65 **EST:** 1978
SQ FT: 11,760
SALES (est): 3.9MM **Privately Held**
WEB: www.calparents.org
SIC: 8299 8351 8322 Educational services; child day care services; family counseling services

(P-17871)
CALIFORNIA YOUNG WORLD CENTER
1110 Fairwood Ave, Sunnyvale (94089-2311)
PHONE..................................408 245-7285
Cathy Boettcher, *Exec Dir*
Angelica Ortiz, *Office Mgr*
Emerson Ventura, *Director*
EMP: 39 **EST:** 1994
SALES (est): 3.6MM **Privately Held**
WEB: www.californiayoungworld.org
SIC: 8351 Preschool center

(P-17872)
CALVARY CHRSTN CH CTR OF SCRMN
Also Called: Calvary Christian Center
2727 Del Paso Blvd, Sacramento (95815-2302)
PHONE..................................916 921-9303
Classic Lane, *Director*
EMP: 40
SALES (corp-wide): 10MM **Privately Held**
WEB: www.calvarychristian.com
SIC: 8211 8351 Private elementary & secondary schools; group day care center
PA: Calvary Christian Church Center Of Sacramento, California, Inc
2665 Del Paso Blvd
Sacramento CA 95815
916 929-5725

(P-17873)
CALVARY CHURCH LOS GATOS CAL (PA)
Also Called: Kiddie Campus Day Care Center
16330 Los Gatos Blvd # 4, Los Gatos (95032-4520)
PHONE..................................408 358-8871
Bob Whitters, *Administration*
Cindy Todd, *Admin Sec*
William Fonda, *Technical Staff*
EMP: 55 **EST:** 1949
SALES (est): 10.1MM **Privately Held**
WEB: www.calvarylg.com
SIC: 8661 8351 Baptist Church; preschool center

(P-17874)
CALVARY CHURCH LOS GATOS CAL
Also Called: Kiddie Kampus Day Care Center
16330 Los Gatos Blvd, Los Gatos (95032-4520)
PHONE..................................408 356-6776
Susan Corey, *Director*
EMP: 58
SALES (corp-wide): 10.1MM **Privately Held**
WEB: www.calvarylg.com
SIC: 8351 Child day care services
PA: Calvary Church Of Los Gatos, California
16330 Los Gatos Blvd # 4
Los Gatos CA 95032
408 358-8871

(P-17875)
CALVARY CHURCH LOS GATOS CAL
Also Called: Calvary Infant Care Center
16330 Los Gatos Blvd, Los Gatos (95032-4520)
PHONE..................................408 356-5126
Bob Thomas, *Principal*
Mark Yoder, *Info Tech Dir*
Haley Green, *Director*
McKenna Raasch, *Director*
Jacob Leung, *Manager*
EMP: 58
SALES (corp-wide): 10.1MM **Privately Held**
WEB: www.calvarylg.com
SIC: 8351 Preschool center
PA: Calvary Church Of Los Gatos, California
16330 Los Gatos Blvd # 4
Los Gatos CA 95032
408 358-8871

(P-17876)
CAMPUS KIDS CONNECTION INC (PA)
Also Called: ASDC
820 Bay Ave Ste 124, Capitola (95010-2165)
PHONE..................................831 462-9822
Joanne Denbow, *Exec Dir*
EMP: 40 **EST:** 1978
SALES: 3.5MM **Privately Held**
WEB: www.campuskidsconnection.com
SIC: 8351 Preschool center

(P-17877)
CAPE INC
Also Called: Community Assoc Pr-School Edca
2406 Armstrong St, Livermore (94551-7617)
PHONE..................................925 443-3434
Rosemary Almand, *Exec Dir*
Heidi Jara, *Administration*
Patricia Martinez, *Administration*
Arlene Raftery, *Administration*
Dan Homerick, *Software Engr*
EMP: 87 **EST:** 1962
SALES (est): 6.1MM **Privately Held**
WEB: www.capeheadstart.org
SIC: 8211 8351 8699 Elementary school; preschool center; charitable organization

(P-17878)
CAPITAL CHRISTIAN CENTER
Also Called: Antelope Christian Academy
4533 Antelope Rd, Sacramento (95843-3947)
PHONE..................................916 722-6169
Karen Clement, *Administration*
William Clement, *Pastor*
EMP: 40 **EST:** 1994
SALES (est): 548.9K **Privately Held**
WEB: www.antelopechristian.org
SIC: 8211 8351 Private elementary school; preschool center

(P-17879)
CATALYST FAMILY INC (PA)
Also Called: Continuing Development
350 Woodview Ave Ste 100, Morgan Hill (95037-8105)
PHONE..................................408 556-7300
Susan Dumars, *President*
Eva Schulte, *COO*
Susan Blake, *Admin Sec*
Mariana Aungurencei, *Controller*
Lisa Coates, *Human Resources*
EMP: 75 **EST:** 1975
SQ FT: 10,000
SALES (est): 53MM **Privately Held**
WEB: www.catalystkids.org
SIC: 8351 8399 Child day care services; social service information exchange

(P-17880)
CENTERVILLE PRESBYTERIAN CH
4360 Central Ave, Fremont (94536-5802)
PHONE..................................510 793-3575
Greg Roth, *Pastor*
Kyle Christie, *Administration*
Sally Suryan, *Finance Mgr*
Chris Anderson, *Director*
David Yim, *Director*
EMP: 42 **EST:** 1945
SQ FT: 47,720
SALES (est): 2.7MM **Privately Held**
WEB: www.cpcfremont.org
SIC: 8661 8351 Presbyterian Church; nursery school

(P-17881)
CENTRAL ASSEMBLY OF GOD
Also Called: El Sobrante Christian School
5100 Argyle Rd, El Sobrante (94803-1343)
PHONE..................................510 223-1966
C Scott Wells, *Principal*
Danny Gomez, *Maintenance Dir*
Orlando Arnold, *Teacher*
Deborah Franklin, *Teacher*
Donna Manguiat, *Teacher*
EMP: 44 **EST:** 1971
SQ FT: 27,086
SALES (est): 3.2MM **Privately Held**
SIC: 8661 8351 Assembly of God Church; child day care services

(P-17882)
CENTURY ASSEMBLY INC (PA)
Also Called: Century Christian School
550 W Century Blvd, Lodi (95240-6602)
PHONE..................................209 334-3230
Richard Dale Edwards, *Pastor*
David A Williams, *General Ptnr*
Nadeen Zerbe, *Principal*
Phillip Orosco, *Admin Sec*
EMP: 76 **EST:** 1930
SQ FT: 10,000
SALES (est): 2.6MM **Privately Held**
WEB: www.centuryassembly.com
SIC: 8661 8351 Assembly of God Church; preschool center

(P-17883)
CENTURY ASSEMBLY INC
Also Called: Century Pre-School
550 W Century Blvd, Lodi (95240-6602)
PHONE..................................209 334-3230
Elizabeth Hernandez, *Director*
EMP: 50
SALES (corp-wide): 2.6MM **Privately Held**
WEB: www.centuryassembly.com
SIC: 8661 8351 Assembly of God Church; preschool center
PA: Century Assembly, Inc.
550 W Century Blvd
Lodi CA 95240
209 334-3230

(P-17884)
CHALLENGER SCHOOLS
4949 Harwood Rd, San Jose (95124-5209)
PHONE..................................408 723-0111

PRODUCTS & SERVICES SECTION
8351 - Child Day Care Svcs County (P-17907)

Josh McKay, *Principal*
Laurie Lingmann, *Vice Pres*
Amy Greenwood, *Office Mgr*
Chade Abplanalp, *CIO*
Camron Chacon, *Maintence Staff*
EMP: 63
SALES (corp-wide): 108.2MM **Privately Held**
WEB: www.challengerschool.com
SIC: 8351 8211 Preschool center; private elementary school
PA: Challenger Schools
9424 S 300 W
Sandy UT 84070
801 569-2700

(P-17885)
CHALLENGER SCHOOLS
3880 Middlefield Rd, Palo Alto (94303-4716)
PHONE.................................650 213-8245
Kamilah Abdul-Haqq, *Principal*
EMP: 63
SALES (corp-wide): 108.2MM **Privately Held**
WEB: www.challengerschool.com
SIC: 8351 8211 Preschool center; elementary & secondary schools
PA: Challenger Schools
9424 S 300 W
Sandy UT 84070
801 569-2700

(P-17886)
CHALLENGER SCHOOLS
39600 Cedar Blvd, Newark (94560-5487)
PHONE.................................510 770-1771
Barbara Baker, *Bd of Directors*
Danica Lacap, *Teacher*
EMP: 63
SALES (corp-wide): 108.2MM **Privately Held**
WEB: www.challengerschool.com
SIC: 8351 Preschool center
PA: Challenger Schools
9424 S 300 W
Sandy UT 84070
801 569-2700

(P-17887)
CHILD ACTION INC (PA)
10540 White Rock Rd # 180, Rancho Cordova (95670-6012)
PHONE.................................916 369-0191
Tracey Strack, *Exec Dir*
Laura Williams, *CFO*
Jaci White, *Director*
Sivar Qazaz, *Case Mgr*
EMP: 163 **EST:** 1976
SALES (est): 88.4MM **Privately Held**
WEB: www.wp.childaction.org
SIC: 8351 Child day care services

(P-17888)
CHILD ACTION INC
2330 Glendale Ln Ste 110, Sacramento (95825-2456)
PHONE.................................916 921-5345
Elaine Arteaga, *Manager*
EMP: 41
SALES (corp-wide): 88.4MM **Privately Held**
WEB: www.wp.childaction.org
SIC: 8351 7299 Child day care services; babysitting bureau
PA: Child Action, Inc.
10540 White Rock Rd # 180
Rancho Cordova CA 95670
916 369-0191

(P-17889)
CHILD ACTION INC
9961 Horn Rd, Sacramento (95827-1946)
PHONE.................................916 369-0191
MAI Pham, *Branch Mgr*
Brian Romine, *Prgrmr*
Maribel Gibbs, *Manager*
Mahmud Maki, *Clerk*
KAO Yang, *Clerk*
EMP: 81
SALES (corp-wide): 88.4MM **Privately Held**
WEB: www.wp.childaction.org
SIC: 8351 Child day care services

PA: Child Action, Inc.
10540 White Rock Rd # 180
Rancho Cordova CA 95670
916 369-0191

(P-17890)
CHILD DEVELOPMENT INCORPORATED (PA)
Also Called: Child Development Centers
350 Woodview Ave, Morgan Hill (95037-8104)
PHONE.................................408 556-7300
Carol Anderson, *CEO*
Patrick McGlashan, *Technology*
Samson Teklu, *Technology*
Anthony Felix, *Recruiter*
Regina Anderson, *Marketing Mgr*
EMP: 50 **EST:** 1979
SALES (est): 28MM **Privately Held**
WEB: www.catalystkids.org
SIC: 8351 Child day care services

(P-17891)
CHILD DEVELOPMENT INCORPORATED
312 Gibson Rd, Woodland (95695-4765)
PHONE.................................530 666-4822
Diana Sorelle, *Branch Mgr*
EMP: 406
SALES (corp-wide): 28MM **Privately Held**
WEB: www.catalystkids.org
SIC: 8351 Preschool center
PA: Child Development Incorporated
350 Woodview Ave
Morgan Hill CA 95037
408 556-7300

(P-17892)
CHILD FAMILY & CMNTY SVCS INC
32980 Alvarado Niles Rd # 856, Union City (94587-3186)
PHONE.................................510 796-9512
Karen Deshayes, *Exec Dir*
John Anthony Borsella, *Finance Dir*
Catherine Clennen Seymour, *Business Mgr*
Cynthia Esquivel-Delgado, *Human Res Mgr*
EMP: 140
SQ FT: 20,000
SALES: 16.5MM **Privately Held**
WEB: www.cfcsinc.org
SIC: 8351 Preschool center

(P-17893)
CHILD START INC
1406 Woolner Ave, Fairfield (94533-5948)
PHONE.................................707 423-4050
Jessica Rivera, *General Mgr*
EMP: 48
SALES (corp-wide): 14.4MM **Privately Held**
WEB: www.childstartinc.org
SIC: 8351 Head start center, except in conjunction with school
PA: Child Start, Inc.
439 Devlin Rd
Napa CA 94558
707 252-8931

(P-17894)
CHILD START INC (PA)
439 Devlin Rd, NAPA (94558-6274)
PHONE.................................707 252-8931
Deborah Peralez, *Exec Dir*
Robert Stalker, *Chairman*
Deborah McGrath, *Business Dir*
Debbie Peralez, *Exec Dir*
Marian Owen, *Technician*
EMP: 45 **EST:** 1965
SQ FT: 13,000
SALES: 14.4MM **Privately Held**
WEB: www.childstartinc.org
SIC: 8351 Head start center, except in conjunction with school

(P-17895)
CHILDCARE FOUNDRY
Also Called: Scuttlebugs Child Dev Ctr
3291 Stevens Creek Blvd, San Jose (95117-1145)
PHONE.................................408 564-5356
Geoff Penman, *Mng Member*
Ashley Chen, *Manager*
EMP: 35 **EST:** 2011

SALES (est): 1.1MM **Privately Held**
WEB: www.scuttlebugscdc.com
SIC: 8351 Preschool center

(P-17896)
CHILDRENS CRATIVE LRNG CTR INC
521 W Capitol Expy, San Jose (95136-3914)
PHONE.................................408 978-1500
Brandie Gonzales, *Manager*
EMP: 429 **Privately Held**
WEB: www.kindercare.com
SIC: 8351 Group day care center
PA: Children's Creative Learning Center, Inc.
794 E Duane Ave
Sunnyvale CA 94085

(P-17897)
CHILDRENS CRATIVE LRNG CTR INC
1625 San Luis Ave, Mountain View (94043-3147)
PHONE.................................650 968-2600
Kadie Albrecht, *Branch Mgr*
EMP: 429 **Privately Held**
WEB: www.kindercare.com
SIC: 8351 Group day care center
PA: Children's Creative Learning Center, Inc.
794 E Duane Ave
Sunnyvale CA 94085

(P-17898)
CHILDRENS CRATIVE LRNG CTR INC
Also Called: Downtown Palo Alto Kindercare
848 Ramona St, Palo Alto (94301-2734)
PHONE.................................650 473-1100
Nicole Ross, *Director*
Sonya Ramsey, *Exec Dir*
EMP: 429 **Privately Held**
WEB: www.kindercare.com
SIC: 8351 Group day care center
PA: Children's Creative Learning Center, Inc.
794 E Duane Ave
Sunnyvale CA 94085

(P-17899)
CHILDRENS CTR OF SAN LRNZO VLY
8500 Highway 9, Ben Lomond (95005-9707)
PHONE.................................831 336-2857
Kelli Polite, *Director*
Shandra Handley, *President*
EMP: 71 **EST:** 1977
SALES (est): 380.9K **Privately Held**
WEB: www.slvusd.org
SIC: 8351 Child day care services

(P-17900)
CHILDRENS DAY SCHOOL
333 Dolores St, San Francisco (94110-1006)
PHONE.................................415 861-5432
Rick Ackerly, *Headmaster*
Diane Larrabee, *Bd of Directors*
Heather Odonnell, *Trustee*
Kamel Zitoun, *Officer*
Tom Farrell, *Vice Pres*
EMP: 50 **EST:** 1983
SQ FT: 22,050
SALES: 19.3MM **Privately Held**
WEB: www.cds-sf.org
SIC: 8351 8211 Preschool center; elementary & secondary schools

(P-17901)
CHILDRENS HOUSE OF LOS ALTOS
770 Berry Ave, Los Altos (94024-5411)
P.O. Box 3040 (94024-0040)
PHONE.................................650 968-9052
Ella M Mayon, *Director*
Beth Burton, *Teacher*
Julie Clark, *Director*
EMP: 39 **EST:** 1995

SALES (est): 529.3K **Privately Held**
WEB: www.emeducation.com
SIC: 8351 Preschool center

(P-17902)
CHRISTIAN BRADSHAW SCHOOL (PA)
8324 Bradshaw Rd, Sacramento (95829-9255)
PHONE.................................916 688-0521
Carl Eastvold, *Superintendent*
Audra Anderson, *Admin Sec*
Sunny Espinoza, *Admin Sec*
Chantil Russo, *Technician*
Star Brewer, *Teacher*
EMP: 68 **EST:** 1992
SALES: 11.1MM **Privately Held**
WEB: www.bradshawchristian.com
SIC: 8211 8351 Private elementary & secondary schools; child day care services

(P-17903)
CHRISTIAN BROOKSIDE SCHOOLS
Also Called: United Chrisitan Schools
3588 Brookside Rd, Stockton (95219-2319)
PHONE.................................209 954-7656
Dennis Gibson, *President*
EMP: 60
SALES (corp-wide): 5.6MM **Privately Held**
WEB: www.brooksidechristian.com
SIC: 8351 Preschool center
PA: Brookside Christian Schools, Inc
3588 Brookside Rd
Stockton CA 95219
209 954-7650

(P-17904)
CHRISTIAN CONCORD CENTER
Also Called: Kings Valley Preschool
4255 Clayton Rd, Concord (94521-2711)
PHONE.................................925 687-2020
Michael Mortune, *Pastor*
Jessica Proia, *Admin Sec*
Joanna Rhodes, *Admin Sec*
Irma Gamez, *Teacher*
Guadalupe Gonzalez, *Teacher*
EMP: 54 **EST:** 1953
SALES (est): 5.9MM **Privately Held**
WEB: www.kingsvalley.org
SIC: 8211 8351 Private elementary & secondary schools; preschool center

(P-17905)
CHRISTIAN EDUCATION DEV CO
Also Called: CELEBRATION CENTER
2260 Jeffrey Way, Brentwood (94513-2432)
PHONE.................................925 240-5437
Jeneane Stevens, *Exec Dir*
Tina Daigre, *Exec Dir*
Terri Hunter, *Director*
EMP: 40 **EST:** 2000
SALES (est): 1.6MM **Privately Held**
WEB: www.celebrationcenter.com
SIC: 8351 Preschool center

(P-17906)
CHRISTIAN MILPITAS SCHOOL (PA)
3435 Birchwood Ln, San Jose (95132-1308)
PHONE.................................408 945-6530
Lu Gilbert, *CFO*
Connie Segreto, *Ch of Bd*
Alesia Williams, *Treasurer*
Pringle Johnston, *Teacher*
Becki Shuler, *Teacher*
EMP: 126 **EST:** 1975
SQ FT: 2,000
SALES (est): 15.9MM **Privately Held**
WEB: www.milpitaschristian.org
SIC: 8211 8351 Private elementary & secondary schools; child day care services

(P-17907)
CHRISTIAN TABERNACLE SCHOOL
Also Called: TABERNACLE CHRISTEN SCHOOL
4380 Concord Blvd, Concord (94521-1155)
PHONE.................................925 685-9169
Bern Taylor, *Principal*

8351 - Child Day Care Svcs County (P-17908)

David Pereira, *Technology*
Tirzah Burke, *Teacher*
Fred Delizo, *Teacher*
Gia Francis, *Teacher*
EMP: 71 **EST:** 1964
SQ FT: 9,960
SALES: 4MM **Privately Held**
WEB: www.tbs.org
SIC: 8211 8351 Private elementary & secondary schools; child day care services

(P-17908)
CITRUS HEIGHTS PRE-SCHOOL INC (PA)
7555 Old Auburn Rd, Citrus Heights (95610-3805)
PHONE................................916 726-1550
Herb Stone, *CEO*
Beverly Stone, *President*
Patty Newton, *Vice Pres*
EMP: 71 **EST:** 1970
SALES (est): 1.6MM **Privately Held**
WEB: www.citrusheightspreschool.com
SIC: 8351 Preschool center

(P-17909)
CLEARVIEW QUEST CORPORATION
Also Called: Serendipity School
3172 Clearview Way, San Mateo (94402-3712)
PHONE................................650 574-7400
Sandra R Carr, *President*
Meaghan Carr, *Admin Sec*
Patrice Warto, *Director*
EMP: 42 **EST:** 1994
SQ FT: 2,500
SALES (est): 5.3MM **Privately Held**
WEB: www.serendipityschool.com
SIC: 8351 Preschool center

(P-17910)
COMMUNITY ACTION PRTNR MDERA C (PA)
1225 Gill Ave, Madera (93637-5234)
PHONE................................559 673-9173
Mattie Mendez, *Exec Dir*
Linda L Wright, *CEO*
Donna Tooley, *CFO*
Maria Castellanos, *Area Mgr*
Jerri Clay, *Technician*
EMP: 200 **EST:** 1965
SQ FT: 18,000
SALES: 29.3MM **Privately Held**
WEB: www.maderacap.org
SIC: 8351 Head start center, except in conjunction with school

(P-17911)
COMMUNITY CHILD CARE CRDNTING (PA)
Also Called: 4 C'S
22351 City Center Dr # 200, Hayward (94541-2805)
PHONE................................510 582-2182
Renee Herzfeld, *Exec Dir*
Jay Perry, *Finance*
Diana Cortes, *Education*
Celia Goetz, *Director*
Paulene Prevatt-Mccarth, *Director*
EMP: 40 **EST:** 1972
SALES: 24.9MM **Privately Held**
WEB: www.4c-alameda.org
SIC: 8351 Child day care services

(P-17912)
COMMUNITY CHLD CRE CNCL SONOMA (PA)
Also Called: 4 Cs
131a Stony Cir Ste 300, Santa Rosa (95401-9507)
PHONE................................707 522-1413
Mary Ann Doan, *Exec Dir*
Ashley Chavez, *Teacher*
Leonor Calderon, *Manager*
Judy Berry, *Supervisor*
EMP: 60 **EST:** 1972
SALES (est): 5MM **Privately Held**
WEB: www.sonoma4cs.org
SIC: 8351 Group day care center

(P-17913)
COMMUNITY PRESBT CH DANVILLE (PA)
222 W El Pintado, Danville (94526-2513)
PHONE................................925 837-5525
Scott Farmer, *Pastor*
Jan Brunkal, *Principal*
Isaac Stokes, *Exec Dir*
Bianca Canales, *Admin Asst*
Heidi Johnson, *Assoc Pastor*
EMP: 120 **EST:** 1928
SQ FT: 140,000
SALES (est): 8.3MM **Privately Held**
WEB: www.cpcdanville.org
SIC: 8661 8351 Presbyterian Church; child day care services

(P-17914)
COMPASS FAMILY SERVICES
Also Called: Compass Children's Center
144 Leavenworth St, San Francisco (94102-3806)
PHONE................................415 644-0504
Mary McNamara, *Director*
EMP: 80
SQ FT: 12,143
SALES (corp-wide): 17.6MM **Privately Held**
WEB: www.compass-sf.org
SIC: 8351 Child day care services
PA: Compass Family Services
37 Grove St
San Francisco CA 94102
415 644-0504

(P-17915)
CONGRGTION BETH JCOB IRVING LV
1550 Almeda De Las Pulgas, Redwood City (94061-2404)
PHONE................................650 366-8481
Gary Geller, *Exec Dir*
Eric Stone, *Exec Dir*
Caroline Geller, *Office Mgr*
Rebecca Schwartz, *CIO*
Laura Bahbout, *Controller*
EMP: 39 **EST:** 1930
SALES (est): 6.6MM **Privately Held**
WEB: www.bethjacobrwc.org
SIC: 8661 8351 Synagogue; child day care services

(P-17916)
COUNTY OF SACRAMENTO
Also Called: William R Ridgeway Family Rela
3341 Power Inn Rd Ste 101, Sacramento (95826-3835)
PHONE................................916 875-3412
Wanda Ferguson, *Manager*
Paul Seave,
Kathleen Kennedy, *Sheriff*
Sharon Lueras, *Legal Staff*
Shavlovsky Yana, *Clerk*
EMP: 38
SALES (corp-wide): 3.1B **Privately Held**
WEB: www.saccounty.net
SIC: 8351 9211 Child day care services; courts;
PA: County Of Sacramento
700 H St Ste 7650
Sacramento CA 95814
916 874-8515

(P-17917)
CREATIVE CHILD CARE INC
17 E Poplar St, Stockton (95202-1607)
PHONE................................209 462-2282
Carolyn Ali, *Director*
EMP: 295 **Privately Held**
WEB: www.cccisj.com
SIC: 8351 Preschool center
PA: Creative Child Care, Inc.
4719 Quail Lakes Dr G-237
Stockton CA 95207

(P-17918)
CREATIVE CHILD CARE INC (PA)
4719 Quail Lakes Dr G-237, Stockton (95207-5267)
PHONE................................209 941-9100
Debbie Eison, *Exec Dir*
Loretta Young, *Human Res Dir*
Janice Marengo, *Human Res Mgr*
EMP: 38 **EST:** 1992
SALES: 18.9MM **Privately Held**
WEB: www.cccisj.com
SIC: 8351 Preschool center

(P-17919)
CREATIVE INSTRUCTIONAL SYSTEMS
Also Called: Hilldale School
79 Florence St, Daly City (94014-2145)
PHONE................................650 756-4737
Elizabeth A O'Donnell, *President*
Kevin O'Donnell, *Vice Pres*
Charles Weinstein, *Admin Sec*
Danielle Bolus, *Teacher*
Nicole Burleson, *Teacher*
EMP: 38 **EST:** 1964
SQ FT: 10,000
SALES (est): 1.4MM **Privately Held**
WEB: www.hilldaleschool.org
SIC: 8211 8351 Private elementary school; preschool center

(P-17920)
CREATIVE LRNG CTR PRESCHOOL
2100 Woods Ln, Los Altos (94024-7154)
P.O. Box 991 (94023-0991)
PHONE................................650 823-1496
Louise Emerson, *Principal*
Noor Albarakat, *Director*
EMP: 35 **EST:** 2009
SALES (est): 6.7MM **Privately Held**
WEB: www.clcsped.com
SIC: 8351 Preschool center

(P-17921)
DIABLO VLY MONTESSORI SCHL INC
Also Called: DVMS
3390 Deer Hill Rd, Lafayette (94549-3258)
PHONE................................925 283-6036
Suzette Smith, *Principal*
Deborah Donnelly, *Executive*
Carly Grote, *Teacher*
Jessica Martin, *Teacher*
Michelle Siegel, *Teacher*
EMP: 40 **EST:** 1965
SQ FT: 5,000
SALES: 2MM **Privately Held**
WEB: www.dvms.org
SIC: 8351 Montessori child development center; nursery school

(P-17922)
DIANNE ADAIR DAY CARE CENTERS (PA)
1862 Bailey Rd, Concord (94521-1349)
PHONE................................925 580-9704
Todd Porter, *CEO*
Brian Carbine, *CFO*
Sheila Bergum, *Principal*
EMP: 100 **EST:** 1982
SALES (est): 7.1MM **Privately Held**
WEB: www.dianneadair.org
SIC: 8351 Group day care center

(P-17923)
DIOCESE STOCKTON EDUCTL OFF
Also Called: Sacred Heart Pre-School
1250 Cooper Ave Ste 3, Turlock (95380-4174)
PHONE................................209 634-8578
Debra Canella, *Director*
Paul Yates, *Principal*
EMP: 174
SALES (corp-wide): 64MM **Privately Held**
WEB: www.stocktondiocese.org
SIC: 8211 8351 Catholic elementary & secondary schools; preschool center
PA: Diocese Of Stockton Educational Office
212 N San Joaquin St
Stockton CA 95202
209 466-0636

(P-17924)
DORRIS EATONS SCHOOL
1 Annabel Ln, San Ramon (94583-4358)
PHONE................................925 930-9000
Nancy Watson, *Partner*
Gerald Ludden, *Partner*
Gloria Aliloupour, *Teacher*
Tracy Bugni, *Teacher*
Mary Dickens, *Teacher*
EMP: 71 **EST:** 1980
SALES (est): 4.2MM **Privately Held**
WEB: www.dorriseaton.com
SIC: 8211 8351 Private elementary school; child day care services

(P-17925)
E CENTER
1506 Starr Dr, Yuba City (95993-2602)
PHONE................................530 634-1200
Kulraj Samra, *CEO*
Amanda Rhyne, *Administration*
Christina Mike, *Human Resources*
Sandra Alcantar, *Director*
Rosalinda Curiel, *Director*
EMP: 150 **EST:** 1973
SQ FT: 4,000
SALES (est): 25.1MM **Privately Held**
WEB: www.ecenter.org
SIC: 8351 Head start center, except in conjunction with school

(P-17926)
EARLY CHILDHOOD EDUCATION SVCS
Also Called: Child Care Development Svcs
365 Nevada St, Auburn (95603-3721)
PHONE................................530 745-1380
EMP: 40
SALES (est): 385.1K **Privately Held**
SIC: 8351 Child Day Care Services

(P-17927)
EAST BAY AGENCY FOR CHILDREN
Also Called: Ebac Therapeutic Nursery Schl
6117 Martin Luther King J, Oakland (94609-1240)
PHONE................................510 655-4896
Timothy Desmond, *Manager*
Vida Bowers, *Admin Asst*
EMP: 36
SALES (corp-wide): 16.6MM **Privately Held**
WEB: www.ebac.org
SIC: 8351 Child day care services
PA: East Bay Agency For Children
2828 Ford St
Oakland CA 94601
510 268-3770

(P-17928)
EASTSIDE UNION HIGH SCHOOL DST
Also Called: Yerba Buena Children's Center
1855 Lucretia Ave, San Jose (95122-3730)
PHONE................................408 347-4700
Carmen Martinez, *Director*
EMP: 41
SALES (corp-wide): 410.1MM **Privately Held**
WEB: www.esuhsd.org
SIC: 8351 Child day care services
PA: Eastside Union High School District
830 N Capitol Ave
San Jose CA 95133
408 347-5000

(P-17929)
EDGEWOOD CTR FOR CHLDREN FMLIE
957 Industrial Rd Ste B, San Carlos (94070-4152)
PHONE................................650 832-6900
Carolina Shahverdiyeva, *Partner*
Robin Randall, *Med Doctor*
EMP: 56
SALES (corp-wide): 30.5MM **Privately Held**
WEB: www.edgewood.org
SIC: 8351 Child day care services
PA: Edgewood Center For Children And Families
1801 Vicente St
San Francisco CA 94116
415 681-3211

(P-17930)
EDUCARE SERVICES INC (PA)
3485 W Ashcroft Ave # 101, Fresno (93722-4249)
PHONE................................559 228-3232
Alvin Vital, *Exec Dir*
Rosemary Avalos, *Program Dir*

PRODUCTS & SERVICES SECTION
8351 - Child Day Care Svcs County (P-17954)

EMP: 45 **EST:** 1983
SALES: 3.6MM **Privately Held**
WEB: www.educareservicesinc.com
SIC: 8351 Preschool center

(P-17931) EL RANCHO SCHOOL INC
Also Called: El Rancho Elementary School
5636 El Camino Ave, Carmichael (95608-5116)
P.O. Box 943 (95609-0943)
PHONE 916 482-8656
Holly Olson, *Principal*
Montgomery Charlene, *Teacher*
Kathy Conroy, *Teacher*
James Coulson, *Teacher*
Milan Djurasovic, *Teacher*
EMP: 40 **EST:** 1965
SALES (est): 3.5MM **Privately Held**
WEB: www.elranchoschool.com
SIC: 8351 8211 Nursery school; elementary & secondary schools

(P-17932) EUREKA UN SCHL DST FING CORP
Also Called: Olive Branch School
5280 Stirling St, Granite Bay (95746-6162)
PHONE 916 774-3437
Teri Louer, *Branch Mgr*
Lisa Cataldo, *Executive Asst*
EMP: 38
SALES (corp-wide): 66.1MM **Privately Held**
WEB: www.eurekausd.org
SIC: 8211 8351 Public elementary & secondary schools; preschool center
PA: Eureka Union School District Financing Corporation
5455 Eureka Rd
Granite Bay CA 95746
916 791-4939

(P-17933) FAIRFX-SAN ANSLMO CHILDREN CTR (PA)
199 Porteous Ave, Fairfax (94930-2022)
PHONE 415 454-1811
Heidi Tomsky, *Director*
EMP: 35 **EST:** 1971
SQ FT: 10,000
SALES (est): 1.3MM **Privately Held**
WEB: www.fsacc.org
SIC: 8351 Group day care center

(P-17934) FIRST BAPTIST CHURCH CROSSWALK
Also Called: Sunnyvale Christian School
445 S Mary Ave, Sunnyvale (94086-7501)
PHONE 408 736-3120
John Christie, *Pastor*
Jerry Inglles, *Principal*
Lisa St Clair, *Principal*
Lorraine McLintock, *Office Mgr*
Lorraine McClintock, *Administration*
EMP: 54 **EST:** 1959
SALES (est): 2.5MM **Privately Held**
WEB: www.sunnyvalechristian.school
SIC: 8661 8351 Child day care services; Baptist Church

(P-17935) FIRST BAPTIST CHURCH LOS ALTOS
Also Called: Altos Oaks Day Care Center
625 Magdalena Ave, Los Altos Hills (94024-5225)
PHONE 650 948-3738
Randy Wilson, *Pastor*
Debra Simmons, *Principal*
Steven Sutjandra, *Teacher*
John Benza, *Director*
EMP: 60 **EST:** 1941
SQ FT: 63,000
SALES (est): 2MM **Privately Held**
WEB: www.lacs.com
SIC: 8661 8211 8351 Baptist Church; private elementary school; child day care services

(P-17936) FIRST BAPTIST HEAD START
3890 Railroad Ave, Pittsburg (94565-6540)
PHONE 925 473-2000
Arika Spencer-Brown, *Exec Dir*
Brenda Battle, *Executive*
Brenda P Battle, *Asst Director*
Ramona Acosta, *Director*
Linda Anderson, *Manager*
EMP: 86 **EST:** 1920
SALES (est): 10.7MM **Privately Held**
WEB: www.firstbaptistheadstart.org
SIC: 8351 Head start center, except in conjunction with school

(P-17937) FRESNO CNTY ECNMIC OPPRTNTIES
1900 Mariposa Mall # 202, Fresno (93721-2514)
PHONE 559 263-1584
Naomi Mizumoto, *Branch Mgr*
EMP: 54
SALES (corp-wide): 108MM **Privately Held**
WEB: www.fresnoeoc.org
SIC: 8351 Child day care services
PA: Fresno County Economic Opportunities Commission
1920 Mariposa Mall # 300
Fresno CA 93721
559 263-1010

(P-17938) FRESNO CNTY ECNMIC OPPRTNTIES
Also Called: Sanger Head Start Center
3037 Orchid Ave, Sanger (93657-3723)
PHONE 559 875-2581
Ramona Sauceda, *Director*
EMP: 54
SALES (corp-wide): 108MM **Privately Held**
WEB: www.fresnoeoc.org
SIC: 8351 Head start center, except in conjunction with school
PA: Fresno County Economic Opportunities Commission
1920 Mariposa Mall # 300
Fresno CA 93721
559 263-1010

(P-17939) FRIENDS TO PARENTS
2525 Wexford Ave, South San Francisco (94080-5518)
P.O. Box 5590 (94083-5590)
PHONE 650 588-8212
Merla Direkze, *Director*
EMP: 40 **EST:** 1971
SALES (est): 1MM **Privately Held**
WEB: www.friendstoparents.org
SIC: 8351 Preschool center

(P-17940) GLENN COUNTY OFFICE EDUCATION
Also Called: Child & Family Services
676 E Walker St Fl 2, Orland (95963-2203)
PHONE 530 865-1145
Tracey Quarne, *Superintendent*
Dezora Jersdal, *Executive*
Bobby Shoutz, *IT Specialist*
Margarita Villalba, *Director*
EMP: 44 **EST:** 1971
SALES (est): 4.4MM **Privately Held**
WEB: www.glenncoe.org
SIC: 8351 8322 Child day care services; family counseling services

(P-17941) GLP
Also Called: Marin Day Schools
2 Harrison St Ste 150, San Francisco (94105-6126)
PHONE 415 777-9696
Danielle C Ober, *Director*
EMP: 144
SALES (corp-wide): 4.7MM **Privately Held**
SIC: 8351 Preschool center
PA: Glp
100 Madowcreek Dr Ste 225
Corte Madera CA

(P-17942) GOLDEN GATE KINDERGARTEN ASSN
Also Called: PHOEBE HEARST PRE SCHOOL
1315 Ellis St, San Francisco (94115-4215)
PHONE 415 931-1018
Irene Byrne, *Exec Dir*
EMP: 40 **EST:** 1879
SALES (est): 2.2MM **Privately Held**
WEB: www.phoebehearstpreschool.org
SIC: 8351 Preschool center

(P-17943) GOLDEN PPPY PRSCHOOL INFANT CT
50 El Camino Dr, Corte Madera (94925-2057)
PHONE 415 924-2828
Gail Reed, *Mng Member*
EMP: 40 **EST:** 1983
SQ FT: 4,000
SALES (est): 1MM **Privately Held**
WEB: www.goldenpoppyschool.com
SIC: 8351 Preschool center; nursery school

(P-17944) GOOD SHEPHERD LUTHERAN SCHOOL
1180 Lynwood Dr, Novato (94947-4846)
PHONE 415 897-2510
Chyrise King, *Principal*
Laura Fitzpatrick, *MIS Dir*
Marlon Morales, *Mktg Dir*
Lora Bluvshteyn, *Teacher*
Forrest Campbell, *Teacher*
EMP: 40 **EST:** 1976
SALES (est): 3.7MM **Privately Held**
WEB: www.gslsnovato.org
SIC: 8211 8351 Elementary & secondary schools; preschool center

(P-17945) GRACE BAPTIST CHURCH INC
Also Called: Grace Christn Academy Pre Schl
1980 S Walton Ave, Yuba City (95993-7011)
PHONE 530 673-6847
Russell Rohleder, *Principal*
Steve Ettles, *President*
Rosemary Denton, *Treasurer*
Lyndell Kuns, *Pastor*
EMP: 35 **EST:** 1968
SQ FT: 16,200
SALES (est): 1.8MM **Privately Held**
WEB: www.graceyc.org
SIC: 8351 Child day care services

(P-17946) GRAND LAKE MONTESSORI
466 Chetwood St, Oakland (94610-2649)
PHONE 510 836-4313
Helen Campbell, *Director*
Somsy Phonexaysitthi, *Teacher*
EMP: 36 **EST:** 1978
SALES: 3.9MM **Privately Held**
WEB: www.grandlakemontessori.com
SIC: 8351 Montessori child development center

(P-17947) H R C CALAVERAS HEAD SRT STATE (PA)
Also Called: Resource Connection
444 E Saint Charles St, San Andreas (95249-9658)
P.O. Box 919 (95249-0919)
PHONE 209 772-3980
Shiela Neyo, *Director*
Celeste Mata, *Manager*
EMP: 44 **EST:** 1985
SALES (est): 2.7MM **Privately Held**
WEB: www.trcac.org
SIC: 8351 Preschool center

(P-17948) HAPPILY EVER LAUGHTER LLC
211 River St, Santa Cruz (95060-2770)
PHONE 831 346-0002
Lacie Gershenson, *CEO*
EMP: 40 **EST:** 2006
SALES (est): 1.1MM **Privately Held**
WEB: www.happilyeverlaughter.com
SIC: 8351 7929 Child day care services; entertainers & entertainment groups

(P-17949) HAPPY HALL PRESCHOOL
Also Called: Happy Hall Schools
233 Santa Inez Ave, San Bruno (94066-5212)
PHONE 650 583-7370
Mary L Johnson, *Owner*
EMP: 35 **EST:** 1951
SALES (est): 4.9MM **Privately Held**
WEB: www.happyhallschools.com
SIC: 8351 Preschool center

(P-17950) HAYWARD UNIFIED SCHOOL DST
Hayward High School
1633 East Ave, Hayward (94541-5314)
PHONE 510 723-3170
David Seymour, *Principal*
Megan Ball, *Ch of Bd*
Kristy Prasad, *Ch of Bd*
Mary Walsh, *Ch of Bd*
Yvonne White, *Ch of Bd*
EMP: 48
SALES (corp-wide): 336.5MM **Privately Held**
WEB: www.husd.us
SIC: 8211 8351 Public junior high school; public elementary school; preschool center
PA: Hayward Unified School District
24411 Amador St
Hayward CA 94544
510 784-2600

(P-17951) HEAD START CHILD DEV CNCIL INC
1425 S Center St, Stockton (95206-2016)
PHONE 209 464-9542
EMP: 60
SALES (corp-wide): 20MM **Privately Held**
SIC: 8211 8351 Elementary/Secondary School Child Day Care Services
PA: Head Start Child Development, Council, Inc.
5361 N Pershing Ave Ste A
Stockton CA 95207

(P-17952) HIS GRWING GROVE CHILD CARE CT
2490 Grove Way, Castro Valley (94546-7106)
PHONE 510 581-5088
Libby Barbaria, *Exec Dir*
EMP: 40 **EST:** 1989
SALES (est): 2.3MM **Privately Held**
WEB: www.hisgrowinggrove.com
SIC: 8351 Preschool center

(P-17953) HOUSE MODESTO (PA)
Also Called: Calvary Temple Academy
1601 Coffee Rd, Modesto (95355-2801)
PHONE 209 529-7346
Glen Berteau, *President*
EMP: 125 **EST:** 1935
SQ FT: 15,000
SALES (est): 6.6MM **Privately Held**
WEB: www.jaredming.org
SIC: 8661 8211 8351 Assembly of God Church; private elementary school; private junior high school; group day care center

(P-17954) IMMACULATE HEART MARY SCHOOL
1000 Almeda De Las Pulgas, Belmont (94002-3508)
PHONE 650 593-2344
Margaret Purcell, *Principal*
Corinne Armstrong, *Admin Sec*
Johanna McCormack, *Administration*
Karen Turner, *Finance*
Claudia Carreno, *Teacher*
EMP: 38 **EST:** 1985

8351 - Child Day Care Svcs County (P-17955)

SALES (est): 4.3MM **Privately Held**
WEB: www.ihmschoolbelmont.org
SIC: **8211** 8661 8351 Catholic elementary & secondary schools; Catholic elementary school; Catholic Church; child day care services

(P-17955)
INSTITUTE FOR HUMN SOCIAL DEV (PA)
Also Called: SAN MATEO HEAD START PROGRAM
155 Bovet Rd Ste 300, San Mateo (94402-3142)
PHONE 650 871-5613
Amy Liew, *Director*
Mayte Reynoso, *Office Mgr*
Ofelia Alfaro, *Opers Mgr*
Dalenna Smith, *Director*
Lupe Ibarra, *Manager*
EMP: 87 **EST:** 1983
SQ FT: 6,000
SALES: 13.3MM **Privately Held**
WEB: www.izziearlyed.org
SIC: **8351** Head start center, except in conjunction with school

(P-17956)
INSTITUTE HUMN BHVIOR RES EDCA
Also Called: Phillips Academy, The
1910 Central Ave, Alameda (94501-2623)
PHONE 510 769-7100
Nicole Barker, *Exec Dir*
Steven Blutink, *President*
Joanna Wong, *Opers Mgr*
EMP: 40 **EST:** 1994
SQ FT: 7,212
SALES (est): 1.6MM **Privately Held**
WEB: www.thephillipsacademy.org
SIC: **8351** Preschool center

(P-17957)
KIDANGO INC
1824 Daytona Dr, San Jose (95122-1719)
PHONE 408 258-9129
Paul Miller, *Branch Mgr*
EMP: 72
SALES (corp-wide): 26MM **Privately Held**
WEB: www.kidango.org
SIC: **8351** Preschool center
PA: Kidango, Inc.
44000 Old Warm Sprng Blvd
Fremont CA 94538
510 897-6900

(P-17958)
KIDANGO INC (PA)
44000 Old Warm Sprng Blvd, Fremont (94538-6145)
PHONE 510 897-6900
Scott Moore, *CEO*
Nereyra Houle, *CFO*
Kate Breitzman, *Officer*
Andrea Garcia, *Officer*
Jennifer Pare, *Officer*
EMP: 80 **EST:** 1979
SQ FT: 5,000
SALES (est): 26MM **Privately Held**
WEB: www.kidango.org
SIC: **8351** Preschool center

(P-17959)
KIDANGO INC
4700 Calaveras Ave, Fremont (94538-1124)
PHONE 510 494-9601
MAI Ton, *Branch Mgr*
EMP: 72
SALES (corp-wide): 26MM **Privately Held**
WEB: www.kidango.org
SIC: **8351** Preschool center
PA: Kidango, Inc.
44000 Old Warm Sprng Blvd
Fremont CA 94538
510 897-6900

(P-17960)
KIDS HAVEN
6056 Montgomery Bnd, San Jose (95135-1429)
PHONE 408 274-8766
EMP: 39 **Privately Held**
SIC: **8351** Child day care services

PA: Kid's Haven
2059 Camden Ave
San Jose CA 95124

(P-17961)
KIDS HAVEN (PA)
2059 Camden Ave, San Jose (95124-2024)
PHONE 408 274-8766
Beth Brady, *Principal*
EMP: 101 **EST:** 1996
SALES (est): 141.4K **Privately Held**
SIC: **8351** Child day care services

(P-17962)
LAFAYETTE ORINDA PRESBT CH
Also Called: Presbyterian Church USA
49 Knox Dr, Lafayette (94549-3322)
PHONE 925 283-8722
Peter Whitelock, *Pastor*
Char Casella, *Treasurer*
Jim Fulford, *Treasurer*
Elizabeth Ball, *Admin Mgr*
David Engelbrekston, *Maintence Staff*
EMP: 67 **EST:** 1954
SALES (est): 7.2MM **Privately Held**
WEB: www.lopc.org
SIC: **8661** 8351 Presbyterian Church; child day care services

(P-17963)
LEARNINGSTAR INC (PA)
571 Tully Rd, San Jose (95111-1904)
PHONE 408 221-4067
Quy Pham, *Principal*
EMP: 50 **EST:** 2009
SALES (est): 402.5K **Privately Held**
WEB: www.vnlearningstar.com
SIC: **8351** Preschool center

(P-17964)
LETTERMAN DIGITAL ARTS LTD
1 Letterman Dr Bldg B, San Francisco (94129-1494)
P.O. Box 29916 (94129-0916)
PHONE 415 746-5044
Ngelo Garcia, *CEO*
Kyle Gibson, *Senior Mgr*
EMP: 71 **EST:** 1998
SALES (est): 570.4K **Privately Held**
WEB: www.onelettermandrive.com
SIC: **8351** Child day care services

(P-17965)
LITTLE BLSSOM MNTSSORI SCHL IN
2075 Arena Blvd, Sacramento (95834-2310)
PHONE 916 515-0550
Lakshman Ranatunga, *President*
Yaowadee Berman, *Teacher*
Mary Davidova, *Teacher*
Katrina Ledet, *Teacher*
Rocio Naranjo, *Teacher*
EMP: 35 **EST:** 2002
SALES (est): 1.7MM **Privately Held**
WEB: www.littleblossom.org
SIC: **8351** Montessori child development center

(P-17966)
LODI UNIFIED SCHOOL DISTRICT
8282 Le Mans Ave, Stockton (95210-2280)
PHONE 209 331-7127
Annette Roberts, *Principal*
Jeff Johnston, *Teacher*
EMP: 52
SALES (corp-wide): 428.1MM **Privately Held**
WEB: www.lodiusd.net
SIC: **8211** 8351 Public elementary school; preschool center
PA: Lodi Unified School District
1305 E Vine St
Lodi CA 95240
209 331-7000

(P-17967)
LOS GATOS SARATOGA DEPT OF COM
Also Called: LGS RECREATION
208 E Main St, Los Gatos (95030-6107)
PHONE 408 354-8700

Nancy Rollett, *Exec Dir*
Harrison Paist, *Finance*
Carly Saletnik, *Analyst*
Manuel Enriquez, *Director*
Stephanie Mekler, *Supervisor*
EMP: 225 **EST:** 1996
SQ FT: 15,000
SALES (est): 8.1MM **Privately Held**
WEB: www.lgsrecreation.org
SIC: **8299** 8351 Educational services; child day care services

(P-17968)
MANTECA UNIFIED SCHOOL DST
Also Called: Manteca Day School
737 W Yosemite Ave, Manteca (95337-5403)
PHONE 209 239-3689
Gerald Braxton, *Principal*
EMP: 35
SALES (corp-wide): 330MM **Privately Held**
WEB: www.mantecausd.net
SIC: **8211** 8351 Public combined elementary & secondary school; group day care center
PA: Manteca Unified School District
2271 W Louise Ave
Manteca CA 95337
209 825-3200

(P-17969)
MARIN COMMUNITY COLLEGE DST
Also Called: Child Development Program
835 College Ave, Kentfield (94904-2590)
PHONE 415 457-8811
EMP: 50
SALES (corp-wide): 54.9MM **Privately Held**
WEB: www.marin.edu
SIC: **8351** Preschool center
PA: Marin Community College District
835 College Ave
Kentfield CA 94904
415 457-8811

(P-17970)
MARIN COMMUNITY COLLEGE DST
Also Called: College Marin Childrens Center
835 College Ave, Kentfield (94904-2590)
PHONE 415 485-9468
Shaquam Edwards, *Manager*
EMP: 57
SALES (corp-wide): 54.9MM **Privately Held**
WEB: www.marin.edu
SIC: **8222** 8351 Community college; child day care services
PA: Marin Community College District
835 College Ave
Kentfield CA 94904
415 457-8811

(P-17971)
MARIN HORIZON SCHOOL INC
305 Montford Ave, Mill Valley (94941-3370)
PHONE 415 388-8408
Rosalind Hamar, *Exec Dir*
Charlie Denby, *Admin Sec*
Tatyana Griffin, *Technology*
Laurie Kelly, *Accounting Mgr*
Lizzie Porter-Roth, *Marketing Staff*
EMP: 50 **EST:** 1977
SQ FT: 20,000
SALES (est): 17.6MM **Privately Held**
WEB: www.marinhorizon.org
SIC: **8351** 8211 Montessori child development center; private elementary school

(P-17972)
MARIN PRIMARY & MIDDLE SCHOOL (PA)
20 Magnolia Ave, Larkspur (94939-2186)
PHONE 415 924-2608
Mark Slavonia, *Ch of Bd*
Linda Franco, *Bd of Directors*
Elizabeth Von Buedingen, *Comms Mgr*
Lisa Ramezzano, *Office Mgr*
David Munson, *Facilities Mgr*
EMP: 35 **EST:** 1975
SQ FT: 25,000

SALES: 12MM **Privately Held**
WEB: www.mpms.org
SIC: **8211** 8351 Public elementary & secondary schools; child day care services

(P-17973)
MERCED CITY SCHOOL DISTRICT
Also Called: Franklin Elementary School
2736 Franklin Rd, Merced (95348-9434)
PHONE 209 385-6364
Lori Slaven, *Principal*
Manola Andrade, *Teacher*
Sara Cardella, *Teacher*
Michele Christiansen, *Teacher*
Catherine Friedman, *Teacher*
EMP: 66
SALES (corp-wide): 169.2MM **Privately Held**
WEB: www.mcsd.k12.ca.us
SIC: **8211** 8351 Public elementary school; preschool center
PA: Merced City School District
444 W 23rd St
Merced CA 95340
209 385-6600

(P-17974)
MILPITAS UNIFIED SCHOOL DST
Also Called: Rose Child Development Center
250a Roswell Dr, Milpitas (95035-5945)
PHONE 408 635-2686
Kathy Lincoln, *Principal*
EMP: 63
SALES (corp-wide): 160.4MM **Privately Held**
WEB: www.musd.org
SIC: **8211** 8351 Public adult education school; child day care services
PA: Milpitas Unified School District
1331 E Calaveras Blvd
Milpitas CA 95035
408 635-2600

(P-17975)
MISSION CHILD CARE CONSORT
Also Called: McCc
4750 Mission St, San Francisco (94112-2745)
PHONE 415 586-6139
Joe Martinez, *Exec Dir*
EMP: 44 **EST:** 1971
SALES (est): 2.7MM **Privately Held**
SIC: **8351** Group day care center

(P-17976)
MODEL SCHL CMPRHNSIVE HMNSTIC
2330 Prince St, Berkeley (94705-1916)
PHONE 510 549-2711
Daisy Mante, *President*
Susan Lee, *Vice Pres*
Marina Barnett, *Office Mgr*
Timothy Van Bourg, *Admin Sec*
Daisy L Mante, *Director*
EMP: 41 **EST:** 1988
SQ FT: 33,150
SALES (est): 1.3MM **Privately Held**
WEB: www.themodelschool.org
SIC: **8351** Preschool center

(P-17977)
MODESTOS NEIGHBORHOOD CHURCH
Also Called: Modesto Christian School
5921 Stoddard Rd, Modesto (95356-9199)
PHONE 209 529-5510
Ralph Sudfeld, *President*
Annie Zonligt, *Ch of Bd*
Kevin Bidlack, *COO*
Paul Andrew, *CFO*
Scott Brown, *CFO*
EMP: 116 **EST:** 1957
SQ FT: 200
SALES (est): 9.8MM **Privately Held**
SIC: **8351** 8211 8661 Group day care center; preschool center; private elementary & secondary schools; Assembly of God Church

PRODUCTS & SERVICES SECTION
8351 - Child Day Care Svcs County (P-18000)

(P-17978)
MONTESSORI SCHOOL SILICON VLY (PA)
630 S Main St, Milpitas (95035-5340)
PHONE..................408 586-8643
Michael Harding, *Exec Dir*
EMP: 40 **EST:** 2002
SALES (est): 167.6K **Privately Held**
WEB: www.msosv.com
SIC: 8351 Montessori child development center

(P-17979)
MONTICELLO CHILD DEVELOPMENT
3401 Monroe St Ste A, Santa Clara (95051-1417)
PHONE..................408 261-0494
Trinh Troung, *President*
David Troung, *Treasurer*
Megan McMahon, *Office Mgr*
Nancy Nguyen, *Nurse*
Darlene Valles, *Asst Director*
EMP: 38 **EST:** 1995
SALES (est): 1.2MM **Privately Held**
WEB: www.monticelloacademy.org
SIC: 8351 Preschool center

(P-17980)
MOUNT MADONNA SCHOOL
491 Summit Rd, Watsonville (95076-9781)
PHONE..................408 847-2717
Judith Diffenbaugh, *Principal*
Jeevani Vince, *Ch of Bd*
Sarojani Rohan, *Exec Dir*
Supriya McDonald, *Admin Sec*
Kami Pacheco, *Admin Sec*
EMP: 117 **EST:** 1980
SALES (est): 4MM **Privately Held**
WEB: www.mountmadonnaschool.org
SIC: 8211 8351 Private combined elementary & secondary school; boarding school; child day care services

(P-17981)
NEW LIFE DISCOVERY SCHOOLS INC (PA)
4926 E Yale Ave Ste 101, Fresno (93727-1561)
PHONE..................559 292-8687
Lynette Ferguson, *President*
EMP: 37 **EST:** 1995
SALES (est): 2.7MM **Privately Held**
WEB: www.newlifediscoveryschools.com
SIC: 8351 Group day care center

(P-17982)
NORTH BAY CHILDRENS CENTER INC (PA)
932 C St, Novato (94949-5060)
PHONE..................415 883-6222
Susan Gilmore, *CEO*
Lisa Butler, *Director*
Molly Fivian, *Director*
Lori Martinez, *Director*
Grace Garrett, *Supervisor*
EMP: 75 **EST:** 1988
SALES: 6.5MM **Privately Held**
WEB: www.nbcc.net
SIC: 8351 Preschool center

(P-17983)
NORTHCOAST CHILDRENS SVCS INC (PA)
1266 9th St, Arcata (95521-5702)
P.O. Box 1165 (95518-1165)
PHONE..................707 822-7206
Kathy Montagne, *Director*
Carol Cuffee, *Technician*
Hollie Miller, *Financial Analy*
Pamela Rex, *Director*
Rodney Oien, *Supervisor*
EMP: 102 **EST:** 1969
SQ FT: 3,500
SALES (est): 11.6MM **Privately Held**
WEB: www.ncsheadstart.org
SIC: 8351 Head start center, except in conjunction with school

(P-17984)
NORTHWEST CHURCH FRESNO CAL
Also Called: Shining Star Preschool
5415 N West Ave, Fresno (93711-2999)
PHONE..................559 435-2200
Scott Gossenberger, *Pastor*
Barbara Pease, *Admin Sec*
Corinne Beatty, *Administration*
Greg Sumii, *Assoc Pastor*
Jared Carl, *Pastor*
EMP: 54 **EST:** 1959
SQ FT: 6,000
SALES (est): 6.8MM **Privately Held**
WEB: www.nwc.org
SIC: 8661 8211 8351 5932 Baptist Church; elementary school; preschool center; clothing & shoes, secondhand

(P-17985)
ODYSSEY LEARNING CENTERS INC
7150 Santa Juanita Ave, Orangevale (95662-2832)
PHONE..................916 988-0258
Doug Norby, *Director*
Cheryl Daly, *Exec Dir*
Shawn Sloane, *Exec Dir*
Shelby Penman, *Controller*
Ryan Sharpe, *Controller*
EMP: 50 **EST:** 1979
SQ FT: 7,000
SALES: 4.5MM **Privately Held**
WEB: www.odysseylearningcenter.org
SIC: 8211 8351 School for the retarded; child day care services

(P-17986)
ONE WORLD MONTESSORI SCHOOL
Also Called: Teacher Training Organization
1170 Foxworthy Ave, San Jose (95118-1209)
PHONE..................408 723-5140
Rebecca Keith, *Principal*
Earl Loomis, *Treasurer*
Janet Montoto, *Admin Sec*
Elizabeth Gomez, *Admin Asst*
Gioia Ingram, *Teacher*
EMP: 36 **EST:** 1979
SALES (est): 5.8MM **Privately Held**
WEB: www.oneworldmontessori.org
SIC: 8211 8351 Private elementary school; Montessori child development center

(P-17987)
ORINDA PRE SCHOOL
Also Called: TOPS
10 Irwin Way, Orinda (94563-2508)
P.O. Box 1 (94563-0001)
PHONE..................925 254-2551
Kristin Armanini, *Director*
Sarah Bossenbroek, *Asst Director*
EMP: 35 **EST:** 1938
SALES (est): 435.8K **Privately Held**
WEB: www.topsonline.org
SIC: 8351 Preschool center

(P-17988)
PALCARE INC
945 California Dr, Burlingame (94010-3605)
PHONE..................650 340-1289
Pettis Perry, *Exec Dir*
Lisa Kiesselbach, *Exec Dir*
Jasmine Hessami, *Office Mgr*
EMP: 50 **EST:** 1987
SQ FT: 12,000
SALES: 3.5MM **Privately Held**
WEB: www.palcare.org
SIC: 8351 Preschool center

(P-17989)
PALO ALTO COMMUNITY CHILD CARE
890 Escondido Rd, Stanford (94305-7101)
PHONE..................650 855-9828
Gary Prehn, *Principal*
EMP: 65
SALES (corp-wide): 8.7MM **Privately Held**
WEB: www.paccc.org
SIC: 8351 Preschool center
PA: Palo Alto Community Child Care Inc
3990 Ventura Ct
Palo Alto CA
650 493-5990

(P-17990)
PENINSULA FAMILY SERVICE (PA)
24 2nd Ave, San Mateo (94401-3828)
PHONE..................650 403-4300
Judy Swanson, *CEO*
Laurie Wishard, *President*
Arne Croce, *CEO*
Kimberly Hines, *Vice Pres*
Susan Houston, *Vice Pres*
EMP: 100 **EST:** 1950
SALES: 14MM **Privately Held**
WEB: www.peninsulafamilyservice.org
SIC: 8351 8322 Group day care center; family (marriage) counseling

(P-17991)
PENINSULA FAMILY SERVICE
2635 N 1st St, San Jose (95134-2026)
PHONE..................650 403-4300
EMP: 74
SALES (corp-wide): 14MM **Privately Held**
WEB: www.peninsulafamilyservice.org
SIC: 8351 Child day care services
PA: Peninsula Family Service
24 2nd Ave
San Mateo CA 94401
650 403-4300

(P-17992)
PENINSULA SCHOOL LTD
920 Peninsula Way, Menlo Park (94025-2300)
PHONE..................650 325-1584
Alison Elliott, *President*
Christine Southgate, *Vice Pres*
Lucille Dacanay, *Office Mgr*
Julie Backlund, *Principal*
Sue Eldredge, *Director*
EMP: 69 **EST:** 1925
SALES: 6.8MM **Privately Held**
WEB: www.peninsulaschool.org
SIC: 8211 8351 Private elementary school; child day care services

(P-17993)
PENINSULA TEMPLE BETH EL
1700 Almeda De Las Pulgas, San Mateo (94403-1223)
PHONE..................650 341-7701
Mike Prozam, *President*
Blair R Brown, *COO*
Blair Brown, *COO*
Adrienne Pryor, *Office Admin*
Mick Chand, *Executive Asst*
EMP: 36 **EST:** 1950
SALES (est): 5.4MM **Privately Held**
WEB: www.ptbe.org
SIC: 8661 8211 8351 Synagogue; private elementary & secondary schools; child day care services

(P-17994)
PHOENIX SCHOOLS INC
2820 Theona Way, Rocklin (95765-5534)
PHONE..................916 415-0780
Staci Patterson, *Director*
Joline Kiser, *Teacher*
Mary Paye, *Teacher*
EMP: 64
SALES (corp-wide): 11.1MM **Privately Held**
WEB: www.phoenixschools.com
SIC: 8351 Preschool center
PA: Phoenix Schools, Inc
8767 E Via De Ventura
Scottsdale AZ 85258
916 488-9066

(P-17995)
PHOENIX SCHOOLS INC
4110 Skyland Ct, Antelope (95843-6122)
PHONE..................916 725-0302
Sandy Dorn, *Exec Dir*
EMP: 64
SALES (corp-wide): 11.1MM **Privately Held**
WEB: www.phoenixschools.com
SIC: 8351 Preschool center
PA: Phoenix Schools, Inc
8767 E Via De Ventura
Scottsdale AZ 85258
916 488-9066

(P-17996)
PHOENIX SCHOOLS INC
Also Called: Broadstone Preschool
76 Clarksville Rd, Folsom (95630-8201)
PHONE..................916 983-0224
Gail Gill, *Administration*
EMP: 64
SALES (corp-wide): 11.1MM **Privately Held**
WEB: www.phoenixschools.com
SIC: 8351 Preschool center
PA: Phoenix Schools, Inc
8767 E Via De Ventura
Scottsdale AZ 85258
916 488-9066

(P-17997)
PHOENIX SCHOOLS INC
Also Called: Lil People's School
600 I St, Sacramento (95814-2414)
PHONE..................916 442-0722
Amy Walker, *Director*
Karin Ho, *Principal*
Afshan Mirza, *Teacher*
Ron Breyne, *Director*
EMP: 64
SALES (corp-wide): 11.1MM **Privately Held**
WEB: www.phoenixschools.com
SIC: 8351 8211 Group day care center; kindergarten
PA: Phoenix Schools, Inc
8767 E Via De Ventura
Scottsdale AZ 85258
916 488-9066

(P-17998)
PHOENIX SCHOOLS INC
Also Called: Phoenix Preschools, The
1820 Alhambra Blvd, Sacramento (95816-7011)
PHONE..................916 452-5150
Kelly Hendrix, *Manager*
EMP: 64
SALES (corp-wide): 11.1MM **Privately Held**
WEB: www.phoenixschools.com
SIC: 8351 Preschool center
PA: Phoenix Schools, Inc
8767 E Via De Ventura
Scottsdale AZ 85258
916 488-9066

(P-17999)
PHOENIX SCHOOLS INC
7998 Old Auburn Rd, Citrus Heights (95610-2434)
PHONE..................916 723-2633
Karla Rader, *Director*
EMP: 64
SALES (corp-wide): 11.1MM **Privately Held**
WEB: www.phoenixschools.com
SIC: 8351 Preschool center
PA: Phoenix Schools, Inc
8767 E Via De Ventura
Scottsdale AZ 85258
916 488-9066

(P-18000)
PHOENIX SCHOOLS INC
650 Willard Dr, Folsom (95630-9543)
PHONE..................916 353-1031
Claudia Sherry, *Principal*
Someca Berchea, *Exec Dir*
Racquel Madson, *CIO*
Marissa Garcia, *Sales Executive*
Seanna Castro, *Teacher*
EMP: 64
SALES (corp-wide): 11.1MM **Privately Held**
WEB: www.phoenixschools.com
SIC: 8351 8211 Preschool center; private elementary & secondary schools
PA: Phoenix Schools, Inc
8767 E Via De Ventura
Scottsdale AZ 85258
916 488-9066

8351 - Child Day Care Svcs County (P-18001)

(P-18001)
PLAY AND LEARN SCHOOL
1898 Pleasant Hill Rd, Pleasant Hill (94523-4056)
PHONE...................................925 947-2820
Sue Houweling, *Exec Dir*
EMP: 39 **EST:** 1999
SALES (est): 1.2MM **Privately Held**
WEB: www.playandlearnschool.com
SIC: 8351 Preschool center

(P-18002)
PLAY N LEARN PRE SCHOOL
3800 Narvaez Ave, San Jose (95136-1210)
PHONE...................................408 269-2338
Adrian Howell, *CEO*
Gloria Howell, *Owner*
Marc Lariz, *Executive*
Tammy L Lariz, *Exec Dir*
Tammy Lariz, *Administration*
EMP: 40 **EST:** 1978
SALES (est): 1.3MM **Privately Held**
WEB: www.playnlearnpreschool.com
SIC: 8351 Preschool center

(P-18003)
PRECIOUS ENTERPRISES INC
Also Called: Clement Preschool
14130 Douglass Ln, Saratoga (95070-5536)
PHONE...................................408 265-2226
Faz Ulla, *Owner*
Shahana Shah, *Co-Owner*
Husna Ulla, *Co-Owner*
Nilu Ulla, *Co-Owner*
EMP: 62 **EST:** 1975
SQ FT: 7,500
SALES (est): 1.3MM **Privately Held**
SIC: 8351 Preschool center

(P-18004)
PRESIDIO HILL SCHOOL
3839 Washington St, San Francisco (94118-1612)
PHONE...................................415 213-8600
Kerry Davis, *Director*
EMP: 120 **EST:** 1918
SQ FT: 6,596
SALES (est): 13.2MM **Privately Held**
WEB: www.presidiohill.org
SIC: 8211 8351 Private combined elementary & secondary school; kindergarten; child day care services

(P-18005)
PRINCE PEACE LUTHERAN CHURCH
Also Called: Prince Peace Lutheran School
38451 Fremont Blvd, Fremont (94536-6030)
PHONE...................................510 797-8186
Dan Dueck, *Principal*
Marcia Houseworth, *Principal*
Robert Marty, *Principal*
David Saver, *Assoc Pastor*
Michelle Esqueda, *Teacher*
EMP: 90 **EST:** 1980
SQ FT: 50,000
SALES (est): 9.3MM **Privately Held**
SIC: 8211 8661 8351 Private elementary & secondary schools; Lutheran Church; preschool center

(P-18006)
RENAISSANCE SCHOOL
Also Called: A Childs World Montessori Schl
3668 Dimond Ave, Oakland (94602-2213)
PHONE...................................510 531-8566
Leslie Hites, *Owner*
Andrea Peto, *Office Mgr*
Richard Barnes, *CIO*
Sophia Gigliotti, *Teacher*
Olga Morataya, *Teacher*
EMP: 38 **EST:** 1992
SALES (est): 2.9MM **Privately Held**
WEB: www.therenaissanceschool.org
SIC: 8351 8211 Preschool center; kindergarten

(P-18007)
RISING STAR MONTESSORI ASSOC
1421 High St, Alameda (94501-3102)
PHONE...................................510 865-4536
Ann Gavey, *President*
Sima Patel, *Hlthcr Dir*
EMP: 44 **EST:** 1981
SQ FT: 7,000
SALES (est): 7.1MM **Privately Held**
WEB: www.risingstarschool.org
SIC: 8211 8351 Private elementary & secondary schools; Montessori child development center

(P-18008)
SACRAMENTO CY UNIFIED SCHL DST
Also Called: Ethel Phillips Elementary Schl
2930 21st Ave, Sacramento (95820-3719)
PHONE...................................916 277-6277
Danny Hernandez, *Principal*
Alfred Moreno, *Principal*
EMP: 53
SALES (corp-wide): 695.4MM **Privately Held**
WEB: www.scusd.edu
SIC: 8211 8351 Public elementary school; preschool center
PA: Sacramento City Unified School District
5735 47th Ave
Sacramento CA 95824
916 643-7400

(P-18009)
SACRAMENTO CY UNIFIED SCHL DST
Also Called: Bret Harte Children's Center
5735 47th Ave, Sacramento (95824-4528)
PHONE...................................916 277-6263
Mary Gary, *Manager*
EMP: 53
SALES (corp-wide): 695.4MM **Privately Held**
WEB: www.scusd.edu
SIC: 8211 8351 Public elementary & secondary schools; child day care services
PA: Sacramento City Unified School District
5735 47th Ave
Sacramento CA 95824
916 643-7400

(P-18010)
SACRAMENTO CY UNIFIED SCHL DST
Also Called: Washington Children's Center
530 18th St, Sacramento (95811-1007)
PHONE...................................916 264-4186
EMP: 53
SALES (corp-wide): 695.4MM **Privately Held**
WEB: www.scusd.edu
SIC: 8211 8351 Public elementary & secondary schools; child day care services
PA: Sacramento City Unified School District
5735 47th Ave
Sacramento CA 95824
916 643-7400

(P-18011)
SACRAMENTO CY UNIFIED SCHL DST
Also Called: Marian Anderson Childrens Ctr
1901 60th Ave, Sacramento (95822-4314)
PHONE...................................916 277-6259
Denise Richardson, *Director*
EMP: 53
SALES (corp-wide): 695.4MM **Privately Held**
WEB: www.scusd.edu
SIC: 8211 8351 Public elementary & secondary schools; child day care services
PA: Sacramento City Unified School District
5735 47th Ave
Sacramento CA 95824
916 643-7400

(P-18012)
SAFARI KID INC (PA)
34899 Newark Blvd, Newark (94560-1203)
PHONE...................................510 739-1511
Deepak Mudakavi, *Principal*
Auxilia William, *Vice Pres*
EMP: 47 **EST:** 2005
SALES (est): 2.2MM **Privately Held**
WEB: www.safarikidusa.com
SIC: 8351 Preschool center

(P-18013)
SAINT VINCENTS DAY HOME
1086 8th St, Oakland (94607-2697)
PHONE...................................510 832-8324
Carol A Corrigan, *President*
Corinne Mohrmann, *Exec Dir*
Jerry Brown, *Mayor*
Matthew Depalm, *Education*
Carmen Baires, *Cust Mgr*
EMP: 36 **EST:** 1911
SQ FT: 3,000
SALES (est): 5MM **Privately Held**
WEB: www.svdh.org
SIC: 8351 Preschool center

(P-18014)
SAKLAN VALLEY SCHOOL
1678 School St, Moraga (94556-1119)
PHONE...................................925 376-7900
Johnathan Martin, *Principal*
Diane Wilcox, *President*
Ruth Bailey, *Treasurer*
Carol Goldman, *Bd of Directors*
Miranda Heerah, *Bd of Directors*
EMP: 35 **EST:** 1978
SQ FT: 7,968
SALES (est): 2.8MM **Privately Held**
WEB: www.saklan.org
SIC: 8211 8351 7032 Elementary school; child day care services; summer camp, except day & sports instructional

(P-18015)
SAN FRANCISCO SCHOOL
300 Gaven St, San Francisco (94134-1113)
PHONE...................................415 239-5065
Steve Morris, *Principal*
Maggie Day, *Ch of Bd*
Terri D Hamer, *CFO*
Melissa Holman, *Technology*
Jalen Allen, *Teacher*
EMP: 55 **EST:** 1966
SQ FT: 16,000
SALES (est): 14.8MM **Privately Held**
WEB: www.sfschool.org
SIC: 8211 8351 Private elementary & secondary schools; preschool center

(P-18016)
SANTA CRUZ CO HEAD START
Also Called: Santa Cruz Cmnty Cnseling Ctr
408 E Lake Ave, Watsonville (95076-4425)
PHONE...................................831 724-3885
Cynthia Sloane, *Director*
Christine Sippl, *Partner*
Kim Morrison, *CFO*
Leelia Franck, *Managing Dir*
Jennifer Hastings, *Managing Dir*
EMP: 36 **EST:** 1965
SALES (est): 490.1K **Privately Held**
WEB: www.encompasscs.org
SIC: 8351 Preschool center

(P-18017)
SANTA CRUZ MONTESSORI SCHOOL
Also Called: Scms
6230 Soquel Dr, Aptos (95003-3118)
PHONE...................................831 476-1646
Kathleen Ann Rideout, *CEO*
Molly Dipiero, *Teacher*
Melissa McGuffin, *Teacher*
EMP: 50 **EST:** 1964
SALES (est): 6.6MM **Privately Held**
WEB: www.scms.org
SIC: 8351 8211 Preschool center; private elementary & secondary schools; private elementary school; private junior high school

(P-18018)
SHASTA COUNTY HEAD START CHILD (PA)
375 Lake Blvd Ste 100, Redding (96003-2557)
PHONE...................................530 241-1036
Carla Clark, *Exec Dir*
EMP: 50
SQ FT: 5,000
SALES (est): 12.9MM **Privately Held**
WEB: www.shastaheadstart.org
SIC: 8351 Head start center, except in conjunction with school

(P-18019)
SIERRA CSCADE FMLY OPPRTNITIES (PA)
Also Called: Head Start
424 N Mill Creek Rd, Quincy (95971-9531)
PHONE...................................530 283-1242
Brenda Poteete, *Director*
Bethany Edholm, *Manager*
EMP: 65 **EST:** 1989
SQ FT: 2,600
SALES (est): 3.3MM **Privately Held**
WEB: www.headstart4u.org
SIC: 8351 Head start center, except in conjunction with school

(P-18020)
SIERRA WALDORF SCHOOL INC
19234 Rawhide Rd, Jamestown (95327-9627)
PHONE...................................209 984-0454
Kim Kendleton, *Director*
Karen Brock, *Principal*
Marcia Williams, *Administration*
Ruth Brickner, *Accounting Dir*
Jennifer Reggiardo, *Teacher*
EMP: 36 **EST:** 1990
SALES (est): 2.5MM **Privately Held**
WEB: www.sierrawaldorf.com
SIC: 8211 8351 Private elementary & secondary schools; child day care services

(P-18021)
SJB CHILD DEVELOPMENT CENTERS (PA)
Also Called: SICK CHILD CARE CENTER, THE
1400 Parkmoor Ave Ste 220, San Jose (95126-3798)
PHONE...................................408 538-0200
Victor Hassan, *CEO*
Kent Williams, *Principal*
Nicholas Puzar, *Assistant*
EMP: 96 **EST:** 1971
SQ FT: 12,840
SALES (est): 12.1MM **Privately Held**
WEB: www.sjbcdc.org
SIC: 8351 Preschool center

(P-18022)
SOLANO FMLY & CHLD COUNCIL INC
Also Called: SOLANO FAMILY & CHILDREN'S SER
421 Executive Ct N, Fairfield (94534-4019)
PHONE...................................707 863-3950
Kathryn Lago, *Exec Dir*
EMP: 74 **EST:** 1978
SALES (est): 30.4MM **Privately Held**
WEB: www.solanofamily.org
SIC: 8351 Child day care services

(P-18023)
SONOMA COUNTRY DAY SCHOOL
Also Called: SCDS
4400 Day School Pl, Santa Rosa (95403-8221)
PHONE...................................707 284-3200
Katie Murphy, *Chairman*
Aly Conway, *Teacher*
Nate Eaton, *Teacher*
Michele Ferretti, *Teacher*
Melissa Kang, *Teacher*
EMP: 116 **EST:** 1983
SALES (est): 9.1MM **Privately Held**
WEB: www.scds.org
SIC: 8211 8351 Private elementary & secondary schools; private elementary school; group day care center

(P-18024)
SOUTH MARKET CHILD CARE INC (PA)
790 Folsom St, San Francisco (94107-1276)
PHONE...................................415 820-3500
Noushin Mofakham, *Exec Dir*
Wendy Aitken, *Treasurer*
Christine Naluz, *Admin Asst*
Dianne Alvarado, *Manager*
EMP: 50 **EST:** 1991
SQ FT: 10,000
SALES: 3.9MM **Privately Held**
WEB: www.somacc.org
SIC: 8351 Group day care center

PRODUCTS & SERVICES SECTION

8351 - Child Day Care Svcs County (P-18047)

(P-18025)
SOUTH PNINSULA HEBREW DAY SCHL
Also Called: SPHDS
1030 Astoria Dr, Sunnyvale (94087-3008)
PHONE.................................408 738-3060
Ann Goewert, *Principal*
Allen Selis, *Principal*
Maya Yaniv, *Exec Dir*
Ruth Burgin, *Admin Sec*
Marisa Carrasco, *Administration*
EMP: 65 **EST:** 1972
SALES (est): 5.6MM **Privately Held**
WEB: www.sphds.org
SIC: 8211 8351 Private elementary & secondary schools; private elementary school; preschool center

(P-18026)
SPRING EDUCATION GROUP INC (PA)
1999 S Bascom Ave Ste 400, Campbell (95008-2219)
PHONE.................................408 973-7351
Shawn Weidmann, *CEO*
EMP: 105 **EST:** 2012
SALES (est): 354.5MM **Privately Held**
WEB: www.discoverypoint.com
SIC: 8351 Child day care services

(P-18027)
SPRINGFIELD MONTESSORI SCHOOL
2780 Mitchell Dr, Walnut Creek (94598-1602)
PHONE.................................925 944-0626
Shashi Lal, *Owner*
EMP: 35 **EST:** 1990
SALES (est): 1.3MM **Privately Held**
WEB: www.springfieldmontessori.com
SIC: 8351 Montessori child development center

(P-18028)
ST ALBANS COUNTRY DAY SCHOOL
2312 Vernon St, Roseville (95678-9701)
PHONE.................................916 782-3557
Laura Bernauer, *Principal*
Jennifer Murrin, *President*
Patricia Gordon, *Principal*
Reed Goodey, *Principal*
Deirdre Lefty, *Director*
EMP: 76 **EST:** 1963
SQ FT: 37,766
SALES (est): 3.4MM **Privately Held**
WEB: www.stalbans.org
SIC: 8211 8351 Private elementary & secondary schools; group day care center

(P-18029)
ST HELENA MONTESSORI SCHL INC
880 College Ave, Saint Helena (94574-1309)
PHONE.................................707 963-1527
Elena O'Heil, *Principal*
Peter White, *Treasurer*
EMP: 49 **EST:** 1981
SALES (est): 3.3MM **Privately Held**
WEB: www.shmontessori.org
SIC: 8351 Montessori child development center

(P-18030)
ST MATTHEWS EPISCOPAL DAY SCHL
16 Baldwin Ave, San Mateo (94401-3807)
PHONE.................................650 342-5436
Mark Hale, *Owner*
Justin Avalos, *Officer*
Martin Otterbach, *Officer*
Marilyn Hundley, *Admin Asst*
Steve Searson, *Info Tech Mgr*
EMP: 168 **EST:** 1952
SALES (est): 15.5MM **Privately Held**
WEB: www.episcopaldaysanmateo.org
SIC: 8211 8351 Private elementary school; preschool center

(P-18031)
ST PHILIP SCHOOL
Also Called: St Philip The Apostle School
665 Elizabeth St, San Francisco (94114-3229)
PHONE.................................415 824-8467
Tony Lescallett, *Principal*
Mary McKeever, *Admin Asst*
Katrina Abbott, *Teacher*
Susan Abellera, *Teacher*
Anne Branch, *Teacher*
EMP: 64 **EST:** 1938
SALES (est): 5.7MM **Privately Held**
SIC: 8211 8661 8351 Catholic elementary school; religious organizations; preschool center

(P-18032)
ST ROSE SCHOOL
4300 Old Redwood Hwy, Santa Rosa (95403-1700)
PHONE.................................707 545-0379
Kathy Ryan, *Principal*
Maggie Casquini, *Admin Sec*
Marika Dueck, *Teacher*
Melanie Haley, *Teacher*
Ron Hill, *Teacher*
EMP: 35 **EST:** 1990
SALES (est): 4.8MM **Privately Held**
WEB: www.strosecatholicschool.org
SIC: 8351 Preschool center

(P-18033)
STAR INC
Also Called: Oakhill Star
9233 Twin School Rd # 505, Granite Bay (95746-7100)
PHONE.................................916 791-8442
Danny Victorin, *Director*
EMP: 563 **Privately Held**
WEB: www.starinc.org
SIC: 8351
PA: Star, Inc.
10101 Jefferson Blvd
Culver City CA 90232

(P-18034)
STATE PRESCHOOL
Also Called: Martin Lthr Kng Chldr Ctr
950 El Pueblo Ave, Pittsburg (94565-4116)
PHONE.................................925 473-4380
EMP: 50
SALES (est): 354.7K **Privately Held**
WEB: www.statepreschool.com
SIC: 8351 Child Day Care Services

(P-18035)
STEP ONE NURSERY SCHOOL
499 Spruce St, Berkeley (94708-1242)
PHONE.................................510 527-9021
Sue Britson, *Director*
Rakhee Sharma, *Bd of Directors*
Jane Lin, *Teacher*
Raquel McKinney, *Teacher*
Eric Peterson, *Co-Director*
EMP: 45 **EST:** 1981
SQ FT: 6,000
SALES (est): 2MM **Privately Held**
WEB: www.steponeschool.org
SIC: 8351 8211 Nursery school; kindergarten

(P-18036)
STRATFORD SCHOOL INC
1999 S Bascom Ave Ste 400, Campbell (95008-2219)
PHONE.................................408 973-7320
Matthew Wulfstat, *CEO*
Saadiya Jamil, *Office Admin*
Pooja Joshi, *Business Anlyst*
Janet Chung, *Technician*
Vanessa Holcomb, *Recruiter*
EMP: 81 **EST:** 2012
SALES (est): 27.7MM **Privately Held**
WEB: www.stratfordschools.com
SIC: 8351 Preschool center

(P-18037)
STRATFORD SCHOOL INC (PA)
870 N California Ave, Palo Alto (94303-3631)
PHONE.................................650 493-1151
Matthew Wulfstat, *CEO*
Joseph Wagner, *President*
Kathleen Hawkins, *Administration*
Delores Williamson, *Administration*
Bea Bacaltos, *Teacher*
EMP: 150 **EST:** 1999
SALES (est): 27.1MM **Privately Held**
WEB: www.stratfordschools.com
SIC: 8351 8211 Preschool center; private elementary school

(P-18038)
TEHIYAH DAY SCHOOL INC
6402 Claremont Ave, Richmond (94805-2041)
PHONE.................................510 233-4405
Steve Tbak, *Director*
Amy Friedman, *Principal*
Elena Givental, *Principal*
Elise Prowse, *Principal*
Joan Ruben, *Principal*
EMP: 73 **EST:** 1979
SALES (est): 11.9K **Privately Held**
WEB: www.tehiyah.org
SIC: 8351 8211 Preschool center; private elementary school

(P-18039)
TRACY UNIFIED SCHOOL DISTRICT
Also Called: Willow Cmty Day School
2525 N Tracy Blvd, Tracy (95376-1768)
PHONE.................................209 830-6054
Joan Check, *Branch Mgr*
Soledad Rodriguez, *Clerk*
EMP: 37
SALES (corp-wide): 200.4MM **Privately Held**
WEB: www.tracy.k12.ca.us
SIC: 8211 8351 Public elementary & secondary schools; group day care center
PA: Tracy Unified School District
1875 W Lowell Ave
Tracy CA 95376
209 830-3200

(P-18040)
TURLOCK CHRISTIAN SCHOOL (PA)
1619 E Monte Vista Ave, Turlock (95382-9184)
P.O. Box 1540 (95381-1540)
PHONE.................................209 632-2337
Karen Winters, *Superintendent*
Dave Schnurstein, *Principal*
Hannah Ewing, *Teacher*
Merri Strand, *Teacher*
Janna Fisher, *Education*
EMP: 80 **EST:** 1979
SALES: 5.8MM **Privately Held**
WEB: www.turlockchristian.com
SIC: 8211 8351 Private elementary & secondary schools; preschool center

(P-18041)
TWIN LAKES BAPTIST CHURCH
Also Called: Children's Enrichment Center
2701 Cabrillo College Dr, Aptos (95003-3199)
PHONE.................................831 465-3302
Suzanne Borreson, *Director*
EMP: 51
SALES (corp-wide): 12.4MM **Privately Held**
WEB: www.tlc.org
SIC: 8661 8351 Baptist Church; preschool center
PA: Twin Lakes Baptist Church
2701 Cabrillo College Dr
Aptos CA 95003
831 465-3300

(P-18042)
VALLEJO CITY UNIFIED SCHL DST
Also Called: Community Edcatn Child Care Ct
1155 Capitol St, Vallejo (94590-6303)
PHONE.................................707 556-8694
John Hillmon, *Branch Mgr*
EMP: 55
SALES (corp-wide): 186.8MM **Privately Held**
WEB: www.vcusd-ca.schoolloop.com
SIC: 8211 8351 Public elementary & secondary schools; child day care services
PA: Vallejo City Unified School District
665 Walnut Ave
Vallejo CA 94592
707 556-8921

(P-18043)
VALLEY MONTESSORI SCHOOL
Also Called: TRY VALLEY MONTESSORI SCHOOL
1273 N Livermore Ave, Livermore (94551-1707)
PHONE.................................925 455-8021
Ann Clark, *Headmaster*
Ann King, *Exec Dir*
Lauren Bullock, *Admin Sec*
Dee Ferro, *Admin Sec*
Kendra Williams, *Admin Sec*
EMP: 80 **EST:** 1976
SALES (est): 7.1MM **Privately Held**
WEB: www.valleymontessorischool.com
SIC: 8211 8351 Private elementary & secondary schools; private elementary school; Montessori child development center

(P-18044)
WALDORF SCHOOL OF MENDOCINO
Also Called: WALDORF SCHOOL OF MENDOCINO CO
6280 3rd St, Calpella (95418)
P.O. Box 349 (95418-0349)
PHONE.................................707 485-8719
Spring Senercha, *Administration*
Kate Stornetta, *President*
David Fissell, *Treasurer*
Kimball Dodge, *Admin Sec*
Star Gilley, *Administration*
EMP: 36 **EST:** 1976
SQ FT: 2,500
SALES: 978.8K **Privately Held**
WEB: www.mendocinowaldorf.org
SIC: 8211 8351 Private combined elementary & secondary school; preschool center

(P-18045)
WASHINGTON UNIFIED SCHOOL DST
Also Called: Westfield Vlg Elementary Schl
508 Poplar Ave, West Sacramento (95691-2555)
PHONE.................................916 375-7720
Crista Koch, *Principal*
Liz Burkholder, *Teacher*
Maria Camargo, *Teacher*
Vanessa Raeder, *Teacher*
EMP: 39
SALES (corp-wide): 120.1MM **Privately Held**
WEB: www.wusd.k12.ca.us
SIC: 8211 8351 Public elementary school; preschool center
PA: Washington Unified School District
930 Westacre Rd
West Sacramento CA 95691
916 375-7600

(P-18046)
WEST PRTAL CTR FOR AFTER SCHL (PA)
1560 Noriega St Ste 206, San Francisco (94122-4462)
PHONE.................................415 753-1113
Arthur Haubenstock, *President*
Simon Lee, *Exec Dir*
EMP: 60 **EST:** 1982
SALES (est): 1.3MM **Privately Held**
WEB: www.westportalschool.com
SIC: 8351 Child day care services

(P-18047)
WU YEE CHILDRENS SERVICES (PA)
827 Broadway, San Francisco (94133-4218)
PHONE.................................415 230-7504
Monica Walters, *CEO*
Shelley Ehret, *Regional Mgr*
Fion Chan, *Office Admin*
Merced Rocha, *Teacher*
Lien Tu, *Teacher*
EMP: 40 **EST:** 1996
SQ FT: 4,000
SALES: 38.1MM **Privately Held**
WEB: www.wuyee.org
SIC: 8351 Group day care center

8351 - Child Day Care Svcs County (P-18048)

(P-18048)
YOLO CO OFFICE OF EDUCATION (PA)
Also Called: YOLO COUNTY SUPERINTENDENT OF
1280 Santa Anita Ct # 10, Woodland (95776-6127)
PHONE.................................530 668-6700
Jeffey Ortiz, *Superintendent*
Jorge Ayala, *Superintendent*
Jorge O Ayala Ed, *Superintendent*
EMP: 45 **EST:** 1852
SALES (est): 45.1MM **Privately Held**
SIC: 8211 8351 Specialty education; head start center, except in conjunction with school

8361 Residential Care

(P-18049)
ADVENT GROUP MINISTRIES INC
90 Great Oaks Blvd # 108, San Jose (95119-1314)
PHONE.................................408 281-0708
Jeff Davis, *Ch of Bd*
Mark Miller, *Exec Dir*
EMP: 63 **EST:** 1985
SQ FT: 4,400
SALES (est): 3.5MM **Privately Held**
WEB: www.adventgm.org
SIC: 8361 Children's home

(P-18050)
AEGIS ASSSTED LIVING PRPTS LLC
Also Called: Aegis of Fremont
3850 Walnut Ave 228, Fremont (94538-2263)
PHONE.................................510 739-1515
Dave Peper, *Exec Dir*
Amita David, *Office Mgr*
Koen Kegelaers, *Food Svc Dir*
Barb Wilson, *Nurse*
Shashi Madahar, *Nursing Dir*
EMP: 125
SALES (corp-wide): 137.2MM **Privately Held**
WEB: www.aegisliving.com
SIC: 8361 Home for the aged
HQ: Aegis Assisted Living Properties, Llc
220 Concourse Blvd
Santa Rosa CA 95403
707 535-3200

(P-18051)
AEGIS OF CARMICHAEL
4050 Walnut Ave, Carmichael (95608-1600)
PHONE.................................916 972-1313
Dwane Clark, *President*
Jerry Myer, *COO*
Angie Snyder, *Chief Mktg Ofcr*
Sandra Preyale, *Officer*
Amy Nelson, *Vice Pres*
EMP: 48 **EST:** 1999
SALES (est): 5.3MM **Privately Held**
WEB: www.aegisliving.com
SIC: 8361 Home for the aged

(P-18052)
AEGIS SENIOR COMMUNITIES LLC
Also Called: Aegis of Moraga
950 Country Club Dr, Moraga (94556-1922)
PHONE.................................925 377-7900
Candice Moses, *General Mgr*
Candace Moses, *General Mgr*
Molly Gleason-Kodama, *Marketing Staff*
Gil Chavez, *Food Svc Dir*
Blanca Melchor, *Nursing Dir*
EMP: 53
SALES (corp-wide): 137.2MM **Privately Held**
WEB: www.aegisliving.com
SIC: 8361 Residential care
PA: Senior Aegis Communities Llc
415 118th Ave Se
Bellevue WA 98005
866 688-5829

(P-18053)
AEGIS SENIOR COMMUNITIES LLC
Also Called: Aegis of NAPA
2100 Redwood Rd, NAPA (94558-3279)
PHONE.................................707 927-3981
Dwayne Clark, *Mng Member*
William Gallaher,
Jerry Meyer,
EMP: 39 **EST:** 2003
SALES (est): 4.2MM **Privately Held**
WEB: www.aegisliving.com
SIC: 8361 Home for the aged

(P-18054)
AEGIS SENIOR COMMUNITIES LLC
Also Called: Aegis Assisted Living
4050 Walnut Ave, Carmichael (95608-1600)
PHONE.................................916 972-1313
Terry Ervin, *Branch Mgr*
Angie Snyder, *Chief Mktg Ofcr*
Sandra Preyale, *Officer*
EMP: 53
SALES (corp-wide): 137.2MM **Privately Held**
WEB: www.aegisliving.com
SIC: 8361 Residential care
PA: Senior Aegis Communities Llc
415 118th Ave Se
Bellevue WA 98005
866 688-5829

(P-18055)
ALTCARE WILLOW CREEK INC (PA)
Also Called: Willow Creek Alzheimer's
22424 Charlene Way, Castro Valley (94546-7102)
PHONE.................................510 527-7282
Terry Carson, *President*
Robert Smith, *Treasurer*
EMP: 40 **EST:** 2006 **Privately Held**
WEB: www.the-creeks.com
SIC: 8361 7389 Home for the aged;

(P-18056)
AMADOR RESIDENTIAL CARE INC
155 Placer Dr, Jackson (95642-2158)
PHONE.................................209 223-4444
Donna Kersh, *General Mgr*
Ron Regan, *Treasurer*
Jerry Jones, *Director*
William Spivey, *Director*
EMP: 36 **EST:** 1983
SALES (est): 4.7MM **Privately Held**
WEB: www.assistcare.com
SIC: 8361 Home for the aged

(P-18057)
ARDEN WOOD INC
445 Wawona St, San Francisco (94116-3058)
PHONE.................................415 681-5500
Ed Sage, *Exec Dir*
Edward Sage, *Exec Dir*
Amy Sparkman, *Corp Comm Staff*
Jocelyne Jam, *Mktg Coord*
Philip Serrano, *Facilities Dir*
EMP: 80 **EST:** 1930
SQ FT: 50,000
SALES (est): 10.1MM **Privately Held**
WEB: www.ardenwood.org
SIC: 8249 8361 Medical training services; residential care

(P-18058)
ARH RECOVERY HOMES INC (PA)
Also Called: House On The Hill
9505 Malech Dr, San Jose (95138-2002)
P.O. Box 21826 (95151-1826)
PHONE.................................408 281-6570
Debby Miranda, *Exec Dir*
Jeff Macredes, *Exec Dir*
Debbie Miranda, *Exec Dir*
EMP: 51 **EST:** 1965
SALES (est): 7.3MM **Privately Held**
SIC: 8361 Rehabilitation center, residential: health care incidental

(P-18059)
ATKINSON YOUTH SERVICES INC
3600 Fair Oaks Blvd, Sacramento (95864-7204)
PHONE.................................916 977-3790
Johann Rubia-Miller, *Principal*
EMP: 36 **Privately Held**
WEB: www.atkinsonfamilyservices.org
SIC: 8361 Group foster home
PA: Atkinson Youth Services Incorporated
1906 El Camino Ave
Sacramento CA 95815

(P-18060)
AVALON AT BRUSH CREEK LLC
4225 Wayvern Dr, Santa Rosa (95409-7108)
PHONE.................................707 538-2590
EMP: 45
SQ FT: 52,150
SALES (est): 2.2MM
SALES (corp-wide): 23.3MM **Privately Held**
SIC: 8361 Residential Care Services
PA: Senior Vintage Housing Llc
23 Corporate Plaza Dr # 190
Newport Beach CA 92660
949 719-4080

(P-18061)
BAYVIEW VILLA
777 Bay View Dr, San Carlos (94070-1667)
PHONE.................................650 596-3489
Violet Loncar, *Owner*
Vivian Fradiacomo, *Director*
EMP: 36 **EST:** 2000
SALES (est): 2.4MM **Privately Held**
WEB: www.bayviewvillaliving.com
SIC: 8361 Home for the aged

(P-18062)
BEYOND EMANCIPATION
675 Hegenberger Rd # 100, Oakland (94621-1973)
PHONE.................................510 667-7694
Jennifer Ling, *Principal*
Maria Luisa Jimenez-Morales, *Principal*
Katherine Westfall, *Principal*
Kate Durham, *Exec Dir*
Vanetta Johnson, *Exec Dir*
EMP: 40 **EST:** 1995
SALES (est): 3.9MM **Privately Held**
WEB: www.beyondemancipation.org
SIC: 8361 Group foster home

(P-18063)
BIDWELL SENIOR CARE SVCS INC
966 Kovak Ct, Chico (95973-0927)
PHONE.................................530 899-3585
Lynette Dorenzo, *President*
Cliff Keene, *Exec Dir*
EMP: 76 **EST:** 2002
SQ FT: 16,000
SALES (est): 4.9MM **Privately Held**
WEB: www.countryvillagecare.com
SIC: 8361 Home for the aged

(P-18064)
BURLINGAME SENIOR CARE LLC
Also Called: Burlingame Skilled Nursing
1100 Trousdale Dr, Burlingame (94010-3207)
PHONE.................................650 692-3758
Marcus Weenig, *CFO*
EMP: 35 **EST:** 2001
SALES (est): 6.4MM **Privately Held**
WEB: www.burlingameseniorhome.com
SIC: 8361 Home for the aged

(P-18065)
CANYON HOUSE RESTHOMES INC (PA)
Also Called: Crescent Villa Care Home
147 Crescent Ave, Sunnyvale (94087-2723)
P.O. Box 640, Menlo Park (94026-0640)
PHONE.................................408 730-4004
Eva Aber, *President*
Steven Aber, *Vice Pres*
EMP: 40 **EST:** 1987
SQ FT: 11,120

SALES (est): 3MM **Privately Held**
SIC: 8361 Residential care

(P-18066)
CARLTON SENIOR LIVING INC
380 Branham Ln Ofc Ofc, San Jose (95136-4302)
PHONE.................................408 972-1400
Mandi Farrell, *Director*
EMP: 96
SALES (corp-wide): 33.6MM **Privately Held**
WEB: www.carltonseniorliving.com
SIC: 8361 Residential care
PA: Senior Carlton Living Inc
4071 Port Chicago Hwy # 130
Concord CA 94520
925 338-2434

(P-18067)
CARLTON SENIOR LIVING INC
Also Called: Senior Asssted Lving Cmnty Cht
175 Cleaveland Rd, Pleasant Hill (94523-3875)
PHONE.................................925 935-1001
Jeffrey Dillon, *Manager*
EMP: 96
SALES (corp-wide): 33.6MM **Privately Held**
WEB: www.carltonseniorliving.com
SIC: 8361 Residential care
PA: Senior Carlton Living Inc
4071 Port Chicago Hwy # 130
Concord CA 94520
925 338-2434

(P-18068)
CARLTON SENIOR LIVING INC
1075 Fulton Ave, Sacramento (95825-4275)
PHONE.................................916 971-4800
Timothy Macdonald, *Branch Mgr*
EMP: 96
SALES (corp-wide): 33.6MM **Privately Held**
WEB: www.carltonseniorliving.com
SIC: 8361 8052 8051 Residential care; intermediate care facilities; skilled nursing care facilities
PA: Senior Carlton Living Inc
4071 Port Chicago Hwy # 130
Concord CA 94520
925 338-2434

(P-18069)
CARMICHAEL OAKS JOINT VENTURE
8350 Fair Oaks Blvd Apt 3, Carmichael (95608-1950)
PHONE.................................916 944-1588
Mike Korin, *Exec Dir*
EMP: 59 **EST:** 1990
SQ FT: 15,000
SALES (est): 1.3MM **Privately Held**
SIC: 8361 Home for the aged

(P-18070)
CARREYS CARE CENTER INC
Also Called: Graves Residential Center
2554 S Barton Ave, Fresno (93725-1502)
PHONE.................................559 444-0151
Lena Graves, *Branch Mgr*
EMP: 63
SALES (corp-wide): 348.2K **Privately Held**
SIC: 8361 7389 Halfway group home, persons with social or personal problems;
PA: Carrey's Care Center, Inc.
5741 E Jensen Ave
Fresno CA

(P-18071)
CASA ALLEGRA COMMUNITY SVCS
35 Mitchell Blvd Ste 11, San Rafael (94903-2065)
PHONE.................................415 499-1116
Chris Bonfiglio, *Administration*
EMP: 43 **EST:** 1975
SQ FT: 500
SALES (est): 709.5K **Privately Held**
WEB: www.casaallegra.org
SIC: 8361 Home for the mentally handicapped

PRODUCTS & SERVICES SECTION
8361 - Residential Care County (P-18093)

(P-18072)
CASA DEL RIOS HBILITATION SVCS
Also Called: Solari Ranch
5541 Solari Ranch Rd, Stockton (95215-9318)
PHONE.....................209 931-1027
Janet Rios, *Owner*
EMP: 39 EST: 1995
SALES (est): 1.6MM **Privately Held**
SIC: 8361 Rehabilitation center, residential: health care incidental

(P-18073)
CENTRAL CAL NIKKEI FOUNDATION
Also Called: VINTAGE GARDENS
540 S Peach Ave, Fresno (93727-3957)
PHONE.....................559 237-4006
Melvin K Renge, *President*
Louis Gebbia, *Exec Dir*
Gale Nakai, *Director*
EMP: 52 EST: 1989
SALES: 3.1MM **Privately Held**
WEB: www.ccnf.org
SIC: 8361 Home for the aged

(P-18074)
CHAMBERLAINS CHILDREN CTR INC
1850 Cienega Rd, Hollister (95023-5516)
P.O. Box 1269 (95024-1269)
PHONE.....................831 636-2121
Robert Freiri, *Exec Dir*
Sarah Garvin, *Office Mgr*
Cristian Sharboneau, *Case Mgr*
Renee Rocha, *Manager*
Brandy Spindel, *Manager*
EMP: 60 EST: 1965
SALES (est): 3.8MM **Privately Held**
WEB: www.chamberlainsyouth.org
SIC: 8361 Residential care for children

(P-18075)
CHILDRENS HOME OF STOCKTON
430 N Pilgrim St, Stockton (95205-4428)
PHONE.....................209 466-0853
Joelle Gomez, *CEO*
Steve Parsons, *Finance*
Laura Pedraza, *Director*
Azzie Smith, *Manager*
EMP: 140 EST: 1882
SQ FT: 10,000
SALES: 10.2MM **Privately Held**
WEB: www.chstockton.org
SIC: 8211 8361 Private combined elementary & secondary school; residential care for children

(P-18076)
CHRISTIAN CHURCH HOMES
Also Called: El-Bethel Terrace
1099 Fillmore St Apt 6h, San Francisco (94115-4796)
PHONE.....................415 814-2670
Babeth Avant, *Manager*
Sidney Stone, *Director*
Siyuan Zhou, *Manager*
EMP: 222
SALES (corp-wide): 11.4MM **Privately Held**
WEB: www.cchnc.org
SIC: 8361 Home for the aged
PA: Christian Church Homes
303 Hegenberger Rd # 201
Oakland CA 94621
510 632-6712

(P-18077)
CHURCH OF VLY RTRMENT HMES INC
Also Called: Valley Village
390 N Winchester Blvd, Santa Clara (95050-6563)
PHONE.....................408 241-7750
Martha Ayala, *President*
Irving Herrera, *Human Res Mgr*
Geno Gacanovic, *Maint Spvr*
EMP: 52 EST: 1961
SALES (est): 5.7MM **Privately Held**
WEB: www.valleyvillageretirement.com
SIC: 8361 Home for the aged

(P-18078)
CLIFF VIEW TERRACE INC
Also Called: Marin Terrace
297 Miller Ave, Mill Valley (94941-2832)
PHONE.....................415 388-9526
Araceli Pareja, *Director*
EMP: 84
SQ FT: 2,534
SALES (corp-wide): 11.7MM **Privately Held**
WEB: www.cliffviewterracesb.com
SIC: 8361 Home for the aged
PA: Cliff View Terrace, Inc.
1020 Cliff Dr
Santa Barbara CA 93109
805 963-7556

(P-18079)
COMMUNITY HOUSING INC
Also Called: Lytton Garden II
437 Webster St, Palo Alto (94301-1242)
PHONE.....................650 328-3300
Gery Yearout, *President*
Jonathan Casey, *Vice Pres*
EMP: 52 EST: 1970
SALES (est): 7.3MM **Privately Held**
WEB: www.community-housing.com
SIC: 8361 Home for the aged

(P-18080)
CONGRGTNAL CH RETIREMENT CMNTY
Also Called: Auburn Ravine Terrace
750 Auburn Ravine Rd, Auburn (95603-3820)
PHONE.....................530 823-6131
Deborah Stouff, *Admin Sec*
Kasey Ridenour, *Marketing Staff*
Mia Peterson, *Nursing Dir*
EMP: 86 EST: 1975
SALES (est): 9.3MM **Privately Held**
WEB: www.auburnravineterrace.org
SIC: 8361 Home for the aged

(P-18081)
CONTINING LF CMMNTIES PLSNTON
Also Called: Stoneridge Creek Pleasanton
3300 Stoneridge Creek Way, Pleasanton (94588-2200)
PHONE.....................925 227-6800
Francis X Rodgers, *Exec Dir*
Troy Bourne, *Vice Pres*
Alicia Pinn, *Human Res Dir*
David Tsan, *Opers Staff*
Susan Filice, *Manager*
EMP: 51 EST: 2007 **Privately Held**
WEB: www.stoneridgecreek.com
SIC: 8361 Home for the aged

(P-18082)
COUNTRY HOUSE
Also Called: Country House & Commons
966 Kovak Ct, Chico (95973-0927)
PHONE.....................530 342-7002
Lynette N Lorenzo, *Owner*
Renee Van Eck, *Hlthcr Dir*
EMP: 35 EST: 1985
SQ FT: 10,000
SALES (est): 2.6MM **Privately Held**
WEB: www.countryvillagecare.com
SIC: 8361 Home for the aged

(P-18083)
COUNTY OF STANISLAUS
Stanislaus Cnty Probation Dept
2215 Blue Gum Ave, Modesto (95358-1052)
PHONE.....................209 525-5400
Linda Duffy, *Director*
Melody Pickford, *Executive Asst*
Brian Krepela, *Auditor*
Rebecca Palacio, *Clerk*
EMP: 41
SALES (corp-wide): 1.2B **Privately Held**
WEB: www.stancounty.com
SIC: 8361 Juvenile correctional facilities
PA: County Of Stanislaus
1010 10th St Ste 5100
Modesto CA 95354
209 525-6398

(P-18084)
COUNTY OF YUBA
Also Called: Yuba County Juvenile Hall
1023 14th St, Marysville (95901-4115)
PHONE.....................530 741-6371
Theresa Dove Weber, *Manager*
Frank Sorgea, *Principal*
EMP: 55
SQ FT: 2,293
SALES (corp-wide): 212MM **Privately Held**
WEB: www.co.yuba.ca.us
SIC: 8361 9111 Juvenile correctional facilities; county supervisors' & executives' offices
PA: County Of Yuba
915 8th St Ste 109
Marysville CA 95901
530 749-7575

(P-18085)
COURTYARD
1240 Williams Way Apt 4, Yuba City (95991-2438)
PHONE.....................530 790-3050
Monica Avalos, *Director*
Gricelda Oregel, *Director*
EMP: 75 EST: 2001
SALES (est): 72K
SALES (corp-wide): 26.9MM **Privately Held**
WEB: www.adventisthealth.org
SIC: 8361 Residential care
PA: Freemont Rideout Health Group
989 Plumas St
Yuba City CA 95991
530 751-4010

(P-18086)
COVELL GARDENS
1111 Alvarado Ave Ofc, Davis (95616-5933)
PHONE.....................530 756-0700
Eric Bresseler, *Business Mgr*
Elmer Mc Nece, *Partner*
Ashlee Sloan, *Director*
EMP: 60 EST: 1987
SALES (est): 5.7MM **Privately Held**
WEB: www.atriaseniorliving.com
SIC: 8361 Home for the aged

(P-18087)
COVIA COMMUNITIES
Also Called: St Paul's Towers
100 Bay Pl Ofc, Oakland (94610-4422)
PHONE.....................510 835-4700
Christopher lechien, *Exec Dir*
Sheba Jenness, *Human Res Dir*
Betsy Baron, *Marketing Staff*
Maria Aina, *Nursing Dir*
EMP: 108
SALES (corp-wide): 133.2MM **Privately Held**
WEB: www.covia.org
SIC: 8361 8052 8051 Home for the aged; intermediate care facilities; skilled nursing care facilities
PA: Covia Communities
2185 N Calif Blvd Ste 215
Walnut Creek CA 94596
925 956-7400

(P-18088)
COVIA COMMUNITIES
Also Called: Los Gatos Meadows
110 Wood Rd Ofc, Los Gatos (95030-6799)
PHONE.....................408 354-0211
Tina Heany, *Exec Dir*
Susan Melin, *Social Dir*
Cheryl Wilson, *Office Mgr*
Connie Yearby-Smith, *Office Mgr*
Rosa Torres, *Human Res Dir*
EMP: 108
SALES (corp-wide): 133.2MM **Privately Held**
WEB: www.covia.org
SIC: 8361 Home for the aged
PA: Covia Communities
2185 N Calif Blvd Ste 215
Walnut Creek CA 94596
925 956-7400

(P-18089)
COVIA COMMUNITIES
Also Called: Spring Lake Village
5555 Montgomery Dr, Santa Rosa (95409-8846)
P.O. Box 1105, Boyes Hot Springs (95416-1105)
PHONE.....................707 538-8400
Sharon York, *Exec Dir*
Sharon D York, *Exec Dir*
Casey O 'neill, *Program Mgr*
Melissa Carr, *Administration*
Maria Buquid,
EMP: 108
SALES (corp-wide): 133.2MM **Privately Held**
WEB: www.covia.org
SIC: 8361 6531 8052 8051 Home for the aged; real estate managers; intermediate care facilities; skilled nursing care facilities
PA: Covia Communities
2185 N Calif Blvd Ste 215
Walnut Creek CA 94596
925 956-7400

(P-18090)
COVIA COMMUNITIES
Also Called: San Francisco Towers
1661 Pine St Apt 911, San Francisco (94109-0410)
PHONE.....................415 776-0500
Donna Teandler, *Branch Mgr*
Tracy Powell, *Vice Pres*
Juan Munoz-Arreola, *Maintence Staff*
Lawrence Brooks, *Food Svc Dir*
Karen Coppock, *Program Dir*
EMP: 108
SALES (corp-wide): 133.2MM **Privately Held**
WEB: www.covia.org
SIC: 8361 8052 8051 Home for the aged; intermediate care facilities; skilled nursing care facilities
PA: Covia Communities
2185 N Calif Blvd Ste 215
Walnut Creek CA 94596
925 956-7400

(P-18091)
CREATIVE ALTERNATIVES
2855 Geer Rd Ste A, Turlock (95382-1133)
PHONE.....................209 668-9361
Stephanie Biddle, *CEO*
EMP: 220 EST: 1976
SQ FT: 40,000
SALES: 21.5MM **Privately Held**
WEB: www.creative-alternatives.org
SIC: 8361 8211 8322 Children's home; private special education school; child related social services

(P-18092)
CREATIVE LIVING OPTIONS INC
2945 Ramco St Ste 120, West Sacramento (95691-5998)
PHONE.....................916 372-2102
Joan Schmidt, *CEO*
Ron Mainini, *Associate Dir*
Amber Cohen, *Admin Asst*
Mary Anne Delaney, *Finance Dir*
EMP: 115 EST: 2001
SALES: 3.3MM **Privately Held**
WEB: www.creativelivingoptions.com
SIC: 8361 Home for the physically handicapped

(P-18093)
CRESTWOOD BEHAVIORAL HLTH INC
Also Called: 1107 San Jose Mhrc
1425 Fruitdale Ave, San Jose (95128-3234)
PHONE.....................408 275-1067
Gail McDonald, *Administration*
John Suggs, *Vice Pres*
EMP: 148
SALES (corp-wide): 238MM **Privately Held**
WEB: www.crestwoodbehavioralhealth.com
SIC: 8361 8063 7389 8059 Halfway group home, persons with social or personal problems; psychiatric hospitals; personal service agents, brokers & bureaus; nursing home, except skilled & intermediate care facility

---

(PA)=Parent Co (HQ)=Headquarters (DH)=Div Headquarters
✿ = New Business established in last 2 years

8361 - Residential Care County (P-18094)

PA: Crestwood Behavioral Health, Inc.
520 Capitol Mall Ste 800
Sacramento CA 95814
510 651-1244

(P-18094)
CRESTWOOD BEHAVIORAL HLTH INC
Also Called: 1122 Redding IMD
3062 Churn Creek Rd, Redding (96002-2124)
PHONE.....................530 221-0976
Jacob Stevens, *Administration*
Nicoletta Groff, *Manager*
EMP: 104
SQ FT: 15,000
SALES (corp-wide): 238MM **Privately Held**
WEB: www.crestwoodbehavioralhealth.com
SIC: 8361 8051 Halfway group home, persons with social or personal problems; skilled nursing care facilities
PA: Crestwood Behavioral Health, Inc.
520 Capitol Mall Ste 800
Sacramento CA 95814
510 651-1244

(P-18095)
CRESTWOOD BEHAVIORAL HLTH INC
Also Called: 1134 Alameda Snf/STP
4303 Stevenson Blvd, Fremont (94538-2645)
PHONE.....................510 651-1244
Leeann Labrie, *Administration*
EMP: 257
SQ FT: 33,790
SALES (corp-wide): 238MM **Privately Held**
WEB: www.crestwoodbehavioralhealth.com
SIC: 8361 8069 8051 Halfway group home, persons with social or personal problems; specialty hospitals, except psychiatric; skilled nursing care facilities
PA: Crestwood Behavioral Health, Inc.
520 Capitol Mall Ste 800
Sacramento CA 95814
510 651-1244

(P-18096)
CRESTWOOD BEHAVIORAL HLTH INC
Also Called: 1120 Fremont Snf
2171 Mowry Ave, Fremont (94538-1717)
PHONE.....................510 793-8383
Kulbinder Hans, *Administration*
EMP: 142
SQ FT: 10,000
SALES (corp-wide): 238MM **Privately Held**
WEB: www.crestwoodbehavioralhealth.com
SIC: 8361 8063 8052 8069 Halfway group home, persons with social or personal problems; psychiatric hospitals; intermediate care facilities; specialty hospitals, except psychiatric
PA: Crestwood Behavioral Health, Inc.
520 Capitol Mall Ste 800
Sacramento CA 95814
510 651-1244

(P-18097)
DAVIS GUEST HOME INC
1878 E Hatch Rd, Modesto (95351-5096)
PHONE.....................209 538-1496
Lonny Davis, *Owner*
Misty Speegle, *Administration*
Heather Closky, *CIO*
EMP: 45 **EST:** 1967
SQ FT: 9,000
SALES (est): 5.4MM **Privately Held**
WEB: www.davisguesthome.com
SIC: 8361 8322 Home for the aged; individual & family services

(P-18098)
DELANCEY STREET FOUNDATION (PA)
Also Called: DELANCEY STREET COACH SERVICE
600 The Embarcadero, San Francisco (94107-2116)
PHONE.....................415 957-9800
Mimi Silbert, *President*
Jerry Raymond, *Treasurer*
Jerri Raymond, *Accounting Mgr*
James Meany, *Marketing Staff*
Abe Irizarry, *Director*
EMP: 400 **EST:** 1971
SQ FT: 325,000
SALES: 10.4MM **Privately Held**
WEB: www.delanceystreetfoundation.org
SIC: 8361 5199 8322 4212 Rehabilitation center, residential: health care incidental; advertising specialties; individual & family services; moving services; eating places; caterers

(P-18099)
DOMINICAN HOSPITAL FOUNDATION
Also Called: Dominican Rehab Services
610 Frederick St, Santa Cruz (95062-2203)
PHONE.....................831 457-7057
Debbie Hite, *Branch Mgr*
EMP: 148 **Privately Held**
WEB: www.supportdominican.org
SIC: 8361 8093 Rehabilitation center, residential: health care incidental; rehabilitation center, outpatient treatment
HQ: Dominican Hospital Foundation
1555 Soquel Dr
Santa Cruz CA 95065
831 462-7700

(P-18100)
DREAMCTCHERS EMPWERMENT NETWRK
Also Called: Rosewood Convalescent Hospital
1911 Oak Park Blvd, Pleasant Hill (94523-4601)
PHONE.....................925 935-6630
Maggie Yousess, *Administration*
EMP: 218
SALES (corp-wide): 2.7MM **Privately Held**
WEB: www.crestwoodbehavioralhealth.com
SIC: 8361 8051 8059 Halfway group home, persons with social or personal problems; skilled nursing care facilities; convalescent home
PA: Dreamcatchers Empowerment Network
7590 Shoreline Dr Ste B
Stockton CA 95219
209 478-5291

(P-18101)
E&S RESIDENTIAL CARE SVCS LLC
Also Called: E & S
6083 N Marks Ave, Fresno (93711-1600)
PHONE.....................559 275-3555
Stephanie Hendricks, *Mng Member*
Eddie Gilbert, *Mng Member*
EMP: 36 **EST:** 1989
SALES (est): 2.8MM **Privately Held**
WEB: www.esrescare.info
SIC: 8361 Residential care for the handicapped

(P-18102)
EDGEWOOD CTR FOR CHLDREN FMLIE (PA)
1801 Vicente St, San Francisco (94116-2923)
PHONE.....................415 681-3211
Lynn Dolce, *CEO*
Julia Timmons, *Partner*
Justine EDM, *Officer*
Justine Underhill, *Officer*
David Ruth, *Vice Pres*
EMP: 224 **EST:** 1850
SQ FT: 100,000
SALES (est): 30.5MM **Privately Held**
WEB: www.edgewood.org
SIC: 8361 8211 8322 8093 Home for the emotionally disturbed; specialty education; child related social services; specialty outpatient clinics

(P-18103)
ELDER CARE ALLIANCE SAN MATEO (HQ)
1301 Marina Vil Pkwy 21 # 210, Alameda (94501)
PHONE.....................510 769-2700
Glen Goddard, *Exec Dir*
Tom Pietrantonio, *Food Svc Dir*
Daphne Kelley, *Nursing Dir*
Kathleen Quinlan, *Director*
EMP: 79 **EST:** 1927
SALES: 4.3MM
SALES (corp-wide): 4.1MM **Privately Held**
WEB: www.eldercarealliance.org
SIC: 8361 8059 8051 Rest home, with health care incidental; convalescent home; skilled nursing care facilities
PA: Elder Care Alliance
1301 Marina Village Pkwy # 210
Alameda CA 94501
510 769-2700

(P-18104)
ELITE FAMILY SYSTEMS
2935 4th St, Ceres (95307-3222)
P.O. Box 490 (95307-0490)
PHONE.....................209 531-2088
Bill Sneed, *President*
Vanita Sneed, *Corp Secy*
EMP: 44
SALES: 2.7MM **Privately Held**
WEB: www.elitefamily.org
SIC: 8361 Residential care

(P-18105)
ESKATON
3421 Palmer Dr, Cameron Park (95682-8200)
PHONE.....................530 672-8900
Orvile Bell, *Branch Mgr*
Carly Amatisto, *Director*
EMP: 171
SQ FT: 23,400
SALES (corp-wide): 148.8MM **Privately Held**
WEB: www.eskaton.org
SIC: 8361 Home for the aged
PA: Eskaton
5105 Manzanita Ave Ste D
Carmichael CA 95608
916 334-0296

(P-18106)
ESKATON
11390 Coloma Rd Ofc, Gold River (95670-6324)
PHONE.....................916 852-7900
Tonae Hasik, *Manager*
Jocelyn Perena, *Office Mgr*
David Van Reusen, *Administration*
Edith Oster, *Nursing Dir*
Paloma Palomares, *Director*
EMP: 171
SALES (corp-wide): 148.8MM **Privately Held**
WEB: www.eskaton.org
SIC: 8361 Home for the aged
PA: Eskaton
5105 Manzanita Ave Ste D
Carmichael CA 95608
916 334-0296

(P-18107)
ESKATON PROPERTIES INC
Also Called: President James Monroe Manor
3225 Freeport Blvd Ofc, Sacramento (95818-4200)
PHONE.....................916 441-1015
Joe Dunham, *President*
EMP: 93 **Privately Held**
WEB: www.eskaton.org
SIC: 8361 Home for the aged
PA: Eskaton Properties Incorporated
5105 Manzanita Ave Ste A
Carmichael CA 95608

(P-18108)
ESKATON PROPERTIES INC
Eskaton Manzanita Manor
5318 Manzanita Ave, Carmichael (95608-0512)
PHONE.....................916 331-8513
Denie Crum, *Administration*
EMP: 93 **Privately Held**
WEB: www.eskaton.org
SIC: 8361 Home for the aged
PA: Eskaton Properties Incorporated
5105 Manzanita Ave Ste A
Carmichael CA 95608

(P-18109)
ESKATON PROPERTIES INC
3421 Palmer Dr, Cameron Park (95682-8200)
PHONE.....................530 677-5066
EMP: 93 **Privately Held**
WEB: www.eskaton.org
SIC: 8361 Home for the aged
PA: Eskaton Properties Incorporated
5105 Manzanita Ave Ste A
Carmichael CA 95608

(P-18110)
ESKATON PROPERTIES INC
Also Called: Eskaton Village Roseville
1650 Eskaton Loop, Roseville (95747-5180)
PHONE.....................916 334-0810
Vicki Cross, *Manager*
Michelle Edmondson, *Food Svc Dir*
Tricia Diaz, *Nursing Dir*
Daisy Absalon,
Savan Rieves, *Director*
EMP: 93 **Privately Held**
WEB: www.eskaton.org
SIC: 8361 Home for the aged
PA: Eskaton Properties Incorporated
5105 Manzanita Ave Ste A
Carmichael CA 95608

(P-18111)
ESKATON PROPERTIES INC
Also Called: Homestead of Fair Oaks
11300 Fair Oaks Blvd, Fair Oaks (95628-5141)
PHONE.....................916 965-4663
Tom Coffey, *Manager*
Danijela Stroud, *Director*
EMP: 93 **Privately Held**
WEB: www.eskaton.org
SIC: 8361 Home for the aged
PA: Eskaton Properties Incorporated
5105 Manzanita Ave Ste A
Carmichael CA 95608

(P-18112)
ESKATON PROPERTIES INC
Also Called: Eskaton Center of Greenhaven
455 Florin Rd, Sacramento (95831-2024)
PHONE.....................916 393-2550
Heather Craig, *Manager*
Anabel Sausman, *Records Dir*
Joelle Courage, *Social Dir*
Sylvia Chu, *Exec Dir*
Vicky Cross, *Exec Dir*
EMP: 93 **Privately Held**
WEB: www.eskaton.org
SIC: 8361 Home for the aged
PA: Eskaton Properties Incorporated
5105 Manzanita Ave Ste A
Carmichael CA 95608

(P-18113)
ESKATON PROPERTIES INC (PA)
Also Called: 0epi
5105 Manzanita Ave Ste A, Carmichael (95608-0523)
PHONE.....................916 334-0810
Todd Murch, *President*
Sheri Peifer, *Officer*
Betsy Donovan, *Senior VP*
Bill Pace, *Senior VP*
Charles Garcia, *Vice Pres*
▲ **EMP:** 60 **EST:** 1983
SQ FT: 27,000
SALES (est): 107MM **Privately Held**
WEB: www.eskaton.org
SIC: 8361 Home for the aged

(P-18114)
ESKATON PROPERTIES INC
Also Called: Eskaton Village Charmichael
3939 Walnut Ave Unit 399, Carmichael (95608-7333)
PHONE.....................916 974-2000
Betsy Donovan, *Exec Dir*
Cain Robles, *Social Dir*
Pristina Zhang, *Director*
EMP: 93 **Privately Held**
WEB: www.eskaton.org
SIC: 8361 Home for the aged

PRODUCTS & SERVICES SECTION
8361 - Residential Care County (P-18139)

PA: Eskaton Properties Incorporated
5105 Manzanita Ave Ste A
Carmichael CA 95608

(P-18115)
FELLOWSHIP HOMES INC
Also Called: Casa De Modesto
1745 Eldena Way, Modesto (95350-3568)
PHONE.................................209 529-4950
Carolyn Amaral, *Administration*
Curt Willems, *Exec Dir*
Joel Merriam, *Opers Staff*
Neelam Nand, *Director*
EMP: 150 **EST:** 1965
SALES (est): 8.4MM **Privately Held**
WEB: www.casademodesto.org
SIC: 8361 Home for the aged

(P-18116)
FORD STREET PROJECT INC
139 Ford St, Ukiah (95482-4011)
PHONE.................................707 462-1934
Jacque Williams, *President*
EMP: 45 **EST:** 1973
SALES (est): 2MM **Privately Held**
WEB: www.fordstreet.org
SIC: 8361 Rehabilitation center, residential: health care incidental

(P-18117)
FOUNTAINWOOD RESIDENTIAL CARE
8773 Oak Ave, Orangevale (95662-2410)
PHONE.................................916 988-2200
Robert Spince, *President*
EMP: 48 **EST:** 1995
SALES (est): 3MM **Privately Held**
WEB: www.fountainwood.org
SIC: 8361 8059 Home for the aged; convalescent home

(P-18118)
FRESNO HERITAGE PARTNERS
Also Called: Somerford Place
6075 N Marks Ave, Fresno (93711-1600)
PHONE.................................559 446-6226
Sharol Hutchison, *Exec Dir*
Fresno Surgery Center, *General Ptnr*
EMP: 50 **EST:** 1996
SQ FT: 26,166
SALES (est): 10.7K **Privately Held**
WEB: www.summerfieldfresno.com
SIC: 8361 Home for the aged

(P-18119)
GENERATION CLOVIS LLC
Also Called: Carmel Village At Clovis
1650 Shaw Ave, Clovis (93611-4201)
PHONE.................................559 297-4900
Erik Schuck, *Administration*
Linda Pope, *Marketing Staff*
Chris Mendez, *Director*
Brandon Montelongo, *Director*
Penny Patlan, *Director*
EMP: 150 **EST:** 2019
SALES (est): 10.7MM **Privately Held**
WEB: www.carmelvillageatclovis.com
SIC: 8361 Home for the aged

(P-18120)
GOLDEN STATE FAMILY SVCS INC (PA)
Also Called: GOLDEN STATE FOSTER FAMILY AGE
4285 N Valentine Ave, Fresno (93722-4148)
P.O. Box 130, Kingsburg (93631-0130)
PHONE.................................559 241-0955
Micki Prins, *CEO*
Erin McCreery, *CFO*
Alexis Hernandez, *Clerk*
EMP: 35 **EST:** 1997
SQ FT: 1,500
SALES (est): 3.8MM **Privately Held**
WEB: www.goldenstatefamily.org
SIC: 8361 Group foster home

(P-18121)
GOOD NEWS RESCUE MISSION
3100 S Market St, Redding (96001-3532)
PHONE.................................530 241-5754
Jim Dahl, *Pastor*
Ken Hadley, *Controller*
Dave Honey, *Pastor*
Ammon Crawford, *Director*
Honey Storlie, *Director*
EMP: 48 **EST:** 1963
SALES (est): 5.2MM **Privately Held**
WEB: www.gnrm.org
SIC: 8361 Self-help group home

(P-18122)
GOOD SHEPHERD LUTHERAN HM OF W
1335 Mowry Ave, Fremont (94538-1701)
PHONE.................................510 505-1244
Nina Bosley, *Manager*
EMP: 65
SQ FT: 16,000
SALES (corp-wide): 14.3MM **Privately Held**
WEB: www.grauranch.com
SIC: 8361 8399 Residential care for the handicapped; fund raising organization, non-fee basis
PA: Good Shepherd Lutheran Home Of The West
24800 Chrisanta Dr # 250
Mission Viejo CA 92691
559 791-2000

(P-18123)
GOOD SHEPHERD LUTHERAN HM OF W
1696 S Helm Ave, Fresno (93727-5111)
PHONE.................................559 454-8514
Roslyn Ward, *Manager*
EMP: 65
SALES (corp-wide): 14.3MM **Privately Held**
WEB: www.grauranch.com
SIC: 8361 8059 Residential care for the handicapped; home for the mentally retarded, exc. skilled or intermediate
PA: Good Shepherd Lutheran Home Of The West
24800 Chrisanta Dr # 250
Mission Viejo CA 92691
559 791-2000

(P-18124)
GRASS VALLEY LLC
Also Called: Quail Ridge Senior Living
150 Sutton Way Ofc, Grass Valley (95945-4104)
PHONE.................................530 272-1055
Mark E Nicol,
Andrew Transleau, *CFO*
Pari Manouchehri, *Exec Dir*
Lacy Ward,
Terresa Ray, *Senior Mgr*
EMP: 45 **EST:** 1995
SALES (est): 11.4MM **Privately Held**
WEB: www.grassvalley.com
SIC: 8361 Home for the aged

(P-18125)
GREENRIDGE SENIOR CARE
2150 Pyramid Dr, El Sobrante (94803-3220)
PHONE.................................510 758-9600
Linda Joseph, *Director*
EMP: 110
SALES: 7.7MM **Privately Held**
WEB: www.greenridgeseniorcare.com
SIC: 8361 Home for the aged

(P-18126)
HANK FISHER PROPERTIES INC
Also Called: Chateau On Capitol Avenue, The
2701 Capitol Ave, Sacramento (95816-6036)
PHONE.................................916 447-4444
Nancy Fisher, *Branch Mgr*
EMP: 36
SALES (corp-wide): 15.8MM **Privately Held**
WEB: www.hankfisherproperties.com
SIC: 8361 Geriatric residential care
PA: Hank Fisher Properties, Inc.
641 Fulton Ave Ste 200
Sacramento CA 95825
916 485-1441

(P-18127)
HANOT FOUNDATION INC (PA)
14373 E Sargent Rd, Lodi (95240-9748)
P.O. Box 950, Lockeford (95237-0950)
PHONE.................................209 334-6454
Nicholas Curtin, *Exec Dir*
Joseph Bertao, *President*
Donald G Schrader, *Treasurer*
Donald Schrader, *Treasurer*
Mike Rolf, *Vice Pres*
EMP: 45 **EST:** 1973
SQ FT: 12,870
SALES (est): 1.4MM **Privately Held**
WEB: www.hanotfoundation.com
SIC: 8361 Home for the mentally retarded

(P-18128)
HARMONY HOME ASSOCIATED
820 Alhambra Ave, Martinez (94553-1604)
PHONE.................................925 256-6303
Cristina Spillett, *CEO*
EMP: 40 **EST:** 1982
SALES: 2.8MM **Privately Held**
SIC: 8361 Residential care for the handicapped

(P-18129)
HARRISON HOME
1755 W Hammer Ln Ste 12, Stockton (95209-2900)
P.O. Box 7356 (95267-0356)
PHONE.................................209 955-2277
EMP: 40
SALES: 1.5MM **Privately Held**
SIC: 8361 Residential Care

(P-18130)
HERITAGE ESTATES INC
Also Called: Locust Home
14012 Castle Rd, Manteca (95336-8752)
P.O. Box 293 (95336-1124)
PHONE.................................209 823-6061
Reba Turnbull, *President*
EMP: 56 **EST:** 1957
SQ FT: 3,900
SALES (est): 6.7MM **Privately Held**
SIC: 8361 7216 Home for the mentally handicapped; drycleaning plants, except rugs

(P-18131)
HOPKINS MANOR
Also Called: M Z R
1235 Hopkins Ave, Redwood City (94062-1519)
PHONE.................................650 368-5656
Travis Wyckoss, *Principal*
Portia Gaddi, *Administration*
Rozz Wycoss, *Info Tech Dir*
Alisa Mallari, *Info Tech Mgr*
Hopkins Manor, *Opers Staff*
EMP: 54 **EST:** 1983
SQ FT: 2,000
SALES (est): 15.8MM **Privately Held**
WEB: www.hmjustlikehome.com
SIC: 8361 Home for the aged

(P-18132)
HORIZON SERVICES INCORPORATED
Also Called: Horizon South
650 S Bascom Ave, San Jose (95128-2601)
P.O. Box 4217, Hayward (94540-4217)
PHONE.................................408 283-8555
Lee Bennett, *President*
EMP: 49
SALES (corp-wide): 17MM **Privately Held**
WEB: www.horizonservices.org
SIC: 8361 Halfway group home, persons with social or personal problems; rehabilitation center, residential: health care incidental
PA: Horizon Services, Incorporated
24051 Amador St
Hayward CA 94544
510 582-2100

(P-18133)
LAKEVIEW LODGE INC
530 Lakeview Way, Emerald Hills (94062-3321)
PHONE.................................650 369-7476
Rosalinda Hartwig, *Owner*
Clarence Balios, *Administration*
EMP: 39 **EST:** 1971
SQ FT: 3,500
SALES (est): 4.1MM **Privately Held**
WEB: www.lakeviewlodgehome.com
SIC: 8361 7011 Home for the aged; vacation lodges

(P-18134)
LASSEN HSE ASSISTED LIVING LLC
705 Luther Rd, Red Bluff (96080-4265)
PHONE.................................530 529-2900
Eric Jacobsen,
EMP: 86 **EST:** 1999
SALES (est): 2.8MM **Privately Held**
SIC: 8361 Home for the aged

(P-18135)
LBN LEISURE CARE LLC
Also Called: Woodlake, The
1445 Expo Pkwy, Sacramento (95815-4230)
PHONE.................................916 604-3780
EMP: 545 **EST:** 2019
SALES (est): 12.4MM
SALES (corp-wide): 175.2MM **Privately Held**
WEB: www.leisurecare.com
SIC: 8361 Home for the aged
HQ: Leisure Care, Llc
999 3rd Ave Ste 4550
Seattle WA 98104
206 436-7827

(P-18136)
LEISURE CARE LLC
Also Called: Heritage Estates-Livermore
800 E Stanley Blvd, Livermore (94550-2800)
PHONE.................................925 371-2300
EMP: 124
SALES (corp-wide): 175.2MM **Privately Held**
WEB: www.leisurecare.com
SIC: 8361 Home for the aged
HQ: Leisure Care, Llc
999 3rd Ave Ste 4550
Seattle WA 98104
206 436-7827

(P-18137)
LEISURE CARE LLC
Also Called: Springfield Place
101 Ely Blvd S, Petaluma (94954-3861)
PHONE.................................707 769-3300
Jeralyn May, *General Mgr*
EMP: 124
SALES (corp-wide): 175.2MM **Privately Held**
WEB: www.leisurecare.com
SIC: 8361 Home for the aged
HQ: Leisure Care, Llc
999 3rd Ave Ste 4550
Seattle WA 98104
206 436-7827

(P-18138)
LEISURE CARE LLC
Also Called: Fairwinds Woodward Park
9525 N Fort Washington Rd, Fresno (93730-0662)
PHONE.................................559 434-1237
Coint Folwer, *Branch Mgr*
Alice Quijano, *Executive*
Isaac Antonio, *Chf Purch Ofc*
Siomn Robinson, *Director*
Edward Varela, *Director*
EMP: 124
SALES (corp-wide): 175.2MM **Privately Held**
WEB: www.leisurecare.com
SIC: 8361 Home for the aged
HQ: Leisure Care, Llc
999 3rd Ave Ste 4550
Seattle WA 98104
206 436-7827

(P-18139)
LINCOLN GLEN MANOR LLC
Also Called: Lincoln Glen Skilled Nursing
2671 Plummer Ave Ste A, San Jose (95125-4877)
PHONE.................................408 267-1492
Loren Kroeker, *Exec Dir*
Norma Rueles, *Records Dir*
Barbara Filler, *Administration*
Richard Barnes, *CIO*
Anne Phoenix, *Info Tech Mgr*
EMP: 108 **EST:** 1965
SQ FT: 68,000
SALES (est): 13.8MM **Privately Held**
WEB: www.lgmanor.org
SIC: 8361 Home for the aged

8361 - Residential Care County (P-18140)

(P-18140)
LITTLE SSTERS OF THE POOR OKLA
Also Called: St Anne's Home
300 Lake St, San Francisco (94118-1357)
PHONE.....................415 751-6510
Patricia Metzgar, President
Steve Lewey, Human Res Dir
Maria Cunningham, Director
EMP: 98 EST: 1902
SQ FT: 110,000
SALES: 7.2MM Privately Held
WEB: www.littlesistersofthepoorsanfrancisco.org
SIC: 8361 8661 Home for the aged; religious organizations

(P-18141)
MAGNOLIA OF MILLBRAE INC
201 Chadbourne Ave, Millbrae (94030-2570)
PHONE.....................650 697-7700
Vincent Muzzi, President
EMP: 93 EST: 1986
SALES (est): 5.6MM Privately Held
WEB: www.themagnolia.com
SIC: 8361 Home for the aged

(P-18142)
MASONIC HOMES OF CALIFORNIA (PA)
1111 California St, San Francisco (94108-2252)
PHONE.....................415 776-7000
David R Doan, President
Tom Boyer, CFO
Timothy A Wood, CFO
Chuck Major, Exec VP
Allan Casalou, Vice Pres
EMP: 375
SQ FT: 8,000
SALES: 69MM Privately Held
WEB: www.masonichome.org
SIC: 8361 Children's home

(P-18143)
MASONIC HOMES OF CALIFORNIA
Also Called: Masonic Home For Adults
34400 Mission Blvd, Union City (94587-3604)
PHONE.....................510 441-3700
Gilbert Smart, Branch Mgr
Soledad Martinez, Social Dir
Tiana Tirona, Admin Asst
Dixie U Reeve, Administration
Brian Pagett, Network Enginr
EMP: 350
SALES (corp-wide): 69MM Privately Held
WEB: www.masonichome.org
SIC: 8361 8051 Rest home, with health care incidental; skilled nursing care facilities
PA: Masonic Homes Of California Inc
1111 California St
San Francisco CA 94108
415 776-7000

(P-18144)
MATHER COMMUNITY CAMPUS (PA)
Also Called: Case Management Team
10626 Schirra Ave, Mather (95655-4121)
PHONE.....................916 228-3100
Beth Maerten, Manager
Linda Grace, Officer
Marsha Lucien, Opers Staff
Elizabeth Sands, Marketing Staff
Chris Stanwick, Program Dir
EMP: 85 EST: 1997
SALES (est): 3MM Privately Held
SIC: 8361 Group foster home

(P-18145)
MERCY RETIREMENT AND CARE CTR
3431 Foothill Blvd, Oakland (94601-3199)
PHONE.....................510 534-8540
Jesse Jantzen, CEO
Maricor Onglatco, Social Dir
Tamra Tsanos, Exec Dir
Tamara Schmutzler, Director
EMP: 95 EST: 1872
SQ FT: 125,000
SALES (est): 24.8MM Privately Held
WEB: www.eldercarealliance.org
SIC: 8361 8051 Home for the aged; skilled nursing care facilities

(P-18146)
MOTHER LODE RHBLTTION ENTPS IN
Also Called: MORE WORKSHOP
399 Placerville Dr, Placerville (95667-3912)
PHONE.....................530 622-4848
Susie Davies, Exec Dir
David Eggerton, Exec Dir
Kelli Nuttall, Director
EMP: 150 EST: 1969
SALES: 3.3MM Privately Held
WEB: www.morerehab.org
SIC: 8361 8322 Rehabilitation center, residential: health care incidental; individual & family services

(P-18147)
NOIA RESIDENTIAL SERVICES INC
606 E Belmont Ave Ste 101, Fresno (93701-1527)
PHONE.....................559 485-5555
Lucia Noia, CEO
Bonda Aranas, Controller
EMP: 96 EST: 1986
SQ FT: 9,767
SALES (est): 4.9MM Privately Held
WEB: www.noia-residential-services-inc.hub.biz
SIC: 8361 Home for destitute men & women

(P-18148)
NORTHERN CA RETIREDD OFCRS
Also Called: PARADISE VALLEY ESTATES
2600 Estates Dr, Fairfield (94533-9711)
PHONE.....................707 432-1200
James G Mertz, CEO
Steve Borostyan, CFO
Neil Calhoun, CFO
Debra Murphy, CFO
Patricia Taylor, Admin Asst
EMP: 225 EST: 1992
SALES: 24.9MM Privately Held
WEB: www.pvestates.com
SIC: 8361 Home for the aged

(P-18149)
NORTHERN CAL YUTH FMLY PRGRAMS (PA)
2577 California Park Dr, Chico (95928-4166)
PHONE.....................530 893-2316
Cheryl Sexton, Office Mgr
Eric James, Asst Director
Ralph Ward, Director
EMP: 71 EST: 1984
SQ FT: 6,000
SALES (est): 7MM Privately Held
WEB: www.ncyfp.org
SIC: 8361 Residential care

(P-18150)
NORTHERN CALIFORNIA PRESBYTERI
Also Called: Sequoias, The
501 Portola Rd, Portola Valley (94028-7654)
PHONE.....................650 851-1501
Jay Sumner, Director
Kelly Augustin, Human Resources
Christina Corodimas, Corp Comm Staff
Sue Horst, Director
Dan Chase, Manager
EMP: 155
SALES (corp-wide): 85.5MM Privately Held
WEB: www.sequoialiving.org
SIC: 8361 Geriatric residential care
PA: Sequoia Living, Inc.
1525 Post St
San Francisco CA 94109
415 202-7808

(P-18151)
ODD FELLOW-REBEKAH CHLD HM CAL (PA)
Also Called: REBEKAH CHILDREN'S SERVICES
290 I O O F Ave, Gilroy (95020-5204)
PHONE.....................408 846-2100
Nancy Johnson, CEO
Christophe Rebboah, CEO
Marjorie Knieriem, Bd of Directors
Sue Nasser, Administration
Jennifer Malone, CTO
EMP: 164 EST: 1897
SQ FT: 46,000
SALES: 22.6MM Privately Held
WEB: www.rcskids.org
SIC: 8361 8093 Home for the emotionally disturbed; mental health clinic, outpatient

(P-18152)
ODD FELLOWS HOME CALIFORNIA
Also Called: Saratoga Retirement Community
14500 Fruitvale Ave # 3000, Saratoga (95070-6169)
PHONE.....................408 741-7100
Cathy Schumacher, Administration
EMP: 275 EST: 1853
SALES (est): 20.6MM Privately Held
SIC: 8361 8051 Home for the aged; skilled nursing care facilities

(P-18153)
PACIFIC AUTISM CTR FOR EDUCATN
Also Called: PACE
1880 Pruneridge Ave, Santa Clara (95050-6514)
PHONE.....................408 245-3400
Kurt Ohlff, Exec Dir
Kurt Ohlfs, Exec Dir
Maureen McNeil, Admin Asst
Nancy Brown, Administration
Manju Prabadaran, Administration
EMP: 165 EST: 1982
SQ FT: 12,250
SALES (est): 10.7MM Privately Held
WEB: www.pacificautism.org
SIC: 8299 8361 Arts & crafts schools; residential care for children

(P-18154)
PACIFIC RETIREMENT SVCS INC
Also Called: University Retirement Cmnty
1515 Shasta Dr Ofc, Davis (95616-6695)
PHONE.....................530 753-1450
Mark Blazer, Exec Dir
Rose Antonio, Records Dir
Susan Scorza, Office Mgr
Natasha Utke, Human Res Dir
Judi Del Ponte, Marketing Staff
EMP: 68 Privately Held
WEB: www.retirement.org
SIC: 8361 Home for the aged
PA: Pacific Retirement Services, Inc.
1 W Main St Ste 303
Medford OR 97501

(P-18155)
PARENTS & FRIENDS INC
Also Called: Cypress Street Center
306 E Redwood Ave, Fort Bragg (95437-3524)
P.O. Box 656 (95437-0656)
PHONE.....................707 964-4940
Mark Hall, President
George Griffith, Exec Dir
Shannan Figueiredo, Program Mgr
Adam Ashford, Program Dir
Lanita Henderson, Director
EMP: 43 EST: 1955
SQ FT: 4,905
SALES (est): 6.4MM Privately Held
WEB: www.parentsandfriends.org
SIC: 8361 5712 Home for the physically handicapped; furniture stores

(P-18156)
PEOPLE SERVICES INC (PA)
Also Called: Konocti Transportation Svcs
4195 Lakeshore Blvd, Lakeport (95453-6411)
PHONE.....................707 263-3810
F Ilene Dumont, Exec Dir
EMP: 44
SQ FT: 13,125
SALES: 4.1MM Privately Held
WEB: www.peopleservices.org
SIC: 8361 Self-help group home

(P-18157)
PREMIER SENIOR LIVING LLC (PA)
206 G St Ste 1, Petaluma (94952-7713)
P.O. Box 259 (94953-0259)
PHONE.....................707 778-6719
Shergosha Mayza,
EMP: 73 EST: 2003
SALES (est): 13.6MM Privately Held
WEB: www.premierseniorliving.com
SIC: 8361 Home for the aged

(P-18158)
PRESIDIO GATE APARTMENTS (PA)
2185 N Calif Blvd Ste 215, Walnut Creek (94596-3566)
PHONE.....................925 956-7400
Kevin Joseph Gerber, CEO
Jonathan Casey, CFO
William Cameron Tobin, Principal
Robert Larson, Manager
EMP: 55 EST: 1982
SALES (est): 1.3MM Privately Held
WEB: www.covia.org
SIC: 8361 Home for the aged

(P-18159)
PRIMROSE ALZHEIMERS LIVING INC (PA)
726 College Ave, Santa Rosa (95404-4107)
PHONE.....................707 568-4355
John Wotring, President
Jack Burton, Food Svc Dir
EMP: 50 EST: 1996
SALES (est): 12.9MM Privately Held
WEB: www.primrosealz.com
SIC: 8361 Home for the aged

(P-18160)
PROMESA BEHAVIORAL HEALTH (PA)
7120 N Marks Ave, Fresno (93711-0268)
PHONE.....................559 439-5437
Lisa Weigant, CEO
Fre Dolmstead, Treasurer
Mary Torre, Executive Asst
Renee Accardo, Administration
Susan Reiss, IT/INT Sup
EMP: 147 EST: 1987
SALES (est): 11MM Privately Held
WEB: www.promesabehavioral.org
SIC: 8361 Residential care

(P-18161)
PROVIDENCE PLACE INC
2456 Geary Blvd, San Francisco (94115-3317)
PHONE.....................415 359-9700
Roman Knop, President
Liz Pushing, CFO
Galina Knop, Administration
Golina Knop, Administration
Catherine Villegas, Business Mgr
EMP: 41 EST: 1999
SQ FT: 8,000
SALES (est): 6.3MM Privately Held
WEB: www.providencecare.com
SIC: 8361 Home for the aged

(P-18162)
PSYNERGY PROGRAMS INC
18225 Hale Ave, Morgan Hill (95037-3547)
PHONE.....................415 590-0579
Christopher Zubaite, President
Arturo Uribe, COO
Michael S Weinstein, CFO
L Jean Edwards, Ch Credit Ofcr
Jean Edwards, Officer
EMP: 55 EST: 2004
SALES (est): 10.8MM Privately Held
WEB: www.psynergy.org
SIC: 8361 Residential care

PRODUCTS & SERVICES SECTION **8361 - Residential Care County (P-18189)**

(P-18163)
RANCHO SAN ANTNIO RTRMENT HSIN
Also Called: Forum At Rancho San Antonio
23500 Cristo Rey Dr, Cupertino (95014-6503)
PHONE..................650 265-2637
Ken Fullmore, *Exec Dir*
EMP: 302 EST: 1990
SALES (est): 23.3MM **Privately Held**
WEB: www.theforum-seniorliving.com
SIC: 8361 8051 Rest home, with health care incidental; skilled nursing care facilities

(P-18164)
REDWOODS
40 Camino Alto Ofc, Mill Valley (94941-2997)
PHONE..................415 383-1600
Barbara Solomon, *Director*
Lorna Wilson, *COO*
Carl Upthegrove, *CFO*
Madeline Rose, *Database Admin*
Barry Schenbaum, *Marketing Staff*
EMP: 41 EST: 2008
SALES (est): 16.6MM **Privately Held**
WEB: www.theredwoods.org
SIC: 8361 Home for the aged

(P-18165)
REGENT ASSISTED LIVING INC
Also Called: Sun Oak Assisted Living
7241 Canelo Hills Dr Ofc, Citrus Heights (95610-3161)
PHONE..................916 722-2800
Sue Cavina, *General Mgr*
EMP: 45 **Privately Held**
SIC: 8361 Residential care
PA: Regent Assisted Living, Inc.
  121 Sw Morrison St # 950
  Portland OR 97204

(P-18166)
REGENT ASSISTED LIVING INC
Also Called: Regent Court
2325 St Pauls Way, Modesto (95355-3309)
PHONE..................209 491-0800
Karen Schemper, *Manager*
EMP: 45 **Privately Held**
SIC: 8361 Residential care
PA: Regent Assisted Living, Inc.
  121 Sw Morrison St # 950
  Portland OR 97204

(P-18167)
REGENT ASSISTED LIVING INC
Also Called: Sunshine Villa Assisted Living
80 Front St, Santa Cruz (95060-5098)
PHONE..................831 459-8400
Deann Daniel, *Manager*
EMP: 45 **Privately Held**
SIC: 8361 8052 Home for the aged; intermediate care facilities
PA: Regent Assisted Living, Inc.
  121 Sw Morrison St # 950
  Portland OR 97204

(P-18168)
REGENT ASSISTED LIVING INC
Also Called: Orchard Park
675 W Alluvial Ave Ofc, Clovis (93611-4403)
PHONE..................559 325-8400
Debbie Aramian, *Manager*
Kara Buck,
Susan Middleton,
Linda Wren, *Manager*
EMP: 45 **Privately Held**
SIC: 8361 8052 Residential care; intermediate care facilities
PA: Regent Assisted Living, Inc.
  121 Sw Morrison St # 950
  Portland OR 97204

(P-18169)
REMI VISTA INC
Also Called: Remi Vista Transitional Hsing
3191 Churn Creek Rd, Redding (96002-2123)
PHONE..................530 222-4561
Jeard Beldon, *Branch Mgr*
EMP: 57
SALES (corp-wide): 12.6MM **Privately Held**
WEB: www.remivistainc.org
SIC: 8361 8322 Residential care for the handicapped; child related social services
PA: Vista Remi Inc
  2701 Park Marina Dr
  Redding CA 96001
  530 245-5805

(P-18170)
REMI VISTA INC
370 9th St, Crescent City (95531-3432)
PHONE..................707 464-4349
Doug Tippman, *Branch Mgr*
EMP: 57
SALES (corp-wide): 12.6MM **Privately Held**
WEB: www.remivistainc.org
SIC: 8361 8063 Residential care for the handicapped; psychiatric hospitals
PA: Vista Remi Inc
  2701 Park Marina Dr
  Redding CA 96001
  530 245-5805

(P-18171)
RES-CARE INC
Also Called: Rcca Gatewood Drvie Home
3408 Gatewood Dr, Modesto (95355-1550)
PHONE..................209 578-1385
EMP: 40
SALES (corp-wide): 24.5B **Privately Held**
SIC: 8361 Residential Care Services
HQ: Res-Care, Inc.
  9901 Linn Station Rd
  Louisville KY 40222
  502 394-2100

(P-18172)
ROHLFFS MEMORIAL MANOR (PA)
Also Called: Concordia Manor
2400 Fair Dr, NAPA (94558-4448)
PHONE..................707 255-9555
Michael Derkacz, *General Mgr*
EMP: 45 EST: 1963
SQ FT: 2,000
SALES (est): 2.8MM **Privately Held**
SIC: 8361 Home for the aged

(P-18173)
ROSS VALLEY HOMES INC
Also Called: Tamalpais
501 Via Casitas, Greenbrae (94904-1901)
PHONE..................415 461-2300
David Berg, *CEO*
Don Meninga, *CFO*
Belinda Ong, *Controller*
EMP: 100 EST: 2002
SALES (est): 24.5MM **Privately Held**
WEB: www.thetam.org
SIC: 8361 Home for the aged

(P-18174)
RVM DAVIS HOUSING CORPORATION
Also Called: Shasta Point Retirement Cmnty
1501 Shasta Dr, Davis (95616-6696)
PHONE..................530 747-7095
EMP: 190 EST: 2007
SALES (est): 3.3MM **Privately Held**
WEB: www.retirement.org
SIC: 8361 Geriatric residential care
PA: Pacific Retirement Services, Inc.
  1 W Main St Ste 303
  Medford OR 97501

(P-18175)
SACRAMENTO CHILDRENS HOME (PA)
2750 Sutterville Rd, Sacramento (95820-1093)
PHONE..................916 452-3981
Roy Alexander, *CEO*
Julia Chubb, *CFO*
Joe Hunt, *Vice Pres*
Laurel Sunderman, *Comms Mgr*
Rebecca Clark, *Executive Asst*
EMP: 125 EST: 1867
SQ FT: 15,500
SALES: 19.9MM **Privately Held**
WEB: www.kidshome.org
SIC: 8361 Children's home

(P-18176)
SAN FRNCSCO LDIES PRTCTION RLI
Also Called: Heritage, The
3400 Laguna St, San Francisco (94123-2271)
PHONE..................415 931-3136
Marla Hastings, *Administration*
Janet Howell, *Bd of Directors*
Joseph Conroy, *Controller*
Raygenia Stewart, *Nursing Dir*
Galina Levinson,
EMP: 207 EST: 1853
SQ FT: 15,000
SALES (est): 49.8MM **Privately Held**
WEB: www.theheritagesf.org
SIC: 8361 Home for the aged

(P-18177)
SEAVIEW HLTHCARE RHBLTTION CTR
6400 Purdue Dr, Eureka (95503-7095)
PHONE..................707 443-5668
Ted Chigaros, *Vice Pres*
EMP: 49 EST: 2003
SALES (est): 2.5MM **Privately Held**
WEB: www.seaviewrehabwc.com
SIC: 8361 Rehabilitation center, residential: health care incidental

(P-18178)
SECOND HOME INC
1797 San Jose Ave, Clovis (93611-3078)
PHONE..................559 298-0699
Darle Stone, *President*
Jennifer Fish, *Administration*
EMP: 35 EST: 1996
SALES (est): 2.1MM **Privately Held**
SIC: 8361 Home for the mentally retarded

(P-18179)
SENIOR MERCY HOUSING INC
Also Called: MERCY MCMAHON TERRACE
3865 J St, Sacramento (95816-5500)
PHONE..................916 733-6510
Mary Francis, *CEO*
EMP: 69 EST: 1989
SALES (est): 7.9MM **Privately Held**
WEB: www.mercymcmahonterrace.org
SIC: 8361 Home for the aged

(P-18180)
SEQUOIA LIVING INC
Also Called: Eastern Park Apts
711 Eddy St Ofc, San Francisco (94109-7853)
PHONE..................415 776-0114
Bob Mompenez, *Manager*
EMP: 36
SALES (corp-wide): 85.5MM **Privately Held**
WEB: www.sequoialiving.org
SIC: 8361 Home for the aged
PA: Sequoia Living, Inc.
  1525 Post St
  San Francisco CA 94109
  415 202-7808

(P-18181)
SHI-III PRRIE CY LNDING OWNER (PA)
645 Willard Dr, Folsom (95630-4048)
PHONE..................916 458-0303
EMP: 45 EST: 2018
SALES (est): 1.1MM **Privately Held**
SIC: 8361 Home for the aged

(P-18182)
SKY PARK GARDENS ASSISTED
5510 Sky Pkwy Ofc, Sacramento (95823-2282)
PHONE..................916 422-5650
Habib Bokhari, *Owner*
EMP: 55 EST: 2001
SALES (est): 5MM **Privately Held**
WEB: www.skyparkgardens.com
SIC: 8361 Home for the aged

(P-18183)
SLOW SCULPTURE
Also Called: BADGER CREEK
5715 Monte Verde Dr, Santa Rosa (95409-3921)
PHONE..................707 537-7024
Patricia Baker, *Administration*
Sarane Collins, *CFO*
EMP: 35 EST: 1991
SALES (est): 1.9MM **Privately Held**
WEB: www.slowsculpture.com
SIC: 8361 8082 Home for the aged; home health care services

(P-18184)
ST REGIS RETIREMENT CTR INC
23950 Mission Blvd, Hayward (94544-1052)
PHONE..................510 881-4240
Roland Rapp, *President*
Sally Rapp, *Treasurer*
Eugene Rapp, *Admin Sec*
EMP: 40 EST: 1977
SQ FT: 100,000
SALES (est): 6.7MM **Privately Held**
WEB: www.stregiscenter.com
SIC: 8361 Home for the aged

(P-18185)
STOCKTON CONGREGATIONAL HOME
Also Called: Plymouth Square
1319 N Madison St Ofc, Stockton (95202-1001)
PHONE..................209 466-4341
Peter Peabody, *Vice Pres*
Stuart Hartman, *Principal*
Eunice Ronquillo, *Nursing Dir*
Quiroga Sarela, *Hlthcr Dir*
Psyche Johnson, *Director*
EMP: 71 EST: 1966
SALES: 5MM **Privately Held**
SIC: 8361 Home for the aged

(P-18186)
SUMMER HOUSE INC (PA)
206 5th St, Woodland (95695-3505)
P.O. Box 1724 (95776-1724)
PHONE..................530 662-8493
Erin Plankryan, *Exec Dir*
Dale Campbell, *Exec Dir*
EMP: 53 EST: 1974
SQ FT: 6,500
SALES: 1.6MM **Privately Held**
WEB: www.summerhouseinc.org
SIC: 8361 8059 8322 Residential care for the handicapped; home for the mentally retarded, exc. skilled or intermediate; social services for the handicapped

(P-18187)
SUN OAK LIMITED PARTNERS
Also Called: Sun Oak Assisted Living
7241 Canelo Hills Dr Ofc, Citrus Heights (95610-3161)
PHONE..................916 722-2800
Ron Seifreid, *Managing Prtnr*
Marissa Mannan, *Food Svc Dir*
Ronald Bailey, *Director*
Kaye Key, *Director*
Amani Kyubwa, *Director*
EMP: 51 EST: 1995
SALES (est): 10.1MM **Privately Held**
WEB: www.sunoakseniorliving.com
SIC: 8361 Home for the aged

(P-18188)
SUNNYSIDE GARDENS
1025 Carson Dr, Sunnyvale (94086-5800)
PHONE..................408 730-4070
Anna Ready, *Director*
Jessie Garcia, *Maintenance Dir*
Ed Bellerive,
Diana Ngo, *Director*
Molly Young, *Director*
EMP: 36 EST: 1998
SALES (est): 13.9MM **Privately Held**
WEB: www.ssgal.com
SIC: 8361 Home for the aged

(P-18189)
SYNERGY LLC (PA)
Also Called: Hayes Valley Care
601 Laguna St, San Francisco (94102-4207)
PHONE..................415 252-1128

8361 - Residential Care County (P-18190)

Gary Low, *Exec Dir*
Synergy LLC, *General Ptnr*
Sal Vaccaro, *Vice Pres*
David C Price, *General Mgr*
Marichel Hilliard, *Admin Asst*
EMP: 35 **EST:** 1997
SALES (est): 2.6MM **Privately Held**
SIC: 8361 Residential care

(P-18190)
TAPESTRY FAMILY SERVICES INC
169 Mason St Ste 300, Ukiah (95482-4483)
PHONE.................................707 463-3300
Sharon Kiichli, *President*
Kevin Powers, *Exec Dir*
Lindsey Wehn, *QC Mgr*
Rebecca Picard, *Internal Med*
EMP: 55 **EST:** 2001
SALES (est): 3.2MM **Privately Held**
WEB: www.tapestryfs.org
SIC: 8361 Group foster home

(P-18191)
TED COLLWELL
Also Called: Californian, The
1224 Cottonwood St Ofc, Woodland (95695-4349)
PHONE.................................530 666-2433
Ted Collwell, *Owner*
Kathy Benson, *Mktg Dir*
EMP: 39 **EST:** 1993
SALES (est): 4.5MM **Privately Held**
WEB: www.thecalifornian.net
SIC: 8361 Home for the aged

(P-18192)
THE REDWOODS A CMNTY SENIORS
Also Called: REDWOODS, THE
40 Camino Alto Ofc, Mill Valley (94941-2997)
PHONE.................................415 383-2741
Barbara Solomon, *CEO*
Susan Badger, *COO*
Alan Kern, *CFO*
Vicki Vestal, *Accountant*
Ron Bruno, *Human Resources*
EMP: 140
SQ FT: 140,000
SALES: 22.1MM **Privately Held**
WEB: www.theredwoods.org
SIC: 8361 Home for the aged

(P-18193)
TRUE HEALTH INC
Also Called: Golden Haven
2324 Lever Blvd, Stockton (95206-2900)
PHONE.................................209 464-4743
Rowena Ramirez, *President*
EMP: 46 **EST:** 1989
SQ FT: 40,000
SALES (est): 8.6MM **Privately Held**
SIC: 8361 Home for the mentally handicapped

(P-18194)
TWELVEACRES INC
286 E Hamilton Ave Ste F, Campbell (95008-0242)
PHONE.................................408 341-0400
Marlie Brooks, *Administration*
EMP: 40 **EST:** 1932
SALES (est): 1.2MM **Privately Held**
WEB: www.twelveacres.org
SIC: 8361 Home for the mentally handicapped

(P-18195)
UNIVERSITY CAL SAN FRNCSCO FND
Also Called: Ucsf Center On Deafness
3333 California St Ste 10, San Francisco (94118-6200)
PHONE.................................415 775-2111
Nancy Moser, *Director*
EMP: 72
SALES (corp-wide): 628.1MM **Privately Held**
WEB: www.ucsf.edu
SIC: 8361 Home for the deaf & blind
PA: University Of California, San Francisco Foundation
220 Montgomery St Ste 500
San Francisco CA 94104
415 476-6922

(P-18196)
VALINE COURT SENIOR CARE INC
Also Called: Waterleaf At Land Park, The
966 43rd Ave, Sacramento (95831-1313)
P.O. Box 7914, Stockton (95267-0914)
PHONE.................................916 394-9400
Paul Cimino, *President*
EMP: 51 **EST:** 2001
SALES (est): 3.8MM **Privately Held**
WEB: www.thewaterleaf.com
SIC: 8361 Home for the aged

(P-18197)
VALLEY HEIGHTS SENIOR CMNTY
925 Freedom Blvd, Watsonville (95076-3804)
PHONE.................................831 722-4884
Richard Murphy, *President*
Kelly Chiolate, *Officer*
Murphy Heidi, *Bookkeeper*
▲ **EMP:** 35 **EST:** 1973
SALES (est): 4.5MM **Privately Held**
WEB: www.informish.com
SIC: 8361 6513 Rest home, with health care incidental; apartment building operators

(P-18198)
VALLEY PINTE NURSING REHAB CTR
20090 Stanton Ave, Castro Valley (94546-5203)
PHONE.................................510 538-8464
Daniel Wittman, *Administration*
EMP: 41 **EST:** 1961
SQ FT: 7,500
SALES (est): 5MM **Privately Held**
WEB: www.valleypointenursing.com
SIC: 8361 Rehabilitation center, residential: health care incidental

(P-18199)
VALLEY TEEN RANCH
2610 W Shaw Ln Ste 105, Fresno (93711-2775)
PHONE.................................559 437-1144
Connie Clendenan, *Exec Dir*
John Addington, *Administration*
David Carrera, *Administration*
Legion Escobar, *Technology*
Miriam Delfin, *Finance Dir*
EMP: 76 **EST:** 1983
SQ FT: 9,996
SALES (est): 4.4MM **Privately Held**
WEB: www.valleyteenranch.org
SIC: 8361 8322 Group foster home; individual & family services

(P-18200)
VICTOR TREATMENT CENTERS INC
Also Called: Willow Creek Treatment Center
341 Irwin Ln, Santa Rosa (95401-5603)
PHONE.................................707 360-1509
Gala Goodwin, *Branch Mgr*
EMP: 43
SQ FT: 3,060
SALES (corp-wide): 61.3MM **Privately Held**
WEB: www.victor.org
SIC: 8361 Home for the emotionally disturbed
PA: Victor Treatment Centers, Inc.
1360 E Lassen Ave
Chico CA 95973
530 893-0758

(P-18201)
VICTOR TREATMENT CENTERS INC
Also Called: North Valley School
12755 N Highway 88, Lodi (95240-9323)
P.O. Box 330, Victor (95253-0330)
PHONE.................................209 465-1080
Terry Crumpacker, *Principal*
Tim Foster, *Principal*
EMP: 129
SALES (corp-wide): 61.3MM **Privately Held**
WEB: www.victor.org
SIC: 8211 8361 Specialty education; home for the emotionally disturbed
PA: Victor Treatment Centers, Inc.
1360 E Lassen Ave
Chico CA 95973
530 893-0758

(P-18202)
VILLA SIENA
1855 Miramonte Ave 117, Mountain View (94040-4029)
PHONE.................................650 961-6484
Corrine Bernard, *CEO*
Scott Johnson, *Marketing Staff*
Filipinas Abad, *Nurse*
Mary Ellen Barber, *Nursing Dir*
Ann Kaye, *Nursing Dir*
EMP: 68 **EST:** 1985
SQ FT: 40,000
SALES: 7.8MM **Privately Held**
WEB: www.villa-siena.org
SIC: 8361 Home for the aged

(P-18203)
VILLAGE AT GRANITE BAY
8550 Barton Rd, Granite Bay (95746-8843)
PHONE.................................916 789-0326
EMP: 68
SALES (est): 579K **Privately Held**
SIC: 8361 Residential Care Services

(P-18204)
VINE VILLAGE INC
4059 Old Sonoma Rd, NAPA (94559-9702)
PHONE.................................707 255-4006
Micheal Kerson, *Exec Dir*
Saanen Kerson, *Associate Dir*
Nancy Kerson, *Asst Director*
EMP: 20 **EST:** 1973
SQ FT: 6,500
SALES (est): 1.1MM **Privately Held**
WEB: www.vinevillage.org
SIC: 8361 8331 2099 Home for the mentally retarded; vocational training agency; vinegar

(P-18205)
WALDEN HOUSE INC (PA)
520 Townsend St, San Francisco (94103-6241)
PHONE.................................415 554-1100
Rod Libbey, *Exec Dir*
Vitka Eisen, *CEO*
David Crawford, *CFO*
EMP: 40 **EST:** 1969
SQ FT: 6,500
SALES: 22.7MM **Privately Held**
WEB: www.waldenhouse.org
SIC: 8361 8322 8331 Group foster home; substance abuse counseling; vocational rehabilitation agency

(P-18206)
WALDEN HOUSE INC
Also Called: Walden House Adolescent
214 Haight St, San Francisco (94102-6127)
PHONE.................................415 554-1480
Bunny Cushman, *Director*
EMP: 130
SQ FT: 24,000
SALES (corp-wide): 22.7MM **Privately Held**
WEB: www.waldenhouse.org
SIC: 8361 Rehabilitation center, residential: health care incidental
PA: Walden House, Inc.
520 Townsend St
San Francisco CA 94103
415 554-1100

(P-18207)
WALDEN HOUSE INC
Also Called: Multi- Services
1735 Mission St, San Francisco (94103-2417)
PHONE.................................415 554-1131
Fermin Loza, *Branch Mgr*
EMP: 130
SALES (corp-wide): 22.7MM **Privately Held**
WEB: www.waldenhouse.org
SIC: 8361 8093 Group foster home; specialty outpatient clinics
PA: Walden House, Inc.
520 Townsend St
San Francisco CA 94103
415 554-1100

(P-18208)
WATERMARK RTRMENT CMMNTIES INC
Also Called: Rosewood Gardens
35 Fenton St, Livermore (94550-4185)
PHONE.................................925 344-5661
Gary Christo, *President*
EMP: 56 **Privately Held**
WEB: www.watermarkcommunities.com
SIC: 8361 Home for the aged
HQ: Watermark Retirement Communities, Inc.
2020 W Rudasill Rd
Tucson AZ 85704

(P-18209)
WATERS EDGE LODGE
801 Island Dr Apt 267, Alameda (94502-6765)
PHONE.................................510 769-6264
Christian Zimmerman, *Partner*
John Zimmerman, *Partner*
Trinh MAI, *Associate*
EMP: 36 **EST:** 1990
SALES (est): 7.3MM **Privately Held**
WEB: www.aecliving.com
SIC: 8361 Home for the aged

(P-18210)
WESTCARE CALIFORNIA INC (HQ)
1900 N Gateway Blvd 100, Fresno (93727-1622)
P.O. Box 12107 (93776-2107)
PHONE.................................559 251-4800
Richard Steinberg, *President*
Jenifer Nolan, *President*
Shawn Jenkins, *Vice Pres*
Maurice Lee, *Vice Pres*
Tina Stiles, *Controller*
EMP: 121 **EST:** 1973
SALES: 29.4MM
SALES (corp-wide): 14.2MM **Privately Held**
WEB: www.westcare.com
SIC: 8361 8093 Rehabilitation center, residential: health care incidental; specialty outpatient clinics
PA: Westcare Foundation, Inc.
1711 Whitney Mesa Dr # 100
Henderson NV 89014
702 385-3330

(P-18211)
WESTERN LIVING CONCEPTS INC (PA)
Also Called: Timber Ridge At Eureka
2740 Timber Ridge Ln Ofc, Eureka (95503-4867)
PHONE.................................707 443-3000
Erica Farnum, *Exec Dir*
Linda Rantz, *Accounting Mgr*
Mindy McGaha, *Teacher*
Lori Owens, *Asst Director*
Ena Burdick, *Director*
EMP: 35 **EST:** 1998
SALES (est): 5MM **Privately Held**
WEB: www.timberridgecare.com
SIC: 8361 Home for the aged

(P-18212)
WESTMONT LIVING INC
Also Called: Terraces of Roseville, The
707 Sunrise Ave, Roseville (95661-4524)
PHONE.................................916 786-3277
Andrew Plant, *President*
Michael O'rourke, *Chairman*
Jodi Ross, *Director*
EMP: 97
SALES (corp-wide): 41MM **Privately Held**
WEB: www.westmontliving.com
SIC: 8361 Home for the aged

PRODUCTS & SERVICES SECTION

8399 - Social Services, NEC County (P-18234)

PA: Westmont Living, Inc.
7660 Fay Ave Ste N
La Jolla CA 92037
858 456-1233

(P-18213)
WILLOW SPRNG ALZHMERS SPCIAL C
191 Churn Creek Rd, Redding (96003-3044)
PHONE.................530 242-0654
Jerry Erwin, *Partner*
EMP: 36 **EST:** 2003
SALES (est): 6MM **Privately Held**
SIC: 8361 8099 Rehabilitation center, residential: health care incidental; blood related health services

(P-18214)
YOUTH HOMES INCORPORATED
Also Called: Anderson House
1159 Everett Ct, Concord (94518-1714)
P.O. Box 5759, Walnut Creek (94596-1759)
PHONE.................925 933-2627
Stuart McCoullough, *Exec Dir*
Linda Callahan, *Director*
Yuliya Korentsvit, *Manager*
EMP: 38
SALES (corp-wide): 8.1MM **Privately Held**
WEB: www.youthhomes.org
SIC: 8361 Home for the emotionally disturbed
PA: Youth Homes Incorporated
1200 Concord Ave Ste 450
Concord CA 94520
925 933-2627

(P-18215)
YUBA CITY MANOR LLC
Also Called: Yuba City Residential Care
1880 Live Oak Blvd, Yuba City (95991-1912)
PHONE.................530 673-6051
Roberto H Ventura, *Partner*
Lynn Ventura, *Co-Owner*
Robert Ventura, *Owner*
EMP: 37 **EST:** 2000
SQ FT: 17,654
SALES (est): 213.8K **Privately Held**
WEB: www.yubacitypostacute.com
SIC: 8361 Home for the aged

8399 Social Services, NEC

(P-18216)
A BETTER WAY INC (PA)
3200 Adeline St, Berkeley (94703-2407)
PHONE.................510 601-0203
Shahnaz Mazandarani, *Exec Dir*
Anne Grascoeur, *Officer*
Cherise Northcutt, *Director*
Sandra Berger, *Supervisor*
EMP: 110 **EST:** 1996
SALES (est): 13.2MM **Privately Held**
WEB: www.abetterwayinc.net
SIC: 8399 Community development groups

(P-18217)
ALAMEDA HEALTH SYSTEM (PA)
Also Called: Highland Hosp Hghland Wellness
1411 E 31st St, Oakland (94602-1018)
PHONE.................510 437-4800
James Jackson, *CEO*
Lynda Wilson, *Ch of Bd*
Mark S Fratzke, *COO*
Peter Hohl, *COO*
David Cox, *CFO*
EMP: 99 **EST:** 2002
SALES (est): 317.8MM **Privately Held**
WEB: www.alamedahealthsystem.org
SIC: 8399 Health systems agency

(P-18218)
AMADOR TLMNE CMNTY ACTION AGCY (PA)
Also Called: Atcaa
10590 State Highway 88, Jackson (95642-9470)
PHONE.................209 296-2785
Shelly Hance, *Exec Dir*
Patty Cunningham, *Deputy Dir*
Pat Porto, *Director*
EMP: 117 **EST:** 1981
SALES (est): 16.7MM **Privately Held**
WEB: www.atcaa.org
SIC: 8399 Community action agency

(P-18219)
ASIAN INC (PA)
1167 Mission St Fl 4, San Francisco (94103-1544)
PHONE.................415 928-5910
Michael Chan, *President*
Yi-Hui Chen, *Officer*
Michael S Chan, *Exec Dir*
Grace Barba, *Admin Asst*
▲ **EMP:** 35 **EST:** 1971
SQ FT: 5,400
SALES (est): 6.6MM **Privately Held**
WEB: www.asianinc.org
SIC: 8399 8699 Neighborhood development group; charitable organization

(P-18220)
ASIAN AMRCANS FOR CMNTY INVLVM (PA)
2400 Moorpark Ave Ste 300, San Jose (95128-2680)
PHONE.................408 975-2730
Michele Lew, *President*
Pancho Chang, *COO*
Brent Copen, *CFO*
Sone Silavong, *Accountant*
▲ **EMP:** 157 **EST:** 1973
SQ FT: 101,753
SALES: 17.4MM **Privately Held**
WEB: www.aaci.org
SIC: 8399 Health & welfare council; health systems agency; social change association

(P-18221)
BANANAS INCORPORATED
Also Called: BANANAS CHILD CARE INFORMATION
5232 Claremont Ave, Oakland (94618-1033)
PHONE.................510 658-7353
Cate Ejjed, *Administration*
Elyce Berrigan-Dunlop, *Corp Comm Staff*
Arlyce Currie, *Director*
Sakshi Pathania, *Director*
Joellen Stencer, *Director*
EMP: 35 **EST:** 1973
SQ FT: 1,500
SALES: 21.4MM **Privately Held**
WEB: www.bananasbunch.org
SIC: 8399 8322 Social service information exchange; referral service for personal & social problems

(P-18222)
CALIFRNIA ATISM FOUNDATION INC
Also Called: Better Chance, A
982 Marlesta Rd, Pinole (94564-2402)
PHONE.................510 724-1751
John Clay, *Director*
EMP: 74
SALES (corp-wide): 8MM **Privately Held**
WEB: www.calautism.org
SIC: 8399 8322 Community development groups; individual & family services
PA: The California Autism Foundation Inc
4138 Lakeside Dr
San Pablo CA 94806
510 758-0433

(P-18223)
CALIFRNIA RUR INDIAN HLTH BD I
1020 Sun Down Way, Roseville (95661-4473)
PHONE.................916 437-0104
James Crouch, *President*
Jason C Lopez, *CFO*
Ronald Moody, *CFO*
Laura Rambeau-Lawson, *Treasurer*
Susan Dahl, *Officer*
EMP: 80
SQ FT: 18,627
SALES (est): 61.2MM **Privately Held**
WEB: www.crihb.org
SIC: 8399 Health & welfare council

(P-18224)
CENTRAL CALIFORNIA FOOD BANK
4010 E Amendola Dr, Fresno (93725-2335)
PHONE.................559 237-3663
Andy Souza, *CEO*
Bob Reyes, *CEO*
Natalie Caples, *COO*
Robert Ojeda, *Vice Pres*
Kym Dildine,
EMP: 44 **EST:** 1992
SQ FT: 45,000
SALES (est): 80.8MM **Privately Held**
WEB: www.ccfoodbank.org
SIC: 8399 Community development groups

(P-18225)
COCOKIDS INC
1035 Detroit Ave Ste 200, Concord (94518-2478)
PHONE.................925 676-5442
John Jones, *Exec Dir*
Jay Perry, *CFO*
John F Jones, *Exec Dir*
Maureen Satcher, *Office Mgr*
Michelle Mortenson, *QC Mgr*
EMP: 105 **EST:** 1976
SALES (est): 43.9MM **Privately Held**
WEB: www.cocokids.org
SIC: 8399 Community action agency

(P-18226)
COLUSA INDIAN CMNTY COUNCIL
Also Called: Colusa Casino
3740 Highway 45, Colusa (95932-4030)
PHONE.................530 458-6572
Laurie Costa, *Director*
Bonnie Pullen, *CFO*
Lance Knapp, *IT/INT Sup*
Tammy Harris, *Human Res Mgr*
Doyle Smotherman, *Opers Staff*
EMP: 118 **Privately Held**
WEB: www.syix.com
SIC: 8399 7991 Community development groups; health club
PA: Colusa Indian Community Council
3730 State Highway 45 B
Colusa CA 95932

(P-18227)
COMMUNITY ACTION PRTNR MDERA C
Also Called: Victims Services Center
1225 Gill Ave, Madera (93637-5234)
PHONE.................559 661-1000
Tina Figueroa, *Office Mgr*
Leticia Murillo, *Program Mgr*
EMP: 53
SALES (corp-wide): 29.3MM **Privately Held**
WEB: www.maderacap.org
SIC: 8399 Community action agency
PA: Community Action Partnership Of Madera County, Inc.
1225 Gill Ave
Madera CA 93637
559 673-9173

(P-18228)
COMMUNITY ACTION PRTNR SNOMA C
141 Stony Cir Ste 210, Santa Rosa (95401-4142)
PHONE.................707 544-0120
Oscar Chavez, *President*
Rupinder Malhi, *CFO*
Karen Erickson, *Vice Pres*
Tim Reese, *Exec Dir*
Marie Ibanez, *Program Mgr*
EMP: 78 **EST:** 1967
SQ FT: 18,000
SALES: 11.7MM **Privately Held**
WEB: www.capsonoma.org
SIC: 8399 Antipoverty board; community action agency

(P-18229)
GLOBAL FUND FOR WOMEN INC
800 Market St Fl 7, San Francisco (94102-3034)
PHONE.................415 248-4800
Latanya Mapp Frett, *President*
Jennifer Quinn, *CFO*
Anil Awasti, *Officer*
Lori Adelman, *Vice Pres*
Janelle Cavanagh, *Vice Pres*
EMP: 44 **EST:** 1987
SQ FT: 5,142
SALES (est): 32.1MM **Privately Held**
WEB: www.globalfundforwomen.org
SIC: 8399 Fund raising organization, non-fee basis

(P-18230)
GREATER SACRAMENTO URBAN LEAG
Also Called: SACRAMENTO URBAN LEAGUE
3725 Marysville Blvd, Sacramento (95838-3738)
PHONE.................916 286-8600
Denelle Ellison, *President*
David B Deluz, *President*
Darsey Varnedoe, *President*
Kevin Daniel, *Vice Pres*
Angelina Garcia, *Vice Pres*
EMP: 40 **EST:** 1968
SQ FT: 1,347
SALES: 1.9MM **Privately Held**
WEB: www.gsul.org
SIC: 8399 Community development groups

(P-18231)
HABITAT FOR HMNITY GRTER SAN F
1 Embarcadero Ctr Sl 12, San Francisco (94111-3628)
PHONE.................415 625-1000
Jen Wilds, *CFO*
Lita Anderson, *Officer*
Rachel Edson, *Officer*
Samantha Ganser, *Officer*
Darrell Byers,
EMP: 87 **EST:** 1989
SALES (est): 7MM **Privately Held**
WEB: www.habitatgsf.org
SIC: 8399 Community development groups

(P-18232)
HEALTHIER KIDS FOUNDATION INC
4040 Moorpark Ave Ste 100, San Jose (95117-1851)
PHONE.................408 564-5114
Kathleen King, *CEO*
Dave Cameron, *CFO*
Beth Paige, *Officer*
Jocelyn MA, *Program Mgr*
Jennifer Shelton, *Admin Asst*
EMP: 35 **EST:** 2000
SALES (est): 3.8MM **Privately Held**
WEB: www.hkidsf.org
SIC: 8399 Fund raising organization, non-fee basis

(P-18233)
HOMELSSNESS SPPRTIVE HSING DEP
440 Turk St, San Francisco (94102-3330)
P.O. Box 427400 (94142-7400)
PHONE.................628 652-7700
Abigail Stewart-Kahn, *Principal*
Derek Chan, *Principal*
EMP: 125 **EST:** 2016
SALES (est): 2.1MM **Privately Held**
WEB: www.hsh.sfgov.org
SIC: 8399 Advocacy group

(P-18234)
INTERNTNAL CHILD RSRCE EXCH IN (PA)
Also Called: INTERNATIONAL CHILD RESOURCE I
125 University Ave # 201, Berkeley (94710-1601)
PHONE.................510 644-1000
Ken Jaffe, *Director*
Sophia Ozburn, *Admin Asst*
Ellie Mashhour, *Senior Mgr*
Victoria Lee, *Director*
Lloyd Muwoni, *Director*
EMP: 123 **EST:** 1981
SALES: 12.1MM **Privately Held**
WEB: www.icrichild.org
SIC: 8399 Social service information exchange

8399 - Social Services, NEC County (P-18235)

(P-18235)
JAPANESE CMNTY YOUTH COUNCIL (PA)
Also Called: Chibi Chan Preschool
2012 Pine St, San Francisco (94115-2899)
PHONE..................................415 202-7905
John Osaki, *Exec Dir*
Julie Matsueda, *Executive*
Arleen Garcia, *Associate Dir*
Gina Gutierrez, *Associate Dir*
Debbie Irawan, *Associate Dir*
EMP: 60
SQ FT: 4,000
SALES: 12.8MM **Privately Held**
WEB: www.jcyc.org
SIC: 8399 Community action agency

(P-18236)
JEWISH CMNTY FDRTION OF SAN FR (PA)
121 Steuart St, San Francisco (94105-1236)
PHONE..................................415 777-0411
Jennifer Gorvitz, *CEO*
Bill Powers, *CFO*
Hallie Baron, *Associate Dir*
Joey Blatt, *Program Mgr*
Carole-Anne Elliott, *Executive Asst*
EMP: 70 **EST:** 1921
SQ FT: 50,000
SALES: 186.3MM **Privately Held**
WEB: www.jewishfed.org
SIC: 8399 Fund raising organization, non-fee basis

(P-18237)
KEYSTONE NPS LLC
Also Called: Keystone Educatn & Youth Svcs
425 Corcoran Ave, Vallejo (94589-1768)
PHONE..................................510 206-8463
Tasha Dean, *Principal*
EMP: 136
SALES (corp-wide): 11.5B **Publicly Held**
SIC: 8399 8211 Advocacy group; private combined elementary & secondary school
HQ: Keystone Nps Llc
11980 Mount Vernon Ave
Grand Terrace CA 92313
909 633-6354

(P-18238)
KIPP FOUNDATION
135 Main St Ste 1875, San Francisco (94105-1955)
PHONE..................................415 399-1556
Richard Barth, *CEO*
Claire Godwin, *CEO*
Amy Hager, *COO*
Tarun Bhatia, *CFO*
Jack Chorowsky, *CFO*
EMP: 110 **EST:** 2000
SALES: 98.6MM **Privately Held**
WEB: www.kipp.org
SIC: 8399 Fund raising organization, non-fee basis

(P-18239)
LASH GROUP LLC
Also Called: Lash Group Healthcare Cons
999 Bayhill Dr Fl 3, San Bruno (94066-3070)
PHONE..................................800 788-9637
Mike Busby, *Manager*
Aimee Bando, *Vice Pres*
Roselle Bartke-Borg, *Human Resources*
EMP: 121
SALES (corp-wide): 189.8B **Publicly Held**
WEB: www.lashgroup.com
SIC: 8399 8742 Health systems agency; hospital & health services consultant
HQ: The Lash Group Llc
1800 Innovation Pt
Fort Mill SC 29715
800 357-5274

(P-18240)
MCCONNELL FOUNDATION
800 Shasta View Dr, Redding (96003-8208)
P.O. Box 492050 (96049-2050)
PHONE..................................530 226-6200
John A Mancasola, *President*
Shannon Phillips, *COO*
Brian Sindt, *Officer*
David Tanner, *Officer*
Rebecca Andrews, *Controller*
EMP: 43 **EST:** 1964
SALES (est): 9.8MM **Privately Held**
WEB: www.mcconnellfoundation.org
SIC: 8399 Fund raising organization, non-fee basis

(P-18241)
MEDICAL AMBASSADORS INTL
Also Called: M A I
5012 Salida Blvd, Salida (95368-9403)
P.O. Box 1302 (95368-1302)
PHONE..................................209 543-7500
Robert Paul, *President*
Michael Carroll, *CFO*
Suzanne Howell, *Executive Asst*
Suzette Montez, *Controller*
Denise Locker, *Corp Comm Staff*
EMP: 42
SQ FT: 9,000
SALES: 2.5MM **Privately Held**
WEB: www.medicalambassadors.org
SIC: 8399 Social change association; health systems agency

(P-18242)
MINORITY VETERANS COALITION
2377 S Attucks Ave, Fresno (93706-4802)
PHONE..................................559 647-3425
Henry A Hendrix, *Principal*
EMP: 45 **EST:** 2012
SALES (est): 434K **Privately Held**
SIC: 8399 Advocacy group

(P-18243)
MISSION MERCED INCORPORATED
644 W 20th St, Merced (95340-3702)
PHONE..................................209 722-9269
Bruce A Metcalf, *CEO*
EMP: 52 **EST:** 2015
SALES (est): 871.9K **Privately Held**
SIC: 8399 Social services

(P-18244)
NORTHERN CAL INST FOR RES EDCA
Also Called: NCIRE
4150 Clement St, San Francisco (94121-1563)
PHONE..................................415 750-6954
Robert Obana, *Exec Dir*
Paul Volberding, *Bd of Directors*
Julianne Todd, *Research*
Chunmiao Feng, *Analyst*
EMP: 300 **EST:** 1988
SQ FT: 1,650
SALES: 44.6MM **Privately Held**
WEB: www.ncire.org
SIC: 8399 8741 Fund raising organization, non-fee basis; management services

(P-18245)
PACE SOLANO
350 Chadbourne Rd, Fairfield (94534-9636)
PHONE..................................707 427-1731
Doniese Roberts, *Branch Mgr*
EMP: 48
SALES (corp-wide): 8.7MM **Privately Held**
WEB: www.pacesolano.org
SIC: 8399 Community development groups
PA: Pace Solano
419 Mason St Ste 118
Vacaville CA 95688
707 448-2283

(P-18246)
PASKENTA BAND NOMLAKI INDIANS
2655 Everett Freeman Way, Corning (96021-9000)
P.O. Box 709 (96021-0709)
PHONE..................................530 528-3538
Andrew Alejandre, *Chairman*
Jeff Realander, *COO*
Gary Poynor, *CFO*
Joshua Morris, *IT/INT Sup*
Jeremy Olson, *Purch Mgr*
EMP: 493 **EST:** 1994
SALES (est): 47.7MM **Privately Held**
WEB: www.paskenta-nsn.gov
SIC: 8399 7011 Council for social agency; casino hotel

(P-18247)
POLL EVERYWHERE INC
639 Howard St, San Francisco (94105-3903)
PHONE..................................800 388-2039
Jeff Vyduna, *CEO*
Nathan Pinsky, *Vice Pres*
Chris Amundson, *Software Engr*
Matt Matt Diebolt, *Software Engr*
Shibo Fang, *Software Engr*
EMP: 60 **EST:** 2012
SALES: 6.7MM **Privately Held**
WEB: www.polleverywhere.com
SIC: 8399 Social service information exchange

(P-18248)
PRC
170 9th St, San Francisco (94103-2603)
PHONE..................................415 777-0333
Brett Andrews, *Exec Dir*
Jude Blackwolf, *Legal Staff*
Lee Harrington, *Director*
Demetri Moshoyannis, *Director*
Pat Riley, *Director*
EMP: 53 **EST:** 1988
SQ FT: 7,000
SALES: 9.7MM **Privately Held**
WEB: www.prcsf.org
SIC: 8399 8322 Council for social agency; individual & family services

(P-18249)
SAN FRNCSCO GEN HOSP FUNDATION
2789 25th St Ste 2028, San Francisco (94110-3582)
P.O. Box 410836 (94141-0836)
PHONE..................................415 206-4478
Stephanie Bray, *CEO*
Gerry Chow, *CFO*
Katie Morris, *Officer*
Judith Guggenhime, *Principal*
Katherine Ripley Williams, *Office Mgr*
EMP: 102 **EST:** 2008
SALES (est): 23.4MM **Privately Held**
WEB: www.sfghf.org
SIC: 8399 Fund raising organization, non-fee basis

(P-18250)
SOURCEAMERICA
Also Called: National Inds For Svrely Hndcp
2633 Camino Ramon Ste 450, San Ramon (94583-2174)
PHONE..................................925 543-5100
David Dubinsky, *Director*
Steve Katsurinis, *Vice Chairman*
Brian Deatley, *Research*
EMP: 58
SALES (corp-wide): 157.8MM **Privately Held**
WEB: www.sourceamerica.org
SIC: 8399 Fund raising organization, non-fee basis
PA: Sourceamerica
8401 Old Courthouse Rd # 110
Vienna VA 22182
888 411-8424

(P-18251)
SPANISH SPKING UNITY CNCIL ALM
Also Called: Thurgood Mrshall Erly Head Sta
1117 10th St, Oakland (94607-2707)
PHONE..................................510 836-0543
Elizabeth Crocker, *Director*
Rosie Jara, *Associate Dir*
Nalleli Albarran, *Program Mgr*
Gloria Benavides, *Property Mgr*
Mirna Gonzalez, *Property Mgr*
EMP: 125
SALES (corp-wide): 36.4MM **Privately Held**
WEB: www.unitycouncil.org
SIC: 8399 8351 Social change association; child day care services
PA: Spanish Speaking Unity Council Of Alameda County, Inc.
1900 Fruitvale Ave Ste 2a
Oakland CA 94601
510 535-6900

(P-18252)
SUPPORTLOGIC INC
2658 Gamblin Dr, Santa Clara (95051-6506)
PHONE..................................408 471-4710
Krishnaraj Raja, *Principal*
Keola Wong, *Director*
EMP: 36 **EST:** 2018
SALES (est): 4MM **Privately Held**
WEB: www.supportlogic.io
SIC: 8399 7371 Advocacy group; computer software development & applications

(P-18253)
TIDES INC (PA)
Also Called: Tides Shared Spaces
1012 Torney Ave, San Francisco (94129-1704)
P.O. Box 29198 (94129-0198)
PHONE..................................415 561-6400
Melissa Bradley, *CEO*
Nick Hodges, *COO*
China Brotsky, *Vice Pres*
Peter Martin, *Director*
EMP: 90 **EST:** 2002
SQ FT: 180,000
SALES: 4.1MM **Privately Held**
WEB: www.tides.org
SIC: 8399 Community development groups

(P-18254)
TIDES CENTER (PA)
The Prsdio 1014 Trney Ave The Presidio, San Francisco (94129)
P.O. Box 29907 (94129-0907)
PHONE..................................415 561-6400
Janiece Evans-Page, *CEO*
Judith Hill, *CFO*
Gary Schwartz, *Principal*
Jain Suneela, *Admin Sec*
Kim Sarnecki, *Director*
EMP: 45 **EST:** 1994
SALES (est): 204MM **Privately Held**
WEB: www.tides.org
SIC: 8399 Community development groups

(P-18255)
TRI VALLEY HAVEN
3663 Pacific Ave, Livermore (94550-7062)
P.O. Box 2190 (94551-2190)
PHONE..................................925 449-1664
Ann King, *Director*
Vicki Thompson, *Associate Dir*
Jose Maguigad, *Store Mgr*
Fay Piovet, *Executive Asst*
Maureen Hamm, *Instructor*
EMP: 35 **EST:** 1977
SQ FT: 6,461
SALES (est): 4.8MM **Privately Held**
WEB: www.trivalleyhaven.org
SIC: 8399 8322 8699 Advocacy group; individual & family services; emergency shelters; charitable organization

(P-18256)
UNITED CRBRAL PLSY ASSN SAN JQ
134 S Pacific Rd, Manteca (95337-5114)
PHONE..................................209 239-3066
Corinne Fielder, *Manager*
EMP: 65
SALES (corp-wide): 4.9MM **Privately Held**
WEB: www.ucpsj.org
SIC: 8399 Fund raising organization, non-fee basis
PA: United Cerebral Palsy Association Of San Joaquin County
333 W Benjamin Holt Dr # 1
Stockton CA 95207
209 956-0290

(P-18257)
UNITED CRBRAL PLSY CNTL CAL IN (PA)
Also Called: U C P-UNITED CEREBAL PALSY ASS
4224 N Cedar Ave, Fresno (93726-3731)
PHONE..................................559 221-8272

PRODUCTS & SERVICES SECTION

8412 - Museums & Art Galleries County (P-18281)

Mark Lanier, *President*
Carol Kloninger, *Vice Pres*
Jamie Marrash, *Exec Dir*
Pat Murphy, *Exec Dir*
Roger Slingerman, *Exec Dir*
EMP: 50 **EST:** 1954
SQ FT: 15,000
SALES: 6.8MM **Privately Held**
WEB: www.ucpcc.org
SIC: 8399 Fund raising organization, non-fee basis

(P-18258)
UNITED WAY SANTA CRUZ COUNTY
4450 Capitola Rd Ste 106, Capitola (95010-3570)
P.O. Box 1458 (95010-1458)
PHONE...........................831 465-2204
Keisha Frost, *CEO*
Dave Mills, *Treasurer*
Lawrence E Donatoni, *Exec Dir*
Mary Goeke, *Exec Dir*
Leon Mattingly, *Admin Sec*
EMP: 43 **EST:** 1974
SALES (est): 6.9MM **Privately Held**
WEB: www.unitedwaysc.org
SIC: 8399 Fund raising organization, non-fee basis

(P-18259)
YUBA CITY UNIFIED SCHOOL
Also Called: Ycusd
750 N Palora Ave, Yuba City (95991-3627)
PHONE...........................530 822-7601
Steven Scriven, *President*
Lonetta Riley, *Vice Pres*
Becki Witzke, *Admin Asst*
Trisha Collier, *Accounting Mgr*
Terry Camburn, *Human Resources*
EMP: 2000 **EST:** 1966
SALES (est): 94.7MM **Privately Held**
WEB: www.ycusd.org
SIC: 8399 Fund raising organization, non-fee basis

8412 Museums & Art Galleries

(P-18260)
ARTCOM INC (PA)
2100 Powell St Fl 10th, Emeryville (94608-1893)
PHONE...........................510 879-4700
Geoffroy Martin, *CEO*
Chuck Kurth, *CFO*
Lisa Sullivan-Cross, *Chief Mktg Ofcr*
Bob Inman, *Senior VP*
Lesa Musatto, *Senior VP*
▼ **EMP:** 200 **EST:** 1995
SALES (est): 206.5MM **Privately Held**
WEB: www.corporate.art.com
SIC: 8412 Art gallery

(P-18261)
ASIAN ART MSEUM FNDTION SAN FR
Also CALLED: ASIAN ART MEUSUEM OF SF
200 Larkin St, San Francisco (94102-4734)
PHONE...........................415 581-3500
Anthony Sun, *CEO*
Akiko Yamazaki, *President*
Timothy F Kahn, *Treasurer*
Nancy Sackson,
Robert L Duffy, *Vice Pres*
▲ **EMP:** 140 **EST:** 1969
SALES (est): 41.5MM **Privately Held**
WEB: www.asianart.org
SIC: 8412 Museum

(P-18262)
BAY AREA DISCOVERY MUSEUM
557 Mcreynolds Rd, Sausalito (94965-2614)
PHONE...........................415 339-3900
Karyn Flynn, *CEO*
Michelle Martinez, *CFO*
Lea Wood, *Officer*
Helen Hadani, *Research*
Zach Deleo, *Controller*
EMP: 40 **EST:** 1986
SQ FT: 35,000

SALES (est): 9.8MM **Privately Held**
WEB: www.bayareadiscoverymuseum.org
SIC: 8412 Museum

(P-18263)
CHABOT SPACE SCNCE CTR FNDTION (PA)
10000 Skyline Blvd, Oakland (94619-2444)
PHONE...........................510 336-7300
Adam Tobin, *Exec Dir*
Julia Taylor, *Accounting Mgr*
Ken Cober, *Analyst*
Amy Callahan, *Sales Staff*
Tara C Holford, *Associate*
EMP: 49 **EST:** 1989
SQ FT: 65,000
SALES (est): 2.7MM **Privately Held**
WEB: www.chabotspace.org
SIC: 8299 8412 Educational services; museums & art galleries

(P-18264)
CHILDRENS CREATIVITY MUSEUM
221 4th St, San Francisco (94103-3116)
PHONE...........................415 820-3320
Adrienne Pon, *CEO*
Laney Whitcanack, *Ch of Bd*
Shanise Mok, *COO*
MAI MAI Wythes, *Chairman*
John Gonzalez, *Treasurer*
EMP: 65 **EST:** 1992
SALES: 1.9MM **Privately Held**
WEB: www.creativity.org
SIC: 8412 5947 Museum; gift shop

(P-18265)
CITY & COUNTY OF SAN FRANCISCO
Also Called: Asian Art Museum
200 Larkin St, San Francisco (94102-4734)
PHONE...........................415 581-3500
Emily Sano, *Director*
Szuhan Chen, *Partner*
Joanne Chou, *COO*
Mara Finerty, *Officer*
Catherine Finn, *Officer*
EMP: 60
SALES (corp-wide): 7.1B **Privately Held**
WEB: www.sf.gov
SIC: 8412 9199 Museum; general government administration; ;
PA: City & County Of San Francisco
1 Dr Carlton B Goodlett P
San Francisco CA 94102
415 554-7500

(P-18266)
COMPUTER HISTORY MUSEUM
1401 N Shoreline Blvd, Mountain View (94043-1311)
PHONE...........................650 810-1010
John C Hollar, *President*
Laurie Yoler, *Trustee*
Gary Matsushita, *Vice Pres*
Michelle Mertz, *Vice Pres*
Kirsten Tashev, *Vice Pres*
▲ **EMP:** 52 **EST:** 1999
SQ FT: 111,670
SALES: 10.6MM **Privately Held**
WEB: www.computerhistory.org
SIC: 8412 Museum

(P-18267)
COPIA THE AMRCN CTR FOR WINE F
500 1st St, NAPA (94559-2642)
PHONE...........................707 259-1600
Peggy Loar, *President*
Kurt Nystrom, *COO*
▼ **EMP:** 41 **EST:** 1989
SQ FT: 80,000
SALES (est): 1.1MM **Privately Held**
WEB: www.ciaatcopia.com
SIC: 8412 Museums & art galleries

(P-18268)
CORPORTION OF FINE ARTS MSEUMS (PA)
Also Called: DEYOUNG MUSEUM
50 Hagiwara Tea Garden Dr, San Francisco (94118-4502)
PHONE...........................415 750-3600
Michelle Gutierrez, *Officer*
Ed Prohaska, *CFO*

Nelson Favenir, *Officer*
Darwin Wong, *Officer*
Suzy Varadi, *Associate Dir*
▲ **EMP:** 510 **EST:** 1987
SQ FT: 300,000
SALES (est): 39.4MM **Privately Held**
WEB: www.famsf.org
SIC: 8412 Museum

(P-18269)
CURIODYSSEY
1651 Coyote Point Dr, San Mateo (94401-1002)
PHONE...........................650 342-7755
Aragon Burlingham, *Exec Dir*
Gisela Paulsen, *Vice Pres*
Rachel Meyer, *Exec Dir*
Audrianna Gonzales, *Executive Asst*
Melvin Buzon, *Buyer*
EMP: 40 **EST:** 1953
SQ FT: 4,000
SALES: 3.4MM **Privately Held**
WEB: www.curiodyssey.org
SIC: 8412 Museum

(P-18270)
DUBLIN HSTRCAL PRSRVATION ASSN
7172 Regional St Pmb 316, Dublin (94568-2324)
PHONE...........................925 785-2898
Steven Minniear, *President*
EMP: 100 **EST:** 1975
SALES (est): 6K **Privately Held**
WEB: www.dhpa.org
SIC: 8412 Museum

(P-18271)
EXPLORATORIUM
17 Pier Ste 100, San Francisco (94111-1455)
PHONE...........................415 528-4462
Chris Flink, *Exec Dir*
Roberta Katz, *Ch of Bd*
Laura Zander, *COO*
Tyler Wanshura, *Sr Corp Ofcr*
Leslie Marks, *Associate Dir*
◆ **EMP:** 401 **EST:** 1968
SQ FT: 200,000
SALES (est): 45.3MM **Privately Held**
WEB: www.exploratorium.edu
SIC: 8412 Museum

(P-18272)
FRESNO ART MUSEUM
2233 N 1st St, Fresno (93703-2364)
PHONE...........................559 441-4221
Carlos Martinez, *Director*
Michele E Pracy, *Exec Dir*
Michele Pracy, *Exec Dir*
Sarah Vargas, *Bookkeeper*
Susan Y Filgate, *Director*
EMP: 46 **EST:** 1948
SQ FT: 28,000
SALES (est): 876.2K **Privately Held**
WEB: www.fresnoartmuseum.org
SIC: 8412 Museum

(P-18273)
HISTORY SAN JOSE
1650 Senter Rd, San Jose (95112-2599)
PHONE...........................408 287-2290
Alida Bray, *President*
Linda Spencer, *Officer*
Reynaldo Foronda, *Accountant*
Roger Lundgren, *Facilities Mgr*
Gillian Farmer, *Education*
EMP: 89 **EST:** 1971
SALES (est): 5.5MM **Privately Held**
WEB: www.historysanjose.org
SIC: 8412 Museum

(P-18274)
LINDSAY WILDLIFE MUSEUM
1931 1st Ave, Walnut Creek (94597-2540)
PHONE...........................925 935-1978
Kramer Klabau, *President*
John Kikuchi, *President*
Loren Behr, *Exec Dir*
Carlos L De La Rosa, *Exec Dir*
Steven Morgan, *Administration*
EMP: 78 **EST:** 1955
SQ FT: 28,000
SALES (est): 5.7MM **Privately Held**
WEB: www.lindsaywildlife.org
SIC: 8412 Museum

(P-18275)
MEXICAN HERITG CTR GALLERY INC
111 S Sutter St, Stockton (95202-3220)
P.O. Box 77985 (95267-1285)
PHONE...........................209 969-9306
Gracie Madrid, *President*
EMP: 75 **EST:** 1997
SQ FT: 6,799
SALES (est): 41.4K **Privately Held**
WEB: www.mexicanheritagecenter.org
SIC: 8412 Museum

(P-18276)
MUSEUM OF ART HSTORY AT MCPHRS
705 Front St, Santa Cruz (95060-4508)
PHONE...........................831 429-1964
Nina Simon, *Exec Dir*
Alison Ruday, *Vice Pres*
Karen Bush, *Research*
Judy Frost, *CPA*
Ashley Holmes, *Marketing Staff*
EMP: 35 **EST:** 1981
SQ FT: 2,500
SALES (est): 1.4MM **Privately Held**
WEB: www.santacruzmah.org
SIC: 8412 Museum

(P-18277)
OAKLAND MUSEUM OF CALIFORNIA
1000 Oak St, Oakland (94607-4892)
PHONE...........................510 318-8400
Lori Fogarty, *CEO*
Lori G Fogarty, *CEO*
Johanna Jones, *Associate Dir*
Erin Lim, *Associate Dir*
Todd Quackenbush, *Associate Dir*
EMP: 100 **EST:** 1969
SQ FT: 150,000
SALES (est): 21.7MM **Privately Held**
WEB: www.museumca.org
SIC: 8412 Museum

(P-18278)
PACIFIC METRO LLC (PA)
Also Called: Thomas Kinkade Company, The
18715 Madrone Pkwy, Morgan Hill (95037-2876)
PHONE...........................408 201-5000
▲ **EMP:** 350 **EST:** 1993
SALES (est): 14.7MM **Privately Held**
SIC: 8412 Art gallery

(P-18279)
SAN FRANCISCO MUSEUM MODRN ART (PA)
Also Called: SFMOMA MUSEUM STORE
151 3rd St, San Francisco (94103-3107)
PHONE...........................415 357-4035
Robert J Fisher, *President*
Charles R Schwab, *Chairman*
Dennis J Wong, *Treasurer*
Samantha Leo, *Officer*
John Robinson, *Officer*
▲ **EMP:** 362 **EST:** 1921
SQ FT: 225,000
SALES: 60.8MM **Privately Held**
WEB: www.sfmoma.org
SIC: 8412 5942 Museum; book stores

(P-18280)
SAN JOSE CHLD DISCOVERY MUSEUM
180 Woz Way, San Jose (95110-2722)
PHONE...........................408 298-5437
William Sullivan, *CEO*
Marilee Jennings, *Exec Dir*
Rick Berg, *Software Dev*
Christine Thalls, *Software Dev*
Celia Vargas, *IT Specialist*
EMP: 85 **EST:** 1983
SQ FT: 52,000
SALES: 5.4MM **Privately Held**
WEB: www.cdm.org
SIC: 8412 Museum

(P-18281)
SAN JOSE MUSEUM OF ART ASSN
110 S Market St, San Jose (95113-2383)
PHONE...........................408 271-6840
Daniel Keegan, *Director*

(PA)=Parent Co (HQ)=Headquarters (DH)=Div Headquarters
✪ = New Business established in last 2 years

8412 - Museums & Art Galleries County (P-18282)

Susan S Batton, *Exec Dir*
Claire Tsai, *Admin Sec*
Karen Rapp, *Asst Director*
Paulina Vu, *Manager*
▲ **EMP:** 70
SQ FT: 80,000
SALES: 5.1MM **Privately Held**
WEB: www.sjmusart.org
SIC: 8412 5942 5947 Museum; book stores; gift shop

(P-18282)
STANSBURY HM PRESERVATION ASSN
307 W 5th St, Chico (95928-5505)
P.O. Box 3262 (95927-3262)
PHONE 530 895-3848
EMP: 50
SQ FT: 3,500
SALES (est): 786.2K **Privately Held**
SIC: 8412 Museum/Art Gallery

(P-18283)
TECH INTERACTIVE (PA)
201 S Market St, San Jose (95113-2008)
PHONE 408 795-6116
Peter Friess, *CEO*
Christopher Digiorgio, *Ch of Bd*
Daniel J Warmenhoven, *Vice Chairman*
Tim Ritchie, *President*
Naresh Kapahi, *CFO*
◆ **EMP:** 154 **EST:** 1983
SQ FT: 130,000
SALES: 24.6MM **Privately Held**
WEB: www.thetech.org
SIC: 8412 Arts or science center; museum

(P-18284)
THE ORIGIN PROJECT INC
2121 Vallejo St, San Francisco (94123-4814)
PHONE 415 601-2409
Nancy Fisher, *Exec Dir*
EMP: 75 **EST:** 2016
SALES (est): 233.1K **Privately Held**
SIC: 8412 Museums & art galleries

(P-18285)
TURTLE BAY EXPLORATION PARK
1335 Arboretum Dr Ste A, Redding (96003-3628)
PHONE 530 242-3186
John C Peterson, *President*
Maggie Redmon, *COO*
Stephen Gaston, *Chairman*
Joanne Crosetti, *Officer*
Jacque Holden, *Officer*
EMP: 50 **EST:** 1984
SALES (est): 4MM **Privately Held**
WEB: www.turtlebay.org
SIC: 8412 Museum

(P-18286)
WALT DISNEY FAMILY MUSEUM
104 Montgomery St, San Francisco (94129-1718)
PHONE 415 345-6800
Ronald W Miller, *President*
Jennifer Miller-Goff, *Corp Secy*
Joanna Miller, *Vice Pres*
Kirsten Komoroske, *Exec Dir*
Alyson Fried, *Executive Asst*
EMP: 60 **EST:** 2007
SALES (est): 12.1MM **Privately Held**
WEB: www.waltdisney.org
SIC: 8412 Museum

8422 Arboreta, Botanical & Zoological Gardens

(P-18287)
AQUARIUM OF BAY (HQ)
Beach Embrcdero Strway 2, San Francisco (94103)
PHONE 415 623-5300
Frtiz Arko, *General Mgr*
▲ **EMP:** 50 **EST:** 1994
SALES (est): 6.8MM
SALES (corp-wide): 7.3MM **Privately Held**
WEB: www.aquariumofthebay.org
SIC: 8422 7999 Aquarium; tourist attraction, commercial
 PA: The Bay Institute Of San Francisco
 695 De Long Ave Ste 100
 Novato CA
 415 898-1376

(P-18288)
BAYORG
Also Called: Aquarium of The Bay, The Embarcadero At Beach St, San Francisco (94133)
PHONE 415 623-5300
John Frawley, *President*
Bobbi Evans, *CFO*
EMP: 99 **EST:** 2010
SALES (est): 11.5MM **Privately Held**
WEB: www.aquariumofthebay.org
SIC: 8422 Aquarium

(P-18289)
CALIFORNIA ACADEMY SCIENCES (PA)
55 Music Concourse Dr, San Francisco (94118-4503)
PHONE 415 379-8000
John Hafernik, *President*
Rebecca Schuett, *Partner*
George Still, *Managing Prtnr*
Alison Brown, *CFO*
Salman Khan, *Trustee*
EMP: 635 **EST:** 1853
SQ FT: 410,000
SALES: 55.8MM **Privately Held**
WEB: www.calacademy.org
SIC: 8422 2721 8412 Aquarium; periodicals: publishing only; museums & art galleries

(P-18290)
CONSERVATION SOCIETY CAL
Also Called: Oakland Zoo In Knowland Park
9777 Golf Links Rd, Oakland (94605-4925)
P.O. Box 5238 (94605-0238)
PHONE 510 632-9525
Joel J Parrott, *CEO*
Steven E Kane, *Ch of Bd*
Kristin Heller, *Vice Pres*
Bob Westfall, *Vice Pres*
William L Marchant, *Admin Sec*
EMP: 165 **EST:** 1936
SQ FT: 1,000
SALES (est): 23.7MM **Privately Held**
WEB: www.oaklandzoo.com
SIC: 8422 Arboreta & botanical or zoological gardens

(P-18291)
FILOLI CENTER
Also Called: Filoli Garden Shop
86 Canada Rd, Woodside (94062-4144)
PHONE 650 364-8300
Kara Newport, *CEO*
Pamela Smith, *President*
Cynthia D'Agosta, *CEO*
Robert Walker, *Principal*
Priya Yadav, *Human Res Dir*
EMP: 55
SQ FT: 1,000
SALES (est): 8.6MM **Privately Held**
WEB: www.filoli.org
SIC: 8422 8412 Botanical garden; museum

(P-18292)
FRESNOS CHAFFEE ZOO CORP
894 W Belmont Ave, Fresno (93728-2807)
PHONE 559 498-5910
Scott Barton, *CEO*
Brian Goldman, *CFO*
Richard Rick Treatch Edd, *CFO*
Merlisa Condoian, *Executive Asst*
Jennifer Winebrenner, *Technician*
◆ **EMP:** 121 **EST:** 2005
SALES (est): 20.4MM **Privately Held**
WEB: www.fresnochaffeezoo.org
SIC: 8422 Animal & reptile exhibit

(P-18293)
MENDOCINO CAST BTNCAL GRDNS CO
Also Called: Mendocino Cast Botanical Grdns
18220 N Highway 1, Fort Bragg (95437-8773)
PHONE 707 964-4352
Molly Barker, *Exec Dir*
Robert Bushansky, *President*
EMP: 45 **EST:** 1986
SQ FT: 2,000
SALES (est): 3.1MM **Privately Held**
WEB: www.gardenbythesea.org
SIC: 8422 Botanical garden

(P-18294)
MONTALVO ASSOCIATION
Also Called: VILLA MONTALVO
15400 Montalvo Rd, Saratoga (95070-6327)
P.O. Box 158 (95071-0158)
PHONE 408 961-5800
Angela McConnell, *CEO*
Glenn Osaka, *Treasurer*
Laura Amador, *Education*
Shruti Murthy, *Research Analys*
Patricia McLeod, *Director*
EMP: 65
SQ FT: 13,000
SALES: 7.6MM **Privately Held**
WEB: www.montalvoarts.org
SIC: 8422 8412 Arboretum; art gallery, noncommercial

(P-18295)
SACRAMENTO ZOOLOGICAL SOCIETY
3930 W Land Park Dr, Sacramento (95822-1123)
PHONE 916 808-5888
Mary Healy, *Exec Dir*
Alison Mott, *Vice Pres*
Kris Yarbery, *Project Mgr*
Robert Churchill, *Finance*
Kathryn Hensley, *Education*
EMP: 50 **EST:** 1956
SALES (est): 8.8MM **Privately Held**
WEB: www.saczoo.org
SIC: 8422 Arboreta & botanical or zoological gardens

8611 Business Associations

(P-18296)
ALMOND BOARD OF CALIFORNIA
1150 9th St Ste 1500, Modesto (95354-0845)
PHONE 209 549-8262
Richard Waycott, *CEO*
Karen Lapsley, *Officer*
Connie Calhoun, *Associate Dir*
Swati Kalgaonkar, *Associate Dir*
Josette Lewis, *Security Dir*
EMP: 50
SQ FT: 10,000
SALES (est): 73MM **Privately Held**
WEB: www.almonds.com
SIC: 8611 Trade associations

(P-18297)
ASSOCIATION CAL WTR AGENCIES (PA)
980 9th St Ste 1000, Sacramento (95814-2736)
PHONE 916 441-4545
Tim Quinn, *Exec Dir*
Glen Peterson, *President*
Soren Nelson, *Analyst*
Stacey Siqueiros, *Marketing Staff*
Kanisha Golden, *Corp Comm Staff*
EMP: 42 **EST:** 1910
SALES (est): 8.6MM **Privately Held**
WEB: www.acwa.com
SIC: 8611 Trade associations

(P-18298)
ASSOCTION ASN/PCFIC CMNTY HLTH
Also Called: Aapcho
2140 Shattuck Ave Ste 203, Berkeley (94704-1211)
PHONE 510 272-9536
Jane Eng, *Treasurer*
Sherry Hirota, *President*
Kazue Shibata, *Vice Pres*
Albert Ayson, *Associate Dir*
Jeff Caballero, *Exec Dir*
EMP: 40 **EST:** 1987
SQ FT: 3,706
SALES: 2.6MM **Privately Held**
WEB: www.aapcho.org
SIC: 8611 Business associations

(P-18299)
BAY MEADOWS RACING ASSOCIATION
2600 S Delaware St, San Mateo (94403-1904)
P.O. Box 1490 (94401-0872)
PHONE 650 573-4500
Fax: 650 573-4677
EMP: 200
SALES (est): 4.5MM **Privately Held**
WEB: www.baymeadows.com
SIC: 8611 Business Association

(P-18300)
BETTER BUSINESS BUREAU INC
1000 Broadway Ste 625, Oakland (94607-4042)
P.O. Box 218, San Leandro (94577-0618)
PHONE 510 844-2000
Lori Wilson, *CEO*
D Patrick Wallace, *President*
Lisa Baldonado, *Vice Pres*
Dubose Scarborough, *Vice Pres*
Kim Sharp, *Vice Pres*
EMP: 37 **EST:** 1927
SQ FT: 3,200
SALES (est): 5.1MM **Privately Held**
SIC: 8611 Better Business Bureau

(P-18301)
CALIFORNIA APARTMENT ASSN
980 9th St Ste 1430, Sacramento (95814-2720)
PHONE 916 447-7881
Thomas K Bannon, *CEO*
Rhovy L Antonio, *Vice Pres*
Anil Babbar, *Vice Pres*
Ben Benoit, *Vice Pres*
Whitney Benzian, *Vice Pres*
EMP: 35 **EST:** 1941
SQ FT: 6,600
SALES (est): 10.3MM **Privately Held**
WEB: www.caanet.org
SIC: 8611 Trade associations

(P-18302)
CALIFORNIA CHAMBER COMMERCE (PA)
Also Called: Cal Chamber
1215 K St Ste 1400, Sacramento (95814-3953)
P.O. Box 1736 (95812-1736)
PHONE 916 444-6670
Allan Zaremberg, *President*
Lawrence M Dicke, *CFO*
Jennifer Barrera, *Exec VP*
Jeanne Cain, *Exec VP*
Dave Kilby, *Exec VP*
EMP: 65 **EST:** 1890
SQ FT: 26,000
SALES (est): 28.2MM **Privately Held**
WEB: www.calchamber.com
SIC: 8611 Chamber of Commerce

(P-18303)
CALIFORNIA RURAL WATER ASSN
1234 N Market Blvd, Sacramento (95834-1906)
PHONE 916 553-4900
Dan Demoss, *Exec Dir*
Dustin Hardwick, *Exec Dir*
Ruby Brungess, *Admin Asst*
Laura Newman, *Admin Asst*
Debra Skelton, *Technician*
EMP: 43 **EST:** 1990
SQ FT: 19,200
SALES: 4MM **Privately Held**
WEB: www.calruralwater.org
SIC: 8611 Trade associations

▲ = Import ▼ = Export
◆ = Import/Export

PRODUCTS & SERVICES SECTION

8621 - Professional Membership Organizations County (P-18327)

(P-18304)
CALIFRNIA ASSN HLTH FACILITIES (PA)
Also Called: CAHF
2201 K St, Sacramento (95816-4922)
PHONE.....................................916 441-6400
James H Gomez, *CEO*
Jason Belden, *Director*
EMP: 42 **EST:** 1950
SQ FT: 1,500
SALES (est): 8.2MM **Privately Held**
WEB: www.cahf.org
SIC: 8611 Trade associations

(P-18305)
CWS UTILITY SERVICES CORP
1720 N 1st St, San Jose (95112-4508)
PHONE.....................................408 367-8200
Robert W Foye, *Principal*
EMP: 235 **EST:** 2005
SALES (est): 1.5MM
SALES (corp-wide): 794.3MM **Publicly Held**
WEB: www.calwatergroup.com
SIC: 8611 Public utility association
PA: California Water Service Group
1720 N 1st St
San Jose CA 95112
408 367-8200

(P-18306)
GREATER FRSNO AREA CHMBER CMMR
2331 Fresno St, Fresno (93721-1801)
PHONE.....................................559 495-4800
Al Smith, *CEO*
Alyssa Stevens, *Manager*
EMP: 37 **EST:** 1895
SQ FT: 1,700
SALES (est): 4.9MM **Privately Held**
WEB: www.fresnochamber.com
SIC: 8611 Chamber of Commerce

(P-18307)
INTERNTNAL ASSN BUS CMMNCATORS
Also Called: Membership Assction-Non-Profit
601 Montgomery St # 1900, San Francisco (94111-2603)
PHONE.....................................415 544-4711
Julie Freeman, *President*
Bonnie Caver, *Ch of Bd*
Maureen Lennon, *Vice Pres*
EMP: 73 **EST:** 1970
SQ FT: 7,740
SALES (est): 2.8MM **Privately Held**
SIC: 8611 Trade associations

(P-18308)
LAKE COUNTY OFFICE EDUCATION (PA)
1152 S Main St, Lakeport (95453-5517)
PHONE.....................................707 262-4102
Brock Falkenberg, *Superintendent*
Kandee Stolesen, *Admin Asst*
Wayne Martin, *IT/INT Sup*
Michelle Buell, *Business Mgr*
Terra Seifert, *Analyst*
EMP: 36 **EST:** 1975
SQ FT: 10,000
SALES (est): 18.1MM **Privately Held**
WEB: www.lakecoe.org
SIC: 8211 8611 Public elementary & secondary schools; business associations

(P-18309)
MERCHANT VALLEY CORPORATION
1808 Avondale Dr, Roseville (95747-8390)
PHONE.....................................916 786-7227
Mahmood Merchant, *Principal*
EMP: 125 **EST:** 1997
SALES (est): 9.9MM **Privately Held**
SIC: 8611 Merchants' association

(P-18310)
NAPA VALLEY VINTNERS
1475 Library Ln, Saint Helena (94574-1144)
P.O. Box 141 (94574-0141)
PHONE.....................................707 963-3388
Linda Reiff, *President*
Steven Tradewell, *CFO*
Joel Coleman-Nakai, *Comms Mgr*
Stacey Capitani, *Managing Dir*
Heather Butler, *Executive Asst*
EMP: 55 **EST:** 1960
SQ FT: 6,900
SALES (est): 10.8MM **Privately Held**
WEB: www.napavintners.com
SIC: 8611 Trade associations

(P-18311)
NEXTFLEX
2244 Blach Pl Ste 150, San Jose (95131-2060)
PHONE.....................................408 435-5523
Malcolm Thompson, *Principal*
Henry Madden, *Program Mgr*
Jeana Lindsley, *Admin Asst*
Robert McManus, *Electrical Engi*
Amy Mueller, *Engineer*
EMP: 37 **EST:** 2016
SALES (est): 10.2MM **Privately Held**
WEB: www.nextflex.us
SIC: 8611 Manufacturers' institute

(P-18312)
NORTH STATE BLDG INDUST ASSN
1536 Eureka Rd, Roseville (95661-3055)
PHONE.....................................916 677-5717
John R Orr, *President*
Deedee Wang, *Admin Asst*
David Darling, *Software Dev*
Jeffrey Klein, *Finance*
Morgan Davis, *Corp Comm Staff*
EMP: 54 **EST:** 1944
SQ FT: 6,000
SALES (est): 5.2MM **Privately Held**
WEB: www.northstatebia.org
SIC: 8611 Contractors' association; trade associations

(P-18313)
PUBLIC POLICY INSTITUTE CAL (PA)
Also Called: PPIC
500 Washington St Ste 600, San Francisco (94111-2907)
PHONE.....................................415 291-4400
David Lyon, *President*
Robert E Obana, *CFO*
Andy Grose, *Principal*
Carlos Torres, *Administration*
Joy Collins, *Research*
EMP: 72 **EST:** 1994
SQ FT: 105,044
SALES (est): 34.3MM **Privately Held**
WEB: www.ppic.org
SIC: 8611 8732 Trade associations; commercial nonphysical research

(P-18314)
RH COMMUNITY BUILDERS LP
2550 W Clinton Ave B-142, Fresno (93705-4206)
PHONE.....................................559 492-1373
Wayne Rutledge, *CEO*
Brad Hardie, *President*
EMP: 100 **EST:** 2019
SALES (est): 4.3MM **Privately Held**
WEB: www.rhcommunitybuilders.com
SIC: 8611 8082 Community affairs & services; home health care services

(P-18315)
SACRAMENTO HARNESS ASSOCIATION
1600 Exposition Blvd, Sacramento (95815-5104)
PHONE.....................................916 239-4040
Ralph Scurfield, *President*
Chris Schick, *Manager*
EMP: 90
SALES: 138.8K **Privately Held**
SIC: 8611 Merchants' association

(P-18316)
SAN FRNCSCO BAR PLOTS BNVLENT
9 Pier Ste 119a, San Francisco (94111-1451)
PHONE.....................................415 362-5436
Peter Mc Isaac, *President*
Capt Peter McIsaac, *President*
Capt Daniel Boriolo, *CFO*
Daniel Boriolo, *Officer*
Anne McIntyre, *Business Dir*
EMP: 52 **EST:** 1835
SQ FT: 20,000
SALES (est): 6.8MM **Privately Held**
WEB: www.sfbarpilots.com
SIC: 8611 Business associations

(P-18317)
SAN JOSE SLCON VLY CHMBER CMMR
Also Called: Chamberpac
101 W Santa Clara St, San Jose (95113-1760)
PHONE.....................................408 291-5250
EMP: 50
SALES (est): 2.2MM **Privately Held**
WEB: www.thesvo.com
SIC: 8611 Business Associations, Nsk

(P-18318)
SEMI (PA)
673 S Milpitas Blvd, Milpitas (95035-5473)
PHONE.....................................408 943-6900
Ajit Manocha, *President*
Bertrand Loy, *Ch of Bd*
Eric Tien, *President*
Richard Salsman, *CFO*
Mary G Puma, *Treasurer*
EMP: 133
SALES (est): 41.7MM **Privately Held**
WEB: www.semi.org
SIC: 8611 Trade associations

(P-18319)
SR HOLDINGS LLC (HQ)
4040 Civic Center Dr, San Rafael (94903-4150)
PHONE.....................................415 927-6400
George Pasha IV, *CEO*
James Britton, *CFO*
Amy Sherburne Manning, *General Counsel*
EMP: 15 **EST:** 2014
SALES (est): 4.5MM
SALES (corp-wide): 632.2MM **Privately Held**
WEB: www.pashagroup.com
SIC: 8611 3443 Shipping & steamship company association; containers, shipping (bombs, etc.): metal plate
PA: The Pasha Group
4040 Civic Center Dr # 350
San Rafael CA 94903
415 927-6400

(P-18320)
SURPLUS LINE ASSOCIATION CAL
12667 Alcosta Blvd # 450, San Ramon (94583-4427)
PHONE.....................................415 434-4900
Ted Pierce, *Exec Dir*
Michael Caturegli, *Vice Pres*
Patricia McAuley, *Data Proc Staff*
Pamela Boyes, *VP Human Res*
Sandhya Dhital, *Education*
EMP: 41 **EST:** 1937
SQ FT: 8,400
SALES (est): 10.2MM **Privately Held**
WEB: www.slacal.com
SIC: 8611 Trade associations

(P-18321)
UNIVERSITY CORP ADVNCD INTERNT
6001 Shellmound St # 850, Emeryville (94608-1968)
PHONE.....................................510 858-0881
David Lambert, *Branch Mgr*
EMP: 44 **Privately Held**
WEB: www.ucaid.com
SIC: 8611 Business associations
PA: University Corporation For Advanced Internet Development
1150 18th St Nw Ste 900
Washington DC 20036

8621 Professional Membership Organizations

(P-18322)
ALAMEDA COUNTY BAR ASSOCIATION
1000 Broadway Ste 480, Oakland (94607-4044)
PHONE.....................................510 302-2222
Donald A McIsaac, *President*
Ming W Chin, *Vice Pres*
Valerie Brown, *Comms Dir*
Ann Wassam, *Exec Dir*
Harold C Norton, *Administration*
EMP: 47 **EST:** 1937
SALES (est): 15.3MM **Privately Held**
WEB: www.acbanet.org
SIC: 8621 Bar association

(P-18323)
AMERICAN ACDEMY OPHTHLMLOGY IN (PA)
655 Beach St, San Francisco (94109-1342)
P.O. Box 7424 (94120-7424)
PHONE.....................................415 561-8500
David W Parke II, *CEO*
Keith Carter, *President*
Jill Boyett, *CFO*
Vicky Loni, *CFO*
Cathy Cohen, *Vice Pres*
EMP: 160 **EST:** 1896
SQ FT: 66,000
SALES (est): 60.4MM **Privately Held**
WEB: www.aao.org
SIC: 8621 Medical field-related associations

(P-18324)
BAR ASSCATION OF SAN FRANCISCO (PA)
201 Mission St Ste 400, San Francisco (94105-1832)
PHONE.....................................415 982-1600
James Donato, *President*
Jonathan Bond, *CFO*
Dan Burkhardt, *Exec Dir*
Samantha Silver, *Admin Asst*
Alvaro Carvajal, *Prgrmr*
EMP: 85 **EST:** 1949
SALES (est): 7.2MM **Privately Held**
WEB: www.sfbar.org
SIC: 8621 Bar association

(P-18325)
BUILD IT GREEN
300 Frank H Ogawa Plz # 620, Oakland (94612-2056)
PHONE.....................................510 590-3360
Karen Kho,
Christopher Becker, *Exec Dir*
Karin Burns, *Exec Dir*
Lawrence J Simi, *Exec Dir*
Lauren Hotell, *Project Mgr*
EMP: 39 **EST:** 2004
SALES: 7.9MM **Privately Held**
WEB: www.builditgreen.org
SIC: 8621 Professional membership organizations

(P-18326)
CALIFORNIA DENTAL ASSOCIATION (PA)
1201 K St Fl 14, Sacramento (95814-3925)
PHONE.....................................916 443-0505
Peter A Dubois, *CEO*
Dennis Kalebjian, *President*
Carol Summerhayes, *President*
Cynthia Schneider, *CFO*
Debi Irwin, *Vice Pres*
EMP: 120 **EST:** 1873
SQ FT: 28,932
SALES (est): 39.5MM **Privately Held**
WEB: www.cda.org
SIC: 8621 Dental association

(P-18327)
CALIFORNIA HEALTH BENEFIT EXCH
Also Called: California Health Insur Exch
1601 Exposition Blvd, Sacramento (95815-5103)
PHONE.....................................916 228-8210

8621 - Professional Membership Organizations County (P-18328)

Peter V Lee, *CEO*
Larry Hicks, *Officer*
Lilly Myers, *Planning*
Linda Anderson, *Opers Staff*
Desi Malone, *Manager*
EMP: 99
SALES (est): 12.8MM **Privately Held**
WEB: www.coveredca.com
SIC: 8621 Health association

(P-18328)
CALIFORNIA MEDICAL ASSOCIATION (PA)
Also Called: C M A
1201 K St Ste 800, Sacramento (95814-3933)
PHONE..................916 444-5532
Dustin Corcoren, *CEO*
Lance Lewis, *COO*
Lance R Lewis, *COO*
Alecia Sanchez, *Officer*
Nick Birtcil, *Vice Pres*
EMP: 73
SALES: 18.3MM **Privately Held**
WEB: www.cmadocs.org
SIC: 8621 Medical field-related associations

(P-18329)
CALIFORNIA NURSES ASSOCIATION (PA)
Also Called: NATIONAL NURSES UNITED
155 Grand Ave Ste 115, Oakland (94612-3758)
PHONE..................510 273-2200
Rose Anne Demoro, *CEO*
Deborah Burger, *President*
Sheila Ibanez, *Executive Asst*
Nikki Dones, *Admin Sec*
Leticia Rodriguez, *Admin Sec*
EMP: 100 **EST:** 1907
SQ FT: 36,000
SALES (est): 56.9MM **Privately Held**
WEB: www.nationalnursesunited.org
SIC: 8621 Nursing association

(P-18330)
CALIFORNIA PRIMARY CARE ASSN
1231 I St Ste 400, Sacramento (95814-2933)
PHONE..................916 440-8170
Carmela Castellano Garcia, *CEO*
Robin Concannon, *CFO*
David Anderson, *Vice Pres*
Robert Beaudry, *Vice Pres*
Andie M Patterson, *Vice Pres*
EMP: 36 **EST:** 1994
SALES: 12.5MM **Privately Held**
WEB: www.cpca.org
SIC: 8621 Health association

(P-18331)
CALIFORNIA SCHOOL BOARDS ASSN
Also Called: CSBA
3251 Beacon Blvd, West Sacramento (95691-3531)
PHONE..................800 266-3382
Vernon M Billy, *CEO*
Cindy Marks, *President*
Stephen Pogemiller, *CFO*
Jesus Holguin, *Vice Pres*
Tamara Otero, *Vice Pres*
EMP: 100
SQ FT: 15,000
SALES: 472K **Privately Held**
WEB: www.csba.org
SIC: 8621 Education & teacher association

(P-18332)
CALIFORNIA TEACHERS ASSN (PA)
1705 Murchison Dr, Burlingame (94010-4583)
P.O. Box 921 (94011-0921)
PHONE..................650 697-1400
Carolyn Doggett, *Exec Dir*
Monica Mora, *Exec Dir*
Sonya Tsujimura, *Exec Dir*
Kim Breen, *Office Mgr*
Ingrid Williams, *Admin Sec*
EMP: 210
SALES: 211.6MM **Privately Held**
WEB: www.cta.org
SIC: 8621 8631 Education & teacher association; labor unions & similar labor organizations

(P-18333)
CALIFRNIA ASSN HSPTALS HLTH SY (PA)
Also Called: California Hospital Assn Cha
1215 K St Ste 800, Sacramento (95814-3946)
PHONE..................916 443-7401
Carmela Coyle, *President*
Lois M Suder, *COO*
Dietmar Grellmann, *Senior VP*
Anne McLeod, *Senior VP*
Patricia L Blaisdell, *Vice Pres*
EMP: 74
SQ FT: 30,000
SALES: 35.7MM **Privately Held**
WEB: www.calhospital.org
SIC: 8621 8011 Health association; group health association

(P-18334)
CALIFRNIA CPA EDCATN FUNDATION
1800 Gateway Dr Ste 200, San Mateo (94404-4072)
PHONE..................800 922-5272
Anthony Pugliese, *CEO*
Dipali Desai, *Technical Staff*
Vinit Shrawagi, *Technical Staff*
EMP: 49 **EST:** 1966
SQ FT: 8,071
SALES (est): 3.2MM **Privately Held**
WEB: www.calcpa.org
SIC: 8621 Professional membership organizations

(P-18335)
CALIFRNIA SOC CRTIF PUB ACCNTN (PA)
Also Called: CALIFORNIA SOCIETY OF CPA'S
1710 Gilbreth Rd Ste 100, Burlingame (94010-1315)
PHONE..................650 522-3000
Anthony Pugliese, *CEO*
Natalie Quan, *CFO*
Emil Redzic, *Info Tech Dir*
Anna Dillig, *Controller*
Tm Sze, *Opers Staff*
EMP: 40
SALES: 14MM **Privately Held**
WEB: www.calcpa.org
SIC: 8621 Professional membership organizations

(P-18336)
CDA HOLDING COMPANY INC (PA)
1201 K St Ste 1400, Sacramento (95814-3925)
PHONE..................916 442-2462
Mark Soth, *CFO*
Richard Krolak, *COO*
Carrie Gordon, *Officer*
Todd Lewis, *Vice Pres*
John McKee, *Vice Pres*
EMP: 51 **EST:** 1996
SALES (est): 34.8MM **Privately Held**
WEB: www.cda.org
SIC: 8621 Dental association

(P-18337)
CENTER FOR CARE INNVATIONS INC (PA)
1438 Webster St Ste 101, Oakland (94612-3229)
PHONE..................415 561-6393
Jane Stafford, *Administration*
Andrea Allen, *Program Mgr*
Jacqueline Nuila, *Program Mgr*
Maria Pelaez, *Finance Mgr*
Angela Liu, *Opers Staff*
EMP: 43 **EST:** 2013
SALES (est): 1.5MM **Privately Held**
WEB: www.careinnovations.org
SIC: 8621 Health association

(P-18338)
HEALTH TRUST (PA)
3180 Newberry Dr Ste 200, San Jose (95118-1566)
PHONE..................408 513-8700
Frederick J Ferrer, *CEO*
Robert Humphreys, *Partner*
Mary Patterson, *Partner*
Gary Allen, *President*
Todd Hansen J D, *COO*
EMP: 135 **EST:** 1996
SALES: 25.5MM **Privately Held**
WEB: www.healthtrust.org
SIC: 8621 8299 Health association; educational services

(P-18339)
LEXISNEXIS COURTLINK INC
2101 K St, Sacramento (95816-4920)
PHONE..................425 974-5000
Michele Vivona, *President*
Nick Baguio, *Manager*
EMP: 56 **EST:** 1977
SQ FT: 40,000
SALES (est): 2.6MM
SALES (corp-wide): 9.4B **Privately Held**
WEB: www.relx.com
SIC: 8621 Professional membership organizations
HQ: Relx Inc.
230 Park Ave Ste 700
New York NY 10169
212 309-8100

(P-18340)
MEDCORE MEDICAL GROUP
Also Called: Omni Ipa/Medcore Medical Group
2609 E Hammer Ln, Stockton (95210-4222)
PHONE..................209 320-2600
Kirit Patel, *Principal*
Jack Dugue, *CIO*
EMP: 51 **EST:** 1985
SALES (est): 1.7MM **Privately Held**
WEB: www.medcoreipa.com
SIC: 8621 Health association

(P-18341)
OAKLAND MLTARY INST CLLEGE PRP
3877 Lusk St, Emeryville (94608-3822)
PHONE..................510 594-3900
Jerry Brown, *Founder*
Bruce Holaday, *Exec Dir*
EMP: 50
SQ FT: 25,000
SALES: 9MM **Privately Held**
WEB: www.oakmil.org
SIC: 8211 8621 Public senior high school; professional membership organizations

(P-18342)
PACIFIC HEALTH ADVANTAGE (HQ)
221 Main St Ste 1500, San Francisco (94105-1940)
PHONE..................415 281-8660
John Grgurina Jr, *President*
Ed Eberhard, *President*
David Greene, *Vice Pres*
EMP: 50 **EST:** 1999
SALES (est): 857K **Privately Held**
WEB: www.pbgh.org
SIC: 8621 Health association

(P-18343)
PENINSULA POST-ACUTE
1609 Trousdale Dr, Burlingame (94010-4520)
PHONE..................650 443-2600
Toby Tilford, *President*
Mary Chesler, *Director*
EMP: 40 **EST:** 2015
SALES (est): 12.2MM **Privately Held**
WEB: www.penpostacute.com
SIC: 8621 Professional membership organizations

(P-18344)
PHYSICANS MED GROUP SANTA CRUZ
Also Called: Physician Services
100 Enterprise Way, Scotts Valley (95066-3248)
PHONE..................831 465-7800
Jeffrey Williams, *President*
Cindy Martin, *Officer*
Lupe Mendoza, *Admin Mgr*
Farhana Basha, *Office Mgr*
D Dawn Motyka, *Admin Sec*
EMP: 43 **EST:** 1985
SQ FT: 9,000
SALES (est): 5.4MM **Privately Held**
WEB: www.dignityhealth.org
SIC: 8621 8011 Medical field-related associations; offices & clinics of medical doctors

(P-18345)
PLACER CO BAR ASSOCIATION (PA)
P.O. Box 4598 (95604-4598)
PHONE..................916 557-9181
David G Cohen, *Principal*
EMP: 172 **EST:** 2009
SALES (est): 64.2K **Privately Held**
WEB: www.placerbar.org
SIC: 8621 Bar association

(P-18346)
SALU BEAUTY INC
Also Called: Salu.net
11344 Coloma Rd Ste 725, Gold River (95670-4464)
PHONE..................916 475-1400
Jim O Steeb, *President*
Steve Brown, *COO*
John V Crisan, *CFO*
Jim Fisher, *Exec Dir*
Denise McDonald, *Prdtn Mgr*
EMP: 55 **EST:** 1995
SALES (est): 10.8MM **Privately Held**
WEB: www.salubeauty.com
SIC: 8621 5961 Health association; general merchandise, mail order
HQ: The Hut.Com Limited
5th Floor Voyager House
Manchester M90 3
161 813-1481

(P-18347)
SAN FRANCISCO HEALTH AUTHORITY (PA)
Also Called: Hsf Programme
50 Beale St Fl 12, San Francisco (94105-1823)
P.O. Box 194247 (94119-4247)
PHONE..................415 615-4407
John Grgurina Jr, *CEO*
Philip Hartman, *President*
John Gregoire, *CFO*
Fiona Donald, *Chief Mktg Ofcr*
James Glauber, *Chief Mktg Ofcr*
EMP: 99 **EST:** 1996
SQ FT: 26,000
SALES (est): 26.6MM **Privately Held**
WEB: www.sfhp.org
SIC: 8621 Health association

(P-18348)
SAN MATEO COUNTY BAR ASSN
Also Called: Release On Rcgnznce For Prvate
333 Bradford St Ste 150, Redwood City (94063-1572)
PHONE..................650 298-4000
John Digiacinto, *President*
Alma D Robles, *Exec Dir*
Susan Espinoza, *Office Mgr*
EMP: 37 **EST:** 1966
SALES (est): 5.4MM **Privately Held**
WEB: www.smcba.org
SIC: 8621 Bar association

(P-18349)
STATE BAR OF CALIFORNIA (PA)
180 Howard St Fl Grnd, San Francisco (94105-6155)
PHONE..................415 538-2000
Bill Hebert, *President*
Peggy Van Horn, *CFO*

PRODUCTS & SERVICES SECTION

8631 - Labor Unions & Similar Organizations County (P-18372)

Juli Finnila, Admin Sec
Martha Munoz, Admin Sec
Sandra Reynolds, Admin Sec
EMP: 296 **EST:** 1927
SQ FT: 72,000
SALES (est): 119.6MM **Privately Held**
WEB: www.calbar.ca.gov
SIC: 8621 Bar association

(P-18350)
STELLAR IT SOLUTIONS LLC
1620 Oakland Rd Ste D200, San Jose (95131-2448)
PHONE 669 250-6837
Krishna Chaitanya Kurnala,
Pandu Semasinghe, Director
EMP: 35 **EST:** 2018
SALES (est): 1.3MM **Privately Held**
WEB: www.stellaritgroup.com
SIC: 8621 Professional membership organizations

(P-18351)
UNITED CEREBRAL PALSY ASSOC (PA)
Also Called: Cerebral Palsy Assn San Joaqui
333 W Benjamin Holt Dr # 1, Stockton (95207-3906)
PHONE 209 956-0290
Ray All, Exec Dir
EMP: 110 **EST:** 1954
SQ FT: 15,000
SALES (est): 4.9MM **Privately Held**
WEB: www.ucpsj.org
SIC: 8621 Professional membership organizations

(P-18352)
WOMENS RCVERY ASSN SAN MTEO CN
Also Called: Womens Recovery Association
2015 Pioneer Ct, San Mateo (94403-1781)
PHONE 650 348-6603
Christina Tufono, Program Dir
Jolie Bou, Finance Dir
EMP: 101 **EST:** 1970
SQ FT: 12,000
SALES (est): 4.3MM
SALES (corp-wide): 96.1MM **Privately Held**
WEB: www.healthright360.org
SIC: 8621 Professional membership organizations
PA: Healthright 360 Foundation
1563 Mission St Fl 1
San Francisco CA 94103
415 762-3700

8631 Labor Unions & Similar Organizations

(P-18353)
AFSCME LOCAL 3299 (PA)
425 15th St, Oakland (94612-2801)
PHONE 510 844-1160
Jane McDonald, Principal
Judy Ashbaugh, Bd of Directors
James L Clark, Bd of Directors
Rosemarie Fejerang, Bd of Directors
Jesse Hernandez, Bd of Directors
EMP: 57 **EST:** 2006
SALES (est): 20.3MM **Privately Held**
WEB: www.afscme3299.org
SIC: 8631 Labor union

(P-18354)
C W A DISTRICT NINE (HQ)
Also Called: Communctons Wkrs Amer AFL-CIO
2870 Gateway Oaks Dr # 100, Sacramento (95833-3577)
PHONE 916 921-4500
Morton Barr, President
Tony Bixler, Vice Pres
EMP: 50 **EST:** 2001
SALES (est): 562.5K
SALES (corp-wide): 164.8MM **Privately Held**
WEB: www.district9.cwa-union.org
SIC: 8631 Labor union

PA: Communications Workers Of America, Afl-Cio, Clc
501 3rd St Nw
Washington DC 20001
202 434-1100

(P-18355)
CALIFORNIA SCHL EMPLOYEES ASSN (PA)
Also Called: Csea
2045 Lundy Ave, San Jose (95131-1865)
PHONE 408 473-1000
Keith Pace, CEO
Steve Brashear, CFO
Monica Esquivel, Admin Asst
Justin Garcia, Graphic Designe
Karin Buckner,
EMP: 180 **EST:** 1927
SQ FT: 65,000
SALES (est): 36.3MM **Privately Held**
WEB: www.csea.com
SIC: 8631 Labor union

(P-18356)
CALIFRNIA CRRCTNAL PACE OFFCER (PA)
Also Called: Ccpoa
755 Riverpoint Dr, West Sacramento (95605-1673)
PHONE 916 372-6060
Chuck Alexander, President
James Martin, Treasurer
Keith Bennett, Vice Pres
Chuck Helton, Vice Pres
Julie Estrella, Executive Asst
EMP: 60
SQ FT: 32,000
SALES (est): 30.4MM **Privately Held**
WEB: www.ccpoa.org
SIC: 8631 8111 Labor union; legal services

(P-18357)
CALIFRNIA STATE EMPLOYEES ASSN (PA)
Also Called: Csea
3000 Advantage Way, Sacramento (95834-9707)
PHONE 916 444-8134
Dave Hart, President
Debbie Cotton, CFO
Dave Okunura, Treasurer
Mark Semo, Bd of Directors
Teresa Schmidt, Comms Mgr
EMP: 80 **EST:** 1932
SQ FT: 30,000
SALES: 3K **Privately Held**
WEB: www.calcsea.org
SIC: 8631 Labor union

(P-18358)
FREIGHT CHCKERS CLRCAL EMPLYEE
Also Called: Teamsters Local 856
453 San Mateo Ave, San Bruno (94066-4415)
PHONE 650 635-0111
Joe Lanthier, President
Michael J McLaughlin, Corp Secy
Kathleen Romero, Trustee
Crystal Young, Corp Comm Staff
Trish Blinstrub, Director
EMP: 48 **EST:** 1949
SALES (est): 9.5MM **Privately Held**
WEB: www.teamsters174.net
SIC: 8631 Labor union

(P-18359)
HOTEL EMPLYEE REST EMPLYEE UN
209 Golden Gate Ave, San Francisco (94102-3705)
PHONE 415 864-8770
Mike Casey, President
Tho Thi Do, Corp Secy
Rafael Espinoza, Vice Pres
EMP: 39 **EST:** 1950
SQ FT: 10,000
SALES (est): 1.6MM **Privately Held**
WEB: www.unitehere.org
SIC: 8631 Labor union

(P-18360)
INDUSTRIAL RELATIONS CAL DEPT
25347 S Schulte Rd, Tracy (95377-9710)
PHONE 209 830-7200
Michael Height, Branch Mgr
EMP: 36 **Privately Held**
SIC: 8631 8249 Labor union; vocational apprentice training
HQ: California Department Of Industrial Relations
455 Golden Gate Ave Fl 10
San Francisco CA 94102

(P-18361)
INDUSTRIAL RELATIONS CAL DEPT
301 Howard St Ste 700, San Francisco (94105-6604)
P.O. Box 420603 (94142-0603)
PHONE 415 703-5133
EMP: 36 **Privately Held**
SIC: 8631 Labor unions & similar labor organizations
HQ: California Department Of Industrial Relations
455 Golden Gate Ave Fl 10
San Francisco CA 94102

(P-18362)
INTERNATIONAL TRANSPORT FEDERA
1188 Franklin St Ste 400, San Francisco (94109-6852)
PHONE 415 440-7043
EMP: 35
SALES (est): 886.7K **Privately Held**
SIC: 8631 Labor Organization

(P-18363)
INTERNTIONAL UN OPER ENGINEERS (PA)
1121 L St Ste 401, Sacramento (95814-3969)
PHONE 916 444-6880
Tim Neep, Director
EMP: 67 **EST:** 2014
SALES (est): 52.1MM **Privately Held**
SIC: 8631 Labor union

(P-18364)
INTERNTNAL BRTHD ELC WKR LCAL (PA)
Also Called: AFL-CIO #1245
30 Orange Tree Cir, Vacaville (95687-3105)
PHONE 707 452-2700
Ed Mallory, President
James McCulley, Vice Pres
Michael J Davis,
Kathy Tindall,
Matthew Locati, Manager
EMP: 64 **EST:** 1948
SALES (est): 49.1MM **Privately Held**
WEB: www.ibew1245.com
SIC: 8631 Labor union

(P-18365)
INTERNTNAL BRTHD ELEC WKRS LCA
55 Fillmore St, San Francisco (94117-3515)
PHONE 415 861-5752
John Orourke, Manager
Rose Dartois, Office Mgr
EMP: 37 **EST:** 1928
SALES (est): 3.8MM **Privately Held**
WEB: www.ibew6.org
SIC: 8631 Trade union

(P-18366)
INTERNTNAL LNGSHRMENS WRHSMEN
Also Called: Longshrmens Wrhsmens Un Lcl 54
22 N Union St, Stockton (95205-4915)
PHONE 209 464-1827
Marc Cuavas, President
Dennis Brueckner, President
Lee Flood, Vice Pres
Frank Aeonis, Admin Sec
Ryan Takas, Representative

EMP: 36 **EST:** 1934
SQ FT: 1,000
SALES (est): 659.1K **Privately Held**
SIC: 8631 Trade union; labor union

(P-18367)
INTERNTNAL UN OPER ENGNERS LCA
Also Called: Operating Engners Lcal Un No 3
1620 S Loop Rd, Alameda (94502-7085)
PHONE 510 748-7400
Dan Reding, Business Mgr
Yu-Ju Wu, CFO
EMP: 300 **EST:** 1896
SALES (est): 60.3MM **Privately Held**
WEB: www.oe3.org
SIC: 8631 Labor union

(P-18368)
IUOE STTONARY ENGINEERS LCL 39
Also Called: Iuoe Local 39
1620 N Market Blvd, Sacramento (95834-1958)
PHONE 916 928-0399
Tony De Marco, President
Jerry Kalmar, Vice Pres
Jim Maple, Training Dir
EMP: 50 **EST:** 1896
SALES (est): 3.4MM **Privately Held**
WEB: www.local39.org
SIC: 8631 Labor union

(P-18369)
LABORERS FNDS ADMNSTRTIVE OFFI (PA)
Also Called: Laborers Trust Funds Nthrn Cal
5672 Stoneridge Dr # 100, Pleasanton (94588-8559)
PHONE 707 864-2800
Edward Smith, Admin Sec
Elena Warner, Auditor
Emily Woods, Payroll Mgr
Matt Clizbe, Opers Staff
Anthony Brooks, Director
EMP: 100 **EST:** 1963
SQ FT: 43,000
SALES (est): 404.6MM **Privately Held**
WEB: www.norcalaborers.org
SIC: 8631 Labor union

(P-18370)
NORTHERN CAL CRPNTERS RGNAL CN
Also Called: Nccrc
265 Hegenberger Rd, Oakland (94621-1443)
PHONE 510 568-4788
Bob Alvarado, Executive Asst
Augie Beltran, Mktg Dir
Tim Lipscomb, Asst Director
Jay Bradshaw, Manager
Samantha Draper, Manager
EMP: 40 **EST:** 2008
SALES (est): 64.6MM **Privately Held**
WEB: www.nccrc.org
SIC: 8631 Labor union

(P-18371)
OPERATING ENGNERS LCAL UN NO 3 (PA)
1620 S Loop Rd, Alameda (94502-7085)
PHONE 510 748-7400
Russ Burns, Business Mgr
Carl Goff, President
Steve Ingersoll, Treasurer
Dan Reding, Treasurer
John Rector, Exec Dir
EMP: 249 **EST:** 1939
SQ FT: 50,000
SALES: 411.3K **Privately Held**
WEB: www.oe3.org
SIC: 8631 Labor unions & similar labor organizations

(P-18372)
SEIU LOCAL 1021
447 29th St, Oakland (94609-3510)
P.O. Box 2077 (94604-2077)
PHONE 510 350-9811
Damita Davis-Howard, Director
Joseph Bryant, Admin Sec
David Canham, Director
EMP: 62 **EST:** 2007

8631 - Labor Unions & Similar Organizations County (P-18373)

(P-18373)
SEIU UNITED HEALTHCARE WORKERS (PA)
560 Thomas L Berkley Way, Oakland (94612-1602)
PHONE...................510 251-1250
Dave Regan, *President*
Sarah Steck, *COO*
Edgard Tajina, *CFO*
Eiseo Medina, *Trustee*
Debbie M Schneider, *Trustee*
EMP: 140
SQ FT: 33,000
SALES (est): 107.3MM **Privately Held**
WEB: www.seiu-uhw.org
SIC: 8631 Labor union

(P-18374)
SEIU UNTD HLTHCARE WRKRS-WEST
Also Called: Seiu Uhw-West
1911 F St, Sacramento (95811-1718)
PHONE...................916 326-5850
Lynn Templeton, *Branch Mgr*
Stan Lyles, *Vice Pres*
Elena Perez, *Corp Comm Staff*
EMP: 37
SALES (corp-wide): 107.3MM **Privately Held**
WEB: www.seiu-uhw.org
SIC: 8631 Labor union
PA: Seiu United Healthcare Workers-West
Local 2005
560 Thomas L Berkley Way
Oakland CA 94612
510 251-1250

(P-18375)
SEIU UNTD HLTHCARE WRKRS-WEST
Also Called: Seiu Uhw West
47 Kearny St Fl 4, San Francisco (94108-5519)
PHONE...................415 441-2500
Sherlina Grimaldo, *Principal*
EMP: 37
SALES (corp-wide): 107.3MM **Privately Held**
WEB: www.seiu-uhw.org
SIC: 8631 Labor union
PA: Seiu United Healthcare Workers-West
Local 2005
560 Thomas L Berkley Way
Oakland CA 94612
510 251-1250

(P-18376)
SEIU UNTD HLTHCARE WRKRS-WEST
Also Called: Seiu Uhw-West
2995 Moorpark Ave, San Jose (95128-2509)
PHONE...................408 557-2835
Sherlina Grimaldo, *Branch Mgr*
EMP: 37
SALES (corp-wide): 107.3MM **Privately Held**
WEB: www.seiu-uhw.org
SIC: 8631 Labor union
PA: Seiu United Healthcare Workers-West
Local 2005
560 Thomas L Berkley Way
Oakland CA 94612
510 251-1250

(P-18377)
SERVICE WORKERS LOCAL 715 (PA)
Also Called: Service Emplyees Intl Un Lcal
2302 Zanker Rd, San Jose (95131-1115)
PHONE...................408 678-3300
Rosemary Romo, *President*
Pamela Rodgers, *Admin Dir*
Kristina Sermersheim, *Exec Sec*
Robert Garner, *Director*
EMP: 39 **EST:** 1955
SQ FT: 1,000
SALES (est): 2.1MM **Privately Held**
WEB: www.seiu521.org
SIC: 8631 8621 Labor union; professional membership organizations

(P-18378)
TEAMSTERS LOCAL UNION 70
Also Called: Brotherhood Teamsters Local 70
400 Roland Way, Oakland (94621-2012)
PHONE...................510 569-9317
Dominic Chivare, *President*
Marty Frates, *Corp Secy*
Daniel Gonsalves Jr, *Vice Pres*
Milton Lewis, *Vice Pres*
Felix Martinez, *Vice Pres*
EMP: 41 **EST:** 1903
SQ FT: 10,000
SALES (est): 9.1MM **Privately Held**
WEB: www.teamsterslocal70.org
SIC: 8631 Labor union

(P-18379)
TRUSTEES OF THE INTRNTNL LNGSH (PA)
Also Called: Trustees of The Ilwu
1188 Franklin St Fl 3, San Francisco (94109-6800)
PHONE...................415 673-8500
Hollis Greenwood, *Exec Dir*
John J Dee, *Exec Dir*
Sam Alvarado, *Director*
Martha Hendricks, *Director*
EMP: 35 **EST:** 1952
SALES (est): 2.7MM **Privately Held**
WEB: www.benefitplans.org
SIC: 8631 Labor union

(P-18380)
UFCW & EMPLOYERS TRUST LLC
Also Called: Valley Clerks Trust Fund
2200 Prfcional Dr Ste 190, Roseville (95661)
PHONE...................916 782-1618
Greg Ritley, *Manager*
EMP: 54
SALES (corp-wide): 555.4MM **Privately Held**
WEB: www.ufcwtrust.com
SIC: 8631 Labor union
PA: Ufcw & Employers Trust Llc
1000 Burnett Ave Ste 110
Concord CA 94520
800 552-2400

(P-18381)
UNITED ASSOCIATION LOCAL 342
Also Called: Plumbers Stmftters Lcal Un 342
935 Detroit Ave, Concord (94518-2501)
PHONE...................925 686-5880
Jay Williams, *Manager*
EMP: 57 **EST:** 1912
SQ FT: 16,000
SALES (est): 12.7MM **Privately Held**
WEB: www.ua342.org
SIC: 8631 Labor union

(P-18382)
UNITED FD COML WKRS UN LCAL 8
Also Called: Ufcw 8 Golden State
2200 Prfcional Dr Ste 100, Roseville (95661)
P.O. Box 619021 (95661-9021)
PHONE...................916 786-0588
Jacques Loveall, *President*
Kirk Vogt, *Sr Exec VP*
Cori Higley, *Office Mgr*
Rauch Donna, *Admin Asst*
Sandy Samoville, *Admin Asst*
EMP: 75 **EST:** 1953
SALES (est): 21.6MM **Privately Held**
WEB: www.ufcw8.org
SIC: 8631 Labor union

(P-18383)
UNITED FD COML WKRS UN LOCAL 5
Also Called: Ufcw 5
240 S Market St, San Jose (95113-2310)
PHONE...................408 998-0428
Ronald J Lind, *Admin Sec*
Roger Vergus, *President*
James Araby, *Exec Dir*
Joanne Los Banos, *Office Mgr*
Teresa Zuniga, *Office Mgr*
EMP: 43 **EST:** 1933
SQ FT: 9,043
SALES (est): 23.5MM **Privately Held**
WEB: www.ufcw5.org
SIC: 8631 Labor union

8641 Civic, Social & Fraternal Associations

(P-18384)
ALPHA DELTA PHI INTERNATIONAL
3871 Piedmont Ave, Oakland (94611-5378)
PHONE...................415 704-1879
Bennet Cox, *Principal*
EMP: 49
SALES (corp-wide): 163.9K **Privately Held**
WEB: www.adps.org
SIC: 8641 University club
PA: Alpha Delta Phi International Inc
2242 N Baldwin Way 5b
Palatine IL 60074
847 581-1992

(P-18385)
AMERICAN ASSN UNIV WOMEN
941 The Alameda, Berkeley (94707-2316)
PHONE...................510 528-3284
EMP: 35
SALES (est): 1.3MM **Privately Held**
SIC: 8641 Civic And Social Associations

(P-18386)
AMERICAN HIGH SCHL BOOSTER CLB
36300 Fremont Blvd, Fremont (94536-3511)
PHONE...................510 796-1776
Thomas Knutson, *President*
Michael Lindsay, *Ch of Bd*
Jerry Losson, *Ch of Bd*
David Takacs, *Ch of Bd*
Jan Cunningham, *Admin Sec*
EMP: 47 **EST:** 1972
SALES (est): 14.9K **Privately Held**
WEB: www.fusd-ca.schoolloop.com
SIC: 8641 Booster club

(P-18387)
AMERICAN LEGION AMBULANCE SVC
Also Called: American Legion Hall
11350 American Legion Dr, Sutter Creek (95685)
P.O. Box 100 (95685-0100)
PHONE...................209 223-2963
Al Lennox, *General Mgr*
EMP: 37 **EST:** 1929
SQ FT: 800
SALES (est): 1.3MM **Privately Held**
WEB: www.alpost108.org
SIC: 8641 Veterans' organization

(P-18388)
ASSOCIATED STUDENTS OF S S U
1801 E Cotati Ave, Rohnert Park (94928-3613)
PHONE...................707 664-2815
Nadier Vissanjy, *President*
Jen Minich, *President*
Mike Blake, *Treasurer*
Margarita Zunita, *Treasurer*
Jamie Holian, *Vice Pres*
EMP: 35 **EST:** 1962
SQ FT: 900
SALES (est): 2.7MM **Privately Held**
WEB: www.sonoma.edu
SIC: 8641 8351 University club; child day care services

(P-18389)
ASSOCIATED STUDENTS S J S U
1 Washington Sq, San Jose (95112-3613)
PHONE...................408 924-6240
Tari Wimbley, *Exec Dir*
Kelli Reid, *Exec Dir*
Michelle Domocol, *Opers Staff*
Edilbert Signey, *Marketing Staff*
Jim Cellini, *Director*
EMP: 39 **EST:** 1898
SQ FT: 1,500
SALES (est): 3.6MM **Privately Held**
WEB: www.sjsu.edu
SIC: 8641 2752 University club; commercial printing, offset

(P-18390)
ASSOCIATED STUDENTS STANFORD (PA)
Also Called: A S S U
201 Tresidder Un, Stanford (94305)
PHONE...................650 723-4331
Linda Whitcomb, *Director*
Chris Middleton, *Vice Pres*
Bikal Sharma, *Vice Pres*
Alice Willoughby, *Principal*
EMP: 63 **EST:** 1914
SALES (est): 1.4MM **Privately Held**
WEB: www.stanford.edu
SIC: 8641 University club

(P-18391)
BAY EAST ASSN RLTORS FUNDATION
7901 Stoneridge Dr # 150, Pleasanton (94588-3677)
PHONE...................925 730-4060
Tricia Thomas, *CEO*
Michael McFann, *CTO*
Toni Wilson, *Director*
Sona Rawat, *Commercial*
EMP: 43 **EST:** 1947
SALES (est): 5.9MM **Privately Held**
WEB: www.bayeast.org
SIC: 8641 Booster club

(P-18392)
BELLEVUE CLUB
525 Bellevue Ave, Oakland (94610-5096)
PHONE...................510 451-1000
Barbara Maroney, *Manager*
Henry Johns, *General Mgr*
Lindsay Clifton, *Editor*
EMP: 79 **EST:** 1926
SQ FT: 1,080,000
SALES (est): 5.7MM **Privately Held**
WEB: www.bellevueoakland.com
SIC: 5812 8641 American restaurant; social club, membership

(P-18393)
BODEGA HARBOUR HOMEOWNERS ASSN
Also Called: Bodega Harbour Golf Links
21301 Heron Dr, Bodega Bay (94923)
P.O. Box 368 (94923-0368)
PHONE...................707 875-3519
Judith A Steeves, *Admin Mgr*
Ken Felker, *Controller*
Brett Fox, *Maint Spvr*
Mary Angelo, *Exec Sec*
Tj Smith, *Manager*
EMP: 65 **EST:** 1971
SQ FT: 10,000
SALES (est): 5.4MM **Privately Held**
WEB: www.bodegaharbourgolf.com
SIC: 8641 5812 5813 7997 Homeowners' association; American restaurant; bars & lounges; yacht club, membership

(P-18394)
BOHEMIAN CLUB (PA)
Also Called: BOHEMIAN GROVE
624 Taylor St, San Francisco (94102-1075)
PHONE...................415 885-2440
Robert L Spence, *CEO*
Matt Ogerio, *General Mgr*
Deena Soulon, *Finance*
Eileen Leong, *Accountant*
Chris Cheeseman, *Manager*
EMP: 100 **EST:** 1872
SQ FT: 20,000
SALES (est): 22.3MM **Privately Held**
SIC: 8641 Social club, membership

(P-18395)
BOYS & GIRLS CLUB NAPA VALLEY
Also Called: BOYS' & GIRLS' CLUB
1515 Pueblo Ave, NAPA (94558-4837)
PHONE...................707 255-8866
Cindy Goodale, *Director*
Mark Kuhnhausen, *Exec Dir*
Camille Ball, *Marketing Staff*
Patrick Smorra,
Van Bui, *Program Dir*

PRODUCTS & SERVICES SECTION

8641 - Civic, Social & Fraternal Associations County (P-18418)

EMP: 44 EST: 1956
SQ FT: 6,500
SALES (est): 3.3MM Privately Held
WEB: www.begreatnv.org
SIC: 8641 Youth organizations

(P-18396)
BOYS & GIRLS CLUB SILICON VLY
518 Valley Way, Milpitas (95035-4106)
PHONE...................408 957-9685
Dana Fraticelli, *Director*
Max Duganne, *Bd of Directors*
Kelly Sandoval, *Exec Dir*
Wendy Plasencia, *Marketing Mgr*
Michelle Albert, *Manager*
EMP: 51 EST: 2001
SALES (est): 4.5MM Privately Held
WEB: www.bgclub.org
SIC: 8641 Youth organizations

(P-18397)
BOYS & GIRLS CLUBS OF N VLY
601 Wall St, Chico (95928-5626)
PHONE...................530 899-0335
Rashell Brobst, *CEO*
Scott Dinits, *Human Res Dir*
Alex Beehner, *Marketing Staff*
Joshua H Campos, *Director*
Sheryl Manies, *Director*
EMP: 80 EST: 1995
SQ FT: 14,000
SALES (est): 5.3MM Privately Held
WEB: www.bgcnv.org
SIC: 8641 Youth organizations

(P-18398)
BOYS GRLS CLUBS SNTA CRUZ CNTY
543 Center St, Santa Cruz (95060-4337)
PHONE...................831 423-3138
Robert Langseth, *Director*
Andrea Tolaio, *Officer*
Rebbie Higgins, *Opers Staff*
Levin Leah, *Education*
Daniel Kumasaka, *Athletic Dir*
EMP: 46 EST: 1969
SALES: 1.7MM Privately Held
WEB: www.boysandgirlsclub.info
SIC: 8641 Youth organizations

(P-18399)
CALCPA INSTITUTE
1710 Gilbreth Rd Ste 100, Burlingame (94010-1315)
PHONE...................800 922-5272
Maria Yarmolinsky, *Principal*
Nastasha Spencer, *Program Mgr*
Gere Cherry, *CPA*
Soco Davenport, *CPA*
David Lo, *CPA*
EMP: 35 EST: 2011
SALES: 591.3K Privately Held
WEB: www.calcpa.org
SIC: 8641 Civic social & fraternal associations

(P-18400)
CALI CALMECAC LANGUAGE ACADEMY
9491 Starr Rd, Windsor (95492-9460)
PHONE...................707 837-7747
Jeanne Acuna, *Principal*
Sharon Ferrer, *Vice Pres*
Hollie Escher, *Admin Sec*
Joel Smith, *Comp Spec*
Patricia Arreguin, *Teacher*
EMP: 60 EST: 2010
SALES: 102.4K Privately Held
WEB: www.ccla.wusd.org
SIC: 8641 8211 Parent-teachers' association; elementary & secondary schools

(P-18401)
CALIFORNIA RESTAURANT ASSN
Also Called: Southern California Rest Assn
621 Capitol Mall Ste 2000, Sacramento (95814-4725)
PHONE...................916 447-5793
Jot Condie, *CEO*
EMP: 35 EST: 1929
SALES (est): 508.4K Privately Held
WEB: www.calrest.org
SIC: 8641 Bars & restaurants, members only

(P-18402)
CALIFORNIA WATERFOWL ASSN
1346 Blue Oaks Blvd, Roseville (95678-7032)
PHONE...................916 648-1406
Yancey Forest-Knowles, *Ch of Bd*
Bob McLandress, *President*
Colby Heaton, *CFO*
Colby K Heaton, *CFO*
Christine Mesaros, *Administration*
EMP: 43
SQ FT: 6,500
SALES: 11.5MM Privately Held
WEB: www.calwaterfowl.org
SIC: 8641 Environmental protection organization

(P-18403)
CALIFRNIA LEAG CNSRVTION VTERS (PA)
350 Frank H Ogawa Plz # 1100, Oakland (94612-2006)
PHONE...................510 271-0900
Sarah Rose, *Director*
Melissa Romero, *Manager*
Sam Shaw, *Associate*
EMP: 45 EST: 1971
SQ FT: 3,500
SALES (est): 733.2K Privately Held
WEB: www.envirovoters.org
SIC: 8641 Environmental protection organization

(P-18404)
CARE2COM INC
3141 Stevens Creek Blvd, San Jose (95117-1141)
PHONE...................650 622-0860
Randy Paynter III, *CEO*
Eric Rardin, *President*
Marlin Miller, *COO*
Geoff Mitchell, *Vice Pres*
EMP: 40 EST: 1997
SALES (est): 5.5MM Privately Held
WEB: www.care2services.com
SIC: 8641 Environmental protection organization

(P-18405)
CENTRAL COAST YMCA
Also Called: YMCA San Benito County
351 Tres Pnos Rd Ste 201a, Hollister (95023)
PHONE...................831 637-8600
Mayra Yerena, *Principal*
Kori Davis, *Director*
EMP: 103
SALES (corp-wide): 7.9MM Privately Held
WEB: www.centralcoastymca.org
SIC: 8641 Youth organizations; recreation association
PA: Central Coast Ymca
600 Camino El Estero
Monterey CA 93940
831 757-4633

(P-18406)
CENTRAL COAST YMCA
27 Sudden St, Watsonville (95076-4322)
PHONE...................831 728-9622
Jeanette Mattos, *Director*
Scott Kurteff, *CFO*
Robert Wollenzien, *Vice Pres*
Joe Gonzales, *Exec Dir*
Robin Schnekenburger, *Exec Dir*
EMP: 103
SALES (corp-wide): 7.9MM Privately Held
WEB: www.centralcoastymca.org
SIC: 8641 7991 8351 7032 Youth organizations; physical fitness facilities; child day care services; youth camps; individual & family services
PA: Central Coast Ymca
600 Camino El Estero
Monterey CA 93940
831 757-4633

(P-18407)
CHICO STATE ENTERPRISES
25 Main St Unit 203, Chico (95928-5388)
PHONE...................530 898-6811
Jessica Bourne, *Exec Dir*
EMP: 2000 EST: 1996
SQ FT: 15,000
SALES: 42.3MM Privately Held
WEB: www.csuchico.edu
SIC: 8641 Civic social & fraternal associations

(P-18408)
COMMUNITY OF HARBOR BAY ISLE
3195 Mecartney Rd, Alameda (94502-6912)
PHONE...................510 865-3363
George Kay, *Exec Dir*
Jen Crook, *Exec Dir*
Kathy Araujo, *Admin Asst*
Samantha Ferris, *Admin Asst*
Javier Silva, *Commander*
EMP: 39 EST: 1977
SQ FT: 12,000
SALES (est): 4.6MM Privately Held
WEB: www.harborbay.org
SIC: 8641 Homeowners' association

(P-18409)
CONTRA COSTA COUNTY EMPLOYEES
Also Called: Cccera
1355 Willow Way Ste 221, Concord (94520-5728)
PHONE...................925 521-3960
Marilyn Leedom, *CEO*
Cary Hally, *CFO*
Wrally Dutkiewicz, *Officer*
Jay Kwon, *Counsel*
David J Macdonald, *Director*
EMP: 40 EST: 2007
SALES (est): 3.2MM Privately Held
WEB: www.cccera.org
SIC: 8641 Social associations

(P-18410)
CORD BLOOD DONOR FOUNDATION
1200 Bayhill Dr Ste 301, San Bruno (94066-3006)
PHONE...................650 635-1420
EMP: 41
SALES (est): 2.9MM Privately Held
WEB: www.cordblood.com
SIC: 8641 Civic/Social Association

(P-18411)
COWELL HOMEOWNERS ASSN INC (PA)
Also Called: Walnut Country
4498 Lawson Ct, Concord (94521-4410)
PHONE...................925 825-0250
Rhinan Harris, *General Mgr*
Michael Demeo, *President*
EMP: 60 EST: 1972
SQ FT: 2,300
SALES (est): 3MM Privately Held
WEB: www.walnutcountry.com
SIC: 8641 8351 Homeowners' association; child day care services

(P-18412)
DUCKS UNLIMITED INC
Also Called: Western Regional Office
3074 Gold Canal Dr, Rancho Cordova (95670-6116)
PHONE...................916 852-2000
Rudy Rosses, *Director*
Nick Wiley, *Officer*
Eric Held, *General Mgr*
Maribeth Lane, *Executive Asst*
Morgan McIntyre, *Executive Asst*
EMP: 50
SALES (corp-wide): 185.3MM Privately Held
WEB: www.ducks.org
SIC: 8641 Environmental protection organization
PA: Ducks Unlimited, Inc.
1 Waterfowl Way
Memphis TN 38120
901 758-3825

(P-18413)
EAST BAY COMMUNITY FOUNDATION
Also Called: E B C F
200 Frank H Ogawa Plz, Oakland (94612-2005)
PHONE...................510 836-3223
Nichole Taylor, *President*
Karen Stevenson, *President*
Valerie Red-Horse Mohl, *CFO*
Theresa Johnson, *Accountant*
Genevieve Zaragoza, *Controller*
EMP: 55 EST: 1928
SQ FT: 15,500
SALES (est): 34.8MM Privately Held
WEB: www.ebcf.org
SIC: 8641 Civic social & fraternal associations

(P-18414)
FISHER HOUSE PALO ALTO
3801 Miranda Ave, Palo Alto (94304-1207)
PHONE...................650 858-3903
Tammie Ridder, *CIO*
Karen Doi, *Project Leader*
Rhonda Thomas, *Recruiter*
Daniel Kulenich, *Deputy Dir*
Anne Jordan, *Pastor Care Dir*
EMP: 37 EST: 2011
SALES (est): 5.5MM Privately Held
WEB: www.meriwest.com
SIC: 8641 Civic social & fraternal associations

(P-18415)
FOUNDTION FOR HISPANIC EDUCATN (PA)
14271 Story Rd, San Jose (95127-3823)
P.O. Box 730453 (95173-0453)
PHONE...................408 585-5022
Edward Alvarez, *CEO*
Terri McCluskey, *Executive Asst*
Michelle Moreno, *Executive Asst*
Cynthia Tapia, *Accountant*
Janice Chavez, *Education*
EMP: 48 EST: 2011
SQ FT: 60
SALES: 16.1MM Privately Held
WEB: www.tfhe.org
SIC: 8641 Civic social & fraternal associations

(P-18416)
FOUNDTION FOR STDNTS RSING ABO
99 The Embarcadero, San Francisco (94105-1214)
P.O. Box 29174 (94129-0174)
PHONE...................415 333-4222
Michael Loughlin, *Exec Dir*
Lynne Martin, *Exec Dir*
Julia Green, *Marketing Staff*
Jennifer Naecker, *Director*
Lauren Brener, *Manager*
EMP: 96 EST: 2003
SALES (est): 11.2MM Privately Held
WEB: www.studentsrisingabove.org
SIC: 8641 8699 Youth organizations; charitable organization

(P-18417)
FRANCISCA CLUB
595 Sutter St, San Francisco (94102-1196)
PHONE...................415 781-1200
Rene De Vos, *Manager*
Drew Gyorke, *Executive*
Rene Devos, *General Mgr*
Shaffer McGee, *Controller*
Nancy Dunn, *Asst Mgr*
EMP: 37 EST: 1910
SQ FT: 12,270
SALES (est): 1.3MM Privately Held
WEB: www.franciscaclub.com
SIC: 8641 Social club, membership

(P-18418)
FRIENDS SANTA CRUZ STATE PARKS
1543 Pacific Ave Ste 206, Santa Cruz (95060-3962)
PHONE...................831 429-1840
Bonny Hawley, *Exec Dir*
Crissy Canlas, *Project Mgr*
Laura Pascal, *Accountant*
Anne Weidlich, *Human Resources*

8641 - Civic, Social & Fraternal Associations County (P-18419)

Jorge Savala, *Director*
EMP: 80 **EST:** 1975
SALES: 5.1MM **Privately Held**
WEB: www.thatsmypark.org
SIC: 8641 Environmental protection organization

(P-18419)
GIRL SCOUTS HEART CENTRAL CAL
6601 Elvas Ave, Sacramento (95819-4339)
PHONE..................916 452-9181
Linda Farley, *CEO*
Kerry Koyasako, *Vice Pres*
Julie O 'donnell, *Vice Pres*
Nena Garcia, *Administration*
Christine Hosford, *Comp Spec*
EMP: 127
SALES: 9.9MM **Privately Held**
WEB: www.girlscoutshcc.org
SIC: 8641 Girl Scout organization

(P-18420)
GIRL SCOUTS NORTHERN CAL
920 Westlake Dr, Kelseyville (95451-7051)
PHONE..................707 279-4689
Andrea Bride, *CFO*
Emily Azevedo, *Bd of Directors*
Sally Biggin, *Bd of Directors*
Patricia Buckley, *Bd of Directors*
Taylor Chin, *Bd of Directors*
EMP: 38
SALES (corp-wide): 24.6MM **Privately Held**
WEB: www.gsnorcal.org
SIC: 8641 Girl Scout organization
PA: Girl Scouts Of Northern California
1650 Harbor Bay Pkwy # 100
Alameda CA 94502
510 562-8470

(P-18421)
GIRL SCOUTS NORTHERN CAL (PA)
1650 Harbor Bay Pkwy # 100, Alameda (94502-3013)
PHONE..................510 562-8470
Marina Park, *CEO*
Robin Macgillivray, *President*
Diana Bell, *Vice Pres*
Ellen Richey, *Vice Pres*
Debra Rossi, *Vice Pres*
EMP: 70 **EST:** 1963
SQ FT: 17,000
SALES: 24.6MM **Privately Held**
WEB: www.gsnorcal.org
SIC: 8641 Girl Scout organization

(P-18422)
GIRL SCOUTS NORTHERN CAL
1310 S Bascom Ave, San Jose (95128-4502)
PHONE..................408 287-4170
Michelle McCormick, *Branch Mgr*
EMP: 38
SALES (corp-wide): 24.6MM **Privately Held**
WEB: www.gsnorcal.org
SIC: 8641 Girl Scout organization
PA: Girl Scouts Of Northern California
1650 Harbor Bay Pkwy # 100
Alameda CA 94502
510 562-8470

(P-18423)
GIRL SCOUTS NORTHERN CAL
4825 Old Redwood Hwy, Santa Rosa (95403-1415)
PHONE..................707 544-5472
Deborah Holden, *Branch Mgr*
EMP: 38
SALES (corp-wide): 24.6MM **Privately Held**
WEB: www.gsnorcal.org
SIC: 8641 Girl Scout organization
PA: Girl Scouts Of Northern California
1650 Harbor Bay Pkwy # 100
Alameda CA 94502
510 562-8470

(P-18424)
GIRL SCOUTS SANTA CLARA COUNTY (PA)
Also Called: Girl Scouts of America
1310 S Bascom Ave, San Jose (95128-4502)
PHONE..................408 287-4170
Joann Neal, *Exec Dir*
EMP: 35 **EST:** 1912
SQ FT: 12,000
SALES (est): 1.1MM **Privately Held**
SIC: 8641 Girl Scout organization

(P-18425)
GLADSTONE FOUNDATION
1650 Owens St, San Francisco (94158-2261)
PHONE..................415 734-2000
R Sanders Williams, *Principal*
EMP: 36 **EST:** 2016
SALES (est): 3.8MM **Privately Held**
WEB: www.gladstone.org
SIC: 8641 Civic social & fraternal associations

(P-18426)
GOLDEN GATE NAT PRKS CNSRVANCY
680 Point Lobos Ave, San Francisco (94121-1477)
PHONE..................415 933-6760
Mark Yanez, *Opers Mgr*
Natalie Yap, *Education*
Niko Bellott, *Director*
Brenda Munive, *Associate*
EMP: 96 **Privately Held**
WEB: www.parksconservancy.org
SIC: 8641 Environmental protection organization
PA: Golden Gate National Parks Conservancy
Fort Mason Bldg 201
San Francisco CA 94123

(P-18427)
GOLDEN RAIN FOUNDATION
800 Rockview Dr, Walnut Creek (94595-3002)
PHONE..................925 988-7800
Warren Thurlow Salmons, *Branch Mgr*
Nancy Bunch, *Opers Staff*
EMP: 35
SQ FT: 24,100
SALES (corp-wide): 33.2MM **Privately Held**
WEB: www.rossmoor.com
SIC: 8641 Homeowners' association
PA: Golden Rain Foundation Of Walnut Creek
1001 Golden Rain Rd
Walnut Creek CA 94595
925 988-7700

(P-18428)
GORDON BETTY MOORE FOUNDATION
1661 Page Mill Rd, Palo Alto (94304-1209)
P.O. Box 29910, San Francisco (94129-0910)
PHONE..................650 213-3000
Steve McCormick, *President*
Sara Bender, *Officer*
Beth Campanella, *Officer*
Gary Greenburg, *Officer*
Adam Jones, *Officer*
EMP: 89 **EST:** 2010
SALES (est): 10.3MM **Privately Held**
WEB: www.moore.org
SIC: 8641 Civic social & fraternal associations

(P-18429)
HANUMAN FELLOWSHIP (PA)
Also Called: Gateway Books
445 Summit Rd, Watsonville (95076-9781)
PHONE..................408 847-0406
Ward Maillard, *President*
EMP: 47 **EST:** 1974
SQ FT: 20,000
SALES: 2.8MM **Privately Held**
WEB: www.mountmadonna.org
SIC: 8299 5942 8641 Educational service, nondegree granting; continuing educ.; book stores; civic social & fraternal associations

(P-18430)
HAYWARD UNIFIED SCHOOL DST
Also Called: Fairview Elementary School
24823 Soto Rd, Hayward (94544-1931)
P.O. Box 5000 (94540-0001)
PHONE..................510 723-3830
John Melvin Jr, *Principal*
Leticia Pajoluk, *Admin Sec*
EMP: 48
SALES (corp-wide): 336.5MM **Privately Held**
WEB: www.husd.us
SIC: 8211 8641 Public elementary school; parent-teachers' association
PA: Hayward Unified School District
24411 Amador St
Hayward CA 94544
510 784-2600

(P-18431)
HIDDEN VALLEY LAKE ASSOCIATION (PA)
Also Called: Hidden Valley Golf Course
18174 Hidden Valley Rd, Hidden Valley Lake (95467-8690)
PHONE..................707 987-3146
Wiliam E Waite, *CEO*
Kim Smith, *Accounting Mgr*
EMP: 81 **EST:** 1968
SQ FT: 1,000
SALES (est): 11.5MM **Privately Held**
WEB: www.hvla.com
SIC: 8641 7997 5813 Homeowners' association; golf club, membership; bar (drinking places)

(P-18432)
HORIZONS 4 CONDOMINIUMS INC
Also Called: Horizon For Hmwners Asscations
2113 Meridan Blvd, Mammoth Lakes (93546)
P.O. Box 175 (93546-0175)
PHONE..................760 934-6779
Fax: 760 934-4224
EMP: 92
SALES (est): 1.1MM **Privately Held**
SIC: 8641 Civic/Social Association

(P-18433)
IDEOORG
444 Spear St Ste 213, San Francisco (94105-1693)
PHONE..................415 426-7080
Stuart Davidson, *CEO*
James McLean, *CFO*
Matt Taylor, *Opers Staff*
Nadia Walker, *Marketing Staff*
Rafael Smith, *Director*
EMP: 70 **EST:** 2011
SALES (est): 13.8MM **Privately Held**
WEB: www.ideo.org
SIC: 8641 Social associations

(P-18434)
INSTITUTE FOR WILDLIFE STUDIES (PA)
835 3rd St, Eureka (95501-0511)
P.O. Box 1104, Arcata (95518-1104)
PHONE..................707 822-4258
David K Garcelon, *President*
Dj Wainman, *Manager*
EMP: 43 **EST:** 1979
SQ FT: 2,300
SALES (est): 3.8MM **Privately Held**
WEB: www.iws.org
SIC: 8641 Environmental protection organization

(P-18435)
LAKE WILDWOOD ASSOCIATION
Also Called: Lake Wildwood Golf Course.
11255 Cottontail Way, Penn Valley (95946-9409)
PHONE..................530 432-1152
Tom Cross, *CEO*
Dustin Wright, *CIO*
Donna Brazil, *Director*
William Haushalter, *Director*
Denise Guy, *Manager*
EMP: 120 **EST:** 1971
SQ FT: 10,000
SALES: 10.6MM **Privately Held**
WEB: www.lwwa.org
SIC: 8641 7997 Homeowners' association; golf club, membership

(P-18436)
LEGION INDUSTRIES
748 Lakemead Way, Emerald Hills (94062-3923)
PHONE..................650 743-6358
Zach Micheletti, *Principal*
Ryan Micheletti, *Principal*
EMP: 50 **EST:** 2014
SALES (est): 598K **Privately Held**
WEB: www.legion.org
SIC: 8641 Veterans' organization

(P-18437)
LELAND STANFORD JUNIOR UNIV
Also Called: Stanford Alumni Association
326 Galvez St, Stanford (94305-6105)
PHONE..................650 723-2021
Howard Wolf, *Branch Mgr*
Subhan Ali, *Bd of Directors*
Roger Melen, *Assoc Prof*
EMP: 250
SALES (corp-wide): 12.4B **Privately Held**
WEB: www.stanford.edu
SIC: 8641 8221 Alumni association; university
PA: Leland Stanford Junior University
450 Jane Stanford Way
Stanford CA 94305
650 723-2300

(P-18438)
LINUX FOUNDATION JAPAN LLC (PA)
548 Market St Pmb 57274, San Francisco (94104-5401)
PHONE..................415 723-9709
Jim Zemlin, *Principal*
Michael Woster, *Officer*
Clyde Seepersad, *Senior VP*
Daniela Barbosa, *Vice Pres*
Michael Dolan, *Vice Pres*
EMP: 104 **EST:** 2008
SALES (est): 4.7MM **Privately Held**
WEB: www.linuxfoundation.org
SIC: 8641 Civic social & fraternal associations

(P-18439)
MISSION NEIGHBORHOOD CTRS INC (PA)
Also Called: PRECITA VALLEY COMMUNITY CENTE
362 Capp St, San Francisco (94110-1808)
PHONE..................415 206-7752
Santiago Ruiz, *CEO*
Tiffany Ann Rasmussen, *President*
George Suncin, *President*
Sebastian Alioto, *Treasurer*
Liliana Carnero-Rossi, *Vice Pres*
EMP: 46 **EST:** 1959
SQ FT: 20,000
SALES: 21.3MM **Privately Held**
WEB: www.mncsf.org
SIC: 8641 Civic social & fraternal associations

(P-18440)
MISSION NEIGHBORHOOD CTRS INC
Also Called: Precita Valley Community Ctr
534 Precita Ave, San Francisco (94110-4720)
PHONE..................415 206-7756
Gloria Romero, *Director*
EMP: 46
SQ FT: 4,050
SALES (corp-wide): 21.3MM **Privately Held**
WEB: www.mncsf.org
SIC: 8641 Youth organizations

PRODUCTS & SERVICES SECTION
8641 - Civic, Social & Fraternal Associations County (P-18463)

PA: Mission Neighborhood Centers, Inc.
362 Capp St
San Francisco CA 94110
415 206-7752

(P-18441)
MOOSE INTERNATIONAL INC
Also Called: Lodge 539 - Newark
6940 Rich Ave, Newark (94560-3614)
P.O. Box 127 (94560-0127)
PHONE.................................510 791-2654
Howard Vrmeer, Manager
EMP: 200
SALES (corp-wide): 48.4MM Privately Held
WEB: www.mooseintl.org
SIC: 8641 Fraternal associations
PA: Moose International, Incorporated
155 S International Dr # 1
Mooseheart IL 60539
630 859-2000

(P-18442)
MXB BATTERY LP
Also Called: Battery The
717 Battery St, San Francisco
(94111-1515)
PHONE.................................415 230-8000
Steven Flowers, Exec Dir
Erik Silverman, Associate Dir
Colleen Gregerson, Exec Dir
Eric Kelly, General Mgr
Gabriel Tam, Meeting Planner
EMP: 100
SALES (corp-wide): 2.5MM Privately Held
SIC: 8641 Social club, membership
PA: Mxb Battery, Lp
387 Tehama St
San Francisco CA 94103
415 896-9200

(P-18443)
NATURE CONSERVANCY
Also Called: California Field Office
201 Mission St Ste 400, San Francisco
(94105-1832)
PHONE.................................415 777-0487
Mark Burget, Exec Dir
Dorothy A Boone, Volunteer Dir
Kim Nye, Officer
Kristy Stoyer, Officer
Jeffrey Burian, Associate Dir
EMP: 80
SQ FT: 2,500
SALES (corp-wide): 992.1MM Privately Held
WEB: www.nature.org
SIC: 8641 Environmental protection organization
PA: The Nature Conservancy
4245 Fairfax Dr Ste 100
Arlington VA 22203
703 841-5300

(P-18444)
OLYMPIC CLUB (PA)
524 Post St, San Francisco (94102-1295)
PHONE.................................415 345-5100
John M Jack, CEO
Andrew Collins, Vice Pres
Traci Mysliwiec, Comms Mgr
Jay Bedsworth, Principal
Patrick Merritt, General Mgr
EMP: 200 EST: 1879
SQ FT: 160,000
SALES: 58.9MM Privately Held
WEB: www.olyclub.com
SIC: 8641 7997 5812 Civic social & fraternal associations; golf club, membership; health food restaurant

(P-18445)
OLYMPIC CLUB
Also Called: Lakeside Clubhouse
599 Skyline Dr, Daly City (94015-4611)
PHONE.................................415 404-4300
Frank Stranzl, Corp Comm Staff
EMP: 63
SALES (corp-wide): 58.9MM Privately Held
WEB: www.olyclub.com
SIC: 8641 5812 Civic social & fraternal associations; health food restaurant

PA: The Olympic Club
524 Post St
San Francisco CA 94102
415 345-5100

(P-18446)
PACIFIC UNION CLUB
1000 California St, San Francisco
(94108-2280)
PHONE.................................415 775-1234
Thomas Gaston, General Mgr
Raveen Singh, Managing Dir
EMP: 61 EST: 1881
SQ FT: 54,000
SALES (est): 3.6MM Privately Held
WEB: www.puclub.org
SIC: 8641 Social club, membership

(P-18447)
PESCADERO CONSERVATION ALIANCE
4100 Cabrillo Hwy, Pescadero
(94060-9724)
P.O. Box 873 (94060-0873)
PHONE.................................650 879-1441
EMP: 50 Privately Held
WEB: www.gazos.org
SIC: 8641 Civic/Social Association

(P-18448)
PINE MOUNTAIN LAKE ASSOCIATION (PA)
19228 Pine Mountain Dr, Groveland
(95321-9581)
PHONE.................................209 962-4080
Brian Sweeney, President
Dana Chavarria, Treasurer
Ian Morcott, Vice Pres
Joe Powell, General Mgr
Jerry Dickson, Admin Sec
EMP: 107 EST: 1969
SQ FT: 20,000
SALES (est): 9.8MM Privately Held
WEB: www.pinemountainlake.com
SIC: 8641 Homeowners' association

(P-18449)
POINT REYES BIRD OBSERVATOR
Also Called: Point Blue Cnservation Science
3820 Cypress Dr Ste 11, Petaluma
(94954-6964)
P.O. Box 69, Bolinas (94924-0069)
PHONE.................................415 868-0371
Allie Cohen, CEO
Grant Ballard, Officer
Lara White, Project Mgr
Todd Greenley, Accountant
Robyn Hettrich, Human Resources
EMP: 45 EST: 2011
SQ FT: 20,000
SALES (est): 8MM Privately Held
SIC: 8641 Environmental protection organization

(P-18450)
POLICE OFFICERS ASSN LODI
215 W Elm St, Lodi (95240-2001)
PHONE.................................209 333-6886
Sierra Brucia, Principal
Gary Benincasa, Facilities Mgr
EMP: 59 EST: 1982
SALES: 81.4K Privately Held
WEB: www.poalodi.com
SIC: 8641 Fraternal associations

(P-18451)
PROFESSIONAL ASSN SVCS INC
42612 Christy St, Fremont (94538-3135)
PHONE.................................510 683-8614
Susan L Hoffman, CEO
EMP: 35 EST: 1993
SALES (est): 2.9MM Privately Held
WEB: www.pas-inc.com
SIC: 8641 Homeowners' association

(P-18452)
PTAC HLEN CARR CSTLLO CAL CNGR
Also Called: Pta Congress
9850 Fire Poppy Dr, Elk Grove
(95757-2851)
PHONE.................................916 686-1725
Ilesha Graham, Principal

Angie Vierra, President
Estela Penney, Treasurer
Heather Baseer, Vice Pres
Lupe Alonzo-Diaz, Admin Sec
EMP: 50 EST: 2010
SALES (est): 549.3K Privately Held
WEB: www.pta.org
SIC: 8641 Parent-teachers' association

(P-18453)
READING AND BEYOND
4670 E Butler Ave, Fresno (93702-4608)
PHONE.................................559 840-1068
Luis Santana, President
Luis C Santana, Exec Dir
Vang Kue, Office Mgr
Alicia Pearce, Executive Asst
Chris Zeitz, Analyst
EMP: 44 EST: 1999
SALES (est): 4MM Privately Held
WEB: www.readingandbeyond.org
SIC: 8641 Youth organizations

(P-18454)
REVEL GATHERINGS INC (PA)
450 Townsend St Ste 225, San Francisco
(94107-1510)
PHONE.................................909 323-0994
Lisa Marrone, CEO
Alexa Wahr, COO
Nina Lorez Collins, Officer
EMP: 54 EST: 2019
SALES (est): 46.1K Privately Held
SIC: 8641 Community membership club

(P-18455)
ROSE FMLY CRTIVE EMPWRMENT CTR
7000 Franklin Blvd # 100, Sacramento
(95823-1820)
PHONE.................................916 376-7916
Jacqueline Rose, CEO
EMP: 99 EST: 2014
SALES (est): 1.7MM Privately Held
SIC: 8641 Civic social & fraternal associations

(P-18456)
ROTARY INTERNATIONAL
Also Called: Rotary Club
9839 Meadowlark Way, Palo Cedro
(96073-8750)
PHONE.................................530 547-5272
EMP: 62
SALES (corp-wide): 355.9MM Privately Held
SIC: 8641 Civic/Social Association
PA: Rotary International
1 Rotary Ctr
Evanston IL 60201
847 866-3000

(P-18457)
SAA SIERRA PROGRAMS LLC
Also Called: Stanford Sierra Camp & Lodge
130 Fallen Leaf Rd, South Lake Tahoe
(96150-6165)
P.O. Box 10618 (96158-3618)
PHONE.................................530 541-1244
David Bunnett, Director
Antja Thompson, Asst Director
Nancy Marzocco, Director
EMP: 62 EST: 1999
SALES (est): 2.6MM
SALES (corp-wide): 12.4B Privately Held
WEB: www.stanfordsierra.com
SIC: 8641 Civic associations
PA: Leland Stanford Junior University
450 Jane Stanford Way
Stanford CA 94305
650 723-2300

(P-18458)
SACRAMENTO CY UNIFIED SCHL DST (PA)
5735 47th Ave, Sacramento (95824-4528)
P.O. Box 246870 (95824-6870)
PHONE.................................916 643-7400
Jose Banda, Superintendent
Tom Barrinson, CFO
Chris Congdon, Teacher
Bre Rizzo, Teacher
Jay Elmquist, Manager
EMP: 300 EST: 1854
SQ FT: 45,000

SALES: 695.4MM Privately Held
WEB: www.scusd.edu
SIC: 8641 Veterans' organization; environmental protection organization; Boy Scout organization

(P-18459)
SACRAMENTO TREE FOUNDATION
191 Lathrop Way Ste D, Sacramento
(95815-4217)
PHONE.................................916 924-8733
Raymond Tretheway III, Exec Dir
Loren O 'rourke, Program Mgr
Stephanie Robinson, CIO
Jordan Cherry, Director
Ray Tretheway, Manager
EMP: 40 EST: 1982
SQ FT: 6,000
SALES (est): 3.3MM Privately Held
WEB: www.sactree.com
SIC: 8641 Civic social & fraternal associations

(P-18460)
SAN FRNCSC-BAY AREA CNCIL BOY
Also Called: SAN FRANCISCO BAY AREA COUNCIL
1001 Davis St, San Leandro (94577-1514)
PHONE.................................510 577-9000
Kenneth Mehlhorn, CEO
EMP: 36 EST: 2008
SALES: 5.3MM Privately Held
WEB: www.sfbac.org
SIC: 8641 Boy Scout organization

(P-18461)
SAN FRNCSCO BAY BIRD OBSRVTORY
524 Valley Way, Milpitas (95035-4106)
PHONE.................................408 946-6548
Cat Burns, Exec Dir
Yiwei Wang, Exec Dir
Kristin Butler, Corp Comm Staff
Benjamin Pearl, Director
Max Tarjan, Director
EMP: 40 EST: 1981
SQ FT: 700
SALES: 1MM Privately Held
WEB: www.sfbbo.org
SIC: 8641 Environmental protection organization

(P-18462)
SAN JQUIN RVER PKWY CNSRVTION
Also Called: River Parkway Trust
11605 Old Friant Rd, Fresno (93730-9701)
P.O. Box 28940 (93729-8940)
PHONE.................................559 248-8480
Coke Hollowell, CEO
George Folsom, President
David Koehler, Exec Dir
Sharon Weaver, Exec Dir
Kennedy Brotemarkle, Technician
EMP: 48 EST: 1988
SQ FT: 2,784
SALES: 3.4MM Privately Held
WEB: www.riverparkway.org
SIC: 8641 Environmental protection organization

(P-18463)
SAN RAMON VLY UNIFIED SCHL DST
Also Called: Montivista
3131 Stone Valley Rd, Danville
(94526-1129)
PHONE.................................925 552-2880
Kevin Ahern, Principal
Cheryl Costello, Ch of Bd
Heather Giovanola, Ch of Bd
Rodger Johnson, Ch of Bd
Gavin Long, Ch of Bd
EMP: 72
SALES (corp-wide): 420.2MM Privately Held
WEB: www.srvusd.net
SIC: 8211 8641 Public elementary school; parent-teachers' association

8641 - Civic, Social & Fraternal Associations County (P-18464)

PA: San Ramon Valley Unified School District
699 Old Orchard Dr
Danville CA 94526
925 552-5500

(P-18464)
SANTA CLARA COUNTY OF
Also Called: SCC Open Space Authority
6980 Santa Teresa Blvd, San Jose (95119-1393)
PHONE..........................408 224-7476
Adrea Manie, *General Mgr*
Matt Freeman, *Manager*
Shashank Ranjan, *Manager*
Lawrence Stone, *Manager*
Jeff Barlow, *Supervisor*
EMP: 41 **Privately Held**
WEB: www.sccgov.org
SIC: 9512 8641 Land conservation agencies; civic social & fraternal associations
PA: County Of Santa Clara
70 W Hedding St 2wing
San Jose CA 95110
408 299-5200

(P-18465)
SAVE REDWOODS LEAGUE
111 Sutter St Fl 11, San Francisco (94104-4541)
PHONE..........................415 362-2352
Sam Hodder, *President*
Rolando Cohen, *CFO*
Jennifer Benito, *Officer*
Corrina Blaney, *CIO*
Rona Kardener, *Human Resources*
EMP: 35
SQ FT: 1,000
SALES: 23.2MM **Privately Held**
WEB: www.savetheredwoods.org
SIC: 8641 Environmental protection organization

(P-18466)
SEQUOIA ELEMENTARY SCHOOL PTA
3333 Rosemont Dr, Sacramento (95826-4099)
PHONE..........................916 228-5850
Cindy Hollander, *Principal*
EMP: 45
SALES: 18.8K **Privately Held**
WEB: www.sequoia.scusd.edu
SIC: 8641 Parent-teachers' association

(P-18467)
SFDPH
1424 18th Ave, San Francisco (94122-3409)
PHONE..........................415 554-2686
Reggie Gage, *Research*
Serlina Cheung, *Opers Mgr*
Jane Bailowitz, *Med Doctor*
Michael Mikolasek, *Nursing Dir*
Maryellen Ryan,
EMP: 48 **EST:** 2009
SALES (est): 1MM **Privately Held**
WEB: www.sfdph.org
SIC: 8641 Civic social & fraternal associations

(P-18468)
SHASTA COUNTY YMCA
Also Called: Shasta Family, The
1155 N Court St, Redding (96001-0437)
PHONE..........................530 605-3330
Al Boren, *Exec Dir*
Bob Wise, *Officer*
James Finck, *Exec Dir*
EMP: 42 **EST:** 1952
SALES (est): 3.8MM **Privately Held**
WEB: www.sfymca.org
SIC: 8641 7991 8351 7032 Youth organizations; physical fitness facilities; child day care services; youth camps; individual & family services

(P-18469)
SIERRA CLUB (PA)
Also Called: SIERRA CLUB BOOKS
2101 Webster St Ste 1300, Oakland (94612-3546)
PHONE..........................415 977-5500
Robin Mann, *President*
Martha Klein, *Ch of Bd*
Cameron Bell, *Vice Chairman*
Julie Levine, *Vice Chairman*
Trey Pollard, *President*
EMP: 175 **EST:** 1892
SQ FT: 43,500
SALES: 141.3MM **Privately Held**
WEB: www.sierraclub.org
SIC: 8641 8399 Environmental protection organization; advocacy group

(P-18470)
SILICON VALLEY MONTEREY BAY CO
29211 Highway 108, Long Barn (95335-9737)
PHONE..........................209 965-3432
Alan Buscaglia, *Branch Mgr*
EMP: 54
SALES (corp-wide): 18MM **Privately Held**
WEB: www.svmbc.org
SIC: 8641 Boy Scout organization
PA: Silicon Valley Monterey Bay Council, Inc., Boy Scouts Of America
970 W Julian St
San Jose CA 95126
408 279-2086

(P-18471)
SILICON VLY CMNTY FOUNDATION (PA)
Also Called: SVCF
2440 W El Cmino Real Ste, Mountain View (94040)
PHONE..........................650 450-5400
Nicole Taylor, *President*
Patrick O'sullivan, *President*
Emmett Carson, *CEO*
Alexandra Bastien, *Officer*
Erica Bleicher, *Officer*
EMP: 118 **EST:** 2006
SALES: 121.2K **Privately Held**
WEB: www.siliconvalleycf.org
SIC: 8641 Civic social & fraternal associations

(P-18472)
SPUR - SAN FRNCSCO BAY AREA PL (PA)
654 Mission St, San Francisco (94105-4015)
PHONE..........................415 781-8726
Jim Chappell, *President*
Alicia John-Baptiste, *President*
Gabriel Metcalf, *President*
Nick Josefowitz, *Officer*
Hannah Schwartz, *Executive*
EMP: 62 **EST:** 1906
SQ FT: 2,000
SALES: 7.4MM **Privately Held**
WEB: www.spur.org
SIC: 8641 Civic associations

(P-18473)
SUTTER CLUB
1220 9th St, Sacramento (95814-4897)
PHONE..........................916 442-0456
Tom Narozonick, *General Mgr*
EMP: 75
SQ FT: 45,000
SALES: 4.1MM **Privately Held**
WEB: www.sutterclub.org
SIC: 8641 Social club, membership

(P-18474)
SWORDS TO PLWSHRES VTRANS RGHT (PA)
1060 Howard St, San Francisco (94103-2820)
PHONE..........................415 252-4788
Michael Blecker, *Exec Dir*
Leon Winston, *COO*
John Beem, *CFO*
Rose Mallamo, *Exec Dir*
Laymer Pamintuan, *Office Mgr*
EMP: 40 **EST:** 1974
SQ FT: 10,000
SALES: 27.1MM **Privately Held**
WEB: www.swords-to-plowshares.org
SIC: 8641 8111 8399 Veterans' organization; legal services; fund raising organization, non-fee basis

(P-18475)
SWORDS TO PLWSHRES VTRANS RGHT
1433 Halibut Ct, San Francisco (94130-1638)
PHONE..........................415 834-0341
Wanda Heffernan, *Branch Mgr*
EMP: 54
SALES (corp-wide): 27.1MM **Privately Held**
WEB: www.swords-to-plowshares.org
SIC: 8641 Veterans' organization
PA: Swords To Plowshares Veterans Rights Organization
1060 Howard St
San Francisco CA 94103
415 252-4788

(P-18476)
TECHSOUP GLOBAL (PA)
Also Called: DISCOUNT TECH
435 Brannan St Ste 100, San Francisco (94107-1780)
PHONE..........................800 659-3579
Rebecca Masisak, *CEO*
Geri Doran, *COO*
James Hebert, *CFO*
Marnie Webb, *Co-CEO*
Joyce Bickford, *Officer*
EMP: 174 **EST:** 1988
SALES: 40.7MM **Privately Held**
WEB: www.techsoupglobal.org
SIC: 8641 Social associations

(P-18477)
THE LINUX FOUNDATION (PA)
548 Market St Pmb 57274, San Francisco (94104-5401)
PHONE..........................415 723-9709
Jim Zemlin, *CEO*
Lisbeth McNabb, *CFO*
Jamie Smith, *Chief Mktg Ofcr*
Clyde Seepersad, *Officer*
Mike Worster, *Officer*
EMP: 219 **EST:** 2007
SALES (est): 57.1MM **Privately Held**
WEB: www.linuxfoundation.org
SIC: 8641 Civic social & fraternal associations

(P-18478)
VANGUARD MUSIC AND PRFRMG ARTS
Also Called: Santa Clara Vanguard
1795 Space Park Dr, Santa Clara (95054-3436)
PHONE..........................408 727-5532
Jeff Fiedler, *CEO*
Marc Hebert, *President*
Sandra Adams, *Treasurer*
Richard Lesher, *Treasurer*
Marie Bienkowski, *Vice Pres*
EMP: 51 **EST:** 1967
SQ FT: 21,000
SALES (est): 7.5MM **Privately Held**
WEB: www.scvanguard.org
SIC: 8641 Youth organizations

(P-18479)
VILLA MARIN HOMEOWNERS ASSN
Also Called: Villa Mrin Rtrement Residences
100 Thorndale Dr, San Rafael (94903-4599)
PHONE..........................415 499-8711
Danel Walker, *CEO*
Dan Walker, *CEO*
Thomas Bucci, *COO*
Doug Kaplan, *Social Dir*
Guillermo Barreto, *Admin Sec*
EMP: 170 **EST:** 1982
SQ FT: 500,000
SALES (est): 17.3MM **Privately Held**
WEB: www.villa-marin.com
SIC: 8641 8051 8059 Homeowners' association; skilled nursing care facilities; personal care home, with health care

(P-18480)
WATERGATE COMMUNITY ASSN (PA)
8 Captain Dr, Emeryville (94608-1744)
PHONE..........................510 428-0118
Tim Sutherland, *General Mgr*
EMP: 36 **EST:** 1979
SQ FT: 1,500
SALES (est): 5.8MM **Privately Held**
WEB: www.websites.vertilinc.com
SIC: 8641 Condominium association

(P-18481)
WOODLAND SWIM TEAM BOSTERS CLB
155 West St, Woodland (95695-3162)
P.O. Box 763 (95776-0763)
PHONE..........................530 662-9783
EMP: 60
SALES: 125.2K **Privately Held**
SIC: 8641 Civic/Social Association

(P-18482)
YMCA OF MID-PENINSULA
1922 The Alameda Ste 300, San Jose (95126-1430)
PHONE..........................650 493-9622
EMP: 300
SQ FT: 6,000
SALES (est): 1.8MM **Privately Held**
WEB: www.ymcasv.org
SIC: 8641 7991 8351 7032 Civic/Social Association Physical Fitness Faclty Child Day Care Services Sport/Recreation Camp Individual/Family Svcs

(P-18483)
YMCA OF SAN JOAQUIN COUNTY
2105 W March Ln Ste 1, Stockton (95207-6422)
PHONE..........................209 472-9622
Dan Chapman, *CEO*
John Acosta, *Technology*
Julia Verduzco, *Finance Dir*
Sam Prak, *Finance*
Jodi Mitchell, *Opers Staff*
EMP: 45 **EST:** 1860
SQ FT: 2,000
SALES (est): 3.3MM **Privately Held**
WEB: www.ymcasjc.org
SIC: 8641 Social club, membership

(P-18484)
YOSEMITE FOUNDATION (PA)
Also Called: YOSEMITE CONSERVANCY
101 Montgomery St # 1700, San Francisco (94104-4129)
PHONE..........................415 434-1782
Micheal Tollesson, *CEO*
Bob Hansen, *President*
Jerry Edelbrock, *CFO*
Alexis Interiano, *Sales Staff*
Matt Adams, *Director*
EMP: 62 **EST:** 1988
SQ FT: 15,000
SALES (est): 18.9MM **Privately Held**
WEB: www.yosemite.org
SIC: 8641 Environmental protection organization

(P-18485)
YOSEMITE LAKES OWNERS ASSN
30250 Yosemite Springs Pk, Coarsegold (93614-9369)
PHONE..........................559 658-7466
Steve Payne, *General Mgr*
Ken Sartain, *Director*
Tammie Damore, *Manager*
EMP: 70 **EST:** 1970
SQ FT: 10,000
SALES (est): 5.9MM **Privately Held**
WEB: www.yosemitelakespark.org
SIC: 8641 Homeowners' association

(P-18486)
YOUNG MENS CHRISTIAN ASSOC SF
3 Hamilton Landing # 140, Novato (94949-8248)
PHONE..........................415 883-9622
EMP: 88
SALES (corp-wide): 82.8MM **Privately Held**
SIC: 8641 7991 8351 7032 Civic/Social Association Physical Fitness Faclty Child Day Care Services Sport/Recreation Camp Individual/Family Svcs

PRODUCTS & SERVICES SECTION
8641 - Civic, Social & Fraternal Associations County (P-18504)

PA: Young Men's Christian Association Of
San Francisco
50 California St Ste 650
San Francisco CA 94111
415 777-9622

(P-18487)
YOUNG MNS CHRSTN ASSN OF E BAY
Also Called: Urban Services YMCA
3265 Market St, Oakland (94608-4332)
PHONE.....................510 654-9622
Chris Chatmon, Exec Dir
EMP: 356
SALES (corp-wide): 65.5MM Privately Held
WEB: www.ymcaeastbay.org
SIC: 8641 7991 8351 7032 Youth organizations; physical fitness facilities; child day care services; youth camps; individual & family services
PA: Young Men's Christian Association Of
The East Bay
2330 Broadway
Oakland CA 94612
510 549-4515

(P-18488)
YOUNG MNS CHRSTN ASSN OF E BAY
200 Lake Ave, Rodeo (94572-1063)
PHONE.....................510 412-5644
Pamela Williams, Branch Mgr
EMP: 356
SALES (corp-wide): 65.5MM Privately Held
WEB: www.ymcaeastbay.org
SIC: 8641 Youth organizations
PA: Young Men's Christian Association Of
The East Bay
2330 Broadway
Oakland CA 94612
510 549-4515

(P-18489)
YOUNG MNS CHRSTN ASSN OF E BAY
1250 23rd St, Richmond (94804-1011)
PHONE.....................510 412-5640
Kathy Hardy, Branch Mgr
EMP: 356
SALES (corp-wide): 65.5MM Privately Held
WEB: www.ymcaeastbay.org
SIC: 8641 Youth organizations
PA: Young Men's Christian Association Of
The East Bay
2330 Broadway
Oakland CA 94612
510 549-4515

(P-18490)
YOUNG MNS CHRSTN ASSN OF E BAY
Also Called: Berkeley Albany YMCA
1705 Thornwood Dr, Concord (94521-1915)
PHONE.....................925 609-7971
EMP: 356
SALES (corp-wide): 65.5MM Privately Held
WEB: www.ymcaeastbay.org
SIC: 8641 Youth organizations
PA: Young Men's Christian Association Of
The East Bay
2330 Broadway
Oakland CA 94612
510 549-4515

(P-18491)
YOUNG MNS CHRSTN ASSN OF E BAY
Also Called: YMCA of East Bay
2350 Broadway, Oakland (94612-2415)
PHONE.....................510 451-8039
Fran Gallati, President
EMP: 852
SALES (corp-wide): 65.5MM Privately Held
WEB: www.ymcaeastbay.org
SIC: 8641 7991 8351 7032 Youth organizations; physical fitness facilities; child day care services; youth camps; individual & family services

PA: Young Men's Christian Association Of
The East Bay
2330 Broadway
Oakland CA 94612
510 549-4515

(P-18492)
YOUNG MNS CHRSTN ASSN OF E BAY
Also Called: Emery Marina
4727 San Pablo Ave, Emeryville (94608-3035)
PHONE.....................510 601-8674
Henry Der, Branch Mgr
EMP: 356
SALES (corp-wide): 65.5MM Privately Held
WEB: www.ymcaeastbay.org
SIC: 8641 7991 8351 7032 Youth organizations; physical fitness facilities; child day care services; youth camps; individual & family services
PA: Young Men's Christian Association Of
The East Bay
2330 Broadway
Oakland CA 94612
510 549-4515

(P-18493)
YOUNG MNS CHRSTN ASSN OF E BAY
Also Called: Y M C A Metro Clinic
2111 Mrtin Lther King Jr, Berkeley (94704-1108)
PHONE.....................510 486-8400
Larry Bush, Manager
EMP: 356
SALES (corp-wide): 65.5MM Privately Held
WEB: www.ymcaeastbay.org
SIC: 8641 7991 8351 7032 Youth organizations; physical fitness facilities; child day care services; youth camps; individual & family services
PA: Young Men's Christian Association Of
The East Bay
2330 Broadway
Oakland CA 94612
510 549-4515

(P-18494)
YOUNG MNS CHRSTN ASSN OF E BAY
Also Called: YMCA Head Start
2009 10th St, Berkeley (94710-2119)
PHONE.....................510 848-9092
Pamela Shaw, Director
Maria Carmona, Exec Dir
EMP: 356
SALES (corp-wide): 65.5MM Privately Held
WEB: www.ymcaeastbay.org
SIC: 8641 7991 8351 7032 Youth organizations; physical fitness facilities; child day care services; youth camps; individual & family services
PA: Young Men's Christian Association Of
The East Bay
2330 Broadway
Oakland CA 94612
510 549-4515

(P-18495)
YOUNG MNS CHRSTN ASSN OF E BAY
Also Called: Downtown Berkeley YMCA
2001 Allston Way, Berkeley (94704-1417)
PHONE.....................510 848-9622
Fran Gallati, Exec Dir
Jennifer Anguella, Director
Sebastian De Rosa, Director
Kisha Hayes, Director
Jocelyn Leche, Director
EMP: 356
SQ FT: 70,135
SALES (corp-wide): 65.5MM Privately Held
WEB: www.ymcaeastbay.org
SIC: 8641 7991 8351 7032 Youth organizations; physical fitness facilities; child day care services; youth camps; individual & family services

PA: Young Men's Christian Association Of
The East Bay
2330 Broadway
Oakland CA 94612
510 549-4515

(P-18496)
YOUNG MNS CHRSTN ASSN OF E BAY
Also Called: YMCA Pre School Hillview
3800 Clark Rd, Richmond (94803-3145)
PHONE.....................510 223-7070
EMP: 356
SALES (corp-wide): 65.5MM Privately Held
WEB: www.ymcaeastbay.org
SIC: 8641 Youth organizations
PA: Young Men's Christian Association Of
The East Bay
2330 Broadway
Oakland CA 94612
510 549-4515

(P-18497)
YOUNG MNS CHRSTN ASSN OF E BAY
Also Called: Kids' Club YMCA Oxford School
1130 Oxford St, Berkeley (94707-2624)
PHONE.....................510 526-2146
Stephanie Hochman, Branch Mgr
EMP: 356
SALES (corp-wide): 65.5MM Privately Held
WEB: www.ymcaeastbay.org
SIC: 8641 7991 8351 7032 Youth organizations; physical fitness facilities; child day care services; youth camps; individual & family services
PA: Young Men's Christian Association Of
The East Bay
2330 Broadway
Oakland CA 94612
510 549-4515

(P-18498)
YOUNG MNS CHRSTN ASSN OF E BAY
Also Called: YMCA Elementary School
505 Escuela Ave, Mountain View (94040-2006)
PHONE.....................650 526-3500
Lucia Medina, Branch Mgr
EMP: 356
SALES (corp-wide): 65.5MM Privately Held
WEB: www.ymcaeastbay.org
SIC: 8641 7991 8351 7032 Youth organizations; physical fitness facilities; child day care services; youth camps; individual & family services
PA: Young Men's Christian Association Of
The East Bay
2330 Broadway
Oakland CA 94612
510 549-4515

(P-18499)
YOUNG MNS CHRSTN ASSN OF E BAY
Also Called: Y M C A
2241 Russell St, Berkeley (94705-1029)
PHONE.....................510 644-6290
Fran Gallati, President
EMP: 356
SALES (corp-wide): 65.5MM Privately Held
WEB: www.ymcaeastbay.org
SIC: 8641 Youth organizations
PA: Young Men's Christian Association Of
The East Bay
2330 Broadway
Oakland CA 94612
510 549-4515

(P-18500)
YOUNG MNS CHRSTN ASSN OF E BAY
Also Called: YMCA Child Care Chadbourne
801 Plymouth Ave, Fremont (94539-4637)
PHONE.....................510 656-7243
Santofh Mahavni, Manager
EMP: 356

SALES (corp-wide): 65.5MM Privately Held
WEB: www.ymcaeastbay.org
SIC: 8641 7991 8351 7032 Youth organizations; physical fitness facilities; child day care services; youth camps; individual & family services
PA: Young Men's Christian Association Of
The East Bay
2330 Broadway
Oakland CA 94612
510 549-4515

(P-18501)
YOUNG MNS CHRSTN ASSN OF E BAY
Also Called: West Contra Costa YMCA
4300 Lakeside Dr Ste 150, Richmond (94806-5717)
PHONE.....................510 222-9622
Bria Cartwright, Exec Dir
EMP: 356
SQ FT: 45,343
SALES (corp-wide): 65.5MM Privately Held
WEB: www.ymcaeastbay.org
SIC: 8641 7991 8351 7032 Youth organizations; physical fitness facilities; child day care services; youth camps; individual & family services
PA: Young Men's Christian Association Of
The East Bay
2330 Broadway
Oakland CA 94612
510 549-4515

(P-18502)
YOUNG MNS CHRSTN ASSN OF E BAY
Also Called: Coronado YMCA
263 S 20th St, Richmond (94804-2709)
PHONE.....................510 412-5647
Don Lau, Branch Mgr
EMP: 356
SQ FT: 16,338
SALES (corp-wide): 65.5MM Privately Held
WEB: www.ymcaeastbay.org
SIC: 8641 Youth organizations; recreation association
PA: Young Men's Christian Association Of
The East Bay
2330 Broadway
Oakland CA 94612
510 549-4515

(P-18503)
YOUNG MNS CHRSTN ASSN OF E BAY
Also Called: Hilltop Family YMCA
4300 Lakeside Dr, Richmond (94806-5717)
PHONE.....................510 222-9622
Linda Cook, Branch Mgr
EMP: 356
SALES (corp-wide): 65.5MM Privately Held
WEB: www.ymcaeastbay.org
SIC: 8641 Youth organizations; recreation association
PA: Young Men's Christian Association Of
The East Bay
2330 Broadway
Oakland CA 94612
510 549-4515

(P-18504)
YOUNG MNS CHRSTN ASSN OF E BAY
Also Called: Tri-Valley YMCA
5000 Pleasanton Ave # 200, Pleasanton (94566-7052)
PHONE.....................925 475-6100
Kelley O'Lague, Branch Mgr
EMP: 356
SALES (corp-wide): 65.5MM Privately Held
WEB: www.ymcaeastbay.org
SIC: 8641 Youth organizations; recreation association
PA: Young Men's Christian Association Of
The East Bay
2330 Broadway
Oakland CA 94612
510 549-4515

8641 - Civic, Social & Fraternal Associations County (P-18505)

(P-18505)
YOUNG MNS CHRSTN ASSN OF E BAY
Also Called: Urban Services Eastlake YMCA
1612 45th Ave, Oakland (94601-4520)
PHONE.................510 534-7441
Chris Chatmon, *Manager*
EMP: 356
SALES (corp-wide): 65.5MM **Privately Held**
WEB: www.ymcaeastbay.org
SIC: **8641** Youth organizations; recreation association
PA: Young Men's Christian Association Of The East Bay
2330 Broadway
Oakland CA 94612
510 549-4515

(P-18506)
YOUNG MNS CHRSTN ASSN OF E BAY
41811 Blacow Rd, Fremont (94538-3352)
PHONE.................510 683-9165
Deepa Meata, *Manager*
EMP: 356
SALES (corp-wide): 65.5MM **Privately Held**
WEB: www.ymcaeastbay.org
SIC: **8641** 7991 8351 7032 Youth organizations; physical fitness facilities; child day care services; youth camps; individual & family services
PA: Young Men's Christian Association Of The East Bay
2330 Broadway
Oakland CA 94612
510 549-4515

(P-18507)
YOUNG MNS CHRSTN ASSN OF E BAY
Also Called: YMCA Sch Age Pgrm Durham
40292 Leslie St 402, Fremont (94538-3520)
PHONE.................510 683-9107
Melda Shaffer, *Director*
EMP: 356
SALES (corp-wide): 65.5MM **Privately Held**
WEB: www.ymcaeastbay.org
SIC: **8641** 7991 8351 7032 Youth organizations; physical fitness facilities; child day care services; youth camps; individual & family services
PA: Young Men's Christian Association Of The East Bay
2330 Broadway
Oakland CA 94612
510 549-4515

(P-18508)
YOUNG MNS CHRSTN ASSN OF E BAY
Also Called: Metro YMCA Leitch
47100 Fernald St 471, Fremont (94539-7005)
PHONE.................510 683-9147
Ericka McKinnon, *Director*
EMP: 356
SALES (corp-wide): 65.5MM **Privately Held**
WEB: www.ymcaeastbay.org
SIC: **8641** 7991 8351 7032 Youth organizations; physical fitness facilities; child day care services; youth camps; individual & family services
PA: Young Men's Christian Association Of The East Bay
2330 Broadway
Oakland CA 94612
510 549-4515

(P-18509)
YOUNG MNS CHRSTN ASSN OF E BAY
Also Called: YMCA
2001 Allston Way, Berkeley (94704-1417)
PHONE.................510 848-6800
Peter Gerharz, *Branch Mgr*
Tracy Rogers, *Diabetes*
EMP: 356
SALES (corp-wide): 65.5MM **Privately Held**
WEB: www.ymcaeastbay.org
SIC: **8641** 7991 8351 7032 Youth organizations; physical fitness facilities; child day care services; youth camps; individual & family services
PA: Young Men's Christian Association Of The East Bay
2330 Broadway
Oakland CA 94612
510 549-4515

(P-18510)
YOUNG MNS CHRSTN ASSN OF E BAY
Also Called: YMCA After School-Olinda
5855 Olinda Rd, Richmond (94803-3543)
PHONE.................510 262-6588
EMP: 356
SALES (corp-wide): 65.5MM **Privately Held**
WEB: www.ymcaeastbay.org
SIC: **8641** 7991 8351 7032 Youth organizations; physical fitness facilities; child day care services; youth camps; individual & family services
PA: Young Men's Christian Association Of The East Bay
2330 Broadway
Oakland CA 94612
510 549-4515

(P-18511)
YOUNG MNS CHRSTN ASSN OF E BAY
Also Called: YMCA
1422 San Pablo Ave, Berkeley (94702-1024)
PHONE.................510 559-2090
Larry Bush, *Branch Mgr*
EMP: 356
SALES (corp-wide): 65.5MM **Privately Held**
WEB: www.ymcaeastbay.org
SIC: **8641** 8322 8351 Youth organizations; individual & family services; head start center, except in conjunction with school
PA: Young Men's Christian Association Of The East Bay
2330 Broadway
Oakland CA 94612
510 549-4515

(P-18512)
YOUNG MNS CHRSTN ASSN SAN FRNC
Also Called: Presidio Community YMCA
57 Post St, San Francisco (94104-5003)
PHONE.................415 447-9602
EMP: 49
SALES (corp-wide): 95MM **Privately Held**
WEB: www.ymcasf.org
SIC: **8641** 7999 Youth organizations; swimming instruction
PA: Young Men's Christian Association Of San Francisco
50 California St Ste 650
San Francisco CA 94111
415 777-9622

(P-18513)
YOUNG MNS CHRSTN ASSN SAN FRNC
Also Called: Presido YMCA
63 Funston Ave, San Francisco (94129-1110)
PHONE.................415 447-9622
Robert Sindelar, *Exec Dir*
Sean Dries, *Director*
EMP: 49
SALES (corp-wide): 95MM **Privately Held**
WEB: www.ymcasf.org
SIC: **8641** 7999 Youth organizations; tennis services & professionals
PA: Young Men's Christian Association Of San Francisco
50 California St Ste 650
San Francisco CA 94111
415 777-9622

(P-18514)
YOUNG MNS CHRSTN ASSN SAN FRNC
Also Called: Peninsula YMCA
1877 S Grant St, San Mateo (94402-2647)
PHONE.................650 286-9622
Rachel Del Monte, *Manager*
Patrizia Guiotto, *Principal*
EMP: 49
SALES (corp-wide): 95MM **Privately Held**
WEB: www.ymcasf.org
SIC: **8641** 7991 8351 Youth organizations; physical fitness facilities; child day care services
PA: Young Men's Christian Association Of San Francisco
50 California St Ste 650
San Francisco CA 94111
415 777-9622

(P-18515)
YOUNG MNS CHRSTN ASSN SAN FRNC
Also Called: Camp Jones Gulch YMCA
11000 Pescadero Creek Rd, La Honda (94020-9711)
PHONE.................650 747-1200
Peter Jones, *Exec Dir*
EMP: 49
SALES (corp-wide): 95MM **Privately Held**
WEB: www.ymcasf.org
SIC: **8641** 8322 Youth organizations; individual & family services
PA: Young Men's Christian Association Of San Francisco
50 California St Ste 650
San Francisco CA 94111
415 777-9622

(P-18516)
YOUNG MNS CHRSTN ASSN SAN FRNC (PA)
Also Called: YMCA OF SAN FRANCISCO
50 California St Ste 650, San Francisco (94111-4607)
PHONE.................415 777-9622
Charles M Collins, *President*
Kathy Cheng, *CFO*
Rachel Del Monte, *Branch Mgr*
Linda Griffith, *Admin Sec*
Maria Catalina Reyes, *Controller*
▲ EMP: 50 EST: 1853
SQ FT: 10,000
SALES: 95MM **Privately Held**
WEB: www.ymcasf.org
SIC: **8641** 7991 8351 7032 Youth organizations; physical fitness facilities; child day care services; youth camps; individual & family services

(P-18517)
YOUNG MNS CHRSTN ASSN SAN FRNC
Also Called: Buchanan YMCA
1530 Buchanan St, San Francisco (94115-3709)
PHONE.................415 931-9622
Maurice Henry, *Director*
Reeshemah Davis, *Principal*
Melissa Langness, *Principal*
EMP: 49
SALES (corp-wide): 95MM **Privately Held**
WEB: www.ymcasf.org
SIC: **8641** 7991 8351 7032 Youth organizations; physical fitness facilities; child day care services; youth camps; individual & family services
PA: Young Men's Christian Association Of San Francisco
50 California St Ste 650
San Francisco CA 94111
415 777-9622

(P-18518)
YOUNG MNS CHRSTN ASSN SAN FRNC
Also Called: Richmond District YMCA
360 18th Ave, San Francisco (94121-2317)
PHONE.................415 666-9622
Tiffany Patterson, *Branch Mgr*
EMP: 49
SALES (corp-wide): 95MM **Privately Held**
WEB: www.ymcasf.org
SIC: **8641** 7991 8351 7032 Youth organizations; physical fitness facilities; child day care services; youth camps; individual & family services
PA: Young Men's Christian Association Of San Francisco
50 California St Ste 650
San Francisco CA 94111
415 777-9622

(P-18519)
YOUNG MNS CHRSTN ASSN SAN FRNC
Also Called: YMCA
169 Steuart St, San Francisco (94105-1206)
PHONE.................415 957-9622
Larry Bush, *Branch Mgr*
EMP: 49
SQ FT: 54,186
SALES (corp-wide): 95MM **Privately Held**
WEB: www.ymcasf.org
SIC: **8641** 7991 8351 7032 Youth organizations; physical fitness facilities; child day care services; youth camps; individual & family services
PA: Young Men's Christian Association Of San Francisco
50 California St Ste 650
San Francisco CA 94111
415 777-9622

(P-18520)
YOUNG MNS CHRSTN ASSN SAN FRNC
Also Called: Shih Yu-Lang Central YMCA
246 Eddy St, San Francisco (94102-2716)
PHONE.................415 885-0460
Carmela Gold, *Exec Dir*
EMP: 49
SALES (corp-wide): 95MM **Privately Held**
WEB: www.ymcasf.org
SIC: **8641** 7997 8322 7999 Youth organizations; membership sports & recreation clubs; senior citizens' center or association; swimming instruction; aerobic dance & exercise classes; hotels
PA: Young Men's Christian Association Of San Francisco
50 California St Ste 650
San Francisco CA 94111
415 777-9622

(P-18521)
YOUNG MNS CHRSTN ASSN SAN FRNC
Also Called: YMCA Pt Bnita Otdoor Cnfrnce C
981 Fort Barry Ggnra, Sausalito (94965)
PHONE.................415 331-9622
Mary Perkins, *Exec Dir*
EMP: 49
SALES (corp-wide): 95MM **Privately Held**
WEB: www.ymcasf.org
SIC: **8641** 7991 8351 7032 Youth organizations; physical fitness facilities; child day care services; youth camps; individual & family services
PA: Young Men's Christian Association Of San Francisco
50 California St Ste 650
San Francisco CA 94111
415 777-9622

(P-18522)
YOUNG MNS CHRSTN ASSN SAN FRNC
Also Called: YMCA NAPA Slano N Bay Gymnstic
415 Mississippi St, Vallejo (94590-3209)
PHONE.................707 643-9622
John Donnham, *President*
EMP: 49
SALES (corp-wide): 95MM **Privately Held**
WEB: www.ymcasf.org
SIC: **8641** 7999 Youth organizations; gymnastic instruction, non-membership

PRODUCTS & SERVICES SECTION
8699 - Membership Organizations, NEC County (P-18540)

PA: Young Men's Christian Association Of
San Francisco
50 California St Ste 650
San Francisco CA 94111
415 777-9622

(P-18523)
YOUNG MNS CHRSTN ASSN SAN FRNC
Also Called: Ymcasf
1500 Los Gamos Dr, San Rafael (94903-1841)
PHONE.....................415 492-9622
Luann Jackman, *Exec Dir*
EMP: 49
SALES (corp-wide): 95MM Privately Held
WEB: www.ymcasf.org
SIC: 8641 8351 7991 Community membership club; child day care services; physical fitness facilities
PA: Young Men's Christian Association Of
San Francisco
50 California St Ste 650
San Francisco CA 94111
415 777-9622

(P-18524)
YOUNG MNS CHRSTN ASSN SAN FRNC
Also Called: Bayview Hunters Point YMCA
1601 Lane St, San Francisco (94124-2732)
PHONE.....................415 822-7728
Kris Lev, *Exec Dir*
Kaia Dutler, *Athletic Dir*
Kyyio Cecil-Raditz, *Program Dir*
Sheriann Chaw, *Director*
Lisa Kruger, *Director*
EMP: 49
SALES (corp-wide): 95MM Privately Held
WEB: www.ymcasf.org
SIC: 8641 Youth organizations
PA: Young Men's Christian Association Of
San Francisco
50 California St Ste 650
San Francisco CA 94111
415 777-9622

(P-18525)
YOUNG MNS CHRSTN ASSN SAN FRNC
Also Called: Mission YMCA
4080 Mission St, San Francisco (94112-1017)
PHONE.....................415 586-6900
Tanya Bouford, *Exec Dir*
EMP: 49
SQ FT: 6,833
SALES (corp-wide): 95MM Privately Held
WEB: www.ymcasf.org
SIC: 8641 7991 8351 7032 Youth organizations; physical fitness facilities; child day care services; youth camps; individual & family services
PA: Young Men's Christian Association Of
San Francisco
50 California St Ste 650
San Francisco CA 94111
415 777-9622

(P-18526)
YOUNG MNS CHRSTN ASSN SLCON VL (PA)
80 Saratoga Ave, Santa Clara (95051-7303)
PHONE.....................408 351-6400
Kathy Riggins, *President*
Tom Nelson, *COO*
Marianne Prum, *COO*
Ed Barrantes, *CFO*
Karla Jessup, *Officer*
EMP: 60 EST: 1867
SQ FT: 5,000
SALES (est): 67.4MM Privately Held
WEB: www.ymcasv.org
SIC: 8641 7991 8351 7032 Youth organizations; physical fitness facilities; child day care services; youth camps; individual & family services

(P-18527)
YOUNG MNS CHRSTN ASSN SLCON VL
Also Called: Young Mens Christn Assocation
1922 The Alameda Ste 300, San Jose (95126-1430)
PHONE.....................650 493-9622
EMP: 157
SALES (corp-wide): 67.4MM Privately Held
WEB: www.ymcasv.org
SIC: 8641 7991 8351 7032 Youth organizations; physical fitness facilities; child day care services; youth camps; individual & family services
PA: Young Men's Christian Association Of
Silicon Valley
80 Saratoga Ave
Santa Clara CA 95051
408 351-6400

(P-18528)
YOUNG MNS CHRSTN ASSN SLCON VL
Also Called: Central Branch YMCA
1717 The Alameda, San Jose (95126-1726)
PHONE.....................408 298-1717
Barbara Cardinez, *Manager*
Jaime Sanchez, *Marketing Staff*
Sarah Shea, *Director*
Nicholas Willford, *Director*
Justin Bryant, *Manager*
EMP: 157
SQ FT: 52,715
SALES (corp-wide): 67.4MM Privately Held
WEB: www.ymcasv.org
SIC: 8641 8351 8322 7997 Youth organizations; child day care services; individual & family services; membership sports & recreation clubs; physical fitness facilities
PA: Young Men's Christian Association Of
Silicon Valley
80 Saratoga Ave
Santa Clara CA 95051
408 351-6400

(P-18529)
YOUNG MNS CHRSTN ASSN SLCON VL
Also Called: El Camino YMCA
2400 Grant Rd, Mountain View (94040-4301)
PHONE.....................650 969-9622
Elaine Glissmeyer, *Director*
Charles West, *Admin Dir*
Julie Griswold, *Exec Dir*
Diego Osorio, *Sales Staff*
Nikita Patel, *Program Dir*
EMP: 157
SALES (corp-wide): 67.4MM Privately Held
WEB: www.ymcasv.org
SIC: 8641 7991 8351 7032 Youth organizations; physical fitness facilities; child day care services; youth camps; individual & family services
PA: Young Men's Christian Association Of
Silicon Valley
80 Saratoga Ave
Santa Clara CA 95051
408 351-6400

(P-18530)
YOUNG MNS CHRSTN ASSN SLCON VL
Also Called: Sequoia YMCA
1445 Hudson St, Redwood City (94061-2925)
PHONE.....................650 368-4168
Julie Wesolek, *Exec Dir*
EMP: 45
SALES (corp-wide): 67.4MM Privately Held
WEB: www.ymcasv.org
SIC: 8641 7991 8351 7032 Youth organizations; physical fitness facilities; child day care services; youth camps; individual & family services
PA: Young Men's Christian Association Of
Silicon Valley
80 Saratoga Ave
Santa Clara CA 95051
408 351-6400

(P-18531)
YOUNG MNS CHRSTN ASSN SLCON VL
Also Called: YMCA of Santa Clara Valley
5632 Santa Teresa Blvd, San Jose (95123-2633)
PHONE.....................408 226-9622
Rick Valdez, *Exec Dir*
EMP: 157
SALES (corp-wide): 67.4MM Privately Held
WEB: www.ymcasv.org
SIC: 8641 7991 8351 7032 Youth organizations; physical fitness facilities; child day care services; youth camps; individual & family services
PA: Young Men's Christian Association Of
Silicon Valley
80 Saratoga Ave
Santa Clara CA 95051
408 351-6400

(P-18532)
YOUNG MNS CHRSTN ASSN SLCON VL
Also Called: YMCA of Santa Clara Valley
1855 Majestic Way, San Jose (95132-1940)
PHONE.....................408 729-4223
Rick Valdez, *Branch Mgr*
EMP: 157
SALES (corp-wide): 67.4MM Privately Held
WEB: www.ymcasv.org
SIC: 8641 7991 8351 7032 Youth organizations; physical fitness facilities; child day care services; youth camps; individual & family services
PA: Young Men's Christian Association Of
Silicon Valley
80 Saratoga Ave
Santa Clara CA 95051
408 351-6400

(P-18533)
YOUNG MNS CHRSTN ASSN SLCON VL
Also Called: YMCA of Redwoods
16275 Highway 9, Boulder Creek (95006-9652)
PHONE.....................831 338-2128
Mike Wentz, *Director*
Laura Peterson, *Exec Dir*
John Rhodes, *Director*
EMP: 157
SALES (corp-wide): 67.4MM Privately Held
WEB: www.ymcasv.org
SIC: 8641 7991 8351 7032 Youth organizations; physical fitness facilities; child day care services; youth camps; individual & family services
PA: Young Men's Christian Association Of
Silicon Valley
80 Saratoga Ave
Santa Clara CA 95051
408 351-6400

(P-18534)
YOUNG WNS CHRSTN ASSN OF WTSNV
Also Called: YWCA of Watsonville
340 E Beach St, Watsonville (95076-4838)
PHONE.....................831 724-6078
Vietta Helmle, *Director*
EMP: 40
SALES: 702.7K Privately Held
WEB: www.ywcawatsonville.org
SIC: 8641 7991 8351 7032 Youth organizations; physical fitness facilities; child day care services; youth camps; individual & family services

(P-18535)
YWCA GOLDEN GATE SILICON VLY
375 S 3rd St, San Jose (95112-3649)
PHONE.....................408 295-4011
Keri Procunier McLain, *President*
Tanis Crosby, *CEO*
Ann Mariepate, *CFO*
Alexandra Lopez, *Bd of Directors*
Jennifer Lopes, *Officer*
EMP: 83 EST: 1905
SALES (est): 14.3MM Privately Held
WEB: www.yourywca.org
SIC: 8641 8322 Community membership club; individual & family services

8651 Political Organizations

(P-18536)
CHINESE FOR AFFIRMATIVE ACTION
17 Walter U Lum Pl, San Francisco (94108-1801)
PHONE.....................415 274-6750
Vincent Pan, *Director*
Lisa K Lee, *Vice Chairman*
Cynthia Choi, *Vice Pres*
Jessie Fernandez, *Program Mgr*
EMP: 36 EST: 1971
SALES (est): 6.2MM Privately Held
WEB: www.caasf.org
SIC: 8651 Political action committee

(P-18537)
LEAGUE OF WOMEN VOTERS CAL (PA)
Also Called: League of Wmen Vters Cal Edcat
921 11th St Ste 700, Sacramento (95814-2821)
PHONE.....................916 442-7215
Helen Hutchinson, *President*
Stephanie Doute, *Exec Dir*
Dora Rose, *Deputy Dir*
Christina Dragonetti, *Director*
Gloria C Hoo, *Director*
EMP: 17 EST: 1939
SALES (est): 2.6MM Privately Held
WEB: www.cavotes.org
SIC: 8651 2741 Political action committee; miscellaneous publishing

(P-18538)
MOVEONORG POLITICAL ACTION
1442 Walnut St Ste 358, Berkeley (94709-1405)
P.O. Box 9218 (94709-0218)
PHONE.....................202 465-4234
Robert Fox, *COO*
Ilya Sheyman, *Exec Dir*
Melissa St Onge, *Exec Dir*
Casey Quirke, *Opers Staff*
Brandon Salesberry, *Opers Staff*
EMP: 50 EST: 2004
SALES (est): 2.6MM Privately Held
WEB: www.front.moveon.org
SIC: 8651 Political action committee

(P-18539)
PEACE ACTION WEST (PA)
2201 Broadway Ste 321, Oakland (94612-3044)
PHONE.....................510 830-3600
Eric See, *Finance Dir*
Jon Rainwater, *Exec Dir*
Jonathan Rainwater, *Exec Dir*
Gabriel Showers, *Asst Director*
Peter Deccy, *Director*
EMP: 43 EST: 1990
SQ FT: 1,600
SALES (est): 999.6K Privately Held
WEB: www.peaceaction.org
SIC: 8651 Political action committee

8699 Membership Organizations, NEC

(P-18540)
AAA CALIFORNIA STATE AUTO ASSN (PA)
Also Called: AAA Northern California
160 Sutter St, San Francisco (94104-4001)
PHONE.....................415 773-1900
William Gee, *Principal*
EMP: 126 EST: 2011
SALES (est): 6.3MM Privately Held
SIC: 8699 6411 Automobile owners' association; insurance agents, brokers & service

8699 - Membership Organizations, NEC County (P-18541)

(P-18541)
ALLIANCE FOR SAFETY & JUSTICE
1624 Franklin St 11, Oakland (94612-2897)
PHONE..................................209 507-6882
Joel Bashevkinn, *Principal*
EMP: 56 **EST:** 2016
SALES (est): 2.3MM **Privately Held**
WEB: www.allianceforsafetyandjustice.org
SIC: 8699 Charitable organization

(P-18542)
ALLIANCE MEMBER SERVICES INC
333 Front St Ste 200, Santa Cruz (95060-4533)
P.O. Box 8507 (95061-8507)
PHONE..................................831 459-0980
Pamela Davis, *President*
A Agarwal, *Chief Mktg Ofcr*
Briane Johnson, *Officer*
David Jolliffe, *Director*
Michele Thomas, *Supervisor*
EMP: 54 **EST:** 2001
SQ FT: 25,000
SALES (est): 17.5MM **Privately Held**
WEB: www.insurancefornonprofits.org
SIC: 8699 Charitable organization

(P-18543)
ALREADY
1801 Marlesta Ct, Pinole (94564-2047)
PHONE..................................510 322-4988
Clarence McGhee, *Principal*
EMP: 50 **EST:** 2020
SALES (est): 248.9K **Privately Held**
SIC: 8699 Charitable organization

(P-18544)
AMERICAN CVIL LBRTIES UN FNDTI
Also Called: ACLU
39 Drumm St, San Francisco (94111-4805)
PHONE..................................415 621-2488
Dorothy Ehrlich, *Exec Dir*
Jennifer Tapken, *CFO*
Courtney Balonek, *Officer*
Danielle Flores, *Litigation*
Erica Ramos, *Legal Staff*
EMP: 40 **EST:** 1958
SALES (est): 14.3MM **Privately Held**
WEB: www.aclunc.org
SIC: 8699 Charitable organization

(P-18545)
ANITA BORG INST FOR WOMEN TECH
1301 Shoreway Rd Ste 425, Belmont (94002-4154)
PHONE..................................650 236-4756
Dr Telle Whitney, *President*
Dr Anita Borg, *President*
Farideh Eshagh, *Vice Pres*
Michelle Flatt, *Vice Pres*
Cindy Georal, *Vice Pres*
EMP: 67
SALES: 22MM **Privately Held**
WEB: www.anitab.org
SIC: 8699 Charitable organization

(P-18546)
ASPHALT COWBOYS OF REDDIN
720 Auditorium Dr, Redding (96001-0919)
PHONE..................................530 244-1117
EMP: 35
SALES: 59.7K **Privately Held**
WEB: www.asphaltcowboys.org
SIC: 8699 Membership Organization

(P-18547)
ASTRONOMICAL SOC OF THE PCF
Also Called: A S P
390 Ashton Ave, San Francisco (94112-1722)
PHONE..................................415 337-1100
William A Gutsch Jr, *President*
Cyrille Betant, *CFO*
Cathy Langridge, *Treasurer*
Michael G Gibbs, *Admin Sec*
Jay Yanos, *Finance*
EMP: 26 **EST:** 1889
SQ FT: 10,000
SALES (est): 2.8MM **Privately Held**
WEB: www.astrosociety.org
SIC: 8699 2721 Personal interest organization; periodicals: publishing only

(P-18548)
ASYLUM ACCESS
344 Thomas L Berkley Way # 111, Oakland (94612-3544)
P.O. Box 14205, San Francisco (94114-0205)
PHONE..................................510 891-8700
Emily Arnold-Fernande, *CEO*
Emily E Arnold-Fernandez, *President*
Michael Diedring, *Bd of Directors*
Niki Fitzgerald, *Opers Mgr*
Lisa Annunzio, *Director*
EMP: 69 **EST:** 2005
SALES (est): 5.3MM **Privately Held**
WEB: www.asylumaccess.org
SIC: 8699 Charitable organization

(P-18549)
AYUSA INTERNATIONAL
600 California St Fl 10, San Francisco (94108-2730)
PHONE..................................888 552-9872
John Wilhelm, *CEO*
Debra Slagle, *Exec Dir*
April Bray, *Regional Mgr*
Kristen Crossland, *Regional Mgr*
Amy Estes, *Regional Mgr*
EMP: 71 **EST:** 1982
SQ FT: 18,000
SALES: 4.5MM **Privately Held**
WEB: www.ayusa.org
SIC: 8299 8699 Student exchange program; charitable organization

(P-18550)
BRIARPATCH COOP NEV CNTY INC
Also Called: Briarpatch Coop-Community Mkt
290 Sierra College Dr, Grass Valley (95945-5762)
PHONE..................................530 272-5333
Christopher Maher, *CEO*
Mike McCary, *Front End Mgr*
Brett Torgrimson, *Manager*
Kirstin Mather, *Clerk*
EMP: 180
SALES (est): 11.8MM **Privately Held**
WEB: www.briarpatch.coop
SIC: 8699 Food co-operative

(P-18551)
BRIDGE HOUSING CORPORATION (PA)
600 California St Fl 9, San Francisco (94108-2706)
PHONE..................................415 989-1111
Cynthia Parker, *President*
Susan Johnson, *Exec VP*
Kimberly McKay, *Exec VP*
Lydia Tan, *Exec VP*
Marco Ramirez, *Manager*
▲ **EMP:** 90
SQ FT: 12,000
SALES: 30.6MM **Privately Held**
WEB: www.bridgehousing.com
SIC: 8699 Civic social & fraternal associations

(P-18552)
CALIF STAT UNIV FRES FOUN
5370 N Chestnut Ave, Fresno (93725)
PHONE..................................559 278-0850
Linda Alatorre, *Branch Mgr*
Jason O 'quin, *Professor*
EMP: 47
SALES (corp-wide): 78MM **Privately Held**
WEB: www.auxiliary.fresnostate.edu
SIC: 8699 Amateur sports promotion
PA: California State University, Fresno Foundation
    4910 N Chestnut Ave
    Fresno CA 93726
    559 278-0850

(P-18553)
CALIFRNIA CHLDREN FMILIES COMM
Also Called: First 5 California
2389 Gateway Oaks Dr # 260, Sacramento (95833-4245)
PHONE..................................916 263-1050
Camille Maben, *Exec Dir*
Oscar Ramirez, *Officer*
Waters Paul, *Administration*
Syphax Vernettia, *CIO*
Erin Dubey, *Consultant*
EMP: 40 **EST:** 2011
SALES (est): 206.4K **Privately Held**
WEB: www.ccfc.ca.gov
SIC: 8699 Charitable organization

(P-18554)
CALIFRNIA YUTH SOCCER ASSN INC
Also Called: Cal North
1767 Tribute Rd Ste F, Sacramento (95815-4409)
PHONE..................................925 426-5437
Kenyatta Scott, *Chairman*
Melinda Rainville, *Vice Chairman*
Larry Svetich, *Vice Chairman*
Doug Couden, *Treasurer*
Gurdev Mann, *General Mgr*
EMP: 87 **EST:** 1972
SALES (est): 4.3MM **Privately Held**
WEB: www.calnorth.org
SIC: 8699 Personal interest organization

(P-18555)
CAMBRIAN SCHOOL DISTRICT
Also Called: Bagby Home and School Club
1840 Harris Ave, San Jose (95124-1125)
PHONE..................................408 377-3882
Leslie Duquette, *President*
EMP: 36
SALES (corp-wide): 43.2MM **Privately Held**
WEB: www.mail.cambriansd.org
SIC: 8211 8699 Public elementary & secondary schools; personal interest organization
PA: Cambrian School District
    4115 Jacksol Dr
    San Jose CA 95124
    408 377-2103

(P-18556)
CARE 2
203 Rdwood Shres Pkwy Ste, Redwood City (94065)
PHONE..................................650 622-0860
Randy Paynter, *Principal*
Ginger Hanssen, *Editor*
EMP: 40 **EST:** 2011
SALES (est): 5.8MM **Privately Held**
WEB: www.care2.com
SIC: 8699 Charitable organization

(P-18557)
CCAPP EDUCATION INSTITUTE
2400 Marconi Ave Ste C, Sacramento (95821-4858)
PHONE..................................916 338-9460
Pete Nielsen, *CEO*
Bob Baillie, *Exec Dir*
Lisa Beintker,
Warren Daniels,
Alan Johnson,
EMP: 57 **EST:** 2015
SALES (est): 725.5K **Privately Held**
WEB: www.ccapp.us
SIC: 8699 Charitable organization

(P-18558)
CHANGELAB SOLUTIONS
2201 Broadway Ste 502, Oakland (94612-3063)
PHONE..................................510 302-3380
Marice Ashe, *CEO*
Dana Serleth, *CFO*
Keith Nagayama,
EMP: 40
SALES: 12.6MM **Privately Held**
WEB: www.changelabsolutions.org
SIC: 8699 Charitable organization

(P-18559)
CHARLES HLEN SCHWAB FOUNDATION
201 Mission St Ste 1960, San Francisco (94105-1880)
P.O. Box 5428, San Mateo (94402-0428)
PHONE..................................415 795-4920
Charles R Schwab, *CEO*
Nancy Bechtle, *Admin Sec*
▲ **EMP:** 40 **EST:** 2001
SALES (est): 2.6MM **Privately Held**
WEB: www.schwabfoundation.org
SIC: 8699 Charitable organization

(P-18560)
CHINESE-AMERICAN BIO PHRM SOC
268 Bush St Ste 1888, San Francisco (94104-3503)
PHONE..................................650 892-6283
Naibo Yang, *President*
EMP: 40 **EST:** 2010
SALES: 83.8K **Privately Held**
WEB: www.cabsweb.org
SIC: 8699 Charitable organization

(P-18561)
COMMON COUNSEL FOUNDATION
1624 Franklin St Ste 1022, Oakland (94612-2824)
PHONE..................................510 834-2995
Peggy Saika, *CEO*
EMP: 36 **EST:** 1994
SALES (est): 8.8MM **Privately Held**
WEB: www.commoncounsel.org
SIC: 8699 Charitable organization

(P-18562)
CROCKER ART MUSEUM ASSOCIATION
Also Called: CROCKER ART MUSEUM
216 O St, Sacramento (95814-5324)
PHONE..................................916 808-7000
Lial Jones, *CEO*
Molly Park, *Officer*
Christine Calvin, *Marketing Staff*
Andy Galloway-Long, *Marketing Staff*
Maria Segoviano, *Pub Rel Staff*
EMP: 66 **EST:** 1875
SQ FT: 150,000
SALES: 12.2MM **Privately Held**
WEB: www.crockerart.org
SIC: 8699 5942 8412 Art council; book stores; museum

(P-18563)
DIRT DGGERS N MTRCYCLE CLB INC
5591 Hwy 49, Pilot Hill (95664)
PHONE..................................916 640-7328
Billy Hilton, *President*
Bob Messer, *Treasurer*
Jeff Krekelberg, *Vice Pres*
EMP: 36 **EST:** 1968
SALES (est): 465K **Privately Held**
SIC: 8699 Personal interest organization

(P-18564)
EARTH ISLAND INSTITUTE INC
2150 Allston Way Ste 460, Berkeley (94704-1375)
PHONE..................................510 859-9100
Michael Mitrani, *CEO*
Sharon Donovan, *Comms Dir*
John A Knox, *Principal*
David Phillips, *Exec Dir*
Shawn Kelly, *Program Mgr*
EMP: 76 **EST:** 1982
SQ FT: 4,400
SALES (est): 16.7MM **Privately Held**
WEB: www.earthisland.org
SIC: 8699 8748 8641 Charitable organization; business consulting; environmental protection organization

(P-18565)
EASY DOES IT EMERG SVCS PROGRM
3271 Adeline St Unit B, Berkeley (94703-2480)
PHONE..................................510 845-5513
Nicole F Brown-Booker, *CEO*
EMP: 53 **EST:** 1995

PRODUCTS & SERVICES SECTION
8699 - Membership Organizations, NEC County (P-18589)

SALES (est): 1.3MM **Privately Held**
WEB: www.easydoesitservices.org
SIC: 8699 Charitable organization

(P-18566)
F50 LEAGUE LLC
Also Called: Sailgp
475 Sansome St Fl 12, San Francisco (94111-3169)
PHONE.................................415 939-4076
EMP: 50
SALES (est): 72MM **Privately Held**
SIC: 8699 Membership Organization

(P-18567)
HAAS JR EVELYN & WALTER FUND
114 Sansome St Fl 6, San Francisco (94104-3814)
P.O. Box 1459, El Cerrito (94530-4459)
PHONE.................................415 856-1400
Ira S Hershfeild, *President*
Cathy Cha, *Officer*
Ramona Rey, *Vice Pres*
Matt Foreman, *Exec Dir*
Maria Zepeda, *Office Mgr*
EMP: 67 **EST:** 1953
SQ FT: 22,000
SALES (est): 8.5MM **Privately Held**
WEB: www.haasjr.org
SIC: 8699 Charitable organization

(P-18568)
HEADLANDS CENTER FOR ARTS
944 Fort Barry, Sausalito (94965-2608)
PHONE.................................415 331-2787
Kathryn Reasoner, *Director*
Sharon Maidenberg, *Exec Dir*
Andrew Niklaus, *Exec Dir*
Betsy Menzel, *Business Mgr*
Adrian Skaj, *Business Mgr*
EMP: 48 **EST:** 1982
SQ FT: 80,000
SALES: 4.9MM **Privately Held**
WEB: www.headlands.org
SIC: 8699 Art council

(P-18569)
HENRY J KAISER FMLY FOUNDATION (PA)
185 Berry St Ste 2000, San Francisco (94107-1704)
PHONE.................................650 854-9400
Drew Altman, *President*
Koonal Gandhi, *Ch Invest Ofcr*
Scott Kim, *Officer*
Trina Scott, *Officer*
Jennifer Kates, *Vice Pres*
EMP: 126 **EST:** 1948
SQ FT: 185,000
SALES: 53.8MM **Privately Held**
WEB: www.kff.org
SIC: 8699 Charitable organization

(P-18570)
HEWLETT WLLIAM FLORA FNDATION
Also Called: Hewlett Foundation
2121 Sand Hill Rd, Menlo Park (94025-6909)
PHONE.................................650 234-4500
Paul Brest, *President*
Suresh Bhat, *CFO*
Althea Anderson, *Officer*
Althea D Anderson, *Officer*
Jean Bordewich, *Officer*
EMP: 60
SALES: 317.4MM **Privately Held**
WEB: www.hewlett.org
SIC: 8699 Charitable organization

(P-18571)
HOMELESS CHILDRENS NETWORK
3450 3rd St Ste 1c, San Francisco (94124-1444)
PHONE.................................415 437-3990
April Silas, *CEO*
Stacy Nicholson, *Executive Asst*
Lyora Zadik, *Opers Spvr*
Mark Jefferson,
Jessica Sandoval, *Assistant*
EMP: 40 **EST:** 1997

SALES (est): 4.7MM **Privately Held**
WEB: www.hcnkids.org
SIC: 8699 Charitable organization

(P-18572)
HOPLAND BAND POMO INDIANS INC (PA)
3000 Shanel Rd, Hopland (95449-9809)
PHONE.................................707 472-2100
Romen Carrillo, *President*
Megan Lotten, *CFO*
Rachel Whetstone, *CFO*
EMP: 170 **EST:** 1976
SQ FT: 3,800
SALES (est): 17.4MM **Privately Held**
WEB: www.hoplandtribe.com
SIC: 8699 Personal interest organization

(P-18573)
HUMANE SOCIETY SILICON VALLEY
Also Called: PET POURRI
901 Ames Ave, Milpitas (95035-6326)
PHONE.................................408 262-2133
Carol Novello, *CEO*
Christine B Arnold, *Exec Dir*
Caroline Alexander, *Executive Asst*
Phyllis Matsuura, *Project Mgr*
Candice Balmaceda, *VP Finance*
EMP: 86 **EST:** 1929
SQ FT: 3,000
SALES: 18.2MM **Privately Held**
WEB: www.hssv.org
SIC: 8699 Animal humane society

(P-18574)
ISLAND CONSERVATION
2100 Delaware Ave Ste A, Santa Cruz (95060-6362)
PHONE.................................831 359-4787
Karen Poiani, *CEO*
Emily Heber, *Comms Mgr*
Richard Griffiths, *Project Dir*
Chad Hanson, *Project Dir*
Wes Jolley, *Project Mgr*
EMP: 38
SALES: 6.1MM **Privately Held**
WEB: www.islandconservation.org
SIC: 8699 Charitable organization

(P-18575)
KAI MING INC (PA)
900 Kearny St Ste 600, San Francisco (94133-5126)
PHONE.................................415 982-4777
Karen Chinn, *Director*
Jerry Yang, *Exec Dir*
Fatima Sequeira, *Executive Asst*
Jeff Dang, *Finance*
Eda WEI, *Finance*
EMP: 47 **EST:** 1975
SQ FT: 3,800
SALES (est): 11.5MM **Privately Held**
WEB: www.kaiming.org
SIC: 8699 8351 Charitable organization; preschool center

(P-18576)
LAKE TAHOE HISTORICAL SOCIETY
3058 Lake Tahoe Blvd, South Lake Tahoe (96150-7810)
P.O. Box 18501 (96151-8501)
PHONE.................................530 541-5458
EMP: 45
SALES: 30K **Privately Held**
SIC: 8699 8412 Membership Organization Museum/Art Gallery

(P-18577)
LAVA BEDS NATIONAL MONUMENTS
Also Called: U S GOVERNMENT
1 Indian Wells Hqtrs, Tulelake (96134-8216)
P.O. Box 1240 (96134-1240)
PHONE.................................530 667-2282
Fax: 530 667-3299
EMP: 50 **EST:** 1963
SALES: 55.2K **Publicly Held**
SIC: 8699 8412 Historic Organization
PA: Government Of The United States
1600 Pennsylvania Ave Nw
Washington DC 20500
202 456-1414

(P-18578)
LIFEMOVES (PA)
181 Constitution Dr, Menlo Park (94025-1106)
PHONE.................................650 685-5880
Bruce Ives, *Principal*
Matthew Bahls, *Vice Chairman*
Pranjal Daga, *Bd of Directors*
Jeff Vanzanten, *Bd of Directors*
Scott Flesher, *Vice Pres*
EMP: 50 **EST:** 1987
SALES (est): 38.8MM **Privately Held**
WEB: www.lifemoves.org
SIC: 8699 Charitable organization

(P-18579)
MARIN HUMANE SOCIETY
171 Bel Marin Keys Blvd, Novato (94949-6183)
PHONE.................................415 883-4621
Suzanne Golt, *Exec Dir*
Anne Oliver, *Volunteer Dir*
John Reese, *COO*
Marilyn Castellblanch, *CFO*
Dave Stapp, *Officer*
EMP: 91 **EST:** 1907
SQ FT: 42,500
SALES: 9.9MM **Privately Held**
WEB: www.marinhumane.org
SIC: 8699 Animal humane society

(P-18580)
MENLO PRK-THRTON EDCATN FNDTIO (PA)
181 Encinal Ave, Atherton (94027-3102)
P.O. Box 584, Menlo Park (94026-0584)
PHONE.................................650 325-0100
Ghysels Maurice, *Superintendent*
Carrie Bildstein, *Exec Dir*
Carrie Chen, *Exec Dir*
EMP: 44 **EST:** 2001
SALES (est): 5.1MM **Privately Held**
WEB: www.mpaef.org
SIC: 8699 Charitable organization

(P-18581)
NATIONAL AUTOMOBILE CLUB (PA)
111 Anza Blvd Ste 109, Burlingame (94010-1918)
PHONE.................................650 294-7000
William Sousa, *CEO*
Carolyn Green,
EMP: 38 **EST:** 1924
SALES (est): 3.8MM **Privately Held**
WEB: www.nacroadservice.com
SIC: 8699 Automobile owners' association

(P-18582)
NORTHERN CAL CTR FOR ARTS
Also Called: Center For The Arts, The
314 W Main St, Grass Valley (95945-6424)
PHONE.................................530 274-8384
Julie Baker, *Exec Dir*
Amber J Manuel, *Exec Dir*
Mikail Graham, *General Mgr*
Shane McKillop, *Prdtn Mgr*
Rachel Conrad, *Production*
EMP: 38 **EST:** 2000
SQ FT: 17,128
SALES: 12.6MM **Privately Held**
WEB: www.thecenterforthearts.org
SIC: 5999 8699 8412 8999 Theater programs; reading rooms & other cultural organizations; charitable organization; museums & art galleries; art related services; property operation, auditoriums & theaters; dance studios, schools & halls

(P-18583)
PENINSULA HUMANE SOC & SPCA
1450 Rollins Rd, Burlingame (94010-2307)
PHONE.................................650 340-7022
Stephen Creager, *Chairman*
Mary Sjostrom, *Vice Pres*
Lisa Van Buskirk, *Vice Pres*
Richard Barnes, *CIO*
Loretta Hoffman, *Finance Mgr*
EMP: 74
SALES (corp-wide): 18MM **Privately Held**
WEB: www.phs-spca.org
SIC: 8699 Animal humane society

PA: Peninsula Humane Society And Spca
12 Airport Blvd
San Mateo CA 94401
650 340-7022

(P-18584)
PETS UNLIMITED
2343 Fillmore St, San Francisco (94115-1812)
PHONE.................................415 563-6700
Suzanne Troxel, *President*
Theresa L Smith, *CFO*
Sally Wortman, *Vice Pres*
Linda Monteferrante, *Practice Mgr*
Brandyn Denico, *Administration*
EMP: 40 **EST:** 1947
SALES: 4.6MM **Privately Held**
WEB: www.sfspca.org
SIC: 8699 Animal humane society

(P-18585)
RUDOLF STEINER FOUNDATION INC
Also Called: RSF SOCIAL FINANCE
1002 Oreilly Ave, San Francisco (94129-5257)
PHONE.................................415 561-3900
Jasper Van Brakel, *President*
Ronald Alston, *Ch of Bd*
Katrina Steffek, *COO*
Christina Cook, *CFO*
John Bloom, *Vice Pres*
EMP: 37 **EST:** 1936
SALES: 36.8MM **Privately Held**
WEB: www.rsfsocialfinance.org
SIC: 8699 Charitable organization

(P-18586)
SACRAMNTO SOC FOR THE PRVNTION
Also Called: Sspca
6201 Florin Perkins Rd, Sacramento (95828-1012)
PHONE.................................916 383-7387
Maryann Subbotin, *Director*
Michele Steiner, *Officer*
Erika Sanders, *Education*
Lety Sanchez,
Marnie Musser, *Manager*
EMP: 76
SQ FT: 40,000
SALES: 8MM **Privately Held**
WEB: www.sspca.org
SIC: 8699 Animal humane society

(P-18587)
SAN FRANCISCO BAY AR TRAN ASSN
915 San Antonio Ave, Alameda (94501-3959)
PHONE.................................510 501-5318
Jahan Byrne, *President*
Monte Boscovich, *Treasurer*
EMP: 150
SALES: 85.5K **Privately Held**
WEB: www.pacifictrans.org
SIC: 8699 7389 Athletic organizations; fund raising organizations

(P-18588)
SAN FRANCISCO FILM SOCIETY
Also Called: San Frncsco Intl Film Festival
39 Mesa St Ste 110, San Francisco (94129-1025)
PHONE.................................415 561-5000
Ted Hope, *Exec Dir*
J Patterson McBaine, *President*
Howard Roffman, *Exec VP*
Noah Cowan, *Executive*
Graham Leggat, *Exec Dir*
EMP: 49 **EST:** 1957
SALES: 7.5MM **Privately Held**
WEB: www.sffs.org
SIC: 8699 7812 Art council; motion picture & video production

(P-18589)
SAN JOSE POLICE OFFICERS ASSN
1151 N 4th St, San Jose (95112-4945)
PHONE.................................408 298-1133
Bobby Lopez, *President*
Jeff Ricketts, *CFO*
Franco Vado, *CFO*
Nicole Decker, *Graphic Designe*

8699 - Membership Organizations, NEC County (P-18590)

PRODUCTS & SERVICES SECTION

Paul Kelly, *Director*
EMP: 43 **EST:** 1961
SQ FT: 10,000
SALES (est): 6.1MM **Privately Held**
WEB: www.sjpoa.com
SIC: 8699 Athletic organizations

(P-18590)
SHEET METAL TRAINING CENTER
1700 Marina Blvd, San Leandro (94577-4203)
PHONE 510 483-9035
Patrick Pico, *Administration*
Dennis Canevari, *District Mgr*
EMP: 51 **EST:** 1991
SALES (est): 1.3MM **Privately Held**
WEB: www.smw104.org
SIC: 8249 8699 Vocational apprentice training; personal interest organization

(P-18591)
SKOLL FOUNDATION
250 University Ave # 200, Palo Alto (94301-1738)
PHONE 650 331-1031
Donald H Gips, *CEO*
Jeffrey S Skoll, *President*
Annalisa Adams-Qualtiere, *Vice Pres*
Sarah Z Borgman, *Vice Pres*
Nadir Shams, *Associate Dir*
EMP: 50 **EST:** 1999
SALES (est): 11.8MM **Privately Held**
WEB: www.skoll.org
SIC: 8699 Charitable organization

(P-18592)
SOCIETY FOR BLIND
1238 S St, Sacramento (95811-7112)
PHONE 916 452-8271
Shari Roeseler, *CEO*
Steve Scott, *President*
Dawn Cornelius, *Principal*
Bryce McAnally, *Principal*
Allison Otto, *Principal*
EMP: 42 **EST:** 1954
SQ FT: 3,000
SALES (est): 2.7MM **Privately Held**
WEB: www.societyfortheblind.org
SIC: 8699 Charitable organization

(P-18593)
SOCIETY FOR SAN FRANCISCO
201 Alabama St, San Francisco (94103-4217)
PHONE 415 554-3000
Katherine Brown, *Ch of Bd*
Jane McHugh-Smith, *President*
David Tateosian, *Treasurer*
Eric Roberts, *Vice Ch Bd*
Alice Jordan, *VP Human Res*
EMP: 200
SQ FT: 57,000
SALES: 34.5MM **Privately Held**
WEB: www.sfspca.org
SIC: 8699 Animal humane society

(P-18594)
SOCIETY OF ST VNCENT DE PAUL A (PA)
2272 San Pablo Ave, Oakland (94612-1321)
PHONE 510 638-7600
Blase Bova, *Exec Dir*
Ron Dean, *Principal*
Gary Flinders, *Human Res Mgr*
EMP: 80 **EST:** 1938
SALES: 4.8MM **Privately Held**
WEB: www.svdp-alameda.org
SIC: 8699 Charitable organization

(P-18595)
SOCIETY OF ST VNCENT DE PAUL P (PA)
134 N Claremont St, San Mateo (94401-1924)
PHONE 650 373-0622
John Lau, *Principal*
Martin Duda, *President*
Anthony Rouse, *CFO*
Deborah Payne, *Vice Pres*
Lorraine Moriarty, *Exec Dir*
EMP: 64 **EST:** 2010
SALES: 2.4MM **Privately Held**
SIC: 8699 Charitable organization

(P-18596)
STUDENT UN OF SAN JOSE STATE U
Also Called: Student Union Building
211 S. 9th Street, San Jose (95192-0001)
PHONE 408 924-6405
Terry Gregory, *Manager*
EMP: 45
SALES (corp-wide): 17.1MM **Privately Held**
WEB: www.sjsu.edu
SIC: 8699 Personal interest organization
PA: The Student Union Of San Jose State University
1 Washington Sq
San Jose CA
408 924-6315

(P-18597)
STUDENT UN OF SAN JOSE STATE U
2160 Lundy Ave Ste 250, San Jose (95131-1862)
PHONE 408 321-8510
Judith Asire, *Manager*
EMP: 45
SALES (corp-wide): 17.1MM **Privately Held**
WEB: www.sjsu.edu
SIC: 8699 Reading rooms & other cultural organizations
PA: The Student Union Of San Jose State University
1 Washington Sq
San Jose CA
408 924-6315

(P-18598)
STUDENT UN OF SAN JOSE STATE U
Also Called: Event Center
290 S 7th St, San Jose (95192-0001)
PHONE 408 924-6371
Cathy Busalacchi, *Branch Mgr*
EMP: 45
SALES (corp-wide): 17.1MM **Privately Held**
WEB: www.sjsu.edu
SIC: 8699 Personal interest organization
PA: The Student Union Of San Jose State University
1 Washington Sq
San Jose CA
408 924-6315

(P-18599)
SUSAN G KOMEN BREAST CANCER
Also Called: Breast Cancer Car Donations
2520 Old Middlefield Way, Mountain View (94043-2319)
PHONE 650 409-2656
EMP: 50
SALES (corp-wide): 74.7MM **Privately Held**
WEB: www.komen.org
SIC: 8699 Charitable organization
PA: The Susan G Komen Breast Cancer Foundation Inc
13770 Noel Rd Unit 801889
Dallas TX 75380
972 855-1600

(P-18600)
SUSTAINABLE SAN MATEO COUNTY (PA)
Also Called: Self-Help For The Elderly
731 Sansome St Ste 100, San Francisco (94111-1725)
PHONE 415 677-7600
Anni Chung, *Principal*
Josephine MA, *Vice Pres*
Christina Kahn, *Program Mgr*
Yicheng Wu, *Manager*
EMP: 40 **EST:** 2011
SALES (est): 123.1K **Privately Held**
WEB: www.selfhelpelderly.org
SIC: 8699 Charitable organization

(P-18601)
THE DAVID LCILE PCKARD FNDTION
300 2nd St, Los Altos (94022-3621)
PHONE 650 917-7167
Carol S Larson, *President*
Emily Bosworth, *Officer*
Ellen Clear, *Officer*
Temple Cooley, *Officer*
Sarah Hogan, *Officer*
▲ **EMP:** 85 **EST:** 1964 **Privately Held**
WEB: www.packard.org
SIC: 8699 Personal interest organization

(P-18602)
TIPPING POINT COMMUNITY
220 Montgomery St Ste 850, San Francisco (94104-3452)
PHONE 415 348-1240
Sam Cobbs, *CEO*
Jonathan Brack, *Partner*
Daniel Lurie, *CEO*
Kara Dukakis, *Officer*
Nora Martin, *Officer*
EMP: 47 **EST:** 2005
SALES: 83.6MM **Privately Held**
WEB: www.tippingpoint.org
SIC: 8699 Personal interest organization

(P-18603)
UC HASTINGS FOUNDATION
200 Mcallister St, San Francisco (94102-4707)
PHONE 415 565-4704
Frank H Wu, *Chancellor*
EMP: 58 **EST:** 2010
SALES (est): 847.7K **Privately Held**
WEB: www.uchastings.edu
SIC: 8699 Charitable organization

(P-18604)
UNITED ANIMAL NATIONS
Also Called: Redrover
3800 J St Ste 100, Sacramento (95816-5551)
P.O. Box 188890 (95818-8890)
PHONE 916 429-2457
Nicole Forsyth, *CEO*
Savannah Verdon, *COO*
Karly Noel, *Vice Pres*
Rachel Stevens, *Program Mgr*
Olivia Carpenter, *Admin Asst*
EMP: 44 **EST:** 1987
SQ FT: 1,900
SALES: 3MM **Privately Held**
WEB: www.redrover.org
SIC: 8699 Animal humane society

(P-18605)
UNITED STATES ENRGY FOUNDATION ◆
301 Battery St Fl 5, San Francisco (94111-3237)
PHONE 415 561-6700
Jason Mark, *Director*
EMP: 80 **EST:** 2021
SALES (est): 441.5K **Privately Held**
SIC: 8699 Charitable organization

(P-18606)
UNITOGETHER INC
1253 Gray Hawk Ln, Suisun City (94585-3789)
PHONE 707 208-7602
Riair Levelle Hamilton, *President*
EMP: 60 **EST:** 2020
SALES (est): 160.1K **Privately Held**
SIC: 8699 Membership organizations

(P-18607)
VILLASPORT LLC (PA)
Also Called: Villa Sport Athletic CLB & Spa
150 Pelican Way, San Rafael (94901-5550)
PHONE 415 448-8300
Tom Lyneis, *Mng Member*
Dan Lopez, *Vice Pres*
Laurie Smith, *Vice Pres*
Lamar Harris, *General Mgr*
Will Pickering, *General Mgr*
EMP: 76 **EST:** 2005
SALES (est): 13.5MM **Privately Held**
WEB: www.villasport.com
SIC: 8699 Athletic organizations

(P-18608)
WIKIMEDIA FOUNDATION INC
1 Montgomery St Ste 1600, San Francisco (94104-5516)
PHONE 415 839-6885
Katherine Maher, *Exec Dir*
V Ronique Kessler, *COO*
Jaime Villagomez, *CFO*
James Heilman, *Trustee*
Chen Almog, *Officer*
EMP: 284
SALES: 89.9MM **Privately Held**
WEB: www.wikimediafoundation.org
SIC: 8699 6732 Charitable organization; trusts: educational, religious, etc.

(P-18609)
YOUNG MNS CHRSTN ASSN SLCON VL
Also Called: Southwest YMCA
13500 Quito Rd, Saratoga (95070-4749)
PHONE 408 370-1877
Maria Drake, *Exec Dir*
Chuck Berls, *Bd of Directors*
Andrea Borch, *Bd of Directors*
Susan Calderon, *Bd of Directors*
Una Daly, *Bd of Directors*
EMP: 118
SALES (corp-wide): 67.4MM **Privately Held**
WEB: www.ymcasv.org
SIC: 8699 8641 Personal interest organization; youth organizations
PA: Young Men's Christian Association Of Silicon Valley
80 Saratoga Ave
Santa Clara CA 95051
408 351-6400

8711 Engineering Services

(P-18610)
A3GEO-CE&G JOINT VENTURE
821 Bancroft Way, Berkeley (94710-2226)
PHONE 510 705-1664
Dona Mann, *Principal*
EMP: 38 **EST:** 2020
SALES (est): 1.4MM **Privately Held**
WEB: www.a3geo.com
SIC: 8711 Consulting engineer

(P-18611)
ABLE SERVICES INC (PA)
868 Folsom St, San Francisco (94107-1123)
PHONE 800 461-9577
Paul Saccone, *CEO*
Mark Kelly, *President*
Jeff Wofford, *CFO*
Luke Wiltshire, *Program Mgr*
Mark Maddox, *Regional Mgr*
EMP: 93 **EST:** 2016
SALES (est): 17.3MM **Privately Held**
WEB: www.ableserve.com
SIC: 8711 7349 Engineering services; building maintenance, except repairs

(P-18612)
ACER CLOUD TECHNOLOGY INC
333 W San Carlos St # 1500, San Jose (95110-2738)
PHONE 408 830-9809
J T Wang, *CEO*
Janet Lee, *Business Anlyst*
Anne Teo, *Credit Staff*
Michael Wagner, *Counsel*
Irene Chan, *Director*
EMP: 3806 **EST:** 2011
SALES (est): 4.3MM **Privately Held**
SIC: 8711 Engineering services
HQ: Acer American Holdings Corp.
1730 N 1st St Ste 400
San Jose CA 95112

(P-18613)
ACHIEVEMENT ENGINEERING CORP
2455 Autumnvale Dr Ste E, San Jose (95131-1839)
PHONE 408 217-9174
Arash Firouzjaei, *President*
Lana Castillo, *Office Mgr*
EMP: 35 **EST:** 2014
SQ FT: 1,800
SALES (est): 4.2MM **Privately Held**
WEB: www.achieveng.com
SIC: 8711 7389 Consulting engineer; inspection & testing services

PRODUCTS & SERVICES SECTION

8711 - Engineering Services County (P-18636)

(P-18614)
ACRONICS SYSTEMS INC
2102 Commerce Dr, San Jose (95131-1804)
PHONE..............................408 432-0888
Kim Tran, *CEO*
Nguyen Michael, *Engineer*
Vivian Nguyen, *Purch Mgr*
Hanh Pham, *Mfg Staff*
Kiem Vo, *Manager*
EMP: 110 **EST:** 1994
SQ FT: 16,000
SALES (est): 16.4MM Privately Held
WEB: www.acronics.com
SIC: 8711 7373 Electrical or electronic engineering; systems engineering, computer related

(P-18615)
ADM ASSOCIATES INCORPORATED
3239 Ramos Cir, Sacramento (95827-2501)
PHONE..............................916 363-8383
Taghi Alereza, *CEO*
Donald Dohrmann, *Corp Secy*
Sasha Baroiant, *Principal*
John Drevenak, *CIO*
Scott Reese, *Info Tech Mgr*
EMP: 120 **EST:** 1979
SQ FT: 8,000
SALES (est): 15.4MM Privately Held
WEB: www.admenergy.com
SIC: 8711 8748 Energy conservation engineering; energy conservation consultant

(P-18616)
ADVENT ENGINEERING SVCS INC (PA)
12647 Alcosta Blvd # 440, San Ramon (94583-4436)
PHONE..............................925 830-4700
Ravi Baliga, *President*
Albert Dyrness, *Vice Pres*
Tom Neal Watts, *Vice Pres*
Kartik Subramanian, *General Mgr*
Jason Devera, *Engineer*
EMP: 35 **EST:** 1988
SQ FT: 3,800
SALES (est): 7.6MM Privately Held
SIC: 8711 Consulting engineer

(P-18617)
AECOM
300 California St Fl 6, San Francisco (94104-1412)
PHONE..............................415 796-8100
William Crockett, *Manager*
Tony Nelson, *Vice Pres*
Russel Rudden, *Vice Pres*
Bruce Allen, *Counsel*
Michael A Arnold, *Sr Associate*
EMP: 40
SALES (corp-wide): 13.2B Publicly Held
WEB: www.aecom.com
SIC: 8711 8712 Consulting engineer; architectural engineering
PA: Aecom
13355 Noel Rd Ste 400
Dallas TX 75240
972 788-1000

(P-18618)
AECOM
Also Called: Aecom Tech
501 2nd St, San Francisco (94107-1469)
PHONE..............................415 908-6135
Tim Phillips, *Engineer*
EMP: 58
SALES (corp-wide): 13.2B Publicly Held
WEB: www.aecom.com
SIC: 8711 Engineering services
PA: Aecom
13355 Noel Rd Ste 400
Dallas TX 75240
972 788-1000

(P-18619)
AECOM INTERNATIONAL INC (DH)
300 California St Ste 600, San Francisco (94104-1407)
PHONE..............................415 716-8100
Mel Dunn, *Vice Pres*
Andrew Miller, *Plant Engr Mgr*
EMP: 223 **EST:** 1990
SALES (est): 7.3MM
SALES (corp-wide): 13.2B Publicly Held
WEB: www.aecom.com
SIC: 8711 Consulting engineer
HQ: Aecom Global Ii, Llc
300 S Grand Ave Ste 900
Los Angeles CA 90071
213 593-8100

(P-18620)
AECOM-TSE JOINT VENTURE
300 Lakeside Dr Ste 400, Oakland (94612-3573)
PHONE..............................510 285-6639
Simon Kim, *Vice Pres*
Etty Mercurio, *Administration*
Paul Van Der Wel, *Administration*
EMP: 99 **EST:** 2017
SQ FT: 150,000
SALES (est): 2.5MM Privately Held
SIC: 8711 Engineering services

(P-18621)
AFFILIATED ENGINEERS W INC (HQ)
123 Mission St Fl 7, San Francisco (94105-5122)
PHONE..............................415 546-3120
Mike Bove, *Principal*
Chris Case, *Project Mgr*
David Nussbaum, *Technology*
Rafi Karim, *Consultant*
EMP: 71 **EST:** 1991
SQ FT: 11,000
SALES (est): 9MM
SALES (corp-wide): 84.2MM Privately Held
WEB: www.aeieng.com
SIC: 8711 Consulting engineer; electrical or electronic engineering
PA: Affiliated Engineers, Inc.
5802 Research Park Blvd
Madison WI 53719
608 238-2616

(P-18622)
AHNTECH INC (PA)
1931 Old Middlefield Way D, Mountain View (94043-2559)
PHONE..............................650 861-3987
Eugene Ahn, *CEO*
Sam Ahn, *President*
Ryan Osborne, *VP Bus Dvlpt*
SOO Myung Ahn, *Principal*
Pat Palas, *Program Mgr*
EMP: 70
SALES (est): 42MM Privately Held
WEB: www.ahntech.com
SIC: 8711 3674 3679 3699 Engineering services; semiconductors & related devices; electronic circuits; recording & playback apparatus, including phonograph; electronic loads & power supplies; electronic crystals; electronic training devices; shooting range operation; calculating & accounting equipment

(P-18623)
ALFA TECH CNSLTING ENGNERS INC (PA)
Also Called: Alfa Tech Consulting Entps
1321 Ridder Park Dr 50, San Jose (95131-2306)
PHONE..............................408 487-1200
Jeff Fini, *Ch of Bd*
Diarmuid Hartley, *Managing Prtnr*
Paul Artelles, *Principal*
Carolyn Keith, *Principal*
Amber Welsh, *Principal*
EMP: 67 **EST:** 1987
SQ FT: 22,000
SALES (est): 48MM Privately Held
WEB: www.atce.com
SIC: 8711 Consulting engineer

(P-18624)
ANDERSON NEIL O AND ASSOC INC (DH)
Also Called: Neil O Anderson Assoc Inc NA
902 Industrial Way, Lodi (95240-3106)
PHONE..............................209 367-3701
Neil O Anderson, *President*
Donald J Vrana, *Treasurer*
E Lynn Price, *Admin Sec*
EMP: 35 **EST:** 1991

SALES (est): 17.9MM Privately Held
WEB: www.terracon.com
SIC: 8711 Consulting engineer

(P-18625)
APCO-ETTNER INC (PA)
1433 W Pine Ave, Fresno (93728-1208)
PHONE..............................559 439-6766
Scott Ettner, *CEO*
EMP: 74 **EST:** 1996
SALES (est): 1.4MM Privately Held
WEB: www.apcoettner.com
SIC: 8711 Mechanical engineering

(P-18626)
AQUATIC DESIGNING INC
4801 West End Rd, Arcata (95521-9242)
PHONE..............................707 822-4629
Paula E Crowley, *President*
EMP: 50 **EST:** 2005
SALES (est): 2.7MM Privately Held
WEB: www.northcoastfabricators.com
SIC: 8711 Engineering services

(P-18627)
ARES HOLDING CORPORATION (PA)
1290 Howard Ave Ste 319, Burlingame (94010-4222)
PHONE..............................650 401-7100
Dr Richard J Stuart, *CEO*
Douglas Schmidt, *CFO*
Geoff Stubson, *CFO*
Larry Shipley, *Exec VP*
Stanley Lynch, *Senior VP*
EMP: 42 **EST:** 1992
SALES (est): 63.2MM Privately Held
WEB: www.arescorporation.com
SIC: 8711 Consulting engineer

(P-18628)
ARES PROJECT MANAGEMENT LLC (HQ)
Also Called: Ares Prism
1290 Howard Ave Ste 319, Burlingame (94010-4222)
PHONE..............................650 401-7100
Stanley C Lynch, *Mng Member*
Joyce Grant, *Controller*
Tiffany Minegar, *Marketing Mgr*
Larry E Shipley,
Chris Donahue, *Director*
EMP: 66 **EST:** 2012
SALES (est): 10.7MM Privately Held
WEB: www.aresprism.com
SIC: 8711 Consulting engineer

(P-18629)
ARMSTRONG MFG & ENGRG INC
12780 Earhart Ave, Auburn (95602-9027)
PHONE..............................530 888-6262
Arthur W Armstrong, *President*
Lisa Kodl, *Office Mgr*
▼ **EMP:** 55 **EST:** 1966
SALES (est): 7MM Privately Held
WEB: www.armstrong-mfg.com
SIC: 8711 5084 Mechanical engineering; industrial machinery & equipment

(P-18630)
ARUP NORTH AMERICA LIMITED (DH)
560 Mission St Fl 7, San Francisco (94105-0915)
PHONE..............................415 957-9445
Mahadev Ramen, *President*
Andrew Howard, *Vice Pres*
James Quiter, *Vice Pres*
Colin Clinton, *Executive*
Anita Daniel, *Executive Asst*
EMP: 200 **EST:** 1987
SALES (est): 322.9MM
SALES (corp-wide): 26.1MM Privately Held
WEB: www.arup.com
SIC: 8711 Consulting engineer

(P-18631)
ATTOCUBE SYSTEMS INC (DH)
2020 Stuart St, Berkeley (94703-2217)
PHONE..............................510 649-9245
Florian Ponnath, *Principal*
Balazs Sipos, *Engineer*
EMP: 50 **EST:** 2009

SALES (est): 2.8MM
SALES (corp-wide): 463.1MM Privately Held
WEB: www.attocube.com
SIC: 8711 Industrial engineers; machine tool design; mechanical engineering
HQ: Attocube Systems Ag
Eglfinger Weg 2
Haar BY 85540
894 207-970

(P-18632)
AUSENCO PSI INC (HQ)
4071 Port Chicago Hwy # 120, Concord (94520-1155)
PHONE..............................925 939-4420
Ed Meka, *President*
Andrew Fletcher, *Treasurer*
Delbert Boyle, *Senior VP*
Craig Allen, *Admin Sec*
Rafael Lima, *Technical Staff*
EMP: 50 **EST:** 2010
SALES (est): 10.1MM Privately Held
WEB: www.ausenco.com
SIC: 8711 Engineering services
PA: Ausenco Usa Inc.
1320 Willow Pass Rd
Concord CA 94520
925 939-4420

(P-18633)
AUTOMATED BLDG SOLUTIONS INC (PA)
Also Called: Automated Bldg Ctrl Solutions
330 Mathew St, Santa Clara (95050-3114)
PHONE..............................408 380-8518
Frank Honesto, *President*
Michael Donovan, *Shareholder*
John Donovan, *Corp Secy*
Kristi Bernardez, *Office Mgr*
Ayshleen Kumar, *Manager*
EMP: 44 **EST:** 2012
SQ FT: 10,000
SALES (est): 7.5MM Privately Held
WEB: www.automatedbldgs.com
SIC: 8711 Engineering services

(P-18634)
B&C TRANSIT INC (HQ)
Also Called: B & C
1924 Franklin St Ste 200, Oakland (94612-2913)
PHONE..............................510 483-3560
Alberto Fernandez, *President*
Tanya Powell, *CFO*
Steven Falk, *Vice Pres*
Jerome S Furman, *Vice Pres*
Jerome Furman, *Vice Pres*
EMP: 60 **EST:** 1999
SQ FT: 25,000
SALES (est): 29MM Privately Held
WEB: www.bnctransit.com
SIC: 8711 Electrical or electronic engineering

(P-18635)
BABCOCK BROWN RNWBLE HLDNGS IN (DH)
1 Letterman Dr Bldg B, San Francisco (94129-1494)
PHONE..............................415 512-1515
Karen R Fagerstrom, *President*
EMP: 50 **EST:** 2006
SALES (est): 219MM Privately Held
SIC: 8711 Energy conservation engineering

(P-18636)
BARA INFOWARE INC (PA)
Also Called: Bara Construction
4115 Blackhawk Plaza Cir, Danville (94506-4901)
PHONE..............................925 790-0130
Elina Singh, *President*
Menginder Singh, *Vice Pres*
EMP: 59 **EST:** 1998
SQ FT: 600
SALES (est): 6.6MM Privately Held
WEB: www.barainfo.com
SIC: 8711 1542 Engineering services; custom builders, non-residential

8711 - Engineering Services County (P-18637)

(P-18637)
BAY-TEC ENGINEERING (PA)
5130 Fulton Dr Ste X, Fairfield (94534-4223)
PHONE..................714 257-1680
John Justus, *President*
Rick Cavalli, *Treasurer*
Adam Beaddy, *Vice Pres*
Alan Kelm, *Admin Sec*
Debbie Le Blanc, *Accountant*
EMP: 53 **EST:** 1983
SQ FT: 22,000
SALES (est): 5.1MM **Privately Held**
SIC: 8711 1731 3823 3829 Engineering services; electronic controls installation; industrial instrmnts msrmnt display/control process variable; measuring & controlling devices

(P-18638)
BDG INNOVATIONS LLC (PA)
6001 Outfall Cir, Sacramento (95828-1066)
PHONE..................855 725-9555
Larry A Devore, *President*
James Brock Littlejohn, *CFO*
Jason Blum,
Jeremy Grosser,
EMP: 40 **EST:** 2016
SALES (est): 160MM **Privately Held**
SIC: 8711 3699 Consulting engineer; electrical equipment & supplies

(P-18639)
BERLOGAR GEOTECHNICAL CONS
5587 Sunol Blvd, Pleasanton (94566-7765)
PHONE..................925 484-0220
Frank Berlogar, *President*
Ranta Wright, *Corp Secy*
Paul Lai, *Vice Pres*
Katie Carey, *Assistant*
EMP: 44 **EST:** 1973
SQ FT: 5,800
SALES (est): 2.7MM **Privately Held**
WEB: www.berlogar.com
SIC: 8711 Consulting engineer

(P-18640)
BIGGS CARDOSA ASSOCIATES INC (PA)
865 The Alameda, San Jose (95126-3133)
PHONE..................408 296-5515
Steven A Biggs, *President*
Mark Cardosa, *Exec VP*
Jake Delgado, *Department Mgr*
Daniel Lazzarini, *Engineer*
Matt Lipa, *Engineer*
EMP: 70 **EST:** 1986
SQ FT: 7,237
SALES (est): 12.4MM **Privately Held**
WEB: www.biggscardosa.com
SIC: 8711 Civil engineering

(P-18641)
BKF ENGINEERS (PA)
255 Shoreline Dr Ste 200, Redwood City (94065-1428)
PHONE..................650 482-6300
Greg Hurd, *CEO*
Maureen Nevin, *CFO*
Max Keech, *Corp Secy*
Todd Adair, *Vice Pres*
Geoff Coleman, *Vice Pres*
EMP: 90 **EST:** 1915
SQ FT: 18,155
SALES (est): 72.8MM **Privately Held**
WEB: www.bkf.com
SIC: 8711 8713 Civil engineering; surveying services

(P-18642)
BLAIR CH FLYNN CNSLTING ENGNER (PA)
451 Clovis Ave Ste 200, Clovis (93612-1376)
PHONE..................559 326-1400
David Mowry, *CEO*
Adam Holt, *CFO*
Jeffrey Brians, *Vice Pres*
Karl Kienow, *Vice Pres*
Cheng Lee, *Technician*
EMP: 135
SQ FT: 15,000

SALES (est): 16MM **Privately Held**
WEB: www.bcf-engr.com
SIC: 8711 8713 Civil engineering; consulting engineer; surveying services

(P-18643)
BOUWMAN ENGINEERING INC
58 Union Way, Vacaville (95687-4104)
PHONE..................707 447-5414
John Bouwman, *President*
EMP: 15 **EST:** 1972
SALES (est): 777.9K **Privately Held**
SIC: 8711 3699 Mechanical engineering; electrical equipment & supplies

(P-18644)
BOWMAN & WILLIAMS A CAL CORP
3949 Res Pk Ct Ste 100, Soquel (95073)
PHONE..................831 426-3560
Joel Ricca, *President*
Curt Dunbar, *Shareholder*
George Dunbar, *Shareholder*
Thomas Mason, *Vice Pres*
Richard Irish, *Principal*
EMP: 52 **EST:** 1908
SQ FT: 3,500
SALES (est): 9.1MM **Privately Held**
WEB: www.bowmanandwilliams.com
SIC: 8711 Civil engineering

(P-18645)
BRELJE RACE CNSLTING ENGINEERS
475 Aviation Blvd Ste 120, Santa Rosa (95403-1062)
PHONE..................707 576-1322
David Long, *President*
Thomas Yokoi, *Admin Sec*
EMP: 40 **EST:** 1954
SQ FT: 7,000
SALES (est): 6.4MM **Privately Held**
WEB: www.brce.com
SIC: 8711 Consulting engineer; civil engineering

(P-18646)
BROSAMER & WALL INC
1777 Oakland Blvd Ste 300, Walnut Creek (94596-4063)
PHONE..................925 932-7900
Robert Brosamer, *Ch of Bd*
Jeffrey Turner, *CFO*
Charles Wall, *Vice Ch Bd*
EMP: 140 **EST:** 2012
SQ FT: 13,000
SALES (est): 25.5MM **Privately Held**
WEB: www.brosamerwall.com
SIC: 8711 Engineering services

(P-18647)
BROWN AND CALDWELL (PA)
201 N Civic Dr Ste 115, Walnut Creek (94596-3865)
P.O. Box 8045 (94596-1220)
PHONE..................925 937-9010
Craig Goehring, *CEO*
Richard D' Amanto, *President*
Marc Damikolas, *COO*
James Miller, *Vice Ch Bd*
Cindy Paulson, *Officer*
▲ **EMP:** 131 **EST:** 1944
SQ FT: 24,000
SALES (est): 374.6MM **Privately Held**
WEB: www.brownandcaldwell.com
SIC: 8711 Civil engineering

(P-18648)
BSI SERVICES & SOLUTIONS W INC (DH)
Also Called: E O R M
2150 N 1st St Ste 450, San Jose (95131-2047)
PHONE..................408 790-9200
Glenn Fishler, *President*
Danielle Reilly Cih, *COO*
Janice McKim, *CFO*
Andy McIntyre, *Exec VP*
Jon Brownstein, *Vice Pres*
EMP: 45 **EST:** 1992

SALES (est): 44.8MM
SALES (corp-wide): 624.9MM **Privately Held**
WEB: www.bsiamericas.com
SIC: 8711 8742 8748 Consulting engineer; industrial hygiene consultant; safety training service

(P-18649)
BSK ASSOCIATES
4230 W Swift Ave Ste 106, Fresno (93722-6339)
PHONE..................559 277-6960
Rob Robbins, *Manager*
EMP: 35
SALES (corp-wide): 37.8MM **Privately Held**
WEB: www.bskassociates.com
SIC: 8711 8734 Professional engineer; testing laboratories
PA: Bsk Associates
550 W Locust Ave
Fresno CA 93650
559 497-2880

(P-18650)
BSK ASSOCIATES
Also Called: B S K Analytical Laboratories
1414 Stanislaus St, Fresno (93706-1623)
PHONE..................559 497-2888
Jeff Koelewyn, *Director*
Kris Morton, *Officer*
EMP: 35
SQ FT: 6,316
SALES (corp-wide): 37.8MM **Privately Held**
WEB: www.bskassociates.com
SIC: 8711 8734 Professional engineer; testing laboratories
PA: Bsk Associates
550 W Locust Ave
Fresno CA 93650
559 497-2880

(P-18651)
BSK ASSOCIATES
3140 Gold Camp Dr Ste 160, Rancho Cordova (95670-6054)
PHONE..................916 853-9293
Dennis Nakamoto, *Manager*
Michelle Harmstead, *Manager*
EMP: 35
SALES (corp-wide): 37.8MM **Privately Held**
WEB: www.bskassociates.com
SIC: 8711 8748 Professional engineer; environmental consultant
PA: Bsk Associates
550 W Locust Ave
Fresno CA 93650
559 497-2880

(P-18652)
BSK ASSOCIATES
1415 Tuolumne St, Fresno (93706-1625)
PHONE..................559 256-2251
Gary Blomgren, *Manager*
Adam Terronez, *Branch Mgr*
EMP: 35
SALES (corp-wide): 37.8MM **Privately Held**
WEB: www.bskassociates.com
SIC: 8711 Civil engineering; consulting engineer
PA: Bsk Associates
550 W Locust Ave
Fresno CA 93650
559 497-2880

(P-18653)
BUEHLER ENGINEERING INC (PA)
600 Q St Ste 200, Sacramento (95811-6353)
PHONE..................916 443-0303
Scott Hooker, *President*
David A Hutchinson, *CEO*
Larry Jones, *Vice Pres*
Lawrence Jones, *Vice Pres*
William Rader, *Principal*
EMP: 48 **EST:** 1946
SALES (est): 4.6MM **Privately Held**
WEB: www.buehlerengineering.com
SIC: 8711 Structural engineering

(P-18654)
BURRELL CONSULTING GROUP INC
Also Called: Burrell Engineering
1001 Entp Way Ste 100, Roseville (95678)
PHONE..................916 783-8898
Jerry V Aplass, *President*
Vanessa Norton, *Vice Pres*
Josie Owens, *Office Mgr*
Dave King, *Technician*
Joe Arino, *Design Engr*
EMP: 48 **EST:** 1990
SQ FT: 4,000
SALES (est): 5.3MM **Privately Held**
WEB: www.burrellcg.com
SIC: 8711 8713 Consulting engineer; surveying services

(P-18655)
CALIFORNIA ENVMTL SYSTEMS INC
12265 Locksley Ln, Auburn (95602-2055)
PHONE..................530 820-3693
Carter Pierce, *Principal*
Jeanette Pierce, *Administration*
David Armenta, *Project Mgr*
Amy Schwartz, *Human Resources*
EMP: 70 **EST:** 2011
SQ FT: 10,000
SALES (est): 6MM **Privately Held**
WEB: www.calenvirosys.com
SIC: 8711 Engineering services

(P-18656)
CAMMISA WIPF CNSLTING ENGNEERS
642 Harrison St Fl 4, San Francisco (94107-1323)
PHONE..................415 863-5740
Robert Boyd, *President*
Mel Cammisa, *Principal*
Daryl Wipf, *Principal*
Victor Wong, *Principal*
Francesca Pruitt, *Admin Asst*
EMP: 40 **EST:** 1965
SQ FT: 6,000
SALES (est): 1MM **Privately Held**
WEB: www.cammisawipf.com
SIC: 8711 Consulting engineer; electrical or electronic engineering

(P-18657)
CAPITAL ENGINEERING CONS INC (PA)
11020 Sun Center Dr # 100, Rancho Cordova (95670-6287)
PHONE..................916 851-3500
Lowell E Shields, *President*
Thomas Duval, *Treasurer*
John Lionakis, *Vice Pres*
Mark Reid, *Info Tech Dir*
Matt Brooks, *Project Mgr*
EMP: 72 **EST:** 1947
SQ FT: 6,800
SALES (est): 10.9MM **Privately Held**
WEB: www.capital-engineering.com
SIC: 8711 Consulting engineer

(P-18658)
CARBON LIGHTHOUSE INC
343 Sansome St Ste 700, San Francisco (94104-5614)
PHONE..................415 787-3550
Brenden Millstein, *Principal*
Matt Ganser, *President*
Jerry Acosta, *COO*
Rick Smith, *Bd of Directors*
Neha Tibrewala, *Exec VP*
EMP: 139 **EST:** 2010
SALES (est): 18.6MM **Privately Held**
WEB: www.carbonlighthouse.com
SIC: 8711 Energy conservation engineering

(P-18659)
CARLILEMACY INC
15 3rd St, Santa Rosa (95401-6204)
PHONE..................707 542-6451
David Hanson, *President*
Mark Hale, *Treasurer*
Curtis Nichols, *Vice Pres*
Bruce Jarvis, *Admin Sec*
Curt Nichols, *Engineer*
EMP: 50 **EST:** 1987
SQ FT: 10,000

PRODUCTS & SERVICES SECTION
8711 - Engineering Services County (P-18681)

SALES (est): 7MM **Privately Held**
WEB: www.carlilemacy.com
SIC: **8711** Civil engineering

(P-18660)
CARLSON BARBEE & GIBSON INC
2633 Camino Ramon, San Ramon (94583-9132)
PHONE..................925 866-0322
David Carlson, *President*
Grant Gibson, *Vice Pres*
Michael Barbee, *Admin Sec*
Christopher Quibol, *Admin Asst*
Lee Rosenblatt, *Project Mgr*
EMP: 100 EST: 1989
SQ FT: 6,800
SALES (est): 11.9MM **Privately Held**
WEB: www.cbandg.com
SIC: **8711** Civil engineering

(P-18661)
CARLTON ENGINEERING INC (PA)
4080 Plaza Goldorado Cir B, Cameron Park (95682-7455)
PHONE..................916 932-7855
Alan V Carlton, *President*
David B Jermstad, *Vice Pres*
Sue Thomson, *General Mgr*
Tom Burkhart, *Admin Sec*
Thomas Burkhart, *Engineer*
EMP: 49 EST: 1983
SQ FT: 25,000
SALES (est): 8.2MM **Privately Held**
WEB: www.carlton-engineering.com
SIC: **8711 8713** Civil engineering; structural engineering; surveying services

(P-18662)
CAROLLO ENGINEERS INC (PA)
2795 Mitchell Dr, Walnut Creek (94598-1601)
PHONE..................925 932-1710
Balakrishnan Narayanan, *President*
Gary Meyerhofer, *Partner*
Rick D Wheadon, *Treasurer*
John Briones, *Assoc VP*
Chris Carvalho, *Assoc VP*
EMP: 100 EST: 2010
SQ FT: 20,000
SALES (est): 198.7MM **Privately Held**
WEB: www.carollo.com
SIC: **8711** Consulting engineer

(P-18663)
CARTER & BURGESS INC
2033 Gateway Pl Fl 6, San Jose (95110-3709)
PHONE..................408 428-2010
Dan Potter, *Branch Mgr*
EMP: 72
SALES (corp-wide): 13.5B **Publicly Held**
WEB: www.c-b.com
SIC: **8711** Civil engineering
HQ: Carter & Burgess, Inc.
777 Main St Ste 2500
Fort Worth TX 76102
817 735-6000

(P-18664)
CB ENGINEERS (PA)
449 10th St, San Francisco (94103-4303)
PHONE..................415 437-7330
Igor Tartakovsky, *President*
Paul O'Neill, *Exec VP*
Enrico S Martin, *Principal*
Jack Mou, *Info Tech Mgr*
Manalee Nabar, *Engineer*
EMP: 40 EST: 1957
SQ FT: 9,500
SALES (est): 11.8MM **Privately Held**
WEB: www.cbengineers.com
SIC: **8711** Consulting engineer

(P-18665)
CB&I GOVERNMENT SOLUTIONS INC
1326 N Market Blvd, Sacramento (95834-1912)
PHONE..................916 928-3300
EMP: 40
SALES (corp-wide): 10.6B **Privately Held**
SIC: **8711** Engineering Services

HQ: Cb&I Government Solutions, Inc.
4171 Essen Ln
Baton Rouge LA 70809
225 932-2500

(P-18666)
CE2 CORPORATION INC
6200 Stnrdge Mall Rd Ste, Pleasanton (94588)
PHONE..................925 463-7301
Clyde Wong, *CEO*
Howard Wong, *General Mgr*
Consuelo Jocson, *Human Res Mgr*
EMP: 43 EST: 1999 **Privately Held**
WEB: www.ce2corp.com
SIC: **8711 8741 7361 7374** Consulting engineer; management services; employment agencies; computer graphics service; engineering help service; computer-aided system services

(P-18667)
CHARLES M SALTER ASSOCIATES (PA)
Also Called: Audio Forensic Center
130 Sutter St Fl 5, San Francisco (94104-4018)
PHONE..................415 470-5461
Charles M Salter, *President*
Trudy J Salter, *Corp Secy*
David Schwind, *Senior VP*
Eva Duesler, *Vice Pres*
Dylan Mills, *Vice Pres*
EMP: 41 EST: 1975
SQ FT: 10,000
SALES (est): 7.7MM **Privately Held**
WEB: www.salter-inc.com
SIC: **8711** Consulting engineer

(P-18668)
CHAUDHARY & ASSOCIATES
211 Gateway Rd W Ste 204, NAPA (94558-6279)
PHONE..................707 255-2729
Arvin Chaudhary, *President*
Gisela D Chaudhary, *Vice Pres*
Sudhir Chaudhary, *Vice Pres*
Elke Chaudhary, *VP Admin*
Erwin Backlin, *Project Mgr*
EMP: 43 EST: 1976
SALES (est): 6.9MM **Privately Held**
WEB: www.chaudhary.com
SIC: **8711 8713 8742** Civil engineering; surveying services; planning consultant

(P-18669)
CHEVRON GLOBAL TECH SVCS CO
6001 Bollinger Canyon Dr, San Ramon (94583-5737)
PHONE..................925 842-1000
Bruce Bowser, *Vice Pres*
EMP: 33 EST: 1976
SALES (est): 2.3MM
SALES (corp-wide): 94.6B **Publicly Held**
WEB: www.chevron.com
SIC: **8711 1382 4924** Energy conservation engineering; oil & gas exploration services; natural gas distribution
PA: Chevron Corporation
6001 Bollinger Canyon Rd
San Ramon CA 94583
925 842-1000

(P-18670)
CIVIL ENGINEERING ASSOC INC
2055 Gateway Pl Ste 550, San Jose (95110-1019)
PHONE..................408 453-1066
Peter McMorrow, *President*
Don Utz, *Vice Pres*
Dennis Gerber, *Engineer*
Addis Ababa, *Senior Mgr*
Angela Ott, *Manager*
EMP: 50 EST: 1983
SQ FT: 1,500
SALES (est): 3.5MM **Privately Held**
WEB: www.civilengineeringassociates.com
SIC: **8711** Civil engineering

(P-18671)
CLARK RICHARDSON AND BISKUP
6001 Shellmound St # 550, Emeryville (94608-1968)
PHONE..................510 907-2700
Trevor Auer, *Branch Mgr*
John Schwaller, *Technology*
EMP: 39
SALES (corp-wide): 128MM **Privately Held**
WEB: www.crbgroup.com
SIC: **8711** Consulting engineer
PA: Clark, Richardson And Biskup Consulting Engineers, Inc.
1251 Nw Briarcliff Pkwy
Kansas City MO 64116
816 880-9800

(P-18672)
CON-QUEST CONTRACTORS INC
290 Toland St, San Francisco (94124-1120)
PHONE..................415 206-0524
Paul N Loukianoff, *CEO*
Alex Loukianoff, *Controller*
Paul Loukianoff, *Opers Mgr*
Rodney Homer, *Superintendent*
EMP: 40 EST: 2008
SALES (est): 16.4MM **Privately Held**
WEB: www.cqcontractors.com
SIC: **8711** Civil engineering

(P-18673)
CONDOR EARTH TECHNOLOGIES INC
17857 High School Rd, Jamestown (95327-9769)
PHONE..................209 984-4593
Robert John Job, *Branch Mgr*
EMP: 45
SALES (corp-wide): 17.1MM **Privately Held**
WEB: www.condorearth.com
SIC: **8711 8713** Consulting engineer; surveying services
PA: Condor Earth Technologies, Inc.
21663 Brian Ln
Sonora CA 95370
209 532-0361

(P-18674)
CONNEXSYS ENGINEERING INC
1320 Willow Pass Rd # 500, Concord (94520-5232)
PHONE..................510 243-2050
Flavio Santini, *CEO*
Frank Baker, *Partner*
Franklin L Baker, *COO*
Shafiq Zainol, *Engineer*
EMP: 50 EST: 1975
SQ FT: 10,000
SALES (est): 5.6MM **Privately Held**
WEB: www.connexsysinc.com
SIC: **8711** Consulting engineer
PA: Versa Engineering & Technology, Inc.
1320 Willow Pass Rd S500
Concord CA 94520

(P-18675)
COOPER THORNE & ASSOCIATES INC
Also Called: C T A
3233 Monier Cir Ste 1, Rancho Cordova (95742-6807)
PHONE..................916 638-0919
David Crosario, *President*
Edgar Brown, *Treasurer*
Brian Allen, *Vice Pres*
Vickey Hillard-Janzen, *General Mgr*
Kevin Heeney, *Engineer*
EMP: 35 EST: 1979
SQ FT: 6,400
SALES (est): 4.2MM **Privately Held**
WEB: www.cooperthorne.com
SIC: **8711 8713** Civil engineering; surveying services

(P-18676)
COOPER VALI & ASSOCIATES INC (HQ)
1850 Gateway Blvd Ste 100, Concord (94520-8447)
PHONE..................510 446-8301
Gary Bedey, *CEO*
Hank Doll, *President*
John Collins, *COO*
Marian Ross, *CFO*
Agnes Weber, *Officer*
EMP: 80 EST: 1987
SQ FT: 3,000
SALES (est): 27.2MM
SALES (corp-wide): 711.8MM **Privately Held**
WEB: www.trccompanies.com
SIC: **8711** Construction & civil engineering; building construction consultant
PA: Trc Companies, L.L.C.
21 Griffin Rd N
Windsor CT 06095
860 298-9692

(P-18677)
COUNTY ENGINEERS ASSN CAL
120 Round Ct, Petaluma (94952-4720)
PHONE..................707 762-3492
EMP: 58
SALES: 353.7K **Privately Held**
SIC: **8711** Engineering Services

(P-18678)
CROWN ENERGY SERVICES INC
Also Called: Able Services
611 Gateway Blvd, South San Francisco (94080-7017)
PHONE..................415 546-6534
EMP: 698 **Privately Held**
WEB: www.ableserve.com
SIC: **8711** Engineering services
PA: Crown Energy Services, Inc.
868 Folsom St
San Francisco CA 94107

(P-18679)
CSG CONSULTANTS INC (PA)
550 Pilgrim Dr, Foster City (94404-1212)
PHONE..................650 522-2500
Cyrus Kianpour, *President*
Khoa Duong, *Vice Pres*
Alison Gray, *Admin Asst*
Peykan Abbassi, *VP Engrg*
Catherine Chan, *Engineer*
EMP: 50 EST: 1991
SQ FT: 16,000
SALES (est): 42MM **Privately Held**
WEB: www.csgengr.com
SIC: **8711** Consulting engineer

(P-18680)
CSW/STBR-STROEH ENGRG GROUP IN (PA)
45 Leveroni Ct, Novato (94949-5721)
PHONE..................415 883-9850
Alan Cornwell, *President*
Kelly Burk, *COO*
Dietrich Stroeh, *Vice Pres*
Kirk Bovitz, *Project Mgr*
Kristine Pillsbury, *Project Mgr*
EMP: 37 EST: 1990
SALES (est): 5.3MM **Privately Held**
WEB: www.cswst2.com
SIC: **8711** Consulting engineer; civil engineering

(P-18681)
CUMMING MANAGEMENT GROUP INC
475 Sansome St Ste 520, San Francisco (94111-3137)
PHONE..................415 748-3080
David Baird, *Director*
EMP: 72
SALES (corp-wide): 191.1MM **Privately Held**
SIC: **8711 8741** Engineering services; management services
PA: Cumming Management Group, Inc.
25220 Hancock Ave Ste 440
Murrieta CA 92562
858 485-6765

(P-18682)
CYGNA GROUP INC
2101 Webster St, Oakland (94612-3011)
PHONE....................................510 419-5000
James Edwards, *CEO*
Marc Tipermas, *President*
Pete Offringa, *Exec VP*
EMP: 250 **EST:** 1974
SALES (est): 10.4MM
SALES (corp-wide): 81.2MM **Publicly Held**
SIC: 8711 8741 8748 Consulting engineer; construction management; business consulting
PA: Kaiser Group Holdings, Inc.
1943 50th St N
Birmingham AL 35212
404 593-1025

(P-18683)
CYPRESS ENVIROSYSTEMS INC
5883 Rue Ferrari Ste 100, San Jose (95138-1861)
PHONE....................................800 544-5411
Harry Sim, *CEO*
Aline Sim, *Manager*
EMP: 25 **EST:** 2007
SQ FT: 14,500
SALES (est): 4.4MM **Privately Held**
WEB: www.cypressenvirosystems.com
SIC: 8711 3822 Energy conservation engineering; auto controls regulating residntl & coml environmt & applncs

(P-18684)
D A WOOD CONSTRUCTION INC
963 Shepard Ct, Oakdale (95361-9392)
P.O. Box 1810, Empire (95319-1810)
PHONE....................................209 491-4970
Danny Wood, *President*
Kristine Wood, *Admin Sec*
Kristine T Wood, *Admin Sec*
Aly Peterson, *Manager*
EMP: 56 **EST:** 2000
SQ FT: 960
SALES (est): 10.3MM **Privately Held**
WEB: www.dawoodinc.com
SIC: 8711 Construction & civil engineering

(P-18685)
DB DESIGN GROUP INC
48507 Milmont Dr, Fremont (94538-7336)
PHONE....................................408 834-1400
Mark Stenholm, *President*
Rennie Bowers, *Vice Pres*
EMP: 23 **EST:** 1989
SQ FT: 25,155
SALES (est): 5.1MM **Privately Held**
WEB: www.dbdesign.com
SIC: 8711 3469 Mechanical engineering; machine parts, stamped or pressed metal
PA: Aem Holdings Ltd.
52 Serangoon North Avenue 4
Singapore 55585

(P-18686)
DEGENKOLB ENGINEERS (PA)
375 Beale St Ste 500, San Francisco (94105-2177)
PHONE....................................415 392-6950
Stacy Bartoletti, *CEO*
Chris Poland, *Ch of Bd*
Maury Ballif, *CFO*
Robert Beggs, *CFO*
David Bonneville, *Principal*
EMP: 66 **EST:** 1940
SQ FT: 22,800
SALES (est): 70.2MM **Privately Held**
WEB: www.degenkolb.com
SIC: 8711 Structural engineering

(P-18687)
DEGENKOLB ENGINEERS
1300 Clay St Ste 9009, Oakland (94612-1425)
PHONE....................................510 272-9040
Jorn Halle, *Branch Mgr*
Carrie Mitchell, *Principal*
Ray Pugliesi, *Principal*
EMP: 41
SALES (corp-wide): 70.2MM **Privately Held**
WEB: www.degenkolb.com
SIC: 8711 Consulting engineer

PA: Degenkolb Engineers
375 Beale St Ste 500
San Francisco CA 94105
415 392-6952

(P-18688)
DELTA PROJECT MANAGEMENT INC
400 Concar Dr, San Mateo (94402-2681)
PHONE....................................415 590-3202
Feras Al-Zubaidy, *Chairman*
Scott Kobayashi, *CEO*
Matthew Snyder, *Principal*
Hannah Sherman, *Opers Mgr*
Leta Sledge, *Manager*
EMP: 60 **EST:** 2006
SALES (est): 5.5MM **Privately Held**
WEB: www.delta-pm.com
SIC: 8711 Consulting engineer

(P-18689)
DESIGNIT GLOBAL LLC
Also Called: Designit Prototype
5935 Labath Ave, Rohnert Park (94928-2089)
PHONE....................................707 584-4000
Larry Childs, *Mng Member*
Bob Lopes, *General Mgr*
Thomas McReynolds,
EMP: 22 **EST:** 2004
SALES (est): 2.8MM **Privately Held**
WEB: www.designitprototype.com
SIC: 8711 3441 Mechanical engineering; fabricated structural metal

(P-18690)
DEWBERRY ENGINEERS INC
Also Called: Drake Haglan & Associates
11060 White Rock Rd Ste 2, Rancho Cordova (95670-6046)
PHONE....................................916 363-4210
Craig C Drake, *Branch Mgr*
Rosina Florez, *Admin Asst*
Dave Richard, *Administration*
Jose Silva, *Engineer*
EMP: 62 **Privately Held**
WEB: www.dewberry.com
SIC: 8711 Civil engineering; consulting engineer
HQ: Dewberry Engineers Inc.
200 Broadacres Dr Ste 410
Bloomfield NJ 07003
973 338-9100

(P-18691)
DJA-MGE JV LLC ◆
7415 Greenhaven Dr # 100, Sacramento (95831-5167)
PHONE....................................916 421-1000
H Fred Huang, *Principal*
Fred Huang, *Principal*
EMP: 40 **EST:** 2021
SALES (est): 1.1MM **Privately Held**
SIC: 8711 Engineering services

(P-18692)
DOKKEN ENGINEERING (PA)
110 Blue Ravine Rd # 200, Folsom (95630-4711)
PHONE....................................916 858-0642
Richard Dokken, *CEO*
Richard Liptak, *President*
Bradley Dokken, *CFO*
Cathy Chan, *Admin Sec*
David Densmore, *Administration*
EMP: 70
SQ FT: 12,931
SALES (est): 28MM **Privately Held**
WEB: www.dokkenengineering.com
SIC: 8711 8741 Civil engineering; construction management

(P-18693)
E E S CORP
Also Called: Enova Engineering Services
39 Quail Ct Ste 100, Walnut Creek (94596-5568)
PHONE....................................925 947-6880
Sohrab Esfandiari, *President*
EMP: 37 **EST:** 1995
SALES (est): 255.5K **Privately Held**
SIC: 8711 Consulting engineer

(P-18694)
E L & ASSOCIATES INC
4900 Hopyard Rd Ste 100, Pleasanton (94588-7101)
PHONE....................................925 249-2300
Edward Toy, *President*
EMP: 36 **EST:** 1992
SALES (est): 601.6K **Privately Held**
WEB: www.ela.com
SIC: 8711 Consulting engineer

(P-18695)
E2 CONSULTING ENGINEERS INC
1900 Powell St Ste 250, Emeryville (94608-1807)
PHONE....................................510 652-1164
Matthew Rindiera, *Office Mgr*
Kimberley Meyers, *Vice Pres*
Tammie Frank, *Office Admin*
Irwin Alvarado, *Sr Software Eng*
Ricardo Carmona, *Business Anlyst*
EMP: 39
SALES (corp-wide): 68MM **Privately Held**
WEB: www.e2.com
SIC: 8711 Consulting engineer
PA: E2 Consulting Engineers, Inc.
450 E 17th Ave Unit 200
Denver CO 80203
510 652-1164

(P-18696)
E2 CONSULTING ENGINEERS INC
2100 Powell St Ste 850, Emeryville (94608-1894)
PHONE....................................510 652-1164
Vinod Badani, *Branch Mgr*
Simon Forder, *Principal*
Theresa Tran, *Technician*
Dhavan Soni, *Controller*
Sarah Mader, *Manager*
EMP: 39
SALES (corp-wide): 68MM **Privately Held**
WEB: www.e2.com
SIC: 8711 Consulting engineer
PA: E2 Consulting Engineers, Inc.
450 E 17th Ave Unit 200
Denver CO 80203
510 652-1164

(P-18697)
EARTH TECH
2101 Webster St Ste 1000, Oakland (94612-3060)
PHONE....................................510 419-6000
Diane Creel, *President*
Bob Cochran, *President*
Shaun Martin, *Treasurer*
John Williams, *Vice Pres*
Paul Weeks, *Admin Sec*
EMP: 110 **EST:** 1982
SQ FT: 225,000
SALES (est): 4.5MM **Privately Held**
SIC: 8711 1629 Construction & civil engineering; industrial plant construction

(P-18698)
EARTHQUAKE PROTECTION SYSTEMS
Also Called: E P S
451 Azuar Ave Bldg 759, Vallejo (94592-1148)
PHONE....................................707 644-5993
Victor Zayas, *President*
Julie Robinson, *CFO*
Stanley Low, *Vice Pres*
Anoop Mokha, *Vice Pres*
▲ **EMP:** 80 **EST:** 1985
SQ FT: 310,000
SALES (est): 17.3MM **Privately Held**
WEB: www.earthquakeprotection.com
SIC: 8711 Structural engineering

(P-18699)
EICHLEAY INC (PA)
1390 Willow Pass Rd # 60, Concord (94520-5200)
PHONE....................................925 689-7000
George F Eichleay Jr, *CEO*
Susan Debock, *Project Mgr*
Thomas Staiano, *Electrical Engi*
Ben Geva, *Engineer*
Brian Harkins, *Engineer*
EMP: 150 **EST:** 2007
SQ FT: 17,000
SALES (est): 67.8MM **Privately Held**
WEB: www.eichleay.com
SIC: 8711 Consulting engineer

(P-18700)
EICHLEAY ENGINEERS INC
1390 Willow Pass Rd # 360, Concord (94520-7936)
P.O. Box 238, Oakdale PA (15071-0238)
PHONE....................................925 689-7000
John Borman, *Vice Pres*
Theodore Nelson Jr, *Treasurer*
William Byers, *Principal*
David F Peck, *Principal*
A Ratowsky, *Principal*
EMP: 94 **EST:** 1945
SALES (est): 2.3MM **Privately Held**
WEB: www.eichleay.com
SIC: 8711 Consulting engineer

(P-18701)
EKI ENVIRONMENT & WATER INC (PA)
2001 Junipero Serra Blvd # 300, Daly City (94014-3887)
PHONE....................................650 292-9100
Michelle King, *President*
Edward P Conti, *Vice Pres*
Theodore Erler, *Vice Pres*
Jenn Hyman, *Vice Pres*
Earl James, *Vice Pres*
EMP: 46 **EST:** 1989
SALES (est): 11.4MM **Privately Held**
WEB: www.ekiconsult.com
SIC: 8711 Consulting engineer

(P-18702)
ENGEO INCORPORATED
6399 San Ignacio Ave # 150, San Jose (95119-1244)
PHONE....................................408 574-4900
Uri Eliahu, *President*
Julia Moriarty, *Senior VP*
Ian McCreery, *Project Engr*
EMP: 84
SALES (corp-wide): 38.5MM **Privately Held**
WEB: www.engeo.com
SIC: 8711 Consulting engineer
PA: Engeo Incorporated
2010 Crow Canyon Pl # 250
San Ramon CA 94583
925 866-9000

(P-18703)
ENGIE SERVICES US INC (HQ)
500 12th St Ste 300, Oakland (94607-4087)
PHONE....................................844 678-3772
John Mahoney, *CEO*
Ryan Blair, *President*
John Sullivan, *CFO*
Mark Emerson, *Chief Mktg Ofcr*
Brad Boerger, *Vice Pres*
EMP: 60 **EST:** 2014
SQ FT: 17,250
SALES (est): 265MM
SALES (corp-wide): 22.7B **Privately Held**
WEB: www.engie.com
SIC: 8711 Energy conservation engineering
PA: Engie
1 Place Samuel De Champlain
Courbevoie
144 220-000

(P-18704)
ENOVITY INC (DH)
100 Montgomery St Ste 600, San Francisco (94104-4333)
PHONE....................................415 974-0390
William Dicroce, *President*
Jonathan Soper, *Vice Pres*
Stephen Casey, *Regional Mgr*
Andrea Kover, *Administration*
Mark Johnson, *Project Mgr*
EMP: 35 **EST:** 2002
SQ FT: 9,500
SALES (est): 25.3MM
SALES (corp-wide): 622.8MM **Privately Held**
WEB: www.enovity.com
SIC: 8711 Consulting engineer

PRODUCTS & SERVICES SECTION

8711 - Engineering Services County (P-18725)

HQ: Veolia Energy North America Holdings, Inc.
53 State St Ste 14
Boston MA 02109
617 849-6600

(P-18705)
ENVIRONMENTAL CHEMICAL CORP (PA)
Also Called: Ecc
1240 Bayshore Hwy, Burlingame (94010-1805)
PHONE..................................650 347-1555
Manjiv S Vohra, *President*
Paul Sabharwal, *Chairman*
Rich Gioscia, *Vice Pres*
August Ochabauer, *Vice Pres*
Bud West, *Vice Pres*
▼ **EMP:** 75 **EST:** 1985
SQ FT: 21,000
SALES (est): 506MM **Privately Held**
WEB: www.ecc.net
SIC: 8711 1542 8744 Engineering services; commercial & office building contractors;

(P-18706)
ERIN ENGINEERING AND RES INC (HQ)
2001 N Main St Ste 510, Walnut Creek (94596-7239)
PHONE..................................925 943-7077
Doug True, *CEO*
Colleen Bernard, *Office Mgr*
Clint Pierce, *Engineer*
Sudharsini Ravikumar, *Analyst*
Sobha Stowell, *Analyst*
EMP: 35 **EST:** 1983
SALES (est): 15.8MM
SALES (corp-wide): 251.1MM **Privately Held**
WEB: www.jensenhughes.com
SIC: 8711 Consulting engineer
PA: Jensen Hughes, Inc.
3610 Commerce Dr Ste 817
Baltimore MD 21227
410 737-8677

(P-18707)
ERM-WEST INC (DH)
Also Called: Environmental Resources MGT
1277 Treat Blvd Ste 500, Walnut Creek (94597-7989)
PHONE..................................925 946-0455
Tim Strawn, *President*
Jeffrey Leety, *Senior Partner*
Jim Warner, *Partner*
John C Stipa, *Treasurer*
Jonathan Beevers, *Vice Pres*
EMP: 106 **EST:** 1984
SQ FT: 19,455
SALES: 20.1MM
SALES (corp-wide): 483.7MM **Privately Held**
WEB: www.erm.com
SIC: 8711 8742 Consulting engineer; management consulting services
HQ: Erm-Delaware, Inc.
1105 N Market St Ste 1300
Wilmington DE 19801
302 651-8300

(P-18708)
EXPONENT INC (PA)
149 Commonwealth Dr, Menlo Park (94025-1133)
PHONE..................................650 326-9400
Toll Free:..........................888 -
Catherine Ford Corrigan, *President*
Paul R Johnston, *Ch of Bd*
Richard L Schlenker Jr, *CFO*
Sally B Shepard, *Officer*
Graeme Fowler, *Vice Pres*
EMP: 475 **EST:** 1967
SQ FT: 153,738
SALES: 399.9MM **Publicly Held**
WEB: www.exponent.com
SIC: 8711 8742 8999 Consulting engineer; management consulting services; scientific consulting

(P-18709)
FBA INC (PA)
1675 Sabre St, Hayward (94545-1013)
PHONE..................................510 265-1888
Waldi Naja, *President*
Judy Fong, *Project Engr*
Amir K Kazemi, *Manager*
EMP: 46 **EST:** 2003
SALES (est): 4.1MM **Privately Held**
WEB: www.fbaengineers.com
SIC: 8711 Civil engineering

(P-18710)
FEHR & PEERS (PA)
100 Pringle Ave Ste 600, Walnut Creek (94596-3582)
PHONE..................................925 977-3200
Matthew Henry, *CEO*
Marion Donnelly, *CFO*
Steven Brown, *Vice Pres*
Alan Telford, *Vice Pres*
EMP: 60 **EST:** 1985
SQ FT: 16,000
SALES (est): 50.9MM **Privately Held**
WEB: www.fehrandpeers.com
SIC: 8711 Consulting engineer

(P-18711)
FOTOWTIO RNEWABLE VENTURES INC
44 Montgomery St Ste 2200, San Francisco (94104-4709)
PHONE..................................415 986-8038
Rafael Benjumea, *CEO*
Jose Luis Blasco, *CFO*
David Fernandez, *Vice Pres*
Erika Daniels, *Admin Asst*
Shannon Shutts, *Human Res Mgr*
EMP: 45 **EST:** 2009
SALES (est): 6MM **Privately Held**
SIC: 8711 Energy conservation engineering

(P-18712)
FUGRO WILLIAM LETTIS ASSOC INC (DH)
Also Called: Fugro USA Land
1777 Botelho Dr Ste 262, Walnut Creek (94596-5132)
PHONE..................................925 256-6070
William Lettis, *President*
Jeff Bachhuber, *Vice Pres*
Keith Kelson, *Vice Pres*
Jeffrey R Unruh, *Vice Pres*
EMP: 50 **EST:** 1990
SQ FT: 5,000
SALES (est): 4MM
SALES (corp-wide): 1B **Privately Held**
WEB: www.fugro.com
SIC: 8711 Engineering services
HQ: Fugro (Usa) Holdings Inc.
6100 Hillcroft St Ste 700
Houston TX 77081
713 772-3700

(P-18713)
FUJITSU ELECTRONICS AMER INC (DH)
Also Called: F E A
1250 E Arques Ave, Sunnyvale (94085-5401)
PHONE..................................408 737-5600
Shinichi Machida, *President*
Victor Kan, *Exec VP*
Doug Saylor, *Senior VP*
Geldsetzer Steffen, *Business Mgr*
Adriana Somariba, *Human Resources*
▲ **EMP:** 84 **EST:** 2001
SQ FT: 49,000
SALES (est): 49.8MM **Privately Held**
WEB: www.kagafei.com
SIC: 8711 5065 Engineering services; electronic parts & equipment

(P-18714)
FUNCTION ENGINEERING INC (PA)
163 Everett Ave, Palo Alto (94301-1033)
PHONE..................................650 326-8834
Sung Kim, *CEO*
Roger Chen, *Engineer*
Kevin Doherty, *Engineer*
Bill Jones, *Engineer*
Will Law, *Engineer*
EMP: 35 **EST:** 1996
SQ FT: 4,500
SALES (est): 5.5MM **Privately Held**
WEB: www.function.com
SIC: 8711 Consulting engineer

(P-18715)
GAS TRANSMISSION SYSTEMS INC
575 Lennon Ln Ste 250, Walnut Creek (94598-2472)
PHONE..................................925 478-8530
Scott Angel, *Project Mgr*
Paul Krum, *Project Mgr*
Coleman Stivers, *Project Mgr*
Ali Ganji, *Project Engr*
Ashley Barks, *Engineer*
EMP: 37
SALES (corp-wide): 249.4MM **Privately Held**
WEB: www.gtsinc.us
SIC: 8711 Consulting engineer
HQ: Gas Transmission Systems, Inc.
130 Amber Grove Dr # 134
Chico CA 95973
530 893-6711

(P-18716)
GAS TRANSMISSION SYSTEMS INC (HQ)
Also Called: GTS
130 Amber Grove Dr # 134, Chico (95973-5880)
PHONE..................................530 893-6711
Ben Campbell, *President*
Scott Clapp, *Senior Partner*
Mark Cabral, *COO*
Morris Biggers, *Executive*
David Alleshouse, *District Mgr*
EMP: 57 **EST:** 2001
SQ FT: 4,500
SALES (est): 5.3MM
SALES (corp-wide): 249.4MM **Privately Held**
WEB: www.gtsinc.us
SIC: 8711 Professional engineer
PA: The Kleinfelder Group Inc
550 W C St Ste 1200
San Diego CA 92101
619 831-4600

(P-18717)
GATAN INC (HQ)
5794 W Las Positas Blvd, Pleasanton (94588-4083)
PHONE..................................925 463-0200
Benjamin Wood, *President*
Ed Morrissey, *Treasurer*
Jack Buhsmer, *Vice Pres*
David Liner, *Admin Sec*
Ray Twesten, *Manager*
EMP: 50 **EST:** 1964
SQ FT: 30,000
SALES (est): 55.2MM
SALES (corp-wide): 4.5B **Publicly Held**
WEB: www.gatan.com
SIC: 8711 3826 Designing: ship, boat, machine & product; analytical optical instruments
PA: Ametek, Inc.
1100 Cassatt Rd
Berwyn PA 19312
610 647-2121

(P-18718)
GAYNER ENGINEERS
1133 Post St, San Francisco (94109-5504)
PHONE..................................415 474-9500
Nick Mironov, *President*
Shuen Lo, *Treasurer*
Grant Wong, *Vice Pres*
John Yee, *Admin Sec*
Raymond Chow, *Electrical Engi*
EMP: 44 **EST:** 1941
SQ FT: 18,000
SALES (est): 4.3MM **Privately Held**
WEB: www.gaynerengineers.com
SIC: 8711 Consulting engineer

(P-18719)
GENER8 LLC (PA)
500 Mercury Dr, Sunnyvale (94085-4018)
PHONE..................................650 940-9898
Jerry Jurkiewicz, *CEO*
Osborne Zoe, *CFO*
Malcolm Minty, *Vice Pres*
William Bischel, *General Mgr*
James Quigley, *Software Engr*
▲ **EMP:** 102 **EST:** 2002
SQ FT: 16,000
SALES (est): 72.2MM **Privately Held**
WEB: www.gener8.net
SIC: 8711 3429 Engineering services; locks or lock sets

(P-18720)
GEOLOGIC ASSOCIATES INC
143 Spring Hill Dr Ste E, Grass Valley (95945-5969)
PHONE..................................530 272-2448
Scott Purdy, *Branch Mgr*
Sarah Battelle, *Vice Pres*
Tony Morgan, *Vice Pres*
Ralph Murphy, *Vice Pres*
Elaine Black, *General Mgr*
EMP: 54 **Privately Held**
WEB: www.geo-logic.com
SIC: 8711 Consulting engineer
PA: Geologic Associates, Inc.
2777 E Guasti Rd Ste 1
Ontario CA 91761

(P-18721)
GHD INC
1735 N 1st St Ste 301, San Jose (95112-4511)
PHONE..................................408 451-9615
EMP: 37
SALES (corp-wide): 877.5MM **Privately Held**
SIC: 8711 Engineering Services
HQ: Ghd Inc.
4747 N 22nd St Ste 200
Phoenix AZ 85016
602 216-7200

(P-18722)
GILBANE FEDERAL (DH)
1655 Grant St Ste 1200, Concord (94520-2790)
PHONE..................................925 946-3100
Sarabjit Singh, *CEO*
Jon Verlinde, *Senior VP*
▲ **EMP:** 110 **EST:** 1994
SALES (est): 9.8MM
SALES (corp-wide): 5.6B **Privately Held**
WEB: www.gilbaneco.com
SIC: 8711 8748 Building construction consultant; environmental consultant
HQ: Gilbane Building Company
7 Jackson Walkway Ste 2
Providence RI 02903
401 456-5800

(P-18723)
GLUMAC INTERNATIONAL (PA)
150 California St Fl 3, San Francisco (94111-4567)
PHONE..................................415 398-7667
EMP: 36
SALES (est): 3.7MM **Privately Held**
SIC: 8711 Engineering Services

(P-18724)
GORDON-PRILL-DRAPES INC
Also Called: Gordon-Pril Drapes
310 E Caribbean Dr, Sunnyvale (94089-1148)
PHONE..................................650 335-1990
Patrick Dolci, *President*
EMP: 48
SALES (corp-wide): 10.2MM **Privately Held**
WEB: www.gordonprill.com
SIC: 8711 Mechanical engineering; electrical or electronic engineering
PA: Gordon-Prill-Drapes, Inc
2291 W Broadway St Ste 4
Missoula MT 59808
406 721-5936

(P-18725)
H M H ENGINEERS
1570 Oakland Rd, San Jose (95131-2430)
P.O. Box 611510 (95151-1510)
PHONE..................................408 487-2200
William J Wagner, *President*
Tom Armstrong, *Vice Pres*
Jake Minnick, *Project Mgr*
Brendin Christolear, *Engineer*
Janet MO, *Marketing Staff*
EMP: 54 **EST:** 1976

(PA)=Parent Co (HQ)=Headquarters (DH)=Div Headquarters
✪ = New Business established in last 2 years

8711 - Engineering Services County (P-18726)

SALES (est): 8.4MM **Privately Held**
WEB: www.hmhca.com
SIC: **8711** 8713 Consulting engineer; surveying services

(P-18726)
HARRIS & ASSOCIATES INC (PA)
Also Called: Harris & Associates Cnstr MGT
1401 Willow Paca Rd Ste 50, Concord (94520)
PHONE..................................925 827-4900
Lisa Larrabee, *CEO*
Carl Harris, *Ch of Bd*
Guy Erickson, *President*
Sherill Conley, *CEO*
Ehab Gerges, *Officer*
▲ EMP: 104 EST: 1974
SQ FT: 23,000
SALES (est): 57.2MM **Privately Held**
WEB: www.weareharris.com
SIC: **8711** 8712 Construction & civil engineering; civil engineering; sanitary engineers; architectural engineering

(P-18727)
HASSELGREN ENGINEERING INC
1221 4th St, Berkeley (94710-1302)
PHONE..................................510 524-2485
Paul Hasselgren, *President*
EMP: 23 EST: 1977
SQ FT: 2,500
SALES (est): 1.5MM **Privately Held**
WEB: www.hasselgren.com
SIC: **8711** 3625 3714 Engineering services; numerical controls; motor vehicle engines & parts

(P-18728)
HDR ENGINEERING INC
Also Called: Hydro Power Service
2379 Gateway Oaks Dr # 200, Sacramento (95833-4238)
PHONE..................................916 564-4214
EMP: 74
SALES (corp-wide): 2.3B **Privately Held**
SIC: **8711** Engineering Services
HQ: Hdr Engineering, Inc.
8404 Indian Hills Dr
Omaha NE 68106
402 399-1000

(P-18729)
HENKEL US OPERATIONS CORP
Also Called: Aerospace Material Division
2850 Willow Pass Rd, Bay Point (94565-3237)
P.O. Box 312 (94565-0031)
PHONE..................................925 458-8086
Sylvie Nicol, *Exec VP*
Rosen Angelov, *Technology*
Tina Miao, *Engineer*
Peter Naye, *Engineer*
Sindhuja Ramnath, *Analyst*
EMP: 170
SQ FT: 6,325
SALES (corp-wide): 22.7B **Privately Held**
WEB: www.henkel.com
SIC: **8711** Engineering services
HQ: Henkel Us Operations Corporation
1 Henkel Way
Rocky Hill CT 06067
860 571-5100

(P-18730)
HENWOOD ENERGY SERVICES INC (DH)
2379 Gateway Oaks Dr # 110, Sacramento (95833-4239)
PHONE..................................916 955-6031
Mark Henwood, *President*
David Branchcomb, *Vice Pres*
EMP: 118 EST: 1985
SALES (est): 14.6MM **Privately Held**
SIC: **8711** Consulting engineer
HQ: Global Energy Decisions Llc
1495 Canyon Blvd Ste 100
Boulder CO 80302
720 221-5200

(P-18731)
HNTB CORPORATION
1735 Tech Dr Ste 650, San Jose (95110)
PHONE..................................408 451-7300
Steve Whitaker, *Branch Mgr*
Tom Donodo, *Engineer*
Stella Joseph, *Engineer*
Steven Grgas, *Financial Analy*
EMP: 51
SALES (corp-wide): 1.2B **Privately Held**
WEB: www.hntb.com
SIC: **8711** Consulting engineer
HQ: Hntb Corporation
715 Kirk Dr
Kansas City MO 64105
816 472-1201

(P-18732)
HNTB CORPORATION
1111 Broadway Ste 900, Oakland (94607-4170)
PHONE..................................510 208-4599
Steve Whitaker, *Manager*
Dan Parkerking, *Assoc VP*
Richard Coffin, *Vice Pres*
Rod Deleon, *Technician*
Oscar Ruiz, *Technical Staff*
EMP: 51
SALES (corp-wide): 1.2B **Privately Held**
WEB: www.hntb.com
SIC: **8711** Consulting engineer
HQ: Hntb Corporation
715 Kirk Dr
Kansas City MO 64105
816 472-1201

(P-18733)
HOLDREGE KULL CNSLTING ENGNERS
792 Searls Ave, Nevada City (95959-3056)
PHONE..................................530 478-1305
Sandy Hakala, *President*
Cheryl Fisk, *Administration*
Kelley Kull, *Administration*
Jason Muir, *Engineer*
EMP: 72 EST: 1993
SQ FT: 10,000
SALES (est): 10.6MM
SALES (corp-wide): 659.3MM **Publicly Held**
WEB: www.nv5.com
SIC: **8711** 8999 8748 1711 Civil engineering; geological consultant; geophysical consultant; environmental consultant; septic system construction
PA: Nv5 Global, Inc.
200 S Park Rd Ste 350
Hollywood FL 33021
954 495-2112

(P-18734)
HYDROSCIENCE ENGINEERS INC (PA)
10569 Old Placerville Rd, Sacramento (95827-2504)
PHONE..................................916 364-1490
George Harris, *President*
Hildegard Harris, *Treasurer*
Jack Grossman, *Vice Pres*
Sim Blake, *Principal*
Mary Hoang, *Principal*
EMP: 35 EST: 1997
SQ FT: 6,400
SALES (est): 11.6MM **Privately Held**
WEB: www.hydroscience.com
SIC: **8711** Consulting engineer

(P-18735)
ICHOR HOLDINGS LTD (PA)
3185 Laurelview Ct, Fremont (94538-6535)
PHONE..................................510 897-5200
Jeffrey S Andreson, *CEO*
Thomas M Rohrs, *Ch of Bd*
Kevin Canty, *COO*
Larry J Sparks, *CFO*
Diana Finucane, *Officer*
EMP: 39 EST: 1999
SQ FT: 62,800
SALES (est): 124.8MM **Publicly Held**
WEB: www.ichorsystems.com
SIC: **8711** 3559 3674 Engineering services; semiconductor manufacturing machinery; wafers (semiconductor devices)

(P-18736)
INDUSTRIAL AUTOMTN GROUP LLC
4400 Sisk Rd, Modesto (95356-8729)
PHONE..................................209 579-7527
Brad Stegmann, *President*
Gaganpreet Pandher, *Engineer*
Nichole Kazynski, *Sales Engr*
Teng Lee, *Manager*
EMP: 75 EST: 2012
SALES (est): 15.3MM **Privately Held**
WEB: www.automationgroup.com
SIC: **8711** Mechanical engineering

(P-18737)
INFINITE TECHNOLOGIES INC (PA)
1264 Hawks Flight Ct # 210, El Dorado Hills (95762-9348)
PHONE..................................916 987-3261
John A Runnberg, *CEO*
Michael P Whittle, *President*
Jenet Taylor, *Administration*
Brian Duby, *Prgrmr*
Nicolas Bailey, *Programmer Anys*
EMP: 56 EST: 1994
SQ FT: 3,450
SALES (est): 10.2MM **Privately Held**
WEB: www.infintech.com
SIC: **8711** 7371 7379 Engineering services; custom computer programming services; computer related maintenance services

(P-18738)
INNOVATE CONCRETE INC
Also Called: Innovate Engineering
2671 Estella Dr, Santa Clara (95051-6515)
PHONE..................................408 497-2000
Ramon Ramirez, *Principal*
EMP: 35 EST: 2007
SALES (est): 2.7MM **Privately Held**
WEB: www.agripolymers.com
SIC: **8711** Engineering services

(P-18739)
INTEGRAL GROUP INC
427 13th St, Oakland (94612-2601)
PHONE..................................510 663-2070
William Overturf III, *CEO*
Rodney Roberts, *CFO*
Doug Kerr, *Officer*
Megan White, *Officer*
Rachel Lieberman, *Principal*
EMP: 114 EST: 2001
SALES (est): 13.5MM **Privately Held**
WEB: www.integralgroup.com
SIC: **8711** Consulting engineer

(P-18740)
INTEGRATION BANKS GROUP LLC
600 E Main St Ste 101, Vacaville (95688-3956)
PHONE..................................707 451-1100
Greg Banks, *President*
Danni Bynum, *Administration*
Angelo Puglisi, *Engineer*
Bessida Taonda, *Engineer*
Jessica Thomas, *Engineer*
EMP: 36 EST: 2003
SALES (est): 6.7MM
SALES (corp-wide): 7.2MM **Privately Held**
WEB: www.banksintegration.com
SIC: **8711** Consulting engineer
HQ: Superior Controls Incorporated
135 Folly Mill Rd
Seabrook NH 03874

(P-18741)
J D PASQUETTI ENGINEERING
3032 Thunder Valley Ct # 200, Lincoln (95648-9395)
PHONE..................................916 543-9401
Jason Pasquetti, *President*
EMP: 70 EST: 2006
SALES (est): 12.2MM **Privately Held**
WEB: www.jdpasquetti.com
SIC: **8711** Engineering services

(P-18742)
JACOBS ENGINEERING GROUP INC
2300 Clayton Rd, Concord (94520-2100)
PHONE..................................925 356-3900
EMP: 92
SALES (corp-wide): 12.7B **Publicly Held**
SIC: **8711** Engineering Services
PA: Jacobs Engineering Group Inc.
155 N Lake Ave
Pasadena CA 75201
626 578-3500

(P-18743)
JACOBS ENGINEERING GROUP INC
1737 N 1st St Ste 300, San Jose (95112-4585)
PHONE..................................408 436-4936
EMP: 88
SALES (corp-wide): 12.7B **Publicly Held**
SIC: **8711** Engineering Services, Nsk
PA: Jacobs Engineering Group Inc.
1999 Bryan St Ste 1200
Dallas TX 75201
214 583-8500

(P-18744)
JTS ENGINEERING CONS INC
1808 J St, Sacramento (95811-3010)
PHONE..................................916 441-6708
Javed Siddiqui, *General Ptnr*
Khalid Siddiqui, *General Ptnr*
EMP: 48 EST: 1977
SALES (est): 2.6MM **Privately Held**
WEB: www.jtsengineering.com
SIC: **8711** Consulting engineer

(P-18745)
KAISER GROUP HOLDINGS INC
Also Called: Earthtech
2101 Webster St Ste 1000, Oakland (94612-3060)
PHONE..................................510 419-6000
EMP: 90
SALES (corp-wide): 527.4MM **Publicly Held**
SIC: **8711** Engineering Consultants
PA: Kaiser Group Holdings, Inc.
9300 Lee Hwy
Fairfax VA 35212
703 934-3000

(P-18746)
KARM INC
5033 Doolan Rd, Livermore (94551-9605)
PHONE..................................650 741-5276
Ravi Randhawa, *President*
EMP: 50 EST: 2010
SALES (est): 3MM **Privately Held**
SIC: **8711** Engineering services

(P-18747)
KENNEDY/JENKS CONSULTANTS INC (PA)
Also Called: Kennedy Jenks
303 2nd St Ste 300s, San Francisco (94107-3632)
PHONE..................................415 243-2150
Gary Carlton, *Chairman*
Keith A London, *President*
Patrick J Courtney, *CFO*
Lynn Takaichi, *Chairman*
George Caraker, *Officer*
EMP: 100 EST: 1919
SQ FT: 45,000
SALES (est): 82.4MM **Privately Held**
WEB: www.kennedyjenks.com
SIC: **8711** Consulting engineer

(P-18748)
KLEINFELDER INC
Also Called: Ganda
1 Saunders Ave, San Anselmo (94960-1719)
PHONE..................................415 458-5803
Louis Armstrong, *Branch Mgr*
EMP: 175
SALES (corp-wide): 249.4MM **Privately Held**
WEB: www.kleinfelder.com
SIC: **8711** Consulting engineer
HQ: Kleinfelder, Inc.
770 First Ave Ste 400
San Diego CA 92101
619 831-4600

(P-18749)
KODIAK ROBOTICS INC
1049 Terra Bella Ave, Mountain View (94043-1829)
PHONE..................................781 626-2729
Paz Eshel, *Principal*
EMP: 80 EST: 2018

▲ = Import ▼ =Export
◆ =Import/Export

PRODUCTS & SERVICES SECTION

8711 - Engineering Services County (P-18772)

SALES (est): 7.8MM **Privately Held**
WEB: www.kodiak.ai
SIC: 8711 Engineering services

(P-18750)
KRATOS UNMNNED ARIAL SYSTEMS I (HQ)
5381 Raley Blvd, Sacramento (95838-1701)
PHONE.................................916 431-7977
Eric M Demarco, *CEO*
Amy Fournier, *President*
Michel M Fournier, *Vice Pres*
Jeff Herro, *Vice Pres*
Peggy McQuillen, *Vice Pres*
▲ EMP: 343 EST: 1963
SQ FT: 60,000
SALES (est): 80.6MM **Publicly Held**
WEB: www.kratosdefense.com
SIC: 8711 3761 Engineering services; guided missiles & space vehicles

(P-18751)
LACO ASSOCIATES (PA)
21 W 4th St, Eureka (95501-0216)
P.O. Box 1023 (95502-1023)
PHONE.................................707 443-5054
Leonard Osborne, *President*
Susanp Clower, *CFO*
Frank Bickner, *Bd of Directors*
John Bergenske, *Vice Pres*
David Lindberg, *Vice Pres*
EMP: 42 EST: 1974
SQ FT: 6,000
SALES (est): 15.4MM **Privately Held**
WEB: www.lacoassociates.us
SIC: 8711 8999 0711 Structural engineering; geological consultant; soil testing services

(P-18752)
LEA & BRAZE ENGINEERING INC (PA)
2495 Industrial Pkwy W, Hayward (94545-5007)
PHONE.................................510 887-4086
Gregory F Braze, *President*
Jeffrey C Lea, *CEO*
Brittney Lee, *Office Mgr*
Will Matthews, *Technician*
Randall West, *Design Engr*
EMP: 83 EST: 1984
SQ FT: 6,000
SALES (est): 15.8MM **Privately Held**
WEB: www.leabraze.com
SIC: 8711 8713 Civil engineering; surveying services

(P-18753)
LELAND SAYLOR & ASSOCIATES INC
Also Called: Leland Saylor Associates
1777 Oakland Blvd Ste 103, Walnut Creek (94596-4096)
PHONE.................................415 291-3200
Leland Saylor, *Chairman*
Brad Saylor, *Managing Dir*
Daniel Tilp, *Analyst*
Rod Raz, *Controller*
Steve Santaguida, *Director*
EMP: 37 EST: 1997
SALES (est): 4.9MM **Privately Held**
WEB: www.lelandsaylor.com
SIC: 8711 Building construction consultant

(P-18754)
LOPEZGARCIA GROUP INC (DH)
300 California St, San Francisco (94104-1407)
PHONE.................................415 796-8100
Rudy M Garcia, *President*
Roger Behgam, *Shareholder*
Juan Cierra, *Shareholder*
Richard Garson, *Shareholder*
Doug Guinn, *Shareholder*
▲ EMP: 148 EST: 1988
SQ FT: 40,345
SALES (est): 45.8MM
SALES (corp-wide): 13.2B **Publicly Held**
WEB: www.aecom.com
SIC: 8711 8713 8741 8748 Consulting engineer; surveying services; management services; environmental consultant
HQ: Aecom Global Ii, Llc
300 S Grand Ave Ste 900
Los Angeles CA 90071
213 593-8100

(P-18755)
LUHDORFF SCLMNINI CNSLTING ENG
500 1st St, Woodland (95695-4026)
PHONE.................................530 661-0109
Joseph C Scalmanini, *Partner*
William Gustavson, *Partner*
Vicki Kretsinger, *Partner*
Till Angermann, *Technical Staff*
Gregory Garrison, *Engineer*
EMP: 56 EST: 1979
SALES (est): 8.8MM **Privately Held**
WEB: www.lsce.com
SIC: 8711 Consulting engineer

(P-18756)
LUND CONSTRUCTION CO
5302 Roseville Rd, North Highlands (95660-5000)
PHONE.................................916 344-5800
Jerry A Lund, *President*
Alta M Lund, *Treasurer*
Jeff Lund, *Vice Pres*
Kevin Lund, *Vice Pres*
Chris Holihan, *Project Engr*
EMP: 155 EST: 1959
SQ FT: 7,500
SALES (est): 23.8MM **Privately Held**
WEB: www.lundconst.com
SIC: 8711 1794 1623 4212 Construction & civil engineering; excavation & grading, building construction; underground utilities contractor; hazardous waste transport

(P-18757)
M NEILS ENGINEERING INC
100 Howe Ave Ste 235n, Sacramento (95825-8217)
PHONE.................................916 923-4400
Michael Neils, *President*
Nancy Neils, *CFO*
Jesse Bastian, *Engineer*
Dakin Chan, *Engineer*
Danielle N Neils, *Manager*
EMP: 55 EST: 1990
SQ FT: 2,000
SALES (est): 8.9MM **Privately Held**
WEB: www.mneilsengineering.com
SIC: 8711 Consulting engineer

(P-18758)
MACAULAY BROWN INC
Also Called: Macb
2933 Bunker Hill Ln # 220, Santa Clara (95054-1124)
PHONE.................................937 426-3421
Vicki Summers, *Exec Dir*
EMP: 1500 EST: 2011
SALES (est): 10.7MM **Privately Held**
SIC: 8711 Consulting engineer

(P-18759)
MACDONALD MOTT LLC (HQ)
12647 Alcosta Blvd, San Ramon (94583-4439)
PHONE.................................925 469-8010
Nicholas Denichilo, *CEO*
EMP: 45 EST: 1972
SQ FT: 9,000
SALES (est): 95.2MM
SALES (corp-wide): 494.8MM **Privately Held**
SIC: 8711 Civil engineering
PA: Macdonald Mott Group Inc
111 Wood Ave S Ste 5
Iselin NJ 08830
973 379-3400

(P-18760)
MACKAY SMPS CVIL ENGINEERS INC (PA)
5142 Franklin Dr Ste C, Pleasanton (94588-3368)
PHONE.................................925 416-1790
James C Ray, *President*
Bob Chan, *Vice Pres*
Steve Smith, *Planning Mgr*
John F Kuzia, *Admin Sec*
Chris Ragan, *Engineer*
EMP: 62 EST: 1953
SALES (est): 10.9MM **Privately Held**
WEB: www.msce.com
SIC: 8711 Civil engineering

(P-18761)
MANUFCTRING ENGRG EXCLLNCE INC
Also Called: M E 2
2597 Flagstone Dr, San Jose (95132-2611)
PHONE.................................408 382-1900
Steve Curtis, *President*
Paul Greenfield, *CFO*
Anita G Greenfield, *Manager*
EMP: 40 EST: 1996
SQ FT: 40,000
SALES (est): 4.9MM **Privately Held**
WEB: www.me2inc.com
SIC: 8711 Electrical or electronic engineering

(P-18762)
MARQUES GEN ENGRG INC A CAL CO
7225 26th St, Rio Linda (95673-1814)
PHONE.................................916 923-3434
Jeremy Jaeger, *CEO*
Laura Coletti, *General Mgr*
Jack Gridley, *Project Mgr*
Warren Rhodes, *Project Mgr*
Garrett Davis, *Project Engr*
EMP: 350 EST: 1999
SQ FT: 2,000
SALES (est): 200MM **Privately Held**
WEB: www.marquespipeline.com
SIC: 8711 Engineering services

(P-18763)
MAZZETTI INC (PA)
220 Montgomery St Ste 650, San Francisco (94104-3491)
PHONE.................................615 579-4375
Walt Vernon, *CEO*
Kurt Messerli, *COO*
Darryl Wandry, *CFO*
Jeff Looney, *Principal*
Takeisha Saunders, *Principal*
EMP: 50 EST: 1962
SQ FT: 17,700
SALES (est): 52.6MM **Privately Held**
WEB: www.mazzetti.com
SIC: 8711 Electrical or electronic engineering

(P-18764)
MBK ENGINEERS
455 University Ave # 100, Sacramento (95825-6513)
PHONE.................................916 456-4400
Lee Bergfeld, *President*
Walter Bourez, *Shareholder*
Darren Cordova, *Shareholder*
Nathan Hershey, *Shareholder*
Gary Kienlen, *Shareholder*
EMP: 47 EST: 1961
SALES (est): 10.1MM **Privately Held**
WEB: www.mbkengineers.com
SIC: 8711 8713 Civil engineering; surveying services

(P-18765)
MCMILLEN JACOBS ASSOCIATES INC (PA)
49 Stevenson St Ste 1200, San Francisco (94105-2974)
PHONE.................................415 434-1822
Daniel Adams, *President*
Mara McMillen, *COO*
Victor Romero, *Exec VP*
Derek Nelson, *Vice Pres*
Frank Pita, *Vice Pres*
EMP: 86 EST: 2014
SALES (est): 126.8MM **Privately Held**
WEB: www.mcmjac.com
SIC: 8711 1629 4911 Construction & civil engineering; civil engineering; structural engineering; dams, waterways, docks & other marine construction; waterway construction; distribution, electric power

(P-18766)
MEYERS+ENGINEERS
98 Battery St Ste 500, San Francisco (94111-5529)
PHONE.................................415 282-4380
Randy Meyers, *President*
Alicia Herrera, *Design Engr*
Richard Somers, *Design Engr*
Simon Gardiner, *Engineer*
Stephen CIA, *Senior Engr*
EMP: 45 EST: 2015
SALES (est): 5.3MM **Privately Held**
WEB: www.meyersplus.com
SIC: 8711 Engineering services

(P-18767)
MEYERS+ENGINEERS
98 Battery St Ste 502, San Francisco (94111-5529)
PHONE.................................415 713-0005
Randy Meyers, *Principal*
EMP: 53 EST: 2015
SALES (est): 2.1MM **Privately Held**
WEB: www.meyersplus.com
SIC: 8711 Engineering services

(P-18768)
MICHAEL BAKER INTL INC
1 Kaiser Plz Ste 1150, Oakland (94612-3601)
PHONE.................................510 879-0950
Mike Conrad, *Branch Mgr*
EMP: 45
SALES (corp-wide): 592.9MM **Privately Held**
WEB: www.mbakerintl.com
SIC: 8711 Civil engineering
HQ: Baker Michael International Inc
500 Grant St Ste 5400
Pittsburgh PA 15219
412 269-6300

(P-18769)
MICHAEL BAKER INTL INC
Also Called: American Engineering Co
500 Ygnacio Valley Rd # 300, Walnut Creek (94596-3840)
PHONE.................................925 949-2452
Garrit Gritz, *Manager*
EMP: 56
SALES (corp-wide): 592.9MM **Privately Held**
WEB: www.mbakerintl.com
SIC: 8711 Consulting engineer
HQ: Baker Michael International Inc
5 Hutton Cntre Dr Ste 500
Santa Ana CA 92707
949 472-3505

(P-18770)
MILLENNIUM ENGRG INTGRTION LLC
350 N Akron Rd, Moffett Field (94035)
P.O. Box 1 (94035-0001)
PHONE.................................703 413-7750
Rick Maurer, *Branch Mgr*
Mike Briggs, *Vice Pres*
EMP: 174
SALES (corp-wide): 103.3MM **Privately Held**
WEB: www.meicompany.com
SIC: 8711 Engineering services
PA: Millennium Engineering And Integration Llc
1400 Crystal Dr Ste 800
Arlington VA 22202
703 413-7750

(P-18771)
MILLERICK ENGINEERING INC
735 E Main St, Turlock (95380-4521)
P.O. Box 3338 (95381-3338)
PHONE.................................209 664-9111
Chris Millerick, *President*
Ciara Millerick, *Shareholder*
Jogre Suasin, *Engineer*
Greg Sessions, *Controller*
Jogre B Suasin, *Director*
EMP: 70 EST: 1997
SALES (est): 7.1MM **Privately Held**
WEB: www.millerickeng.com
SIC: 8711 Industrial engineers

(P-18772)
MIYAMOTO INTERNATIONAL INC (PA)
1450 Halyard Dr Ste 1, West Sacramento (95691-5038)
PHONE.................................916 373-1995
Hideki Kit Miyamoto, *President*
Lon Determan, *Bd of Directors*
Diana Erwin, *Comms Dir*

(PA)=Parent Co (HQ)=Headquarters (DH)=Div Headquarters
✪ = New Business established in last 2 years

8711 - Engineering Services County (P-18773)

Andrew Kim, *Project Engr*
Jonathan Lo, *Project Engr*
EMP: 63 **EST:** 1946
SQ FT: 6,000
SALES (est): 11.2MM **Privately Held**
WEB: www.miyamotointernational.com
SIC: 8711 Consulting engineer; structural engineering

(P-18773)
MORPHICS TECHNOLOGY INC
1730 N 1st St Ms-13305, San Jose (95112-4642)
PHONE................................408 369-7227
Colin Macnab, *President*
Dale Lindly, *CFO*
Barry L Cox, *Chairman*
Arup Gupta, *Vice Pres*
Ted Williams, *Vice Pres*
EMP: 80 **EST:** 1998
SALES (est): 1.8MM **Privately Held**
SIC: 8711 3674 Designing: ship, boat, machine & product; semiconductors & related devices

(P-18774)
MORTON & PITALO INC (PA)
600 Coolidge Dr Ste 140, Folsom (95630-4211)
PHONE................................916 984-7621
Eddie Kho, *President*
Chris Buckley, *COO*
Vincent Doyle, *CFO*
Gregory J Bardini, *Vice Pres*
Christopher J Gorges, *Vice Pres*
EMP: 64 **EST:** 1977
SALES (est): 12.1MM **Privately Held**
WEB: www.mpengr.com
SIC: 8711 Civil engineering

(P-18775)
MVE INC (PA)
Also Called: M V E
1117 L St, Modesto (95354-0833)
PHONE................................209 526-4214
Kirk Delamare, *CEO*
Catherine De La Mare, *Vice Pres*
Sean Tobin, *Vice Pres*
EMP: 52 **EST:** 1969
SQ FT: 10,000
SALES (est): 10.6MM **Privately Held**
WEB: www.mve.net
SIC: 8711 8713 Civil engineering; surveying services

(P-18776)
NATIONAL SECURITY TECH LLC
Also Called: Bechtel
161 S Vasco Rd Ste A, Livermore (94551-5131)
PHONE................................925 960-2500
Gary Still, *Branch Mgr*
EMP: 545
SALES (corp-wide): 414MM **Privately Held**
WEB: www.nnss.gov
SIC: 8711 1629 Civil engineering; industrial plant construction
PA: National Security Technologies, Llc
2621 Losee Rd
North Las Vegas NV 89030
702 295-1000

(P-18777)
NATIONWIDE ENVMTL CNSTR SVCS I
Also Called: Nationwide Sun
4470 Yankee Hill Rd # 200, Rocklin (95677-1632)
PHONE................................916 708-7445
Frank Dasmacci, *President*
EMP: 41 **EST:** 2014
SALES (est): 17.1MM **Privately Held**
WEB: www.environation.us
SIC: 8711 1731 Electrical or electronic engineering; electrical work

(P-18778)
NEW ENGLAND SHTMTL WORKS INC
2731 S Cherry Ave, Fresno (93706-5423)
P.O. Box 4287 (93744-4287)
PHONE................................559 268-7375
Michael Hensley, *CEO*
EMP: 150 **EST:** 1920
SQ FT: 43,000
SALES (est): 21MM **Privately Held**
WEB: www.nesmw.com
SIC: 8711 8741 1542 Engineering services; construction management; commercial & office building, new construction

(P-18779)
NMI INDUSTRIAL HOLDINGS INC
8503 Weyand Ave, Sacramento (95828-2610)
PHONE................................916 635-7030
Majid Rahimian, *President*
Steve Mathias, *COO*
Javad Rahimian, *Treasurer*
Alex Elmendorf, *Project Mgr*
Todd Krevitsky, *Technology*
EMP: 90 **EST:** 2010
SALES (est): 16.6MM **Privately Held**
WEB: www.nmiindustrial.com
SIC: 8711 1799 Construction & civil engineering; building site preparation

(P-18780)
NOVARIANT INC (PA)
Also Called: Autofarm
46610 Landing Pkwy, Fremont (94538-6420)
PHONE................................510 933-4800
Dave Vaughn, *President*
Mike Manning, *CFO*
Dennis Connor, *Vice Pres*
Husam Kal, *Vice Pres*
Gregory Park, *Info Tech Dir*
EMP: 60 **EST:** 1994
SQ FT: 20,000
SALES (est): 21.7MM **Privately Held**
WEB: www.agjunction.com
SIC: 8711 Engineering services

(P-18781)
NV5 INC (DH)
Also Called: Nolte Associates
2525 Natomas Park Dr # 300, Sacramento (95833-2933)
PHONE................................916 641-9100
Dickerson Wright, *CEO*
Brad Riel, *Vice Pres*
Melannie Turner, *Human Res Mgr*
Patrick Dunn, *Director*
Robert Van Uffelen, *Director*
EMP: 80 **EST:** 1949
SQ FT: 27,000
SALES (est): 48.1MM
SALES (corp-wide): 659.3MM **Publicly Held**
WEB: www.nv5.com
SIC: 8711 Civil engineering

(P-18782)
OPERATING ENGINEERS LOCA
325 Digital Dr, Morgan Hill (95037-2878)
PHONE................................408 782-9803
Lisa Kunkel, *Branch Mgr*
EMP: 35
SALES (corp-wide): 411.3K **Privately Held**
WEB: www.oe3.org
SIC: 8711 Engineering services
PA: Operating Engineers Local Union No. 3 Scholarship Foundation
1620 S Loop Rd
Alameda CA 94502
510 748-7400

(P-18783)
OPTOFIDELITY INC
20863 Stevns Crk Blvd, Cupertino (95014-2113)
PHONE................................669 241-8383
Lasse Lepisto, *CEO*
Hans Kuosmanen, *Vice Pres*
EMP: 32 **EST:** 2017
SALES (est): 4.5MM **Privately Held**
WEB: www.optofidelity.com
SIC: 8711 3827 Engineering services; optical instruments & lenses

(P-18784)
OSI ENGINEERING INC
901 Campisi Way Ste 160, Campbell (95008-2365)
PHONE................................408 550-2800
Javier Diaz, *President*
Odi Banuelos, *CEO*
EMP: 120 **EST:** 2010

SALES (est): 5MM **Privately Held**
WEB: www.osiengineering.com
SIC: 8711 Consulting engineer

(P-18785)
PACIFIC CIVIL & STRL CONS LLC
7415 Greenhaven Dr # 100, Sacramento (95831-5167)
PHONE................................916 421-1000
Fred Huang, *Partner*
EMP: 50 **EST:** 2010
SALES (est): 5MM **Privately Held**
SIC: 8711 Structural engineering

(P-18786)
PACIFIC COAST GEN ENGRG INC
12 Industry Rd, Pittsburg (94565-2700)
PHONE................................925 252-0214
Henry Sam Baugh III, *President*
Eric Morgan Kavert, *Vice Pres*
EMP: 35 **EST:** 2007
SQ FT: 2,000
SALES (est): 5.5MM **Privately Held**
WEB: www.pcge.biz
SIC: 8711 Civil engineering

(P-18787)
PACIFIC ENVIRONMENTAL GROUP
1921 Ringwood Ave, San Jose (95131-1721)
PHONE................................408 453-7500
Barbara Heineman, *CFO*
Debra Moser, *President*
Erin Garner, *Vice Pres*
Lance Geselbracht, *Vice Pres*
Bob Wenzlau, *Vice Pres*
EMP: 90 **EST:** 1987
SQ FT: 20,000
SALES (est): 3.5MM **Privately Held**
SIC: 8711 Engineering services

(P-18788)
PCH INTERNATIONAL USA INC
Also Called: Pch Lime Lab
135 Mississippi St, San Francisco (94107-2536)
PHONE................................415 643-5463
William Casey, *CEO*
Zixiao Pan, *Officer*
Chaz Flexman, *Vice Pres*
Sean Peters, *Vice Pres*
Matt Crichton, *Business Dir*
EMP: 44 **EST:** 2002
SALES (est): 8.1MM **Privately Held**
WEB: www.pchintl.com
SIC: 8711 Engineering services

(P-18789)
PCH LABS INC
Also Called: Pch Innovation Hub
135 Mississippi St, San Francisco (94107-2536)
PHONE................................415 643-5463
William G Casey, *CEO*
Jonathan Naseath, *CFO*
Gary Rabkin, *Vice Pres*
Andre Yousafi, *Vice Pres*
Albert Ho, *Program Mgr*
EMP: 41
SQ FT: 28,000
SALES (est): 10.5MM **Privately Held**
WEB: www.pchintl.com
SIC: 8711 8734 Electrical or electronic engineering; testing laboratories
HQ: P.C.H. International Unlimited Company
Heritage Business Park
Blackrock

(P-18790)
PGH WONG ENGINEERING (PA)
182 2nd St Fl 5, San Francisco (94105-3800)
PHONE................................415 284-0800
Peter Wong, *Owner*
Jeffery Katz, *Principal*
Linda Tang, *Office Mgr*
Ronald Wong, *Office Mgr*
Nadia Alarcon, *Administration*
EMP: 45 **EST:** 1985
SQ FT: 5,000

SALES (est): 16.5MM **Privately Held**
WEB: www.pghwong.com
SIC: 8711 Consulting engineer

(P-18791)
PHANTOM AUTO INC
601 Dna Way Unit C, South San Francisco (94080-4908)
PHONE................................510 284-9898
Shay Magzimof, *CEO*
Gia Afzal, *Manager*
EMP: 45 **EST:** 2017
SALES (est): 3.3MM **Privately Held**
WEB: www.phantom.auto
SIC: 8711 Engineering services

(P-18792)
POWER CONSTRUCTORS INC
Also Called: PCI
2934 Gold Pan Ct Ste 4, Rancho Cordova (95670-6136)
PHONE................................916 858-8601
Chris Kayne, *Manager*
EMP: 305
SALES (corp-wide): 509.6MM **Privately Held**
SIC: 8711 1623 1731 Consulting engineer; water, sewer & utility lines; communications specialization
HQ: Power Constructors, Inc
3940 Glenbrook Dr
Hailey ID 83333
208 788-3456

(P-18793)
POWER ENGINEERS INCORPORATED
218 Loreto Ct, Martinez (94553-3551)
P.O. Box 2037 (94553-0203)
PHONE................................925 372-9284
EMP: 52
SALES (corp-wide): 298.6MM **Privately Held**
SIC: 8711 Engineering Services
PA: Power Engineers, Incorporated
3940 Glenbrook Dr
Hailey ID 83333
208 788-3456

(P-18794)
PRINCIPAL SVC SOLUTIONS INC
4285 Spyres Way Ste 2, Modesto (95356-9270)
PHONE................................209 408-1982
Timothy Wylie, *President*
Jeff Hamilton, *CFO*
Gina Wylie, *Exec VP*
Neal Landsburgh, *Vice Pres*
Matt Farriba, *Sales Mgr*
EMP: 200 **EST:** 2010
SALES (est): 14.3MM **Privately Held**
WEB: www.psstechnical.com
SIC: 8711 Engineering services

(P-18795)
PT SYSTEMS INC
2350 Whitman Rd Ste B, Concord (94518-2541)
PHONE................................925 676-0709
Peter Tchan, *President*
Adele Oakes, *CFO*
EMP: 28 **EST:** 1974
SQ FT: 30,000
SALES (est): 1.8MM **Privately Held**
WEB: www.ptsystemsinc.com
SIC: 8711 7373 3823 3625 Electrical or electronic engineering; computer integrated systems design; industrial instrmnts msrmnt display/control process variable; relays & industrial controls

(P-18796)
QUASAR ENGINEERING INC
1301 Shoreway Rd Ste 425, Belmont (94002-4154)
PHONE................................650 508-6600
EMP: 100
SQ FT: 13,000
SALES (est): 16MM **Privately Held**
WEB: www.quasarusa.com
SIC: 8711 1541 Construction Design Engineers

PRODUCTS & SERVICES SECTION
8711 - Engineering Services County (P-18820)

(P-18797)
QUINCY ENGINEERING INC (PA)
11017 Cobblerock Dr # 100, Rancho Cordova (95670-6286)
PHONE..................916 368-9181
John S Quincy, *CEO*
Jeff Olson, *CFO*
Steve Mellon, *Vice Pres*
Carolyn Davis, *Creative Dir*
Bobbi Gallagher, *Office Mgr*
EMP: 41 **EST:** 1989 **Privately Held**
WEB: www.quincyeng.com
SIC: 8711 Civil engineering

(P-18798)
R & R PACIFIC CONSTRUCTION
619 1/2 Main St Ste 7, Woodland (95695-3296)
P.O. Box 1029 (95776-1029)
PHONE..................530 668-7525
Raul Melendez, *CEO*
EMP: 40 **EST:** 2012
SALES (est): 9.3MM **Privately Held**
SIC: 8711 Construction & civil engineering

(P-18799)
R JOY INC
Also Called: Richard Joy Engineering
1584 Wolf Meadows Ln, Portola (96122-7080)
PHONE..................530 832-5760
Richard Joy, *Owner*
EMP: 100 **EST:** 2009
SALES (est): 1.7MM **Privately Held**
WEB: www.joyengineering.com
SIC: 8711 Engineering services

(P-18800)
RAJAPPAN MYER CNSLTING ENGNERS (PA)
1038 Leigh Ave Ste 100, San Jose (95126-4129)
PHONE..................408 280-2772
Bala Rajappan, *President*
Keith Myers, *Vice Pres*
Suneeta Ayyalasomayajul, *Accountant*
EMP: 40 **EST:** 1992
SQ FT: 10,000
SALES (est): 4.7MM **Privately Held**
WEB: www.rmengineers.com
SIC: 8711 Consulting engineer

(P-18801)
RAXIUM INC
1250 Reliance Way, Fremont (94539-6100)
PHONE..................510 296-9935
Rick Dodd, *CEO*
Scott Craig, *Vice Pres*
Carlos Osuna, *Planning*
EMP: 70 **EST:** 2018
SALES (est): 6.5MM **Privately Held**
SIC: 8711 Engineering services

(P-18802)
RELIANT ENGRG & MFG SVCS INC
Also Called: Reliant Ems
47366 Fremont Blvd, Fremont (94538-6501)
PHONE..................510 252-1973
Kamran Honardoost, *President*
Tho Nguyen, *Vice Pres*
Ali Alian, *Engineer*
Bryan Sumoba, *Director*
EMP: 38 **EST:** 2009
SQ FT: 10,000
SALES (est): 3.1MM **Privately Held**
SIC: 8711 3841 3444 3824 Engineering services; surgical & medical instruments; sheet metalwork; mechanical & electro-mechanical counters & devices; harness assemblies for electronic use: wire or cable

(P-18803)
RIPCORD INC
30955 Huntwood Ave, Hayward (94544-7005)
PHONE..................408 838-7446
Alex Fielding, *CEO*
Ronald Sorisho, *COO*
Ahson Ahmad, *Officer*
Wasim Khan, *Officer*
Jens Hurley, *Exec VP*
EMP: 60 **EST:** 2015
SALES (est): 19.1MM **Privately Held**
WEB: www.ripcord.com
SIC: 8711 7374 Engineering services; data processing & preparation

(P-18804)
RMC WATER AND ENVIRONMENT
101 Montgomery St # 1850, San Francisco (94104-4151)
PHONE..................415 321-3400
Alison Watson, *Principal*
EMP: 38
SALES (corp-wide): 252.4MM **Privately Held**
SIC: 8711 Consulting engineer
HQ: Rmc Water And Environment
2175 N Calif Blvd Ste 315
Walnut Creek CA 94596
925 627-4100

(P-18805)
ROSS F CARROLL INC
8873 Warnerville Rd, Oakdale (95361-9411)
P.O. Box 1308 (95361-1308)
PHONE..................209 848-5959
Sean Carroll, *President*
Sheila M Carroll, *Corp Secy*
Don Ingram, *Vice Pres*
Monica Aguiar, *Administration*
EMP: 50 **EST:** 1989
SALES (est): 12.3MM **Privately Held**
WEB: www.rossfcarrollinc.com
SIC: 8711 Engineering services

(P-18806)
RUGGERI-JENSEN-AZAR & ASSOC
4690 Chabot Dr Ste 200, Pleasanton (94588-2777)
PHONE..................925 227-9100
Piero Ruggeri, *President*
Rosanna Patton, *Executive Asst*
Ross Doyle, *Planning*
Elizabeth Chan, *Engineer*
EMP: 40 **Privately Held**
WEB: www.rja-gps.com
SIC: 8711 Civil engineering
PA: Ruggeri-Jensen-Azar & Associates
8055 Camino Arroyo
Gilroy CA 95020

(P-18807)
SACRAMENTO ENGINEERING CONS
10555 Old Placerville Rd, Sacramento (95827-2503)
PHONE..................916 368-4468
Rickert Henriksen, *Owner*
Judy G Gregory, *General Mgr*
Jose Hernandez, *Project Mgr*
Scott Mendonsa, *Engineer*
Chris Gilland, *Manager*
EMP: 39 **EST:** 1980
SQ FT: 2,400
SALES (est): 5.3MM **Privately Held**
WEB: www.saceng.com
SIC: 8711 Consulting engineer

(P-18808)
SALAS OBRIEN ENGINEERS INC (PA)
305 S 11th St, San Jose (95112-2218)
PHONE..................408 282-1700
Paul Silva, *CEO*
Chris Cox, *Vice Pres*
Bi Nguyen, *Vice Pres*
Brenda Ross, *Vice Pres*
John Thomson, *Vice Pres*
▲ **EMP:** 50 **EST:** 1976
SQ FT: 10,000
SALES (est): 91.7MM **Privately Held**
WEB: www.salasobrien.com
SIC: 8711 Consulting engineer

(P-18809)
SALEM ENGINEERING GROUP INC (PA)
4729 W Jacquelyn Ave, Fresno (93722-6438)
PHONE..................559 271-9700
Sammy Salem, *President*
George Winters, *Info Tech Dir*
Arcadia Williams, *Project Mgr*
Bruce Myers, *Engineer*
Melaina Dibuduo, *Human Res Mgr*
EMP: 36 **EST:** 2004
SALES (est): 7.5MM **Privately Held**
WEB: www.salem.net
SIC: 8711 Engineering services

(P-18810)
SENSOR CONCEPTS LLC
7950 National Dr, Livermore (94550-8811)
P.O. Box 2657 (94551-2657)
PHONE..................925 443-9001
John Ashton, *Mng Member*
Michael Sanders, *President*
George Blenis, *COO*
Bradie Rosa, *Admin Asst*
Ron Chong, *Software Engr*
EMP: 70 **EST:** 1995
SALES (est): 11.9MM **Privately Held**
WEB: www.sensorconcepts.com
SIC: 8711 3812 Engineering services; radar systems & equipment

(P-18811)
SHALLEY-DIBBLE INCORPORATED
Also Called: Engineering Enterprise, The
1305 Marina Village Pkwy # 1, Alameda (94501-1100)
PHONE..................510 769-7600
Brian Smith, *President*
Johnathan Freedman, *Treasurer*
Scott Wheeler, *Vice Pres*
Kristina Martin, *Admin Sec*
Paul Miller, *Project Mgr*
EMP: 39 **EST:** 1974
SQ FT: 8,000
SALES (est): 5MM **Privately Held**
SIC: 8711 Electrical or electronic engineering

(P-18812)
SHN CNSLTING ENGNERS GLGSTS IN (PA)
812 W Wabash Ave, Eureka (95501-2138)
PHONE..................707 441-8855
Michael Foget, *CEO*
Brenda Sigler, *CFO*
Anders Rasmussen, *Engineer*
Charles Swanson, *Engineer*
Gary Simpson, *Director*
EMP: 60
SQ FT: 14,000
SALES (est): 15.7MM **Privately Held**
WEB: www.shn-engr.com
SIC: 8711 8999 Consulting engineer; geological consultant

(P-18813)
SIEMENS INDUSTRY SOFTWARE INC
46871 Bayside Pkwy, Fremont (94538-6572)
PHONE..................510 445-1836
Frank Schellenberg, *Manager*
Veronica Watson, *President*
Burak Aytuna, *Technical Mgr*
Mehrdad Nouralishahi, *Software Engr*
Bill Au, *Technology*
EMP: 36
SALES (corp-wide): 67.4B **Privately Held**
WEB: www.siemens.com
SIC: 8711 Electrical or electronic engineering
HQ: Siemens Industry Software Inc.
5800 Granite Pkwy Ste 600
Plano TX 75024
972 987-3000

(P-18814)
SIX3 ADVANCED SYSTEMS INC
2933 Bunker Hill Ln, Santa Clara (95054-1124)
PHONE..................408 878-4920
Robert A Coleman, *Branch Mgr*
EMP: 38
SALES (corp-wide): 6B **Publicly Held**
SIC: 8711 Engineering services
HQ: Six3 Advanced Systems, Inc.
45200 Business Ct Ste 100
Dulles VA 20166
703 742-7660

(P-18815)
SOF-TEK INTEGRATORS INC
4712 Mtn Lakes Blvd # 200, Redding (96003-1479)
PHONE..................530 242-0527
Jay Dunlap, *CEO*
Daniel C Morrow, *President*
Meredith Morrow, *CFO*
S Curt Dodds, *Vice Pres*
Morrow Annmary, *Admin Sec*
EMP: 40 **EST:** 2000
SQ FT: 5,000
SALES (est): 5.4MM **Privately Held**
WEB: www.sof-tek.com
SIC: 8711 Engineering services

(P-18816)
SOHA ENGINEERS (PA)
48 Colin P Kelly Jr St, San Francisco (94107-2008)
PHONE..................415 989-9900
Stephen Lau, *President*
Tim Bernard, *Partner*
Larry Chambers, *Project Mgr*
Gary Anderson, *Controller*
EMP: 35 **EST:** 1965
SQ FT: 10,000
SALES (est): 3.3MM **Privately Held*
WEB: www.soha.com
SIC: 8711 Consulting engineer

(P-18817)
SPAN DIGITAL INC
333 Bryant St Ste 140, San Francisco (94107-4144)
PHONE..................415 484-9269
Chris Lyon, *CEO*
Andrew Sather,
EMP: 40 **EST:** 2013
SALES (est): 2.5MM **Privately Held**
WEB: www.spandigital.com
SIC: 8711 Engineering services

(P-18818)
STANTEC ARCHITECTURE INC
100 California St # 1000, San Francisco (94111-4505)
PHONE..................415 882-9500
Michael Gambucci, *CEO*
Annie Coull, *Vice Pres*
Roger Swanson, *Vice Pres*
Meri Melani, *Administration*
Lori Van Dermark, *Marketing Staff*
EMP: 214
SALES (corp-wide): 3.6B **Privately Held**
WEB: www.stantec.com
SIC: 8711 8712 Engineering services; architectural services
HQ: Stantec Architecture Inc.
224 S Michigan Ave # 1400
Chicago IL 60604
336 714-7413

(P-18819)
STANTEC CONSULTING SVCS INC
1340 Treat Blvd Ste 300, Walnut Creek (94597-7966)
PHONE..................925 627-4500
Stacey Robinson, *Office Mgr*
Maria Chryssofos, *Technology*
EMP: 170
SALES (corp-wide): 3.6B **Privately Held**
WEB: www.stantec.com
SIC: 8711 Consulting engineer
HQ: Stantec Consulting Services Inc.
475 5th Ave Fl 12
New York NY 10017
212 352-5160

(P-18820)
STATCOMM INC
939 San Rafael Ave Ste C, Mountain View (94043-1941)
PHONE..................408 734-0440
Richard Schwanck, *President*
William Wood, *Corp Secy*
Rich Schwank, *Vice Pres*
Mark Andrade, *Admin Sec*
EMP: 47 **EST:** 1991
SQ FT: 5,000
SALES (est): 17.9MM **Privately Held**
WEB: www.statcomm.com
SIC: 8711 Engineering services

8711 - Engineering Services County (P-18821)

(P-18821)
STEVENS FRRONE BILEY ENGRG INC (PA)
1600 Willow Pass Ct, Concord (94520-1010)
P.O. Box 815 (94522-0815)
PHONE..................925 688-1001
Patrick Stevens, *President*
Jonathan Bailey, *Vice Pres*
Ken Ferrone, *Vice Pres*
Marty Babione, *Technician*
Matt Minor, *Technician*
EMP: 35 **EST:** 2000 **Privately Held**
WEB: www.sfbengineering.com
SIC: 8711 Consulting engineer

(P-18822)
STOKES VANNOY INC
1560 Drew Ave, Davis (95618-6320)
PHONE..................530 747-2026
Tobin Booth, *CEO*
Ryan Zahner, *COO*
Janie Booth, *CFO*
Cherie Garrett, *Officer*
Danny Lee, *Vice Pres*
EMP: 43 **EST:** 2004
SQ FT: 11,837
SALES (est): 5.9MM **Privately Held**
SIC: 8711 7389 Engineering services; design services

(P-18823)
STRUCTURAL INTEGRITY ASSOC INC (PA)
5215 Hellyer Ave Ste 210, San Jose (95138-1079)
PHONE..................408 978-8200
Mark W Marano, *President*
David Stager, *CFO*
Darren Gale, *Vice Pres*
Andy Jensen, *Vice Pres*
Sean Fuller, *Exec Dir*
EMP: 65 **EST:** 1983
SQ FT: 17,000
SALES (est): 52MM **Privately Held**
WEB: www.structint.com
SIC: 8711 Consulting engineer

(P-18824)
SUMMIT ENGINEERING INC
463 Aviation Blvd Ste 200, Santa Rosa (95403-1092)
PHONE..................707 527-0775
Gregory Swaffar, *President*
Jasper Lewis-Gehring, *Vice Pres*
Yi Yang, *Vice Pres*
Zak Zakalik, *Vice Pres*
Jim Macdougald, *Technology*
EMP: 39 **EST:** 1975
SQ FT: 12,000
SALES (est): 5.9MM **Privately Held**
WEB: www.summit-sr.com
SIC: 8711 Civil engineering

(P-18825)
T Y LIN INTERNATIONAL (HQ)
345 California St Fl 23, San Francisco (94104-2646)
PHONE..................415 291-3700
Man Chung Tang, *Chairman*
Robert A Peterson, *CFO*
Veronica Fennie, *Officer*
Michael Fitzpatrick, *Assoc VP*
Stephen Smith, *Assoc VP*
EMP: 84 **EST:** 1964
SQ FT: 30,159
SALES (est): 117MM
SALES (corp-wide): 123.3MM **Privately Held**
WEB: www.tylin.com
SIC: 8711 Consulting engineer
PA: T.Y.Lin International Group, Ltd.
345 California St Fl 23
San Francisco CA 94104
415 291-3700

(P-18826)
TAIT & ASSOCIATES INC
2880 Sunrise Blvd, Rancho Cordova (95742-6547)
PHONE..................916 635-2444
Stan Iverson, *Vice Pres*
Dennis Tweedy, *Director*
Chandra Miehe, *Manager*
EMP: 49

SALES (corp-wide): 30.1MM **Privately Held**
WEB: www.tait.com
SIC: 8711 Civil engineering
PA: Tait & Associates, Inc.
701 Parkcenter Dr
Santa Ana CA 92705
866 584-0283

(P-18827)
TANNER PACIFIC INC
261 Oakview Dr, San Carlos (94070-4536)
PHONE..................650 585-4484
William Tanner, *CEO*
Demi Pacifuentes, *Treasurer*
Sarah Lucere, *Project Engr*
Andrew Matey, *Manager*
Amelia Wheeler, *Manager*
EMP: 38 **EST:** 2016
SALES (est): 2.9MM **Privately Held**
WEB: www.tannerpacific.com
SIC: 8711 Engineering services

(P-18828)
TECHNICON ENGINEERING SVCS INC
4539 N Brawley Ave # 108, Fresno (93722-3950)
PHONE..................559 276-9311
Darren Williams, *President*
Kent Baucher, *Vice Pres*
EMP: 48 **EST:** 1989
SQ FT: 1,800
SALES (est): 8.1MM **Privately Held**
WEB: www.technicon.net
SIC: 8711 Consulting engineer

(P-18829)
TECTONIC ENGRG SRVYING CONS PC
2855 Mitchell Dr Ste 227, Walnut Creek (94598-1630)
PHONE..................925 357-8236
EMP: 35
SALES (corp-wide): 93.8MM **Privately Held**
WEB: www.tectonicengineering.com
SIC: 8711 8713 Civil engineering; surveying services
PA: Tectonic Engineering Consultants, Geologists & Land Surveyors, D.P.C.
70 Pleasant Hill Rd
Mountainville NY 10953
845 534-5959

(P-18830)
TED JACOB ENGRG GROUP INC (PA)
1763 Broadway, Oakland (94612-2105)
PHONE..................510 763-4880
Ted Jacob, *President*
Shad Shabbas, *CFO*
Atur Shabbas, *Executive*
Atur Chabbes, *Office Mgr*
Tupou Fakava, *Administration*
EMP: 40 **EST:** 1985
SQ FT: 12,000
SALES (est): 15MM **Privately Held**
WEB: www.tjeg.com
SIC: 8711 Mechanical engineering; electrical or electronic engineering

(P-18831)
TEECOM
50 California St Ste 1500, San Francisco (94111-4612)
PHONE..................510 337-2800
David Marks, *CEO*
Jerry Dreiling, *CFO*
Randy Gruberman, *Vice Pres*
Ben Shemuel, *Vice Pres*
Jim Graham, *Business Dir*
EMP: 87 **EST:** 1997
SQ FT: 12,600
SALES (est): 14.9MM **Privately Held**
WEB: www.teecom.com
SIC: 8711 Consulting engineer

(P-18832)
TERMINAL INC (PA)
1 Letterman Dr Bldg C, San Francisco (94129-2402)
PHONE..................281 682-8294
Jennifer Farris, *Officer*
Scott Shirk, *Exec VP*

Nabil Fahel, *Director*
Jordan Caviness, *Manager*
EMP: 92 **EST:** 2018
SALES (est): 4.7MM **Privately Held**
WEB: www.terminal.io
SIC: 8711 Engineering services

(P-18833)
TESSOLVEDTS INC (PA)
226 Airport Pkwy Ste 300, San Jose (95110-3700)
PHONE..................408 865-0873
Pakkirisamy Rajamanickam, *CEO*
EMP: 46 **EST:** 2014
SALES (est): 1.4MM **Privately Held**
WEB: www.tessolve.com
SIC: 8711 Consulting engineer

(P-18834)
TESTING ENGINEERS INCORPORATED (PA)
2811 Teagarden St, San Leandro (94577-5716)
PHONE..................510 835-3142
Gary Snyder, *President*
Terry Egland, *Vice Pres*
Colin Stock, *Division Mgr*
Wayne Wicker, *Info Tech Mgr*
Debbie Myers, *Human Res Mgr*
EMP: 40
SQ FT: 10,000
SALES (est): 7MM **Privately Held**
WEB: www.testing-engineers.com
SIC: 8711 Consulting engineer

(P-18835)
TETER LLP (PA)
7535 N Palm Ave Ste 201, Fresno (93711-5504)
PHONE..................559 437-0887
Glen Teter, *Partner*
Clay Davis, *Partner*
Byron Dietrich, *Partner*
Paul Halajian, *Partner*
Jamie Hickman, *Partner*
EMP: 50 **EST:** 1979
SALES (est): 10.2MM **Privately Held**
WEB: www.teterae.com
SIC: 8711 8712 Structural engineering; architectural services

(P-18836)
TGCON INC (HQ)
50 Contractors St, Livermore (94551-4863)
PHONE..................925 449-5764
William L Gates, *President*
John Copriviza, *President*
Brian L Gates, *COO*
Scott Blaine, *CFO*
Brian Gates, *Exec VP*
EMP: 294 **EST:** 1989
SQ FT: 25,000
SALES (est): 44.7MM
SALES (corp-wide): 203MM **Privately Held**
WEB: www.goodfellowbros.com
SIC: 8711 Construction & civil engineering
PA: Goodfellow Bros. Llc
135 N Wenatchee Ave
Wenatchee WA 98801
509 662-7111

(P-18837)
THOMAS MARK & COMPANY INC (PA)
2833 Junction Ave Ste 110, San Jose (95134-1920)
PHONE..................408 453-5373
Mike Lohman, *President*
Robert A Himes, *President*
Richard K Tanaka, *Chairman*
Sasha D Dansky, *Principal*
David E Ross, *Principal*
EMP: 50 **EST:** 1927
SALES (est): 30.6MM **Privately Held**
WEB: www.markthomas.com
SIC: 8711 8713 Consulting engineer; surveying services

(P-18838)
TIPPING MAR & ASSOCIATES
1906 Shattuck Ave, Berkeley (94704-1022)
PHONE..................510 549-1906
Marc Steyer, *President*
Leo Panian, *Treasurer*
Gina Phelan, *General Mgr*

Susan Papps, *Office Mgr*
Mike Korolyc, *Admin Sec*
EMP: 38 **EST:** 1983
SQ FT: 5,000
SALES (est): 6MM **Privately Held**
WEB: www.tippingmar.com
SIC: 8711 Structural engineering

(P-18839)
TREADWELL & ROLLO INC (DH)
555 Montgomery St # 1300, San Francisco (94111-2541)
PHONE..................415 955-9040
Philip Ttringale, *Director*
Philip G Smith, *Exec VP*
Maria G Flessas, *Vice Pres*
Patrick B Hubbard, *Vice Pres*
Richard D Rodgers, *Vice Pres*
EMP: 50 **EST:** 1988
SQ FT: 12,500
SALES (est): 10.9MM
SALES (corp-wide): 177.9MM **Privately Held**
WEB: www.langan.com
SIC: 8711 Consulting engineer
HQ: Langan Engineering And Environmental Services, Inc.
300 Kimball Dr
Parsippany NJ 07054
973 560-4900

(P-18840)
TRINITY ENGINEERING
583 Martin Ave, Rohnert Park (94928-2060)
PHONE..................707 585-2959
Bruce D Omholt, *CEO*
Michael Johnston, *President*
Ronald R Milard, *President*
Denise R Palmer, *CFO*
Christopher Prochazka, *Technician*
EMP: 40 **EST:** 1980
SQ FT: 18,000
SALES (est): 5.9MM **Privately Held**
WEB: www.trinityengineering.com
SIC: 8711 2542 Designing; ship, boat, machine & product; fixtures: display, office or store: except wood

(P-18841)
TURLOCK SHEET METAL & WLDG INC
Also Called: P & F Metals
301 S Broadway, Turlock (95380-5414)
PHONE..................209 667-4716
Jim Vieira, *CEO*
Sarah Snyder, *Office Mgr*
Gary Pinheiro, *Admin Sec*
Keith Valenzuela, *Engineer*
Terra Krigbaum, *Accounting Mgr*
EMP: 45 **EST:** 1956
SQ FT: 12,000
SALES (est): 9.9MM **Privately Held**
SIC: 8711 Engineering services; mechanical engineering

(P-18842)
TYLIN INTL GROUP LTD (PA)
345 California St Fl 23, San Francisco (94104-2646)
PHONE..................415 291-3700
Matthew G Cummings, *President*
Sheila Jordan, *Chief Mktg Ofcr*
Maribel Castillo, *Vice Pres*
Veronica Fennie, *Vice Pres*
John Flint, *Vice Pres*
EMP: 109 **EST:** 1961
SQ FT: 34,000
SALES (est): 123.3MM **Privately Held**
WEB: www.tylin.com
SIC: 8711 Consulting engineer

(P-18843)
UNICO ENGINEERING INC
110 Blue Ravine Rd, Folsom (95630-4711)
PHONE..................916 293-8953
C Antonio Montes De Oca, *Principal*
Lisa McClintock, *Business Dir*
EMP: 46 **EST:** 2014
SALES (est): 4.8MM **Privately Held**
WEB: www.unicoengineering.com
SIC: 8711 Civil engineering

PRODUCTS & SERVICES SECTION
8711 - Engineering Services County (P-18867)

(P-18844)
URS ALASKA LLC (HQ)
600 Montgomery St Fl 25, San Francisco (94111-2724)
PHONE................415 774-2700
EMP: 50 EST: 2013
SALES (est): 2.7MM
SALES (corp-wide): 13.2B Publicly Held
WEB: www.aecom.com
SIC: 8711 Engineering services
PA: Aecom
  13355 Noel Rd Ste 400
  Dallas TX 75240
  972 788-1000

(P-18845)
URS CORPORATION (HQ)
300 California St Fl 4, San Francisco (94104-1414)
PHONE................213 593-8100
Peter James Holland, CEO
Josimar Thomas, Training Spec
EMP: 50 EST: 1970
SALES (est): 12.5MM
SALES (corp-wide): 13.2B Publicly Held
WEB: www.aecom.com
SIC: 8711 Consulting engineer
PA: Aecom
  13355 Noel Rd Ste 400
  Dallas TX 75240
  972 788-1000

(P-18846)
URS CORPORATION
300 Lakeside Dr Ste 400, Oakland (94612-3573)
PHONE................510 893-3600
Bob Snyder, President
David Colley, Vice Pres
Daniel Curry, Vice Pres
John Debruin, Vice Pres
Dwayne H Deutscher, Vice Pres
EMP: 46 EST: 2015
SALES (est): 3.1MM Privately Held
WEB: www.aecom.com
SIC: 8711 Consulting engineer

(P-18847)
URS GROUP INC
300 Lakeside Dr Ste 400, Oakland (94612-3573)
PHONE................510 893-3600
Louise Armstrong, Manager
John Bischoff, Vice Pres
Linda Pappas, Vice Pres
Robert K Green, Engineer
Robert Michna, Manager
EMP: 90
SALES (corp-wide): 13.2B Publicly Held
WEB: www.aecom.com
SIC: 8711 4953 Consulting engineer; refuse systems
HQ: Urs Group, Inc.
  300 S Grand Ave Ste 900
  Los Angeles CA 90071
  213 593-8000

(P-18848)
URS GROUP INC
300 Lakeside Dr Ste 400, Oakland (94612-3573)
PHONE................925 446-3800
Sam Capps, Branch Mgr
EMP: 90
SALES (corp-wide): 13.2B Publicly Held
WEB: www.aecom.com
SIC: 8711 8712 8741 Consulting engineer; architectural engineering; construction management
HQ: Urs Group, Inc.
  300 S Grand Ave Ste 900
  Los Angeles CA 90071
  213 593-8000

(P-18849)
URS GROUP INC
4 N 2nd St, San Jose (95113-1308)
PHONE................408 297-9585
William Hadaya, Branch Mgr
James Hawald, Project Leader
Ramsey Hissen, Sr Project Mgr
EMP: 90
SALES (corp-wide): 13.2B Publicly Held
WEB: www.aecom.com
SIC: 8711 Consulting engineer

HQ: Urs Group, Inc.
  300 S Grand Ave Ste 900
  Los Angeles CA 90071
  213 593-8000

(P-18850)
URS GROUP INC
1360 E Spruce Ave Ste 101, Fresno (93720-3378)
PHONE................559 255-2541
Ralph Boyakin, Manager
EMP: 90
SALES (corp-wide): 13.2B Publicly Held
WEB: www.aecom.com
SIC: 8711 Consulting engineer
HQ: Urs Group, Inc.
  300 S Grand Ave Ste 900
  Los Angeles CA 90071
  213 593-8000

(P-18851)
URS HOLDINGS INC (DH)
600 Montgomery St Fl 25, San Francisco (94111-2724)
PHONE................415 774-2700
Thomas W Bishop, CEO
Martin M Koffel, Ch of Bd
Kim Long, Admin Asst
Carol Frieda Brandenburg-Smith, Asst Sec
EMP: 470 EST: 1991
SALES (est): 1.5B
SALES (corp-wide): 13.2B Publicly Held
WEB: www.aecom.com
SIC: 8711 7389 6531 8249 Consulting engineer; financial services; real estate agents & managers; aviation school; aircraft maintenance & repair services
HQ: Aecom Global Ii, Llc
  300 S Grand Ave Ste 900
  Los Angeles CA 90071
  213 593-8100

(P-18852)
US INTERACTIVE DELAWARE (PA)
1270 Oakmead Pkwy Ste 318, Sunnyvale (94085-4044)
PHONE................408 863-7500
Sunil Mathur, CEO
Tom Morris, President
Rashmi Srivastava, Treasurer
Kekin Dand, Administration
EMP: 117 EST: 1994
SALES (est): 9.8MM Privately Held
WEB: www.usinteractive.com
SIC: 8711 Consulting engineer

(P-18853)
VALLEY TECH SYSTEMS INC
160 Blue Ravine Rd Ste A, Folsom (95630-4718)
PHONE................916 760-1025
Russell Carlson, CEO
Joe Viola, CFO
Joseph Viola, CFO
Ragan Wilkinson, CTO
EMP: 40 EST: 2006
SALES (est): 2MM Privately Held
WEB: www.vts-i.com
SIC: 8711 Consulting engineer

(P-18854)
VERSA ENGINEERING & TECH INC (PA)
1320 Willow Pass Rd S500, Concord (94520-5232)
PHONE................925 405-4505
Fred Fong, President
Flavio Santini, Chairman
Tom Nollie, Principal
Shaan Mustafa, Project Mgr
EMP: 55 EST: 2005
SALES (est): 12.9MM Privately Held
WEB: www.versaet.com
SIC: 8711 Consulting engineer

(P-18855)
WALLACE-KUHL INVESTMENTS LLC
3422 W Hammer Ln Ste G, Stockton (95219-5493)
PHONE................209 234-7722
Doug Kuhl, Owner
Andrew Wallace, Officer
Kevin Watson, Project Engr

Edward Mak, Senior Engr
EMP: 35 Privately Held
WEB: www.wallace-kuhl.com
SIC: 8711 Civil engineering
PA: Wallace-Kuhl Investments, Llc
  3050 Industrial Blvd
  West Sacramento CA 95691

(P-18856)
WALLACE-KUHL INVESTMENTS LLC (PA)
3050 Industrial Blvd, West Sacramento (95691-3470)
P.O. Box 1137 (95691-1137)
PHONE................916 372-1434
Douglas J Kuhl,
Mike Soto, Technician
Steve French, Engineer
David A Redford, Engineer
Thomas S Wallace,
EMP: 65 EST: 1984
SQ FT: 11,300
SALES (est): 11MM Privately Held
WEB: www.wallace-kuhl.com
SIC: 8711 8748 Civil engineering; business consulting

(P-18857)
WARREN CNSULTING ENGINEERS INC
1117 Windfield Way # 110, El Dorado Hills (95762-9834)
PHONE................916 985-1870
George Warren, CEO
Kacey Cook, Accounts Mgr
EMP: 49 EST: 2002
SALES (est): 3.9MM Privately Held
WEB: www.wceinc.com
SIC: 8711 Civil engineering

(P-18858)
WATLOW ELECTRIC MFG CO
6781 Via Del Oro, San Jose (95119-1360)
PHONE................408 776-6646
EMP: 85
SALES (corp-wide): 586.3MM Privately Held
WEB: www.watlow.com
SIC: 8711 Engineering services
PA: Watlow Electric Manufacturing Company
  12001 Lackland Rd
  Saint Louis MO 63146
  314 878-4600

(P-18859)
WEST YOST & ASSOCIATES INC (PA)
2020 Res Pk Dr Ste 100, Davis (95618)
PHONE................530 756-5905
Charles Duncan, President
Bruce West, President
Steven R Dalrymple, Corp Secy
Jim Yost, Vice Pres
Christine Encelan, Admin Asst
EMP: 76 EST: 1990
SQ FT: 25,000
SALES (est): 17.7MM Privately Held
WEB: www.westyost.com
SIC: 8711 Civil engineering

(P-18860)
WHIPSAW INC
434 S 1st St, San Jose (95113-2815)
P.O. Box 758 (95106-0758)
PHONE................408 297-9771
Dan Harden, President
Robert Riccomini, CEO
Heidi Schwank, Treasurer
Jane Moynihan, Program Mgr
Julie Riccomini, Admin Sec
EMP: 50 EST: 1999
SQ FT: 6,240
SALES (est): 3.4MM Privately Held
WEB: www.whipsaw.com
SIC: 8711 Mechanical engineering

(P-18861)
WILLDAN ENGINEERING
9281 Office Park Cir # 10, Elk Grove (95758-8068)
PHONE................916 661-3520
Rachel Trinh, Manager
EMP: 57

SALES (corp-wide): 390.9MM Publicly Held
WEB: www.willdan.com
SIC: 8711 Civil engineering
HQ: Willdan Engineering
  2401 E Katella Ave # 300
  Anaheim CA 92806
  714 978-8200

(P-18862)
WILLDAN ENGINEERING
2240 Douglas Blvd Ste 270, Roseville (95661-3874)
PHONE................916 924-7000
Robert Keefe, Branch Mgr
Banwait Avtar, Engineer
EMP: 57
SALES (corp-wide): 390.9MM Publicly Held
WEB: www.willdan.com
SIC: 8711 8742 Civil engineering; business planning & organizing services
HQ: Willdan Engineering
  2401 E Katella Ave # 300
  Anaheim CA 92806
  714 978-8200

(P-18863)
WMH CORPORATION
55 S Market St Ste 1200, San Jose (95113-2365)
PHONE................408 971-7300
William M Hadaya, President
EMP: 45 EST: 2007
SALES (est): 2.6MM Privately Held
WEB: www.wmhcorporation.com
SIC: 8711 Consulting engineer

(P-18864)
WOOD RODGERS INC (PA)
3301 C St Ste 100b, Sacramento (95816-3350)
PHONE................916 341-7760
Mark Rodgers, President
Martin Rodriguez, Officer
Steve Balbierz, Vice Pres
Gerardo Calvillo, Vice Pres
Shyamal Chowdhury, Vice Pres
EMP: 120 EST: 1996
SQ FT: 5,500
SALES (est): 47.5MM Privately Held
WEB: www.woodrodgers.com
SIC: 8711 Civil engineering

(P-18865)
YERBA BUENA ENGRG & CNSTR INC (PA)
1340 Egbert Ave, San Francisco (94124-3617)
PHONE................415 822-4400
Miguel Galarza, CEO
EMP: 36 EST: 2002
SQ FT: 5,000
SALES (est): 8.6MM Privately Held
WEB: www.yerba-buena.net
SIC: 8711 Construction & civil engineering

(P-18866)
YOUNGDAHL CONSULTING GROUP INC
1234 Glenhaven Ct, El Dorado Hills (95762-5709)
PHONE................916 933-0633
John Youngdahl, President
Scott Youngdahl, Treasurer
Jeffry Cannon, Dept Chairman
Katherine Gallagher, Assistant
EMP: 38 EST: 1984
SQ FT: 9,500
SALES (est): 5.7MM Privately Held
WEB: www.youngdahl.net
SIC: 8711 8748 Consulting engineer; environmental consultant

(P-18867)
YUPANA INC (PA)
4020 Nelson Ave Ste 200, Concord (94520-8526)
PHONE................925 482-0657
Muzaffer Mete Dalan, CEO
John McWeeny, Admin Sec
Cary Workmon, Technician
Manuel Hernandez, Technical Staff
Onur Yildirim, Technical Staff
EMP: 49 EST: 2011

8711 - Engineering Services County (P-18868)

SALES (est): 10.2MM **Privately Held**
WEB: www.yupanatech.com
SIC: 8711 Engineering services

(P-18868)
ZOHO CORPORATION
Also Called: Manageengine
4900 Hopyard Rd Ste 310, Pleasanton (94588-7100)
PHONE.....................925 924-9500
Sridhar Vembu, *CEO*
Sridhar Iyengar, *Vice Pres*
Anand Raman, *CIO*
Saravanan Moorthy, *Technical Staff*
Gobi Subash, *Manager*
EMP: 395 **Privately Held**
WEB: www.site24x7.com
SIC: 8711 Engineering services
HQ: Zoho Corporation
4141 Hacienda Dr
Pleasanton CA 94588

8712 Architectural Services

(P-18869)
ANDERSON BRULE ARCHITECTS INC
Also Called: A B A
325 S 1st St Fl 4, San Jose (95113-2826)
PHONE.....................408 298-1885
Pamela Anderson-Brule, *President*
Pierre Brule, *Principal*
Amy Ford, *Office Mgr*
Emily Conant, *Office Admin*
Kim McAfee, *Accountant*
EMP: 35 **EST:** 1984
SQ FT: 17,000
SALES (est): 5.8MM **Privately Held**
WEB: www.aba-arch.com
SIC: 8712 Architectural engineering

(P-18870)
ARCHITCTRAL RSOURCES GROUP INC (PA)
9 Pier Ste 107, San Francisco (94111-1451)
PHONE.....................415 421-1680
Stephen Farneth, *Partner*
Bruce Judd, *Principal*
Andrew Blyholder, *Info Tech Dir*
Robert Preciado, *Technician*
Naomi Miroglio, *Engineer*
EMP: 43 **EST:** 1980
SQ FT: 4,700
SALES (est): 9MM **Privately Held**
WEB: www.argcreate.com
SIC: 8712 Architectural engineering

(P-18871)
ARCHITECTURE PLUS INC
4335 N Star Way Ste B, Modesto (95356-8628)
PHONE.....................209 577-4661
Frank Boots, *President*
Rod Alonvo, *Vice Pres*
Joseph Smith, *Vice Pres*
EMP: 39 **EST:** 1982
SQ FT: 4,080
SALES (est): 2.6MM **Privately Held**
WEB: www.apiarc.com
SIC: 8712 Architectural engineering

(P-18872)
BAR ARCHITECTS
77 Geary St Ste 200, San Francisco (94108-5724)
PHONE.....................415 293-5700
Robert Hunter, *President*
Earl Wilson, *Principal*
Sam Chan, *Project Mgr*
Christine Phoen, *Accountant*
Michele Fazio, *Controller*
EMP: 80 **EST:** 1966
SALES (est): 13MM **Privately Held**
WEB: www.bararch.com
SIC: 8712 Architectural engineering

(P-18873)
BAUM THORNLEY ARCHITECTS
95 Brady St, San Francisco (94103-1241)
PHONE.....................415 503-1411
Robert Baum, *Owner*
Douglas Thornley, *Partner*
EMP: 53 **EST:** 1991
SQ FT: 4,600
SALES (est): 1.3MM **Privately Held**
WEB: www.gouldevans.com
SIC: 8712 7389 Architectural engineering; interior designer

(P-18874)
BRERETON ARCHITECTS INC
909 Montgomery St Ste 260, San Francisco (94133-4650)
PHONE.....................415 546-1212
Ashley Miller, *President*
Nick Brereton, *President*
David Peebles, *Engineer*
Joseph Bowe, *Accountant*
Michael Castro, *Architect*
EMP: 40 **EST:** 1978
SALES (est): 5.7MM **Privately Held**
WEB: www.brereton.com
SIC: 8712 7389 Architectural engineering; interior designer

(P-18875)
CALPO HOM DONG ARCHITECTS INC
2120 20th St Ste 1, Sacramento (95818-1760)
PHONE.....................916 446-7741
Alan Hom, *President*
Rudy Calpo, *President*
Dennis Dong, *Vice Pres*
Andy Kwong, *Vice Pres*
Jill Haw, *Director*
EMP: 77 **EST:** 1984
SQ FT: 7,000
SALES (est): 8.1MM **Privately Held**
WEB: www.chdarchitects.com
SIC: 8712 7389 Architectural engineering; interior design services

(P-18876)
CARTER & BURGESS INC
300 Frank H Ogawa Plz, Oakland (94612-2037)
PHONE.....................510 457-0027
Robert Turley, *Branch Mgr*
EMP: 72
SALES (corp-wide): 13.5B **Publicly Held**
WEB: www.c-b.com
SIC: 8712 8713 8711 Architectural engineering; surveying services; civil engineering
HQ: Carter & Burgess, Inc.
777 Main St Ste 2500
Fort Worth TX 76102
817 735-6000

(P-18877)
CAW ARCHITECTS INC
455 Lambert Ave, Palo Alto (94306-2220)
PHONE.....................650 328-1818
Montgomery Anderson, *President*
Christopher Wasney, *Vice Pres*
Monique Wood, *Project Mgr*
Dane Borda, *Manager*
EMP: 66 **EST:** 1968
SQ FT: 4,000
SALES (est): 4.4MM **Privately Held**
WEB: www.cawarchitects.com
SIC: 8712 Architectural engineering

(P-18878)
CGL COMPANIES LLC
2260 Del Paso Rd Ste 100, Sacramento (95834-9713)
PHONE.....................916 678-7890
Robert Glass, *Exec VP*
Jami Godkin, *Vice Pres*
EMP: 70 **EST:** 2017
SALES (est): 4.4MM **Privately Held**
WEB: www.cglcompanies.com
SIC: 8712 Architectural services

(P-18879)
COACT DESIGNWORKS
Also Called: Stafford-King-Wiese Architects
3348 Montclaire St, Sacramento (95821-3738)
PHONE.....................916 930-5900
Pat Derickson, *President*
Kelly Reynolds, *Vice Pres*
Kirby Perkins, *Administration*
Rebecca Weldon, *Business Mgr*
Christopher Garcia, *Education*
EMP: 50 **EST:** 1945
SALES (est): 9MM **Privately Held**
WEB: www.coactdesignworks.com
SIC: 8712 Architectural engineering

(P-18880)
DAHLIN GROUP INC (PA)
5865 Owens Dr, Pleasanton (94588-3942)
PHONE.....................925 251-7200
Nancy K Keenan, *President*
Tim Williams, *CFO*
Mark Day, *Officer*
Karl Danielson, *Vice Pres*
Charles Meyer, *Vice Pres*
EMP: 60 **EST:** 1972
SQ FT: 300,000
SALES (est): 17.1MM **Privately Held**
WEB: www.dahlingroup.com
SIC: 8712 Architectural engineering

(P-18881)
DARDEN ARCHITECTS INC
6790 N West Ave Ste 104, Fresno (93711-4306)
PHONE.....................559 448-8051
Martin Dietz, *President*
Tricia Sanger, *Executive Asst*
Alfredo Rodriguez, *Project Mgr*
Ivette Ledesma, *Marketing Staff*
Kari Trenhaile, *Manager*
EMP: 75 **EST:** 1959
SQ FT: 5,000
SALES (est): 6.8MM **Privately Held**
WEB: www.dardenarchitects.com
SIC: 8712 7389 Architectural engineering; interior designer

(P-18882)
DES ARCHITECTS ENGINEERS INC
399 Bradford St Ste 300, Redwood City (94063-1585)
P.O. Box 3599 (94064-3599)
PHONE.....................650 364-6453
Thomas Gilman, *President*
Stephen D Mincey, *CFO*
Craig Ivancovich, *Corp Secy*
Melanie Rogers, *Executive*
Karen Withers, *Executive Asst*
EMP: 115 **EST:** 1973
SQ FT: 35,000
SALES (est): 17.9MM **Privately Held**
WEB: www.des-ae.com
SIC: 8712 8711 Architectural engineering; engineering services

(P-18883)
DG ARCHITECTS INC (PA)
Also Called: Dga Plnning L Arch L Interiors
550 Ellis St, Mountain View (94043-2236)
PHONE.....................650 943-1660
Randall Dowler, *President*
Nancy Escano, *Treasurer*
Trey Post, *Planning*
Rachel Santos, *CIO*
Mark Davis, *CTO*
EMP: 49 **EST:** 1995
SQ FT: 15,000
SALES (est): 10.3MM **Privately Held**
WEB: www.dgaonline.com
SIC: 8712 Architectural engineering

(P-18884)
FIELD PAOLI ARCHITECTS PC
711 Market St 2, San Francisco (94103-2101)
PHONE.....................415 788-6606
David Paoli, *President*
John Field, *Corp Secy*
Wilmer Mendiola, *Info Tech Dir*
Paulynn Ortiz, *Technology*
Christen Soares, *Sr Associate*
▲ **EMP:** 45 **EST:** 1986
SALES (est): 7MM **Privately Held**
WEB: www.fieldpaoli.com
SIC: 8712 House designer

(P-18885)
FORGE ARCHITECTURE
Also Called: Fee Munson Ebert Architects
500 Montgomery St, San Francisco (94111-6523)
PHONE.....................415 434-0320
Jack Munson, *Partner*
Andrew Wilson, *Principal*
Noelle Narez, *Office Admin*
Richard Barnes, *Project Mgr*
Anthia Wong, *Project Mgr*
EMP: 51 **EST:** 1980
SQ FT: 6,800
SALES (est): 8.8MM **Privately Held**
SIC: 8712 7389 Architectural services; interior design services

(P-18886)
GELFLAND PARTNERS ARCHITECTS
165 10th St Ste 100, San Francisco (94103-2659)
PHONE.....................415 346-4040
Lisa Gelfand, *President*
Nunn Yang Kang, *Treasurer*
Ralph Rosling, *Vice Pres*
Chris Duncan, *Principal*
Kotro Nakmura, *Admin Sec*
EMP: 46 **EST:** 1997
SALES (est): 6.5MM **Privately Held**
WEB: www.gelfand-partners.com
SIC: 8712 Architectural engineering

(P-18887)
GENSLER ASSCTS/NTRNATIONAL LTD (HQ)
45 Fremont St Ste 1500, San Francisco (94105-2214)
PHONE.....................415 433-3700
Arthur Gensler Jr, *President*
EMP: 339 **EST:** 1988
SALES (est): 25.1MM
SALES (corp-wide): 1.2B **Privately Held**
WEB: www.gensler.com
SIC: 8712 Architectural engineering
PA: M. Arthur Gensler Jr. & Associates, Inc.
45 Fremont St Ste 1500
San Francisco CA 94105
415 433-3700

(P-18888)
HELLMUTH OBATA & KASSABAUM INC (DH)
Also Called: H O K
1 Bush St Ste 200, San Francisco (94104-4404)
PHONE.....................415 243-0555
Patrick Macleamy, *CEO*
William Hellmuth, *President*
Lisa Green, *Treasurer*
Thomas Robson, *Officer*
John Bartolomi, *CIO*
EMP: 193 **EST:** 1966
SALES (est): 118.7MM
SALES (corp-wide): 457.5MM **Privately Held**
WEB: www.hok.com
SIC: 8712 8711 8742 7389 Architectural engineering; engineering services; management consulting services; interior design services; landscape architects

(P-18889)
HERMAN COLIVER LOCUS ARCH
Also Called: Hcla
423 Tehama St, San Francisco (94103-4111)
PHONE.....................415 495-1776
Robert Gerald Herman, *President*
Susan Coliver, *Vice Pres*
Steven Rajninger, *Vice Pres*
Lila Cohen, *Project Mgr*
Gretchen Mokry, *Project Mgr*
EMP: 36 **EST:** 1969
SQ FT: 3,800
SALES (est): 3.8MM **Privately Held**
WEB: www.hclarchitecture.com
SIC: 8712 Architectural services

(P-18890)
HMR ARCHITECTS INC
2130 21st St, Sacramento (95818-1708)
PHONE.....................916 736-2724
Scott Pullen, *President*
Richard Barnes, *CIO*
Bryan Fawkes, *Project Mgr*
Suzanne Reiss, *Business Mgr*
EMP: 45 **EST:** 1963
SQ FT: 10,000
SALES (est): 4.6MM **Privately Held**
WEB: www.hmrarchitects.com
SIC: 8712 Architectural engineering

PRODUCTS & SERVICES SECTION
8712 - Architectural Services County (P-18913)

(P-18891)
HORNBERGER WORSTELL ASSOC INC
Also Called: Hornberger, Mark R
170 Maiden Ln Ste 700, San Francisco (94108-5335)
PHONE..............................415 391-1080
Mark Hornberger, *President*
Francine Larose, *CFO*
Jack Worstell, *Exec VP*
John Davis, *Senior VP*
Karen Bass, *Finance Mgr*
EMP: 50 **EST:** 1980
SALES (est): 6.5MM **Privately Held**
WEB: www.hornbergerworstell.com
SIC: 8712 Architectural engineering

(P-18892)
HUNTSMAN ARCHITECTURAL GROUP (PA)
50 California St Fl 7, San Francisco (94111-4624)
PHONE..............................415 394-1212
Sascha Wagner, *President*
Linda H Parker, *President*
Susan Williams, *CFO*
Bill Puetz, *Principal*
Kenneth Fout, *Info Tech Dir*
EMP: 83 **EST:** 1981
SQ FT: 19,000
SALES (est): 21MM **Privately Held**
WEB: www.huntsmanag.com
SIC: 8712 Architectural engineering

(P-18893)
KELLY & STONE ARCHITECTS INC
11209 Brockway Rd Ste 211, Truckee (96161-2219)
PHONE..............................530 214-8896
Keith Kelly, *President*
Lacey Hoffmann, *Controller*
EMP: 35 **Privately Held**
WEB: www.kellyandstonearchitects.com
SIC: 8712 Architectural engineering
PA: Kelly & Stone Architects Inc
465 Anglers Dr
Steamboat Springs CO 80487

(P-18894)
KMD ARCHITECTS (PA)
417 Montgomery St Ste 200, San Francisco (94104-1107)
PHONE..............................415 398-5191
Paul Ryan Stevens, *CEO*
Robert Matthew, *Ch of Bd*
Kavinder Singh, *President*
Nathan Galloway, *Admin Sec*
Dawnee Hahn, *Human Res Mgr*
▲ **EMP:** 84 **EST:** 1963
SQ FT: 35,000
SALES (est): 24.6MM **Privately Held**
WEB: www.kmdarchitects.com
SIC: 8712 Architectural services

(P-18895)
LIONAKIS (PA)
Also Called: Architecture
1919 19th St, Sacramento (95811-6714)
PHONE..............................916 558-1901
Andrew Deeble, *Exec Dir*
Tim Fry, *President*
Nick Docous, *Vice Pres*
David Younger, *Vice Pres*
Maynard Feist, *Social Dir*
EMP: 150
SQ FT: 38,000
SALES (est): 29.9MM **Privately Held**
WEB: www.lionakis.com
SIC: 8712 7389 8711 Architectural services; interior design services; structural engineering

(P-18896)
LOVING CAMPOS ASSOCIATES (PA)
Also Called: Lca Architects
245 Ygnacio Valley Rd # 200, Walnut Creek (94596-7029)
PHONE..............................925 944-1626
Jerry P Loving, *CEO*
Carl Campos, *President*
David Bogstad, *Vice Pres*
Terry Benson, *Office Mgr*

Loren Gachen, *Project Mgr*
EMP: 47 **EST:** 1974
SQ FT: 6,300
SALES (est): 5.6MM **Privately Held**
WEB: www.lca-architects.com
SIC: 8712 Architectural engineering

(P-18897)
LPAS INC
2484 Natomas Park Dr # 100, Sacramento (95833-2928)
PHONE..............................916 443-0335
Theressa Page, *Owner*
David Brady Smith, *President*
Ronald Metzker, *Treasurer*
Curtis Owyang, *Admin Sec*
Michael Millett, *CIO*
EMP: 61 **EST:** 1975
SQ FT: 12,000
SALES (est): 8.5MM **Privately Held**
WEB: www.lpas.com
SIC: 8712 Architectural engineering

(P-18898)
M ARTHUR GENSLER JR ASSOC INC
225 W Santa Clara St # 1, San Jose (95113-1723)
PHONE..............................408 885-8100
Kevin Schaeffer, *Branch Mgr*
Laura Latham, *Director*
EMP: 38
SALES (corp-wide): 1.2B **Privately Held**
WEB: www.gensler.com
SIC: 8712 Architectural engineering
PA: M. Arthur Gensler Jr. & Associates, Inc.
45 Fremont St Ste 1500
San Francisco CA 94105
415 433-3700

(P-18899)
M ARTHUR GENSLER JR ASSOC INC (PA)
45 Fremont St Ste 1500, San Francisco (94105-2214)
PHONE..............................415 433-3700
Andy Cohen, *Co-CEO*
Robin Klehr Avia, *Ch of Bd*
Linda Havard, *CFO*
Diane Hoskins, *Co-CEO*
John Adams, *Principal*
EMP: 360 **EST:** 1965
SQ FT: 57,000
SALES: 1.2B **Privately Held**
WEB: www.gensler.com
SIC: 8712 Architectural services

(P-18900)
M ARTHUR GENSLER JR ASSOC INC
2101 Webster St Ste 2000, Oakland (94612-3032)
PHONE..............................510 625-7400
EMP: 207
SALES (corp-wide): 915.3MM **Privately Held**
SIC: 8712 Architectural Services
PA: M. Arthur Gensler Jr. & Associates, Inc.
2 Harrison St Fl 4
San Francisco CA 94105
415 433-3700

(P-18901)
MARTIN ATI-AC INC (PA)
Also Called: ATI Architects & Engineers
4750 Willow Rd Ste 250, Pleasanton (94588-2962)
PHONE..............................925 648-8800
Paul Didonato, *President*
Olliver Santos, *CFO*
Bruce Gillings, *Vice Pres*
Gmichael Goldsworthy, *Vice Pres*
Ysenia Cooper, *Administration*
EMP: 74 **EST:** 1989
SQ FT: 14,000
SALES (est): 12MM **Privately Held**
WEB: www.acmartin.com
SIC: 8712 8711 Architectural engineering; structural engineering

(P-18902)
MBH ARCHITECTS INC
960 Atlantic Ave Ste 100, Alameda (94501-1066)
PHONE..............................510 865-8663

Dennis Heath, *President*
Clay Fry, *Treasurer*
Joseph Smart, *Vice Pres*
John McNulty, *Principal*
Reena Nadkarni, *Principal*
EMP: 210 **EST:** 1989
SQ FT: 55,000
SALES (est): 36.8MM **Privately Held**
WEB: www.mbharch.com
SIC: 8712 Architectural engineering

(P-18903)
PEDRO MCCRCKEN DSIGN GROUP INC (PA)
Also Called: PM Design Group
6930 Destiny Dr Ste 100, Rocklin (95677-2989)
PHONE..............................916 415-5358
Roy Pedro, *President*
Jesse Macias, *Vice Pres*
Ken McCracken, *Vice Pres*
Ernest Wuethrich, *Program Mgr*
Andy Hellner, *Regional Mgr*
EMP: 35 **EST:** 2009
SQ FT: 4,000
SALES (est): 6.3MM **Privately Held**
WEB: www.pmdginc.com
SIC: 8712 Architectural services

(P-18904)
PERKINS + WILL INC
Also Called: Perkins & Will
2 Bryant St Ste 300, San Francisco (94105-1641)
PHONE..............................415 856-3000
Russ Drinker, *Branch Mgr*
Julia Decker-Steinkra, *Admin Asst*
EMP: 60
SALES (corp-wide): 606MM **Privately Held**
WEB: www.perkinswill.com
SIC: 8712 Architectural services
HQ: Will Perkins Inc
1222 22nd St Nw Ste 200
Washington DC 20037

(P-18905)
QUATTROCCHI KWOK ARCHITECTS
636 5th St, Santa Rosa (95404-4411)
PHONE..............................707 576-0829
Mark Quattrocchi, *President*
Steve Kwok, *CFO*
Terry Calder, *Admin Asst*
Craig Gaevert, *Project Mgr*
Paul Gard, *Project Mgr*
EMP: 48 **EST:** 1986
SQ FT: 6,000
SALES (est): 6.7MM **Privately Held**
WEB: www.qka.com
SIC: 8712 Architectural engineering

(P-18906)
RAINFORTH GRAU ARCHITECTS
2101 Capitol Ave Ste 100, Sacramento (95816-5781)
PHONE..............................916 368-7990
Jeffrey A Grau, *CEO*
Tim Dewitt, *COO*
Steve Smith, *QA Dir*
Timothy Dewitt, *Project Mgr*
Francis Mendez, *Project Mgr*
EMP: 37 **EST:** 2008
SALES (est): 6MM **Privately Held**
WEB: www.rainforthgrau.com
SIC: 8712 Architectural engineering

(P-18907)
RATCLIFF ARCHITECTS
5856 Doyle St, Emeryville (94608-2520)
PHONE..............................510 899-6400
Dan Wetherell, *President*
Scott Haney, *COO*
David Dersch, *CFO*
Derrick Barron, *Executive*
Joseph Nicola, *Business Dir*
EMP: 58 **EST:** 1906
SQ FT: 20,000
SALES (est): 11.6MM **Privately Held**
WEB: www.ratcliffarch.com
SIC: 8712 Architectural engineering

(P-18908)
REVEL ARCH & DESIGN INC (PA)
417 Montgomery St, San Francisco (94104-1129)
PHONE..............................415 230-7010
Gary Nichols, *CEO*
Kevin Likens, *Project Mgr*
Diego Garcia, *Manager*
James Hua, *Manager*
EMP: 63 **EST:** 2017
SALES (est): 5.3MM **Privately Held**
WEB: www.revelers.com
SIC: 8712 Architectural services

(P-18909)
RICHARD AVLAR ASSOC A CAL CORP
590 Ygnacio Valley Rd # 200, Walnut Creek (94596-3889)
PHONE..............................510 893-5501
Richard Avelar, *President*
Joseph G Garcia, *Architect*
EMP: 35 **EST:** 1976
SALES (est): 6.3MM **Privately Held**
SIC: 8712 Architectural engineering

(P-18910)
ROBINSON MILLS + WILLIAMS (PA)
Also Called: Rmw Architecture & Interiors
160 Pine St Ste 400, San Francisco (94111-5504)
PHONE..............................415 781-9800
Thomas B Gerfen, *Chairman*
Steven Worthington, *Partner*
Russ Nichols, *President*
Glenn Bauer, *Chairman*
Steve Guest, *Treasurer*
EMP: 35 **EST:** 1970
SQ FT: 12,870
SALES (est): 10.6MM **Privately Held**
SIC: 8712 7389 Architectural engineering; interior design services

(P-18911)
SB ARCHITECTS (PA)
415 Jackson St Ste 100, San Francisco (94111-1629)
PHONE..............................415 673-8990
Scott Lee, *CEO*
John Cisco, *CFO*
Joroy Friedman, *Vice Pres*
Pinar Harris, *Vice Pres*
Matt Page, *Vice Pres*
EMP: 41 **EST:** 1960
SALES (est): 16MM **Privately Held**
WEB: www.sb-architects.com
SIC: 8712 Architectural engineering

(P-18912)
SDG ARCHITECTS INC
3361 Walnut Blvd Ste 120, Brentwood (94513-4489)
PHONE..............................925 634-7000
Ralph Strauss, *President*
Jonathan Strauss, *CFO*
Gwyn Lewis, *Info Tech Mgr*
Scott Prickett, *Design Engr*
Roger Strauss, *Project Mgr*
EMP: 50 **EST:** 1993
SALES (est): 6.6MM **Privately Held**
WEB: www.sdgarchitectsinc.com
SIC: 8712 Architectural engineering

(P-18913)
SKIDMORE OWINGS & MERRILL LLP
1 Maritime Plz Fl 5, San Francisco (94111-3408)
PHONE..............................415 981-1555
Gene Schnair, *Partner*
Peter Jackson, *Partner*
John Kriken, *Partner*
Jana Huey, *Office Mgr*
Anne Scallan, *Executive Asst*
EMP: 240
SALES (corp-wide): 104.2MM **Privately Held**
WEB: www.som.com
SIC: 8712 Architectural engineering
PA: Skidmore, Owings & Merrill Llp
224 S Michigan Ave # 1000
Chicago IL 60604
312 554-9090

(PA)=Parent Co (HQ)=Headquarters (DH)=Div Headquarters
✪ = New Business established in last 2 years

8712 - Architectural Services

(P-18914)
SMITHGROUP INC
Also Called: Smithgroupjjr
301 Battery St Fl 7, San Francisco
(94111-3237)
PHONE.................................313 442-8351
Michael Medici, *President*
Russ Sykes, *Managing Prtnr*
Troy Thompson, *Managing Prtnr*
Kevin Piontkowski, *Treasurer*
Vince Avallone, *Vice Pres*
EMP: 146
SALES (corp-wide): 210.4MM **Privately Held**
WEB: www.smithgroup.com
SIC: 8712 Architectural engineering
HQ: Smithgroup, Inc.
 1700 New York Ave Nw # 100
 Washington DC 20006
 202 842-2100

(P-18915)
STANTEC ARCHITECTURE INC
1383 N Mcdowell Blvd # 25, Petaluma
(94954-1187)
PHONE.................................707 765-1660
Ike Tolks, *Branch Mgr*
James Thompson, *Info Tech Mgr*
Lori Van Dermark, *Marketing Staff*
EMP: 214
SALES (corp-wide): 3.6B **Privately Held**
WEB: www.stantec.com
SIC: 8712 8711 Architectural services; engineering services
HQ: Stantec Architecture Inc.
 224 S Michigan Ave # 1400
 Chicago IL 60604
 336 714-7413

(P-18916)
STV INCORPORATED
505 14th St Ste 1060, Oakland
(94612-1406)
PHONE.................................510 763-1313
EMP: 96
SALES (corp-wide): 261MM **Privately Held**
WEB: www.stvinc.com
SIC: 8712 Architectural engineering
HQ: Stv Incorporated
 225 Park Ave S Fl 5
 New York NY 10003
 212 529-2722

(P-18917)
WARNER WALKER ARCHITECTS
353 Folsom St Fl 1, San Francisco
(94105-2306)
PHONE.................................415 318-8900
Brooks Walker, *Partner*
Greg Warner, *Partner*
Canner Charlotte, *Office Mgr*
Sandrine Carmantrand, *Administration*
Hana Bittner, *Project Mgr*
EMP: 40 EST: 1994
SALES (est): 5.2MM **Privately Held**
WEB: www.walkerwarner.com
SIC: 8712 Architectural engineering

(P-18918)
WATRY DESIGN INC (PA)
2099 Gateway Pl Ste 550, San Jose
(95110-1051)
PHONE.................................408 392-7900
John D Purinton, *CEO*
Michelle Wendler, *President*
Elisabeth Blanton, *CFO*
David Lococo, *Vice Pres*
Anju Ram, *Admin Asst*
EMP: 41 EST: 1975
SQ FT: 1,600
SALES (est): 6.8MM **Privately Held**
WEB: www.watrydesign.com
SIC: 8712 Architectural engineering

(P-18919)
WRNS STUDIO (PA)
501 2nd St Ste 402, San Francisco
(94107-4132)
PHONE.................................415 489-2224
Jeff Warner, *CEO*
Adam Woltag, *COO*
David Englund, *CFO*
Sam Nunes, *Senior VP*
John Ruffo, *Senior VP*
EMP: 49 EST: 2005
SALES (est): 11.5MM **Privately Held**
WEB: www.wrnsstudio.com
SIC: 8712 Architectural engineering

8713 Surveying Services

(P-18920)
ANDREGG GEOMATICS
11661 Blocker Dr Ste 200, Auburn
(95603-4649)
PHONE.................................530 885-7072
Dennis Meyer, *President*
Mark Bardakjian, *COO*
Christine Johnson, *Admin Sec*
EMP: 52 EST: 1946
SALES (est): 3.5MM **Privately Held**
WEB: www.andregg.com
SIC: 8713 Surveying services

(P-18921)
BKF ENGINEERS
4670 Willow Rd Ste 250, Pleasanton
(94588-8589)
PHONE.................................925 396-7700
Natalina Bernardi, *Vice Pres*
Alonso Hernandez, *Technician*
Nguyen Kevin, *Design Engr*
Devon Kurcina, *Business Mgr*
EMP: 95
SALES (corp-wide): 72.8MM **Privately Held**
WEB: www.bkf.com
SIC: 8713 Surveying services
PA: Bkf Engineers
 255 Shoreline Dr Ste 200
 Redwood City CA 94065
 650 482-6300

(P-18922)
ETRAC INC
637 Lindaro St Ste 100, San Rafael
(94901-6027)
PHONE.................................415 462-0421
Michael Mueller, *President*
Erik Mueller, *Vice Pres*
Amit Jayakaran, *CTO*
Greg Gibson, *Manager*
Amanda Best, *Accounts Mgr*
EMP: 45 EST: 2011
SQ FT: 4,000
SALES (est): 5.2MM **Privately Held**
WEB: www.etracinc.com
SIC: 8713 Surveying services

(P-18923)
F3 AND ASSOCIATES INC (PA)
701 E H St, Benicia (94510-3567)
P.O. Box 5099, Petaluma (94955-5099)
PHONE.................................707 748-4300
Fred Feickert, *President*
Gene Feickert, *Partner*
Sean Finn, *Partner*
Michael Ferreira, *Project Mgr*
Chris Reis, *Project Mgr*
EMP: 70
SALES (est): 13MM **Privately Held**
WEB: www.f3-inc.com
SIC: 8713 Surveying services

(P-18924)
KIER WRGHT CVIL ENGNERS SRVYOR
2850 Collier Canyon Rd, Livermore
(94551-9201)
PHONE.................................925 245-8788
Tony McCants, *Manager*
Colin Clements, *CFO*
Joe Thompson, *Vice Pres*
Lea Ambler, *Administration*
Adam Carvalho, *Project Engr*
EMP: 50
SALES (corp-wide): 13.1MM **Privately Held**
WEB: www.kierwright.com
SIC: 8713 8711 Surveying services; civil engineering
PA: Kier & Wright Civil Engineers & Surveyors Inc
 3350 Scott Blvd Bldg 22
 Santa Clara CA 95054
 408 727-6665

(P-18925)
SANDIS CIVIL ENGINEERS (PA)
1700 Winchester Blvd, Campbell
(95008-1163)
PHONE.................................408 636-0900
Ken Olcott, *President*
Tony Brubaker, *Treasurer*
Jeff Setera, *Vice Pres*
Roy Latess, *Department Mgr*
Edrianne Aguilar, *Design Engr*
EMP: 61
SQ FT: 12,000
SALES (est): 17.9MM **Privately Held**
WEB: www.sandis.net
SIC: 8713 8711 Surveying services; civil engineering

(P-18926)
STANTEC ENERGY & RESOURCES INC
1340 Treat Blvd Ste 300, Walnut Creek
(94597-7966)
PHONE.................................925 627-4508
Gary Grelli, *Branch Mgr*
Graham Carey, *Project Mgr*
EMP: 144
SALES (corp-wide): 31.9MM **Privately Held**
SIC: 8713 Surveying services
HQ: Stantec Energy & Resources Inc.
 5500 Ming Ave Ste 410
 Bakersfield CA 93309
 661 396-3770

(P-18927)
SUBDYNAMIC LOCATING SVCS INC
274 Hillsdale Ave, San Jose (95136-1352)
P.O. Box 28827 (95159-8827)
PHONE.................................408 723-4191
Anthony Lobue, *CEO*
Lu Anne Lobue, *Corp Secy*
Chris Brunin, *Technician*
EMP: 36 EST: 1992
SQ FT: 3,000
SALES (est): 1.5MM **Privately Held**
WEB: www.subdynamic.com
SIC: 8713 7389 Surveying services; safety inspection service

(P-18928)
TOWILL INC (HQ)
Also Called: Swinerton
2300 Clayton Rd Ste 1200, Concord
(94520-2176)
PHONE.................................925 682-6976
Dennis Curtin, *President*
Aaron Badavinac, *CFO*
Aaron Bagger, *CFO*
Ken Meme, *Chairman*
Dawn Antonucci, *Vice Pres*
EMP: 35 EST: 1968
SQ FT: 18,000
SALES (est): 18.3MM **Privately Held**
WEB: www.towill.com
SIC: 8713 Photogrammetric engineering

8721 Accounting, Auditing & Bookkeeping Svcs

(P-18929)
ABBOTT STRNGHAM LYNCH A PROF A
1530 Meridian Ave 2, San Jose
(95125-5350)
PHONE.................................408 377-8700
Morgan Lynch, *President*
Ray Scheaffer, *President*
Franceen Borrillo, *Principal*
Bill Melton, *Principal*
Todd Robinson, *Principal*
EMP: 98 EST: 1977
SALES (est): 15.2MM **Privately Held**
WEB: www.aslcpa.com
SIC: 8721 Accounting services, except auditing; certified public accountant

(P-18930)
ALLEVITY HR INC
870 Manzanita Ct Ste A, Chico
(95926-2392)
PHONE.................................530 345-2486
Craig Ahlswede, *CEO*
Kevin Ahlswede, *Division Mgr*
Richard Barnes, *CIO*
Michelle Niven, *Human Resources*
Cassandra Ganzer, *Supervisor*
EMP: 55 EST: 2006
SALES (est): 3.9MM **Privately Held**
WEB: www.allevity.com
SIC: 8721 Payroll accounting service

(P-18931)
ARMANINO LLP
50 W San Fernando St, San Jose
(95113-2429)
PHONE.................................408 200-6400
Surbhi Bordia, *Managing Dir*
Rob Johnson, *Manager*
Laura Shannon, *Associate*
EMP: 45
SALES (corp-wide): 350MM **Privately Held**
WEB: www.armaninollp.com
SIC: 8721 8742 Certified public accountant; management consulting services
PA: Armanino Llp
 12657 Alcosta Blvd # 500
 San Ramon CA 94583
 925 790-2600

(P-18932)
ARMANINO LLP (PA)
12657 Alcosta Blvd # 500, San Ramon
(94583-4406)
PHONE.................................925 790-2600
Matt Armanino, *Managing Prtnr*
Linda Antonelli, *Partner*
David Greenamyre, *Partner*
Tim Hourigan, *Partner*
Robert Larue, *Partner*
EMP: 160 EST: 1969
SQ FT: 5,500
SALES (est): 350MM **Privately Held**
WEB: www.armaninollp.com
SIC: 8721 8742 Certified public accountant; management consulting services

(P-18933)
ARMANINO LLP
50 W San Fernando St # 60, San Jose
(95113-2429)
PHONE.................................408 200-6400
Gary Jones, *President*
Nghi Huynh, *Partner*
Ryan Teed, *Office Mgr*
Patrick Hall, *Senior Mgr*
David Meharg, *Senior Mgr*
EMP: 45
SALES (corp-wide): 350MM **Privately Held**
WEB: www.armaninollp.com
SIC: 8721 8742 Certified public accountant; management consulting services
PA: Armanino Llp
 12657 Alcosta Blvd # 500
 San Ramon CA 94583
 925 790-2600

(P-18934)
BOWMAN & CO LLP
10100 Trinity Pkwy # 310, Stockton
(95219-7240)
PHONE.................................209 473-1040
Taylor Welz, *Partner*
Herbert H Bowman, *Partner*
Richard D Cline, *Partner*
Gary R Daniel, *Partner*
Tara E Eastwood, *Partner*
EMP: 35 EST: 1949
SQ FT: 10,000
SALES (est): 3.6MM **Privately Held**
WEB: www.cpabowman.com
SIC: 8721 Certified public accountant

(P-18935)
BPM LLP
10 Almaden Blvd Ste 1000, San Jose
(95113-2238)
PHONE.................................408 961-6300
James Wallace, *Partner*
EMP: 100 EST: 2017
SALES (est): 5.3MM **Privately Held**
SIC: 8721 Accounting, auditing & bookkeeping

PRODUCTS & SERVICES SECTION
8721 - Accounting, Auditing & Bookkeeping Svcs County (P-18956)

(P-18936)
BPM LLP (PA)
Also Called: B P M
600 California St Fl 6, San Francisco (94108-2733)
PHONE.................................415 421-5757
Mark Berger, *Managing Prtnr*
Kenneth Dansie, *Partner*
Philip Leibowitz, *Partner*
Sandy Murray, *Partner*
Jackie Matsumura, *Shareholder*
EMP: 55 **EST:** 2016
SALES (est): 38.7MM **Privately Held**
WEB: www.bpmcpa.com
SIC: 8721 Certified public accountant

(P-18937)
BURR PILGER MAYER INC
110 Stony Point Rd # 210, Santa Rosa (95401-4189)
PHONE.................................707 544-4078
Carolyn Amster, *Principal*
Craig Hamm, *Partner*
Joseph C Kitts, *Shareholder*
Carol S O'Hara, *Shareholder*
Beth Baldwin, *Officer*
EMP: 51
SALES (corp-wide): 42.6MM **Privately Held**
WEB: www.bpmcpa.com
SIC: 8721 Certified public accountant
PA: Burr Pilger Mayer, Inc.
  600 California St Fl 6
  San Francisco CA 94108
  415 421-5757

(P-18938)
BURR PILGER MAYER INC (PA)
600 California St Fl 6, San Francisco (94108-2733)
PHONE.................................415 421-5757
James Wallace, *CEO*
Rich Bellucci, *Partner*
Norm Bustamante, *Partner*
Brian Finnegan, *Partner*
Terry Hill, *Partner*
EMP: 110 **EST:** 1986
SQ FT: 20,824
SALES (est): 42.6MM **Privately Held**
WEB: www.bpmcpa.com
SIC: 8721 Certified public accountant

(P-18939)
BURR PILGER MAYER INC
2001 N Main St Ste 360, Walnut Creek (94596-7253)
PHONE.................................925 296-1040
Marc Berger, *Branch Mgr*
Brad Holsworth, *Shareholder*
Cecilia Albay, *Admin Asst*
Michael Lawrence Jr, *Network Enginr*
EMP: 51
SALES (corp-wide): 42.6MM **Privately Held**
WEB: www.bpmcpa.com
SIC: 8721 Certified public accountant
PA: Burr Pilger Mayer, Inc.
  600 California St Fl 6
  San Francisco CA 94108
  415 421-5757

(P-18940)
BURR PILGER MAYER INC
10 Almaden Blvd Ste 1000, San Jose (95113-2238)
PHONE.................................408 961-6300
Mark Loveless, *Manager*
Michael Schaffer, *Accountant*
Maggie Vuong, *Marketing Staff*
Carl Hu, *Director*
Brian Finnegan, *Manager*
EMP: 51
SALES (corp-wide): 42.6MM **Privately Held**
WEB: www.bpmcpa.com
SIC: 8721 Certified public accountant
PA: Burr Pilger Mayer, Inc.
  600 California St Fl 6
  San Francisco CA 94108
  415 421-5757

(P-18941)
BURR PILGER MAYER INC
4200 Bohannon Dr Ste 250, Menlo Park (94025-1021)
PHONE.................................650 855-6800
Mark Loveless, *Branch Mgr*
Sharon Selleck, *QA Dir*
Rich McDonnell, *CPA*
Eugene Pong, *Manager*
EMP: 51
SALES (corp-wide): 42.6MM **Privately Held**
WEB: www.bpmcpa.com
SIC: 8721 Certified public accountant
PA: Burr Pilger Mayer, Inc.
  600 California St Fl 6
  San Francisco CA 94108
  415 421-5757

(P-18942)
CALIFRNIA STATE TCHERS RTRMENT
915 L St Fl 7, Sacramento (95814-3705)
PHONE.................................916 445-0211
Freda Luan-Dun, *Branch Mgr*
Ricardo Duran, *Officer*
Gabriel Juarez, *Officer*
Nicolas Kimmie, *Officer*
Chris Moore, *Officer*
EMP: 50 **Privately Held**
WEB: www.calstrs.com
SIC: 8721 Accounting, auditing & bookkeeping
HQ: California State Teachers Retirement System
  100 Waterfront Pl
  West Sacramento CA 95605

(P-18943)
CAPINCROUSE LLP
5990 Stoneridge Dr, Pleasanton (94588-4517)
PHONE.................................925 201-1187
EMP: 88
SALES (corp-wide): 10.3MM **Privately Held**
WEB: www.capincrouse.com
SIC: 8721 Certified public accountant
PA: Capincrouse Llp
  9511 Angola Ct Ste 221
  Indianapolis IN 46268
  317 885-2620

(P-18944)
CHERRY BEKAERT LLP
1676 N Calif Blvd Fl 3, Walnut Creek (94596-4144)
PHONE.................................925 954-0100
Wallace F Helin, *Partner*
EMP: 41
SALES (corp-wide): 194.7MM **Privately Held**
WEB: www.cbh.com
SIC: 8721 Certified public accountant
PA: Cherry Bekaert Llp
  200 S 10th St Ste 900
  Richmond VA 23219
  804 673-5700

(P-18945)
CLIFTONLARSONALLEN LLP
925 Highland Pointe Dr # 450, Roseville (95678-5427)
PHONE.................................916 784-7800
Mark Walker, *CPA*
Patrick Risse, *Director*
EMP: 300
SALES (corp-wide): 755.1MM **Privately Held**
WEB: www.blogs.claconnect.com
SIC: 8721 Certified public accountant
PA: Cliftonlarsonallen Llp
  220 S 6th St Ste 300
  Minneapolis MN 55402
  612 376-4500

(P-18946)
COLLABRUS INC
Also Called: M Squared Consulting
180 Montgomery St # 2380, San Francisco (94104-4228)
PHONE.................................415 288-1826
Alex Todd, *CEO*
Anna Araman, *Partner*
Russel Orelowitz, *CFO*
Rhonelle Deleon, *Opers Staff*
Mike Horwath, *Opers Staff*
EMP: 240 **EST:** 1995
SALES (est): 11.7MM
SALES (corp-wide): 77.7MM **Privately Held**
WEB: www.collabrus.com
SIC: 8721 Billing & bookkeeping service
HQ: M Squared Consulting, Inc.
  180 Montgomery St # 2380
  San Francisco CA 94104
  415 391-1038

(P-18947)
DE GREGORI GORMSEN RINGER LLP
1401 N Hunter St, Stockton (95202-1105)
P.O. Box 8540 (95208-0540)
PHONE.................................209 944-0740
John H Degregori, *Partner*
Peter Gormsen, *Partner*
Bill Ringer, *Partner*
John H De Gregori, *CPA*
Gabrielle Hartzler, *CPA*
EMP: 42 **EST:** 1963
SQ FT: 5,000
SALES (est): 2.4MM **Privately Held**
WEB: www.dgr-cpas.com
SIC: 8721 Certified public accountant

(P-18948)
DELOITTE & TOUCHE LLP
225 W Santa Clara St # 600, San Jose (95113-1728)
PHONE.................................408 704-4000
Jonathan Tharmapalan, *Manager*
Sam Parikh, *Managing Dir*
Matthew Thoma Collins, *Partner*
Tracey Parry, *Corp Comm Staff*
Edgar Meza,
EMP: 450
SALES (corp-wide): 768.6K **Privately Held**
WEB: www.deloitte.com
SIC: 8721 8742 6282 Certified public accountant; management consulting services; investment advice
HQ: Deloitte & Touche Llp
  30 Rockefeller Plz # 4350
  New York NY 10112
  212 492-4000

(P-18949)
DELOITTE TAX LLP
555 Mission St Ste 1400, San Francisco (94105-0942)
PHONE.................................415 783-4000
Mark Edmunds, *Branch Mgr*
Kirby Rattenbury, *Partner*
Donna Bernal-Silva, *CFO*
Jon Contreras, *Managing Dir*
Michele Ruskin, *Managing Dir*
EMP: 294
SALES (corp-wide): 768.6K **Privately Held**
WEB: www.deloitte.com
SIC: 8721 Auditing services; certified public accountant
HQ: Deloitte Tax Llp
  30 Rockefeller Plz
  New York NY 10112
  212 492-4000

(P-18950)
DEMERA DMERA CMRON AN ACCNTNCY
5080 N Fruit Ave Ste 101, Fresno (93711-3062)
PHONE.................................559 226-9200
Howard J Demera, *President*
Evin Edwards, *Department Mgr*
John Houlihan, *Admin Sec*
Shelly Broadstreet, *Administration*
Lisa Kjar, *Administration*
EMP: 35 **EST:** 1960
SQ FT: 12,000
SALES (est): 589.6K **Privately Held**
WEB: www.ddccpa.com
SIC: 8721 Certified public accountant

(P-18951)
DRISAS GROOM MCCORMICK
7511 N Remington Ave, Fresno (93711-5757)
PHONE.................................559 447-8484
Ken Groom, *Partner*
Denise Waite, *CTO*
Natalie Hinds, *Accountant*
David Mendoza, *Accountant*
James Enns, *CPA*
EMP: 60 **EST:** 1981
SALES (est): 3.3MM **Privately Held**
WEB: www.dgmcpa.com
SIC: 8721 5734 Accounting services, except auditing; modems, monitors, terminals & disk drives: computers

(P-18952)
EIDE BAILLY LLP
2151 River Plaza Dr # 308, Sacramento (95833-3881)
PHONE.................................916 570-1880
Kevin Pulliam, *Managing Prtnr*
EMP: 41
SALES (corp-wide): 339.7MM **Privately Held**
WEB: www.eidebailly.com
SIC: 8721 Certified public accountant
PA: Eide Bailly Llp
  4310 17th Ave S
  Fargo ND 58103
  701 239-8500

(P-18953)
EIDE BAILLY LLP
1900 S Norfolk St Ste 225, San Mateo (94403-1166)
PHONE.................................650 462-0400
Richard Blake, *Partner*
Sandy Donnell, *Office Mgr*
Susan Nazari, *Accountant*
Andrea Williams, *Accountant*
Dennis Mydlowski, *CPA*
EMP: 41
SALES (corp-wide): 339.7MM **Privately Held**
WEB: www.eidebailly.com
SIC: 8721 Certified public accountant
PA: Eide Bailly Llp
  4310 17th Ave S
  Fargo ND 58103
  701 239-8500

(P-18954)
EIDE BAILLY LLP
Also Called: Vavrinek Trine Day & Co
6051 N Fresno St Ste 101, Fresno (93710-5280)
PHONE.................................559 248-0871
Bill Williams, *Partner*
David Ruiz, *Accountant*
Sandra Gallegos, *Bookkeeper*
Danni Guo, *Manager*
Tim Haynes, *Manager*
EMP: 41
SALES (corp-wide): 339.7MM **Privately Held**
WEB: www.eidebailly.com
SIC: 8721 Certified public accountant
PA: Eide Bailly Llp
  4310 17th Ave S
  Fargo ND 58103
  701 239-8500

(P-18955)
EISNERAMPER LLP
1 Market Ste 620, San Francisco (94105-5105)
PHONE.................................415 974-6000
John Williamson, *Managing Prtnr*
Mahi Saraf, *Human Res Mgr*
Aleena Herrera, *Marketing Staff*
Kelly Mattner, *Senior Mgr*
EMP: 225
SALES (corp-wide): 383.2MM **Privately Held**
WEB: www.eisneramper.com
SIC: 8721 Certified public accountant
PA: Eisneramper Llp
  733 3rd Ave Fl 9
  New York NY 10017
  212 949-8700

(P-18956)
EISNERAMPER LLP
3001 Douglas Blvd Ste 350, Roseville (95661-4230)
PHONE.................................916 563-7790
Sarah Mossman, *Administration*
EMP: 225
SALES (corp-wide): 383.2MM **Privately Held**
WEB: www.eisneramper.com
SIC: 8721 Certified public accountant

8721 - Accounting, Auditing & Bookkeeping Svcs County (P-18957)

PA: Eisneramper Llp
733 3rd Ave Fl 9
New York NY 10017
212 949-8700

(P-18957)
ERNEST J WINTTER
Also Called: Ernst Wintter and Assoc
675 Ygnacio Valley Rd A200, Walnut Creek (94596-3860)
PHONE.....................925 933-2626
Ernest Wintter, *Owner*
Ernst Wintter, *Owner*
Ming An, *Accountant*
Benjamin Lesser, *CPA*
EMP: 45 **EST:** 1987
SALES (est): 3.4MM **Privately Held**
WEB: www.ewallp.com
SIC: 8721 Certified public accountant

(P-18958)
ERNST & YOUNG LLP
560 Mission St Ste 1600, San Francisco (94105-0911)
PHONE.....................415 894-8000
EMP: 700
SALES (corp-wide): 3B **Privately Held**
SIC: 8721 Accounting/Auditing/Bookkeeping
PA: Ernst & Young Llp
5 Times Sq Fl Conlv1
New York NY 10001
212 773-3000

(P-18959)
GILBERT ASSOCIATES INC
2880 Gateway Oaks Dr # 100, Sacramento (95833-4329)
PHONE.....................916 646-6464
David L June, *President*
David Ljung, *President*
Sarah Ellis, *CFO*
Linda Geery, *Vice Pres*
Kevin Wong, *Admin Sec*
EMP: 35 **EST:** 2010
SALES (est): 5.2MM **Privately Held**
WEB: www.gilbertcpa.com
SIC: 8721 Certified public accountant

(P-18960)
GRIMBLEBY CLMAN CRTIF PUB ACCN
200 W Roseburg Ave, Modesto (95350-5255)
PHONE.....................209 527-4220
Clive T Grimbleby, *President*
Clayton Hobbs, *Accountant*
Connie Kendall, *Accountant*
Nathan Miller, *Client Mgr*
EMP: 71 **EST:** 1981
SQ FT: 1,000
SALES (est): 2.5MM **Privately Held**
WEB: www.grimbleby-coleman.com
SIC: 8721 Certified public accountant

(P-18961)
GRYPHON FINANCIAL GROUP INC
855 Jarvis Dr Ste 70, Morgan Hill (95037-2858)
P.O. Box 2110 (95038-2110)
PHONE.....................408 825-2500
Sean A Rositano, *President*
Stephen Bashada, *Exec VP*
Bernd Haetzel, *Exec VP*
Robert Jones, *Exec VP*
Craigj Berry, *Vice Pres*
EMP: 50 **EST:** 2005
SQ FT: 11,700
SALES (est): 8.1MM **Privately Held**
WEB: www.gryphonfg.com
SIC: 8721 Auditing services

(P-18962)
HOOD & STRONG LLP (PA)
275 Battery St Ste 900, San Francisco (94111-3332)
PHONE.....................415 781-0793
Robert Raffo, *Managing Prtnr*
Raul Hernandez, *Partner*
Steve Piuma, *Partner*
Yvette Rangel, *Executive Asst*
Claudia Perez-Valdez, *Accountant*
EMP: 75 **EST:** 1917
SQ FT: 13,000
SALES (est): 13.9MM **Privately Held**
WEB: www.hoodstrong.com
SIC: 8721 Certified public accountant

(P-18963)
INTERPACIFIC GROUP INC
576 Beale St, San Francisco (94105-2019)
PHONE.....................415 442-0711
Dave Smith, *President*
Megan Devlin-Preiksa, *VP Mktg*
EMP: 1306 **EST:** 1986
SALES (est): 9.1MM **Privately Held**
WEB: www.inter-pacific.com
SIC: 8721 Accounting, auditing & bookkeeping

(P-18964)
KPMG LLP
55 2nd St Ste 1400, San Francisco (94105-4557)
PHONE.....................415 963-5100
Louis P Miramontes, *Managing Prtnr*
Barbara Carbone, *Partner*
Alan Chinn, *Partner*
Glenn M Farrell, *Partner*
Brad Fisher, *Partner*
EMP: 50
SQ FT: 4,325
SALES (corp-wide): 1.3B **Privately Held**
WEB: www.kpmg.us
SIC: 8721 Certified public accountant
PA: Kpmg Llp
345 Park Ave
New York NY 10154
212 758-9700

(P-18965)
LINDQUIST LLP (PA)
5000 Executive Pkwy # 400, San Ramon (94583-4210)
PHONE.....................925 277-9100
Barry Omahen, *Partner*
James Browning, *Partner*
Mark Flanagan, *Partner*
Alan C Lindquist, *Partner*
Kimberly Ray, *Partner*
EMP: 57 **EST:** 1994
SALES (est): 11.4MM **Privately Held**
WEB: www.lindquistcpa.com
SIC: 8721 Certified public accountant

(P-18966)
LINDQUIST VON HUSEN & JOYCE
301 Howard St Ste 850, San Francisco (94105-6672)
PHONE.....................415 957-9999
Scott Seamands, *Partner*
Paul Cameron, *Partner*
Duane Frisbey, *Partner*
Stephen Hinshaw, *Partner*
Rod Johnson, *Partner*
EMP: 40 **EST:** 1935
SQ FT: 8,000
SALES (est): 4.6MM **Privately Held**
WEB: www.lvhj.com
SIC: 8721 Certified public accountant

(P-18967)
LINKENHMER LLT CPAS ADVSORS LL
187 Concourse Blvd, Santa Rosa (95403-8217)
PHONE.....................707 546-0272
Cecil Humes, *Managing Prtnr*
Timothy Delaney, *Partner*
John Jones, *Partner*
Jennifer Brown, *Accountant*
Rodrigo Nunez, *Accountant*
EMP: 46 **EST:** 1956
SQ FT: 6,000
SALES (est): 1.6MM **Privately Held**
WEB: www.linkcpa.com
SIC: 8721 Certified public accountant

(P-18968)
LLP MOSS ADAMS
2882 Prospect Park Dr # 300, Rancho Cordova (95670-6059)
PHONE.....................916 503-8100
Robert Ahern, *Branch Mgr*
Barbara Collom, *Executive Asst*
Coleman Jane, *Tax Mgr*
Irene Lewis, *Marketing Staff*
Bob Sullivan, *Director*
EMP: 67
SALES (corp-wide): 317.2MM **Privately Held**
WEB: www.mossadams.com
SIC: 8721 Certified public accountant
PA: Moss Adams Llp
999 3rd Ave Ste 2800
Seattle WA 98104
206 302-6800

(P-18969)
LLP MOSS ADAMS
3121 W March Ln Ste 100, Stockton (95219-2367)
PHONE.....................209 955-6100
David Gellerman, *Principal*
Chad Duval, *Partner*
Lorrie Bernstein, *Senior Mgr*
Adam Hite, *Manager*
EMP: 67
SALES (corp-wide): 317.2MM **Privately Held**
WEB: www.mossadams.com
SIC: 8721 Certified public accountant
PA: Moss Adams Llp
999 3rd Ave Ste 2800
Seattle WA 98104
206 302-6800

(P-18970)
LLP MOSS ADAMS
101 2nd St Ste 900, San Francisco (94105-3650)
PHONE.....................415 956-1500
Joy Robinson, *Branch Mgr*
Dan Cheyney, *Partner*
Caryl Thorp, *Partner*
Eric Tostenrud, *Partner*
Paul Tucci, *Partner*
EMP: 67
SALES (corp-wide): 317.2MM **Privately Held**
WEB: www.mossadams.com
SIC: 8721 Certified public accountant
PA: Moss Adams Llp
999 3rd Ave Ste 2800
Seattle WA 98104
206 302-6800

(P-18971)
LLP MOSS ADAMS
635 Campbell Tech Pkwy, Campbell (95008-5071)
PHONE.....................408 369-2400
Vid Lock, *Partner*
Mary Martin, *Admin Asst*
Wendy Couch, *Technician*
Melissa Geow, *Accountant*
Simran Kaur, *Accountant*
EMP: 67
SALES (corp-wide): 317.2MM **Privately Held**
WEB: www.mossadams.com
SIC: 8721 Certified public accountant
PA: Moss Adams Llp
999 3rd Ave Ste 2800
Seattle WA 98104
206 302-6800

(P-18972)
LLP MOSS ADAMS
3558 Round Barn Blvd # 300, Santa Rosa (95403-0992)
PHONE.....................707 527-0800
Jeff Gutsch, *Branch Mgr*
EMP: 67
SALES (corp-wide): 317.2MM **Privately Held**
WEB: www.mossadams.com
SIC: 8721 Certified public accountant
PA: Moss Adams Llp
999 3rd Ave Ste 2800
Seattle WA 98104
206 302-6800

(P-18973)
MACIAS GINI & OCONNELL LLP (PA)
500 Capitol Mall Ste 2200, Sacramento (95814-4759)
PHONE.....................916 928-4600
Kevin O'Connell, *Partner*
Kevin O Connell, *Partner*
Ernest Gini, *Partner*
Jim Godsey, *Partner*
Rick Green, *Partner*
EMP: 75 **EST:** 1992
SQ FT: 12,000
SALES (est): 78.5MM **Privately Held**
WEB: www.mgocpa.com
SIC: 8721 Certified public accountant

(P-18974)
MARCUM LLP
111 W Saint John St # 1010, San Jose (95113-1113)
PHONE.....................408 918-0900
George Uccelli, *Branch Mgr*
Judy Lee-Strain, *Executive*
Stacy McGoldrick, *Accountant*
Yifan Y Zhang, *CPA*
EMP: 47
SALES (corp-wide): 212.1MM **Privately Held**
WEB: www.marcumllp.com
SIC: 8721 Certified public accountant
PA: Marcum Llp
730 3rd Ave Fl 11
New York NY 10017
212 485-5500

(P-18975)
MARCUM LLP
1 Montgomery St Ste 1700, San Francisco (94104-5517)
PHONE.....................415 432-6200
Hugh Tama, *Manager*
EMP: 47
SALES (corp-wide): 212.1MM **Privately Held**
WEB: www.marcumllp.com
SIC: 8721 Certified public accountant
PA: Marcum Llp
730 3rd Ave Fl 11
New York NY 10017
212 485-5500

(P-18976)
MARKETMILE INC
3965 Freedom Cir Fl 11 Flr 11, Mountain View (94043)
PHONE.....................650 903-5600
Stephen Savignano, *CEO*
Mark Kelly, *CFO*
John M Corsi, *Vice Pres*
Elizabeth George, *Controller*
Steven D Levine, *VP Mktg*
EMP: 41 **EST:** 2000
SQ FT: 5,000
SALES (est): 751.7K **Privately Held**
SIC: 8721 8742 Accounting, auditing & bookkeeping; management consulting services

(P-18977)
MAZE & ASSOC ACCOUNTING CORP
3478 Buskirk Ave Ste 215, Pleasant Hill (94523-4346)
PHONE.....................925 930-0902
Timothy Kirsch, *CEO*
Timothy J Krisch, *CEO*
Chris Hunt, *COO*
Katherine Yuen, *Vice Pres*
David Alvey, *Principal*
EMP: 60 **EST:** 1979
SALES (est): 8.1MM **Privately Held**
WEB: www.mazeassociates.com
SIC: 8721 7299 Accounting services, except auditing; information services, consumer

(P-18978)
MED-DATA INCORPORATED
3741 Douglas Blvd Ste 170, Roseville (95661-4271)
PHONE.....................916 771-1362
Bruce Stewart, *Branch Mgr*
Emily Arias, *Vice Pres*
Julie Diaz, *Vice Pres*
Robert J Wagner, *Vice Pres*
Alma Guerra, *Exec Dir*
EMP: 100
SALES (corp-wide): 9.1MM **Privately Held**
WEB: www.meddata.com
SIC: 8721 Accounting services, except auditing
PA: Med-Data, Incorporated
3326 160th Ave Se Ste 440
Bellevue WA 98008
800 261-0048

PRODUCTS & SERVICES SECTION
8721 - Accounting, Auditing & Bookkeeping Svcs County (P-19000)

(P-18979)
MEDAMERICA BILLING SVCS INC (HQ)
Also Called: California Emergency Physician
1601 Cummins Dr Ste D, Modesto (95358-6411)
PHONE..................................209 491-7710
Michael F Harrington, *CEO*
Erik Davenport, *Partner*
James V Proffitt, *Officer*
Shawn Wood, *Administration*
Tony Carolla, *Programmer Anys*
EMP: 393 **EST:** 1993
SQ FT: 75,000
SALES (est): 37MM
SALES (corp-wide): 500MM **Privately Held**
WEB: www.vituity.com
SIC: 8721 Billing & bookkeeping service
PA: Cep America-California
2100 Powell St Ste 900
Emeryville CA 94608
510 350-2700

(P-18980)
NIGRO KRLIN SGAL FLDSTEIN BLNO
1 Embarcadero Ctr # 3840, San Francisco (94111-3628)
PHONE..................................415 463-1300
EMP: 257
SALES (corp-wide): 213.2K **Privately Held**
WEB: www.nksfb.com
SIC: 8721 Certified public accountant
PA: Nigro Karlin Segal Feldstein & Bolno, Llc.
10960 Wilshire Blvd Fl 5
Los Angeles CA 90024
310 277-4657

(P-18981)
PAIGE PRICE & CO
Also Called: Hinojosa, Fausto CPA
570 N Magnolia Ave # 100, Clovis (93611-9209)
PHONE..................................559 299-9540
Robert Price, *President*
Henry Oum, *Partner*
Fausto Jinojosa, *Principal*
Bennie Neal, *Admin Asst*
Andrea Gutierrez, *Administration*
EMP: 85 **EST:** 1976
SALES (est): 5.5MM **Privately Held**
WEB: www.ppcpas.com
SIC: 8721 Accounting services, except auditing

(P-18982)
PAYCHEX INC
50 Iron Point Cir Ste 200, Folsom (95630-8594)
PHONE..................................916 983-0303
Anita Mc Afee, *Branch Mgr*
Vickie Franklin, *Human Resources*
Danita McAfee, *Accounts Mgr*
EMP: 70
SALES (corp-wide): 3.3B **Publicly Held**
WEB: www.paychex.com
SIC: 8721 Payroll accounting service
PA: Paychex, Inc.
911 Panorama Trl S
Rochester NY 14625
585 385-6666

(P-18983)
PERRY-SMITH LLP
400 Capitol Mall Ste 1400, Sacramento (95814-4498)
PHONE..................................916 441-1000
Gary A Fox, *Managing Prtnr*
David T Becker, *Partner*
Jeffrey A Bertleson, *Partner*
Jeffrey Claire, *Partner*
Sue Cordonnier, *Partner*
EMP: 39 **EST:** 1985
SALES (est): 4.4MM **Privately Held**
WEB: www.perry-smith.com
SIC: 8721 Certified public accountant

(P-18984)
PETRINOVICH PUGH & COMPANY
Also Called: Petrinovich Pugh & Company
333 W Santa Clara St # 830, San Jose (95113-1716)
PHONE..................................408 287-7911
Marc Parkinson, *Managing Prtnr*
Tom Wagstaff, *Partner*
Laurie Campbell, *Accountant*
Kevin Kong, *Accountant*
Alyssa Campbell, *CPA*
EMP: 45 **EST:** 1951
SQ FT: 9,000
SALES (est): 7.5MM **Privately Held**
WEB: www.ppandco.com
SIC: 8721 Certified public accountant

(P-18985)
PRICEWATERHOUSECOOPERS LLP
488 Almaden Blvd Ste 1800, San Jose (95110-2768)
PHONE..................................408 817-3700
Don McGovern, *Branch Mgr*
Jeff Hersh, *Partner*
Marc Suidan, *Partner*
Trudy Doucet, *Executive*
Christine Galloni, *Executive Asst*
EMP: 700
SALES (corp-wide): 6.7B **Privately Held**
WEB: www.pwc.com
SIC: 8721 Certified public accountant
PA: Pricewaterhousecoopers Llp
300 Madison Ave
New York NY 10017
646 471-4000

(P-18986)
PROFESSNAL BLLING MGT SVCS INC
220 Standiford Ave Ste F, Modesto (95350-1159)
PHONE..................................209 579-5628
Janet Selover, *President*
EMP: 35 **EST:** 1987
SQ FT: 3,300
SALES (est): 2.5MM **Privately Held**
WEB: www.professionalbilling.net
SIC: 8721 Billing & bookkeeping service

(P-18987)
PROMERIO INC (PA)
Also Called: California Payroll
1240 Central Blvd Ste B, Brentwood (94513-2247)
PHONE..................................925 240-2400
Henry Lonsdale, *President*
Lindsey Gardiner, *Sales Staff*
Sandy Rodriguez, *Manager*
EMP: 77 **EST:** 2004
SALES (est): 6.9MM **Privately Held**
WEB: www.californiapayroll.com
SIC: 8721 Payroll accounting service

(P-18988)
ROSERYAN INC
35473 Dumbarton Ct, Newark (94560-1100)
PHONE..................................510 456-3056
Kathleen M Ryan, *President*
David Roberson, *Vice Pres*
Cody Strub, *Vice Pres*
Pat Voll, *Vice Pres*
Stan Fels, *Business Dir*
EMP: 60 **EST:** 2004
SALES (est): 5.8MM **Privately Held**
WEB: www.roseryan.com
SIC: 8721 Accounting, auditing & bookkeeping

(P-18989)
RSM US LLP
100 W San Fernando St, San Jose (95113-2219)
PHONE..................................408 572-4440
EMP: 84
SALES (corp-wide): 2.4B **Privately Held**
SIC: 8721 Accounting, Auditing, And Bookkeeping
PA: Rsm Us Llp
1 S Wacker Dr Ste 800
Chicago IL 60606
312 384-6000

(P-18990)
SCOTT BALDWIN CPAS A PROF CORP
990 Reserve Dr Ste 120, Roseville (95678-1391)
PHONE..................................916 722-2524
David Scott, *President*
EMP: 46 **EST:** 1991
SALES (est): 6.2MM **Privately Held**
SIC: 8721 Certified public accountant

(P-18991)
SEILER LLP (PA)
3 Lagoon Dr Ste 400, Redwood City (94065-5157)
P.O. Box 8043 (94063-0943)
PHONE..................................650 365-4646
George Marinos, *Partner*
Mark Berryman, *Partner*
James G B Demartini III, *Partner*
Brian J Dinsmore, *Partner*
Kenneth Everett, *Partner*
EMP: 102 **EST:** 1957
SQ FT: 31,142
SALES (est): 28.5MM **Privately Held**
WEB: www.seiler.com
SIC: 8721 Certified public accountant

(P-18992)
SEILER LLP
220 Montgomery St Ste 300, San Francisco (94104-3436)
PHONE..................................415 392-2123
Brian Jeffs, *Manager*
Arlan Kertz, *Partner*
Debra McCall, *Partner*
Jim Boyle, *Managing Dir*
Jose Aleman, *Analyst*
EMP: 57
SQ FT: 10,230
SALES (corp-wide): 28.5MM **Privately Held**
WEB: www.seiler.com
SIC: 8721 Certified public accountant
PA: Seiler Llp
3 Lagoon Dr Ste 400
Redwood City CA 94065
650 365-4646

(P-18993)
SENSIBA SAN FILIPPO LLP (PA)
5960 Inglewood Dr Ste 201, Pleasanton (94588-8611)
P.O. Box 11897 (94588-1897)
PHONE..................................925 271-8700
John Sansiba, *Managing Prtnr*
Robert De Marta, *Partner*
Stephen De Martini, *Partner*
Gordon Dito, *Partner*
Maurice Eckley, *Partner*
EMP: 35 **EST:** 1975
SALES (est): 21.9MM **Privately Held**
WEB: www.ssfllp.com
SIC: 8721 Accounting services, except auditing

(P-18994)
SHEA LBAGH DBBRSTEIN CRTIF PUB (PA)
44 Montgomery St Ste 3200, San Francisco (94104-4805)
PHONE..................................415 308-1368
James Dobberstein, *President*
Ron Simonian, *Treasurer*
Gregory T Labagh, *Vice Pres*
Tom Jackson, *Admin Sec*
Karen Salinas, *Admin Asst*
EMP: 50 **EST:** 1944
SQ FT: 15,000
SALES (est): 11.3MM **Privately Held**
WEB: www.sldcpa.com
SIC: 8721 Certified public accountant

(P-18995)
SQUAR MILNER PETERSON
135 Main St Fl 9, San Francisco (94105-1815)
PHONE..................................415 781-2500
Christine Tsoi, *Sr Associate*
Patricia Gayler, *Manager*
Kevin Oconnell, *Manager*
Angela Fong, *Supervisor*
Roxanne Magpantay, *Supervisor*
EMP: 35
SALES (corp-wide): 45.8MM **Privately Held**
WEB: www.bakertilly.com
SIC: 8721 Certified public accountant
PA: Squar, Milner, Peterson, Miranda & Williamson, Certified Public Accountants, Llp
18500 Von Karman Ave # 10
Irvine CA 92612
949 222-2999

(P-18996)
STAMPLI INC
191 Castro St Fl 2, Mountain View (94041-1201)
PHONE..................................650 963-9429
Eyal Feldman, *CEO*
Shane Hamby, *Vice Pres*
Tiffaney Quintana, *Vice Pres*
Tiffaney F Quintana, *Vice Pres*
Lisa Elie, *Executive*
EMP: 46 **EST:** 2016
SALES (est): 3.4MM **Privately Held**
WEB: www.stampli.com
SIC: 8721 Accounting, auditing & bookkeeping
PA: Stampli Ltd
144 Begin Menachem Rd
Tel Aviv-Jaffa

(P-18997)
STATE CENTER CMNTY COLLEGE DST
Also Called: Fresno City College Bus Off
1101 E University Ave, Fresno (93741-0001)
PHONE..................................559 442-4600
Carole Goldsmith, *President*
Cathy Kozielski, *Technician*
Darren Adams, *Instructor*
Brian Gallo, *Instructor*
CAM Olson, *Director*
EMP: 64
SALES (corp-wide): 114.5MM **Privately Held**
WEB: www.scccd.edu
SIC: 8222 8721 Community college; accounting, auditing & bookkeeping
PA: State Center Community College District
1171 Fulton St
Fresno CA 93721
559 226-0720

(P-18998)
SURGICAL CARE AFFILIATE
Also Called: TAC Rbo
2450 Venture Oaks Way # 120, Sacramento (95833-3292)
PHONE..................................916 529-4590
EMP: 50 **EST:** 2011
SALES (est): 2.7MM **Privately Held**
SIC: 8721 Accounting/Auditing/Bookkeeping

(P-18999)
SYMED CORPORATION
215 Gateway Rd W Ste 101, NAPA (94558-7593)
P.O. Box 238 (94559-0238)
PHONE..................................707 255-3300
Arthur Roosa, *CEO*
EMP: 31
SQ FT: 14,400
SALES: 3.2MM **Privately Held**
WEB: www.symed.net
SIC: 8721 7372 Billing & bookkeeping service; prepackaged software

(P-19000)
TEAMWORKS INC (PA)
2398 Walsh Ave, Santa Clara (95051-1301)
PHONE..................................408 243-3970
Carol Hower, *President*
Beatrice Karadeema, *Exec Dir*
EMP: 40 **EST:** 1994
SQ FT: 1,000
SALES (est): 2.7MM **Privately Held**
WEB: www.teamworksinc.net
SIC: 8721 7389 Certified public accountant; office facilities & secretarial service rental

8721 - Accounting, Auditing & Bookkeeping Svcs County (P-19001)

(P-19001)
THOMAS WIRIG DOLL & CO CPAS
Also Called: Thomas Doll & Company
165 Lennon Ln Ste 200, Walnut Creek (94598-2447)
P.O. Box 30307 (94598-9307)
PHONE.....................925 939-2500
Brent P Thomas, *President*
Sylvie Castaniada, *Executive Asst*
Sherman Doll, *Admin Sec*
Connie Privett, *Payroll Mgr*
Kathy Larson, *Human Resources*
EMP: 66 **EST:** 1988
SQ FT: 9,000
SALES (est): 8.5MM **Privately Held**
WEB: www.thomasdoll.com
SIC: 8721 Certified public accountant

(P-19002)
UC DAVIS SHARED SERVICES CTR
260 Cousteau Pl Ste 150, Davis (95618-5497)
PHONE.....................530 754-4772
Terry Sugai, *Manager*
EMP: 36 **EST:** 2013
SALES (est): 4.8MM **Privately Held**
WEB: www.ucdavis.edu
SIC: 8721 8742 Payroll accounting service; human resource consulting services

(P-19003)
WEAVER CRLSON MC CRTNEY ACCNTN
2117 4th St, Livermore (94550-4551)
PHONE.....................925 447-2010
Timothy Weaver, *President*
Kenneth L Mc Cartney, *Treasurer*
Richard Carlson, *Admin Sec*
Timothy A Weaver, *CPA*
EMP: 44 **EST:** 1970
SQ FT: 2,500
SALES (est): 901.5K **Privately Held**
WEB: www.wcmcpa.com
SIC: 8721 Accounting services, except auditing; certified public accountant

(P-19004)
WILLIAMS ADLEY & COMPANY L L P (PA)
7677 Oakport St Ste 1000, Oakland (94621-1950)
PHONE.....................510 893-8114
Robert Griffin, *General Ptnr*
Tom W Williams Jr, *General Ptnr*
Mary Butler, *Partner*
Kola Isiaq, *Partner*
Williams Adley, *Government*
EMP: 45 **EST:** 1982
SQ FT: 6,000
SALES (est): 4.3MM **Privately Held**
WEB: www.wacllp.com
SIC: 8721 8742 Certified public accountant; management consulting services

(P-19005)
WITHUMSMITH+BROWN PC
601 California St # 1800, San Francisco (94108-2834)
PHONE.....................415 434-3744
EMP: 68
SALES (corp-wide): 132.8K **Privately Held**
WEB: www.withum.com
SIC: 8721 Certified public accountant
PA: Withumsmith+Brown, Pc
506 Carnegie Ctr Ste 400
Princeton NJ 08540
609 520-1188

(P-19006)
WITTMAN ENTERPRISES LLC
21 Blue Sky Ct Ste Ab, Sacramento (95828-1015)
P.O. Box 269110 (95826-9110)
PHONE.....................916 381-6552
Donna Wittman, *Owner*
David Wittman, *Officer*
Dave Wittman, *Vice Pres*
Jennifer Bump, *Division Mgr*
Jennifer Gentry, *Production*
EMP: 40 **EST:** 1991
SALES (est): 1.7MM **Privately Held**
WEB: www.webillems.com
SIC: 8721 Billing & bookkeeping service

8731 Commercial Physical & Biological Research

(P-19007)
10X GENOMICS INC (PA)
6230 Stoneridge Mall Rd, Pleasanton (94588-3260)
PHONE.....................925 401-7300
Serge Saxonov, *CEO*
John R Stuelpnagel, *Ch of Bd*
Benjamin J Hindson, *President*
Justin J McAnear, *CFO*
Bradford J Crutchfield, *Ch Credit Ofcr*
EMP: 407 **EST:** 2012
SQ FT: 200,000
SALES (est): 298.8MM **Publicly Held**
WEB: www.10xgenomics.com
SIC: 8731 Commercial physical research

(P-19008)
4D MOLECULAR THERAPEUTICS INC
5858 Horton St Ste 455, Emeryville (94608-2072)
PHONE.....................510 505-2680
David Kirn, *CEO*
John F Milligan, *Ch of Bd*
Fred Kamal, *COO*
August Moretti, *CFO*
Robert Fishman, *Chief Mktg Ofcr*
EMP: 78 **EST:** 2013
SALES (est): 13.6MM **Privately Held**
WEB: www.4dmoleculartherapeutics.com
SIC: 8731 Biological research

(P-19009)
A3 LABS LLC (PA)
130 Webster St, Oakland (94607-3756)
PHONE.....................925 274-8503
Sheila Gibson,
Kamili Moreland, *Admin Sec*
EMP: 36 **EST:** 2016
SALES (est): 7.5MM **Privately Held**
WEB: www.a3ventures.co
SIC: 8731 Commercial physical research

(P-19010)
ACME BIOSCIENCE INC
3941 E Bayshore Rd, Palo Alto (94303-4313)
PHONE.....................650 969-8000
Jason Zhang, *President*
EMP: 237 **EST:** 2001
SALES (est): 4.8MM **Privately Held**
WEB: www.acmeca.com
SIC: 8731 Biotechnical research, commercial
HQ: Frontage Laboratories, Inc.
700 Pennsylvania Dr
Exton PA 19341
610 232-0100

(P-19011)
ADVANCED CELL DIAGNOSTICS INC
Also Called: Acd
7707 Gateway Blvd Ste 200, Newark (94560-1268)
PHONE.....................510 576-8800
Yuling Luo, *President*
Steve Chen, *COO*
Jessie Qian Wang, *CFO*
Rob Monroe, *Chief Mktg Ofcr*
Xiao-Jun MA, *Officer*
EMP: 90 **EST:** 2006
SQ FT: 2,500
SALES (est): 10.3MM
SALES (corp-wide): 931MM **Publicly Held**
WEB: www.bio-techne.com
SIC: 8731 2835 Biotechnical research, commercial; microbiology & virology diagnostic products
PA: Bio-Techne Corporation
614 Mckinley Pl Ne
Minneapolis MN 55413
612 379-8854

(P-19012)
ADVANCED MCRGRID SOLUTIONS INC
986 Mission St Fl 4, San Francisco (94103-2970)
PHONE.....................415 638-6146
Seyed Madaeni, *CEO*
Carlo Woods, *CFO*
Matt Penfold, *Ch Credit Ofcr*
Carroll Ayana, *Vice Pres*
Yanni Kapranos, *Vice Pres*
EMP: 81 **EST:** 2013
SALES (est): 5.8MM **Privately Held**
WEB: www.advancedmicrogridsolutions.com
SIC: 8731 Energy research

(P-19013)
ALECTOR LLC (HQ)
131 Oyster Point Blvd # 60, South San Francisco (94080-2029)
PHONE.....................415 231-5660
Arnon Rosenthal, *President*
Tillman Gerngross, *Ch of Bd*
Robert Paul, *Chief Mktg Ofcr*
Sabah Oney, *Vice Pres*
Charles Wolfus, *Vice Pres*
EMP: 75 **EST:** 2013
SALES (est): 21.1MM
SALES (corp-wide): 27.6MM **Publicly Held**
WEB: www.alector.com
SIC: 8731 Biotechnical research, commercial
PA: Alector, Inc.
131 Oyster Point Blvd # 60
South San Francisco CA 94080
415 231-5660

(P-19014)
ALKAHEST INC
125 Shoreway Rd Ste D, San Carlos (94070-2789)
PHONE.....................650 801-0474
Karoly Nikolich, *CEO*
Helen Jenkins, *COO*
Michael Byrnes, *CFO*
Cesar Cerezo, *Chief Mktg Ofcr*
Sam Jackson, *Chief Mktg Ofcr*
EMP: 95 **EST:** 2014
SALES (est): 10.5MM **Privately Held**
WEB: www.alkahest.com
SIC: 8731 Biotechnical research, commercial

(P-19015)
ALLAKOS INC
975 Island Dr Ste 201, Redwood City (94065-5173)
PHONE.....................650 597-5002
Robert Alexander, *President*
Daniel Janney, *Ch of Bd*
Adam Tomasi, *COO*
Baird Radford, *CFO*
Henrik Rasmussen, *Chief Mktg Ofcr*
EMP: 44 **EST:** 2012
SQ FT: 10,142 **Privately Held**
WEB: www.allakos.com
SIC: 8731 Biotechnical research, commercial

(P-19016)
ALLCELLS LLC
1301 Harbor Bay Pkwy # 200, Alameda (94502-6528)
PHONE.....................510 521-2600
Jie Tong,
Robert Wong, *General Mgr*
John Ng, *Info Tech Mgr*
Erin Douglas, *Development*
Lisa Tsang, *Technology*
▲ **EMP:** 52 **EST:** 1997
SALES (est): 23.6MM **Privately Held**
WEB: www.allcells.com
SIC: 8731 Biotechnical research, commercial

(P-19017)
ALLOGENE THERAPEUTICS INC
210 E Grand Ave, South San Francisco (94080-4811)
PHONE.....................650 457-2700
David Chang, *President*
Debbie Messemer, *Partner*
Arie Belldegrun, *Ch of Bd*
Eric Schmidt, *CFO*
Christopher Corcoran, *Chairman*
EMP: 122 **EST:** 2017
SQ FT: 68,000 **Privately Held**
WEB: www.allogene.com
SIC: 8731 2836 Biological research; biological products, except diagnostic

(P-19018)
ALTOS LABS INC (PA) ◆
2000 Bridge Pkwy, Redwood City (94065-1182)
PHONE.....................650 438-7055
Ann Lee-Karlon, *CEO*
EMP: 92 **EST:** 2021
SALES (est): 263.7K **Privately Held**
SIC: 8731 Biological research

(P-19019)
ALVEO TECHNOLOGIES INC
1000 Atlantic Ave Ste 114, Alameda (94501-1112)
PHONE.....................510 851-5314
Ronald Phillip Chiarello, *CEO*
Mike Aicher, *President*
EMP: 45 **EST:** 2014
SALES (est): 3.6MM **Privately Held**
WEB: www.alveotechnologies.com
SIC: 8731 Biotechnical research, commercial

(P-19020)
ALVEO TECHNOLOGIES INC
1000 Atlantic Ave, Alameda (94501-1147)
PHONE.....................510 749-4895
Ronald Chiarello, *CEO*
Julianne Averill, *CFO*
Johnson Chiang, *Officer*
Donald Green, *Engineer*
Kevin Gunning, *Director*
EMP: 45 **EST:** 2015
SALES (est): 3.5MM **Privately Held**
WEB: www.alveotechnologies.com
SIC: 8731 Commercial physical research

(P-19021)
ALZETA CORPORATION
1968 Hartog Dr, San Jose (95131-2200)
PHONE.....................408 727-8282
John D Sullivan, *President*
Angela R Kendall, *Shareholder*
John E Kendall, *Ch of Bd*
Stephen G Egli, *CFO*
James Gotterba, *Regional Mgr*
▲ **EMP:** 15 **EST:** 1982
SALES (est): 4.7MM **Privately Held**
WEB: www.alzeta.com
SIC: 8731 3433 Energy research; heating equipment, except electric

(P-19022)
AMBYS MEDICINES INC
131 Oyster Point Blvd # 20, South San Francisco (94080-2029)
PHONE.....................650 481-7662
Ronald Park, *CEO*
Jeffrey K Tong, *Ch of Bd*
Amanda Valentino,
Deidre Roniger, *Senior VP*
Nancy Shulman, *Vice Pres*
EMP: 43 **EST:** 2016
SALES (est): 6.4MM **Privately Held**
WEB: www.ambys.com
SIC: 8731 Biological research

(P-19023)
AMPRIUS INC (PA)
1180 Page Ave, Fremont (94538-7342)
PHONE.....................800 425-8803
Kang Sun, *CEO*
Richard Barnes, *CFO*
Bill Deihl, *CFO*
Ionel Stefan, *Officer*
Aaron Bakke, *Surgery Dir*
EMP: 44 **EST:** 2008
SALES (est): 7.2MM **Privately Held**
WEB: www.amprius.com
SIC: 8731 Commercial physical research

PRODUCTS & SERVICES SECTION
8731 - Commercial Physical & Biological Research County (P-19045)

(P-19024)
AMUNIX PHARMACEUTICAL INC
Also Called: Amunix Operating
2 Tower Pl Ste 1100, South San Francisco (94080-1842)
PHONE..................650 428-1800
Angie You, *CEO*
Volker Schellenberger, *President*
David Nathan Harris, *COO*
Frederick Hausheer, *Chief Mktg Ofcr*
Bryan Irving, *Officer*
EMP: 38 **EST:** 2009
SALES (est): 9.5MM **Privately Held**
WEB: www.amunix.com
SIC: 8731 Biotechnical research, commercial

(P-19025)
ANASPEC INC (HQ)
Also Called: Anaspec Egt Group
34801 Campus Dr, Fremont (94555-3606)
PHONE..................510 791-9560
Philippe Cronet, *President*
Masatoshi Yoshimatsu, *CFO*
Raman Afshar, *Vice Pres*
Susan Garcia, *Vice Pres*
Masanobu Sugawara, *Vice Pres*
▲ **EMP:** 50 **EST:** 1993
SALES (est): 12MM **Privately Held**
WEB: www.anaspec.com
SIC: 8731 Biotechnical research, commercial

(P-19026)
APPLIED STEMCELL INC
521 Cottonwood Dr Ste 111, Milpitas (95035-7467)
PHONE..................408 773-8007
Ruhong Jiang, *President*
Nicole Ha, *CIO*
Lizvette Ayala-Valdez, *Research*
Ll Barie, *Research*
Kevin Yoon, *Research*
▼ **EMP:** 41 **EST:** 2008
SQ FT: 1,000
SALES (est): 6.5MM **Privately Held**
WEB: www.appliedstemcell.com
SIC: 8731 Biotechnical research, commercial

(P-19027)
ARAGEN BIOSCIENCE INC
380 Woodview Ave, Morgan Hill (95037-2823)
PHONE..................408 779-1700
Axel Schleyer, *CEO*
Manmahesh Kantipudi, *Ch of Bd*
Manni Kantipudi, *CEO*
Malavika Ghosh, *Vice Pres*
David Driedger, *IT/INT Sup*
EMP: 50 **EST:** 2004
SALES (est): 9MM **Privately Held**
WEB: www.aragen.com
SIC: 8731 Biotechnical research, commercial; medical research, commercial
HQ: Aragen Life Sciences Private Limited
Plot No. 28a
Hyderabad TG

(P-19028)
ARCUS BIOSCIENCES INC (PA)
3928 Point Eden Way, Hayward (94545-3719)
PHONE..................510 694-6200
Terry Rosen, *Ch of Bd*
Juan Carlos Jaen, *President*
Rekha Hemrajani, *COO*
Eric Hoefer, *Ch Credit Ofcr*
Jennifer Jarrett, *Bd of Directors*
EMP: 107 **EST:** 2015
SQ FT: 70,100
SALES (est): 77.5MM **Publicly Held**
WEB: www.arcusbio.com
SIC: 8731 Biotechnical research, commercial

(P-19029)
ARIOSA DIAGNOSTICS INC
5945 Optical Ct, San Jose (95138-1400)
PHONE..................408 229-7500
Kenneth Song MD, *CEO*
Dave Mullarkey, *COO*
Thomas Musci MD, *Chief Mktg Ofcr*
Thomas J Musci, *Vice Pres*
Arnold Oliphant, *Security Dir*
EMP: 140 **EST:** 2008
SALES (est): 28.5MM **Publicly Held**
WEB: www.harmonytest.com
SIC: 8731 Biotechnical research, commercial
HQ: Bio-Reference Laboratories, Inc.
481 Edward H Ross Dr
Elmwood Park NJ 07407
201 791-2600

(P-19030)
ARSENAL BIOSCIENCES INC
Also Called: Arsenalbio
2 Tower Pl Ste 700, South San Francisco (94080-1848)
PHONE..................858 945-3091
Ken Drazan, *CEO*
EMP: 51 **EST:** 2018
SALES (est): 14.9MM **Privately Held**
SIC: 8731 Biotechnical research, commercial

(P-19031)
ASTERIAS BIOTHERAPEUTICS INC
1010 Atlantic Ave Ste 102, Alameda (94501-1258)
PHONE..................510 456-3800
Michael H Mulroy, *President*
Jane S Lebkowski, *President*
Katharine E Spink, *COO*
Ryan D Chavez, *CFO*
Stephen Cartt, *Bd of Directors*
EMP: 55
SALES: 4MM **Publicly Held**
WEB: www.asteriasbiotherapeutics.com
SIC: 8731 2836 Biotechnical research, commercial; biological products, except diagnostic
PA: Lineage Cell Therapeutics, Inc.
2173 Salk Ave Ste 200
Carlsbad CA 92008

(P-19032)
AZURE BIOSYSTEMS INC
6747 Sierra Ct Ste A, Dublin (94568-2651)
PHONE..................925 307-7127
Alnoor Mohamedali Shivji, *CEO*
Lisa Isailovic, *Vice Pres*
Ghazvini Sia, *Vice Pres*
David Grothen, *Technical Staff*
Danny Obregon, *Technical Staff*
▲ **EMP:** 40 **EST:** 2013
SALES (est): 8.2MM **Privately Held**
WEB: www.azurebiosystems.com
SIC: 8731 Biotechnical research, commercial

(P-19033)
BIO-VED PHARMACEUTICALS INC
1929 Otoole Way, San Jose (95131-2238)
PHONE..................408 432-4020
Deepa Chitre, *CEO*
Katki Sawant, *Controller*
EMP: 27 **EST:** 1994
SQ FT: 1,000
SALES (est): 2.5MM **Privately Held**
WEB: www.bioved.com
SIC: 8731 2834 Biotechnical research, commercial; druggists' preparations (pharmaceuticals)

(P-19034)
BIONETICS CORPORATION
Mercury Consolidated Div
P.O. Box 115, Moffett Field (94035-0115)
PHONE..................650 604-5327
Charles Spectre, *Branch Mgr*
EMP: 62
SALES (corp-wide): 52.2MM **Privately Held**
WEB: www.bionetics.com
SIC: 8731 Commercial research laboratory
PA: The Bionetics Corporation
101 Production Dr Ste 100
Yorktown VA 23693
757 873-0900

(P-19035)
BIONOVA SCIENTIFIC LLC
3100 W Warren Ave, Fremont (94538-6423)
PHONE..................510 305-8048
Haiyan Kong, *Mng Member*
Ling-Ling Kang, *Director*
EMP: 50 **EST:** 2013
SALES (est): 5.8MM **Privately Held**
WEB: www.bionovascientific.com
SIC: 8731 Biotechnical research, commercial

(P-19036)
BOLT THREADS INC (PA)
Also Called: Refactored Materials
5858 Horton St Ste 400, Emeryville (94608-2046)
PHONE..................415 279-5585
Daniel Widmaier, *CEO*
Ethan Mirsky, *CFO*
Jamie Bainbridge, *Vice Pres*
Sholeh Esmaili-Montoya, *Vice Pres*
Troy Rhonemus, *Vice Pres*
EMP: 52 **EST:** 2009
SQ FT: 32,000
SALES (est): 17.6MM **Privately Held**
WEB: www.boltthreads.com
SIC: 8731 Biotechnical research, commercial

(P-19037)
BRIDGEBIO SERVICES INC
421 Kipling St, Palo Alto (94301-1530)
PHONE..................650 438-1302
Neil Kumar, *CEO*
Brian Stolz, *COO*
Brian Stephenson, *CFO*
Frank McCormick, *Chairman*
Richard Scheller, *Chairman*
EMP: 96 **EST:** 2015
SALES (est): 2MM
SALES (corp-wide): 8.2MM **Publicly Held**
WEB: www.bridgebio.com
SIC: 8731 Biotechnical research, commercial
PA: Bridgebio Pharma, Inc.
421 Kipling St
Palo Alto CA 94301
650 391-9740

(P-19038)
CALICO LIFE SCIENCES LLC
Also Called: California Life Company
1170 Veterans Blvd, South San Francisco (94080-1985)
PHONE..................650 754-6200
Arthur Levinson, *CEO*
Hal Barron, *President*
Jing Yuan, *Associate Dir*
Gail Brady, *Admin Asst*
Dan Gottschling, *Admin Asst*
EMP: 73 **EST:** 2013
SALES (est): 17.2MM
SALES (corp-wide): 182.5B **Publicly Held**
WEB: www.calicolabs.com
SIC: 8731 Biotechnical research, commercial
HQ: Google Llc
1600 Amphitheatre Pkwy
Mountain View CA 94043
650 253-0000

(P-19039)
CALIFRNIA COOP RICE RES FNDTIO
Also Called: Rice Experiment Station
955 Butt City Hwy, Biggs (95917-9634)
P.O. Box 306 (95917-0306)
PHONE..................530 868-5481
Kent Mekinsey, *Director*
Marlin Brandon, *Admin Sec*
Kent McKenzie, *Director*
EMP: 35 **EST:** 1912
SQ FT: 3,000
SALES (est): 1.4MM **Privately Held**
WEB: www.crrf.org
SIC: 8731 Commercial physical research

(P-19040)
CCINTEGRATION INC (PA)
2060 Corporate Ct, San Jose (95131-1753)
PHONE..................408 228-1314
Anna Hung, *CEO*
Kelly Styskal, *CFO*
Linh Diep, *Technical Staff*
Stacey Moore, *Buyer*
Hoai Ta, *Opers Staff*
EMP: 84 **EST:** 1988
SQ FT: 235,000
SALES (est): 17.9MM **Privately Held**
WEB: www.ccintegration.com
SIC: 8731 7371 Computer (hardware) development; computer software development

(P-19041)
CENTER FOR CULINARY DEV INC
Also Called: Ccd Innovation
1201 Park Ave Ste 101, Emeryville (94608-3632)
PHONE..................415 693-8900
Ruth Halpern, *CEO*
James Reiter, *President*
Marc Halperin, *Treasurer*
Tracy Scala, *Advisor*
EMP: 56 **EST:** 1991
SALES (est): 10.6MM **Privately Held**
WEB: www.ccdinnovation.com
SIC: 8731 Commercial physical research; food research

(P-19042)
CHECKPOINT TECHNOLOGIES LLC
66 Bonaventura Dr, San Jose (95134-2123)
PHONE..................408 321-9780
Guoquing Xiao,
Miroslav Saraivanov, *Engineer*
Robert Hand, *Marketing Staff*
Horst Groneberg,
David Morgan, *Manager*
EMP: 39 **EST:** 1996
SQ FT: 12,000
SALES (est): 7.9MM **Privately Held**
WEB: www.checkpointtechnologies.com
SIC: 8731 Biotechnical research, commercial

(P-19043)
COBALT TECHNOLOGIES INC
Also Called: Cobalt Biofuels
500 Clyde Ave Ste 500 # 500, Mountain View (94043-2212)
PHONE..................650 230-0722
Robert Mayers, *CEO*
Andy Meyer, *President*
Carole Cobb, *COO*
David Walther, *Vice Pres*
EMP: 38
SALES (est): 4.1MM **Privately Held**
WEB: www.cobalttech.com
SIC: 8731 Biotechnical research, commercial

(P-19044)
COHERE TECHNOLOGIES INC
2550 Walsh Ave Ste 150, Santa Clara (95051-1345)
PHONE..................408 246-1277
Shlomo Rakib, *CEO*
Perry Tanner, *Exec VP*
Jake Katz, *Vice Pres*
Anton Monk, *Vice Pres*
Richard Lynch, *Principal*
EMP: 51 **EST:** 2010
SALES (est): 6.5MM **Privately Held**
WEB: www.cohere-tech.com
SIC: 8731 Electronic research

(P-19045)
COHERUS BIOSCIENCES INC (PA)
333 Twin Dolphin Dr # 60, Redwood City (94065-1401)
PHONE..................650 649-3530
Dennis M Lanfear, *Ch of Bd*
Vincent Aniceti, *COO*
Jean-Frederic Viret, *CFO*
Rich Hameister, *Exec VP*
Susy Chen, *Vice Pres*
EMP: 215 **EST:** 2010
SALES (est): 475.8MM **Publicly Held**
WEB: www.coherus.com
SIC: 8731 2836 Biological research; biological products, except diagnostic

8731 - Commercial Physical & Biological Research County (P-19046)

(P-19046)
COMPARENETWORKS INC (PA)
Also Called: Biocompare
395 Oyster Point Blvd # 300, South San Francisco (94080-1931)
PHONE.....................................650 873-9031
Brian Cowley, *CEO*
Paul Gatti, *President*
Mike Okimoto, *Officer*
Bo Purtic, *Officer*
Joan Boyce, *Vice Pres*
EMP: 73 **EST:** 2000
SQ FT: 16,152
SALES (est): 13.2MM **Privately Held**
WEB: www.corp.comparenetworks.com
SIC: 8731 Biotechnical research, commercial

(P-19047)
CPU TECHNOLOGY INC
5753 W Las Positas Blvd, Pleasanton (94588-4084)
PHONE.....................................925 398-7659
Chris D Wedewer, *President*
Dan Jurchenko, *President*
Maria Grabowski, *Purch Mgr*
EMP: 60 **EST:** 1989
SALES (est): 5.2MM
SALES (corp-wide): 58.1B **Publicly Held**
WEB: www.cputech.com
SIC: 8731 8711 3674 3672 Computer (hardware) development; engineering services; semiconductors & related devices; printed circuit boards
PA: The Boeing Company
100 N Riverside Plz
Chicago IL 60606
312 544-2000

(P-19048)
CUBERG INC
1198 65th St Ste 170, Emeryville (94608-1474)
PHONE.....................................510 725-4200
Richard Wang, *CEO*
Mauro Pasta, *President*
David Koo, *Engineer*
Russell Debi, *Sales Staff*
Andrew Karp, *Manager*
EMP: 35 **EST:** 2015
SALES (est): 3.4MM **Privately Held**
WEB: www.cuberg.net
SIC: 8731 Commercial physical research

(P-19049)
DEPOSITION SCIENCES INC
Also Called: D S I
3300 Coffey Ln, Santa Rosa (95403-1917)
PHONE.....................................707 573-6700
Lee Bartolomei, *President*
Lee A Bartolomei, *Vice Pres*
Thomas Chambers, *Director*
EMP: 96 **EST:** 1985
SQ FT: 8,400
SALES (est): 16.5MM **Publicly Held**
WEB: www.depsci.com
SIC: 8731 3827 Industrial laboratory, except testing; lens coating equipment
PA: Lockheed Martin Corporation
6801 Rockledge Dr
Bethesda MD 20817

(P-19050)
DIAGNOSTIC BIOSYSTEMS INC
6616 Owens Dr, Pleasanton (94588-3334)
PHONE.....................................925 484-3350
Bipin Gupta, *President*
Nancy Hui, *Associate Dir*
Pathanjaly Hariharan, *Sales Staff*
Ananda Kumar, *Sales Staff*
Simi Narindray, *Manager*
EMP: 46 **EST:** 1994
SQ FT: 2,000
SALES (est): 5.4MM **Privately Held**
WEB: www.dbiosys.com
SIC: 8731 Biotechnical research, commercial

(P-19051)
DNA TWOPOINTO INC
Also Called: Dna2.0
37950 Central Ct, Newark (94560-3463)
PHONE.....................................650 853-8347
Jeremy Minshull, *CEO*
Claes Gustafsson, *Officer*
Sridhar Govindarajan, *Vice Pres*
Jon Ness, *Vice Pres*
Walter Tian, *Vice Pres*
▼ **EMP:** 68 **EST:** 2003
SQ FT: 40,000
SALES (est): 14.6MM **Privately Held**
WEB: www.atum.bio
SIC: 8731 Biotechnical research, commercial

(P-19052)
DOCOMO INNOVATIONS INC
3301 Hillview Ave, Palo Alto (94304-1204)
PHONE.....................................650 493-9600
Tak Inagawa, *CEO*
Hongfeng Yin, *Engineer*
Mayumi Kamihata, *Accounting Mgr*
Fujio Watanabe, *Director*
EMP: 45 **EST:** 1999
SALES (est): 13.2MM **Privately Held**
WEB: www.docomoinnovations.com
SIC: 8731 Electronic research
HQ: Ntt Docomo, Inc.
2-11-1, Nagatacho
Chiyoda-Ku TKY 100-0

(P-19053)
DSM BIOMEDICAL INC
Also Called: Polymer Technology Group, The
2810 7th St, Berkeley (94710-2703)
PHONE.....................................510 841-8800
EMP: 120
SQ FT: 55,000
SALES (est): 19.8MM
SALES (corp-wide): 9.9B **Privately Held**
WEB: www.dsm.com
SIC: 8731 2836 Commercial Physical Research, Nsk
PA: Koninklijke Dsm N.V.
Het Overloon 1
Heerlen 6411
455 788-111

(P-19054)
EIDOS THERAPEUTICS INC
1800 Owens St, San Francisco (94158-2388)
PHONE.....................................415 887-1471
Neil Kumar, *CEO*
Christine Siu, *CFO*
Eric Aguiar, *Bd of Directors*
Jonathan C Fox, *Chief Mktg Ofcr*
John Grimaldi, *Officer*
EMP: 45 **EST:** 2014
SALES (corp-wide): 8.2MM **Publicly Held**
WEB: www.eidostx.com
SIC: 8731 Biotechnical research, commercial
PA: Bridgebio Pharma, Inc.
421 Kipling St
Palo Alto CA 94301
650 391-9740

(P-19055)
EMERALD CLOUD LAB INC
844 Dubuque Ave, South San Francisco (94080-1804)
PHONE.....................................650 257-7554
Daniel Kleinbaum, *President*
Brian Frezza, *Co-CEO*
Daniel Jerome Kleinbaum, *Co-CEO*
EMP: 90 **EST:** 2009
SALES (est): 14.5MM **Privately Held**
WEB: www.emeraldcloudlab.com
SIC: 8731 Biotechnical research, commercial

(P-19056)
ENVIRONMENTAL SCIENCE ASSOC
Also Called: E S A
350 Frank H Ogawa Plz, Oakland (94612-2006)
PHONE.....................................510 839-5066
Annette Bonilla, *Branch Mgr*
EMP: 94
SALES (corp-wide): 80K **Privately Held**
WEB: www.esassoc.com
SIC: 8731 8748 Environmental research; environmental consultant
PA: Environmental Science Associates
550 Kearny St Ste 800
San Francisco CA 94108
415 896-5900

(P-19057)
ENVIRONMENTAL SCIENCE ASSOC (PA)
Also Called: ESA
550 Kearny St Ste 800, San Francisco (94108-2512)
PHONE.....................................415 896-5900
Leslie Moulton, *President*
Gary Oates, *Senior VP*
Brian Pittman, *Fmly & Gen Dent*
EMP: 65
SQ FT: 20,000
SALES (est): 80K **Privately Held**
WEB: www.esassoc.com
SIC: 8731 8748 Environmental research; environmental consultant

(P-19058)
EPITOMICS INC (HQ)
863 Mitten Rd Ste 103, Burlingame (94010-1311)
PHONE.....................................650 583-6688
Guo-Liang Yu, *Ch of Bd*
Zhiqiang An, *Officer*
Brad S Lee, *Exec VP*
Weimin Zhu, *Vice Pres*
Robert Pytela, *Security Dir*
EMP: 108 **EST:** 2001
SALES (est): 16.9MM
SALES (corp-wide): 316.8MM **Privately Held**
WEB: www.abcam.com
SIC: 8731 Biotechnical research, commercial
PA: Abcam Plc
Discovery Drive
Cambridge CAMBS CB2 0
122 369-6000

(P-19059)
EUREKA THERAPEUTICS INC
5858 Horton St Ste 170, Emeryville (94608-2007)
PHONE.....................................510 654-7045
Cheng Liu, *President*
Diana Chen, *Project Mgr*
Ziyou Cui, *Research*
Hong Liu, *Research*
Jianying Liu, *Research*
EMP: 40 **EST:** 2006
SALES (est): 6MM **Privately Held**
WEB: www.eurekatherapeutics.com
SIC: 8731 Biotechnical research, commercial

(P-19060)
EUROFINS DISCOVERX PDTS LLC
42501 Albrae St, Fremont (94538-3394)
PHONE.....................................510 979-1415
Sailaja Kuchibhatla,
EMP: 60 **EST:** 2020
SALES (est): 1.6MM **Privately Held**
WEB: www.discoverx.com
SIC: 8731 Biotechnical research, commercial

(P-19061)
FUJIFILM DIMATIX INC
2230 Martin Ave, Santa Clara (95050-2704)
PHONE.....................................408 565-0670
John McDonald, *Branch Mgr*
Chris Torrey, *Vice Pres*
Eunice Wang, *Info Tech Mgr*
Fred Amidon, *Engineer*
Henry Mossell, *Engineer*
EMP: 64 **Privately Held**
WEB: www.dimatix.com
SIC: 8731 Commercial physical research
HQ: Fujifilm Dimatix, Inc.
2250 Martin Ave
Santa Clara CA 95050
408 565-9150

(P-19062)
FUJITSU RESEARCH AMERICA INC (HQ)
Also Called: Fujitsu Laboratories Amer Inc
350 Cobalt Way, Sunnyvale (94085)
PHONE.....................................408 530-4500
Hiromu Hayashi, *President*
Nobuaki Kawato, *Exec VP*
Dave Marvit, *Vice Pres*
Hitoshi Matsumoto, *VP Bus Dvlpt*
Masami Yamamoto, *Principal*
EMP: 80 **EST:** 1994
SALES (est): 224.3MM **Privately Held**
WEB: www.fujitsu.com
SIC: 8731 Commercial physical research

(P-19063)
GENIA TECHNOLOGIES INC
2841 Scott Blvd, Santa Clara (95050-2549)
PHONE.....................................650 300-5970
Stefan Roever, *CEO*
Pratima RAO, *COO*
Randy Davis, *Vice Pres*
Hui Tian, *Vice Pres*
Markus Wallgren, *Vice Pres*
EMP: 41 **EST:** 2009
SALES (est): 8MM
SALES (corp-wide): 69.8B **Privately Held**
WEB: www.cialis-online-rezept.com
SIC: 8731 Biotechnical research, commercial
HQ: F. Hoffmann-La Roche Ag
Grenzacherstrasse 124
Basel BS 4058
616 881-111

(P-19064)
GREENVENUS LLC
1910 5th St, Davis (95616-4018)
PHONE.....................................530 648-9985
Sebastian Langbehn, *CEO*
Sekhar Boddupalli,
EMP: 35 **EST:** 2019
SALES (est): 1.3MM **Privately Held**
WEB: www.greenvenus.com
SIC: 8731 Biotechnical research, commercial

(P-19065)
HARPOON THERAPEUTICS INC
131 Oyster Point Blvd # 100, South San Francisco (94080-2030)
PHONE.....................................650 443-7400
Gerald McMahon, *President*
Luke Evnin, *Ch of Bd*
Georgia Erbez, *CFO*
Georgia L Erbez, *CFO*
Natalie Sacks, *Chief Mktg Ofcr*
EMP: 45 **EST:** 2015
SQ FT: 13,500
SALES (est): 17.4MM **Privately Held**
WEB: www.harpoontx.com
SIC: 8731 Biotechnical research, commercial

(P-19066)
HELIX HOLDINGS I LLC
1 Circle Star Way Fl 2, San Carlos (94070-6234)
PHONE.....................................415 805-3360
Robin Thurston, *CEO*
EMP: 100 **EST:** 2015
SALES (est): 2.1MM **Privately Held**
SIC: 8731 Biological research

(P-19067)
HELIX OPCO LLC
101 S Ellsworth Ave # 350, San Mateo (94401-3964)
PHONE.....................................415 805-3360
Marc Stapley, *CEO*
Robin Thurston, *CEO*
Nicole Washington, *Manager*
EMP: 106 **EST:** 2015
SALES (est): 18.9MM **Privately Held**
WEB: www.helix.com
SIC: 8731 Biotechnical research, commercial

(P-19068)
HOWARD HUGHES MEDICAL INST
Also Called: H H M I
279 Campus Dr Rm B202, Stanford (94305-5101)
PHONE.....................................650 725-8252
EMP: 100
SALES (corp-wide): 2.3B **Privately Held**
SIC: 8731 6732 Commercial Physical Research Nonprofit Trust Management
PA: Howard Hughes Medical Institute Inc
4000 Jones Bridge Rd
Chevy Chase MD 20815
301 215-8500

PRODUCTS & SERVICES SECTION
8731 - Commercial Physical & Biological Research County (P-19090)

(P-19069)
HOWARD HUGHES MEDICAL INST
1550 4th St Rm 190, San Francisco (94143-2324)
PHONE 415 476-9668
John Flickinger, *Branch Mgr*
Patricia Soochan, *Officer*
Kevin Moses, *Executive*
Anne Tarrant, *Managing Dir*
Erik Fuss, *Office Mgr*
EMP: 63
SALES (corp-wide): 1.7B **Privately Held**
WEB: www.hhmi.org
SIC: 8731 Biological research
PA: Howard Hughes Medical Institute Inc
 4000 Jones Bridge Rd
 Chevy Chase MD 20815
 301 215-8500

(P-19070)
IGM BIOSCIENCES INC
325 E Middlefield Rd, Mountain View (94043-4003)
PHONE 650 965-7873
Fred Schwarzer, *President*
Michael Loberg, *Ch of Bd*
Misbah Tahir, *CFO*
Daniel Chen, *Chief Mktg Ofcr*
Chris H Takimoto, *Chief Mktg Ofcr*
EMP: 51 **EST:** 1993
SQ FT: 34,000
SALES (corp-wide): 981.5MM **Publicly Held**
WEB: www.igmbio.com
SIC: 8731 Biotechnical research, commercial
PA: Topsoe Holding A/S
 Haldor Topsoes Alle 1
 Kongens Lyngby 2800
 458 784-94

(P-19071)
IMMUNOSCIENCE LLC (PA)
6780 Sierra Ct Ste M, Dublin (94568-2630)
P.O. Box 3279, Danville (94526-9479)
PHONE 925 460-8111
Sateesh Apte MD, *Med Doctor*
Hector Bonilla, *Vice Pres*
Robert J Nagy, *Branch Mgr*
Sara Mestas, *Technology*
Raquel Biascoechea, *Controller*
EMP: 42 **EST:** 1995
SQ FT: 7,120
SALES (est): 4.2MM **Privately Held**
WEB: www.immunoscience.com
SIC: 8731 Biotechnical research, commercial

(P-19072)
IMS - INSURANCE MED SVCS INC
37600 Central Ct Ste 201, Newark (94560-3456)
PHONE 510 490-6211
Saeed Uddin, *CEO*
Rina Albelda, *COO*
Bilal Saeed, *Vice Pres*
Mia McDaniels, *Sales Staff*
Christian Ojas, *Case Mgr*
EMP: 124 **EST:** 1993
SALES (est): 9.1MM **Privately Held**
WEB: www.imsparamed.com
SIC: 8731 Commercial physical research

(P-19073)
INCLIN INC (PA)
2929 Campus Dr Ste 230, San Mateo (94403-2534)
PHONE 650 961-3422
Taylor Kilfoil, *CEO*
Dirk Thye, *CEO*
Tony Pantuso, *COO*
Arnold Wong, *CFO*
Charles Du Mond, *Senior VP*
EMP: 74 **EST:** 1998
SALES (est): 5.1MM **Privately Held**
WEB: www.inclin.com
SIC: 8731 Biotechnical research, commercial

(P-19074)
INSITRO INC
279 E Grand Ave Ste 200, South San Francisco (94080-4804)
PHONE 650 488-1789
Daphne Koller, *CEO*
Mary M Rozenman, *CFO*
Keith James, *Senior VP*
Allison Lai, *Vice Pres*
Matthew Rasmussen, *Vice Pres*
EMP: 100 **EST:** 2018
SALES (est): 22.4MM **Privately Held**
WEB: www.insitro.com
SIC: 8731 Commercial physical research

(P-19075)
INTERNATIONAL BUS MCHS CORP
Also Called: IBM
650 Harry Rd, San Jose (95120-6001)
PHONE 408 927-1080
Mark Dean, *Vice Pres*
Arnon Amir, *Vice Pres*
Yvonne Paxton, *Admin Asst*
Anthony Chang, *Software Dev*
Jeannette Garcia, *Research*
EMP: 500
SALES (corp-wide): 73.6B **Publicly Held**
WEB: www.ibm.com
SIC: 8731 Commercial research laboratory
PA: International Business Machines Corporation
 1 New Orchard Rd Ste 1 # 1
 Armonk NY 10504
 914 499-1900

(P-19076)
JANSSEN ALZHEIMER IMMUNOTHERA
700 Gateway Blvd, South San Francisco (94080-7020)
PHONE 650 794-2500
Dr Stefaan Heylen, *President*
Anh Dang, *Engineer*
Chris Nebel, *Marketing Staff*
Joe Warlow, *Director*
Nadine De Leeuw, *Manager*
EMP: 100 **EST:** 2009
SALES (est): 14.4MM
SALES (corp-wide): 82.5B **Publicly Held**
WEB: www.janssenlabs.com
SIC: 8731 Commercial physical research
HQ: Janssen Research & Development, Llc
 920 Us Highway 202
 Raritan NJ 08869
 908 704-4000

(P-19077)
KARIUS INC
975 Island Dr Ste 100, Redwood City (94065-5173)
PHONE 866 452-7487
Michael Kertesz, *President*
Stacy Solorio, *Vice Pres*
Sivan Bercovici, *CTO*
Fred Christians, *Research*
Karen To, *Finance Dir*
EMP: 58 **EST:** 2015
SALES (est): 7.1MM **Privately Held**
WEB: www.kariusdx.com
SIC: 8731 Biotechnical research, commercial

(P-19078)
KIOXIA AMERICA INC
35 Iron Point Cir Ste 100, Folsom (95630-8588)
PHONE 916 986-4707
Robert Beard, *Branch Mgr*
Chuck Piercey, *Director*
EMP: 50
SALES (corp-wide): 100.6MM **Privately Held**
SIC: 8731 Electronic research
PA: Kioxia America, Inc.
 2610 Orchard Pkwy
 San Jose CA 95134
 408 526-2400

(P-19079)
L3 APPLIED TECHNOLOGIES INC
2700 Merced St, San Leandro (94577-5602)
PHONE 510 577-7100
Janet Luna, *Director*
Diana Tow, *Controller*
EMP: 109
SALES (corp-wide): 18.1B **Publicly Held**
SIC: 8731 Commercial physical research
HQ: L3 Applied Technologies, Inc.
 10180 Barnes Canyon Rd # 10
 San Diego CA 92121
 858 404-7824

(P-19080)
LAB-GISTICS LLC
885 Pacific Ave, San Jose (95126-4821)
PHONE 650 309-2627
Minh Phan,
EMP: 200 **EST:** 2012
SQ FT: 60,000
SALES (est): 25MM **Privately Held**
SIC: 8731 Computer (hardware) development

(P-19081)
LABCYTE INC (DH)
Also Called: Echo
170 Rose Orchard Way # 200, San Jose (95134-1374)
PHONE 408 747-2000
Mark F Colbrie, *President*
Richard Ellson, *Officer*
Mathew Bramwell, *Vice Pres*
Michael F Miller, *Vice Pres*
Nick Samaras, *Managing Dir*
EMP: 73 **EST:** 2000
SQ FT: 19,200
SALES: 25.4K
SALES (corp-wide): 22.2B **Publicly Held**
WEB: www.labcyte.com
SIC: 8731 Biotechnical research, commercial
HQ: Beckman Coulter, Inc.
 250 S Kraemer Blvd
 Brea CA 92821
 714 993-5321

(P-19082)
LIGHTWAVES 2020 INC
1323 Great Mall Dr, Milpitas (95035-8013)
PHONE 408 503-8888
J J Pan, *Ch of Bd*
Jewel Chang, *Principal*
EMP: 50 **EST:** 1997
SALES (est): 6.2MM **Privately Held**
WEB: www.lightwaves2020.com
SIC: 8731 Electronic research

(P-19083)
LIVELEAF INC (PA)
Also Called: Liveleaf Bioscience
1160 Industrial Rd Ste 11, San Carlos (94070-4128)
PHONE 650 722-2984
Alex Warren, *CEO*
Chloe Chan, *CFO*
Jeff Bruton, *Info Tech Mgr*
Philip Ho, *Technology*
Fabien Lubais, *VP Mktg*
EMP: 41 **EST:** 2010
SALES (est): 1.6MM **Privately Held**
WEB: www.liveleaf.com
SIC: 8731 Biotechnical research, commercial

(P-19084)
LUIDIA INC
591 W Hamilton Ave # 205, Campbell (95008-0566)
PHONE 650 413-7500
C K Kim, *CEO*
Chris Choi, *Sales Mgr*
Steve Pimentel, *Manager*
▲ **EMP:** 47 **EST:** 2003
SALES (est): 8.3MM **Privately Held**
WEB: www.luidia.com
SIC: 8731 3577 Electronic research; computer peripheral equipment

(P-19085)
LUMIATA INC
Also Called: Medgle
489 S El Camino Real, San Mateo (94402-1727)
PHONE 916 607-2442
Dilawar Syed, *CEO*
Derek Gordon, *COO*
Miguel Alvarado, *Chief Engr*
Emad Khan, *Finance*
Bob Lehto, *Human Res Dir*
EMP: 46 **EST:** 2013
SALES (est): 5.6MM **Privately Held**
WEB: www.lumiata.com
SIC: 8731 7372 Medical research, commercial; application computer software

(P-19086)
LYELL IMMUNOPHARMA INC (PA)
Also Called: LYELL BIOTECH
201 Haskins Way, South San Francisco (94080-6215)
PHONE 650 695-0677
Elizabeth Homans, *CEO*
Richard D Klausner, *Ch of Bd*
Charles Newton, *CFO*
Tina Albertson, *Officer*
Stephen Hill, *Officer*
EMP: 148 **EST:** 2018
SQ FT: 40,000
SALES (est): 1.2MM **Publicly Held**
WEB: www.lyell.com
SIC: 8731 Biological research

(P-19087)
MAMMOTH BIOSCIENCES INC
1000 Marina Blvd Ste 600, Brisbane (94005-1842)
PHONE 770 655-1937
Trevor Martin, *CEO*
Janice Chen, *Principal*
Jennifer Doudna, *Principal*
Lucas Harrington, *Principal*
Ashley Tehranchi, *Principal*
EMP: 67 **EST:** 2017
SALES (est): 6.6MM **Privately Held**
WEB: www.mammoth.bio
SIC: 8731 Biotechnical research, commercial

(P-19088)
MEMBRANE TECHNOLOGY & RES INC (PA)
Also Called: M T R
39630 Eureka Dr, Newark (94560-4805)
PHONE 650 328-2228
Colin Bailey, *Chairman*
Hans Wijmans, *President*
Nicolas Wynn, *COO*
Meryl Rains, *CFO*
Janet Farrant, *Exec VP*
◆ **EMP:** 69 **EST:** 1982
SQ FT: 60,000
SALES (est): 17.9MM **Privately Held**
WEB: www.mtrinc.com
SIC: 8731 3823 Commercial research laboratory; on-stream gas/liquid analysis instruments, industrial

(P-19089)
MERCEDES-BENZ RES DEV N AMER IN (DH)
Also Called: Mbrdna
309 N Pastoria Ave, Sunnyvale (94085-4109)
PHONE 650 845-2500
Akhtar Jameel, *President*
Wilson Chris, *Vice Pres*
Reckels Dieter, *Vice Pres*
Holfelder Wieland, *Vice Pres*
Hondson Kuang, *Software Engr*
EMP: 45 **EST:** 1994
SQ FT: 15,000
SALES (est): 29.5MM
SALES (corp-wide): 182.4B **Privately Held**
WEB: www.mbrdna.com
SIC: 8731 Commercial physical research

(P-19090)
NANOSCALE CMBNTRIAL SYNTHSIS I (PA)
Also Called: Nanosyn
3100 Central Expy, Santa Clara (95051-0801)
PHONE 408 987-2004
Nikolai Sepetov, *CEO*
Olga Isskova, *Vice Pres*
Zeeshan Kamal, *Associate Dir*
Benjie Reyes, *CIO*
Jacob Macdonald, *Research*
EMP: 74 **EST:** 1998
SQ FT: 30,000

8731 - Commercial Physical & Biological Research County (P-19091)

SALES (est): 21.3MM **Privately Held**
WEB: www.nanosyn.com
SIC: **8731** Biotechnical research, commercial

(P-19091)
NAUTILUS BIOTECHNOLOGY INC
201 Industrial Rd Ste 310, San Carlos (94070-2396)
PHONE..................................206 333-2001
Sujal Patel, *CEO*
Matt Murphy, *General Counsel*
EMP: 106 EST: 2016
SALES (est): 16.9MM **Publicly Held**
WEB: www.nautilus.bio
SIC: **8731** Biotechnical research, commercial
PA: Nautilus Biotechnology, Inc.
425 Pontius Ave N Ste 202
Seattle WA 98109
206 333-2001

(P-19092)
NEURONA THERAPEUTICS INC
170 Harbor Way Ste 200, South San Francisco (94080-6102)
PHONE..................................510 366-1177
Tim Kutzkey, *Principal*
Gautam Banik, *Vice Pres*
Joanne Tin, *Admin Asst*
Hubert Nethercott, *Research*
Lauren Budesheim, *Human Resources*
EMP: 44 EST: 2008
SALES (est): 5.2MM **Privately Held**
WEB: www.neuronatherapeutics.com
SIC: **8731** Medical research, commercial

(P-19093)
NOON HOME INC
20400 Stevens Creek Blvd # 370, Cupertino (95014-2257)
PHONE..................................650 242-7565
Erik Charlton, *CEO*
Johnny Gilmore, *COO*
Kate Bessonova, *Web Dvlpr*
Andrew Chalker, *Software Engr*
David Boone, *Technical Staff*
EMP: 47 EST: 2015
SALES (est): 4.5MM **Privately Held**
WEB: www.noonhome.com
SIC: **8731** Computer (hardware) development

(P-19094)
NOVODIAX INC
3517 Breakwater Ave, Hayward (94545-3610)
PHONE..................................510 342-3043
Jianfu Wang, *CEO*
Paul Kortschak, *Vice Pres*
Jin Wu, *Vice Pres*
Zhiqing Zhang, *Vice Pres*
Peter Le, *CIO*
EMP: 40 EST: 2010
SALES (est): 4.2MM **Privately Held**
WEB: www.novodiax.com
SIC: **8731** Biotechnical research, commercial

(P-19095)
NURIX THERAPEUTICS INC (PA)
1700 Owens St Ste 205, San Francisco (94158-0006)
PHONE..................................415 660-5320
Arthur T Sands, *President*
David Lacey, *Ch of Bd*
Stefani A Wolff, *COO*
Hans Van Houte, *CFO*
Gwenn Hansen, *Officer*
EMP: 114 EST: 2009
SQ FT: 49,991
SALES (est): 17.8MM **Publicly Held**
WEB: www.nurixtx.com
SIC: **8731** Biotechnical research, commercial

(P-19096)
ONEPOINTONE INC ◆
1185 Campbell Ave Unit G1, San Jose (95126-1068)
PHONE..................................855 346-5964
Samuel Bertram, *CEO*
John Bertram, *Principal*
Christopher Kitts, *Principal*
Raymond Levitt, *Principal*
Michael Steep, *Principal*
EMP: 70 EST: 2021
SALES (est): 5.7MM **Privately Held**
WEB: www.onepointone.com
SIC: **8731** 0182 Agricultural research; food crops grown under cover

(P-19097)
PALO ALTO RESEARCH CENTER INC
Also Called: Parc
3333 Coyote Hill Rd, Palo Alto (94304-1314)
PHONE..................................650 812-4000
Tolga Kurtoglu, *CEO*
Mark Bernstein, *President*
John Knights, *President*
John Pauksta, *CFO*
Jonathan R Wolter, *CFO*
EMP: 250 EST: 1998
SQ FT: 200,000
SALES (est): 80.8MM
SALES (corp-wide): 7B **Publicly Held**
WEB: www.parc.com
SIC: **8731** Medical research, commercial
HQ: Xerox Corporation
201 Merritt 7
Norwalk CT 06851
800 835-6100

(P-19098)
PAX WATER TECHNOLOGIES INC
550 Sycamore Dr, Milpitas (95035-7412)
PHONE..................................866 729-6493
Peter Fiske, *CEO*
EMP: 38 EST: 2006 **Privately Held**
SIC: **8731** Commercial physical research

(P-19099)
PENDULUM THERAPEUTICS INC
2001 Bryant St, San Francisco (94110-2125)
PHONE..................................844 912-2256
Colleen Cutcliffe, *CEO*
Brendon Stoneburner, *Research*
Surabhi Tyagi, *Research*
Fanny Perraudeau, *Senior Mgr*
David Raksin, *Director*
EMP: 55 EST: 2012
SALES (est): 98.2K **Privately Held**
WEB: www.pendulumlife.com
SIC: **8731** Biotechnical research, commercial

(P-19100)
PERSEID THERAPEUTICS LLC
515 Galveston Dr, Redwood City (94063-4720)
PHONE..................................650 298-5800
EMP: 48
SALES (est): 2.8MM
SALES (corp-wide): 12.2B **Privately Held**
SIC: **8731** Commercial Physical Research
HQ: Astellas Us Holding, Inc.
1 Astellas Way
Northbrook IL 60062
224 205-8800

(P-19101)
PETER H MATTSON & CO INC
343 Hatch Dr, Foster City (94404-1162)
PHONE..................................650 356-2500
Steve Gundrum, *President*
Peter H Mattson, *Chairman*
Patricia Mattson, *Corp Secy*
Barbara Stuckey, *Officer*
Al Banisch, *Exec VP*
EMP: 70 EST: 1977
SQ FT: 20,000
SALES (est): 15.6MM **Privately Held**
WEB: www.mattsonco.com
SIC: **8731** Food research

(P-19102)
PHARMATECH ASSOCIATES INC
22320 Fthill Blvd Ste 330, Hayward (94541)
PHONE..................................510 732-0177
Warren G Baker, *CEO*
Michaela Mueller, *CFO*
Calvin Wong, *Chairman*
Warford S Reaney, *Exec VP*
Warford Reaney, *Exec VP*
EMP: 39 EST: 1995
SALES (est): 10.7MM
SALES (corp-wide): 318.6MM **Privately Held**
WEB: www.pharmatechassociates.com
SIC: **8731** 8999 8748 7379 Biotechnical research, commercial; scientific consulting; systems analysis & engineering consulting services; computer related consulting services; chemical engineering
PA: The United States Pharmacopeial Convention Inc
12601 Twinbrook Pkwy
Rockville MD 20852
301 881-0666

(P-19103)
PLANT SCIENCES INC (PA)
342 Green Valley Rd, Watsonville (95076-1305)
PHONE..................................831 728-7771
Steven D Nelson, *CEO*
Richard Nelson, *President*
Michael D Nelson, *Vice Pres*
Vicki Nelson, *Admin Sec*
Daniel Nelson, *Director*
◆ EMP: 45 EST: 1985
SQ FT: 28,000
SALES (est): 22.2MM **Privately Held**
WEB: www.plantsciences.com
SIC: **8731** 8748 Agricultural research; biological research; agricultural consultant

(P-19104)
POLYFUEL INC
1245 Terra Bella Ave, Mountain View (94043-1849)
PHONE..................................650 429-4700
Jim Balcom, *President*
Frederick Cooper, *Vice Pres*
Phil Cox, *Vice Pres*
Henry Voss, *Vice Pres*
Daney Densin, *Accounts Mgr*
EMP: 37 EST: 1999
SQ FT: 15,500
SALES (est): 2.8MM **Privately Held**
WEB: www.polyfuel.com
SIC: **8731** Natural resource research

(P-19105)
PORTOLA PHARMACEUTICALS INC (DH)
270 E Grand Ave, South San Francisco (94080-4811)
PHONE..................................650 246-7300
Scott Garland, *CEO*
Hollings Renton, *Ch of Bd*
Dan Chen, *CFO*
Mardi Dier, *CFO*
Sheldon Koenig, *Ch Credit Ofcr*
EMP: 403 EST: 2003
SQ FT: 74,000
SALES (est): 116.6MM
SALES (corp-wide): 26.6B **Privately Held**
WEB: www.alexion.com
SIC: **8731** Biotechnical research, commercial

(P-19106)
PROMAB BIOTECHNOLOGIES INC
2600 Hilltop Dr, San Pablo (94806-1971)
PHONE..................................510 860-4615
Lijun Wu, *President*
Vita Golubovskaya, *Business Dir*
Van Dang, *Technical Staff*
EMP: 80 EST: 2001
SALES (est): 7.2MM **Privately Held**
WEB: www.promab.com
SIC: **8731** Biotechnical research, commercial

(P-19107)
PROTEINSIMPLE (HQ)
3001 Orchard Pkwy, San Jose (95134-2017)
PHONE..................................408 510-5500
Timothy Harkness, *President*
Robert Gavin, *Vice Pres*
Jason Novi, *Vice Pres*
Martin Putnam, *Vice Pres*
Marty Putnam, *Vice Pres*
▼ EMP: 45 EST: 2000
SALES (est): 37.9MM
SALES (corp-wide): 931MM **Publicly Held**
WEB: www.proteinsimple.com
SIC: **8731** Biotechnical research, commercial
PA: Bio-Techne Corporation
614 Mckinley Pl Ne
Minneapolis MN 55413
612 379-8854

(P-19108)
PROZYME INC
3832 Bay Center Pl, Hayward (94545-3619)
PHONE..................................510 638-6900
Sergey Vlasenko, *President*
Bruce Amsden, *Admin Sec*
C Richard Hutchinson, *VP Info Sys*
Justin Hyche, *Marketing Staff*
EMP: 47 EST: 1990
SQ FT: 20,000
SALES (est): 16.7MM
SALES (corp-wide): 5.3B **Publicly Held**
WEB: www.explore.agilent.com
SIC: **8731** Biotechnical research, commercial
PA: Agilent Technologies, Inc.
5301 Stevens Creek Blvd
Santa Clara CA 95051
800 227-9770

(P-19109)
PSIQUANTUM CORP (PA)
700 Hansen Way, Palo Alto (94304-1016)
PHONE..................................650 427-0000
Jeremy O'Brien, *CEO*
Nicholas Licausi, *Research*
Bradley Snyder, *Research*
Michael Johnson, *Accountant*
Jonathan Tsai, *Purchasing*
EMP: 41 EST: 2015
SALES (est): 3.8MM **Privately Held**
SIC: **8731** Commercial physical research

(P-19110)
PULSE BIOSCIENCES INC
3957 Point Eden Way, Hayward (94545-3720)
PHONE..................................510 906-4600
Darrin R Uecker, *President*
Robert W Duggan, *Ch of Bd*
Brian B Dow, *CFO*
Sandra Gardiner, *CFO*
Kenneth Clark, *Bd of Directors*
EMP: 54 EST: 2014
SQ FT: 15,700 **Privately Held**
WEB: www.pulsebiosciences.com
SIC: **8731** Biotechnical research, commercial

(P-19111)
Q BIO INC
1411 Industrial Rd, San Carlos (94070-4139)
PHONE..................................415 967-7622
Jeffrey Howard Kaditz, *CEO*
Chelsea Schlunt, *COO*
Amy Cray, *Director*
EMP: 42 EST: 2015
SALES (est): 2.8MM **Privately Held**
WEB: www.q.bio
SIC: **8731** Biotechnical research, commercial

(P-19112)
QUANTICEL PHARMACEUTICALS INC (PA)
1500 Owens St Ste 500, San Francisco (94158-2339)
PHONE..................................415 358-7609
Steve Kaldor, *President*
Jeffrey Stafford, *Admin Sec*
EMP: 40 EST: 2009
SQ FT: 9,000
SALES (est): 6.4MM **Privately Held**
SIC: **8731** Biotechnical research, commercial

(P-19113)
QURASENSE INC (PA)
3517 Edison Way Ste A, Menlo Park (94025-1876)
PHONE..................................415 702-8935
Soren R Therkelsen, *COO*
Marissa Letendre, *Vice Pres*

PRODUCTS & SERVICES SECTION **8731 - Commercial Physical & Biological Research County (P-19135)**

Brian Weinberg, *Research*
EMP: 56 **EST:** 2017
SALES (est): 739.8K **Privately Held**
WEB: www.qurasense.com
SIC: 8731 3821 Commercial research laboratory; clinical laboratory instruments, except medical & dental

(P-19114)
RADWARE INC
100 Mathilda Pl Ste 170, Sunnyvale (94086-6085)
PHONE..................650 627-4672
EMP: 57
SALES (corp-wide): 211.3MM **Privately Held**
WEB: www.radware.com
SIC: 8731 Computer (hardware) development
HQ: Radware Inc.
575 Corporate Dr Ste 205
Mahwah NJ 07430

(P-19115)
RAVEN BIOTECHNOLOGIES INC
1 Corporate Dr, South San Francisco (94080-7043)
PHONE..................650 624-2600
George Schreiner, *CEO*
Michael Kranda, *Ch of Bd*
John B Whelan, *COO*
William R Rohn, *Vice Ch Bd*
Lucille W S Chang, *Vice Pres*
EMP: 102 **EST:** 1999
SQ FT: 68,000
SALES (est): 8.3MM
SALES (corp-wide): 104.8MM **Publicly Held**
WEB: www.ravenbio.com
SIC: 8731 Biotechnical research, commercial; commercial research laboratory
PA: Macrogenics, Inc.
9704 Medical Center Dr
Rockville MD 20850
301 251-5172

(P-19116)
REGENTS OF THE UNIV OF CAL
Also Called: Division of Agriculture
1111 Franklin St Fl 10, Oakland (94607-5201)
PHONE..................510 987-0043
Glenda Humiston, *Vice Pres*
Wendy Ernst, *Officer*
Alan Wong, *Accountant*
EMP: 45 **Privately Held**
WEB: www.universityofcalifornia.edu
SIC: 8731 8221 9411 Commercial physical research; university; administration of educational programs;
HQ: The Regents Of The University Of California
1111 Franklin St Fl 12
Oakland CA 94607
510 987-0700

(P-19117)
REVOLUTION MEDICINES INC (PA)
700 Saginaw Dr, Redwood City (94063-4752)
PHONE..................650 481-6801
Mark A Goldsmith, *President*
Steve Kelsey, *President*
Margaret Horn, *COO*
Jack Anders, *Vice Pres*
Zhengping Wang, *Vice Pres*
EMP: 55 **EST:** 2014
SQ FT: 42,000
SALES (est): 42.9MM **Publicly Held**
WEB: www.revmed.com
SIC: 8731 Biotechnical research, commercial

(P-19118)
RIPPLE FOODS PBC
901 Gilman St Ste A, Berkeley (94710-1467)
PHONE..................510 269-2563
Laura Flanagan, *CEO*
Steve Orcutt, *CFO*
Eva Guilmo, *Associate Dir*
Jerome Edesan, *Engineer*
Ana Craig, *QC Mgr*
EMP: 82 **EST:** 2015

SQ FT: 10,000
SALES (est): 17.3MM **Privately Held**
WEB: www.ripplefoods.com
SIC: 8731 Food research

(P-19119)
ROCHE MOLECULAR SYSTEMS INC
1 Dna Way, South San Francisco (94080-4918)
P.O. Box 45090, San Francisco (94145-0090)
PHONE..................650 225-1000
Peng Zhang, *Analyst*
Lauren Wu, *Counsel*
Milan Crnogorac, *Senior Mgr*
Desai Ankita, *Manager*
EMP: 51
SALES (corp-wide): 69.8B **Privately Held**
WEB: www.diagnostics.roche.com
SIC: 8731 Biotechnical research, commercial
HQ: Roche Molecular Systems, Inc.
4300 Hacienda Dr
Pleasanton CA 94588

(P-19120)
ROCHE MOLECULAR SYSTEMS INC
2821 Scott Blvd, Santa Clara (95050-2549)
PHONE..................925 523-8099
EMP: 51
SALES (corp-wide): 69.8B **Privately Held**
WEB: www.diagnostics.roche.com
SIC: 8731 Biotechnical research, commercial
HQ: Roche Molecular Systems, Inc.
4300 Hacienda Dr
Pleasanton CA 94588

(P-19121)
ROCHE MOLECULAR SYSTEMS INC (DH)
4300 Hacienda Dr, Pleasanton (94588-2722)
P.O. Box 9002 (94566-9002)
PHONE..................925 730-8000
Paul Brown, *President*
Nick Solimo, *Vice Pres*
Priya Ratnam, *General Mgr*
Annie LI, *Planning*
Donald Cole, *Information Mgr*
◆ **EMP:** 400 **EST:** 1991
SALES (est): 435.5MM
SALES (corp-wide): 69.8B **Privately Held**
WEB: www.diagnostics.roche.com
SIC: 8731 Biotechnical research, commercial
HQ: Roche Holdings, Inc.
1 Dna Way
South San Francisco CA 94080
650 225-1000

(P-19122)
ROCHE NIMBLEGEN INC
4300 Hacienda Dr, Pleasanton (94588-2722)
PHONE..................608 316-3890
Frank Pitzer, *President*
Rebecca Selzer, *President*
Thomas M Palay, *CFO*
Robert J Palay, *Chairman*
Mark Schaller, *Treasurer*
EMP: 121 **EST:** 2000
SALES (est): 25.2MM
SALES (corp-wide): 69.8B **Privately Held**
WEB: www.sequencing.roche.com
SIC: 8731 Biotechnical research, commercial
PA: Roche Holding Ag
Grenzacherstrasse 124
Basel BS 4058
616 881-1011

(P-19123)
SAMSUNG RESEARCH AMERICA INC (DH)
Also Called: Sisa
665 Clyde Ave, Mountain View (94043-2235)
PHONE..................650 210-1001
Joonhyun Lee, *President*
Sungyu Hahm, *CFO*

Seungbeom Choi, *Senior VP*
Eyal Miller, *Vice Pres*
Woo-Young Yoon, *Executive*
◆ **EMP:** 805 **EST:** 1977
SQ FT: 130,000
SALES (est): 241MM **Privately Held**
WEB: www.sra.samsung.com
SIC: 8731 7371 Computer (hardware) development; computer software development & applications
HQ: Samsung Electronics America, Inc.
85 Challenger Rd
Ridgefield Park NJ 07660
201 229-4000

(P-19124)
SANSA TECHNOLOGY LLC
6990 Village Pkwy, Dublin (94568-2438)
PHONE..................866 204-3710
EMP: 50
SALES (est): 2.6MM **Privately Held**
SIC: 8731 Commercial Physical Research

(P-19125)
SILLAJEN BIOTHERAPEUTICS INC
450 Sansome St Ste 650, San Francisco (94111-3380)
PHONE..................415 281-8886
Laurent Fischer, *President*
David H Kirn, *Chief Mktg Ofcr*
James M Burke, *Vice Pres*
Deborah Campagna, *Senior Mgr*
Laurent Fanget, *Director*
EMP: 37 **EST:** 2008
SALES (est): 1.3MM
SALES (corp-wide): 1.4MM **Privately Held**
WEB: www.jennerex.com
SIC: 8731 Biotechnical research, commercial
PA: Sillajen Usa, Inc.
450 Sansome St Ste 650
San Francisco CA 94111
415 281-8886

(P-19126)
SIMBOL INC
Also Called: Simbol Materials
6920 Koll Center Pkwy # 216, Pleasanton (94566-3156)
PHONE..................925 226-7400
Luka Erceg, *President*
EMP: 100 **EST:** 2007
SALES (est): 7.9MM **Privately Held**
WEB: www.simbolinc.com
SIC: 8731 Natural resource research

(P-19127)
SOFAR OCEAN TECHNOLOGIES INC (PA)
Also Called: Spoondrift Technologies
Shed B Blkhead Of Pier 50 St Pier, San Francisco (94158)
P.O. Box 1533, El Granada (94018-1533)
PHONE..................415 230-2299
Tim Janssen, *CEO*
Evan Shapiro, *CTO*
Cameron Dunning, *Opers Staff*
EMP: 41 **EST:** 2015
SALES (est): 2.6MM **Privately Held**
WEB: www.sofarocean.com
SIC: 8731 Environmental research

(P-19128)
SONY BIOTECHNOLOGY INC
1730 N 1st St Fl 2, San Jose (95112-4642)
PHONE..................408 352-4257
EMP: 50
SALES (est): 875.4K **Privately Held**
WEB: www.sonybiotechnology.com
SIC: 8731 Commercial Physical Research

(P-19129)
SPRING BIOSCIENCE CORP
4300 Hacienda Dr, Pleasanton (94588-2722)
PHONE..................925 474-8463
Meghan Lehrkamp, *Manager*
EMP: 824 **EST:** 2002
SALES (est): 2.7MM
SALES (corp-wide): 69.8B **Privately Held**
WEB: www.diagnostics.roche.com
SIC: 8731 Biotechnical research, commercial

HQ: Ventana Medical Systems, Inc.
1910 E Innovation Park Dr
Oro Valley AZ 85755
520 887-2155

(P-19130)
STELLARTECH RESEARCH CORP (PA)
560 Cottonwood Dr, Milpitas (95035-7403)
PHONE..................408 331-3134
Roger A Stern, *President*
Jerome Jackson, *Vice Pres*
Jerry Smith, *Vice Pres*
Vincent Sullivan, *Vice Pres*
My Duong, *Engineer*
EMP: 99 **EST:** 1988
SQ FT: 20,000
SALES (est): 19.4MM **Privately Held**
WEB: www.stellartechresearch.com
SIC: 8731 3842 Medical research, commercial; surgical appliances & supplies

(P-19131)
SUN INNOVATIONS INC
43241 Osgood Rd, Fremont (94539-5657)
PHONE..................510 573-3913
Ted Sun, *President*
Priti Shah, *Training Spec*
George Donna, *Marketing Staff*
EMP: 50 **EST:** 2002
SQ FT: 2,200
SALES (est): 3.5MM **Privately Held**
WEB: www.sun-innovations.com
SIC: 8731 Commercial physical research

(P-19132)
SUNSYSTEM TECHNOLOGY LLC
2025 N Gateway Blvd # 112, Fresno (93727-1619)
PHONE..................559 412-7870
Kurtis Bank, *Branch Mgr*
EMP: 157
SALES (corp-wide): 28.3MM **Privately Held**
WEB: www.sstsolar.com
SIC: 8731 7374 Commercial physical research; data processing & preparation
PA: Sunsystem Technology, Llc
2731 Citrus Rd Ste D
Rancho Cordova CA 95742
916 671-3351

(P-19133)
SUNSYSTEM TECHNOLOGY LLC (PA)
2731 Citrus Rd Ste D, Rancho Cordova (95742-6303)
PHONE..................916 671-3351
Derek Chase, *CEO*
Jeff Hammer, *COO*
Mehrad Saidi, *CFO*
Darrell Hurley, *Vice Pres*
Greg Sellers, *Vice Pres*
EMP: 96 **EST:** 2014
SALES (est): 28.3MM **Privately Held*
WEB: www.sstsolar.com
SIC: 8731 4911 Commercial physical research; transmission, electric power

(P-19134)
TAKARA BIO USA INC (DH)
Also Called: Clontech
2560 Orchard Pkwy, San Jose (95131-1033)
PHONE..................650 919-7300
Carol Lou, *President*
Leslee McLennan Bonino, *Vice Pres*
Lorna Neilson, *Vice Pres*
Michael Rechsteiner, *Vice Pres*
Magnolia Bostick, *Associate Dir*
EMP: 174 **EST:** 1984
SQ FT: 100,000
SALES (est): 95.6MM **Privately Held**
WEB: www.takarabio.com
SIC: 8731 2836 Biotechnical research, commercial; biological products, except diagnostic

(P-19135)
TEGILE SYSTEMS INC
7999 Gateway Blvd Ste 120, Newark (94560-1144)
PHONE..................510 791-7900
Rohit Kshetrapal, *CEO*

(PA)=Parent Co (HQ)=Headquarters (DH)=Div Headquarters
✪ = New Business established in last 2 years

2022 Northern California Business Directory and Buyers Guide

8731 - Commercial Physical & Biological Research County (P-19136)

Tim Lewis, *Partner*
James Yu, *President*
Ian Edmundson, *CFO*
Michael Morgan, *CFO*
EMP: 130 **EST:** 2010
SQ FT: 6,500
SALES (est): 22.2MM Privately Held
WEB: www.tintri.com
SIC: 8731 3572 Computer (hardware) development; computer storage devices

(P-19136)
TIGO ENERGY INC (PA)
655 Campbell Tech Pkwy # 150, Campbell (95008-5061)
PHONE...............................408 402-0802
Zvi Alon, *CEO*
Ron Hadar, *President*
Jurgen Krehnke, *Ch Credit Ofcr*
George B Holmes, *Officer*
Jeffrey Krisa, *Senior VP*
▲ **EMP:** 42 **EST:** 2007
SALES (est): 9.9MM Privately Held
WEB: www.tigoenergy.com
SIC: 8731 1796 Energy research; power generating equipment installation

(P-19137)
TIZONA THERAPEUTICS INC
4000 Shoreline Ct Ste 200, South San Francisco (94080-2005)
PHONE...............................650 383-0800
Christine Obrien, *CEO*
Joyson Karakunnel, *Chief Mktg Ofcr*
Courtney Beers, *Officer*
Christine O 'brien, *Exec Dir*
Shelly Pinto, *Controller*
EMP: 42 **EST:** 2014
SALES (est): 6.3MM Privately Held
WEB: www.tizonatx.com
SIC: 8731 Biotechnical research, commercial

(P-19138)
TOSOH BIOSCIENCE INC
Also Called: Tosoh USA
6000 Shoreline Ct Ste 101, South San Francisco (94080-7606)
PHONE...............................650 615-4970
Max Yamata, *President*
Masanobu Kasai, *Vice Pres*
Bernadette Oconnell, *Technical Staff*
Benoit Maag, *VP Sls/Mktg*
◆ **EMP:** 75 **EST:** 1989
SQ FT: 13,917
SALES (est): 14.1MM Privately Held
WEB: www.diagnostics.us.tosohbioscience.com
SIC: 8731 Biotechnical research, commercial
HQ: Tosoh America, Inc.
3600 Gantz Rd
Grove City OH 43123

(P-19139)
TRACE GENOMICS INC
303 Twin Dolphin Dr # 600, Redwood City (94065-1422)
PHONE...............................650 332-6661
Dan Vradenburg, *CEO*
Brenda Rogers, *Vice Pres*
Ron Zink, *Principal*
Poornima Parameswaran, *Exec Dir*
Richard Barnes, *CIO*
EMP: 47 **EST:** 2015
SALES (est): 7.5MM Privately Held
WEB: www.tracegenomics.com
SIC: 8731 Biotechnical research, commercial

(P-19140)
TWIST BIOSCIENCE CORPORATION (PA)
681 Gateway Blvd, South San Francisco (94080-7015)
PHONE...............................800 719-0671
Emily M Leproust, *Ch of Bd*
Patrick Weiss, *COO*
James M Thorburn, *CFO*
Patrick Finn, *Ch Credit Ofcr*
Mark Daniels,
EMP: 413 **EST:** 2013
SQ FT: 60,963
SALES: 90.1MM Publicly Held
WEB: www.twistbioscience.com
SIC: 8731 Biotechnical research, commercial

(P-19141)
ULTIMA GENOMICS INC
7979 Gateway Blvd Ste 101, Newark (94560-1157)
P.O. Box 3760, Los Altos (94024-0760)
PHONE...............................650 861-1194
Tilad Almogi, *CEO*
Toni Lin, *Controller*
EMP: 40 **EST:** 2016
SQ FT: 5,000
SALES (est): 5.5MM Privately Held
SIC: 8731 Biotechnical research, commercial

(P-19142)
UNITED STATES DEPT OF ENERGY
1 Cyclotron Rd, Berkeley (94720-8099)
PHONE...............................510 486-4936
Fax: 510 486-7192
EMP: 2351 Publicly Held
SIC: 8731 Commercial Physical Research
HQ: United States Dept Of Energy
1000 Independence Ave Sw
Washington DC 20585
202 586-5000

(P-19143)
UNITED STATES DEPT OF ENERGY
Also Called: Lawrence Livermore Nat Lab
7000 East Ave, Livermore (94550-9698)
P.O. Box 808 (94551-0808)
PHONE...............................925 422-1100
Fax: 925 423-3597
EMP: 7000 Publicly Held
SIC: 8731 9611 Commercial Physical Research Administrative General Economic Programs
HQ: United States Dept Of Energy
1000 Independence Ave Sw
Washington DC 20585
202 586-5000

(P-19144)
UNITY BIOTECHNOLOGY INC
285 E Grand Ave, South San Francisco (94080-4804)
PHONE...............................650 416-1192
Anirvan Ghosh, *CEO*
Nathaniel E David, *President*
Robert C Goeltz II, *CFO*
Lynne Sullivan, *CFO*
Jamie Dananberg, *Chief Mktg Ofcr*
EMP: 106 **EST:** 2009 Privately Held
WEB: www.unitybiotechnology.com
SIC: 8731 Medical research, commercial

(P-19145)
UNIVERSITY CALIFORNIA DAVIS
Division of Agriculture
2801 2nd St, Davis (95618-7717)
PHONE...............................530 750-1313
Barbara Allen-Diaz, *Vice Pres*
EMP: 37 Privately Held
WEB: www.ucdavis.edu
SIC: 8731 8221 9411 Agricultural research; university; administration of educational programs;
HQ: University Of California, Davis
1 Shields Ave
Davis CA 95616

(P-19146)
VACUUM PROCESS ENGINEERING INC
150 Commerce Cir, Sacramento (95815-4208)
PHONE...............................916 925-6100
Carl P Schalansky, *Branch Mgr*
Dean Misajon, *Manager*
EMP: 84
SALES (corp-wide): 15.7MM Privately Held
WEB: www.vpei.com
SIC: 8731 Commercial physical research
PA: Vacuum Process Engineering, Inc.
110 Commerce Cir
Sacramento CA 95815
916 925-6100

(P-19147)
VERINATA HEALTH INC
Also Called: Illumina-Redwood City
200 Lincoln Centre Dr, Foster City (94404-1122)
PHONE...............................650 632-1680
Jeff Bird, *CEO*
Vance Vanier, *President*
William Chen, *Senior Mgr*
EMP: 55 **EST:** 2002
SALES (est): 12MM
SALES (corp-wide): 3.2B Publicly Held
WEB: www.illumina.com
SIC: 8731 2835 Biotechnical research, commercial; in vitro & in vivo diagnostic substances
PA: Illumina, Inc.
5200 Illumina Way
San Diego CA 92122
858 202-4500

(P-19148)
VIR BIOTECHNOLOGY INC (PA)
499 Illinois St Ste 500, San Francisco (94158-2521)
PHONE...............................415 906-4324
George Scangos, *President*
Vicki Sato, *Ch of Bd*
Howard Horn, *CFO*
Phil Pang, *Chief Mktg Ofcr*
Jay Parrish, *Officer*
EMP: 159 **EST:** 2016
SALES (est): 76.3MM Publicly Held
WEB: www.vir.bio
SIC: 8731 Biotechnical research, commercial

(P-19149)
VIRIDENT SYSTEMS INC
1745 Tech Dr Ste 700, San Jose (95110)
PHONE...............................408 573-5000
Mike Gustafson, *Senior VP*
Bruce Horn, *CFO*
Steven Campbell, *Officer*
Mark Delsman, *Vice Pres*
Kumar Ganapathy, *Vice Pres*
EMP: 110 **EST:** 2006
SALES (est): 24.5MM
SALES (corp-wide): 16.9B Publicly Held
WEB: www.westerndigital.com
SIC: 8731 Computer (hardware) development
HQ: Hgst, Inc.
5601 Great Oaks Pkwy
San Jose CA 95119
408 717-6000

(P-19150)
ZINFI TECHNOLOGIES INC
6200 Stnrdge Mall Rd Ste, Pleasanton (94588)
PHONE...............................925 251-0332
Sugata Sanyal, *CEO*
Seah K Leng, *President*
Kaushik Basu, *Executive*
Debasish Mete, *Web Dvlpr*
Surajit Ghosh, *Software Engr*
EMP: 42 **EST:** 2002
SALES (est): 5.9MM Privately Held
WEB: www.zinfi.com
SIC: 8731 Commercial physical research

(P-19151)
ZYMERGEN INC (PA)
5980 Horton St Ste 105, Emeryville (94608-2056)
PHONE...............................415 801-8073
Jay Flatley, *CEO*
Jay T Flatley, *Ch of Bd*
Enakshi Singh, *CFO*
Lincoln Germain, *Ch Credit Ofcr*
Mina Kim,
EMP: 620 **EST:** 2013
SQ FT: 252,000
SALES (est): 13.2MM Publicly Held
WEB: www.zymergen.com
SIC: 8731 Biotechnical research, commercial

8732 Commercial Economic, Sociological & Educational Research

(P-19152)
ANSWERLAB LLC (PA)
700 Larkspur Landing Cir, Larkspur (94939-1715)
PHONE...............................415 814-9910
Amy Buckner, *CEO*
Scott Gunter, *Vice Pres*
Isabel Klint, *Vice Pres*
Jennifer Scheer, *Vice Pres*
Edward Cruz, *Executive*
EMP: 35 **EST:** 2004
SQ FT: 7,600
SALES (est): 26.3MM Privately Held
WEB: www.answerlab.com
SIC: 8732 Market analysis, business & economic research

(P-19153)
BERKELEY NUTRITIONAL MFG CORP
Also Called: Protein Research
1852 Rutan Dr, Livermore (94551-7635)
PHONE...............................925 243-6300
Robert Matheson, *President*
Melissa Dethardt, *Vice Pres*
Ashley Matheson, *Vice Pres*
Melissa Matheson, *Vice Pres*
Gary Troxel, *Vice Pres*
▲ **EMP:** 60 **EST:** 1972
SQ FT: 53,900
SALES (est): 11.1MM Privately Held
WEB: www.proteinresearch.com
SIC: 8732 Market analysis or research

(P-19154)
C3 NANO INC
3988 Trust Way, Hayward (94545-3716)
PHONE...............................510 259-9650
Cliff Morris, *CEO*
Paul Larose, *CFO*
Ajay Virkar, *CTO*
Faraz Azadi, *Research*
Yadong Cao, *Engineer*
EMP: 87 **EST:** 2010
SALES (est): 6.8MM Privately Held
WEB: www.c3nano.com
SIC: 8732 Research services, except laboratory

(P-19155)
CAPITOL CORPORATE SERVICES INC (PA)
455 Capitol Mall Ste 217, Sacramento (95814-4405)
PHONE...............................916 444-6787
John H Robinson, *Vice Pres*
Cheryl Roberts, *President*
EMP: 99 **EST:** 1996
SALES (est): 327.9K Privately Held
SIC: 8732 Research services, except laboratory

(P-19156)
CLAS INFORMATION SERVICES
2020 Hurley Way Ste 350, Sacramento (95825-3214)
PHONE...............................916 564-7800
Judith Kahler, *CEO*
EMP: 56 **EST:** 1980
SALES (est): 4.7MM Privately Held
WEB: www.clasinfo.com
SIC: 8732 8111 Research services, except laboratory; legal services

(P-19157)
ECKER CONSUMER RECRUITING INC
Also Called: Ecker & Associates
1303 Melbourne St, Foster City (94404-3739)
PHONE...............................650 871-6800
Leon Ecker, *President*
Bette Rosenthal, *Vice Pres*
EMP: 51 **EST:** 1969
SQ FT: 5,300
SALES (est): 2.2MM Privately Held
SIC: 8732 Opinion research

PRODUCTS & SERVICES SECTION **8732 - Commercial Economic, Sociological & Educational Research County (P-19182)**

(P-19158)
ELLIOTT BENSON
1226 H St, Sacramento (95814-1911)
PHONE...................................916 325-1670
Jaclyn Benson, *Partner*
Patti Plymesser, *Purchasing*
Bryce Potter, *Purchasing*
Mildred Santos, *Opers Staff*
EMP: 50 **EST:** 1997
SALES (est): 3.3MM **Privately Held**
WEB: www.elliottbenson.com
SIC: 8732 Market analysis or research

(P-19159)
FX PALO ALTO LABORATORY INC
3174 Porter Dr, Palo Alto (94304-1212)
PHONE...................................650 842-4800
James Baker, *President*
Hiro Kabasawa, *CFO*
Hideh Takahashi, *Chairman*
Tsutomu G Abe, *Vice Pres*
Ram Sriram, *Vice Pres*
EMP: 45 **EST:** 1995
SALES (est): 10.4MM **Privately Held**
WEB: www.fxpal.com
SIC: 8732 Research services, except laboratory
HQ: Fujifilm Bi International Operations Corp.
 2100 Geng Rd Ste 210
 Palo Alto CA 94303

(P-19160)
GATOR BIO INC
2454 Embarcadero Way, Palo Alto (94303-3313)
PHONE...................................650 800-7651
Hong Tan, *CEO*
EMP: 100 **EST:** 2017
SALES (est): 3MM **Privately Held**
WEB: www.gatorbio.com
SIC: 8732 Business research service

(P-19161)
GFK CUSTOM RESEARCH LLC
360 Pine St Fl 6, San Francisco (94104-3226)
PHONE...................................415 398-2812
EMP: 54
SALES (corp-wide): 536.6K **Privately Held**
SIC: 8732 8713 Commercial Nonphysical Research Surveying Services
HQ: Gfk Custom Research, Llc
 200 Liberty St Fl 4
 New York NY 10281
 973 599-3540

(P-19162)
GLASS LEWIS & CO LLC (HQ)
255 California St # 1100, San Francisco (94111-4904)
PHONE...................................415 678-4110
Carrie Busch, *President*
John Wieck, *COO*
Stephen Gray, *CFO*
Dan Concannon, *Ch Credit Ofcr*
Nichol Garzon-Mitchell, *Senior VP*
EMP: 60 **EST:** 2003
SALES (est): 39.1MM **Privately Held**
WEB: www.glasslewis.com
SIC: 8732 Business analysis

(P-19163)
GOTION INC
48660 Kato Rd, Fremont (94538-7319)
PHONE...................................510 249-5610
Chen LI, *CEO*
Julie Sukey, *Admin Asst*
Wubing Ye, *Engineer*
Meimei Fu, *Controller*
EMP: 50 **EST:** 2014
SALES (est): 5.3MM **Privately Held**
WEB: www.gotion.com
SIC: 8732 Business research service

(P-19164)
GREENBERG INC (PA)
1250 53rd St Ste 5, Emeryville (94608-2965)
PHONE...................................510 446-8200
Andrew Greenberg, *President*
Philip Heuring,
Nick Collins, *Officer*
Iwan Thomis, *Officer*
Nicola Finnerty, *Vice Pres*
EMP: 48 **EST:** 1992
SQ FT: 5,500
SALES (est): 12.3MM **Privately Held**
WEB: www.greenberginc.com
SIC: 8732 Market analysis or research

(P-19165)
HALFZEEZ LLC
Also Called: Tailor Research
1990 N California Blvd, Walnut Creek (94596-3742)
PHONE...................................833 824-5675
George Schmilinsky, *CEO*
EMP: 50 **EST:** 2007
SALES (est): 1.8MM **Privately Held**
WEB: www.halfzeez.com
SIC: 8732 8713 Market analysis or research; surveying services

(P-19166)
IMAGINE EASY SOLUTIONS LLC (HQ)
3990 Freedom Cir, Santa Clara (95054-1204)
PHONE...................................212 675-6738
Neal Taparia, *CEO*
Bob Petrie, *COO*
Lindsey Palmer, *Executive*
Till Klampaeckel, *CTO*
Patricia Lu, *Human Res Mgr*
EMP: 50 **EST:** 2003
SALES (est): 2.4MM **Publicly Held**
WEB: www.chegg.com
SIC: 8732 Educational research

(P-19167)
INTERNATIONAL SOCIETY FOR
2861 Buena Vista Way, Berkeley (94708)
PHONE...................................510 680-6126
Kathryn Dumbleton, *Admin Sec*
EMP: 36 **EST:** 1978
SALES (est): 17.5K **Privately Held**
WEB: www.isclr.org
SIC: 8732 7371 Educational research; computer software development & applications

(P-19168)
IQVIA INC
135 Main St Fl 22, San Francisco (94105-1856)
PHONE...................................415 692-9898
Telia Mangrai, *Manager*
Anilkumar Kapu, *Associate Dir*
EMP: 100 **Publicly Held**
WEB: www.iqvia.com
SIC: 8732 Market analysis or research
HQ: Iqvia Inc.
 83 Wooster Hts Fl 5
 Danbury CT 06810
 203 448-4600

(P-19169)
MARKOV CORPORATION
1225 Magdalena Ct, Los Altos (94024-5205)
PHONE...................................650 207-9445
Lenard Spicer, *CEO*
EMP: 20 **EST:** 2016
SALES (est): 590.5K **Privately Held**
WEB: www.level.ai
SIC: 8732 3634 Market analysis, business & economic research; housewares, excluding cooking appliances & utensils

(P-19170)
MATHEMATICA INC
505 14th St Ste 800, Oakland (94612-1475)
PHONE...................................510 830-3700
Paul Decker, *Manager*
Debbie Reed, *Vice Pres*
Susie Clausen, *Office Admin*
Caitlin Matolka, *Project Mgr*
Jody Schimmel Hyde, *Deputy Dir*
EMP: 94
SALES (corp-wide): 290MM **Privately Held**
WEB: www.mathematica.org
SIC: 8732 Market analysis or research
HQ: Mathematica Inc.
 600 Alexander Park # 100
 Princeton NJ 08540
 609 799-3535

(P-19171)
NATIONAL OPINION RESEARCH CTR
50 California St Ste 1500, San Francisco (94111-4612)
PHONE...................................415 315-2000
EMP: 77
SALES (corp-wide): 237.7MM **Privately Held**
WEB: www.norc.org
SIC: 8732 Research services, except laboratory
PA: National Opinion Research Center
 55 E Monroe St Fl 30
 Chicago IL 60603
 312 759-4266

(P-19172)
NATIONAL OPINION RESEARCH CTR
1250 Borregas Ave, Sunnyvale (94089-1309)
PHONE...................................415 315-3800
EMP: 77
SALES (corp-wide): 237.7MM **Privately Held**
WEB: www.norc.org
SIC: 8732 Research services, except laboratory
PA: National Opinion Research Center
 55 E Monroe St Fl 30
 Chicago IL 60603
 312 759-4266

(P-19173)
NIELSEN COMPANY (US) LLC
Also Called: Neilsen TV Ratings
1001 Madison St Fl 2, Benicia (94510-2931)
PHONE...................................707 746-6905
EMP: 45 **Privately Held**
SIC: 8732 Commercial Nonphysical Research
HQ: The Nielsen Company Us Llc
 85 Broad St
 New York NY 10004
 646 654-5000

(P-19174)
NIELSEN MOBILE LLC (DH)
1010 Battery St, San Francisco (94111-1224)
PHONE...................................917 435-9301
Sid Gorham, *President*
Tom Stahl, *COO*
Jim Wandrey, *Treasurer*
Ryan O 'hearn, *Vice Pres*
Jagdish Patil, *Vice Pres*
EMP: 180 **EST:** 2000
SQ FT: 38,000
SALES (est): 41.2MM
SALES (corp-wide): 3.3B **Privately Held**
WEB: www.nielsen.com
SIC: 8732 Market analysis or research

(P-19175)
NOVOZYMES INC (DH)
Also Called: Novo Nordisk Biotech
1445 Drew Ave, Davis (95618-4880)
PHONE...................................530 757-8100
Peder Holk Nielsen, *CEO*
Ejner B Jensen, *President*
Melanie Allen, *Office Mgr*
Julia Waterson, *Executive Asst*
Miranda Warrick, *Admin Asst*
EMP: 62 **EST:** 1994
SQ FT: 64,000
SALES (est): 31.3MM
SALES (corp-wide): 23.2B **Privately Held**
WEB: www.novozymes.com
SIC: 8732 Commercial nonphysical research
HQ: Novozymes North America, Inc.
 77 Perry Chapel Church Rd
 Franklinton NC 27525
 919 494-2014

(P-19176)
NUEVORA
5000 Executive Pkwy # 515, San Ramon (94583-4210)
PHONE...................................925 967-2000
Phani K Nagarjuna, *CEO*
KS Kumar, *Officer*
Hari Hariharan, *Vice Pres*

Sastry Penumarthy, *Vice Pres*
Grant Anderson, *Marketing Staff*
EMP: 39 **EST:** 2005
SALES (est): 1.4MM
SALES (corp-wide): 1.6B **Privately Held**
WEB: www.sutherlandglobal.com
SIC: 8732 Business economic service; business research service
PA: Sutherland Global Services Inc.
 1160 Pittsford Victor Rd A
 Pittsford NY 14534
 585 586-5757

(P-19177)
ORANGE SILICON VALLEY LLC
Also Called: France Telecom RES & Dev LLC
60 Spear St Ste 1100, San Francisco (94105-1599)
PHONE...................................415 284-9765
Elie Girard,
Matthieu Cordier, *Vice Pres*
Michael Daride, *Vice Pres*
Jaline Davidson, *Vice Pres*
Timothy Ecton, *Vice Pres*
EMP: 65 **EST:** 1999
SALES (est): 26.6MM
SALES (corp-wide): 26.7B **Privately Held**
WEB: www.orangesv.com
SIC: 8732 Market analysis or research
PA: Orange
 111 Quai Du President Roosevelt
 Issy Les Moulineaux 92130

(P-19178)
OTR GLOBAL HOLDINGS II INC
155 Montgomery St Ste 501, San Francisco (94104-4110)
PHONE...................................415 675-7660
EMP: 51 **Privately Held**
WEB: www.otrglobal.com
SIC: 8732 Market analysis or research
PA: Otr Global Holdings Ii, Inc.
 4 Manhattanville Rd
 Purchase NY 10577

(P-19179)
PACIFIC RES INST FOR PUB PLICY (PA)
1 Embarcadero Ctr Ste 350, San Francisco (94111-3631)
PHONE...................................415 989-0833
Sally Pipes, *President*
Keith Chreston, *COO*
Christine Hughes, *Vice Pres*
Rowena Itchon, *Vice Pres*
Evan Harris, *Relations*
EMP: 19 **EST:** 1979
SALES (est): 6.1MM **Privately Held**
WEB: www.pacificresearch.org
SIC: 8732 2731 Economic research; books; publishing only

(P-19180)
PULSE Q&A INC
795 Folsom St Ste 1104, San Francisco (94107-1243)
PHONE...................................215 908-0199
Mayank Mehta, *CEO*
EMP: 50 **EST:** 2017
SQ FT: 1,000
SALES (est): 4.7MM **Privately Held**
WEB: www.pulse.qa
SIC: 8732 Market analysis, business & economic research

(P-19181)
QURI INC
655 Montgomery St Lbby 1, San Francisco (94111-2638)
PHONE...................................415 413-0100
EMP: 50
SALES (est): 5MM **Privately Held**
WEB: www.quri.com
SIC: 8732 Commercial Nonphysical Research

(P-19182)
RAYDIANCE INC
1100 La Avenida St, Mountain View (94043-1452)
PHONE...................................408 764-4000
Richard Pierce, *CEO*
John H N Fisher, *Principal*
Mike Mielke, *Security Dir*

8732 - Commercial Economic, Sociological & Educational Research County (P-19183)

▼ **EMP:** 22 **EST:** 2003
SQ FT: 42,000
SALES (est): 3.6MM **Privately Held**
SIC: 8732 3826 3821 Research services, except laboratory; laser scientific & engineering instruments; laser beam alignment devices

(P-19183)
REPUTATIONDEFENDER LLC (HQ)
1400a Saport Blvd Ste 401, Redwood City (94063)
PHONE.................................888 851-9609
Richard Matta,
EMP: 62 **EST:** 2018
SALES (est): 545.5K
SALES (corp-wide): 199.1K **Privately Held**
WEB: www.reputationdefender.com
SIC: 8732 Market analysis or research
PA: The Stagwell Group Llc
 1808 Eye St Nw Ste 600
 Washington DC 20006
 917 765-2638

(P-19184)
SK TELECOM AMERICAS INC
100 Mathilda Pl Ste 230, Sunnyvale (94086-6078)
PHONE.................................408 328-2900
Min Hyung Park, *President*
Joon Lee, *Vice Pres*
Paul Moon, *Vice Pres*
Sanjiv Parikh, *Vice Pres*
Hee Chung, *VP Bus Dvlpt*
EMP: 49 **EST:** 2000
SQ FT: 22,465
SALES (est): 5.5MM **Privately Held**
WEB: www.skta.com
SIC: 8732 Market analysis or research
PA: Sk Telecom Co.,Ltd.
 65 Eulji-Ro, Jung-Gu
 Seoul 04539

(P-19185)
SMARTREVENUECOM INC
101 Cooper St Ste 205, Santa Cruz (95060-4526)
PHONE.................................203 733-9156
John Dranow, *CEO*
EMP: 492
SALES (corp-wide): 22.8MM **Privately Held**
SIC: 8732 Market analysis or research
PA: Smartrevenue.Com, Inc.
 60 Twin Ridge Rd
 Ridgefield CT 06877
 203 733-9156

(P-19186)
SOCRATIC TECHNOLOGIES INC (PA)
245 N Main St, Sebastopol (95472-3435)
P.O. Box 411587, San Francisco (94141-1587)
PHONE.................................415 430-2200
Bill Macelroy, *President*
Chris Davis, *Exec VP*
Lee Streu, *Exec VP*
Michael Gray, *Vice Pres*
Laurie Matschoss, *Vice Pres*
EMP: 40 **EST:** 1994
SQ FT: 14,000
SALES (est): 6.3MM **Privately Held**
WEB: www.sotech.com
SIC: 8732 Market analysis or research

(P-19187)
SPHERE INSTITUTE
500 Airport Blvd Ste 340, Burlingame (94010-1934)
PHONE.................................650 558-3980
Thomas MA Curdy, *President*
Ellen Banh, *COO*
Greg Boro, *Treasurer*
Kyle Dobitz, *Software Dev*
Nathaniel Luders, *Software Dev*
EMP: 290 **EST:** 1996
SQ FT: 2,000
SALES (est): 29.2MM **Privately Held**
WEB: www.sphereinstitute.org
SIC: 8732 Market analysis or research

(P-19188)
SUNING CMMERCE R D CTR USA INC
Also Called: Suning USA
845 Page Mill Rd, Palo Alto (94304-1011)
PHONE.................................650 834-9800
Enlong Hou, *CEO*
Jin Ming, *President*
Leon Liu, *IT Specialist*
Yichao Chen, *Marketing Staff*
EMP: 60 **EST:** 2013
SQ FT: 9,800
SALES (est): 7MM **Privately Held**
WEB: www.ussuning.com
SIC: 8732 Commercial nonphysical research
PA: Suning.Com Co., Ltd.
 1-5/F, Jinshan Building, No. 8, Shanxi Road
 Nanjing 21000

(P-19189)
SURVEYSPARROW INC
2345 Yale St Fl 1, Palo Alto (94306-1449)
PHONE.................................800 481-0410
Muhammed Shihab Puthukkudi, *President*
EMP: 55 **EST:** 2018
SALES (est): 1.9MM **Privately Held**
WEB: www.surveysparrow.com
SIC: 8732 Survey service: marketing, location, etc.

(P-19190)
TIGER ANALYTICS INC (PA)
2350 Mission College Blvd # 495, Santa Clara (95054-1534)
PHONE.................................408 508-4430
Mahesh Kumar, *President*
Kishor Gummaraju, *Vice Pres*
Jinendra Jain, *Vice Pres*
Prashant Kabade, *Vice Pres*
Naveed Farhan, *Analyst*
EMP: 52 **EST:** 2011
SALES (est): 22.3MM **Privately Held**
WEB: www.tigeranalytics.com
SIC: 8732 8742 Business analysis; management consulting services

(P-19191)
VIZU CORPORATION (DH)
1010 Battery St, San Francisco (94111-1202)
PHONE.................................415 362-8498
Dan Beltramo, *CEO*
Sean O'Neal, *President*
John Moffett, *CFO*
Jeff Smith, *Vice Pres*
EMP: 78 **EST:** 2005
SALES (est): 1.1MM
SALES (corp-wide): 3.3B **Privately Held**
WEB: www.nielsen.com
SIC: 8732 Market analysis or research

8733 Noncommercial Research Organizations

(P-19192)
A 3 BY AIRBUS LLC
601 W California Ave, Sunnyvale (94086-4831)
PHONE.................................650 660-5809
Mark Cousin, *CEO*
Eduardo Dominguez-Puerta, *COO*
Trusten Allan McArtor,
EMP: 100 **EST:** 2014
SALES (est): 10.3MM
SALES (corp-wide): 59B **Privately Held**
WEB: www.airbus.com
SIC: 8733 Noncommercial research organizations
HQ: Airbus Americas, Inc.
 2550 Wasser Ter Ste 9000
 Herndon VA 20171
 703 834-3400

(P-19193)
ABBVIE STEMCENTRX LLC
1000 Gateway Blvd, South San Francisco (94080-7028)
PHONE.................................415 298-9242
Brian Slingerland, *CEO*
James N Strabridge, *COO*
Scott J Dylla, *Officer*
Hetal Sarvaiya, *Associate Dir*
Catherine Torres, *General Mgr*
EMP: 190 **EST:** 2008
SALES (est): 12.6MM
SALES (corp-wide): 45.8B **Publicly Held**
WEB: www.abbvie.com
SIC: 8733 2834 Medical research; proprietary drug products
PA: Abbvie Inc.
 1 N Waukegan Rd
 North Chicago IL 60064
 847 932-7900

(P-19194)
AFFYMAX RESEARCH INSTITUTE
4001 Miranda Ave, Palo Alto (94304-1218)
PHONE.................................650 812-8700
Gordon Ringold PHD, *CEO*
Lauren Stevens, *President*
Helen S Kim, *Officer*
Emily Lee Kelly, *Vice Pres*
EMP: 69 **EST:** 1988
SQ FT: 103,000
SALES (est): 6.9MM
SALES (corp-wide): 45.3B **Privately Held**
WEB: www.affymax.com
SIC: 8733 8732 8731 Medical research; commercial nonphysical research; commercial physical research
PA: Glaxosmithkline Plc
 G S K House
 Brentford MIDDX TW8 9
 208 047-5000

(P-19195)
AMERICAN CANCER SOC CAL DIV (PA)
1001 Marina Village Pkwy, Alameda (94501-1091)
PHONE.................................510 893-7900
Carolyn F Katzin, *CEO*
Marilyn Broussard, *CFO*
David Veneziano, *Exec VP*
Gina Mayfield, *Admin Asst*
Patrice Lestrange, *Corp Comm Staff*
EMP: 100 **EST:** 1946
SQ FT: 47,000
SALES (est): 73.6MM **Privately Held**
SIC: 8733 Noncommercial research organizations

(P-19196)
APPLIED EARTHWORKS INC (PA)
1391 W Shaw Ave Ste C, Fresno (93711-3600)
PHONE.................................559 229-1856
E A Johansen, *President*
S K Goldberg, *Ch of Bd*
Andrew Monastero, *Vice Pres*
William Borkan, *Executive*
Vanessa Mirro, *Regional Mgr*
EMP: 49 **EST:** 1995
SALES (est): 9.2MM **Privately Held**
WEB: www.appliedearthworks.com
SIC: 8733 8748 Archeological expeditions; business consulting

(P-19197)
ASIA FOUNDATION (PA)
465 California St Fl 9, San Francisco (94104-1892)
P.O. Box 193223 (94119-3223)
PHONE.................................415 982-4640
David D Arnold, *President*
Suzanne Siskel, *COO*
Ken Krug, *CFO*
Alexander D Calhoun, *Bd of Directors*
Scott Cook, *Trustee*
◆ **EMP:** 90 **EST:** 1951
SQ FT: 17,207
SALES (est): 104.7MM **Privately Held**
WEB: www.asiafoundation.org
SIC: 8733 Noncommercial research organizations

(P-19198)
BAY AREA ENVMTL RES INST
Also Called: Baer Institute
Nasa Res Pk Bldg 18 Rm 10, Moffett Field (94035)
P.O. Box 25 (94035-0025)
PHONE.................................707 938-9387
Robert W Bergstrom, *President*

Mark Sittloh, *Exec Dir*
Gailynne Bouret, *Administration*
Thomas Hartlep, *Research*
Cindy Schmidt, *Research*
▲ **EMP:** 50 **EST:** 1993
SQ FT: 750
SALES: 21.8MM **Privately Held**
WEB: www.baeri.org
SIC: 8733 Medical research

(P-19199)
BIOMEDICAN INC (PA)
40471 Encyclopedia Cir, Fremont (94538-2452)
PHONE.................................412 475-8886
Maxim Mikheev, *President*
EMP: 54 **EST:** 2017
SALES (est): 463.3K **Privately Held**
WEB: www.biomedican.com
SIC: 8733 Medical research

(P-19200)
BUCK INST FOR RES ON AGING (PA)
8001 Redwood Blvd, Novato (94945-1400)
PHONE.................................415 209-2000
Eric M Verdin, *President*
Dale Bredesen MD, *President*
Nancy Derr, *CFO*
Meagan Moore, *Officer*
Raja Kamal, *Senior VP*
EMP: 139 **EST:** 1986
SQ FT: 185,000
SALES (est): 50.4MM **Privately Held**
WEB: www.buckinstitute.org
SIC: 8733 Medical research

(P-19201)
CALIFORNIA CMPLTE CNT CNSUS
400 R St Ste 350, Sacramento (95811-6233)
PHONE.................................916 852-2020
Ditas Katague, *Principal*
Dorothy Johnson, *Asst Director*
Sara Murillo, *Manager*
Thuong Pham, *Manager*
EMP: 60 **EST:** 2018
SALES (est): 2.9MM **Privately Held**
WEB: www.counties.org
SIC: 8733 Noncommercial research organizations

(P-19202)
CALIFORNIA IMAGING INST LLC (PA)
1867 E Fir Ave Ste 101, Fresno (93720-3808)
PHONE.................................559 325-5810
Mariela Resendes, *Principal*
Frank Chang, *Risk Mgmt Dir*
Jason Roberts, *Nuclear Medcne*
Jeffrey Saavedra, *Radiology*
EMP: 48 **EST:** 2005
SALES (est): 6.4MM **Privately Held**
WEB: www.caimaginginstitute.com
SIC: 8733 Noncommercial research organizations

(P-19203)
CAMBRIOS TECHNOLOGIES CORP
930 E Arques Ave, Sunnyvale (94085-4520)
PHONE.................................408 738-7400
John Lemoncheck, *CEO*
Michael Knapp, *President*
Vinod Mahendroo, *COO*
Michael Spaid, *Vice Pres*
David Yao, *Vice Pres*
EMP: 35 **EST:** 2002
SQ FT: 1,000
SALES (est): 5MM **Privately Held**
WEB: www.cambrios.com
SIC: 8733 Scientific research agency

(P-19204)
CANCER PREVENTION INST CAL
2001 Center St Ste 700, Berkeley (94704-1242)
PHONE.................................510 608-5000
Susan Hurley, *Branch Mgr*
EMP: 35

PRODUCTS & SERVICES SECTION
8733 - Noncommercial Research Organizations County (P-19227)

SALES (corp-wide): 13.2K **Privately Held**
WEB: www.cpic.org
SIC: **8733** Medical research
PA: Cancer Prevention Institute Of California
39141 Civic Center Dr # 425
Fremont CA 94538
510 608-5000

(P-19205)
CANCER PREVENTION INST CAL (PA)
Also Called: GREATER BAY AREA CANCER REGIST
39141 Civic Center Dr # 425, Fremont (94538-5818)
P.O. Box 4120, San Mateo (94404-0120)
PHONE 510 608-5000
Matt O'Grady, *CEO*
Jay Yu, *Vice Pres*
Rita Leung, *Programmer Anys*
Sally Glaser, *Research*
Ingrid Oakley-Girvan, *Research*
EMP: 115 EST: 1974
SALES: 13.2K **Privately Held**
WEB: www.cpic.org
SIC: **8733** Medical research

(P-19206)
CARNEGIE INSTITUTION WASH
Also Called: Department of Global Ecology
260 Panama St, Stanford (94305-4150)
PHONE 650 319-8904
Chris Field, *Director*
Jennifer Brophy, *Research*
EMP: 73
SALES (corp-wide): 73.9MM **Privately Held**
WEB: www.carnegiescience.edu
SIC: **8733** Scientific research agency
PA: Carnegie Institution Of Washington
5251 Broad Branch Rd Nw
Washington DC 20015
202 387-6400

(P-19207)
CG2 INC
Also Called: Quantum3d Government Systems
1759 Mccarthy Blvd, Milpitas (95035-7416)
PHONE 407 737-8800
EMP: 69
SALES (est): 3.2MM **Privately Held**
SIC: **8733** Noncommercial Research Organization

(P-19208)
CHAN ZUCKERBERG BIOHUB INC
499 Illinois St, San Francisco (94158-2518)
PHONE 628 200-3246
Stephen Quake, *President*
Bryant Chhun, *Research*
Syuan-Ming Guo, *Research*
Merlin Lange, *Research*
Maureen Sheehy, *General Counsel*
EMP: 68 EST: 2017
SALES (est): 11.1MM **Privately Held**
WEB: www.czbiohub.org
SIC: **8733** Medical research

(P-19209)
CHRONO THERAPEUTICS INC (PA)
3953 Point Eden Way, Hayward (94545-3720)
PHONE 510 362-7788
David A Happel, *CEO*
James Young, *Ch of Bd*
David Matly, *President*
Tony Rimac, *CFO*
Guy Dipierro, *Senior VP*
EMP: 37 EST: 2003
SQ FT: 10,000
SALES (est): 5MM **Privately Held**
WEB: www.chronothera.com
SIC: **8733** Medical research

(P-19210)
COAGUSENSE INC
48377 Fremont Blvd # 113, Fremont (94538-6565)
PHONE 510 270-5442
Doug Patterson, *CEO*
Duane Yamasaki, *Vice Pres*
Nandita Bhatnagar, *Technical Staff*
Van Chang, *Prdtn Mgr*
Walter Martinez, *Production*
EMP: 43 EST: 2011
SALES (est): 13.8MM **Privately Held**
WEB: www.coag-sense.com
SIC: **8733** **8621** Noncommercial biological research organization; medical field-related associations
PA: I-Sens, Inc.
43 Banpo-Daero 28-Gil, Seocho-Gu
Seoul 06646

(P-19211)
COMENTIS INC
400 Oyster Point Blvd # 226, South San Francisco (94080-1904)
PHONE 650 869-7600
Terence Kelly, *President*
Daniel Hunt, *President*
EMP: 35 EST: 2005
SALES (est): 3.8MM **Privately Held**
WEB: www.comentis.com
SIC: **8733** Medical research

(P-19212)
COMPLETE GENOMICS INC
2904 Orchard Pkwy, San Jose (95134-2009)
PHONE 408 648-2560
Clifford A Reid PHD, *Ch of Bd*
Ajay Bansal, *CFO*
Keith Raffel, *Ch Credit Ofcr*
Arthur W Homan, *Senior VP*
Ethan Knowlden, *Senior VP*
EMP: 255 EST: 2005
SQ FT: 66,000
SALES (est): 34.6MM **Privately Held**
WEB: www.completegenomics.com
SIC: **8733** Biotechnical research, noncommercial
PA: Beijing Genomics Institute At Shenzhen
Comprehensive Building, Beishan Industrial Zone, Yantian Street, Shenzhen 51800

(P-19213)
DISHCRAFT ROBOTICS INC
611 Taylor Way Ste 1, San Carlos (94070-6305)
PHONE 888 231-3318
Linda Hirschhorn Pouliot, *CEO*
Michelle Berry, *Officer*
Steven Hung, *CIO*
Brett Lee, *Engineer*
Disha Samaiyar, *Engineer*
EMP: 52 EST: 2016
SALES (est): 7.9MM **Privately Held**
WEB: www.dishcraft.com
SIC: **8733** Research institute

(P-19214)
ELECTRIC POWER RES INST INC (PA)
3420 Hillview Ave, Palo Alto (94304-1382)
P.O. Box 10412 (94303-0813)
PHONE 650 855-2000
Michael Howard, *CEO*
Pedro J Pizarro, *Ch of Bd*
Terry Boston, *President*
Stanley W Connally Jr, *Chairman*
Patricia Vincent-Collawn, *Vice Ch Bd*
EMP: 600 EST: 1973
SQ FT: 300,000
SALES (est): 420.2MM **Privately Held**
WEB: www.epri.com
SIC: **8733** Research institute

(P-19215)
ELEMENT SCIENCE INC
200 Kansas St Ste 210, San Francisco (94103-5146)
PHONE 415 872-6500
Uday N Kumar, *President*
Megan Steck, *Mfg Staff*
Sidney Negus, *Opers Staff*
Chris Leano, *Manager*
EMP: 72 EST: 2011
SALES (est): 5.1MM **Privately Held**
WEB: www.elementscience.com
SIC: **8733** **8011** Medical research; surgeon

(P-19216)
ENERGY BERKELEY OFFICE US DEPT
Also Called: Lawrence Berkeley National Lab
1226 Cornell Ave, Albany (94706-2308)
PHONE 510 701-1089
EMP: 135 **Publicly Held**
WEB: www.es.net
SIC: **8733** **9611** Noncommercial research organizations; energy development & conservation agency, government
HQ: United States Department Of Energy Berkeley Office
1 Cyclotron Rd
Berkeley CA 94720
510 486-5784

(P-19217)
ENERGY BERKELEY OFFICE US DEPT
Also Called: Lawrence Berkeley National Lab
419 Latimer Hall, Berkeley (94720-1461)
PHONE 510 486-4033
EMP: 135 **Publicly Held**
WEB: www.lbl.gov
SIC: **8733** **9611** Noncommercial research organizations; energy development & conservation agency, government;
HQ: United States Department Of Energy Berkeley Office
1 Cyclotron Rd
Berkeley CA 94720
510 486-5784

(P-19218)
HAKOMI INSTITUTE OF CAL LLC
5874b Vallejo St, Oakland (94608-2626)
PHONE 415 839-6788
Robert Fisher, *Branch Mgr*
EMP: 35
SALES (corp-wide): 236.6K **Privately Held**
SIC: **8733** Noncommercial research organizations
PA: The Hakomi Institute Of California Llc
5758 Geary Blvd
San Francisco CA

(P-19219)
INSTITUTE FOR FUTURE
201 Hamilton Ave, Palo Alto (94301-2530)
PHONE 650 854-6322
Ellen Marram, *Ch of Bd*
Daria Lamb, *Partner*
Martin Low, *CFO*
Marty Low, *Officer*
Michael Ness, *Business Dir*
EMP: 38 EST: 1968
SQ FT: 13,000
SALES (est): 13.9MM **Privately Held**
WEB: www.iftf.org
SIC: **8733** **8742** Medical research; management consulting services

(P-19220)
INSTITUTE OF HEARTMATH
14700 W Park Ave, Boulder Creek (95006-9673)
P.O. Box 1463 (95006-1463)
PHONE 831 338-8500
Sara Paddison, *President*
Brian Kabaker, *CFO*
Rollin McCraty, *Senior VP*
Katherine Floriano, *Exec Dir*
EMP: 37 EST: 1985
SQ FT: 23,910
SALES: 2.5MM **Privately Held**
WEB: www.heartmath.org
SIC: **8733** Research institute

(P-19221)
INSTITUTE OF NOETIC SCIENCES
101 San Antonio Rd, Petaluma (94952-9524)
PHONE 707 775-3500
James O' DEA, *President*
Rolando Pintro, *Info Tech Dir*
Jenny Mathews, *Research*
Kerstin Sjoquist, *Director*
Deborah Day, *Manager*
EMP: 36 EST: 1972
SQ FT: 4,750
SALES (est): 5.3MM **Privately Held**
WEB: www.noetic.org
SIC: **8733** Research institute

(P-19222)
INTERNTIONAL CMPT SCIENCE INST
Also Called: I C S I
2150 Shattuck Ave # 1100, Berkeley (94704-1345)
PHONE 510 643-9153
Rebecca Pieraccini, *President*
Robin Sommer, *Executive*
Maria Quintana, *Exec Dir*
Maria Eugenia Quintana, *Exec Dir*
Cindy Ngu, *Admin Asst*
EMP: 45 EST: 1986
SQ FT: 26,000
SALES (est): 9.2MM **Privately Held**
WEB: www.icsi.berkeley.edu
SIC: **8733** Research institute

(P-19223)
JACKSON LABORATORY
1650 Santa Ana Ave, Sacramento (95838-1752)
PHONE 916 373-5905
EMP: 38
SALES (corp-wide): 440.7MM **Privately Held**
SIC: **8733** Noncommercial Research Organization
PA: The Jackson Laboratory
600 Main St
Bar Harbor ME 04609
207 288-6000

(P-19224)
MIDEA EMERGING TECH CO LTD
250 W Tasman Dr, San Jose (95134-1714)
PHONE 973 539-5330
Kurt Jovais, *President*
Chunwei Qiu, *Admin Sec*
EMP: 39 EST: 2017
SQ FT: 1,000
SALES (est): 1.6MM **Privately Held**
SIC: **8733** Physical research, noncommercial

(P-19225)
NATIONAL FOOD LABORATORY LLC
365 N Canyons Pkwy # 201, Livermore (94551-7703)
PHONE 925 828-1440
Austin Sharp, *President*
Carla Mitchell, *Senior VP*
Jena Roberts, *Vice Pres*
James Skiles, *Vice Pres*
Eden Legesse, *Analyst*
EMP: 62 EST: 1991
SQ FT: 21,000
SALES (est): 7.2MM **Privately Held**
WEB: www.thenfl.com
SIC: **8733** Scientific research agency

(P-19226)
NEUMORA THERAPEUTICS INC
8000 Marina Blvd Ste 700, Brisbane (94005-1888)
PHONE 510 828-4062
Paul Berns, *CEO*
EMP: 100 EST: 2019
SALES (est): 2.3MM **Privately Held**
SIC: **8733** Biotechnical research, noncommercial

(P-19227)
OPENAI INC
3180 18th St Ste 100, San Francisco (94110-2042)
PHONE 650 387-6701
Bob McGrew, *Vice Pres*
Mario Saltarelli, *Info Tech Mgr*
Jakub Pachocki, *Research*
Peter Welinder, *Research*
Lei Zhang, *Research*
EMP: 50 EST: 2017
SALES (est): 6MM **Privately Held**
WEB: www.openai.com
SIC: **8733** Biotechnical research, noncommercial

8733 - Noncommercial Research Organizations County (P-19228)

(P-19228)
PALO ALTO VTERANS INST FOR RES
Also Called: PAVIR
3801 Miranda Ave 101a, Palo Alto (94304-1207)
PHONE....................650 858-3970
Kerstin Lynam, *CEO*
Mary Thornton, *COO*
Nga Phan, *Admin Sec*
Joseph Garrido, *Administration*
Margaret Hinebaugh, *Administration*
EMP: 218 EST: 1988
SQ FT: 5,500
SALES: 29.5MM **Privately Held**
WEB: www.pavir.org
SIC: 8733 Medical research; noncommercial biological research organization; scientific research agency

(P-19229)
POINT REYES BIRD OBSERVATORY
Also Called: Point Blue Cnservation Science
3820 Cypress Dr Ste 11, Petaluma (94954-6964)
PHONE....................707 781-2555
Ellie M Cohen, *President*
Kate Howard, *Partner*
Luke Petersen, *Partner*
Corey Shake, *Partner*
Carrie Wendt, *Partner*
EMP: 85
SQ FT: 2,000
SALES: 11.9MM **Privately Held**
WEB: www.pointblue.org
SIC: 8733 8748 Noncommercial biological research organization; business consulting

(P-19230)
PREMIER SOURCE LLC
999 Bayhill Dr Fl 3, San Bruno (94066-3070)
PHONE....................415 349-2010
EMP: 65
SQ FT: 13,000
SALES (est): 3.4MM
SALES (corp-wide): 153.1B **Publicly Held**
SIC: 8733 Scientific Research Agency
PA: Amerisourcebergen Corporation
1300 Morris Dr Ste 100
Chesterbrook PA 19428
610 727-7000

(P-19231)
PROTHENA BIOSCIENCES INC
331 Oyster Point Blvd, South San Francisco (94080-1913)
PHONE....................650 837-8550
Gene Kinney, *CEO*
Carol Karp, *Officer*
Karin Walker, *Officer*
Pam Farmer, *Vice Pres*
Ria Palarca, *Associate Dir*
EMP: 50 EST: 2012
SALES (est): 9.9MM **Privately Held**
WEB: www.prothena.com
SIC: 8733 Medical research

(P-19232)
PUBLIC HEALTH INSTITUTE (PA)
555 12th St Ste 290, Oakland (94607-3601)
PHONE....................510 285-5500
Mary Pittman, *President*
Melange Matthews, *COO*
Bob Wolfson, *COO*
Tamar Dorfman, *CFO*
M L Matthews, *Exec VP*
EMP: 100 EST: 1964
SQ FT: 50,000
SALES: 112.1MM **Privately Held**
WEB: www.phi.org
SIC: 8733 Scientific research agency; medical research

(P-19233)
PUBLIC HEALTH INSTITUTE
1683 Shattuck Ave Ste B, Berkeley (94709-1611)
PHONE....................510 285-5500
Dileep Bal, *Chairman*
Matthew Marsom, *Vice Pres*
Janet Eadie, *Benefits Mgr*
EMP: 53
SALES (corp-wide): 112.1MM **Privately Held**
WEB: www.phi.org
SIC: 8733 8299 Scientific research agency; educational service, nondegree granting: continuing educ.
PA: Public Health Institute
555 12th St Ste 290
Oakland CA 94607
510 285-5500

(P-19234)
SAN FRANCISCO ESTUARY INST
4911 Central Ave, Richmond (94804-5803)
P.O. Box 632, Pinole (94564-0632)
PHONE....................510 746-7334
Jim Kelly, *Exec Dir*
Warner Chabot, *Exec Dir*
Jennifer Hunt, *Program Mgr*
Patrick Walsh, *Finance*
Amy Richey, *Analyst*
EMP: 49 EST: 1983
SQ FT: 24,366
SALES (est): 13.2MM **Privately Held**
WEB: www.sfei.org
SIC: 8733 Scientific research agency

(P-19235)
SEARCH GROUP INCORPORATED
Also Called: NATIONAL CONSORTIUM FOR JUSTIC
1900 Point West Way # 161, Sacramento (95815-4705)
PHONE....................916 392-2550
Scott Came, *Exec Dir*
Timothy Lott,
EMP: 72 EST: 1974
SQ FT: 3,700
SALES (est): 3.7MM **Privately Held**
WEB: www.search.org
SIC: 8733 Noncommercial research organizations

(P-19236)
SETI INSTITUTE
Also Called: Seti Institute, The
339 Bernardo Ave Ste 200, Mountain View (94043-5232)
PHONE....................650 961-6633
Matthew Doan, *President*
Dr John Billingham, *Vice Chairman*
Edna Devor, *CEO*
Shannon Atkinson, *CFO*
Dr Greg Papadopolous, *Chairman*
EMP: 115 EST: 1984
SQ FT: 19,737
SALES (est): 22.6MM **Privately Held**
WEB: www.seti.org
SIC: 8733 Research institute

(P-19237)
SRI INTERNATIONAL (PA)
333 Ravenswood Ave, Menlo Park (94025-3493)
P.O. Box 2203 (94026-2203)
PHONE....................650 859-2000
William Jeffrey, *CEO*
Denise Glyn Borders, *President*
Stephen Ciesinski, *President*
Manish Kothari, *President*
Greg Kovacs, *President*
▲ EMP: 1430 EST: 1946
SQ FT: 1,300,000
SALES: 461.4MM **Privately Held**
WEB: www.sri.com
SIC: 8733 8748 Scientific research agency; noncommercial social research organization; business consulting

(P-19238)
STANFORD UNIV FRMAN SPGLI INST
616 Jane Stanford Way, Stanford (94305-6008)
PHONE....................650 723-8681
Michael McFaul, *Director*
Lisa Krauss, *Associate*
EMP: 250 EST: 2017
SALES (est): 14MM **Privately Held**
WEB: www.stanford.edu
SIC: 8733 Research institute

(P-19239)
TRANSFAIR USA
Also Called: Fair Trade USA
1901 Harrison St Ste 1700, Oakland (94612-3635)
PHONE....................510 663-5260
Paul Rice, *President*
Dave Rochlin, *COO*
Joan Catherine Braun, *CFO*
Clay Brown, *Officer*
Mark Gunton, *Officer*
EMP: 144 EST: 1996
SALES (est): 21.6MM **Privately Held**
WEB: www.fairtradecertified.org
SIC: 8733 Noncommercial social research organization

(P-19240)
UNITED STATES DEPT OF ENERGY
Also Called: Lawrence Berkeley National Lab
1 Cyclotron Rd, Berkeley (94720-8099)
PHONE....................510 486-4000
EMP: 5000 **Publicly Held**
SIC: 8733 9611 Research Laboratory
HQ: United States Dept Of Energy
1000 Independence Ave Sw
Washington DC 20585
202 586-5000

(P-19241)
UNIVERSITY CAL SAN FRANCISCO
Also Called: Uscf Caps Department Medicine
500 Parnassus Ave, San Francisco (94143-2203)
PHONE....................415 476-9000
EMP: 87
SALES (corp-wide): 9.5B **Privately Held**
SIC: 8733 8221 9411 Noncommercial Research Organization
HQ: University Of California, San Francisco
505 Parnassus Ave
San Francisco CA 94143
415 476-9000

(P-19242)
UNIVERSITY CAL SAN FRANCISCO
Also Called: Ucsf Neuro Epidemiology Lab
1450 3rd St St230, San Francisco (94143-2197)
PHONE....................415 476-9323
EMP: 51 **Privately Held**
WEB: www.ucsf.edu
SIC: 8733 8221 9411 Medical research; university; administration of educational programs
HQ: University Cal San Francisco
513 Parnassus Ave 115f
San Francisco CA 94143

(P-19243)
URS GROUP INC
1550 Humboldt Rd Ste 2, Chico (95928-9115)
PHONE....................530 893-9675
Elena Nilsson, *Branch Mgr*
EMP: 90
SALES (corp-wide): 13.2B **Publicly Held**
WEB: www.aecom.com
SIC: 8733 Archeological expeditions
HQ: Urs Group, Inc.
300 S Grand Ave Ste 900
Los Angeles CA 90071
213 593-8000

(P-19244)
VIOPTIX INC
39655 Eureka Dr, Newark (94560-4806)
PHONE....................510 226-5860
Larry C Heaton II, *President*
Mark Lonsinger, *Vice Pres*
Derek Lee, *Technician*
Melissa Liu, *Controller*
Dan Barry, *Regl Sales Mgr*
EMP: 18 EST: 1999
SQ FT: 11,000
SALES (est): 2.9MM **Privately Held**
WEB: www.vioptix.com
SIC: 8733 3841 Medical research; diagnostic apparatus, medical

(P-19245)
WATER RESOURCES CAL DEPT
Division of Flood Management
3310 El Cmino Ave Ste 200, Sacramento (95821)
PHONE....................916 574-1423
Sandra Layne, *Exec Dir*
Janiene Friend, *Admin Asst*
Dee Alstatt, *Administration*
Michael Barentson, *Administration*
Michael Hom, *Info Tech Mgr*
EMP: 100 **Privately Held**
WEB: www.ca.gov
SIC: 8733 Research institute
HQ: California Department Of Water Resources
1416 9th St
Sacramento CA 95814
916 653-9394

(P-19246)
WESTED
300 Lakeside Dr Fl 25th, Oakland (94612-3534)
PHONE....................510 302-4200
Teresa Johnson, *Branch Mgr*
Joaquin Petersen, *IT/INT Sup*
Marycruz Diaz, *Research*
Yvonne KAO, *Research*
Robert Montgomery, *Sr Project Mgr*
EMP: 48
SALES (corp-wide): 71.6MM **Privately Held**
WEB: www.wested.org
SIC: 8733 8732 Educational research agency; commercial nonphysical research
PA: Wested
730 Harrison St Ste 500
San Francisco CA 94107
415 565-3000

(P-19247)
WESTED
180 Harbor Dr Ste 112, Sausalito (94965-2845)
PHONE....................415 289-2300
Peter Mangione, *Branch Mgr*
Erin Freschi, *Program Mgr*
Tran Keys, *Research*
Jaclyn Tejwani, *Research*
Staci Wendt, *Research*
EMP: 48
SALES (corp-wide): 71.6MM **Privately Held**
WEB: www.wested.org
SIC: 8733 8732 Educational research agency; commercial nonphysical research
PA: Wested
730 Harrison St Ste 500
San Francisco CA 94107
415 565-3000

(P-19248)
WESTED (PA)
730 Harrison St Ste 500, San Francisco (94107-1242)
PHONE....................415 565-3000
Glen H Harvey, *CEO*
Beverly Hurley, *Bd of Directors*
Sabrina Laine, *Officer*
Robin M Montoya, *Managing Dir*
Mary Peterson, *Managing Dir*
EMP: 115 EST: 1995
SQ FT: 85,000
SALES (est): 71.6MM **Privately Held**
WEB: www.wested.org
SIC: 8733 Educational research agency

(P-19249)
WESTED
400 Seaport Ct Ste 222, Redwood City (94063-2767)
PHONE....................650 381-6400
Steve Schneider, *Branch Mgr*
Kellie Kim, *Research*
Ellen Mandinach, *Research*
Ryan Miskell, *Research*
Darius Taylor, *Research*
EMP: 48
SALES (corp-wide): 71.6MM **Privately Held**
WEB: www.wested.org
SIC: 8733 8732 Educational research agency; educational research

PRODUCTS & SERVICES SECTION
8734 - Testing Laboratories County (P-19271)

PA: Wested
730 Harrison St Ste 500
San Francisco CA 94107
415 565-3000

(P-19250)
WESTED
1550 The Alameda Ste 201, San Jose (95126-2304)
PHONE..............................408 299-1700
Yolanda Garcia, *Director*
EMP: 48
SALES (corp-wide): 71.6MM **Privately Held**
WEB: www.wested.org
SIC: **8733** 8299 Educational research agency; educational services
PA: Wested
730 Harrison St Ste 500
San Francisco CA 94107
415 565-3000

(P-19251)
WESTERN STATES INFO NETWRK INC
1825 Bell St Ste 205, Sacramento (95825-1020)
PHONE..............................916 263-1188
Karen Aumond, *Exec Dir*
EMP: 78 EST: 2009
SALES (est): 5.4MM **Privately Held**
SIC: **8733** Noncommercial research organizations

(P-19252)
ZONARE MEDICAL SYSTEMS INC
420 Bernardo Ave, Mountain View (94043-5209)
P.O. Box 760, Alviso (95002-0760)
PHONE..............................650 230-2800
Donald Southard, *CEO*
Timothy A Marcotte, *President*
Steve Edwards, *Vice Pres*
Michael Gabler, *Vice Pres*
Glen W McLaughlin, *Vice Pres*
EMP: 65 EST: 1999
SALES (est): 14.5MM **Privately Held**
WEB: www.mindraynorthamerica.com
SIC: **8733** 5047 Research institute; hospital equipment & supplies
PA: Mindray Medical International Limited
C/O: Conyers Trust Company (Cayman) Limited
George Town GR CAYMAN

8734 Testing Laboratories

(P-19253)
ACCION LABS US INC
4633 Old Ironsides Dr # 304, Santa Clara (95054-1807)
PHONE..............................408 970-9809
William Flavin, *General Mgr*
Jignasha Patel, *Finance Mgr*
Jennifer Wells, *Opers Mgr*
Gary Krofcheck, *Sales Staff*
EMP: 162
SALES (corp-wide): 48.9MM **Privately Held**
WEB: www.accionlabs.com
SIC: **8734** Testing laboratories
PA: Accion Labs Us, Inc.
1225 Wash Pike Ste 401
Bridgeville PA 15017
724 260-5139

(P-19254)
AGRICLTURE PRRITY PLLTNTS LABS (PA)
Also Called: Appl
908 N Temperance Ave, Clovis (93611-8606)
PHONE..............................559 275-2175
Diane Anderson, *President*
Bradford Anderson, *Treasurer*
Sue Bonds, *Admin Sec*
Rene Patterson, *Safety Mgr*
Robb Pendergrass, *Marketing Staff*
EMP: 48 EST: 1983
SQ FT: 8,000
SALES (est): 10.8MM **Privately Held**
WEB: www.applinc.com
SIC: **8734** Pollution testing

(P-19255)
ALPHA ANALYTICAL LABS INC (PA)
Also Called: Beta Partnership
208 Mason St, Ukiah (95482-4407)
PHONE..............................707 468-0401
Bruce Gove, *President*
Robert Phillips, *Vice Pres*
Rob Phillips, *General Mgr*
Robbie Phillips, *General Mgr*
Karen Lantz, *Project Mgr*
EMP: 57 EST: 1980
SALES (est): 9.5MM **Privately Held**
WEB: www.alpha-labs.com
SIC: **8734** 8071 Water testing laboratory; medical laboratories

(P-19256)
AMAZON
905 Eleventh Ave, Sunnyvale (94089-4757)
PHONE..............................510 676-6906
Kristi Macmillan, *Program Mgr*
Mary Lou Maitoga, *Opers Staff*
Sarah Kensler, *Senior Mgr*
Mandy Schort, *Senior Mgr*
EMP: 39 EST: 2018
SALES (est): 14.6MM **Privately Held**
SIC: **8734** Testing laboratories

(P-19257)
ANN BREZNOCK
Also Called: Winters Veterinary Clinic
27956 State Highway 128, Winters (95694-9079)
PHONE..............................530 795-2356
Ann Breznock, *Owner*
EMP: 39 EST: 1979
SQ FT: 10,000
SALES (est): 1.8MM **Privately Held**
SIC: **8734** 0742 Testing laboratories; animal hospital services, pets & other animal specialties

(P-19258)
ARCEO LABS INC (PA)
1612 Castro St, San Francisco (94114-3707)
PHONE..............................628 222-3622
Raj Shah, *CEO*
EMP: 67 EST: 2016
SALES (est): 2.8MM **Privately Held**
WEB: www.resilienceinsurance.com
SIC: **8734** Testing laboratories

(P-19259)
AVA FOOD LABS INC
Also Called: Endless West
1150 Illinois St, San Francisco (94107-3105)
PHONE..............................415 806-3914
Alec Lee, *Principal*
EMP: 37 EST: 2016
SALES (est): 5.3MM
SALES (corp-wide): 8.6B **Publicly Held**
WEB: www.endlesswest.com
SIC: **8734** Testing laboratories
PA: Constellation Brands, Inc.
207 High Point Dr # 100
Victor NY 14564
585 678-7100

(P-19260)
BRELJE AND RACE LABS INC
425 S E St, Santa Rosa (95404-5192)
PHONE..............................707 544-8807
William Race, *President*
EMP: 39 EST: 1967
SQ FT: 5,500
SALES (est): 3.8MM **Privately Held**
WEB: www.brlabsinc.com
SIC: **8734** Water testing laboratory

(P-19261)
CELO LABS INC (PA)
500 Treat Ave Ste 101, San Francisco (94110-2068)
PHONE..............................415 942-4178
Rene Reinsberg, *CEO*
Marek Olszewski, *CTO*
Sepandar Kamvar, *Director*
EMP: 39 EST: 2019
SALES (est): 1.4MM **Privately Held**
SIC: **8734** Testing laboratories

(P-19262)
CENTRAL COUNTIES
241 Business Park Way, Atwater (95301-9487)
PHONE..............................209 356-0355
Christine Hackler, *Principal*
Ryan Dorman, *Technology*
Amy Land, *Human Res Dir*
Mary Pickel, *Mktg Coord*
Daniel Krutoy, *Director*
EMP: 70 EST: 2005
SALES (est): 5.1MM **Privately Held**
WEB: www.valleytechlogic.com
SIC: **8734** Testing laboratories

(P-19263)
CONSTRUCTION TSTG & ENGRG INC
Also Called: C T E
3628 Madison Ave Ste 22, North Highlands (95660-5071)
PHONE..............................916 331-6030
Terry Haagensen, *Manager*
EMP: 38
SALES (corp-wide): 85.6MM **Privately Held**
WEB: www.cte-inc.net
SIC: **8734** Testing laboratories
HQ: Construction Testing & Engineering, Inc.
1441 Montiel Rd Ste 115
Escondido CA 92026

(P-19264)
EAG HOLDINGS LLC
2710 Walsh Ave, Santa Clara (95051-0963)
PHONE..............................408 530-3500
Siddhartha Kadia, *CEO*
Patricia M Lindley, *Exec VP*
Troy Devault, *Vice Pres*
Kristein King, *Vice Pres*
Albert Lee, *Vice Pres*
EMP: 700 EST: 2006
SQ FT: 70,000
SALES (est): 54.5MM **Privately Held**
WEB: www.eag.com
SIC: **8734** Testing laboratories

(P-19265)
ENTHALPY ANALYTICAL LLC
Also Called: Curtis & Tompkins
2323 5th St, Berkeley (94710-2407)
PHONE..............................510 486-0900
Steven Eckard, *President*
Ryan Brokamp, *Vice Pres*
Jeremy Clark, *Vice Pres*
Bob Finken, *Vice Pres*
Peter Arth, *Lab Dir*
EMP: 47
SALES (corp-wide): 328.2MM **Publicly Held**
WEB: www.enthalpy.com
SIC: **8734** Testing laboratories
HQ: Enthalpy Analytical, Llc
800 Capitola Dr Ste 1
Durham NC 27713

(P-19266)
EUROFINS AIR TOXICS LLC
180 Blue Ravine Rd Ste B, Folsom (95630-4703)
PHONE..............................916 985-1000
J Wilson Hershey, *Ch of Bd*
Robert Mitzel, *President*
Coleen Wollam, *CFO*
Thomas E Wolgemuth, *Corp Secy*
Melony Levesque, *Vice Pres*
EMP: 55 EST: 1989
SQ FT: 24,000
SALES (est): 11.4MM
SALES (corp-wide): 29.4MM **Privately Held**
WEB: www.eurofinsus.com
SIC: **8734** Water testing laboratory
PA: Eurofins Environment Testing Us Holdings, Inc.
2200 Rittenhouse St # 175
Des Moines IA 50321
515 698-5039

(P-19267)
EUROFINS EAG AGROSCIENCE LLC
675 Alfred Nobel Dr, Hercules (94547-1815)
PHONE..............................510 741-3000
EMP: 40
SALES (corp-wide): 367.9K **Privately Held**
WEB: www.eurofinsus.com
SIC: **8734** Testing laboratories
HQ: Eurofins Eag Agroscience, Llc
2425 New Holland Pike
Lancaster PA 17601
717 658-2300

(P-19268)
EUROFINS EAG ENGRG SCIENCE LLC (DH)
2710 Walsh Ave, Santa Clara (95051-0963)
PHONE..............................408 588-0050
Stefan Karnavas, *President*
EMP: 100 EST: 2018
SALES (est): 25.6MM
SALES (corp-wide): 367.9K **Privately Held**
WEB: www.eag.com
SIC: **8734** Testing laboratories
HQ: Eurofins Eag Materials Science Us Holding, Inc.
4747 Executive Dr Ste 700
San Diego CA 92121
949 521-6200

(P-19269)
EUROFINS EAG MTLS SCIENCE LLC (DH)
Also Called: Eurofins Eag Laboratories
810 Kifer Rd, Sunnyvale (94086-5203)
PHONE..............................408 454-4600
Stefan Karnavas, *President*
Pat Lindley, *Exec VP*
Tomoya Aoyama, *Vice Pres*
Thomas Byrd, *Vice Pres*
Carey Lewis, *Vice Pres*
EMP: 429 EST: 2008
SQ FT: 70,000
SALES (est): 118.7MM
SALES (corp-wide): 367.9K **Privately Held**
WEB: www.eag.com
SIC: **8734** Product testing laboratories
HQ: Eurofins Eag Materials Science Us Holding, Inc.
4747 Executive Dr Ste 700
San Diego CA 92121
949 521-6200

(P-19270)
EUROFINS FD CHMSTRY TSTG MDSON
Covance Food Solutions
2441 Constitution Dr, Livermore (94551-7573)
PHONE..............................609 452-4440
EMP: 4167
SALES (corp-wide): 189.2MM **Privately Held**
WEB: www.eurofinsus.com
SIC: **8734** Testing laboratories
PA: Eurofins Food Chemistry Testing Madison, Inc.
6304 Ronald Reagan Ave
Madison WI 53704
717 656-2300

(P-19271)
EUROFINS NANOLAB TECH INC (PA)
1708 Mccarthy Blvd, Milpitas (95035-7454)
PHONE..............................408 433-3320
Stefan Karnavas, *President*
Patricia Lindley, *CEO*
Carol Traub, *Treasurer*
Xiu Han, *Vice Pres*
Jein Shyue, *Vice Pres*
EMP: 84 EST: 2007
SQ FT: 15,000
SALES (est): 12MM **Privately Held**
WEB: www.nanolabtechnologies.com
SIC: **8734** Water testing laboratory

8734 - Testing Laboratories County (P-19272)

(P-19272)
EVANS ANALYTICAL GROUP LLC
Also Called: Wildlife International
2710 Walsh Ave, Santa Clara
(95051-0963)
PHONE.................................408 454-4600
Siddhartha C Kadia, *Principal*
Tomoya Aoyama, *Vice Pres*
Zhiguo Z Is, *Vice Pres*
Zhiguo Zhang, *Vice Pres*
Zhiguo Z Zz, *Vice Pres*
EMP: 81 **EST:** 2012
SALES (est): 16.5MM
SALES (corp-wide): 367.9K **Privately Held**
WEB: www.eag.com
SIC: 8734 Assaying service
PA: Eurofins Eag Materials Science, Llc
810 Kifer Rd
Sunnyvale CA 94086
408 454-4600

(P-19273)
FCL TECH INC
Also Called: Facebook Connectivity Lab
1601 Willow Rd, Menlo Park (94025-1452)
PHONE.................................650 656-7570
David Kling, *CEO*
EMP: 41 **EST:** 2016
SALES (est): 9.7MM
SALES (corp-wide): 85.9B **Publicly Held**
WEB: www.facebook.com
SIC: 8734 Testing laboratories
PA: Meta Platforms, Inc.
1601 Willow Rd
Menlo Park CA 94025
650 543-4800

(P-19274)
FOUND HEALTH INC
1 Letterman Dr Ste C3500, San Francisco
(94129-1494)
PHONE.................................415 854-3296
Sarah Jones Simmer, *CEO*
Andrew Dudum, *Principal*
Chester Ng, *Principal*
Teresa Starin, *Principal*
Emily Yudofsky, *Principal*
EMP: 70 **EST:** 2019
SALES (est): 1.5MM **Privately Held**
SIC: 8734 Testing laboratories

(P-19275)
IDEAL AEROSMITH INC
155 Constitution Dr, Menlo Park
(94025-1106)
PHONE.................................650 353-3641
Bill Meckfessel, *Branch Mgr*
EMP: 15
SALES (corp-wide): 30.5MM **Privately Held**
WEB: www.ideal-aerosmith.com
SIC: 8734 3826 3545 3494 Testing laboratories; analytical instruments; machine tool accessories; valves & pipe fittings; aircraft & motor vehicle measurement equipment
PA: Ideal Aerosmith, Inc.
3001 S Washington St
Grand Forks ND 58201
701 757-3400

(P-19276)
INTERNATIONAL PROCESS SOLUTION
1300 Industrial Rd Ste 22, San Carlos
(94070-4141)
PHONE.................................310 432-0665
Thomas Main, *CEO*
Jim Tomlin, *Sales Executive*
EMP: 52
SALES (est): 6MM **Privately Held**
WEB: www.ips-us.com
SIC: 8734 Calibration & certification

(P-19277)
ISE LABS INC (DH)
46800 Bayside Pkwy, Fremont
(94538-6592)
PHONE.................................510 687-2500
Tien Wu, *CEO*
Jeff Thompson, *Vice Pres*
Wennie Nie, *Sales Engr*
Marco Zavala, *Supervisor*
EMP: 200 **EST:** 1999
SQ FT: 69,000
SALES (est): 43.9MM **Privately Held**
WEB: www.iselabs.com
SIC: 8734 3672 Calibration & certification; printed circuit boards

(P-19278)
MCCAMPBELL ANALYTICAL INC
1534 Willow Pass Rd, Pittsburg
(94565-1701)
PHONE.................................925 252-9262
Edward Hamilton, *CEO*
Jill Miller, *Officer*
Ed Hamilton, *Lab Dir*
Blake Brown, *Project Mgr*
Heidi Fruhlinger, *Project Mgr*
EMP: 63 **EST:** 1991
SQ FT: 12,896
SALES (est): 10.2MM **Privately Held**
WEB: www.mccampbell.com
SIC: 8734 Testing laboratories

(P-19279)
MICRO PRCISION CALIBRATION INC (PA)
Also Called: Micro Precision Test Equipment
22835 Industrial Pl, Grass Valley
(95949-6326)
PHONE.................................530 268-1860
Jerry Trammell, *CEO*
Ysmael Gonzales, *COO*
Judy Trammell, *CFO*
Deana Gold, *Principal*
Julian Contreras, *Division Mgr*
EMP: 43 **EST:** 1969
SQ FT: 12,000
SALES (est): 66.3MM **Privately Held**
WEB: www.microprecision.com
SIC: 8734 Calibration & certification

(P-19280)
MOORE TWINING ASSOCIATES INC (PA)
2527 Fresno St, Fresno (93721-1804)
PHONE.................................559 268-7021
Harry D Moore, *President*
Ruth E Moore, *Corp Secy*
EMP: 85
SQ FT: 22,500
SALES (est): 15.2MM **Privately Held**
WEB: www.mooretwining.com
SIC: 8734 8711 Testing laboratories; engineering services

(P-19281)
NTS TECHNICAL SYSTEMS
41039 Boyce Rd, Fremont (94538-2434)
PHONE.................................510 578-3500
Anuj Kumar, *Branch Mgr*
Vishal Narayan, *Engineer*
Ben Anderson, *Regl Sales Mgr*
EMP: 50
SALES (corp-wide): 1.2B **Privately Held**
WEB: www.nts.com
SIC: 8734 8742 Testing laboratories; quality assurance consultant
HQ: Nts Technical Systems
2125 E Katella Ave # 250
Anaheim CA 92806
714 450-9100

(P-19282)
PRO-FORM MANUFACTURING LLC
Also Called: Pro-Form Laboratories
5001 Industrial Way, Benicia (94510-1017)
P.O. Box 626, Orinda (94563-0576)
PHONE.................................707 752-9010
Nicholas Gillespie, *CEO*
Melinda Gillespie, *Ch Invest Ofcr*
Joann Gillespie, *Administration*
Alanna Hernaez, *Technician*
Ryan Gillespie, *Design Engr*
EMP: 195 **EST:** 1980
SALES (est): 34.3MM **Privately Held**
SIC: 8734 Product testing laboratory, safety or performance

(P-19283)
SE LABORATORIES INC
Also Called: S E Labs
1065 Comstock St, Santa Clara
(95054-3439)
PHONE.................................408 727-3286
Anil R Singh, *President*
Marilyn Singh, *Treasurer*
Christopher Lewis, *Officer*
Dan Turgeon, *Executive*
Agnes Lewis, *Principal*
EMP: 79 **EST:** 1978
SQ FT: 11,450
SALES (est): 8.6MM **Privately Held**
WEB: www.trescal.us
SIC: 8734 7629 Calibration & certification; electronic equipment repair

(P-19284)
SGS SA
Also Called: SGS Forensic Laboratories
3777 Depot Rd Ste 409, Hayward
(94545-2761)
PHONE.................................800 827-3274
EMP: 52
SALES (corp-wide): 6.1B **Privately Held**
WEB: www.sgs.com
SIC: 8734 Forensic laboratory
PA: Sgs Sa
Place Des Alpes 1
GenCve GE 1201
227 399-111

(P-19285)
SIGNET TESTING LABS INC (HQ)
3526 Breakwater Ct, Hayward
(94545-3611)
PHONE.................................510 887-8484
Robert V Tadlock, *President*
EMP: 50 **EST:** 1994
SALES (est): 15.7MM
SALES (corp-wide): 26.3MM **Privately Held**
WEB: www.signettesting.com
SIC: 8734 Testing laboratories
PA: United Engineering Resources, Inc.
498 N 3rd St
Sacramento CA 95811
916 375-6700

(P-19286)
STEEP HILL INC (PA)
2448 6th St, Berkeley (94710-2414)
PHONE.................................510 562-7400
Andrew Rosenstein, *CEO*
David Lampach, *President*
Reggie Gaudino, *Officer*
Anthony Torres, *Research*
Austin Ali, *Sales Staff*
EMP: 105 **EST:** 2014
SALES (est): 6.1MM **Privately Held**
WEB: www.steephill.com
SIC: 8734 Testing laboratories

(P-19287)
TESTAMERICA LABORATORIES INC
Also Called: Eurofins Testamerica
880 Riverside Pkwy, West Sacramento
(95605-1500)
PHONE.................................916 373-5600
Roger Freize, *Manager*
Isabel Enfinger, *Project Mgr*
Nicole McCabe, *Project Mgr*
Diana Crisp, *Credit Mgr*
William Sullivan, *Director*
EMP: 31
SALES (corp-wide): 367.9K **Privately Held**
WEB: www.testamericainc.com
SIC: 8734 8731 2899 Testing laboratories; commercial physical research; chemical preparations
HQ: Testamerica Laboratories, Inc.
4101 Shuffel St Nw # 100
North Canton OH 44720
800 456-9396

(P-19288)
TREVI SYSTEMS INC
1500 Valley House Dr # 130, Rohnert Park
(94928-4937)
PHONE.................................707 992-0567
John Webley, *President*
Karen Godfrey, *CFO*
Jerry Bauer, *Engineer*
Serguei Charamko, *Engineer*
Victor Ivashin, *Engineer*
EMP: 40 **EST:** 2011
SALES (est): 5.5MM **Privately Held**
WEB: www.trevisystems.com
SIC: 8734 Water testing laboratory

(P-19289)
UNDERWRITERS LABORATORIES INC
4510 Riding Club Ct, Hayward
(94542-2238)
PHONE.................................408 754-6500
EMP: 180
SALES (corp-wide): 22.6MM **Privately Held**
SIC: 8734 Testing Laboratory
PA: Underwriters Laboratories Inc.
333 Pfingsten Rd
Northbrook IL 60062
847 272-8800

(P-19290)
UNITED MFG ASSEMBLY INC
44169 Fremont Blvd, Fremont
(94538-6044)
PHONE.................................510 490-4680
Yonwen Chou, *President*
Jack Stewart, *Vice Pres*
May Mah, *Finance*
May Wah, *Controller*
Margie Vo, *Human Res Mgr*
EMP: 95 **EST:** 1987
SALES (est): 9.1MM **Privately Held**
WEB: www.umai.com
SIC: 8734 3672 Testing laboratories; printed circuit boards

(P-19291)
VITISYSTEMS INC
Also Called: Caltest Analytical Laboratory
1885 N Kelly Rd, NAPA (94558-6219)
PHONE.................................707 258-4000
Karen Albertson, *President*
Todd Albertson, *Vice Pres*
Shawna Rees, *Lab Dir*
EMP: 44 **EST:** 1982
SQ FT: 20,000
SALES (est): 6.8MM **Privately Held**
WEB: www.caltestlabs.com
SIC: 8734 Water testing laboratory; hazardous waste testing

(P-19292)
X-SCAN IMAGING CORPORATION
107 Bonaventura Dr, San Jose
(95134-2106)
PHONE.................................408 432-9888
Chinlee Wang, *President*
Linbo Yang, *Info Tech Dir*
Nguyen Luu, *Electrical Engi*
Michelle Elles, *Accounting Mgr*
EMP: 25 **EST:** 2006
SALES (est): 3.5MM **Privately Held**
WEB: www.x-scanimaging.com
SIC: 8734 3827 3829 X-ray inspection service, industrial; optical test & inspection equipment; thermometers & temperature sensors; scintillation detectors

8741 Management Services

(P-19293)
A-1 ROOF MGT & CNSTR INC
14100 Doolittle Dr, San Leandro
(94577-5540)
PHONE.................................510 347-5400
Andrew Triphon, *CEO*
Esaul Diaz, *Maintence Staff*
EMP: 55 **EST:** 2008
SALES (est): 12.2MM **Privately Held**
WEB: www.roofmanage.com
SIC: 8741 1761 1521 Business management; roofing contractor; single-family housing construction

(P-19294)
ACTIVE WELLNESS LLC
600 California St Fl 11, San Francisco
(94108-2727)
P.O. Box 2358 (94126-2358)
PHONE.................................415 741-3300
Jill Stevens Kinney, *Chairman*
William Joseph McBride III, *President*
Carey White, *CFO*
Michael Rucker, *Vice Pres*
Erika Eugenio, *General Mgr*
EMP: 1100 **EST:** 2015
SQ FT: 1,000 **Privately Held**
WEB: www.activewellness.com

PRODUCTS & SERVICES SECTION

8741 - Management Services County (P-19318)

SIC: 8741 7991 Hospital management; nursing & personal care facility management; health club

(P-19295)
ALLCARE HSPTLIST MED GROUP INC
3320 Tully Rd Ste 1, Modesto (95350-0800)
PHONE 209 550-5200
Randy Winter MD, *CEO*
Tina Scharli, *Executive Asst*
Carolyn Ogden, *Director*
EMP: 36 EST: 1999
SALES (est): 9.6MM **Privately Held**
WEB: www.allcareipa.com
SIC: 8741 Financial management for business

(P-19296)
AMERICAN BUILDING SUPPLY INC
Also Called: Abs-American Building Supply
6300 S Watt Ave, Sacramento (95829-1303)
PHONE 916 387-4101
EMP: 57 **Publicly Held**
WEB: www.abs-abs.com
SIC: 8741 Construction management
HQ: American Building Supply, Inc.
8360 Elder Creek Rd
Sacramento CA 95828
916 503-4100

(P-19297)
ANGLEPOINT GROUP INC (PA)
3945 Freedom Cir Ste 360, Santa Clara (95054-1267)
PHONE 855 512-6453
Ron Brill, *Ch of Bd*
Ravi Kohli, *COO*
Brian Papay, *COO*
Johnson Kris, *Exec VP*
Selina Baranowski, *Vice Pres*
EMP: 142 EST: 2009
SQ FT: 4,000
SALES (est): 15.6MM **Privately Held**
WEB: www.anglepoint.com
SIC: 8741 Business management

(P-19298)
ARCHIVES MANAGEMENT CORP (PA)
Also Called: Bay Management
2301 S El Camino Real, San Mateo (94403-2213)
PHONE 650 544-2200
Harlan Shapers, *President*
EMP: 180 EST: 1981
SQ FT: 12,000
SALES (est): 8.3MM **Privately Held**
SIC: 8741 8742 Business management; management consulting services

(P-19299)
ARNOLD PALMER GOLF MGT LLC
300 Finley Rd, San Francisco (94129-1196)
P.O. Box 29063 (94129-0063)
PHONE 415 561-4670
EMP: 70
SALES (corp-wide): 48.4MM **Privately Held**
SIC: 8741 7992 Management Services Public Golf Course
HQ: Arnold Palmer Golf Management, Llc
5430 Lbj Fwy Ste 1400
Dallas TX 75240
972 419-1400

(P-19300)
AXIS APPRAISAL MGT SOLUTIONS (PA)
1101 5th Ave Ste 210, San Rafael (94901-2903)
PHONE 888 806-2947
Janette Miller, *CEO*
Michael Simmons, *Vice Pres*
Kim Perotti, *Principal*
Kimberly Perotti, *Principal*
Jennifer Wojslaw, *Analyst*
EMP: 82 EST: 2011

SALES (est): 9.9MM **Privately Held**
WEB: www.axis-amc.com
SIC: 8741 6531 Management services; appraiser, real estate

(P-19301)
BAY AREA AIR QUALITY MGT DST
375 Beale St Ste 600, San Francisco (94105-2097)
PHONE 415 749-4900
Jack Broadbent, *Principal*
EMP: 400 EST: 2014 **Privately Held**
WEB: www.baaqmd.gov
SIC: 9511 8741 5722 Air pollution control agency, government; business management; electric household appliances

(P-19302)
BECHTEL CAPITAL MGT CORP
50 Beale St, San Francisco (94105-1813)
PHONE 415 768-1234
Riley Bechtel, *Chairman*
Brendan Bechtel, *President*
Bill Dudley, *CEO*
Peter Dawson, *CFO*
Anshul Maheshwari, *Treasurer*
EMP: 68 EST: 1987
SQ FT: 600,000
SALES (est): 4.6MM
SALES (corp-wide): 5B **Privately Held**
WEB: www.bechtel.com
SIC: 8741 Financial management for business
PA: Bechtel Group, Inc.
12011 Sunset Hills Rd # 1
Reston VA 20190
571 392-6300

(P-19303)
BELLEVUE UN ELMENTARY SCHL DST (PA)
3150 Education Dr, Santa Rosa (95407-2767)
PHONE 707 542-5197
Armando S Flores, *Superintendent*
Roy Camarillo, *Principal*
Yancy Forest-Knowles, *Principal*
Nancy Rogers-Zigarra, *Principal*
Moriah Hart, *Executive Asst*
EMP: 50 EST: 1949
SALES (est): 29.3MM **Privately Held**
WEB: www.busd.org
SIC: 8211 8741 Public elementary & secondary schools; school board; management services

(P-19304)
BON APPETIT MANAGEMENT CO
4125 Hopyard Rd, Pleasanton (94588-8534)
PHONE 925 730-3653
EMP: 132
SALES (corp-wide): 26B **Privately Held**
WEB: www.eatlowcarbon.org
SIC: 8741 Management services
HQ: Bon Appetit Management Co.
201 Rdwood Shres Pkwy Ste
Redwood City CA 94065
650 798-8000

(P-19305)
BON APPETIT MANAGEMENT CO
500 El Camino Real 500 # 500, Santa Clara (95050-4345)
PHONE 408 554-2728
Cathy Staub, *Manager*
EMP: 132
SALES (corp-wide): 26B **Privately Held**
WEB: www.eatlowcarbon.org
SIC: 8741 Management services
HQ: Bon Appetit Management Co.
201 Rdwood Shres Pkwy Ste
Redwood City CA 94065
650 798-8000

(P-19306)
BON APPETIT MANAGEMENT CO
383 E Grand Ave, South San Francisco (94080-6234)
PHONE 650 467-3767
EMP: 132

SALES (corp-wide): 26B **Privately Held**
WEB: www.eatlowcarbon.org
SIC: 8741 Restaurant management
HQ: Bon Appetit Management Co.
201 Rdwood Shres Pkwy Ste
Redwood City CA 94065
650 798-8000

(P-19307)
BON APPETIT MANAGEMENT CO
301 Market St, Santa Clara (95053-0001)
PHONE 408 554-5771
EMP: 132
SALES (corp-wide): 26B **Privately Held**
WEB: www.eatlowcarbon.org
SIC: 8741 Management services
HQ: Bon Appetit Management Co.
201 Rdwood Shres Pkwy Ste
Redwood City CA 94065
650 798-8000

(P-19308)
BPG STORAGE SOLUTIONS INC
2033 N Main St Ste 340, Walnut Creek (94596-3727)
PHONE 562 467-2000
Michael Barker, *President*
EMP: 46 EST: 2006
SALES (est): 1.8MM
SALES (corp-wide): 44.8MM **Privately Held**
WEB: www.storagesolutionsca.com
SIC: 8741 Management services
PA: Barker Pacific Group, Inc.
1800 Sutter St Ste 775
Concord CA 94520
415 884-9977

(P-19309)
BUCKINGHAM STRATEGIC PARTNERS
Also Called: Loring Ward
10 Almaden Blvd Fl 15, San Jose (95113-2226)
PHONE 800 366-7266
John Avilla, *Vice Pres*
Brian Margrave, *Technical Mgr*
Megan Costa, *Human Resources*
Beau Barnett, *Director*
Sean Brooks, *Director*
EMP: 41 EST: 1998
SALES (est): 600.5K **Privately Held**
WEB: www.buckinghamstrategicpartners.com
SIC: 8741 Business management

(P-19310)
BUCKLAND VINEYARD MGT INC
4560 Slodusty Rd, Garden Valley (95633-9244)
PHONE 530 333-1534
Alfred Buckland, *President*
EMP: 65 EST: 1984
SALES (est): 1.7MM **Privately Held**
WEB: www.bucklandvineyards.com
SIC: 8741 Management services

(P-19311)
BUTTE BASIN MANAGEMENT CO
1624 Poole Blvd, Yuba City (95993-2610)
P.O. Box 3775 (95992-3775)
PHONE 530 674-2060
Samuel Neves, *President*
Dominic Neves, *Vice Pres*
EMP: 50 EST: 2012
SALES (est): 5MM **Privately Held**
WEB: www.buttebasin.com
SIC: 8741 Management services

(P-19312)
CAL CARE INC
Also Called: Atherton Healthcare
1275 Crane St, Menlo Park (94025-4212)
PHONE 650 325-8600
Chris Green, *Administration*
Nana Cocachvili, *Administration*
Bin Jin, *Human Resources*
EMP: 74 EST: 2005
SALES (est): 6.3MM **Privately Held**
WEB: www.athertonregency.com
SIC: 8741 Nursing & personal care facility management

(P-19313)
CALIFRNIA STATE UNIV E BAY FND
25800 Carlos Bee Blvd, Hayward (94542-3000)
PHONE 510 885-2700
Curt Robinson, *Director*
EMP: 44 EST: 1959
SQ FT: 32,500
SALES (est): 13.4MM **Privately Held**
WEB: www.csueastbay.edu
SIC: 5942 8741 Book stores; administrative management

(P-19314)
CAMBRIDGE CM INC
420 Olive Ave, Palo Alto (94306-2225)
PHONE 650 543-3030
William Hammerson, *President*
Peyton Riley, *Project Mgr*
Jake White, *Project Engr*
Daniel Connelly, *Opers Staff*
Jana Aubert, *Sr Project Mgr*
EMP: 45 EST: 2002
SALES (est): 6.2MM **Privately Held**
WEB: www.cambridge-cm.com
SIC: 8741 Construction management

(P-19315)
CHICK-FIL-A INC
5080 Redwood Dr, Rohnert Park (94928-7905)
PHONE 707 585-7462
James Bains, *Branch Mgr*
EMP: 83
SALES (corp-wide): 1.2B **Privately Held**
WEB: www.chick-fil-a.com
SIC: 5812 8741 Fast-food restaurant, chain; restaurant management
PA: Chick-Fil-A, Inc.
5200 Buffington Rd
Atlanta GA 30349
404 765-8038

(P-19316)
CLARIZEN INC
691 S Milpitas Blvd # 212, Milpitas (95035-5478)
PHONE 866 502-9813
Boaz Chalamish, *CEO*
RAO Adavikolanu, *Chief Mktg Ofcr*
Anne Catambay, *Vice Pres*
Meir Uziel, *Vice Pres*
Veno Bender, *Sales Staff*
EMP: 55 EST: 2007
SALES (est): 15.7MM **Privately Held**
WEB: www.clarizen.com
SIC: 8741 Management services
HQ: Clarizen Ltd
4 Hacharash, Floor 10
Hod Hasharon
979 443-00

(P-19317)
CLOROX SERVICES COMPANY
4900 Johnson Dr, Pleasanton (94588-3308)
PHONE 925 368-6000
R A Llenado, *Ch of Bd*
EMP: 167
SALES (corp-wide): 7.3B **Publicly Held**
WEB: www.thecloroxcompany.com
SIC: 8741 Management services
HQ: Clorox Services Company
1221 Broadway
Oakland CA 94612

(P-19318)
CONSTRUCTION TESTING SERVICES (PA)
2118 Rheem Dr, Pleasanton (94588-2775)
PHONE 925 462-5151
Patrick Greenan, *President*
John G Dooling, *Principal*
Yate Chhoun-Le, *Project Mgr*
Tom Wipfli, *Project Mgr*
Brian Situ, *Engineer*
EMP: 78 EST: 1994
SQ FT: 5,000
SALES (est): 12.6MM **Privately Held**
WEB: www.cts-1.com
SIC: 8741 Construction management

8741 - Management Services County (P-19319)

(P-19319)
CONTRA COSTA CNTY OFF EDUCATN (PA)
77 Santa Barbara Rd, Pleasant Hill (94523-4215)
PHONE 925 942-3388
Karen Sakata, *Superintendent*
Anica Bilisoly, *Exec Dir*
Wren Maletsky, *Exec Dir*
Michelle Kiernan, *Executive Asst*
Danielle Davies, *Admin Asst*
EMP: 419 EST: 1950
SALES (est): 120.7MM **Privately Held**
WEB: www.cccoe.k12.ca.us
SIC: **8211** 8741 8331 Public elementary & secondary schools; management services; job training & vocational rehabilitation services

(P-19320)
CORNERSTONE HOTEL MANAGEMENT (DH)
222 Kearny St Ste 200, San Francisco (94108-4537)
PHONE 415 397-5572
Tom La Tour, *President*
J Kirke Wrench, *CFO*
Nir Margalit, *Admin Sec*
EMP: 75 EST: 1985
SALES (est): 44.8MM **Privately Held**
WEB: www.cornerstonehotels.com
SIC: **8741** Management services

(P-19321)
CPM ASSOCIATES INC
65 Mccoppin St, San Francisco (94103-1235)
PHONE 415 543-6515
Wendy Glassett, *Vice Pres*
EMP: 44 EST: 2018
SALES (est): 2.9MM **Privately Held**
WEB: www.cpmservices.com
SIC: **8741** Construction management

(P-19322)
CUMMING MANAGEMENT GROUP INC
2495 Natomas Park Dr, Sacramento (95833-2935)
PHONE 916 779-7140
Brooks Rehkopf, *Principal*
Gary Todd, *Sr Project Mgr*
Kathryn Defay, *Senior Mgr*
EMP: 72
SALES (corp-wide): 191.1MM **Privately Held**
SIC: **8741** 1522 1521 Business management; residential construction; single-family housing construction
PA: Cumming Management Group, Inc.
  25220 Hancock Ave Ste 440
  Murrieta CA 92562
  858 485-6765

(P-19323)
DELTA ELECTRONICS AMERICAS LTD (DH)
46101 Fremont Blvd, Fremont (94538-6468)
PHONE 510 668-5100
Kelvin Huang, *CEO*
Jiashien Chen, *CFO*
Tran Lam, *Administration*
Wenli Fang, *Sr Software Eng*
Christopher Yang, *Marketing Staff*
◆ EMP: 100 EST: 1985
SALES (est): 101.4MM **Privately Held**
WEB: www.deltabreez.com
SIC: **8741** 3577 5065 5063 Management services; computer peripheral equipment; electronic parts & equipment; electrical apparatus & equipment; computer peripheral equipment

(P-19324)
DEWOLF REALTY CO INC
4330 California St, San Francisco (94118-1316)
P.O. Box 591540 (94159-1540)
PHONE 415 221-2032
William A Talmage, *President*
Marie Wayne, *Corp Secy*
Aaron Sinel, *Vice Pres*
EMP: 60 EST: 1879
SALES (est): 5.3MM **Privately Held**
WEB: www.dewolfsf.com
SIC: **8741** 6531 Management services; appraiser, real estate; real estate brokers & agents

(P-19325)
DFA OF CALIFORNIA
Also Called: American Cncil For Fd Sfety Ql
2037 Morgan Dr, Kingsburg (93631-2753)
PHONE 559 233-7249
Michael Hurley, *Director*
Hugh Riedle, *Manager*
EMP: 62 **Privately Held**
WEB: www.dfaofcalifornia.com
SIC: **8741** 8734 Administrative management; food testing service
PA: Dfa Of California
  710 Striker Ave
  Sacramento CA 95834
  916 561-5900

(P-19326)
EDUCATION FOR CHANGE (PA)
333 Hegenberger Rd # 600, Oakland (94621-1462)
PHONE 510 568-7936
Hae S Thomas, *CEO*
Sudhir Aggarwal, *Bd of Directors*
Mike Barr, *Bd of Directors*
Anain Arciga, *Office Mgr*
Ana Buenrostro, *Office Mgr*
EMP: 43 EST: 2005
SALES (est): 46.4MM **Privately Held**
WEB: www.efcps.org
SIC: **8741** Management services

(P-19327)
ENERGY SALVAGE INC
8231 Alpine Ave Ste 3, Sacramento (95826-4746)
P.O. Box 255009 (95865-5009)
PHONE 916 737-8640
EMP: 50
SALES (est): 2.1MM **Privately Held**
SIC: **8741** 6512 Management Services, Nsk

(P-19328)
EPICUREAN GROUP
111 Main St Ste 3, Los Altos (94022-2914)
PHONE 650 947-6800
Mary Clark Bartlett, *CEO*
Marvin Rodriguez, *CFO*
Reynaldo Hernandez, *Vice Pres*
Phil Wright, *Vice Pres*
James Cruz, *District Mgr*
EMP: 500 EST: 2003
SALES (est): 76.6MM **Privately Held**
WEB: www.epicurean-group.com
SIC: **5812** 8741 Contract food services; business management

(P-19329)
ESHARES INC
Also Called: Carta
333 Bush St Fl 23, San Francisco (94104-2851)
PHONE 650 669-8381
Henry Ward, *CEO*
Vinson Quiris, *Partner*
Jean-Pierre Bitchoka, *Officer*
Tim Gunderson, *Vice Pres*
Jenny Kim, *Vice Pres*
EMP: 73 EST: 2012
SALES (est): 26.4MM **Privately Held**
SIC: **8741** Business management

(P-19330)
ET CAPITAL SOLAR PARTNERS USA
4900 Hopyard Rd Ste 2, Pleasanton (94588-3344)
PHONE 925 460-9898
Boris Schubert, *CEO*
Elaine Jones, *President*
Wenli Yang, *Human Res Mgr*
EMP: 50 EST: 2013
SALES (est): 4.1MM **Privately Held**
WEB: www.etintegration.com
SIC: **8741** 3674 Financial management for business; solar cells
PA: Et Solar Group

(P-19331)
EVEREST SILICON VALLEY MGT LP
8200 Gateway Blvd, Newark (94560-8000)
PHONE 510 494-8800
Marshall Young, *CEO*
LI Hui Lo, *COO*
EMP: 54 EST: 2018
SQ FT: 7,500
SALES (est): 450K
SALES (corp-wide): 1.2MM **Privately Held**
SIC: **8741** Hotel or motel management
PA: Everest Hotel Group, Llc
  2140 S Dupont Hwy
  Camden DE 19934
  213 272-0088

(P-19332)
EXECUTIVE SCHEDULING ASSOC
215 Lake Blvd Ste 367, Redding (96003-2506)
PHONE 877 315-3689
EMP: 120
SALES (est): 44.8K **Privately Held**
WEB: www.esasolutions.com
SIC: **8741** Management Services

(P-19333)
FAMILY CHRISTIAN STORES LLC (PA)
3945 Freedom Cir Ste 560, Santa Clara (95054-1269)
PHONE 616 554-8700
Charles Bengochea, *CEO*
Chuck Bengochea, *President*
Eric V Veen, *Director*
▲ EMP: 100 EST: 1994
SQ FT: 61,212
SALES (est): 133.7MM **Privately Held**
SIC: **5942** 5735 5947 5699 Books, religious; compact discs; greeting cards; customized clothing & apparel; management services

(P-19334)
FIRSTSERVICE RESIDENTIAL
12009 Foundation Pl, Gold River (95670-4533)
PHONE 916 293-4740
Leon Castiaux, *Branch Mgr*
Stephanie Parker, *Vice Pres*
EMP: 72
SALES (corp-wide): 2.4B **Privately Held**
WEB: www.fsresidential.com
SIC: **8741** 6531 Business management; real estate managers
HQ: Firstservice Residential
  15241 Laguna Canyon Rd
  Irvine CA 92618
  949 448-6000

(P-19335)
FLATIRON CONSTRUCTION CORP
2100 Goodyear Rd, Benicia (94510-1216)
PHONE 707 742-6270
John Diedurcio, *CEO*
Blair Brandon, *President*
Bob French, *COO*
Paul Driscoll, *CFO*
Lars Leitner, *CFO*
EMP: 281 EST: 1990
SALES (est): 22.8MM **Privately Held**
WEB: www.flatironcorp.com
SIC: **8741** Construction management

(P-19336)
FORT JAMES CORPORATION
Also Called: Fort James Communications Pprs
2000 Powell St, Emeryville (94608-1804)
PHONE 510 594-4900
Miles Marsh, *Branch Mgr*
EMP: 2019
SALES (corp-wide): 36.9B **Privately Held**
SIC: **8741** Administrative management
HQ: Fort James Corporation
  133 Peachtree St Ne
  Atlanta GA 30303
  404 652-4000

(P-19337)
FORTE ENTERPRISES INC (PA)
Also Called: St Francis Pavillion
99 Escuela Dr, Daly City (94015-4003)
PHONE 650 994-3200
Thomas J Nico, *President*
Remy Bamba, *Director*
Jose Fajardo, *Director*
Martin Moskowitz, *Director*
EMP: 240 EST: 1982
SQ FT: 14,000
SALES (est): 19.9MM **Privately Held**
SIC: **8741** 8721 Nursing & personal care facility management; accounting, auditing & bookkeeping

(P-19338)
FORTY NINERS STADIUM MGT LLC
4949 Mrie P Debartolo Way, Santa Clara (95054-1156)
PHONE 408 562-4949
EMP: 38 EST: 2012
SALES (est): 6MM **Privately Held**
SIC: **8741** 7941 Management services; sports field or stadium operator, promoting sports events

(P-19339)
FPI MANAGEMENT INC
1107 Luchessi Dr, San Jose (95118-3739)
PHONE 408 267-3952
EMP: 184
SALES (corp-wide): 249.9MM **Privately Held**
WEB: www.fpimgt.com
SIC: **8741** 6513 Business management; apartment building operators
PA: Fpi Management, Inc.
  800 Iron Point Rd
  Folsom CA 95630
  916 357-5300

(P-19340)
GILARDI & CO LLC
Also Called: K C C
1 Mcinnis Pkwy, San Rafael (94903-2764)
PHONE 415 798-5900
Eric Barberio, *President*
Bryan Butvick, *CEO*
Daniel Burke, *Exec VP*
Lara McDermott, *Exec VP*
Kim Wagner, *Exec VP*
EMP: 80 EST: 1997
SQ FT: 16,000
SALES: 530.8K **Privately Held**
WEB: www.kccllc.com
SIC: **8741** 8111 Management services; legal services
HQ: Kurtzman Carson Consultants, Inc
  2335 Alaska Ave
  El Segundo CA 90245
  310 823-9000

(P-19341)
GILBANE AECOM JV
1655 Grant St Fl 12, Concord (94520-2600)
PHONE 925 946-3100
Eric Banks, *Manager*
Jonathan May, *Project Engr*
Harvey Coppage, *Manager*
Natalia Rahkman, *Manager*
Matt Tierney, *Manager*
EMP: 59 EST: 2016
SALES (est): 9.5MM
SALES (corp-wide): 5.6B **Privately Held**
WEB: www.gilbaneco.com
SIC: **8741** Construction management
HQ: Gilbane Federal
  1655 Grant St Ste 1200
  Concord CA 94520

(P-19342)
GLOBALITY INC
2555 Park Blvd, Palo Alto (94306-1924)
PHONE 650 352-8900
Joel Hyatt, *CEO*
Lior Delgo, *President*
Erik Bardman, *CFO*
York Poon, *Officer*
Robert Casamento, *Senior VP*
EMP: 36 EST: 2015

PRODUCTS & SERVICES SECTION

8741 - Management Services County (P-19365)

SALES (est): 124.4K **Privately Held**
WEB: www.globality.com
SIC: 8741 Business management

(P-19343)
GRANITE POWER INC
580 W Beach St, Watsonville (95076-5107)
P.O. Box 50085 (95077-5085)
PHONE 831 724-1011
EMP: 300 **EST:** 2019
SALES (est): 6.7MM **Publicly Held**
WEB: www.graniteconstruction.com
SIC: 8741 Construction management
PA: Granite Construction Incorporated
585 W Beach St
Watsonville CA 95076

(P-19344)
GREENFLDS INTRMDATE CARE FCLTY
Also Called: Greenfields Icf-Ddn
400 Santa Clara St # 200, Vallejo (94590-5900)
PHONE 707 553-2935
Jasmine Badillo, *Administration*
EMP: 38 **EST:** 1997
SALES (est): 557.4K **Privately Held**
SIC: 8741 8051 Nursing & personal care facility management; skilled nursing care facilities

(P-19345)
GREYSTAR LP
821 W El Camino Real, Mountain View (94040-2511)
PHONE 650 386-6438
EMP: 68
SALES (corp-wide): 117.7K **Privately Held**
SIC: 8741 Management services
PA: Greystar, Lp
465 Meeting St Ste 500
Charleston SC 29403
843 579-9400

(P-19346)
HALL MANAGEMENT CORP
Also Called: Land & Personnel Management
759 S Madera Ave, Kerman (93630-1744)
PHONE 559 846-7382
Stacy Hampton, *President*
James Randles, *Vice Pres*
EMP: 2000 **EST:** 2001
SQ FT: 5,000
SALES (est): 77.2MM **Privately Held**
SIC: 8741 Personnel management

(P-19347)
HEALTH EVOLUTION PARTNERS (PA)
555 Mission St Ste 2300, San Francisco (94105-0925)
PHONE 415 362-5800
David J Brailer, *Ch of Bd*
Ned Brown, *Partner*
David A Smith, *Partner*
Kay Yun, *Partner*
Richard Schwartz, *President*
EMP: 100 **EST:** 2007
SALES (est): 25.2MM **Privately Held**
WEB: www.healthevolutionpartners.com
SIC: 8741 Management services

(P-19348)
HOLLINS CONSULTING INC
870 Market St Ste 700, San Francisco (94102-2902)
PHONE 415 238-1300
Guy Hollins, *CEO*
Kali Futnani, *Project Engr*
Auzja Mendoza, *Manager*
EMP: 35 **EST:** 2008
SALES (est): 1.5MM **Privately Held**
WEB: www.hollinsconsult.com
SIC: 8741 Construction management

(P-19349)
HOSPI COMM FOR THE L-P AREA T (DH)
Also Called: Valley Care Health System, The
5555 W Las Positas Blvd, Pleasanton (94588-4000)
PHONE 925 847-3000
Scott Gregerson, *CEO*
Kyle Wichelmann, *CFO*
Gina Teeples, *Officer*
Cindy Noonan, *Vice Pres*
Dennis Ong, *Pharmacy Dir*
EMP: 500 **EST:** 1958
SALES: 315.5MM
SALES (corp-wide): 12.4B **Privately Held**
WEB: www.valleycare.com
SIC: 8741 8062 Hospital management; general medical & surgical hospitals
HQ: Stanford Health Care
300 Pasteur Dr
Stanford CA 94305
650 723-4000

(P-19350)
HOSPI COMM FOR THE L-P AREA T
Also Called: Stanford Hlth Care-Valleycare
1111 E Stanley Blvd, Livermore (94550-4115)
PHONE 925 447-7000
Marcelina L Feit, *CEO*
Richard Shumway, *Officer*
Isabel Chen, *Exec Dir*
Tony Washington, *Exec Dir*
Virgil De Leon, *Network Analyst*
EMP: 1000
SALES (est): 272.7MM
SALES (corp-wide): 12.4B **Privately Held**
WEB: www.valleycare.com
SIC: 8741 Administrative management; hospital management
HQ: The Hospital Committee For The Livermore-Pleasanton Areas
5555 W Las Positas Blvd
Pleasanton CA 94588
925 847-3000

(P-19351)
HOSTMARK INVESTORS LTD PARTNR
Also Called: Santa Clara Hilton, The
4949 Great America Pkwy, Santa Clara (95054-1216)
PHONE 408 330-0001
Roy Truitt, *General Mgr*
EMP: 36 **Privately Held**
WEB: www.hostmark.squarespace.com
SIC: 8741 7991 5813 5812 Hotel or motel management; physical fitness facilities; drinking places; eating places; hotel, franchised
PA: Hostmark Investors Limited Partnership
1300 E Wdfield Rd Ste 400
Schaumburg IL 60173

(P-19352)
HUMANGOOD AFFORDABLE HOUSING (DH)
Also Called: Beacon Communities, Inc.
6120 Stoneridge Mall Rd # 100, Pleasanton (94588-3296)
PHONE 925 924-7163
David B Ferguson, *CEO*
John M Elliston, *COO*
Pamela Polley, *Controller*
Mark Sanderson, *Marketing Staff*
Brenda Kennedy,
EMP: 256 **EST:** 2015
SALES (est): 11.9MM
SALES (corp-wide): 25.9MM **Privately Held**
WEB: www.humangood.org
SIC: 8741 Business management
HQ: Humangood Norcal
6120 Stnrdge Mall Rd Ste
Pleasanton CA 94588
925 924-7100

(P-19353)
IMAGINE H20 INC
88 Kearny St Ste 2100, San Francisco (94108-5547)
PHONE 415 828-6344
Scott Bryan, *President*
Tom Ferguson, *Vice Pres*
Nimesh Modak, *Vice Pres*
Brian Matthay, *Managing Dir*
Ellie Barker, *Program Mgr*
EMP: 36 **EST:** 2011
SALES (est): 1.7MM **Privately Held**
WEB: www.imagineh2o.org
SIC: 8741 Management services

(P-19354)
INNOVATIVE EDUCATION MGT INC (PA)
4535 Missouri Flat Rd 1a, Placerville (95667-6808)
P.O. Box 2252 (95667-2252)
PHONE 530 295-3566
Randy Gaschler, *President*
Kirstine Bowers, *Executive Asst*
Denise Williams, *Executive Asst*
Linette Harris, *Admin Asst*
John Wilberger, *Info Tech Mgr*
EMP: 53 **EST:** 1998
SQ FT: 2,000
SALES (est): 21.8MM **Privately Held**
WEB: www.ieminc.org
SIC: 8741 Management services

(P-19355)
JSR NORTH AMERICA HOLDINGS INC
1280 N Mathilda Ave, Sunnyvale (94089-1213)
PHONE 408 543-8800
Eric Johnson, *President*
EMP: 37 **EST:** 2019
SALES (est): 3.1MM **Privately Held**
WEB: www.jsrmicro.com
SIC: 8741 Management services

(P-19356)
JT2 INTEGRATED RESOURCES (PA)
333 Hegenberger Rd # 650, Oakland (94621-1463)
P.O. Box 8021, Pleasanton (94588-8604)
PHONE 925 556-7012
Jeff Sandford, *Ch of Bd*
John Casas, *President*
Tabatha Bettencourt, *Senior VP*
Theresa Fernandez, *Vice Pres*
Carmen Angeles, *Program Mgr*
EMP: 65 **EST:** 1989
SQ FT: 4,200
SALES (est): 6.7MM **Privately Held**
WEB: www.jt2.com
SIC: 8741 Administrative management

(P-19357)
KAISER HLTH PLAN ASSET MGT INC
1 Kaiser Plz Ste 1333, Oakland (94612-3604)
PHONE 510 271-5910
Thomas R Meier, *President*
Megan Gannaway, *Officer*
Terry Anderson, *Med Doctor*
Rafael Barajas, *Manager*
Maryam Fakhari, *Consultant*
EMP: 50 **EST:** 1998
SALES: 51MM
SALES (corp-wide): 30.5B **Privately Held**
WEB: www.healthy.kaiserpermanente.org
SIC: 8741 Hospital management
PA: Kaiser Foundation Health Plan, Inc.
1 Kaiser Plz
Oakland CA 94612
510 271-5800

(P-19358)
KELLEYAMERIT HOLDINGS INC (PA)
Also Called: Kelleyamerit Fleet Services
1331 N Calif Blvd Ste 150, Walnut Creek (94596-4535)
PHONE 877 512-6374
Dan Williams, *CEO*
Amein Punjani, *COO*
Kent Bates, *CFO*
Salim Elmahmoud, *Business Mgr*
Robert Brauer, *VP Sales*
EMP: 956 **EST:** 2010
SQ FT: 10,000
SALES (est): 180MM **Privately Held**
SIC: 8741 Management services

(P-19359)
KISCO SENIOR LIVING LLC
Also Called: Bridgepoint At San Francisco
1601 19th Ave Ofc, San Francisco (94122-3478)
PHONE 415 664-6264
Susan Edwards, *Branch Mgr*
EMP: 249
SALES (corp-wide): 138.2MM **Privately Held**
WEB: www.kiscoseniorliving.com
SIC: 8741 Nursing & personal care facility management
PA: Senior Kisco Living Llc
5790 Fleet St Ste 300
Carlsbad CA 92008
760 804-5900

(P-19360)
KRM RISK MANAGEMENT SVCS INC
4270 W Richert Ave # 101, Fresno (93722-6334)
P.O. Box 9549 (93793-9549)
PHONE 559 277-4800
Steve Wigh, *Vice Pres*
EMP: 46 **Privately Held**
WEB: www.risico.com
SIC: 8741 Management services
PA: Krm Risk Management Services, Inc.
4270 W Richert Ave 101
Fresno CA 93722

(P-19361)
LAKE MRRITT HEALTHCARE CTR LLC
309 Macarthur Blvd, Oakland (94610-3233)
PHONE 510 227-1806
Edna Cortez, *Administration*
EMP: 80 **EST:** 2016
SALES (est): 2.7MM **Privately Held**
SIC: 8741 Hospital management

(P-19362)
LEGACY PRTNERS RESIDENTIAL INC (PA)
950 Tower Ln Ste 900, Foster City (94404-2125)
PHONE 650 571-2250
C Preston Butcher, *Ch of Bd*
Gary J Rossi, *CFO*
John Faust, *Managing Dir*
Jonathan Figone, *General Mgr*
Amelia Johnson, *VP Human Res*
EMP: 180 **EST:** 1995
SALES (est): 49.6MM **Privately Held**
WEB: www.legacypartners.com
SIC: 8741 Management services

(P-19363)
LENDLEASE US CONSTRUCTION INC
71 Stevenson St Ste 800, San Francisco (94105-2919)
PHONE 415 512-0586
EMP: 40 **Privately Held**
WEB: www.lendlease.com
SIC: 8741 8742 1541 1542 Management Services Mgmt Consulting Svcs Industrial Bldg Cnstn Nonresidential Cnstn
HQ: Lendlease (Us) Construction Inc.
200 Park Ave Fl 9
New York NY 10166
212 592-6700

(P-19364)
MANAGED FCLITIES SOLUTIONS LLC
128 Component Dr, San Jose (95131-1119)
PHONE 408 920-0110
Tom Spies, *Mng Member*
David Borrison, *Senior VP*
Isaac Rodriguez, *Opers Staff*
EMP: 37 **EST:** 2016
SALES (est): 6.1MM **Privately Held**
WEB: www.mfs.team
SIC: 8741 Management services

(P-19365)
MARIN MED PRCTICE CONCEPTS INC
Also Called: M M P
100 Rowland Way Ste 201, Novato (94945-5041)
PHONE 415 493-3300
Joel Sklar MD, *President*
EMP: 35 **EST:** 1996
SALES (est): 4.8MM **Privately Held**
SIC: 8741 Management services

8741 - Management Services County (P-19366) — PRODUCTS & SERVICES SECTION

(P-19366)
MATRIC ABSENCE MANAGEMENT
2208 Plaza Dr Ste 100, Rocklin (95765-4418)
PHONE 916 773-5737
Jose Reynoso, *Principal*
Gwen Cristiano, *Manager*
Pamela Mehiel, *Manager*
Elizabeth Echon, *Assistant*
Frank Malizia, *Supervisor*
EMP: 36 **EST:** 2004
SALES (est): 2.6MM **Privately Held**
SIC: 8741 Business management

(P-19367)
MATRIX ABSENCE MANAGEMENT INC
1420 Rocky Ridge Dr # 270, Roseville (95661-2830)
PHONE 916 773-5737
EMP: 62 **Privately Held**
WEB: www.matrixcos.com
SIC: 8741 Management services
HQ: Matrix Absence Management, Inc.
2421 W Peoria Ave Ste 200
Phoenix AZ 85029

(P-19368)
MAX SPORTSTERS INC
Also Called: Wheeler and Company
10050 N Foothill Blvd # 200, Cupertino (95014-5661)
PHONE 408 446-8330
David Wheeler, *President*
EMP: 50
SALES (est): 1.3MM **Privately Held**
SIC: 8741 Restaurant management

(P-19369)
MAXISCALE INC
1100 La Avenida St Ste A, Mountain View (94043-1453)
PHONE 408 962-6000
EMP: 15
SALES (est): 730.6K
SALES (corp-wide): 329.1K **Privately Held**
WEB: www.maxiscale.com
SIC: 8741 7372 Management Services Prepackaged Software Services
HQ: Overland Storage, Inc.
9112 Spectrum Center Blvd
San Diego CA 94583
858 571-5555

(P-19370)
MENDOZA & ASSOCIATES (PA)
1390 Market St Ste 200, San Francisco (94102-5404)
PHONE 415 644-0180
Richard Mendoza, *Owner*
Michelle Dugentas, *Admin Asst*
Joseph Saunders, *Administration*
Patricia Watson, *Contract Mgr*
John Volpp, *Manager*
EMP: 46 **EST:** 1992
SALES (est): 7.2MM **Privately Held**
SIC: 8741 Construction management

(P-19371)
MERITAGE GROUP LP
1 Ferry Building, San Francisco (94111-4289)
PHONE 415 399-5330
Mark Mindich,
EMP: 1500 **EST:** 2007
SALES (est): 25.6MM **Privately Held**
SIC: 8741 Management services

(P-19372)
MOTIVATE INTERNATIONAL INC (HQ)
185 Berry St Ste 5000, San Francisco (94107-2503)
P.O. Box 320592, Brooklyn NY (11232-0592)
PHONE 347 916-0210
Jay Walder, *CEO*
Jules Flynn, *Exec VP*
Justine Lee, *Vice Pres*
Jean-Sebastien Bettez, *CTO*
James Paulson, *Human Res Dir*
EMP: 50 **EST:** 2015

SALES (est): 20.8MM **Publicly Held**
WEB: www.motivateco.com
SIC: 8741 8742 5941 Management services; management consulting services; bicycle & bicycle parts

(P-19373)
NETWORK MANAGEMENT & CTRL CORP
529 Rock Oak Rd, Walnut Creek (94598-2735)
PHONE 319 483-1123
Mark D Hearn, *Branch Mgr*
Tanya Seda, *Officer*
EMP: 57
SALES (corp-wide): 6.2MM **Privately Held**
WEB: www.network-control.com
SIC: 8741 Management services
PA: Network Management & Control Corporation
215 20th St Nw
Waverly IA 50677
319 483-1100

(P-19374)
NORDSTROM INC
1200 Broadway Plz, Walnut Creek (94596-5115)
PHONE 925 930-7959
Brian Lee, *Branch Mgr*
Jonathan Ortiz, *Department Mgr*
Johanna Titus, *Department Mgr*
Julie Vu, *Admin Sec*
Nyesha Rayford, *Administration*
EMP: 163
SALES (corp-wide): 10.7B **Publicly Held**
WEB: www.nordstrom.com
SIC: 5651 8741 Family clothing stores; restaurant management
PA: Nordstrom, Inc.
1617 6th Ave
Seattle WA 98101
206 628-2111

(P-19375)
NORTHSTAR SENIOR LIVING INC
2334 Washington Ave Ste A, Redding (96001-2159)
PHONE 530 242-8300
Rick Jensen, *CEO*
Brian Uhlir, *CFO*
Tonya Glass, *Vice Pres*
Kasey Segerstrom, *Vice Pres*
Patty King, *Exec Dir*
EMP: 586 **EST:** 2008
SALES (est): 22.6MM **Privately Held**
WEB: www.northstarseniorliving.com
SIC: 8741 Nursing & personal care facility management

(P-19376)
PACIFIC FOUNDATION SVCS LLC
1660 Bush St 300, San Francisco (94109-5308)
PHONE 415 561-6540
Charles R Casey, *President*
Frank Buenrostro, *Officer*
Ash McNeely, *Officer*
Emily Schroeder, *Officer*
Leslie Griep, *Vice Pres*
EMP: 53 **EST:** 1989
SQ FT: 4,000
SALES (est): 9.8MM **Privately Held**
WEB: www.pfs-llc.net
SIC: 8741 Management services

(P-19377)
PACIFIC PARK MANAGEMENT
1300 Fillmore St, San Francisco (94115-4113)
PHONE 415 440-4840
EMP: 85 **Privately Held**
WEB: www.pacificparkonline.com
SIC: 8741 7521 Business management; indoor parking services
PA: Pacific Park Management Inc
311 California St Ste 310
San Francisco CA 94104

(P-19378)
PACIFIC PARTNERS MGT SVCS INC
Also Called: Pacific Partners MSI
1051 E Hillsdale Blvd, Foster City (94404-1640)
P.O. Box 5860, San Mateo (94402-5860)
PHONE 650 358-5804
Lori Vatcher, *CEO*
M L Bonham MD, *President*
EMP: 100 **EST:** 1997
SALES (est): 12.7MM **Publicly Held**
WEB: www.ppmsi.com
SIC: 8741 8748 Business management; business consulting
PA: Hca Healthcare, Inc.
1 Park Plz
Nashville TN 37203

(P-19379)
PAVILIONS MANAGEMENT LLC (PA)
8450 Wood Thrush Way, Granite Bay (95746-6120)
P.O. Box 2456 (95746-2456)
PHONE 916 782-8822
Kenneth Ristuben, *Principal*
EMP: 37 **EST:** 2007
SALES (est): 584.2K **Privately Held**
SIC: 8741 Management services

(P-19380)
PEARL MANAGEMENT GROUP INC (PA)
2150 Bluebell Dr, Santa Rosa (95403-2508)
PHONE 818 383-0095
Michael B Perlman, *Principal*
EMP: 72 **EST:** 2008
SALES (est): 1.1MM **Privately Held**
SIC: 8741 Management services

(P-19381)
PEN-CAL ADMINISTRATORS INC
Also Called: P C A
7633 Suthfront Rd Ste 120, Livermore (94551)
PHONE 925 251-3400
Kirk Penland, *CEO*
Jon Van Oosbree, *Info Tech Mgr*
Sergio Amiri, *Technology*
Christian Penland, *Analyst*
Hunter Penland, *Analyst*
EMP: 75 **EST:** 1980
SQ FT: 15,000
SALES (est): 10.3MM
SALES (corp-wide): 7.6B **Publicly Held**
WEB: www.voya.com
SIC: 8741 Financial management for business
PA: Voya Financial, Inc.
230 Park Ave Fl 14
New York NY 10169
212 309-8200

(P-19382)
PRIMED MGT CONSULTING SVCS INC
2409 Camino Ramon, San Ramon (94583-4285)
P.O. Box 5080 (94583-0980)
PHONE 925 327-6710
David Joyner, *CEO*
Steve McDermott, *President*
Tim Richards, *CFO*
Mitra Javidi, *Vice Pres*
Khanh Nguyen, *Vice Pres*
EMP: 488 **EST:** 1984
SQ FT: 30,000
SALES (est): 53.8MM **Privately Held**
WEB: www.hillphysicians.com
SIC: 8741 8742 Management services; management consulting services
PA: Hill Physicians Medical Group, Inc.
2409 Camino Ramon
San Ramon CA 94583

(P-19383)
PROACTIVE BUS SOLUTIONS INC
410 7th St 205, Oakland (94607-3928)
PHONE 510 302-0120
Deidrie Towery, *CEO*
Larry Hall, *Officer*
Renee Holloman, *VP Bus Dvlpt*
Bill Riley, *Info Tech Dir*
Hatim Nasher, *Info Tech Mgr*
EMP: 250 **EST:** 1998
SQ FT: 3,000
SALES (est): 12.4MM **Privately Held**
WEB: www.proactiveok.com
SIC: 8741 8742 Business management; business consultant

(P-19384)
PS24 INC
Also Called: Grove - Design District, The
65 Division St, San Francisco (94103-5215)
PHONE 415 834-5105
Kenneth Zankel, *CEO*
Charles Baldwin, *General Mgr*
Anna Zankel, *Admin Sec*
EMP: 100 **EST:** 2017
SALES (est): 4.5MM **Privately Held**
SIC: 8741 Restaurant management

(P-19385)
RAISIN ADM COMMITTEE
2445 Capitol St Ste 200, Fresno (93721-2236)
PHONE 559 225-0520
Ron Worthley, *President*
Chris Gunland, *Chairman*
Debbie Pilloud, *Opers Staff*
EMP: 35 **EST:** 1949
SALES (est): 3.3MM **Privately Held**
WEB: www.raisins.org
SIC: 8741 Administrative management

(P-19386)
RAPID VALUE SOLUTIONS INC
Also Called: Miller's Rent All
7901 Stoneridge Dr # 225, Pleasanton (94588-3677)
PHONE 925 398-3344
Rajesh Pandijaremadam, *CEO*
Sivakumar Nair, *President*
Sirish Kosaraju, *COO*
Anil Pillai, *Vice Pers*
Sundar Rengamani, *Vice Pres*
EMP: 50 **EST:** 2008
SALES (est): 10.8MM **Privately Held**
WEB: www.rapidvaluesolutions.com
SIC: 8741 Business management
PA: Rapidvalue It Services Private Limited
3c, 3rd Floor, Phase-2, Carnival Leela Infopark, Infopark Road
Ernakulam KL 68204

(P-19387)
REMODELORS INC
Also Called: North State Solar Energy
15523 Nopel Ave, Forest Ranch (95942-9679)
P.O. Box 899 (95942-0899)
PHONE 530 893-4741
Michael Houar, *CEO*
EMP: 35 **EST:** 2002
SALES (est): 2.4MM **Privately Held**
SIC: 8741 Construction management

(P-19388)
REPUBLIC DOCUMENT MANAGEMENT
6377 Clark Ave Ste 250, Dublin (94568-3014)
PHONE 925 551-4747
Tessa Widman, *Branch Mgr*
Todd McDonald, *Opers Mgr*
James Tuthill, *Manager*
EMP: 38
SALES (corp-wide): 8.1MM **Privately Held**
WEB: www.gorepublic.com
SIC: 8741 Management services
PA: Republic Document Management, Inc
660 N Diamond Bar Blvd # 258
Diamond Bar CA 91765
909 718-1421

PRODUCTS & SERVICES SECTION
8741 - Management Services County (P-19413)

(P-19389)
ROBERTSON STPHENS WLTH MGT LLC (PA)
455 Market St Ste 1600, San Francisco (94105-2444)
PHONE..................415 500-6810
Ren Riley, *CEO*
Erik Boe, *Officer*
Dan Barth, *Vice Pres*
Raymond Lang, *Vice Pres*
Molly Wallace, *Vice Pres*
EMP: 55 **EST:** 2018
SALES (est): 6.8MM **Privately Held**
WEB: www.rscapital.com
SIC: 8741 Business management

(P-19390)
RUBY BURMA INVESTMENT LLC
612 El Camino Real, San Carlos (94070-3104)
PHONE..................650 590-0545
Max Lee, *Mng Member*
Justin Kwok, *Accountant*
EMP: 51 **EST:** 2014
SALES (est): 3.4MM **Privately Held**
SIC: 8741 Restaurant management

(P-19391)
RW3 TECHNOLOGIES INC (PA)
Also Called: R W Information Technologies
1601 Cornell Way, Auburn (95603-3063)
PHONE..................925 743-7703
Bruce Nagle, *CEO*
Deepika Kurl, *Controller*
Aimee Brown, *Director*
EMP: 41 **EST:** 1992
SQ FT: 4,500 **Privately Held**
WEB: www.rw3.com
SIC: 8741 Management services

(P-19392)
SALAS OBRIEN LLC (PA)
305 S 11th St, San Jose (95112-2218)
PHONE..................408 282-1500
Paul Silva, *CEO*
Jesse Naughton, *Assoc VP*
Eric Anest, *Vice Pres*
Carl Crizer, *Vice Pres*
Brian Smith, *Vice Pres*
EMP: 60 **EST:** 2011
SALES (est): 19.7MM **Privately Held**
WEB: www.salasobrien.com
SIC: 8741 Construction management

(P-19393)
SAN FRANCISCO UNIFIED SCHL DST (PA)
Also Called: Adminstrtion Offces For Schl D
555 Franklin St, San Francisco (94102-4414)
PHONE..................415 241-6000
Arlene Ackerman, *Superintendent*
Betty Hong, *Executive*
Angie Sagastume, *Exec Dir*
Janet Schulze, *Branch Mgr*
Maryline Hee, *Admin Sec*
▲ **EMP:** 250 **EST:** 1856
SQ FT: 14,000
SALES (est): 918.7MM **Privately Held**
WEB: www.sfusd.edu
SIC: 8211 8741 Public elementary & secondary schools; administrative management

(P-19394)
SAN FRNCSCO CMNTY CLNIC CNSRTI
Also Called: SFCCC
2720 Taylor St Ste 430, San Francisco (94133-1231)
PHONE..................415 355-2222
John Gressman, *President*
Pat Dunn, *COO*
Maria Powers, *CFO*
Patricia Dunn, *Vice Pres*
Jim Jarvenpaa, *Executive Asst*
EMP: 71 **EST:** 1983
SQ FT: 7,000
SALES (est): 9.5MM **Privately Held**
WEB: www.sfccc.org
SIC: 8741 Management services

(P-19395)
SAN JOSE ARENA MANAGEMENT LLC (PA)
525 W Santa Clara St, San Jose (95113-1500)
PHONE..................408 287-7070
Greg Jamison,
Erik Taubman, *Sales Staff*
EMP: 151 **EST:** 2001
SALES (est): 22.8MM **Privately Held**
WEB: www.sapcenter.com
SIC: 8741 Management services

(P-19396)
SAN JOSE EARTHQUAKES MGT LLC
451 El Cmino Real Ste 220, Santa Clara (95050)
PHONE..................408 556-7700
Lew Wolff, *Owner*
Keith Wolff, *Managing Prtnr*
John Fisher, *Shareholder*
Dave Kaval, *President*
Jared Shawlee, *COO*
EMP: 51 **EST:** 2011
SALES (est): 5.6MM **Privately Held**
WEB: www.sjearthquakes.com
SIC: 8741 Management services

(P-19397)
SFNY GROUP INC ✪
1901 Harrison St Ste 1100, Oakland (94612-3648)
PHONE..................510 646-1360
Antoine Keane, *CEO*
EMP: 35 **EST:** 2021
SALES (est): 1.3MM **Privately Held**
SIC: 8741 Management services

(P-19398)
SHAREHLDER RPRSNTTIVE SVCS LLC (PA)
Also Called: SRS
601 Montgomery St Ste 750, San Francisco (94111-2611)
PHONE..................303 648-4085
Mark Vogel, *Mng Member*
Andrew Hyde, *CFO*
Andrew P Hyde, *CFO*
Debbie Wapensky, *CFO*
Andrew Hyde, *Vice Pres*
EMP: 35 **EST:** 2007
SQ FT: 10,000
SALES (est): 11.7MM **Privately Held**
WEB: www.srsacquiom.com
SIC: 8741 Management services

(P-19399)
SODEXO MANAGEMENT INC
Also Called: Cific Energy Center
851 Howard St, San Francisco (94103-3009)
PHONE..................925 325-9657
Jim Wasley, *Branch Mgr*
EMP: 414
SALES (corp-wide): 158.5MM **Privately Held**
WEB: www.sodexo.com
SIC: 8741 Management services
HQ: Sodexo Management Inc.
9801 Washingtonian Blvd
Gaithersburg MD 20878

(P-19400)
SODEXO MANAGEMENT INC
1 University Cir, Turlock (95382-3200)
PHONE..................209 667-3634
Tom Welton, *Manager*
EMP: 414
SALES (corp-wide): 158.5MM **Privately Held**
WEB: www.sodexo.com
SIC: 8741 Management services
HQ: Sodexo Management Inc.
9801 Washingtonian Blvd
Gaithersburg MD 20878

(P-19401)
STANDISH MANAGEMENT LLC (PA)
750 Battery St Ste 600, San Francisco (94111-1567)
PHONE..................415 391-7225
Robert A Raynard, *Managing Prtnr*
Susan Gillick, *President*
Alexander D'eletto, *Controller*
Zan Zuna, *Controller*
Judy Dickinson, *Director*
EMP: 54 **EST:** 2014
SALES (est): 27.3MM **Privately Held**
WEB: www.standishmanagement.com
SIC: 8741 Business management

(P-19402)
STELLAR ENTERPRISE ASSOC INC
2300 Stanwell Dr Ste A, Concord (94520-4841)
PHONE..................510 662-3333
Michael Parker, *President*
Darral Brown, *CFO*
Chris Pratt, *Vice Pres*
Grant Allen, *Admin Sec*
EMP: 45 **EST:** 2001
SQ FT: 7,000
SALES (est): 2MM **Privately Held**
SIC: 8741 Management services

(P-19403)
STITCH LABS INC
1455 Market St Ste 600, San Francisco (94103-1332)
PHONE..................415 323-0630
Brandon Levey, *CEO*
Charles Michael, *Partner*
Mavian Ruiz, *Partner*
Jill Richards, *Chief Mktg Ofcr*
Yvonne KAO, *Controller*
EMP: 47 **EST:** 2011
SALES (est): 1MM **Privately Held**
WEB: www.stitchlabs.com
SIC: 8741 7372 Business management; application computer software

(P-19404)
SUNHILL CORP
147 Lomita Dr Ste G, Mill Valley (94941-1462)
PHONE..................415 383-9100
Hameed S Faidi, *President*
Zach Faidi, *Treasurer*
Inam Faidi, *Vice Pres*
EMP: 69 **EST:** 1981
SALES (est): 2.7MM **Privately Held**
SIC: 8741 Management services

(P-19405)
SUTTER VALLEY MED FOUNDATION
3707 Schriever Ave, Mather (95655-4202)
PHONE..................916 454-8449
Brian Johnson, *Branch Mgr*
Joyce Swan, *Director*
EMP: 54 **Privately Held**
WEB: www.sutterhealth.org
SIC: 8741 8082 Hospital management; home health care services
PA: Sutter Valley Medical Foundation
2700 Gateway Oaks Dr
Sacramento CA 95833

(P-19406)
SUTTER VALLEY MED FOUNDATION
Also Called: Padilla, David A MD
568 N Sunrise Ave Ste 250, Roseville (95661-3097)
PHONE..................916 865-1140
Susan Paez, *Manager*
EMP: 54 **Privately Held**
WEB: www.sutterhealth.org
SIC: 8741 8011 Hospital management; internal medicine, physician/surgeon
PA: Sutter Valley Medical Foundation
2700 Gateway Oaks Dr
Sacramento CA 95833

(P-19407)
TCV MANAGEMENT 2004 LLC
528 Ramona St, Palo Alto (94301-1709)
PHONE..................650 614-8200
Jay C Hoag, *Manager*
Nathan Sanders, *IT Executive*
EMP: 35 **EST:** 2004
SALES (est): 557K **Privately Held**
SIC: 8741 Management services

(P-19408)
TEXTAINER GROUP HOLDINGS LTD (DH)
650 California St Fl 16, San Francisco (94108-2720)
PHONE..................415 434-0551
John A Maccarone, *CEO*
John Simmons, *Vice Pres*
Kenneth Chow, *Network Enginr*
Joseph Tilelli, *Opers-Prdtn-Mfg*
Cathy Dudley, *Opers Staff*
EMP: 55 **EST:** 1994
SALES (est): 27.5MM **Privately Held**
WEB: www.textainer.com
SIC: 8741 Business management

(P-19409)
TILTON PACIFIC CNSTR INC
940 Saratoga Ave Ste 105, San Jose (95129-3409)
PHONE..................408 551-0492
James Tilton, *Branch Mgr*
Meile Pochy, *Administration*
Kevin Matthiessen, *Info Tech Mgr*
Kimberly Fox, *Project Mgr*
Gregoire Zaldua, *Project Mgr*
EMP: 37 **Privately Held**
WEB: www.tiltonpacific.com
SIC: 8741 1521 Construction management; single-family housing construction
PA: Tilton Pacific Construction, Inc.
4150 Citrus Ave
Rocklin CA 95677

(P-19410)
TRAFFIC MANAGEMENT INC
8399 Edgewater Dr, Oakland (94621-1401)
PHONE..................415 370-7916
Mark Coleman, *Principal*
EMP: 36 **Privately Held**
WEB: www.trafficmanagement.com
SIC: 8741 7389 Business management; flagging service (traffic control)
PA: Traffic Management, Inc.
4900 Arprt Plz Dr Ste 300
Long Beach CA 90815

(P-19411)
TRAFFIC MANAGEMENT INC
5806 Perrin Ave, McClellan (95652-2410)
PHONE..................916 394-2200
Chris Spano, *Branch Mgr*
Jonathan Castro, *Accounts Mgr*
EMP: 36 **Privately Held**
WEB: www.trafficmanagement.com
SIC: 8741 Business management
PA: Traffic Management, Inc.
4900 Arprt Plz Dr Ste 300
Long Beach CA 90815

(P-19412)
TRI-STATE ENTERPRISES INC
2133 Leghorn St, Mountain View (94043-1605)
PHONE..................650 210-0085
Nagi Chami, *President*
Donald Cox, *Ch of Bd*
EMP: 37 **EST:** 1999
SQ FT: 7,500
SALES (est): 1.1MM **Privately Held**
WEB: www.3state.net
SIC: 8741 Construction management; business management

(P-19413)
UNITED BEHAVIORAL HEALTH (HQ)
425 Market St Fl 18, San Francisco (94105-2532)
PHONE..................415 547-1403
Saul Feldman, *Ch of Bd*
Keith Dickson, *President*
Ann Mc Clanathan, *COO*
Karen Schievelbein, *CFO*
William Goldman Sr, *Exec VP*
EMP: 250 **EST:** 1979
SQ FT: 20,000

(PA)=Parent Co (HQ)=Headquarters (DH)=Div Headquarters
✪ = New Business established in last 2 years

8741 - Management Services County (P-19414)

SALES (est): 32.7MM
SALES (corp-wide): 257.1B **Publicly Held**
WEB: www.unitedhealthgroup.com
SIC: 8741 8742 Management services; management consulting services
PA: Unitedhealth Group Incorporated
   9900 Bren Rd E Ste 300w
   Minnetonka MN 55343
   952 936-1300

(P-19414)
UNIVERSITY ENTERPRISES INC
Also Called: SACRAMENTO STATE SPONSORED RES
6000 J St, Sacramento (95819-2605)
PHONE..................................916 278-7001
James Reinhart, *Exec Dir*
Craig Barth, *CFO*
Alexander Gonzalez, *Chairman*
Crystal Sims, *Treasurer*
Nathan Dietrich, *Assoc VP*
EMP: 1856 EST: 1951
SQ FT: 22,931
SALES: 101.6MM **Privately Held**
WEB: www.enterprises.csus.edu
SIC: 8299 8741 Educational services; management services

(P-19415)
UNIVERSITY OF CALIFORNIA
1 Shields Ave, Davis (95616-8500)
PHONE..................................530 752-0503
Georgette M Handal, *President*
Dorsey Griffith, *Officer*
Lorie Trapani, *Officer*
Anna Lawrence, *Associate Dir*
Trina Wiggins, *Associate Dir*
EMP: 75 EST: 2019
SALES (est): 10.5MM **Privately Held**
WEB: www.ucdavis.edu
SIC: 8741 Management services

(P-19416)
VANIR CONSTRUCTION MGT INC (PA)
4540 Duckhorn Dr Ste 300, Sacramento (95834-2597)
PHONE..................................916 444-3700
Dorene C Dominguez, *Ch of Bd*
John Kuprenas, *CEO*
Alex Leon, *CFO*
Ray Nez, *CFO*
Bruce Hart, *Chief Mktg Ofcr*
EMP: 70 EST: 1980
SQ FT: 16,000
SALES (est): 47.8MM **Privately Held**
WEB: www.vanir.com
SIC: 8741 Construction management

(P-19417)
VETERANS HEALTH ADMINISTRATION
Also Called: VA Palo Alto Healthcare System
3801 Miranda Ave, Palo Alto (94304-1207)
PHONE..................................650 493-5000
Vanessa Amasol, *Branch Mgr*
Tammy Linton, *CIO*
Nancy Clum, *Prgrmr*
Gerwin Legaspi, *Technician*
Lisa Kinoshita, *Psychologist*
EMP: 49 **Publicly Held**
WEB: www.benefits.va.gov
SIC: 8741 9451 Hospital management;
HQ: Veterans Health Administration
   810 Vermont Ave Nw
   Washington DC 20420

(P-19418)
VICTUS GROUP INC
2377 W Shaw Ave Ste 201, Fresno (93711-3438)
PHONE..................................559 429-8080
Bob Young Yoon, *CEO*
Doreen Lopez, *Vice Pres*
Braxton Myers, *Vice Pres*
Timothy Clark, *Manager*
EMP: 176 EST: 2012
SALES (est): 2.8MM **Privately Held**
WEB: www.thevictusgroup.com
SIC: 8741 Hotel or motel management

(P-19419)
VIVA SOMA LESSEE INC
Also Called: Park Central Ht San Francisco
50 3rd St, San Francisco (94103-3106)
PHONE..................................415 974-6400
John Anderson, *Branch Mgr*
Binyam Tarekegn, *Accounting Mgr*
Yu Nakanishi, *Analyst*
John Carrillo, *Opers Staff*
Sou Kotaki, *Sales Staff*
EMP: 511 **Publicly Held**
SIC: 8741 Hotel or motel management; restaurant management
HQ: Viva Soma Lessee, Inc.
   7550 Wisconsin Ave Fl 10
   Bethesda MD

(P-19420)
WASTEXPERTS INCORPORATED
901 Howe Rd, Martinez (94553-3443)
P.O. Box 2099 (94553-0209)
PHONE..................................925 484-1057
David Lentz, *President*
EMP: 80 EST: 2012
SALES (est): 10.7MM **Privately Held**
WEB: www.wastexperts.net
SIC: 8741 Management services

(P-19421)
WBB MANAGEMENT COMPANY INC
Also Called: West Bay Builders
250 Bel Marin Keys Blvd A, Novato (94949-5727)
P.O. Box 6115 (94948-6115)
PHONE..................................415 456-8972
Paul Thompson, *President*
Joe Haas, *Vice Pres*
Clayton Fraser, *VP Bus Dvlpt*
Alex Diaz, *Project Mgr*
Peter Hopkins, *Project Mgr*
EMP: 50 EST: 1999
SALES (est): 2.3MM **Privately Held**
WEB: www.tbcorp.com
SIC: 8741 Management services

(P-19422)
WENDT INDUSTRIES INC
Also Called: Club Resource Group
1875 N Macarthur Dr, Tracy (95376-2820)
PHONE..................................209 836-4100
Michael Wendt, *CEO*
Bill Ladouceur, *General Mgr*
Richard Barnes, *CIO*
Jeff Palma, *Project Mgr*
Katie Kovenich, *Controller*
▲ EMP: 40 EST: 1995
SALES (est): 6.7MM **Privately Held**
SIC: 8741 Construction management

(P-19423)
WESTERN HEALTH RESOURCES
100 San Hedrin Cir, Willits (95490-8753)
PHONE..................................707 459-1818
William G Wiedemann, *Manager*
EMP: 82
SALES (corp-wide): 57MM **Privately Held**
SIC: 8741 8742 Administrative management; business planning & organizing services
PA: Western Health Resources
   2100 Douglas Blvd
   Roseville CA
   916 781-2000

(P-19424)
WESTLAKE DEVELOPMENT GROUP LLC
520 El Camino Real Fl 9, Belmont (94002-2121)
PHONE..................................650 579-1010
T M Chang, *Branch Mgr*
EMP: 47
SQ FT: 600
SALES (corp-wide): 17.8MM **Privately Held**
WEB: www.westlake-realty.com
SIC: 8741 Administrative management
PA: Westlake Development Group, Llc
   520 S El Camino Real # 900
   San Mateo CA 94402
   650 579-1010

(P-19425)
WHISPERAI INC
260 8th St, San Francisco (94103-3923)
PHONE..................................855 765-0088
Dwight Crow, *CEO*
Andrew Song, *Principal*
EMP: 50 EST: 2017
SALES (est): 5.1MM **Privately Held**
WEB: www.whisper.ai
SIC: 8741 7371 Management services; computer software development & applications

(P-19426)
WILLIAM L LYON & ASSOC INC (HQ)
Also Called: Lyon Real Estate
3640 Amrcn Rver Dr Ste 10, Sacramento (95864)
PHONE..................................916 978-4200
Patrick M Shea, *President*
Michael Levedahl, *CFO*
Jean LI, *CFO*
Paula Colombo, *Vice Pres*
Casey Schumacher, *Office Mgr*
EMP: 43 EST: 1946
SQ FT: 5,000
SALES (est): 75.3MM
SALES (corp-wide): 164.4MM **Privately Held**
WEB: www.golyon.com
SIC: 8741 Management services
PA: Windermere Real Estate Services Company
   5424 Sand Point Way Ne
   Seattle WA 98105
   206 527-3801

(P-19427)
WOOD AG MANAGEMENT INC
652 W Cromwell Ave # 103, Fresno (93711-5747)
PHONE..................................559 432-5164
EMP: 35 EST: 2019
SALES (est): 2.5MM **Privately Held**
SIC: 8741 Management services

(P-19428)
WURL INC (PA)
591 Lytton Ave, Palo Alto (94301-1538)
PHONE..................................662 649-8825
Sean P Doherty, *CEO*
Craig Heiting, *Senior VP*
Yuval Fisher, *Vice Pres*
Karl Forsman, *Software Engr*
EMP: 105 EST: 2011
SALES (est): 3.7MM **Privately Held**
WEB: www.wurl.com
SIC: 8741 Management services

(P-19429)
ZMC HOTELS LLC (HQ)
1855 Olympic Blvd Ste 300, Walnut Creek (94596-5019)
PHONE..................................925 933-4000
Mark D Hall, *President*
Dan Sicotte, *CFO*
Tonya Houdyshell, *Manager*
EMP: 50 EST: 1982
SALES (est): 33MM
SALES (corp-wide): 36.8MM **Privately Held**
WEB: www.zmchotels.com
SIC: 8741 Hotel or motel management
PA: Hall Equities Group
   1855 Olympic Blvd Ste 300
   Walnut Creek CA
   925 933-4000

8742 Management Consulting Services

(P-19430)
101MFG LLC
107 Dublin Ct, Petaluma (94952-7511)
PHONE..................................415 828-9015
Richard Herman,
EMP: 40 EST: 2003
SALES (est): 1.4MM **Privately Held**
WEB: www.101mfg.com
SIC: 8742 Marketing consulting services

(P-19431)
ABACUS INFORMATION TECH LLC (HQ)
101 California St Fl 10, San Francisco (94111-5813)
PHONE..................................415 517-8005
Peter Bergman,
Frank Kim, *Vice Pres*
Christopher Grandi,
Jason Hasday, *Manager*
EMP: 70 EST: 2009
SALES (est): 9.8MM
SALES (corp-wide): 48.6MM **Privately Held**
WEB: www.abacusgroupllc.com
SIC: 8742 Management information systems consultant
PA: Abacus Group Llc
   655 3rd Ave Ste 801
   New York NY 10017
   212 812-8444

(P-19432)
ACCOUNTNOW INC
2603 Camino Ramon Ste 485, San Ramon (94583-9131)
P.O. Box 5100, Pasadena (91117-0100)
PHONE..................................925 498-1800
James G Jones, *CEO*
David J Petrini, *CFO*
Paul Rosenfeld, *Chief Mktg Ofcr*
Jenn Cordeiro, *Technology*
Slava Ostrovsky, *Technology*
EMP: 63 EST: 2003
SALES (est): 7.2MM
SALES (corp-wide): 1.1B **Publicly Held**
WEB: www.accountnow.com
SIC: 8742 Financial consultant
PA: Green Dot Corporation
   3465 E Foothill Blvd
   Pasadena CA 91107
   626 765-2000

(P-19433)
ACTION PROPERTY MANAGEMENT INC
850 Montgomery St Ste 150, San Francisco (94133-5120)
PHONE..................................800 400-2284
Kimber Matthews, *Manager*
EMP: 40
SALES (corp-wide): 107.1MM **Privately Held**
WEB: www.actionlife.com
SIC: 8742 Management consulting services
PA: Action Property Management, Inc.
   2603 Main St Ste 500
   Irvine CA 92614
   949 450-0202

(P-19434)
ADIVO ASSOCIATES LLC
44 Montgomery St Ste 4050, San Francisco (94104-4824)
PHONE..................................415 992-1449
Maik Klasen, *Branch Mgr*
Xianglong Zhu, *Consultant*
Aaron Aho, *Associate*
Brandi Baughman, *Associate*
Jason Bruton, *Associate*
EMP: 90
SALES (corp-wide): 1.5MM **Privately Held**
WEB: www.adivoassociates.com
SIC: 8742 Business consultant
PA: Adivo Associates Llc
   1429 Plymouth Ave
   San Francisco CA 94112
   650 743-6226

(P-19435)
AG & ASSOCIATES INC (PA)
2208 Camino Ramon Ste A, San Ramon (94583-1328)
P.O. Box 2700 (94583-7700)
PHONE..................................925 327-0804
Anselmo Antonio Goulart, *Principal*
EMP: 37 EST: 2015

▲ = Import ▼ = Export
◆ = Import/Export

PRODUCTS & SERVICES SECTION

8742 - Management Consulting Services County (P-19457)

SALES (est): 1MM **Privately Held**
WEB: www.agassociatesinc.com
SIC: 8742 Management consulting services

(P-19436)
AGAMA SOLUTIONS INC
39159 Paseo Padre Pkwy # 216, Fremont (94538-1689)
PHONE 510 796-9300
Pankaj Kalra, *CEO*
Tanu Kalra, *President*
Shivani G Sanan, *CEO*
Ashish Sanan, *Vice Pres*
Aman Sharma, *Technical Staff*
EMP: 40 **EST:** 2006
SQ FT: 9,000
SALES (est): 2.3MM **Privately Held**
WEB: www.agamasolutions.com
SIC: 8742 7371 Business consultant; computer software development

(P-19437)
AGREEYA SOLUTIONS INC (PA)
605 Coolidge Dr Ste 200, Folsom (95630-4210)
PHONE 916 294-0075
Neerja Khosla, *President*
Sangeeta Khazanchi, *CFO*
Sanjay Khosla, *Vice Pres*
Brian Pugh, *Vice Pres*
Kempf Rick, *Vice Pres*
EMP: 55 **EST:** 1999
SQ FT: 14,000
SALES (est): 55.3MM **Privately Held**
WEB: www.agreeya.com
SIC: 8742 7371 Management consulting services; computer software systems analysis & design, custom

(P-19438)
AKI TECHNOLOGIES INC
912 Cole St, San Francisco (94117-4316)
PHONE 415 462-4254
Scott Swanson, *CEO*
Todd Benedict, *Officer*
Matt Knust, *Vice Pres*
Faridh Mendoza, *Software Dev*
Khin Thomson, *Opers Staff*
EMP: 38
SALES (corp-wide): 4.2MM **Privately Held**
WEB: www.a.ki
SIC: 8742 Marketing consulting services
PA: Aki Technologies, Inc.
  760 Church St
  San Francisco CA 94114
  415 462-4254

(P-19439)
AKQA INC (HQ)
360 3rd St Ste 500, San Francisco (94107-2165)
PHONE 415 645-9400
Tom Bedecarre, *CEO*
Rei Inamoto, *Ch Credit Ofcr*
Mark Kramer, *Vice Pres*
Matt Bennett, *Creative Dir*
Eamonn Dixon, *Creative Dir*
EMP: 400 **EST:** 1990
SQ FT: 28,000
SALES (est): 349.9MM
SALES (corp-wide): 15.9B **Privately Held**
WEB: www.akqa.com
SIC: 8742 Marketing consulting services
PA: Wpp Plc
  13 Castle Street
  Jersey JE1 1
  207 282-4600

(P-19440)
ALIBABACOM US LLC (DH)
Also Called: Alibaba Group
525 Almanor Ave Ste 400, Sunnyvale (94085-3542)
PHONE 408 785-5580
Jack MA, *Principal*
Jessie Zheng, *Officer*
Paul Fu, *Surgery Dir*
Jun Hu, *Sr Ntwrk Engine*
Jian Wang, *CTO*
EMP: 102 **EST:** 2000
SALES (est): 73.6MM **Privately Held**
WEB: www.alibabagroup.com
SIC: 8742 Marketing consulting services

(P-19441)
ALLIED ADMINISTRATORS INC
825 Battery St Fl 1, San Francisco (94111-1829)
PHONE 415 989-7443
Somanicheada Lao, *President*
Arthur Mathews, *Vice Pres*
Ben Tidball, *Vice Pres*
Danielle Lundbaek, *Executive Asst*
Mark Waldrip, *Administration*
EMP: 36 **EST:** 1952
SQ FT: 5,000
SALES (est): 5.1MM **Privately Held**
WEB: www.alliedadministrators.com
SIC: 8742 Administrative services consultant

(P-19442)
ALPHADETAIL INC
777 Mariners Island Blvd # 700, San Mateo (94404-5008)
PHONE 650 581-3100
Rishi Varma, *President*
Tassos Nicolaou, *Ch of Bd*
Roger Jensen, *CEO*
Felix Yang, *Director*
EMP: 45 **EST:** 2001
SQ FT: 10,000
SALES (est): 9.5MM **Publicly Held**
WEB: www.alphadetail.com
SIC: 8742 Marketing consulting services
HQ: Alphaimpactrx, Inc.
  550 Blair Mill Rd Ste 100
  Horsham PA 19044
  215 444-8900

(P-19443)
AMMUNITION LLC
1500 Sansome St Ste 110, San Francisco (94111-1015)
PHONE 415 632-1170
Peter Rack, *Managing Dir*
Darcy Dinucci, *Vice Pres*
Christopher Kuh, *Vice Pres*
Victoria Slaker, *Vice Pres*
Brett Wickens, *Creative Dir*
EMP: 38 **EST:** 2007
SQ FT: 5,200
SALES (est): 6.9MM **Privately Held**
WEB: www.ammunitiongroup.com
SIC: 8742 Industrial consultant

(P-19444)
AMS VENTURES INC
Also Called: Nichols Research
39055 Hastings St Ste 205, Fremont (94538-1599)
PHONE 301 980-5087
Stephen Zuppas, *CFO*
EMP: 70 **EST:** 2018
SALES (est): 5MM **Privately Held**
WEB: www.nicholsresearch.com
SIC: 8742 Marketing consulting services

(P-19445)
APERIAN GLOBAL INC (PA)
555 12th St Ste 1670, Oakland (94607-3623)
PHONE 628 222-3773
Ernest Gundling, *President*
Dave Eaton, *President*
Theodore Dale, *COO*
David Reilly, *CFO*
Felicia Gonzalez, *Admin Asst*
EMP: 58 **EST:** 1990
SALES (est): 10.4MM **Privately Held**
WEB: www.aperianglobal.com
SIC: 8742 Business consultant

(P-19446)
APEX SITE SOLUTIONS INC
9749 Kent St, Elk Grove (95624-2416)
PHONE 916 685-8619
Kenny Blakeslee, *President*
Brooke Blakeslee, *CFO*
Mark Blakeslee, *Project Mgr*
EMP: 67 **EST:** 2010
SQ FT: 12,100
SALES (est): 11.5MM **Privately Held**
WEB: www.apexsitesolutions.com
SIC: 8742 Management consulting services

(P-19447)
APRIL SIX INC
900 Kearny St Ste 700, San Francisco (94133-5100)
PHONE 415 363-6070
Fiona Shepherd, *CEO*
Jill Melchionda, *Managing Dir*
Edward Fung, *Director*
Allan Johnson, *Director*
Maia Mileff, *Manager*
EMP: 36 **EST:** 2014
SALES: 6MM
SALES (corp-wide): 162.1MM **Privately Held**
WEB: www.aprilsix.com
SIC: 8742 Marketing consulting services
HQ: April Six Limited
  Chaplin House
  Uxbridge MIDDX UB9 6
  189 582-5599

(P-19448)
ARES TECHNICAL SERVICES CORP
1290 Howard Ave Ste 319, Burlingame (94010-4222)
PHONE 650 401-7100
Richard J Stuart, *CEO*
Stanley Lynch, *Vice Pres*
James Custodio, *Sr Consultant*
EMP: 589 **EST:** 2011
SALES (est): 1.4MM **Privately Held**
WEB: www.arescorporation.com
SIC: 8742 Construction project management consultant
PA: Ares Holding Corporation
  1290 Howard Ave Ste 319
  Burlingame CA 94010

(P-19449)
ASPIREIQ INC
550 Montgomery St Ste 800, San Francisco (94111-6548)
PHONE 415 445-3567
Anand Kishore, *CEO*
Shawn Silverstein, *Executive*
Samir Chugh, *Engineer*
Nicole Farray, *Marketing Staff*
Melissa Muncy, *Marketing Staff*
EMP: 100 **EST:** 2013
SALES (est): 7MM **Privately Held**
WEB: www.aspireiq.com
SIC: 8742 Marketing consulting services

(P-19450)
ASSET PRESERVATION INC (DH)
Also Called: Asset Preservation of Texas
1420 Rocky Ridge Dr # 380, Roseville (95661-2830)
PHONE 916 791-5991
Javier Vandesteeg, *President*
Kayla Franklin, *Division Mgr*
Leslie Moodie, *Admin Asst*
Rosie Niebolt, *Admin Asst*
Jennifer Westlund, *Administration*
EMP: 35 **EST:** 1990
SALES (est): 8MM
SALES (corp-wide): 2.2B **Publicly Held**
WEB: www.apiexchange.com
SIC: 8742 Real estate consultant
HQ: Stewart Title Company
  1360 Post Oak Blvd Ste 10
  Houston TX 77056
  800 501-2766

(P-19451)
AURRERA HEALTH GROUP LLC
1400 K St Ste 204, Sacramento (95814-3916)
PHONE 916 662-7930
Hilary Haycock, *President*
Jennifer Ryan, *Exec VP*
Carri Ziegler, *Vice Pres*
Allison Valentine, *Associate Dir*
Rajveer Rakkar, *Regional Mgr*
EMP: 49 **EST:** 2008
SALES (est): 5.3MM **Privately Held**
WEB: www.harbageconsulting.com
SIC: 8742 General management consultant

(P-19452)
AVISO INC
805 Veterans Blvd Ste 300, Redwood City (94063-1737)
PHONE 650 567-5470
K V RAO, *CEO*
Stephen D Angelo, *President*
Mandar Parikh, *Vice Pres*
Rahul Pathak, *Vice Pres*
Jeff Stout, *Vice Pres*
EMP: 69 **EST:** 2011
SALES (est): 2MM **Privately Held**
WEB: www.aviso.com
SIC: 8742 8748 8732 Marketing consulting services; business consulting; business research service

(P-19453)
BBCERT
510 Hwy 1, Bodega Bay (94923)
P.O. Box 6 (94923-0006)
PHONE 480 220-3799
Linda Stout, *President*
EMP: 50 **EST:** 2017
SALES (est): 1.2MM **Privately Held**
SIC: 8742 Training & development consultant

(P-19454)
BERGERSON GROUP
Also Called: Channel Impact
1030 Country Club Dr B, Moraga (94556-1950)
PHONE 925 948-8110
Laura Bergerson, *President*
Andi Christenson, *Project Mgr*
EMP: 70 **EST:** 2005
SALES (est): 5.2MM **Privately Held**
WEB: www.channel-impact.com
SIC: 8742 Marketing consulting services

(P-19455)
BETTERUP INC (PA)
1200 Folsom St, San Francisco (94103-3817)
PHONE 415 862-0708
Alexi Robichaux, *CEO*
Marc Maloy, *President*
Eduardo Medina, *COO*
Vinh Le, *CFO*
Katie Coupe, *Vice Pres*
EMP: 298 **EST:** 2013
SALES (est): 40.3MM **Privately Held**
WEB: www.betterup.com
SIC: 8742 Training & development consultant

(P-19456)
BIRDLY INC
Also Called: Plato Hq
34 Harriet St, San Francisco (94103-4006)
PHONE 650 942-9388
Quang Hoang, *CEO*
Jean-Baptiste Coger, *Principal*
EMP: 41 **EST:** 2015
SALES (est): 1.7MM **Privately Held**
SIC: 8742 Business consultant

(P-19457)
BITE COMMUNICATIONS LLC (HQ)
100 Montgomery St # 1101, San Francisco (94104-4388)
PHONE 415 365-0222
Tim Dyson, *Mng Member*
Andrea Cunningham, *President*
Alisa Macdonnell, *Senior VP*
Will Willis, *Senior VP*
Molly Stein, *Vice Pres*
EMP: 75 **EST:** 1992
SQ FT: 10,000
SALES (est): 21.3MM
SALES (corp-wide): 435.2MM **Privately Held**
WEB: www.bitecommunications.com
SIC: 8742 8743 Marketing consulting services; public relations services
PA: Next Fifteen Communications Group Plc
  75 Bermondsey Street
  London SE1 3
  207 908-6444

8742 - Management Consulting Services County (P-19458)

(P-19458)
BOSPAR LLC
1835 Franklin St, San Francisco (94109-3483)
PHONE 415 913-7528
Curtis Sparrer,
Mick Emmett, *Vice Pres*
Lauren Essex, *Vice Pres*
Gabrielle Jasinski, *Vice Pres*
Alessandra Nagy, *Vice Pres*
EMP: 35
SALES (est): 3.5MM **Privately Held**
WEB: www.bospar.com
SIC: 8742 Marketing consulting services

(P-19459)
BRANDWATCH LLC
445 Bush St Fl 8, San Francisco (94108-3729)
PHONE 415 429-5800
Dan Freund, *Officer*
Dylan Marvin, *Officer*
Michael D`aloia, *Vice Pres*
Ellen Matsell, *Vice Pres*
Emelie Swerre, *Analyst*
EMP: 205
SALES (corp-wide): 671.3MM **Privately Held**
WEB: www.brandwatch.com
SIC: 8742 Marketing consulting services
HQ: Brandwatch Llc
145 Sherman Ave
Merrick NY 11566
212 229-2240

(P-19460)
BROADSPECTRUM AMERICAS INC
155 Corporate Pl, Vallejo (94590-6968)
PHONE 707 642-2222
Lou Hall, *President*
Javier Garcia, *Supervisor*
EMP: 39 **Privately Held**
SIC: 8742 Business consultant
HQ: Ferrovial Services U.S., Inc.
1330 Post Oak Blvd # 1250
Houston TX 77056

(P-19461)
BROKER SOLUTIONS INC
Also Called: New American Funding
3558 Round Barn Blvd, Santa Rosa (95403-1780)
PHONE 707 392-4354
EMP: 69 **Privately Held**
WEB: www.newamericanfunding.com
SIC: 8742 6162 Financial consultant; bond & mortgage companies
PA: Broker Solutions, Inc.
14511 Myford Rd Ste 100
Tustin CA 92780

(P-19462)
BUSINESS FOR SCIAL RSPNSBILITY (PA)
Also Called: B S R
220 Montgomery St # 1700, San Francisco (94104-3402)
PHONE 415 984-3200
Aron Cramer, *CEO*
Kate E Brandt, *Officer*
Jeff Seabright, *Officer*
Magali Barraja, *Associate Dir*
Giulio Berruti, *Associate Dir*
EMP: 40 **EST:** 1991
SALES (est): 31.3MM **Privately Held**
WEB: www.bsr.org
SIC: 8742 General management consultant

(P-19463)
CADATASOFT INC (PA)
3350 Scott Blvd Ste 5502, Santa Clara (95054-3124)
PHONE 214 935-1355
Harsha Pamulaparthi, *President*
EMP: 66 **EST:** 2006
SQ FT: 2,500
SALES (est): 4.9MM **Privately Held**
WEB: www.cadatasoft.com
SIC: 8742 7371 Business consultant; computer software development

(P-19464)
CALCERTS INC
31 Natoma St Ste 120, Folsom (95630-2658)
PHONE 916 985-3400
Michael E Bachand, *President*
Holly Walsh, *Program Mgr*
Richard Barnes, *CIO*
Kamiya Chaudhary, *Prgrmr*
Roy Mittleider, *Project Mgr*
EMP: 43 **EST:** 2005
SALES (est): 2.8MM **Privately Held**
WEB: www.calcerts.com
SIC: 8742 Training & development consultant

(P-19465)
CAPITOL SERVICES INC
3609 Bradshaw Rd Ste H, Sacramento (95827-3275)
PHONE 916 443-0657
Shauna Krause, *CEO*
Taura Oleuricy, *Manager*
EMP: 158 **EST:** 1982
SALES (est): 3.4MM **Privately Held**
WEB: www.capitolservices.org
SIC: 8742 Industry specialist consultants

(P-19466)
CARBON HEALTH TECHNOLOGIES INC
55 Pacific Ave Ste 160, San Francisco (94111-2009)
PHONE 415 223-2858
Eren Bali, *CEO*
Scott Cheeseman, *COO*
John Frager, *Vice Pres*
Kerem Ozkay, *Vice Pres*
Baris Taze, *Vice Pres*
EMP: 52 **EST:** 2015
SALES (est): 4.9MM **Privately Held**
WEB: www.carbonhealth.com
SIC: 8742 Business consultant

(P-19467)
CELERITY CONSULTING GROUP INC (PA)
2 Gough St Ste 300, San Francisco (94103-5420)
PHONE 415 986-8850
Rachelle Yowell, *CEO*
Christopher Yowell, *President*
Norman Yee, *COO*
Steffani Aranas, *Vice Pres*
Kevin Liu, *Vice Pres*
EMP: 61 **EST:** 2001
SQ FT: 28,000
SALES (est): 14.6MM **Privately Held**
WEB: www.consultcelerity.com
SIC: 8742 7371 7379 7375 Management consulting services; management information systems consultant; computer software development & applications; data processing consultant; on-line data base information retrieval; data processing service

(P-19468)
CENTRIC SOFTWARE INC (PA)
655 Campbell Tech Pkwy # 200, Campbell (95008-5062)
P.O. Box 111330 (95011-1330)
PHONE 408 574-7802
Chris Groves, *President*
Alice Goff, *CFO*
Stacey Charbin, *Chief Mktg Ofcr*
Fabrice Canonge, *Vice Pres*
Laurent Dubuisson, *Vice Pres*
EMP: 42 **EST:** 1989
SQ FT: 10,000
SALES (est): 43.8MM **Privately Held**
WEB: www.centricsoftware.com
SIC: 8742 7372 Management consulting services; prepackaged software

(P-19469)
CERTIFIEDSAFETY INC
3070 Bay Vista Courtste B, Benicia (94510)
PHONE 707 747-9400
Amanda Tucker, *COO*
Jason Durkee, *Info Tech Mgr*
Quincy Daniels, *Project Mgr*
Benny Soto, *Opers Staff*
Jamie Soape, *Advisor*
EMP: 78
SALES (corp-wide): 14MM **Privately Held**
WEB: www.certifiedsafety.net
SIC: 8742 Business consultant
PA: Certifiedsafety, Llc
906 W 13th St
Deer Park TX 77536
281 680-1200

(P-19470)
CHRISTIE BRYANT INC
2005 I St Ste 200, Sacramento (95811-3167)
PHONE 916 492-7062
James C Christie, *Branch Mgr*
Luke Bohlinger, *Research*
Mary Little, *Research*
Kristen Ford, *Bookkeeper*
Luke Moderhack, *Research Analys*
EMP: 35 **Privately Held**
WEB: www.bryantchristie.com
SIC: 8742 Foreign trade consultant
PA: Christie Bryant Inc
1418 3rd Ave Ste 300
Seattle WA 98101

(P-19471)
COBALTIX LLC
1095 Folsom St, San Francisco (94103-4025)
PHONE 415 322-1025
Steve Walker, *CEO*
Jay Goldberg, *President*
Robert Wambaugh, *Administration*
Michael Miller, *Sr Ntwrk Engine*
Chito Arguelles, *Network Enginr*
EMP: 35 **EST:** 2012
SALES (est): 4.8MM **Privately Held**
WEB: www.cobaltix.com
SIC: 8742 Management consulting services

(P-19472)
CODE FOR AMERICA LABS INC
972 Mission St Fl 5, San Francisco (94103-2994)
PHONE 415 816-1286
Amanda Renteria, *CEO*
Lizzy Gilbert, *Associate Dir*
Tom Dooner, *Sr Software Eng*
Benjamin Golder, *Web Dvlpr*
Fritz Jooste, *Software Dev*
EMP: 80
SALES: 15.1MM **Privately Held**
WEB: www.codeforamerica.org
SIC: 8742 Marketing consulting services

(P-19473)
COLLEGE TRACK
112 Linden St, Oakland (94607-2538)
PHONE 510 834-3295
Elissa Salas, *CEO*
Jonas Aquino, *Info Tech Mgr*
Scott Minkow, *Development*
Oliver Huang, *Technology*
Margaret Winnen, *Human Resources*
EMP: 191 **EST:** 1997
SALES (est): 30.4MM **Privately Held**
WEB: www.collegetrack.org
SIC: 8742 School, college, university consultant

(P-19474)
COMPENSIA INC
125 S Market St Ste 1000, San Jose (95113-2234)
P.O. Box 1059 (95108-1059)
PHONE 408 876-4025
Timothy Sparks, *CEO*
Barbara Rix, *Controller*
Jason LI, *Sr Associate*
Susan E Gellen, *Director*
Jasper Luong, *Consultant*
EMP: 43 **EST:** 2003
SQ FT: 2,586
SALES (est): 5.4MM **Privately Held**
WEB: www.compensia.com
SIC: 8742 Business consultant

(P-19475)
CONFIG CONSULTANTS LLC
Also Called: A5
4900 Hopyard Rd Ste 100, Pleasanton (94588-7101)
PHONE 844 852-2525
Vinay Kruttiventi, *Partner*
EMP: 50 **EST:** 2015
SALES (est): 2.7MM **Privately Held**
WEB: www.config-consultants.com
SIC: 8742 Management consulting services

(P-19476)
CONSOL
1610 R St Ste 200 Scrmnto, Sacramento (95811)
PHONE 209 474-8446
Michael G Hodgson, *President*
David Meyers, *COO*
Jason Lenzmeier, *CFO*
Rob Hammon, *Principal*
EMP: 35 **EST:** 1982
SQ FT: 10,200
SALES (est): 3.1MM **Privately Held**
WEB: www.consol.org
SIC: 8742 General management consultant

(P-19477)
CONSUMER HLTH INTERACTIVE LLC
436 14th St Ste 1500, Oakland (94612-2797)
PHONE 415 537-0735
Daniel A Segedin, *President*
▲ **EMP:** 40 **EST:** 2000
SALES (est): 3.8MM
SALES (corp-wide): 268.7B **Publicly Held**
SIC: 8742 Hospital & health services consultant
HQ: Caremarkpcs Health, L.L.C.
211 Commerce St Ste 800
Nashville TN 37201

(P-19478)
CONTENTSTACK LLC
49 Geary St Ste 238, San Francisco (94108-5727)
PHONE 415 255-5955
Neha Sampat, *CEO*
David Overmyer, *CFO*
Jun Feng, *Controller*
Louie Beltran, *Sales Staff*
Andrew Lachman, *Legal Staff*
EMP: 37 **EST:** 2018
SALES (est): 5.1MM **Privately Held**
WEB: www.contentstack.com
SIC: 8742 Business consultant

(P-19479)
CONTINUUMGLOBAL INC (PA)
3723 Haven Ave, Menlo Park (94025-1011)
PHONE 415 685-3302
Suresh Mathai, *CEO*
Dora Hsia, *VP Opers*
Sarah Oelschig, *Opers Staff*
EMP: 594 **EST:** 2009
SALES (est): 11.2MM **Privately Held**
SIC: 8742 Marketing consulting services

(P-19480)
CONTINUUMGLOBAL INC
1200 Gough St Unit 3a, San Francisco (94109-6613)
PHONE 415 685-3301
EMP: 206
SALES (corp-wide): 11.2MM **Privately Held**
SIC: 8742 Marketing consulting services
PA: Continuumglobal, Inc.
3723 Haven Ave
Menlo Park CA 94025
415 685-3302

(P-19481)
COOPERATIVE PERSONNEL SERVICES (PA)
Also Called: CPS Hr Consulting
2450 Del Paso Rd Ste 220, Sacramento (95834-9711)
PHONE 916 263-3600
Jerry Greenwell, *CEO*

▲ = Import ▼ = Export
◆ = Import/Export

PRODUCTS & SERVICES SECTION
8742 - Management Consulting Services County (P-19503)

Tim Howard, *CFO*
Sandy Macdonald-Hopp, *CFO*
Karina Mendez, *Technician*
Heather Moore, *Technician*
EMP: 139 **EST:** 1985
SQ FT: 34,000
SALES (est): 24.4MM **Privately Held**
WEB: www.cpshr.us
SIC: 8742 Personnel management consultant

(P-19482)
CORNAMI INC
300 Orchard Cy Dr Ste 131, Campbell (95008)
PHONE 408 337-0070
Gordon Campbell, *CEO*
Syed Ahmed, *Vice Pres*
Denoid Tucker, *Vice Pres*
EMP: 48 **EST:** 2011
SALES (est): 3.7MM **Privately Held**
WEB: www.cornami.com
SIC: 8742 Business consultant

(P-19483)
CORNERSTONE CONCILIUM INC
241 5th St, San Francisco (94103-4102)
PHONE 415 705-7800
Wayne H Perry, *CEO*
Charles Jones, *Bd of Directors*
Derek Lawson, *Vice Pres*
Ming Ng, *Vice Pres*
Martin Banas, *Office Mgr*
EMP: 50 **EST:** 1986
SQ FT: 2,000
SALES (est): 3.4MM **Privately Held**
WEB: www.cornerstoneconcilium.com
SIC: 8742 7379 Business consultant; computer related consulting services

(P-19484)
CPRIME INC (HQ)
107 S B St Ste 200, San Mateo (94401-3993)
P.O. Box 4777, Foster City (94404-0777)
PHONE 650 931-1650
Zubin Irani, *CEO*
Niles Love, *Vice Pres*
Brandon Huff, *Managing Dir*
Swati Jain, *Managing Dir*
Marc Rehberger, *Managing Dir*
EMP: 74 **EST:** 2003
SALES (est): 23.7MM
SALES (corp-wide): 603.3MM **Privately Held**
WEB: www.cprime.com
SIC: 8742 8331 8748 Business consultant; manpower training; systems engineering consultant, ex. computer or professional
PA: Alten
  40 Avenue Andre Morizet
  Boulogne Billancourt 92100
  146 056-673

(P-19485)
CRAWFORD COMMUNICATIONS GROUP
3190 S Bascom Ave Ste 230, San Jose (95124-2510)
PHONE 408 343-0200
Judy Crawford, *President*
Robert Whit, *CFO*
Trisha Gouveia, *Vice Pres*
Laurie Stein, *Vice Pres*
Nic Jasso, *Recruiter*
EMP: 45 **EST:** 2003
SALES (est): 5.1MM **Privately Held**
WEB: www.crawfordgroup.com
SIC: 8742 Marketing consulting services

(P-19486)
CRETELLIGENT INC
11344 Coloma Rd Ste 870, Gold River (95670-6308)
PHONE 916 288-8177
Anthony Romano, *CEO*
Chris Barry, *Officer*
Megan Mauer, *Analyst*
Abraham Serrato, *Analyst*
John Heath, *Production*
EMP: 40 **EST:** 2014
SALES (est): 7.3MM **Privately Held**
WEB: www.escreenlogic.com
SIC: 8742 Real estate consultant

(P-19487)
CSUS
Also Called: Dr. Brostrand
6000 J St Ereka Hall 420b, Sacramento (95819)
PHONE 916 278-4489
Brostrand, *Project Mgr*
Daisy Yepez, *Accountant*
David Gibbs, *Manager*
EMP: 86 **EST:** 2015
SALES (est): 7.7MM **Privately Held**
WEB: www.csus.edu
SIC: 8742 School, college, university consultant

(P-19488)
DATACARE CORPORATION
992 S De Anza Blvd, San Jose (95129-2777)
PHONE 866 834-2334
Eunhee Kim Rn Msn, *CEO*
Dr Paulo Franca, *President*
Rob Roj, *Vice Pres*
Lou George, *Software Engr*
Larry Nguyen, *Business Anlyst*
EMP: 43 **EST:** 2003
SALES (est): 4.4MM **Privately Held**
WEB: www.datacare.com
SIC: 8742 Management consulting services

(P-19489)
DELOITTE CONSULTING LLP
Also Called: Bersin By Deloitte
555 Mission St, San Francisco (94105-0920)
PHONE 510 251-4400
Joshua Bersin, *Principal*
Melody Phipps, *Managing Dir*
Kathy Sobrero, *Planning*
Katharine Caputo, *Analyst*
Bhanu Rasala, *Human Resources*
EMP: 39
SALES (corp-wide): 768.6K **Privately Held**
WEB: www.deloitte.com
SIC: 8742 Financial consultant
HQ: Deloitte Consulting Llp
  30 Rockefeller Plz
  New York NY 10112
  212 492-4000

(P-19490)
DELOITTE CONSULTING LLP
225 W Santa Clara St, San Jose (95113-1723)
PHONE 212 492-4000
Tom Dong, *Partner*
James Parkin, *Partner*
Daniel Reaugh, *Partner*
Wen H Chow, *Admin Asst*
Lokesh Kedia,
EMP: 39
SALES (corp-wide): 768.6K **Privately Held**
WEB: www.deloitte.com
SIC: 8742 Financial consultant
HQ: Deloitte Consulting Llp
  30 Rockefeller Plz
  New York NY 10112
  212 492-4000

(P-19491)
DELOITTE CONSULTING LLP
600 Yosemite Blvd, Modesto (95354-2760)
PHONE 212 492-4000
EMP: 39
SALES (corp-wide): 768.6K **Privately Held**
WEB: www.deloitte.com
SIC: 8742 Financial consultant
HQ: Deloitte Consulting Llp
  30 Rockefeller Plz
  New York NY 10112
  212 492-4000

(P-19492)
DEVCOOL INC
5890 Stoneridge Dr # 107, Pleasanton (94588-5818)
PHONE 408 372-4313
Sandeep Deokule, *President*
Rohith Nampally, *Recruiter*
Dipa Rangarajan, *VP Opers*
EMP: 100 **EST:** 2006
SQ FT: 1,400
SALES (est): 6MM **Privately Held**
WEB: www.devcool.com
SIC: 8742 Management consulting services

(P-19493)
DIGITAL NIRVANA INC (PA)
3984 Washington Blvd # 355, Fremont (94538-4954)
PHONE 510 226-9000
Hirendra Hindocha, *President*
Vishnu Beri, *COO*
Michael Collins, *Cust Svc Dir*
EMP: 439 **EST:** 2002
SQ FT: 4,000
SALES (est): 42.9MM **Privately Held**
WEB: www.digital-nirvana.com
SIC: 8742 Business consultant

(P-19494)
DIGITALTHINK INC (DH)
601 Brannan St, San Francisco (94107-1511)
PHONE 415 625-4000
Michael W Pope, *President*
Jon Madonna, *Ch of Bd*
Robert J Krolik, *CFO*
Adam D Levy, *Vice Pres*
EMP: 250 **EST:** 1996
SQ FT: 51,000
SALES (est): 40.6MM
SALES (corp-wide): 3B **Publicly Held**
WEB: www.andrecoelho.com
SIC: 8742 Marketing consulting services
HQ: Convergys Customer Management Group Inc.
  201 E 4th St Bsmt
  Cincinnati OH 45202
  513 723-6104

(P-19495)
DRAWBRIDGE INC
479 N Pastoria Ave, Sunnyvale (94085-4112)
PHONE 650 513-2323
Kamakshi Sivaramakrishnan, *CEO*
EMP: 85 **EST:** 2010
SALES (est): 8.9MM
SALES (corp-wide): 168B **Publicly Held**
WEB: www.linkedin.com
SIC: 8742 Marketing consulting services
HQ: Linkedin Corporation
  1000 W Maude Ave
  Sunnyvale CA 94085
  650 687-3600

(P-19496)
ECORP CONSULTING INC (PA)
2525 Warren Dr, Rocklin (95677-2167)
PHONE 916 782-9100
James Stewart, *President*
James D Stewart, *CEO*
Bjorn Gregersen, *CFO*
Peter Balfour, *Vice Pres*
Brant Brechbiel, *Vice Pres*
EMP: 55
SQ FT: 6,950
SALES (est): 18.8MM **Privately Held**
WEB: www.ecorpconsulting.com
SIC: 8742 8748 Industry specialist consultants; business consulting

(P-19497)
EDELMAN FINANCIAL ENGINES LLC (HQ)
1050 Entp Way Fl 3 Flr 3, Sunnyvale (94089)
PHONE 408 498-6000
Lawrence M Raffone, *President*
John B Bunch, *COO*
Debra Babbitt, *Officer*
Lewis E Antone Jr, *Exec VP*
Hamesh Chawla, *Exec VP*
EMP: 170 **EST:** 1996
SQ FT: 80,995
SALES (est): 480.5MM **Privately Held**
WEB: www.edelmanfinancialengines.com
SIC: 8742 6282 6411 Financial consultant; investment advice; pension & retirement plan consultants
PA: Financial Engines Edelman, L.P.
  6500 Sheridan Dr Ste 110
  Buffalo NY 14221
  800 706-3916

(P-19498)
EK HEALTH SERVICES INC (PA)
992 S De Anza Blvd Ste 10, San Jose (95129-2777)
PHONE 408 973-0888
Eunhee Kim, *President*
Kerri Wilson, *President*
Douglas Benner, *Chief Mktg Ofcr*
Joseph N Desantis, *Vice Pres*
Mark Hostetler, *Vice Pres*
EMP: 152 **EST:** 1998
SQ FT: 6,500
SALES (est): 11.9MM **Privately Held**
WEB: www.ekhealth.com
SIC: 8742 Hospital & health services consultant; human resource consulting services; personnel management consultant

(P-19499)
EMPLOYEE BNEFT SPECIALISTS INC
Also Called: E B S
5675 Gibraltar Dr, Pleasanton (94588-8547)
P.O. Box 11675 (94588-1675)
PHONE 925 460-3910
Joan L Rhodes, *President*
Chimane Rhodes, *Vice Pres*
Ann Mary Atencio, *Executive Asst*
EMP: 41 **EST:** 1987
SQ FT: 2,200
SALES (est): 2.9MM **Privately Held**
SIC: 8742 8748 Compensation & benefits planning consultant; employee programs administration

(P-19500)
ENDORS TOI PBC
Also Called: Western Flower Company
600 F St Ste 3, Arcata (95521-6301)
PHONE 434 987-0919
Arthur Lichtenberger, *CEO*
EMP: 60 **EST:** 2019
SALES (est): 2.6MM **Privately Held**
SIC: 8742 Business consultant

(P-19501)
ENERGY EXPERTS INTERNATIONAL (PA)
555 Twin Dolphin Dr # 150, Redwood City (94065-2139)
PHONE 650 593-4261
Michael Watanabe, *CEO*
Kim Anderson, *Vice Pres*
Robert Becken, *Vice Pres*
Lana Carlson, *Vice Pres*
Steve Gauthier, *Vice Pres*
EMP: 230 **EST:** 1999
SQ FT: 4,000
SALES: 43.8MM **Privately Held**
WEB: www.eeintl.com
SIC: 8742 Business consultant

(P-19502)
ENGAGE3 INC
501 2nd St, Davis (95616-4618)
PHONE 530 231-5485
Jonah Ellin, *Vice Pres*
Marielle Fong, *Marketing Staff*
Kevin Johnson, *Marketing Staff*
James Holliday, *Director*
Bill Senn, *Director*
EMP: 36 **EST:** 2012
SALES (est): 946K **Privately Held**
WEB: www.engage3.com
SIC: 8742 Marketing consulting services

(P-19503)
ENSIGHTEN INC (HQ)
887 Oak Grove Ave Ste 203, Menlo Park (94025-4430)
PHONE 650 249-4712
Josh Manion, *CEO*
Alex Rodriguez, *Partner*
Varun Sekhri, *Partner*
Tim Benhart, *Officer*
Ian Woolley, *Officer*
EMP: 175 **EST:** 2012
SALES (est): 31MM **Privately Held**
WEB: www.ensighten.com
SIC: 8742 8741 Management consulting services; management services

8742 - Management Consulting Services County (P-19504)

(P-19504)
ENTERPRISE EVENTS GROUP INC
950 Northgate Dr Ste 100, San Rafael (94903-3430)
PHONE.....................................415 499-4444
Matt Gillam, *CEO*
Rich A Calcaterra, *Vice Pres*
Joanne Bain, *Executive*
Michael Gill, *Branch Mgr*
Allison Biel, *General Mgr*
EMP: 150 **EST:** 1995
SQ FT: 18,000
SALES (est): 29MM **Privately Held**
WEB: www.eeginc.com
SIC: 8742 8743 Incentive or award program consultant; promotion service

(P-19505)
EPIXEL SOLUTIONS
1001 Bayhill Dr, San Bruno (94066-3062)
PHONE.....................................650 616-4488
Sajin Rajan, *Principal*
EMP: 80 **EST:** 2019
SALES (est): 1.5MM **Privately Held**
WEB: www.epixelsolutions.com
SIC: 8742 Marketing consulting services

(P-19506)
EQECAT INC (DH)
475 14th St Ste 550, Oakland (94612-1938)
PHONE.....................................415 817-3100
Paul C Little, *President*
Rodney Griffin, *Senior VP*
Ray Kincaid, *Senior VP*
Thomas Larsen, *Senior VP*
Mahmoud Khater, *CTO*
EMP: 96 **EST:** 1994
SALES (est): 5.1MM
SALES (corp-wide): 1.6B **Privately Held**
WEB: www.corelogic.com
SIC: 8742 Training & development consultant
HQ: Corelogic, Inc.
40 Pacifica Ste 900
Irvine CA 92618
866 873-3651

(P-19507)
EQUILIBRIUM MANAGEMENT LLC
2443 Fillmore St Ste 345, San Francisco (94115-1814)
PHONE.....................................415 516-2930
Gabriel Hulls, *Mng Member*
EMP: 25 **EST:** 2017
SALES (est): 1.5MM **Privately Held**
SIC: 8742 7372 Business planning & organizing services; application computer software

(P-19508)
ESSEX NATIONAL SECURITIES LLC
550 Gateway Dr Ste 210, NAPA (94558-7578)
PHONE.....................................707 258-5000
Stephen Amarante, *President*
EMP: 101 **Privately Held**
WEB: www.ensinet.com
SIC: 8742 Financial consultant
HQ: Essex National Securities, Llc
538 Preston Ave
Meriden CT 06450

(P-19509)
EVA AUTOMATION INC
3945 Freedom Cir Ste 560, Santa Clara (95054-1269)
PHONE.....................................650 513-6875
David Liu, *Principal*
EMP: 400 **EST:** 2014
SALES (est): 14.1MM **Privately Held**
SIC: 8742 Automation & robotics consultant

(P-19510)
EXCEL MANAGED CARE DISA
3840 Watt Ave Bldg C, Sacramento (95821-2640)
PHONE.....................................916 944-7185
Brenda Smith, *President*
Steve Smetana, *Vice Pres*
EMP: 125 **EST:** 1992
SQ FT: 3,600
SALES (est): 12.9MM **Publicly Held**
WEB: www.genexservices.com
SIC: 8742 Hospital & health services consultant
HQ: Genex Services, Llc
440 E Swedesford Rd Ste 1
Wayne PA 19087
610 964-5100

(P-19511)
EXPONENT PARTNERS
201 Mission St Ste 1200, San Francisco (94105-1888)
P.O. Box 347537 (94134-7537)
PHONE.....................................800 918-2917
Rembert Hoffmann, *CEO*
Michael Hassid, *Vice Pres*
Bruce Irving, *Vice Pres*
Tucker Maclean, *Vice Pres*
EMP: 49 **EST:** 2005
SALES (est): 5.5MM **Privately Held**
WEB: www.exponentpartners.com
SIC: 8742 7371 Marketing consulting services; computer software development & applications

(P-19512)
EXPONENTIAL INTERACTIVE INC (HQ)
1111 Broadway Ste 300, Oakland (94607-4167)
PHONE.....................................510 250-5500
Dilip Dasilva, *President*
Tim Brown, *Officer*
Philip Buxton, *Officer*
Hani Elnaggar, *Vice Pres*
Evan Kramer, *Vice Pres*
EMP: 79 **EST:** 2000
SALES (est): 36.6MM
SALES (corp-wide): 2.9MM **Privately Held**
WEB: www.exponential.com
SIC: 8742 Marketing consulting services
PA: Exponential Interactive Uk Limited
C/O Thomas Alexander & Company L
London N13 5
203 411-7401

(P-19513)
EXPRESSWORKS INTERNATIONAL LLC (PA)
2410 Camino Ramon Ste 167, San Ramon (94583-4328)
PHONE.....................................925 244-0900
John Quereto, *Managing Prtnr*
Debby Bernardi, *Info Tech Mgr*
Giovanna Jimenez, *Marketing Staff*
Stephen Zaruba, *Mng Member*
Shanna Brewer, *Manager*
EMP: 100 **EST:** 1984
SQ FT: 12,000
SALES (est): 13.2MM **Privately Held**
WEB: www.expressworks.com
SIC: 8742 Marketing consulting services

(P-19514)
EXTOLE INC
350 Sansome St Ste 700, San Francisco (94104-1316)
PHONE.....................................415 625-0411
EMP: 41 **EST:** 2009
SALES (est): 1.2MM **Privately Held**
WEB: www.extole.com
SIC: 8742 Marketing consulting services

(P-19515)
FIREWOOD MARKETING INC
23 Geary St Ste 7, San Francisco (94108-5751)
PHONE.....................................415 872-5132
Lanya Zambrano, *Principal*
Loni Knepper, *CFO*
Erica Carmel, *Vice Pres*
Alyssa Boisson, *Creative Dir*
Juan Zambrano, *Principal*
EMP: 70 **EST:** 2011
SQ FT: 5,000
SALES (est): 12.6MM **Privately Held**
WEB: www.firewoodmarketing.com
SIC: 8742 Marketing consulting services

(P-19516)
FNI INTERNATIONAL INC
1300 Ethan Way, Sacramento (95825-2211)
PHONE.....................................916 643-1400
Bob Taylor, *Manager*
Robert Taylor, *Agent*
EMP: 87
SALES (corp-wide): 14.3MM **Privately Held**
SIC: 8742 Financial consultant
PA: Fni International, Inc.
200 N Pacific Coast Hwy
El Segundo CA 90245
310 326-3100

(P-19517)
FORESIGHT ANALYTICS LLC
1330 Broadway Ste 428, Oakland (94612-2504)
P.O. Box 2878, Alameda (94501-0878)
PHONE.....................................510 893-1760
EMP: 56
SALES (est): 181.8K
SALES (corp-wide): 1.7MM **Privately Held**
WEB: www.foresight-analytics.com
SIC: 8742 Management Consulting Services
HQ: Trepp, Llc
600 5th Ave Fl 7
New York NY 10020
212 754-1010

(P-19518)
FRANK GATES SERVICE COMPANY
1107 Investment Blvd, El Dorado Hills (95762-5736)
PHONE.....................................916 934-0812
Chanteo Kvigne, *Manager*
EMP: 39 **Privately Held**
SIC: 8742 Management consulting services
HQ: The Frank Gates Service Company
5000 Bradenton Ave # 100
Dublin OH 43017
614 793-8000

(P-19519)
GATEWAY FINANCIAL ADVISORS INC (PA)
Also Called: Quality Life Insurance Agency
4101 Crw Cnyn Pl 100, San Ramon (94583)
PHONE.....................................925 999-8699
Shane Westhoelter, *President*
Steve Doman, *Vice Pres*
Michael Bivens, *Manager*
Michelle Cheah, *Manager*
Jeffrey Coleman, *Manager*
EMP: 58 **EST:** 2000 **Privately Held**
WEB: www.gfainvestments.com
SIC: 8742 Banking & finance consultant

(P-19520)
GOLDEN STATE RESTAURANT GROUP
4502 Georgetown Pl, Stockton (95207-6202)
PHONE.....................................209 478-0234
EMP: 48 **EST:** 2017
SALES (est): 1MM **Privately Held**
WEB: www.goldenstatemcd.com
SIC: 8742 Restaurant & food services consultants

(P-19521)
GREENOAKS OPPORTUNITY I LLC
101 Mission St Ste 1630, San Francisco (94105-1730)
PHONE.....................................415 805-8922
Peretz Benjamin, *President*
EMP: 50 **EST:** 2004
SALES (est): 1.9MM **Privately Held**
SIC: 8742 Business consultant

(P-19522)
GREENOUGH CONSULTING GROUP LLC
1350 Bayshore Hwy Ste 920, Burlingame (94010-1818)
PHONE.....................................650 548-6900
Mark Greenough, *President*
Marjorie Bailey, *CFO*
Ed Canty, *CFO*
Chuong Tran, *Controller*
Yin Tseng, *Mktg Dir*
EMP: 37 **EST:** 1999
SALES (est): 5.1MM **Privately Held**
WEB: www.greenoughgroup.com
SIC: 8742 Business consultant
PA: Apex Fund Services Ltd
C/O Apex Corporate Services Ltd
Hamilton

(P-19523)
GREYLINE PARTNERS LLC (PA)
109 Stevenson St Fl 4, San Francisco (94105-3478)
PHONE.....................................415 604-9527
Matthew Okolita, *Mng Member*
Annie Kong, *Vice Pres*
Joseph Frost, *Sr Associate*
EMP: 35 **EST:** 2011
SALES (est): 3MM **Privately Held**
WEB: www.greyline.co
SIC: 8742 Business consultant

(P-19524)
GROW WEST LLC (PA)
201 East St, Woodland (95776-3523)
PHONE.....................................530 662-5442
Ernie Roncoroni,
Gary Silveria, *Vice Pres*
Fred Freitas,
Shani Smith, *Manager*
EMP: 66 **EST:** 2019
SALES (est): 12.1MM **Privately Held**
SIC: 8742 7389 2873 8711 Management consulting services; financial services; fertilizers: natural (organic), except compost; engineering services; fertilizers & agricultural chemicals; trucking, except local

(P-19525)
GROWTHPOINT TECH PARTNERS LLC (PA)
2208 Seminole Ct, Santa Rosa (95405-8044)
PHONE.....................................650 322-2500
John Savage, *Mng Member*
Nick Derose, *Vice Pres*
Anson Kwan, *Vice Pres*
Rishi Mehta, *Vice Pres*
John Cromwell, *Managing Dir*
EMP: 56 **EST:** 2005
SALES (est): 2.9MM **Privately Held**
WEB: www.growthpoint.com
SIC: 8742 Financial consultant

(P-19526)
H R OPTIONS INC
1401 Willow Pass Rd # 820, Concord (94520-7934)
PHONE.....................................800 777-8944
Gordon Lovett, *CEO*
Laura Remy, *Human Resources*
Kristin Dorado, *Opers Staff*
Nunzio Presta, *Sales Staff*
Sandra B Paredes, *Director*
EMP: 35 **EST:** 1989
SQ FT: 3,000
SALES (est): 5MM **Privately Held**
WEB: www.hroptions.com
SIC: 8742 7361 Human resource consulting services; employment agencies

(P-19527)
H&H CATERING LP
111 Pine St, San Francisco (94111-5602)
PHONE.....................................408 354-1964
Patti Wilson, *Branch Mgr*
EMP: 39
SALES (corp-wide): 14MM **Privately Held**
WEB: www.wolfgangpuck.com
SIC: 8742 Human resource consulting services
PA: H&H Catering, L.P.
6801 Hollywood Blvd
Los Angeles CA 90028
323 491-1250

PRODUCTS & SERVICES SECTION
8742 - Management Consulting Services County (P-19550)

(P-19528)
HAMILTON PARTNERS
1301 Shoreway Rd Ste 250, Burlingame (94010)
PHONE.................................650 347-8800
EMP: 55
SALES (est): 293.1K Privately Held
WEB: www.hamiltonpartners.com
SIC: 8742 Management Consulting Services

(P-19529)
HAPAG-LLOYD (AMERICA) LLC
180 Grand Ave Ste 1535, Oakland (94612-3702)
PHONE.................................510 286-1940
Manfred Braun, Manager
Shelly Krizmanic, Sales Staff
Siafa Dorley, Consultant
EMP: 60
SALES (corp-wide): 15.1B Privately Held
WEB: www.hapag-lloyd.com
SIC: 8742 4499 Transportation consultant; marine salvaging & surveying services
HQ: Hapag-Lloyd (America) Llc
   399 Hoes Ln Ste 101
   Piscataway NJ 08854
   732 562-1800

(P-19530)
HARBOR INDUSTRIES INC
74 W Neal St Ste 102, Pleasanton (94566-6661)
PHONE.................................925 461-1366
Shane Pickett, Principal
EMP: 192
SALES (corp-wide): 55.6MM Privately Held
WEB: www.harborretail.com
SIC: 8742 Marketing consulting services
PA: Harbor Industries, Inc.
   14130 172nd Ave
   Grand Haven MI 49417
   616 842-5330

(P-19531)
HARRIS MYCFO INC
2200 Geng Rd Ste 100, Palo Alto (94303-3358)
PHONE.................................480 348-7725
Michael Montogomery, President
John Benevides, President
Craig Rawlins, President
Jeff Leonard, Executive
Harvey Armstrong, Exec Dir
EMP: 90 EST: 2003
SALES (est): 7.4MM Privately Held
SIC: 8742 Financial consultant

(P-19532)
HDD CO INC
4525 Serrano Pkwy Ste 210, El Dorado Hills (95762-7572)
PHONE.................................530 676-5705
EMP: 49 EST: 2018
SALES (est): 9.6MM Privately Held
WEB: www.crossinggroup.com
SIC: 8742 Business consultant

(P-19533)
HDS MERCURY INC
Also Called: Hds Global
870 E Charleston Rd # 210, Palo Alto (94303-4611)
PHONE.................................650 800-7701
Louis Borders, CEO
Aravind Durai, Vice Pres
Jacqueline Ho, Opers Staff
EMP: 41 EST: 2018
SALES (est): 3.5MM Privately Held
WEB: www.mercurystartups.com
SIC: 5961 8742 7371 Fruit, mail order; general merchandise, mail order; automation & robotics consultant; computer software development & applications; computer software systems analysis & design, custom

(P-19534)
ICON INTERNET VENTURES INC
505 Montgomery St 10t, San Francisco (94111-6529)
PHONE.................................415 874-3397
EMP: 38
SQ FT: 7,000
SALES: 12MM Privately Held
SIC: 8742 Management Consulting Services

(P-19535)
INDUCTIVE AUTOMATION LLC
90 Blue Ravine Rd, Folsom (95630-4715)
PHONE.................................800 266-7798
Steve Hechtman, President
Jason Waits, Officer
Katharina Robinett, Exec VP
Colby Clegg, Vice Pres
Wendi-Lynn Hechtman, Vice Pres
EMP: 100 EST: 2011
SALES (est): 17.7MM Privately Held
WEB: www.inductiveautomation.com
SIC: 8742 5734 Automation & robotics consultant; computer software & accessories

(P-19536)
INFOR500 LLC
2350 Mission College Blvd, Santa Clara (95054-1532)
PHONE.................................408 209-6837
Vijay Caveripakkam,
Ward Karson,
EMP: 42 EST: 2012
SALES (est): 2.5MM Privately Held
WEB: www.infor500.com
SIC: 8742 Management consulting services

(P-19537)
INGENIO LLC
182 Howard St Unit 826, San Francisco (94105-1611)
PHONE.................................415 992-8218
Devina Whitley, Mng Member
Natalie Rusnak, Partner
EMP: 57 EST: 2013
SALES (est): 5.2MM Privately Held
WEB: www.ingenio.com
SIC: 8742 Management consulting services

(P-19538)
INKLING SYSTEMS INC
343 Sansome St 8, San Francisco (94104-1303)
PHONE.................................415 975-4420
Jeff Carr, CEO
Rob Cromwell, President
Charles Macinnis, President
Matt Macinnis, Founder
John Crowther, Vice Pres
EMP: 66 EST: 2009
SALES (est): 11MM Privately Held
WEB: www.inkling.com
SIC: 8742 Management consulting services
PA: Marlin Equity Partners, Llc
   338 Pier Ave
   Hermosa Beach CA 90254

(P-19539)
INNOWAVE MARKETING GROUP LLC
533 Airport Blvd Ste 400, Burlingame (94010-2013)
PHONE.................................650 454-4952
Stuart Birger,
Jim Gaspa, Opers Staff
Lynn Campana-Lee Ip, Director
EMP: 42
SALES (corp-wide): 8.8MM Privately Held
WEB: www.innowavemarketing.com
SIC: 8742 Marketing consulting services
PA: Innowave Marketing Group Llc
   60 Roberts Way
   Hillsborough CA 94010
   650 627-4212

(P-19540)
INTEGRATED ARCHIVE SYSTEMS INC (PA)
Also Called: I A S
1121 San Antonio Rd D100, Palo Alto (94303-4311)
PHONE.................................650 390-9995
Amy Joyce RAO, CEO
Anna Borden, CFO
John Woodall, Vice Pres
Linda Lagarejos, CIO
Bob Elsey, Info Tech Mgr
EMP: 36 EST: 1994
SQ FT: 90,400
SALES (est): 14.1MM Privately Held
WEB: www.itshot.com
SIC: 8742 5045 Management information systems consultant; computer software

(P-19541)
INTERACTION ASSOCIATES INC (PA)
2310 Oregon St, Berkeley (94705-1107)
PHONE.................................617 234-2700
Barry Rosen, CEO
Timothy Swords, Ch of Bd
Jen Cebrero, Controller
Jake Blocker, Marketing Staff
Kaitlyn Labbe, Client Mgr
EMP: 50
SALES (est): 8.4MM Privately Held
WEB: www.interactionassociates.com
SIC: 8742 Training & development consultant

(P-19542)
INTERMOTIVE INC
12840 Earhart Ave, Auburn (95602-9003)
PHONE.................................530 823-1048
Greg Schafer, President
Marc Ellison, Vice Pres
Wes Rodgers, Program Mgr
Linda Johnston, Admin Asst
Shaun Baye, Technical Staff
EMP: 25 EST: 1996
SQ FT: 11,000
SALES (est): 5.7MM Privately Held
WEB: www.intermotive.net
SIC: 8742 3559 5531 8748 Training & development consultant; automotive related machinery; automotive accessories; systems analysis or design

(P-19543)
IQMS
Also Called: Iot and Automation Product Dev
4309 Hacienda Dr Ste 550, Pleasanton (94588-2794)
PHONE.................................805 227-1122
Trevor Diehl, Manager
Ben Jacobus,
Kristen Couto, Engineer
EMP: 48
SALES (corp-wide): 2B Privately Held
WEB: www.iqms.com
SIC: 8742 Automation & robotics consultant
HQ: Iqms, Llc
   2231 Wisteria Ln
   Paso Robles CA 93446

(P-19544)
IRON HORSE VENTURES LLC
Also Called: Iron Horse Interactive
6111 Bollinger Canyon Rd # 555, San Ramon (94583-5186)
PHONE.................................925 415-6141
Uzair Dada, CEO
Wendy Haig, COO
Nitesh Mehta, Vice Pres
Samir Mehta, Vice Pres
Nora Maus, General Mgr
EMP: 30 EST: 2001
SALES (est): 4.9MM Privately Held
WEB: www.ironhorse.io
SIC: 8742 7372 Marketing consulting services; business oriented computer software

(P-19545)
IT MANAGEMENT CORP
Also Called: 101 Voice
5201 Great America Pkwy # 320, Santa Clara (95054-1140)
PHONE.................................408 739-1100
EMP: 35 EST: 2009
SALES: 40MM Privately Held
SIC: 8742 It Telecommunication Sales And Services

(P-19546)
ITRADENETWORK INC (HQ)
4160 Dublin Blvd Ste 300, Dublin (94568-7756)
PHONE.................................925 660-1100
Robert Bonavito, CEO
Rhonda Bassett-Spiers, President
Liam Taylor, COO
Marie-France Nelson, CFO
Pete Reuling, CFO
EMP: 43 EST: 1999
SALES (est): 20.9MM
SALES (corp-wide): 5.5B Publicly Held
WEB: www.itradenetwork.com
SIC: 8742 Retail trade consultant
PA: Roper Technologies, Inc.
   6901 Prof Pkwy E Ste 200
   Sarasota FL 34240
   941 556-2601

(P-19547)
JUMPSTART DIGITAL MKTG INC (DH)
Also Called: Jumpstart Automotive Media
550 Kearny St Ste 500, San Francisco (94108-2595)
PHONE.................................415 844-6336
Nick Matarazzo, CEO
Denise Rasmussen, Pub Rel Mgr
EMP: 80 EST: 1996
SQ FT: 3,600
SALES (est): 23.9MM
SALES (corp-wide): 4.2B Privately Held
WEB: www.hearst.com
SIC: 8742 7311 Marketing consulting services; advertising agencies
HQ: Hearst Communications, Inc.
   300 W 57th St
   New York NY 10019
   212 649-2000

(P-19548)
KAISER FOUNDATION HOSPITALS
3200 Arden Way, Sacramento (95825-2015)
PHONE.................................916 974-6211
Erick Berry, Admin Asst
Ryan Pauline, Technology
Gary Besinque, Pharmacist
Jeff Murray, Director
EMP: 784
SALES (corp-wide): 30.5B Privately Held
WEB: www.kaisercenter.com
SIC: 9224 9221 8742 8699 Fire protection; police protection; hospital & health services consultant; charitable organization
HQ: Kaiser Foundation Hospitals Inc
   1 Kaiser Plz
   Oakland CA 94612
   510 271-6611

(P-19549)
KENSHOO INC (HQ)
22 4th St Fl 7, San Francisco (94103-3141)
PHONE.................................877 536-7462
Yoav Izhar-Prato, CEO
Shirley Grill-Rachman, COO
Sarit Firon, CFO
Igal Shany, CFO
Sandy Shanman, Officer
EMP: 101 EST: 2008
SALES (est): 22.9MM
SALES (corp-wide): 39MM Privately Held
WEB: www.skai.io
SIC: 8742 Marketing consulting services
PA: Kenshoo Ltd
   30 Habarzel
   Tel Aviv-Jaffa 69710
   732 862-507

(P-19550)
KINSALE HOLDINGS INC (PA)
Also Called: Validant
388 Market St Ste 860, San Francisco (94111-5314)
PHONE.................................415 400-2600
Patrick Ronan, CEO
Stephanie Colotti, Senior Partner
Kimberly Snyder, Senior Partner
Mohsen Eghbal, Managing Prtnr
John McShane, Managing Prtnr
EMP: 196 EST: 2005
SALES (est): 28.5MM Privately Held
WEB: www.validant.com
SIC: 8742 Management consulting services

8742 - Management Consulting Services County (P-19551)

(P-19551)
KYO AUTISM THERAPY LLC
1155 Broadway St Ste 218, Redwood City (94063-3127)
PHONE..................................877 264-6747
Melissa Willa, *Branch Mgr*
Johanna Adams, *Technician*
Vienna Beck, *Technician*
Sean Espinal, *Technician*
Galen Lew, *Technician*
EMP: 59 **Privately Held**
WEB: www.kyocare.com
SIC: 8742 Hospital & health services consultant
PA: Kyo Autism Therapy, Llc
1663 Mission St Ste 400
San Francisco CA 94103

(P-19552)
KYO AUTISM THERAPY LLC
121 Paul Dr, San Rafael (94903-2047)
PHONE..................................877 264-6747
Melissa Willa, *Branch Mgr*
EMP: 59 **Privately Held**
WEB: www.kyocare.com
SIC: 8742 Hospital & health services consultant
PA: Kyo Autism Therapy, Llc
1663 Mission St Ste 400
San Francisco CA 94103

(P-19553)
KYO AUTISM THERAPY LLC (PA)
Also Called: Educatnal Cnslting Thrapy For
1663 Mission St Ste 400, San Francisco (94103-2485)
PHONE..................................877 264-6747
Melissa Willa, *Mng Member*
Julius Schillinger, *Vice Pres*
Antisha Partee, *Administration*
Annika Daley, *Technician*
Matthew Durham, *Technician*
EMP: 414 **EST:** 2005
SALES (est): 35.4MM **Privately Held**
WEB: www.kyocare.com
SIC: 8742 8748 Hospital & health services consultant; educational consultant

(P-19554)
LANCASHIRE GROUP INCORPORATED
Also Called: Tlg
37053 Cherry St Ste 210, Newark (94560-3782)
P.O. Box 1138 (94560-6138)
PHONE..................................510 792-9384
Ian McDonnell, *President*
Johnny Lambert, *COO*
John Lambert, *Senior VP*
EMP: 40 **EST:** 1989
SQ FT: 2,400
SALES (est): 1.2MM **Privately Held**
SIC: 8742 Industry specialist consultants

(P-19555)
LANDMARK WORLDWIDE LLC (PA)
353 Sacramento St Ste 200, San Francisco (94111-3639)
PHONE..................................415 981-8850
Arthur Schreiber,
Anna Nemchenko, *Executive Asst*
Tina Renschen, *Technology*
Jim Golding, *Finance Dir*
Tsivya Frieder, *Production*
EMP: 163 **EST:** 2002
SQ FT: 15,000
SALES (est): 80.9MM **Privately Held**
WEB: www.landmarkworldwide.com
SIC: 8742 Training & development consultant

(P-19556)
LATENTVIEW ANALYTICS CORP
2540 N 1st St Ste 108, San Jose (95131-1016)
PHONE..................................408 493-6653
Venkat Viswanathan, *President*
Krishnan Venkata, *President*
Dhuwaaragesh Sivaraman, *Business Anlyst*
Avnish Kumar, *Analyst*
Priya Balakrishnan, *Manager*
EMP: 35 **Privately Held**
WEB: www.latentview.com
SIC: 8742 Marketing consulting services
HQ: Latentview Analytics Corporation
5 Independence Way # 418
Princeton NJ 08540

(P-19557)
LEGACY MARKETING GROUP (PA)
5341 Old Redwood Hwy # 400, Petaluma (94954-7127)
PHONE..................................707 778-8638
Lynda R Pitts, *CEO*
Preston Pitts, *President*
Chris Eaken, *Vice Pres*
Dayna Wells, *Vice Pres*
Eric James, *Sales Mgr*
EMP: 215 **EST:** 1993
SALES (est): 10.7MM **Privately Held**
WEB: www.legacynet.com
SIC: 8742 Marketing consulting services

(P-19558)
LEIGHFISHER INC (HQ)
4 Embarcadero Ctr # 3800, San Francisco (94111-5974)
PHONE..................................650 579-7722
Nick Davidson, *President*
Michael Hanowsky, *Associate Dir*
Brett Simon, *Associate Dir*
Stephen Van Beek, *Exec Dir*
Felicia Simmons, *Executive Asst*
EMP: 58 **EST:** 2009
SALES (est): 12.8MM
SALES (corp-wide): 13.5B **Publicly Held**
WEB: www.leighfisher.com
SIC: 8742 Management consulting services
PA: Jacobs Engineering Group Inc.
1999 Bryan St Ste 1200
Dallas TX 75201
214 583-8500

(P-19559)
LENDING EXPRESS INC
400 Concar Dr, San Mateo (94402-2681)
PHONE..................................838 800-0644
Moshe Kazimirsky, *Vice Pres*
EMP: 40 **EST:** 2019
SALES (est): 1.7MM **Privately Held**
WEB: www.become.co
SIC: 8742 Financial consultant

(P-19560)
LIFTOPIA INC (PA)
350 Sansome St Ste 925, San Francisco (94104-1314)
PHONE..................................415 728-0444
Evan V Reece, *CEO*
Danielle Billelo, *Office Mgr*
Conrad Chan, *Software Engr*
Brian Patzin, *Software Engr*
Darrell Ten, *IT/INT Sup*
EMP: 56 **EST:** 2005
SALES (est): 5.2MM **Privately Held**
WEB: www.liftopia.com
SIC: 8742 Management consulting services

(P-19561)
LINARDOS ENTERPRISES INC
75 Broadway, San Francisco (94111-1422)
PHONE..................................415 644-0827
EMP: 58
SQ FT: 800
SALES (est): 5.7MM **Privately Held**
WEB: www.leicontractors.com
SIC: 8742 Management Consulting Services

(P-19562)
LINQIA INC
965 Mission St, San Francisco (94103-2921)
PHONE..................................415 913-7179
Nader Alizadeh, *CEO*
Nicole Dalton, *Partner*
Tim Richards, *Officer*
Mohammed Pedhiwala, *Vice Pres*
Saurabh Singh, *Software Engr*
EMP: 100 **EST:** 2012
SALES (est): 9.8MM **Privately Held**
WEB: www.linqia.com
SIC: 8742 Marketing consulting services

(P-19563)
LYLES SERVICES CO
Also Called: WM LYLES CO
525 W Alluvial Ave Ste C, Fresno (93711-5521)
P.O. Box 4348 (93744-4348)
PHONE..................................559 441-1900
Richard Nemmer, *CEO*
Richard E Amigh, *Vice Pres*
Todd K Sheller, *Vice Pres*
John Driscoll, *CIO*
EMP: 54 **EST:** 2007
SALES: 14.3MM
SALES (corp-wide): 17.8MM **Privately Held**
WEB: www.lylesgroup.com
SIC: 8742 Construction project management consultant
PA: Lyles Diversified, Inc.
525 W Alluvial Ave
Fresno CA 93711
559 441-1900

(P-19564)
MAGNETIC MICHIGAN (PA)
167 2nd Ave, San Mateo (94401-3801)
PHONE..................................650 544-2400
Rita Brogley, *President*
Robert Cell, *Ch of Bd*
Ainslie Mayberry, *CFO*
Anu Shukla, *Chairman*
Chip Overstreet, *Senior VP*
EMP: 41 **EST:** 2001
SQ FT: 22,000
SALES (est): 17.9MM **Privately Held**
SIC: 8742 Marketing consulting services

(P-19565)
MAKANI TECHNOLOGIES LLC (PA)
2175 Monarch St, Alameda (94501-5096)
PHONE..................................503 939-5359
Fort Felker, *Mng Member*
Darren Woulfe, *Mng Member*
EMP: 49 **EST:** 2019
SALES (est): 2.4MM **Privately Held**
SIC: 8742 Business consultant

(P-19566)
MARKET FORCE INFORMATION INC
2037 Hwy 4 Ste C, Arnold (95223)
PHONE..................................209 795-0830
EMP: 38
SALES (corp-wide): 55.3MM **Privately Held**
SIC: 8742 8748 Management Consulting Services Business Consulting Services
PA: Market Force Information, Inc.
6025 The Corners Pkwy # 200
Peachtree Corners GA 30092
303 536-1924

(P-19567)
MARKSYS LLC
3725 Cincinnati Ave # 200, Rocklin (95765-1220)
PHONE..................................916 745-4883
Jerod Meents, *Principal*
Brad Eickmann, *Vice Pres*
Jasdeep Singh, *Principal*
Doug Philbin, *Branch Mgr*
Tabrez Rajani, *General Mgr*
EMP: 60 **EST:** 2012
SQ FT: 45,000
SALES (est): 34MM **Privately Held**
WEB: www.themarksys.com
SIC: 8742 Marketing consulting services

(P-19568)
MARKSYS HOLDINGS LLC
3725 Cincinnati Ave # 200, Rocklin (95765-1220)
PHONE..................................916 745-4883
Tabrez Rajani, *Mng Member*
Julie Moeller, *Opers Staff*
EMP: 60 **EST:** 2018
SALES (est): 3.5MM **Privately Held**
WEB: www.themarksys.com
SIC: 8742 Marketing consulting services

(P-19569)
MCCLELLAN BUSINESS PARK LLC
Also Called: Mp Holdings
3140 Peacekeeper Way, McClellan (95652-2508)
PHONE..................................916 965-7100
Larry Kelley, *President*
Adam Schwartz, *CFO*
Jay Heckliventy, *Exec VP*
Debra Compton, *Senior VP*
Ken Giannotti, *Senior VP*
EMP: 99 **EST:** 1999
SQ FT: 22,000
SALES (est): 16.9MM **Privately Held**
WEB: www.mcclellanpark.com
SIC: 8742 Real estate consultant

(P-19570)
MCINTYRE
14680 Wicks Blvd, San Leandro (94577-6716)
PHONE..................................510 614-5890
Jo Farsight, *Owner*
EMP: 96 **EST:** 2019
SALES (est): 4.9MM **Privately Held**
WEB: www.mcintyre-industries.com
SIC: 8742 Manufacturing management consultant

(P-19571)
MCKINSEY & COMPANY INC
555 California St # 4800, San Francisco (94104-1779)
PHONE..................................415 981-0250
Gary Pinkus, *Manager*
Oscar Boldt-Christmas, *Senior Partner*
Kenneth Bonheure, *Senior Partner*
Laura Furstenthal, *Senior Partner*
Endre Holen, *Senior Partner*
EMP: 300
SALES (corp-wide): 2B **Privately Held**
WEB: www.mckinsey.com
SIC: 8742 Business consultant
PA: Mckinsey & Company, Inc.
3 World Trade Ctr
New York NY 10007
212 446-7000

(P-19572)
MELDISCO K-M RANCHO CORDOVA CA
2344 Sunrise Blvd, Gold River (95670-4343)
PHONE..................................916 635-3400
EMP: 40
SALES (est): 1.8MM
SALES (corp-wide): 396MM **Privately Held**
SIC: 5661 8742 Ret Shoes Management Consulting Services
PA: Xstelos Corp.
45 Rockefeller Plz # 2260
New York NY 10111
201 934-2000

(P-19573)
MENTOR TCHNICAL GROUP INTL LLC
601 Gateway Blvd Ste 1210, South San Francisco (94080-7044)
P.O. Box 6857, Caguas PR (00726-6857)
PHONE..................................787 743-0897
Flavia Tejada,
EMP: 50 **EST:** 2009
SALES (est): 4.8MM **Privately Held**
WEB: www.mentortg.com
SIC: 8742 Management consulting services

(P-19574)
MERIDIAN KNWLDGE SOLUTIONS LLC (DH)
80 Iron Point Cir Ste 100, Folsom (95630-8592)
PHONE..................................916 985-9625
Jonna Ward, *CEO*
Sean Osborne, *Senior VP*
EMP: 50 **EST:** 2006
SQ FT: 32,481
SALES (est): 13.9MM **Privately Held**
WEB: www.meridianks.com
SIC: 8742 Training & development consultant

PRODUCTS & SERVICES SECTION

8742 - Management Consulting Services County (P-19598)

HQ: Visionary Integration Professionals, Llc
80 Iron Point Cir Ste 100
Folsom CA 95630
916 985-9625

(P-19575)
MESMERIZE LLC
Also Called: Brite Media
350 Frank H Ogawa Plz # 310, Oakland (94612-2084)
PHONE..................415 374-8298
Gregory Park, *Vice Pres*
EMP: 106
SALES (corp-wide): 22.5MM **Privately Held**
WEB: www.mesmerize.com
SIC: 8742 Sales (including sales management) consultant
HQ: Mesmerize, Llc
505 8th Ave
New York NY 10018

(P-19576)
MINDSTRONG INC
Also Called: Mindstrong Health
303 Bryant St Ste 300, Mountain View (94041-1554)
PHONE..................650 850-7050
Daniel Graf, *CEO*
Phuong Quach, *CFO*
Leo Dagum, *VP Engrg*
Fidaa Alaraj, *Accountant*
EMP: 41 **EST:** 2016
SALES (est): 6.5MM **Privately Held**
WEB: www.mindstrong.com
SIC: 8742 Business consultant

(P-19577)
MISSION ECONOMIC DEV AGCY
2301 Mission St Ste 301, San Francisco (94110-1900)
PHONE..................415 282-3334
Luis Granados, *Director*
Libardo Clavijo, *CFO*
Gladys Castro, *Officer*
Liz Cortez, *Associate Dir*
Johnny Oliver, *Associate Dir*
EMP: 35 **EST:** 1973
SALES: 12.7MM **Privately Held**
WEB: www.medasf.org
SIC: 8742 8331 Business planning & organizing services; job training & vocational rehabilitation services

(P-19578)
MLSLISTINGS INC
Also Called: RE Infolink
740 Kifer Rd, Sunnyvale (94086-5121)
PHONE..................408 874-0200
Gerald J Harrison, *President*
Leann Connell, *Vice Pres*
Steve Fast, *Office Mgr*
Tracy Qi, *Executive Asst*
Richard Jacinto, *Administration*
EMP: 58 **EST:** 2007
SALES (est): 14MM **Privately Held**
WEB: www.mlslistings.com
SIC: 8742 Real estate consultant

(P-19579)
MODSQUAD INC (PA)
Also Called: Metaverse Mod Squad
1300 S St Ste B, Sacramento (95811-7142)
PHONE..................916 913-4465
Amelia Pritchard, *CEO*
Michael Pinkerton, *COO*
Mike Pinkerton, *COO*
Amy Kennedy, *Chief Mktg Ofcr*
Stephen Henry, *Vice Pres*
EMP: 239 **EST:** 2009
SALES (est): 25MM **Privately Held**
WEB: www.modsquad.com
SIC: 8742 7389 Management consulting services; telephone answering service

(P-19580)
MOTISTA LLC
2 Embarcadero Ctr Fl 8, San Francisco (94111-3833)
PHONE..................650 204-7976
Scott Magids, *CEO*
Michael Mathias, *President*
Tom O'Sullivan, *Exec VP*
Ed Kuderna, *Senior VP*
Michelle Bold, *Vice Pres*
EMP: 59 **EST:** 2011
SALES (est): 1.9MM **Privately Held**
WEB: www.motista.com
SIC: 8742 Marketing consulting services

(P-19581)
MT DIABLO UNIFIED SCHOOL DST
Also Called: Willow Creek Center
1026 Mohr Ln, Concord (94518-3833)
PHONE..................925 685-1011
Stephanie Roberts, *Principal*
EMP: 57
SALES (corp-wide): 431.8MM **Privately Held**
WEB: www.mdusd.org
SIC: 8211 Public elementary & secondary schools; training & development consultant
PA: Mt. Diablo Unified School District
1936 Carlotta Dr
Concord CA 94519
925 682-8000

(P-19582)
MTC RESTURANT GROUP INC
Also Called: Togo's Eatery
1777 S Bascom Ave Ste D, Campbell (95008-0635)
PHONE..................408 371-3806
Mike Cobler, *President*
Mark Boeckman, *Vice Pres*
Andy Sinisi, *Project Mgr*
Simona Krebs, *Manager*
Sandra Reese, *Manager*
EMP: 48 **EST:** 1998
SALES (est): 1.5MM **Privately Held**
WEB: www.togos.com
SIC: 5812 8742 8741 Sandwiches & submarines shop; management consulting services; management services

(P-19583)
MUNISERVICES LLC (DH)
Also Called: Avenu Muniservices
7625 N Palm Ave Ste 108, Fresno (93711-5785)
PHONE..................800 800-8181
Steve Roberts, *President*
Doug Jensen, *Vice Pres*
Mark Bryson, *Business Anlyst*
Timothy Olson, *Auditor*
Ray Beye, *Opers Staff*
EMP: 113 **EST:** 1978
SQ FT: 16,000
SALES (est): 13.6MM
SALES (corp-wide): 47.8MM **Privately Held**
WEB: www.avenuinsights.com
SIC: 8742 Industry specialist consultants
HQ: Avenu Insights & Analytics, Llc
555 Madison Ave Fl 16
New York NY 10022
757 519-9300

(P-19584)
MYERS-BRIGGS COMPANY (PA)
185 N Wolfe Rd, Sunnyvale (94086-5212)
PHONE..................650 969-8901
Jeffrey Hayes, *CEO*
Marion McGovern, *Ch of Bd*
Carl Thoresen, *Ch of Bd*
Calvin W Finch, *Senior VP*
Andrew Bell, *Vice Pres*
EMP: 100 **EST:** 1956
SQ FT: 16,000
SALES (est): 25.1MM **Privately Held**
WEB: www.themyersbriggs.com
SIC: 8742 5999 Management consulting services; educational aids & electronic training materials

(P-19585)
MYTHIC INC
805 Veterans Blvd Ste 228, Redwood City (94063-1737)
PHONE..................734 707-7339
Frederick SOO, *Director*
EMP: 43
SALES (corp-wide): 17.3MM **Privately Held**
WEB: www.mythic-ai.com
SIC: 8742 Management consulting services

PA: Mythic Inc.
1905 Kramer Ln Ste A200
Austin TX 78758
650 388-0824

(P-19586)
NATIONAL FNCL SRVCS CNSRTM LLC
3161 Los Prados St, San Mateo (94403-2013)
PHONE..................650 572-2872
EMP: 99
SALES (est): 2.6MM **Privately Held**
SIC: 8742 Management Consulting Services

(P-19587)
NELSON/NYGARD CNSLTING ASSOC I (PA)
2 Bryant St Ste 300, San Francisco (94105-1641)
PHONE..................415 284-1544
Paul Jewel, *COO*
Bonnie Nelson, *President*
Emmanuel Garcia, *COO*
Jeanne Martin, *Mktg Dir*
Anne Le-Reiver, *Marketing Staff*
EMP: 38 **EST:** 1987
SALES (est): 13.5MM **Privately Held**
WEB: www.nelsonnygaard.com
SIC: 8742 Transportation consultant

(P-19588)
NETLINE CORPORATION (PA)
900 E Hamilton Ave # 100, Campbell (95008-0664)
PHONE..................408 340-2200
Robert Alvin, *CEO*
Werner Mansfeld, *President*
David Fortino, *Vice Pres*
Jayaram Kalpathy, *Vice Pres*
Mitchell Wright, *Vice Pres*
EMP: 51 **EST:** 1994
SALES (est): 11.3MM **Privately Held**
WEB: www.netline.com
SIC: 8742 Marketing consulting services

(P-19589)
NETWORK CONFERENCE CO INC
Also Called: Network Meeting Center
5201 Great America Pkwy # 122, Santa Clara (95054-1122)
PHONE..................408 562-6205
Fax: 408 562-5703
EMP: 40
SQ FT: 146,000
SALES (est): 2.4MM **Privately Held**
WEB: www.networkmeetingcenter.com
SIC: 8742 Management Consulting Services

(P-19590)
NEXTNAV LLC
484 Oakmead Pkwy, Sunnyvale (94085-4708)
PHONE..................800 775-0982
Ganesh Pattabiraman, *Branch Mgr*
Christian Gates, *Vice Pres*
David Knutson, *Vice Pres*
Eric Swank, *Vice Pres*
Warren Low, *Network Enginr*
EMP: 38
SALES (corp-wide): 11.8MM **Privately Held**
WEB: www.nextnav.com
SIC: 8742 Marketing consulting services
PA: Nextnav, Llc
484 Oakmead Pkwy
Sunnyvale CA 94085
571 765-3637

(P-19591)
NINJA CREDIT CONSULTANTS LLC
71 1st Ave Ste 662, Lewiston (96052)
PHONE..................888 646-5282
Ian Lacovara, *Mng Member*
EMP: 39 **EST:** 2010
SALES (est): 250K **Privately Held**
WEB: www.ninja-credit-consultants.business.site
SIC: 8742 Management consulting services

(P-19592)
NORTHBOUND LLC
961 E Arques Ave, Sunnyvale (94085-4521)
PHONE..................408 333-9780
Hetel Mehta, *Mng Member*
Leena Menon, *Mng Member*
Ryan Haire, *Director*
Britney Barnes, *Manager*
Mala Mukundan, *Manager*
EMP: 128 **EST:** 2003
SQ FT: 20,000
SALES (est): 12.2MM **Privately Held**
WEB: www.northboundllc.com
SIC: 8742 Management information systems consultant

(P-19593)
NUVOLUM INC
1450 Tech Ln Ste 150, Petaluma (94954)
PHONE..................415 413-4999
Jeffrey Thompson, *Principal*
Jock Putney, *Managing Prtnr*
John Putney, *Principal*
Anthony Zheng, *Web Dvlpr*
Sarah Babac, *Research*
EMP: 35 **EST:** 2013
SALES (est): 3.5MM **Privately Held**
WEB: www.nuvolum.com
SIC: 8742 Marketing consulting services

(P-19594)
OMEGA WASTE MANAGEMENT INC
Also Called: Omega Management Services
957 Colusa St, Corning (96021-2224)
P.O. Box 495 (96021-0495)
PHONE..................530 824-1890
Robert O'Conner, *President*
Karen O'Conner, *Vice Pres*
Dan O'Connor, *Vice Pres*
Laurie Spindler, *Human Res Mgr*
Laura Bachelor, *Manager*
EMP: 68 **EST:** 1989
SQ FT: 6,000
SALES (est): 10.9MM **Privately Held**
WEB: www.omegawaste.com
SIC: 8742 Management consulting services

(P-19595)
ONE10 LLC
180 Montgomery St, San Francisco (94104-4205)
PHONE..................415 398-3534
EMP: 100
SALES (corp-wide): 1.8B **Privately Held**
SIC: 8742 Management Consulting Services
HQ: One10 Llc
100 N 6th St Ste 700b
Minneapolis MN 55403
763 445-3000

(P-19596)
ONE10 LLC
735 Battery St Fl 1, San Francisco (94111-1535)
PHONE..................415 844-2200
Fax: 415 844-2248
EMP: 70
SALES (corp-wide): 1.8B **Privately Held**
SIC: 8742 Management Consulting Services
HQ: One10 Llc
100 N 6th St Ste 700b
Minneapolis MN 55403
763 445-3000

(P-19597)
ONEVALLEY INC
2955 Campus Dr Ste 110, San Mateo (94403-2563)
PHONE..................650 421-2000
Nikhil Sinha, *CEO*
EMP: 35 **EST:** 2012
SALES (est): 2.5MM **Privately Held**
SIC: 8742 Business planning & organizing services

(P-19598)
ONFIDO INC
995 Market St Fl 2, San Francisco (94103-1732)
PHONE..................844 663-4366
Husayn Kassai, *CEO*

8742 - Management Consulting Services County (P-19599)

Thomas Ammirati, *CTO*
Steve Durkee, *Business Mgr*
Katie Burns, *Marketing Staff*
Yannick Concordel, *Accounts Mgr*
EMP: 82 **EST:** 2015
SALES (est): 7.7MM
SALES (corp-wide): 60.3MM **Privately Held**
WEB: www.onfido.com
SIC: 8742 Management information systems consultant
PA: Onfido Ltd
3 Finsbury Avenue
London EC2M
208 133-3628

(P-19599)
P K B INVESTMENTS INC
Also Called: Home Instead Senior Care
745 E Locust Ave Ste 105, Fresno (93720-3000)
PHONE.................................559 243-1224
David Phillips, *President*
April Cavanaugh, *CFO*
Patrick Cavanaugh, *Admin Sec*
Sherri Woods, *Manager*
EMP: 140 **EST:** 1995
SALES (est): 8.2MM **Privately Held**
WEB: www.homeinstead.com
SIC: 8742 8322 Management consulting services; individual & family services

(P-19600)
PACIFIC MARKET INTERNATIONAL (PA)
Also Called: PMI San Fran Export
395 Oyster Point Blvd # 225, South San Francisco (94080-1930)
PHONE.................................650 238-1059
EMP: 91 **EST:** 2002
SALES (est): 1MM **Privately Held**
SIC: 8742 Marketing consulting services

(P-19601)
PACIFIC SECURED EQUITIES INC
Also Called: Intercare Holdings Insur Svcs
6020 West Oaks Blvd # 100, Rocklin (95765-5472)
P.O. Box 579, Roseville (95661-0579)
PHONE.................................916 677-2500
George W McCleary Jr, *CEO*
Agnes Hoeberling, *COO*
Don Nguyen, *CFO*
Gabriella Hubbard, *Assoc VP*
Lanai P Phun, *Assoc VP*
EMP: 300 **EST:** 1994
SQ FT: 21,000
SALES (est): 23.5MM **Privately Held**
SIC: 8742 Administrative services consultant

(P-19602)
PEER SERVICES INC
1396 W Sequoia Cir, Reedley (93654-2776)
P.O. Box 1286 (93654-1286)
PHONE.................................559 970-1240
David Reimer, *CEO*
Darren Trisel, *Vice Pres*
Dale Torry, *Managing Dir*
EMP: 35 **EST:** 2014
SALES (est): 1.8MM **Privately Held**
WEB: www.peerservicesinc.com
SIC: 8742 Management consulting services

(P-19603)
PERMANENTE FEDERATION LLC
1 Kaiser Plz Fl 27, Oakland (94612-3610)
PHONE.................................510 625-6920
Cal James, *CEO*
Claire Tamo, *CFO*
Nolan Chang, *Exec VP*
Nancy Gin, *Exec VP*
Edward Lee, *Exec VP*
EMP: 80 **EST:** 1997
SQ FT: 18,663
SALES (est): 7.2MM **Privately Held**
WEB: www.permanente.org
SIC: 8742 Management consulting services

(P-19604)
PG&E CAPITAL LLC
1 Market St, San Francisco (94105-1420)
PHONE.................................415 321-4600
Anthony Earley, *Chairman*
EMP: 497 **EST:** 1998
SALES (est): 1.2MM **Publicly Held**
WEB: www.pgecorp.com
SIC: 8742 Marketing consulting services
PA: Pg&E Corporation
77 Beale St
San Francisco CA 94105

(P-19605)
PHOENIX AMERICAN INCORPORATED (PA)
2401 Kerner Blvd, San Rafael (94901-5569)
PHONE.................................415 485-4500
Gus Constantin, *Ch of Bd*
Andrew N Gregson, *CFO*
Easha Anantha, *Executive*
Karen Gooding, *Executive*
Lisa A Olsen, *Admin Sec*
EMP: 100 **EST:** 1972
SQ FT: 60,000
SALES (est): 40MM **Privately Held**
WEB: www.phxa.com
SIC: 8742 Financial consultant

(P-19606)
PLAYER IN GAME INC (PA)
1625 E Shaw Ave Ste 122, Fresno (93710-8100)
PHONE.................................559 905-6217
Amar Daroch, *CEO*
EMP: 38 **EST:** 2010
SALES (est): 514.8K **Privately Held**
SIC: 8742 Business consultant

(P-19607)
POSITION2 INC (PA)
333 W Maude Ave Ste 207, Sunnyvale (94085-4373)
PHONE.................................650 618-8900
Rajiv Parikh, *CEO*
Jaideep Gopinath, *Vice Pres*
Suraj Hattangadi, *Vice Pres*
Sajjan Kanukolanu, *Vice Pres*
Vinita Soin, *Vice Pres*
EMP: 37 **EST:** 2005
SALES (est): 5.9MM **Privately Held**
WEB: www.position2.com
SIC: 8742 Marketing consulting services

(P-19608)
PREALIZE HEALTH INC
745 Emerson St, Palo Alto (94301-2411)
PHONE.................................650 690-5300
Linda Hand, *CEO*
Timothy Dwight, *Vice Pres*
Alan Glaseroff, *Med Doctor*
EMP: 40 **EST:** 2018
SALES (est): 3.1MM **Privately Held**
WEB: www.prealizehealth.com
SIC: 8742 Management consulting services

(P-19609)
PREVENTION INSTITUTE
221 Oak St Ste A, Oakland (94607-4595)
PHONE.................................510 444-4133
Larry Cohen, *Exec Dir*
Emily Kemp, *Officer*
Veonna Washington, *Officer*
Rachel Davis, *Exec Dir*
Ruben Cantu, *Program Mgr*
EMP: 56
SQ FT: 2,612
SALES (est): 4.7MM **Privately Held**
WEB: www.preventioninstitute.org
SIC: 8742 Training & development consultant

(P-19610)
PROCUREABILITY INC
11260 Donner Pass Rd C, Truckee (96161-4848)
PHONE.................................904 432-7001
John Evans, *President*
Conrad Snover, *Exec VP*
Marrena Anderson, *Vice Pres*
Don Dougherty, *Vice Pres*
Robin Harris, *Office Mgr*
EMP: 42 **EST:** 2011
SALES (est): 3.7MM **Privately Held**
WEB: www.procureability.com
SIC: 8742 Business consultant

(P-19611)
PROPHET BRAND STRATEGY (PA)
1 Bush St Fl 7, San Francisco (94104-4413)
PHONE.................................415 677-0909
Michael Dunn, *President*
Mike Fleming, *Senior Partner*
Thomas Han, *Partner*
Bernhard Schaar, *Partner*
Oscar Wang, *Partner*
EMP: 50 **EST:** 1992
SQ FT: 1,744
SALES (est): 84.7MM **Privately Held**
WEB: www.prophet.com
SIC: 8742 Marketing consulting services

(P-19612)
PROTAGONIST TECHNOLOGY LLC (PA)
345 California St Ste 600, San Francisco (94104-2657)
PHONE.................................415 967-5530
Douglas Randall,
Aaron Harms, *Exec VP*
Emily Keane, *Vice Pres*
Chris Pelletier, *Office Mgr*
Marissa Ticas, *Executive Asst*
EMP: 37 **EST:** 2003
SQ FT: 6,700
SALES (est): 8.1MM **Privately Held**
WEB: www.protagonist.io
SIC: 8742 8748 8732 8731 Management consulting services; economic consultant; commercial sociological & educational research; commercial physical research

(P-19613)
PROTIVITI INC (HQ)
2884 Sand Hill Rd Ste 200, Menlo Park (94025-7072)
PHONE.................................650 234-6000
Joseph Tarantino, *President*
Brian Christensen, *Exec VP*
Andrew Clinton, *Exec VP*
James Pajakowski, *Exec VP*
Seth Cox, *Associate Dir*
EMP: 100 **EST:** 2002
SALES (est): 630.9MM
SALES (corp-wide): 5.1B **Publicly Held**
WEB: www.protiviti.com
SIC: 8742 8721 Industry specialist consultants; auditing services
PA: Robert Half International Inc.
2884 Sand Hill Rd Ste 200
Menlo Park CA 94025
650 234-6000

(P-19614)
Q ANALYSTS LLC (PA)
4320 Stevens Creek Blvd, San Jose (95129-1202)
PHONE.................................408 907-8500
Ross Fernandes,
Joe Lawlor, *President*
Jason R Knight, *Vice Pres*
Debbie McGarvey, *Vice Pres*
Patrick Yaguchi, *Vice Pres*
EMP: 70
SALES (est): 14.2MM **Privately Held**
WEB: www.qanalysts.com
SIC: 8742 7379 Quality assurance consultant; computer related consulting services

(P-19615)
QB3 LLC
29 Hunter Crk, Fairfax (94930-1355)
PHONE.................................415 515-3595
Andrew Kimball, *Branch Mgr*
EMP: 35
SALES (corp-wide): 277.4K **Privately Held**
WEB: www.qb3.org
SIC: 8742 Management consulting services
PA: Qb3, Llc
824 E St
San Rafael CA 94901
415 459-7459

(P-19616)
QB3 LLC (PA)
Also Called: Q B International
824 E St, San Rafael (94901-2819)
PHONE.................................415 459-7459
Andrew Kimball,
Janet Chino,
EMP: 37 **EST:** 1996
SQ FT: 4,500
SALES (est): 277.4K **Privately Held**
WEB: www.qb3.org
SIC: 8249 8742 Business training services; business consultant

(P-19617)
QUALITY PLANNING CORPORATION
388 Market St Ste 750, San Francisco (94111-5352)
PHONE.................................415 369-0707
Raj Bhat, *President*
EMP: 56 **EST:** 1985
SALES (est): 8.2MM **Publicly Held**
WEB: www.verisk.com
SIC: 8742 Financial consultant
HQ: Insurance Services Office, Inc.
545 Wshngton Blvd Fl 14-2 Flr 14
Jersey City NJ 07310
201 469-2153

(P-19618)
RAMSEY MARKETING & MGT CO (PA)
Also Called: Murphy's Market
785 Bayside Rd, Arcata (95521-6723)
PHONE.................................707 822-7665
Pat Murphy, *President*
Cody Bunnell, *Manager*
Nelson Fagundes, *Manager*
Nicholas Painter, *Manager*
EMP: 82 **EST:** 1982
SALES (est): 9.1MM **Privately Held**
WEB: www.murphysmarkets.net
SIC: 8742 Marketing consulting services

(P-19619)
RAVIX FINANCIAL INC
Also Called: Ravix Group
226 Airport Pkwy Ste 400, San Jose (95110-1027)
PHONE.................................408 216-0656
Daniel Saccani, *President*
Ingrid Glazebrook, *Vice Pres*
Andrea Vanegas, *Accountant*
Jill Howard, *Manager*
Lance Chu, *Consultant*
EMP: 40 **EST:** 2000
SALES (est): 5.4MM **Privately Held**
WEB: www.ravixgroup.com
SIC: 8742 Financial consultant

(P-19620)
RED DOOR GROUP
Also Called: Red Door Catering, The
2925 Adeline St, Oakland (94608-4422)
PHONE.................................510 339-2320
Reign Free, *Mng Member*
EMP: 35 **EST:** 2006
SQ FT: 2,000
SALES (est): 2.4MM **Privately Held**
WEB: www.reddoorcatering.com
SIC: 5812 8742 Caterers; planning consultant

(P-19621)
REDSTONE PRINT & MAIL INC
910 Riverside Pkwy Ste 40, West Sacramento (95605-1510)
PHONE.................................916 318-6450
Ledi Cody, *President*
EMP: 60 **EST:** 2015
SALES (est): 20MM **Privately Held**
WEB: www.redstoneprintmail.com
SIC: 8742 Marketing consulting services

(P-19622)
RENOVITE TECHNOLOGIES INC (PA)
39785 Paseo Padre Pkwy, Fremont (94538-2926)
PHONE.................................510 771-9200
Virendar Rana, *CEO*
Mark Green, *Sr Software Eng*
Anton Godfrey, *Senior Mgr*
David Lock, *Senior Mgr*

PRODUCTS & SERVICES SECTION 8742 - Management Consulting Services County (P-19645)

Sukhi Kaur, *Manager*
EMP: 56 **EST:** 2014
SALES (est): 1.3MM **Privately Held**
WEB: www.renovite.com
SIC: 8742 Business consultant

(P-19623)
RK LOGISTICS GROUP INC (PA)
41707 Christy St, Fremont (94538-4195)
P.O. Box 610670, San Jose (95161-0670)
PHONE.....................................408 942-8107
Rodney F Kalune, *President*
Keoki Kaluna, *Bd of Directors*
Rock Magnan, *Officer*
Kip Shepard, *Vice Pres*
Victoria Jones, *Finance*
EMP: 144 **EST:** 2004
SQ FT: 180,000
SALES (est): 29MM **Privately Held**
WEB: www.rklogisticsgroup.com
SIC: 8742 4214 4225 Transportation consultant; local trucking with storage; general warehousing & storage

(P-19624)
ROHNERT PARK HOUSING FING AUTH
30 Avram Ave, Rohnert Park (94928)
PHONE.....................................707 588-2226
David Mitchell, *Principal*
EMP: 45 **EST:** 2013
SALES (est): 67.4K
SALES (corp-wide): 76.2MM **Privately Held**
WEB: www.ci.rohnert-park.ca.us
SIC: 8742 Financial consultant
PA: City Of Rohnert Park
130 Avram Ave
Rohnert Park CA 94928
707 588-2200

(P-19625)
ROI COMMUNICATIONS INC (PA)
5274 Scotts Valley Dr # 107, Scotts Valley (95066-3538)
PHONE.....................................831 430-0170
Barbara Fagan Smith, *President*
Rory Macleod, *Owner*
Charlie Wrench, *President*
Sheryl Lewis, *COO*
Joann Webster, *Officer*
EMP: 64 **EST:** 2001
SALES (est): 14.3MM **Privately Held**
WEB: www.roico.com
SIC: 8742 Marketing consulting services

(P-19626)
S P S INC
245 Medio Ave, Half Moon Bay (94019-5335)
PHONE.....................................650 685-5913
Steve Semprevivo, *President*
EMP: 70 **EST:** 1997
SALES (est): 1.3MM **Privately Held**
SIC: 8742 Marketing consulting services

(P-19627)
SCHOOL INNVTONS ACHEVEMENT INC
Also Called: School Innvations Advocacy
5200 Golden Foothill Pkwy, El Dorado Hills (95762-9610)
PHONE.....................................800 487-9234
EMP: 36 **Privately Held**
SIC: 8742 Management Consulting Services
PA: School Innovations And Achievement
5200 Golden Foothill Pkwy
El Dorado Hills CA 95762

(P-19628)
SCHOOL SERVICES CALIFORNIA INC
1121 L St Ste 1060, Sacramento (95814-3944)
PHONE.....................................916 446-7517
Kenneth Hall, *Chairman*
Ron Bennett, *President*
Paul M Goldfinger, *Vice Pres*
Sheila Vickers, *Admin Sec*
Gina Sherman Will, *Controller*
EMP: 38 **EST:** 1975
SQ FT: 7,500
SALES (est): 2.5MM **Privately Held**
WEB: www.sscal.com
SIC: 8742 School, college, university consultant

(P-19629)
SELLANDS BROADWAY INC
Also Called: Selland's Market Cafe
915 Broadway Ste 300, Sacramento (95818-2166)
PHONE.....................................916 732-3390
EMP: 35 **EST:** 2019
SALES (est): 1.6MM **Privately Held**
WEB: www.sellands.com
SIC: 8742 5812 Marketing consulting services; eating places

(P-19630)
SENSE TALENT LABS INC (PA)
225 Bush St Ste 1350, San Francisco (94104-4287)
PHONE.....................................408 674-5180
Anil Dharni, *CEO*
Ram Gudavalli, *Treasurer*
Sanjay Dharmani, *Managing Dir*
EMP: 45 **EST:** 2015
SALES (est): 3.7MM **Privately Held**
WEB: www.sensehq.com
SIC: 8742 8741 Training & development consultant; personnel management

(P-19631)
SHANNON RANCHES INC
12601 E Highway 20, Clearlake Oaks (95423-8312)
P.O. Box 2037 (95423-2037)
PHONE.....................................707 998-9656
Clay Shannon, *President*
Margarita Shannon, *Corp Secy*
Brian Altomari, *Vice Pres*
Craig Shannon, *Vice Pres*
Roxanne Jackson, *Marketing Staff*
EMP: 250 **EST:** 1993
SQ FT: 2,100
SALES (est): 22.5MM **Privately Held**
SIC: 8742 Administrative services consultant

(P-19632)
SHOPALYST INC (PA)
38350 Fremont Blvd # 203, Fremont (94536-6060)
PHONE.....................................949 583-0507
Girish Ramachandra, *President*
EMP: 85 **EST:** 2018
SALES (est): 669.4K **Privately Held**
WEB: www.shopalyst.com
SIC: 8742 Business consultant

(P-19633)
SIGMAWAYS INC
39737 Paseo Padre Pkwy C1, Fremont (94538-2957)
PHONE.....................................510 573-4208
Prakash Sadasivam, *CEO*
Bhuvana Ravikumar, *Technology*
Sudha Kadirvelu, *Human Res Mgr*
David Donnelly, *Director*
EMP: 60 **EST:** 2006
SQ FT: 5,000
SALES (est): 5.9MM **Privately Held**
WEB: www.sigmaways.com
SIC: 8742 7379 7373 Management consulting services; computer related consulting services; systems software development services

(P-19634)
SIMBE ROBOTICS INC
385 Oyster Point Blvd # 2, South San Francisco (94080-1934)
PHONE.....................................415 625-8555
Brooks Augustine, *Senior VP*
Tom Gehani, *Vice Pres*
Richard Barnes, *CIO*
Jeremy Nolan, *Engineer*
EMP: 42 **EST:** 2014
SALES (est): 4.3MM **Privately Held**
WEB: www.simberobotics.com
SIC: 8742 Automation & robotics consultant

(P-19635)
SLALOM LLC
100 Pine St Ste 2500, San Francisco (94111-5211)
PHONE.....................................415 593-3450
Pat Meade, *General Mgr*
EMP: 113 **Privately Held**
WEB: www.slalom.com
SIC: 8742 Business consultant
PA: Slalom, Llc
821 2nd Ave Ste 1900
Seattle WA 98104

(P-19636)
SMARTZIP ANALYTICS INC
6200 Stnrdge Mall Rd Ste, Pleasanton (94588)
PHONE.....................................855 661-1064
Tom Glassanos, *President*
Scott Baumgartner, *CFO*
Frank Richards, *Chairman*
Peter Grace, *Exec VP*
Matt Grant, *Executive*
EMP: 77 **EST:** 2008
SALES (est): 12.1MM **Privately Held**
WEB: www.app.smartzip.com
SIC: 8742 Marketing consulting services; real estate consultant

(P-19637)
SOLOPOINT SOLUTIONS INC (PA)
3350 Scott Blvd Bldg 2, Santa Clara (95054-3108)
PHONE.....................................408 246-5945
Dinh Le, *President*
Anthony Snow, *Tech Recruiter*
Sara Almario, *Opers Staff*
EMP: 69 **EST:** 2006
SALES (est): 8.4MM **Privately Held**
WEB: www.solopointsolutions.com
SIC: 8742 Management consulting services

(P-19638)
STAGE 4 SOLUTIONS INCORPORATED
19200 Portos Dr, Saratoga (95070-5123)
PHONE.....................................408 868-9739
Niti Agrawal, *CEO*
Akansha Singh, *Technical Staff*
Jane Rayskaya, *Director*
EMP: 50 **EST:** 2003
SALES (est): 5.7MM **Privately Held**
WEB: www.stage4solutions.com
SIC: 8742 New products & services consultants

(P-19639)
STERLING CONSULTING GROUP LLC
Also Called: Sterling Brand
600 California St Fl 8, San Francisco (94108-2726)
PHONE.....................................415 248-7900
Austin McGhie, *Manager*
Corey Allen, *Accountant*
EMP: 84 **Privately Held**
WEB: www.sterlingbrands.com
SIC: 8742 Marketing consulting services
PA: Sterling Consulting Group Llc
75 Varick St Fl 8
New York NY 10013

(P-19640)
STERLING MKTG & FINCL CORP
Also Called: T3 Direct
4660 Spyres Way Ste 1, Modesto (95356-9801)
PHONE.....................................209 593-1140
Albert W Dadesho, *President*
Susie Dadesho, *Vice Pres*
EMP: 50 **EST:** 2008
SQ FT: 8,000
SALES (est): 5.5MM **Privately Held**
WEB: www.t3direct.com
SIC: 8742 Marketing consulting services

(P-19641)
STERLING STAMOS ACCELERATION
2498 Sand Hill Rd, Menlo Park (94025-6940)
PHONE.....................................650 233-5000
Peter Stamos, *President*
Kevin Barcelona, *Partner*
EMP: 35 **EST:** 2004
SALES (est): 4MM **Privately Held**
WEB: www.stamoscapital.com
SIC: 8742 Financial consultant

(P-19642)
STRATEGIC BUS INSIGHTS INC (PA)
333 Ravenswood Ave, Menlo Park (94025-3453)
PHONE.....................................650 859-4600
William Guns, *CEO*
William Ralston, *CFO*
Larry Cohen, *Vice Pres*
Chulho Park, *Principal*
Kimberley Evans, *Office Mgr*
EMP: 63
SQ FT: 10,000
SALES (est): 7.9MM **Privately Held**
WEB: www.strategicbusinessinsights.com
SIC: 8742 Business consultant

(P-19643)
STRATEGIC CAPITAL INCORPORATED
Also Called: Pezzi King Vineyards
3225 W Dry Creek Rd, Healdsburg (95448-9724)
PHONE.....................................707 473-4310
James P Rowe Sr, *CEO*
Tom Rowe, *President*
Sharon Bilbro, *Sales Staff*
Sharon Bro, *Sales Staff*
Kristina D'Angelo, *Manager*
EMP: 30 **EST:** 1982
SQ FT: 6,000
SALES (est): 3.7MM
SALES (corp-wide): 4.3MM **Privately Held**
WEB: www.pezziking.com
SIC: 8742 6282 0172 2084 Marketing consulting services; investment advisory service; grapes; wine cellars, bonded: engaged in blending wines
PA: Wilson Winery
1960 Dry Creek Rd
Healdsburg CA 95448
707 433-4355

(P-19644)
STRATEOS INC (PA)
3565 Haven Ave Ste 3, Menlo Park (94025-1065)
PHONE.....................................650 763-8432
Mark Colbrie, *CEO*
Max Hodak, *President*
Christopher Krueger, *CFO*
Jaimie Cravens, *Executive Asst*
Peter Lee, *Technical Staff*
EMP: 57 **EST:** 2012
SALES (est): 8.2MM **Privately Held**
WEB: www.strateos.com
SIC: 8742 7371 8731 Automation & robotics consultant; computer software development & applications; biological research

(P-19645)
SUTTER PHYSICIAN SERVICES (HQ)
10470 Old Placerville Rd, Sacramento (95827-2539)
P.O. Box 211584, Saint Paul MN (55121-2884)
PHONE.....................................916 854-6600
Jeremy Eaves, *CEO*
Mitch Proaps, *Comms Mgr*
Sharon Prewitt, *Executive Asst*
Aneel Mandava, *CIO*
Damon Lang, *Client Mgr*
EMP: 800 **EST:** 1989
SQ FT: 87,000

8742 - Management Consulting Services County (P-19646)

SALES (est): 146.4MM
SALES (corp-wide): 13.2B **Privately Held**
WEB: www.sutterphysicianservices.org
SIC: 8742 8741 8721 Hospital & health services consultant; management information systems consultant; management services; accounting, auditing & bookkeeping
PA: Sutter Health
2200 River Plaza Dr
Sacramento CA 95833
916 733-8800

(P-19646)
SWIG COMPANY LLC
Also Called: Mills Building
220 Montgomery St Ste 950, San Francisco (94104-3441)
PHONE..................................415 291-1100
Kennard Perry, *President*
Jenne Myerson, *President*
Sunita Bayley, *Treasurer*
Connor Kidd, *Exec VP*
Tomas Schoenberg, *Exec VP*
EMP: 40 **EST:** 1950
SQ FT: 535,000
SALES: 160.5K **Privately Held**
WEB: www.swigco.com
SIC: 8742 Management consulting services

(P-19647)
SWINERTON MGT & CONSULTING INC (HQ)
260 Townsend St, San Francisco (94107-1761)
PHONE..................................415 984-1261
Linda Schowalter, *Senior VP*
Jeffrey Gee, *Vice Pres*
George Hershman, *Vice Pres*
Cheryl Johnson, *Vice Pres*
James O'Reilly, *Vice Pres*
EMP: 45 **EST:** 1995
SQ FT: 10,000
SALES (est): 12.8MM **Privately Held**
WEB: www.swinertonmc.com
SIC: 8742 Management consulting services

(P-19648)
SYNOPTEK INC
930 Alabama St, San Francisco (94110-2707)
PHONE..................................415 651-4236
Matt McGraw, *Manager*
EMP: 148 **Privately Held**
WEB: www.synoptek.com
SIC: 8742 New business start-up consultant
PA: Synoptek, Inc.
19520 Jamboree Rd Ste 110
Irvine CA 92612

(P-19649)
TEKNOS ASSOCIATES LLC
548 Market St, San Francisco (94104-5401)
PHONE..................................650 330-8800
James Timmins, *Principal*
Sean Gilbert, *Assoc VP*
Alex Salvadori, *Assoc VP*
Adam Hibble, *Vice Pres*
Isaac Salem, *Vice Pres*
EMP: 50 **EST:** 2008
SALES (est): 3.8MM **Privately Held**
WEB: www.teknosassociates.com
SIC: 8742 Financial consultant

(P-19650)
TELEGRAPH HILL PARTNERS INVEST (PA)
360 Post St Ste 601, San Francisco (94108-4909)
PHONE..................................415 765-6980
J Matthew Mackowski, *Chairman*
Rob C Hart Cfa, *Vice Pres*
M Celeste Salvatto, *Administration*
Deval A Lashkari PHD,
Jeanette M Welsh JD,
EMP: 50
SALES (est): 35MM **Privately Held**
WEB: www.thpartners.net
SIC: 8742 6799 Management consulting services; investors

(P-19651)
TOPDOWN CONSULTING INC
530 Divisadero St Ste 310, San Francisco (94117-2213)
PHONE..................................888 644-8445
EMP: 80 **EST:** 2000
SALES (est): 8.6MM **Privately Held**
WEB: www.topdownconsulting.com
SIC: 8742 Management Consulting Services

(P-19652)
TRANSIRIS CORPORATION
Also Called: Retina Communications
555 Airport Blvd Ste 325, Burlingame (94010-2062)
PHONE..................................650 303-3495
Ted Kohnen, *CEO*
Silvian Centiu, *Principal*
Simona Nan, *General Mgr*
Rebecca Falk, *Director*
Fabian Moldoveanu, *Director*
EMP: 60 **EST:** 2012
SALES (est): 7.3MM **Privately Held**
WEB: www.retinab2.com
SIC: 8742 Marketing consulting services

(P-19653)
TRANZEAL INC
2107 N 1st St Ste 500, San Jose (95131-2028)
PHONE..................................408 834-8711
Akhil Khera, *Partner*
Murali Kolli, *COO*
Ajay Singh, *Tech Recruiter*
Praveen Kumar, *Opers Staff*
EMP: 42 **EST:** 2011
SQ FT: 2,200
SALES (est): 1.3MM **Privately Held**
WEB: www.tranzeal.com
SIC: 8742 Management consulting services

(P-19654)
TRIAGE CONSULTING GROUP LLC (PA)
221 Main St Ste 1100, San Francisco (94105-1927)
PHONE..................................415 512-9400
Brian Neece, *President*
Damon Lewis, *CFO*
Joyce Balistreri, *Office Mgr*
Kim Mc Lemore, *Office Mgr*
Sean Alavi, *Admin Sec*
EMP: 280 **EST:** 1994
SQ FT: 21,665 **Privately Held**
WEB: www.cloudmed.com
SIC: 8742 8748 Hospital & health services consultant; business consulting

(P-19655)
TRIPLE RING TECHNOLOGIES INC
39655 Eureka Dr, Newark (94560-4806)
PHONE..................................510 592-3000
Joseph A Heanue, *CEO*
Marc Whyte, *Ch of Bd*
Philip Devlin, *Officer*
Barclay Dorman, *Vice Pres*
Ryan Gaunt, *Vice Pres*
EMP: 50
SALES (est): 11.8MM **Privately Held**
WEB: www.tripleringtech.com
SIC: 8742 Business consultant

(P-19656)
TROVE RECOMMERCE INC
240 Valley Dr, Brisbane (94005-1241)
PHONE..................................925 726-3316
Andrew Ruben, *CEO*
EMP: 200 **EST:** 2019
SALES (est): 14.2MM **Privately Held**
WEB: www.trove.co
SIC: 8742 Business consultant

(P-19657)
TRUSTARC INC (HQ)
Also Called: Truste
2121 N Calif Blvd Ste 290, Walnut Creek (94596-7351)
PHONE..................................415 520-3400
Christopher Babel, *CEO*
Tim Sullivan, *CFO*
Dave Deasy, *Chief Mktg Ofcr*
Hilary Wandall, *Officer*
Michelle Hines, *Vice Pres*
EMP: 98 **EST:** 2008
SALES (est): 19.6MM
SALES (corp-wide): 96.4K **Privately Held**
WEB: www.trustarc.com
SIC: 8742 7379 Management consulting services; marketing consulting services; computer related consulting services

(P-19658)
TSMC NORTH AMERICA (HQ)
2851 Junction Ave, San Jose (95134-1910)
PHONE..................................408 382-8000
Richard B Cassidy II, *CEO*
Rick Cassidy, *President*
Jerry Tai, *COO*
Harvey Chang, *CFO*
Peter Bonfield, *Bd of Directors*
EMP: 971 **EST:** 1987
SALES (est): 183.1MM **Privately Held**
WEB: www.tsmc.com
SIC: 8742 8711 5065 3674 Marketing consulting services; consulting engineer; electronic parts & equipment; semiconductor circuit networks

(P-19659)
UNDERGRUND SVC ALERT NTHRN CAL
Also Called: USA North 811
4005 Port Chicago Hwy, Concord (94520-1180)
PHONE..................................800 640-5137
James Wingate, *CEO*
Ryan White, *Managing Dir*
Rita Hughes, *Admin Asst*
Stephen Baker, *Administration*
Dillon Estates, *Bookkeeper*
EMP: 42 **EST:** 1986
SQ FT: 9,200
SALES (est): 7.1MM **Privately Held**
WEB: www.usanorth811.org
SIC: 8742 8611 Construction project management consultant; public utility association

(P-19660)
UNITED ENGRG RESOURCES INC (PA)
498 N 3rd St, Sacramento (95811-0215)
PHONE..................................916 375-6700
Robert V Tadlock, *CEO*
Scott Warady, *Controller*
Dominic D Zovi, *Opers Mgr*
EMP: 62 **EST:** 2014
SALES (est): 26.3MM **Privately Held**
WEB: www.uercorp.com
SIC: 8742 Business planning & organizing services

(P-19661)
UNITED INNOVATION SERVICES INC
950 Tower Ln, Foster City (94404-2121)
PHONE..................................831 334-0673
Tingting Du, *CEO*
EMP: 84 **EST:** 2017
SALES (est): 1.8MM **Privately Held**
WEB: www.uisus.com
SIC: 8742 Management consulting services

(P-19662)
UNIVERSITY EAST-WEST MEDICINE
595 Lawrence Expy, Sunnyvale (94085-3922)
PHONE..................................408 992-0218
Ying Wang, *President*
Jerry Wang, *CEO*
Su Fang Tong, *CFO*
Richard Friberg, *Vice Pres*
Kenneth Fu, *Admin Director*
EMP: 45 **EST:** 1999
SQ FT: 27,007
SALES (est): 5.8MM **Privately Held**
WEB: www.uewm.edu
SIC: 8742 School, college, university consultant

(P-19663)
VARIS LLC
3915 Security Park Dr B, Rancho Cordova (95742-6903)
PHONE..................................916 294-0860
Dean B Wilkie, *Manager*
Lisa Polte, *Vice Pres*
Fran Degregorio, *Auditor*
Christy Jamison, *Manager*
Anthony Tomasello, *Manager*
EMP: 70
SALES (corp-wide): 9.9MM **Privately Held**
WEB: www.varis1.com
SIC: 8742 Hospital & health services consultant
PA: Varis Llc
9245 Sierra College Blvd
Roseville CA 95661
916 294-0860

(P-19664)
VARIS LLC (PA)
9245 Sierra College Blvd, Roseville (95661-5919)
PHONE..................................916 294-0860
Joy A Wilkie, *Mng Member*
Dean Wilkie, *General Mgr*
Adriana Velasquez, *Admin Asst*
Marlana Hill, *Administration*
Amaniese Roberts, *Administration*
EMP: 40 **EST:** 2004
SQ FT: 5,600
SALES (est): 9.9MM **Privately Held**
WEB: www.varis1.com
SIC: 8742 Hospital & health services consultant

(P-19665)
VELOCITI PARTNERS INC
712 Bancroft Rd 124, Walnut Creek (94598-1531)
PHONE..................................866 300-2925
Alison Moore, *President*
EMP: 50 **EST:** 2005
SALES (est): 2.3MM **Privately Held**
WEB: www.velociti.partners
SIC: 8742 Marketing consulting services

(P-19666)
VERITAS MEDIA GROUP LLC
1111 Broadway Ste 300, Oakland (94607-4167)
PHONE..................................510 867-4699
Jason Ballance, *CEO*
Zach Luechauer, *President*
EMP: 50 **EST:** 2018
SALES (est): 4.5MM **Privately Held**
SIC: 8742 7319 Marketing consulting services; media buying service

(P-19667)
WAGEWORKS INC (HQ)
1100 Park Pl Fl 4, San Mateo (94403-1599)
PHONE..................................650 577-5200
Edgar Montes, *President*
Colm Callan, *CFO*
Bruce Bodaken, *Bd of Directors*
Carol Goode, *Bd of Directors*
Jerome Gramaglia, *Bd of Directors*
EMP: 113 **EST:** 2000
SQ FT: 37,937
SALES: 472.1MM **Publicly Held**
WEB: www.wageworks.com
SIC: 8742 Compensation & benefits planning consultant

(P-19668)
WAYPOINT BUILDING GROUP INC
847 Sansome St Fl 3, San Francisco (94111-1529)
P.O. Box 1226, Sparta NJ (07871-5226)
PHONE..................................415 738-4730
Diane Vrkic, *President*
Alex Holt, *Engineer*
Susan Gutierrez Simon, *Manager*
Laura Suttie, *Manager*
Matt Tschirgi, *Accounts Exec*
EMP: 51 **EST:** 2009
SALES (est): 4MM **Privately Held**
WEB: www.waypointbuilding.com
SIC: 8742 8748 8732 Business consultant; urban planning & consulting services; market analysis or research

PRODUCTS & SERVICES SECTION

8743 - Public Relations Svcs County (P-19691)

(P-19669)
WHITE OAK GLOBAL ADVISORS LLC (PA)
3 Embarcadero Ctr Ste 550, San Francisco (94111-4048)
PHONE.....................415 644-4100
Andre Amin Hakkak, *Mng Member*
Jon Patty, *Partner*
David M Lund, *CFO*
Bob Defazio, *Treasurer*
Kenneth Wendler, *Ch Credit Ofcr*
EMP: 36 **EST:** 2007
SQ FT: 2,000
SALES (est): 66.7MM **Privately Held**
WEB: www.whiteoaksf.com
SIC: 8742 Financial consultant

(P-19670)
WIND RIVER SYSTEMS INTL INC (DH)
500 Wind River Way, Alameda (94501-1162)
PHONE.....................510 748-4100
Barry Mainz, *CEO*
Andra Cristea, *Engineer*
Sandra Tan, *Human Res Dir*
Bonnie Coker, *Sr Project Mgr*
John Templin, *Manager*
EMP: 97 **EST:** 1997
SALES (est): 6.3MM **Privately Held**
WEB: www.windriver.com
SIC: 8742 Management consulting services
HQ: Wind River Systems, Inc.
500 Wind River Way
Alameda CA 94501
510 748-4100

(P-19671)
WORK HEALTH
Also Called: Queen of The Valley Hospital
3421 Villa Ln Ste 2a, NAPA (94558-3060)
P.O. Box 2340 (94558-0688)
PHONE.....................707 257-4084
Deborah Morrissey, *Owner*
Robert Eisen, *Vice Pres*
Mary Dominguez, *Radiology*
Jeffery Lundeen, *Nurse*
Pamela Contos, *Manager*
EMP: 78 **EST:** 1999
SALES (est): 7.2MM **Privately Held**
WEB: www.thequeen.org
SIC: 8742 8049 8011 Compensation & benefits planning consultant; occupational therapist; occupational & industrial specialist, physician/surgeon

(P-19672)
WORLD FINANCIAL GROUP (PA)
2099 Gold St, Alviso (95002-3601)
P.O. Box 730 (95002-0730)
PHONE.....................408 941-1838
Gabriel Gancayco, *Principal*
Richa Jethwa, *Mktg Dir*
Fu Yang, *Marketing Staff*
EMP: 47 **EST:** 2005
SALES (est): 1.9MM **Privately Held**
SIC: 8742 Financial consultant

(P-19673)
YODLEE INC (HQ)
999 Baker Way Ste 100, San Mateo (94404-1580)
PHONE.....................650 980-3600
Anil Arora, *President*
Brian Buan, *Partner*
Jeff Cain, *Partner*
Ambermarie Roy, *Partner*
Mike Armsby, *CFO*
▲ **EMP:** 146 **EST:** 1999
SALES (est): 74.4MM
SALES (corp-wide): 998.2MM **Publicly Held**
WEB: www.envestnet.com
SIC: 8742 Banking & finance consultant
PA: Envestnet, Inc.
35 E Wacker Dr Ste 2400
Chicago IL 60601
312 827-2800

(P-19674)
YOUAPPI INC
2 Embarcadero Ctr # 2310, San Francisco (94111-3823)
PHONE.....................646 854-3390
EMP: 70 **EST:** 2011
SALES (est): 176.4K **Privately Held**
SIC: 8742 7313 Management Consulting Services Advertising Representative

(P-19675)
ZENDAR INC (PA)
1110 Euclid Ave, Berkeley (94708-1603)
PHONE.....................510 590-8060
EMP: 48 **EST:** 2017
SALES (est): 3.6MM **Privately Held**
WEB: www.zendar.io
SIC: 8742 Business consultant

(P-19676)
ZIFF DAVIS B2B FOCUS INC (DH)
625 2nd St, San Francisco (94107-2014)
PHONE.....................415 696-5453
Vivek Shah, *CEO*
Andy Johns, *CFO*
Asada Krengvithaya, *Executive*
Asif Ahmed, *Manager*
EMP: 50 **EST:** 2011
SALES (est): 214.4MM
SALES (corp-wide): 1.4B **Publicly Held**
WEB: www.ziffdavis.com
SIC: 8742 Marketing consulting services

(P-19677)
ZIPLINE INTERNATIONAL INC
333 Corey Way, South San Francisco (94080-6706)
PHONE.....................415 993-0604
Keller Rinaudo, *CEO*
Keenan Wyrobek, *CTO*
Stefan Aprodu, *Engineer*
Marina Yang, *Director*
EMP: 150 **EST:** 2012
SALES (est): 25.7MM **Privately Held**
SIC: 8742 Automation & robotics consultant

(P-19678)
ZOHO CORPORATION
Manage Engine
4141 Hacienda Dr, Pleasanton (94588-8566)
PHONE.....................925 924-9500
Sridhar Vembu, *CEO*
Arvind Parthiban, *Sr Consultant*
EMP: 395 **Privately Held**
WEB: www.site24x7.com
SIC: 8742 Management information systems consultant
HQ: Zoho Corporation
4141 Hacienda Dr
Pleasanton CA 94588

(P-19679)
ZONIC DESIGN & IMAGING LLC
875 Mahler Rd Ste 238, Burlingame (94010-1612)
PHONE.....................415 643-3700
Brian Ramphal,
Mark Altieri, *President*
George Chou, *Info Tech Dir*
Tom Brown, *Mktg Dir*
Eric Gille, *Marketing Staff*
EMP: 40
SQ FT: 3,300
SALES (est): 8.4MM **Privately Held**
WEB: www.zonicdesign.com
SIC: 8742 Marketing consulting services

8743 Public Relations Svcs

(P-19680)
10 FOLD COMMUNICATIONS INC
800 S Broadway Ste 309, Walnut Creek (94596-5218)
PHONE.....................925 271-8205
Susan Thomas, *CEO*
EMP: 36 **EST:** 1999
SALES (est): 8MM **Privately Held**
SIC: 8743 Public relations services

(P-19681)
ACCESS PUBLIC RELATIONS LLC
Also Called: Access Brand Communications
720 California St Fl 5, San Francisco (94108-2453)
PHONE.....................415 904-7070
Susan Butenhoff,
Danielle Caff, *Senior VP*
Matt Afflixio,
Jennifer Sims-Fellner,
EMP: 64 **EST:** 1982
SQ FT: 17,000
SALES (est): 20MM
SALES (corp-wide): 13.1B **Publicly Held**
WEB: www.accesstheagency.com
SIC: 8743 Public relations & publicity
HQ: Ketchum Incorporated
1285 Avenue Of The Americ
New York NY 10019
646 935-3900

(P-19682)
AMF MEDIA GROUP
12657 Alcosta Blvd # 500, San Ramon (94583-4438)
PHONE.....................925 790-2662
Vintage Foster, *President*
Kayla Cash, *Executive*
Joe Lopez, *Creative Dir*
Lauren Finley, *Director*
Tia Daniel, *Supervisor*
EMP: 38
SALES (est): 5.2MM **Privately Held**
WEB: www.amfmediagroup.com
SIC: 8743 8742 8748 Public relations & publicity; marketing consulting services; communications consulting

(P-19683)
ATOMIC PUBLIC RELATIONS (HQ)
Also Called: Atomic P R
735 Market St Fl 4, San Francisco (94103-2034)
PHONE.....................415 402-0230
Andy Getsey, *CEO*
Annette Wiedemann, *Vice Pres*
James Hannon, *CIO*
EMP: 85 **EST:** 1991
SALES (est): 1.2MM
SALES (corp-wide): 5.8MM **Privately Held**
WEB: www.huntsworth.com
SIC: 8743 Public relations & publicity

(P-19684)
CALIFRNIA ASSN PUB HSPTALS HLT
Also Called: C A P H
70 Washington St Ste 215, Oakland (94607-3795)
PHONE.....................510 874-7100
Erica Murray, *President*
Megan Renfrew, *Comms Dir*
Leossie Hernandez, *Accounting Mgr*
EMP: 47 **EST:** 1984
SALES (est): 2.6MM **Privately Held**
WEB: www.caph.org
SIC: 8743 Lobbyist

(P-19685)
CITIGATE CUNNINGHAM INC (PA)
1530 Page Mill Rd Ste 3, Palo Alto (94304-1134)
PHONE.....................650 858-3700
Paul Bergevin, *President*
Ron Ricci, *Principal*
EMP: 40 **EST:** 1985
SALES (est): 2.7MM **Privately Held**
SIC: 8743 Public relations services

(P-19686)
GLODOW NEAD COMMUNICATIONS LLC
1700 Montgomery St # 203, San Francisco (94111-1023)
PHONE.....................415 394-6500
John Glodow,
Jeff Nead,
Jane Chung, *Asst Mgr*
EMP: 43 **EST:** 1973
SQ FT: 1,200
SALES (est): 4.9MM **Privately Held**
WEB: www.glodownead.com
SIC: 8743 Public relations services

(P-19687)
GMR MARKETING LLC
Also Called: Gmr - San Francisco
600 California St Fl 7, San Francisco (94108-2731)
PHONE.....................415 229-7733
Zaileen Janmohmad, *Branch Mgr*
Mariana Alvaro, *Production*
Victoria Montague, *Director*
Stephanie Lee, *Manager*
EMP: 43
SALES (corp-wide): 13.1B **Publicly Held**
WEB: www.gmrmarketing.com
SIC: 8743 Promotion service
HQ: Gmr Marketing Llc
5000 S Towne Dr
New Berlin WI 53151
800 447-8560

(P-19688)
HIGHWIRE PUBLIC RELATIONS INC (HQ)
727 Sansome St, San Francisco (94111-1736)
PHONE.....................415 963-4174
Kathleen E Gratehouse, *CEO*
Nitin Walia, *Officer*
James Beechinor-Collins, *Exec VP*
James Holland, *Exec VP*
Christine M Elswick, *Vice Pres*
EMP: 68 **EST:** 2013
SALES (est): 9.5MM **Privately Held**
WEB: www.highwirepr.com
SIC: 8743 Public relations & publicity
PA: Inner Circle Labs Llc
333 1st St Ste A
San Francisco CA 94105
415 684-9400

(P-19689)
HOFFMAN AGENCY (PA)
325 S 1st St Ste 300, San Jose (95113-2830)
PHONE.....................408 286-2611
Lou Hoffman, *CEO*
Leon Hunt, *CFO*
Pouneh Lechner, *Vice Pres*
Tom Peterson, *Vice Pres*
Mandy Heiser, *Executive*
EMP: 45 **EST:** 1987
SQ FT: 23,000
SALES (est): 5.4MM **Privately Held**
WEB: www.hoffman.com
SIC: 8743 Public relations & publicity

(P-19690)
KETCHUM INCORPORATED
600 California St Fl 1, San Francisco (94108-2734)
PHONE.....................415 984-6100
Melissa Kinch, *Director*
Shawn McBride, *Exec VP*
Courtney Nally, *Exec VP*
Kate Durkin, *Senior VP*
Maxine Enciso, *Senior VP*
EMP: 75
SALES (corp-wide): 13.1B **Publicly Held**
WEB: www.ketchum.com
SIC: 8743 Public relations & publicity
HQ: Ketchum Incorporated
1285 Avenue Of The Americ
New York NY 10019
646 935-3900

(P-19691)
LEAGUE OF CALIFORNIA CITIES (PA)
Also Called: Western City Magazine
1400 K St Fl 4, Sacramento (95814-3916)
PHONE.....................916 658-8200
Carolyn Coleman, *Exec Dir*
Norman Coppinger, *CFO*
Randall Stone, *Bd of Directors*
Pam Herrera, *Exec Dir*
Erica Manuel, *Exec Dir*
EMP: 65 **EST:** 1932
SQ FT: 32,000
SALES: 300.6K **Privately Held**
WEB: www.calcities.org
SIC: 8743 2721 Lobbyist; magazines: publishing only, not printed on site

8743 - Public Relations Svcs

(P-19692)
OGILVY PUB RLATIONS WORLD WIDE
800 El Camino Real, Menlo Park (94025-4887)
PHONE..................................650 324-7015
Kate Osullivan, *Vice Pres*
EMP: 105
SALES (corp-wide): 15.9B **Privately Held**
SIC: 8743 Public relations & publicity
HQ: Ogilvy Public Relations World Wide
3340 Peachtree Rd Ne # 300
Atlanta GA 30326

(P-19693)
OUTCAST AGENCY LLC
100 Montgomery St # 1201, San Francisco (94104-4331)
PHONE..................................415 392-8282
Tim Dyson,
Tj Snyder, *Partner*
Darlyn Phillips, *CFO*
Mindy Whittington, *Exec VP*
Rachel McFarland, *Senior VP*
EMP: 120 EST: 2012
SALES (est): 10.3MM **Privately Held**
WEB: www.thisisoutcast.com
SIC: 8743 Public relations services

(P-19694)
PEDERSEN MEDIA GROUP INC
Also Called: Intrepid
1115 3rd St, San Rafael (94901-3017)
PHONE..................................415 512-9800
Mark Pedersen, *President*
Maureen Maloney, *CFO*
Maureen Kumar, *Treasurer*
Julie Nelson, *Prdtn Mgr*
Lori Wright, *Producer*
EMP: 38 EST: 1982
SALES (est): 4.7MM **Privately Held**
WEB: www.pedersen.com
SIC: 8743 7812 Public relations services; video tape production

(P-19695)
PRX INC
991 W Hedding St Ste 201, San Jose (95126-1248)
PHONE..................................408 287-1700
Brenna Bolger, *President*
Steve Mangold, *COO*
Thuy Nguyen, *CFO*
Daniel Garza, *Vice Pres*
Bill Kugler, *Vice Pres*
EMP: 42 EST: 1975
SQ FT: 4,500
SALES (est): 5MM **Privately Held**
WEB: www.prxdigital.com
SIC: 8743 8399 7311 Public relations & publicity; fund raising organization, non-fee basis; advertising agencies

(P-19696)
R/GA MEDIA GROUP INC
35 Park St, San Francisco (94110-5833)
PHONE..................................415 913-7531
Barry Wacksman, *Branch Mgr*
Cara Watson, *Managing Dir*
Brian Sullivan, *Technology*
Lisa LI, *Marketing Staff*
Ben Pirotte, *Director*
EMP: 77
SALES (corp-wide): 9B **Publicly Held**
WEB: www.rga.com
SIC: 8743 Public relations & publicity
HQ: R/Ga Media Group, Inc.
450 W 33rd St Fl 12
New York NY 10001
212 946-4000

(P-19697)
RURAL COUNTY REP CAL
1215 K St Ste 1650, Sacramento (95814-3998)
PHONE..................................916 447-4806
Greg Norton, *President*
EMP: 48 EST: 1972
SALES (est): 5.6MM **Privately Held**
WEB: www.rcrcnet.org
SIC: 8743 Lobbyist

(P-19698)
VOCE COMMUNICATIONS INC
550 3rd St, San Francisco (94107-1805)
PHONE..................................415 975-2200
Richard Cline, *Director*
EMP: 40
SALES (corp-wide): 13.1B **Publicly Held**
SIC: 8743 Public relations services
HQ: Voce Communications, Inc.
298 S Sunnyvale Ave # 101
Sunnyvale CA
408 738-7840

(P-19699)
YOUNG & RUBICAM LLC
Also Called: Burson Marsteller
100 Pine St Ste 2300, San Francisco (94111-5209)
PHONE..................................650 287-4000
Dave Chapman, *General Mgr*
Bews Alan William, *IT/INT Sup*
Darcy Harrison, *Project Mgr*
EMP: 150
SALES (corp-wide): 15.9B **Privately Held**
WEB: www.vmlyr.com
SIC: 8743 Public relations services
HQ: Young & Rubicam Llc
3 Columbus Cir Frnt 3 # 3
New York NY 10019
212 210-3000

8744 Facilities Support Mgmt Svcs

(P-19700)
AGUATIERRA ASSOCIATES INC (PA)
Also Called: Weiss Associates
2000 Powell St Ste 555, Emeryville (94608-1838)
PHONE..................................510 450-6000
Michael D Dresen, *President*
Richard B Weiss, *CFO*
Scott Bourne, *Vice Pres*
Robert Devany, *Vice Pres*
Tom Fojut, *Engineer*
EMP: 46 EST: 1980
SQ FT: 13,000
SALES (est): 10MM **Privately Held**
SIC: 8744 4959 8748 Facilities support services; environmental cleanup services; environmental consultant

(P-19701)
AMERICAN REPROGRAPHICS CO LLC (HQ)
Also Called: A R C
1981 N Broadway Ste 385, Walnut Creek (94596-8214)
PHONE..................................925 949-5100
K Suriyakumar, *CEO*
Dilantha Wijesuriya, *COO*
John E D Toth, *CFO*
Ted Buscaglia, *Exec VP*
Jorge Avalos, *Vice Pres*
▲ EMP: 35 EST: 1997
SQ FT: 10,000
SALES (est): 173.6MM
SALES (corp-wide): 289.4MM **Publicly Held**
WEB: www.ryansallans.com
SIC: 8744 7334 Facilities support services; photocopying & duplicating services
PA: Arc Document Solutions, Inc.
12657 Alcosta Blvd # 200
San Ramon CA 94583
925 949-5100

(P-19702)
AMERIT FLEET SOLUTIONS INC
1331 N Calif Blvd Ste 150, Walnut Creek (94596-4535)
PHONE..................................877 512-6374
Dan Williams, *CEO*
Amein Punjani, *COO*
Matt Lavay, *CFO*
Bob Brauer, *Risk Mgmt Dir*
EMP: 200 EST: 2010
SALES (est): 5.8MM **Privately Held**
WEB: www.ameritfleetsolutions.com
SIC: 8744 Base maintenance (providing personnel on continuing basis)

(P-19703)
JLS ENVIRONMENTAL SERVICES INC
3460 Swetzer Rd, Loomis (95650-7624)
PHONE..................................916 660-1525
John Sheehan, *President*
Larry Walker, *President*
John G Sheehan, *CEO*
David Locke, *CFO*
Shane Lesher, *General Mgr*
EMP: 86 EST: 2002
SALES (est): 10.6MM **Privately Held**
WEB: www.jlsinc.com
SIC: 8744 8999 ; earth science services

(P-19704)
LINDEN UNIFIED SCHOOL DISTRICT
100 N Jack Tone Rd, Stockton (95215-9575)
PHONE..................................209 946-0707
Dr Ronald Estes, *Administration*
Dena Acuna, *Teacher*
Sara Alonso, *Teacher*
Jennifer Burkland, *Teacher*
Rob Chase, *Teacher*
EMP: 98
SALES (corp-wide): 27.1MM **Privately Held**
WEB: www.lindenusd.com
SIC: 8211 8744 Public elementary & secondary schools; base maintenance (providing personnel on continuing basis)
PA: Linden Unified School District
18527 E Highway 26
Linden CA 95236
209 887-3894

(P-19705)
NUGATE GROUP LLC (PA)
619 N 1st St, San Jose (95112-5110)
PHONE..................................408 278-9911
Jamila Stanford,
Oscar Estrada, *Opers Staff*
EMP: 244 EST: 2007 **Privately Held**
WEB: www.nugategroup.com
SIC: 8744 7349 Base maintenance (providing personnel on continuing basis); building maintenance services; building & office cleaning services; hospital housekeeping; janitorial service, contract basis

(P-19706)
SMG
Also Called: Smg Stockton
3445 S El Dorado St, Stockton (95206)
PHONE..................................209 937-7433
Kandra Clark, *General Mgr*
EMP: 400 EST: 2010
SQ FT: 25,000
SALES (est): 21MM
SALES (corp-wide): 1.1B **Privately Held**
WEB: www.stocktonlive.com
SIC: 8744 Facilities support services
HQ: Smg Holdings, Llc
300 Cnshohckn State Rd # 450
Conshohocken PA 19428

(P-19707)
ZERO WASTE SOLUTIONS INC
1850 Gateway Blvd # 1030, Concord (94520-3279)
P.O. Box 5097 (94524-0097)
PHONE..................................925 270-3339
Shavila Singh, *President*
Crystel Castillo, *Opers Mgr*
Lonnie Mt-Home, *Manager*
EMP: 200 EST: 2002
SQ FT: 3,000
SALES (est): 19.4MM **Privately Held**
WEB: www.zerowastesolutions.com
SIC: 8744 Facilities support services

8748 Business Consulting Svcs, NEC

(P-19708)
3DEGREES GROUP INC (PA)
235 Montgomery St Ste 320, San Francisco (94104-3121)
PHONE..................................415 561-6852
Dan Kalafatas, *Chairman*
Stasia Brownell, *Partner*
Steve McDougal, *CEO*
Sumit Kapur,
Adam Capage, *Vice Pres*
EMP: 40 EST: 2007
SALES (est): 24.6MM **Privately Held**
WEB: www.3degreesinc.com
SIC: 8748 6799 Environmental consultant; investors

(P-19709)
AC SQUARE INC
4590 Qantas Ln, Stockton (95206-3903)
PHONE..................................650 293-2730
EMP: 239
SALES (corp-wide): 43.7MM **Privately Held**
SIC: 8748 Business Consulting, Nec, Nsk
PA: Ac Square, Inc.
371 Foster City Blvd
Foster City CA 94404
650 293-2730

(P-19710)
ACC-GWG LLC
Also Called: American Commodity Co.
6133 Abel Rd, Williams (95987-5816)
P.O. Box 236 (95987-0236)
PHONE..................................530 473-2827
Chris Crutchfield, *President*
Bob Watts, *Vice Pres*
Nicole Montna Van Vleck, *Admin Sec*
Paul Crutchfield,
Al Montna,
EMP: 60 EST: 2005
SALES (est): 10.4MM **Privately Held**
WEB: www.accrice.com
SIC: 8748 Agricultural consultant

(P-19711)
ACRT PACIFIC LLC
3443 Deer Park Dr Ste B, Stockton (95219-2306)
PHONE..................................330 945-7500
Brad S Schroeder,
Alan Rothenbuecher,
EMP: 450 EST: 2017
SALES (est): 50MM **Privately Held**
SIC: 8748 Business consulting

(P-19712)
ACTELIS NETWORKS INC (PA)
Also Called: Actelis USA
47800 Westinghouse Dr, Fremont (94539-7469)
PHONE..................................510 545-1045
T Barlev, *Founder*
Stephen Cordial, *COO*
Tuvia Barlev, *Founder*
AVI Moyal, *Senior VP*
Bruce Hammergren, *Vice Pres*
EMP: 143 EST: 1998
SALES (est): 20.7MM **Privately Held**
WEB: www.actelis.com
SIC: 8748 Telecommunications consultant

(P-19713)
ADDFORCE INC (PA)
1470 Civic Ct Ste 309, Concord (94520-5230)
PHONE..................................415 738-6469
Elena Florova, *Vice Pres*
EMP: 43 EST: 2006
SALES (est): 312.2K **Privately Held**
WEB: www.addforce.com
SIC: 8748 8742 Business consulting; construction project management consultant; business consultant; sales (including sales management) consultant

(P-19714)
ADVISORYCLOUD INC
7 Hamilton Landing # 100, Novato (94949-8209)
PHONE..................................415 289-7115
John Thompson, *Managing Prtnr*
Debra Shumar, *Executive*
Elicia Bansuelo, *Analyst*
Rallie Black, *Analyst*
Lisa Brayer, *Analyst*
EMP: 156 EST: 2018
SALES (est): 9.1MM **Privately Held**
WEB: www.advisorycloud.com
SIC: 8748 Business consulting

PRODUCTS & SERVICES SECTION
8748 - Business Consulting Svcs, NEC County (P-19739)

(P-19715)
AECOM USA INC
100 W San Fernando St, San Jose (95113-2219)
PHONE..................408 392-0670
EMP: 104
SALES (corp-wide): 17.4B Publicly Held
SIC: 8748 Business Consulting Services
HQ: Aecom Usa, Inc.
605 3rd Ave
New York NY 10158
212 973-2900

(P-19716)
ALL ENVIRONMENTAL INC (PA)
Also Called: Aei Consultants
2500 Camino Diablo, Walnut Creek (94597-3998)
PHONE..................925 746-6000
Craig Hertz, CEO
Holly Neber, President
Peter F Millar, Exec VP
Kathleen Baxter, Vice Pres
Paul Hinkston, Vice Pres
EMP: 45 EST: 1992
SQ FT: 1,200
SALES (est): 28.5MM Privately Held
WEB: www.aeiconsultants.com
SIC: 8748 Environmental consultant

(P-19717)
ALLIANCES MGT CONSULTING INC
544 Hillside Rd, Redwood City (94062-3345)
PHONE..................650 780-0466
Charles Anthony Aspinall, CEO
EMP: 50 EST: 2012
SALES (est): 2.5MM Privately Held
WEB: www.am.consulting
SIC: 8748 Business consulting

(P-19718)
ALMENDARIZ CONSULTING INC
1136 Suncast Ln Ste 9, El Dorado Hills (95762-9311)
PHONE..................916 939-3392
Mateo Almendariz, President
Matt Mateo Almendariz, President
Kirk Ridgley, Vice Pres
EMP: 40 EST: 2011
SQ FT: 3,000
SALES (est): 2.7MM Privately Held
WEB: www.almendarizconsulting.com
SIC: 8748 7389 Traffic consultant; flagging service (traffic control)

(P-19719)
AMERICAN INFRASTRUCTURE MLP FU
950 Tower Ln Ste 800, Foster City (94404-2191)
PHONE..................650 854-6000
George McCown, Partner
Judy Bornstein, CFO
Anita Amershi, Vice Pres
Paul Gurm, Vice Pres
Tina Eagle, Executive Asst
EMP: 46 EST: 2007
SALES (est): 4.9MM Privately Held
WEB: www.aimlp.com
SIC: 8748 Business consulting

(P-19720)
AMTEL INC
950 S Bascom Ave Ste 2002, San Jose (95128-3538)
PHONE..................408 615-0522
Pankaj Gupta, CEO
Chet Jackson, President
EMP: 50 EST: 2001
SALES (est): 9.9MM Privately Held
WEB: www.amtelnet.com
SIC: 8748 7371 Telecommunications consultant; computer software development
HQ: Netplus Buyer, Inc.
9707 Key West Ave Ste 202
Rockville MD 20850
800 989-5566

(P-19721)
APX INC (PA)
2150 N 1st St Ste 200, San Jose (95131-2020)
PHONE..................408 517-2100
Joseph Varnas, CEO
Hung Chau, Software Dev
Elena Shulepov, Software Dev
Kent Liang, Finance
Adam Barrett, Manager
EMP: 41 EST: 1996
SALES (est): 14.6MM Privately Held
WEB: www.apx.com
SIC: 8748 Energy conservation consultant

(P-19722)
ASSOCTED LRNG LNGAGE SPCILIST (PA)
1060 Twin Dolphin Dr # 1, Redwood City (94065-1133)
P.O. Box 1389, San Carlos (94070-7389)
PHONE..................650 631-9999
Pamela Joy, Director
Liz Field, Director
EMP: 46 EST: 1982
SQ FT: 9,400
SALES (est): 3MM Privately Held
WEB: www.allsinc.com
SIC: 8748 8049 Educational consultant; speech pathologist

(P-19723)
ATLAS TECHNICAL CONS LLC
Also Called: Consolidated Engineering Labs
2001 Crow Canyon Rd # 110, San Ramon (94583-5368)
PHONE..................925 314-7100
L Boyer, Branch Mgr
EMP: 350
SALES (corp-wide): 533.8MM Privately Held
WEB: www.oneatlas.com
SIC: 8748 Testing services
PA: Atlas Technical Consultants Llc
13215 Bee Cave Pkwy B230
Austin TX 78738
866 858-4499

(P-19724)
AVA THE RABBIT HAVEN INC
Also Called: RABBIT HAVEN THE
1261 S Mary St, Scotts Valley (95067)
P.O. Box 66594 (95067-6594)
PHONE..................831 600-7479
Heather Bechtel, Director
Richard Jacobel, President
EMP: 80 EST: 2010
SALES: 90.3K Privately Held
WEB: www.therabbithaven.org
SIC: 8748 Testing service, educational or personnel

(P-19725)
AXIOM GLOBAL TECHNOLOGIES INC
220 N Wiget Ln, Walnut Creek (94598-2404)
PHONE..................925 393-5800
Mohit Sishu Arora, CEO
Priya Arora, Ch of Bd
Raj Singh, Vice Pres
Vikas Gupta, Executive
Sean Innerst, Project Mgr
EMP: 125 EST: 2001
SALES (est): 10.2MM Privately Held
WEB: www.axiomglobal.com
SIC: 8748 Business consulting

(P-19726)
BARGAS ENVMTL CONSULTING LLC
3604 Fair Oaks Blvd # 180, Sacramento (95864-7256)
PHONE..................916 993-9218
Angela Depaoli,
David Carr, Project Mgr
James Stewart, Sr Consultant
Maggie Snelgrove, Assistant
EMP: 50 EST: 2012
SALES (est): 6.7MM Privately Held
WEB: www.bargasconsulting.com
SIC: 8748 8711 Environmental consultant; engineering services

(P-19727)
BAY AREA AIR QUALITY (PA)
375 Beale St Ste 600, San Francisco (94105-2097)
P.O. Box 420434 (94142-0434)
PHONE..................415 749-4900
Jack Broadbent, CEO
Andrea Academia, Officer
Ralph Borrmann, Officer
Tina McRee, Vice Pres
Vanessa Johnson, Executive
EMP: 250 EST: 1955
SQ FT: 101,000
SALES (est): 60.1MM Privately Held
WEB: www.baaqmd.gov
SIC: 8748 Environmental consultant

(P-19728)
BEHAVRAL EDCTL STRTGIES TRNING
Also Called: Behavrl/Dctnal Strtgs/Training
2630 W Rumble Rd, Modesto (95350-0155)
PHONE..................209 579-9444
Sally Grevemberg, President
Jonathan Bryant, Supervisor
EMP: 42 EST: 2007
SALES (est): 2.6MM Privately Held
WEB: www.bestforautism.com
SIC: 8748 Educational consultant

(P-19729)
BEST CONSULTING INC
8795 Folsom Blvd Ste 103, Sacramento (95826-3720)
PHONE..................916 448-2050
Sergio E Pinto, President
Danielle Nuzum, COO
Jaclyn Shandy-Pinto, Vice Pres
Sergio Pinto, Principal
EMP: 50 EST: 2003
SALES (est): 2.7MM Privately Held
WEB: www.bestconsultinginc.com
SIC: 8748 Educational consultant

(P-19730)
BIDDLE CONSULTING GROUP INC
Also Called: Criticall
193 Blue Ravine Rd # 270, Folsom (95630-4756)
PHONE..................916 294-4250
Daniel Biddle, President
Patrick Nooren, Exec VP
Dan Kuang, Vice Pres
Daniel Kuang, Vice Pres
Nick Brown, Executive
EMP: 50 EST: 2000
SQ FT: 4,000
SALES (est): 10.7MM Privately Held
WEB: www.biddle.com
SIC: 5734 8748 Computer software & accessories; business consulting

(P-19731)
BIOLA FRESH INC
5887 N Sycamore Ave, Fresno (93723-8111)
PHONE..................559 970-8881
Sandra Olds, CEO
EMP: 60 EST: 2018
SALES (est): 2.5MM Privately Held
SIC: 8748 Agricultural consultant

(P-19732)
BIOMAAS INC
1278 Indiana St Unit 300, San Francisco (94107-7436)
PHONE..................415 255-8077
Hillary Hodge, Principal
Steve Powell, Principal
Cullen Wilkerson, Principal
EMP: 35 EST: 2006
SALES (est): 2.9MM Privately Held
WEB: www.biomaas.com
SIC: 8748 Environmental consultant

(P-19733)
BOOST HALTHCARE CONSULTING LLC
1320 Harbor Bay Pkwy # 220, Alameda (94502-6578)
PHONE..................415 377-7589
Liana Hamilton, President
Liana Hans, Principal
Nelie Sithong, Sr Consultant
Hannah Gannon, Associate
Johnathon Tuttle, Associate
EMP: 40 EST: 2013
SALES (est): 3MM Privately Held
WEB: www.boosthealthcare.com
SIC: 8748 Business consulting

(P-19734)
BPO SYSTEMS INC (PA)
1700 Ygnacio Valley Rd # 205, Walnut Creek (94598-3191)
PHONE..................925 478-4299
Rambabu Yarlagadda, CEO
Rambabu V Yarlagadda, CEO
EMP: 38 EST: 2000
SQ FT: 4,000
SALES (est): 3.8MM Privately Held
WEB: www.bposystems.com
SIC: 8748 Systems analysis or design

(P-19735)
BROCADE CMMNCTIONS SYSTEMS INC
110 Holger Way, San Jose (95134-1376)
PHONE..................408 333-4300
EMP: 71
SALES (corp-wide): 13.2B Privately Held
SIC: 8748 Business Consulting Services
HQ: Brocade Communications Systems Llc
130 Holger Way
San Jose CA 95131

(P-19736)
BUXTON CONSULTING
2010 Crow Canyon Pl # 100, San Ramon (94583-1344)
PHONE..................925 467-0700
James T Buxton, President
Chandra Reddy, Vice Pres
Arno Fritz, Human Resources
EMP: 90 EST: 1981
SALES (est): 10.8MM Privately Held
WEB: www.buxtonconsulting.com
SIC: 8748 Systems engineering consultant, ex. computer or professional

(P-19737)
CALIFORNIA DEPARTMENT TRNSP
Also Called: Caltrans District 1
1656 Union St, Eureka (95501-2229)
P.O. Box 3700 (95502-3700)
PHONE..................707 445-6600
Charlie Fielder, Director
David Tompkins, Info Tech Mgr
Tim Day, IT/INT Sup
Jose Moreno, Graphic Designe
Wayne Smith, Engineer
EMP: 43 Privately Held
WEB: www.dot.ca.gov
SIC: 8748 4789 9621 Business consulting; railroad maintenance & repair services;
HQ: California, Department Of Transportation
1120 N St
Sacramento CA 95814

(P-19738)
CAMBRIA SOLUTIONS INC (PA)
731 K St Ste 300, Sacramento (95814-3416)
PHONE..................916 326-4446
Robert J Rodriguez, President
Suzanne Vitale, President
Anand Adoni, Vice Pres
Henk Keukenkamp, Executive
Kristen Dronberger, Executive Asst
EMP: 105 EST: 2003 Privately Held
WEB: www.cambriasolutions.com
SIC: 8748 8742 Systems analysis & engineering consulting services; management consulting services

(P-19739)
CARDNO CHEMRISK LLC (DH)
235 Pine St Ste 2300, San Francisco (94104-2700)
PHONE..................415 896-2400
Mark Swatek, Manager
Mark Garavaglia, CFO
Dennis J Paustenbach,
David Blakenhorn, Manager
Brent Finley, Manager
EMP: 93 EST: 2009

8748 - Business Consulting Svcs, NEC County (P-19740)

SALES (est): 8.7MM **Privately Held**
WEB: www.cardnochemrisk.com
SIC: **8748** Environmental consultant
HQ: Cardno, Inc.
  8310 S Valley Hwy Ste 300
  Englewood CO 80112
  720 257-5800

(P-19740)
CAVISSON SYSTEMS INC
5201 Great America Pkwy, Santa Clara (95054-1122)
PHONE.....................................800 701-6125
Anil Kumar, *President*
Neeraj Jain, *Vice Pres*
Neil Pande, *Associate Dir*
Richa Garg, *Software Dev*
Kunal Sharma, *Software Engr*
EMP: 500
SQ FT: 10,000
SALES (est): 20MM **Privately Held**
WEB: www.cavisson.com
SIC: **8748** Systems analysis & engineering consulting services

(P-19741)
CBA SITE SERVICES INC
11387 Pyrites Way, Rancho Cordova (95670-4595)
PHONE.....................................925 754-7633
Michael McWhirter, *President*
David Cyr, *Controller*
Toccara Shepherd,
Mary McGee, *Manager*
Kc Shackelford, *Manager*
EMP: 62 EST: 1980
SQ FT: 70,000
SALES (est): 20.2MM **Privately Held**
WEB: www.legacy-wireless.com
SIC: **8748** Telecommunications consultant

(P-19742)
CETECOM INC
411 Dixon Landing Rd, Milpitas (95035-2579)
PHONE.....................................408 586-6200
Maan Ghanma, *CEO*
Willfried Klassmann, *President*
Heiko Strehlow, *COO*
Clorinda Sammis, *Treasurer*
Praveena Anandkumar, *Administration*
EMP: 110 EST: 1998
SQ FT: 48,000
SALES (est): 24.9MM
SALES (corp-wide): 300.2MM **Privately Held**
WEB: www.cetecom.com
SIC: **8748** **8734** Telecommunications consultant; testing laboratories
HQ: Cetecom Gmbh
  Im Teelbruch 116
  Essen NW 45219
  205 495-190

(P-19743)
CITY OF PLEASANTON
Also Called: Livermore Pleasanton Fire Dept
3560 Nevada St, Pleasanton (94566-6267)
PHONE.....................................925 454-2341
Bill Cody, *Superintendent*
James Miguel, *Top Exec*
Deborah Espinoza, *IT/INT Sup*
Steven Martin, *Opers Spvr*
Jason Solak, *Chief*
EMP: 129
SALES (corp-wide): 142.6MM **Privately Held**
WEB: www.covid19.cityofpleasantonca.gov
SIC: **9224** **8748** ; business consulting
PA: City Of Pleasanton
  123 Main St
  Pleasanton CA 94566
  925 931-5002

(P-19744)
CLEAN HARBORS ENVMTL SVCS INC
4101 Industrial Way, Benicia (94510-1211)
PHONE.....................................707 747-6699
Kevin Carnahan, *President*
Brian P Tobin, *Branch Mgr*
Taylor Foy, *Administration*
Monica M Williams, *Administration*
Michael Clark, *Manager*
EMP: 100
SALES (corp-wide): 3.1B **Publicly Held**
WEB: www.cleanharbors.com
SIC: **8748** Environmental consultant
HQ: Clean Harbors Environmental Services, Inc.
  42 Longwater Dr
  Norwell MA 02061
  781 792-5000

(P-19745)
COBEAL
1941 Park Oak Dr, Roseville (95661-4056)
PHONE.....................................916 622-7330
Sophy Laughing, *CEO*
Erik Gustav Hollsten, *President*
EMP: 50 EST: 2020
SALES (est): 31.1K **Privately Held**
SIC: **8748** Business consulting

(P-19746)
COHEN VENTURES INC (PA)
Also Called: Energy Solutions
449 15th St 400, Oakland (94612-2821)
PHONE.....................................510 482-4420
Samuel D Cohen, *President*
Chris Burmester, *Vice Pres*
Kevin Cornish, *Vice Pres*
Mike Laffey, *Vice Pres*
Ted Pope, *Vice Pres*
EMP: 74 EST: 1995
SQ FT: 11,000
SALES (est): 13.5MM **Privately Held**
WEB: www.energy-solution.com
SIC: **8748** Energy conservation consultant

(P-19747)
COMMUNITY COLLEGE FOUNDATION (PA)
1901 Royal Oaks Dr # 100, Sacramento (95815-4235)
PHONE.....................................916 418-5100
Richard Fowler, *President*
Kirk Turner, *CFO*
Beck Edwards, *Principal*
Gordon Dorff, *CIO*
Kathy Lee, *HR Admin*
EMP: 75 EST: 1983
SALES: 4.5MM **Privately Held**
WEB: www.communitycollege.org
SIC: **8299** **8748** Educational services; business consulting

(P-19748)
COMMUNITY HSING IMPRV PRGRAM I (PA)
1001 Willow St, Chico (95928-5958)
PHONE.....................................530 891-6931
Seana O'Shaughnessy, *President*
James W Jessee, *President*
Tom Simenc, *Treasurer*
Steve Troester, *Vice Pres*
David Ferrier, *Exec Dir*
EMP: 44
SQ FT: 6,000
SALES (est): 7.4MM **Privately Held**
WEB: www.chiphousing.org
SIC: **8748** Urban planning & consulting services

(P-19749)
CONCENTRIC POWER INC
1550 Dell Ave Ste I, Campbell (95008-6912)
PHONE.....................................888 321-0620
Brian Curtis, *CEO*
Chad Forrest, *CFO*
Theresa Armstrong, *Office Mgr*
Theresa Olson Van Eeghe, *Office Mgr*
Jamey Wyman, *General Counsel*
EMP: 55 EST: 2013
SALES (est): 5.2MM **Privately Held**
WEB: www.concentricpower.com
SIC: **8748** Energy conservation consultant

(P-19750)
CONDOR EARTH TECHNOLOGIES INC
188 Frank West Cir Ste I, Stockton (95206-4010)
PHONE.....................................209 388-9601
Alex Dewitt, *Vice Pres*
Rebecca Selvage, *General Mgr*
Ron Skaggs, *Sales Executive*
Micheline Kipf, *Manager*
John Lane, *Manager*
EMP: 45
SALES (corp-wide): 17.1MM **Privately Held**
WEB: www.condorearth.com
SIC: **8748** Environmental consultant
PA: Condor Earth Technologies, Inc.
  21663 Brian Ln
  Sonora CA 95370
  209 532-0361

(P-19751)
CONTROLLER CONSULTING SVCS INC
1577 Aldacourrou St, Tracy (95304-5872)
PHONE.....................................408 221-2492
Eric Fan, *President*
EMP: 150 EST: 2007
SALES (est): 5.4MM **Privately Held**
WEB: www.controllerconsulting.com
SIC: **8748** Business consulting

(P-19752)
CORNERSTONE CNSULTING TECH INC
241 5th St, San Francisco (94103-4102)
PHONE.....................................415 705-7800
Wayne Perry, *CEO*
Charles Jones, *Officer*
Ming Ng, *General Mgr*
EMP: 38 EST: 1987
SQ FT: 1,400
SALES (est): 1MM **Privately Held**
WEB: www.cornerstoneconcilium.com
SIC: **8748** **8742** **7379** Educational consultant; management consulting services; computer related consulting services

(P-19753)
CORNERSTONE RESEARCH INC
353 Sacramento St Ste 19, San Francisco (94111-3620)
PHONE.....................................617 927-3000
John Jankowski, *Branch Mgr*
Michael Lindh, *Senior Mgr*
Laura Londa, *Director*
Russ Molter, *Manager*
EMP: 45
SALES (corp-wide): 84MM **Privately Held**
WEB: www.cornerstone.com
SIC: **8748** Economic consultant
PA: Cornerstone Research, Inc.
  1000 El Camino Real # 250
  Menlo Park CA 94025
  650 853-1660

(P-19754)
CORNERSTONE RESEARCH INC (PA)
1000 El Camino Real # 250, Menlo Park (94025-4315)
PHONE.....................................650 853-1660
Cynthia Zollinger, *Chairman*
Michael E Burton, *President*
Susan M Wittner, *Chief Mktg Ofcr*
Alexander Aganin, *Senior VP*
Catherine Galley, *Senior VP*
EMP: 100 EST: 1989
SQ FT: 40,000
SALES (est): 84MM **Privately Held**
WEB: www.cornerstone.com
SIC: **8748** **7389** Economic consultant; financial services

(P-19755)
CORNERSTONE RESEARCH INC
2 Embarcadero Ctr Fl 20, San Francisco (94111-3922)
PHONE.....................................415 229-8100
Cynthia Zollinger, *CEO*
Gregory L Negus, *COO*
Abe Chernin, *Vice Pres*
Greg Leonard, *Vice Pres*
Robert Majure, *Vice Pres*
EMP: 52
SALES (corp-wide): 84MM **Privately Held**
WEB: www.cornerstone.com
SIC: **8748** Economic consultant
PA: Cornerstone Research, Inc.
  1000 El Camino Real # 250
  Menlo Park CA 94025
  650 853-1660

(P-19756)
CVE CONTRACTING GROUP INC
Also Called: Central Valley Environmental
4263 N Selland Ave, Fresno (93722-7803)
PHONE.....................................559 222-1122
Tim Williamson, *President*
Dustin Drake, *Vice Pres*
Greg Paul, *Manager*
EMP: 45 EST: 2011
SALES (est): 2MM **Privately Held**
WEB: www.cvecorp.com
SIC: **8748** Environmental consultant

(P-19757)
CVE NB CONTRACTING GROUP INC
Also Called: Central Valley Environmental
135 Utility Ct A, Rohnert Park (94928-1616)
PHONE.....................................707 584-1900
Tim Williamson, *CEO*
Glenn Accornero, *COO*
EMP: 42 EST: 2015
SQ FT: 4,700
SALES (est): 5.5MM **Privately Held**
WEB: www.cvecorp.com
SIC: **8748** Environmental consultant

(P-19758)
CWES INC
Also Called: Califrnia Workforce Enrgy Svcs
3055 N Sunnyside Ave # 101, Fresno (93727-1343)
PHONE.....................................559 346-1251
Michael Williams, *President*
EMP: 32
SALES (est): 2.7MM **Privately Held**
WEB: www.princeofpalletees.com
SIC: **8748** **1389** **1521** Business consulting; construction, repair & dismantling services; new construction, single-family houses

(P-19759)
D2M INC
Also Called: D2m Trading Limited
935 Benecia Ave, Sunnyvale (94085-2805)
PHONE.....................................650 567-9995
Andrew Butler, *President*
Matt Vargas, *Engineer*
Qian LI, *Controller*
Hugues Gervaise, *Opers Mgr*
John Tompain,
▼ EMP: 38 EST: 1994
SQ FT: 3,000
SALES (est): 2.5MM **Privately Held**
WEB: www.d2m-inc.com
SIC: **8748** Business consulting

(P-19760)
DESIGN COMMUNITY & ENVMT INC (PA)
1625 Shattuck Ave Ste 300, Berkeley (94709-16E7)
PHONE.....................................510 848-3815
David Early, *President*
Nancy Graham, *COO*
EMP: 52 EST: 1995
SALES (est): 5MM **Privately Held**
WEB: www.placeworks.com
SIC: **8748** City planning

(P-19761)
DETECON INC
33 New Montgomery St # 2000, San Francisco (94105-4532)
PHONE.....................................415 549-6999
Daniel Kellmereit, *President*
Jochen Dinger, *Managing Prtnr*
Carsten Glohr, *Managing Prtnr*
Steffen Kuhn, *Managing Prtnr*
Steffen Roos, *Managing Prtnr*
EMP: 35 EST: 2008
SALES (est): 5.8MM
SALES (corp-wide): 119.4B **Privately Held**
WEB: www.detecon.com
SIC: **8748** Telecommunications consultant
HQ: Detecon International Gmbh
  Sternengasse 14-16
  Koln NW 50676
  221 916-10

▲ = Import ▼=Export
◆ =Import/Export

8748 - Business Consulting Svcs, NEC County (P-19784)

(P-19762)
DRISHTICON INC (PA)
39899 Balentine Dr # 200, Newark (94560-5361)
PHONE.................510 402-4515
Manoj Vidyarthi, *CEO*
Suraksha Vidyarthi, *Vice Pres*
Senthil Murugesan, *Project Mgr*
EMP: 49 **EST:** 2006
SALES (est): 6.4MM **Privately Held**
WEB: www.drishticon.com
SIC: 8748 7373 7371 Systems engineering consultant, ex. computer or professional; systems software development services; computer software development & applications; computer software development

(P-19763)
DUCTTESTERS INC
336 W Main St, Ripon (95366-2424)
P.O. Box 266 (95366-0266)
PHONE.................209 579-5000
Dave Hegarty, *President*
Shelby Pettus, *Administration*
Richard Swingle, *IT/INT Sup*
Tony Souza, *Manager*
Don Hegarty, *Consultant*
EMP: 38 **EST:** 2007
SALES (est): 6MM **Privately Held**
WEB: www.ducttesters.com
SIC: 8748 Testing services

(P-19764)
ECO BAY SERVICES INC
1501 Minnesota St, San Francisco (94107-3521)
PHONE.................415 643-7777
Trent Scott Michels, *CEO*
Padraic Ryan, *Vice Pres*
Mike Bellamy, *Division Mgr*
Saul Bravo, *Opers Staff*
Chris Davini, *Manager*
EMP: 150 **EST:** 2007
SQ FT: 80,000
SALES (est): 51.1MM **Privately Held**
WEB: www.ecobayservices.com
SIC: 8748 Environmental consultant

(P-19765)
END TO END ANALYTICS LLC
2595 E Byshore Rd Ste 150, Palo Alto (94303)
PHONE.................650 331-9659
Robert Hall,
Gianpaolo Callioni,
Allan Gray,
Russell Halper,
Colin Kessinger,
EMP: 60 **EST:** 2005
SQ FT: 3,200
SALES (est): 20MM **Privately Held**
WEB: www.e2eanalytics.com
SIC: 8748 Systems analysis & engineering consulting services
HQ: Accenture Inc.
161 N Clark St Ste 1100
Chicago IL 60601
312 693-0161

(P-19766)
ENOVITY INC
11180 Sun Center Dr, Rancho Cordova (95670-6167)
PHONE.................916 853-1718
Gregory Cunningham, *President*
Zhan Wang, *Technical Mgr*
Tim Huang, *Project Mgr*
Mark Johnson, *Project Mgr*
Dan Morelock, *Technical Staff*
EMP: 48
SALES (corp-wide): 622.8MM **Privately Held**
WEB: www.enovity.com
SIC: 8748 5211 8742 Energy conservation consultant; energy conservation products; automation & robotics consultant
HQ: Enovity, Inc.
100 Montgomery St Ste 600
San Francisco CA 94104
415 974-0390

(P-19767)
ENTERPRISE SOLUTIONS INC
2855 Kifer Rd, Santa Clara (95051-0814)
PHONE.................408 727-3637
Lucy Phang, *CFO*
Joshua Rosenthal, *VP Bus Dvlpt*
Vaibhav Chaudhary, *IT/INT Sup*
Atiya Subhani, *IT/INT Sup*
Amit Dubey, *Tech Recruiter*
EMP: 344 **Privately Held**
WEB: www.enterprisesolutioninc.com
SIC: 8748 Systems engineering consultant, ex. computer or professional
PA: Enterprise Solutions, Inc.
500 E Diehl Rd Ste 130
Naperville IL 60563

(P-19768)
ENVIRONMENTAL INCENTIVES LLC (PA)
3351 Lake Tahoe Blvd # 2, South Lake Tahoe (96150-7977)
PHONE.................530 541-2980
Jeremy Sokulsky, *CEO*
Chad Praul, *COO*
Ellen Christen, *Executive Asst*
Cameryn Brock, *Research*
Molly Armanino, *Opers Staff*
EMP: 97 **EST:** 2006
SQ FT: 1,500
SALES (est): 6.2MM **Privately Held**
WEB: www.enviroincentives.com
SIC: 8748 Environmental consultant

(P-19769)
ENVIRONMENTAL SCIENCE ASSOC
Also Called: ESA
2600 Capitol Ave Ste 200, Sacramento (95816-5929)
PHONE.................916 564-4500
Steve Alverson, *Branch Mgr*
Catherine Leblanc, *Sr Associate*
Matt Morales, *Manager*
EMP: 40
SALES (corp-wide): 80K **Privately Held**
WEB: www.esassoc.com
SIC: 8748 Environmental consultant
PA: Environmental Science Associates
550 Kearny St Ste 800
San Francisco CA 94108
415 896-5900

(P-19770)
ESTRADA CONSULTING INC
1221 18th St, Sacramento (95811-4112)
PHONE.................916 473-7493
Rafael Estrada, *President*
Mark McDonell, *Vice Pres*
Rajesh Durai, *Software Dev*
Venkat Gujapaneni, *Software Dev*
Summer Shan, *Marketing Staff*
EMP: 42 **EST:** 2000
SALES (est): 3MM **Privately Held**
WEB: www.estradaci.com
SIC: 8748 Business consulting

(P-19771)
ETIC (PA)
2285 Morello Ave, Pleasant Hill (94523-1850)
PHONE.................925 602-4710
Christa Marting, *President*
Alan Anselmo, *COO*
James Norwood, *CFO*
Karthika Thurairajah, *Program Mgr*
Lance Beezley, *Technician*
EMP: 45 **EST:** 1991
SQ FT: 12,000
SALES (est): 28MM **Privately Held**
WEB: www.eticeng.com
SIC: 8748 8711 Environmental consultant; consulting engineer

(P-19772)
F R O INC
2003 1st St Ste 100, Selma (93662-3519)
PHONE.................559 891-0237
Oscar F Ramos, *President*
Jose Lemus, *Manager*
EMP: 20 **EST:** 2000
SQ FT: 1,500
SALES (est): 1.2MM **Privately Held**
SIC: 8748 3315 Agricultural consultant; steel wire & related products

(P-19773)
FAMILY AND CHILDREN SERVICES
950 W Julian St, San Jose (95126-2719)
PHONE.................408 292-9353
Diana Nemen, *CEO*
Lauren Grey, *Exec Dir*
Cristina Trujillo, *Admin Asst*
Julie Daul, *Director*
Howard Lagoze, *Director*
EMP: 36 **EST:** 1948
SQ FT: 9,500
SALES (est): 1.4MM **Privately Held**
WEB: www.fcservices.org
SIC: 8748 Business consulting

(P-19774)
FAR WSTERN ANTHRPLGCAL RES GRO (PA)
2727 Del Rio Pl Ste A, Davis (95618-7729)
PHONE.................530 756-3941
William Hildebrandt, *President*
Kelly McGuire, *CFO*
Kim Carpenter, *Vice Pres*
Jeff Rosenthal, *Vice Pres*
D Craig Young Jr, *Vice Pres*
EMP: 37 **EST:** 1979
SQ FT: 2,000
SALES (est): 8.5MM **Privately Held**
WEB: www.farwestern.com
SIC: 8748 Environmental consultant

(P-19775)
FIRST STEP HOUSING
Also Called: First Step Communities
139 Blakeslee Way, Folsom (95630-4629)
PHONE.................916 769-8877
Stephen Watters, *CEO*
EMP: 77 **EST:** 2015
SALES (est): 331.3K **Privately Held**
SIC: 8748 Urban planning & consulting services

(P-19776)
FISHBIO ENVIRONMENTAL LLC (PA)
1617 S Yosemite Ave, Oakdale (95361-9387)
PHONE.................209 847-6300
Doug Demko, *Mng Member*
Erin Loury, *Comms Dir*
Andrea Fuller,
EMP: 35 **EST:** 2006
SQ FT: 20,000
SALES (est): 3.5MM **Privately Held**
WEB: www.fishbio.com
SIC: 8748 Environmental consultant

(P-19777)
FORGEN LLC (PA)
6558 Lonetree Blvd, Rocklin (95765-5874)
PHONE.................916 462-6400
Chris Shea, *Mng Member*
Bruce Diettert, *CFO*
Matt Marks, *Senior VP*
Kevin Corradino, *VP Bus Dvlpt*
Jodi Rufino, *Admin Asst*
EMP: 63 **EST:** 2009
SQ FT: 7,310
SALES (est): 104.5MM **Privately Held**
WEB: www.forgen.com
SIC: 8748 1629 Environmental consultant; earthmoving contractor

(P-19778)
FRANCSCO PRTNERS III CAYMAN LP
1 Letterman Dr Bldg C, San Francisco (94129-2402)
PHONE.................415 418-2900
Dipanjan Deb, *CEO*
Chris Adams, *Partner*
Jason Brein, *Partner*
Lyndon Cantor, *Partner*
Peter Christodoulo, *Partner*
EMP: 64 **EST:** 2016
SALES (est): 3.1MM **Privately Held**
WEB: www.franciscopartners.com
SIC: 8748 Business consulting

(P-19779)
FREMOUW ENVIRONMENTAL SVCS INC
6940 Tremont Rd, Dixon (95620-9603)
PHONE.................707 448-3700
Ted Fremouw, *CEO*
Nancy Fremouw, *CFO*
Phillip A Fremouw, *Vice Pres*
Stu E Jordan, *Vice Pres*
Marty Mosley, *Vice Pres*
EMP: 60 **EST:** 1996
SQ FT: 4,000
SALES (est): 12.9MM **Privately Held**
WEB: www.fremouwenvironmental.com
SIC: 8748 4212 Environmental consultant; hazardous waste transport

(P-19780)
FTI CONSULTING INC
50 California St Ste 1900, San Francisco (94111-4620)
PHONE.................415 283-4200
Jerry Keeler, *Manager*
John Cartoux, *Managing Dir*
Robert Clover, *Managing Dir*
Glen Greenland, *Managing Dir*
Alok Khare, *Managing Dir*
EMP: 80
SALES (corp-wide): 2.4B **Publicly Held**
WEB: www.fticonsulting.com
SIC: 8748 Business consulting
PA: Fti Consulting, Inc.
555 12th St Nw Ste 3
Washington DC 20004
202 312-9100

(P-19781)
FUNGIBLE INC
3201 Scott Blvd, Santa Clara (95054-3008)
PHONE.................669 292-5522
Pradeep Sindhu, *CEO*
Brian McCloskey, *Officer*
Toby Owen, *Vice Pres*
Norma Castro, *Executive Asst*
Jialin Song, *Technical Staff*
EMP: 80 **EST:** 2015
SALES (est): 9.3MM **Privately Held**
WEB: www.fungible.com
SIC: 8748 Business consulting

(P-19782)
FUSE PROJECT LLC
1401 16th St, San Francisco (94103-5109)
PHONE.................415 908-1492
Yves Behar, *President*
Logan Ray, *Partner*
Mitch Pergola, *Managing Prtnr*
Helen Fu Thomas, *Ch of Bd*
Galen Myers, *Vice Pres*
▲ **EMP:** 60 **EST:** 1998
SQ FT: 22,000
SALES (est): 12.8MM **Privately Held**
WEB: www.fuseproject.com
SIC: 8748 Business consulting

(P-19783)
GENPACT LLC
3300 Hillview Ave, Palo Alto (94304-1203)
PHONE.................203 690-9308
Sanjay Srivastava, *Principal*
Achin Kishore, *Vice Pres*
EMP: 50 **Privately Held**
WEB: www.genpact.com
SIC: 8748 Business consulting
HQ: Genpact Llc
1155 Ave Of The Amrcas Fl
New York NY 10036
212 896-6600

(P-19784)
GLASSFAB TEMPERING SVCS INC (PA)
Also Called: Glass Fab Tempering Sv
1448 Mariani Ct, Tracy (95376-2825)
PHONE.................209 229-1060
Jagmohan Singh, *CEO*
Surinderpal Bains, *President*
Usha Mhay, *CFO*
Terry Arslanian, *Credit Mgr*
Deanna Biring, *Plant Mgr*
EMP: 56 **EST:** 2005
SQ FT: 60,000
SALES (est): 11.5MM **Privately Held**
WEB: www.glassfabusa.com
SIC: 8748 Business consulting

8748 - Business Consulting Svcs, NEC County (P-19785)

(P-19785)
GLOBAL INFOTECH CORPORATION
2890 Zanker Rd Ste 202, San Jose (95134-2118)
PHONE 408 567-0600
Atul Sharma, *President*
Nitin Prasad, *Vice Pres*
Malay Das, *Manager*
Malay Thakur, *Manager*
EMP: 550 EST: 1995
SQ FT: 3,000 **Privately Held**
WEB: www.global-infotech.com
SIC: 8748 Systems analysis & engineering consulting services

(P-19786)
GORDON E BTTY I MORE FUNDATION
1661 Page Mill Rd, Palo Alto (94304-1209)
PHONE 650 213-3000
Lewis W Coleman, *President*
John Hennessy, *Vice Chairman*
Bruce Alberts, *Trustee*
Denise Strack, *Ch Invest Ofcr*
Genevieve Biggs, *Officer*
EMP: 75
SALES: 451.9MM **Privately Held**
WEB: www.moore.org
SIC: 8748 Economic consultant

(P-19787)
GOYETTE RUANO & THOMPSON INC (PA)
2366 Gold Meadow Way A, Gold River (95670-4471)
PHONE 916 851-1900
Paul Q Goyette, *Owner*
EMP: 64 EST: 2003
SALES (est): 4.7MM **Privately Held**
WEB: www.goyetteassociates.com
SIC: 8748 8111 Business consulting; legal services

(P-19788)
HARRIS & SLOAN CONSULTING
2295 Gateway Oaks Dr # 165, Sacramento (95833-4211)
PHONE 916 921-2800
Timothy Sloan, *President*
Scott Meyer, *Technician*
Cree Farnes, *Design Engr*
Alyssa Gutierrez, *Design Engr*
Corey Stevens, *Design Engr*
EMP: 50 EST: 2002
SALES (est): 5.3MM **Privately Held**
WEB: www.harrisandsloan.com
SIC: 8748 Business consulting

(P-19789)
HERO DIGITAL LLC (PA)
555 Montgomery St # 1250, San Francisco (94111-6510)
PHONE 415 230-0724
David Kilimnik, *CEO*
Patrick Frend, *President*
Nick Gerostathos, *CFO*
Kenneth Parks, *Chief Mktg Ofcr*
Jef Bekes, *Exec VP*
EMP: 200 EST: 2014
SALES (est): 42.7MM **Privately Held**
WEB: www.herodigital.com
SIC: 8748 Business consulting

(P-19790)
HUMBOLDT STATE UNIV SPNSRED PR
Also Called: HSU FOUNDATION
1 Harpst St Sbs Bldg Rm 4, Arcata (95521)
P.O. Box 1185 (95518-1185)
PHONE 707 826-4189
Steven Karp, *Exec Dir*
Sharon Tuttle, *Professor*
Arne Jacobson, *Assoc Prof*
EMP: 100 EST: 1952
SALES: 34.9MM **Privately Held**
WEB: www.humboldt.edu
SIC: 8748 Educational consultant

(P-19791)
IDEO PARTNERS LLC
715 Alma St, Palo Alto (94301-2403)
PHONE 650 289-3400
David Blakely,
Whitney Mortimer, *Partner*
Joe Gerber, *Managing Dir*
Travis Lee, *Managing Dir*
Christina Segeler, *Executive Asst*
EMP: 41 EST: 2007
SALES (est): 1.1MM **Privately Held**
WEB: www.ideo.com
SIC: 8748 Systems analysis or design

(P-19792)
INFLECTIONCOM INC (PA)
303 Twin Dolphin Dr # 600, Redwood City (94065-1497)
PHONE 650 618-9910
Michale Steven Grossman, *CEO*
Jared Waterman, *CFO*
Brian Kielian, *Vice Pres*
Max Wesman, *Vice Pres*
EMP: 115 EST: 2014
SQ FT: 7,000
SALES: 33.2MM **Privately Held**
WEB: www.inflection.com
SIC: 8748 Business consulting

(P-19793)
INFOSOFT INC
7891 Westwood Dr Ste 113, Gilroy (95020-4786)
PHONE 408 659-4326
Ashish Chopra, *President*
Raj Chopra, *Vice Pres*
Alex Pandey, *Recruiter*
Eric Parker, *Recruiter*
Ashley Puri, *Recruiter*
EMP: 80 EST: 2005
SALES (est): 5.5MM **Privately Held**
WEB: www.infosoft-inc.com
SIC: 8748 7361 Systems engineering consultant, ex. computer or professional; placement agencies

(P-19794)
INNOVATIVE CIRCUITS ENGRG INC
2310 Lundy Ave, San Jose (95131-1827)
PHONE 408 955-9505
Narendra Narayan, *President*
Kevin Nguyen, *Vice Pres*
Gustovo Ortega, *Vice Pres*
Tristan Stephan, *Engineer*
Monju Shariff, *Human Res Mgr*
EMP: 46 EST: 1991
SQ FT: 4,800
SALES (est): 10.4MM **Privately Held**
WEB: www.icenginc.com
SIC: 8748 Systems analysis & engineering consulting services

(P-19795)
INNOVTIVE INTLLGENT SLTONS LLC (PA)
42480 Christy St Ste 108, Fremont (94538-3141)
PHONE 408 332-5736
Praveen Chintha, *CEO*
Karthik Pichai, *COO*
Rajesh Pulipati, *Business Mgr*
Kavitha Rikebi, *Opers Staff*
EMP: 99 EST: 2006
SQ FT: 5,000
SALES (est): 15MM **Privately Held**
WEB: www.iis-it.com
SIC: 8748 7371 7363 Systems analysis & engineering consulting services; computer software development; employee leasing service

(P-19796)
INSIGNIA ENVIRONMENTAL
545 Middlefield Rd # 210, Menlo Park (94025-3400)
PHONE 650 321-6787
Anne Marie McGraw, *President*
Alex McGraw, *Vice Pres*
EMP: 65 EST: 2004
SALES (est): 16.2MM **Privately Held**
WEB: www.insigniaenvironmental.com
SIC: 8748 Environmental consultant

(P-19797)
INTEGRATED BLDG SOLUTIONS INC
Also Called: Ibs
2000 Crow Canyon Pl # 440, San Ramon (94583-1383)
P.O. Box 2698 (94583-7698)
PHONE 925 244-1900
Eugene Gutkin, *President*
Sergey Gutkin, *Project Mgr*
Don Snell, *Engineer*
Joshua Daniels, *Internal Med*
Bobby Coucoules, *Manager*
EMP: 15 EST: 1998
SALES (est): 2MM **Privately Held**
WEB: www.ibismsi.com
SIC: 8748 3822 1731 Energy conservation consultant; building services monitoring controls, automatic; energy management controls

(P-19798)
INTEGRTED RSRCE SLTONS GROUP L
1100 Grundy Ln Ste 100, San Bruno (94066-3066)
PHONE 650 726-7628
Lauren Casentini, *President*
David Casentini, *Vice Pres*
Alison Ten Cate, *Vice Pres*
Lorna Rushforth, *Vice Pres*
EMP: 36 EST: 2006
SQ FT: 5,000
SALES (est): 2.1MM
SALES (corp-wide): 323.8MM **Privately Held**
WEB: www.clearesult.com
SIC: 8748 Environmental consultant
PA: Clearesult Consulting Inc.
6504 Bridge Point Pkwy # 42
Austin TX 78730
512 327-9200

(P-19799)
IRIS ENVIRONMENTAL
1814 Franklin St Ste 505, Oakland (94612-3461)
PHONE 510 834-4747
Adrienne Lapierre, *President*
Christopher S Alger, *Principal*
Robert B Balas, *Principal*
Todd Bernhardt, *Principal*
Phillip L Fitzwater, *Principal*
EMP: 35 EST: 2015
SALES (est): 5.8MM
SALES (corp-wide): 720.8MM **Privately Held**
WEB: www.irisenv.com
SIC: 8748 Environmental consultant
HQ: Rps Group, Inc.
20405 Tomball Pkwy # 200
Houston TX 77070

(P-19800)
ITC SRVICE GROUP ACQSITION LLC (DH)
Also Called: I T C
7777 Greenback Ln Ste 201, Citrus Heights (95610-5800)
PHONE 877 370-4482
Jim Rush,
Seneca Mullins, *President*
Kristin Edwards, *Exec VP*
John Carrazco, *Vice Pres*
Michael Fulton, *Vice Pres*
EMP: 50
SQ FT: 11,843
SALES (est): 76.7MM **Privately Held**
WEB: www.callitc.com
SIC: 8748 Telecommunications consultant
HQ: America Fujikura Ltd
170 Ridgeview Cir
Duncan SC 29334
800 235-3423

(P-19801)
JP RESEARCH INC
5050 El Cmino Real Ste 20, Los Altos (94022)
PHONE 650 559-5999
Ajit Dandapani, *President*
Jeya Padmanaban, *Vice Pres*
William Bussone, *Senior Engr*
Jon Garcia, *Sr Consultant*
▲ EMP: 35 EST: 1995
SALES (est): 4MM **Privately Held**
WEB: www.jpresearch.com
SIC: 8748 Economic consultant

(P-19802)
JUMP ASSOCIATES LLC (PA)
1825 S Grant St Ste 9-12, San Mateo (94402-2655)
PHONE 650 373-7200
Dev Patnaik,
Colleen Murray, *Vice Pres*
Sean Young, *Vice Pres*
Nealm Moore,
Neal Moore, *Director*
EMP: 44 EST: 1998
SALES (est): 10.2MM **Privately Held**
WEB: www.jumpassociates.com
SIC: 8748 Business consulting

(P-19803)
KADIANT LLC
155 Grand Ave Ste 500, Oakland (94612-3747)
P.O. Box 399318, San Francisco (94139-9318)
PHONE 209 521-4791
Valerie Spyksma, *Director*
Natalia Szmacinski, *Supervisor*
EMP: 40 EST: 2019
SALES (est): 8.1MM **Privately Held**
WEB: www.kadiant.com
SIC: 8748 Business consulting

(P-19804)
KCCTECH LLC
1630 N Main St Ste 305, Walnut Creek (94596-4609)
PHONE 628 400-2420
Ahmet Cark, *Mng Member*
Hakan Kavlak, *Managing Prtnr*
Farid Shidiq, *Technology*
EMP: 150 EST: 2016
SQ FT: 2,500
SALES: 8.1MM **Privately Held**
WEB: www.kcctech.com
SIC: 8748 8742 8711 1799 Telecommunications consultant; management consulting services; engineering services; construction site cleanup; transmitting tower (telecommunication) construction

(P-19805)
KEYSTONE STRATEGY LLC
150 Spear St Ste 1750, San Francisco (94105-1541)
PHONE 877 419-2623
Henry Liu, *Principal*
Sue Porter, *Human Resources*
Bennett Winton, *Sr Associate*
Catherine Poirier, *Consultant*
EMP: 80 **Privately Held**
WEB: www.keystonestrategy.com
SIC: 8748 Business consulting
PA: Keystone Strategy, Llc
150 Cambridgepark Dr # 704
Cambridge MA 02140

(P-19806)
KLH CONSULTING INC
2324 Bethards Dr, Santa Rosa (95405-8537)
PHONE 707 575-9986
Soni Lampert, *CEO*
Hub Lampert, *CFO*
Kavitha Selvaraj, *Software Dev*
Alexander Sanville, *Network Enginr*
Kevin Kiesel, *Manager*
EMP: 55 EST: 1978
SALES (est): 8.2MM **Privately Held**
WEB: www.klhconsulting.com
SIC: 8748 7371 7372 Systems engineering consultant, ex. computer or professional; custom computer programming services; business oriented computer software

(P-19807)
KOCHERGEN FARMS COMPOSTING INC (PA)
Also Called: Green Valley Recycling
523 N Brawley Ave Ste B, Fresno (93706-1015)
P.O. Box 11006 (93771-1006)
PHONE 559 498-0900

PRODUCTS & SERVICES SECTION **8748 - Business Consulting Svcs, NEC County (P-19831)**

Mike J Kochergen, *President*
EMP: 63 **EST:** 2001
SQ FT: 42,785
SALES (est): 6.5MM **Privately Held**
WEB:
www.kochergenfarmscomposting.com
SIC: 8748 Environmental consultant

(P-19808)
KRAZAN & ASSOCIATES (PA)
215 W Dakota Ave, Clovis (93612-5608)
PHONE.................................559 348-2200
Dean L Alexander, *President*
Dean Alexander, *COO*
Jodi Ragsdale, *CFO*
Emilo Vargas, *CFO*
Thomas P Krazan, *Chairman*
EMP: 68 **EST:** 1982
SQ FT: 21,000
SALES (est): 35MM **Privately Held**
WEB: www.krazan.com
SIC: 8748 8734 8742 Environmental consultant; product testing laboratory, safety or performance; management engineering

(P-19809)
KYNDI INC
1300 S El Cmino Real Ste, San Mateo (94402)
PHONE.................................917 374-5531
James Ryan Welsh, *Principal*
Dan Gartung, *CTO*
Shimul Chaudhary, *Engineer*
Brendan Wagner, *Mktg Coord*
Sharon Santos, *Manager*
EMP: 35 **EST:** 2015
SALES (est): 1MM **Privately Held**
WEB: www.kyndi.com
SIC: 8748 Business consulting

(P-19810)
LESLEY FOUNDATION
701 Arnold Way Bldg A, Half Moon Bay (94019-2199)
PHONE.................................650 726-4888
Catherine Evans, *Exec Dir*
Jenny Carrington, *Administration*
Mary Cheung, *Director*
EMP: 73
SALES: 8.3MM **Privately Held**
SIC: 8748 Urban planning & consulting services

(P-19811)
LETTIS CONSULTANTS INTL INC (PA)
1000 Burnett Ave Ste 350, Concord (94520-2000)
PHONE.................................925 482-0360
Jeffrey Unruh, *President*
Serkan Bozkurt, *Partner*
John Baldwin, *CFO*
Kevin Clahan, *Engineer*
Andrew Seifried, *Engineer*
EMP: 38 **EST:** 2011 **Privately Held**
WEB: www.lettisci.com
SIC: 8748 Environmental consultant

(P-19812)
LIVEVOX INC (PA)
655 Montgomery St # 1000, San Francisco (94111-2635)
PHONE.................................415 671-6000
Louis Summe, *CEO*
Larry Siegel, *COO*
Michael Leraris, *CFO*
Randall Nelson, *Senior VP*
David D'Antonio, *Vice Pres*
EMP: 142 **EST:** 2000
SALES (est): 45.9MM **Privately Held**
WEB: www.livevox.com
SIC: 8748 7371 Telecommunications consultant; software programming applications

(P-19813)
LUMETRA HEALTHCARE SOLUTIONS
300 Montgomery St Ste 639, San Francisco (94104-1908)
PHONE.................................415 677-2000
Patricia Daniel, *CEO*
Lewy Roth, *Office Mgr*
Richard Barnes, *CIO*
Annie Auyeung, *Accountant*
Danielle Smith, *Recruiter*
EMP: 50 **EST:** 1984
SALES (est): 3.9MM **Privately Held**
WEB: www.lumetrasolutions.com
SIC: 8748 Business consulting

(P-19814)
LYLE COMPANY
3140 Gold Camp Dr Ste 30, Rancho Cordova (95670-6192)
P.O. Box 2255 (95741-2255)
PHONE.................................916 266-7000
Lanny G Lyle, *Ch of Bd*
Thu Nguyen, *CFO*
Matt Johnson, *Director*
EMP: 60 **EST:** 1989
SALES (est): 8.6MM **Privately Held**
WEB: www.lyleco.com
SIC: 8748 Business consulting

(P-19815)
MACDONALDS RESTAURANTS
Also Called: McDonald's
7065 N Ingram Ave, Fresno (93650-1083)
PHONE.................................559 440-9206
EMP: 43
SALES (est): 556.8K **Privately Held**
WEB: www.mcdonalds.com
SIC: 8748 5812 Eating Place Business Consulting Services

(P-19816)
MACKIN CONSULTANCY LLC
2880 Zanker Rd Ste 203, San Jose (95134-2122)
PHONE.................................828 755-4073
Andy Mackin, *CEO*
Fiona Donnelly, *COO*
Leniece Lane, *Chief Mktg Ofcr*
Claire Goulding, *Administration*
Barry Crowley, *Consultant*
EMP: 150 **EST:** 2014
SALES (est): 2.9MM **Privately Held**
WEB: www.mackinconsultancy.com
SIC: 8748 Business consulting

(P-19817)
MAXVAL GROUP INC (PA)
2251 Grant Rd Ste B, Los Altos (94024-6958)
PHONE.................................650 472-0644
D Bommi Bommannan, *President*
Stuart Recher, *President*
Jaya Bommannan, *CFO*
Kurt Wedel, *Officer*
Savi Gupta, *Vice Pres*
EMP: 69 **EST:** 2004
SALES (est): 7.6MM **Privately Held**
WEB: www.maxval.com
SIC: 8748 Business consulting

(P-19818)
MENKE & ASSOCIATES INC (PA)
1 Kaiser Plz Ste 505, Oakland (94612-3611)
PHONE.................................415 362-5200
John Menke, *President*
W Kyle Coltman, *CEO*
Sherman Coultas, *Senior VP*
Nancy Menke, *Admin Sec*
Patricia Barnes, *CIO*
EMP: 35 **EST:** 1974
SQ FT: 12,500
SALES (est): 10.4MM **Privately Held**
WEB: www.menke.com
SIC: 8748 Employee programs administration

(P-19819)
MERCED COUNTY ASSN GOVERNMENTS
369 W 18th St, Merced (95340-4801)
PHONE.................................209 723-3153
Marjorie Kirn, *Exec Dir*
Navneet Mattu, *Analyst*
Marli Foster, *Accountant*
Alicia Ochoa-Jones, *Purchasing*
Sue Speer, *Purchasing*
EMP: 45 **EST:** 1967
SALES (est): 5.3MM **Privately Held**
WEB: www.mcagov.org
SIC: 8748 Urban planning & consulting services

(P-19820)
MICHAEL BAKER INTL INC
2729 Prospect Park Dr # 220, Rancho Cordova (95670-6291)
PHONE.................................916 361-8384
Phil Carter, *Manager*
Kurt Bergman, *CEO*
Bowen Yang, *Technical Staff*
Lindsey Viersen, *Business Mgr*
Melody Haigh, *Sr Consultant*
EMP: 45
SALES (corp-wide): 592.9MM **Privately Held**
WEB: www.mbakerintl.com
SIC: 8748 Business consulting
HQ: Baker Michael International Inc
  500 Grant St Ste 5400
  Pittsburgh PA 15219
  412 269-6300

(P-19821)
MICHAEL BAKER INTL INC
140 Independence Cir C, Chico (95973-4963)
PHONE.................................530 894-3469
Phil Carter, *Manager*
EMP: 45
SALES (corp-wide): 592.9MM **Privately Held**
WEB: www.mbakerintl.com
SIC: 8748 Business consulting
HQ: Baker Michael International Inc
  500 Grant St Ste 5400
  Pittsburgh PA 15219
  412 269-6300

(P-19822)
MODULAR POWER SOLUTIONS LLC (HQ)
880 Mabury Rd, San Jose (95133-1021)
PHONE.................................408 321-2270
Lawrence L Beltramo, *Partner*
EMP: 50 **EST:** 2011
SALES (est): 3.8MM
SALES (corp-wide): 175.1MM **Privately Held**
SIC: 8748 Business consulting
PA: Rosendin Holdings, Inc.
  400 S Hope St
  Los Angeles CA 90071
  213 891-9619

(P-19823)
MONTROSE ENVIRONMENTAL CORP
2825 Verne Roberts Cir, Antioch (94509-7902)
PHONE.................................925 680-4300
WEI Marcus Tan, *Principal*
EMP: 172 **Privately Held**
WEB: www.montrose-env.com
SIC: 8748 Environmental consultant
PA: Montrose Environmental Corporation
  1 Park Plz Ste 1000
  Irvine CA 92614

(P-19824)
MOORE IACOFANO GOLTSMAN INC (PA)
Also Called: M I G
800 Hearst Ave, Berkeley (94710-2018)
PHONE.................................510 845-7549
Susan M Goltsman, *President*
Daniel Iacofano, *CEO*
Carolyn Verheyen, *COO*
Marlee Ehrenfeld, *Officer*
Tim Carroll, *Social Dir*
EMP: 63 **EST:** 1981
SQ FT: 6,000
SALES (est): 22.2MM **Privately Held**
WEB: www.migcom.com
SIC: 8748 Environmental consultant

(P-19825)
MULTIPLIER
780 Glendome Cir, Oakland (94602-1410)
PHONE.................................415 421-3774
Laura Deaton, *Exec Dir*
Mellissa Clack, *President*
Jill K Johnson, *Principal*
Carolyn Schour, *Director*
Katharine McCallie, *Manager*
EMP: 70 **EST:** 2001
SALES (est): 6.8MM **Privately Held**
WEB: www.trustforconservationinnovation.org
SIC: 8748 8699 Environmental consultant; animal humane society

(P-19826)
MUTUAL AID RESPONSE SVCS INC
88 Emery Bay Dr, Emeryville (94608-2938)
P.O. Box 99408 (94662-9408)
PHONE.................................866 627-7911
Joseph Pred, *President*
EMP: 48 **EST:** 2000
SALES (est): 1.1MM **Privately Held**
WEB: www.mars911.info
SIC: 8748 Business consulting

(P-19827)
NAVIS CORPORATION (PA)
55 Harrison St Ste 600, Oakland (94607-3776)
PHONE.................................510 267-5000
Rob Dillon, *CEO*
Andy Barrons, *Officer*
Younus Aftab, *Senior VP*
Raj Gupta, *Senior VP*
Robert Dillon, *Vice Pres*
EMP: 281 **EST:** 1988
SALES (est): 28.6MM **Privately Held**
WEB: www.navis.com
SIC: 8748 7371 Systems analysis & engineering consulting services; custom computer programming services

(P-19828)
NEWFIELD WIRELESS INC (DH)
2855 Telg Ave Ste 200, Berkeley (94705)
PHONE.................................510 848-8248
Marc Bensadoun, *CEO*
Matthew Ehrenman, *Senior VP*
Chris Haidet, *Senior VP*
Kethees Ketheesan, *Vice Pres*
Petrit Nahi, *Vice Pres*
EMP: 84 **EST:** 1995
SALES (est): 21.8MM
SALES (corp-wide): 831.2MM **Publicly Held**
SIC: 8748 7361 Telecommunications consultant; employment agencies
HQ: Netscout Systems Texas, Llc
  2200 Penn Ave Nw Ste 800w
  Washington DC 20037
  202 828-0850

(P-19829)
NORTH STATE RESOURCES INC
376 Hartnell Ave Ste B, Redding (96002-1881)
PHONE.................................530 222-5347
Laura F Kuh, *President*
Benjamin Wiechman, *Info Tech Mgr*
Charles Shoemaker, *Project Mgr*
Connie Carpenter, *Project Engr*
Kathryn McDonald, *Analyst*
EMP: 50 **EST:** 1986
SALES (est): 6.4MM
SALES (corp-wide): 3.6B **Privately Held**
WEB: www.stantec.com
SIC: 8748 Environmental consultant
PA: Stantec Inc
  10220 103 Ave Nw Suite 400
  Edmonton AB T5J 0
  780 917-7000

(P-19830)
NORTHROP GRUMMAN SYSTEMS CORP
Also Called: Northrop Grumman Info Tech
49 Stevenson St Ste 1400, San Francisco (94105-2976)
PHONE.................................415 281-4600
EMP: 40
SQ FT: 800 **Publicly Held**
SIC: 8748 Business Consulting Services
HQ: Northrop Grumman Systems Corporation
  2980 Fairview Park Dr
  Falls Church VA 22042
  703 280-2900

(P-19831)
NU REV COMMUNICATIONS INC
2428 Research Dr, Livermore (94550-3850)
PHONE.................................925 980-2799

8748 - Business Consulting Svcs, NEC County (P-19832)

Roberto Galicha, *President*
EMP: 47 **EST:** 2009
SQ FT: 9,000 **Privately Held**
WEB: www.nurevcommunications.wordpress.com
SIC: 8748 Telecommunications consultant

(P-19832)
O C JONES & SONS INC
155 Filbert St Ste 209, Oakland (94607-2524)
PHONE 510 663-6911
Carla Radosta, *Branch Mgr*
Rob Layne, *Vice Pres*
Victor Babbitt, *Project Mgr*
EMP: 100
SALES (corp-wide): 58.3MM **Privately Held**
WEB: www.ocjones.com
SIC: 8748 Business consulting
PA: O. C. Jones & Sons, Inc.
1520 4th St
Berkeley CA 94710
510 526-3424

(P-19833)
ONE DIVERSIFIED LLC
3275 Edward Ave, Santa Clara (95054-2340)
PHONE 408 969-1972
EMP: 91
SALES (corp-wide): 1.2B **Privately Held**
WEB: www.onediversified.com
SIC: 8748 7373 Systems analysis & engineering consulting services; systems integration services
PA: One Diversified, Llc
2975 Northwoods Pkwy
Peachtree Corners GA 30071
770 447-1001

(P-19834)
ORANGE SILICON VALLEY
60 Spear St Ste 1100, San Francisco (94105-1599)
PHONE 415 243-1500
EMP: 60 **EST:** 2012
SALES (est): 3.6MM **Privately Held**
SIC: 8748 Business Consulting, Nec, Nsk

(P-19835)
PACIRA CRYOTECH INC
46400 Fremont Blvd, Fremont (94538-6469)
PHONE 800 442-0989
Timothy Still, *President*
Brian Farley, *Ch of Bd*
Peter Osborne, *CFO*
Michelle MAI, *Research*
Alan Dazo, *Engineer*
EMP: 50 **EST:** 2005
SALES (est): 12.1MM **Publicly Held**
WEB: www.pacira.com
SIC: 8748 Business consulting
PA: Pacira Biosciences, Inc.
5 Sylvan Way Ste 300
Parsippany NJ 07054

(P-19836)
PACKET FUSION INC (PA)
4301 Hacienda Dr Ste 400, Pleasanton (94588-2816)
PHONE 650 292-6000
Matthew Pingatore, *President*
Steven Hastings, *COO*
Kevin Sewell, *Executive*
Matt Herman, *Managing Dir*
Benny Martinez, *IT/INT Sup*
EMP: 42 **EST:** 2002
SALES (est): 8MM **Privately Held**
WEB: www.packetfusion.com
SIC: 8748 Telecommunications consultant

(P-19837)
PARTNERS IN SCHOOL INNOVATION
1060 Tennessee St, San Francisco (94107-3016)
PHONE 415 824-6196
Julien R Phillips, *Exec Dir*
Amanda Bachelor, *Partner*
Tim Burke, *Partner*
Amanda Faulkner, *Partner*
Melissa Shaughnessy, *Partner*
EMP: 76 **EST:** 1994
SALES (est): 7.7MM **Privately Held**
WEB: www.partnersinschools.org
SIC: 8748 Educational consultant

(P-19838)
PCS MOBILE SOLUTIONS LLC
888 Blossom Hill Rd, San Jose (95123-1201)
PHONE 408 229-8900
Saad Nadhir, *Branch Mgr*
EMP: 71
SALES (corp-wide): 86MM **Privately Held**
WEB: www.sprint.com
SIC: 8748 5065 4813 4812 Telecommunications consultant; telephone & telegraphic equipment; local & long distance telephone communications; cellular telephone services
PA: Pcs Mobile Solutions, Llc
32000 Northwestern Hwy # 279
Farmington Hills MI 48334
248 539-2221

(P-19839)
PONDER ENVIRONMENTAL SVCS INC (PA)
4563 E 2nd St, Benicia (94510-1032)
P.O. Box 1427 (94510-4427)
PHONE 707 748-7775
Jim Ponder, *President*
Curtis Fox, *Area Mgr*
Sam Hoang, *Controller*
Sharon Taylor, *Safety Dir*
Justin Ponder, *Opers Mgr*
EMP: 50 **EST:** 2001
SQ FT: 15,000
SALES (est): 16.1MM **Privately Held**
WEB: www.ponderenvironmentalservices.com
SIC: 8748 Environmental consultant

(P-19840)
PROJECT SENTINEL INC (PA)
1490 El Camino Real, Santa Clara (95050-4609)
PHONE 650 321-6291
Ann Marquart, *Exec Dir*
Michael Dittmer, *Analyst*
EMP: 36 **EST:** 1990
SALES (est): 2.7MM **Privately Held**
WEB: www.housing.org
SIC: 8748 Urban planning & consulting services

(P-19841)
QMETRY INC
3200 Patrick Henry Dr # 2, Santa Clara (95054-1875)
PHONE 408 727-1101
Agnelo Rodrigues, *Mng Member*
Ashish Katrekar, *Vice Pres*
Harshal Vora, *Executive*
EMP: 110 **EST:** 2018
SALES (est): 3MM **Privately Held**
WEB: www.qmetry.com
SIC: 8748 Testing services

(P-19842)
QUALIA LABS INC
201 Mission St Ste 1800, San Francisco (94105-1858)
PHONE 440 477-5625
Nathan Baker, *President*
Stuart Watts, *Finance*
EMP: 216 **EST:** 2015
SQ FT: 3,700
SALES (est): 25.7MM **Privately Held**
WEB: www.qualia.com
SIC: 8748 Business consulting

(P-19843)
QUARTERWAVE CORP
1500 Valley House Dr # 100, Rohnert Park (94928-4939)
PHONE 707 793-9105
Steven Price, *CEO*
Steven C Price, *CTO*
Peggy Wise, *Human Res Dir*
EMP: 26 **EST:** 1987
SQ FT: 7,250
SALES (est): 5.5MM **Privately Held**
WEB: www.quarterwave.com
SIC: 8748 3663 3679 Telecommunications consultant; amplifiers, RF power & IF; microwave components

(P-19844)
QUOVA INC
401 Castro St Fl 3, Mountain View (94041-2089)
PHONE 650 965-2898
Marie Alexander, *President*
Gary P Jackson, *COO*
Jean-Louis Casabonne, *CFO*
EMP: 60 **EST:** 2000
SQ FT: 10,000
SALES (est): 6MM
SALES (corp-wide): 606.2MM **Privately Held**
WEB: www.risk.neustar.biz
SIC: 8748 Business consulting
HQ: Neustar, Inc.
1906 Reston Metro Plz # 5
Reston VA 20190
571 434-5400

(P-19845)
RAHI SYSTEMS INC (PA)
48303 Fremont Blvd, Fremont (94538-6580)
PHONE 510 651-2205
Tarun Raisoni, *CEO*
Kelly Yagi, *CFO*
Alison Lolis, *Vice Pres*
Jennifer Merritt, *Vice Pres*
Bruce Moore, *Vice Pres*
EMP: 330 **EST:** 2013
SALES (est): 165.6MM **Privately Held**
WEB: www.rahisystems.com
SIC: 8748 Telecommunications consultant

(P-19846)
RANEY PLANNING & MGT INC
1501 Sports Dr, Sacramento (95834-2035)
PHONE 916 372-6100
Tim Raney, *President*
Cindy Gnos, *Vice Pres*
Tina Doyle, *Bookkeeper*
Zachary Dahla, *Mktg Coord*
Stefanie Williams, *Manager*
EMP: 35 **EST:** 1999
SQ FT: 6,000
SALES (est): 4.2MM **Privately Held**
WEB: www.raneymanagement.com
SIC: 8748 Environmental consultant

(P-19847)
REDEVELOPMENT AGENCY OF THE CI
Also Called: SUISUN REDEVELOPMENT AGENCY
701 Civic Center Blvd, Suisun City (94585-2617)
PHONE 707 421-7309
Suzanne Bragdon, *Manager*
Pete Sanchez, *Mayor*
Jason Garben, *Director*
EMP: 68
SALES (est): 12.6MM **Privately Held**
WEB: www.suisun.com
SIC: 8748 Urban planning & consulting services

(P-19848)
RESOURCE INNOVATIONS INC (HQ)
719 Main St, Half Moon Bay (94019-1924)
PHONE 415 369-1000
Lauren Casentini, *CEO*
Sunil Bhardwaj, *CFO*
Samuel Mueller, *Exec VP*
Eric Bober, *Vice Pres*
Luther Dow, *Vice Pres*
EMP: 80 **EST:** 1999
SALES (est): 74.9MM **Privately Held**
WEB: www.resource-innovations.com
SIC: 8748 Energy conservation consultant
PA: Bv Ri Acquisitionco, Llc
125 High St Fl 17
Boston MA 02110
617 224-0057

(P-19849)
RIDGE COMMUNICATIONS INC
12919 Alcosta Blvd Ste 1, San Ramon (94583-1340)
PHONE 925 498-2340
Russ Patridge, *CEO*
Michael Patridge, *President*
Wes Rigsby, *General Mgr*
Leslie Robinson, *Human Res Mgr*
David Haddock, *Site Mgr*
EMP: 47 **EST:** 2002
SQ FT: 4,200
SALES (est): 13.1MM **Privately Held**
WEB: www.ridgecommunicate.com
SIC: 8743 Telecommunications consultant

(P-19850)
ROSE INTERNATIONAL INC
5000 Executive Pkwy # 430, San Ramon (94583-4282)
PHONE 636 812-4000
Mary Coats, *Branch Mgr*
Larry Crane, *Vice Pres*
Lauri Buchmeier, *Associate Dir*
Sharon Leath, *Accountant*
Mandi Ashby, *Hum Res Coord*
EMP: 107 **Privately Held**
WEB: www.roseint.com
SIC: 8748 7371 7363 7361 Systems engineering consultant, ex. computer or professional; computer software development; help supply services; employment agencies
PA: Rose International, Inc.
16305 Swingley Ridge Rd # 350
Chesterfield MO 63017

(P-19851)
SA PHOTONICS INC
120 Knowles Dr, Los Gatos (95032-1828)
PHONE 408 560-3500
James Coward, *President*
Cynthia Gamble, *CFO*
Andrea Singewald, *CFO*
David Upham, *Vice Pres*
Angela Bents, *Program Mgr*
EMP: 110 **EST:** 2002
SQ FT: 30,000
SALES (est): 22.3MM **Privately Held**
WEB: www.saphotonics.com
SIC: 8748 Business consulting

(P-19852)
SACRAMENTO HOUSING DEV CORP (PA)
Also Called: HOUSING AUTHORITY OF SACRAMENT
801 12th St, Sacramento (95814-2947)
P.O. Box 1834 (95812-1834)
PHONE 916 440-1333
David Ossont, *President*
Cari Scott, *Admin Sec*
EMP: 90 **EST:** 1951
SQ FT: 33,000 **Privately Held**
WEB: www.shra.org
SIC: 8748 Urban planning & consulting services

(P-19853)
SACRAMNTO MTRO A QULTY MGT DST
777 12th St Ste 300, Sacramento (95814-1928)
PHONE 916 874-4800
Larry Greene, *Network Enginr*
Lauren Neves, *Officer*
Albertc Ayala, *Exec Dir*
Patrick Smith, *Program Mgr*
Charles Wilmoth, *Information Mgr*
EMP: 60 **EST:** 2012
SALES (est): 51.9MM **Privately Held**
WEB: www.airquality.org
SIC: 8748 Environmental consultant

(P-19854)
SAINTS CAPITAL DAKOTA LLC (PA)
2020 Union St, San Francisco (94123-4103)
PHONE 415 395-2897
Ghia Griarte,
David P Quinlivan,
Kenneth B Sawyer,
EMP: 84 **EST:** 2008

PRODUCTS & SERVICES SECTION
8748 - Business Consulting Svcs, NEC County (P-19877)

SALES (est): 46MM Privately Held
WEB: www.saintscapital.com
SIC: 8748 Business consulting

(P-19855)
SALABER ASSOCIATES INC
180 S 1st St Ste 10, Dixon (95620-3439)
PHONE.................................707 693-8800
Robert Salaber, *President*
EMP: 37 EST: 1999
SALES (est): 2.8MM Privately Held
WEB: www.saiservices.com
SIC: 8748 Systems analysis & engineering consulting services

(P-19856)
SAN JOAQUIN VAL UNI AIR POL (PA)
Also Called: Valley Air District
1990 E Gettysburg Ave, Fresno (93726-0244)
PHONE.................................559 230-6000
Seyed Sadredin, *Exec Dir*
Jaime Holt, *Officer*
Jonathan Klassen, *Program Mgr*
Jessica Olsen, *Program Mgr*
Christal Martinez, *General Mgr*
EMP: 200 EST: 1992
SQ FT: 60,000
SALES (est): 31MM Privately Held
WEB: www.valleyair.org
SIC: 8748 Environmental consultant

(P-19857)
SAN JOSE REDEVELOPMENT AGENCY
200 E Santa Clara St 14th, San Jose (95113-1903)
PHONE.................................408 535-8500
Harry Mavrogenes, *Exec Dir*
Julie Amato, *Officer*
John Wise, *Deputy Dir*
EMP: 140 EST: 1987
SQ FT: 10,045
SALES: 243.2MM
SALES (corp-wide): 1.8B Privately Held
WEB: www.sjredevelopment.com
SIC: 8748 Urban planning & consulting services
PA: City Of San Jose
    200 E Santa Clara St 13th
    San Jose CA 95113
    408 535-3500

(P-19858)
SASCO
2400 Del Paso Rd Ste 200, Sacramento (95834-9631)
PHONE.................................916 565-4120
Glen Kucera, *Manager*
Larry Kirkenslager, *Vice Pres*
Jeff Farr, *Executive*
John Whitlow, *CTO*
Bryan Friend, *Project Mgr*
EMP: 451
SALES (corp-wide): 519.2MM Privately Held
WEB: www.sasco.com
SIC: 8748 Communications consulting
PA: Sasco
    2750 Moore Ave
    Fullerton CA 92833
    714 870-0217

(P-19859)
SENSITY SYSTEMS INC (HQ)
1237 E Arques Ave, Sunnyvale (94085-4701)
PHONE.................................408 841-4200
Hugh Martin, *CEO*
Sean Harrington, *COO*
Phil Rehkemper, *CFO*
Scott Shipman,
Geoff Arnold, *CTO*
EMP: 50 EST: 2010
SALES (est): 15.4MM
SALES (corp-wide): 128.2B Publicly Held
WEB: www.verizon.com
SIC: 8748 Lighting consultant
PA: Verizon Communications Inc.
    1095 Ave Of The Americas
    New York NY 10036
    212 395-1000

(P-19860)
SILICON VLY ABA CNSULTING SVCS
1295 E Dunne Ave, Morgan Hill (95037-7065)
P.O. Box 2701, Cupertino (95015-2701)
PHONE.................................408 913-5019
Alma Guinto, *Exec Dir*
Lui Bayani, *Administration*
EMP: 50 EST: 2010
SALES (est): 3MM Privately Held
WEB: www.siliconvalleyaba.com
SIC: 8748 8093 Business consulting; mental health clinic, outpatient

(P-19861)
SMART SFTWR TSTG SOLUTIONS INC
2450 Peralta Blvd Ste 202, Fremont (94536-3826)
PHONE.................................833 778-7872
Pankaj Goel, *CEO*
Amit Kumar, *Officer*
Victor Khan, *Asst Mgr*
EMP: 60 EST: 2016
SALES (est): 1.2MM Privately Held
SIC: 8748 7371 Testing services; computer software development & applications

(P-19862)
SOLUTIONSATI CONSULTING INC
19925 Stevns Crk Blvd, Cupertino (95014-2300)
PHONE.................................408 655-0224
Edward W Porta, *Principal*
EMP: 37 EST: 2007
SALES (est): 2.8MM Privately Held
WEB: www.solutionsati.com
SIC: 8748 7389 Business consulting;

(P-19863)
SONOMA TECHNOLOGY INC
1450 N Mcdowell Blvd # 2, Petaluma (94954-6515)
PHONE.................................707 665-9900
Lyle R Chinkin, *President*
Fred Lurmann, *Chairman*
Barbara A Austin, *Exec VP*
Paul T Roberts, *Exec VP*
Paul Roberts, *Exec VP*
EMP: 65 EST: 1982
SQ FT: 29,011
SALES (est): 9.9MM Privately Held
WEB: www.sonomatech.com
SIC: 8748 Environmental consultant

(P-19864)
SOUTHEAST FRESNO RAD LP
4430 E Hamilton Ave, Fresno (93702-4535)
PHONE.................................559 443-8400
Preston Prince, *CEO*
EMP: 225 EST: 2014
SALES (est): 11.3MM Privately Held
WEB: www.fresnohousing.org
SIC: 8748 Urban planning & consulting services

(P-19865)
SPECTRUM SERVICES GROUP INC
3841 N Freeway Blvd # 120, Sacramento (95834-1968)
PHONE.................................916 760-7913
Tasawwar Ali, *CEO*
Shane Ali, *President*
Shannon Dawson, *Office Mgr*
Hasnain Ali, *Project Mgr*
Robert Liles, *Project Mgr*
EMP: 85 EST: 1999
SQ FT: 2,000
SALES (est): 9.3MM Privately Held
WEB: www.spectrum-inc.net
SIC: 8748 8744 8741 Business consulting; facilities support services; construction management

(P-19866)
STILLWTER ECSYSTEM WTRSHED RVR (PA)
Also Called: Stillwater Sciences
2855 Telg Ave Ste 400, Berkeley (94705)
PHONE.................................510 848-8098
Christine Champe, *CEO*
Chris Lyle, *Engineer*
EMP: 60 EST: 1996
SALES (est): 9.1MM Privately Held
WEB: www.stillwatersci.com
SIC: 8748 Environmental consultant

(P-19867)
SYMBIOSYS INC (HQ)
2055 Gateway Pl Ste 350, San Jose (95110-1060)
PHONE.................................408 996-9700
Jacob Hsu, *CEO*
Baoguo Zhou, *COO*
Qing Lu, *CFO*
Yuting Hung, *Vice Pres*
Mika Muukkonen, *Managing Dir*
EMP: 1314 EST: 1994
SALES (est): 100.3MM
SALES (corp-wide): 321.7MM Privately Held
WEB: www.symbio.com
SIC: 8748 8742 7371 8731 Business consulting; quality assurance consultant; computer software development & applications; commercial physical research
PA: Vxi Global Solutions, Llc
    220 W 1st St Fl 3
    Los Angeles CA 90012
    213 739-4720

(P-19868)
SYMPHONY TECHNOLOGY GROUP LLC (PA)
428 University Ave, Palo Alto (94301-1812)
P.O. Box 51770 (94303-0720)
PHONE.................................650 935-9500
Jim Obsitnik, *CEO*
Stephen Henkenmeier, *CFO*
William Chisholm,
Bill Diaz,
Romesh Wadhwani,
EMP: 5775 EST: 2000
SQ FT: 15,000
SALES (est): 191.2MM Privately Held
WEB: www.stgpartners.com
SIC: 8748 6719 Business consulting; investment holding companies, except banks

(P-19869)
SYNAGRO WEST LLC
1499 Bayshore Hwy Ste 111, Burlingame (94010-1723)
PHONE.................................650 652-6531
EMP: 99
SALES: 950K
SALES (corp-wide): 43.6K Privately Held
SIC: 8748 Residuals Management Services
HQ: Synagro Technologies, Inc.
    435 Williams Ct Ste 100
    Baltimore MD 21220

(P-19870)
SYPARTNERS LLC (HQ)
475 Brannan St Ste 100, San Francisco (94107-5419)
PHONE.................................415 536-6600
Susan Schuman, *CEO*
Kendra Cooke, *Partner*
Sabrina Clark, *Managing Prtnr*
Nicolas Maitret, *Managing Prtnr*
Lisa Maulhardt, *Exec VP*
EMP: 55 EST: 2012
SALES (est): 17.9MM Privately Held
WEB: www.sypartners.com
SIC: 8748 Business consulting

(P-19871)
SYSTEM OPERATION SERVICES INC (PA)
Also Called: SOS
200 Martinique Ave, Belvedere Tiburon (94920-1013)
PHONE.................................800 699-7674
Grace Livingston, *President*
EMP: 62 EST: 1993

SALES (est): 950.3K Privately Held
SIC: 8748 Environmental consultant

(P-19872)
TAGIT SOLUTIONS INC (PA)
5201 Great America Pkwy, Santa Clara (95054-1122)
PHONE.................................888 518-8710
Ryan Scott, *Vice Pres*
Renato Jovic, *General Mgr*
Bill Lundy, *CTO*
Dimitris Spanos, *CTO*
Dave Roberts, *Software Dev*
EMP: 52 EST: 2009
SALES (est): 527.7K Privately Held
WEB: www.tagitsolutions.com
SIC: 8748 Business consulting

(P-19873)
TELECOM TECHNOLOGY SVCS INC
Also Called: Tts
7901 Stoneridge Dr # 500, Pleasanton (94588-3969)
PHONE.................................925 224-7812
Shuky Sheffer, *President*
Al Tavalaro, *Project Mgr*
Ravi Desai, *Engineer*
Tuna Kuru, *Engineer*
Omer Mohammed, *Engineer*
EMP: 130 EST: 1999
SQ FT: 7,102
SALES (est): 39.9MM
SALES (corp-wide): 3.5B Privately Held
WEB: www.ttswireless.com
SIC: 8748 Telecommunications consultant
HQ: Amdocs, Inc.
    1390 Tmberlake Manor Pkwy
    Chesterfield MO 63017
    314 212-7000

(P-19874)
TETRA TECH EC INC
3101 Zinfandel Dr Ste 200, Rancho Cordova (95670-6398)
PHONE.................................916 852-8300
Anh Nghiem, *Manager*
EMP: 49
SALES (corp-wide): 2.9B Publicly Held
SIC: 8748 Environmental consultant
HQ: Tetra Tech Ec, Inc.
    6 Century Dr Ste 3
    Parsippany NJ 07054
    973 630-8000

(P-19875)
TM FINANCIAL FORENSICS LLC (PA)
3595 Mt Diablo Blvd 250, Lafayette (94549-3851)
PHONE.................................415 692-6350
Paul Meyer, *President*
Cheryl A Leevan, *Treasurer*
Jeff Colditz, *Vice Pres*
Elizabeth Dean, *Vice Pres*
Rob Dwyer, *Vice Pres*
EMP: 36 EST: 2009
SALES (est): 9.3MM Privately Held
WEB: www.tmfin.com
SIC: 8748 Communications consulting

(P-19876)
TRANSSIGHT LLC
7599 Balmoral Way, San Ramon (94582-5971)
PHONE.................................510 415-6301
Arvinder Bhalla, *CEO*
Satinder Bhalla, *President*
Bimesh Giri, *Vice Pres*
EMP: 25 EST: 2014
SALES (est): 1.4MM Privately Held
WEB: www.transsight.com
SIC: 8748 8742 7371 7372 Systems engineering consultant, ex. computer or professional; business consultant; computer software systems analysis & design, custom; application computer software; systems software development services;

(P-19877)
TRC SOLUTIONS
10680 White Rock Rd # 100, Rancho Cordova (95670-6175)
PHONE.................................916 962-7001
Lisa Heschong, *Principal*
Douglas Mahone, *Principal*

8748 - Business Consulting Svcs, NEC County (P-19878)

Acker Russell, *Comp Spec*
Stephen Huvane, *Project Mgr*
Todd Shannon, *Project Mgr*
EMP: 106 **EST:** 1993
SALES (est): 1.9MM
SALES (corp-wide): 711.8MM **Privately Held**
WEB: www.h-m-g.com
SIC: 8748 Environmental consultant
PA: Trc Companies, L.L.C.
21 Griffin Rd N
Windsor CT 06095
860 298-9692

(P-19878)
TRIMARK ASSOCIATES INC
2365 Iron Point Rd # 100, Folsom (95630-8714)
PHONE..................916 357-5970
Mark J Morosky, *President*
Dean Schoeder, *COO*
Robert Wood, *COO*
Bob Wood, *CTO*
Mario Marquez, *Info Tech Dir*
EMP: 53 **EST:** 2000
SQ FT: 108,000
SALES (est): 10.5MM **Privately Held**
WEB: www.trimarkassoc.com
SIC: 8748 Energy conservation consultant

(P-19879)
TRITON ENTERPRISES LLC
5638 Wells Ln, San Ramon (94582-3079)
PHONE..................925 230-8395
Lawrence Kodiyanplakkal, *Partner*
EMP: 20 **EST:** 2014
SALES (est): 1.1MM **Privately Held**
SIC: 8748 2024 Business consulting; yogurt desserts, frozen

(P-19880)
UNIVERSAL NETWORK DEV CORP (PA)
Also Called: Undc
2555 3rd St Ste 112, Sacramento (95810-1100)
PHONE..................916 475-1200
Cinthia Larkin Kazee, *President*
Jim McDermott, *Engineer*
Randolph Pearson, *Engineer*
Dennis Kazee, *Manager*
EMP: 115 **EST:** 1980
SQ FT: 1,600
SALES (est): 9.3MM **Privately Held**
WEB: www.undc.com
SIC: 8748 8711 Telecommunications consultant; professional engineer

(P-19881)
V2SOLUTIONS INC (PA)
2340 Walsh Ave, Santa Clara (95051-1328)
PHONE..................408 550-2340
Vijay Shah, *President*
Teresa Phillips, *Vice Pres*
Jon Hall, *CIO*
Sachin Rohra, *Project Mgr*
Gerald Hensley, *Sales Mgr*
EMP: 108 **EST:** 2003
SALES (est): 4.1MM **Privately Held**
WEB: www.v2solutions.com
SIC: 8748 Environmental consultant

(P-19882)
VALLEJO FLOOD & WASTEWATER DST
450 Ryder St, Vallejo (94590-7217)
PHONE..................707 644-8949
Melissa Morton, *Manager*
Alexandria Bell, *Principal*
Mj Brown, *Principal*
Jeff Tucker, *Director*
Mark Tomko, *Manager*
EMP: 96 **EST:** 2018
SALES (est): 36.1MM **Privately Held**
WEB: www.vallejowastewater.org
SIC: 8748 Environmental consultant

(P-19883)
VALLEJO FLOOD WSTWTER DST FING
450 Ryder St, Vallejo (94590-7217)
PHONE..................707 644-8949
Melissa Morton, *CEO*
Mary A Morris, *CFO*

Holly M Charlety, *Admin Sec*
Erika Sheetenhelm, *Technician*
Mark Tomko, *Engineer*
EMP: 86
SQ FT: 10,000
SALES (est): 32.7MM **Privately Held**
WEB: www.vallejowastewater.org
SIC: 8748 Environmental consultant; traffic consultant; economic consultant

(P-19884)
VEGA ECONOMIC CONSULTING
Also Called: Vega Economics
2040 Bancroft Way Ste 200, Berkeley (94704-1495)
PHONE..................510 280-5520
Ethan Cohen-Cole, *Director*
Daphne Chen, *Managing Dir*
Joe Pollack, *Administration*
Shivprasad Gunjal, *Sr Associate*
Dylan Jaggar, *Sr Associate*
EMP: 35 **EST:** 2017
SALES (est): 1.9MM **Privately Held**
WEB: www.vegaeconomics.com
SIC: 8748 8721 8713 8111 Business consulting; accounting, auditing & bookkeeping; surveying services; legal services

(P-19885)
VILLA REAL INC
421 S El Dorado St Unit D, Stockton (95203-3459)
P.O. Box 447 (95201-0447)
PHONE..................209 460-5069
Greg Arnaudo, *Ch of Bd*
Ludmila George, *Property Mgr*
EMP: 35 **EST:** 1999
SALES (est): 2.3MM **Privately Held**
SIC: 8748 Urban planning & consulting services

(P-19886)
VIMO INC (PA)
Also Called: Getinsured.com
1305 Terra Bella Ave, Mountain View (94043-1851)
PHONE..................650 618-4600
Srinivasan Krishnan, *CEO*
Paul Neutz, *President*
Shankar Srinivasan, *COO*
Daniel Wolf, *Vice Pres*
Whitney Chang, *Admin Sec*
EMP: 305 **EST:** 2005
SQ FT: 20,000
SALES (est): 102.9K **Privately Held**
WEB: www.getinsured.com
SIC: 8748 6411 7371 7373 Business consulting; insurance brokers; computer software development & applications; systems software development services

(P-19887)
VIRTUOZ INC (HQ)
6001 Shellmound St # 500, Emeryville (94608-1968)
PHONE..................415 202-5709
Steve L Adams, *CEO*
Karen Camp, *CFO*
Alexandre Lebrun, *Vice Pres*
EMP: 49 **EST:** 2009
SALES (est): 1.2MM **Publicly Held**
WEB: www.nuance.com
SIC: 8748 Business consulting

(P-19888)
VSC SPORTS INC
Also Called: Yorba Bena Ice Skting Bowl Ctr
750 Folsom St, San Francisco (94107-1276)
PHONE..................415 820-3525
Michael Paikin, *Owner*
Robyn Marlinski, *Director*
EMP: 60
SALES (corp-wide): 5.3MM **Privately Held**
SIC: 8748 Business consulting
PA: Vsc Sports Inc
11401 Topanga Canyon Blvd # 125
Chatsworth CA 91311
818 994-3229

(P-19889)
WEISSCOMM GROUP LTD (PA)
Also Called: Wcg World
50 Francisco St Ste 400, San Francisco (94133-2114)
PHONE..................415 362-5018
James Weiss, *CEO*
Mary Corcoran, *President*
Chris Deri, *President*
Diane Weiser, *President*
Richard Neave, *CFO*
EMP: 75 **EST:** 2001
SQ FT: 16,000
SALES (est): 90.7MM **Privately Held**
WEB: www.w2ogroup.com
SIC: 8748 Communications consulting

(P-19890)
WEST VLLY-MSSION CMNTY CLLEGE
Also Called: Mission College
3000 Mission College Blvd, Santa Clara (95054-1804)
PHONE..................408 988-2200
Linda Wilczewski, *Exec Dir*
Rick Bennett, *Vice Pres*
Leandra Martin, *Vice Pres*
Danny Nguyen, *Vice Pres*
Linda Angelotti, *Executive Asst*
EMP: 400
SALES (corp-wide): 12.1MM **Privately Held**
WEB: www.westvalley.edu
SIC: 8222 8748 8221 Community college; business consulting; colleges universities & professional schools
PA: West Valley-Mission Community College District
14000 Fruitvale Ave
Saratoga CA 95070
408 867-2200

(P-19891)
WESTED
1000 G St Ste 500, Sacramento (95814-0892)
PHONE..................916 492-9999
Donald Hum, *Branch Mgr*
May Chan, *Officer*
Sheyanne Johnson, *Executive*
Mary Stump, *Associate Dir*
Julie J Colton, *Admin Asst*
EMP: 48
SALES (corp-wide): 71.6MM **Privately Held**
WEB: www.wested.org
SIC: 8748 Educational consultant
PA: Wested
730 Harrison St Ste 500
San Francisco CA 94107
415 565-3000

(P-19892)
WESTERVELT COMPANY
Westervelt Ecological Services
600 N Market Blvd Ste 3, Sacramento (95834-1257)
PHONE..................916 646-3644
Greg Sutter, *Vice Pres*
Greg Deyoung, *Vice Pres*
Hal Holland, *Manager*
EMP: 36
SALES (corp-wide): 130MM **Privately Held**
WEB: www.westerveltproperties.com
SIC: 8748 Environmental consultant
PA: Westervelt Company
1400 Jack Warner Pkwy Ne
Tuscaloosa AL 35404
205 562-5295

(P-19893)
ZEALTECH INC
39111 Paseo Padre Pkwy, Fremont (94538-1672)
PHONE..................510 797-7006
Sunil Palamuttam, *CEO*
EMP: 36 **EST:** 2005
SALES (est): 2.8MM **Privately Held**
WEB: www.zealtechus.com
SIC: 8748 7373 8742 7371 Business consulting; computer integrated systems design; management consulting services; computer software development; software programming applications

(P-19894)
ZEST CONSULTING LLC
5000 Hopyard Rd Ste 165, Pleasanton (94588-3348)
PHONE..................415 361-5696
Jayashree Pawar, *President*
EMP: 46 **EST:** 2016
SALES (est): 1.6MM **Privately Held**
SIC: 8748 Business consulting

(P-19895)
ZGLOBAL INC (PA)
604 Sutter St Ste 250, Folsom (95630-2694)
PHONE..................916 985-9461
Ziad Alaywan, *President*
Kevin Coffee, *Vice Pres*
Jamie Nagel, *Intrm Mgr*
Omar Itani, *Engineer*
Dhayanesh Velusamy, *Engineer*
EMP: 47 **EST:** 2005
SALES (est): 9MM **Privately Held**
WEB: www.zglobal.biz
SIC: 8748 Energy conservation consultant

8999 Services Not Elsewhere Classified

(P-19896)
ADANTA INC
1100 Lincoln Ave Ste 206, NAPA (94558-4956)
PHONE..................707 709-8894
Kimberly Patz, *President*
EMP: 52 **EST:** 2008
SALES (est): 2.7MM **Privately Held**
WEB: www.adanta-inc.com
SIC: 8999 Earth science services

(P-19897)
ARDOR LEARNING INC (PA)
1027 Amarillo Ave, Palo Alto (94303-3706)
PHONE..................650 245-6300
Deepak Desai, *CEO*
Bob Leman, *Consultant*
EMP: 45 **EST:** 2014
SALES (est): 3MM **Privately Held**
WEB: www.ardorlearning.com
SIC: 8999 7389 7372 Lecturing services; ; prepackaged software

(P-19898)
CALIFORNIA TAHOE CONSERVANCY
1061 3rd St, South Lake Tahoe (96150-3475)
PHONE..................530 542-5580
Patrick Wright, *Exec Dir*
Russell Maloney, *Principal*
Jane Freeman, *Exec Dir*
David Gregorich, *Administration*
EMP: 50 **EST:** 1984
SALES (est): 5.2MM **Privately Held**
WEB: www.tahoe.ca.gov
SIC: 8999 Natural resource preservation service
HQ: California Natural Resources Agency
1416 9th St Ste 1311
Sacramento CA 95814

(P-19899)
CITY OF REDDING (PA)
777 Cypress Ave, Redding (96001-2718)
P.O. Box 496071 (96049-6071)
PHONE..................530 225-4079
Kristen Schreder, *Council Mbr*
Ray Duryee, *COO*
Allyn F Clark, *Treasurer*
John Dobson, *Vice Pres*
Charles Aukland, *General Mgr*
▲ **EMP:** 802
SQ FT: 105,000
SALES: 107.1MM **Privately Held**
WEB: www.cityofredding.org
SIC: 9111 8999 8399 City & town managers' offices; ; search & rescue service; community action agency

PRODUCTS & SERVICES SECTION

8999 - Services Not Elsewhere Classified County (P-19923)

(P-19900)
ENVIRONMENTAL REMEDIES INC
1999 Alpine Way, Hayward (94545-1701)
P.O. Box 10416, Pleasanton (94588-0416)
PHONE 925 461-3285
Scott Tamayo, Exec Dir
EMP: 65 EST: 2004
SALES (est): 4.2MM Privately Held
WEB: www.environmentalremediesinc.com
SIC: 8999 Earth science services

(P-19901)
FORT MASON CENTER
2 Marina Blvd Bldg A, San Francisco (94123-1284)
PHONE 415 345-7500
Caroline Werth, President
Rich Hillis, Exec Dir
Matt Sauerman, Info Tech Mgr
Virgilio Capistrano, Technician
Mauricio Ramirez, Technician
EMP: 56
SQ FT: 300,000
SALES: 13.8MM Privately Held
WEB: www.fortmason.org
SIC: 8999 Art related services

(P-19902)
GLOBAL BUILDING SERVICES INC
17618 Murphy Pkwy, Lathrop (95330-8629)
PHONE 209 858-9501
Mario Belloso, Representative
EMP: 193
SALES (corp-wide): 19.7MM Privately Held
WEB: www.globalbuildingservices.com
SIC: 8999 Actuarial consultant
PA: Global Building Services, Inc.
27433 Tourney Rd Ste 280
Valencia CA 91355
800 675-6643

(P-19903)
GOLDEN GATE NAT PRKS CNSRVANCY
1 Presidio Ave, San Francisco (94115-1017)
PHONE 415 440-4068
EMP: 120 Privately Held
WEB: www.parksconservancy.org
SIC: 8999 Natural resource preservation service
PA: Golden Gate National Parks Conservancy
Fort Mason Bldg 201
San Francisco CA 94123

(P-19904)
GOLDEN GATE NAT PRKS CNSRVANCY
Also Called: Golden Gate Nat Prks Cnsrvancy
1600 Los Gamos Dr, San Rafael (94903-1806)
PHONE 415 785-4787
EMP: 120 Privately Held
WEB: www.parksconservancy.org
SIC: 8999 Natural resource preservation service
PA: Golden Gate National Parks Conservancy
Fort Mason Bldg 201
San Francisco CA 94123

(P-19905)
GOLDEN GATE NAT PRKS CNSRVANCY (PA)
Fort Mason Bldg 201, San Francisco (94123)
PHONE 415 561-3000
Greg Moore, CEO
Staci Slaughter, Vice Chairman
Nicolas Elsishans, Exec VP
Cathie Barner, Vice Pres
Sharon Farrell, Vice Pres
▲ EMP: 70 EST: 1981
SQ FT: 5,000
SALES: 67.5MM Privately Held
WEB: www.parksconservancy.org
SIC: 8999 Natural resource preservation service

(P-19906)
INTERNET STORE INC
Also Called: Cruzio
903 Pacific Ave Ste 101, Santa Cruz (95060-4460)
PHONE 831 459-6301
Christopher Neklason, President
Margaret Collins, Technology
Nikkie Lanctot, Finance Mgr
Alan Goldstein, Manager
Steve Soskin, Consultant
EMP: 36 EST: 1989
SQ FT: 6,500
SALES (est): 1MM Privately Held
WEB: www.cruzio.com
SIC: 8999 Personal services

(P-19907)
JAQUI FOUNDATION INC
675 Hegenberger Rd # 209, Oakland (94621-1973)
P.O. Box 4938 (94605-6938)
PHONE 510 562-4721
Robert L Porter Jr, CEO
Dorothy M Jones, Treasurer
Dawson Andrews, Admin Sec
EMP: 50 EST: 2005
SQ FT: 600
SALES (est): 1.5MM Privately Held
WEB: www.jaquifoundation.org
SIC: 8999 Personal services

(P-19908)
KINGS RIVER CONSERVATION DST
4886 E Jensen Ave, Fresno (93725-1899)
PHONE 559 237-5567
Mark McKean, President
Brent Graham, Vice Pres
Corey McLaughlin, Executive Asst
Soua Lee, Analyst
Gregory Beberian, Director
EMP: 64 EST: 1952
SQ FT: 8,500
SALES (est): 10.2MM Privately Held
WEB: www.krcd.org
SIC: 8999 Natural resource preservation service

(P-19909)
KLINGSTUBBINS INC
160 Spear St Ste 330, San Francisco (94105-1543)
PHONE 415 356-2040
Peter Dugo, Manager
EMP: 71
SALES (corp-wide): 13.5B Publicly Held
SIC: 8999 Artists & artists' studios
HQ: Klingstubbins, Inc.
2301 Chestnut St
Philadelphia PA 19103
215 569-2900

(P-19910)
LINE2 INC
535 Mission St Fl 14, San Francisco (94105-3253)
PHONE 415 223-5811
Doug Brackbill, CEO
Mark Pengelski, Analyst
Angelica Navarro, Controller
Anthony Razouk, Sales Staff
Raymond Castro, Manager
EMP: 35 EST: 2006
SQ FT: 3,500
SALES (est): 6.5MM Privately Held
WEB: www.line2.com
SIC: 8999 Communication services

(P-19911)
MCCLATCHY COMPANY
2100 Q St, Sacramento (95816-6816)
PHONE 916 321-1941
EMP: 10000
SALES (est): 72.8K Privately Held
SIC: 8999 Services-Misc

(P-19912)
MIDPENNSULA RGNAL OPEN SPACE D
330 Distel Cir, Los Altos (94022-1404)
PHONE 650 691-1200
Craig Britton, President
EMP: 65 EST: 1972
SQ FT: 12,000
SALES: 65.7MM Privately Held
WEB: www.openspace.org
SIC: 8999 Natural resource preservation service

(P-19913)
MILLIMAN INC
650 California St Fl 21, San Francisco (94108-2602)
PHONE 415 403-1333
Steve White, Manager
Bob Helliesen, Principal
Jim Walbridge, Principal
Rich Wright, General Mgr
Cindy Legassie, Admin Asst
EMP: 50
SALES (corp-wide): 1.1B Privately Held
WEB: www.us.milliman.com
SIC: 8999 6411 Actuarial consultant; ratemaking organizations, insurance
PA: Milliman, Inc.
1301 5th Ave Ste 3800
Seattle WA 98101
206 624-7940

(P-19914)
NATURENER GLACIER WIND ENERGY
394 Pacific Ave Ste 300, San Francisco (94111-1718)
PHONE 415 217-5500
EMP: 40
SALES (est): 1.2MM
SALES (corp-wide): 2MM Privately Held
SIC: 8999 Independent Power Producer
HQ: Naturener Usa, Llc
394 Pacific Ave Ste 300
San Francisco CA 94133
415 217-5500

(P-19915)
NORCAL GEOPHYSICAL CONS INC
Also Called: Norcal Gphysical Cons Inc NS
321 Blodgett St Ste A, Cotati (94931-8710)
PHONE 707 796-7170
Kenneth Blom, President
William Black, Vice Pres
EMP: 57 EST: 1983
SQ FT: 4,200
SALES (est): 1MM Privately Held
WEB: www.norcalgeophysical.com
SIC: 8999 Geological consultant; geophysical consultant
HQ: Terracon Consultants, Inc.
10841 S Ridgeview Rd
Olathe KS 66061

(P-19916)
SACRAMNTO CMNTY CBLE FUNDATION
Also Called: Access Sacramento
4623 T St Ste A, Sacramento (95819-4700)
PHONE 916 456-8600
Donna Girot, Exec Dir
Don Henkle, Ch of Bd
Bob Smith, Vice Chairman
Robert Morin, CFO
Gary Martin, Exec Dir
EMP: 36 EST: 1985
SQ FT: 2,800
SALES (est): 4.5MM Privately Held
WEB: www.accesssacramento.org
SIC: 8999 Radio & television announcing

(P-19917)
STORMGEO (DH)
Also Called: Applied Weather Technology Inc
140 Kifer Ct, Sunnyvale (94086-5120)
PHONE 408 731-8600
Robert Haydn Jones, CEO
Haydn Jones, President
William Lapworth, CFO
John Eaton, General Mgr
Neill Moseley, General Mgr
EMP: 166 EST: 1996
SQ FT: 19,000
SALES (est): 13.6MM
SALES (corp-wide): 2.6MM Privately Held
WEB: www.stormgeo.com
SIC: 8999 Weather forecasting

(P-19918)
TRIPLE HS INC (PA)
Also Called: H. T. Harvey & Associates
983 University Ave Bldg D, Los Gatos (95032-7637)
PHONE 408 458-3200
Karin Hunsicker, CEO
Ronald R Duke, President
Steve Rottenborn, Vice Pres
Daniel Stephens, Vice Pres
Yuliya Kulchitskiy, Admin Asst
EMP: 55 EST: 1971
SQ FT: 15,000
SALES (est): 11.2MM Privately Held
WEB: www.harveyecology.com
SIC: 8999 8731 8748 Scientific consulting; environmental research; environmental consultant

(P-19919)
VERIZON MEDIA INC
701 First Ave, Sunnyvale (94089-1019)
PHONE 310 907-3016
EMP: 720 Publicly Held
SIC: 8999 Communication services
HQ: Verizon Media Inc.
11995 Bluff Creek Dr
Los Angeles CA 90094
310 907-3016

(P-19920)
WEATHERFLOW-TEMPEST INC ✪
108 Whispering Pines Dr, Scotts Valley (95066-4791)
PHONE 831 438-9742
Daniel C Lyones, CEO
EMP: 36 EST: 2021
SALES (est): 438K Privately Held
SIC: 8999 Weather related services

(P-19921)
WOODMONT REAL ESTATE SVCS LP
3883 Airway Dr, Santa Rosa (95403-1670)
PHONE 707 569-0582
Ron Granville, Branch Mgr
EMP: 43 Privately Held
WEB: www.wres.com
SIC: 8999 Artists & artists' studios
PA: Woodmont Real Estate Services, L.P.
1050 Ralston Ave
Belmont CA 94002

(P-19922)
ZENO GROUP INC
275 Shoreline Dr Ste 530, Redwood City (94065-1413)
PHONE 650 801-7950
Todd Irwin, Branch Mgr
Michael Brito, Exec VP
Reagan Crossley, Vice Pres
Sophie Isacowitz, Vice Pres
Brian Devenny, Supervisor
EMP: 52
SALES (corp-wide): 1.5B Privately Held
WEB: www.zenogroup.com
SIC: 8999 Personal services
HQ: Zeno Group, Inc.
130 E Randolph St # 3000
Chicago IL 60601
312 396-9700

(P-19923)
ZOE HOLDING COMPANY INC
44 Montgomery St, San Francisco (94104-4602)
PHONE 415 421-4900
John Unick, Branch Mgr
EMP: 90
SALES (corp-wide): 36.9MM Privately Held
WEB: www.zoeholding.com
SIC: 8999 Artists & artists' studios
PA: Zoe Holding Company, Inc.
7025 N Scottsdale Rd # 200
Scottsdale AZ 85253
602 508-1883

ALPHABETIC SECTION

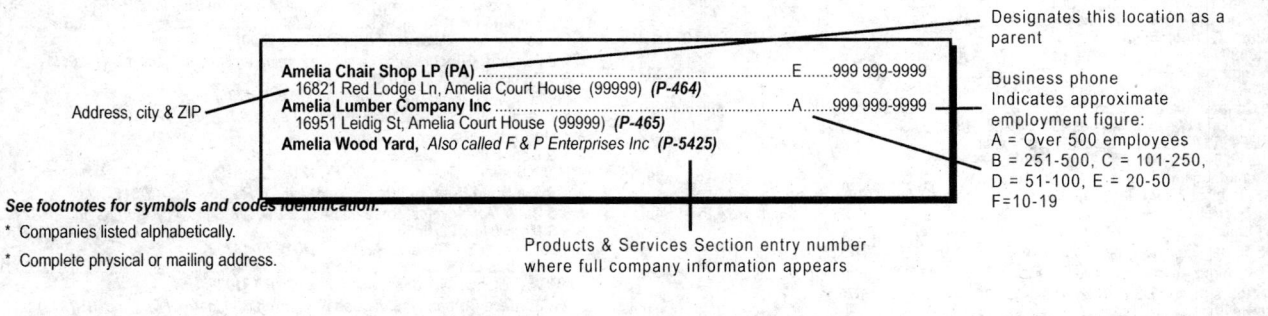

See footnotes for symbols and codes identification.
* Companies listed alphabetically.
* Complete physical or mailing address.

(a) Tool Shed Inc (PA) .... E 831 477-7133
  3700 Soquel Ave Santa Cruz (95062) *(P-12025)*
0epi, Carmichael *Also called Eskaton Properties Inc* *(P-18113)*
1-800 Radiator & A/C (HQ) .... D 707 747-7400
  4401 Park Rd Benicia (94510) *(P-8435)*
1-800-Radiator, Benicia *Also called 1-800 Radiator & A/C* *(P-8435)*
10 Fold Communications Inc .... E 925 271-8205
  800 S Broadway Ste 309 Walnut Creek (94596) *(P-19680)*
1000 Executive Parkway LLC .... C 530 533-7335
  1000 Executive Pkwy Oroville (95966) *(P-15903)*
1000 Sansome Associates LLC .... E 415 233-8357
  1000 Sansome St Ste 200 San Francisco (94111) *(P-13546)*
101 Voice, Santa Clara *Also called It Management Corp* *(P-19545)*
101mfg Llc .... E 415 828-9015
  107 Dublin Ct Petaluma (94952) *(P-19430)*
10up Inc (PA) .... D 888 571-7130
  2765 Carradale Dr Roseville (95661) *(P-13547)*
10x Genomics Inc (PA) .... B 925 401-7300
  6230 Stoneridge Mall Rd Pleasanton (94588) *(P-19007)*
11 Main Inc. .... C 530 892-9191
  527 Flume St Chico (95928) *(P-7918)*
1101 Corporate-Sacramento, Sacramento *Also called Crestwood Behavioral Hlth Inc* *(P-16735)*
1101 Stockton Accounting Off, Stockton *Also called Crestwood Behavioral Hlth Inc* *(P-16740)*
1106 Sacramento Mhrc, Sacramento *Also called Crestwood Behavioral Hlth Inc* *(P-16736)*
1107 San Jose Mhrc, San Jose *Also called Crestwood Behavioral Hlth Inc* *(P-18093)*
1110 Eureka Mhrc, Eureka *Also called Crestwood Behavioral Hlth Inc* *(P-16230)*
1112 Modesto Snf/STP, Modesto *Also called Crestwood Behavioral Hlth Inc* *(P-16734)*
1120 Fremont Snf, Fremont *Also called Crestwood Behavioral Hlth Inc* *(P-18096)*
1122 Redding IMD, Redding *Also called Crestwood Behavioral Hlth Inc* *(P-18094)*
1125 Sir Frncis Drake Blvd Ope .... C 415 456-9680
  1125 Sir Frncis Drake Blv Kentfield (94904) *(P-16285)*
1134 Alameda Snf/STP, Fremont *Also called Crestwood Behavioral Hlth Inc* *(P-18095)*
1140 Kingsburg Mhrc, Kingsburg *Also called Crestwood Behavioral Hlth Inc* *(P-16229)*
1143 Pleasant Hill Bridge, Pleasant Hill *Also called Crestwood Behavioral Hlth Inc* *(P-15976)*
1153 American River PHF, Carmichael *Also called Crestwood Behavioral Hlth Inc* *(P-16741)*
1156 Sacramento PHF, Sacramento *Also called Crestwood Behavioral Hlth Inc* *(P-16737)*
1157 San Jose PHF, San Jose *Also called Crestwood Behavioral Hlth Inc* *(P-16738)*
1159 Solano PHF, Vallejo *Also called Crestwood Behavioral Hlth Inc* *(P-16739)*
1166 San Francisco Mhrc, San Francisco *Also called Crestwood Behavioral Hlth Inc* *(P-16231)*
1172 Solano Csu, Fairfield *Also called Crestwood Behavioral Hlth Inc* *(P-17524)*
14766 Wash Ave Operations LLC .... D 510 352-2211
  14766 Washington Ave San Leandro (94578) *(P-16212)*
150 The Tunnel Center For Reha .... E 415 673-8405
  1359 Pine St San Francisco (94109) *(P-15904)*
15th & L Investors LLC. .... D 916 267-6805
  1121 15th St Sacramento (95814) *(P-10900)*
16500 Sixteen Five Hundred .... E 510 208-5005
  2001 Broadway Fl 4th Oakland (94612) *(P-8835)*
1651 Tiburon Hotel LLC .... D 401 946-4600
  1651 Tiburon Blvd Belvedere Tiburon (94920) *(P-10901)*
18 Rabbits Inc (PA) .... F 415 922-6006
  995 Market St Fl 2 San Francisco (94103) *(P-2424)*
1849 Condominiums Rentals, Mammoth Lakes *Also called 1849 Homeowners Association* *(P-11623)*
1849 Homeowners Association .... E 760 934-7525
  826 Lakeview Blvd Mammoth Lakes (93546) *(P-11623)*
1919 Investment Counsel LLC .... E 415 500-6707
  49 Stevenson St Ste 1075 San Francisco (94105) *(P-4339)*
1healthio Inc .... E 208 681-4058
  388 Market St San Francisco (94111) *(P-7919)*
1life Healthcare Inc .... B 415 814-0927
  1 Embarcadero Ctr # 1900 San Francisco (94111) *(P-15266)*
1st Chice HM Halthcare Hospice .... E 650 393-5936
  1291 E Hillsdale Blvd Foster City (94404) *(P-16825)*
1st Class Laundry Services, Union City *Also called Specialized Laundry Svcs Inc* *(P-11670)*
1st Light Energy Inc (PA) .... E 209 824-5500
  1869 Moffat Blvd Manteca (95336) *(P-1996)*
1st Pacific Credit Union (PA) .... E 707 552-4550
  536 Santa Clara St Vallejo (94590) *(P-9773)*

1st Quality Produce Inc .... E 559 442-1932
  2445 S Gearhart Ave Fresno (93725) *(P-9385)*
1st United Credit Union (PA) .... D 800 649-0193
  5901 Gibraltar Dr Pleasanton (94588) *(P-9774)*
1STNORCAL, Martinez *Also called Contra Costa Federal Credit Un* *(P-9781)*
2-G Enterprises, Mountain View *Also called Applied Physics Systems* *(P-6892)*
205 Kentucky Street LLC .... E 707 559-3393
  205 Kentucky St Petaluma (94952) *(P-10902)*
2150 N Frst Nvel Coworking LLC 312 283-3683
  2150 N 1st St San Jose (95131) *(P-10374)*
21st Century Health Club (PA) .... E 707 795-0400
  680a E Cotati Ave Cotati (94931) *(P-16982)*
22 Miles Inc .... E 408 933-3000
  1595 Mccarthy Blvd Milpitas (95035) *(P-13776)*
22nd Century Technologies Inc 866 537-9191
  6203 San Ignacio Ave # 1 San Jose (95119) *(P-12211)*
23andme Inc (HQ) .... B 650 961-7152
  223 N Mathilda Ave Sunnyvale (94086) *(P-13777)*
24 Hour Fitness Usa Inc .... E 209 951-5999
  3137 W Benjamin Holt Dr Stockton (95219) *(P-14919)*
24 Hour Fitness Usa Inc .... E 408 923-2639
  375 N Capitol Ave Ste A San Jose (95133) *(P-14920)*
24 Hour Fitness Usa Inc .... E 650 343-7922
  500 El Camino Real Burlingame (94010) *(P-14921)*
24 Hour Fitness Usa Inc .... E 510 524-4583
  1775 Solano Ave Berkeley (94707) *(P-14922)*
24 Hour In Motion Fitness, Chico *Also called B A M I Inc* *(P-14927)*
24/7 Medstaff, Sacramento *Also called Epn Enterprises Inc* *(P-12170)*
247ai Inc (PA) .... A 650 385-2247
  2001 All Programable # 200 San Jose (95124) *(P-13826)*
24hr Homecare LLC .... D 650 209-3295
  228 Hamilton Ave Ste 300 Palo Alto (94301) *(P-16826)*
24hr Homecare LLC .... D 650 209-3248
  951 Mariners Island Blvd San Mateo (94404) *(P-16827)*
24hr Homecare LLC .... D 408 550-8295
  4675 Stevens Creek Blvd # 121 Santa Clara (95051) *(P-16828)*
24hr Homecare LLC .... D 925 322-8627
  1399 Ygnacio Valley Rd # 35 Walnut Creek (94598) *(P-16829)*
24i Unit Media Inc .... C 818 802-9995
  1633 Bayshore Hwy Ste 338 Burlingame (94010) *(P-12212)*
28 Sasf Owner LLC. .... E 415 276-9888
  222 Sansome St San Francisco (94104) *(P-10903)*
280 Capmarkets LLC (PA) .... E 628 231-2390
  220 Montgomery St # 1060 San Francisco (94104) *(P-14185)*
2crsi Corporation .... F 408 598-3176
  894 Faulstich Ct Ste B San Jose (95112) *(P-5280)*
2dream Inc 650 943-2366
  5729 Sonoma Dr Ste Z Pleasanton (94566) *(P-14186)*
2k Marin Inc .... E 646 536-2898
  10 Hamilton Landing Novato (94949) *(P-12213)*
2wire Inc (HQ) .... C 408 235-5500
  2450 Walsh Ave Santa Clara (95051) *(P-7920)*
3 Badge Beverage Corporation .... F 707 343-1167
  32 Patten St Sonoma (95476) *(P-2500)*
3 Ink Productions Inc. 559 275-4565
  4790 W Jacquelyn Ave Fresno (93722) *(P-2966)*
3-Way Farms (PA). .... E 831 722-0748
  428 Browns Valley Rd Watsonville (95076) *(P-115)*
314e Corporation .... C 510 371-6736
  6701 Koll Center Pkwy # 34 Pleasanton (94566) *(P-12214)*
35-A District AG Assn .... E 209 966-2432
  5007 Fairgrounds Rd Mariposa (95338) *(P-14187)*
360 Media Direct, Fresno *Also called Subdirect LLC* *(P-3516)*
360 Viansa LLC .... E 707 935-4700
  25200 Arnold Dr Sonoma (95476) *(P-11704)*
3d Data Com (PA) .... E 916 573-3720
  11365 Sunrise Gold Cir Rancho Cordova (95742) *(P-1086)*
3d Robotics Inc (PA) .... D 415 599-1404
  1165 Miller Ave Berkeley (94708) *(P-6508)*
3d Technology Services, Rancho Cordova *Also called 3d Data Com* *(P-1086)*
3dconnexion Inc 510 713-6000
  6505 Kaiser Dr Fremont (94555) *(P-5338)*
3degrees Group Inc (PA) .... E 415 561-6852
  235 Montgomery St Ste 320 San Francisco (94104) *(P-19708)*
3jam Inc .... F 415 867-1339
  2108 Sand Hill Rd Menlo Park (94025) *(P-5783)*

3k Technologies LLC C 408 716-5900
1114 Cadillac Ct Milpitas (95035) ***(P-12215)***
3par Inc (HQ) **C 510 445-1046**
4209 Technology Dr Fremont (94538) ***(P-5236)***
3plus1 Technology Inc E 408 374-1111
18809 Cox Ave Ste 250 Saratoga (95070) ***(P-6005)***
3q Digital Inc (HQ) **C 650 539-4124**
155 Bovet Rd Ste 480 San Mateo (94402) ***(P-11737)***
3s Communications Inc E 408 505-9517
105 Serra Way 312 Milpitas (95035) ***(P-1439)***
3scale Inc (PA) **E 415 349-5187**
995 Market St San Francisco (94103) ***(P-14113)***
3stonedeggs Inc E 541 225-7491
840 Embarcadero Dr Ste 40 West Sacramento (95605) ***(P-9344)***
3vr Security Inc D 415 513-4577
1 Kaiser Plz Ste 1030 Oakland (94612) ***(P-14114)***
4 C'S, Hayward *Also called Community Child Care Crdnting* ***(P-17911)***
4 Cs, Santa Rosa *Also called Community Chld Cre Cncl Sonoma* ***(P-17912)***
40 Hours Staffing, San Jose *Also called 40 Hrs Inc* ***(P-12067)***
40 Hrs Inc A 408 414-0158
1669 Flanigan Dr San Jose (95121) ***(P-12067)***
425 North Point Street LLC E 800 648-4626
101 California St Ste 950 San Francisco (94111) ***(P-10904)***
4290 El Camino Properties LP C 650 857-0787
4290 El Camino Real Palo Alto (94306) ***(P-10905)***
4505 Meats Inc E 415 255-3094
548 Market St San Francisco (94104) ***(P-2851)***
478826 Limited E 916 933-5280
5050 Hillsdale Cir El Dorado Hills (95762) ***(P-5455)***
4961 North Cdr LLC D 559 224-4200
4961 N Cedar Ave Fresno (93726) ***(P-10906)***
4d Inc C 408 557-4600
95 S Market St Ste 240 San Jose (95113) ***(P-12216)***
4d Molecular Therapeutics Inc D 510 505-2680
5858 Horton St Ste 455 Emeryville (94608) ***(P-19008)***
4d Sight Inc E 415 425-1321
2150 Shattuck Ave Berkeley (94704) ***(P-12944)***
4info Inc E 650 350-4800
4 N 2nd St Ste 1150 San Jose (95113) ***(P-11799)***
4into1 Inc F 650 741-6175
280 Wattis Way B South San Francisco (94080) ***(P-6646)***
4leaf Inc (PA) **D 925 462-5959**
2126 Rheem Dr Pleasanton (94588) ***(P-14188)***
4th & Folsom Associates LP B 415 417-3086
201 Eddy St San Francisco (94102) ***(P-10416)***
5 Palms LLC C 650 457-0539
800 S B St Fl 1 San Mateo (94401) ***(P-14189)***
5 Star Service, Sacramento *Also called Borge Construction Inc* ***(P-621)***
5-Stars Engineering Associates E 408 380-4849
3393 De La Cruz Blvd Santa Clara (95054) ***(P-5106)***
500 Startups Management Co LLC C 650 743-4738
3478 Buskirk Ave Ste 1000 Pleasant Hill (94523) ***(P-10827)***
501 C Services, San Jose *Also called 501(c Insurance Programs Inc* ***(P-10223)***
501(c Insurance Programs Inc E 408 216-9796
400 Race St Ste 200 San Jose (95126) ***(P-10223)***
643 Capital Management Inc (PA) **E 650 759-0599**
2001 Broadway Fl 4th Oakland (94612) ***(P-9954)***
6wind Usa Inc D 408 816-1366
2445 Augustine Dr Ste 150 Santa Clara (95054) ***(P-12217)***
7 Flags Car Wash, Vacaville *Also called Jack Anthony Industries Inc* ***(P-14642)***
7 Flags Car Wash - Fairfield, Fairfield *Also called Jack Anthony Industries Inc* ***(P-14643)***
7 Flags Car Wash - Plaza, Vallejo *Also called Jack Anthony Industries Inc* ***(P-14644)***
7 Up, Stockton *Also called Varni Brothers Corporation* ***(P-2817)***
765 Airport Boulevard Partnr E 650 347-7800
765 Airport Blvd Burlingame (94010) ***(P-10907)***
7th Avenue Center LLC E 831 476-1700
1171 7th Ave Santa Cruz (95062) ***(P-16731)***
7x7, San Francisco *Also called Hartle Media Ventures LLC* ***(P-3502)***
8181 LLC E 303 779-3053
2570 W El Camino Real Mountain View (94040) ***(P-10375)***
85 C Bakery Cafe, Stockton *Also called Golden 85 Investments Corp* ***(P-10849)***
89bio Inc E 415 500-4614
142 Sansome St Fl 2 San Francisco (94104) ***(P-3823)***
8minute Solar Energy LLC (PA) **E 916 608-9060**
4370 Town Center Blvd # 11 El Dorado Hills (95762) ***(P-1185)***
8minutenergy Renewables, El Dorado Hills *Also called 8minute Solar Energy LLC* ***(P-1185)***
8x8 Inc (PA) **A 408 727-1885**
675 Creekside Way Campbell (95008) ***(P-7921)***
99designs Inc (PA) **C 415 539-1088**
2201 Broadway Ste 815 Oakland (94612) ***(P-11856)***
A & A A/C Heating & Shtmtl, Grass Valley *Also called A & A AC Htg & Shtmtl* ***(P-1186)***
A & A AC Htg & Shtmtl E 530 273-1301
763 S Auburn St Grass Valley (95945) ***(P-1186)***
A & A Portables Inc E 209 524-0401
201 Roscoe Rd Modesto (95357) ***(P-12026)***
A & A Stepping Stone Mfg Inc (PA) **E 530 885-7481**
10291 Ophir Rd Newcastle (95658) ***(P-4416)***
A & B Construction, Berkeley *Also called Andrew M Jordan Inc* ***(P-1950)***
A & B Die Casting Co Inc E 877 708-0009
900 Alfred Nobel Dr Hercules (94547) ***(P-4574)***
A & B Diecasting, Hercules *Also called Benda Tool & Model Works Inc* ***(P-5081)***
A & D Precision Machining Inc E 510 657-6781
4155 Business Center Dr Fremont (94538) ***(P-5456)***
A & D Rubber Products Co Inc (PA) **E 209 941-0100**
1438 Bourbon St Stockton (95204) ***(P-4201)***
A & E Anodizing Inc F 408 297-5910
652 Charles St Ste A San Jose (95112) ***(P-4890)***
A & E Arborists Tree Care Inc C 530 790-5312
225 Butte Ave Yuba City (95993) ***(P-511)***
A & I Transportation, Watsonville *Also called A & I Trucking Inc* ***(P-7500)***
A & I Trucking Inc (PA) **E 831 763-7805**
123 Lee Rd Ste E Watsonville (95076) ***(P-7500)***
A & J Fencing, Concord *Also called California Lumber Company Inc* ***(P-2015)***
A & J Precision Sheetmetal Inc D 408 885-9134
2233 Paragon Dr Ste A San Jose (95131) ***(P-4735)***
A & L Ready Mix, Sonora *Also called L K Lehman Trucking* ***(P-4490)***
A & M Printing, Pleasanton *Also called Leo Lam Inc* ***(P-3672)***
A & R Doors Inc E 831 637-8139
41 5th St Frnt Hollister (95023) ***(P-3121)***
A & R Pre-Hung Door, Hollister *Also called A & R Doors Inc* ***(P-3121)***
A & S BMW Motorcycles, Roseville *Also called A & S Motorcycle Parts Inc* ***(P-14732)***
A & S Motorcycle Parts Inc E 916 726-7334
1125 Orlando Ave Ste A Roseville (95661) ***(P-14732)***
A 3 By Airbus LLC D 650 660-5809
601 W California Ave Sunnyvale (94086) ***(P-19192)***
A A A Furnace Company, San Jose *Also called Rando AAA Hvac Inc* ***(P-1343)***
A A Label Inc (PA) **E 925 803-5709**
6958 Sierra Ct Dublin (94568) ***(P-3400)***
A and G News Papers, Hayward *Also called Daily Review* ***(P-3431)***
A B & I, Fowler *Also called McWane Inc* ***(P-4550)***
A B A, San Jose *Also called Anderson Brule Architects Inc* ***(P-18869)***
A B Boyd Co (PA) **A 888 244-6931**
5960 Inglewood Dr Ste 115 Pleasanton (94588) ***(P-4211)***
A B C D Associates C 916 363-4843
10410 Coloma Rd Rancho Cordova (95670) ***(P-15905)***
A B C Pediatrics E 650 579-6500
50 S San Mateo Dr Ste 260 San Mateo (94401) ***(P-15267)***
A B M, Pittsburg *Also called Antioch Building Materials Co* ***(P-8617)***
A Better Way Inc (PA) **C 510 601-0203**
3200 Adeline St Berkeley (94703) ***(P-18216)***
A C L, Santa Clara *Also called Advanced Component Labs Inc* ***(P-6012)***
A C M, Burlingame *Also called Advanced Components Mfg* ***(P-5465)***
A C T, San Francisco *Also called American Cnsrvtory Thtre Fndti* ***(P-14835)***
A C Trucking Inc E 209 823-3224
1974 E Yosemite Ave Manteca (95336) ***(P-7501)***
A Career Apparel, Burlingame *Also called School Apparel Inc* ***(P-3006)***
A Ccess (PA) **D 209 383-7147**
1850 Wardrobe Ave Merced (95341) ***(P-17851)***
A Childs World Montessori Schl, Oakland *Also called Renaissance School* ***(P-18006)***
A Company In Development Stage, South San Francisco *Also called Aclara Biosciences Inc* ***(P-6890)***
A D Bilich Inc D 925 820-5557
11 Crow Canyon Ct Ste 100 San Ramon (94583) ***(P-9889)***
A Development Stage Company, San Francisco *Also called Brience Inc* ***(P-12308)***
A F Evans Company Inc D 925 937-1700
1700 Tice Valley Blvd Ofc Walnut Creek (94595) ***(P-14190)***
A G A, Fremont *Also called Homelegance Inc* ***(P-8494)***
A Grace Sub Acute Skilled Care, San Jose *Also called Lita & Ava Inc* ***(P-16910)***
A H K Electronic Shtmtl Inc E 408 778-3901
875 Jarvis Dr Ste 120 Morgan Hill (95037) ***(P-4736)***
A Is For Apple Inc D 877 991-0009
1485 Saratoga Ave Ste 200 San Jose (95129) ***(P-15877)***
A J Excavation Inc C 559 408-5908
514 N Brawley Ave Fresno (93706) ***(P-1949)***
A K M, San Jose *Also called Akm Semiconductor Inc* ***(P-6017)***
A L Gilbert Company F 530 934-2157
504 S Tehama St Willows (95988) ***(P-2337)***
A M T, San Jose *Also called Advance Modular Technology Inc* ***(P-5341)***
A Pet Emrgncy & Specialty Ctr E 415 456-7372
901 Francisco Blvd E San Rafael (94901) ***(P-318)***
A Plus Signs Inc E 559 275-0700
4270 N Brawley Ave Fresno (93722) ***(P-7213)***
A R C, Walnut Creek *Also called American Reprographics Co LLC* ***(P-19701)***
A Rpac Ltd Liability Company E 209 826-0272
21490 Ortigalita Rd Los Banos (93635) ***(P-266)***
A Ruiz Cnstr Co & Assoc Inc E 415 647-4010
1601 Cortland Ave San Francisco (94110) ***(P-819)***
A S I, Fremont *Also called Asi Computer Technologies Inc* ***(P-8670)***
A S I, San Pablo *Also called Analytcal Scentific Instrs Inc* ***(P-6808)***
A S P, San Francisco *Also called Astronomical Soc of The PCF* ***(P-18547)***
A S S U, Stanford *Also called Associated Students Stanford* ***(P-18390)***
A S U C, Berkeley, Berkeley *Also called Assoc Students University CA* ***(P-15176)***
A T Associates Inc E 510 649-6670
2223 Ashby Ave Berkeley (94705) ***(P-16213)***
A T Associates Inc D 510 261-8564
2919 Fruitvale Ave Oakland (94602) ***(P-16214)***
A T Associates Inc (PA) **D 925 808-6540**
535 School St Pittsburg (94565) ***(P-16215)***
A Teichert & Son Inc E 530 587-3811
13879 Butterfield Dr Truckee (96161) ***(P-582)***
A Teichert & Son Inc E 209 983-2300
265 Val Dervin Pkwy Stockton (95206) ***(P-997)***
A Teichert & Son Inc E 209 832-4150
36314 S Bird Rd Tracy (95304) ***(P-583)***
A Teichert & Son Inc E 530 406-4200
24207 County Road 100a Davis (95616) ***(P-998)***
A Teichert & Son Inc E 530 787-3468
27944 County Road 19a Esparto (95627) ***(P-584)***
A Teichert & Son Inc E 916 645-4800
4401 Duluth Ave Roseville (95678) ***(P-999)***
A Teichert & Son Inc E 530 885-4244
2601 State Highway 49 Cool (95614) ***(P-585)***

A Teichert & Son Inc ....E....916 386-6974
8609 Jackson Rd Sacramento (95826) ***(P-4456)***

A Teichert & Son Inc ....E....530 749-1230
3331 Walnut Ave Marysville (95901) ***(P-586)***

A Teichert & Son Inc (HQ) ....**A....916 484-3011**
5200 Franklin Dr Ste 115 Pleasanton (94588) ***(P-8614)***

A Teichert & Son Inc ....E....559 813-3100
5771 S Toyota Ave Fresno (93725) ***(P-1000)***

A Teichert & Son Inc ....E....209 461-3700
1801 El Pinal Dr Ste B Stockton (95205) ***(P-1001)***

A Teichert & Son Inc ....E....530 743-6111
4249 Hmmnton Smrtville Rd Marysville (95901) ***(P-587)***

A Teichert & Son Inc ....E....916 783-7132
721 Berry St Roseville (95678) ***(P-4457)***

A Teichert & Son Inc ....E....916 351-0123
3417 Grant Line Rd Rancho Cordova (95742) ***(P-588)***

A Teichert & Son Inc ....E....916 386-6900
8760 Kiefer Blvd Sacramento (95826) ***(P-589)***

A To Z Tree Nursery Inc (PA) ....**E....510 651-9021**
3225 Auto Mall Pkwy Fremont (94538) ***(P-9621)***

A Tool Shed Equipment Rentals, Santa Cruz *Also called (a) Tool Shed Inc* ***(P-12025)***

A&A Metal Finishing Entps LLC ....E....916 442-1063
8290 Alpine Ave Sacramento (95826) ***(P-4891)***

A&M Products Manufacturing Co (HQ) ....**D....510 271-7000**
1221 Broadway Ste 51 Oakland (94612) ***(P-4527)***

A&S Floors, Benicia *Also called Anthony Trevino* ***(P-1764)***

A&T Precision Machining ....E....408 363-1198
330 Piercy Rd San Jose (95138) ***(P-5457)***

A&W Restaurant, Campbell *Also called Harman Management Corporation* ***(P-8765)***

A-1 Advantage Asphalt Inc ....D....916 388-2020
10308 Placer Ln Ste 100 Sacramento (95827) ***(P-1002)***

A-1 Jays Machining Inc (PA) ....**D....408 262-1845**
2228 Oakland Rd San Jose (95131) ***(P-5458)***

A-1 Machine Manufacturing Inc (PA) ....**C....408 727-0880**
490 Gianni St Santa Clara (95054) ***(P-5459)***

A-1 Modular Inc ....E....408 393-8808
1514 Mono Ave San Leandro (94578) ***(P-14708)***

A-1 Roof MGT & Cnstr Inc ....D....510 347-5400
14100 Doolittle Dr San Leandro (94577) ***(P-19293)***

A-1 Ruiz & Sons Inc ....E....408 293-0909
460 W Taylor St San Jose (95110) ***(P-3491)***

A-A Lock & Alarm Inc (PA) ....**E....650 326-9020**
1251 El Camino Real Menlo Park (94025) ***(P-9140)***

A-C Electric Company ....D....559 233-2208
2560 S East Ave Fresno (93706) ***(P-1440)***

A-Mark T-Shirts Inc ....E....559 227-6370
3 E Shields Ave Fresno (93704) ***(P-3717)***

A-Para Transit Corp ....C....510 562-5500
1400 Doolittle Dr San Leandro (94577) ***(P-7320)***

A-Pro Pest Control Inc ....E....408 559-0933
75 Cristich Ln Campbell (95008) ***(P-11877)***

A.C.T., Sacramento *Also called Aluminum Coating Tech Inc* ***(P-4895)***

A1 Protective Services Inc ....D....415 467-7200
5 Thomas Mellon Cir San Francisco (94134) ***(P-14022)***

A1 Protective Services LLC ....E....916 421-3000
7000 Franklin Blvd # 410 Sacramento (95823) ***(P-14023)***

A10 Networks Inc (PA) ....**A....408 325-8668**
2300 Orchard Pkwy San Jose (95131) ***(P-13827)***

A2, Sunnyvale *Also called Westak Inc* ***(P-5998)***

A29 Funding LLC ....C....916 446-0100
300 J St Sacramento (95814) ***(P-10908)***

A3 Labs LLC (PA) ....**E....925 274-8503**
130 Webster St Oakland (94607) ***(P-19009)***

A3 Smart Home LP ....D....925 830-4777
2440 Camino Ramon Ste 200 San Ramon (94583) ***(P-14024)***

A3Geo-Ce&g Joint Venture ....E....510 705-1664
821 Bancroft Way Berkeley (94710) ***(P-18610)***

A5, Pleasanton *Also called Config Consultants LLC* ***(P-19475)***

AA Portable Power Corporation ....E....510 525-2328
825 S 19th St Richmond (94804) ***(P-6484)***

AA Production Services Inc ....E....530 982-0123
8032 County Road 61 Princeton (95970) ***(P-553)***

Aa/Acme Locksmiths Inc ....D....510 483-6584
1660 Factor Ave San Leandro (94577) ***(P-1441)***

AAA California State Auto Assn (PA) ....**C....415 773-1900**
160 Sutter St San Francisco (94104) ***(P-18540)***

AAA Fire Protection Service, Union City *Also called AAA Restaurant Fire Ctrl Inc* ***(P-14191)***

AAA Northern California, San Francisco *Also called AAA California State Auto Assn* ***(P-18540)***

AAA Restaurant Fire Ctrl Inc ....D....510 786-9555
30113 Union City Blvd Union City (94587) ***(P-14191)***

AAA Signs Inc ....D....916 568-3456
1834 Auburn Blvd Sacramento (95815) ***(P-14537)***

Aaaaa Rent-A-Space, Castro Valley *Also called Ras Management Inc* ***(P-7700)***

AAC Glass Inc ....E....909 214-4049
31044 San Antonio St Hayward (94544) ***(P-1934)***

AAC Technologies Holdings Inc (HQ) ....**E....408 490-4263**
20380 Town Center Ln Cupertino (95014) ***(P-8882)***

Aae Systems Inc ....F....408 732-1710
5150 El Cmino Real Ste B3 Los Altos (94022) ***(P-13548)***

Aai Termite Pest Control, Salida *Also called Royce Corporation* ***(P-11907)***

Aanw Inc ....E....707 428-1623
2400 Cordelia Rd Fairfield (94534) ***(P-14543)***

Aapcho, Berkeley *Also called Assoction Asn/Pcfic Cmnty Hlth* ***(P-18298)***

Aardvark Woodcraft Inc (PA) ....**E....916 230-3518**
8283 Branchoak Ct Elk Grove (95758) ***(P-3255)***

Aarki Inc (PA) ....**C....408 382-1180**
530 Lakeside Dr Ste 260 Sunnyvale (94085) ***(P-12218)***

Aaron Dowling Incorporated ....D....559 432-4500
8080 N Palm Ave Ste 300 Fresno (93711) ***(P-17196)***

Aasc, Stockton *Also called Applied Arospc Structures Corp* ***(P-6631)***

AB Sciex LLC (HQ) ....**D....877 740-2129**
1201 Radio Rd Redwood City (94065) ***(P-6802)***

Abacus Information Tech LLC (HQ) ....**D....415 517-8005**
101 California St Fl 10 San Francisco (94111) ***(P-19431)***

Abacus Service Corporation ....B....916 288-8948
1725 23rd St Sacramento (95816) ***(P-12219)***

Abaqus Inc ....E....415 496-9436
972 N California Ave Palo Alto (94303) ***(P-12945)***

Abaxis Inc (HQ) ....**C....510 675-6500**
3240 Whipple Rd Union City (94587) ***(P-6889)***

Abb Inc ....D....808 497-7240
6650 Goodyear Rd Benicia (94510) ***(P-8836)***

ABB - Los Gatos Research, San Jose *Also called ABB Enterprise Software Inc* ***(P-8800)***

ABB Enterprise Software Inc ....D....408 770-8968
3055 Orchard Dr San Jose (95134) ***(P-8800)***

ABB Inc ....D....510 987-7111
1321 Harbor Bay Pkwy # 101 Alameda (94502) ***(P-5645)***

ABB Optical Group, Alameda *Also called Abb/Con-Cise Optical Group LLC* ***(P-8798)***

Abb/Con-Cise Optical Group LLC ....D....800 852-8089
1750 N Loop Rd Ste 150 Alameda (94502) ***(P-8797)***

Abb/Con-Cise Optical Group LLC ....C....510 483-9400
1750 N Loop Rd Ste 150 Alameda (94502) ***(P-8798)***

Abbett Electric Corporation ....E....415 864-7500
1850 Bryant St San Francisco (94110) ***(P-1442)***

Abbey Carpet, San Jose *Also called Conklin Bros San Jose Inc* ***(P-8509)***

Abbey Carpet, Fairfield *Also called Gillespies Carpet Center Inc* ***(P-11653)***

Abbey Wtznberg Wrren Emery A P ....E....415 986-3103
100 Stony Point Rd # 200 Santa Rosa (95401) ***(P-17197)***

Abbott Diabetes Care Inc (HQ) ....**C....510 749-5400**
1420 Harbor Bay Pkwy Alameda (94502) ***(P-4014)***

Abbott Diabetes Care Sls Corp ....D....510 749-5400
1360 S Loop Rd Alameda (94502) ***(P-3824)***

Abbott Diagnostics Division, Santa Clara *Also called Abbott Laboratories* ***(P-6930)***

Abbott Laboratories ....B....408 330-0057
4551 Great America Pkwy Santa Clara (95054) ***(P-6930)***

Abbott Laboratories ....A....408 845-3000
3200 Lakeside Dr Santa Clara (95054) ***(P-6931)***

Abbott Nutrition ....F....707 399-1100
2302 Courage Dr Fairfield (94533) ***(P-3825)***

Abbott Nutrition Mfg Inc (HQ) ....**C....707 399-1100**
2351 N Watney Way Ste C Fairfield (94533) ***(P-3826)***

Abbott Strngham Lynch A Prof A ....D....408 377-8700
1530 Meridian Ave 2 San Jose (95125) ***(P-18929)***

Abbott Vascular, Santa Clara *Also called Abbott Laboratories* ***(P-6931)***

Abbott Vascular Inc (HQ) ....**A....408 845-3000**
3200 Lakeside Dr Santa Clara (95054) ***(P-6932)***

Abbvie Biotherapeutics Inc ....D....650 454-1000
1500 Seaport Blvd Redwood City (94063) ***(P-3827)***

Abbvie Stemcentrx LLC ....C....415 298-9242
1000 Gateway Blvd South San Francisco (94080) ***(P-19193)***

Abbyy USA Software House Inc (HQ) ....**C....408 457-9777**
890 Hillview Ct Ste 300 Milpitas (95035) ***(P-12220)***

ABC 30, Fresno *Also called Kfsn Television LLC* ***(P-8047)***

ABC Bus Inc ....D....650 368-3364
3508 Haven Ave Redwood City (94063) ***(P-8420)***

ABC Cable Networks Group ....C....415 954-7911
900 Front St San Francisco (94111) ***(P-8038)***

ABC Imaging of Washington ....E....415 869-1669
679 Bryant St San Francisco (94107) ***(P-11857)***

ABC Imaging of Washington ....F....202 429-8870
2327 Union St Oakland (94607) ***(P-3718)***

ABC Imaging of Washington ....F....415 525-3874
832 Folsom St San Francisco (94107) ***(P-3719)***

ABC Printing Inc ....F....408 263-1118
1090 S Milpitas Blvd Milpitas (95035) ***(P-3613)***

ABC Sacramento Striker, Sacramento *Also called Amerisourcebergen Drug Corp* ***(P-9222)***

ABC Security Service Inc (PA) ....**C....510 436-0666**
1840 Embarcadero Oakland (94606) ***(P-14025)***

Abco Laboratories Inc (PA) ....**D....707 432-2200**
2450 S Watney Way Fairfield (94533) ***(P-3828)***

Abcsp LLC ....C....855 470-2273
1406 Blue Oaks Blvd Ste 1 Roseville (95747) ***(P-16830)***

Abd Insurance & Fincl Svcs Inc (PA) ....**D....650 488-8565**
777 Mariners Island Blvd # 250 San Mateo (94404) ***(P-10224)***

Abel, Gregory C, Walnut Creek *Also called Whiting Fallon & Ross* ***(P-17396)***

Abel, Michael E MD, San Francisco *Also called Volpe Chiu Abel Sternberg* ***(P-15810)***

Abelisk Inc (PA) ....**E....559 227-1000**
7060 N Fresno St Ste 210 Fresno (93720) ***(P-12221)***

Abgenix Inc (PA) ....**C....510 608-6500**
6701 Kaiser Dr Fremont (94555) ***(P-3829)***

ABI Document Support Svcs LLC ....D....909 793-0613
11010 White Rock Rd Ste 1 Rancho Cordova (95670) ***(P-14192)***

ABI Mastermind R, Sacramento *Also called Advanced Bus Integrators Inc* ***(P-13832)***

Abilities United, Redwood City *Also called Abilitypath Housing* ***(P-17405)***

Abilitypath ....C....650 259-8500
350 Twin Dolphin Dr # 12 Redwood City (94065) ***(P-17404)***

Abilitypath Housing (PA) ....**D....650 494-0550**
350 Twin Dolphin Dr # 12 Redwood City (94065) ***(P-17405)***

Abjayon Inc ....C....510 824-3260
42808 Christy St Ste 228 Fremont (94538) ***(P-12222)***

Able Building Maintenance, Sacramento *Also called Crown Building Maintenance Co* ***(P-11940)***

Able Metal Plating Inc ....E....510 569-6539
932 86th Ave Oakland (94621) ***(P-4892)***

Able Services, South San Francisco *Also called Crown Energy Services Inc* ***(P-18678)***

A
L
P
H
A
B
E
T
I
C

Employee Codes: A=Over 500 employees, B=251-500
C=101-250, D=51-100, E=20-50 F=10-19

Able Services Inc (PA)...D...**800 461-9577**
868 Folsom St San Francisco (94107) ***(P-18611)***
ABM Aviation Inc...D...650 872-5400
601 Gateway Blvd Ste 1145 South San Francisco (94080) ***(P-7762)***
ABM Elctrcal Ltg Solutions Inc...D...408 399-3030
6940 Koll Center Pkwy # 100 Pleasanton (94566) ***(P-11912)***
ABM Industry Groups LLC...E...916 443-9094
414 J St Sacramento (95814) ***(P-14497)***
ABM Security Services Inc...D...916 614-9571
830 Riverside Pkwy Ste 30 West Sacramento (95605) ***(P-14115)***
Abode Services (PA)...D...**510 657-7409**
40849 Fremont Blvd Fremont (94538) ***(P-17406)***
Abound Logic Inc...E...408 873-3400
19200 Stevens Creek Blvd # 200 Cupertino (95014) ***(P-6006)***
ABS Capital Partners III LP...B...415 617-2800
101 California St Fl 24 San Francisco (94111) ***(P-10828)***
ABS Direct Inc...E...209 545-6090
4724 Enterprise Way Modesto (95356) ***(P-11834)***
ABS- American Building Supply, Sacramento *Also called American Building Supply Inc* ***(P-8525)***
Abs-American Building Supply, Sacramento *Also called American Building Supply Inc* ***(P-19296)***
Abs-American Building Supply, Sacramento *Also called American Building Supply Inc* ***(P-8524)***
Abs-American Building Supply, Sacramento *Also called American Building Supply Inc* ***(P-8527)***
ABS-Cbn International (HQ)...C...**800 527-2820**
432 N Canal St Ste 21 South San Francisco (94080) ***(P-8058)***
Abshear Landscape Development...E...916 660-1617
3171b Rippey Rd Loomis (95650) ***(P-392)***
Absinthe Group Inc...E...530 823-8527
2043 Airpark Ct Ste 30 Auburn (95602) ***(P-2210)***
Absl Construction...E...510 727-0900
29393 Pacific St Hayward (94544) ***(P-1003)***
Absolutdata Technologies Inc...D...510 748-9922
1320 Harbor Bay Pkwy # 170 Alameda (94502) ***(P-14193)***
Absolute Machine Inc...F...530 242-6840
5020 Mountain Lakes Blvd Redding (96003) ***(P-5460)***
Absolute Roofing CA, Fresno *Also called Absolute Urethane* ***(P-1779)***
Absolute Turnkey Services Inc...E...408 850-7530
555 Aldo Ave Santa Clara (95054) ***(P-5905)***
Absolute Urethane...E...877 471-3626
6614 S Elm Ave Fresno (93706) ***(P-1779)***
Abstract, San Francisco *Also called Elastic Projects Inc* ***(P-12417)***
Abundant Robotics...F...510 274-5846
3521 Investment Blvd Hayward (94545) ***(P-5223)***
Abx Engineering Inc...D...650 552-2300
875 Stanton Rd Burlingame (94010) ***(P-8888)***
Abzooba Inc (HQ)...C...**650 453-8760**
1551 Mccarthy Blvd # 204 Milpitas (95035) ***(P-12223)***
AC By Marriott Palo Alto, Palo Alto *Also called M10 Dev LLC* ***(P-11279)***
AC Enterprises, Hayward *Also called Andrew Chekene Enterprises Inc* ***(P-611)***
AC Hotel San Jose Downtown, San Jose *Also called Avr San Jose Downtown Ht LLC* ***(P-10938)***
AC Hotel San Jose Snnyvale Cpr, Sunnyvale *Also called K3 Dev LLC* ***(P-11225)***
AC Hotel Santa Rosa Downtown, Santa Rosa *Also called MB Hosptlity Srosa AC 2018 LLC* ***(P-11291)***
AC Hotel Sunnyvale, Sunnyvale *Also called K3 Dev LLC* ***(P-11226)***
AC Photonics Inc...E...408 986-9838
2701 Northwestern Pkwy Santa Clara (95051) ***(P-5138)***
AC Square Inc...C...650 293-2730
4590 Qantas Ln Stockton (95206) ***(P-19709)***
AC TRANSIT, Oakland *Also called Alameda-Contra Costa Trnst Dst* ***(P-7324)***
Acacia Communications Inc...D...212 331-8417
2700 Zanker Rd Ste 160 San Jose (95134) ***(P-6007)***
Academic Therapy Publications, Novato *Also called Arena Press* ***(P-3555)***
Acalvio Technologies Inc...D...408 931-6160
2520 Mission College Blvd # 110 Santa Clara (95054) ***(P-14116)***
Acampo Grape Harvesting LLC...E...209 333-7072
2551 E Acampo Rd Acampo (95220) ***(P-259)***
ACC West Coast, Benicia *Also called American Civil Const* ***(P-1007)***
ACC-Gwg LLC...D...530 473-2827
6133 Abel Rd Williams (95987) ***(P-19710)***
Accel Manufacturing Inc...F...408 727-5883
1709 Grant St Santa Clara (95050) ***(P-5070)***
Accel-KKR Capitl Partners V LP (PA)...B...**650 289-2460**
2180 Sand Hill Rd Ste 300 Menlo Park (94025) ***(P-10829)***
Accel-KKR Company LLC (PA)...A...**650 289-2460**
2180 Sand Hill Rd Ste 300 Menlo Park (94025) ***(P-10830)***
Accela Inc (PA)...C...**925 659-3200**
2633 Camino Ramon Ste 500 San Ramon (94583) ***(P-12946)***
Acceldata Inc...C...650 450-3423
3031 Tisch Way San Jose (95128) ***(P-14117)***
Accelerance Inc...F...650 472-3785
303 Twin Dolphin Dr # 60 Redwood City (94065) ***(P-12947)***
Accelerite (PA)...D...**408 216-7010**
2055 Laurelwood Rd Santa Clara (95054) ***(P-12948)***
Accellion Inc...C...650 485-4300
1804 Embarcadero Rd # 200 Palo Alto (94303) ***(P-13828)***
Accent Hospitality Group LLC...C...415 286-2867
2830 I St Ste 104 Sacramento (95816) ***(P-7812)***
Accent Manufacturing Inc...E...408 846-9993
105 Leavesley Rd Bldg 3d Gilroy (95020) ***(P-3333)***
Accentcare HM Hlth Scrmnto Inc...A...916 852-5888
2880 Sunrise Blvd Ste 218 Rancho Cordova (95742) ***(P-16831)***
Access Brand Communications, San Francisco *Also called Access Public Relations LLC* ***(P-19681)***
Access Capital Services Inc (PA)...D...**559 627-5221**
1625 E Shaw Ave Ste 137 Fresno (93710) ***(P-11821)***
Access Closure Inc...B...408 610-6500
5452 Betsy Ross Dr Santa Clara (95054) ***(P-6933)***
Access Communications, San Jose *Also called Access Telecomm Systems Inc* ***(P-1443)***
Access Electric, Ceres *Also called Access To Power Inc* ***(P-1444)***
Access International Company (HQ)...E...**510 226-1000**
45630 Northport Loop E Fremont (94538) ***(P-8658)***
Access Public Relations LLC...D...415 904-7070
720 California St Fl 5 San Francisco (94108) ***(P-19681)***
Access Sacramento, Sacramento *Also called Sacramnto Cmnty Cble Fundation* ***(P-19916)***
Access Systems Inc...E...916 941-8099
4947 Hillsdale Cir El Dorado Hills (95762) ***(P-6803)***
Access Systems Americas Inc...D...408 400-3000
3965 Freedom Cir Ste 200 Santa Clara (95054) ***(P-12224)***
Access Telecomm Systems Inc...E...800 342-4439
976 Rincon Cir San Jose (95131) ***(P-1443)***
Access To Power Inc...E...209 577-1491
1990 Foundry Ct Ceres (95307) ***(P-1444)***
Accion Labs Us Inc...C...408 970-9809
4633 Old Ironsides Dr # 304 Santa Clara (95054) ***(P-19253)***
Acclamation Insurance Mgt Svcs...D...559 227-9891
4450 N Brawley Ave Fresno (93722) ***(P-10225)***
Acco Brands USA LLC...D...650 572-2700
1500 Fashion Island Blvd # 300 San Mateo (94404) ***(P-5328)***
Acco Engineered Systems Inc...C...510 346-4300
1133 Aladdin Ave San Leandro (94577) ***(P-1187)***
Acco Management Company...C...408 241-3000
100 Buckingham Dr Ofc Santa Clara (95051) ***(P-10487)***
Accor Services US LLC (HQ)...A...**415 772-5000**
950 Mason St San Francisco (94108) ***(P-10909)***
Accordent Technologies Inc...F...310 374-7491
1846 Schooldale Dr San Jose (95124) ***(P-12949)***
Accountants International, San Jose *Also called Randstad Professionals Us LLC* ***(P-12126)***
Accountble Hlthcare Stffing In...C...916 286-7667
7777 Greenback Ln Ste 205 Citrus Heights (95610) ***(P-12068)***
Accountble Hlthcare Stffing In...C...408 377-9960
1999 S Bascom Ave Ste 590 Campbell (95008) ***(P-12069)***
Accountmate Software Corp (PA)...E...**707 774-7500**
1445 Technology Ln Ste A5 Petaluma (94954) ***(P-12950)***
Accountnow Inc...D...925 498-1800
2603 Camino Ramon Ste 485 San Ramon (94583) ***(P-19432)***
Accounts Payable, San Jose *Also called Mellanox Technologies Inc* ***(P-6197)***
Accrete Solutions LLC...B...877 849-5838
3350 Scott Blvd Bldg 34a Santa Clara (95054) ***(P-13829)***
Accrualify Inc...F...650 437-7225
14 N San Mateo Dr San Mateo (94401) ***(P-5775)***
Acct Holdings LLC...A...916 971-1981
5949 Fair Oaks Blvd Carmichael (95608) ***(P-14194)***
Accu-Image Inc...E...408 736-9066
330 Tennant Ave Morgan Hill (95037) ***(P-12225)***
Accu-Swiss Inc (PA)...F...**209 847-1016**
544 Armstrong Way Oakdale (95361) ***(P-4865)***
Accuracy Screw Machine Pdts, San Carlos *Also called Pencom/Accuracy Inc* ***(P-4868)***
Accurate Always Inc...E...650 728-9428
127 Ocean Ave Half Moon Bay (94019) ***(P-5237)***
Accurate Firestop Inc...C...510 886-1169
1057 Serpentine Ln Ste A Pleasanton (94566) ***(P-14195)***
Accurate Heating & Cooling Inc...E...209 858-4125
3515 Yosemite Ave Lathrop (95330) ***(P-4737)***
Accurate Technology Mfg Inc...D...408 733-4344
930 Thompson Pl Sunnyvale (94085) ***(P-5461)***
Accurate Tube Bending Inc...E...510 790-6500
37770 Timber St Newark (94560) ***(P-4973)***
Accuray Incorporated (PA)...C...**408 716-4600**
1310 Chesapeake Ter Sunnyvale (94089) ***(P-6934)***
Accusplit (PA)...F...**925 290-1900**
1262 Quarry Ln Ste B Pleasanton (94566) ***(P-7160)***
Acd, Newark *Also called Advanced Cell Diagnostics Inc* ***(P-19011)***
Ace Composites Inc...E...530 743-1885
1394 Sky Harbor Dr Olivehurst (95961) ***(P-4252)***
Ace Hardware, Fresno *Also called Fresno Plumbing & Heating Inc* ***(P-1269)***
Ace Hardware, Hilmar *Also called Hilmar Lumber Inc* ***(P-8551)***
Ace Hardware, Vacaville *Also called McKenzie Hardware Inc* ***(P-8987)***
Ace Hardware, Scotts Valley *Also called Scarborough Lbr & Bldg Sup Inc* ***(P-8606)***
Ace Hardware, San Jose *Also called County Building Materials Inc* ***(P-8539)***
Ace Hardware, Morgan Hill *Also called D & J Lumber Co Inc* ***(P-8540)***
Ace Mailing & Data Processing...E...415 863-4223
2736 16th St San Francisco (94103) ***(P-11835)***
Ace Parking Management Inc...D...510 589-2313
1901 Harrison St Ste 102 Oakland (94612) ***(P-14498)***
Ace Parking Management Inc...D...415 398-1900
235 Montgomery St Lbby San Francisco (94104) ***(P-14499)***
Ace Parking Management Inc...D...916 497-0222
900 13th St Sacramento (95814) ***(P-14500)***
Ace Parking Management Inc...D...510 251-0509
1330 Broadway Ste 915 Oakland (94612) ***(P-14501)***
Ace Parking Management Inc...D...415 749-1949
415 Taylor St San Francisco (94102) ***(P-14502)***
Ace Parking Management Inc...D...415 674-1799
1776 Sacramento St San Francisco (94109) ***(P-14503)***
Ace Parking Management Inc...D...408 437-2185
2050 Gateway Pl San Jose (95110) ***(P-14504)***
Ace Parking Management Inc...D...415 421-8800
350 Bush St San Francisco (94104) ***(P-14505)***
Ace Parking Management Inc...D...925 295-3283
2185 N Calif Blvd Ste 212 Walnut Creek (94596) ***(P-14506)***

Ace Products Enterprises Inc....E....707 765-1500
3920 Cypress Dr Ste B Petaluma (94954) *(P-4346)*
Ace Products Group, Petaluma *Also called Ace Products Enterprises Inc (P-4346)*
Ace USA....D....510 790-4695
39300 Civic Center Dr # 290 Fremont (94538) *(P-10226)*
Ace Usa Inc....E....415 773-6500
275 Battery St Ste 1500 San Francisco (94111) *(P-10160)*
Acelrx Pharmaceuticals Inc (PA)....E....**650 216-3500**
25821 Industrial Blvd # 400 Hayward (94545) *(P-3830)*
Acemij Farms Inc....E....559 842-7766
3621 N Howard Ave Kerman (93630) *(P-145)*
Acer America Corporation (HQ)....D....**408 533-7700**
1730 N 1st St Ste 400 San Jose (95112) *(P-13830)*
Acer American Holdings Corp (HQ)....A....**408 533-7700**
1730 N 1st St Ste 400 San Jose (95112) *(P-5339)*
Acer Cloud Technology Inc....A....408 830-9809
333 W San Carlos St # 1500 San Jose (95110) *(P-18612)*
Acera, Oakland *Also called Alameda Cnty Emplyees Rtrment (P-10227)*
Acertus....E....916 331-2355
3044 Elkhorn Blvd Ste J North Highlands (95660) *(P-7873)*
Aces Waste Services Inc....E....209 274-2237
6500 Buena Vista Rd Ione (95640) *(P-8297)*
Acf Components & Fasteners Inc (PA)....E....**510 487-2100**
2512 Tripaldi Way Hayward (94545) *(P-8978)*
Acf Industrial Solutions, Hayward *Also called Acf Components & Fasteners Inc (P-8978)*
Acfn Franchised Inc....E....888 794-2236
4 N 2nd St Ste 1240 San Jose (95113) *(P-9839)*
Achaogen Inc....C....650 800-3636
1 Tower Pl Ste 300 South San Francisco (94080) *(P-3831)*
Achievement Engineering Corp....E....408 217-9174
2455 Autumnvale Dr Ste E San Jose (95131) *(P-18613)*
Achievemint, San Mateo *Also called Evidation Health Inc (P-12434)*
Achievo Corporation (PA)....D....**925 498-8864**
1400 Terra Bella Ave E Mountain View (94043) *(P-12226)*
Achronix Semiconductor Corp....D....408 889-4100
2903 Bunker Hill Ln # 200 Santa Clara (95054) *(P-6008)*
Aci Alloys Inc....F....408 259-7337
1458 Seareel Pl San Jose (95131) *(P-4924)*
Acl Digital, San Jose *Also called Calsoft Labs Inc (P-13563)*
Aclara Biosciences Inc....E....800 297-2728
345 Oyster Point Blvd South San Francisco (94080) *(P-6890)*
ACLU, San Francisco *Also called American Cvil Lbrties Un Fndti (P-18544)*
Acm Machining Inc....E....916 804-9489
240 State Highway 16 # 18 Plymouth (95669) *(P-5462)*
Acm Machining Inc (PA)....E....**916 852-8600**
11390 Gold Dredge Way Rancho Cordova (95742) *(P-5463)*
Acm Research Inc (PA)....A....**510 445-3700**
42307 Osgood Rd Ste I Fremont (94539) *(P-5437)*
Acma Computers Inc....E....510 497-8626
1565 Reliance Way Fremont (94539) *(P-8659)*
Acme Bag Co Inc (PA)....F....**530 662-6130**
440 N Pioneer Ave Ste 300 Woodland (95776) *(P-3390)*
Acme Bioscience Inc....C....650 969-8000
3941 E Bayshore Rd Palo Alto (94303) *(P-19010)*
Acme Bread Co....F....650 938-2978
362 E Grand Ave South San Francisco (94080) *(P-2359)*
Acme Bread Co Div II, Berkeley *Also called Doughtronics Inc (P-2378)*
Acme Bread Company, Berkeley *Also called Doughtronics Inc (P-2377)*
Acme Building Maint Co Inc (HQ)....D....**408 263-5911**
941 Catherine St Alviso (95002) *(P-11913)*
Acme Construction Company Inc....E....209 523-2674
1565 Cummins Dr Modesto (95358) *(P-787)*
Acme Electric Co, Turlock *Also called Oliveira-Lucas Enterprises Inc (P-1556)*
Acme Press Inc....D....925 682-1111
2312 Stanwell Dr Concord (94520) *(P-3614)*
Acme Printing Co, Modesto *Also called Pinnacle Solutions Inc (P-14365)*
Acme Roofing Co, San Francisco *Also called Dissmeyer Corporation (P-1798)*
Acosta Sheet Metal Mfg Co, San Jose *Also called Sal J Acsta Sheetmetal Mfg Inc (P-4814)*
Acoustic Guitar Magazine, Richmond *Also called String Letter Publishing Inc (P-3603)*
Acp Composites, Livermore *Also called Aerospace Composite Products (P-6630)*
Acp Ventures....F....925 297-0100
3340 Mt Diablo Blvd Ste B Lafayette (94549) *(P-3615)*
Acqua Hotel, Mill Valley *Also called Joie De Vivre Hospitality LLC (P-11216)*
Acqua Hotel The, Mill Valley *Also called Przm LLC (P-11377)*
ACR Solar International Corp....E....916 481-7200
5840 Gibbons Dr Ste H Carmichael (95608) *(P-4624)*
Acrobat Staffing, Rocklin *Also called SE Scher Corporation (P-12134)*
Acronics Systems Inc....C....408 432-0888
2102 Commerce Dr San Jose (95131) *(P-18614)*
Acrt Pacific LLC....B....330 945-7500
3443 Deer Park Dr Ste B Stockton (95219) *(P-19711)*
ACS, Antioch *Also called Allied Container Systems Inc (P-4844)*
ACS Instrumentation Valves Inc....D....510 262-1880
3065 Richmond Pkwy # 106 Richmond (94806) *(P-6710)*
Act Associates, Folsom *Also called Matthew Burns (P-919)*
Actagro LLC (HQ)....C....**559 369-2222**
4516 N Howard Ave Kerman (93630) *(P-9593)*
Actcm, San Francisco *Also called American Clg Trdtnl Chnse Mdcn (P-16987)*
Actega Wit, Fairfield *Also called Water Ink Technology (P-4155)*
Actelis Networks Inc (PA)....C....**510 545-1045**
47800 Westinghouse Dr Fremont (94539) *(P-19712)*
Actelis USA, Fremont *Also called Actelis Networks Inc (P-19712)*
Actiance, Redwood City *Also called Smarsh Inc (P-13447)*
Actiance Inc....E....650 631-6300
1400 Seaport Blvd Redwood City (94063) *(P-4832)*
Action Gypsum Supply West LP (PA)....E....**510 259-1965**
21040 Forbes Ave Hayward (94545) *(P-9106)*
Action Property Management Inc....E....800 400-2284
850 Montgomery St Ste 150 San Francisco (94133) *(P-19433)*
Action Sign Systems, Redwood City *Also called D N G Cummings Inc (P-7227)*
Action Urgent Care Inc (PA)....D....**408 440-8335**
1375 Blossom Hill Rd # 49 San Jose (95118) *(P-15268)*
Active Wellness LLC....A....415 741-3300
600 California St Fl 11 San Francisco (94108) *(P-19294)*
Activevideo Networks LLC (HQ)....D....**408 931-9200**
333 W San Carlos St # 90 San Jose (95110) *(P-13549)*
Activewire Inc (PA)....D....**650 969-4000**
895 Commercial St Ste 700 Palo Alto (94303) *(P-5340)*
Actsolar Inc....E....408 721-5000
2900 Semiconductor Dr Santa Clara (95051) *(P-6009)*
Actuate Corporation (HQ)....B....**650 645-3000**
951 Mariners Island Blvd # 7 San Mateo (94404) *(P-12227)*
Acumen LLC....C....650 558-8882
500 Airport Blvd Ste 100 Burlingame (94010) *(P-13550)*
Acura of Stockton, Stockton *Also called Quality Motor Cars Stockton (P-14619)*
Acura Pleasanton, Pleasanton *Also called Hendrick Automotive Group (P-8425)*
Acwa Jpia, Roseville *Also called Assoc CA Wtr AGC/Jt Pw Ins (P-10239)*
Acwd, Fremont *Also called Alameda County Water District (P-8218)*
Ad Art Inc (PA)....D....**415 869-6460**
150 Executive Park Blvd # 2100 San Francisco (94134) *(P-7214)*
Ad Art Sign Company, San Francisco *Also called Ad Art Inc (P-7214)*
Ad Spcial TS EMB Scrnprnting I....F....707 452-7272
202 Bella Vista Rd Ste B Vacaville (95687) *(P-3044)*
Ad-In Incorporated....E....510 656-6700
42200 Boscell Rd Fremont (94538) *(P-1655)*
Adamas Pharmaceuticals Inc (PA)....C....**510 450-3500**
1900 Powell St Ste 1000 Emeryville (94608) *(P-3832)*
Adams Label Company LLC (PA)....E....**925 371-5393**
6052 Industrial Way Ste G Livermore (94551) *(P-3720)*
Adams Pool Specialties, Sacramento *Also called Dave Gross Enterprises Inc (P-2028)*
Adams Winery LLC (PA)....E....**707 395-6126**
9711 W Dr Creek Rd Healdsburg (95448) *(P-2501)*
Adams Winery LLC....E....508 648-2505
9711 W Dry Creek Rd Healdsburg (95448) *(P-2502)*
Adanta Inc....D....707 709-8894
1100 Lincoln Ave Ste 206 NAPA (94558) *(P-19896)*
Adaps Photonics Inc (PA)....D....**650 521-3925**
252 Corral Ave Sunnyvale (94086) *(P-5784)*
Adaptive Electronics, San Jose *Also called Infiniti Solutions Usa Inc (P-5940)*
Adaptive Insights LLC....D....408 656-4229
14 W Central Ave Los Gatos (95030) *(P-2986)*
Adaptive Insights LLC (HQ)....C....**650 528-7500**
2300 Geng Rd Ste 100 Palo Alto (94303) *(P-12951)*
Adaptive Spctrum Signal Algnmt (PA)....D....**650 654-3400**
203 Rdwood Shres Pkwy Ste Redwood City (94065) *(P-7922)*
Adaptive Spctrum Signal Algnmt, Redwood City *Also called Adaptive Spctrum Sgnal Algnmt (P-7922)*
Adara Inc (PA)....C....**408 876-6360**
2625 Middlefield Rd # 827 Palo Alto (94306) *(P-12952)*
Adara Power Inc....F....844 223-2969
15466 Los Gatos Blvd 10 Los Gatos (95032) *(P-6485)*
Adco Manufacturing....C....559 875-5563
2170 Academy Ave Sanger (93657) *(P-5194)*
Adco/Grier Inc....E....916 631-7010
11242 Pyrites Way Gold River (95670) *(P-1656)*
Addappt Inc....F....408 402-5468
15680 Loma Vista Ave Los Gatos (95032) *(P-12953)*
Addepar Inc (PA)....D....**855 464-6268**
303 Bryant St Mountain View (94041) *(P-12228)*
Addforce Inc (PA)....E....**415 738-6469**
1470 Civic Ct Ste 309 Concord (94520) *(P-19713)*
Addisn-Pnzak Jwish Cmnty Ctr S....C....408 358-3636
14855 Oka Rd Ste 201 Los Gatos (95032) *(P-14923)*
Addison Engineering, San Jose *Also called Addison Technology Inc (P-5906)*
Addison Technology Inc....E....408 749-1000
150 Nortech Pkwy San Jose (95134) *(P-5906)*
Addlife....E....650 556-9430
1190 Kern Ave Sunnyvale (94085) *(P-12027)*
Addus Healthcare, Modesto *Also called Addus Homecare Corporation (P-16835)*
Addus Healthcare Inc....D....209 526-8451
817 Coffee Rd Ste B1 Modesto (95355) *(P-16832)*
Addus Healthcare Inc....D....530 566-0405
196 Cohasset Rd Ste 200 Chico (95926) *(P-16833)*
Addus Healthcare Inc....D....650 638-7943
1730 S Amphlett Blvd San Mateo (94402) *(P-16834)*
Addus Healthcare Inc....E....530 247-0858
2851 Park Marina Dr # 150 Redding (96001) *(P-15878)*
Addus Homecare Corporation (HQ)....E....**209 526-8451**
817 Coffee Rd Ste B Modesto (95355) *(P-16835)*
Adecco Employment Services....D....209 474-0443
1231 W Robinhood Dr Stockton (95207) *(P-12156)*
Adem LLC....E....408 727-8955
1040 Di Giulio Ave # 160 Santa Clara (95050) *(P-5464)*
Adept Technology, San Ramon *Also called Omron Robotics Safety Tech Inc (P-5053)*
Adesto Technologies Corp (HQ)....C....**408 400-0578**
3600 Peterson Way Santa Clara (95054) *(P-6010)*
Adeza Biomedical Corporation....A....408 745-6491
1240 Elko Dr Sunnyvale (94089) *(P-4015)*
Adiana Inc....B....650 421-2900
1240 Elko Dr Sunnyvale (94089) *(P-3833)*
Adivo Associates LLC....D....415 992-1449
44 Montgomery St Ste 4050 San Francisco (94104) *(P-19434)*
Adler & Colvin A Law Corp....E....415 421-7555
135 Main St Ste 2000 San Francisco (94105) *(P-17198)*

ALPHABETIC

ADM Associates Incorporated....C....916 363-8383
3239 Ramos Cir Sacramento (95827) ***(P-18615)***
ADM Garage Doors (PA)....**E....916 595-5355**
4185 69th St Sacramento (95820) ***(P-1728)***
Admail West Inc....D....916 554-5755
800 N 10th St Ste F Sacramento (95811) ***(P-3367)***
Admail-Express Inc....E....510 471-6200
31640 Hayman St Hayward (94544) ***(P-3616)***
Admedes Inc (HQ)....**E....925 417-0778**
2800 Collier Canyon Rd Livermore (94551) ***(P-8771)***
Admi Inc....E....408 776-0060
18525 Sutter Blvd Ste 290 Morgan Hill (95037) ***(P-12954)***
Administrative Systems Inc....D....916 563-1121
1651 Response Rd Ste 350 Sacramento (95815) ***(P-14196)***
Adminstrtion Offces For Schl D, San Francisco *Also called San Francisco Unified Schl Dst* ***(P-19393)***
Admiral Security Services Inc....B....888 471-1128
2151 Salvio St Ste 260 Concord (94520) ***(P-14118)***
Adobe....E....415 832-7791
601 Townsend St Fl 1 San Francisco (94103) ***(P-3552)***
Adobe Animal Hospital....D....650 948-9661
4470 El Camino Real Los Altos (94022) ***(P-319)***
Adobe Inc....E....408 536-6000
321 Park Ave San Jose (95110) ***(P-12955)***
Adobe Inc (PA)....**A....408 536-6000**
345 Park Ave San Jose (95110) ***(P-12956)***
Adobe Macromedia Software LLC (HQ)....**A....415 832-2000**
601 Townsend St San Francisco (94103) ***(P-12957)***
Adobe Road Investment Group....E....530 529-4178
520 Adobe Rd Red Bluff (96080) ***(P-10910)***
Adonai Enterprises Inc (PA)....**E....510 475-9950**
7752 Enterprise Dr Newark (94560) ***(P-14733)***
Adoption Clinical Services LLC....E....405 476-1983
510 3rd St Ste 9 Eureka (95501) ***(P-17407)***
Adoptions, Fresno *Also called Social Services Cal Dept* ***(P-17746)***
Adorno Construction Inc....D....408 369-8675
520 Westchester Dr Ste A Campbell (95008) ***(P-1848)***
ADP, Novato *Also called Automatic Data Processing Inc* ***(P-13694)***
Adrenas Therapeutics Inc....E....408 899-9018
421 Kipling St Palo Alto (94301) ***(P-15879)***
Adrienne Mattos Swim Schl Inc (PA)....**E....866 633-4147**
2203 Mariner Square Loop Alameda (94501) ***(P-15169)***
Adroit Resources Inc (HQ)....**E....510 344-8797**
46231 Landing Pkwy Fremont (94538) ***(P-13831)***
Adroll, San Francisco *Also called Nextroll Inc* ***(P-13332)***
ADS Solutions....F....415 897-3700
10 Commercial Blvd # 208 Novato (94949) ***(P-12958)***
Adsmart Digital Prepress, San Francisco *Also called Gumas Advertising LLC* ***(P-11759)***
Adswizz Inc (HQ)....**D....408 674-4355**
210 S Ellsworth Ave San Mateo (94401) ***(P-11800)***
Adswood Trs LLC....E....408 247-0800
1085 E El Camino Real Sunnyvale (94087) ***(P-10911)***
Adtech Computers, Ceres *Also called Advanced Technology Distrs Inc* ***(P-8661)***
Adtek Inc....E....209 634-0300
1460 Ellerd Dr Turlock (95380) ***(P-4641)***
Adult Mddlhlth Otptient Clinic, Fairfield *Also called County of Solano* ***(P-16179)***
Adult Probation Department, San Jose *Also called Santa Clara County of* ***(P-17716)***
Adult Services Division, Marysville *Also called County of Yuba* ***(P-17520)***
Aduro Gvax Inc....E....510 848-4400
740 Heinz Ave Berkeley (94710) ***(P-3834)***
Advance Carbon Products Inc....E....510 293-5930
2036 National Ave Hayward (94545) ***(P-5669)***
Advance Construction Tech Inc....D....408 658-3682
23575 Cabot Blvd Ste 206 Hayward (94545) ***(P-604)***
Advance Day Care Center Inc....E....510 434-9288
2236 International Blvd Oakland (94606) ***(P-17852)***
Advance Elctro Polishing, Santa Clara *Also called Process Stainless Lab Inc* ***(P-4917)***
Advance Modular Technology Inc....E....408 453-9880
2075 Bering Dr Ste C San Jose (95131) ***(P-5341)***
Advance Semiconductor Engrg, Sunnyvale *Also called Ase (us)inc* ***(P-8892)***
Advance Services Inc....A....408 767-2797
8021 Kern Ave Gilroy (95020) ***(P-14707)***
Advance Staffing Inc....B....408 205-6154
2060 Walsh Ave Ste 101 Santa Clara (95050) ***(P-12070)***
Advanced Analogic Tech Inc....C....408 330-1400
2740 Zanker Rd San Jose (95134) ***(P-6011)***
Advanced Asphalt, Truckee *Also called Advanced Companies Inc* ***(P-8615)***
Advanced Bus Integrators Inc....E....916 381-3809
8413 Jackson Rd Ste C Sacramento (95826) ***(P-13832)***
Advanced Cell Diagnostics Inc....D....510 576-8800
7707 Gateway Blvd Ste 200 Newark (94560) ***(P-19011)***
Advanced Circuits Inc....F....415 602-6834
1602 Tacoma Way Redwood City (94063) ***(P-5907)***
Advanced Companies Inc....E....530 582-0800
40165 Trk Arpt Rd 30 Truckee (96161) ***(P-8615)***
Advanced Component Labs Inc....E....408 327-0200
990 Richard Ave Ste 118 Santa Clara (95050) ***(P-6012)***
Advanced Components Mfg....E....650 344-6272
1415 N Carolan Ave Burlingame (94010) ***(P-5465)***
Advanced Crdvsclar Spclsts Inc....E....650 962-4690
2490 Hospital Dr Ste 311 Mountain View (94040) ***(P-15269)***
Advanced Design Engrg & Mfg, Santa Clara *Also called Adem LLC* ***(P-5464)***
Advanced Dgital Solutions Intl....E....510 490-6667
7026 Koll Center Pkwy # 21 Pleasanton (94566) ***(P-8660)***
Advanced Fabrication Tech, Hayward *Also called R2g Enterprises Inc* ***(P-1833)***
Advanced Gases and Eqp Inc....D....530 344-0771
4639 Missouri Flat Rd Placerville (95667) ***(P-9050)***
Advanced Grinding Incorporated....E....510 536-3465
812 49th Ave Oakland (94601) ***(P-4925)***
Advanced Helicopter Svs, Woodland *Also called Dfc Inc* ***(P-6609)***
Advanced Home Health Inc....D....916 978-0744
4354 Auburn Blvd Sacramento (95841) ***(P-16836)***
Advanced Indus Coatings Inc....D....209 234-2700
950 Industrial Dr Stockton (95206) ***(P-4926)***
Advanced Industrial Ceramics....E....408 955-9990
2449 Zanker Rd San Jose (95131) ***(P-5139)***
Advanced Integration Tech, Hayward *Also called Integrated Flow Systems LLC* ***(P-6722)***
Advanced Ipm....E....916 759-1570
205 Kenroy Ln Roseville (95678) ***(P-11878)***
Advanced Linear Dvcs RES Inc....E....408 747-1155
415 Tasman Dr Sunnyvale (94089) ***(P-6013)***
Advanced McHning Tchniques Inc....E....408 778-4500
16205 Vineyard Blvd Morgan Hill (95037) ***(P-5466)***
Advanced McRgrid Solutions Inc....D....415 638-6146
986 Mission St Fl 4 San Francisco (94103) ***(P-19012)***
Advanced Metal Finishing LLC....E....530 888-7772
2130 March Rd Roseville (95747) ***(P-4893)***
Advanced Mfg & Dev Inc....C....707 459-9451
200 N Lenore Ave Willits (95490) ***(P-4738)***
Advanced Micro Devices Inc (PA)....**A....408 749-4000**
2485 Augustine Dr Santa Clara (95054) ***(P-6014)***
Advanced Microtechnology....F....408 945-9191
3511 Thomas Rd Ste 8 Santa Clara (95054) ***(P-6742)***
Advanced Pressure Technology....D....707 259-0102
687 Technology Way NAPA (94558) ***(P-6711)***
Advanced Roof Design Inc (PA)....**E....916 381-2266**
4 Wayne Ct Ste 10 Sacramento (95829) ***(P-1780)***
Advanced Software Design Inc....D....925 457-8540
58 Van Tassel Ln Orinda (94563) ***(P-12229)***
Advanced Software Dynamics, Orinda *Also called Advanced Software Design Inc* ***(P-12229)***
Advanced Technology Distrs Inc....E....209 541-1111
1571 E Whitmore Ave Ceres (95307) ***(P-8661)***
Advanced Ti Inc....E....925 299-0515
1553 3rd Ave Walnut Creek (94597) ***(P-734)***
Advanced Viticulture Inc....E....707 838-3805
930 Shiloh Rd Bldg 44-E Windsor (95492) ***(P-366)***
Advancedcath Technologies LLC (HQ)....**E....408 433-9505**
176 Component Dr San Jose (95131) ***(P-6935)***
Advantage Framing Solutions....E....530 742-7660
1965 N Beale Rd Marysville (95901) ***(P-820)***
Advantage Metal Products, Livermore *Also called Segundo Metal Products Inc* ***(P-4816)***
Advantage Route Systems Inc....E....209 632-1122
3201 Liberty Square Pkwy Turlock (95380) ***(P-12230)***
Advantage Sales & Marketing....E....925 463-5600
5064 Franklin Dr Pleasanton (94588) ***(P-9261)***
Advantage Truss Company LLC....E....831 635-0377
2025 San Juan Rd Hollister (95023) ***(P-3198)***
Advantage Workforce Svcs LLC....C....415 212-6464
39 Stillman St San Francisco (94107) ***(P-12157)***
Advantech Corporation (HQ)....**B....408 519-3800**
380 Fairview Way Milpitas (95035) ***(P-12231)***
Advantek Taping Systems Inc (HQ)....**D....510 623-1877**
6839 Mowry Ave Newark (94560) ***(P-9107)***
Advantest America Inc (HQ)....**D....408 456-3600**
3061 Zanker Rd San Jose (95134) ***(P-6015)***
Advantis Global Inc (PA)....**C....415 612-3338**
20 Sunnyside Ave Ste E Mill Valley (94941) ***(P-13833)***
Advent Engineering Svcs Inc (PA)....**E....925 830-4700**
12647 Alcosta Blvd # 440 San Ramon (94583) ***(P-18616)***
Advent Group Ministries Inc....D....408 281-0708
90 Great Oaks Blvd # 108 San Jose (95119) ***(P-18049)***
Advent Software Inc (HQ)....**A....415 543-7696**
600 Townsend St Fl 4 San Francisco (94103) ***(P-12232)***
Adventist Health Lodi Memorial, Lodi *Also called Lodi Memorial Hosp Assn Inc* ***(P-16427)***
Adventist Health Selma....B....559 891-1000
1141 Rose Ave Selma (93662) ***(P-16286)***
Adventist Health Sonora....E....209 536-5000
179 Fairview Ln Sonora (95370) ***(P-16287)***
Adventist Health Sonora....E....209 536-5070
690 Guzzi Ln Ste A Sonora (95370) ***(P-16288)***
Adventist Health Sonora....E....209 532-0126
680 Guzzi Ln Sonora (95370) ***(P-16289)***
Adventist Health Sonora....E....209 532-3167
14540 Mono Way Sonora (95370) ***(P-16290)***
Adventist Health Sonora....E....209 795-1270
2037 Hwy 4 Arnold (95223) ***(P-16291)***
Adventist Health Sonora (HQ)....**A....209 532-5000**
1000 Greenley Rd Sonora (95370) ***(P-16292)***
Adventist Health Sonora....E....209 536-5770
680 Guzzi Ln Ste 101 Sonora (95370) ***(P-16293)***
Adventist Health Sonora....E....209 536-3900
14542 Lolly Ln Sonora (95370) ***(P-16294)***
Adventist Health Sonora....E....209 536-5060
690 Guzzi Ln Ste B Sonora (95370) ***(P-16295)***
Adventist Health Sonora....E....209 536-2665
1000 Greenley Rd Sonora (95370) ***(P-16296)***
Adventist Health System/West....D....530 342-4576
111 Raley Blvd Chico (95928) ***(P-16297)***
Adventist Health System/West....D....707 987-8344
18990 Coyote Valley Rd # 11 Hidden Valley Lake (95467) ***(P-16298)***
Adventist Health System/West....D....559 626-0882
1455 Park Blvd Orange Cove (93646) ***(P-16299)***
Adventist Health System/West....D....209 532-3161
1000 Greenley Rd Sonora (95370) ***(P-16300)***
Adventist Health System/West....D....530 473-5641
501 E St Ste B Williams (95987) ***(P-16301)***

ALPHABETIC SECTION Agari Data Inc

Adventist Health System/West ... D ... 209 536-5043
13808 Mono Way Sonora (95370) *(P-16302)*
Adventist Health System/West ... E ... 559 638-2154
1150 E Washington Ave Reedley (93654) *(P-15880)*
Adventist Hlth Clrlake Hosp In (HQ) ... **B ... 707 994-6486**
15630 18th Ave Clearlake (95422) *(P-16303)*
Adventist Hlth Clrlake Hosp In ... C ... 707 994-6486
15140 Lakeshore Dr Clearlake (95422) *(P-16304)*
Adventist Hlth Cmnty Cr-Prlier, Parlier *Also called Adventist Hlth Systm/West Corp* *(P-16306)*
Adventist Hlth Systm/West Corp ... D ... 559 856-6110
2141 High St Ste E Selma (93662) *(P-16305)*
Adventist Hlth Systm/West Corp ... D ... 559 646-1200
155 S Newmark Ave Parlier (93648) *(P-16306)*
Adventist Hlth Systm/West Corp ... D ... 559 645-4191
11976 Road 37 Madera (93636) *(P-16307)*
Adventist Hlth Systm/West Corp ... D ... 559 834-1614
300 S Leon S. Peters Blvd Fowler (93625) *(P-16308)*
Adventist Hlth Systm/West Corp ... D ... 707 995-4888
14880 Olympic Dr Clearlake (95422) *(P-16309)*
Adventist Hlth Systm/West Corp (PA) ... **B ... 844 574-5686**
1 Adventist Health Way Roseville (95661) *(P-16310)*
Adventist Hlth Systm/West Corp ... D ... 559 864-3212
2440 W Tahoe Ave Caruthers (93609) *(P-16311)*
Adventist Hlth Systm/West Corp ... D ... 707 995-4500
15230 Lakeshore Dr Clearlake (95422) *(P-16312)*
Adventist Hlth Systm/West Corp ... D ... 559 846-9370
1000 S Madera Ave Kerman (93630) *(P-16313)*
Adventist Hlth Systm/West Corp ... D ... 559 875-6900
1939 Academy Ave Sanger (93657) *(P-16314)*
Adventist Hlth Systm/West Corp ... D ... 559 856-6090
1041 Rose Ave Selma (93662) *(P-16315)*
Adventist Hlth Systm/West Corp ... D ... 707 994-6486
18th Ave Hwy 53 Clearlake (95422) *(P-16316)*
Adventist Hlth Systm/West Corp ... D ... 209 536-5700
20100 Cedar Rd N Sonora (95370) *(P-16317)*
Adventist Med Center-Reedley, Reedley *Also called Reedley Community Hospital* *(P-16489)*
Adventres Rlling Cross-Country ... E ... 415 332-5075
242 Rdwood Hwy Frntage Rd Mill Valley (94941) *(P-11596)*
Adventst Hlth Cmmnty Cre-or, Orange Cove *Also called Adventist Health System/West* *(P-16299)*
Adventures Cross-Country, Mill Valley *Also called Adventres Rlling Cross-Country* *(P-11596)*
Advertiser, The, Oakdale *Also called Morris Publications* *(P-3463)*
Adverum Biotechnologies Inc ... D ... 650 656-9323
800 Saginaw Dr Redwood City (94063) *(P-4031)*
Advintist Hlth Clearlake Hosp ... D ... 707 994-6486
18th Ave & Hwy 53 Clearlake (95422) *(P-16318)*
Advisor Software Inc (PA) ... **E ... 925 299-7782**
2185 N Calif Blvd Ste 290 Walnut Creek (94596) *(P-12959)*
Advisorycloud Inc ... C ... 415 289-7115
7 Hamilton Landing # 100 Novato (94949) *(P-19714)*
Advolife Inc (HQ) ... **D ... 408 879-1835**
828 S Bascom Ave Ste 280 San Jose (95128) *(P-16837)*
Aea Pharmaceuticals Inc ... E ... 650 996-5895
351 Galveston Dr Redwood City (94063) *(P-3835)*
Aechelon Technology Inc (PA) ... **C ... 415 255-0120**
888 Brannan St Ste 210 San Francisco (94103) *(P-5238)*
Aeco Systems Inc ... E ... 510 342-0008
3512 Breakwater Ct Hayward (94545) *(P-1445)*
Aecom ... E ... 415 796-8100
300 California St Fl 6 San Francisco (94104) *(P-18617)*
Aecom ... D ... 415 908-6135
501 2nd St San Francisco (94107) *(P-18618)*
Aecom International Inc (HQ) ... **C ... 415 716-8100**
300 California St Ste 600 San Francisco (94104) *(P-18619)*
Aecom Tech, San Francisco *Also called Aecom* *(P-18618)*
Aecom Usa Inc ... C ... 408 392-0670
100 W San Fernando St San Jose (95113) *(P-19715)*
Aecom-TSE Joint Venture ... D ... 510 285-6639
300 Lakeside Dr Ste 400 Oakland (94612) *(P-18620)*
Aee Solar Inc ... D ... 800 777-6609
1227 Striker Ave Ste 200 Sacramento (95834) *(P-8837)*
AEG Industries Inc ... E ... 707 575-0697
1219 Briggs Ave Santa Rosa (95401) *(P-6625)*
Aegea Medical Inc ... E ... 650 701-1125
4055 Campbell Ave Menlo Park (94025) *(P-6936)*
Aegis Assisted Living, Aptos *Also called Aegis Senior Communities LLC* *(P-16840)*
Aegis Assisted Living, Carmichael *Also called Aegis Senior Communities LLC* *(P-18054)*
Aegis Asssted Living Prpts LLC ... C ... 510 739-1515
3850 Walnut Ave 228 Fremont (94538) *(P-18050)*
Aegis Fire Systems LLC ... D ... 925 417-5550
500 Boulder Ct Ste A Pleasanton (94566) *(P-1188)*
Aegis Gardens, Fremont *Also called Aegis Senior Communities LLC* *(P-16838)*
Aegis Living, Pleasant Hill *Also called Aegis Senior Communities LLC* *(P-16839)*
AEgis of Carmichael ... E ... 916 972-1313
4050 Walnut Ave Carmichael (95608) *(P-18051)*
Aegis of Fremont, Fremont *Also called Aegis Asssted Living Prpts LLC* *(P-18050)*
Aegis of Moraga, Moraga *Also called Aegis Senior Communities LLC* *(P-18052)*
Aegis of NAPA, NAPA *Also called Aegis Senior Communities LLC* *(P-18053)*
Aegis of South San Francisco, South San Francisco *Also called Aegis Senior Communities LLC* *(P-16841)*
Aegis Senior Communities LLC ... D ... 925 377-7900
950 Country Club Dr Moraga (94556) *(P-18052)*
Aegis Senior Communities LLC ... C ... 510 739-0909
36281 Fremont Blvd Fremont (94536) *(P-16838)*
Aegis Senior Communities LLC ... D ... 925 588-7030
1660 Oak Park Blvd Pleasant Hill (94523) *(P-16839)*
Aegis Senior Communities LLC ... C ... 831 684-2700
125 Heather Ter Aptos (95003) *(P-16840)*
Aegis Senior Communities LLC ... E ... 707 927-3981
2100 Redwood Rd NAPA (94558) *(P-18053)*
Aegis Senior Communities LLC ... D ... 916 972-1313
4050 Walnut Ave Carmichael (95608) *(P-18054)*
Aegis Senior Communities LLC ... C ... 650 952-6100
2280 Gellert Blvd South San Francisco (94080) *(P-16841)*
Aegis Treatment Centers ... E ... 209 565-5982
1947 N California St Stockton (95204) *(P-17408)*
Aehr Test Systems (PA) ... **D ... 510 623-9400**
400 Kato Ter Fremont (94539) *(P-6743)*
Aei Consultants, Walnut Creek *Also called All Environmental Inc* *(P-19716)*
Aei Electech Corp ... F ... 510 489-5088
33485 Western Ave Union City (94587) *(P-6395)*
Aemetis Inc (PA) ... **F ... 408 213-0940**
20400 Stevns Crk Blvd # 700 Cupertino (95014) *(P-4117)*
Aemetis Advnced Fels Keyes Inc ... E ... 209 632-4511
4209 Jessup Rd Ceres (95307) *(P-4118)*
AEP Span Inc ... C ... 916 372-0933
2110 Enterprise Blvd West Sacramento (95691) *(P-1781)*
Aer Electronics Inc (PA) ... **D ... 510 300-0500**
42744 Boscell Rd Fremont (94538) *(P-8298)*
Aera Energy, Rio Vista *Also called Dick Brown Technical Services* *(P-555)*
Aera Energy Services Company ... E ... 559 935-7418
29010 Shell Rd Coalinga (93210) *(P-5044)*
Aera Technology Inc (PA) ... **C ... 408 524-2222**
707 California St Mountain View (94041) *(P-12233)*
Aerelectronics, Fremont *Also called Aer Electronics Inc* *(P-8298)*
Aerial Applicators, Biggs *Also called Chuck Jones Flying Service* *(P-251)*
Aerial Topco LP (PA) ... **E ... 415 983-2700**
1 Embarcadero Ctr Ste 390 San Francisco (94111) *(P-13778)*
Aeris Communications Inc (PA) ... **C ... 408 557-1900**
2099 Gateway Pl Ste 600 San Jose (95110) *(P-7923)*
Aero Precision Holdings LP ... C ... 925 455-9900
2525 Collier Canyon Rd Livermore (94551) *(P-6626)*
Aero Precision Industries LLC (PA) ... **C ... 424 252-8294**
2525 Collier Canyon Rd Livermore (94551) *(P-9149)*
Aero Technologies Inc (PA) ... **E ... 415 314-7479**
555 Mission St San Francisco (94105) *(P-7321)*
Aero Turbine Inc ... D ... 209 983-1112
6800 Lindbergh St Stockton (95206) *(P-4990)*
Aeroground Inc (HQ) ... **A ... 650 266-6965**
270 Lawrence Ave South San Francisco (94080) *(P-7763)*
Aerohive Networks Inc (HQ) ... **A ... 408 510-6100**
1011 Mccarthy Blvd Milpitas (95035) *(P-13551)*
Aerojet Rocketdyne Inc (HQ) ... **A ... 916 355-4000**
2001 Aerojet Rd Rancho Cordova (95742) *(P-6655)*
Aerojet Rocketdyne Inc ... E ... 916 355-4000
1180 Iron Point Rd # 350 Folsom (95630) *(P-6627)*
Aerojet Rocketdyne Inc ... E ... 916 355-4000
160 Blue Ravine Rd Ste C Folsom (95630) *(P-6628)*
Aerometals Inc (PA) ... **D ... 916 939-6888**
3920 Sandstone Dr El Dorado Hills (95762) *(P-6629)*
Aerospace Composite Products (PA) ... **F ... 925 443-5900**
78 Lindbergh Ave Livermore (94551) *(P-6630)*
Aerospace Material Division, Bay Point *Also called Henkel US Operations Corp* *(P-18729)*
AES, Chico *Also called Alternative Energy Systems Inc* *(P-1198)*
AES, Palo Alto *Also called Applied Expert Systems Inc* *(P-12980)*
AES Networks, San Jose *Also called Thales Esecurity Inc* *(P-13997)*
Aesyntix Health Inc (HQ) ... **D ... 916 791-9500**
3300 Douglas Blvd Ste 100 Roseville (95661) *(P-17098)*
Aetna Health California Inc (HQ) ... **C ... 925 543-9223**
1401 Willow Pass Rd # 600 Concord (94520) *(P-10089)*
Aeva Technologies Inc (PA) ... **E ... 650 481-7070**
555 Ellis St Mountain View (94043) *(P-6571)*
Afc First Consumer Discount Co, Oakland *Also called Renew Financial Corp II* *(P-9925)*
Affiliated Engineers W Inc (HQ) ... **D ... 415 546-3120**
123 Mission St Fl 7 San Francisco (94105) *(P-18621)*
Affinity Inc ... E ... 650 380-9305
121 2nd St Fl 6 San Francisco (94105) *(P-12234)*
Affinity Truck Center, Fresno *Also called Central Valley GMC* *(P-14552)*
Affirm Inc (HQ) ... **C ... 415 984-0490**
650 California St Fl 12 San Francisco (94108) *(P-9866)*
Affirm Holdings Inc (PA) ... **C ... 415 984-0490**
650 California St Fl 12 San Francisco (94108) *(P-9867)*
Affirm Identity, San Francisco *Also called Affirm Inc* *(P-9866)*
Affymax Research Institute ... D ... 650 812-8700
4001 Miranda Ave Palo Alto (94304) *(P-19194)*
Affymetrix Inc (HQ) ... **A ... 408 731-5000**
3380 Central Expy Santa Clara (95051) *(P-6804)*
AFL-CIO #1245, Vacaville *Also called Interntnal Brthd Elc Wkr Lcal* *(P-18364)*
Afn Services LLC ... E ... 408 364-1564
368 E Campbell Ave Campbell (95008) *(P-3334)*
Afresh Technologies Inc ... D ... 805 551-9245
116 New Montgomery St # 4 San Francisco (94105) *(P-12960)*
Afscme Local 3299 (PA) ... **D ... 510 844-1160**
425 15th St Oakland (94612) *(P-18353)*
After-Party2 Inc ... D ... 408 457-1187
22674 Broadway A Sonoma (95476) *(P-12028)*
AG & Associates Inc (PA) ... **E ... 925 327-0804**
2208 Camino Ramon Ste A San Ramon (94583) *(P-19435)*
AG Neovo Technology Corp ... F ... 408 321-8210
48501 Warm Springs Blvd # 114 Fremont (94539) *(P-5329)*
AG Spanos Companies (PA) ... **D ... 209 478-7954**
10100 Trinity Pkwy Fl 5 Stockton (95219) *(P-735)*
Agama Solutions Inc ... E ... 510 796-9300
39159 Paseo Padre Pkwy # 216 Fremont (94538) *(P-19436)*
Agari Data Inc (HQ) ... **C ... 650 627-7667**
950 Tower Ln Ste 2000 Foster City (94404) *(P-12235)*

ALPHABETIC

Agc Inc.....D.....408 369-6305
745 Camden Ave Ste B Campbell (95008) ***(P-1189)***
Age Defy Dermatology Wellness.....E.....408 559-0988
3803 S Bascom Ave Ste 200 Campbell (95008) ***(P-15270)***
Age Defying Dermatology, Campbell *Also called Age Defy Dermatology Wellness* ***(P-15270)***
Agemark Corporation (PA).....C.....925 257-4671
25 Avenida De Orinda Orinda (94563) ***(P-15906)***
Agent Iq Inc.....E.....844 243-6847
95 3rd St San Francisco (94103) ***(P-8662)***
Agenus West LLC.....E.....781 674-4400
793 Heinz Ave Berkeley (94710) ***(P-4032)***
Aggregate -Eliot Quarry, Pleasanton *Also called Cemex Cnstr Mtls PCF LLC* ***(P-4465)***
Aggregate Clayton Quarry, Clayton *Also called Cemex Cnstr Mtls PCF LLC* ***(P-8621)***
Aggrigator Inc.....E.....831 728-2824
350 W Beach St Watsonville (95076) ***(P-12961)***
Agh, Fresno *Also called American Grape Harvesters Inc* ***(P-9030)***
Agi Publishing Inc (PA).....E.....559 251-8888
1850 N Gateway Blvd # 152 Fresno (93727) ***(P-11738)***
Agilent Tech Foundation.....E.....408 345-8886
5301 Stevens Creek Blvd Santa Clara (95051) ***(P-6744)***
Agilent Tech World Trade Inc (HQ).....A.....408 345-8886
5301 Stevens Creek Blvd Santa Clara (95051) ***(P-6745)***
Agilent Technologies Inc (PA).....A.....800 227-9770
5301 Stevens Creek Blvd Santa Clara (95051) ***(P-6805)***
Agilepoint Inc (PA).....C.....650 968-6789
1916 Old Middlefield Way Mountain View (94043) ***(P-12962)***
Agiliance Inc (PA).....E.....408 200-0400
845 Stewart Dr Ste D Sunnyvale (94085) ***(P-13834)***
Agiloft Inc.....E.....650 587-8615
460 Seaport Ct Ste 200 Redwood City (94063) ***(P-12963)***
Aging California Department.....E.....530 898-5923
2491 Carmichael Dr Chico (95928) ***(P-17409)***
Agraquest Inc (HQ).....C.....866 992-2937
890 Embarcadero Dr West Sacramento (95605) ***(P-3836)***
Agreeya Solutions Inc (PA).....D.....916 294-0075
605 Coolidge Dr Ste 200 Folsom (95630) ***(P-19437)***
Agri Technovation Inc.....C.....559 931-3332
516 Villa Ave Clovis (93612) ***(P-4128)***
Agri-Comm Express Inc.....E.....209 854-2474
3915 S Hunt Rd Gustine (95322) ***(P-7446)***
Agrian Inc (PA).....D.....559 437-5700
352 W Spruce Ave Clovis (93611) ***(P-13835)***
Agribag Inc.....E.....510 533-2388
3925 Alameda Ave Oakland (94601) ***(P-2983)***
Agrichem, Fowler *Also called Kandarian Agri Enterprises* ***(P-59)***
Agriclture Prrity Plltnts Labs (PA).....E.....559 275-2175
908 N Temperance Ave Clovis (93611) ***(P-19254)***
Agriculture Bag Manufacturing,, Oakland *Also called Agriculture Bag Mfg USA Inc* ***(P-2967)***
Agriculture Bag Mfg USA Inc (PA).....E.....510 632-5637
960 98th Ave Oakland (94603) ***(P-2967)***
Agrifim Irrigation Pdts Inc.....F.....559 443-6680
2855 S East Ave Fresno (93725) ***(P-4994)***
Agrinos Inc (PA).....D.....888 706-9505
279 Cousteau Pl Ste 100 Davis (95618) ***(P-267)***
Agromillora California.....E.....530 846-0404
612 E Gridley Rd Gridley (95948) ***(P-9622)***
AGS, Fresno *Also called Ameriguard Security Svcs Inc* ***(P-14029)***
Aguatierra Associates Inc (PA).....E.....510 450-6000
2000 Powell St Ste 555 Emeryville (94608) ***(P-19700)***
Ah Parallel Fund V LP.....E.....650 798-3900
2865 Sand Hill Rd Ste 101 Menlo Park (94025) ***(P-10831)***
Ah Wines Inc.....F.....209 625-8170
27 E Vine St Lodi (95240) ***(P-2503)***
Aha Labs Inc.....D.....650 575-1425
20 Gloria Cir Menlo Park (94025) ***(P-12964)***
Aharoni & Steele Inc.....F.....408 451-9585
1855 Norman Ave Santa Clara (95054) ***(P-2441)***
Ahead Magnetics Inc.....D.....408 226-9800
6410 Via Del Oro San Jose (95119) ***(P-6396)***
Aheadtek, San Jose *Also called Ahead Magnetics Inc* ***(P-6396)***
Ahlborn Companies, Santa Rosa *Also called Ahlborn Fence & Steel Inc* ***(P-1997)***
Ahlborn Fence & Steel Inc (PA).....E.....707 573-0742
1230 Century Ct Santa Rosa (95403) ***(P-1997)***
Ahlborn Structural Steel Inc.....E.....707 573-0742
1230 Century Ct Santa Rosa (95403) ***(P-4642)***
Ahn Enterprises LLC.....F.....408 734-1878
1240 Birchwood Dr Ste 2 Sunnyvale (94089) ***(P-6375)***
Ahntech Inc (PA).....D.....650 861-3987
1931 Old Middlefield Way D Mountain View (94043) ***(P-18622)***
Aho Enterprises Inc.....E.....650 593-1019
956 Bransten Rd San Carlos (94070) ***(P-14516)***
Ahoy-Hoy Inc (PA).....E.....415 669-6902
6116 N Rockridge Blvd Oakland (94618) ***(P-12965)***
Ahtna Facility Services Inc.....C.....916 375-0199
3100 Beacon Blvd West Sacramento (95691) ***(P-11914)***
Ai Industries LLC (PA).....D.....650 366-4099
1725 E Byshore Rd Ste 101 Redwood City (94063) ***(P-4894)***
Aidells Sausage Company Inc.....A.....510 614-5450
2411 Baumann Ave San Lorenzo (94580) ***(P-2109)***
Aids Lifecycle, San Francisco *Also called San Francisco Aids Foundation* ***(P-17709)***
AIG, Walnut Creek *Also called Western National Life Insur Co* ***(P-10368)***
Aiken Underground Inc.....E.....925 776-4600
3000 Wilbur Ave Ste A Antioch (94509) ***(P-605)***
Aim Higher Incorporated (PA).....D.....916 786-0351
1132 Smith Ln Roseville (95661) ***(P-17410)***
Aim Mail Centers, Woodland *Also called American International Mfg Co* ***(P-4995)***
Aimmune Therapeutics Inc.....C.....650 614-5220
8000 Marina Blvd Ste 300 Brisbane (94005) ***(P-3837)***
Ainor Signs Inc.....E.....916 348-4370
5443 Stationers Way Sacramento (95842) ***(P-7215)***
Air & Lube Systems Inc (PA).....E.....916 381-5588
8353 Demetre Ave Sacramento (95828) ***(P-1998)***
Air Bearing Technology, Hayward *Also called KLA Tencor* ***(P-5222)***
Air Blown Concrete.....E.....916 991-1738
601 W Delano St Elverta (95626) ***(P-1999)***
Air Blown Concrete & Ready Mix, Elverta *Also called Air Blown Concrete* ***(P-1999)***
Air Cargo Handling Service, South San Francisco *Also called Aeroground Inc* ***(P-7763)***
Air Factors Inc.....F.....925 579-0040
4771 Arroyo Vis Ste D Livermore (94551) ***(P-5189)***
Air Liquide Electronics US LP.....A.....510 624-4338
46401 Landing Pkwy Fremont (94538) ***(P-3777)***
Air Monitor Corporation (PA).....D.....707 544-2706
1050 Hopper Ave Santa Rosa (95403) ***(P-6712)***
Air Systems Inc.....B.....408 280-1666
940 Remillard Ct Frnt San Jose (95122) ***(P-1190)***
Air Systems Service & Cnstr.....C.....916 368-0336
10381 Old Placerville Rd # 100 Sacramento (95827) ***(P-1191)***
Air Vapor System, Concord *Also called Airvapor LLC* ***(P-3373)***
Airbnb Inc (PA).....A.....415 510-4027
888 Brannan St Fl 3 San Francisco (94103) ***(P-14197)***
Airbnb Payments Inc.....E.....415 861-2325
888 Brannan St San Francisco (94103) ***(P-9840)***
Airborne Security Patrol Inc (PA).....D.....916 394-2400
10481 Grant Line Rd # 175 Elk Grove (95624) ***(P-14026)***
Aircargo Communities Inc.....E.....650 952-9050
41 Margaret Ave Brisbane (94005) ***(P-13692)***
Airco Commercial Services Inc (HQ).....E.....866 731-4458
5725 Alder Ave Sacramento (95828) ***(P-1192)***
Airco Mechanical Inc (PA).....C.....916 381-4523
8210 Demetre Ave Sacramento (95828) ***(P-1193)***
Aircraft Covers Inc.....E.....408 738-3959
18850 Adams Ct Morgan Hill (95037) ***(P-3036)***
Aircraft Technical Publishers (PA).....E.....415 330-9500
2000 Sierra Point Pkwy # 501 Brisbane (94005) ***(P-3553)***
Airdrome Orchards Inc (PA).....E.....408 297-6461
111 E Alma Ave San Jose (95112) ***(P-95)***
Aire Sheet Metal Inc.....E.....650 364-8081
1973 E Bayshore Rd Redwood City (94063) ***(P-1194)***
Airfield Supply Co.....D.....408 320-0230
1190 Coleman Ave San Jose (95110) ***(P-9187)***
Airgard Inc (PA).....E.....408 573-0701
1755 Mccarthy Blvd Milpitas (95035) ***(P-5190)***
Airline Coach Service, Burlingame *Also called Jeremiah Phillips LLC* ***(P-7337)***
Airline Coach Service Inc.....E.....650 697-7733
San Francisco Intl Arprt San Francisco (94125) ***(P-7322)***
Airline Coach Service Inc (PA).....E.....650 697-7733
863 Malcolm Rd Burlingame (94010) ***(P-7323)***
Airmagnet Inc.....E.....408 571-5000
178 E Tasman Dr San Jose (95134) ***(P-8663)***
Airport, San Jose *Also called City of San Jose* ***(P-7769)***
Airport Auto Parts Inc.....F.....650 952-1135
520 San Mateo Ave San Bruno (94066) ***(P-8436)***
Airport Cinemas 12, Santa Rosa *Also called North American Cinemas Inc* ***(P-14814)***
Airport Club.....D.....707 528-2582
432 Aviation Blvd Santa Rosa (95403) ***(P-15048)***
Airport Health Club, Santa Rosa *Also called Airport Club* ***(P-15048)***
Airport Parking Service Inc.....D.....650 875-6655
630 N San Mateo Dr San Mateo (94401) ***(P-14507)***
Airport Specialty Products Inc.....E.....559 439-9737
2531 W Paul Ave Fresno (93711) ***(P-606)***
Airports Dept, Sacramento *Also called County of Sacramento* ***(P-7772)***
Airspace Systems Inc.....E.....415 226-7779
1933 Davis St Ste 229 San Leandro (94577) ***(P-5674)***
Airtronics Metal Products Inc (PA).....C.....408 977-7800
140 San Pedro Ave Morgan Hill (95037) ***(P-4739)***
Airvapor LLC.....F.....925 405-5582
200 Mason Cir Concord (94520) ***(P-3373)***
Aisera Inc.....D.....650 667-4308
1121 San Antonio Rd C202 Palo Alto (94303) ***(P-12236)***
Aisha Academy.....D.....310 908-1962
706 S Pershing Ave Stockton (95203) ***(P-11588)***
Aisin Electronics Inc.....C.....209 983-4988
199 Frank West Cir Stockton (95206) ***(P-6572)***
Aixtron Inc.....C.....669 228-3759
1700 Wyatt Dr Ste 15 Santa Clara (95054) ***(P-6016)***
Aja Video Systems Inc (PA).....E.....530 274-2048
180 Litton Dr Grass Valley (95945) ***(P-5817)***
Ajax - Untd Pttrns & Molds Inc.....C.....510 476-8000
34585 7th St Union City (94587) ***(P-4253)***
Ajax Custom Manufacturing, Union City *Also called Ajax - Untd Pttrns & Molds Inc* ***(P-4253)***
Ajilon LLC.....C.....408 367-2592
2055 Gateway Pl Ste 300 San Jose (95110) ***(P-12158)***
Ajinomoto Foods North Amer Inc.....C.....510 293-1838
2395 American Ave Hayward (94545) ***(P-2301)***
AJPJ II LLC.....C.....707 972-9563
1140 Airport Park Blvd Ukiah (95482) ***(P-10912)***
AJW Construction.....E.....510 568-2300
966 81st Ave Oakland (94621) ***(P-4186)***
AK Mak Bakeries Division, Sanger *Also called Soojians Inc* ***(P-2418)***
Akas Manufacturing Corporation.....E.....510 786-3200
3200 Investment Blvd Hayward (94545) ***(P-4740)***
Akash Systems Inc (PA).....F.....408 887-6682
600 California St Fl 11 San Francisco (94108) ***(P-6397)***
Akero Therapeutics Inc (PA).....F.....650 487-6488
601 Gateway Blvd Ste 350 South San Francisco (94080) ***(P-3838)***
Aki Technologies Inc.....E.....415 462-4254
912 Cole St San Francisco (94117) ***(P-19438)***

Akido Printing Inc ...F....510 357-0238
2096 Merced St San Leandro (94577) ***(P-3617)***
Akira Seiki USA Inc ...E....925 443-1200
255 Capitol St Livermore (94551) ***(P-5071)***
Akm Semiconductor Inc ...E....408 436-8580
1731 Tech Dr Ste 500 San Jose (95110) ***(P-6017)***
Akon Incorporated ...D....408 432-8039
2135 Ringwood Ave San Jose (95131) ***(P-7267)***
Akoonu Inc ...F....844 425-6668
350 Townsend St Ste 402 San Francisco (94107) ***(P-12966)***
Akqa Inc (HQ) ...**B....415 645-9400**
360 3rd St Ste 500 San Francisco (94107) ***(P-19439)***
Akraya Inc ...E....408 907-6400
2933 Bunker Hill Ln # 100 Santa Clara (95054) ***(P-12071)***
Akribis Systems Incorporated ...F....408 913-1300
780 Montague Expy Ste 508 San Jose (95131) ***(P-5657)***
Akshaya Inc (PA) ...**C....925 914-7395**
415 Boulder Ct Ste 100 Pleasanton (94566) ***(P-13836)***
Akt America Inc (HQ) ...**B....408 563-5455**
3101 Scott Blvd Bldg 91 Santa Clara (95054) ***(P-6018)***
Akt America Inc ...B....408 563-5455
1245 Walsh Ave Santa Clara (95050) ***(P-6019)***
Aktana Inc (PA) ...**B....888 707-3125**
207 Powell St Fl 8 San Francisco (94102) ***(P-12967)***
Akzo Nobel Coatings Inc ...E....510 562-8812
2100 Adams Ave San Leandro (94577) ***(P-4101)***
Al Kramp Specialties ...F....209 464-7539
1707 El Pinal Dr Stockton (95205) ***(P-5741)***
Al Lamm Ranch Inc ...E....559 638-3204
42902 Road 56 Reedley (93654) ***(P-200)***
Al Stockwell Inc ...E....510 269-7423
405 14th St Fl 7 Oakland (94612) ***(P-12237)***
Al Tabase Summit Hospital ...D....510 869-6600
350 Hawthorne Ave Oakland (94609) ***(P-16983)***
Al-Tar Services Inc ...D....866 522-3499
823 Kifer Rd Sunnyvale (94086) ***(P-14734)***
Ala Csta Ctr Prgram For The Dv (PA) ...**E....510 527-2550**
1300 Rose St Berkeley (94702) ***(P-17853)***
Alacritech Inc ...E....408 867-3809
1995 N 1st St Ste 200 San Jose (95112) ***(P-6020)***
Alameda Alliance For Health ...C....510 747-4555
1240 S Loop Rd Alameda (94502) ***(P-10090)***
Alameda Bureau Elec Imprv Corp (HQ) ...**D....510 748-3902**
2000 Grand St Alameda (94501) ***(P-8089)***
Alameda Chapel of The Chimes, Hayward *Also called Chapel of Chimes* ***(P-10724)***
Alameda Cnty Cmnty Fd Bnk Inc ...D....510 635-3663
7900 Edgewater Dr Oakland (94621) ***(P-17411)***
Alameda Cnty Employees Rtrment ...D....510 628-3000
475 14th St Ste 1000 Oakland (94612) ***(P-10227)***
Alameda Cnty Mental Hlth Assn ...D....510 835-5010
954 60th St Ste 10 Oakland (94608) ***(P-16984)***
Alameda County AG Fair Assn ...D....925 426-7600
4501 Pleasanton Ave Pleasanton (94566) ***(P-15170)***
Alameda County Bar Association ...E....510 302-2222
1000 Broadway Ste 480 Oakland (94607) ***(P-18322)***
Alameda County Fair, Pleasanton *Also called Alameda County AG Fair Assn* ***(P-15170)***
Alameda County Industries Inc ...E....510 357-7282
610 Aladdin Ave San Leandro (94577) ***(P-8299)***
Alameda County Water District (PA) ...**C....510 668-4200**
43885 S Grimmer Blvd Fremont (94538) ***(P-8218)***
Alameda County Water District ...E....510 668-6631
42436 Mission Blvd Fremont (94539) ***(P-8219)***
Alameda Electric Supply (HQ) ...**E....510 786-1400**
3875 Bay Center Pl Hayward (94545) ***(P-8838)***
Alameda Electrical Distrs, Hayward *Also called Alameda Electric Supply* ***(P-8838)***
Alameda Family Services ...C....510 629-6300
2325 Clement Ave Alameda (94501) ***(P-17854)***
Alameda Halthcare Wellness Ctr, Alameda *Also called Alameda Hlthcare & Wellnss Ctr* ***(P-15907)***
Alameda Health System (PA) ...**D....510 437-4800**
1411 E 31st St Oakland (94602) ***(P-18217)***
Alameda Hlthcare & Wellnss Ctr ...D....510 523-8857
430 Willow St Alameda (94501) ***(P-15907)***
Alameda Hospital, Alameda *Also called City Alameda Health Care Corp* ***(P-16333)***
Alameda Hospitality LLC ...E....510 522-1000
1628 Webster St Alameda (94501) ***(P-10913)***
Alameda Municipal Power, Alameda *Also called Alameda Bureau Elec Imprv Corp* ***(P-8089)***
Alameda Newspapers Inc (HQ) ...**C....510 783-6111**
22533 Foothill Blvd Hayward (94541) ***(P-3411)***
Alameda Newspapers Inc ...C....650 348-4321
1080 S Amphlett Blvd San Mateo (94402) ***(P-3412)***
Alameda Office Edction Opprtni, Oakland *Also called Youth Employment Partnr Inc* ***(P-17850)***
Alameda-Contra Costa Trnst Dst (PA) ...**C....510 891-4777**
1600 Franklin St Oakland (94612) ***(P-7324)***
Alameda-Contra Costa Trnst Dst ...A....510 577-8816
10626 International Blvd Oakland (94603) ***(P-7444)***
Alamo Capital ...E....925 472-5700
201 N Civic Dr Ste 180 Walnut Creek (94596) ***(P-9955)***
Alan J Vallarine DDS Inc ...E....209 669-8120
1840 N Olive Ave Ste 4 Turlock (95382) ***(P-15820)***
Alaniz Construction Inc ...E....510 770-5000
7160 Stevenson Blvd Fremont (94538) ***(P-1004)***
Alarcon Bohm Corp ...D....510 893-4405
5301 Adeline St Oakland (94608) ***(P-1977)***
Alarmwatch, Atwater *Also called Hoffmans Electronic Systems* ***(P-14136)***
Alasco Rubber & Plastics Corp ...F....707 823-5270
1250 Enos Ave Sebastopol (95472) ***(P-4212)***
Alation Inc (PA) ...**D....650 779-4440**
3 Lagoon Dr Ste 300 Redwood City (94065) ***(P-12968)***
Albano Dale Dunn & Lewis Insur ...E....916 988-0214
9197 Greenback Ln Ste E Orangevale (95662) ***(P-10228)***
Albany Ford Inc (PA) ...**D....510 528-1244**
718 San Pablo Ave Albany (94706) ***(P-14544)***
Albany Subaru, Albany *Also called Albany Ford Inc* ***(P-14544)***
Albeco Inc ...D....415 461-1164
270 Bon Air Ctr Greenbrae (94904) ***(P-2360)***
Albert D Seeno Cnstr Co Inc ...D....925 671-7711
4021 Port Chicago Hwy Concord (94520) ***(P-607)***
Albert Nahman Plumbing & Htg ...E....510 843-6904
3333 Mrtin Lther King Jr Berkeley (94703) ***(P-1195)***
Albion River Inn Incorporated ...D....707 937-1919
3790 N Highway 1 Albion (95410) ***(P-10914)***
Alcal Industries Inc (PA) ...**E....510 786-1400**
25823 Clawiter Rd Hayward (94545) ***(P-8839)***
Alcal Specialty Contg Inc (HQ) ...**B....916 929-3100**
946 N Market Blvd Sacramento (95834) ***(P-1782)***
Alcan Packg Capsules Cal LLC ...E....707 257-6481
5425 Broadway St American Canyon (94503) ***(P-9108)***
Alcatel-Lucent USA Inc ...D....650 623-3300
777 E Middlefield Rd Mountain View (94043) ***(P-5785)***
Alcatel-Lucent USA Inc ...E....510 475-5000
30971a San Benito St Hayward (94544) ***(P-5786)***
Alcatraz Ai Inc ...D....650 600-0197
1808 El Camino Real Redwood City (94063) ***(P-14119)***
Alcatraz Cruises LLC ...D....415 981-7625
Hrnblwer Alctraz Pier 33 St Pier San Francisco (94111) ***(P-7813)***
Alccon General Engineering ...E....916 381-4600
6060 Mortono St Sacramento (95828) ***(P-1005)***
Alchemy Cafe Inc (PA) ...**E....925 825-8400**
746 French Gulch Rd Murphys (95247) ***(P-13818)***
Alco Iron & Metal Co (PA) ...**D....510 562-1107**
2140 Davis St San Leandro (94577) ***(P-9172)***
Alco Iron & Metal Co ...E....510 562-1107
1091 Doolittle Dr C San Leandro (94577) ***(P-8300)***
Alcohol & Drug Svcs Dept, Palo Alto *Also called Santa Clara County of* ***(P-17067)***
Alcohol DRG Awareness Program ...E....209 870-6500
1981 Cherokee Rd Stockton (95205) ***(P-17412)***
Aldea Inc ...E....925 577-3102
470 Chadbourne Rd Ste F Fairfield (94534) ***(P-17413)***
Alderman Logging, Sonora *Also called Alderman Timber Company Inc* ***(P-3054)***
Alderman Timber Company Inc ...E....209 532-9636
17180 Alderman Rd Sonora (95370) ***(P-3054)***
Alderson Construction Inc ...E....510 841-7159
2944 Elmwood Ct Berkeley (94705) ***(P-736)***
Alderson Convalescent Hospital, Woodland *Also called United Health Systems Inc* ***(P-16148)***
Aldetec Inc ...E....916 453-3382
3560 Business Dr Ste 100 Sacramento (95820) ***(P-5818)***
Alector LLC (HQ) ...**D....415 231-5660**
131 Oyster Point Blvd # 60 South San Francisco (94080) ***(P-19013)***
Alegre Trucking, Stockton *Also called California Bulk Inc* ***(P-7518)***
Alembic Inc ...F....707 523-2611
240 Classic Ct Rohnert Park (94928) ***(P-7169)***
Alemeda County Industries LLC ...D....510 357-7282
610 Aladdin Ave San Leandro (94577) ***(P-8301)***
Alertenterprise Inc ...C....510 440-0840
4350 Starboard Dr Fremont (94538) ***(P-12969)***
Alessandro Electric Inc ...D....916 283-6966
11335 Sunrise Gold Cir Rancho Cordova (95742) ***(P-1446)***
Alex Tronix, Fresno *Also called GNA Industries Inc* ***(P-5679)***
Alex's Dry Cleaning Valet, San Rafael *Also called Fcsi Inc* ***(P-11628)***
Alexa Alborzi DDS Mds Inc (PA) ...**E....650 342-4171**
235 N San Mateo Dr # 300 San Mateo (94401) ***(P-15271)***
Alexander Company, Burlingame *Also called J J J & K Inc* ***(P-1744)***
Alexander Valley Gourmet LLC ...E....707 473-0116
140 Grove Ct B Healdsburg (95448) ***(P-2866)***
Alexander Valley Healthcare, Cloverdale *Also called Coppertower Family Medical Ctr* ***(P-15366)***
Alexander Valley Vineyards, Healdsburg *Also called AVV Winery Co LLC* ***(P-2507)***
Alexander Valley Winery, Healdsburg *Also called Silver Oak Wine Cellars LLC* ***(P-2717)***
Alexza Pharmaceuticals Inc (HQ) ...**E....650 944-7000**
2091 Stierlin Ct Mountain View (94043) ***(P-3839)***
Aleyegn Inc (PA) ...**D....301 758-2949**
23600 Big Basin Way Saratoga (95070) ***(P-6937)***
Alfa Tech Cnslting Engners Inc (PA) ...**D....408 487-1200**
1321 Ridder Park Dr 50 San Jose (95131) ***(P-18623)***
Alfa Tech Consulting Entps, San Jose *Also called Alfa Tech Cnslting Engners Inc* ***(P-18623)***
Alfred Conhagen Inc California ...E....707 746-4848
3900 Oregon St Ste 1 Benicia (94510) ***(P-9109)***
Alfred's Machining, Plymouth *Also called Acm Machining Inc* ***(P-5462)***
Algo Technologies Inc ...F....608 332-9716
2025 Geri Ln Hillsborough (94010) ***(P-12970)***
Algolia Inc (PA) ...**D....415 366-9672**
301 Howard St Ste 300 San Francisco (94105) ***(P-12971)***
Algomedica Inc (PA) ...**E....650 857-0116**
440 N Wolfe Rd Sunnyvale (94085) ***(P-15272)***
Algonquin Power Sanger LLC ...E....559 875-0800
1125 Muscat Ave Sanger (93657) ***(P-5646)***
Alibaba Group, Sunnyvale *Also called Alibabacom US LLC* ***(P-19440)***
Alibabacom US LLC (HQ) ...**C....408 785-5580**
525 Almanor Ave Ste 400 Sunnyvale (94085) ***(P-19440)***
Alice Gray ...E....415 388-5060
36 Tiburon Blvd Mill Valley (94941) ***(P-10488)***
Alice Manner, Fowler *Also called Nia Healthcare Services Inc* ***(P-16068)***
Alice Manor, Fowler *Also called Nia Healthcare Services Inc* ***(P-16070)***

ALPHABETIC

Alien Technology LLC ....D....408 782-3900
845 Embedded Way Ste 100 San Jose (95138) ***(P-12238)***
Alien Technology LLC (PA) ....E....**408 782-3900**
845 Embedded Way Ste 100 San Jose (95138) ***(P-5819)***
Alienvault LLC (HQ) ....B....**650 713-3333**
1100 Park Pl Ste 300 San Mateo (94403) ***(P-12972)***
Aligntech ....E....714 605-7114
2820 Orchard Pkwy San Jose (95134) ***(P-14545)***
Aligos Therapeutics Inc (PA) ....D....**800 466-6059**
1 Corporate Dr Fl 2 South San Francisco (94080) ***(P-4033)***
Alion Energy Inc ....D....510 965-0868
2200 Central St D Richmond (94801) ***(P-6021)***
Alivecor Inc (PA) ....D....**650 396-8650**
189 Bernardo Ave Ste 100 Mountain View (94043) ***(P-12973)***
Alkahest Inc ....D....650 801-0474
125 Shoreway Rd Ste D San Carlos (94070) ***(P-19014)***
Alkira Inc ....F....408 654-9696
2811 Mission College Blvd F Santa Clara (95054) ***(P-12974)***
All American Fence Corporation ....E....925 275-5110
568 Mcgraw Ave Livermore (94551) ***(P-2000)***
All American Label, Dublin *Also called A A Label Inc* ***(P-3400)***
All Bates Summit Medical Ctr, Berkeley *Also called Sutter Health* ***(P-16648)***
All Bay Mechanical Inc ....E....408 280-5558
2033 Gateway Pl Ste 500 San Jose (95110) ***(P-1196)***
All Bay Pallet Company Inc (PA) ....E....**510 636-4131**
24993 Tarman Ave Hayward (94544) ***(P-3217)***
All Commercial Landscape Svc ....E....559 453-1670
5213 E Pine Ave Fresno (93727) ***(P-445)***
All Environmental Inc (PA) ....E....**925 746-6000**
2500 Camino Diablo Walnut Creek (94597) ***(P-19716)***
All Fab Prcsion Sheetmetal Inc ....D....408 279-1099
1015 Timothy Dr San Jose (95133) ***(P-1783)***
All Fence Company Inc ....E....650 369-4556
1900 Spring St Redwood City (94063) ***(P-2001)***
All Frign Dmestics Auto Bdy Sp, Stockton *Also called B T Automotive Inc* ***(P-9173)***
All Good Pallets Inc ....E....209 467-7000
1055 Diamond St Stockton (95205) ***(P-3218)***
All Guard Alarm Systems Inc (PA) ....D....**800 255-4273**
1306 Stealth St Livermore (94551) ***(P-1447)***
All Klin Corporation (PA) ....E....**408 327-1000**
1432 Old Bayshore Hwy San Jose (95112) ***(P-8437)***
All Metals Inc (PA) ....E....**408 200-7000**
705 Reed St Santa Clara (95050) ***(P-4556)***
All Phase Security Inc ....D....916 919-3859
2959 Promenade St Ste 200 West Sacramento (95691) ***(P-14027)***
All Pro Drywall ....E....530 722-5182
22148 Buckeye Pl Cottonwood (96022) ***(P-1657)***
All Quality & Services Inc ....C....510 249-5800
47817 Fremont Blvd Fremont (94538) ***(P-5908)***
All Saintsidence Opco LLC ....E....510 481-3200
1652 Mono Ave San Leandro (94578) ***(P-15908)***
All Sensors Corporation ....E....408 776-9434
16035 Vineyard Blvd Morgan Hill (95037) ***(P-6022)***
All Snts Sbcute Trnstonal Care, San Leandro *Also called All Saintsidence Opco LLC* ***(P-15908)***
All Star Rentals, Fairfield *Also called Fairfield Rental Service Inc* ***(P-12020)***
All Things Video, Sacramento *Also called Atv Video Center Inc* ***(P-14786)***
All Turtles Corporation (PA) ....E....**609 352-3172**
1266 Harrison St San Francisco (94103) ***(P-12239)***
All Weather Inc ....D....916 928-1000
1065 National Dr Ste 1 Sacramento (95834) ***(P-6891)***
All Weather Insulated Panels, Vacaville *Also called Pre-Insulated Metal Tech Inc* ***(P-4855)***
All West Coast Shipping Inc (PA) ....D....**510 236-3008**
1200 Wright Ave Richmond (94804) ***(P-7447)***
All West Container, Madera *Also called Packageone Inc* ***(P-3361)***
All West Fabricators Inc ....F....510 623-1200
44875 Fremont Blvd Fremont (94538) ***(P-4643)***
All-American Lumping LLC ....D....209 715-0309
5665 N Pershing Ave A1 Stockton (95207) ***(P-5060)***
All-American Prtg Svcs Corp (PA) ....E....**707 762-2500**
1324 Rand St Petaluma (94954) ***(P-11844)***
All-Battery.com, Fremont *Also called Tenergy Corporation* ***(P-6491)***
All-In Machining LLC ....E....209 839-8672
157 Sloan Ct Ste B Tracy (95304) ***(P-5467)***
All-Points Petroleum LLC ....D....707 745-1116
640 Noyes Ct Benicia (94510) ***(P-9527)***
All-Rite, Hollister *Also called Associated R V Ent Inc* ***(P-8439)***
All-Tech Machine & Engrg Inc ....E....510 353-2000
2700 Prune Ave Fremont (94539) ***(P-5468)***
All-Truss Inc ....E....707 938-5595
22700 Broadway Sonoma (95476) ***(P-3199)***
Allakos Inc ....E....650 597-5002
975 Island Dr Ste 201 Redwood City (94065) ***(P-19015)***
Allay Therapeutics Inc ....E....650 514-6284
4040 Campbell Ave Ste 110 Menlo Park (94025) ***(P-6938)***
Allbirds Inc ....A....628 225-4848
730 Montgomery St San Francisco (94111) ***(P-4340)***
Allcare Hsptlist Med Group Inc ....E....209 550-5200
3320 Tully Rd Ste 1 Modesto (95350) ***(P-19295)***
Allcells LLC ....D....510 521-2600
1301 Harbor Bay Pkwy # 200 Alameda (94502) ***(P-19016)***
Alldata LLC ....B....916 684-5200
9650 W Taron Dr Ste 100 Elk Grove (95757) ***(P-12975)***
Alldragon International Inc ....E....408 410-6248
4285 Payne Ave 10028 San Jose (95117) ***(P-12240)***
Alldrin Brothers Inc ....E....855 667-4231
584 Hi Tech Pkwy Oakdale (95361) ***(P-268)***
Alldrin Brothers Almonds, Oakdale *Also called Alldrin Brothers Inc* ***(P-268)***
Allegro Copy & Print, Lafayette *Also called Acp Ventures* ***(P-3615)***
Allen David & Assoc Lm 724, Sacramento *Also called David Allen & Associates* ***(P-17246)***
Allen Drywall & Associates ....D....650 579-0664
380 Lang Rd Burlingame (94010) ***(P-1658)***
Allen Matkins, San Francisco *Also called Eileen Nottoli* ***(P-17261)***
Allen Property Group Inc ....E....831 688-5100
347 Spreckels Dr Aptos (95003) ***(P-10376)***
Allen Transportation Co, Sacramento *Also called Amador Stage Lines Inc* ***(P-7420)***
Allens Press Clipping Bureau (PA) ....E....**415 392-2353**
55 New Montgomery St # 31 San Francisco (94105) ***(P-14198)***
Allergy Asthma Assoc Snta Clar (PA) ....E....**408 243-2700**
4050 Moorpark Ave San Jose (95117) ***(P-15273)***
Allevity Hr Inc ....D....530 345-2486
870 Manzanita Ct Ste A Chico (95926) ***(P-18930)***
Alliance Fiber Optic Pdts Inc ....A....408 736-6900
445 Lakeside Dr Sunnyvale (94085) ***(P-4368)***
Alliance For Safety & Justice ....D....209 507-6882
1624 Franklin St 11 Oakland (94612) ***(P-18541)***
Alliance For Workforce Dev Inc ....E....530 283-3933
76 Crescent St Quincy (95971) ***(P-12072)***
Alliance Ground Intl LLC ....C....650 821-0855
648 Rest Field Rd San Francisco (94128) ***(P-7764)***
Alliance Hospital Services ....B....650 697-6900
100 S San Mateo Dr San Mateo (94401) ***(P-16842)***
Alliance Info Tech Cmpt Sftwr (PA) ....F....**925 462-9787**
7041 Koll Center Pkwy # 140 Pleasanton (94566) ***(P-12241)***
Alliance Medical Center Inc ....D....707 431-8234
1381 University St Healdsburg (95448) ***(P-15274)***
Alliance Member Services Inc ....D....831 459-0980
333 Front St Ste 200 Santa Cruz (95060) ***(P-18542)***
Alliance Rdwods Cnfrnce Grunds ....C....707 874-3507
6250 Bohemian Hwy Occidental (95465) ***(P-11597)***
Alliance Roofing Company Inc ....E....800 579-2595
630 Martin Ave Santa Clara (95050) ***(P-1784)***
Allianceit, Pleasanton *Also called Alliance Info Tech Cmpt Sftwr* ***(P-12241)***
Alliances MGT Consulting Inc ....E....650 780-0466
544 Hillside Rd Redwood City (94062) ***(P-19717)***
Alliant International Univ Inc ....D....559 456-2777
5130 E Clinton Way Fresno (93727) ***(P-16985)***
Alliant Tchsystems Oprtons LLC ....E....408 513-3271
151 Martinvale Ln Ste 150 San Jose (95119) ***(P-6660)***
Allianz Global Corporate &, Mill Valley *Also called Allianz Technology America Inc* ***(P-13837)***
Allianz Globl Risks US Insur ....B....415 899-3758
1465 N Mcdowell Blvd Petaluma (94954) ***(P-10161)***
Allianz Insurance Company, Petaluma *Also called Allianz Globl Risks US Insur* ***(P-10161)***
Allianz Reinsurance Amer Inc ....A....415 899-2000
1465 N Mcdowell Blvd Petaluma (94954) ***(P-10081)***
Allianz Technology America Inc ....C....415 899-4110
1 Belvedere Dr Mill Valley (94941) ***(P-13837)***
Allied Administrators Inc ....E....415 989-7443
825 Battery St Fl 1 San Francisco (94111) ***(P-19441)***
Allied Auto Store, Fremont *Also called Serrato-Mcdermott Inc* ***(P-8466)***
Allied Aviation Fueling Co Inc ....D....916 924-1002
7330 Earhart Dr Sacramento (95837) ***(P-7765)***
Allied Concrete and Supply Co ....E....209 524-3177
440 Mitchell Rd Ste B Modesto (95354) ***(P-4458)***
Allied Container Systems Inc ....C....925 944-7600
511 Wilbur Ave Ste B4 Antioch (94509) ***(P-4844)***
Allied Crane Inc ....E....925 427-9200
855 N Parkside Dr Pittsburg (94565) ***(P-14735)***
Allied Electric Motor Svc Inc (PA) ....D....**559 486-4222**
4690 E Jensen Ave Fresno (93725) ***(P-8840)***
Allied Exhaust Systems Inc (PA) ....E....**707 745-0506**
3928 Oregon St Benicia (94510) ***(P-8438)***
Allied Fire Protection ....C....510 533-5516
555 High St Oakland (94601) ***(P-1197)***
Allied Framers Inc ....C....707 452-7050
4990 Allison Pkwy Vacaville (95688) ***(P-1729)***
Allied Intl San Franisco, Hayward *Also called Nor-Cal Moving Services* ***(P-7630)***
Allied Janitorial Maint Inc ....E....209 992-6687
16925 S Harlan Rd Ste 205 Lathrop (95330) ***(P-11915)***
Allied Landscape Services, Morgan Hill *Also called New Path Landscape Svcs Inc* ***(P-427)***
Allied Lube Inc ....D....408 779-8969
17010 Walnut Grove Dr Morgan Hill (95037) ***(P-14654)***
Allied Telesis Inc ....E....408 519-8700
3041 Orchard Pkwy San Jose (95134) ***(P-5342)***
Allied Waste, Stockton *Also called Sunset Disposal Service Inc* ***(P-7492)***
Alling Iron Works, West Sacramento *Also called Carter Group* ***(P-4651)***
Allmodular Systems Inc ....E....510 887-9000
21005 Cabot Blvd Hayward (94545) ***(P-8651)***
Allogene Therapeutics Inc ....C....650 457-2700
210 E Grand Ave South San Francisco (94080) ***(P-19017)***
Alloy Metal Products, Livermore *Also called Fred Matter Inc* ***(P-5528)***
Alloy Technologies Inc (PA) ....D....**415 990-5140**
528 Folsom St San Francisco (94105) ***(P-8664)***
Allred Edward C, Fresno *Also called Family Plg Assoc Med Group* ***(P-15403)***
Allstate Plastics LLC ....F....510 783-9600
1763 Sabre St Hayward (94545) ***(P-4254)***
Allstripes Research Inc ....F....415 404-9287
121 2nd St Ste 700 San Francisco (94105) ***(P-3840)***
Allteq Industries Inc ....F....925 833-7666
215 Rustic Pl San Ramon (94582) ***(P-6023)***
Allure Labs Inc ....E....510 489-8896
30901 Wiegman Ct Hayward (94544) ***(P-4079)***
Allvia Inc ....E....408 234-8778
445 Fairway Dr Half Moon Bay (94019) ***(P-6024)***
Allworth Financial LP ....D....888 577-2489
135 Camino Dorado Ste 1 NAPA (94558) ***(P-10026)***

Allyn James Inc....F....925 828-5530
6575 Trinity Ct Ste B Dublin (94568) ***(P-3618)***
Allyo, Sunnyvale *Also called Sass Labs Inc* ***(P-13427)***
Almaden, Santa Clara *Also called Stone Publishing Inc* ***(P-3602)***
Almaden Golf & Country Club....D....408 323-4812
6663 Hampton Dr San Jose (95120) ***(P-15049)***
Almaden Health & Rehab Ctr, San Jose *Also called Mariner Health Care Inc* ***(P-16056)***
Almaden Valley Athletic Club....D....408 445-4900
5400 Camden Ave San Jose (95124) ***(P-14924)***
Almaden Vly Counseling Svc Inc....E....408 997-0200
6529 Crown Blvd Ste D San Jose (95120) ***(P-17414)***
Almanor Dock Supply, Westwood *Also called Brett Lee Womack* ***(P-2011)***
Almavia of San Francisco, San Francisco *Also called Elder Care Alnce San Francisco* ***(P-15983)***
Almendariz Consulting Inc....E....916 939-3392
1136 Suncast Ln Ste 9 El Dorado Hills (95762) ***(P-19718)***
Almond Board of California....E....209 549-8262
1150 9th St Ste 1500 Modesto (95354) ***(P-18296)***
Almond Company....E....559 665-4405
22782 Road 9 Chowchilla (93610) ***(P-2442)***
Almost Famous Wine Company, Livermore *Also called Darcie Kent Winery LLC* ***(P-9573)***
Alms Company, Gold River *Also called Markes International Inc* ***(P-6836)***
Aloft Hotel Santa Clara....C....408 263-3900
510 America Ctr Ct Alviso (95002) ***(P-10915)***
Aloft Ht San Francisco Arprt....D....650 443-5500
401 E Millbrae Ave Millbrae (94030) ***(P-10916)***
Aloft Mountain View, Mountain View *Also called Camino Real Group LLC* ***(P-10985)***
Aloft Sfo, Millbrae *Also called Millbrae Wcp Hotel II LLC* ***(P-11301)***
Aloft Silicon Valley....D....510 494-8800
8200 Gateway Blvd Newark (94560) ***(P-10917)***
Aloha, Fremont *Also called Air Liquide Electronics US LP* ***(P-3777)***
Aloha Bay....E....707 994-3267
16275 A Main St Lower Lake (95457) ***(P-7268)***
Aloha Beach Resort, San Francisco *Also called Equinox Hotel Management Inc* ***(P-11083)***
Aloha Seafood Inc....E....415 441-4484
Shed D6 Pier 45 San Francisco (94133) ***(P-9358)***
Alois LLC....C....215 297-4492
548 Market St Ste 47970 San Francisco (94104) ***(P-12073)***
Alois Staffing, San Francisco *Also called Alois LLC* ***(P-12073)***
Alom Technologies Corporation (PA)....**C....510 360-3600**
48105 Warm Springs Blvd Fremont (94539) ***(P-14199)***
Alpenglow Expeditions LLC....E....877 873-5376
1985 Squaw Valley Rd # 23 Olympic Valley (96146) ***(P-15171)***
Alpha Agency Inc....E....415 421-6272
23 Grant Ave Fl 4 San Francisco (94108) ***(P-12074)***
Alpha Analytical Labs Inc (PA)....**D....707 468-0401**
208 Mason St Ukiah (95482) ***(P-19255)***
Alpha and Omega Semicdtr Inc (HQ)....**C....408 789-0008**
475 Oakmead Pkwy Sunnyvale (94085) ***(P-6025)***
Alpha Delta PHI International....E....415 704-1879
3871 Piedmont Ave Oakland (94611) ***(P-18384)***
Alpha Dyno Nobel (PA)....**E....916 645-3377**
3400 Nader Rd Lincoln (95648) ***(P-9516)***
Alpha Ems Corporation....C....510 498-8788
44193 S Grimmer Blvd Fremont (94538) ***(P-5909)***
Alpha Explosives, Lincoln *Also called Alpha Dyno Nobel* ***(P-9516)***
Alpha Granite & Marble Inc....E....303 373-4911
2303 Merced St San Leandro (94577) ***(P-8616)***
Alpha Innotech Corp (HQ)....**C....510 483-9620**
81 Daggett Dr San Jose (95134) ***(P-8772)***
Alpha Machine Company Inc....F....831 462-7400
933 Chittenden Ln Ste A Capitola (95010) ***(P-5469)***
Alpha Net Consulting Llc....D....408 330-0896
3080 Olcott St Ste C235 Santa Clara (95054) ***(P-12242)***
Alpha Pet Grooming Salon LLC....E....650 271-4282
1325 Howard Ave Burlingame (94010) ***(P-350)***
Alpha Research & Tech Inc....D....916 431-9340
5175 Hillsdale Cir # 100 El Dorado Hills (95762) ***(P-5239)***
Alpha Rstoration Waterproofing....E....650 875-7500
218 Littlefield Ave South San Francisco (94080) ***(P-821)***
Alpha Teknova Inc....C....831 637-1100
2290 Bert Dr Hollister (95023) ***(P-4034)***
Alphabet Inc (PA)....**A....650 253-0000**
1600 Amphitheatre Pkwy Mountain View (94043) ***(P-12243)***
Alphadetail Inc....E....650 581-3100
777 Mariners Island Blvd # 700 San Mateo (94404) ***(P-19442)***
Alphagem Bio Inc....F....510 999-1153
4201 Business Center Dr Fremont (94538) ***(P-4255)***
AlphaGraphics, Sunnyvale *Also called Jsl Partners Inc* ***(P-3663)***
AlphaGraphics, San Francisco *Also called Integrated Digital Media* ***(P-3659)***
AlphaGraphics, San Francisco *Also called Califrnia Integrated Media Inc* ***(P-3632)***
AlphaGraphics, Modesto *Also called Batchlder Bus Cmmnications Inc* ***(P-3629)***
Alphonso Inc (PA)....**E....415 223-2112**
331 Castro St Ste 200 Mountain View (94041) ***(P-12244)***
Alpine Allrgy Asthma Assoc Inc....D....530 888-1016
3254 Professional Dr Auburn (95602) ***(P-15275)***
Alpine Animal Hospital, Union City *Also called Animus Inc* ***(P-15281)***
Alpine Biomed Corp....D....650 802-0400
1501 Industrial Rd San Carlos (94070) ***(P-6939)***
Alpine Carpet One Floor & Home, South Lake Tahoe *Also called Alpine Carpets Corporation* ***(P-1763)***
Alpine Carpets Corporation (PA)....**D....530 541-6171**
2212 Lake Tahoe Blvd South Lake Tahoe (96150) ***(P-1763)***
Alpine Hlls Tnnis Swmming CLB....E....650 851-1591
4139 Alpine Rd Portola Valley (94028) ***(P-15050)***
Alpine Land Info Svcs Inc (PA)....**E....530 222-8100**
4451 Caterpillar Rd Ste 6 Redding (96003) ***(P-533)***
Alpine Meadows Ski Area....E....530 583-4232
2600 Alpine Meadows Rd Alpine Meadows (96146) ***(P-10918)***
Alpine Meadows Ski Resort, Alpine Meadows *Also called Alpine Meadows Ski Area* ***(P-10918)***
Alpine Meats Inc....E....209 477-2691
9850 Lower Sacramento Rd Stockton (95210) ***(P-2110)***
Alpine Orthopedic Med Group, Stockton *Also called Gary M Alegre MD* ***(P-15413)***
Alpine Pacific Nut Co Inc....E....209 667-8688
6413 E Keyes Rd Hughson (95326) ***(P-260)***
Alps Group Inc....E....760 500-4490
1100 Cadillac Ct Milpitas (95035) ***(P-10919)***
Already....E....510 322-4988
1801 Marlesta Ct Pinole (94564) ***(P-18543)***
ALS Interiors Inc....E....916 344-2942
5710 Auburn Blvd Ste 14 Sacramento (95841) ***(P-608)***
Alsco - Geyer Irrigation Inc....D....530 476-2253
700 5th St Arbuckle (95912) ***(P-9029)***
Alsco Inc....D....510 237-9634
1009 Factory St Richmond (94801) ***(P-11630)***
Alston & Bird LLP....D....415 243-3440
560 Mission St San Francisco (94105) ***(P-17199)***
Alston & Bird LLP....D....650 838-2000
1950 University Ave # 500 East Palo Alto (94303) ***(P-17200)***
Alston Construction Co Inc (PA)....**D....916 340-2400**
8775 Folsom Blvd Ste 201 Sacramento (95826) ***(P-822)***
Alta Bates Medical Center, Berkeley *Also called Ocadian Care Centers LLC* ***(P-16083)***
Alta Bates Summit Foundation....D....510 204-1667
2450 Ashby Ave Ste 601 Berkeley (94705) ***(P-15276)***
Alta Bates Summit Medical Ctr, Berkeley *Also called Surgery Ctr of Alta Btes Smmit* ***(P-16564)***
Alta Bates Summit Medical Ctr, Berkeley *Also called Sutter Bay Hospitals* ***(P-16569)***
Alta Bates Summit Medical Ctr, Oakland *Also called Sutter Bay Hospitals* ***(P-16571)***
Alta Bates Summit Medical Ctr, Berkeley *Also called Sutter Bay Hospitals* ***(P-16574)***
Alta Btes Cmprhnsive Cncer Ctr, Berkeley *Also called Surgery Ctr of Alta Btes Smmit* ***(P-16566)***
Alta Cal Regional Ctr Inc....C....530 666-3391
283 W Court St Woodland (95695) ***(P-17415)***
Alta Cal Regional Ctr Inc....C....916 786-8110
807 Douglas Blvd Roseville (95678) ***(P-17416)***
Alta Cal Regional Ctr Inc....C....530 674-3070
950 Tharp Rd Yuba City (95993) ***(P-17417)***
Alta California Regional Ctr, Roseville *Also called Alta Cal Regional Ctr Inc* ***(P-17416)***
Alta Devices Inc....C....408 988-8600
545 Oakmead Pkwy Sunnyvale (94085) ***(P-6026)***
Alta Industries, Santa Rosa *Also called Stx Inc* ***(P-7201)***
Alta Manufacturing Inc....E....510 668-1870
47650 Westinghouse Dr Fremont (94539) ***(P-5910)***
Alta Mira Hotel & Restaurant, Sausalito *Also called Alta Mira Recovery Ctrs LLC* ***(P-10920)***
Alta Mira Recovery Ctrs LLC....D....415 332-1350
125 Bulkley Ave Sausalito (94965) ***(P-10920)***
Alta Motors, Brisbane *Also called Faster Faster Inc* ***(P-6579)***
Alta Partners Management Corp....E....415 362-4022
1 Embarcadero Ctr Fl 37 San Francisco (94111) ***(P-10832)***
Alta PCF Tech Solutions Group, Fresno *Also called Altapacific Inc* ***(P-12245)***
Alta Sierra Country Club Inc....E....530 273-2041
11897 Tammy Way Grass Valley (95949) ***(P-14986)***
Altaflex....D....408 727-6614
336 Martin Ave Santa Clara (95050) ***(P-5911)***
Altamedix Corporation....D....916 648-3999
4234 N Freeway Blvd # 500 Sacramento (95834) ***(P-17418)***
Altamont Capital Partners LLC (PA)....**B....650 264-7750**
400 Hamilton Ave Ste 230 Palo Alto (94301) ***(P-10833)***
Altamont Manufacturing Inc....F....925 371-5401
241 Rickenbacker Cir Livermore (94551) ***(P-5470)***
Altapacific Inc....E....559 439-5700
1525 E Shaw Ave Ste 201 Fresno (93710) ***(P-12245)***
Altcare Willow Creek Inc (PA)....**E....510 527-7282**
22424 Charlene Way Castro Valley (94546) ***(P-18055)***
Alten Construction Inc....D....510 234-4200
1141 Marina Way S Richmond (94804) ***(P-609)***
Altep California LLC (HQ)....**D....650 691-4500**
2479 E Bayshore Rd # 215 Palo Alto (94303) ***(P-7924)***
Altera Corporation (HQ)....**A....408 544-7000**
101 Innovation Dr San Jose (95134) ***(P-6027)***
Alterg Inc....D....510 270-5900
48368 Milmont Dr Fremont (94538) ***(P-7185)***
Altergy Systems....E....916 458-8590
140 Blue Ravine Rd Folsom (95630) ***(P-5692)***
Alternative Energy Engineering, Sacramento *Also called Aee Solar Inc* ***(P-8837)***
Alternative Energy Systems Inc....D....530 345-6980
13620 State Highway 99 N Chico (95973) ***(P-1198)***
Alterra Spcalty Insur Svcs Ltd....D....415 490-4615
201 California St San Francisco (94111) ***(P-10075)***
Altest Corporation....E....408 436-9900
898 Faulstich Ct San Jose (95112) ***(P-5471)***
Altexsoft Inc....C....877 777-9097
6590 Lockheed Dr Redding (96002) ***(P-13838)***
Altia Systems Inc....E....408 996-9710
20400 Stevns Crk Blvd # 750 Cupertino (95014) ***(P-7148)***
Altierre Corporation....E....408 435-7343
1980 Concourse Dr San Jose (95131) ***(P-6028)***
Altigen Communications Inc....C....408 597-9000
670 N Mccarthy Blvd # 20 Milpitas (95035) ***(P-5787)***
Altium Packaging LLC....F....209 820-1700
75 W Valpico Rd Tracy (95376) ***(P-4256)***
Altium Packaging LLC....F....209 531-9180
1620 Gobel Way Modesto (95358) ***(P-4237)***
Alto Counseling Center, Santa Cruz *Also called Encompass Community Services* ***(P-17547)***

ALPHABETIC

Alto International School ....E....650 324-8617
475 Pope St Menlo Park (94025) ***(P-17855)***
Altos Labs Inc (PA) ....**D....650 438-7055**
2000 Bridge Pkwy Redwood City (94065) ***(P-19018)***
Altos Oaks Day Care Center, Los Altos Hills *Also called First Baptist Church Los Altos* ***(P-17935)***
Altos Pedia Assoc A Prof Corp ....E....650 941-0550
842 Altos Oaks Dr Los Altos (94024) ***(P-15277)***
Altran, Santa Clara *Also called Aricent NA Inc* ***(P-12271)***
Altrubio Inc (PA) ....**E....650 453-3462**
455 Margarita Ave Palo Alto (94306) ***(P-3841)***
Altus Health Inc ....C....916 781-6500
151 N Sunrise Ave # 1011 Roseville (95661) ***(P-16843)***
Alum Rock Counseling Ctr Inc (PA) ....**E....408 240-0070**
777 N 1st St Ste 444 San Jose (95112) ***(P-17419)***
Aluma USA Inc ....E....707 545-9344
435 Tesconi Cir Santa Rosa (95401) ***(P-7163)***
Alumawall Inc ....D....408 275-7165
1701 S 7th St Ste 9 San Jose (95112) ***(P-4845)***
Aluminum Coating Tech Inc ....E....916 442-1063
8290 Alpine Ave Sacramento (95826) ***(P-4895)***
Alvah Contractors Inc ....B....650 741-6785
263 S Maple Ave South San Francisco (94080) ***(P-1448)***
Alvarez Industries ....E....831 423-5515
116 Hubbard St Santa Cruz (95060) ***(P-11916)***
Alvellan Inc ....E....925 689-2421
1030 Shary Ct Concord (94518) ***(P-5472)***
Alveo Technologies Inc ....E....510 851-5314
1000 Atlantic Ave Ste 114 Alameda (94501) ***(P-19019)***
Alveo Technologies Inc ....E....510 749-4895
1000 Atlantic Ave Alameda (94501) ***(P-19020)***
Alves, Robert L, Selma *Also called Robert Alves Farms Inc* ***(P-72)***
Alviso Health Center, Alviso *Also called Gardner Family Hlth Netwrk Inc* ***(P-15412)***
Alw Enterprises Inc ....E....559 275-2828
8727 W Herndon Ave Fresno (93723) ***(P-1978)***
Alward Construction Company ....E....510 527-6498
1035 Carleton St Berkeley (94710) ***(P-610)***
Always Be Learning Inc ....E....650 450-2603
156 2nd St Ste 100 San Francisco (94105) ***(P-17856)***
Always Best Care Senior Svcs, Vacaville *Also called Thriving Seniors LLC* ***(P-16277)***
Always Best Care Senior Svcs, Roseville *Also called Abcsp LLC* ***(P-16830)***
Always Home Nursing Svc Inc ....C....916 989-6420
7777 Greenback Ln Ste 208 Citrus Heights (95610) ***(P-16844)***
Alx Oncology Holdings Inc (PA) ....**E....650 466-7125**
323 Allerton Ave South San Francisco (94080) ***(P-3842)***
Alza Corporation (HQ) ....**A....707 453-6400**
700 Eubanks Dr Vacaville (95688) ***(P-3843)***
Alza Corporation ....A....650 564-5000
1010 Joaquin Rd Mountain View (94043) ***(P-6806)***
Alza Corporation ....A....707 453-6400
700 Eubanks Dr Vacaville (95688) ***(P-6807)***
Alza Pharmaceuticals, Vacaville *Also called Alza Corporation* ***(P-3843)***
Alzeta Corporation ....F....408 727-8282
1968 Hartog Dr San Jose (95131) ***(P-19021)***
ALZHEIMER'S SERVICES OF THE EA, Berkeley *Also called Alzheimers Svcs of East Bay* ***(P-17420)***
Alzheimers Svcs of East Bay (PA) ....**E....510 644-3181**
2320 Channing Way Berkeley (94704) ***(P-17420)***
AM & S Transportation Co ....D....510 208-0271
1700 24th St Oakland (94607) ***(P-7502)***
AM and S Mfg Inc ....F....408 396-3027
1394 Tully Rd Ste 203 San Jose (95122) ***(P-4711)***
AM&s Mnufactruing Design Group, San Jose *Also called AM and S Mfg Inc* ***(P-4711)***
Amadeus Spa NAPA Vly Marriott ....E....707 254-3330
3425 Solano Ave NAPA (94558) ***(P-14925)***
Amador County Landfill, Ione *Also called Amador Disposal Service Inc* ***(P-8302)***
Amador Disposal Service Inc ....D....209 274-4095
6500 Buena Vista Rd Ione (95640) ***(P-8302)***
Amador Home Care Service ....E....209 223-3866
245 New York Ranch Rd A Jackson (95642) ***(P-16845)***
Amador Residential Care Inc ....E....209 223-4444
155 Placer Dr Jackson (95642) ***(P-18056)***
Amador Stage Lines Inc ....D....916 444-7880
1331 C St Sacramento (95814) ***(P-7420)***
Amador Tlmne Cmnty Action Agcy (PA) ....**C....209 296-2785**
10590 State Highway 88 Jackson (95642) ***(P-18218)***
Amador Valley Medical Clinic, Tracy *Also called Amador Vly Med Group Ltd A CA* ***(P-16319)***
Amador Vly Med Group Ltd A CA ....D....925 828-9211
3253 Patina Ct Tracy (95377) ***(P-16319)***
Amador Water Agency ....D....209 223-3018
12800 Ridge Rd Sutter Creek (95685) ***(P-8220)***
Amalgamated Bank ....E....415 995-8157
255 California St Ste 600 San Francisco (94111) ***(P-9755)***
Amar Transportation Inc (PA) ....**C....831 728-8209**
144 W Lake Ave Ste C Watsonville (95076) ***(P-7503)***
Amaranth Medical Inc ....E....650 965-3830
600 California St Fl 6 San Francisco (94108) ***(P-15278)***
Amat ....F....408 563-5385
3101 Scott Blvd Santa Clara (95054) ***(P-6029)***
Amato Industries Incorporated ....E....650 697-5548
1550 Gilbreth Rd Burlingame (94010) ***(P-7367)***
Amax Computer, Fremont *Also called Amax Engineering Corporation* ***(P-8665)***
Amax Engineering Corporation (PA) ....**C....510 651-8886**
1565 Reliance Way Fremont (94539) ***(P-8665)***
Amazing Facts International ....D....916 434-3880
6615 Sierra College Blvd Roseville (95746) ***(P-8015)***
Amazing Facts Ministries, Roseville *Also called Amazing Facts International* ***(P-8015)***
Amazon ....E....510 676-6906
905 Eleventh Ave Sunnyvale (94089) ***(P-19256)***
Amazon Prsrvation Partners Inc ....E....415 775-6355
1550 Leigh Ave San Jose (95125) ***(P-2211)***
Ambarella Inc (PA) ....**A....408 734-8888**
3101 Jay St Santa Clara (95054) ***(P-6030)***
Ambarella Corporation ....E....408 734-8888
3101 Jay St Santa Clara (95054) ***(P-6031)***
Amber Holdings Inc ....D....415 765-6500
150 California St San Francisco (94111) ***(P-12246)***
Amberwood Gardens ....D....408 253-7502
1601 Petersen Ave San Jose (95129) ***(P-16986)***
Ambios Technology Inc (PA) ....**E....831 427-1160**
1 Technology Dr Milpitas (95035) ***(P-6032)***
Ambius, Hayward *Also called Rentokil North America Inc* ***(P-12059)***
Ambr Inc (PA) ....**E....530 221-4759**
1160 Industrial St Redding (96002) ***(P-10229)***
Ambrose Recreation & Park Dst ....E....925 458-1601
3105 Willow Pass Rd Bay Point (94565) ***(P-15172)***
Ambultory Surgery Ctr Stockton, Stockton *Also called Stockton Ambltory Srgery Ctr L* ***(P-15705)***
Ambys Medicines Inc ....E....650 481-7662
131 Oyster Point Blvd # 20 South San Francisco (94080) ***(P-19022)***
Amcan Beverages Inc ....B....707 557-0500
1201 Commerce Blvd American Canyon (94503) ***(P-2781)***
Amcor Flexibles LLC ....D....530 671-9000
800 N Walton Ave Yuba City (95993) ***(P-3721)***
Amcor Flexibles LLC ....C....707 257-6481
5425 Broadway St American Canyon (94503) ***(P-3374)***
Amcor Manufacturing Inc ....F....209 581-9687
500 Winmoore Way Modesto (95358) ***(P-3778)***
Amcs Inc ....E....408 846-9274
200 Mayock Rd Gilroy (95020) ***(P-8475)***
AMD, Santa Clara *Also called Advanced Micro Devices Inc* ***(P-6014)***
AMD Far East Ltd (HQ) ....**B....408 749-4000**
1 Amd Pl Sunnyvale (94085) ***(P-6033)***
AMD Metal Works Inc ....E....916 465-8185
8155 Belvedere Ave # 100 Sacramento (95826) ***(P-1785)***
Amdocs Bcs Inc ....B....916 934-7000
1104 Investment Blvd El Dorado Hills (95762) ***(P-12247)***
Amedica Biotech Inc ....F....510 785-5980
28301 Industrial Blvd K Hayward (94545) ***(P-6940)***
Amen Clinics Inc A Med Corp ....E....650 416-7830
350 N Wiget Ln Ste 105 Walnut Creek (94598) ***(P-17099)***
Ameri-Kleen ....C....831 722-8888
313 W Beach St Watsonville (95076) ***(P-11917)***
Ameri-Kleen Building Services, Watsonville *Also called Ameri-Kleen* ***(P-11917)***
America Printing, Burlingame *Also called Asia America Enterprise Inc* ***(P-3621)***
American Acdemy Ophthlmlogy In (PA) ....**C....415 561-8500**
655 Beach St San Francisco (94109) ***(P-18323)***
American Agcredit Flca (PA) ....**D....707 545-1200**
400 Aviation Blvd Ste 100 Santa Rosa (95403) ***(P-9879)***
American Air Conditioning Co, San Leandro *Also called Heathorn & Assoc Contrs Inc* ***(P-1277)***
American Air Liquide Inc (HQ) ....**D....510 624-4000**
46409 Landing Pkwy Fremont (94538) ***(P-3770)***
American Airlines/Eagle, Fresno *Also called Piedmont Airlines Inc* ***(P-7739)***
American Ambulance, Fresno *Also called KWPH Enterprises* ***(P-7385)***
American Asp Repr Rsrfcing Inc (PA) ....**D....510 723-0280**
24200 Clawiter Rd Hayward (94545) ***(P-1006)***
American Assn Univ Women ....E....510 528-3284
941 The Alameda Berkeley (94707) ***(P-18385)***
American Avk Co ....F....559 452-4305
5286 E Home Ave Fresno (93727) ***(P-4958)***
American Baptist Homes of West, Pleasanton *Also called Humangood Norcal* ***(P-10440)***
American Biodiesel Inc ....F....209 466-4823
809 Snedeker Ave Ste C Stockton (95203) ***(P-4119)***
American Bldg Maint Co of Ill ....B....510 573-1618
44870 Osgood Rd Fremont (94539) ***(P-11918)***
American Bldg Maint Co-West (HQ) ....**C....415 733-4000**
75 Broadway Ste 111 San Francisco (94111) ***(P-11919)***
American Blinds and Drap Inc ....E....510 487-3500
30776 Huntwood Ave Hayward (94544) ***(P-3021)***
American Building Maint Co NY ....D....415 733-4000
101 California St San Francisco (94111) ***(P-11920)***
American Building Service Inc ....D....510 483-5120
4578 Crow Canyon Pl Castro Valley (94552) ***(P-11921)***
American Building Supply Inc ....D....916 387-4101
6300 S Watt Ave Sacramento (95829) ***(P-19296)***
American Building Supply Inc (HQ) ....**C....916 503-4100**
8360 Elder Creek Rd Sacramento (95828) ***(P-8524)***
American Building Supply Inc ....D....916 387-4101
8920 43rd Ave Sacramento (95828) ***(P-8525)***
American Building Supply Inc ....D....209 941-8852
1488 Tillie Lewis Dr Stockton (95206) ***(P-8526)***
American Building Supply Inc ....D....916 503-4100
1 Wayne Ct Sacramento (95829) ***(P-8527)***
American Cancer Soc Cal Div (PA) ....**D....510 893-7900**
1001 Marina Village Pkwy Alameda (94501) ***(P-19195)***
American Carequest Inc (PA) ....**E....415 885-9100**
819 Cowan Rd Ste C Burlingame (94010) ***(P-16846)***
American Carports Inc (PA) ....**E....866 730-9865**
1415 Clay St Colusa (95932) ***(P-4846)***
American Carrier Systems ....E....559 442-1500
2285 E Date Ave Fresno (93706) ***(P-6548)***
American Casting Co, Hollister *Also called Reed Manufacturing Inc* ***(P-4552)***
American Civil Const ....D....707 746-8028
2990 Bay Vista Ct Ste D Benicia (94510) ***(P-1007)***

American Civil Constrs LLC ....D....707 746-8028
3701 Mallard Dr Benicia (94510) *(P-1145)*
American Clg Trdtnl Chnse Mdcn (PA) ....D....**415 282-0316**
455 Arkansas St San Francisco (94107) *(P-16987)*
American Cncil For Fd Sfety Ql, Kingsburg *Also called Dfa of California (P-19325)*
American Cnsrvtory Thtre Fndti (PA) ....D....**415 834-3200**
415 Geary St San Francisco (94102) *(P-14835)*
American Commodity Co., Williams *Also called ACC-Gwg LLC (P-19710)*
American Concrete Washouts Inc (PA) ....C....**916 990-0842**
7013 Folsom Auburn Rd Folsom (95630) *(P-1849)*
American Conservatory Theater (PA) ....C....**415 749-2228**
30 Grant Ave Fl 7 San Francisco (94108) *(P-11705)*
American Crane Rental Inc ....D....209 838-8815
17800 Comconex Rd Manteca (95336) *(P-12016)*
American Crier Eqp Trlr Sls LL ....E....559 442-1500
2285 E Date Ave Fresno (93706) *(P-14655)*
American Cstm Private SEC Inc ....E....209 369-1200
446 E Vine St Ste A Stockton (95202) *(P-14028)*
American Custom Meats LLC ....D....209 839-8800
4276 N Tracy Blvd Tracy (95304) *(P-2111)*
American Cvil Lbrties Un Fndti ....E....415 621-2488
39 Drumm St San Francisco (94111) *(P-18544)*
American Cylnder Head Repr Exc ....E....510 536-1764
499 Lesser St Oakland (94601) *(P-6573)*
American Emperor Inc ....E....713 478-5973
888 Doolittle Dr San Leandro (94577) *(P-4613)*
American Engineering Co, Walnut Creek *Also called Michael Baker Intl Inc (P-18769)*
American Engrg Contrs Inc ....C....209 229-1591
25445 S Schulte Rd Tracy (95377) *(P-1449)*
American Etal Technology, Fremont *Also called Axt Inc (P-6061)*
American Etc Inc ....B....650 873-5353
1140 San Mateo Ave South San Francisco (94080) *(P-11626)*
American Fencing, Fresno *Also called A J Excavation Inc (P-1949)*
American Financial Network Inc ....D....925 705-7710
2125 Oak Grove Rd Walnut Creek (94598) *(P-10027)*
American Financial Network Inc ....E....209 238-3210
3300 Tully Rd Ste C6 Modesto (95350) *(P-10028)*
American Golf Corporation ....D....925 672-9737
1001 Peacock Creek Dr Clayton (94517) *(P-15051)*
American Grape Harvesters Inc ....E....559 277-7380
5778 W Barstow Ave Fresno (93722) *(P-9030)*
American Hard Bag LLC ....F....707 484-1283
1467 Stoney Cross Ln Lincoln (95648) *(P-6647)*
American Health Care, Rocklin *Also called American Hlthcare ADM Svcs Inc (P-17100)*
American Herbs & Specialties, South San Francisco *Also called Bay Area Herbs & Spc LLC (P-9388)*
American HI Security Inc ....E....209 518-9207
8156 S El Dorado St French Camp (95231) *(P-1450)*
American High Schl Booster CLB ....E....510 796-1776
36300 Fremont Blvd Fremont (94536) *(P-18386)*
American Histology Reagent Co, Lodi *Also called American Mstr Tech Scntfic Inc (P-6941)*
American Hlthcare ADM Svcs Inc ....B....916 773-7227
3850 Atherton Rd Rocklin (95765) *(P-17100)*
American Hospital Mgt Corp (PA) ....B....**707 822-3621**
3800 Janes Rd Arcata (95521) *(P-16320)*
American Hospital Mgt Corp ....E....707 826-8420
4605 Valley West Blvd Arcata (95521) *(P-16321)*
American Hotel Inc ....E....650 323-5101
235 Hamilton Ave Palo Alto (94301) *(P-10921)*
American Infrastructure Mlp Fu ....E....650 854-6000
950 Tower Ln Ste 800 Foster City (94404) *(P-19719)*
American International Mfg Co ....E....530 666-2446
1230 Fortna Ave Woodland (95776) *(P-4995)*
American Legion Ambulance Svc ....E....209 223-2963
11350 American Legion Dr Sutter Creek (95685) *(P-18387)*
American Legion Hall, Sutter Creek *Also called American Legion Ambulance Svc (P-18387)*
American Leisure Company (PA) ....F....**831 427-4270**
135 Ingalls St Santa Cruz (95060) *(P-5722)*
American Leisure Patio, Santa Cruz *Also called American Leisure Company (P-5722)*
American Licorice Company ....B....510 487-5500
2477 Liston Way Union City (94587) *(P-2425)*
American Lithographers Inc ....D....916 441-5392
1281 National Dr Sacramento (95834) *(P-3619)*
American Marketing Systems Inc ....D....800 747-7784
2800 Van Ness Ave San Francisco (94109) *(P-10489)*
American Mechanical Inc ....E....925 946-9101
1275 Boulevard Way Walnut Creek (94595) *(P-1199)*
American Med Rspnse Inland Emp ....B....916 563-0600
1041 Fee Dr Sacramento (95815) *(P-7368)*
American Med Rspnse Inland Emp ....B....530 246-9111
4451 Caterpillar Rd Ste 1 Redding (96003) *(P-7369)*
American Med Rspnse Inland Emp ....B....415 922-9400
1300 Illinois St San Francisco (94107) *(P-7370)*
American Med Rspnse Inland Emp ....B....831 423-7030
116 Hubbard St Santa Cruz (95060) *(P-7371)*
American Media Corp ....F....800 652-0778
150 Harbor Dr 2442 Sausalito (94965) *(P-3554)*
American Medical Bill Review, Redding *Also called Ambr Inc (P-10229)*
American Medical Response Inc ....C....415 794-9204
13992 Catalina St San Leandro (94577) *(P-7372)*
American Modular Systems Inc ....D....209 825-1921
787 Spreckels Ave Manteca (95336) *(P-3248)*
American Mstr Tech Scntfic Inc ....C....209 368-4031
1330 Thurman St Lodi (95240) *(P-6941)*
American Nat Red Cross - Blood, Stockton *Also called Delta Blood Bank LLC (P-17134)*
American Nat Red Cross - Blood, Pleasant Hill *Also called American National Red Cross (P-17421)*
American Nat Red Cross - Blood, Oakland *Also called American National Red Cross (P-17422)*
American National Red Cross ....E....925 602-1460
140 Gregory Ln Ste 120 Pleasant Hill (94523) *(P-17421)*
American National Red Cross ....E....510 594-5100
6230 Claremont Ave Oakland (94618) *(P-17422)*
American National Red Cross ....E....510 595-4400
6230 Claremont Ave Oakland (94618) *(P-17423)*
American National Red Cross ....E....209 533-1513
850 Sanguinetti Rd Sonora (95370) *(P-17424)*
American National Red Cross ....E....415 371-1740
569 Terry A Francois Blvd San Francisco (94158) *(P-17425)*
American National Red Cross ....E....800 733-2767
5880 W Las Psts Blvd # 34 Pleasanton (94588) *(P-17426)*
American National Red Cross ....E....800 733-2767
5665 Power Inn Rd Sacramento (95824) *(P-17427)*
American National Red Cross ....E....925 603-7400
1300 Alberta Way Concord (94521) *(P-17428)*
American Pacific Mortgage Corp (PA) ....C....**916 960-1325**
3000 Lava Ridge Ct # 200 Roseville (95661) *(P-9890)*
American Packaging Co, San Leandro *Also called Italian American Corp (P-9664)*
American Pavement Systems Inc ....E....209 522-2277
1012 11th St Ste 1000 Modesto (95354) *(P-1008)*
American Paving Co ....E....559 268-9886
315 N Thorne Ave Fresno (93706) *(P-1009)*
American Plastic, Tracy *Also called AP Unlimited Corporation (P-9240)*
American Poly-Foam Company Inc ....E....510 786-3626
1455 Crocker Ave Hayward (94544) *(P-4238)*
American Portwell Tech Inc (PA) ....D....**510 403-3399**
44200 Christy St Fremont (94538) *(P-8666)*
American Precision Gear Co ....E....650 627-8060
365 Foster City Blvd Foster City (94404) *(P-5210)*
American Precision Spring Corp ....E....408 986-1020
1513 Arbuckle Ct Santa Clara (95054) *(P-4963)*
American Production Co Inc ....E....650 368-5334
2734 Spring St Redwood City (94063) *(P-4596)*
American Property Management ....C....925 463-8000
7050 Johnson Dr Pleasanton (94588) *(P-10922)*
American Pwr & Communications ....E....209 833-1369
1416 Mariani Ct Ste 130 Tracy (95376) *(P-1451)*
American Recovery Service, El Dorado Hills *Also called Patrick K Willis and Co Inc (P-14353)*
American Red Cross, Sonora *Also called American National Red Cross (P-17424)*
American Red Cross, San Francisco *Also called American National Red Cross (P-17425)*
American Red Cross, Pleasanton *Also called American National Red Cross (P-17426)*
American Red Cross, Sacramento *Also called American National Red Cross (P-17427)*
American Red Cross, Concord *Also called American National Red Cross (P-17428)*
American Reprographics Co LLC (HQ) ....E....**925 949-5100**
1981 N Broadway Ste 385 Walnut Creek (94596) *(P-19701)*
American Restoration Services, Hayward *Also called ATI Restoration LLC (P-2007)*
American Rice Inc ....D....530 438-2265
1 Comet Ln Maxwell (95955) *(P-2315)*
American River Bank (PA) ....E....**916 565-6100**
1545 River Park Dr # 107 Sacramento (95815) *(P-9698)*
American River Dental Center, Rancho Cordova *Also called Holm McHael B DDS John C Rach (P-15836)*
American River Hospice Svcs ....E....229 255-4609
1451 River Park Dr # 241 Sacramento (95815) *(P-16169)*
American River Packaging, Sacramento *Also called Pk1 Inc (P-3364)*
American Rsdntial Svcs Ind Inc ....C....650 409-1986
1618 Doolittle Dr San Leandro (94577) *(P-1200)*
American Rver Care Rhblttion C, Carmichael *Also called Sunbrdge Brttany Rhblttion Ctr (P-16134)*
American Scence Tech As T Corp (PA) ....C....**415 251-2800**
50 California St Fl 21 San Francisco (94111) *(P-6606)*
American Seals West, Ceres *Also called McMillan - Hendryx Inc (P-4203)*
American Securities Company ....E....415 396-4566
464 California St Ste 100 San Francisco (94104) *(P-10834)*
American Skynet Electronics, Milpitas *Also called Silicon Vly World Trade Corp (P-5654)*
American Steel & Stairways Inc ....E....408 848-2992
8525 Forest St Ste A Gilroy (95020) *(P-4833)*
American Synrgy Asb Rmval Svcs ....E....510 444-2333
28436 Satellite St Hayward (94545) *(P-2002)*
American Tech Netwrk Corp (PA) ....E....**800 910-2862**
1341 San Mateo Ave South San Francisco (94080) *(P-6865)*
American Technologies Network, South San Francisco *Also called American Tech Netwrk Corp (P-6865)*
American Telesource Inc ....E....510 428-1111
1311 63rd St Ste B Emeryville (94608) *(P-8889)*
American Trck Trlr Bdy Co Inc (PA) ....E....**209 836-8985**
100 W Valpico Rd Ste D Tracy (95376) *(P-6563)*
American Underwater Products (HQ) ....D....**800 435-3483**
2002 Davis St San Leandro (94577) *(P-7186)*
American Wholesale Ltg Inc ....D....510 252-1088
1725 Rutan Dr Livermore (94551) *(P-8841)*
American Whtwter Expdtions Inc ....E....530 642-0804
6019 New River Rd Coloma (95613) *(P-15173)*
American Woodmark Corporation ....C....916 851-7400
3146 Gold Camp Dr Rancho Cordova (95670) *(P-3166)*
American Zoetrope, San Francisco *Also called Francis Ford Coppola Inc (P-14791)*
Americana Vacation Resorts Inc (PA) ....E....**530 544-8463**
1156 Ski Run Blvd Ste 1 South Lake Tahoe (96150) *(P-10490)*
Americas Best Beverage Inc ....E....800 723-8808
600 50th Ave Oakland (94601) *(P-2834)*
Americom Central Station Inc ....D....415 550-7100
1355 Fairfax Ave Ste 6 San Francisco (94124) *(P-14120)*

ALPHABETIC

Americore Inc ALPHABETIC SECTION

Americore Inc ....E....209 632-5679
19705 August Ave Hilmar (95324) *(P-4847)*
Ameriflight LLC ....D....510 569-6000
21889 Skywest Dr Hayward (94541) *(P-7737)*
AmeriGas Propane LP ....D....916 852-7400
11030 White Rock Rd # 100 Rancho Cordova (95670) *(P-9528)*
Ameriguard Security Svcs Inc ....D....559 271-5984
5470 W Spruce Ave Ste 102 Fresno (93722) *(P-14029)*
Amerimade Technology Inc ....E....925 243-9090
449 Mountain Vista Pkwy Livermore (94551) *(P-4257)*
Amerine Systems Incorporated ....E....209 847-5968
10866 Cleveland Ave Oakdale (95361) *(P-393)*
Amerisourcebergen Drug Corp ....C....916 830-4500
1325 Striker Ave Sacramento (95834) *(P-9222)*
Amerit Fleet Solutions Inc (HQ) ....**D....877 512-6374**
1331 N Calif Blvd Ste 150 Walnut Creek (94596) *(P-14656)*
Amerit Fleet Solutions Inc ....C....877 512-6374
1331 N Calif Blvd Ste 150 Walnut Creek (94596) *(P-19702)*
Ameritech Mortgage, Walnut Creek *Also called Izt Mortgage Inc (P-9942)*
Ames 1 LLC ....E....907 344-0067
2371 Washington Ave Ste G Oroville (95966) *(P-823)*
Ames Fire Waterworks ....D....530 666-2493
1485 Tanforan Ave Woodland (95776) *(P-5675)*
Ames-Grenz Insurance Svcs Inc ....E....916 486-2900
3435 American River Dr C Sacramento (95864) *(P-10230)*
Ametek Inc ....E....510 431-6718
1288 San Luis Obispo St Hayward (94544) *(P-8667)*
Amex Plating Incorporated ....E....408 986-8222
3333 Woodward Ave Santa Clara (95054) *(P-4896)*
AMF, Roseville *Also called Advanced Metal Finishing LLC (P-4893)*
AMF Media Group ....E....925 790-2662
12657 Alcosta Blvd # 500 San Ramon (94583) *(P-19682)*
Amgen Inc ....E....650 244-2000
1120 Veterans Blvd South San Francisco (94080) *(P-3844)*
AMI Manufacturing, Sacramento *Also called Airco Mechanical Inc (P-1193)*
Amick Brown LLC (PA) ....**D....925 820-2000**
2500 Old Crow Canyon Rd San Ramon (94583) *(P-12248)*
Amin-Oakland LLC ....E....510 568-1500
8452 Edes Ave Oakland (94621) *(P-10923)*
Amino Technologies (us) LLC (HQ) ....**E....408 861-1400**
20823 Stevens Creek Blvd Cupertino (95014) *(P-5820)*
Amity Home Health Care Inc ....E....510 785-9088
27001 Calaroga Ave Hayward (94545) *(P-16847)*
Amlogic Inc ....E....408 850-9688
2518 Mission College Blvd Santa Clara (95054) *(P-6034)*
Ammunition LLC ....E....415 632-1170
1500 Sansome St Ste 110 San Francisco (94111) *(P-19443)*
Amobee Inc (HQ) ....**B....650 353-4399**
100 Redwood Shores Pkwy # 300 Redwood City (94065) *(P-11739)*
Amos & Andrews Inc ....E....707 422-4844
1801 Walters Ct Fairfield (94533) *(P-1201)*
Amour Vert Inc ....D....650 388-4284
1278 Minnesota St Ste A San Francisco (94107) *(P-9250)*
AMP Technologies LLC ....C....877 442-2824
445 Melrose Ct San Ramon (94582) *(P-12249)*
Ampac Analytical, El Dorado Hills *Also called Ampac Fine Chemicals LLC (P-3845)*
Ampac Fine Chemicals LLC (HQ) ....**B....916 357-6880**
Hwy 50 Hzel Ave Bldg 0501 Rancho Cordova (95741) *(P-3779)*
Ampac Fine Chemicals LLC ....E....916 357-6221
12295 Hartford St Rancho Cordova (95742) *(P-3780)*
Ampac Fine Chemicals LLC ....E....916 245-6500
1100 Windfield Way El Dorado Hills (95762) *(P-3845)*
Ampac Technology Corporation ....F....415 912-2838
425 Market St Fl 22 San Francisco (94105) *(P-6035)*
Ampex Data Systems Corporation (HQ) ....**D....650 367-2011**
26460 Corporate Ave Hayward (94545) *(P-5281)*
Amphenol DC Electronics Inc ....B....408 947-4500
1870 Little Orchard St San Jose (95125) *(P-5709)*
Ampine LLC ....D....209 223-1690
11610 Ampine Fibreform Rd Sutter Creek (95685) *(P-3300)*
Ampine LLC (HQ) ....**F....209 223-6091**
11300 Ridge Rd Martell (95654) *(P-3197)*
Ampla Health (PA) ....**C....530 674-4261**
935 Market St Yuba City (95991) *(P-15821)*
Ample Inc ....D....617 504-3557
100 Hooper St Ste 25 San Francisco (94107) *(P-14200)*
Amplitude Inc (PA) ....**B....650 988-5131**
201 3rd St Ste 200 San Francisco (94103) *(P-12250)*
Amplitude Analytics, San Francisco *Also called Amplitude Inc (P-12250)*
Amprius Inc (PA) ....**E....800 425-8803**
1180 Page Ave Fremont (94538) *(P-19023)*
Amprius Technologies Inc ....E....800 425-8803
1180 Page Ave Fremont (94538) *(P-8842)*
Ampro Adlink Technology Inc ....D....408 360-0200
6450 Via Del Oro San Jose (95119) *(P-5240)*
Ampro Systems Inc ....E....510 624-9000
1000 Page Ave Fremont (94538) *(P-5912)*
AMR Appraisals Inc ....D....925 400-6066
4000 Executive Pkwy # 230 San Ramon (94583) *(P-10491)*
AMS, Manteca *Also called American Modular Systems Inc (P-3248)*
AMS Bekins Van Lines, Burlingame *Also called AMS Relocation Incorporated (P-7448)*
AMS Electric Inc ....D....925 961-1600
6905 Sierra Ct Ste A Dublin (94568) *(P-1452)*
AMS Heating Inc ....E....209 466-6692
3602 Munford Ave Stockton (95215) *(P-1202)*
AMS Relocation Incorporated ....D....650 697-3530
1873 Rollins Rd Burlingame (94010) *(P-7448)*
AMS Ventures Inc ....D....301 980-5087
39055 Hastings St Ste 205 Fremont (94538) *(P-19444)*
Amsi Real Estate Services, San Francisco *Also called American Marketing Systems Inc (P-10489)*
Amsnet Inc (PA) ....**E....925 245-6100**
502 Commerce Way Livermore (94551) *(P-13552)*
Amsurg, Fresno *Also called Herndon Surgery Center Inc (P-15430)*
Amt Metal Fabricators Inc ....E....510 236-1414
211 Parr Blvd Richmond (94801) *(P-4644)*
Amtech Microelectronics Inc ....E....408 612-8888
485 Cochrane Cir Morgan Hill (95037) *(P-5913)*
Amtek Electronic Inc ....F....408 971-8787
1150 N 5th St San Jose (95112) *(P-5241)*
Amtel Inc ....E....408 615-0522
950 S Bascom Ave Ste 2002 San Jose (95128) *(P-19720)*
Amunix Operating, South San Francisco *Also called Amunix Pharmaceutical Inc (P-19024)*
Amunix Pharmaceutical Inc ....E....650 428-1800
2 Tower Pl Ste 1100 South San Francisco (94080) *(P-19024)*
Amwins Connect Insur Svcs LLC (PA) ....**D....650 348-4131**
1600 W Hillsdale Blvd San Mateo (94402) *(P-10231)*
Amyris Inc (PA) ....**A....510 450-0761**
5885 Hollis St Ste 100 Emeryville (94608) *(P-4120)*
Amyris Clean Beauty Inc ....E....510 450-0761
5885 Hollis St Ste 100 Emeryville (94608) *(P-4080)*
Amyris Fuels LLC ....E....510 450-0761
5885 Hollis St Ste 100 Emeryville (94608) *(P-9529)*
Amys Kitchen Inc (PA) ....**A....707 578-7188**
1650 Corporate Cir Petaluma (94954) *(P-2302)*
Amzn Mobile LLC ....B....925 348-4580
525 Market St Fl 19 San Francisco (94105) *(P-12251)*
Anacom Inc ....E....408 519-2062
11682 Vineyard Spring Ct Cupertino (95014) *(P-5821)*
Anacor Pharmaceuticals Inc ....E....650 543-7500
1020 E Meadow Cir Palo Alto (94303) *(P-3846)*
Analog Bits ....E....650 279-9323
945 Stewart Dr Sunnyvale (94085) *(P-6036)*
Analogix Semiconductor Inc ....E....408 988-8848
3211 Scott Blvd Ste 100 Santa Clara (95054) *(P-6037)*
Analytcal Scentific Instrs Inc ....E....510 669-2250
3023 Research Dr San Pablo (94806) *(P-6808)*
Anand Software Inc ....D....209 287-1708
4719 Quail Lakes Dr Stockton (95207) *(P-12252)*
Ananda Church of Self-Realztn (PA) ....**D....530 478-7560**
14618 Tyler Foote Rd Nevada City (95959) *(P-3522)*
Anaplan Inc (PA) ....**A....415 742-8199**
50 Hawthorne St San Francisco (94105) *(P-13839)*
Anaspec Egt Group, Fremont *Also called Anaspec Inc (P-19025)*
Anaspec Inc (HQ) ....**E....510 791-9560**
34801 Campus Dr Fremont (94555) *(P-19025)*
Anatomage Inc (PA) ....**D....408 885-1474**
303 Almaden Blvd Ste 100 San Jose (95110) *(P-12253)*
Anatometal Inc ....E....831 454-9880
165 Dubois St Santa Cruz (95060) *(P-7164)*
Anberry Physcl Rhblttion Ctr I ....D....209 357-5121
1685 Shaffer Rd Atwater (95301) *(P-15881)*
Anberry Rehabilitation Hosp, Atwater *Also called Tjd LLC (P-16279)*
Anchor Brewers & Distlrs LLC (HQ) ....**D....415 892-4569**
4 Rebelo Ln Novato (94947) *(P-2470)*
Anchor Distilling Company ....E....415 863-8350
1705 Mariposa St San Francisco (94107) *(P-2504)*
Anchor J Dairy, Stevinson *Also called James J Stevinson A Corp (P-215)*
Ancient Harvest, Ukiah *Also called Quinoa Corporation (P-2400)*
Ancil Hoffman Golf Course, Carmichael *Also called Empire Golf Inc (P-15001)*
Ancora Heart Inc ....E....408 727-1105
4001 Burton Dr Santa Clara (95054) *(P-6942)*
Andapt Inc (PA) ....**E....408 931-4898**
950 S Bascom Ave Ste 3012 San Jose (95128) *(P-12976)*
Andersen & Sons Shelling Inc ....D....530 839-2236
4530 Rowles Rd Vina (96092) *(P-269)*
Andersen Nut Company ....E....209 854-6820
3050 S Hunt Rd Gustine (95322) *(P-270)*
Andersen Tax LLC ....D....650 289-5700
2121 S El Camino Real # 1100 San Mateo (94403) *(P-11701)*
Andersncttonwood Disposal Svcs (PA) ....**E....530 221-6510**
8592 Commercial Way Redding (96002) *(P-7449)*
Andersncttonwood Disposal Svcs ....D....530 824-4700
3281 State Highway 99w S Corning (96021) *(P-7450)*
Anderson Rowe & Buckley Inc ....C....415 282-1625
2833 3rd St San Francisco (94107) *(P-1203)*
Anderson Zeigler Disharoon (PA) ....**E....707 545-4910**
50 Old Courthouse Sq # 500 Santa Rosa (95404) *(P-17201)*
Anderson Brule Architects Inc ....E....408 298-1885
325 S 1st St Fl 4 San Jose (95113) *(P-18869)*
Anderson House, Concord *Also called Youth Homes Incorporated (P-18214)*
Anderson Logging Inc ....D....707 964-2770
1296 N Main St Fort Bragg (95437) *(P-3055)*
Anderson Moulds Incorporated ....F....209 943-1145
3131 E Anita St Stockton (95205) *(P-4258)*
Anderson Neil O and Assoc Inc (HQ) ....**E....209 367-3701**
902 Industrial Way Lodi (95240) *(P-18624)*
Anderson PCF Engrg Cnstr Inc ....D....408 970-9900
1370 Norman Ave Santa Clara (95054) *(P-1146)*
Anderson Physical Therapy ....E....530 265-8100
202 Prvdnce Mine Rd # 206 Nevada City (95959) *(P-15882)*
Anderson Pump Company ....D....559 665-4477
24719 Robertson Blvd Chowchilla (93610) *(P-8221)*
Anderson Valley Brewing Inc ....E....707 895-2337
17700 Hwy 253 Boonville (95415) *(P-2471)*
Anderson Valley Brewing Co, Boonville *Also called Anderson Valley Brewing Inc (P-2471)*
Anderson's Carpet & Linoleum, Oakland *Also called Linoleum Sales Co Inc (P-4361)*

Andpak Inc (PA) ....E....**408 776-1072**
400 Jarvis Dr Ste A Morgan Hill (95037) ***(P-14201)***
Andrade Electric Inc ....E....916 635-4082
3245 Fitzgerald Rd Ste A Rancho Cordova (95742) ***(P-1453)***
Andre-Boudin Bakeries Inc ....E....925 935-4375
67 Broadwalk Ln Walnut Creek (94596) ***(P-2361)***
Andre-Boudin Bakeries Inc ....E....415 283-1230
619 Market St San Francisco (94105) ***(P-2362)***
Andregg Geomatics ....D....530 885-7072
11661 Blocker Dr Ste 200 Auburn (95603) ***(P-18920)***
Andreini & Company (PA) ....D....**650 573-1111**
220 W 20th Ave San Mateo (94403) ***(P-10232)***
Andresen, South San Francisco *Also called Clic LLC* ***(P-3636)***
Andrew Chekene Enterprises Inc ....C....650 588-1001
21965 Meekland Ave Hayward (94541) ***(P-611)***
Andrew F Calman, Md, PHD, San Francisco *Also called Premier Eyecare San Francisco* ***(P-15634)***
Andrew M Jordan Inc ....D....510 999-6000
1350 4th St Berkeley (94710) ***(P-1950)***
Andrews Hotel (PA) ....E....**415 563-6877**
624 Post St San Francisco (94109) ***(P-10924)***
Andrian ....E....408 434-0730
1935 Lundy Ave San Jose (95131) ***(P-2003)***
Andrighetto Produce Inc (PA) ....C....**650 588-0930**
155 Terminal Ct 15-33 South San Francisco (94080) ***(P-9386)***
Andros Incorporated ....F....510 837-3525
3301 Leonard Ct Santa Clara (95054) ***(P-6713)***
Andrus Sheet Metal Inc ....E....510 232-8687
5021 Seaport Ave Richmond (94804) ***(P-4741)***
Andys Produce Market Inc ....E....707 823-8661
1691 Gravenstein Hwy N Sebastopol (95472) ***(P-9387)***
Andys Roofing Co Inc ....E....510 777-1100
2161 Adams Ave San Leandro (94577) ***(P-1786)***
Andytown Coffee Roasters, San Francisco *Also called Andytown LLC* ***(P-2835)***
Andytown LLC (PA) ....E....**415 702-9859**
3016 Taraval St San Francisco (94116) ***(P-2835)***
Anesthsia Anlgsia Med Group In ....E....707 522-1800
2455 Bennett Valley Rd C2 Santa Rosa (95404) ***(P-15279)***
Anesthsia Cons of Frsno A Med ....D....559 436-0871
7417 N Cedar Ave Fresno (93720) ***(P-15280)***
Anfield Insurance Service ....D....415 439-5750
433 California St Ste 820 San Francisco (94104) ***(P-10233)***
Angad Corp ....E....650 743-0461
950 Tower Ln Ste 1975 Foster City (94404) ***(P-12254)***
Angaza Design Inc ....D....415 993-5595
315 Montgomery St Fl 10 San Francisco (94104) ***(P-12255)***
Angel Island Co, Red Bluff *Also called Concessionaires Urban Park* ***(P-15195)***
Angel Island-Tiburon Ferry Inc ....E....415 435-2131
21 Main St Belvedere Tiburon (94920) ***(P-7734)***
Angeleno Magazine, San Francisco *Also called Modern Luxury Media LLC* ***(P-3509)***
Angelo Kilday & Kilduff ....D....916 564-6100
601 University Ave # 150 Sacramento (95825) ***(P-17202)***
Anglepoint Group Inc (PA) ....C....**855 512-6453**
3945 Freedom Cir Ste 360 Santa Clara (95054) ***(P-19297)***
Angotti & Reilly Inc ....E....415 575-3700
2200 Jerrold Ave Ste E San Francisco (94124) ***(P-824)***
Angular Machining Inc ....E....408 954-8326
2040 Hartog Dr San Jose (95131) ***(P-5473)***
Anheuser-Busch, Rocklin *Also called Bi Warehousing Inc* ***(P-8443)***
Anheuser-Busch LLC ....B....707 429-7595
3101 Busch Dr Fairfield (94534) ***(P-2472)***
Ani Private SEC & Patrol Inc ....E....510 652-6833
4122 Broadway Oakland (94611) ***(P-14030)***
Animal Clinic of Santa Cruz ....E....831 427-3345
815 Mission St Santa Cruz (95060) ***(P-320)***
Animoto LLC ....D....415 987-3139
333 Kearny St Fl 6 San Francisco (94108) ***(P-12256)***
Animus Inc (PA) ....C....**800 306-7910**
34501 7th St Union City (94587) ***(P-15281)***
Anita Borg Inst For Women Tech ....D....650 236-4756
1301 Shoreway Rd Ste 425 Belmont (94002) ***(P-18545)***
Anixter Inc ....E....925 469-8500
5000 Franklin Dr 200 Pleasanton (94588) ***(P-8843)***
Ankar Cycles Inc ....D....510 657-7200
151 Hegenberger Rd Oakland (94621) ***(P-14736)***
Ankoor Financial Llc ....E....530 724-3471
3930 County Rd 89 Dunnigan (95937) ***(P-10925)***
Anlin Industries ....C....800 287-7996
1665 Tollhouse Rd Clovis (93611) ***(P-3122)***
Anlin Window Systems, Clovis *Also called Anlin Industries* ***(P-3122)***
Anlin Windows & Doors ....C....800 287-7996
1665 Tollhouse Rd Clovis (93611) ***(P-4696)***
Ann Breznock ....E....530 795-2356
27956 State Highway 128 Winters (95694) ***(P-19257)***
Ann Lilli Corp (PA) ....D....**415 482-9444**
1010 B St Ste 333 San Rafael (94901) ***(P-3004)***
Annabelles Bar & Bistro, San Francisco *Also called Mosser Vctrian Ht Arts Mus Inc* ***(P-11313)***
Annexon Inc (PA) ....E....**650 822-5500**
180 Kimball Way Ste 200 South San Francisco (94080) ***(P-3847)***
Annieglass Inc (PA) ....F....**831 761-2041**
310 Harvest Dr Watsonville (95076) ***(P-4369)***
Annies Inc (HQ) ....C....**510 558-7500**
1610 5th St Berkeley (94710) ***(P-2867)***
Annies Annuals Perennials LLC ....E....510 215-3301
801 Chesley Ave Richmond (94801) ***(P-9623)***
Anning-Johnson Company ....C....510 670-0100
22955 Kidder St Hayward (94545) ***(P-1659)***
Ano-Tech Metal Finishing, Clovis *Also called Atmf Inc* ***(P-4899)***
Anomali Incorporated ....D....408 800-4050
808 Winslow St Redwood City (94063) ***(P-14121)***
Anomalies International Inc ....D....800 855-1113
2833 Mission St Santa Cruz (95060) ***(P-2782)***
Another Corporate Isp LLC ....E....415 974-1313
286 12th St San Francisco (94103) ***(P-7925)***
Anrak Corporation ....E....916 383-5030
5820 Mayhew Rd Sacramento (95827) ***(P-1010)***
Anritsu Americas Sales Company ....A....408 778-2000
490 Jarvis Dr Morgan Hill (95037) ***(P-9051)***
Anritsu Company, Morgan Hill *Also called Anritsu US Holding Inc* ***(P-6746)***
Anritsu Company (HQ) ....B....**800 267-4878**
490 Jarvis Dr Morgan Hill (95037) ***(P-5822)***
Anritsu US Holding Inc (HQ) ....B....**408 778-2000**
490 Jarvis Dr Morgan Hill (95037) ***(P-6746)***
Answerlab LLC (PA) ....E....**415 814-9910**
700 Larkspur Landing Cir Larkspur (94939) ***(P-19152)***
Antelope Christian Academy, Sacramento *Also called Capital Christian Center* ***(P-17878)***
Anthem Insurance Companies Inc ....B....559 230-6200
5260 N Palm Ave Ste 215 Fresno (93704) ***(P-10091)***
Anthem Insurance Companies Inc ....B....415 617-1700
2 Embarcadero Ctr # 1310 San Francisco (94111) ***(P-10092)***
Anthony Leonardo Logging, Fortuna *Also called Leonardo Logging and Cnstr Inc* ***(P-3068)***
ANTHONY SOTO EMPLOYMENT TRAINI, Santa Rosa *Also called California Human Dev Corp* ***(P-17798)***
Anthony Trevino ....D....707 747-4776
938 Adams St Ste A Benicia (94510) ***(P-1764)***
Anthonys Auto Craft Inc (PA) ....D....**415 456-7591**
111 Verdi St San Rafael (94901) ***(P-14517)***
Anthonys Industrial Rents ....F....916 373-5320
2999 Promenade St Ste 100 West Sacramento (95691) ***(P-558)***
Antibodies Incorporated ....F....800 824-8540
25242 County Road 95 Davis (95616) ***(P-4016)***
Antica NAPA Valley, NAPA *Also called Antinori California* ***(P-2505)***
Antinori California ....E....707 265-8866
3149 Soda Canyon Rd NAPA (94558) ***(P-2505)***
Antioch Building Materials Co (PA) ....E....**925 432-0171**
1375 California Ave Pittsburg (94565) ***(P-8617)***
Antioch Convalescent Hospital, Antioch *Also called Norcal Care Centers Inc* ***(P-16072)***
Antioch Public Golf Corp ....D....925 706-4220
4800 Golf Course Rd Antioch (94531) ***(P-14987)***
Antioch Rotary Club ....E....925 757-1800
324 G St Antioch (94509) ***(P-15052)***
Antipodean Pharmaceuticals Inc (PA) ....D....**866 749-3338**
1700 Montgomery St # 209 San Francisco (94111) ***(P-3848)***
Anvil Builders Inc ....C....415 285-5000
1475 Donner Ave San Francisco (94124) ***(P-1011)***
Anza Park & Sky, Burlingame *Also called Anza Parking Corporation* ***(P-14508)***
Anza Parking Corporation ....E....650 348-8800
615 Airport Blvd Burlingame (94010) ***(P-14508)***
Ao Sky Corporation ....F....415 717-9901
4989 Pedro Hill Rd Pilot Hill (95664) ***(P-6661)***
AOC Technologies Inc ....B....925 875-0808
5960 Inglewood Dr Pleasanton (94588) ***(P-8805)***
AON Consulting & Insur Svcs ....C....415 486-7500
199 Fremont St Fl 14 San Francisco (94105) ***(P-10234)***
AON Risk Insurance Svcs W Inc (HQ) ....E....**415 486-7000**
425 Market St Ste 2800 San Francisco (94105) ***(P-10235)***
Aopen America Incorporated ....D....408 586-1200
2150 N 1st St Ste 400 San Jose (95131) ***(P-8668)***
AP Tech, Fremont *Also called American Portwell Tech Inc* ***(P-8666)***
AP Tech, NAPA *Also called Advanced Pressure Technology* ***(P-6711)***
AP Unlimited Corporation ....F....209 834-0287
1225 N Macarthur Dr # 200 Tracy (95376) ***(P-9240)***
APA Family Support Services ....E....415 617-0061
10 Nottingham Pl San Francisco (94133) ***(P-17429)***
Apacer Memory America Inc ....E....408 518-8699
46732 Lakeview Blvd Fremont (94538) ***(P-8890)***
Apache Computer Retail, San Jose *Also called Apache Design Inc* ***(P-12257)***
Apache Design Inc (HQ) ....C....**408 457-2000**
2645 Zanker Rd San Jose (95134) ***(P-12257)***
Apartment List Inc ....E....415 817-1068
475 Brannan St Ste 410 San Francisco (94107) ***(P-10470)***
Apco-Ettner Inc (PA) ....D....**559 439-6766**
1433 W Pine Ave Fresno (93728) ***(P-18625)***
Apct Inc (HQ) ....C....**408 727-6442**
3495 De La Cruz Blvd Santa Clara (95054) ***(P-5914)***
Apct Holdings LLC (PA) ....E....**408 727-6442**
3495 De La Cruz Blvd Santa Clara (95054) ***(P-5915)***
Apellis Pharmaceuticals Inc ....E....415 872-9970
720 Market St Fl 5 San Francisco (94102) ***(P-3849)***
Aperia Technologies Inc ....E....415 494-9624
1616 Rollins Rd Burlingame (94010) ***(P-5140)***
Aperian Global Inc (PA) ....D....**628 222-3773**
555 12th St Ste 1670 Oakland (94607) ***(P-19445)***
Aperture Aviation, San Jose *Also called McClelland Aviation Inc* ***(P-7776)***
Apex Die Corporation ....D....650 592-6350
840 Cherry Ln San Carlos (94070) ***(P-3393)***
Apex Fence Co Inc ....E....530 365-3316
19896 Alexander Ave Anderson (96007) ***(P-2004)***
Apex Healthcare Services LLC ....D....925 922-3525
2120 Rosswood Dr San Jose (95124) ***(P-16848)***
Apex Machining Inc ....E....408 441-1335
1997 Hartog Dr San Jose (95131) ***(P-5474)***
Apex Rail Automation, Grass Valley *Also called Vossloh Signaling LLC* ***(P-12915)***
Apex Site Solutions Inc ....D....916 685-8619
9749 Kent St Elk Grove (95624) ***(P-19446)***
Apexcare, Sacramento *Also called Support For Family LLC* ***(P-17762)***

ALPHABETIC

Apexcare Inc (PA) .... A 916 924-9111
1418 Howe Ave Ste B Sacramento (95825) ***(P-16849)***

Apexigen Inc .... E 650 931-6236
75 Shoreway Rd Ste C San Carlos (94070) ***(P-3850)***

API Marketing .... F 916 632-1946
13020 Earhart Ave Auburn (95602) ***(P-3620)***

Apigee Corporation .... B 408 343-7300
1600 Amphitheatre Pkwy Mountain View (94043) ***(P-12258)***

APM Terminals Pacific Ltd .... B 510 992-6430
5801 Christie Ave Emeryville (94608) ***(P-7823)***

Apn Software Services Inc (PA) .... C 510 623-5050
39899 Balentine Dr # 385 Newark (94560) ***(P-13840)***

Apolent Corporation (PA) .... E 408 203-6828
2570 N 1st St Ste 200 San Jose (95131) ***(P-13841)***

Apollo Graph Inc .... E 206 225-9488
37 Oceanview Dr Pittsburg (94565) ***(P-12259)***

Aporeto Inc .... D 408 472-7648
10 Almaden Blvd Ste 400 San Jose (95113) ***(P-12977)***

App Annie Inc (HQ) .... B 844 277-2664
23 Geary St Ste 8 San Francisco (94108) ***(P-12260)***

Appdirect Inc (PA) .... D 415 852-3924
650 California St Fl 25 San Francisco (94108) ***(P-12978)***

Appdynamics LLC (HQ) .... A 415 442-8400
303 2nd St Fl 8 San Francisco (94107) ***(P-12261)***

Appellation Tours Inc .... E 707 938-8001
21707 8th St E Sonoma (95476) ***(P-7814)***

Appex Networks Corporation .... E 408 973-7898
4010 Moorpark Ave Ste 212 San Jose (95117) ***(P-12979)***

Appl, Clovis *Also called Agriclture Prrity Plltnts Labs* ***(P-19254)***

Apple Inc (PA) .... A 408 996-1010
1 Apple Park Way Cupertino (95014) ***(P-5823)***

Apple Inns Inc .... E 510 895-1311
68 Monarch Bay Dr San Leandro (94577) ***(P-10926)***

Apple Six Hospitality MGT .... E 650 872-1515
670 Gateway Blvd South San Francisco (94080) ***(P-10927)***

Apple Valley Care & Rehab, Sebastopol *Also called Apple Vly Cnvalescent Hosp Inc* ***(P-15909)***

Apple Vly Cnvalescent Hosp Inc .... D 707 823-7675
1035 Gravenstein Hwy N Sebastopol (95472) ***(P-15909)***

Appleby & Company Inc (PA) .... E 559 222-8402
2828 N Wishon Ave Fresno (93704) ***(P-14202)***

Applied Anodize Inc .... E 408 435-9191
622 Charcot Ave Ste D San Jose (95131) ***(P-4897)***

Applied Arospc Structures Corp (PA) .... C 209 982-0160
3437 S Airport Way Stockton (95206) ***(P-6631)***

Applied Biosystems Inc .... E 800 327-3002
850 Lincoln Centre Dr Foster City (94404) ***(P-13693)***

Applied Cells Inc .... E 800 960-3004
3350 Scott Blvd Bldg 6 Santa Clara (95054) ***(P-6690)***

Applied Ceramics Inc (PA) .... C 510 249-9700
48630 Milmont Dr Fremont (94538) ***(P-6038)***

Applied Control Electronics .... F 530 626-5181
5480 Merchant Cir Placerville (95667) ***(P-5676)***

Applied Earthworks Inc (PA) .... E 559 229-1856
1391 W Shaw Ave Ste C Fresno (93711) ***(P-19196)***

Applied Engineering, San Jose *Also called Electronic Interface Co Inc* ***(P-6516)***

Applied Expert Systems Inc .... E 650 617-2400
999 Commercial St Ste 201 Palo Alto (94303) ***(P-12980)***

Applied Extracts Inc .... F 415 260-9786
1027 S Claremont St San Mateo (94402) ***(P-4035)***

Applied Films Corporation .... C 408 727-5555
3050 Bowers Ave Santa Clara (95054) ***(P-6039)***

Applied Intuition Inc (PA) .... E 630 935-8986
145 E Dana St Mountain View (94041) ***(P-12262)***

Applied Materials, Roseville *Also called Cokeva Inc* ***(P-13820)***

Applied Materials Inc (PA) .... A 408 727-5555
3050 Bowers Ave Bldg 1 Santa Clara (95054) ***(P-5141)***

Applied Materials Inc .... D 408 727-5555
3340 Scott Blvd Santa Clara (95054) ***(P-6040)***

Applied Materials Inc .... E 408 679-2925
1700 E Pescadero Ave Tracy (95304) ***(P-6041)***

Applied Materials Inc .... E 408 727-5555
974 E Arques Ave Sunnyvale (94085) ***(P-6042)***

Applied Materials (holdings) (HQ) .... C 408 727-5555
3050 Bowers Ave Santa Clara (95054) ***(P-6043)***

Applied Mfr Group Inc .... E 408 855-8857
941 George St Santa Clara (95054) ***(P-6044)***

Applied Micro Circuits Corp (HQ) .... B 408 542-8600
4555 Great America Pkwy # 6 Santa Clara (95054) ***(P-6045)***

Applied Molecular Trnspt Inc .... D 650 392-0420
450 E Jamie Ct South San Francisco (94080) ***(P-3851)***

Applied Mtls Asia-Pacific LLC (HQ) .... A 408 727-5555
3050 Bowers Ave Santa Clara (95054) ***(P-6046)***

Applied Photon Technology Inc .... E 510 780-9500
3346 Arden Rd Hayward (94545) ***(P-5708)***

Applied Physics Systems (PA) .... C 650 965-0500
425 Clyde Ave Mountain View (94043) ***(P-6892)***

Applied Process Equipment .... E 650 365-6895
2620 Bay Rd Redwood City (94063) ***(P-5475)***

Applied Science Inc (PA) .... F 530 273-8299
983 Golden Gate Ter Grass Valley (95945) ***(P-6943)***

Applied Sewing Resources Inc .... E 707 748-1614
6440 Goodyear Rd Benicia (94510) ***(P-2963)***

Applied Silver Inc .... F 888 939-4747
26254 Eden Landing Rd Hayward (94545) ***(P-3264)***

Applied Stemcell Inc .... E 408 773-8007
521 Cottonwood Dr Ste 111 Milpitas (95035) ***(P-19026)***

Applied Systems Engrg Inc .... F 408 364-0500
2105 S Bascom Ave Ste 155 Campbell (95008) ***(P-13842)***

Applied Thin-Film Products (HQ) .... C 510 661-4287
3620 Yale Way Fremont (94538) ***(P-6398)***

Applied Thin-Film Products .... F 510 661-4287
3439 Edison Way Fremont (94538) ***(P-6399)***

Applied Weather Technology Inc, Sunnyvale *Also called Stormgeo* ***(P-19917)***

Applied Wireless Identific (PA) .... E 408 779-1929
18300 Sutter Blvd Morgan Hill (95037) ***(P-8891)***

Applitools Inc .... E 650 680-1000
155 Bovet Rd Ste 600 San Mateo (94402) ***(P-12263)***

Applovin Corporation (PA) .... B 800 839-9646
1100 Page Mill Rd Palo Alto (94304) ***(P-12981)***

Appodeal Inc (PA) .... D 415 996-6877
575 Market St Fl 4 San Francisco (94105) ***(P-9645)***

Apporto Corporation .... E 650 326-0920
200 Hamilton Ave Palo Alto (94301) ***(P-12982)***

Appro International Inc (HQ) .... D 408 941-8100
220 Devcon Dr San Jose (95112) ***(P-5282)***

Appsflyer Inc .... E 408 367-9938
100 1st St Ste 2500 San Francisco (94105) ***(P-12264)***

Appsflyer Ltd .... D 415 636-9430
111 New Montgomery St San Francisco (94105) ***(P-11801)***

Appsroi Inc .... D 510 470-0095
1765 Landess Ave 121 Milpitas (95035) ***(P-8669)***

Appvance Inc .... E 408 871-0122
3080 Olcott St Ste B240 Santa Clara (95054) ***(P-12983)***

April Six Inc .... E 415 363-6070
900 Kearny St Ste 700 San Francisco (94133) ***(P-19447)***

Apriori Cellar LLC (PA) .... F 707 512-0606
1432 Main St Saint Helena (94574) ***(P-2506)***

Apstra Inc (HQ) .... D 650 307-3245
1137 Innovation Way Sunnyvale (94089) ***(P-13843)***

Apteligent Inc .... D 415 371-1402
1100 La Avenida St Ste A Mountain View (94043) ***(P-12265)***

Aptim Federal Services LLC .... C 925 288-9898
4005 Port Chicago Hwy Concord (94520) ***(P-612)***

Aptiv Digital LLC .... D 818 295-6789
2160 Gold St San Jose (95002) ***(P-12984)***

Apttus Corporation (PA) .... A 650 445-7700
1840 Gateway Dr Ste 300 San Mateo (94404) ***(P-13553)***

Apx Inc (PA) .... E 408 517-2100
2150 N 1st St Ste 200 San Jose (95131) ***(P-19721)***

Aqs, Fremont *Also called All Quality & Services Inc* ***(P-5908)***

Aqua Gunite Inc .... E 408 271-2782
5830 S Naylor Rd Livermore (94551) ***(P-2005)***

Aqua Metals Inc .... E 510 479-7635
1010 Atlantic Ave Alameda (94501) ***(P-4557)***

Aqualine Piping Inc .... D 408 745-7100
2108 Bering Dr Ste C San Jose (95131) ***(P-1204)***

Aquamatic Cover Systems, Gilroy *Also called Amcs Inc* ***(P-8475)***

Aquamatic Fire Protection Inc (PA) .... E 925 753-0420
540 Garcia Ave Ste A Pittsburg (94565) ***(P-1205)***

Aquantia Corp (HQ) .... B 408 228-8300
5488 Marvell Ln Santa Clara (95054) ***(P-6047)***

Aquarium of Bay (HQ) .... E 415 623-5300
Beach Embrcdero Strway 2 San Francisco (94103) ***(P-18287)***

Aquarium of The Bay, The, San Francisco *Also called Bayorg* ***(P-18288)***

Aquatek Plumbing Inc .... E 408 354-5885
1236 N 5th St San Jose (95112) ***(P-1206)***

Aquatic Designing Inc .... E 707 822-4629
4801 West End Rd Arcata (95521) ***(P-18626)***

Aquatic Environments Inc .... E 925 521-0400
345 Industrial Way Benicia (94510) ***(P-1147)***

Aquera Inc .... E 650 618-6442
2100 Geng Rd Ste 210 Palo Alto (94303) ***(P-12266)***

Aquinas Corporation .... C 408 248-7100
3580 Payne Ave San Jose (95117) ***(P-15910)***

ARA Technology .... E 408 734-8131
1286 Anvilwood Ave Sunnyvale (94089) ***(P-4898)***

Aradigm Corporation .... E 510 265-9000
1613 Lyon St San Francisco (94115) ***(P-3852)***

Aragen Bioscience Inc .... E 408 779-1700
380 Woodview Ave Morgan Hill (95037) ***(P-19027)***

Aragon Commercial Ldscpg Inc .... C 408 998-0600
2305 S Vasco Rd Livermore (94550) ***(P-446)***

Aramark Spt & Entrmt Group LLC .... B 408 999-5735
525 W Santa Clara St San Jose (95113) ***(P-14867)***

Aramark Spt & Entrmt Group LLC .... B 408 748-7030
5001 Great America Pkwy Santa Clara (95054) ***(P-14868)***

Aramark Unf & Career AP LLC .... D 916 286-4100
1419 National Dr Sacramento (95834) ***(P-11631)***

Aramark Uniform Services, Sacramento *Also called Aramark Unf & Career AP LLC* ***(P-11631)***

Arandas Tortilla Company Inc .... E 209 464-8675
1318 E Scotts Ave Stockton (95205) ***(P-2868)***

Arangodb Inc .... E 415 992-7801
548 Market St 61436 San Francisco (94104) ***(P-12985)***

Aras Power Technologies (PA) .... E 408 935-8877
371 Fairview Way Milpitas (95035) ***(P-6376)***

Arbor Fence Inc .... E 707 938-3133
22660 Broadway Sonoma (95476) ***(P-4834)***

Arbor Vly Nrsing Rhblttion Ctr, Modesto *Also called Kissito Healthcare Inc* ***(P-16032)***

Arboricultural Specialties Inc .... E 510 549-3954
2828 8th St Berkeley (94710) ***(P-512)***

Arborwell Inc (PA) .... C 510 881-4260
2337 American Ave Hayward (94545) ***(P-513)***

ARC Document Solutions Inc (PA) .... E 925 949-5100
12657 Alcosta Blvd # 200 San Ramon (94583) ***(P-11854)***

ARC Fresno/Madera Counties (PA) .... C 559 226-6268
4490 E Ashlan Ave Fresno (93726) ***(P-17793)***

ARC of Butte County (PA) .... C 530 891-5865
2030 Park Ave Chico (95928) ***(P-17430)***

ALPHABETIC SECTION

ARC of The East Bay (PA) ..... E 510 357-3569
  1101 Walpert St Hayward (94541) (P-17431)
ARC San Francisco (PA) ..... C 415 255-7200
  1500 Howard St San Francisco (94103) (P-17794)
ARC USA, Fremont Also called Mirror Plus Technologies Inc (P-12610)
Arcade Belts Inc (PA) ..... D 530 580-8089
  150 Alpine Meadows Rd Alpine Meadows (96146) (P-3019)
Arcadia Inc ..... E 916 375-1478
  2324 Del Monte St West Sacramento (95691) (P-4562)
Arcadia Services Inc ..... E 248 352-7530
  4340 Redwood Hwy Ste 123 San Rafael (94903) (P-12159)
Arcata Garbage Co ..... E 707 822-0304
  30 S G St Arcata (95521) (P-8303)
Arcbyt Inc (PA) ..... E 415 449-4852
  548 Market St Pmb 39975 San Francisco (94104) (P-5024)
Arceo Labs Inc (PA) ..... D 628 222-3622
  1612 Castro St San Francisco (94114) (P-19258)
Arch Foods Inc (PA) ..... E 510 331-8352
  25817 Clawiter Rd Hayward (94545) (P-4603)
Arch US MI Holdings Inc (HQ) ..... C 800 909-4264
  Pmi Plaza 3003 Oak Rd Walnut Creek (94597) (P-10191)
Archer Aviation Inc (PA) ..... C 650 272-3233
  1880 Embarcadero Rd Palo Alto (94303) (P-6607)
Archer Aviation Operating Corp ..... C 650 272-3233
  1880 Embarcadero Rd Palo Alto (94303) (P-6608)
Archerhall LLC ..... E 916 449-2820
  2081 Arena Blvd Ste 200 Sacramento (95834) (P-13844)
Archeyy & Friends LLC ..... E 703 579-7649
  3630 Andrews Dr Apt 114 Pleasanton (94588) (P-2332)
Archipelago Analytics Holdings (PA) ..... E 415 696-4896
  165 Buena Vista Ave E San Francisco (94117) (P-12267)
Architctral Coml Glzing Alum P, Fremont Also called National Glass Systems Inc (P-1939)
Architctral Fcdes Unlmited Inc ..... D 408 846-5350
  600 E Luchessa Ave Gilroy (95020) (P-4417)
Architctral Rsources Group Inc (PA) ..... E 415 421-1680
  9 Pier Ste 107 San Francisco (94111) (P-18870)
Architectural Blomberg LLC ..... E 916 428-8060
  1453 Blair Ave Sacramento (95822) (P-4697)
Architectural GL & Alum Co Inc (PA) ..... C 925 583-2460
  6400 Brisa St Livermore (94550) (P-8806)
Architectural Plastics Inc ..... E 707 765-9898
  1299 N Mcdowell Blvd Petaluma (94954) (P-4259)
Architectural Wood Design Inc ..... E 559 292-9104
  5672 E Dayton Ave Fresno (93727) (P-3167)
Architecture, Sacramento Also called Lionakis (P-18895)
Architecture Plus Inc ..... E 209 577-4661
  4335 N Star Way Ste B Modesto (95356) (P-18871)
Archives Management Corp (PA) ..... C 650 544-2200
  2301 S El Camino Real San Mateo (94403) (P-19298)
Archway Insurance Brokers LLC ..... E 408 441-2000
  1731 Tech Dr Ste 250 San Jose (95110) (P-10236)
Arcline Elvtion Svcs Hldngs LL ..... A 860 805-2025
  4 Embarcadero Ctr # 3460 San Francisco (94111) (P-14737)
Arcline Investment MGT LP (PA) ..... F 415 801-4570
  4 Embarcadero Ctr # 3460 San Francisco (94111) (P-3815)
Arcsoft Inc (PA) ..... A 510 440-9901
  46605 Fremont Blvd Fremont (94538) (P-12268)
Arctic Express Norcal LLC ..... E 925 553-3681
  3130 Crow Canyon Pl # 210 San Ramon (94583) (P-9333)
Arctouch LLC ..... E 415 944-2000
  1001 Front St San Francisco (94111) (P-12269)
Arcus Biosciences Inc (PA) ..... C 510 694-6200
  3928 Point Eden Way Hayward (94545) (P-19028)
Ardelyx Inc ..... C 510 745-1700
  34175 Ardenwood Blvd Fremont (94555) (P-3853)
Arden Health & Rehab Ctr, Sacramento Also called Mariner Health Care Inc (P-16044)
Arden Hills Country Club Inc ..... D 916 482-6111
  1220 Arden Hills Ln Sacramento (95864) (P-14926)
Arden Little League Snack Bar (PA) ..... E 916 359-6379
  1150 Eastern Ave Sacramento (95864) (P-15053)
Arden Wood Inc ..... D 415 681-5500
  445 Wawona St San Francisco (94116) (P-18057)
Ardenbrook Inc ..... D 510 794-1020
  5016 Paseo Padre Pkwy Fremont (94555) (P-10492)
Ardent Mills LLC ..... F 209 983-6551
  3939 Producers Dr Stockton (95206) (P-2308)
Ardent Systems Inc ..... E 408 526-0100
  2040 Ringwood Ave San Jose (95131) (P-5916)
Ardenwood Rental Condominiums, Fremont Also called Ardenbrook Inc (P-10492)
Ardor Learning Inc (PA) ..... E 650 245-6300
  1027 Amarillo Ave Palo Alto (94303) (P-19897)
Area 1 Security Inc ..... D 650 924-1637
  15 N Ellsworth Ave # 102 San Mateo (94401) (P-12986)
Area Wide Exterminators Inc ..... E 209 464-4731
  2239 Country Club Blvd Stockton (95204) (P-11879)
Arena Press ..... F 415 883-3314
  20 Leveroni Ct Novato (94949) (P-3555)
Arena Stuart Rentals Inc ..... C 408 856-3232
  454 S Abbott Ave Milpitas (95035) (P-12029)
Ares Holding Corporation (PA) ..... E 650 401-7100
  1290 Howard Ave Ste 319 Burlingame (94010) (P-18627)
Ares Prism, Burlingame Also called Ares Project Management LLC (P-18628)
Ares Project Management LLC (HQ) ..... D 650 401-7100
  1290 Howard Ave Ste 319 Burlingame (94010) (P-18628)
Ares Technical Services Corp ..... A 650 401-7100
  1290 Howard Ave Ste 319 Burlingame (94010) (P-19448)
Arete Hotels LLC ..... D 209 602-7952
  2229 Den Helder Dr Modesto (95356) (P-10928)
Argent Hotel, The, San Francisco Also called L-O Soma Hotel Inc (P-11240)
Argo Insurance Brokers Inc (HQ) ..... E 925 682-7001
  2300 Contra Costa Blvd # 375 Pleasant Hill (94523) (P-10237)
Argonaut Constructors Inc ..... C 707 542-4862
  360 Sutton Pl Santa Rosa (95407) (P-1012)
Argonaut Hotel ..... E 415 563-0800
  495 Jefferson St San Francisco (94109) (P-10929)
Argonaut Kensington Associates ..... E 925 943-1121
  1580 Geary Rd Ofc Walnut Creek (94597) (P-17432)
Argonaut Window & Door Inc ..... D 408 376-4018
  1901 S Bascom Ave Ste 800 Campbell (95008) (P-8528)
Argos Software, Fresno Also called Abelisk Inc (P-12221)
Arguello Pet Hospital Inc ..... E 415 751-3242
  530 Arguello Blvd San Francisco (94118) (P-321)
Argus Courier, Petaluma Also called St Louis Post-Dispatch LLC (P-3483)
Arh Recovery Homes Inc (PA) ..... D 408 281-6570
  9505 Malech Dr San Jose (95138) (P-18058)
Aria Systems Inc (PA) ..... C 415 852-7250
  100 Pine St Ste 2450 San Francisco (94111) (P-12270)
Aria Technologies Inc ..... E 925 292-1616
  102 Wright Brothers Ave Livermore (94551) (P-4567)
Ariat International Inc (PA) ..... C 510 477-7000
  3242 Whipple Rd Union City (94587) (P-4352)
Ariba Inc (HQ) ..... C 650 849-4000
  3420 Hillview Ave Palo Alto (94304) (P-12987)
Aricent NA Inc (HQ) ..... D 408 324-1800
  3979 Freedom Cir Ste 950 Santa Clara (95054) (P-12271)
Aricent Technologies, Santa Clara Also called Aricent US Inc (P-12272)
Aricent US Inc (HQ) ..... E 408 329-7400
  3979 Freedom Cir Ste 950 Santa Clara (95054) (P-12272)
Aricent US Inc ..... C 650 632-4310
  303 Twin Dolphin Dr # 600 Redwood City (94065) (P-12273)
Aridis Pharmaceuticals Inc ..... E 408 385-1742
  983 University Ave Bldg B Los Gatos (95032) (P-3854)
Aries Industries Inc ..... C 559 291-0383
  5748 E Shields Ave # 101 Fresno (93727) (P-8278)
Aries Research Inc ..... E 925 818-1078
  46750 Fremont Blvd # 107 Fremont (94538) (P-5343)
Aries Solutions, Fremont Also called Aries Research Inc (P-5343)
Ariosa Diagnostics Inc ..... C 408 229-7500
  5945 Optical Ct San Jose (95138) (P-19029)
Arista Networks ..... F 408 547-5725
  1390 Market St Ste 800 San Francisco (94102) (P-12988)
Arizona Tile LLC ..... E 916 853-0100
  11115 Folsom Blvd Rancho Cordova (95670) (P-8618)
Arizona Tile LLC ..... E 916 782-3200
  10576 Industrial Ave Roseville (95678) (P-8619)
Arkose Labs Holdings Inc (PA) ..... C 415 917-8701
  250 Montgomery St # 1000 San Francisco (94104) (P-14122)
Arleen Logistics Inc (PA) ..... D 916 514-9746
  5556 Honor Pkwy Sacramento (95835) (P-7874)
Arm Inc (HQ) ..... B 408 576-1500
  150 Rose Orchard Way San Jose (95134) (P-6048)
Armanino Foods Distinction Inc ..... E 510 441-9300
  30588 San Antonio St Hayward (94544) (P-2303)
Armanino LLP ..... E 408 200-6400
  50 W San Fernando St San Jose (95113) (P-18931)
Armanino LLP (PA) ..... C 925 790-2600
  12657 Alcosta Blvd # 500 San Ramon (94583) (P-18932)
Armanino LLP ..... E 408 200-6400
  50 W San Fernando St # 60 San Jose (95113) (P-18933)
Armed Guard Private SEC Inc ..... D 530 751-3218
  50 Landing Cir Chico (95973) (P-14031)
Armey, Rutter, Fresno Also called Rutter Armey Inc (P-14621)
Armin Maier and Associates Inc (PA) ..... E 415 332-6467
  2149 Powell St San Francisco (94133) (P-8505)
Armo Biosciences Inc ..... E 650 779-5075
  575 Chesapeake Dr Redwood City (94063) (P-3855)
Armor Brer Protective Svcs Inc ..... E 833 692-2774
  2701 Del Paso Rd Ste 130 Sacramento (95835) (P-14032)
Armorous ..... D 707 387-4400
  1360 19th Hole Dr Ste 207 Windsor (95492) (P-14033)
Armstrng/Robitaille Insur Svcs, Pleasanton Also called BB&T Insurance Svcs Cal Inc (P-10245)
Armstrong Construction Company, Emeryville Also called Armstrong Instlltion Svc A Cal (P-1403)
Armstrong Instlltion Svc A Cal ..... C 408 777-1234
  4575 San Pablo Ave Emeryville (94608) (P-1403)
Armstrong Mfg & Engrg Inc ..... D 530 888-6262
  12780 Earhart Ave Auburn (95602) (P-18629)
Armstrong Technology Sv Inc ..... F 408 734-4434
  1271 Anvilwood Ave Sunnyvale (94089) (P-5476)
Armstrong Technology Sv Inc ..... F 530 888-6262
  12780 Earhart Ave Auburn (95602) (P-5477)
Arnaudo Bros Transport Inc (PA) ..... D 209 835-0406
  16505 S Tracy Blvd Tracy (95304) (P-146)
Arnaudo Bros Trucking, Tracy Also called Arnaudo Bros Transport Inc (P-146)
Arnold & Porter PC ..... B 415 434-1600
  3 Embarcadero Ctr Fl 7 San Francisco (94111) (P-17203)
Arnold Family Medical Center, Arnold Also called Adventist Health Sonora (P-16291)
Arnold Medical Clinic, Arnold Also called Mark Twain Medical Center (P-16439)
Arnold Palmer Golf MGT LLC ..... D 415 561-4670
  300 Finley Rd San Francisco (94129) (P-19299)
Arntz Builders Inc ..... E 415 382-1188
  431 Payran St Ste A Petaluma (94952) (P-788)
Arraycon ..... D 916 925-0201
  1143 Blumenfeld Dr # 200 Sacramento (95815) (P-1207)
Arraycon LLC (PA) ..... E 916 925-0201
  1143 Blumenfeld Dr # 200 Sacramento (95815) (P-1208)

Arrcus Inc...E...408 884-1965
2077 Gateway Pl Ste 400 San Jose (95110) *(P-12274)*
Arreolas Complete Ldscp Svc, Sacramento *Also called Arreolas Complete Ldscp Svc (P-447)*
Arreolas Complete Ldscp Svc...D...916 387-6777
8671 Morrison Creek Dr Sacramento (95828) *(P-447)*
Arrhenius, Santa Clara *Also called Prodigy Surface Tech Inc (P-4918)*
Arriba Juntos (PA)...**E...415 487-3240**
1850 Mission St San Francisco (94103) *(P-17795)*
Arrive Technologies Inc...F...916 715-9775
3693 Westchester Dr Roseville (95747) *(P-6049)*
Arrow Construction, Sacramento *Also called Arrow Drillers Inc (P-1087)*
Arrow Drillers Inc (PA)...**E...916 640-0600**
1850 Diesel Dr Sacramento (95838) *(P-1087)*
Arrow Electric Motor Service...E...559 266-0104
645 Broadway St Fresno (93721) *(P-14727)*
Arrow Fence Co, Sacramento *Also called Rowar Corporation (P-2063)*
Arrow Sign Co (PA)...**E...209 931-5522**
1051 46th Ave Oakland (94601) *(P-7216)*
Arrow Sign Co...E...209 931-7852
3133 N Ad Art Rd Stockton (95215) *(P-7217)*
Arrow Sign Company, Oakland *Also called Arrow Sign Co (P-7216)*
Arrow Surf Products (PA)...**F...831 462-2791**
1115 Thompson Ave Ste 7 Santa Cruz (95062) *(P-7187)*
Arrow Systems Integration Inc...F...510 897-2900
46425 Landing Pkwy Fremont (94538) *(P-7926)*
Arrowhead Mountain Winery Corp (PA)...**E...707 938-3254**
2352 Thornsberry Rd Sonoma (95476) *(P-9565)*
Arsenal Biosciences Inc...D...858 945-3091
2 Tower Pl Ste 700 South San Francisco (94080) *(P-19030)*
Arsenalbio, South San Francisco *Also called Arsenal Biosciences Inc (P-19030)*
Arstasis Inc...F...650 508-1549
6500 Kaiser Dr Ste 120 Fremont (94555) *(P-6944)*
Art, El Dorado Hills *Also called Alpha Research & Tech Inc (P-5239)*
Art Brand Studios LLC (PA)...**E...408 201-5000**
18715 Madrone Pkwy Morgan Hill (95037) *(P-3556)*
Art Craft Staturary Inc...E...510 633-1411
10441 Edes Ave Oakland (94603) *(P-4515)*
Art Hild Body and Frame Inc...E...530 222-6828
1579 E Cypress Ave Redding (96002) *(P-14518)*
Art of Muse LLC...E...510 644-2100
2222 5th St Berkeley (94710) *(P-3273)*
Art of Yoga Project...E...650 924-9222
330 Twin Dolphin Dr # 13 Redwood City (94065) *(P-15174)*
Art Piccadilly Shaw LLC (PA)...**C...559 348-5520**
2305 W Shaw Ave Fresno (93711) *(P-10930)*
Art Piccadilly Shaw LLC...D...559 375-7760
5115 E Mckinley Ave Fresno (93727) *(P-10931)*
Art Piccadilly Shaw LLC...D...559 224-4200
4961 N Cedar Ave Fresno (93726) *(P-10932)*
Art Robbins Instruments LLC...E...408 734-8400
1293 Mountain View Alviso Sunnyvale (94089) *(P-6809)*
Art Sign Company...E...510 632-6353
732 Kevin Ct Oakland (94621) *(P-14203)*
Art Supply Enterprises Inc (PA)...**E...800 289-9800**
1375 Ocean Ave Emeryville (94608) *(P-9646)*
Artcom Inc (PA)...**C...510 879-4700**
2100 Powell St Fl 10th Emeryville (94608) *(P-18260)*
Artehouse, San Rafael *Also called One Bella Casa Inc (P-3029)*
Arteris Inc (PA)...**E...408 470-7300**
595 Millich Dr Ste 200 Campbell (95008) *(P-6050)*
Arteris Holdings Inc...E...408 470-7300
591 W Hamilton Ave # 250 Campbell (95008) *(P-6051)*
Arterys Inc...D...650 319-7230
2021 Fillmore St 100 San Francisco (94115) *(P-8773)*
Artesa Winery, NAPA *Also called Codorniu Napa Inc (P-2537)*
Artesian Home Products, Granite Bay *Also called New Cal Metals Inc (P-4793)*
Arthur Kunde & Sons Inc...E...707 833-5501
9825 Sonoma Hwy Kenwood (95452) *(P-367)*
Arthur Schawlow Center, Chico *Also called California Vocations Inc (P-16223)*
Artic Aire of Chico Inc...E...530 895-3330
2530 Zanella Way Ste A Chico (95928) *(P-1209)*
Artichoke Joe's Casino, San Bruno *Also called Artichoke Joes (P-15175)*
Artichoke Joes...B...650 589-8812
659 Huntington Ave San Bruno (94066) *(P-15175)*
Artificial Intelligence Lab, San Francisco *Also called Goldenspear LLC (P-14286)*
Artisan Bakers...D...707 939-1765
21684 8th St E Ste 400 Sonoma (95476) *(P-9437)*
Artisan Brewers LLC...E...510 567-4926
1933 Davis St Ste 177 San Leandro (94577) *(P-2473)*
Artisan Partners Ltd Partnr...D...415 283-2444
100 Pine St Ste 2950 San Francisco (94111) *(P-10024)*
Aruba Networks Inc...A...408 227-4500
1322 Crossman Ave Sunnyvale (94089) *(P-5344)*
Aruba Networks Inc (HQ)...**B...408 227-4500**
3333 Scott Blvd Santa Clara (95054) *(P-5345)*
Aruba Networks Inc...E...408 227-4500
392 Acoma Way Fremont (94539) *(P-5824)*
Aruba Networks Inc...A...408 227-4500
634 E Caribbean Dr Sunnyvale (94089) *(P-5346)*
Aruba Networks Inc...A...408 227-4500
390 W Caribbean Dr Sunnyvale (94089) *(P-5825)*
Aruba Networks Cafe, Santa Clara *Also called Aruba Networks Inc (P-5345)*
Arundo Analytics Inc (PA)...**E...713 256-7584**
470 Ramona St Palo Alto (94301) *(P-5224)*
Arup North America Limited (HQ)...**C...415 957-9445**
560 Mission St Fl 7 San Francisco (94105) *(P-18630)*

Arvee Bros Inc...D...650 583-3935
1375 El Camino Real Millbrae (94030) *(P-10933)*
Arvi Manufacturing Inc...E...408 734-4776
1256 Birchwood Dr Ste B Sunnyvale (94089) *(P-4980)*
Arxan Technologies Inc...E...301 968-4290
760 Market St Ste 709 San Francisco (94102) *(P-12275)*
Aryaka Networks Inc (PA)...**B...888 692-7925**
1850 Gateway Dr Ste 500 San Mateo (94404) *(P-13554)*
Asa Computers Inc...E...650 230-8000
48761 Kato Rd Fremont (94538) *(P-13555)*
Asa Corporation...F...530 305-3720
3111 Sunset Blvd Ste V Rocklin (95677) *(P-6810)*
Asa Eden LLC...E...510 653-7227
2044 Edison Ave San Leandro (94577) *(P-9624)*
Asa Floral, San Leandro *Also called Asa Eden LLC (P-9624)*
Asana Inc (PA)...**A...415 525-3888**
633 Folsom St Ste 100 San Francisco (94107) *(P-13845)*
Asante Technologies Inc (PA)...**E...408 435-8388**
2223 Oakland Rd San Jose (95131) *(P-5347)*
Asbestos MGT Group of Cal...E...510 654-8441
3438 Helen St Oakland (94608) *(P-2006)*
Asbury Pk Nrsing Rhblttion Ctr...C...916 649-2000
2257 Fair Oaks Blvd Sacramento (95825) *(P-16216)*
ASC Building Products, West Sacramento *Also called ASC Profiles LLC (P-8807)*
ASC Profiles LLC (HQ)...**D...916 376-2800**
2110 Enterprise Blvd West Sacramento (95691) *(P-8807)*
Ascend Clinical LLC (PA)...**D...800 800-5655**
1400 Industrial Way Redwood City (94063) *(P-16772)*
Ascend.io, Palo Alto *Also called Ascension Labs Inc (P-12277)*
Ascendify Corporation...E...415 528-5503
30 Castlewood Dr Pleasanton (94566) *(P-12276)*
Ascendis Pharma Inc...F...650 352-8389
1000 Page Mill Rd Palo Alto (94304) *(P-3856)*
Ascension Labs Inc...E...650 898-9798
541 Cowper St Palo Alto (94301) *(P-12277)*
Ascent Services Group Inc...B...925 627-4900
1001 Galaxy Way Ste 408 Concord (94520) *(P-12160)*
Ascent Technology Inc...F...408 213-1080
838 Jury Ct San Jose (95112) *(P-4742)*
Ascor Inc (HQ)...**D...925 328-4650**
4650 Norris Canyon Rd San Ramon (94583) *(P-5677)*
Asd Global Inc...E...925 975-0690
1371 Oakland Blvd Ste 100 Walnut Creek (94596) *(P-13556)*
ASDC, Capitola *Also called Campus Kids Connection Inc (P-17876)*
Ase (us)inc (HQ)...**D...408 636-9500**
1255 E Arques Ave Sunnyvale (94085) *(P-8892)*
ASG, San Jose *Also called Automated Solutions Group Inc (P-6699)*
Ashbury Market Inc...D...650 952-8889
179 Starlite St South San Francisco (94080) *(P-9438)*
Ashby Lumber Company (PA)...**D...510 843-4832**
824 Ashby Ave Berkeley (94710) *(P-14468)*
Ashby Lumber Concord, Berkeley *Also called Ashby Lumber Company (P-14468)*
Ashen Company Ltd (PA)...**D...916 487-0117**
3901 Marconi Ave Sacramento (95821) *(P-15822)*
Ashford Trs Fremont LLC...C...510 413-3700
46100 Landing Pkwy Fremont (94538) *(P-10934)*
Ashok N Veeranki DDS A Pro (PA)...**D...209 836-3870**
620 W Eaton Ave Tracy (95376) *(P-15823)*
Ashwood Construction Inc...E...559 253-7240
5755 E Kings Canyon Rd # 11 Fresno (93727) *(P-737)*
Asi Computer Technologies Inc (PA)...**D...510 226-8000**
48289 Fremont Blvd Fremont (94538) *(P-8670)*
Asia America Enterprise Inc...E...650 348-2333
1321 N Carolan Ave Burlingame (94010) *(P-3621)*
Asia Foundation (PA)...**D...415 982-4640**
465 California St Fl 9 San Francisco (94104) *(P-19197)*
Asia Network Pacific Home Care (PA)...**E...510 268-1118**
212 9th St Ste 205 Oakland (94607) *(P-16850)*
Asia Pacific Groups, San Francisco *Also called HMw and Jk Enterprises Inc (P-9941)*
Asiainfo-Linkage Inc...A...408 970-9788
5201 Great America Pkwy # 356 Santa Clara (95054) *(P-7927)*
Asian Inc (PA)...**E...415 928-5910**
1167 Mission St Fl 4 San Francisco (94103) *(P-18219)*
Asian Amercn Recovery Svcs Inc...C...408 271-3900
1340 Tully Rd Ste 304 San Jose (95122) *(P-16751)*
Asian Amrcans For Cmnty Invlvm (PA)...**C...408 975-2730**
2400 Moorpark Ave Ste 300 San Jose (95128) *(P-18220)*
ASIAN ART MEUSUEM OF SF, San Francisco *Also called Asian Art Mseum Fndtion San Fr (P-18261)*
Asian Art Mseum Fndtion San Fr...C...415 581-3500
200 Larkin St San Francisco (94102) *(P-18261)*
Asian Art Museum, San Francisco *Also called City & County of San Francisco (P-18265)*
Asian Cmnty Mental Hlth Svcs, Oakland *Also called Asian Community Mental Hlth Bd (P-16988)*
Asian Community Center of Sac...E...916 393-9020
7801 Rush River Dr Sacramento (95831) *(P-15911)*
Asian Community Mental Hlth Bd...D...510 869-6003
310 8th St Ste 303 Oakland (94607) *(P-16988)*
Asian Health Services (PA)...**C...510 986-6800**
101 8th St Oakland (94607) *(P-15282)*
Asian PCF Islnder Wllness Ctr...E...415 292-3400
730 Polk St Fl 4 San Francisco (94109) *(P-17433)*
Asic Advantage Inc...D...408 541-8686
3850 N 1st St San Jose (95134) *(P-6052)*
Ask Media Group LLC...F...510 985-7400
555 12th St Ste 500 Oakland (94607) *(P-3557)*
Ask.com, Oakland *Also called IAC Search & Media Inc (P-13794)*

Asl Print Fx ....F....707 927-3096
871 Latour Ct NAPA (94558) **(P-3622)**
Asm America Inc ....C....408 451-0830
97 E Brokaw Rd Ste 100 San Jose (95112) **(P-14690)**
Asm Precision Inc ....F....707 584-7950
613 Martin Ave Ste 106 Rohnert Park (94928) **(P-4743)**
Asomeo Envmtl Rstrtion Indust ....D....530 434-6869
2151 River Plaza Dr # 105 Sacramento (95833) **(P-9018)**
Aspen Apts I ....D....415 673-5879
165 Eddy St San Francisco (94102) **(P-10417)**
Asphalt Cowboys of Reddin ....E....530 244-1117
720 Auditorium Dr Redding (96001) **(P-18546)**
Aspira Wellness, Turlock *Also called Aspiranet* **(P-16851)**
Aspiranet ....E....209 669-2583
440 E Canal Dr Turlock (95380) **(P-16851)**
Aspire Bakeries LLC ....D....510 494-1700
6500 Overlake Pl Newark (94560) **(P-9439)**
Aspire Bakeries LLC ....D....209 469-4920
920 Shaw Rd Stockton (95215) **(P-2363)**
Aspire General Insurance Co ....E....877 789-4742
2721 Citrus Rd Ste B Rancho Cordova (95742) **(P-10238)**
Aspireiq Inc ....D....415 445-3567
550 Montgomery St Ste 800 San Francisco (94111) **(P-19449)**
Asrc Aerospace Corp ....C....650 604-5946
Nasa Ames Research Ctr Mountain View (94035) **(P-6662)**
Assay Technology Inc ....E....925 461-8880
1382 Stealth St Livermore (94551) **(P-14204)**
Assembly Biosciences Inc (PA) ....D....833 509-4583
331 Oyster Point Blvd # 4 South San Francisco (94080) **(P-3857)**
Assembly Systems (PA) ....E....408 395-5313
16595 Englewood Ave Los Gatos (95032) **(P-4604)**
Asset Preservation Inc (HQ) ....E....916 791-5991
1420 Rocky Ridge Dr # 380 Roseville (95661) **(P-19450)**
Asset Preservation of Texas, Roseville *Also called Asset Preservation Inc* **(P-19450)**
Assetmark Inc (HQ) ....E....925 521-1040
1655 Grant St Ste 1000 Concord (94520) **(P-10029)**
Assetmark Financial Inc (HQ) ....B....925 521-2200
1655 Grant St Fl 10 Concord (94520) **(P-10030)**
Assetmark Fincl Holdings Inc (PA) ....D....925 521-2200
1655 Grant St Fl 10 Concord (94520) **(P-10031)**
Assoc CA Wtr AGC/Jt Pw Ins ....E....916 786-5742
2100 Professional Dr Roseville (95661) **(P-10239)**
Assoc Students University CA (PA) ....C....510 642-5420
Bancroft Way 400 Eshleman St Bancroft W Berkeley (94704) **(P-15176)**
Associated Builders, San Francisco *Also called Associated Building Entp Inc* **(P-825)**
Associated Building Entp Inc ....E....415 285-6200
4026 3rd St San Francisco (94124) **(P-825)**
Associated Feed & Supply Co (PA) ....C....209 667-2708
5213 W Main St Turlock (95380) **(P-9594)**
Associated Fmly Physicians Inc ....D....916 689-4111
8110 Timberlake Way Sacramento (95823) **(P-15283)**
Associated Indemnity Corp ....C....415 899-2000
1465 N Mcdowell Blvd # 100 Petaluma (94954) **(P-10076)**
Associated Lighting Rep Inc (PA) ....E....510 638-3800
7777 Pardee Ln Oakland (94621) **(P-8844)**
Associated Materials Inc ....A....415 788-5111
1 Maritime Plz Fl 12 San Francisco (94111) **(P-4260)**
Associated Pathology Med Group ....D....408 399-5010
459 Monterey Ave Los Gatos (95030) **(P-16773)**
Associated Pension Cons Inc (PA) ....D....530 343-4233
2035 Forest Ave Chico (95928) **(P-10211)**
Associated R V Ent Inc ....E....831 636-9566
1500 Shelton Dr Frnt Hollister (95023) **(P-8439)**
Associated Students of S S U ....E....707 664-2815
1801 E Cotati Ave Rohnert Park (94928) **(P-18388)**
Associated Students S J S U ....E....408 924-6240
1 Washington Sq San Jose (95112) **(P-18389)**
Associated Students Stanford (PA) ....D....650 723-4331
201 Tresidder Un Stanford (94305) **(P-18390)**
Associated Trucking Inc ....E....650 652-3960
1065 San Mateo Ave San Bruno (94066) **(P-7504)**
Associates In Womens Hlth Care ....E....916 782-2229
2 Medical Plaza Dr # 205 Roseville (95661) **(P-15284)**
Association Cal Wtr Agencies (PA) ....E....916 441-4545
980 9th St Ste 1000 Sacramento (95814) **(P-18297)**
Assocted Intrnal Mdcine Med Gr (PA) ....E....510 465-6700
5800 Hollis St Emeryville (94608) **(P-15285)**
Assocted Lrng Lngage Spcialist (PA) ....E....650 631-9999
1060 Twin Dolphin Dr # 1 Redwood City (94065) **(P-19722)**
Assocted Stdnts Cal State Univ (PA) ....A....530 898-6815
101 Hazel St Rm 218 Chico (95928) **(P-15177)**
Assocted Stdnts of The Univ CA ....D....510 590-7874
112 Hearst Gym Rm 4520 Berkeley (94720) **(P-3558)**
Assocted Vtrnary Practices Inc ....E....925 634-1177
4519 Ohara Ave Brentwood (94513) **(P-322)**
Assoction Asn/Pcfic Cmnty Hlth ....E....510 272-9536
2140 Shattuck Ave Ste 203 Berkeley (94704) **(P-18298)**
Assured Care Enterprises Inc ....E....408 379-7000
1361 S Wnchester Blvd San Jose (95128) **(P-17101)**
Assured Insurance Technologies ....D....424 781-7123
650 Page Mill Rd Palo Alto (94304) **(P-10240)**
Assured Relocation Inc ....E....888 670-9700
50 Woodside Plz Ste 441 Redwood City (94061) **(P-14205)**
Assuredpartners Inc ....D....916 443-0200
1455 Response Rd Ste 260 Sacramento (95815) **(P-10241)**
Assurx Inc ....D....408 778-1376
18525 Sutter Blvd Ste 150 Morgan Hill (95037) **(P-12278)**
Asta Construction Co Inc (PA) ....E....707 374-6472
1090 Saint Francis Way Rio Vista (94571) **(P-554)**
Asteel Flash USA Corp (HQ) ....C....510 440-2840
4211 Starboard Dr Fremont (94538) **(P-5917)**
Asteelflash Fremont, Fremont *Also called Asteel Flash USA Corp* **(P-5917)**
Asterias Biotherapeutics Inc ....D....510 456-3800
1010 Atlantic Ave Ste 102 Alameda (94501) **(P-19031)**
Astero Bio Corporation ....E....800 749-0898
3475 Edison Way Ste A Menlo Park (94025) **(P-6945)**
Astex Pharmaceuticals Inc (HQ) ....C....925 560-0100
4420 Rosewood Dr Ste 200 Pleasanton (94588) **(P-3858)**
Astound Commerce Corporation (HQ) ....B....800 591-4710
1611 Telegraph Ave # 400 Oakland (94612) **(P-13846)**
Astranis Space Tech Corp ....C....415 854-0586
420 Bryant St San Francisco (94107) **(P-5826)**
Astrazeneca LP ....E....650 634-0103
121 Oyster Point Blvd South San Francisco (94080) **(P-3859)**
Astrazeneca Pharmaceuticals LP ....E....650 305-2600
200 Cardinal Way Redwood City (94063) **(P-3860)**
Astro Digital US Inc ....E....650 804-3210
3171 Jay St Santa Clara (95054) **(P-6663)**
Astronomical Soc of The PCF ....E....415 337-1100
390 Ashton Ave San Francisco (94112) **(P-18547)**
Astute Business Solutions ....C....925 997-3267
11501 Dublin Blvd Ste 200 Dublin (94568) **(P-12279)**
Asus Computer International ....C....510 739-3777
48720 Kato Rd Fremont (94538) **(P-8671)**
Asylum Access ....D....510 891-8700
344 Thomas L Berkley Way # 111 Oakland (94612) **(P-18548)**
At Home Caregivers, Novato *Also called Bear Flag Marketing Corp* **(P-16856)**
AT&T Corp ....B....925 823-6949
330 R San Ramon (94583) **(P-7896)**
AT&T Long Distance, Pleasanton *Also called SBC Long Distance LLC* **(P-7911)**
AT&T Mobility LLC ....C....650 638-1188
3 Bay View Dr San Carlos (94070) **(P-8069)**
AT&T Services Inc ....C....415 545-9051
610 Brannan St San Francisco (94107) **(P-7928)**
AT&T Services Inc ....D....415 545-9058
666 Folsom St Rm 1132 San Francisco (94107) **(P-7929)**
AT&T Services Inc ....C....408 554-3335
485 S Monroe St 13a San Jose (95128) **(P-7930)**
At-Bay Inc (PA) ....E....888 338-9522
196 Castro St Ste A Mountain View (94041) **(P-10242)**
Atac (PA) ....D....408 736-2822
2770 De La Cruz Blvd Santa Clara (95050) **(P-13557)**
Atara Biotherapeutics Inc (PA) ....C....650 278-8930
611 Gateway Blvd Ste 900 South San Francisco (94080) **(P-4036)**
Atari Corporation, San Jose *Also called Jts Corporation* **(P-5297)**
Atcaa, Jackson *Also called Amador Tlmne Cmnty Action Agcy* **(P-18218)**
Atcg Technology Solutions Inc (HQ) ....E....916 850-2620
785 Orchard Dr Ste 150 Folsom (95630) **(P-12280)**
Atech Logistics Inc ....C....707 526-1910
7 College Ave Santa Rosa (95401) **(P-7824)**
Atech Manufacturing, San Jose *Also called T&S Manufacturing Tech LLC* **(P-4688)**
Atech Warehousing & Dist Inc (PA) ....D....707 526-1910
7 College Ave Santa Rosa (95401) **(P-7505)**
Atel 12 LLC ....C....415 989-8800
600 California St Fl 6 San Francisco (94108) **(P-9880)**
Atel 14 LLC ....E....415 989-8800
600 California St Fl 6 San Francisco (94108) **(P-9881)**
Atel Associates 14 LLC (PA) ....D....415 989-8800
600 California St Fl 9 San Francisco (94108) **(P-9882)**
Atel Capital Group, San Francisco *Also called Atel Financial Services LLC* **(P-9884)**
Atel Capital Group (PA) ....D....800 543-2835
600 Montgomery St Fl 9 San Francisco (94111) **(P-9883)**
Atel Corporation ....D....415 989-8800
600 Montgomery St Ste 900 San Francisco (94111) **(P-14206)**
Atel Financial Services LLC (HQ) ....D....415 989-8800
600 Montgomery St Fl 9 San Francisco (94111) **(P-9884)**
Atempo Americas Inc (HQ) ....E....650 494-2600
2465 E Byshore Rd Ste 400 Palo Alto (94303) **(P-12281)**
Atg-Wci Inc (HQ) ....C....916 489-3651
1650 Tribute Rd Sacramento (95815) **(P-14738)**
Atharwa Investments LLC ....E....209 474-3301
111 E March Ln Stockton (95207) **(P-10935)**
Athelas Inc ....E....408 603-1954
10209 Danube Dr Cupertino (95014) **(P-6946)**
Athens Administrators, Concord *Also called Athens Insurance Service Inc* **(P-10243)**
Athens Insurance, Concord *Also called James C Jenkins Insur Svc Inc* **(P-10302)**
Athens Insurance Service Inc ....C....925 826-1000
2552 Stanwell Dr Ste 100 Concord (94520) **(P-10243)**
Atherton Healthcare, Menlo Park *Also called Cal Care Inc* **(P-19312)**
Athleta LLC ....E....707 559-2200
1 Harrison St Lbby San Francisco (94105) **(P-2991)**
Athletic Media Company (PA) ....B....415 891-7354
332 Pine St Ph San Francisco (94104) **(P-11809)**
Athletic Sports LLC ....E....310 709-3944
11327 Trade Center Dr # 33 Rancho Cordova (95742) **(P-7218)**
Athletics Investment Group LLC (PA) ....C....510 638-4900
7000 Coliseum Way Ste 3 Oakland (94621) **(P-14903)**
Athoc Inc (HQ) ....D....925 242-5660
3001 Bishop Dr Ste 400 San Ramon (94583) **(P-12989)**
Athos, Redwood City *Also called Mad Apparel Inc* **(P-2994)**
ATI, Emeryville *Also called American Telesource Inc* **(P-8889)**
ATI Architects & Engineers, Pleasanton *Also called Martin ATI-AC Inc* **(P-18901)**
ATI Machinery Inc ....E....559 884-2471
21436 S Lassen Ave Five Points (93624) **(P-9031)**
ATI Restoration LLC ....D....510 429-5000
25000 Industrial Blvd Hayward (94545) **(P-2007)**

ALPHABETIC

Atkinson Youth Services Inc............E.......916 977-3790
3600 Fair Oaks Blvd Sacramento (95864) ***(P-18059)***
Atlantic Aviation Svc............D.......408 297-7552
1250 Aviation Ave Ste 235 San Jose (95110) ***(P-7766)***
Atlantic Trust Wlfare Prvate M, San Francisco *Also called Stein Roe Inv Counsel Inc* ***(P-10061)***
Atlas Disposal Industries LLC............D.......916 455-2800
3035 Prospect Park Dr # 40 Rancho Cordova (95670) ***(P-8304)***
Atlas Heating, South San Francisco *Also called Tuck Aire Heating & AC Corp* ***(P-1387)***
Atlas Heating and AC Co, Oakland *Also called Your Warm Friend Inc* ***(P-1402)***
Atlas Lift Tech Inc............C.......415 283-1804
210 Porter Dr Ste 300 San Ramon (94583) ***(P-17102)***
Atlas Pest Control, Concord *Also called Atlas Tree Service Inc* ***(P-514)***
Atlas Private Security Inc............E.......408 613-0668
888 N 1st St Ste 222 San Jose (95112) ***(P-14034)***
Atlas Shower Door Co, Sacramento *Also called Atlas Specialties Corporation* ***(P-4383)***
Atlas Specialties Corporation (PA)............**E.......503 636-8182**
4337 Astoria St Sacramento (95838) ***(P-4383)***
Atlas Technical Cons LLC............B.......925 314-7100
2001 Crow Canyon Rd # 110 San Ramon (94583) ***(P-19723)***
Atlas Tree Service Inc............E.......925 687-3631
150 Medburn St Concord (94520) ***(P-514)***
Atlas Van Lines Agent, San Rafael *Also called Johnson & Daly Moving & Strg* ***(P-7557)***
Atlassian Inc (HQ)............**D.......415 701-1110**
350 Bush St Fl 13 San Francisco (94104) ***(P-12990)***
Atlaz Inc............D.......415 671-6142
10721 Fair Oaks Blvd Fair Oaks (95628) ***(P-12282)***
Atmf Inc............E.......559 299-6836
807 Lincoln Ave Clovis (93612) ***(P-4899)***
Atmos Engineering Inc............F.......650 879-1674
443 Dearborn Park Rd Pescadero (94060) ***(P-6893)***
Atmosic Technologies Inc............E.......650 678-7864
2105 S Bascom Ave Ste 220 Campbell (95008) ***(P-8893)***
Atomic Fiction Inc (HQ)............**E.......510 488-6641**
160 Pacific Ave Ste 204 San Francisco (94111) ***(P-14800)***
Atomic Labs LLC (PA)............**D.......415 896-4148**
1 Letterman Dr Ste 702 San Francisco (94129) ***(P-10774)***
Atomic P R, San Francisco *Also called Atomic Public Relations* ***(P-19683)***
Atomic Public Relations (HQ)............**D.......415 402-0230**
735 Market St Fl 4 San Francisco (94103) ***(P-19683)***
Atomic Training, Folsom *Also called Hoonuit LLC* ***(P-13211)***
Atonarp Us Inc............E.......650 714-6290
46653 Fremont Blvd Fremont (94538) ***(P-6811)***
Atoptech Inc............E.......408 550-2600
2111 Tasman Dr Santa Clara (95054) ***(P-12283)***
Atp, Brisbane *Also called Aircraft Technical Publishers* ***(P-3553)***
Atp, Fremont *Also called Applied Thin-Film Products* ***(P-6398)***
Atp Electronics Inc............E.......408 732-5000
2590 N 1st St Ste 150 San Jose (95131) ***(P-6053)***
Atr International Inc (PA)............**E.......408 328-8000**
2804 Mission College Blvd # 120 Santa Clara (95054) ***(P-12075)***
Atreca Inc............D.......650 595-2595
835 Industrial Rd Ste 400 San Carlos (94070) ***(P-4037)***
Atrenta Inc (HQ)............**D.......408 453-3333**
690 E Middlefield Rd Mountain View (94043) ***(P-12284)***
Atrium Finance I LP............B.......916 446-0100
300 J St Sacramento (95814) ***(P-10936)***
Atrium Plaza LLC............D.......650 653-6000
1770 S Amphlett Blvd San Mateo (94402) ***(P-10937)***
Attackiq Inc (PA)............**C.......858 228-0864**
171 Main St 656 Los Altos (94022) ***(P-13847)***
Attainia Inc............F.......866 288-2464
1503 Grant Rd Ste 200 Mountain View (94040) ***(P-12991)***
Attainit............E.......916 325-7800
2555 3rd St Ste 100 Sacramento (95818) ***(P-11922)***
Attic, Oroville *Also called Oroville Hospital* ***(P-16475)***
Attivo Networks Inc (PA)............**D.......510 623-1000**
46601 Fremont Blvd Fremont (94538) ***(P-8672)***
Attocube Systems Inc (HQ)............**E.......510 649-9245**
2020 Stuart St Berkeley (94703) ***(P-18631)***
Attorneys At Law, Fresno *Also called Lang Richert & Patch* ***(P-17308)***
Atv Video Center Inc............E.......916 973-9100
2424 Glendale Ln Sacramento (95825) ***(P-14786)***
Atwater Medical Group............D.......209 358-5611
1775 3rd St Atwater (95301) ***(P-15286)***
Atypon Systems LLC (PA)............**D.......408 988-1240**
5201 Great America Pkwy # 215 Santa Clara (95054) ***(P-12992)***
Auberge Du Soleil, Rutherford *Also called Terre Du Soleil Ltd* ***(P-11529)***
Aubin Industries Inc............F.......800 324-0051
23833 S Chrisman Rd Tracy (95304) ***(P-4247)***
Auburn Ale House, Auburn *Also called Auburn Alehouse LP* ***(P-9543)***
Auburn Alehouse LP............E.......530 885-2537
289 Washington St Auburn (95603) ***(P-9543)***
Auburn Associates Inc............D.......530 823-7234
1801 Grass Valley Hwy Auburn (95603) ***(P-14546)***
Auburn Constructors LLC............D.......916 924-0344
730 W Stadium Ln Sacramento (95834) ***(P-1148)***
Auburn Dermatology Center, Auburn *Also called Alpine Allrgy Asthma Assoc Inc* ***(P-15275)***
Auburn Honda, Auburn *Also called Auburn Associates Inc* ***(P-14546)***
Auburn Journal Inc (HQ)............**C.......530 885-5656**
1030 High St Auburn (95603) ***(P-3413)***
Auburn Oaks Care Center............D.......650 949-7777
3400 Bell Rd Auburn (95603) ***(P-15912)***
Auburn Otptent Srgery Dgnstc C............D.......530 888-8899
3123 Prfcional Dr Ste 100 Auburn (95603) ***(P-16322)***
Auburn Printers and Mfg, Auburn *Also called API Marketing* ***(P-3620)***
Auburn Ravine Terrace, Auburn *Also called Congrgtnal Ch Retirement Cmnty* ***(P-18080)***
Auburn Surgery Center, Auburn *Also called Auburn Otptent Srgery Dgnstc C* ***(P-16322)***
Auburn Trader Inc (HQ)............**E.......530 888-7653**
1115 Grass Valley Hwy Auburn (95603) ***(P-3414)***
Auctions By Bay Inc............E.......510 740-0220
2701 Monarch St Alameda (94501) ***(P-14207)***
Audentes Therapeutics Inc (HQ)............**C.......415 818-1001**
600 California St Fl 17 San Francisco (94108) ***(P-4038)***
Audentes Therapeutics Inc............E.......415 818-1001
201 Gateway Blvd South San Francisco (94080) ***(P-4039)***
Audio Forensic Center, San Francisco *Also called Charles M Salter Associates* ***(P-18667)***
Audio Visual MGT Solutions............E.......707 254-3395
3425 Solano Ave NAPA (94558) ***(P-5751)***
Augmedix Inc (PA)............**A.......888 669-4885**
111 Sutter St Ste 1300 San Francisco (94104) ***(P-12993)***
Augmedix Operating Corporation............D.......855 720-2929
111 Sutter St Fl 13 San Francisco (94104) ***(P-14208)***
August Hall & Fifth Arrow, San Francisco *Also called Jasper Hall LLC* ***(P-11722)***
August Home Inc............E.......415 891-0866
657 Bryant St San Francisco (94107) ***(P-4614)***
Augustine Ideas, Roseville *Also called D Augustine & Associates* ***(P-11748)***
AUL Corp (PA)............**E.......707 257-9700**
1250 Main St Ste 300 NAPA (94559) ***(P-14728)***
Aurionpro, San Ramon *Also called Cyberinc Corporation* ***(P-13104)***
Auris Health Inc (HQ)............**D.......650 610-0750**
150 Shoreline Dr Redwood City (94065) ***(P-6947)***
Aurora Bhvral Hlthcare - STA R............D.......707 800-7700
1287 Fulton Rd Santa Rosa (95401) ***(P-16989)***
Aurora Innovation Inc............D.......646 725-4999
77 Stillman St San Francisco (94107) ***(P-12994)***
Aurora Operations Inc (PA)............**A.......888 583-9506**
280 Bernardo Ave Mountain View (94043) ***(P-12995)***
Aurrera Health Group LLC............E.......916 662-7930
1400 K St Ste 204 Sacramento (95814) ***(P-19451)***
Aus Decking Inc............D.......916 373-5320
2999 Promenade St Ste 100 West Sacramento (95691) ***(P-1850)***
Ausenco Psi Inc (HQ)............**E.......925 939-4420**
4071 Port Chicago Hwy # 120 Concord (94520) ***(P-18632)***
Austn Creek Materials, Santa Rosa *Also called Bohan Cnlis - Astin Creek Rdym* ***(P-4460)***
Authentica Solutions LLC (PA)............**F.......614 296-6479**
717 Market St Ste 300 San Francisco (94103) ***(P-12996)***
Auto Clerk Inc............E.......925 284-1005
1981 N Broadway Ste 430 Walnut Creek (94596) ***(P-12285)***
Auto Ex Towing & Recovery LLC............E.......415 846-2262
2594 Oakdale Ave San Francisco (94124) ***(P-14657)***
Auto Parts Group, Rancho Cordova *Also called Pick Pull Auto Dismantling Inc* ***(P-8487)***
Auto World Car Wash LLC............A.......408 345-6532
15951 Los Gatos Blvd Los Gatos (95032) ***(P-14628)***
Auto-Chlor System NY Cy Inc (PA)............**C.......650 967-3085**
450 Ferguson Dr Mountain View (94043) ***(P-5438)***
Autocom Power LLC............F.......510 350-1030
2735 Broadway Oakland (94612) ***(P-4261)***
Autodesk Inc............D.......415 356-0700
1 Market St San Francisco (94105) ***(P-12997)***
Autodesk Inc (PA)............**B.......415 507-5000**
111 Mcinnis Pkwy San Rafael (94903) ***(P-12998)***
Autodesk Global Inc (HQ)............**B.......415 507-5000**
1111 Mcinnis Pkwy San Rafael (94903) ***(P-12999)***
Autofarm, Fremont *Also called Novariant Inc* ***(P-18780)***
Autogrid Systems Inc (PA)............**F.......650 461-9038**
255 Shoreline Dr Ste 350 Redwood City (94065) ***(P-13000)***
Autohaus Automotive Inc (PA)............**E.......510 881-1915**
21650 Mission Blvd Hayward (94541) ***(P-8440)***
Automated Bldg Components Inc............E.......559 485-8232
2853 S Orange Ave Fresno (93725) ***(P-3200)***
Automated Bldg Ctrl Solutions, Santa Clara *Also called Automated Bldg Solutions Inc* ***(P-18633)***
Automated Bldg Solutions Inc (PA)............**E.......408 380-8518**
330 Mathew St Santa Clara (95050) ***(P-18633)***
Automated Solutions Group Inc............E.......408 432-0300
2150 Bering Dr San Jose (95131) ***(P-6699)***
Automatic Control Engrg Corp............E.......510 293-6040
20788 Corsair Blvd Hayward (94545) ***(P-6894)***
Automatic Data Processing Inc............C.......415 899-7300
505 San Marin Dr Ste A110 Novato (94945) ***(P-13694)***
Automation & Entertainment Inc............E.......408 353-4223
25870 Soquel San Jose Rd Los Gatos (95033) ***(P-4953)***
Automation Anywhere Inc (PA)............**B.......888 484-3535**
633 River Oaks Pkwy San Jose (95134) ***(P-12286)***
Automation Technology Inc............E.......408 350-7020
2001 Gateway Pl Ste 100w San Jose (95110) ***(P-12287)***
Automattic Inc (PA)............**D.......877 273-3049**
2601 Mission St Ste 900 San Francisco (94110) ***(P-7931)***
Autometrix Inc............F.......530 477-5065
12098 Charles Dr Grass Valley (95945) ***(P-5142)***
Automobile Accessories Company............E.......530 223-1561
2304 Churn Creek Rd Redding (96002) ***(P-8441)***
Automotivemastermind Inc............D.......646 679-3441
201 Mission St Fl 10 San Francisco (94105) ***(P-12288)***
Automted Mdia Proc Sltions Inc............E.......415 332-4343
500 Tamal Plz Ste 520 Corte Madera (94925) ***(P-7932)***
Autonomic LLC (PA)............**D.......650 823-1806**
3251 Hillview Ave 200 Palo Alto (94304) ***(P-12289)***
Autonomy Inc (HQ)............**E.......415 243-9955**
1 Market Plz Fl 19 San Francisco (94105) ***(P-13001)***
Autoreturn, San Francisco *Also called Tegsco LLC* ***(P-14676)***
Autowest Collision Repairs Inc............E.......408 392-1200
1729 Junction Ave San Jose (95112) ***(P-14519)***
Autox Technologies Inc............E.......650 492-8869
441 W Trimble Rd San Jose (95131) ***(P-12290)***

Autumn Press Inc ....E....510 654-4545
945 Camelia St Berkeley (94710) *(P-3623)*
Auxin Solar Inc ....E....408 225-4380
6835 Via Del Oro San Jose (95119) *(P-6054)*
AV Brands Inc ....E....410 884-9463
635 Broadway Ste 2 Sonoma (95476) *(P-9566)*
AV Now Inc ....E....831 425-2500
225 Technology Cir Scotts Valley (95066) *(P-5752)*
Ava Food Labs Inc ....E....415 806-3914
1150 Illinois St San Francisco (94107) *(P-19259)*
Ava The Rabbit Haven Inc ....D....831 600-7479
1261 S Mary St Scotts Valley (95067) *(P-19724)*
Avac, San Jose *Also called Almaden Valley Athletic Club (P-14924)*
Avago Tech Wreless USA Mfg LLC ....E....800 433-8778
1320 Ridder Park Dr San Jose (95131) *(P-6055)*
Avago Technologies US Inc ....A....408 433-4068
1730 Fox Dr San Jose (95131) *(P-6056)*
Avago Technologies US Inc ....F....408 435-7400
350 W Trimble Rd San Jose (95131) *(P-6057)*
Avago Technologies US Inc (HQ) ....B....800 433-8778
1320 Ridder Park Dr San Jose (95131) *(P-6058)*
Avail Medsystems Inc ....E....650 772-1529
2953 Bunker Hill Ln # 101 Santa Clara (95054) *(P-6948)*
Avalanche Technology Inc ....E....510 438-0148
3450 W Warren Ave Fremont (94538) *(P-6059)*
Avalon At Brush Creek LLC ....E....707 538-2590
4225 Wayvern Dr Santa Rosa (95409) *(P-18060)*
Avalon Care Cen ....E....209 723-1056
3170 M St Merced (95348) *(P-15913)*
Avalon Care Center - Modesto ....C....209 526-1775
1900 Coffee Rd Modesto (95355) *(P-15914)*
Avalon Care Ctr - Chwchlla LLC ....D....559 665-4826
1010 Ventura Ave Chowchilla (93610) *(P-15915)*
Avalon Care Ctr - Modesto LLC ....D....209 529-0516
515 E Orangeburg Ave Modesto (95350) *(P-15916)*
Avalon Care Ctr - Mrced Frncsc ....D....209 722-6231
3169 M St Merced (95348) *(P-15917)*
Avalon Care Ctr - Newman LLC ....D....209 862-2862
709 N St Newman (95360) *(P-15918)*
Avalon Care Ctr - San Andreas ....C....209 754-3823
900 Mountain Ranch Rd San Andreas (95249) *(P-15919)*
Avalon Care Ctr - Sonora LLC ....C....209 533-2500
19929 Greenley Rd Sonora (95370) *(P-15920)*
Avalon Graphics, Roseville *Also called Kkp - Roseville Inc (P-3664)*
AVALON HEALTH CARE GROUP, Sonora *Also called Avalon Care Ctr - Sonora LLC (P-15920)*
Avanquest Publishing Usa Inc (HQ) ....D....925 474-1700
7031 Koll Center Pkwy # 150 Pleasanton (94566) *(P-12291)*
Avanquest Software USA, Pleasanton *Also called Bvrp America Inc (P-13041)*
Avanta Inc (HQ) ....E....925 818-4760
1470 Civic Ct Ste 309 Concord (94520) *(P-12292)*
Avantec Vascular Corporation ....E....408 329-5400
870 Hermosa Ave Sunnyvale (94085) *(P-6949)*
Avantica Technologies, Mountain View *Also called Group Avantica Inc (P-12492)*
Avantis Medical Systems Inc ....E....408 733-1901
2367 Bering Dr San Jose (95131) *(P-7096)*
Avatier Corporation (PA) ....E....925 217-5170
4733 Chabot Dr Ste 201 Pleasanton (94588) *(P-13002)*
Avaya Inc ....E....408 437-2504
1030 Commercial St San Jose (95112) *(P-7933)*
Avegant Corp ....E....800 270-0760
37 E 4th Ave 1 San Mateo (94401) *(P-12293)*
Avenidas (PA) ....E....650 289-5400
4000 Middlefield Rd Ste I Palo Alto (94303) *(P-17434)*
AVENIDAS SENIOR HEALTH DAY HEA, Palo Alto *Also called Avenidas (P-17434)*
Aveniu Brands, Sonoma *Also called AV Brands Inc (P-9566)*
Avenu Muniservices, Fresno *Also called Muniservices LLC (P-19583)*
Aver Information Inc ....E....408 263-3828
668 Mission Ct Fremont (94539) *(P-8673)*
Avermedia Technologies Inc ....E....510 403-0006
4038 Clipper Ct Fremont (94538) *(P-5348)*
Avg Technologies Usa Inc (HQ) ....E....978 319-4460
2100 Powell St Emeryville (94608) *(P-13848)*
AVI Systems Inc ....D....415 915-2070
44150 S Grimmer Blvd Fremont (94538) *(P-8894)*
Aviate Enterprises Inc ....E....916 993-4000
5844 Price Ave McClellan (95652) *(P-5428)*
Aviatrix Systems Inc ....D....844 262-3100
2901 Tasman Dr Ste 109 Santa Clara (95054) *(P-13849)*
Avicenatech Corp (PA) ....D....919 376-6258
1130 Independence Ave Mountain View (94043) *(P-14209)*
Avid Systems Inc (HQ) ....C....650 526-1600
280 Bernardo Ave Mountain View (94043) *(P-5827)*
Avidbank (PA) ....D....408 200-7390
1732 N 1st St Fl 6 San Jose (95112) *(P-9699)*
Avidbank Holdings Inc ....C....408 200-7390
1732 N 1st St Fl 6 San Jose (95112) *(P-9700)*
Avinger Inc ....D....650 241-7900
400 Chesapeake Dr Redwood City (94063) *(P-6950)*
Aviso Inc ....D....650 567-5470
805 Veterans Blvd Ste 300 Redwood City (94063) *(P-19452)*
Avistar Communications Corp (PA) ....E....650 525-3300
1875 S Grant St Fl 10 San Mateo (94402) *(P-5349)*
Avitas Systems Inc ....D....650 233-3900
2882 Sand Hill Rd Ste 240 Menlo Park (94025) *(P-14210)*
Avoy Corp ....E....510 295-8055
114 Greenbank Ave Piedmont (94611) *(P-3624)*
Avp Technology LLC ....E....510 683-0157
4140 Business Center Dr Fremont (94538) *(P-5195)*
Avr San Jose Downtown Ht LLC ....D....408 924-0900
350 W Santa Clara St San Jose (95113) *(P-10938)*
AVV Winery Co LLC ....E....707 433-7209
8644 Highway 128 Healdsburg (95448) *(P-2507)*
Awake Security Inc ....E....833 292-5348
5453 Great America Pkwy Santa Clara (95054) *(P-13003)*
Awards By Wilson, Sacramento *Also called Wilson Trophy Co California (P-9186)*
Aweta-Autoline Inc (HQ) ....E....559 244-8340
4516 E Citron Fresno (93725) *(P-4996)*
AWI, Sacramento *Also called All Weather Inc (P-6891)*
Awid, Morgan Hill *Also called Applied Wireless Identific (P-8891)*
Awt Construction Group Inc ....D....707 746-7500
4740 E 2nd St Ste 22 Benicia (94510) *(P-613)*
Axcess Financial Services Inc ....E....916 424-4180
4241 Florin Rd Sacramento (95823) *(P-9841)*
Axcess Financial Services Inc ....E....916 783-0173
3981 Foothills Blvd Roseville (95747) *(P-9842)*
Axiad Ids Inc (HQ) ....E....408 841-4670
900 Lafayette St Ste 600 Santa Clara (95050) *(P-8895)*
Axiom Inc ....E....415 392-9466
28 Cyril Magnin St San Francisco (94102) *(P-10939)*
Axiom Global Technologies Inc ....C....925 393-5800
220 N Wiget Ln Walnut Creek (94598) *(P-19725)*
Axiom Hotel, San Francisco *Also called Axiom Inc (P-10939)*
Axiom Industries Inc ....E....559 276-1310
4202 W Sierra Madre Ave Fresno (93722) *(P-7066)*
Axis Appraisal MGT Solutions (PA) ....D....888 806-2947
1101 5th Ave Ste 210 San Rafael (94901) *(P-19300)*
Axis Community Health Inc ....D....925 462-1755
4361 Railroad Ave Pleasanton (94566) *(P-16990)*
Axis Construction, Hayward *Also called Axis Services Inc (P-738)*
Axis Group Inc ....E....510 487-7393
1220 Whipple Rd Union City (94587) *(P-6060)*
Axis Jet, Sacramento *Also called Eldorado Air LLC (P-7756)*
Axis Services Inc ....C....510 732-6111
2544 Barrington Ct Hayward (94545) *(P-738)*
Axl Musical Instruments Co Ltd (PA) ....E....415 508-1398
401 Forbes Blvd South San Francisco (94080) *(P-7170)*
Axt Inc ....A....510 683-5900
4311 Solar Way Fremont (94538) *(P-6061)*
Axt Inc (PA) ....E....510 438-4700
4281 Technology Dr Fremont (94538) *(P-6062)*
Axt-Tongmei Inc ....E....510 438-4700
4281 Technology Dr Fremont (94538) *(P-6063)*
Axygen Inc (HQ) ....C....510 494-8900
33210 Central Ave Union City (94587) *(P-6812)*
Axygen Scientific, Union City *Also called Axygen Inc (P-6812)*
Ayala and Son Pallets, Sanger *Also called Tripie A Pallets Inc (P-3231)*
Ayantra Inc ....F....510 623-7526
47873 Fremont Blvd Fremont (94538) *(P-5788)*
Ayar Labs Inc (PA) ....E....650 963-7200
3351 Olcott St Santa Clara (95054) *(P-5242)*
Ayehu Inc (HQ) ....D....800 652-5601
99 Almaden Blvd Fl 6 San Jose (95113) *(P-13004)*
Ayehu Software Technologies, San Jose *Also called Ayehu Inc (P-13004)*
Ayoob & Peery Plumbing Co Inc ....D....415 550-0975
975 Indiana St San Francisco (94107) *(P-1210)*
Ayusa International ....D....888 552-9872
600 California St Fl 10 San Francisco (94108) *(P-18549)*
Azalea Holdings LLC ....D....916 452-3592
3700 H St Sacramento (95816) *(P-15921)*
Azazie Inc ....E....650 963-9420
148 E Brokaw Rd San Jose (95112) *(P-3000)*
Azimuth Industrial Co Inc ....E....510 441-6000
30593 Un Cy Blvd Ste 110 Union City (94587) *(P-6064)*
Azimuth Semiconductor Assembly, Union City *Also called Azimuth Industrial Co Inc (P-6064)*
Aztec Machine Co Inc ....F....916 638-4894
3156 Fitzgerald Rd Ste A Rancho Cordova (95742) *(P-5478)*
Azuga Inc (HQ) ....B....888 790-0715
42840 Christy St Ste 205 Fremont (94538) *(P-13558)*
Azul Systems Inc (PA) ....C....650 230-6500
385 Moffett Park Dr # 115 Sunnyvale (94089) *(P-13005)*
Azulworks Inc ....C....415 558-1507
1400 Egbert Ave San Francisco (94124) *(P-8222)*
Azuma Foods Intl Inc USA, Hayward *Also called Azuma Foods Intl Inc USA (P-2829)*
Azuma Foods Intl Inc USA (HQ) ....D....510 782-1112
20201 Mack St Hayward (94545) *(P-2829)*
Azumio Inc (PA) ....C....719 310-3774
255 Shoreline Dr Ste 130 Redwood City (94065) *(P-12294)*
Azumo LLC ....C....415 610-7002
3130 Alpine Rd Ste 288 Portola Valley (94028) *(P-12295)*
Azure Biosystems Inc ....E....925 307-7127
6747 Sierra Ct Ste A Dublin (94568) *(P-19032)*
Azusa Rock LLC ....E....209 826-5066
22101 Sunset Dr Los Banos (93635) *(P-4459)*
B & B Concrete, Santa Clara *Also called Robert A Bothman Inc (P-1907)*
B & B Mfg Co, Turlock *Also called Rose Joaquin Inc (P-9091)*
B & B Travelware LLC ....F....408 564-7569
5700 Stnrdge Mall Rd Ste Pleasanton (94588) *(P-4347)*
B & C, Oakland *Also called B&C Transit Inc (P-18634)*
B & C Chandler Trucking Inc ....E....559 674-7181
16930 Road 26 Ste C Madera (93638) *(P-7451)*
B & C Painting Solutions Inc ....E....209 982-0422
107 Val Dervin Pkwy Stockton (95206) *(P-4927)*
B & C Trucking, Madera *Also called B & C Chandler Trucking Inc (P-7451)*
B & F Logistics LLC (PA) ....E....707 720-6101
175 Santa Barbara Way Fairfield (94533) *(P-7875)*

ALPHABETIC

B & G Precision Inc.....F.....510 438-9785
45450 Industrial Pl Ste 9 Fremont (94538) *(P-5479)*
B & H Engineering Company, San Carlos *Also called Begovic Industries Inc (P-5483)*
B & H Labeling Systems, Ceres *Also called B & H Manufacturing Co Inc (P-5196)*
B & H Manufacturing Co Inc (PA).....C.....**209 537-5785**
3461 Roeding Rd Ceres (95307) *(P-5196)*
B & J Body Shop Inc (PA).....E.....**916 635-4400**
11000 Folsom Blvd Rancho Cordova (95670) *(P-14520)*
B & L Mechanical Inc.....E.....559 268-2727
3218 N Marks Ave 3220 Fresno (93722) *(P-1211)*
B & N Industries Inc (PA).....D.....**650 593-4127**
1409 Chapin Ave Fl 2nd Burlingame (94010) *(P-8764)*
B & R Farms LLC.....E.....831 637-9168
5280 Fairview Rd Hollister (95023) *(P-2250)*
B & W Resort Marina.....E.....916 777-6161
964 Brannan Island Rd Isleton (95641) *(P-10940)*
B A M I Inc.....D.....530 343-5678
1293 E 1st Ave Chico (95926) *(P-14927)*
B B C, San Jose *Also called Babbitt Bearing Co Inc (P-5481)*
B C C S Inc (PA).....C.....**408 379-5500**
1711 Dell Ave Campbell (95008) *(P-614)*
B F C Inc.....C.....415 495-3085
675 Davis St San Francisco (94111) *(P-1454)*
B H R Operations LLC.....A.....408 321-9500
777 Bellew Dr Milpitas (95035) *(P-10941)*
B I A, Emeryville *Also called Behavioral Intervention Assn (P-12161)*
B Js Heating & AC Inc.....E.....530 662-8601
1240 Wilson Way Woodland (95776) *(P-1212)*
B K D Holdings.....E.....650 704-3454
800 Mason St Vacaville (95688) *(P-10942)*
B M B, Rancho Cordova *Also called Bmb Metal Products Corporation (P-4744)*
B M D, Galt *Also called Building Material Distrs Inc (P-8532)*
B M D Enterprises Inc.....F.....559 291-7708
4959 E Dakota Ave Ste A Fresno (93727) *(P-5439)*
B Metal Fabrication Inc.....E.....650 615-7705
318 S Maple Ave South San Francisco (94080) *(P-4645)*
B P M, San Francisco *Also called Bpm LLP (P-18936)*
B R & F Spray Inc.....E.....408 988-7582
3380 De La Cruz Blvd Santa Clara (95054) *(P-4928)*
B R Funsten & Co.....D.....209 825-5375
105 Lndustrial Park Manteca (95337) *(P-8506)*
B R Printers Inc (PA).....D.....**408 278-7711**
665 Lenfest Rd San Jose (95133) *(P-3625)*
B S A, Fremont *Also called Ball Screws & Actuators Co Inc (P-5220)*
B S K Analytical Laboratories, Fresno *Also called BSK Associates (P-18650)*
B S R, San Francisco *Also called Business For Scial Rspnsbility (P-19462)*
B T Automotive Inc.....E.....209 462-4444
1917 Navy Dr Stockton (95206) *(P-9173)*
B T Mancini Co Inc.....C.....916 381-3660
8571 23rd Ave Sacramento (95826) *(P-8507)*
B T Mancini Co Inc (PA).....D.....**408 942-7900**
876 S Milpitas Blvd Milpitas (95035) *(P-1765)*
B T W, West Sacramento *Also called Bytheways Manufacturing Inc (P-3330)*
B W Padilla Inc.....E.....408 275-9834
197 Ryland St San Jose (95110) *(P-14709)*
B Z Plumbing Company Inc.....E.....916 645-1600
1901 Aviation Blvd Lincoln (95648) *(P-1213)*
B&C Transit Inc (HQ).....D.....**510 483-3560**
1924 Franklin St Ste 200 Oakland (94612) *(P-18634)*
B&R Maintenance Inc.....E.....650 589-0331
90 S Spruce Ave Ste Us South San Francisco (94080) *(P-11923)*
B&Z Manufacturing Company Inc.....E.....408 943-1117
1478 Seareel Ln San Jose (95131) *(P-5480)*
B-K Lighting Inc.....D.....559 438-5800
40429 Brickyard Dr Madera (93636) *(P-5723)*
B.T. Mancini Company, Milpitas *Also called B T Mancini Co Inc (P-1765)*
B12 Drywall Inc.....E.....916 635-3600
11467 Sunrise Gold Cir # 8 Rancho Cordova (95742) *(P-1660)*
B2 Machining LLC.....F.....510 668-1360
4255 Business Center Dr Fremont (94538) *(P-14739)*
B44 Catalan Bistro.....E.....415 986-6287
44 Belden Pl San Francisco (94104) *(P-2169)*
Ba Leasing & Capital Corp (HQ).....C.....**415 765-1804**
555 California St Fl 4 San Francisco (94104) *(P-12030)*
Baart Behavioral Hlth Svcs Inc (HQ).....E.....**415 552-7914**
1145 Market St Fl 10 San Francisco (94103) *(P-16991)*
Bab Acquisition Corp.....F.....408 267-7214
3670 Charter Park Dr A San Jose (95136) *(P-6813)*
Babbitt Bearing Co Inc.....E.....408 298-1101
1170 N 5th St San Jose (95112) *(P-5481)*
Babcock Brown Rnwble Hldngs In (HQ).....E.....**415 512-1515**
1 Letterman Dr Bldg B San Francisco (94129) *(P-18635)*
Babette (PA).....E.....**510 625-8500**
867 Newton Carey Jr Way Oakland (94607) *(P-3007)*
Babycenter LLC (HQ).....D.....**415 537-0900**
163 Freelon St San Francisco (94107) *(P-11706)*
Babyganics, San Francisco *Also called Kas Direct LLC (P-3396)*
Babylon Printing Inc.....E.....408 519-5000
15850 Concord Cir Ste B Morgan Hill (95037) *(P-3626)*
Bacchus Press Inc (PA).....E.....**510 420-5800**
1287 66th St Emeryville (94608) *(P-3627)*
Bace Manufacturing Inc.....D.....510 657-5800
45581 Northport Loop W Fremont (94538) *(P-4262)*
Back Street Fitness Inc.....E.....707 254-7200
3175 California Blvd NAPA (94558) *(P-14928)*
Backblaze Inc.....C.....650 352-3738
500 Ben Franklin Ct San Mateo (94401) *(P-13779)*
Backbone Software Inc.....E.....415 993-2468
490 43rd St Unit 132 Oakland (94609) *(P-13559)*
Backroads (PA).....D.....**510 527-1555**
801 Cedar St Berkeley (94710) *(P-7815)*
Backyard Unlimited.....E.....707 447-7433
5119 Quinn Rd Vacaville (95688) *(P-826)*
Baco Realty Corporation.....D.....916 974-9898
6310 Stockton Blvd Sacramento (95824) *(P-14035)*
Baco Realty Corporation.....D.....925 275-0100
2071 Camino Ramon San Ramon (94583) *(P-7681)*
Bacon's Multivision, Oakland *Also called Multivision Inc (P-14335)*
Bacs Adult Day Care, Oakland *Also called Bay Area Community Svcs Inc (P-17439)*
Bad Boys Bail Bonds Inc (PA).....D.....**408 298-3333**
595 Park Ave Ste 200 San Jose (95110) *(P-14211)*
Badass Beard Care, Granite Bay *Also called Badass Brand Inc (P-9223)*
Badass Brand Inc.....E.....916 990-3873
8400 Moss Ct Granite Bay (95746) *(P-9223)*
BADGER CREEK, Santa Rosa *Also called Slow Sculpture (P-18183)*
Badger Maps Inc.....E.....415 592-5909
539 Broadway San Francisco (94133) *(P-13006)*
Badgeville Inc.....E.....650 323-6668
805 Veterans Blvd Ste 307 Redwood City (94063) *(P-13007)*
Bae Systems Imging Sltions Inc.....D.....408 433-2500
1841 Zanker Rd Ste 50 San Jose (95112) *(P-6065)*
Bae Systems Land Armaments LP.....B.....408 289-0111
6331 San Ignacio Ave San Jose (95119) *(P-6664)*
Bae Systems Srra Dtroit Desl A (HQ).....D.....**510 635-8991**
1755 Adams Ave San Leandro (94577) *(P-14547)*
Baer Institute, Moffett Field *Also called Bay Area Envmtl Res Inst (P-19198)*
Baffle Inc.....E.....408 663-6737
2811 Mission College Blvd F Santa Clara (95054) *(P-13008)*
Bagatelos Glass Systems Inc (PA).....D.....**916 364-3600**
2750 Redding Ave Sacramento (95820) *(P-1935)*
Bagatlos Archtctral GL Systems, Sacramento *Also called Bagatelos Glass Systems Inc (P-1935)*
Bagby Home and School Club, San Jose *Also called Cambrian School District (P-18555)*
Bagelry Inc (PA).....E.....**831 429-8049**
320 Cedar St Ste A Santa Cruz (95060) *(P-2364)*
Baggage & Air Freight Service, Fresno *Also called Skywest Airlines Inc (P-7740)*
Baggie Farms Express Inc.....E.....559 486-7330
6385 E North Ave Fresno (93725) *(P-7506)*
Bagley, William T, San Francisco *Also called Nossaman LLP (P-17346)*
Baidu USA LLC.....C.....669 224-6400
1195 Bordeaux Dr Sunnyvale (94089) *(P-13850)*
Bailard Inc (HQ).....E.....**650 571-5800**
950 Tower Ln Ste 1900 Foster City (94404) *(P-10032)*
Bailey Creek Golf Course, Westwood *Also called Bailey Creek Investors A Cali (P-14988)*
Bailey Creek Investors A Cali.....E.....530 259-4653
433 Durkin Dr Westwood (96137) *(P-14988)*
Bailey Creek Invstors A Cal Lt (PA).....E.....**530 891-6753**
1766 Bidwell Ave Chico (95926) *(P-10695)*
Bailey Fence Company Inc.....E.....510 538-1175
3205 Baumberg Ct Hayward (94545) *(P-2008)*
Bailey Valve Inc.....E.....559 434-2838
264 W Fallbrook Ave # 105 Fresno (93711) *(P-4954)*
Bainbridge and Associates Inc.....E.....408 356-5040
805 University Ave Ste I Los Gatos (95032) *(P-615)*
Bains Woodward Insur Svcs Inc.....D.....530 534-6600
2260 Oro Dam Blvd E Ste C Oroville (95966) *(P-10244)*
Baja Construction Co Inc (PA).....D.....**925 229-0732**
223 Foster St Martinez (94553) *(P-1921)*
Baker & McKenzie LLP.....C.....415 576-3000
2 Embarcadero Ctr # 1100 San Francisco (94111) *(P-17204)*
Baker & McKenzie LLP.....D.....650 856-2400
660 Hansen Way Ste 1 Palo Alto (94304) *(P-17205)*
Baker Avenue Asset MGT LP (PA).....D.....**415 986-1110**
301 Battery St Fl 2 San Francisco (94111) *(P-10033)*
Baker Commodities Inc.....E.....559 237-4320
16801 W Jensen Ave Kerman (93630) *(P-2457)*
Baker Custom Cabinets Inc.....F.....559 675-1395
455 S Pine St Ste 2 Madera (93637) *(P-3168)*
Baker Farming.....E.....559 659-3942
45499 W Panoche Rd Firebaugh (93622) *(P-43)*
Baker Manock & Jensen Pc.....D.....559 432-5400
5260 N Palm Ave Ste 201 Fresno (93704) *(P-17206)*
Baker Mnock Jnsen Attys At Law, Fresno *Also called Baker Manock & Jensen Pc (P-17206)*
Baker Places Inc.....D.....415 503-3137
101 Gough St San Francisco (94102) *(P-16992)*
Baker Places Inc.....D.....415 387-2275
2157 Grove St San Francisco (94117) *(P-17435)*
Balaji Alameda LLC.....E.....510 521-4500
1700 Harbor Bay Pkwy Alameda (94502) *(P-10943)*
Balance, Concord *Also called Consumer Cr Cnsling Svc San Fr (P-11713)*
Balance Staffing Workforce LLC.....E.....209 215-4188
2800 N Cherryland Ave Stockton (95215) *(P-12076)*
Balanced Rock Inc.....D.....408 374-8692
1190 Dell Ave Ste I Campbell (95008) *(P-15178)*
Balbix Inc.....D.....866 936-3180
3031 Tisch Way Ste 800 San Jose (95128) *(P-12296)*
Balboa Enterprises Inc.....C.....650 961-6161
2530 Solace Pl Mountain View (94040) *(P-15922)*
Balch Petro Contrs & Bldrs Inc.....D.....408 942-8686
930 Ames Ave Milpitas (95035) *(P-1088)*
Baldocchi and Sons Inc.....E.....650 755-2330
2499 Hillside Blvd Colma (94014) *(P-9625)*
Baldwin Contracting Co Inc.....F.....209 460-3785
400 S Lincoln St Stockton (95203) *(P-590)*

Baldwin Contracting Co Inc (HQ).....E.....530 891-6555
1764 Skyway Chico (95928) *(P-1013)*

Baldwin Hotel, San Francisco *Also called Sing Seng Hing Co Ltd (P-11482)*

Baldwin-Minkler Farms.....E.....530 865-7676
320 E South St Orland (95963) *(P-82)*

Ball Corporation.....B.....209 848-6500
300 Greger St Oakdale (95361) *(P-4597)*

Ball Rig Welding LLC.....E.....530 990-5795
4801 Fther Rver Blvd Ste Oroville (95965) *(P-14710)*

Ball Screws & Actuators Co Inc (HQ).....D.....510 770-5932
48767 Kato Rd Fremont (94538) *(P-5220)*

Balletto Vineyards, Santa Rosa *Also called Laguna Oaks Vnyards Winery Inc (P-2646)*

Balliet Bros Construction Corp.....E.....650 871-9000
390 Swift Ave Ste 14 South San Francisco (94080) *(P-827)*

Balloons Above Valley Ltd.....E.....707 253-2222
603 California Blvd NAPA (94559) *(P-15179)*

Baloian Farm, Fresno *Also called Baloian Packing Co Inc (P-24)*

Baloian Packing Co Inc (PA).....C.....559 485-9200
446 N Blythe Ave Fresno (93706) *(P-24)*

Balsam Brands Inc (PA).....D.....877 442-2572
50 Woodside Plz Ste 111 Redwood City (94061) *(P-7269)*

Balsam Hill, Redwood City *Also called Balsam Brands Inc (P-7269)*

Baltimore Aircoil Company Inc.....C.....559 673-9231
15341 Road 28 1/2 Madera (93638) *(P-5429)*

Bam Advisor Services LLC.....D.....800 366-7266
10 Almaden Blvd Fl 15 San Jose (95113) *(P-10034)*

Bambacigno Steel Company.....E.....209 524-9681
4930 Mchenry Ave Modesto (95356) *(P-4539)*

Bamford Equipment, Oroville *Also called J W Bamford Inc (P-3066)*

Bana Solomon LLC.....E.....707 867-1770
703 2nd St Ste 306 Santa Rosa (95404) *(P-16852)*

Bananas Incorporated.....E.....510 658-7353
5232 Claremont Ave Oakland (94618) *(P-18221)*

BANANAS CHILD CARE INFORMATION, Oakland *Also called Bananas Incorporated (P-18221)*

Banc America Lsg & Capitl LLC (HQ).....C.....415 765-7349
555 California St Fl 4 San Francisco (94104) *(P-9677)*

Bancorp Financial Services Inc (HQ).....D.....916 641-2000
9343 Tech Center Dr # 160 Sacramento (95826) *(P-9885)*

Bancroft Club.....E.....510 549-0152
2680 Bancroft Way Berkeley (94704) *(P-10944)*

Bancroft Hotel, Berkeley *Also called Bancroft Club (P-10944)*

Bancwest Corporation.....A.....415 765-4800
180 Montgomery St San Francisco (94104) *(P-9701)*

Bandai Namco Entrtmt Amer Inc.....C.....408 235-2000
2051 Mission College Blvd Santa Clara (95054) *(P-9164)*

Bandmerch LLC.....E.....818 736-4800
3945 Freedom Cir Ste 560 Santa Clara (95054) *(P-3045)*

Bandpage Inc.....E.....415 800-6614
901 Cherry Ave San Bruno (94066) *(P-13851)*

Bangs Avenue Medical Offices, Modesto *Also called Kaiser Foundation Hospitals (P-15462)*

Banh An Binh.....E.....408 935-8950
1965 Stonewood Ln San Jose (95132) *(P-6400)*

Banister Electrical Inc.....D.....925 778-7801
2532 Verne Roberts Cir Antioch (94509) *(P-1455)*

Banjo, Redwood City *Also called Safexai Inc (P-13421)*

Bank America National Assn.....E.....650 960-4701
444 Castro St Ste 100 Mountain View (94041) *(P-9678)*

Bank America National Assn.....E.....209 578-6006
1601 I St Frnt Modesto (95354) *(P-9679)*

Bank America National Assn.....E.....530 226-6172
1300 Hilltop Dr Redding (96003) *(P-9680)*

Bank of America, San Francisco *Also called Bankamerica Financial Inc (P-9868)*

Bank of Marin.....D.....415 472-2265
4460 Redwood Hwy Ste 1 San Rafael (94903) *(P-9702)*

Bank of Marin Bancorp (PA).....C.....415 763-4520
504 Redwood Blvd Ste 100 Novato (94947) *(P-9703)*

Bank of Orient Foundation (HQ).....D.....415 338-0668
100 Pine St Ste 600 San Francisco (94111) *(P-9704)*

Bank of San Francisco.....E.....415 744-6700
575 Market St Ste 900 San Francisco (94105) *(P-9705)*

Bank of Stockton (HQ).....C.....209 929-1600
301 E Miner Ave Stockton (95202) *(P-9706)*

BANK OF THE ORIENT, San Francisco *Also called Orient Bancorporation (P-9740)*

BANK OF THE WEST (HQ).....A.....415 765-4800
180 Montgomery St # 1400 San Francisco (94104) *(P-9707)*

Bank Up, Alameda *Also called Business Recovery Services Inc (P-13700)*

Bankamerica Financial Inc.....D.....415 622-3521
315 Montgomery St San Francisco (94104) *(P-9868)*

Banks & Co, Fresno *Also called W Banks Moore Inc (P-2085)*

Banks Glass, Jamestown *Also called V B Glass Co Inc (P-1947)*

Banksia Landscape.....E.....408 617-7100
1055 E Brokaw Rd 30-34 San Jose (95131) *(P-394)*

Banner Health.....C.....530 251-3147
1800 Spring Ridge Dr Susanville (96130) *(P-16323)*

Banner Lssen Med Ctr Fndtion I.....C.....530 252-2000
1800 Spring Ridge Dr Susanville (96130) *(P-16324)*

Banuelos, Jose L Jr MD, Modesto *Also called Orangeburg Medical Group (P-15570)*

Bar 20 Dairy LLC.....D.....559 846-7095
25000 W Whitesbridge Ave Kerman (93630) *(P-205)*

Bar Architects.....D.....415 293-5700
77 Geary St Ste 200 San Francisco (94108) *(P-18872)*

Bar Asscation of San Francisco (PA).....D.....415 982-1600
201 Mission St Ste 400 San Francisco (94105) *(P-18324)*

Bar Media Inc.....F.....415 861-5019
44 Gough St Ste 204 San Francisco (94103) *(P-3415)*

Bar-S Foods Co.....D.....408 941-9958
392 Railroad Ct Milpitas (95035) *(P-2112)*

Bara Construction, Danville *Also called Bara Infoware Inc (P-18636)*

Bara Infoware Inc (PA).....D.....925 790-0130
4115 Blackhawk Plaza Cir Danville (94506) *(P-18636)*

Barbara-Hoffman Inc.....D.....916 635-9767
3780 Happy Ln Ste A Sacramento (95827) *(P-11924)*

Barbee Elc.....D.....916 884-1983
1406 Blue Oaks Blvd Ste 1 Roseville (95747) *(P-16853)*

Barber Beale, Marysville *Also called Gino Morena Enterprises LLC (P-11698)*

Barbier Security Group.....C.....415 747-8473
20 Galli Dr 9-10 Novato (94949) *(P-14036)*

Barbosa Cabinets Inc.....B.....209 836-2501
2020 E Grant Line Rd Tracy (95304) *(P-3169)*

Barbour Vineyards LLC.....E.....707 257-1829
104 Camino Dorado NAPA (94558) *(P-2508)*

Barcelon Associates MGT Corp.....C.....925 627-7000
590 Lennon Ln Ste 110 Walnut Creek (94598) *(P-10493)*

Barebottle Brewing Company Inc.....F.....415 926-8617
1525 Cortland Ave San Francisco (94110) *(P-2474)*

Barefoot Cellars, Santa Rosa *Also called Grape Links Inc (P-2604)*

Bargas Envmtl Consulting LLC.....E.....916 993-9218
3604 Fair Oaks Blvd # 180 Sacramento (95864) *(P-19726)*

Barkerblue Inc.....E.....650 696-2100
363 N Amphlett Blvd San Mateo (94401) *(P-3763)*

Barlow and Sons Printing Inc.....F.....707 664-9773
481 Aaron St Cotati (94931) *(P-3628)*

Barlow Printing, Cotati *Also called Barlow and Sons Printing Inc (P-3628)*

Barnard Bessac Joint Venture.....D.....650 212-8957
395 Shoreway Rd Redwood City (94065) *(P-1149)*

Barnes Welding Supply, Fresno *Also called Fresno Oxgn Wldg Suppliers Inc (P-9067)*

Barney & Co California LLC.....F.....559 442-1752
2925 S Elm Ave Ste 101 Fresno (93706) *(P-2869)*

Barnum & Celillo Electric Inc (PA).....C.....916 646-4661
135 Main Ave Sacramento (95838) *(P-1456)*

Baron, Roseville *Also called Empire Paper Corporation (P-9207)*

Baron Brand Spices, Fairfield *Also called Abco Laboratories Inc (P-3828)*

Barra LLC (HQ).....B.....510 548-5442
2100 Milvia St Berkeley (94704) *(P-13009)*

Barracuda Networks Inc (HQ).....C.....408 342-5400
3175 Winchester Blvd Campbell (95008) *(P-13010)*

Barrel Merchants, Saint Helena *Also called Red River Lumber Co (P-3239)*

Barrel Ten Qarter Cir Land Inc.....F.....209 538-3131
33 Harlow Ct NAPA (94558) *(P-2509)*

Barrera Adolfo DDS (PA).....E.....408 871-2885
40 Jeffers Way Campbell (95008) *(P-15824)*

Barrett Business Services Inc.....A.....650 653-7588
1840 Gateway Dr San Mateo (94404) *(P-12077)*

Barrett SF.....E.....415 986-2960
250 Sutter St Ste 200 San Francisco (94108) *(P-11740)*

Barri Electric Company Inc.....E.....415 468-6477
61 Napoleon St San Francisco (94124) *(P-1457)*

Barricade Co & Traffic Sup Inc (PA).....F.....707 523-2350
3963 Santa Rosa Ave Santa Rosa (95407) *(P-4981)*

Barrier Spclty Rofg Ctings Inc.....E.....559 233-1680
2671 S Cherry Ave Fresno (93706) *(P-1787)*

Barrx Medical Inc.....D.....408 328-7300
540 Oakmead Pkwy Sunnyvale (94085) *(P-6951)*

Barry Bishop.....D.....510 596-0888
6001 Shellmound St # 875 Emeryville (94608) *(P-17207)*

Barry Callebaut USA LLC.....C.....707 642-8200
1175 Commerce Blvd Ste D American Canyon (94503) *(P-2435)*

Barry Swenson Builders, Santa Cruz *Also called Green Valley Corporation (P-649)*

Barrys Cultured Marble Inc.....F.....707 745-3444
866 Teal Dr Benicia (94510) *(P-4516)*

Bart, Oakland *Also called San Frncsco Bay Area Rpid Trns (P-7349)*

Bart Manufacturing Inc (PA).....D.....408 320-4373
3787 Spinnaker Ct Fremont (94538) *(P-7270)*

Bartholomew Park Winery, Sonoma *Also called Vineburg Wine Company Inc (P-2758)*

Bartko Zankel Tarrant & Mil.....D.....415 956-1900
1 Embarcadero Ctr Ste 800 San Francisco (94111) *(P-17208)*

Barton Memorial Hospital (HQ).....A.....530 541-3420
2170 South Ave South Lake Tahoe (96150) *(P-16325)*

Barton Overhead Door Inc.....E.....209 571-3667
1132 N Carpenter Rd Modesto (95351) *(P-1730)*

Barton Ranch Inc.....E.....209 838-8930
22398 Mcbride Rd Escalon (95320) *(P-245)*

Basalite Building Products LLC (HQ).....E.....707 678-1901
2150 Douglas Blvd Ste 260 Roseville (95661) *(P-4418)*

BASF Venture Capital Amer Inc.....E.....510 445-6140
46820 Fremont Blvd Fremont (94538) *(P-4121)*

Basic American Inc (PA).....D.....925 472-4438
2999 Oak Rd Ste 800 Walnut Creek (94597) *(P-2251)*

Basic American Foods, Walnut Creek *Also called Basic American Inc (P-2251)*

Basic Resources Inc (PA).....E.....209 521-9771
928 12th St Ste 700 Modesto (95354) *(P-1014)*

Basic Solutions Corp.....C.....510 573-3658
46724 Fremont Blvd Fremont (94538) *(P-13852)*

Basis Science Inc.....E.....415 367-7477
150 Chestnut St San Francisco (94111) *(P-8774)*

Basque French Bakery, Fresno *Also called Fresno French Bread Bakery Inc (P-2384)*

Basquez Tiburcio Health Center.....E.....510 471-5907
33255 9th St Union City (94587) *(P-16993)*

Bass Electric, South San Francisco *Also called Bay Area Systems Solutions Inc (P-1460)*

Bass Medical Group, Walnut Creek *Also called Brian D Hopkins MD (P-15302)*

Bass Tickets, Concord *Also called Bay Area Seating Service Inc (P-15181)*

Bassard Cnvalescent Med HM Inc (PA).....D.....510 537-6700
3269 D St Hayward (94541) *(P-16217)*

Bassard Convalscent Home, Hayward *Also called Bassard Cnvalescent Med HM Inc (P-16217)*

Employee Codes: A=Over 500 employees, B=251-500 C=101-250, D=51-100, E=20-50 F=10-19
2022 Northern California Business Directory and Buyers Guide
© Mergent Inc. 1-800-342-5647
907

Bassian Farms Inc ALPHABETIC SECTION

Bassian Farms Inc ....E....408 286-6262
4051 Seaport Blvd West Sacramento (95691) *(P-9375)*
Batchlder Bus Cmmnications Inc ....E....209 577-2222
2900 Standiford Ave Ste 5 Modesto (95350) *(P-3629)*
Battery The, San Francisco *Also called Mxb Battery LP (P-18442)*
Batth Dehydrator LLC ....E....559 864-3501
4624 W Nebraska Ave Caruthers (93609) *(P-2252)*
Batth Farms, Caruthers *Also called Charanjit Singh Batth (P-85)*
Bauers Intelligent Trnsp Inc (PA) ....**C....415 263-4020**
50 Pier San Francisco (94158) *(P-7373)*
Baum Thornley Architects ....D....415 503-1411
95 Brady St San Francisco (94103) *(P-18873)*
Bausch Health Americas Inc ....C....707 793-2600
1330 Redwood Way Ste C Petaluma (94954) *(P-3861)*
Bavarian Lion Company Cal (PA) ....**C....707 545-8530**
2777 4th St Santa Rosa (95405) *(P-10945)*
Bavc, San Francisco *Also called Bay Area Video Coalition Inc (P-14801)*
Bay 101, San Jose *Also called Sutters Place Inc (P-15248)*
Bay Advanced Tech 0045, Newark *Also called Bay Advanced Technologies LLC (P-9052)*
Bay Advanced Technologies LLC ....E....510 857-0900
8100 Central Ave Newark (94560) *(P-9052)*
Bay Alarm Company (PA) ....**D....925 935-1100**
5130 Commercial Cir Concord (94520) *(P-1458)*
Bay Alarm Company ....E....209 465-1986
3819 Duck Creek Dr Stockton (95215) *(P-1459)*
Bay Area Air Quality (PA) ....**C....415 749-4900**
375 Beale St Ste 600 San Francisco (94105) *(P-19727)*
Bay Area Air Quality MGT Dst ....B....415 749-4900
375 Beale St Ste 600 San Francisco (94105) *(P-19301)*
Bay Area Airstream Adventures, Fairfield *Also called Aanw Inc (P-14543)*
Bay Area At Home, Belmont *Also called Silverado Senior Living Inc (P-16120)*
Bay Area Beverage Company, Richmond *Also called T F Louderback Inc (P-9563)*
Bay Area Builders Inc ....E....408 648-4500
3360 De La Cruz Blvd Santa Clara (95054) *(P-616)*
Bay Area Circuits Inc ....E....510 933-9000
44358 Old Warm Sprng Blvd Fremont (94538) *(P-5918)*
Bay Area Cmnty Resources Inc ....E....510 559-3000
11175 San Pablo Ave El Cerrito (94530) *(P-17436)*
Bay Area Cnstr Framers Inc ....C....925 454-8514
1150 W Center St Ste 105 Manteca (95337) *(P-1731)*
Bay Area Community Health (PA) ....**C....510 770-8040**
40910 Fremont Blvd Fremont (94538) *(P-15287)*
Bay Area Community Svcs Inc ....D....510 656-7742
40963 Grimmer Blvd Fremont (94538) *(P-17437)*
Bay Area Community Svcs Inc (PA) ....**E....510 613-0330**
390 40th St Oakland (94609) *(P-17438)*
Bay Area Community Svcs Inc ....D....510 601-1074
5714 Mrtin Lther King Jr Oakland (94609) *(P-17439)*
Bay Area Concrete LLC ....D....510 294-0220
1580 Chabot Ct Hayward (94545) *(P-8305)*
Bay Area Discovery Museum ....E....415 339-3900
557 Mcreynolds Rd Sausalito (94965) *(P-18262)*
Bay Area Distributing Coinc ....E....510 232-8554
1061 Factory St Richmond (94801) *(P-9544)*
Bay Area Envmtl Res Inst ....E....707 938-9387
Nasa Res Pk Bldg 18 Rm 10 Moffett Field (94035) *(P-19198)*
Bay Area Healthcare Center ....E....510 536-6512
1833 10th Ave Oakland (94606) *(P-17103)*
Bay Area Herbs & Spc LLC ....E....650 583-0857
155 Terminal Ct Ste G South San Francisco (94080) *(P-9388)*
Bay Area Hospice, Brisbane *Also called Silverado Senior Living Inc (P-16203)*
Bay Area Hspano Inst For Advnc ....D....510 525-1463
1000 Camelia St Berkeley (94710) *(P-17857)*
Bay Area Indus Filtration Inc ....E....510 562-6373
6355 Coliseum Way Oakland (94621) *(P-5225)*
Bay Area Installations Inc (PA) ....**D....510 895-8196**
2481 Verna Ct San Leandro (94577) *(P-2009)*
Bay Area Kenworth, San Leandro *Also called Ssmb Pacific Holding Co Inc (P-8429)*
Bay Area Legal Aid (PA) ....**E....510 663-4755**
1735 Telegraph Ave Oakland (94612) *(P-17209)*
Bay Area Motorcycle Training ....E....925 677-7408
5100 Clayton Rd 311 Concord (94521) *(P-15180)*
Bay Area News Group E Bay LLC (HQ) ....**E....925 302-1683**
6270 Houston Pl Ste A Dublin (94568) *(P-11810)*
Bay Area Obstetrics Gynecology ....E....650 756-2404
1850 Sullivan Ave Ste 550 Daly City (94015) *(P-15288)*
Bay Area Pdatric Med Group Inc ....D....650 343-4200
123 S San Mateo Dr San Mateo (94401) *(P-15289)*
Bay Area Reporter, San Francisco *Also called Bar Media Inc (P-3415)*
Bay Area Rescue Mission (PA) ....**D....510 215-4555**
2114 Macdonald Ave Richmond (94801) *(P-17440)*
Bay Area Seafood Inc (PA) ....**E....510 475-7100**
30248 Santucci Ct Hayward (94544) *(P-9359)*
Bay Area Seating Service Inc ....B....925 671-4000
1855 Gateway Blvd Ste 630 Concord (94520) *(P-15181)*
Bay Area Senior Services Inc ....C....650 579-5500
1 Baldwin Ave Ofc San Mateo (94401) *(P-17441)*
Bay Area Srgcal Spclsts Inc A ....C....925 350-4044
2637 Shadelands Dr Walnut Creek (94598) *(P-15290)*
Bay Area Systems Solutions Inc ....E....650 295-1600
390 Swift Ave Ste 12 South San Francisco (94080) *(P-1460)*
Bay Area Techworkers (PA) ....**A....925 359-2200**
2000 Crow Canyon Pl # 150 San Ramon (94583) *(P-12078)*
Bay Area Traffic Solutions Inc ....C....510 657-2543
44800 Industrial Dr Fremont (94538) *(P-14212)*
Bay Area Underpinning Inc (PA) ....**D....707 310-0602**
2333 Courage Dr Ste C Fairfield (94533) *(P-1851)*
Bay Area Video Coalition Inc ....D....415 861-3282
2727 Mariposa St Fl 2 San Francisco (94110) *(P-14801)*
Bay Area/Diablo Petroleum Co ....E....925 228-2222
1800 Sutter St Concord (94520) *(P-9530)*
Bay Associates Wire Tech Corp (HQ) ....**A....510 988-3800**
46840 Lakeview Blvd Fremont (94538) *(P-2981)*
Bay Bolt Inc ....F....510 532-1188
4610 Malat St Oakland (94601) *(P-8979)*
Bay Bread LLC ....D....415 440-0356
2325 Pine St San Francisco (94115) *(P-9440)*
Bay Center, Eureka *Also called Humboldt Cmnty Access Rsrce CT (P-17608)*
Bay Cities Crane & Rigging Inc (PA) ....**E....510 232-7222**
457 Parr Blvd Richmond (94801) *(P-12031)*
Bay Cities Pav & Grading Inc ....C....925 687-6666
1450 Civic Ct Ste 400 Concord (94520) *(P-1951)*
Bay Cities Refuse Service Inc ....D....510 237-4614
2525 Garden Tract Rd Richmond (94801) *(P-8306)*
Bay City Capital MGT LLC (PA) ....**C....415 676-3830**
3001 Bridgeway Sausalito (94965) *(P-9956)*
Bay City Flower Co (PA) ....**D....650 726-5535**
2265 Cabrillo Hwy S Half Moon Bay (94019) *(P-9626)*
Bay City Mechanical Inc (PA) ....**C....510 233-7000**
870 Harbour Way S Richmond (94804) *(P-1214)*
Bay Club America Inc ....C....415 781-1874
1 Lombard St Ste 201 San Francisco (94111) *(P-15054)*
Bay Club Golden Gateway LLC ....E....415 616-8800
370 Drumm St San Francisco (94111) *(P-15055)*
Bay Club Peninsula LLC ....E....650 593-2800
200 Redwood Shores Pkwy Redwood City (94065) *(P-15056)*
Bay Company, The, San Francisco *Also called Portco Inc (P-9161)*
Bay Contract Maintenance Inc ....E....650 737-5902
1129 Airport Blvd South San Francisco (94080) *(P-11925)*
Bay Counties Investments Inc ....E....510 538-8100
3501 Village Dr Castro Valley (94546) *(P-14885)*
Bay Counties Waste Svcs Inc ....D....408 565-9900
3355 Thomas Rd Santa Clara (95054) *(P-8307)*
Bay Dynamics Inc ....E....415 912-3130
1320 Ridder Park Dr San Jose (95131) *(P-12297)*
Bay East Assn Rltors Fundation ....E....925 730-4060
7901 Stoneridge Dr # 150 Pleasanton (94588) *(P-18391)*
Bay Elctrnic Spport Trnics Inc ....C....408 432-3222
2090 Fortune Dr San Jose (95131) *(P-5919)*
Bay Equipment Co Inc ....E....510 226-8800
44221 S Grimmer Blvd Fremont (94538) *(P-4874)*
Bay Federal Credit Union (PA) ....**D....831 479-6000**
3333 Clares St Capitola (95010) *(P-9775)*
Bay Grove Capital Group LLC (PA) ....**E....415 229-7953**
801 Montgomery St Fl 5 San Francisco (94133) *(P-10748)*
Bay Guardian Company ....E....415 255-3100
135 Micaicaippi St San Francisco (94107) *(P-3416)*
Bay Imaging Cons Med Group Inc (PA) ....**D....925 296-7150**
2125 Oak Grove Rd Ste 200 Walnut Creek (94598) *(P-15291)*
Bay Management, San Mateo *Also called Archives Management Corp (P-19298)*
Bay Marine & Indus Sup LLC ....E....510 337-9122
2900 Main St Alameda (94501) *(P-9188)*
Bay Marine Boatworks Inc ....E....510 237-0140
310 W Cutting Blvd Richmond (94804) *(P-14740)*
Bay Maritime Corp (PA) ....**E....510 337-9122**
2900 Main St Ste 2100 Alameda (94501) *(P-7717)*
Bay Meadows Racing Association ....C....650 573-4500
2600 S Delaware St San Mateo (94403) *(P-18299)*
Bay Medic Transportation Inc ....D....800 689-9511
959 Detroit Ave Concord (94518) *(P-7374)*
Bay Medical Management LLC ....C....925 296-7150
2125 Oak Grove Rd Ste 200 Walnut Creek (94598) *(P-15292)*
Bay Photo Inc ....C....831 475-6090
2959 Park Ave Ste A Soquel (95073) *(P-11672)*
Bay Point Control Inc ....E....510 614-3500
799 Thornton St San Leandro (94577) *(P-14682)*
Bay Polymers Corp ....E....510 490-1791
44530 S Grimmer Blvd Fremont (94538) *(P-8308)*
Bay Precision Machining Inc ....E....650 365-3010
815 Sweeney Ave Ste D Redwood City (94063) *(P-5482)*
Bay Print Solutions Inc ....F....408 579-6640
161 W San Fernando St San Jose (95113) *(P-3630)*
Bay Respite Care, Benicia *Also called Sonia Corina Inc (P-17181)*
Bay Ship & Yacht, Alameda *Also called Bay Maritime Corp (P-7717)*
Bay Ship & Yacht Co (PA) ....**C....510 337-9122**
2900 Main St Ste 2100 Alameda (94501) *(P-6638)*
Bay Sleep Clinic, Los Gatos *Also called Qualium Corp (P-15636)*
Bay Sport, Redwood City *Also called Bay Club Peninsula LLC (P-15056)*
Bay Standard Inc ....D....925 634-1181
24485 Marsh Creek Rd Brentwood (94513) *(P-9110)*
Bay Standard Manufacturing Inc (PA) ....**E....925 634-1181**
24485 Marsh Creek Rd Brentwood (94513) *(P-4871)*
Bay State Milling Company ....E....530 666-6565
360 Hanson Way Woodland (95776) *(P-2309)*
Bay Systems Consulting Inc (PA) ....**E....650 960-3310**
3600 W Byshore Rd Ste 204 Palo Alto (94303) *(P-13560)*
Bay Valley Medical Group Inc (PA) ....**D....510 785-5000**
319 Diablo Rd Ste 105 Danville (94526) *(P-15293)*
Bay Vave Service & Engineering ....D....925 849-8600
3948 Teal Ct Benicia (94510) *(P-14741)*
Bay View Hnters Pt Sbstnce Abu, San Francisco *Also called Bayview Hnters Pt Fndtion For (P-16994)*
Bay View Refuse & Recycling, Richmond *Also called Bay Cities Refuse Service Inc (P-8306)*
Bay View Rhbilitation Hosp LLC ....D....510 521-5600
516 Willow St Alameda (94501) *(P-15923)*
Bay Vista Senior Housing ....A....925 924-7100
6120 Stnrdge Mall Rd 3rd Pleasanton (94588) *(P-10418)*

Bay West Shwplace Invstors LLC (PA)....E....**415 490-5800**
2 Henry Adams St Ste 450 San Francisco (94103) ***(P-10377)***
Bay-TEC Engineering (PA)....D....**714 257-1680**
5130 Fulton Dr Ste X Fairfield (94534) ***(P-18637)***
Bayberry Inc....D....707 995-1643
15120 Lakeshore Dr C Clearlake (95422) ***(P-15924)***
Baybridge Employment Services, Eureka *Also called Humboldt Cmnty Access Rsrce CT* ***(P-17609)***
Baychildrens Physicians....E....510 428-3460
747 52nd St Oakland (94609) ***(P-15294)***
Baycorr Packaging LLC (PA)....C....**925 449-1148**
6850 Brisa St Livermore (94550) ***(P-3353)***
Bayer Cropscience, West Sacramento *Also called Agraquest Inc* ***(P-3836)***
Bayer Healthcare LLC....C....510 597-6150
5885 Hollis St Emeryville (94608) ***(P-3862)***
Bayer Healthcare LLC....C....510 705-7545
800 Dwight Way Berkeley (94710) ***(P-3863)***
Bayer Protective Services Inc....C....916 486-5800
3436 Amrcn Rver Dr Ste 10 Sacramento (95864) ***(P-14037)***
Bayfab Metals Inc....E....510 568-8950
870 Doolittle Dr San Leandro (94577) ***(P-4698)***
Baylands Soil Processing LLC (PA)....E....**415 956-4157**
712 Sansome St San Francisco (94111) ***(P-4137)***
Bayline, Union City *Also called Compro Packaging LLC* ***(P-3356)***
Baynetwork Inc (PA)....D....**650 561-8120**
961 Hamilton Ave Menlo Park (94025) ***(P-8674)***
Bayone Solutions....C....408 930-1600
4637 Chabot Dr Ste 250 Pleasanton (94588) ***(P-12298)***
Bayorg....D....415 623-5300
Embarcadero At Beach St San Francisco (94133) ***(P-18288)***
Baypoint Trading, San Francisco *Also called Btig LLC* ***(P-9959)***
Bayscape Management Inc....D....408 288-2940
1350 Pacific Ave Alviso (95002) ***(P-395)***
Bayshore Ambulance Inc (PA)....D....**650 525-9700**
370 Hatch Dr Foster City (94404) ***(P-7375)***
Bayshore Lights, San Francisco *Also called Ijk & Co Inc* ***(P-6525)***
Bayshore Metals....E....415 647-7981
4240 San Andres Way El Dorado Hills (95762) ***(P-8808)***
Bayside Insulation & Cnstr Inc....D....925 288-8960
1635 Challenge Dr Concord (94520) ***(P-828)***
Bayside Interiors Inc (PA)....C....**510 438-9171**
3220 Darby Cmn Fremont (94539) ***(P-1661)***
Bayspec Inc....E....408 512-5928
1101 Mckay Dr San Jose (95131) ***(P-6814)***
Baysport Inc....C....650 593-2800
200 Redwood Shores Pkwy Redwood City (94065) ***(P-15295)***
Baysport Physical Therapy, Redwood City *Also called Baysport Inc* ***(P-15295)***
Baytech Webs Inc....E....408 533-8519
1798 Tech Dr Ste 178 San Jose (95110) ***(P-13695)***
Bayview Demolition Svcs Inc....E....510 544-5270
6925 San Leandro St Oakland (94621) ***(P-1979)***
Bayview Engrg & Cnstr Co Inc....D....916 939-8986
5040 Rbert J Mathews Pkwy El Dorado Hills (95762) ***(P-1215)***
Bayview Environmental Svcs Inc....C....510 562-6181
6925 San Leandro St Oakland (94621) ***(P-2010)***
Bayview General Engrg Inc....E....925 447-6600
658 N L St Livermore (94551) ***(P-1015)***
Bayview Hnters Pt Fndtion For....E....415 822-8200
1625 Carroll Ave San Francisco (94124) ***(P-16994)***
Bayview Hunters Point YMCA, San Francisco *Also called Young MNS Chrstn Assn San Frnc* ***(P-18524)***
Bayview Plastic Solutions Inc....E....510 360-0001
43651 S Grimmer Blvd Fremont (94538) ***(P-4263)***
Bayview Services Inc (PA)....E....**510 562-6181**
6925 San Leandro St Oakland (94621) ***(P-1980)***
Bayview Villa....E....650 596-3489
777 Bay View Dr San Carlos (94070) ***(P-18061)***
Baywood Cellars Inc....E....415 606-4640
5573 W Woodbridge Rd Lodi (95242) ***(P-2510)***
Baywood Court (PA)....C....**510 733-2102**
21966 Dolores St Apt 143 Castro Valley (94546) ***(P-16854)***
Baywood Court Retirement Ctr, Castro Valley *Also called Baywood Court* ***(P-16854)***
Baywood Golf and Country Club....D....707 822-3686
3600 Buttermilk Ln Arcata (95521) ***(P-15057)***
Bb Franchising LLC....D....510 817-2786
1777 N Calif Blvd Ste 330 Walnut Creek (94596) ***(P-10803)***
BB&T Insurance Svcs Cal Inc (HQ)....E....**925 463-9672**
4480 Willow Rd Pleasanton (94588) ***(P-10245)***
Bbam Arcft Holdings 139 Labuan, San Francisco *Also called Bbam US LP* ***(P-9957)***
Bbam US LP....B....415 267-1600
50 California St Fl 14 San Francisco (94111) ***(P-9957)***
Bbcert....E....480 220-3799
510 Hwy 1 Bodega Bay (94923) ***(P-19453)***
Bbhs, San Francisco *Also called Baart Behavioral Hlth Svcs Inc* ***(P-16991)***
Bbt Health LLC....D....559 248-0131
5105 E Dakota Ave Fresno (93727) ***(P-16855)***
Bbva USA....C....925 947-3434
2536 N Main St Ste 100 Walnut Creek (94597) ***(P-9768)***
Bbva USA....C....209 239-1381
201 N Main St Manteca (95336) ***(P-9708)***
Bbva USA....C....209 473-6925
2427 W Hammer Ln Stockton (95209) ***(P-9709)***
Bbva USA....C....209 939-3288
202 N Hunter St Stockton (95202) ***(P-9710)***
Bcci Builders, San Francisco *Also called Bcci Construction LLC* ***(P-829)***
Bcci Construction LLC (HQ)....C....**415 817-5100**
1160 Battery St Ste 250 San Francisco (94111) ***(P-829)***
Bcj Sand and Rock Inc....F....707 544-0303
3388 Regional Pkwy Ste A Santa Rosa (95403) ***(P-601)***
BCM Construction Company Inc....E....530 342-1722
2990 California 32 Chico (95973) ***(P-789)***
BCT Consulting Inc (PA)....E....**559 579-1400**
7910 N Ingram Ave Ste 101 Fresno (93711) ***(P-13853)***
Bd Biscnces Systems Rgents Inc....C....408 518-5024
2350 Qume Dr San Jose (95131) ***(P-3781)***
Bdg Innovations LLC (PA)....E....**855 725-9555**
6001 Outfall Cir Sacramento (95828) ***(P-18638)***
Bdp Bowl Inc....D....650 878-0300
900 King Plz Daly City (94015) ***(P-14886)***
BDS Plumbing Inc....E....925 939-1004
2125 Youngs Ct Walnut Creek (94596) ***(P-1216)***
Bea Systems Inc (HQ)....A....**650 506-7000**
2315 N 1st St San Jose (95131) ***(P-12299)***
Beach House Ht - Half Moon Bay, Half Moon Bay *Also called Pacific Beach House LLC* ***(P-11343)***
Beach Retreat & Lodge At Tahoe, South Lake Tahoe *Also called Lcof Lake Tahoe Operating LLC* ***(P-11259)***
Beachcomber Motel, Fort Bragg *Also called Rap Investors LP* ***(P-11383)***
Beacon Communities, Inc., Pleasanton *Also called Humangood Affordable Housing* ***(P-19352)***
Beacon Restaurant, South Lake Tahoe *Also called Richardson Camp Resort Inc* ***(P-11593)***
Beam "easy Living" Center, Grass Valley *Also called Beam Vacuums California Inc* ***(P-1461)***
Beam Dynamics Inc....E....408 764-4805
5100 Patrick Henry Dr Santa Clara (95054) ***(P-5089)***
Beam On Technology Corporation....E....408 982-0161
317 Brokaw Rd Santa Clara (95050) ***(P-5226)***
Beam Vacuums California Inc....E....916 564-3279
422 Henderson St Grass Valley (95945) ***(P-1461)***
Beamery Inc (PA)....D....**866 473-7136**
353 Sacramento St Ste 800 San Francisco (94111) ***(P-13011)***
BEANSTALK, Sacramento *Also called BJ Jrdan Child Care Prgrams* ***(P-17863)***
Bear Creek Winery, Lodi *Also called Goldstone Land Company LLC* ***(P-2602)***
Bear Flag Marketing Corp....C....415 899-8466
7599 Redwood Blvd Ste 200 Novato (94945) ***(P-16856)***
Bear River Casino....C....707 733-9644
11 Bear Paws Way Loleta (95551) ***(P-10946)***
Bear River Casino (PA)....D....**707 733-9644**
27 Bear River Dr Loleta (95551) ***(P-10947)***
Bear River Casino Hotel, Loleta *Also called Bear River Casino* ***(P-10946)***
Bear River Gaming Agency, Loleta *Also called Bear River Casino* ***(P-10947)***
Bear River Lake Resort Inc....E....209 295-4868
40800 State Highway 88 Pioneer (95666) ***(P-10948)***
Bear Valley Mountain Resort, Bear Valley *Also called Bear Valley Ski Co* ***(P-15182)***
Bear Valley Ski Co....B....209 753-2301
2280 State Rte 207 Bear Valley (95223) ***(P-15182)***
Beards Custom Cabinets, Redding *Also called David Beard* ***(P-3178)***
Bears For Humanity Inc....E....866 325-1668
841 Ocean View Ave San Mateo (94401) ***(P-4122)***
Beats Music LLC....D....415 590-5104
235 2nd St San Francisco (94105) ***(P-13012)***
Beau Pre Corporation....E....707 839-2342
1777 Norton Rd McKinleyville (95519) ***(P-15058)***
Beau Pre Golf Course, McKinleyville *Also called Beau Pre Corporation* ***(P-15058)***
Beau Wine Tours, Sonoma *Also called Appellation Tours Inc* ***(P-7814)***
Beaulieu Vineyard, Rutherford *Also called Diageo North America Inc* ***(P-2768)***
Beauty Bazar Inc....D....650 326-8522
36 Stanford Shopping Ctr Palo Alto (94304) ***(P-11675)***
Beauty Craft Furniture Corp....E....916 428-2238
3316 51st Ave Sacramento (95823) ***(P-3274)***
Beaver Dam Health Care Center....E....559 834-2542
1306 E Sumner Ave Fowler (93625) ***(P-15925)***
Beaver Dam Health Care Center....E....707 546-0471
1221 Rosemarie Ln Stockton (95207) ***(P-15926)***
Beaver Dam Health Care Center....E....559 275-4785
925 N Cornelia Ave Fresno (93706) ***(P-15927)***
Beaver Dam Health Care Center....E....408 356-8136
14966 Terreno De Flores Los Gatos (95032) ***(P-15928)***
Beaver Dam Health Care Center....E....559 226-9401
2984 N Maroa Ave Fresno (93704) ***(P-15929)***
Beaver Dam Health Care Center....E....209 368-0693
950 S Fairmont Ave Lodi (95240) ***(P-15930)***
Beaver Dam Health Care Center....E....707 546-0471
4650 Hoen Ave Santa Rosa (95405) ***(P-15931)***
Beaver Dam Health Care Center....E....408 366-6510
5425 Mayme Ave San Jose (95129) ***(P-15932)***
Beaver Dam Health Care Center....E....707 763-4109
217 Lakeville St Apt 3 Petaluma (94952) ***(P-15933)***
Beaver Dam Health Care Center....E....559 673-9278
1700 Howard Rd Madera (93637) ***(P-15934)***
Beaver Dam Health Care Center....E....408 923-7232
401 Ridge Vista Ave San Jose (95127) ***(P-15935)***
Beaver Dam Health Care Center....E....559 222-4807
3510 E Shields Ave Fresno (93726) ***(P-15936)***
Beaver Dam Health Care Center....E....559 299-2591
111 Barstow Ave Clovis (93612) ***(P-15937)***
Beaver Dam Health Care Center....E....559 227-5383
3672 N 1st St Fresno (93726) ***(P-15938)***
Beaver Dam Health Care Center....E....559 638-3577
1090 E Dinuba Ave Reedley (93654) ***(P-15939)***
Beaver Dam Health Care Center....E....209 548-0318
1900 Coffee Rd Modesto (95355) ***(P-15940)***
Beaver Dam Health Care Center....E....408 356-9151
350 De Soto Dr Los Gatos (95032) ***(P-15941)***
Beaver Dam Health Care Center....E....209 466-3522
2740 N California St Stockton (95204) ***(P-15942)***

ALPHABETIC

Beaver Dam Health Care Center.....E.....707 938-1096
678 2nd St W Sonoma (95476) *(P-15943)*
Beaver Dam Health Care Center.....E.....530 343-6084
188 Cohasset Ln Chico (95926) *(P-15944)*
Beaver Dam Health Care Center.....E.....209 862-2862
709 N St Newman (95360) *(P-15945)*
Bebop Sensors Inc (PA).....**E.....503 875-4990**
970 Miller Ave Berkeley (94708) *(P-2980)*
Bechtel, Livermore *Also called National Security Tech LLC (P-18776)*
Bechtel Capital MGT Corp.....D.....415 768-1234
50 Beale St San Francisco (94105) *(P-19302)*
Beckmann's Bakery, Santa Cruz *Also called Beckmanns Old World Bakery Ltd (P-2365)*
Beckmanns Old World Bakery Ltd.....D.....831 423-9242
1053 17th Ave Santa Cruz (95062) *(P-2365)*
Becks Motor Lodge.....E.....415 621-8212
2222 Market St San Francisco (94114) *(P-10949)*
Becton Dickinson and Company.....B.....408 432-9475
2350 Qume Dr San Jose (95131) *(P-6952)*
Bed and Breakfast, Mendocino *Also called Maccallum House Restaurant (P-11280)*
Bedrosian's Tiles & Stone, Fresno *Also called Paragon Industries Inc (P-4519)*
Bee Content Design Inc.....D.....888 962-4587
450 Townsend St San Francisco (94107) *(P-13013)*
Beechwood Computing Limited (PA).....**C.....408 496-2900**
4677 Old Ironsides Dr Santa Clara (95054) *(P-13854)*
Beeline Group LLC.....D.....510 477-5400
30941 San Clemente St Hayward (94544) *(P-7219)*
Beer Beer & More Beer, Pittsburg *Also called Moreflavor Inc (P-9081)*
Beezwax Datatools Inc.....E.....510 835-4483
200 Frank H Ogawa Plz 7th Oakland (94612) *(P-12300)*
Beezy Inc (PA).....**D.....510 567-7110**
548 Market St 76279 San Francisco (94104) *(P-13561)*
Begovic Industries Inc.....E.....650 594-2861
1725 Old County Rd San Carlos (94070) *(P-5483)*
Behavior Frontiers LLC.....E.....310 856-0800
4030 Moorpark Ave Ste 105 San Jose (95117) *(P-16995)*
Behavioral Intervention Assn.....E.....510 652-7445
2354 Powell St A Emeryville (94608) *(P-12161)*
Behaviosec USA Inc.....E.....833 248-6732
535 Mission St Fl 14 San Francisco (94105) *(P-13014)*
Behavral Edctl Strtgies Trning.....E.....209 579-9444
2630 W Rumble Rd Modesto (95350) *(P-19728)*
Behavrl/Dctnal Strtgs/Training, Modesto *Also called Behavral Edctl Strtgies Trning (P-19728)*
Beigene Usa Inc.....D.....619 733-1842
1900 Powell St Ste 500 Emeryville (94608) *(P-14213)*
Beigene Usa Inc.....D.....877 828-5568
2955 Campus Dr Fl 2 San Mateo (94403) *(P-3864)*
Beko Radiator Cores LLC.....F.....925 671-2975
2322 Bates Ave Ste A Concord (94520) *(P-6574)*
Bel Air Market 501, Sacramento *Also called Bel Air Mart (P-2367)*
Bel Air Market 502, Sacramento *Also called Bel Air Mart (P-2413)*
Bel Air Market 509, Roseville *Also called Bel Air Mart (P-2366)*
Bel Air Market 510, Sacramento *Also called Bel Air Mart (P-2368)*
Bel Air Market 525, Elk Grove *Also called Bel Air Mart (P-9843)*
Bel Air Mart.....C.....916 786-6101
1039 Sunrise Ave Roseville (95661) *(P-2366)*
Bel Air Mart.....C.....916 714-6996
9435 Elk Grove Blvd Elk Grove (95624) *(P-9843)*
Bel Air Mart.....C.....916 739-8647
6231 Fruitridge Rd Sacramento (95820) *(P-2367)*
Bel Air Mart.....C.....916 920-2493
1540 W El Camino Ave Sacramento (95833) *(P-2368)*
Bel Air Mart.....C.....916 972-0555
4320 Arden Way Sacramento (95864) *(P-2413)*
Bel Aire Engineering Inc.....F.....510 538-6950
22740 Alice St Hayward (94541) *(P-8809)*
Bel Power Solutions Inc.....A.....866 513-2839
2390 Walsh Ave Santa Clara (95051) *(P-6377)*
Belcampo Group Inc.....D.....530 842-5200
329 N Phillipe Ln Yreka (96097) *(P-11707)*
Belcampo Group Inc (PA).....**D.....510 250-7810**
65 Webster St Oakland (94607) *(P-242)*
Belcampo Meat, Yreka *Also called Belcampo Group Inc (P-11707)*
Belco Cabinets Inc.....F.....209 334-5437
1109 Black Diamond Way Lodi (95240) *(P-4699)*
Belkasoft LLC.....E.....650 272-0384
702 San Conrado Ter # 1 Sunnyvale (94085) *(P-13015)*
Bell Electrical Supply Inc (PA).....**E.....408 727-2355**
316 Mathew St Santa Clara (95050) *(P-8845)*
Bell Products Inc.....D.....707 255-1811
722 Soscol Ave NAPA (94559) *(P-1217)*
Bell Sports Inc (HQ).....**D.....469 417-6600**
5550 Scotts Valley Dr Scotts Valley (95066) *(P-7188)*
Bell-Carter Foods Inc.....E.....209 549-5939
4207 Finch Rd Modesto (95357) *(P-2212)*
Bell-Carter Foods LLC (PA).....**B.....209 549-5939**
590 Ygnacio Valley Rd # 300 Walnut Creek (94596) *(P-2213)*
Bell-Carter Foods LLC.....B.....530 528-4820
1012 2nd St Corning (96021) *(P-2276)*
Bell-Carter Olive Company, Walnut Creek *Also called Bell-Carter Foods LLC (P-2213)*
Bell-Carter Olive Packing Co, Corning *Also called Bell-Carter Foods LLC (P-2276)*
Bell-Carter Packaging, Modesto *Also called Bell-Carter Foods Inc (P-2212)*
Bella Circus.....E.....415 205-8355
231 Mullen Ave San Francisco (94110) *(P-14836)*
Bella Terra Technologies Inc.....D.....650 316-6660
1600 Amphitheatre Pkwy Mountain View (94043) *(P-8070)*
Bella Viva Orchards Inc.....F.....209 883-9015
7030 Hughson Ave Hughson (95326) *(P-147)*
Bellabeat Inc.....E.....415 317-6153
16 Merced Ave San Francisco (94127) *(P-7208)*
Bellagrace Vineyards (PA).....**E.....209 681-2103**
22715 Upton Rd Plymouth (95669) *(P-44)*
Bellavista Landscape Svcs Inc (PA).....**D.....408 410-6000**
1165 Lincoln Ave Ste 200 San Jose (95125) *(P-396)*
Bellevue Club.....D.....510 451-1000
525 Bellevue Ave Oakland (94610) *(P-18392)*
Bellevue Un Elmentary Schl Dst (PA).....**E.....707 542-5197**
3150 Education Dr Santa Rosa (95407) *(P-19303)*
Bellingham Marine Inds Inc.....E.....707 678-2385
8810 Sparling Ln Dixon (95620) *(P-1150)*
Bells Haldsburg Ambulance Svc.....E.....707 433-1114
438 Powell Ave Healdsburg (95448) *(P-7376)*
Belmont Bruns Construction Inc.....D.....408 977-1708
1125 Mabury Rd San Jose (95133) *(P-830)*
Belmont Car Wash, Fresno *Also called Swartout Inc (P-14652)*
Belmont Corporation.....D.....530 542-1101
901 Park Ave South Lake Tahoe (96150) *(P-10950)*
Belmont Hlls Memory Care Cmnty, Belmont *Also called Silverado Senior Living Inc (P-16121)*
Belmont Oaks Academy.....D.....650 593-6175
2200 Carlmont Dr Belmont (94002) *(P-17858)*
Bema Electronic Mfg Inc.....D.....510 490-7770
4545 Cushing Pkwy Fremont (94538) *(P-5920)*
Ben Myerson Candy Co Inc.....D.....510 236-2233
912 Harbour Way S Richmond (94804) *(P-9567)*
Benchmark Elec Mfg Sltions Inc (HQ).....**D.....805 222-1303**
5550 Hellyer Ave San Jose (95138) *(P-5921)*
Benchmark Thermal, Grass Valley *Also called Manufacturers Coml Fin LLC (P-4631)*
Benchmark Thermal Corporation.....D.....530 477-5011
13185 Nevada City Ave Grass Valley (95945) *(P-4625)*
Benchmark Wine Group Inc.....E.....707 255-3500
445 Devlin Rd NAPA (94558) *(P-9568)*
Benda Tool & Model Works Inc.....E.....510 741-3170
900 Alfred Nobel Dr Hercules (94547) *(P-5081)*
Beneficent Technology Inc.....E.....650 644-3400
480 California Ave # 201 Palo Alto (94306) *(P-14214)*
Benefit & Risk Management Svcs.....C.....916 467-1200
80 Iron Point Cir Ste 200 Folsom (95630) *(P-10246)*
Benefit Cosmetics LLC (HQ).....**D.....415 781-8153**
225 Bush St Fl 20 San Francisco (94104) *(P-9224)*
Benefitstreet Inc.....D.....925 831-0800
12677 Alcosta Blvd San Ramon (94583) *(P-10247)*
Benetech, Palo Alto *Also called Beneficent Technology Inc (P-14214)*
Benetech Inc (PA).....**D.....916 484-6811**
3841 N Freeway Blvd # 185 Sacramento (95834) *(P-10248)*
Benicia Fabrication & Mch Inc.....C.....707 745-8111
101 E Channel Rd Benicia (94510) *(P-4712)*
Benicia Herald, Benicia *Also called Gibson Printing & Pubg Inc (P-3441)*
Benicia Plumbing Inc.....D.....707 745-2930
265 W Channel Rd Benicia (94510) *(P-1218)*
Benjamin Holt Sport Club, Stockton *Also called 24 Hour Fitness Usa Inc (P-14919)*
Bennathon Corp (PA).....**E.....916 405-2100**
10278 Iron Rock Way Elk Grove (95624) *(P-831)*
Bennett Ranch, Firebaugh *Also called JFB Ranch Inc (P-175)*
Bennett's Bakery, Sacramento *Also called Bennetts Baking Company (P-2420)*
Bennetts Baking Company.....F.....916 481-3349
2530 Tesla Way Sacramento (95825) *(P-2420)*
Bentec Medical Opco LLC.....E.....530 406-3333
1380 E Beamer St Woodland (95776) *(P-6953)*
Bentek Corporation.....D.....408 954-9600
1991 Senter Rd San Jose (95112) *(P-6401)*
Bentek Solar, San Jose *Also called Bentek Corporation (P-6401)*
Bentley Systems Incorporated.....D.....925 933-2525
1600 Riviera Ave Ste 300 Walnut Creek (94596) *(P-12301)*
Bento Merge Enterprises, San Francisco *Also called Bento Technologies Inc (P-13016)*
Bento Technologies Inc.....E.....415 887-2028
221 Main St Ste 1325 San Francisco (94105) *(P-13016)*
Benton Enterprises LLC.....E.....559 664-0800
18252 Avenue 20 Madera (93637) *(P-83)*
Benz Engineering, Fremont *Also called Compressed A Benz Systems Inc (P-5182)*
Benziger Family Winery, Glen Ellen *Also called Bfw Associates LLC (P-2511)*
Berber Food Manufacturing Inc.....C.....510 553-0444
10115 Iron Rock Way Ste 1 Elk Grove (95624) *(P-2870)*
Berberian Bros Inc.....D.....209 944-5514
3755 West Ln Stockton (95204) *(P-14548)*
Berding & Weil LLP (PA).....**D.....925 838-2090**
2175 N Calif Blvd Ste 500 Walnut Creek (94596) *(P-17210)*
Beresford Arms, The, San Francisco *Also called Beresford Corporation (P-10951)*
Beresford Corporation.....E.....415 673-9900
635 Sutter St San Francisco (94102) *(P-10951)*
Berg Injury Lawyers, Alameda *Also called Berg William L Attorney At Law (P-17211)*
Berg William L Attorney At Law (PA).....**E.....510 523-3200**
2440 Santa Clara Ave Alameda (94501) *(P-17211)*
Bergelectric Corp.....D.....916 636-1880
11333 Sunrise Park Dr Rancho Cordova (95742) *(P-1462)*
Berger Steel Corporation.....E.....916 640-8778
4728 Kilzer Ave 692 McClellan (95652) *(P-4646)*
Bergerson Group.....D.....925 948-8110
1030 Country Club Dr B Moraga (94556) *(P-19454)*
Berk Street Enterprises Inc.....D.....916 370-6179
2377 Gold Meadow Way # 100 Gold River (95670) *(P-16857)*
Berke Door & Hardware Inc.....F.....916 452-7331
8255 Belvedere Ave Sacramento (95826) *(P-8529)*
Berkel & Company Contrs Inc.....D.....415 495-3627
81 Langton St Unit 15 San Francisco (94103) *(P-1852)*

Berkeley......E......510 845-7300
2086 Allston Way Berkeley (94704) *(P-10952)*
Berkeley Albany YMCA, Concord *Also called Young MNS Chrstn Assn of E Bay (P-18490)*
Berkeley Cement Inc......C......510 525-8175
1200 6th St Berkeley (94710) *(P-1853)*
Berkeley Communications Corp......E......510 644-1599
801 Addison St Berkeley (94710) *(P-13855)*
Berkeley Community Health Prj......E......510 548-2570
2339 Durant Ave Berkeley (94704) *(P-16858)*
Berkeley Concrete Pumping, Berkeley *Also called Fadelli Concrete Pumping (P-1868)*
Berkeley Country Club......C......510 233-7550
7901 Cutting Blvd El Cerrito (94530) *(P-15059)*
Berkeley Design Automation Inc......E......408 496-6600
46871 Bayside Pkwy Fremont (94538) *(P-6066)*
Berkeley Dog & Cat Hosp Inc......D......510 848-5041
2126 Haste St Berkeley (94704) *(P-323)*
Berkeley Downtown Ht Owner LLC......D......510 982-2100
2121 Center St Berkeley (94704) *(P-10953)*
Berkeley Electronic Press, Berkeley *Also called Internet-Journals LLC (P-13918)*
Berkeley Emrgncy Med Group Inc......D......925 962-1067
2000 Crow Canyon Pl San Ramon (94583) *(P-17104)*
Berkeley Forge & Tool, Berkeley *Also called Bierwith Forge & Tool Inc (P-4875)*
BERKELEY FREE CLINIC, Berkeley *Also called Berkeley Community Health Prj (P-16858)*
Berkeley Lights Inc (PA)......C......510 858-2855
5858 Horton St Ste 320 Emeryville (94608) *(P-6815)*
Berkeley Mills, Berkeley *Also called Berkeley Mllwk & Furn Co Inc (P-3275)*
Berkeley Mllwk & Furn Co Inc......E......510 549-2854
2830 7th St Berkeley (94710) *(P-3275)*
Berkeley Montessori School Inc......D......510 843-9374
2030 Francisco St Berkeley (94709) *(P-17859)*
Berkeley Nutritional Mfg Corp......D......925 243-6300
1852 Rutan Dr Livermore (94551) *(P-19153)*
Berkeley Pediatric Med Group......E......510 848-2566
1650 Walnut St Berkeley (94709) *(P-15296)*
Berkeley Pines Care Center, Berkeley *Also called A T Associates Inc (P-16213)*
Berkeley Repertory Theatre (PA)......D......510 204-8901
2025 Addison St Berkeley (94704) *(P-14837)*
Berkeley Sport Club, Berkeley *Also called 24 Hour Fitness Usa Inc (P-14922)*
Berkeley Student Coop Inc......D......510 848-1936
2424 Ridge Rd Berkeley (94709) *(P-11624)*
Berkeley Symphony Orchestra......E......510 841-2800
1919 Addison St Ste 104 Berkeley (94704) *(P-14869)*
Berkeley Therapy Institute......D......510 841-8484
1749 Mrtin Lther King Jr Berkeley (94709) *(P-15883)*
Berkeley Touchless Carwash, San Francisco *Also called Canadian American Oil Co Inc (P-14633)*
Berkeley Youth Alternatives (PA)......D......510 845-9010
1255 Allston Way Berkeley (94702) *(P-17442)*
Berkeleyside LLC......F......510 671-0380
2120 University Ave Berkeley (94704) *(P-3417)*
Berkely/Rchmond Jwish Cmnty Ct, Berkeley *Also called Jewish Cmnty Fdrtion of Grter (P-17622)*
Berkley Crdovascular Med Group......E......510 204-1691
2450 Ashby Ave Ste 2785 Berkeley (94705) *(P-15297)*
Berkshire Hathaway Homestates (HQ)......C......415 433-1650
1 California St Ste 600 San Francisco (94111) *(P-10249)*
Berkshire Hathaway Inc......E......510 651-6500
43225 Mission Blvd Fremont (94539) *(P-10494)*
Berkwood Hedge School......D......510 883-6990
1809 Bancroft Way Berkeley (94703) *(P-17860)*
Berlin Food & Lab Equipment Co......E......650 589-4231
43 S Linden Ave South San Francisco (94080) *(P-6691)*
Berliner Cohen LLP......E......209 385-0700
2844 Park Ave Merced (95348) *(P-17212)*
Berliner Cohen LLP......E......209 576-1197
1601 I St Ste 150 Modesto (95354) *(P-17213)*
Berlogar Geotechnical Cons......E......925 484-0220
5587 Sunol Blvd Pleasanton (94566) *(P-18639)*
Bermad Inc (PA)......E......877 577-4283
3816 S Willow Ave Ste 101 Fresno (93725) *(P-4959)*
Bermad Control Valves, Fresno *Also called Bermad Inc (P-4959)*
Bernard Osher Mrin Jwish Cmnty......C......415 444-8000
200 N San Pedro Rd San Rafael (94903) *(P-17443)*
Bernstein Orthodontics, Santa Rosa *Also called Rael Bernstein DDS A Prof Corp (P-15855)*
Berrett-Koehler Publishers Inc (PA)......F......510 817-2277
1333 Broadway Ste 1000 Oakland (94612) *(P-3523)*
Berryman Health Inc......E......707 462-8864
1349 S Dora St Ukiah (95482) *(P-15946)*
Berrys Sawmill Inc......E......707 865-2365
405 Cazadero Hwy Cazadero (95421) *(P-3090)*
Bersin By Deloitte, San Francisco *Also called Deloitte Consulting LLP (P-19489)*
Bert E Jessup Transportation......D......408 848-3390
641 Old Gilroy St Gilroy (95020) *(P-7507)*
Bert Williams and Sons Inc......E......707 255-7003
525 Northbay Dr NAPA (94559) *(P-8442)*
Bertagna Orchards Inc......E......530 343-8014
3329 Hegan Ln Chico (95928) *(P-96)*
Bertetta Tanklines Inc......E......650 872-2900
1486 Huntington Ave # 300 South San Francisco (94080) *(P-7508)*
Bertolotti Disposal Inc......E......209 537-1500
231 Flamingo Dr Modesto (95358) *(P-8309)*
Bertram Capital Management LLC (PA)......C......650 358-5000
950 Tower Ln Ste 1000 Foster City (94404) *(P-10835)*
Bes Concrete Products, Tracy *Also called Bescal Inc (P-4419)*
Bescal Inc......E......209 836-3492
10304 W Linne Rd Tracy (95377) *(P-4419)*
Bespoke Inc......E......612 201-6800
3260 19th St San Francisco (94110) *(P-7137)*
Bess Testlab Inc......E......408 988-0101
2463 Tripaldi Way Hayward (94545) *(P-1089)*
Best Choice LLC......E......510 862-4989
22568 Mssion Blvd Ste 344 Hayward (94541) *(P-14215)*
BEST Consulting Inc......E......916 448-2050
8795 Folsom Blvd Ste 103 Sacramento (95826) *(P-19729)*
Best Contracting Services Inc......D......510 886-7240
4301 Bettencourt Way Union City (94587) *(P-1788)*
Best Electric, Merced *Also called Bestco Electric Inc (P-1464)*
Best Event Staffing Team, San Jose *Also called Ophelia Quinones (P-12186)*
Best Express Foods Inc......B......209 490-2612
1718 Boeing Way Ste 100 Stockton (95206) *(P-2369)*
Best Sanitizers Inc......D......530 265-1800
310 Prvdnce Mine Rd # 120 Nevada City (95959) *(P-4066)*
Best Supplement Guide LLC (PA)......E......209 366-2800
512 N Cherokee Ln Lodi (95240) *(P-14929)*
Best USA, West Sacramento *Also called Tomra Sorting Inc (P-8368)*
Best Value Textbooks LLC......E......800 646-7782
410 Hemsted Dr Ste 100 Redding (96002) *(P-3559)*
Best Western, South Lake Tahoe *Also called Belmont Corporation (P-10950)*
Best Western, Santa Rosa *Also called Bromley Properties Inc (P-10978)*
Best Western, Chico *Also called Emerald Investments Inc (P-11081)*
Best Western, Garberville *Also called Humboldt House Inn LLC (P-11176)*
Best Western, Aptos *Also called Seacliff Inn Inc (P-11448)*
Best Western, NAPA *Also called NAPA Motel and Restaurant (P-11321)*
Best Western, Milpitas *Also called West Coast Property Management (P-11570)*
Best Western, South San Francisco *Also called Grosvenor Properties Ltd (P-11122)*
Best Western, Stockton *Also called Atharwa Investments LLC (P-10935)*
Best Western, Fortuna *Also called Fortuna Country Inn Corp (P-11099)*
Best Western Amador Inn, Jackson *Also called Sita Ram LLC (P-11484)*
Best Western Bayshore Inn......E......707 268-8005
3500 Broadway Eureka (95503) *(P-10954)*
Best Western Civic Ctr Mtr Inn......E......415 621-2826
364 9th St San Francisco (94103) *(P-10955)*
Best Western Concord, Concord *Also called Heritage Invstmnts Concord LLC (P-11135)*
Best Western Country, Dunnigan *Also called Ankoor Financial Llc (P-10925)*
Best Western Dry Creek Inn, Healdsburg *Also called Dry Creek Inn Ltd Partnership (P-11062)*
Best Western Garden Court Inn, Fremont *Also called Thundrbird Ldge Frmont A Cal L (P-11532)*
Best Western Half Moon Bay, Half Moon Bay *Also called Pacifica Hotel Company (P-11350)*
Best Western Hillside Inn Mtl, Santa Rosa *Also called Hillside Inn Inc (P-11138)*
Best Western Hotel Tomo......E......415 921-4000
1800 Sutter St San Francisco (94115) *(P-10956)*
Best Western Inn Inc......E......831 438-6666
6020 Scotts Valley Dr Scotts Valley (95066) *(P-10957)*
Best Western Petaluma Inn, Petaluma *Also called Petaluma Properties Inc (P-11364)*
Best Western Plus-Heritage Inn......D......209 474-3301
111 E March Ln Stockton (95207) *(P-10958)*
Best Western Silicon Vly Inn......E......408 735-7800
600 N Mathilda Ave Sunnyvale (94085) *(P-10959)*
Best Western Tree Hse Mtr Inn, Mount Shasta *Also called Six CS Enterprises Inc (P-11487)*
Best Western-Bristol Hotel, San Jose *Also called Bristol Hotel (P-10974)*
Best Wstn El Rancho Inn Suites, Millbrae *Also called El Rancho Motel Inc (P-11076)*
Best Wstn Half Moon Bay Lodge, Half Moon Bay *Also called Half Moon Bay Lodge (P-11123)*
Best Wstn Plus Clnga Inn Sites, Coalinga *Also called Merchant Valley Corp (P-11296)*
Bestco Electric Inc (PA)......E......209 569-0120
1322 7th St Modesto (95354) *(P-1463)*
Bestco Electric Inc......E......209 723-2061
2160 Wardrobe Ave Merced (95341) *(P-1464)*
Bestek Manufacturing Inc......E......408 321-8834
675 Sycamore Dr Ste 170 Milpitas (95035) *(P-5350)*
Bestliving Care LLC......D......510 862-3508
2401 Merced St Ste 300 San Leandro (94577) *(P-16859)*
Bestronics, San Jose *Also called Bay Elctrnic Spport Trnics Inc (P-5919)*
Bestronics Holdings Inc (PA)......D......408 385-7777
2090 Fortune Dr San Jose (95131) *(P-6370)*
Beta Healthcare Group (PA)......E......925 838-6070
1443 Danville Blvd Alamo (94507) *(P-10082)*
Beta Partnership, Ukiah *Also called Alpha Analytical Labs Inc (P-19255)*
Betawave Corporation (PA)......E......415 738-8706
706 Mission St Fl 10 San Francisco (94103) *(P-13696)*
Bethany Adult Day Care, Ripon *Also called Bethany HM Soc San Jquin Cnty (P-15947)*
Bethany HM Soc San Jquin Cnty......D......209 599-7670
368 S Wilma Ave Ripon (95366) *(P-15947)*
Bethel Church of San Jose......D......408 246-6790
1201 S Winchester Blvd San Jose (95128) *(P-17861)*
Bethel Lutheran Home Inc......D......559 896-4900
2280 Dockery Ave Selma (93662) *(P-16218)*
Bethel Pre School, San Jose *Also called Bethel Church of San Jose (P-17861)*
Bethel Rtrment Cmnty A Cal Ltd......E......209 577-1901
2345 Scenic Dr Ofc C Modesto (95355) *(P-16219)*
Bettendorf Enterprises Inc (PA)......E......707 822-0173
4545 West End Rd Arcata (95521) *(P-7509)*
Bettendorf Trucking, Arcata *Also called Bettendorf Enterprises Inc (P-7509)*
Better Builders Cnstr Inc......E......530 589-2574
5263 Royal Oaks Dr Oroville (95966) *(P-617)*
Better Built Truss Inc......E......209 869-4545
251 E 4th St Ripon (95366) *(P-3201)*
Better Business Bureau Inc......E......510 844-2000
1000 Broadway Ste 625 Oakland (94607) *(P-18300)*
Better Chance, A, Pinole *Also called Califrnia Atism Foundation Inc (P-18222)*

ALPHABETIC

Better Cleaning Systems Inc ....E.......559 673-5700
1122 Maple St Madera (93637) ***(P-5707)***
Better Homes and Gardens, Walnut Creek *Also called Mason-Mcduffie Real Estate Inc* ***(P-10614)***
Better Therapeutics Inc....................E.......415 887-2311
548 Market St 49404 San Francisco (94104) ***(P-3865)***
Better Way Fster Fmly Adption....................E.......510 601-0203
3200 Adeline St Berkeley (94703) ***(P-17444)***
Betterup Inc (PA)....................B.......415 862-0708**
1200 Folsom St San Francisco (94103) ***(P-19455)***
Betts Company (PA) ....D.......559 498-3304**
2843 S Maple Ave Fresno (93725) ***(P-4964)***
Betts Company....................D.......209 599-1824
3025 E Palm Ave Ste 104 Manteca (95337) ***(P-4956)***
Betts Company....................F.......559 498-8624
2867 S Maple Ave Fresno (93725) ***(P-6564)***
Betts Spring Manufacturing, Fresno *Also called Betts Company* ***(P-4964)***
Betty K Ng....................E.......415 364-7600
1490 Mason St San Francisco (94133) ***(P-15298)***
Beutler Heating & AC, Fairfield *Also called Villara Corporation* ***(P-1844)***
Beutler Heating & AC, Manteca *Also called Villara Corporation* ***(P-1392)***
Beveled Edge Inc....................F.......408 467-9900
1740 Junction Ave Ste D San Jose (95112) ***(P-4384)***
Beverly, Fowler *Also called Beaver Dam Health Care Center* ***(P-15925)***
Beverly, Fresno *Also called Beaver Dam Health Care Center* ***(P-15929)***
Beverly, San Jose *Also called Beaver Dam Health Care Center* ***(P-15932)***
Beverly Healthcare, Los Gatos *Also called Beaver Dam Health Care Center* ***(P-15928)***
Beverly Healthcare, Lodi *Also called Beaver Dam Health Care Center* ***(P-15930)***
Beverly Healthcare, Madera *Also called Beaver Dam Health Care Center* ***(P-15934)***
Beverly Healthcare, Fresno *Also called Beaver Dam Health Care Center* ***(P-15938)***
Beverly Healthcare, Modesto *Also called Beaver Dam Health Care Center* ***(P-15940)***
Beverly Healthcare, Los Gatos *Also called Beaver Dam Health Care Center* ***(P-15941)***
Beverly Healthcare, Chico *Also called Beaver Dam Health Care Center* ***(P-15944)***
Beverly Healthcare, Newman *Also called Beaver Dam Health Care Center* ***(P-15945)***
Bevill Vineyard Management LLC ....E.......707 433-1101
4724 Dry Creek Rd Healdsburg (95448) ***(P-45)***
Beyond Emancipation....................E.......510 667-7694
675 Hegenberger Rd # 100 Oakland (94621) ***(P-18062)***
Beyond Pool Care Inc (PA) ....D.......707 535-6463**
7911 Redwood Dr Ste 201 Cotati (94931) ***(P-14216)***
Beyond Security Inc....................D.......279 201-7150
2267 Lava Ridge Ct # 100 Roseville (95661) ***(P-8896)***
Beyondid Inc....................D.......415 878-6210
535 Mission St Fl 14 San Francisco (94105) ***(P-13856)***
BFI Waste Systems N Amer Inc....................E.......408 432-1234
1601 Dixon Landing Rd Milpitas (95035) ***(P-7452)***
Bfl Transportation LLC (PA)....................E.......510 727-0900**
29393 Pacific St Hayward (94544) ***(P-1016)***
Bfp Fire Protection Inc ....D.......831 461-1100
17 Janis Way Scotts Valley (95066) ***(P-1219)***
Bfw Associates LLC (HQ)....................E.......707 935-3000**
1883 London Ranch Rd Glen Ellen (95442) ***(P-2511)***
Bgm, San Jose *Also called Brilliant General Maint Inc* ***(P-11929)***
Bhandal Bros Inc ....E.......831 728-2691
2490 San Juan Rd Hollister (95023) ***(P-7510)***
Bhandal Bros Trucking Inc ....D.......831 728-2691
2490 San Juan Rd Hollister (95023) ***(P-7511)***
Bhatnagar Law Office....................E.......408 564-8051
84 W Santa Clara St # 560 San Jose (95113) ***(P-17214)***
Bhd Information Systems, Sacramento *Also called Big Hairy Dog Info Systems* ***(P-8675)***
Bhogart LLC....................E.......855 553-3887
1919 Monterey Hwy Ste 80 San Jose (95112) ***(P-9053)***
Bhr Operations LLC....................C.......415 771-9000
495 Bay St San Francisco (94133) ***(P-10960)***
Bhr Trs Tahoe LLC....................C.......530 562-3045
13031 Ritz Crlton Hghlnds Truckee (96161) ***(P-10961)***
Bi Cmos Foundry, Santa Clara *Also called Onspec Technology Partners Inc* ***(P-6244)***
Bi Warehousing Inc (PA) ....D.......916 624-0654**
5404 Pacific St Rocklin (95677) ***(P-8443)***
Bi Warehousing Inc ....D.......916 652-4433
3865 Taylor Rd Ste A Loomis (95650) ***(P-8444)***
Bi Warehousing Inc ....D.......916 624-0654
5404 Pacific St Ste B Rocklin (95677) ***(P-8445)***
Bi Warehousing Inc ....E.......530 671-8787
1490 Bridge St Yuba City (95993) ***(P-8446)***
Bi-County Ambulance Svc Inc....................E.......530 674-2780
1700 Poole Blvd Yuba City (95993) ***(P-7377)***
Bi-Jamar Inc ....E.......209 948-2104
2010 E Fremont St Stockton (95205) ***(P-1465)***
Bi-Rite Foodservice Distrs, Brisbane *Also called Bi-Rite Restaurant Sup Co Inc* ***(P-9262)***
Bi-Rite Restaurant Sup Co Inc....................B.......415 656-0187
123 S Hill Dr Brisbane (94005) ***(P-9262)***
Bianchi AG Services Inc (PA) ....C.......530 882-4575**
1210 Richvale Hwy Richvale (95974) ***(P-9032)***
Bianchi-Amaker, San Jose *Also called George Bianchi Cnstr Inc* ***(P-1647)***
Bianco Landscape Management....................D.......916 521-1314
1524 Vista Ridge Way Roseville (95661) ***(P-448)***
Biarca Inc (PA) ....D.......408 564-4465**
333 W San Carlos St # 600 San Jose (95110) ***(P-13857)***
Bibbero Systems Inc (HQ)....................E.......800 242-2376**
1425 N Mcdowell Blvd # 211 Petaluma (94954) ***(P-3631)***
Bickmore and Associates Inc (HQ) ....D.......916 244-1100**
1750 Creekside Oaks Dr # 200 Sacramento (95833) ***(P-10250)***
Bickmore Risk Svcs Consulting, Sacramento *Also called Bickmore and Associates Inc* ***(P-10250)***
Biddle Consulting Group Inc ....E.......916 294-4250
193 Blue Ravine Rd # 270 Folsom (95630) ***(P-19730)***
Bidgely, Sunnyvale *Also called Myenersave Inc* ***(P-13320)***
Bidwell Senior Care Svcs Inc ....D.......530 899-3585
966 Kovak Ct Chico (95973) ***(P-18063)***
Bidwell Title and Escrow Co (PA)....................E.......530 894-2612**
500 Wall St Chico (95928) ***(P-10195)***
Bien Padre Foods Inc ....F.......707 442-4585
1459 Railroad St Eureka (95501) ***(P-2196)***
Bierwith Forge & Tool Inc ....D.......510 526-5034
1331 Eastshore Hwy Berkeley (94710) ***(P-4875)***
Big Accessories, Petaluma *Also called Gmpc LLC* ***(P-7231)***
Big Basin Foods, Scotts Valley *Also called Tradin Organics USA LLC* ***(P-2948)***
Big C Athletic Club, Concord *Also called C Big Corporation* ***(P-14933)***
Big Creek Lumber Company (PA) ....D.......831 457-5015**
3564 Highway 1 Davenport (95017) ***(P-3091)***
Big D Products, Fairfield *Also called Drake Enterprises Incorporated* ***(P-3050)***
Big Four Restaurant, San Francisco *Also called Nob Hill Properties Inc* ***(P-11329)***
Big Fresno Fair, The, Fresno *Also called Twenty First District AG Assn* ***(P-15259)***
Big Hairy Dog Info Systems....................E.......916 368-3939
3205 Ramos Cir Sacramento (95827) ***(P-8675)***
Big Health Inc....................D.......415 867-3473
461 Bush St Ste 200 San Francisco (94108) ***(P-16170)***
Big Heart Pet Brands Inc (HQ)....................B.......415 247-3000**
1 Maritime Plz Fl 2 San Francisco (94111) ***(P-2333)***
Big Hill Logging & Rd Building (PA) ....E.......530 673-4155**
680 Sutter St Yuba City (95991) ***(P-3056)***
Big Joe California North Inc (PA)....................C.......510 785-6900**
25932 Eden Landing Rd Hayward (94545) ***(P-9054)***
Big Joe Handling Systems, Hayward *Also called Big Joe California North Inc* ***(P-9054)***
Big Lgue Dreams Consulting LLC ....C.......530 223-1177
20155 Viking Way Redding (96003) ***(P-15060)***
Big O Tires, Dublin *Also called CCM Partnership* ***(P-14608)***
Big O Tires, Woodland *Also called Tire Store 40 Inc* ***(P-14598)***
Big Oak Hardwood Floor Co Inc....................D.......650 591-8651
1731 Leslie St San Mateo (94402) ***(P-1766)***
Big Poppy Holdings Inc ....C.......707 636-9020
6580 Oakmont Dr Ste A Santa Rosa (95409) ***(P-9711)***
Big Poppy Holdings Inc ....C.......707 836-1588
9230 Old Redwood Hwy Windsor (95492) ***(P-9712)***
Big River Lodge, Mendocino *Also called Big River Ltd-Design* ***(P-10962)***
Big River Ltd-Design ....D.......707 937-5615
44850 Comptche Ukiah Rd Mendocino (95460) ***(P-10962)***
Big Sandy Rancheria, Auberry *Also called Mono Wind Casino* ***(P-11308)***
Big Switch Networks LLC ....C.......650 322-6510
5453 Great America Pkwy Santa Clara (95054) ***(P-13017)***
Big Valley Christian School, Modesto *Also called Big Valley Grace Cmnty Ch Inc* ***(P-17862)***
Big Valley Ford Inc....................C.......209 870-4400
3282 Auto Center Cir Stockton (95212) ***(P-14549)***
Big Valley Grace Cmnty Ch Inc (PA) ....C.......209 577-1604**
4040 Tully Rd Ste D Modesto (95356) ***(P-17862)***
Big Valley Metals LP ....F.......916 372-2383
620 Houston St Ste 1 West Sacramento (95691) ***(P-4647)***
BIG VALLEY MORTGAGE, Roseville *Also called American Pacific Mortgage Corp* ***(P-9890)***
Big-D Construction, Pleasanton *Also called Big-D Pacific Builders LP* ***(P-618)***
Big-D Pacific Builders LP....................D.......925 460-3232
6210 Stoneridge Mall Rd Pleasanton (94588) ***(P-618)***
Biggie Crane and Ritting, San Leandro *Also called Galena Equipment Rental LLC* ***(P-12021)***
Biggs Cardosa Associates Inc (PA) ....D.......408 296-5515**
865 The Alameda San Jose (95126) ***(P-18640)***
Bigham Taylor Roofing Corp ....D.......510 886-0197
22721 Alice St Hayward (94541) ***(P-1789)***
Bigstepcom ....C.......415 229-8500
2601 Mission St Ste 500 San Francisco (94110) ***(P-7934)***
Bill Brown Construction Co....................E.......408 297-3738
242 Phelan Ave San Jose (95112) ***(P-619)***
Bill Hamilton Roofing Inc ....E.......408 379-1303
230 Harrison Ave Campbell (95008) ***(P-1790)***
Bill Sharp Electrical Contr....................E.......530 338-1735
5136 Caterpillar Rd Redding (96003) ***(P-1466)***
Bill Wilson Center (PA)....................D.......408 243-0222**
3490 The Alameda Santa Clara (95050) ***(P-17445)***
Billcom LLC (HQ)....................C.......650 353-3301**
1800 Embarcadero Rd Palo Alto (94303) ***(P-13018)***
Billcom Holdings Inc (PA)....................B.......650 621-7700**
6220 America Center Dr # 100 San Jose (95002) ***(P-13019)***
Billet Transportation Inc (PA)....................E.......707 649-9200**
255 Lombard Rd Ste B American Canyon (94503) ***(P-7512)***
Billing & Registration, Oakland *Also called La Clinica De La Raza Inc* ***(P-17158)***
Billing Services Plus DBA Apex....................D.......415 604-3515
70 Dorman Ave San Francisco (94124) ***(P-11926)***
Billington Welding & Mfg Inc....................D.......209 526-0846
1442 N Emerald Ave Modesto (95351) ***(P-5125)***
Billiontoone Inc....................D.......650 666-6443
1035 Obrien Dr Menlo Park (94025) ***(P-16774)***
Bimbo Bakeries Usa Inc ....F.......209 825-8647
2007 N Main St Manteca (95336) ***(P-2370)***
Bimbo Bakeries Usa Inc ....F.......559 498-3632
1836 G St Fresno (93706) ***(P-2371)***
Binbin Windows Inc (PA)....................D.......415 282-1688**
272 Bay Shore Blvd San Francisco (94124) ***(P-8530)***
Binti Inc....................E.......844 424-6844
1212 Broadway Ste 200 Oakland (94612) ***(P-13020)***
Bio Behavioral Medical Clinics....................E.......559 437-1111
1060 W Sierra Ave 105 Fresno (93711) ***(P-15299)***
Bio-RAD Laboratories Inc (PA)....................A.......510 724-7000**
1000 Alfred Nobel Dr Hercules (94547) ***(P-6816)***
Bio-RAD Laboratories Inc ....A.......510 741-6916
225 Linus Pauling Dr Hercules (94547) ***(P-6817)***

Bio-Ved Pharmaceuticals Inc.....E.....408 432-4020
1929 Otoole Way San Jose (95131) *(P-19033)*
Biocare Medical LLC.....C.....925 603-8000
60 Berry Dr Pacheco (94553) *(P-6954)*
Biocentury Inc (PA).....E.....650 595-5333
1235 Radio Rd Ste 100 Redwood City (94065) *(P-3418)*
Biocheck Inc (HQ).....D.....650 573-1968
425 Eccles Ave South San Francisco (94080) *(P-6955)*
Bioclinica, San Mateo *Also called Synarc Inc (P-12840)*
Biocompare, South San Francisco *Also called Comparenetworks Inc (P-19046)*
Bioelectron Technology Corp (PA).....F.....650 641-9200
350 Bernardo Ave Mountain View (94043) *(P-3866)*
Biogenex Laboratories (PA).....E.....510 824-1400
48810 Kato Rd Ste 200 Fremont (94538) *(P-6956)*
Biointellisense Inc.....E.....650 481-8140
570 El Cmino Real Ste 200 Redwood City (94063) *(P-7097)*
Biokey Inc.....E.....510 668-0881
44370 Old Warm Springs Bl Fremont (94538) *(P-3867)*
Biola Fresh Inc.....D.....559 970-8881
5887 N Sycamore Ave Fresno (93723) *(P-19731)*
Biolog Inc.....E.....510 785-2564
21124 Cabot Blvd Hayward (94545) *(P-6818)*
Biomaas Inc.....E.....415 255-8077
1278 Indiana St Unit 300 San Francisco (94107) *(P-19732)*
Biomarin Pharmaceutical Inc (PA).....B.....415 506-6700
770 Lindaro St San Rafael (94901) *(P-3868)*
Biomedican Inc (PA).....D.....412 475-8886
40471 Encyclopedia Cir Fremont (94538) *(P-19199)*
Biomicrolab Inc.....E.....925 689-1200
2500 Dean Lesher Dr Ste A Concord (94520) *(P-5454)*
Bionetics Corporation.....D.....650 604-5327
P.O. Box 115 Moffett Field (94035) *(P-19034)*
Bionova Scientific LLC.....E.....510 305-8048
3100 W Warren Ave Fremont (94538) *(P-19035)*
Bioq Pharma Incorporated (PA).....F.....415 336-6496
1325 Howard St San Francisco (94103) *(P-3869)*
Biosearch Technologies Inc (HQ).....C.....415 883-8400
2199 S Mcdowell Blvd Petaluma (94954) *(P-4040)*
Biossance, Emeryville *Also called Amyris Clean Beauty Inc (P-4080)*
Biotherm Hydronic Inc.....F.....707 794-9660
476 Primero Ct Cotati (94931) *(P-4626)*
Biotricity Inc.....E.....650 832-1626
275 Shoreline Dr Ste 150 Redwood City (94065) *(P-6957)*
Biotronics, Anderson *Also called Visioncare Devices Inc (P-8796)*
Bioware Sacramento (HQ).....E.....916 403-3500
1015 20th St Sacramento (95811) *(P-9165)*
Bipolarics Inc.....F.....408 372-7574
45920 Sentinel Pl Fremont (94539) *(P-6067)*
Birdeye Inc (PA).....C.....800 561-3357
2479 E Byshore Rd Ste 175 Palo Alto (94303) *(P-3560)*
Birdly Inc.....E.....650 942-9388
34 Harriet St San Francisco (94103) *(P-19456)*
Birds Lnding Hnting Prsrve Inc.....E.....707 374-5092
2099 Collinsville Rd Rio Vista (94571) *(P-15061)*
Birkenstock Usa Lp (HQ).....E.....415 884-3200
8171 Redwood Blvd Novato (94945) *(P-9258)*
Birst Inc.....B.....415 766-4800
45 Fremont St Ste 1800 San Francisco (94105) *(P-12302)*
Biscotti and Kate Mack, Oakland *Also called Mack & Reiss Inc (P-3016)*
Bishop Ranch, San Ramon *Also called Sunset Development Company (P-10410)*
Bishop Ranch Veterinary Center (PA).....D.....925 743-9300
2000 Bishop Dr San Ramon (94583) *(P-324)*
Bishop-Wisecarver Corporation (PA).....D.....925 439-8272
2104 Martin Way Pittsburg (94565) *(P-4982)*
Bissell Bros Bldg Maint Servic, Rancho Cordova *Also called Bissell Brothers Janitorial (P-11927)*
Bissell Brothers Janitorial.....D.....916 635-1852
3207 Luyung Dr Rancho Cordova (95742) *(P-11927)*
Bitalign Inc.....D.....415 395-9525
95 Minna St Fl 4 San Francisco (94105) *(P-12303)*
Bite Communications LLC (HQ).....D.....415 365-0222
100 Montgomery St # 1101 San Francisco (94104) *(P-19457)*
Bitmicro Networks Inc (PA).....F.....510 743-3124
47929 Fremont Blvd Fremont (94538) *(P-5283)*
Bittorrent Inc.....E.....408 641-4219
612 Howard St Ste 400 San Francisco (94105) *(P-12304)*
Bitzer Mobile Inc.....E.....866 603-8392
4230 Leonard Stocking Dr Santa Clara (95054) *(P-13021)*
Biz Performance Solutions Inc.....F.....408 844-4284
840 Loma Vista St Moss Beach (94038) *(P-13022)*
Bizcom Electronics Inc (HQ).....C.....408 262-7877
1361 El Camino Real Santa Clara (95050) *(P-8676)*
Bizlink Technology Inc (HQ).....D.....510 252-0786
47211 Bayside Pkwy Fremont (94538) *(P-5710)*
Bizps, Moss Beach *Also called Biz Performance Solutions Inc (P-13022)*
Biztek Innovations, San Jose *Also called Global Technology Services Inc (P-13902)*
BJ Jrdan Child Care Prgrams (PA).....E.....916 344-6259
1771 Tribute Rd Ste A Sacramento (95815) *(P-17863)*
Bjj Company LLC (PA).....D.....209 941-8361
1040 W Kettleman Ln Lodi (95240) *(P-7513)*
Bjork Construction Company Inc (PA).....C.....510 656-4688
4420 Enterprise Pl Fremont (94538) *(P-832)*
BJs Restaurants Inc.....E.....209 526-8850
3401 Dale Rd Ste 840 Modesto (95356) *(P-9179)*
Bkf Engineers.....D.....925 396-7700
4670 Willow Rd Ste 250 Pleasanton (94588) *(P-18921)*
Bkf Engineers (PA).....D.....650 482-6300
255 Shoreline Dr Ste 200 Redwood City (94065) *(P-18641)*
Blach Construction Company (PA).....D.....408 244-7100
2244 Blach Pl Ste 100 San Jose (95131) *(P-790)*
Black Bear Security Svcs Inc.....E.....415 559-5159
2016 Oakdale Ave Ste B San Francisco (94124) *(P-14038)*
Black Car Network LLC (PA).....E.....877 277-0208
1184 San Mateo Ave South San Francisco (94080) *(P-7325)*
Black Diamond Electric Inc.....D.....925 777-3440
2595 W 10th St Antioch (94509) *(P-1467)*
Black Diamond Video Inc.....D.....510 439-4500
503 Canal Blvd Richmond (94804) *(P-5351)*
Black Knight Infoserv LLC.....C.....415 989-9800
601 California St Ste 980 San Francisco (94108) *(P-14217)*
Black Oak Casino.....D.....209 928-9300
19400 Tuolumne Rd N Tuolumne (95379) *(P-15183)*
Black Point Products Inc.....E.....510 232-7723
2700 Rydin Rd Ste G Richmond (94804) *(P-5789)*
Black Tie Transportation LLC.....C.....925 847-0747
7080 Commerce Dr Pleasanton (94588) *(P-7378)*
Black's Irrigation Systems, Chowchilla *Also called Blacks Irrigations Systems (P-4420)*
Blackbeard's Family Fun Center, Fresno *Also called GLad Entertainment Inc (P-15206)*
Blackberry Corporation (HQ).....A.....972 650-6126
3001 Bishop Dr San Ramon (94583) *(P-13023)*
Blackburn Farming Company Inc.....E.....559 659-3753
43940 W North Ave Firebaugh (93622) *(P-368)*
Blackhawk Country Club.....C.....925 736-6500
599 Blackhawk Club Dr Danville (94506) *(P-15062)*
Blackhawk Engagement Solution.....D.....925 226-9990
6220 Stoneridge Mall Rd Pleasanton (94588) *(P-13780)*
Blackhawk Network Inc (HQ).....A.....925 226-9990
6220 Stoneridge Mall Rd Pleasanton (94588) *(P-9844)*
Blackhawk Network Holdings Inc (HQ).....B.....925 226-9990
6220 Stoneridge Mall Rd Pleasanton (94588) *(P-9845)*
Blackline Manufacturing, Chico *Also called Mtech Inc (P-4305)*
Blackrock Global Investors.....A.....415 670-2000
400 Howard St San Francisco (94105) *(P-10749)*
Blackrock Instnl Tr Nat Assn (HQ).....A.....415 597-2000
400 Howard St San Francisco (94105) *(P-10750)*
Blackrock Logistics Inc (PA).....C.....925 523-3878
7031 Koll Center Pkwy # 250 Pleasanton (94566) *(P-7825)*
Blacks Irrigations Systems.....E.....559 665-4891
144 N Chowchilla Blvd Chowchilla (93610) *(P-4420)*
Blackstone Gaming LLC.....D.....424 488-0505
1887 Matrix Blvd San Jose (95110) *(P-9166)*
Blackstone Technology Group (PA).....D.....415 837-1400
33 New Montgomery St # 850 San Francisco (94105) *(P-9958)*
Blacktalon Industries Inc.....F.....707 256-1812
481 Technology Way NAPA (94558) *(P-4966)*
Blackthorn Therapeutics Inc.....E.....415 548-5401
780 Brannan St San Francisco (94103) *(P-3870)*
Blackwater Cellular Corp.....C.....415 526-2200
125 E Sir Frncis Drake Bl Larkspur (94939) *(P-7897)*
Blackwell General Engrg Inc.....E.....408 441-1120
1199 E Taylor St San Jose (95133) *(P-1090)*
Blackwell Solar Park LLC.....E.....650 539-3380
1777 Borel Pl Ste 102 San Mateo (94402) *(P-1220)*
Blade Therapeutics Inc.....E.....650 334-2079
442 Littlefield Ave South San Francisco (94080) *(P-3871)*
Bladium Inc (PA).....D.....510 814-4999
800 W Tower Ave Bldg 40 Alameda (94501) *(P-14930)*
Bladium Sports Clubs, Alameda *Also called Bladium Inc (P-14930)*
Blair Ch Flynn Cnslting Engner (PA).....C.....559 326-1400
451 Clovis Ave Ste 200 Clovis (93612) *(P-18642)*
Blaize Inc (PA).....B.....916 347-0050
4370 Town Center Blvd # 24 El Dorado Hills (95762) *(P-6068)*
Blameless Inc.....E.....425 749-8859
500 University Ave Palo Alto (94301) *(P-13024)*
Blanding Boyer & Rockwell LLP.....E.....925 954-0113
1676 N Calif Blvd Fl 3 Walnut Creek (94596) *(P-10419)*
Blazer Exhibits & Graphics Inc.....F.....408 263-7000
4227 Technology Dr Fremont (94538) *(P-7220)*
Blazona Concrete Cnstr Inc.....D.....916 375-8337
525 Harbor Blvd Ste 10 West Sacramento (95691) *(P-833)*
Blc Wc Inc.....E.....510 489-5400
2900 Faber St Union City (94587) *(P-5197)*
Bleacher Report Inc.....D.....415 777-5505
609 Mission St San Francisco (94105) *(P-13697)*
Bleacher Report Inc.....E.....415 777-5505
153 Kearny St Fl 2 San Francisco (94108) *(P-14803)*
Bledsoe Cthcart Dstel Peterson.....E.....415 981-5411
601 California St Fl 16 San Francisco (94108) *(P-17215)*
Blend Insurance Agency Inc.....C.....650 550-4810
415 Kearny St San Francisco (94108) *(P-9891)*
Blend Labs Inc.....A.....650 550-4810
415 Kearny St San Francisco (94108) *(P-13025)*
Blentech Corporation.....D.....707 523-5949
2899 Dowd Dr Santa Rosa (95407) *(P-5126)*
Bliss Eye Associates, Sacramento *Also called Lewis S Bliss MD (P-15504)*
Bliss World LLC.....D.....415 217-7047
39 Pier San Francisco (94133) *(P-9180)*
Blize Healthcare Cal Inc.....D.....800 343-2549
750 Alfred Nobel Dr # 202 Hercules (94547) *(P-16860)*
Blocka Construction Inc.....D.....510 657-3686
445 Boulder Ct Pleasanton (94566) *(P-1221)*
Blockfreight Inc.....E.....415 815-3924
535 Mission St Fl 14 San Francisco (94105) *(P-13026)*
Blomberg Building Materials (PA).....D.....916 428-8060
1453 Blair Ave Sacramento (95822) *(P-4700)*
Blomberg Window Systems, Sacramento *Also called Blomberg Building Materials (P-4700)*
Blomberg Window Systems, Sacramento *Also called Architectural Blomberg LLC (P-4697)*

Employee Codes: A=Over 500 employees, B=251-500
C=101-250, D=51-100, E=20-50 F=10-19
2022 Northern California Business Directory and Buyers Guide
© Mergent Inc. 1-800-342-5647
913

Blommer Chocolate Company Cal — C — 510 471-4300
  1515 Pacific St Union City (94587) *(P-2436)*
Blood Bank of Redwoods (PA) — C — 707 545-1222
  3505 Industrial Dr Santa Rosa (95403) *(P-17105)*
Blood Center of The Pacific, Santa Rosa Also called Blood Bank of Redwoods *(P-17105)*
Bloodsource Inc (PA) — B — 916 456-1500
  10536 Peter A Mccuen Blvd Mather (95655) *(P-17106)*
Bloodsource Inc — E — 209 724-0428
  382 E Yosemite Ave Merced (95340) *(P-17107)*
Bloodsource Inc — E — 916 488-1701
  3099 Fair Oaks Blvd Sacramento (95864) *(P-17108)*
Bloodsource Inc — E — 530 893-5433
  555 Rio Lindo Ave Chico (95926) *(P-17109)*
Bloodsource North Valley, Chico Also called Bloodsource Inc *(P-17109)*
Bloom Energy Corporation (PA) — B — 408 543-1500
  4353 N 1st St San Jose (95134) *(P-6069)*
Bloom-Rite, Half Moon Bay Also called Tally One Inc *(P-141)*
Bloomlife Inc — E — 415 215-4251
  181 2nd St San Francisco (94105) *(P-6958)*
Bloomreach Inc (PA) — C — 650 964-1541
  82 Pioneer Way Mountain View (94041) *(P-7935)*
Blooms Wholesale Nursery Inc — E — 707 935-0606
  15079 Trestle Glen Dr Glen Ellen (95442) *(P-9627)*
Blossom Valley Cnstr Inc — D — 408 993-0766
  1125 Mabury Rd San Jose (95133) *(P-449)*
Blossom Valley Foods Inc — E — 408 848-5520
  20 Casey Ln Gilroy (95020) *(P-2819)*
Blu Homes Inc (PA) — C — 866 887-7997
  1015 Walnut Ave Vallejo (94592) *(P-620)*
Blue and Gold Fleet — D — 415 705-8200
  Marine Terminal Pier 41 St Pier San Francisco (94133) *(P-7718)*
Blue Beacon Truck Wash, Corning Also called Blue Beacon USA LP *(P-14629)*
Blue Beacon USA LP — E — 530 824-0474
  3000 Highway 99w Corning (96021) *(P-14629)*
Blue Bus Tours LLC — C — 415 353-5310
  216 Ryan Way South San Francisco (94080) *(P-7816)*
Blue Cedar Networks Inc — E — 415 329-0401
  325 Pacific Ave Fl 1 San Francisco (94111) *(P-5352)*
Blue Coat, Fremont Also called Mitac Information Systems Corp *(P-5261)*
Blue Coat LLC — A — 408 220-2200
  350 Ellis St Mountain View (94043) *(P-13027)*
Blue Coat Systems LLC (HQ) — A — 650 527-8000
  420 N Mary Ave Sunnyvale (94085) *(P-13028)*
Blue Diamond, Turlock Also called Blue Diamond Growers *(P-2872)*
Blue Diamond Growers — C — 209 545-6221
  4800 Sisk Rd Modesto (95356) *(P-271)*
Blue Diamond Growers — C — 916 446-8464
  1701 C St Sacramento (95811) *(P-2871)*
Blue Diamond Growers — C — 559 251-4044
  10840 E Mckinley Ave Sanger (93657) *(P-272)*
Blue Diamond Growers — C — 209 604-1501
  1300 N Washington Rd Turlock (95380) *(P-2872)*
Blue Eagle Contracting Inc — D — 530 272-0287
  113 Presley Way Ste 8 Grass Valley (95945) *(P-7453)*
Blue Jeans Network Inc (HQ) — C — 408 550-2828
  3098 Olsen Dr San Jose (95128) *(P-8071)*
Blue Lake Casino — D — 707 668-5101
  777 Casino Way Blue Lk Blue Lake Blue Lake (95525) *(P-10963)*
Blue Line Transfer Inc — E — 650 589-5511
  500 E Jamie Ct South San Francisco (94080) *(P-8310)*
Blue Mountain Air, Vacaville Also called Blue Mountain Cnstr Svcs Inc *(P-1222)*
Blue Mountain Cnstr Svcs Inc — C — 800 889-2085
  707 Aldridge Rd Vacaville (95688) *(P-1222)*
Blue Mtn Ctr of Meditation Inc — E — 707 878-2369
  3600 Tomales Rd Tomales (94971) *(P-3524)*
Blue Oak Dental Group, Roseville Also called Blue Oak Dental Group *(P-15825)*
Blue Oak Dental Group — E — 916 786-6777
  15 Sierra Gate Plz Roseville (95678) *(P-15825)*
Blue Ribbon Supply Company Brs, South San Francisco Also called Lenaco Corporation *(P-9121)*
Blue Ring Stencils LLC — F — 866 763-3873
  675 Trade Zone Blvd Milpitas (95035) *(P-7204)*
Blue River Seafood Inc — D — 510 300-6800
  25447 Industrial Blvd Hayward (94545) *(P-9360)*
Blue Sheild of California, Walnut Creek Also called California Physicians Service *(P-10094)*
Blue Shield Cal Lf Hlth Insur — A — 800 660-3007
  4005 Manzanita Ave Ste 6 Carmichael (95608) *(P-10093)*
Blue Shield of California, Oakland Also called California Physicians Service *(P-10096)*
Blue Shield of California, NAPA Also called California Physicians Service *(P-10098)*
Blue Shield of California, Rancho Cordova Also called California Physicians Service *(P-10099)*
Blue Shield of California, Fresno Also called California Physicians Service *(P-10100)*
Blue Skies For Children — E — 510 261-1076
  3021 Brookdale Ave Oakland (94602) *(P-17864)*
Blue Sky Research Incorporated (PA) — E — 408 941-6068
  510 Alder Dr Milpitas (95035) *(P-6866)*
Bluedata Software Inc — F — 650 450-4067
  3979 Freedom Cir Ste 850 Santa Clara (95054) *(P-13029)*
Blueline Associates Inc — E — 925 462-2200
  2134 Rheem Dr Ste 100 Pleasanton (94588) *(P-834)*
Blueline Construction, Rancho Cordova Also called Ron Nurss Inc *(P-1908)*
Bluescape, Redwood City Also called Thought Stream LLC *(P-12863)*
Blueshift Labs Inc — C — 844 258-3735
  433 California St Ste 600 San Francisco (94104) *(P-13030)*
Bluestack Systems Inc — E — 408 412-9439
  2105 S Bascom Ave Ste 380 Campbell (95008) *(P-13031)*
Bluevine Capital Inc — B — 888 216-9619
  401 Warren St Ste 300 Redwood City (94063) *(P-9936)*

Bluewater Envmtl Svcs Inc — D — 510 346-8800
  2075 Williams St San Leandro (94577) *(P-1981)*
Bluewave Express LLC (PA) — E — 877 503-0008
  2175 Francisco Blvd E G San Rafael (94901) *(P-14630)*
Blum Capital Partners T LP — E — 415 645-0092
  909 Montgomery St Ste 400 San Francisco (94133) *(P-10035)*
Blum Construction Co Inc — F — 408 629-3740
  404a Umbarger Rd A San Jose (95111) *(P-4701)*
Blurb Inc — D — 415 364-6300
  580 California St Fl 3 San Francisco (94104) *(P-3525)*
BM Lynn Painting Inc — E — 916 920-4000
  4324 Pinell St Sacramento (95838) *(P-1404)*
Bmb Metal Products Corporation — E — 916 631-9120
  11460 Elks Cir Rancho Cordova (95742) *(P-4744)*
BMC Stock Holdings Inc — B — 916 481-5030
  4300 Jetway Ct North Highlands (95660) *(P-8531)*
Bme Electrical Construction — E — 510 208-1967
  1281 30th St Oakland (94608) *(P-1468)*
Bmf - Baktek Metal Fabrication — F — 925 245-0200
  290 Lindbergh Ave Livermore (94551) *(P-4983)*
Bmi Imaging Systems Inc (PA) — E — 916 924-6666
  1115 E Arques Ave Sunnyvale (94085) *(P-13698)*
BMW Fresno, Fresno Also called Weber Motors Fresno Inc *(P-14678)*
BMW of San Francisco, San Francisco Also called German Motors Corporation *(P-14525)*
Bnnv LLC — E — 707 880-2300
  1030 Main St NAPA (94559) *(P-14838)*
BNP Lodging LLC — E — 559 251-5200
  1551 N Peach Ave Fresno (93727) *(P-10964)*
Bo Dean Co Inc (PA) — E — 707 576-8205
  1060 N Dutton Ave Santa Rosa (95401) *(P-575)*
Bobby Salazar Corporate, Fowler Also called Bobby Slzars Mxcan Fd Pdts Inc *(P-2197)*
Bobby Slzars Mxcan Fd Pdts Inc (PA) — E — 559 834-4787
  2810 San Antonio Dr Fowler (93625) *(P-2197)*
Bobs Iron Inc — C — 510 567-8983
  629 Whitney St San Leandro (94577) *(P-4648)*
Bockmon & Woody Elc Co Inc — C — 209 464-4878
  1528 El Pinal Dr Stockton (95205) *(P-1469)*
Bodega Bay Associates — D — 650 330-8888
  1100 Alma St Ste 106 Bodega Bay (94923) *(P-10965)*
Bodega Bay Lodge, Bodega Bay Also called NAPA Valley Lodge LP *(P-11324)*
Bodega Bay Lodge, Bodega Bay Also called Bodega Bay Associates *(P-10965)*
Bodega Coast Inn, Bodega Also called Pacific Lodging Group *(P-11349)*
Bodega Harbour Golf Links, Bodega Bay Also called Bodega Harbour Homeowners Assn *(P-18393)*
Bodega Harbour Homeowners Assn — D — 707 875-3519
  21301 Heron Dr Bodega Bay (94923) *(P-18393)*
Bodies In Motion — E — 415 897-2185
  351 San Andreas Dr Novato (94945) *(P-14931)*
Body Kinetics (PA) — E — 415 895-5965
  1530 Center Rd Ste 11 Novato (94947) *(P-14932)*
Boeger Winery Inc — E — 530 622-8094
  1709 Carson Rd Placerville (95667) *(P-2512)*
Boething Treeland Farms Inc — D — 650 851-4770
  2923 Alpine Rd Portola Valley (94028) *(P-528)*
Boething Treeland Farms Inc — D — 209 727-3741
  20601 E Kettleman Ln Lodi (95240) *(P-529)*
Boething Treeland Nursery, Lodi Also called Boething Treeland Farms Inc *(P-529)*
Boghosian Raisin Pkg Co Inc — E — 559 834-5348
  726 S 8th St Fowler (93625) *(P-273)*
Bogle Vineyards Inc — E — 916 744-1139
  37783 County Road 144 Clarksburg (95612) *(P-46)*
Bogle Winery, Clarksburg Also called Bogle Vineyards Inc *(P-46)*
Bogner Sheet Metal — E — 831 423-4322
  142 Benito Ave Santa Cruz (95062) *(P-1223)*
Bohan Cnlis - Astin Creek Rdym — D — 707 632-5296
  1528 Copperhill Pkwy F Santa Rosa (95403) *(P-4460)*
Bohannan Concrete Inc — E — 925 932-2192
  1553 3rd Ave Walnut Creek (94597) *(P-1854)*
Bohemian Club (PA) — D — 415 885-2440
  624 Taylor St San Francisco (94102) *(P-18394)*
BOHEMIAN GROVE, San Francisco Also called Bohemian Club *(P-18394)*
Bohm Law Group Inc (PA) — E — 916 927-5574
  4600 Northgate Blvd # 210 Sacramento (95834) *(P-17216)*
Boise Cascade Company — E — 209 983-4114
  12030 S Harlan Rd Lathrop (95330) *(P-3342)*
Boku Inc (PA) — D — 415 375-3160
  660 Market St Ste 400 San Francisco (94104) *(P-12305)*
Bolb Inc — F — 925 453-6293
  52 Wright Brothers Ave Livermore (94551) *(P-6070)*
Bold Data Technology Inc — E — 510 490-8296
  47540 Seabridge Dr Fremont (94538) *(P-5243)*
Boldt Company — C — 415 762-8300
  375 Beale St Ste 500 San Francisco (94105) *(P-835)*
Bollman Treatment Plant, Concord Also called Contra Costa Water District *(P-8231)*
Bolt Biotherapeutics Inc — D — 650 260-9295
  900 Chesapeake Dr Redwood City (94063) *(P-3872)*
Bolt Threads Inc (PA) — D — 415 279-5585
  5858 Horton St Ste 400 Emeryville (94608) *(P-19036)*
Boltbus, Fresno Also called Greyhound Lines Inc *(P-7336)*
Bolton Rsnbaum Brnsten Pdtric — E — 415 666-1860
  3838 California St Rm 111 San Francisco (94118) *(P-15300)*
Bon Appetit Management Co — C — 925 730-3653
  4125 Hopyard Rd Pleasanton (94588) *(P-19304)*
Bon Appetit Management Co — C — 408 554-2728
  500 El Camino Real 500 # 500 Santa Clara (95050) *(P-19305)*
Bon Appetit Management Co — C — 650 467-3767
  383 E Grand Ave South San Francisco (94080) *(P-19306)*

Bon Appetit Management Co....C....408 554-5771
301 Market St Santa Clara (95053) *(P-19307)*
Bona Furtuna LLC (PA)....D....**800 380-8819**
20 N Santa Cruz Ave Ste B Los Gatos (95030) *(P-9647)*
Bonander Pontiac Inc (PA)....D....**209 632-8871**
231 S Center St Turlock (95380) *(P-14607)*
Bonander Pontiac-Buick-Gmc, Turlock *Also called Bonander Pontiac Inc (P-14607)*
Bonanza Inn Magnuson Grand Ht....D....530 674-8824
1001 Clark Ave Yuba City (95991) *(P-10966)*
Bond Manufacturing Co Inc (PA)....D....**866 771-2663**
2516 Verne Roberts Cir H3 Antioch (94509) *(P-4421)*
Bondline Elctrnic Adhsive Corp....D....408 830-9200
777 N Pastoria Ave Sunnyvale (94085) *(P-4149)*
Bonetti Frank Plumbing Company....E....510 582-0934
20878 Rutledge Rd Castro Valley (94546) *(P-1224)*
Bongmi Inc....E....415 823-8595
68 Harriet St Unit 3 San Francisco (94103) *(P-8775)*
Bonita House Inc....D....510 923-0180
6333 Telg Ave Ste 102 Oakland (94609) *(P-17446)*
Bonner Processing Inc....E....925 455-3833
6052 Industrial Way Ste A Livermore (94551) *(P-4900)*
Bonnie Plants Inc....B....541 441-2847
729 Green Valley Rd Watsonville (95076) *(P-9595)*
Bonny Doon Vineyard (PA)....E....**831 425-3625**
328 Ingalls St Santa Cruz (95060) *(P-2513)*
Bonny Doon Winery Inc....F....831 425-3625
328 Ingalls St Santa Cruz (95060) *(P-2514)*
Bonsai Ai Inc....E....510 900-1112
2150 Shattuck Ave # 1200 Berkeley (94704) *(P-13032)*
Book Sellers & Publishers, San Francisco *Also called City Lights Books (P-3529)*
Bookheaded Learning LLC....D....707 996-3427
610 Daniel Young Dr Sonoma (95476) *(P-17865)*
Boole Inc....E....408 368-2515
2979 Basil Cmn Livermore (94551) *(P-8677)*
Boost Halthcare Consulting LLC....E....415 377-7589
1320 Harbor Bay Pkwy # 220 Alameda (94502) *(P-19733)*
Boosted Inc (PA)....E....**650 933-5151**
400 Oyster Point Blvd # 229 South San Francisco (94080) *(P-7189)*
Boosted Boards, South San Francisco *Also called Boosted Inc (P-7189)*
Booth Ranches LLC (PA)....C....**559 626-4732**
12201 Avenue 480 Orange Cove (93646) *(P-246)*
Bora Bora Residential Coml Cle....E....925 243-5992
3135 Clayton Rd Ste 208 Concord (94519) *(P-11928)*
Borden Decal Company Inc....F....415 431-1587
11760 San Pablo Ave Ste B El Cerrito (94530) *(P-3722)*
Borden Lighting....E....510 357-0171
2355 Verna Ct San Leandro (94577) *(P-5732)*
Bordenaves, San Rafael *Also called Bordenaves Marin Baking (P-9441)*
Bordenaves Marin Baking....D....415 453-2957
1512 4th St San Rafael (94901) *(P-9441)*
Borderx Lab Inc (PA)....D....**408 746-5462**
111 W Evelyn Ave Ste 202 Sunnyvale (94086) *(P-12306)*
Boreal Ridge Corporation....C....530 426-1012
19749 Boreal Ridge Rd Soda Springs (95728) *(P-10967)*
Boreal Ski Area, Soda Springs *Also called Boreal Ridge Corporation (P-10967)*
Boresha International Inc....E....925 676-1400
7041 Koll Center Pkwy # 100 Pleasanton (94566) *(P-2836)*
Borg Redwood Fences, Livermore *Also called Selex Inc (P-2066)*
Borga Stl Bldngs Cmponents Inc....D....559 834-5375
300 W Peach St Fowler (93625) *(P-4835)*
Borge Construction Inc (PA)....E....**916 927-4800**
975 Fee Dr Sacramento (95815) *(P-621)*
Borgens & Borgens Inc....E....209 547-2980
141 E Acacia St Ste D Stockton (95202) *(P-14039)*
Borqs International Holdg Corp....E....619 363-3168
5201 Great America Pkwy Santa Clara (95054) *(P-6499)*
Bosco Oil Inc....E....650 967-2253
785 Yuba Dr Mountain View (94041) *(P-9523)*
Bospar LLC....E....415 913-7528
1835 Franklin St San Francisco (94109) *(P-19458)*
Bossa Nova Robotics Inc (HQ)....D....**415 234-5136**
610 22nd St Ste 250 San Francisco (94107) *(P-9189)*
Bossa Nova Robotics Inc....C....415 234-5136
709 N Shoreline Blvd Mountain View (94043) *(P-9190)*
Boston Properties Ltd Partnr....D....415 772-0700
4 Embarcadero Ctr Lvel San Francisco (94111) *(P-10696)*
Boston Scientific Corporation....C....408 935-3400
150 Baytech Dr San Jose (95134) *(P-7067)*
Botanica Landscapes, Yuba City *Also called United Landscape Resource Inc (P-507)*
Bottling Group LLC....A....559 485-5050
1150 E North Ave Fresno (93725) *(P-2783)*
Bottling Group LLC....A....914 767-6000
3440 S East Ave Fresno (93725) *(P-2784)*
Bottomley Distributing Co Inc....D....408 945-0660
755 Yosemite Dr Milpitas (95035) *(P-9545)*
Bouchaine Vineyards Inc....F....707 252-9065
1075 Buchli Station Rd NAPA (94559) *(P-2515)*
Bouchaine Wineary, NAPA *Also called Bouchaine Vineyards Inc (P-2515)*
Boulevard Cinemas, Petaluma *Also called Petaluma Cinemas LLC (P-14815)*
Bounce A Rama Inc....D....510 754-8799
1450 Great Mall Dr Milpitas (95035) *(P-14870)*
Boundary Bend Inc....E....844 626-2726
455 Harter Ave Woodland (95776) *(P-2461)*
Boundary Bend Olives, Woodland *Also called Boundary Bend Inc (P-2461)*
Boundless Care Inc....E....408 363-8900
5988 Silver Creek Valley San Jose (95138) *(P-16220)*
Bourdolan 25 Lusk LLC....E....415 495-5875
25 Lusk St San Francisco (94107) *(P-10968)*
Boutique Air Inc (PA)....B....**415 449-0505**
5 3rd St Ste 925 San Francisco (94103) *(P-7755)*
Bouton Construction Inc....D....408 375-0829
420 E Mcglincy Ln Campbell (95008) *(P-9019)*
Bouwman Engineering Inc....F....707 447-5414
58 Union Way Vacaville (95687) *(P-18643)*
Bowie Enterprises (PA)....D....**559 227-6221**
4411 N Blackstone Ave Fresno (93726) *(P-14631)*
Bowie Enterprises....D....559 292-6565
801 W Shaw Ave Clovis (93612) *(P-14632)*
Bowlero Corp....D....201 797-5400
6450 N Blackstone Ave Fresno (93710) *(P-14887)*
Bowlero Corp....D....510 523-6767
300 Park St Alameda (94501) *(P-14888)*
Bowles & Verna....E....925 935-3300
2121 N Calif Blvd Ste 875 Walnut Creek (94596) *(P-17217)*
Bowles Farming Company Inc....D....209 827-3000
11609 Hereford Rd Los Banos (93635) *(P-148)*
Bowman & Co LLP....E....209 473-1040
10100 Trinity Pkwy # 310 Stockton (95219) *(P-18934)*
Bowman & Williams A Cal Corp....D....831 426-3560
3949 Res Pk Ct Ste 100 Soquel (95073) *(P-18644)*
Box Inc (PA)....A....**877 729-4269**
900 Jefferson Ave Redwood City (94063) *(P-13033)*
Box Lunch Company Inc....E....650 589-1886
319 S Maple Ave Ste 206 South San Francisco (94080) *(P-9263)*
Boyd, Pleasanton *Also called LTI Flexible Products Inc (P-4202)*
Boyd, Pleasanton *Also called LTI Holdings Inc (P-3814)*
Boyd Corporation (HQ)....A....**209 236-1111**
5960 Inglewood Dr Ste 115 Pleasanton (94588) *(P-4150)*
Boyd Lighting Fixture Company (PA)....E....**415 778-4300**
200a Harbor Dr Sausalito (94965) *(P-5733)*
Boyer Inc....E....831 724-0123
105 Thompson Rd Watsonville (95076) *(P-4129)*
Boyett Construction Inc (PA)....D....**510 264-9100**
2404 Tripaldi Way Hayward (94545) *(P-1662)*
Boyett Petroleum, Modesto *Also called Stan Boyett & Son Inc (P-9539)*
Boykin Mgt Co Ltd Lblty Co....D....510 548-7920
200 Marina Blvd Berkeley (94710) *(P-10969)*
Boys & Girls CLB of Peninsula....D....650 322-6255
401 Pierce Rd Menlo Park (94025) *(P-15063)*
Boys & Girls Club NAPA Valley....E....707 255-8866
1515 Pueblo Ave NAPA (94558) *(P-18395)*
Boys & Girls Club Silicon Vly....D....408 957-9685
518 Valley Way Milpitas (95035) *(P-18396)*
Boys & Girls Clubs of N Vly....D....530 899-0335
601 Wall St Chico (95928) *(P-18397)*
Boys and Girls Homes Shelter, San Francisco *Also called Catholic Chrties Cyo of The AR (P-17464)*
Boys Grls Clubs Snta Cruz Cnty....E....831 423-3138
543 Center St Santa Cruz (95060) *(P-18398)*
BOYS' & GIRLS' CLUB, NAPA *Also called Boys & Girls Club NAPA Valley (P-18395)*
BP, Fremont *Also called Bay Polymers Corp (P-8308)*
Bpaz Holdings 18 LLC....D....972 354-6250
1 Sansome St Fl 15 San Francisco (94104) *(P-10728)*
Bpaz Holdings 2 LLC....E....972 354-6250
1 Sansome St Ste 1500 San Francisco (94104) *(P-10495)*
Bpaz Holdings 6 LLC....D....415 295-8080
1 Sansome St Ste 1500 San Francisco (94104) *(P-10729)*
Bpg Storage Solutions Inc....E....562 467-2000
2033 N Main St Ste 340 Walnut Creek (94596) *(P-19308)*
Bpm LLP....D....408 961-6300
10 Almaden Blvd Ste 1000 San Jose (95113) *(P-18935)*
Bpm LLP (PA)....D....**415 421-5757**
600 California St Fl 6 San Francisco (94108) *(P-18936)*
Bpo Systems Inc (PA)....E....**925 478-4299**
1700 Ygnacio Valley Rd # 205 Walnut Creek (94598) *(P-19734)*
Bpr Properties Berkeley LLC....C....650 424-1400
953 Industrial Ave # 100 Palo Alto (94303) *(P-10378)*
BR Funsten, Manteca *Also called B R Funsten & Co (P-8506)*
Bracut International Corp....E....707 826-9850
4949 West End Rd Arcata (95521) *(P-3092)*
Braddock & Logan Services Inc....C....925 736-4000
4155 Blackhawk Plaza Cir # 201 Danville (94506) *(P-836)*
Braddock Logan Ventr Group LP (PA)....A....**925 736-4000**
4155 Blackhawk Plaza Cir Danville (94506) *(P-778)*
Braden Prtners LP A Cal Ltd PR (HQ)....D....**415 893-1518**
1304 Sthpint Blvd Ste 130 Petaluma (94954) *(P-8776)*
Bradford & Barthel LLP (PA)....E....**916 569-0790**
2518 River Plaza Dr Sacramento (95833) *(P-17218)*
Bradford Messenger Service....D....559 252-0775
4955 E Andersen Ave # 118 Fresno (93727) *(P-14218)*
Braemac (ca) LLC....D....510 687-1000
43134 Osgood Rd Fremont (94539) *(P-8897)*
Bragg Crane & Rigging, Richmond *Also called Bay Cities Crane & Rigging Inc (P-12031)*
Braid Logistics, Mountain View *Also called Hansen Medical Inc (P-6980)*
Brain Balance Franchising, Walnut Creek *Also called Bb Franchising LLC (P-10803)*
Brain Technologies Inc....B....650 918-2245
400 S El Cmino Real Ste 2 San Mateo (94402) *(P-12307)*
Braintree, Palo Alto *Also called Paypal Inc (P-14357)*
Braintree, San Francisco *Also called Paypal Inc (P-14358)*
Bramasol Inc....D....408 831-0046
3979 Freedom Cir Ste 620 Santa Clara (95054) *(P-8678)*
Brampton Mthesen Fabr Pdts Inc....E....510 483-7771
1688 Abram Ct San Leandro (94577) *(P-3037)*
Branch Metrics Inc (PA)....B....**650 209-6491**
1400 Sport Blvd Bldg Bfl Redwood City (94063) *(P-13699)*
Brandel Manor, Turlock *Also called Covenant Living West (P-16343)*

Brandelli Arts Inc ....E....714 537-0969
1250 Shaws Flat Rd Sonora (95370) ***(P-4535)***
Brandt Electronics Inc ....E....408 240-0004
1971 Tarob Ct Milpitas (95035) ***(P-6402)***
Brandvia Alliance Inc (PA) ....**C....408 955-0500**
2159 Bering Dr San Jose (95131) ***(P-11741)***
Brandwatch LLC ....C....415 429-5800
445 Bush St Fl 8 San Francisco (94108) ***(P-19459)***
Brantner Holding LLC (HQ) ....**D....650 361-5292**
501 Oakside Ave Redwood City (94063) ***(P-6389)***
Brass Engineering Intl ....C....925 867-1000
2551 San Ramon Valley Blv San Ramon (94583) ***(P-7793)***
Braunhagey & Borden LLP ....E....415 599-0210
351 California St Fl 10 San Francisco (94104) ***(P-17219)***
Brava Home Inc ....E....408 675-2569
312 Chestnut St Redwood City (94063) ***(P-5703)***
Bravante Produce, Reedley *Also called Cal Packing & Storage LP* ***(P-7677)***
Bravo Fono, Palo Alto *Also called Fono Unlimited* ***(P-2173)***
Bravo Personal Care Services, Gold River *Also called Berk Street Enterprises Inc* ***(P-16857)***
Brayton Purcell ....E....801 521-1712
222 Rush Landing Rd Novato (94945) ***(P-17220)***
Brayton Purcell APC (PA) ....**C....415 898-1555**
222 Rush Landing Rd Novato (94945) ***(P-17221)***
Bre Select Hotels Oper LLC ....E....916 773-7171
1951 Taylor Rd Roseville (95661) ***(P-10970)***
Bre Select Hotels Oper LLC ....E....916 353-1717
221 Iron Point Rd Folsom (95630) ***(P-10971)***
Bre/Japantown Owner LLC ....D....415 922-3200
1625 Post St San Francisco (94115) ***(P-10972)***
Bread Basket, Daly City *Also called Westlake Bakery Inc* ***(P-2411)***
Breakfast Club At Midtown ....E....408 280-0688
1432 W San Carlos St # 8 San Jose (95126) ***(P-15064)***
Breakthrough Behavioral Inc ....C....888 282-2522
702 Marshall St Ste 340 Redwood City (94063) ***(P-17447)***
Breaktime Studios Inc (PA) ....**E....415 290-4900**
100 Montgomery St # 1900 San Francisco (94104) ***(P-13034)***
Breast Cancer Car Donations, Mountain View *Also called Susan G Komen Breast Cancer* ***(P-18599)***
Breast Imaging Center, Sacramento *Also called Sutter Health* ***(P-15721)***
Brelje and Race Labs Inc ....E....707 544-8807
425 S E St Santa Rosa (95404) ***(P-19260)***
Brelje Race Cnslting Engineers ....E....707 576-1322
475 Aviation Blvd Ste 120 Santa Rosa (95403) ***(P-18645)***
Brenden Theatre Corporation ....D....707 469-0180
531 Davis St Vacaville (95688) ***(P-14804)***
Brenden Theatre Corporation ....D....209 491-7770
1021 10th St Frnt Modesto (95354) ***(P-14805)***
Brenden Theatre Corporation (PA) ....**C....925 677-0462**
1985 Willow Pass Rd Ste C Concord (94520) ***(P-14806)***
Brent Redmond Trnsp Inc ....E....831 637-5342
1800 Lana Way Hollister (95023) ***(P-7514)***
Brentwood Press & Pubg Co LLC ....E....925 516-4757
248 Oak St Brentwood (94513) ***(P-3419)***
Brentwood Sklled Nrsing Rhbltt, Red Bluff *Also called Brentwood Sklled Nrsing Rhbltt* ***(P-16221)***
Brentwood Sklled Nrsing Rhbltt ....D....530 527-2046
1795 Walnut St Red Bluff (96080) ***(P-16221)***
Brentwood Veterinary Hospital, Brentwood *Also called Assocted Vtrnary Practices Inc* ***(P-322)***
Brentwood Yellow Pages, Brentwood *Also called Brentwood Press & Pubg Co LLC* ***(P-3419)***
Brereton Architects Inc ....E....415 546-1212
909 Montgomery St Ste 260 San Francisco (94133) ***(P-18874)***
Bret Harte Children's Center, Sacramento *Also called Sacramento Cy Unified Schl Dst* ***(P-18009)***
Brett Lee Womack (PA) ....**E....530 596-3358**
461 Firehouse Rd Westwood (96137) ***(P-2011)***
Brett V Crtis MD A Prof Corp I ....E....415 924-4525
101 Casa Buena Dr Corte Madera (94925) ***(P-15301)***
Brew Building, Fort Bragg *Also called North Coast Brewing Co Inc* ***(P-2488)***
Brewer Brewer Lofgren LLP (PA) ....**E....916 550-1482**
650 University Ave # 220 Sacramento (95825) ***(P-2873)***
Brewery On Half Moon Bay Inc ....C....650 728-2739
390 Capistrano Rd Half Moon Bay (94019) ***(P-2475)***
Brex Inc (PA) ....**B....650 250-6428**
110 S Park St San Francisco (94107) ***(P-14219)***
Brex Technologies, San Francisco *Also called Brex Inc* ***(P-14219)***
Brian D Hopkins MD ....E....925 378-4517
365 Lennon Ln Ste 250 Walnut Creek (94598) ***(P-15302)***
Brian's Welding, San Jose *Also called B W Padilla Inc* ***(P-14709)***
Briarpatch Coop Nev Cnty Inc ....C....530 272-5333
290 Sierra College Dr Grass Valley (95945) ***(P-18550)***
Briarpatch Coop-Community Mkt, Grass Valley *Also called Briarpatch Coop Nev Cnty Inc* ***(P-18550)***
Brichetto Bros ....E....209 847-2775
8700 Crane Rd Oakdale (95361) ***(P-7271)***
Bridge Bank, San Jose *Also called Western Alliance Bank* ***(P-9754)***
Bridge Bay Resort & Marina ....D....530 275-3021
10300 Bridge Bay Rd Redding (96003) ***(P-10973)***
Bridge Economic Dev Corp (PA) ....**D....415 989-1111**
345 Spear St Ste 700 San Francisco (94105) ***(P-622)***
Bridge Housing Corporation (PA) ....**D....415 989-1111**
600 California St Fl 9 San Francisco (94108) ***(P-18551)***
Bridgebio Pharma Inc (PA) ....**C....650 391-9740**
421 Kipling St Palo Alto (94301) ***(P-3873)***
Bridgebio Services Inc ....D....650 438-1302
421 Kipling St Palo Alto (94301) ***(P-19037)***

Bridgecrew Inc ....E....510 304-4622
1 Market St San Francisco (94105) ***(P-5353)***
Bridgeford Flying Services, NAPA *Also called NAPA Jet Center Inc* ***(P-7777)***
Bridgelux Inc ....D....925 583-8400
46410 Fremont Blvd Fremont (94538) ***(P-6071)***
Bridgene Biosciences Inc ....F....626 632-3188
75 Nicholson Ln San Jose (95134) ***(P-3874)***
Bridgepoint At San Francisco, San Francisco *Also called Kisco Senior Living LLC* ***(P-19359)***
Bridger Technologies Inc ....E....406 556-0300
1000 Alfred Nobel Dr Hercules (94547) ***(P-6819)***
Bridges At Gale Ranch LLC ....D....925 735-4253
9000 S Gale Ridge Rd San Ramon (94582) ***(P-14989)***
Bridges Golf Club, The, San Ramon *Also called Bridges At Gale Ranch LLC* ***(P-14989)***
Bridgestone Americas ....D....925 372-9056
4575 Pacheco Blvd Martinez (94553) ***(P-14550)***
Bridgstone Amrcas Tire Oprtons ....D....916 447-4220
1401 Richards Blvd Sacramento (95811) ***(P-8476)***
Brience Inc (HQ) ....**D....415 974-5300**
128 Spear St Fl 3 San Francisco (94105) ***(P-12308)***
Bright Development ....E....209 526-8242
1620 N Carpenter Rd Modesto (95351) ***(P-623)***
Bright Event Rentals LLC ....D....310 202-0011
22674 Broadway Ste A Sonoma (95476) ***(P-12032)***
Bright Lights Candle Company, Lower Lake *Also called Aloha Bay* ***(P-7268)***
Bright Machines Inc (PA) ....**B....415 867-4402**
132 Hawthorne St San Francisco (94107) ***(P-5107)***
Bright Path Therapists Inc ....E....415 689-1700
49 Bennit Ave San Anselmo (94960) ***(P-15884)***
Bright People Foods Inc (PA) ....**E....530 669-6870**
1640 Tide Ct Woodland (95776) ***(P-2874)***
Brightedge Technologies Inc (PA) ....**C....800 578-8023**
989 E Hillsdale Blvd # 3 Foster City (94404) ***(P-12309)***
Brighten Academy Preschool Inc ....E....559 299-8100
1825 Austin Ave Clovis (93611) ***(P-17866)***
Brighter Beginnings (PA) ....**E....510 903-7503**
2727 Macdonald Ave Richmond (94804) ***(P-17448)***
Brighterion Inc ....D....415 986-5600
123 Mission St Ste 1700 San Francisco (94105) ***(P-12310)***
Brightidea Incorporated ....E....415 814-1387
255 California St # 1100 San Francisco (94111) ***(P-13035)***
Brightmark LLC (PA) ....**C....415 964-4411**
1725 Montgomery St Fl 3 San Francisco (94111) ***(P-545)***
BRIGHTON, Modesto *Also called Del Rio Golf & Country Club* ***(P-15085)***
Brightseed Bio ....E....415 965-7778
201 Haskins Way Ste 310 South San Francisco (94080) ***(P-16775)***
Brightside Health Inc ....E....415 662-8618
2471 Peralta St Unit A Oakland (94607) ***(P-17110)***
Brightsign LLC ....D....408 852-9263
983 University Ave Bldg A Los Gatos (95032) ***(P-7221)***
Brightstar Healthcare, Roseville *Also called Altus Health Inc* ***(P-16843)***
Brighttalk Inc (HQ) ....**E....415 625-1500**
703 Market St Ste 15 San Francisco (94103) ***(P-12311)***
Brightview Landscape Dev Inc ....D....925 463-0700
7039 Commerce Cir Ste A Pleasanton (94588) ***(P-1151)***
Brightview Landscape Dev Inc ....C....916 386-4875
20 Business Pkwy Ste 200 Sacramento (95828) ***(P-397)***
Brightview Landscape Svcs Inc ....C....510 487-4826
20551b Corsair Blvd Hayward (94545) ***(P-398)***
Brightview Landscape Svcs Inc ....C....916 415-1004
4030 Alvis Ct Rocklin (95677) ***(P-399)***
Brightview Landscape Svcs Inc ....C....925 957-8831
4677 Pacheco Blvd Martinez (94553) ***(P-400)***
Brightview Landscape Svcs Inc ....C....650 289-9324
4055 Bohannon Dr Menlo Park (94025) ***(P-401)***
Brightview Landscape Svcs Inc ....C....925 243-0288
5779 Preston Ave Livermore (94551) ***(P-402)***
Brightview Landscape Svcs Inc ....C....408 453-5904
825 Mabury Rd San Jose (95133) ***(P-403)***
Brightview Landscape Svcs Inc ....C....916 381-2800
5745 Alder Ave Sacramento (95828) ***(P-404)***
Brightview Landscape Svcs Inc ....C....925 924-8900
7039 Commerce Cir Ste B Pleasanton (94588) ***(P-405)***
Brightview Tree Company ....D....925 862-2485
8501 Calaveras Rd Sunol (94586) ***(P-530)***
Brightview Tree Company ....D....209 886-5511
28915 E Funck Rd Farmington (95230) ***(P-406)***
Brilliant General Maint Inc (PA) ....**C....408 287-6708**
954 Chestnut St San Jose (95110) ***(P-11929)***
Brilliant Home Technology Inc ....E....650 539-5320
155 Bovet Rd Ste 500 San Mateo (94402) ***(P-5649)***
Brilliant Lighting Products, Livermore *Also called American Wholesale Ltg Inc* ***(P-8841)***
Brilliant Worldwide Inc ....E....650 468-2966
200 Pine St Fl 8 San Francisco (94104) ***(P-13036)***
Brillio LLC ....A....800 317-0575
5201 Great America Pkwy # 100 Santa Clara (95054) ***(P-12312)***
Brisbane Mechanical, Brisbane *Also called F W Spencer & Son Inc* ***(P-1259)***
Bristlecone Incorporated ....A....650 386-4000
10 Almaden Blvd Ste 600 San Jose (95113) ***(P-12313)***
Bristol Hospice Foundation Cal ....D....661 670-8000
4568 Feather River Dr Stockton (95219) ***(P-16171)***
Bristol Hospice Foundation Cal ....D....209 338-3000
1101 Sylvan Ave Ste B10 Modesto (95350) ***(P-16172)***
Bristol Hospice Foundation Cal ....E....408 207-9222
3375 Scott Blvd Ste 410 Santa Clara (95054) ***(P-16861)***
Bristol Hotel ....E....408 559-3330
3341 S Bascom Ave San Jose (95124) ***(P-10974)***
Bristol Hspice - Scramento LLC ....D....916 782-5511
2140 Prof Dr Ste 210 Roseville (95661) ***(P-16173)***

Bristol-Myers Squibb Company ... D ... 800 332-2056
700 Bay Rd Redwood City (94063) *(P-3875)*

Brita Products Company ... D ... 510 271-7000
1221 Broadway Ste 290 Oakland (94612) *(P-8992)*

Britannia Construction Inc ... E ... 650 742-6490
925 Terminal Way San Carlos (94070) *(P-624)*

Brite Industries Inc ... D ... 510 250-9330
1746 13th St Oakland (94607) *(P-7272)*

Brite Labs, Oakland *Also called Brite Industries Inc (P-7272)*

Brite Media, Oakland *Also called Mesmerize LLC (P-19575)*

Brite Media Group LLC (PA) ... E ... 877 479-7777
50 1st St Ste 600 San Francisco (94105) *(P-11802)*

Brite Media LLC (PA) ... C ... 877 479-7777
350 Frank Ogawa Plz Ste 3 Oakland (94612) *(P-11742)*

Britelab Inc ... D ... 650 961-0671
6341 San Ignacio Ave San Jose (95119) *(P-6739)*

Britevision Media, Oakland *Also called Brite Media LLC (P-11742)*

Britz Fertilizers Inc ... E ... 559 884-2421
21817 S Frsno Coalinga Rd Five Points (93624) *(P-9596)*

Brix Group Inc ... E ... 800 726-2333
4762 W Jennifer Ave # 103 Fresno (93722) *(P-7898)*

Brix Group Inc (PA) ... D ... 559 457-4700
838 N Laverne Ave Fresno (93727) *(P-8898)*

Brix Group Inc ... E ... 559 457-4750
80 Van Ness Ave Fresno (93721) *(P-6509)*

Brix Group Inc ... E ... 559 457-4794
80 Van Ness Ave Fresno (93721) *(P-8883)*

Broach Masters Inc ... E ... 530 885-1939
2160 Precision Pl Auburn (95603) *(P-5090)*

Broadcom, San Jose *Also called LSI Corporation (P-6182)*

Broadcom Corporation ... E ... 408 922-7000
250 Innovation Dr San Jose (95134) *(P-6072)*

Broadcom Corporation (HQ) ... A ... 408 433-8000
1320 Ridder Park Dr San Jose (95131) *(P-6073)*

Broadcom Inc (PA) ... B ... 408 433-8000
1320 Ridder Park Dr San Jose (95131) *(P-6074)*

Broadcom Technologies Inc (HQ) ... A ... 408 433-8000
1320 Ridder Park Dr San Jose (95131) *(P-6075)*

Broadlight Inc ... D ... 408 982-4210
2901 Tasman Dr Ste 218 Santa Clara (95054) *(P-6076)*

Broadly Inc ... E ... 510 400-6039
409 13th St Fl 3 Oakland (94612) *(P-13037)*

Broadmoor Hotel (PA) ... D ... 415 776-7034
1499 Sutter St San Francisco (94109) *(P-10975)*

Broadmoor Hotel ... D ... 415 673-8445
1465 65th St Apt 274 Emeryville (94608) *(P-10976)*

Broadmoor Hotel ... D ... 415 673-2511
1000 Sutter St San Francisco (94109) *(P-10977)*

Broadrach Cpitl Prtners Fund I ... A ... 650 331-2500
248 Homer Ave Palo Alto (94301) *(P-10751)*

Broadreach Capitl Partners LLC (PA) ... D ... 650 331-2500
855 El Cmino Real Bldg 5 Palo Alto (94301) *(P-10836)*

Broadreach Capitl Partners LLC ... A ... 415 354-4640
235 Montgomery St # 1018 San Francisco (94104) *(P-10837)*

Broadspectrum Americas Inc ... E ... 707 642-2222
155 Corporate Pl Vallejo (94590) *(P-19460)*

Broadstone Preschool, Folsom *Also called Phoenix Schools Inc (P-17996)*

Broadstone Raquet Club, Folsom *Also called Spare-Time Inc (P-15149)*

Broadway By Bay ... C ... 650 579-5565
1972 2nd Ave Walnut Creek (94597) *(P-14839)*

Broadway Management Co Inc ... E ... 925 820-7292
8 Crow Canyon Ct Ste 100 San Ramon (94583) *(P-10496)*

Broadway Mech - Contrs Inc ... C ... 510 746-4000
873 81st Ave Oakland (94621) *(P-1225)*

Broadway Sacramento ... C ... 916 446-5880
1419 H St Sacramento (95814) *(P-10379)*

Broadway Sacramento (PA) ... C ... 916 446-5880
1510 J St Ste 200 Sacramento (95814) *(P-14840)*

Broadway Sheet Metal & Mfg, South San Francisco *Also called Fonco Inc (P-1803)*

Broadway Villa Post Acute, Sonoma *Also called Ensign Sonoma LLC (P-15992)*

Brocade Cmmnctions Systems Inc ... D ... 408 333-4300
110 Holger Way San Jose (95134) *(P-19735)*

Brocade Cmmnctions Systems LLC (HQ) ... A ... 408 333-8000
1320 Ridder Park Dr San Jose (95131) *(P-5354)*

Brocap Vineyard Company, NAPA *Also called Twin Creeks Vineyard Company (P-78)*

Brocchini Farms Inc ... E ... 209 599-4229
27011 S Austin Rd Ripon (95366) *(P-47)*

Brock LLC (PA) ... D ... 925 371-2184
3025 Independence Dr C Livermore (94551) *(P-7826)*

Brock Transportation, Livermore *Also called Brock LLC (P-7826)*

Broderick General Engineering ... E ... 707 996-7809
21750 8th St E Ste B Sonoma (95476) *(P-1017)*

Broderick General Engineering ... D ... 707 996-7809
21750 8th St E Ste B Sonoma (95476) *(P-5025)*

Broker Solutions Inc ... D ... 707 392-4254
3558 Round Barn Blvd Santa Rosa (95403) *(P-19461)*

Broker Solutions Inc ... D ... 408 429-2085
55 S Market St Ste 1600 San Jose (95113) *(P-9869)*

Bromley Properties Inc ... D ... 707 546-4031
1500 Santa Rosa Ave Santa Rosa (95404) *(P-10978)*

Bronco Concrete Inc ... E ... 559 323-5005
3197 E North Ave Ste 101 Fresno (93725) *(P-1855)*

Brondell Inc ... E ... 415 315-9000
1830 Harrison St San Francisco (94103) *(P-9225)*

Brookdale Inn and Spa ... D ... 831 588-6609
11570 Highway 9 Brookdale (95007) *(P-10979)*

Brookfeld Bay Area Hldings LLC ... D ... 925 743-8000
500 La Gonda Way Ste 100 Danville (94526) *(P-10697)*

Brookfield Homes, Danville *Also called Brookfeld Bay Area Hldings LLC (P-10697)*

Brooks Home Health Care ... E ... 559 221-4800
5070 N 6th St Ste 169 Fresno (93710) *(P-17111)*

Brookside Cmnty Hlth Ctr Inc (PA) ... D ... 510 215-9092
2023 Vale Rd San Pablo (94806) *(P-15303)*

Brookside Country Club ... D ... 209 956-6200
3603 Saint Andrews Dr Stockton (95219) *(P-15065)*

Brookside Optometric Group ... E ... 209 951-0820
3133 W March Ln Ste 2020 Stockton (95219) *(P-15867)*

Brooktrails Resort Golf Course ... E ... 707 459-6761
24860 Birch St Willits (95490) *(P-14990)*

Brosamer & Wall Inc ... C ... 925 932-7900
1777 Oakland Blvd Ste 300 Walnut Creek (94596) *(P-18646)*

Brosamer & Wall LLC ... E ... 925 932-7900
1777 Oakland Blvd Ste 300 Walnut Creek (94596) *(P-10497)*

Brotherhood Teamsters Local 70, Oakland *Also called Teamsters Local Union 70 (P-18378)*

Brothers Pride Produce Inc (PA) ... E ... 650 368-6993
2345 Middlefield Rd Redwood City (94063) *(P-2253)*

Broward Builders Inc ... D ... 530 666-5635
1200 E Kentucky Ave Woodland (95776) *(P-837)*

Brower Mechanical Inc ... D ... 530 749-0808
4060 Alvis Ct Rocklin (95677) *(P-14683)*

Brown & Toland Medical Group ... C ... 415 923-3015
2100 Webster St Ste 117 San Francisco (94115) *(P-15304)*

Brown & Toland Medical Group ... C ... 415 752-8038
3905 Sacramento St # 301 San Francisco (94118) *(P-15305)*

Brown and Caldwell (PA) ... C ... 925 937-9010
201 N Civic Dr Ste 115 Walnut Creek (94596) *(P-18647)*

Brown Brown Insur Brks Scrmnto ... E ... 916 630-8643
5750 West Oaks Blvd # 140 Rocklin (95765) *(P-10251)*

Brown Brown Insur Svcs Cal Inc ... E ... 925 416-1692
5890 Stoneridge Dr # 209 Pleasanton (94588) *(P-10252)*

Brown Construction Inc ... D ... 916 374-8616
1465 Entp Blvd Ste 100 West Sacramento (95691) *(P-838)*

Brown Estate Vineyards LLC (PA) ... E ... 707 963-2435
3233 Sage Canyon Rd Saint Helena (94574) *(P-2516)*

Brown Tland Physcn Svcs Orgnzt (HQ) ... C ... 415 972-4162
1221 Broadway Ste 700 Oakland (94612) *(P-15306)*

Brownie Baker Inc ... D ... 559 277-7070
4870 W Jacquelyn Ave Fresno (93722) *(P-2414)*

Browning-Ferris Inds Cal Inc ... E ... 650 726-1819
12310 San Mateo Rd Half Moon Bay (94019) *(P-8311)*

Browning-Ferris Inds Cal Inc ... E ... 925 313-8901
951 Waterbird Way Martinez (94553) *(P-8312)*

Bruce Carone Grading & Pav Inc ... D ... 510 787-4070
2294 Vista Del Rio St Crockett (94525) *(P-1018)*

Bruce Tucker Construction Inc ... E ... 707 255-1587
2260 Brown St NAPA (94558) *(P-839)*

Bruce's Custom Covers, Morgan Hill *Also called Aircraft Covers Inc (P-3036)*

Bruder Industry ... D ... 916 939-6888
3920 Sandstone Dr El Dorado Hills (95762) *(P-5484)*

Bruni Glass Packaging Inc ... E ... 707 752-6200
2750 Maxwell Way Fairfield (94534) *(P-9191)*

Brunos Iron & Metal LP ... E ... 559 233-6543
3211 S Golden State Blvd Fresno (93725) *(P-8313)*

Brutocao Vineyards ... E ... 707 744-1320
1400 Highway 175 Hopland (95449) *(P-2517)*

Brutocaosellers.com, Hopland *Also called Brutocao Vineyards (P-2517)*

Bryant Estate ... E ... 707 963-0483
1567 Sage Canyon Rd Saint Helena (94574) *(P-2518)*

Bsgs Five Points, Five Points *Also called Britz Fertilizers Inc (P-9596)*

BSI Services & Solutions W Inc (HQ) ... E ... 408 790-9200
2150 N 1st St Ste 450 San Jose (95131) *(P-18648)*

BSK Associates ... E ... 559 277-6960
4230 W Swift Ave Ste 106 Fresno (93722) *(P-18649)*

BSK Associates ... E ... 559 497-2888
1414 Stanislaus St Fresno (93706) *(P-18650)*

BSK Associates ... E ... 916 853-9293
3140 Gold Camp Dr Ste 160 Rancho Cordova (95670) *(P-18651)*

BSK Associates ... E ... 559 256-2251
1415 Tuolumne St Fresno (93706) *(P-18652)*

Bsm, Concord *Also called Building Srvcs/System Mint Inc (P-843)*

Bsmi, Brentwood *Also called Bay Standard Manufacturing Inc (P-4871)*

Bsr, Berkeley *Also called Assocted Stdnts of The Univ CA (P-3558)*

Bssp, Sausalito *Also called Butler Shine Stern Prtners LLC (P-11743)*

BT Holdings Inc ... E ... 707 279-4317
4150 Soda Bay Rd Kelseyville (95451) *(P-97)*

Bti, Hercules *Also called Bridger Technologies Inc (P-6819)*

Btig LLC (PA) ... D ... 415 248-2200
600 Montgomery St Fl 6 San Francisco (94111) *(P-9959)*

Buchanan YMCA, San Francisco *Also called Young MNS Chrstn Assn San Frnc (P-18517)*

Buck Inst For RES On Aging (PA) ... C ... 415 209-2000
8001 Redwood Blvd Novato (94945) *(P-19200)*

Buckelew Programs (PA) ... C ... 415 457-6964
201 Alameda Del Prado # 103 Novato (94949) *(P-16996)*

Buckeye Fire Equipment Company ... B ... 510 483-1815
2416 Teagarden St San Leandro (94577) *(P-9055)*

Buckhorn Cafe Inc (PA) ... D ... 530 795-1319
2 Main St Winters (95694) *(P-2113)*

Buckingham Property Management ... D ... 559 322-1105
12609 Moffatt Ln Fresno (93730) *(P-11708)*

Buckingham Strategic Partners ... E ... 800 366-7266
10 Almaden Blvd Fl 15 San Jose (95113) *(P-19309)*

Buckland Vineyard MGT Inc ... D ... 530 333-1534
4560 Slodusty Rd Garden Valley (95633) *(P-19310)*

Buckles-Smith Electric Company (PA) ... D ... 408 280-7777
540 Martin Ave Santa Clara (95050) *(P-9056)*

Budget Electric, Tracy *Also called American Engrg Contrs Inc (P-1449)*

Buehler Engineering Inc (PA) ... E ... 916 443-0303
600 Q St Ste 200 Sacramento (95811) *(P-18653)*

ALPHABETIC

Employee Codes: A=Over 500 employees, B=251-500
C=101-250, D=51-100, E=20-50 F=10-19

2022 Northern California Business
Directory and Buyers Guide

© Mergent Inc. 1-800-342-5647
917

Buena Vista Business Svcs LP ....D....908 452-9002
1276 Lincoln Ave Ste 107 San Jose (95125) **(P-11676)**
Buena Vista Gaming Authority ....B....866 915-0777
4640 Coal Mine Rd Ione (95640) **(P-10980)**
Buffalo Bills Brewery, Hayward *Also called Steinbeck Brewing Company* **(P-2494)**
Buffalo Distribution Inc ....F....510 324-3800
30750 San Clemente St Hayward (94544) **(P-5650)**
Bugcrowd Inc (PA) ....C....650 260-8443
921 Front St Ste 100 San Francisco (94111) **(P-13858)**
Bugsnag Inc ....E....415 484-8664
110 Sutter St Fl 10 San Francisco (94104) **(P-13038)**
Build Group Inc (PA) ....C....415 367-9399
160 S Van Ness Ave San Francisco (94103) **(P-840)**
Build Group Inc ....D....408 986-8711
1210 Coleman Ave Santa Clara (95050) **(P-841)**
Build It Green ....E....510 590-3360
300 Frank H Ogawa Plz # 620 Oakland (94612) **(P-18325)**
Build Sjc, Santa Clara *Also called Build Group Inc* **(P-841)**
Build Your Own Garment, Dublin *Also called Print Ink Inc* **(P-3746)**
Buildcom Inc ....B....800 375-3403
402 Otterson Dr Ste 100 Chico (95928) **(P-8993)**
Builder Inc ....E....530 691-4354
1445 Grange St Redding (96001) **(P-842)**
Builders & Tradesmens ....D....916 772-9200
6610 Sierra College Blvd Rocklin (95677) **(P-10253)**
Builders & Tradesmens Insur ....E....916 772-9200
6610 Sierra College Blvd Rocklin (95677) **(P-10077)**
Builders Concrete Inc (HQ) ....E....559 225-3667
3664 W Ashlan Ave Fresno (93722) **(P-4461)**
Builders Concrete Inc (HQ) ....F....209 388-0183
3169 Beachwood Dr Merced (95348) **(P-4462)**
Builders Concrete Inc ....E....559 787-3117
17041 E Kings Canyon Rd Sanger (93657) **(P-4463)**
Builders Concrete - Merced, Merced *Also called Builders Concrete Inc* **(P-4462)**
Building & Facilities Svcs LLC (PA) ....C....650 458-9083
63 Bovet Rd Ste 334 San Mateo (94402) **(P-11930)**
Building Blocks, Oakland *Also called Seneca Family of Agencies* **(P-17732)**
Building Inspection Division, Stockton *Also called County of San Joaquin* **(P-14238)**
Building Material Distrs Inc (PA) ....C....209 745-3001
225 Elm Ave Galt (95632) **(P-8532)**
Building Robotics Inc ....D....510 972-9709
1504 Franklin St Ste 200 Oakland (94612) **(P-9057)**
Building Services/System Inc ....E....925 688-1234
2575 Stanwell Dr Concord (94520) **(P-11931)**
Building Srvcs/System Mint Inc ....D....925 688-1234
2575 Stanwell Dr Concord (94520) **(P-843)**
Buildingminds Inc (PA) ....E....973 397-6510
1200 Seaport Blvd Redwood City (94063) **(P-12314)**
Buildings & Grounds, Sacramento *Also called General Services Cal Dept* **(P-877)**
Builtio LLC ....E....415 255-5955
49 Geary St Ste 238 San Francisco (94108) **(P-12315)**
Bull Outdoor Products Inc ....E....909 770-8626
1011 E Pine St Ste A Lodi (95240) **(P-5700)**
Bulldog Reporter ....F....510 596-9300
124 Linden St Oakland (94607) **(P-3420)**
Bumblebee Spaces Inc (PA) ....E....415 624-3785
1004 Treat Ave San Francisco (94110) **(P-14220)**
Bundy and Sons Inc ....F....530 246-3868
15196 Mountain Shadows Dr Redding (96001) **(P-3057)**
Bungalow Living Inc ....D....415 501-0981
1 Letterman Dr Ste Cp500 San Francisco (94129) **(P-10498)**
Bunge Milling Inc ....D....530 666-1691
845 Kentucky Ave Woodland (95695) **(P-9500)**
Bunge North America, Modesto *Also called Bunge Oils Inc* **(P-2462)**
Bunge Oils Inc ....D....209 574-9981
436 S Mcclure Rd Modesto (95357) **(P-2462)**
Buoncristiani Wine Co LLC ....F....707 259-1681
2275 Soda Canyon Rd NAPA (94558) **(P-2519)**
Buoy Labs Inc ....F....855 481-7112
125 Mcpherson St Santa Cruz (95060) **(P-13039)**
Burbank Housing Dev Corp (PA) ....C....707 526-9782
1425 Corporate Cntr Pkwy Santa Rosa (95407) **(P-10698)**
Burdick Painting ....D....408 567-1330
705 Nuttman St Santa Clara (95054) **(P-2012)**
Bureau of Narcotic Enforcement, Stockton *Also called County of San Joaquin* **(P-17009)**
Bureau of Reclamation ....E....916 777-6992
2420 W Brannan Island Rd Isleton (95641) **(P-17449)**
Burger King, Menlo Park *Also called Whitevale Co Inc* **(P-10723)**
Burger Physcl Therapy Svcs Inc (HQ) ....C....916 983-5900
1301 E Bidwell St Ste 201 Folsom (95630) **(P-15885)**
Burger Physcl Therapy Svcs Inc ....E....530 626-4734
4250 Fowler Ln Ste 101 Diamond Springs (95619) **(P-15886)**
Burger Physcl Therapy Svcs Inc ....E....530 823-6835
11990 Heritage Oak Pl # 8 Auburn (95603) **(P-15887)**
Burger Physcl Thrapy Rhblttion, Folsom *Also called Burger Physcl Therapy Svcs Inc* **(P-15885)**
Burger Rhblitation Systems Inc (PA) ....C....800 900-8491
1301 E Bidwell St Ste 201 Folsom (95630) **(P-15888)**
Burgess Cellars Inc ....E....707 963-4766
1108 Deer Park Rd Saint Helena (94574) **(P-2520)**
Burgess Lumber (PA) ....F....707 542-5091
3610 Copperhill Ln Santa Rosa (95403) **(P-3093)**
Burgess Lumber ....E....707 485-8072
8800 West Rd Redwood Valley (95470) **(P-3094)**
Burgett Incorporated (PA) ....D....916 567-9999
4111a N Freeway Blvd Sacramento (95834) **(P-9192)**
Burke Industries Delaware Inc (HQ) ....C....408 297-3500
2250 S 10th St San Jose (95112) **(P-4213)**

Burky, Robert E Jr MD, Yuba City *Also called North Vly Orthpd Hand Srgery A* **(P-16464)**
Burlingame Country Club ....D....650 696-8100
80 New Place Rd Hillsborough (94010) **(P-15066)**
Burlingame Htg Ventilation Inc ....E....650 697-9142
821 Malcolm Rd Burlingame (94010) **(P-4745)**
Burlingame Industries Inc ....C....209 464-9001
4555 Mckinley Ave Stockton (95206) **(P-8639)**
BURLINGAME SENIOR CARE LLC ....E....650 692-3758
1100 Trousdale Dr Burlingame (94010) **(P-18064)**
Burlingame Skilled Nursing, Burlingame *Also called BURLINGAME SENIOR CARE LLC* **(P-18064)**
Burn Unit Ucd Medical Center ....E....916 734-3637
2315 Stockton Blvd Sacramento (95817) **(P-16752)**
Burnett Sons Planing Mill Lbr ....E....916 442-0493
214 11th St Sacramento (95814) **(P-3170)**
Burnham & Brown, Oakland *Also called Burnham Brown A Prof Corp* **(P-17222)**
Burnham Brown A Prof Corp ....C....510 444-6800
1901 Harrison St Ste 1100 Oakland (94612) **(P-17222)**
Burr Pilger Mayer Inc ....D....707 544-4078
110 Stony Point Rd # 210 Santa Rosa (95401) **(P-18937)**
Burr Pilger Mayer Inc (PA) ....C....415 421-5757
600 California St Fl 6 San Francisco (94108) **(P-18938)**
Burr Pilger Mayer Inc ....D....925 296-1040
2001 N Main St Ste 360 Walnut Creek (94596) **(P-18939)**
Burr Pilger Mayer Inc ....D....408 961-6300
10 Almaden Blvd Ste 1000 San Jose (95113) **(P-18940)**
Burr Pilger Mayer Inc ....D....650 855-6800
4200 Bohannon Dr Ste 250 Menlo Park (94025) **(P-18941)**
Burrell Consulting Group Inc ....E....916 783-8898
1001 Entp Way Ste 100 Roseville (95678) **(P-18654)**
Burrell Engineering, Roseville *Also called Burrell Consulting Group Inc* **(P-18654)**
Burson Marsteller, San Francisco *Also called Young & Rubicam LLC* **(P-19699)**
Bushnell Gardens ....D....916 791-4199
5255 Douglas Blvd Granite Bay (95746) **(P-9628)**
Bushnell's Landscape Creations, Granite Bay *Also called Bushnell Gardens* **(P-9628)**
Business Extension Bureau Ltd ....E....650 737-5700
500 S Airport Blvd South San Francisco (94080) **(P-3492)**
Business For Scial Rspnsbility (PA) ....E....415 984-3200
220 Montgomery St # 1700 San Francisco (94104) **(P-19462)**
Business Industry & Envmt Inc ....D....916 481-0268
3720 Madison Ave 210 North Highlands (95660) **(P-11880)**
Business Journal ....E....559 490-3400
1315 Van Ness Ave Ste 200 Fresno (93721) **(P-3493)**
Business Jrnl Publications Inc ....B....408 295-3800
125 S Market St 11 San Jose (95113) **(P-3421)**
Business Point Impressions, Concord *Also called Hnc Printing Services LLC* **(P-3655)**
Business Recovery Services Inc ....D....510 522-9700
1301 Marina Village Pkwy # 2 Alameda (94501) **(P-13700)**
Business Services Network ....D....415 282-8161
1275 Fairfax Ave Ste 103 San Francisco (94124) **(P-11836)**
Busseto Foods Inc (PA) ....C....559 485-9882
1351 N Crystal Ave Fresno (93728) **(P-2875)**
Butcher's Brand, San Leandro *Also called Webers Quality Meats Inc* **(P-9382)**
Butler Shine Stern Prtners LLC ....C....415 331-6049
20 Liberty Ship Way Sausalito (94965) **(P-11743)**
Butte Auto, Marysville *Also called Hust Brothers Inc* **(P-10578)**
Butte Basin Management Co ....E....530 674-2060
1624 Poole Blvd Yuba City (95993) **(P-19311)**
Butte Fics, Chico *Also called Victor Cmnty Support Svcs Inc* **(P-17089)**
Butte Home Health Inc ....D....530 895-0462
10 Constitution Dr Chico (95973) **(P-16862)**
Butte Home Health & Hospice, Chico *Also called Butte Home Health Inc* **(P-16862)**
Butte Sand and Gravel ....E....530 755-0225
10373 S Butte Rd Sutter (95982) **(P-591)**
Butterfield Electric Inc ....C....530 666-2116
2101 Freeway Dr Ste A Woodland (95776) **(P-1470)**
Button Transportation Inc ....C....707 678-7434
7000 Button Ln Dixon (95620) **(P-7515)**
Buxton Consulting ....D....925 467-0700
2010 Crow Canyon Pl # 100 San Ramon (94583) **(P-19736)**
Buy 4 Less ....D....209 368-3614
401 W Lockeford St Lodi (95240) **(P-8846)**
Buycoins Inc ....E....650 278-7402
2261 Market St San Francisco (94114) **(P-12316)**
Buyerlink, Walnut Creek *Also called One Planet Ops Inc* **(P-11776)**
Buyersroad Inc ....F....937 313-4466
3000 Executive Pkwy # 315 San Ramon (94583) **(P-13040)**
Buzz Converting Inc ....E....209 948-1341
4343 E Fremont St Stockton (95215) **(P-3350)**
Buzz Oates Management Services ....E....916 381-3843
555 Capitol Mall Ste 900 Sacramento (95814) **(P-10499)**
Bvk Gaming Inc ....D....707 644-8853
3466 Broadway St American Canyon (94503) **(P-15184)**
Bvrp America Inc ....E....303 450-1139
7031 Koll Center Pkwy # 15 Pleasanton (94566) **(P-13041)**
BVT Publishing, Redding *Also called Best Value Textbooks LLC* **(P-3559)**
Bw Integrated Systems ....F....559 638-8484
1949 E Manning Ave Reedley (93654) **(P-5198)**
BWC Weststeyn Dairy LP ....E....209 886-5334
1763 S Hewitt Rd Linden (95236) **(P-206)**
Bwdixon LLC (PA) ....E....707 678-1400
1345 Commercial Way Dixon (95620) **(P-10981)**
Bwm, Modesto *Also called Billington Welding & Mfg Inc* **(P-5125)**
By Quest LLC ....F....209 234-0202
2518 Boeing Way Stockton (95206) **(P-3723)**
By The Bay Health (PA) ....C....415 927-2273
17 E Sir Francis Drake Bl Larkspur (94939) **(P-16863)**

By The Bay Health ...E...415 626-5900
1540 Market St Ste 350 San Francisco (94102) *(P-16864)*
Byer California (PA) ...**A...415 626-7844**
66 Potrero Ave San Francisco (94103) *(P-2997)*
Byer California ...D...925 245-0184
3740 Livermore Outlets Dr Livermore (94551) *(P-2998)*
Byer California ...C...707 259-1225
811 Factory Stores Dr NAPA (94558) *(P-9251)*
Byers Enterprises Inc ...D...530 272-7777
11773 Slow Poke Ln Grass Valley (95945) *(P-1791)*
Byers Leafguard Gutter Systems, Grass Valley *Also called Byers Enterprises Inc (P-1791)*
Bynd LLC ...D...415 944-2293
100 Montgomery St # 1102 San Francisco (94104) *(P-12317)*
Byron Bethany Irrigation Dst ...D...209 835-0375
7995 Bruns Rd Byron (94514) *(P-8223)*
Byron Park, Walnut Creek *Also called A F Evans Company Inc (P-14190)*
Byte Mobile, Santa Clara *Also called Bytemobile Inc (P-8072)*
Bytemobile Inc (HQ) ...**B...408 327-7788**
2860 De La Cruz Blvd # 200 Santa Clara (95050) *(P-8072)*
Bytheways Manufacturing Inc ...D...916 453-1212
2080 Enterprise Blvd West Sacramento (95691) *(P-3330)*
Byton North America Corp ...C...408 966-5078
4201 Burton Dr Santa Clara (95054) *(P-6549)*
Bz - Bee Pollination Inc ...E...530 787-3044
24204 Rd 23 Esparto (95627) *(P-249)*
C & C Security Patrol Inc (PA) ...**C...510 713-1260**
4615 Enterprise Cmn Fremont (94538) *(P-14040)*
C & D Construction, Nevada City *Also called C & D Contractors Inc (P-625)*
C & D Contractors Inc ...E...530 264-7074
12803 Sneath Clay Rd Nevada City (95959) *(P-625)*
C & D Semiconductor Svcs Inc (PA) ...**E...408 383-1888**
2031 Concourse Dr San Jose (95131) *(P-6077)*
C & H Enterprises, Fremont *Also called Colleen & Herb Enterprises Inc (P-5494)*
C & J Contracting Inc ...E...408 374-6025
331 Commercial St San Jose (95112) *(P-844)*
C & O Painting Inc ...E...408 279-8011
1500 N 4th St San Jose (95112) *(P-1405)*
C & P Microsystems, Petaluma *Also called Colter & Peterson Microsystems (P-6714)*
C & S Draperies Inc ...C...209 466-5371
4210 Kiernan Ave Modesto (95356) *(P-11657)*
C 5 Children School ...E...415 626-4880
525 Golden Gate Ave San Francisco (94102) *(P-17867)*
C 5 Childrens School ...D...415 703-1277
455 Golden Gate Ave # 2400 San Francisco (94102) *(P-17868)*
C A P H, Oakland *Also called Califrnia Assn Pub Hsptals HLT (P-19684)*
C and C Wine Services Inc ...E...707 546-5712
2134 Olivet Rd Santa Rosa (95401) *(P-2521)*
C B S Marketwatch, San Francisco *Also called Marketwatch Inc (P-14155)*
C Big Corporation ...D...925 671-2110
1381 Galaxy Way Concord (94520) *(P-14933)*
C C S Medical Service, Modesto *Also called County of Stanislaus (P-12168)*
C Case Company Inc ...E...559 867-3912
7010 W Cerini Ave Riverdale (93656) *(P-561)*
C D I, Sacramento *Also called Creative Design Interiors Inc (P-1767)*
C D International Tech Inc ...F...408 986-0725
695 Pinnacle Pl Livermore (94550) *(P-6403)*
C D Simonian Insurance Inc ...E...559 834-5333
503 N 7th St Fowler (93625) *(P-10254)*
C D Simonian Insurance Agency, Fowler *Also called C D Simonian Insurance Inc (P-10254)*
C E I, Oakland *Also called Center For Elders Independence (P-10102)*
C E T, San Jose *Also called Center For Employment Training (P-17801)*
C E Toland & Son ...C...707 747-1000
5300 Industrial Way Benicia (94510) *(P-2013)*
C G A, Concord *Also called Concord Graphic Arts Inc (P-11858)*
C H I, Modesto *Also called Community Hospice Inc (P-16178)*
C H Reynolds Electric Inc ...B...408 436-9280
1281 Wayne Ave San Jose (95131) *(P-1471)*
C I W, Pittsburg *Also called Concord Iron Works Inc (P-4654)*
C J Health Services Inc ...D...510 793-3000
38650 Mission Blvd Fremont (94536) *(P-15948)*
C L Hann Industries Inc ...F...408 293-4800
1020 Timothy Dr San Jose (95133) *(P-5485)*
C L S Woodside Mgt Group (PA) ...**E...209 577-4181**
1620 N Carptr Rd Ste C28 Modesto (95351) *(P-10500)*
C Line Express ...E...707 553-6041
75 Mezzetta Ct American Canyon (94503) *(P-7516)*
C M A, Sacramento *Also called California Medical Association (P-18328)*
C M C, Fremont *Also called Content Management Corporation (P-3726)*
C M D Products, Roseville *Also called Cmd Products (P-4240)*
C M P, San Leandro *Also called Peggy S Lane Inc (P-4251)*
C M Service, San Carlos *Also called Commercial Mechanical Svc Inc (P-14686)*
C Mondavi & Family (PA) ...**D...707 967-2200**
2800 Main St Saint Helena (94574) *(P-2522)*
C N C Solutions (PA) ...**E...408 586-8236**
945 Ames Ave Milpitas (95035) *(P-9058)*
C O R A, San Mateo *Also called Cora Cmnty Ovrcming Rltnship A (P-17507)*
C Overaa & Co (PA) ...**B...510 234-0926**
200 Parr Blvd Richmond (94801) *(P-845)*
C P Shades Inc ...C...510 647-9605
2633 Ashby Ave Berkeley (94705) *(P-14221)*
C P Shades Inc (PA) ...**F...415 331-4581**
403 Coloma St Sausalito (94965) *(P-3008)*
C R I, San Francisco *Also called Coordnted Rsrces Inc San Frncs (P-8493)*
C R Martin Auctioneers Inc ...E...510 428-0100
5644 Telegraph Ave Oakland (94609) *(P-14222)*
C R S Drywall Inc ...D...408 998-4360
135 San Jose Ave San Jose (95125) *(P-1663)*
C S T I, San Jose *Also called Chemical Safety Technology Inc (P-4267)*
C T A, Rancho Cordova *Also called Cooper Thorne & Associates Inc (P-18675)*
C T E, North Highlands *Also called Construction Tstg & Engrg Inc (P-19263)*
C T R, Healdsburg *Also called Cooling Tower Resources Inc (P-3267)*
C V S Optical Lab Div, Rancho Cordova *Also called Vision Service Plan Inc (P-10157)*
C W A District Nine (HQ) ...**E...916 921-4500**
2870 Gateway Oaks Dr # 100 Sacramento (95833) *(P-18354)*
C W Brower Inc (PA) ...**D...209 523-1828**
413 S Riverside Dr Ste A Modesto (95354) *(P-9264)*
C W C, San Leandro *Also called Continental Western Corp (P-9115)*
C Y S, Fresno *Also called Comprhnsive Yuth Svcs Frsno In (P-17505)*
C&C Building Automation Co Inc ...E...650 292-7450
26062 Eden Landing Rd # 8 Hayward (94545) *(P-6895)*
C&D Precision Machining, San Jose *Also called C & D Semiconductor Svcs Inc (P-6077)*
C&H Sugar, Crockett *Also called C&H Sugar Company Inc (P-2423)*
C&H Sugar Company Inc ...A...510 787-2121
830 Loring Ave Crockett (94525) *(P-2423)*
C&N Reinforcing Inc ...E...209 399-2022
2194 Gibralter Dr Manteca (95337) *(P-1922)*
C&S Global Foods Inc ...F...209 392-2223
1651 Reynolds Ave Dos Palos (93620) *(P-2876)*
C&S Wholesale Grocers Inc ...D...916 383-5275
8301 Fruitridge Rd Sacramento (95826) *(P-7682)*
C&S Wholesale Grocers Inc ...C...559 442-4700
2797 S Orange Ave Fresno (93725) *(P-9265)*
C&T Publishing Inc ...E...925 677-0377
1651 Challenge Dr Concord (94520) *(P-3561)*
C.O.M.P.A.S.S., Redding *Also called Care Optons MGT Plans Spprtive (P-16868)*
C2 Financial Corporation ...C...925 938-1300
3000 Citrus Cir Ste 118 Walnut Creek (94598) *(P-10036)*
C2 Financial Corporation ...C...559 824-2300
978 Burlingame Ave Clovis (93612) *(P-10037)*
C3 Delaware Inc ...F...650 503-2200
1300 Seaport Blvd Ste 500 Redwood City (94063) *(P-13042)*
C3 Nano Inc ...D...510 259-9650
3988 Trust Way Hayward (94545) *(P-19154)*
C3-Ilex LLC (PA) ...**E...510 659-8300**
46609 Fremont Blvd Fremont (94538) *(P-6700)*
C3AI INC (PA) ...**C...650 503-2200**
1300 Seaport Blvd Ste 500 Redwood City (94063) *(P-13043)*
Ca Inc ...C...800 225-5224
3965 Freedom Cir Fl 6 Santa Clara (95054) *(P-13044)*
Ca Inc ...D...408 433-8000
1320 Ridder Park Dr San Jose (95131) *(P-6078)*
Caban Systems Inc ...E...831 245-1608
858 Stanton Rd Burlingame (94010) *(P-6486)*
Cabana Hotel, Palo Alto *Also called 4290 El Camino Properties LP (P-10905)*
Cabinetry, Sacramento *Also called Premier Woodworking LLC (P-3147)*
Cabinets By Andy Inc ...F...707 839-0220
2411 Central Ave McKinleyville (95519) *(P-3171)*
Cable Car Partners LLC (PA) ...**E...415 922-2425**
190 Napoleon St San Francisco (94124) *(P-15185)*
Cable Com, Fresno *Also called Cablecom LLC (P-14692)*
Cable Connection Inc ...D...510 249-9000
1035 Mission Ct Fremont (94539) *(P-5711)*
Cable Moore Inc (PA) ...**E...510 436-8000**
4700 Coliseum Way Oakland (94601) *(P-4967)*
Cable Wholesalecom Inc (PA) ...**E...925 455-0800**
1200 Voyager St Livermore (94551) *(P-8679)*
Cable-Cisco, San Francisco *Also called Carpenter Group (P-5059)*
Cablecom LLC ...E...916 891-2400
5337 Luce Ave McClellan (95652) *(P-14691)*
Cablecom LLC ...E...559 412-8720
5745 E Fountain Way Fresno (93727) *(P-14692)*
Cabrera Painting Inc ...E...408 998-4789
1262 Shortridge Ave San Jose (95116) *(P-1406)*
Cabrillo Cmnty Cllege Dst Fing (PA) ...**A...831 479-6100**
6500 Soquel Dr Aptos (95003) *(P-14841)*
Cabrillo College, Aptos *Also called Cabrillo Cmnty Cllege Dst Fing (P-14841)*
Cabrillo College Children Ctr ...E...831 479-6352
6500 Soquel Dr Aptos (95003) *(P-17869)*
Cabrillo Fitness Club ...E...831 475-5979
6200 Soquel Dr Aptos (95003) *(P-15067)*
Cache Creek Casino Resort ...A...530 796-3118
14455 State Highway 16 Brooks (95606) *(P-10982)*
Cache Creek Foods LLC ...F...530 662-1764
411 N Pioneer Ave Woodland (95776) *(P-2877)*
Cadatasoft Inc (PA) ...**D...214 935-1355**
3350 Scott Blvd Ste 5502 Santa Clara (95054) *(P-19463)*
Cade Corporation ...D...310 539-2508
100 Lewis St San Jose (95112) *(P-4156)*
Cadence Design Systems Inc (PA) ...**A...408 943-1234**
2655 Seely Ave Bldg 5 San Jose (95134) *(P-13045)*
Cadent Inc ...C...408 470-1000
2560 Orchard Pkwy San Jose (95131) *(P-13562)*
Cadent Tech Inc (HQ) ...**D...408 642-6400**
4 N 2nd St Ste 1100 San Jose (95113) *(P-12318)*
Cae Online, Palo Alto *Also called Capital Asset Exch & Trdg LLC (P-9059)*
Cafe Chromatic ...D...510 220-1341
460 Lincoln Ave Ste 10 San Jose (95126) *(P-2837)*
Cafe Niebaum Coppola, San Francisco *Also called Niebam-Cppola Estate Winery LP (P-2669)*
Cafe Villa, San Rafael *Also called Villa Inn (P-11558)*
CAHF, Sacramento *Also called Califrnia Assn Hlth Facilities (P-18304)*
Cahill Contractors Inc (PA) ...**C...415 986-0600**
425 California St # 2200 San Francisco (94104) *(P-846)*

ALPHABETIC

Cahill Contractors LLC D 415 986-0600
425 California St # 2200 San Francisco (94104) *(P-847)*

Cai International Inc (PA) E **415 788-0100**
1 Market Plz Ste 2400 San Francisco (94105) *(P-12033)*

Caitcon LLC A 925 314-7100
2001 Crow Canyon Rd # 110 San Ramon (94583) *(P-12017)*

Caito Fisheries Inc (PA) D **707 964-6368**
19400 Harbor Ave Fort Bragg (95437) *(P-9361)*

Cake Corporation D 650 215-7777
1528 S El Cmino Real Ste San Mateo (94402) *(P-12319)*

Cakebread Cellar Vineyards, Rutherford *Also called Cakebread Cellars (P-2523)*

Cakebread Cellars D 707 963-5221
8300 Saint Helena Hwy Rutherford (94573) *(P-2523)*

Cal Care Inc D 650 325-8600
1275 Crane St Menlo Park (94025) *(P-19312)*

Cal Central Catering Trailers, Modesto *Also called Golden Valley & Associates Inc (P-5063)*

Cal Chamber, Sacramento *Also called California Chamber Commerce (P-18302)*

Cal Coast Financial Inc D 510 683-9850
39355 California St # 101 Fremont (94538) *(P-9892)*

Cal Coast Financial Corp (PA) D **510 683-9850**
5960 Stoneridge Dr # 101 Pleasanton (94588) *(P-9893)*

Cal Coast Telecom, San Jose *Also called Radonich Corp (P-1573)*

Cal Consoldated Communications B 916 786-6141
211 Lincoln St Roseville (95678) *(P-7936)*

Cal Courts, Eureka *Also called Nor-Wall Inc (P-15115)*

Cal Crush, Ripon *Also called California Rock Crushers (P-1153)*

Cal Custom Enterprises Inc F 530 774-2621
792 Durham Dayton Hwy Durham (95938) *(P-14711)*

Cal Custom Tile D 559 875-1460
1300 Commerce Way Sanger (93657) *(P-1711)*

Cal Inc E 707 446-7996
2040 Peabody Rd Ste 400 Vacaville (95687) *(P-848)*

Cal Insurance and Assoc Inc D 415 661-6500
2311 Taraval St San Francisco (94116) *(P-10255)*

Cal Land Title E 707 361-5760
497 Walnut St NAPA (94559) *(P-10256)*

Cal Lighting, San Ramon *Also called Califrnia Architectural Ltg Inc (P-8847)*

Cal Nor Trucking Inc (PA) D **530 695-9219**
2670 Apricot St Live Oak (95953) *(P-7517)*

Cal North, Sacramento *Also called Califrnia Yuth Soccer Assn Inc (P-18554)*

Cal Packing & Storage LP D 559 638-2929
1356 S Buttonwillow Ave Reedley (93654) *(P-7677)*

Cal Ranch Inc (PA) D **925 429-2900**
2628 Concord Blvd Concord (94519) *(P-2254)*

Cal Saw, San Francisco *Also called Sawbirds Inc (P-4612)*

Cal Shakes, Orinda *Also called California Shakespeare Theater (P-14842)*

Cal Sheets LLC D 209 234-3300
1212 Performance Dr Stockton (95206) *(P-3354)*

Cal Southern Seafood Inc (PA) D **805 698-8262**
125 Salinas Rd Ste 5b Royal Oaks (95076) *(P-9362)*

Cal Strs, West Sacramento *Also called Califrnia State Tchers Rtrment (P-10213)*

Cal Trans, San Leandro *Also called California Government Trnsp (P-7869)*

Cal Valley Construction Inc E 559 274-0300
5125 N Gates Ave Ste 102 Fresno (93722) *(P-1152)*

Cal Vsta Erosion Ctrl Pdts LLC E 530 476-0706
459 Country Rd 99w 99 W Arbuckle (95912) *(P-5026)*

Cal Yuba Investments, Olivehurst *Also called Yuba Rver Mlding Mill Work Inc (P-3165)*

Cal-Asia Truss Inc E 916 685-5648
10547 E Stockton Blvd Elk Grove (95624) *(P-3202)*

Cal-Coast Dairy Systems Inc E 209 634-9026
424 S Tegner Rd Turlock (95380) *(P-4997)*

Cal-Pacific Construction Inc E 650 557-1238
1009 Terra Nova Blvd Pacifica (94044) *(P-849)*

Cal-Sierra Technologies Inc E 510 742-9996
39055 Hastings St Ste 103 Fremont (94538) *(P-12320)*

Cal-Sign Wholesale Inc F 209 523-7446
5260 Jerusalem Ct Modesto (95356) *(P-7222)*

Cal-Spray Inc F 650 325-0096
1905 Bay Rd East Palo Alto (94303) *(P-4929)*

Cal-Weld Inc C 510 226-0100
4308 Solar Way Fremont (94538) *(P-4984)*

Cal-West Concrete Cutting Inc C 209 823-2236
1153 Vanderbilt Cir Manteca (95337) *(P-1856)*

Cal-West Precision Solutions F 408 988-8069
3485 Edward Ave Santa Clara (95054) *(P-5072)*

Cala Health Inc D 415 890-3961
875 Mahler Rd Ste 168 Burlingame (94010) *(P-7098)*

Calaveras County Water Dst D 209 754-3543
120 Toma Ct San Andreas (95249) *(P-8224)*

Calaveras Enterprise, San Andreas *Also called Calaveras First Co Inc (P-3422)*

Calaveras First Co Inc E 209 754-3861
15 Main St San Andreas (95249) *(P-3422)*

Calaveras Materials Inc (HQ) E **209 883-0448**
1100 Lowe Rd Hughson (95326) *(P-4464)*

Calaveras Materials Inc E 559 233-2311
2095 E Central Ave Fresno (93725) *(P-8620)*

Calbee North America LLC E 707 427-2500
2600 Maxwell Way Fairfield (94534) *(P-9324)*

Calcerts Inc E 916 985-3400
31 Natoma St Ste 120 Folsom (95630) *(P-19464)*

Calchef Foods LLC E 888 638-7083
4221 E Mariposa Rd Ste B Stockton (95215) *(P-2277)*

Calcom Energy, Fresno *Also called California Coml Solar Inc (P-1226)*

Calcpa Institute E 800 922-5272
1710 Gilbreth Rd Ste 100 Burlingame (94010) *(P-18399)*

Calculex E 707 578-2307
131 Stony Cir Ste 500a Santa Rosa (95401) *(P-6390)*

Caldwell Vineyard LLC F 707 255-1294
169 Kreuzer Ln NAPA (94559) *(P-2524)*

Caledonian Building Svcs Inc E 925 803-3500
47 Rickenbacker Cir Livermore (94551) *(P-11932)*

Calex Mfg Co Inc E 925 687-4411
2401 Stanwell Dr Frnt Concord (94520) *(P-8899)*

Cali Calmecac Language Academy D 707 837-7747
9491 Starr Rd Windsor (95492) *(P-18400)*

Cali Food Company Inc (PA) F **408 515-3178**
45401 Research Ave Fremont (94539) *(P-2198)*

Caliber Bodyworks Texas Inc D 408 972-0300
3517 Hillcap Ave San Jose (95136) *(P-14521)*

Caliber Bodyworks Texas Inc E 559 435-9900
125 E Auto Center Dr Fresno (93710) *(P-14522)*

Caliber Collision Centers, San Jose *Also called Caliber Bodyworks Texas Inc (P-14521)*

Caliber Home Loans Inc E 925 417-3491
6600 Koll Center Pkwy Pleasanton (94566) *(P-9894)*

Caliber Home Loans Inc E 530 894-6418
2101 Forest Ave Ste 150 Chico (95928) *(P-9895)*

Caliber Home Loans Inc E 707 432-1000
3700 Hilborn Rd Ste 700 Fairfield (94534) *(P-9896)*

Caliber Home Loans Inc E 707 834-6094
527 D St Eureka (95501) *(P-9897)*

Calico Hardwoods Inc D 707 546-4045
3580 Westwind Blvd Santa Rosa (95403) *(P-3120)*

Calico Life Sciences LLC D 650 754-6200
1170 Veterans Blvd South San Francisco (94080) *(P-19038)*

Calidad Industries Inc B 510 698-7200
1301 30th Ave Oakland (94601) *(P-17796)*

Calif Stat Univ Fres Foun E 559 278-0850
5370 N Chestnut Ave Fresno (93725) *(P-18552)*

California 5 Minute Car Wash, Modesto *Also called Charles Fenley Enterprises (P-14636)*

California Academy Sciences (PA) A **415 379-8000**
55 Music Concourse Dr San Francisco (94118) *(P-18289)*

California Advncd Imaging Med E 415 884-3413
504 Redwood Blvd Ste 300 Novato (94947) *(P-17112)*

California Amercn Exterminator, Boulder Creek *Also called Godfathers Exterminator Inc (P-11899)*

California Apartment Assn E 916 447-7881
980 9th St Ste 1430 Sacramento (95814) *(P-18301)*

California Appellate Project (PA) E **415 495-0500**
345 California St # 1400 San Francisco (94104) *(P-17223)*

CALIFORNIA ARMENIAN HOME, Fresno *Also called California HM For The Aged Inc (P-16222)*

California Autism Center D 559 475-7860
1630 E Shaw Ave Ste 190 Fresno (93710) *(P-17450)*

California Backyard Inc (PA) E **916 543-1900**
130 Cyber Ct Rocklin (95765) *(P-8508)*

California Bag, Woodland *Also called Acme Bag Co Inc (P-3390)*

California Brazing, Newark *Also called Nevada Heat Treating LLC (P-14718)*

California Bulk Inc C 209 983-1069
3939 Producers Dr Stockton (95206) *(P-7518)*

California Cab & Store Fix E 916 386-1340
8472 Carbide Ct Sacramento (95828) *(P-3123)*

California Cabinet & Storage, Sacramento *Also called California Cabinet & Str Fixs (P-3172)*

California Cabinet & Str Fixs E 916 681-0901
8472 Carbide Ct Sacramento (95828) *(P-3172)*

California Cascade Industries C 916 736-3353
7512 14th Ave Sacramento (95820) *(P-3256)*

California Cascade-Woodland E 530 666-1261
1492 Churchill Downs Ave Woodland (95776) *(P-3257)*

CALIFORNIA CASUALITY, San Mateo *Also called California Casualty Mgt Co (P-10162)*

California Casualty Mgt Co (HQ) C **650 574-4000**
1875 S Grant St Ste 800 San Mateo (94402) *(P-10162)*

California Cedar Products Co (PA) E **209 932-5002**
2385 Arch Airport Rd # 50 Stockton (95206) *(P-3265)*

California Cereal Products Inc (PA) D **510 452-4500**
1267 14th St Oakland (94607) *(P-9501)*

California Chamber Commerce (PA) D **916 444-6670**
1215 K St Ste 1400 Sacramento (95814) *(P-18302)*

California Closet Co, Concord *Also called Closet Innovation Inc (P-2021)*

California Closet Company Inc (HQ) E **510 763-2033**
1414 Harbour Way S Richmond (94804) *(P-2014)*

California Cmplte CNT Cnsus D 916 852-2020
400 R St Ste 350 Sacramento (95811) *(P-19201)*

California Coastal Insurance (PA) E **925 866-7050**
3000 Executive Pkwy # 300 San Ramon (94583) *(P-10257)*

California Coml Solar Inc D 559 667-9200
9479 N Fort Washington Rd # 105 Fresno (93730) *(P-1226)*

California Concentrate Company E 209 334-9112
18678 N Highway 99 Acampo (95220) *(P-2290)*

California Concrete Pipe Corp D 209 466-4212
2960 S Highway 99 Stockton (95215) *(P-4422)*

California Convalescent Hosp, San Francisco *Also called Timberlake-Forrest Inc (P-16278)*

California Cryobank Inc B 650 635-1420
611 Gateway Blvd Ste 820 South San Francisco (94080) *(P-17113)*

California Cslty Fire Insur Co E 650 574-4000
1900 Alameda De Las Pulga San Mateo (94403) *(P-10163)*

California Cslty Gen Insur Co (HQ) C **650 574-4000**
1900 Alameda De Las Pulga San Mateo (94403) *(P-10164)*

California Custom Proc LLC E 559 416-5122
3211 Aviation Dr Madera (93637) *(P-791)*

California Dairies Inc C 559 233-5154
755 F St Fresno (93706) *(P-2186)*

California Dairies Inc C 209 656-1942
475 S Tegner Rd Turlock (95380) *(P-2141)*

California Dental Arts LLC D 408 255-1020
20421 Pacifica Dr Cupertino (95014) *(P-16823)*

California Dental Association (PA)..........C.......**916 443-0505**
1201 K St Fl 14 Sacramento (95814) ***(P-18326)***
California Department Tech..........E.......916 464-3747
10860 Gold Center Dr # 100 Rancho Cordova (95670) ***(P-13701)***
California Department Tech (HQ)..........C.......**916 319-9223**
1325 J St Ste 1600 Sacramento (95814) ***(P-13859)***
California Department Trnsp..........D.......707 762-6641
611 Payran St Petaluma (94952) ***(P-1019)***
California Department Trnsp..........E.......707 445-6600
1656 Union St Eureka (95501) ***(P-19737)***
California Department Trnsp..........D.......707 428-2031
2019 W Texas St Fairfield (94533) ***(P-1020)***
California Department Trnsp..........D.......530 842-2723
1745 S Main St Yreka (96097) ***(P-1021)***
California Dept of Pub Hlth..........C.......510 231-7408
850 Marina Bay Pkwy F175 Richmond (94804) ***(P-15307)***
California Door, Morgan Hill *Also called California Kit Cab Door Corp* ***(P-3173)***
California Drywall Co (PA)..........C.......**408 292-7500**
2290 S 10th St San Jose (95112) ***(P-1664)***
California Ear Institute Inc..........E.......650 494-1000
844 Portola Rd Portola Valley (94028) ***(P-15308)***
California Eastern Labs Inc (PA)..........D.......**408 919-2500**
5201 Great America Pkwy Santa Clara (95054) ***(P-8900)***
California Emergency Physician, Modesto *Also called Medamerica Billing Svcs Inc* ***(P-18979)***
California Endive Farm, Rio Vista *Also called California Vegetable Spc Inc* ***(P-9390)***
California Envmtl Systems Inc..........D.......530 820-3693
12265 Locksley Ln Auburn (95602) ***(P-18655)***
California Expanded Met Pdts..........F.......925 473-9340
1001a Pttsburg Antoch Hwy Pittsburg (94565) ***(P-4848)***
California Eye Institute..........C.......559 449-5000
Low Vsion Dept St Agnes H Fresno (93720) ***(P-15309)***
California Family Foods LLC..........D.......530 476-3326
6550 Struckmeyer Rd Arbuckle (95912) ***(P-2316)***
California Field Office, San Francisco *Also called Nature Conservancy* ***(P-18443)***
California Fire Fghtrs Apprent..........E.......916 648-1717
1780 Creekside Oaks Dr Sacramento (95833) ***(P-17797)***
California Fruit Basket, Sanger *Also called Melkonian Enterprises Inc* ***(P-2263)***
California Fruit Exchange LLC (PA)..........C.......**209 334-2988**
6011 E Pine St Lodi (95240) ***(P-9389)***
California Gold Dev Corp..........E.......209 533-3333
133 Old Wards Ferry Rd G Sonora (95370) ***(P-850)***
California Government Trnsp..........E.......510 614-5942
600 Lewelling Blvd San Leandro (94579) ***(P-7869)***
California Grand Casino..........D.......925 685-8397
5988 Pacheco Blvd Pacheco (94553) ***(P-15186)***
California Health Benefit Exch..........D.......916 228-8210
1601 Exposition Blvd Sacramento (95815) ***(P-18327)***
California Health Insur Exch, Sacramento *Also called California Health Benefit Exch* ***(P-18327)***
California Heritage Mills Inc..........E.......530 438-2100
1 Comet Ln Maxwell (95955) ***(P-2317)***
California Hlth Collaborative (PA)..........D.......**559 221-6315**
1680 W Shaw Ave Fresno (93711) ***(P-14223)***
California HM For The Aged Inc..........C.......559 251-8414
6720 E Kings Canyon Rd Fresno (93727) ***(P-16222)***
California Hospital Assn Cha, Sacramento *Also called Califrnia Assn Hsptals Hlth Sy* ***(P-18333)***
California House, Sacramento *Also called Beauty Craft Furniture Corp* ***(P-3274)***
California Human Dev Corp (PA)..........C.......**707 523-1155**
3315 Airway Dr Santa Rosa (95403) ***(P-17798)***
California Hydronics Corp (PA)..........E.......**510 293-1993**
2293 Tripaldi Way Hayward (94545) ***(P-9007)***
California Imaging Inst LLC (PA)..........E.......**559 325-5810**
1867 E Fir Ave Ste 101 Fresno (93720) ***(P-19202)***
California Industrial Mfg LLC (PA)..........F.......**530 846-9960**
1221 Independence Pl Gridley (95948) ***(P-7273)***
California Industrial Rbr Co (PA)..........E.......**559 268-7321**
2539 S Cherry Ave Fresno (93706) ***(P-9111)***
California Industrial Rbr Co..........F.......530 674-2444
1690 Sierra Ave Yuba City (95993) ***(P-3813)***
California ISO, Folsom *Also called Califrnia Ind Sys Oprator Corp* ***(P-8090)***
California Kit Cab Door Corp (PA)..........B.......**408 782-5700**
400 Cochrane Cir Morgan Hill (95037) ***(P-3173)***
California Life Company, South San Francisco *Also called Calico Life Sciences LLC* ***(P-19038)***
California Lithographers, Concord *Also called Acme Press Inc* ***(P-3614)***
California Lumber Company Inc..........E.......925 939-2105
2336 Bates Ave Concord (94520) ***(P-2015)***
California Materials Inc..........E.......209 472-7422
3736 S Highway 99 Stockton (95215) ***(P-7454)***
California Medical Association (PA)..........D.......**916 444-5532**
1201 K St Ste 800 Sacramento (95814) ***(P-18328)***
California Mfg & Engrg Co LLC..........C.......559 842-1500
1401 S Madera Ave Kerman (93630) ***(P-5027)***
California Mrtg Advisors Inc..........E.......415 451-4888
4304 Redwood Hwy 100 San Rafael (94903) ***(P-9898)***
California Natural Color, Modesto *Also called E & J Gallo Winery* ***(P-2558)***
California Natural Products..........B.......209 858-2525
1250 Lathrop Rd Lathrop (95330) ***(P-2878)***
California Newspapers Inc..........A.......415 883-8600
150 Alameda Del Prado Novato (94949) ***(P-3423)***
California Newspapers Partnr (PA)..........E.......**408 920-5333**
4 N 2nd St Ste 700 San Jose (95113) ***(P-3424)***
California Nuggets Inc..........E.......209 599-7131
23073 S Frederick Rd Ripon (95366) ***(P-2852)***
California Nurses Association (PA)..........D.......**510 273-2200**
155 Grand Ave Ste 115 Oakland (94612) ***(P-18329)***
California Olive and Vine LLC..........F.......530 763-7921
1670 Poole Blvd Yuba City (95993) ***(P-2463)***
California Olive Ranch Inc (PA)..........E.......**530 846-8000**
265 Airpark Blvd Ste 200 Chico (95973) ***(P-2464)***
California Oregon Broadcasting (HQ)..........D.......**530 243-7777**
755 Auditorium Dr Redding (96001) ***(P-8039)***
California Overnight, Sacramento *Also called Express Messenger Systems Inc* ***(P-7644)***
California Overnight, San Francisco *Also called Express Messenger Systems Inc* ***(P-7646)***
California Paint Company, Fairfield *Also called LB Ford Painting Inc* ***(P-1420)***
California Pajarosa Floral..........E.......831 722-6374
133 Hughes Rd Watsonville (95076) ***(P-116)***
California Parenting Institute..........D.......707 585-6108
3650 Standish Ave Santa Rosa (95407) ***(P-17870)***
California Park Rehab Hos..........E.......530 894-1010
2850 Sierra Sunrise Ter Chico (95928) ***(P-15949)***
California Parking Company (PA)..........D.......**415 781-4896**
768 Sansome St San Francisco (94111) ***(P-10476)***
California Pavement Maint Inc..........C.......916 381-8033
9390 Elder Creek Rd Sacramento (95829) ***(P-1022)***
California Paving Company, Oakhurst *Also called Persson Inc* ***(P-1070)***
California Payroll, Brentwood *Also called Promerio Inc* ***(P-18987)***
California PCF Med Ctr Depts, San Francisco *Also called Sutter Health* ***(P-16649)***
California Performance Packg..........D.......909 390-4422
33200 Lewis St Union City (94587) ***(P-4239)***
California Physicians Service..........D.......925 927-7419
2066 Camel Ln Apt 24 Walnut Creek (94596) ***(P-10094)***
California Physicians Service..........D.......530 668-2986
6300 Canoga Ave Woodland (95695) ***(P-10095)***
California Physicians Service (PA)..........A.......**510 607-2000**
601 12th St Oakland (94607) ***(P-10096)***
California Physicians Service..........D.......530 351-6115
4700 Bechelli Ln Redding (96002) ***(P-10097)***
California Physicians Service..........D.......949 859-6303
1915 Laurel St NAPA (94559) ***(P-10098)***
California Physicians Service..........D.......916 350-7730
10834 International Dr Rancho Cordova (95670) ***(P-10099)***
California Physicians Service..........D.......559 440-4000
5250 N Palm Ave Ste 120 Fresno (93704) ***(P-10100)***
CALIFORNIA PINES LODGE, Alturas *Also called Califrnia Property Owners Assn* ***(P-10984)***
California Primary Care Assn..........E.......916 440-8170
1231 I St Ste 400 Sacramento (95814) ***(P-18330)***
California Restaurant Assn..........E.......916 447-5793
621 Capitol Mall Ste 2000 Sacramento (95814) ***(P-18401)***
California Rock Crushers..........E.......209 599-9941
339 Doak Blvd Ripon (95366) ***(P-1153)***
California Royale LLC..........E.......209 874-1866
5043 N Montpelier Rd Denair (95316) ***(P-274)***
California Rural Water Assn..........E.......916 553-4900
1234 N Market Blvd Sacramento (95834) ***(P-18303)***
California Sandwich Company, West Sacramento *Also called 3stonedeggs Inc* ***(P-9344)***
California Schl Employees Assn (PA)..........C.......**408 473-1000**
2045 Lundy Ave San Jose (95131) ***(P-18355)***
California School Boards Assn..........D.......800 266-3382
3251 Beacon Blvd West Sacramento (95691) ***(P-18331)***
California School of Mech Arts..........D.......415 333-4021
755 Ocean Ave San Francisco (94112) ***(P-10380)***
California Security Alarms Inc (PA)..........E.......**800 669-7779**
2440 Camino Ramon Ste 200 San Ramon (94583) ***(P-14123)***
California Security Svcs Inc (PA)..........E.......**530 749-0280**
5548 Feather River Blvd Olivehurst (95961) ***(P-14041)***
California Security Svcs Inc..........E.......530 899-3751
35 Heritage Ln Ste 6 Chico (95926) ***(P-14042)***
California Seniors Care, Campbell *Also called Natalie Dstiny Entps Ltd Lblty* ***(P-17653)***
California Shakespeare Theater (PA)..........C.......**510 548-3422**
100 Clfrnia Shkspear Thte Orinda (94563) ***(P-14842)***
California Shellfish Co Inc..........C.......707 542-9490
1280 Columbus Ave 300r San Francisco (94133) ***(P-9363)***
California Sierra Express Inc..........E.......916 375-7070
2975 Oates St Ste 30 West Sacramento (95691) ***(P-7827)***
California Sierra Express Inc..........E.......510 786-9974
2720 W Winton Ave Hayward (94545) ***(P-7828)***
California Sierra Express Inc..........E.......559 441-1300
1842 G St Fresno (93725) ***(P-7738)***
California Skin Institute..........D.......650 969-5600
6399 San Ignacio Ave San Jose (95119) ***(P-15310)***
CALIFORNIA SOCIETY OF CPA'S, Burlingame *Also called Califrnia Soc Crtif Pub Accntn* ***(P-18335)***
California State Univ Long Bch..........C.......559 278-2216
5201 N Maple Ave Fresno (93740) ***(P-14843)***
California Stl Fabricators Inc..........E.......209 566-0629
1120 Reno Ave Modesto (95351) ***(P-4649)***
California Stl Stair Rail Mfr..........E.......209 824-1785
587 Carnegie St Manteca (95337) ***(P-4540)***
California Suites (PA)..........E.......**916 941-7970**
4970 Windplay Dr El Dorado Hills (95762) ***(P-10477)***
California Sun Inc..........D.......916 789-1034
8265 Sierra College Blvd Roseville (95661) ***(P-11709)***
California Sun Rooms, Rancho Cordova *Also called Califrnia Cstm Snroms Ptio Cve* ***(P-2016)***
California Tahoe Conservancy..........E.......530 542-5580
1061 3rd St South Lake Tahoe (96150) ***(P-19898)***
California Teachers Assn (PA)..........C.......**650 697-1400**
1705 Murchison Dr Burlingame (94010) ***(P-18332)***
California Tile Installers, San Jose *Also called U S Perma Inc* ***(P-1727)***
California Tiny House Inc..........F.......559 316-4500
3337 W Sussex Way Fresno (93722) ***(P-3247)***
California Track & Engineering..........E.......559 237-2590
4668 N Sonora Ave Ste 101 Fresno (93722) ***(P-7190)***

A L P H A B E T I C

California Trenchless Inc ALPHABETIC SECTION

California Trenchless Inc ....E 510 782-5335
2315 Dunn Rd Hayward (94545) ***(P-1091)***
California Tribal Tanf Partnr (PA) ....**D 707 262-4404**
991 Parallel Dr Ste B Lakeport (95453) ***(P-17451)***
California Trvl & Tourism Comm ....E 916 444-4429
555 Capitol Mall Ste 1100 Sacramento (95814) ***(P-7794)***
California United Mech Inc (PA) ....**B 408 232-9000**
2185 Oakland Rd San Jose (95131) ***(P-1227)***
California Vacation Club ....E 707 252-4200
500 Lincoln Ave NAPA (94558) ***(P-10983)***
California Valley Land Co Inc (PA) ....**D 559 945-9292**
18036 Gale Huron (93234) ***(P-250)***
California Valley Products, Hughson *Also called Mid Valley Nut Company Inc* ***(P-293)***
California Vegetable Spc Inc ....D 707 374-2111
15 Poppy House Rd Rio Vista (94571) ***(P-9390)***
California Vocations Inc ....C 530 877-0937
564 Rio Lindo Ave Ste 204 Chico (95926) ***(P-16223)***
California Waste Solutions Inc (PA) ....**D 510 832-8111**
1005 Timothy Dr San Jose (95133) ***(P-8314)***
California Water Service Co (HQ) ....**C 408 367-8200**
1720 N 1st St San Jose (95112) ***(P-8225)***
California Water Service Group (PA) ....**C 408 367-8200**
1720 N 1st St San Jose (95112) ***(P-8226)***
California Waterfowl Assn ....E 916 648-1406
1346 Blue Oaks Blvd Roseville (95678) ***(P-18402)***
California Young World Center ....E 408 245-7285
1110 Fairwood Ave Sunnyvale (94089) ***(P-17871)***
California-American Water Co ....E 916 568-4216
4701 Beloit Dr Sacramento (95838) ***(P-8227)***
Californian, The, Woodland *Also called Ted Collwell* ***(P-18191)***
Califrnia Archtectural Ltg Inc (PA) ....**E 925 242-0111**
4000 Executive Pkwy # 350 San Ramon (94583) ***(P-8847)***
Califrnia Assn Hlth Facilities (PA) ....**E 916 441-6400**
2201 K St Sacramento (95816) ***(P-18304)***
Califrnia Assn Hsptals Hlth Sy (PA) ....**D 916 443-7401**
1215 K St Ste 800 Sacramento (95814) ***(P-18333)***
Califrnia Assn Pub Hsptals HLT ....E 510 874-7100
70 Washington St Ste 215 Oakland (94607) ***(P-19684)***
Califrnia Atism Foundation Inc ....D 510 724-1751
982 Marlesta Rd Pinole (94564) ***(P-18222)***
Califrnia Child Care Rsrce Rfr ....E 510 658-0381
5232 Claremont Ave Oakland (94618) ***(P-17452)***
Califrnia Chldren Fmilies Comm ....E 916 263-1050
2389 Gateway Oaks Dr # 260 Sacramento (95833) ***(P-18553)***
Califrnia Cncer Assoc For RES (PA) ....**D 800 456-5860**
7130 N Millbrook Ave Fresno (93720) ***(P-15311)***
Califrnia Cncer Care A Med Gro ....D 415 925-5000
1350 S Eliseo Dr Ste 200 Greenbrae (94904) ***(P-15312)***
Califrnia Coop Rice RES Fndtio ....E 530 868-5481
955 Butt City Hwy Biggs (95917) ***(P-19039)***
Califrnia CPA Edcatn Fundation ....E 800 922-5272
1800 Gateway Dr Ste 200 San Mateo (94404) ***(P-18334)***
Califrnia Crdvsclar Cons Med A (PA) ....**D 510 796-0222**
2333 Mowry Ave Fremont (94538) ***(P-15313)***
Califrnia Crrctnal Pace Offcer (PA) ....**D 916 372-6060**
755 Riverpoint Dr West Sacramento (95605) ***(P-18356)***
Califrnia Cryobank Lf Sciences, South San Francisco *Also called California Cryobank Inc* ***(P-17113)***
Califrnia Cslty Indemnity Exch (PA) ....**C 650 574-4000**
1900 Almeda De Las Pulgas San Mateo (94403) ***(P-10165)***
Califrnia Cstm Snroms Ptio Cve ....F 800 834-3211
3160 Gold Valley Dr # 300 Rancho Cordova (95742) ***(P-2016)***
Califrnia Elctrnic Asset Rcver ....E 916 388-1777
3678 Lemay St Mather (95655) ***(P-8315)***
Califrnia Emrgncy Physcans Med ....E 510 350-2777
2100 Powell St Ste 400 Emeryville (94608) ***(P-15314)***
Califrnia Erctors Bay Area Inc ....C 707 746-1990
4500 California Ct Benicia (94510) ***(P-1923)***
Califrnia Fire Fghtr Joint App, Sacramento *Also called California Fire Fghtrs Apprent* ***(P-17797)***
Califrnia Fire Rscue Trning Au ....C 916 475-1660
3121 Gold Canal Dr Rancho Cordova (95670) ***(P-17799)***
Califrnia Frnsic Med Group Inc ....D 530 573-3035
300 Forni Rd Kelsey (95667) ***(P-17114)***
Califrnia Frnsic Med Group Inc ....C 209 525-5670
200 E Hackett Rd Modesto (95358) ***(P-15315)***
Califrnia Golf CLB San Frncsco ....D 650 588-9021
844 W Orange Ave South San Francisco (94080) ***(P-15068)***
Califrnia High Rach Eqp Rntl I ....E 209 577-0515
531 Bitritto Way Modesto (95356) ***(P-12018)***
Califrnia High Speed Rail Auth ....D 916 324-1541
770 L St Ste 620 Sacramento (95814) ***(P-7318)***
Califrnia Ind Sys Oprator Corp (PA) ....**B 916 351-4400**
250 Outcropping Way Folsom (95630) ***(P-8090)***
Califrnia Indian Mnpwer Cnsrti (PA) ....**E 916 920-0285**
738 N Market Blvd Sacramento (95834) ***(P-17800)***
Califrnia Integrated Media Inc ....F 415 627-8310
14 Avila St San Francisco (94123) ***(P-3632)***
Califrnia Leag Cnsrvtion Vters (PA) ....**E 510 271-0900**
350 Frank H Ogawa Plz # 1100 Oakland (94612) ***(P-18403)***
Califrnia Mantel Fireplace Inc (PA) ....**E 916 925-5775**
4141 N Freeway Blvd Sacramento (95834) ***(P-3124)***
Califrnia Mrtime Acdemy Fndtio ....C 707 654-1000
200 Maritime Academy Dr Vallejo (94590) ***(P-10785)***
Califrnia Nwspapers Ltd Partnr ....C 530 877-4413
5399 Clark Rd Paradise (95969) ***(P-3425)***
Califrnia Odd Fllows Hsing Nap (PA) ....**D 707 257-7885**
1800 Atrium Pkwy NAPA (94559) ***(P-10420)***
Califrnia Odd Fllows Hsing Nap ....D 707 257-7885
1800 Atrium Pkwy NAPA (94559) ***(P-10421)***
Califrnia PCF Med Ctr RES Inst, San Francisco *Also called Sutter Bay Hospitals* ***(P-16568)***
Califrnia PCF Rice Mil A CA LP ....E 530 661-1923
194 W Main St Woodland (95695) ***(P-2318)***
Califrnia Property Owners Assn ....E 530 233-5842
750 Shasta View Dr Alturas (96101) ***(P-10984)***
Califrnia Prson Hlthcare Rcvrs ....D 916 691-6721
501 J St Ste 100 Sacramento (95814) ***(P-16865)***
Califrnia Psychtric Trnsitions ....D 209 667-9304
9234n Hinton Ave Delhi (95315) ***(P-15316)***
Califrnia Pub Emplyees Rtrment (HQ) ....**A 916 795-3000**
400 Q St Sacramento (95811) ***(P-10212)***
Califrnia Rur Indian Hlth Bd I ....D 916 437-0104
1020 Sun Down Way Roseville (95661) ***(P-18223)***
Califrnia Shock Truma A Rescue (PA) ....**D 916 921-4000**
4933 Bailey Loop McClellan (95652) ***(P-7379)***
Califrnia Soc Crtif Pub Accntn (PA) ....**E 650 522-3000**
1710 Gilbreth Rd Ste 100 Burlingame (94010) ***(P-18335)***
Califrnia Solar Innovators Inc ....E 209 596-0350
580 N Wilma Ave Ste H Ripon (95366) ***(P-1228)***
Califrnia Srvying Drftg Sup In (PA) ....**E 916 344-0232**
4733 Auburn Blvd Sacramento (95841) ***(P-12019)***
Califrnia State Employees Assn (PA) ....**D 916 444-8134**
3000 Advantage Way Sacramento (95834) ***(P-18357)***
Califrnia State Tchers Rtrment (HQ) ....**B 800 228-5453**
100 Waterfront Pl West Sacramento (95605) ***(P-10213)***
Califrnia State Tchers Rtrment ....E 916 445-0211
915 L St Fl 7 Sacramento (95814) ***(P-18942)***
Califrnia State Univ E Bay Fnd ....E 510 885-2700
25800 Carlos Bee Blvd Hayward (94542) ***(P-19313)***
Califrnia Sthern Bptst Cnvntio ....D 209 965-3735
29005 Highway 108 Long Barn (95335) ***(P-11598)***
Califrnia Workforce Enrgy Svcs, Fresno *Also called Cwes Inc* ***(P-19758)***
Califrnia Wste Rcvery Systems ....E 209 369-6887
175 Enterprise Ct Ste A Galt (95632) ***(P-8316)***
Califrnia Yuth Soccer Assn Inc ....D 925 426-5437
1767 Tribute Rd Ste F Sacramento (95815) ***(P-18554)***
Califrnia-Nevada Methdst Homes ....C 510 835-5511
1850 Alice St Ofc Oakland (94612) ***(P-16224)***
Califrnias Gnite Pool Plst Inc ....D 925 960-9500
510 Greenville Rd Livermore (94550) ***(P-2017)***
Calistoga Inn, Calistoga *Also called NAPA Valley Brewing Co Inc* ***(P-11323)***
Calistoga Spa Inc ....D 707 942-6269
1006 Washington St Calistoga (94515) ***(P-14934)***
Calistoga Spa Hot Springs, Calistoga *Also called Calistoga Spa Inc* ***(P-14934)***
Calithera Biosciences Inc ....D 650 870-1000
343 Oyster Point Blvd # 20 South San Francisco (94080) ***(P-3876)***
Calix Inc (PA) ....**A 408 514-3000**
2777 Orchard Pkwy San Jose (95134) ***(P-8073)***
Callan LLC (PA) ....**C 415 974-5060**
600 Montgomery St Ste 800 San Francisco (94111) ***(P-10038)***
Calliber Collision, Fresno *Also called Caliber Bodyworks Texas Inc* ***(P-14522)***
Callidus Software Inc (HQ) ....**A 925 251-2200**
2700 Camino Ramon 400 San Ramon (94583) ***(P-12321)***
Calliduscloud, San Ramon *Also called Callidus Software Inc* ***(P-12321)***
Callisto Media Inc ....D 510 253-0500
1955 Broadway 400 Oakland (94612) ***(P-3526)***
Callsign Inc (PA) ....**E 650 320-1710**
2225 E Bayshore Rd Palo Alto (94303) ***(P-12322)***
Calmar Laser, Palo Alto *Also called Calmar Optcom Inc* ***(P-5790)***
Calmar Optcom Inc ....E 408 733-7800
951 Commercial St Palo Alto (94303) ***(P-5790)***
Calmax Technology Inc ....E 408 748-8600
3491 Lafayette St Santa Clara (95054) ***(P-5486)***
Calmax Technology Inc ....F 408 506-2035
558 Laurelwood Rd Santa Clara (95054) ***(P-5487)***
Calmax Technology Inc (PA) ....**E 408 748-8660**
526 Laurelwood Rd Santa Clara (95054) ***(P-5488)***
Calmcom Inc (PA) ....**E 415 278-0991**
77 Geary St 3 San Francisco (94108) ***(P-13046)***
Calnet Inc ....D 530 672-1078
4101 Wild Chaparral Dr Shingle Springs (95682) ***(P-7937)***
Calogic (PA) ....**E 510 656-2900**
237 Whitney Pl Fremont (94539) ***(P-6747)***
Calpella Distribution Center, Calpella *Also called Mendocino Forest Pdts Co LLC* ***(P-8592)***
Calpers, Sacramento *Also called Public Employees Retirement* ***(P-10218)***
Calpico Inc ....E 650 588-2241
1387 San Mateo Ave South San Francisco (94080) ***(P-5712)***
Calpine Containers Inc (PA) ....**F 559 519-7199**
380 W Spruce Ave Clovis (93611) ***(P-9212)***
Calpine Corporation ....E 530 821-2075
5029 S Township Rd Yuba City (95993) ***(P-8091)***
Calplant I LLC ....E 530 361-0003
6101 State Highway 162 Willows (95988) ***(P-3262)***
Calplant I Holdco LLC (PA) ....**E 530 570-0542**
6101 State Highway 162 Willows (95988) ***(P-3263)***
Calpo Hom Dong Architects Inc ....D 916 446-7741
2120 20th St Ste 1 Sacramento (95818) ***(P-18875)***
Calsoft Labs Inc (HQ) ....**C 408 755-3000**
2890 Zanker Rd Ste 200 San Jose (95134) ***(P-13563)***
Calstar, McClellan *Also called Califrnia Shock Truma A Rescue* ***(P-7379)***
Calstar Products Inc ....F 262 752-9131
3945 Freedom Cir Ste 560 Santa Clara (95054) ***(P-4398)***
Calstone Company ....E 408 686-9627
13755 Llagas Ave San Martin (95046) ***(P-4410)***
Calstone Company ....E 209 745-2981
421 Crystal Way Galt (95632) ***(P-4411)***
Caltest Analytical Laboratory, NAPA *Also called Vitisystems Inc* ***(P-19291)***
Caltrain, San Carlos *Also called Peninsula Crrdor Jint Pwers Bd* ***(P-7344)***
Caltrans, Fairfield *Also called California Department Trnsp* ***(P-1020)***

ALPHABETIC SECTION **Capital Corrugated LLC**

Caltrans District 1, Eureka *Also called California Department Trnsp* ***(P-19737)***

Caltronics Business Systems, Sacramento *Also called JJR Enterprises Inc* ***(P-14701)***

Calva Products LLC (PA)...E...**800 328-9680**
4351 E Winery Rd Acampo (95220) ***(P-2338)***

Calva Products Co Inc...E...209 339-1516
4351 E Winery Rd Acampo (95220) ***(P-2339)***

Calvac Inc...E...408 262-1162
2645 Pacer Ln San Jose (95111) ***(P-1023)***

Calvac Paving & Sealing, San Jose *Also called Calvac Inc* ***(P-1023)***

Calvada Sales Company (PA)...E...**916 441-6290**
450 Richards Blvd Sacramento (95811) ***(P-9376)***

Calvary Christian Center, Sacramento *Also called Calvary Chrstn Ch Ctr of Scrmn* ***(P-17872)***

Calvary Chrstn Ch Ctr of Scrmn...E...916 921-9303
2727 Del Paso Blvd Sacramento (95815) ***(P-17872)***

Calvary Church Los Gatos Cal (PA)...D...**408 358-8871**
16330 Los Gatos Blvd # 4 Los Gatos (95032) ***(P-17873)***

Calvary Church Los Gatos Cal...D...408 356-6776
16330 Los Gatos Blvd Los Gatos (95032) ***(P-17874)***

Calvary Church Los Gatos Cal...D...408 356-5126
16330 Los Gatos Blvd Los Gatos (95032) ***(P-17875)***

Calvary Cross Ch of Highlands (PA)...C...**650 873-4095**
1900 Monterey Dr San Bruno (94066) ***(P-17453)***

Calvary Infant Care Center, Los Gatos *Also called Calvary Church Los Gatos Cal* ***(P-17875)***

Calvary Temple Academy, Modesto *Also called House Modesto* ***(P-17953)***

Calvey Incorporated...D...916 681-4800
8670 Fruitridge Rd # 300 Sacramento (95826) ***(P-9648)***

Calwest Steel Detailing, Pleasanton *Also called Future Innovations Inc* ***(P-14281)***

Calypto Design Systems Inc...E...408 850-2300
2099 Gateway Pl Ste 550 San Jose (95110) ***(P-13047)***

Calysta Inc (PA)...F...**650 492-6880**
1900 Alameda De Las Pulga San Mateo (94403) ***(P-4123)***

Calyx Software, San Jose *Also called Calyx Technology Inc* ***(P-12323)***

Calyx Technology Inc (PA)...E...**408 997-5525**
6475 Camden Ave Ste 207 San Jose (95120) ***(P-12323)***

Camanche Nrthshore Str/Cffee S, Ione *Also called Concessionaires Urban Park* ***(P-15197)***

Camanche Recreation-North, Ione *Also called Concessionaires Urban Park* ***(P-15196)***

Camarena Health (PA)...C...**559 664-4000**
344 E 6th St Madera (93638) ***(P-15317)***

Cambria Solutions Inc (PA)...C...**916 326-4446**
731 K St Ste 300 Sacramento (95814) ***(P-19738)***

Cambrian School District...E...408 377-3882
1840 Harris Ave San Jose (95124) ***(P-18555)***

Cambridge Cm Inc...E...650 543-3030
420 Olive Ave Palo Alto (94306) ***(P-19314)***

Cambridge Homes (HQ)...D...**559 447-3400**
8080 N Palm Ave Ste 110 Fresno (93711) ***(P-10699)***

Cambrios Technologies Corp...E...408 738-7400
930 E Arques Ave Sunnyvale (94085) ***(P-19203)***

Camelbak Acquisition Corp...E...707 792-9700
2000 S Mcdwell Blvd Ste 2 Petaluma (94954) ***(P-7191)***

Camelbak Products LLC (HQ)...D...**707 792-9700**
2000 S Mcdwell Blvd Ste 2 Petaluma (94954) ***(P-7192)***

Cameo Crafts...D...513 381-1480
4995 Hillsdale Cir El Dorado Hills (95762) ***(P-3724)***

Cameron & Lisa Palmer...E...650 726-5705
1410 Cabrillo Hwy S Half Moon Bay (94019) ***(P-10381)***

Cameron International Corp...D...530 242-6965
562 River Park Dr Redding (96003) ***(P-5045)***

Cameron Park Country Club Inc...D...530 672-9840
3201 Royal Dr Cameron Park (95682) ***(P-15069)***

Cameron Park Firefighters Assn...D...530 677-6190
3200 Country Club Dr Cameron Park (95682) ***(P-15187)***

Cameron's Restaurant & Inn, Half Moon Bay *Also called Cameron & Lisa Palmer* ***(P-10381)***

Cameroncompany, Petaluma *Also called Robert W Cameron & Co Inc* ***(P-3544)***

Camflor Inc...C...831 726-1330
2364 Riverside Rd Watsonville (95076) ***(P-9629)***

Camico Mutual Insurance Co (PA)...D...**650 378-6874**
1800 Gateway Dr Ste 200 San Mateo (94404) ***(P-10258)***

Camico Services Inc...E...800 652-1772
1800 Gateway Dr Ste 200 San Mateo (94404) ***(P-9854)***

Caminar...E...530 343-4421
376 Rio Lindo Ave Chico (95926) ***(P-16997)***

Caminar...E...707 648-8121
902 Tuolumne St Vallejo (94590) ***(P-16998)***

Camino Real Group LLC...E...650 964-1700
840 E El Camino Real Mountain View (94040) ***(P-10985)***

Cammisa Wipf Cnslting Engneers...E...415 863-5740
642 Harrison St Fl 4 San Francisco (94107) ***(P-18656)***

Camp Jones Gulch YMCA, La Honda *Also called Young MNS Chrstn Assn San Frnc* ***(P-18515)***

Camp Latieze, Redding *Also called Shasta County Office Education* ***(P-11610)***

Camp Wellspring LLC (HQ)...E...**559 638-5374**
42675 Road 44 Reedley (93654) ***(P-17454)***

CAMP WINNARAINBOW, Berkeley *Also called Winnarainbow Inc* ***(P-11616)***

Campaign Monitor USA Inc (HQ)...D...**888 533-8098**
55 2nd St Ste 1925 San Francisco (94105) ***(P-12324)***

Campanella Corporation...E...510 536-4800
2216 Dunn Rd Hayward (94545) ***(P-1982)***

Campbell Christian School...D...408 370-4900
1075 W Campbell Ave Campbell (95008) ***(P-11599)***

Campbell Grinding Inc...E...209 339-8838
1003 E Vine St Lodi (95240) ***(P-5489)***

Campbell Hhg Hotel Dev LLP...D...408 626-9590
655 Creekside Way Campbell (95008) ***(P-10986)***

Campos Family Farms LLC...D...559 275-3000
4726 W Jacquelyn Ave Fresno (93722) ***(P-149)***

Campton Place Hotel, San Francisco *Also called Southbourne Inc* ***(P-11494)***

Campton Place, A Taj Hotel, San Francisco *Also called Ihms (sf) LLC* ***(P-11187)***

Campus Commons Imaging, Sacramento *Also called Sutter Health* ***(P-15723)***

Campus Kids Connection Inc (PA)...E...**831 462-9822**
820 Bay Ave Ste 124 Capitola (95010) ***(P-17876)***

Campus Pointe Cinemas Oper LLC...E...213 805-5333
3090 E Campus Pointe Dr Fresno (93710) ***(P-14807)***

Camtek Usa Inc...E...510 624-9905
48389 Fremont Blvd # 112 Fremont (94538) ***(P-6079)***

Can-AM Plumbing Inc...C...925 846-1833
151 Wyoming St Pleasanton (94566) ***(P-1229)***

Canaan Company, Fresno *Also called DV Kap Inc* ***(P-3024)***

Canaccord Genuity LLC...D...415 229-7171
44 Montgomery St Ste 1600 San Francisco (94104) ***(P-9960)***

Canadian American Oil Co Inc (PA)...D...**415 621-8676**
444 Divisadero St 100 San Francisco (94117) ***(P-10382)***

Canadian American Oil Co Inc...E...510 644-8229
444 Divisadero St 100 San Francisco (94117) ***(P-14633)***

Canadian American Oil Co Inc...D...415 621-8676
444 Divisadero St San Francisco (94117) ***(P-14634)***

Canal Alliance...D...415 485-3074
91 Larkspur St San Rafael (94901) ***(P-17224)***

Canal Farm Motel, Los Banos *Also called Espanas Mexican Restaurant* ***(P-11084)***

Canandaigua Wine Company Inc...C...559 673-7071
12667 Road 24 Madera (93637) ***(P-9569)***

Canary Communications Inc...F...408 365-0609
6040 Hellyer Ave Ste 150 San Jose (95138) ***(P-5828)***

Canary Technologies Corp...E...415 578-1414
450 9th St Fl 1 San Francisco (94103) ***(P-13048)***

Cancer Prevention Inst Cal...E...510 608-5000
2001 Center St Ste 700 Berkeley (94704) ***(P-19204)***

Cancer Prevention Inst Cal (PA)...C...**510 608-5000**
39141 Civic Center Dr # 425 Fremont (94538) ***(P-19205)***

Cancer Resource Center, Cameron Park *Also called Marshall Medical Center* ***(P-16452)***

Cancom USA, Fremont *Also called HPM Incorporated* ***(P-8710)***

Candle3 LLC...E...415 365-9679
101 California St # 2710 San Francisco (94111) ***(P-8848)***

Candlewood Pleasanton, Pleasanton *Also called Larkspur Hsptality Dev MGT LLC* ***(P-11253)***

Candlewood Suites, Turlock *Also called Turlock Hospitality LLC* ***(P-11546)***

Canepa Design, Scotts Valley *Also called Canepa Group Inc* ***(P-14523)***

Canepa Group Inc...E...831 430-9940
4900 Scotts Valley Dr Scotts Valley (95066) ***(P-14523)***

Canepas Car Wash...E...209 478-5516
6230 Pacific Ave Stockton (95207) ***(P-14635)***

Canine Cmpnons For Indpendence (PA)...D...**707 577-1700**
2965 Dutton Ave Santa Rosa (95407) ***(P-351)***

Canon Financial Services Inc...E...916 368-7610
3265 Ramos Cir Ste 200 Sacramento (95827) ***(P-8680)***

Canon Solutions America Inc...E...707 442-9397
1651 Myrtle Ave Ste C Eureka (95501) ***(P-9205)***

Canteen Refreshment Services, Hayward *Also called Compass Group Usa Inc* ***(P-14232)***

Canterbury Hotel Corp...D...415 345-3200
750 Sutter St San Francisco (94109) ***(P-10987)***

Canto Inc...D...415 495-6545
625 Market St Ste 600 San Francisco (94105) ***(P-13049)***

Cantor Ftzgrald Asset MGT Hldn, Redwood City *Also called Fintan Partners LLC* ***(P-9968)***

Canyon House Resthomes Inc (PA)...E...**408 730-4004**
147 Crescent Ave Sunnyvale (94087) ***(P-18065)***

Canyon Mnor Rsdntial Trtmnt Ct, Novato *Also called Marin County Sart Program* ***(P-16743)***

Canyon Road Winery, NAPA *Also called Geyser Peak Winery* ***(P-2593)***

Canyon Rock Co Inc...E...707 887-2207
7525 Hwy 116 Forestville (95436) ***(P-592)***

Canyon Springs Post-Acute...E...408 259-8700
180 N Jackson Ave San Jose (95116) ***(P-15950)***

Canyon View Capital Inc...D...831 480-6335
331 Soquel Ave Ste 100 Santa Cruz (95062) ***(P-10815)***

Capax Management & Insur Svcs (HQ)...E...**209 526-3110**
4335 N Star Way Ste D Modesto (95356) ***(P-10259)***

Capay Fruits and Vegetables, West Sacramento *Also called Capay Incorporated* ***(P-9391)***

Capay Incorporated (PA)...D...**530 796-0730**
3880 Seaport Blvd West Sacramento (95691) ***(P-9391)***

Capay Organic, West Sacramento *Also called Farm Fresh To You LLC* ***(P-167)***

Capcom Entertainment Inc...D...650 350-6500
185 Berry St Ste 1200 San Francisco (94107) ***(P-9167)***

Capcom U S A Inc (HQ)...C...**650 350-6500**
185 Berry St Ste 1200 San Francisco (94107) ***(P-9168)***

Capcom U.S.a, San Francisco *Also called Capcom Entertainment Inc* ***(P-9167)***

Cape Inc...D...925 443-3434
2406 Armstrong St Livermore (94551) ***(P-17877)***

Capella Photonics Inc...E...408 360-4240
1100 La Avenida St Ste A Mountain View (94043) ***(P-6500)***

Capella Space Corp...D...650 334-7734
438 Shotwell St San Francisco (94110) ***(P-8849)***

Capgemini America Inc...D...415 796-6777
427 Brannan St San Francisco (94107) ***(P-13860)***

Capincrouse LLP...D...925 201-1187
5990 Stoneridge Dr Pleasanton (94588) ***(P-18943)***

Capital Asset Exch & Trdg LLC (PA)...E...**650 326-3313**
870 E Charleston Rd # 210 Palo Alto (94303) ***(P-9059)***

Capital Athletic Club Inc...E...916 442-3927
1515 8th St Sacramento (95814) ***(P-14935)***

Capital Beverage Company (PA)...C...**916 371-8164**
2500 Del Monte St West Sacramento (95691) ***(P-9546)***

Capital Christian Center...E...916 722-6169
4533 Antelope Rd Sacramento (95843) ***(P-17878)***

Capital City Drywall Inc...D...916 331-9200
6525 32nd St Ste B1 North Highlands (95660) ***(P-1665)***

Capital Corrugated and Carton, Sacramento *Also called Capital Corrugated LLC* ***(P-3355)***

Capital Corrugated LLC...D...916 388-7848
8333 24th Ave Sacramento (95826) ***(P-3355)***

A L P H A B E T I C

Capital Engineering Cons Inc (PA)...D...916 851-3500
11020 Sun Center Dr # 100 Rancho Cordova (95670) ***(P-18657)***
Capital Eye Medical Group...D...916 241-9378
6620 Coyle Ave Ste 408 Carmichael (95608) ***(P-15318)***
Capital Lumber...F...916 922-8861
160 Commerce Cir Sacramento (95815) ***(P-8533)***
Capital Lumber Company...E...707 433-7070
13480 Old Redwood Hwy Healdsburg (95448) ***(P-8534)***
Capital Obgyn (PA)...D...916 920-2082
77 Cadillac Dr Ste 230 Sacramento (95825) ***(P-15319)***
Capital Public Radio Inc...E...916 278-8900
7055 Folsom Blvd Sacramento (95826) ***(P-8016)***
Capital Transitional Care, Sacramento *Also called Covenant Care California LLC* ***(P-15969)***
Capitol Administrators Inc...E...916 669-2463
10951 White Rock Rd # 100 Rancho Cordova (95670) ***(P-10083)***
Capitol Barricade Inc (PA)...D...916 451-5176
6001 Elvas Ave Sacramento (95819) ***(P-9060)***
Capitol Beverage Packers...E...916 929-7777
2670 Land Ave Sacramento (95815) ***(P-2785)***
Capitol Builders Hardware Inc (HQ)...D...916 451-2821
4699 24th St Sacramento (95822) ***(P-1732)***
Capitol Casino...C...916 446-0700
411 N 16th St Sacramento (95811) ***(P-15188)***
Capitol Clutch & Brake Inc...E...916 371-5970
3100 Duluth St West Sacramento (95691) ***(P-8447)***
Capitol Communications Inc...E...415 861-1727
480 9th St San Francisco (94103) ***(P-1472)***
Capitol Components, Sacramento *Also called Capitol Store Fixtures* ***(P-3301)***
Capitol Corporate Services Inc (PA)...D...916 444-6787
455 Capitol Mall Ste 217 Sacramento (95814) ***(P-19155)***
Capitol Door Service, Sacramento *Also called Capitol Builders Hardware Inc* ***(P-1732)***
Capitol Drive-In, San Jose *Also called Century Theatres Inc* ***(P-14809)***
Capitol Intrventional Crdiolgy...E...916 967-0115
6347 Coyle Ave Carmichael (95608) ***(P-15320)***
Capitol Iron Works Inc...E...916 381-1554
7009 Power Inn Rd Sacramento (95828) ***(P-4650)***
Capitol Regency LLC...B...916 443-1234
1209 L St Sacramento (95814) ***(P-10988)***
Capitol Services Inc...C...916 443-0657
3609 Bradshaw Rd Ste H Sacramento (95827) ***(P-19465)***
Capitol Sport Club, San Jose *Also called 24 Hour Fitness Usa Inc* ***(P-14920)***
Capitol Steel Company...E...916 924-3195
1932 Auburn Blvd Sacramento (95815) ***(P-8810)***
Capitol Store Fixtures...E...916 646-9096
4220 Pell Dr Ste C Sacramento (95838) ***(P-3301)***
Capitol Tarpaulin Co, Sacramento *Also called Philip A Stitt Agency* ***(P-3041)***
Capitol Valley Electric Inc...E...916 686-3244
8550 Thys Ct Sacramento (95828) ***(P-1473)***
Capitola Imports Inc...C...831 462-4200
4200 Auto Plaza Dr Capitola (95010) ***(P-14658)***
Capnia Inc (PA)...D...650 213-8444
1101 Chess Dr Foster City (94404) ***(P-3877)***
Cappstone Inc...C...415 821-6757
1699 Valencia St San Francisco (94110) ***(P-11933)***
Caps Oak Street Bar and Grill...E...925 634-1025
144 Oak St Brentwood (94513) ***(P-11710)***
Capstone Health Inc (PA)...D...408 667-6004
5424 Sunol Blvd Pleasanton (94566) ***(P-17115)***
Capstone Logistics LLC...A...209 858-1401
16888 Mckinley Ave Lathrop (95330) ***(P-7876)***
Captivateiq Inc...D...650 930-0619
480 2nd St Ste 100 San Francisco (94107) ***(P-12325)***
Captive Plastics LLC...D...209 858-9188
601 Tesla Dr Lathrop (95330) ***(P-4264)***
Captive-Aire Systems Inc...C...530 351-7150
6856 Lockheed Dr Redding (96002) ***(P-4746)***
Caracal Enterprises LLC...E...707 773-3373
1260 Holm Rd Ste A Petaluma (94954) ***(P-5426)***
Carando Technologies Inc...E...209 948-6500
345 N Harrison St Stockton (95203) ***(P-5078)***
Caravali Coffees Inc (HQ)...D...916 565-5500
1300 Del Paso Rd Sacramento (95834) ***(P-9442)***
Caravan Bakery Inc...F...510 487-2600
33300 Western Ave Union City (94587) ***(P-2372)***
Caravan Foods II Inc...F...510 487-2600
33300 Western Ave Union City (94587) ***(P-2421)***
Caravan Trading, Union City *Also called Caravan Foods II Inc* ***(P-2421)***
Carbon Inc...C...650 285-6307
1089 Mills Way Redwood City (94063) ***(P-5355)***
Carbon Design Innovations Inc (PA)...E...650 697-7070
1745 Adrian Rd Ste 20 Burlingame (94010) ***(P-5670)***
Carbon Five, San Francisco *Also called Carbonfive Incorporated* ***(P-12326)***
Carbon Health Technologies Inc...D...415 223-2858
55 Pacific Ave Ste 160 San Francisco (94111) ***(P-19466)***
Carbon Lighthouse Inc...C...415 787-3550
343 Sansome St Ste 700 San Francisco (94104) ***(P-18658)***
Carbonfive Incorporated...D...415 546-0500
585 Howard St Fl 2 San Francisco (94105) ***(P-12326)***
Carbonic Service...E...408 727-8835
1920 De La Cruz Blvd Santa Clara (95050) ***(P-9112)***
Cardiac Surgery West Med Corp...E...916 733-6850
3941 J St Ste 270 Sacramento (95819) ***(P-15321)***
Cardinal Cg Company, Galt *Also called Cardinal Glass Industries Inc* ***(P-4355)***
Cardinal Glass Industries Inc...C...209 744-8940
680 Industrial Dr Galt (95632) ***(P-4355)***
Cardinal Hotel, Palo Alto *Also called American Hotel Inc* ***(P-10921)***
Cardinal Paint and Powder Inc...D...408 452-8522
890 Commercial St San Jose (95112) ***(P-4102)***
Cardio Vascular Associates...D...559 439-6808
1313 E Herndon Ave # 203 Fresno (93720) ***(P-15322)***
Cardiovascular Cons Med Group...E...925 277-1900
5201 Norris Canyon Rd # 220 San Ramon (94583) ***(P-15323)***
Cardiovascular Cons Med Group...E...510 537-3556
20126 Stanton Ave Ste 100 Castro Valley (94546) ***(P-15324)***
Cardiovascular Consultants Hea...D...559 432-4303
1207 E Herndon Ave Fresno (93720) ***(P-15325)***
Cardiva Medical Inc...C...408 470-7100
1615 Wyatt Dr Santa Clara (95054) ***(P-6959)***
Cardivascular Assoc of Peninsu, Burlingame *Also called Cardivsclar Assoc of Peninsula* ***(P-15326)***
Cardivsclar Assoc of Peninsula...E...650 652-8600
1501 Trousdale Dr Fl 2 Burlingame (94010) ***(P-15326)***
Cardivsclar Mdcine Crnary Intr...C...650 306-2300
2900 Whipple Ave Ste 230 Redwood City (94062) ***(P-16326)***
Cardno Chemrisk LLC (HQ)...D...415 896-2400
235 Pine St Ste 2300 San Francisco (94104) ***(P-19739)***
Care 2...E...650 622-0860
203 Rdwood Shres Pkwy Ste Redwood City (94065) ***(P-18556)***
Care At Home...E...707 579-6822
5555 Montgomery Dr Santa Rosa (95409) ***(P-16225)***
Care At Home Inc...E...408 379-3990
1333 Bush St San Francisco (94109) ***(P-16866)***
Care Indeed Inc (PA)...D...650 800-7645
890 Santa Cruz Ave Ste A Menlo Park (94025) ***(P-16867)***
Care Innovations LLC...E...800 450-0970
950 Iron Point Rd Ste 160 Folsom (95630) ***(P-7099)***
Care Management Services, Sacramento *Also called Davis Uc Medical Center* ***(P-16345)***
Care Network, NAPA *Also called Queen of Vly Med Ctr Fundation* ***(P-16487)***
Care Optons MGT Plans Spprtive (PA)...C...530 242-8580
1020 Market St Redding (96001) ***(P-16868)***
Care Zone Inc...E...206 707-9127
121 Capp St Ste 200 San Francisco (94110) ***(P-13050)***
Care2com Inc...E...650 622-0860
3141 Stevens Creek Blvd San Jose (95117) ***(P-18404)***
Careage Inc...E...408 238-9751
2501 Alvin Ave San Jose (95121) ***(P-15951)***
Caredx Inc (PA)...B...415 287-2300
1 Tower Pl Fl 9 South San Francisco (94080) ***(P-16776)***
Career Group Inc...C...415 781-8188
345 California St # 1650 San Francisco (94104) ***(P-12079)***
Caremark Rx LLC...E...209 957-7050
800 Douglas Rd Stockton (95207) ***(P-15327)***
Caremore Health Plan...E...408 963-2400
4855 Atherton Ave San Jose (95130) ***(P-16327)***
Careone HM Hlth & Hospice Inc...E...209 632-8888
2813 Coffee Rd Ste C1 Modesto (95355) ***(P-16174)***
Careonsite Inc...D...562 437-0381
1805 Arnold Dr Martinez (94553) ***(P-15328)***
Careray USA, Santa Clara *Also called Compass Innovations Inc* ***(P-4229)***
Cares Community Health...C...916 443-3299
1500 21st St Sacramento (95811) ***(P-15329)***
Carezone, San Francisco *Also called Care Zone Inc* ***(P-13050)***
Cargill Meat Solutions Corp...B...559 875-2232
2350 Academy Ave Sanger (93657) ***(P-2090)***
Cargill Meat Solutions Corp...B...559 268-5586
3115 S Fig Ave Fresno (93706) ***(P-2091)***
Caribou Biosciences Inc...D...510 982-6030
2929 7th St Ste 105 Berkeley (94710) ***(P-4041)***
Caritas Management Corporation...D...415 647-7191
1358 Valencia St San Francisco (94110) ***(P-10501)***
Carl J Kruppa...E...209 358-1759
9575 Walnut Ave Winton (95388) ***(P-150)***
Carl Zeiss Meditec Inc (HQ)...B...925 557-4100
5300 Central Pkwy Dublin (94568) ***(P-6867)***
Carl Zeiss Ophthalmic Systems...E...925 557-4100
5300 Central Pkwy Dublin (94568) ***(P-6960)***
Carl Ziss X-Ray Microscopy Inc...D...925 701-3600
5300 Central Pkwy Dublin (94568) ***(P-7091)***
Carlilemacy Inc...E...707 542-6451
15 3rd St Santa Rosa (95401) ***(P-18659)***
Carlmont Gardens LLC...D...650 591-9601
2140 Carlmont Dr Belmont (94002) ***(P-16226)***
Carlson Barbee & Gibson Inc...D...925 866-0322
2633 Camino Ramon San Ramon (94583) ***(P-18660)***
Carlson Wireless Tech Inc...F...707 443-0100
3134 Jacobs Ave Ste C Eureka (95501) ***(P-5829)***
Carlton Engineering Inc (PA)...E...916 932-7855
4080 Plaza Goldorado Cir B Cameron Park (95682) ***(P-18661)***
Carlton Ht Prpts A Cal Ltd Prt...D...415 673-0242
1075 Sutter St San Francisco (94109) ***(P-10989)***
Carlton Plaza of San Leandro, San Leandro *Also called Carlton Senior Living Inc* ***(P-10504)***
Carlton Senior Living Inc...D...408 972-1400
380 Branham Ln Ofc Ofc San Jose (95136) ***(P-18066)***
Carlton Senior Living Inc...D...925 935-1001
175 Cleaveland Rd Pleasant Hill (94523) ***(P-18067)***
Carlton Senior Living Inc...D...916 714-2404
6915 Elk Grove Blvd Elk Grove (95758) ***(P-10502)***
Carlton Senior Living Inc (PA)...E...925 338-2434
4071 Port Chicago Hwy # 130 Concord (94520) ***(P-10503)***
Carlton Senior Living Inc...D...510 636-0660
1000 E 14th St San Leandro (94577) ***(P-10504)***
Carlton Senior Living Inc...D...916 971-4800
1075 Fulton Ave Sacramento (95825) ***(P-18068)***
Carlton Senior Living Inc...E...925 935-1660
2770 Pleasant Hill Rd Ofc Concord (94523) ***(P-10700)***
Carmel Village At Clovis, Clovis *Also called Generation Clovis LLC* ***(P-18119)***
Carmichael Adult Day Hlth Ctr, Carmichael *Also called Eskaton Properties Inc* ***(P-17554)***

Carmichael Care Inc ....E....916 483-8103
6041 Fair Oaks Blvd Carmichael (95608) ***(P-15952)***
Carmichael Imaging, Carmichael *Also called Sutter Health* ***(P-16652)***
Carmichael Oaks Joint Venture ....D....916 944-1588
8350 Fair Oaks Blvd Apt 3 Carmichael (95608) ***(P-18069)***
Carmichael Recreation & Pk Dst ....D....916 485-5322
5750 Grant Ave Carmichael (95608) ***(P-15189)***
Carnegie Institution Wash ....D....650 319-8904
260 Panama St Stanford (94305) ***(P-19206)***
Carneros Inn LLC ....B....707 299-4880
4048 Sonoma Hwy NAPA (94559) ***(P-10990)***
Carneros Ranching Inc ....F....707 253-9464
1134 Dealy Ln NAPA (94559) ***(P-2525)***
Carneros Resort and Spa, NAPA *Also called GF Carneros Tenant LLC* ***(P-11681)***
Carneros Vintners Inc ....F....707 933-9349
4202 Stage Gulch Rd Sonoma (95476) ***(P-261)***
Caro Nut Company ....E....559 475-5400
2885 S Cherry Ave Fresno (93706) ***(P-2255)***
Carollo Engineers Inc (PA) ....**D....925 932-1710**
2795 Mitchell Dr Walnut Creek (94598) ***(P-18662)***
Caron Compactor Co ....E....800 448-8236
1204 Ullrey Ave Escalon (95320) ***(P-5028)***
Caron's Auto Supply, Fair Oaks *Also called Carons Service Center Inc* ***(P-14551)***
Carone & Company Inc ....D....925 602-8800
5009 Forni Dr Ste A Concord (94520) ***(P-1952)***
Carons Service Center Inc ....F....916 444-3713
4301 Castleglen Way Fair Oaks (95628) ***(P-14551)***
Carpenter Fnds Admnstrtive Off ....D....510 633-0333
265 Hegenberger Rd # 100 Oakland (94621) ***(P-10792)***
Carpenter Group (PA) ....**E....415 285-1954**
222 Napoleon St San Francisco (94124) ***(P-5059)***
Carpentry Millwork, Fresno *Also called Architectural Wood Design Inc* ***(P-3167)***
Carquest Auto Parts, Fresno *Also called Sebring-West Automotive* ***(P-14591)***
Carquinez Dental Group, Benicia *Also called Patrick L Roetzer DDS Inc* ***(P-15854)***
Carr & Ferrell LLP (PA) ....**D....650 812-3400**
120 Constitution Dr Menlo Park (94025) ***(P-17225)***
Carr Mc Clellan Ingersoll Thom (PA) ....**D....650 342-9600**
216 Park Rd Burlingame (94010) ***(P-17226)***
Carr, McClellan, Burlingame *Also called Carr Mc Clellan Ingersoll Thom* ***(P-17226)***
Carrera Auto Body, San Francisco *Also called Shing Tai Corporation* ***(P-14532)***
Carreys Care Center Inc ....D....559 444-0151
2554 S Barton Ave Fresno (93725) ***(P-18070)***
Carriage Inn, Daly City *Also called Reneson Hotels Inc* ***(P-11396)***
Carrier Commercial Service, Sacramento *Also called Carrier Corporation* ***(P-14684)***
Carrier Corporation ....E....916 928-9500
1168 National Dr Ste 60 Sacramento (95834) ***(P-14684)***
Carriere Family Farms LLC ....E....530 934-8200
1640 State Highway 45 Glenn (95943) ***(P-84)***
Carriere Farms LLC ....E....530 934-8200
1640 State Highway 45 Glenn (95943) ***(P-4)***
Carris Reels California Inc (HQ) ....**E....802 733-9111**
2100 W Almond Ave Madera (93637) ***(P-3266)***
Carroll Burdick Mc Donough LLP (PA) ....**C....415 989-5900**
275 Battery St Ste 2600 San Francisco (94111) ***(P-17227)***
Carroll Inn, Sunnyvale *Also called Midpen Property MGT Corp* ***(P-11592)***
Carrollco Inc ....E....559 396-3939
3104 N Miami Ave Fresno (93727) ***(P-450)***
Carros Sensors Systems Co LLC ....B....925 979-4400
355 Lennon Ln Walnut Creek (94598) ***(P-6896)***
Carson House Inn ....E....707 443-1601
1209 4th St Eureka (95501) ***(P-10991)***
Carson Landscape Industries, Sacramento *Also called Frank Carson Ldscp & Maint Inc* ***(P-415)***
Carsons Coatings Inc ....E....209 745-2387
550 Industrial Dr Ste 200 Galt (95632) ***(P-4879)***
Carta, San Francisco *Also called Eshares Inc* ***(P-19329)***
Cartel Transport LLC (PA) ....**C....559 659-3981**
1487 13th St Firebaugh (93622) ***(P-7455)***
Cartel Transport LLC ....E....209 892-3880
154 Poppy Ave Patterson (95363) ***(P-7456)***
Carter & Burgess Inc ....D....510 457-0027
300 Frank H Ogawa Plz Oakland (94612) ***(P-18876)***
Carter & Burgess Inc ....D....408 428-2010
2033 Gateway Pl Fl 6 San Jose (95110) ***(P-18663)***
Carter Group (PA) ....**E....916 373-0148**
3709 Seaport Blvd West Sacramento (95691) ***(P-4651)***
Carter House, Eureka *Also called Mark Carter* ***(P-11285)***
Carter W Neal MD, Atwater *Also called Atwater Medical Group* ***(P-15286)***
Cartwright Hotel ....E....415 421-2865
524 Sutter St San Francisco (94102) ***(P-10992)***
Caruthers Raisin Pkg Co Inc (PA) ....**D....559 864-9448**
12797 S Elm Ave Caruthers (93609) ***(P-2256)***
Casa Allegra Community Svcs ....E....415 499-1116
35 Mitchell Blvd Ste 11 San Rafael (94903) ***(P-18071)***
Casa Allegra Community Svcs ....D....415 499-1116
35 Mitchell Blvd Ste 8 San Rafael (94903) ***(P-17455)***
Casa Coloma Health Care Center, Rancho Cordova *Also called A B C D Associates* ***(P-15905)***
Casa De Modesto, Modesto *Also called Fellowship Homes Inc* ***(P-18115)***
Casa Del Rios Hbilitation Svcs ....E....209 931-1027
5541 Solari Ranch Rd Stockton (95215) ***(P-18072)***
Casa Lupe Inc (PA) ....**D....530 846-3218**
130 Magnolia St Gridley (95948) ***(P-2879)***
Casa Lupe Market & Restaurants, Gridley *Also called Casa Lupe Inc* ***(P-2879)***
Casa Madrona Hotel and Spa LLC ....A....415 332-0502
801 Bridgeway Sausalito (94965) ***(P-10993)***
Casa Sanchez, San Francisco *Also called Sanchez Business Inc* ***(P-2208)***
Casa Sanchez Foods, Hayward *Also called Fante Inc* ***(P-2855)***
Casa Sandoval LLC ....D....510 727-1700
1200 Russell Way Hayward (94541) ***(P-10422)***
Casahl Technology Inc ....E....925 328-2828
2400 Cmino Rmon Bldg K St San Ramon (94583) ***(P-12327)***
Casaone, Emeryville *Also called La Casa Ventures Inc* ***(P-12051)***
Casavina Foundation Corp ....C....408 238-9751
2501 Alvin Ave San Jose (95121) ***(P-15953)***
Cascade Comfort Service Inc ....E....530 365-5350
5203 Industrial Way Anderson (96007) ***(P-1230)***
Cascade Filtration Inc ....E....530 529-1212
205 Kimball Rd Red Bluff (96080) ***(P-1991)***
Case Dealer Holding Co LLC (HQ) ....**D....916 649-0096**
1751 Bell Ave Sacramento (95838) ***(P-9020)***
Case Management Team, Mather *Also called Mather Community Campus* ***(P-18144)***
Case Medical Group, Sacramento *Also called Central Ansthsia Svc Exch Med* ***(P-15333)***
Case Vlott Cattle ....E....559 665-7399
20330 Road 4 Chowchilla (93610) ***(P-207)***
Case's Oil, Riverdale *Also called C Case Company Inc* ***(P-561)***
Casemaker Inc ....F....408 261-8265
1680 Civic Center Dr Frnt Santa Clara (95050) ***(P-13051)***
Casetext Inc ....E....317 407-0790
330 Townsend St Ste 100 San Francisco (94107) ***(P-12328)***
Casey Securities Inc (PA) ....**D....415 544-5030**
301 Pine St San Francisco (94104) ***(P-9961)***
Casey-Fogli Con Contrs Inc (PA) ....**D....510 887-0837**
1970 National Ave Hayward (94545) ***(P-1857)***
Cashedge Inc ....D....408 541-3900
525 Almanor Ave Ste 150 Sunnyvale (94085) ***(P-14224)***
Cashew Farm, Fresno *Also called Dan On & Associates (usa) Ltd* ***(P-2887)***
Cashnet, Oakland *Also called Higher One Payments Inc* ***(P-13210)***
Casini Enterprises Inc ....E....707 865-2255
22855 Moscow Rd Duncans Mills (95430) ***(P-11617)***
Casini Ranch Family Campground, Duncans Mills *Also called Casini Enterprises Inc* ***(P-11617)***
Casino Real Inc ....E....209 239-1455
1355 N Main St Manteca (95336) ***(P-10994)***
Casino Real Card Room, Manteca *Also called Casino Real Inc* ***(P-10994)***
Casino San Pablo, San Pablo *Also called Lytton Rancheria* ***(P-11276)***
Cason Engineering Inc ....E....916 939-9311
4952 Windplay Dr Ste D El Dorado Hills (95762) ***(P-5490)***
Caspers, San Leandro *Also called Spar Sausage Co* ***(P-2125)***
Caspian Networks Inc ....E....408 382-5200
101 University Ave # 100 Palo Alto (94301) ***(P-5356)***
Caspio Inc (PA) ....**E....650 691-0900**
1286 Kifer Rd Ste 107 Sunnyvale (94086) ***(P-13052)***
Cass Inc (PA) ....**D....510 893-6476**
2730 Peralta St Oakland (94607) ***(P-9174)***
Cassidy Trly Prop MGT Sn Frncs ....D....415 781-8100
201 California St Ste 800 San Francisco (94111) ***(P-10505)***
Castelanelli Brothers ....E....209 369-9218
401 W Armstrong Rd Lodi (95242) ***(P-208)***
Castello Diamorosa, Calistoga *Also called Villa Amorosa* ***(P-2756)***
Castle Dental Surgery Centre ....E....209 381-2047
3605 Hospital Rd Ste H Atwater (95301) ***(P-15826)***
Castle Distribution Svcs Inc ....E....559 665-3716
16505 Avenue 24 1/2 Chowchilla (93610) ***(P-7683)***
Castle Family Health Ctrs Inc (PA) ....**D....209 381-2000**
3605 Hospital Rd Ste H Atwater (95301) ***(P-15330)***
Castle Global Inc ....C....401 523-9531
575 Market St Fl 15 San Francisco (94105) ***(P-12329)***
Castle Medical Center ....E....808 263-5182
2100 Douglas Blvd Roseville (95661) ***(P-15331)***
Castle Oaks Golf Club, Ione *Also called Portlock International Ltd* ***(P-15017)***
Castle Rock Spring Water Co ....E....530 678-4444
4121 Dunsmuir Ave Dunsmuir (96025) ***(P-2786)***
Castlehill Properties Inc (PA) ....**D....209 472-9800**
3240 W March Ln Stockton (95219) ***(P-10995)***
Castlehill Properties Inc ....E....209 472-9700
3252 W March Ln Stockton (95219) ***(P-10996)***
Castlelite Block LLC (PA) ....**E....707 678-3465**
8615 Robben Rd Dixon (95620) ***(P-4412)***
Castlewood Country Club ....C....925 846-2871
707 Country Club Cir Pleasanton (94566) ***(P-15070)***
Castlight Health Inc (PA) ....**B....415 829-1400**
150 Spear St Ste 400 San Francisco (94105) ***(P-13702)***
Castro Valley Health Inc ....C....510 690-1930
39 Beta Ct San Ramon (94583) ***(P-16869)***
Castro Village Bowl, Castro Valley *Also called Bay Counties Investments Inc* ***(P-14885)***
Catalyst Bio Inc (HQ) ....**F....650 871-0761**
611 Gateway Blvd Ste 710 South San Francisco (94080) ***(P-3878)***
Catalyst Biosciences Inc (PA) ....**D....650 871-0761**
611 Gateway Blvd Ste 710 South San Francisco (94080) ***(P-3879)***
Catalyst Family Inc (PA) ....**D....408 556-7300**
350 Woodview Ave Ste 100 Morgan Hill (95037) ***(P-17879)***
Catalyst Mortgage ....E....916 283-9922
3013 Douglas Blvd Ste 135 Roseville (95661) ***(P-9899)***
Catamorphic Co (PA) ....**C....415 579-3275**
1999 Harrison St Ste 1100 Oakland (94612) ***(P-12330)***
Catamunt Brdcstg Chc-Rdding In (PA) ....**C....530 893-2424**
3460 Silverbell Rd Chico (95973) ***(P-8040)***
Cataphora Inc (PA) ....**D....650 622-9840**
3425 Edison Way Menlo Park (94025) ***(P-12331)***
Caterpillar Authorized Dealer, West Sacramento *Also called Holt of California* ***(P-9023)***
Cathedral Pioneer Church Homes (PA) ....**D....916 442-4906**
415 P St Ofc Sacramento (95814) ***(P-15954)***
Catherine-Elizabeth Inc (PA) ....**E....707 827-1655**
4707 Vine Hill Rd Sebastopol (95472) ***(P-2526)***

A L P H A B E T I C

CATHOLIC CHARITIES OF EAST BAY, Oakland *Also called Catholic Chrties of The Dcese* ***(P-17467)***
Catholic Chrties Cyo of The AR.....E.....415 743-0017
810 Avenue D San Francisco (94130) ***(P-17456)***
Catholic Chrties Cyo of The AR.....E.....415 405-2000
141 Leland Ave San Francisco (94134) ***(P-17457)***
Catholic Chrties Cyo of The AR.....E.....415 863-1141
1390 Mission St San Francisco (94103) ***(P-17458)***
Catholic Chrties Cyo of The AR.....D.....650 757-2110
699 Serramonte Blvd 210 Daly City (94015) ***(P-7424)***
Catholic Chrties Cyo of The AR.....E.....415 334-5550
1111 Junipero Serra Blvd San Francisco (94132) ***(P-17459)***
Catholic Chrties Cyo of The AR.....E.....415 553-8700
20 Franklin St San Francisco (94102) ***(P-17460)***
Catholic Chrties Cyo of The AR (PA).....**D.....415 972-1200**
1 Saint Vincents Dr San Rafael (94903) ***(P-17461)***
Catholic Chrties Cyo of The AR.....E.....415 507-2000
1 Saint Vincents Dr San Rafael (94903) ***(P-17462)***
Catholic Chrties Cyo of The AR.....E.....415 452-3500
50 Broad St San Francisco (94112) ***(P-17463)***
Catholic Chrties Cyo of The AR.....E.....415 668-9543
750 33rd Ave San Francisco (94121) ***(P-17464)***
Catholic Chrties Cyo of The AR.....E.....415 206-1467
899 Guerrero St San Francisco (94110) ***(P-17465)***
Catholic Chrties of The Dcese.....D.....209 529-3784
2351 Tenaya Dr D Modesto (95354) ***(P-17466)***
Catholic Chrties of The Dcese (PA).....**D.....510 768-3100**
433 Jefferson St Oakland (94607) ***(P-17467)***
Catholic Chrties Snta Clara CN.....D.....408 282-8600
195 E San Fernando St San Jose (95112) ***(P-17468)***
Catholic Chrties Snta Clara CN (PA).....**C.....408 468-0100**
2625 Zanker Rd Ste 200 San Jose (95134) ***(P-17469)***
Catholic Health Care West, San Francisco *Also called Saint Francis Memorial Hosp* ***(P-16497)***
Catholic Social Service, Vallejo *Also called Roman Cathlic Bishp Sacramento* ***(P-17695)***
Cato Networks Inc.....E.....646 975-9243
3031 Tisch Way San Jose (95128) ***(P-13053)***
Caton Moving & Storage, Alameda *Also called Chipman Corporation* ***(P-7519)***
Catta Verdera Country Club LLC.....D.....916 645-7200
1111 Catta Verdera Lincoln (95648) ***(P-15071)***
Cattleman's Restaurant, Roseville *Also called Cattlemens* ***(P-11711)***
Cattlemens.....D.....916 782-5587
2000 Taylor Rd Roseville (95678) ***(P-11711)***
Cavallo Point LLC (PA).....**D.....415 339-4700**
601 Murray Cir Sausalito (94965) ***(P-10997)***
Cavendish Kinetics Inc.....E.....408 627-4504
2960 N 1st St San Jose (95134) ***(P-8901)***
Cavisson Systems Inc.....B.....800 701-6125
5201 Great America Pkwy Santa Clara (95054) ***(P-19740)***
Cavium LLC (HQ).....**B.....408 222-2500**
5488 Marvell Ln Santa Clara (95054) ***(P-6080)***
Cavium Networks Intl Inc (HQ).....**D.....650 625-7000**
2315 N 1st St San Jose (95131) ***(P-6081)***
Caw Architects Inc.....D.....650 328-1818
455 Lambert Ave Palo Alto (94306) ***(P-18877)***
Caylym Holdings, Fresno *Also called Caylym Technologies Intl LLC* ***(P-13564)***
Caylym Technologies Intl LLC.....E.....209 322-9596
5340 E Home Ave Fresno (93727) ***(P-13564)***
CB Engineers (PA).....**E.....415 437-7330**
449 10th St San Francisco (94103) ***(P-18664)***
CB Mill Inc.....F.....415 386-5309
1232 Connecticut St San Francisco (94107) ***(P-3276)***
CB&i Government Solutions Inc.....E.....916 928-3300
1326 N Market Blvd Sacramento (95834) ***(P-18665)***
Cb-1 Hotel.....D.....415 633-3838
757 Market St San Francisco (94103) ***(P-10998)***
CBA Site Services Inc.....D.....925 754-7633
11387 Pyrites Way Rancho Cordova (95670) ***(P-19741)***
Cbc Steel Buildings LLC.....C.....209 858-2425
1700 E Louise Ave Lathrop (95330) ***(P-4849)***
Cbem LLC Corporate Office (PA).....**D.....925 283-9000**
270 Lafayette Cir Lafayette (94549) ***(P-17470)***
Cbf Electric & Data, San Francisco *Also called B F C Inc* ***(P-1454)***
Cbiz Inc.....E.....925 956-0505
2300 Contra Costa Blvd Pleasant Hill (94523) ***(P-10260)***
Cbre Inc.....D.....916 446-6800
500 Capitol Mall Ste 2400 Sacramento (95814) ***(P-10506)***
CBS, Fresno *Also called Entercom Media Corp* ***(P-8021)***
CBS, San Francisco *Also called Entercom Media Corp* ***(P-8022)***
CBS, Sacramento *Also called Entercom Media Corp* ***(P-8023)***
CBS Farms LLC.....E.....831 724-0700
80 Sakata Ln Watsonville (95076) ***(P-39)***
CBS Interactive Inc (HQ).....**A.....415 344-2000**
235 2nd St San Francisco (94105) ***(P-11811)***
CBS Maxpreps Inc.....E.....530 676-6440
4364 Town Center Blvd # 320 El Dorado Hills (95762) ***(P-7938)***
Cbsi, San Francisco *Also called CBS Interactive Inc* ***(P-11811)***
Cbx Technologies Inc.....E.....510 729-7130
642 N L St Apt B Livermore (94551) ***(P-13861)***
CC Co Health Cntr Information.....D.....925 431-2300
2311 Loveridge Rd Pittsburg (94565) ***(P-15332)***
Cc-Palo Alto Inc.....D.....650 853-5000
620 Sand Hill Rd Palo Alto (94304) ***(P-16175)***
Ccapp Education Institute.....D.....916 338-9460
2400 Marconi Ave Ste C Sacramento (95821) ***(P-18557)***
CCARE, Fresno *Also called Califrnia Cncer Assoc For RES* ***(P-15311)***
Ccbc Reference Lab, Fresno *Also called Central California Blood Ctr* ***(P-17120)***
Cccera, Concord *Also called Contra Costa County Employees* ***(P-18409)***
Cccs Inc.....E.....916 457-6111
5061 24th St Sacramento (95822) ***(P-1024)***
Ccd Innovation, Emeryville *Also called Center For Culinary Dev Inc* ***(P-19041)***
Cchp, San Francisco *Also called Chinese Community Health Plan* ***(P-15349)***
CCI Financial and Insur Svcs, San Ramon *Also called California Coastal Insurance* ***(P-10257)***
Ccintegration Inc (PA).....**D.....408 228-1314**
2060 Corporate Ct San Jose (95131) ***(P-19040)***
CCM Partnership.....E.....925 829-1950
7121 Dublin Blvd Dublin (94568) ***(P-14608)***
Ccpoa, West Sacramento *Also called Califrnia Crrctnal Pace Offcer* ***(P-18356)***
Ccv Engineering & Mfg, Fresno *Also called Aries Industries Inc* ***(P-8278)***
Ccwd, Concord *Also called Contra Costa Water District* ***(P-8230)***
Cda Holding Company Inc (PA).....**D.....916 442-2462**
1201 K St Ste 1400 Sacramento (95814) ***(P-18336)***
Cdc San Francisco LLC.....D.....415 616-6512
888 Howard St San Francisco (94103) ***(P-10999)***
Cdg Technology LLC.....E.....530 243-4451
779 Twin View Blvd Redding (96003) ***(P-5671)***
CDI, Fresno *Also called Construction Developers Inc* ***(P-858)***
Ce2 Corporation Inc.....E.....925 463-7301
6200 Stnrdge Mall Rd Ste Pleasanton (94588) ***(P-18666)***
Cecelia Packing Corporation.....C.....559 626-5000
24780 E South Ave Orange Cove (93646) ***(P-9392)***
Cedar Creek Corporation.....D.....530 364-2143
15875 Jellys Ferry Rd Red Bluff (96080) ***(P-1092)***
Cedar Crest Nrsing Rhbltion C, Sunnyvale *Also called Ghc of Sunnyvale LLC* ***(P-16235)***
Cedar Fair LP.....C.....408 988-1776
4701 Great America Pkwy Santa Clara (95054) ***(P-15040)***
Cedar Knoll Vineyards Inc.....E.....707 226-5587
4029 Hagen Rd NAPA (94558) ***(P-2527)***
Cedar Lane North, South San Francisco *Also called Cedarlane Natural Foods North* ***(P-2880)***
Cedarlane Natural Foods North.....E.....650 742-0444
150 Airport Blvd South San Francisco (94080) ***(P-2880)***
Cedars of Marin (PA).....**D.....415 454-5310**
115 Upper Rd Ross (94957) ***(P-16176)***
Cederlind Farms LP.....D.....209 606-8586
2514 Kenney Ave Winton (95388) ***(P-48)***
Cei, San Jose *Also called Cupertino Electric Inc* ***(P-1491)***
CELEBRATION CENTER, Brentwood *Also called Christian Education Dev Co* ***(P-17905)***
Celerity Consulting Group Inc (PA).....**D.....415 986-8850**
2 Gough St Ste 300 San Francisco (94103) ***(P-19467)***
Celestica LLC.....C.....510 770-5100
49235 Milmont Dr Fremont (94538) ***(P-6404)***
Celestica Prcsion McHining Ltd (PA).....**E.....510 742-0500**
49235 Milmont Dr Fremont (94538) ***(P-5211)***
Celestica Prcsion McHining Ltd.....F.....510 252-2100
40725 Encyclopedia Cir Fremont (94538) ***(P-5491)***
Celestix Networks Inc.....D.....510 668-0700
4125 Hopyard Rd Ste 225 Pleasanton (94588) ***(P-13565)***
Celigo Inc (PA).....**C.....650 579-0210**
1820 Gateway Dr Ste 260 San Mateo (94404) ***(P-13054)***
Cell Biosciences, San Jose *Also called Alpha Innotech Corp* ***(P-8772)***
Cell Design Labs Inc.....E.....510 398-0501
5858 Horton St Ste 240 Emeryville (94608) ***(P-3880)***
Cell Marque Corporation.....E.....916 746-8900
6600 Sierra College Blvd Rocklin (95677) ***(P-4017)***
Cellarpro Cooling Systems, Petaluma *Also called Planet One Products Inc* ***(P-3319)***
Cellco Partnership.....D.....530 477-8042
682 Freeman Ln Grass Valley (95949) ***(P-7899)***
Cellco Partnership.....D.....916 838-9525
5815 Stockton Blvd Ste D Sacramento (95824) ***(P-7900)***
Cellco Partnership.....D.....559 321-8116
300 W Shaw Ave Clovis (93612) ***(P-7901)***
Cellco Partnership.....D.....925 743-9327
18012 Bollinger Canyon Rd San Ramon (94583) ***(P-7902)***
Cellco Partnership.....D.....209 474-9071
10952 Trinity Pkwy Stockton (95219) ***(P-7903)***
Cellfusion Inc (PA).....**E.....650 347-4000**
2033 Gateway Pl Fl 5 San Jose (95110) ***(P-13055)***
Cellink Corporation.....E.....650 799-3018
610 Quarry Rd San Carlos (94070) ***(P-6405)***
Cellmark Inc (HQ).....**D.....415 927-1700**
88 Rowland Way Ste 300 Novato (94945) ***(P-9193)***
Cellmobility Inc.....E.....510 549-3300
808 Gilman St Berkeley (94710) ***(P-4589)***
Cello & Maudru Cnstr Co Inc.....E.....707 257-0454
2505 Oak St NAPA (94559) ***(P-851)***
Cellotape Inc (HQ).....**C.....510 651-5551**
39611 Eureka Dr Newark (94560) ***(P-7223)***
Cellphone-Mate Inc.....D.....510 770-0469
48346 Milmont Dr Fremont (94538) ***(P-5830)***
Celltheon Corporation.....F.....650 743-3672
32980 Alvarado Niles Rd Union City (94587) ***(P-3881)***
Cellular One, Larkspur *Also called Blackwater Cellular Corp* ***(P-7897)***
Cellulo Co Division, Fresno *Also called Gusmer Enterprises Inc* ***(P-5229)***
Celo Labs Inc (PA).....**E.....415 942-4178**
500 Treat Ave Ste 101 San Francisco (94110) ***(P-19261)***
Celona Inc.....E.....408 839-7625
10080 N Wolfe Rd Sw3250 Cupertino (95014) ***(P-13056)***
Cemco, Pittsburg *Also called California Expanded Met Pdts* ***(P-4848)***
Cemex, Pleasanton *Also called RMC Pacific Materials LLC* ***(P-4397)***
Cemex California Cement LLC.....B.....760 381-7616
8251 Power Ridge Rd Sacramento (95826) ***(P-4394)***
Cemex Cnstr Mtls PCF LLC.....E.....925 672-4900
515 Mitchell Canyon Rd Clayton (94517) ***(P-8621)***
Cemex Cnstr Mtls PCF LLC.....E.....925 846-2824
1544 Stanley Blvd Pleasanton (94566) ***(P-4465)***

Cemex Cnstr Mtls PCF LLC ....E....707 422-2520
1601 Cement Hill Rd Fairfield (94533) *(P-4466)*
Cemex Cnstr Mtls PCF LLC ....E....209 862-0182
3407 W Stuhr Rd Newman (95360) *(P-4467)*
Cemex Cnstr Mtls PCF LLC ....E....855 292-8453
900 Whipple Rd Union City (94587) *(P-4468)*
Cemex Cnstr Mtls PCF LLC ....E....855 292-8453
1290 E Turner Rd Lodi (95240) *(P-4469)*
Cemex Cnstr Mtls PCF LLC ....E....800 992-3639
4132 Cordelia Rd Suisun City (94585) *(P-4423)*
Cemex Corp ....C....800 992-3639
22101 W Sunset Ave Los Banos (93635) *(P-8622)*
Cemex Corp ....C....800 992-3639
808 Gilman St Berkeley (94710) *(P-8623)*
Cemex Materials LLC ....D....707 678-4311
7059 Tremont Rd Dixon (95620) *(P-4470)*
Cemex Materials LLC ....E....855 292-8453
1645 Stanley Blvd Pleasanton (94566) *(P-4471)*
Cemex Materials LLC ....D....510 234-3616
401 Wright Ave Richmond (94804) *(P-4472)*
Cemex Materials LLC ....D....707 255-3035
385 Tower Rd NAPA (94558) *(P-4473)*
Cemex Materials LLC ....D....559 275-2241
4150 N Brawley Ave Fresno (93722) *(P-4474)*
Cen Cal Plastering Inc (PA) ....B....209 858-1045
1256 W Lathrop Rd Manteca (95336) *(P-1666)*
Cen Cal Plastering Inc ....D....209 981-5265
15300 E Wyman Rd Lathrop (95330) *(P-1667)*
Cen-Cal Fire Systems Inc ....E....209 334-9166
1615 S Stockton St Lodi (95240) *(P-1231)*
Cencal Cnc Inc ....E....559 897-8706
2491 Simpson St Kingsburg (93631) *(P-5492)*
Cencal Recycling LLC ....F....209 546-8000
501 Port Road 22 Stockton (95203) *(P-3340)*
Cenpatico Behavioral Hlth LLC ....C....877 858-3855
1740 Creekside Oaks Dr Sacramento (95833) *(P-17116)*
Centen AG LLC ....F....925 432-5000
901 Loveridge Rd Pittsburg (94565) *(P-4141)*
Centene Corporation ....E....314 505-6689
12033 Foundation Pl Gold River (95670) *(P-10101)*
Center For Care Innvations Inc (PA) ....E....415 561-6393
1438 Webster St Ste 101 Oakland (94612) *(P-18337)*
Center For Cllbrtive Classroom ....D....510 533-0213
1001 Marina Village Pkwy # 1 Alameda (94501) *(P-3527)*
Center For Culinary Dev Inc ....D....415 693-8900
1201 Park Ave Ste 101 Emeryville (94608) *(P-19041)*
Center For Domestic Peace ....E....415 457-2464
734 A St San Rafael (94901) *(P-17471)*
Center For Elders Independence ....C....510 433-1150
510 17th St Ste 400 Oakland (94612) *(P-10102)*
Center For Employment Training (PA) ....D....408 287-7924
701 Vine St San Jose (95110) *(P-17801)*
Center For Fathers & Families ....E....916 568-3237
920 Del Paso Blvd Sacramento (95815) *(P-17472)*
Center For Human Services (PA) ....C....209 526-1476
2000 W Briggsmore Ave I Modesto (95350) *(P-17473)*
Center For Lrng Atism Spport S ....B....800 538-8365
424 Peninsula Ave San Mateo (94401) *(P-17474)*
Center For Social Dynamics LLC (PA) ....B....510 268-8120
1025 Atlantic Ave Ste 101 Alameda (94501) *(P-17475)*
Center For The Arts, The, Grass Valley *Also called Northern Cal Ctr For Arts* *(P-18582)*
Center For Women's Health Care, Eureka *Also called St Joseph Hospital* *(P-16542)*
Center For Youth Wellness ....E....415 684-9520
3450 3rd St Ste 201 San Francisco (94124) *(P-17117)*
Center Point Inc (PA) ....C....415 492-4444
135 Paul Dr San Rafael (94903) *(P-17476)*
Center State Pipe and Sup Co ....F....209 466-0871
2750 Cherokee Rd Stockton (95205) *(P-8994)*
Center To Prmote Hlthcare Acce ....D....916 563-4004
1 Capitol Mall Ste 300 Sacramento (95814) *(P-17118)*
Center To Prmote Hlthcare Acce (PA) ....D....510 273-4651
1951 Webster St Fl 2 Oakland (94612) *(P-17119)*
Centerism Memorial Hospital, Rohnert Park *Also called Santa Rosa Memorial Hospital* *(P-17070)*
Centerplate, San Francisco *Also called Volume Services Inc* *(P-15262)*
Centerra Solutions Inc ....E....408 791-6188
368 Fairview Way Milpitas (95035) *(P-13862)*
Centerville Presbyterian Ch ....E....510 793-3575
4360 Central Ave Fremont (94536) *(P-17880)*
Centra Freight Services Inc (PA) ....D....650 873-8147
279 Lawrence Ave South San Francisco (94080) *(P-7865)*
Centra Software Inc ....E....650 378-1363
1840 Gateway Dr Fl 2 San Mateo (94404) *(P-13057)*
Central Ansthsia Svc Exch Med ....D....916 481-6800
3315 Watt Ave Sacramento (95821) *(P-15333)*
Central Assembly of God ....E....510 223-1966
5100 Argyle Rd El Sobrante (94803) *(P-17881)*
Central Branch YMCA, San Jose *Also called Young MNS Chrstn Assn Slcon Vl* *(P-18528)*
Central Business Forms Inc ....E....650 548-0918
289 Foster City Blvd B Foster City (94404) *(P-3633)*
Central Business Solutions Inc ....D....510 573-5500
37600 Central Ct Ste 214 Newark (94560) *(P-13863)*
Central Cal Almond Grwers Assn (PA) ....E....559 846-5377
8325 S Madera Ave Kerman (93630) *(P-275)*
Central Cal Dar Cnstr Inc ....C....209 667-0381
2700 Lassiter Ln Turlock (95380) *(P-852)*
Central Cal Dntl Surgicenter, Atwater *Also called Castle Dental Surgery Centre* *(P-15826)*
Central Cal Ear Nose Throat ME ....C....559 432-3724
1351 E Spruce Ave Fresno (93720) *(P-15334)*
Central Cal Fclty Med Group In ....D....559 435-6600
2335 E Kashian Ln Ste 220 Fresno (93701) *(P-15335)*
Central Cal Fclty Med Group In ....D....559 266-4100
2335 E Kashian Ln Fresno (93701) *(P-15336)*
Central Cal Fclty Med Group In ....D....559 320-1090
2828 Fresno St Ste 203 Fresno (93721) *(P-15337)*
Central Cal Fclty Med Group In ....D....559 435-4700
6311 N Fresno St Fresno (93710) *(P-15338)*
Central Cal Healthcare Sys, Fresno *Also called Veterans Health Administration* *(P-15790)*
Central Cal Metals, Fresno *Also called Robert J Alandt & Sons* *(P-4682)*
Central Cal Nikkei Foundation ....D....559 237-4006
540 S Peach Ave Fresno (93727) *(P-18073)*
Central California Blood Ctr ....D....559 389-5433
4343 W Herndon Ave Fresno (93722) *(P-17120)*
Central California Blood Ctr (PA) ....C....559 389-5433
4343 W Herndon Ave Fresno (93722) *(P-17121)*
Central California Cont Mfg ....E....559 665-7611
800 Commerce Dr Chowchilla (93610) *(P-4265)*
Central California Faculty Med ....D....209 620-6937
1085 W Minnesota Ave Turlock (95382) *(P-17122)*
Central California Faculty Med (PA) ....D....559 453-5200
2625 E Divisadero St Fresno (93721) *(P-15339)*
Central California Food Bank ....E....559 237-3663
4010 E Amendola Dr Fresno (93725) *(P-18224)*
Central City Hospitality House ....E....415 749-2100
290 Turk St San Francisco (94102) *(P-17477)*
Central Coast Wine Company (HQ) ....C....707 745-8500
4301 Industrial Way Benicia (94510) *(P-9570)*
Central Coast YMCA ....C....831 637-8600
351 Tres Pnos Rd Ste 201a Hollister (95023) *(P-18405)*
Central Coast YMCA ....C....831 728-9622
27 Sudden St Watsonville (95076) *(P-18406)*
Central Concrete Supply Co Inc (HQ) ....D....408 293-6272
755 Stockton Ave San Jose (95126) *(P-4475)*
Central Contra Costa Sani Dst ....B....925 228-9500
5019 Imhoff Pl Martinez (94553) *(P-8279)*
Central Counties ....D....209 356-0355
241 Business Park Way Atwater (95301) *(P-19262)*
Central Fish Inc ....D....559 237-2049
1535 Kern St Fresno (93706) *(P-9364)*
Central Garden & Pet Company (PA) ....E....925 948-4000
1340 Treat Blvd Ste 600 Walnut Creek (94597) *(P-9649)*
Central Garden & Pet Company ....E....925 964-9879
38 Pheasant Run Pl Danville (94506) *(P-9650)*
Central Irrigation Inc ....E....209 262-3723
2941 N Highway 59 Merced (95348) *(P-4998)*
Central Marin Sanitation Agcy ....E....415 459-1455
1301 Andersen Dr San Rafael (94901) *(P-8393)*
Central Parking Corporation ....D....510 832-7227
1624 Franklin St Ste 722 Oakland (94612) *(P-14509)*
Central Parking System Inc ....D....916 441-1074
716 10th St Ste 101 Sacramento (95814) *(P-14510)*
Central Plastics and Mfg, Tracy *Also called Mother Lode Plas Molding Inc* *(P-4304)*
Central Precast Concrete Inc ....D....925 417-6854
3500 Boulder St Pleasanton (94566) *(P-4424)*
Central Printing Group, Foster City *Also called Central Business Forms Inc* *(P-3633)*
Central Sanitary Supply LLC (HQ) ....E....209 523-3002
416 N 9th St Ste A Modesto (95350) *(P-9141)*
Central Striping Service Inc ....E....916 635-5175
3489 Luyung Dr Rancho Cordova (95742) *(P-1025)*
Central Supply Co, Fresno *Also called San Joaquin Hydraulic Inc* *(P-9132)*
Central Tech Inc ....E....408 955-0919
2271 Ringwood Ave San Jose (95131) *(P-6510)*
Central Valley AG Grinding Inc (PA) ....E....209 869-1721
5509 Langworth Rd Oakdale (95361) *(P-276)*
Central Valley AG Transload, Modesto *Also called Central Valley AG Trnspt Inc* *(P-7864)*
Central Valley AG Transload, Oakdale *Also called Central Valley AG Trnspt Inc* *(P-277)*
Central Valley AG Trnspt Inc ....E....209 544-9246
330 Codoni Ave Modesto (95357) *(P-7864)*
Central Valley AG Trnspt Inc ....D....209 544-9246
5509 Langworth Rd Oakdale (95361) *(P-277)*
Central Valley Builders Supply ....E....707 963-3622
1100 Vintage Ave Saint Helena (94574) *(P-9033)*
Central Valley Cheese Inc ....D....209 664-1080
115 S Kilroy Rd Turlock (95380) *(P-9334)*
Central Valley Cmnty Bancorp (PA) ....C....559 298-1775
7100 N Fincl Dr Ste 101 Fresno (93720) *(P-9713)*
Central Valley Community Bank ....E....916 985-8700
905 Sutter St Ste 100 Folsom (95630) *(P-9714)*
Central Valley Community Bank (HQ) ....C....800 298-1775
7100 N Fincl Dr Ste 101 Fresno (93720) *(P-9715)*
Central Valley Concrete Inc (PA) ....C....209 723-8846
3823 N State Highway 59 Merced (95348) *(P-7457)*
Central Valley Concrete Inc ....D....209 667-0161
4200 Lester Rd Denair (95316) *(P-1232)*
Central Valley Electric Inc ....E....209 531-2470
24 Frazine Rd Ste A Modesto (95357) *(P-1474)*
Central Valley Engrg & Asp Inc ....E....916 791-1609
216 Kenroy Ln Roseville (95678) *(P-1026)*
Central Valley Environmental, Fresno *Also called Cve Contracting Group Inc* *(P-19756)*
Central Valley Environmental, Rohnert Park *Also called Cve Nb Contracting Group Inc* *(P-19757)*
Central Valley Eye, Stockton *Also called R Scott Foster MD* *(P-15638)*
Central Valley Fund, The, Davis *Also called Cvf Capital Partners Inc* *(P-10840)*
Central Valley Gaming LLC ....F....209 668-1010
2321 W Main St Ste C Turlock (95380) *(P-15190)*
Central Valley GMC (PA) ....D....559 334-3496
2707 S East Ave Fresno (93725) *(P-14552)*

ALPHABETIC

Central Valley Indian Hlth Inc (PA) ....D....**559 299-2578**
2740 Herndon Ave Clovis (93611) ***(P-15340)***
Central Valley Injured (PA) ....D....**209 522-2777**
3101 Mchenry Ave Modesto (95350) ***(P-17228)***
Central Valley Machining Inc ....E....559 291-7749
5820 E Harvard Ave Fresno (93727) ***(P-4652)***
Central Valley Oprtnty Ctr Inc (PA) ....D....**209 357-0062**
6838 Bridget Ct Winton (95388) ***(P-17802)***
Central Valley Party Supply ....E....209 569-0399
3250 Dale Rd Ste I Modesto (95356) ***(P-12034)***
Central Valley Pizza LLC ....E....209 589-9633
2930 Geer Rd Ste 174 Turlock (95382) ***(P-10804)***
Central Valley Tank of Cal ....F....559 456-3500
4752 E Carmen Ave Fresno (93703) ***(P-4713)***
Central Valley Trlr Repr Inc ....D....559 233-8444
2974 S East Ave Fresno (93725) ***(P-14553)***
Central Valley Trucking, Merced *Also called Central Valley Concrete Inc* ***(P-7457)***
Central Vly Assembly Packg Inc ....E....559 486-4260
5515 E Lamona Ave 103 Fresno (93727) ***(P-4623)***
Central Vly Chld Svcs Netwrk ....D....559 456-1100
1911 N Helm Ave Fresno (93727) ***(P-17478)***
Central Vly Ctr For Arts Inc (PA) ....E....**209 338-2100**
1000 I St Modesto (95354) ***(P-14844)***
Central Vly Fmly Health-Kerman, Kerman *Also called Adventist Hlth Systm/West Corp* ***(P-16313)***
Central Vly Fmly Health-Sanger, Sanger *Also called Adventist Hlth Systm/West Corp* ***(P-16314)***
Central Vly Fmly Health-Selma, Selma *Also called Adventist Hlth Systm/West Corp* ***(P-16315)***
Central Vly Fmly Hlth-Cruthers, Caruthers *Also called Adventist Hlth Systm/West Corp* ***(P-16311)***
Central Vly Fmly Hlth-Slma Cnt, Selma *Also called Adventist Hlth Systm/West Corp* ***(P-16305)***
Central Vly Specialty Hosp Inc ....C....209 248-7700
730 17th St Modesto (95354) ***(P-16328)***
Centric Software Inc (PA) ....E....**408 574-7802**
655 Campbell Tech Pkwy # 200 Campbell (95008) ***(P-19468)***
Centrify Corporation (PA) ....A....**669 444-5200**
201 Rdwood Shres Pkwy Ste Redwood City (94065) ***(P-12332)***
Centrix Builders Inc ....D....650 876-9400
160 S Linden Ave Ste 100 South San Francisco (94080) ***(P-626)***
Centrl Inc ....E....650 641-7092
257 Castro St Ste 215 Mountain View (94041) ***(P-13058)***
Centro La Familia Advacasy Svc ....E....559 237-2961
302 Fresno St Ste 102 Fresno (93706) ***(P-17479)***
CENTRO LA FAMILIA ADVOCACY, Fresno *Also called Centro La Familia Advacasy Svc* ***(P-17479)***
CENTRO VIDA, Berkeley *Also called Bay Area Hspano Inst For Advnc* ***(P-17857)***
Centrro Inc (PA) ....E....**510 891-7500**
2418 Teal Ln Alameda (94501) ***(P-13781)***
Centurion, Merced *Also called Fineline Industries Inc* ***(P-6642)***
Centurioni Industries Inc ....F....858 213-7433
580 Crespi Dr Pacifica (94044) ***(P-7274)***
Century 14, Vallejo *Also called Century Theatres Inc* ***(P-14808)***
Century 20, Milpitas *Also called Century Theatres Inc* ***(P-14820)***
Century 21, Sunnyvale *Also called Sunmar Corporation* ***(P-10666)***
Century 21, Merced *Also called M A D Inc* ***(P-10609)***
Century 21, Turlock *Also called Premier Valley Inc A Cal Corp* ***(P-10647)***
Century 21 Showcase, Boulder Creek *Also called Cortlandt Liquidating LLC* ***(P-10526)***
Century 21 Wildwood Properties ....E....209 586-3258
22910 Twain Harte Dr Twain Harte (95383) ***(P-10507)***
Century Assembly Inc (PA) ....D....**209 334-3230**
550 W Century Blvd Lodi (95240) ***(P-17882)***
Century Assembly Inc ....E....209 334-3230
550 W Century Blvd Lodi (95240) ***(P-17883)***
Century Christian School, Lodi *Also called Century Assembly Inc* ***(P-17882)***
Century Cinema, Mountain View *Also called Century Theatres Inc* ***(P-14826)***
Century Cinema, Corte Madera *Also called Century Theatres Inc* ***(P-14828)***
Century Commercial Service ....E....530 823-1004
12820 Earhart Ave Auburn (95602) ***(P-8850)***
Century Laguna 16, Elk Grove *Also called Century Theatres Inc* ***(P-14819)***
Century Pk Capitl Partners LLC ....D....650 324-1956
1010 Coleman Ave Ste 30 Menlo Park (94025) ***(P-10838)***
Century Pre-School, Lodi *Also called Century Assembly Inc* ***(P-17883)***
Century Presidio, San Francisco *Also called Century Theatres Inc* ***(P-14825)***
Century Theatres, San Francisco *Also called Syufy Century Corporation* ***(P-14818)***
Century Theatres Inc ....C....916 683-5290
9349 Big Horn Blvd Elk Grove (95758) ***(P-14819)***
Century Theatres Inc ....C....408 942-7441
1010 Great Mall Dr Milpitas (95035) ***(P-14820)***
Century Theatres Inc ....E....916 442-7000
445 Downtown Plz Sacramento (95814) ***(P-14821)***
Century Theatres Inc ....C....707 648-3456
109 Plaza Dr Vallejo (94591) ***(P-14808)***
Century Theatres Inc ....C....866 322-4547
825 Middlefield Rd Redwood City (94063) ***(P-14822)***
Century Theatres Inc ....C....510 758-9626
3200 Klose Way Richmond (94806) ***(P-14823)***
Century Theatres Inc ....E....925 681-2000
125 Crescent Dr Pleasant Hill (94523) ***(P-14824)***
Century Theatres Inc ....C....415 776-2388
2340 Chestnut St San Francisco (94123) ***(P-14825)***
Century Theatres Inc ....C....650 961-3828
1500 N Shoreline Blvd Mountain View (94043) ***(P-14826)***
Century Theatres Inc ....C....408 226-2251
3630 Hillcap Ave San Jose (95136) ***(P-14809)***
Century Theatres Inc ....E....650 340-1516
1304 Bayshore Hwy Burlingame (94010) ***(P-14827)***
Century Theatres Inc ....E....415 924-6505
41 Tamal Vista Blvd Corte Madera (94925) ***(P-14828)***
Century Theatres Inc ....C....916 332-2622
6233 Garfield Ave Sacramento (95841) ***(P-14829)***
Century Theatres Inc ....C....415 661-2539
85 West Portal Ave San Francisco (94127) ***(P-14830)***
Century Theatres Inc ....C....916 363-6572
9616 Oates Dr Sacramento (95827) ***(P-14831)***
Cenveo Worldwide Limited ....C....415 821-7171
665 3rd St Ste 505 San Francisco (94107) ***(P-3634)***
Cenzic Inc ....D....408 200-0700
655 Campbell Tech Pkwy # 100 Campbell (95008) ***(P-8902)***
Cep America - Anesthesia PC ....E....510 350-2842
2100 Powell St Ste 400 Emeryville (94608) ***(P-15341)***
Cep America - Illinois LLP ....D....510 350-2777
2100 Powell St Ste 400 Emeryville (94608) ***(P-15342)***
Cep America - Illinois Snf LLP ....E....510 350-2777
2100 Powell St Ste 400 Emeryville (94608) ***(P-15955)***
Cep America - Intensivists PC ....E....510 350-2777
2100 Powell St Ste 400 Emeryville (94608) ***(P-15343)***
Cep America - Kansas LLC ....E....510 350-2777
2100 Powell St Ste 400 Emeryville (94608) ***(P-15344)***
Cep America LLC ....D....510 350-2691
2100 Powell St 400 Emeryville (94608) ***(P-15345)***
Cep Amrc-Llnois Hsptalists LLP ....E....510 350-2777
2100 Powell St Ste 400 Emeryville (94608) ***(P-15346)***
Cephas Enterprises Inc ....E....650 244-0310
1365 Lowrie Ave South San Francisco (94080) ***(P-11934)***
Cepheid ....F....408 548-9104
632 E Caribbean Dr Sunnyvale (94089) ***(P-4018)***
Cepheid (HQ) ....A....**408 541-4191**
904 E Caribbean Dr Sunnyvale (94089) ***(P-6820)***
Ceps, Sacramento *Also called Consultnts In Edctl Per Skills* ***(P-17506)***
Cequent Towing Products, Fresno *Also called Horizon Global Americas Inc* ***(P-14661)***
Ceramic Tech Inc ....E....510 252-8500
46211 Research Ave Fremont (94539) ***(P-5493)***
Cerebral Palsy Assn San Joaqui, Stockton *Also called United Cerebral Palsy Assoc* ***(P-18351)***
Cerebras Systems Inc ....C....650 933-4980
1237 E Arques Ave Sunnyvale (94085) ***(P-13566)***
Cerium Systems Inc ....D....408 623-0787
1735 Tech Dr Ste 575 San Jose (95110) ***(P-13864)***
Cernex Inc ....E....408 541-9226
1710 Zanker Rd Ste 103 San Jose (95112) ***(P-6406)***
Certain Inc (PA) ....E....**415 353-5330**
75 Hawthorne St Ste 550 San Francisco (94105) ***(P-13059)***
Certent Inc (HQ) ....E....**925 730-4300**
1548 Eureka Rd Ste 100 Roseville (95661) ***(P-12333)***
Certified Coatings Company ....D....707 639-4414
2320 Cordelia Rd Fairfield (94534) ***(P-1407)***
Certified Foods Inc ....D....530 666-6565
41970 E Main St Woodland (95776) ***(P-2310)***
Certified Meat Products Inc ....D....559 256-1433
4586 E Commerce Ave Fresno (93725) ***(P-2092)***
Certified Stainless Svc Inc ....D....209 356-3300
441 Business Park Way Atwater (95301) ***(P-4714)***
Certified Stainless Svc Inc (PA) ....E....**209 537-4747**
2704 Railroad Ave Ceres (95307) ***(P-4715)***
Certified Stainless Svc Inc ....D....209 537-4747
581 Industry Way Atwater (95301) ***(P-4716)***
Certifiedsafety Inc ....D....707 747-9400
3070 Bay Vista Courtste B Benicia (94510) ***(P-19469)***
Cerus Corporation (PA) ....B....**925 288-6000**
1220 Concord Ave Ste 600 Concord (94520) ***(P-4042)***
Cerutti & Sons Trnsp Co ....E....559 275-6608
750 N Valentine Ave Fresno (93706) ***(P-7458)***
Ces Electric Inc ....E....530 636-4257
632 Entler Ave Chico (95928) ***(P-1475)***
CESCA THERAPEUTICS, Rancho Cordova *Also called Thermogenesis Holdings Inc* ***(P-7050)***
Cetas Inc ....F....847 530-5785
3260 Hillview Ave Palo Alto (94304) ***(P-13060)***
Cetec Automation Inc ....E....650 570-7557
553 Pilgrim Dr Ste A Foster City (94404) ***(P-12334)***
Cetecom Inc ....C....408 586-6200
411 Dixon Landing Rd Milpitas (95035) ***(P-19742)***
Ceterix Orthopaedics Inc ....E....650 241-1748
6500 Kaiser Dr Ste 120 Fremont (94555) ***(P-6961)***
CF Merced La Sierra LLC ....D....209 723-4224
2424 M St Merced (95340) ***(P-15956)***
CF Susanville LLC ....D....530 257-5341
2005 River St Susanville (96130) ***(P-15957)***
Cfarms Inc ....E....916 375-3000
1244 E Beamer St Woodland (95776) ***(P-2881)***
Cfarms Inc (PA) ....E....**916 375-3000**
1330 N Dutton Ave Ste 100 Santa Rosa (95401) ***(P-2882)***
Cfkba Inc (PA) ....E....**650 847-3900**
150 Jefferson Dr Menlo Park (94025) ***(P-4568)***
Cfkba Inc ....F....650 302-6331
508 2nd Ave Redwood City (94063) ***(P-4569)***
CFM Equipment Distributors Inc (PA) ....E....**916 447-7022**
1644 Main Ave Ste 1 Sacramento (95838) ***(P-9008)***
Cfmg, Kelsey *Also called Califrnia Frnsic Med Group Inc* ***(P-17114)***
Cfr Rinkens LLC ....E....310 297-8488
2875 Prune Ave Fremont (94539) ***(P-7684)***
Cfr San Francisco, Fremont *Also called Cfr Rinkens LLC* ***(P-7684)***

Cg Roxane LLC ....E....415 339-9521
10 Pimentel Ct Novato (94949) *(P-2787)*
Cg2 Inc ....D....407 737-8800
1759 Mccarthy Blvd Milpitas (95035) *(P-19207)*
Cgl Companies LLC ....D....916 678-7890
2260 Del Paso Rd Ste 100 Sacramento (95834) *(P-18878)*
Ch Cupertino Owner LLC ....D....408 253-8900
10050 S De Anza Blvd Cupertino (95014) *(P-11000)*
Ch Industrial Technology Inc ....F....559 485-8011
3160 E California Ave Fresno (93702) *(P-4653)*
Ch Reynolds, San Jose *Also called C H Reynolds Electric Inc (P-1471)*
Cha Industries Inc ....E....510 683-8554
250 S Vasco Rd Livermore (94551) *(P-5143)*
Cha Vacuum Technology, Livermore *Also called Cha Industries Inc (P-5143)*
Cha-Dor Realty LLC ....C....530 544-2237
2763 Lake Tahoe Blvd South Lake Tahoe (96150) *(P-8535)*
Chabot Space Scnce Ctr Fndtion (PA) ....**E....510 336-7300**
10000 Skyline Blvd Oakland (94619) *(P-18263)*
CHAC, Mountain View *Also called Community Hlth Awrness Council (P-17496)*
Chai DDS Inc ....C....909 810-7287
3514 Verona Ter Davis (95618) *(P-15827)*
Chalcedon Inc ....F....209 736-4365
3756 Highway 4 Vallecito (95251) *(P-10786)*
CHALCEDON FOUNDATION, Vallecito *Also called Chalcedon Inc (P-10786)*
Chalgren Enterprises ....F....408 847-3994
380 Tomkins Ct Gilroy (95020) *(P-7100)*
Challenge Dairy Products Inc (HQ) ....**D....925 828-6160**
6701 Donlon Way Dublin (94568) *(P-9335)*
Challenger Schools ....D....408 723-0111
4949 Harwood Rd San Jose (95124) *(P-17884)*
Challenger Schools ....D....650 213-8245
3880 Middlefield Rd Palo Alto (94303) *(P-17885)*
Challenger Schools ....D....510 770-1771
39600 Cedar Blvd Newark (94560) *(P-17886)*
Chamberlains Children Ctr Inc ....D....831 636-2121
1850 Cienega Rd Hollister (95023) *(P-18074)*
Chamberpac, San Jose *Also called San Jose Slcon Vly Chmber Cmmr (P-18317)*
Chambers & Chambers Inc (PA) ....**E....415 642-5500**
511 Alexis Ct NAPA (94558) *(P-9571)*
Chameleon Books & Journals, Gilroy *Also called Chameleon Like Inc (P-3760)*
Chameleon Like Inc ....D....408 847-3661
345 Kishimura Dr Gilroy (95020) *(P-3760)*
Chaminade Ltd ....C....831 475-5600
1 Chaminade Ln Santa Cruz (95065) *(P-11001)*
Chaminade At Santa Cruz, Santa Cruz *Also called Chaminade Ltd (P-11001)*
Champ Co, Campbell *Also called Consoldted Hnge Mnfctured Pdts (P-5495)*
Champagne Landscape Nurs Inc ....D....559 277-8188
3233 N Cornelia Ave Fresno (93722) *(P-451)*
Champion Industrial Contrs Inc (PA) ....**E....209 524-6601**
1420 Coldwell Ave Modesto (95350) *(P-1233)*
Champion Industrial Contrs Inc ....E....209 579-5478
451 Tully Rd Modesto (95350) *(P-1234)*
Champion Installs Inc ....E....916 627-0929
9631 Elk Grove Florin Rd Elk Grove (95624) *(P-3174)*
Champion Scaffold Services Inc ....D....510 788-4731
112 Railroad Ave Richmond (94801) *(P-2018)*
Champs Sports, Newark *Also called Foot Locker Retail Inc (P-4345)*
Chan Zuckerberg Biohub Inc ....D....628 200-3246
499 Illinois St San Francisco (94158) *(P-19208)*
Chanate Ldge Assoc A Cal Ltd P ....E....707 575-7503
3250 Chanate Rd Santa Rosa (95404) *(P-10423)*
Chance 4 Change Inc (PA) ....**E....707 443-8601**
525 2nd St Ste 213 Eureka (95501) *(P-17480)*
Chancellor Hlth Care of Cal IV ....B....209 367-8870
2220 W Kettleman Ln Ofc Lodi (95242) *(P-15958)*
Chancellor Hotel Associates A ....E....415 362-2004
433 Powell St San Francisco (94102) *(P-11002)*
Chancellor Place of Lodi, Lodi *Also called Chancellor Hlth Care of Cal IV (P-15958)*
Change Lending LLC ....D....707 596-5111
100 Stony Point Rd # 290 Santa Rosa (95401) *(P-9937)*
Changelab Solutions ....E....510 302-3380
2201 Broadway Ste 502 Oakland (94612) *(P-18558)*
Changeorg Inc (PA) ....**C....415 817-1840**
383 Rhode Island St # 300 San Francisco (94103) *(P-13782)*
Changing Future Outcome ....E....415 901-7000
372 Hanover St A41 San Francisco (94112) *(P-11677)*
Channel 40 Inc ....C....916 454-4422
4655 Fruitridge Rd Sacramento (95820) *(P-8041)*
Channel Impact, Moraga *Also called Bergerson Group (P-19454)*
Channel Medical Center, Stockton *Also called Community Medical Centers Inc (P-15358)*
Channel Systems Inc ....E....510 568-7170
74 98th Ave Oakland (94603) *(P-4425)*
Channing House ....D....650 327-0950
850 Webster St Ofc Palo Alto (94301) *(P-16227)*
Chapa-De Indian Hlth Prgram In (PA) ....**D....530 887-2800**
11670 Atwood Rd Auburn (95603) *(P-15347)*
Chapa-De Indian Hlth Prgram In ....D....530 477-8545
1350 E Main St Grass Valley (95945) *(P-15828)*
Chaparral Foundation ....D....510 848-8774
1309 Allston Way Berkeley (94702) *(P-15959)*
Chaparral House, Berkeley *Also called Chaparral Foundation (P-15959)*
Chapel of Chimes (HQ) ....**D....510 471-3363**
32992 Mission Blvd Hayward (94544) *(P-10724)*
Chapel of Chimes ....D....650 349-4411
100 Lifemark Rd Redwood City (94062) *(P-10725)*
Chappellet Vineyard ....E....707 286-4219
1581 Sage Canyon Rd Saint Helena (94574) *(P-2528)*
Chappellet Winery Inc (PA) ....**E....707 286-4268**
1581 Sage Canyon Rd Saint Helena (94574) *(P-2529)*
Charanjit Singh Batth ....D....559 864-9421
5434 W Kamm Ave Caruthers (93609) *(P-85)*
Chardnnay Golf CLB Vnyrds - NA, NAPA *Also called NAPA Golf Associates LLC (P-15113)*
Chardonnay Golf Club, NAPA *Also called Chardonnay/ Club Shakespeare (P-15072)*
Chardonnay/ Club Shakespeare ....E....707 257-1900
2555 Jamieson Canyon Rd NAPA (94558) *(P-15072)*
Chargepoint Inc (PA) ....**A....408 841-4500**
254 E Hacienda Ave Campbell (95008) *(P-5693)*
Chargepoint Holdings Inc (PA) ....**A....408 841-4500**
240 E Hacienda Ave Campbell (95008) *(P-5658)*
Charging Tree Corporation ....F....559 760-5473
35788 Highway 41 Coarsegold (93614) *(P-562)*
Charis Youth Center ....E....530 477-9800
714 W Main St Grass Valley (95945) *(P-17481)*
Charles Culberson Inc ....C....650 335-4730
1084 Allen Way Campbell (95008) *(P-1668)*
Charles Fenley Enterprises (PA) ....**E....209 576-0381**
1121 Oakdale Rd Ste 7 Modesto (95355) *(P-14636)*
Charles Fenley Enterprises ....E....209 523-2832
1109 Oakdale Rd Modesto (95355) *(P-14637)*
Charles Fenley Enterprises ....E....209 576-0381
1115 Oakdale Rd Modesto (95355) *(P-14638)*
Charles Hlen Schwab Foundation ....E....415 795-4920
201 Mission St Ste 1960 San Francisco (94105) *(P-18559)*
Charles Krug Winery, Saint Helena *Also called C Mondavi & Family (P-2522)*
Charles M Salter Associates (PA) ....**E....415 470-5461**
130 Sutter St Fl 5 San Francisco (94104) *(P-18667)*
Charles Matoian Entps Inc (PA) ....**C....559 445-8600**
1888 S East Ave Fresno (93721) *(P-7685)*
Charles McMurray Co (PA) ....**D....559 292-5751**
2520 N Argyle Ave Fresno (93727) *(P-8980)*
Charles McMurray Co ....E....916 929-9560
2601 Land Ave Sacramento (95815) *(P-8981)*
Charles Pnkow Bldrs Ltd A Cal ....B....510 893-5170
1111 Broadway Ste 200 Oakland (94607) *(P-853)*
Charles Schwab & Co Inc (HQ) ....**B....415 636-7000**
211 Main St Fl 17 San Francisco (94105) *(P-9962)*
Charles Schwab Corporation (PA) ....**A....415 667-7000**
211 Main St Fl 17 San Francisco (94105) *(P-9963)*
Charlie Mitchell Chld Clinic, Madera *Also called Valley Childrens Hospital (P-16704)*
Charming Trim & Packaging ....A....415 302-7021
28 Brookside Ct Novato (94947) *(P-9241)*
Charolais Care V Inc ....E....415 921-5038
1426 Fillmore St Ste 207 San Francisco (94115) *(P-16870)*
Chart Inc ....E....408 371-3303
46441 Landing Pkwy Fremont (94538) *(P-4717)*
Chartboost Inc (HQ) ....**C....415 493-0727**
1 Sansome St Fl 21 San Francisco (94104) *(P-12335)*
Chase Inc (PA) ....**D....559 277-2828**
3754 W Holland Ave Fresno (93722) *(P-9681)*
Chase Chevrolet Co Inc ....D....209 475-6600
6441 Holman Rd Stockton (95212) *(P-14554)*
Chase Chvrlet Chevy Trck World, Stockton *Also called Chase Chevrolet Co Inc (P-14554)*
Chase Manhattan Mortgage Corp ....C....858 605-3300
560 Mission St Fl 2 San Francisco (94105) *(P-9900)*
Chase Manhattan Mortgage Corp ....C....707 525-5060
2245 Mendocino Ave # 202 Santa Rosa (95403) *(P-9901)*
Chasen (usa) Inc ....E....408 725-7571
19925 Stevns Crk Blvd Cupertino (95014) *(P-10730)*
Chateau At River's Edge, Sacramento *Also called Hank Fisher Properties Inc (P-16237)*
Chateau Construction, Los Gatos *Also called Bainbridge and Associates Inc (P-615)*
Chateau Diana LLC (PA) ....**F....707 433-6992**
6195 Dry Creek Rd Healdsburg (95448) *(P-2530)*
Chateau La Salle, San Jose *Also called Mobilehome Communities America (P-10473)*
Chateau Masson LLC ....E....408 741-7002
14831 Pierce Rd Saratoga (95070) *(P-2531)*
Chateau Montelena LLC ....E....707 942-5105
1429 Tubbs Ln Calistoga (94515) *(P-2532)*
Chateau Montelena Winery, Calistoga *Also called Chateau Montelena LLC (P-2532)*
Chateau On Capitol Avenue, The, Sacramento *Also called Hank Fisher Properties Inc (P-18126)*
Chateau Pleasant Hill 2, Concord *Also called Carlton Senior Living Inc (P-10700)*
Chateau Woltner, Angwin *Also called Ladera Winery LLC (P-2645)*
Chatterbug Inc (PA) ....**E....415 957-9000**
995 Market St San Francisco (94103) *(P-12336)*
Chaudhary & Associates ....E....707 255-2729
211 Gateway Rd W Ste 204 NAPA (94558) *(P-18668)*
Chavez & Sons Trucking LLC ....F....707 999-1409
6692 Pedrick Rd Dixon (95620) *(P-6600)*
Chawk Technology Intl Inc (PA) ....**C....510 330-5299**
31033 Huntwood Ave Hayward (94544) *(P-4266)*
Chay & Harris Pntg Contrs Inc ....E....650 966-1472
2520 Wyandotte St Ste E Mountain View (94043) *(P-1408)*
Chayachitra Media LLC (PA) ....**E....510 397-8344**
38713 Chimaera Cir Fremont (94536) *(P-8074)*
Chdc, Santa Rosa *Also called Hdc Business Development Inc (P-10572)*
Checchi Enterprises Inc ....F....530 378-1207
19849 Riverside Ave Anderson (96007) *(P-3635)*
Check Point Software Tech Inc (HQ) ....**C....650 628-2000**
959 Skyway Rd Ste 300 San Carlos (94070) *(P-13061)*
Checkpoint Cloudguard Dome9, Mountain View *Also called Dome9 Security Inc (P-8694)*
Checkpoint Technologies LLC ....E....408 321-9780
66 Bonaventura Dr San Jose (95134) *(P-19042)*
Checkr Inc ....C....844 824-3257
1 Montgomery St Ste 2400 San Francisco (94104) *(P-11832)*

ALPHABETIC

Employee Codes: A=Over 500 employees, B=251-500 C=101-250, D=51-100, E=20-50 F=10-19
2022 Northern California Business Directory and Buyers Guide
© Mergent Inc. 1-800-342-5647
929

Cheema Logistics ....D....559 702-1444
968 Sierra St Ste 130 Kingsburg (93631) ***(P-7715)***
Cheema Transport Inc ....E....559 634-9109
1483 Avenue 396 Kingsburg (93631) ***(P-7877)***
Cheese Administrative Corp Inc ....E....209 826-3744
429 H St Los Banos (93635) ***(P-2144)***
Chef's Cut Real Jerky, Sonoma *Also called Rsj Ventures LLC* ***(P-2122)***
Chelbay Schuler & Chelbay (PA) ....**D....408 288-4400**
6800 Santa Teresa Blvd # 100 San Jose (95119) ***(P-10214)***
Chelsio Communications Inc ....C....408 962-3600
735 N Pastoria Ave Sunnyvale (94085) ***(P-12337)***
Chem Quip Inc ....D....800 821-1678
2551 Land Ave Sacramento (95815) ***(P-9154)***
Chemetall Oakite, Fremont *Also called Chemetall US Inc* ***(P-4067)***
Chemetall US Inc ....E....408 387-5340
46716 Lakeview Blvd Fremont (94538) ***(P-4067)***
Chemical Safety Technology Inc ....E....408 263-0984
2461 Autumnvale Dr San Jose (95131) ***(P-4267)***
Chemical Technologies Intl Inc ....F....916 638-1315
2747 Merc Dr Ste 200 Rancho Cordova (95742) ***(P-5440)***
Chemocentryx Inc (PA) ....**D....650 210-2900**
835 Industrial Rd Ste 600 San Carlos (94070) ***(P-3882)***
Chemsw Inc ....F....707 864-0845
2480 Burskirk Ste 300 Pleasant Hill (94523) ***(P-13062)***
Cher Ae Heights Casino, Trinidad *Also called Cher-Ae Heights Indian Cmnty* ***(P-15191)***
Cher-Ae Heights Indian Cmnty ....C....707 677-3611
27 Scenic Dr Trinidad (95570) ***(P-15191)***
Cherokee Freight Lines, Stockton *Also called Scan-Vino LLC* ***(P-7591)***
Cherry Bekaert LLP ....E....925 954-0100
1676 N Calif Blvd Fl 3 Walnut Creek (94596) ***(P-18944)***
Cherry Pie, Saint Helena *Also called One True Vine LLC* ***(P-2673)***
Chesapeake Lodging Trust ....C....415 296-2900
333 Battery St Lbby San Francisco (94111) ***(P-11003)***
Chester C Lehmann Co Inc (PA) ....**D....408 293-5818**
1135 Auzerais Ave San Jose (95126) ***(P-8851)***
Chevron, Fresno *Also called Bowie Enterprises* ***(P-14631)***
Chevron, Modesto *Also called Charles Fenley Enterprises* ***(P-14637)***
Chevron, San Jose *Also called Lark Avenue Car Wash* ***(P-14648)***
Chevron, Campbell *Also called Lark Avenue Car Wash* ***(P-14649)***
Chevron, Stockton *Also called Canepas Car Wash* ***(P-14635)***
Chevron Corporation (PA) ....**A....925 842-1000**
6001 Bollinger Canyon Rd San Ramon (94583) ***(P-4170)***
Chevron Federal Credit Union (PA) ....**D....888 884-4630**
500 12th St Ste 200 Oakland (94607) ***(P-9776)***
Chevron Global Energy Inc (HQ) ....**D....925 842-1000**
6001 Bollinger Canyon Rd San Ramon (94583) ***(P-4171)***
Chevron Global Lubricants, San Ramon *Also called Chevron Global Energy Inc* ***(P-4171)***
Chevron Global Tech Svcs Co ....E....925 842-1000
6001 Bollinger Canyon Rd San Ramon (94583) ***(P-18669)***
Chevron Munaigas Inc (HQ) ....**D....925 842-1000**
6001 Bollinger Canyon Rd San Ramon (94583) ***(P-546)***
Chevron Oronite Company LLC (HQ) ....**E....925 842-1000**
6001 Bollinger Canyon Rd San Ramon (94583) ***(P-4157)***
Chevron Shipping Company LLC ....D....925 842-1000
6001 Bollinger Canyon Rd San Ramon (94583) ***(P-7829)***
Chevron Stations Inc ....C....209 830-0370
755 S Tracy Blvd Tracy (95376) ***(P-9345)***
Chevron Stations Inc ....C....925 328-0292
18060 San Ramon Vly Blvd San Ramon (94583) ***(P-9346)***
Chevron Trading LLC (HQ) ....**C....925 842-1000**
6001 Bollinger Canyon Rd San Ramon (94583) ***(P-9531)***
Chevron USA Inc ....D....510 242-3000
841 Chevron Way Richmond (94801) ***(P-4172)***
Chevron USA Inc ....D....925 842-0855
6001 Bollinger Canyon Rd San Ramon (94583) ***(P-4173)***
CHi Doors Holdings Inc ....C....209 229-5663
3748 Zephyr Ct Stockton (95206) ***(P-1733)***
CHI MEI Optelectronics USA Inc, San Jose *Also called Innolux Optoelectronic Inc* ***(P-11962)***
CHI West LLC (HQ) ....**D....415 608-8757**
660 4th St San Francisco (94107) ***(P-5659)***
Chia Network Inc ....F....628 222-5925
44 Montgomery St Ste 2310 San Francisco (94104) ***(P-13063)***
Chiala, George Packing, Morgan Hill *Also called George Chiala Farms Inc* ***(P-31)***
Chibi Chan Preschool, San Francisco *Also called Japanese Cmnty Youth Council* ***(P-18235)***
Chicago Title Company ....C....408 292-4212
675 N 1st St Ste 400 San Jose (95112) ***(P-10196)***
Chicago Title Insurance Co ....A....408 371-4100
1500 E Hamilton Ave # 104 Campbell (95008) ***(P-10197)***
Chick-Fil-A Inc ....D....707 585-7462
5080 Redwood Dr Rohnert Park (94928) ***(P-19315)***
Chicken Rnch Economic Dev Corp ....E....209 984-9066
16929 Chicken Ranch Rd Jamestown (95327) ***(P-3426)***
Chico Area Recreation & Pk Dst (PA) ....**C....530 895-4711**
545 Vallombrosa Ave Chico (95926) ***(P-15192)***
Chico Community Publishing (PA) ....**E....530 894-2300**
353 E 2nd St Chico (95928) ***(P-3427)***
Chico Community Publishing ....C....916 498-1234
1124 Del Paso Blvd Sacramento (95815) ***(P-3428)***
Chico Creek Care Rhabilitation, Chico *Also called Helios Healthcare LLC* ***(P-16022)***
Chico Electric Inc ....D....530 891-1933
36 W Eaton Rd Chico (95973) ***(P-1476)***
Chico Enterprise Record, Chico *Also called Gatehouse Media LLC* ***(P-3440)***
Chico Eye Center, Chico *Also called James Hazlehurst* ***(P-15870)***
Chico Immdate Care Med Ctr Inc (PA) ....**E....530 891-1676**
376 Vallombrosa Ave Chico (95926) ***(P-15348)***
Chico Lodging LLC ....E....318 635-8000
2481 Carmichael Dr Chico (95928) ***(P-11004)***
Chico Lodging LLC ....E....530 894-5500
2485 Carmichael Dr Chico (95928) ***(P-11005)***
Chico Municipal Airport, Chico *Also called City of Chico* ***(P-7767)***
Chico Produce Inc (PA) ....**C....530 893-0596**
70 Pepsi Way Durham (95938) ***(P-9393)***
Chico Produce Inc ....E....530 241-1124
70 Pepsi Way Durham (95938) ***(P-9394)***
Chico Sports Club, Chico *Also called Jeff Stover Inc* ***(P-14955)***
Chico State Enterprises ....A....530 898-6811
25 Main St Unit 203 Chico (95928) ***(P-18407)***
Chico V A Outpatient Clinic, Chico *Also called Veterans Health Administration* ***(P-15797)***
Chicobag, Chico *Also called Chicoeco Inc* ***(P-3031)***
Chicoeco Inc ....E....530 342-4426
747 Fortress St Chico (95973) ***(P-3031)***
Child & Family Services, Orland *Also called Glenn County Office Education* ***(P-17940)***
Child Abuse Prvntion Cncil SCR ....E....916 244-1900
4700 Roseville Rd Ste 102 North Highlands (95660) ***(P-17482)***
Child Action Inc (PA) ....**C....916 369-0191**
10540 White Rock Rd # 180 Rancho Cordova (95670) ***(P-17887)***
Child Action Inc ....E....916 921-5345
2330 Glendale Ln Ste 110 Sacramento (95825) ***(P-17888)***
Child Action Inc ....D....916 369-0191
9961 Horn Rd Sacramento (95827) ***(P-17889)***
Child Care Development Svcs, Auburn *Also called Early Childhood Education Svcs* ***(P-17926)***
CHILD CARE FOOD PROGRAM, Watsonville *Also called Community Bridges* ***(P-17493)***
Child Dev Enrollment Off, Menlo Park *Also called Redwood City School District* ***(P-17683)***
Child Development Centers, Morgan Hill *Also called Child Development Incorporated* ***(P-17890)***
Child Development Incorporated (PA) ....**E....408 556-7300**
350 Woodview Ave Morgan Hill (95037) ***(P-17890)***
Child Development Incorporated ....B....530 666-4822
312 Gibson Rd Woodland (95695) ***(P-17891)***
Child Development Program, Kentfield *Also called Marin Community College Dst* ***(P-17969)***
Child Family & Cmnty Svcs Inc ....C....510 796-9512
32980 Alvarado Niles Rd # 856 Union City (94587) ***(P-17892)***
Child Family Health Inter (PA) ....**D....415 957-9000**
400 29th St Ste 508 Oakland (94609) ***(P-17123)***
CHILD PARENT INSTITUTE, Santa Rosa *Also called California Parenting Institute* ***(P-17870)***
Child Start Inc ....E....707 423-4050
1406 Woolner Ave Fairfield (94533) ***(P-17893)***
Child Start Inc (PA) ....**E....707 252-8931**
439 Devlin Rd NAPA (94558) ***(P-17894)***
Child Support Svcs Cal Dept (HQ) ....**B....916 464-5000**
11150 International Dr Rancho Cordova (95670) ***(P-17483)***
Childcare Careers LLC ....A....650 372-0211
2000 Sierra Point Pkwy # 702 Brisbane (94005) ***(P-12162)***
Childcare Foundry ....E....408 564-5356
3291 Stevens Creek Blvd San Jose (95117) ***(P-17895)***
Children & Families First Comm, San Jose *Also called First 5 Santa Clara County* ***(P-17570)***
Children Health Care, Stockton *Also called County of San Joaquin* ***(P-15368)***
Children's Choice, Danville *Also called Choice Foodservices Inc* ***(P-4583)***
Children's Enrichment Center, Aptos *Also called Twin Lakes Baptist Church* ***(P-18041)***
Children's Health Center, Chico *Also called Enloe Medical Center* ***(P-16369)***
Children's Home Care, Fresno *Also called Valley Childrens Hospital* ***(P-16706)***
Childrens Crative Lrng Ctr Inc ....B....408 978-1500
521 W Capitol Expy San Jose (95136) ***(P-17896)***
Childrens Crative Lrng Ctr Inc ....B....650 968-2600
1625 San Luis Ave Mountain View (94043) ***(P-17897)***
Childrens Crative Lrng Ctr Inc ....B....650 473-1100
848 Ramona St Palo Alto (94301) ***(P-17898)***
Childrens Creativity Museum ....D....415 820-3320
221 4th St San Francisco (94103) ***(P-18264)***
Childrens Crsis Ctr Stnslaus C ....E....209 577-4413
1244 Fiori Ave Modesto (95350) ***(P-17484)***
Childrens Ctr of San Lrnzo Vly ....D....831 336-2857
8500 Highway 9 Ben Lomond (95005) ***(P-17899)***
Childrens Cuncil San Francisco (PA) ....**D....415 343-3378**
445 Church St San Francisco (94114) ***(P-17485)***
Childrens Day School ....E....415 861-5432
333 Dolores St San Francisco (94110) ***(P-17900)***
Childrens Hlth Cncil of The MD ....C....650 326-5530
650 Clark Way Palo Alto (94304) ***(P-17486)***
Childrens Home of Stockton ....C....209 466-0853
430 N Pilgrim St Stockton (95205) ***(P-18075)***
Childrens Hosp RES Ctr At Okla (PA) ....**A....510 428-3000**
747 52nd St Oakland (94609) ***(P-16329)***
Childrens House of Los Altos ....E....650 968-9052
770 Berry Ave Los Altos (94024) ***(P-17901)***
Childrens Protective Services ....D....530 749-6311
5730 Packard Ave Marysville (95901) ***(P-17487)***
Childrens Rcvery Ctr Nthrn Cal, Campbell *Also called Childrens Recovery Ctr 1 LLC* ***(P-16753)***
Childrens Recovery Ctr 1 LLC ....D....408 558-3640
3777 S Bascom Ave Campbell (95008) ***(P-16753)***
Childrens Recvg Hm Sacramento ....C....916 482-2370
3555 Auburn Blvd Sacramento (95821) ***(P-17488)***
Childrens Therapeutic Services, Ukiah *Also called Redwood Community Services Inc* ***(P-17685)***
Childrens Vlg of Sonoma Cnty ....E....707 566-7044
1321 Lia Ln Santa Rosa (95404) ***(P-17489)***
Chili Bar LLC ....E....530 622-3325
11380 State Highway 193 Placerville (95667) ***(P-578)***
Chili Bar Slate, Placerville *Also called Chili Bar LLC* ***(P-578)***
Chilisin America Ltd ....E....408 954-7389
2880 Zanker Rd Ste 203 San Jose (95134) ***(P-6378)***

China Custom Manufacturing Ltd ....A....510 979-1920
44843 Fremont Blvd Fremont (94538) ***(P-4268)***
China Peak Mountain Resort LLC ....D....559 233-2500
59265 Hwy 168 Lakeshore (93634) ***(P-11006)***
Chinatown Cmnty Dev Ctr Inc (PA) ....**E....415 984-1450**
1525 Grant Ave San Francisco (94133) ***(P-10424)***
Chinchiolo Stemilt Cal LLC ....C....209 931-7000
4799 N Jack Tone Rd Stockton (95215) ***(P-278)***
Chinese Community Health Plan ....E....415 955-8800
445 Grant Ave Ste 700 San Francisco (94108) ***(P-15349)***
Chinese Consumer Yellow Pages, Fremont *Also called Chinese Overseas Mktg Svc Corp* ***(P-3563)***
Chinese For Affirmative Action ....E....415 274-6750
17 Walter U Lum Pl San Francisco (94108) ***(P-18536)***
Chinese Hospital Association (PA) ....**B....415 982-2400**
845 Jackson St San Francisco (94133) ***(P-16330)***
Chinese Overseas Mktg Svc Corp ....E....510 476-0880
33420 Alvarado Niles Rd Union City (94587) ***(P-3562)***
Chinese Overseas Mktg Svc Corp ....E....626 280-8588
46292 Warm Springs Blvd Fremont (94539) ***(P-3563)***
Chinese Times, San Francisco *Also called Gum Sun Times Inc* ***(P-3444)***
Chinese-American Bio Phrm Soc ....E....650 892-6283
268 Bush St Ste 1888 San Francisco (94104) ***(P-18560)***
Chiodo Candy Co ....F....510 464-2977
2923 Adeline St Oakland (94608) ***(P-2426)***
Chip Arasan Systems Inc ....D....408 282-1616
2150 N 1st St San Jose (95131) ***(P-10508)***
Chip Estimate Corporation ....E....408 943-1234
2655 Seely Ave San Jose (95134) ***(P-13064)***
Chipestimate.com, San Jose *Also called Chip Estimate Corporation* ***(P-13064)***
Chipman Corporation (PA) ....**E....510 748-8700**
1040 Marina Village Pkwy # 100 Alameda (94501) ***(P-7519)***
Chiron Corporation ....A....510 655-8730
4560 Horton St Emeryville (94608) ***(P-3883)***
Choice Food Products Inc ....E....559 266-1674
1822 W Hedges Ave Fresno (93728) ***(P-2114)***
Choice Foodservices Inc ....D....925 837-0104
569 San Ramon Valley Blvd Danville (94526) ***(P-4583)***
Choice In Aging (PA) ....**D....925 682-6330**
490 Golf Club Rd Pleasant Hill (94523) ***(P-16999)***
Chooljian & Sons Inc (PA) ....**D....559 888-2031**
5287 S Del Rey Ave Del Rey (93616) ***(P-279)***
Chooljian Bros Packing Co Inc ....E....559 875-5501
3192 S Indianola Ave Sanger (93657) ***(P-9443)***
Chouinard & Myhre Inc ....E....415 480-3636
655 Redwood Hwy Frontage # 102 Mill Valley (94941) ***(P-13567)***
Chowchilla Conv. Center, Chowchilla *Also called Avalon Care Ctr - Chwchlla LLC* ***(P-15915)***
Chowchilla Medical Center, Chowchilla *Also called Madera Community Hospital* ***(P-16435)***
Chowchilla Mem Hlth Care Dst (PA) ....**D....559 665-3781**
1104 Ventura Ave Chowchilla (93610) ***(P-15960)***
Chrisad, San Rafael *Also called Christensen Advertising* ***(P-11744)***
Chrisp Company (PA) ....**C....510 656-2840**
43650 Osgood Rd Fremont (94539) ***(P-1027)***
Chrissa Imports Ltd ....E....650 877-8460
280 Harbor Way South San Francisco (94080) ***(P-9547)***
Christensen Advertising ....E....415 924-8575
11 Professional Ctr Pkwy San Rafael (94903) ***(P-11744)***
Christian Bradshaw School (PA) ....**D....916 688-0521**
8324 Bradshaw Rd Sacramento (95829) ***(P-17902)***
Christian Brookside Schools ....D....209 954-7656
3588 Brookside Rd Stockton (95219) ***(P-17903)***
Christian Church Homes (PA) ....**E....510 632-6712**
303 Hegenberger Rd # 201 Oakland (94621) ***(P-10425)***
Christian Church Homes ....C....415 814-2670
1099 Fillmore St Apt 6h San Francisco (94115) ***(P-18076)***
Christian Church Homes ....E....510 420-8802
6400 San Pablo Ave Oakland (94608) ***(P-10426)***
Christian Church Homes ....E....510 893-2998
251 28th St Oakland (94611) ***(P-10427)***
Christian Concord Center ....D....925 687-2020
4255 Clayton Rd Concord (94521) ***(P-17904)***
Christian Conference Grounds, Mount Hermon *Also called Mount Hermon Association Inc* ***(P-11609)***
Christian Education Dev Co ....E....925 240-5437
2260 Jeffrey Way Brentwood (94513) ***(P-17905)***
Christian Evang Chrches Amer I ....E....510 533-8300
2433 Coolidge Ave Oakland (94601) ***(P-14845)***
Christian Milpitas School (PA) ....**C....408 945-6530**
3435 Birchwood Ln San Jose (95132) ***(P-17906)***
Christian Tabernacle School ....D....925 685-9169
4380 Concord Blvd Concord (94521) ***(P-17907)***
Christie Bryant Inc ....E....916 492-7062
2005 I St Ste 200 Sacramento (95811) ***(P-19470)***
Christopher Ranch LLC (PA) ....**C....408 847-1100**
305 Bloomfield Ave Gilroy (95020) ***(P-15)***
Christopher Ransom LLC ....D....510 345-9144
1300 Clay St Oakland (94612) ***(P-10509)***
Christy Vault Company (PA) ....**E....650 994-1378**
1000 Collins Ave Colma (94014) ***(P-4426)***
Chrome Craft, Sacramento *Also called Mencarini & Jarwin Inc* ***(P-4912)***
Chrome Deposit Corp ....E....925 432-4507
900 Loveridge Rd Pittsburg (94565) ***(P-4901)***
Chronicle Books LLC (HQ) ....**C....415 537-4200**
680 2nd St San Francisco (94107) ***(P-3528)***
Chronicle Broadcasting Co ....B....415 561-8000
900 Front St San Francisco (94111) ***(P-8042)***
Chronicle LLC (HQ) ....**D....650 214-5199**
250 Mayfield Ave Mountain View (94043) ***(P-14124)***
Chronicled Inc ....E....415 355-4681
116 Natoma St Fl 2 San Francisco (94105) ***(P-8681)***
Chrono Therapeutics Inc (PA) ....**E....510 362-7788**
3953 Point Eden Way Hayward (94545) ***(P-19209)***
Chrontel Inc (PA) ....**D....408 383-9328**
2210 Otoole Ave Ste 100 San Jose (95131) ***(P-6082)***
Chsp Trs Fisherman Wharf LLC ....B....415 563-1234
555 N Point St San Francisco (94133) ***(P-11007)***
Chuck Jones Flying Service (PA) ....**E....530 868-5798**
216 W Hamilton Rd Biggs (95917) ***(P-251)***
Chukchansi Gold Resort Casino ....A....866 794-6946
711 Lucky Ln Coarsegold (93614) ***(P-11008)***
Church of Vly Rtrment Hmes Inc ....D....408 241-7750
390 N Winchester Blvd Santa Clara (95050) ***(P-18077)***
Chw Mrcy Mrced Cmnty Hosp Kids ....E....209 564-4500
1260 D St Merced (95341) ***(P-16331)***
Ci, Mather *Also called Construction Innovations LLC* ***(P-6511)***
Ciarra Construction, San Jose *Also called Walt Oxley Enterprises Inc* ***(P-983)***
Ciasom LLC (PA) ....**E....408 560-2990**
1040 Richard Ave Santa Clara (95050) ***(P-11745)***
Cibo, San Francisco *Also called 1000 Sansome Associates LLC* ***(P-13546)***
Cielo House Inc (HQ) ....**E....650 292-0253**
750 El Camino Real Burlingame (94010) ***(P-17000)***
Cific Energy Center, San Francisco *Also called Sodexo Management Inc* ***(P-19399)***
Ciking Steel, Sacramento *Also called Hansford Industries Inc* ***(P-8818)***
Cim/Oakland City Center LLC ....D....510 451-4000
1001 Broadway Oakland (94607) ***(P-11009)***
Cimas Landscape & Maint Inc ....E....916 635-2462
3181 Luyung Dr Ste B Rancho Cordova (95742) ***(P-452)***
Cimc, Sacramento *Also called Califrnia Indian Mnpwer Cnsrti* ***(P-17800)***
Cinedome 9, Sacramento *Also called Century Theatres Inc* ***(P-14829)***
Cingular Wireless, San Carlos *Also called AT&T Mobility LLC* ***(P-8069)***
Cinnabar Hills Golf Club, San Jose *Also called Traditions Golf LLC* ***(P-15034)***
Cinta Salon Inc ....E....415 989-1000
23 Grant Ave Fl 2 San Francisco (94108) ***(P-11678)***
Cintas Corporation No 3 ....E....510 352-6330
777 139th Ave San Leandro (94578) ***(P-11712)***
Cintas Corporation No 3 ....C....209 922-0500
1877 Industrial Dr Stockton (95206) ***(P-11632)***
Cintas Corporation No 3 ....C....925 692-5860
1229 California Ave Pittsburg (94565) ***(P-11633)***
Cintas Corporation No 3 ....E....650 589-4300
220 Demeter St East Palo Alto (94303) ***(P-11663)***
Ciphercloud Inc (HQ) ....**D....408 687-4350**
2581 Junction Ave Ste 200 San Jose (95134) ***(P-13065)***
Circle G Ranch Inc ....D....530 666-0979
30479 County Road 24 Woodland (95695) ***(P-151)***
Circle Internet Services Inc (PA) ....**E....707 731-4912**
201 Spear St Fl 12 San Francisco (94105) ***(P-13066)***
Circle K Ranch (PA) ....**D....559 834-1571**
8640 E Manning Ave Selma (93662) ***(P-98)***
Circleci, San Francisco *Also called Circle Internet Services Inc* ***(P-13066)***
Circosta Iron and Metal Co Inc ....E....415 282-8568
1801 Evans Ave San Francisco (94124) ***(P-8317)***
Circus Center ....E....415 759-8123
755 Frederick St San Francisco (94117) ***(P-15193)***
Circus Ice Cream ....F....408 977-1134
345 N Montgomery St San Jose (95110) ***(P-9336)***
Cirexx Corporation ....E....408 988-3980
791 Nuttman St Santa Clara (95054) ***(P-5922)***
Cirexx International Inc (PA) ....**C....408 988-3980**
791 Nuttman St Santa Clara (95054) ***(P-5923)***
Cirimele Electrical Works Inc ....E....510 620-1150
607 Marina Way S Richmond (94804) ***(P-1477)***
Cirks Construction Inc ....C....916 362-5460
3300 Industrial Blvd West Sacramento (95691) ***(P-854)***
Cirtec Medical Corp ....D....408 395-0443
101b Cooper Ct Los Gatos (95032) ***(P-6962)***
CIS Security, Fresno *Also called Geil Enterprises Inc* ***(P-14064)***
Cisco Meraki, San Francisco *Also called Meraki LLC* ***(P-13935)***
Cisco Systems Inc (PA) ....**A....408 526-4000**
170 W Tasman Dr San Jose (95134) ***(P-5357)***
Cisco Systems Capital Corp (HQ) ....**A....610 386-5870**
170 W Tasman Dr San Jose (95134) ***(P-14225)***
Cisco Systems LLC (HQ) ....**B....650 989-6500**
170 W Tasman Dr San Jose (95134) ***(P-13067)***
Cisco Technology Inc (HQ) ....**D....408 526-4000**
170 W Tasman Dr San Jose (95134) ***(P-5358)***
Cisco Webex LLC (HQ) ....**A....408 435-7000**
170 W Tasman Dr San Jose (95134) ***(P-14226)***
Citadel Roofing and Solar, Vacaville *Also called Jaj Roofing* ***(P-1813)***
Citcon USA LLC (PA) ....**E....888 254-4887**
2001 Gateway Pl Ste 410w San Jose (95110) ***(P-9846)***
Citibank FSB (HQ) ....**B....415 627-6000**
1 Sansome St San Francisco (94104) ***(P-9682)***
Citibank FSB ....C....415 817-9111
590 Market St San Francisco (94104) ***(P-9769)***
Citibank FSB ....C....415 649-6971
2000 Irving St San Francisco (94122) ***(P-9683)***
Citicorp Select Investments ....E....650 353-2765
250 University Ave Lbby Palo Alto (94301) ***(P-10039)***
Citicorp Select Investments ....E....415 658-4468
1 Sansome St Fl 22 San Francisco (94104) ***(P-10040)***
Citifinancial Credit Company ....C....530 671-7970
1054 Harter Pkwy Ste 4 Yuba City (95993) ***(P-9855)***
Citigate Cunningham Inc (PA) ....**E....650 858-3700**
1530 Page Mill Rd Ste 3 Palo Alto (94304) ***(P-19685)***

ALPHABETIC

Employee Codes: A=Over 500 employees, B=251-500 C=101-250, D=51-100, E=20-50 F=10-19
2022 Northern California Business Directory and Buyers Guide
© Mergent Inc. 1-800-342-5647
931

Citigroup Global Markets Inc.....D.....408 947-2200
225 W Santa Clara St # 9 San Jose (95113) ***(P-9964)***
Citiscape Prprty MGT Group LLC.....D.....415 401-2000
3450 3rd St Ste 1a San Francisco (94124) ***(P-10510)***
Citizen Corporation.....E.....209 537-6334
340 Spenker Ave Modesto (95354) ***(P-1478)***
Citizen Electric, Modesto *Also called Citizen Corporation* ***(P-1478)***
Citizens Telecom Co Cal Inc (HQ).....**B.....317 208-3567**
9260 E Stockton Blvd Elk Grove (95624) ***(P-7939)***
Citragen Pharmaceuticals Inc.....F.....510 249-9066
3789 Spinnaker Ct Fremont (94538) ***(P-3884)***
Citrix Systems Inc.....D.....408 790-8000
4988 Great America Pkwy Santa Clara (95054) ***(P-12338)***
Citrus Heights Pre-School Inc (PA).....**D.....916 726-1550**
7555 Old Auburn Rd Citrus Heights (95610) ***(P-17908)***
Citrusbits Inc.....E.....925 452-6012
5994 W Las Psts Blvd Pleasanton (94588) ***(P-12339)***
City & County of San Francisco.....D.....415 581-3500
200 Larkin St San Francisco (94102) ***(P-18265)***
City & County of San Francisco.....A.....415 206-8000
1001 Potrero Ave San Francisco (94110) ***(P-16332)***
City Alameda Health Care Corp.....A.....510 522-3700
2070 Clinton Ave Alameda (94501) ***(P-16333)***
City and County of San Francis.....E.....415 557-5000
170 Otis St San Francisco (94103) ***(P-17490)***
City Baking Company.....D.....650 332-8730
1373 Lowrie Ave South San Francisco (94080) ***(P-2373)***
City Beach Inc.....E.....408 654-9330
4020 Technology Pl Fremont (94538) ***(P-11600)***
City Building Inc.....E.....415 285-1711
212 N San Mateo Dr San Mateo (94401) ***(P-855)***
City Canvas.....E.....408 287-2688
1381 N 10th St San Jose (95112) ***(P-3038)***
City Center Grill, Oakland *Also called Cim/Oakland City Center LLC* ***(P-11009)***
City Club LLC.....E.....415 362-2480
155 Sansome St Fl 9 San Francisco (94104) ***(P-15073)***
City Club of San Francisco, San Francisco *Also called City Club LLC* ***(P-15073)***
City Electric Supply.....E.....707 523-4600
360 Tesconi Cir Santa Rosa (95401) ***(P-8852)***
City II Enterprises Inc.....E.....408 275-1200
845 Earle Ave San Jose (95126) ***(P-453)***
City Lights Books.....E.....415 362-8193
261 Columbus Ave San Francisco (94133) ***(P-3529)***
City Lights Lighting Showroom.....E.....415 863-2020
1585 Folsom St San Francisco (94103) ***(P-8853)***
City Mechanical Inc.....D.....510 724-9088
724 Alfred Nobel Dr Hercules (94547) ***(P-14685)***
City of Burlingame.....E.....650 558-7670
1361 N Carolan Ave Burlingame (94010) ***(P-1028)***
City of Chico.....D.....530 896-7699
150 Airpark Blvd Ste 20 Chico (95973) ***(P-7767)***
City of Fairfield.....E.....707 428-7680
5110 Peabody Rd Fairfield (94533) ***(P-8228)***
City of Folsom.....D.....916 355-7272
50 Natoma St Folsom (95630) ***(P-5886)***
City of Folsom.....C.....916 355-8395
1300 Leidesdorff St Folsom (95630) ***(P-7326)***
City of Fresno.....B.....559 621-7433
2223 G St Fresno (93706) ***(P-7327)***
City of Fresno.....C.....559 621-5300
1910 E University Ave Fresno (93703) ***(P-8229)***
City of Hayward.....E.....510 293-8678
20301 Skywest Dr Hayward (94541) ***(P-7768)***
City of Lodi (PA).....**D.....209 333-6700**
221 W Pine St Lodi (95240) ***(P-14227)***
City of Pleasanton.....C.....925 454-2341
3560 Nevada St Pleasanton (94566) ***(P-19743)***
City of Redding (PA).....**A.....530 225-4079**
777 Cypress Ave Redding (96001) ***(P-19899)***
City of Rio Vista.....E.....707 374-5337
1 Main St Rio Vista (94571) ***(P-7328)***
City of Sacramento.....E.....916 808-4949
2812 Meadowview Rd Sacramento (95832) ***(P-8318)***
City of San Jose.....D.....650 965-4156
801 N 1st St San Jose (95110) ***(P-7769)***
City of Santa Clara, Santa Clara *Also called Community Recreation Center* ***(P-11618)***
City of Vallejo.....E.....707 648-4361
111 Amador St Vallejo (94590) ***(P-17229)***
City of Woodland.....D.....530 668-5287
140c Tony Diaz Way Woodland (95776) ***(P-352)***
City of Woodland.....C.....530 661-5860
1000 Lincoln Ave Woodland (95695) ***(P-7275)***
City of Yuba City.....D.....530 822-4601
1201 Civic Center Blvd Yuba City (95993) ***(P-17803)***
City Park, San Francisco *Also called Imperial Parking (us) LLC* ***(P-14513)***
City Rise LLC.....D.....209 334-2703
18826 N Lwer Ste Escrmnt Woodbridge (95258) ***(P-14228)***
City San Jose Animal Care Ctr.....E.....408 794-7297
2750 Monterey Hwy San Jose (95111) ***(P-325)***
City Snta Cruz Mncpl Utilities, Santa Cruz *Also called Santa Cruz City of* ***(P-8270)***
City Towel & Dust Service Inc.....D.....707 542-0391
3016 Dutton Ave Santa Rosa (95407) ***(P-11634)***
City View At Metreon.....E.....415 369-6142
135 4th St Ste 4000 San Francisco (94103) ***(P-14904)***
Cityaid First Aid Direct, San Francisco *Also called Safetymax Corporation* ***(P-9201)***
Cityteam Ministries (PA).....**E.....408 885-8080**
2304 Zanker Rd San Jose (95131) ***(P-17804)***
Civicactions Inc.....D.....510 408-7510
3527 Mt Diablo Blvd # 269 Lafayette (94549) ***(P-13865)***
Civicorps.....E.....510 992-7800
6315 San Leandro St Oakland (94621) ***(P-8319)***
Civicsolar Inc (PA).....**E.....800 409-2257**
304 12th St Ste 3b Oakland (94607) ***(P-8995)***
Civil Engineering Assoc Inc.....E.....408 453-1066
2055 Gateway Pl Ste 550 San Jose (95110) ***(P-18670)***
Civil Svc Employees Insur Co (PA).....**E.....800 282-6848**
2121 N Calif Blvd Ste 900 Walnut Creek (94596) ***(P-10261)***
Ciwp, Merced *Also called Community Intgrted Work Prgram* ***(P-17497)***
CJ Logistics America LLC.....D.....209 362-2232
1565 N Macarthur Dr Tracy (95376) ***(P-7686)***
CJ Model Home Maintenance Inc.....D.....925 485-3280
240 Spring St Pleasanton (94566) ***(P-11935)***
CJS Lighting Inc.....E.....916 774-6888
300 Derek Pl Roseville (95678) ***(P-8854)***
Claims Management Inc.....E.....916 631-1250
1101 Crkside Rdg Dr Roseville (95678) ***(P-10262)***
Claims Services Group LLC (HQ).....**D.....925 866-1100**
6111 Bollinger Canyon Rd # 2 San Ramon (94583) ***(P-10263)***
Clamp Swing Pricing Co Inc.....E.....510 567-1600
8386 Capwell Dr Oakland (94621) ***(P-7276)***
Clapp Moroney (PA).....**E.....925 734-0990**
5860 Owens Dr Ste 410 Pleasanton (94588) ***(P-17230)***
Clara Foods Co.....E.....415 570-1535
1 Tower Pl Fl 8 South San Francisco (94080) ***(P-2257)***
Claremont Country Club.....D.....510 653-6789
5295 Broadway Ter Oakland (94618) ***(P-15074)***
Claremont Hotel Properties LLC.....A.....510 843-3000
41 Tunnel Rd Berkeley (94705) ***(P-11010)***
Claremont Ht Prpts Ltd Partnr, Berkeley *Also called Claremont Hotel Properties LLC* ***(P-11010)***
Claremont Rsort Spa Tennis CLB, Berkeley *Also called Harsch Investment Realty LLC* ***(P-11130)***
Clarion Hotel, Concord *Also called Clarion Inn* ***(P-11012)***
Clarion Hotel San Jose Airport.....E.....408 453-5340
1355 N 4th St San Jose (95112) ***(P-11011)***
Clarion Inn.....E.....925 566-8820
1050 Burnett Ave Concord (94520) ***(P-11012)***
Clarion Resort.....E.....707 442-3261
2223 4th St Eureka (95501) ***(P-11013)***
Claris International Inc (HQ).....**C.....408 987-7000**
1 Apple Park Way 104-1g Cupertino (95014) ***(P-12340)***
Clarity Consultants, Campbell *Also called Pacific Netsoft Inc* ***(P-12116)***
Clarizen Inc.....D.....866 502-9813
691 S Milpitas Blvd # 212 Milpitas (95035) ***(P-19316)***
Clark Richardson and Biskup.....E.....510 907-2700
6001 Shellmound St # 550 Emeryville (94608) ***(P-18671)***
Clark & Sullivan Constrs Inc.....C.....916 338-7707
2024 Opportunity Dr # 150 Roseville (95678) ***(P-856)***
Clark - Pacific Corporation (PA).....**B.....916 371-0305**
710 Riverpoint Ct Ste 100 West Sacramento (95605) ***(P-8624)***
Clark Harry Plumbing & Heating.....E.....510 444-1776
3026 Broadway Oakland (94611) ***(P-1235)***
Clark Pacific, West Sacramento *Also called Clark - Pacific Corporation* ***(P-8624)***
Clark Pest Control 11, Santa Rosa *Also called Clark Pest Ctrl Stockton Inc* ***(P-11896)***
Clark Pest Ctrl Stockton Inc.....E.....209 826-6051
1370 Merced Ave Merced (95341) ***(P-11881)***
Clark Pest Ctrl Stockton Inc.....E.....209 483-4043
595 Pomona Dr Brentwood (94513) ***(P-11882)***
Clark Pest Ctrl Stockton Inc (HQ).....**D.....209 368-7152**
555 N Guild Ave Lodi (95240) ***(P-11883)***
Clark Pest Ctrl Stockton Inc.....E.....530 235-6101
1288 Garden Hwy Yuba City (95991) ***(P-11884)***
Clark Pest Ctrl Stockton Inc.....E.....209 524-6384
480 E Service Rd Modesto (95358) ***(P-11885)***
Clark Pest Ctrl Stockton Inc.....E.....925 935-5077
4045 Nelson Ave Ste B Concord (94520) ***(P-11886)***
Clark Pest Ctrl Stockton Inc.....E.....916 925-7000
5822 Roseville Rd Sacramento (95842) ***(P-11887)***
Clark Pest Ctrl Stockton Inc.....E.....707 446-9748
811 U Banks Vacaville (95688) ***(P-11888)***
Clark Pest Ctrl Stockton Inc.....E.....209 532-3464
429 Mono Way Sonora (95370) ***(P-11889)***
Clark Pest Ctrl Stockton Inc.....E.....209 474-3204
4816 Clowes St Stockton (95210) ***(P-11890)***
Clark Pest Ctrl Stockton Inc.....E.....650 596-1270
485 Oneill Ave Belmont (94002) ***(P-11891)***
Clark Pest Ctrl Stockton Inc.....E.....408 866-2278
2030 Fortune Dr Ste 100 San Jose (95131) ***(P-11892)***
Clark Pest Ctrl Stockton Inc.....E.....925 449-6203
2313 Research Dr Livermore (94550) ***(P-11893)***
Clark Pest Ctrl Stockton Inc.....E.....925 757-5890
4045 Nelson Ave Concord (94520) ***(P-11894)***
Clark Pest Ctrl Stockton Inc.....E.....916 635-7770
11285 White Rock Rd Rancho Cordova (95742) ***(P-11895)***
Clark Pest Ctrl Stockton Inc.....E.....707 571-0414
3215 Brickway Blvd Santa Rosa (95403) ***(P-11896)***
Clark Sllvan Bldrs Inc DBA Clr.....C.....916 338-7707
1340 Blue Oaks Blvd Ste 1 Roseville (95678) ***(P-857)***
Clarmil Manufacturing Corp (PA).....**D.....510 476-0700**
30865 San Clemente St Hayward (94544) ***(P-2883)***
Clas Information Services.....D.....916 564-7800
2020 Hurley Way Ste 350 Sacramento (95825) ***(P-19156)***
Class, San Mateo *Also called Center For Lrng Atism Spport S* ***(P-17474)***
Class a Powdercoat Inc.....E.....916 681-7474
7506 Henrietta Dr Sacramento (95822) ***(P-4930)***
Class Act Hair & Nail Salon.....D.....530 223-3442
2795 Bechelli Ln Redding (96002) ***(P-11679)***
Classic Bowling Center, Daly City *Also called Bdp Bowl Inc* ***(P-14886)***

Classic Custom Vacations, San Jose *Also called Classic Vacations LLC (P-7817)*
Classic Custom Vacations Inc..........D.......800 221-3949
5893 Rue Ferrari San Jose (95138) *(P-7795)*
Classic Innovations, Cloverdale *Also called Classic Mill & Cabinet LLC (P-3175)*
Classic Mill & Cabinet LLC..........E.......707 894-9800
590 Santana Dr Cloverdale (95425) *(P-3175)*
Classic Parking Inc..........A.......408 278-1444
34 S Autumn St San Jose (95110) *(P-14511)*
Classic Party Rentals, Sonoma *Also called CP Opco LLC (P-12037)*
Classic Party Rentals, Sonoma *Also called CP Opco LLC (P-12038)*
Classic Party Rentals, Sonoma *Also called CP Opco LLC (P-12039)*
Classic Salads LLC..........E.......831 763-4520
100 Harrington Rd Royal Oaks (95076) *(P-2884)*
Classic Sightseeing Adventures, San Francisco *Also called Cable Car Partners LLC (P-15185)*
Classic Vacations LLC..........C.......408 287-4550
5893 Rue Ferrari San Jose (95138) *(P-7817)*
Claude Lambert..........D.......415 421-3154
715 Bush St San Francisco (94108) *(P-11014)*
Clausen Meat Company Inc..........E.......209 667-8690
19455 W Clausen Rd Turlock (95380) *(P-2093)*
Clay Miranda Trucking Inc..........E.......559 275-6250
3220 W Belmont Ave Fresno (93722) *(P-7459)*
Clay Mix LLC (PA)..........**E.......559 485-0065**
1003 N Abby St Fresno (93701) *(P-4476)*
Clay Sherman & Co (PA)..........**E.......650 952-2300**
1111 Bayhill Dr Ste 450 San Bruno (94066) *(P-10511)*
Clay, Kenneth MD, Davis *Also called Sutter Health (P-16612)*
Clayborn Lab, Truckee *Also called Horvath Holdings Inc (P-2970)*
CLC Incorporated (PA)..........**E.......916 789-7600**
3001 Lava Ridge Ct # 250 Roseville (95661) *(P-12080)*
Cleaire Advanced Emission (PA)..........**E.......510 347-6103**
1001 42nd St Emeryville (94608) *(P-4174)*
Clean Harbors Envmtl Svcs Inc..........D.......707 747-6699
4101 Industrial Way Benicia (94510) *(P-19744)*
Clean Hrbors Es Indus Svcs Inc..........E.......510 979-9210
3789 Spinnaker Ct Fremont (94538) *(P-2019)*
Clean Power Research LLC..........E.......707 258-2765
1541 Third St NAPA (94559) *(P-13866)*
Clean Roofing..........E.......408 472-7378
1445 Koll Cir Ste 109 San Jose (95112) *(P-14742)*
Cleanair Image Inc..........D.......510 352-2480
2334 Stagecoach Rd Ste J Stockton (95215) *(P-11936)*
CLEANERIFIC, San Francisco *Also called Jewish Family and Chld Svcs (P-17625)*
Cleanpartset Inc..........C.......408 886-3300
3530 Bassett St Santa Clara (95054) *(P-5144)*
Cleanrite Inc..........E.......800 870-0030
2684 State Highway 32 # 100 Chico (95973) *(P-11658)*
Cleanrite Inc..........E.......916 381-1321
814 Striker Ave Ste B Sacramento (95834) *(P-11897)*
Cleanrite Inc..........E.......530 246-4886
5601 Cedars Rd Ste I Redding (96001) *(P-11659)*
Cleansmart Solutions Inc..........E.......650 871-9123
47422 Kato Rd Fremont (94538) *(P-3397)*
Cleantech Group Inc (PA)..........**D.......415 684-1020**
33 New Montgomery St # 22 San Francisco (94105) *(P-10041)*
Cleantech Network, San Francisco *Also called Cleantech Group Inc (P-10041)*
Cleanworld..........F.......916 635-7300
2330 Gold Meadow Way Gold River (95670) *(P-7193)*
Clear Image Inc (PA)..........**E.......916 933-4700**
4949 Windplay Dr Ste 100 El Dorado Hills (95762) *(P-3383)*
Clear Shape Technologies Inc..........F.......408 943-1234
2655 Seely Ave Bldg 5 San Jose (95134) *(P-5694)*
Clear Skye Inc..........E.......415 619-5001
2340 Powell St Ste 325 Emeryville (94608) *(P-13068)*
Clear View LLC..........F.......408 271-2734
1650 Las Plumas Ave Ste A San Jose (95133) *(P-4702)*
Clear-Com Communications, Alameda *Also called Clear-Com LLC (P-5831)*
Clear-Com LLC (HQ)..........**A.......510 337-6600**
1301 Marina Village Pkwy # 105 Alameda (94501) *(P-5831)*
Clearbags, El Dorado Hills *Also called Clear Image Inc (P-3383)*
Clearcapitalcom Inc..........C.......530 550-2500
10266 Truckee Airport Rd Truckee (96161) *(P-10512)*
Clearcaptions LLC..........E.......866 868-8695
3001 Lava Ridge Ct # 100 Roseville (95661) *(P-7940)*
Clearedge Solutions Inc..........E.......408 262-2800
1020 Rock Ave San Jose (95131) *(P-4370)*
Clearist Inc..........F.......408 835-8620
2105 Lundy Ave San Jose (95131) *(P-7224)*
Clearlake Family Health Center, Clearlake *Also called Adventist Hlth Systm/West Corp (P-16312)*
Clearpath Management Group Inc..........E.......650 691-4140
1928 Old Middlefield Way A Mountain View (94043) *(P-12163)*
Clearpath Workforce MGT Inc..........C.......209 239-8700
1215 W Center St Ste 102 Manteca (95337) *(P-12164)*
Clearslide Inc (HQ)..........**D.......877 360-3366**
45 Fremont St Fl 32 San Francisco (94105) *(P-13069)*
Clearview Quest Corporation..........E.......650 574-7400
3172 Clearview Way San Mateo (94402) *(P-17909)*
Clearway Energy Group LLC (PA)..........**B.......415 627-1600**
100 California St Ste 400 San Francisco (94111) *(P-8092)*
Clearway Renew LLC (HQ)..........**E.......415 627-1600**
100 California St Ste 400 San Francisco (94111) *(P-8093)*
Clearwell Systems Inc..........C.......877 253-2793
350 Ellis St Mountain View (94043) *(P-13070)*
Clearxchange LLC..........D.......415 813-4801
275 Sacramento St 400 San Francisco (94111) *(P-14229)*

Cleary Bros Landscape Inc..........C.......925 838-2551
4115 Blackhawk Plaza Cir Danville (94506) *(P-407)*
Cleasby Manufacturing Co Inc (PA)..........**E.......415 822-6565**
1414 Bancroft Ave San Francisco (94124) *(P-5029)*
Clement Preschool, Saratoga *Also called Precious Enterprises Inc (P-18003)*
Cleveland Wrecking Company..........A.......510 674-2600
1580 Chabot Ct Hayward (94545) *(P-1983)*
Clever Girls Collective Inc..........E.......408 676-6428
2415 San Rmon Vly Blvd St San Ramon (94583) *(P-11746)*
Clfrn/Clrd/Flrd/rgon I Comcast..........C.......925 424-0273
3011 Comcast Pl Livermore (94551) *(P-7904)*
Cli Liquidating Corporation..........D.......510 354-0300
47266 Benicia St Fremont (94538) *(P-7101)*
Cli-Metrics Inc..........E.......408 886-3800
382 Martin Ave Santa Clara (95050) *(P-1236)*
Cli-Metrics Service Company, Santa Clara *Also called Cli-Metrics Inc (P-1236)*
Clic LLC..........E.......415 421-2900
396 Forbes Blvd Ste D South San Francisco (94080) *(P-3636)*
Click Labs Inc..........E.......415 658-5227
315 Montgomery St Fl 8 San Francisco (94104) *(P-12341)*
Clickaway Corporation..........E.......408 626-9400
457 E Mcglincy Ln Ste 1 Campbell (95008) *(P-13819)*
Clickhouse Inc..........E.......408 915-6542
4113 Alpine Rd Portola Valley (94028) *(P-14230)*
Clicktale Inc (PA)..........**D.......800 807-2117**
2 Embarcadero Ctr San Francisco (94111) *(P-13703)*
Client First Home Loans, San Jose *Also called Customer Service Realty (P-10534)*
Clif Bar & Company (PA)..........**A.......510 596-6300**
1451 66th St Emeryville (94608) *(P-2427)*
Cliff House Restaurant, Fort Bragg *Also called Tradewinds Lodge (P-11539)*
Cliff Lede Vineyards, Yountville *Also called Twin Teaks Winery (P-79)*
Cliff View Terrace Inc..........D.......415 388-9526
297 Miller Ave Mill Valley (94941) *(P-18078)*
Clift Royal Sonesta Hotel, The, San Francisco *Also called Sonesta Intl Hotels Corp (P-11490)*
Cliftonlarsonallen LLP..........B.......916 784-7800
925 Highland Pointe Dr # 450 Roseville (95678) *(P-18945)*
Climate Corporation (HQ)..........**E.......415 363-0500**
201 3rd St Ste 1010 San Francisco (94103) *(P-13071)*
Climate Fieldview, San Francisco *Also called Climate Corporation (P-13071)*
Climb Real Estate (HQ)..........**D.......415 431-8888**
251 Rhode Island St Ste 1 San Francisco (94103) *(P-10513)*
Clinica Sierra Vista..........E.......559 457-5200
2790 S Elm Ave Fresno (93706) *(P-15350)*
Clinica Sierra Vista..........E.......559 457-5292
1945 N Fine Ave Ste 100 Fresno (93727) *(P-15351)*
Clinica Sierra Vista..........E.......559 457-5500
2505 E Divisadero St # 100 Fresno (93721) *(P-15352)*
Clinical Pharmacy, San Francisco *Also called University Cal San Francisco (P-16697)*
Cliosoft Inc..........E.......510 790-4732
39500 Stevenson Pl # 110 Fremont (94539) *(P-13072)*
Clonetab Inc..........E.......209 292-5663
1660 W Linne Rd Ste 214 Tracy (95377) *(P-13073)*
Clontech, San Jose *Also called Takara Bio Usa Inc (P-19134)*
Clorox Company (PA)..........**A.......510 271-7000**
1221 Broadway Ste 1300 Oakland (94612) *(P-4068)*
Clorox Company..........F.......925 368-6000
4900 Johnson Dr Pleasanton (94588) *(P-4069)*
Clorox International Company (HQ)..........**D.......510 271-7000**
1221 Broadway Fl 13 Oakland (94612) *(P-4142)*
Clorox Manufacturing Company..........D.......707 437-1051
2600 Huntington Dr Fairfield (94533) *(P-4070)*
Clorox Manufacturing Company..........E.......925 425-6040
11950 S Harlan Rd Lathrop (95330) *(P-3769)*
Clorox Manufacturing Company (HQ)..........**C.......510 271-7000**
1221 Broadway Oakland (94612) *(P-4071)*
Clorox Services Company..........C.......925 368-6000
4900 Johnson Dr Pleasanton (94588) *(P-19317)*
Clorox Services Company (HQ)..........**D.......510 271-7000**
1221 Broadway Oakland (94612) *(P-4072)*
Clos Du Bois Wines Inc..........E.......707 857-1651
19410 Geyserville Ave Geyserville (95441) *(P-2533)*
Clos Du Val Wine Company Ltd..........E.......707 259-2200
5330 Silverado Trl NAPA (94558) *(P-2534)*
Clos La Chance Wines Inc..........E.......408 686-1050
1 Hummingbird Ln San Martin (95046) *(P-2535)*
Clos Pegase Winery Inc..........E.......707 942-4981
1060 Dunaweal Ln Calistoga (94515) *(P-2536)*
Closet Dimension (PA)..........**E.......650 594-1155**
23768 Eichler St Ste A Hayward (94545) *(P-2020)*
Closet Innovation Inc..........E.......925 687-5033
2956 Treat Blvd Ste D Concord (94518) *(P-2021)*
Cloud Destinations Inc..........E.......510 715-7044
2603 Camino Ramon Ste 200 San Ramon (94583) *(P-13867)*
Cloud9 Charts Inc..........F.......510 507-3661
1528 Webster St Oakland (94612) *(P-13074)*
Cloudcar Inc..........E.......650 946-1236
2560 N 1st St Ste 100 San Jose (95131) *(P-13075)*
Cloudely Inc (PA)..........**E.......800 797-8608**
2880 Zanker Rd Ste 203 San Jose (95134) *(P-12342)*
Cloudera Inc (PA)..........**A.......650 362-0488**
5470 Great America Pkwy Santa Clara (95054) *(P-13076)*
Cloudflare Inc (PA)..........**A.......888 993-5273**
101 Townsend St San Francisco (94107) *(P-13077)*
Cloudian Inc..........E.......650 227-2380
177 Bovet Rd Ste 450 San Mateo (94402) *(P-13568)*
Cloudinary Inc..........D.......650 772-1833
3400 Central Expy Ste 110 Santa Clara (95051) *(P-13868)*

ALPHABETIC

Cloudious LLC ALPHABETIC SECTION

Cloudious LLC (PA)..........C.......**732 666-2468**
2833 Junction Ave Ste 206 San Jose (95134) ***(P-13869)***
Cloudjee Inc..........E.......866 660-6099
1975 W El Cmino Real 30 Mountain View (94040) ***(P-13078)***
Cloudknox Security Inc..........E.......408 647-5515
333 Camarillo Ter Ste 3 Sunnyvale (94085) ***(P-14043)***
Cloudpassage Inc..........D.......800 838-4098
180 Townsend St Fl 3 San Francisco (94107) ***(P-12343)***
Cloudpeople Global..........E.......530 591-7028
2485 Notre Dame Blvd Chico (95928) ***(P-12344)***
Cloudphysics Inc..........E.......650 646-4616
2010 El Camino Real Santa Clara (95050) ***(P-13870)***
Cloudradiant Corp..........A.......408 256-1527
1111 Di Napoli Dr San Jose (95129) ***(P-9651)***
Cloudshield Technologies LLC..........C.......408 331-6640
212 Gibraltar Dr Sunnyvale (94089) ***(P-13079)***
Cloudsimple Inc..........D.......412 568-3487
1600 Amphitheatre Pkwy Mountain View (94043) ***(P-13080)***
Cloudwick Technologies Inc (PA)..........D.......**650 346-5788**
39899 Balentine Dr # 350 Newark (94560) ***(P-13871)***
Clover Health Labs LLC..........E.......415 548-6456
22 4th St Fl 6 San Francisco (94103) ***(P-17124)***
Clover Network Inc..........D.......650 210-7888
415 N Mathilda Ave Sunnyvale (94085) ***(P-7941)***
Clover Sonoma, Petaluma *Also called Clover-Stornetta Farms Inc* ***(P-9444)***
Clover-Stornetta Farms Inc (PA)..........C.......**707 769-3282**
1800 S Mcdowell Blvd Ext Petaluma (94954) ***(P-9444)***
Cloverdale Healthcare Center, Cloverdale *Also called Ensign Cloverdale LLC* ***(P-15989)***
Cloverleaf Bowl, Fremont *Also called Fremont Sports Inc* ***(P-14893)***
Clovis Community Living, Fresno *Also called Community Medical Center* ***(P-16337)***
Clovis Community Medical Ctr, Clovis *Also called Fresno Cmnty Hosp & Med Ctr* ***(P-16375)***
Clovis Hotels Inc..........E.......559 323-8080
50 N Clovis Ave Clovis (93612) ***(P-11015)***
Clovis Independent, Sacramento *Also called El Dorado Newspapers* ***(P-3434)***
Clovis Oncology Inc..........D.......415 409-5440
499 Illinois St Ste 230 San Francisco (94158) ***(P-15353)***
Clp Apg LLC..........C.......510 528-1444
1700 4th St Berkeley (94710) ***(P-3530)***
Clp Resources Inc..........D.......916 788-0300
1000 Sunrise Ave Ste 8a Roseville (95661) ***(P-12165)***
Clp Resources Inc..........E.......415 446-7000
4460 Redwood Hwy Ste 14 San Rafael (94903) ***(P-12166)***
Club At Los Gatos Inc..........D.......408 867-5110
14428 Big Basin Way Ste A Saratoga (95070) ***(P-14936)***
Club Corp Incorporated..........D.......925 240-2990
120 Guthrie Ln Brentwood (94513) ***(P-14937)***
Club Donatello Owners Assn..........E.......415 474-7333
501 Post St San Francisco (94102) ***(P-7161)***
Club One Casino Inc..........B.......559 497-3000
3950 N Cedar Ave Ste 101 Fresno (93726) ***(P-11016)***
Club Quarters San Francisco..........E.......415 268-3606
424 Clay St San Francisco (94111) ***(P-11017)***
Club Resource Group, Tracy *Also called Wendt Industries Inc* ***(P-19422)***
Club Sanctuary Video Prod, Fresno *Also called Sanctuary* ***(P-17715)***
Club Sport of Fremont..........E.......510 226-8500
46650 Landing Pkwy Fremont (94538) ***(P-14938)***
Clubsport of Fremont, Fremont *Also called Leisure Sports Inc* ***(P-14957)***
Clubsport of Pleasanton, Pleasanton *Also called Cs-Pleasanton LLC* ***(P-15081)***
Clubsport San Ramon LLC..........D.......925 283-4000
4000 Mt Diablo Blvd Lafayette (94549) ***(P-14939)***
Clubsport San Ramon LLC (PA)..........C.......**925 735-1182**
350 Bollinger Canyon Ln San Ramon (94582) ***(P-14940)***
Clustrix Inc..........E.......415 501-9560
699 Veterans Blvd Redwood City (94063) ***(P-12345)***
CLY Incorporated..........E.......707 763-5591
121 Lakeville St Petaluma (94952) ***(P-1029)***
Clyde Ned Construction Inc..........E.......925 689-5411
159 Mason Cir Concord (94520) ***(P-1953)***
Clyde Wheeler Pipeline Inc..........D.......209 848-0809
509 Hi Tech Pkwy Oakdale (95361) ***(P-1093)***
Cmat, Stockton *Also called California Materials Inc* ***(P-7454)***
CMC Rebar West..........C.......707 863-3933
1060 Kaiser Rd NAPA (94558) ***(P-792)***
CMC Rebar West..........D.......707 759-1400
5160 Fulton Dr Fairfield (94534) ***(P-8811)***
Cmd Products..........F.......916 434-0228
1130 Conroy Ln Ste 301 Roseville (95661) ***(P-4240)***
Cmg Financial Services..........C.......925 983-3073
3160 Crow Canyon Rd # 400 San Ramon (94583) ***(P-9902)***
Cmg Mortgage Inc (PA)..........B.......**619 554-1327**
3160 Crow Canyon Rd # 400 San Ramon (94583) ***(P-9938)***
CMI, Hughson *Also called Calaveras Materials Inc* ***(P-4464)***
Cmor Manufacturing Inc..........D.......916 626-3100
3625 Cincinnati Ave Rocklin (95765) ***(P-5713)***
Cmp I Fremont Owner LP..........D.......510 656-1800
47000 Lakeview Blvd Fremont (94538) ***(P-11018)***
Cmt, Camino *Also called Coastal Mountain Timber Inc* ***(P-515)***
Cmy Image Corporation..........F.......510 516-6668
33268 Central Ave Union City (94587) ***(P-3637)***
Cnc Noodle Corporation..........F.......510 835-2269
325 Fallon St Oakland (94607) ***(P-2885)***
Cnc Solutions Inc..........E.......408 586-8236
1011 Pecten Ct Milpitas (95035) ***(P-14743)***
Cncml A California Ltd Partnr..........D.......530 583-1578
1920 Squaw Valley Rd Olympic Valley (96146) ***(P-11019)***
Cnet Networks Inc..........A.......415 344-2000
235 2nd St San Francisco (94105) ***(P-13569)***
Cnet Technology Corporation (HQ)..........C.......**408 392-9966**
26291 Prod Ave Ste 205 Hayward (94545) ***(P-8903)***
Cnex Labs Inc (PA)..........E.......**408 695-1045**
2880 Stevens Creek Blvd # 300 San Jose (95128) ***(P-6083)***
Cni Thl Ops LLC..........D.......916 772-3500
1910 Taylor Rd Roseville (95661) ***(P-11020)***
Cni Thl Ops LLC..........E.......925 460-8800
5115 Hopyard Rd Pleasanton (94588) ***(P-11021)***
Cni Thl Ops LLC..........D.......916 638-4800
10755 Gold Center Dr. Gold River (95670) ***(P-11022)***
Cni Thl Ops LLC..........D.......408 782-6034
18610 Madrone Pkwy Morgan Hill (95037) ***(P-11023)***
Cni Thl Ops LLC..........E.......916 772-3404
301 Creekside Ridge Ct Roseville (95678) ***(P-11024)***
Cni Thl Ops LLC..........E.......916 984-7624
2575 Iron Point Rd Folsom (95630) ***(P-11025)***
Cntry Vlla Merced Hlthcre Cntr, Merced *Also called Country Villa Service Corp* ***(P-17508)***
Coact Designworks..........E.......916 930-5900
3348 Montclaire St Sacramento (95821) ***(P-18879)***
Coadna Holdings Inc..........D.......408 736-1100
1020 Stewart Dr Sunnyvale (94085) ***(P-10731)***
Coadna Photonics Inc (HQ)..........D.......**408 736-1100**
1012 Stewart Dr Sunnyvale (94085) ***(P-5791)***
Coagusense Inc..........E.......510 270-5442
48377 Fremont Blvd # 113 Fremont (94538) ***(P-19210)***
Coalinga Dstngished Cmnty Care..........D.......559 935-5939
834 Maple Rd Coalinga (93210) ***(P-15961)***
Coalinga Feed Yard Inc..........D.......559 935-0836
35244 Oil City Rd Coalinga (93210) ***(P-199)***
Coalinga Regional Med Ctr Aux..........C.......559 935-6400
1191 Phelps Ave Coalinga (93210) ***(P-16334)***
Coalinga State Hospital, Coalinga *Also called State Hospitals Cal Dept* ***(P-16745)***
Coalition Inc (PA)..........D.......**833 866-1337**
1160 Battery St Ste 350 San Francisco (94111) ***(P-10264)***
Coast Central Credit Union (PA)..........D.......**707 445-8801**
2650 Harrison Ave Eureka (95501) ***(P-9777)***
Coast Central Credit Union..........E.......707 445-8801
1968 Central Ave McKinleyville (95519) ***(P-9778)***
Coast Citrus Distributors..........E.......213 955-3448
2885 Volpey Way Union City (94587) ***(P-9395)***
Coast Creative Nameplates, San Jose *Also called Coast Engraving Companies Inc* ***(P-3768)***
Coast Engraving Companies Inc..........E.......408 297-2555
1097 N 5th St San Jose (95112) ***(P-3768)***
Coast Landscape Management, American Canyon *Also called Coast Lm Inc* ***(P-408)***
Coast Landscape Management, Alviso *Also called Bayscape Management Inc* ***(P-395)***
Coast Lm Inc (PA)..........C.......**707 251-8872**
4100 Paoli Loop Rd American Canyon (94503) ***(P-408)***
Coast Personnel Services Inc (PA)..........A.......**408 653-2100**
2295 De La Cruz Blvd Santa Clara (95050) ***(P-12167)***
Coast Tropical, Union City *Also called Coast Citrus Distributors* ***(P-9395)***
Coastal Circuit, Redwood City *Also called Advanced Circuits Inc* ***(P-5907)***
Coastal Construction Svcs LLC..........E.......510 785-9220
1633 Industrial Pkwy W Hayward (94544) ***(P-8642)***
Coastal Intl Holdings LLC (PA)..........C.......**415 339-1700**
3 Harbor Dr Ste 211 Sausalito (94965) ***(P-14231)***
Coastal Mountain Timber Inc..........D.......530 303-3378
3737 Carson Rd Unit A Camino (95709) ***(P-515)***
Coastal Pacific Fd Distrs Inc (PA)..........C.......**909 947-2066**
1015 Performance Dr Stockton (95206) ***(P-9266)***
Coastal Pacific Fd Distrs Inc..........D.......650 692-8211
1801 Murchison Dr Ste 300 Burlingame (94010) ***(P-9267)***
Coastal PVA Opco LLC..........F.......530 406-3303
2929 Grandview St Placerville (95667) ***(P-5244)***
COASTLINE ENTERPRISES, Crescent City *Also called Del Norte Assoc For Dvlpmntl S* ***(P-17811)***
Coastwide Envmtl Tech Inc..........E.......831 761-5511
170 2nd St Watsonville (95076) ***(P-2022)***
Cobalt Biofuels, Mountain View *Also called Cobalt Technologies Inc* ***(P-19043)***
Cobalt Labs Inc (PA)..........F.......**415 651-7028**
575 Market St Fl 4 San Francisco (94105) ***(P-13081)***
Cobalt Power Systems Inc..........E.......650 938-9574
2557 Wyandotte St Mountain View (94043) ***(P-1237)***
Cobalt Robotics Inc..........D.......650 781-3626
4019 Transport St Ste De Palo Alto (94303) ***(P-5245)***
Cobalt Robotics Inc..........D.......650 315-4314
2121 S El Cmino Real Ste San Mateo (94403) ***(P-12346)***
Cobalt Technologies Inc..........E.......650 230-0722
500 Clyde Ave Ste 500 # 500 Mountain View (94043) ***(P-19043)***
Cobaltix LLC..........E.......415 322-1025
1095 Folsom St San Francisco (94103) ***(P-19471)***
Cobeal..........E.......916 622-7330
1941 Park Oak Dr Roseville (95661) ***(P-19745)***
Cobham Adv Elec Sol Inc..........B.......408 624-3000
5300 Hellyer Ave San Jose (95138) ***(P-6665)***
Coblentz Patch Duffy Bass LLP..........D.......510 655-4598
1 Montgomery St Ste 3000 San Francisco (94104) ***(P-17231)***
Coca-Cola Company American Cyn..........F.......707 556-1220
1201 Commerce Blvd American Canyon (94503) ***(P-2788)***
Cocokids Inc..........C.......925 676-5442
1035 Detroit Ave Ste 200 Concord (94518) ***(P-18225)***
Codding Construction, Rohnert Park *Also called Codding Enterprises LP* ***(P-10383)***
Codding Enterprises LP (PA)..........E.......**707 795-3550**
1400 Valley House Dr # 100 Rohnert Park (94928) ***(P-10383)***
Coddington Hcks Dnfrth A Prof..........E.......650 592-5400
555 Twin Dolphin Dr # 30 Redwood City (94065) ***(P-17232)***
Code For America Labs Inc..........D.......415 816-1286
972 Mission St Fl 5 San Francisco (94103) ***(P-19472)***
Code Green Networks Inc..........E.......408 498-8413
385 Moffett Park Dr # 105 Sunnyvale (94089) ***(P-12347)***

Codefast Inc ....E....408 687-4700
21170 Canyon Oak Way Cupertino (95014) **(P-13082)**
Codexis Inc (PA) ....**C....650 421-8100**
200 Penobscot Dr Redwood City (94063) **(P-3782)**
Codility US Inc ....C....415 568-5055
1355 Market St Ste 488 San Francisco (94103) **(P-12348)**
Codorniu Napa Inc ....D....707 254-2148
1345 Henry Rd NAPA (94559) **(P-2537)**
Coe Orchard Equipment Inc ....D....530 695-5121
3453 Riviera Rd Live Oak (95953) **(P-4999)**
Coelho West Custom Farming ....D....559 884-2566
26979 S Butte Ave Five Points (93624) **(P-152)**
Coen Company Inc (HQ) ....**E....650 522-2100**
951 Mariners Island Blvd San Mateo (94404) **(P-4627)**
Cofan Usa Inc ....E....510 490-7533
48664 Milmont Dr Fremont (94538) **(P-9113)**
Coffee Works Inc ....F....916 452-1086
3418 Folsom Blvd Sacramento (95816) **(P-2838)**
Cog Group LLC (PA) ....**D....408 213-1790**
1731 Tech Dr Ste 100 San Jose (95110) **(P-8490)**
Cognex, Hayward *Also called Ametek Inc* **(P-8667)**
Cognician Inc (HQ) ....**E....858 997-6732**
535 Mission St Ste 1628 San Francisco (94105) **(P-12349)**
Cognifit Inc ....D....646 340-1740
600 California St Fl 11 San Francisco (94108) **(P-17805)**
Cognitiveclouds Software Inc ....D....415 234-3611
5433 Ontario Cmn Fremont (94555) **(P-12350)**
Cognix Automation Inc ....E....925 464-8822
4900 Hopyard Rd Ste 100 Pleasanton (94588) **(P-13570)**
Cohen Ventures Inc (PA) ....**D....510 482-4420**
449 15th St 400 Oakland (94612) **(P-19746)**
Cohere Technologies Inc ....D....408 246-1277
2550 Walsh Ave Ste 150 Santa Clara (95051) **(P-19044)**
Coherent Inc (PA) ....**A....408 764-4000**
5100 Patrick Henry Dr Santa Clara (95054) **(P-6821)**
Coherent Asia Inc ....D....408 764-4000
5100 Patrick Henry Dr Santa Clara (95054) **(P-6407)**
Coherus Biosciences Inc (PA) ....**C....650 649-3530**
333 Twin Dolphin Dr # 60 Redwood City (94065) **(P-19045)**
Cohesity Inc (PA) ....**B....855 926-4374**
300 Park Ave Ste 1700 San Jose (95110) **(P-12351)**
Cohesity Inc ....B....650 968-4470
1880 Fallen Leaf Ln Los Altos (94024) **(P-10793)**
Coit Restoration Services, Modesto *Also called C & S Draperies Inc* **(P-11657)**
Coit Services Inc ....D....650 697-6190
865 Hinckley Rd Burlingame (94010) **(P-11660)**
Coit Services Inc ....D....916 731-7006
3499 Business Dr Sacramento (95820) **(P-11661)**
Cokeva Inc ....C....916 462-6001
9000 Foothills Blvd Roseville (95747) **(P-13820)**
Colabo Inc ....E....650 288-6649
751 Laurel St Ste 840 San Carlos (94070) **(P-13083)**
Cold Creek Compost Inc ....E....707 485-5966
6000 Potter Valley Rd Ukiah (95482) **(P-4138)**
Cold Springs Golf & Cntry CLB ....E....530 622-4567
6500 Clubhouse Dr Placerville (95667) **(P-15075)**
Cold Stone Creamery, Vallejo *Also called Park Management Corp* **(P-15045)**
Coldwell Banker, Pleasanton *Also called Katie Minor* **(P-10592)**
Coldwell Banker, Grass Valley *Also called Grass Roots Realty* **(P-10563)**
Coldwell Banker, Davis *Also called Doug Arnold Real Estate Inc* **(P-10541)**
Coldwell Banker ....D....650 596-5400
580 El Camino Real San Carlos (94070) **(P-10265)**
Coldwell Banker Residential BR, Mill Valley *Also called Alice Gray* **(P-10488)**
Coldwell Banker Residential RE, San Jose *Also called Terry Meyer* **(P-10672)**
Coldwell Bnkr Amral Assoc Rlto ....D....925 439-7400
3775 Main St Ste E Oakley (94561) **(P-10514)**
Coldwell Bnkr Residential Brkg (HQ) ....**D....925 275-3000**
1855 Gateway Blvd Ste 750 Concord (94520) **(P-10515)**
Coldwell Bnkr Residential Brkg ....E....650 558-4200
1427 Chapin Ave Burlingame (94010) **(P-10516)**
Coldwell Bnkr Residential Brkg ....E....831 462-9000
124 Rancho Del Mar Aptos (95003) **(P-10517)**
Coldwell Bnkr Residential Brkg ....E....510 608-7600
3340 Walnut Ave Ste 110 Fremont (94538) **(P-10518)**
Coldwell Bnkr Rsdntial RE Svcs ....B....415 461-2020
500 Sir Frncis Drake Blvd Greenbrae (94904) **(P-10519)**
Coleman Chavez & Assoc LLP ....D....916 787-2310
1731 E Rsvlle Pkwy Ste 20 Roseville (95661) **(P-17233)**
Coleman Company Inc ....C....650 837-9178
27 Idlewood Dr South San Francisco (94080) **(P-4241)**
Colfax International ....E....408 730-2275
2805 Bowers Ave Ste 230 Santa Clara (95051) **(P-5246)**
Colinas Farming Company ....E....707 963-2053
990 Rutherford Rutherford (94573) **(P-369)**
Collabrative DRG Discovery Inc ....E....650 204-3084
1633 Bayshore Hwy Ste 342 Burlingame (94010) **(P-13084)**
Collabria Care ....D....707 258-9080
414 S Jefferson St NAPA (94559) **(P-16871)**
Collabrus Inc ....C....415 288-1826
180 Montgomery St # 2380 San Francisco (94104) **(P-18946)**
Collaris Defense, Morgan Hill *Also called Collaris LLC* **(P-6408)**
Collaris LLC ....D....510 825-9995
685 Jarvis Dr Ste C Morgan Hill (95037) **(P-6408)**
Collective Health, San Francisco *Also called Collectivehealth Inc* **(P-10266)**
Collectivehealth Inc ....B....650 376-3804
85 Bluxome St San Francisco (94107) **(P-10266)**
Colleen & Herb Enterprises Inc ....C....510 226-6083
46939 Bayside Pkwy Fremont (94538) **(P-5494)**
Colleen Strawberries Inc (PA) ....**E....831 724-0700**
80 Sakata Ln Watsonville (95076) **(P-40)**
College Marin Childrens Center, Kentfield *Also called Marin Community College Dst* **(P-17970)**
College Track ....C....510 834-3295
112 Linden St Oakland (94607) **(P-19473)**
Collette Foods LLC ....D....209 487-1260
7251 Galilee Rd Ste 180 Roseville (95678) **(P-2278)**
Collier Warehouse Inc ....E....415 920-9720
90 Dorman Ave San Francisco (94124) **(P-8536)**
Colliers International ....D....415 788-3100
101 2nd St Ste 1100 San Francisco (94105) **(P-10520)**
Collimated Holes Inc ....E....408 374-5080
460 Division St Campbell (95008) **(P-6868)**
Collins Electrical Company Inc (PA) ....**C....209 466-3691**
3412 Metro Dr Stockton (95215) **(P-1479)**
Collins Electrical Company Inc ....E....209 466-3691
1902 Channel Dr West Sacramento (95691) **(P-1480)**
Collins Electrical Company Inc ....E....559 454-8164
1809 N Helm Ave Ste 7 Fresno (93727) **(P-1481)**
Collins Pine Company ....E....530 258-2111
500 Main St Chester (96020) **(P-3095)**
Collins Pine Company ....E....530 258-2131
540 Main St Chester (96020) **(P-3096)**
Collotype Labels USA Inc (HQ) ....**D....707 603-2500**
21 Executive Way NAPA (94558) **(P-3725)**
Colonial Van & Storage Inc (PA) ....**E....916 546-3600**
6001 88th St Ste A Sacramento (95828) **(P-7520)**
Colony Landscape & Maint Inc ....E....408 941-1090
4911 Spreckles Ave Alviso (95002) **(P-454)**
Color Genomic Danny, Burlingame *Also called Color Health Inc* **(P-8777)**
Color Health Inc (PA) ....**B....650 651-7116**
831 Mitten Rd Ste 100 Burlingame (94010) **(P-8777)**
Color Spot Lodi, Lodi *Also called Csn Winddown Inc* **(P-117)**
Colortokens Inc (PA) ....**E....408 341-6030**
2101 Tasman Dr Ste 201 Santa Clara (95054) **(P-13085)**
Coloserve, San Jose *Also called Gogrid LLC* **(P-7956)**
Colter & Peterson Microsystems ....E....707 776-4500
1260 Holm Rd Ste C Petaluma (94954) **(P-6714)**
Columbia City Hotel LLC ....E....209 532-5341
22768 Main St Columbia (95310) **(P-11026)**
Columbia Cosmetics Mfrs Inc (PA) ....**D....510 562-5900**
1661 Timothy Dr San Leandro (94577) **(P-4081)**
Columbia Electric Inc ....E....510 430-9505
1980 Davis St San Leandro (94577) **(P-1482)**
Columbia Hospitality Inc ....D....415 362-8878
665 Bush St San Francisco (94108) **(P-11027)**
Columbia Hydronics Co., Hayward *Also called California Hydronics Corp* **(P-9007)**
Columbus Foods LLC ....B....510 921-3400
30977 San Antonio St Hayward (94544) **(P-2094)**
Columbus Manufacturing Inc (HQ) ....**D....510 921-3423**
30977 San Antonio St Hayward (94544) **(P-2115)**
Colusa Casino, Colusa *Also called Colusa Indian Cmnty Council* **(P-18226)**
Colusa Casino Resort, Colusa *Also called New Colusa Indian Bingo* **(P-15223)**
Colusa Indian Cmnty Council ....B....530 458-5787
3720 State Highway 45 Colusa (95932) **(P-15354)**
Colusa Indian Cmnty Council ....C....530 458-6572
3740 Highway 45 Colusa (95932) **(P-18226)**
Colusa Indian Cmnty Council ....B....530 458-5501
3710 Highway 45 Ste A Colusa (95932) **(P-15355)**
Colusa Produce Corporation ....D....530 696-0121
1954 Progress Rd Meridian (95957) **(P-9445)**
Colvin-Friedman LLC ....E....707 769-4488
1311 Commerce St Petaluma (94954) **(P-4269)**
Comba Telecom Inc ....F....408 526-0180
568 Gibraltar Dr Milpitas (95035) **(P-8904)**
Comcast California Ix Inc ....E....215 286-3345
1111 Andersen Dr San Rafael (94901) **(P-8059)**
Comcast Slcon Vly Innvtion Ctr, Sunnyvale *Also called Plaxo Inc* **(P-8064)**
Comcast Spotlight ....E....415 264-6267
4733 Chabot Dr Ste 101 Pleasanton (94588) **(P-5742)**
Comcast Sprtsnet Bay Area Hldn ....E....415 896-2557
360 3rd St Fl 2 San Francisco (94107) **(P-8043)**
Comco Sheet Metal Company ....F....510 832-6433
237 Southbrook Pl Clayton (94517) **(P-4747)**
Comcore Opcital Communication, Fremont *Also called Comcore Technologies Inc* **(P-6869)**
Comcore Technologies Inc ....E....408 623-9704
48834 Kato Rd Ste 108a Fremont (94538) **(P-6869)**
Comentis Inc ....E....650 869-7600
400 Oyster Point Blvd # 226 South San Francisco (94080) **(P-19211)**
Comerit Inc ....E....888 556-5990
2201 Francisco Dr 140-2 El Dorado Hills (95762) **(P-13872)**
Comet Building Maintenance Inc ....D....415 382-1150
21 Commercial Blvd Ste 12 Novato (94949) **(P-409)**
Comet Technologies USA Inc ....C....408 325-8770
2360 Bering Dr San Jose (95131) **(P-6897)**
Comfort Air Inc ....D....209 466-4601
1607 French Camp Tpke Stockton (95206) **(P-1238)**
Comfort California Inc ....C....415 928-5000
2775 Van Ness Ave San Francisco (94109) **(P-11028)**
Comfort Energy Inc ....E....408 263-3100
1465 N Milpitas Blvd Milpitas (95035) **(P-1239)**
Comfort Inn, Hayward *Also called Vishnu Hotel LLC* **(P-11563)**
Comfort Inn, San Francisco *Also called Comfort California Inc* **(P-11028)**
Comfort Inn, Fresno *Also called Sethi Conglomerate LLC* **(P-11463)**
Comfort Inn, South San Francisco *Also called Comfort Suites* **(P-11029)**
Comfort Inn, Oakland *Also called Amin-Oakland LLC* **(P-10923)**
Comfort Inn, Modesto *Also called Vipa Hospitality Inc* **(P-11561)**

ALPHABETIC

Comfort Inn, Morgan Hill *Also called Marutiz Inc (P-11288)*
Comfort Keepers, Kingsburg *Also called In Home Services LLC (P-16899)*
Comfort Keepers, Citrus Heights *Also called Fortune Senior Enterprises (P-16884)*
Comfort Suites, Fresno *Also called Jai Jai Mata Inc (P-11205)*
Comfort Suites..........E.......650 589-7100
121 E Grand Ave South San Francisco (94080) ***(P-11029)***
Comfort Zone Mechanical Air, Milpitas *Also called Comfort Energy Inc (P-1239)*
Comfy, Oakland *Also called Building Robotics Inc (P-9057)*
Comglobal Systems Inc (HQ)..........**D.......619 321-6000**
1315 Dell Ave Campbell (95008) ***(P-13571)***
Comity Designs Inc..........D.......415 967-1530
41 Marvin Ave Los Altos (94022) ***(P-13873)***
Commerce Home Mortgage LLC..........D.......831 460-0202
523 Capitola Ave Capitola (95010) ***(P-9903)***
Commerce Home Mortgage LLC..........D.......530 282-1166
970 Executive Way Redding (96002) ***(P-9904)***
Commercial Casework Inc (PA)..........**D.......510 657-7933**
41780 Christy St Fremont (94538) ***(P-3125)***
Commercial Energy California, Oakland *Also called Commercial Energy Montana Inc (P-547)*
Commercial Energy Montana Inc..........F.......510 567-2700
7677 Oakport St Ste 525 Oakland (94621) ***(P-547)***
Commercial Manufacturing..........E.......559 237-1855
2432 S East Ave Fresno (93706) ***(P-5127)***
Commercial Mechanical Svc Inc (PA)..........**E.......650 610-8440**
981 Bing St San Carlos (94070) ***(P-14686)***
Commercial Patterns Inc..........F.......510 784-1014
260 Bridgehead Ln Hayward (94544) ***(P-4270)***
Commercial Restaurant Service, Auburn *Also called Tf Welch Enterprises Inc (P-1380)*
Commercial Sting Spcalists Inc..........E.......408 453-8983
481 Laurelwood Rd Santa Clara (95054) ***(P-8491)***
Committee On Shelterless..........E.......707 765-6530
900 Hopper St Petaluma (94952) ***(P-17491)***
Commodore Dining Cruises Inc..........D.......510 337-9000
Mainers Sq Alameda (94501) ***(P-7719)***
Common Counsel Foundation..........E.......510 834-2995
1624 Franklin St Ste 1022 Oakland (94612) ***(P-18561)***
Common Ground Ldscp MGT Inc..........E.......408 278-9807
1127 Mockingbird Ct San Jose (95120) ***(P-455)***
Commonweal..........D.......415 868-0970
451 Mesa Rd Bolinas (94924) ***(P-17492)***
Commonwealth Central Credit Un (PA)..........**D.......408 531-3100**
5890 Silver Creek Vly Rd San Jose (95138) ***(P-9779)***
Communctons Wkrs Amer AFL-CIO, Sacramento *Also called C W A District Nine (P-18354)*
Communicare Health Centers..........C.......530 758-2060
2051 John Jones Rd Davis (95616) ***(P-15356)***
Communication Arts, Menlo Park *Also called Coyne & Blanchard Inc (P-3495)*
Communications & Pwr Inds LLC..........A.......650 846-3729
811 Hansen Way Palo Alto (94304) ***(P-5832)***
Communications & Pwr Inds LLC..........D.......530 662-7553
1318 Commerce Ave Woodland (95776) ***(P-14693)***
Communications & Pwr Inds LLC (HQ)..........**A.......650 846-2900**
811 Hansen Way Palo Alto (94304) ***(P-5900)***
Communigate Systems, Belvedere Tiburon *Also called Stalker Software Inc (P-13465)*
Community Access Program, Auburn *Also called RES-Care Inc (P-16936)*
Community Action Marin..........C.......415 459-6330
1108 Tamalpais Ave San Rafael (94901) ***(P-17001)***
Community Action Marine, San Rafael *Also called Community Action Marin (P-17001)*
Community Action Prtnr Mdera C (PA)..........**C.......559 673-9173**
1225 Gill Ave Madera (93637) ***(P-17910)***
Community Action Prtnr Mdera C..........D.......559 661-1000
1225 Gill Ave Madera (93637) ***(P-18227)***
Community Action Prtnr Snoma C..........D.......707 544-0120
141 Stony Cir Ste 210 Santa Rosa (95401) ***(P-18228)***
Community Assoc Pr-School Edca, Livermore *Also called Cape Inc (P-17877)*
Community Behavioral Health, San Francisco *Also called State Hospitals Cal Dept (P-17075)*
Community Bridges (PA)..........**E.......831 688-8840**
519 Main St Watsonville (95076) ***(P-17493)***
Community Bridges..........D.......831 724-2024
114 E 5th St Watsonville (95076) ***(P-17494)***
Community Care Licensing Div, Sacramento *Also called Social Services Cal Dept (P-17748)*
Community Child Care Crdnting (PA)..........**E.......510 582-2182**
22351 City Center Dr # 200 Hayward (94541) ***(P-17911)***
Community Chld Cre Cncl Sonoma (PA)..........**D.......707 522-1413**
131a Stony Cir Ste 300 Santa Rosa (95401) ***(P-17912)***
Community College Foundation (PA)..........**D.......916 418-5100**
1901 Royal Oaks Dr # 100 Sacramento (95815) ***(P-19747)***
Community Edcatn Child Care Ct, Vallejo *Also called Vallejo City Unified Schl Dst (P-18042)*
Community Facilities District, Yuba City *Also called City of Yuba City (P-17803)*
Community First Credit Union (PA)..........**C.......707 546-6000**
1105 N Dutton Ave Ste A Santa Rosa (95401) ***(P-9780)***
Community Forward Sf Inc (PA)..........**D.......415 241-1199**
1171 Mission St Fl 2 San Francisco (94103) ***(P-17495)***
Community Fuels, Stockton *Also called American Biodiesel Inc (P-4119)*
Community Health Partnr Inc..........E.......408 556-6605
408 N Capitol Ave San Jose (95133) ***(P-17125)***
COMMUNITY HEALTH SYSTEM, Fresno *Also called Community Hospitals Centl Cal (P-16335)*
Community Hlth Awrness Council..........E.......650 965-2020
590 W El Camino Real Mountain View (94040) ***(P-17496)***
Community Hlth For Asian Amrca..........E.......925 778-1667
1141 Harbor Bay Pkwy # 103 Alameda (94502) ***(P-17002)***
Community Home Partners LLC..........D.......408 985-5252
2384 Pacific Dr Santa Clara (95051) ***(P-16177)***
Community Hospice Inc (PA)..........**C.......209 578-6300**
4368 Spyres Way Modesto (95356) ***(P-16178)***
Community Hospitals Centl Cal (PA)..........**A.......559 459-6000**
2823 Fresno St Fresno (93721) ***(P-16335)***
Community Hospitals Centl Cal..........A.......559 459-6000
2823 Fresno St Fresno (93721) ***(P-16336)***
Community Housing Inc..........D.......650 328-3300
437 Webster St Palo Alto (94301) ***(P-18079)***
Community Hsing Imprv Prgram I (PA)..........**E.......530 891-6931**
1001 Willow St Chico (95928) ***(P-19748)***
Community Integration Program, Sacramento *Also called Develop Disabilities Svc Org (P-17530)*
Community Intgrted Work Prgram, Madera *Also called Community Intgrted Work Prgram (P-17807)*
Community Intgrted Work Prgram..........E.......408 871-9680
651 Division St Campbell (95008) ***(P-17806)***
Community Intgrted Work Prgram..........E.......559 673-5174
980 Emily Way Ste A Madera (93637) ***(P-17807)***
Community Intgrted Work Prgram..........E.......209 723-4025
1735 Ashby Rd Ste D Merced (95348) ***(P-17497)***
Community Intgrted Work Prgram..........E.......559 276-8564
4623 W Jacquelyn Ave Fresno (93722) ***(P-17498)***
Community Management Svcs Inc..........E.......408 559-1977
1935 Dry Creek Rd Ste 203 Campbell (95008) ***(P-10521)***
Community Medical Center..........E.......209 944-4705
131 W A St Ste 1 Dixon (95620) ***(P-15357)***
Community Medical Center..........C.......559 222-7416
3003 N Mariposa St Fresno (93703) ***(P-16337)***
Community Medical Centers, Fresno *Also called Pediatric Anesthesia Assoc Med (P-16478)*
Community Medical Centers Inc..........E.......209 944-4700
701 E Channel St Stockton (95202) ***(P-15358)***
Community Medical Centers Inc..........E.......209 940-5600
1031 Waterloo Rd Stockton (95205) ***(P-15359)***
Community Medical Centers Inc..........E.......209 331-8019
721 Calaveras St Lodi (95240) ***(P-15360)***
Community Medical Centers Inc (PA)..........**D.......209 373-2800**
7210 Murray Dr Stockton (95210) ***(P-17003)***
Community Medical Centers Inc..........E.......707 359-1800
600 Nut Tree Rd Ste 260 Vacaville (95687) ***(P-15361)***
Community Medical Centers Inc..........E.......209 368-2212
2401 W Turner Rd Ste 450 Lodi (95242) ***(P-15362)***
Community Medical Centers Inc..........E.......209 373-2800
7210 Murray Dr Stockton (95210) ***(P-15363)***
Community of Harbor Bay Isle..........E.......510 865-3363
3195 Mecartney Rd Alameda (94502) ***(P-18408)***
Community Partners Intl..........C.......510 225-9676
580 California St Fl 16 San Francisco (94104) ***(P-10787)***
Community Presbt Ch Danville (PA)..........**C.......925 837-5525**
222 W El Pintado Danville (94526) ***(P-17913)***
Community Printers Inc..........E.......831 426-4682
1827 Soquel Ave Santa Cruz (95062) ***(P-3638)***
Community Rcnstrction Slutions..........E.......650 692-3030
855 Hinckley Rd Burlingame (94010) ***(P-739)***
Community Recreation Center..........E.......408 615-3140
969 Kiely Blvd Santa Clara (95051) ***(P-11618)***
Community Regional Medical Ctr, Fresno *Also called Community Hospitals Centl Cal (P-16336)*
Community Services, Modesto *Also called County of Stanislaus (P-17514)*
Community Skating Inc..........E.......650 493-4566
3009 Middlefield Rd Palo Alto (94306) ***(P-15194)***
Community Sltons For Chldren F (PA)..........**C.......408 842-7138**
9015 Murray Ave Ste 100 Gilroy (95020) ***(P-17499)***
Community Support Services, Santa Cruz *Also called Encompass Community Services (P-17552)*
Community Svcs Agcy Mtn View L..........C.......650 968-0836
204 Stierlin Rd Mountain View (94043) ***(P-17500)***
Community Vocational Svcs LLC..........E.......559 227-8287
3419 W Shaw Ave Fresno (93711) ***(P-17501)***
Commure Inc (PA)..........**D.......415 741-1114**
376 Brannan St San Francisco (94107) ***(P-12352)***
Compac Engineering Inc..........E.......530 872-2042
1111 Noffsinger Ln Paradise (95969) ***(P-6701)***
Compactor Management Co LLC..........E.......510 623-2323
32420 Central Ave Union City (94587) ***(P-4748)***
Compandsave, Union City *Also called Cmy Image Corporation (P-3637)*
Comparenetworks Inc (PA)..........**D.......650 873-9031**
395 Oyster Point Blvd # 300 South San Francisco (94080) ***(P-19046)***
Compass Bank, Manteca *Also called Bbva USA (P-9708)*
Compass Bank, Stockton *Also called Bbva USA (P-9709)*
Compass Bank, Stockton *Also called Bbva USA (P-9710)*
Compass Children's Center, San Francisco *Also called Compass Family Services (P-17914)*
Compass Clara House, San Francisco *Also called Compass Family Services (P-17504)*
Compass Components Inc (PA)..........**C.......510 656-4700**
48133 Warm Springs Blvd Fremont (94539) ***(P-6409)***
Compass Container Group Inc (PA)..........**E.......510 839-7500**
6345 Coliseum Way Oakland (94621) ***(P-9114)***
Compass Equipment Inc (PA)..........**E.......530 533-7284**
4688 Pacific Heights Rd Oroville (95965) ***(P-5050)***
Compass Family Services (PA)..........**E.......415 644-0504**
37 Grove St San Francisco (94102) ***(P-17502)***
Compass Family Services..........D.......415 644-0504
144 Leavenworth St San Francisco (94102) ***(P-17914)***
Compass Family Services..........D.......415 644-0504
626 Polk St San Francisco (94102) ***(P-17503)***
Compass Family Services..........D.......415 644-0504
111 Page St San Francisco (94102) ***(P-17504)***
Compass Family Shelter, San Francisco *Also called Compass Family Services (P-17503)*
Compass Group Usa Inc..........C.......510 259-0416
20929 Cabot Blvd Hayward (94545) ***(P-14232)***

Compass Innovations Inc............C.......408 418-3985
2352 Walsh Ave Santa Clara (95051) ***(P-4229)***
Compass Manufacturing Service, Fremont *Also called Compass Components Inc* ***(P-6409)***
Compass Marketing Inc............E.......925 299-7878
3447 Mt Diablo Blvd Lafayette (94549) ***(P-11747)***
Compass Transportation Charter, San Jose *Also called Sfo Airporter Inc* ***(P-7358)***
Compassionate Health Options (PA)............**D.......415 255-1200**
755 29th Ave San Francisco (94121) ***(P-17126)***
Compensia Inc............E.......408 876-4025
125 S Market St Ste 1000 San Jose (95113) ***(P-19474)***
Compex Legal Services LLC............C.......650 833-0460
1225 Pear Ave 110 Mountain View (94043) ***(P-11845)***
Complete Building Services, San Mateo *Also called Building & Facilities Svcs LLC* ***(P-11930)***
Complete Genomics Inc............B.......408 648-2560
2904 Orchard Pkwy San Jose (95134) ***(P-19212)***
Complete Linen Services, South San Francisco *Also called Medical Linen Service Inc* ***(P-11637)***
Complete Millwork Services Inc............E.......408 567-9664
405 Aldo Ave Santa Clara (95054) ***(P-8537)***
Complianceonline, San Jose *Also called Metricstream Inc* ***(P-13306)***
Compose Inc............F.......415 574-7038
273 S Railroad Ave Ste A San Mateo (94401) ***(P-13086)***
Composite Software LLC (HQ)............**D.......800 553-6387**
755 Sycamore Dr Milpitas (95035) ***(P-13087)***
Composite Technology Intl, Sacramento *Also called Composite Technology Intl Inc* ***(P-3126)***
Composite Technology Intl Inc............E.......916 551-1850
1730 I St Ste 100 Sacramento (95811) ***(P-3126)***
Comprehensive SEC Svcs Inc (PA)............**D.......916 683-3605**
10535 E Stockton Blvd G Elk Grove (95624) ***(P-14044)***
Compressed A Benz Systems Inc (HQ)............**D.......510 413-5200**
48434 Milmont Dr Fremont (94538) ***(P-5182)***
Comprhnsive Yuth Svcs Frsno In............D.......559 229-3561
4545 N West Ave Ste 101 Fresno (93705) ***(P-17505)***
Compro Packaging LLC............E.......510 475-0118
1600 Atlantic St Union City (94587) ***(P-3356)***
Compserv Inc............F.......415 331-4571
42 Golf Rd Pleasanton (94566) ***(P-6410)***
Compu Tech Lumber Products............E.......707 437-6683
1980 Huntington Ct Fairfield (94533) ***(P-3203)***
Compugraphics USA Inc (HQ)............**D.......510 249-2600**
43455 Osgood Rd Fremont (94539) ***(P-6084)***
Compumail Information Svcs Inc............D.......925 689-7100
4057 Port Chicago Hwy # 300 Concord (94520) ***(P-14233)***
Computer, San Francisco *Also called Zazmic Inc* ***(P-12934)***
Computer Access Tech Corp............D.......408 727-6600
3385 Scott Blvd Santa Clara (95054) ***(P-5247)***
Computer Exchange, The, Sacramento *Also called Raymar Information Tech Inc* ***(P-5807)***
Computer History Museum............D.......650 810-1010
1401 N Shoreline Blvd Mountain View (94043) ***(P-18266)***
Computer Media Technology, San Jose *Also called Dataendure* ***(P-8690)***
Computer Performance Inc............E.......408 330-5599
2695 Walsh Ave Santa Clara (95051) ***(P-8682)***
Computer Plastics............E.......510 785-3600
1914 National Ave Hayward (94545) ***(P-5082)***
Computer Power Sftwr Group Inc (PA)............**F.......916 985-4445**
716 Figueroa St Folsom (95630) ***(P-12353)***
Compwest Insurance Company............C.......415 593-5100
100 Pringle Ave Ste 515 Walnut Creek (94596) ***(P-10166)***
Comstock Mortgage, Sacramento *Also called Sacramento 1st Mortgage Inc* ***(P-9947)***
Comstock Publishing Inc............F.......916 364-1000
2335 Amrcn Rver Dr Ste 30 Sacramento (95825) ***(P-3494)***
Comstock's Magazine, Sacramento *Also called Comstock Publishing Inc* ***(P-3494)***
Comtech Communications Inc............E.......800 377-7422
120 Main Ave Ste J Sacramento (95838) ***(P-14679)***
Comtech Stllite Ntwrk Tech Inc............C.......408 213-3000
3550 Bassett St Santa Clara (95054) ***(P-5833)***
Comtel Systems Technology Inc............D.......408 543-5600
1292 Hammerwood Ave Sunnyvale (94089) ***(P-1483)***
Con J Franke Electric Inc............D.......209 462-0717
317 N Grant St Stockton (95202) ***(P-1484)***
Con-Cise Contact Lens Co, Alameda *Also called Lens C-C Inc* ***(P-7143)***
Con-Fab California Corporation (PA)............**F.......209 249-4700**
1910 Lathrop Rd Lathrop (95330) ***(P-4427)***
Con-Quest Contractors Inc............E.......415 206-0524
290 Toland St San Francisco (94124) ***(P-18672)***
Con-Way, Lakeport *Also called Xpo Enterprise Services Inc* ***(P-7613)***
Con-Way, Santa Rosa *Also called Xpo Logistics Freight Inc* ***(P-7616)***
Con-Way Freight, Redding *Also called Xpo Logistics Freight Inc* ***(P-7863)***
Concannon Vineyard, Livermore *Also called Tesla Vineyards Lp* ***(P-2738)***
Concealed Carrier LLC............E.......916 530-6205
11315 Sunrise Gold Cir F Rancho Cordova (95742) ***(P-4952)***
Concentra Medical Center............C.......909 558-2273
2970 Hilltop Mall Rd # 2 Richmond (94806) ***(P-15364)***
Concentra Medical Center A Med, Richmond *Also called Concentra Medical Center* ***(P-15364)***
Concentric Power Inc............D.......888 321-0620
1550 Dell Ave Ste I Campbell (95008) ***(P-19749)***
Concentric Software Inc............E.......408 816-7068
4750 Blue Ridge Dr San Jose (95129) ***(P-13088)***
Concentrix Corporation............E.......510 668-3717
44201 Nobel Dr Fremont (94538) ***(P-13874)***
Concentrix Corporation (PA)............**A.......800 747-0583**
44111 Nobel Dr Fremont (94538) ***(P-14234)***
Concept Hotels LLC (PA)............**E.......650 600-8257**
260 Main St Ste E Redwood City (94063) ***(P-11030)***
Concept Part Solutions Inc............E.......408 748-1244
2047 Zanker Rd San Jose (95131) ***(P-5091)***
Concept Systems Mfg Inc............E.......408 855-8595
2047 Zanker Rd San Jose (95131) ***(P-6085)***
Concessionaires Urban Park (PA)............**B.......530 529-1512**
2150 Main St Ste 5 Red Bluff (96080) ***(P-15195)***
Concessionaires Urban Park............D.......209 763-5121
2000 Camanche Rd Ofc Ofc Ione (95640) ***(P-15196)***
Concessionaires Urban Park............D.......209 763-5166
2000 Camanche Rd Ofc Ofc Ione (95640) ***(P-15197)***
Concessionaires Urban Park............D.......530 529-1596
34600 Ardenwood Blvd Fremont (94555) ***(P-15198)***
Concessionaires Urban Park............D.......530 529-1513
18013 Bollinger Canyon Rd San Ramon (94583) ***(P-15199)***
Conco Cement Company, Concord *Also called Gonsalves & Santucci Inc* ***(P-1875)***
Conco Companies............E.......925 685-6799
5141 Commercial Cir Concord (94520) ***(P-1858)***
Concord Graphic Arts Inc............E.......925 682-9670
3270 Monument Way Concord (94518) ***(P-11858)***
Concord Hotel LLC............D.......925 521-3751
45 John Glenn Dr Concord (94520) ***(P-11031)***
Concord Iron Works Inc............E.......925 432-0136
1 Leslie Dr Pittsburg (94565) ***(P-4654)***
Concord Jet Service Inc............E.......925 825-2980
3000 Oak Rd Ste 200 Walnut Creek (94597) ***(P-12035)***
Concord Sheet Metal, Pittsburg *Also called Levmar Inc* ***(P-4777)***
Concord Toyota, Concord *Also called FAA Concord T Inc* ***(P-14562)***
Concord Veranda Cinema LLC............C.......707 762-0990
2035 Diamond Blvd Ste 150 Concord (94520) ***(P-14787)***
Concord Vet Center, Concord *Also called Veterans Health Administration* ***(P-15805)***
Concord Worldwide Inc............D.......415 689-5488
177 Post St Ph Ste 910 San Francisco (94108) ***(P-12354)***
Concordia Manor, NAPA *Also called Rohlffs Memorial Manor* ***(P-18172)***
Concrete Inc (HQ)............**D.......209 933-6999**
400 S Lincoln St Stockton (95203) ***(P-4477)***
Concrete Craft, San Rafael *Also called Ghilotti Bros Inc* ***(P-1961)***
Concrete North Inc............D.......209 745-7400
10274 Iron Rock Way Elk Grove (95624) ***(P-1859)***
Concrete Ready Mix Inc............E.......408 224-2452
33 Hillsdale Ave San Jose (95136) ***(P-4478)***
Concreteworks Studio Inc............D.......510 534-7141
1998 Republic Ave San Leandro (94577) ***(P-8812)***
Condeco Software Inc (HQ)............**F.......917 677-7600**
2105 S Bascom Ave Ste 150 Campbell (95008) ***(P-13089)***
Condit Inn GP LLC............E.......408 779-7666
16115 Condit Rd Morgan Hill (95037) ***(P-11032)***
Condon-Johnson & Assoc Inc (PA)............**E.......510 636-2100**
480 Roland Way Ste 200 Oakland (94621) ***(P-1860)***
Condor Earth Technologies Inc............E.......209 984-4593
17857 High School Rd Jamestown (95327) ***(P-18673)***
Condor Earth Technologies Inc............E.......209 388-9601
188 Frank West Cir Ste I Stockton (95206) ***(P-19750)***
Condor Reliability Svcs Inc............E.......408 486-9600
2175 De La Cruz Blvd Santa Clara (95050) ***(P-6086)***
Condor Trading LP............A.......415 248-2200
600 Montgomery St Fl 6 San Francisco (94111) ***(P-10732)***
Conduent State Lcal Sltons Inc............A.......415 486-2409
455 The Embarcadero # 103 San Francisco (94111) ***(P-13572)***
Conetech Custom Services LLC............F.......707 823-2404
2191 Laguna Rd Santa Rosa (95401) ***(P-2538)***
Confab, Lathrop *Also called Con-Fab California Corporation* ***(P-4427)***
Confidential Canine Services............E.......800 574-5545
8094 Langham Way Sacramento (95829) ***(P-353)***
Config Consultants LLC............E.......844 852-2525
4900 Hopyard Rd Ste 100 Pleasanton (94588) ***(P-19475)***
Confluent Inc (PA)............**A.......800 439-3207**
899 W Evelyn Ave Mountain View (94041) ***(P-13090)***
Conforti Plumbing Inc............E.......530 622-0202
6080 Pleasant Valley Rd C El Dorado (95623) ***(P-1240)***
Congregation Emanu-El............C.......650 755-4700
1299 El Camino Real Colma (94014) ***(P-10522)***
Congrgtion Beth Jcob Irving Lv............E.......650 366-8481
1550 Almeda De Las Pulgas Redwood City (94061) ***(P-17915)***
Congrgtnal Ch Retirement Cmnty............D.......530 823-6131
750 Auburn Ravine Rd Auburn (95603) ***(P-18080)***
Conifer Financial Services LLC (HQ)............**D.......415 677-1500**
1 Ferry Building Ste 255 San Francisco (94111) ***(P-9965)***
Conifer Fund Services LLC............E.......415 677-5979
1 Ferry Plz Ste 255 San Francisco (94111) ***(P-9966)***
Conifer Securities, San Francisco *Also called Conifer Fund Services LLC* ***(P-9966)***
Conklin & Conklin Incorporated............E.......510 489-5500
34201 7th St Union City (94587) ***(P-4872)***
Conklin Bros San Jose Inc (PA)............**E.......408 266-2250**
2250 Almaden Expy San Jose (95125) ***(P-8509)***
Connealy Chiropractic Inc (PA)............**E.......913 669-8023**
930 Detroit Ave Ste A Concord (94518) ***(P-15864)***
Connected Cannabis............E.......916 308-4175
2831 Fruitridge Rd Sacramento (95820) ***(P-7277)***
Conner Logistics Inc............D.......888 939-4637
4069 W Shaw Ave Ste 103 Fresno (93722) ***(P-7830)***
Conners Oro-Cal Mfg Co............F.......530 533-5065
1720 Bird St Oroville (95965) ***(P-7165)***
Connexsys Engineering Inc............E.......510 243-2050
1320 Willow Pass Rd # 500 Concord (94520) ***(P-18674)***
Conquest Imaging, Stockton *Also called Conrad Corporation* ***(P-8778)***
Conrad Corporation............E.......209 942-2654
1815 Industrial Dr # 100 Stockton (95206) ***(P-8778)***
Conrad Lab, The, Lodi *Also called Lodi Memorial Hosp Assn Inc* ***(P-16428)***
Conrad Wood Preserving Co............F.......530 476-2894
7085 Eddy Rd Unit C Arbuckle (95912) ***(P-3258)***

ALPHABETIC

Conservation Corps N Bay Inc ....E....415 454-4554
11 Pimentel Ct Novato (94949) *(P-17808)*
Conservation Society Cal ....C....510 632-9525
9777 Golf Links Rd Oakland (94605) *(P-18290)*
Consol ....E....209 474-8446
1610 R St Ste 200 Scrmnto Sacramento (95811) *(P-19476)*
Consoldted Hnge Mnfctured Pdts ....F....408 379-6550
1150b Dell Ave Campbell (95008) *(P-5495)*
Consoldted Metal Fbrctng Coinc ....E....559 268-7887
2780 S Cherry Ave Fresno (93706) *(P-8813)*
Consoldted Protective Svcs Inc ....E....916 483-2500
3307 Watt Ave Ste 3 Sacramento (95821) *(P-14045)*
Consoldted Tribal Hlth Prj Inc ....D....707 485-5115
6991 N State St Redwood Valley (95470) *(P-17004)*
Console (PA) ....E....855 858-5497
3131 Jay St Ste 210 Santa Clara (95054) *(P-7942)*
Consolidated Engineering Labs, San Ramon *Also called Atlas Technical Cons LLC (P-19723)*
Consolidated Pallet Company ....F....916 381-8123
4400 Florin Perkins Rd Sacramento (95826) *(P-8538)*
Consolidated Printers Inc ....E....510 843-8524
2630 8th St Berkeley (94710) *(P-3551)*
Consolidated Training LLC ....E....831 768-8888
144 Holm Rd Spc 47 Watsonville (95076) *(P-7278)*
Consortium For Community Svcs, Fresno *Also called Quality Group Homes Inc (P-690)*
Constllion Brnds US Oprations, Geyserville *Also called Clos Du Bois Wines Inc (P-2533)*
Constllion Brnds US Oprtons I ....A....559 485-0141
12667 Road 24 Madera (93637) *(P-9572)*
Construction, Loomis *Also called Sierra Trim Inc (P-1758)*
Construction, Fresno *Also called Quiring General LLC (P-940)*
Construction Developers Inc ....E....559 277-4700
5755 W Barstow Ave # 103 Fresno (93722) *(P-858)*
Construction Electrical Pdts, Livermore *Also called R K Larrabee Company Inc (P-5667)*
Construction Innovations LLC ....C....855 725-9555
10630 Mather Blvd Ste 200 Mather (95655) *(P-6511)*
Construction Testing Services (PA) ....D....925 462-5151
2118 Rheem Dr Pleasanton (94588) *(P-19318)*
Construction Tstg & Engrg Inc ....E....916 331-6030
3628 Madison Ave Ste 22 North Highlands (95660) *(P-19263)*
Consultnts In Edctl Per Skills (PA) ....D....916 348-1890
5825 Auburn Blvd Ste 1 Sacramento (95841) *(P-17506)*
Consumer Cr Cnsling Svc San Fr (PA) ....D....888 456-2227
1655 Grant St Ste 1300 Concord (94520) *(P-11713)*
Consumer Hlth Interactive LLC ....E....415 537-0735
436 14th St Ste 1500 Oakland (94612) *(P-19477)*
Contactual Inc ....D....650 292-4408
810 W Maude Ave Sunnyvale (94085) *(P-13091)*
Contadina Foods, Woodland *Also called Pacific Coast Producers (P-2239)*
Containment Consultants Inc ....F....408 848-6998
110 Old Gilroy St Gilroy (95020) *(P-4718)*
Contech Solutions Incorporated ....E....510 357-7900
631 Montague St San Leandro (94577) *(P-6087)*
Contemporary Records, Berkeley *Also called Fantasy Inc (P-5777)*
Content Guru Inc ....B....408 559-3988
900 E Hamilton Ave # 510 Campbell (95008) *(P-13573)*
Content Management Corporation ....F....510 505-1100
4287 Technology Dr Fremont (94538) *(P-3726)*
Contentstack LLC ....E....415 255-5955
49 Geary St Ste 238 San Francisco (94108) *(P-19478)*
Context Engineering Co ....E....408 748-9112
1043 Di Giulio Ave Santa Clara (95050) *(P-4880)*
Contextlogic Inc (PA) ....B....415 795-8061
1 Sansome St Fl 33 San Francisco (94104) *(P-11812)*
Continental Enterprises, Fowler *Also called Pps Packaging Company (P-3348)*
Continental Sales & Mktg Inc (PA) ....E....510 895-1881
2360 Alvarado St San Leandro (94577) *(P-8855)*
Continental Terminals Inc ....E....510 746-1100
300 Mitchell Ave Alameda (94501) *(P-7687)*
Continental Western Corp (PA) ....E....510 352-3133
2950 Merced St Ste 200 San Leandro (94577) *(P-9115)*
Contining Lf Cmmnties Plsnton ....D....925 227-6800
3300 Stoneridge Creek Way Pleasanton (94588) *(P-18081)*
Continntal Intllgent Trnsp Sys ....E....408 391-9008
3901 N 1st St San Jose (95134) *(P-4197)*
Continuing Development, Morgan Hill *Also called Catalyst Family Inc (P-17879)*
Continuum Electro-Optics Inc ....D....408 727-3240
532 Gibraltar Dr Milpitas (95035) *(P-6822)*
Continuum Estate Winery Co, Saint Helena *Also called Tmr Wine Company LLC (P-2744)*
Continuumglobal Inc (PA) ....A....415 685-3302
3723 Haven Ave Menlo Park (94025) *(P-19479)*
Continuumglobal Inc ....C....415 685-3301
1200 Gough St Unit 3a San Francisco (94109) *(P-19480)*
Contra Costa Cnty Off Educatn (PA) ....B....925 942-3388
77 Santa Barbara Rd Pleasant Hill (94523) *(P-19319)*
Contra Costa Country Club ....D....925 798-7135
801 Golf Club Rd Pleasant Hill (94523) *(P-15076)*
Contra Costa County ....C....925 313-1323
30 Douglas Dr Martinez (94553) *(P-7905)*
Contra Costa County Employees ....E....925 521-3960
1355 Willow Way Ste 221 Concord (94520) *(P-18409)*
Contra Costa Door Co ....E....925 671-7888
145 Mason Cir Concord (94520) *(P-1734)*
Contra Costa Electric Inc (HQ) ....B....925 229-4250
825 Howe Rd Martinez (94553) *(P-1485)*
Contra Costa Federal Credit Un (PA) ....E....925 228-7550
1111 Pine St Martinez (94553) *(P-9781)*
Contra Costa Metal Fabricators, Oakland *Also called Monterey Mechanical Co (P-1168)*
Contra Costa Newspapers Inc (HQ) ....A....925 935-2525
175 Lennon Ln Ste 100 Walnut Creek (94598) *(P-3429)*
Contra Costa Newspapers Inc ....D....510 758-8400
4301 Lakeside Dr San Pablo (94806) *(P-3430)*
Contra Costa Times, Walnut Creek *Also called Contra Costa Newspapers Inc (P-3429)*
Contra Costa Water District (PA) ....C....925 688-8000
1331 Concord Ave Concord (94520) *(P-8230)*
Contra Costa Water District ....E....925 688-8090
2015 Bates Ave Concord (94520) *(P-8231)*
Contra Costa Water District ....E....925 383-2576
3760 Neroly Rd Oakley (94561) *(P-8232)*
Contra Csta Msqito Vctor Ctrl ....E....925 685-9301
155 Mason Cir Concord (94520) *(P-8394)*
Contra Csta Rgonal Med Ctr Aux ....D....925 370-5000
2500 Alhambra Ave Martinez (94553) *(P-15365)*
Contract Interiors San Diego ....D....559 276-0561
4450 N Brawley Ave # 125 Fresno (93722) *(P-8492)*
Contract Metal Products Inc ....E....510 979-0000
6451 W Schulte Rd Ste 110 Tracy (95377) *(P-4749)*
Contract Office Group, San Jose *Also called Cog Group LLC (P-8490)*
Contract Sweeping Services LLC ....E....408 828-5280
760 E Capitol Ave Milpitas (95035) *(P-8395)*
Contract Sweeping Services LLC ....E....408 828-5280
1113 Shaw Rd Stockton (95215) *(P-8396)*
Contract Wrangler Inc ....E....408 472-6898
1840 Gateway Dr Ste 300 San Mateo (94404) *(P-13092)*
Contractors Scaffold Sup Inc ....D....650 871-8190
229 Harbor Way South San Francisco (94080) *(P-12036)*
Contrctor Cmpliance Monitoring (PA) ....E....650 522-4403
635 Mariners Island Blvd San Mateo (94404) *(P-2023)*
Control Air North Inc ....D....510 441-1800
30655 San Clemente St Hayward (94544) *(P-1241)*
Controller Consulting Svcs Inc ....C....408 221-2492
1577 Aldacourrou St Tracy (95304) *(P-19751)*
Convergent Laser Technologies, Alameda *Also called Xintec Corporation (P-7135)*
Convergent Manufacturing Tech ....E....408 987-2770
966 Shulman Ave Santa Clara (95050) *(P-5359)*
Conversica Inc (PA) ....F....650 290-7674
950 Tower Ln Ste 1200 Foster City (94404) *(P-8683)*
Convertly, San Jose *Also called Medianews Group Inc (P-3459)*
Convict Lake Resort Inc ....E....760 934-3800
2000 Convict Lake Rd Crowley Lake (93546) *(P-11033)*
Convrgd Data Tech Inc ....C....650 461-4488
999 Commercial St Ste 202 Palo Alto (94303) *(P-8684)*
Conxtech Inc ....C....510 264-9111
6600 Koll Center Pkwy # 210 Pleasanton (94566) *(P-4655)*
Cook Cabinets Inc ....E....530 621-0851
6428 Capitol Ave Diamond Springs (95619) *(P-1735)*
Cook Concrete Products Inc ....E....530 243-2562
5461 Eastside Rd Redding (96001) *(P-4428)*
Cook Engineering, Rancho Cordova *Also called Cook General Engineering Inc (P-1954)*
Cook General Engineering Inc ....E....916 631-1365
3203 Fitzgerald Rd Rancho Cordova (95742) *(P-1954)*
Cook Realty Inc ....E....916 451-6702
4305 Freeport Blvd Sacramento (95822) *(P-10523)*
Cook Realty Sales, Sacramento *Also called Cook Realty Inc (P-10523)*
Cooke & Associates Inc (PA) ....E....408 842-0602
145 Town And Country Dr # 108 Danville (94526) *(P-14046)*
Cooks Communications Corp ....E....559 233-8818
160 N Broadway St Fresno (93701) *(P-14694)*
Cooks Truck Body Mfg Inc ....E....916 784-3220
9600 Del Rd Roseville (95747) *(P-6565)*
Cooley Godward Kronish, San Francisco *Also called Cooley LLP (P-17234)*
Cooley LLP ....D....415 693-2000
3 Embarcadero Ctr Fl 20 San Francisco (94111) *(P-17234)*
Cooley LLP (PA) ....B....650 843-5000
3175 Hanover St Palo Alto (94304) *(P-17235)*
Cooling Source Inc ....C....925 292-1293
2021 Las Positas Ct # 101 Livermore (94551) *(P-4575)*
Cooling Tower Resources Inc (PA) ....E....707 433-3900
1470 Grove St Healdsburg (95448) *(P-3267)*
Coolisys, Milpitas *Also called Turnongreen Inc (P-6798)*
Coolsculpting, Pleasanton *Also called Zeltiq Aesthetics Inc (P-7064)*
Cooltouch, Roseville *Also called New Star Lasers Inc (P-7117)*
Cooman, Lynn W Jr, Merced *Also called Merced Orthopedic Med Group (P-15533)*
Cooper Cameron Valves, Redding *Also called Cameron International Corp (P-5045)*
Cooper Companies Inc (PA) ....A....925 460-3600
6101 Bollinger Canyon Rd # 5 San Ramon (94583) *(P-7138)*
Cooper Medical Inc (HQ) ....D....925 460-3600
6140 Stnrdge Mall Rd Ste Pleasanton (94588) *(P-6963)*
Cooper Software, Inc., San Francisco *Also called Designit North America Inc (P-12384)*
Cooper Thorne & Associates Inc ....E....916 638-0919
3233 Monier Cir Ste 1 Rancho Cordova (95742) *(P-18675)*
Cooper Vali & Associates Inc (HQ) ....D....510 446-8301
1850 Gateway Blvd Ste 100 Concord (94520) *(P-18676)*
Cooper White & Cooper LLP (PA) ....C....415 433-1900
201 California St Fl 17 San Francisco (94111) *(P-17236)*
Cooperative Personnel Services (PA) ....C....916 263-3600
2450 Del Paso Rd Ste 220 Sacramento (95834) *(P-19481)*
Coordnted Rsrces Inc San Frncs ....E....415 989-0773
130 Sutter St Fl 3 San Francisco (94104) *(P-8493)*
Coors Brewing Company ....E....916 786-2666
3001 Douglas Blvd Ste 200 Roseville (95661) *(P-2476)*
Cope Manufacturing Co, Acampo *Also called Engineered Automation LLC (P-5520)*
Copia The Amrcn Ctr For Wine F ....E....707 259-1600
500 1st St NAPA (94559) *(P-18267)*
Copper Harbor Company Inc ....F....510 639-4670
2300 Davis St San Leandro (94577) *(P-4158)*

ALPHABETIC SECTION County of Alameda

Copper River Country Club LP (PA) ....E....559 434-5200
2140 E Clubhouse Dr Fresno (93730) *(P-15077)*

Copperfields Books Inc (PA) ....E....707 823-8991
139 Edman Way Sebastopol (95472) *(P-10384)*

Copperflds Petaluma Gold Bkstr, Sebastopol *Also called Copperfields Books Inc (P-10384)*

Coppertower Family Medical Ctr ....E....707 894-4229
100 W 3rd St Cloverdale (95425) *(P-15366)*

Copy Rite, Danville *Also called Razvi Inc (P-13751)*

Copymat, San Francisco *Also called Digital Mania Inc (P-3640)*

Cora Cmnty Ovrcming Rltnship A ....E....650 652-0800
2211 Palm Ave San Mateo (94403) *(P-17507)*

Coraid Inc (PA) ....D....650 517-9300
255 Shoreline Dr Ste 650 Redwood City (94065) *(P-5284)*

Coral Reef Motel & Suites, Alameda *Also called Coral Reef Motel LLC (P-11034)*

Coral Reef Motel LLC ....E....510 521-2330
400 Park St Alameda (94501) *(P-11034)*

Coraltree Inc ....E....408 215-1441
6120 Hellyer Ave Ste 100 San Jose (95138) *(P-13093)*

Coram Halthcare Corp Nthrn Cal ....A....415 292-6811
3160 Corporate Pl Hayward (94545) *(P-16872)*

Corbin Willits Systems Inc ....F....510 979-5600
3755 Washington Blvd # 204 Fremont (94538) *(P-12355)*

Corbion Biotech Inc (HQ) ....E....650 780-4777
1 Tower Pl Ste 600 South San Francisco (94080) *(P-2886)*

Corcept Therapeutics Inc ....C....650 327-3270
149 Commonwealth Dr Menlo Park (94025) *(P-3885)*

Cord Blood Donor Foundation ....E....650 635-1420
1200 Bayhill Dr Ste 301 San Bruno (94066) *(P-18410)*

Cordelia Winery LLC (PA) ....E....707 286-1764
2650 Cordelia Rd Fairfield (94534) *(P-14235)*

Cordevalle Golf Club LLC ....A....408 695-4500
1 Cordevalle Club Dr San Martin (95046) *(P-15078)*

Cordis Corporation ....E....408 273-3700
5452 Betsy Ross Dr Santa Clara (95054) *(P-6964)*

Cordova Printed Circuits Inc ....F....408 942-1100
1648 Watson Ct Milpitas (95035) *(P-5924)*

Core Diagnostics Inc ....F....650 561-4176
3535 Breakwater Ave Hayward (94545) *(P-4019)*

Core Group, The, Milpitas *Also called Tcg Builders Inc (P-971)*

Core Medical Clinic Inc ....E....916 796-0020
3990 Industrial Blvd West Sacramento (95691) *(P-17005)*

Core Mobility Inc (PA) ....E....650 603-6600
2023 Stierlin Ct 2 Mountain View (94043) *(P-12356)*

Core Systems Incorporated ....E....510 933-2300
47757 Warm Springs Blvd Fremont (94539) *(P-6088)*

Core+data Corporation ....E....510 540-0168
37 Roble Rd Berkeley (94705) *(P-7943)*

Core-Mark Holding Company Inc ....E....866 791-4210
2959 Thomas Pl Ste 150 West Sacramento (95691) *(P-9268)*

Corelogic Inc ....E....714 250-6400
201 Spear St Fl 4 San Francisco (94105) *(P-10524)*

Corelogic Inc ....D....916 431-2146
11010 White Rock Rd Rancho Cordova (95670) *(P-11833)*

Corelogic Inc ....E....925 676-0225
555 12th St Ste 1100 Oakland (94607) *(P-14236)*

Corelogic Dorado, Oakland *Also called Dorado Network Systems Corp (P-13122)*

Corelogic Info Solutions, Rancho Cordova *Also called Corelogic Inc (P-11833)*

Coreos LLC ....D....888 733-4281
101 New Montgomery St # 5 San Francisco (94105) *(P-12357)*

Coretech Fitness, San Francisco *Also called Tempo Interactive Inc (P-14980)*

Corinthian Intl Prkg Svcs Inc ....B....408 867-7275
19925 Stevns Crk Blvd Cupertino (95014) *(P-14125)*

Corinthian Parking Services, Cupertino *Also called Corinthian Intl Prkg Svcs Inc (P-14125)*

Corinthian Realty LLC ....D....510 487-8653
3902 Smith St Union City (94587) *(P-10525)*

Cork Supply Usa Inc ....E....707 746-0353
531 Stone Rd Benicia (94510) *(P-9652)*

Corn Products Development Inc (HQ) ....A....209 982-1920
1021 Industrial Dr Stockton (95206) *(P-2331)*

Cornami Inc ....E....408 337-0070
300 Orchard Cy Dr Ste 131 Campbell (95008) *(P-19482)*

Cornell Hotel, San Francisco *Also called Claude Lambert (P-11014)*

Cornerstone Cnsulting Tech Inc ....E....415 705-7800
241 5th St San Francisco (94103) *(P-19752)*

Cornerstone Concilium Inc ....E....415 705-7800
241 5th St San Francisco (94103) *(P-19483)*

Cornerstone Hotel Management (HQ) ....D....415 397-5572
222 Kearny St Ste 200 San Francisco (94108) *(P-19320)*

Cornerstone Research Inc ....E....617 927-3000
353 Sacramento St Ste 19 San Francisco (94111) *(P-19753)*

Cornerstone Research Inc (PA) ....D....650 853-1660
1000 El Camino Real # 250 Menlo Park (94025) *(P-19754)*

Cornerstone Research Inc ....D....415 229-8100
2 Embarcadero Ctr Fl 20 San Francisco (94111) *(P-19755)*

Cornerstone Select Bldrs Inc ....E....510 490-7911
5542 Brisa St Ste F Livermore (94550) *(P-627)*

Corning Head Start Center, Corning *Also called Northern Cal Child Dev Inc (P-17658)*

Coronado YMCA, Richmond *Also called Young MNS Chrstn Assn of E Bay (P-18502)*

Corovan ....E....415 934-1600
901 16th St San Francisco (94107) *(P-14237)*

Corp Couch, San Francisco *Also called Corporatecouch (P-6089)*

Corporate Construction Svcs, Sacramento *Also called Cccs Inc (P-1024)*

Corporate Interior Solutions ....E....510 670-8800
25546 Seaboard Ln Hayward (94545) *(P-2024)*

Corporate Sign Systems Inc ....E....408 292-1600
2464 De La Cruz Blvd Santa Clara (95050) *(P-7225)*

Corporatecouch ....E....415 312-6078
260 Vicente St San Francisco (94127) *(P-6089)*

Corportion of Fine Arts Mseums (PA) ....A....415 750-3600
50 Hagiwara Tea Garden Dr San Francisco (94118) *(P-18268)*

Corr, Grass Valley *Also called Granite Wellness Centers (P-17020)*

Corralitos Market & Sausage Co ....E....831 722-2633
569 Corralitos Rd Watsonville (95076) *(P-2116)*

Corrugated Packaging Pdts Inc ....E....650 615-9180
21615 Hesperian Blvd B Hayward (94541) *(P-3357)*

Corsair Gaming Inc (PA) ....B....510 657-8747
47100 Bayside Pkwy Fremont (94538) *(P-5360)*

Corsair Memory Inc ....C....510 657-8747
47100 Bayside Pkwy Fremont (94538) *(P-6090)*

Corsair Memory Inc (HQ) ....C....510 657-8747
47100 Bayside Pkwy Fremont (94538) *(P-6091)*

Cort Yard Creamery Inc ....E....916 729-4021
7910 Antelope Rd Citrus Heights (95610) *(P-9446)*

Cortec Precision Shtmtl Inc (PA) ....C....408 278-8540
2231 Will Wool Dr San Jose (95112) *(P-4750)*

Cortexyme Inc (PA) ....F....415 910-5717
269 E Grand Ave South San Francisco (94080) *(P-4043)*

Cortina Systems Inc (HQ) ....C....408 481-2300
2953 Bunker Hill Ln # 300 Santa Clara (95054) *(P-6092)*

Cortlandt Liquidating LLC ....D....831 338-4500
13117 Highway 9 Boulder Creek (95006) *(P-10526)*

Corvus Pharmaceuticals Inc ....D....650 900-4520
863 Mitten Rd Ste 102 Burlingame (94010) *(P-3886)*

Cosco Fire Protection Inc ....D....925 455-2751
7455 Longard Rd Livermore (94551) *(P-1486)*

Cosco Fire Protection Inc ....E....916 652-2210
4320 Anthony Ct Ste 8 Rocklin (95677) *(P-1242)*

Cosco Fire Protection Inc ....E....559 275-3795
4223 W Srra Mdre Ave # 108 Fresno (93722) *(P-1243)*

Cosentino Signature Wineries ....E....707 921-2809
7415 St Helena Hwy Yountville (94599) *(P-2539)*

Cosentino Winery, Yountville *Also called Cosentino Signature Wineries (P-2539)*

Cosmo Import & Export LLC ....E....916 209-5500
3771 Channel Dr West Sacramento (95691) *(P-3294)*

Costa View Farms ....E....559 675-3131
16800 Road 15 Madera (93637) *(P-209)*

Costa View Farms Shop, Madera *Also called Costa View Farms (P-209)*

Costal Brands, Manteca *Also called Delicato Vineyards LLC (P-2548)*

Costanoa, Pescadero *Also called King-Reynolds Ventures LLC (P-14317)*

Costco Depot 179, Tracy *Also called Costco Wholesale Corporation (P-7688)*

Costco Wholesale Corporation ....B....209 835-5222
25501 S Gateway Blvd Tracy (95377) *(P-7688)*

Cosumnes Community Svcs Dst ....B....916 405-7150
9355 E Stockton Blvd Elk Grove (95624) *(P-15200)*

Cosyns Farms ....E....559 674-6283
15310 Road 19 Madera (93637) *(P-86)*

Cotchett Pitre & McCarthy LLP ....E....650 697-6000
840 Malcolm Rd Ste 200 Burlingame (94010) *(P-17237)*

Cothera Biopharma Inc ....E....510 364-1930
1960 Noel Dr Los Altos (94024) *(P-3887)*

COTS, Petaluma *Also called Committee On Shelterless (P-17491)*

Couch Distributing Company Inc ....C....831 724-0649
104 Lee Rd Watsonville (95076) *(P-9548)*

Couchbase Inc (PA) ....A....650 417-7500
3250 Olcott St Santa Clara (95054) *(P-12358)*

Coughran Mechanical Svcs Inc ....E....707 374-2100
3053 Liberty Island Rd Rio Vista (94571) *(P-5496)*

Coulter Forge Technology Inc ....F....510 420-3500
1494 67th St Emeryville (94608) *(P-4876)*

Coulter Steel and Forge, Emeryville *Also called Coulter Forge Technology Inc (P-4876)*

Counter Hospitality Group LLC ....D....559 228-9735
8398 N Fresno St Ste 101 Fresno (93720) *(P-13094)*

Countertop Designs Inc ....D....916 929-4562
1522 Silica Ave Sacramento (95815) *(P-2025)*

Countis Industries Inc ....E....530 272-8334
12295 Charles Dr Grass Valley (95945) *(P-4407)*

Country Almanac, Palo Alto *Also called Embarcadero Publishing Company (P-3435)*

Country Builders Inc ....C....925 373-1020
5915 Graham Ct Livermore (94550) *(P-740)*

Country Builders Construction, Livermore *Also called Country Builders Inc (P-740)*

Country Club Lanes, Sacramento *Also called Pinsetters Inc (P-14897)*

Country Connection Inc (PA) ....F....530 589-5176
2805 Richter Ave Oroville (95966) *(P-3234)*

Country House ....E....530 342-7002
966 Kovak Ct Chico (95973) *(P-18082)*

Country House & Commons, Chico *Also called Country House (P-18082)*

Country Villa Service Corp ....D....209 723-2911
510 W 26th St Merced (95340) *(P-17508)*

Country Vlla Rvrview Rhab Hlth, Susanville *Also called CF Susanville LLC (P-15957)*

Countryman Associates Inc ....F....650 364-9988
195 Constitution Dr Menlo Park (94025) *(P-5753)*

Countryside Mushrooms Inc ....E....408 683-2748
11300 Center Ave Gilroy (95020) *(P-142)*

County Building Materials Inc ....D....408 274-4920
2927 S King Rd San Jose (95122) *(P-8539)*

County Engineers Assn Cal ....D....707 762-3492
120 Round Ct Petaluma (94952) *(P-18677)*

County of Alameda ....E....510 346-1300
2060 Fairmont Dr San Leandro (94578) *(P-16732)*

County of Alameda ....D....510 272-6222
1401 Lakeside Dr Ste 802 Oakland (94612) *(P-17238)*

County of Alameda ....D....510 895-4200
15400 Foothill Blvd San Leandro (94578) *(P-16338)*

County of Alameda ....D....510 437-4190
1411 E 31st St Oakland (94602) *(P-16873)*

ALPHABETIC

County of Contra Costa ....C....925 370-5000
2500 Alhambra Ave Martinez (94553) ***(P-16339)***
County of Contra Costa ....E....510 463-7325
50 Douglas Dr Martinez (94553) ***(P-17127)***
County of El Dorado, Placerville *Also called El Dorado County Health Dept* ***(P-15388)***
County of Humboldt ....E....707 839-5402
3561 Boeing Ave Eureka (95501) ***(P-7770)***
County of Los Angeles ....E....559 675-7739
209 W Yosemite Ave Madera (93637) ***(P-17509)***
County of Medocina Dept of Mnt, Ukiah *Also called County of Mendocino* ***(P-17006)***
County of Mendocino ....E....707 463-4363
340 Lake Mendocino Dr Ukiah (95482) ***(P-7771)***
County of Mendocino ....C....707 463-4396
860a N Bush St Ukiah (95482) ***(P-17006)***
County of Placer ....D....916 791-7059
6900 Eureka Rd Granite Bay (95746) ***(P-17510)***
County of Sacramento ....E....916 875-3412
3341 Power Inn Rd Ste 101 Sacramento (95826) ***(P-17916)***
County of Sacramento ....E....916 874-9670
2921 Stockton Blvd Sacramento (95817) ***(P-17128)***
County of Sacramento ....D....916 875-2711
9700 Goethe Rd Ste D Sacramento (95827) ***(P-1081)***
County of Sacramento ....C....916 875-0900
9616 Micron Ave Ste 750 Sacramento (95827) ***(P-15962)***
County of Sacramento ....E....916 875-5701
7001 East Pkwy A Sacramento (95823) ***(P-15367)***
County of Sacramento ....D....916 874-1953
1000 River Walk Way Carmichael (95608) ***(P-17239)***
County of Sacramento ....E....916 575-4653
4103 Eagles Nest Rd Sacramento (95830) ***(P-14991)***
County of Sacramento ....D....916 874-0912
6900 Airport Blvd Sacramento (95837) ***(P-7772)***
County of Sacramento ....E....916 482-9792
6341 Tarshes Dr Carmichael (95608) ***(P-14992)***
County of San Benito ....D....831 389-4591
25820 Airline Hwy Paicines (95043) ***(P-5227)***
County of San Joaquin ....E....209 468-3460
1601 E Hazelton Ave Stockton (95205) ***(P-16777)***
County of San Joaquin ....E....209 468-6280
500 W Hospital Rd French Camp (95231) ***(P-17007)***
County of San Joaquin ....E....209 468-8750
1212 N California St Stockton (95202) ***(P-17008)***
County of San Joaquin ....D....209 468-3123
1810 E Hazelton Ave Stockton (95205) ***(P-14238)***
County of San Joaquin ....D....209 468-3720
1201 N El Dorado St Stockton (95202) ***(P-17511)***
County of San Joaquin ....D....209 468-3357
4520 W Eight Mile Rd Stockton (95209) ***(P-11937)***
County of San Joaquin ....D....209 468-3090
1702 E Scotts Ave Stockton (95205) ***(P-1094)***
County of San Joaquin ....E....209 468-2385
1414 N California St Stockton (95202) ***(P-15368)***
County of San Joaquin ....C....209 468-3500
56 S Lincoln St Stockton (95203) ***(P-17809)***
County of San Joaquin ....E....209 468-3983
1414 N California St Fl 1 Stockton (95202) ***(P-15369)***
County of San Joaquin ....D....209 948-3612
P.O. Box 7838 Stockton (95267) ***(P-17009)***
County of San Mateo ....A....650 208-3480
222 W 39th Ave San Mateo (94403) ***(P-15370)***
County of Solano ....D....707 784-6570
740 Beck Ave Fairfield (94533) ***(P-17512)***
County of Solano ....E....707 553-5029
355 Tuolumne St Vallejo (94590) ***(P-16778)***
County of Solano ....D....707 784-2080
2101 Courage Dr Fairfield (94533) ***(P-16179)***
County of Sonoma ....E....707 433-0728
3333 Skaggs Springs Rd Geyserville (95441) ***(P-15889)***
County of Sonoma ....E....707 565-4963
2350 Professional Dr Santa Rosa (95403) ***(P-16874)***
County of Sonoma ....D....707 565-4711
1450 Neotomas Ave Ste 200 Santa Rosa (95405) ***(P-17513)***
County of Sonoma ....C....707 823-8511
501 Petaluma Ave Sebastopol (95472) ***(P-16340)***
County of Sonoma ....D....707 565-4850
2227 Capricorn Way # 207 Santa Rosa (95407) ***(P-16733)***
County of Stanislaus ....C....209 525-7000
830 Scenic Dr Modesto (95350) ***(P-16341)***
County of Stanislaus ....E....209 522-4098
2000 Santa Fe Ave Modesto (95357) ***(P-8397)***
County of Stanislaus ....E....209 558-8828
830 Scenic Dr Modesto (95350) ***(P-17514)***
County of Stanislaus ....E....209 567-4120
801 11th St Modesto (95354) ***(P-17515)***
County of Stanislaus ....E....209 558-7377
108 Campus Way Modesto (95350) ***(P-17516)***
County of Stanislaus ....D....209 558-7377
108 Campus Way Modesto (95350) ***(P-17129)***
County of Stanislaus ....E....209 558-9675
251 E Hackett Rd Modesto (95358) ***(P-17517)***
County of Stanislaus ....D....209 558-5312
1209 Woodrow Ave Ste B10 Modesto (95350) ***(P-15371)***
County of Stanislaus ....D....209 525-7423
800 Scenic Dr Bldg B Modesto (95350) ***(P-17010)***
County of Stanislaus ....E....209 558-2500
108 Campus Way Modesto (95350) ***(P-17518)***
County of Stanislaus ....E....209 558-2100
251 E Hackett Rd Ste 2 Modesto (95358) ***(P-17810)***
County of Stanislaus ....E....209 558-8118
1325 Sonoma Ave Modesto (95355) ***(P-12168)***
County of Stanislaus ....D....209 664-8044
2101 Geer Rd Ste 120 Turlock (95382) ***(P-17011)***
County of Stanislaus ....E....209 525-5400
2215 Blue Gum Ave Modesto (95358) ***(P-18083)***
County of Yuba ....D....530 741-6275
209 6th St Marysville (95901) ***(P-17519)***
County of Yuba ....D....530 749-6471
5730 Packard Ave Ste 100 Marysville (95901) ***(P-17520)***
County of Yuba ....D....530 749-7550
215 5th St Ste 154 Marysville (95901) ***(P-17521)***
County of Yuba ....D....530 741-6371
1023 14th St Marysville (95901) ***(P-18084)***
County of Yuba ....D....530 749-7770
215 5th St Ste 152 Marysville (95901) ***(P-17240)***
County Quarry Products ....E....925 682-0707
5501 Imhoff Pl Martinez (94553) ***(P-8320)***
Coupa Software Incorporated (PA) ....A....650 931-3200
1855 S Grant St San Mateo (94402) ***(P-13095)***
Courage Production LLC ....D....707 422-6300
2475 Courage Dr Fairfield (94533) ***(P-2117)***
Course At Wente Vineyards, The, Livermore *Also called Cresta Blanca Golf LLC* ***(P-14995)***
Courseco Inc ....B....707 255-4333
2295 Streblow Dr NAPA (94558) ***(P-14993)***
Coursera Inc (PA) ....A....650 963-9884
381 E Evelyn Ave Mountain View (94041) ***(P-13096)***
Court House Athletic Club (PA) ....E....530 885-1964
2514 Bell Rd Auburn (95603) ***(P-14941)***
Court Street Surgery Center ....E....530 246-4444
2184 Court St Redding (96001) ***(P-15372)***
Courtesy Motors Auto Ctr Inc ....D....530 345-9444
2520 Cohasset Rd Chico (95973) ***(P-14555)***
Courtesy Moving and Storage, Fresno *Also called Rich Harvest Inc* ***(P-112)***
Courtesy Security Inc ....D....888 572-5545
2252 Erie Ct Tracy (95304) ***(P-14047)***
Courtney Aviation Inc ....E....209 532-2345
10747 Airport Rd Columbia (95310) ***(P-534)***
Courtside Club, Los Gatos *Also called Courtside Tennis Club* ***(P-15079)***
Courtside Tennis Club ....D....408 395-7111
14675 Winchester Blvd Los Gatos (95032) ***(P-15079)***
Courtyard ....D....530 790-3050
1240 Williams Way Apt 4 Yuba City (95991) ***(P-18085)***
Courtyard By Marriott, Cupertino *Also called Courtyard Management Corp* ***(P-11037)***
Courtyard By Marriott, Richmond *Also called Pacific Hotel Management LLC* ***(P-11347)***
Courtyard By Marriott, Fresno *Also called Courtyard Management Corp* ***(P-11038)***
Courtyard By Marriott, San Jose *Also called Sontesta Select San Jose Arprt* ***(P-11493)***
Courtyard By Marriott, Larkspur *Also called Courtyard Management Corp* ***(P-11039)***
Courtyard By Marriott, Foster City *Also called Courtyard Management Corp* ***(P-11040)***
Courtyard By Marriott ....E....510 568-7600
350 Hegenberger Rd Oakland (94621) ***(P-11035)***
Courtyard By Marriott ....C....925 866-2900
18090 San Ramon Vly Blvd San Ramon (94583) ***(P-11036)***
Courtyard By Marriott Merced, Merced *Also called Maxs Partnership A Gen Partnr* ***(P-11290)***
Courtyard By Marriott Stockton, Stockton *Also called Castlehill Properties Inc* ***(P-10996)***
Courtyard By Mrrott San Frncsc, San Francisco *Also called Rlj C San Francisco Lessee LP* ***(P-11413)***
Courtyard By Mrrott San Jose C, Campbell *Also called Campbell Hhg Hotel Dev LLP* ***(P-10986)***
Courtyard Care Center, San Jose *Also called SSC San Jose Operating Co LP* ***(P-16127)***
Courtyard Chico, Chico *Also called Chico Lodging LLC* ***(P-11004)***
Courtyard Folsom, Folsom *Also called Cni Thl Ops LLC* ***(P-11025)***
Courtyard Fremont Silicon Vly, Fremont *Also called Cmp I Fremont Owner LP* ***(P-11018)***
Courtyard Healthcare, Davis *Also called Covenant Care Courtyard LLC* ***(P-15973)***
Courtyard Little Chico Creek, Chico *Also called Hignell Incorporated* ***(P-10704)***
Courtyard Management Corp ....E....408 252-9100
10605 N Wolfe Rd Cupertino (95014) ***(P-11037)***
Courtyard Management Corp ....D....559 221-6000
140 E Shaw Ave Fresno (93710) ***(P-11038)***
Courtyard Management Corp ....D....415 925-1800
2500 Larkspur Landing Cir Larkspur (94939) ***(P-11039)***
Courtyard Management Corp ....E....650 377-0600
550 Shell Blvd Foster City (94404) ***(P-11040)***
Courtyard Marriott, Fairfield *Also called Embassy Investments LLC* ***(P-11080)***
Courtyard Morgan Hill, Morgan Hill *Also called Cni Thl Ops LLC* ***(P-11023)***
Courtyard Oakland Downtown, Oakland *Also called Cy Oakland Operator LLC* ***(P-11044)***
Courtyard Roseville 2, Roseville *Also called Cni Thl Ops LLC* ***(P-11024)***
Courtyard Sacramento-Midtown, Sacramento *Also called Cy Sac Operator LLC* ***(P-11045)***
Covad Communications Group Inc (HQ) ....C....408 952-6400
6800 Koll Center Pkwy # 20 Pleasanton (94566) ***(P-7944)***
Covanta Stanislaus Inc ....E....209 837-4423
4040 Fink Rd Crows Landing (95313) ***(P-8321)***
Covell Gardens ....D....530 756-0700
1111 Alvarado Ave Ofc Davis (95616) ***(P-18086)***
Covello Group Inc ....E....925 933-2300
1660 Olympic Blvd Ste 300 Walnut Creek (94596) ***(P-8280)***
Covenant Aviation Security LLC ....A....650 219-3473
1000 Marina Blvd Ste 100 Brisbane (94005) ***(P-14048)***
Covenant Care LLC ....D....831 476-0770
1935 Wharf Rd Capitola (95010) ***(P-15963)***
Covenant Care California LLC ....D....209 477-5252
9289 Branstetter Pl Stockton (95209) ***(P-15964)***
Covenant Care California LLC ....D....415 327-0511
911 Bryant St Palo Alto (94301) ***(P-15965)***
Covenant Care California LLC ....D....408 248-3736
410 N Winchester Blvd Santa Clara (95050) ***(P-15966)***
Covenant Care California LLC ....D....510 261-2628
2124 57th Ave Oakland (94621) ***(P-15967)***

Covenant Care California LLC ....D....559 251-8463
577 S Peach Ave Fresno (93727) *(P-15968)*
Covenant Care California LLC ....D....209 667-8409
1101 E Tuolumne Rd Turlock (95382) *(P-16180)*
Covenant Care California LLC ....D....916 391-6011
6821 24th St Sacramento (95822) *(P-15969)*
Covenant Care California LLC ....D....209 632-3821
1111 E Tuolumne Rd Turlock (95382) *(P-15970)*
Covenant Care California LLC ....D....408 842-9311
8170 Murray Ave Gilroy (95020) *(P-15971)*
Covenant Care California LLC ....E....209 521-2094
3620 Dale Rd Ste B Modesto (95356) *(P-16228)*
Covenant Care California LLC ....D....650 964-0543
1949 Grant Rd Mountain View (94040) *(P-16342)*
Covenant Care California LLC ....D....650 941-5255
809 Fremont Ave Los Altos (94024) *(P-15972)*
Covenant Care Courtyard LLC ....C....530 756-1800
1850 E 8th St Davis (95616) *(P-15973)*
Covenant Living West ....D....209 667-5600
1801 N Olive Ave Turlock (95382) *(P-16343)*
Coventina-Gse Jv LLC ....E....813 509-0669
6950 Preston Ave Livermore (94551) *(P-1095)*
Coventry Cove Apartments, Fresno *Also called Buckingham Property Management* *(P-11708)*
Coveo Software Corp ....D....800 635-5476
44 Montgomery St San Francisco (94104) *(P-12359)*
Coverity LLC (HQ) ....D....415 321-5200
185 Berry St Ste 6500 San Francisco (94107) *(P-12360)*
Covey Auto Express Inc (PA) ....C....253 826-0461
1444 El Pinal Dr Stockton (95205) *(P-14659)*
Covia Affordable Communities ....C....925 956-7400
2185 N Calif Blvd Ste 215 Walnut Creek (94596) *(P-17522)*
Covia Communities ....C....510 835-4700
100 Bay Pl Ofc Oakland (94610) *(P-18087)*
Covia Communities ....C....408 354-0211
110 Wood Rd Ofc Los Gatos (95030) *(P-18088)*
Covia Communities ....C....707 538-8400
5555 Montgomery Dr Santa Rosa (95409) *(P-18089)*
Covia Communities ....C....415 776-0500
1661 Pine St Apt 911 San Francisco (94109) *(P-18090)*
Covidien, Sunnyvale *Also called Barrx Medical Inc* *(P-6951)*
Covidien Holding Inc ....C....408 585-7700
540 Oakmead Pkwy Sunnyvale (94085) *(P-6965)*
Covidien Holding Inc ....C....510 456-1500
6531 Dumbarton Cir Fremont (94555) *(P-6966)*
Cowboy Concrete Pumping LLC (PA) ....E....925 350-2700
5082 Fernwood Ct Oakley (94561) *(P-1861)*
Cowell Homeowners Assn Inc (PA) ....D....925 825-0250
4498 Lawson Ct Concord (94521) *(P-18411)*
Cowell Student Health Center, Davis *Also called University California Davis* *(P-15779)*
Cox & Cox Construction Inc ....E....530 243-6016
8837 Airport Rd Ste A Redding (96002) *(P-1096)*
Cox & Perez ....E....209 894-3741
5807 Highway 33 Westley (95387) *(P-153)*
Cox & Perez Farms, Westley *Also called Cox & Perez* *(P-153)*
Cox Enterprises Inc ....E....559 432-3947
1549 W Menlo Ave Fresno (93711) *(P-8060)*
Cox Wtton Grffin Hnsen Plos LL ....D....415 438-4600
900 Front St San Francisco (94111) *(P-17241)*
Coyne & Blanchard Inc ....D....650 326-6040
110 Constitution Dr Menlo Park (94025) *(P-3495)*
Coyote Creek Consulting Inc ....E....408 383-9200
1057 Cochrane Rd Morgan Hill (95037) *(P-13875)*
Coyote Creek Golf Club ....E....408 463-1400
1 Coyote Creek Golf Dr Morgan Hill (95037) *(P-14994)*
Cozad Trailer Sales LLC ....D....209 931-3000
4907 E Waterloo Rd Stockton (95215) *(P-6601)*
CP Employer Inc (PA) ....C....415 273-2900
1000 Sansome St Fl 1 San Francisco (94111) *(P-741)*
CP Multifamily Cnstr Cal Inc ....C....415 273-2900
1000 Sansome St Fl 1 San Francisco (94111) *(P-742)*
CP Opco LLC ....D....707 253-2332
22674 Broadway A Sonoma (95476) *(P-12037)*
CP Opco LLC ....D....650 652-0300
22674 Broadway A Sonoma (95476) *(P-12038)*
CP Opco LLC ....E....916 444-6120
22674 Broadway A Sonoma (95476) *(P-12039)*
Cpacket Networks Inc ....E....650 969-9500
2130 Gold St 200 San Jose (95002) *(P-5361)*
CPI, Palo Alto *Also called Communications & Pwr Inds LLC* *(P-5832)*
CPI, Palo Alto *Also called Communications & Pwr Inds LLC* *(P-5900)*
CPI International ....D....707 521-6327
5580 Skylane Blvd Santa Rosa (95403) *(P-8801)*
CPI International Holding Corp ....C....650 846-2900
811 Hansen Way Palo Alto (94304) *(P-6411)*
CPI International Holding LLC ....D....650 846-2900
811 Hansen Way Palo Alto (94304) *(P-6412)*
CPI Satcom & Antenna Tech Inc ....D....408 955-1900
2205 Fortune Dr San Jose (95131) *(P-5834)*
CPI Subsidiary Holdings LLC (HQ) ....C....650 846-2900
811 Hansen Way Palo Alto (94304) *(P-6413)*
Cpk Manufacturing Inc ....F....408 971-4019
2188 Del Franco St Ste 70 San Jose (95131) *(P-5497)*
CPM Associates Inc ....E....415 543-6515
65 Mccoppin St San Francisco (94103) *(P-19321)*
Cpmc, San Francisco *Also called Sutter Health* *(P-16585)*
Cpmc Mission Bernal Campus, San Francisco *Also called Sutter Health* *(P-16632)*
Cpmc Van Ness Campus, San Francisco *Also called Sutter Health* *(P-16616)*
Cpp Inc ....F....650 969-8901
185 N Wolfe Rd Sunnyvale (94086) *(P-3531)*
Cprime Inc (HQ) ....D....650 931-1650
107 S B St Ste 200 San Mateo (94401) *(P-19484)*
CPS, San Mateo *Also called Kotobuki-Ya Inc* *(P-7338)*
CPS Hr Consulting, Sacramento *Also called Cooperative Personnel Services* *(P-19481)*
CPS Security Solutions Inc ....D....510 806-7227
799 Fletcher Ln Ste 201 Hayward (94544) *(P-14049)*
Cpsg, Folsom *Also called Computer Power Sftwr Group Inc* *(P-12353)*
Cpu Technology Inc ....D....925 398-7659
5753 W Las Positas Blvd Pleasanton (94588) *(P-19047)*
Cr Drywall, San Jose *Also called C R S Drywall Inc* *(P-1663)*
Crafton Carton ....E....510 441-5985
31790 Hayman St Hayward (94544) *(P-3370)*
Craftsman Printing, San Jose *Also called United Craftsmen Priniting* *(P-3707)*
Craigo Investments Inc ....E....559 222-9293
2745 W Shaw Ave Ste 120 Fresno (93711) *(P-7226)*
Crain Cutter Company Inc ....D....408 946-6100
1155 Wrigley Way Milpitas (95035) *(P-4615)*
Crane Acquisition Inc ....A....415 922-1666
2700 Geary Blvd San Francisco (94118) *(P-11898)*
Crane Mills ....D....530 824-5427
22938 South Ave Corning (96021) *(P-87)*
Crane Pest Control, San Francisco *Also called Crane Acquisition Inc* *(P-11898)*
Crawford Communications Group ....E....408 343-0200
3190 S Bascom Ave Ste 230 San Jose (95124) *(P-19485)*
Cray Cluster Solutions, San Jose *Also called Appro International Inc* *(P-5282)*
CRAYCROFT YOUTH CENTER, Fresno *Also called Rescue Children Inc* *(P-17690)*
Crazy Maple Studio Inc (PA) ....E....972 757-1283
1277 Borregas Ave Ste A Sunnyvale (94089) *(P-3564)*
CRC Health Corporate (HQ) ....D....408 367-0044
20400 Stevns Crk Blvd Cupertino (95014) *(P-17012)*
CRC Health Group Inc ....D....408 866-8167
256 E Hamilton Ave Ste I Campbell (95008) *(P-17013)*
CRC Health LLC (HQ) ....D....877 272-8668
20400 Stevns Crk Blvd # 600 Cupertino (95014) *(P-16754)*
CRC Roofing Inc ....E....916 362-4373
3774 Bradview Dr Sacramento (95827) *(P-1792)*
Createpros LLC ....C....844 752-7328
4353 N 1st St San Jose (95134) *(P-8905)*
Creation Networks Inc ....F....925 446-4332
1001 Shary Cir Ste 1 Concord (94518) *(P-1487)*
Creation Tech Santa Clara Inc ....D....408 235-7500
2801 Northwestern Pkwy Santa Clara (95051) *(P-5925)*
Creative Alternatives ....C....209 668-9361
2855 Geer Rd Ste A Turlock (95382) *(P-18091)*
Creative Child Care Inc ....B....209 462-2282
17 E Poplar St Stockton (95202) *(P-17917)*
Creative Child Care Inc (PA) ....E....209 941-9100
4719 Quail Lakes Dr G-237 Stockton (95207) *(P-17918)*
Creative Design Interiors Inc (PA) ....D....916 641-1121
737 Del Paso Rd Sacramento (95834) *(P-1767)*
Creative Dmnsions In Dentistry, Castro Valley *Also called Creative Dmnsions In Dentistry* *(P-15829)*
Creative Dmnsions In Dentistry (PA) ....E....510 881-8010
20265 Lake Chabot Rd Castro Valley (94546) *(P-15829)*
Creative Energy Foods Inc ....D....510 638-8668
9957 Medford Ave Ste 4 Oakland (94603) *(P-9447)*
Creative Environments, Sebastopol *Also called North Landscaping Inc* *(P-428)*
Creative Instructional Systems ....E....650 756-4737
79 Florence St Daly City (94014) *(P-17919)*
Creative Labs Inc (HQ) ....C....408 428-6600
1901 Mccarthy Blvd Milpitas (95035) *(P-8685)*
Creative Living Options Inc ....C....916 372-2102
2945 Ramco St Ste 120 West Sacramento (95691) *(P-18092)*
Creative Lrng Ctr Preschool ....E....650 823-1496
2100 Woods Ln Los Altos (94024) *(P-17920)*
Creative Metal Products Corp ....E....408 281-0797
6284 San Ignacio Ave D San Jose (95119) *(P-5498)*
Creative Mfg Solutions Inc ....E....408 327-0600
18400 Sutter Blvd Morgan Hill (95037) *(P-4751)*
Creative Plant Design Inc ....F....408 452-1444
1670 Las Plumas Ave Ste C San Jose (95133) *(P-9630)*
Creative Recrtl Systems Inc ....D....916 638-5375
2377 Gold Meadow Way # 10 Gold River (95670) *(P-9155)*
Creative Security Company Inc ....B....408 295-2600
150 S Autumn St Ste B San Jose (95110) *(P-14050)*
Creative Shower Door Corp ....F....510 623-9000
43652 S Grimmer Blvd Fremont (94538) *(P-4248)*
Creative Wood Products Inc ....C....510 635-5399
900 77th Ave Oakland (94621) *(P-3302)*
Cred-Corp, Jamestown *Also called Chicken Rnch Economic Dev Corp* *(P-3426)*
Credence Id LLC ....E....888 243-5452
2335 Broadway Ste 100 Oakland (94612) *(P-5835)*
Credence Medsystems Inc ....F....844 263-3797
1430 Obrien Dr Ste D Menlo Park (94025) *(P-6967)*
Credit Karma LLC (HQ) ....A....415 510-5059
1100 Broadway Ste 1800 Oakland (94607) *(P-14239)*
Creditors Bureau of California, Fresno *Also called Fresno Credit Bureau* *(P-11822)*
Credo Mobile Inc ....D....415 369-2000
101 Market St Ste 700 San Francisco (94105) *(P-7906)*
Credo Semiconductor Inc ....E....408 664-9329
1600 Technology Dr Fl 5 San Jose (95110) *(P-14240)*
Creekside Center, Stockton *Also called Genesis Healthcare LLC* *(P-16012)*
Creekside Cnvalescent Hosp Inc ....E....707 544-7750
850 Sonoma Ave Santa Rosa (95404) *(P-15974)*
Creekside Convalescent Hosp, Santa Rosa *Also called Nadhan Inc* *(P-16064)*

ALPHABETIC

Creekside Counseling Ctr Inc..........E.......530 722-9957
1170 Industrial St Redding (96002) ***(P-17523)***
Creekside Farming Company..........E.......559 674-9999
30814 Avenue 9 Madera (93637) ***(P-370)***
Creekside Healthcare Center, San Pablo *Also called Summerville Senior Living Inc* ***(P-16132)***
Creekside Healthcare Ctr..........E.......510 235-5514
1900 Church Ln San Pablo (94806) ***(P-15975)***
Creekside Inn In Palo Alto, Palo Alto *Also called Interntional Ht Assoc No 3 LLC* ***(P-11196)***
Creekside Rhblttion Bhvral HLT..........D.......707 524-7030
850 Sonoma Ave Santa Rosa (95404) ***(P-17014)***
Creganna - Tactx Medical, Campbell *Also called Tactx Medical Inc* ***(P-7047)***
Creganna Medical Devices Inc (HQ)..........**E.......408 364-7100**
1353 Dell Ave Campbell (95008) ***(P-6968)***
Creganna-Tactx Medical, Campbell *Also called Creganna Medical Devices Inc* ***(P-6968)***
Crescent Cy Convalescent Hosp, Crescent City *Also called North Shore Investment Inc* ***(P-16075)***
Crescent Healthcare Inc..........D.......510 264-5454
25901 Industrial Blvd Hayward (94545) ***(P-16875)***
Crescent Healthcare Inc..........D.......707 543-5822
131 Stony Cir Ste 200 Santa Rosa (95401) ***(P-16876)***
Crescent Villa Care Home, Sunnyvale *Also called Canyon House Resthomes Inc* ***(P-18065)***
Cresta Blanca Golf LLC..........D.......925 456-2475
5050 Arroyo Rd Livermore (94550) ***(P-14995)***
Crestmark Millwork Inc..........E.......707 822-4034
5640 West End Rd Arcata (95521) ***(P-3127)***
Crestwood Behavioral Hlth Inc..........B.......209 526-8050
1400 Celeste Dr Modesto (95355) ***(P-16734)***
Crestwood Behavioral Hlth Inc..........D.......559 238-6981
1200 Smith St Kingsburg (93631) ***(P-16229)***
Crestwood Behavioral Hlth Inc..........E.......707 442-5721
2370 Buhne St Eureka (95501) ***(P-16230)***
Crestwood Behavioral Hlth Inc (PA)..........**D.......510 651-1244**
520 Capitol Mall Ste 800 Sacramento (95814) ***(P-16735)***
Crestwood Behavioral Hlth Inc..........C.......408 275-1067
1425 Fruitdale Ave San Jose (95128) ***(P-18093)***
Crestwood Behavioral Hlth Inc..........C.......530 221-0976
3062 Churn Creek Rd Redding (96002) ***(P-18094)***
Crestwood Behavioral Hlth Inc..........B.......510 651-1244
4303 Stevenson Blvd Fremont (94538) ***(P-18095)***
Crestwood Behavioral Hlth Inc..........D.......916 452-1431
2600 Stockton Blvd Sacramento (95817) ***(P-16736)***
Crestwood Behavioral Hlth Inc..........C.......510 793-8383
2171 Mowry Ave Fremont (94538) ***(P-18096)***
Crestwood Behavioral Hlth Inc..........D.......916 452-1431
2600 Stockton Blvd Sacramento (95817) ***(P-16737)***
Crestwood Behavioral Hlth Inc..........E.......408 275-1067
1425 Fruitdale Ave San Jose (95128) ***(P-16738)***
Crestwood Behavioral Hlth Inc..........E.......707 428-1131
2101 Courage Dr Fairfield (94533) ***(P-17524)***
Crestwood Behavioral Hlth Inc..........D.......707 234-2222
2201 Tuolumne St Vallejo (94589) ***(P-16739)***
Crestwood Behavioral Hlth Inc..........D.......415 213-7993
450 Stanyan St Fl 5 San Francisco (94117) ***(P-16231)***
Crestwood Behavioral Hlth Inc..........E.......925 938-8050
550 Blvd Pleasant Hill (94523) ***(P-15976)***
Crestwood Behavioral Hlth Inc..........D.......209 478-5291
7590 Shoreline Dr Stockton (95219) ***(P-16740)***
Crestwood Behavioral Hlth Inc..........E.......916 977-0949
4741 Engle Rd Carmichael (95608) ***(P-16741)***
Cretelligent Inc..........E.......916 288-8177
11344 Coloma Rd Ste 870 Gold River (95670) ***(P-19486)***
Cricket Company LLC..........E.......415 475-4150
68 Leveroni Ct Ste 200 Novato (94949) ***(P-4214)***
Cricket Wireless, Oakland *Also called Tks Wireless Inc* ***(P-7916)***
Crime Prevention Patrol, Sacramento *Also called Wade Casey* ***(P-14110)***
Crimetek Security..........D.......209 668-6208
3448 N Golden State Blvd Turlock (95382) ***(P-14051)***
Crimson Sv LLC (PA)..........**D.......415 970-5800**
601 California St # 1450 San Francisco (94108) ***(P-10775)***
Crimson Wine Group Ltd (PA)..........**C.......800 486-0503**
5901 Silverado Trl NAPA (94558) ***(P-2540)***
Crinklaw Farm Services Inc..........E.......559 897-1077
13837 S Zediker Ave Kingsburg (93631) ***(P-252)***
Crisis Spport Svcs Almeda Cnty..........E.......510 420-2460
6117 Mrtin Lther King Jr Oakland (94609) ***(P-14241)***
Crist Group Inc..........E.......530 661-0700
1324 E Beamer St Woodland (95776) ***(P-5145)***
Critchfield Mechanical Inc..........B.......650 321-7801
4085 Campbell Ave Menlo Park (94025) ***(P-1244)***
Criticall, Folsom *Also called Biddle Consulting Group Inc* ***(P-19730)***
Crittenden Publishing Inc (HQ)..........**D.......415 475-1522**
45 Leveroni Ct Ste 204 Novato (94949) ***(P-3565)***
Criveller California Corp..........F.......707 431-2211
185 Grant Ave Healdsburg (95448) ***(P-5128)***
Crl Systems Inc..........C.......510 351-3500
14798 Wicks Blvd San Leandro (94577) ***(P-5836)***
Crmc, Coalinga *Also called Coalinga Regional Med Ctr Aux* ***(P-16334)***
CROCKER ART MUSEUM, Sacramento *Also called Crocker Art Museum Association* ***(P-18562)***
Crocker Art Museum Association..........D.......916 808-7000
216 O St Sacramento (95814) ***(P-18562)***
Crockett Garbage Service, Richmond *Also called Richmond Sanitary Service Inc* ***(P-14772)***
Crocus Holdings LLC..........D.......916 782-1238
1161 Cirby Way Roseville (95661) ***(P-15977)***
Cromer Clarklift, Oakland *Also called East Bay Clarklift Inc* ***(P-9065)***
Crooks, Jerry C MD, Stockton *Also called Stockton Orthpd Med Group Inc* ***(P-16561)***
Crop Care Associates Inc..........E.......707 258-2998
851 Napa Vly Corp Way Ste NAPA (94558) ***(P-253)***
Cross Install, San Francisco *Also called Crossinstall Inc* ***(P-12362)***
Cross Link Inc..........D.......415 495-3191
50 Pier Bldg C San Francisco (94158) ***(P-7727)***
Cross Match Inc..........C.......650 474-4000
6607 Kaiser Dr Fremont (94555) ***(P-12361)***
Crossbar Inc..........E.......408 884-0281
3200 Patrick Henry Dr # 110 Santa Clara (95054) ***(P-6093)***
Crossing Automation Inc (HQ)..........**A.......510 661-5000**
46702 Bayside Pkwy Fremont (94538) ***(P-9061)***
Crossinstall Inc..........E.......415 425-5929
650 California St Fl 30 San Francisco (94108) ***(P-12362)***
Crosslink Capital Inc..........E.......415 617-1800
2180 Sand Hill Rd Ste 200 Menlo Park (94025) ***(P-10839)***
Crosslink Prof Tax Sltions LLC (PA)..........**D.......209 835-2720**
16916 S Harlan Rd Lathrop (95330) ***(P-12363)***
Crossroad Services Inc..........B.......714 728-3915
2360 Alvarado St San Leandro (94577) ***(P-9653)***
Crossroads Diversfd Svcs Inc..........D.......916 676-2540
7011 Sylvan Rd Ste A Citrus Heights (95610) ***(P-12081)***
Crothall Services Group..........A.......909 991-4887
8190 Murray Ave Gilroy (95020) ***(P-11648)***
CROW CANYON COUNTRY CLUB, Danville *Also called Crow Canyon Management Corp* ***(P-15080)***
Crow Canyon Management Corp..........D.......925 735-5700
711 Silver Lake Dr Danville (94526) ***(P-15080)***
Crowdcircle Inc..........E.......206 853-7560
1810 Gateway Dr Ste 200 San Mateo (94404) ***(P-13097)***
Crowdoptic, San Francisco *Also called Kba2 Inc* ***(P-13260)***
Crowdstrike Inc (HQ)..........**C.......888 512-8906**
150 Mathilda Pl Ste 300 Sunnyvale (94086) ***(P-13876)***
Crowdstrike Holdings Inc (PA)..........**C.......888 512-8906**
150 Mathilda Pl Ste 300 Sunnyvale (94086) ***(P-13098)***
Crown Bay Nrsing Rhblttion Ctr, Alameda *Also called G&R Almeda Healthcare Svcs LLC* ***(P-17587)***
Crown Building Maintenance Co..........B.......916 920-9556
1832 Tribute Rd Ste H Sacramento (95815) ***(P-11938)***
Crown Building Maintenance Co..........B.......303 680-3713
235 Pine St Ste 600 San Francisco (94104) ***(P-11939)***
Crown Building Maintenance Co..........B.......415 546-6534
1143 N Market Blvd Ste 3 Sacramento (95834) ***(P-11940)***
Crown Electric Inc (PA)..........**E.......415 559-7432**
85 Columbia Sq San Francisco (94103) ***(P-1488)***
Crown Energy Services Inc..........A.......415 546-6534
611 Gateway Blvd South San Francisco (94080) ***(P-18678)***
Crown Management Services Inc..........E.......510 537-8470
22660 Main St Hayward (94541) ***(P-11041)***
Crown Mfg Co Inc..........E.......510 742-8800
37625 Sycamore St Newark (94560) ***(P-4271)***
Crown Micro, Fremont *Also called Bold Data Technology Inc* ***(P-5243)***
Crown Painting Inc..........D.......209 322-3275
4210 Kiernan Ave Modesto (95356) ***(P-1409)***
Crown Plaza, Milpitas *Also called B H R Operations LLC* ***(P-10941)***
Crown Shtmtl & Skylights Inc..........F.......415 467-5008
855 Stanton Rd Burlingame (94010) ***(P-1793)***
Crown Worldwide Moving & Stor, San Leandro *Also called Crown Worldwide Mvg & Stor LLC* ***(P-7521)***
Crown Worldwide Mvg & Stor LLC (PA)..........**E.......510 895-8050**
14826 Wicks Blvd San Leandro (94577) ***(P-7521)***
Crowne Plaza Concord, Concord *Also called Concord Hotel LLC* ***(P-11031)***
Crowne Plaza Hotel, Foster City *Also called Founders Management II Corp* ***(P-11100)***
Crowne Plz Scramento Northeast, Sacramento *Also called Khanna Entps - II Ltd Partnr* ***(P-11228)***
Crucible..........C.......510 444-0919
1260 7th St Oakland (94607) ***(P-17525)***
Cruise LLC..........D.......415 787-2346
333 Brannan St San Francisco (94107) ***(P-6550)***
Cruise LLC (HQ)..........**D.......415 335-4097**
1201 Bryant St San Francisco (94103) ***(P-7380)***
Crunch LLC..........D.......415 346-0222
1725 Union St San Francisco (94123) ***(P-14942)***
Crunch LLC..........D.......650 257-8000
1190 Saratoga Ave San Jose (95129) ***(P-14943)***
Crunch LLC..........D.......415 543-1110
61 New Montgomery St San Francisco (94105) ***(P-14944)***
Crunch LLC..........D.......415 495-1939
345 Spear St Ste 104 San Francisco (94105) ***(P-14945)***
Crunch Fitness, San Francisco *Also called Crunch LLC* ***(P-14942)***
Crunch Fitness, San Francisco *Also called Crunch LLC* ***(P-14944)***
Crunchyroll, San Francisco *Also called Ellation LLC* ***(P-12419)***
Crusader Fence Company Inc..........E.......916 631-9191
3115 Gold Valley Dr Ste B Rancho Cordova (95742) ***(P-2026)***
Crushvirus, Hayward *Also called Twin Bridges Technologies LLC* ***(P-8757)***
Crux Informatics Inc (PA)..........**E.......415 614-4400**
201 California St # 1300 San Francisco (94111) ***(P-13704)***
Cruzio, Santa Cruz *Also called Internet Store Inc* ***(P-19906)***
Cryowest Inc..........E.......831 786-9721
25 Hangar Way Watsonville (95076) ***(P-4719)***
Cryptic Studios Inc..........D.......408 399-1969
980 University Ave Los Gatos (95032) ***(P-7175)***
Cryptography Research Inc..........E.......408 462-8000
4453 N 1st St San Jose (95134) ***(P-13877)***
Crystal Basin Cellars..........F.......530 303-3749
3550 Carson Rd Camino (95709) ***(P-2541)***
Crystal Cream & Butter Co (HQ)..........**D.......916 444-7200**
8340 Belvedere Ave Sacramento (95826) ***(P-2187)***
Crystal Creamery, Modesto *Also called Foster Dairy Farms* ***(P-9338)***

Crystal Dynamics Inc (HQ)......D......650 421-7600
1400a Saport Blvd Ste 300 Redwood City (94063) *(P-13099)*
Crystal Geyser Water Company......E......707 647-4410
5001 Fermi Dr Fairfield (94534) *(P-2789)*
Crystal Graphics, Campbell *Also called Crystalgraphics Inc (P-12364)*
Crystal Springs Golf Course, Burlingame *Also called Crystal Springs Golf Partners (P-14996)*
Crystal Springs Golf Partners......E......650 342-4188
6650 Golf Course Dr Burlingame (94010) *(P-14996)*
Crystal Springs Landscape Co, San Jose *Also called Stevenson-Smith Enterprises (P-503)*
Crystal Springs Water Co, Santa Cruz *Also called Dtj Inc (P-9449)*
Crystal Technology, Fremont *Also called Gooch & Housego Palo Alto LLC (P-6431)*
Crystalgraphics Inc......F......800 394-0700
1999 S Bascom Ave Ste 700 Campbell (95008) *(P-12364)*
Cs-Pleasanton LLC......A......925 463-2822
7090 Johnson Dr Pleasanton (94588) *(P-15081)*
Csaa Insurance Exchange (PA)......A......925 279-2300
3055 Oak Rd Walnut Creek (94597) *(P-10267)*
Csaa Insurance Group, Walnut Creek *Also called Csaa Insurance Services Inc (P-10268)*
Csaa Insurance Services Inc (HQ)......D......925 279-3153
3055 Oak Rd Walnut Creek (94597) *(P-10268)*
Csac Excess Insurance Auth......D......916 850-7300
75 Iron Point Cir Ste 200 Folsom (95630) *(P-10269)*
CSBA, West Sacramento *Also called California School Boards Assn (P-18331)*
CSC Corporation......E......510 430-0399
9835 Kitty Ln Oakland (94603) *(P-1489)*
CSC Covansys Corporation......B......510 304-3430
34740 Tuxedo Cmn Fremont (94555) *(P-12365)*
Csd Autism Services, Alameda *Also called Center For Social Dynamics LLC (P-17475)*
CSDS, Sacramento *Also called Califrnia Srvying Drftg Sup In (P-12019)*
Cse Insurance Group, Walnut Creek *Also called Civil Svc Employees Insur Co (P-10261)*
Csea, Sacramento *Also called Califrnia State Employees Assn (P-18357)*
Csea, San Jose *Also called California Schl Employees Assn (P-18355)*
Csg Consultants Inc (PA)......E......650 522-2500
550 Pilgrim Dr Foster City (94404) *(P-18679)*
Csn Winddown Inc......C......209 369-3018
5400 E Harney Ln Lodi (95240) *(P-117)*
Csr Technology Inc (HQ)......B......408 523-6500
1060 Rincon Cir San Jose (95131) *(P-6414)*
CSS, Oakland *Also called Crisis Spport Svcs Almeda Cnty (P-14241)*
CSS, San Jose *Also called Slashsupport Inc (P-7992)*
Csus......D......916 278-4489
6000 J St Ereka Hall 420b Sacramento (95819) *(P-19487)*
Csw/Stbr-Stroeh Engrg Group In (PA)......E......415 883-9850
45 Leveroni Ct Novato (94949) *(P-18680)*
Ctc Services Inc......E......916 434-0195
3144 Venture Dr Ste 100 Lincoln (95648) *(P-14242)*
Ctdn - Redding, Redding *Also called Donor Network West (P-17137)*
Cthulhu Ventures LLC (PA)......E......415 444-9602
184 Bulkley Ave Sausalito (94965) *(P-10042)*
CTI, Rancho Cordova *Also called Chemical Technologies Intl Inc (P-5440)*
Cti-Controltech Inc......F......925 208-4250
22 Beta Ct San Ramon (94583) *(P-5678)*
CTT Inc (PA)......D......408 541-0596
5870 Hellyer Ave Ste 70 San Jose (95138) *(P-5837)*
Cttp, Lakeport *Also called California Tribal Tanf Partnr (P-17451)*
Ctu Precast, Olivehurst *Also called Precast Con Tech Unlimited LLC (P-4448)*
Cuberg Inc......E......510 725-4200
1198 65th St Ste 170 Emeryville (94608) *(P-19048)*
Cubeware Inc......E......650 847-8345
1735 Technology Dr # 430 San Jose (95110) *(P-14243)*
Culberson Drywall, Campbell *Also called Charles Culberson Inc (P-1668)*
Culinary Farms, Santa Rosa *Also called Cfarms Inc (P-2882)*
Culinary Farms Inc......E......916 375-3000
1244 E Beamer St Woodland (95776) *(P-2258)*
Culligan, Fresno *Also called Walter C Voigt Inc (P-9499)*
Culligan Partners Ltd Partnrs......E......650 573-1500
3700 S El Camino Real San Mateo (94403) *(P-14244)*
Cultured Stone Corporation (PA)......A......707 255-1727
Hwy 29 & Tower Rd NAPA (94559) *(P-4429)*
Cumming Management Group Inc......D......916 779-7140
2495 Natomas Park Dr Sacramento (95833) *(P-19322)*
Cumming Management Group Inc......D......415 748-3080
475 Sansome St Ste 520 San Francisco (94111) *(P-18681)*
Cummings-Violich Inc......E......530 894-5494
1750 Dayton Rd Chico (95928) *(P-371)*
Cummings-Vlich Inc-Orchard MGT, Chico *Also called Cummings-Violich Inc (P-371)*
Cummins Pacific LLC......F......916 371-0630
875 Riverside Pkwy West Sacramento (95605) *(P-4991)*
Cummins Pacific LLC......E......559 277-6760
2755 S Cherry Ave Fresno (93706) *(P-6575)*
Cumulus Networks Inc (PA)......C......650 383-6700
185 E Dana St Mountain View (94041) *(P-13100)*
Cuneo Black Ward Missler A Law......E......916 363-8822
700 University Ave # 110 Sacramento (95825) *(P-17242)*
Cuneo, Black, Ward & Missler, Sacramento *Also called Cuneo Black Ward Missler A Law (P-17242)*
Cunha Draying Inc......D......209 858-1400
1500 Madruga Rd Lathrop (95330) *(P-7522)*
Cunningham Legal, Auburn *Also called James Cunningham (P-17296)*
Cup4cup LLC (PA)......E......707 754-4263
840 Latour Ct Ste B NAPA (94558) *(P-2853)*
Cupertino Dental Group......D......408 257-3031
10383 Torre Ave Ste I Cupertino (95014) *(P-15830)*
Cupertino Electric Inc......A......408 808-8260
350 Lenore Way Felton (95018) *(P-1490)*
Cupertino Electric Inc (PA)......B......408 808-8000
1132 N 7th St San Jose (95112) *(P-1491)*
Cupertino Electric Inc......A......415 970-3400
1740 Cesar Chavez Fl 2 San Francisco (94124) *(P-1492)*
Cupertino Healthcare......D......408 253-9034
22590 Voss Ave Cupertino (95014) *(P-15978)*
Cupertino Hlthcare Wllness Ctr, Cupertino *Also called Cupertino Healthcare (P-15978)*
Cupertino Hspitality Assoc LLC......C......408 777-8787
10741 N Wolfe Rd Cupertino (95014) *(P-11042)*
Cupertino Inn, Cupertino *Also called Forge-Vdvich Mtl Ltd Prtnr A C (P-11098)*
Cupertino Lessee LLC......C......908 253-8900
10050 S De Anza Blvd Cupertino (95014) *(P-11043)*
Curacubby Inc......F......415 200-3373
2120 University Ave Berkeley (94704) *(P-13101)*
Curated Inc......D......415 855-1825
638 4th St San Francisco (94107) *(P-12366)*
Curebase Inc......E......248 978-3541
145 Gardenside Dr Apt 9 San Francisco (94131) *(P-12367)*
Curiodyssey......E......650 342-7755
1651 Coyote Point Dr San Mateo (94401) *(P-18269)*
Curology Inc (PA)......B......858 859-1188
353 Sacramento St # 2000 San Francisco (94111) *(P-17130)*
Curology Medical Group, San Francisco *Also called Curology Inc (P-17130)*
Current Tv LLC......C......415 995-8328
118 King St San Francisco (94107) *(P-14245)*
CURRY SENIOR CENTER, San Francisco *Also called Curry Senior Center (P-17526)*
Curry Senior Center (PA)......E......415 885-2274
333 Turk St San Francisco (94102) *(P-17526)*
Curtis & Tompkins, Berkeley *Also called Enthalpy Analytical Llc (P-19265)*
Curtis Lgal Group A Prof Law C......E......209 521-1800
1300 K St Fl 2 Modesto (95354) *(P-17243)*
Cushman & Wakefield Cal Inc (HQ)......C......408 275-6730
1 Maritime Plz Ste 900 San Francisco (94111) *(P-10527)*
Cushman & Wakefield Cal Inc......A......408 572-4134
1357 Hillcrest Dr San Jose (95120) *(P-10528)*
Cushman & Wakefield Cal Inc......A......510 763-4900
555 12th St Ste 1400 Oakland (94607) *(P-10529)*
Cushman & Wakefield Cal Inc......A......408 436-5500
560 S Wnchester Blvd # 200 San Jose (95128) *(P-10530)*
Cushman & Wakefield Cal Inc......A......925 935-0770
1333 N Calif Blvd Ste 550 Walnut Creek (94596) *(P-10531)*
Cushman & Wakefield Cal Inc......A......415 397-1700
2125 Hamilton Ave San Jose (95125) *(P-10532)*
Cushman & Wakefield Cal Inc......A......415 828-1923
455 Market St Ste 530 San Francisco (94105) *(P-10533)*
Custom AG Formulators Inc (PA)......D......559 435-1052
3430 S Willow Ave Fresno (93725) *(P-9597)*
Custom Alloy Scrap Sales Inc (HQ)......E......510 893-6476
2730 Peralta St Oakland (94607) *(P-9175)*
Custom Building Products Inc......E......209 983-8322
3525 Zephyr Ct Stockton (95206) *(P-5030)*
Custom Chrome Manufacturing......B......408 825-5000
15750 Vineyard Blvd # 100 Morgan Hill (95037) *(P-8448)*
Custom Cmpstes Fbrgls Fbrction, Olivehurst *Also called Ace Composites Inc (P-4252)*
Custom Coils Inc......F......707 752-8633
4000 Industrial Way Benicia (94510) *(P-6379)*
Custom Cooperage Innerstave, Sonoma *Also called Innerstave LLC (P-3236)*
Custom Crushing Industries Inc......E......530 842-5544
2409 E Oberlin Rd Yreka (96097) *(P-543)*
Custom Drywall Inc......D......408 263-1616
1570 Gladding Ct Milpitas (95035) *(P-1669)*
Custom Exteriors Inc......E......925 249-2280
2142 Rheem Dr Ste E Pleasanton (94588) *(P-2027)*
Custom Exteriors Windors Door, Pleasanton *Also called Custom Exteriors Inc (P-2027)*
Custom Freight Systems Inc (PA)......E......510 728-7515
2484 Baumann Ave San Lorenzo (94580) *(P-7618)*
Custom Furniture Design Inc......F......916 631-6300
3340 Sunrise Blvd Ste F Rancho Cordova (95742) *(P-3176)*
Custom Home Accessories, Rancho Cordova *Also called Penfield Products Inc (P-4802)*
Custom Label, Woodland *Also called Sachs Industries Inc (P-3405)*
Custom Label & Decal LLC......E......510 876-0000
3392 Investment Blvd Hayward (94545) *(P-3727)*
Custom Marble & Onyx, Modesto *Also called Sharcar Enterprises Inc (P-4522)*
Custom Micro Machining Inc......E......510 651-9434
707 Brown Rd Fremont (94539) *(P-5499)*
Custom Pad and Partition Inc......D......408 970-9711
1100 Richard Ave Santa Clara (95050) *(P-3358)*
Custom Paper Products LP......D......510 352-6880
2360 Teagarden St San Leandro (94577) *(P-3352)*
Custom Produce Sales (PA)......C......559 254-5800
13475 E Progress Dr Parlier (93648) *(P-9396)*
Custom Product Dev Corp......D......925 960-0577
4603 Las Positas Rd Ste A Livermore (94551) *(P-1794)*
Custom Wood Products, Parlier *Also called John Daniel Gonzalez (P-3237)*
Customer Service Realty (PA)......E......408 558-5000
5330 Canton Ave San Jose (95123) *(P-10534)*
Cut Loose (PA)......D......415 822-2031
101 Williams Ave San Francisco (94124) *(P-3009)*
Cutera Inc (PA)......B......415 657-5500
3240 Bayshore Blvd Brisbane (94005) *(P-7102)*
Cutie Pie Snack Pies, Lathrop *Also called Horizon Snack Foods Inc (P-2422)*
Cutler Group LP......E......415 645-6745
101 Montgomery St Ste 700 San Francisco (94104) *(P-14246)*
Cutter Lumber Products......E......209 982-4477
4004 S El Dorado St Stockton (95206) *(P-3219)*
Cutting Edge Machining Inc (PA)......E......408 738-8677
1331 Old County Rd Belmont (94002) *(P-5500)*

ALPHABETIC

Cv Starr Community Center ....D.......707 964-9446
300 S Lincoln St Fort Bragg (95437) ***(P-17527)***
Cvag, Oakdale *Also called Central Valley AG Grinding Inc* ***(P-276)***
Cvc Construction Corp (HQ) ....**B.......916 852-6030**
530 Bercut Dr Ste G Sacramento (95811) ***(P-1862)***
Cve Contracting Group Inc ....E.......559 222-1122
4263 N Selland Ave Fresno (93722) ***(P-19756)***
Cve Nb Contracting Group Inc ....E.......707 584-1900
135 Utility Ct A Rohnert Park (94928) ***(P-19757)***
Cvf Capital Partners Inc ....C.......530 757-7004
1590 Drew Ave Ste 110 Davis (95618) ***(P-10840)***
Cvh Care ....E.......650 393-5657
39 Beta Ct San Ramon (94583) ***(P-16877)***
Cvh Home Health Services, San Ramon *Also called Castro Valley Health Inc* ***(P-16869)***
Cvoc, Winton *Also called Central Valley Oprtnty Ctr Inc* ***(P-17802)***
Cvpartners Inc (HQ) ....**C.......415 543-8600**
655 Montgomery St # 1200 San Francisco (94111) ***(P-12082)***
CVS, Grass Valley *Also called Longs Drug Stores Cal Inc* ***(P-14159)***
CVS, Daly City *Also called Longs Drug Stores Cal LLC* ***(P-14174)***
CVS, Antioch *Also called Longs Drug Stores Cal Inc* ***(P-14161)***
CVS Health Corporation ....B.......415 348-1814
995 Market St San Francisco (94103) ***(P-17131)***
Cvtr, Fresno *Also called Central Valley Trlr Repr Inc* ***(P-14553)***
CW Horton General Contr Inc ....E.......510 780-0949
3295 Depot Rd Hayward (94545) ***(P-628)***
Cwes Inc ....E.......559 346-1251
3055 N Sunnyside Ave # 101 Fresno (93727) ***(P-19758)***
Cwi, San Francisco *Also called Collier Warehouse Inc* ***(P-8536)***
Cwip, Fresno *Also called Community Intgrted Work Prgram* ***(P-17498)***
Cwr Labs, San Jose *Also called Cpacket Networks Inc* ***(P-5361)***
Cws Utility Services Corp ....C.......408 367-8200
1720 N 1st St San Jose (95112) ***(P-18305)***
Cy Oakland Operator LLC ....E.......510 625-8282
988 Broadway Oakland (94607) ***(P-11044)***
Cy Sac Operator LLC ....D.......916 455-6800
4422 Y St Sacramento (95817) ***(P-11045)***
Cy Truss ....E.......559 888-2160
10715 E American Ave Del Rey (93616) ***(P-3204)***
Cyara Inc (PA) ....**C.......650 549-8522**
805 Veterans Blvd Ste 105 Redwood City (94063) ***(P-13102)***
Cyara Solutions Corp ....C.......650 549-8522
805 Veterans Blvd Ste 105 Redwood City (94063) ***(P-8686)***
Cyber Inc ....F.......925 242-0777
4000 Executive Pkwy # 250 San Ramon (94583) ***(P-13103)***
Cyber Press, Santa Clara *Also called Nss Enterprises* ***(P-3679)***
Cybercsi Inc ....D.......408 727-2900
3511 Thomas Rd Ste 5 Santa Clara (95054) ***(P-8687)***
Cyberguys Inc ....E.......800 892-1010
11321 White Rock Rd Rancho Cordova (95742) ***(P-8688)***
Cyberinc Corporation (HQ) ....**E.......925 242-0777**
4000 Executive Pkwy # 250 San Ramon (94583) ***(P-13104)***
Cybernet Entertainment LLC (PA) ....**C.......415 865-0230**
1800 Mission St San Francisco (94103) ***(P-14788)***
Cybernet Software Systems Inc ....B.......972 792-7597
75 E Santa Clara St # 900 San Jose (95113) ***(P-12368)***
Cybernetic Micro Systems Inc ....E.......650 726-3000
3000 La Honda Rd San Gregorio (94074) ***(P-5330)***
Cybersource Corporation (HQ) ....**A.......650 432-7350**
900 Metro Center Blvd Foster City (94404) ***(P-13705)***
Cycle Shack ....F.......650 583-7014
816 Murchison Dr Millbrae (94030) ***(P-6648)***
Cygna Group Inc ....C.......510 419-5000
2101 Webster St Oakland (94612) ***(P-18682)***
Cygnus Home Service LLC ....F.......916 686-8662
9919 Kent St Elk Grove (95624) ***(P-2170)***
Cylance Inc (HQ) ....**A.......949 375-3380**
3001 Bishop Dr Ste 400 San Ramon (94583) ***(P-13105)***
Cymabay Therapeutics Inc (PA) ....**E.......510 293-8800**
7575 Gateway Blvd Ste 110 Newark (94560) ***(P-3888)***
Cymmetrik Usa Inc ....E.......408 205-1114
62 Bonaventura Dr San Jose (95134) ***(P-3728)***
Cynthia Dunlap Dutra ....E.......209 456-1531
5030 E Peach Ave Manteca (95337) ***(P-410)***
Cyoptics Inc ....F.......408 433-7343
1320 Ridder Park Dr San Jose (95131) ***(P-6094)***
Cypress Creek Renewables LLC ....D.......415 306-5300
445 Bush St Fl 7 San Francisco (94108) ***(P-8094)***
Cypress Envirosystems Inc ....E.......800 544-5411
5883 Rue Ferrari Ste 100 San Jose (95138) ***(P-18683)***
Cypress Green ....E.......510 861-2214
5219 N Forestdale Cir Dublin (94568) ***(P-372)***
Cypress Grove Chevre Inc ....D.......707 825-1100
1330 Q St Arcata (95521) ***(P-2145)***
Cypress Hotel, Cupertino *Also called Ch Cupertino Owner LLC* ***(P-11000)***
Cypress Lawn Cemetery Assn ....C.......650 755-0580
1370 El Camino Real Colma (94014) ***(P-10726)***
CYPRESS LAWN MEMORIAL PARK, Colma *Also called Cypress Lawn Cemetery Assn* ***(P-10726)***
Cypress Private Security LP (HQ) ....**B.......866 345-1277**
478 Tehama St San Francisco (94103) ***(P-14052)***
Cypress Semiconductor Corp (HQ) ....**A.......408 943-2600**
198 Champion Ct San Jose (95134) ***(P-6095)***
Cypress Semiconductor Intl Inc (HQ) ....**C.......408 943-2600**
4001 N 1st St San Jose (95134) ***(P-6096)***
Cypress Street Center, Fort Bragg *Also called Parents & Friends Inc* ***(P-18155)***
Cyral Inc ....E.......310 689-8512
691 S Milpitas Blvd # 212 Milpitas (95035) ***(P-12369)***
Cytek Biosciences Inc (PA) ....**B.......877 922-9835**
46107 Landing Pkwy Fremont (94538) ***(P-6823)***
Cytokinetics Incorporated (PA) ....**C.......650 624-3000**
280 E Grand Ave South San Francisco (94080) ***(P-3889)***
Cytomx Therapeutics Inc ....C.......650 515-3185
151 Oyster Point Blvd # 40 South San Francisco (94080) ***(P-3890)***
Cytosport, Walnut Creek *Also called Gmp Manufacturing Inc* ***(P-2162)***
Cytosport Inc ....C.......707 751-3942
1340 Treat Blvd Ste 350 Walnut Creek (94597) ***(P-2158)***
D & D Cbnets - Svage Dsgns Inc ....E.......530 634-9713
1478 Sky Harbor Dr Olivehurst (95961) ***(P-3177)***
D & F Standler Inc ....E.......408 226-8188
195 Lewis Rd Ste 39 San Jose (95111) ***(P-5501)***
D & J Lumber Co Inc (PA) ....**D.......408 778-1550**
600 Tennant Ave Morgan Hill (95037) ***(P-8540)***
D & J Plumbing Inc ....E.......916 922-4888
4341 Winters St Sacramento (95838) ***(P-1245)***
D & J Tile Company Inc ....D.......650 632-4000
1045 Terminal Way San Carlos (94070) ***(P-1712)***
D & K Leather Corporation ....D.......415 433-9320
3001 Ponderosa Dr Concord (94520) ***(P-9654)***
D & T Fiberglass Inc ....E.......916 383-9012
8900 Osage Ave Sacramento (95828) ***(P-4272)***
D & T Foods Company, Santa Clara *Also called D and T Foods Inc* ***(P-9325)***
D & T Machining Inc ....F.......408 486-6035
3360 Victor Ct Santa Clara (95054) ***(P-5502)***
D A Financial Group California ....D.......925 254-7100
3470 Mt Diablo Blvd A100 Lafayette (94549) ***(P-10270)***
D A McCosker Construction Co ....E.......925 686-1780
3911 Laura Alice Way Concord (94520) ***(P-1030)***
D A Pope Incorporated ....E.......650 349-5086
1160 Chess Dr Ste 11 Foster City (94404) ***(P-859)***
D A Wood Construction Inc ....D.......209 491-4970
963 Shepard Ct Oakdale (95361) ***(P-18684)***
D and T Foods Inc ....E.......408 727-8331
1261 Martin Ave Santa Clara (95050) ***(P-9325)***
D Augustine & Associates ....D.......916 774-9600
3017 Douglas Blvd Ste 200 Roseville (95661) ***(P-11748)***
D C M, Menlo Park *Also called Dcm Management Inc* ***(P-10776)***
D C M Data Systems, Fremont *Also called Dcm Technologies Inc* ***(P-12376)***
D C Taylor Co ....D.......925 603-1100
5060 Forni Dr Ste B Concord (94520) ***(P-1795)***
D C Vient Inc (PA) ....**D.......209 578-1224**
1556 Cummins Dr Modesto (95358) ***(P-1410)***
D Carlson Construction Inc (PA) ....**E.......408 354-2893**
236 N Santa Cruz Ave # 244 Los Gatos (95030) ***(P-629)***
D Davis Enterprise, Davis *Also called McNaughton Newspapers* ***(P-3457)***
D E M Enterprises Inc ....E.......650 401-6200
15 S Bayshore Blvd San Mateo (94401) ***(P-13706)***
D E Shaw Valence LLC ....C.......650 926-9460
2735 Sand Hill Rd Ste 105 Menlo Park (94025) ***(P-10841)***
D F P F Corporation ....E.......415 512-7677
15 Brush Pl San Francisco (94103) ***(P-860)***
D K Express, Stockton *Also called DK Express Cargo Inc* ***(P-7526)***
D M Jepsen Inc ....E.......925 455-0872
295 Boeing Ct Livermore (94551) ***(P-1493)***
D M S, Fremont *Also called DMS Facility Services Inc* ***(P-11944)***
D N G Cummings Inc ....F.......650 593-8974
3580 Haven Ave Ste 1 Redwood City (94063) ***(P-7227)***
D O Neronde Inc ....D.......530 823-6591
1650 Grass Valley Hwy Auburn (95603) ***(P-14556)***
D P Nicoli Inc ....F.......650 873-2999
266 Harbor Way South San Francisco (94080) ***(P-8814)***
D R C, Sacramento *Also called Disability Rights California* ***(P-17253)***
D S I, Santa Rosa *Also called Deposition Sciences Inc* ***(P-19049)***
D W Nicholson Corporation (PA) ....**C.......510 887-0900**
24747 Clawiter Rd Hayward (94545) ***(P-1246)***
D W Young Cnstr Co Inc ....D.......925 743-1536
333 Camille Ave Alamo (94507) ***(P-1097)***
D Zelinsky & Sons Inc ....E.......510 215-5253
5301 Adeline St Oakland (94608) ***(P-1411)***
D&H / R&D, Fremont *Also called D&H Manufacturing Company* ***(P-7279)***
D&H Manufacturing, Fremont *Also called Celestica LLC* ***(P-6404)***
D&H Manufacturing Company ....E.......510 770-5100
49235 Milmont Dr Fremont (94538) ***(P-7279)***
D&M Manufacturing Co LLC ....F.......559 834-4668
5400 S Villa Ave Fresno (93725) ***(P-5000)***
D-K-P Inc ....F.......559 266-2695
275 N Marks Ave Fresno (93706) ***(P-5001)***
D-Tek Manufacturing ....E.......408 588-1574
3245 Woodward Ave Santa Clara (95054) ***(P-6097)***
D2m Inc ....E.......650 567-9995
935 Benecia Ave Sunnyvale (94085) ***(P-19759)***
D2m Trading Limited, Sunnyvale *Also called D2m Inc* ***(P-19759)***
D3 Led Llc (PA) ....**E.......916 669-7408**
11370 Sunrise Park Dr Rancho Cordova (95742) ***(P-7228)***
D7 Roofing Services Inc ....D.......916 447-2175
2851 Gold Tailings Ct Rancho Cordova (95670) ***(P-1796)***
Daca, San Jose *Also called De Anza Cupertino Aquatics* ***(P-15082)***
Dacast ....E.......510 619-4857
1175 Folsom St San Francisco (94103) ***(P-14789)***
Dado Inc ....E.......510 364-6263
248 3rd St Ste 938 Oakland (94607) ***(P-13106)***
Daggett Solar Power 3 LLC ....C.......415 627-1600
100 California St Ste 400 San Francisco (94111) ***(P-1247)***
Dahl-Beck Electric Co ....D.......510 237-2325
2775 Goodrick Ave Richmond (94801) ***(P-8856)***

Dahlhauser Mfg Co Inc ....E....408 988-3717
1855 Russell Ave Santa Clara (95054) ***(P-4968)***
Dahlin Group Inc (PA) ....**D....925 251-7200**
5865 Owens Dr Pleasanton (94588) ***(P-18880)***
DAILY CALIFORNIAN, Berkeley *Also called Indepndent Brkley Stdnt Pubg I* ***(P-3448)***
Daily Republic, Fairfield *Also called McNaughton Newspapers Inc* ***(P-3458)***
Daily Review ....F....510 783-6111
3317 Arden Rd Hayward (94545) ***(P-3431)***
Dairy Farmers America Inc ....D....209 667-9627
600 Trade Way Turlock (95380) ***(P-2146)***
Dakota AG Welding, Ripon *Also called Jackrabbit* ***(P-5009)***
Dakota AG Welding, Modesto *Also called Jackrabbit* ***(P-5010)***
Dakota Press Inc ....F....510 895-1300
14400 Doolittle Dr San Leandro (94577) ***(P-3639)***
Dale Brisco Inc ....F....559 834-5926
2132 S Temperance Ave Fowler (93625) ***(P-4752)***
Dale Grove Corporation ....F....408 251-7220
1501 Stone Creek Dr San Jose (95132) ***(P-5129)***
Dale Road Nursery, Modesto *Also called Nagel Landscaping* ***(P-487)***
Daleo Inc ....D....408 846-9621
550 E Luchessa Ave Gilroy (95020) ***(P-1098)***
Daleys Drywall and Taping Inc ....B....408 378-9500
960 Camden Ave Campbell (95008) ***(P-1670)***
Dameron Hospital Association (HQ) ....**A....209 944-5550**
525 W Acacia St Stockton (95203) ***(P-16344)***
Damrell Nelson Schrimp Pall (PA) ....**E....209 526-3500**
1601 I St Ste 500 Modesto (95354) ***(P-17244)***
Dan Avila & Sons Farms Inc ....D....209 495-3899
2718 Roberts Rd Ceres (95307) ***(P-25)***
Dan Fitzgerald & Assoc Inc ....E....530 592-6500
2910 State Highway 32 # 2200 Chico (95973) ***(P-14247)***
Dan On & Associates (usa) Ltd (PA) ....**E....559 233-2828**
2628 S Cherry Ave Fresno (93706) ***(P-2887)***
Dan R Costa Inc ....C....209 234-2004
17239 Louise Ave Escalon (95320) ***(P-154)***
Dana Estates Inc (PA) ....**E....707 963-4365**
1500 Whitehall Ln Saint Helena (94574) ***(P-2542)***
Dana Kitchens & Associates Inc ....E....707 571-8326
5464 Skylane Blvd Santa Rosa (95403) ***(P-1671)***
Dana Motors Inc (PA) ....**F....916 920-0150**
901 Arden Way Sacramento (95815) ***(P-8449)***
Dana, Steven M Dvm, San Rafael *Also called A Pet Emrgncy & Specialty Ctr* ***(P-318)***
Danco Builders ....D....707 822-9000
5251 Ericson Way Ste A Arcata (95521) ***(P-743)***
Danco Machine, Santa Clara *Also called P M S D Inc* ***(P-5585)***
Daniel Larratt Plumbing Inc ....E....415 553-6011
944 Terminal Way San Carlos (94070) ***(P-1248)***
Danisco US Inc (HQ) ....**C....650 846-7500**
925 Page Mill Rd Palo Alto (94304) ***(P-4020)***
Dannis Wlver Klley A Prof Corp (PA) ....**D....415 543-4111**
275 Battery St Ste 1150 San Francisco (94111) ***(P-17245)***
Danoc Embroidery, Sacramento *Also called Danoc Manufacturing Corp Inc* ***(P-3005)***
Danoc Manufacturing Corp Inc ....F....916 455-2876
6015 Power Inn Rd Ste A Sacramento (95824) ***(P-3005)***
Dantel Inc ....E....559 292-1111
4210 N Brawley Ave 108 Fresno (93722) ***(P-5792)***
Danville Long-Term Care Inc ....D....925 837-4566
336 Diablo Rd Danville (94526) ***(P-15979)***
Danville Post Acute Rehab, Danville *Also called Danville Long-Term Care Inc* ***(P-15979)***
Dapper Tire Co Inc ....F....510 780-1616
20380 Corsair Blvd Hayward (94545) ***(P-6576)***
Daratel Ltd (PA) ....**E....925 825-1443**
1975 Diamond Blvd E260 Concord (94520) ***(P-11714)***
Darcie Kent Vineyards ....E....925 243-9040
4590 Tesla Rd Livermore (94550) ***(P-2543)***
Darcie Kent Winery LLC ....E....925 443-5368
7000 Tesla Rd Livermore (94550) ***(P-9573)***
Darcoid Company of California ....E....510 836-2449
950 3rd St Oakland (94607) ***(P-9116)***
Darcoid Nor-Cal Seal, Oakland *Also called Darcoid Company of California* ***(P-9116)***
Darden Architects Inc ....D....559 448-8051
6790 N West Ave Ste 104 Fresno (93711) ***(P-18881)***
Daregal Inc ....C....209 633-3600
300 Dianne Dr Turlock (95380) ***(P-16)***
Darioush Khaledi Winery LLC ....E....707 257-2345
4240 Silverado Trl NAPA (94558) ***(P-2544)***
Darkhorse Golf Club ....E....530 269-7900
24150 Darkhorse Dr Auburn (95602) ***(P-14997)***
Darko Precision Inc ....D....408 988-6133
470 Gianni St Santa Clara (95054) ***(P-5503)***
Darktrace Inc (PA) ....**D....415 229-9100**
555 Mission St Ste 3225 San Francisco (94105) ***(P-13574)***
Darrell Herzog Enterprises ....E....559 307-4566
14028 Skyview Rd Madera (93636) ***(P-1797)***
Dart Container Corp Calif, Lodi *Also called Dart Container Corp California* ***(P-4242)***
Dart Container Corp California ....D....209 333-8088
1400 E Victor Rd Lodi (95240) ***(P-4242)***
Dasher Technologies Inc (HQ) ....**E....408 409-2607**
675 Campbell Tech Pkwy Campbell (95008) ***(P-12370)***
Dassels Petroleum Inc (PA) ....**E....831 636-5100**
31 Wright Rd Hollister (95023) ***(P-9532)***
Data Advantage Group Inc ....F....415 947-0400
145 Natoma St Fl 5 San Francisco (94105) ***(P-13107)***
Data Center Gear, Cupertino *Also called Mirapath Inc* ***(P-8728)***
Data Consultants, Fresno *Also called T B B Inc* ***(P-8753)***
Data Domain LLC ....A....408 980-4800
2421 Mission College Blvd Santa Clara (95054) ***(P-13575)***
Data Physics Corporation (PA) ....**F....408 437-0100**
3100 De La Cruz Blvd # 101 Santa Clara (95054) ***(P-8689)***
Database Specialists Inc (HQ) ....**D....415 344-0500**
580 California St 500 San Francisco (94104) ***(P-13783)***
Databricks Inc (PA) ....**D....415 494-7672**
160 Spear St Fl 13 San Francisco (94105) ***(P-12371)***
Datacare Corporation ....E....866 834-2334
992 S De Anza Blvd San Jose (95129) ***(P-19488)***
Dataendure ....E....408 734-3339
1960 Zanker Rd 10 San Jose (95112) ***(P-8690)***
Datafox Intelligence Inc ....F....415 969-2144
475 Sansome St Fl 15 San Francisco (94111) ***(P-13108)***
Datalogix Texas Inc ....E....510 475-8787
33250 Central Ave Union City (94587) ***(P-1494)***
Datamax Software Group Inc ....E....916 939-4065
1101 Inv Blvd Ste 250 El Dorado Hills (95762) ***(P-12372)***
Datameer Inc (PA) ....**C....650 286-9100**
535 Mission St Ste 2602 San Francisco (94105) ***(P-12373)***
Datapipe, Mountain View *Also called Rackspace Hosting Inc* ***(P-13749)***
Datapipe, San Jose *Also called Rackspace Hosting Inc* ***(P-13750)***
Datasafe Inc (PA) ....**E....650 875-3800**
2237 Palou Ave San Francisco (94124) ***(P-7707)***
Dataself Corp ....E....888 910-9802
1200 Franklin Mall Santa Clara (95050) ***(P-12374)***
Datastax Inc (PA) ....**A....650 389-6000**
3975 Freedom Cir Fl 4 Santa Clara (95054) ***(P-12375)***
Datavisor Inc ....D....408 331-9886
967 N Shoreline Blvd Mountain View (94043) ***(P-13109)***
Datera Inc ....D....844 432-8372
2811 Mission College Blvd F Santa Clara (95054) ***(P-13110)***
Datrium Inc ....D....650 485-2165
385 Moffett Park Dr # 205 Sunnyvale (94089) ***(P-8691)***
Daughters Charity Health Sys, Los Altos Hills *Also called Ministry Services of The Daugh* ***(P-10799)***
Dav El Chuffeured Trnsp Networ, San Francisco *Also called Dav-El Reservations System Inc* ***(P-7381)***
Dav-El Reservations System Inc ....D....415 206-7950
2025 Mckinnon Ave San Francisco (94124) ***(P-7381)***
Dave Calhoun and Assoc LLC ....C....925 688-1234
2575 Stanwell Dr Ste 100 Concord (94520) ***(P-11941)***
Dave Drunker ....E....650 853-4827
795 El Camino Real Palo Alto (94301) ***(P-16779)***
Dave Gross Enterprises Inc ....D....916 388-2000
7 Wayne Ct Sacramento (95829) ***(P-2028)***
Dave J Mendrin Inc ....F....559 352-1700
4876 W Athens Ave Fresno (93722) ***(P-49)***
Dave Wilson Nursery (PA) ....**E....209 874-1821**
19701 Lake Rd Hickman (95323) ***(P-118)***
Davey Tree Surgery Company ....D....530 378-2674
6915 Eastside Rd Ste 94 Anderson (96007) ***(P-516)***
Davey Tree Surgery Company (HQ) ....**A....925 443-1723**
2617 S Vasco Rd Livermore (94550) ***(P-517)***
David Allen & Associates (PA) ....**E....916 455-4800**
5230 Folsom Blvd Sacramento (95819) ***(P-17246)***
David Beard ....F....530 244-1248
821 Twin View Blvd Redding (96003) ***(P-3178)***
David Bruce Winery Inc ....F....408 354-4214
21439 Bear Creek Rd Los Gatos (95033) ***(P-2545)***
David D Bohannon Organization (PA) ....**D....650 345-8222**
60 31st Ave San Mateo (94403) ***(P-10385)***
David Darroch ....E....510 835-9100
300 Lakeside Dr Fl 24 Oakland (94612) ***(P-17247)***
David Knott Inc ....E....559 449-8935
4711 N Blythe Ave Fresno (93722) ***(P-1984)***
David L Gates & Associates Inc ....D....925 736-8176
1655 N Main St Ste 365 Walnut Creek (94596) ***(P-411)***
David P Enfield MD, Stockton *Also called Mark H Nishiki MD* ***(P-15521)***
David Powell Inc (PA) ....**D....650 357-6000**
3190 Clearview Way # 100 San Mateo (94402) ***(P-12083)***
David Smith ....E....916 570-1460
7423 Winding Way Fair Oaks (95628) ***(P-630)***
Davids Bridal Inc ....F....530 342-5914
1515 Springfield Dr # 100 Chico (95928) ***(P-3001)***
Davis Cmnty Clnic Dntl Program, Davis *Also called Davis Community Clinic* ***(P-15373)***
Davis Community Clinic (PA) ....**D....530 758-2060**
2040 Sutter Pl Davis (95616) ***(P-15373)***
Davis Community Clinic ....E....916 403-2970
500 Jefferson Blvd B195 West Sacramento (95605) ***(P-16755)***
Davis Community Meals Inc ....D....530 756-4008
202 F St Davis (95616) ***(P-17528)***
Davis Drier & Elevator N F ....E....559 659-3035
9421 N Dos Palos Hwy Firebaugh (93622) ***(P-155)***
Davis Golf Course Inc ....E....530 756-0647
24439 Fairway Dr Davis (95616) ***(P-14998)***
Davis Guest Home Inc ....E....209 538-1496
1878 E Hatch Rd Modesto (95351) ***(P-18097)***
Davis Instruments Corporation ....D....510 732-9229
3465 Diablo Ave Hayward (94545) ***(P-6666)***
Davis Machine Shop Inc ....E....530 696-2577
15805 Central St Meridian (95957) ***(P-5002)***
Davis Medical Group, Sacramento *Also called University California Davis* ***(P-15775)***
Davis Medical Offices, Davis *Also called Kaiser Foundation Hospitals* ***(P-15477)***
Davis Polk & Wardwell LLP ....D....650 752-2000
1600 El Camino Real # 100 Menlo Park (94025) ***(P-17248)***
Davis Street Community Center (PA) ....**D....510 347-4620**
3081 Teagarden St San Leandro (94577) ***(P-17529)***
DAVIS STREET FAMILY RESOURCE C, San Leandro *Also called Davis Street Community Center* ***(P-17529)***

Davis Uc Medical Center ....B....916 734-2011
4800 2nd Ave 3010 Sacramento (95817) ***(P-16345)***
Davis Wright Tremaine LLP ....D....415 276-6500
505 Montgomery St Ste 800 San Francisco (94111) ***(P-17249)***
Davison Iron Works Inc ....E....916 381-2121
8845 Elder Creek Rd Ste A Sacramento (95828) ***(P-4656)***
Davita Health Care, San Pablo *Also called Davita Inc* ***(P-16972)***
Davita Inc ....E....510 234-0835
14020 San Pablo Ave Ste B San Pablo (94806) ***(P-16972)***
Dawn VME Products ....E....510 657-4444
47915 Westinghouse Dr Fremont (94539) ***(P-6415)***
Daylight Foods Inc ....C....510 931-4207
30200 Whipple Rd Union City (94587) ***(P-9397)***
Days Inn, Novato *Also called Novato Management Group Inc* ***(P-11332)***
Days Inn, Palo Alto *Also called Palo Alto Inn* ***(P-11351)***
Days Inn ....E....408 737-1177
590 N Mathilda Ave Sunnyvale (94085) ***(P-11046)***
Days Inn By Wyndham San Frncsc ....D....415 766-0678
2358 Lombard St San Francisco (94123) ***(P-11047)***
Days Inn Oakland Airport, Oakland *Also called Jalaram Investment LLC* ***(P-11207)***
Daystar Technologies Inc ....D....408 582-7100
1010 S Milpitas Blvd Milpitas (95035) ***(P-6098)***
Db Design Group Inc ....E....408 834-1400
48507 Milmont Dr Fremont (94538) ***(P-18685)***
Dbi Beverage San Francisco ....C....415 643-9900
245 S Spruce Ave Ste 100 South San Francisco (94080) ***(P-9549)***
DC Electronics Inc ....D....408 947-4531
1870 Little Orchard St San Jose (95125) ***(P-5714)***
DC Valve Mfg & Precision Mchs, Morgan Hill *Also called Dcpm Inc* ***(P-5504)***
Dcatalog Inc ....E....408 824-5648
956 Larkspur Ave Sunnyvale (94086) ***(P-13111)***
Dcg Systems, Fremont *Also called Fei Efa Inc* ***(P-6828)***
DCI Donor Services Inc ....D....877 401-2546
3940 Industrial Blvd West Sacramento (95691) ***(P-17132)***
DCI Donor Services Inc ....D....916 567-1600
3940 Industrial Blvd # 100 West Sacramento (95691) ***(P-17133)***
Dcl, Fremont *Also called Discopylabs* ***(P-7832)***
Dcl, Fremont *Also called Discopylabs* ***(P-13883)***
Dcm Management Inc ....E....650 233-1400
2420 Sand Hill Rd Ste 200 Menlo Park (94025) ***(P-10776)***
Dcm Technologies Inc ....E....510 494-2321
39159 Paseo Padre Pkwy # 303 Fremont (94538) ***(P-12376)***
Dco Environmental & Recycl LLC ....F....573 204-3844
300 Montgomery St Ste 421 San Francisco (94104) ***(P-4273)***
Dcpm Inc ....E....408 928-2510
885 Jarvis Dr Morgan Hill (95037) ***(P-5504)***
DCS, Lathrop *Also called Performant Recovery Inc* ***(P-11827)***
DCs Asphalt Maintenance ....E....415 577-6705
1470 Warrington Rd Santa Rosa (95404) ***(P-11942)***
Dcss, Modesto *Also called County of Stanislaus* ***(P-17517)***
DDB Worldwide ....C....415 732-3600
600 California St Fl 7 San Francisco (94108) ***(P-11749)***
DDS, Hayward *Also called Detention Device Systems* ***(P-5507)***
DDSO, Sacramento *Also called Develpmntal Dsblties Svc Orgnz* ***(P-17531)***
De Anza Cupertino Aquatics ....E....408 446-5600
1080 S De Anza Blvd Ste B San Jose (95129) ***(P-15082)***
De Anza Manufacturing Svcs Inc ....D....408 734-2020
1271 Reamwood Ave Sunnyvale (94089) ***(P-6416)***
De Benedetto AG, Chowchilla *Also called J & R Debenedetto Orchards Inc* ***(P-103)***
De Gregori Gormsen Ringer LLP ....E....209 944-0740
1401 N Hunter St Stockton (95202) ***(P-18947)***
De La Cruz Lath and Plaster Co ....E....209 368-8658
3480 Carpenter Rd Stockton (95215) ***(P-1863)***
De Mattei Construction Inc ....D....408 295-7516
1794 The Alameda San Jose (95126) ***(P-631)***
De Ruosi Group LLC ....E....209 838-8307
25055 Arthur Rd Escalon (95320) ***(P-280)***
De Ruosi Nut, Escalon *Also called De Ruosi Group LLC* ***(P-280)***
Dealertrack Clltral MGT Svcs I ....C....916 368-5300
9750 Goethe Rd Sacramento (95827) ***(P-12377)***
Dean Moon ....E....916 387-1339
9373 Elder Creek Rd Sacramento (95829) ***(P-456)***
Deans & Homer (PA) ....**E....415 421-8332**
340 Pine St Fl 2 San Francisco (94104) ***(P-10167)***
Decathalon Club, San Francisco *Also called Executives Outlet Inc* ***(P-14949)***
Decathlon Club Inc ....D....408 738-2582
3250 Central Expy Santa Clara (95051) ***(P-14946)***
Decentral TV Corporation ....D....415 480-6800
442 Post St Fl 10 San Francisco (94102) ***(P-7945)***
Decimal Inc ....D....855 980-6612
1160 Battery St Ste 350 San Francisco (94111) ***(P-14248)***
Decision Minds ....C....408 309-8051
1525 Mccarthy Blvd # 224 Milpitas (95035) ***(P-13707)***
Deck West Inc ....E....209 939-9700
1900 Sanguinetti Ln Stockton (95205) ***(P-4753)***
Decker Landscaping Inc ....D....916 652-1780
13265 Bill Francis Dr Auburn (95603) ***(P-457)***
Declara Inc ....D....877 216-0604
977 Commercial St Palo Alto (94303) ***(P-13878)***
Decore-Ative Spc NC LLC ....C....916 686-4700
104 Gate Eats Stock Blvd Elk Grove (95624) ***(P-3128)***
Decrevel Incorporated ....E....707 258-8065
1836 Soscol Ave NAPA (94559) ***(P-5083)***
Dedicated Management Group LLC ....C....209 385-0694
3876 E Childs Ave Merced (95341) ***(P-14249)***
Deem Inc (HQ) ....**D....415 590-8300**
1330 Broadway Fl 7 Oakland (94612) ***(P-13112)***
Deep Labs Inc (PA) ....**E....877 504-4544**
101 2nd St Ste 375 San Francisco (94105) ***(P-13113)***
Deep North Inc (PA) ....**D....650 781-1550**
303 Twin Dolphin Dr # 600 Redwood City (94065) ***(P-12378)***
Deep Ocean Engineering Inc ....F....408 436-1102
2403 Qume Dr San Jose (95131) ***(P-6641)***
Deep Sentinel Corp ....E....415 858-4688
1249 Quarry Ln Ste 147 Pleasanton (94566) ***(P-14126)***
Deer Creek Broadcasting LLC ....E....530 345-0021
2654 Cramer Ln Chico (95928) ***(P-8017)***
Deer Park Pharmacy, Saint Helena *Also called St Helena Hospital* ***(P-16536)***
Dees-Hennessey Inc ....E....650 595-8933
200 Industrial Rd Ste 190 San Carlos (94070) ***(P-793)***
Degenkolb Engineers (PA) ....**D....415 392-6952**
375 Beale St Ste 500 San Francisco (94105) ***(P-18686)***
Degenkolb Engineers ....E....510 272-9040
1300 Clay St Ste 9009 Oakland (94612) ***(P-18687)***
Dehlinger Winery, Sebastopol *Also called Thomas Dehlinger* ***(P-2740)***
Del Castillo Foods Inc ....E....209 369-2877
2346 Maggio Cir Lodi (95240) ***(P-2888)***
Del Contes Landscaping Inc ....D....510 353-6030
41900 Boscell Rd Fremont (94538) ***(P-412)***
Del Dotto, NAPA *Also called Hedgeside Vintners* ***(P-2615)***
Del Logging Inc ....F....530 294-5492
101 Punkin Center Rd Bieber (96009) ***(P-3058)***
Del Mar Farms Partners Ltd (PA) ....**E....209 894-5555**
9843 Cox Rd Patterson (95363) ***(P-156)***
Del Mar Food Products Corp ....B....831 722-3516
1720 Beach Rd Watsonville (95076) ***(P-2214)***
Del Mar Seed Processing, Patterson *Also called Del Mar Farms Partners Ltd* ***(P-156)***
Del Monte Capitol Meat Co LLC (HQ) ....**D....916 927-0595**
4051 Seaport Blvd West Sacramento (95691) ***(P-9269)***
Del Monte Corporation (PA) ....**C....415 247-3000**
1 Maritime Plz Ste 700 San Francisco (94111) ***(P-2889)***
Del Monte Electric Co Inc (PA) ....**E....925 829-6000**
6998 Sierra Ct Ste A Dublin (94568) ***(P-1495)***
Del Monte Foods Inc (HQ) ....**C....925 949-2772**
205 N Wiget Ln Walnut Creek (94598) ***(P-9448)***
Del Norte Assoc For Dvlpmntl S ....E....707 464-8338
838 4th St Crescent City (95531) ***(P-17811)***
Del Norte Club Inc ....E....916 483-5111
3040 Becerra Way Sacramento (95821) ***(P-15083)***
DEL NORTE WORKFORCE CENTER, Crescent City *Also called Rural Human Services* ***(P-17697)***
Del Paso Country Club ....C....916 489-3681
3333 Marconi Ave Sacramento (95821) ***(P-15084)***
Del Paso Health Center, Sacramento *Also called County of Sacramento* ***(P-15367)***
Del Puerto Health Care Dst ....D....209 892-9100
875 E St Patterson (95363) ***(P-15374)***
Del Puerto Health Center, Patterson *Also called Del Puerto Health Care Dst* ***(P-15374)***
Del Rey Juice Co ....D....559 888-8533
5286 S Del Rey Ave Del Rey (93616) ***(P-2291)***
Del Rey Packing Co, Del Rey *Also called Chooljian & Sons Inc* ***(P-279)***
Del Rio Golf & Country Club ....C....209 341-2414
801 Stewart Rd Modesto (95356) ***(P-15085)***
Del Rio West Pallets ....E....209 983-8215
3845 S El Dorado St Stockton (95206) ***(P-3220)***
Del Rosario Rene DMD (PA) ....**E....510 324-2000**
32364 Dyer St Union City (94587) ***(P-15831)***
DELANCEY STREET COACH SERVICE, San Francisco *Also called Delancey Street Foundation* ***(P-18098)***
Delancey Street Foundation (PA) ....**B....415 957-9800**
600 The Embarcadero San Francisco (94107) ***(P-18098)***
Delave Inc (PA) ....**D....408 293-7200**
311 E Reed St Apt 13 San Jose (95112) ***(P-9655)***
Delave Periodicals, San Jose *Also called Delave Inc* ***(P-9655)***
Delaware G3 Enterprises, El Dorado Hills *Also called G3 Enterprises Inc* ***(P-7690)***
Delegat Usa Inc ....D....415 538-7988
555 Mission St Ste 2625 San Francisco (94105) ***(P-2546)***
Delegata Corporation ....D....916 609-5400
2450 Venture Oaks Way # 40 Sacramento (95833) ***(P-13576)***
Deleon Realty Inc ....E....650 543-8500
1717 Embarcadero Rd # 500 Palo Alto (94303) ***(P-10535)***
Delicato Vineyards ....E....707 265-1700
455 Devlin Rd Ste 201 NAPA (94558) ***(P-2547)***
Delicato Vineyards LLC (PA) ....**C....209 824-3600**
12001 S Highway 99 Manteca (95336) ***(P-2548)***
Deliverimates LLC ....D....857 445-7736
5311 Escover Ln San Jose (95118) ***(P-7878)***
Dell, San Jose *Also called Force10 Networks Global Inc* ***(P-13590)***
Della Maggiore Tile Inc ....D....408 286-3991
87 N 30th St San Jose (95116) ***(P-1713)***
Deloitte & Touche LLP ....B....408 704-4000
225 W Santa Clara St # 600 San Jose (95113) ***(P-18948)***
Deloitte Consulting LLP ....E....510 251-4400
555 Mission St San Francisco (94105) ***(P-19489)***
Deloitte Consulting LLP ....E....212 492-4000
225 W Santa Clara St San Jose (95113) ***(P-19490)***
Deloitte Consulting LLP ....E....212 492-4000
600 Yosemite Blvd Modesto (95354) ***(P-19491)***
Deloitte Tax LLP ....B....415 783-4000
555 Mission St Ste 1400 San Francisco (94105) ***(P-18949)***
Delong Manufacturing Co Inc ....F....408 727-3348
967 Parker Ct Santa Clara (95050) ***(P-5505)***
Delphi Productions Inc (PA) ....**C....510 748-7494**
950 W Tower Ave Alameda (94501) ***(P-14250)***
Delphix Corp (PA) ....**E....650 494-1645**
1400 Saport Blvd Ste 200a Redwood City (94063) ***(P-12379)***

Delphon Industries LLC (PA) ....C....510 576-2220
31398 Huntwood Ave Hayward (94544) *(P-4274)*
Delta America Ltd (HQ) ....C....510 668-5100
46101 Fremont Blvd Fremont (94538) *(P-8906)*
Delta Blood Bank LLC (HQ) ....D....800 244-6794
65 N Commerce St Stockton (95202) *(P-17134)*
Delta Blue Grass, Stockton *Also called Zuckerman-Heritage Inc (P-198)*
Delta Boatworks, Isleton *Also called Ken & Laura Scheidegger (P-7731)*
Delta Charter Service Inc ....E....209 465-1053
4900 E Mariposa Rd Stockton (95215) *(P-7421)*
Delta Dental of California (PA) ....B....415 972-8300
560 Mission St Ste 1300 San Francisco (94105) *(P-10103)*
Delta Dental of California ....E....916 853-7373
11155 International Dr Sacramento (95826) *(P-10104)*
Delta Dental of California ....E....916 381-4054
7801 Folsom Blvd Sacramento (95826) *(P-10105)*
Delta Dental Plan, Sacramento *Also called Delta Dental of California (P-10104)*
Delta Disposal Service Co, Tracy *Also called Tracy Dlta Solid Waste Mgt Inc (P-8369)*
Delta Electronics Americas Ltd (HQ) ....D....510 668-5100
46101 Fremont Blvd Fremont (94538) *(P-19323)*
Delta Grinding Company Inc ....E....925 778-3939
5131 Lone Tree Way Antioch (94531) *(P-1154)*
Delta Hawkeye Security Inc ....D....209 957-3333
7400 Shoreline Dr Ste 2 Stockton (95219) *(P-14053)*
DELTA HEALTH SYSTEMS, Stockton *Also called Wm Michael Stemler Inc (P-10370)*
Delta Machine, San Jose *Also called Delta Matrix Inc (P-5506)*
Delta Marina Yacht Harbor ....E....707 374-2315
100 Marina Dr Rio Vista (94571) *(P-7728)*
Delta Matrix Inc ....E....408 955-9140
2180 Oakland Rd San Jose (95131) *(P-5506)*
Delta Network Solutions, Stockton *Also called Delta Wireless Inc (P-14680)*
Delta Pacific Products, Union City *Also called Delta Yimin Technologies Inc (P-4275)*
Delta Personnel Services Inc ....D....925 356-3034
1820 Galindo St Ste 3 Concord (94520) *(P-14054)*
Delta Products, Fremont *Also called Delta America Ltd (P-8906)*
Delta Project Management Inc ....D....415 590-3202
400 Concar Dr San Mateo (94402) *(P-18688)*
Delta Protective Services, Stockton *Also called Borgens & Borgens Inc (P-14039)*
Delta Radiology Medical Group ....D....209 334-4416
1031 S Fairmont Ave Lodi (95240) *(P-15375)*
Delta Signs, Stockton *Also called Street Graphics Inc (P-7255)*
Delta Specialties Inc ....F....209 937-9650
1250 S Wilson Way Ste C1 Stockton (95205) *(P-1936)*
Delta Tech Service Inc (PA) ....E....707 745-2080
397 W Channel Rd Benicia (94510) *(P-11943)*
Delta Truck Center, French Camp *Also called Fresno Truck Center (P-8423)*
Delta Valley Athletic Club, Brentwood *Also called Club Corp Incorporated (P-14937)*
Delta Web Printing Inc ....E....916 375-0044
4251 Gateway Park Blvd Sacramento (95834) *(P-3729)*
Delta Web Printing & Bindery, Sacramento *Also called Delta Web Printing Inc (P-3729)*
Delta Wireless Inc ....E....209 948-9611
1700 W Fremont St Stockton (95203) *(P-14680)*
Delta Yimin Technologies Inc ....E....510 487-4411
33170 Central Ave Union City (94587) *(P-4275)*
Deltatrak Inc ....E....209 579-5343
1236 Doker Dr Modesto (95351) *(P-6898)*
Deltatrak Inc (PA) ....E....925 249-2250
6801 Koll Center Pkwy # 120 Pleasanton (94566) *(P-6899)*
Delu Vineyards Inc ....D....209 334-6660
15175 N Devries Rd Lodi (95242) *(P-50)*
Demand Known Inc ....F....310 929-5930
943 Addison Ave Palo Alto (94301) *(P-5776)*
Demandbase Inc (PA) ....C....415 683-2660
680 Folsom St Ste 400 San Francisco (94107) *(P-13114)*
Demandforce Inc ....E....800 246-9853
600 Harrison St Ste 601 San Francisco (94107) *(P-12380)*
Demandtec LLC ....B....914 499-1900
1 Franklin Pkwy Bldg 910 San Mateo (94403) *(P-12381)*
Demera Dmera Cmron An Accntncy ....E....559 226-9200
5080 N Fruit Ave Ste 101 Fresno (93711) *(P-18950)*
Demptos NAPA Cooperage (HQ) ....E....707 257-2628
1050 Soscol Ferry Rd NAPA (94558) *(P-3235)*
Demtech Services Inc ....E....530 621-3200
6414 Capitol Ave Diamond Springs (95619) *(P-4276)*
Denalect Inc ....D....925 935-2680
1309 Pine St Walnut Creek (94596) *(P-14127)*
Denalect Alarm Company, Walnut Creek *Also called Denalect Inc (P-14127)*
Denali Software Inc (HQ) ....E....408 943-1234
2655 Seely Ave San Jose (95134) *(P-13115)*
Denali Therapeutics Inc (PA) ....C....650 866-8548
161 Oyster Point Blvd South San Francisco (94080) *(P-4044)*
Denham Sj Inc (PA) ....E....530 241-1756
772 N Market St Redding (96003) *(P-14524)*
Denios Rsvlle Frmrs Mkt Actn I ....C....916 782-2704
2013 Opportunity Dr Roseville (95678) *(P-14251)*
Dennis Blazona Construction ....E....916 375-8337
525 Harbor Blvd Ste 10 West Sacramento (95691) *(P-1864)*
Dennis Design & Mfg Inc ....E....209 632-9956
4202 Jessup Rd Ceres (95307) *(P-9062)*
Dennis Zai MD Inc ....E....925 754-8710
3903 Lone Tree Way Antioch (94509) *(P-15376)*
Denny's, Los Banos *Also called JN Restaurants Inc (P-9144)*
Denodo Technologies Inc (PA) ....D....650 566-8833
525 University Ave Ste 31 Palo Alto (94301) *(P-12382)*
Denova Home Sales Inc ....D....925 852-0545
1500 Willow Pass Ct Concord (94520) *(P-10536)*
Denova Homes, Concord *Also called Denova Home Sales Inc (P-10536)*

Denron Inc ....B....408 435-8588
2135 Ringwood Ave San Jose (95131) *(P-6417)*
Density Inc ....E....888 990-2253
369 Sutter St San Francisco (94108) *(P-12383)*
Dental Bneft Providers Cal Inc ....E....415 778-3800
425 Market St Fl 12 San Francisco (94105) *(P-15832)*
Dentists Insurance Company (HQ) ....C....916 443-4567
1201 K St Ste 1600 Sacramento (95814) *(P-10271)*
Dentists Supply Company ....E....888 253-1223
1201 K St Ste 740 Sacramento (95814) *(P-7083)*
Dentonis Spring and Suspension, Stockton *Also called Dentonis Welding Works Inc (P-14712)*
Dentonis Welding Works Inc (PA) ....E....209 464-4930
801 S Airport Way Stockton (95205) *(P-14712)*
Department Ansthslogy Pain Mdc, Sacramento *Also called University California Davis (P-16703)*
Department of Allergy, San Francisco *Also called Kaiser Foundation Hospitals (P-15491)*
Department of Global Ecology, Stanford *Also called Carnegie Institution Wash (P-19206)*
Department of Health Services, Martinez *Also called County of Contra Costa (P-16339)*
Department of Mental Health, Turlock *Also called County of Stanislaus (P-17011)*
Department of Neurology, Sacramento *Also called University California Davis (P-15780)*
Department of Public Works, Sacramento *Also called City of Sacramento (P-8318)*
Department of Transportation, Ukiah *Also called County of Mendocino (P-7771)*
Department of Urology, San Francisco *Also called University Cal San Francisco (P-16696)*
Department Workforce Dev, Modesto *Also called County of Stanislaus (P-17810)*
Dependable Furniture Mfg Co, San Francisco *Also called Van Sark Inc (P-3293)*
Dependable Heating & AC, Dixon *Also called Dependable Sheet Metal (P-1249)*
Dependable Highway Express Inc ....D....209 342-0184
1343 Lone Palm Ave Modesto (95351) *(P-7523)*
Dependable Highway Express Inc ....D....510 357-2223
3012 Alvarado St San Leandro (94577) *(P-7524)*
Dependable Highway Express Inc ....D....510 357-2223
3199 Alvarado St San Leandro (94577) *(P-7525)*
Dependable Highway Express Inc ....E....916 374-0782
830 E St West Sacramento (95605) *(P-7460)*
Dependable Plas & Pattern Inc ....E....707 863-4900
4900 Fulton Dr Fairfield (94534) *(P-4277)*
Dependable Precision Mfg Inc ....F....209 369-1055
1111 S Stockton St Ste A Lodi (95240) *(P-4754)*
Dependable Sheet Metal ....E....707 678-9600
1855 N 1st St Unit A Dixon (95620) *(P-1249)*
Deplabs Inc ....D....415 456-5600
2872 Ygnacio Valley Rd # 24 Walnut Creek (94598) *(P-13879)*
Deposition Sciences Inc ....D....707 573-6700
3300 Coffey Ln Santa Rosa (95403) *(P-19049)*
Depuy Synthes Products Inc ....F....408 246-4300
130 Knowles Dr Ste E Los Gatos (95032) *(P-6969)*
Der Manouel Insurance Group, Fresno *Also called Hub Intrntional Insur Svcs Inc (P-10295)*
Derco Inc ....E....415 626-7442
888 Brannan St Ste 137 San Francisco (94103) *(P-9181)*
Derco Jewelers, San Francisco *Also called Derco Inc (P-9181)*
Derek Silva Community, San Francisco *Also called Catholic Chrties Cyo of The AR (P-17460)*
Dermira Inc ....B....650 421-7200
275 Middlefield Rd # 150 Menlo Park (94025) *(P-3891)*
Derosa Sales, Woodland *Also called Volume Snacks (P-9381)*
Derouen Enterprises LLC ....D....925 360-5743
1547 Palos Verdes Mall Walnut Creek (94597) *(P-14252)*
Des Architects Engineers Inc ....C....650 364-6453
399 Bradford St Ste 300 Redwood City (94063) *(P-18882)*
Design Community & Envmt Inc (PA) ....D....510 848-3815
1625 Shattuck Ave Ste 300 Berkeley (94709) *(P-19760)*
Design Industries Inc ....D....559 675-3535
17918 Brook Dr W Madera (93638) *(P-4430)*
Design Machine and Mfg ....E....559 897-7374
2491 Simpson St Kingsburg (93631) *(P-14744)*
Design Octaves ....E....831 464-8500
2701 Research Park Dr Soquel (95073) *(P-4278)*
Design Veronique, Richmond *Also called My True Image Mfg Inc (P-8788)*
Design Woodworking Inc (PA) ....E....209 334-6674
709 N Sacramento St Lodi (95240) *(P-3129)*
Designed MBL Systems Inds Inc ....F....209 892-6298
800 S State Highway 33 Patterson (95363) *(P-861)*
Designit Global LLC ....E....707 584-4000
5935 Labath Ave Rohnert Park (94928) *(P-18689)*
Designit North America Inc ....E....415 267-3500
450 Sansome St Fl 9 San Francisco (94111) *(P-12384)*
Designit Prototype, Rohnert Park *Also called Designit Global LLC (P-18689)*
Designs Metals, Ceres *Also called Dennis Design & Mfg Inc (P-9062)*
Designs With Fabric, South San Francisco *Also called Magnolia Lane Soft HM Furn Inc (P-3028)*
Desilva Gates Construction LP (PA) ....D....925 361-1380
11555 Dublin Blvd Dublin (94568) *(P-1031)*
Desserts On Us Inc ....F....707 822-0160
57 Belle Falor Ct Arcata (95521) *(P-2374)*
Destefano Design Group, Sacramento *Also called John C Destefano (P-3182)*
Destiny Arts Center ....E....510 597-1619
970 Grace Ave Oakland (94608) *(P-15201)*
Destiny Tool, Morgan Hill *Also called Step Tools Unlimited Inc (P-5099)*
Detecon Inc ....E....415 549-6999
33 New Montgomery St # 2000 San Francisco (94105) *(P-19761)*
Detention Device Systems ....E....510 783-0771
25545 Seaboard Ln Hayward (94545) *(P-5507)*
Devcon Construction Inc (PA) ....B....408 942-8200
690 Gibraltar Dr Milpitas (95035) *(P-862)*
Devcool Inc ....D....408 372-4313
5890 Stoneridge Dr # 107 Pleasanton (94588) *(P-19492)*

ALPHABETIC

Develop Disabilities Svc Org — 2331 Saint Marks Way G1 Sacramento (95864) *(P-17530)* ....D.......916 973-1951
Developmental Svcs Cal Dept — 15000 Arnold Dr Eldridge (95431) *(P-16756)* ....A.......707 938-6000
Develpmntal Dsblties Svc Orgnz (PA) — 5051 47th Ave Sacramento (95824) *(P-17531)* ....D.......916 456-5166
Device Anywhere — 777 Mariners Isl Blvd # 250 San Mateo (94404) *(P-12385)* ....D.......650 655-6400
Devil Mountain Whl Nurs LLC (PA) — 9885 Alcosta Blvd San Ramon (94583) *(P-9631)* ....D.......925 829-6006
Devincenzi Concrete Cnstr — 3276 Dutton Ave Santa Rosa (95407) *(P-1865)* ....E.......707 568-4370
Devincenzi Metal Products Inc — 1809 Castenada Dr Burlingame (94010) *(P-4755)* ....E.......650 692-5800
Devine & Son Trucking Co Inc (PA) — 3870 Channel Dr West Sacramento (95691) *(P-7716)* ....C.......559 486-7440
Devine Intermodal, West Sacramento *Also called Devine & Son Trucking Co Inc (P-7716)*
Devine Organics LLC (PA) — 684 W Cromwell Ave # 107 Fresno (93711) *(P-157)* ....E.......559 573-7500
Devonway Inc (PA) — 601 California St Ste 210 San Francisco (94108) *(P-12386)* ....D.......415 904-4000
Devron H Char MD — 45 Castro St Ste 309 San Francisco (94114) *(P-15377)* ....E.......415 522-0700
Dewberry Engineers Inc — 11060 White Rock Rd Ste 2 Rancho Cordova (95670) *(P-18690)* ....D.......916 363-4210
Deweyl Tool Co Inc — 959 Transport Way Petaluma (94954) *(P-5092)* ....E.......707 765-5779
Dewolf Realty Co Inc — 4330 California St San Francisco (94118) *(P-19324)* ....D.......415 221-2032
Dexta Corporation — 957 Enterprise Way NAPA (94558) *(P-7084)* ....D.......707 255-2454
DEYOUNG MUSEUM, San Francisco *Also called Corportion of Fine Arts Mseums (P-18268)*
Dfa of California — 2037 Morgan Dr Kingsburg (93631) *(P-19325)* ....D.......559 233-7249
Dfa of California — 1050 Diamond St Stockton (95205) *(P-14253)* ....D.......209 465-2289
Dfc Inc — 17986 County Road 94b Woodland (95695) *(P-6609)* ....D.......530 669-7115
DFI Technologies LLC — 5501 Monte Claire Ln Loomis (95650) *(P-8692)* ....D.......916 378-4166
Dfine Inc (HQ) — 3047 Orchard Pkwy San Jose (95134) *(P-6970)* ....C.......408 321-9999
Dfj Management LLC — 2882 Sand Hill Rd Ste 150 Menlo Park (94025) *(P-10842)* ....E.......650 233-9000
Dg Architects Inc (PA) — 550 Ellis St Mountain View (94043) *(P-18883)* ....E.......650 943-1660
Dg Mountz Associates, San Jose *Also called Mountz Inc (P-6728)*
Dga Plnning L Arch L Interiors, Mountain View *Also called Dg Architects Inc (P-18883)*
Dga Services Inc (PA) — 1075 Montague Expy Milpitas (95035) *(P-7619)* ....D.......408 232-4800
Dgn Technologies Inc (PA) — 46500 Fremont Blvd # 708 Fremont (94538) *(P-12387)* ....C.......510 252-0346
DH Smith Company Inc — 6000 Hellyer Ave Ste 150 San Jose (95138) *(P-1672)* ....D.......408 532-7617
Dharma Mudranalaya (PA) — 35788 Hauser Bridge Rd Cazadero (95421) *(P-3532)* ....E.......707 847-3380
DHARMA PUBLISHING, Cazadero *Also called Dharma Mudranalaya (P-3532)*
Dhe, San Leandro *Also called Dependable Highway Express Inc (P-7525)*
Dhillon Bros Trucking Inc — 6251 E American Ave Fresno (93725) *(P-7461)* ....E.......559 834-5600
Dhl Express (usa) Inc — 401 23rd St San Francisco (94107) *(P-7745)* ....D.......415 826-7338
Dhm Enterprises Inc — 7609 Wilbur Way Sacramento (95828) *(P-6658)* ....F.......916 688-7767
DHR Construction Inc — 860 Green Island Rd American Canyon (94503) *(P-1155)* ....E.......707 552-6500
Dhx-Dependable Hawaiian Ex Inc — 3623 Munster St Hayward (94545) *(P-7831)* ....D.......510 686-2600
Dhyan Infotech Inc — 160 Stanford Ave Fremont (94539) *(P-13880)* ....E.......510 589-7875
Dhyan Networks and Tech Inc, Fremont *Also called Dhyan Infotech Inc (P-13880)*
Diablo Ballet — 1646 N Calif Blvd Ste 109 Walnut Creek (94596) *(P-14846)* ....E.......925 943-1775
Diablo Cardiology Med Group, Walnut Creek *Also called Diablo Crdiolgy Med Group Inc (P-15378)*
Diablo Clinical Research Inc — 2255 Ygnacio Valley Rd M Walnut Creek (94598) *(P-3892)* ....E.......925 930-7267
Diablo Country Club — 1700 Clubhouse Rd Diablo (94528) *(P-15086)* ....E.......925 837-4221
Diablo Country Magazine Inc — 2520 Camino Diablo Walnut Creek (94597) *(P-3496)* ....E.......925 943-1111
Diablo Crdiolgy Med Group Inc — 1450 Treat Blvd Walnut Creek (94597) *(P-15378)* ....E.......925 933-6981
Diablo Creek Information LLC — 4057 Port Chicago Hwy # 100 Concord (94520) *(P-13784)* ....E.......925 330-3200
Diablo Custom Publishing, Walnut Creek *Also called Diablo Country Magazine Inc (P-3496)*
Diablo Grande Golf Resort, Patterson *Also called Sgm Inc (P-15025)*
Diablo Landscape Inc — 1655 Berryessa Rd San Jose (95133) *(P-458)* ....D.......408 487-9620
Diablo Lodge Partnership, Danville *Also called Braddock Logan Ventr Group LP (P-778)*
Diablo Molding & Trim Company — 5600 Sunol Blvd Ste C Pleasanton (94566) *(P-4703)* ....F.......925 417-0663
Diablo Realty — 975 Ygnacio Valley Rd Walnut Creek (94596) *(P-10537)* ....E.......925 933-9300
Diablo Subaru of Walnut Creek, Walnut Creek *Also called Lithia of Walnut Creek Inc (P-14664)*
Diablo Valley Eye Center, Walnut Creek *Also called Diablo Valley Eye Medical Ctr (P-15379)*
Diablo Valley Eye Medical Ctr — 112 La Casa Via Ste 260 Walnut Creek (94598) *(P-15379)* ....E.......925 934-6300
Diablo Valley Rock, Concord *Also called Carone & Company Inc (P-1952)*
Diablo Vly College Foundation (PA) — 321 Golf Club Rd Pleasant Hill (94523) *(P-14254)* ....A.......925 685-1230
Diablo Vly Montessori Schl Inc — 3390 Deer Hill Rd Lafayette (94549) *(P-17921)* ....E.......925 283-6036
Diageo North America Inc — 21468 8th St E Ste 1 Sonoma (95476) *(P-2549)* ....D.......707 939-6200
Diageo North America Inc — 1960 Saint Helena Hwy Rutherford (94573) *(P-2768)* ....D.......707 967-5200
Diageo North America Inc — 1160 Battery St Ste 30 San Francisco (94111) *(P-2550)* ....E.......415 835-7300
Diageo North America Inc — 6130 Stoneridge Mall Rd Pleasanton (94588) *(P-2769)* ....E.......925 520-3116
Diageo North America Inc — 151 Commonwealth Dr Menlo Park (94025) *(P-2770)* ....E.......650 329-3220
Diagnostic Biosystems Inc — 6616 Owens Dr Pleasanton (94588) *(P-19050)* ....E.......925 484-3350
Dialog Semiconductor, Campbell *Also called Iwatt Inc (P-6167)*
Dialog Semiconductor Inc (HQ) — 2560 Mission College Blvd # 110 Santa Clara (95054) *(P-6099)* ....C.......408 845-8500
Dialog Semiconductor Inc — 1515 Wyatt Dr Santa Clara (95054) *(P-8907)* ....C.......408 327-8800
Dialpad Inc — 1 Letterman Dr Bldg C San Francisco (94129) *(P-8693)* ....B.......760 648-3282
Diamanti Inc (PA) — 111 N Market St Ste 800 San Jose (95113) *(P-5331)* ....E.......408 645-5111
Diamond Communications Inc — 124 S C St Ste C Madera (93638) *(P-14128)* ....E.......559 673-5925
Diamond Foods LLC (PA) — 1050 Diamond St Stockton (95205) *(P-2443)* ....A.......209 467-6000
Diamond Learning Center Inc — 1620 W Fairmont Ave Fresno (93705) *(P-17532)* ....D.......559 241-0580
Diamond Mountain Casino — 900 Skyline Dr Susanville (96130) *(P-11048)* ....C.......530 252-1100
Diamond of California, Stockton *Also called Diamond Foods LLC (P-2443)*
Diamond Pet Fd Prcssors Cal LL — 250 Roth Rd Lathrop (95330) *(P-2334)* ....E.......209 983-4900
Diamond Ridge Healthcare Ctr, Pittsburg *Also called SSC Pittsburg Operating Co LP (P-16271)*
Diamond Sales & Services Inc — 1505 N 4th St San Jose (95112) *(P-14557)* ....E.......408 263-8997
Diamond Tool and Die Inc — 508 29th Ave Oakland (94601) *(P-5508)* ....E.......510 534-7050
Diamond Touch Inc — 1625 Trancas St Unit 2280 NAPA (94558) *(P-12388)* ....D.......707 253-7450
Diamond Youth Shelter, San Francisco *Also called Larkin Street Youth Services (P-17634)*
Dianne Adair Day Care Centers (PA) — 1862 Bailey Rd Concord (94521) *(P-17922)* ....D.......925 580-9704
Dibuduo Dfendis Insur Brks LLC (PA) — 6873 N West Ave Fresno (93711) *(P-10272)* ....E.......559 432-0222
Dicalite Minerals Corp (HQ) — 36994 Summit Lake Rd Burney (96013) *(P-4528)* ....E.......530 335-5451
Dicar Inc — 1285 Alma Ct San Jose (95112) *(P-4570)* ....E.......408 295-1106
Dice Molecules Sv Inc — 279 E Grand Ave Ste 300 South San Francisco (94080) *(P-3893)* ....F.......650 566-1402
Dick Anderson & Sons Farming — 15900 W Dorris Ave Huron (93234) *(P-158)* ....C.......559 945-2511
Dick Brown Technical Services — 553 Airport Rd Ste B Rio Vista (94571) *(P-555)* ....F.......707 374-2133
Dick James & Associates Inc — 2990 Lava Ridge Ct Ste 24 Roseville (95661) *(P-10538)* ....C.......916 332-7430
Dickenson Ptman Fgrty Inc A PR (PA) — 1455 1st St Ste 301 NAPA (94559) *(P-17250)* ....E.......707 252-7122
Dickinson, Diane MD, Arcata *Also called Northcountry Clinic (P-15554)*
Dicom Systems Inc — 119 University Ave Los Gatos (95030) *(P-12389)* ....F.......415 684-8790
Dicon Fiberoptics Inc — 1689 Regatta Blvd Richmond (94804) *(P-6418)* ....B.......510 620-5000
Die and Tool Products Inc — 1842 Sabre St Hayward (94545) *(P-4881)* ....F.......415 822-2888
Diede Construction Inc — 12393 N Hwy 99 Lodi (95240) *(P-863)* ....D.......209 369-8255
Diepenbrock Elkin LLP — 555 University Ave # 200 Sacramento (95825) *(P-17251)* ....E.......916 492-5000
Diestel Turkey Ranch — 14111 High Tech Dr C Jamestown (95327) *(P-235)* ....E.......209 984-0826
Diestel Turkey Ranch (PA) — 22200 Lyons Bald Mtn Rd Sonora (95370) *(P-236)* ....C.......209 532-4950
Dietrich Industries Inc — 2525 S Airport Way Stockton (95206) *(P-4541)* ....D.......209 547-9066
Dietrich Post Co Inc — 945 Bryant St San Francisco (94103) *(P-9206)* ....E.......510 596-0080
Diez & Leis RE Group Inc — 5120 Manzanita Ave # 120 Carmichael (95608) *(P-10539)* ....A.......916 487-4287
Digestive Disease Consultants — 1187 E Herndon Ave # 101 Fresno (93720) *(P-15380)* ....E.......559 440-0450
Digicom Electronics Inc — 7799 Pardee Ln Oakland (94621) *(P-5926)* ....E.......510 639-7003
Digilens Inc — 1288 Hammerwood Ave Sunnyvale (94089) *(P-6870)* ....E.......408 734-0219
Digilock, Petaluma *Also called Security People Inc (P-6468)*
Digital Chocolate Inc — 1855 S Grant St Ste 200 San Mateo (94402) *(P-12390)* ....E.......650 372-1600
Digital Doc LLC — 4789 Golden Foothill Pkwy El Dorado Hills (95762) *(P-8779)* ....E.......916 941-8010

Digital Dynamics Inc...E...831 438-4444
5 Victor Sq Scotts Valley (95066) *(P-6715)*
DIGITAL FIRST MEDIA, San Jose *Also called San Jose Mercury-News LLC* ***(P-3476)***
Digital Foundry Inc...E...415 789-1600
1707 Tiburon Blvd Belvedere Tiburon (94920) *(P-13881)*
Digital Insight Corporation (HQ)...**C...818 879-1010**
1300 Seaport Blvd Ste 300 Redwood City (94063) *(P-13785)*
Digital Japan LLC (HQ)...**D...415 738-6500**
4 Embarcadero Ctr San Francisco (94111) *(P-10816)*
Digital Loggers, Santa Clara *Also called Computer Performance Inc* ***(P-8682)***
Digital Loggers Inc...E...408 330-5599
2695 Walsh Ave Santa Clara (95051) *(P-5651)*
Digital Mania Inc...E...415 896-0500
455 Market St Ste 180 San Francisco (94105) *(P-3640)*
Digital Media Publishing, Sausalito *Also called American Media Corp* ***(P-3554)***
Digital Nirvana Inc (PA)...**B...510 226-9000**
3984 Washington Blvd # 355 Fremont (94538) *(P-19493)*
Digital Onus Inc (PA)...**C...408 228-3490**
84 W Santa Clara St # 74 San Jose (95113) *(P-12391)*
Digital Path Inc...E...800 676-7284
1065 Marauder St Chico (95973) *(P-7946)*
Digital Prototype Systems Inc...E...559 454-1600
4955 E Yale Ave Fresno (93727) *(P-5838)*
Digital Shadows Inc (PA)...**C...888 889-4143**
3046a Polk St San Francisco (94109) *(P-14129)*
Digital Storm, Gilroy *Also called Hanaps Enterprises* ***(P-5372)***
Digitalist USA Ltd...A...949 278-1354
611 Gateway Blvd Ste 120 South San Francisco (94080) *(P-13577)*
Digitalthink Inc (HQ)...**C...415 625-4000**
601 Brannan St San Francisco (94107) *(P-19494)*
Digite Inc...C...408 418-3834
21060 Homestead Rd # 220 Cupertino (95014) *(P-12392)*
Digits Financial Inc...E...814 634-4487
1015 Fillmore St San Francisco (94115) *(P-13116)*
Dignity Community Care (PA)...**E...415 438-5500**
185 Berry St Ste 300 San Francisco (94107) *(P-16346)*
Dignity Health...E...916 965-1936
1380 Lead Hill Blvd # 110 Roseville (95661) *(P-15381)*
Dignity Health (HQ)...**C...415 438-5500**
185 Berry St Ste 200 San Francisco (94107) *(P-16347)*
Dignity Health...A...916 537-5000
6501 Coyle Ave Carmichael (95608) *(P-16348)*
Dignity Health...C...916 423-5940
7500 Hospital Dr Sacramento (95823) *(P-16349)*
Dignity Health...A...415 668-1000
450 Stanyan St San Francisco (94117) *(P-16350)*
Dignity Health...E...209 943-4663
2333 W March Ln Ste B Stockton (95207) *(P-16878)*
Dignity Health Med Foundation...D...831 475-8834
1667 Dominican Way # 134 Santa Cruz (95065) *(P-16351)*
Dignity Health Med Foundation...D...916 379-2840
3400 Data Dr Rancho Cordova (95670) *(P-16352)*
Dignity Health Med Foundation...D...916 450-2600
9837 Folsom Blvd Ste F Sacramento (95827) *(P-16353)*
Dignity Health Med Foundation (HQ)...**C...916 379-2840**
3400 Data Dr Rancho Cordova (95670) *(P-16354)*
Dignity Health Med Foundation...D...831 475-1111
1595 Soquel Dr Ste 140 Santa Cruz (95065) *(P-16355)*
Dignity Hlth Med Group - Dmnca, Santa Cruz *Also called Dignity Health Med Foundation* ***(P-16351)***
Dignity Hlth Med Grp-Dominican, Rancho Cordova *Also called Dignity Health Med Foundation* ***(P-16352)***
Dignity Hlth Med Grp-Dominican, Rancho Cordova *Also called Dignity Health Med Foundation* ***(P-16354)***
Diligence Security Group...C...510 710-5806
66 Franklin St Ste 300 Oakland (94607) *(P-1496)*
Diligente Technologies LLC...B...510 304-0852
2350 Mission College Blvd Santa Clara (95054) *(P-13578)*
Dillingham & Murphy LLP (PA)...**E...415 397-2700**
353 Sacramento St # 2000 San Francisco (94111) *(P-17252)*
Dillingham Construction NA...A...925 249-8850
1020 Serpentine Ln # 110 Pleasanton (94566) *(P-1156)*
Dimare Company, Newman *Also called Dimare Enterprises Inc* ***(P-26)***
Dimare Enterprises Inc (PA)...**C...209 827-2900**
1406 N St Newman (95360) *(P-26)*
Dimaxx Technologies LLC...F...530 888-1942
11838 Kemper Rd Auburn (95603) *(P-6871)*
Dimension Data Cloud, Santa Clara *Also called Ntt Cloud Infrastructure Inc* ***(P-12639)***
Dimensions Unlimited, Vallejo *Also called Jbe Inc* ***(P-3315)***
Dinahs Garden Hotel Inc...C...650 493-2844
4261 El Camino Real Palo Alto (94306) *(P-11049)*
Dinostor, Mountain View *Also called Global Automation Inc* ***(P-13900)***
Diocese Stockton Eductl Off...C...209 634-8578
1250 Cooper Ave Ste 3 Turlock (95380) *(P-17923)*
Dionex Corporation (HQ)...**B...408 737-0700**
1228 Titan Way Ste 1002 Sunnyvale (94085) *(P-6824)*
Direct Commerce Inc...E...415 288-9700
25 Martling Rd San Anselmo (94960) *(P-13708)*
Direct Line Inc...E...510 843-3900
2847 Shattuck Ave Berkeley (94705) *(P-14255)*
Direct Line Tele Response, Berkeley *Also called Direct Line Inc* ***(P-14255)***
Direct Stone Tool Supply Inc (PA)...**F...510 747-9720**
2400 Teagarden St San Leandro (94577) *(P-4605)*
Direct Technology, Roseville *Also called Directapps Inc* ***(P-13882)***
Direct Urgent Care Inc...E...510 686-3621
2920 Telegraph Ave Berkeley (94705) *(P-15382)*
Directapps Inc (PA)...**C...916 787-2200**
3009 Douglas Blvd Ste 300 Roseville (95661) *(P-13882)*
Directed Light Inc...E...408 321-8500
74 Bonaventura Dr San Jose (95134) *(P-9063)*
Directly Inc...D...650 714-7334
333 Bryant St Ste 250 San Francisco (94107) *(P-12393)*
Directv Group Inc...C...707 452-7409
340 Commerce Ave Fairfield (94533) *(P-8061)*
Directv Group Inc...C...510 481-1324
1129 B St San Lorenzo (94580) *(P-8062)*
Dirt Dggers N Mtrcycle CLB Inc...E...916 640-7328
5591 Hwy 49 Pilot Hill (95664) *(P-18563)*
Dirt Dynasty Inc...E...209 623-1141
4110 Meadow Oaks Dr Valley Springs (95252) *(P-1032)*
Dirt Movers...E...209 461-7111
1930 W Fremont St Stockton (95203) *(P-1955)*
Disability Rights California (PA)...**D...916 488-9950**
1831 K St Sacramento (95811) *(P-17253)*
Discopylabs (PA)...**E...510 651-5100**
48641 Milmont Dr Fremont (94538) *(P-7832)*
Discopylabs...E...510 651-5100
48819 Kato Rd Fremont (94539) *(P-13883)*
Discord Inc...C...650 389-2453
444 De Haro St Ste 200 San Francisco (94107) *(P-12394)*
Discount Builders Supply...D...415 285-2800
1695 Mission St San Francisco (94103) *(P-8541)*
DISCOUNT TECH, San Francisco *Also called Techsoup Global* ***(P-18476)***
Discovery Cnsling Ctr of San R...D...925 837-0505
115 Town And Country Dr A Danville (94526) *(P-17533)*
Dishcraft Robotics Inc...D...888 231-3318
611 Taylor Way Ste 1 San Carlos (94070) *(P-19213)*
Disney Construction Inc...D...650 689-5149
533 Airport Blvd Ste 120 Burlingame (94010) *(P-1033)*
Dispatch Office, Oakland *Also called First Transit Inc* ***(P-7333)***
Dispatcher Newspaper...F...415 775-0533
1188 Franklin St Fl 4 San Francisco (94109) *(P-3432)*
Displaylink Corp (HQ)...**F...650 838-0481**
1251 Mckay Dr San Jose (95131) *(P-12395)*
Dissmeyer Corporation...E...415 587-5869
1400 Wallace Ave San Francisco (94124) *(P-1798)*
Distel Family Ranch, Sonora *Also called Diestel Turkey Ranch* ***(P-236)***
Distinctive Corporation...E...408 568-5598
14413 Big Basin Way Saratoga (95070) *(P-14256)*
District Attorney, Oakland *Also called County of Alameda* ***(P-17238)***
Ditech Networks Inc (HQ)...**D...408 883-3636**
3099 N 1st St San Jose (95134) *(P-5793)*
Divco West Acquisitions LLC (PA)...**E...415 284-5700**
301 Howard St Ste 2100 San Francisco (94105) *(P-10752)*
Divco West RE Svcs Inc...E...415 284-5700
301 Howard St Ste 2100 San Francisco (94105) *(P-10540)*
Diverse Steel Sales Inc (PA)...**F...925 756-0555**
1666 Willow Pass Rd Pittsburg (94565) *(P-8815)*
Divine Home Care, Oakland *Also called Wild Karma Inc* ***(P-16160)***
Divisadero 500 LLC...F...415 572-6062
502 Divisadero St San Francisco (94117) *(P-3335)*
Divisadero Touchless Car Wash, San Francisco *Also called Canadian American Oil Co Inc* ***(P-10382)***
Divisadero Touchless Carwash, San Francisco *Also called Canadian American Oil Co Inc* ***(P-14634)***
Division of Agriculture, Oakland *Also called Regents of The Univ of Cal* ***(P-19116)***
Dixie SC Dst Maint Dept, San Rafael *Also called Miller Creek School District* ***(P-11973)***
Dixon Corp...E...510 366-6697
35182 Santiago St Fremont (94536) *(P-11859)*
Dixon Ridge Farms, Winters *Also called Russell Wayne Lester* ***(P-113)***
Diy Co...F...844 564-6349
3360 20th St San Francisco (94110) *(P-6512)*
Diy Drones, Berkeley *Also called 3d Robotics Inc* ***(P-6508)***
DJ Grey Company Inc...F...707 431-2779
455 Allan Ct Healdsburg (95448) *(P-6419)*
Dja-Mge JV LLC...E...916 421-1000
7415 Greenhaven Dr # 100 Sacramento (95831) *(P-18691)*
Djont Operations LLC...C...650 342-4600
150 Anza Blvd Burlingame (94010) *(P-11050)*
Djont Operations LLC...C...408 942-0400
901 E Calaveras Blvd Milpitas (95035) *(P-11051)*
Djont/Cmb Ssf Leasing LLC...E...650 589-3400
250 Gateway Blvd South San Francisco (94080) *(P-11052)*
Djont/Cmb Ssf Leasing LLC...D...650 589-3400
250 Gateway Blvd South San Francisco (94080) *(P-11053)*
DK Enterprises Inc...E...209 892-3386
520 S 3rd St Patterson (95363) *(P-1799)*
DK Express Cargo Inc...E...209 954-9354
2000 W Charter Way Stockton (95206) *(P-7526)*
Dkd Property Management, San Jose *Also called Property Maintenance Company* ***(P-11987)***
Dki, Fresno *Also called David Knott Inc* ***(P-1984)***
Dkw Precision Machining Inc...E...209 824-7899
17731 Ideal Pkwy Manteca (95336) *(P-5509)*
DLa Colmena Inc...E...831 724-4544
129 W Lake Ave Watsonville (95076) *(P-2375)*
Dli Mechanical, San Carlos *Also called Daniel Larratt Plumbing Inc* ***(P-1248)***
Dlight Design Inc...A...415 872-6136
2100 Geng Rd Ste 210 Palo Alto (94303) *(P-1250)*
Dlive Inc...E...650 491-9555
3390 Octavius Dr Apt 438 Santa Clara (95054) *(P-3566)*
Dmg Mori Digital Tech Lab Corp...E...530 746-7400
3601 Faraday Ave Davis (95618) *(P-5093)*
Dmg Mori Manufacturing USA Inc (HQ)...**C...530 746-7400**
3601 Faraday Ave Davis (95618) *(P-5073)*
Dmh - Frnsic Assrtive Cmmnty T, Santa Rosa *Also called County of Sonoma* ***(P-16874)***

ALPHABETIC

DMS Facility Services Inc......A......510 656-9400
3137 Skyway Ct Fremont (94539) *(P-11944)*
Dna Twopointo Inc......D......650 853-8347
37950 Central Ct Newark (94560) *(P-19051)*
Dna2.0, Newark *Also called Dna Twopointo Inc (P-19051)*
DNC Prks Resorts At Tenaya Inc (HQ)......C......877 247-9241
1122 Highway 41 Fish Camp (93623) *(P-11054)*
DNC Prks Rsrts At Yosemite Inc......A......209 372-1001
9001 Village Dr Yosemite Ntpk (95389) *(P-11055)*
Dnfcs Inc (PA)......E......510 201-9809
2150 N 1st St Ste 400 San Jose (95131) *(P-12396)*
Dnj Parking, San Francisco *Also called California Parking Company (P-10476)*
Dns Electronics, Sunnyvale *Also called Screen Spe Usa LLC (P-14704)*
Dnt In Home Care Inc......E......530 556-4030
3440 Palmer Dr Ste 8h Cameron Park (95682) *(P-16879)*
Do Arellanes Holdings......E......415 472-5700
899 Northgate Dr Ste 304 San Rafael (94903) *(P-12084)*
Do Big Things LLC......E......415 806-3423
147 Buckelew St Sausalito (94965) *(P-12397)*
Do Dine Inc......F......510 583-7546
24052 Mission Blvd Hayward (94544) *(P-13117)*
Do It Best, Saint Helena *Also called Central Valley Builders Supply (P-9033)*
Docker Inc (PA)......B......800 764-4847
3790 Corina Way 1052 Palo Alto (94303) *(P-12398)*
Docomo Innovations Inc......E......650 493-9600
3301 Hillview Ave Palo Alto (94304) *(P-19052)*
Docphin, Mountain View *Also called Healthtap Inc (P-15428)*
Docsend Inc......D......888 258-5951
351 California St # 1200 San Francisco (94104) *(P-13118)*
Doctors Company Foundation......A......800 421-2368
185 Greenwood Rd NAPA (94558) *(P-10084)*
Doctors Company Insurance Svcs......B......707 226-0100
185 Greenwood Rd NAPA (94558) *(P-10192)*
Doctors Hospital Manteca Inc......B......209 823-3111
1205 E North St Manteca (95336) *(P-16356)*
Doctors Management Company (HQ)......C......707 226-0100
185 Greenwood Rd NAPA (94558) *(P-10273)*
Document Proc Solutions Inc......E......925 839-1182
535 Main St Ste 317 Martinez (94553) *(P-3343)*
Docusign Inc (PA)......B......415 489-4940
221 Main St Ste 1550 San Francisco (94105) *(P-13119)*
Dodge & Cox......C......415 981-1710
555 California St Fl 40 San Francisco (94104) *(P-10753)*
Dodge Ridge Corporation......B......209 536-5300
1 Dodge Ridge Rd Pinecrest (95364) *(P-11056)*
Dodge Ridge Winter Sports Area, Pinecrest *Also called Dodge Ridge Corporation (P-11056)*
Dokken Engineering (PA)......D......916 858-0642
110 Blue Ravine Rd # 200 Folsom (95630) *(P-18692)*
Dolan Concrete Construction......D......408 869-3250
3045 Alfred St Santa Clara (95054) *(P-1866)*
Dolans Pinole Lbr Bldg Mtls Co......E......925 927-4662
2750 Camino Diablo Lafayette (94597) *(P-8542)*
Dolby Laboratories Inc (PA)......A......415 558-0200
1275 Market St Fl 15 San Francisco (94103) *(P-5754)*
Dolby Labs Licensing Corp......C......415 558-0200
100 Potrero Ave San Francisco (94103) *(P-5755)*
Dole Food Company Inc......C......559 843-2504
12840 W Shields Ave Kerman (93630) *(P-2259)*
Dole Packaged Foods LLC......B......559 875-3354
1117 K St Sanger (93657) *(P-2292)*
Dolk Tractor Company......E......707 374-6438
242 N Front St Rio Vista (94571) *(P-14745)*
Dolphin Technology Inc......E......408 392-0012
333 W Santa Clara St # 9 San Jose (95113) *(P-6100)*
Domain Hotel, The, Sunnyvale *Also called Adswood Trs LLC (P-10911)*
Domaine Carneros Ltd......D......707 257-0101
1240 Duhig Rd NAPA (94559) *(P-51)*
Domaine Chandon Inc (HQ)......D......707 944-8844
1 California Dr Yountville (94599) *(P-2551)*
Domaine St George Winery, Healdsburg *Also called Pan Magna Group (P-2677)*
Dome Printing and Lithograph, McClellan *Also called Meriliz Incorporated (P-3676)*
Dome9 Security Inc......E......831 212-2353
800 W El Cmino Real Ste 1 Mountain View (94040) *(P-8694)*
Domico Software......F......510 841-4155
1220 Oakland Blvd Ste 300 Walnut Creek (94596) *(P-13120)*
Dominguez Landscape Svcs Inc......D......916 381-8855
8376 Rovana Cir Sacramento (95828) *(P-459)*
Dominican Hospital Foundation......C......831 457-7057
610 Frederick St Santa Cruz (95062) *(P-18099)*
Dominican Hospital Foundation (HQ)......C......831 462-7700
1555 Soquel Dr Santa Cruz (95065) *(P-16357)*
Dominican Medical Foundation, Santa Cruz *Also called Dignity Health Med Foundation (P-16355)*
Dominican Oaks Corporation......D......831 462-6257
3400 Paul Sweet Rd Ofc Santa Cruz (95065) *(P-10428)*
Dominican Rehab Services, Santa Cruz *Also called Dominican Hospital Foundation (P-18099)*
Dominics Orgnal Gnova Deli Inc......D......707 253-8686
1550 Trancas St NAPA (94558) *(P-2376)*
Dominion International Inc......E......916 683-9545
2305 Longport Ct Elk Grove (95758) *(P-11057)*
Domino Data Lab Inc (PA)......C......415 570-2425
548 Market St 72800 San Francisco (94104) *(P-13121)*
Domino's, Turlock *Also called Central Valley Pizza LLC (P-10804)*
Dominus Estate Corporation......F......707 944-8954
2570 Napa Nook Rd Yountville (94599) *(P-2552)*
Domries Enterprises Inc......E......559 485-4306
12281 Road 29 Madera (93638) *(P-5003)*
Domus Construction & Design......E......916 381-7500
8864 Fruitridge Rd Sacramento (95826) *(P-632)*
Don Beeman Farms, Woodland *Also called Donald W Beeman (P-27)*
Don Berry Construction Inc......D......559 896-5700
13701 Golden State Blvd Kingsburg (93631) *(P-1034)*
Don Francisco Cheese, Modesto *Also called Rizo Lopez Foods Inc (P-2153)*
Don Gragnani Farms......D......559 693-4352
12910 S Napa Ave Tranquillity (93668) *(P-159)*
Don Ramatici Insurance Inc......E......707 782-9200
731 Southpoint Blvd A Petaluma (94954) *(P-10274)*
Don Sbstani Sons Intl Wine Ngc......E......707 337-1961
520 Airpark Rd NAPA (94558) *(P-2553)*
Don Turner and Associates, Fresno *Also called Turner Camera SEC Systems Inc (P-14151)*
Don Vito Ozuna Foods Corp......E......408 465-2010
180 Cochrane Cir Morgan Hill (95037) *(P-2854)*
Donaghy Sales Inc......A......559 486-0901
2363 S Cedar Ave Fresno (93725) *(P-9550)*
Donahue & Davies LLP......E......916 817-2900
1 Natoma St Folsom (95630) *(P-17254)*
Donahue Fitzgerald LLP......E......510 451-3300
1999 Harrison St Ste 2600 Oakland (94612) *(P-17255)*
Donahue Gallager Woods LLP (PA)......D......415 381-4161
1999 Harrison St Ste 2500 Oakland (94612) *(P-17256)*
Donal Machine Inc......E......707 763-6625
591 N Mcdowell Blvd Petaluma (94954) *(P-5510)*
Donald P Dick AC Inc (PA)......E......559 255-1644
1444 N Whitney Ave Fresno (93703) *(P-1251)*
Donald W Beeman......E......530 662-3012
37190 County Road 24 Woodland (95695) *(P-27)*
Donaldson Arthur M D Inc......D......209 532-0966
940 Sylva Ln Ste G Sonora (95370) *(P-15383)*
Donations With Care......D......916 544-3080
6220 Winding Way Carmichael (95608) *(P-17534)*
Dongalen Enterprises Inc (PA)......E......916 422-3110
330 Commerce Cir Sacramento (95815) *(P-9513)*
Donner Lake Village Resort......D......530 587-6081
15695 Dnner Paca Rd Ste 1 Truckee (96161) *(P-11058)*
Donor Network West......E......510 418-0336
6721 N Willow Ave Ste 104 Fresno (93710) *(P-17135)*
Donor Network West (PA)......C......925 480-3100
12667 Alcosta Blvd # 500 San Ramon (94583) *(P-17136)*
Donor Network West......E......510 418-0336
5800 Airport Rd Ste B Redding (96002) *(P-17137)*
Dons Mobile Glass Inc (PA)......D......209 548-7000
3800 Finch Rd Modesto (95357) *(P-8643)*
Doors Unlimited......E......707 822-5959
1685 Sutter Rd McKinleyville (95519) *(P-8543)*
Dorado Network Systems Corp......C......650 227-7300
555 12th St Ste 1100 Oakland (94607) *(P-13122)*
Dorado Software Inc......D......916 673-1100
4805 Golden Foothill Pkwy El Dorado Hills (95762) *(P-12399)*
Doremus & Company......E......415 273-7800
720 California St Fl 6 San Francisco (94108) *(P-11750)*
Dorfman Pacific, Stockton *Also called Dorfman-Pacific Co (P-9243)*
Dorfman-Pacific Co (HQ)......C......209 982-1400
2615 Boeing Way Stockton (95206) *(P-9243)*
Dorothy Johnson Center, Chico *Also called Chico Area Recreation & Pk Dst (P-15192)*
Dorris Eatons School......D......925 930-9000
1 Annabel Ln San Ramon (94583) *(P-17924)*
Dorris Lumber and Moulding Co (PA)......D......916 452-7531
3453 Ramona Ave Ste 5 Sacramento (95826) *(P-3130)*
Dorsey, D J MD, Fremont *Also called South E Bay Pdtric Med Group I (P-15697)*
Dos Palos Mem Rur Hlth Clinic, Dos Palos *Also called Dos Palos Memorial Hosp Inc (P-15384)*
Dos Palos Memorial Hosp Inc......D......209 392-6121
2118 Marguerite St Dos Palos (93620) *(P-15384)*
Dostal Studio......F......415 721-7080
17 Woodland Ave San Rafael (94901) *(P-7203)*
DOT Foods Inc......C......209 581-9090
2200 Nickerson Dr Modesto (95358) *(P-9270)*
Double D Farms (PA)......E......559 573-7500
29191 Fresno Coalinga Rd Coalinga (93210) *(P-160)*
Double Decker Corporation......E......707 585-0226
300 Golf Course Dr Rohnert Park (94928) *(P-14889)*
Double Decker Lanes, Rohnert Park *Also called Double Decker Corporation (P-14889)*
Double Diamond Dairy & Ranch......D......209 722-8505
729 E Jefferson Rd El Nido (95317) *(P-210)*
Double Eagle Resort......E......760 648-7004
5587 Boulder Drv Hwy 158 June Lake (93529) *(P-11059)*
Double Eagle Resort & Spa, June Lake *Also called Double Eagle Resort (P-11059)*
Double Tree By Hlton Sfo Arprt, South San Francisco *Also called Lotus Hospitality Inc (P-11270)*
Double Tree Past Acute, Sacramento *Also called Sacramento Operating Co LP (P-16105)*
Doubledutch Inc (HQ)......C......800 748-9024
44 Tehama St Ste 504 San Francisco (94105) *(P-13123)*
Doubletree By Hilton Fresno, Fresno *Also called Uniwell Fresno Hotel LLC (P-11551)*
Doubletree By Hilton San Jose, San Jose *Also called San Jose Lessee LLC (P-11439)*
Doubletree Hotel, San Jose *Also called HLT San Jose LLC (P-11145)*
Doubletree Hotel Modesto, Modesto *Also called Modesto Hospitality Lessee LLC (P-11307)*
Doubltree By Hilton Ht Modesto, Modesto *Also called Modesto Hospitality LLC (P-11306)*
Doubltree By Hlton Brkley Mrin, Berkeley *Also called Westpost Berkeley LLC (P-11574)*
Doubltree By Hlton Ht Snoma Wi, Rohnert Park *Also called Park US Lessee Holdings LLC (P-11357)*
Doudell Trucking Company (PA)......D......408 263-7300
1505 N 4th St San Jose (95112) *(P-7527)*
Doug Arnold Real Estate Inc (PA)......E......530 758-3080
505 2nd St Davis (95616) *(P-10541)*

ALPHABETIC SECTION
Duckhorn Portfolio Inc

Doughtronics Inc (PA).....E.....510 524-1327
1601 San Pablo Ave Berkeley (94702) *(P-2377)*
Doughtronics Inc.....E.....510 843-2978
2730 9th St Berkeley (94710) *(P-2378)*
Douglas Ross Construction Inc.....D.....408 429-7700
900 E Hamilton Ave # 140 Campbell (95008) *(P-744)*
Doulas By Bay LLC.....D.....415 510-9736
1201 Liberty St El Cerrito (94530) *(P-17138)*
Dow Jones Lmg Stockton Inc.....A.....209 943-6397
530 E Market St Stockton (95202) *(P-3433)*
Downey Brand LLP (PA).....C.....916 444-1000
621 Capitol Mall Fl 18 Sacramento (95814) *(P-17257)*
Downtown Berkeley YMCA, Berkeley *Also called Young MNS Chrstn Assn of E Bay (P-18495)*
Downtown Joe's, NAPA *Also called Joes Dwntwn Brewry & Rest Inc (P-2482)*
Downtown Palo Alto Kindercare, Palo Alto *Also called Childrens Crative Lrng Ctr Inc (P-17898)*
Doximity Inc.....A.....650 549-4330
500 3rd St Ste 510 San Francisco (94107) *(P-12400)*
Dp, Santa Clara *Also called Data Physics Corporation (P-8689)*
Dpp Tech Inc.....E.....415 754-9170
1390 Market St Ste 200 San Francisco (94102) *(P-12401)*
Dppm Inc.....D.....415 695-7707
4040 24th St San Francisco (94114) *(P-10542)*
Dpr Construction Inc (PA).....A.....650 474-1450
1450 Veterans Blvd Redwood City (94063) *(P-864)*
Dpr Construction A Gen Partnr.....C.....408 370-2322
1510 S Winchester Blvd San Jose (95128) *(P-865)*
Dpr Construction A Gen Partnr.....C.....916 568-3434
1801 J St Sacramento (95811) *(P-866)*
Dpr Construction A Gen Partnr (HQ).....A.....650 474-1450
1450 Veterans Blvd Redwood City (94063) *(P-867)*
Dpr Skanska A Joint Venture.....E.....650 306-7671
1450 Veterans Blvd Redwood City (94063) *(P-868)*
Dps Telecom, Fresno *Also called Digital Prototype Systems Inc (P-5838)*
Dpss Lasers Inc.....E.....408 988-4300
2525 Walsh Ave Santa Clara (95051) *(P-6513)*
Dpw Inc.....E.....650 588-8482
203 E Harris Ave South San Francisco (94080) *(P-1252)*
Dr Earth Inc.....F.....707 448-4676
4021 Devon Ct Vacaville (95688) *(P-4130)*
Dr McDougall's Right Foods, Woodland *Also called Bright People Foods Inc (P-2874)*
Dr Pepper/Seven Up Inc.....F.....707 545-7797
1901 Russell Ave Santa Rosa (95403) *(P-2790)*
Dr Ross, Wan & Taylor, Campbell *Also called Family Eye Care Optometry Corp (P-15868)*
Dr. Brostrand, Sacramento *Also called Csus (P-19487)*
Dr. Yelena L Krijanovski, Fairfield *Also called Sutter Regional Med Foundation (P-15732)*
Dragon Engineering, Chowchilla *Also called Anderson Pump Company (P-8221)*
Dragonfly Investments Group, San Mateo *Also called Veev Group Inc (P-10020)*
Drakaina Logistics.....D.....559 765-1347
958 Ryan Ave Clovis (93611) *(P-7879)*
Drake Enterprises Incorporated.....D.....707 864-3077
490 Watt Dr Fairfield (94534) *(P-3050)*
Drake Haglan & Associates, Rancho Cordova *Also called Dewberry Engineers Inc (P-18690)*
Drake Terrace, San Rafael *Also called Kisco Senior Living LLC (P-10444)*
Drake's Brewing Company, San Leandro *Also called Artisan Brewers LLC (P-2473)*
Drawbridge Inc.....D.....650 513-2323
479 N Pastoria Ave Sunnyvale (94085) *(P-19495)*
Drd Hospitality Inc.....E.....916 952-6552
179 Commerce Ave Manteca (95336) *(P-11060)*
Drd Hospitality Inc.....E.....916 952-6552
9950 Koa Ln Elk Grove (95624) *(P-11061)*
Dreamalliance Entrmt Inc (PA).....E.....510 270-8693
20236 Santa Maria Ave Castro Valley (94546) *(P-14871)*
Dreambig Semiconductor Inc.....D.....408 839-1232
2860 Zanker Rd Ste 210 San Jose (95134) *(P-6101)*
Dreamctchers Empwerment Netwrk.....C.....925 935-6630
1911 Oak Park Blvd Pleasant Hill (94523) *(P-18100)*
Dreamctchers Empwerment Netwrk.....E.....707 558-1775
2201 Tuolumne St Vallejo (94589) *(P-6420)*
Dreamhome Remodeling and Bldrs, San Jose *Also called Eli Kiselman (P-565)*
Dreams Duvets & Bed Linens Inc.....F.....415 543-1800
921 Howard St San Francisco (94103) *(P-3023)*
Dreams Duvets & Linens, San Francisco *Also called Dreams Duvets & Bed Linens Inc (P-3023)*
Dreisbach Enterprises Inc.....E.....510 533-6600
2530 E 11th St Oakland (94601) *(P-10478)*
Dremio Corporation (PA).....E.....408 882-3569
3970 Freedom Cir Ste 110 Santa Clara (95054) *(P-12402)*
Dresick Farms Inc (PA).....C.....559 945-2513
19536 Jayne Ave Huron (93234) *(P-28)*
Dresser/Areia Construction.....C.....800 392-9891
3940 Valley Ave Pleasanton (94566) *(P-1099)*
Dreyer Bbich Bccola Cllham LLP.....D.....916 379-3500
20 Bicentennial Cir Sacramento (95826) *(P-17258)*
Dreyer Bbich Bccola WD Cmpora (PA).....D.....916 379-3500
20 Bicentennial Cir Sacramento (95826) *(P-17259)*
Dreyers Grand Ice Cream Inc (HQ).....C.....510 594-9466
5929 College Ave Oakland (94618) *(P-2171)*
Dreyers Grand Ice Cream Inc.....A.....510 652-8187
5929 College Ave Oakland (94618) *(P-2172)*
Dreyers Grnd Ice Cream Hldngs (HQ).....C.....510 652-8187
5929 College Ave Oakland (94618) *(P-9337)*
Dri Clean & Restoration.....E.....559 292-1100
2890 N Sunnyside Ave U114 Fresno (93727) *(P-563)*
Driftwood Convalescent Hosp, Davis *Also called Mariner Health Care Inc (P-16051)*
Driftwood Healthcare Center, Hayward *Also called Mariner Health Care Inc (P-16054)*
Drilling & Trenching Sup Inc (PA).....F.....510 895-1650
1458 Mariani Ct Tracy (95376) *(P-5094)*
Drilling World, Tracy *Also called Drilling & Trenching Sup Inc (P-5094)*
Dripworks Inc.....E.....707 459-6323
190 San Hedrin Cir Willits (95490) *(P-9034)*
Drisas Groom McCormick.....D.....559 447-8484
7511 N Remington Ave Fresno (93711) *(P-18951)*
Driscolls Inc (PA).....D.....831 424-0506
345 Westridge Dr Watsonville (95076) *(P-9398)*
Driscolls Inc.....D.....800 871-3333
150 Westridge Dr Watsonville (95076) *(P-9399)*
Drishti Technologies Inc.....C.....669 273-9090
1975 W El Cmino Real Ste Mountain View (94040) *(P-12403)*
Drishticon Inc (PA).....E.....510 402-4515
39899 Balentine Dr # 200 Newark (94560) *(P-19762)*
Drive Line Service Sacramento, West Sacramento *Also called Scoggan Co Inc (P-8465)*
Driveai Inc.....C.....408 693-0765
365 Ravendale Dr Mountain View (94043) *(P-13124)*
Driver Inc.....D.....415 999-4960
438 Shotwell St San Francisco (94110) *(P-13125)*
Drivesavers Inc.....D.....415 382-2000
400 Bel Marin Keys Blvd Novato (94949) *(P-13786)*
Drivesavers Data Recovery, Novato *Also called Drivesavers Inc (P-13786)*
Drivescale Inc.....E.....408 849-4651
1320 Hillview Dr Menlo Park (94025) *(P-13126)*
Drivewyze Inc.....E.....888 988-1590
398 Primrose Rd Burlingame (94010) *(P-12404)*
Drobo Inc (HQ).....D.....408 454-4200
1289 Anvilwood Ave Sunnyvale (94089) *(P-8695)*
Droisys Inc (PA).....B.....408 874-8333
46540 Fremont Blvd # 516 Fremont (94538) *(P-13579)*
Dropbox Inc (PA).....A.....415 857-6800
1800 Owens St Ste 200 San Francisco (94158) *(P-13127)*
Drug Abuse Alternatives Center.....C.....707 571-2233
2403 Prof Dr Ste 103 Santa Rosa (95403) *(P-17015)*
Druva Inc (HQ).....D.....650 241-3501
800 W California Ave # 100 Sunnyvale (94086) *(P-13128)*
Dry Creek Band of Pomo Indians, Geyserville *Also called Dry Creek Rancheria (P-11063)*
Dry Creek Inn Ltd Partnership.....D.....707 433-0300
200 Dry Creek Rd Healdsburg (95448) *(P-11062)*
Dry Creek Rancheria.....E.....707 857-1266
3250 Highway 128 Geyserville (95441) *(P-11063)*
Dry Creek Vineyard Inc.....E.....707 433-1000
3770 Lambert Bridge Rd Healdsburg (95448) *(P-2554)*
Dry Farm Wines Inc (PA).....D.....707 944-1500
3149 California Blvd C NAPA (94558) *(P-2555)*
Dry Launch Light Co, Livermore *Also called Sierra Design Mfg Inc (P-5740)*
Dry Vac Environmental Inc (PA).....E.....707 374-7500
864 Saint Francis Way Rio Vista (94571) *(P-6825)*
Dryco Construction Inc (PA).....C.....510 438-6500
42745 Boscell Rd Fremont (94538) *(P-1035)*
Dryden Construction Inc.....E.....925 243-8750
72 Rickenbacker Cir Ste A Livermore (94551) *(P-745)*
DS Baxley Inc.....E.....925 371-3950
6571 Las Positas Rd Livermore (94551) *(P-1768)*
Dsb Inc.....E.....408 228-3000
2157 Otoole Ave Ste 20 San Jose (95131) *(P-8510)*
DSB Commercial Floor Finishes, San Jose *Also called Dsb Inc (P-8510)*
Dsd Merchandisers Inc.....E.....925 449-2044
6226 Industrial Way Ste A Livermore (94551) *(P-2444)*
DSM Biomedical Inc.....C.....510 841-8800
2810 7th St Berkeley (94710) *(P-19053)*
Dsp Group Inc (PA).....D.....408 986-4300
2055 Gateway Pl Ste 480 San Jose (95110) *(P-6102)*
Dst Controls, Benicia *Also called Dusouth Industries (P-6716)*
Dst Output California Inc.....C.....916 939-4617
5220 Rbert J Mathews Pkwy El Dorado Hills (95762) *(P-13821)*
DTE Stockton LLC.....E.....209 467-3838
2526 W Washington St Stockton (95203) *(P-564)*
Dten Inc (PA).....E.....866 936-3836
97 E Brokaw Rd Ste 180 San Jose (95112) *(P-5362)*
Dtex Systems Inc.....E.....408 418-3786
19630 Allendale Ave # 22 Saratoga (95070) *(P-12405)*
Dtj Inc.....E.....831 423-8956
2151-B Delaware Ave Santa Cruz (95060) *(P-9449)*
DTL Mori Seiki, Davis *Also called Dmg Mori Digital Tech Lab Corp (P-5093)*
DTL Research & Technical Ctr, Davis *Also called Dmg Mori Manufacturing USA Inc (P-5073)*
Dtrs St Francis LLC.....D.....415 397-7000
335 Powell St San Francisco (94102) *(P-11064)*
Dts, Sacramento *Also called California Department Tech (P-13859)*
Du-All Anodizing Inc.....E.....408 275-6694
730 Chestnut St San Jose (95110) *(P-4902)*
Duarte Nursery Inc.....B.....209 887-3409
23456 E Flood Rd Linden (95236) *(P-119)*
Duarte Nursery Inc (PA).....E.....209 531-0351
1555 Baldwin Rd Hughson (95326) *(P-120)*
Duarte Properties, Hughson *Also called Duarte Nursery Inc (P-120)*
Dublin Honda, Dublin *Also called Harvey & Madding Inc (P-14570)*
Dublin Hstrcal Prsrvation Assn.....D.....925 785-2898
7172 Regional St Pmb 316 Dublin (94568) *(P-18270)*
Dublin San Ramon Services Dst (PA).....C.....925 875-2276
7051 Dublin Blvd Dublin (94568) *(P-8233)*
Dublin Volkswagen.....D.....925 829-0800
6085 Scarlett Ct Dublin (94568) *(P-14558)*
Ducey's On The Lake, Bass Lake *Also called Pines Resorts of California (P-11370)*
Duckhorn Portfolio Inc (HQ).....C.....707 302-2658
1201 Dowdell Ln Saint Helena (94574) *(P-2556)*

ALPHABETIC

Duckhorn Wine Company (HQ) ....E....**707 963-7108**
1000 Lodi Ln Saint Helena (94574) ***(P-2557)***
Ducks Unlimited Inc....E....916 852-2000
3074 Gold Canal Dr Rancho Cordova (95670) ***(P-18412)***
Duckys Car Wash (PA)....E....**650 637-1301**
1301 Old County Rd San Carlos (94070) ***(P-14639)***
Ducttesters Inc....E....209 579-5000
336 W Main St Ripon (95366) ***(P-19763)***
Duda Mobile Inc....D....855 790-0003
577 College Ave Palo Alto (94306) ***(P-13129)***
Dudleys Excavating Inc....E....530 385-1445
209 San Benito Ave Gerber (96035) ***(P-1956)***
Duel Systems Inc....D....408 453-9500
2025 Gateway Pl Ste 235 San Jose (95110) ***(P-6391)***
Duetto Research Inc....D....415 968-9389
333 Bush St Fl 12 San Francisco (94104) ***(P-12406)***
Duffys Myrtledale....D....707 942-6888
3076 Myrtledale Rd Calistoga (94515) ***(P-17016)***
Duggans Serra Mortuary....D....650 756-4500
500 Westlake Ave Daly City (94014) ***(P-11699)***
Duke Empirical Inc....D....831 420-1104
2829 Mission St Santa Cruz (95060) ***(P-6971)***
Duke Scientific Corporation....D....650 424-1177
46360 Fremont Blvd Fremont (94538) ***(P-6826)***
Duleys Landscape Inc....E....559 855-5090
28876 Topaz Rd Tollhouse (93667) ***(P-460)***
Dumont Printing Inc....E....559 485-6311
1333 G St Fresno (93706) ***(P-3641)***
Dumont Printing & Mailing, Fresno *Also called Dumont Printing Inc* ***(P-3641)***
Dunamis Center Inc....D....530 338-0087
1465 Victor Ave Ste B Redding (96003) ***(P-17017)***
Dunamis Ctr Cunseling Wellness, Redding *Also called Dunamis Center Inc* ***(P-17017)***
Dunan Sensing LLC....E....408 613-1015
1953 Concourse Dr San Jose (95131) ***(P-6514)***
Duncan Enterprises (HQ)....C....**559 291-4444**
5673 E Shields Ave Fresno (93727) ***(P-4103)***
Dunlop Manufacturing Inc (PA)....D....**707 745-2722**
150 Industrial Way Benicia (94510) ***(P-7171)***
Dupont Market Inc (PA)....D....**510 562-3593**
8612 Younger Creek Dr Sacramento (95828) ***(P-9377)***
Dura Chemicals Inc (PA)....E....**510 658-1987**
1901 Harrison St Ste 1100 Oakland (94612) ***(P-4159)***
Dura-Metrics Inc (PA)....D....**707 546-5138**
2628 El Camino Ave Ste B1 Sacramento (95821) ***(P-16824)***
Duracite, Fairfield *Also called Halabi Inc* ***(P-4518)***
Duran & Venables Inc....E....408 741-9883
748 S Hillview Dr Milpitas (95035) ***(P-1957)***
Duravent Inc (HQ)....B....**800 835-4429**
877 Cotting Ct Vacaville (95688) ***(P-4756)***
Durden Construction Inc....E....831 623-1200
410 3rd St Ste A San Juan Bautista (95045) ***(P-633)***
Durect Corporation (PA)....D....**408 777-1417**
10260 Bubb Rd Cupertino (95014) ***(P-3894)***
Durham School Services L P....C....925 606-0871
379 Earhart Way Livermore (94551) ***(P-7425)***
Durham School Services L P....C....510 887-6005
27577 Industrial Blvd A Hayward (94545) ***(P-7426)***
Durham School Services L P....C....530 273-7282
10701 E Bennett Rd Grass Valley (95945) ***(P-7427)***
Durham School Services L P....C....925 686-3391
2121 Piedmont Way Pittsburg (94565) ***(P-7428)***
Durie Tangri LLP....E....415 362-6666
217 Leidesdorff St San Francisco (94111) ***(P-17260)***
Durkee Drayage Company....D....510 970-7550
539 Stone Rd Benicia (94510) ***(P-7620)***
Dusouth Industries....E....707 745-5117
651 Stone Rd Benicia (94510) ***(P-6716)***
Dust Networks Inc....D....510 400-2900
32990 Alvarado Niles Rd Union City (94587) ***(P-6103)***
Dutra Construction Co Inc (HQ)....D....**415 258-6876**
2350 Kerner Blvd Ste 200 San Rafael (94901) ***(P-1157)***
Dutra Dredging Company (HQ)....D....**415 721-2131**
2350 Kerner Blvd Ste 200 San Rafael (94901) ***(P-1158)***
Dutra Dredging Company....E....707 374-5127
615 River Rd Rio Vista (94571) ***(P-1159)***
Dutra Group (PA)....D....**415 258-6876**
2350 Kerner Blvd Ste 200 San Rafael (94901) ***(P-1160)***
Dutra Materials, Richmond *Also called San Rafael Rock Quarry Inc* ***(P-4190)***
Dutra Materials, San Rafael *Also called San Rafael Rock Quarry Inc* ***(P-581)***
Dutra's Dreamscape, Manteca *Also called Cynthia Dunlap Dutra* ***(P-410)***
Dutton Ranch Corp....D....707 823-0448
10717 Graton Rd Sebastopol (95472) ***(P-99)***
DV Kap Inc....E....559 435-5575
426 W Bedford Ave Fresno (93711) ***(P-3024)***
Dvbe Technology Group....E....916 565-7610
333 University Ave # 200 Sacramento (95825) ***(P-13884)***
DVMS, Lafayette *Also called Diablo Vly Montessori Schl Inc* ***(P-17921)***
DW Morgan LLC....D....925 460-2700
4185 Blackhawk Plaza Cir # 260 Danville (94506) ***(P-7880)***
Dwayne Nash Industries Inc....C....916 253-1900
8825 Washington Blvd # 100 Roseville (95678) ***(P-1800)***
Dwell Life Inc....F....212 382-2010
548 Market St San Francisco (94104) ***(P-3567)***
Dwell Life Inc (PA)....E....**415 373-5100**
595 Pacific Ave Fl 4 San Francisco (94133) ***(P-3497)***
Dwell Store The, San Francisco *Also called Dwell Life Inc* ***(P-3567)***
Dwn, Hickman *Also called Dave Wilson Nursery* ***(P-118)***
Dybeck Inc (PA)....E....**559 299-7696**
7094 N Cedar Ave Fresno (93720) ***(P-11680)***
Dycora Trnsitional Hlth Living, Fresno *Also called Williams-Foster Group LLC* ***(P-16161)***
Dylern Incorporated....E....530 470-8785
14444 Greenwood Cir Nevada City (95959) ***(P-5511)***
Dynamex Inc....D....209 464-7008
4790 Frontier Way Ste A Stockton (95215) ***(P-7642)***
Dynamic Digital Displays, Rancho Cordova *Also called D3 Led Llc* ***(P-7228)***
Dynamic Graphics Inc (PA)....E....**510 522-0700**
1015 Atlantic Ave Alameda (94501) ***(P-12407)***
Dynamic Intgrted Solutions LLC....F....408 727-3400
1710 Fortune Dr San Jose (95131) ***(P-6104)***
Dynamic Intgrted Solutions LLC (PA)....E....**408 727-3400**
3964 Rivermark Plz # 104 Santa Clara (95054) ***(P-6105)***
Dynamic Pre-Cast Co Inc....E....707 573-1110
5300 Sebastopol Rd Santa Rosa (95407) ***(P-4431)***
Dynamic Security Tech Inc....E....510 786-1121
28301 Industrial Blvd B Hayward (94545) ***(P-8908)***
Dynamic Signal Inc (PA)....B....**650 231-2550**
851 Traeger Ave Ste 200 San Bruno (94066) ***(P-13709)***
Dynamic Staffing Inc (PA)....C....**916 773-3900**
920 Reserve Dr Ste 150 Roseville (95678) ***(P-12085)***
Dynatect Ro-Lab Inc....E....262 786-1500
8830 W Linne Rd Tracy (95304) ***(P-4208)***
Dynatex International....E....707 542-4227
5577 Skylane Blvd Santa Rosa (95403) ***(P-5095)***
Dynavax Technologies Corp (PA)....D....**510 848-5100**
2100 Powell St Ste 900 Emeryville (94608) ***(P-4045)***
Dyned International Inc (PA)....D....**650 375-7011**
1350 Bayshore Hwy Ste 850 Burlingame (94010) ***(P-12408)***
E & B Marine Inc (HQ)....D....**831 728-2700**
500 Westridge Dr Watsonville (95076) ***(P-9150)***
E & E Co Ltd....B....530 669-5991
2222 E Beamer St Woodland (95776) ***(P-634)***
E & E Co Ltd (PA)....C....**510 490-9788**
45875 Northport Loop E Fremont (94538) ***(P-8511)***
E & J Gallo Winery (PA)....A....**209 341-3111**
600 Yosemite Blvd Modesto (95354) ***(P-2558)***
E & J Gallo Winery....E....707 963-2736
254 Saint Helena Hwy S Saint Helena (94574) ***(P-2559)***
E & M Electric and McHy Inc (PA)....E....**707 433-5578**
126 Mill St Healdsburg (95448) ***(P-9064)***
E & S, Fresno *Also called E&S Residential Care Svcs LLC* ***(P-18101)***
E & S Precision Machine Inc....F....209 545-6161
4631 Enterprise Way Modesto (95356) ***(P-5512)***
E & S Westcoast LLC (PA)....E....**209 870-1900**
7100 Longe St Ste 300 Stockton (95206) ***(P-8857)***
E A Davidovits & Co Inc....E....650 366-6068
555 Price Ave Ste 200 Redwood City (94063) ***(P-869)***
E B C F, Oakland *Also called East Bay Community Foundation* ***(P-18413)***
E B S, Pleasanton *Also called Employee Bneft Specialists Inc* ***(P-19499)***
E B Stone & Son Inc....D....707 426-2500
6111 Lambie Rd Suisun City (94585) ***(P-9598)***
E C S-Elitegroup Cmpt Systems, Newark *Also called Elitegroup Computer Systems Ho* ***(P-8698)***
E Center....C....530 634-1200
1506 Starr Dr Yuba City (95993) ***(P-17925)***
E D G, Novato *Also called EDG Interior Arch & Design Inc* ***(P-14260)***
E D M Sacramento Inc....E....916 851-9285
11341 Sunrise Park Dr Rancho Cordova (95742) ***(P-5513)***
E E G and E P, Chico *Also called Enloe Medical Center* ***(P-16365)***
E E S Corp....E....925 947-6880
39 Quail Ct Ste 100 Walnut Creek (94596) ***(P-18693)***
E G Ayers Distributing Inc....E....707 445-2077
5819 S Broadway St Eureka (95503) ***(P-9271)***
E J Masonry Inc....E....916 941-8760
3195 Luyung Dr Rancho Cordova (95742) ***(P-1645)***
E K C Technology/Burmar Chem, Hayward *Also called Ekc Technology Inc* ***(P-3784)***
E L & Associates Inc....E....925 249-2300
4900 Hopyard Rd Ste 100 Pleasanton (94588) ***(P-18694)***
E La Carte Inc....D....650 468-0680
810 Hamilton St Redwood City (94063) ***(P-12409)***
E O R M, San Jose *Also called BSI Services & Solutions W Inc* ***(P-18648)***
E P, Union City *Also called Emerald Packaging Inc* ***(P-9656)***
E P I, Milpitas *Also called Envision Peripherals Inc* ***(P-8701)***
E P S, Vallejo *Also called Earthquake Protection Systems* ***(P-18698)***
E P U, Fresno *Also called Exceptnal Prents Unlimited Inc* ***(P-17556)***
E R T Inc....E....408 986-9920
306 Mathew St Santa Clara (95050) ***(P-5514)***
E S A, Oakland *Also called Environmental Science Assoc* ***(P-19056)***
E T Horn Company....C....510 532-8689
2135 Frederick St Oakland (94606) ***(P-9517)***
E Z 8 Motels Inc....E....925 674-0888
1581 Concord Ave Concord (94520) ***(P-11065)***
E Z 8 Motels Inc....E....510 794-7775
5555 Cedar Ct Newark (94560) ***(P-11066)***
E Z 8 Motels Inc....E....408 246-3119
3550 El Camino Real Santa Clara (95051) ***(P-11067)***
E Z Electric, Sunnyvale *Also called Vexillum Inc* ***(P-1630)***
E&M, Healdsburg *Also called E & M Electric and McHy Inc* ***(P-9064)***
E&S Residential Care Svcs LLC....E....559 275-3555
6083 N Marks Ave Fresno (93711) ***(P-18101)***
E-3 Systems....E....510 487-9195
1220 Whipple Rd Union City (94587) ***(P-794)***
E-Base Technologies Inc (PA)....E....**510 790-2547**
39159 Paseo Padre Pkwy # 206 Fremont (94538) ***(P-12410)***
E-Fab Inc....E....408 727-5218
1075 Richard Ave Santa Clara (95050) ***(P-4931)***
E-Filliate Inc....E....916 858-1000
11321 White Rock Rd Rancho Cordova (95742) ***(P-8696)***

E-Fuel Corporation ....E....408 267-2667
15466 Los Gatos Blvd 37 Los Gatos (95032) ***(P-6515)***
E-Loan Inc (HQ) ....A....**925 847-6200**
6230 Stoneridge Mall Rd Pleasanton (94588) ***(P-9939)***
E-M Manufacturing Inc ....F....209 825-1800
1290 Dupont Ct Manteca (95336) ***(P-4757)***
E-Solutions, San Jose *Also called Vidhwan Inc* ***(P-12151)***
E-Z 8 Motel, Concord *Also called E Z 8 Motels Inc* ***(P-11065)***
E-Z 8 Motel, Newark *Also called E Z 8 Motels Inc* ***(P-11066)***
E-Z 8 Motels, Santa Clara *Also called E Z 8 Motels Inc* ***(P-11067)***
E-Z Haul Ready Mix Inc ....E....559 233-6603
1538 N Blackstone Ave Fresno (93703) ***(P-4479)***
E2 Consulting Engineers Inc ....E....510 652-1164
1900 Powell St Ste 250 Emeryville (94608) ***(P-18695)***
E2 Consulting Engineers Inc ....E....510 652-1164
2100 Powell St Ste 850 Emeryville (94608) ***(P-18696)***
E2e Mfg LLC ....E....925 862-2057
3500 Yale Way Fremont (94538) ***(P-4882)***
EA, Redwood City *Also called Electronic Arts Inc* ***(P-13138)***
Ea Sports, Redwood City *Also called Electronic Arts Redwood Inc* ***(P-6501)***
Eag Holdings LLC ....A....408 530-3500
2710 Walsh Ave Santa Clara (95051) ***(P-19264)***
Eagle Building Materials, Fresno *Also called Sequoia Steel and Supply Co* ***(P-8634)***
Eagle Canyon Capital LLC (PA) ....A....**925 884-0800**
3130 Crow Canyon Pl # 240 San Ramon (94583) ***(P-2830)***
Eagle Paving & Grading ....E....530 221-4194
2848 Tarmac Rd Redding (96003) ***(P-1036)***
Eagle Ridge Construction, Fair Oaks *Also called David Smith* ***(P-630)***
Eagle Ridge Golf Club, Gilroy *Also called Eagle Ridge Golf Cntry CLB LLC* ***(P-15087)***
Eagle Ridge Golf Cntry CLB LLC ....D....408 846-4531
2951 Club Dr Gilroy (95020) ***(P-15087)***
Eagle Rock Incorporated ....F....530 623-4444
40029 La Grange Rd Junction City (96048) ***(P-5031)***
Eagle Roofing Products, Stockton *Also called Burlingame Industries Inc* ***(P-8639)***
Eagle Systems Intl Inc ....B....510 259-1700
28436 Satellite St Hayward (94545) ***(P-1253)***
Eagle Tech Manufacturing Inc ....E....831 768-7467
841 Walker St Watsonville (95076) ***(P-6717)***
Eagle Transportation Co Inc ....E....707 586-9766
4325 Santa Rosa Ave Santa Rosa (95407) ***(P-7528)***
Eagle Trs 3 LLC ....E....650 418-2444
330 N Bayshore Blvd San Mateo (94401) ***(P-11068)***
Eagle Trs 4 LLC ....E....916 443-8400
4800 Riverside Blvd Sacramento (95822) ***(P-11069)***
Eagle Vnes Vnyrds Golf CLB LLC ....D....707 257-4470
580 S Kelly Rd American Canyon (94503) ***(P-14999)***
Eah Elena Gardens LP ....D....415 295-8840
1902 Lakewood Dr San Jose (95132) ***(P-10429)***
EAH HOUSING, San Rafael *Also called Eah Inc* ***(P-10471)***
Eah Inc (PA) ....D....**415 258-1800**
22 Pelican Way San Rafael (94901) ***(P-10471)***
Eandm ....F....707 473-3137
126 Mill St Healdsburg (95448) ***(P-14729)***
Eargo Inc (PA) ....D....**650 351-7700**
1600 Technology Dr Fl 6 San Jose (95110) ***(P-7068)***
Earl's Organic Produce, San Francisco *Also called Earls Organic* ***(P-9400)***
Earls Organic ....D....415 824-7419
2101 Jerrold Ave Ste 100 San Francisco (94124) ***(P-9400)***
Early Childhood Education Svcs ....E....530 745-1380
365 Nevada St Auburn (95603) ***(P-17926)***
Earth Island Institute Inc ....D....510 859-9100
2150 Allston Way Ste 460 Berkeley (94704) ***(P-18564)***
Earth Tech ....C....510 419-6000
2101 Webster St Ste 1000 Oakland (94612) ***(P-18697)***
Earthbound Farm LLC (PA) ....A....**831 623-7880**
1721 San Juan Hwy San Juan Bautista (95045) ***(P-281)***
Earthpro Inc ....E....408 294-1920
2010 El Camino Real Santa Clara (95050) ***(P-4413)***
Earthquake Protection Systems ....D....707 644-5993
451 Azuar Ave Bldg 759 Vallejo (94592) ***(P-18698)***
Earthtech, Oakland *Also called Kaiser Group Holdings Inc* ***(P-18745)***
Eascare Products USA, Fresno *Also called McGrayel Company* ***(P-4164)***
East Area Office, Walnut Creek *Also called East Bay Municipl Utilty Distr* ***(P-8245)***
East Bay Agency For Children ....E....510 655-4896
6117 Martin Luther King J Oakland (94609) ***(P-17927)***
East Bay Arrhythmia Elctrphysl, Castro Valley *Also called Cardiovascular Cons Med Group* ***(P-15324)***
East Bay Asian Local Dev Corp ....C....510 267-1917
1825 San Pablo Ave # 200 Oakland (94612) ***(P-10430)***
East Bay Asian Youth Center (PA) ....E....**510 533-1092**
2025 E 12th St Oakland (94606) ***(P-17535)***
East Bay Asian Youth Center ....D....510 533-1092
2025 E 12th St Oakland (94606) ***(P-17536)***
East Bay Brass Foundry Inc ....E....510 233-7171
1200 Chesley Ave Richmond (94801) ***(P-4576)***
East Bay Cardiology Med Group ....E....510 233-9300
2101 Vale Rd Ste 201 San Pablo (94806) ***(P-15385)***
East Bay Clarklift Inc (PA) ....E....**510 534-6566**
4701 Oakport St Oakland (94601) ***(P-9065)***
East Bay Community Foundation ....D....510 836-3223
200 Frank H Ogawa Plz Oakland (94612) ***(P-18413)***
East Bay Endoscopy Center LP ....D....510 654-4554
5858 Horton St Ste 100 Emeryville (94608) ***(P-16358)***
East Bay Fixture Company ....E....510 652-4421
941 Aileen St Oakland (94608) ***(P-3259)***
East Bay Fmly Prctice Med Grou ....E....510 645-9900
3100 Telg Ave Ste 2109 Oakland (94609) ***(P-16359)***
East Bay Innovations ....D....510 618-1580
2450 Washington Ave # 240 San Leandro (94577) ***(P-14257)***
East Bay Machine and Shtmtl, Concord *Also called Alvellan Inc* ***(P-5472)***
East Bay Mncpl Utility Dst Wstw (HQ) ....E....**866 403-2683**
375 11th St Oakland (94607) ***(P-8281)***
East Bay Mncpl Utility Dst Wstw ....C....209 772-8204
15083 Camanche Pkwy S Valley Springs (95252) ***(P-8234)***
East Bay Mncpl Utility Dst Wtr ....E....866 403-2683
3999 Lakeside Dr Richmond (94806) ***(P-8235)***
East Bay Mncpl Utility Dst Wtr (PA) ....A....**866 403-2683**
375 11th St Oakland (94607) ***(P-8236)***
East Bay Mncpl Utility Dst Wtr ....E....866 403-2683
6921 Chabot Rd Oakland (94618) ***(P-8237)***
East Bay Mncpl Utility Dst Wtr ....E....209 333-2095
1 Winemaster Way Ste K Lodi (95240) ***(P-8238)***
East Bay Mncpl Utility Dst Wtr ....E....925 254-3778
500 San Pablo Dam Rd Orinda (94563) ***(P-8239)***
East Bay Mncpl Utility Dst Wtr ....E....209 772-8200
Pardee Ctr Valley Springs (95252) ***(P-8240)***
East Bay Mncpl Utility Dst Wtr ....E....209 946-8000
1804 W Main St Stockton (95203) ***(P-8241)***
East Bay Mncpl Utility Dst Wtr ....E....510 287-0600
375 11th St Oakland (94607) ***(P-8242)***
East Bay Municipl Utilty Distr ....E....866 403-2683
3849 Mount Diablo Blvd Lafayette (94549) ***(P-8243)***
East Bay Municipl Utilty Distr ....E....866 403-2683
1100 21st St Oakland (94607) ***(P-8244)***
East Bay Municipl Utilty Distr ....E....866 403-2683
2551 N Main St Walnut Creek (94597) ***(P-8245)***
East Bay Municipl Utilty Distr ....E....866 403-2683
2020 Wake Ave Oakland (94607) ***(P-8322)***
East Bay Municipl Utilty Distr ....D....866 403-2683
2149 Union St Oakland (94607) ***(P-8246)***
East Bay Nephrology ....E....510 235-1057
2089 Vale Rd Ste 32 San Pablo (94806) ***(P-15386)***
East Bay Pump & Equipment Co ....F....510 532-1800
4900 E 12th St Oakland (94601) ***(P-9066)***
East Bay Tire Co ....F....707 747-5613
4961 Park Rd Benicia (94510) ***(P-4198)***
EAST BAY TRANSITIONAL HOMES, Oakland *Also called Bay Area Community Svcs Inc* ***(P-17438)***
East Bay Water, Orinda *Also called East Bay Mncpl Utlty Dst Wtr* ***(P-8239)***
East Electronics, Fremont *Also called Myntahl Corporation* ***(P-6459)***
East Lawn Inc (PA) ....E....**916 732-2000**
4300 Folsom Blvd Sacramento (95819) ***(P-10727)***
East Lawn Memorial Park, Sacramento *Also called East Lawn Inc* ***(P-10727)***
East Palo Alto Hotel Dev Inc ....C....650 566-1200
2050 University Ave East Palo Alto (94303) ***(P-11070)***
East Private Holdings II LLC (PA) ....E....**650 357-3500**
6750 Dumbarton Cir Fremont (94555) ***(P-3730)***
East Side Msqito Abatement Dst, Modesto *Also called County of Stanislaus* ***(P-8397)***
Eastbay Express, Oakland *Also called Village Voice Media* ***(P-3488)***
Easter Seal Soc Superior Cal (PA) ....D....**916 485-6711**
3205 Hurley Way Sacramento (95864) ***(P-17139)***
Easter Seals Central Cal ....D....831 684-2166
9010 Soquel Dr Aptos (95003) ***(P-17537)***
Easter Seals Main Office, Sacramento *Also called Easter Seal Soc Superior Cal* ***(P-17139)***
Eastern Cntra Costa Trnst Auth ....E....925 754-6622
801 Wilbur Ave Antioch (94509) ***(P-7329)***
Eastern Park Apts, San Francisco *Also called Sequoia Living Inc* ***(P-18180)***
Eastern Plmas Hlth Care Fndtio (PA) ....C....**530 832-4277**
500 1st Ave Portola (96122) ***(P-17140)***
Eastern Plumas Health Care ....D....530 993-1225
700 3rd St Loyalton (96118) ***(P-15980)***
EASTERN PLUMAS HOSPITAL, Portola *Also called Eastern Plmas Hlth Care Fndtio* ***(P-17140)***
Easton Bell Sports, Scotts Valley *Also called Bell Sports Inc* ***(P-7188)***
Eastside Management Co Inc ....C....209 578-9852
1131 12th St Ste C Modesto (95354) ***(P-373)***
Eastside Management Co Inc (PA) ....C....**209 578-9852**
1518 K St Modesto (95354) ***(P-374)***
Eastside Union High School Dst ....E....408 347-4700
1855 Lucretia Ave San Jose (95122) ***(P-17928)***
Easun Inc ....E....916 929-8855
2001 Point West Way Sacramento (95815) ***(P-11071)***
Easy Does It Emerg Svcs Progrm ....D....510 845-5513
3271 Adeline St Unit B Berkeley (94703) ***(P-18565)***
Eat Just Inc (PA) ....D....**844 423-6637**
2000 Folsom St San Francisco (94110) ***(P-2279)***
Eaton Drilling Co Inc ....E....530 402-1143
20 W Kentucky Ave Woodland (95695) ***(P-1919)***
Eb, Santa Rosa *Also called Exchange Bank* ***(P-9771)***
Eb Sav Inc ....E....303 635-4500
1721 San Juan Hwy San Juan Bautista (95045) ***(P-282)***
Ebac Therapeutic Nursery Schl, Oakland *Also called East Bay Agency For Children* ***(P-17927)***
Ebara Technologies Inc (HQ) ....D....**916 920-5451**
51 Main Ave Sacramento (95838) ***(P-5183)***
Ebayc, Oakland *Also called East Bay Asian Youth Center* ***(P-17535)***
Ebit-Golf Inc ....D....559 275-5900
7492 N Bryan Ave Fresno (93722) ***(P-15000)***
Ebmc, Rohnert Park *Also called Eugene Burger Management Corp* ***(P-10546)***
Ebmud, Lafayette *Also called East Bay Municipl Utilty Distr* ***(P-8243)***
Ebmud, Oakland *Also called East Bay Municipl Utilty Distr* ***(P-8244)***
Ebmud, Richmond *Also called East Bay Mncpl Utlty Dst Wtr* ***(P-8235)***
Ebmud, Oakland *Also called East Bay Municipl Utilty Distr* ***(P-8322)***
EBMUD, Oakland *Also called East Bay Mncpl Utlty Dst Wtr* ***(P-8236)***

ALPHABETIC

Ebmud, Oakland *Also called East Bay Mncpl Utility Dst Wtr* ***(P-8237)***
Ebmud, Lodi *Also called East Bay Mncpl Utility Dst Wtr* ***(P-8238)***
Ebmud, Valley Springs *Also called East Bay Mncpl Utility Dst Wtr* ***(P-8240)***
Ebmud, Valley Springs *Also called East Bay Mncpl Utility Dst Wstw* ***(P-8234)***
Ebmud - Construction and Maint, Oakland *Also called East Bay Municipl Utilty Distr* ***(P-8246)***
EBMUD - SPECIAL DISTRICT NO. 1, Oakland *Also called East Bay Mncpl Utility Dst Wstw* ***(P-8281)***
Ebr Systems Inc (PA)....E....**408 720-1906**
480 Oakmead Pkwy Sunnyvale (94085) ***(P-7103)***
Ebrary....D....650 475-8700
161 E Evelyn Ave Mountain View (94041) ***(P-13787)***
Ebreastimaging LLC (PA)....E....**408 800-5247**
15195 National Ave # 201 Los Gatos (95032) ***(P-16780)***
EBSC LP....D....510 547-2244
3875 Telegraph Ave Oakland (94609) ***(P-15387)***
ECB Corp....E....916 492-8900
1650 Parkway Blvd West Sacramento (95691) ***(P-4758)***
Ecc, Burlingame *Also called Environmental Chemical Corp* ***(P-18705)***
Echelon Corporation (HQ)....D....**408 938-5200**
3600 Peterson Way Santa Clara (95054) ***(P-6748)***
Echo, San Jose *Also called Labcyte Inc* ***(P-19081)***
Echo Chalet Inc....E....530 659-7207
9900 Echo Lakes Rd Echo Lake (95721) ***(P-11072)***
Ecker & Associates, Foster City *Also called Ecker Consumer Recruiting Inc* ***(P-19157)***
Ecker Consumer Recruiting Inc....D....650 871-6800
1303 Melbourne St Foster City (94404) ***(P-19157)***
Eckert Cold Storage Company....C....209 823-3181
757 Moffat Blvd Manteca (95336) ***(P-7678)***
Eclipse Mdi, San Jose *Also called Eclipse Microwave Inc* ***(P-6421)***
Eclipse Metal Fabrication Inc....E....650 298-8731
17700 Shideler Pkwy Lathrop (95330) ***(P-4759)***
Eclipse Microwave Inc....F....408 806-8938
4425 Fortran Dr Ste 40 San Jose (95134) ***(P-6421)***
Ecmd Inc....E....530 741-0769
4722 Skyway Dr Marysville (95901) ***(P-3131)***
Ecms Inc (HQ)....E....**510 986-0131**
1809 Peralta St Oakland (94607) ***(P-11627)***
Eco Bay Services Inc....C....415 643-7777
1501 Minnesota St San Francisco (94107) ***(P-19764)***
Eco Farm Holdings Pbc....E....707 485-3035
465 Stony Point Rd # 144 Santa Rosa (95401) ***(P-161)***
Eco Sensors, Newark *Also called Kwj Engineering Inc* ***(P-6907)***
Eco Services Operations Corp....E....925 313-8224
100 Mococo Rd Martinez (94553) ***(P-3783)***
Eco-Shell Inc....E....530 824-8794
5230 Grange Rd Corning (96021) ***(P-7280)***
Ecolab....F....408 928-8100
640 Lenfest Rd San Jose (95133) ***(P-4062)***
Econo Lodge....E....916 443-6631
711 16th St Sacramento (95814) ***(P-11073)***
Econoday Inc....F....925 299-5350
3730 Mt Diablo Blvd # 340 Lafayette (94549) ***(P-3568)***
Econolite....E....408 577-1733
4120 Business Center Dr Fremont (94538) ***(P-14258)***
Economy Stock Feed Company Inc....E....559 888-2187
10508 E Central Ave Del Rey (93616) ***(P-2340)***
Econosoft Inc....D....408 442-3663
2375 Zanker Rd Ste 250 San Jose (95131) ***(P-12411)***
Econtactlive Inc....D....209 548-4300
6436 Oakdale Rd Riverbank (95367) ***(P-14259)***
Ecorp Consulting Inc (PA)....D....**916 782-9100**
2525 Warren Dr Rocklin (95677) ***(P-19496)***
Ecrio Inc....D....408 973-7290
19925 Stevns Crk Blvd Cupertino (95014) ***(P-13130)***
ECS, San Francisco *Also called Episcpal Cmnty Svcs San Frncsc* ***(P-17553)***
Ecs Refining, Santa Clara *Also called All Metals Inc* ***(P-4556)***
Ecullet Inc....D....650 493-7300
1 Vintage Ct Woodside (94062) ***(P-8323)***
Ed Rocha Livestock Trnsp Inc....D....209 538-1302
2400 Nickerson Dr Modesto (95358) ***(P-7529)***
Ed Supports LLC....D....201 478-8711
3240 Lone Tree Way Ste 10 Antioch (94509) ***(P-17538)***
Ed Supports LLC....D....201 478-8711
1710 Pririe Cy Rd Ste 100 Folsom (95630) ***(P-17539)***
Ed Supports LLC....D....201 478-8711
1045 Willow St San Jose (95125) ***(P-17018)***
Ed Supports LLC....D....201 478-8711
6001 Telegraph Ave Oakland (94609) ***(P-17019)***
Edata Solutions Inc....A....510 574-5380
2450 Peralta Blvd Ste 202 Fremont (94536) ***(P-13710)***
Edaw Inc (HQ)....C....**415 955-2800**
300 California St Fl 5 San Francisco (94104) ***(P-10701)***
Edc-Biosystems Inc (PA)....E....**510 257-1500**
170 Rose Orchard Way # 200 San Jose (95134) ***(P-6718)***
Edcast Inc (PA)....E....**650 823-3511**
1901 Old Middlefield Way Mountain View (94043) ***(P-13131)***
Edelman Financial Engines LLC (HQ)....C....**408 498-6000**
1050 Entp Way Fl 3 Flr 3 Sunnyvale (94089) ***(P-19497)***
Edelman Productions, San Francisco *Also called New Paradigm Productions Inc* ***(P-14794)***
Edelstein Printing Co....E....510 352-7890
2725 Miller St San Leandro (94577) ***(P-3642)***
Eden Area Rgnal Occptnal Prgra....D....510 293-2900
26316 Hesperian Blvd Hayward (94545) ***(P-17812)***
Eden Area Rop School, Hayward *Also called Eden Area Rgnal Occptnal Prgra* ***(P-17812)***
Eden Home Health Elk Grove LLC....E....916 681-4949
9299 E Stockton Blvd # 10 Elk Grove (95624) ***(P-17141)***
Eden Housing Inc (PA)....C....**510 582-1460**
22645 Grand St Hayward (94541) ***(P-746)***
Eden Housing Management, San Leandro *Also called Eden Lodge LP* ***(P-10432)***
Eden Housing Resident Svcs Inc....D....510 582-1460
22645 Grand St Hayward (94541) ***(P-10431)***
Eden Labs Med Group Inc....C....510 537-1234
20103 Lake Chabot Rd Castro Valley (94546) ***(P-16360)***
Eden Lodge LP (HQ)....E....**510 352-7008**
400 Springlake Dr San Leandro (94578) ***(P-10432)***
Eden Medical Center, Castro Valley *Also called Sutter Health* ***(P-16608)***
Eden Medical Center, Sacramento *Also called Sutter Health* ***(P-16650)***
Eden Technologies Inc....D....800 754-3166
54 Jeff Adachi Way San Francisco (94103) ***(P-12412)***
Eden Villa, Redding *Also called Ku Kyoung* ***(P-16034)***
EDG Interior Arch & Design Inc (PA)....D....**415 454-2277**
7 Hamilton Landing # 200 Novato (94949) ***(P-14260)***
Edge Electronics Corporation....E....510 614-7988
164 21st Ave San Francisco (94121) ***(P-4720)***
Edgeq Inc....E....408 209-0368
2550 Great America Way # 3 Santa Clara (95054) ***(P-6106)***
Edges Electrical Group LLC (HQ)....D....**408 293-5818**
1135 Auzerais Ave San Jose (95126) ***(P-8858)***
Edgewater Networks Inc....D....408 351-7200
5225 Hellyer Ave Ste 100 San Jose (95138) ***(P-13885)***
Edgewood Ctr For Chldren Fmlie....D....650 832-6900
957 Industrial Rd Ste B San Carlos (94070) ***(P-17929)***
Edgewood Ctr For Chldren Fmlie (PA)....C....**415 681-3211**
1801 Vicente St San Francisco (94116) ***(P-18102)***
Edgewood Partners Insur Ctr (HQ)....D....**415 356-3900**
1 California St Ste 400 San Francisco (94111) ***(P-10275)***
Edmodo Inc (HQ)....E....**310 614-6868**
400 Concar Dr San Mateo (94402) ***(P-13132)***
Edmodo Inc....E....202 489-8129
400 Concar Dr San Mateo (94402) ***(P-13133)***
EDS Manufacturing....E....408 982-3688
1494 Gladding Ct Milpitas (95035) ***(P-7281)***
EDS Mfg Inc....F....408 900-8941
1725 De La Cruz Blvd # 5 Santa Clara (95050) ***(P-7282)***
Edtuit Inc (PA)....E....**415 269-4471**
3527 Hamlin Rd Lafayette (94549) ***(P-8075)***
Educare Services Inc (PA)....E....**559 228-3232**
3485 W Ashcroft Ave # 101 Fresno (93722) ***(P-17930)***
Education Elements Inc....E....650 440-7860
101 Hickey Blvd Ste A South San Francisco (94080) ***(P-13134)***
Education For Change (PA)....E....**510 568-7936**
333 Hegenberger Rd # 600 Oakland (94621) ***(P-19326)***
Education Training & RES Assoc (PA)....D....**831 438-4060**
5619 Scotts Valley Dr # 140 Scotts Valley (95066) ***(P-3533)***
Educational Employees Cr Un (PA)....C....**559 437-7700**
2222 W Shaw Ave Fresno (93711) ***(P-9782)***
Educational Employees Cr Un....D....559 896-0222
3488 W Shaw Ave Fresno (93711) ***(P-9783)***
Educational Employees Cr Un....D....559 437-7700
455 E Barstow Ave Fresno (93710) ***(P-9784)***
Educational Media Foundation (PA)....C....**916 251-1600**
5700 West Oaks Blvd Rocklin (95765) ***(P-8018)***
Educatnal Cnslting Thrapy For, San Francisco *Also called Kyo Autism Therapy LLC* ***(P-19553)***
Edulastic, Fremont *Also called Snapwiz Inc* ***(P-13450)***
Edward B Ward & Company Inc (HQ)....E....**415 330-6600**
99 S Hill Dr Ste B Brisbane (94005) ***(P-9009)***
Edward B Ward & Company Inc....D....559 487-1860
2345 Los Angeles St Fresno (93721) ***(P-9010)***
Edward Silveira (PA)....E....**209 394-8656**
4174 Sultana Ave Atwater (95301) ***(P-17)***
Edward W Scott Electric Co Inc....E....415 206-7120
1555 Burke Ave Ste L San Francisco (94124) ***(P-8095)***
Edwards & Anderson Inc (PA)....D....**510 581-0230**
3649 Jamison Way Castro Valley (94546) ***(P-14640)***
Edwards & Anderson Inc....E....408 847-6770
2845 Day Rd Gilroy (95020) ***(P-5422)***
Edwards Lock and Safe, Fresno *Also called Havens For Total Security Inc* ***(P-14754)***
Edwards Theatres Circuit Inc....D....707 432-2121
1549 Gateway Blvd Fairfield (94533) ***(P-14810)***
Edwards Vacuum LLC (PA)....E....**978 658-5410**
2041 Mission College Blvd Santa Clara (95054) ***(P-5184)***
Eel River Brewing Co Inc (PA)....E....**707 725-2739**
1777 Alamar Way Fortuna (95540) ***(P-2477)***
Eero LLC....E....415 738-7972
660 3rd St Fl 4 San Francisco (94107) ***(P-13580)***
Eezer Products Inc....E....559 255-4140
4734 E Home Ave Fresno (93703) ***(P-3801)***
Eff Aero, Stockton *Also called Wkf (friedman Enterprises Inc* ***(P-6624)***
Effort, The, Sacramento *Also called Wellspace Health* ***(P-17091)***
Efi, Fremont *Also called Electronics For Imaging Inc* ***(P-3731)***
Efront Financial Solutions Inc....D....415 653-3239
135 Main St Ste 1330 San Francisco (94105) ***(P-12413)***
Eg Systems LLC (PA)....D....**510 324-0126**
6200 Village Pkwy Dublin (94568) ***(P-6107)***
Egain Corporation (PA)....B....**408 636-4500**
1252 Borregas Ave Sunnyvale (94089) ***(P-13135)***
Egomotion Corp (PA)....E....**415 849-4662**
888 Marin St Ste B San Francisco (94124) ***(P-10543)***
EH Suda Inc (PA)....F....**650 622-9700**
611 Industrial Rd Ste 3 San Carlos (94070) ***(P-5515)***
EH Suda Inc....E....530 778-9830
210 Texas Ave Lewiston (96052) ***(P-5516)***
EHC LIFEBUILDERS, Milpitas *Also called Homefrst Svcs Santa Clara Cnty* ***(P-17603)***
Ehealth Inc (PA)....C....**650 584-2700**
2625 Augustine Dr Ste 125 Santa Clara (95054) ***(P-10276)***
Ehealth Insurance.com, Gold River *Also called Ehealthinsurance Services Inc* ***(P-12414)***

Ehealthinsurance Services Inc (HQ)....D....**650 584-2700**
2625 Augustine Dr Ste 201 Santa Clara (95054) ***(P-10277)***
Ehealthinsurance Services Inc....C....916 608-6101
11919 Foundation Pl # 100 Gold River (95670) ***(P-12414)***
Ehealthwirecom Inc....C....916 924-8092
2450 Venture Oaks Way # 100 Sacramento (95833) ***(P-17142)***
Ehlers Estate, Saint Helena *Also called New Vavin Inc* ***(P-2667)***
Ehren Jordan Wine Cellars LLC....F....707 963-0530
3530 Silverado Trl N Saint Helena (94574) ***(P-2560)***
Eht Wsac LLC....E....916 443-8400
4800 Riverside Blvd Sacramento (95822) ***(P-11074)***
Ei Corp....E....530 274-1240
13355 Grass Valley Ave A Grass Valley (95945) ***(P-5756)***
Eichleay Inc (PA)....C....**925 689-7000**
1390 Willow Pass Rd # 60 Concord (94520) ***(P-18699)***
Eichleay Engineers Inc....D....925 689-7000
1390 Willow Pass Rd # 360 Concord (94520) ***(P-18700)***
Eide Bailly LLP....E....916 570-1880
2151 River Plaza Dr # 308 Sacramento (95833) ***(P-18952)***
Eide Bailly LLP....E....650 462-0400
1900 S Norfolk St Ste 225 San Mateo (94403) ***(P-18953)***
Eide Bailly LLP....E....559 248-0871
6051 N Fresno St Ste 101 Fresno (93710) ***(P-18954)***
Eidos Therapeutics Inc....E....415 887-1471
1800 Owens St San Francisco (94158) ***(P-19054)***
Eiger Biopharmaceuticals Inc (PA)....E....**650 272-6138**
2155 Park Blvd Palo Alto (94306) ***(P-4046)***
Eightfold Ai Inc (PA)....C....**650 265-7380**
2625 Augustine Dr Fl 6th Santa Clara (95054) ***(P-13136)***
Eileen Nottoli....D....415 837-1515
3 Embarcadero Ctr # 1200 San Francisco (94111) ***(P-17261)***
Einfochips Inc (HQ)....C....**408 496-1882**
2025 Gateway Pl Ste 270 San Jose (95110) ***(P-12415)***
Einstein Brothers Bagels, Greenbrae *Also called Einstein Noah Rest Group Inc* ***(P-2381)***
Einstein Noah Rest Group Inc....C....408 358-5895
15996 Los Gatos Blvd Los Gatos (95032) ***(P-2147)***
Einstein Noah Rest Group Inc....D....415 731-1700
1521 Sloat Blvd San Francisco (94132) ***(P-2379)***
Einstein Noah Rest Group Inc....D....650 299-9050
1067 El Camino Real Redwood City (94063) ***(P-2380)***
Einstein Noah Rest Group Inc....C....415 925-9971
170 Bon Air Ctr Greenbrae (94904) ***(P-2381)***
Eis Group Inc....C....415 402-2622
731 Sansome St Fl 4 San Francisco (94111) ***(P-13137)***
Eisneramper LLP....C....415 974-6000
1 Market Ste 620 San Francisco (94105) ***(P-18955)***
Eisneramper LLP....C....916 563-7790
3001 Douglas Blvd Ste 350 Roseville (95661) ***(P-18956)***
Ej Plumbing....E....650 520-8718
1170 Martin Ave Santa Clara (95050) ***(P-1254)***
EJ Weber Electric Co Inc....E....415 641-9300
895 Innes Ave San Francisco (94124) ***(P-1497)***
Ejs Pizza Co....D....916 989-1133
9500 Greenback Ln Ste 1 Folsom (95630) ***(P-11715)***
Ek Health Services Inc (PA)....C....**408 973-0888**
992 S De Anza Blvd Ste 10 San Jose (95129) ***(P-19498)***
Ekc Technology Inc (HQ)....C....**510 784-9105**
2520 Barrington Ct Hayward (94545) ***(P-3784)***
EKI Environment & Water Inc (PA)....E....**650 292-9100**
2001 Junipero Serra Blvd # 300 Daly City (94014) ***(P-18701)***
Eko Devices Inc....D....844 356-3384
1212 Broadway Ste 100 Oakland (94612) ***(P-7104)***
Ekso Bionics Inc (PA)....D....**510 984-1761**
1414 Hrbour Way S Ste 120 Richmond (94804) ***(P-5146)***
Ekso Bionics Holdings Inc....D....510 984-1761
1414 Hrbour Way S Ste 120 Richmond (94804) ***(P-7069)***
El & El Wood Products Corp....E....916 685-1855
10149 Iron Rock Way Elk Grove (95624) ***(P-8544)***
El Avisador Magazine, San Jose *Also called A-1 Ruiz & Sons Inc* ***(P-3491)***
El Bonita Motel, Saint Helena *Also called Warren Resorts Inc* ***(P-11565)***
El Camino Care Center, Carmichael *Also called Helios Healthcare LLC* ***(P-16021)***
El Camino Hospital Auxiliary....A....650 940-7214
2500 Grant Rd Mountain View (94040) ***(P-16880)***
El Camino Hospital District RE (PA)....C....**650 940-7000**
2500 Grant Rd Mountain View (94040) ***(P-10794)***
EL CAMINO HOSPITAL MOUNTAIN VI, Mountain View *Also called El Camino Hospital District RE* ***(P-10794)***
El Camino Surgery Center LLC....D....650 961-1200
15046 Karl Ave Monte Sereno (95030) ***(P-16361)***
El Camino YMCA, Mountain View *Also called Young MNS Chrstn Assn Slcon Vl* ***(P-18529)***
El Cerrito Ryale Retirement HM, El Cerrito *Also called Summerville Senior Living Inc* ***(P-16133)***
El Charro Mexican Dining....E....925 283-2345
16 Saint Louis Ln Pleasant Hill (94523) ***(P-11716)***
El Concilio California (PA)....C....**209 644-2600**
445 N San Joaquin St A Stockton (95202) ***(P-17540)***
El Dorado Center, Santa Cruz *Also called Encompass Community Services* ***(P-17546)***
El Dorado County, Placerville *Also called Health and Humn Svcs Agcy Hhsa* ***(P-11134)***
El Dorado County Health Dept....D....530 621-6100
931 Spring St Placerville (95667) ***(P-15388)***
El Dorado Hills Cmnty Svcs Dst....C....916 933-6624
1021 Harvard Way El Dorado Hills (95762) ***(P-15202)***
El Dorado Hills County Wtr Dst....D....916 933-6623
1050 Wilson Blvd El Dorado Hills (95762) ***(P-8247)***
El Dorado Hills Fire Dept, El Dorado Hills *Also called El Dorado Hills County Wtr Dst* ***(P-8247)***
El Dorado Irrigation District....B....530 622-4513
2890 Mosquito Rd Placerville (95667) ***(P-8248)***
El Dorado Newspapers (HQ)....C....**916 321-1826**
2100 Q St Sacramento (95816) ***(P-3434)***
El Dorado Savings Bank (PA)....D....**530 622-1492**
4040 El Dorado Rd Placerville (95667) ***(P-9770)***
El Dorado Truss Co Inc....E....530 622-1264
300 Industrial Dr Placerville (95667) ***(P-3205)***
El Macero Country Club Inc....D....530 753-3363
44571 Clubhouse Dr El Macero (95618) ***(P-15088)***
El Monte Motor Inn, Concord *Also called The Inn* ***(P-11531)***
El Pueblo Inn, Sonoma *Also called El Pueblo Motel Inc* ***(P-11075)***
El Pueblo Motel Inc....D....707 996-3651
896 W Napa St Sonoma (95476) ***(P-11075)***
El Rancho Elementary School, Carmichael *Also called El Rancho School Inc* ***(P-17931)***
El Rancho Motel Inc....C....650 588-8500
1100 El Camino Real Millbrae (94030) ***(P-11076)***
El Rancho School Inc....E....916 482-8656
5636 El Camino Ave Carmichael (95608) ***(P-17931)***
El Sobrante Christian School, El Sobrante *Also called Central Assembly of God* ***(P-17881)***
El-Bethel Terrace, San Francisco *Also called Christian Church Homes* ***(P-18076)***
Elance Inc (HQ)....C....**650 316-7500**
2625 Augustine Dr Ste 601 Santa Clara (95054) ***(P-11751)***
Elastic Beam LLC....E....925 963-8122
497 Seaport Ct Ste 101 Redwood City (94063) ***(P-12416)***
Elastic Projects Inc....D....415 857-1593
255 Golden Gate Ave San Francisco (94102) ***(P-12417)***
Elation Health Inc....D....415 213-5164
530 Divisadero St Ste 872 San Francisco (94117) ***(P-14261)***
Elb Global, Pleasanton *Also called Elb US Inc* ***(P-3336)***
Elb US Inc....E....925 400-6175
415 Boulder Ct Ste 500 Pleasanton (94566) ***(P-3336)***
Elcon Inc....E....408 292-7800
1009 Timothy Dr San Jose (95133) ***(P-6422)***
Elcon Precision LLC....E....408 292-7800
1009 Timothy Dr San Jose (95133) ***(P-5096)***
Elcor Electric Inc....C....408 986-1320
3310 Bassett St Santa Clara (95054) ***(P-1498)***
Elder Care Alliance San Mateo (HQ)....D....**510 769-2700**
1301 Marina Vil Pkwy 21 # 210 Alameda (94501) ***(P-18103)***
Elder Care Alliance San Mateo....D....650 212-4400
4000 S El Camino Real San Mateo (94403) ***(P-15981)***
Elder Care Alliance San Rafael....E....510 769-2700
1301 Marina Village Pkwy # 2 Alameda (94501) ***(P-15982)***
Elder Care Alnce San Francisco....D....415 337-1339
1 Thomas More Way San Francisco (94132) ***(P-15983)***
Elder Options (PA)....E....**530 626-6939**
82 Main St Placerville (95667) ***(P-17541)***
Eldorado Air LLC....D....916 391-5000
6133 Freport Blvd Ste 300 Sacramento (95822) ***(P-7756)***
Elecraft Incorporated....E....831 763-4211
125 Westridge Dr Watsonville (95076) ***(P-6749)***
Electric Cloud Inc (HQ)....C....**408 419-4300**
125 S Market St Ste 400 San Jose (95113) ***(P-8697)***
Electric Innovations Inc....D....530 222-3366
3711 Meadow View Dr # 100 Redding (96002) ***(P-1499)***
Electric Motor & Supply, Fresno *Also called Electric Motor Shop* ***(P-8859)***
Electric Motor & Supply Co., Fresno *Also called Electric Motor Shop* ***(P-8860)***
Electric Motor Shop (PA)....E....**559 233-1153**
253 Fulton St Fresno (93721) ***(P-8859)***
Electric Motor Shop....C....559 233-1153
250 Broadway St Fresno (93721) ***(P-8860)***
Electric Power RES Inst Inc (PA)....A....**650 855-2000**
3420 Hillview Ave Palo Alto (94304) ***(P-19214)***
Electric Tech Construction Inc....D....925 849-5324
1910 Mark Ct Ste 130 Concord (94520) ***(P-1100)***
Electric USA....E....800 921-1151
480 Aldo Ave Santa Clara (95054) ***(P-1500)***
Electrical Distributors Co, San Jose *Also called Chester C Lehmann Co Inc* ***(P-8851)***
Electrical Service Company, San Jose *Also called Rpd Electrical Service Co Inc* ***(P-1594)***
Electrical Services Company, Oakland *Also called CSC Corporation* ***(P-1489)***
Electriq Power Inc....F....833 462-2883
1937 Davis St Unit A1 San Leandro (94577) ***(P-6750)***
Electrnic Rcyclers Intl - Ind....D....317 522-1414
7815 N Palm Ave Ste 140 Fresno (93711) ***(P-8324)***
Electrnic Rcyclers Intl - Wash....E....253 736-2627
7815 N Palm Ave Ste 140 Fresno (93711) ***(P-8325)***
Electro Star Indus Coating Inc....F....530 527-5400
1945 Airport Blvd Red Bluff (96080) ***(P-4932)***
Electro Star Powder Coatings, Red Bluff *Also called Electro Star Indus Coating Inc* ***(P-4932)***
Electro-Plating Spc Inc....E....510 786-1881
2436 American Ave Hayward (94545) ***(P-4903)***
Electrochem Solutions Inc....B....510 476-1840
32500 Central Ave Union City (94587) ***(P-4904)***
Electrochem Solutions LLC....E....510 476-1840
32500 Central Ave Union City (94587) ***(P-4905)***
Electroglas, Dublin *Also called Eg Systems LLC* ***(P-6107)***
Electromax Inc....E....408 428-9474
1960 Concourse Dr San Jose (95131) ***(P-5927)***
Electroneek Robotics Inc....D....650 600-9550
611 Gateway Blvd Ste 120 South San Francisco (94080) ***(P-12418)***
Electronic Arts Inc (PA)....B....**650 628-1500**
209 Redwood Shores Pkwy Redwood City (94065) ***(P-13138)***
Electronic Arts Redwood Inc (HQ)....A....**650 628-1500**
209 Redwood Shores Pkwy Redwood City (94065) ***(P-6501)***
Electronic Cooling Solutions....F....408 738-8331
2344 Walsh Ave Ste B Santa Clara (95051) ***(P-5248)***
Electronic Interface Co Inc....D....408 286-2134
6341 San Ignacio Ave # 10 San Jose (95119) ***(P-6516)***
Electronic Recyclers America, Fresno *Also called Electronic Recyclers Intl Inc* ***(P-8326)***

Electronic Recyclers Intl Inc (PA)....A....**800 374-3473**
7815 N Palm Ave Ste 140 Fresno (93711) ***(P-8326)***
Electronic Resources Network....E....530 758-0180
1950 5th St Davis (95616) ***(P-5363)***
Electronic Systems Co Esco, Sunnyvale *Also called Northrop Grumman Systems Corp* ***(P-6616)***
Electronics For Imaging Inc (HQ)....E....**650 357-3500**
6453 Kaiser Dr Fremont (94555) ***(P-3731)***
Elegant Surfaces....E....209 823-9388
3640 Amrcn Rver Dr Ste 15 Sacramento (95864) ***(P-8625)***
Elekta Inc....E....408 830-8000
100 Mathilda Pl Fl 5 Sunnyvale (94086) ***(P-13139)***
Elekta / Impac Medical Systems, Sunnyvale *Also called Impac Medical Systems Inc* ***(P-13224)***
Element Analytics Inc....E....415 483-0310
564 Market St Ste 316 San Francisco (94104) ***(P-13581)***
Element Critical, San Francisco *Also called New Cch LLC* ***(P-13735)***
Element Santa Clara, Santa Clara *Also called Mission Park Hotel LP* ***(P-3792)***
Element Science Inc....D....415 872-6500
200 Kansas St Ste 210 San Francisco (94103) ***(P-19215)***
Element Six Tech US Corp....F....408 986-8184
3901 Burton Dr Santa Clara (95054) ***(P-3785)***
Elementcxi....E....408 935-8090
25 E Trimble Rd San Jose (95131) ***(P-6108)***
Elements By Grapevine Inc....F....209 727-3711
18251 N Highway 88 Lockeford (95237) ***(P-3277)***
Elements Manufacturing Inc....E....831 421-9440
115 Harvey West Blvd C Santa Cruz (95060) ***(P-3313)***
Elements Mountain Company....E....530 582-0300
17356 Northwoods Blvd Truckee (96161) ***(P-11945)***
Elena Gardens Apartments, San Jose *Also called Eah Elena Gardens LP* ***(P-10429)***
Elevate Addiction Services, Aptos *Also called Enlighticare Inc* ***(P-16758)***
Elevate Labs LLC....E....415 875-9817
1390 Market St Ste 200 San Francisco (94102) ***(P-13140)***
Elevator Industries Inc....F....916 921-1495
110 Main Ave Sacramento (95838) ***(P-5046)***
Eleven Inc....C....415 707-1111
500 Sansome St Ste 100 San Francisco (94111) ***(P-11752)***
ELF Beauty Inc (PA)....C....**510 210-8602**
570 10th St Oakland (94607) ***(P-4082)***
Eli Kiselman....E....832 886-3743
98 N 1st St Unit 725 San Jose (95113) ***(P-565)***
Elica Health Centers....E....916 454-2345
3701 J St Ste 201 Sacramento (95816) ***(P-15389)***
Elica Health Centers....E....916 275-3747
155 15th St West Sacramento (95691) ***(P-15390)***
Eligius Manufacturing Inc....E....408 437-0337
1177 N 15th St San Jose (95112) ***(P-4657)***
Elijah House SLe....E....530 370-8386
1980 Arnold Ave Oroville (95966) ***(P-17542)***
Elisity Inc....F....408 839-3971
100 Century Center Ct # 710 San Jose (95112) ***(P-5364)***
Elite Biomechanical Design (PA)....E....**530 894-6913**
9 Governors Ln Chico (95926) ***(P-7070)***
Elite E/M Inc....E....408 988-3505
340 Martin Ave Santa Clara (95050) ***(P-4760)***
Elite Family Systems....E....209 531-2088
2935 4th St Ceres (95307) ***(P-18104)***
Elite Landscaping Inc....C....559 292-7760
2972 Larkin Ave Clovis (93612) ***(P-461)***
Elite Metal Fabrication Inc....F....408 433-9926
2299 Ringwood Ave Ste C1 San Jose (95131) ***(P-5517)***
Elite Power Inc....D....916 739-1580
6530 Asher Ln Sacramento (95828) ***(P-1501)***
Elite Ready-Mix LLC....E....916 366-4627
6790 Bradshaw Rd Sacramento (95829) ***(P-4480)***
Elite Security Group Inc....E....925 597-8852
640 Bailey Rd 124 Bay Point (94565) ***(P-14130)***
Elite Service Experts Inc (PA)....D....**916 568-1400**
725 Del Paso Rd Sacramento (95834) ***(P-5147)***
Elite Universal Security, Olivehurst *Also called California Security Svcs Inc* ***(P-14041)***
Elite Universal Security, Chico *Also called California Security Svcs Inc* ***(P-14042)***
Elitecare Medical Staffing LLC....D....559 438-7700
761 E Locust Ave Ste 103 Fresno (93720) ***(P-12086)***
Elitegroup Cmpt Systems Inc....C....510 226-7333
6851 Mowry Ave Newark (94560) ***(P-5365)***
Elitegroup Computer Systems Ho....C....510 794-2952
6851 Mowry Ave Newark (94560) ***(P-8698)***
Elitigation Solutions, Palo Alto *Also called Altep California LLC* ***(P-7924)***
Elizabeth Headrick....E....530 247-8000
7194 Bridge St Anderson (96007) ***(P-3059)***
Elizabethan Inn Associates LP....E....916 448-1300
1935 Wright St Apt 231 Sacramento (95825) ***(P-11077)***
Elk Grove Milling Inc....E....916 684-2056
8320 Eschinger Rd Elk Grove (95757) ***(P-2341)***
Elk Grove Unified School Dst....E....916 686-7733
8421 Gerber Rd Sacramento (95828) ***(P-7429)***
Elk Ridge Almonds, Madera *Also called Benton Enterprises LLC* ***(P-83)***
Elk Valley Casino Inc....C....707 464-1020
2500 Howland Hill Rd Crescent City (95531) ***(P-11078)***
Elk Valley Rancheria Cal, Crescent City *Also called Elk Valley Casino Inc* ***(P-11078)***
Elkhorn Berry Farms LLC....E....831 722-2472
262 E Lake Ave Watsonville (95076) ***(P-162)***
Ellation LLC (HQ)....C....**415 796-3560**
444 Bush St San Francisco (94108) ***(P-12419)***
Ellensburg Lamb Company Inc....D....707 678-3091
7390 Rio Dixon Rd Dixon (95620) ***(P-2095)***
Ellensburg Lamb Company Inc (HQ)....F....**530 758-3091**
2530 River Plaza Dr # 200 Sacramento (95833) ***(P-2096)***
Ellie Mae, Pleasanton *Also called Ice Mortgage Technology Inc* ***(P-13222)***
Elliott Benson....E....916 325-1670
1226 H St Sacramento (95814) ***(P-19158)***
Elliott Manufacturing Co Inc....F....559 233-6235
2664 S Cherry Ave Fresno (93706) ***(P-5518)***
Ellis and Ellis Sign, Sacramento *Also called Illuminated Creations Inc* ***(P-7233)***
Elliston Vineyards Inc....D....925 862-2377
463 Kilkare Rd Sunol (94586) ***(P-2561)***
Elm Ford, Woodland *Also called Elm Ford Inc* ***(P-14559)***
Elm Ford Inc (PA)....E....**530 662-2817**
346 Main St Woodland (95695) ***(P-14559)***
Elma Electronic Inc (HQ)....C....**510 656-3400**
44350 S Grimmer Blvd Fremont (94538) ***(P-5249)***
Elmco & Assoc (PA)....E....**916 383-0110**
11225 Trade Center Dr # 100 Rancho Cordova (95742) ***(P-4249)***
Elmech Inc....F....408 782-2990
195 San Pedro Ave Ste E15 Morgan Hill (95037) ***(P-6423)***
Elmwood Care Center, Berkeley *Also called Shattuck Health Care Inc* ***(P-16114)***
Elo Touch Solutions Inc (HQ)....B....**408 597-8000**
670 N Mccarthy Blvd # 100 Milpitas (95035) ***(P-8699)***
Els Investments....C....916 388-0308
2701 Citrus Rd Ste A Rancho Cordova (95742) ***(P-413)***
Elsa L Inc....E....415 472-8388
800 A St San Rafael (94901) ***(P-9194)***
Elson Electric Holdings Inc....E....925 464-7461
3440 Vincent Rd Pleasant Hill (94523) ***(P-1502)***
Emagia Corporation....E....408 654-6575
4701 P Henry Dr Bldg 20 Santa Clara (95054) ***(P-14262)***
Emagined Security Inc....E....415 944-2977
2816 San Simeon Way San Carlos (94070) ***(P-14131)***
Emanio Inc (PA)....C....**510 849-9300**
832 Bancroft Way Berkeley (94710) ***(P-12420)***
Emanuel Medical Center Inc (HQ)....A....**209 667-4200**
825 Delbon Ave Turlock (95382) ***(P-16362)***
Embarcadero Inn Associates....D....415 495-2100
155 Steuart St San Francisco (94105) ***(P-11079)***
Embarcadero Publishing Company (PA)....D....**650 964-6300**
450 Cambridge Ave Palo Alto (94306) ***(P-3435)***
Embarcadero, The, San Francisco *Also called Crunch LLC* ***(P-14945)***
Embark Trucks Inc....E....765 409-4499
424 Townsend St San Francisco (94107) ***(P-7462)***
Embassador Private Securities....D....415 822-8811
1341 Evans Ave San Francisco (94124) ***(P-9967)***
Embassy Investments LLC....D....707 422-4111
1350 Holiday Ln Fairfield (94534) ***(P-11080)***
Embassy Sites-So San Francisco, South San Francisco *Also called Djont/Cmb Ssf Leasing LLC* ***(P-11053)***
Embassy Stes - Mlpts/Slcon Vly, Milpitas *Also called Djont Operations LLC* ***(P-11051)***
Embassy Stes - So San Frncisco, South San Francisco *Also called Djont/Cmb Ssf Leasing LLC* ***(P-11052)***
Embassy Suites, NAPA *Also called NAPA Es Leasing LLC* ***(P-11319)***
Embassy Suites, Burlingame *Also called Djont Operations LLC* ***(P-11050)***
Embassy Suites, San Rafael *Also called Hotel McInnis Marin LLC* ***(P-11167)***
Embassy Suites- Santa Clara, Santa Clara *Also called Msr Hotels & Resorts Inc* ***(P-10870)***
Ember Industries....F....310 490-8926
812 Barstow Ave Clovis (93612) ***(P-5928)***
Embroker Insurance Svcs LLC (PA)....C....**844 436-2765**
24 Shotwell St San Francisco (94103) ***(P-10278)***
Emburse LLC....E....415 766-2012
548 Market St 27197 San Francisco (94104) ***(P-14263)***
Emco High Voltage, Jackson *Also called Xp Power LLC* ***(P-8975)***
Eme Technologies Inc....E....408 720-8817
3485 Victor St Santa Clara (95054) ***(P-5519)***
Emerald Cloud Lab Inc....D....650 257-7554
844 Dubuque Ave South San Francisco (94080) ***(P-19055)***
Emerald Farms LLC....E....530 438-2133
4599 Mcdermott Rd Maxwell (95955) ***(P-163)***
Emerald Hlls Asssted Lving Fcl, Auburn *Also called Emeritus Corporation* ***(P-16181)***
Emerald Investments Inc....E....530 894-8600
25 Heritage Ln Chico (95926) ***(P-11081)***
Emerald Kingdom Greenhouse LLC (PA)....E....**530 215-5670**
104 Masonic Ln Weaverville (96093) ***(P-4850)***
Emerald Landscape Company Inc (HQ)....E....**925 449-4743**
2265 Research Dr Livermore (94550) ***(P-414)***
Emerald Packaging Inc....C....510 429-5700
33050 Western Ave Union City (94587) ***(P-9656)***
Emerald Site Services Inc....D....916 685-7211
9190 Jackson Rd Sacramento (95826) ***(P-1958)***
Emerald Triangle MGT Group Inc....F....707 630-5040
5550 West End Rd Ste 11 Arcata (95521) ***(P-7283)***
Emergency Housing Chld Program, Sacramento *Also called Sacramento Area Emerg Housing* ***(P-17698)***
Emergency Physicians, Pleasanton *Also called Quantum Hlthcare Med Assoc Inc* ***(P-15637)***
Emergent Payments Inc....D....646 867-7200
2445 Augustine Dr Ste 460 Santa Clara (95054) ***(P-12421)***
Emeritus Corporation....C....510 797-4011
38035 Martha Ave Fremont (94536) ***(P-15984)***
Emeritus Corporation....C....530 653-1974
11550 Education St # 212 Auburn (95602) ***(P-16181)***
Emeritus Corporation....C....707 552-3336
2261 Tuolumne St Vallejo (94589) ***(P-15985)***
Emeritus Corporation....C....707 996-7101
800 Oregon St Sonoma (95476) ***(P-16182)***
Emeritus Corporation....C....707 324-7087
300 Fountaingrove Pkwy Santa Rosa (95403) ***(P-16183)***

Emerson Collective LLC ....C.......650 422-2152
555 Bryant St Ste 259 Palo Alto (94301) *(P-12422)*
Emery Marina, Emeryville *Also called Young MNS Chrstn Assn of E Bay (P-18492)*
Emerzian Woodworking Inc ....E.......559 292-2448
2555 N Argyle Ave Fresno (93727) *(P-3314)*
Emeter Corporation ....C.......650 227-7770
4000 E 3rd Ave Ste 400 Foster City (94404) *(P-12423)*
Emf Broadcasting ....D.......601 992-6988
5700 West Oaks Blvd Rocklin (95765) *(P-8019)*
Emg Inc ....D.......707 525-9941
675 Aviation Blvd Ste B Santa Rosa (95403) *(P-7172)*
Emile's Table Wines, Morgan Hill *Also called Guglielmo Emilo Winery Inc (P-54)*
Emilio Guglielmo Winery Inc ....F.......408 779-2145
1480 E Main Ave Morgan Hill (95037) *(P-2562)*
Emilykate LLC ....F.......916 761-6261
8336 Valdez Ave Sacramento (95828) *(P-12424)*
Emkay Mfg., Redwood City *Also called Bay Precision Machining Inc (P-5482)*
Emmett W McCrkle Inc Insur Svc ....E.......650 349-2364
700 Airport Blvd Ste 300 Burlingame (94010) *(P-10279)*
Empire Cinema, San Francisco *Also called Century Theatres Inc (P-14830)*
Empire Elevator, Sebastopol *Also called Kone Inc (P-14758)*
Empire Golf Inc ....E.......916 482-3284
6700 Tarshes Dr Carmichael (95608) *(P-15001)*
Empire Paper Corporation ....E.......510 534-2700
4930 Waterstone Dr Roseville (95747) *(P-9207)*
Empire Realty Associates Inc ....A.......925 217-5000
380 Diablo Rd Danville (94526) *(P-10544)*
Empire Shower Doors Inc ....E.......707 773-2898
1217 N Mcdowell Blvd Petaluma (94954) *(P-4385)*
Empire Waste Management ....D.......707 462-2063
450 Orr Springs Rd Ukiah (95482) *(P-8327)*
Empire West Inc ....E.......707 823-1190
9270 Graton Rd Graton (95444) *(P-4279)*
Empire West Plastics, Graton *Also called Empire West Inc (P-4279)*
Employee Bneft Specialists Inc ....E.......925 460-3910
5675 Gibraltar Dr Pleasanton (94588) *(P-19499)*
Employee Health Services, Davis *Also called University California Davis (P-15782)*
Employerware LLC ....E.......925 283-9735
350 N Wiget Ln Ste 200 Walnut Creek (94598) *(P-3569)*
Empower Yolo Inc ....E.......530 662-1133
175 Walnut St Woodland (95695) *(P-17543)*
Empres Financial Services LLC ....A.......707 643-2793
1527 Springs Rd Vallejo (94591) *(P-15986)*
Empres Post Acute Rhbilitation, Petaluma *Also called Evergreen At Petaluma LLC (P-15999)*
Empresas Del Bosque Inc ....B.......209 364-6428
51481 W Shields Ave Firebaugh (93622) *(P-164)*
Empress Care Center LLC ....E.......408 287-0616
1299 S Bascom Ave San Jose (95128) *(P-15987)*
Emq Families First (PA) ....D.......**408 379-3790**
251 Llewellyn Ave Campbell (95008) *(P-17544)*
EMQ FAMILIESFIRST, Campbell *Also called Uplift Family Services (P-17778)*
Emq Familiesfirst ....E.......408 354-0149
499 Loma Alta Ave Los Gatos (95030) *(P-17545)*
EMR Cpr LLC ....B.......408 471-6804
32970 Alvarado Niles Rd # 736 Union City (94587) *(P-13582)*
Emtec Engineering ....E.......408 779-5800
16840 Joleen Way Ste F1 Morgan Hill (95037) *(P-4761)*
Emvco LLC ....E.......650 432-3149
900 Metro Center Blvd Foster City (94404) *(P-6424)*
Enablence Systems Inc (HQ) ....D.......**510 226-8900**
2933 Bayview Dr Fremont (94538) *(P-13141)*
Enablence USA Components Inc ....D.......510 226-8900
2933 Bayview Dr Fremont (94538) *(P-5794)*
Enact Systems Inc ....F.......510 828-2701
6200 Stnrdge Mall Rd Ste Pleasanton (94588) *(P-13142)*
Enartis Usa Inc (PA) ....E.......**707 838-6312**
7795 Bell Rd Windsor (95492) *(P-9450)*
Enartis Vinquiry, Windsor *Also called Enartis Usa Inc (P-9450)*
Enbiz International, San Jose *Also called Cloudradiant Corp (P-9651)*
Encinal Yacht Club ....E.......510 522-3272
1251 Pacific Marina Alameda (94501) *(P-15089)*
Enclipse Corp ....E.......866 261-3503
2410 Camino Ramon Ste 320 San Ramon (94583) *(P-13886)*
Encompass, Sacramento *Also called Laser Recharge Inc (P-7207)*
Encompass Community Services ....D.......831 688-6293
2716 Freedom Blvd Watsonville (95076) *(P-16757)*
Encompass Community Services ....E.......831 479-9494
941 El Dorado Ave Santa Cruz (95062) *(P-17546)*
Encompass Community Services ....E.......831 423-2003
716 Ocean St Ste 230 Santa Cruz (95060) *(P-17547)*
Encompass Community Services ....E.......831 423-3890
125 Rigg St Santa Cruz (95060) *(P-17548)*
Encompass Community Services ....E.......831 425-0771
380 Encinal St Ste 200 Santa Cruz (95060) *(P-17549)*
Encompass Community Services ....E.......831 728-2226
241 E Lake Ave Watsonville (95076) *(P-17550)*
Encompass Community Services ....E.......831 724-3885
225 Westridge Dr Watsonville (95076) *(P-17551)*
Encompass Community Services ....E.......831 459-6644
716 Ocean St Ste 200 Santa Cruz (95060) *(P-17552)*
Encore Events Rentals Inc ....D.......707 431-3500
1001 American Way Windsor (95492) *(P-12040)*
Encore Industries ....E.......408 416-0501
597 Brennan St San Jose (95131) *(P-4762)*
Encore Technical Staffing LLC (PA) ....E.......**541 396-1885**
1134 Crane St Ste 216 Menlo Park (94025) *(P-12169)*
End Timey Industries LLC (PA) ....F.......**202 550-7570**
250 Fell St San Francisco (94102) *(P-7284)*
End To End Analytics LLC ....D.......650 331-9659
2595 E Byshore Rd Ste 150 Palo Alto (94303) *(P-19765)*
Endeavor Homes Inc ....E.......530 534-0300
655 Cal Oak Rd Oroville (95965) *(P-5032)*
Endless West, San Francisco *Also called Ava Food Labs Inc (P-19259)*
Endodontics Associates ....E.......408 294-4149
2000 Forest Ave Ste D San Jose (95128) *(P-15833)*
Endors Toi Pbc ....D.......434 987-0919
600 F St Ste 3 Arcata (95521) *(P-19500)*
Endorse Corp ....D.......617 470-8332
60 E 3rd Ave San Mateo (94401) *(P-8700)*
Endrun Technologies LLC ....F.......707 573-8633
2270 Northpoint Pkwy Santa Rosa (95407) *(P-6692)*
Endsight ....D.......510 280-2019
1440 4th St Ste B Berkeley (94710) *(P-13887)*
Endurance Lending Network, San Francisco *Also called Funding Circle Usa Inc (P-9870)*
Endwave Corporation (HQ) ....B.......**408 522-3100**
6024 Silver Creek Vly Rd San Jose (95138) *(P-5839)*
Endwave Defense Systems Inc (HQ) ....D.......**408 522-3180**
130 Baytech Dr San Jose (95134) *(P-6109)*
Energous Corporation ....D.......408 963-0200
3590 N 1st St Ste 210 San Jose (95134) *(P-5840)*
Energy Berkeley Office US Dept ....C.......510 701-1089
1226 Cornell Ave Albany (94706) *(P-19216)*
Energy Berkeley Office US Dept ....C.......510 486-4033
419 Latimer Hall Berkeley (94720) *(P-19217)*
Energy Experts International (PA) ....C.......**650 593-4261**
555 Twin Dolphin Dr # 150 Redwood City (94065) *(P-19501)*
Energy Performance Intl ....E.......916 995-1511
3844 Lynwood Way Sacramento (95864) *(P-14746)*
Energy Recovery Inc (PA) ....C.......**510 483-7370**
1717 Doolittle Dr San Leandro (94577) *(P-5148)*
Energy Salvage Inc ....E.......916 737-8640
8231 Alpine Ave Ste 3 Sacramento (95826) *(P-19327)*
Energy Saving Pros LLC ....E.......916 259-2501
3334 Swetzer Rd Loomis (95650) *(P-1255)*
Energy Solutions, Oakland *Also called Cohen Ventures Inc (P-19746)*
Energy Star Construction Inc (PA) ....E.......**559 231-5998**
2767 E Shaw Ave Ste 103 Fresno (93710) *(P-635)*
Energy Systems, Stockton *Also called ES West Coast LLC (P-5660)*
Enerparc Ca3 LLC ....F.......844 367-7272
1999 Harrison St Ste 830 Oakland (94612) *(P-6110)*
Enervenue Inc ....E.......408 664-0355
47621 Westinghouse Dr Fremont (94539) *(P-4565)*
Enexus Global Inc ....D.......510 936-4044
39510 Paseo Padre Pkwy # 390 Fremont (94538) *(P-13888)*
Enfabrica Corporation ....E.......650 206-8533
295 Bernardo Ave Ste 200 Mountain View (94043) *(P-6111)*
Enflick, San Francisco *Also called Textnow Inc (P-7999)*
Engage3 Inc ....E.......530 231-5485
501 2nd St Davis (95616) *(P-19502)*
Engagio Inc ....E.......650 265-2264
181 2nd Ave Ste 200 San Mateo (94401) *(P-13143)*
Engeo Incorporated ....D.......408 574-4900
6399 San Ignacio Ave # 150 San Jose (95119) *(P-18702)*
Engie Services US Inc (HQ) ....D.......**844 678-3772**
500 12th St Ste 300 Oakland (94607) *(P-18703)*
Engine No 1 LP ....E.......628 251-1222
710 Sansome St San Francisco (94111) *(P-14264)*
Engine World LLC ....E.......510 653-4444
1487 67th St Emeryville (94608) *(P-6577)*
Engineered Automation LLC ....F.......209 368-6363
20400 N Kennefick Rd Acampo (95220) *(P-5520)*
Engineered Plastic Division, San Jose *Also called Triad Tool & Engineering Inc (P-4327)*
Engineered Soil Repairs Inc (PA) ....D.......**408 297-2150**
1267 Springbrook Rd Walnut Creek (94597) *(P-1646)*
Engineering Enterprise, The, Alameda *Also called Shalley-Dibble Incorporated (P-18811)*
Enginrng/Rmdtion Rsrces Group (PA) ....D.......**925 839-2200**
4585 Pacheco Blvd Ste 200 Martinez (94553) *(P-8398)*
English Garden Care Inc ....E.......916 635-4275
3294 Luyung Dr Rancho Cordova (95742) *(P-462)*
English Oaks Cnvlscent Rhbltti, Modesto *Also called English Oaks Convalescent (P-15988)*
English Oaks Convalescent ....D.......209 577-1001
2633 W Rumble Rd Modesto (95350) *(P-15988)*
Enjoy Technology Inc (PA) ....B.......**650 488-7676**
3240 Hillview Ave Palo Alto (94304) *(P-13889)*
Enki Technology Inc ....E.......408 383-9034
1035 Walsh Ave Santa Clara (95050) *(P-3786)*
Enlighted Inc ....D.......650 964-1094
3979 Freedom Cir Ste 210 Santa Clara (95054) *(P-5734)*
Enlighticare Inc ....D.......831 750-3546
138 Victoria Ln Aptos (95003) *(P-16758)*
Enloe Homecare Services, Chico *Also called Enloe Medical Center (P-16881)*
Enloe Hospice Program, Chico *Also called Enloe Medical Center (P-16367)*
Enloe Hospt-Phys Thrpy (PA) ....B.......**530 891-7300**
1600 Esplanade Chico (95926) *(P-16363)*
Enloe Hospt-Phys Thrpy ....C.......530 891-7300
1444 Magnolia Ave Chico (95926) *(P-16364)*
Enloe Medical Center ....C.......530 891-7347
W 5th Av & Esplanade Chico (95926) *(P-7382)*
Enloe Medical Center ....C.......530 332-4111
560 Cohasset Rd Chico (95926) *(P-16365)*
Enloe Medical Center ....C.......530 332-7522
175 W 5th Ave Chico (95926) *(P-16366)*
Enloe Medical Center ....C.......530 332-6050
1390 E Lassen Ave Chico (95973) *(P-16881)*

A L P H A B E T I C

Enloe Medical Center ....D....530 332-6138
340 W East Ave Chico (95926) ***(P-15890)***
Enloe Medical Center ....C....530 332-5520
1536 Arcadian Ave Chico (95926) ***(P-16367)***
Enloe Medical Center ....C....530 332-6400
888 Lakeside Vlg Cmns Chico (95928) ***(P-16368)***
Enloe Medical Center ....C....530 332-6000
1515 Sprngfeld Dr Ste 175 Chico (95928) ***(P-16369)***
Enloe Outpatient Center, Chico *Also called Enloe Medical Center* ***(P-16368)***
Enloe Rehabilitation Center, Chico *Also called Enloe Medical Center* ***(P-15890)***
Enova Engineering Services, Walnut Creek *Also called E E S Corp* ***(P-18693)***
Enovity Inc ....E....916 853-1718
11180 Sun Center Dr Rancho Cordova (95670) ***(P-19766)***
Enovity Inc (HQ) ....E....415 974-0390
100 Montgomery St Ste 600 San Francisco (94104) ***(P-18704)***
Enovix Corporation ....C....510 695-2350
3501 W Warren Ave Fremont (94538) ***(P-6493)***
Enovix Corporation ....C....510 695-2399
3501 W Warren Ave Fremont (94538) ***(P-6494)***
Enphase Energy Inc (PA) ....A....707 774-7000
47281 Bayside Pkwy Fremont (94538) ***(P-6112)***
Enpower Management Corp ....D....925 244-1100
2603 Camino Ramon Ste 263 San Ramon (94583) ***(P-8096)***
Enquero Inc ....D....408 406-3203
1551 Mccarthy Blvd # 207 Milpitas (95035) ***(P-13583)***
Enquero, A Genpact Company, Milpitas *Also called Enquero Inc* ***(P-13583)***
Enray Inc., Livermore *Also called Truroots Inc* ***(P-2951)***
Ensher Alexander & Barsoom Inc (PA) ....E....916 443-6875
926 J St Ste 503 Sacramento (95814) ***(P-165)***
Ensighten Inc (HQ) ....C....650 249-4712
887 Oak Grove Ave Ste 203 Menlo Park (94025) ***(P-19503)***
Ensign Cloverdale LLC ....C....707 894-5201
300 Cherry Creek Rd Cloverdale (95425) ***(P-15989)***
Ensign Group Inc ....D....707 525-1250
3751 Montgomery Dr Santa Rosa (95405) ***(P-15990)***
Ensign Pleasanton LLC ....C....707 462-8864
1349 S Dora St Ukiah (95482) ***(P-15991)***
Ensign Sonoma LLC ....C....707 938-8406
1250 Broadway Sonoma (95476) ***(P-15992)***
Ensign Willits LLC ....C....707 459-5592
64 Northbrook Way Willits (95490) ***(P-15993)***
Ensurge Micropower Inc ....D....408 503-7300
2581 Junction Ave San Jose (95134) ***(P-6425)***
Ent Facial Surgery Center, Fresno *Also called Central Cal Ear Nose Throat ME* ***(P-15334)***
Entco Holdings Inc ....E....650 687-5817
3000 Hanover St Palo Alto (94304) ***(P-13144)***
Entekra LLC ....E....209 624-1630
945 E Whitmore Ave Modesto (95358) ***(P-3249)***
Entercom Communications Corp ....C....916 766-5000
5345 Madison Ave Sacramento (95841) ***(P-8020)***
Entercom Media Corp ....D....559 490-0106
1071 W Shaw Ave Fresno (93711) ***(P-8021)***
Entercom Media Corp ....D....415 765-4097
865 Battery St Fl 3 San Francisco (94111) ***(P-8022)***
Entercom Media Corp ....D....916 923-6800
280 Commerce Cir Sacramento (95815) ***(P-8023)***
Enterprise Auto Parts, Redding *Also called Automobile Accessories Company* ***(P-8441)***
Enterprise Events Group Inc ....C....415 499-4444
950 Northgate Dr Ste 100 San Rafael (94903) ***(P-19504)***
Enterprise Ntwrking Sltons Inc ....D....916 369-7567
2860 Gold Tailings Ct Rancho Cordova (95670) ***(P-13890)***
Enterprise Protective Svcs Inc (PA) ....E....408 840-2680
777 1st St Gilroy (95020) ***(P-14055)***
Enterprise Rent-A-Car Co ....E....415 330-0290
50 Elmira St San Francisco (94124) ***(P-14476)***
Enterprise Rnt—car San Frncsc ....E....415 882-9440
687 Folsom St San Francisco (94107) ***(P-14477)***
Enterprise Rnt—car San Frncsc ....E....707 462-2200
2800 N State St Ukiah (95482) ***(P-14478)***
Enterprise Rnt—car San Frncsc ....E....510 223-6444
2940 Hilltop Mall Rd Richmond (94806) ***(P-14479)***
Enterprise Rnt—car San Frncsc ....E....510 271-4160
3030 Broadway Oakland (94611) ***(P-14480)***
Enterprise Rnt—car San Frncsc ....E....650 697-9200
780 Mcdonnell Rd San Francisco (94128) ***(P-14481)***
Enterprise Rnt—car San Frncsc ....E....408 450-6000
1659 Airport Blvd Ste 7 San Jose (95110) ***(P-14482)***
Enterprise Rnt—car Scrmnto LL ....C....916 576-3164
6320 Mcnair Cir Sacramento (95837) ***(P-14483)***
Enterprise Rnt—car Scrmnto LL ....C....916 934-0783
7034 Rossmore Ln El Dorado Hills (95762) ***(P-14484)***
Enterprise Rnt—car Scrmnto LL ....C....916 648-1725
3216 Palm St McClellan (95652) ***(P-14485)***
Enterprise Rnt—car Scrmnto LL (HQ) ....E....916 787-4500
150 N Sunrise Ave Roseville (95661) ***(P-14486)***
Enterprise Rnt—car Scrmnto LL ....C....530 223-0700
217 E Cypress Ave Redding (96002) ***(P-14487)***
Enterprise Roofing Service Inc ....D....925 689-8100
2400 Bates Ave Concord (94520) ***(P-1801)***
Enterprise Solutions Inc ....B....408 727-3627
2855 Kifer Rd Santa Clara (95051) ***(P-19767)***
Enterprise Vineyards Inc ....E....707 996-6513
16600 Norrbom Rd Sonoma (95476) ***(P-52)***
Entertainment Centers Plus, Rancho Cordova *Also called Custom Furniture Design Inc* ***(P-3176)***
Enthalpy Analytical Llc ....E....510 486-0900
2323 5th St Berkeley (94710) ***(P-19265)***
Envelope Products Co ....E....925 939-5173
2882 W Cromwell Ave Fresno (93711) ***(P-3344)***
Envestment Management Inc (HQ) ....E....408 962-7878
160 W Santa Clara St Fl 8 San Jose (95113) ***(P-10043)***
Envia Systems Inc ....E....510 509-1367
7979 Gateway Blvd Ste 101 Newark (94560) ***(P-6517)***
Envirnmental Trnsp Specialists ....D....916 442-4971
4343 Chiles Rd Davis (95618) ***(P-14560)***
Envirnmntal Cmpliance Pros Inc ....E....916 953-9006
2701 Del Paso Rd Ste 130 Sacramento (95835) ***(P-4073)***
Envirnmntal Systems Inc Nthrn (PA) ....D....408 980-1711
3353 De La Cruz Blvd Santa Clara (95054) ***(P-1256)***
Enviro Tech Chemical Svcs Inc (PA) ....C....209 581-9576
500 Winmoore Way Modesto (95358) ***(P-9518)***
Envirocare International Inc ....E....707 638-6800
507 Green Island Rd American Canyon (94503) ***(P-5191)***
Environ Clean Technology, San Jose *Also called Environ-Clean Technology Inc* ***(P-6113)***
Environ-Clean Technology Inc ....F....408 487-1770
1710 Ringwood Ave San Jose (95131) ***(P-6113)***
Environment Control ....E....559 456-9791
3065 N Sunnyside Ave # 101 Fresno (93727) ***(P-11946)***
Environmental Chemical Corp (PA) ....D....650 347-1555
1240 Bayshore Hwy Burlingame (94010) ***(P-18705)***
Environmental Dynamics, Petaluma *Also called James Furuli Investment Co* ***(P-11963)***
Environmental Incentives LLC (PA) ....D....530 541-2980
3351 Lake Tahoe Blvd # 2 South Lake Tahoe (96150) ***(P-19768)***
Environmental Ldscp Solutions, Rancho Cordova *Also called Els Investments* ***(P-413)***
Environmental Remedies Inc ....D....925 461-3285
1999 Alpine Way Hayward (94545) ***(P-19900)***
Environmental Resources MGT, Walnut Creek *Also called Erm-West Inc* ***(P-18707)***
Environmental Sampling Sup Inc ....C....510 465-4988
640 143rd Ave San Leandro (94578) ***(P-4280)***
Environmental Science Assoc ....D....510 839-5066
350 Frank H Ogawa Plz Oakland (94612) ***(P-19056)***
Environmental Science Assoc (PA) ....D....415 896-5900
550 Kearny St Ste 800 San Francisco (94108) ***(P-19057)***
Environmental Science Assoc ....E....916 564-4500
2600 Capitol Ave Ste 200 Sacramento (95816) ***(P-19769)***
Environmental Technology Inc ....E....707 443-9323
300 S Bay Depot Rd Fields Landing (95537) ***(P-3802)***
Enviroplex Inc ....D....209 466-8000
4777 Carpenter Rd Stockton (95215) ***(P-4851)***
Envise ....C....510 447-3300
33333 Western Ave Union City (94587) ***(P-1257)***
Envision Peripherals Inc (PA) ....E....510 770-9988
490 N Mccarthy Blvd # 12 Milpitas (95035) ***(P-8701)***
Envivio Inc ....C....650 243-2700
2795 Augustine Dr Santa Clara (95054) ***(P-7947)***
Envoy Inc (PA) ....E....415 787-7871
410 Townsend St Ste 410 # 410 San Francisco (94107) ***(P-12425)***
Eo Products, San Rafael *Also called Small World Trading Co* ***(P-9237)***
Eo Products LLC ....C....415 945-1900
90 Windward Way San Rafael (94901) ***(P-9226)***
Eoc Resource Development, Fresno *Also called Fresno Cnty Ecnmic Opprtnties* ***(P-17581)***
Eoplex Inc ....E....408 638-5100
1321 Ridder Park Dr 10 San Jose (95131) ***(P-6518)***
Eoplex Technologies Inc ....E....408 638-5100
2940 N 1st St San Jose (95134) ***(P-6519)***
Eos Healthcare, Novato *Also called True North Ar LLC* ***(P-11831)***
Eos Software Inc ....E....408 439-2903
900 E Hamilton Ave # 100 Campbell (95008) ***(P-13145)***
Ep Executive Press Inc ....F....925 685-5111
201 Stonewall Rd Berkeley (94705) ***(P-3570)***
Epac Technologies Inc (PA) ....C....510 317-7979
2561 Grant Ave San Leandro (94579) ***(P-3643)***
Epco, Fresno *Also called Envelope Products Co* ***(P-3344)***
Epg Gym LLC ....E....707 964-6290
401 Cypress St Fort Bragg (95437) ***(P-14947)***
Epibiome Inc (HQ) ....F....650 825-1600
201 Gateway Blvd Ste 2061 South San Francisco (94080) ***(P-4021)***
Epic Creations Inc ....C....650 918-7327
702 Marshall St Ste 280 Redwood City (94063) ***(P-12426)***
Epic Holdings Inc (PA) ....D....650 295-4600
1390 Willow Pass Rd # 80 Concord (94520) ***(P-10280)***
Epic Hospitality Inc ....E....707 725-5500
1859 Alamar Way Fortuna (95540) ***(P-11082)***
Epic Tech Inc (PA) ....D....877 627-2215
12177 Bus Park Dr Ste 10 Truckee (96161) ***(P-14265)***
Epic Ventures Inc (PA) ....E....844 824-0422
200 Concourse Blvd Santa Rosa (95403) ***(P-9574)***
Epic War, Palo Alto *Also called Machine Zone Inc* ***(P-12591)***
Epic Wines & Spirits, Santa Rosa *Also called Epic Ventures Inc* ***(P-9574)***
Epicor Software Corporation ....C....925 361-9900
4120 Dublin Blvd Ste 300 Dublin (94568) ***(P-13146)***
Epicurean Group ....B....650 947-6800
111 Main St Ste 3 Los Altos (94022) ***(P-19328)***
Epidendio Construction Inc ....E....707 994-5100
11325 Highway 29 Lower Lake (95457) ***(P-1867)***
Epignosis LLC ....E....646 797-2799
315 Montgomery St Fl 9 San Francisco (94104) ***(P-13147)***
Episcpal Cmnty Svcs San Frncsc (PA) ....E....415 487-3300
165 8th St Fl 3 San Francisco (94103) ***(P-17553)***
Epitomics Inc (HQ) ....C....650 583-6688
863 Mitten Rd Ste 103 Burlingame (94010) ***(P-19058)***
Epixel Solutions ....D....650 616-4488
1001 Bayhill Dr San Bruno (94066) ***(P-19505)***
EPLP, San Mateo *Also called Essex Portfolio LP* ***(P-10817)***
Epmware Inc ....E....408 614-0442
333 W San Carlos St # 60 San Jose (95110) ***(P-8702)***
Epn Enterprises Inc ....D....888 788-5424
1900 Point West Way # 171 Sacramento (95815) ***(P-12170)***

Epoch International Entps Inc (PA).....C.....510 556-1225
46583 Fremont Blvd Fremont (94538) ***(P-5149)***
Epocrates Inc (HQ).....B.....650 227-1700
50 Hawthorne St San Francisco (94105) ***(P-17143)***
Epson Research and Dev Inc (HQ).....D.....408 952-6000
214 Devcon Dr San Jose (95112) ***(P-13584)***
Epstein Becker & Green PC.....D.....415 398-3500
655 Montgomery St # 1150 San Francisco (94111) ***(P-17262)***
Eqecat Inc (HQ).....D.....415 817-3100
475 14th St Ste 550 Oakland (94612) ***(P-19506)***
Equal Rights Advocates Inc.....E.....415 621-0672
611 Mission St Fl 4 San Francisco (94105) ***(P-17263)***
Equilar Inc.....C.....877 441-6090
1100 Marshall St Redwood City (94063) ***(P-14266)***
Equilibrium Management LLC.....E.....415 516-2930
2443 Fillmore St Ste 345 San Francisco (94115) ***(P-19507)***
Equilibrium Solutions Group, Corte Madera *Also called Automted Mdia Proc Sltions Inc* ***(P-7932)***
Equinix Inc (PA).....C.....650 598-6000
1 Lagoon Dr Ste 400 Redwood City (94065) ***(P-13711)***
Equinix (us) Enterprises Inc (HQ).....D.....650 598-6363
1 Lagoon Dr Redwood City (94065) ***(P-8076)***
Equinix Pacific LLC (HQ).....B.....650 598-6000
1 Lagoon Dr Ste 400 Redwood City (94065) ***(P-7948)***
Equinix Pacific, Inc., Redwood City *Also called Equinix Pacific LLC* ***(P-7948)***
Equinix Professional Svcs Inc.....E.....800 322-9280
1 Lagoon Dr Redwood City (94065) ***(P-7949)***
Equinox Hotel Management Inc.....D.....415 668-6887
2422 Lake St San Francisco (94121) ***(P-11083)***
Equinox-76th Street Inc.....D.....415 398-0747
301 Pine St San Francisco (94104) ***(P-14948)***
Equitex, NAPA *Also called Lixit Corporation* ***(P-7296)***
ERC Concepts Co Inc.....E.....408 734-5345
1255 Birchwood Dr Sunnyvale (94089) ***(P-5521)***
Erepublic Inc (PA).....C.....916 932-1300
100 Blue Ravine Rd Folsom (95630) ***(P-14267)***
Erg Aerospace Corporation.....D.....510 658-9785
964 Stanford Ave Oakland (94608) ***(P-3787)***
Erg Materials and Aerospace, Oakland *Also called Erg Aerospace Corporation* ***(P-3787)***
Eric Electronics Inc.....E.....408 432-1111
2220 Lundy Ave San Jose (95131) ***(P-8909)***
Eric Ladenheim MD Inc.....E.....559 446-1065
6145 N Thesta St Fresno (93710) ***(P-15391)***
Eric Stark Interiors Inc.....D.....408 441-6136
2284 Paragon Dr San Jose (95131) ***(P-1673)***
Ericsson Inc.....A.....408 750-5000
2755 Augustine Dr Santa Clara (95054) ***(P-7950)***
Ericsson Inc.....E.....408 970-2000
250 Holger Way San Jose (95134) ***(P-5841)***
Eride Inc.....F.....415 848-7800
1 Letterman Dr Ste 310 San Francisco (94129) ***(P-13148)***
Eriks North America Inc.....D.....916 366-9340
10182 Croydon Way Sacramento (95827) ***(P-9117)***
Erin Engineering and RES Inc (HQ).....E.....925 943-7077
2001 N Main St Ste 510 Walnut Creek (94596) ***(P-18706)***
Erm-West Inc (HQ).....C.....925 946-0455
1277 Treat Blvd Ste 500 Walnut Creek (94597) ***(P-18707)***
Ermico Enterprises Inc.....D.....415 822-6776
1111 17th St Ste B San Francisco (94107) ***(P-7194)***
Ernest J Wintter.....E.....925 933-2626
675 Ygnacio Valley Rd A200 Walnut Creek (94596) ***(P-18957)***
Ernest Ongaro & Sons Inc.....E.....707 579-3511
2995 Dutton Ave Santa Rosa (95407) ***(P-1258)***
Ernest Packaging Solutions, Sacramento *Also called Calvey Incorporated* ***(P-9648)***
Ernie & Sons Scaffolding.....C.....925 446-4442
1960 Olivera Rd Concord (94520) ***(P-2029)***
Ernst & Young LLP.....A.....415 894-8000
560 Mission St Ste 1600 San Francisco (94105) ***(P-18958)***
Ernst Benary of America Inc.....E.....831 288-2803
195 Paulsen Rd Watsonville (95076) ***(P-121)***
Ernst Development Inc.....E.....650 368-4539
937 Lakeview Way Emerald Hills (94062) ***(P-636)***
Ernst Publishing Co, Half Moon Bay *Also called Ucc Guide Inc* ***(P-3609)***
Ernst Wintter and Assoc, Walnut Creek *Also called Ernest J Wintter* ***(P-18957)***
Errg, Martinez *Also called Enginrng/Rmdtion Rsrces Group* ***(P-8398)***
Errotabere Ranches.....D.....559 867-4461
22895 S Dickenson Ave Riverdale (93656) ***(P-166)***
Ert Operating Company.....A.....412 390-3000
5615 Scotts Valley Dr # 150 Scotts Valley (95066) ***(P-12427)***
ES West Coast LLC.....E.....209 870-1900
7100 Longe St Ste 300 Stockton (95206) ***(P-5660)***
ESA, San Francisco *Also called Environmental Science Assoc* ***(P-19057)***
ESA, Sacramento *Also called Environmental Science Assoc* ***(P-19769)***
ESA Risk Management, San Jose *Also called SCC ESA Dept of Risk Mgmt* ***(P-10342)***
Esau Concrete Inc DBA Pcs Con.....D.....209 357-7601
101 Business Park Way Atwater (95301) ***(P-779)***
Escrowcom Inc.....E.....949 635-3800
180 Montgomery St Ste 650 San Francisco (94104) ***(P-9847)***
Escue and Associates Inc.....E.....510 924-7422
745 85th Ave Ste M-N Oakland (94621) ***(P-2030)***
Escueta Care Home 3 Inc (PA).....D.....510 785-0203
23571 Ronald Ln Hayward (94541) ***(P-16232)***
Esg Consulting Inc (PA).....E.....408 970-8595
4040 Clipper Ct Fremont (94538) ***(P-13891)***
Eshares Inc.....D.....650 669-8381
333 Bush St Fl 23 San Francisco (94104) ***(P-19329)***
Esilicon Corporation (HQ).....C.....408 217-7300
2953 Bunker Hill Ln # 300 Santa Clara (95054) ***(P-6114)***

Eskaton.....C.....530 672-8900
3421 Palmer Dr Cameron Park (95682) ***(P-18105)***
Eskaton (PA).....D.....916 334-0296
5105 Manzanita Ave Ste D Carmichael (95608) ***(P-10386)***
Eskaton.....C.....916 852-7900
11390 Coloma Rd Ofc Gold River (95670) ***(P-18106)***
Eskaton.....C.....916 395-1722
5701 Falconer Way Sacramento (95824) ***(P-10387)***
Eskaton.....B.....916 536-3750
9722 Fair Oaks Blvd Ste A Fair Oaks (95628) ***(P-16882)***
Eskaton Center of Greenhaven, Sacramento *Also called Eskaton Properties Inc* ***(P-18112)***
Eskaton Properties Inc.....D.....916 441-1015
3225 Freeport Blvd Ofc Sacramento (95818) ***(P-18107)***
Eskaton Properties Inc.....B.....916 974-2060
3847 Walnut Ave Carmichael (95608) ***(P-15994)***
Eskaton Properties Inc.....D.....916 331-8513
5318 Manzanita Ave Carmichael (95608) ***(P-18108)***
Eskaton Properties Inc.....D.....530 677-5066
3421 Palmer Dr Cameron Park (95682) ***(P-18109)***
Eskaton Properties Inc.....D.....916 334-0810
1650 Eskaton Loop Roseville (95747) ***(P-18110)***
Eskaton Properties Inc.....D.....916 965-4663
11300 Fair Oaks Blvd Fair Oaks (95628) ***(P-18111)***
Eskaton Properties Inc.....D.....916 393-2550
455 Florin Rd Sacramento (95831) ***(P-18112)***
Eskaton Properties Inc (PA).....D.....916 334-0810
5105 Manzanita Ave Ste A Carmichael (95608) ***(P-18113)***
Eskaton Properties Inc.....C.....916 334-0296
5105 Manzanita Ave Ste D Carmichael (95608) ***(P-17554)***
Eskaton Properties Inc.....D.....916 974-2000
3939 Walnut Ave Unit 399 Carmichael (95608) ***(P-18114)***
Eskaton Village Care Center, Carmichael *Also called Eskaton Properties Inc* ***(P-15994)***
Eskaton Village Charmichael, Carmichael *Also called Eskaton Properties Inc* ***(P-18114)***
Eskaton Village Roseville, Roseville *Also called Eskaton Properties Inc* ***(P-18110)***
Esl Technologies Inc.....B.....916 677-4500
8875 Washington Blvd B Roseville (95678) ***(P-13822)***
Esmart Source Inc.....F.....408 739-3500
5159 Commercial Cir Ste H Concord (94520) ***(P-13149)***
Espanas Mexican Restaurant.....D.....209 826-4041
1460 E Pacheco Blvd Los Banos (93635) ***(P-11084)***
Esparto Family Practice, Dixon *Also called Community Medical Center* ***(P-15357)***
Esparza Inc.....E.....209 358-4944
1500 Sycamore Ave Atwater (95301) ***(P-14561)***
Espe Machine Work / Ver Mfg, San Jose *Also called Neodora LLC* ***(P-4306)***
Esperanto Technologies Inc (PA).....D.....650 319-7357
800 W El Cmino Real Ste 4 Mountain View (94040) ***(P-6115)***
Espressive Inc.....E.....408 753-8766
5201 Great America Pkwy # 110 Santa Clara (95054) ***(P-13150)***
Esquivel Grading & Paving Inc.....E.....415 822-5400
918 Ingerson Ave San Francisco (94124) ***(P-1037)***
Ess Technology Holdings Inc (HQ).....E.....408 643-8818
109 Bonaventura Dr San Jose (95134) ***(P-6116)***
Essai Inc (HQ).....C.....510 580-1700
48580 Kato Rd Fremont (94538) ***(P-6751)***
Essence Printing Inc (PA).....D.....650 952-5072
270 Oyster Point Blvd South San Francisco (94080) ***(P-3644)***
Essential Products Inc.....D.....650 300-0000
380 Portage Ave Palo Alto (94306) ***(P-12428)***
Essex Management Corporation (HQ).....D.....650 494-3700
925 E Meadow Dr Palo Alto (94303) ***(P-10433)***
Essex National Securities LLC.....C.....707 258-5000
550 Gateway Dr Ste 210 NAPA (94558) ***(P-19508)***
Essex Portfolio LP (HQ).....B.....650 655-7800
1100 Park Pl Ste 200 San Mateo (94403) ***(P-10817)***
Essex Property Trust Inc (PA).....B.....650 655-7800
1100 Park Pl Ste 200 San Mateo (94403) ***(P-10434)***
Esterle LLC.....E.....415 673-0691
1450 Lombard St San Francisco (94123) ***(P-11085)***
Estes Commercial Rfrgn Inc.....E.....510 232-5464
1400 Potrero Ave Richmond (94804) ***(P-14687)***
Estes Express Lines.....D.....530 895-5123
2100 Fair St Chico (95928) ***(P-7530)***
Estes Express Lines.....D.....559 441-0915
4355 S Chestnut Ave Fresno (93725) ***(P-7531)***
Estes Express Lines.....D.....707 585-7961
650 Carlson Ct Rohnert Park (94928) ***(P-7532)***
Estes Express Lines.....D.....408 286-3894
1634 S 7th St San Jose (95112) ***(P-7533)***
Estes Express Lines.....D.....510 635-0165
1750 Adams Ave San Leandro (94577) ***(P-7534)***
Estes Express Lines.....D.....209 982-1841
7611 S Airport Way Stockton (95206) ***(P-7535)***
Estes Refrigeration, Richmond *Also called Estes Commercial Rfrgn Inc* ***(P-14687)***
Estrada Consulting Inc.....E.....916 473-7493
1221 18th St Sacramento (95811) ***(P-19770)***
Estuate Inc.....D.....408 946-0002
830 Hillview Ct Ste 280 Milpitas (95035) ***(P-12429)***
Esurance Insurance Svcs Inc (HQ).....C.....415 875-4500
650 Davis St San Francisco (94111) ***(P-10281)***
Et Capital Solar Partners USA.....E.....925 460-9898
4900 Hopyard Rd Ste 2 Pleasanton (94588) ***(P-19330)***
Et Water Systems LLC.....E.....415 945-9383
384 Bel Marin Keys Blvd Novato (94949) ***(P-6900)***
Etech-360 Inc.....A.....714 900-3486
1141 Folsom St San Francisco (94103) ***(P-12430)***
Ethan Conrad Properties Inc (PA).....D.....916 779-1000
1300 National Dr Ste 100 Sacramento (95834) ***(P-10545)***
Ethel Phillips Elementary Schl, Sacramento *Also called Sacramento Cy Unified Schl Dst* ***(P-18008)***

ALPHABETIC

Eti, Fields Landing *Also called Environmental Technology Inc* ***(P-3802)***
Etic (PA) ....E........**925 602-4710**
2285 Morello Ave Pleasant Hill (94523) ***(P-19771)***
Etm—Electromatic Inc (PA) ....D........**510 797-1100**
35451 Dumbarton Ct Newark (94560) ***(P-5842)***
Eton Corporation ....E........650 903-3866
1015 Corporation Way Palo Alto (94303) ***(P-6520)***
Etouch Systems Corp ....A........510 795-4800
39899 Balentine Dr # 200 Newark (94560) ***(P-13892)***
ETR, Scotts Valley *Also called Education Training & RES Assoc* ***(P-3533)***
Etr Associates Inc ....D........831 438-4060
100 Enterprise Way Scotts Valley (95066) ***(P-17555)***
Etrac Inc ....E........415 462-0421
637 Lindaro St Ste 100 San Rafael (94901) ***(P-18922)***
Ets-Esc Holdings LLC ....B........925 314-7100
2001 Crow Canyon Rd # 110 San Ramon (94583) ***(P-10733)***
Ettore Products Co ....D........510 748-4130
2100 N Loop Rd Alameda (94502) ***(P-9142)***
Etude Wines Inc ....E........707 299-3057
1250 Cuttings Wharf Rd NAPA (94559) ***(P-2563)***
Eugene Burger Management Corp (PA) ....E........**707 584-5123**
6600 Hunter Dr Rohnert Park (94928) ***(P-10546)***
Eugenus Inc (HQ) ....D........**669 235-8244**
677 River Oaks Pkwy San Jose (95134) ***(P-6752)***
Euphonix Inc (HQ) ....D........**650 526-1600**
280 Bernardo Ave Mountain View (94043) ***(P-5843)***
Eureka, Willows *Also called Calplant I LLC* ***(P-3262)***
Eureka District Office, Eureka *Also called State Compensation Insur Fund* ***(P-10185)***
Eureka Freightliner Parts, Redding *Also called Redding Freightliner Inc* ***(P-8427)***
Eureka Rehab & Wellness Center ....D........707 445-3261
2353 23rd St Eureka (95501) ***(P-15995)***
Eureka Super 8 Motel ....E........707 443-3193
1304 4th St Eureka (95501) ***(P-11086)***
Eureka Therapeutics Inc ....E........510 654-7045
5858 Horton St Ste 170 Emeryville (94608) ***(P-19059)***
Eureka Times-Standard, Eureka *Also called Pasadena Newspapers Inc* ***(P-3473)***
Eureka Un Schl Dst Fing Corp ....E........916 774-3437
5280 Stirling St Granite Bay (95746) ***(P-17932)***
Eurodrip USA Inc ....D........559 674-2670
1850 W Almond Ave Madera (93637) ***(P-9035)***
Eurofins Air Toxics LLC ....D........916 985-1000
180 Blue Ravine Rd Ste B Folsom (95630) ***(P-19266)***
Eurofins Discoverx Pdts LLC ....D........510 979-1415
42501 Albrae St Fremont (94538) ***(P-19060)***
Eurofins Eag Agroscience LLC ....E........510 741-3000
675 Alfred Nobel Dr Hercules (94547) ***(P-19267)***
Eurofins Eag Engrg Science LLC (HQ) ....D........**408 588-0050**
2710 Walsh Ave Santa Clara (95051) ***(P-19268)***
Eurofins Eag Laboratories, Sunnyvale *Also called Eurofins Eag Mtls Science LLC* ***(P-19269)***
Eurofins Eag Mtls Science LLC (HQ) ....B........**408 454-4600**
810 Kifer Rd Sunnyvale (94086) ***(P-19269)***
Eurofins Fd Chmstry Tstg Mdson ....A........609 452-4440
2441 Constitution Dr Livermore (94551) ***(P-19270)***
Eurofins Nanolab Tech Inc (PA) ....D........**408 433-3320**
1708 Mccarthy Blvd Milpitas (95035) ***(P-19271)***
Eurofins Testamerica, West Sacramento *Also called Testamerica Laboratories Inc* ***(P-19287)***
European Paving Designs Inc ....D........408 283-5230
1474 Berger Dr San Jose (95112) ***(P-1412)***
European Rolling Shutters, San Jose *Also called Blum Construction Co Inc* ***(P-4701)***
Euv Tech Inc ....F........925 229-4388
2830 Howe Rd A Martinez (94553) ***(P-6827)***
Eva Automation Inc ....B........650 513-6875
3945 Freedom Cir Ste 560 Santa Clara (95054) ***(P-19509)***
Evalve Inc ....D........650 330-8100
4045 Campbell Ave Menlo Park (94025) ***(P-4960)***
Evans Analytical Group LLC ....D........408 454-4600
2710 Walsh Ave Santa Clara (95051) ***(P-19272)***
Evb LLC ....E........415 281-3950
29 Park Way Piedmont (94611) ***(P-11753)***
Evehrtay LLC (PA) ....E........**707 293-3033**
421 1st St W Sonoma (95476) ***(P-2564)***
Event and Labor Services ....C........650 723-2285
340 Bonair Siding Rd Stanford (94305) ***(P-14790)***
Event Center, San Jose *Also called Student Un of San Jose State U* ***(P-18598)***
Eventbrite Inc (PA) ....B........**415 692-7779**
155 5th St Fl 7 San Francisco (94103) ***(P-13893)***
Eventbrite International Inc (PA) ....E........**415 692-7779**
155 5th St Fl 7 San Francisco (94103) ***(P-13894)***
Events Management Inc ....B........415 487-9114
1798 Bryant St San Francisco (94110) ***(P-11717)***
Eventure Cpitl Partners II LLC ....E........415 869-5200
600 Montgomery St Fl 43 San Francisco (94111) ***(P-10843)***
Everactive Inc ....D........517 256-0679
2986 Oakmead Village Ct Santa Clara (95051) ***(P-6753)***
Everest Consulting Group Inc ....D........510 494-8440
39650 Mission Blvd Fremont (94539) ***(P-12431)***
Everest Networks Inc ....F........408 300-9236
205 Ravendale Dr Mountain View (94043) ***(P-5366)***
Everest Silicon Valley MGT LP ....D........510 494-8800
8200 Gateway Blvd Newark (94560) ***(P-19331)***
Everest Wtrprfing Rstrtion Inc ....D........415 282-9800
1270 Missouri St San Francisco (94107) ***(P-11718)***
Everett Graphics Inc ....D........510 577-6777
7300 Edgewater Dr Oakland (94621) ***(P-3371)***
Everflow Technologies Inc ....E........408 479-9405
530 Showers Dr Ste 7-302 Mountain View (94040) ***(P-13585)***
Evergent Technologies Inc ....B........877 897-1240
1250 Borregas Ave Sunnyvale (94089) ***(P-12432)***
Evergreen At Chico LLC ....C........530 342-4885
1200 Springfield Dr Chico (95928) ***(P-15996)***
Evergreen At Heartwood Ave LLC ....E........707 643-2267
1044 Heartwood Ave Vallejo (94591) ***(P-15997)***
Evergreen At Lakeport LLC (PA) ....D........**707 263-6382**
1291 Craig Ave Lakeport (95453) ***(P-15998)***
Evergreen At Petaluma LLC ....D........707 763-6887
300 Douglas St Petaluma (94952) ***(P-15999)***
Evergreen At Springs Road LLC ....D........360 892-6628
1527 Springs Rd Vallejo (94591) ***(P-16000)***
Evergreen Co ....E........916 923-9000
2485 Natomas Park Dr # 360 Sacramento (95833) ***(P-10702)***
Evergreen Dstntion Hldings LLC ....D........209 379-2606
33160 Evergreen Rd Groveland (95321) ***(P-11087)***
Evergreen Envmtl Svcs Inc ....C........510 795-4400
6880 Smith Ave Newark (94560) ***(P-8328)***
Evergreen Lkport Halthcare Ctr, Lakeport *Also called Evergreen At Lakeport LLC* ***(P-15998)***
Evergreen Lodge, Groveland *Also called Evergreen Dstntion Hldings LLC* ***(P-11087)***
Evergreen Packaging LLC ....C........209 664-3426
1500 W Main St Turlock (95380) ***(P-9657)***
Evergreen Paper and Energy LLC (PA) ....D........**802 357-1003**
353 Rio Del Oro Ln Sacramento (95825) ***(P-3341)***
Evergreen-Energy, Sacramento *Also called Evergreen Paper and Energy LLC* ***(P-3341)***
Everliner, Willits *Also called Dripworks Inc* ***(P-9034)***
Evernote Corporation (PA) ....B........**650 216-7700**
305 Walnut St Redwood City (94063) ***(P-12433)***
Everycaronline Inc ....E........650 284-0497
4040 Moorpark Ave Ste 128 San Jose (95117) ***(P-13712)***
Everyday Health Care Fresno ....E........559 225-4706
392 S Richelle Ave Fresno (93727) ***(P-15392)***
Eviction Def Cllbrtive Inc A C ....D........415 947-0797
1338 Mission St Fl 4 San Francisco (94103) ***(P-6667)***
Evidation Health Inc (PA) ....C........**833 234-7048**
63 Bovet Rd 146 San Mateo (94402) ***(P-17144)***
Evidation Health Inc ....B........650 727-5557
400 Concar Dr Rm 3-109 San Mateo (94402) ***(P-12434)***
Evidentio Inc (HQ) ....D........**855 933-1337**
7901 Stoneridge Dr # 150 Pleasanton (94588) ***(P-12435)***
Evolent Health Inc ....B........571 389-6000
1 Kearny St Ste 300 San Francisco (94108) ***(P-17145)***
Evolphin Software Inc (PA) ....E........**888 386-4114**
6101 Bollinger Canyon Rd # 3 San Ramon (94583) ***(P-13151)***
Evolution Bureau, Piedmont *Also called Evb LLC* ***(P-11753)***
Evolv Surfaces Inc ....C........415 767-4600
825 Potter St Berkeley (94710) ***(P-3324)***
Evolv Technology Solutions Inc (PA) ....E........**415 444-9040**
611 Mission St Fl 6 San Francisco (94105) ***(P-13152)***
Evolva Nutrition Inc ....F........415 374-0785
101 Larkspur Landing Cir # 222 Larkspur (94939) ***(P-2890)***
Evolve Manufacturing Tech Inc ....D........650 968-9292
47300 Bayside Pkwy Fremont (94538) ***(P-6972)***
Evolveware Inc ....D........408 748-8301
4677 Old Ironsides Dr # 240 Santa Clara (95054) ***(P-12436)***
Ewing-Foley Inc (PA) ....E........**408 342-1201**
10061 Bubb Rd Ste 100 Cupertino (95014) ***(P-8910)***
Exabeam Inc (PA) ....C........**844 392-2326**
1051 E Hillsdale Blvd # 400 Foster City (94404) ***(P-14132)***
Exablox Corporation ....E........408 773-8477
1156 Sonora Ct Sunnyvale (94086) ***(P-13153)***
Exact Corp ....E........209 544-8600
5143 Blue Gum Ave Modesto (95358) ***(P-9036)***
Exactacator Inc (PA) ....E........**209 464-8979**
2237 Stagecoach Rd Stockton (95215) ***(P-7195)***
Exacttarget LLC (HQ) ....E........**415 901-7000**
415 Mission St Fl 3 San Francisco (94105) ***(P-13154)***
Exadel Inc (PA) ....C........**925 363-9510**
1340 Treat Blvd Ste 375 Walnut Creek (94597) ***(P-13155)***
Exar Corporation (HQ) ....C........**669 265-6100**
1060 Rincon Cir San Jose (95131) ***(P-6117)***
Exatron Inc ....E........408 629-7600
2842 Aiello Dr San Jose (95111) ***(P-6754)***
Excel Building Services LLC ....A........925 474-1080
1061 Serpentine Ln Ste H Pleasanton (94566) ***(P-11947)***
Excel Cnc Machining Inc ....E........408 970-9460
3185 De La Cruz Blvd Santa Clara (95054) ***(P-5522)***
Excel Machining, Santa Clara *Also called Excel Cnc Machining Inc* ***(P-5522)***
Excel Managed Care Disa ....C........916 944-7185
3840 Watt Ave Bldg C Sacramento (95821) ***(P-19510)***
Excel Precision Corp USA ....E........408 727-4260
3350 Scott Blvd Bldg 62 Santa Clara (95054) ***(P-6755)***
Excel Restoration Inc ....D........559 903-8902
1369 E Waldon Way Fresno (93730) ***(P-14268)***
Excelfore Corporation (PA) ....E........**510 868-2500**
39650 Liberty St Ste 255 Fremont (94538) ***(P-13586)***
Excell Care Ctr, Oakland *Also called Mariner Health Care Inc* ***(P-16057)***
Excellence Magazine Inc ....F........415 382-0582
42 Digital Dr Ste 5 Novato (94949) ***(P-3498)***
Excelsior Inc ....E........559 346-0932
2681 N Business Park Ave Fresno (93727) ***(P-4658)***
Exceptnal Prents Unlimited Inc ....C........559 229-2000
4440 N 1st St Fresno (93726) ***(P-17556)***
Exchange Bank (PA) ....C........**707 524-3000**
545 4th St Santa Rosa (95401) ***(P-9771)***
Excite Credit Union (PA) ....D........**800 232-8669**
265 Curtner Ave San Jose (95125) ***(P-9785)***
Exclara Inc ....F........408 329-9319
4701 Patrick Henry Dr Santa Clara (95054) ***(P-6118)***
Exclusive Fresh Inc ....E........650 728-7321
165 Airport St El Granada (94018) ***(P-9365)***

Exclusive Networks Usa Inc ....E....408 943-9193
2075 Zanker Rd San Jose (95131) ***(P-8703)***
Executive Inn Inc ....D....408 245-5330
1217 Wildwood Ave Sunnyvale (94089) ***(P-11088)***
Executive Scheduling Assoc ....C....877 315-3689
215 Lake Blvd Ste 367 Redding (96003) ***(P-19332)***
Executive System Group, Fremont *Also called Esg Consulting Inc* ***(P-13891)***
Executives Outlet Inc ....D....415 433-6044
1 Lombard St Lbby San Francisco (94111) ***(P-14949)***
Exelixis Inc ....C....650 837-8254
169 Harbor Way South San Francisco (94080) ***(P-3895)***
Exelixis Inc ....B....650 837-7000
1851 Harbor Bay Pkwy Alameda (94502) ***(P-6740)***
Exelixis Inc ....C....650 837-7000
1851 Harbor Bay Pkwy Alameda (94502) ***(P-3896)***
Exelixis Inc (PA) ....**D....650 837-7000**
1851 Harbor Bay Pkwy Alameda (94502) ***(P-4047)***
Exigen (usa) Inc (PA) ....**B....415 402-2600**
345 California St Fl 22 San Francisco (94104) ***(P-12437)***
Exigen Group, San Francisco *Also called Exigen (usa) Inc* ***(P-12437)***
Exin LLC ....F....415 359-2600
1213 Evans Ave San Francisco (94124) ***(P-3436)***
Exis Inc ....E....408 944-4600
1590 The Alameda Ste 110 San Jose (95126) ***(P-8911)***
Exit Realty Consultants, Ceres *Also called Klair Real Estate Inc* ***(P-10597)***
Expandable Software Inc (PA) ....**E....408 261-7880**
900 Lafayette St Ste 400 Santa Clara (95050) ***(P-13156)***
EXPANDING LIGHT, THE, Nevada City *Also called Ananda Church of Self-Realztn* ***(P-3522)***
Expanse LLC ....C....415 590-0129
425 Market St Fl 8 San Francisco (94105) ***(P-12438)***
Expanse, Inc., San Francisco *Also called Expanse LLC* ***(P-12438)***
Expedite Precision Works Inc ....E....408 437-1893
931 Berryessa Rd San Jose (95133) ***(P-5523)***
Expeditors Intl Wash Inc ....E....415 657-3600
425 Valley Dr Brisbane (94005) ***(P-7833)***
Experian Health Inc ....D....415 716-6633
2233 Watt Ave Ste 275 Sacramento (95825) ***(P-13587)***
Expert Dry Wall Systems Inc ....D....408 271-5044
1141 Old Byshore Hwy Ste San Jose (95112) ***(P-8545)***
Expert Semiconductor Tech Inc ....E....831 439-9300
10 Victor Sq Ste 100 Scotts Valley (95066) ***(P-5150)***
Expertech, Scotts Valley *Also called Expert Semiconductor Tech Inc* ***(P-5150)***
Exploramed Nc7 Inc ....D....650 559-5805
1975 W El Cmino Real Ste Mountain View (94040) ***(P-7105)***
Exploratorium ....B....415 528-4462
17 Pier Ste 100 San Francisco (94111) ***(P-18271)***
Exploring New Horizons Inc ....E....831 338-3013
6265 Highway 9 Felton (95018) ***(P-11601)***
Expo Decor, Fresno *Also called Expo Marketing & Services Inc* ***(P-14269)***
Expo Marketing & Services Inc ....E....559 495-3300
3714 N Valentine Ave Fresno (93722) ***(P-14269)***
Exponent Inc (PA) ....**B....650 326-9400**
149 Commonwealth Dr Menlo Park (94025) ***(P-18708)***
Exponent Partners ....E....800 918-2917
201 Mission St Ste 1200 San Francisco (94105) ***(P-19511)***
Exponential Interactive Inc (HQ) ....**D....510 250-5500**
1111 Broadway Ste 300 Oakland (94607) ***(P-19512)***
Express Messenger Systems Inc ....E....707 773-1564
3830 Cypress Dr Petaluma (94954) ***(P-7643)***
Express Messenger Systems Inc ....D....916 921-6016
1635 Main Ave Ste 3 Sacramento (95838) ***(P-7644)***
Express Messenger Systems Inc ....D....559 277-4910
4603 N Brawley Ave # 103 Fresno (93722) ***(P-7645)***
Express Messenger Systems Inc ....D....415 495-7300
101 Spear St Ste A1 San Francisco (94105) ***(P-7646)***
Express Personnel Services ....D....530 671-9202
870 W Onstott Frontage Rd E Yuba City (95991) ***(P-12171)***
Express Sewer & Drain Inc ....E....916 858-0220
3300 Fitzgerald Rd Rancho Cordova (95742) ***(P-14747)***
Express System Intermodal Inc ....E....801 302-6625
2633 Camino Ramon Ste 400 San Ramon (94583) ***(P-7834)***
Expression Systems LLC (PA) ....**E....877 877-7421**
2537 2nd St Davis (95618) ***(P-4048)***
Expresso, Santa Clara *Also called Interctive Fitnes Holdings LLC* ***(P-10739)***
Expressworks International LLC (PA) ....**D....925 244-0900**
2410 Camino Ramon Ste 167 San Ramon (94583) ***(P-19513)***
Extend Inc (PA) ....**E....650 270-9184**
301 Howard St Ste 1410 San Francisco (94105) ***(P-13895)***
Extole Inc ....E....415 625-0411
350 Sansome St Ste 700 San Francisco (94104) ***(P-19514)***
Extrateam, Inc. ....E....925 398-4400
7031 Koll Center Pkwy # 250 Pleasanton (94566) ***(P-14695)***
Extraview Corporation ....E....831 461-7100
100 Enterprise Way C210 Scotts Valley (95066) ***(P-12439)***
Extreme Networks Inc ....D....630 288-3665
3585 Monroe St Santa Clara (95051) ***(P-12440)***
Extreme Networks Inc (PA) ....**B....408 579-2800**
6480 Via Del Oro San Jose (95119) ***(P-5795)***
Extreme Precision Inc ....F....408 275-8365
1717 Little Orchard St B San Jose (95125) ***(P-5524)***
Extron Contract Mfg Inc ....E....510 353-0177
496 S Abbott Ave Milpitas (95035) ***(P-7176)***
Extron Contract Packaging, Milpitas *Also called Extron Contract Mfg Inc* ***(P-7176)***
Exxact Corporation ....D....510 226-7366
46221 Landing Pkwy Fremont (94538) ***(P-8704)***
Eye Care Institute ....D....707 546-9800
1017 2nd St Santa Rosa (95404) ***(P-15393)***
Eye Design Optometry, Sacramento *Also called Thomas H Murphy Od* ***(P-15874)***
Eye Mdcal Clnic Snta Clara Vly ....D....408 869-3400
220 Meridian Ave San Jose (95126) ***(P-15394)***
Eye Medical Center of Fresno, Fresno *Also called Eye Medical Clinic Fresno Inc* ***(P-15395)***
Eye Medical Clinic Fresno Inc ....D....559 486-5000
1360 E Herndon Ave # 301 Fresno (93720) ***(P-15395)***
Eye Q Vision Care ....E....559 673-8055
2339 W Cleveland Ave Madera (93637) ***(P-15396)***
Eye Q Vision Care (PA) ....**C....559 486-2000**
7075 N Sharon Ave Fresno (93720) ***(P-15397)***
Eyecarelive Inc ....E....415 329-7848
5201 Great America Pkwy Santa Clara (95054) ***(P-12441)***
Eyefluence Inc ....E....408 586-8632
1600 Amphitheatre Pkwy Mountain View (94043) ***(P-7139)***
Ezrez Software, San Francisco *Also called Topguest Inc* ***(P-13495)***
F & H Construction (PA) ....**D....209 931-3738**
1115 E Lockeford St Lodi (95240) ***(P-870)***
F C Bickert Company Inc ....E....530 529-3575
1315 Vista Way Red Bluff (96080) ***(P-1674)***
F E A, Sunnyvale *Also called Fujitsu Electronics Amer Inc* ***(P-18713)***
F F L, San Francisco *Also called Ffl Partners LLC* ***(P-10777)***
F Korbel & Bros (PA) ....**C....707 824-7000**
13250 River Rd Guerneville (95446) ***(P-2565)***
F M G Company, San Jose *Also called Fonseca/Mcelroy Grinding Inc* ***(P-1040)***
F M G Enterprises ....E....408 982-0110
1125 Memorex Dr Santa Clara (95050) ***(P-14748)***
F R O Inc ....E....559 891-0237
2003 1st St Ste 100 Selma (93662) ***(P-19772)***
F S I, Sonoma *Also called Fastening Systems Intl* ***(P-8982)***
F W Spencer & Son Inc ....C....415 468-5000
99 S Hill Dr Brisbane (94005) ***(P-1259)***
F-P Press, Union City *Also called Fricke-Parks Press Inc* ***(P-3650)***
F-Secure Inc (HQ) ....**E....888 432-8233**
470 Ramona St Palo Alto (94301) ***(P-8705)***
F3 and Associates Inc (PA) ....**D....707 748-4300**
701 E H St Benicia (94510) ***(P-18923)***
F50 League LLC ....E....415 939-4076
475 Sansome St Fl 12 San Francisco (94111) ***(P-18566)***
FAA Concord T Inc ....D....925 682-7131
1090 Concord Ave Concord (94520) ***(P-14562)***
Fab-9 Corporation ....D....408 667-2448
5400 Hellyer Ave San Jose (95138) ***(P-13896)***
Fabco Holdings Inc ....A....925 454-9500
151 Lawrence Dr Livermore (94551) ***(P-6578)***
Fabri-Tech Components Inc ....F....510 249-2000
49038 Milmont Dr Fremont (94538) ***(P-6426)***
Fabricated Extrusion Co LLC (PA) ....**E....209 529-9200**
2331 Hoover Ave Modesto (95354) ***(P-4281)***
Fabricated Glass Spc Inc ....E....707 429-6160
2350 S Watney Way Ste E Fairfield (94533) ***(P-4386)***
Fabrinet West Inc ....C....408 748-0900
4900 Patrick Henry Dr Santa Clara (95054) ***(P-5929)***
Fabrique Delices, Hayward *Also called Sapar Usa Inc* ***(P-2124)***
Fabritec Precision Inc ....E....209 529-8504
1060 Reno Ave Modesto (95351) ***(P-4763)***
Fabtron, San Carlos *Also called EH Suda Inc* ***(P-5515)***
Fabtron, Lewiston *Also called EH Suda Inc* ***(P-5516)***
Facebook, Menlo Park *Also called Meta Platforms Inc* ***(P-13800)***
Facebook ....D....650 823-7128
1105 Hamilton Ct Menlo Park (94025) ***(P-13788)***
Facebook Connectivity Lab, Menlo Park *Also called Fcl Tech Inc* ***(P-19273)***
Facebook Park Tower ....A....949 725-8637
250 Howard St San Francisco (94105) ***(P-13789)***
Faces SF Fmly Child Empwrment ....E....415 567-2357
1101 Masonic Ave San Francisco (94117) ***(P-17557)***
Facilities MGT Div Bldg Maint, Stockton *Also called County of San Joaquin* ***(P-11937)***
Facilitron Inc (PA) ....**E....800 272-2962**
485 Alberto Way Ste 210 Los Gatos (95032) ***(P-13157)***
Facility Masters Inc (PA) ....**C....408 436-9090**
1604 Kerley Dr San Jose (95112) ***(P-11948)***
Fadelli Concrete Pumping (PA) ....**E....510 525-4111**
1200 6th St Berkeley (94710) ***(P-1868)***
Fafco Inc (PA) ....**E....530 332-2100**
435 Otterson Dr Chico (95928) ***(P-4628)***
FAI Electronics Corp ....E....408 434-0369
690 N Mccarthy Blvd Ste 2 Milpitas (95035) ***(P-8912)***
FAI Electronics Corp ....E....408 829-7581
2220 Otoole Ave San Jose (95131) ***(P-8913)***
Failla Wines, Saint Helena *Also called Ehren Jordan Wine Cellars LLC* ***(P-2560)***
Fair Isaac Corporation (PA) ....**C....408 535-1500**
181 Metro Dr Ste 700 San Jose (95110) ***(P-14270)***
Fair Isaac International Corp (HQ) ....**A....415 446-6000**
200 Smith Ranch Rd San Rafael (94903) ***(P-13158)***
Fair Oaks Water District ....E....916 967-5723
10326 Fair Oaks Blvd Fair Oaks (95628) ***(P-8249)***
Fair Trade USA, Oakland *Also called Transfair USA* ***(P-19239)***
Fairchild Med Ctr Fndation Inc ....D....530 842-4121
444 Bruce St Yreka (96097) ***(P-17146)***
Fairchild Medical Center, Yreka *Also called Siskiyou Hospital Inc* ***(P-15688)***
Fairchild Medical Center, Yreka *Also called Siskiyou Hospital Inc* ***(P-16527)***
Fairchild Semicdtr Intl Inc (HQ) ....**A....408 822-2000**
1272 Borregas Ave Sunnyvale (94089) ***(P-6119)***
Fairfeld Inn By Mrrott Vcville ....D....707 469-0800
370 Orange Dr Vacaville (95687) ***(P-11089)***
Fairfeld V A Outpatient Clinic, Fairfield *Also called Veterans Health Administration* ***(P-15798)***
Fairfield Health Care Inc ....C....707 425-0623
1255 Travis Blvd Fairfield (94533) ***(P-16001)***
Fairfield Inn, Kingsburg *Also called Superb Hospitality LLC* ***(P-11521)***

ALPHABETIC

Fairfield Inn, Rancho Cordova *Also called Presidio Hotel Group LLC* ***(P-11376)***
Fairfield Inn, Clovis *Also called Clovis Hotels Inc* ***(P-11015)***
Fairfield Inn By Marr, Sacramento *Also called Welcome Group Inc* ***(P-11568)***
Fairfield Inn Roseville, Roseville *Also called Cni Thl Ops LLC* ***(P-11020)***
Fairfield Medical Offices, Fairfield *Also called Kaiser Foundation Hospitals* ***(P-15458)***
Fairfield Post-Acute Rehab, Fairfield *Also called Fairfield Health Care Inc* ***(P-16001)***
Fairfield Rental Service Inc..........F.......707 422-2270
2525 Clay Bank Rd Fairfield (94533) ***(P-12020)***
Fairfield Stadium Cinema, Fairfield *Also called Edwards Theatres Circuit Inc* ***(P-14810)***
Fairfield-Suisun Sewer Dst..........D.......707 429-8930
1010 Chadbourne Rd Fairfield (94534) ***(P-8282)***
Fairfld-Sisun Unified Schl Dst..........D.......707 421-4253
1650 Fairfield Ave Fairfield (94533) ***(P-11949)***
Fairfx-San Anslmo Children Ctr (PA)..........**E.......415 454-1811**
199 Porteous Ave Fairfax (94930) ***(P-17933)***
Fairmont Hospital- Regist, San Leandro *Also called County of Alameda* ***(P-16338)***
Fairmont Hotel, San Francisco *Also called Accor Services US LLC* ***(P-10909)***
Fairmont Hotel Guest)..........D.......615 578-2670
170 S Market St Lbby San Jose (95113) ***(P-11090)***
Fairmont Hritg Pl Ghrrdelli Sq..........C.......415 268-9900
900 N Point St Ste E204 San Francisco (94109) ***(P-11091)***
Fairmont San Francisco, San Francisco *Also called Mason Street Opco LLC* ***(P-11289)***
Fairmont Snoma Mission Inn Spa, Sonoma *Also called Sonoma Hotel Operator Inc* ***(P-11491)***
Fairview Elementary School, Hayward *Also called Hayward Unified School Dst* ***(P-18430)***
Fairweather & Associates Inc..........E.......707 829-2922
140 Todd Rd Santa Rosa (95407) ***(P-637)***
Fairwinds Woodward Park, Fresno *Also called Leisure Care LLC* ***(P-18138)***
Fairwood Apartments, Carmichael *Also called Fairwood Associates Apts* ***(P-10435)***
Fairwood Associates Apts..........D.......916 944-0152
8893 Fair Oaks Blvd Ofc Carmichael (95608) ***(P-10435)***
Fairytale Town Inc..........D.......916 808-7462
3901 Land Park Dr Sacramento (95822) ***(P-15041)***
Falcon Critical Care Trans A..........E.......510 223-1171
3508 San Pablo Dam Rd El Sobrante (94803) ***(P-17147)***
Falcon Trading Company (PA)..........**C.......831 786-7000**
423 Salinas Rd Royal Oaks (95076) ***(P-2891)***
Falconer House, Sacramento *Also called Eskaton* ***(P-10387)***
Falkonry Inc..........D.......408 761-7108
10020 N De Anza Blvd Cupertino (95014) ***(P-12442)***
Fallon Hotel, Columbia *Also called Columbia City Hotel LLC* ***(P-11026)***
Famand Inc..........D.......707 255-9295
1604 Airport Blvd Santa Rosa (95403) ***(P-1260)***
Famand Inc (PA)..........**E.......916 988-8808**
1512 Silica Ave Sacramento (95815) ***(P-1261)***
Familiar Srrndings HM Care LLC..........E.......408 979-9990
1568 Meridian Ave San Jose (95125) ***(P-16883)***
Family & Children Services..........D.......650 326-6576
375 Cambridge Ave Palo Alto (94306) ***(P-17558)***
Family and Children Services..........E.......408 292-9353
950 W Julian St San Jose (95126) ***(P-19773)***
Family Bridges Inc..........C.......510 839-2270
168 11th St Oakland (94607) ***(P-17559)***
Family Caregiver Alliance..........E.......415 434-3388
101 Montgomery St # 2150 San Francisco (94104) ***(P-17560)***
Family Christian Stores LLC (PA)..........**D.......616 554-8700**
3945 Freedom Cir Ste 560 Santa Clara (95054) ***(P-19333)***
Family Eye Care Optometry Corp..........D.......408 379-2020
338 E Hamilton Ave Campbell (95008) ***(P-15868)***
Family Health Care Med Group..........E.......209 527-6900
1320 Celeste Dr Modesto (95355) ***(P-15398)***
Family Health Services Clinic, Madera *Also called Madera Community Hospital* ***(P-16434)***
Family Healthcare Network..........C.......559 528-2804
12586 Ave 408 Orange Cove (93646) ***(P-15399)***
Family House Inc (PA)..........**E.......415 476-8321**
540 Mission Bay Blvd N San Francisco (94158) ***(P-17561)***
Family Intrnal Mdcn-Plcerville, Placerville *Also called Marshall Medical Center* ***(P-16450)***
Family Med Group San Leandro..........D.......510 351-2100
13851 E 14th St Ste 102 San Leandro (94578) ***(P-15400)***
Family Medical Group..........D.......209 668-4101
911 E Tuolumne Rd Turlock (95382) ***(P-15401)***
Family Paths Inc..........E.......510 582-0148
22320 Fthill Blvd Ste 400 Hayward (94541) ***(P-17562)***
Family Physcans Inc A Med Corp..........D.......530 671-2020
1530 N Township Rd Yuba City (95993) ***(P-15402)***
Family Plg Assoc Med Group..........E.......559 233-8657
165 N Clark St Fresno (93701) ***(P-15403)***
Family Plg Assoc Med Group..........E.......209 578-0443
2030 Coffee Rd Ste A1 Modesto (95355) ***(P-15404)***
Family Radio, Alameda *Also called Family Stations Inc* ***(P-8024)***
Family Resource & Referral Ctr..........D.......209 948-1553
509 W Weber Ave Ste 101 Stockton (95203) ***(P-17563)***
Family Service Agency, San Rafael *Also called Family Svcs Agcy Marin Cnty* ***(P-17566)***
FAMILY SERVICE AGENCY OF SAN F, San Francisco *Also called Felton Institute* ***(P-12172)***
Family Stations Inc (PA)..........**C.......510 568-6200**
1350 S Loop Rd Alameda (94502) ***(P-8024)***
Family Support Division, Modesto *Also called County of Stanislaus* ***(P-17518)***
Family Support Services (PA)..........**E.......510 834-2443**
303 Hegenberger Rd # 400 Oakland (94621) ***(P-17564)***
Family Svc Agcy of Centl Coast..........D.......831 423-9444
104 Walnut Ave Ste 208 Santa Cruz (95060) ***(P-17565)***
Family Svcs Agcy Marin Cnty (PA)..........**D.......415 491-5700**
555 Northgate Dr San Rafael (94903) ***(P-17566)***
Family Tree Farms Mktg LLC..........E.......559 591-6280
41646 Road 62 Reedley (93654) ***(P-9401)***
Famous Amos Chclat Chip Cookie, Stockton *Also called Murray Biscuit Company LLC* ***(P-2417)***
Famous Software II LLC (PA)..........**D.......559 438-3600**
8080 N Palm Ave Ste 210 Fresno (93711) ***(P-12443)***
Famsoft Corporation..........E.......510 683-3940
44946 Osgood Rd Fremont (94539) ***(P-13159)***
Fandom Inc (PA)..........**D.......415 762-0780**
130 Sutter St Ste 400 San Francisco (94104) ***(P-13790)***
Faneuil Inc..........B.......757 722-4095
5012 Dudley Blvd McClellan (95652) ***(P-12087)***
Fanfa Inc..........E.......510 278-8410
2401 Grant Ave San Lorenzo (94580) ***(P-1038)***
Fantasy Inc..........D.......510 486-2038
2600 10th St Ste 100 Berkeley (94710) ***(P-5777)***
Fante Inc (PA)..........**E.......650 697-7525**
2898 W Winton Ave Hayward (94545) ***(P-2855)***
Far Niente Wine Estates, Oakville *Also called Far Niente Winery Inc* ***(P-2566)***
Far Niente Winery Inc..........D.......707 944-2861
1350 Acacia Dr Oakville (94562) ***(P-2566)***
FAR NORTHERN REGIONAL CENTER, Redding *Also called Far Nrthern Crdnting Cncil On* ***(P-17568)***
Far Nrthern Crdnting Cncil On..........D.......530 895-8633
1377 E Lassen Ave Chico (95973) ***(P-17567)***
Far Nrthern Crdnting Cncil On (PA)..........**D.......530 222-4791**
1900 Churn Creek Rd # 114 Redding (96002) ***(P-17568)***
Far West Rice Inc..........E.......530 891-1339
3455 Nelson Rd Nelson (95958) ***(P-2319)***
Far Wstern Anthrplgcal RES Gro (PA)..........**E.......530 756-3941**
2727 Del Rio Pl Ste A Davis (95618) ***(P-19774)***
Farallon Brands Inc (PA)..........**F.......510 550-4299**
33300 Central Ave Union City (94587) ***(P-3025)***
Farallon Capital Partners LP (PA)..........**D.......415 421-2132**
1 Maritime Plz Ste 2100 San Francisco (94111) ***(P-10754)***
Farasis Energy Usa Inc..........D.......510 732-6600
21363 Cabot Blvd Hayward (94545) ***(P-5661)***
Farlows Scientific Glassblowing, Grass Valley *Also called Farlows Scntfic Glssblwing Inc* ***(P-4371)***
Farlows Scntfic Glssblwing Inc..........E.......530 477-5513
200 Litton Dr Ste 234 Grass Valley (95945) ***(P-4371)***
Farm Credit West..........D.......530 671-1420
939 Live Oak Blvd Yuba City (95991) ***(P-9886)***
Farm Fresh To You LLC (PA)..........**C.......916 303-7145**
3880 Seaport Blvd West Sacramento (95691) ***(P-167)***
Farmers & Merchants Bancorp (PA)..........**B.......209 367-2300**
111 W Pine St Lodi (95240) ***(P-9716)***
Farmers Business Network, San Carlos *Also called Fbn Inputs LLC* ***(P-376)***
Farmers Insurance Exchange..........B.......510 895-6000
2344 Merced St San Leandro (94577) ***(P-10282)***
Farmers International Inc..........E.......530 566-1405
1260 Muir Ave Chico (95973) ***(P-88)***
Farmers Rice Cooperative (PA)..........**E.......916 923-5100**
2566 River Plaza Dr Sacramento (95833) ***(P-2320)***
Farmers Rice Cooperative..........D.......916 373-5549
1800 Terminal Rd Sacramento (95820) ***(P-2321)***
Farmers Rice Cooperative..........D.......530 666-1691
845 Kentucky Ave Woodland (95695) ***(P-2322)***
Farmers Rice Cooperative..........D.......530 439-2244
4937 Highway 45 Colusa (95932) ***(P-283)***
Farmers Rice Cooperative..........D.......916 373-5500
2224 Industrial Blvd West Sacramento (95691) ***(P-2323)***
Farmers Rice Cooperative..........D.......530 666-1691
845 Kentucky Ave Woodland (95695) ***(P-9502)***
Farmhouse Inn & Restaurant LLC..........E.......707 887-3300
7871 River Rd Forestville (95436) ***(P-11092)***
Farmland Management Services..........E.......559 674-4305
17486 Road 23 Madera (93637) ***(P-375)***
Farmstead Gourmet, Lodi *Also called California Fruit Exchange LLC* ***(P-9389)***
Farmstead Long Meadow Ranch, Saint Helena *Also called Long Meadow Ranch Partners LP* ***(P-11268)***
Farwest Safety Inc..........E.......209 339-8085
226 N Main St Lodi (95240) ***(P-1039)***
Farwest Sanitation and Storage..........E.......925 686-1625
2625 E 18th St Antioch (94509) ***(P-12041)***
Farwest Trading, Turlock *Also called Associated Feed & Supply Co* ***(P-9594)***
Fashion Cleaners (PA)..........**E.......925 672-5505**
318 Montecillo Dr Walnut Creek (94595) ***(P-11652)***
Fast AG Svcs Trnspt Inc (PA)..........**E.......559 233-0970**
1303 S Cornelia Ave Fresno (93706) ***(P-7881)***
Fast Pro Inc..........D.......408 566-0200
2555 Lafayette St Ste 103 Santa Clara (95050) ***(P-8450)***
Fast Undercar, Santa Clara *Also called Fast Pro Inc* ***(P-8450)***
Fastening Systems Intl..........E.......707 935-1170
1206 E Macarthur St Ste 1 Sonoma (95476) ***(P-8982)***
Faster Faster Inc..........E.......323 839-0654
185 Valley Dr Brisbane (94005) ***(P-6579)***
Fastly Inc (PA)..........**A.......844 432-7859**
475 Brannan St Ste 300 San Francisco (94107) ***(P-12444)***
Fastrak Manufacturing Svcs Inc..........E.......408 298-6414
1275 Alma Ct San Jose (95112) ***(P-6427)***
Fastramp, Fremont *Also called Stats Chippac Test Svcs Inc* ***(P-6313)***
Fastsigns, Fresno *Also called Craigo Investments Inc* ***(P-7226)***
Fastsigns, Hayward *Also called Justipher Inc* ***(P-7240)***
Fastsigns..........E.......415 537-6900
650 Harrison St San Francisco (94107) ***(P-7229)***
Fatcat Scones, Sacramento *Also called Van Wolfs LLC* ***(P-9331)***
Fathom, Oakland *Also called Kemeera LLC* ***(P-8718)***
Faucetdirect.com, Chico *Also called Buildcom Inc* ***(P-8993)***

Fault Line Plumbing Inc ....E....925 443-6450
7640 National Dr Livermore (94550) *(P-1262)*
Faultline Harley-Davidson, Oakland *Also called Ankar Cycles Inc (P-14736)*
Faurot Ranch LLC ....E....831 722-1346
703 Hall Rd Royal Oaks (95076) *(P-29)*
Fba Inc (PA) ....**E....510 265-1888**
1675 Sabre St Hayward (94545) *(P-18709)*
Fbd Vanguard Construction Inc ....C....925 245-1300
550 Greenville Rd Livermore (94550) *(P-1869)*
Fbn Inputs LLC ....D....844 200-3276
388 El Camino Real San Carlos (94070) *(P-376)*
Fcl Tech Inc ....E....650 656-7570
1601 Willow Rd Menlo Park (94025) *(P-19273)*
Fcs Software Solutions Limited ....C....408 324-1203
2375 Zanker Rd Ste 250 San Jose (95131) *(P-12445)*
Fcsi Inc ....E....415 457-8000
628 Lindaro St San Rafael (94901) *(P-11628)*
Fdc Aerofilter, El Dorado Hills *Also called Filtration Development Co LLC (P-6380)*
Fdi, San Francisco *Also called Fisher Development Inc (P-873)*
Fdi Collateral Management, Sacramento *Also called Dealertrack Clltral MGT Svcs I (P-12377)*
Feather Falls Casino, Oroville *Also called Mooretown Rancheria (P-15038)*
Feather Falls Casino, Oroville *Also called Mooretown Rancheria (P-15220)*
Feather Publishing Company Inc (PA) ....**E....530 283-0800**
287 Lawrence St Quincy (95971) *(P-3437)*
Feather River Bulletin, Quincy *Also called Feather Publishing Company Inc (P-3437)*
Feather River Disposal Inc ....A....530 283-2065
1166 Industrial Way Quincy (95971) *(P-7463)*
Feather River Surgery Center ....C....530 751-4800
370 Del Norte Ave Ste 101 Yuba City (95991) *(P-15405)*
Feather Rver Recreation Pk Dst ....D....530 533-2011
1875 Feather River Blvd Oroville (95965) *(P-15203)*
Federal Express Corporation ....D....800 463-3339
3541 Regional Pkwy Petaluma (94954) *(P-7746)*
Federal Express Corporation ....C....510 347-2430
1601 Aurora Dr San Leandro (94577) *(P-7747)*
Federal Express Corporation ....B....510 382-2344
9190 Edes Ave Oakland (94603) *(P-7647)*
Federal Express Corporation ....C....510 465-5209
500 12th St Ste 139 Oakland (94607) *(P-7748)*
Federal Express Corporation ....D....916 361-5500
8950 Cal Center Dr # 370 Sacramento (95826) *(P-7749)*
Federal Hm Ln Bnk San Frncisco (PA) ....**C....415 616-1000**
333 Bush St Ste 2700 San Francisco (94104) *(P-9851)*
Federal HM Ln Bnk San Frncisco ....E....916 851-6900
11050 White Rock Rd Rancho Cordova (95670) *(P-9856)*
Federal Land Bnk Assn Nthrn CA ....D....530 895-8698
3435 Silverbell Rd Chico (95973) *(P-9756)*
Federal Realty Investment Tr ....E....408 551-4600
356 Santana Row Ste 1005 San Jose (95128) *(P-10818)*
Federal Solutions Group ....E....510 775-9068
2303 Camino Ramon San Ramon (94583) *(P-11876)*
Federated Insurance, Rancho Cordova *Also called Federated Mutual Insurance Co (P-10168)*
Federated Mutual Insurance Co ....E....916 631-0345
10850 Gold Center Dr # 100 Rancho Cordova (95670) *(P-10168)*
Federted Indans Grton Rncheria ....D....707 588-7100
630 Park Ct Rohnert Park (94928) *(P-11093)*
Fedex, Petaluma *Also called Federal Express Corporation (P-7746)*
Fedex, San Leandro *Also called Federal Express Corporation (P-7747)*
Fedex, Oakland *Also called Federal Express Corporation (P-7647)*
Fedex, Oakland *Also called Federal Express Corporation (P-7748)*
Fedex, Sacramento *Also called Federal Express Corporation (P-7749)*
Fedex Corporation ....E....415 657-0403
50 Cypress Ln Brisbane (94005) *(P-14271)*
Fedex Freight West Inc ....D....650 244-9522
3050 Teagarden St San Leandro (94577) *(P-7536)*
Fedex Freight West Inc ....C....559 266-0732
4570 S Maple Ave Fresno (93725) *(P-7537)*
Fedex Freight West Inc ....E....707 778-3191
1230 N Mcdowell Blvd Petaluma (94954) *(P-7538)*
Fee Munson Ebert Architects, San Francisco *Also called Forge Architecture (P-18885)*
Feedzai Inc ....B....650 649-9486
1875 S Grant St Ste 950 San Mateo (94402) *(P-12446)*
Feeney Inc ....E....510 893-9473
2603 Union St Oakland (94607) *(P-4969)*
Fehr & Peers (PA) ....**D....925 977-3200**
100 Pringle Ave Ste 600 Walnut Creek (94596) *(P-18710)*
Fei Efa Inc (HQ) ....**D....510 897-6800**
3400 W Warren Ave Fremont (94538) *(P-6828)*
Feist Cabinets & Woodworks Inc ....E....916 686-8230
9930 Kent St Elk Grove (95624) *(P-1736)*
Felcor Union Square Lessee LLC ....D....415 398-8900
480 Sutter St San Francisco (94108) *(P-11094)*
Fellowship Homes Inc ....C....209 529-4950
1745 Eldena Way Modesto (95350) *(P-18115)*
Felson Companies Inc ....D....510 538-1150
1290 B St Ste 210 Hayward (94541) *(P-10547)*
Felton Institute (PA) ....**D....415 474-7310**
1500 Franklin St San Francisco (94109) *(P-12172)*
Femco, Hollister *Also called Food Equipment Mfg Co (P-5130)*
Fencecorp Inc ....D....916 388-0887
6837 Power Inn Rd Sacramento (95828) *(P-2031)*
Fenwick & West LLP (PA) ....**B....650 988-8500**
801 California St Mountain View (94041) *(P-17264)*
Fenwick & West LLP ....C....415 875-2300
555 California St # 1200 San Francisco (94104) *(P-17265)*
Feral Productions LLC ....E....510 791-5392
1935 N Macarthur Dr Tracy (95376) *(P-5525)*
Ferguson & Brewer Inv Co (PA) ....**E....530 872-1810**
2565 Zanella Way Ste C Chico (95928) *(P-10548)*
Ferguson Family Entps Inc ....E....530 273-0686
12911 Loma Rica Dr Grass Valley (95945) *(P-1503)*
Ferma Corporation ....C....510 794-0414
6655 Smith Ave Ste A Newark (94560) *(P-1985)*
Fern Electric & Control Inc ....E....650 952-3203
6 S Linden Ave Ste 2 South San Francisco (94080) *(P-1504)*
Fern Ldge Chrstn Scnce Nursing, Castro Valley *Also called Fern Lodge Inc (P-16002)*
Fern Lodge Inc ....E....510 886-2448
18457 Madison Ave Castro Valley (94546) *(P-16002)*
Fernqvist Labeling Solutions, Mountain View *Also called Fernqvist Retail Systems Inc (P-3716)*
Fernqvist Retail Systems Inc (HQ) ....**F....650 428-0330**
2544 Leghorn St Mountain View (94043) *(P-3716)*
Ferrar-Crano Vnyrds Winery LLC (PA) ....**C....707 433-6700**
8761 Dry Creek Rd Healdsburg (95448) *(P-2567)*
Ferrari-Carano Winery, Healdsburg *Also called Ferrar-Crano Vnyrds Winery LLC (P-2567)*
Ferrosaur Inc ....E....530 246-7843
4821 Mountain Lakes Blvd Redding (96003) *(P-4659)*
Ferrotec (usa) Corporation (HQ) ....**D....408 964-7700**
3945 Freedom Cir Ste 450 Santa Clara (95054) *(P-5221)*
Fertility Physicians Northe (PA) ....**D....408 356-5000**
2581 Samaritan Dr Ste 302 San Jose (95124) *(P-15406)*
Fetters U.S.A., San Francisco *Also called Mr S Leather (P-3018)*
Fetzer Vineyards (HQ) ....**C....707 744-1250**
12901 Old River Rd Hopland (95449) *(P-2568)*
Ffl Partners LLC (PA) ....**D....415 402-2100**
1 Maritime Plz Fl 22 San Francisco (94111) *(P-10777)*
Fiber Optic Cable Shop, Richmond *Also called Support Systems Intl Corp (P-6472)*
Fiber Systems Inc ....E....831 430-0700
101 Soquel Ave Apt 418 Santa Cruz (95060) *(P-5796)*
Fiberlite Centrifuge LLC ....D....408 492-1109
422 Aldo Ave Santa Clara (95054) *(P-6829)*
Fibres Internation Recycling, Novato *Also called Fibres International Inc (P-8329)*
Fibres International Inc ....E....425 455-9811
88 Rowland Way Ste 300 Novato (94945) *(P-8329)*
Fibres International Inc ....E....425 455-9811
88 Rowland Way Ste 300 Novato (94945) *(P-8330)*
Fibrogen Inc (PA) ....**A....415 978-1200**
409 Illinois St San Francisco (94158) *(P-3897)*
Fico, San Jose *Also called Fair Isaac Corporation (P-14270)*
Fictiv Inc ....C....415 580-2509
168 Welsh St San Francisco (94107) *(P-12447)*
Fidelity Nat HM Warranty Co ....C....925 356-0194
1850 Gateway Blvd Ste 400 Concord (94520) *(P-10198)*
Fidelity Roof Company (PA) ....**D....510 547-6330**
1075 40th St Oakland (94608) *(P-1802)*
Field Construction Inc (PA) ....**E....415 648-8140**
490 2nd St Ste 100 San Francisco (94107) *(P-871)*
Field Fresh Farms LLC ....D....831 722-1422
320 Industrial Rd Watsonville (95076) *(P-9402)*
Field Paoli Architects PC ....E....415 788-6606
711 Market St 2 San Francisco (94103) *(P-18884)*
Field Sales Office, San Mateo *Also called Centra Software Inc (P-13057)*
Field Stone Winery Vinyrd Inc ....F....707 433-7266
10075 Highway 128 Healdsburg (95448) *(P-2569)*
Fieldwirelabs Inc ....E....415 234-3050
85 2nd St Fl 6 San Francisco (94105) *(P-12448)*
Fierce Wombat Games Inc ....E....408 745-5400
910 E Hamilton Ave Fl 6 Campbell (95008) *(P-13713)*
Fife Metal Fabricating Inc ....E....530 243-4696
2305 Radio Ln Redding (96001) *(P-4660)*
Fifer Street Fitness Inc ....E....415 927-4653
2 Fifer Ave Ste 250 Corte Madera (94925) *(P-14950)*
Fifteen Dollar Sewer Drain Svc, San Jose *Also called Great American Plumbing Co Inc (P-14751)*
Fifth Sun, Chico *Also called Gonzales Park LLC (P-9244)*
Fifth Sun LLC ....D....530 343-8725
495 Ryan Ave Chico (95973) *(P-3010)*
Fig Holdings LLC ....D....209 524-4817
1310 W Granger Ave Modesto (95350) *(P-16003)*
Figma Inc (PA) ....**D....888 236-4310**
760 Market St Fl 10 San Francisco (94102) *(P-12449)*
Figure Eight Technologies Inc ....D....415 471-1920
940 Howard St San Francisco (94103) *(P-13714)*
Figure Technologies Inc (PA) ....**B....888 819-6388**
650 California St Fl 2700 San Francisco (94108) *(P-14272)*
Filice Insurance Agency, San Jose *Also called Ron Filice Enterprises Inc (P-10339)*
Filoli Center ....D....650 364-8300
86 Canada Rd Woodside (94062) *(P-18291)*
Filoli Garden Shop, Woodside *Also called Filoli Center (P-18291)*
Filtration Development Co LLC ....E....415 884-0555
3920 Sandstone Dr El Dorado Hills (95762) *(P-6380)*
Fime USA Inc ....E....408 228-4040
1737 N 1st St Ste 410 San Jose (95112) *(P-12450)*
Finance Department, Hercules *Also called Bio-RAD Laboratories Inc (P-6817)*
Financial Center Credit Union ....E....209 462-2807
2405 S Airport Way Stockton (95206) *(P-9786)*
Financial Center Credit Union (PA) ....**E....209 948-6024**
18 S Center St Stockton (95202) *(P-9787)*
Financial Pacific Insur Group (HQ) ....**D....916 630-5000**
3880 Atherton Rd Rocklin (95765) *(P-10283)*
Financial Pacific Insurance Co, Rocklin *Also called Financial Pacific Insur Group (P-10283)*
Financial Technology Ventures, San Francisco *Also called Ftv Management Company LP (P-10761)*

ALPHABETIC

Employee Codes: A=Over 500 employees, B=251-500 C=101-250, D=51-100, E=20-50 F=10-19
2022 Northern California Business Directory and Buyers Guide
© Mergent Inc. 1-800-342-5647
963

Financialforcecom Inc (HQ)....A....**866 743-2220**
595 Market St Ste 2700 San Francisco (94105) *(P-12451)*

Finastra Merchant Services Inc (PA)....D....**415 277-9900**
333 Bush St Fl 26 San Francisco (94104) *(P-9848)*

Findly, San Francisco *Also called First Advntage Tlent MGT Svcs (P-13161)*

Findora, Palo Alto *Also called Temujin Labs Inc (P-12858)*

Fine Chemicals Holdings Corp....B....916 357-6880
Hwy 50 Hzel Ave Bldg 0501 Rancho Cordova (95741) *(P-10734)*

Fine Line Construction, San Francisco *Also called D F P F Corporation (P-860)*

Fine Line Group Inc....E....415 777-4070
457 Minna St San Francisco (94103) *(P-872)*

Fine Line Sawing & Drlg Inc....E....510 793-6700
37651 Sycamore St Newark (94560) *(P-1870)*

Fine Northern Oak, NAPA *Also called Seguin Mreau NAPA Coperage Inc (P-9133)*

Fineline Carpentry Inc....E....650 592-2442
1297 Old County Rd Belmont (94002) *(P-3179)*

Fineline Industries Inc (PA)....D....**209 384-0255**
2047 Grogan Ave Merced (95341) *(P-6642)*

Finelite Inc (PA)....C....**510 441-1100**
30500 Whipple Rd Union City (94587) *(P-5735)*

Fingerprint Digital Inc....E....415 497-2611
4220 Shelter Bay Ave Mill Valley (94941) *(P-3645)*

Finis Inc (PA)....E....**925 454-0111**
5849 W Schulte Rd Ste 104 Tracy (95377) *(P-7196)*

Finis USA, Tracy *Also called Finis Inc (P-7196)*

Finisar Corporation (HQ)....E....**408 548-1000**
1389 Moffett Park Dr Sunnyvale (94089) *(P-5797)*

Finlink Inc (PA)....C....**888 999-5467**
241 Center St Ste B Healdsburg (95448) *(P-12452)*

Finsix Corporation....E....650 285-6400
3565 Haven Ave Ste 1 Menlo Park (94025) *(P-13588)*

Fintan Partners LLC....E....650 687-3400
203 Rdwood Shres Pkwy Ste Redwood City (94065) *(P-9968)*

Fior Di Sole LLC....C....707 259-1477
2511 Napa Valley Corp Dr NAPA (94558) *(P-2570)*

Fior Di Sole LLC....E....707 259-1477
2511 Napa Valley Corp Dr NAPA (94558) *(P-2571)*

Fiorano Software Inc....D....650 326-1136
230 California Ave # 103 Palo Alto (94306) *(P-13160)*

Fiore Di Pasta Inc....D....559 457-0431
4776 E Jensen Ave Fresno (93725) *(P-2892)*

Fire Dept, Cameron Park *Also called Cameron Park Firefighters Assn (P-15187)*

Fire Recovery Usa LLC....D....916 200-3999
2271 Lava Ridge Ct # 120 Roseville (95661) *(P-14273)*

Fire System Solutions Inc....E....559 275-4894
4277 W Richert Ave # 103 Fresno (93722) *(P-14274)*

Fireeye International LLC (HQ)....D....**408 321-6300**
601 Mccarthy Blvd Milpitas (95035) *(P-13589)*

Firelight Glass, San Leandro *Also called Vitrico Corp (P-4381)*

Fireside Lanes Inc....E....916 725-2101
7901 Auburn Blvd Citrus Heights (95610) *(P-14890)*

Firestone, Atwater *Also called Esparza Inc (P-14561)*

Firetide Inc (HQ)....D....**408 399-7771**
2105 S Bascom Ave Ste 220 Campbell (95008) *(P-5367)*

Firewood Marketing Inc....D....415 872-5132
23 Geary St Ste 7 San Francisco (94108) *(P-19515)*

First Last & Always Inc....E....415 541-7978
1311 22nd St San Francisco (94107) *(P-1769)*

First 5 Alameda County....D....510 227-6900
1115 Atlantic Ave Alameda (94501) *(P-17569)*

First 5 California, Sacramento *Also called Califrnia Chldren Fmilies Comm (P-18553)*

First 5 Santa Clara County....E....408 260-3700
4000 Moorpark Ave Ste 200 San Jose (95117) *(P-17570)*

First Advntage Tlent MGT Svcs....E....415 446-3930
98 Battery St Ste 400 San Francisco (94111) *(P-13161)*

First Alarm (PA)....C....**831 476-1111**
1111 Estates Dr Aptos (95003) *(P-14133)*

First Alarm SEC & Patrol Inc....B....209 473-1110
5250 Claremont Ave Stockton (95207) *(P-14134)*

First Alarm SEC & Patrol Inc....B....925 295-1260
1801 Oakland Blvd Ste 315 Walnut Creek (94596) *(P-14056)*

First Alarm SEC & Patrol Inc....B....707 584-1110
1240 Briggs Ave Santa Rosa (95401) *(P-14057)*

First Alarm SEC & Patrol Inc (PA)....C....**408 866-1111**
1731 Tech Dr Ste 800 San Jose (95110) *(P-14058)*

First American Title Co NAPA (PA)....E....**707 254-4500**
497 Walnut St Ste A NAPA (94559) *(P-10692)*

First American Title Insur Co (HQ)....A....**714 250-3109**
330 Soquel Ave Santa Cruz (95062) *(P-10199)*

First Baptist Church Crosswalk....D....408 736-3120
445 S Mary Ave Sunnyvale (94086) *(P-17934)*

First Baptist Church Los Altos....D....650 948-3738
625 Magdalena Ave Los Altos Hills (94024) *(P-17935)*

First Baptist Head Start....D....925 473-2000
3890 Railroad Ave Pittsburg (94565) *(P-17936)*

First Call Nursing Svcs Inc....E....408 262-1533
1313 N Milpitas Blvd # 15 Milpitas (95035) *(P-12088)*

First Class Svc Trckg Co Inc....E....209 832-4669
400 Gandy Dancer Dr Tracy (95377) *(P-7464)*

First Data Bank, South San Francisco *Also called First Databank Inc (P-3571)*

First Databank Inc (HQ)....D....**800 633-3453**
701 Gateway Blvd Ste 600 South San Francisco (94080) *(P-3571)*

First Impressions Printing Inc....E....510 784-0811
25030 Viking St Hayward (94545) *(P-3646)*

First Northern Bank of Dixon (HQ)....D....**707 678-4422**
195 N 1st St Dixon (95620) *(P-9717)*

First Northern Cmnty Bancorp (PA)....D....**707 678-3041**
195 N 1st St Dixon (95620) *(P-9718)*

FIRST NORTHERN COMMUNITY, Dixon *Also called First Northern Bank of Dixon (P-9717)*

First Orleans Hotel Assoc LP....C....415 397-5572
222 Kearny St Ste 200 San Francisco (94108) *(P-11095)*

First Place For Youth (PA)....E....**510 272-0979**
426 17th St Ste 100 Oakland (94612) *(P-17571)*

First Priority Financial Inc....B....707 432-1000
3700 Hilborn Rd Ste 700 Fairfield (94534) *(P-9905)*

First Republic Bank....D....415 389-0880
750 Redwood Hwy Frontage Mill Valley (94941) *(P-9719)*

First Republic Bank....D....415 392-3888
44 Montgomery St Ste 110 San Francisco (94104) *(P-9720)*

First Republic Bank....D....650 233-8880
2550 Sand Hill Rd Ste 100 Menlo Park (94025) *(P-9721)*

First Republic Bank....D....415 561-2988
558 Presidio Blvd Ste A San Francisco (94129) *(P-9722)*

First Republic Bank....D....925 846-8811
249 Main St Pleasanton (94566) *(P-9723)*

First Republic Bank....D....925 254-8993
224 Brookwood Rd Orinda (94563) *(P-9724)*

First Republic Bank....D....415 564-8881
653 Irving St San Francisco (94122) *(P-9725)*

First Republic Bank....D....415 487-0888
1355 Market St Ste 140 San Francisco (94103) *(P-9726)*

First Republic Bank....D....415 975-3877
405 Howard St Ste 110 San Francisco (94105) *(P-9727)*

First Republic Bank....D....650 383-2888
401 San Antonio Rd Ste 68 Mountain View (94040) *(P-9728)*

First Republic Bank (PA)....B....**415 392-1400**
111 Pine St Fl 2 San Francisco (94111) *(P-9757)*

First Republic Bank....D....650 470-8888
1215 El Camino Real Menlo Park (94025) *(P-9729)*

First Republic Inv MGT Inc....E....415 296-5727
111 Pine St San Francisco (94111) *(P-9730)*

First Responder Ems Inc....D....530 897-6345
333 Huss Dr Ste 100 Chico (95928) *(P-7383)*

First Round Capital LLC....E....415 646-0072
595 Pacific Ave Fl 4 San Francisco (94133) *(P-10844)*

First Security Services, San Jose *Also called First Alarm SEC & Patrol Inc (P-14058)*

First Step Communities, Folsom *Also called First Step Housing (P-19775)*

First Step Housing....D....916 769-8877
139 Blakeslee Way Folsom (95630) *(P-19775)*

First Student Inc....C....510 237-6677
436 Parr Blvd Richmond (94801) *(P-7430)*

First Student Inc....C....415 455-9098
59 Jordan St San Rafael (94901) *(P-7431)*

First Student Inc....C....510 628-0014
2368 Bates Ave Concord (94520) *(P-7432)*

First Student Inc....C....650 685-8245
520 Bragato Rd San Carlos (94070) *(P-7433)*

First Student Inc....C....209 466-7737
2005 Navy Dr Stockton (95206) *(P-7434)*

First Student Inc....C....559 268-4077
2805 S East Ave Fresno (93725) *(P-7435)*

First Student Inc....C....415 647-9012
2270 Jerrold Ave San Francisco (94124) *(P-7436)*

First Student Inc....C....408 971-3466
931 Remillard Ct San Jose (95122) *(P-7437)*

First Student Inc....C....925 754-4878
801 Wilbur Ave Antioch (94509) *(P-7438)*

First Student Inc....C....559 661-7433
123 N E St Ste 102 Madera (93638) *(P-7439)*

First Tactical LLC....A....855 665-3410
4300 Spyres Way Modesto (95356) *(P-2984)*

First Tech Federal Credit Un, San Jose *Also called First Technology Federal Cr Un (P-9789)*

First Technology Federal Cr Un....D....408 863-6240
19960 Stevens Creek Blvd Cupertino (95014) *(P-9788)*

First Technology Federal Cr Un (PA)....D....**855 855-8805**
2702 Orchard Pkwy San Jose (95134) *(P-9789)*

First Technology Federal Cr Un....D....855 855-8805
1011 Sunset Blvd Ste 210 Rocklin (95765) *(P-9790)*

First Transit Inc....C....209 385-1226
2047 Grogan Ave Merced (95341) *(P-7330)*

First Transit Inc....C....831 460-9911
117 Fern St Ste 100 Santa Cruz (95060) *(P-7331)*

First Transit Inc....C....866 244-6383
500 W Hospital Rd French Camp (95231) *(P-7332)*

First Transit Inc....C....510 437-8990
407 High St Oakland (94601) *(P-7333)*

First US Community Credit Un (PA)....E....**916 576-5700**
580 University Ave # 100 Sacramento (95825) *(P-9791)*

Firstcall (PA)....C....**415 781-4300**
1 Sansome St Ste 3500 San Francisco (94104) *(P-14059)*

Firstservice Residential....D....916 293-4740
12009 Foundation Pl Gold River (95670) *(P-19334)*

Firstup Inc (PA)....C....**415 655-2700**
123 Mission St Fl 25 San Francisco (94105) *(P-13162)*

Fiscalini Cheese Company LP....F....209 346-0384
7206 Kiernan Ave Modesto (95358) *(P-2188)*

Fischer Tile and Marble Inc....C....916 452-1426
1800 23rd St Sacramento (95816) *(P-1714)*

Fischl Tibor (HQ)....E....**707 529-9350**
1030 Winding Ridge Ct Santa Rosa (95404) *(P-9451)*

Fish Mkt Rstrants- San Jose LP....D....650 349-3474
1855 S Norfolk St San Mateo (94403) *(P-9366)*

Fishbio Environmental LLC (PA)....E....**209 847-6300**
1617 S Yosemite Ave Oakdale (95361) *(P-19776)*

Fishel Company....E....209 207-9068
5431 W Grant Line Rd Tracy (95304) *(P-1505)*

Fisher Development Inc....E....415 228-3060
601 California St Ste 300 San Francisco (94108) *(P-873)*

Fisher Graphic Inds A Cal Corp.....E.....209 577-0181
1137 Graphics Dr Modesto (95351) *(P-5119)*
Fisher House Palo Alto.....E.....650 858-3903
3801 Miranda Ave Palo Alto (94304) *(P-18414)*
Fisher Nut Company.....F.....209 527-0108
137 N Hart Rd Modesto (95358) *(P-2893)*
Fishers Nursery.....D.....209 599-3412
24081 S Austin Rd Ripon (95366) *(P-9632)*
Fisk Demolition Inc (PA).....**E.....209 323-8999**
8507 Goggin St Valley Springs (95252) *(P-1986)*
Fitbit LLC (HQ).....**A.....415 513-1000**
199 Fremont St Fl 14 San Francisco (94105) *(P-6901)*
Fitness Systems, Lodi *Also called Best Supplement Guide LLC (P-14929)*
Fitness Together, Sanger *Also called R Thunder Inc (P-14966)*
Fitstar Inc.....E.....415 409-8348
80 Langton St San Francisco (94103) *(P-13163)*
Fitz Fresh Inc.....D.....831 763-4440
211 Lee Rd Watsonville (95076) *(P-143)*
Fitzgerald Designers & Mfrs, South San Francisco *Also called J F Fitzgerald Company Inc (P-3288)*
Fitzgrald Abbott Beardsley LLP.....E.....510 451-3300
1221 Broadway Fl 21 Oakland (94612) *(P-17266)*
Fitzgrald Alvrez Cmmo A Prof L.....E.....559 674-4696
221 N I St Madera (93637) *(P-17267)*
Five Flavors Herbs Inc.....F.....510 923-0178
344 40th St Oakland (94609) *(P-2159)*
Five Keys Inc.....F.....209 358-7971
152 E Broadway Ave Atwater (95301) *(P-2992)*
Five Keys Schools and Programs.....E.....415 734-3310
70 Oak Grove St San Francisco (94107) *(P-17572)*
Five Point Holdings LLC.....E.....415 344-8865
1 Sansome St Ste 3200 San Francisco (94104) *(P-10549)*
Five Prime Therapeutics Inc.....D.....415 365-5600
111 Oyster Point Blvd South San Francisco (94080) *(P-3898)*
Five River Trucking Inc.....E.....530 212-4477
1020 Oswald Rd Yuba City (95991) *(P-7465)*
Five Star Auto Repair and Wash, Rocklin *Also called Jkf Auto Service Inc (P-14646)*
Five Star Lumber Company LLC (PA).....**E.....510 795-7204**
6899 Smith Ave Newark (94560) *(P-3221)*
Five Star Pallet Co, Newark *Also called Five Star Lumber Company LLC (P-3221)*
Five Star Quality Care Inc.....E.....559 446-6226
6075 N Marks Ave Fresno (93711) *(P-16004)*
Five Star Qulty Care-CA II LLC.....C.....209 466-2066
537 E Fulton St Stockton (95204) *(P-16005)*
Five9 Inc (PA).....**A.....925 201-2000**
3001 Bishop Dr Ste 350 San Ramon (94583) *(P-13164)*
Fix Air, San Jose *Also called Pacific Coast Sales & Svc Inc (P-9012)*
Fixstream Networks Inc.....E.....408 921-0200
2001 Gateway Pl Ste 520w San Jose (95110) *(P-12453)*
Fixture-Pro Inc.....E.....707 545-3901
2344 Bluebell Dr Ste A Santa Rosa (95403) *(P-1737)*
Fja Industries Inc.....F.....408 727-0100
1230 Coleman Ave Santa Clara (95050) *(P-5228)*
Fjellbo & Son Construction Inc.....E.....925 363-3000
1717 Solano Way Ste 20 Concord (94520) *(P-638)*
FL Service Team Inc.....E.....559 647-5120
2491 Alluvial Ave Ste 440 Clovis (93611) *(P-14696)*
Flagship Airport Services Inc (HQ).....**B.....408 977-0155**
1050 N 5th St Ste E San Jose (95112) *(P-11950)*
Flagship Enterprises Holdg Inc (PA).....**C.....408 977-0155**
1050 N 5th St Ste E San Jose (95112) *(P-11951)*
Flagship Sweeping Services Inc (HQ).....**E.....408 977-0155**
1050 N 5th St San Jose (95112) *(P-8399)*
Flair, San Francisco *Also called Standard Euler Inc (P-12815)*
Flair Building Maintanance, Santa Clara *Also called Flair Building Services Inc (P-11952)*
Flair Building Services Inc.....D.....408 987-4040
3470 Edward Ave Santa Clara (95054) *(P-11952)*
Flake R Recycling.....E.....559 233-9361
1710 W Pine Ave Fresno (93728) *(P-1161)*
Flamingo Resort Hotel, Santa Rosa *Also called Bavarian Lion Company Cal (P-10945)*
Flanzbaum, Jonathan M MD, Livermore *Also called Livermore Pediatrics (P-15506)*
Flashco Manufacturing Inc (PA).....**E.....707 824-4448**
150 Todd Rd Ste 400 Santa Rosa (95407) *(P-4566)*
Flatiron Construction Corp.....B.....707 742-6270
2100 Goodyear Rd Benicia (94510) *(P-19335)*
Flatiron West Inc.....C.....707 742-6000
2100 Goodyear Rd Benicia (94510) *(P-1082)*
Flea Market Inc.....E.....408 453-1110
1590 Berryessa Rd Frnt San Jose (95133) *(P-10479)*
Fleenor Company Inc (PA).....**E.....800 433-2531**
2225 Harbor Bay Pkwy Alameda (94502) *(P-3401)*
Fleenor Paper Company, Alameda *Also called Fleenor Company Inc (P-3401)*
Fleet Maintenance Dept, Santa Cruz *Also called Santa Cruz Metro Trnst Dst (P-7356)*
Fleetpride Inc.....E.....408 286-9200
1164 Old Bayshore Hwy San Jose (95112) *(P-8451)*
Fletcher Dors Windows Trim Inc.....F.....209 632-3610
1720 Paulson Rd Turlock (95380) *(P-3132)*
Fletcher Plumbing Inc.....E.....916 652-9769
3237 Rippey Rd Ste 150 Loomis (95650) *(P-1263)*
Fletchers Plumbing & Contg Inc (PA).....**E.....530 673-2489**
219 Burns Dr Unit 2 Yuba City (95991) *(P-1264)*
Flex Interconnect Tech Inc.....E.....408 956-8204
1603 Watson Ct Milpitas (95035) *(P-5930)*
Flex Products Inc.....C.....707 525-9200
1402 Mariner Way Santa Rosa (95407) *(P-6872)*
Flexcare LLC.....A.....866 564-3589
532 Gibson Dr Ste 100 Roseville (95678) *(P-12089)*
Flexcare Medical Staffing, Roseville *Also called Flexcare LLC (P-12089)*
Flexilis, San Francisco *Also called Lookout Inc (P-13627)*
Flexon Technologies Inc.....C.....925 398-8280
7901 Stoneridge Dr # 390 Pleasanton (94588) *(P-12454)*
Flexport Inc (PA).....**A.....415 231-5252**
760 Market St Fl 8 San Francisco (94102) *(P-13165)*
Flextronics America LLC (HQ).....**C.....408 576-7000**
6201 America Center Dr San Jose (95002) *(P-5931)*
Flextronics Corporation (HQ).....**C.....803 936-5200**
6201 America Center Dr Alviso (95002) *(P-6428)*
Flextronics Intl USA Inc.....A.....408 576-7000
6201 America Center Dr San Jose (95002) *(P-5932)*
Flextronics Intl USA Inc (HQ).....**A.....408 576-7000**
6201 America Center Dr San Jose (95002) *(P-5933)*
Flextronics Logistics USA Inc (HQ).....**B.....408 576-7000**
6201 America Center Dr # 6 San Jose (95002) *(P-5934)*
Flextronics Semiconductor (HQ).....**E.....408 576-7000**
2241 Lundy Ave Bldg 2 San Jose (95131) *(P-6120)*
Flickr Inc.....E.....650 265-0396
390 Fremont St San Francisco (94105) *(P-12455)*
Flint Builders Inc.....D.....916 757-1000
401 Derek Pl Roseville (95678) *(P-874)*
Flip Hospitality & Entrmt LLC (PA).....**D.....707 584-1405**
101 Golf Course Dr A220 Rohnert Park (94928) *(P-9143)*
Flipcause Inc.....F.....800 523-1950
101 Broadway Fl 3 Oakland (94607) *(P-13166)*
Flo Stor Engineering Inc (PA).....**E.....510 887-7179**
21371 Cabot Blvd Hayward (94545) *(P-5051)*
Flock Is Inc.....E.....415 851-2376
350 Townsend St Ste 402 San Francisco (94107) *(P-12456)*
Floor & Decor Outlets Amer Inc.....D.....510 394-9976
1700 Fairway Dr San Leandro (94577) *(P-1871)*
Floor Seal Technology Inc (PA).....**E.....408 436-8181**
1005 Ames Ave Milpitas (95035) *(P-1770)*
Flora Springs Wine Company.....F.....707 963-5711
677 Saint Helena Hwy S Saint Helena (94574) *(P-2572)*
Flora Terra Landscape MGT, San Jose *Also called City II Enterprises Inc (P-453)*
Florence & New Itln Art Co Inc.....E.....510 785-9674
27735 Industrial Blvd Hayward (94545) *(P-4432)*
Florence Villa Hotel.....C.....415 397-7700
225 Powell St San Francisco (94102) *(P-11096)*
Florence Villa Hotel LLC.....D.....415 397-7700
225 Powell St San Francisco (94102) *(P-11097)*
Florestone Products Co (PA).....**E.....559 661-4171**
2851 Falcon Dr Madera (93637) *(P-4250)*
Florian Industries Inc.....F.....415 330-9000
151 Industrial Way Brisbane (94005) *(P-4661)*
Flory Construction Inc.....E.....510 483-6860
2325 Verna Ct San Leandro (94577) *(P-795)*
Flory Industries.....D.....209 545-1167
4737 Toomes Rd Salida (95368) *(P-5004)*
Flostor, Hayward *Also called Flo Stor Engineering Inc (P-5051)*
Flowers Baking Co Modesto LLC (HQ).....**D.....209 857-4600**
736 Mariposa Rd Modesto (95354) *(P-2382)*
Flowers Vineyard & Winery LLC.....F.....707 847-3661
28500 Seaview Rd Cazadero (95421) *(P-2573)*
Floyd Johnston Cnstr Co Inc.....D.....559 299-7373
2301 Herndon Ave Clovis (93611) *(P-1101)*
Flt Inc.....C.....916 355-1500
12747 Folsom Blvd Folsom (95630) *(P-14563)*
Fluent Speech Technologies, Santa Clara *Also called Sensory Inc (P-12771)*
Fluid Inc (HQ).....**D.....877 343-3240**
1611 Telegraph Ave # 400 Oakland (94612) *(P-12457)*
Fluid Industrial Mfg Inc.....F.....408 782-9900
340 S Milpitas Blvd Milpitas (95035) *(P-5430)*
Fluid Tech Hydraulics Inc.....E.....916 681-0888
8432 Tiogawoods Dr Sacramento (95828) *(P-14749)*
Fluidigm Corporation (PA).....**A.....650 266-6000**
2 Tower Pl Ste 2000 South San Francisco (94080) *(P-6830)*
Fluidigm Sciences Inc.....E.....408 900-7205
2 Tower Pl Fl 20 South San Francisco (94080) *(P-6831)*
Fluidix Inc (PA).....**E.....760 935-2016**
1422 Mammoth Tav Rd C6 Mammoth Lakes (93546) *(P-5215)*
Fluor Facility & Plant Svcs.....C.....408 256-1333
124 Blossom Hill Rd Ste H San Jose (95123) *(P-11953)*
Flurish Inc.....D.....855 253-6387
1750 Broadway 300 Oakland (94612) *(P-9857)*
Fluxion Biosciences Inc.....E.....650 241-4777
1600 Harbor Bay Pkwy # 150 Alameda (94502) *(P-6973)*
Fluxx Labs Inc.....D.....408 981-7080
67 Carmel St San Francisco (94117) *(P-12458)*
Fly With Y LLC.....D.....844 435-9948
611 Gateway Blvd Ste 120 South San Francisco (94080) *(P-10550)*
Flyex Inc.....E.....650 646-3339
4000 E 3rd Ave Ste 650 Foster City (94404) *(P-12459)*
Flyleaf Windows Inc.....E.....925 344-1181
11040 Bollinger Canyon Rd # 40 San Ramon (94582) *(P-4387)*
Flynn Properties Inc.....E.....415 835-0225
225 Bush St Ste 1470 San Francisco (94104) *(P-10551)*
Flytbase Inc.....E.....805 470-8985
1900 Camden Ave San Jose (95124) *(P-7796)*
Flywheel Software Inc.....E.....650 260-1700
816 Hamilton St Redwood City (94063) *(P-13167)*
FM Industries Inc (HQ).....**C.....510 668-1900**
221 E Warren Ave Fremont (94539) *(P-5526)*
Fmg Vacuum Pump & Blower Repr, Santa Clara *Also called F M G Enterprises (P-14748)*
Fmw Machine Shop.....E.....650 363-1313
519 Claire St Hayward (94541) *(P-5527)*
Fni International Inc.....D.....916 643-1400
1300 Ethan Way Sacramento (95825) *(P-19516)*

ALPHABETIC

Foam Distributors Incorporated.....D.....510 441-8377
31009 San Antonio St Hayward (94544) *(P-9658)*
Foam Fabrication For Packaging, Hayward *Also called Foam Distributors Incorporated (P-9658)*
Foamex, San Leandro *Also called Fxi Inc (P-4243)*
Focus Enhancements Inc (HQ).....D.....**650 230-2400**
931 Benecia Ave Sunnyvale (94085) *(P-6121)*
Focus Enhncments Systems Group, Sunnyvale *Also called Focus Enhancements Inc (P-6121)*
Foley Family Wines Inc (HQ).....D.....**707 708-7600**
200 Concourse Blvd Santa Rosa (95403) *(P-2574)*
Foley Fmly Wines Holdings Inc (PA).....D.....**707 708-7600**
200 Concourse Blvd Santa Rosa (95403) *(P-2575)*
Foley Wine Group, Santa Rosa *Also called Foley Family Wines Inc (P-2574)*
Folgergraphics Inc.....E.....510 293-2294
21093 Forbes Ave Hayward (94545) *(P-3764)*
Folio Wine Company LLC (PA).....E.....**707 256-2700**
550 Gateway Dr Ste 220 NAPA (94558) *(P-9575)*
Folio Wine Company LLC.....D.....707 256-2757
1285 Dealy Ln NAPA (94559) *(P-9576)*
Folio Wine Company Imports, NAPA *Also called Folio Wine Company LLC (P-9575)*
Folio3 Software Inc.....E.....650 802-8668
1301 Shoreway Rd Ste 160 Belmont (94002) *(P-13168)*
Folkmanis Inc.....E.....510 658-7677
1219 Park Ave Emeryville (94608) *(P-7285)*
Folsom Ambulatory Surgery Ctr, Folsom *Also called Kaiser Foundation Hospitals (P-15459)*
Folsom Care Center.....E.....916 985-3641
510 Mill St Folsom (95630) *(P-17148)*
Folsom Lake Appliance Inc.....D.....916 985-3426
8146 Greenback Ln Ste 102 Fair Oaks (95628) *(P-14697)*
Folsom Lake Bank, Folsom *Also called Central Valley Community Bank (P-9714)*
Folsom Lake Toyota, Folsom *Also called Flt Inc (P-14563)*
Folsom Outpatient Surgery Ctr, Folsom *Also called Folsom Surgery Center Inc (P-15407)*
Folsom Psychiatry Associates, Folsom *Also called Soliman Hisham M D Inc (P-15692)*
Folsom Ready Mix Inc (PA).....E.....**916 851-8300**
3401 Fitzgerald Rd Rancho Cordova (95742) *(P-4481)*
Folsom Recreation Corp.....D.....916 983-4411
511 E Bidwell St Folsom (95630) *(P-14891)*
Folsom Surgery Center Inc.....D.....916 673-1990
1651 Creekside Dr Ste 100 Folsom (95630) *(P-15407)*
Fonco Inc.....F.....650 873-4585
133 Starlite St South San Francisco (94080) *(P-1803)*
Fonexperts Inc.....E.....707 303-8200
1650 Northpoint Pkwy F Santa Rosa (95407) *(P-1506)*
Fong & Chan Architect Inc.....E.....415 931-8600
1361 Bush St San Francisco (94109) *(P-14275)*
Fong & Chan Architects, San Francisco *Also called Fong & Chan Architect Inc (P-14275)*
Fong Brothers Printing Inc (PA).....C.....**415 467-1050**
320 Valley Dr Brisbane (94005) *(P-3647)*
Fong Fong Prtrs Lthgrphers Inc.....E.....916 739-1313
3009 65th St Sacramento (95820) *(P-3648)*
Fono Unlimited (PA).....E.....**650 322-4664**
99 Stanford Shopping Ctr Palo Alto (94304) *(P-2173)*
Fonseca/Mcelroy Grinding Inc.....E.....408 573-9364
5225 Hellyer Ave Ste 220 San Jose (95138) *(P-1040)*
Food Bank For Humboldt County, Eureka *Also called Food For People Inc (P-17573)*
Food Equipment Mfg Co.....E.....831 637-1624
175 Mitchell Rd Hollister (95023) *(P-5130)*
Food For People Inc.....D.....707 445-3166
307 W 14th St Eureka (95501) *(P-17573)*
Food Services Division, Fresno *Also called Fresno Cnty Ecnmic Opprtnties (P-17583)*
Food Specialists Inc.....B.....510 444-3456
2 Broadway Oakland (94607) *(P-10480)*
Food Stamp Office, Auburn *Also called Social Services Cal Dept (P-17747)*
Foodliner Inc.....D.....209 941-8361
2431 E Mariposa Rd Stockton (95205) *(P-7539)*
Foodlink Online LLC.....E.....408 395-7280
475 Alberto Way Ste 100 Los Gatos (95032) *(P-13169)*
Foodmaxx, Redding *Also called Save Mart Supermarkets Disc (P-2404)*
Foodmaxx, Antelope *Also called Save Mart Supermarkets (P-2403)*
Foodmaxx, Citrus Heights *Also called Save Mart Supermarkets Disc (P-9301)*
Foot Locker Retail Inc.....E.....510 797-5750
2059 Newpark Mall Fl 2 Newark (94560) *(P-4345)*
Foothill Fire Protection Inc (PA).....E.....**916 663-3582**
4000 Alvis Ct Rocklin (95677) *(P-1265)*
Foothill Oaks Care Center Inc.....E.....530 888-6257
3400 Bell Rd Auburn (95603) *(P-16006)*
Foothill Ready Mix Inc.....F.....530 527-2565
11415 State Highway 99w Red Bluff (96080) *(P-4482)*
Foothll-De Anza Cmnty Cllege D.....B.....650 949-7260
12345 S El Monte Rd # 6202 Los Altos Hills (94022) *(P-8025)*
Footloose Incorporated.....E.....760 934-2400
3043 Main St Mammoth Lakes (93546) *(P-15204)*
Footloose Sports, Mammoth Lakes *Also called Footloose Incorporated (P-15204)*
Foppiano Vineyards, Healdsburg *Also called L Foppiano Wine Co (P-2643)*
Forager Project LLC (PA).....D.....**855 729-5253**
235 Montgomery St Ste 420 San Francisco (94104) *(P-2293)*
Force10 Networks Global Inc.....A.....800 289-3355
350 Holger Way San Jose (95134) *(P-13590)*
Ford Construction Company Inc.....D.....209 333-1116
300 W Pine St Lodi (95240) *(P-1162)*
Ford Lincoln Fairfield, Fairfield *Also called Price-Simms Ford LLC (P-14584)*
Ford Logging Inc.....E.....707 840-9442
1225 Central Ave Ste 11 McKinleyville (95519) *(P-3060)*
Ford Store Morgan Hill Inc.....D.....408 782-8201
17045 Condit Rd Morgan Hill (95037) *(P-14491)*
Ford Store San Leandro, San Leandro *Also called Nicholas K Corporation (P-14493)*
Ford Street Project Inc.....E.....707 462-1934
139 Ford St Ukiah (95482) *(P-18116)*
Foreal Spectrum Inc.....E.....408 923-1675
2370 Qume Dr Ste A San Jose (95131) *(P-6873)*
Forensic Logic Inc.....E.....415 810-2114
712 Bancroft Rd 423 Walnut Creek (94598) *(P-13170)*
Forescout Technologies Inc (PA).....A.....**408 213-3191**
190 W Tasman Dr San Jose (95134) *(P-12460)*
Foresight Analytics LLC.....D.....510 893-1760
1330 Broadway Ste 428 Oakland (94612) *(P-19517)*
Forest Investment Group Inc.....F.....415 459-2330
83 Hamilton Dr Ste 100 Novato (94949) *(P-3649)*
Forest Park Cabana Club.....E.....408 244-1884
2911 Pruneridge Ave Santa Clara (95051) *(P-15090)*
Forethought Technologies Inc.....E.....415 994-9706
150 Spear St Ste 350 San Francisco (94105) *(P-4388)*
Forever Firewood Inc (PA).....E.....**831 461-0634**
46 El Pueblo Rd Ste A Santa Cruz (95066) *(P-1804)*
Forever Young.....E.....650 355-5481
208 Palmetto Ave Pacifica (94044) *(P-2894)*
Forge Architecture.....D.....415 434-0320
500 Montgomery St San Francisco (94111) *(P-18885)*
Forge Global Inc (PA).....C.....**415 881-1612**
415 Mission St Ste 5510 San Francisco (94105) *(P-13171)*
Forge-Vdvich Mtl Ltd Prtnr A C.....D.....408 996-7700
10889 N De Anza Blvd Cupertino (95014) *(P-11098)*
Forgen LLC (PA).....D.....**916 462-6400**
6558 Lonetree Blvd Rocklin (95765) *(P-19777)*
Forgerock Inc (PA).....A.....**415 599-1100**
201 Mission St Ste 2900 San Francisco (94105) *(P-8706)*
Forgerock Us Inc (HQ).....D.....**415 599-1100**
201 Mission St Ste 2900 San Francisco (94105) *(P-13172)*
Form & Fiction LLC (PA).....E.....**415 802-2000**
1935 Lawton St San Francisco (94122) *(P-11860)*
Form & Fusion Mfg Inc (PA).....E.....**916 638-8576**
11261 Trade Center Dr Rancho Cordova (95742) *(P-4883)*
Formac Inc.....C.....510 379-9027
3155 Kearney St Ste 210 Fremont (94538) *(P-13591)*
Formation Inc.....D.....650 257-2277
315 Montgomery St Fl 10 San Francisco (94104) *(P-13173)*
Formation Systems, San Francisco *Also called Formation Inc (P-13173)*
Formatop, Campbell *Also called Teammate Builders Inc (P-3329)*
Formax LLC.....E.....800 800-1822
305 S Soderquist Rd Turlock (95380) *(P-14698)*
Formax Technologies, Turlock *Also called Formax LLC (P-14698)*
Formax Technologies Inc.....F.....209 668-1001
305 S Soderquist Rd Turlock (95380) *(P-6521)*
Formfactor Inc (PA).....C.....**925 290-4000**
7005 Southfront Rd Livermore (94551) *(P-6122)*
Formulation Technology Inc.....E.....209 847-0331
571 Armstrong Way Oakdale (95361) *(P-3899)*
Forsys Inc.....E.....408 409-2567
691 S Milpitas Blvd # 213 Milpitas (95035) *(P-13715)*
Fort Bragg Advocate-News, Ukiah *Also called Gatehouse Media LLC (P-3438)*
Fort James Communications Pprs, Emeryville *Also called Fort James Corporation (P-19336)*
Fort James Corporation.....A.....510 594-4900
2000 Powell St Emeryville (94608) *(P-19336)*
Fort Mason Center.....D.....415 345-7500
2 Marina Blvd Bldg A San Francisco (94123) *(P-19901)*
Fort Point Beer Company, San Francisco *Also called June Sf LLC (P-2483)*
Fort Point Beer Company (PA).....C.....**415 336-3596**
644 Mason St San Francisco (94129) *(P-2478)*
Fort Sutter Diagnostic Imaging, Sacramento *Also called Sutter Health (P-15724)*
Fort Wash Golf & Cntry CLB.....D.....559 434-1702
10272 N Millbrook Ave Fresno (93730) *(P-15091)*
Fort, The, Fresno *Also called Fort Wash Golf & Cntry CLB (P-15091)*
Fortanix Inc (PA).....C.....**650 943-2484**
800 W El Cmino Real Ste 1 Mountain View (94040) *(P-13174)*
Fortasa Memory Systems Inc.....E.....888 367-8588
1670 S Amphlett Blvd San Mateo (94402) *(P-5285)*
Forte Enterprises Inc (PA).....C.....**650 994-3200**
99 Escuela Dr Daly City (94015) *(P-19337)*
Fortemedia Inc (PA).....E.....**408 716-8028**
4051 Burton Dr Santa Clara (95054) *(P-6123)*
Forterra Pipe & Precast LLC.....E.....916 379-9695
7020 Tokay Ave Sacramento (95828) *(P-4433)*
Fortex Technologies Inc (PA).....D.....**650 591-8822**
203 Rdwood Shres Pkwy Ste Redwood City (94065) *(P-12461)*
Fortezza Iridium Holdings Inc.....A.....415 765-6500
150 California St San Francisco (94111) *(P-13175)*
Fortier & Fortier Inc.....E.....559 638-5774
1260 S Buttonwillow Ave Reedley (93654) *(P-9037)*
Fortify Infrstructure Svcs Inc (HQ).....E.....**408 850-3119**
2340 Walsh Ave Ste A Santa Clara (95051) *(P-13897)*
Fortinet Inc (PA).....A.....**408 235-7700**
899 Kifer Rd Sunnyvale (94086) *(P-5368)*
Fortis Solutions Group LLC.....E.....707 256-6343
535 Airpark Rd NAPA (94558) *(P-3732)*
Fortis Solutions Group LLC.....E.....800 388-1990
1870 Wardrobe Ave Merced (95341) *(P-3733)*
Fortrend Engineering Corp.....E.....408 734-9311
2220 Otoole Ave San Jose (95131) *(P-6719)*
Fortuna Country Inn Corp.....E.....707 725-6822
2025 Riverwalk Dr Fortuna (95540) *(P-11099)*
Fortuna Rhbltion Wellness Ctr, Fortuna *Also called Fortuna Rhbltion Wllness Ctr (P-16007)*
Fortuna Rhbltion Wllness Ctr.....E.....707 725-4467
2321 Newburg Rd Fortuna (95540) *(P-16007)*
Fortune Brands Windows Inc.....C.....707 446-7600
2019 E Monte Vista Ave Vacaville (95688) *(P-4282)*

Fortune Senior Enterprises ....C.......916 560-9100
6060 Sunrise Vista Dr # 1180 Citrus Heights (95610) ***(P-16884)***
Forty Four Group LLC (PA) ....**D.......949 407-6360**
600 San Ramon Valley Blvd # 200 Danville (94526) ***(P-11754)***
Forty Niners Football Co LLC ....D.......408 562-4949
4949 Mrie P Debartolo Way Santa Clara (95054) ***(P-14905)***
Forty Niners SC Stadium Co LLC ....E.......408 562-4949
4949 Mrie P Debartolo Way Santa Clara (95054) ***(P-14906)***
Forty Niners Stadium MGT LLC ....E.......408 562-4949
4949 Mrie P Debartolo Way Santa Clara (95054) ***(P-19338)***
Forty Seven Inc (HQ) ....**D.......650 352-4150**
333 Lakeside Dr Foster City (94404) ***(P-3900)***
Forum At Rancho San Antonio, Cupertino *Also called Rancho San Antnio Rtrment Hsin* ***(P-18163)***
Forum Healthcare Center ....D.......650 944-0200
23600 Via Esplendor Cupertino (95014) ***(P-16008)***
Forward Inc (HQ) ....**E.......209 466-4482**
1145 W Charter Way Stockton (95206) ***(P-8331)***
Forward Inc ....C.......209 982-4298
9999 S Austin Rd Manteca (95336) ***(P-8332)***
Forward Air Inc ....E.......415 570-6040
30108 Eigenbrodt Way # 100 Union City (94587) ***(P-7835)***
Forward Management LLC ....D.......415 869-6300
101 California St Fl 16 San Francisco (94111) ***(P-10044)***
Forward Networks Inc ....D.......844 393-6389
2390 Mission College Blvd Santa Clara (95054) ***(P-13176)***
Foster Commodities ....E.......559 897-1081
1900 Kern St Kingsburg (93631) ***(P-2342)***
Foster Dairy Farms (PA) ....**A.......209 576-3400**
529 Kansas Ave Modesto (95351) ***(P-9338)***
Foster Dairy Farms ....F.......209 576-2300
415 Kansas Ave Modesto (95351) ***(P-2189)***
Foster Dairy Farms ....F.......707 725-6182
572 State Highway 1 Fortuna (95540) ***(P-2160)***
Foster Dairy Products Distrg (PA) ....**E.......209 576-3400**
529 Kansas Ave Modesto (95351) ***(P-9339)***
Foster Farms, Waterford *Also called Foster Poultry Farms* ***(P-2131)***
Foster Farms, Kingsburg *Also called Foster Commodities* ***(P-2342)***
Foster Farms, Livingston *Also called Foster Poultry Farms* ***(P-2132)***
Foster Farms, Fresno *Also called Foster Poultry Farms* ***(P-2135)***
Foster Farms ....D.......559 265-2000
900 W Belgravia Ave Fresno (93706) ***(P-168)***
Foster Farms LLC ....D.......559 897-1081
1900 Kern St Kingsburg (93631) ***(P-2129)***
Foster Farms Dairy, Modesto *Also called Foster Dairy Farms* ***(P-2189)***
Foster Poultry Farms (PA) ....**C.......209 394-7901**
1000 Davis St Livingston (95334) ***(P-2130)***
Foster Poultry Farms ....B.......209 394-7901
1307 Ellenwood Rd Waterford (95386) ***(P-2131)***
Foster Poultry Farms ....B.......209 394-7901
1333 Swan St Livingston (95334) ***(P-2132)***
Foster Poultry Farms ....C.......209 394-7950
221 Stefani Ave Livingston (95334) ***(P-2343)***
Foster Poultry Farms ....C.......209 394-7901
834 Davis St Livingston (95334) ***(P-240)***
Foster Poultry Farms ....D.......209 668-5922
1033 S Center St Turlock (95380) ***(P-2133)***
Foster Poultry Farms ....B.......559 265-2000
900 W Belgravia Ave Fresno (93706) ***(P-2134)***
Foster Poultry Farms ....B.......559 442-3771
2960 S Cherry Ave Fresno (93706) ***(P-2135)***
Foster Turkey Live Haul, Turlock *Also called Foster Poultry Farms* ***(P-2133)***
Foster Turkey Products ....A.......209 394-7901
1000 Davis St Livingston (95334) ***(P-237)***
Fotonation Corporation (PA) ....**D.......650 843-9025**
3025 Orchard Pkwy San Jose (95134) ***(P-6429)***
Fotowtio Rnewable Ventures Inc ....E.......415 986-8038
44 Montgomery St Ste 2200 San Francisco (94104) ***(P-18711)***
Found Health Inc ....D.......415 854-3296
1 Letterman Dr Ste C3500 San Francisco (94129) ***(P-19274)***
Foundation Building Material, San Jose *Also called Railway Distributing Inc* ***(P-8632)***
Foundation Capital LLC ....E.......650 614-0500
550 High St Ste 300 Palo Alto (94301) ***(P-10845)***
Foundation Constructors Inc (PA) ....**D.......925 754-6633**
81 Big Break Rd Oakley (94561) ***(P-1163)***
Foundation For Educational ADM ....E.......916 444-3216
1575 Bayshore Hwy Ste 300 Burlingame (94010) ***(P-10788)***
Foundation For Nat Progress ....E.......415 321-1700
222 Sutter St Ste 600 San Francisco (94108) ***(P-3499)***
Founders Fund LLC ....E.......415 359-1922
1 Letterman Dr Ste 500 San Francisco (94129) ***(P-14276)***
Founders Management II Corp ....B.......650 570-5700
1221 Chess Dr Foster City (94404) ***(P-11100)***
Foundtion For Hispanic Educatn (PA) ....**E.......408 585-5022**
14271 Story Rd San Jose (95127) ***(P-18415)***
Foundtion For Stdnts Rsing ABO ....D.......415 333-4222
99 The Embarcadero San Francisco (94105) ***(P-18416)***
Fountain, San Francisco *Also called Onboardiq Inc* ***(P-12645)***
Fountain Grove Golf & Athc CLB ....D.......707 701-3050
1525 Fountaingrove Pkwy Santa Rosa (95403) ***(P-15002)***
Fountaingrove Inn LLC ....D.......707 578-6101
101 Fountaingrove Pkwy Santa Rosa (95403) ***(P-11101)***
Fountains, The, Yuba City *Also called United Com Serve* ***(P-16147)***
Fountainwood Residential Care ....E.......916 988-2200
8773 Oak Ave Orangevale (95662) ***(P-18117)***
Fountngrove Inn Conference Ctr, Santa Rosa *Also called Fountaingrove Inn LLC* ***(P-11101)***
Four Corners Property Tr Inc (PA) ....**C.......415 965-8030**
591 Redwood Hwy Frontage # 3215 Mill Valley (94941) ***(P-10819)***
Four CS Service Inc ....D.......559 237-3990
1560 H St Fresno (93721) ***(P-1805)***
Four D Imaging ....F.......510 290-3533
808 Gilman St Berkeley (94710) ***(P-6902)***
Four D Metal Finishing ....E.......408 730-5722
1065 Memorex Dr Santa Clara (95050) ***(P-4906)***
Four Dimensions Inc ....F.......510 782-1843
3140 Diablo Ave Hayward (94545) ***(P-6756)***
Four In One Company, San Jose *Also called Lee Brothers Inc* ***(P-2282)***
Four Pnts By Shrton Ht Stes Sa, South San Francisco *Also called Summit Hotel Trs 115 LLC* ***(P-11515)***
Four Pnts By Shrton Scrmnto In, Sacramento *Also called G B Commercial LLC* ***(P-11109)***
Four Points Pleasanton, Pleasanton *Also called Cni Thl Ops LLC* ***(P-11021)***
Four Points San Jose Downtown ....E.......408 282-8800
211 S 1st St San Jose (95113) ***(P-11102)***
Four Points San Rafael, San Rafael *Also called San Rafael Hillcrest LLC* ***(P-11441)***
Four Season, San Francisco *Also called 28 Sasf Owner LLC* ***(P-10903)***
Four Seasons Hotel, San Francisco *Also called Cb-1 Hotel* ***(P-10998)***
Four Seasons Hotel Inc ....C.......415 633-3441
735 Market St Fl 6 San Francisco (94103) ***(P-11103)***
Four Seasons Hotel Silicon Vly, East Palo Alto *Also called East Palo Alto Hotel Dev Inc* ***(P-11070)***
Four Sisters Inns ....D.......707 939-1340
630 Broadway Sonoma (95476) ***(P-11104)***
Four Ssons Hotel-San Francisco, San Francisco *Also called Four Seasons Hotel Inc* ***(P-11103)***
Four Star Recovery Inc ....E.......209 524-2854
1228 Doker Dr Modesto (95351) ***(P-14277)***
Four Tribes Enterprises LLC ....E.......530 317-2500
1516 Main St Susanville (96130) ***(P-1041)***
Four Wheel Campers Inc ....E.......530 666-1442
1400 Churchill Downs Ave A Woodland (95776) ***(P-6656)***
Fourth Street Bowl Inc ....E.......408 453-5555
1441 N 4th St San Jose (95112) ***(P-14892)***
Fowler Labor Service Inc ....B.......559 834-3723
633 W Fresno St Fowler (93625) ***(P-12090)***
Fowler Packing Company Inc ....C.......559 834-5911
8570 S Cedar Ave Fresno (93725) ***(P-284)***
Fowles Wine (usa) Inc ....F.......703 975-8093
230 Colfax Ave Ste A Grass Valley (95945) ***(P-2576)***
Fox Barrel Cider Company Inc ....E.......530 346-9699
1213 S Auburn St Ste A Colfax (95713) ***(P-2577)***
Fox Factory Inc (HQ) ....**C.......831 274-6500**
130 Hangar Way Watsonville (95076) ***(P-6580)***
Fox Factory Inc ....E.......831 274-6545
200 El Pueblo Rd Scotts Valley (95066) ***(P-6581)***
Fox Marble & Granite, Berkeley *Also called Evolv Surfaces Inc* ***(P-3324)***
Fox Paine & Company LLC (PA) ....**C.......650 235-2075**
2105 Woodside Rd Ste D Woodside (94062) ***(P-9969)***
Fox Racing Shox, Watsonville *Also called Fox Factory Inc* ***(P-6580)***
Fox Rent A Car Inc ....D.......408 210-2208
7600 Earhart Rd Ste 9o Oakland (94621) ***(P-14488)***
Fox Rent-A-Car & Truck, Oakland *Also called Fox Rent A Car Inc* ***(P-14488)***
Fox Rothschild LLP ....D.......415 539-3336
1 Sansome St Ste 2850 San Francisco (94104) ***(P-17268)***
Fox Tail Golf Course ....D.......707 584-7766
100 Golf Course Dr Rohnert Park (94928) ***(P-15003)***
Foxfarm Soil & Fertilizer, Samoa *Also called United Compost & Organics Inc* ***(P-9614)***
Foxpass Inc ....F.......415 805-6350
548 Market St San Francisco (94104) ***(P-13177)***
FP, San Francisco *Also called Francisco Partners GP III LP* ***(P-13592)***
FPI Management Inc ....C.......408 267-3952
1107 Luchessi Dr San Jose (95118) ***(P-19339)***
FPI Management Inc ....C.......530 756-5332
1124 F St Davis (95616) ***(P-10552)***
FPI Management Inc (PA) ....**E.......916 357-5300**
800 Iron Point Rd Folsom (95630) ***(P-10553)***
FPI Management Inc ....C.......530 272-5274
131 Eureka St Ofc Grass Valley (95945) ***(P-10554)***
Framehawk Inc ....F.......415 371-9110
650 Townsend St Ste 325 San Francisco (94103) ***(P-13178)***
France Telecom RES & Dev LLC, San Francisco *Also called Orange Silicon Valley LLC* ***(P-19177)***
Franchise Update Inc ....F.......408 402-5681
6489 Camden Ave Ste 204 San Jose (95120) ***(P-3500)***
Franchise Update Media Group, San Jose *Also called Franchise Update Inc* ***(P-3500)***
Francis Classic Cars, Fresno *Also called L J Inc* ***(P-14529)***
Francis Coppola Winery LLC ....E.......707 857-1400
300 Via Archimedes Geyserville (95441) ***(P-2578)***
Francis Ford Coppola Inc ....D.......415 788-7500
916 Kearny St San Francisco (94133) ***(P-14791)***
Francis Ford Coppola Winery, Geyserville *Also called Francis Ford Cppola Prsnts LLC* ***(P-2579)***
Francis Ford Cppola Prsnts LLC ....E.......707 251-3200
300 Via Archimedes Geyserville (95441) ***(P-2579)***
Francisca Club ....E.......415 781-1200
595 Sutter St San Francisco (94102) ***(P-18417)***
Franciscan Conv. Hospital, Merced *Also called Avalon Care Ctr - Mrced Frncsc* ***(P-15917)***
Franciscan Vineyards Inc ....D.......707 933-2332
18701 Gehricke Rd Sonoma (95476) ***(P-2580)***
Franciscan Vineyards Inc ....D.......209 369-5861
5950 E Woodbridge Rd Acampo (95220) ***(P-2581)***
Franciscan Vineyards Inc (HQ) ....**D.......707 963-7111**
1178 Galleron Rd Saint Helena (94574) ***(P-2582)***
Franciscan Vinyards Inc ....E.......707 433-6981
16275 Healdsburg Ave Healdsburg (95448) ***(P-2583)***

ALPHABETIC

Francisco Partners Agility LP (PA)....C....**415 418-2900**
1 Letterman Dr Bldg C San Francisco (94129) ***(P-10755)***

Francisco Partners GP III LP (HQ)....D....**415 418-2900**
1 Letterman Dr Bldg C San Francisco (94129) ***(P-13592)***

Francisco Partners Iv-A LP....E....415 418-2900
1 Letterman Dr San Francisco (94129) ***(P-10756)***

Francisco Partners MGT LP (PA)....E....**415 418-2900**
1 Letterman Dr Ste 410 San Francisco (94129) ***(P-10846)***

Francisco Partners Vi LP (PA)....C....**415 418-2900**
1 Letterman Dr Bldg Cs San Francisco (94129) ***(P-14278)***

Francsco Prtners III Cayman LP....D....415 418-2900
1 Letterman Dr Bldg C San Francisco (94129) ***(P-19778)***

Frangadakis, Kenneth DDS, Cupertino *Also called Cupertino Dental Group* ***(P-15830)***

Frank and Patricia Maggiore (PA)....E....**925 634-4176**
820 Quiet Gable Ct Brentwood (94513) ***(P-30)***

Frank C Alegre Trucking Inc (PA)....C....**209 334-2112**
5100 W Highway 12 Lodi (95242) ***(P-7540)***

Frank Carson Ldscp & Maint Inc....C....916 856-5400
9530 Elder Creek Rd Sacramento (95829) ***(P-415)***

Frank Coelho & Sons LP....E....209 722-6843
12775 Anchor St El Nido (95317) ***(P-211)***

Frank Gates Service Company....E....916 934-0812
1107 Investment Blvd El Dorado Hills (95762) ***(P-19518)***

Frank Ghiglione Inc (PA)....D....**510 483-7000**
1622 Moreland Dr Alameda (94501) ***(P-7466)***

Frank Ghiglione Inc....D....510 483-2063
2972 Alvarado St Ste H San Leandro (94577) ***(P-7467)***

Frank M Booth Inc (PA)....E....**530 742-7134**
222 3rd St Marysville (95901) ***(P-1266)***

Frank M Booth Inc....C....650 871-8292
251 Michelle Ct South San Francisco (94080) ***(P-1267)***

Frank Toste....E....559 233-4329
11900 W Lincoln Ave Fresno (93706) ***(P-212)***

Frank-Lin Distillers Pdts Ltd (PA)....C....**408 259-8900**
2455 Huntington Dr Fairfield (94533) ***(P-9577)***

Franklin Advisers Inc (HQ)....A....**650 312-2000**
1 Franklin Pkwy San Mateo (94403) ***(P-10757)***

Franklin Elementary School, Merced *Also called Merced City School District* ***(P-17973)***

Franklin Logging, Burney *Also called Shasta Green Inc* ***(P-3078)***

Franklin Logging Inc....D....530 549-4924
11906 Wilson Way Redding (96003) ***(P-3061)***

Franklin Resources Inc (PA)....A....**650 312-2000**
1 Franklin Pkwy Bldg 920 San Mateo (94403) ***(P-10045)***

Franklin Templeton Instnl LLC (HQ)....D....**650 312-2000**
1 Franklin Pkwy San Mateo (94403) ***(P-10758)***

Franklin Templeton Investment, Rancho Cordova *Also called Franklin Tmpleton Inv Svcs LLC* ***(P-9970)***

Franklin Templeton Svcs LLC....A....650 312-3000
1 Franklin Pkwy Bldg 970 San Mateo (94403) ***(P-10759)***

Franklin Tmpleton Inv Svcs LLC....C....650 312-2000
3366 Quality Dr Rancho Cordova (95670) ***(P-10760)***

Franklin Tmpleton Inv Svcs LLC....C....925 875-2619
5130 Hacienda Dr Fl 4 Dublin (94568) ***(P-10046)***

Franklin Tmpleton Inv Svcs LLC (HQ)....A....**916 463-1500**
3344 Quality Dr Rancho Cordova (95670) ***(P-9970)***

Franks Heating & Refrigeration, Crescent City *Also called Orca Heating and Rfrgn Inc* ***(P-1329)***

Franks Janitorial Service....E....707 226-1848
2400 Oak St NAPA (94559) ***(P-11954)***

Frantz Wholesale Nursery LLC....C....209 874-1459
12161 Delaware Rd Hickman (95323) ***(P-122)***

Franz Inc....E....510 452-2000
3685 Mt Diablo Blvd # 300 Lafayette (94549) ***(P-13179)***

Franzia Winery, Ripon *Also called Franzia/Sanger Winery* ***(P-2586)***

Franzia Winery LP....F....209 599-4111
17000 E State Highway 120 Ripon (95366) ***(P-2584)***

Franzia Winery LLC....E....209 599-4111
17000 E State Highway 120 Ripon (95366) ***(P-2585)***

Franzia/Sanger Winery....D....209 599-4111
17000 E State Highway 120 Ripon (95366) ***(P-2586)***

Frase Enterprises....E....510 856-3600
2261 Carion Ct Pittsburg (94565) ***(P-5721)***

Fray Logging....E....209 984-5968
10619 Jim Brady Rd Jamestown (95327) ***(P-3062)***

Frazier Nut Farms Inc....E....209 522-1406
10830 Yosemite Blvd Waterford (95386) ***(P-89)***

Frc, Sacramento *Also called Farmers Rice Cooperative* ***(P-2320)***

FReal Foods LLC....D....800 483-3218
6121 Hollis St Ste 500 Emeryville (94608) ***(P-2161)***

Fred Matter Inc....E....925 371-1234
7801 Las Positas Rd Livermore (94551) ***(P-5528)***

Frederick L Richter & Son Inc....E....530 458-3180
707 Main St Colusa (95932) ***(P-8)***

Fredericksen Tank Lines Inc (PA)....E....**916 371-4960**
840 Delta Ln West Sacramento (95691) ***(P-7541)***

Free Flow Medical Inc (PA)....D....**717 669-2566**
44380 S Grimmer Blvd Fremont (94538) ***(P-16370)***

Free Hot Water, San Jose *Also called Gemtech Sales Corp* ***(P-4629)***

Free Stream Media Corp (PA)....D....**415 854-0073**
123 Townsend St Fl 5 San Francisco (94107) ***(P-9659)***

Freedom Debt Relief, San Mateo *Also called Freedom Financial Network LLC* ***(P-11719)***

Freedom Financial Network LLC (PA)....A....**650 393-6619**
1875 S Grant St Ste 400 San Mateo (94402) ***(P-11719)***

Freedom of Press Foundation....F....510 995-0780
601 Van Ness Ave Ste E731 San Francisco (94102) ***(P-3501)***

Freeman Brown Sperry & D Aiuto, Stockton *Also called Freeman D Aiuto Prof Law Corp* ***(P-17269)***

Freeman D Aiuto Prof Law Corp....D....209 474-1818
1818 Grand Canal Blvd # 4 Stockton (95207) ***(P-17269)***

Freeman Motors Inc....C....707 542-1791
2875 Corby Ave Santa Rosa (95407) ***(P-14564)***

Freeman Toyota Rent-A-Car, Santa Rosa *Also called Freeman Motors Inc* ***(P-14564)***

Freemark Abbey Wnery Ltd Prtnr....E....707 963-9694
3022 Saint Helena Hwy N Saint Helena (94574) ***(P-2587)***

Freemont Health Care Center, Fremont *Also called Mariner Health Care Inc* ***(P-16045)***

Freemont Rideout Health Group....D....530 751-4270
726 4th St Marysville (95901) ***(P-16371)***

Freemont Rideout Health Group....D....530 671-2883
481 Plumas Blvd Ste 105 Yuba City (95991) ***(P-16372)***

Freenome Holdings Inc....C....650 446-6630
279 E Grand Ave South San Francisco (94080) ***(P-4022)***

Freeport Bakery Inc....F....916 442-4256
2966 Freeport Blvd Sacramento (95818) ***(P-2383)***

Freewire Technologies Inc....E....415 779-5515
1933 Davis St Ste 301a San Leandro (94577) ***(P-5662)***

Freight Chckers Clrcal Emplyee....E....650 635-0111
453 San Mateo Ave San Bruno (94066) ***(P-18358)***

Freixenet Sonoma Caves Inc....E....707 996-4981
23555 Arnold Dr Sonoma (95476) ***(P-2588)***

Freixenet Usa Inc....D....707 996-7256
23555 Arnold Dr Sonoma (95476) ***(P-9578)***

Fremont Ambltory Srgery Ctr LP....D....510 456-4600
39350 Civic Center Dr Fremont (94538) ***(P-15408)***

Fremont Amgen Inc (HQ)....C....**510 284-6500**
6397 Kaiser Dr Fremont (94555) ***(P-3901)***

Fremont Bank (HQ)....C....**510 505-5226**
39150 Fremont Blvd Fremont (94538) ***(P-9731)***

Fremont Bank....D....510 512-1900
1679 Industrial Pkwy W Hayward (94544) ***(P-9732)***

Fremont Bank....D....925 314-1420
210 Railroad Ave Danville (94526) ***(P-9733)***

Fremont Ford, Newark *Also called J & S Operations LLC* ***(P-14572)***

Fremont Group LLC (PA)....C....**415 284-8500**
199 Fremont St Fl 19 San Francisco (94105) ***(P-10047)***

Fremont Hills Country Club....E....650 948-8261
12889 Viscaino Pl Los Altos Hills (94022) ***(P-15092)***

Fremont Hospital, Mariposa *Also called John C Fremont Healthcare Dst* ***(P-16389)***

Fremont Hospital....C....530 751-4000
620 J St Marysville (95901) ***(P-16373)***

Fremont Marriott....E....510 413-3700
46100 Landing Pkwy Fremont (94538) ***(P-11105)***

Fremont Marriott Silicon Vly, Fremont *Also called Ashford Trs Fremont LLC* ***(P-10934)***

Fremont Medical Center, Marysville *Also called Fremont Hospital* ***(P-16373)***

Fremont Mutual Funds Inc....D....800 548-4539
333 Market St Ste 2600 San Francisco (94105) ***(P-9971)***

Fremont Package Express....F....916 541-1812
734 Still Breeze Way Sacramento (95831) ***(P-5061)***

Fremont Paving Company Inc....D....510 797-3553
38370 Cedar Blvd Newark (94560) ***(P-1042)***

Fremont Properties Inc....E....415 284-8500
199 Fremont St Ste 1900 San Francisco (94105) ***(P-10388)***

Fremont Rideout Comp Clinic....D....530 749-4411
1531 Plumas Ct Yuba City (95991) ***(P-16374)***

Fremont Sports Inc....E....510 656-4411
40645 Fremont Blvd Ste 3 Fremont (94538) ***(P-14893)***

Fremont Surgery Center, Fremont *Also called Fremont Ambltory Srgery Ctr LP* ***(P-15408)***

Fremont-Rdout Occpational Hlth, Yuba City *Also called Fremont Rideout Comp Clinic* ***(P-16374)***

Fremont-Rideout Health Group, Marysville *Also called Freemont Rideout Health Group* ***(P-16371)***

Fremouw Environmental Svcs Inc....D....707 448-3700
6940 Tremont Rd Dixon (95620) ***(P-19779)***

French Redwood Inc....C....650 598-9000
223 Twin Dolphin Dr Redwood City (94065) ***(P-11106)***

Freschi Air Systems Inc....D....925 827-9761
715 Fulton Shipyard Rd Antioch (94509) ***(P-1268)***

Freschi Service Experts, Antioch *Also called Freschi Air Systems Inc* ***(P-1268)***

Fresenius Kidney Care Clovis, Clovis *Also called Fresenius Med Care Clovis LLC* ***(P-16973)***

Fresenius Med Care Clovis LLC....A....559 324-8023
2585 Alluvial Ave Clovis (93611) ***(P-16973)***

Fresenius Med Care Slano Cnty....D....707 678-6433
125 N Lincoln St Ste B Dixon (95620) ***(P-16974)***

Fresenius Med Care Solano Cnty, Dixon *Also called Fresenius Med Care Slano Cnty* ***(P-16974)***

Fresenius Med Care Wdlnd Cal L....D....530 668-4503
35 W Main St Woodland (95695) ***(P-16975)***

Fresenius Medical Care Wdlnd, Woodland *Also called Fresenius Med Care Wdlnd Cal L* ***(P-16975)***

Fresh Innovations Cal LLC....C....209 983-9700
7735 S Highway 99 Stockton (95215) ***(P-9403)***

Fresh Pick Produce....E....408 315-4612
195 San Pedro Ave Ste D Morgan Hill (95037) ***(P-9195)***

Fresh Start Bakeries, Stockton *Also called Aspire Bakeries LLC* ***(P-2363)***

Freshdesk Inc (HQ)....E....**866 832-3090**
1250 Bayhill Dr Ste 315 San Bruno (94066) ***(P-13898)***

Freshko Produce Services Inc....C....559 497-7000
2155 E Muscat Ave Fresno (93725) ***(P-9404)***

Freshpoint Central California....C....209 216-0200
5900 N Golden State Blvd Turlock (95382) ***(P-9405)***

Freshworks Inc (PA)....E....**650 513-0514**
2950 S Del St Ste 201 San Mateo (94403) ***(P-13180)***

Fresn-Mdera Fdral Land Bnk Ass (HQ)....E....**559 277-7000**
4635 W Spruce Ave Fresno (93722) ***(P-9852)***

Fresno - Rgnal Med Cmnty Hlth, Fresno *Also called Clinica Sierra Vista* ***(P-15352)***

Fresno Airport Hotel, Fresno *Also called BNP Lodging LLC* ***(P-10964)***
Fresno Airport Hotels LLC..........D.......559 252-3611
5090 E Clinton Way Fresno (93727) ***(P-11107)***
FRESNO ART MUSEUM..........E.......559 441-4221
2233 N 1st St Fresno (93703) ***(P-18272)***
Fresno Auto Dealers Auction..........A.......559 268-8051
278 N Marks Ave Fresno (93706) ***(P-8421)***
Fresno Baseball Club LLC..........E.......559 320-4487
1800 Tulare St Fresno (93721) ***(P-15093)***
Fresno Beverage Company Inc..........C.......559 650-1500
3525 S East Ave Fresno (93725) ***(P-9551)***
Fresno Business Journal, Fresno *Also called Business Journal* ***(P-3493)***
Fresno Chrysler Ddge Jeep Ram, Fresno *Also called Fresno Chrysler Jeep Inc* ***(P-14565)***
Fresno Chrysler Jeep Inc..........D.......559 431-4000
6162 N Blackstone Ave Fresno (93710) ***(P-14565)***
Fresno City College Bus Off, Fresno *Also called State Center Cmnty College Dst* ***(P-18997)***
Fresno Cmnty Hosp & Med Ctr..........D.......559 324-4000
2755 Herndon Ave Clovis (93611) ***(P-16375)***
Fresno Cmnty Hosp & Med Ctr (HQ)..........A.......559 459-3948
2823 Fresno St Fresno (93721) ***(P-16376)***
Fresno Cnty Ecnmic Opprtnties..........E.......559 486-6587
3120 W Neilson Fresno (93706) ***(P-17574)***
Fresno Cnty Ecnmic Opprtnties..........D.......559 263-1584
1900 Mariposa Mall # 202 Fresno (93721) ***(P-17937)***
Fresno Cnty Ecnmic Opprtnties..........E.......559 935-2058
311 Coalinga Plz Coalinga (93210) ***(P-17575)***
Fresno Cnty Ecnmic Opprtnties..........E.......559 263-1000
1900 Mariposa Mall # 300 Fresno (93721) ***(P-17576)***
Fresno Cnty Ecnmic Opprtnties (PA)..........A.......559 263-1010
1920 Mariposa Mall # 300 Fresno (93721) ***(P-17577)***
Fresno Cnty Ecnmic Opprtnties..........E.......559 637-0025
1240 E Washington Ave Reedley (93654) ***(P-17578)***
Fresno Cnty Ecnmic Opprtnties..........E.......559 896-0142
1325 Stillman St Selma (93662) ***(P-17579)***
Fresno Cnty Ecnmic Opprtnties..........E.......559 485-3733
3120 W Nielsen Ave Fresno (93706) ***(P-17580)***
Fresno Cnty Ecnmic Opprtnties..........D.......559 875-2581
3037 Orchid Ave Sanger (93657) ***(P-17938)***
Fresno Cnty Ecnmic Opprtnties..........E.......559 263-1013
1920 Mariposa Mall Fresno (93721) ***(P-17581)***
Fresno Cnty Ecnmic Opprtnties..........E.......559 485-3733
3120 W Nielsen Ave # 102 Fresno (93706) ***(P-17582)***
Fresno Cnty Ecnmic Opprtnties..........E.......559 266-3663
3100 W Nielsen Ave Fresno (93706) ***(P-17583)***
Fresno Credit Bureau..........E.......559 650-7177
757 L St Fresno (93721) ***(P-11822)***
Fresno D", Fresno *Also called Fresno Distributing Co* ***(P-5757)***
Fresno Distributing Co..........E.......559 442-8800
2055 E Mckinley Ave Fresno (93703) ***(P-5757)***
Fresno District Office, Fresno *Also called State Compensation Insur Fund* ***(P-10181)***
Fresno Eoc, Fresno *Also called Fresno Cnty Ecnmic Opprtnties* ***(P-17576)***
FRESNO EOC, Fresno *Also called Fresno Cnty Ecnmic Opprtnties* ***(P-17577)***
Fresno Fab-Tech Inc..........E.......559 875-9800
1035 K St Sanger (93657) ***(P-4662)***
Fresno Ford Tractor Inc..........E.......559 485-9090
3040 S Parkway Dr Fresno (93725) ***(P-5023)***
Fresno French Bread Bakery Inc..........E.......559 268-7088
2625 Inyo St Fresno (93721) ***(P-2384)***
Fresno Glass Plant, Fresno *Also called Vitro Flat Glass LLC* ***(P-4364)***
Fresno Grizzlies Baseball, Fresno *Also called Fresno Baseball Club LLC* ***(P-15093)***
Fresno Heart Hospital LLC..........B.......559 433-8000
15 E Audubon Dr Fresno (93720) ***(P-16377)***
Fresno Heritage Partners..........E.......559 446-6226
6075 N Marks Ave Fresno (93711) ***(P-18118)***
Fresno Imaging Center (PA)..........E.......559 447-2600
6191 N Thesta St Fresno (93710) ***(P-15409)***
Fresno Irrigation District..........D.......559 233-7161
2907 S Maple Ave Fresno (93725) ***(P-8410)***
Fresno Metro Flood Ctrl Dst..........D.......559 456-3292
5469 E Olive Ave Fresno (93727) ***(P-14279)***
Fresno Oral Mxllfcial Srgery D..........E.......559 226-2722
1903 E Fir Ave Ste 101 Fresno (93720) ***(P-15834)***
Fresno Oxgn Wldg Suppliers Inc (PA)..........E.......559 233-6684
2825 S Elm Ave Ste 101 Fresno (93706) ***(P-9067)***
Fresno Paper Express, Fresno *Also called Paper Pulp & Film* ***(P-3404)***
Fresno Pipe & Supply Inc (PA)..........E.......559 233-0500
4696 E Commerce Ave Fresno (93725) ***(P-8996)***
Fresno Plumbing & Heating Inc (PA)..........C.......559 294-0200
2585 N Larkin Ave Fresno (93727) ***(P-1269)***
Fresno Precision Plastics Inc..........D.......916 689-5284
8456 Carbide Ct Sacramento (95828) ***(P-4283)***
Fresno Produce Inc..........E.......559 495-0143
1415 B St Fresno (93706) ***(P-9406)***
Fresno Rescue Mission Inc (PA)..........E.......559 268-0839
263 G St Fresno (93706) ***(P-17584)***
Fresno Respite Companion Svcs, Fresno *Also called Maxim Healthcare Services Inc* ***(P-16912)***
Fresno Roofing Co Inc..........D.......559 255-8377
5950 E Olive Ave Fresno (93727) ***(P-1806)***
Fresno Skilled Nursing..........D.......559 268-5361
1665 M St Fresno (93721) ***(P-16009)***
Fresno Staffing, Fresno *Also called Maxim Healthcare Services Inc* ***(P-12182)***
Fresno Surgery Center LP (PA)..........C.......559 431-8000
6125 N Fresno St Fresno (93710) ***(P-16378)***
Fresno Surgical Hospital, Fresno *Also called Fresno Surgery Center LP* ***(P-16378)***
Fresno Truck Center..........D.......559 486-4310
2727 E Central Ave Fresno (93725) ***(P-8422)***
Fresno Truck Center..........C.......209 983-2400
10182 S Harlan Rd French Camp (95231) ***(P-8423)***
Fresno Valves & Castings Inc (PA)..........C.......559 834-2511
7736 E Springfield Ave Selma (93662) ***(P-8411)***
Fresno-Madera Farm Credit, Fresno *Also called Fresn-Mdera Fdral Land Bnk Ass* ***(P-9852)***
Fresnos Chaffee Zoo Corp..........C.......559 498-5910
894 W Belmont Ave Fresno (93728) ***(P-18292)***
Freund Baking Co, Hayward *Also called Oakhurst Industries Inc* ***(P-9281)***
Frey Vineyards Ltd..........F.......707 485-5177
14000 Tomki Rd Redwood Valley (95470) ***(P-2589)***
Friant & Associates LLC (PA)..........D.......510 535-5113
1980 W Avenue 140th San Leandro (94577) ***(P-2032)***
Fricke-Parks Press Inc..........E.......510 489-6543
33250 Transit Ave Union City (94587) ***(P-3650)***
Friedman Bros Home Imprv Ctr, Santa Rosa *Also called Friedmans Home Improvement* ***(P-8983)***
Friedmans Home Improvement..........D.......707 584-7811
4055 Santa Rosa Ave Santa Rosa (95407) ***(P-8983)***
Friends Outside..........D.......209 955-0701
1148 W Fremont St Stockton (95203) ***(P-17585)***
Friends Santa Cruz State Parks..........D.......831 429-1840
1543 Pacific Ave Ste 206 Santa Cruz (95060) ***(P-18418)***
Friends To Parents..........E.......650 588-8212
2525 Wexford Ave South San Francisco (94080) ***(P-17939)***
Frito-Lay North America Inc..........B.......209 544-5400
600 Garner Rd Modesto (95357) ***(P-2856)***
Frog Design Inc (HQ)..........B.......415 442-4804
427 Brannan St San Francisco (94107) ***(P-11861)***
Frogs Leap Winery..........E.......707 963-4704
8815 Conn Creek Rd Rutherford (94573) ***(P-2590)***
Front Porch Inc (PA)..........D.......209 288-5500
905 Mono Way Sonora (95370) ***(P-12462)***
Front St Inc..........C.......831 420-0120
2115 7th Ave Santa Cruz (95062) ***(P-16233)***
Front St Residential Care, Santa Cruz *Also called Front St Inc* ***(P-16233)***
Frontage Laboratories Inc..........E.......510 626-9993
3825 Bay Center Pl Hayward (94545) ***(P-3902)***
Frontapp Inc..........D.......415 680-3048
1455 Market St Fl 19 San Francisco (94103) ***(P-13181)***
Frontier, Elk Grove *Also called Citizens Telecom Co Cal Inc* ***(P-7939)***
Frontier AG Co Inc (PA)..........E.......530 297-1020
46735 County Road 32b Davis (95618) ***(P-2344)***
Frontier California Inc..........B.......209 239-4128
525 E Yosemite Ave Manteca (95336) ***(P-7951)***
Frontier California Inc..........B.......212 395-1000
295 Parkshore Dr Folsom (95630) ***(P-7952)***
Frontier Ford (PA)..........C.......408 241-1800
3701 Stevens Creek Blvd Santa Clara (95051) ***(P-8424)***
Frontier Land Companies..........E.......209 957-8112
10100 Trinity Pkwy # 420 Stockton (95219) ***(P-639)***
Frontier Medicines..........E.......650 457-1005
151 Oyster Point Blvd # 200 South San Francisco (94080) ***(P-3903)***
Frontier Performance Lubr Inc..........E.......209 334-6353
816 Black Diamond Way A Lodi (95240) ***(P-9533)***
Frontier Rent-A-Car, Santa Clara *Also called Frontier Ford* ***(P-8424)***
Frontier Semiconductor (PA)..........E.......408 432-8338
165 Topaz St Milpitas (95035) ***(P-6124)***
Frontier Transportation Inc..........E.......209 836-0251
425 W Larch Rd Tracy (95304) ***(P-7621)***
Frontline Envmtl Tech Group In..........E.......707 745-1116
3195 Park Rd Ste C Benicia (94510) ***(P-6720)***
Frontline Technologies, Benicia *Also called Frontline Envmtl Tech Group In* ***(P-6720)***
Frontrs-Frnters Land Companies, Stockton *Also called Frontier Land Companies* ***(P-639)***
Frt of America LLC..........F.......408 261-2632
1101 S Winchester Blvd San Jose (95128) ***(P-5097)***
Fruehe Design, Fresno *Also called Simply Smashing Inc* ***(P-7254)***
Fruitridge Prtg Lithograph Inc (PA)..........E.......916 452-9213
3258 Stockton Blvd Sacramento (95820) ***(P-3651)***
Fruitvale Healthcare Center, Oakland *Also called SSC Oakland Fruitvale Oper LP* ***(P-16270)***
Fryes Printing Inc..........E.......707 253-1114
1050 Lincoln Ave NAPA (94558) ***(P-11846)***
Fsm, Milpitas *Also called Frontier Semiconductor* ***(P-6124)***
Fsq Rio Las Palmas Business Tr..........C.......209 957-4711
877 E March Ln Apt 378 Stockton (95207) ***(P-16010)***
Ftg Builders Inc (PA)..........E.......408 564-1534
384 Breen Rd San Juan Bautista (95045) ***(P-640)***
FTg Construction Mtls Inc..........C.......209 334-4038
5100 W Highway 12 Lodi (95242) ***(P-7542)***
Fti, Turlock *Also called Formax Technologies Inc* ***(P-6521)***
Fti Consulting Inc..........D.......415 283-4200
50 California St Ste 1900 San Francisco (94111) ***(P-19780)***
Ftv Management Company LP (PA)..........C.......415 229-3000
555 California St # 2900 San Francisco (94104) ***(P-10761)***
Fuddruckers, Concord *Also called Daratel Ltd* ***(P-11714)***
Fuel Delivery Services Inc..........D.......209 751-2185
4895 S Airport Way Stockton (95206) ***(P-7543)***
Fugro USA Land, Walnut Creek *Also called Fugro William Lettis Assoc Inc* ***(P-18712)***
Fugro William Lettis Assoc Inc (HQ)..........E.......925 256-6070
1777 Botelho Dr Ste 262 Walnut Creek (94596) ***(P-18712)***
Fuji Xerox, Palo Alto *Also called Xerox International Partners* ***(P-5124)***
Fujifilm Bi Intrntnal Oprtons..........E.......650 240-3740
3174 Porter Dr Palo Alto (94304) ***(P-8707)***
Fujifilm Dimatix Inc (HQ)..........A.......408 565-9150
2250 Martin Ave Santa Clara (95050) ***(P-5369)***
Fujifilm Dimatix Inc..........D.......408 565-0670
2230 Martin Ave Santa Clara (95050) ***(P-19061)***
Fujitsu America Inc..........E.......925 327-0050
5000 Executive Pkwy # 290 San Ramon (94583) ***(P-12463)***

A L P H A B E T I C

Employee Codes: A=Over 500 employees, B=251-500
C=101-250, D=51-100, E=20-50 F=10-19

Fujitsu Components America Inc (HQ)......E......**408 745-4900**
1230 E Arques Ave Ms160 Sunnyvale (94085) ***(P-8914)***
Fujitsu Computer Pdts Amer Inc (HQ)......B......**800 626-4686**
1250 E Arques Ave Sunnyvale (94085) ***(P-13593)***
Fujitsu Consulting (canada) (PA)......C......**732 549-4100**
1250 E Arques Ave Sunnyvale (94085) ***(P-13594)***
Fujitsu Consulting LLC (HQ)......D......**408 746-6000**
1250 E Arques Ave Sunnyvale (94085) ***(P-13595)***
Fujitsu Electronics Amer Inc (HQ)......D......**408 737-5600**
1250 E Arques Ave Sunnyvale (94085) ***(P-18713)***
Fujitsu Laboratories Amer Inc, Sunnyvale *Also called Fujitsu Research America Inc* ***(P-19062)***
Fujitsu Research America Inc (HQ)......D......**408 530-4500**
350 Cobalt Way Sunnyvale (94085) ***(P-19062)***
Fujitsu Retirement MGT Inc (HQ)......B......**408 746-6000**
1250 E Arques Ave Sunnyvale (94085) ***(P-13596)***
Fujitsu Tech & Bus Amer Inc......E......408 746-6000
1250 E Arques Ave Sunnyvale (94085) ***(P-4372)***
Fulfillment Whsng Slutions Inc......E......760 685-5388
31137 Wiegman Rd Hayward (94544) ***(P-7882)***
Full Circle Brewing Co Ltd LLC......F......559 264-6323
620 F St Fresno (93706) ***(P-2479)***
Full Service Janitorial Inc......E......408 227-0600
350 Piercy Rd San Jose (95138) ***(P-11955)***
Full Service Maintenance Inc......E......408 227-2400
350 Piercy Rd San Jose (95138) ***(P-11956)***
Fullbloom Baking Company Inc......A......510 456-3638
6500 Overlake Pl Newark (94560) ***(P-2385)***
Fullcontact Inc......E......415 366-6587
535 Mission St Fl 14 San Francisco (94105) ***(P-12464)***
Fuller Manufacturing Inc......F......209 267-5071
130 Ridge Rd Sutter Creek (95685) ***(P-6522)***
Fullpower Technologies Inc......E......831 459-0447
1200 Pacific Ave Ste 300 Santa Cruz (95060) ***(P-12465)***
Fullstack Labs LLC (PA)......E......**415 609-2453**
9719 Village Center Dr # 100 Granite Bay (95746) ***(P-12466)***
Fun To Stay Lessee Inc......E......415 882-1300
165 Steuart St San Francisco (94105) ***(P-11108)***
Function Engineering Inc (PA)......E......**650 326-8834**
163 Everett Ave Palo Alto (94301) ***(P-18714)***
Fundex Investment Group, San Francisco *Also called Fundx Investment Group LLC* ***(P-3572)***
Funding Circle Usa Inc......D......855 385-5356
85 2nd St Ste 400 San Francisco (94105) ***(P-9870)***
Funding Pace Group LLC......E......844 873-7223
750 University Ave # 240 Los Gatos (95032) ***(P-9871)***
Fundx Investment Group LLC......F......415 986-7979
235 Montgomery St # 1049 San Francisco (94104) ***(P-3572)***
Fungible Inc......D......669 292-5522
3201 Scott Blvd Santa Clara (95054) ***(P-19781)***
Funtopia Inc......D......510 246-3098
3700 Brookstone Dr Turlock (95382) ***(P-15205)***
Funworks, Modesto *Also called Putt-Putt of Modesto Inc* ***(P-15229)***
Fuse Project LLC......D......415 908-1492
1401 16th St San Francisco (94103) ***(P-19782)***
Fusion Cloud Company LLC (HQ)......D......**925 201-2500**
6800 Koll Center Pkwy # 20 Pleasanton (94566) ***(P-7953)***
Fusion Coatings Inc......F......925 443-8083
6589 Las Positas Rd Livermore (94551) ***(P-4933)***
Fusion Mphc Holding Corp (HQ)......E......**925 201-2500**
6800 Koll Center Pkwy Pleasanton (94566) ***(P-13182)***
Fusion Ranch Inc......E......650 589-8899
405 S Airport Blvd South San Francisco (94080) ***(P-2118)***
Fusion Real Estate Network Inc......D......916 448-3174
1300 National Dr Ste 170 Sacramento (95834) ***(P-10555)***
Fusionone Inc......E......408 282-1200
55 Almaden Blvd Ste 500 San Jose (95113) ***(P-12467)***
Futurama, San Mateo *Also called Bears For Humanity Inc* ***(P-4122)***
Future Active Industrial Elec, Milpitas *Also called FAI Electronics Corp* ***(P-8912)***
Future Dial Incorporated......D......408 245-8880
392 Potrero Ave Sunnyvale (94085) ***(P-12468)***
Future Energy Corporation (PA)......C......**800 985-0733**
8980 Grant Line Rd Elk Grove (95624) ***(P-1675)***
Future Energy Savers, Elk Grove *Also called Future Energy Corporation* ***(P-1675)***
Future Fast Inc......D......559 813-0113
5081 W Brown Ave Fresno (93722) ***(P-14280)***
Future Ford Lncoln Mrcury Cnco, Concord *Also called Future Ford of Concord LLC* ***(P-14609)***
Future Ford of Concord LLC......D......925 686-5000
2285 Diamond Blvd Concord (94520) ***(P-14609)***
Future Innovations Inc......E......925 485-2000
4495 Stoneridge Dr Pleasanton (94588) ***(P-14281)***
Future State......C......925 956-4200
415 Mission St Ste 3300 San Francisco (94105) ***(P-13899)***
Futureadvisor, San Francisco *Also called Xulu Inc* ***(P-10074)***
Futures Explored......C......925 332-7183
2150 John Glenn Dr Ste 30 Concord (94520) ***(P-17586)***
Futurewei Technologies Inc......C......469 277-5700
2330 Central Expy Santa Clara (95050) ***(P-7954)***
Fuzebox Software Corporation (HQ)......D......**415 692-4800**
150 Spear St Ste 900 San Francisco (94105) ***(P-13183)***
Fx Palo Alto Laboratory Inc......E......650 842-4800
3174 Porter Dr Palo Alto (94304) ***(P-19159)***
Fxi Inc......D......510 357-2600
2451 Polvorosa Ave San Leandro (94577) ***(P-4243)***
G & G Construction Co, Atwater *Also called Gino/Giuseppe Inc* ***(P-1873)***
G & R Wholesale Distribution, Lodi *Also called Buy 4 Less* ***(P-8846)***
G and H Vineyards, Rutherford *Also called Grgich Hills Cellar* ***(P-2605)***
G and L Brock Cnstr Co Inc......E......209 931-3626
4145 Calloway Ct Stockton (95215) ***(P-1959)***
G B Commercial LLC......D......916 263-9000
4900 Duckhorn Dr Sacramento (95834) ***(P-11109)***
G B Group Inc (PA)......D......**408 848-8118**
8921 Murray Ave Gilroy (95020) ***(P-747)***
G C Micro Corporation......E......707 789-0600
3910 Cypress Dr Petaluma (94954) ***(P-8708)***
G D B, San Rafael *Also called Guide Dogs For Blind Inc* ***(P-354)***
G D M Electronic Assembly Inc......D......408 945-4100
2070 Ringwood Ave San Jose (95131) ***(P-5715)***
G L Mezzetta Inc......D......707 648-1050
105 Mezzetta Ct American Canyon (94503) ***(P-2215)***
G M Quartz, Oakland *Also called GM Associates Inc* ***(P-6430)***
G Pallets Inc......E......209 814-2250
2200 Hoover Ave Modesto (95354) ***(P-3222)***
G S I, Alameda *Also called Golden State Imports Intl Inc* ***(P-9182)***
G S R, Pleasanton *Also called Global Software Resources Inc* ***(P-13901)***
G&R Almeda Healthcare Svcs LLC......D......510 521-5765
508 Westline Dr Alameda (94501) ***(P-17587)***
G-Elk Grove LP......D......916 478-9000
9175 W Stockton Blvd Elk Grove (95758) ***(P-11110)***
G.I.M.S., San Francisco *Also called Galindo Instltion Mvg Svcs In* ***(P-3325)***
G2 Metal Fab......E......925 443-7903
4205 S B St Ste A Stockton (95206) ***(P-4663)***
G3 Enterprises, Modesto *Also called United Sttes Intrmdal Svcs LLC* ***(P-7855)***
G3 Enterprises Inc (PA)......C......**209 341-7515**
502 E Whitmore Ave Modesto (95358) ***(P-7689)***
G3 Enterprises Inc......E......209 341-3441
1300 Camino Diablo Rd Byron (94514) ***(P-7836)***
G3 Enterprises Inc......E......209 341-4045
500 S Santa Rosa Ave Modesto (95354) ***(P-7837)***
G3 Enterprises Inc......E......209 341-8670
4995 Hillsdale Cir El Dorado Hills (95762) ***(P-7690)***
G3 Enterprises Inc......E......209 341-5265
2612 Crows Landing Rd Modesto (95358) ***(P-11862)***
G4s Secure Solutions (usa)......C......925 543-0008
1 Annabel Ln Ste 208 San Ramon (94583) ***(P-14060)***
G4s Tchnology Holdings USA Inc......B......510 633-1300
3073 Teagarden St San Leandro (94577) ***(P-14061)***
Gachina Landscape MGT Inc......B......650 853-0400
1130 Obrien Dr Menlo Park (94025) ***(P-416)***
Gaddis Nursery Inc......E......707 542-2202
3050 Piner Rd Santa Rosa (95401) ***(P-123)***
Gaelco Leasing Inc (PA)......E......**707 678-4404**
8656 Sparling Ln Dixon (95620) ***(P-9887)***
Gaffar Enterprise Inc......E......510 834-9880
1901 3rd Ave Oakland (94606) ***(P-16234)***
Gahvejian Enterprises Inc......E......559 834-5956
2004 S Temperance Ave Fowler (93625) ***(P-9213)***
Gainsight Inc......B......888 623-8562
350 Bay St Ste 100 San Francisco (94133) ***(P-12469)***
Gala Therapeutics Inc (PA)......C......**628 800-1154**
1531 Industrial Rd San Carlos (94070) ***(P-6974)***
Galante Brothers Gen Engrg Inc......D......408 291-0100
291 Barnard Ave San Jose (95125) ***(P-1043)***
Galaxy Desserts......C......510 439-3160
1100 Marina Way S Ste D Richmond (94804) ***(P-2386)***
Galaxy Medical Inc......E......510 847-5189
1531 Industrial Rd San Carlos (94070) ***(P-6975)***
Galaxy Patterson Road LLC......D......209 863-9012
2525 Patterson Rd Riverbank (95367) ***(P-10389)***
Galena Equipment Rental LLC......D......510 638-8100
10700 Bigge St San Leandro (94577) ***(P-12021)***
Galil Motion Control Inc......E......800 377-6329
270 Technology Way Rocklin (95765) ***(P-6721)***
Galileo Learning LLC (PA)......E......**510 595-7293**
1021 3rd St Oakland (94607) ***(P-11602)***
Galindo Instltion Mvg Svcs In......F......415 861-4230
2901 Mariposa St Ste 3 San Francisco (94110) ***(P-3325)***
Gallagher Inc......E......530 414-0267
11198 Trails End Ct Ste 3 Truckee (96161) ***(P-641)***
Gallagher & Burk, Dublin *Also called Oliver De Silva Inc* ***(P-580)***
Gallagher & Lindsey Inc (PA)......E......**510 521-8181**
2424 Central Ave Alameda (94501) ***(P-10556)***
Gallagher Bassett Services Inc......E......916 929-7581
1451 River Park Dr # 220 Sacramento (95815) ***(P-10284)***
Gallagher Construction, Truckee *Also called Gallagher Inc* ***(P-641)***
Gallagher Properties Inc (PA)......E......**510 261-0466**
344 High St Oakland (94601) ***(P-1960)***
Galleria Park Associates LLC......D......415 781-3060
191 Sutter St San Francisco (94104) ***(P-11111)***
Galleria Park Hotel, San Francisco *Also called Galleria Park Associates LLC* ***(P-11111)***
Galli Produce Company......D......408 436-6100
1650 Old Bayshore Hwy San Jose (95112) ***(P-9407)***
Gallien Technology Inc (PA)......D......**209 234-7300**
2234 Industrial Dr Stockton (95206) ***(P-5758)***
Galliien Krueger, Stockton *Also called Gallien Technology Inc* ***(P-5758)***
Gallo Cattle Co A Ltd Partnr......B......209 394-7984
10561 State Highway 140 Atwater (95301) ***(P-213)***
GALLO CENTER FOR THE ARTS, Modesto *Also called Central Vly Ctr For Arts Inc* ***(P-14844)***
Gallo Glass Company (HQ)......A......**209 341-3710**
605 S Santa Cruz Ave Modesto (95354) ***(P-4366)***
Gallo Global Nutrition LLC......C......209 394-7984
10561 Highway 140 Atwater (95301) ***(P-2148)***
Gallo Sales Company Inc (HQ)......C......**510 476-5000**
30825 Wiegman Rd Hayward (94544) ***(P-2591)***

Galloway Lucchese Everson ....E....925 930-9090
2300 Contra Costa Blvd Walnut Creek (94596) ***(P-17270)***
Galt Herald, Galt *Also called Herburger Publications Inc* ***(P-3445)***
Galt Steel Foundry, Lodi *Also called Lodi Iron Works Inc* ***(P-4548)***
Gambrel Companies Inc ....F....209 274-0150
6780 Martin Ln Ione (95640) ***(P-4483)***
Gameplay Inc ....E....415 617-1550
50 California St Ste 1500 San Francisco (94111) ***(P-15037)***
Gamus LLC ....E....408 441-0170
3286 Victor St Santa Clara (95054) ***(P-9660)***
Gamut Smart Media From Cox LLC ....E....650 392-6238
611 Gateway Blvd South San Francisco (94080) ***(P-8077)***
Ganda, San Anselmo *Also called Kleinfelder Inc* ***(P-18748)***
Garabedian Bros Inc (PA) ....**E....559 268-5014**
2543 S Orange Ave Fresno (93725) ***(P-5529)***
Garage Cabinet Warehouse Inc (PA) ....**E....916 638-0123**
2700 Merc Dr Ste 800 Rancho Cordova (95742) ***(P-1738)***
Garage Champs, Sacramento *Also called Hironaka Promotions LLC* ***(P-3736)***
Garage Door Specialists, West Sacramento *Also called Singley Enterprises* ***(P-1759)***
Garage Doors, Brentwood *Also called Nor-Cal Overhead Inc* ***(P-4706)***
Garage Doors Incorporated ....E....408 293-7443
147 Martha St San Jose (95112) ***(P-3133)***
Garcia Pallet, Fresno *Also called Garcias Pallets Inc* ***(P-3223)***
Garcias Pallets Inc ....E....559 485-8182
4125 S Golden State Blvd Fresno (93725) ***(P-3223)***
Garda CL West Inc ....E....707 591-0282
1650 Northpoint Pkwy B Santa Rosa (95407) ***(P-14062)***
Garda CL West Inc ....E....650 617-4548
1320 Willow Rd Menlo Park (94025) ***(P-14063)***
Gardelle Cnstr & Ldscp Inc ....E....925 680-6425
2625 Sinclair Ave Concord (94519) ***(P-463)***
Garden City Inc ....A....408 244-3333
1887 Matrix Blvd San Jose (95110) ***(P-11112)***
Garden City Casino & Rest, San Jose *Also called Garden City Inc* ***(P-11112)***
Garden City Construction Inc ....E....408 289-8807
1010 S 1st St San Jose (95110) ***(P-875)***
GARDEN CITY HEALTHCARE CENTER, Modesto *Also called Fig Holdings LLC* ***(P-16003)***
Garden Highway, Rancho Cordova *Also called Renaissance Food Group LLC* ***(P-2937)***
Garden Plus Pest Control, Pleasanton *Also called McCauley Brothers Inc* ***(P-11903)***
Gardeners Guild Inc ....C....415 457-0400
2780 Goodrick Ave Richmond (94801) ***(P-464)***
Gardenworks Inc ....D....707 857-2050
20325 Geyserville Ave Geyserville (95441) ***(P-465)***
Gardner Family Hlth Netwrk Inc ....C....408 254-5197
3030 Alum Rock Ave San Jose (95127) ***(P-15410)***
Gardner Family Hlth Netwrk Inc (PA) ....**E....408 457-7100**
160 E Virginia St Ste 100 San Jose (95112) ***(P-15411)***
Gardner Family Hlth Netwrk Inc ....C....408 457-7100
1621 Gold St Alviso (95002) ***(P-15412)***
Gardner Family Ltd Partnership ....E....559 675-8149
300 Commerce Dr Madera (93637) ***(P-4616)***
GARDNER HEALTH SERVICES, San Jose *Also called Gardner Family Hlth Netwrk Inc* ***(P-15411)***
Garfield Nursing Home Inc ....C....510 582-7676
1100 Marina Village Pkwy # 100 Alameda (94501) ***(P-16011)***
Garner Products Inc ....F....916 784-0200
10620 Industrial Ave # 100 Roseville (95678) ***(P-6668)***
Garnett Sign Studio, Fremont *Also called Garnett Signs LLC* ***(P-7230)***
Garnett Signs LLC ....F....650 871-9518
48531 Warm Springs Blvd # 412 Fremont (94539) ***(P-7230)***
Garratt-Callahan Company (PA) ....**D....650 697-5811**
50 Ingold Rd Burlingame (94010) ***(P-4160)***
Garton Tractor Inc (PA) ....**D....209 632-3931**
2400 N Golden State Blvd Turlock (95382) ***(P-9038)***
Gary Beebe Industries Inc ....E....916 645-6073
500 Wise Rd Lincoln (95648) ***(P-7468)***
Gary D Nelson Associates Inc (PA) ....**E....707 935-6113**
19080 Lomita Ave Sonoma (95476) ***(P-12091)***
Gary Doupnik Manufacturing Inc ....E....916 652-9291
3237 Rippey Rd Loomis (95650) ***(P-3250)***
Gary M Alegre MD ....E....209 946-7162
2488 N California St Stockton (95204) ***(P-15413)***
Gary McDonald Development Co ....E....559 436-1700
11326 N Glencastle Way Fresno (93730) ***(P-642)***
Gas Transmission Systems Inc ....E....925 478-8530
575 Lennon Ln Ste 250 Walnut Creek (94598) ***(P-18715)***
Gas Transmission Systems Inc (HQ) ....**D....530 893-6711**
130 Amber Grove Dr # 134 Chico (95973) ***(P-18716)***
Gasna 10p LLC ....E....775 562-4104
50 California St Ste 820 San Francisco (94111) ***(P-8097)***
Gasna 36p LLC ....E....775 562-4104
50 California St Ste 820 San Francisco (94111) ***(P-8098)***
Gasna 38p LLC ....E....775 562-4104
50 California St Ste 820 San Francisco (94111) ***(P-8099)***
Gasna 39p LLC ....E....415 230-5601
50 California St Ste 820 San Francisco (94111) ***(P-8100)***
Gasna 44p LLC ....E....415 230-5601
50 California St Ste 820 San Francisco (94111) ***(P-8101)***
Gasna 45p LLC ....E....415 230-5601
50 California St Ste 820 San Francisco (94111) ***(P-8102)***
Gasna 57p LLC ....E....415 230-5601
50 California St Ste 820 San Francisco (94111) ***(P-8103)***
Gasna 60p LLC ....E....415 230-5601
50 California St Ste 820 San Francisco (94111) ***(P-8104)***
Gasna 61p LLC ....E....415 230-5601
50 California St Ste 820 San Francisco (94111) ***(P-8105)***
Gasna 65p LLC ....E....775 562-4104
50 California St Ste 820 San Francisco (94111) ***(P-8106)***
Gasna 69p LLC ....E....415 230-5601
50 California St Ste 820 San Francisco (94111) ***(P-8107)***
Gasna 75p LLC ....E....775 562-4104
50 California St Ste 820 San Francisco (94111) ***(P-8108)***
Gasna 76p LLC ....E....775 562-4104
50 California St Ste 820 San Francisco (94111) ***(P-8109)***
Gasna 78p LLC ....E....415 230-5601
50 California St Ste 820 San Francisco (94111) ***(P-8110)***
Gasna 79p LLC ....E....415 230-5601
50 California St Ste 820 San Francisco (94111) ***(P-8111)***
Gasna 81p LLC ....E....775 562-4104
50 California St Ste 820 San Francisco (94111) ***(P-8112)***
Gastroenterology Division ....D....415 206-8823
1001 Potrero Ave Ste 1e21 San Francisco (94110) ***(P-15414)***
Gat - Arln Ground Support Inc ....B....916 923-2349
6701 Lindbergh Dr Sacramento (95837) ***(P-7773)***
Gatan Inc (HQ) ....**E....925 463-0200**
5794 W Las Positas Blvd Pleasanton (94588) ***(P-18717)***
Gatan International Inc ....E....925 463-0200
5794a W Las Positas Blvd Pleasanton (94588) ***(P-6832)***
Gate Five Group LLC ....E....415 339-9500
200 Gate 5 Rd Ste 116 Sausalito (94965) ***(P-8512)***
Gate-Or-Door Inc ....F....209 751-4881
14811 Leroy Ave Ripon (95366) ***(P-13184)***
Gatehouse Media LLC ....E....707 964-5642
617 S State St Ukiah (95482) ***(P-3438)***
Gatehouse Media LLC ....E....530 842-5777
309 S Broadway St Yreka (96097) ***(P-3439)***
Gatehouse Media LLC ....E....530 891-1234
400 E Park Ave Chico (95928) ***(P-3440)***
Gates, David L & Associates, Walnut Creek *Also called David L Gates & Associates Inc* ***(P-411)***
Gateway Books, Watsonville *Also called Hanuman Fellowship* ***(P-18429)***
Gateway Financial Advisors Inc (PA) ....**D....925 999-8699**
4101 Crw Cnyn Pl 100 San Ramon (94583) ***(P-19519)***
Gateway Landscape Cnstr Inc ....D....925 875-0000
6735 Sierra Ct Ste A Dublin (94568) ***(P-466)***
Gateway Limousine, Burlingame *Also called Amato Industries Incorporated* ***(P-7367)***
Gateway Precision Inc ....F....408 855-8849
480 Vista Way Milpitas (95035) ***(P-5530)***
Gateway Residential Programs ....E....916 782-1111
1780 Vernon St Ste 1&5 Roseville (95678) ***(P-17588)***
Gator Bio Inc ....D....650 800-7651
2454 Embarcadero Way Palo Alto (94303) ***(P-19160)***
Gatsby Inc ....E....650 468-0587
2055 Center St Apt 311 Berkeley (94704) ***(P-12470)***
Gauss Surgical Inc ....E....650 949-4153
4085 Campbell Ave Menlo Park (94025) ***(P-6976)***
Gavin Atwood Coombs (PA) ....**D....415 292-2384**
1400 Van Ness Ave San Francisco (94109) ***(P-10557)***
Gaw Van Male Smith Myers ....D....707 425-1250
1411 Oliver Rd Ste 300 Fairfield (94534) ***(P-17271)***
Gayner Engineers ....E....415 474-9500
1133 Post St San Francisco (94109) ***(P-18718)***
Gazzalis Supermarket Inc ....E....510 569-8159
7000 Bancroft Ave Oakland (94605) ***(P-9408)***
Gb Sport Sf LLC ....E....415 863-6171
200 Potrero Ave San Francisco (94103) ***(P-3017)***
Gbk Corporation (PA) ....**E....530 241-2337**
2245 Eureka Way Redding (96001) ***(P-11649)***
GBS Pest Control, San Mateo *Also called Genesis Building Services Inc* ***(P-11957)***
GBT, South San Francisco *Also called Global Blood Therapeutics Inc* ***(P-3919)***
Gc Products Inc ....E....916 645-3870
601 7th St Lincoln (95648) ***(P-4434)***
Gca Law Partners LLP ....E....650 428-3900
2570 W El Cmino Real Ste Mountain View (94040) ***(P-17272)***
Gcc, Santa Rosa *Also called Ghilotti Construction Co Inc* ***(P-1164)***
Gci Inc ....E....415 978-2790
875 Battery St Fl 1 San Francisco (94111) ***(P-876)***
GCI General Contractors ....D....415 978-2790
875 Battery St Fl 1 San Francisco (94111) ***(P-2033)***
Gcl Solar Energy Inc ....D....415 362-2601
1 Market Er 00 Steuart Tow San Francisco (94105) ***(P-1270)***
Gcm Holding Corporation ....B....510 475-0404
1350 Atlantic St Union City (94587) ***(P-10735)***
Gcm Medical & Oem Inc (PA) ....**D....510 475-0404**
1350 Atlantic St Union City (94587) ***(P-4764)***
Gco Inc (PA) ....**E....510 786-3333**
27750 Industrial Blvd Hayward (94545) ***(P-8997)***
Gco Inc ....E....707 584-3333
4130 S Moorland Ave Santa Rosa (95407) ***(P-9118)***
GCR Tires & Service 853, Martinez *Also called Bridgestone Americas* ***(P-14550)***
Gct Semiconductor Inc (PA) ....**E....408 434-6040**
2121 Ringwood Ave Ste A San Jose (95131) ***(P-6125)***
Gcu Trucking Inc ....D....209 845-2117
7819 Crane Rd Oakdale (95361) ***(P-7544)***
GD Long Electric Company ....E....707 252-3512
450 Technology Way NAPA (94558) ***(P-1507)***
GD Nielson Construction Inc ....D....707 253-8774
147 Camino Oruga NAPA (94558) ***(P-1102)***
Gdas-Lincoln Inc ....E....916 645-8961
1501 Aviation Blvd Lincoln (95648) ***(P-6610)***
Gdc, San Jose *Also called Dale Grove Corporation* ***(P-5129)***
Gdca Inc ....E....925 456-9900
1799 Portola Ave Ste 1 Livermore (94551) ***(P-5370)***
Gdm Electronic & Medical, San Jose *Also called G D M Electronic Assembly Inc* ***(P-5715)***
Gdsa-Lincoln Inc (PA) ....**D....916 645-8961**
1501 Aviation Blvd Lincoln (95648) ***(P-14699)***
Gdsi, San Jose *Also called Grinding & Dicing Services Inc* ***(P-6134)***

ALPHABETIC

GE Digital LLC ALPHABETIC SECTION

GE Digital LLC (HQ)...B...925 242-6200
2623 Camino Ramon San Ramon (94583) **(P-13185)**
GE Digital LLC...E...925 242-6200
2700 Camino Ramon San Ramon (94583) **(P-13186)**
GE Vallecitos Nuclear Center, Sunol *Also called Ge-Hitachi Nuclear Energy* **(P-3788)**
GE Ventures Inc...F...650 233-3900
3000 Sand Hill Rd 2-160 Menlo Park (94025) **(P-6977)**
Ge-Hitachi Nuclear Energy...D...925 862-4382
6705 Vallecitos Rd Sunol (94586) **(P-3788)**
Gea Farm Technologies Inc...E...559 497-5074
2717 S 4th St Fresno (93725) **(P-4074)**
Geary Darling Lessee Inc...C...415 292-0100
501 Geary St San Francisco (94102) **(P-11113)**
Gefen LLC...E...818 772-9100
1800 S Mcdowell Blvd Ext Petaluma (94954) **(P-6523)**
Geico General Insurance Co...B...916 923-5050
5211 Madison Ave Sacramento (95841) **(P-10285)**
Geiger Manufacturing Inc...F...209 464-7746
1110 E Scotts Ave Stockton (95205) **(P-5531)**
Geil Enterprises Inc...A...559 495-3000
1945 N Helm Ave Ste 102 Fresno (93727) **(P-14064)**
Gekkeikan Sake USAinC...E...916 985-3111
1136 Sibley St Folsom (95630) **(P-2592)**
Gel Pak LLC...D...510 576-2220
31398 Huntwood Ave Hayward (94544) **(P-11863)**
Gelateria Naia, Hercules *Also called Naia Inc* **(P-2181)**
Gelfland Partners Architects...E...415 346-4040
165 10th St Ste 100 San Francisco (94103) **(P-18886)**
Gelston, Willis L MD, San Leandro *Also called Family Med Group San Leandro* **(P-15400)**
Gemperle Enterprises...D...209 667-2651
10218 Lander Ave Turlock (95380) **(P-230)**
Gemperle Farms, Turlock *Also called Gemperle Enterprises* **(P-230)**
Gemtech Sales Corp...E...408 432-9900
2146 Bering Dr San Jose (95131) **(P-4629)**
Genelabs Technologies Inc (HQ)...D...415 297-2901
505 Penobscot Dr Redwood City (94063) **(P-3904)**
Genencor International, Palo Alto *Also called Danisco US Inc* **(P-4020)**
Genentech Inc...E...707 454-1000
1000 New Horizons Way Vacaville (95688) **(P-3905)**
Genentech Inc...C...650 225-2791
530 Forbes Blvd South San Francisco (94080) **(P-3906)**
Genentech Inc (HQ)...A...650 225-1000
1 Dna Way South San Francisco (94080) **(P-3907)**
Genentech Inc...C...408 963-8759
465 E Grand Ave Ms432 South San Francisco (94080) **(P-3908)**
Genentech Inc...C...650 216-2900
550 Broadway St Redwood City (94063) **(P-3909)**
Genentech Inc...C...650 225-3214
431 Grandview Dr Bldg 2 South San Francisco (94080) **(P-3910)**
Genentech Inc...C...650 225-1000
1 Dna Way South San Francisco (94080) **(P-3911)**
Genentech Inc...F...650 438-7573
220 Miramontes Ave Half Moon Bay (94019) **(P-3912)**
Genentech Usa Inc...A...650 225-1000
1 Dna Way South San Francisco (94080) **(P-3913)**
Gener8 LLC (PA)...C...650 940-9898
500 Mercury Dr Sunnyvale (94085) **(P-18719)**
General Auto Repair Inc...E...510 533-3333
4425 International Blvd Oakland (94601) **(P-8452)**
General Coatings, Fresno *Also called Walton Industries Inc* **(P-4114)**
General Coatings Corporation...D...559 495-4004
1220 E North Ave Fresno (93725) **(P-1413)**
General Dynamics Mission...B...408 908-7300
2688 Orchard Pkwy San Jose (95134) **(P-5887)**
General Dynmics Ots Ncvlle Inc (HQ)...D...707 473-9200
511 Grove St Healdsburg (95448) **(P-6632)**
General Dynmics Ots Vrstron In...D...916 355-7700
950 Iron Point Rd Ste 110 Folsom (95630) **(P-6669)**
General Elec Assembly Inc...E...408 980-8819
1525 Atteberry Ln San Jose (95131) **(P-5935)**
General Foundry Service Corp...D...510 297-5040
1390 Business Center Pl San Leandro (94577) **(P-4584)**
General Grinding Inc...E...510 261-5557
801 51st Ave Oakland (94601) **(P-4907)**
General Internal Medicine, San Francisco *Also called University Cal San Francisco* **(P-15761)**
General Lgstics Systems US Inc...C...800 322-5555
4601 Malat St Oakland (94601) **(P-7648)**
General Lgstics Systems US Inc...C...415 492-1112
760 Cabin Dr Mill Valley (94941) **(P-7649)**
General Mills Inc...E...209 334-7061
2000 W Turner Rd Lodi (95242) **(P-2314)**
General Mortgage Capital Corp (PA)...D...650 340-7800
1350 Bayshore Hwy Ste 740 Burlingame (94010) **(P-9906)**
General Motors LLC...E...408 529-6794
955 Benecia Ave Sunnyvale (94085) **(P-12471)**
General Petroleum Corporation...D...209 537-1056
237 E Whitmore Ave Modesto (95358) **(P-9524)**
General Plumbing Supply Co Inc (PA)...E...925 939-4622
1530 San Luis Rd Walnut Creek (94597) **(P-8998)**
General Pool & Spa Supply Inc (PA)...D...916 853-2401
11285 Sunco Dr Rancho Cordova (95742) **(P-9156)**
General Prod A Cal Ltd Partnr (PA)...C...916 441-6431
1330 N B St Sacramento (95811) **(P-9409)**
General Radar Corp...E...626 319-5827
616 Mountain View Ave Belmont (94002) **(P-6670)**
General RE Corporation...E...415 781-1700
555 California St # 3400 San Francisco (94104) **(P-10169)**
General Services Cal Dept...E...916 376-5330
707 3rd St Fl 1 West Sacramento (95605) **(P-12092)**
General Services Cal Dept...E...916 322-3880
625 Q St Sacramento (95811) **(P-877)**
General Trailer Inc...E...209 948-6090
2150 E Fremont St Stockton (95205) **(P-14610)**
Generate Capital Inc...D...415 360-3063
560 Davis St Ste 250 San Francisco (94111) **(P-10847)**
Generation Clovis LLC...C...559 297-4900
1650 Shaw Ave Clovis (93611) **(P-18119)**
Genesis Building Services Inc...D...650 375-5935
916 S Claremont St San Mateo (94402) **(P-11957)**
Genesis Healthcare LLC...C...209 478-6488
9107 Davis Rd Stockton (95209) **(P-16012)**
Genesis Logistics Inc...E...510 476-0790
4013 Whipple Rd Union City (94587) **(P-7691)**
Genesys Cloud Services Inc (HQ)...B...650 466-1100
2001 Junipero Serra Blvd Daly City (94014) **(P-13187)**
Genesys Logic America Inc...E...408 435-8899
2880 Zanker Rd Ste 105 San Jose (95134) **(P-6126)**
Genesys Telecom Labs, Daly City *Also called Genesys Cloud Services Inc* **(P-13187)**
Genetic Dsase Screning Program, Richmond *Also called California Dept of Pub Hlth* **(P-15307)**
Gengo Inc...E...650 585-4390
204 E 2nd Ave 736 San Mateo (94401) **(P-14282)**
Genia Technologies Inc...E...650 300-5970
2841 Scott Blvd Santa Clara (95050) **(P-19063)**
Genium Inc...C...415 935-3593
2955 Campus Dr Ste 110 San Mateo (94403) **(P-12472)**
Genmark Automation (HQ)...D...510 897-3400
46723 Lakeview Blvd Fremont (94538) **(P-9068)**
Genmark Diagnostics Inc (HQ)...A...650 225-1000
1 Dna Way South San Francisco (94080) **(P-6978)**
Genomic Health Inc (HQ)...A...650 556-9300
301 Penobscot Dr Redwood City (94063) **(P-16781)**
Genpact LLC...E...203 690-9308
3300 Hillview Ave Palo Alto (94304) **(P-19783)**
Gensler Asscts/Ntrnational Ltd (HQ)...B...415 433-3700
45 Fremont St Ste 1500 San Francisco (94105) **(P-18887)**
Genstar Capital LLC (PA)...E...415 834-2350
4 Embarcadero Ctr # 1900 San Francisco (94111) **(P-9972)**
Genstar Capital Partners Ix LP...E...415 834-2350
4 Embarcadero Ctr # 1900 San Francisco (94111) **(P-10762)**
Gentec Manufacturing Inc...F...408 432-6220
2241 Ringwood Ave San Jose (95131) **(P-5532)**
Gentiva Health Services Inc...D...707 545-7114
1260 N Dutton Ave Ste 150 Santa Rosa (95401) **(P-16885)**
Gentle Dental...A...650 341-8008
853 Middlefield Rd Ste 1 Palo Alto (94301) **(P-15835)**
Geo M Martin Company (PA)...D...510 652-2200
1250 67th St Emeryville (94608) **(P-5118)**
Geo Semiconductor Inc (PA)...D...408 638-0400
101 Metro Dr Ste 620 San Jose (95110) **(P-6127)**
Geographic Expeditions Inc...D...415 922-0448
1016 Lincoln Blvd Ste 316 San Francisco (94129) **(P-7797)**
Geologic Associates Inc...D...530 272-2448
143 Spring Hill Dr Ste E Grass Valley (95945) **(P-18720)**
Geometrics Inc...D...408 428-4244
2190 Fortune Dr San Jose (95131) **(P-6903)**
George Bianchi Cnstr Inc...E...408 453-3037
775a Mabury Rd San Jose (95133) **(P-1647)**
George Chiala Farms Inc...C...408 778-0562
15500 Hill Rd Morgan Hill (95037) **(P-31)**
George E Masker Inc...D...510 568-1206
7699 Edgewater Dr Oakland (94621) **(P-1414)**
George Family Enterprises...D...415 884-0399
32 Pamaron Way Ste A Novato (94949) **(P-1676)**
George Hills Company Inc...C...916 859-4800
3017 Gold Canal Dr 400 Rancho Cordova (95670) **(P-10286)**
George Kishida Inc...D...209 368-0603
1725 Ackerman Dr Lodi (95240) **(P-7469)**
George M Robinson & Co (PA)...E...510 632-7017
1461 Atteberry Ln San Jose (95131) **(P-1271)**
George Reed Inc (HQ)...E...877 823-2305
140 Empire Ave Modesto (95354) **(P-1872)**
Georgetown Pre-Cast Inc...F...530 333-4404
2420 Georgia Slide Rd Georgetown (95634) **(P-4435)**
Geovera Specialty Insurance Co...D...707 863-3700
1455 Oliver Rd Fairfield (94534) **(P-10287)**
Gerawan Enterprises, Fresno *Also called Gerawan Ranches* **(P-101)**
Gerawan Farming LLC...C...559 638-9281
1467 E Dinuba Ave Reedley (93654) **(P-100)**
Gerawan Farming Partners Inc...D...559 787-8780
7108 N Fresno St Ste 450 Fresno (93720) **(P-254)**
Gerawan Ranches (PA)...E...559 787-8780
7108 N Fresno St Ste 450 Fresno (93720) **(P-101)**
Gerawan Ranches...C...559 787-8780
10045 W Lincoln Ave Fresno (93706) **(P-102)**
Gerlinger Fndry Mch Works Inc (PA)...E...530 243-1053
1527 Sacramento St Redding (96001) **(P-4664)**
Gerlinger Fndry Mch Works Inc...F...530 243-1053
1510 Tanforan Ave Woodland (95776) **(P-8816)**
Gerlinger Steel & Supply Co, Woodland *Also called Gerlinger Fndry Mch Works Inc* **(P-8816)**
Germains Seed Technology Inc...E...408 848-8120
8333 Swanston Ln Gilroy (95020) **(P-9599)**
German Motors Corporation (PA)...C...415 590-3773
1675 Howard St San Francisco (94103) **(P-14525)**
Geron Corporation (PA)...D...650 473-7700
919 E Hillsdale Blvd # 250 Foster City (94404) **(P-3914)**
Gerson Bakar & Associates, Palo Alto *Also called Oak Creek Apartments* **(P-10451)**

Get Fit Modesto, Modesto *Also called J&T Crenshaw Inc* ***(P-14954)***
Getaround Inc (PA)..........C.......**866 438-2768**
55 Green St Fl 4 San Francisco (94111) ***(P-14489)***
Getfeedback Inc..........D.......888 684-8821
1 Curiosity Way San Mateo (94403) ***(P-12473)***
Getinsured.com, Mountain View *Also called Vimo Inc* ***(P-19886)***
Getright Ventures Inc..........D.......510 402-4816
3675 Rocky Shore Ct Vallejo (94591) ***(P-9940)***
Gettler-Ryan Inc (PA)..........D.......**925 551-7555**
6805 Sierra Ct Ste G Dublin (94568) ***(P-2034)***
Gexpro, Livermore *Also called Rexel Usa Inc* ***(P-8874)***
Geyser Peak Winery..........E.......707 857-9463
1300 1st St Ste 368 NAPA (94559) ***(P-2593)***
Geysers Power Company LLC..........E.......707 431-6000
10350 Socrates Mine Rd Middletown (95461) ***(P-8113)***
Geyserville Inn, Geyserville *Also called Iav Inc* ***(P-11186)***
GF Carneros Tenant LLC..........E.......707 299-4900
4048 Sonoma Hwy NAPA (94559) ***(P-11681)***
Gfk Custom Research LLC..........D.......415 398-2812
360 Pine St Fl 6 San Francisco (94104) ***(P-19161)***
Ggc Administration LLC..........A.......415 983-2700
1 Embarcadero Ctr Fl 39 San Francisco (94111) ***(P-10736)***
GGF Marble & Supply Inc..........E.......925 676-8385
1375 Franquette Ave Ste F Concord (94520) ***(P-4517)***
Ggrc, San Rafael *Also called Golden Gate Regional Ctr Inc* ***(P-17591)***
Gh Foods Ca LLC (HQ)..........B.......**916 844-1140**
8425 Carbide Ct Sacramento (95828) ***(P-2895)***
Ghangor Cloud Inc..........D.......408 713-3303
2001 Gateway Pl Ste 710w San Jose (95110) ***(P-6524)***
Ghc of Sunnyvale LLC..........C.......408 738-4880
797 E Fremont Ave Sunnyvale (94087) ***(P-16235)***
Ghd Inc..........E.......408 451-9615
1735 N 1st St Ste 301 San Jose (95112) ***(P-18721)***
Ghilotti Bros Inc..........B.......415 454-7011
525 Jacoby St San Rafael (94901) ***(P-1961)***
Ghilotti Brothers Cnstr Inc..........D.......415 454-7011
525 Jacoby St San Rafael (94901) ***(P-643)***
Ghilotti Construction Co Inc (PA)..........B.......**707 585-1221**
246 Ghillotti Ave Santa Rosa (95407) ***(P-1164)***
Ghirardelli Chocolate Co (HQ)..........B.......**510 483-6970**
1111 139th Ave San Leandro (94578) ***(P-2437)***
Ghiringhlli Spcialty Foods Inc..........C.......707 561-7670
101 Benicia Rd Vallejo (94590) ***(P-2896)***
Gl GP IV LLC (PA)..........E.......**415 688-4800**
188 The Embarcadero # 700 San Francisco (94105) ***(P-9973)***
Gl Partners, San Francisco *Also called Global Innovation Partners LLC* ***(P-14284)***
Gl Partners, San Francisco *Also called Gl GP IV LLC* ***(P-9973)***
Giampolini & Co..........C.......415 673-1236
1482 67th St Emeryville (94608) ***(P-1415)***
Giampolini/Courtney, Emeryville *Also called Giampolini & Co* ***(P-1415)***
Gianelli & Associates..........E.......209 521-6260
1014 16th St Modesto (95354) ***(P-17273)***
Giannini Garden Ornaments Inc..........E.......650 873-4493
225 Shaw Rd South San Francisco (94080) ***(P-4436)***
Giant Creative Strategy Llc..........C.......415 655-5200
1700 Montgomery St # 485 San Francisco (94111) ***(P-11755)***
Giant Horse Printing Inc..........F.......650 875-7137
1336 San Mateo Ave South San Francisco (94080) ***(P-3652)***
Gibbs Plastic & Rubber LLC..........F.......707 746-7300
3959 Teal Ct Benicia (94510) ***(P-4215)***
Gibson Printing & Pubg Inc..........E.......707 745-0733
820 1st St Benicia (94510) ***(P-3441)***
Gibson Wine Company..........E.......559 875-2505
1720 Academy Ave Sanger (93657) ***(P-2594)***
Gic Real Estate Inc..........E.......415 229-1800
1 Bush St Ste 1100 San Francisco (94104) ***(P-10820)***
Gic Real Estate Inc (HQ)..........D.......**415 229-1800**
1 Bush St Ste 1100 San Francisco (94104) ***(P-10558)***
Gidel & Kocal Cnstr Co Inc..........E.......408 370-0280
574 Division St Campbell (95008) ***(P-878)***
Giga Omni Media Inc..........D.......415 974-6355
1613a Lyon St San Francisco (94115) ***(P-14154)***
Giga-Tronics Incorporated (PA)..........F.......**925 328-4650**
5990 Gleason Dr Dublin (94568) ***(P-6757)***
Gigamat Technologies Inc..........F.......510 770-8008
47269 Fremont Blvd Fremont (94538) ***(P-6128)***
Gigamon Inc (HQ)..........A.......**408 831-4000**
3300 Olcott St Santa Clara (95054) ***(P-5371)***
Gigpeak Inc (HQ)..........C.......**408 546-3316**
6024 Silver Creek Vly Rd San Jose (95138) ***(P-6129)***
Gigster Inc..........C.......941 888-4447
301 Howard St Ste 1800 San Francisco (94105) ***(P-12474)***
Gilardi & Co LLC..........D.......415 798-5900
1 Mcinnis Pkwy San Rafael (94903) ***(P-19340)***
Gilbane Aecom JV..........D.......925 946-3100
1655 Grant St Fl 12 Concord (94520) ***(P-19341)***
Gilbane Federal (HQ)..........C.......**925 946-3100**
1655 Grant St Ste 1200 Concord (94520) ***(P-18722)***
Gilbert Associates Inc..........E.......916 646-6464
2880 Gateway Oaks Dr # 100 Sacramento (95833) ***(P-18959)***
Gilbert Smolin MD Inc..........E.......650 697-3200
1720 El Camino Real Burlingame (94010) ***(P-15415)***
Gilbert Spray Coat Inc..........E.......408 988-0747
300 Laurelwood Rd Santa Clara (95054) ***(P-4934)***
Gilead Colorado Inc..........D.......650 574-3000
333 Lakeside Dr Foster City (94404) ***(P-3915)***
Gilead Palo Alto Inc (HQ)..........B.......**650 384-8500**
333 Lakeside Dr Foster City (94404) ***(P-3916)***
Gilead Sciences Inc (PA)..........B.......**650 574-3000**
333 Lakeside Dr Foster City (94404) ***(P-3917)***
Gill Grove Electric Company..........E.......510 451-2929
909 7th St Oakland (94607) ***(P-1508)***
Gillespies Carpet Center Inc..........E.......707 427-3773
360 Chadbourne Rd Fairfield (94534) ***(P-11653)***
Gillies Trucking Inc..........E.......209 948-6268
3931 Newton Rd Stockton (95205) ***(P-7470)***
Gillig LLC (HQ)..........A.......**510 264-5000**
451 Discovery Dr Livermore (94551) ***(P-6566)***
Gillson Trucking Inc..........C.......925 400-9094
1801 E Dr Mrtn Lther King Stockton (95205) ***(P-7545)***
Gilroy Buck GMC, Gilroy *Also called Gilroy Im Automotive LLC* ***(P-14566)***
Gilroy Dispatch..........F.......408 842-6400
6400 Monterey Rd Gilroy (95020) ***(P-3442)***
Gilroy Gardens Family Theme Pk..........C.......408 840-7100
3050 Hecker Pass Rd Gilroy (95020) ***(P-15042)***
Gilroy Health & Rehab Ctr, Gilroy *Also called Mariner Health Care Inc* ***(P-16046)***
Gilroy Health Care, Gilroy *Also called Covenant Care California LLC* ***(P-15971)***
Gilroy Im Automotive LLC..........E.......408 713-3200
6600 Automall Pkwy Gilroy (95020) ***(P-14566)***
Gilroy Motorcycle Center Inc..........E.......408 842-9955
7661 Monterey St Gilroy (95020) ***(P-6649)***
Gilton Rsrce Rcvery Trnsf Fclt (PA)..........D.......**209 527-3781**
755 S Yosemite Ave Oakdale (95361) ***(P-8333)***
Gilton Solid Waste MGT Inc..........C.......209 527-3781
755 S Yosemite Ave Oakdale (95361) ***(P-8334)***
Gilwin Company..........E.......209 522-9775
2354 Lapham Dr Modesto (95354) ***(P-4704)***
Gingerio Inc..........D.......408 455-0574
116 New Montgomery St # 5 San Francisco (94105) ***(P-12475)***
Gino Morena Enterprises LLC (PA)..........E.......**800 227-6905**
111 Starlite St South San Francisco (94080) ***(P-11682)***
Gino Morena Enterprises LLC..........B.......530 788-0053
Bldg 2434 Marysville (95903) ***(P-11698)***
Gino Rinaldi Inc..........D.......831 761-0195
51 Fremont St Royal Oaks (95076) ***(P-1715)***
Gino/Giuseppe Inc..........C.......209 358-0556
700 Enterprise Ct Ste A Atwater (95301) ***(P-1873)***
Ginsberg Holdco Inc..........B.......408 831-4000
3300 Olcott St Santa Clara (95054) ***(P-13188)***
Giorgios Restaurant Italiano..........E.......415 925-0808
99 Rock Rd Greenbrae (94904) ***(P-2199)***
Giovannetti Equipment Sales, Woodland *Also called Half Moon Fruit & Produce Co* ***(P-5)***
Girl Scouts Heart Central Cal..........C.......916 452-9181
6601 Elvas Ave Sacramento (95819) ***(P-18419)***
Girl Scouts Northern Cal..........E.......707 279-4689
1920 Westlake Dr Kelseyville (95451) ***(P-18420)***
Girl Scouts Northern Cal (PA)..........D.......**510 562-8470**
1650 Harbor Bay Pkwy # 100 Alameda (94502) ***(P-18421)***
Girl Scouts Northern Cal..........E.......408 287-4170
1310 S Bascom Ave San Jose (95128) ***(P-18422)***
Girl Scouts Northern Cal..........E.......707 544-5472
4825 Old Redwood Hwy Santa Rosa (95403) ***(P-18423)***
Girl Scouts of America, San Jose *Also called Girl Scouts Santa Clara County* ***(P-18424)***
Girl Scouts Santa Clara County (PA)..........E.......**408 287-4170**
1310 S Bascom Ave San Jose (95128) ***(P-18424)***
Gist Inc..........D.......530 644-8000
4385 Pleasant Valley Rd Placerville (95667) ***(P-7211)***
Gist Silversmiths, Placerville *Also called Gist Inc* ***(P-7211)***
Gitlab Inc (PA)..........F.......**415 829-2854**
268 Bush St 350 San Francisco (94104) ***(P-13189)***
Giustos Specialty Foods LLC (PA)..........E.......**650 873-6566**
344 Littlefield Ave South San Francisco (94080) ***(P-2311)***
GK Transport Inc..........E.......559 275-3628
2175 N Brawley Ave Fresno (93722) ***(P-7546)***
Gla Morris Construction Inc..........E.......530 448-1613
10330 Donner Pass Rd A Truckee (96161) ***(P-644)***
Glacier Foods Division, Sanger *Also called Dole Packaged Foods LLC* ***(P-2292)***
Glacier Ice Company, Elk Grove *Also called Glacier Valley Ice Company LP* ***(P-2860)***
Glacier Valley Ice Company LP (PA)..........E.......**916 394-2939**
8580 Laguna Station Rd Elk Grove (95758) ***(P-2860)***
GLad Entertainment Inc (PA)..........D.......**559 292-9000**
4055 N Chestnut Ave Fresno (93726) ***(P-15206)***
Glad Products Company (HQ)..........C.......**510 271-7000**
1221 Broadway Ste A Oakland (94612) ***(P-4230)***
Gladding McBean, Lincoln *Also called Pabco Clay Products LLC* ***(P-4399)***
Gladding McBean, Lincoln *Also called Pabco Building Products LLC* ***(P-4405)***
Gladiolus Holdings LLC..........E.......530 622-3400
1040 Marshall Way Placerville (95667) ***(P-16013)***
Gladly Software Inc..........D.......650 387-8485
60 29th St Ste 125 San Francisco (94110) ***(P-12476)***
Gladstone Foundation..........E.......415 734-2000
1650 Owens St San Francisco (94158) ***(P-18425)***
Glasforms Inc..........F.......408 297-9300
271 Barnard Ave San Jose (95125) ***(P-3803)***
Glaspy & Glaspy A Prof Corp..........E.......408 279-8844
100 Pringle Ave Ste 750 Walnut Creek (94596) ***(P-17274)***
Glass Lewis & Co LLC (HQ)..........D.......**415 678-4110**
255 California St # 1100 San Francisco (94111) ***(P-19162)***
Glass & Sash Inc (PA)..........E.......**415 456-2240**
425 Irwin St San Rafael (94901) ***(P-8644)***
Glass Fab Tempering Sv, Tracy *Also called Glassfab Tempering Svcs Inc* ***(P-19784)***
Glass House, The, San Jose *Also called Glasshouse Sj LLC* ***(P-15207)***
Glass Jar Inc..........F.......831 427-9946
125 Beach St Santa Cruz (95060) ***(P-2174)***
Glass Jar Inc (PA)..........D.......**831 227-2247**
913 Cedar St Santa Cruz (95060) ***(P-2175)***
Glassbeam Inc..........D.......408 740-4600
2033 Gateway Pl Ste 658 San Jose (95110) ***(P-12477)***

ALPHABETIC

Employee Codes: A=Over 500 employees, B=251-500
C=101-250, D=51-100, E=20-50 F=10-19
2022 Northern California Business
Directory and Buyers Guide
© Mergent Inc. 1-800-342-5647
973

Glassdoor Inc ALPHABETIC SECTION

Glassdoor Inc (HQ)....C....415 275-7411
50 Beale St Ste 1600 San Francisco (94105) *(P-12093)*

Glassfab Tempering Svcs Inc (PA)....D....209 229-1060
1448 Mariani Ct Tracy (95376) *(P-19784)*

Glasshouse Sj LLC....E....408 606-8148
84 W Santa Clara St # 10 San Jose (95113) *(P-15207)*

Glasslab Inc....E....415 244-5584
209 Redwood Shores Pkwy Redwood City (94065) *(P-13190)*

Glaxosmthkline Cnsmr Hlthcare....C....559 650-1550
2020 E Vine Ave Fresno (93706) *(P-3918)*

Glazier Steel Inc....D....510 471-5300
650 Sandoval Way Hayward (94544) *(P-4665)*

Glen Ellen Carneros Winery, Sonoma *Also called Diageo North America Inc (P-2549)*

Glenborough LLC (PA)....D....650 343-9300
400 S El Camino Real # 1100 San Mateo (94402) *(P-10559)*

Glenmoor Realty Inc....E....510 793-4030
5255 Mowry Ave Ste L Fremont (94538) *(P-10560)*

Glenn County Office Education....E....530 865-1145
676 E Walker St Fl 2 Orland (95963) *(P-17940)*

Glenn Medical Center Inc....D....530 934-4681
1133 W Sycamore St Willows (95988) *(P-16379)*

Glenn-Colusa Irrigation Dst (PA)....D....530 934-8881
344 E Laurel St Willows (95988) *(P-8412)*

Glenrock Group....E....408 323-9900
1000 Old Quarry Rd San Jose (95123) *(P-15094)*

Glesby Building Mtls Co Inc....E....510 639-9350
2015 W Avenue 140th San Leandro (94577) *(P-8546)*

Glesby Wholesale, San Leandro *Also called Glesby Building Mtls Co Inc (P-8546)*

Glf Integrated Power Inc (PA)....E....408 239-4326
4500 Great America Pkwy Santa Clara (95054) *(P-14283)*

Glide-Write, Milpitas *Also called Marburg Technology Inc (P-5397)*

Glint Inc....D....650 817-7240
1000 W Maude Ave Sunnyvale (94085) *(P-13716)*

Global Automation Inc (PA)....E....650 316-5900
1388 Terra Bella Ave Mountain View (94043) *(P-13900)*

Global Blood Therapeutics Inc (PA)....B....650 741-7700
181 Oyster Point Blvd South San Francisco (94080) *(P-3919)*

Global Blue Dvbe Inc....D....916 632-2583
4470 Yankee Hill Rd # 160 Rocklin (95677) *(P-13814)*

Global Building Services Inc....C....209 858-9501
17618 Murphy Pkwy Lathrop (95330) *(P-19902)*

Global Contract Manufacturing, Union City *Also called Gcm Medical & Oem Inc (P-4764)*

Global Defense Group LLC....E....530 510-5204
395 S State Highway 65 A-271 Lincoln (95648) *(P-14065)*

Global Diversified Inds Inc (PA)....E....559 665-5800
1200 Airport Dr Chowchilla (93610) *(P-3251)*

Global Diving & Salvage Inc....F....707 561-6810
1280 Terminal St West Sacramento (95691) *(P-566)*

Global Equipment Rental Co, Dixon *Also called Global Rental Co Inc (P-14469)*

Global Equipment Services, San Jose *Also called Kimball Electronics Ind Inc (P-5944)*

Global Foundries, Santa Clara *Also called Globalfoundries US Inc (P-5901)*

Global Fund For Women Inc....E....415 248-4800
800 Market St Fl 7 San Francisco (94102) *(P-18229)*

Global Grid For Learning Pbc (PA)....F....888 904-9773
1101 Marina Village Pkwy # 201 Alameda (94501) *(P-13191)*

Global Healthcare Services LLC....D....209 549-9875
400 12th St Ste 25 Modesto (95354) *(P-16886)*

Global Information Dist Inc....F....408 232-5500
2635 Zanker Rd San Jose (95134) *(P-7149)*

Global Infotech Corporation....A....408 567-0600
2890 Zanker Rd Ste 202 San Jose (95134) *(P-19785)*

Global Innovation Partners LLC....E....650 233-3600
188 The Embarcadero # 700 San Francisco (94105) *(P-14284)*

Global Meddata Inc (PA)....D....650 369-9734
3705 Haven Ave 124 Menlo Park (94025) *(P-17149)*

Global Modular Inc (HQ)....E....209 676-8029
1120 Commerce Ave Atwater (95301) *(P-3252)*

Global Motorsport Parts Inc....C....408 778-0500
15750 Vineyard Blvd # 100 Morgan Hill (95037) *(P-6650)*

Global Plating Inc....E....510 659-8764
44620 S Grimmer Blvd Fremont (94538) *(P-4908)*

Global Precision Manufacturing, Grass Valley *Also called Taylor Investments LLC (P-5188)*

Global Printing Sourcing & Dev, San Rafael *Also called Goff Investment Group LLC (P-3573)*

Global Rental Co Inc....C....707 693-2520
325 Industrial Way Dixon (95620) *(P-14469)*

Global Software Resources Inc (PA)....E....925 249-2200
4447 Stoneridge Dr Ste 1 Pleasanton (94588) *(P-13901)*

Global Specialties Direct, Oakland *Also called Global Steel Products Corp (P-3326)*

Global Steel Products Corp....E....510 652-2060
936 61st St Oakland (94608) *(P-3326)*

Global Technology Services Inc....E....408 333-9639
6120 Hellyer Ave Ste 100 San Jose (95138) *(P-13902)*

Global Testing Corporation....E....408 745-0718
225 Pamela Dr Apt 205 Mountain View (94040) *(P-6130)*

Global Touchpoints Inc....D....916 878-5954
3017 Douglas Blvd Ste 300 Roseville (95661) *(P-12478)*

Global Upside Inc (PA)....E....650 964-4820
4300 Stevens Creek Blvd # 270 San Jose (95129) *(P-9858)*

Global V R, Milpitas *Also called Virtual Technologies Inc (P-7315)*

Global Valley Networks Inc....E....209 892-4100
515 Keystone Blvd Patterson (95363) *(P-7955)*

Global Wine Group....E....209 340-8500
3750 E Woodbridge Rd Acampo (95220) *(P-2595)*

Globalfoundries Dresden....A....408 462-3900
1050 E Arques Ave Sunnyvale (94085) *(P-6131)*

Globalfoundries US Inc....D....408 462-3900
1278 Reamwood Ave Sunnyvale (94089) *(P-6132)*

Globalfoundries US Inc (HQ)....A....408 462-3900
2600 Great America Way Santa Clara (95054) *(P-5901)*

Globality Inc....E....650 352-8900
2555 Park Blvd Palo Alto (94306) *(P-19342)*

Globallogic Inc (HQ)....C....408 273-8900
1741 Tech Dr Ste 400 San Jose (95110) *(P-12479)*

Globalridge LLC....F....800 225-4345
865 Parallel Dr Lakeport (95453) *(P-3816)*

Globant LLC (HQ)....A....877 215-5230
875 Howard St Fl 3 San Francisco (94103) *(P-12480)*

GLOBE BUSINESS SERVICE'S, San Jose *Also called San Jose Mailing Inc (P-11841)*

Glocol Inc....E....650 224-2108
980 9th St Fl 16 Sacramento (95814) *(P-7334)*

Glodow Nead Communications LLC....E....415 394-6500
1700 Montgomery St # 203 San Francisco (94111) *(P-19686)*

Glodyne Technoserve Inc (PA)....A....408 340-5017
2700 Augustine Dr Ste 190 Santa Clara (95054) *(P-13597)*

Gloria Ferrer, Sonoma *Also called Freixenet Usa Inc (P-9578)*

Gloria Ferrer Winery, Sonoma *Also called Freixenet Sonoma Caves Inc (P-2588)*

Gloriann Farms Inc (PA)....C....209 834-0010
4598 S Tracy Blvd Ste 160 Tracy (95377) *(P-285)*

Glorystar Satellite Systems, Rocklin *Also called Satellite Av LLC (P-5866)*

Glovefit International Corp....F....559 243-1110
4705 N Sonora Ave Ste 108 Fresno (93722) *(P-4284)*

Glp....C....415 777-9696
2 Harrison St Ste 150 San Francisco (94105) *(P-17941)*

GLS US Freight Inc (PA)....D....209 823-2168
6750 Longe St Ste 100 Stockton (95206) *(P-7547)*

Glu Mobile Inc (PA)....B....415 800-6100
875 Howard St Ste 100 San Francisco (94103) *(P-13192)*

Glue Networks Group, Sacramento *Also called Gluware Inc (P-13598)*

Glumac International (PA)....E....415 398-7667
150 California St Fl 3 San Francisco (94111) *(P-18723)*

Gluware Inc (PA)....E....916 877-8224
2020 L St Ste 130 Sacramento (95811) *(P-13598)*

Glyntai Inc....F....650 386-6932
705 N Shoreline Blvd Mountain View (94043) *(P-13193)*

GM Associates Inc....D....510 430-0806
9824 Kitty Ln Oakland (94603) *(P-6430)*

Gmj Air Shuttle LLC....D....916 884-2001
5411 Luce Ave 201 McClellan (95652) *(P-7335)*

Gmp Manufacturing Inc....E....707 751-3942
1340 Treat Blvd Ste 350 Walnut Creek (94597) *(P-2162)*

Gmpc LLC....F....707 766-1702
2180 S Mcdwell Blvd Ext S Petaluma (94954) *(P-7231)*

Gmr - San Francisco, San Francisco *Also called Gmr Marketing LLC (P-19687)*

Gmr Marketing LLC....E....415 229-7733
600 California St Fl 7 San Francisco (94108) *(P-19687)*

Gmr Northern California LLC....E....925 294-9074
7150 Patterson Pass Rd G Livermore (94550) *(P-14750)*

Gmw Associates....F....650 802-8292
951 Industrial Rd Ste D San Carlos (94070) *(P-9069)*

Gmw Associates....E....650 802-8292
955 Industrial Rd San Carlos (94070) *(P-6671)*

GNA Industries Inc....E....559 276-0953
4761 W Jacquelyn Ave Fresno (93722) *(P-5679)*

GNB Corporation....D....916 233-3543
3200 Dwight Rd Ste 100 Elk Grove (95758) *(P-5074)*

GNB Vacuum Excellence Defined, Elk Grove *Also called GNB Corporation (P-5074)*

Gnekow Family Winery LLC....E....209 463-0697
17347 E Gawne Rd Stockton (95215) *(P-2596)*

Go Capital, Roseville *Also called Nations First Capital LLC (P-9888)*

Go Express LLC....E....559 274-0168
4067 W Shaw Ave Fresno (93722) *(P-7471)*

Go Risk Vision....F....925 271-8227
845 Stewart Dr Ste D Sunnyvale (94085) *(P-13194)*

Go West Holdings LLC....C....888 670-0080
795 Folsom St San Francisco (94107) *(P-14285)*

Goalsr Inc....F....650 453-5844
933 Berryessa Rd Ste 10 San Jose (95133) *(P-13195)*

Gobble Inc....C....650 847-1258
282 2nd St Ste 300 San Francisco (94105) *(P-2897)*

Gobig Inc....E....415 513-3029
3185 Kipling St Palo Alto (94306) *(P-13599)*

Gobp Holdings Inc....C....510 845-1999
2000 5th St Berkeley (94710) *(P-10848)*

Godfathers Exterminator Inc....E....831 338-4800
13350 W Park Ave Ste E Boulder Creek (95006) *(P-11899)*

Godfrey Dadich Partners LLC....E....415 217-2800
140 New Montgomery St # 7 San Francisco (94105) *(P-11756)*

Goebel Construction Inc....E....707 763-0088
227 Howard St Petaluma (94952) *(P-1044)*

Goff Investment Group LLC....E....415 456-2934
135 3rd St Ste 150 San Rafael (94901) *(P-3573)*

Gogreen Roofing Corporation (PA)....D....408 343-8495
3315 Woodward Ave Santa Clara (95054) *(P-1807)*

Gogrid LLC....C....415 869-7444
150 S 1st St Ste 101 San Jose (95113) *(P-7956)*

Goji Farm USA, Santa Rosa *Also called Fischl Tibor (P-9451)*

Gold & Sons Ready Mix, Ione *Also called Gambrel Companies Inc (P-4483)*

Gold Club Centerfolds, Rancho Cordova *Also called Gold Club Inc (P-14847)*

Gold Club Inc....E....916 442-3111
11363 Folsom Blvd Rancho Cordova (95742) *(P-14847)*

Gold Club, The, San Francisco *Also called Solid Gold Inc (P-14878)*

Gold Country Casino, Oroville *Also called Tyme Maidu Tribe-Berry Creek (P-11549)*

Gold Country Health Center Inc (PA)....C....530 621-1100
4301 Golden Center Dr Placerville (95667) *(P-16014)*

Gold River Mills LLC (PA)....E....530 661-1923
1620 E Kentucky Ave Woodland (95776) *(P-2324)*

Gold River Racquet Club, Gold River *Also called Spare-Time Inc (P-15152)*

Gold Rush Chevrolet Inc....D....530 885-0471
570 Grass Valley Hwy Auburn (95603) ***(P-14567)***
Gold Rush Chevrolet-Subaru, Auburn *Also called Gold Rush Chevrolet Inc* ***(P-14567)***
Gold Rush Energy Solutions....E....530 334-0676
4911 Windplay Dr Ste 4 El Dorado Hills (95762) ***(P-1272)***
Gold Rush Kettle Korn Llc....E....707 747-6773
4690 E 2nd St Ste 9 Benicia (94510) ***(P-2428)***
Gold Standard Diagnostics Corp (PA)....D....530 759-8000
2795 2nd St Ste 300 Davis (95618) ***(P-8780)***
Gold Star Gymnastics....E....650 694-7827
240 S Whisman Rd Mountain View (94041) ***(P-14951)***
Gold Star Painting, Modesto *Also called R & M Painting Inc* ***(P-1426)***
Gold Technologies Inc....E....408 321-9568
1648 Mabury Rd Ste A San Jose (95133) ***(P-5716)***
Gold's Gym Marin, Corte Madera *Also called Fifer Street Fitness Inc* ***(P-14950)***
Golden 1 Credit Union....D....916 732-2900
5901 Sunrise Blvd Citrus Heights (95610) ***(P-9829)***
Golden 1 Credit Union....D....916 732-2900
7770 College Town Dr Sacramento (95826) ***(P-9830)***
Golden 1 Credit Union....D....877 465-3361
1282 Stabler Ln Ste 640 Yuba City (95993) ***(P-9831)***
Golden 1 Credit Union (PA)....B....916 732-2900
8945 Cal Center Dr Sacramento (95826) ***(P-9832)***
Golden 1 Credit Union....D....530 251-0205
2942 Main St Susanville (96130) ***(P-9833)***
Golden 1 Credit Union....D....916 784-9226
1701 Santa Clara Dr # 120 Roseville (95661) ***(P-9834)***
Golden 85 Investments Corp....E....209 242-2916
878 W Benjamin Holt Dr Stockton (95207) ***(P-10849)***
Golden Age Cnvlescent Hosp Inc....E....831 475-0722
523 Burlingame Ave Capitola (95010) ***(P-16236)***
Golden Age Nutrition Program, Watsonville *Also called Community Bridges* ***(P-17494)***
Golden Altos Corporation....E....408 956-1010
402 S Hillview Dr Milpitas (95035) ***(P-6758)***
Golden Bay Construction Inc....E....510 783-2960
3826 Depot Rd Hayward (94545) ***(P-1874)***
Golden Bay Insulation Inc (PA)....E....650 743-1628
652 Scofield Ave E Palo Alto (94303) ***(P-1677)***
Golden Bear Sportswear, San Francisco *Also called Gb Sport Sf LLC* ***(P-3017)***
Golden Brands, West Sacramento *Also called Harbor Distributing LLC* ***(P-9552)***
Golden Brands, Santa Cruz *Also called Reyes Holdings LLC* ***(P-9561)***
Golden Cellars LLC....E....707 528-8500
14251 Old River Rd Hopland (95449) ***(P-2597)***
Golden Coast Cnstr Restoration....D....916 955-7461
4811 Chippendale Dr # 301 Sacramento (95841) ***(P-645)***
Golden Eagle Distributing Corp....C....916 645-6600
1251 Tinker Rd Rocklin (95765) ***(P-9070)***
Golden Empire Convalescent Hos....C....530 273-1316
121 Dorsey Dr Grass Valley (95945) ***(P-16380)***
Golden Empire Mortgage Inc....E....916 576-7919
601 University Ave # 105 Sacramento (95825) ***(P-9907)***
Golden Gate Brdge Hwy Trnsp Ds (PA)....C....415 921-5858
Toll Plz San Francisco (94129) ***(P-7870)***
Golden Gate Brdge Hwy Trnsp Ds....D....415 455-2000
101 E Sir Frncis Drake Bl Larkspur (94939) ***(P-7871)***
Golden Gate Bridge High....A....415 457-3110
1011 Andersen Dr San Rafael (94901) ***(P-7872)***
Golden Gate Capital, San Francisco *Also called Golden Gate Private Equity Inc* ***(P-10850)***
Golden Gate Capital, San Francisco *Also called Ggc Administration LLC* ***(P-10736)***
Golden Gate Cncil Amrcn Yuth H....E....415 474-5721
685 Ellis St San Francisco (94109) ***(P-11114)***
Golden Gate Cncil Amrcn Yuth H....E....415 771-7277
240 Fort Mason San Francisco (94123) ***(P-11115)***
Golden Gate Debris Box Service (HQ)....E....415 626-4000
515 Tunnel Ave San Francisco (94134) ***(P-9214)***
Golden Gate Ferry, Larkspur *Also called Golden Gate Brdge Hwy Trnsp Ds* ***(P-7871)***
Golden Gate Fields, Albany *Also called Pacific Racing Association* ***(P-14917)***
Golden Gate Freightliner Inc (HQ)....C....559 486-4310
8200 Baldwin St Oakland (94621) ***(P-14568)***
Golden Gate Freightliner Inc....B....559 486-4310
2727 E Central Ave Fresno (93725) ***(P-5062)***
Golden Gate Kindergarten Assn....E....415 931-1018
1315 Ellis St San Francisco (94115) ***(P-17942)***
Golden Gate Meat Company Inc (PA)....E....415 861-3800
803 Wright Ave Richmond (94804) ***(P-9378)***
Golden Gate Nat Prks Cnsrvancy, San Rafael *Also called Golden Gate Nat Prks Cnsrvancy* ***(P-19904)***
Golden Gate Nat Prks Cnsrvancy....C....415 440-4068
1 Presidio Ave San Francisco (94115) ***(P-19903)***
Golden Gate Nat Prks Cnsrvancy....C....415 785-4787
1600 Los Gamos Dr San Rafael (94903) ***(P-19904)***
Golden Gate Nat Prks Cnsrvancy....D....415 933-6760
680 Point Lobos Ave San Francisco (94121) ***(P-18426)***
Golden Gate Nat Prks Cnsrvancy (PA)....D....415 561-3000
Fort Mason Bldg 201 San Francisco (94123) ***(P-19905)***
Golden Gate Private Equity Inc (PA)....A....415 983-2706
1 Embarcadero Ctr Fl 39 San Francisco (94111) ***(P-10850)***
Golden Gate Regional Ctr Inc (PA)....C....415 546-9222
1355 Market St Ste 220 San Francisco (94103) ***(P-17589)***
Golden Gate Regional Ctr Inc....E....650 574-9232
3130 La Selva St Ste 202 San Mateo (94403) ***(P-17590)***
Golden Gate Regional Ctr Inc....E....415 446-3000
4000 Civic Center Dr # 310 San Rafael (94903) ***(P-17591)***
Golden Gate Scnic Stmship Corp....E....415 901-5249
Shed C Pier 45 St Pier San Francisco (94133) ***(P-7720)***
Golden Gate Transit, San Rafael *Also called Golden Gate Bridge High* ***(P-7872)***
Golden Gate Truck Center, Oakland *Also called Golden Gate Freightliner Inc* ***(P-14568)***
Golden Gate Truck Center, Fresno *Also called Golden Gate Freightliner Inc* ***(P-5062)***

Golden Gate Urology Inc (PA)....D....415 543-2830
1661 Mission St San Francisco (94103) ***(P-15416)***
Golden Gateidence Opco LLC....C....415 922-5085
2121 Pine St San Francisco (94115) ***(P-16184)***
Golden Gtwy Tennis & Swim CLB, San Francisco *Also called Bay Club Golden Gateway LLC* ***(P-15055)***
Golden Haven, Stockton *Also called True Health Inc* ***(P-18193)***
Golden Key Motel, Auburn *Also called M Rothrock Properties Inc* ***(P-11277)***
Golden Living Center - Chateau, Stockton *Also called Beaver Dam Health Care Center* ***(P-15926)***
Golden Livingcenter - Clovis, Clovis *Also called Beaver Dam Health Care Center* ***(P-15937)***
Golden Livingcenter - Petaluma, Petaluma *Also called Beaver Dam Health Care Center* ***(P-15933)***
Golden Livingcenter - Portside, Stockton *Also called Beaver Dam Health Care Center* ***(P-15942)***
Golden Livingcenter - Reedley, Reedley *Also called Beaver Dam Health Care Center* ***(P-15939)***
Golden Livingcenter - San Jose, San Jose *Also called Beaver Dam Health Care Center* ***(P-15935)***
Golden Lvngcenter - Santa Rosa, Santa Rosa *Also called Beaver Dam Health Care Center* ***(P-15931)***
Golden Lvngcnter - Cntry View, Fresno *Also called Beaver Dam Health Care Center* ***(P-15927)***
Golden Lvngcnter - Lndon Hse S, Sonoma *Also called Beaver Dam Health Care Center* ***(P-15943)***
Golden N-Life Diamite Intl Inc (PA)....D....510 651-0405
3500 Gateway Blvd Fremont (94538) ***(P-9227)***
Golden Optical Corporation....D....408 246-4500
2855 Stevens Creek Blvd Santa Clara (95050) ***(P-15869)***
Golden Pacific Bank Nat Assn (HQ)....E....916 288-1069
1409 28th St Sacramento (95816) ***(P-9734)***
Golden Phoenix Bakery, San Leandro *Also called Triple C Foods Inc* ***(P-2419)***
Golden Plastics Corporation....E....510 569-6465
8465 Baldwin St Oakland (94621) ***(P-4285)***
Golden Pppy Prschool Infant CT....E....415 924-2828
50 El Camino Dr Corte Madera (94925) ***(P-17943)***
Golden Rain Foundation (PA)....B....925 988-7700
1001 Golden Rain Rd Walnut Creek (94595) ***(P-10561)***
Golden Rain Foundation....E....925 988-7800
800 Rockview Dr Walnut Creek (94595) ***(P-18427)***
Golden State Assembly Inc....F....408 438-0314
18220 Butterfield Blvd Morgan Hill (95037) ***(P-4558)***
Golden State Assembly Inc (PA)....C....510 226-8155
47823 Westinghouse Dr Fremont (94539) ***(P-4559)***
Golden State Donor Services, West Sacramento *Also called DCI Donor Services Inc* ***(P-17133)***
Golden State Family Svcs Inc (PA)....E....559 241-0955
4285 N Valentine Ave Fresno (93722) ***(P-18120)***
Golden State Fire Appratus Inc....F....916 330-1638
7400 Reese Rd Sacramento (95828) ***(P-6551)***
GOLDEN STATE FOSTER FAMILY AGE, Fresno *Also called Golden State Family Svcs Inc* ***(P-18120)***
Golden State Imports Intl Inc (PA)....F....510 995-1320
2417 Mariner Square Loop # 25 Alameda (94501) ***(P-9182)***
Golden State Landscaping, Livermore *Also called J Redfern Inc* ***(P-471)***
Golden State Mixing Inc....E....209 632-3656
415 D St Turlock (95380) ***(P-2190)***
Golden State Restaurant Group....E....209 478-0234
4502 Georgetown Pl Stockton (95207) ***(P-19520)***
Golden State Utility Co....E....408 982-5420
5275 Central Ave Fremont (94536) ***(P-1103)***
Golden State Utility Co....E....916 387-6255
8766 Fruitridge Rd Sacramento (95826) ***(P-1104)***
Golden State Utility Co....E....559 896-6690
10600 E Mountain View Ave Selma (93662) ***(P-1105)***
Golden State Vintners (PA)....F....707 254-4900
4596 S Tracy Blvd Tracy (95377) ***(P-2598)***
Golden State Vintners....E....707 254-1985
1075 Golden Gate Dr NAPA (94558) ***(P-2599)***
Golden State Vintners....E....707 553-6480
1175 Commmerce Blvd Vallejo (94503) ***(P-2600)***
Golden State Warriors LLC....D....415 388-0100
1 Warriors Way San Francisco (94158) ***(P-14907)***
Golden Valley & Associates Inc....E....209 549-1549
3511 Finch Rd A Modesto (95357) ***(P-5063)***
Golden Valley Health Centers (PA)....C....209 383-1848
737 W Childs Ave Merced (95341) ***(P-15417)***
Golden Valley Industries Inc....E....209 939-3370
960 Lone Palm Ave Modesto (95351) ***(P-2097)***
Golden Vly Grape Jice Wine LLC (PA)....E....559 661-4657
11770 Road 27 1/2 Madera (93637) ***(P-2601)***
Golden Vly Occpational Therapy, Oroville *Also called Oroville Hospital* ***(P-15893)***
Golden W Ppr Converting Corp....E....510 317-0646
2480 Grant Ave San Lorenzo (94580) ***(P-3372)***
Golden West Envelope Corp....E....510 452-5419
1009 Morton St Alameda (94501) ***(P-3398)***
Goldeneye, Saint Helena *Also called Duckhorn Wine Company* ***(P-2557)***
Goldenspear LLC....E....415 643-0100
729b Douglass St San Francisco (94114) ***(P-14286)***
Goldfarb & Lipman LLP (PA)....E....510 836-6336
1300 Clay St Fl 11th Oakland (94612) ***(P-17275)***
Goldfire Corporation....F....510 354-3666
4882 Davenport Pl Fremont (94538) ***(P-1739)***
Goldilocks, Hayward *Also called Clarmil Manufacturing Corp* ***(P-2883)***
Goldilocks Bakeshop and Rest, Hayward *Also called Goldilocks Corporation Calif* ***(P-2387)***

ALPHABETIC

Employee Codes: A=Over 500 employees, B=251-500
C=101-250, D=51-100, E=20-50 F=10-19
2022 Northern California Business
Directory and Buyers Guide
© Mergent Inc. 1-800-342-5647
975

Goldilocks Corporation Calif (PA) ....E....**510 476-0700**
30865 San Clemente St Hayward (94544) ***(P-2387)***
Goldman Enterprises....E....415 821-7726
1150 Phelps St San Francisco (94124) ***(P-124)***
Goldrush Getaways, Citrus Heights *Also called Travelmasters Inc* ***(P-7808)***
Goldstein Dmchak Bller Brgen D ....E....510 763-9800
300 Lakeside Dr Ste 1000 Oakland (94612) ***(P-17276)***
Goldstone Land Company LLC ....E....209 368-3113
11900 Furry Rd Lodi (95240) ***(P-2602)***
Goldtec USA, San Jose *Also called Gold Technologies Inc* ***(P-5716)***
Golet Wine Estates, NAPA *Also called Clos Du Val Wine Company Ltd* ***(P-2534)***
Golf Club At Boulder Ridge, San Jose *Also called Glenrock Group* ***(P-15094)***
Golf Pro. Shop, Diablo *Also called Diablo Country Club* ***(P-15086)***
Golfland Entrmt Ctrs Inc ....C....408 263-4330
1199 Jacklin Rd Milpitas (95035) ***(P-15208)***
Golfland-Sunsplash, Roseville *Also called Roseville Golfland Ltd Partnr* ***(P-15232)***
Gong's Ventures, Sanger *Also called Gongs Market of Sanger Inc* ***(P-10390)***
Gongio Inc ....E....415 412-0214
265 Cmbrdge Ave Ste 60717 Palo Alto (94306) ***(P-12481)***
Gongs Market of Sanger Inc (PA) ....E....**559 875-5576**
1825 Academy Ave Sanger (93657) ***(P-10390)***
Gonsalves & Santucci Inc (PA) ....E....**925 685-6799**
5141 Commercial Cir Concord (94520) ***(P-1875)***
Gonzales Park LLC ....C....530 343-8725
495 Ryan Ave Chico (95973) ***(P-9244)***
Gonzalez Pallets Inc (PA) ....E....**408 999-0280**
1261 Yard Ct San Jose (95133) ***(P-3224)***
Gooch & Housego Palo Alto LLC (HQ) ....D....**650 856-7911**
44247 Nobel Dr Fremont (94538) ***(P-6431)***
Good Neighbor Pharmacy, Fresno *Also called Northwest Medical Group Inc* ***(P-15558)***
Good News Rescue Mission ....E....530 241-5754
3100 S Market St Redding (96001) ***(P-18121)***
Good Samaritan Breastcare Ctr, Los Gatos *Also called Good Samaritan Hospital LP* ***(P-16382)***
Good Samaritan Hospital LP (HQ) ....A....**408 559-2011**
2425 Samaritan Dr San Jose (95124) ***(P-16381)***
Good Samaritan Hospital LP ....C....408 358-8414
15400 National Ave # 200 Los Gatos (95032) ***(P-16382)***
Good Samaritan Hospital LP ....C....408 356-4111
15891 Los Gtos Almaden Rd Los Gatos (95032) ***(P-16383)***
GOOD SAMARITAN REHAB AND CARE, Stockton *Also called Stockton Edson Healthcare Corp* ***(P-16275)***
Good Shepherd Lutheran HM of W ....D....510 505-1244
1335 Mowry Ave Fremont (94538) ***(P-18122)***
Good Shepherd Lutheran HM of W ....D....559 454-8514
1696 S Helm Ave Fresno (93727) ***(P-18123)***
Good Shepherd Lutheran School ....E....415 897-2510
1180 Lynwood Dr Novato (94947) ***(P-17944)***
Good Smritan Fmly Resource Ctr ....E....415 401-4253
1294 Potrero Ave Unit 1 San Francisco (94110) ***(P-17592)***
Good Technology Corporation (HQ) ....C....**408 352-9102**
3001 Bishop Dr Ste 400 San Ramon (94583) ***(P-12482)***
Good View Future Group Inc ....F....408 834-5698
277 S B St San Mateo (94401) ***(P-2898)***
Goodby Slverstein Partners Inc ....C....415 392-0669
720 California St San Francisco (94108) ***(P-11757)***
Goode Company, The, Cotati *Also called Goode Printing and Mailing LLC* ***(P-11837)***
Goode Printing and Mailing LLC ....E....707 588-8028
361 Blodgett St Cotati (94931) ***(P-11837)***
Goodfellow Bros California LLC ....B....925 245-2111
50 Contractors St Livermore (94551) ***(P-646)***
Goodhire, Redwood City *Also called Inflection Risk Solutions LLC* ***(P-13722)***
Goodland Landscape Cnstr Inc ....E....209 835-9956
2455 Naglee Rd 402 Tracy (95304) ***(P-467)***
Goodman Manufacturing Co LP ....B....510 265-1212
3018 Alvarado St Ste C San Leandro (94577) ***(P-5431)***
Goodwill Cntl Southern Ind Inc ....E....925 631-0148
566 Center St Moraga (94556) ***(P-17593)***
Goodwill Inds of Grter E Bay I (PA) ....D....**510 698-7200**
1301 30th Ave Oakland (94601) ***(P-17813)***
Goodwill Inds of Rdwood Empire ....E....707 546-4481
1033 4th St Santa Rosa (95404) ***(P-17594)***
Goodwill Inds of Rdwood Empire (PA) ....D....**707 523-0550**
651 Yolanda Ave Santa Rosa (95404) ***(P-17814)***
Goodwill Inds San Frncsco San (PA) ....B....**415 575-2101**
750 Post St San Francisco (94109) ***(P-17815)***
Goodwill Inds San Jquin Vly FN (PA) ....D....**209 466-2311**
129 S Grant St Stockton (95202) ***(P-17595)***
Goodwill Industries, Moraga *Also called Goodwill Cntl Southern Ind Inc* ***(P-17593)***
Goodwill Silicon Valley LLC (PA) ....D....**408 998-5774**
1080 N 7th St San Jose (95112) ***(P-12173)***
Goodwill Silicon Valley LLC ....E....831 634-0960
550 Tres Pnos Rd Frnt Frn Hollister (95023) ***(P-12174)***
Goodwill Silicon Valley LLC ....E....408 281-1449
7098 Santa Teresa Blvd San Jose (95139) ***(P-12175)***
Goodwin-Cole Company Inc ....E....916 381-8888
8320 Belvedere Ave Sacramento (95826) ***(P-12042)***
Goodyear, Pinole *Also called Jarvis & Jarvis Inc* ***(P-14614)***
Goodyear Coml Tire & Svc Ctrs, West Sacramento *Also called Goodyear Coml Tire & Svc Ctrs* ***(P-14569)***
Goodyear Coml Tire & Svc Ctrs ....C....479 788-6400
3085 W Capitol Ave West Sacramento (95691) ***(P-14569)***
Google Checkout, Mountain View *Also called Google Payment Corp* ***(P-14287)***
Google LLC ....E....415 546-3149
345 Spear St Fl 2-4 San Francisco (94105) ***(P-12483)***
Google LLC (HQ) ....C....**650 253-0000**
1600 Amphitheatre Pkwy Mountain View (94043) ***(P-12484)***
Google Payment Corp ....E....650 253-0000
1600 Amphitheatre Pkwy Mountain View (94043) ***(P-14287)***
Goosecross Cellars A Cal Corp ....E....707 944-1986
1119 State Ln Yountville (94599) ***(P-2603)***
Gopro Inc (PA) ....B....**650 332-7600**
3000 Clearview Way San Mateo (94402) ***(P-7150)***
Gordon & Rees, Oakland *Also called Gordon Rees Scully Mansukhani* ***(P-17278)***
Gordon and Schwenkmeyer Inc ....C....916 569-1740
1860 Howe Ave Ste 300 Sacramento (95825) ***(P-14288)***
Gordon Betty Moore Foundation ....D....650 213-3000
1661 Page Mill Rd Palo Alto (94304) ***(P-18428)***
Gordon Biersch Brewing Company ....D....408 792-1546
357 E Taylor St San Jose (95112) ***(P-2480)***
Gordon Biersch Brewing Company (PA) ....F....**408 278-1008**
357 E Taylor St San Jose (95112) ***(P-2481)***
Gordon E Btty I More Fundation ....D....650 213-3000
1661 Page Mill Rd Palo Alto (94304) ***(P-19786)***
Gordon Prill Inc ....E....408 745-7164
310 E Caribbean Dr Sunnyvale (94089) ***(P-879)***
Gordon Rees Scully Mansukhani ....E....916 830-6900
655 University Ave # 200 Sacramento (95825) ***(P-17277)***
Gordon Rees Scully Mansukhani ....E....510 463-8600
1111 Broadway Ste 1700 Oakland (94607) ***(P-17278)***
Gordon Rees Scully Mansukhani (PA) ....B....**415 986-5900**
275 Battery St Ste 2000 San Francisco (94111) ***(P-17279)***
Gordon-Prill Drapes, Sunnyvale *Also called Gordon-Prill-Drapes Inc* ***(P-18724)***
Gordon-Prill-Drapes Inc ....E....650 335-1990
310 E Caribbean Dr Sunnyvale (94089) ***(P-18724)***
Gorilla Circuits (PA) ....C....**408 294-9897**
1445 Oakland Rd San Jose (95112) ***(P-5936)***
Gospel Center Rescue Mission I, Stockton *Also called Gospel Ctr Rescue Mission Inc* ***(P-17596)***
Gospel Ctr Rescue Mission Inc ....E....209 466-2138
343 S San Joaquin St # 111 Stockton (95203) ***(P-17596)***
Got Appraisals, San Ramon *Also called AMR Appraisals Inc* ***(P-10491)***
Gothic Landscaping Inc ....D....661 857-9020
29240 Pacific St Hayward (94544) ***(P-417)***
Gotion Inc ....E....510 249-5610
48660 Kato Rd Fremont (94538) ***(P-19163)***
Gott's Roadside, Saint Helena *Also called Gotts Partners LP* ***(P-13196)***
Gotts Partners LP ....E....415 213-2992
1344 Adams St Saint Helena (94574) ***(P-13196)***
Gourmet Plus Inc ....E....415 643-9945
1201 Minnesota St San Francisco (94107) ***(P-9354)***
Government App Solutions Inc ....E....833 538-2220
980 9th St Ste 1601 Sacramento (95814) ***(P-12485)***
Government Technology, Folsom *Also called Erepublic Inc* ***(P-14267)***
Goyard Miami LLC ....E....415 398-1110
345 Powell St San Francisco (94102) ***(P-4348)***
Goyette Ruano & Thompson Inc (PA) ....D....**916 851-1900**
2366 Gold Meadow Way A Gold River (95670) ***(P-19787)***
Grace Baptist Church Inc ....E....530 673-6847
1980 S Walton Ave Yuba City (95993) ***(P-17945)***
Grace Christn Academy Pre Schl, Yuba City *Also called Grace Baptist Church Inc* ***(P-17945)***
Gracenote Inc (HQ) ....B....**510 428-7200**
2000 Powell St Ste 1500 Emeryville (94608) ***(P-12486)***
Graham & James LLP ....A....415 954-0200
1 Maritime Plz Fl 3 San Francisco (94111) ***(P-17280)***
Graham Concrete Cnstr Inc ....D....559 292-6571
1323 Dayton Ave Ste 103 Clovis (93612) ***(P-1876)***
Graham Contractors Inc ....E....408 293-9516
860 Lonus St San Jose (95126) ***(P-1045)***
Graham-Prewett Inc ....E....559 291-3741
2773 N Bus Park Ave # 101 Fresno (93727) ***(P-1808)***
Grail LLC (HQ) ....B....**833 694-2553**
1525a Obrien Dr Menlo Park (94025) ***(P-3920)***
Grammarly Inc (PA) ....C....**888 318-6146**
548 Market St Ste 35410 San Francisco (94104) ***(P-13600)***
Granada Bowl Inc ....E....925 447-5600
1620 Railroad Ave Livermore (94550) ***(P-14894)***
Granada Hotel, San Francisco *Also called Broadmoor Hotel* ***(P-10977)***
Granberg International, Pittsburg *Also called Granberg Pump and Meter Ltd* ***(P-5102)***
Granberg Pump and Meter Ltd ....F....707 562-2099
1051 Los Medanos St Pittsburg (94565) ***(P-5102)***
Grand Cabinets and Stone Inc (PA) ....F....**916 270-7207**
10368 Hite Cir Elk Grove (95757) ***(P-3180)***
GRAND CENTRAL STATION, Livermore *Also called All Guard Alarm Systems Inc* ***(P-1447)***
Grand Events, Modesto *Also called Central Valley Party Supply* ***(P-12034)***
Grand Hotel The, Sunnyvale *Also called Selvi-Vidovich LP* ***(P-11460)***
Grand Hyatt San Francisco, San Francisco *Also called Hyatt Corporation* ***(P-11180)***
Grand Hyatt Sf LLC ....E....415 398-1234
345 Stockton St San Francisco (94108) ***(P-11116)***
Grand Lake Montessori ....E....510 836-4313
466 Chetwood St Oakland (94610) ***(P-17946)***
Grand Prix Belmont LLC ....E....650 591-8600
400 Concourse Dr Belmont (94002) ***(P-11117)***
Grand Rounds Inc (PA) ....C....**800 929-0926**
1 California St Ste 2300 San Francisco (94111) ***(P-17150)***
Grande Vitesse Systems, San Francisco *Also called Insignia* ***(P-13612)***
Granit-Bayashi 3 A Joint Ventr ....E....831 724-1011
585 W Beach St Watsonville (95076) ***(P-1046)***
Granite Bay Golf Club Inc ....D....916 791-5379
9600 Golf Club Dr Granite Bay (95746) ***(P-15095)***
Granite Bay Technologies, Rocklin *Also called Morrow Snowboards Inc* ***(P-6456)***
Granite Cnstr Northeast Inc ....E....831 724-1011
585 W Beach St Watsonville (95076) ***(P-1047)***
Granite Construction Co Guam (HQ) ....D....**831 724-1011**
585 W Beach St Watsonville (95076) ***(P-647)***

Granite Construction Company (HQ).....C.....**831 724-1011**
585 W Beach St Watsonville (95076) ***(P-1048)***
Granite Construction Company.....C.....209 982-4750
10500 S Harlan Rd French Camp (95231) ***(P-1049)***
Granite Construction Inc (PA).....A.....**831 724-1011**
585 W Beach St Watsonville (95076) ***(P-1083)***
Granite Payment Alliance LLC (PA).....E.....**916 580-6285**
3400 Douglas Blvd Ste 150 Roseville (95661) ***(P-14289)***
Granite Peak Management (PA).....E.....**530 583-7545**
150 Alpine Meadows Rd 1 Alpine Meadows (96146) ***(P-10562)***
Granite Power Inc.....B.....831 724-1011
580 W Beach St Watsonville (95076) ***(P-19343)***
Granite Rick Co.....C.....831 768-2000
5225 Hellyer Ave Ste 220 San Jose (95138) ***(P-10851)***
Granite Rock Co (PA).....D.....**831 768-2000**
350 Technology Dr Watsonville (95076) ***(P-593)***
Granite Rock Co.....E.....650 482-3800
365 Blomquist St Redwood City (94063) ***(P-4187)***
Granite Rock Co.....E.....831 471-3440
303 Coral St Santa Cruz (95060) ***(P-8626)***
Granite Rock Co.....E.....831 724-3847
540 W Beach St Watsonville (95076) ***(P-8627)***
Granite Rock Co.....E.....650 869-3370
355 Blomquist St Redwood City (94063) ***(P-1050)***
Granite Solutions Groupe Inc (PA).....C.....**415 963-3999**
235 Montgomery St Ste 430 San Francisco (94104) ***(P-12094)***
Granite Wellness Centers.....C.....530 878-5166
180 Sierra College Dr Grass Valley (95945) ***(P-17020)***
Granlbakken Ski Racquet Resort, Tahoe City *Also called Granlibakken Management Co Ltd* ***(P-11118)***
Granlibakken Management Co Ltd.....D.....800 543-3221
725 Granlibakken Rd Tahoe City (96145) ***(P-11118)***
Grant-Cuesta Nursing Center, Mountain View *Also called Covenant Care California LLC* ***(P-16342)***
Granville Homes Inc.....D.....559 268-2000
1396 W Herndon Ave # 101 Fresno (93711) ***(P-648)***
Grape Links Inc.....E.....707 524-8000
420 Aviation Blvd Ste 106 Santa Rosa (95403) ***(P-2604)***
Graphiant Inc (PA).....E.....**510 676-5916**
760 Navajo Way Fremont (94539) ***(P-14290)***
Graphic Packaging Intl LLC.....C.....530 533-1058
525 Airport Pkwy Oroville (95965) ***(P-3734)***
Graphic Reproduction (PA).....D.....**925 674-0900**
1381 Franquette Ave B1 Concord (94520) ***(P-11847)***
Graphic Sportswear LLC.....D.....415 206-7200
173 Utah Ave South San Francisco (94080) ***(P-3735)***
Graphics Microsystems Inc (HQ).....D.....**408 731-2000**
484 Oakmead Pkwy Sunnyvale (94085) ***(P-5120)***
Grappa Software Inc.....D.....925 818-4760
1470 Civic Ct Ste 309 Concord (94520) ***(P-12487)***
Grass Roots Realty.....E.....530 273-7293
1012 Sutton Way Grass Valley (95945) ***(P-10563)***
Grass Valley Inc.....C.....530 478-3000
125 Crown Point Ct Grass Valley (95945) ***(P-5844)***
Grass Valley Inc (HQ).....D.....**530 265-1000**
125 Crown Point Ct Grass Valley (95945) ***(P-5845)***
Grass Valley LLC.....E.....530 272-1055
150 Sutton Way Ofc Grass Valley (95945) ***(P-18124)***
Grass Valley Nissan, Auburn *Also called D O Neronde Inc* ***(P-14556)***
Grass Valley Surgery Ctr LLC.....D.....530 271-2282
408 Sierra College Dr Grass Valley (95945) ***(P-15418)***
Grass Valley Usa LLC (PA).....B.....**800 547-8949**
125 Crown Point Ct Grass Valley (95945) ***(P-5798)***
Graton Spirits Company LLC (PA).....E.....**707 829-6100**
617 2nd St Ste C Petaluma (94952) ***(P-2771)***
Graves 6 Inc (PA).....D.....**916 348-3098**
3437 Myrtle Ave Ste 440 North Highlands (95660) ***(P-1273)***
Graves Residential Center, Fresno *Also called Carreys Care Center Inc* ***(P-18070)***
Gray Eagle Lodge, Blairsden *Also called Territory Designs Inc* ***(P-11530)***
Gray Electric Company, Grass Valley *Also called Ferguson Family Entps Inc* ***(P-1503)***
Graybug Vision Inc (PA).....E.....**650 487-2800**
275 Shoreline Dr Ste 450 Redwood City (94065) ***(P-3921)***
Grayline of San Francisco, South San Francisco *Also called Blue Bus Tours LLC* ***(P-7816)***
Graysix Company.....E.....510 845-5936
2427 4th St Berkeley (94710) ***(P-4765)***
Great American Dry Cleaners, San Pablo *Also called Ratnakar & Sons* ***(P-11655)***
Great American Plumbing Co Inc.....E.....408 279-1515
166 Graham Ave San Jose (95110) ***(P-14751)***
Great Clips, San Jose *Also called Buena Vista Business Svcs LP* ***(P-11676)***
Great Northern Wheels Deals.....E.....530 533-2134
810 Lake Blvd Ste C Redding (96003) ***(P-3443)***
Great Spaces USA, Merced *Also called Olde World Corporation* ***(P-3317)***
GREATER BAY AREA CANCER REGIST, Fremont *Also called Cancer Prevention Inst Cal* ***(P-19205)***
Greater Bay Construction, San Jose *Also called Pan-Cal Investment Company Inc* ***(P-784)***
Greater Frsno Area Chmber Cmmr.....E.....559 495-4800
2331 Fresno St Fresno (93721) ***(P-18306)***
Greater Mdsto Med Srgcal Assoc (HQ).....E.....**209 577-3388**
1541 Florida Ave Modesto (95350) ***(P-15419)***
Greater Sacramento Sur.....D.....916 929-7229
2288 Auburn Blvd Ste 201 Sacramento (95821) ***(P-17021)***
Greater Sacramento Surgery Ctr, Sacramento *Also called Greater Sacramento Sur* ***(P-17021)***
Greater Sacramento Urban Leag.....E.....916 286-8600
3725 Marysville Blvd Sacramento (95838) ***(P-18230)***
Greater Secrement Pediatrics (PA).....E.....**916 965-4612**
6555 Coyle Ave Ste 310 Carmichael (95608) ***(P-15420)***
Greater Vallejo Recreation Dst.....D.....707 648-4600
395 Amador St Vallejo (94590) ***(P-15209)***
Greatlink International Inc.....A.....510 657-1667
44168 S Grimmer Blvd Fremont (94538) ***(P-8861)***
Gree International Inc.....C.....415 409-5200
275 Battery St Ste 1700 San Francisco (94111) ***(P-12488)***
Gree International Entrmt Inc.....C.....415 409-5200
185 Berry St Ste 590 San Francisco (94107) ***(P-12489)***
Green Acres Nursery & Sup LLC.....D.....916 673-9720
604 Sutter St Ste 350 Folsom (95630) ***(P-9039)***
Green Acres Nursery and Supply, Sacramento *Also called Matsudas By Green Acres LLC* ***(P-130)***
Green Catalysts Inc (PA).....D.....**415 271-0675**
870 Market St Ste 659 San Francisco (94102) ***(P-3789)***
Green Circuits Inc.....C.....408 526-1700
1130 Ringwood Ct San Jose (95131) ***(P-5937)***
Green Hills Retirement Center, Millbrae *Also called Hillsdale Group LP* ***(P-16239)***
Green Lake Investors LLC.....E.....707 577-1301
3310 Coffey Ln Santa Rosa (95403) ***(P-7205)***
Green Leaf Produce, Brisbane *Also called Oakville Produce Partners LLC* ***(P-9422)***
Green Living Planet LLC.....D.....415 715-4718
44 Montgomery St 4-101 San Francisco (94104) ***(P-11958)***
Green Mattress Recycling, Livermore *Also called Gmr Northern California LLC* ***(P-14750)***
Green Rush Group Inc.....E.....650 762-5474
714 N San Mateo Dr San Mateo (94401) ***(P-11758)***
Green Shutter Plaza, Hayward *Also called Crown Management Services Inc* ***(P-11041)***
Green Tree Nursery.....E.....209 874-9100
23979 Lake Rd La Grange (95329) ***(P-9633)***
Green Valley Corporation (PA).....E.....**408 287-0246**
777 N 1st St Fl 5 San Jose (95112) ***(P-880)***
Green Valley Corporation.....D.....831 475-7100
740 Front St Ste 315 Santa Cruz (95060) ***(P-649)***
Green Valley Country Club.....D.....707 864-1101
35 Country Club Dr Fairfield (94534) ***(P-15096)***
Green Valley Labor Inc.....E.....209 358-2851
1851 Freedom Ln Ste C Atwater (95301) ***(P-358)***
Green Valley Recycling, Fresno *Also called Kochergen Farms Composting Inc* ***(P-19807)***
Green Valley Trnsp Corp.....E.....209 836-5192
30131 Highway 33 Tracy (95304) ***(P-7548)***
Green Wall Tech Inc.....E.....510 252-1170
2020 Warm Springs Ct # 2 Fremont (94539) ***(P-1678)***
Greenall, Suisun City *Also called E B Stone & Son Inc* ***(P-9598)***
Greenan Pffer Sllnder Llly LLP.....E.....925 866-1000
6111 Bollinger Canyon Rd # 500 San Ramon (94583) ***(P-17281)***
Greenberg Inc (PA).....E.....**510 446-8200**
1250 53rd St Ste 5 Emeryville (94608) ***(P-19164)***
Greenberg Traurig LLP.....D.....650 328-8500
1900 University Ave Fl 5 East Palo Alto (94303) ***(P-17282)***
Greenbrae Management Inc (PA).....E.....**415 461-0200**
50 Bon A Shopg Ctr Ste 20 Greenbrae (94904) ***(P-10436)***
Greenbrea Care Center, Greenbrae *Also called Ocadian Care Centers LLC* ***(P-16084)***
Greenbriar Homes Community, Fremont *Also called Greenbriar Management Company* ***(P-10564)***
Greenbriar Management Company.....D.....510 497-8200
43160 Osgood Rd Fremont (94539) ***(P-10564)***
Greene Rdvsky Maloney Share LP.....D.....415 981-1400
4 Embarcadero Ctr # 4000 San Francisco (94111) ***(P-17283)***
Greener Printer, Richmond *Also called Tulip Pubg & Graphics Inc* ***(P-3705)***
Greenfields Icf-Ddn, Vallejo *Also called Greenflds Intrmdate Care Fclty* ***(P-19344)***
Greenflds Intrmdate Care Fclty.....E.....707 553-2935
400 Santa Clara St # 200 Vallejo (94590) ***(P-19344)***
Greenhorn Creek Associates LP (PA).....D.....**209 729-8111**
711 Mccauley Ranch Rd Angels Camp (95222) ***(P-15097)***
Greenhorn Creek Golf Course, Angels Camp *Also called Greenhorn Creek Associates LP* ***(P-15097)***
Greenhorn Creek Guest Ranch.....E.....530 283-0930
2116 Greenhorn Rd Quincy (95971) ***(P-11119)***
Greenhouse System USA.....E.....831 722-1188
512 Casserly Rd Watsonville (95076) ***(P-881)***
Greenlaw Grupe Jr Operating Co, Angels Camp *Also called Motherlode Investors LLC* ***(P-15014)***
Greenleaf Power LLC (PA).....E.....**916 596-2500**
2600 Capitol Ave Sacramento (95816) ***(P-8114)***
Greenley Primary Care Center, Sonora *Also called Adventist Health Sonora* ***(P-16296)***
Greenliant Systems Inc.....C.....408 217-7400
3970 Freedom Cir Ste 100 Santa Clara (95054) ***(P-6133)***
Greenoaks Opportunity I LLC.....E.....415 805-8922
101 Mission St Ste 1630 San Francisco (94105) ***(P-19521)***
Greenough Consulting Group LLC.....E.....650 548-6900
1350 Bayshore Hwy Ste 920 Burlingame (94010) ***(P-19522)***
Greenridge Senior Care.....C.....510 758-9600
2150 Pyramid Dr El Sobrante (94803) ***(P-18125)***
Greenteam of San Jose, San Jose *Also called Waste Connections Cal Inc* ***(P-8380)***
Greentree Property MGT Inc.....E.....415 347-8600
1 Bush St Fl 9 San Francisco (94104) ***(P-10391)***
Greenvenus LLC.....E.....530 648-9985
1910 5th St Davis (95616) ***(P-19064)***
Greenwaste Recovery Inc (PA).....D.....**408 283-4800**
1500 Berger Dr Watsonville (95077) ***(P-8335)***
Greenwaste Recovery Inc.....E.....408 283-4800
610 E Gish Rd San Jose (95112) ***(P-4286)***
Greenwood Ford, Hollister *Also called Tiffany Motor Company* ***(P-14597)***
Greg H Carpenter Concrete Inc.....E.....209 367-4224
955 N Guild Ave Lodi (95240) ***(P-1877)***
Gregory Associates Inc.....E.....408 446-5725
1233 Belknap Ct Cupertino (95014) ***(P-6759)***

ALPHABETIC

Gregory B Bragg & Associates ... E ... 209 956-2119
4512 Feather River Dr B Stockton (95219) (P-10288)
Greiner Heating & AC, Dixon Also called Greiner Htg - A - Slar Enrgy I (P-1274)
Greiner Htg - A - Slar Enrgy I ... E ... 707 678-1784
8235 Pedrick Rd Dixon (95620) (P-1274)
Gremlin Inc ... E ... 408 214-9885
55 S Market St Ste 1205 San Jose (95113) (P-13197)
Grewal Bros Trucking Inc ... E ... 209 678-2557
515 E Greenway Ave Turlock (95380) (P-7472)
Grey Bears ... E ... 831 479-1055
2710 Chanticleer Ave Santa Cruz (95065) (P-8336)
Greyhound Lines Inc ... D ... 559 268-1829
5275 W Shaw Ave Fresno (93722) (P-7336)
Greyline Partners LLC (PA) ... E ... 415 604-9527
109 Stevenson St Fl 4 San Francisco (94105) (P-19523)
Greystar LP ... D ... 650 386-6438
821 W El Camino Real Mountain View (94040) (P-19345)
Grgich Hills Cellar ... E ... 707 963-2784
1829 St Helena Hwy Rutherford (94573) (P-2605)
Grid Alternative ... B ... 510 731-1310
1171 Ocean Ave Ste 200 Emeryville (94608) (P-1275)
Grid Dynamics Holdings Inc (PA) ... C ... 650 523-5000
5000 Executive Pkwy # 520 San Ramon (94583) (P-13198)
Grid Dynamics Intl LLC (HQ) ... B ... 650 523-5000
5000 Executive Pkwy # 520 San Ramon (94583) (P-13903)
Grid Modernization Division, San Jose Also called Networked Energy Services Corp (P-6534)
Grid Net Inc (PA) ... E ... 415 419-6632
909 Montgomery St Ste 104 San Francisco (94133) (P-12490)
Gridbright Inc ... F ... 925 899-9025
618 Oakshire Pl Alamo (94507) (P-13601)
Gridgain Systems Inc (PA) ... C ... 650 241-2281
1065 E Hillsdale Blvd # 410 Foster City (94404) (P-13199)
Gridley Hlthcare & Wellnss Cen ... D ... 530 846-6266
246 Spruce St Gridley (95948) (P-16015)
Griffin & Reed A Medical Corp ... F ... 916 483-2525
651 Fulton Ave Sacramento (95825) (P-7140)
Grigsby & Associates Inc (PA) ... D ... 214 522-4664
2406 Saddleback Dr Danville (94506) (P-9974)
Grimaud Farms, Sacramento Also called Dupont Market Inc (P-9377)
Grimaud Farms California (HQ) ... E ... 209 466-3200
1320 S Aurora St Ste A Stockton (95206) (P-2136)
Grimbleby Clman Crtif Pub Accn ... D ... 209 527-4220
200 W Roseburg Ave Modesto (95350) (P-18960)
Grinding & Dicing Services Inc ... E ... 408 451-2000
925 Berryessa Rd San Jose (95133) (P-6134)
Grindstone Wines LLC ... D ... 530 393-2162
130 Cortina School Rd Arbuckle (95912) (P-2606)
Grio, San Francisco Also called Bitalign Inc (P-12303)
Gritstone Bio Inc (PA) ... C ... 510 871-6100
5959 Horton St Ste 300 Emeryville (94608) (P-4049)
Grm Byshore Property Owner LLC ... E ... 650 347-2381
1250 Bayshore Hwy Burlingame (94010) (P-11120)
Grm Information MGT Svcs Inc (PA) ... B ... 201 798-7100
41099 Boyce Rd Fremont (94538) (P-7708)
Grm Infrmtion MGT Svcs San Frn ... E ... 888 907-9687
41099 Boyce Rd Fremont (94538) (P-14291)
Grocery Outlet Holding Corp (PA) ... B ... 510 845-1999
5650 Hollis St Emeryville (94608) (P-9272)
Groq Inc ... E ... 650 521-9007
400 Castro St Ste 600 Mountain View (94041) (P-12491)
Groskopf Warehouse & Logistics ... E ... 707 939-3100
20580 8th St E Sonoma (95476) (P-2607)
Grossi Fabrication Inc ... E ... 209 883-2817
3200 Tully Rd Hughson (95326) (P-4970)
Grosvenor House, San Francisco Also called Grosvenor Properties Ltd (P-10565)
Grosvenor Inv MGT US Inc ... D ... 415 773-0275
155 Montgomery St Ste 611 San Francisco (94104) (P-10289)
Grosvenor Properties Ltd (PA) ... E ... 415 421-5940
222 Front St Fl 7 San Francisco (94111) (P-11121)
Grosvenor Properties Ltd ... B ... 415 421-1899
899 Pine St Apt 103 San Francisco (94108) (P-10565)
Grosvenor Properties Ltd ... C ... 650 873-3200
380 S Airport Blvd South San Francisco (94080) (P-11122)
Groth Vineyards and Winery ... E ... 707 944-0290
750 Oakville Cross Rd Oakville (94562) (P-53)
Ground Control Inc ... E ... 415 508-8589
1485 Bay Shore Blvd Ste 4 San Francisco (94124) (P-5846)
Groundlvel - Ovraa Joint Ventr ... D ... 925 446-6084
5013 Forni Dr Ste C Concord (94520) (P-882)
Groundworks Inc ... D ... 925 513-0300
2145 Elkins Way Ste C Brentwood (94513) (P-1878)
Group Avantica Inc ... E ... 650 248-9678
2680 Bayshore Pkwy Ste 4 Mountain View (94043) (P-12492)
Group Delphi, Alameda Also called Delphi Productions Inc (P-14250)
Group Delphi, Alameda Also called Icon Exhibits LLC (P-14300)
Group Insurance Programs, Sacramento Also called State Compensation Insur Fund (P-10182)
Group Manufacturing Svcs Inc (PA) ... D ... 408 436-1040
1928 Hartog Dr San Jose (95131) (P-4766)
Group Manufacturing Svcs Inc ... F ... 916 858-3270
2751 Merc Dr Ste 900 Rancho Cordova (95742) (P-4767)
Groupware Technology Inc (HQ) ... E ... 408 540-0090
541 Division St Campbell (95008) (P-13602)
Grove - Design District, The, San Francisco Also called Ps24 Inc (P-19384)
Grove Street, San Francisco Also called Baker Places Inc (P-17435)
Grover Landscape Services Inc ... D ... 209 545-4401
6224 Stoddard Rd Modesto (95356) (P-125)

Groves/Eden Corporation (PA) ... C ... 209 894-2481
534 S Del Puerto Ave Patterson (95363) (P-11683)
Grow West LLC (PA) ... D ... 530 662-5442
201 East St Woodland (95776) (P-19524)
Grower Direct Nut Company Inc ... E ... 209 883-4890
2288 Geer Rd Hughson (95326) (P-286)
Growers Transplanting Inc ... E ... 209 854-3702
27630 Carnation Rd Gustine (95322) (P-126)
Growing Company Inc ... D ... 916 379-9088
4 Wayne Ct Ste 3 Sacramento (95829) (P-468)
Growthpoint Tech Partners LLC (PA) ... D ... 650 322-2500
2208 Seminole Ct Santa Rosa (95405) (P-19525)
Grubb Co Inc ... D ... 510 339-0400
1960 Mountain Blvd Oakland (94611) (P-10566)
Gruendl Inc ... E ... 510 577-7700
411 Pendleton Way Ste B Oakland (94621) (P-1509)
Grunsky Ebey Farrar & Howel ... E ... 831 688-1180
240 Westgate Dr Ste 100 Watsonville (95076) (P-17284)
Grupe Commercial Company ... D ... 209 473-6000
1203 N Grant St Stockton (95202) (P-10703)
Grupe Company ... D ... 209 473-6000
3255 W March Ln Ste 400 Stockton (95219) (P-10567)
Grupe Dev Companynorthern Cal ... D ... 209 473-6000
3255 W March Ln Ste 400 Stockton (95219) (P-780)
Grupe Huber Company, Stockton Also called Grupe Commercial Company (P-10703)
Grutzmacher & Lewis Med Corp ... E ... 916 649-1515
1515 River Park Dr # 100 Sacramento (95815) (P-15421)
Gryphon Financial Group Inc ... E ... 408 825-2500
855 Jarvis Dr Ste 70 Morgan Hill (95037) (P-18961)
Gryphon Investors Inc (PA) ... A ... 415 217-7400
1 Maritime Plz Ste 2300 San Francisco (94111) (P-10852)
GS Cosmeceutical Usa Inc ... D ... 925 371-5000
131 Pullman St Livermore (94551) (P-4083)
Gsa Media, San Francisco Also called Brite Media Group LLC (P-11802)
GSC Logistics Inc (PA) ... C ... 510 844-3700
530 Water St Fl 5 Oakland (94607) (P-7622)
GSe Construction Company Inc (PA) ... C ... 925 447-0292
7633 Suthfront Rd Ste 160 Livermore (94551) (P-1106)
Gsi Technology Inc ... D ... 408 980-8388
2360 Owen St Santa Clara (95054) (P-6135)
Gsi Technology Inc (PA) ... D ... 408 331-8800
1213 Elko Dr Sunnyvale (94089) (P-6136)
Gsl Fine Lithographers ... E ... 916 231-1410
1281 National Dr Sacramento (95834) (P-3653)
Gsvlabs, San Mateo Also called Nestgsv Silicon Valley LLC (P-13322)
Gt Nexus Inc (HQ) ... D ... 510 808-2222
1111 Broadway Ste 700 Oakland (94607) (P-12493)
GTM Technologies Inc (PA) ... F ... 415 856-0570
1619 Shattuck Ave Berkeley (94709) (P-4721)
GTS, Chico Also called Gas Transmission Systems Inc (P-18716)
GTS Distribution- Northern Cal, Santa Clara Also called Gamus LLC (P-9660)
Gtt Communications (mp) Inc (HQ) ... C ... 415 687-3870
6700 Koll Center Pkwy # 33 Pleasanton (94566) (P-7957)
Gu ... F ... 510 527-4664
1204 10th St Berkeley (94710) (P-3922)
Guadalupe Associates Inc (PA) ... F ... 415 387-2324
1348 10th Ave San Francisco (94122) (P-3574)
Guarantee Real Estate Corp ... D ... 559 321-6040
180 W Bullard Ave Ste 101 Clovis (93612) (P-10568)
Guarantee Records Management, Fremont Also called Grm Information MGT Svcs Inc (P-7708)
Guaranteed Rate Inc ... C ... 916 501-3919
915 Highland Pointe Dr Roseville (95678) (P-9908)
Guard Force Inc ... E ... 951 233-0206
6135 Tam O Shanter Dr 2 Stockton (95210) (P-14135)
Guard Force International, Stockton Also called Guard Force Inc (P-14135)
Guardant Health Inc (PA) ... B ... 855 698-8887
505 Penobscot Dr Redwood City (94063) (P-16782)
Guardian Analytics Inc ... E ... 650 383-9200
2465 Latham St Ste 200 Mountain View (94040) (P-13200)
Guardian Industries LLC ... B ... 559 891-8867
11535 E Mountain View Ave Kingsburg (93631) (P-4356)
Guardian Industries Corp ... D ... 559 891-8867
11535 E Mountain View Ave Kingsburg (93631) (P-4357)
Guardian Industries Corp ... D ... 559 638-3588
11535 E Mountain View Ave Kingsburg (93631) (P-4358)
Guardian Security Agency, Concord Also called Delta Personnel Services Inc (P-14054)
Guardian-Kingsburg, Kingsburg Also called Guardian Industries LLC (P-4356)
Guardsmark LLC ... C ... 650 652-9130
1601 Bayshore Hwy Ste 350 Burlingame (94010) (P-14066)
Guava Holdings LLC ... E ... 530 671-0550
1220 Plumas St Yuba City (95991) (P-16759)
Guavus Inc (HQ) ... D ... 650 243-3400
2125 Zanker Rd San Jose (95131) (P-13201)
Guayaki Sstnble Rnfrest Pdts I ... E ... 888 482-9254
6782 Sebastopol Ave # 100 Sebastopol (95472) (P-9452)
Guayaki Yerba Mate, Sebastopol Also called Guayaki Sstnble Rnfrest Pdts I (P-9452)
Gudgel Roofing Inc ... E ... 916 387-6900
5321 84th St Sacramento (95826) (P-1809)
Guerra Nut Shelling Company ... D ... 831 637-4471
190 Hillcrest Rd Hollister (95023) (P-287)
Guglielmo Emilo Winery Inc ... F ... 408 779-2145
1480 E Main Ave Morgan Hill (95037) (P-54)
Guidant Sales LLC ... B ... 650 965-2634
825 E Middlefield Rd Mountain View (94043) (P-6979)
Guide Dogs For Blind Inc (PA) ... C ... 415 499-4000
350 Los Ranchitos Rd San Rafael (94903) (P-354)
Guided Wave Inc ... E ... 916 638-4944
3033 Gold Canal Dr Rancho Cordova (95670) (P-6874)

Guidetech Inc ....E....408 733-6555
774 Charcot Ave San Jose (95131) *(P-6760)*
Guidewire Software Inc (PA) ....A....650 357-9100
2850 S Del St Ste 400 San Mateo (94403) *(P-13202)*
Guitons Pool Center Inc ....E....530 221-6656
2305 Larkspur Ln Redding (96002) *(P-2035)*
Guittard Chocolate Holdings Co ....C....650 697-4427
10 Guittard Rd Burlingame (94010) *(P-2438)*
Gulfstream California, Lincoln *Also called Gdas-Lincoln Inc (P-6610)*
Gulshan International Corp ....E....408 745-6090
1355 Geneva Dr Sunnyvale (94089) *(P-6137)*
Gum Moon RES Hall, San Francisco *Also called Gum Moon Residence Hall (P-11589)*
Gum Moon Residence Hall ....E....415 421-8827
940 Washington St San Francisco (94108) *(P-11589)*
Gum Sun Times Inc (PA) ....E....415 379-6788
625 Kearny St San Francisco (94108) *(P-3444)*
Gumas Advertising LLC ....E....415 621-7575
99 Shotwell St San Francisco (94103) *(P-11759)*
GUN ACCESSORY SUPPLY, Oakdale *Also called Infinity Sports Inc (P-539)*
Gunderson Dettmer Stough Ville (PA) ....C....650 321-2400
550 Allerton St Redwood City (94063) *(P-17285)*
Gunnebo Entrance Control Inc (HQ) ....F....707 748-0885
535 Getty Ct Ste F Benicia (94510) *(P-6904)*
Gunter Enterprises, Pioneer *Also called Bear River Lake Resort Inc (P-10948)*
Guntert Sales Div Inc ....E....209 599-6131
222 E 4th St Ripon (95366) *(P-8817)*
Guntert Steel, Ripon *Also called Guntert Sales Div Inc (P-8817)*
Guntert Zmmerman Const Div Inc ....E....209 599-0066
222 E 4th St Ripon (95366) *(P-5033)*
Gupshup Inc (PA) ....B....415 506-9095
415 Jackson St San Francisco (94111) *(P-13203)*
Gupta Technologies LLC ....D....916 928-6400
2101 Arena Blvd Ste 100 Sacramento (95834) *(P-8709)*
Gusmer Enterprises Inc ....D....908 301-1811
81 M St Fresno (93721) *(P-5229)*
Guss Automation LLC ....F....559 897-0245
2545 Simpson St Kingsburg (93631) *(P-5005)*
Gustine Mini Storage, Gustine *Also called Andersen Nut Company (P-270)*
Gustine Ready Mix, Gustine *Also called Legacy Vulcan LLC (P-4442)*
Gusto Inc (PA) ....C....800 936-0383
525 20th St San Francisco (94107) *(P-13204)*
Gutterglove Inc ....D....916 624-5000
8860 Industrial Ave # 140 Roseville (95678) *(P-1810)*
Guy Chaddock & Company (PA) ....C....408 907-9200
1100 La Avenida St Mountain View (94043) *(P-3287)*
Guy Plumbing & Heating Inc ....E....650 323-8415
1265 El Camino Real Menlo Park (94025) *(P-1276)*
Guynn Inc (PA) ....E....530 566-9292
2452 Notre Dame Blvd Chico (95928) *(P-14660)*
Guzik Technical Enterprises (PA) ....E....650 625-8000
2443 Wyandotte St Mountain View (94043) *(P-6761)*
Guzzardo and Associates Inc ....E....510 923-1677
836 Montgomery St San Francisco (94133) *(P-418)*
Gvn, Patterson *Also called Global Valley Networks Inc (P-7955)*
Gym Doctors, Hayward *Also called Gymdoc Inc (P-14752)*
Gymdoc Inc ....F....510 886-4321
3488 Arden Rd Hayward (94545) *(P-14752)*
Gymguyz Santa Clara Valley, San Jose *Also called Syndicate Corp (P-14422)*
Gymstars Gymnastics Inc (PA) ....E....209 955-7595
1740 W Hammer Ln Stockton (95209) *(P-14908)*
Gyrfalcon Technology Inc (PA) ....E....408 944-9219
1900 Mccarthy Blvd # 412 Milpitas (95035) *(P-6138)*
H & B, Petaluma *Also called Hunt & Behrens Inc (P-9600)*
H & D Electric ....B....916 332-0794
5237 Walnut Ave Ste 100 Sacramento (95841) *(P-1510)*
H & M Precision Machining, Santa Clara *Also called H&M Precision Machining (P-4866)*
H & R Block, Twain Harte *Also called M E Prigmore & Co (P-11702)*
H & R Gunlund Ranches Inc ....C....559 864-8186
3510 W Saginaw Ave Caruthers (93609) *(P-55)*
H A Bowen Electric Inc ....D....510 483-0500
2055 Williams St San Leandro (94577) *(P-1511)*
H and H Drug Stores Inc ....D....209 931-5200
4692 E Waterloo Rd Stockton (95215) *(P-8781)*
H C C S Inc ....D....916 454-5752
4700 Elvas Ave Sacramento (95819) *(P-16016)*
H C I, Rocklin *Also called Hugin Components Inc (P-4884)*
H C Muddox, Sacramento *Also called Pabco Clay Products LLC (P-4400)*
H De V LLC ....E....541 386-9119
588 Trancas St NAPA (94558) *(P-2608)*
H H M I, Stanford *Also called Howard Hughes Medical Inst (P-19068)*
H Lima Company Inc ....E....209 239-6787
704 E Yosemite Ave Manteca (95336) *(P-602)*
H M H Engineers ....D....408 487-2200
1570 Oakland Rd San Jose (95131) *(P-18725)*
H M T, Madera *Also called Horn Machine Tools Inc (P-5079)*
H N Lockwood Inc ....E....650 366-9557
880 Sweeney Ave Redwood City (94063) *(P-4287)*
H O K, San Francisco *Also called Hellmuth Obata & Kassabaum Inc (P-18888)*
H R C Calaveras Head Srt State (PA) ....E....209 772-3980
444 E Saint Charles St San Andreas (95249) *(P-17947)*
H R Options Inc ....E....800 777-8944
1401 Willow Pass Rd # 820 Concord (94520) *(P-19526)*
H V Food Products Company ....B....510 271-7612
1221 Broadway Oakland (94612) *(P-2280)*
H V Welker Co Inc ....D....408 263-4400
970 S Milpitas Blvd Milpitas (95035) *(P-1771)*
H&Gbygiselleco ....F....415 829-3867
626 Mssion Bay Blvd N Apt San Francisco (94158) *(P-469)*
H&H Catering LP ....E....408 354-1964
111 Pine St San Francisco (94111) *(P-19527)*
H&H Resolution LLC ....D....408 362-2293
151 Bernal Rd Ste 6 San Jose (95119) *(P-11823)*
H&L Partners, Oakland *Also called Hoffman/Lewis (P-11760)*
H&M Precision Machining ....F....408 982-9184
504 Robert Ave Santa Clara (95050) *(P-4866)*
H-Square Corporation ....E....408 732-1240
3100 Patrick Henry Dr Santa Clara (95054) *(P-6139)*
H. T. Harvey & Associates, Los Gatos *Also called Triple Hs Inc (P-19918)*
H2 Co, Santa Clara *Also called H-Square Corporation (P-6139)*
H2o Plus LLC ....E....415 964-5100
727 Sansome St Fl 2 San Francisco (94111) *(P-11684)*
H2o Plus LLC (PA) ....D....800 242-2284
111 Sutter St Fl 22 San Francisco (94104) *(P-4084)*
H2o.ai, Mountain View *Also called H2oai Inc (P-12494)*
H2oai Inc ....C....650 429-8337
2307 Leghorn St Mountain View (94043) *(P-12494)*
HA Rider & Sons Inc ....E....831 722-3882
2482 Freedom Blvd Watsonville (95076) *(P-2791)*
Ha-Le Aloha Convalescent Hosp, Ceres *Also called Mark One Corporation (P-16251)*
Haagen-Dazs, Oakland *Also called Dreyers Grand Ice Cream Inc (P-2171)*
Haart, Oakland *Also called Humanstic Altrntves To Addctio (P-17025)*
Haas Jr Evelyn & Walter Fund ....D....415 856-1400
114 Sansome St Fl 6 San Francisco (94104) *(P-18567)*
Habitat For Hmnity Grter San F ....D....415 625-1000
1 Embarcadero Ctr Sl12 San Francisco (94111) *(P-18231)*
Hacienda Surgery Center LLC (PA) ....C....925 734-6744
4626 Willow Rd Ste 100 Pleasanton (94588) *(P-15422)*
Hackerearth Inc (PA) ....C....650 461-4192
550 Bryant St Ste 2k San Francisco (94107) *(P-12495)*
Hackerone Inc (PA) ....B....415 891-0777
22 4th St Fl 5 San Francisco (94103) *(P-13904)*
Hackett Industries Inc ....E....209 955-8220
4445 E Fremont St Stockton (95215) *(P-5131)*
Hackworth Imax Dome, San Jose *Also called Imax Corporation (P-14811)*
Haeger Incorporated (HQ) ....E....209 848-4000
811 Wakefield Dr Oakdale (95361) *(P-5108)*
Hagadone Directories Inc ....C....707 444-0255
555 H St Ste E Eureka (95501) *(P-3575)*
Hagafen Cellars Inc ....F....707 252-0781
4160 Silverado Trl NAPA (94558) *(P-2609)*
Hagensen Pacific Cnstr Inc ....E....408 961-8656
2033 Gateway Pl Ste 600 San Jose (95110) *(P-883)*
Haggerty Construction Inc ....E....209 475-9898
2474 Wigwam Dr Ste A Stockton (95205) *(P-650)*
Haggin Oaks Golf Shop, Sacramento *Also called Morton Golf Management LLC (P-15013)*
Haig Precision Mfg Corp ....D....408 378-4920
3616 Snell Ave San Jose (95136) *(P-5533)*
Haigs Delicacies LLC ....E....510 782-6285
25673 Nickel Pl Hayward (94545) *(P-2899)*
Hair ACC By Mia Minnelli, Pleasant Hill *Also called Mosaic Brands Inc (P-7300)*
Haisch Construction Co Inc ....F....530 378-6800
1800 S Barney Rd Anderson (96007) *(P-3206)*
Hakomi Institute of Cal LLC ....E....415 839-6788
5874b Vallejo St Oakland (94608) *(P-19218)*
Hal-Mar-Jac Enterprises ....C....415 467-1470
1044 Potrero Cir Suisun City (94585) *(P-14067)*
Halabi Inc (PA) ....C....707 402-1600
4447 Green Valley Rd Fairfield (94534) *(P-4518)*
Hale Aloha Convalescent, Turlock *Also called Mark One Corporation (P-16250)*
Haley Brothers, Stockton *Also called T M Cobb Company (P-3156)*
Half Moon Bay Brewing Company, Half Moon Bay *Also called Brewery On Half Moon Bay Inc (P-2475)*
Half Moon Bay Golf Links, Half Moon Bay *Also called Ocean Colony Partners LLC (P-10711)*
Half Moon Bay Lodge ....D....650 726-9000
2400 Cabrillo Hwy S Half Moon Bay (94019) *(P-11123)*
Half Moon Bay Review, Half Moon Bay *Also called Wick Communications Co (P-3489)*
Half Moon Fruit & Produce Co (PA) ....E....530 662-1727
403 Court St Woodland (95695) *(P-5)*
Halfzeez LLC ....E....833 824-5675
1990 N California Blvd Walnut Creek (94596) *(P-19165)*
Halio Inc (PA) ....C....650 416-5200
3955 Trust Way Hayward (94545) *(P-4389)*
Hall Capital Partners LLC (PA) ....D....415 288-0544
1 Maritime Plz Fl 5 San Francisco (94111) *(P-10763)*
Hall Management Corp ....A....559 846-7382
759 S Madera Ave Kerman (93630) *(P-19346)*
Hall Wines LLC ....E....707 967-2626
401 Saint Helena Hwy S Saint Helena (94574) *(P-2610)*
Halo Neuro Inc ....F....415 851-3338
735 Market St Fl 4 San Francisco (94103) *(P-7106)*
Halo Neuroscience, San Francisco *Also called Halo Neuro Inc (P-7106)*
Halrec Inc ....C....408 984-1234
4202 Stevens Creek Blvd San Jose (95129) *(P-14611)*
Halsen Healthcare LLC ....A....831 724-4741
75 Nielson St Watsonville (95076) *(P-16384)*
Halstead Partnership ....D....916 830-8000
2850 Gateway Oaks Dr # 450 Sacramento (95833) *(P-884)*
Ham Delles Company Inc (PA) ....E....707 578-8840
386 Tesconi Ct Santa Rosa (95401) *(P-10569)*
Hamilton and Dillon Elc Inc ....D....209 529-6292
1128 Reno Ave Modesto (95351) *(P-1512)*
Hamilton Avenue Med Group Inc ....D....408 279-0548
295 Oconnor Dr San Jose (95128) *(P-15423)*
Hamilton Families ....D....415 409-2100
1631 Hayes St San Francisco (94117) *(P-17597)*
Hamilton Medical Group, San Jose *Also called Hamilton Avenue Med Group Inc (P-15423)*

ALPHABETIC

Hamilton Partners......D......650 347-8800
1301 Shoreway Rd Ste 250 Burlingame (94010) ***(P-19528)***
Hamilton Tree Service Inc......E......925 228-1010
4949 Pacheco Blvd Martinez (94553) ***(P-518)***
Hamlin Hotel LP......D......415 984-1450
1525 Grant Ave San Francisco (94133) ***(P-11124)***
Hammon Plating Corporation......E......650 494-2691
890 Commercial St Palo Alto (94303) ***(P-4909)***
Hammond Enterprises Inc......E......925 432-3537
549 Garcia Ave Ste C Pittsburg (94565) ***(P-5534)***
Hammonds Ranch Inc......D......209 364-6185
47375 W Dakota Ave Firebaugh (93622) ***(P-247)***
Hampton By Hilton, Manteca *Also called Manteca Hampton Inn & Suites* ***(P-11283)***
Hampton Inn, Elk Grove *Also called Dominion International Inc* ***(P-11057)***
Hampton Inn, Alameda *Also called Balaji Alameda LLC* ***(P-10943)***
Hampton Inn, Woodland *Also called Sunrise Hospitality Inc* ***(P-11518)***
Hampton Inn, Daly City *Also called Shyam Lodging Group II LLC* ***(P-11475)***
Hampton Inn, San Jose *Also called Miramar Hospitality Consulting* ***(P-11304)***
Hampton Inn, Vacaville *Also called B K D Holdings* ***(P-10942)***
Hampton Inn, Red Bluff *Also called Adobe Road Investment Group* ***(P-10910)***
Hampton Inn, San Francisco *Also called Suisun City Hotel LLC* ***(P-11514)***
Hampton Inn & Suites By Hilton, Redding *Also called Larkspur Group LLC* ***(P-11246)***
Hampton Inn Rancho Cordova, Gold River *Also called Cni Thl Ops LLC* ***(P-11022)***
Hampton Inn Vallejo, Vallejo *Also called Sak Hospitality Inc* ***(P-11428)***
Hana Microelectronics Inc......E......408 452-7474
3100 De La Cruz Blvd Santa Clara (95054) ***(P-8915)***
Hanaps Enterprises......D......669 235-3810
8100 Camino Arroyo Gilroy (95020) ***(P-5372)***
Hand Biomechanics Lab Inc......F......916 923-5073
77 Scripps Dr Ste 104 Sacramento (95825) ***(P-7071)***
Hand Crfted Dutchman Doors Inc......E......209 833-7378
770 Stonebridge Dr Tracy (95376) ***(P-3134)***
Hand Surgery Associates......E......916 457-4263
1201 Alhambra Blvd # 410 Sacramento (95816) ***(P-15424)***
Handle Inc......E......650 863-6113
251 Tennyson Ave Palo Alto (94301) ***(P-3268)***
Handlery Hotels Inc......C......415 781-7800
351 Geary St San Francisco (94102) ***(P-11125)***
Handlery Union Square Hotel, San Francisco *Also called Handlery Hotels Inc* ***(P-11125)***
Handley Cellars Ltd......E......707 895-3876
3151 Highway 128 Philo (95466) ***(P-2611)***
Handley Cellars Winery, Philo *Also called Handley Cellars Ltd* ***(P-2611)***
Handpick Inc (PA)......E......415 859-8955
215 Red Rock Way Apt 206j San Francisco (94131) ***(P-12496)***
Hands-On Mobile Inc (PA)......E......415 580-6400
208 Utah St Ste 300 San Francisco (94103) ***(P-13603)***
Handshake, San Francisco *Also called Stryder Corp* ***(P-13469)***
Hane and Hane Inc......E......408 292-2140
303 Piercy Rd San Jose (95138) ***(P-4910)***
Hanergy Holding (america) LLC (HQ)......C......650 288-3722
1350 Bayshore Hwy Burlingame (94010) ***(P-6140)***
Hanergy Holding America Inc......B......650 288-3722
1350 Bayshore Hwy Ste 825 Burlingame (94010) ***(P-8115)***
Hanes Floor Incorporated......E......530 221-6544
870 Commerce St Redding (96002) ***(P-1772)***
Hanford Hotels......E......510 732-6300
20777 Hesperian Blvd Hayward (94541) ***(P-11126)***
Hanford Ready-Mix Inc......E......916 405-1918
9800 Kent St Elk Grove (95624) ***(P-4484)***
Hank Fisher Properties Inc......E......916 447-4444
2701 Capitol Ave Sacramento (95816) ***(P-18126)***
Hank Fisher Properties Inc......C......916 921-1970
641 Feature Dr Apt 233 Sacramento (95825) ***(P-16237)***
Hanna Brphy McLean Mcleer Jnse (PA)......E......510 839-1180
1956 Webster St Ste 450 Oakland (94612) ***(P-17286)***
Hanot Foundation Inc (PA)......E......209 334-6454
14373 E Sargent Rd Lodi (95240) ***(P-18127)***
Hansel - Prestige Inc......E......707 578-4717
2925 Corby Ave Santa Rosa (95407) ***(P-8453)***
Hansel BMW of Santa Rosa, Santa Rosa *Also called Hansel - Prestige Inc* ***(P-8453)***
Hansen Adkins Auto Trnspt Inc......E......408 514-2345
650 Hammond Way Milpitas (95035) ***(P-7549)***
Hansen Bros Enterprises (PA)......D......530 273-3100
11727 La Barr Meadows Rd Grass Valley (95949) ***(P-594)***
Hansen Medical Inc......C......650 404-5800
800 E Middlefield Rd Mountain View (94043) ***(P-6980)***
Hansford Industries Inc (PA)......E......916 379-0210
8610 Elder Creek Rd Sacramento (95828) ***(P-8818)***
Hanson & Fitch Inc......E......408 778-0499
3458 Enterprise Ave Hayward (94545) ***(P-12043)***
Hanson & Fitch Inc......D......800 847-7037
342 Railroad Ave Danville (94526) ***(P-14292)***
Hanson Aggrgtes Md-Pacific Inc......F......925 862-2236
7999 Athenour Way Sunol (94586) ***(P-4485)***
Hanson Aggrgtes Md-Pacific Inc......F......510 526-1611
699 Virginia St Berkeley (94710) ***(P-4486)***
Hanson Bridgett LLP (PA)......B......415 543-2055
425 Market St Fl 26 San Francisco (94105) ***(P-17287)***
Hanson Drywall......D......831 297-4581
7180 Forest St Gilroy (95020) ***(P-1679)***
Hanson Lehigh Inc......E......972 653-5603
3000 Executive Pkwy # 240 San Ramon (94583) ***(P-4487)***
Hanson McClain Advisors, NAPA *Also called Allworth Financial LP* ***(P-10026)***
Hanson Truss Components Inc......D......530 740-7750
4476 Skyway Dr Olivehurst (95961) ***(P-3207)***
Hantel Technologies Inc......E......510 400-1164
3496 Breakwater Ct Hayward (94545) ***(P-6981)***
Hantronix Inc......E......408 252-1100
10080 Bubb Rd Cupertino (95014) ***(P-5151)***
Hanuman Fellowship (PA)......E......408 847-0406
445 Summit Rd Watsonville (95076) ***(P-18429)***
Hanzell Vineyards......F......707 996-3860
18596 Lomita Ave Sonoma (95476) ***(P-2612)***
Hapag-Lloyd (america) LLC......D......510 286-1940
180 Grand Ave Ste 1535 Oakland (94612) ***(P-19529)***
Happily Ever Laughter LLC......E......831 346-0002
211 River St Santa Cruz (95060) ***(P-17948)***
Happy Company, The, Hayward *Also called Tender Loving Things Inc* ***(P-4096)***
Happy Hall Preschool......E......650 583-7370
233 Santa Inez Ave San Bruno (94066) ***(P-17949)***
Happy Hall Schools, San Bruno *Also called Happy Hall Preschool* ***(P-17949)***
Happy Team Inc......E......209 257-1500
101 Clinton Rd Jackson (95642) ***(P-11127)***
Happy Valley I.C.F., Walnut Creek *Also called Nic USA Inc* ***(P-17655)***
Harbert Roofing Inc......D......530 223-3251
19799 Hirsch Ct Anderson (96007) ***(P-1811)***
Harbin Hot Springs, Middletown *Also called Heart Consciousness Church Inc* ***(P-11625)***
Harbor Court Hotel, San Francisco *Also called Steuart Street Venture LP* ***(P-11509)***
Harbor Distributing LLC......B......916 373-5700
3500 Carlin Dr West Sacramento (95691) ***(P-9552)***
Harbor Distributing LLC......D......530 691-5811
6450 Lockheed Dr Redding (96002) ***(P-9553)***
Harbor Electronics Inc (PA)......C......408 988-6544
3021 Kenneth St Santa Clara (95054) ***(P-5938)***
Harbor Industries Inc......C......925 461-1366
74 W Neal St Ste 102 Pleasanton (94566) ***(P-19530)***
Harbor Lite Lodge LLC......E......707 964-0221
120 N Harbor Dr Fort Bragg (95437) ***(P-11128)***
Harbor Ready Mix, San Carlos *Also called Norcal Materials Inc* ***(P-4499)***
Hard Rock Cafe Intl Inc......D......530 633-6938
3317 Forty Mile Rd Wheatland (95692) ***(P-11129)***
Hard Rock Ht Csino Scrmnto At, Wheatland *Also called Hard Rock Cafe Intl Inc* ***(P-11129)***
Hardcraft Industries Inc......D......408 432-8340
2221 Ringwood Ave San Jose (95131) ***(P-4768)***
Harding & Associates, San Jose *Also called Harding Mktg Cmmunications Inc* ***(P-11864)***
Harding Mktg Cmmunications Inc (PA)......D......408 345-4545
377 S Daniel Way San Jose (95128) ***(P-11864)***
Hardrock Concrete Inc......E......408 481-4990
241 Commercial St Sunnyvale (94085) ***(P-1879)***
Hardware Express, Redding *Also called Gbk Corporation* ***(P-11649)***
Hardwoods Specialty Pdts US LP......D......408 275-1990
620 Quinn Ave San Jose (95112) ***(P-8547)***
Harley Murray Inc......E......209 466-0266
1754 E Mariposa Rd Stockton (95205) ***(P-6602)***
Harley-Davidson, Sacramento *Also called Westbrook Enterprises Inc* ***(P-14785)***
Harley-Davidson Fresno Inc......E......559 275-8586
4345 W Shaw Ave Fresno (93722) ***(P-14753)***
Harman Cnncted Svcs Holdg Corp (HQ)......A......650 623-9400
636 Ellis St Mountain View (94043) ***(P-13604)***
Harman Connected Services Inc (HQ)......E......650 623-9400
636 Ellis St Mountain View (94043) ***(P-13605)***
Harman Management Corporation (PA)......B......650 941-5681
595 Millich Dr Ste 106 Campbell (95008) ***(P-8765)***
Harmless Harvest Inc (PA)......E......347 688-6286
1814 Franklin St Ste 1000 Oakland (94612) ***(P-2900)***
Harmonic Drive LLC......F......800 921-3332
333 W San Carlos St # 10 San Jose (95110) ***(P-5212)***
Harmonic Inc (PA)......A......408 542-2500
2590 Orchard Pkwy San Jose (95131) ***(P-5847)***
Harmony Home Associated......E......925 256-6303
820 Alhambra Ave Martinez (94553) ***(P-18128)***
Harold A Steuber Entps Inc......E......707 586-5205
553 Martin Ave Rohnert Park (94928) ***(P-14293)***
Harold E Nutter Inc......E......916 334-4343
5934 Rosebud Ln Sacramento (95841) ***(P-1513)***
Harold Reichs Pharmacy......F......209 835-1832
39 W 10th St Tracy (95376) ***(P-6982)***
Harold Smith & Son Inc......E......707 963-7977
800 Crane Ave Saint Helena (94574) ***(P-1165)***
Harper's Model Homes Services, Shingle Springs *Also called Harpers Model Home Services* ***(P-11959)***
Harpers Model Home Services......E......916 335-0282
4900 Cothrin Ranch Rd Shingle Springs (95682) ***(P-11959)***
Harpoon Therapeutics Inc......E......650 443-7400
131 Oyster Point Blvd # 100 South San Francisco (94080) ***(P-19065)***
Harrah's Northern California, Ione *Also called Buena Vista Gaming Authority* ***(P-10980)***
Harrell Remodeling Inc......E......650 230-2900
944 Industrial Ave Palo Alto (94303) ***(P-651)***
Harris & Associates Inc (PA)......C......925 827-4900
1401 Willow Paca Rd Ste 50 Concord (94520) ***(P-18726)***
Harris & Associates Cnstr MGT, Concord *Also called Harris & Associates Inc* ***(P-18726)***
Harris & Bruno International, Roseville *Also called Harris & Bruno Machine Co Inc* ***(P-5121)***
Harris & Bruno Machine Co Inc (PA)......D......916 781-7676
8555 Washington Blvd Roseville (95678) ***(P-5121)***
Harris & Sloan Consulting......E......916 921-2800
2295 Gateway Oaks Dr # 165 Sacramento (95833) ***(P-19788)***
Harris Company Concrete Cnstr......E......707 246-5697
1129 Industrial Ave # 204 Petaluma (94952) ***(P-1880)***
Harris Construction Co Inc......C......559 251-0301
5286 E Home Ave Fresno (93727) ***(P-885)***
Harris Farms Inc......B......559 935-0717
24505 W Dorris Ave Coalinga (93210) ***(P-169)***
Harris Lorenzo......E......916 993-5863
4704 Roseville Rd Ste 112 North Highlands (95660) ***(P-11960)***

Harris Mycfo Inc...D.......480 348-7725
2200 Geng Rd Ste 100 Palo Alto (94303) **(P-19531)**
Harris Ranch Beef Company...A.......559 896-3081
16277 S Mccall Ave Selma (93662) **(P-2098)**
Harris Rebar Northern Cal Inc...C.......925 373-0733
355 S Vasco Rd Livermore (94550) **(P-1924)**
Harris Woolf Cal Almonds LLC...C.......559 884-2147
26060 Colusa Ave Coalinga (93210) **(P-288)**
Harrison Con Ctng Inc A Cal Co...D.......530 662-2185
33522 County Road 24 Woodland (95695) **(P-1881)**
Harrison Drywall Inc...E.......415 821-9584
447 10th St San Francisco (94103) **(P-1680)**
Harrison Home...E.......209 955-2277
1755 W Hammer Ln Ste 12 Stockton (95209) **(P-18129)**
Harry Clark Sewers, Oakland *Also called Clark Harry Plumbing & Heating* **(P-1235)**
Harsch Investment Realty LLC...E.......510 475-0755
32970 Alvarado Niles Rd # 740 Union City (94587) **(P-10570)**
Harsch Investment Realty LLC...C.......510 843-3000
41 Tunnel Rd Berkeley (94705) **(P-11130)**
Harsch Investment Realty LLC...E.......415 673-6757
325 Mason St San Francisco (94102) **(P-14512)**
Hart Howerton Ltd (PA)...**D.......415 439-2200**
1 Union St Fl 3 San Francisco (94111) **(P-419)**
Hartford Family Winery, Forestville *Also called Hartford Jackson LLC* **(P-2613)**
Hartford Jackson LLC...E.......707 887-1756
8075 Martinelli Rd Forestville (95436) **(P-2613)**
Hartle Media Ventures LLC...E.......415 362-7797
680 2nd St San Francisco (94107) **(P-3502)**
Hartmann Studios Inc...C.......510 232-5030
1150 Brickyard Cove Rd # 202 Point Richmond (94801) **(P-14294)**
Harvest Food Products Co Inc...D.......510 675-0383
710 Sandoval Way Hayward (94544) **(P-2901)**
Harvest Inn Investors I LLC...D.......707 963-9463
1 Main St Saint Helena (94574) **(P-11131)**
Harvest Park Bowl...D.......925 516-1221
5000 Balfour Rd Brentwood (94513) **(P-14895)**
Harvest Printing Company, Anderson *Also called Checchi Enterprises Inc* **(P-3635)**
Harvest Technical Service Inc...C.......925 937-4874
1839 Ygnacio Valley Rd # 390 Walnut Creek (94598) **(P-12095)**
Harvey & Madding Inc...D.......925 828-8030
6300 Dublin Blvd Dublin (94568) **(P-14570)**
Harvey Clars State Actn Gllery, Oakland *Also called C R Martin Auctioneers Inc* **(P-14222)**
Harwood Products...C.......707 984-1601
Branscomb Rd Branscomb (95417) **(P-3135)**
Haseeb Al-Mufti MD Inc (PA)...**E.......510 604-6012**
660 4th St Unit 349 San Francisco (94107) **(P-15425)**
Hasel Hawkins Clinic, Hollister *Also called Hazel Hawkins Memorial Hosp* **(P-15426)**
Hashicorp Inc (PA)...**A.......415 301-3250**
101 2nd St Ste 700 San Francisco (94105) **(P-12497)**
Hashicorp Federal Inc...A.......415 672-0721
101 2nd St Ste 700 San Francisco (94105) **(P-12498)**
Hassard Bonnington LLP (PA)...**D.......415 288-9800**
275 Battery St Ste 1600 San Francisco (94111) **(P-17288)**
Hasselgren Engineering Inc...E.......510 524-2485
1221 4th St Berkeley (94710) **(P-18727)**
Hastings Enterprises, San Mateo *Also called HE Inc* **(P-10573)**
Hasura Inc...E.......833 690-2124
355 Bryant St Unit 403 San Francisco (94107) **(P-13606)**
Hat Creek Cnstr & Mtls Inc (PA)...**E.......530 335-5501**
24339 State Highway 89 Burney (96013) **(P-1166)**
Hathaway Dinwiddie Cnstr Co...D.......415 986-2718
565 Laurelwood Rd Santa Clara (95054) **(P-886)**
Hathaway Dinwiddie Cnstr Co...B.......415 986-2718
275 Battery St Ste 300 San Francisco (94111) **(P-887)**
Hathaway Dinwiddie Cnstr Group (PA)...**D.......415 986-2718**
275 Battery St Ste 300 San Francisco (94111) **(P-888)**
Haus Beverage Inc...E.......503 939-5298
1377 Grove St Ste D Healdsburg (95448) **(P-2614)**
Haven Wns Ctr Stanislaus Cnty...E.......209 524-4331
618 13th St Modesto (95354) **(P-17598)**
Haven Womens Center Stanislaus, Modesto *Also called Haven Wns Ctr Stanislaus Cnty* **(P-17598)**
Havens For Total Security Inc...E.......559 432-7600
459 N Blackstone Ave Fresno (93701) **(P-14754)**
Hawk Crest, NAPA *Also called Stags Leap Wine Cellars* **(P-2724)**
Hawthorn Suites, Alameda *Also called Alameda Hospitality LLC* **(P-10913)**
Hawthorn Suites, Santa Clara *Also called Santa Clara Suites LP* **(P-11442)**
Hawthorn Suites...E.......916 441-1200
321 Bercut Dr Sacramento (95811) **(P-11132)**
Hawthorn Suites Fremont Newark, Newark *Also called Pacific Hotel Management LLC* **(P-11345)**
Hawthorne Group Inc...E.......530 672-1330
1010 Camerado Dr Ste 108 Cameron Park (95682) **(P-12096)**
Hawthorne Hydroponics LLC...E.......800 221-1760
2877 Giffen Ave Santa Rosa (95407) **(P-4131)**
Hawthrn/Stone RE Invstmnts Inc...E.......415 441-8400
1704 Union St San Francisco (94123) **(P-10571)**
Hayes Brothers Collision, Elk Grove *Also called Hayes Family Enterprises Inc* **(P-14526)**
Hayes Convalescent Hospital...E.......415 931-8806
1250 Hayes St San Francisco (94117) **(P-16017)**
Hayes Family Enterprises Inc...D.......916 686-8454
9141 Elkmont Dr Elk Grove (95624) **(P-14526)**
Hayes Mansion Conference Ctr...C.......408 226-3200
200 Edenvale Ave San Jose (95136) **(P-11133)**
Hayes Scott Bnino Ellngson McL...E.......650 551-8929
999 Skyway Rd Ste 310 San Carlos (94070) **(P-17289)**
Hayes Valley Care, San Francisco *Also called Synergy LLC* **(P-18189)**
Hayward Air Terminal, Hayward *Also called City of Hayward* **(P-7768)**
Hayward Area Recreation & Park...E.......510 881-6721
1099 E St Hayward (94541) **(P-11673)**
Hayward Convalescent Hospital, Hayward *Also called Hillsdale Group LP* **(P-16240)**
Hayward Enterprises Inc...E.......707 261-5100
2700 Napa Valley Corp Dr NAPA (94558) **(P-2294)**
Hayward Ford Inc...E.......510 352-2000
1111 Marina Blvd San Leandro (94577) **(P-14571)**
Hayward Hills Health Care Ctr, Hayward *Also called Mariner Health Care Inc* **(P-16053)**
Hayward Quartz Machining Co, Fremont *Also called Hayward Quartz Technology Inc* **(P-6141)**
Hayward Quartz Technology Inc...C.......510 657-9605
1700 Corporate Way Fremont (94539) **(P-6141)**
Hayward Sisters Hospital (HQ)...**A.......510 264-4000**
27200 Calaroga Ave Hayward (94545) **(P-16385)**
Hayward Unified School Dst...E.......510 723-3830
24823 Soto Rd Hayward (94544) **(P-18430)**
Hayward Unified School Dst...E.......510 723-3170
1633 East Ave Hayward (94541) **(P-17950)**
Hazel Creek Assisted Living, Orangevale *Also called Summerville At Hazel Creek LLC* **(P-16131)**
Hazel Hawkins Memorial Hosp, Hollister *Also called Hazel Hawkins Memorial Hosp* **(P-16386)**
Hazel Hawkins Memorial Hosp...E.......831 636-2664
930 Sunset Dr Ste 3 Hollister (95023) **(P-15426)**
Hazel Hawkins Memorial Hosp (PA)...**B.......831 637-5711**
911 Sunset Dr Ste A Hollister (95023) **(P-16386)**
Hazel Health Services, Truckee *Also called Telehealth Services USA* **(P-15738)**
Hazelcast Inc (PA)...**D.......650 521-5453**
2 W 5th Ave Ste 300 San Mateo (94402) **(P-13205)**
Haztech Systems Inc...E.......209 966-8088
4996 Gold Leaf Dr Mariposa (95338) **(P-4116)**
HB, San Francisco *Also called Hassard Bonnington LLP* **(P-17288)**
HB Animal Clinics Inc...E.......408 227-3717
955 Blossom Hill Rd San Jose (95123) **(P-326)**
Hbe Rental, Grass Valley *Also called Hansen Bros Enterprises* **(P-594)**
Hbno, Chico *Also called IL Helth Buty Natural Oils Inc* **(P-4162)**
Hci, Chowchilla *Also called Winnresidential Ltd Partnr* **(P-10469)**
Hcl America Inc (HQ)...**C.......408 733-0480**
330 Potrero Ave Sunnyvale (94085) **(P-13815)**
Hcla, San Francisco *Also called Herman Coliver Locus Arch* **(P-18889)**
Hcr Manorcare Inc...D.......408 450-7850
2005 De La Cruz Blvd Santa Clara (95050) **(P-16018)**
Hcr Manorcare Inc...D.......419 252-5743
1575 Bayshore Hwy Ste 200 Burlingame (94010) **(P-16019)**
Hd Supply Facilities Maint Ltd...D.......510 783-4019
2754 W Winton Ave Hayward (94545) **(P-12044)**
Hdc Business Development Inc (HQ)...**D.......707 523-1155**
3315 Airway Dr Santa Rosa (95403) **(P-10572)**
Hdd Co Inc...E.......530 676-5705
4525 Serrano Pkwy Ste 210 El Dorado Hills (95762) **(P-19532)**
Hdp Enterprises Inc...E.......707 763-7388
2237 S Mcdowell Blvd Ext Petaluma (94954) **(P-9340)**
HDR Engineering Inc...D.......916 564-4214
2379 Gateway Oaks Dr # 200 Sacramento (95833) **(P-18728)**
Hds Global, Palo Alto *Also called Hds Mercury Inc* **(P-19533)**
Hds Mercury Inc...E.......650 800-7701
870 E Charleston Rd # 210 Palo Alto (94303) **(P-19533)**
Hdx International Inc (PA)...**E.......925 922-1448**
2036 Avanti Ave Dublin (94568) **(P-8916)**
HE Inc...D.......650 794-1128
3 E 3rd Ave San Mateo (94401) **(P-10573)**
Head Over Heels...E.......510 655-1265
4701 Doyle St Ste F Emeryville (94608) **(P-15210)**
Head Over Heels Athletic Art, Emeryville *Also called Head Over Heels* **(P-15210)**
Head Start, Quincy *Also called Sierra Cscade Fmly Opprtnities* **(P-18019)**
Head Start Child Dev Cncil Inc...D.......209 464-9542
1425 S Center St Stockton (95206) **(P-17951)**
Headlands Center For Arts...E.......415 331-2787
944 Fort Barry Sausalito (94965) **(P-18568)**
Headrick Logging, Anderson *Also called Elizabeth Headrick* **(P-3059)**
Headstart, Watsonville *Also called Encompass Community Services* **(P-17551)**
Headstart Nursery Inc (PA)...**D.......408 842-3030**
4860 Monterey Rd Gilroy (95020) **(P-9634)**
Headway Technologies Inc...B.......408 934-5660
678 S Hillview Dr Milpitas (95035) **(P-12045)**
Headway Technologies Inc...A.......408 935-1020
463 S Milpitas Blvd Milpitas (95035) **(P-5286)**
Headway Technologies Inc (HQ)...**C.......408 934-5300**
682 S Hillview Dr Milpitas (95035) **(P-5287)**
Headway Technologies Inc...A.......425 503-2131
39639 Leslie St Apt 135 Fremont (94538) **(P-11685)**
Headway Technologies Inc...A.......408 934-5300
497 S Hillview Dr Milpitas (95035) **(P-5288)**
Headway Technologies Inc...A.......408 934-3262
550 S Hillview Dr Milpitas (95035) **(P-5289)**
Healdsburg District Hospital, Healdsburg *Also called North Sonoma County Hosp Dst* **(P-16463)**
Healdsburg Golf Club, Healdsburg *Also called Tayman Park Golf Group Inc* **(P-15033)**
Healdsburg Lumber Company Inc...D.......707 431-9663
359 Hudson St Healdsburg (95448) **(P-3136)**
Healdsburg Primary Care Inc...E.......707 433-3383
1312 Prentice Dr Healdsburg (95448) **(P-15427)**
Health & Human Care, San Jose *Also called Santa Clara County of* **(P-17722)**
Health and Humn Svcs Agcy Hhsa...E.......530 621-5834
3057 Briw Rd Ste A Placerville (95667) **(P-11134)**
Health Care Fund, Oakland *Also called County of Alameda* **(P-16873)**

ALPHABETIC

Employee Codes: A=Over 500 employees, B=251-500 C=101-250, D=51-100, E=20-50 F=10-19
2022 Northern California Business Directory and Buyers Guide
© Mergent Inc. 1-800-342-5647
981

Health Care Workers Union (PA) ....D....510 251-1250
560 Thomas L Berkley Way Oakland (94612) *(P-10392)*
Health Comp Administrators (PA) ....C....559 499-2450
621 Santa Fe Ave Fresno (93721) *(P-10290)*
Health Education, Oakland *Also called La Clinica De La Raza Inc (P-17159)*
Health Evolution Partners (PA) ....D....415 362-5800
555 Mission St Ste 2300 San Francisco (94105) *(P-19347)*
Health Financial Systems, Elk Grove *Also called International Micro Design Inc (P-12534)*
Health Gorilla Inc (PA) ....C....844 446-7455
228 Hamilton Ave Palo Alto (94301) *(P-13206)*
Health Iq ....D....917 770-2190
2513 Charleston Rd # 102 Mountain View (94043) *(P-17151)*
Health Lf Orgnization Inc Halo ....D....916 428-3788
3030 Explorer Dr Sacramento (95827) *(P-17152)*
Health Net Federal Svcs LLC (HQ) ....A....916 935-5000
10730 International Dr Rancho Cordova (95670) *(P-10106)*
Health Net Pharmaceutical Svcs ....C....800 977-7532
2868 Prospect Park Dr Rancho Cordova (95670) *(P-10107)*
Health Plan of San Joaquin ....C....209 942-6300
7751 S Manthey Rd French Camp (95231) *(P-10108)*
Health Plan of San Mateo, South San Francisco *Also called San Mateo Health Commission (P-17174)*
Health Quest, NAPA *Also called Back Street Fitness Inc (P-14928)*
Health Svcs Bneft Admnstrtors (PA) ....D....925 833-7300
4160 Dublin Blvd Dublin (94568) *(P-10215)*
Health Trust (PA) ....C....408 513-8700
3180 Newberry Dr Ste 200 San Jose (95118) *(P-18338)*
Health Trust ....D....408 513-8700
3180 Newberry Dr Ste 200 San Jose (95118) *(P-17599)*
Health Ventures Inc (HQ) ....E....510 869-6703
350 Hawthorne Ave Oakland (94609) *(P-16783)*
Healthcare Barton System (PA) ....A....530 541-3420
2170 South Ave South Lake Tahoe (96150) *(P-16387)*
Healthcare Centre of Fresno, Fresno *Also called Fresno Skilled Nursing (P-16009)*
Healthcare Centre of Fresno ....C....559 268-5361
1665 M St Fresno (93721) *(P-16760)*
Healthcare Clinical Labs (PA) ....D....209 467-6330
1800 N California St Stockton (95204) *(P-16784)*
Healthcare Services, French Camp *Also called San Jquin Gen Hosp Fndtion A C (P-16505)*
Healthcare Staffing, Fresno *Also called Recruitment Alley LLC (P-17171)*
Healthcomp ....B....559 499-2450
621 Santa Fe Ave Fresno (93721) *(P-10291)*
Healthcomp Administrators, Fresno *Also called Healthcomp (P-10291)*
Healthcrowd, San Mateo *Also called Crowdcircle Inc (P-13097)*
Healthier Kids Foundation Inc ....E....408 564-5114
4040 Moorpark Ave Ste 100 San Jose (95117) *(P-18232)*
Healthline Media Inc (PA) ....B....415 281-3100
660 3rd St San Francisco (94107) *(P-3576)*
Healthline Networks Inc ....E....415 281-3100
660 3rd St San Francisco (94107) *(P-13791)*
Healthpocket Inc ....C....800 984-8015
444 Castro St Ste 710 Mountain View (94041) *(P-10085)*
Healthsport Ltd A Ltd Partnr (PA) ....C....707 822-3488
300 Dr Martin Luther Arcata (95521) *(P-14952)*
Healthsport-Arcata, Arcata *Also called Healthsport Ltd A Ltd Partnr (P-14952)*
Healthtap Inc ....D....650 268-9806
2465 Latham St Fl 3 Mountain View (94040) *(P-15428)*
Healthy Beginning, Stockton *Also called County of San Joaquin (P-15369)*
Healthy Living Enterprise Inc ....E....916 296-0228
900 E Bidwell St Ste 700 Folsom (95630) *(P-14295)*
Hearsay Social Inc (PA) ....C....888 399-2280
600 Harrison St Ste 120 San Francisco (94107) *(P-13207)*
Hearst Stations Inc ....C....916 446-3333
3 Television Cir Sacramento (95814) *(P-8044)*
Hearst Stations Inc ....C....916 447-5858
3 Television Cir Sacramento (95814) *(P-8045)*
Hearst Stations Inc (HQ) ....D....916 446-3333
3 Television Cir Sacramento (95814) *(P-8046)*
Heart Consciousness Church Inc (PA) ....C....707 987-2477
18424 Harbin Springs Rd Middletown (95461) *(P-11625)*
Heart Group, The, Fresno *Also called Cardio Vascular Associates (P-15322)*
Heart Humanity Health Svcs Inc (PA) ....D....415 898-4278
1400 Grant Ave Ste 203 Novato (94945) *(P-16887)*
Heart Wood Manufacturing Inc ....F....408 848-9750
5860 Obata Way Gilroy (95020) *(P-3181)*
Heartflow Inc (PA) ....D....650 241-1221
1400 Seaport Blvd Bldg B Redwood City (94063) *(P-13607)*
Hearthco Inc ....E....530 622-3877
5781 Pleasant Valley Rd El Dorado (95623) *(P-4617)*
HEARTLAND, Fresno *Also called Premier Valley Bank (P-9760)*
Heartland Child & Family Svcs ....D....916 922-9868
811 Grand Ave Ste D Sacramento (95838) *(P-17600)*
Heartmath LLC ....E....831 338-8700
14700 W Park Ave Boulder Creek (95006) *(P-10805)*
Heartwood Cabinets, Gilroy *Also called Heart Wood Manufacturing Inc (P-3181)*
Heat, San Francisco *Also called Hvsf Transition LLC (P-11762)*
Heath Ceramics Ltd ....E....415 399-9284
101 The Embarcadero San Francisco (94105) *(P-8628)*
Heath Ceramics Ltd ....E....415 361-5552
2900 18th St San Francisco (94110) *(P-4409)*
Heathorn & Assoc Contrs Inc ....E....510 351-7578
2799 Miller St San Leandro (94577) *(P-1277)*
Heatwave Labs Inc ....F....831 722-9081
195 Aviation Way Ste 100 Watsonville (95076) *(P-5902)*
Heavenly Construction Inc ....D....408 723-4954
370 Umbarger Rd Ste A San Jose (95111) *(P-420)*
Heavenly Greens, San Jose *Also called Heavenly Construction Inc (P-420)*

Hebrew Home For Aged Disabled ....A....415 334-2500
302 Silver Ave San Francisco (94112) *(P-16020)*
Heco Inc ....E....916 372-5411
2350 Del Monte St West Sacramento (95691) *(P-5213)*
Heco-Pacific Manufacturing Inc ....E....510 487-1155
1510 Pacific St Union City (94587) *(P-5052)*
Hedgeside Vintners ....E....707 963-2134
540 Technology Way NAPA (94558) *(P-2615)*
Heighten America Inc ....E....209 845-0455
1144 Post Rd Oakdale (95361) *(P-5535)*
Heighten Manfacturing, Oakdale *Also called Heighten America Inc (P-5535)*
Heights Capital Management Inc ....D....415 403-6500
101 California St # 3250 San Francisco (94111) *(P-9975)*
Heirloom, Fresno *Also called Counter Hospitality Group LLC (P-13094)*
Heirloom Computing Inc ....E....510 709-7245
3000 Dnville Blvd Ste 148 Alamo (94507) *(P-13208)*
Helados La Tapatia Inc ....E....559 441-1105
4495 W Shaw Ave Fresno (93722) *(P-2176)*
Helena Industries LLC ....C....559 846-5303
1075 S Vineland Ave Kerman (93630) *(P-4139)*
Helios Healthcare LLC ....D....916 482-0465
2540 Carmichael Way Carmichael (95608) *(P-16021)*
Helios Healthcare LLC ....D....530 345-1306
587 Rio Lindo Ave Chico (95926) *(P-16022)*
Helios Healthcare LLC ....E....707 644-7401
2200 Tuolumne St Vallejo (94589) *(P-16238)*
Heliotrope Technologies Inc ....E....510 871-3980
850 Marina Village Pkwy # 10 Alameda (94501) *(P-4359)*
Heliovolt Corporation ....E....512 767-6079
3945 Freedom Cir Ste 560 Santa Clara (95054) *(P-6432)*
Helitek Company Ltd ....D....510 933-7688
4033 Clipper Ct Fremont (94538) *(P-6142)*
Helix Holdings I LLC ....D....415 805-3360
1 Circle Star Way Fl 2 San Carlos (94070) *(P-19066)*
Helix Medical Comm LLC (HQ) ....E....650 357-0958
1400 Fashion Island Blvd San Francisco (94104) *(P-8782)*
Helix Opco LLC ....C....415 805-3360
101 S Ellsworth Ave # 350 San Mateo (94401) *(P-19067)*
Helix Re Inc (PA) ....D....415 254-2724
4055 Happy Valley Rd Lafayette (94549) *(P-4161)*
Hellmuth Obata & Kassabaum Inc (HQ) ....C....415 243-0555
1 Bush St Ste 200 San Francisco (94104) *(P-18888)*
Hellosign, San Francisco *Also called Jn Projects Inc (P-11723)*
Helmer and Sons Inc (PA) ....E....707 965-2425
910 Howell Mountain Rd Angwin (94508) *(P-889)*
Help & Care LLC (PA) ....D....408 384-4412
14417 Big Basin Way Ste B Saratoga (95070) *(P-16888)*
Helping Hearts Foundation Inc ....D....916 368-7200
3050 Fite Cir Ste 108 Sacramento (95827) *(P-16889)*
Helpware Inc (PA) ....E....949 273-2824
548 Market St San Francisco (94104) *(P-12499)*
Hemington Landscape Svcs Inc ....D....530 677-9290
4170 Business Dr Cameron Park (95682) *(P-421)*
Hemostat Laboratories Inc (PA) ....E....707 678-9594
515 Industrial Way Dixon (95620) *(P-4050)*
Hendrick Automotive Group ....D....925 463-4700
4355 Rosewood Dr Pleasanton (94588) *(P-8425)*
Hendrickson Truck Lines Inc ....C....916 387-9614
7080 Florin Perkins Rd Sacramento (95828) *(P-7550)*
Hendrickson Trucking Inc ....B....916 387-9614
7080 Florin Perkins Rd Sacramento (95828) *(P-7551)*
Henkel US Operations Corp ....C....925 458-8086
2850 Willow Pass Rd Bay Point (94565) *(P-18729)*
Henris Supply Inc ....E....707 763-1535
741 Petaluma Blvd S Petaluma (94952) *(P-1812)*
Henry Broadcasting Co ....E....415 285-1133
2277 Jerrold Ave San Francisco (94124) *(P-8026)*
Henry J Kaiser Fmly Foundation (PA) ....C....650 854-9400
185 Berry St Ste 2000 San Francisco (94107) *(P-18569)*
Henry Mechanical Inc ....E....707 838-3311
7656 Bell Rd Windsor (95492) *(P-1278)*
Henry Plastic Molding Inc ....C....510 490-7993
41703 Albrae St Fremont (94538) *(P-4288)*
Henry Wine Group LLC (HQ) ....B....707 745-8500
4301 Industrial Way Benicia (94510) *(P-9579)*
Henry Wine Group of C.A., The, Benicia *Also called Henry Wine Group LLC (P-9579)*
Henry Wine Group, The, Benicia *Also called Central Coast Wine Company (P-9570)*
Henry's Pub, Berkeley *Also called Hotel Durant A Ltd Partnership (P-11163)*
Hensel Phelps Construction Co ....C....408 452-1800
4750 Willow Rd Ste 100 Pleasanton (94588) *(P-890)*
Hensly Event Resources, Brisbane *Also called Michaael S Hensley (P-11725)*
Henwood Energy Services Inc (HQ) ....C....916 955-6031
2379 Gateway Oaks Dr # 110 Sacramento (95833) *(P-18730)*
Herbs Pool Service Inc ....D....415 479-4040
3769 Redwood Hwy San Rafael (94903) *(P-14296)*
Herburger Publications Inc (PA) ....D....916 685-5533
604 N Lincoln Way Galt (95632) *(P-3445)*
Herdell Prtg & Lithography Inc ....E....707 963-3634
340 Mccormick St Saint Helena (94574) *(P-3654)*
Heritage 1 Window and Building ....C....916 481-5030
4300 Jetway Ct North Highlands (95660) *(P-8548)*
Heritage Bank of Commerce (HQ) ....C....408 947-6900
224 Airport Pkwy Ste 100 San Jose (95110) *(P-9735)*
Heritage Commerce Corp (PA) ....D....408 947-6900
224 Airport Pkwy Ste 100 San Jose (95110) *(P-9736)*
Heritage Community Credit Un (PA) ....E....916 364-1700
10415 Old Placerville Rd Sacramento (95827) *(P-9792)*
Heritage Conalescent Hospital, Sacramento *Also called Horizon West Inc (P-16026)*

Heritage Estates Inc ....D....209 823-6061
14012 Castle Rd Manteca (95336) *(P-18130)*
Heritage Estates-Livermore, Livermore *Also called Leisure Care LLC (P-18136)*
Heritage Interests LLC (PA) ....D....916 481-5030
4300 Jetway Ct North Highlands (95660) *(P-1740)*
Heritage Invstmnts Concord LLC ....E....925 686-4466
4600 Clayton Rd Concord (94521) *(P-11135)*
Heritage One Door & Carpentry, North Highlands *Also called BMC Stock Holdings Inc (P-8531)*
Heritage One Door Crpentry LLC ....D....916 481-5030
4300 Jetway Ct North Highlands (95660) *(P-8549)*
Heritage Paper Co, Livermore *Also called Baycorr Packaging LLC (P-3353)*
Heritage Realty ....E....650 349-9300
1107 S B St San Mateo (94401) *(P-10574)*
Heritage, The, San Francisco *Also called San Frncsco Ldies Prtction Rli (P-18176)*
Herman Coliver Locus Arch ....E....415 495-1776
423 Tehama St San Francisco (94103) *(P-18889)*
Herman Health Care Center, San Jose *Also called Herman Sanitarium (P-16023)*
Herman Produce Sales LLC ....D....559 661-8253
2370 W Cleveland Ave # 108 Madera (93637) *(P-9410)*
Herman Produce Sales LLC (PA) ....E....559 871-3161
2985 Airport Dr Madera (93637) *(P-9411)*
Herman Sanitarium ....D....408 269-0701
2295 Plummer Ave San Jose (95125) *(P-16023)*
Hermes-Microvision Inc ....E....408 597-8600
1762 Automation Pkwy San Jose (95131) *(P-6143)*
Hermsmeyer Painting Co Inc (PA) ....E....707 575-4549
19005 Hwy 89 Hat Creek (96040) *(P-1416)*
Herndon Investors ....D....559 435-2630
1515 E Alluvial Ave 101 Fresno (93720) *(P-15429)*
Herndon Recovery Center LLC (PA) ....E....559 472-3669
7361 N Sierra Vista Ave Fresno (93720) *(P-17022)*
Herndon Surgery Center Inc ....D....559 323-6611
1843 E Fir Ave Ste 104 Fresno (93720) *(P-15430)*
Hero Arts Rubber Stamps Inc ....D....510 232-4200
1200 Hrbour Way S Ste 201 Richmond (94804) *(P-7206)*
Hero Digital LLC (PA) ....C....415 230-0724
555 Montgomery St # 1250 San Francisco (94111) *(P-19789)*
Heroku Inc ....E....650 704-6107
1 Market St Ste 300 San Francisco (94105) *(P-13209)*
Herotek Inc ....E....408 941-8399
155 Baytech Dr San Jose (95134) *(P-5848)*
Herrero Builders Incorporated (PA) ....C....415 824-7675
2100 Oakdale Ave San Francisco (94124) *(P-796)*
Herrick Corporation (PA) ....E....209 956-4751
3003 E Hammer Ln Stockton (95212) *(P-4666)*
Hertz, San Jose *Also called Enterprise Rnt—car San Frncsc (P-14482)*
HEs Transportation Svcs Inc ....E....510 783-6100
3623 Munster St Hayward (94545) *(P-7838)*
Hesperian Health Guides (PA) ....E....510 845-1447
1919 Addison St Ste 304 Berkeley (94704) *(P-3534)*
Hess Collection Import Co, NAPA *Also called Hess Collection Winery (P-2617)*
Hess Collection Winery ....D....707 255-1144
1166 Commerce Blvd American Canyon (94503) *(P-2616)*
Hess Collection Winery (HQ) ....E....707 255-1144
4411 Redwood Rd NAPA (94558) *(P-2617)*
Hester Fabrication Inc ....E....530 227-6867
20876 Corsair Blvd Hayward (94545) *(P-14713)*
Hewlett Foundation, Menlo Park *Also called Hewlett Wlliam Flora Fndation (P-18570)*
Hewlett Packard ....A....650 857-1501
3000 Hanover St Palo Alto (94304) *(P-12500)*
Hewlett Packard Enterprise Co ....A....408 914-2390
4555 Great America Pkwy Santa Clara (95054) *(P-13717)*
Hewlett Wlliam Flora Fndation ....D....650 234-4500
2121 Sand Hill Rd Menlo Park (94025) *(P-18570)*
Hexaware Technologies Inc ....B....609 409-6950
2603 Camino Ramon Ste 200 San Ramon (94583) *(P-13905)*
Hg Holdings Inc ....E....916 944-2828
924 Enterprise Dr Sacramento (95825) *(P-14068)*
Hggc LLC (PA) ....B....650 321-4910
1950 University Ave # 350 East Palo Alto (94303) *(P-10853)*
HGH Electric Inc ....E....510 923-1859
3032 Market St Oakland (94608) *(P-1514)*
Hgst Inc ....E....408 954-8100
5601 Great Oaks Pkwy San Jose (95119) *(P-5290)*
Hgst Inc (HQ) ....A....408 717-6000
5601 Great Oaks Pkwy San Jose (95119) *(P-5291)*
HI Lo Motel, Edgewood *Also called Siskiyou Development Company (P-11483)*
HI Relblity McRelectronics Inc ....D....408 764-5500
1804 Mccarthy Blvd Milpitas (95035) *(P-6144)*
Hi-Grade Foods Co, Hayward *Also called Hong Kong Evrgrn Trdg Co Inc (P-9453)*
Hickman Plrmo Trong Becker LLP ....E....408 414-1080
1 Almaden Blvd 12 San Jose (95113) *(P-17290)*
Hid Global Safe Inc ....D....408 453-1008
6607 Kaiser Dr Fremont (94555) *(P-13608)*
Hidden Valley Golf Course, Hidden Valley Lake *Also called Hidden Valley Lake Association (P-18431)*
Hidden Valley Lake Association (PA) ....D....707 987-3146
18174 Hidden Valley Rd Hidden Valley Lake (95467) *(P-18431)*
Hidden Vly Lk Cmnty Svcs Dst ....E....707 987-9201
19400 Hartmann Rd Hidden Valley Lake (95467) *(P-8283)*
Hiddenbrook Golf Club (PA) ....D....707 558-0330
1095 Hddnbroke Pkwy Ste A Vallejo (94591) *(P-15098)*
Hiddenbrook Pro Shop, Vallejo *Also called Hiddenbrook Golf Club (P-15098)*
Hiep Nguyen Corporation ....E....408 451-9042
1641 Rogers Ave San Jose (95112) *(P-5536)*
High Camp Home, Truckee *Also called Recycled Spaces Inc (P-3299)*
High Connection Density Inc ....E....408 743-9700
820 Kifer Rd Ste A Sunnyvale (94086) *(P-6392)*
High End Development Inc ....C....925 687-2540
665 Stone Rd Benicia (94510) *(P-2036)*
High Quality Alfalfa Yields, Dos Palos *Also called James Carollo & Co (P-264)*
High Ranch Nursery Inc ....E....916 652-9261
3800 Delmar Ave Loomis (95650) *(P-9635)*
High Sierra Electronics, Grass Valley *Also called Slouber Enterprises Inc (P-6853)*
High Summit LLC ....E....925 605-2900
174 Lawrence Dr Ste A Livermore (94551) *(P-14612)*
High Tek Usa Inc ....F....800 504-7120
12420 Gold Flake Ct Rancho Cordova (95742) *(P-3384)*
Highcom Security Services ....D....510 893-7600
1900 Webster St Ste B Oakland (94612) *(P-14069)*
Higher One Payments Inc ....C....510 769-9888
80 Swan Way Ste 200 Oakland (94621) *(P-13210)*
Higherring ....E....415 272-6948
17 Seadrift Lndg Belvedere Tiburon (94920) *(P-14297)*
Highland Hosp Hghland Wellness, Oakland *Also called Alameda Health System (P-18217)*
Highland Hospital, Oakland *Also called Ucsf East Bay Surgery Program (P-16690)*
Highland Technology ....E....415 551-1700
650 Potrero Ave San Francisco (94110) *(P-6905)*
Highland Wholesale Foods Inc ....D....209 933-0580
1604 Tillie Lewis Dr Stockton (95206) *(P-9273)*
Highlands Water Company ....E....707 994-2393
14580 Lakeshore Dr Clearlake (95422) *(P-8250)*
Highmark Capital MGT Inc ....D....800 582-4734
350 California St Fl 22 San Francisco (94104) *(P-10048)*
Highpoint Technologies Inc ....E....408 942-5800
41650 Christy St Fremont (94538) *(P-5292)*
Hightail, San Mateo *Also called Open Text Inc (P-12651)*
Highwire Public Relations Inc (HQ) ....D....415 963-4174
727 Sansome St San Francisco (94111) *(P-19688)*
Hignell Incorporated ....D....530 342-0707
1770 Humboldt Rd Chico (95928) *(P-10704)*
Hignell Incorporated ....E....530 345-1965
1836 Laburnum Ave Chico (95926) *(P-10437)*
Hilb Rgal Hobbs Insur Svcs Inc (HQ) ....E....212 915-8084
525 Market St Ste 3400 San Francisco (94105) *(P-10292)*
Hilbers Inc ....D....530 673-2947
770 N Walton Ave Ste 100 Yuba City (95993) *(P-891)*
Hilbers Contractors & Engrg, Yuba City *Also called Hilbers Inc (P-891)*
Hilbert, Diana L MD, San Francisco *Also called Mercy Doctors Med Group Inc (P-15535)*
Hild Collision Center, Redding *Also called Art Hild Body and Frame Inc (P-14518)*
Hildebrand & Sons Trucking Inc (PA) ....D....831 722-3006
6 Lewis Rd Royal Oaks (95076) *(P-7473)*
Hilfiker Pipe Co ....E....707 443-5091
1902 Hilfiker Ln Eureka (95503) *(P-4437)*
Hilfiker Retaining Walls, Eureka *Also called Hilfiker Pipe Co (P-4437)*
Hill & Co Real Estate Inc (HQ) ....E....415 921-6000
1880 Lombard St San Francisco (94123) *(P-10575)*
Hill Country Community Clinic ....E....530 337-6243
29632 E Highway 299 Round Mountain (96084) *(P-15431)*
Hill House Associates ....E....707 937-0554
10701 Palette Dr Mendocino (95460) *(P-11136)*
Hill House of Mendocino, Mendocino *Also called Hill House Associates (P-11136)*
Hill Manufacturing Company LLC ....E....408 988-4744
3363 Edward Ave Santa Clara (95054) *(P-4769)*
Hill Physicians Med Group Inc (PA) ....B....800 445-5747
2409 Camino Ramon San Ramon (94583) *(P-15432)*
Hill Top Hospitality LLC ....E....530 888-7441
8801 Folsom Blvd Ste 150 Sacramento (95826) *(P-11137)*
Hill View Dairy Farm, Fresno *Also called Frank Toste (P-212)*
Hillcrest Post Acute, Petaluma *Also called Trestles Holdings LLC (P-10745)*
Hillcrest Senior Housing Corp ....A....650 757-1737
35 Hillcrest Dr Daly City (94014) *(P-10438)*
Hilldale School, Daly City *Also called Creative Instructional Systems (P-17919)*
Hiller Aircraft Corporation ....E....559 659-5959
925 M St Firebaugh (93622) *(P-6633)*
Hillhouse Construction Co Inc ....E....408 467-1000
140 Charcot Ave San Jose (95131) *(P-797)*
Hills Flat Lumber Co (PA) ....D....530 273-6171
380 Railroad Ave Grass Valley (95945) *(P-8550)*
Hillsdale Group LP ....C....650 742-9150
1201 Broadway Ofc Millbrae (94030) *(P-16239)*
Hillsdale Group LP ....C....510 538-3866
1832 B St Hayward (94541) *(P-16240)*
Hillsdale Inn, San Mateo *Also called Sam Bennion (P-11430)*
Hillside Inn Inc ....E....707 546-9353
2901 4th St Santa Rosa (95409) *(P-11138)*
Hillside Internal Medicine, Sonora *Also called Adventist Health Sonora (P-16295)*
Hilltop Commons Senior Living, Grass Valley *Also called Ray Stone Incorporated (P-17681)*
Hilltop Estates, Grass Valley *Also called FPI Management Inc (P-10554)*
Hilltop Family YMCA, Richmond *Also called Young MNS Chrstn Assn of E Bay (P-18503)*
Hilltop Inn Redding LLC ....D....530 221-6100
2300 Hilltop Dr Redding (96002) *(P-11139)*
Hilltop Ranch Inc ....C....209 874-1875
13890 Looney Rd Ballico (95303) *(P-289)*
Hilltop Trading, Ballico *Also called Hilltop Ranch Inc (P-289)*
Hillview Convalescent Hospital ....E....408 779-3633
530 W Dunne Ave Morgan Hill (95037) *(P-16024)*
Hilmar Cheese Company Inc ....D....209 667-6076
3600 W Canal Dr Turlock (95380) *(P-2149)*
Hilmar Cheese Company Inc (PA) ....A....209 667-6076
8901 Lander Ave Hilmar (95324) *(P-2150)*
Hilmar Ingredients, Hilmar *Also called Hilmar Cheese Company Inc (P-2150)*

ALPHABETIC

Hilmar Lumber Inc ....E....209 668-8123
8150 Lander Ave Hilmar (95324) ***(P-8551)***
Hilmar Oaks LLC ....E....209 668-0867
23546 American Ave Hilmar (95324) ***(P-2969)***
Hilmar Whey Protein Inc (PA) ....**B....209 667-6076**
9001 Lander Ave Hilmar (95324) ***(P-2163)***
Hilton, Stockton *Also called Stockton Hotel Ltd* ***(P-11510)***
Hilton, Oakland *Also called Park Hotels & Resorts Inc* ***(P-11354)***
Hilton, San Francisco *Also called Parc 55 Lessee LLC* ***(P-11352)***
Hilton, Roseville *Also called Bre Select Hotels Oper LLC* ***(P-10970)***
Hilton, Folsom *Also called Bre Select Hotels Oper LLC* ***(P-10971)***
Hilton, Scotts Valley *Also called Inn At Scotts Valley LLC* ***(P-11191)***
Hilton, Redding *Also called Win River Hotel Corporation* ***(P-11578)***
Hilton, Emeryville *Also called Rljhgn Emeryville Lessee LP* ***(P-11414)***
Hilton, Burlingame *Also called 765 Airport Boulevard Partnr* ***(P-10907)***
Hilton, San Jose *Also called West Hotel Partners LP* ***(P-11571)***
Hilton, Santa Clara *Also called Ontario Airport Hotel Corp* ***(P-11340)***
Hilton Concord, Concord *Also called Vwi Concord LLC* ***(P-11564)***
Hilton Garden, South San Francisco *Also called Apple Six Hospitality MGT* ***(P-10927)***
Hilton Garden Hotel, Foster City *Also called Hilton Garden In San Mateo* ***(P-11140)***
Hilton Garden In San Mateo ....D....650 522-9000
2000 Bridgepointe Pkwy Foster City (94404) ***(P-11140)***
Hilton Garden Inn ....D....510 346-5533
510 Lewelling Blvd San Leandro (94579) ***(P-11141)***
Hilton Garden Inn Cupertino, Cupertino *Also called Cupertino Hspitality Assoc LLC* ***(P-11042)***
Hilton Garden Inn Roseville, Roseville *Also called Inn Ventures Inc* ***(P-11192)***
Hilton Garden Inn Roseville, Roseville *Also called Larkspur Hsptality Dev MGT LLC* ***(P-11249)***
Hilton Garden Inns MGT LLC ....D....408 840-7000
6070 Monterey Rd Gilroy (95020) ***(P-11142)***
Hilton Garden Inns MGT LLC ....D....925 292-2000
2801 Constitution Dr Fl 2 Livermore (94551) ***(P-11143)***
Hilton Grdn Inn San Frncsco Ar, South San Francisco *Also called Larkspur Hsptality Dev MGT LLC* ***(P-11255)***
Hilton San Francisco Fincl Dst ....D....415 433-6600
750 Kearny St San Francisco (94108) ***(P-11144)***
Hilton Santa Clara, Santa Clara *Also called Stanford Hotels Corporation* ***(P-11500)***
Hims Inc (HQ) ....**C....415 851-0195**
2269 Chestnut St 523 San Francisco (94123) ***(P-4085)***
Hims & Hers Health Inc (PA) ....**E....415 851-0195**
2269 Chestnut St 523 San Francisco (94123) ***(P-3923)***
Hinds Hospice (PA) ....**C....559 674-0407**
2490 W Shaw Ave Ste 100a Fresno (93711) ***(P-16185)***
Hines Interests Ltd Partnr ....C....650 518-6139
1 Hacker Way Bldg 10 Menlo Park (94025) ***(P-10576)***
Hinge Health Inc (PA) ....**A....855 902-7777**
455 Market St Fl 7 San Francisco (94105) ***(P-17153)***
Hinode, Woodland *Also called Sunfoods LLC* ***(P-9313)***
Hinojosa, Fausto CPA, Clovis *Also called Paige Price & Co* ***(P-18981)***
Hint Inc ....E....415 513-4051
2124 Union St Ste D San Francisco (94123) ***(P-2792)***
Hipcamp Inc ....C....242 377-8982
965 Market St Ste 480 San Francisco (94103) ***(P-7798)***
Hiplink Software, Los Gatos *Also called Semotus Inc* ***(P-13435)***
Hippo Analytics Inc (PA) ....**B....925 895-9184**
150 Forest Ave Palo Alto (94301) ***(P-10293)***
Hippo Insurance Service, Palo Alto *Also called Hippo Analytics Inc* ***(P-10293)***
Hire Up Staffing Service ....B....559 579-1331
155 E Shaw Ave Ste 108 Fresno (93710) ***(P-12097)***
Hired Hands Home Care, Novato *Also called Hired Hands Inc* ***(P-16890)***
Hired Hands Inc (PA) ....**D....415 884-4343**
1744 Novato Blvd Ste 200 Novato (94947) ***(P-16890)***
Hironaka Promotions LLC ....E....916 631-8470
2608 R St Sacramento (95816) ***(P-3736)***
Hirsch Machine Inc ....E....408 738-8844
1030 Autumn Ln Los Altos (94024) ***(P-5537)***
His Grwing Grove Child Care CT ....E....510 581-5088
2490 Grove Way Castro Valley (94546) ***(P-17952)***
History San Jose ....D....408 287-2290
1650 Senter Rd San Jose (95112) ***(P-18273)***
Hitachi High-Tech America Inc ....D....925 218-2800
5960 Inglewood Dr Ste 200 Pleasanton (94588) ***(P-8917)***
Hitachi Metals America Ltd ....D....408 467-8900
880 N Mccarthy Blvd # 200 Milpitas (95035) ***(P-8819)***
Hitachi Vantara Corporation (HQ) ....**B....408 970-1000**
2535 Augustine Dr Santa Clara (95054) ***(P-5293)***
Hitech Global Distribution LLC ....E....408 781-8043
2059 Camden Ave Ste 160 San Jose (95124) ***(P-6145)***
Hive, San Francisco *Also called Castle Global Inc* ***(P-12329)***
Hl Power Company ....E....530 254-6161
732-025 Wendel Rd Wendel (96136) ***(P-8116)***
Hlc, Healdsburg *Also called Healdsburg Lumber Company Inc* ***(P-3136)***
HLT San Jose LLC ....E....408 437-2103
2050 Gateway Pl San Jose (95110) ***(P-11145)***
Hmb Investors LLC ....D....415 474-5400
1075 California St San Francisco (94108) ***(P-11146)***
HMC Display, Madera *Also called Gardner Family Ltd Partnership* ***(P-4616)***
Hmclause Inc (HQ) ....**C....800 320-4672**
260 Cousteau Pl Ste 210 Davis (95618) ***(P-127)***
Hmclause Inc ....D....530 713-5838
42 Glenshire Ln Chico (95973) ***(P-128)***
Hmh Builders, Sacramento *Also called Swinerton Builders Hc* ***(P-969)***
Hmi Cardinal, Livermore *Also called Hoskin & Muir Inc* ***(P-8552)***
Hmi Industrial Contractors Inc ....D....916 386-2586
3899 Security Park Dr Rancho Cordova (95742) ***(P-1992)***
Hmr Architects Inc ....E....916 736-2724
2130 21st St Sacramento (95818) ***(P-18890)***
HMw and Jk Enterprises Inc (PA) ....**E....415 731-3100**
1290 24th Ave San Francisco (94122) ***(P-9941)***
Hnc Printing Services LLC ....F....925 771-2080
5125 Port Chicago Hwy Concord (94520) ***(P-3655)***
Hntb Corporation ....D....408 451-7300
1735 Tech Dr Ste 650 San Jose (95110) ***(P-18731)***
Hntb Corporation ....D....510 208-4599
1111 Broadway Ste 900 Oakland (94607) ***(P-18732)***
Hoc Holdings Inc (PA) ....**C....916 921-8950**
7310 Pacific Ave Pleasant Grove (95668) ***(P-9021)***
Hodges Electric Inc ....E....559 298-5533
1239 Hoblitt Ave Clovis (93612) ***(P-1515)***
Hoefer & Arnett Inc (PA) ....**E....415 538-5700**
555 Market St Ste 1800 San Francisco (94105) ***(P-9976)***
Hoem & Associates Inc ....C....650 871-5194
951 Linden Ave South San Francisco (94080) ***(P-1773)***
Hoffman Agency (PA) ....**E....408 286-2611**
325 S 1st St Ste 300 San Jose (95113) ***(P-19689)***
Hoffman/Lewis (PA) ....**E....415 434-8500**
100 Webster St Ste 100 # 100 Oakland (94607) ***(P-11760)***
Hoffmans Electronic Systems ....D....209 723-2667
2301 Aviation Dr Atwater (95301) ***(P-14136)***
Hofmann Company, Walnut Creek *Also called Hofmann Construction Co* ***(P-781)***
Hofmann Construction Co (PA) ....**E....925 478-2000**
3000 Oak Rd Ste 300 Walnut Creek (94597) ***(P-781)***
Hogan Lovells US LLP ....D....415 374-2300
3 Embarcadero Ctr # 1500 San Francisco (94111) ***(P-17291)***
Hogan Lovells US LLP ....D....650 463-4000
4085 Campbell Ave Menlo Park (94025) ***(P-17292)***
Hogan Mfg Inc (PA) ....**C....209 838-7323**
1638 Main St Escalon (95320) ***(P-7286)***
Hogan Mfg Inc ....C....209 838-2400
1520 1st St Escalon (95320) ***(P-7287)***
Holbrooke Hotel LLC ....E....530 273-2300
212 W Main St Grass Valley (95945) ***(P-11147)***
Holder Corporation ....D....408 516-4401
2033 Gateway Pl Fl 6 San Jose (95110) ***(P-892)***
Holdrege Kull Cnslting Engners ....D....530 478-1305
792 Searls Ave Nevada City (95959) ***(P-18733)***
Holiday Garden Wc Corp ....E....925 932-3332
2730 N Main St Walnut Creek (94597) ***(P-11148)***
Holiday Harbor Inc (PA) ....**E....530 238-2383**
20061 Shasta Caverns Rd Lakehead (96051) ***(P-7729)***
Holiday Inn, San Pablo *Also called Lotus Hotels Inc* ***(P-11271)***
Holiday Inn, Union City *Also called Lotus Hotels - Union City LLC* ***(P-11272)***
Holiday Inn, Williams *Also called Kosmadi Brothers* ***(P-11238)***
Holiday Inn, Jackson *Also called Happy Team Inc* ***(P-11127)***
Holiday Inn, Elk Grove *Also called Drd Hospitality Inc* ***(P-11061)***
Holiday Inn, Redwood City *Also called Shiva Enterprises Inc* ***(P-11473)***
Holiday Inn, Mountain View *Also called Kirosh Inc* ***(P-11236)***
Holiday Inn, San Francisco *Also called Six Continents Hotels Inc* ***(P-11486)***
Holiday Inn, Newark *Also called Raps Hospitality Group* ***(P-11385)***
Holiday Inn, Concord *Also called Montclair Hotels Mb LLC* ***(P-11309)***
Holiday Inn, Stockton *Also called Best Western Plus-Heritage Inn* ***(P-10958)***
Holiday Inn, Sacramento *Also called Atrium Finance I LP* ***(P-10936)***
Holiday Inn, San Francisco *Also called Bhr Operations LLC* ***(P-10960)***
Holiday Inn, Milpitas *Also called Alps Group Inc* ***(P-10919)***
Holiday Inn, Vacaville *Also called Jbr Associates Inc* ***(P-11210)***
Holiday Inn, Dublin *Also called Trevi Partners A Calif LP* ***(P-11541)***
Holiday Inn, Burlingame *Also called Trevi Partners A Calif LP* ***(P-11542)***
Holiday Inn, Elk Grove *Also called G-Elk Grove LP* ***(P-11110)***
Holiday Inn, San Francisco *Also called Todays Hotel Corporation* ***(P-11538)***
Holiday Inn, San Jose *Also called San Jose Airport Hotel LLC* ***(P-11436)***
Holiday Inn, Chico *Also called Jai Shri Ram Hospitali* ***(P-11206)***
Holiday Inn, Willows *Also called Kumar Hotels Inc* ***(P-11239)***
Holiday Inn, Mill Valley *Also called Trevi Partners A Calif LP* ***(P-11544)***
Holiday Inn, Sacramento *Also called A29 Funding LLC* ***(P-10908)***
Holiday Inn, Fortuna *Also called Epic Hospitality Inc* ***(P-11082)***
Holiday Inn Ex Ht & Suites ....E....510 548-1700
1175 University Ave Berkeley (94702) ***(P-11149)***
Holiday Inn Ex San Frncsco - A, Burlingame *Also called Grm Byshore Property Owner LLC* ***(P-11120)***
Holiday Inn Ex Walnut Creek, Walnut Creek *Also called Holiday Garden Wc Corp* ***(P-11148)***
Holiday Inn Express ....E....650 863-8771
4525 Howard Rd Westley (95387) ***(P-11150)***
Holiday Inn Express ....D....530 544-5900
3961 Lake Tahoe Blvd South Lake Tahoe (96150) ***(P-11151)***
Holiday Inn Express ....D....888 803-5176
600 Riverside Ave Santa Cruz (95060) ***(P-11152)***
Holiday Inn Express ....E....209 826-8282
28976 Plaza Dr Gustine (95322) ***(P-11153)***
Holiday Inn Express & Suites ....D....559 297-0555
650 W Shaw Ave Clovis (93612) ***(P-11154)***
Holiday Inn Express Manteca, Manteca *Also called Drd Hospitality Inc* ***(P-11060)***
Holiday Inn Express Merced ....D....209 383-0333
730 Motel Dr Merced (95341) ***(P-11155)***
Holiday Inn Great America ....D....408 235-8900
4200 Great America Pkwy Santa Clara (95054) ***(P-11156)***
Holiday Inn San Js-Silicon Vly, San Jose *Also called Sj 1st Street Hotel LLC* ***(P-11488)***
Holiday Inn Suites ....E....559 277-5700
5046 N Barcus Ave Fresno (93722) ***(P-11157)***
Holistic Homecare, Clovis *Also called Well Being Senior Solutions* ***(P-16969)***

Hollins Consulting Inc.....E.....415 238-1300
870 Market St Ste 700 San Francisco (94102) *(P-19348)*
Hollister Landscape Supply Inc.....D.....831 636-8750
2410 San Juan Rd Hollister (95023) *(P-4488)*
Holly Yashi Inc.....D.....707 822-0389
1300 9th St Arcata (95521) *(P-7166)*
Holm McHael B DDS John C Rach.....E.....916 362-9247
10350 Coloma Rd Rancho Cordova (95670) *(P-15836)*
Holo Inc.....E.....510 221-4177
39684 Eureka Dr Newark (94560) *(P-6762)*
Holophane Corporation.....C.....510 540-0156
2231 4th St Berkeley (94710) *(P-5736)*
Holt CA, Pleasant Grove *Also called Holt of California (P-9022)*
Holt Lumber Inc (PA).....**E.....559 233-3291**
1916 S Cherry Ave Fresno (93721) *(P-3208)*
Holt of California (HQ).....**C.....916 991-8200**
7310 Pacific Ave Pleasant Grove (95668) *(P-9022)*
Holt of California.....C.....916 373-4100
3850 Channel Dr West Sacramento (95691) *(P-9023)*
Holt Rental Services.....D.....916 921-8800
7310 Pacific Ave Pleasant Grove (95668) *(P-9024)*
Holt Tool & Machine Inc.....E.....650 364-2547
2909 Middlefield Rd Redwood City (94063) *(P-4542)*
Holz Rubber Company Inc.....C.....209 368-7171
1129 S Sacramento St Lodi (95240) *(P-4216)*
Holzmueller Corporation.....E.....415 826-8383
1000 25th St San Francisco (94107) *(P-12046)*
Holzmueller Productions, San Francisco *Also called Holzmueller Corporation (P-12046)*
Home Away Inc.....D.....559 642-3121
54432 Road 432 Bass Lake (93604) *(P-11158)*
Home Care Assistance LLC (PA).....**A.....650 462-9501**
1808 Tice Valley Blvd Walnut Creek (94595) *(P-16891)*
Home Depot USA Inc.....C.....510 533-7379
4000 Alameda Ave Oakland (94601) *(P-12047)*
Home Depot USA Inc.....C.....916 983-0401
2675 E Bidwell St Folsom (95630) *(P-12048)*
Home Depot, The, Oakland *Also called Home Depot USA Inc (P-12047)*
Home Depot, The, Folsom *Also called Home Depot USA Inc (P-12048)*
Home First.....E.....408 539-2125
507 Valley Way Milpitas (95035) *(P-17601)*
Home Health Care MGT Inc.....D.....530 343-0727
1398 Ridgewood Dr Chico (95973) *(P-16892)*
Home Helpers of Santa Rosa, Santa Rosa *Also called Bana Solomon LLC (P-16852)*
Home Instead Senior Care, Rancho Cordova *Also called Scott Shaw Entrprises Inc (P-16940)*
Home Instead Senior Care, Fresno *Also called P K B Investments Inc (P-19599)*
Home of Peace Cemetery, Colma *Also called Congregation Emanu-El (P-10522)*
Home Sweet Home, Daly City *Also called Nediljka Colma Inc (P-16067)*
Homebridge Inc.....B.....415 255-2079
1035 Market St Ste L1 San Francisco (94103) *(P-17602)*
Homeenergy Inc.....D.....707 200-8287
2930 Domingo Ave Berkeley (94705) *(P-1279)*
Homefrst Svcs Santa Clara Cnty.....C.....408 539-2100
507 Valley Way Milpitas (95035) *(P-17603)*
Homegaincom Inc.....D.....925 983-2852
12667 Alcosta Blvd # 200 San Ramon (94583) *(P-10577)*
Homegrown Naturals, Berkeley *Also called Annies Inc (P-2867)*
Homeguard Incorporated (PA).....**D.....408 993-1900**
510 Madera Ave San Jose (95112) *(P-11900)*
Homelegance Inc (PA).....**D.....510 933-6888**
48200 Fremont Blvd Fremont (94538) *(P-8494)*
Homeless Childrens Network.....E.....415 437-3990
3450 3rd St Ste 1c San Francisco (94124) *(P-18571)*
Homeless Prenatal Program.....E.....415 546-6756
33 Middle Point Rd San Francisco (94124) *(P-17604)*
Homelssness Spprtive Hsing Dep.....C.....628 652-7700
440 Turk St San Francisco (94102) *(P-18233)*
Homepointe Property Management, Sacramento *Also called Ram Commercial Enterprises Inc (P-10652)*
Homeq Servicing Corporation (HQ).....**A.....916 339-6192**
4837 Watt Ave North Highlands (95660) *(P-9909)*
Homesite Svcs Inc A Cal Corp (PA).....**D.....925 237-3050**
6611 Preston Ave Ste E Livermore (94551) *(P-8513)*
Homestar Systems Inc.....D.....415 323-4008
251 Post St Ste 302 San Francisco (94108) *(P-13906)*
Homestead Fine Foods, South San Francisco *Also called Homestead Ravioli Company (P-2200)*
Homestead of Fair Oaks, Fair Oaks *Also called Eskaton Properties Inc (P-18111)*
Homestead Ravioli Company.....F.....910 755-6802
315 S Maple Ave Ste 106 South San Francisco (94080) *(P-2200)*
Homestore Apartments & Rentals, Santa Clara *Also called Move Sales Inc (P-10624)*
Homewood Care Center, San Jose *Also called Ocadian Care Centers LLC (P-16086)*
Homewood Components Inc.....E.....530 743-8855
5033 Feather River Blvd Marysville (95901) *(P-3209)*
Homewood Mountain Resort, Homewood *Also called Homewood Village Resorts LLC (P-11160)*
Homewood Stes Hlton Sfo Arprt, Brisbane *Also called Sage Hospitality Resources LLC (P-11426)*
Homewood Suites, Fresno *Also called Homwood Suites By Hilton (P-11161)*
Homewood Suites, Fairfield *Also called Hotel NAPA II Opco LP (P-11169)*
Homewood Suites Management LLC.....E.....510 663-2700
1103 Embarcadero Oakland (94606) *(P-11159)*
Homewood Truss, Marysville *Also called Homewood Components Inc (P-3209)*
Homewood Village Resorts LLC.....E.....530 525-2992
5145 W Lake Blvd Homewood (96141) *(P-11160)*
Homwood Suites By Hilton.....D.....559 440-0801
6820 N Fresno St Fresno (93710) *(P-11161)*
Hon Hai Precision Industry, San Jose *Also called Nsg Technology Inc (P-14702)*
Honda of Motor Creek, San Jose *Also called Santa Clara Imported Cars Inc (P-14589)*
Honeybook Inc.....D.....770 403-9234
539 Bryant St Ste 200 San Francisco (94107) *(P-12501)*
Honeywell Authorized Dealer, Berkeley *Also called L J Kruse Co (P-1299)*
Honeywell Authorized Dealer, Windsor *Also called Henry Mechanical Inc (P-1278)*
Honeywell Authorized Dealer, San Jose *Also called J & J Air Conditioning Inc (P-1288)*
Honeywell Authorized Dealer, Santa Clara *Also called Envirnmntal Systems Inc Nthrn (P-1256)*
Honeywell Authorized Dealer, Fresno *Also called Linkus Enterprises LLC (P-1114)*
Honeywell Authorized Dealer, Rocklin *Also called Brower Mechanical Inc (P-14683)*
Honeywell Authorized Dealer, Hollister *Also called San Benito Htg & Shtmtl Inc (P-1353)*
Honeywell Authorized Dealer, Fresno *Also called B & L Mechanical Inc (P-1211)*
Honeywell Authorized Dealer, Yuba City *Also called R B Spencer Inc (P-1341)*
Honeywell Authorized Dealer, Anderson *Also called Linkus Enterprises LLC (P-1115)*
Hong Kong Evrgrn Trdg Co Inc.....E.....510 476-1881
30988 San Benito St Hayward (94544) *(P-9453)*
Honig Cellars, Rutherford *Also called Honig Vineyard and Winery LLC (P-56)*
Honig Vineyard and Winery LLC.....E.....707 963-5618
850 Rutherford Rd Rutherford (94573) *(P-56)*
Honolua Bay Holdings LLC.....E.....530 243-6317
2120 Benton Dr Redding (96003) *(P-10737)*
Honor Technology Inc (PA).....**D.....415 999-0555**
2151 Salvio St Ste 310 Concord (94520) *(P-12502)*
Hood & Strong LLP (PA).....**D.....415 781-0793**
275 Battery St Ste 900 San Francisco (94111) *(P-18962)*
Hood Exhibits.....E.....510 965-9999
1001 Canal Blvd Ste C Richmond (94804) *(P-14298)*
Hook & Ladder Winery, Santa Rosa *Also called C and C Wine Services Inc (P-2521)*
Hook or Crook Cellars, Lodi *Also called Baywood Cellars Inc (P-2510)*
Hoonuit LLC (HQ).....**E.....320 631-5900**
150 Parkshore Dr Folsom (95630) *(P-13211)*
Hoopa Forest Industries.....E.....530 625-4281
778 Marshall Ln Hoopa (95546) *(P-3063)*
Hoopa Modular Building Entp (PA).....**E.....530 625-4551**
151 Cal Pac Rd Hoopa (95546) *(P-782)*
Hoopla Software Inc.....E.....408 498-9600
84 W Santa Clara St # 460 San Jose (95113) *(P-13212)*
Hootsuite Media US Inc.....E.....206 519-5705
535 Mission St Fl 14 San Francisco (94105) *(P-13792)*
Hoover Institution.....C.....650 723-0603
434 Galvez Mall Stanford (94305) *(P-14299)*
Hoover Little League Stockt.....D.....209 467-7271
P.O. Box 7191 Stockton (95267) *(P-15099)*
HOPE COOPERATIVE, Sacramento *Also called Tlcs Inc (P-17769)*
Hope Hospice Inc.....C.....925 829-8770
6377 Clark Ave Ste 100 Dublin (94568) *(P-11590)*
HOPE HOUSE, Redwood City *Also called Service League San Mateo Cnty (P-17735)*
Hope Services (PA).....**E.....408 284-2849**
30 Las Colinas Ln San Jose (95119) *(P-17816)*
Hopkins & Carley A Law Corp (PA).....**D.....408 286-9800**
70 S 1st St San Jose (95113) *(P-17293)*
Hopkins Manor.....D.....650 368-5656
1235 Hopkins Ave Redwood City (94062) *(P-18131)*
Hopland Band Pomo Indians Inc (PA).....**C.....707 472-2100**
3000 Shanel Rd Hopland (95449) *(P-18572)*
Hopland Sho-Ka-Wah Casino, Hopland *Also called Shokawah Casino (P-11474)*
Hoppy Brewing Co Inc.....E.....916 451-4677
2425 24th St Ste B Sacramento (95818) *(P-2772)*
Horizon Cal Publications Inc.....E.....760 934-3929
452 Old Mammoth Rd Mammoth Lakes (93546) *(P-3446)*
Horizon Contract Glazing Inc.....E.....916 373-9900
1200 Triangle Ct West Sacramento (95605) *(P-1937)*
Horizon For Hmwners Asscations, Mammoth Lakes *Also called Horizons 4 Condominiums Inc (P-18432)*
Horizon Glass Company, West Sacramento *Also called Horizon Contract Glazing Inc (P-1937)*
Horizon Global Americas Inc.....C.....559 266-9000
3181 S Willow Ave Ste 104 Fresno (93725) *(P-14661)*
Horizon Health & Subacute Ctr, Fresno *Also called Tdc Convalescent Inc (P-16142)*
Horizon Home Care LLC.....E.....559 840-1559
255 W Fllbrook Ave Ste Fresno (93711) *(P-16893)*
Horizon Services Incorporated.....E.....408 283-8555
650 S Bascom Ave San Jose (95128) *(P-18132)*
Horizon Snack Foods Inc.....D.....925 373-7700
197 Darcy Pkwy Lathrop (95330) *(P-2422)*
Horizon South, San Jose *Also called Horizon Services Incorporated (P-18132)*
Horizon West Inc.....E.....916 488-8601
3529 Walnut Ave Carmichael (95608) *(P-16025)*
Horizon West Inc.....E.....916 331-4590
5255 Hemlock St Sacramento (95841) *(P-16026)*
Horizon West Inc (PA).....**E.....916 624-6230**
4020 Sierra College Blvd Rocklin (95677) *(P-16027)*
Horizon West Healthcare Inc (HQ).....**E.....916 624-6230**
4020 Sierra College Blvd # 190 Rocklin (95677) *(P-16028)*
Horizons 4 Condominiums Inc.....D.....760 934-6779
2113 Meridan Blvd Mammoth Lakes (93546) *(P-18432)*
Horizons Unlmted San Frncsco I.....D.....415 487-6700
440 Potrero Ave San Francisco (94110) *(P-17605)*
Horn Electric.....E.....209 339-4278
1008 Black Diamond Way A Lodi (95240) *(P-1516)*
Horn Group Inc.....E.....415 905-4000
101 Montgomery St Fl 15 San Francisco (94104) *(P-11761)*

ALPHABETIC

Horn Machine Tools Inc (PA) ....E....**559 431-4131**
40455 Brickyard Dr # 101 Madera (93636) ***(P-5079)***
Hornberger Worstell Assoc Inc ....E....415 391-1080
170 Maiden Ln Ste 700 San Francisco (94108) ***(P-18891)***
Hornberger, Mark R, San Francisco *Also called Hornberger Worstell Assoc Inc* ***(P-18891)***
Hornblower Cruises & Event, San Francisco *Also called Hornblower Yachts LLC* ***(P-7800)***
Hornblower Energy LLC ....F....415 788-7020
The Embarcadero Pier 3 St Pier San Francisco (94111) ***(P-3771)***
Hornblower Group Inc (PA) ....B....**415 635-2210**
The Embarcadero Pier 3 St Pier San Francisco (94111) ***(P-7799)***
Hornblower Yachts LLC ....D....916 446-1185
200 Marina Blvd Berkeley (94710) ***(P-7721)***
Hornblower Yachts LLC (PA) ....C....**415 788-8866**
On The Embarcadero Pier 3 St Pier San Francisco (94111) ***(P-7800)***
Horsley Bridge Partners Inc (PA) ....E....**415 986-7733**
505 Montgomery St # 2100 San Francisco (94111) ***(P-10854)***
Horsley Bridge Partners LLC ....D....415 986-7733
505 Montgomery St # 2100 San Francisco (94111) ***(P-10855)***
Hortonworks Inc (HQ) ....A....**408 916-4121**
5470 Great America Pkwy Santa Clara (95054) ***(P-13213)***
Horvath Holdings Inc ....F....530 587-4700
40173 Trk Arpt Rd Truckee (96161) ***(P-2970)***
Hoskin & Muir Inc ....E....925 373-1135
6611 Preston Ave Ste C Livermore (94551) ***(P-8552)***
Hospi Comm For The L-P Area T (HQ) ....B....**925 847-3000**
5555 W Las Positas Blvd Pleasanton (94588) ***(P-19349)***
Hospi Comm For The L-P Area T ....A....925 447-7000
1111 E Stanley Blvd Livermore (94550) ***(P-19350)***
Hospice & Home Health of E Bay ....E....510 632-4390
333 Hegenberger Rd # 700 Oakland (94621) ***(P-16894)***
Hospice and Palliative Care ....D....925 945-8924
2849 Miranda Ave Alamo (94507) ***(P-16186)***
HOSPICE CARING PROJECT, Scotts Valley *Also called Hospice of Santa Cruz County* ***(P-16896)***
Hospice Caring Project, Watsonville *Also called Hospice of Santa Cruz County* ***(P-16897)***
Hospice of Foothills (PA) ....D....**530 272-5739**
11270 Rough And Ready Hwy Grass Valley (95945) ***(P-16895)***
Hospice of Humboldt Inc (PA) ....E....**707 445-8443**
3327 Timber Fall Ct Eureka (95503) ***(P-17023)***
HOSPICE OF MARIN, Larkspur *Also called By The Bay Health* ***(P-16863)***
Hospice of San Joaquin ....D....209 957-3888
3888 Pacific Ave Stockton (95204) ***(P-16029)***
Hospice of Santa Cruz County (PA) ....C....**831 430-3000**
940 Disc Dr Scotts Valley (95066) ***(P-16896)***
Hospice of Santa Cruz County ....D....831 430-3000
65 Nielson St Ste 121 Watsonville (95076) ***(P-16897)***
Hospice of The East Bay, Alamo *Also called Hospice and Palliative Care* ***(P-16186)***
Hospice of Valley (PA) ....E....**408 947-1233**
4850 Union Ave San Jose (95124) ***(P-16898)***
Hospice Services Lake County ....E....707 263-6222
1862 Parallel Dr Lakeport (95453) ***(P-16187)***
Hospital Systems Inc ....D....925 427-7800
750 Garcia Ave Pittsburg (94565) ***(P-7107)***
Host International Inc ....C....408 294-1702
1661 Airport Blvd Ste 3e San Jose (95110) ***(P-11162)***
Hostelling International, San Francisco *Also called Golden Gate Cncil Amrcn Yuth H* ***(P-11114)***
Hostmark Investors Ltd Partnr ....E....408 330-0001
4949 Great America Pkwy Santa Clara (95054) ***(P-19351)***
Hot Line Construction Inc ....A....925 634-9333
9020 Brentwood Blvd Ste H Brentwood (94513) ***(P-1517)***
Hotaling & Co LLC (PA) ....E....**415 630-5910**
550 Montgomery St Ste 300 San Francisco (94111) ***(P-2773)***
Hotan Corp ....E....925 290-1000
630 Hardcastle Ct San Ramon (94583) ***(P-8918)***
Hotbox, Campbell *Also called Streamray Inc* ***(P-14880)***
Hotdoodle.com, Fremont *Also called Metabyte Inc* ***(P-13937)***
Hotel Abri, San Francisco *Also called Monticello Hotel LLC* ***(P-11310)***
Hotel Adagio, San Francisco *Also called SC Hotel Partners LLC* ***(P-11447)***
Hotel Avante, Mountain View *Also called Joie De Vivre Hospitality LLC* ***(P-11220)***
Hotel Britton, San Francisco *Also called Reneson Hotels Inc* ***(P-11397)***
Hotel California, San Francisco *Also called Jame Hotel Corporation* ***(P-11208)***
Hotel Citrine, Palo Alto *Also called M10 Dev LLC* ***(P-11278)***
Hotel Del Sol, San Francisco *Also called Joie De Vivre Hospitality LLC* ***(P-11218)***
Hotel Durant A Ltd Partnership ....D....510 845-8981
2600 Durant Ave Berkeley (94704) ***(P-11163)***
Hotel Emplyee Rest Emplyee Un ....E....415 864-8770
209 Golden Gate Ave San Francisco (94102) ***(P-18359)***
Hotel Griffon, San Francisco *Also called Embarcadero Inn Associates* ***(P-11079)***
Hotel Healdsburg LLC (PA) ....D....**707 431-2800**
25 Matheson St Healdsburg (95448) ***(P-11164)***
Hotel Kabuki, San Francisco *Also called Bre/Japantown Owner LLC* ***(P-10972)***
Hotel La Rose ....D....707 284-2879
308 Wilson St Santa Rosa (95401) ***(P-11165)***
Hotel Leger LLC ....E....209 286-1401
83047 Main St Burlingame (94010) ***(P-11166)***
Hotel Mark Twain, San Francisco *Also called Jbear Associates LLC* ***(P-11209)***
Hotel McInnis Marin LLC ....D....415 499-9222
101 Mcinnis Pkwy San Rafael (94903) ***(P-11167)***
Hotel Moneco, San Francisco *Also called Kimpton Hotel & Rest Group LLC* ***(P-11235)***
Hotel NAPA I Opco L P ....D....707 863-0900
4775 Business Center Dr Fairfield (94534) ***(P-11168)***
Hotel NAPA II Opco LP ....E....707 863-0300
4755 Business Center Dr Fairfield (94534) ***(P-11169)***
Hotel Nikko San Francisco Inc ....B....415 394-1111
222 Mason St San Francisco (94102) ***(P-11170)***
Hotel Petaluma, Petaluma *Also called 205 Kentucky Street LLC* ***(P-10902)***
Hotel Prdox Autograph Collectn ....E....831 425-7100
611 Ocean St Santa Cruz (95060) ***(P-11171)***
Hotel Sfitel San Francisco Bay, Redwood City *Also called French Redwood Inc* ***(P-11106)***
Hotel Spero Jspers Crnr Tap Ki, San Francisco *Also called Serenity Now Lessee Inc* ***(P-11461)***
Hotel Tomo, San Francisco *Also called Khp III SF Sutter LLC* ***(P-11229)***
Hotel Tonight Inc (PA) ....B....**800 208-2949**
888 Brannan St Fl 3 San Francisco (94103) ***(P-11172)***
Hotel Tonight LLC (PA) ....D....**248 525-3814**
888 Brannan St Fl 3 San Francisco (94103) ***(P-11173)***
Hotel Trio, Healdsburg *Also called Svi Healdsburg LLC* ***(P-11522)***
Hotel Vitale, San Francisco *Also called Joie De Vivre Hospitality LLC* ***(P-11214)***
Hotel Vitale, San Francisco *Also called Mission Stuart Ht Partners LLC* ***(P-11305)***
Hotel Whitcomb ....D....415 626-8000
1231 Market St San Francisco (94103) ***(P-11174)***
Hotel Yountville LLC ....E....707 967-7900
6462 Washington St Yountville (94599) ***(P-11175)***
Hotwire Inc ....C....415 343-8400
114 Sansome St Ste 400 San Francisco (94104) ***(P-7958)***
House Modesto (PA) ....C....**209 529-7346**
1601 Coffee Rd Modesto (95355) ***(P-17953)***
House of Bagels Inc (PA) ....F....**650 595-4700**
1007 Washington St San Carlos (94070) ***(P-2388)***
House On The Hill, San Jose *Also called Arh Recovery Homes Inc* ***(P-18058)***
Housecanary Inc (PA) ....B....**866 729-7770**
201 Spear St San Francisco (94105) ***(P-13718)***
Housing Auth of The Cy Scrmnto, Sacramento *Also called Sacramnto Hsing Rdvlpment Agcy* ***(P-10657)***
HOUSING AUTHORITY OF SACRAMENT, Sacramento *Also called Sacramento Housing Dev Corp* ***(P-19852)***
Housing Matters ....D....831 458-6020
115b Coral St Santa Cruz (95060) ***(P-17606)***
Houston Mfg & Installation Inc ....E....209 556-0163
520 E Service Rd Modesto (95358) ***(P-9071)***
Houzz Inc (PA) ....D....**650 326-3000**
285 Hamilton Ave Fl 4 Palo Alto (94301) ***(P-12503)***
Howard Frank R Memorial Hosp, Willits *Also called Willits Hospital Inc* ***(P-16724)***
Howard Hughes Medical Inst ....D....650 725-8252
279 Campus Dr Rm B202 Stanford (94305) ***(P-19068)***
Howard Hughes Medical Inst ....D....415 476-9668
1550 4th St Rm 190 San Francisco (94143) ***(P-19069)***
Howard Johnson, Redding *Also called Trigild International Inc* ***(P-11545)***
Howard Prep (PA) ....E....**209 538-2431**
1424 Stonum Rd Modesto (95351) ***(P-17817)***
Howard Prep ....E....209 521-9877
4801 Stratos Way Ste A Modesto (95356) ***(P-17818)***
Howe Electric Inc (PA) ....E....**559 255-8992**
4682 E Olive Ave Fresno (93702) ***(P-1518)***
Howe Electric Inc ....C....559 255-8992
4690 E Olive Ave Fresno (93702) ***(P-1519)***
Howe Electric Construction Inc ....C....559 255-8992
4682 E Olive Ave Fresno (93702) ***(P-1520)***
Howk Systems, Modesto *Also called Howk Well & Equipment Co Inc* ***(P-1107)***
Howk Well & Equipment Co Inc ....E....209 529-4110
1825 Yosemite Blvd Modesto (95354) ***(P-1107)***
Hoya Holdings Inc (HQ) ....C....**408 654-2300**
680 N Mccarthy Blvd # 120 Milpitas (95035) ***(P-7151)***
Hoya Optical Inc (PA) ....D....**209 579-7739**
1400 Carpenter Ln Modesto (95351) ***(P-7141)***
Hp Inc ....D....415 979-3700
303 2nd St Ste S500 San Francisco (94107) ***(P-5250)***
HP Hewlett Packard Group LLC ....D....650 857-1501
1501 Page Mill Rd Palo Alto (94304) ***(P-13719)***
HP Hood LLC ....B....916 379-9266
8340 Belvedere Ave Sacramento (95826) ***(P-2191)***
HP Inc (PA) ....A....**650 857-1501**
1501 Page Mill Rd Palo Alto (94304) ***(P-5251)***
HP Pavillion At San Jose, San Jose *Also called San Jose Sharks LLC* ***(P-14914)***
HP R&D Holding LLC (HQ) ....D....**650 857-1501**
1501 Page Mill Rd Palo Alto (94304) ***(P-5252)***
HP Water Systems Inc ....E....559 268-4751
9338 W Whites Bridge Ave Fresno (93706) ***(P-5176)***
Hpe Enterprises LLC (HQ) ....A....**650 857-5817**
6280 America Center Dr San Jose (95002) ***(P-13214)***
Hpe Government Llc ....D....916 435-9200
46600 Landing Pkwy Fremont (94538) ***(P-5332)***
Hpi Cchgpii LLC ....E....650 687-5817
1501 Page Mill Rd Palo Alto (94304) ***(P-13215)***
Hpi Federal LLC (HQ) ....C....**650 857-1501**
1501 Page Mill Rd Palo Alto (94304) ***(P-5253)***
Hpl Contract Inc ....F....209 892-1717
525 Baldwin Rd Patterson (95363) ***(P-3303)***
HPM Incorporated ....D....510 353-0770
850 Auburn Ct Fremont (94538) ***(P-8710)***
Hpmi, Fremont *Also called Henry Plastic Molding Inc* ***(P-4288)***
Hr, Lodi *Also called Holz Rubber Company Inc* ***(P-4216)***
Hr-Oakmont F/C 5212 ....E....530 895-0123
2801 Cohasset Rd Chico (95973) ***(P-17607)***
Hrn Services, Citrus Heights *Also called Accountble Hlthcare Stffing In* ***(P-12068)***
Hrn Services, Campbell *Also called Accountble Hlthcare Stffing In* ***(P-12069)***
Hsba, Dublin *Also called Health Svcs Bneft Admnstrtors* ***(P-10215)***
Hsf Programme, San Francisco *Also called San Francisco Health Authority* ***(P-18347)***
Hsi Mechanical Inc ....E....209 408-0183
1013 N Emerald Ave Modesto (95351) ***(P-4770)***
Hsq Technology A Corporation ....E....510 259-1334
26227 Research Pl Hayward (94545) ***(P-13609)***
HSU FOUNDATION, Arcata *Also called Humboldt State Univ Spnsred PR* ***(P-19790)***

Hti Turnkey Manufacturing Svcs E 408 955-0807
2200 Zanker Rd Ste A San Jose (95131) ***(P-6433)***
Huawei Enterprise USA Inc D 408 394-4295
20400 Stevens Creek Blvd Cupertino (95014) ***(P-7959)***
Hub Intrntional Insur Svcs Inc E 415 512-2100
44 2nd St San Francisco (94105) ***(P-10294)***
Hub Intrntional Insur Svcs Inc D 559 447-4600
548 W Cromwell Ave # 101 Fresno (93711) ***(P-10295)***
Hudson & Company LLC F 916 774-6465
100 Irene Ave Roseville (95678) ***(P-3026)***
Hudson Excavation Inc E 925 250-1990
570 Valdry Ct Ste C10 Brentwood (94513) ***(P-1962)***
Huey Construction MGT Co Inc E 415 558-9806
266 5th Ave Apt 1 San Francisco (94118) ***(P-652)***
Huffman Logging Co Inc E 707 725-4335
1155 Huffman Dr Fortuna (95540) ***(P-3064)***
Hughes Dental Group, Campbell *Also called John A Hughes DDS Incorporated* ***(P-15842)***
Hughson Nut Inc F 209 394-6005
11173 Mercedes Ave Livingston (95334) ***(P-2902)***
Hughson Nut Inc (HQ) **B 209 883-0403**
1825 Verduga Rd Hughson (95326) ***(P-2445)***
Hugin Components Inc E 916 652-1070
4231 Pacific St Ste 23 Rocklin (95677) ***(P-4884)***
Huhtamaki Inc D 916 688-4938
8450 Gerber Rd Sacramento (95828) ***(P-9661)***
Hula Networks Inc (PA) **F 866 485-2638**
929 Berryessa Rd Ste 10 San Jose (95133) ***(P-8711)***
Hulft Inc (PA) **D 650 393-4930**
1820 Gateway Dr Ste 120 San Mateo (94404) ***(P-13216)***
Hulling Company E 559 674-1896
2900 Airport Dr Madera (93637) ***(P-290)***
Human Resource Consultants E 916 485-6500
3727 Marconi Ave Sacramento (95821) ***(P-17024)***
Human Resource Solutions, Chico *Also called Roy Carrington Inc* ***(P-12131)***
Humanapi Inc D 650 542-9800
951 Mariners Island Blvd # 300 San Mateo (94404) ***(P-12504)***
Humanconcepts LLC E 650 581-2500
3 Harbor Dr Ste 200 Sausalito (94965) ***(P-13217)***
Humane Society Silicon Valley D 408 262-2133
901 Ames Ave Milpitas (95035) ***(P-18573)***
Humangear Inc F 415 580-7553
2962 Fillmore St San Francisco (94123) ***(P-4289)***
Humangood (PA) **B 602 906-4024**
6120 Stoneridge Mall Rd Pleasanton (94588) ***(P-16241)***
Humangood Affordable Housing D 925 924-7100
6120 Stoneridge Mall Rd Pleasanton (94588) ***(P-10439)***
Humangood Affordable Housing (HQ) **B 925 924-7163**
6120 Stoneridge Mall Rd # 100 Pleasanton (94588) ***(P-19352)***
Humangood Norcal (HQ) **D 925 924-7100**
6120 Stnrdge Mall Rd Ste Pleasanton (94588) ***(P-10440)***
Humangood Norcal D 650 948-8291
373 Pine Ln Los Altos (94022) ***(P-16242)***
Humangood Norcal D 408 357-1100
800 Blossom Hill Rd Ofc Los Gatos (95032) ***(P-16243)***
Humanstic Altrntves To Addctio E 510 875-2300
10850 Macarthur Blvd # 20 Oakland (94605) ***(P-17025)***
Humboldt Bay Fire Jint Pwers A D 707 441-4000
533 C St Eureka (95501) ***(P-17154)***
Humboldt Bay Harbor, The, Eureka *Also called Humboldt Bay Hbr Rcrtion Cnsrv* ***(P-7730)***
Humboldt Bay Hbr Rcrtion Cnsrv D 707 443-0801
601 Startare Dr Eureka (95501) ***(P-7730)***
Humboldt Bottling LLC F 707 725-4119
517 7th St Fortuna (95540) ***(P-2793)***
Humboldt Bottling Co., Fortuna *Also called Humboldt Bottling LLC* ***(P-2793)***
Humboldt Cmnty Access Rsrce CT D 707 441-8625
1001 Searles St Eureka (95501) ***(P-17608)***
Humboldt Cmnty Access Rsrce CT D 707 443-7077
1707 E St Ste 2 Eureka (95501) ***(P-17609)***
Humboldt Commnty Accss Resrc (PA) **C 707 443-7077**
1707 E St Ste 2 Eureka (95501) ***(P-17610)***
Humboldt Community Service Dst E 707 443-4558
5055 Walnut Dr Eureka (95503) ***(P-8251)***
Humboldt Dev LLC D 213 295-2890
2804 Gateway Oaks Dr # 100 Sacramento (95833) ***(P-13907)***
Humboldt Dog Obedience Group E 707 444-3862
P.O. Box 6733 Eureka (95502) ***(P-355)***
Humboldt House Inn LLC E 707 923-2771
701 Redwood Dr Garberville (95542) ***(P-11176)***
Humboldt Newspaper Inc D 707 442-1711
930 6th St Eureka (95501) ***(P-3447)***
Humboldt Redwood Company LLC (HQ) **C 707 764-4472**
125 Main St Scotia (95565) ***(P-8553)***
Humboldt Sanitatation & Recycl, McKinleyville *Also called Humboldt Sanitation Co* ***(P-7474)***
Humboldt Sanitation Co D 707 839-3285
2585 Central Ave McKinleyville (95519) ***(P-7474)***
Humboldt Senior Resource Ctr (PA) **D 707 443-9747**
1910 California St Eureka (95501) ***(P-17611)***
Humboldt State Univ Spnsred PR D 707 826-4189
1 Harpst St Sbs Bldg Rm 4 Arcata (95521) ***(P-19790)***
Humdog, Eureka *Also called Humboldt Dog Obedience Group* ***(P-355)***
Hume Lake Christian Camps Inc E 559 305-7770
64144 Hume Lake Rd Ofc Miramonte (93628) ***(P-11603)***
Humphrey Plumbing Inc D 209 634-4626
880 S Kilroy Rd Turlock (95380) ***(P-1280)***
Humu Inc (PA) **D 669 241-4868**
100 View St Ste 101 Mountain View (94041) ***(P-12505)***
Huneeus Vintners LLC (PA) **E 707 286-2724**
1040 Main St Ste 204 NAPA (94559) ***(P-2618)***
Hunt & Behrens Inc E 707 762-4594
30 Lakeville St Petaluma (94952) ***(P-9600)***
Hunt & Sons Inc (PA) **E 916 383-4868**
5750 S Watt Ave Sacramento (95829) ***(P-9525)***
Hunter Douglas Fabrications C 408 435-8844
842 Charcot Ave San Jose (95131) ***(P-3331)***
Huntford Printing E 408 957-5000
275 Dempsey Rd Milpitas (95035) ***(P-3656)***
Huntford Printing & Graphics, Milpitas *Also called Huntford Printing* ***(P-3656)***
Huntington Mechanical Labs, Grass Valley *Also called Huntington Mechanical Labs Inc* ***(P-5185)***
Huntington Mechanical Labs Inc E 530 273-9533
13355 Nevada City Ave Grass Valley (95945) ***(P-5185)***
Huntsman Architectural Group (PA) **D 415 394-1212**
50 California St Fl 7 San Francisco (94111) ***(P-18892)***
Hupp Signs & Lighting Inc F 530 345-7078
70 Loren Ave Chico (95928) ***(P-7232)***
Hurley Construction Inc D 916 446-7599
1801 I St Ste 200 Sacramento (95811) ***(P-748)***
Hurricane Electric LLC (PA) **E 510 580-4100**
760 Mission Ct Fremont (94539) ***(P-13793)***
Husch Vineyards Inc (PA) **E 707 895-3216**
4400 Highway 128 Philo (95466) ***(P-2619)***
Huskies Lessee LLC C 415 392-7755
450 Powell St San Francisco (94102) ***(P-11177)***
Hust Brothers Inc (PA) **E 530 743-1561**
710 3rd St Marysville (95901) ***(P-10578)***
Hustle Inc E 415 851-4878
595 Market St Ste 920 San Francisco (94105) ***(P-12506)***
Hutchs Car Washes Inc E 510 538-9274
17945 Hesperian Blvd San Lorenzo (94580) ***(P-14641)***
Hv-Houston Development Inc E 916 638-1100
11211 Point East Dr Rancho Cordova (95742) ***(P-11178)***
Hvr Software Inc (PA) **E 415 655-6361**
135 Main St Ste 850 San Francisco (94105) ***(P-13218)***
Hvr Software Usa Inc D 415 489-3427
44 Montgomery St Ste 3 San Francisco (94104) ***(P-13219)***
Hvsf Transition LLC B 415 477-1999
1100 Sansome St San Francisco (94111) ***(P-11762)***
Hwang LLC D 408 435-8800
2585 Seaboard Ave San Jose (95131) ***(P-11179)***
Hy-Lond Hlth Care Cnter-Merced, Merced *Also called Avalon Care Cen* ***(P-15913)***
Hy-Lond Hlth Care Cntr-Modesto, Modesto *Also called Avalon Care Center - Modesto* ***(P-15914)***
Hy-Tech Plating Inc F 650 593-4566
1011 American St San Carlos (94070) ***(P-4911)***
Hyatt Cinema 3, Burlingame *Also called Century Theatres Inc* ***(P-14827)***
Hyatt Corporation B 415 848-6050
345 Stockton St San Francisco (94108) ***(P-11180)***
Hyatt Corporation B 925 743-1882
2323 San Ramon Vly Blvd San Ramon (94583) ***(P-11181)***
Hyatt Corporation C 650 452-1234
55 S Mcdonnell Rd San Francisco (94128) ***(P-11182)***
Hyatt Corporation A 415 788-1234
5 Embarcadero Ctr San Francisco (94111) ***(P-11183)***
Hyatt Die Cast Engrg Corp - S E 408 523-7000
1250 Kifer Rd Sunnyvale (94086) ***(P-4577)***
Hyatt Die Casting, Sunnyvale *Also called Hyatt Die Cast Engrg Corp - S* ***(P-4577)***
Hyatt Fshrmans Wharf San Frncs, San Francisco *Also called Chsp Trs Fisherman Wharf LLC* ***(P-11007)***
Hyatt Hotel, San Francisco *Also called Hyatt Corporation* ***(P-11182)***
Hyatt Hotel, Santa Clara *Also called Hyatt Regency Santa Clara* ***(P-11184)***
Hyatt Hotel, Santa Rosa *Also called Noble Aew Vineyard Creek LLC* ***(P-11330)***
Hyatt House Rancho Cordova, Rancho Cordova *Also called Select Hotels Group LLC* ***(P-11457)***
Hyatt House San Ramon, San Ramon *Also called Select Hotels Group LLC* ***(P-11453)***
Hyatt House San Ramon, San Ramon *Also called Hyatt Corporation* ***(P-11181)***
Hyatt House Santa Clara, Santa Clara *Also called Select Hotels Group LLC* ***(P-11456)***
Hyatt Hse Blmnt/Redwood Shores, Belmont *Also called Grand Prix Belmont LLC* ***(P-11117)***
Hyatt Hse Blmnt/Redwood Shores, Belmont *Also called Island Hospitality MGT LLC* ***(P-11202)***
Hyatt Hse Emryvll/San Frncsco, Emeryville *Also called Select Hotels Group LLC* ***(P-11454)***
Hyatt Hse San Jose Silicon Vly, San Jose *Also called Select Hotels Group LLC* ***(P-11459)***
Hyatt Pl Fremont/Silicon Vly, Fremont *Also called Select Hotels Group LLC* ***(P-11455)***
Hyatt Pl Sacramento/Roseville, Roseville *Also called Select Hotels Group LLC* ***(P-11458)***
Hyatt Place San Jose/Downtown, San Jose *Also called West San Crlos Ht Partners LLC* ***(P-11572)***
Hyatt Place Vacaville, Vacaville *Also called Sunrise Palace Inc* ***(P-11519)***
Hyatt Regency Sacramento, Sacramento *Also called Capitol Regency LLC* ***(P-10988)***
Hyatt Regency San Francisco Ht, San Francisco *Also called Hyatt Corporation* ***(P-11183)***
Hyatt Regency Santa Clara D 408 200-1234
5101 Great America Pkwy Santa Clara (95054) ***(P-11184)***
Hydrapak Inc E 510 632-8318
6605 San Leandro St Oakland (94621) ***(P-7197)***
Hydratech LLC (HQ) **D 559 233-0876**
453 Pollasky Ave Ste 106 Clovis (93612) ***(P-14755)***
Hydro Division, Snelling *Also called Merced Irrigation District* ***(P-8124)***
Hydro Power Service, Sacramento *Also called HDR Engineering Inc* ***(P-18728)***
Hydrofarm LLC (HQ) **E 707 765-9990**
2249 S Mcdowell Blvd Ext Petaluma (94954) ***(P-5743)***
Hydropoint Data Systems Inc E 707 769-9696
1720 Corporate Cir Petaluma (94954) ***(P-5006)***
Hydroscience Engineers Inc (PA) **E 916 364-1490**
10569 Old Placerville Rd Sacramento (95827) ***(P-18734)***
Hye Quality Bakery Inc E 559 445-1511
2222 Santa Clara St Fresno (93721) ***(P-2415)***

A L P H A B E T I C

Hygieia Biological Labs ALPHABETIC SECTION

Hygieia Biological Labs ...E...530 661-1442
1240 Commerce Ave Ste B Woodland (95776) ***(P-4051)***
Hyland LLC ...F...440 788-5045
12919 Earhart Ave Auburn (95602) ***(P-12507)***
Hylton Security Inc ...E...916 442-1000
2045 Hallmark Dr Ste 6 Sacramento (95825) ***(P-14070)***
Hypergrid Inc ...D...650 316-5524
425 Tasso St Palo Alto (94301) ***(P-12508)***
Hyperion Therapeutics Inc ...E...650 492-1385
2000 Sierra Point Pkwy # 400 Brisbane (94005) ***(P-3924)***
Hyperwallet, San Francisco *Also called Paypal Inc* ***(P-14359)***
Hyponex Corporation ...E...209 887-3845
23390 E Flood Rd Linden (95236) ***(P-4132)***
Hypower Hydraulics, Turlock *Also called Turlock Machine Works* ***(P-5453)***
Hytek R&D Inc (PA) ...**E...408 761-5266**
2044 Corporate Ct Milpitas (95035) ***(P-5939)***
Hytrust Inc (HQ) ...**D...650 681-8100**
1975 W El Cmino Real Ste Mountain View (94040) ***(P-12509)***
I & A Inc ...E...408 432-8340
2221 Ringwood Ave San Jose (95131) ***(P-4771)***
I & E Lath Mill ...E...707 895-3380
8701 Philo School Rd Philo (95466) ***(P-3097)***
I A S, Palo Alto *Also called Integrated Archive Systems Inc* ***(P-19540)***
I AM Activity, Dunsmuir *Also called Saint Germain Foundation* ***(P-3513)***
I B S, Roseville *Also called Iptor Supply Chain Systems USA* ***(P-12538)***
I C Refrigeration Svc Inc ...E...209 538-8271
2216 Rockefeller Dr Ceres (95307) ***(P-1281)***
I C S, San Rafael *Also called Integrated Community Services* ***(P-17617)***
I C S I, Berkeley *Also called Interntional Cmpt Science Inst* ***(P-19222)***
I Can Do That Theatre Company ...E...415 264-2518
194 Diablo Rd Danville (94526) ***(P-14848)***
I G S Inc ...E...408 733-4621
916 E California Ave Sunnyvale (94085) ***(P-4360)***
I Manageproperty Inc ...E...510 665-0665
1400 Shattuck Ave Ste 2 Berkeley (94709) ***(P-13220)***
I Merit Inc (PA) ...**E...650 777-7857**
985 University Ave Ste 8 Los Gatos (95032) ***(P-13720)***
I Merit Inc ...A...504 226-2427
14435c Big Basin Way Saratoga (95070) ***(P-13721)***
I Merit USA, Los Gatos *Also called I Merit Inc* ***(P-13720)***
I S A Contracting Svcs Inc ...A...559 659-1080
958 O St Firebaugh (93622) ***(P-262)***
I S T, Santa Clara *Also called Information Scan Tech Inc* ***(P-6763)***
I T C, Citrus Heights *Also called Itc Srvice Group Acqsition LLC* ***(P-19800)***
I T C, Fresno *Also called Interntnal Trque Cnverters Inc* ***(P-14540)***
I T M Software Corp ...F...650 864-2500
1030 W Maude Ave Sunnyvale (94085) ***(P-13221)***
I Trovatori Opera Inc ...E...925 246-9360
2097 Olivera Rd Apt C Concord (94520) ***(P-14872)***
I-5 Rentals Inc ...E...530 226-8081
8443 Commercial Way Redding (96002) ***(P-12049)***
I2c Inc ...B...650 593-5400
100 Redwood Shores Pkwy # 100 Redwood City (94065) ***(P-8712)***
IA Lodging NAPA Solano Trs LLC ...C...707 253-8600
3425 Solano Ave NAPA (94558) ***(P-11185)***
Iab Brands Inc ...F...844 426-2634
4060 Clarewood Way Sacramento (95835) ***(P-7288)***
Iab Mfg, Sacramento *Also called Iab Brands Inc* ***(P-7288)***
IAC Publishing LLC ...D...510 985-7400
555 12th St Ste 300 Oakland (94607) ***(P-7960)***
IAC Search & Media Inc (HQ) ...**C...510 985-7400**
555 12th St Ste 500 Oakland (94607) ***(P-13794)***
Iav Inc ...E...707 857-4343
21714 Geyserville Ave Geyserville (95441) ***(P-11186)***
Iberia Catering Inc ...E...415 587-5117
139 20th Ave San Francisco (94121) ***(P-11720)***
Ibex Enterprises ...E...415 777-0202
350 Brannan St Fl 1 San Francisco (94107) ***(P-8495)***
IBM, San Jose *Also called International Bus Mchs Corp* ***(P-12533)***
IBM, San Francisco *Also called International Bus Mchs Corp* ***(P-8652)***
IBM, San Jose *Also called International Bus Mchs Corp* ***(P-19075)***
Ibs, San Ramon *Also called Integrated Bldg Solutions Inc* ***(P-19797)***
IC Ink Image Co Inc ...E...209 931-3040
4627 E Fremont St Stockton (95215) ***(P-3737)***
Ic Sensors Inc ...D...510 498-1570
45738 Northport Loop W Fremont (94538) ***(P-6146)***
Ice Consulting Inc (PA) ...**D...408 701-5700**
1900 Mccarthy Blvd # 300 Milpitas (95035) ***(P-13908)***
Ice Mortgage Technology Inc (HQ) ...**A...855 224-8572**
4420 Rosewood Dr Ste 500 Pleasanton (94588) ***(P-13222)***
Ichor Holdings Ltd (PA) ...**E...510 897-5200**
3185 Laurelview Ct Fremont (94538) ***(P-18735)***
Ichor Systems Inc (HQ) ...**E...510 897-5200**
3185 Laurelview Ct Fremont (94538) ***(P-6147)***
ICO Rally, Palo Alto *Also called Insulation Sources Inc* ***(P-8863)***
Icom Mechanical Inc ...C...408 292-4968
477 Burke St San Jose (95112) ***(P-1282)***
Icon Aircraft Inc (PA) ...**C...707 564-4000**
2141 Icon Way Vacaville (95688) ***(P-6634)***
Icon Apparel Group LLC ...E...916 372-4266
2989 Promenade St Ste 100 West Sacramento (95691) ***(P-2968)***
Icon Design and Display Inc ...E...707 416-0230
17740 Shideler Pkwy Lathrop (95330) ***(P-3304)***
Icon Exhibits LLC ...E...260 482-8700
950 W Tower Ave Alameda (94501) ***(P-14300)***
Icon Internet Ventures Inc ...E...415 874-3397
505 Montgomery St 10t San Francisco (94111) ***(P-19534)***
Icracked Inc (HQ) ...**E...877 700-0349**
690 Broadway St Redwood City (94063) ***(P-14700)***
Ics Integrated Comm Systems ...D...408 491-6000
6680 Via Del Oro San Jose (95119) ***(P-1521)***
Ics-CA North, Roseville *Also called Industrial Cont Svcs - CA N LL* ***(P-9120)***
Icu Medical Inc ...D...408 284-7064
5729 Fontanoso Way San Jose (95138) ***(P-6983)***
ID Tech Camps, Campbell *Also called Internal Drive* ***(P-11604)***
Idc Technologies Inc (PA) ...**C...408 376-0212**
920 Hillview Ct Ste 250 Milpitas (95035) ***(P-12098)***
Idea Travel Company ...A...650 948-0207
13145 Byrd Ln Ste 101 Los Altos Hills (94022) ***(P-7801)***
Ideal Aerosmith Inc ...F...650 353-3641
155 Constitution Dr Menlo Park (94025) ***(P-19275)***
Ideal Envmtl Pdts & Svcs, Gilroy *Also called Containment Consultants Inc* ***(P-4718)***
Ideaya Biosciences Inc ...D...650 443-6209
7000 Shoreline Ct Ste 350 South San Francisco (94080) ***(P-3925)***
Idec Corporation (HQ) ...**D...408 747-0550**
1175 Elko Dr Sunnyvale (94089) ***(P-8919)***
Identiv Inc (PA) ...**C...949 250-8888**
2201 Walnut Ave Ste 100 Fremont (94538) ***(P-5373)***
Ideo LP (PA) ...**C...650 289-3400**
780 High St Palo Alto (94301) ***(P-11865)***
Ideo Partners LLC ...E...650 289-3400
715 Alma St Palo Alto (94301) ***(P-19791)***
Ideoorg ...D...415 426-7080
444 Spear St Ste 213 San Francisco (94105) ***(P-18433)***
Idex Global Services Inc ...C...415 482-4242
2301 Kerner Blvd Ste D San Rafael (94901) ***(P-1522)***
Idex Health & Science LLC (HQ) ...**D...707 588-2000**
600 Park Ct Rohnert Park (94928) ***(P-6693)***
Idg Consumer & Smb Inc (HQ) ...**C...415 243-0500**
501 2nd St San Francisco (94107) ***(P-3503)***
Idt Telecomm Data, San Rafael *Also called Installtion Dgtal Trnsmssons I* ***(P-2038)***
Iest Family Farms ...D...559 674-9417
14576 Avenue 14 Madera (93637) ***(P-214)***
If Copack LLC ...E...559 875-3354
1912 Industrial Way Sanger (93657) ***(P-2201)***
If Holding Inc (PA) ...**C...559 875-3354**
1912 Industrial Way Sanger (93657) ***(P-2903)***
Ifeatu Nnebe DDS Inc (PA) ...**E...916 299-9487**
2700 E Bidwell St Ste 300 Folsom (95630) ***(P-15837)***
Ifwe Inc (HQ) ...**C...415 946-1850**
848 Battery St San Francisco (94111) ***(P-13223)***
Igenex Inc ...E...650 424-1191
556 Gibraltar Dr Milpitas (95035) ***(P-16785)***
Igenex Reference Laboratory, Milpitas *Also called Igenex Inc* ***(P-16785)***
Igm Biosciences Inc ...D...650 965-7873
325 E Middlefield Rd Mountain View (94043) ***(P-19070)***
Ignatius Press, San Francisco *Also called Guadalupe Associates Inc* ***(P-3574)***
Ignite Lending, Roseville *Also called Catalyst Mortgage* ***(P-9899)***
Ignyta Inc (HQ) ...**C...858 255-5959**
1 Dna Way South San Francisco (94080) ***(P-3926)***
Igraphics (PA) ...**E...530 273-2200**
165 Spring Hill Dr Grass Valley (95945) ***(P-3738)***
Igt Interactive Inc (HQ) ...**D...415 625-8300**
300 California St Fl 8 San Francisco (94104) ***(P-15211)***
Iguard Security Services Inc (PA) ...**E...650 714-1884**
2850 Stevens Creek Blvd San Jose (95128) ***(P-14137)***
Iheartcommunications Inc ...D...559 230-4300
83 E Shaw Ave Ste 150 Fresno (93710) ***(P-8027)***
Ihms (sf) LLC ...C...415 781-5555
340 Stockton St San Francisco (94108) ***(P-11187)***
IHSS CONSORTIUM, THE, San Francisco *Also called Homebridge Inc* ***(P-17602)***
Iitjobs Inc ...D...510 509-9368
1340 S De Anza Blvd # 208 San Jose (95129) ***(P-12099)***
Iix Peering, Santa Clara *Also called Console* ***(P-7942)***
Ijk & Co Inc ...E...415 826-8899
225 Industrial St San Francisco (94124) ***(P-6525)***
Ikes Landscaping & Maintenance ...D...530 758-1698
2700 Tiber Ave Davis (95616) ***(P-470)***
IL Fornaio (america) LLC (HQ) ...**E...415 945-0500**
770 Tamalpais Dr Ste 208 Corte Madera (94925) ***(P-9454)***
IL Fornaio Cucina Italiana, Corte Madera *Also called IL Fornaio (america) LLC* ***(P-9454)***
IL Helth Buty Natural Oils Inc ...E...530 358-0222
2644 Hegan Ln Chico (95928) ***(P-4162)***
Illinois Tool Works Inc ...D...916 939-4332
5000 Hillsdale Cir El Dorado Hills (95762) ***(P-6148)***
Illumina-Redwood City, Foster City *Also called Verinata Health Inc* ***(P-19147)***
Illuminated Creations Inc ...E...916 924-1936
1111 Joellis Way Sacramento (95815) ***(P-7233)***
Illumio Inc ...C...669 800-5000
920 De Guigne Dr Sunnyvale (94085) ***(P-12510)***
Ilovetocreate A Duncan Entps, Fresno *Also called Duncan Enterprises* ***(P-4103)***
Imacc Corporation ...E...510 233-4865
2200 Central St Richmond (94801) ***(P-9119)***
Image Masters, Merced *Also called On Target Marketing* ***(P-11872)***
Image Technology, Palo Alto *Also called Suss McRtec Prcsion Phtmask In* ***(P-7158)***
Imagex Inc ...F...925 474-8100
5990 Stoneridge Dr # 112 Pleasanton (94588) ***(P-3657)***
Imagine Easy Solutions LLC (HQ) ...**E...212 675-6738**
3990 Freedom Cir Santa Clara (95054) ***(P-19166)***
Imagine H20 Inc ...E...415 828-6344
88 Kearny St Ste 2100 San Francisco (94108) ***(P-19353)***
Imagine Your Photos, Fremont *Also called Iyp Inc* ***(P-11674)***
Imax Corporation ...D...408 294-8324
201 S Market St San Jose (95113) ***(P-14811)***

Imerys Filtration Minerals Inc (HQ)......E......**805 562-0200**
1732 N 1st St Ste 450 San Jose (95112) ***(P-4529)***
IMG Altair LLC......D......650 508-8700
41970 Christy St Fremont (94538) ***(P-5152)***
IMG Companies LLC (PA)......D......**925 273-1100**
225 Mountain Vista Pkwy Livermore (94551) ***(P-5538)***
Imidomics Inc......F......415 652-4963
541 Jefferson Ave Ste 100 Redwood City (94063) ***(P-3927)***
Immaculate Heart Mary School......E......650 593-2344
1000 Almeda De Las Pulgas Belmont (94002) ***(P-17954)***
Immecor......E......707 636-2550
1650 Northpoint Pkwy C Santa Rosa (95407) ***(P-12511)***
Immersion Corporation (PA)......E......**408 467-1900**
330 Townsend St Ste 234 San Francisco (94107) ***(P-5374)***
Immigration Inst of Bay Area (PA)......E......**415 538-8100**
1111 Market St Fl 4 San Francisco (94103) ***(P-17612)***
Immunoscience LLC (PA)......E......**925 460-8111**
6780 Sierra Ct Ste M Dublin (94568) ***(P-19071)***
Impac Medical Systems Inc (HQ)......E......**408 830-8000**
100 Mathilda Pl Fl 5 Sunnyvale (94086) ***(P-13224)***
Impact Business Service, Redwood City *Also called Abilitypath* ***(P-17404)***
Impact Destinations & Events......E......415 766-4170
26338 Esperanza Dr Los Altos Hills (94022) ***(P-11721)***
Impact Displays, Santa Clara *Also called Impact Marketing Displays LLC* ***(P-7234)***
Impact Events, Los Altos Hills *Also called Impact Destinations & Events* ***(P-11721)***
Impact Marketing Displays LLC......F......408 217-6850
1725 De La Cruz Blvd Santa Clara (95050) ***(P-7234)***
Impakt Holdings LLC......E......408 727-0880
490 Gianni St Santa Clara (95054) ***(P-4772)***
Impec Group Inc (PA)......C......**408 330-9350**
3350 Scott Blvd Bldg 8 Santa Clara (95054) ***(P-11961)***
Imperative Care Inc (PA)......E......**669 228-3814**
1359 Dell Ave Campbell (95008) ***(P-7072)***
Imperfect Foods Inc (PA)......A......**415 829-2262**
1616 Donner Ave San Francisco (94124) ***(P-2904)***
Imperfect Produce, San Francisco *Also called Imperfect Foods Inc* ***(P-2904)***
Imperial Die Cutting Inc......E......916 443-6142
300 N 12th St Sacramento (95811) ***(P-3394)***
Imperial Parking (us) LLC......A......415 495-3909
1740 Cesar Chavez Fl 2 San Francisco (94124) ***(P-14513)***
Imperial System, Union City *Also called Blc Wc Inc* ***(P-5197)***
Imperial Western Products Inc......D......559 891-2600
3766 E Conejo Ave Selma (93662) ***(P-9507)***
Imperva Inc (HQ)......A......**650 345-9000**
1 Curiosity Way Ste 203 San Mateo (94403) ***(P-12512)***
Implus LLC......C......408 796-7739
1610 Dell Ave Ste S Campbell (95008) ***(P-4199)***
Imply Data Inc (PA)......C......**415 685-8187**
1633 Old Byshore Hwy Ste Burlingame (94010) ***(P-13225)***
Importers Software, Santa Clara *Also called Laxmi Group Inc* ***(P-12570)***
Impossible Aerospace Corp......F......707 293-9367
1709 Junction Ct San Jose (95112) ***(P-6611)***
Impossible Foods Inc (PA)......B......**650 461-4385**
400 Saginaw Dr Redwood City (94063) ***(P-2905)***
Imprint Energy Inc......F......510 847-7027
1320 Harbor Bay Pkwy # 110 Alameda (94502) ***(P-6495)***
IMS - Insurance Med Svcs Inc......C......510 490-6211
37600 Central Ct Ste 201 Newark (94560) ***(P-19072)***
IMT, Milpitas *Also called Integrated Mfg Tech Inc* ***(P-5541)***
IMT Associates......E......510 352-6000
1850 San Leandro Blvd San Leandro (94577) ***(P-17294)***
IMT Precision Inc......E......510 324-8926
31902 Hayman St Hayward (94544) ***(P-5539)***
Imtec Acculine LLC......E......510 770-1800
49036 Milmont Dr Fremont (94538) ***(P-5153)***
Imusti Inc (PA)......D......**510 453-1864**
48371 Fremont Blvd # 103 Fremont (94538) ***(P-12513)***
In Front Enterprises......E......510 799-9018
1877 Redwood Rd Hercules (94547) ***(P-12514)***
In Home Health, Burlingame *Also called Hcr Manorcare Inc* ***(P-16019)***
In Home Services LLC......E......559 897-5161
1673 Lewis St Kingsburg (93631) ***(P-16899)***
In-Shape City, Stockton *Also called In-Shape Health Clubs LLC* ***(P-14953)***
In-Shape Health Clubs LLC (PA)......E......**209 472-2231**
6507 Pacific Ave 344 Stockton (95207) ***(P-14953)***
Ina, Michael T Dvm, San Francisco *Also called Arguello Pet Hospital Inc* ***(P-321)***
Inaudr LLC (PA)......E......**707 585-2718**
5460 State Farm Dr Rohnert Park (94928) ***(P-3658)***
Inbenta Technologies Inc (PA)......E......**408 213-8771**
440 N Wolfe Rd Sunnyvale (94085) ***(P-13226)***
Incal Technology Inc......E......510 657-8405
46420 Fremont Blvd Fremont (94538) ***(P-5375)***
Incalus Inc......E......510 209-4064
41829 Albrae St Ste 212 Fremont (94538) ***(P-13909)***
Incarda Therapeutics Inc......E......510 422-5522
39899 Balentine Dr # 185 Newark (94560) ***(P-3928)***
Inclin Inc (PA)......D......**650 961-3422**
2929 Campus Dr Ste 230 San Mateo (94403) ***(P-19073)***
Incline Therapeutics Inc......F......650 241-6800
900 Saginaw Dr Ste 200 Redwood City (94063) ***(P-3929)***
Incognia US Inc......D......650 463-9280
2479 E Byshore Rd Ste 150 East Palo Alto (94303) ***(P-12515)***
Incom Mechanical Inc......D......707 586-0511
975 Transport Way Ste 5 Petaluma (94954) ***(P-1283)***
Incountry Inc......D......415 323-0322
2443 Fillmore St 380-1 San Francisco (94115) ***(P-13227)***
Incube Labs LLC......E......847 565-9506
518 Sycamore Dr Milpitas (95035) ***(P-10856)***
Independent Construction Co, Concord *Also called D A McCosker Construction Co* ***(P-1030)***
Independent Electric Sup Inc (HQ)......C......**510 877-9850**
2001 Marina Blvd San Leandro (94577) ***(P-8862)***
Independent Quality Care Inc (PA)......D......**925 855-0881**
3 Crow Canyon Ct San Ramon (94583) ***(P-16244)***
Independent Quality Care Inc......D......415 479-1230
40 Professional Ctr Pkwy San Rafael (94903) ***(P-16245)***
Independent Quality Care Inc......E......650 583-7768
890 El Camino Real San Bruno (94066) ***(P-16246)***
Independent Quality Care Inc......D......510 836-3677
2910 Mcclure St Oakland (94609) ***(P-16247)***
Independent Quality Care Inc......D......925 284-5544
3721 Mt Diablo Blvd Lafayette (94549) ***(P-16248)***
Independent, The, Livermore *Also called Inland Valley Publishing Co* ***(P-3450)***
Indepndent Brkley Stdnt Pubg I......D......510 548-8300
2483 Hearst Ave Berkeley (94709) ***(P-3448)***
Indepndent Flr Tstg Insptn Inc......F......925 676-7682
1390 Willow Pass Rd # 1010 Concord (94520) ***(P-4438)***
Indepndnt Onlne Dstribution (PA)......D......**415 777-4632**
539 Bryant St Ste 303 San Francisco (94107) ***(P-14301)***
India-West Publications Inc (PA)......E......**510 383-1140**
933 Macarthur Blvd San Leandro (94577) ***(P-3449)***
Indian Head Industries Inc......D......707 894-3333
1184 S Cloverdale Blvd Cloverdale (95425) ***(P-6582)***
Indian Hill Processing......F......209 274-9164
2201 Michigan Bar Rd Ione (95640) ***(P-603)***
Indian Hlth Ctr Snta Clara Vly......C......408 445-3400
1333 Meridian Ave San Jose (95125) ***(P-15433)***
Indian Rock Universal Inc......E......916 696-6973
4132 Manzanita Ave # 400 Carmichael (95608) ***(P-7907)***
Indian Springs Resort & Spa, Calistoga *Also called Resort At Indian Springs LLC* ***(P-11406)***
Indian Valley Golf Club Inc......E......415 897-1118
3035 Novato Blvd Novato (94947) ***(P-15004)***
Indian Valley Health Care Dist......E......530 284-7191
184 Hot Springs Rd Greenville (95947) ***(P-16388)***
Indian Valley Hospital, Greenville *Also called Indian Valley Health Care Dist* ***(P-16388)***
Indiegogo Inc......C......866 641-4646
965 Mission St Fl 7 San Francisco (94103) ***(P-7961)***
Indigo America Inc......C......650 857-1501
1501 Page Mill Rd Palo Alto (94304) ***(P-5254)***
Indium Software Inc......E......408 501-8844
19925 Stevns Crk Blvd Cupertino (95014) ***(P-13228)***
Individual Software Inc......E......925 734-6767
3049 Independence Dr E Livermore (94551) ***(P-13229)***
Individuals Now......D......707 544-3299
2447 Summerfield Rd Santa Rosa (95405) ***(P-17613)***
Indoor Environmental Services, Sacramento *Also called Famand Inc* ***(P-1261)***
Inductive Automation LLC......D......800 266-7798
90 Blue Ravine Rd Folsom (95630) ***(P-19535)***
Indus Corporation......D......415 202-1830
1275 Columbus Ave San Francisco (94133) ***(P-12516)***
Induspac California Inc (HQ)......E......**510 324-3626**
6818 Patterson Pass Rd A Livermore (94550) ***(P-3804)***
Industrial Automtn Group LLC......D......209 579-7527
4400 Sisk Rd Modesto (95356) ***(P-18736)***
Industrial Carting, Santa Rosa *Also called Industrial Wste Dbris Box Rnta* ***(P-7475)***
Industrial Cont Svcs - CA N LL......D......916 781-2775
749 Galleria Blvd Roseville (95678) ***(P-9120)***
Industrial Control Components, Santa Clara *Also called Bell Electrical Supply Inc* ***(P-8845)***
Industrial Elec Systems Inc (PA)......E......**916 638-1000**
3250 Monier Cir Ste F Rancho Cordova (95742) ***(P-1523)***
Industrial Electric Mfg, Fremont *Also called New Iem LLC* ***(P-5652)***
Industrial Glass Service, Sunnyvale *Also called I G S Inc* ***(P-4360)***
Industrial Grwth Partners V LP......C......415 882-4550
101 Mission St Ste 1500 San Francisco (94105) ***(P-10738)***
Industrial Lght Mgic Vncver LL......C......415 292-4671
1110 Gorgas Ave San Francisco (94129) ***(P-14792)***
Industrial Metal Recycling Inc......E......408 294-2334
260 Phelan Ave San Jose (95112) ***(P-8337)***
Industrial Relations Cal Dept......E......209 830-7200
25347 S Schulte Rd Tracy (95377) ***(P-18360)***
Industrial Relations Cal Dept......D......510 286-7000
1515 Clay St Ste 1201 Oakland (94612) ***(P-7883)***
Industrial Relations Cal Dept......E......415 703-5133
301 Howard St Ste 700 San Francisco (94105) ***(P-18361)***
Industrial Welding, Redding *Also called Ferrosaur Inc* ***(P-4659)***
Industrial Wiper & Supply Inc......F......408 286-4752
1025 98th Ave A Oakland (94603) ***(P-2971)***
Industrial Wste Dbris Box Rnta......E......707 585-0511
3911 Santa Rosa Ave Santa Rosa (95407) ***(P-7475)***
Industry Ventures LLC (PA)......D......**415 273-4201**
30 Hotaling Pl 3 San Francisco (94111) ***(P-10857)***
Indusys Technology Inc......E......408 321-2888
210 Baypointe Pkwy San Jose (95134) ***(P-13610)***
Ineda Systems Inc (PA)......E......**408 400-7375**
5201 Great America Pkwy # 532 Santa Clara (95054) ***(P-5294)***
Inevit Inc......C......650 298-6001
541 Jefferson Ave Ste 100 Redwood City (94063) ***(P-6487)***
Infant/Toddler Consort, Oakland *Also called Califrnia Child Care Rsrce Rfr* ***(P-17452)***
Infineon Raceway, Sonoma *Also called Speedway Sonoma LLC* ***(P-14918)***
Infineon Tech Americas Corp......A......866 951-9519
640 N Mccarthy Blvd Milpitas (95035) ***(P-6149)***
Infineon Tech N Amer Corp (HQ)......B......**408 503-2642**
640 N Mccarthy Blvd Milpitas (95035) ***(P-6150)***
Infineon Tech N Amer Corp......C......919 768-0315
30805 Santana St Hayward (94544) ***(P-6151)***
Infineon Tech US Holdco Inc (HQ)......D......**866 951-9519**
640 N Mccarthy Blvd Milpitas (95035) ***(P-6152)***
Infineon Technologies AG, Milpitas *Also called Infineon Tech US Holdco Inc* ***(P-6152)***

ALPHABETIC

Employee Codes: A=Over 500 employees, B=251-500
C=101-250, D=51-100, E=20-50 F=10-19
2022 Northern California Business Directory and Buyers Guide
© Mergent Inc. 1-800-342-5647
989

Infinera Corporation   ALPHABETIC SECTION

Infinera Corporation (PA) .... B 408 572-5200
  6373 San Ignacio Ave San Jose (95119) *(P-5799)*
Infinite Solutions Inc (PA) .... E 916 641-0500
  1687 Eureka Rd Ste 200 Roseville (95661) *(P-13611)*
Infinite Technologies Inc (PA) .... D 916 987-3261
  1264 Hawks Flight Ct # 210 El Dorado Hills (95762) *(P-18737)*
Infiniti Solutions Usa Inc (PA) .... C 408 923-7300
  3910 N 1st St San Jose (95134) *(P-5940)*
Infinity Energy Inc .... C 916 474-4723
  3825 Atherton Rd Ste 101 Rocklin (95765) *(P-1284)*
Infinity Sports Inc .... E 209 845-3940
  900 Wakefield Dr Oakdale (95361) *(P-539)*
Inflection Risk Solutions LLC .... C 650 618-9910
  555 Twin Dolphin Dr # 63 Redwood City (94065) *(P-13722)*
Inflectioncom Inc (PA) .... C 650 618-9910
  303 Twin Dolphin Dr # 600 Redwood City (94065) *(P-19792)*
Influxdata Inc .... C 415 295-1901
  799 Market St Ste 400 San Francisco (94103) *(P-12517)*
Info Plus International, San Mateo Also called Ip International Inc *(P-13921)*
Infobahn Softworld Inc (PA) .... C 408 855-9616
  2010 N 1st St Ste 470 San Jose (95131) *(P-13910)*
Infoblox International Inc (HQ) .... B 408 986-4000
  2390 Mission College Blvd Santa Clara (95054) *(P-5376)*
Infocus Jupiter, Hayward Also called Jupiter Systems Inc *(P-5333)*
Infogain Corporation (PA) .... C 408 355-6000
  485 Alberto Way Ste 100 Los Gatos (95032) *(P-13911)*
Infogroup Inc .... D 650 389-0700
  951 Mariners Island Blvd # 130 San Mateo (94404) *(P-11838)*
Infoimage of California Inc (PA) .... D 650 473-6388
  175 S Hill Dr Brisbane (94005) *(P-3739)*
Infor Public Sector Inc (HQ) 916 921-0883
  11092 Sun Center Dr Rancho Cordova (95670) *(P-13230)*
Infor500 LLC .... E 408 209-6837
  2350 Mission College Blvd Santa Clara (95054) *(P-19536)*
Informatica Holdco Inc .... A 650 385-5000
  2100 Seaport Blvd Redwood City (94063) *(P-13231)*
Informatica Inc .... A 650 385-5000
  2100 Seaport Blvd Redwood City (94063) *(P-13232)*
Informatica International Inc (HQ) .... C 650 385-5000
  2100 Seaport Blvd Redwood City (94063) *(P-13233)*
Informatica LLC (HQ) .... A 650 385-5000
  2100 Seaport Blvd Redwood City (94063) *(P-13234)*
Information Scan Tech Inc .... F 408 988-1908
  487 Gianni St Santa Clara (95054) *(P-6763)*
Infosoft Inc .... D 408 659-4326
  7891 Westwood Dr Ste 113 Gilroy (95020) *(P-19793)*
Infostar LLC (PA) .... F 650 288-6717
  779 Sunny Brook Way Pleasanton (94566) *(P-13235)*
Infostretch Corporation (PA) .... E 408 727-1100
  3200 Patrick Henry Dr # 2 Santa Clara (95054) *(P-13912)*
Infotech Consulting LLC .... E 415 986-5400
  340 Pine St Ste 504 San Francisco (94104) *(P-12100)*
Infotech Global Services, San Francisco Also called Infotech Consulting LLC *(P-12100)*
Infotech Sourcing .... E 415 986-5400
  2069 Green St San Francisco (94123) *(P-13913)*
Infovie Inc .... E 551 214-8745
  1390 Market St Ste 200 San Francisco (94102) *(P-13914)*
Infoworksio Inc .... D 408 899-4687
  490 California Ave # 200 Palo Alto (94306) *(P-12518)*
Infoworld Media Group Inc (HQ) .... D 415 243-4344
  501 2nd St Ste 500 San Francisco (94107) *(P-3504)*
Infrastructureworld LLC .... E 415 699-1543
  377 Margarita Dr San Rafael (94901) *(P-6833)*
Infrrd Inc .... E 844 446-3773
  2001 Gateway Pl Ste 301e San Jose (95110) *(P-12519)*
Ingenio Inc .... C 415 248-4000
  182 Howard St 826 San Francisco (94105) *(P-7962)*
Ingenio LLC .... D 415 992-8218
  182 Howard St Unit 826 San Francisco (94105) *(P-19537)*
Ingenious Packaging Group (HQ) .... E 707 252-8300
  580 Gateway Dr NAPA (94558) *(P-14302)*
Inglenook .... E 707 968-1100
  1991 St Helena Hwy Rutherford (94573) *(P-2620)*
Ingomar Packing Company LLC (PA) .... D 209 826-9494
  9950 S Ingomar Grade Los Banos (93635) *(P-2216)*
Ingram Entertainment Inc .... F 916 235-5400
  1130 Iron Point Rd Folsom (95630) *(P-9196)*
Ingrasys Technology USA Inc 863 271-8266
  2025 Gateway Pl Ste 190 San Jose (95110) *(P-6764)*
Ingrooves, San Francisco Also called Isolation Network Inc *(P-5759)*
Initiative Food Company, Sanger Also called If Holding Inc *(P-2903)*
Initiative Foods, Sanger Also called If Copack LLC *(P-2201)*
Initiative Foods LLC .... C 559 875-3354
  1912 Industrial Way Sanger (93657) *(P-2202)*
Inititive Rvtlztion Cmmunities, Hayward Also called IROC *(P-14310)*
Inkling Systems Inc .... D 415 975-4420
  343 Sansome St 8 San Francisco (94104) *(P-19538)*
Inko Industrial Corporation .... D 408 830-1040
  695 Vaqueros Ave Sunnyvale (94085) *(P-13723)*
Inktomi Corporation (HQ) .... E 650 653-2800
  701 First Ave Sunnyvale (94089) *(P-13236)*
Inland Business Machines Inc (HQ) .... D 916 928-0770
  1326 N Market Blvd Sacramento (95834) *(P-14756)*
Inland Marine Industries Inc .... C 510 785-5555
  3245 Depot Rd Hayward (94545) *(P-4773)*
Inland Metal Technologies, Hayward Also called Inland Marine Industries Inc *(P-4773)*
Inland Star Dist Ctrs Inc (PA) .... D 559 237-2052
  3146 S Chestnut Ave Fresno (93725) *(P-7552)*

Inland Valley Publishing Co .... E 925 243-8000
  2250 1st St Livermore (94550) *(P-3450)*
Inland Valley Truss Inc .... F 209 943-4710
  150 N Sinclair Ave Stockton (95215) *(P-3210)*
Inmage Systems Inc .... D 408 200-3840
  1065 La Avenida St Mountain View (94043) *(P-13237)*
Inmobi Inc (HQ) .... D 650 269-5173
  475 Brannan St Ste 420 San Francisco (94107) *(P-11763)*
Inmotion, Sonoma Also called Monica Bruce Designs Inc *(P-3046)*
Inn At Depot Hill .... E 831 462-3376
  250 Monterey Ave Capitola (95010) *(P-11188)*
Inn At Jack London Square LLC .... E 510 452-4565
  1000 Marina Village Pkwy # 100 Alameda (94501) *(P-11189)*
Inn At Morgan Hill The, Morgan Hill Also called Condit Inn GP LLC *(P-11032)*
Inn At Opera A Cal Ltd Partnr .... E 415 863-8400
  333 Fulton St San Francisco (94102) *(P-11190)*
Inn At Pasatiempo, Santa Cruz Also called Pasatiempo III Investments *(P-11361)*
Inn At Scotts Valley LLC .... D 831 440-1000
  6001 La Madrona Dr Scotts Valley (95060) *(P-11191)*
Inn Ventures Inc .... D 916 773-7171
  1951 Taylor Rd Roseville (95661) *(P-11192)*
Inn Vision Homeless Shelter, San Jose Also called Innvision Way Home *(P-17614)*
Inncal Incorporated .... D 209 477-5576
  2717 W March Ln Stockton (95219) *(P-11193)*
Inneos LLC .... E 925 226-0138
  5700 Stoneridge Dr # 200 Pleasanton (94588) *(P-6875)*
Innerasia Travel Group, San Francisco Also called Geographic Expeditions Inc *(P-7797)*
Innerscope Hearing Tech Inc .... F 916 218-4100
  2151 Professional Dr Fl 2 Roseville (95661) *(P-7073)*
Innerstave LLC .... E 707 996-8781
  21660 8th St E Ste B Sonoma (95476) *(P-3236)*
Innodisk Usa Corporation .... E 510 770-9421
  42996 Osgood Rd Fremont (94539) *(P-6153)*
Innogrit Corporation .... E 408 785-3678
  1735 Technology Dr San Jose (95110) *(P-6154)*
Innolux Optoelectronic Inc .... D 408 573-8438
  101 Metro Dr Ste 510 San Jose (95110) *(P-11962)*
Innomedia Inc .... E 408 943-8604
  1901 Mccarthy Blvd Milpitas (95035) *(P-12520)*
Innominds Software Inc (PA) .... E 408 434-6463
  2055 Junction Ave Ste 122 San Jose (95131) *(P-12521)*
Innosys Incorporated .... E 510 594-1034
  1555 3rd Ave Walnut Creek (94597) *(P-12522)*
Innova Solutions Inc .... A 408 889-2020
  3211 Scott Blvd Ste 202 Santa Clara (95054) *(P-13915)*
Innovaccer Inc (PA) .... B 650 479-4891
  535 Mission St Fl 18 San Francisco (94105) *(P-12523)*
Innovalight Inc .... E 408 419-4400
  965 W Maude Ave Sunnyvale (94085) *(P-5744)*
Innovate Concrete Inc .... E 408 497-2000
  2671 Estella Dr Santa Clara (95051) *(P-18738)*
Innovate Engineering, Santa Clara Also called Innovate Concrete Inc *(P-18738)*
Innovated Packaging Co Inc .... D 510 745-8180
  38505 Cherry St Ste C Newark (94560) *(P-7866)*
Innovative Circuits Engrg Inc .... E 408 955-9505
  2310 Lundy Ave San Jose (95131) *(P-19794)*
Innovative Combustion Tech (PA) .... F 510 652-6000
  5160 Fulton Dr Fairfield (94534) *(P-4630)*
Innovative Education MGT Inc (PA) .... D 530 295-3566
  4535 Missouri Flat Rd 1a Placerville (95667) *(P-19354)*
Innovative Installers Inc (PA) .... E 510 651-9890
  43134 Osgood Rd Fremont (94539) *(P-2037)*
Innovative Integrated Hlth Inc .... C 949 228-5577
  2042 Kern St Fresno (93721) *(P-17155)*
Innovative Machining Inc .... D 408 262-2270
  845 Yosemite Way Milpitas (95035) *(P-5540)*
Innovative Molding (HQ) .... D 707 238-9250
  1200 Valley House Dr # 100 Rohnert Park (94928) *(P-4290)*
Innovative Pathways Inc .... D 510 346-7100
  14895 E 14th St San Leandro (94578) *(P-17026)*
Innovative Silicon Inc .... D 408 572-8700
  4800 Great America Pkwy # 500 Santa Clara (95054) *(P-14303)*
Innovative Solutions, Sacramento Also called Is Inc *(P-13614)*
Innovative Steel Structures, Modesto Also called JR Daniels Commercial Bldrs *(P-4857)*
Innovel Solutions Inc .... A 707 748-1940
  521 Stone Rd Benicia (94510) *(P-7839)*
Innovtive Intllgent Sltons LLC (PA) .... D 408 332-5736
  42480 Christy St Ste 108 Fremont (94538) *(P-19795)*
Innovtive Rttional Molding Inc .... E 559 673-4764
  2300 W Pecan Ave Madera (93637) *(P-4291)*
Innowave Marketing Group LLC .... E 650 454-4952
  533 Airport Blvd Ste 400 Burlingame (94010) *(P-19539)*
Innowi Inc .... E 408 609-9404
  3240 Scott Blvd Santa Clara (95054) *(P-5255)*
Inns At Sonoma, Sonoma Also called Four Sisters Inns *(P-11104)*
Innvision Way Home .... D 408 271-5160
  358 N Montgomery St San Jose (95110) *(P-17614)*
Ino-Tech Laser Processing Inc .... E 408 262-1845
  2228 Oakland Rd San Jose (95131) *(P-6526)*
Inolux Corporation .... F 650 483-6227
  619 Bainbridge St Foster City (94404) *(P-6155)*
Inovative Packaging, Newark Also called Integrated Pkg & Crating Svcs *(P-7867)*
Inoxpa Usa Inc .... B 707 585-3900
  3721 Santa Rosa Ave B4 Santa Rosa (95407) *(P-9072)*
Inpatient Psychiatric Services, Yuba City Also called Sutter/Yuba B-Cnty Mntal Hlth *(P-15735)*
Inphenix Inc .... E 925 606-8809
  250 N Mines Rd Livermore (94551) *(P-6156)*

Inphi Corporation (HQ)..........C.......**408 217-7300**
110 Rio Robles San Jose (95134) ***(P-6157)***
Inpixon (PA)..........E.......**408 702-2167**
2479 E Byshore Rd Ste 195 Palo Alto (94303) ***(P-13916)***
Inpowered Inc..........E.......415 796-7800
129 Marina Blvd San Francisco (94123) ***(P-11764)***
Inreach Internet LLC (HQ)..........D.......**888 467-3224**
4635 Georgetown Pl Stockton (95207) ***(P-7963)***
Inscopix Inc..........F.......650 600-3886
2462 Embarcadero Way Palo Alto (94303) ***(P-6876)***
Insideview Technologies Inc..........C.......415 728-9309
444 De Haro St Ste 210 San Francisco (94107) ***(P-8713)***
Insieme Networks LLC..........E.......408 424-1227
210 W Tasman Dr Bldg F San Jose (95134) ***(P-5800)***
Insight Editions LP..........D.......415 526-1370
800 A St San Rafael (94901) ***(P-3535)***
Insight Mfg Services, Murphys *Also called Kaiser Enterprises Inc* ***(P-4975)***
Insight Wealth Strategies LLC..........E.......925 659-0251
5000 Executive Pkwy # 420 San Ramon (94583) ***(P-10049)***
Insignia..........E.......415 777-0320
390 Fremont St San Francisco (94105) ***(P-13612)***
Insignia Capital Partners LP (PA)..........D.......**925 399-8900**
1333 N Calif Blvd Ste 520 Walnut Creek (94596) ***(P-9355)***
Insignia Environmental..........D.......650 321-6787
545 Middlefield Rd # 210 Menlo Park (94025) ***(P-19796)***
Insignia/Esg Ht Partners Inc..........B.......408 288-2900
225 W Santa Clara St # 2 San Jose (95113) ***(P-10579)***
Insignia/Esg Ht Partners Inc..........B.......415 772-0123
101 California St San Francisco (94111) ***(P-10580)***
Insite Digestive Health Care..........D.......408 471-2222
200 Jose Figueres Ave San Jose (95116) ***(P-15434)***
Insitesource Inc..........F.......510 263-9157
203 Carol Ct Alamo (94507) ***(P-13238)***
Insitro Inc..........D.......650 488-1789
279 E Grand Ave Ste 200 South San Francisco (94080) ***(P-19074)***
Inspira Inc..........E.......408 247-9500
4125 Blackford Ave # 255 San Jose (95117) ***(P-12524)***
Inspro Corporation..........D.......925 685-1600
2300 Clayton Rd Ste 1100 Concord (94520) ***(P-10296)***
Inspur Systems Inc (HQ)..........E.......**800 697-5893**
1501 Mccarthy Blvd Milpitas (95035) ***(P-5256)***
Inspur Systems Inc..........E.......510 400-7599
3347 Gateway Blvd Fremont (94538) ***(P-5257)***
Inspur US R&D Technology Ctr, Fremont *Also called Inspur Systems Inc* ***(P-5257)***
Instabase Inc (PA)..........C.......**213 453-0488**
220 Montgomery St Ste 991 San Francisco (94104) ***(P-14304)***
Instabug Inc..........D.......650 422-9555
855 El Cmino Real St Ste Palo Alto (94301) ***(P-12525)***
Instacart, San Francisco *Also called Maplebear Inc* ***(P-7482)***
Instagis Inc (PA)..........F.......**415 527-6636**
218 9th St San Francisco (94103) ***(P-13239)***
Installtion Dgtal Trnsmssons I..........F.......415 226-0020
517 Jacoby St Ste C San Rafael (94901) ***(P-2038)***
Instant Algae, Campbell *Also called Reed Mariculture Inc* ***(P-2354)***
Instant Systems Inc..........D.......510 657-8100
447 King Ave Fremont (94536) ***(P-12526)***
Instantsys, Fremont *Also called Instant Systems Inc* ***(P-12526)***
Instart Logic Inc..........E.......888 576-3166
3945 Freedom Cir Ste 560 Santa Clara (95054) ***(P-12527)***
Institute For Future..........E.......650 854-6322
201 Hamilton Ave Palo Alto (94301) ***(P-19219)***
Institute For Humn Social Dev (PA)..........D.......**650 871-5613**
155 Bovet Rd Ste 300 San Mateo (94402) ***(P-17955)***
Institute For Wildlife Studies (PA)..........E.......**707 822-4258**
835 3rd St Eureka (95501) ***(P-18434)***
Institute Humn Bhvior RES Edca..........E.......510 769-7100
1910 Central Ave Alameda (94501) ***(P-17956)***
Institute of Heartmath..........E.......831 338-8500
14700 W Park Ave Boulder Creek (95006) ***(P-19220)***
Institute of Noetic Sciences..........E.......707 775-3500
101 San Antonio Rd Petaluma (94952) ***(P-19221)***
Institute On Aging..........C.......510 536-3377
2880 Zanker Rd San Jose (95134) ***(P-16249)***
Institute On Aging..........D.......415 600-2690
3698 California St San Francisco (94118) ***(P-17615)***
Institute On Aging (PA)..........D.......**415 750-4101**
3575 Geary Blvd San Francisco (94118) ***(P-17616)***
Institutional Real Estate Inc (PA)..........E.......**925 933-4040**
1475 N Broadway Ste 300 Walnut Creek (94596) ***(P-3577)***
Institutional Ventr MGT X LLC..........E.......650 854-0132
3000 Sand Hill Rd Bldg 2 Menlo Park (94025) ***(P-14305)***
Institutional Venture Partners..........E.......415 432-4660
607 Front St San Francisco (94111) ***(P-10858)***
Instituto Familiar De La Raza..........E.......415 229-0500
2919 Mission St San Francisco (94110) ***(P-17156)***
Insul-Flow Inc..........D.......559 456-1105
2684 N Fordham Ave Fresno (93727) ***(P-1882)***
Insulation Sources Inc (PA)..........E.......**650 856-8378**
2575 E Bayshore Rd Palo Alto (94303) ***(P-8863)***
Insurnce Svcs San Frncisco Inc..........D.......415 788-9810
201 California St Ste 200 San Francisco (94111) ***(P-10297)***
Insync Software Inc..........E.......408 352-0600
181 Metro Dr Ste 540 San Jose (95110) ***(P-13240)***
Intake Screens Inc..........F.......916 665-2727
8417 River Rd Sacramento (95832) ***(P-4971)***
Intapp Us Inc (HQ)..........C.......**650 852-0400**
3101 Park Blvd Palo Alto (94306) ***(P-12528)***
Intech Mechanical Company LLC..........C.......916 797-4900
7501 Galilee Rd Roseville (95678) ***(P-1285)***
Integenx Inc (HQ)..........D.......**925 701-3400**
5720 Stoneridge Dr # 300 Pleasanton (94588) ***(P-6834)***
Integra Tech Silicon Vly LLC (HQ)..........C.......**408 618-8700**
1635 Mccarthy Blvd Milpitas (95035) ***(P-6158)***
Integral Group Inc..........C.......510 663-2070
427 13th St Oakland (94612) ***(P-18739)***
Integrated Archive Systems Inc (PA)..........E.......**650 390-9995**
1121 San Antonio Rd D100 Palo Alto (94303) ***(P-19540)***
Integrated Bldg Solutions Inc..........F.......925 244-1900
2000 Crow Canyon Pl # 440 San Ramon (94583) ***(P-19797)***
Integrated Community Services..........D.......415 455-8481
3020 Kerner Blvd Ste A San Rafael (94901) ***(P-17617)***
Integrated Designs By Somam, Fresno *Also called Somam Inc* ***(P-14409)***
Integrated Digital Media (PA)..........D.......**415 986-4091**
840 Sansome St San Francisco (94111) ***(P-3659)***
Integrated Flow Systems LLC (HQ)..........D.......**510 659-4900**
26462 Corporate Ave Hayward (94545) ***(P-6722)***
Integrated Mfg Tech Inc..........E.......510 659-9770
1477 N Milpitas Blvd Milpitas (95035) ***(P-14714)***
Integrated Mfg Tech Inc..........F.......510 366-8793
1477 N Milpitas Blvd Milpitas (95035) ***(P-5541)***
Integrated Optical Svcs Corp..........E.......408 982-9510
3270 Keller St Ste 102 Santa Clara (95054) ***(P-4104)***
Integrated Pain Management..........D.......925 691-9806
450 N Wiget Ln Walnut Creek (94598) ***(P-15435)***
Integrated Pkg & Crating Svcs..........E.......510 745-8180
38505 Cherry St Newark (94560) ***(P-7867)***
Integration Banks Group LLC..........E.......707 451-1100
600 E Main St Ste 101 Vacaville (95688) ***(P-18740)***
Integrity Cnstr Maint Inc..........E.......707 829-5300
3531 Gravenstein Hwy S Sebastopol (95472) ***(P-893)***
Integrity Technology Corp..........F.......270 812-8867
2505 Technology Dr Hayward (94545) ***(P-6434)***
Integrted Rsrce Sltons Group L..........E.......650 726-7628
1100 Grundy Ln Ste 100 San Bruno (94066) ***(P-19798)***
Integrted Silicon Solution Inc (PA)..........A.......**408 969-6600**
1623 Buckeye Dr Milpitas (95035) ***(P-6159)***
Intel Americas Inc (HQ)..........C.......**408 765-8080**
2200 Mission College Blvd Santa Clara (95054) ***(P-5377)***
INTEL Corporation..........F.......408 765-2508
3065 Bowers Ave Santa Clara (95054) ***(P-5378)***
Intel Corporation (PA)..........A.......**408 765-8080**
2200 Mission College Blvd Santa Clara (95054) ***(P-6160)***
Intel Corporation..........C.......408 425-8398
2300 Mission College Blvd Santa Clara (95054) ***(P-5379)***
Intel Corporation..........A.......408 544-7000
101 Innovation Dr Bldg 1 San Jose (95134) ***(P-5380)***
Intel Corporation..........D.......916 356-8080
1900 Prairie City Rd Folsom (95630) ***(P-6161)***
Intel International Inc..........E.......408 765-8080
2200 Mission College Blvd Santa Clara (95054) ***(P-5381)***
INTEL International Limited (HQ)..........F.......**408 765-8080**
2200 Mission College Blvd Santa Clara (95054) ***(P-6162)***
Intel McRoelectronics Asia Ltd (HQ)..........D.......**408 765-8080**
2200 Mission College Blvd Santa Clara (95054) ***(P-5382)***
Intel Media Inc..........B.......408 765-0063
2200 Mission College Blvd Santa Clara (95054) ***(P-8063)***
Intel Overseas Corporation..........F.......408 765-8080
2200 Mission College Blvd Santa Clara (95054) ***(P-5383)***
Intel Phils Holding LLC (HQ)..........B.......**408 765-8080**
2200 Mission Blvd Santa Clara (95054) ***(P-5384)***
INTEL Puerto Rico Inc..........D.......408 765-8080
2200 Mission College Blvd Santa Clara (95054) ***(P-6163)***
INTEL Resale Corporation..........E.......408 765-8080
2200 Mission College Blvd Santa Clara (95054) ***(P-5385)***
Intel Semiconductor (us) LLC (HQ)..........D.......**408 765-8080**
2200 Mission College Blvd Santa Clara (95054) ***(P-6164)***
Intel Services LLC (HQ)..........A.......**408 765-8080**
2200 Mission College Blvd Santa Clara (95054) ***(P-5386)***
Intel Technologies Inc (HQ)..........B.......**408 765-8080**
2200 Mission College Blvd Santa Clara (95054) ***(P-5387)***
Intelenex Inc (HQ)..........E.......**415 367-4871**
2455 Bennett Valley Rd C2 Santa Rosa (95404) ***(P-12529)***
Intella Interventional Systems..........D.......650 269-1375
605 W California Ave Sunnyvale (94086) ***(P-6984)***
Intelligent Energy Inc..........E.......562 997-3600
1731 Tech Dr Ste 755 San Jose (95110) ***(P-4618)***
Intelligent Photonics, San Francisco *Also called Invuity Inc* ***(P-6989)***
Intelligent Quartz Solutions, Fremont *Also called Imtec Acculine LLC* ***(P-5153)***
Intelligent Storage Solution..........E.......408 428-0105
2073 Otoole Ave San Jose (95131) ***(P-5295)***
Intellipro Group Inc..........B.......408 200-9891
3120 Scott Blvd 301 Santa Clara (95054) ***(P-13917)***
Intelliswift Software Inc (PA)..........C.......**510 490-9240**
39600 Balentine Dr # 200 Newark (94560) ***(P-12530)***
Intellisync Corporation (HQ)..........D.......**650 625-2185**
313 Fairchild Dr Mountain View (94043) ***(P-12531)***
Intelpeer Cloud Cmmnctions LLC..........C.......650 525-9200
155 Bovet Rd Ste 405 San Mateo (94402) ***(P-8078)***
Inteltec Alarm Technologies, Lincoln *Also called Global Defense Group LLC* ***(P-14065)***
Inter Continental, Fresno *Also called Six Continents Hotels Inc* ***(P-11485)***
Inter Star Inc..........D.......530 224-6866
833 Mistletoe Ln Ste A1 Redding (96002) ***(P-7964)***
Inter-City Cleaners..........D.......650 875-9200
438 S Airport Blvd South San Francisco (94080) ***(P-11654)***
Inter-City Printing Co Inc..........F.......510 451-4775
614 Madison St Oakland (94607) ***(P-3660)***
Inter-Muntain Truss Girder Inc..........E.......209 847-9184
9604 Allende Ln Oakdale (95361) ***(P-3211)***

A L P H A B E T I C

Inter-Tribal Council Cal Inc (PA) ....E....**916 973-9581**
3400 Douglas Blvd Ste 230 Roseville (95661) ***(P-17618)***
Interaction Associates Inc (PA) ....E....**617 234-2700**
2310 Oregon St Berkeley (94705) ***(P-19541)***
Interactive Solutions Inc (HQ) ....D....**510 214-9002**
283 4th St Ste 301 Oakland (94607) ***(P-13241)***
Intercare Holdings Insur Svcs, Rocklin *Also called Pacific Secured Equities Inc* ***(P-19601)***
Intercare Spclty Risk Insur Sv (PA) ....E....**916 757-1200**
140 Diamond Creek Pl Roseville (95747) ***(P-10298)***
Intercntinental Hotels Resorts, San Francisco *Also called Intercntnntal Htels San Frncsc* ***(P-11194)***
Intercntnntal Htels San Frncsc ....C....415 616-6500
888 Howard St San Francisco (94103) ***(P-11194)***
Intercom Inc ....B....831 920-7088
55 2nd St Fl 4 San Francisco (94105) ***(P-12532)***
Intercontinental Mark Hopkins, San Francisco *Also called One Nob Hill Associates LLC* ***(P-11339)***
Intercontinental San Francisco, San Francisco *Also called Cdc San Francisco LLC* ***(P-10999)***
Intercontinental Services, Concord *Also called Carlton Senior Living Inc* ***(P-10503)***
Interctive Fitnes Holdings LLC ....E....888 528-8589
2225 Martin Ave Ste I Santa Clara (95050) ***(P-10739)***
Interctive Med Specialists Inc ....D....415 472-4204
252 Waterside Cir San Rafael (94903) ***(P-12176)***
Interdent Service Corporation ....C....707 528-7000
1421 Guerneville Rd # 102 Santa Rosa (95403) ***(P-15838)***
Interface Masters Inc ....F....408 441-9341
150 E Brokaw Rd San Jose (95112) ***(P-5388)***
Interface Masters Tech Inc ....E....408 441-9341
150 E Brokaw Rd San Jose (95112) ***(P-6435)***
Interform Commercial Interiors ....E....925 867-1001
3000 Executive Pkwy # 175 San Ramon (94583) ***(P-8496)***
Intergen Inc ....F....408 245-2737
1145 Tasman Dr Sunnyvale (94089) ***(P-6527)***
Interim Asssted Care E Bay Inc ....E....925 944-5779
91 Gregory Ln Ste 7 Pleasant Hill (94523) ***(P-16900)***
Interim Healthcare of Jackson, Jackson *Also called K&B Pichette Enterprises Inc* ***(P-16901)***
Interior Plant Design ....E....408 286-1367
1950 Monterey Hwy San Jose (95112) ***(P-14306)***
Interior Specialists Inc ....E....916 779-1666
1164 National Dr Ste 10 Sacramento (95834) ***(P-14307)***
Interior Specialists Inc ....E....925 416-0408
4511 Willow Rd Pleasanton (94588) ***(P-14308)***
Interior United States Dept ....D....530 752-6745
1 Shields Ave Davis (95616) ***(P-15436)***
Interket Enterprise, Fremont *Also called Unitek Inc* ***(P-13685)***
Interlink Self-Help Center, Santa Rosa *Also called Goodwill Inds of Rdwood Empire* ***(P-17594)***
Intermdia Cloud Cmmnctions Inc ....A....650 641-4000
100 Mathilda Pl Ste 600 Sunnyvale (94086) ***(P-13242)***
Intermedia Communications Inc (HQ) ....C....**800 940-0011**
100 Mathilda Pl Ste 600 Sunnyvale (94086) ***(P-7965)***
Intermolecular Inc (HQ) ....C....**408 582-5700**
3011 N 1st St San Jose (95134) ***(P-6165)***
Intermotive Inc ....E....530 823-1048
12840 Earhart Ave Auburn (95602) ***(P-19542)***
Intermountain Electric Company ....E....650 591-7118
947 Washington St San Carlos (94070) ***(P-1524)***
Intermune Inc (HQ) ....C....**415 466-4383**
1 Dna Way South San Francisco (94080) ***(P-3930)***
Internal Drive ....B....408 871-2227
910 E Hamilton Ave # 300 Campbell (95008) ***(P-11604)***
Internal Medicine, Fresno *Also called Herndon Investors* ***(P-15429)***
Internal Revenue Service ....C....510 576-7589
2469 Arf Ave Hayward (94545) ***(P-15437)***
Internal Revenue Service ....C....916 974-5678
9006 Morganfield Pl Elk Grove (95624) ***(P-15438)***
International Building Inv Inc ....D....916 716-9565
6117 Grant Ave Carmichael (95608) ***(P-749)***
International Bus Mchs Corp ....A....408 463-2000
555 Bailey Ave San Jose (95141) ***(P-12533)***
International Bus Mchs Corp ....C....415 545-4747
425 Market St San Francisco (94105) ***(P-8652)***
International Bus Mchs Corp ....B....408 927-1080
650 Harry Rd San Jose (95120) ***(P-19075)***
INTERNATIONAL CHILD RESOURCE I, Berkeley *Also called Interntnal Child Rsrce Exch In* ***(P-18234)***
International Co-Packing Co, Fresno *Also called Lidestri Foods Inc* ***(P-2221)***
International Glace Inc (PA) ....E....**559 385-7675**
4067 W Shaw Ave Fresno (93722) ***(P-2429)***
International Group Inc ....C....510 232-8704
102 Cutting Blvd Richmond (94804) ***(P-4175)***
International Hort Tech LLC ....E....831 637-1800
150 Acquistapace Rd Hollister (95023) ***(P-5007)***
International Hotel Assoc LLC ....E....415 283-4832
334 Mason St San Francisco (94102) ***(P-11195)***
International House ....C....510 642-9490
2299 Piedmont Ave Ste 535 Berkeley (94720) ***(P-11591)***
INTERNATIONAL HOUSE AT U C BER, Berkeley *Also called International House* ***(P-11591)***
International Inst of Bay Area, San Francisco *Also called Immigration Inst of Bay Area* ***(P-17612)***
International Micro Design Inc ....E....888 216-6041
8109 Laguna Blvd Elk Grove (95758) ***(P-12534)***
International Process Solution ....D....310 432-0665
1300 Industrial Rd Ste 22 San Carlos (94070) ***(P-19276)***
International Society For ....E....510 680-6126
2861 Buena Visa Way Berkeley (94708) ***(P-19167)***

International Transport Federa ....E....415 440-7043
1188 Franklin St Ste 400 San Francisco (94109) ***(P-18362)***
Internet Archive ....C....415 561-6767
300 Funston Ave San Francisco (94118) ***(P-13795)***
Internet Escrow Services Inc ....D....888 511-8600
180 Montgomery St Ste 650 San Francisco (94104) ***(P-10581)***
Internet Store Inc ....E....831 459-6301
903 Pacific Ave Ste 101 Santa Cruz (95060) ***(P-19906)***
Internet-Journals LLC ....D....510 665-1200
2100 Milvia St Ste 300 Berkeley (94704) ***(P-13918)***
Interntional Cmpt Science Inst ....E....510 643-9153
2150 Shattuck Ave # 1100 Berkeley (94704) ***(P-19222)***
Interntional Horticulture Tech, Hollister *Also called International Hort Tech LLC* ***(P-5007)***
Interntional Ht Assoc No 3 LLC ....D....650 493-2411
3400 El Camino Real Palo Alto (94306) ***(P-11196)***
Interntional Un Oper Engineers (PA) ....D....**916 444-6880**
1121 L St Ste 401 Sacramento (95814) ***(P-18363)***
Interntnal Assn Bus Cmmncators ....D....415 544-4711
601 Montgomery St # 1900 San Francisco (94111) ***(P-18307)***
Interntnal Brthd Elc Wkr Lcal (PA) ....D....**707 452-2700**
30 Orange Tree Cir Vacaville (95687) ***(P-18364)***
Interntnal Brthd Elec Wkrs Lca ....E....415 861-5752
55 Fillmore St San Francisco (94117) ***(P-18365)***
Interntnal Ch of Frsqare Gospl ....E....209 532-4295
15250 Old Oak Ranch Rd Sonora (95370) ***(P-11605)***
Interntnal Child Rsrce Exch In (PA) ....C....**510 644-1000**
125 University Ave # 201 Berkeley (94710) ***(P-18234)***
Interntnal Elctrnic Cmpnnts US (HQ) ....F....**408 477-2755**
809 Aldo Ave Ste 104 Santa Clara (95054) ***(P-8920)***
Interntnal Lngshrmens Wrhsmen ....E....209 464-1827
22 N Union St Stockton (95205) ***(P-18366)***
Interntnal Ptro Pdts Addtves I ....F....925 556-5530
7600 Dublin Blvd Ste 240 Dublin (94568) ***(P-4194)***
Interntnal Trque Cnverters Inc ....E....559 266-7471
712 N Abby St Fresno (93701) ***(P-14540)***
Interntnal Un Oper Engners Lca ....B....510 748-7400
1620 S Loop Rd Alameda (94502) ***(P-18367)***
Interpac Distribution Center, Woodland *Also called Interpac Technologies Inc* ***(P-14309)***
Interpac Technologies Inc ....D....530 662-6363
260 N Pioneer Ave Woodland (95776) ***(P-14309)***
Interpacific Group Inc ....A....415 442-0711
576 Beale St San Francisco (94105) ***(P-18963)***
Interpet Usa LLC (HQ) ....E....**925 948-4000**
1340 Treat Blvd Ste 4600 Walnut Creek (94597) ***(P-9662)***
Interpress Technologies Inc (HQ) ....E....**916 929-9771**
1120 Del Paso Rd Sacramento (95834) ***(P-9663)***
Intersect Ent Inc (PA) ....B....**650 641-2100**
1555 Adams Dr Menlo Park (94025) ***(P-6985)***
Intershop Communications Inc ....E....415 844-1500
461 2nd St Apt 151 San Francisco (94107) ***(P-13243)***
Intersil Quellan, Milpitas *Also called Quellan Inc* ***(P-6265)***
Intersil Techwell, South San Francisco *Also called Renesas Electronics Amer Inc* ***(P-6273)***
Interstate Con Pmpg Co Inc ....D....209 983-3092
11180 Vallejo Ct French Camp (95231) ***(P-1883)***
Interstate Grading and Pav Inc ....E....650 952-7333
128 S Maple Ave South San Francisco (94080) ***(P-1051)***
Interstate Plastics, Sacramento *Also called Dongalen Enterprises Inc* ***(P-9513)***
Interstate Truck Center LLC (PA) ....D....**209 944-5821**
2110 S Sinclair Ave Stockton (95215) ***(P-8426)***
Intertrust Technologies Corp (PA) ....E....**408 616-1600**
920 Stewart Dr Sunnyvale (94085) ***(P-12535)***
Interwest Insurance Svcs LLC (PA) ....C....**916 488-3100**
8950 Cal Center Dr Bldg 3 Sacramento (95826) ***(P-10299)***
Interwest Insurance Svcs LLC ....D....916 784-1008
5 Sierra Gate Plz Fl 2nd Roseville (95678) ***(P-10300)***
Intevac Inc (PA) ....C....**408 986-9888**
3560 Bassett St Santa Clara (95054) ***(P-5154)***
Intevac Photonics Inc (HQ) ....D....**408 986-9888**
3560 Bassett St Santa Clara (95054) ***(P-6877)***
Intex Auto Parts, San Jose *Also called All Klin Corporation* ***(P-8437)***
Intime Infotech Inc ....E....650 396-4319
39962 Cedar Blvd Ste 185 Newark (94560) ***(P-12536)***
Intrado Interactive Svcs Corp ....D....888 527-5225
100 Enterprise Way A-3 Scotts Valley (95066) ***(P-8013)***
Intraop Medical Services, Sunnyvale *Also called Mc Liquidation Inc* ***(P-7112)***
Intrawest NAPA Rvrbend Hsptlit ....D....408 829-4141
1314 Mckinstry St NAPA (94559) ***(P-11197)***
Intrepid, San Rafael *Also called Pedersen Media Group Inc* ***(P-19694)***
Intrinsyx Technologies Corp ....E....650 210-9220
350 N Akron Rd M S 19 102 Ms Moffett Field (94035) ***(P-12537)***
Introlligent Inc (PA) ....E....**916 436-8889**
1425 River Park Dr # 401 Sacramento (95815) ***(P-13919)***
Intuit Financial Services, Redwood City *Also called Digital Insight Corporation* ***(P-13785)***
Intuit Financing Inc ....E....605 944-6000
2700 Coast Ave Mountain View (94043) ***(P-13244)***
Intuit Inc (PA) ....D....**650 944-6000**
2700 Coast Ave Mountain View (94043) ***(P-13245)***
Intuit Inc ....C....650 944-6000
2535 Garcia Ave Mountain View (94043) ***(P-13246)***
Intuitive Srgcal Oprations Inc (HQ) ....A....**408 523-2100**
1020 Kifer Rd Sunnyvale (94086) ***(P-6986)***
Intuitive Srgical Holdings LLC (HQ) ....D....**408 523-2100**
1020 Kifer Rd Sunnyvale (94086) ***(P-6987)***
Intuitive Surgical Inc (PA) ....C....**408 523-2100**
1020 Kifer Rd Sunnyvale (94086) ***(P-7074)***
Intuity Medical Inc ....D....408 530-1700
3500 W Warren Ave Fremont (94538) ***(P-6988)***
Invarian, Santa Clara *Also called Silvaco Inc* ***(P-13663)***
Invax Technologies, Sunnyvale *Also called Gulshan International Corp* ***(P-6137)***

ALPHABETIC SECTION
ITW Semisystems Inc

Invecas Inc (PA) E 408 758-5636
2350 Mission College Blvd # 777 Santa Clara (95054) *(P-6166)*
Invensense Inc (HQ) A 408 501-2200
1745 Tech Dr Ste 200 San Jose (95110) *(P-6672)*
Inverse Solutions Inc E 925 931-9500
3922 Valley Ave Ste A Pleasanton (94566) *(P-5542)*
Investment Retrievers Inc E 916 941-8851
950 Glenn Dr Ste 160 Folsom (95630) *(P-11824)*
Invitae Corporation (PA) D 415 374-7782
1400 16th St San Francisco (94103) *(P-16786)*
Invoice 2go LLC (HQ) C 650 300-5180
2317 Broadway St Fl 2 Redwood City (94063) *(P-13247)*
Invuity Inc C 415 665-2100
444 De Haro St Ste 110 San Francisco (94107) *(P-6989)*
Inxeption Corporation C 888 852-4783
185 Valley Dr Brisbane (94005) *(P-13920)*
Ioda, San Francisco *Also called Indepndnt Onlne Dstribution (P-14301)*
Iogyn Inc E 408 996-2517
150 Baytech Dr San Jose (95134) *(P-6990)*
Ione Primemed Clinic, Ione *Also called Lodi Memorial Hosp Assn Inc (P-16429)*
Ionetix Corporation (PA) F 415 944-1440
101 The Embarcadero # 210 San Francisco (94105) *(P-6528)*
Ios Optics, Santa Clara *Also called Integrated Optical Svcs Corp (P-4104)*
Iosafe Inc F 888 984-6723
10600 Industrial Ave # 120 Roseville (95678) *(P-5296)*
Iot and Automation Product Dev, Pleasanton *Also called Iqms (P-19543)*
Iovance Biotherapeutics Inc (PA) C 650 260-7120
999 Skyway Rd Ste 150 San Carlos (94070) *(P-3931)*
Ip Infusion Inc (HQ) D 408 400-1900
3965 Freedom Cir Ste 200 Santa Clara (95054) *(P-13613)*
Ip International Inc E 650 403-7800
1510 Fashion Island Blvd # 104 San Mateo (94404) *(P-13921)*
Ip Portfolio I LLC E 510 260-2192
548 Market St 68743 San Francisco (94104) *(P-8117)*
Ipac, Dublin *Also called Interntnal Ptro Pdts Addtves I (P-4194)*
Ipac Inc F 925 556-5530
7600 Dublin Blvd Ste 240 Dublin (94568) *(P-4195)*
Ipass Inc (HQ) C 650 232-4100
3800 Bridge Pkwy Redwood City (94065) *(P-7966)*
Ipolipo Inc D 408 916-5290
440 N Wolfe Rd Sunnyvale (94085) *(P-13248)*
Ips Printing Inc F 916 442-8961
1730 Lathrop Way Sacramento (95815) *(P-3661)*
Iptor Supply Chain Systems USA (HQ) C 916 542-2820
915 Highland Pointe Dr # 250 Roseville (95678) *(P-12538)*
Ipull U Pull Auto Parts, Fresno *Also called Vehicle Recycling Services LLC (P-8378)*
Iqms E 805 227-1122
4309 Hacienda Dr Ste 550 Pleasanton (94588) *(P-19543)*
Iqvia Inc D 415 692-9898
135 Main St Fl 22 San Francisco (94105) *(P-19168)*
Ira Services Trust Company E 650 591-3335
1160 Industrial Rd Ste 1 San Carlos (94070) *(P-10795)*
IRD Acquisitions LLC F 530 210-2966
12810 Earhart Ave Auburn (95602) *(P-7142)*
Irdeto Usa Inc (HQ) D 818 508-2313
3255 Scott Blvd Ste 3-101 Santa Clara (95054) *(P-12539)*
Irene Swndlls Adult Day Care P, San Francisco *Also called Institute On Aging (P-17615)*
Irhythm Technologies Inc (PA) E 415 632-5700
699 8th St Ste 600 San Francisco (94103) *(P-6991)*
Iridex, Mountain View *Also called Iris Medical Instruments Inc (P-7109)*
Iridex Corporation (PA) D 650 940-4700
1212 Terra Bella Ave Mountain View (94043) *(P-7108)*
Iris Environmental E 510 834-4747
1814 Franklin St Ste 505 Oakland (94612) *(P-19799)*
Iris Medical Instruments Inc E 650 940-4700
1212 Terra Bella Ave Mountain View (94043) *(P-7109)*
Iris Usa Inc C 209 982-9100
3021 Boeing Way Stockton (95206) *(P-9455)*
IRM, Madera *Also called Innovtive Rttional Molding Inc (P-4291)*
IROC E 510 706-8669
20993 Foothill Blvd 208 Hayward (94541) *(P-14310)*
Iron Construction Inc E 408 282-1080
1955 The Alameda Fl 2 San Jose (95126) *(P-653)*
Iron Dog Fabrication Inc F 707 579-7831
3450 Regional Pkwy Ste E Santa Rosa (95403) *(P-4667)*
Iron Horse Interactive, San Ramon *Also called Iron Horse Ventures LLC (P-19544)*
Iron Horse Ranch & Vineyard E 707 887-1507
9786 Ross Station Rd Sebastopol (95472) *(P-57)*
Iron Horse Ventures LLC E 925 415-6141
6111 Bollinger Canyon Rd # 555 San Ramon (94583) *(P-19544)*
Iron Horse Vineyards E 707 887-1909
9786 Ross Station Rd Sebastopol (95472) *(P-2621)*
Iron Mechanical Inc (PA) D 916 341-3530
721 N B St Ste 100 Sacramento (95811) *(P-1286)*
Iron Oak Plumbing Inc E 916 782-9565
3825 Cincinnati Ave Ste A Rocklin (95765) *(P-1287)*
Iron Ox Inc E 281 381-0409
955 Terminal Way San Carlos (94070) *(P-9197)*
Iron Systems Inc D 408 943-8000
980 Mission Ct Fremont (94539) *(P-8714)*
Iron Works Enterprises Inc E 209 572-7450
801 S 7th St Modesto (95351) *(P-6603)*
Ironclad Inc (PA) C 855 999-4766
71 Stevenson St Ste 600 San Francisco (94105) *(P-12540)*
Ironies E 510 644-2100
2200 Central St Ste D Richmond (94801) *(P-3305)*
Ironridge Inc (HQ) E 800 227-9523
28357 Industrial Blvd Hayward (94545) *(P-8999)*
Ironsource, San Francisco *Also called Supersonic ADS Inc (P-7256)*

Irritec Usa Inc D 559 275-8825
1420 N Irritec Way Fresno (93703) *(P-5008)*
Irvine APT Communities LP C 408 943-1595
39 Rio Robles E San Jose (95134) *(P-10441)*
Is Inc E 916 920-1700
2554 Millcreek Dr Sacramento (95833) *(P-13614)*
Isbell Construction Inc D 530 587-0230
11090 Trails End Ct Truckee (96161) *(P-894)*
Iscience Interventional Corp E 650 421-2700
41316 Christy St Fremont (94538) *(P-6992)*
Iscs Inc C 408 362-3000
100 Great Oaks Blvd # 100 San Jose (95119) *(P-12541)*
ISE Labs Inc (HQ) C 510 687-2500
46800 Bayside Pkwy Fremont (94538) *(P-19277)*
Isec Incorporated D 650 872-1391
395 Oyster Point Blvd # 21 South San Francisco (94080) *(P-1741)*
Isec Incorporated E 510 490-1333
7077 Koll Center Pkwy # 200 Pleasanton (94566) *(P-1742)*
Isec Incorporated D 707 693-6555
1855 N 1st St Unit D Dixon (95620) *(P-1743)*
Ishares, San Francisco *Also called Blackrock Instnl Tr Nat Assn (P-10750)*
Ishares Inc (PA) A 415 597-2000
400 Howard St San Francisco (94105) *(P-10764)*
Isheriff Inc C 650 412-4300
555 Twin Dolphin Dr # 135 Redwood City (94065) *(P-12542)*
ISI Inspection Services Inc (PA) D 510 900-2101
1798 University Ave Berkeley (94703) *(P-14311)*
Island Conservation E 831 359-4787
2100 Delaware Ave Ste A Santa Cruz (95060) *(P-18574)*
Island Hospitality MGT LLC E 408 226-7676
6111 San Ignacio Ave San Jose (95119) *(P-11198)*
Island Hospitality MGT LLC E 408 720-1000
750 Lakeway Dr Sunnyvale (94085) *(P-11199)*
Island Hospitality MGT LLC E 650 574-4700
2000 Winward Way San Mateo (94404) *(P-11200)*
Island Hospitality MGT LLC E 408 720-8893
1080 Stewart Dr Sunnyvale (94085) *(P-11201)*
Island Hospitality MGT LLC E 650 591-8600
400 Concourse Dr Belmont (94002) *(P-11202)*
Island Hospitality MGT LLC E 650 940-1300
1854 W El Camino Real Mountain View (94040) *(P-11203)*
Island Water Park Inc E 559 277-6800
6099 W Barstow Ave Fresno (93723) *(P-15043)*
Isolation Network Inc (PA) E 415 489-7000
55 Francisco St Ste 350 San Francisco (94133) *(P-5759)*
Isolink Inc E 408 946-1968
880 Yosemite Way Milpitas (95035) *(P-6436)*
Isomedia LLC E 510 668-1656
43297 Osgood Rd Fremont (94539) *(P-5778)*
Isp Granule Products Inc C 209 274-2930
1900 Hwy 104 Ione (95640) *(P-4530)*
Isr Holdings, Roseville *Also called Intercare Spclty Risk Insur Sv (P-10298)*
Isrs/Aao E 415 447-0369
655 Beach St San Francisco (94109) *(P-15439)*
Issuu Inc (PA) D 844 477-8800
131 Lytton Ave Palo Alto (94301) *(P-3578)*
It Management Corp E 408 739-1100
5201 Great America Pkwy # 320 Santa Clara (95054) *(P-19545)*
Ita-Med Co E 510 200-9249
25377 Huntwood Ave Hayward (94544) *(P-8783)*
Italent Corporation (PA) C 408 496-6200
300 Orchard Cy Dr Ste 136 Campbell (95008) *(P-13922)*
Italent Digital, Campbell *Also called Italent Corporation (P-13922)*
Italfoods Inc D 650 877-0724
205 Shaw Rd South San Francisco (94080) *(P-9274)*
Italian American Corp E 510 877-9000
1515 Alvarado St San Leandro (94577) *(P-9664)*
Italix Company Inc F 408 988-2487
120 Mast St Ste A Morgan Hill (95037) *(P-4935)*
Itapp Inc F 415 786-3455
4633 Old Ironsides Dr # 280 Santa Clara (95054) *(P-13249)*
Itc Srvice Group Acqsition LLC (HQ) E 877 370-4482
7777 Greenback Ln Ste 201 Citrus Heights (95610) *(P-19800)*
Itco Solutions Inc B 650 367-0514
1003 Whitehall Ln Redwood City (94061) *(P-13923)*
Itouchless Housewares Pdts Inc E 650 578-0578
777 Mariners Island Blvd San Mateo (94404) *(P-4292)*
Itradenetwork Inc (HQ) E 925 660-1100
4160 Dublin Blvd Ste 300 Dublin (94568) *(P-19546)*
Itrenew Inc (HQ) E 408 744-9600
7575 Gateway Blvd Ste 100 Newark (94560) *(P-13924)*
Itron Networked Solutions Inc (HQ) B 669 770-4000
230 W Tasman Dr San Jose (95134) *(P-8079)*
Itsago Builders Inc E 916 496-2316
11928 Silver Cliff Way Gold River (95670) *(P-654)*
Itsj Group Inc E 408 609-6392
490 Parrott St San Jose (95112) *(P-5543)*
Itsourcetek, Inc., San Rafael *Also called Do Arellanes Holdings (P-12084)*
ITT LLC C 707 523-2300
500 Tesconi Cir Santa Rosa (95401) *(P-5680)*
Ittavi Inc E 866 246-4408
1100 La Avenida St Ste A Mountain View (94043) *(P-13250)*
Ituner Networks Corporation F 510 573-0783
44244 Fremont Blvd Fremont (94538) *(P-5389)*
ITW Alpine, Sacramento *Also called ITW Blding Cmponents Group Inc (P-4722)*
ITW Blding Cmponents Group Inc E 916 387-0116
8801 Folsom Blvd Ste 107 Sacramento (95826) *(P-4722)*
ITW Semisystems Inc E 408 350-0244
625 Wool Creek Dr Ste G San Jose (95112) *(P-4560)*

ALPHABETIC

Iunlimited Incorporated C 916 218-6198
7801 Folsom Blvd Ste 203 Sacramento (95826) ***(P-14071)***

Iuoe Local 39, Sacramento *Also called Iuoe Sttonary Engineers Lcl 39* ***(P-18368)***

Iuoe Sttonary Engineers Lcl 39 E 916 928-0399
1620 N Market Blvd Sacramento (95834) ***(P-18368)***

Ivalua Inc (HQ) **E 650 930-9710**
805 Veterans Blvd Ste 203 Redwood City (94063) ***(P-12543)***

Ivp, San Francisco *Also called Institutional Venture Partners* ***(P-10858)***

Ivu Traffic Technologies Inc F 415 655-2200
2612 8th St Ste A Berkeley (94710) ***(P-6583)***

Iwatt Inc (HQ) **E 408 374-4200**
675 Campbell Tech Pkwy # 150 Campbell (95008) ***(P-6167)***

Iwi, Sunnyvale *Also called Intella Interventional Systems* ***(P-6984)***

Ix Layer Inc E 408 594-7586
440 N Wolfe Rd Sunnyvale (94085) ***(P-12544)***

Ix Systems, San Jose *Also called Ixsystems Inc* ***(P-12545)***

Ixerv Americas Inc E 786 542-9744
785 Orchard Dr Ste 140 Folsom (95630) ***(P-13925)***

Ixia, Santa Clara *Also called Net Optics Inc* ***(P-13323)***

Ixsystems Inc (PA) **D 408 943-4100**
2490 Kruse Dr San Jose (95131) ***(P-12545)***

Ixys LLC (HQ) **B 408 457-9000**
1590 Buckeye Dr Milpitas (95035) ***(P-6168)***

Iyp Inc E 305 593-1211
46595 Landing Pkwy Fremont (94538) ***(P-11674)***

Izmocars, San Francisco *Also called Homestar Systems Inc* ***(P-13906)***

Izt Mortgage Inc (PA) **E 925 946-1858**
3011 Citrus Cir Ste 202 Walnut Creek (94598) ***(P-9942)***

J & A Jeffery Inc E 707 678-0369
395 Industrial Way Ste B Dixon (95620) ***(P-7289)***

J & C Custom Cabinets Inc F 916 638-3400
11451 Elks Cir Rancho Cordova (95742) ***(P-3306)***

J & D Meat Company C 559 445-1123
4671 E Edgar Ave Fresno (93725) ***(P-9456)***

J & J Acoustics Inc C 408 275-9255
2260 De La Cruz Blvd Santa Clara (95050) ***(P-1681)***

J & J Air Conditioning Inc D 408 920-0662
1086 N 11th St San Jose (95112) ***(P-1288)***

J & J Quality Door Inc E 209 948-5013
741 S Airport Way Stockton (95205) ***(P-3137)***

J & L Digital Precision Inc F 650 592-0170
551 Taylor Way Ste 15 San Carlos (94070) ***(P-6437)***

J & M Inc E 925 724-0300
6700 National Dr Livermore (94550) ***(P-1108)***

J & O'S Commercial Tire Center, Richmond *Also called Rubber Dust Inc* ***(P-14539)***

J & R Debenedetto Orchards Inc E 559 665-1712
26393 Road 22 1/2 Chowchilla (93610) ***(P-103)***

J & R Logging Inc F 209 245-5540
9252 Bush St Plymouth (95669) ***(P-3065)***

J & S Operations LLC D 510 360-7165
39700 Balentine Dr Newark (94560) ***(P-14572)***

J & S Stakes Inc F 707 668-5647
3157 Greenwood Heights Dr Kneeland (95549) ***(P-3269)***

J A-Co Machine Works LLC E 877 429-8175
4 Carbonero Way Scotts Valley (95066) ***(P-5544)***

J B Company D 916 929-3003
1825 Bell St Ste 100 Sacramento (95825) ***(P-895)***

J B Enterprises, Sacramento *Also called John Boyd Enterprises Inc* ***(P-6584)***

J B Hunt Transport Inc C 209 235-1371
2660 Loomis Rd Stockton (95205) ***(P-7553)***

J B Hunt Transport Inc C 866 759-1127
3170 Crow Canyon Pl # 180 San Ramon (94583) ***(P-7554)***

J B Hunt Transport Svcs Inc A 559 834-3852
3124 E Manning Ave Fowler (93625) ***(P-7555)***

J B Precision, Campbell *Also called Jessee Brothers Machine Sp Inc* ***(P-5547)***

J Bender Company F 916 462-7900
4491 Pacific St Ste B Rocklin (95677) ***(P-896)***

J C C, San Rafael *Also called Bernard Osher Mrin Jwish Cmnty* ***(P-17443)***

J C Heating & Air Conditioning, Santa Cruz *Also called JC Heating & AC Inc* ***(P-1292)***

J Crecelius Inc D 209 883-4826
5043 N Montpelier Rd Denair (95316) ***(P-170)***

J D I, Newcastle *Also called Jim Dobbas Inc* ***(P-14313)***

J D Pasquetti Engineering D 916 543-9401
3032 Thunder Valley Ct # 200 Lincoln (95648) ***(P-18741)***

J F Fitzgerald Company Inc E 415 648-6161
429 Cabot Rd South San Francisco (94080) ***(P-3288)***

J F Hillebrand Usa Inc E 707 996-5686
5325 Industrial Way Benicia (94510) ***(P-7840)***

J F Lighting & Design, Santa Rosa *Also called Wiggins Enterprises LLC* ***(P-1637)***

J Flores Construction Co Inc E 415 337-2934
4229 Mission St San Francisco (94112) ***(P-1109)***

J Ginger Masonry LP E 209 229-1581
9850 Hillview Rd B Newcastle (95658) ***(P-1648)***

J H Meek & Sons Inc E 530 662-1106
22075 County Road 99 Woodland (95695) ***(P-171)***

J H Simpson Company Inc D 209 466-1477
4025 Coronado Ave Stockton (95204) ***(P-1289)***

J I T Transportation, Milpitas *Also called Dga Services Inc* ***(P-7619)***

J J J & K Inc E 650 373-3900
1322 Marsten Rd Burlingame (94010) ***(P-1744)***

J K Lighting Systems, Stockton *Also called Al Kramp Specialties* ***(P-5741)***

J L C, Santa Rosa *Also called Jl Construction Inc* ***(P-901)***

J L G Enterprises Inc E 209 847-4797
11116 Sierra Rd Oakdale (95361) ***(P-348)***

J L Precision Sheet Metal, San Jose *Also called Laptalo Enterprises Inc* ***(P-4776)***

J Lohr Viney, San Jose *Also called J Lohr Winery Corporation* ***(P-2622)***

J Lohr Warehouse, San Jose *Also called J Lohr Winery Corporation* ***(P-2623)***

J Lohr Winery Corporation (PA) **E 408 288-5057**
1000 Lenzen Ave San Jose (95126) ***(P-2622)***

J Lohr Winery Corporation E 408 293-1345
1935 S 10th St San Jose (95112) ***(P-2623)***

J M Custom Cabinets, Fresno *Also called JM Custom Cabinets & Furniture* ***(P-3278)***

J M D Enterprises (PA) **D 925 935-4780**
1434 N Main St Walnut Creek (94596) ***(P-11686)***

J M Equipment Company Inc (PA) **D 209 522-3271**
321 Spreckels Ave Manteca (95336) ***(P-12050)***

J M Fremont Motors LLC D 510 403-3700
43191 Boscell Rd Fremont (94538) ***(P-14573)***

J M I, Union City *Also called Jenson Mechanical Inc* ***(P-5546)***

J M K Investments Inc E 408 263-2626
1724 Sunnyhills Dr Milpitas (95035) ***(P-10582)***

J M ONeill Inc E 925 225-1200
354 Earhart Way Livermore (94551) ***(P-798)***

J Marchini & Son Inc D 559 665-2944
12000 Le Grand Rd Le Grand (95333) ***(P-172)***

J Milano Co Inc F 209 944-0902
910 W Charter Way Stockton (95206) ***(P-8984)***

J P Graphics Inc E 408 235-8821
3310 Woodward Ave Santa Clara (95054) ***(P-3662)***

J P L, Fresno *Also called J P Lamborn Co* ***(P-5432)***

J P Lamborn Co (PA) **B 559 650-2120**
3663 E Wawona Ave Fresno (93725) ***(P-5432)***

J Pedroncelli Winery E 707 857-3531
1220 Canyon Rd Geyserville (95441) ***(P-2624)***

J R Pierce Plumbing Company E 510 483-5473
14481 Wicks Blvd San Leandro (94577) ***(P-1290)***

J R Roberts Corp (HQ) **D 916 729-5600**
7745 Greenback Ln Ste 300 Citrus Heights (95610) ***(P-897)***

J R Roberts Enterprises Inc C 916 729-5600
7745 Greenback Ln Ste 300 Citrus Heights (95610) ***(P-898)***

J Redfern Inc D 925 371-3300
164 N L St Livermore (94550) ***(P-471)***

J S Hckley Archtctral Sgnage E 510 940-2608
1999 Alpine Way Hayward (94545) ***(P-7235)***

J S West and Company (PA) **C 209 577-3221**
501 9th St Modesto (95354) ***(P-9534)***

J S West Milling Co Inc E 209 529-4232
501 9th St Modesto (95354) ***(P-2345)***

J W Bamford Inc F 530 533-0732
4288 State Highway 70 Oroville (95965) ***(P-3066)***

J W Floor Covering Inc C 858 444-1214
3401 Enterprise Ave Hayward (94545) ***(P-2906)***

J W Wood Co Inc (PA) **E 530 894-1325**
3676 Old Hwy 44 Dr Redding (96003) ***(P-9000)***

J&M Manufacturing Inc E 707 795-8223
430 Aaron St Cotati (94931) ***(P-6438)***

J&N Engineering Inc E 408 680-1810
1310 N 4th St San Jose (95112) ***(P-5075)***

J&T Crenshaw Inc E 209 606-8256
2801 Mchenry Ave Modesto (95350) ***(P-14954)***

J.B. Hunt Transport Services, Fowler *Also called J B Hunt Transport Svcs Inc* ***(P-7555)***

J.L. Haley, Rancho Cordova *Also called Vander-Bend Manufacturing Inc* ***(P-5635)***

J4 Systems, Rocklin *Also called Joseph Systems Inc* ***(P-13615)***

Ja Apparel Corp (HQ) **E 877 986-9669**
6100 Stevenson Blvd Fremont (94538) ***(P-9245)***

Jabil Circuit, San Jose *Also called Jabil Inc* ***(P-5941)***

Jabil Inc B 408 361-3200
30 Great Oaks Blvd San Jose (95119) ***(P-5941)***

Jabil Silver Creek Inc C 669 255-2900
4050 Technology Pl Fremont (94538) ***(P-14715)***

Jac Logistics LLC E 954 881-2231
1750 Pririe Cy Rd Ste 130 Folsom (95630) ***(P-7884)***

Jack Anthony Industries Inc E 707 448-0104
108 Elmira Rd Vacaville (95687) ***(P-14642)***

Jack Anthony Industries Inc E 707 426-2000
2270 N Texas St Fairfield (94533) ***(P-14643)***

Jack Anthony Industries Inc E 707 557-5353
135 Valle Vista Ave Vallejo (94590) ***(P-14644)***

Jack Hunt Automotive, San Rafael *Also called Jack L Hunt Inc* ***(P-14613)***

Jack James Tow Svc E 510 581-1950
549 C St Hayward (94541) ***(P-14662)***

Jack Klein Trust Partnership E 209 956-8800
3101 W March Ln Ste B Stockton (95219) ***(P-263)***

Jack L Hunt Inc E 415 453-1611
1714 4th St San Rafael (94901) ***(P-14613)***

Jack Neal & Son Inc C 707 963-7303
360 Lafata St Saint Helena (94574) ***(P-58)***

Jack Plump Inc E 415 346-5712
3138 Fillmore St San Francisco (94123) ***(P-11204)***

Jack Sparrowk E 209 759-3530
18780 E Hwy 88 Clements (95227) ***(P-201)***

Jackrabbit (PA) **D 209 599-6118**
471 Industrial Ave Ripon (95366) ***(P-5009)***

Jackrabbit F 209 521-9325
1318 Dakota Ave Modesto (95358) ***(P-5010)***

Jacks Car Wash 3 D 559 438-8201
6745 N West Ave Fresno (93711) ***(P-14645)***

Jackson & Hertogs LLP E 415 986-4559
909 Montgomery St Ste 200 San Francisco (94133) ***(P-17295)***

Jackson Construction (PA) **E 916 381-8113**
155 Cadillac Dr Sacramento (95825) ***(P-799)***

Jackson Creek Dental Group E 209 223-2712
100 French Bar Rd Ste 101 Jackson (95642) ***(P-15839)***

Jackson Family Farms LLC (PA) **C 707 837-1000**
425 Aviation Blvd Santa Rosa (95403) ***(P-2625)***

Jackson Family Farms LLC ....D....707 836-2047
5660 Skylane Blvd Santa Rosa (95403) *(P-2626)*
Jackson Family Wines Inc ....E....707 836-2035
1190 Kittyhawk Blvd Santa Rosa (95403) *(P-2627)*
Jackson Family Wines Inc (PA) ....D....707 544-4000
421 And 425 Aviation Blvd Santa Rosa (95403) *(P-2628)*
Jackson Laboratory ....E....916 373-5905
1650 Santa Ana Ave Sacramento (95838) *(P-19223)*
Jackson-Mitchell Inc (PA) ....E....209 667-0786
1240 South Ave Turlock (95380) *(P-2192)*
Jacksons Hardware Inc ....D....415 870-4083
435 Du Bois St San Rafael (94901) *(P-8985)*
Jacmar Ddc LLC ....D....916 372-9795
3057 Promenade St West Sacramento (95691) *(P-9457)*
Jacmar Food Service Dist, West Sacramento *Also called Jacmar Ddc LLC (P-9457)*
Jaco Machine Works, Scotts Valley *Also called J A-Co Machine Works LLC (P-5544)*
Jacob's Farm, Santa Cruz *Also called Jacobs Farm/Del Cabo Inc (P-173)*
Jacobs Engineering Group Inc ....D....925 356-3900
2300 Clayton Rd Concord (94520) *(P-18742)*
Jacobs Engineering Group Inc ....D....408 436-4936
1737 N 1st St Ste 300 San Jose (95112) *(P-18743)*
Jacobs Farm/Del Cabo Inc ....D....831 421-9171
1751 Coast Rd Santa Cruz (95060) *(P-173)*
Jacobs Farm/Del Cabo Inc ....D....650 827-1133
390 Swift Ave Ste 8 South San Francisco (94080) *(P-174)*
Jacobsen Trailer Inc ....E....559 834-5971
1128 E South Ave Fowler (93625) *(P-6604)*
Jacquard Products, Healdsburg *Also called Rupert Gibbon & Spider Inc (P-4110)*
Jacuzzi Family Vineyards LLC ....E....707 931-7500
24724 Arnold Dr Sonoma (95476) *(P-2629)*
Jad Construction Inc ....E....916 408-6850
1019 Nichols Ct Rocklin (95765) *(P-750)*
Jade Global Inc (PA) ....D....408 899-7200
1731 Tech Dr Ste 350 San Jose (95110) *(P-13926)*
Jae Properties Inc ....E....707 747-2861
801 1st St Ste F Benicia (94510) *(P-10583)*
Jagdeep Singh Insur Agcy Inc ....E....559 277-5580
4185 W Figarden Dr # 101 Fresno (93722) *(P-10301)*
Jagpreet Enterprises LLC ....C....510 336-8376
25823 Clawiter Rd Hayward (94545) *(P-9458)*
JAGUAR ANIMAL HEALTH, San Francisco *Also called Jaguar Health Inc (P-3932)*
Jaguar Health Inc (PA) ....E....415 371-8300
200 Pine St Fl 4 San Francisco (94104) *(P-3932)*
Jai Inc ....E....408 383-0300
6800 Santa Teresa Blvd # 175 San Jose (95119) *(P-8921)*
Jai Jai Mata Inc ....E....559 435-5650
102 E Herndon Ave Fresno (93720) *(P-11205)*
Jai Shri Ram Hospitali ....D....530 345-2491
685 Manzanita Ct Chico (95926) *(P-11206)*
Jain Farm Fresh Foods Inc (HQ) ....E....541 481-2522
2525 Cooper Ave Merced (95348) *(P-2260)*
Jaj Roofing (PA) ....B....707 446-5500
4980 Allison Pkwy Vacaville (95688) *(P-1813)*
Jalaram Investment LLC ....E....510 568-1880
8350 Edes Ave Oakland (94621) *(P-11207)*
Jamcor Corporation ....E....916 652-7713
6261 Angelo Ct Loomis (95650) *(P-8986)*
Jame Hotel Corporation ....D....415 885-2500
405 Taylor St San Francisco (94102) *(P-11208)*
Jameco Electronics, Belmont *Also called James Electronics Limited (P-8922)*
James C Jenkins Insur Svc Inc ....C....925 798-3334
1390 Willow Pass Rd Concord (94520) *(P-10302)*
James Carollo & Co ....F....209 392-3737
1618 Redfern Ave Dos Palos (93620) *(P-264)*
James Cunningham ....E....530 269-1515
200 Auburn Folsom Rd # 106 Auburn (95603) *(P-17296)*
James E Roberts-Obayashi Corp ....C....925 820-0600
20 Oak Ct Danville (94526) *(P-751)*
James Electronics Limited ....D....650 592-6718
1355 Shoreway Rd Belmont (94002) *(P-8922)*
James Furuli Investment Co ....D....707 778-7102
1320 Commerce St Ste T Petaluma (94954) *(P-11963)*
James G Parker Insurance Assoc (PA) ....D....559 222-7722
1753 E Fir Ave Fresno (93720) *(P-10303)*
James Hazlehurst ....E....530 895-1727
605 W East Ave Chico (95926) *(P-15870)*
James J Stevinson A Corp (PA) ....E....209 632-1681
25079 River Rd Stevinson (95374) *(P-215)*
James L Hall Co Incorporated ....D....707 544-2436
218 Roberts Ave Santa Rosa (95401) *(P-6381)*
James Nevada Properties, Roseville *Also called Dick James & Associates Inc (P-10538)*
James Taylor Roberts Inc ....E....707 895-2500
9000 Highway 128 Philo (95466) *(P-14312)*
Jamestown Hlth Med Sup Co LLC (PA) ....E....916 431-8046
879 F St Ste 120 West Sacramento (95605) *(P-8784)*
Jamestown Motor Corporation ....E....209 984-5272
18475 5th Ave Jamestown (95327) *(P-14663)*
Jamie G Watt ....F....925 580-2805
833 Curlew Rd Livermore (94551) *(P-5034)*
Jampro Antennas Inc ....D....916 383-1177
6340 Sky Creek Dr Sacramento (95828) *(P-5849)*
Janco Airless Center, Berkeley *Also called Janco Chemical Corporation (P-4105)*
Janco Chemical Corporation ....E....510 527-9770
1235 5th St Berkeley (94710) *(P-4105)*
Jane Technologies Inc ....D....617 285-2466
1347 Pacific Ave Ste 201 Santa Cruz (95060) *(P-8715)*
Jani-King of California Inc ....E....925 688-1120
5050 Hopyard Rd Ste 225 Pleasanton (94588) *(P-11964)*
Janico Building Services, North Highlands *Also called Harris Lorenzo (P-11960)*
Janssen Alzheimer Immunothera ....D....650 794-2500
700 Gateway Blvd South San Francisco (94080) *(P-19076)*
Janssen Biopharma Inc ....E....650 635-5500
260 E Grand Ave South San Francisco (94080) *(P-3933)*
Janus Corporation (PA) ....C....925 969-9200
1081 Shary Cir Concord (94518) *(P-2039)*
Janus of Santa Cruz ....D....831 462-1060
200 7th Ave Ste 150 Santa Cruz (95062) *(P-16761)*
Japan Engine Inc ....F....510 532-7878
2131 Williams St San Leandro (94577) *(P-6497)*
Japanese Cltral Cmnty N Cali C ....E....415 567-5505
1840 Sutter St Ste 202 San Francisco (94115) *(P-10393)*
Japanese Cmnty Youth Council (PA) ....D....415 202-7905
2012 Pine St San Francisco (94115) *(P-18235)*
Japanese Community Center, San Francisco *Also called Japanese Cltral Cmnty N Cali C (P-10393)*
Japanese Weekend Inc (PA) ....E....415 621-0555
496 S Airport Blvd South San Francisco (94080) *(P-3011)*
Japonesque LLC ....F....925 866-6670
12647 Alcosta Blvd # 375 San Ramon (94583) *(P-4086)*
Jaqui Foundation Inc ....E....510 562-4721
675 Hegenberger Rd # 209 Oakland (94621) *(P-19907)*
Jar Ventures Inc ....F....530 224-9655
4351 Caterpillar Rd Redding (96003) *(P-7236)*
Jared G Dnielson DDS Dntl Corp (PA) ....D....916 230-8837
3628 Walker Park Dr El Dorado Hills (95762) *(P-15840)*
Jari Electro Supply, Gilroy *Also called Chalgren Enterprises (P-7100)*
Jarka Enterprises Inc (PA) ....D....408 325-5700
675 Brennan St San Jose (95131) *(P-2040)*
Jaroth Inc ....C....925 553-3650
2001 Crow Canyon Rd # 200 San Ramon (94583) *(P-1525)*
Jarvis ....E....707 255-5280
2970 Monticello Rd NAPA (94558) *(P-2630)*
Jarvis & Jarvis Inc ....E....510 222-0431
1520 Fitzgerald Dr Pinole (94564) *(P-14614)*
Jarvis Manufacturing Inc ....F....408 226-2600
210 Hillsdale Ave San Jose (95136) *(P-5545)*
Jarvis Winery, NAPA *Also called Jarvis (P-2630)*
Jason Abel Construction Inc ....E....530 824-2022
23333 Neva Ave Corning (96021) *(P-1884)*
Jason Mechanical Inc ....E....916 638-8763
1379 Fitzgerald Rd Rancho Cordova (95742) *(P-1291)*
Jasper Display Corp ....E....408 831-5788
3235 Kifer Rd Ste 150 Santa Clara (95051) *(P-5155)*
Jasper Hall LLC ....D....415 872-5745
420 Mason St San Francisco (94102) *(P-11722)*
Jasper Ridge Partners ....E....650 494-4800
2885 Sand Hill Rd Ste 100 Menlo Park (94025) *(P-10778)*
Jaton Corporation ....D....510 933-8888
47677 Lakeview Blvd Fremont (94538) *(P-5942)*
Jaunt Inc ....E....650 618-6579
951 Mariners Island Blvd # 500 San Mateo (94404) *(P-13251)*
Jaunt Xr, San Mateo *Also called Jaunt Inc (P-13251)*
Java City, Sacramento *Also called Caravali Coffees Inc (P-9442)*
Java City (HQ) ....D....916 565-5500
717 Del Paso Rd Sacramento (95834) *(P-9459)*
Javad Ems Inc ....D....408 770-1700
900 Rock Ave San Jose (95131) *(P-6439)*
Javelin Logistics Company Inc ....C....800 577-1060
7025 Central Ave Newark (94560) *(P-7841)*
Javelin Logistics Corporation (PA) ....E....510 795-7287
7025 Central Ave Newark (94560) *(P-7623)*
Jay Nolan Community Svcs Inc ....C....408 293-5002
1190 S Bascom Ste 240 Campbell (95008) *(P-17619)*
Jay Nolan Community Svcs Inc ....C....408 293-5002
1190 S Bastom San Jose (95128) *(P-17620)*
Jaylaneentertainment Corp ....D....707 820-2773
585 Fernando Dr Novato (94945) *(P-11803)*
Jazz Pharmaceuticals Inc (HQ) ....A....650 496-3777
3170 Porter Dr Palo Alto (94304) *(P-3934)*
JB&a Distribution, San Rafael *Also called Jeff Burgess & Associates Inc (P-5760)*
Jbe Inc ....F....707 552-6800
1080 Nimitz Ave Ste 400 Vallejo (94592) *(P-3315)*
Jbear Associates LLC ....D....415 673-2332
345 Taylor St San Francisco (94102) *(P-11209)*
Jbr Inc (PA) ....C....916 258-8000
1731 Aviation Blvd Lincoln (95648) *(P-2907)*
Jbr Associates Inc ....D....707 451-3500
151 Lawrence Dr Vacaville (95687) *(P-11210)*
Jbt Food Tech Madera, Madera *Also called John Bean Technologies Corp (P-5132)*
JC Heating & AC Inc (PA) ....E....831 475-6538
1900 Commercial Way Ste E Santa Cruz (95065) *(P-1292)*
JC Metal Specialists Inc (PA) ....F....415 822-3878
220 Michelle Ct San Francisco (94124) *(P-4668)*
JC Penney, Sacramento *Also called Penney Opco LLC (P-11691)*
JC Penney, Stockton *Also called Penney Opco LLC (P-11692)*
JC Penney, Chico *Also called Penney Opco LLC (P-11693)*
JCCEB, Berkeley *Also called Jewish Community Ctr of E Bay (P-17623)*
Jck Legacy Company (HQ) ....C....916 321-1844
1601 Alhambra Blvd # 100 Sacramento (95816) *(P-3451)*
JD Fine & Company Inc ....E....925 521-3300
2304 Willow Pass Rd Concord (94520) *(P-9252)*
JD Food, Fresno *Also called J & D Meat Company (P-9456)*
Jdi Display America Inc (PA) ....E....408 501-3720
1740 Tech Dr Ste 460 San Jose (95110) *(P-6440)*
Jdj Semiconductor LLC ....E....408 542-9430
1249 Reamwood Ave Sunnyvale (94089) *(P-6169)*

ALPHABETIC

Jeff Burgess & Associates Inc (HQ) ....E....415 256-2800
1050 Northgate Dr Ste 200 San Rafael (94903) ***(P-5760)***

Jeff Frank ....F....831 469-8208
120 Encinal St Santa Cruz (95060) ***(P-7237)***

Jeff Stover Inc ....D....530 345-9427
260 Cohasset Rd Ste 190 Chico (95926) ***(P-14955)***

Jeffco Painting & Coating Inc ....D....707 562-1900
1260 Railroad Ave Vallejo (94592) ***(P-1417)***

Jefferson Head Start, Reedley *Also called Fresno Cnty Ecnmic Opprtnties* ***(P-17578)***

Jeffrey Hung-Yip Lee DDS Inc (PA) ....E....650 325-2496
615 Arcadia Ter Unit 304 Sunnyvale (94085) ***(P-15841)***

Jei, Cameron Park *Also called JEI* ***(P-8923)***

JEI ....F....530 677-3210
3087 Alhambra Dr Cameron Park (95682) ***(P-8923)***

Jei Corporate Services, San Jose *Also called Jarka Enterprises Inc* ***(P-2040)***

Jem America Corp ....E....510 683-9234
3000 Laurelview Ct Fremont (94538) ***(P-8924)***

Jemstep Inc ....E....650 966-6500
5150 El Camino Real B16 Los Altos (94022) ***(P-13252)***

Jennifer Lee MD Inc (PA) ....D....408 866-1135
700 W Parr Ave Ste A Los Gatos (95032) ***(P-15440)***

Jennings Technology Co LLC (HQ) ....D....408 292-4025
970 Mclaughlin Ave San Jose (95122) ***(P-6371)***

Jensen & Pilegard (PA) ....E....559 268-9221
1739 E Terrace Ave Fresno (93703) ***(P-9040)***

Jensen Corp Landscape Contr ....C....408 446-4881
1983 Concourse Dr San Jose (95131) ***(P-472)***

Jensen Corp Landscape Contrs, San Jose *Also called Jensen Landscape Services Inc* ***(P-474)***

Jensen Corporate Holdings Inc (PA) ....C....408 446-1118
1250 Ames Ave Ste 104 Milpitas (95035) ***(P-473)***

Jensen Enterprises Inc ....E....530 865-4277
7210 State Highway 32 Orland (95963) ***(P-4439)***

Jensen Enterprises Inc ....D....916 992-8301
5400 Raley Blvd Sacramento (95838) ***(P-8645)***

Jensen Landscape Services Inc ....C....408 446-1118
1983 Concourse Dr San Jose (95131) ***(P-474)***

Jensen Precast, Sacramento *Also called Jensen Enterprises Inc* ***(P-8645)***

Jenson Mechanical Inc ....E....510 429-8078
32420 Central Ave Union City (94587) ***(P-5546)***

Jeppesen Dataplan Inc ....A....408 961-2825
225 W Santa Clara St # 1600 San Jose (95113) ***(P-13796)***

Jepsen Electric, Livermore *Also called D M Jepsen Inc* ***(P-1493)***

Jepson Vineyard Ltd ....F....707 468-8936
10400 S Highway 101 Ukiah (95482) ***(P-2631)***

Jepson Vnyrds-Wnery-Distillery, Ukiah *Also called Jepson Vineyard Ltd* ***(P-2631)***

Jeremiah Phillips LLC ....D....650 697-7733
863 Malcolm Rd Burlingame (94010) ***(P-7337)***

Jeremiahs Pick Coffee Company ....F....415 206-9900
1495 Evans Ave San Francisco (94124) ***(P-2839)***

Jericho Canyon Vineyards LLC ....E....707 942-9665
3292 Old Lawley Toll Rd Calistoga (94515) ***(P-2632)***

Jerico Fire Protection Co Inc ....E....559 255-6446
1380 N Hulbert Ave Fresno (93728) ***(P-1293)***

Jerry Thompson & Sons Pntg Inc ....C....415 454-1500
3 Simms St San Rafael (94901) ***(P-1418)***

Jerrys Trenching Service Inc ....E....559 275-1520
3096 W Belmont Ave # 106 Fresno (93722) ***(P-1110)***

Jessee Brothers Machine Sp Inc ....F....408 866-1755
1640 Dell Ave Campbell (95008) ***(P-5547)***

Jessee Heating & AC ....E....530 891-4926
3025 Southgate Ln Chico (95928) ***(P-1294)***

Jessica McClintock Inc (PA) ....C....415 553-8200
2307 Broadway St San Francisco (94115) ***(P-3015)***

Jessie A Laurent, San Rafael *Also called Laurent Culinary Service* ***(P-2915)***

Jessie Steele Inc ....F....510 204-0991
1020 The Alameda San Jose (95126) ***(P-3051)***

Jessies Grove Winery ....E....209 368-0880
1973 W Turner Rd Lodi (95242) ***(P-2633)***

Jetlore LLC ....E....650 485-1822
1528 S El Cmino Real Ste San Mateo (94402) ***(P-13253)***

Jetronics Company, Santa Rosa *Also called James L Hall Co Incorporated* ***(P-6381)***

Jetstream Software Inc ....E....408 766-1775
2550 N 1st St Ste 420 San Jose (95131) ***(P-12546)***

Jewelry Supply Inc ....E....916 780-9610
301 Derek Pl Roseville (95678) ***(P-9183)***

Jewelrysupply.com, Roseville *Also called Jewelry Supply Inc* ***(P-9183)***

Jewish Cmnty Ctr San Francisco (PA) ....C....415 292-1200
3200 California St San Francisco (94118) ***(P-11606)***

Jewish Cmnty Fdrtion of Grter (PA) ....E....510 839-2900
300 Grand Ave Oakland (94610) ***(P-17621)***

Jewish Cmnty Fdrtion of Grter ....D....510 848-0237
1414 Walnut St Berkeley (94709) ***(P-17622)***

Jewish Cmnty Fdrtion of San Fr (PA) ....D....415 777-0411
121 Steuart St San Francisco (94105) ***(P-18236)***

Jewish Cmnty Relations Council, Oakland *Also called Jewish Cmnty Fdrtion of Grter* ***(P-17621)***

Jewish Community Ctr of E Bay ....E....510 848-0237
1414 Walnut St Berkeley (94709) ***(P-17623)***

Jewish Family and Chld Svcs ....C....650 931-1860
200 Channing Ave Palo Alto (94301) ***(P-17624)***

Jewish Family and Chld Svcs (PA) ....D....415 449-1200
2150 Post St San Francisco (94115) ***(P-17625)***

Jewish Family and Chld Svcs ....C....650 688-3030
200 Channing Ave Palo Alto (94301) ***(P-17626)***

Jewish Family and Chld Svcs ....C....415 449-3862
600 5th Ave San Rafael (94901) ***(P-17627)***

Jewish Fmly & Cmnty Svcs E Bay (PA) ....E....510 704-7475
2484 Shattuck Ave Ste 210 Berkeley (94704) ***(P-17628)***

JEWISH HOME FOR THE AGED, San Francisco *Also called Hebrew Home For Aged Disabled* ***(P-16020)***

Jewish Senior Living Group ....D....415 562-2600
302 Silver Ave San Francisco (94112) ***(P-10442)***

Jewish Vctnal Creer Cnsling Sv ....D....415 391-3600
5106 Camden St Oakland (94619) ***(P-17819)***

JF Shea Construction Inc ....D....530 246-4292
17400 Clear Creek Rd Redding (96001) ***(P-655)***

JFB Ranch Inc ....E....209 364-6149
51170 W Althea Ave Firebaugh (93622) ***(P-175)***

Jfc Electric Inc ....E....916 789-9311
7451 Galilee Rd Ste 130 Roseville (95678) ***(P-1526)***

JFCS/EAST BAY, Berkeley *Also called Jewish Fmly & Cmnty Svcs E Bay* ***(P-17628)***

Jfrog Ltd (PA) ....D....408 329-1540
270 E Caribbean Dr Sunnyvale (94089) ***(P-13254)***

Jiangsu Juwang Info Tech Co (PA) ....E....510 967-3729
195 Recino St Fremont (94539) ***(P-12547)***

JIC Industrial Co Inc ....E....408 935-9880
978 Hanson Ct Milpitas (95035) ***(P-6441)***

Jifco Inc (PA) ....D....925 449-4665
571 Exchange Ct Livermore (94550) ***(P-4974)***

Jifco Fabaricated Piping, Livermore *Also called Jifco Inc* ***(P-4974)***

Jiff Inc (HQ) ....B....415 829-1400
150 Spear St Ste 400 San Francisco (94105) ***(P-12548)***

Jiff Inc ....C....510 844-4139
1999 Harrison St Ste 2070 Oakland (94612) ***(P-13797)***

Jifflenow, Sunnyvale *Also called Ipolipo Inc* ***(P-13248)***

Jiffy Lube, Morgan Hill *Also called Allied Lube Inc* ***(P-14654)***

Jiffy Lube, Chico *Also called Guynn Inc* ***(P-14660)***

Jighi Inc ....E....408 332-1262
2005 De La Cruz Blvd # 295 Santa Clara (95050) ***(P-12549)***

Jigsaw Data Corporation ....E....650 235-8400
900 Concar Dr San Mateo (94402) ***(P-3579)***

Jigsaw Operations LLC (PA) ....E....212 565-8046
1600 Amphitheatre Pkwy Mountain View (94043) ***(P-7967)***

Jim Crawford Cnstr Co Inc ....E....559 299-0306
1189 Hoblitt Ave Clovis (93612) ***(P-1052)***

Jim Dobbas Inc (PA) ....E....916 663-3363
300 Taylor Rd Newcastle (95658) ***(P-14313)***

Jim Jonas Inc ....E....707 994-5911
9125 Hwy 53 Lower Lake (95457) ***(P-9526)***

Jim Little Raymonds Print Shop, Fremont *Also called Raymonds Little Print Shop Inc* ***(P-3690)***

Jim Murphy & Associates, Santa Rosa *Also called Murphy-True Inc* ***(P-928)***

Jim Walters Construction Inc (PA) ....D....650 596-9751
1042 Terminal Way San Carlos (94070) ***(P-899)***

Jinkosolar (us) Holding Inc (PA) ....C....415 402-0502
595 Market St Ste 2200 San Francisco (94105) ***(P-1295)***

Jinkosolar (us) Inc ....D....415 402-0502
595 Market St Ste 2200 San Francisco (94105) ***(P-6170)***

Jisco, Fresno *Also called Johnston Industrial Supply Inc* ***(P-9073)***

Jiseki Health Inc ....E....408 763-7264
10 Rollins Rd Ste 209 Millbrae (94030) ***(P-13255)***

Jit Transportation Inc ....B....408 232-4800
1075 Montague Expy Milpitas (95035) ***(P-7885)***

Jive Software Inc ....F....503 295-3700
735 Emerson St Palo Alto (94301) ***(P-13256)***

Jivox Corporation (HQ) ....D....650 412-1125
1810 Gateway Dr Ste 280 San Mateo (94404) ***(P-8716)***

Jj Barn Transport Inc ....E....916 371-5800
3030 Morrow Bay St West Sacramento (95691) ***(P-7556)***

JJ Charles Inc ....E....559 264-6664
4115 S Orange Ave Fresno (93725) ***(P-3260)***

Jj Express Freight Inc ....E....916 914-3231
4196 Valtara Rd Cameron Park (95682) ***(P-7886)***

Jj Pfister Distilling Co LLC ....F....503 939-9535
9819 Business Park Dr # 3 Sacramento (95827) ***(P-2774)***

JJ Rios Farm Services Inc ....D....209 333-7467
4890 E Acampo Rd Acampo (95220) ***(P-359)***

Jjk Hotels LP (PA) ....D....707 441-4721
1929 4th St Eureka (95501) ***(P-11211)***

JJR Enterprises Inc (HQ) ....D....916 363-2666
10491 Old Placerville Rd # 150 Sacramento (95827) ***(P-14701)***

Jkb Homes Corp ....E....209 668-5303
2370 W Monte Vista Ave Turlock (95382) ***(P-656)***

Jkf Auto Service Inc ....D....916 315-0555
6818 Five Star Blvd Rocklin (95677) ***(P-14646)***

JL Bray & Son Inc ....D....209 545-2856
4501 Broadway Salida (95368) ***(P-900)***

Jl Construction Inc ....E....707 527-5788
70 Stony Point Rd Ste D Santa Rosa (95401) ***(P-901)***

JL Haley Enterprises Inc ....C....916 631-6375
3510 Luyung Dr Rancho Cordova (95742) ***(P-5548)***

Jla Home, Woodland *Also called E & E Co Ltd* ***(P-634)***

Jla Home, Fremont *Also called E & E Co Ltd* ***(P-8511)***

Jls Environmental Services Inc ....D....916 660-1525
3460 Swetzer Rd Loomis (95650) ***(P-19703)***

JM Custom Cabinets & Furniture ....E....559 291-6638
3848 N Winery Ave Fresno (93726) ***(P-3278)***

JM Huber Corporation ....D....209 549-9771
700 Kiernan Ave Ste D Modesto (95356) ***(P-3790)***

JM Streamline Inc ....D....530 272-6806
154 Scandling Ave Grass Valley (95945) ***(P-902)***

JMB Construction Inc ....D....650 267-5300
132 S Maple Ave South San Francisco (94080) ***(P-903)***

JMEKM Enterprises ....E....866 370-0419
1072 S De Anza Blvd San Jose (95129) *(P-11965)*
Jmp Group Inc (HQ)....D....415 835-8900
600 Montgomery St # 1100 San Francisco (94111) *(P-9977)*
Jmp Securities LLC (HQ)....C....415 835-8900
600 Montgomery St # 1100 San Francisco (94111) *(P-9978)*
JMS Realtors Ltd (PA)....C....559 490-1500
575 E Alluvial Ave # 101 Fresno (93720) *(P-10584)*
Jn Projects Inc ....D....415 766-0273
333 Brannan St San Francisco (94107) *(P-11723)*
JN Restaurants Inc (PA)....B....209 710-8385
933 6th St Ste B Los Banos (93635) *(P-9144)*
Jobs Plus, Chico *Also called Caminar (P-16997)*
Jobs Plus, San Ramon *Also called Plus Group Inc (P-12189)*
Jobtrain Inc ....E....650 330-6429
1200 Obrien Dr Menlo Park (94025) *(P-17820)*
Joby Aviation Inc ....A....831 426-3733
2155 Delaware Ave Ste 225 Santa Cruz (95060) *(P-6612)*
Joe Heidrick Enterprises Inc ....E....530 662-2339
36826 County Road 24 Woodland (95695) *(P-7)*
Joe Lunardi Electric Inc ....D....707 545-4755
5334 Sebastopol Rd Santa Rosa (95407) *(P-1527)*
Joe Pucci & Sons Seafoods, Hayward *Also called Blue River Seafood Inc (P-9360)*
Joes Dwntwn Brewry & Rest Inc ....E....707 258-2337
902 Main St NAPA (94559) *(P-2482)*
Joguru Inc ....D....855 526-4332
2600 El Camino Real Ste 4 Palo Alto (94306) *(P-7818)*
Johanson Transportation Svc (PA)....E....559 458-2200
5583 E Olive Ave Fresno (93727) *(P-7842)*
John A Hughes DDS Incorporated ....D....408 378-3489
1580 Winchester Blvd # 30 Campbell (95008) *(P-15842)*
John Aguilar & Company Inc ....D....209 546-0171
1505 Navy Dr Stockton (95206) *(P-7476)*
John B Sanfilippo & Son Inc ....C....209 854-2455
29241 Cottonwood Rd Gustine (95322) *(P-2446)*
John Bean Technologies Corp ....C....559 661-3200
2300 W Industrial Ave Madera (93637) *(P-5132)*
John Boyd Enterprises Inc (PA)....C....916 381-4790
8401 Specialty Cir Sacramento (95828) *(P-6584)*
John C Destefano ....E....916 276-4056
7325 Reese Rd Sacramento (95828) *(P-3182)*
John C Fremont Healthcare Dst ....B....209 966-3631
5189 Hospital Rd Mariposa (95338) *(P-16389)*
John C Fremont Hosp Foundation ....E....209 966-0850
5189 Hospital Rd Mariposa (95338) *(P-16390)*
John Chailch, San Francisco *Also called Hayes Convalescent Hospital (P-16017)*
John Daniel Gonzalez ....E....559 646-6621
13458 E Industrial Dr Parlier (93648) *(P-3237)*
John Deere Authorized Dealer, Fresno *Also called Vucovich Inc (P-9049)*
John Deere Authorized Dealer, Manteca *Also called J M Equipment Company Inc (P-12050)*
John Deere Authorized Dealer, Robbins *Also called Valley Truck and Tractor Inc (P-9048)*
John Deere Authorized Dealer, Firebaugh *Also called Thomason Tractor Co California (P-9044)*
John Deere Authorized Dealer, Stockton *Also called E & S Westcoast LLC (P-8857)*
John Deere Authorized Dealer, San Leandro *Also called Valley Power Systems Inc (P-9103)*
John F Otto Inc ....C....916 441-6870
1717 2nd St Sacramento (95811) *(P-904)*
John Fitzpatrick & Sons ....E....530 241-3216
1480 Beltline Rd Redding (96003) *(P-2794)*
John George Psychiatric, San Leandro *Also called County of Alameda (P-16732)*
John Gore Organization Inc ....D....650 340-0469
255 S B St San Mateo (94401) *(P-14849)*
John H Jones Community Clinic, West Sacramento *Also called Davis Community Clinic (P-16755)*
John H Kautz Farms ....E....209 334-4786
5490 Bear Creek Rd Lodi (95240) *(P-255)*
John Jackson Masonry ....D....916 381-8021
5691 Power Inn Rd Ste B Sacramento (95824) *(P-1649)*
John L Sllivan Investments Inc (PA)....C....916 969-5911
6200 Northfront Rd Livermore (94551) *(P-14574)*
John L Sullivan Chevrolet Inc ....C....916 782-1243
350 Automall Dr Roseville (95661) *(P-14615)*
John Muir Behavioral Hlth Ctr ....D....925 674-4100
2740 Grant St Concord (94520) *(P-16742)*
John Muir Diabetes Cntr Walnut ....E....925 952-2944
175 La Casa Via Walnut Creek (94598) *(P-16391)*
John Muir Health (HQ)....A....925 947-4449
1601 Ygnacio Valley Rd Walnut Creek (94598) *(P-16392)*
John Muir Health ....A....925 939-3000
1601 Ygnacio Valley Rd Walnut Creek (94598) *(P-16393)*
John Muir Inptient Therapy Ctr, Walnut Creek *Also called Muir John Mgntic Imging Ctr L (P-16461)*
JOHN MUIR MEDICAL CENTER, Walnut Creek *Also called John Muir Physician Network (P-16394)*
John Muir Medical Center, Walnut Creek *Also called John Muir Health (P-16393)*
John Muir Physician Network ....E....925 988-7580
1914 Tice Valley Blvd Walnut Creek (94595) *(P-15441)*
John Muir Physician Network (PA)....A....925 296-9700
1450 Treat Blvd Walnut Creek (94597) *(P-16394)*
John Naimi Inc ....E....408 280-7433
2410 Monterey Hwy San Jose (95111) *(P-657)*
John Paul USA (PA)....C....415 905-6088
575 Market St Ste 720 San Francisco (94105) *(P-12177)*
John Plane Construction Inc ....C....415 468-0555
661 Hayne Rd Hillsborough (94010) *(P-905)*
John Russo Industrial Metal, Newark *Also called Jri Inc (P-4774)*
John Sikkema Construction Inc ....E....209 599-1573
26126 S Curtis Ave Ripon (95366) *(P-906)*
John Stewart Company ....E....707 676-5660
191 Heritage Ln Dixon (95620) *(P-10585)*
John Stewart Company ....E....916 561-0323
1455 Response Rd Ste 140 Sacramento (95815) *(P-10586)*
John Stewart Company ....E....831 438-5725
104 Whispering Pines Dr # 200 Scotts Valley (95066) *(P-10587)*
John Stewart Company (PA)....D....415 345-4400
1388 Sutter St Ste 1100 San Francisco (94109) *(P-10588)*
John Stewart Company ....E....415 621-6258
370 Valencia St San Francisco (94103) *(P-10589)*
John Taylor Fertilizers Co (HQ)....B....916 991-9840
841 W Elkhorn Blvd Rio Linda (95673) *(P-9601)*
John Vellequette DDS ....E....408 245-7500
877 W Fremont Ave Ste L3 Sunnyvale (94087) *(P-15843)*
John Wheeler Logging Inc ....C....530 527-2993
13570 State Highway 36 E Red Bluff (96080) *(P-3067)*
John Xxiii Snior Ntrtn Site Ct, San Jose *Also called Catholic Chrties Snta Clara CN (P-17468)*
John Zink Company LLC ....E....918 234-1884
2151 River Plaza Dr # 200 Sacramento (95833) *(P-6723)*
John's Formica Shop, Santa Rosa *Also called Johns Formica Inc (P-3327)*
Johns Formica Inc ....E....707 544-8585
2439 Piner Rd Santa Rosa (95403) *(P-3327)*
Johnson & Daly Moving & Strg ....E....415 435-1192
110 Belvedere St Ste 200 San Rafael (94901) *(P-7557)*
Johnson & Johnson ....D....650 237-4878
3509 Langdon Cmn Fremont (94538) *(P-3395)*
Johnson Air, Clovis *Also called Ladell Inc (P-1300)*
Johnson Contrls Authorized Dlr, Hayward *Also called Automatic Control Engrg Corp (P-6894)*
Johnson Matthey Inc ....E....408 727-2221
1070 Coml St Ste 110 San Jose (95112) *(P-6993)*
Johnson Ranch Racquet Club, Roseville *Also called Spare-Time Inc (P-15151)*
Johnson Schchter Lwis A Prof L ....E....916 921-5800
2180 Harvard St Ste 560 Sacramento (95815) *(P-17297)*
Johnson Service Group Inc ....A....408 728-9510
950 S Bascom Ave San Jose (95128) *(P-10394)*
Johnson United Inc (PA)....E....209 543-1320
5201 Pentecost Dr Modesto (95356) *(P-7238)*
Johnson, David L MD, Fremont *Also called Washington Rdologist Med Group (P-16723)*
Johnston Industrial Supply Inc (PA)....E....559 233-1822
2433 S Cherry Ave Fresno (93706) *(P-9073)*
Johnstons Trading Post Inc ....E....530 661-6152
11 N Pioneer Ave Woodland (95776) *(P-3238)*
Joie De Vivre Hospitality LLC ....D....408 335-1700
210 E Main St Los Gatos (95030) *(P-11212)*
Joie De Vivre Hospitality LLC (PA)....E....415 922-6000
1750 Geary Blvd San Francisco (94115) *(P-11213)*
Joie De Vivre Hospitality LLC ....D....415 278-3700
8 Mission St San Francisco (94105) *(P-11214)*
Joie De Vivre Hospitality LLC ....D....415 567-8467
444 Presidio Ave San Francisco (94115) *(P-11215)*
Joie De Vivre Hospitality LLC ....D....415 380-0400
555 Redwood Hwy Frontage Mill Valley (94941) *(P-11216)*
Joie De Vivre Hospitality LLC ....D....415 441-2700
580 Geary St San Francisco (94102) *(P-11217)*
Joie De Vivre Hospitality LLC ....D....415 921-5520
3100 Webster St San Francisco (94123) *(P-11218)*
Joie De Vivre Hospitality LLC ....D....415 776-1380
601 Eddy St San Francisco (94109) *(P-11219)*
Joie De Vivre Hospitality LLC ....D....650 940-1000
860 E El Camino Real Mountain View (94040) *(P-11220)*
Joie De Vivre Hospitality LLC ....D....415 775-1755
845 Bush St San Francisco (94108) *(P-11221)*
Joie De Vivre Hospitality Inc ....D....408 738-0500
910 E Fremont Ave Sunnyvale (94087) *(P-11222)*
Joie De Vivre Hotels ....D....415 776-1380
601 Eddy St San Francisco (94109) *(P-11223)*
Jomu Mist Incorporated ....F....415 448-7273
309 Chapman Dr Corte Madera (94925) *(P-13257)*
Jon K Takata Corporation (PA)....D....510 315-5400
4142 Point Eden Way Hayward (94545) *(P-17629)*
Jonas Heating & Cooling, Lower Lake *Also called Jim Jonas Inc (P-9526)*
Jones Hall A Prof Law Corp ....E....415 391-5780
475 Sansome St Ste 1700 San Francisco (94111) *(P-17298)*
Jones Rest HM Cnvalescent Hosp, San Leandro *Also called Sanhyd Inc (P-16266)*
Jonna Corp Inc ....E....408 297-7910
348 Phelan Ave San Jose (95112) *(P-4723)*
Joong-Ang Daily News Cal Inc ....E....510 487-3333
23575 Cabot Blvd Ste 201 Hayward (94545) *(P-3452)*
Jopari Solutions Inc ....D....925 459-5200
1855 Gateway Blvd Ste 500 Concord (94520) *(P-14314)*
Joplin Inc (PA)....E....707 847-3494
34285 Kruse Ranch Rd Cazadero (95421) *(P-11607)*
Jordan Vineyard & Winery, Healdsburg *Also called Jvw Corporation (P-2636)*
Jordan Vineyard & Winery LP ....E....707 431-5250
1474 Alexander Valley Rd Healdsburg (95448) *(P-2634)*
Jorgensen & Co, Fresno *Also called Jorgensen & Sons Inc (P-9198)*
Jorgensen & Sons Inc (PA)....D....559 268-6241
2467 Foundry Park Ave Fresno (93706) *(P-9198)*
Jorgensen Sgel Mc Clure Flgel ....E....650 324-9300
1100 Alma St Ste 210 Menlo Park (94025) *(P-17299)*
Joroda Inc (PA)....E....925 930-0122
1559 Botelho Dr Walnut Creek (94596) *(P-2389)*
Jose Vramontes ....E....209 810-5384
14345 N Highway 88 Lodi (95240) *(P-176)*

ALPHABETIC

Joseph B Hawkins Jr MD Inc......E......559 431-6197
7230 N Millbrook Ave Fresno (93720) ***(P-15442)***
Joseph Bui Dmd Inc (PA)......**E......209 224-8104**
1110 W Kettleman Ln # 47 Lodi (95240) ***(P-15844)***
Joseph Cozza Salon Inc (PA)......**E......415 433-3030**
77 Maiden Ln Fl 2 San Francisco (94108) ***(P-11687)***
Joseph Farms, Atwater *Also called Gallo Global Nutrition LLC* ***(P-2148)***
Joseph Farms Cheese, Atwater *Also called Gallo Cattle Co A Ltd Partnr* ***(P-213)***
Joseph J Albanese Inc......A......408 727-5700
851 Martin Ave Santa Clara (95050) ***(P-1885)***
Joseph Phelps Vineyards, Saint Helena *Also called Stone Bridge Cellars Inc* ***(P-2730)***
Joseph Phelps Vineyards LLC......D......707 963-2745
200 Taplin Rd Saint Helena (94574) ***(P-2635)***
Joseph R Martel MD Inc......E......916 635-6161
11216 Trinity River Dr Rancho Cordova (95670) ***(P-15443)***
Joseph Systems Inc......E......916 303-7200
2521 Warren Dr Ste A Rocklin (95677) ***(P-13615)***
Josephine's Personnel Services, San Jose *Also called Josephines Prof Staffing Inc* ***(P-12101)***
Josephines Prof Staffing Inc (PA)......**C......408 943-0111**
2158 Ringwood Ave San Jose (95131) ***(P-12101)***
Joshua H Hoffman MD, Sacramento *Also called Sutter Inc* ***(P-15728)***
Jostens Inc......E......916 408-2295
P.O. Box 1747 Rocklin (95677) ***(P-7167)***
Journey Inc......E......916 780-7000
2211 Plaza Dr Ste 100 Rocklin (95765) ***(P-10304)***
Journeyworks Publishing......F......831 423-1400
763 Chestnut St Santa Cruz (95060) ***(P-3580)***
Joveo Inc (PA)......**D......408 896-9030**
1047 Whipple Ave Ste B Redwood City (94062) ***(P-12550)***
Joy Engineering, Portola *Also called R & J Joy Inc* ***(P-1972)***
Joy Signal Technology LLC......E......530 891-3551
1020 Marauder St Ste A Chico (95973) ***(P-5717)***
Joyent Inc......C......415 400-0600
655 Montgomery St # 1600 San Francisco (94111) ***(P-13927)***
JP, Santa Clara *Also called J P Graphics Inc* ***(P-3662)***
JP Research Inc......E......650 559-5999
5050 El Cmino Real Ste 20 Los Altos (94022) ***(P-19801)***
Jpa Landscape & Cnstr Inc......D......925 960-9602
256 Boeing Ct Livermore (94551) ***(P-475)***
Jpmorgan Chase Bank Nat Assn......C......559 449-0632
6495 N Palm Ave Ste 101 Fresno (93704) ***(P-9684)***
JR Daniels Commercial Bldrs......E......209 545-6040
907 Maze Blvd Modesto (95351) ***(P-4857)***
JR Perce Plbg Inc Sacramento......C......916 434-9554
3610 Cincinnati Ave Rocklin (95765) ***(P-1296)***
JR Stephens Company......E......707 825-0100
5208 Boyd Rd Arcata (95521) ***(P-3183)***
JR Watkins LLC......E......415 477-8500
101 Mission St San Francisco (94105) ***(P-3027)***
Jri Inc......E......510 494-5300
38021 Cherry St Newark (94560) ***(P-4774)***
JRP Hospitality Inc......E......408 569-2911
309 Prosperity Blvd Chowchilla (93610) ***(P-11224)***
Js Contracting Services Inc......E......916 625-1690
3129 Swetzer Rd Ste E Loomis (95650) ***(P-752)***
JS Homen Trucking Inc......D......209 723-9559
4224 Turlock Rd Snelling (95369) ***(P-7477)***
JS Trade Bindery Services Inc......E......650 486-1475
209 Oxford Way Belmont (94002) ***(P-3761)***
Js Trucking Inc......E......209 252-0007
2930 Geer Rd Turlock (95382) ***(P-5064)***
Jsdu, Santa Rosa *Also called Viavi Solutions Inc* ***(P-6546)***
Jsj Electrical Display Corp......F......707 747-5595
340 Via Palo Linda Fairfield (94534) ***(P-7239)***
Jsl Partners Inc......E......408 747-9000
1294 Anvilwood Ct Sunnyvale (94089) ***(P-3663)***
Jsr Micro Inc (HQ)......**C......408 543-8800**
1280 N Mathilda Ave Sunnyvale (94089) ***(P-4124)***
Jsr North America Holdings Inc......E......408 543-8800
1280 N Mathilda Ave Sunnyvale (94089) ***(P-19355)***
Jt2 Integrated Resources (PA)......**D......925 556-7012**
333 Hegenberger Rd # 650 Oakland (94621) ***(P-19356)***
Jts Communities Inc (PA)......**E......916 487-3434**
11249 Gold Country Blvd # 180 Gold River (95670) ***(P-658)***
Jts Corporation......A......408 468-1800
166 Baypointe Pkwy San Jose (95134) ***(P-5297)***
Jts Engineering Cons Inc......E......916 441-6708
1808 J St Sacramento (95811) ***(P-18744)***
Jts Sports Services Inc......E......916 390-0829
10556 Industrial Ave # 130 Roseville (95678) ***(P-15212)***
Judson Enterprises Inc (PA)......**B......916 596-6721**
2440 Gold River Rd # 100 Rancho Cordova (95670) ***(P-753)***
Julie Pearl A Prof Corp......D......415 771-7500
560 Miramonte Ave Palo Alto (94306) ***(P-17300)***
July Systems Inc (PA)......**D......650 685-2460**
533 Airport Blvd Ste 395 Burlingame (94010) ***(P-6502)***
Jumbo Logistics LLC......E......216 662-5420
801 E Roth Rd French Camp (95231) ***(P-7843)***
Jumio Corporation (HQ)......**E......650 424-8545**
395 Page Mill Rd Ste 150 Palo Alto (94306) ***(P-12551)***
Jumio Software & Dev LLC......E......650 388-0264
1971 Landings Dr Mountain View (94043) ***(P-13258)***
Jump Associates LLC (PA)......**E......650 373-7200**
1825 S Grant St Ste 9-12 San Mateo (94402) ***(P-19802)***
Jumpshot Inc......D......415 212-9250
333 Bryant St Ste 240 San Francisco (94107) ***(P-12552)***
Jumpstart Automotive Media, San Francisco *Also called Jumpstart Digital Mktg Inc* ***(P-19547)***
Jumpstart Digital Mktg Inc (HQ)......**D......415 844-6336**
550 Kearny St Ste 500 San Francisco (94108) ***(P-19547)***
June Sf LLC......E......415 906-4021
644 Old Mason St San Francisco (94129) ***(P-2483)***
Jungsten Construction......E......415 381-3162
495 Miller Ave Mill Valley (94941) ***(P-659)***
Juniper Hotel, Cupertino *Also called Cupertino Lessee LLC* ***(P-11043)***
Juniper Networks Inc......A......408 745-2000
1137 Innovation Way B Sunnyvale (94089) ***(P-13616)***
Juniper Networks Inc (PA)......**B......408 745-2000**
1133 Innovation Way Sunnyvale (94089) ***(P-5390)***
Juniper Networks (us) Inc (HQ)......**C......408 745-2000**
1133 Innovation Way Sunnyvale (94089) ***(P-13617)***
Juniper Networks Intl LLC......F......408 745-2000
1133 Innovation Way Sunnyvale (94089) ***(P-13618)***
Juniper Square Inc......B......415 841-2722
343 Sansome St Ste 600 San Francisco (94104) ***(P-8717)***
Junk King LLC (PA)......**C......888 888-5865**
389 Oyster Point Blvd # 6 South San Francisco (94080) ***(P-7478)***
Junopacific Inc......C......831 462-1141
2840 Res Pk Dr Ste 160 Soquel (95073) ***(P-4293)***
Jupiter Intelligence Inc......E......650 255-7122
181 2nd Ave Ste 300 San Mateo (94401) ***(P-1528)***
Jupiter Systems Inc......E......510 675-1000
31015 Huntwood Ave Hayward (94544) ***(P-5333)***
Just Desserts, Fairfield *Also called New Desserts Inc* ***(P-9469)***
Just Tomatoes Inc......D......209 894-5371
2103 W Hamilton Rd Westley (95387) ***(P-291)***
Justanswer LLC......E......800 785-2305
38 Keyes Ave Ste 150 San Francisco (94129) ***(P-7968)***
Justice Dvrsity Ctr of The Bar......D......415 575-3130
1360 Mission St San Francisco (94103) ***(P-17301)***
Justice United States Dept......E......559 251-4040
2500 Tulare St Ste 4401 Fresno (93721) ***(P-12102)***
Justin Carey Enterprises Inc......E......559 213-4731
703 N Abby St Fresno (93701) ***(P-1774)***
Justipher Inc......F......510 918-6800
1248 W Winton Ave Hayward (94545) ***(P-7240)***
Juul Labs Inc (PA)......**B......415 829-2336**
560 20th St San Francisco (94107) ***(P-7290)***
Juut Midwest Inc......E......650 328-4067
240 University Ave Palo Alto (94301) ***(P-11688)***
Juut Salonspa, Palo Alto *Also called Juut Midwest Inc* ***(P-11688)***
Juvo Atism Bhavioral Hlth Svcs, Antioch *Also called Ed Supports LLC* ***(P-17538)***
Juvo Atism Bhavioral Hlth Svcs, Folsom *Also called Ed Supports LLC* ***(P-17539)***
Juvo Atism Bhavioral Hlth Svcs, San Jose *Also called Ed Supports LLC* ***(P-17018)***
Juvo Atism Bhavioral Hlth Svcs, Oakland *Also called Ed Supports LLC* ***(P-17019)***
Jvw Corporation......D......707 431-5250
1474 Alexander Valley Rd Healdsburg (95448) ***(P-2636)***
JWP Manufacturing LLC......E......408 970-0641
3500 De La Cruz Blvd Santa Clara (95054) ***(P-5549)***
K & D Landscaping Inc......D......831 728-4018
62-C Hngar Way Wtsonville Watsonville (95076) ***(P-422)***
K B M Office Equipment Inc (PA)......**D......408 351-7100**
225 W Santa Clara St San Jose (95113) ***(P-8497)***
K B R Inc (PA)......**D......707 454-2000**
190 S Orchard Ave A200 Vacaville (95688) ***(P-11825)***
K B W Inc......E......559 233-2591
2660 S Dearing Ave Fresno (93725) ***(P-4585)***
K C C, San Rafael *Also called Gilardi & Co LLC* ***(P-19340)***
K Darpinian & Sons Inc......D......209 524-4442
5913 Coffee Rd Modesto (95357) ***(P-104)***
K G O T V News Bureau......D......510 451-4772
520 3rd St Ste 200 Oakland (94607) ***(P-8028)***
K G Walters Cnstr Co Inc......D......707 527-9968
195 Concourse Blvd Ste A Santa Rosa (95403) ***(P-907)***
K J Woods Construction Inc......E......415 759-0506
1485 Bay Shore Blvd # 149 San Francisco (94124) ***(P-1111)***
K K R, Menlo Park *Also called Kohlberg Kravis Roberts Co LP* ***(P-10863)***
K P Graphics, Stockton *Also called Kp LLC* ***(P-3667)***
K P I, Fremont *Also called Knightsbridge Plastics Inc* ***(P-4296)***
K R Anderson Inc (PA)......**D......408 825-1800**
18330 Sutter Blvd Morgan Hill (95037) ***(P-9519)***
K W Construction, West Sacramento *Also called Krw Enterprises* ***(P-910)***
K W Emerson Inc......E......209 754-3839
413 W Saint Charles St San Andreas (95249) ***(P-1112)***
K X T V Channel 10, Sacramento *Also called Kxtv Inc* ***(P-8052)***
K&B Pichette Enterprises Inc......D......209 452-5999
11992 State Highway 88 # 20 Jackson (95642) ***(P-16901)***
K&I International Trade Inc......E......320 228-2788
1267 Willis St Ste 200 Redding (96001) ***(P-8498)***
K-Designers, Rancho Cordova *Also called Judson Enterprises Inc* ***(P-753)***
K-Fab, Santa Clara *Also called P M S D Inc* ***(P-5586)***
K-Love Radio Network, Rocklin *Also called Educational Media Foundation* ***(P-8018)***
K2 Pure Slutions Nocal Salt LP......F......925 297-4901
950 Loveridge Rd Pittsburg (94565) ***(P-4163)***
K3 Dev LLC......D......408 733-7950
725 S Fair Oaks Ave Sunnyvale (94086) ***(P-11225)***
K3 Dev LLC......D......408 733-7950
597 E El Camino Real Sunnyvale (94087) ***(P-11226)***
K9 Activity Club Inc (PA)......**E......707 569-1394**
4340 Occidental Rd Santa Rosa (95401) ***(P-15100)***
Kabam Inc (HQ)......**A......604 256-0054**
575 Market St Ste 2450 San Francisco (94105) ***(P-12553)***
Kabuki Springs & Spa, San Francisco *Also called Joie De Vivre Hospitality LLC* ***(P-11213)***
Kadiant LLC......E......209 521-4791
155 Grand Ave Ste 500 Oakland (94612) ***(P-19803)***

ALPHABETIC SECTION
Kaiser Foundation Hospitals

Kae Properties (PA)..........E......510 276-2635
2033 Miramonte Ave San Leandro (94578) ***(P-10443)***
Kagome Inc (HQ)..........C......209 826-8850
333 Johnson Rd Los Banos (93635) ***(P-2217)***
Kahn Rennaissance LLC..........C......510 260-3161
640 Bailey Rd Ste 509 Bay Point (94565) ***(P-11635)***
Kai Ming Inc (PA)..........E......415 982-4777
900 Kearny St Ste 600 San Francisco (94133) ***(P-18575)***
Kaiam Corp..........D......650 344-2231
39677 Eureka Dr Newark (94560) ***(P-1529)***
Kaidan Hospitality LP..........D......530 221-8700
1830 Hilltop Dr Redding (96002) ***(P-11227)***
Kainos Dental Technologies LLC (PA)..........E......800 331-4834
2975 Treat Blvd Ste A3 Concord (94518) ***(P-6994)***
Kainos HM Trning Ctr For Dvlpm..........D......650 361-1355
2761 Fair Oaks Ave Ste A Redwood City (94063) ***(P-17630)***
Kainos Work Activity Ctr, Redwood City *Also called Kainos HM Trning Ctr For Dvlpm* ***(P-17630)***
Kaise Perma San Franc Medic Ce..........E......415 833-2000
2425 Geary Blvd San Francisco (94115) ***(P-7075)***
Kaiser Aluminum Intl Corp..........C......949 614-1740
6177 Sunal Blvd Pleasanton (94566) ***(P-4554)***
Kaiser Enterprises Inc..........D......209 728-2091
798 Murphys Creek Rd Murphys (95247) ***(P-4975)***
Kaiser Foundation Health Plan, Vacaville *Also called Kaiser Foundation Hospitals* ***(P-16396)***
Kaiser Foundation Health Plan, Union City *Also called Kaiser Foundation Hospitals* ***(P-10109)***
Kaiser Foundation Health Plan, San Francisco *Also called Kaiser Foundation Hospitals* ***(P-15447)***
Kaiser Foundation Health Plan, Elk Grove *Also called Kaiser Foundation Hospitals* ***(P-10111)***
Kaiser Foundation Health Plan, Vallejo *Also called Kaiser Foundation Hospitals* ***(P-10112)***
Kaiser Foundation Health Plan, San Rafael *Also called Kaiser Foundation Hospitals* ***(P-10113)***
Kaiser Foundation Health Plan, Oakland *Also called Kaiser Foundation Hospitals* ***(P-10114)***
Kaiser Foundation Health Plan, Fresno *Also called Kaiser Foundation Hospitals* ***(P-10115)***
Kaiser Foundation Health Plan, Elk Grove *Also called Kaiser Foundation Hospitals* ***(P-10116)***
Kaiser Foundation Health Plan, Hayward *Also called Kaiser Foundation Hospitals* ***(P-10117)***
Kaiser Foundation Health Plan, Vallejo *Also called Kaiser Foundation Hospitals* ***(P-10119)***
Kaiser Foundation Health Plan, Walnut Creek *Also called Kaiser Foundation Hospitals* ***(P-10123)***
Kaiser Foundation Health Plan, Clovis *Also called Kaiser Foundation Hospitals* ***(P-10124)***
Kaiser Foundation Health Plan, Roseville *Also called Kaiser Foundation Hospitals* ***(P-10125)***
Kaiser Foundation Health Plan, San Rafael *Also called Kaiser Foundation Hospitals* ***(P-10126)***
Kaiser Foundation Health Plan, Oakhurst *Also called Kaiser Foundation Hospitals* ***(P-10127)***
Kaiser Foundation Health Plan, Daly City *Also called Kaiser Foundation Hospitals* ***(P-10128)***
Kaiser Foundation Health Plan, Union City *Also called Kaiser Foundation Hospitals* ***(P-10129)***
Kaiser Foundation Health Plan, Tracy *Also called Kaiser Foundation Hospitals* ***(P-10130)***
Kaiser Foundation Health Plan, San Bruno *Also called Kaiser Foundation Hospitals* ***(P-10131)***
Kaiser Foundation Health Plan, Santa Rosa *Also called Kaiser Foundation Hospitals* ***(P-10132)***
Kaiser Foundation Health Plan, Santa Rosa *Also called Kaiser Foundation Hospitals* ***(P-10133)***
Kaiser Foundation Health Plan, Modesto *Also called Kaiser Foundation Hospitals* ***(P-10134)***
Kaiser Foundation Health Plan, Rohnert Park *Also called Kaiser Foundation Hospitals* ***(P-10135)***
Kaiser Foundation Health Plan, Alameda *Also called Kaiser Foundation Hospitals* ***(P-15487)***
Kaiser Foundation Health Plan, Oakland *Also called Kaiser Foundation Hospitals* ***(P-10136)***
Kaiser Foundation Health Plan, Selma *Also called Kaiser Foundation Hospitals* ***(P-10137)***
Kaiser Foundation Health Plan, Sacramento *Also called Kaiser Foundation Hospitals* ***(P-10139)***
Kaiser Foundation Health Plan, San Jose *Also called Kaiser Foundation Hospitals* ***(P-10140)***
Kaiser Foundation Health Plan, Gilroy *Also called Kaiser Foundation Hospitals* ***(P-10141)***
Kaiser Foundation Health Plan, Fresno *Also called Kaiser Foundation Hospitals* ***(P-10142)***
Kaiser Foundation Health Plan, Modesto *Also called Kaiser Foundation Hospitals* ***(P-10143)***
Kaiser Foundation Hospitals..........C......916 482-1132
2829 Watt Ave Ste 150 Sacramento (95821) ***(P-17027)***
Kaiser Foundation Hospitals..........A......707 393-4633
3559 Round Barn Blvd Santa Rosa (95403) ***(P-16395)***
Kaiser Foundation Hospitals..........A......707 624-4000
1 Quality Dr Fl A1 Vacaville (95688) ***(P-16396)***
Kaiser Foundation Hospitals..........C......510 675-5777
30116 Eigenbrodt Way Union City (94587) ***(P-10109)***
Kaiser Foundation Hospitals..........B......408 361-2100
50 Great Oaks Blvd San Jose (95119) ***(P-16902)***
Kaiser Foundation Hospitals..........A......916 746-3937
1680 E Roseville Pkwy Roseville (95661) ***(P-16397)***
Kaiser Foundation Hospitals..........C......916 771-2871
504 Gibson Dr Roseville (95678) ***(P-15444)***
Kaiser Foundation Hospitals..........C......707 393-4000
401 Bicentennial Way Santa Rosa (95403) ***(P-15445)***
Kaiser Foundation Hospitals..........C......925 813-6500
4501 Sand Creek Rd Antioch (94531) ***(P-15446)***
Kaiser Foundation Hospitals..........A......925 906-2380
320 Lennon Ln Walnut Creek (94598) ***(P-16398)***
Kaiser Foundation Hospitals..........C......559 448-4620
4785 N 1st St Fl 2 Fresno (93726) ***(P-10110)***
Kaiser Foundation Hospitals..........C......415 833-2616
2350 Geary Blvd Fl 2 San Francisco (94115) ***(P-15447)***
Kaiser Foundation Hospitals..........C......925 295-4145
710 S Broadway Walnut Creek (94596) ***(P-15448)***
Kaiser Foundation Hospitals..........C......916 478-5000
9201 Big Horn Blvd Elk Grove (95758) ***(P-10111)***
Kaiser Foundation Hospitals..........C......408 439-6808
1721 Technology Dr San Jose (95110) ***(P-15449)***
Kaiser Foundation Hospitals..........C......510 675-2377
3551 Whipple Rd Bldg C Union City (94587) ***(P-17028)***
Kaiser Foundation Hospitals..........D......925 372-1000
200 Muir Rd Martinez (94553) ***(P-10796)***
Kaiser Foundation Hospitals..........A......510 752-1000
3600 Broadway Oakland (94611) ***(P-15450)***
Kaiser Foundation Hospitals..........A......415 833-2000
2425 Geary Blvd San Francisco (94115) ***(P-15451)***
Kaiser Foundation Hospitals..........A......650 299-2234
901 Marshall St Redwood City (94063) ***(P-16399)***
Kaiser Foundation Hospitals..........C......415 491-1164
1650 Los Gamos Dr San Rafael (94903) ***(P-15452)***
Kaiser Foundation Hospitals (HQ)..........C......510 271-6611
1 Kaiser Plz Oakland (94612) ***(P-16400)***
Kaiser Foundation Hospitals..........A......415 833-2200
2200 Ofarrell St San Francisco (94115) ***(P-16401)***
Kaiser Foundation Hospitals..........C......916 525-6790
8247 E Stockton Blvd Sacramento (95828) ***(P-17029)***
Kaiser Foundation Hospitals..........A......510 752-1000
280 W Macarthur Blvd Oakland (94611) ***(P-16402)***
Kaiser Foundation Hospitals..........A......916 558-6520
501 J St Sacramento (95814) ***(P-16403)***
Kaiser Foundation Hospitals..........C......707 645-2720
1761 Broadway St Ste 210 Vallejo (94589) ***(P-10112)***
Kaiser Foundation Hospitals..........A......415 444-2000
99 Montecillo Rd San Rafael (94903) ***(P-15453)***
Kaiser Foundation Hospitals..........C......510 307-1500
901 Nevin Ave Richmond (94801) ***(P-15454)***
Kaiser Foundation Hospitals..........A......408 972-6010
280 Hospital Pkwy San Jose (95119) ***(P-16404)***
Kaiser Foundation Hospitals..........C......415 444-3522
820 Las Gallinas Ave San Rafael (94903) ***(P-10113)***
Kaiser Foundation Hospitals..........C......510 752-7864
255 W Macarthur Blvd Oakland (94611) ***(P-10114)***
Kaiser Foundation Hospitals..........C......559 448-4555
4785 N 1st St Fresno (93726) ***(P-10115)***
Kaiser Foundation Hospitals..........C......916 544-6000
10305 Promenade Pkwy Elk Grove (95757) ***(P-10116)***
Kaiser Foundation Hospitals..........D......510 454-1000
27303 Sleepy Hollow Ave S Hayward (94545) ***(P-10117)***
Kaiser Foundation Hospitals..........C......707 624-4000
1 Quality Dr Vacaville (95688) ***(P-15455)***
Kaiser Foundation Hospitals..........C......209 839-3200
2185 W Grant Line Rd Tracy (95377) ***(P-15456)***
Kaiser Foundation Hospitals..........C......510 675-4010
3555 Whipple Rd Union City (94587) ***(P-15457)***
Kaiser Foundation Hospitals..........C......707 427-4000
1550 Gateway Blvd Fairfield (94533) ***(P-15458)***
Kaiser Foundation Hospitals..........C......916 986-4178
285 Palladio Pkwy Folsom (95630) ***(P-15459)***
Kaiser Foundation Hospitals..........C......916 543-5153
1900 Dresden Dr Lincoln (95648) ***(P-15460)***
Kaiser Foundation Hospitals..........C......209 735-5000
4601 Dale Rd Modesto (95356) ***(P-15461)***
Kaiser Foundation Hospitals..........C......415 209-2444
100 Rowland Way Ste 125 Novato (94945) ***(P-15891)***
Kaiser Foundation Hospitals..........C......209 735-5000
4125 Bangs Ave Modesto (95356) ***(P-15462)***
Kaiser Foundation Hospitals..........C......510 243-4000
1301 Pinole Valley Rd Pinole (94564) ***(P-15463)***
Kaiser Foundation Hospitals..........C......650 358-7000
1000 Franklin Pkwy San Mateo (94403) ***(P-15464)***
Kaiser Foundation Hospitals..........C......510 454-1000
2500 Merced St San Leandro (94577) ***(P-15465)***
Kaiser Foundation Hospitals..........C......925 244-7600
2300 Camino Ramon San Ramon (94583) ***(P-10118)***
Kaiser Foundation Hospitals..........C......408 851-1000
1263 E Arques Ave Sunnyvale (94085) ***(P-15466)***
Kaiser Foundation Hospitals..........C......510 752-6808
275 W Macarthur Blvd Oakland (94611) ***(P-8785)***
Kaiser Foundation Hospitals..........C......510 752-1000
280 W Macarthur Blvd Oakland (94611) ***(P-15467)***
Kaiser Foundation Hospitals..........A......925 598-2799
5820 Owens Dr Bldg E-2 Pleasanton (94588) ***(P-16405)***
Kaiser Foundation Hospitals..........C......408 972-7000
250 Hospital Pkwy San Jose (95119) ***(P-15468)***
Kaiser Foundation Hospitals..........C......707 651-2311
975 Sereno Dr Vallejo (94589) ***(P-10119)***
Kaiser Foundation Hospitals..........A......408 235-4005
3900 Freedom Cir Ste 201 Santa Clara (95054) ***(P-16406)***
Kaiser Foundation Hospitals..........C......415 216-5853
2238 Geary Blvd Fl 3 San Francisco (94115) ***(P-15469)***
Kaiser Foundation Hospitals..........A......510 749-3021
1451 Harbor Bay Pkwy Alameda (94502) ***(P-16407)***
Kaiser Foundation Hospitals..........A......916 974-6211
3200 Arden Way Sacramento (95825) ***(P-19548)***
Kaiser Foundation Hospitals..........C......650 299-2000
1100 Veterans Blvd Redwood City (94063) ***(P-15470)***
Kaiser Foundation Hospitals..........C......925 295-4000
1425 S Main St Walnut Creek (94596) ***(P-15471)***
Kaiser Foundation Hospitals..........C......916 614-4350
1001 Riverside Ave Roseville (95678) ***(P-15472)***
Kaiser Foundation Hospitals..........C......415 833-9688
601 Van Ness Ave Ste 2008 San Francisco (94102) ***(P-15473)***
Kaiser Foundation Hospitals..........A......916 973-5000
1650 Response Rd Sacramento (95815) ***(P-16408)***

ALPHABETIC

Kaiser Foundation Hospitals.....C.....831 430-2700
5615 Scotts Valley Dr Scotts Valley (95066) ***(P-15474)***
Kaiser Foundation Hospitals.....C.....408 945-2900
770 E Calaveras Blvd Milpitas (95035) ***(P-15475)***
Kaiser Foundation Hospitals.....A.....510 987-1000
1950 Franklin St Oakland (94612) ***(P-15476)***
Kaiser Foundation Hospitals.....C.....530 757-7100
1955 Cowell Blvd Davis (95618) ***(P-15477)***
Kaiser Foundation Hospitals.....A.....916 631-3088
10725 International Dr Rancho Cordova (95670) ***(P-16409)***
Kaiser Foundation Hospitals.....C.....707 765-3900
3900 Lakeville Hwy Petaluma (94954) ***(P-15478)***
Kaiser Foundation Hospitals.....C.....415 899-7400
97 San Marin Dr Novato (94945) ***(P-15479)***
Kaiser Foundation Hospitals.....C.....707 624-4000
1 Quality Dr Vacaville (95688) ***(P-10120)***
Kaiser Foundation Hospitals.....C.....510 678-4000
27400 Hesperian Blvd Hayward (94545) ***(P-15480)***
Kaiser Foundation Hospitals.....A.....650 903-3000
555 Castro St Fl 3 Mountain View (94041) ***(P-16410)***
Kaiser Foundation Hospitals.....C.....916 784-4000
1001 Riverside Ave Roseville (95678) ***(P-15481)***
Kaiser Foundation Hospitals.....C.....415 833-3450
2241 Geary Blvd Ste 118 San Francisco (94115) ***(P-15482)***
Kaiser Foundation Hospitals.....A.....925 906-2000
501 Lennon Ln Walnut Creek (94598) ***(P-16411)***
Kaiser Foundation Hospitals.....A.....925 847-5000
7601 Stoneridge Dr Pleasanton (94588) ***(P-16412)***
Kaiser Foundation Hospitals.....C.....510 559-5362
1795 2nd St Berkeley (94710) ***(P-10121)***
Kaiser Foundation Hospitals.....C.....916 817-5200
2155 Iron Point Rd Folsom (95630) ***(P-15483)***
Kaiser Foundation Hospitals.....C.....510 891-3400
2000 Brdwy Oakland (94612) ***(P-10122)***
Kaiser Foundation Hospitals.....D.....925 926-3000
25 N Via Monte Walnut Creek (94598) ***(P-10123)***
Kaiser Foundation Hospitals.....C.....650 742-2000
1200 El Camino Real South San Francisco (94080) ***(P-15484)***
Kaiser Foundation Hospitals.....E.....510 625-3431
1800 Harrison St Fl 16 Oakland (94612) ***(P-16413)***
Kaiser Foundation Hospitals.....A.....916 688-2000
6600 Bruceville Rd Sacramento (95823) ***(P-15485)***
Kaiser Foundation Hospitals.....C.....925 779-5000
3400 Delta Fair Blvd Antioch (94509) ***(P-17030)***
Kaiser Foundation Hospitals.....C.....510 248-3000
39400 Paseo Padre Pkwy Fremont (94538) ***(P-15486)***
Kaiser Foundation Hospitals.....D.....707 258-2500
3285 Claremont Way NAPA (94558) ***(P-10797)***
Kaiser Foundation Hospitals.....A.....707 651-1000
975 Sereno Dr Vallejo (94589) ***(P-16414)***
Kaiser Foundation Hospitals.....C.....559 324-5100
2071 Herndon Ave Clovis (93611) ***(P-10124)***
Kaiser Foundation Hospitals.....C.....916 784-4050
1840 Sierra Gardens Dr Roseville (95661) ***(P-10125)***
Kaiser Foundation Hospitals.....C.....415 482-6800
1033 3rd St San Rafael (94901) ***(P-10126)***
Kaiser Foundation Hospitals.....C.....559 658-8388
40595 Westlake Dr Oakhurst (93644) ***(P-10127)***
Kaiser Foundation Hospitals.....C.....650 301-5860
395 Hickey Blvd Daly City (94015) ***(P-10128)***
Kaiser Foundation Hospitals.....C.....510 675-2170
3553 Whipple Rd Union City (94587) ***(P-10129)***
Kaiser Foundation Hospitals.....C.....209 832-6339
2417 Naglee Rd Tracy (95304) ***(P-10130)***
Kaiser Foundation Hospitals.....C.....650 742-2100
901 El Camino Real San Bruno (94066) ***(P-10131)***
Kaiser Foundation Hospitals.....C.....707 571-3835
3554 Round Barn Blvd Santa Rosa (95403) ***(P-10132)***
Kaiser Foundation Hospitals.....C.....707 393-4033
3925 Old Redwood Hwy Santa Rosa (95403) ***(P-10133)***
Kaiser Foundation Hospitals.....C.....855 268-4096
1320 Standiford Ave Modesto (95350) ***(P-10134)***
Kaiser Foundation Hospitals.....C.....707 206-3000
5900 State Farm Dr # 100 Rohnert Park (94928) ***(P-10135)***
Kaiser Foundation Hospitals.....C.....510 752-1190
2417 Central Ave Alameda (94501) ***(P-15487)***
Kaiser Foundation Hospitals.....C.....510 251-0121
969 Broadway Oakland (94607) ***(P-10136)***
Kaiser Foundation Hospitals.....C.....559 898-6000
2651 Highland Ave Selma (93662) ***(P-10137)***
Kaiser Foundation Hospitals.....C.....209 825-3700
1777 W Yosemite Ave Manteca (95337) ***(P-10138)***
Kaiser Foundation Hospitals.....C.....916 973-5000
2345 Fair Oaks Blvd Sacramento (95825) ***(P-10139)***
Kaiser Foundation Hospitals.....C.....408 972-3000
250 Hospital Pkwy Bldg D San Jose (95119) ***(P-15488)***
Kaiser Foundation Hospitals.....A.....415 833-2000
2425 Geary Blvd San Francisco (94115) ***(P-15489)***
Kaiser Foundation Hospitals.....C.....408 972-3376
5755 Cottle Rd San Jose (95123) ***(P-10140)***
Kaiser Foundation Hospitals.....A.....408 972-6700
275 Hospital Pkwy 765a San Jose (95119) ***(P-16415)***
Kaiser Foundation Hospitals.....C.....408 848-4600
7520 Arroyo Cir Gilroy (95020) ***(P-10141)***
Kaiser Foundation Hospitals.....A.....510 434-5835
5800 Coliseum Way Oakland (94621) ***(P-16416)***
Kaiser Foundation Hospitals.....D.....916 784-5081
1840 Sierra Gardens Dr Roseville (95661) ***(P-10798)***
Kaiser Foundation Hospitals.....C.....925 432-6000
3000 Las Positas Rd Livermore (94551) ***(P-15490)***
Kaiser Foundation Hospitals.....C.....415 833-3780
1635 Divisadero St Fl 1 San Francisco (94115) ***(P-15491)***
Kaiser Foundation Hospitals.....A.....916 784-4000
1600 Eureka Rd Roseville (95661) ***(P-16417)***
Kaiser Foundation Hospitals.....C.....916 817-5651
2155 Iron Point Rd Folsom (95630) ***(P-16787)***
Kaiser Foundation Hospitals.....C.....559 448-4500
7300 N Fresno St Fresno (93720) ***(P-10142)***
Kaiser Foundation Hospitals.....C.....559 448-4500
7300 N Fresno St Fresno (93720) ***(P-15492)***
Kaiser Foundation Hospitals.....A.....916 525-6300
7300 Wyndham Dr Sacramento (95823) ***(P-16418)***
Kaiser Foundation Hospitals.....A.....209 476-3101
7373 West Ln Stockton (95210) ***(P-16419)***
Kaiser Foundation Hospitals.....C.....209 557-1000
1625 I St Modesto (95354) ***(P-10143)***
Kaiser Foundation Hospitals.....A.....408 851-1000
710 Lawrence Expy Santa Clara (95051) ***(P-16420)***
Kaiser Fundation Hlth Plan Inc (PA).....**B.....510 271-5800**
1 Kaiser Plz Oakland (94612) ***(P-15493)***
Kaiser Fundation Hlth Plan Inc.....D.....510 271-5800
4460 Hacienda Dr Pleasanton (94588) ***(P-10144)***
Kaiser Group Holdings Inc.....D.....510 419-6000
2101 Webster St Ste 1000 Oakland (94612) ***(P-18745)***
Kaiser Hlth Plan Asset MGT Inc.....E.....510 271-5910
1 Kaiser Plz Ste 1333 Oakland (94612) ***(P-19357)***
Kaiser Permanente, San Jose *Also called Kaiser Foundation Hospitals* ***(P-16902)***
Kaiser Permanente, Stockton *Also called Tpmg Laboratory Stockton* ***(P-16810)***
Kaiser Permanente, Walnut Creek *Also called Kaiser Foundation Hospitals* ***(P-15448)***
Kaiser Permanente, Oakland *Also called Kaiser Foundation Hospitals* ***(P-16400)***
Kaiser Permanente, San Francisco *Also called Kaiser Foundation Hospitals* ***(P-16401)***
Kaiser Permanente, Oakland *Also called Kaiser Foundation Hospitals* ***(P-16402)***
Kaiser Permanente, Sacramento *Also called Kaiser Foundation Hospitals* ***(P-16403)***
Kaiser Permanente, San Rafael *Also called Kaiser Foundation Hospitals* ***(P-15453)***
Kaiser Permanente, Richmond *Also called Kaiser Foundation Hospitals* ***(P-15454)***
Kaiser Permanente, San Jose *Also called Kaiser Foundation Hospitals* ***(P-15468)***
Kaiser Permanente, Santa Clara *Also called Kaiser Foundation Hospitals* ***(P-16406)***
Kaiser Permanente, Redwood City *Also called Kaiser Foundation Hospitals* ***(P-15470)***
Kaiser Permanente, Walnut Creek *Also called Kaiser Foundation Hospitals* ***(P-15471)***
Kaiser Permanente, Sacramento *Also called Kaiser Foundation Hospitals* ***(P-16408)***
Kaiser Permanente, San Francisco *Also called Kaiser Foundation Hospitals* ***(P-15482)***
Kaiser Permanente, Walnut Creek *Also called Kaiser Foundation Hospitals* ***(P-16411)***
Kaiser Permanente, Pleasanton *Also called Kaiser Foundation Hospitals* ***(P-16412)***
Kaiser Permanente, Berkeley *Also called Kaiser Foundation Hospitals* ***(P-10121)***
Kaiser Permanente, South San Francisco *Also called Kaiser Foundation Hospitals* ***(P-15484)***
Kaiser Permanente, Oakland *Also called Kaiser Foundation Hospitals* ***(P-16413)***
Kaiser Permanente, Antioch *Also called Kaiser Foundation Hospitals* ***(P-17030)***
Kaiser Permanente, Fremont *Also called Kaiser Foundation Hospitals* ***(P-15486)***
Kaiser Permanente, NAPA *Also called Kaiser Foundation Hospitals* ***(P-10797)***
Kaiser Permanente, San Francisco *Also called Kaiser Foundation Hospitals* ***(P-15489)***
Kaiser Permanente, Roseville *Also called Kaiser Foundation Hospitals* ***(P-16417)***
Kaiser Permanente, Folsom *Also called Kaiser Foundation Hospitals* ***(P-16787)***
Kaiser Permanente, Fresno *Also called Kaiser Foundation Hospitals* ***(P-15492)***
Kaiser Permanente, Stockton *Also called Kaiser Foundation Hospitals* ***(P-16419)***
Kaiser Permanente.....E.....510 450-2109
3505 Broadway Oakland (94611) ***(P-16421)***
Kaiser Permanente - Hr Svc Ctr, Alameda *Also called Kaiser Foundation Hospitals* ***(P-16407)***
Kaiser Permanente Chemical Dep, Union City *Also called Kaiser Foundation Hospitals* ***(P-17028)***
Kaiser Permanente Division RES, Oakland *Also called Kaiser Foundation Hospitals* ***(P-10122)***
Kaiser Permanente Med Ctr S, Sacramento *Also called Kaiser Foundation Hospitals* ***(P-17029)***
Kaiser Permanente San, San Francisco *Also called Kaiser Foundation Hospitals* ***(P-15451)***
Kaiser Permanente Santa Clara, Santa Clara *Also called Peter Castillo Md PA* ***(P-15627)***
Kaiser Perminente, Folsom *Also called Kaiser Foundation Hospitals* ***(P-15483)***
Kaiser Prmanente Internet Svcs, Pleasanton *Also called Kaiser Foundation Hospitals* ***(P-16405)***
Kaiser Prmnnte Advice Ctr - Al, Sacramento *Also called Kaiser Foundation Hospitals* ***(P-16418)***
Kaiser Prmnnte Antioch Med Ctr, Antioch *Also called Kaiser Foundation Hospitals* ***(P-15446)***
Kaiser Prmnnte Eye Svcs - Optm, Roseville *Also called Kaiser Foundation Hospitals* ***(P-16397)***
Kaiser Prmnnte Hayward Med Ctr, Hayward *Also called Kaiser Foundation Hospitals* ***(P-15480)***
Kaiser Prmnnte Lvrmore Med Ctr, Livermore *Also called Kaiser Foundation Hospitals* ***(P-15490)***
Kaiser Prmnnte Manteca Med Ctr, Manteca *Also called Kaiser Foundation Hospitals* ***(P-10138)***
Kaiser Prmnnte Modesto Med Ctr, Modesto *Also called Permanente Medical Group Inc* ***(P-15625)***
Kaiser Prmnnte Oakland Med Ctr, Oakland *Also called Kaiser Foundation Hospitals* ***(P-15467)***
Kaiser Prmnnte S Scrmnto Med C, Sacramento *Also called Kaiser Foundation Hospitals* ***(P-15485)***
Kaiser Prmnnte San Frncsco Med, San Francisco *Also called Kaiser Foundation Hospitals* ***(P-15473)***
Kaiser Prmnnte San Jose Med Ct, San Jose *Also called Kaiser Foundation Hospitals* ***(P-15488)***

Kaiser Prmnnte San Jose Med Ct, San Jose *Also called Kaiser Foundation Hospitals* ***(P-16415)***
Kaiser Prmnnte San Lndro Med C, San Leandro *Also called Kaiser Foundation Hospitals* ***(P-15465)***
Kaiser Prmnnte San Mteo Med Ct, San Mateo *Also called Kaiser Foundation Hospitals* ***(P-15464)***
Kaiser Prmnnte Snta Clara Med, Santa Clara *Also called Kaiser Foundation Hospitals* ***(P-16420)***
Kaiser Prmnnte Snta Rosa Med C, Santa Rosa *Also called Kaiser Foundation Hospitals* ***(P-15445)***
Kaiser Prmnnte Vallejo Med Ctr, Vallejo *Also called Kaiser Foundation Hospitals* ***(P-16414)***
Kaiserair Inc ....E....707 528-7400
2240 Airport Blvd Santa Rosa (95403) ***(P-7774)***
Kaiserair Inc (PA) ....**C....510 569-9622**
8735 Earhart Rd Oakland (94621) ***(P-7757)***
Kaizen Technology Partners LLC ....E....415 515-1909
981 Mission St San Francisco (94103) ***(P-12554)***
Kal Machining Inc ....E....408 782-8989
18450 Sutter Blvd Morgan Hill (95037) ***(P-5550)***
Kal-Kustom Enterprises (PA) ....**F....510 651-8400**
43289 Osgood Rd Fremont (94539) ***(P-9157)***
Kalila Medical Inc ....E....408 819-5175
1400 Dell Ave Ste C Campbell (95008) ***(P-6906)***
Kalkai Advance Mfg Inc ....E....707 588-9906
630 Martin Ave Rohnert Park (94928) ***(P-5943)***
Kallidus Inc ....D....877 554-2176
555 Mission St Ste 1950 San Francisco (94105) ***(P-12555)***
Kalman Manufacturing Inc ....E....408 776-7664
780 Jarvis Dr Ste 150 Morgan Hill (95037) ***(P-5551)***
Kamet, Milpitas *Also called Khuus Inc* ***(P-5553)***
Kamper Fabrication Inc ....E....209 599-7137
20107 N Ripon Rd Ripon (95366) ***(P-5011)***
Kana Software Inc (HQ) ....**D....650 614-8300**
2550 Walsh Ave Ste 120 Santa Clara (95051) ***(P-13259)***
Kandarian Agri Enterprises ....E....559 834-1501
116 W Adams Ave Fowler (93625) ***(P-59)***
Kandy Investments LLC ....E....707 584-8363
3205 Dutton Ave Santa Rosa (95407) ***(P-7692)***
Kanrad Technologies Inc ....E....408 615-8880
4340 Stevens Creek Blvd San Jose (95129) ***(P-12556)***
Kanthal Thermal Process Inc ....D....209 533-1990
19500 Nugget Blvd Sonora (95370) ***(P-5156)***
Kap LP ....D....559 897-5132
10363 Davis Ave Kingsburg (93631) ***(P-105)***
Kapcsandy Family LLC ....F....707 948-3100
1001 State Ln Yountville (94599) ***(P-377)***
Kapcsandy Family Winery, Yountville *Also called Kapcsandy Family LLC* ***(P-377)***
Kappel & Kappel Mortgage & Inv, Vacaville *Also called Kappel and Kappel Inc* ***(P-10590)***
Kappel & Kappel Mortgage & Inv, Fairfield *Also called Kappel and Kappel Inc* ***(P-10591)***
Kappel and Kappel Inc (PA) ....**E....707 446-0600**
355 Main St Vacaville (95688) ***(P-10590)***
Kappel and Kappel Inc ....D....707 429-2922
1300 Oliver Rd Ste 105 Fairfield (94534) ***(P-10591)***
Kapsch Trafficcom Usa Inc ....C....925 225-1600
4256 Hacienda Dr Ste 100 Pleasanton (94588) ***(P-5681)***
Karcher Environmental Inc ....D....510 297-0180
1718 Fairway Dr San Leandro (94577) ***(P-2041)***
Kargo Master Inc ....E....916 638-8703
11261 Trade Center Dr Rancho Cordova (95742) ***(P-4775)***
Karius Inc ....D....866 452-7487
975 Island Dr Ste 100 Redwood City (94065) ***(P-19077)***
Karm Inc ....E....650 741-5276
5033 Doolan Rd Livermore (94551) ***(P-18746)***
Karma Inc ....C....209 239-1222
410 Eastwood Ave Manteca (95336) ***(P-16030)***
Karssli Corporation ....E....831 420-8900
901 Corcoran Ave Santa Cruz (95062) ***(P-7650)***
Karsyn Construction Inc ....D....559 271-2900
4697 W Jacquelyn Ave Fresno (93722) ***(P-908)***
Karthikeya Devireddy MD Inc ....D....209 826-2222
311 W I St Los Banos (93635) ***(P-15494)***
Kas Direct LLC ....E....516 934-0541
637 Commercial St Fl 3 San Francisco (94111) ***(P-3396)***
Kasco Fab Inc ....D....559 442-1018
4529 S Chestnut Ave Lowr Fresno (93725) ***(P-4669)***
Kaspick & Co LLC (HQ) ....**D....650 585-4100**
203 Redwood Shores Pkwy # 300 Redwood City (94065) ***(P-10305)***
Kasra Investments LLC ....E....408 464-0074
1480 Saratoga Ave Saratoga (95070) ***(P-14315)***
Katadyn Desalination LLC ....E....415 526-2780
2220 S Mcdowell Blvd Ext Petaluma (94954) ***(P-5704)***
Kateeva Inc ....C....800 385-7802
7015 Gateway Blvd Newark (94560) ***(P-5850)***
Katie Minor ....E....925 847-2200
5980 Stoneridge Dr # 122 Pleasanton (94588) ***(P-10592)***
Kaufman Building & MGT Inc ....F....707 732-3770
1834 Soscol Ave Ste C NAPA (94559) ***(P-595)***
Kautz Ironstone Vineyards, Murphys *Also called Kautz Vineyards Inc* ***(P-60)***
Kautz Vineyards Inc ....E....209 369-1911
6111 E Armstrong Rd Lodi (95240) ***(P-2637)***
Kautz Vineyards Inc (PA) ....**D....209 728-1251**
1894 6 Mile Rd Murphys (95247) ***(P-60)***
Kawahara Nursery Inc ....C....408 779-2400
698 Burnett Ave Morgan Hill (95037) ***(P-129)***
Kay Chesterfield Inc ....E....510 533-5565
6365 Coliseum Way Oakland (94621) ***(P-3289)***
Kay Dix Inc ....E....916 776-1701
14400 Andrus Island Rd Isleton (95641) ***(P-106)***
Kaye Sandy Enterprises Inc ....E....650 961-5334
1074 Independence Ave Mountain View (94043) ***(P-6643)***
Kazan McClain Sttrley Grnwood ....C....877 995-6372
55 Harrison St Ste 400 Oakland (94607) ***(P-17302)***
Kazeon Systems Inc ....D....650 641-8100
2841 Mission College Blvd Santa Clara (95054) ***(P-12557)***
KB Home South Bay Inc ....C....925 983-2500
5000 Executive Pkwy # 125 San Ramon (94583) ***(P-754)***
Kba Docusys Inc (PA) ....**E....510 214-4040**
32900 Alvarado Niles Rd # 1 Union City (94587) ***(P-9074)***
Kba2 Inc ....E....415 528-5500
55 New Montgomery St # 606 San Francisco (94105) ***(P-13260)***
Kbi Painting Inc ....E....707 795-4955
866 Palm Ave Penngrove (94951) ***(P-1419)***
Kbl Associates, Hayward *Also called Krug Associates Inc* ***(P-1533)***
Kbm-Hogue, San Jose *Also called K B M Office Equipment Inc* ***(P-8497)***
KC Metal Products Inc (PA) ....**D....408 436-8754**
1960 Hartog Dr San Jose (95131) ***(P-4670)***
Kc Metals, San Jose *Also called KC Metal Products Inc* ***(P-4670)***
Kcctech LLC ....C....628 400-2420
1630 N Main St Ste 305 Walnut Creek (94596) ***(P-19804)***
Kcra, Sacramento *Also called Hearst Stations Inc* ***(P-8044)***
Kdc Construction, West Sacramento *Also called Cirks Construction Inc* ***(P-854)***
Kdf Enterprises LLC ....C....803 928-7073
3941 Park Dr El Dorado Hills (95762) ***(P-5035)***
KDF Inc ....E....408 779-3731
15875 Concord Cir Morgan Hill (95037) ***(P-5552)***
Kdr Holding Inc (PA) ....**E....510 230-2777**
47448 Fremont Blvd Fremont (94538) ***(P-10859)***
Kds Nail Products ....E....916 381-9358
8580 Younger Creek Dr Sacramento (95828) ***(P-7291)***
Kearneys Aluminum Foundry Inc (PA) ....**E....559 233-2591**
2660 S Dearing Ave Fresno (93725) ***(P-4578)***
Kearneys Metals Inc ....E....559 233-2591
4731 E Vine Ave Fresno (93725) ***(P-8820)***
Keebler Company ....C....209 836-0302
1550 N Chrisman Rd Tracy (95304) ***(P-2416)***
Keegan & Coppin Company Inc (PA) ....**E....707 528-1400**
1355 N Dutton Ave Ste 100 Santa Rosa (95401) ***(P-10593)***
Keegan & Coppin Property MGT, Santa Rosa *Also called Keegan & Coppin Company Inc* ***(P-10593)***
Keep Truckin Inc (PA) ....**E....855 434-3564**
55 Hawthorne St Ste 400 San Francisco (94105) ***(P-12558)***
Kehe Distributors LLC ....E....209 467-1962
4650 Newcastle Rd Stockton (95215) ***(P-9460)***
Keiser Corporation (PA) ....**D....559 256-8000**
2470 S Cherry Ave Fresno (93706) ***(P-7198)***
Keiser Sports Health Equipment, Fresno *Also called Keiser Corporation* ***(P-7198)***
Keker Van Nest & Peters LLP ....D....415 391-5400
633 Battery St Bsmt 91 San Francisco (94111) ***(P-17303)***
Kelleher Corporation ....E....916 561-2860
201 Opportunity St Sacramento (95838) ***(P-8554)***
Kelleher Corporation ....E....415 898-8440
10 Grandview Ave Novato (94945) ***(P-8555)***
Keller Canyon Landfill Company ....A....925 458-9800
901 Bailey Rd Bay Point (94565) ***(P-8338)***
Kelleyamerit Fleet Services, Walnut Creek *Also called Kelleyamerit Holdings Inc* ***(P-19358)***
Kelleyamerit Holdings Inc (PA) ....**A....877 512-6374**
1331 N Calif Blvd Ste 150 Walnut Creek (94596) ***(P-19358)***
Kellogg Garden Product, Lockeford *Also called Kellogg Supply Inc* ***(P-4133)***
Kellogg Supply Inc ....E....209 727-3130
12686 Locke Rd Lockeford (95237) ***(P-4133)***
Kelly & Stone Architects Inc ....E....530 214-8896
11209 Brockway Rd Ste 211 Truckee (96161) ***(P-18893)***
Kelly Computer Systems Inc ....E....650 960-1010
1060 La Avenida St Mountain View (94043) ***(P-5391)***
Kelly-Moore Paint Company Inc (PA) ....**C....650 592-8337**
1390 El Cmino Real Ste 30 San Carlos (94070) ***(P-4106)***
Kelly-Moore Paints, San Carlos *Also called Kelly-Moore Paint Company Inc* ***(P-4106)***
Kelytech Corporation ....E....408 935-0888
1482 Gladding Ct Milpitas (95035) ***(P-6442)***
Kemeera LLC (PA) ....**E....510 281-9000**
620 3rd St Oakland (94607) ***(P-8718)***
Kemper & Sons Masonry Inc ....E....530 600-3697
2083 James Ave Unit A South Lake Tahoe (96150) ***(P-1650)***
Kemper Independence Insur Co ....E....559 326-2551
2565 Alluvial Ave Ste 182 Clovis (93611) ***(P-10306)***
Kemper Insurance, San Jose *Also called Thoits Insurance Service Inc* ***(P-10359)***
Kemper Insurance, Kingsburg *Also called Van Beurden Insurance Svcs Inc* ***(P-10365)***
Kemper Insurance, Sacramento *Also called Interwest Insurance Svcs LLC* ***(P-10299)***
Kemper Insurance, Walnut Creek *Also called Northstar Risk MGT Insur Svcs* ***(P-10323)***
Kemper Insurance, Clovis *Also called Kemper Independence Insur Co* ***(P-10306)***
Ken & Laura Scheidegger ....E....916 777-6462
106 W Brannan Island Rd Isleton (95641) ***(P-7731)***
Ken Fulk Inc ....E....415 285-1164
310 7th St San Francisco (94103) ***(P-14316)***
Kenco Engineering Inc ....E....916 782-8494
2155 Pfe Rd Roseville (95747) ***(P-5036)***
Kendall-Jackson Wine Center ....E....707 571-7500
5007 Fulton Rd Fulton (95439) ***(P-378)***
Kendall-Jackson Wine Estates (HQ) ....**B....707 544-4000**
425 Aviation Blvd Santa Rosa (95403) ***(P-2638)***
Kendo Holdings Inc (HQ) ....**B....415 284-6000**
425 Market St Fl 19 San Francisco (94105) ***(P-9228)***
Kenefick Ranches LLC ....E....707 942-6175
2200 Pickett Rd Calistoga (94515) ***(P-2639)***
Keney Manufacturing Co (PA) ....**F....209 358-6474**
586 Broadway Ave Atwater (95301) ***(P-3184)***

ALPHABETIC

Employee Codes: A=Over 500 employees, B=251-500 C=101-250, D=51-100, E=20-50 F=10-19
2022 Northern California Business Directory and Buyers Guide
© Mergent Inc. 1-800-342-5647
1001

Keney's Cabinets, Atwater *Also called Keney Manufacturing Co (P-3184)*
Kenna Security Inc (HQ)......C......855 474-7546
3945 Freedom Cir Ste 300 Santa Clara (95054) *(P-13928)*
Kennedy Jenks, San Francisco *Also called Kennedy/Jenks Consultants Inc (P-18747)*
Kennedy/Jenks Consultants Inc (PA)......D......415 243-2150
303 2nd St Ste 300s San Francisco (94107) *(P-18747)*
Kennerley-Spratling Inc (PA)......C......510 351-8230
2116 Farallon Dr San Leandro (94577) *(P-4294)*
Kennerley-Spratling Inc......C......408 944-9407
2308 Zanker Rd San Jose (95131) *(P-4295)*
Kenneth Allen Rush......E......559 224-3976
3030 N Maroa Ave Fresno (93704) *(P-9665)*
Kennie C Knowles Trucking......E......530 243-1366
3411 S Market St Redding (96001) *(P-7479)*
Kennolyn Camp Inc......E......831 479-6714
8205 Glen Haven Rd Soquel (95073) *(P-11608)*
Kenshoo Inc (HQ)......C......877 536-7462
22 4th St Fl 7 San Francisco (94103) *(P-19549)*
Kensington Laboratories LLC (PA)......F......510 324-0126
6200 Village Pkwy Dublin (94568) *(P-5682)*
Kensington Place, Walnut Creek *Also called Argonaut Kensington Associates (P-17432)*
Kentfield Hospital, Kentfield *Also called Vibra Healthcare LLC (P-16717)*
Kentfield Rehabilitation Hosp, Kentfield *Also called 1125 Sir Frncis Drake Blvd Ope (P-16285)*
Kenwood Vineyards, Kenwood *Also called Pernod Ricard Usa LLC (P-2680)*
Kenyon Construction Inc......D......707 528-1906
364 Bellevue Ave Santa Rosa (95407) *(P-14527)*
Kenyon Construction Inc......E......800 949-4319
63 Trevarno Rd Livermore (94551) *(P-1682)*
Kenyon Construction Inc......E......559 277-5645
4667 N Blythe Ave Fresno (93722) *(P-1683)*
Kenyon Construction Inc......E......916 514-9502
3223 E St North Highlands (95660) *(P-1684)*
Kenyon Construction Inc......E......209 462-4060
1286 N Broadway Ave Stockton (95205) *(P-1685)*
Kenyon Plastering, Livermore *Also called Kenyon Construction Inc (P-1682)*
Kenyon Plastering, North Highlands *Also called Kenyon Construction Inc (P-1684)*
Kenyon Plastering, Stockton *Also called Kenyon Construction Inc (P-1685)*
Kenzo Estate Inc......E......707 254-7572
3200 Monticello Rd NAPA (94558) *(P-379)*
Keri Systems Inc (PA)......D......408 435-8400
302 Enzo Dr Ste 190 San Jose (95138) *(P-6529)*
Kerio Technologies Inc......F......409 880-7011
111 W Saint John St # 1100 San Jose (95113) *(P-13261)*
Kernen Construction......D......707 826-8686
2350 Glendale Dr McKinleyville (95519) *(P-800)*
Kerrock Countertops Inc (PA)......F......510 441-2300
1450 Dell Ave Ste C Campbell (95008) *(P-3279)*
Kertel Communications Inc (HQ)......D......559 432-5800
7600 N Palm Ave Ste 101 Fresno (93711) *(P-1530)*
Kessil, Richmond *Also called Dicon Fiberoptics Inc (P-6418)*
Ketchum Incorporated......D......415 984-6100
600 California St Fl 1 San Francisco (94108) *(P-19690)*
Ketera Technologies Inc (HQ)......E......408 572-9500
3055 Olin Ave Ste 2200 San Jose (95128) *(P-13262)*
Ketos Inc......D......408 550-2162
420 S Hillview Dr Milpitas (95035) *(P-13619)*
Kettle Pop, Benicia *Also called Gold Rush Kettle Korn Llc (P-2428)*
Kevala Inc......E......415 712-7829
55 Francisco St Ste 350 San Francisco (94133) *(P-13263)*
Key Business Solutions Inc (PA)......E......916 646-2080
4738 Duckhorn Dr Sacramento (95834) *(P-12559)*
Keypoint Credit Union (PA)......C......408 731-4100
2805 Bowers Ave Ste 105 Santa Clara (95051) *(P-9793)*
Keysight Technologies Inc (PA)......A......800 829-4444
1400 Fountaingrove Pkwy Santa Rosa (95403) *(P-6724)*
Keyspan, Walnut Creek *Also called Innosys Incorporated (P-12522)*
Keyssa Inc (PA)......E......408 637-2300
3945 Freedom Cir Ste 560 Santa Clara (95054) *(P-6171)*
Keystone Door & Bldg Sup Inc......E......916 623-8100
1037 N Market Blvd Ste 9 Sacramento (95834) *(P-1745)*
Keystone Educatn & Youth Svcs, Vallejo *Also called Keystone NPS LLC (P-18237)*
Keystone NPS LLC......C......510 206-8463
425 Corcoran Ave Vallejo (94589) *(P-18237)*
Keystone Strategy LLC......D......877 419-2623
150 Spear St Ste 1750 San Francisco (94105) *(P-19805)*
Kezar Life Sciences Inc......E......650 822-5600
4000 Shoreline Ct Ste 300 South San Francisco (94080) *(P-3935)*
Kfjc FM, Los Altos Hills *Also called Foothll-De Anza Cmnty Cllege D (P-8025)*
Kfsn Television LLC......C......559 442-1170
1777 G St Fresno (93706) *(P-8047)*
KG Oldco Inc (HQ)......E......408 980-8550
2270 Martin Ave Santa Clara (95050) *(P-13620)*
KG Technologies Inc......F......888 513-1874
6028 State Farm Dr Rohnert Park (94928) *(P-6443)*
KG Vineyard Management LLC......E......209 367-8996
9077 W Cotta Rd Lodi (95242) *(P-380)*
Kgo 810am, San Francisco *Also called San Francisco Radio Assets LLC (P-8034)*
Kh Construction, Fresno *Also called Nevocal Enterprises Inc (P-596)*
Khalsa Transportation Inc......E......559 697-6557
13371 S Fowler Ave Selma (93662) *(P-7558)*
Khamishon, Ilya MD, Folsom *Also called University California Davis (P-15771)*
Khan Academy Inc......D......650 336-5426
1200 Villa St Ste 200 Mountain View (94041) *(P-13264)*
Khanna Entps - II Ltd Partnr......E......916 338-5800
5321 Date Ave Sacramento (95841) *(P-11228)*
Khosla Ventures LLC......E......650 376-8500
2128 Sand Hill Rd Menlo Park (94025) *(P-10860)*
Khp III SF Sutter LLC (PA)......D......415 921-4000
1800 Sutter St San Francisco (94115) *(P-11229)*
Khsl TV, Chico *Also called Catamunt Brdcstg Chc-Rdding In (P-8040)*
Khuus Inc......D......408 522-8000
1778 Mccarthy Blvd Milpitas (95035) *(P-5553)*
Kibblwhite Prcsion McHning Inc......E......650 359-4704
580 Crespi Dr Ste H Pacifica (94044) *(P-6651)*
Kickfire, San Jose *Also called Visistat Inc (P-12909)*
Kidango Inc......D......408 258-9129
1824 Daytona Dr San Jose (95122) *(P-17957)*
Kidango Inc (PA)......D......510 897-6900
44000 Old Warm Sprng Blvd Fremont (94538) *(P-17958)*
Kidango Inc......D......510 494-9601
4700 Calaveras Ave Fremont (94538) *(P-17959)*
Kidder Mathews California Inc (HQ)......E......415 229-8888
101 Mission St Ste 1800 San Francisco (94105) *(P-10594)*
Kidder Mathews Inc......E......408 970-9400
10 Almaden Blvd Ste 550 San Jose (95113) *(P-10595)*
Kidder Mathews Inc......E......415 229-8888
101 Mission St Fl 21 San Francisco (94105) *(P-10596)*
Kiddie Campus Day Care Center, Los Gatos *Also called Calvary Church Los Gatos Cal (P-17873)*
Kiddie Kampus Day Care Center, Los Gatos *Also called Calvary Church Los Gatos Cal (P-17874)*
Kids Care, Merced *Also called Chw Mrcy Mrced Cmnty Hosp Kids (P-16331)*
Kids Haven......E......408 274-8766
6056 Montgomery Bnd San Jose (95135) *(P-17960)*
Kids Haven (PA)......C......408 274-8766
2059 Camden Ave San Jose (95124) *(P-17961)*
Kids Overcoming LLC......D......415 748-8052
40029 St Ste 204 Oakland (94609) *(P-16903)*
Kids' Club YMCA Oxford School, Berkeley *Also called Young MNS Chrstn Assn of E Bay (P-18497)*
Kie-Con Inc......D......925 754-9494
3551 Wilbur Ave Antioch (94509) *(P-4440)*
Kier Wrght Cvil Engners Srvyor......E......925 245-8788
2850 Collier Canyon Rd Livermore (94551) *(P-18924)*
Kieu Hoang Winery LLC......F......707 253-1615
1285 Dealy Ln NAPA (94559) *(P-2640)*
Kiid, Roseville *Also called Walt Disney Company (P-8036)*
Kikkoman Sales Usa Inc (HQ)......E......415 956-7750
50 California St Ste 3600 San Francisco (94111) *(P-9461)*
Kilam Inc......C......510 943-4040
39678 Mission Blvd Fremont (94539) *(P-9246)*
Kilgore Enterprises Llc......E......925 885-8999
2005 San Jose Dr Unit 258 Antioch (94509) *(P-567)*
Klma W Medical Center......D......530 625-4114
535 Airport Rd Hoopa (95546) *(P-17031)*
Kimball Electronics Ind Inc......E......669 234-1110
5215 Hellyer Ave Ste 130 San Jose (95138) *(P-5944)*
KIMBERLEY WINE VINEGARS, Acampo *Also called California Concentrate Company (P-2290)*
Kimberlite Corporation (PA)......D......559 264-9730
3621 W Beechwood Ave Fresno (93711) *(P-14138)*
Kimco Staffing Services Inc......A......925 945-1444
1801 Oakland Blvd Ste 220 Walnut Creek (94596) *(P-17157)*
Kimmel Construction Inc......D......916 927-3118
10 Main Ave Ste 2 Sacramento (95838) *(P-909)*
Kimpton Hotel & Rest Group LLC......C......415 885-2500
405 Taylor St San Francisco (94102) *(P-11230)*
Kimpton Hotel & Rest Group LLC (HQ)......D......415 397-5572
222 Kearny St Ste 200 San Francisco (94108) *(P-11231)*
Kimpton Hotel & Rest Group LLC......C......415 561-1100
425 N Point St San Francisco (94133) *(P-11232)*
Kimpton Hotel & Rest Group LLC......C......415 392-8800
127 Ellis St San Francisco (94102) *(P-11233)*
Kimpton Hotel & Rest Group LLC......C......415 561-1111
2455 Mason St San Francisco (94133) *(P-11234)*
Kimpton Hotel & Rest Group LLC......C......415 292-0100
501 Geary St San Francisco (94102) *(P-11235)*
Kimpton Hotels, Sacramento *Also called Sg Downtown LLC (P-11466)*
Kimzey Welding Works......F......530 662-9331
164 Kentucky Ave Woodland (95695) *(P-5554)*
Kind Homecare Inc......D......888 885-5463
3705 Haven Ave Ste 104 Menlo Park (94025) *(P-16904)*
Kind Led Grow Lights, Santa Rosa *Also called Supercloset (P-4609)*
Kinder's, Walnut Creek *Also called PK Kinder Co Inc (P-9288)*
Kindred Biosciences Inc (HQ)......C......650 701-7901
1555 Bayshore Hwy Ste 200 Burlingame (94010) *(P-3936)*
Kindred Healthcare LLC......C......209 474-7884
10100 Trinity Pkwy Stockton (95219) *(P-16422)*
Kindred Healthcare LLC......D......408 871-9860
901 Campisi Way Ste 205 Campbell (95008) *(P-16905)*
Kindred Healthcare LLC......C......408 261-6943
4030 Moorpark Ave Ste 251 San Jose (95117) *(P-16423)*
Kindred Healthcare LLC......D......707 639-4155
4820 Bus Center Dr # 105 Fairfield (94534) *(P-16906)*
Kindred Healthcare Oper LLC......B......510 357-8300
2800 Benedict Dr San Leandro (94577) *(P-16424)*
Kindred Hospital, San Leandro *Also called Kindred Healthcare Oper LLC (P-16424)*
Kinematic Automation Inc......D......209 532-3200
21085 Longeway Rd Sonora (95370) *(P-6995)*
Kinesso LLC......C......415 262-5900
600 Battery St San Francisco (94111) *(P-11765)*
Kinetic Farm Inc......F......650 503-3279
210 Industrial Rd Ste 102 San Carlos (94070) *(P-13265)*
Kinetics Mechanical Svc Inc......D......925 245-6200
6336 Patterson Pass Rd H Livermore (94550) *(P-1297)*

ALPHABETIC SECTION

Kona Prince Food, Roseville

Kinetix Technology Svcs LLC....E....650 454-8850
2261 Market St Ste 4163 San Francisco (94114) ***(P-13929)***
King's Roofing, Patterson *Also called DK Enterprises Inc* ***(P-1799)***
King-Reynolds Ventures LLC....D....650 879-2136
2001 Rossi Rd Pescadero (94060) ***(P-14317)***
Kingfish Group Inc (PA)....D....650 980-0200
601 California St # 1250 San Francisco (94108) ***(P-10861)***
Kings Arena Ltd Partnership....D....916 928-0000
1 Sports Pkwy Sacramento (95834) ***(P-14909)***
Kings Asian Gourmet Inc....E....415 222-6100
683 Brannan St Unit 304 San Francisco (94107) ***(P-2203)***
Kings River Casting Inc....E....559 875-8250
1350 North Ave Sanger (93657) ***(P-3312)***
Kings River Conservation Dst....D....559 237-5567
4886 E Jensen Ave Fresno (93725) ***(P-19908)***
Kings River Packing LP....E....559 787-2056
21083 E Trimmer Sprng Rd Sanger (93657) ***(P-177)***
Kings Valley Preschool, Concord *Also called Christian Concord Center* ***(P-17904)***
Kings View....E....559 673-0167
126 N D St Madera (93638) ***(P-14873)***
Kings View....E....559 641-2805
49269 Golden Oak Dr 204b Oakhurst (93644) ***(P-16762)***
Kingsbarns Golf Links LLC....C....800 441-1391
239 Main St Ste E Pleasanton (94566) ***(P-15213)***
Kingsburg Apple Packers Inc....B....559 897-5132
10363 Davis Ave Kingsburg (93631) ***(P-9412)***
Kingsburg Center, Kingsburg *Also called Sunbridge Care Entps W LLC* ***(P-16136)***
Kingsburg Center, Kingsburg *Also called Sunbridge Care Entps W LLC* ***(P-16137)***
Kingsburg Cultivator Inc....E....559 897-3662
40190 Road 36 Kingsburg (93631) ***(P-5012)***
Kingsburg Orchards, Kingsburg *Also called Kingsburg Apple Packers Inc* ***(P-9412)***
Kingsburg Orchards....D....559 897-2986
10363 Davis Ave Kingsburg (93631) ***(P-9413)***
Kingsford Manufacturing Co....F....510 271-7000
1221 Broadway Ste 1300 Oakland (94612) ***(P-4075)***
Kingsford Products Company LLC (HQ)....D....510 271-7000
1221 Broadway Ste 1300 Oakland (94612) ***(P-4115)***
Kingspan Insulated Panels Inc....D....209 531-9091
2000 Morgan Rd Modesto (95358) ***(P-4852)***
Kingsview Corp....E....209 533-6245
2 S Green St Sonora (95370) ***(P-17032)***
Kinsa Inc....D....347 405-4315
535 Mission St Fl 18 San Francisco (94105) ***(P-16907)***
Kinsale Holdings Inc (PA)....C....415 400-2600
388 Market St Ste 860 San Francisco (94111) ***(P-19550)***
Kintara Therapeutics Inc....F....650 269-1984
3475 Edison Way Ste R Menlo Park (94025) ***(P-3937)***
Kinwai USA Inc....E....510 780-9388
2951 Whipple Rd Union City (94587) ***(P-3280)***
Kion Technology Inc....E....408 435-3008
2190 Oakland Rd San Jose (95131) ***(P-4936)***
Kioxia America Inc (PA)....C....408 526-2400
2610 Orchard Pkwy San Jose (95134) ***(P-8925)***
Kioxia America Inc....E....916 986-4707
35 Iron Point Cir Ste 100 Folsom (95630) ***(P-19078)***
Kipp Foundation....C....415 399-1556
135 Main St Ste 1875 San Francisco (94105) ***(P-18238)***
Kirby Manufacturing Inc (PA)....D....209 723-0778
484 S St 59 Merced (95341) ***(P-5013)***
Kirkland & Ellis LLP....C....415 439-1400
555 California St # 2700 San Francisco (94104) ***(P-17304)***
Kirkwood Asssted Lving Rsdence....E....530 241-2900
395 Hilltop Dr Redding (96003) ***(P-16031)***
Kirosh Inc....D....650 595-2847
93 W El Camino Real Mountain View (94040) ***(P-11236)***
Kis, Fremont *Also called Sable Computer Inc* ***(P-13658)***
Kisco Senior Living LLC....C....415 664-6264
1601 19th Ave Ofc San Francisco (94122) ***(P-19359)***
Kisco Senior Living LLC....D....415 491-1935
275 Los Ranchitos Rd San Rafael (94903) ***(P-10444)***
Kisco Senior Living LLC....D....559 449-8070
1100 E Spruce Ave Ofc Fresno (93720) ***(P-10445)***
Kisco Senior Living LLC....D....707 585-1800
1350 Oak View Cir Rohnert Park (94928) ***(P-10446)***
Kisco Senior Living LLC....D....650 948-7337
1174 Los Altos Ave Ofc Los Altos (94022) ***(P-10447)***
Kishida Geo Trucking, Lodi *Also called George Kishida Inc* ***(P-7469)***
Kissito Health Case Inc....D....925 689-9222
3318 Willow Pass Rd Concord (94519) ***(P-16908)***
Kissito Healthcare Inc....E....209 524-4817
1310 W Granger Ave Modesto (95350) ***(P-16032)***
Kit Carson Nursing & Rehab....E....209 223-2231
811 Court St Jackson (95642) ***(P-16033)***
Kitanica LLC....F....707 272-7286
867 Isabella St Oakland (94607) ***(P-7292)***
Kitchencraft of Marin, San Rafael *Also called Lamperti Associates* ***(P-662)***
Kitchens Now Inc....E....916 229-8222
20 Blue Sky Ct Sacramento (95828) ***(P-3185)***
Kite Hill, Hayward *Also called Lyrical Foods Inc* ***(P-2920)***
Kiva Confections, Oakland *Also called Kiva Manufacturing Inc* ***(P-7293)***
Kiva Designs, Benicia *Also called Applied Sewing Resources Inc* ***(P-2963)***
Kiva Manufacturing Inc....E....510 780-0777
445 Lesser St Oakland (94601) ***(P-7293)***
Kkp - Roseville Inc....E....916 786-8573
106 N Sunrise Ave Ste B2 Roseville (95661) ***(P-3664)***
KKR Financial Corporation (HQ)....D....415 315-3620
555 California St # 5000 San Francisco (94104) ***(P-10821)***
KLA Corporation (PA)....B....408 875-3000
1 Technology Dr Milpitas (95035) ***(P-6878)***
KLA Corporation....F....408 986-5600
5451 Patrick Henry Dr Santa Clara (95054) ***(P-6172)***
KLA Tencor....E....510 887-2647
2260 American Ave Ste 1 Hayward (94545) ***(P-5222)***
KLA-Tencor Asia-Pac Dist Corp....D....408 875-4144
1 Technology Dr Milpitas (95035) ***(P-6173)***
Klair Real Estate Inc....C....209 484-8075
3018 E Svc Rd Ste 104105 Ceres (95307) ***(P-10597)***
Klean Kanteen Inc....D....530 592-4552
3960 Morrow Ln Chico (95928) ***(P-4598)***
Kleary Masonry Inc....C....916 869-6835
4612 Auburn Blvd Ste 2 Sacramento (95841) ***(P-1651)***
Kleenrite, Madera *Also called Better Cleaning Systems Inc* ***(P-5707)***
Klein Bros Holdings Ltd....E....209 465-5033
3101 W March Ln Ste B Stockton (95219) ***(P-2447)***
Klein Bros Snacks, Stockton *Also called Klein Bros Holdings Ltd* ***(P-2447)***
Klein Family Farms, Stockton *Also called Jack Klein Trust Partnership* ***(P-263)***
Klein Foods Inc....D....707 431-1533
11455 Old Redwood Hwy Healdsburg (95448) ***(P-61)***
Kleiner Prkins Cfeld Byers LLC (PA)....E....650 233-2750
2750 Sand Hill Rd Menlo Park (94025) ***(P-10862)***
Kleinfelder Inc....C....415 458-5803
1 Saunders Ave San Anselmo (94960) ***(P-18748)***
Klh Consulting Inc....D....707 575-9986
2324 Bethards Dr Santa Rosa (95405) ***(P-19806)***
Klingstubbins Inc....D....415 356-2040
160 Spear St Ste 330 San Francisco (94105) ***(P-19909)***
Klippenstein Corporation....E....559 834-4258
2246 E Date Ave Fresno (93706) ***(P-5199)***
Kloudgin Inc....C....877 256-8303
440 N Wolfe Rd Sunnyvale (94085) ***(P-13266)***
Kloves Inc (PA)....E....408 768-5966
6203 San Ignacio Ave # 1 San Jose (95119) ***(P-13621)***
Klutz....E....650 687-2650
1450 Veterans Blvd Redwood City (94063) ***(P-3536)***
KMA Emergency Services Inc....D....510 614-1420
14275 Wicks Blvd San Leandro (94577) ***(P-7384)***
Kmax TV, West Sacramento *Also called Sacramento Television Stns Inc* ***(P-8054)***
Kmbc/Kcwe, Sacramento *Also called Hearst Stations Inc* ***(P-8046)***
KMD Architects (PA)....D....415 398-5191
417 Montgomery St Ste 200 San Francisco (94104) ***(P-18894)***
Kmic Technology Inc....E....408 240-3600
2095 Ringwood Ave Ste 10 San Jose (95131) ***(P-5851)***
Kmph Fox 26....C....559 255-2600
5111 E Mckinley Ave Fresno (93727) ***(P-8048)***
Kms Fishermans Wharf LP....D....415 561-1100
425 N Point St San Francisco (94133) ***(P-11237)***
Kms Technology Inc (PA)....E....925 828-1906
6098 Kingsmill Ter Dublin (94568) ***(P-12560)***
Knapp, James C MD, Turlock *Also called Family Medical Group* ***(P-15401)***
Knauf Insulation Inc....C....530 275-9665
3100 Ashby Rd Shasta Lake (96019) ***(P-4533)***
Knife River Construction, Chico *Also called Baldwin Contracting Co Inc* ***(P-1013)***
Knight Farms....E....530 934-9536
7920 County Road 29 Glenn (95943) ***(P-9)***
Knight Roofing Co (PA)....D....510 438-9077
3240 Darby Cmn Fremont (94539) ***(P-1814)***
Knights Electric Incorporated....D....707 433-6931
11410 Old Redwood Hwy Windsor (95492) ***(P-1531)***
Knightsbridge Plastics Inc....D....510 440-8444
3075 Osgood Ct Fremont (94539) ***(P-4296)***
Knightscope Inc....D....650 924-1025
1070 Terra Bella Ave Mountain View (94043) ***(P-6530)***
Knisley Aircraft Exhaust, Loomis *Also called Knisley Welding Inc* ***(P-14716)***
Knisley Welding Inc....E....916 652-5891
3450 Swetzer Rd Loomis (95650) ***(P-14716)***
Kno Inc....D....408 844-8120
2200 Mission College Blvd Santa Clara (95054) ***(P-13267)***
Knob Hill Oil & Gas Co....E....650 328-0820
1143 Crane St Ste 200 Menlo Park (94025) ***(P-178)***
Knobbe Martens Olson Bear LLP....E....415 954-4114
333 Bush St Fl 21 San Francisco (94104) ***(P-17305)***
Knt Inc....C....510 651-7163
39760 Eureka Dr Newark (94560) ***(P-5555)***
Knt Manufacturing, Newark *Also called Knt Inc* ***(P-5555)***
Knt Manufacturing Inc....D....510 896-1699
39760 Eureka Dr Newark (94560) ***(P-7294)***
Kochergen Farms Composting Inc (PA)....D....559 498-0900
523 N Brawley Ave Ste B Fresno (93706) ***(P-19807)***
Koda Farms Inc....E....209 392-2191
22540 Russell Ave South Dos Palos (93665) ***(P-2325)***
Kodiak Cartoners Inc....E....559 266-4844
2550 S East Ave Ste 101 Fresno (93706) ***(P-5200)***
Kodiak Precision Inc (PA)....F....510 234-4165
444 S 1st St Richmond (94804) ***(P-5556)***
Kodiak Robotics Inc....D....781 626-2729
1049 Terra Bella Ave Mountain View (94043) ***(P-18749)***
Kodiak Roofing & Waterproofing, Roseville *Also called Dwayne Nash Industries Inc* ***(P-1800)***
Koehler Lefforge Inc....E....916 381-9333
2647 Mercantile Dr Ste B Rancho Cordova (95742) ***(P-8514)***
Koffler Elec Mech Apprtus Repr....D....510 567-0630
527 Whitney St San Leandro (94577) ***(P-8864)***
Kohlberg Kravis Roberts Co LP....D....650 233-6560
2800 Sand Hill Rd Ste 200 Menlo Park (94025) ***(P-10863)***
Kokatat Inc....D....707 822-7621
5350 Ericson Way Arcata (95521) ***(P-2993)***
Kona Prince Food, Roseville *Also called Collette Foods LLC* ***(P-2278)***

ALPHABETIC

Kone Inc ALPHABETIC SECTION

Kone Inc..........E.......510 351-5141
15021 Wicks Blvd San Leandro (94577) *(P-14757)*
Kone Inc..........E.......707 778-2247
1031 Laurel Ct Sebastopol (95472) *(P-14758)*
Kong Inc..........E.......415 754-9283
251 Post St Ste 200 San Francisco (94108) *(P-12561)*
Kong Hq, San Francisco *Also called Kong Inc (P-12561)*
Kong Inc..........E.......415 754-9283
150 Spear St Ste 1600 San Francisco (94105) *(P-12562)*
Koning & Associates Inc (PA)..........E.......408 265-3800
1631 Willow St Ste 220 San Jose (95125) *(P-10307)*
Konocti Transportation Svcs, Lakeport *Also called People Services Inc (P-18156)*
Konocti Vista Casino (PA)..........C.......707 262-1900
2755 Mission Rancheria Rd Lakeport (95453) *(P-15214)*
Korbel Champagne Cellers, Guerneville *Also called F Korbel & Bros (P-2565)*
Kortick Manufacturer Co, Pittsburg *Also called Frase Enterprises (P-5721)*
Kosan Biosciences Incorporated..........D.......650 995-7356
3832 Bay Center Pl Hayward (94545) *(P-3938)*
Kositch Enterprises Inc..........D.......510 657-4460
5700 Boscell Cmn Fremont (94538) *(P-1532)*
Kosmadi Brothers..........D.......530 473-5120
374 Ruggieri Way Williams (95987) *(P-11238)*
Kosta Browne Winery, Sebastopol *Also called Kosta Browne Wines LLC (P-2641)*
Kosta Browne Wines LLC..........E.......707 823-7430
220 Morris St Sebastopol (95472) *(P-2641)*
Kotobuki-Ya Inc..........D.......650 344-7955
720 Woodside Way San Mateo (94401) *(P-7338)*
Kountable Inc (PA)..........D.......310 613-5481
321 Pacific Ave Fl 3 San Francisco (94111) *(P-14318)*
Kozlowski Farms A Corporation..........E.......707 887-1587
5566 Hwy 116 Forestville (95436) *(P-2218)*
Kozuki Farming Inc..........D.......559 646-2652
16518 E Adams Ave Parlier (93648) *(P-107)*
Kp International, Oakland *Also called Permanente Kaiser Intl (P-10149)*
Kp LLC (PA)..........D.......510 346-0729
13951 Washington Ave San Leandro (94578) *(P-3665)*
Kp LLC..........E.......510 346-0729
13951 Washington Ave San Leandro (94578) *(P-3666)*
Kp LLC..........E.......209 466-6761
1134 Enterprise St Stockton (95204) *(P-3667)*
Kp Research Services Inc..........E.......530 878-5390
11818 Kemper Rd Auburn (95603) *(P-14072)*
Kpcb, Menlo Park *Also called Kleiner Prkins Cfeld Byers LLC (P-10862)*
Kpcb Holdings Inc (PA)..........E.......650 233-2750
2750 Sand Hill Rd Menlo Park (94025) *(P-10864)*
Kpi Partners Inc..........E.......510 818-9480
39899 Balentine Dr # 375 Newark (94560) *(P-12563)*
Kpisoft Inc..........D.......415 439-5228
50 California St Ste 1500 San Francisco (94111) *(P-13268)*
Kpmg LLP..........E.......415 963-5100
55 2nd St Ste 1400 San Francisco (94105) *(P-18964)*
Kqca, Sacramento *Also called Hearst Stations Inc (P-8045)*
Kqed Inc (PA)..........B.......415 864-2000
2601 Mariposa St San Francisco (94110) *(P-8049)*
Kqed Public Media, San Francisco *Also called Kqed Inc (P-8049)*
Kr Subsidiary Inc (HQ)..........E.......915 320-7033
1050 Diamond St Stockton (95205) *(P-9508)*
Kraemer & Co Mfg Inc..........E.......530 865-7982
3778 County Road 99w Orland (95963) *(P-4853)*
Kraft Heinz Foods Company..........F.......925 242-4504
2603 Camino Ramon Ste 180 San Ramon (94583) *(P-2219)*
Krafts Body Shop..........E.......831 476-2440
6100 Soquel Ave Santa Cruz (95062) *(P-14528)*
Kranem Corporation..........C.......650 319-6743
560 S Wnchester Blvd # 5 San Jose (95128) *(P-13269)*
Kratos Unmnned Arial Systems I (HQ)..........B.......916 431-7977
5381 Raley Blvd Sacramento (95838) *(P-18750)*
Krave Jerky, Sonoma *Also called Krave Pure Foods Inc (P-2119)*
Krave Pure Foods Inc..........D.......707 939-9176
117 W Napa St Ste A Sonoma (95476) *(P-2119)*
Krayden, Morgan Hill *Also called K R Anderson Inc (P-9519)*
Krazan & Associates (PA)..........D.......559 348-2200
215 W Dakota Ave Clovis (93612) *(P-19808)*
KRC Los Altos, Los Altos *Also called Kisco Senior Living LLC (P-10447)*
Krcr TV, Redding *Also called California Oregon Broadcasting (P-8039)*
Krisalis Precision Machining..........F.......209 296-6866
3366 Golden Gate Ct San Andreas (95249) *(P-5557)*
Krish Compusoft Services Inc..........C.......855 527-7890
1525 Mccarthy Blvd # 212 Milpitas (95035) *(P-12564)*
Kristich-Monterey Pipe Co Inc..........E.......831 724-4186
225 Salinas Rd Ste B Royal Oaks (95076) *(P-4441)*
Kriya Therapeutics Inc..........E.......833 574-9289
1100 Island Dr Ste 203 Redwood City (94065) *(P-4052)*
Krm Risk Management Svcs Inc..........E.......559 277-4800
4270 W Richert Ave # 101 Fresno (93722) *(P-19360)*
Kroeger Eqp Sup Co A Cal Corp..........E.......559 485-9900
2645 S Chestnut Ave Fresno (93725) *(P-8454)*
Kroeker Inc..........C.......559 237-3764
4627 S Chestnut Ave Fresno (93725) *(P-1987)*
Krohn Division, Fair Oaks *Also called Rice Corporation (P-2326)*
Kron-TV, San Francisco *Also called Chronicle Broadcasting Co (P-8042)*
Kron-TV, San Francisco *Also called Young Brdcstg of San Francisco (P-8057)*
Kronick Mskvitz Tdmann Grard A (PA)..........C.......916 321-4500
1331 Garden Hwy Ste 350 Sacramento (95833) *(P-17306)*
Kronos Bio Inc (PA)..........D.......650 781-5200
1300 S El Camino Real Ste 400 San Mateo (94402) *(P-3939)*
Krueger Bros Builders Inc..........E.......415 863-5846
535 Alabama St San Francisco (94110) *(P-660)*
Krug Associates Inc..........D.......510 887-1117
26269 Research Pl Hayward (94545) *(P-1533)*
Kruger Foods Inc..........C.......209 941-8518
18362 E Highway 4 Stockton (95215) *(P-2281)*
Kruppa Farms, Winton *Also called Carl J Kruppa (P-150)*
Krw Enterprises..........E.......916 372-8600
841 F St West Sacramento (95605) *(P-910)*
Krytar Inc..........E.......408 734-5999
1288 Anvilwood Ave Sunnyvale (94089) *(P-6444)*
Krzr 103 7 FM, Fresno *Also called Iheartcommunications Inc (P-8027)*
KS Trans Service Co..........D.......559 264-5650
3190 S Elm Ave Fresno (93706) *(P-7559)*
Kseg-FM, Sacramento *Also called Entercom Communications Corp (P-8020)*
Ksi Corp (PA)..........D.......650 952-0815
839 Mitten Rd San Bruno (94066) *(P-7844)*
Ksm Corp..........D.......408 514-2400
1959 Concourse Dr San Jose (95131) *(P-6174)*
Ksm Vacuum Products Inc..........F.......408 514-2400
102 Persian Dr Ste 203 Sunnyvale (94089) *(P-4724)*
Ktay Kmxi Khsl Kwe Khhz Krer, Chico *Also called Deer Creek Broadcasting LLC (P-8017)*
Ktvu Partnership Inc..........C.......510 834-1212
2 Jack London Sq Oakland (94607) *(P-8050)*
Ktvu Television Fox 2, Oakland *Also called Ktvu Partnership Inc (P-8050)*
Ktxl-Fox 40, Sacramento *Also called Channel 40 Inc (P-8041)*
Ku Kyoung..........C.......510 582-2765
Unknown Redding (96003) *(P-16034)*
Kubota Authorized Dealer, Rio Vista *Also called Dolk Tractor Company (P-14745)*
Kubota Authorized Dealer, Turlock *Also called Garton Tractor Inc (P-9038)*
Kuckenbecker Tractor Co, Fresno *Also called Fresno Ford Tractor Inc (P-5023)*
KUDos&co Inc..........F.......650 799-9104
470 Ramona St Palo Alto (94301) *(P-3581)*
Kugga Inc..........D.......925 639-0721
1841 Sunnyvale Ave Walnut Creek (94597) *(P-12565)*
Kuic Inc..........D.......707 446-0200
555 Mason St Ste 245 Vacaville (95688) *(P-8029)*
Kuic-FM, Vacaville *Also called Kuic Inc (P-8029)*
Kumar Hotels Inc (PA)..........C.......530 934-8900
545 N Humboldt Ave Willows (95988) *(P-11239)*
Kunde Enterprises Inc..........D.......707 833-5501
9825 Sonoma Hwy Kenwood (95452) *(P-2642)*
Kunde Estate Winery, Kenwood *Also called Arthur Kunde & Sons Inc (P-367)*
Kunde Estate Winery, Kenwood *Also called Kunde Enterprises Inc (P-2642)*
Kuprion Inc..........E.......650 223-1600
4425 Fortran Dr San Jose (95134) *(P-4154)*
Kurt Meiswinkel Inc..........E.......650 344-7200
1407 E 3rd Ave San Mateo (94401) *(P-1686)*
Kuykendall Solar Corporation..........E.......559 658-2525
2840 Yosemite Spgs Coarsegold (93614) *(P-1298)*
Kval Inc..........C.......707 762-4363
825 Petaluma Blvd S Petaluma (94952) *(P-5115)*
Kval Machinery Co, Petaluma *Also called Kval Inc (P-5115)*
Kvie Inc (PA)..........D.......916 929-5843
2030 W El Cmino Ave Ste 1 Sacramento (95833) *(P-8051)*
KVIE CHANNEL 6, Sacramento *Also called Kvie Inc (P-8051)*
Kw Automotive North Amer Inc..........E.......800 445-3767
300 W Pontiac Way Clovis (93612) *(P-6585)*
Kwan Software Engineering Inc..........E.......408 496-1200
849 Lakechime Dr Sunnyvale (94089) *(P-13270)*
Kwan Wo Ironworks Inc..........C.......415 822-9628
31628 Hayman St Hayward (94544) *(P-1925)*
Kwik Bond Polymers LLC..........E.......866 434-1772
923 Teal Dr Ste A Benicia (94510) *(P-4151)*
Kwj Engineering Inc (PA)..........E.......510 794-4296
8430 Central Ave Ste C Newark (94560) *(P-6907)*
KWPH Enterprises..........A.......559 443-5900
2911 E Tulare St Fresno (93721) *(P-7385)*
Kxtv Inc..........C.......916 441-2345
400 Broadway Sacramento (95818) *(P-8052)*
Kyakamena Sklled Nrsing Fcilty, Berkeley *Also called Sanhyd Inc (P-16111)*
Kycon Inc..........E.......408 494-0330
305 Digital Dr Morgan Hill (95037) *(P-8926)*
Kyles Rock & Redi-Mix Inc..........F.......916 681-4848
1221 San Simeon Dr Roseville (95661) *(P-4489)*
Kyma Medical Technologies Inc..........F.......650 386-5089
2000 Ringwood Ave San Jose (95131) *(P-7110)*
Kyndi Inc..........E.......917 374-5531
1300 S El Cmino Real Ste San Mateo (94402) *(P-19809)*
Kyo Autism Therapy LLC..........D.......877 264-6747
1155 Broadway St Ste 218 Redwood City (94063) *(P-19551)*
Kyo Autism Therapy LLC..........D.......877 264-6747
121 Paul Dr San Rafael (94903) *(P-19552)*
Kyo Autism Therapy LLC (PA)..........B.......877 264-6747
1663 Mission St Ste 400 San Francisco (94103) *(P-19553)*
Kyocera Sld Laser Inc..........E.......805 696-6999
6500 Kaiser Dr Fremont (94555) *(P-6531)*
Kyte, San Francisco *Also called Decentral TV Corporation (P-7945)*
Kzst Radio, Santa Rosa *Also called Redwood Empire Stereocasters (P-8031)*
L & B Laboratories Inc..........E.......408 251-7888
1660 Mabury Rd San Jose (95133) *(P-7295)*
L & D Construction Co Inc..........E.......408 292-0128
255 W Julian St Ste 200 San Jose (95110) *(P-661)*
L & H Airco, Rocklin *Also called Sacramento Cooling Systems Inc (P-1596)*
L & H Iron Inc..........E.......408 287-8797
1049 Felipe Ave San Jose (95122) *(P-4671)*
L & L Logic and Logistics LP..........E.......707 795-2475
6 Hamilton Landing # 250 Novato (94949) *(P-9259)*
L & T Precision Engrg Inc..........E.......408 441-1890
2395 Qume Dr San Jose (95131) *(P-5558)*

L A S Transportation Inc..........E.......559 264-6583
250 E Belmont Ave Fresno (93701) ***(P-7560)***
L and C Cook Spcalty Foods Inc..........E.......530 587-3939
10607 W River St Ste 2f Truckee (96161) ***(P-9462)***
L B C Holdings U S A Corp (PA)..........C.......650 873-0750
362 E Grand Ave South San Francisco (94080) ***(P-7802)***
L B Construction, Roseville *Also called Lancaster Burns Cnstr Inc* ***(P-1687)***
L Foppiano Wine Co..........E.......707 433-2736
12707 Old Redwood Hwy Healdsburg (95448) ***(P-2643)***
L J E Enterprises, Manteca *Also called Lee Jennings Target Ex Inc* ***(P-7845)***
L J Inc..........E.......559 485-1413
2420 E Mckinley Ave Fresno (93703) ***(P-14529)***
L J Kruse Co..........D.......510 644-0260
920 Pardee St Berkeley (94710) ***(P-1299)***
L K Lehman Trucking..........E.......209 532-5586
19333 Industrial Dr Sonora (95370) ***(P-4490)***
L P Glassblowing Inc..........E.......408 988-7561
2322 Calle Del Mundo Santa Clara (95054) ***(P-6445)***
L P McNear Brick Co Inc..........D.......415 453-7702
1 Mcnear Brickyard Rd San Rafael (94901) ***(P-4414)***
L R Enterprises, Milpitas *Also called Lre Silicon Services* ***(P-6181)***
L Y Z Ltd (PA)..........F.......415 445-9505
210 Post St San Francisco (94108) ***(P-3002)***
L-3 Cmmnications Sonoma Eo Inc..........C.......707 568-3000
428 Aviation Blvd Santa Rosa (95403) ***(P-7152)***
L-3 Communications Wescam..........D.......707 568-3000
428 Aviation Blvd Ste 3l Santa Rosa (95403) ***(P-6673)***
L-O Soma Hotel Inc..........A.......415 974-6400
50 3rd St San Francisco (94103) ***(P-11240)***
L3 Applied Technologies Inc..........C.......510 577-7100
2700 Merced St San Leandro (94577) ***(P-19079)***
L3 Technologies Inc..........C.......650 326-9500
130 Constitution Dr Menlo Park (94025) ***(P-5852)***
La Belle Days Spas and Salons, Palo Alto *Also called Beauty Bazar Inc* ***(P-11675)***
La Boulange, San Francisco *Also called Bay Bread LLC* ***(P-9440)***
La Boulangerie French Bky Cafe..........E.......559 222-0555
730 W Shaw Ave Fresno (93704) ***(P-2390)***
La Brothers Enterprise Inc..........E.......415 626-8818
57 Columbia Sq San Francisco (94103) ***(P-3668)***
La Campana Tortilla Factory, Lodi *Also called Del Castillo Foods Inc* ***(P-2888)***
La Casa De Las Madres..........E.......415 503-0500
1269 Howard St San Francisco (94103) ***(P-17631)***
La Casa Ventures Inc..........E.......415 272-3147
1900 Powell St Ste 150 Emeryville (94608) ***(P-12051)***
La Cascada Inc..........F.......510 452-3663
1940 Union St Ste 10 Oakland (94607) ***(P-2204)***
La Clinica De La Raza Inc..........C.......510 535-6300
1515 Fruitvale Ave Oakland (94601) ***(P-15495)***
La Clinica De La Raza Inc..........C.......707 556-8100
243 Georgia St Vallejo (94590) ***(P-15496)***
La Clinica De La Raza Inc..........C.......510 535-3500
3451 E 12th St Oakland (94601) ***(P-17158)***
La Clinica De La Raza Inc..........C.......510 535-4110
1450 Fruitvale Ave B Oakland (94601) ***(P-15497)***
La Clinica De La Raza Inc..........C.......510 535-4130
1537 Fruitvale Ave Oakland (94601) ***(P-17159)***
La Clinica De La Raza Inc (PA)..........E.......510 535-4000
1450 Fruitvale Ave Fl 3 Oakland (94601) ***(P-15498)***
La Clinica De La Raza Inc..........C.......510 535-4700
3050 E 16th St Oakland (94601) ***(P-15499)***
La Clinica De La Raza Inc..........C.......510 535-6200
1601 Fruitvale Ave Oakland (94601) ***(P-15500)***
La Clinica De La Raza Inc..........C.......925 431-1250
337 E Leland Rd Pittsburg (94565) ***(P-15501)***
La Colonial, San Jose *Also called Robles Bros Inc* ***(P-2939)***
La Contenta Golf Club, Valley Springs *Also called La Contenta Investors Ltd* ***(P-15005)***
La Contenta Investors Ltd..........E.......209 772-1081
1653 S Highway 26 Valley Springs (95252) ***(P-15005)***
La Estrellita Restaurant, Redwood City *Also called La Estrellita Tizapan Mercado* ***(P-2908)***
La Estrellita Tizapan Mercado (PA)..........E.......650 369-3877
2205 Middlefield Rd Redwood City (94063) ***(P-2908)***
La Familia Counseling Ctr Inc..........D.......916 452-3601
5523 34th St Sacramento (95820) ***(P-17632)***
La Follette Enterprises Inc..........E.......209 632-1385
3312 S Blaker Rd Turlock (95380) ***(P-265)***
La Hacienda Inn Hotel, Campbell *Also called Morosin Enterprises Inc* ***(P-11311)***
La Pachanga Foods Inc..........E.......209 522-2222
708 L St Modesto (95354) ***(P-2099)***
La Fetite Baleen (PA)..........E.......650 726-7166
775 Main St Half Moon Bay (94019) ***(P-15215)***
La Quinta Inn, Hayward *Also called Hanford Hotels* ***(P-11126)***
La Quinta Inn, Dublin *Also called Raps Dublin LLC* ***(P-11384)***
La Quinta Inn, San Francisco *Also called Mile Post Properties LLC* ***(P-11299)***
La Quinta Inn..........D.......510 632-8900
8465 Enterprise Way Oakland (94621) ***(P-11241)***
La Quinta Inn San Jose, San Jose *Also called Hwang LLC* ***(P-11179)***
La Quinta Inn Suites Airport W, Millbrae *Also called Ramkabir LLC* ***(P-11382)***
La Raza Centro Legal SF..........E.......415 575-3500
474 Valencia St Ste 295 San Francisco (94103) ***(P-17307)***
La Rinconada Country Club Inc (PA)..........C.......408 395-4181
14595 Clearview Dr Los Gatos (95032) ***(P-15101)***
LA RINCONADA GOLF AND COUNTRY, Los Gatos *Also called La Rinconada Country Club Inc* ***(P-15101)***
La Rosa Tortilla Factory Inc..........C.......831 728-5332
26 Menker St Watsonville (95076) ***(P-2909)***
La Salette Rehab Convlesc Hos, Stockton *Also called Mariner Health Care Inc* ***(P-16058)***
La Sierra Care Center, Merced *Also called CF Merced La Sierra LLC* ***(P-15956)***

La Tapatia - Norcal Inc..........F.......510 783-2045
23423 Cabot Blvd Hayward (94545) ***(P-2910)***
La Tapatia Tortilleria Inc..........C.......559 441-1030
104 E Belmont Ave Fresno (93701) ***(P-2911)***
La Terra Fina Usa Inc..........D.......510 404-5888
1300 Atlantic St Union City (94587) ***(P-2912)***
La Tortilla Factory Inc (PA)..........B.......707 586-4000
3300 Westwind Blvd Santa Rosa (95403) ***(P-9463)***
La Tortilla Factory Inc..........E.......707 586-4000
3645 Standish Ave Santa Rosa (95407) ***(P-2913)***
La- Rochelle, Livermore *Also called Steven Kent LLC* ***(P-2728)***
Lab Clear, Oakland *Also called Diamond Tool and Die Inc* ***(P-5508)***
Lab-Gistics LLC..........C.......650 309-2627
885 Pacific Ave San Jose (95126) ***(P-19080)***
Labcon North America..........C.......707 766-2100
3700 Lakeville Hwy # 200 Petaluma (94954) ***(P-4297)***
Labcyte Inc (HQ)..........D.......408 747-2000
170 Rose Orchard Way # 200 San Jose (95134) ***(P-19081)***
Label Art - HM Es-E Stik Lbels..........E.......510 465-1125
290 27th St Oakland (94612) ***(P-3669)***
Label Art of California, Oakland *Also called Label Art - HM Es-E Stik Lbels* ***(P-3669)***
Label Division, Modesto *Also called G3 Enterprises Inc* ***(P-11862)***
Label Technology Inc..........E.......209 384-1000
2050 Wardrobe Ave Merced (95341) ***(P-3402)***
Labelbox Inc (PA)..........E.......415 294-0791
510 Treat Ave San Francisco (94110) ***(P-13271)***
Labor One Inc..........D.......559 430-4202
575 Minnewawa Ave Ste 3 Clovis (93612) ***(P-360)***
Laborer, San Francisco *Also called H&Gbygisellecо* ***(P-469)***
Laborers Fnds Admnstrtive Offi (PA)..........D.......707 864-2800
5672 Stoneridge Dr # 100 Pleasanton (94588) ***(P-18369)***
Laborers Trust Funds Nthrn Cal, Pleasanton *Also called Laborers Fnds Admnstrtive Offi* ***(P-18369)***
Labratory, San Francisco *Also called Permanente Medical Group Inc* ***(P-15598)***
Labtronix, Hayward *Also called Akas Manufacturing Corporation* ***(P-4740)***
Lace House Ldry & Lin Sup Inc..........E.......707 763-1515
949 Lindberg Ln Petaluma (94952) ***(P-11636)***
Lacework Inc (PA)..........B.......888 292-5027
6201 America Center Dr # 200 San Jose (95002) ***(P-13622)***
Lackey Woodworking Inc..........E.......831 462-0528
2730 Chanticleer Ave Santa Cruz (95065) ***(P-3186)***
Laclinica, Pittsburg *Also called La Clinica De La Raza Inc* ***(P-15501)***
Laco Inc..........E.......775 461-2960
6767 Preston Ave Livermore (94551) ***(P-6393)***
Laco Associates (PA)..........E.......707 443-5054
21 W 4th St Eureka (95501) ***(P-18751)***
Ladder Financial Inc..........E.......844 533-7206
555 University Ave Palo Alto (94301) ***(P-12566)***
Ladell Inc..........E.......559 650-2000
605 N Halifax Ave Clovis (93611) ***(P-1300)***
Ladenheim Dialysis Access Ctrs, Fresno *Also called Eric Ladenheim MD Inc* ***(P-15391)***
Ladera Oaks..........D.......650 854-3101
3249 Alpine Rd Portola Valley (94028) ***(P-15102)***
Ladera Oaks Swim & Tennis Club, Portola Valley *Also called Ladera Oaks* ***(P-15102)***
Ladera Vineyards LLC..........D.......707 965-2445
150 White Cottage Rd S Angwin (94508) ***(P-2644)***
Ladera Winery LLC..........E.......707 965-2445
150 White Cottage Rd S Angwin (94508) ***(P-2645)***
Lady Shaw Activity Center, San Francisco *Also called Self-Help For Elderly* ***(P-15240)***
Lafayette Orinda Presbt Ch..........D.......925 283-8722
49 Knox Dr Lafayette (94549) ***(P-17962)***
Lafayette Park Hotel Corp..........E.......925 283-3700
3287 Mt Diablo Blvd Lafayette (94549) ***(P-11242)***
Laguna Creek Racquet Club, Elk Grove *Also called Spare-Time Inc* ***(P-15153)***
Laguna Oaks Vnyards Winery Inc..........E.......707 568-2455
5700 Occidental Rd Santa Rosa (95401) ***(P-2646)***
Lahlouh Inc..........C.......650 692-6600
1649 Adrian Rd Burlingame (94010) ***(P-3670)***
Lahontan Golf Club, Truckee *Also called Lahontan LLC* ***(P-10705)***
Lahontan Golf Club..........C.......530 550-2400
12700 Lodgetrail Dr Truckee (96161) ***(P-15103)***
Lahontan LLC..........D.......530 550-2990
11253 Brockway Rd Ste 201 Truckee (96161) ***(P-10705)***
Laidlaw Transit Services, Santa Cruz *Also called First Transit Inc* ***(P-7331)***
Laidlaw Transit Services, Madera *Also called First Student Inc* ***(P-7439)***
Laird Family Estate LLC (PA)..........E.......707 257-0360
5055 Solano Ave NAPA (94558) ***(P-2647)***
Laird Manufacturing, Merced *Also called Laird Mfg LLC* ***(P-5014)***
Laird Mfg LLC (PA)..........E.......209 722-4145
531 S State Highway 59 Merced (95341) ***(P-5014)***
Laird Technologies Inc..........F.......408 726-5329
2755 Great America Way Santa Clara (95054) ***(P-5683)***
Lake Bowl, Folsom *Also called Folsom Recreation Corp* ***(P-14891)***
Lake Cnty Fire Protection Dst..........D.......707 994-2170
14815 Olympic Dr Clearlake (95422) ***(P-17633)***
Lake Cnty Trbal Hlth Cnsrtium..........D.......707 263-8382
925 Bevins Ct Lakeport (95453) ***(P-15845)***
Lake County Office Education (PA)..........E.......707 262-4102
1152 S Main St Lakeport (95453) ***(P-18308)***
Lake County Publishing Co Inc (HQ)..........D.......707 263-5636
617 S State St Ukiah (95482) ***(P-3453)***
Lake County Record-Bee, Ukiah *Also called Lake County Publishing Co Inc* ***(P-3453)***
Lake County Walnut Inc..........F.......707 279-1200
4545 Loasa Dr Kelseyville (95451) ***(P-2448)***
Lake Merced Golf Club..........D.......650 755-2233
2300 Junipero Serra Blvd Daly City (94015) ***(P-15104)***

ALPHABETIC

Lake Mrritt Healthcare Ctr LLC.....D.....510 227-1806
309 Macarthur Blvd Oakland (94610) *(P-19361)*
Lake Natoma Inn, Folsom *Also called Lake Natoma Lodging LP (P-11243)*
Lake Natoma Lodging LP.....D.....916 351-1500
702 Gold Lake Dr Folsom (95630) *(P-11243)*
Lake of Pines Association.....E.....530 268-1141
11665 Lakeshore N Auburn (95602) *(P-15006)*
Lake of The Pines Homeowners, Auburn *Also called Lake of Pines Association (P-15006)*
Lake Park Retirment Residence, Oakland *Also called Califrnia-Nevada Methdst Homes (P-16224)*
Lake Shore Convalescent Hosp, Oakland *Also called Gaffar Enterprise Inc (P-16234)*
Lake Shstina Golf Cntry CLB In.....D.....530 938-3201
5925 Country Club Dr Weed (96094) *(P-15007)*
Lake Tahoe Historical Society.....E.....530 541-5458
3058 Lake Tahoe Blvd South Lake Tahoe (96150) *(P-18576)*
Lake Tahoe Resort Hotel, South Lake Tahoe *Also called Roppong-Thoe LP A Cal Ltd Prtn (P-11418)*
Lake Wildwood Association.....C.....530 432-1152
11255 Cottontail Way Penn Valley (95946) *(P-18435)*
Lake Wildwood Golf Course., Penn Valley *Also called Lake Wildwood Association (P-18435)*
Lakeport Post Acute LLC.....D.....707 263-6382
1291 Craig Ave Lakeport (95453) *(P-16188)*
Lakeshore Fire Dept, Clearlake *Also called Lake Cnty Fire Protection Dst (P-17633)*
Lakeshore Resort.....D.....559 893-3193
61953 Huntington Lake Rd Lakeshore (93634) *(P-11244)*
Lakeshore Supply, Lakeshore *Also called Lakeshore Resort (P-11244)*
Lakeside Clubhouse, Daly City *Also called Olympic Club (P-18445)*
Lakeview Lodge Inc.....E.....650 369-7476
530 Lakeview Way Emerald Hills (94062) *(P-18133)*
Lakos Corporation.....D.....559 255-1601
1365 N Clovis Ave Fresno (93727) *(P-9075)*
Lam Research Corporation (PA).....**D.....510 572-0200**
4650 Cushing Pkwy Fremont (94538) *(P-6175)*
Lam Research Corporation.....E.....510 572-8400
1 Portola Ave Livermore (94551) *(P-6176)*
Lam Research Corporation.....E.....209 597-2194
1201 Voyager St Livermore (94550) *(P-6177)*
Lamanuzzi & Pantaleo LLC (PA).....**D.....559 432-3170**
11767 Road 27 1/2 Madera (93637) *(P-62)*
Lamar Tool & Die Casting Inc.....E.....209 545-5525
4230 Technology Dr Modesto (95356) *(P-4543)*
Lamart Corporation.....C.....510 489-8100
2600 Central Ave Ste E Union City (94587) *(P-4526)*
Lamassu Utility Services Inc.....E.....707 750-5130
536 Stone Rd Ste D Benicia (94510) *(P-14759)*
Lambdatest Inc.....C.....866 430-7087
1390 Market St Ste 200 San Francisco (94102) *(P-13623)*
Lamon Construction Company Inc.....E.....530 671-1370
871 Von Geldern Way Yuba City (95991) *(P-911)*
Lamperti Associates.....E.....415 454-1623
1241 Andersen Dr Ste A San Rafael (94901) *(P-662)*
Lanai Garden Corporation.....E.....408 929-8100
1575 Tully Rd San Jose (95122) *(P-11245)*
Lanai Garden Inn & Suites, San Jose *Also called Lanai Garden Corporation (P-11245)*
Lancashire Group Incorporated.....E.....510 792-9384
37053 Cherry St Ste 210 Newark (94560) *(P-19554)*
Lancaster Burns Cnstr Inc.....C.....916 624-8404
8655 Washington Blvd Roseville (95678) *(P-1687)*
Land & Personnel Management, Kerman *Also called Hall Management Corp (P-19346)*
Land Home Financial Svcs Inc (PA).....**E.....925 676-7038**
1355 Willow Way Ste 250 Concord (94520) *(P-9910)*
Land OLakes Inc.....E.....530 865-7626
3601 County Road C Orland (95963) *(P-2151)*
Land Services Ldscp Contrs Inc.....D.....510 656-8101
901 Brown Rd Fremont (94539) *(P-10706)*
Landacorp Inc.....E.....530 891-0853
500 Orient St Ste 110 Chico (95928) *(P-12567)*
Landavazo Bros Inc (PA).....**C.....510 888-1043**
29280 Pacific St Hayward (94544) *(P-1886)*
Landcare USA LLC.....D.....707 836-1460
930 Shiloh Rd Bldg 44 Windsor (95492) *(P-476)*
Landcare USA LLC.....D.....916 635-0936
3213 Fitzgerald Rd Rancho Cordova (95742) *(P-477)*
Landcare USA LLC.....D.....925 462-2193
1064 Serpentine Ln Ste A Pleasanton (94566) *(P-478)*
Landcare USA LLC.....D.....408 727-4099
85 Old Tully Rd San Jose (95111) *(P-479)*
Landec Corporation (PA).....**C.....650 306-1650**
5201 Great America Pkwy # 232 Santa Clara (95054) *(P-2220)*
Landmark Capital Inc.....E.....209 242-8880
2311 W Alpine Ave Stockton (95204) *(P-1301)*
Landmark Event Staffing.....A.....510 632-9000
1965 Adams Ave San Leandro (94577) *(P-12178)*
Landmark Healthcare Svcs Inc (HQ).....**C.....800 638-4557**
1610 Arden Way Ste 280 Sacramento (95815) *(P-15865)*
Landmark Technology Inc.....E.....408 435-8890
1660 Mckee Rd San Jose (95116) *(P-6446)*
Landmark Worldwide LLC (PA).....**C.....415 981-8850**
353 Sacramento St Ste 200 San Francisco (94111) *(P-19555)*
Landor LLC.....D.....415 365-1700
360 3rd St 5 San Francisco (94107) *(P-14319)*
Landor Associates, San Francisco *Also called Landor LLC (P-14319)*
Landor Associates Intl Ltd (HQ).....**C.....415 365-1700**
360 3rd St 5 San Francisco (94107) *(P-11866)*
Landscape & Tree Company Inc (HQ).....**D.....916 246-9987**
9350 Viking Pl Roseville (95747) *(P-423)*
Landscape Maintenance Services, Roseville *Also called Optima Ldscp Sacramento Inc (P-429)*

Lane International Trading Inc (PA).....**D.....510 489-7364**
33155 Transit Ave Union City (94587) *(P-4341)*
Lane Safety Co Inc.....E.....707 746-4820
340 W Channel Rd Ste F Benicia (94510) *(P-12179)*
Lang Richert & Patch.....E.....559 228-6700
5200 N Palm Ave Ste 401 Fresno (93704) *(P-17308)*
Langetwins Inc.....E.....209 339-4055
1298 E Jahant Rd Acampo (95220) *(P-2648)*
Langetwins Wine Company Inc.....E.....209 334-9780
1525 E Jahant Rd Acampo (95220) *(P-2649)*
Langetwins Winery & Vineyards, Acampo *Also called Langetwins Wine Company Inc (P-2649)*
Langills General Machine Inc.....E.....916 452-0167
7850 14th Ave Sacramento (95826) *(P-5559)*
Langley Hill Quarry.....E.....650 851-0179
12 Langley Hill Rd Woodside (94062) *(P-579)*
Langtry Farms LLC.....F.....707 987-2772
21000 Butts Canyon Rd Middletown (95461) *(P-2650)*
Lanlogic Inc (HQ).....**E.....925 273-2300**
248 Rickenbacker Cir Livermore (94551) *(P-13624)*
Lanner Electronics Usa Inc.....E.....510 979-0688
47790 Westinghouse Dr Fremont (94539) *(P-8719)*
Lanner USA, Fremont *Also called Lanner Electronics Usa Inc (P-8719)*
Lansas Products, Lodi *Also called Vander Lans & Sons Inc (P-5450)*
Lansing Farming Co, Fresno *Also called Woolf Farming Co Cal Inc (P-197)*
Lansky Sharpeners, Oakland *Also called Levine Arthur Lansky & Assoc (P-4606)*
Lanterns At The Ridge, Auburn *Also called Ridge Golf Course LLC (P-15020)*
Lanza Vineyards Inc (PA).....**D.....707 864-0730**
4756 Suisun Valley Rd Fairfield (94534) *(P-63)*
Lapham Company Inc.....D.....510 531-6000
4844 Telegraph Ave Oakland (94609) *(P-10598)*
Lapham Company Management, Oakland *Also called Lapham Company Inc (P-10598)*
Laptalo Enterprises Inc.....D.....408 727-6633
2360 Zanker Rd San Jose (95131) *(P-4776)*
Lares Research.....E.....530 345-1767
295 Lockheed Ave Chico (95973) *(P-7085)*
Largo Concrete Inc.....B.....408 874-2500
891 W Hamilton Ave Campbell (95008) *(P-1887)*
Lark Ave Classic Car Wash, Los Gatos *Also called Lark Avenue Car Wash (P-14647)*
Lark Avenue Car Wash.....D.....408 356-2525
16500 Lark Ave Los Gatos (95032) *(P-14647)*
Lark Avenue Car Wash.....D.....408 371-2565
5005 Almaden Expy San Jose (95118) *(P-14648)*
Lark Avenue Car Wash.....D.....408 377-2525
981 E Hamilton Ave Campbell (95008) *(P-14649)*
Lark Creek Inn Prtners L P A C.....E.....415 924-7767
234 Magnolia Ave Larkspur (94939) *(P-11724)*
Lark Technologies Inc.....D.....650 300-1750
2570 W El Cmino Real Ste Mountain View (94040) *(P-12568)*
Larkin Street Youth Services.....D.....415 567-1020
6324 Geary Blvd San Francisco (94121) *(P-17634)*
Larkspur Group LLC.....D.....530 223-9344
2160 Larkspur Ln Redding (96002) *(P-11246)*
Larkspur Group LLC (PA).....**D.....530 224-1001**
2160 Larkspur Ln Redding (96002) *(P-11247)*
Larkspur Hsptality Dev MGT LLC.....E.....916 773-1717
1931 Taylor Rd Roseville (95661) *(P-11248)*
Larkspur Hsptality Dev MGT LLC.....E.....916 773-7171
1951 Taylor Rd Roseville (95661) *(P-11249)*
Larkspur Hsptality Dev MGT LLC.....E.....916 355-1616
121 Iron Point Rd Folsom (95630) *(P-11250)*
Larkspur Hsptality Dev MGT LLC.....E.....650 827-1515
690 Gateway Blvd South San Francisco (94080) *(P-11251)*
Larkspur Hsptality Dev MGT LLC.....E.....916 646-1212
555 Howe Ave Sacramento (95825) *(P-11252)*
Larkspur Hsptality Dev MGT LLC.....E.....925 463-1212
5535 Johnson Ct Pleasanton (94588) *(P-11253)*
Larkspur Hsptality Dev MGT LLC.....E.....408 885-1234
302 S Market St San Jose (95113) *(P-11254)*
Larkspur Hsptality Dev MGT LLC.....E.....650 872-1515
670 Gateway Blvd South San Francisco (94080) *(P-11255)*
Larkspur Hsptality Dev MGT LLC (PA).....**E.....415 945-5000**
125 E Sir Frncis Drake Bl Larkspur (94939) *(P-11256)*
Larkspur Landing, Folsom *Also called Larkspur Hsptality Dev MGT LLC (P-11250)*
Larkspur Landing Home Sweet Ht, South San Francisco *Also called Larkspur Hsptality Dev MGT LLC (P-11251)*
Larkspur Landing Hotel, Sacramento *Also called Larkspur Hsptality Dev MGT LLC (P-11252)*
Larry Fisher & Sons Ltd Partnr.....F.....559 252-2575
5242 E Home Ave Fresno (93727) *(P-8499)*
Larry Hopkins Honda, Sunnyvale *Also called Larry Hopkins Inc (P-14575)*
Larry Hopkins Inc.....D.....408 720-1888
1048 W El Camino Real Sunnyvale (94087) *(P-14575)*
Larry Mthvin Installations Inc.....D.....209 368-2105
128 N Cluff Ave Lodi (95240) *(P-4390)*
Larry Schlussler.....F.....707 822-9095
824 L St Ste 7 Arcata (95521) *(P-5702)*
Larsens Inc.....F.....831 476-3009
1041 17th Ave Ste A Santa Cruz (95062) *(P-3039)*
Larson Automation Inc.....D.....408 432-4800
960 Rincon Cir San Jose (95131) *(P-12569)*
Larson Packaging Company LLC.....E.....408 946-4971
1000 Yosemite Dr Milpitas (95035) *(P-3098)*
Lartech, San Jose *Also called L & H Iron Inc (P-4671)*
Las Alcobas Hotel.....E.....707 963-7000
1485 Main St Ste 201 Saint Helena (94574) *(P-11257)*
Las Animas Con & Bldg Sup Inc.....E.....831 425-4084
146 Encinal St Santa Cruz (95060) *(P-4491)*
Lasaltte Hlth Rhbilitation Ctr, Stockton *Also called Five Star Qulty Care-CA II LLC (P-16005)*

Lasar, Lakeport *Also called Paul Loewen* ***(P-7779)***
Lasar Underground Cnstr Inc....E....559 291-1024
2929 N Burl Ave Fresno (93727) ***(P-1113)***
Laselva Beach Spice Co Inc....F....831 724-4500
453 Mcquaide Dr Watsonville (95076) ***(P-2914)***
Laser Division, Milpitas *Also called Spectra-Physics Inc* ***(P-6543)***
Laser Excel, Santa Rosa *Also called Green Lake Investors LLC* ***(P-7205)***
Laser Recharge Inc (PA)....E....916 813-2717
8250 Belvedere Ave Ste C Sacramento (95826) ***(P-7207)***
Laser Reference Inc....E....408 361-0220
151 Martinvale Ln San Jose (95119) ***(P-6694)***
Laser Skin Srgery Ctr Nthrn Ca, Sacramento *Also called Laser Skin Srgery Med Group In* ***(P-15502)***
Laser Skin Srgery Med Group In....E....916 456-0400
3835 J St Sacramento (95816) ***(P-15502)***
Laserbeam Software LLC....F....925 459-2595
1647 Willow Pass Rd # 40 Concord (94520) ***(P-13272)***
Lasertec USA Inc (HQ)....E....408 437-1441
2107 N 1st St Ste 210 San Jose (95131) ***(P-14760)***
Lash Group LLC....C....800 788-9637
999 Bayhill Dr Fl 3 San Bruno (94066) ***(P-18239)***
Lash Group Healthcare Cons, San Bruno *Also called Lash Group LLC* ***(P-18239)***
Lasher Wes ADI/ Ddg/Volkswagen, Sacramento *Also called Wesley B Lasher Inv Corp* ***(P-14604)***
Lassen Canyon Nursery Inc (PA)....C....530 223-1075
10364 Salmon Creek Rd Redding (96003) ***(P-9275)***
Lassen Forest Products Inc....E....530 527-7677
22829 Casale Rd Red Bluff (96080) ***(P-3212)***
Lassen Hse Assisted Living LLC....D....530 529-2900
705 Luther Rd Red Bluff (96080) ***(P-18134)***
Lassen Medical Group Inc (PA)....E....530 527-0414
2450 Sster Mary Clumba Dr Red Bluff (96080) ***(P-15503)***
Lassen Municipal Utility Dst....E....530 257-4174
65 S Roop St Susanville (96130) ***(P-8118)***
Last Frontier Healthcare Dst....C....530 708-8800
1111 N Nagle St Alturas (96101) ***(P-16425)***
Lastline Inc (PA)....C....877 671-3239
3401 Hillview Ave Palo Alto (94304) ***(P-13273)***
Latch So Chropractic Prof Corp....E....415 775-4204
1237 Van Ness Ave Ste 300 San Francisco (94109) ***(P-15866)***
Latentview Analytics Corp....E....408 493-6653
2540 N 1st St Ste 108 San Jose (95131) ***(P-19556)***
Lathrop Construction Assoc Inc (PA)....D....707 746-8000
4001 Park Rd Benicia (94510) ***(P-912)***
Lathrop Engineering, Morgan Hill *Also called Paramit Corporation* ***(P-5957)***
Lathrop Woodworks, Lathrop *Also called Rafael Sandoval* ***(P-3101)***
Latino Comm On Alchol DRG Abus (PA)....E....650 244-1444
1001 Sneath Ln Ste 307 San Bruno (94066) ***(P-17033)***
Latino Family Center, San Francisco *Also called Mission Cncil Alchol Abuse Spn* ***(P-17650)***
Lattice Data Inc....E....650 800-7262
801 El Camino Real Menlo Park (94025) ***(P-13274)***
Lattice Engines Inc (HQ)....C....877 460-0010
1820 Gateway Dr Ste 200 San Mateo (94404) ***(P-13625)***
Lattice Semiconductor Corp....B....408 826-6000
2115 Onel Dr San Jose (95131) ***(P-6178)***
LAuberge De Sonoma LLC....C....707 938-2929
29 E Macarthur St Sonoma (95476) ***(P-11258)***
Laughlin Falbo Levy Moresi LLP (PA)....D....510 628-0496
1001 Galaxy Way Ste 200 Concord (94520) ***(P-17309)***
Launchdarkly, Oakland *Also called Catamorphic Co* ***(P-12330)***
Laurel Inn, San Francisco *Also called Joie De Vivre Hospitality LLC* ***(P-11215)***
Laurent Culinary Service....F....415 485-1122
1945 Francisco Blvd E # 4 San Rafael (94901) ***(P-2915)***
Lava Beds National Monuments....E....530 667-2282
1 Indian Wells Hqtrs Tulelake (96134) ***(P-18577)***
Lava Cap Winery, Placerville *Also called Lava Springs Inc* ***(P-2651)***
Lava Springs Inc....E....530 621-0175
2221 Fruitridge Rd Placerville (95667) ***(P-2651)***
Lavender Hill Spa....E....707 942-4495
1015 Foothill Blvd Calistoga (94515) ***(P-14956)***
Law Foundation Silicon Valley....E....408 293-4790
4 N 2nd St Ste 1350 San Jose (95113) ***(P-17310)***
Law Offces Rudy Exlrod Zeff LL....E....415 434-9800
351 California St Ste 700 San Francisco (94104) ***(P-17311)***
Law Office Robert B Jobe PC....D....415 956-5513
100 Bush St Ste 1250 San Francisco (94104) ***(P-17312)***
Lawley's Trucking, Stockton *Also called Lawleys Inc* ***(P-2346)***
Lawleys Inc....E....209 337-1170
4554 Qantas Ln Stockton (95206) ***(P-2346)***
Lawrence Berkeley National Lab, Albany *Also called Energy Berkeley Office US Dept* ***(P-19216)***
Lawrence Berkeley National Lab, Berkeley *Also called United States Dept of Energy* ***(P-19240)***
Lawrence Berkeley National Lab, Berkeley *Also called Energy Berkeley Office US Dept* ***(P-19217)***
Lawrence Livermore Nat Lab, Livermore *Also called United States Dept of Energy* ***(P-19143)***
Lawson Mechanical Contractors (PA)....D....916 381-5000
6090 S Watt Ave Sacramento (95829) ***(P-1302)***
Lawson Roofing Co Inc....D....415 285-1661
1495 Tennessee St San Francisco (94107) ***(P-1815)***
Lawsons Landing Inc....E....707 878-2443
137 Marine View Dr Dillon Beach (94929) ***(P-11619)***
Lawyers Title Insurance Corp....C....650 445-6300
530 El Camino Real Ste A San Carlos (94070) ***(P-10200)***
Lawyers Title Insurance Corp....C....510 733-2250
20630 Patio Dr Castro Valley (94546) ***(P-10201)***

Laxmi Group Inc....D....408 329-7733
4701 Patrick Henry Dr # 25 Santa Clara (95054) ***(P-12570)***
Lazestar Inc....E....925 443-5293
6956 Preston Ave Livermore (94551) ***(P-3138)***
LB Ford Painting Inc....E....707 447-5274
4325 Abernathy Rd Fairfield (94534) ***(P-1420)***
LBC Mundial Corporation (HQ)....D....650 873-0750
3563 Inv Blvd Ste 3 Hayward (94545) ***(P-7750)***
LBC North America, Hayward *Also called LBC Mundial Corporation* ***(P-7750)***
Lbn Leisure Care LLC....A....916 604-3780
1445 Expo Pkwy Sacramento (95815) ***(P-18135)***
Lca Architects, Walnut Creek *Also called Loving Campos Associates* ***(P-18896)***
Lcof Lake Tahoe Operating LLC....E....530 541-6722
3411 Lake Tahoe Blvd South Lake Tahoe (96150) ***(P-11259)***
Lcr-Dixon Corporation....F....404 307-1695
2048 Union St Apt 4 San Francisco (94123) ***(P-13275)***
LD Strobel Co Inc....E....925 686-3241
1022 Shary Cir Ste 9 Concord (94518) ***(P-2042)***
Le Belge Chocolatier Inc....E....707 258-9200
761 Skyway Ct NAPA (94558) ***(P-2430)***
Le Meridian Hotel, San Francisco *Also called Chesapeake Lodging Trust* ***(P-11003)***
Lea & Braze Engineering Inc (PA)....D....510 887-4086
2495 Industrial Pkwy W Hayward (94545) ***(P-18752)***
Lead Genius....E....415 969-2915
2054 University Ave Berkeley (94704) ***(P-11766)***
Leadspace Inc (HQ)....E....855 532-3772
445 Bush St Ste 900 San Francisco (94108) ***(P-13930)***
Leadstack Inc....D....628 200-3063
611 Gateway Blvd Ste 120 South San Francisco (94080) ***(P-12103)***
League of California Cities (PA)....D....916 658-8200
1400 K St Fl 4 Sacramento (95814) ***(P-19691)***
League of Wmen Vters Cal Edcat, Sacramento *Also called League of Women Voters Cal* ***(P-18537)***
League of Women Voters Cal (PA)....F....916 442-7215
921 11th St Ste 700 Sacramento (95814) ***(P-18537)***
Leandata Inc....D....669 600-5676
2901 Patrick Henry Dr Santa Clara (95054) ***(P-8720)***
Leantaas Inc....C....650 409-3501
471 El Cmino Real Ste 230 Santa Clara (95050) ***(P-12571)***
Leapfrog Enterprises Inc (HQ)....B....510 420-5000
2200 Powell St Ste 500 Emeryville (94608) ***(P-7177)***
Leapyear Technologies Inc....E....510 542-9193
612 Howard St San Francisco (94105) ***(P-12572)***
Learning Services Corporation....E....408 848-4379
10855 De Bruin Way Gilroy (95020) ***(P-17034)***
Learning Services Northern Cal, Gilroy *Also called Learning Services Corporation* ***(P-17034)***
Learning Squared Inc (PA)....C....650 567-9995
935 Benecia Ave Sunnyvale (94085) ***(P-7178)***
Learningstar Inc (PA)....E....408 221-4067
571 Tully Rd San Jose (95111) ***(P-17963)***
Leasing Equipment, San Francisco *Also called Atel Capital Group* ***(P-9883)***
Leatherby's Family Creamery, Citrus Heights *Also called Cort Yard Creamery Inc* ***(P-9446)***
Leavitt Pacific Insur Brks Inc....E....408 288-6262
1330 S Bascom Ave Ste A San Jose (95128) ***(P-10308)***
Lee & Associates Central Vly....E....209 983-1111
241 Frank West Cir # 300 Stockton (95206) ***(P-10599)***
Lee Bros Foodservices Inc (PA)....D....408 275-0700
660 E Gish Rd San Jose (95112) ***(P-9276)***
Lee Brothers Inc....E....650 964-9650
1011 Timothy Dr San Jose (95133) ***(P-2282)***
Lee Industrial Catering, San Jose *Also called Lee Bros Foodservices Inc* ***(P-9276)***
Lee Jennings Target Ex Inc....D....209 823-0071
815 Moffat Blvd Manteca (95336) ***(P-7845)***
Leemah Corporation (PA)....C....415 394-1288
155 S Hill Dr Brisbane (94005) ***(P-5903)***
Leemah Electronics Inc....E....415 394-1288
1080 Sansome St San Francisco (94111) ***(P-8119)***
Leeman Brothers Drywall Inc....E....916 652-9019
3851 Taylor Rd Loomis (95650) ***(P-1688)***
Leena Ai Inc....C....332 232-9740
3260 Hillview Ave Palo Alto (94304) ***(P-8014)***
Lees Concrete Materials Inc....D....559 486-2440
200 S Pine St Madera (93637) ***(P-4492)***
Lees Imperial Welding Inc....C....510 657-4900
3300 Edison Way Fremont (94538) ***(P-4672)***
Lees Sandwiches Intl Inc....E....408 280-1595
660 E Gish Rd San Jose (95112) ***(P-10806)***
Leewood Press Inc....E....415 896-0513
1407 Indiana St San Francisco (94107) ***(P-3671)***
Leeyo Software Inc (HQ)....E....408 988-5800
2841 Junction Ave Ste 201 San Jose (95134) ***(P-13276)***
Legacy and Nursing Rehab....D....925 228-8383
1790 Muir Rd Martinez (94553) ***(P-16035)***
Legacy Global Logistics Svcs, San Jose *Also called Legacy Transportation Svcs Inc* ***(P-7624)***
Legacy Marketing Group (PA)....C....707 778-8638
5341 Old Redwood Hwy # 400 Petaluma (94954) ***(P-19557)***
Legacy Mech & Enrgy Svcs Inc....D....925 820-6938
3130 Crow Canyon Pl # 410 San Ramon (94583) ***(P-1303)***
Legacy Prtners Residential Inc (PA)....C....650 571-2250
950 Tower Ln Ste 900 Foster City (94404) ***(P-19362)***
Legacy Roofg Waterproofing Inc (PA)....E....408 451-9785
1698 Rogers Ave Ste 10 San Jose (95112) ***(P-1816)***
Legacy Transportation Svcs Inc (PA)....C....408 294-9800
935 Mclaughlin Ave San Jose (95122) ***(P-7624)***
Legacy Vulcan LLC....F....209 854-3088
28525 Bambouer Rd Gustine (95322) ***(P-4442)***
Legal Services Northern Cal (PA)....E....916 551-2150
517 12th St Sacramento (95814) ***(P-17313)***

A L P H A B E T I C

Legalmatchcom (PA) ..... E 415 946-0800
395 Oyster Point Blvd # 55 South San Francisco (94080) *(P-17314)*
Legend Silicon Corp ..... E 510 656-9888
440 Mission Ct Fremont (94539) *(P-5853)*
Legend Transpotation, Yuba City *Also called New Legend Inc (P-7570)*
Legends Apparel & I C Ink, Stockton *Also called IC Ink Image Co Inc (P-3737)*
Leggett & Platt Incorporated ..... D 510 487-8063
31023 Huntwood Ave Hayward (94544) *(P-11813)*
Legion Corporation (PA) ..... D 800 750-0062
784 Geary St San Francisco (94109) *(P-14073)*
Legion Industries ..... E 650 743-6358
748 Lakemead Way Emerald Hills (94062) *(P-18436)*
Lehar Sales Co ..... D 510 465-3255
477 Forbes Blvd South San Francisco (94080) *(P-9347)*
Lehigh Southwest Cement Co ..... F 408 996-4271
24001 Stevens Creek Blvd Cupertino (95014) *(P-4395)*
Lehigh Southwest Cement Co (HQ) ..... F 972 653-5500
2300 Clayton Rd Ste 300 Concord (94520) *(P-4396)*
Lehmans Manufacturing Co Inc ..... F 559 486-1700
4960 E Jensen Ave Fresno (93725) *(P-4673)*
Lehr, Sacramento *Also called Stommel Inc (P-1614)*
Leica Geosystems Hds LLC ..... D 925 790-2300
5000 Executive Pkwy # 500 San Ramon (94583) *(P-6908)*
Leighfisher Inc (HQ) ..... D 650 579-7722
4 Embarcadero Ctr # 3800 San Francisco (94111) *(P-19558)*
Leisure Care, Livermore *Also called Livermore Snior Lving Assoc LP (P-10448)*
Leisure Care LLC ..... C 925 371-2300
800 E Stanley Blvd Livermore (94550) *(P-18136)*
Leisure Care LLC ..... E 707 769-3300
101 Ely Blvd S Petaluma (94954) *(P-18137)*
Leisure Care LLC ..... C 559 434-1237
9525 N Fort Washington Rd Fresno (93730) *(P-18138)*
Leisure Gardens Retirement HM, Vacaville *Also called Westlake Development Group LLC (P-16283)*
Leisure Sports Inc ..... D 510 226-8500
46650 Landing Pkwy Fremont (94538) *(P-14957)*
Leisure Sports Inc ..... B 925 938-3058
2805 Jones Rd Walnut Creek (94597) *(P-11260)*
Leiter's Compounding, San Jose *Also called Wedgewood Connect (P-4007)*
Lek Enterprises Inc ..... E 916 985-4102
12175 Folsom Blvd Ste B Rancho Cordova (95742) *(P-1304)*
Leland House, San Francisco *Also called Catholic Chrties Cyo of The AR (P-17457)*
Leland Prchini Stnberg Mtzger ..... E 415 957-1800
199 Fremont St Fl 21 San Francisco (94105) *(P-17315)*
Leland Saylor & Associates Inc ..... E 415 291-3200
1777 Oakland Blvd Ste 103 Walnut Creek (94596) *(P-18753)*
Leland Saylor Associates, Walnut Creek *Also called Leland Saylor & Associates Inc (P-18753)*
Leland Stanford Junior Univ (PA) ..... C 650 723-2300
450 Jane Stanford Way Stanford (94305) *(P-16763)*
Leland Stanford Junior Univ ..... A 650 935-5365
505 Broadway St Fl 4 Redwood City (94063) *(P-16764)*
Leland Stanford Junior Univ ..... C 650 723-2021
326 Galvez St Stanford (94305) *(P-18437)*
Lembi Group Inc (PA) ..... D 415 861-1111
2101 Market St San Francisco (94114) *(P-10600)*
Lemo USA Inc ..... D 707 206-3700
635 Park Ct Rohnert Park (94928) *(P-8927)*
Lemore Transportation Inc (PA) ..... D 925 689-6444
1420 Royal Industrial Way Concord (94520) *(P-7561)*
Lemtech USA Inc ..... F 408 824-5352
185 Estancia Dr Unit 117 San Jose (95134) *(P-4885)*
Lenaco Corporation ..... E 650 873-3500
451 E Jamie Ct South San Francisco (94080) *(P-9121)*
Lencioni Construction Co Inc ..... E 650 216-9900
420 Maple St Redwood City (94063) *(P-663)*
Lending Express Inc ..... E 838 800-0644
400 Concar Dr San Mateo (94402) *(P-19559)*
Lendingclub Corporation (PA) ..... A 415 632-5600
595 Market St Fl 4 San Francisco (94105) *(P-9859)*
Lendlease US Construction Inc ..... E 415 512-0586
71 Stevenson St Ste 800 San Francisco (94105) *(P-19363)*
Lendup, Oakland *Also called Flurish Inc (P-9857)*
Lendup Card Services Inc ..... C 855 253-6387
225 Bush St Ste 1150 San Francisco (94104) *(P-14320)*
Lendus LLC ..... A 925 295-9300
3240 Stone Valley Rd W Alamo (94507) *(P-9911)*
Lendusa LLC (PA) ..... C 925 295-9300
3240 Stone Valley Rd W Alamo (94507) *(P-9912)*
Lennar Mltfmily Cmmunities LLC ..... A 415 975-4980
492 9th St Ste 300 Oakland (94607) *(P-783)*
Lenovo (united States) Inc ..... D 510 813-3331
602 Charcot Ave San Jose (95131) *(P-5258)*
Lens C-C Inc (PA) ..... D 800 772-3911
1750 N Loop Rd Ste 150 Alameda (94502) *(P-7143)*
Lensa Inc (PA) ..... E 415 528-8467
541 Jefferson Ave Ste 100 Redwood City (94063) *(P-12104)*
Lensvector Inc ..... D 408 542-0300
6203 San Ignacio Ave San Jose (95119) *(P-7144)*
Lent Burden Farming Company ..... E 209 847-3276
250 S Oak Ave Ste C1 Oakdale (95361) *(P-381)*
Lenz Precision Technology Inc ..... E 650 966-1784
355 Pioneer Way Ste A Mountain View (94041) *(P-5560)*
Lenz Technology, Mountain View *Also called Lenz Precision Technology Inc (P-5560)*
Leo J Ryan Child Care Ctr, South San Francisco *Also called Peninsula Family Service (P-17671)*
Leo Lam Inc ..... E 925 484-3690
3589 Nevada St Ste A Pleasanton (94566) *(P-3672)*

Leonardo Logging and Cnstr Inc ..... E 707 725-1809
604 L St Fortuna (95540) *(P-3068)*
Leopard Imaging Inc (PA) ..... D 408 263-0988
48820 Kato Rd Ste 100b Fremont (94538) *(P-7153)*
Leotek Electronics USA LLC ..... E 408 380-1788
1955 Lundy Ave San Jose (95131) *(P-7241)*
Leprino Foods Company ..... B 209 835-8340
2401 N Macarthur Dr Tracy (95376) *(P-2152)*
Lescure Company Inc ..... D 925 283-2528
2301 Arnold Industrial Wa Concord (94520) *(P-1305)*
Lesley Foundation ..... D 650 726-4888
701 Arnold Way Bldg A Half Moon Bay (94019) *(P-19810)*
Leslie Heavy Haul LLC ..... E 209 840-1664
18971 Hess Ave Sonora (95370) *(P-14321)*
Let It Flho Lessee Inc ..... E 415 397-7700
225 Powell St San Francisco (94102) *(P-11261)*
Letterman Digital Arts Ltd ..... D 415 746-5044
1 Letterman Dr Bldg B San Francisco (94129) *(P-17964)*
Lettieri & Co Ltd ..... E 415 657-3392
120 Park Ln Brisbane (94005) *(P-9464)*
Lettis Consultants Intl Inc (PA) ..... E 925 482-0360
1000 Burnett Ave Ste 350 Concord (94520) *(P-19811)*
Levan Auto Body Parts, Sacramento *Also called Levan Import-Export Inc (P-8455)*
Levan Import-Export Inc ..... E 916 381-5712
6935 Stockton Blvd Sacramento (95823) *(P-8455)*
Level 1 Roofing Inc ..... E 888 505-0878
3350 Swetzer Ct Loomis (95650) *(P-1817)*
Level 10 Construction LP ..... C 408 747-5000
1050 Entp Way Ste 250 Sunnyvale (94089) *(P-913)*
Level 5 Inc ..... E 669 263-6292
1210 Coleman Ave Santa Clara (95050) *(P-1053)*
Level 5 Drywall Inc ..... D 650 486-1657
70 Glenn Way Ste 4 San Carlos (94070) *(P-1689)*
Level Labs LP ..... F 408 499-6839
530 Lytton Ave Lbby Palo Alto (94301) *(P-13277)*
Level-It Installations Group ..... D 604 942-2022
3700 Yale Way Fremont (94538) *(P-914)*
Level-It Installations Ltd ..... E 604 942-2022
2443 Fillmore St San Francisco (94115) *(P-915)*
Lever Inc ..... D 415 458-2731
1125 Mission St San Francisco (94103) *(P-12573)*
Levi Stadium ..... E 408 757-1156
4900 Mrie P Debartolo Way Santa Clara (95054) *(P-14910)*
Levi Strauss & Co (PA) ..... A 415 501-6000
1155 Battery St San Francisco (94111) *(P-2987)*
Levin-Richmond Terminal Corp ..... E 510 232-4422
402 Wright Ave Richmond (94804) *(P-7722)*
Levine Arthur Lansky & Assoc (PA) ..... F 415 234-6020
3914 Delmont Ave Oakland (94605) *(P-4606)*
Levmar Inc ..... F 925 680-8723
1666 Willow Pass Rd Pittsburg (94565) *(P-4777)*
Lewis & Lewis Inc ..... E 209 474-1777
5757 Pacific Ave 5 Stockton (95207) *(P-15216)*
Lewis & Taylor LLC ..... C 415 781-3496
440 Bryant St San Francisco (94107) *(P-11966)*
Lewis & Taylor Bldg Svc Contrs, San Francisco *Also called Lewis & Taylor LLC (P-11966)*
Lewis Brsbois Bsgard Smith LLP ..... E 415 362-2580
333 Bush St San Francisco (94104) *(P-17316)*
Lewis John Glass Studio ..... E 510 635-4607
10229 Pearmain St Oakland (94603) *(P-4373)*
Lewis Logging ..... E 707 722-1975
3897 Rohnerville Rd Fortuna (95540) *(P-3069)*
Lewis Rents, San Lorenzo *Also called Neff Corporation (P-12056)*
Lewis Rents Inc ..... E 510 276-3080
15740 Hesperian Blvd San Lorenzo (94580) *(P-12052)*
Lewis S Bliss MD ..... E 916 863-3143
5773 Greenback Ln Sacramento (95841) *(P-15504)*
Lexisnexis Courtlink Inc ..... D 425 974-5000
2101 K St Sacramento (95816) *(P-18339)*
Lexus of Roseville, Roseville *Also called RPM Luxury Auto Sales Inc (P-14620)*
Lftm Inc ..... F 510 249-0900
49035 Milmont Dr Fremont (94538) *(P-8500)*
Lg, San Francisco *Also called Little Giant Bldg Maint Inc (P-11967)*
Lg Display America Inc (HQ) ..... D 408 350-0190
2540 N 1st St Ste 400 San Jose (95131) *(P-8928)*
Lg Innotek Usa Inc ..... E 408 234-6356
2540 N 1st St Ste 400 San Jose (95131) *(P-6674)*
Lg Innotek Usa Inc (HQ) ..... C 408 955-0364
2540 N 1st St Ste 400 San Jose (95131) *(P-6447)*
Lgc Biosearch Technologies, Petaluma *Also called Biosearch Technologies Inc (P-4040)*
Lge Electrical Sales Inc ..... C 408 992-4145
755 E Evelyn Ave Sunnyvale (94086) *(P-8865)*
LGS RECREATION, Los Gatos *Also called Los Gatos Saratoga Dept of Com (P-17967)*
Lgsrc, Los Gatos *Also called Los Gatos Swim and Racquet CLB (P-14961)*
Lhl Construction Inc ..... E 916 782-9001
1370 Furneaux Rd Olivehurst (95961) *(P-1926)*
Libby Laboratories Inc ..... E 510 527-5400
1700 6th St Berkeley (94710) *(P-4087)*
Liberty American Mortgage Corp (PA) ..... D 916 780-3000
193 Blue Ravine Rd # 240 Folsom (95630) *(P-9943)*
Liberty Bank (PA) ..... E 650 871-2400
500 Linden Ave South San Francisco (94080) *(P-9737)*
LIBERTY ENERGY, South Lake Tahoe *Also called Liberty Utlties Clpeco Elc LLC (P-8120)*
Liberty Fresh Foods LLC ..... E 916 638-8825
11020 White Rock Rd # 100 Rancho Cordova (95670) *(P-2916)*
Liberty Laboratories Inc ..... E 408 262-6633
10869 Sycamore Ct Cupertino (95014) *(P-6765)*
Liberty Packing Company LLC ..... E 209 826-7100
12045 Ingomar Grade Los Banos (93635) *(P-14322)*

Liberty Packing Company LLC (PA)....E....**209 826-7100**
724 Main St Woodland (95695) **(P-9414)**
Liberty Utlties Clpeco Elc LLC....D....800 782-2506
933 Eloise Ave South Lake Tahoe (96150) **(P-8120)**
Licap Technologies Inc....D....916 329-8099
9795 Business Park Dr A Sacramento (95827) **(P-3791)**
Lick Wilmerding High School, San Francisco *Also called California School of Mech Arts* **(P-10380)**
Lidestri Foods Inc....D....559 251-1000
568 S Temperance Ave Fresno (93727) **(P-2221)**
Lieff Cbrser Hmann Brnstein LL (PA)....C....**415 788-0245**
275 Battery St Fl 29 San Francisco (94111) **(P-17317)**
Life Gnerations Healthcare LLC....E....925 937-7450
1224 Rossmoor Pkwy Walnut Creek (94595) **(P-16036)**
Life Street Corporation....E....415 757-0497
981 Industrial Rd Ste D San Carlos (94070) **(P-11767)**
Life Time Inc....C....916 472-2000
1435 E Roseville Pkwy Roseville (95661) **(P-14958)**
Life-Assist Incorporated (PA)....E....**916 635-3822**
11277 Sunrise Park Dr Rancho Cordova (95742) **(P-8786)**
Lifeaid Beverage Company LLC (PA)....D....**888 558-1113**
2833 Mission St Santa Cruz (95060) **(P-2795)**
Lifearound2angels, Sacramento *Also called Emilykate LLC* **(P-12424)**
Lifehouse Inc (PA)....B....**415 472-2373**
18 Prfssnal Ctr Pkwy Fl 2 San Rafael (94903) **(P-17635)**
Lifekind Products Inc....F....530 477-5395
333 Crown Point Cir # 225 Grass Valley (95945) **(P-4063)**
Lifeline SEC & Automtn Inc....D....916 285-9078
2081 Arena Blvd Ste 260 Sacramento (95834) **(P-6532)**
Lifelong Medical Care (PA)....E....**510 704-6010**
2344 6th St Berkeley (94710) **(P-15505)**
Lifemoves (PA)....E....**650 685-5880**
181 Constitution Dr Menlo Park (94025) **(P-18578)**
Lifescan Products LLC (HQ)....B....**408 719-8443**
1000 Gibraltar Dr Milpitas (95035) **(P-6996)**
Lifestreet Corporation....D....650 508-2220
98 Battery St St 504 San Carlos (94070) **(P-9666)**
Lifestreet Media, San Carlos *Also called Lifestreet Corporation* **(P-9666)**
Lifi Labs Inc (PA)....E....**650 739-5563**
350 Townsend St Ste 830 San Francisco (94107) **(P-4374)**
Liftopia Inc (PA)....D....**415 728-0444**
350 Sansome St Ste 925 San Francisco (94104) **(P-19560)**
Lifx, San Francisco *Also called Lifi Labs Inc* **(P-4374)**
Ligand Pharmaceuticals Inc (PA)....E....**858 550-7500**
5980 Horton St Ste 405 Emeryville (94608) **(P-3940)**
Light Labs Inc....D....650 257-8100
725 Shasta St Redwood City (94063) **(P-6879)**
Lightbend Inc....D....877 989-7372
625 Market St Ste 1000 San Francisco (94105) **(P-12574)**
Lightech Fiberoptic Inc....F....510 567-8700
1987 Adams Ave San Leandro (94577) **(P-6448)**
Lightera, Sunnyvale *Also called Luminus Inc* **(P-5745)**
Lighthuse For Blind Vslly Impr (PA)....E....**415 431-1481**
1155 Market St Fl 10 San Francisco (94103) **(P-17636)**
Lights Fantastic....F....408 266-2787
2408 Lincoln Village Dr San Jose (95125) **(P-3673)**
Lightwaves 2020 Inc....E....408 503-8888
1323 Great Mall Dr Milpitas (95035) **(P-19082)**
Lil People's School, Sacramento *Also called Phoenix Schools Inc* **(P-17997)**
Lilien LLC (HQ)....E....**415 389-7500**
17 E Sir Francis Drake Bl Larkspur (94939) **(P-13626)**
Lilt Inc (PA)....D....**650 530-7180**
550 15th St Ste 39 San Francisco (94103) **(P-12575)**
Lily Development Inc (PA)....E....**209 527-2010**
1230 E Orangeburg Ave A Modesto (95350) **(P-10601)**
Lily Holdings LLC....E....559 222-4807
3510 E Shields Ave Fresno (93726) **(P-16037)**
Lily Samii Collection, San Francisco *Also called L Y Z Ltd* **(P-3002)**
Limagrain Sunflowers Inc....C....530 661-0756
71 W Kentucky Ave Woodland (95695) **(P-9602)**
Lime Light Crm Inc....E....800 455-9645
89 De Boom St San Francisco (94107) **(P-4511)**
Limelight Bar & Cafe, Sacramento *Also called Limelight Bar and Cafe LLC* **(P-15217)**
Limelight Bar and Cafe LLC....E....916 446-2208
1014 Alhambra Blvd Sacramento (95816) **(P-15217)**
Limitless Kitchen and Bath Inc....F....925 238-0046
1201 Auto Center Dr Antioch (94509) **(P-3316)**
Lin Engineering Inc....C....408 919-0200
16245 Vineyard Blvd Morgan Hill (95037) **(P-5663)**
Lin Frank Distillers....E....707 437-1092
2455 Huntington Dr Fairfield (94533) **(P-2775)**
Lin-Zhi International Inc....E....408 970-8811
2945 Oakmead Village Ct Santa Clara (95051) **(P-8787)**
Linardos Enterprises Inc....D....415 644-0827
75 Broadway San Francisco (94111) **(P-19561)**
Lincare Inc....D....559 435-6379
7545 N Del Mar Ave # 102 Fresno (93711) **(P-16909)**
Lincoln (PA)....C....**510 273-4700**
1266 14th St Oakland (94607) **(P-17035)**
Lincoln Aquatics, Concord *Also called Scp Distributors LLC* **(P-9162)**
Lincoln Brdcstg A Cal Ltd Prtn (PA)....D....**415 508-1056**
100 Valley Dr Brisbane (94005) **(P-8053)**
Lincoln Glen Manor LLC....C....408 267-1492
2671 Plummer Ave Ste A San Jose (95125) **(P-18139)**
Lincoln Glen Skilled Nursing, San Jose *Also called Lincoln Glen Manor LLC* **(P-18139)**
Lincoln Hills Golf Club....E....916 543-9200
1005 Sun City Ln Lincoln (95648) **(P-15008)**
Lincoln Medical Offices, Lincoln *Also called Kaiser Foundation Hospitals* **(P-15460)**

Lind Marine Inc (PA)....E....**707 762-7251**
100 E D St Petaluma (94952) **(P-2347)**
Linda Mar Care Center, Pacifica *Also called Pacifica Linda Mar Inc* **(P-16090)**
Linda Terra Farms (PA)....C....**559 867-3473**
5494 W Mount Whitney Ave Riverdale (93656) **(P-204)**
Linde Gas & Equipment Inc....E....800 225-8247
203 Golden State Blvd Turlock (95380) **(P-3772)**
Linde Inc....C....510 451-4100
901 Embarcadero Oakland (94606) **(P-3773)**
Linde Inc....E....510 223-9593
2995 Atlas Rd San Pablo (94806) **(P-3774)**
Lindeburg & Co....E....650 592-6275
758 Industrial Rd San Carlos (94070) **(P-7209)**
Lindeburg Jewelers, San Carlos *Also called Lindeburg & Co* **(P-7209)**
Linden Lab, San Francisco *Also called Linden Research Inc* **(P-12576)**
Linden Nut, Stockton *Also called Pearl Crop Inc* **(P-301)**
Linden Nut, Linden *Also called Pearl Crop Inc* **(P-2932)**
Linden Research Inc....B....415 243-9000
945 Battery St San Francisco (94111) **(P-12576)**
Linden Steel & Cnstr Inc....E....209 239-2160
17863 Ideal Pkwy Manteca (95336) **(P-568)**
Linden Unified School District....D....209 946-0707
100 N Jack Tone Rd Stockton (95215) **(P-19704)**
Lindquist LLP (PA)....D....**925 277-9100**
5000 Executive Pkwy # 400 San Ramon (94583) **(P-18965)**
Lindquist Von Husen & Joyce....E....415 957-9999
301 Howard St Ste 850 San Francisco (94105) **(P-18966)**
Lindsay Wildlife Museum....D....925 935-1978
1931 1st Ave Walnut Creek (94597) **(P-18274)**
Lindstrom Co....E....650 343-4542
1121 Bayswater Ave San Mateo (94401) **(P-1306)**
Line2 Inc....E....415 223-5811
535 Mission St Fl 14 San Francisco (94105) **(P-19910)**
Lineage Logistics Holdings LLC....D....209 942-2323
2323 Port Road A Stockton (95203) **(P-7679)**
Linear Integrated Systems Inc....E....510 490-9160
4042 Clipper Ct Fremont (94538) **(P-6179)**
Linear Technology LLC (HQ)....A....**408 432-1900**
1630 Mccarthy Blvd Milpitas (95035) **(P-6180)**
Linkedin Corporation (HQ)....A....**650 687-3600**
1000 W Maude Ave Sunnyvale (94085) **(P-13798)**
Linkenhmer LLT Cpas Advsors LL....E....707 546-0272
187 Concourse Blvd Santa Rosa (95403) **(P-18967)**
Linkus Enterprises LLC....C....559 256-6600
5595 W San Madele Ave Fresno (93722) **(P-1114)**
Linkus Enterprises LLC (PA)....A....**530 229-9197**
18631 Lloyd Ln Anderson (96007) **(P-1115)**
Linoleum Sales Co Inc (PA)....C....**510 652-1032**
1000 W Grand Ave Oakland (94607) **(P-4361)**
Linqia Inc....D....415 913-7179
965 Mission St San Francisco (94103) **(P-19562)**
Linux Foundation Japan LLC (PA)....C....**415 723-9709**
548 Market St Pmb 57274 San Francisco (94104) **(P-18438)**
Linwood Nursery, La Grange *Also called Green Tree Nursery* **(P-9633)**
Lion Brothers Farms-Newstone, Madera *Also called Lion Raisins Inc* **(P-179)**
Lion Packing Co, Selma *Also called Lion Raisins Inc* **(P-2261)**
Lion Raisins Inc (PA)....C....**559 834-6677**
9500 S De Wolf Ave Selma (93662) **(P-2261)**
Lion Raisins Inc....C....559 662-8686
12555 Road 9 Madera (93637) **(P-179)**
Lion Trading Company LLC (PA)....D....**408 946-0888**
1838 N Milpitas Blvd Milpitas (95035) **(P-8515)**
Lionakis (PA)....C....**916 558-1901**
1919 19th St Sacramento (95811) **(P-18895)**
Lionsgate Ht & Conference Ctr....D....916 643-6222
3410 Westover St McClellan (95652) **(P-11262)**
Lipman Company Inc....E....510 796-4676
3340 Walnut Ave Ste 290 Fremont (94538) **(P-10309)**
Lipman Insur Admnistrators Inc (PA)....D....**510 796-4676**
39420 Liberty St Ste 260 Fremont (94538) **(P-10216)**
Liquid Robotics Inc (HQ)....D....**408 636-4200**
1329 Moffett Park Dr Sunnyvale (94089) **(P-6586)**
Lisac Construction, Campbell *Also called Kerrock Countertops Inc* **(P-3279)**
List Biological Labs Inc....E....408 866-6363
540 Division St Campbell (95008) **(P-4053)**
List Labs, Campbell *Also called List Biological Labs Inc* **(P-4053)**
Lita & Ava Inc....E....408 241-3844
1250 S Winchester Blvd San Jose (95128) **(P-16910)**
Lite-On Inc (HQ)....E....**408 946-4873**
720 S Hillview Dr Milpitas (95035) **(P-8929)**
Lite-On Technology Intl Inc (HQ)....D....**408 945-0222**
720 S Hillview Dr Milpitas (95035) **(P-5392)**
Lite-On Trading Usa Inc (PA)....E....**408 946-4873**
720 S Hillview Dr Milpitas (95035) **(P-8721)**
Lite-On U S A, Milpitas *Also called Lite-On Inc* **(P-8929)**
Lithia Ford Mzda Suzuki Fresno, Fresno *Also called Lithia Motors Inc* **(P-14492)**
Lithia Mazda of Fresno....E....559 256-0700
5200 N Blackstone Ave Fresno (93710) **(P-14576)**
Lithia Motors Inc....C....559 435-8400
195 E Auto Center Dr Fresno (93710) **(P-14492)**
Lithia of Walnut Creek Inc....E....925 937-6900
2646 N Main St Walnut Creek (94597) **(P-14664)**
Lithos Energy Inc....E....415 944-5482
1281 Andersen Dr Ste A San Rafael (94901) **(P-3674)**
Lithotype Company Inc (PA)....D....**650 871-1750**
333 Point San Bruno Blvd South San Francisco (94080) **(P-3675)**
Litmus Automation Inc....E....765 418-7405
2107 N 1st St Ste 440 San Jose (95131) **(P-8722)**

ALPHABETIC

Employee Codes: A=Over 500 employees, B=251-500
C=101-250, D=51-100, E=20-50 F=10-19
2022 Northern California Business
Directory and Buyers Guide

1009

Little Blssom Mntssori Schl In...E...916 515-0550
2075 Arena Blvd Sacramento (95834) ***(P-17965)***
Little Giant Bldg Maint Inc (PA)...**D...415 508-0282**
1485 Bay Shore Blvd # 117 San Francisco (94124) ***(P-11967)***
Little Giant Bldg Maint Inc...C...415 508-0282
15 Brooks Pl Pacifica (94044) ***(P-11968)***
Little Passports Inc...E...415 874-9577
27 Maiden Ln Fl 4 San Francisco (94108) ***(P-7179)***
Little River Inn Inc...C...707 937-5942
7901 N Highway 1 Little River (95456) ***(P-11263)***
Little River Inn and Golf Crse, Little River *Also called Little River Inn Inc* ***(P-11263)***
Little Ssters of The Poor Okla...D...415 751-6510
300 Lake St San Francisco (94118) ***(P-18140)***
Littler Mendelson PC (PA)...**B...415 433-1940**
333 Bush St Fl 34 San Francisco (94104) ***(P-17318)***
Littlethings Inc...D...917 364-9277
642 Harrison St Fl 3 San Francisco (94107) ***(P-13931)***
Live Action General Engrg Inc...E...559 564-3444
2972 Larkin Ave Clovis (93612) ***(P-1307)***
Live Fit Gym Inc (PA)...**D...415 525-4364**
301 Fell St San Francisco (94102) ***(P-14959)***
Live Gamer, Santa Clara *Also called Emergent Payments Inc* ***(P-12421)***
Live Journal Inc...E...415 230-3600
6363 Skyline Blvd Oakland (94611) ***(P-3454)***
Live Oak Adult Day Services...E...408 971-9363
1147 Minnesota Ave San Jose (95125) ***(P-17637)***
Live2kite LLC (PA)...**E...415 924-9463**
44 Industrial Way Greenbrae (94904) ***(P-7180)***
Liveaction Inc (PA)...**E...415 837-3303**
960 San Antonio Rd # 200 Palo Alto (94303) ***(P-13278)***
Liveleaf Inc (PA)...**E...650 722-2984**
1160 Industrial Rd Ste 11 San Carlos (94070) ***(P-19083)***
Liveleaf Bioscience, San Carlos *Also called Liveleaf Inc* ***(P-19083)***
Liveramp Holdings Inc (PA)...**B...866 352-3267**
225 Bush St Ste 1700 San Francisco (94104) ***(P-13724)***
Livermore Amdor Vly Trnst Auth...E...925 455-7555
1362 Rutan Dr Ste 100 Livermore (94551) ***(P-7339)***
Livermore Area Rcration Pk Dst (PA)...**B...925 373-5700**
4444 East Ave Livermore (94550) ***(P-15218)***
Livermore Casino, Livermore *Also called Sidjon Corporation* ***(P-11476)***
Livermore Pediatrics...E...925 455-5050
1171 Murrieta Blvd Livermore (94550) ***(P-15506)***
Livermore Pleasanton Fire Dept, Pleasanton *Also called City of Pleasanton* ***(P-19743)***
Livermore Snior Lving Assoc LP...E...925 371-2300
900 E Stanley Blvd # 38 Livermore (94550) ***(P-10448)***
Livermore Software Tech LLC (HQ)...**D...925 449-2500**
7374 Las Positas Rd Livermore (94551) ***(P-12577)***
Livermore VA Medical Center, Livermore *Also called Veterans Health Administration* ***(P-15803)***
Livermore Valley Tennis Club...D...925 443-7700
2000 Arroyo Rd Livermore (94550) ***(P-14960)***
Livevox Inc (PA)...**C...415 671-6000**
655 Montgomery St # 1000 San Francisco (94111) ***(P-19812)***
Liveworld Inc (PA)...**D...800 301-9507**
2105 S Bascom Ave Ste 159 Campbell (95008) ***(P-7969)***
Living Centers, Vallejo *Also called Empres Financial Services LLC* ***(P-15986)***
Livingston Community Health (PA)...**D...209 394-7913**
600 B St Bldg A Livingston (95334) ***(P-15507)***
Livingston Farmers Association...E...209 394-7941
11019 Eucalyptus Ave Livingston (95334) ***(P-9415)***
LIVINGSTON HEALTH CENTER, Livingston *Also called Livingston Community Health* ***(P-15507)***
Livingstons Concrete Svc Inc (PA)...**E...916 334-4313**
5416 Roseville Rd North Highlands (95660) ***(P-4493)***
Livingstons Concrete Svc Inc...E...916 334-4313
5416 Roseville Rd North Highlands (95660) ***(P-4494)***
Livingstons Concrete Svc Inc...E...916 334-4313
2915 Lesvos Ct Lincoln (95648) ***(P-4495)***
Livongo Health Inc (HQ)...**E...866 435-5643**
150 W Evelyn Ave Ste 150 # 150 Mountain View (94041) ***(P-16765)***
Lixit Corporation (PA)...**C...800 358-8254**
100 Coombs St NAPA (94559) ***(P-7296)***
Liz Palacios Designs Ltd...F...628 444-3339
1 Stanton Way Mill Valley (94941) ***(P-7210)***
LJ Walch Co Inc...D...925 449-9252
6600 Preston Ave Livermore (94551) ***(P-9151)***
LL Sunnyvale LP...E...408 733-1212
748 N Mathilda Ave Sunnyvale (94085) ***(P-11264)***
Llano Seco Rancho, Chico *Also called Parrott Investment Company Inc* ***(P-185)***
LLC Baker Cummins...D...925 732-9338
580 Garcia Ave Pittsburg (94565) ***(P-4088)***
LLC Lyons Magnus (PA)...**B...559 268-5966**
3158 E Hamilton Ave Fresno (93702) ***(P-2222)***
LLC Lyons Magnus...F...559 268-5966
1636 S 2nd St Fresno (93702) ***(P-2223)***
LLC Merritt West...F...209 334-6674
709 N Sacramento St Lodi (95240) ***(P-3139)***
LLC Noble Rider (PA)...**D...209 566-7800**
4300 Spyres Way Modesto (95356) ***(P-9247)***
Lloyds Custom Woodwork Inc...E...925 680-6600
1012 Shary Cir Concord (94518) ***(P-3140)***
LLP Moss Adams...D...916 503-8100
2882 Prospect Park Dr # 300 Rancho Cordova (95670) ***(P-18968)***
LLP Moss Adams...D...209 955-6100
3121 W March Ln Ste 100 Stockton (95219) ***(P-18969)***
LLP Moss Adams...D...415 956-1500
101 2nd St Ste 900 San Francisco (94105) ***(P-18970)***
LLP Moss Adams...D...408 369-2400
635 Campbell Tech Pkwy Campbell (95008) ***(P-18971)***
LLP Moss Adams...D...707 527-0800
3558 Round Barn Blvd # 300 Santa Rosa (95403) ***(P-18972)***
LMC West Inc...E...209 869-0144
5300 Claus Rd Riverbank (95367) ***(P-9076)***
LMI, Windsor *Also called Luthiers Mercantile Intl Inc* ***(P-3270)***
LMI, Lodi *Also called Larry Mthvin Installations Inc* ***(P-4390)***
LN Curtis and Sons (PA)...**D...510 839-5111**
185 Lennon Ln 110 Walnut Creek (94598) ***(P-9145)***
Loandepotcom LLC...A...209 846-6400
1020 15th St Ste 20 Modesto (95354) ***(P-9913)***
Loanpal LLC (PA)...**B...916 290-9999**
8781 Sierra College Blvd Roseville (95661) ***(P-9914)***
Loard's Ice Cream and Candies, San Leandro *Also called Loco Ventures Inc* ***(P-2177)***
Loayzas Ldscpg Pools Spas Inc...E...408 297-5555
2096 Stone Ave Ste 1 San Jose (95125) ***(P-480)***
Lobo Services Ltd...E...916 660-9909
3298 Swetzer Rd Loomis (95650) ***(P-755)***
Lobob Laboratories Inc...F...408 324-0381
1440 Atteberry Ln San Jose (95131) ***(P-3941)***
Loc-Aid Technologies Inc (PA)...**E...415 666-2370**
101 Clay St San Francisco (94111) ***(P-12578)***
Locaid, San Francisco *Also called Loc-Aid Technologies Inc* ***(P-12578)***
Local 250 Health Care Wkrs Un, Oakland *Also called Health Care Workers Union* ***(P-10392)***
Localmind Corp...A...858 382-4809
300 Brannan St Ste 201 San Francisco (94107) ***(P-12579)***
Location Services LLC (PA)...**D...800 588-0097**
2365 Iron Point Rd # 160 Folsom (95630) ***(P-7887)***
Lock-N-Stitch Inc...E...209 632-2345
1015 S Soderquist Rd Turlock (95380) ***(P-5561)***
Lockheed Martin (HQ)...**D...408 834-9741**
1111 Lockheed Martin Way Sunnyvale (94089) ***(P-6613)***
Lockheed Martin Corporation...B...408 756-3008
2655 S Macarthur Dr Tracy (95376) ***(P-6614)***
Lockheed Martin Corporation...B...408 742-5219
1374 Holland Ct San Jose (95118) ***(P-6615)***
Lockwood Seed & Grain, Willows *Also called A L Gilbert Company* ***(P-2337)***
Loco Ventures Inc...E...510 351-0405
2000 Wayne Ave San Leandro (94577) ***(P-2177)***
Locust Home, Manteca *Also called Heritage Estates Inc* ***(P-18130)***
Loda Mem Hosp Occpational Hlth, Lodi *Also called Lodi Memorial Hosp Assn Inc* ***(P-16426)***
Lodge 539 - Newark, Newark *Also called Moose International Inc* ***(P-18441)***
Lodge At The Bear Valley Inc...E...209 753-2325
3 Bear Valley Rd Bear Valley (95223) ***(P-11265)***
Lodge At Tiburon, Belvedere Tiburon *Also called 1651 Tiburon Hotel LLC* ***(P-10901)***
Lodge At Tiburon, The, Belvedere Tiburon *Also called Tiburon Hotel LLC* ***(P-11533)***
Lodgeworks LP...D...707 690-9800
1230 1st St NAPA (94559) ***(P-11266)***
Lodi Farming Inc...E...209 948-4022
11292 N Alpine Rd Stockton (95212) ***(P-64)***
Lodi Iron Works Inc (PA)...**E...209 368-5395**
820 S Sacramento St Lodi (95240) ***(P-4548)***
Lodi Mail Express, Lodi *Also called Lodi News Sentinel* ***(P-3455)***
Lodi Memorial Hosp Assn Inc...D...209 339-7441
975 S Fairmont Ave Ste 8 Lodi (95240) ***(P-16426)***
Lodi Memorial Hosp Assn Inc (HQ)...**A...209 334-3411**
975 S Fairmont Ave Lodi (95240) ***(P-16427)***
Lodi Memorial Hosp Assn Inc...D...209 339-7583
1200 W Vine St Lodi (95240) ***(P-16428)***
Lodi Memorial Hosp Assn Inc...D...209 274-2183
395 Preston Ave Ione (95640) ***(P-16429)***
Lodi Memorial Hosp Assn Inc...E...209 333-3100
800 S Lower Sacramento Rd Lodi (95242) ***(P-15508)***
Lodi News Sentinel...E...209 369-2761
125 N Church St Lodi (95240) ***(P-3455)***
Lodi Nut Company Inc...E...209 334-2081
1230 S Fairmont Ave Lodi (95240) ***(P-9509)***
Lodi Regional Hlth Systems Inc (PA)...**D...800 323-3360**
975 S Fairmont Ave Lodi (95240) ***(P-16430)***
Lodi Regional Hlth Systems Inc...C...209 948-0808
10200 Trinity Pkwy # 102 Stockton (95219) ***(P-16431)***
Lodi Unified School District...D...209 331-7127
8282 Le Mans Ave Stockton (95210) ***(P-17966)***
Lodi Unified School District...E...209 331-7169
820 S Cuff Ave Lodi (95240) ***(P-7440)***
Loews Regency San Francisco, San Francisco *Also called San Francisco Hotel Group LLC* ***(P-11434)***
Logans Gap B Member LLC (HQ)...**D...415 283-4000**
1088 Sansome St San Francisco (94111) ***(P-8214)***
Logicbio Therapeutics Inc...F...415 710-8265
815 Perseus Ln Foster City (94404) ***(P-3942)***
Logicool Inc...E...408 907-1344
1825 De La Cruz Blvd # 201 Santa Clara (95050) ***(P-13279)***
Logictier Inc...C...650 235-6600
7 41st Ave 76 San Mateo (94403) ***(P-13932)***
Logigear Corporation (PA)...**A...650 572-1400**
1730 S Amphlett Blvd San Mateo (94402) ***(P-12580)***
Logik Systems Inc (PA)...**D...844 363-3347**
111 Sutter St San Francisco (94104) ***(P-13799)***
Logikcull, San Francisco *Also called Logik Systems Inc* ***(P-13799)***
Loginext Solutions Inc...D...339 244-0380
5002 Spring Crest Ter Fremont (94536) ***(P-13280)***
Logistics, Fresno *Also called Service Express Inc* ***(P-3598)***
Logitech Inc (HQ)...**B...510 795-8500**
7700 Gateway Blvd Newark (94560) ***(P-5393)***
Logitech Latin America Inc...F...510 795-8500
7700 Gateway Blvd Newark (94560) ***(P-5394)***
Logitech Streaming Media Inc...D...510 795-8500
7600 Gateway Blvd Newark (94560) ***(P-5395)***

ALPHABETIC SECTION

Lowes Home Centers LLC

Lohika Systems Inc ....D....650 636-6993
1825 S Grant St Ste 400 San Mateo (94402) *(P-12581)*

Lok Redwood Empire Prpts Inc ....D....707 584-8280
5100 Montero Way Petaluma (94954) *(P-11267)*

Loma Vista Medical Inc ....E....650 490-4747
863a Mitten Rd Ste 100a Burlingame (94010) *(P-6997)*

Lombardi Loper & Conant LLP ....E....510 433-2600
2030 Franklin St Fl 7th Oakland (94612) *(P-17319)*

Lombardo Diamnd Core Drlg Inc ....D....408 727-7922
2225 De La Cruz Blvd Santa Clara (95050) *(P-1888)*

Lomeli's Gardens, Lockeford *Also called Lomelis Statuary Inc (P-4536)*

Lomelis Statuary Inc (PA) ....**E....209 367-1131**
11921 E Brandt Rd Lockeford (95237) *(P-4536)*

Lone Star Landscape Inc ....E....408 682-0100
1910 E San Martin Ave San Martin (95046) *(P-481)*

Lone Tree Cnvalescent Hosp Inc ....C....925 754-0470
4001 Lone Tree Way Antioch (94509) *(P-16038)*

LONE TREE GOLF COURSE, Antioch *Also called Antioch Public Golf Corp (P-14987)*

Long & Levit LLP ....D....415 397-2222
465 California St Ste 500 San Francisco (94104) *(P-17320)*

Long Meadow Ranch Partners LP ....E....707 963-4555
738 Main St Saint Helena (94574) *(P-11268)*

Long Valley Health Center ....E....707 984-6131
50 Branscomb Rd Laytonville (95454) *(P-15509)*

Longevity Global Inc ....F....877 566-4462
23591 Foley St Hayward (94545) *(P-5104)*

Longs Drug Stores Cal Inc ....E....530 823-0922
388 Elm Ave Auburn (95603) *(P-14157)*

Longs Drug Stores Cal Inc ....E....925 676-4700
4424 Treat Blvd Concord (94521) *(P-14158)*

Longs Drug Stores Cal Inc ....E....530 272-6611
1005 Sutton Way Grass Valley (95945) *(P-14159)*

Longs Drug Stores Cal Inc ....E....916 408-0209
63 Lincoln Blvd Lincoln (95648) *(P-14160)*

Longs Drug Stores Cal Inc ....E....925 754-4600
2511 Somersville Rd Antioch (94509) *(P-14161)*

Longs Drug Stores Cal Inc ....D....650 873-9363
851 Cherry Ave Ste 10 San Bruno (94066) *(P-14162)*

Longs Drug Stores Cal Inc ....E....559 897-0116
929 Sierra St Kingsburg (93631) *(P-14163)*

Longs Drug Stores Cal Inc ....E....916 334-7170
5333 Elkhorn Blvd Sacramento (95842) *(P-14164)*

Longs Drug Stores Cal Inc ....D....916 391-1200
7465 Rush Rver Dr Ste 500 Sacramento (95831) *(P-14165)*

Longs Drug Stores Cal Inc ....E....916 624-8288
4785 Granite Dr Rocklin (95677) *(P-14166)*

Longs Drug Stores Cal Inc ....E....925 439-7288
230 Atlantic Ave Pittsburg (94565) *(P-14167)*

Longs Drug Stores Cal Inc ....E....925 370-8075
560 Center Ave Martinez (94553) *(P-14168)*

Longs Drug Stores Cal Inc ....E....530 885-8783
2140 Grass Valley Hwy Auburn (95603) *(P-14169)*

Longs Drug Stores Cal Inc ....E....925 284-7177
3625 Mt Diablo Blvd Lafayette (94549) *(P-14170)*

Longs Drug Stores Cal Inc ....E....916 989-2212
8861 Greenback Ln Orangevale (95662) *(P-14171)*

Longs Drug Stores Cal Inc ....E....916 783-1350
5090 Foothills Blvd Roseville (95747) *(P-14172)*

Longs Drug Stores Cal LLC ....C....707 938-4734
201 W Napa St Ste 35 Sonoma (95476) *(P-14173)*

Longs Drug Stores Cal LLC ....C....650 994-0752
348 Gellert Blvd Daly City (94015) *(P-14174)*

Longs Drug Stores Cal LLC ....C....209 723-3292
300 Merced Mall Merced (95348) *(P-14175)*

Longs Drug Stores Cal LLC ....C....916 726-4433
6197 Sunrise Blvd Citrus Heights (95610) *(P-14176)*

Longs Drug Stores Cal LLC ....C....916 684-6811
5040 Laguna Blvd Elk Grove (95758) *(P-14177)*

Longs Drug Stores Cal LLC ....C....925 938-7616
738 Bancroft Rd Walnut Creek (94598) *(P-14178)*

Longs Drug Stores Cal LLC ....C....209 522-1047
2900 Standiford Ave Modesto (95350) *(P-14179)*

Longs Drug Stores Cal LLC ....C....925 672-0547
5408 Ygnacio Valley Rd Concord (94521) *(P-14180)*

Longs Drug Stores Cal LLC ....C....209 895-7839
2400 Keystone Pcf Pkwy Patterson (95363) *(P-7693)*

Longshrmens Wrhsmens Un Lcl 54, Stockton *Also called Interntnal Lngshrmens Wrhsmen (P-18366)*

Lonza Biologics Inc ....D....510 731-3500
1978 W Winton Ave Hayward (94545) *(P-3943)*

Looker Data Sciences Inc (HQ) ....**D....831 244-0340**
101 Church St Fl 4 Santa Cruz (95060) *(P-12582)*

Lookout Inc (PA) ....**B....650 241-2358**
275 Battery St Ste 200 San Francisco (94111) *(P-13627)*

Loomis Bsin Equine Med Ctr Inc ....E....916 652-7645
2973 Penryn Rd Penryn (95663) *(P-327)*

Loomis Bsin Vtrnary Clinic Inc ....E....916 652-5816
3901 Sierra College Blvd Loomis (95650) *(P-328)*

Loon LLC ....C....310 625-3449
100 Mayfield Ave Mountain View (94043) *(P-14323)*

Loop, Mountain View *Also called Samsung Pay Inc (P-14394)*

Loopnet Inc (HQ) ....**C....415 243-4200**
101 California St # 4300 San Francisco (94111) *(P-10602)*

Loopup, San Francisco *Also called Ring2 Communications LLC (P-8084)*

Lopezgarcia Group Inc (HQ) ....**C....415 796-8100**
300 California St San Francisco (94104) *(P-18754)*

Lor-Van Manufacturing LLC ....E....408 980-1045
3307 Edward Ave Santa Clara (95054) *(P-4778)*

Lora H Costa DDS Inc (PA) ....**E....408 774-1200**
1286 Kifer Rd Ste 110 Sunnyvale (94086) *(P-15846)*

Loral Landscaping ....E....650 340-6940
704 S Amphlett Blvd San Mateo (94402) *(P-482)*

Lore Io Inc ....E....415 691-9680
557 Croyden Ct Sunnyvale (94087) *(P-13281)*

Lorin Robinson Center, Redding *Also called Shascade Community Svcs Inc (P-17737)*

Loring Smart Roast Inc ....D....707 526-7215
3200 Dutton Ave Ste 413 Santa Rosa (95407) *(P-9077)*

Loring Ward, San Jose *Also called Bam Advisor Services LLC (P-10034)*

Loring Ward, San Jose *Also called Buckingham Strategic Partners (P-19309)*

Lorom West, Fremont *Also called Cable Connection Inc (P-5711)*

Los Altos Golf and Country CLB ....D....650 947-3100
1560 Country Club Dr Los Altos (94024) *(P-15105)*

Los Altos Hotel Associates LLC ....E....650 559-7890
4460 El Camino Real Los Altos (94022) *(P-11269)*

Los Altos Sb-Cute Rhbltion Ct, Los Altos *Also called Covenant Care California LLC (P-15972)*

Los Altos Town Crier, Los Altos *Also called Select Communications Inc (P-3514)*

Los Bagels Inc (PA) ....**E....707 822-3150**
1061 I St Ste 101 Arcata (95521) *(P-2391)*

Los Banos Abattoir Co ....E....209 826-2212
1312 W Pacheco Blvd Los Banos (93635) *(P-2100)*

Los Banos Nursing and Rehab, Los Banos *Also called Para & Palli Inc (P-16092)*

Los Banos Racquet Club, Los Banos *Also called Turlock Hlth & Fitnes Ctr Inc (P-14982)*

Los Banos Rock and Ready Mix, Los Banos *Also called Azusa Rock LLC (P-4459)*

Los Banos Veterinary Clinic ....E....209 826-5860
1900 E Pacheco Blvd Los Banos (93635) *(P-317)*

Los Californias Winery, Fresno *Also called Full Circle Brewing Co Ltd LLC (P-2479)*

Los Gatos Dog & Cat Hospital ....E....408 354-6474
17480 Shelburne Way Los Gatos (95030) *(P-329)*

Los Gatos Imaging Center Ltd ....D....408 374-8897
800 Pollard Rd Ste B101 Los Gatos (95032) *(P-15510)*

Los Gatos Meadows, Los Gatos *Also called Covia Communities (P-18088)*

Los Gatos Saratoga Dept of Com ....C....408 354-8700
208 E Main St Los Gatos (95030) *(P-17967)*

Los Gatos Swim and Racquet CLB ....D....408 356-2136
14700 Oka Rd Los Gatos (95032) *(P-14961)*

Los Gatos Tomato Products LLC (PA) ....**F....559 945-2700**
7041 N Van Ness Blvd Fresno (93711) *(P-2224)*

Los Olivos Wns Med Group Inc (PA) ....**E....408 356-0431**
15151 National Ave Ste 1 Los Gatos (95032) *(P-15511)*

Los Robles Proffessional Group, Los Gatos *Also called Lrimg Inc (P-15512)*

Loss Prevention Group Inc ....E....510 836-6011
524 7th St Oakland (94607) *(P-14074)*

Lost Coast Brewery & Cafe, Eureka *Also called Table Bluff Brewing Inc (P-2496)*

Lotus Bed Solutions LLC ....F....415 756-5099
4600 Greenholme Dr Apt 3 Sacramento (95842) *(P-3281)*

Lotus Hospitality Inc ....E....650 873-3550
275 S Airport Blvd South San Francisco (94080) *(P-11270)*

Lotus Hotels Inc ....D....510 965-1900
2525 San Pablo Dam Rd San Pablo (94806) *(P-11271)*

Lotus Hotels - Union City LLC ....E....510 475-0600
31140 Alvarado Niles Rd Union City (94587) *(P-11272)*

Lotusflare Inc ....E....626 695-5634
2880 Lakeside Dr Ste 331 Santa Clara (95054) *(P-13282)*

Louie Foods International ....E....559 264-2745
471 S Teilman Ave Fresno (93706) *(P-2917)*

Louis M. Martini Winery, Saint Helena *Also called E & J Gallo Winery (P-2559)*

Loupe, San Francisco *Also called Plangrid Inc (P-13372)*

Lovazzano Mechanical Inc ....D....650 367-6216
189 Constitution Dr Menlo Park (94025) *(P-1308)*

Loving Campos Associates (PA) ....**E....925 944-1626**
245 Ygnacio Valley Rd # 200 Walnut Creek (94596) *(P-18896)*

Low Ball & Lynch A Prof Corp (PA) ....**D....415 981-6630**
505 Montgomery St Fl 7 San Francisco (94111) *(P-17321)*

Lowe Enterprises ....E....530 581-6628
400 Squaw Creek Rd Olympic Valley (96146) *(P-11273)*

Lowery-Pena Cnstr Co Inc ....E....209 328-2050
1509 W Yosemite Ave A1 Manteca (95337) *(P-756)*

Lowes Home Centers LLC ....C....559 436-6266
7651 N Blackstone Ave Fresno (93720) *(P-8556)*

Lowes Home Centers LLC ....C....209 545-7676
3801 Plndale Ave Side Frn Side Frnt Modesto (95356) *(P-8557)*

Lowes Home Centers LLC ....C....415 486-8611
491 Bay Shore Blvd San Francisco (94124) *(P-8558)*

Lowes Home Centers LLC ....C....916 984-7979
800 E Bidwell St Folsom (95630) *(P-8559)*

Lowes Home Centers LLC ....C....408 518-4165
775 Ridder Park Dr San Jose (95131) *(P-8560)*

Lowes Home Centers LLC ....C....707 207-2070
3400 N Texas St Fairfield (94533) *(P-8884)*

Lowes Home Centers LLC ....C....707 455-4400
1751 E Monte Vista Ave Vacaville (95688) *(P-8561)*

Lowes Home Centers LLC ....C....925 756-0370
1951 Auto Center Dr Antioch (94509) *(P-8562)*

Lowes Home Centers LLC ....C....510 476-0600
32040 Union Lndg Union City (94587) *(P-8563)*

Lowes Home Centers LLC ....C....650 616-7800
1340 El Camino Real San Bruno (94066) *(P-8564)*

Lowes Home Centers LLC ....C....916 771-7111
10201 Fairway Dr Roseville (95678) *(P-8565)*

Lowes Home Centers LLC ....C....925 245-2440
4255 First St Livermore (94551) *(P-8566)*

Lowes Home Centers LLC ....C....916 688-1922
8369 Power Inn Rd Elk Grove (95624) *(P-8567)*

Lowes Home Centers LLC ....C....530 895-5130
2350 Forest Ave Chico (95928) *(P-8568)*

Lowes Home Centers LLC ....C....209 956-7200
3645 E Hammer Ln Stockton (95212) *(P-8569)*

ALPHABETIC

Lowes Home Centers LLC.....C.....408 413-6000
7151 Camino Arroyo Gilroy (95020) ***(P-8570)***
Lowes Home Centers LLC.....C.....916 728-7800
7840 Greenback Ln Citrus Heights (95610) ***(P-8571)***
Lowes Home Centers LLC.....C.....209 385-5000
1750 W Olive Ave Merced (95348) ***(P-8572)***
Lowes Home Centers LLC.....C.....559 322-3000
875 Shaw Ave Clovis (93612) ***(P-8573)***
Lowes Home Centers LLC.....C.....209 339-2600
1389 S Lwer Sacramento Rd Lodi (95242) ***(P-8574)***
Lowes Home Centers LLC.....C.....510 344-4920
43612 Pcf Commons Blvd Fremont (94538) ***(P-8575)***
Lowes Home Centers LLC.....C.....925 779-4560
5503 Lone Tree Way Antioch (94531) ***(P-8576)***
Lowes Home Centers LLC.....C.....209 513-9843
10342 Trinity Pkwy Stockton (95219) ***(P-8577)***
Lowes Home Centers LLC.....C.....707 242-5000
7921 Redwood Dr Cotati (94931) ***(P-8578)***
Lowes Home Centers LLC.....C.....209 223-6140
12071 Industry Blvd Jackson (95642) ***(P-8579)***
Lowes Home Centers LLC.....C.....408 470-1680
811 E Arques Ave Sunnyvale (94085) ***(P-8580)***
Lowes Home Centers LLC.....C.....530 351-0181
1200 E Cypress Ave Redding (96002) ***(P-8581)***
Lowes Home Centers LLC.....C.....530 844-5000
935 Tharp Rd Yuba City (95993) ***(P-8582)***
Lowes Home Centers LLC.....C.....209 656-3020
3303 Entertainment Way Turlock (95380) ***(P-8583)***
Lowes Home Centers LLC.....C.....916 267-2850
3251 Zinfandel Dr Rancho Cordova (95670) ***(P-8584)***
Lowes Home Centers LLC.....C.....925 241-3082
3750 Dublin Blvd Dublin (94568) ***(P-8585)***
Lowes Home Centers LLC.....C.....559 416-4000
2100 W Cleveland Ave Madera (93637) ***(P-8586)***
Lowes Home Centers LLC.....C.....925 566-9000
1935 Arnold Indus Way Concord (94520) ***(P-8587)***
Lowpensky Moulding.....F.....415 822-7422
900 Palou Ave San Francisco (94124) ***(P-3141)***
Loyal3 Holdings Inc.....D.....415 981-0700
150 California St Ste 400 San Francisco (94111) ***(P-14324)***
Loyalty Juggernaut Inc.....F.....650 283-5081
5216 Ashley Way San Jose (95135) ***(P-13283)***
Lozano Car Wash, Mountain View *Also called Lozano Inc* ***(P-14650)***
Lozano Inc.....C.....650 941-0590
2690 W El Camino Real Mountain View (94040) ***(P-14650)***
Lozano Smith LLP.....C.....559 431-5600
7404 N Spalding Ave Fresno (93720) ***(P-17322)***
Lozano Smith A Prof Corp (PA).....**D.....559 431-5600**
7404 N Spalding Ave Fresno (93720) ***(P-17323)***
Lpa Insurance Agency Inc.....D.....916 286-7850
3800 Watt Ave Ste 147 Sacramento (95821) ***(P-13284)***
Lpas Inc.....D.....916 443-0335
2484 Natomas Park Dr # 100 Sacramento (95833) ***(P-18897)***
Lr Leasing Inc.....E.....916 438-0888
5411 Raley Blvd Sacramento (95838) ***(P-7562)***
Lre Silicon Services.....F.....408 262-8725
1235 Torres Ave Milpitas (95035) ***(P-6181)***
Lrg Builder Services Inc.....E.....209 894-7100
26 S 3rd St Ste E Patterson (95363) ***(P-801)***
Lrimg Inc.....D.....408 358-2479
15215 National Ave # 200 Los Gatos (95032) ***(P-15512)***
LSI Corporation (HQ).....**A.....408 433-8000**
1320 Ridder Park Dr San Jose (95131) ***(P-6182)***
LTI Boyd.....A.....800 554-0200
600 S Mcclure Rd Modesto (95357) ***(P-5109)***
LTI Flexible Products Inc.....E.....209 491-4797
5960 Inglewood Dr Ste 115 Pleasanton (94588) ***(P-4202)***
LTI Holdings Inc (PA).....**F.....925 271-8041**
5960 Inglewood Dr Ste 115 Pleasanton (94588) ***(P-3814)***
LTS Rentals LLC (PA).....**E.....209 334-4100**
927 Black Diamond Way Lodi (95240) ***(P-14470)***
Luca International Group LLC (PA).....**F.....510 498-8829**
39650 Liberty St Ste 490 Fremont (94538) ***(P-559)***
Lucas Digital Ltd (HQ).....**B.....415 258-2000**
3155 Kerner Blvd San Rafael (94901) ***(P-14850)***
Lucas Labs, Gilroy *Also called Lucas/Signatone Corporation* ***(P-6766)***
Lucas Learning Ltd.....E.....415 662-1927
5858 Lucas Valley Rd Nicasio (94946) ***(P-12583)***
Lucas/Signatone Corporation (PA).....**E.....408 848-2851**
393 Tomkins Ct Ste J Gilroy (95020) ***(P-6766)***
Lucasfilm Coml Productions, San Francisco *Also called Lucasfilm Ltd* ***(P-14793)***
Lucasfilm Ltd (HQ).....**C.....415 623-1000**
1110 Gorgas Ave Bldg C-Hr San Francisco (94129) ***(P-14793)***
Lucerne Foods Inc.....A.....925 951-4724
5918 Stoneridge Mall Rd Pleasanton (94588) ***(P-2918)***
Lucero Cables Inc.....C.....408 536-0340
193 Stauffer Blvd San Jose (95125) ***(P-6449)***
Lucid Design Group Inc.....D.....510 907-0400
55 Harrison St 200 Oakland (94607) ***(P-13628)***
Lucid Group Inc (PA).....**E.....510 648-3553**
7373 Gateway Blvd Newark (94560) ***(P-6552)***
Lucid Motors, Newark *Also called Lucid Usa Inc* ***(P-6553)***
Lucid Usa Inc (HQ).....**C.....510 648-3553**
7373 Gateway Blvd Newark (94560) ***(P-6553)***
Lucid Vr Inc (PA).....**D.....408 391-0506**
63 Bettencourt Way Milpitas (95035) ***(P-12584)***
Lucidworks Inc (PA).....**B.....415 329-6515**
235 Montgomery St Ste 500 San Francisco (94104) ***(P-13629)***
Lucile Packard Childrens Hosp, Palo Alto *Also called Lucile Slter Pckard Chld Hosp* ***(P-16766)***
Lucile Packard Childrens Hosp.....D.....650 321-2545
730 Welch Rd Ste B Palo Alto (94304) ***(P-16432)***
Lucile Pckard Fndtion For Chld (PA).....**E.....650 497-8365**
400 Hamilton Ave Ste 240 Palo Alto (94301) ***(P-17638)***
Lucile Slter Pckard Chld Hosp (HQ).....**A.....650 497-8000**
725 Welch Rd Palo Alto (94304) ***(P-16766)***
Lucira Health Inc.....D.....510 350-8071
1412 62nd St Emeryville (94608) ***(P-4023)***
Lucky Bear Casino.....E.....530 625-5198
Hwy 96 Hoopa (95546) ***(P-11274)***
Lucky Bear Casino and Bingo, Hoopa *Also called Lucky Bear Casino* ***(P-11274)***
Lucky Chances Inc.....A.....650 758-2237
1700 Hillside Blvd Colma (94014) ***(P-11275)***
Lucky Chances Casino, Colma *Also called Lucky Chances Inc* ***(P-11275)***
Lucky Stores II LLC.....D.....209 830-1977
875 S Tracy Blvd Tracy (95376) ***(P-9229)***
Luhdorff Sclmnini Cnslting Eng.....D.....530 661-0109
500 1st St Woodland (95695) ***(P-18755)***
Luidia Inc.....E.....650 413-7500
591 W Hamilton Ave # 205 Campbell (95008) ***(P-19084)***
Luis A Agurto.....E.....925 238-0744
1555 Yosemite Ave Ste 46 San Francisco (94124) ***(P-11901)***
Lukes Local Inc (PA).....**D.....415 643-4510**
960 Cole St San Francisco (94117) ***(P-2919)***
Luma Health Inc.....E.....415 741-3377
3 E 3rd Ave San Mateo (94401) ***(P-12585)***
Lumasense Technologies Inc (HQ).....**D.....408 727-1600**
888 Tasman Dr 100 Milpitas (95035) ***(P-7111)***
Lumedx Corporation (PA).....**F.....510 419-1000**
555 12th St Ste 2060 Oakland (94607) ***(P-12586)***
Lumen Tech Gvrnment Sltons Inc.....A.....916 781-7772
2240 Douglas Blvd Ste 250 Roseville (95661) ***(P-7970)***
Lumen Technologies Inc.....E.....925 974-0200
1085 Marguerite Ct Lafayette (94549) ***(P-7971)***
Lumenis, Livermore *Also called Rh USA Inc* ***(P-7027)***
Lumenis Be Inc.....C.....408 764-3000
2077 Gateway Pl Ste 300 San Jose (95110) ***(P-6998)***
Lumenis Inc (HQ).....**C.....408 764-3000**
2077 Gateway Pl Ste 300 San Jose (95110) ***(P-6999)***
Lumens Integration Inc.....E.....510 657-8367
4116 Clipper Ct Fremont (94538) ***(P-7154)***
Lumens LLC (HQ).....**E.....916 444-5585**
2020 L St Ste Ll10 Sacramento (95811) ***(P-8866)***
Lumentum Holdings Inc (PA).....**A.....408 546-5483**
1001 Ridder Park Dr San Jose (95131) ***(P-5888)***
Lumentum Inc.....E.....408 546-5483
400 N Mccarthy Blvd Milpitas (95035) ***(P-5889)***
Lumetra Healthcare Solutions.....E.....415 677-2000
300 Montgomery St Ste 639 San Francisco (94104) ***(P-19813)***
Lumewave Inc (HQ).....**C.....916 400-3535**
550 Meridian Ave San Jose (95126) ***(P-1534)***
Lumiata Inc.....E.....916 607-2442
489 S El Camino Real San Mateo (94402) ***(P-19085)***
Lumigrow Inc.....E.....800 514-0487
6550 Vallejo St Ste 200 Emeryville (94608) ***(P-5737)***
Lumileds LLC (HQ).....**E.....408 964-2900**
370 W Trimble Rd San Jose (95131) ***(P-6767)***
Lumin Digital LLC.....D.....727 561-2227
3001 Bishop Dr Ste 110 San Ramon (94583) ***(P-12587)***
Lumina Networks Inc (PA).....**E.....800 430-7321**
2077 Gateway Pl Ste 500 San Jose (95110) ***(P-12588)***
Luminostics Inc.....E.....760 709-2230
446 S Hillview Dr Milpitas (95035) ***(P-7000)***
Luminus Inc (HQ).....**C.....408 708-7000**
1145 Sonora Ct Sunnyvale (94086) ***(P-5745)***
Luminus Devices Inc.....C.....978 528-8000
1145 Sonora Ct Sunnyvale (94086) ***(P-5746)***
Lumity Inc.....D.....844 258-6489
71 E 3rd Ave San Mateo (94401) ***(P-10145)***
Lunar Design Incorporated (HQ).....**E.....415 252-4388**
537 Hamilton Ave Palo Alto (94301) ***(P-14325)***
Lunas Sheet Metal Inc.....F.....408 492-1260
3125 Molinaro St Ste 102 Santa Clara (95054) ***(P-4779)***
Lund Construction Co.....C.....916 344-5800
5302 Roseville Rd North Highlands (95660) ***(P-18756)***
Lundberg Designs, San Francisco *Also called Thomas Lundberg* ***(P-3295)***
Lundberg Family Farms, Richvale *Also called Wehah Farm Inc* ***(P-2330)***
Lundi Inc.....E.....415 735-0101
548 Market St San Francisco (94104) ***(P-13725)***
Lupton Excavation Inc.....D.....916 387-1104
8467 Florin Rd Sacramento (95828) ***(P-1963)***
Lusamerica Foods Inc (PA).....**C.....408 778-7200**
16480 Railroad Ave Morgan Hill (95037) ***(P-9367)***
Lusardi Construction Co.....C.....925 829-1114
6376 Clark Ave Dublin (94568) ***(P-916)***
Lustre-Cal LLC.....D.....206 370-1600
715 S Guild Ave Lodi (95240) ***(P-3740)***
Lustre-Cal Nameplate Corp.....D.....209 370-1600
715 S Guild Ave Lodi (95240) ***(P-3741)***
Luther Burbank Corporation (PA).....**D.....844 446-8201**
520 3rd St Fl 4 Santa Rosa (95401) ***(P-9758)***
Luther Burbank Mem Foundation.....D.....707 546-3600
50 Mark West Springs Rd Santa Rosa (95403) ***(P-14851)***
Luther Burbank Savings (HQ).....**E.....707 578-9216**
500 3rd St Santa Rosa (95401) ***(P-9772)***
Luthiers Mercantile Intl Inc.....F.....707 433-1823
7975 Cameron Dr Ste 1600 Windsor (95492) ***(P-3270)***
Luxer Corporation.....C.....415 390-0123
5040 Dudley Blvd McClellan (95652) ***(P-3307)***
Luxer One, McClellan *Also called Luxer Corporation* ***(P-3307)***

Luxfer-GTM, Berkeley *Also called GTM Technologies LLC (P-4721)*
Luxor Cabs Inc ....E....415 282-4141
531 Bay Shore Blvd San Francisco (94124) *(P-7413)*
Luxshare-Ict Inc ....E....408 957-0535
890 Hillview Ct Ste 200 Milpitas (95035) *(P-7297)*
Lvmh Moet Hnnssy Louis Vuitton, San Francisco *Also called Benefit Cosmetics LLC (P-9224)*
Ly Brothers Corporation (PA) ....C....510 782-2118
1963 Sabre St Hayward (94545) *(P-2392)*
Lydia C Gonzalez ....E....650 299-4707
1400 Veterans Blvd Redwood City (94063) *(P-17639)*
LYELL BIOTECH, South San Francisco *Also called Lyell Immunopharma Inc (P-19086)*
Lyell Immunopharma Inc (PA) ....C....650 695-0677
201 Haskins Way South San Francisco (94080) *(P-19086)*
Lyft Inc (PA) ....A....844 250-2773
185 Berry St Ste 5000 San Francisco (94107) *(P-7386)*
Lyle Company ....D....916 266-7000
3140 Gold Camp Dr Ste 30 Rancho Cordova (95670) *(P-19814)*
Lyles Services Co ....D....559 441-1900
525 W Alluvial Ave Ste C Fresno (93711) *(P-19563)*
Lyman Group Inc (PA) ....E....530 662-5442
201 East St Woodland (95776) *(P-9603)*
Lyncean Technologies Inc ....F....650 320-8300
47633 Westinghouse Dr Fremont (94539) *(P-7092)*
Lynch Gilardi & Grummer LLP ....E....415 397-2800
170 Columbus Ave Fl 5 San Francisco (94133) *(P-17324)*
Lyngso Garden Materials Inc ....E....650 364-1730
345 Shoreway Rd San Carlos (94070) *(P-8629)*
Lynx Enterprises Inc ....D....209 833-3400
724 E Grant Line Rd Ste B Tracy (95304) *(P-4780)*
Lynx Software Technologies Inc (PA) ....D....408 979-3900
855 Embedded Way San Jose (95138) *(P-13285)*
Lyon & Associates Realtors, Sacramento *Also called William L Lyon & Assoc Inc (P-10687)*
Lyon Medical Construction Inc ....E....415 508-1970
100 N Hill Dr Ste 52 Brisbane (94005) *(P-917)*
Lyon Real Estate, Sacramento *Also called William L Lyon & Assoc Inc (P-19426)*
Lyon Realtors, Fair Oaks *Also called William L Lyon & Assoc Inc (P-10688)*
Lyon Realty ....C....916 784-1500
2220 Douglas Blvd Ste 100 Roseville (95661) *(P-10603)*
Lyon Realty ....C....916 481-3840
2580 Fair Oaks Blvd # 20 Sacramento (95825) *(P-10604)*
Lyon Realty ....C....916 787-7700
851 Pleasant Grove Blvd # 150 Roseville (95678) *(P-10605)*
Lyon Realty ....C....916 962-0111
8814 Madison Ave Fair Oaks (95628) *(P-10606)*
Lyon Realty ....C....530 295-4444
4340 Golden Center Dr A Placerville (95667) *(P-10481)*
Lyon Realty ....C....916 939-5300
3900 Park Dr El Dorado Hills (95762) *(P-10607)*
Lyon Realty (PA) ....D....916 574-8800
2280 Del Paso Rd Ste 100 Sacramento (95834) *(P-10608)*
Lyon-Martin Wns Hlth Svcs Inc ....E....415 565-7667
1735 Mission St San Francisco (94103) *(P-15513)*
Lyons Transportation Inc (PA) ....E....559 299-0123
3198 Willow Ave Ste 104 Clovis (93612) *(P-7563)*
Lyra Health Inc ....C....650 477-2991
287 Lorton Ave 2 Burlingame (94010) *(P-15514)*
Lyric Recovery Services Inc ....E....408 219-4681
1210 S Bascom Ave Ste 205 San Jose (95128) *(P-17036)*
Lyrical Foods Inc ....C....510 784-0955
3180 Corporate Pl Hayward (94545) *(P-2920)*
Lyru Engineering Inc ....E....510 357-5951
965 San Leandro Blvd San Leandro (94577) *(P-5562)*
Lystek International Inc ....F....707 419-0084
1014 Chadbourne Rd Fairfield (94534) *(P-7298)*
Lytton Garden II, Palo Alto *Also called Community Housing Inc (P-18079)*
Lytton Rancheria ....A....510 215-7888
13255 San Pablo Ave San Pablo (94806) *(P-11276)*
M & C Restoration Inc ....D....530 273-1957
11229 Mccourtney Rd Grass Valley (95949) *(P-11969)*
M & H Realty Partners LP ....D....415 693-9000
353 Sacramento St Fl 21 San Francisco (94111) *(P-10865)*
M & H Uniforms, Burlingame *Also called Murphy HARtelius/M&h Uniforms (P-9249)*
M & L Precision Machining Inc (PA) ....E....408 436-3955
18665 Madrone Pkwy Morgan Hill (95037) *(P-5563)*
M & M Bakery Products Inc ....D....510 235-0274
1900 Garden Tract Rd Richmond (94801) *(P-2393)*
M & M Electric, Sacramento *Also called May-Han Electric Inc (P-1537)*
M & M Materials, Roseville *Also called Universal Plastics Inc (P-1435)*
M & M Services Inc (PA) ....E....707 838-2597
590 Caletti Ave Windsor (95492) *(P-8339)*
M & W Engineering Inc ....E....530 676-7185
3880 Dividend Dr Ste 100 Shingle Springs (95682) *(P-5564)*
M A D Inc (PA) ....E....209 383-6475
3500 G St Merced (95340) *(P-10609)*
M A I, Salida *Also called Medical Ambassadors Intl (P-18241)*
M Arthur Gensler Jr Assoc Inc ....E....408 885-8100
225 W Santa Clara St # 1 San Jose (95113) *(P-18898)*
M Arthur Gensler Jr Assoc Inc (PA) ....B....415 433-3700
45 Fremont St Ste 1500 San Francisco (94105) *(P-18899)*
M Arthur Gensler Jr Assoc Inc ....C....510 625-7400
2101 Webster St Ste 2000 Oakland (94612) *(P-18900)*
M B, San Jose *Also called Marquez Brothers Intl Inc (P-9277)*
M B I Ready-Mix L L C ....F....530 346-2432
44 Central St Colfax (95713) *(P-4496)*
M B M, Pleasanton *Also called McLane Foodservice Dist Inc (P-9326)*
M C I Manufacturing Inc (PA) ....E....408 456-2700
1020 Rock Ave San Jose (95131) *(P-4781)*
M Calosso & Son ....E....209 466-8994
1947 E Miner Ave Stockton (95205) *(P-9604)*
M Construction & Design Inc ....E....510 651-6981
43126 Osgood Rd Fremont (94539) *(P-1116)*
M D S I, Chowchilla *Also called Madera Disposal Systems Inc (P-8340)*
M E 2, San Jose *Also called Manufctring Engrg Exclnce Inc (P-18761)*
M E Prigmore & Co (PA) ....E....530 223-6672
22922 Huston Ave Twain Harte (95383) *(P-11702)*
M F A Incorporated (PA) ....D....510 547-8444
5530 Moraga Ave Piedmont (94611) *(P-5761)*
M F Maher Inc ....D....707 552-2774
490 Ryder St Vallejo (94590) *(P-1889)*
M H Construction, San Francisco *Also called Huey Construction MGT Co Inc (P-652)*
M I G, Berkeley *Also called Moore Iacofano Goltsman Inc (P-19824)*
M J&C Holding Inc ....E....916 635-9090
11277 Trade Center Dr Rancho Cordova (95742) *(P-8588)*
M M P, Novato *Also called Marin Med Prctice Concepts Inc (P-19365)*
M Neils Engineering Inc ....D....916 923-4400
100 Howe Ave Ste 235n Sacramento (95825) *(P-18757)*
M Nexon Inc ....D....805 448-3351
6121 Hollis St Ste 6 Emeryville (94608) *(P-12589)*
M Nunes Inc ....E....209 722-7943
3990 Thrift Rd Merced (95341) *(P-180)*
M O S Plastics, San Jose *Also called Kennerley-Spratling Inc (P-4295)*
M P A, Ione *Also called Mp Associates Inc (P-4152)*
M Park Inc ....E....559 626-5057
630 W Railroad Ave Orange Cove (93646) *(P-14326)*
M R C, Fremont *Also called Manufacturing Resource Corp (P-14328)*
M Rothrock Properties Inc ....D....530 885-8611
13450 Lincoln Way Auburn (95603) *(P-11277)*
M S, Pleasant Hill *Also called Mark Scott Construction Inc (P-918)*
M S I, Rancho Cordova *Also called Mailing Systems Inc (P-11839)*
M Squared Consulting, San Francisco *Also called Collabrus Inc (P-18946)*
M T C, San Francisco *Also called Metropolitan Trnsp Comm (P-7342)*
M T R, Newark *Also called Membrane Technology & RES Inc (P-19088)*
M Tek Corporation ....E....530 888-9609
169 Borland Ave Auburn (95603) *(P-14761)*
M V E, Modesto *Also called Mve Inc (P-18775)*
M Z R, Redwood City *Also called Hopkins Manor (P-18131)*
M&L Refrigerated Terminal, Stockton *Also called Lineage Logistics Holdings LLC (P-7679)*
M-Pulse Microwave Inc ....E....408 432-1480
576 Charcot Ave San Jose (95131) *(P-6183)*
M-T Metal Fabrications Inc ....E....510 357-5262
536 Lewelling Blvd Ste A San Leandro (94579) *(P-4782)*
M/H Vccp LLC (HQ) ....E....415 255-6363
220 Sansome St Fl 15 San Francisco (94104) *(P-11768)*
M10 Dev LLC (PA) ....C....650 424-8991
750 San Antonio Rd Palo Alto (94303) *(P-11278)*
M10 Dev LLC ....E....650 565-8100
744 San Antonio Rd Palo Alto (94303) *(P-11279)*
M2 Antenna Systems Inc ....F....559 221-2271
4402 N Selland Ave Fresno (93722) *(P-6450)*
M4 Concrete and Drywall Inc (PA) ....D....209 850-9250
2930 Geer Rd Turlock (95382) *(P-1890)*
M4 Concrete and Drywall Inc ....E....209 850-9250
11380 Early Dawn Rd Turlock (95380) *(P-1891)*
MA Steiner Construction Inc ....D....916 988-6300
8854 Greenback Ln Ste 1 Orangevale (95662) *(P-802)*
Maana Inc (PA) ....D....888 956-2262
524 Hamilton Ave Ste 201 Palo Alto (94301) *(P-12590)*
Maas Brothers Inc ....D....925 294-8200
285 S Vasco Rd Livermore (94551) *(P-4937)*
Maas Brothers Powder Coating, Livermore *Also called Maas Brothers Inc (P-4937)*
Mabrey Products Inc ....F....530 895-3799
200 Ryan Ave Chico (95973) *(P-3142)*
Mac Cal Company ....D....408 441-1435
2520 Zanker Rd San Jose (95131) *(P-4783)*
Mac Cal Manufacturing, San Jose *Also called Mac Cal Company (P-4783)*
Mac Kenzie Warehouse, San Francisco *Also called S F Auto Parts Whse Inc (P-8462)*
Mac Publishing LLC (HQ) ....E....415 243-0505
501 2nd St Ste 600 San Francisco (94107) *(P-3505)*
Mac Thin Films Inc ....E....707 791-1656
2721 Giffen Ave Santa Rosa (95407) *(P-4391)*
Macarthur Trnst Cmnty Prtners ....D....415 989-1111
345 Spear St Ste 700 San Francisco (94105) *(P-664)*
Macaulay Brown Inc ....A....937 426-3421
2933 Bunker Hill Ln # 220 Santa Clara (95054) *(P-18758)*
Macb, Santa Clara *Also called Macaulay Brown Inc (P-18758)*
Maccallum House Restaurant ....E....707 937-0289
45020 Albion St Mendocino (95460) *(P-11280)*
Macchia Inc ....F....209 333-2600
7099 E Peltier Rd Acampo (95220) *(P-2652)*
Maccorkle Insurance Service, Burlingame *Also called Emmett W McCrkle Inc Insur Svc (P-10279)*
Macdonald Mott LLC (HQ) ....E....925 469-8010
12647 Alcosta Blvd San Ramon (94583) *(P-18759)*
Macdonald Screen Print, Modesto *Also called Sign Designs Inc (P-7252)*
Macdonalds Restaurants ....E....559 440-9206
7065 N Ingram Ave Fresno (93650) *(P-19815)*
Mace Meadow Golf Cntry CLB Inc ....E....209 295-7020
26570 Fairway Dr Pioneer (95666) *(P-15009)*
Machado & Sons Cnstr Inc ....E....209 632-5260
1000 S Kilroy Rd Turlock (95380) *(P-665)*
Machado Backhoe Inc ....E....209 634-4836
22332 Third Ave Stevinson (95374) *(P-1964)*
Machine Zone Inc (HQ) ....D....650 320-1678
1050 Page Mill Rd Palo Alto (94304) *(P-12591)*

Employee Codes: A=Over 500 employees, B=251-500 C=101-250, D=51-100, E=20-50 F=10-19
2022 Northern California Business Directory and Buyers Guide
© Mergent Inc. 1-800-342-5647
1013

Machine Zone LLC..........D.......650 320-1678
2225 E Byshore Rd Ste 200 East Palo Alto (94303) ***(P-13286)***
Machining and Frame Division, San Jose *Also called Mass Precision Inc* ***(P-4785)***
Macias Gini & OConnell LLP (PA)..........**D.......916 928-4600**
500 Capitol Mall Ste 2200 Sacramento (95814) ***(P-18973)***
Macintyre Corp..........E.......800 229-3560
27403 Industrial Blvd Hayward (94545) ***(P-5433)***
Mack & Reiss Inc..........D.......510 434-9122
5601 San Leandro St Ste 3 Oakland (94621) ***(P-3016)***
Mackay Smps Cvil Engineers Inc (PA)..........**D.......925 416-1790**
5142 Franklin Dr Ste C Pleasanton (94588) ***(P-18760)***
Mackevision LLC..........C.......248 656-6566
1255 Treat Blvd Ste 250 Walnut Creek (94597) ***(P-13630)***
Mackin Consultancy LLC..........C.......828 755-4073
2880 Zanker Rd Ste 203 San Jose (95134) ***(P-19816)***
Maclac Co, San Francisco *Also called R J McGlennon Company Inc* ***(P-4109)***
Macmurray Pacific, San Francisco *Also called Wildenradt-Mcmurray Inc* ***(P-8991)***
Macom Cnnctivity Solutions LLC..........E.......408 542-8686
4555 Great America Pkwy Santa Clara (95054) ***(P-6184)***
Macpherson Wstn Tl Sup Co LLC (PA)..........**E.......925 443-8665**
203 Lawrence Dr Ste D Livermore (94551) ***(P-9122)***
Macpherson's, Emeryville *Also called Art Supply Enterprises Inc* ***(P-9646)***
Macquarie Electronics Inc..........E.......408 965-3860
2153 Otoole Ave Ste 20 San Jose (95131) ***(P-6185)***
Macqurie Arcft Lsg Svcs US Inc..........D.......415 829-6600
2 Embarcadero Ctr Ste 200 San Francisco (94111) ***(P-12053)***
Macro Plastics Inc (PA)..........**E.......707 437-1200**
2250 Huntington Dr Fairfield (94533) ***(P-4298)***
Macrogenics West Inc..........E.......650 624-2600
3280 Byshore Blvd Ste 200 Brisbane (94005) ***(P-3944)***
Macronix America Inc (HQ)..........**D.......408 262-8887**
680 N Mccarthy Blvd # 200 Milpitas (95035) ***(P-8930)***
Macs Equip Repair..........E.......559 846-6534
3690 S Madera Ave Kerman (93630) ***(P-14762)***
Macworld Magazine, San Francisco *Also called Mac Publishing LLC* ***(P-3505)***
Macys Inc..........D.......415 951-5700
22 4th St Fl 7 San Francisco (94103) ***(P-11689)***
Mad Apparel Inc..........E.......650 503-3386
201 Arch St Redwood City (94062) ***(P-2994)***
Mad Dog Express Inc (PA)..........**D.......650 588-1900**
299 Lawrence Ave South San Francisco (94080) ***(P-7480)***
Mad Oak, Oakland *Also called Mad Oak Bar and Yard* ***(P-3337)***
Mad Oak Bar and Yard..........F.......510 924-2047
135 12th St Oakland (94607) ***(P-3337)***
Mad River Brewing Company Inc..........E.......707 668-4151
101 Taylor Way Blue Lake (95525) ***(P-2484)***
Mad River Community Hospital, Arcata *Also called American Hospital Mgt Corp* ***(P-16320)***
Maddox Dairy LLC..........D.......559 866-5308
12863 W Kamm Ave Spc 2 Riverdale (93656) ***(P-216)***
Maddox Dairy A Ltd Partnership (PA)..........**D.......559 867-3545**
12863 W Kamm Ave Spc 2 Riverdale (93656) ***(P-217)***
Maddox Farms LLC..........D.......559 866-5308
12840 W Kamm Ave Riverdale (93656) ***(P-181)***
Madera Cmnty Hosp Foundation..........D.......559 673-5101
1250 E Almond Ave Madera (93637) ***(P-16433)***
Madera Cnty Msqito Vctor Ctrl..........E.......559 662-8880
3105 Airport Dr Madera (93637) ***(P-11902)***
Madera Community Hospital..........E.......559 675-5530
1210 E Almond Ave Ste A Madera (93637) ***(P-16434)***
Madera Community Hospital..........E.......559 665-3768
285 Hospital Dr Chowchilla (93610) ***(P-16435)***
Madera Community Hospital (PA)..........**A.......559 675-5555**
1250 E Almond Ave Madera (93637) ***(P-16436)***
Madera Convalescent Hosp Inc (PA)..........**C.......559 673-9228**
517 S A St Madera (93638) ***(P-16039)***
Madera County Probation Dept, Madera *Also called County of Los Angeles* ***(P-17509)***
Madera Disposal Systems Inc (HQ)..........**D.......559 665-3099**
21739 Road 19 Chowchilla (93610) ***(P-8340)***
Madera Family Med Group Inc..........D.......559 673-3000
1111 W 4th St Madera (93637) ***(P-15515)***
Madera Fina, Fremont *Also called Commercial Casework Inc* ***(P-3125)***
Madera Industrial Med Group, Madera *Also called Madera Family Med Group Inc* ***(P-15515)***
Madera Irrigation District..........E.......559 673-3514
12152 Road 28 1/4 Madera (93637) ***(P-8252)***
Madera Public Defender Office, Madera *Also called Fitzgrald Alvrez Cmmo A Prof L* ***(P-17267)***
Madera Village Suites, Corte Madera *Also called Marin Suites Hotel LLC* ***(P-11284)***
Madison Reed Inc..........E.......415 225-0872
430 Shotwell St San Francisco (94110) ***(P-4089)***
Madison Street Press, Oakland *Also called Inter-City Printing Co Inc* ***(P-3660)***
Madison Vineyard Holdings LLC..........E.......707 254-8673
1 Kirkland Ranch Rd American Canyon (94503) ***(P-9580)***
Madrona Mnor Wine Cntry Inn RE..........D.......707 433-4231
1001 Westside Rd Healdsburg (95448) ***(P-11281)***
Madrone Art Bar, San Francisco *Also called Divisadero 500 LLC* ***(P-3335)***
Madrone Hospice Inc (PA)..........**E.......530 842-3160**
255 Collier Cir Yreka (96097) ***(P-16189)***
Madruga Iron Works Inc..........E.......209 832-7003
305 Gandy Dancer Dr Tracy (95377) ***(P-4674)***
Madsen Roofg Waterproofing Inc..........E.......916 361-3327
5960 Bradshaw Rd Sacramento (95829) ***(P-1818)***
Magagnini, Newark *Also called Intelliswift Software Inc* ***(P-12530)***
Magave Tequila Inc..........E.......415 515-3536
6 Park Pl Belvedere Tiburon (94920) ***(P-9581)***
Magento, San Jose *Also called Xcommerce Inc* ***(P-14014)***
Maggiora Baking Co, Richmond *Also called M & M Bakery Products Inc* ***(P-2393)***
Maggiora Bros Drilling Inc (PA)..........**E.......831 724-1338**
595 Airport Blvd Watsonville (95076) ***(P-1920)***
Magico LLc..........E.......510 649-9700
3170 Corporate Pl Hayward (94545) ***(P-5762)***
Magito & Company LLC..........F.......707 567-1521
1446 Industrial Ave Sebastopol (95472) ***(P-2653)***
Magma Design Automation Inc (HQ)..........**B.......408 565-7500**
1650 Tech Dr Ste 100 San Jose (95110) ***(P-12592)***
Magma Design Automation Inc..........E.......408 432-7288
2880 Zanker Rd Ste 203 San Jose (95134) ***(P-8723)***
Magnatrans LLC..........E.......916 969-6300
8620 Antelope North Rd A Antelope (95843) ***(P-7481)***
Magnet Systems Inc..........E.......650 329-5904
2300 Geng Rd Ste 100 Palo Alto (94303) ***(P-13287)***
Magnetic Coils Inc..........D.......707 459-5994
150 San Hedrin Cir Willits (95490) ***(P-6382)***
Magnetic Imaging Affilates..........E.......510 204-1820
5730 Telegraph Ave Oakland (94609) ***(P-16788)***
Magnetic Michigan (PA)..........**E.......650 544-2400**
167 2nd Ave San Mateo (94401) ***(P-19564)***
Magnetic Rcrding Solutions Inc..........F.......408 970-8266
3080 Oakmead Village Dr Santa Clara (95051) ***(P-6768)***
Magnitude Electronics LLC..........F.......650 551-1850
926 Bransten Rd San Carlos (94070) ***(P-6451)***
Magnolia Lane Soft HM Furn Inc..........E.......650 624-0700
187 Utah Ave South San Francisco (94080) ***(P-3028)***
Magnolia of Millbrae Inc..........D.......650 697-7700
201 Chadbourne Ave Millbrae (94030) ***(P-18141)***
Magnum Drywall Inc..........D.......510 979-0420
42027 Boscell Rd Fremont (94538) ***(P-1690)***
Magnum Semiconductor Inc..........C.......408 934-3700
6024 Silver Creek Vly Rd San Jose (95138) ***(P-6186)***
Maher M F Concrete Cnstr, Vallejo *Also called M F Maher Inc* ***(P-1889)***
Mahony, John MD, San Pablo *Also called Brookside Cmnty Hlth Ctr Inc* ***(P-15303)***
MAI Construction Inc..........C.......408 434-9880
50 Bonaventura Dr San Jose (95134) ***(P-666)***
Maier Manufacturing Inc..........E.......530 272-9036
416 Crown Point Cir Ste 1 Grass Valley (95945) ***(P-6652)***
Maier Racing Enterprises Inc..........E.......510 581-7600
22215 Meekland Ave Hayward (94541) ***(P-6587)***
Mailboxes and Bus Svcs Inc..........E.......916 971-4957
2443 Fair Oaks Blvd Sacramento (95825) ***(P-14327)***
Mailcentro Inc..........C.......916 985-4445
715 Sutter St Ste B Folsom (95630) ***(P-7972)***
Mailing Systems Inc..........E.......916 266-2285
2431 Mercantile Dr Ste A Rancho Cordova (95742) ***(P-11839)***
Maintance, Fairfield *Also called Fairfld-Sisun Unified Schl Dst* ***(P-11949)***
Maintenance Department, Petaluma *Also called California Department Trnsp* ***(P-1019)***
Maintenance Dept, Santa Cruz *Also called Santa Cruz Metro Trnst Dst* ***(P-7355)***
Maintenance Office, NAPA *Also called NAPA Valley Unified School Dst* ***(P-11977)***
Maintenancenet LLC..........D.......408 526-4000
170 W Tasman Dr San Jose (95134) ***(P-13726)***
Maison Goyard, San Francisco *Also called Goyard Miami LLC* ***(P-4348)***
Maitri Compassionate Care..........E.......415 558-3000
401 Duboce Ave San Francisco (94117) ***(P-16767)***
Majestic Floors Inc..........E.......925 825-0771
5111 Port Chicago Hwy Concord (94520) ***(P-8516)***
Major Transportation Svcs Inc..........E.......559 485-5949
3342 N Weber Ave Fresno (93722) ***(P-7564)***
MAK Associates Inc..........E.......408 244-9848
980 Memorex Dr Santa Clara (95050) ***(P-2043)***
Makani Technologies LLC (PA)..........**E.......503 939-5359**
2175 Monarch St Alameda (94501) ***(P-19565)***
Make Community LLC..........E.......707 200-3714
150 Todd Rd Ste 100 Santa Rosa (95407) ***(P-3506)***
Makena Capital Management LLC..........D.......650 926-0510
2755 Sand Hill Rd Ste 200 Menlo Park (94025) ***(P-10866)***
Makersights Inc..........E.......415 658-7709
435 Pacific Ave Ste 350 San Francisco (94133) ***(P-12593)***
Making It Big Inc..........F.......707 795-1995
1375 Corp Ctr Pkwy Ste A Santa Rosa (95407) ***(P-2999)***
Malaga County Water District..........E.......559 485-7353
3580 S Frank Ave Fresno (93725) ***(P-8284)***
Malcolm Drilling Company Inc (PA)..........**A.......415 901-4400**
92 Natoma St Ste 400 San Francisco (94105) ***(P-2044)***
Malibu Compost LLC (PA)..........**E.......800 282-6676**
1442a Walnut St Ste 80 Berkeley (94709) ***(P-4140)***
Malik Dental Corp (PA)..........**E.......925 692-2010**
15051 Hesperian Blvd San Leandro (94578) ***(P-15847)***
Malikco LLC..........E.......925 974-3555
2121 N Calif Blvd Ste 290 Walnut Creek (94596) ***(P-13288)***
Mallar Industrial Finshg Inc..........F.......510 651-6694
4500 Enterprise St Fremont (94538) ***(P-4107)***
Mallard Holdco LLC (PA)..........**E.......707 302-2658**
1201 Dowdell Ln Saint Helena (94574) ***(P-2654)***
Maloof Sport Entertainment, Sacramento *Also called Kings Arena Ltd Partnership* ***(P-14909)***
Maloof Sports & Entertainment, Sacramento *Also called Sacramento Kings Ltd Partnr* ***(P-14911)***
Maltby Electric Supply Co Inc (PA)..........**E.......415 863-5000**
336 7th St San Francisco (94103) ***(P-8867)***
Malwarebytes Inc..........A.......408 852-4336
3979 Freedom Cir Fl 12 Santa Clara (95054) ***(P-13289)***
Mammoth Biosciences Inc..........D.......770 655-1937
1000 Marina Blvd Ste 600 Brisbane (94005) ***(P-19087)***
Mammoth Community Water Dst..........E.......760 934-2596
1315 Meridian Blvd Mammoth Lakes (93546) ***(P-8253)***
Mammoth Disposal Company..........D.......760 934-2201
59 Commerce Dr Mammoth Lakes (93546) ***(P-8341)***
MAMMOTH HOSPITAL, Mammoth Lakes *Also called Southern Mono Healthcare Dst* ***(P-16533)***

Mammoth Mountain Inn, Mammoth Lakes *Also called Mammoth Mountain Ski Area LLC* ***(P-11282)***
Mammoth Mountain Ski Area LLC (HQ) ....B....**760 934-2571**
10001 Minaret Rd Mammoth Lakes (93546) ***(P-11282)***
Mammoth Times, Mammoth Lakes *Also called Horizon Cal Publications Inc* ***(P-3446)***
Mamone James M, Roseville *Also called Sutter Health* ***(P-16584)***
Managed Fclities Solutions LLC ....E....408 920-0110
128 Component Dr San Jose (95131) ***(P-19364)***
Managed Health Network (HQ) ....B....**415 460-8168**
2370 Kerner Blvd San Rafael (94901) ***(P-10146)***
Manageengine, Pleasanton *Also called Zoho Corporation* ***(P-18868)***
Management Associates, Saint Helena *Also called Silverado Orchards LLC* ***(P-10459)***
Managment Rcrters Grass Vly In ....E....530 432-1966
426 Sutton Way Ste 108 Grass Valley (95945) ***(P-12105)***
Manchester Band Pomo Indians ....D....707 882-2788
24 Mamie Laiwa Dr Point Arena (95468) ***(P-17640)***
Manchster Pt Arena Band Pomo I, Point Arena *Also called Manchester Band Pomo Indians* ***(P-17640)***
Mandego Apparel, Hollister *Also called Mandego Inc* ***(P-2976)***
Mandego Inc ....F....831 637-5241
2300 Tech Pkwy Ste 2 Hollister (95023) ***(P-2976)***
Mandiant Inc (PA) ....A....**408 321-6300**
601 Mccarthy Blvd Milpitas (95035) ***(P-5396)***
Mango Materials Inc ....F....650 440-0430
800 Buchanan St Berkeley (94710) ***(P-3805)***
Mangrove Lab & X-Ray, Chico *Also called Mangrove Medical Group* ***(P-15516)***
Mangrove Medical Group ....E....530 345-0064
1040 Mangrove Ave Chico (95926) ***(P-15516)***
Maniglia Landscape Inc ....E....408 487-9620
1655 Berryessa Rd Ste A San Jose (95133) ***(P-424)***
Manning Gardens Care Ctr Inc ....D....559 834-2586
2113 E Manning Ave Fresno (93725) ***(P-16040)***
Manor Care Sunnyvale Ca LLC ....C....408 735-7200
1150 Tilton Dr Sunnyvale (94087) ***(P-16041)***
Manorcare Hlth Svcs Sunnyvale, Sunnyvale *Also called Manor Care Sunnyvale Ca LLC* ***(P-16041)***
Manson Construction Co ....D....510 232-6319
1401 Marina Way S F Richmond (94804) ***(P-1167)***
Manteca Bulletin, Manteca *Also called Morris Newspaper Corp Cal* ***(P-3462)***
Manteca Care Rhabilitation Ctr, Manteca *Also called Karma Inc* ***(P-16030)***
Manteca Day School, Manteca *Also called Manteca Unified School Dst* ***(P-17968)***
Manteca Ford-Mercury Inc ....E....209 239-3561
555 N Main St Manteca (95336) ***(P-14577)***
Manteca Hampton Inn & Suites ....E....209 823-1926
1461 Bass Pro Dr Manteca (95337) ***(P-11283)***
Manteca Unified School Dst ....E....209 239-3689
737 W Yosemite Ave Manteca (95337) ***(P-17968)***
Manticore Games Inc ....E....650 799-6145
1390 Buckingham Way Hillsborough (94010) ***(P-13290)***
Manuel Bros Inc ....D....530 272-4213
908 Taylorville Rd # 104 Grass Valley (95949) ***(P-1117)***
Manufacturer, Hollister *Also called Advantage Truss Company LLC* ***(P-3198)***
Manufacturer, Roseville *Also called Swiss-Tech Machining LLC* ***(P-4870)***
Manufacturers Coml Fin LLC ....E....530 477-5011
13185 Nevada City Ave Grass Valley (95945) ***(P-4631)***
Manufacturers Import & Export, San Jose *Also called Amtek Electronic Inc* ***(P-5241)***
Manufacturing Resource Corp ....E....510 438-9600
44853 Fremont Blvd Fremont (94538) ***(P-14328)***
Manufctring Engrg Exclince Inc ....E....408 382-1900
2597 Flagstone Dr San Jose (95132) ***(P-18761)***
Manutronics Inc ....F....408 262-6579
736 S Hillview Dr Milpitas (95035) ***(P-6452)***
Manzana Products Co Inc ....E....707 823-5313
9141 Green Valley Rd Sebastopol (95472) ***(P-2225)***
Map Energy LLC ....D....650 324-9095
3000 El Camino Real Palo Alto (94306) ***(P-9979)***
Map Royalty Inc (PA) ....E....**650 324-9095**
3000 El Cmino Real Ste 5 Palo Alto (94306) ***(P-10802)***
Mapbox Inc ....E....202 250-3633
50 Beale St Ste 900 San Francisco (94105) ***(P-13291)***
Maplebear Inc (PA) ....A....**888 246-7822**
50 Beale St Ste 600 San Francisco (94105) ***(P-7482)***
Maplelabs Inc ....C....408 743-4414
1248 Reamwood Ave Sunnyvale (94089) ***(P-12594)***
Mar Cor Purification Inc ....E....510 397-0025
2606 Barrington Ct Hayward (94545) ***(P-5441)***
Marathon Business Group Inc ....D....707 575-8252
3210 Coffey Ln Ste A Santa Rosa (95403) ***(P-7483)***
Marathon Express, Santa Rosa *Also called Marathon Business Group Inc* ***(P-7483)***
Marathon Products Incorporated ....E....510 562-6450
14500 Doolittle Dr San Leandro (94577) ***(P-6909)***
Marathon Staffing Solutions ....D....978 649-6230
2950 Beacon Blvd Ste 45 West Sacramento (95691) ***(P-12106)***
Marburg Technology Inc ....D....408 262-8400
304 Turquoise St Milpitas (95035) ***(P-5397)***
Marc Jacobs Beauty, San Francisco *Also called Kendo Holdings Inc* ***(P-9228)***
March Plasma Systems, Concord *Also called Nordson March Inc* ***(P-5187)***
Marco Fine Furniture Inc ....E....415 285-3235
650 Potrero Ave San Francisco (94110) ***(P-3290)***
Marco Roofing, Fremont *Also called Milan Corporation* ***(P-1822)***
Marcolin USA Inc ....D....415 383-6348
6 Janet Way Apt 116 Belvedere Tiburon (94920) ***(P-8799)***
Marcucci Heating and AC Inc ....E....650 556-1882
2400 Bay Rd Redwood City (94063) ***(P-1309)***
Marcum LLP ....E....408 918-0900
111 W Saint John St # 1010 San Jose (95113) ***(P-18974)***
Marcum LLP ....E....415 432-6200
1 Montgomery St Ste 1700 San Francisco (94104) ***(P-18975)***
Marcus Millichap Corp RE Svcs (HQ) ....D....**650 391-1700**
2626 Hanover St Palo Alto (94304) ***(P-10610)***
Marcus Mllchap RE Inv Svcs Inc ....E....650 494-8900
2626 Hanover St Palo Alto (94304) ***(P-10611)***
Mare Island Dry Dock LLC ....D....707 652-7356
1180 Nimitz Ave Vallejo (94592) ***(P-6639)***
Mare Island Outpatient Clinic, Vallejo *Also called Veterans Health Administration* ***(P-15787)***
Marelich Mechanical Co Inc (HQ) ....D....**510 785-5500**
24041 Amador St Hayward (94544) ***(P-1310)***
Margaret OLeary Inc (PA) ....D....**415 354-6663**
50 Dorman Ave San Francisco (94124) ***(P-3012)***
Mariadb Usa Inc ....E....847 562-9000
350 Bay St Ste 100-319 San Francisco (94133) ***(P-8724)***
Marian Anderson Childrens Ctr, Sacramento *Also called Sacramento Cy Unified Schl Dst* ***(P-18011)***
Mariani Bros, Marysville *Also called Mariani Packing Co Inc* ***(P-2262)***
Mariani Packing Co Inc (PA) ....B....**707 452-2800**
500 Crocker Dr Vacaville (95688) ***(P-292)***
Mariani Packing Co Inc ....E....530 749-6565
9281 Highway 70 Marysville (95901) ***(P-2262)***
Mariani Packing Partnership LP ....E....707 452-2864
500 Crocker Dr Vacaville (95688) ***(P-3375)***
Mariani Winery, Saratoga *Also called Savannah Chanelle Vineyards* ***(P-2709)***
Mariannes Ice Cream LLC (PA) ....E....**831 457-1447**
2100 Delaware Ave Ste B Santa Cruz (95060) ***(P-2178)***
Marich Confectionery Co Inc ....C....831 634-4700
2101 Bert Dr Hollister (95023) ***(P-2431)***
MARIN ABUSED WOMEN'S SERVICES, San Rafael *Also called Center For Domestic Peace* ***(P-17471)***
Marin Acura, Corte Madera *Also called Ted Stevens Inc* ***(P-14495)***
Marin Airporter Inc ....D....415 884-2878
1455 N Hamilton Pkwy Novato (94949) ***(P-7340)***
Marin Beauty Company (PA) ....E....**415 454-4500**
417 3rd St San Rafael (94901) ***(P-11690)***
Marin Brewing Co Inc ....D....415 461-4677
1809 Larkspur Landing Cir Larkspur (94939) ***(P-2485)***
Marin Buty Cmpny-Beauty Sups S, San Rafael *Also called Marin Beauty Company* ***(P-11690)***
Marin Cancer Care Inc ....E....415 925-5000
1350 S Eliseo Dr Ste 200 Greenbrae (94904) ***(P-15517)***
Marin Clean Energy ....D....415 464-6028
1125 Tamalpais Ave San Rafael (94901) ***(P-8121)***
Marin Cnvlscent Rhblttion Hosp ....D....415 435-4554
30 Hacienda Dr Belvedere Tiburon (94920) ***(P-16042)***
Marin Community Clinic ....D....415 448-1500
9 Commercial Blvd Ste 100 Novato (94949) ***(P-15518)***
MARIN COMMUNITY CLINICS, Novato *Also called Marin Community Clinic* ***(P-15518)***
Marin Community College Dst ....E....415 457-8811
835 College Ave Kentfield (94904) ***(P-17969)***
Marin Community College Dst ....D....415 485-9468
835 College Ave Kentfield (94904) ***(P-17970)***
Marin Community Food Bank ....E....415 883-1302
2550 Kerner Blvd San Rafael (94901) ***(P-17641)***
Marin Country Club Inc ....D....415 382-6700
500 Country Club Dr Novato (94949) ***(P-15106)***
Marin County Office Education (PA) ....B....**415 472-4110**
1111 Las Gallinas Ave San Rafael (94903) ***(P-17821)***
Marin County Sart Program ....E....415 892-1628
655 Canyon Rd Novato (94947) ***(P-16743)***
Marin Day Schools, San Francisco *Also called Glp* ***(P-17941)***
Marin Eyes, San Rafael *Also called Marin Ophthlmic Cons A Med Cor* ***(P-15519)***
Marin Food Specialties Inc ....E....925 634-6126
14800 Byron Hwy Byron (94514) ***(P-2205)***
Marin General Hospital ....A....415 925-7000
250 Bon Air Rd Kentfield (94904) ***(P-16437)***
Marin Healthcare District (PA) ....D....**415 464-2090**
100 Drakes Landing Rd B Greenbrae (94904) ***(P-16438)***
Marin Horizon School Inc ....E....415 388-8408
305 Montford Ave Mill Valley (94941) ***(P-17971)***
Marin Humane Society ....D....415 883-4621
171 Bel Marin Keys Blvd Novato (94949) ***(P-18579)***
Marin Independent Journal, Novato *Also called California Newspapers Inc* ***(P-3423)***
Marin Industrial Distributors, San Rafael *Also called Jacksons Hardware Inc* ***(P-8985)***
Marin Magazine Inc ....E....415 332-4800
1 Harbor Dr Ste 208 Sausalito (94965) ***(P-3507)***
Marin Manufacturing Inc ....E....415 453-1825
195 Mill St San Rafael (94901) ***(P-4675)***
Marin Med Prctice Concepts Inc ....E....415 493-3300
100 Rowland Way Ste 201 Novato (94945) ***(P-19365)***
Marin Medical Laboratories, Novato *Also called Pathgroup San Francisco LLC* ***(P-15586)***
Marin Mountain Bikes (PA) ....F....**415 382-6000**
1450 Tech Ln Ste 100 Petaluma (94954) ***(P-9158)***
Marin Municipal Water District (PA) ....C....**415 945-1455**
220 Nellen Ave Corte Madera (94925) ***(P-8413)***
Marin Ophthlmic Cons A Med Cor ....D....415 454-5565
901 E St Ste 285 San Rafael (94901) ***(P-15519)***
Marin Primary & Middle School (PA) ....E....**415 924-2608**
20 Magnolia Ave Larkspur (94939) ***(P-17972)***
Marin Resource Recovery Center, San Rafael *Also called Marin Sanitary Service* ***(P-8342)***
Marin Sanitary Service (PA) ....D....**415 456-2601**
1050 Andersen Dr San Rafael (94901) ***(P-8342)***
Marin Sanitary Service ....D....415 485-5646
565 Jacoby St San Rafael (94901) ***(P-8343)***
Marin Software Incorporated (PA) ....C....**415 399-2580**
123 Mission St Fl 27 San Francisco (94105) ***(P-13727)***
Marin Storage & Trucking Inc (PA) ....E....**707 778-8313**
801 Lindberg Ln Petaluma (94952) ***(P-7625)***

A L P H A B E T I C

Employee Codes: A=Over 500 employees, B=251-500 C=101-250, D=51-100, E=20-50 F=10-19
2022 Northern California Business Directory and Buyers Guide
© Mergent Inc. 1-800-342-5647
1015

Marin Suites Hotel LLC ....D....415 924-3608
45 Tamal Vista Blvd Corte Madera (94925) *(P-11284)*

Marin Terrace, Mill Valley *Also called Cliff View Terrace Inc* *(P-18078)*

Marin Treatment Center ....D....415 457-3755
1466 Lincoln Ave San Rafael (94901) *(P-17037)*

Marina Breeze, San Leandro *Also called Vasona Management Inc* *(P-10466)*

Marina Convalescent Center, Fremont *Also called C J Health Services Inc* *(P-15948)*

Marina Garden Nursing Ctr Inc ....E....510 523-2363
3201 Fernside Blvd Alameda (94501) *(P-16043)*

Marina Inn, San Leandro *Also called Apple Inns Inc* *(P-10926)*

Marina Mechanical, San Leandro *Also called Bay Point Control Inc* *(P-14682)*

Marina Security Services Inc ....C....415 773-2300
465 California St Ste 609 San Francisco (94104) *(P-14075)*

Marine & Industrial Svcs Inc ....F....925 757-8791
2391 W 10th St Antioch (94509) *(P-4976)*

Marine Mammal Center (PA) ....**E....415 339-0430**
2000 Bunker Rd Sausalito (94965) *(P-330)*

Marine Spill Response Corp ....E....707 442-6087
990 W Waterfront Dr Eureka (95501) *(P-6835)*

Mariner Health Care Inc ....E....916 481-5500
3400 Alta Arden Expy Sacramento (95825) *(P-16044)*

Mariner Health Care Inc ....E....510 792-3743
39022 Presidio Way Fremont (94538) *(P-16045)*

Mariner Health Care Inc ....E....408 842-9311
8170 Murray Ave Gilroy (95020) *(P-16046)*

Mariner Health Care Inc ....E....408 298-3950
2065 Forest Ave San Jose (95128) *(P-16047)*

Mariner Health Care Inc ....E....916 422-4825
7400 24th St Sacramento (95822) *(P-16048)*

Mariner Health Care Inc ....E....510 783-8150
27350 Tampa Ave Hayward (94544) *(P-16049)*

Mariner Health Care Inc ....E....510 232-5945
13484 San Pablo Ave San Pablo (94806) *(P-16050)*

Mariner Health Care Inc ....E....530 756-1800
1850 E 8th St Davis (95616) *(P-16051)*

Mariner Health Care Inc ....E....831 475-6323
675 24th Ave Santa Cruz (95062) *(P-16052)*

Mariner Health Care Inc ....E....510 538-4424
1768 B St Hayward (94541) *(P-16053)*

Mariner Health Care Inc ....E....510 785-2880
19700 Hesperian Blvd Hayward (94541) *(P-16054)*

Mariner Health Care Inc ....E....415 479-3610
45 Professional Ctr Pkwy San Rafael (94903) *(P-16055)*

Mariner Health Care Inc ....E....408 377-9275
2065 Los Gatos Almaden Rd San Jose (95124) *(P-16056)*

Mariner Health Care Inc ....E....510 261-5200
3025 High St Oakland (94619) *(P-16057)*

Mariner Health Care Inc ....E....209 466-2066
537 E Fulton St Stockton (95204) *(P-16058)*

Mariner Square Athletic Inc ....D....510 523-8011
2227 Mariner Square Loop Alameda (94501) *(P-14962)*

Mariner's Point Golf Course, Foster City *Also called Vb Golf LLC* *(P-15035)*

Marinship Dev Interest LLC (PA) ....**E....415 282-5160**
1485 Bay Shore Blvd Ste 2 San Francisco (94124) *(P-10707)*

Mariposa Market, Willits *Also called Mariposa Natural Foods* *(P-9416)*

Mariposa Natural Foods ....E....707 459-9630
500 S Main St Willits (95490) *(P-9416)*

Mark Carter ....E....707 444-8062
301 L St Eureka (95501) *(P-11285)*

Mark E Jacobson M D ....D....707 571-4022
1260 N Dutton Ave Ste 230 Santa Rosa (95401) *(P-15520)*

Mark H Nishiki MD ....D....209 465-6221
1800 N California St Stockton (95204) *(P-15521)*

Mark III Construction Inc (PA) ....**D....916 381-8080**
5101 Florin Perkins Rd Sacramento (95826) *(P-1535)*

Mark III Dvlpers Dsgn/Builders, Sacramento *Also called Mark III Construction Inc* *(P-1535)*

Mark Nicholson Inc ....D....831 637-5728
701 Mccray St Hollister (95023) *(P-1054)*

Mark One Corporation ....C....209 667-2484
812 W Main St Turlock (95380) *(P-16250)*

Mark One Corporation ....E....209 537-4581
1711 Richland Ave Ceres (95307) *(P-16251)*

Mark Scott Construction Inc ....E....707 864-8880
2250 Boynton Ave Fairfield (94533) *(P-757)*

Mark Scott Construction Inc ....E....209 982-0502
2835 Contra Costa Blvd A Pleasant Hill (94523) *(P-758)*

Mark Scott Construction Inc (PA) ....**E....925 944-0502**
2835 Contra Costa Blvd A Pleasant Hill (94523) *(P-918)*

Mark Tanner Construction Inc ....E....530 587-4000
10603 E River St Truckee (96161) *(P-667)*

Mark Twain Conv. Hospital, San Andreas *Also called Avalon Care Ctr - San Andreas* *(P-15919)*

Mark Twain Medical Center ....E....209 795-4193
2182 Hwy 4 Ste A100 Arnold (95223) *(P-16439)*

Mark Twain Medical Center (HQ) ....**C....209 754-3521**
768 Mountain Ranch Rd San Andreas (95249) *(P-16440)*

Mark Twain Medical Center ....E....209 754-1487
768 Mountain Ranch Rd San Andreas (95249) *(P-16441)*

MARK TWAIN ST JOSEPH'S HOSPITAL, San Andreas *Also called Mark Twain Medical Center* *(P-16440)*

Mark/Space Inc (PA) ....**D....408 399-5300**
654 N Santa Cruz Ave C Los Gatos (95030) *(P-13292)*

Marker Hotel, The, San Francisco *Also called Geary Darling Lessee Inc* *(P-11113)*

Markes International Inc ....F....513 745-0241
2355 Gold Meadow Way # 120 Gold River (95670) *(P-6836)*

Market Force Information Inc ....E....209 795-0830
2037 Hwy 4 Ste C Arnold (95223) *(P-19566)*

Market Hall Foods, Oakland *Also called Pasta Shop* *(P-9474)*

Market One Builders, Sacramento *Also called Marketone Builders Inc* *(P-668)*

Marketmile Inc ....E....650 903-5600
3965 Freedom Cir Fl 11 Flr 11 Mountain View (94043) *(P-18976)*

Marketo Inc (HQ) ....**A....650 376-2300**
901 Mariners Island Blvd # 200 San Mateo (94404) *(P-12595)*

Marketone Builders Inc ....E....916 928-7474
1200 R St Ste 150 Sacramento (95811) *(P-668)*

Marketshare Inc (PA) ....**D....408 262-0677**
2001 Tarob Ct Milpitas (95035) *(P-7242)*

Marketwatch Inc (HQ) ....**D....415 439-6400**
201 California St Fl 13 San Francisco (94111) *(P-14155)*

Marki Microwave Inc ....E....408 778-4200
345 Digital Dr Morgan Hill (95037) *(P-8931)*

Marklogic Corporation (PA) ....**B....650 655-2300**
999 Skyway Rd Ste 200 San Carlos (94070) *(P-12596)*

Markmonitor (all-D) Inc ....D....415 278-8400
425 Market St Ste 500 San Francisco (94105) *(P-17325)*

Markov Corporation ....E....650 207-9445
1225 Magdalena Ct Los Altos (94024) *(P-19169)*

Markstein Bev Co Sacramento ....C....916 920-3911
60 Main Ave Sacramento (95838) *(P-9554)*

Markstein Beverage Co, Antioch *Also called Markstein Sales Company* *(P-9555)*

Markstein Beverage Company, Sacramento *Also called Markstein Bev Co Sacramento* *(P-9554)*

Markstein Sales Company ....C....925 755-1919
1645 Drive In Way Antioch (94509) *(P-9555)*

Marksys LLC ....D....916 745-4883
3725 Cincinnati Ave # 200 Rocklin (95765) *(P-19567)*

Marksys Holdings LLC ....D....916 745-4883
3725 Cincinnati Ave # 200 Rocklin (95765) *(P-19568)*

Maroevich Oshea Cghlan Insur S ....D....415 957-0600
44 Montgomery St Ste 1700 San Francisco (94104) *(P-10310)*

Marqeta Inc ....A....888 462-7738
180 Grand Ave Ste 600 Oakland (94612) *(P-13293)*

Marquee Fire Protection LLC (PA) ....**E....916 641-7997**
710 W Stadium Ln Sacramento (95834) *(P-1311)*

Marques Gen Engrg Inc A Cal Co ....B....916 923-3434
7225 26th St Rio Linda (95673) *(P-18762)*

Marquez & Associates RE Inc ....E....510 863-0081
1630 N Main St 196 Walnut Creek (94596) *(P-10612)*

Marquez Brothers Intl Inc (PA) ....**C....408 960-2700**
5801 Rue Ferrari San Jose (95138) *(P-9277)*

Marquis Care At Shasta, Redding *Also called Marquis Companies I Inc* *(P-16059)*

Marquis Companies I Inc ....E....530 222-3630
3550 Churn Creek Rd Redding (96002) *(P-16059)*

Marr B Olsen Inc ....E....707 763-9707
320 1st St Petaluma (94952) *(P-1892)*

Marriots Tmber Ldge At Lk Thoe ....D....530 542-8416
4100 Lake Tahoe Blvd South Lake Tahoe (96150) *(P-11286)*

Marriott, Ukiah *Also called AJPJ II LLC* *(P-10912)*

Marriott, San Jose *Also called Host International Inc* *(P-11162)*

Marriott, Scotts Valley *Also called Sheraton LLC* *(P-11468)*

Marriott, Pleasanton *Also called Pleasanton Project Owner LLC* *(P-11372)*

Marriott, Rancho Cordova *Also called Hv-Houston Development Inc* *(P-11178)*

Marriott, San Francisco *Also called Renaissance Hotel Operating Co* *(P-11395)*

Marriott - Un Sq San Francisco, San Francisco *Also called Felcor Union Square Lessee LLC* *(P-11094)*

Marriott Downtown ....E....415 896-1600
55 4th St San Francisco (94103) *(P-11287)*

Marriott Vacation Club Pulse, San Francisco *Also called PHF Ruby LLC* *(P-11365)*

Marrone Bio Innovations Inc (PA) ....**C....530 750-2800**
1540 Drew Ave Davis (95618) *(P-4143)*

MArs Engineering Company Inc ....E....510 483-0541
699 Montague St San Leandro (94577) *(P-5565)*

Marseille Inc ....E....408 855-9003
3211 Scott Blvd Ste 205 Santa Clara (95054) *(P-6187)*

Marshall Brothers Entps Inc ....E....925 449-4020
5783 Preston Ave Livermore (94551) *(P-1055)*

Marshall Hospital, Placerville *Also called Marshall Medical Center* *(P-16451)*

Marshall Hospital Home Care, Placerville *Also called Marshall Medical Center* *(P-16444)*

Marshall Medical Center ....E....530 626-3682
941 Spring St Ste A Placerville (95667) *(P-16442)*

Marshall Medical Center ....E....530 344-5400
5137 Golden Foothill Pkwy # 120 El Dorado Hills (95762) *(P-16443)*

Marshall Medical Center ....E....530 626-2900
681 Main St Ste 206 Placerville (95667) *(P-16444)*

Marshall Medical Center ....E....530 626-2616
Marshall Way Placerville (95667) *(P-16445)*

Marshall Medical Center ....E....530 344-5470
1095 Marshall Way Fl 2 Placerville (95667) *(P-16446)*

Marshall Medical Center ....E....530 672-7040
3501 Palmer Dr Cameron Park (95682) *(P-16447)*

Marshall Medical Center ....E....530 621-3600
4341b Golden Center Dr Placerville (95667) *(P-16448)*

Marshall Medical Center ....E....916 933-2273
1100 Marshall Way El Dorado Hills (95762) *(P-16449)*

Marshall Medical Center ....E....530 626-2920
1095 Marshall Way Placerville (95667) *(P-16450)*

Marshall Medical Center (PA) ....**A....530 622-1441**
1100 Marshall Way Placerville (95667) *(P-16451)*

Marshall Medical Center ....E....530 672-7050
3581 Palmer Dr Ste 202 Cameron Park (95682) *(P-16452)*

Marshall Ob/Gyn, Placerville *Also called Marshall Medical Center* *(P-16446)*

Martech, Lodi *Also called Mechanical Analysis/Repair Inc* *(P-14763)*

Martel Eye Medical Group, Rancho Cordova *Also called Joseph R Martel MD Inc* *(P-15443)*

Marticus Electric Inc ....E....916 368-2186
9266 Beatty Dr Ste D Sacramento (95826) *(P-1536)*

Martin ATI-AC Inc (PA)......D......**925 648-8800**
4750 Willow Rd Ste 250 Pleasanton (94588) ***(P-18901)***
Martin Brothers Cnstr LLC (PA)......D......**916 386-1600**
8801 Folsom Blvd Ste 260 Sacramento (95826) ***(P-1056)***
Martin Fischer Logging Co Inc......F......209 293-4847
1165 Skull Flat Rd West Point (95255) ***(P-3070)***
Martin Lthr Kng Chldr Ctr, Pittsburg *Also called State Preschool* ***(P-18034)***
Martin Ragno & Associates Inc......E......650 325-4996
1303 Elmer St Belmont (94002) ***(P-483)***
Martin, Steve DDS, Santa Rosa *Also called Interdent Service Corporation* ***(P-15838)***
Martina Landscape Inc......D......408 871-8800
811 Camden Ave Campbell (95008) ***(P-484)***
Martinelli Envmtl Graphics, San Francisco *Also called Martinelli Envmtl Graphics* ***(P-7243)***
Martinelli Envmtl Graphics......F......415 468-4000
1829 Egbert Ave San Francisco (94124) ***(P-7243)***
Martinez Center For Rehab, Martinez *Also called Veterans Health Administration* ***(P-15806)***
Martinez Cogen Ltd Partnership......D......925 313-0800
550 Solano Way Pacheco (94553) ***(P-8122)***
Martinez Medical Offices, Martinez *Also called Kaiser Foundation Hospitals* ***(P-10796)***
Martinez Outpatient Clinic, Martinez *Also called Veterans Health Administration* ***(P-15796)***
Martinez Pallets Inc......F......916 238-4548
6541 26th St Rio Linda (95673) ***(P-3225)***
Martinez Ranches Inc......E......530 795-2957
8777 Halley Rd Winters (95694) ***(P-531)***
Martini Prati Winery, Santa Rosa *Also called Conetech Custom Services LLC* ***(P-2538)***
Martinlli Orchrd Oprations LLC......E......831 724-1126
227 E Beach St Watsonville (95076) ***(P-2921)***
Martis Camp Club......B......530 550-6000
7951 Fleur Du Lac Ct Truckee (96161) ***(P-17642)***
Marutiz Inc......E......408 778-3400
16225 Condit Rd Morgan Hill (95037) ***(P-11288)***
Marvac Scientific Mfg Co......F......925 825-4636
3231 Monument Way Ste I Concord (94518) ***(P-6695)***
Marvel Parent LLC (HQ)......E......**650 321-4910**
1950 University Ave # 350 East Palo Alto (94303) ***(P-12597)***
Marvell Semiconductor......E......408 222-2500
700 First Ave Sunnyvale (94089) ***(P-6188)***
Marvell Semiconductor Inc......C......916 605-3700
890 Glenn Dr Folsom (95630) ***(P-6189)***
Marvell Semiconductor Inc......E......408 855-8839
5450 Bayfront Plz Santa Clara (95054) ***(P-6769)***
Marvell Semiconductor Inc (HQ)......A......**408 222-2500**
5488 Marvell Ln Santa Clara (95054) ***(P-6190)***
Marvell Technology Group Ltd......D......408 222-2500
5488 Marvell Ln Santa Clara (95054) ***(P-6191)***
Marvin Gardens Real Estate, El Cerrito *Also called Marvin Gardens Real Property* ***(P-10613)***
Marvin Gardens Real Property......E......510 527-9111
7502 Fairmount Ave El Cerrito (94530) ***(P-10613)***
Marx Digital Cnc Machine Shop, Santa Clara *Also called Marx Digital Mfg Inc* ***(P-5566)***
Marx Digital Mfg Inc (PA)......D......**408 748-1783**
3551 Victor St Santa Clara (95054) ***(P-5566)***
Mary Anns Baking Co Inc......C......916 681-7444
8371 Carbide Ct Sacramento (95828) ***(P-2394)***
Marymount Villa LLC......D......510 895-5007
345 Davis St Ofc San Leandro (94577) ***(P-16190)***
Marysville Post-Acute, Marysville *Also called Melon Holdings LLC* ***(P-16063)***
Masa's, San Francisco *Also called San Francisco Hotel Associates* ***(P-11433)***
Masco, San Jose *Also called Topbuild Services Group Corp* ***(P-2076)***
Mashgin Inc......F......650 847-8050
849 E Charleston Rd Palo Alto (94303) ***(P-5334)***
Masker Painting, Oakland *Also called George E Masker Inc* ***(P-1414)***
Mason Bpp Inc......E......925 256-1092
837 Arnold Dr Ste 4 Martinez (94553) ***(P-669)***
Mason McDuffie Mortgage Corp (PA)......D......**925 242-4400**
2010 Crow Canyon Pl # 400 San Ramon (94583) ***(P-9915)***
Mason Street Opco LLC......A......415 772-5000
950 Mason St San Francisco (94108) ***(P-11289)***
Mason-Mcduffie Real Estate Inc (PA)......E......**925 924-4600**
1555 Riviera Ave Ste E Walnut Creek (94596) ***(P-10614)***
Masonic Home For Adults, Union City *Also called Masonic Homes of California* ***(P-18143)***
Masonic Homes of California (PA)......B......**415 776-7000**
1111 California St San Francisco (94108) ***(P-18142)***
Masonic Homes of California......B......510 441-3700
34400 Mission Blvd Union City (94587) ***(P-18143)***
Mass Microsystems Inc......F......408 522-1200
810 W Maude Ave Sunnyvale (94085) ***(P-5298)***
Mass Precision Inc......C......408 954-0200
46555 Landing Pkwy Fremont (94538) ***(P-4784)***
Mass Precision Inc......D......408 786-0378
2070 Oakland Rd San Jose (95131) ***(P-1819)***
Mass Precision Inc (PA)......C......**408 954-0200**
2110 Oakland Rd San Jose (95131) ***(P-4785)***
Massdrop Inc (PA)......D......**415 340-2999**
1390 Market St Ste 200 San Francisco (94102) ***(P-14329)***
Massingham & Assoc MGT Inc (PA)......E......**510 896-2634**
8000 Jarvis Ave 2 Newark (94560) ***(P-10615)***
Master of Code Global......F......650 200-8490
541 Jefferson Ave Ste 104 Redwood City (94063) ***(P-13294)***
Master Plastics Incorporated......E......707 451-3168
820 Eubanks Dr Ste I Vacaville (95688) ***(P-4299)***
Master Precision Machining......E......408 727-0185
2199 Ronald St Santa Clara (95050) ***(P-5567)***
Master Suites, Fresno *Also called Preferred Corporate Svcs Inc* ***(P-10455)***
Masterank Wax Incorporated (PA)......F......**925 998-2186**
2221 Carion Ct Pittsburg (94565) ***(P-4176)***
Masterclass, San Francisco *Also called Yanka Industries Inc* ***(P-14884)***
Masters Group, The, San Jose *Also called Trans Pacific Inc* ***(P-10673)***
Masters Whosales, Rancho Cordova *Also called Novo Masters Wholesale Inc* ***(P-8885)***

Matagrano Inc......C......650 829-4829
440 Forbes Blvd South San Francisco (94080) ***(P-9556)***
Matanzas Creek Winery......F......707 528-6464
6097 Bennett Valley Rd Santa Rosa (95404) ***(P-2655)***
Matarzzi / Pelsinger Bldrs Inc......E......415 285-6930
355 11th St Ste 200 San Francisco (94103) ***(P-670)***
Mater Misericordiae Hospital (PA)......A......**209 564-5000**
333 Mercy Ave Merced (95340) ***(P-16453)***
Material Technology Intl, Richmond *Also called MTI Corporation* ***(P-6457)***
Materials Innovation, Sunnyvale *Also called Jsr Micro Inc* ***(P-4124)***
Maternal Cnnctons El Cmino Hos......E......650 988-8287
2110 Forest Ave Ste B San Jose (95128) ***(P-16454)***
Mathematica Inc......D......510 830-3700
505 14th St Ste 800 Oakland (94612) ***(P-19170)***
Matheny Sars Linkert Jaime LLP......D......916 978-3434
3638 American River Dr Sacramento (95864) ***(P-17326)***
Mather Aviation LLC (PA)......E......**916 364-4711**
10360 Macready Ave Mather (95655) ***(P-7775)***
Mather Community Campus (PA)......D......**916 228-3100**
10626 Schirra Ave Mather (95655) ***(P-18144)***
Matheson Fast Freight Inc......B......209 342-0184
9785 Goethe Rd Sacramento (95827) ***(P-7565)***
Matheson Fast Freight Inc (HQ)......D......**916 686-4600**
9780 Dino Dr Elk Grove (95624) ***(P-7566)***
Matheson Trucking Inc (PA)......E......**916 685-2330**
9785 Goethe Rd Sacramento (95827) ***(P-7567)***
Mathews Mechanical, Newark *Also called Adonai Enterprises Inc* ***(P-14733)***
Mathews Ready Mix LLC......E......530 893-8856
1619 Skyway Chico (95928) ***(P-4497)***
Mathews Ready Mix LLC......E......530 671-2400
249 Lamon St Yuba City (95991) ***(P-4498)***
Mathews Readymix, Yuba City *Also called Mathews Ready Mix LLC* ***(P-4498)***
Matric Absence Management......E......916 773-5737
2208 Plaza Dr Ste 100 Rocklin (95765) ***(P-19366)***
Matrix Absence Management Inc......D......916 773-5737
1420 Rocky Ridge Dr # 270 Roseville (95661) ***(P-19367)***
Matrix Logic Corporation......E......415 893-9897
1380 East Ave Ste 124240 Chico (95926) ***(P-13295)***
Matrix Resources Inc......D......415 644-0642
1 Embarcadero Ctr Ste 500 San Francisco (94111) ***(P-12107)***
Matrixx Software Inc (PA)......B......**408 215-9344**
1098 Fster Cy Blvd Ste 10 Foster City (94404) ***(P-13631)***
Matson Alarm Co Inc (PA)......E......**559 438-8000**
581 W Fllbrook Ave Ste 10 Fresno (93711) ***(P-14139)***
Matson Alaska Inc......E......704 973-7000
555 12th St Ste 700 Oakland (94607) ***(P-7735)***
Matson Logistics Inc......E......925 887-6207
1855 Gateway Blvd Ste 550 Concord (94520) ***(P-7846)***
Matson Navigation Co Alsk LLC......D......510 628-4000
555 12th St Ste 700 Oakland (94607) ***(P-7736)***
Matson Navigation Company......E......209 577-1081
1710 Springwood Dr Modesto (95350) ***(P-7712)***
Matson Navigation Company Inc (HQ)......C......**510 628-4000**
555 12th St Fl 7 Oakland (94607) ***(P-7713)***
Matsudas By Green Acres LLC......C......916 673-9290
10600 Florin Rd Sacramento (95830) ***(P-130)***
Matteoli Brothers......E......530 738-4201
17580 Cranmore Rd Knights Landing (95645) ***(P-182)***
Matter LLC......E......415 589-7036
22 Shotwell St San Francisco (94103) ***(P-11867)***
Matterhorn Ice Cream Inc......F......208 287-8916
1221 66th St Sacramento (95819) ***(P-2179)***
Mattermark, San Francisco *Also called Fullcontact Inc* ***(P-12464)***
Mattermost Inc (PA)......C......**650 667-8512**
530 Lytton Ave Fl 2 Palo Alto (94301) ***(P-12598)***
Matternet Inc (PA)......E......**650 260-2727**
185 E Dana St Mountain View (94041) ***(P-6635)***
Matterport Inc (PA)......E......**650 641-2241**
352 E Java Dr Sunnyvale (94089) ***(P-13296)***
Matterport Operating LLC (HQ)......C......**650 641-2241**
352 E Java Dr Sunnyvale (94089) ***(P-8725)***
Matthew Burns......D......209 676-4940
617 Flower Dr Folsom (95630) ***(P-919)***
Matthews Skyline Logging Inc......E......707 743-2890
10100 East Rd Potter Valley (95469) ***(P-3071)***
Mattson Technology Inc (HQ)......B......**510 657-5900**
47131 Bayside Pkwy Fremont (94538) ***(P-6192)***
Mavens Creamery LLC......E......408 216-9270
1701 S 7th St Ste 7 San Jose (95112) ***(P-2180)***
Maverick Enterprises Inc......C......707 463-5591
751 E Gobbi St Ukiah (95482) ***(P-4561)***
Maverick Therapeutics Inc......E......650 684-7140
3260 Bayshore Blvd Brisbane (94005) ***(P-3945)***
Max Machinery Inc......E......707 433-2662
33 Healdsburg Ave Ste A Healdsburg (95448) ***(P-6725)***
Max Process Equipment LLC......E......707 433-7281
1420 Healdsburg Ave Healdsburg (95448) ***(P-8766)***
Max Sportsters Inc......E......408 446-8330
10050 N Foothill Blvd # 200 Cupertino (95014) ***(P-19368)***
Maxar Space LLC (HQ)......D......**650 852-4000**
3825 Fabian Way Palo Alto (94303) ***(P-8080)***
Maxar Space LLC......A......916 605-5448
5130 Rbert J Mathews Pkwy El Dorado Hills (95762) ***(P-5854)***
Maxar Space LLC......A......650 852-4000
1140 Hamilton Ct Menlo Park (94025) ***(P-7694)***
Maxco Supply Inc (PA)......E......**559 646-8449**
605 S Zediker Ave Parlier (93648) ***(P-9215)***
Maxco Supply Inc......D......559 638-8449
2059 E Olsen Ave Reedley (93654) ***(P-3351)***

A L P H A B E T I C

Maxim Equipment Inc ....F....209 649-7225
339 Doak Blvd Ripon (95366) *(P-4188)*
Maxim Healthcare Services Inc ....C....408 914-7478
631 River Oaks Pkwy San Jose (95134) *(P-16911)*
Maxim Healthcare Services Inc ....D....916 614-9539
1050 Fulton Ave Ste 230 Sacramento (95825) *(P-12180)*
Maxim Healthcare Services Inc ....D....510 873-0700
6475 Christie Ave Ste 350 Emeryville (94608) *(P-12181)*
Maxim Healthcare Services Inc ....D....559 224-0299
5066 N Fresno St Ste 103 Fresno (93710) *(P-12182)*
Maxim Healthcare Services Inc ....D....916 771-7444
151 N Sunrise Ave Ste 905 Roseville (95661) *(P-12183)*
Maxim Healthcare Services Inc ....D....410 910-1500
1101 S Wnchster Blvd Ste San Mateo (94403) *(P-12184)*
Maxim Healthcare Services Inc ....C....559 227-2250
6051 N Fresno St Ste 102 Fresno (93710) *(P-16912)*
Maxim Integrated Products Inc (HQ) ....A....**408 601-1000**
160 Rio Robles San Jose (95134) *(P-6193)*
Maximum Games Inc (PA) ....E....**925 708-3242**
590 Ygnacio Valley Rd # 220 Walnut Creek (94596) *(P-12599)*
Maximus Holdings Inc ....A....650 935-9500
2475 Hanover St Palo Alto (94304) *(P-13297)*
Maximus Real Estate Partners ....D....415 584-4832
1 Maritime Plz Ste 1900 San Francisco (94111) *(P-10482)*
Maxiscale Inc ....F....408 962-6000
1100 La Avenida St Ste A Mountain View (94043) *(P-19369)*
Maxonic Inc ....D....408 739-4900
2542 S Bascom Ave Ste 190 Campbell (95008) *(P-13933)*
Maxplore Technologies Inc ....D....925 621-1400
4450 Rosewood Dr Ste 200 Pleasanton (94588) *(P-12600)*
Maxs Partnership A Gen Partnr ....E....209 725-1221
750 Motel Dr Merced (95341) *(P-11290)*
Maxtor Corporation (HQ) ....D....**831 438-6550**
4575 Scotts Valley Dr Scotts Valley (95066) *(P-5299)*
Maxval Group Inc (PA) ....D....**650 472-0644**
2251 Grant Rd Ste B Los Altos (94024) *(P-19817)*
Maxx Metals Inc ....D....650 654-1500
355 Quarry Rd San Carlos (94070) *(P-8821)*
May-Han Electric Inc ....D....916 929-0150
1600 Auburn Blvd Sacramento (95815) *(P-1537)*
Maya Cinemas Pittsburg, Pittsburg *Also called Maya Pittsburg Cinemas LLC (P-14812)*
Maya Fresno Cinemas, Fresno *Also called Campus Pointe Cinemas Oper LLC (P-14807)*
Maya Pittsburg Cinemas LLC ....E....213 805-5333
4085 Century Blvd Pittsburg (94565) *(P-14812)*
Mayacama Golf Club LLC ....C....707 569-2900
1240 Mayacama Club Dr Santa Rosa (95403) *(P-15107)*
Mayall Hrley Kntsen Smith Gree ....E....209 465-8733
2453 Grand Canal Blvd # 2 Stockton (95207) *(P-17327)*
Mayfield Equipment Company (PA) ....E....**707 462-2404**
235 E Perkins St Ukiah (95482) *(P-9605)*
Mayfield Fund ....E....650 854-5560
2484 Sand Hill Rd Menlo Park (94025) *(P-10867)*
Mayview Community Hlth Ctr Inc (PA) ....E....**650 327-8717**
270 Grant Ave Ste 102 Palo Alto (94306) *(P-15522)*
Maze & Assoc Accounting Corp ....D....925 930-0902
3478 Buskirk Ave Ste 215 Pleasant Hill (94523) *(P-18977)*
Mazzetti Inc (PA) ....E....**615 579-4375**
220 Montgomery St Ste 650 San Francisco (94104) *(P-18763)*
MB Hosptlity Srosa AC 2018 LLC ....E....707 527-1075
300 Davis St Santa Rosa (95401) *(P-11291)*
MB Sports Inc ....E....209 357-4153
280 Airpark Rd Atwater (95301) *(P-6644)*
MBA Electronics, Fremont *Also called William Ho (P-6001)*
Mbanq, Healdsburg *Also called Finlink Inc (P-12452)*
Mbh Architects Inc ....C....510 865-8663
960 Atlantic Ave Ste 100 Alameda (94501) *(P-18902)*
MBI, Stockton *Also called Midstate Barrier Inc (P-1060)*
MBK Engineers ....E....916 456-4400
455 University Ave # 100 Sacramento (95825) *(P-18764)*
Mbkt Corp ....E....408 212-0230
2372 Qume Dr Ste A San Jose (95131) *(P-1538)*
Mbrdna, Sunnyvale *Also called Mercedes-Benz RES Dev N Amer In (P-19089)*
Mbtechnology ....E....559 233-2181
188 S Teilman Ave Fresno (93706) *(P-4191)*
Mc Donald Sloan M DDS Rbrto J ....E....925 778-2100
5201 Deer Valley Rd 2b Antioch (94531) *(P-15848)*
Mc Electronics LLC ....B....831 637-1651
1891 Airway Dr Hollister (95023) *(P-5945)*
Mc Entire Landscaping, Redding *Also called McEntire Landscaping Inc (P-485)*
Mc Graw Commercial Insur Svc (PA) ....D....**650 780-4800**
3601 Haven Ave Menlo Park (94025) *(P-10311)*
Mc Intyre Coil, San Francisco *Also called Edge Electronics Corporation (P-4720)*
Mc Ivor, William MD, Walnut Creek *Also called Muir Orthopedics Inc (P-15543)*
Mc Leas Tire & Automotive Svc, Santa Rosa *Also called Mc Leas Tire Service Inc (P-8477)*
Mc Leas Tire Service Inc (PA) ....E....**707 542-0363**
800 Piner Rd Santa Rosa (95403) *(P-8477)*
Mc Liquidation Inc ....D....408 636-1020
570 Del Rey Ave Sunnyvale (94085) *(P-7112)*
MC Metal Inc ....F....415 822-2288
1347 Donner Ave San Francisco (94124) *(P-4836)*
Mc Namara Dodge Ney Beatt (PA) ....D....**925 939-5330**
3480 Buskirk Ave Ste 250 Pleasant Hill (94523) *(P-17328)*
McAfee LLC (HQ) ....A....**888 847-8766**
6220 America Center Dr San Jose (95002) *(P-13298)*
McAfee Corp (PA) ....B....**866 622-3911**
6220 America Center Dr San Jose (95002) *(P-13299)*
McAfee Finance 1 LLC (HQ) ....E....**888 847-8766**
2821 Mission College Blvd Santa Clara (95054) *(P-13300)*
McAfee Finance 2 LLC ....A....888 847-8766
2821 Mission College Blvd Santa Clara (95054) *(P-13301)*
McAfee Public Sector LLC (HQ) ....E....**888 847-8766**
6220 America Center Dr San Jose (95002) *(P-14140)*
McAfee Security LLC ....D....866 622-3911
2821 Mission College Blvd Santa Clara (95054) *(P-13302)*
McC Controls LLC ....E....218 847-1317
859 Cotting Ct Ste G Vacaville (95688) *(P-5442)*
McCalls Catering, San Francisco *Also called Events Management Inc (P-11717)*
McCalls Nurseries Inc ....E....559 255-7679
8151 E Olive Ave Fresno (93737) *(P-9636)*
McCampbell Analytical Inc ....D....925 252-9262
1534 Willow Pass Rd Pittsburg (94565) *(P-19278)*
McCann-Erickson Corporation (HQ) ....D....**415 348-5600**
135 Main St Fl 21 San Francisco (94105) *(P-11769)*
McCarthy Bldg Companies Inc ....D....408 908-7005
3975 Freedom Cir Ste 950 Santa Clara (95054) *(P-920)*
McCarthy Ranch ....F....408 356-2300
15425 Los Gatos Blvd # 102 Los Gatos (95032) *(P-3253)*
McCauley Brothers Inc (PA) ....E....**925 439-1000**
6678 Owens Dr Ste 100 Pleasanton (94588) *(P-11903)*
McCc, San Francisco *Also called Mission Child Care Consort (P-17975)*
McClatchy Company ....A....916 321-1941
2100 Q St Sacramento (95816) *(P-19911)*
McClatchy Newspapers Inc (HQ) ....A....**916 321-1855**
1601 Alhambra Blvd # 100 Sacramento (95816) *(P-3456)*
McClellan Business Park LLC ....D....916 965-7100
3140 Peacekeeper Way McClellan (95652) *(P-19569)*
McClellan Hospitality Svcs LLC ....D....916 965-7100
3140 Peacekeeper Way McClellan (95652) *(P-11292)*
McClellan Realty LLC ....E....916 965-7100
3140 Peacekeeper Way McClellan (95652) *(P-10616)*
McClelland Aviation Inc ....E....408 258-4075
2500 Robert Fowler Way San Jose (95148) *(P-7776)*
McClenahan S P Co Tree Service, Portola Valley *Also called SP McClenahan Co (P-522)*
McClone Construction Company ....C....559 431-9411
4340 Product Dr Cameron Park (95682) *(P-671)*
McClone Construction Company ....C....916 358-5495
3880 El Dorado Hills Blvd El Dorado Hills (95762) *(P-1893)*
McClure Convalescent Hospital, Oakland *Also called Independent Quality Care Inc (P-16247)*
McConnell Foundation ....E....530 226-6200
800 Shasta View Dr Redding (96003) *(P-18240)*
McCormick Barstow, Fresno *Also called McCormick Brstow Shppard Wyte (P-17329)*
McCormick Brstow Shppard Wyte (PA) ....C....**559 433-1300**
7647 N Fresno St Fresno (93720) *(P-17329)*
McCourtney Road Transfer Stn ....E....530 274-2215
14741 Wolf Mountain Rd Grass Valley (95949) *(P-8344)*
McCown De Leeuw & Co ....E....650 854-6000
950 Tower Ln Ste 800 Foster City (94404) *(P-10779)*
McCoy's Patrol Service, Suisun City *Also called Hal-Mar-Jac Enterprises (P-14067)*
McCullough Construction Inc ....D....707 825-1014
57 Aldergrove Rd Arcata (95521) *(P-1057)*
McCutcheon Construction Co Inc ....E....925 280-0083
1280 6th St Berkeley (94710) *(P-672)*
McDaniel Manufacturing Inc ....F....530 626-6336
6180 Enterprise Dr Ste D Diamond Springs (95619) *(P-4619)*
McDonald's, Fresno *Also called Macdonalds Restaurants (P-19815)*
McE, Rancho Cordova *Also called Nidec Motor Corporation (P-5047)*
McE, San Rafael *Also called Marin Clean Energy (P-8121)*
McE Corporation (PA) ....D....**925 803-4111**
4000 Industrial Way Concord (94520) *(P-1058)*
McElvany Inc ....D....209 826-1102
13343 Johnson Rd Los Banos (93635) *(P-1118)*
McEntire Landscaping Inc ....E....530 245-4590
4475 Tenaya Ct Ste B Redding (96003) *(P-485)*
McEvoy of Marin LLC ....D....707 778-2307
5935 Red Hill Rd Petaluma (94952) *(P-2465)*
McEvoy Properties LLC ....F....415 537-4200
680 2nd St San Francisco (94107) *(P-3537)*
McEvoy Ranch, Petaluma *Also called McEvoy of Marin LLC (P-2465)*
McFadden Farm ....E....707 743-1122
16000 Powerhouse Rd Potter Valley (95469) *(P-6)*
McGrath Rentcorp ....C....877 221-2813
5700 Las Positas Rd Livermore (94551) *(P-9078)*
McGrath Rentcorp (PA) ....B....**925 606-9200**
5700 Las Positas Rd Livermore (94551) *(P-9079)*
McGrayel Company ....E....559 299-7660
5361 S Villa Ave Fresno (93725) *(P-4164)*
McGuire and Hester (PA) ....B....**510 632-7676**
2810 Harbor Bay Pkwy Alameda (94502) *(P-1119)*
McGuire Real Estate, San Francisco *Also called Walter E Mc Guire RE Inc (P-10681)*
MCH, Madera *Also called Madera Community Hospital (P-16436)*
Mch Electric Inc (PA) ....C....**925 453-5041**
7693 Longard Rd Livermore (94551) *(P-1539)*
MCHC, Ukiah *Also called Mendocino Cmnty Hlth Clnic Inc (P-15529)*
McHenry Medical Group Inc ....D....209 577-3388
1541 Florida Ave Ste 200 Modesto (95350) *(P-15523)*
McInerney & Dillon PC ....E....510 465-7100
180 Grand Ave Ste 1390 Oakland (94612) *(P-17330)*
McInnis Park Golf Center Ltd (PA) ....E....**415 492-1800**
14 Commercial Blvd # 119 Novato (94949) *(P-15010)*
McIntyre ....D....510 614-5890
14680 Wicks Blvd San Leandro (94577) *(P-19570)*
McKee and Company Electric ....D....415 724-2738
594 Monterey Blvd San Francisco (94127) *(P-1540)*
McKenzie Hardware Inc ....E....707 448-2978
627 Merchant St Vacaville (95688) *(P-8987)*

McKenzie Machining Inc....F....408 748-8885
481 Perry Ct Santa Clara (95054) *(P-5568)*
McKesson Corporation....D....510 666-0854
3000 Colby St Berkeley (94705) *(P-9230)*
McKesson Corporation....F....916 372-4600
3775 Seaport Blvd West Sacramento (95691) *(P-7001)*
McKesson Medical Surgical, San Francisco *Also called McKesson Medical-Surgical Inc (P-9231)*
McKesson Medical-Surgical Inc....D....415 983-8300
1 Post St Fl 18 San Francisco (94104) *(P-9231)*
McKesson Spclty Hlth Tech Pdts (HQ)....E....415 983-8300
1 Post St Fl 18 San Francisco (94104) *(P-9232)*
McKinley Park Care Center, Sacramento *Also called Azalea Holdings LLC (P-15921)*
McKinleyville Cmnty Svcs Dst....E....707 839-3251
1656 Sutter Rd McKinleyville (95519) *(P-8285)*
McKinsey & Company Inc....B....415 981-0250
555 California St # 4800 San Francisco (94104) *(P-19571)*
McLane Foodservice Dist Inc....C....209 823-7157
800 Mellon Ave Manteca (95337) *(P-9278)*
McLane Foodservice Dist Inc....D....252 985-7200
5675 Sunol Blvd Pleasanton (94566) *(P-9326)*
McLane/Pacific Inc....B....209 725-2500
3876 E Childs Ave Merced (95341) *(P-9279)*
McLarney Construction Inc....E....408 246-8600
355 S Daniel Way San Jose (95128) *(P-921)*
McLaughlin Waste Equipment Inc (PA)....D....209 367-8810
11900 Locke Rd Lockeford (95237) *(P-9080)*
MCM Construction Inc (PA)....D....916 334-1221
6413 32nd St North Highlands (95660) *(P-1084)*
McManis Family Vineyards, Ripon *Also called R J M Enterprises Inc (P-70)*
McManis Family Vineyards Inc....E....209 599-1186
18700 E River Rd Ripon (95366) *(P-2656)*
McManis Faulkner A Prof Corp....E....408 279-8700
50 W San Fernando St # 1000 San Jose (95113) *(P-17331)*
McMillan - Hendryx Inc....F....209 538-2300
3924 Starlite Dr Ste B Ceres (95307) *(P-4203)*
McMillan Data Cmmnications Inc....D....415 992-6582
1823 Egbert Ave San Francisco (94124) *(P-1541)*
McMillan Electric....B....415 826-5100
1950 Cesar Chavez San Francisco (94124) *(P-1542)*
McMillen Jacobs Associates Inc (PA)....D....415 434-1822
49 Stevenson St Ste 1200 San Francisco (94105) *(P-18765)*
McNab Ridge Winery, Ukiah *Also called Plc LLC (P-2686)*
McNab Ridge Winery LLC....F....707 462-2423
2350 Mcnab Ranch Rd Ukiah (95482) *(P-2657)*
McNaughton Newspapers....D....530 756-0800
315 G St Davis (95616) *(P-3457)*
McNaughton Newspapers Inc (PA)....D....707 425-4646
1250 Texas St Fairfield (94533) *(P-3458)*
McNeal Enterprises Inc....D....408 922-7290
2031 Ringwood Ave San Jose (95131) *(P-4300)*
McNear Brick & Block, San Rafael *Also called L P McNear Brick Co Inc (P-4414)*
MCS Opco LLC....E....203 740-4236
905 Cottinlane Vacaville (95688) *(P-8868)*
McUbe Inc (PA)....D....408 637-5503
2570 N 1st St Ste 300 San Jose (95131) *(P-6194)*
McV Group Inc (PA)....E....559 431-3142
7045 N Fruit Ave Fresno (93711) *(P-13934)*
McWane Inc....C....510 632-3467
7825 San Leandro St Oakland (94621) *(P-4549)*
McWane Inc....F....559 834-4630
2581 S Golden State Blvd Fowler (93625) *(P-4550)*
McWealth Care Inc....E....559 293-3174
1616 W Shaw Ave Ste B4 Fresno (93711) *(P-16252)*
MD Imaging Inc A Prof Med Corp....D....530 243-1249
2020 Court St Redding (96001) *(P-15524)*
Mda Cmmunications Holdings LLC....E....650 852-4000
3825 Fabian Way Palo Alto (94303) *(P-5855)*
Mdc Precision, Hayward *Also called Mdc Vacuum Products LLC (P-5186)*
Mdc Vacuum Products LLC (PA)....D....510 265-3500
30962 Santana St Hayward (94544) *(P-5186)*
Mdc Vacuum Products LLC....C....510 265-3500
23874b Cabot Blvd Hayward (94545) *(P-4955)*
MDE Electric, Sunnyvale *Also called MDE Electric Company Inc (P-1543)*
MDE Electric Company Inc....E....408 738-8600
152 Commercial St Sunnyvale (94086) *(P-1543)*
Mdusd....E....925 682-8000
1936 Carlotta Dr Concord (94519) *(P-17160)*
Mdv Management Company LLC....E....650 233-9301
3000 Sand Hill Rd 3-290 Menlo Park (94025) *(P-10868)*
ME-N-ED'S PIZZERIA, Fresno *Also called Milano Restaurants Intl Corp (P-10807)*
Meadow Club....D....415 453-3274
1001 Bolinas Rd Fairfax (94930) *(P-15108)*
Meadowood Assoc A Ltd Partnr (PA)....C....707 963-3646
900 Meadowood Ln Saint Helena (94574) *(P-11293)*
Meadowood Associates LP....D....707 968-3190
900 Silverado Trl N Saint Helena (94574) *(P-15219)*
Meadowood Care Center, Stockton *Also called Meadowood Hlth Rehabilitation (P-16060)*
Meadowood Hlth Rehabilitation....E....209 956-3444
3110 Wagner Heights Rd Stockton (95209) *(P-16060)*
Meadowood Nursing Center, Clearlake *Also called Vindra Inc (P-16154)*
Meadowood Resort and Cntry CLB, Saint Helena *Also called Meadowood Assoc A Ltd Partnr (P-11293)*
Meadows Nappa Valley Care Ctr, NAPA *Also called Califrnia Odd Fllows Hsing Nap (P-10421)*
Meadows of NAPA Valley, NAPA *Also called Califrnia Odd Fllows Hsing Nap (P-10420)*
Meals On Wheels, San Jose *Also called Health Trust (P-17599)*
MEALS ON WHEELS, San Leandro *Also called Service Opprtunity For Seniors (P-17736)*
Meals On Wheels By ACC....E....916 444-9533
7375 Park City Dr Sacramento (95831) *(P-17643)*
Meals On Wheels Diablo Region (PA)....E....925 937-8311
1300 Civic Dr Fl 1 Walnut Creek (94596) *(P-17644)*
Meals On Whels San Frncsco Inc....E....415 920-1111
1375 Fairfax Ave San Francisco (94124) *(P-17645)*
Meals On Whels Solano Cnty Inc....D....707 426-3079
95 Marina Ctr Suisun City (94585) *(P-17646)*
Meany Wilson L P....E....415 905-5300
4 Embarcadero Ctr # 3330 San Francisco (94111) *(P-10708)*
Measurement Specialties Inc....D....530 273-4608
424 Crown Point Cir Grass Valley (95945) *(P-6770)*
Mechanical Analysis/Repair Inc....E....209 333-8478
142 N Cluff Ave Lodi (95240) *(P-14763)*
Mechanics Bank (HQ)....C....800 797-6324
1111 Civic Dr Ste 290 Walnut Creek (94596) *(P-9738)*
Mecoptron Inc....F....510 226-9966
3115 Osgood Ct Fremont (94539) *(P-5569)*
Mecpro Inc....D....408 727-9757
980 George St Santa Clara (95054) *(P-5570)*
Med-Data Incorporated....D....916 771-1362
3741 Douglas Blvd Ste 170 Roseville (95661) *(P-18978)*
Medallia Inc (PA)....C....650 321-3000
575 Market St Ste 1850 San Francisco (94105) *(P-13303)*
Medallion Cnstr Clean-Up, Mountain View *Also called Service By Medallion (P-11996)*
Medallion Industries Inc....F....925 449-9040
4771 Arroyo Vis Ste F Livermore (94551) *(P-8589)*
Medallion Landscape MGT Inc (PA)....D....408 782-7500
10 San Bruno Ave Morgan Hill (95037) *(P-425)*
Medamerica Inc....E....408 281-2772
554 Blossom Hill Rd San Jose (95123) *(P-15525)*
Medamerica Billing Svcs Inc (HQ)....B....209 491-7710
1601 Cummins Dr Ste D Modesto (95358) *(P-18979)*
Medconx Inc....D....408 330-0003
2901 Tasman Dr Ste 211 Santa Clara (95054) *(P-4217)*
Medcore Medical Group....D....209 320-2600
2609 E Hammer Ln Stockton (95210) *(P-18340)*
Medeonbio Inc....E....650 397-5100
452 Oakmead Pkwy Sunnyvale (94085) *(P-7002)*
Medgle, San Mateo *Also called Lumiata Inc (P-19085)*
Medi-Flight Northern Cal, Modesto *Also called Sutter Central Vly Hospitals (P-16578)*
Media News, Paradise *Also called Califrnia Nwspapers Ltd Partnr (P-3425)*
Media News Groups, Vacaville *Also called Reporter (P-3475)*
Media Print Services Inc....F....866 935-5077
10012 Del Almendra Dr Oakdale (95361) *(P-11868)*
Mediajel Inc (PA)....E....925 393-0444
1601 N Main St Ste 101 Walnut Creek (94596) *(P-12601)*
Medianews Group Inc....B....408 920-5713
4 N 2nd St Ste 800 San Jose (95113) *(P-3459)*
Mediatek USA Inc (PA)....C....408 526-1899
2840 Junction Ave San Jose (95134) *(P-5259)*
Medic Ambulance Service Inc (PA)....C....707 644-1761
506 Couch St Vallejo (94590) *(P-7387)*
Medic Ambulance Service Inc....E....916 564-9011
1001 Texas St Ste C Fairfield (94533) *(P-7388)*
Medical Ambassadors Intl....E....209 543-7500
5012 Salida Blvd Salida (95368) *(P-18241)*
Medical Analysis Systems Inc (HQ)....C....510 979-5000
46360 Fremont Blvd Fremont (94538) *(P-6837)*
Medical Anesthesia Cons LLC....C....925 287-1505
100 N Wiget Ln Ste 160 Walnut Creek (94598) *(P-15526)*
Medical Anesthesia Cons LLC (HQ)....E....925 543-0140
2175 N Calif Blvd Ste 425 Walnut Creek (94596) *(P-15527)*
Medical Billing Services, Hercules *Also called West Coast Pathology Lab (P-16821)*
Medical Blling Intgration Svcs, Fresno *Also called Anesthsia Cons of Frsno A Med (P-15280)*
Medical Care Professionals Inc....E....650 583-9898
363 El Cmino Real Ste 215 South San Francisco (94080) *(P-16061)*
Medical Center Mgntic Imaging, Oakland *Also called Health Ventures Inc (P-16783)*
Medical Center of Marin, Corte Madera *Also called Brett V Crtis MD A Prof Corp I (P-15301)*
Medical Centre, Sacramento *Also called University California Davis (P-16701)*
Medical Eye Group, Grass Valley *Also called Sierra View Medical Eye Inc (P-15687)*
Medical Hill Healthcare Center, Oakland *Also called Oaklandidence Opco LLC (P-16195)*
Medical Hill Rehabilitation, Oakland *Also called Ocadian Care Centers LLC (P-16082)*
Medical HM Care Professionals, Redding *Also called Medical Home Specialists Inc (P-16913)*
Medical Home Specialists Inc....D....530 226-5577
2115 Churn Creek Rd Redding (96002) *(P-16913)*
Medical Instr Dev Labs Inc....E....510 357-3952
557 Mccormick St San Leandro (94577) *(P-7003)*
Medical Insurance Exchange, Oakland *Also called Medical Underwriters Cal Inc (P-10313)*
Medical Insurance Exchange Cal....D....510 596-4935
6250 Claremont Ave Oakland (94618) *(P-10312)*
Medical Linen Service Inc....D....650 873-1221
290 S Maple Ave South San Francisco (94080) *(P-11637)*
Medical Surgery Unit, Placerville *Also called Marshall Medical Center (P-16445)*
Medical Underwriters Cal Inc (PA)....D....510 428-9411
6250 Claremont Ave Oakland (94618) *(P-10313)*
Medical Vision Technology Inc (PA)....E....916 731-8040
1700 Alhambra Blvd # 202 Sacramento (95816) *(P-15528)*
Medisense, Alameda *Also called Abbott Diabetes Care Inc (P-4014)*
Meditab Software Inc....D....510 201-0130
1420 River Park Dr Sacramento (95815) *(P-13304)*
Medius, Morgan Hill *Also called Babylon Printing Inc (P-3626)*
Medivation Inc....F....415 812-6345
499 Illinois St San Francisco (94158) *(P-3946)*
Medivation Inc (HQ)....A....415 543-3470
525 Market St Ste 2800 San Francisco (94105) *(P-3947)*

ALPHABETIC

Employee Codes: A=Over 500 employees, B=251-500
C=101-250, D=51-100, E=20-50 F=10-19
2022 Northern California Business Directory and Buyers Guide
© Mergent Inc. 1-800-342-5647
1019

Medmark Trtmnt Ctrs - Scrmnto — E — 916 391-4293
7240 E Southgate Dr Ste G Sacramento (95823) (P-17038)
Medric, Burlingame Also called Acumen LLC (P-13550)
Medrio Inc (PA) — C — 415 963-3700
345 California St Ste 325 San Francisco (94104) (P-13305)
Medstar LLC — D — 916 669-0550
20 Business Park Way # 100 Sacramento (95828) (P-7389)
Medstar Amblnce Mndcino Cnty I — E — 707 462-3808
130 Ford St Ukiah (95482) (P-7390)
Medtronic Inc — E — 707 541-3144
5345 Skyllane Blvd Santa Rosa (95403) (P-7004)
Medtronic Spine LLC — A — 408 548-6500
1221 Crossman Ave Sunnyvale (94089) (P-7005)
Meeder Equipment Company (PA) — E — 559 485-0979
3495 S Maple Ave Fresno (93725) (P-5157)
Meek's, South Lake Tahoe Also called Cha-Dor Realty LLC (P-8535)
Meek's Lumber & Hardware, Roseville Also called Western Buyers LLC (P-8612)
Mees Moving & Storage Inc (PA) — E — 916 635-8262
2561 Grennan Ct Rancho Cordova (95742) (P-7626)
Mega Creation Inc — E — 510 741-9998
228 Linus Pauling Dr Hercules (94547) (P-4090)
Mega Force Corporation — E — 408 956-9989
2035 Otoole Ave San Jose (95131) (P-5398)
Mega Herbal Products Inc — E — 516 996-7770
2f Ocean Ave San Francisco (94112) (P-3817)
Megachips LSI USA Corporation — D — 408 570-0555
910 E Hamilton Ave # 120 Campbell (95008) (P-6195)
Megacycle Cams, San Rafael Also called Megacycle Engineering Inc (P-6653)
Megacycle Engineering Inc — E — 415 472-3195
90 Mitchell Blvd San Rafael (94903) (P-6653)
Megaforce, San Jose Also called Mega Force Corporation (P-5398)
Megapath, Pleasanton Also called Covad Communications Group Inc (P-7944)
Megapath, Pleasanton Also called Gtt Communications (mp) Inc (P-7957)
Mehus Construction Inc — E — 408 395-2388
211 San Mateo Ave Los Gatos (95030) (P-673)
Meivac Incorporated — E — 408 362-1000
5830 Hellyer Ave San Jose (95138) (P-6196)
Mek Norwood Pines LLC — D — 916 922-7177
500 Jessie Ave Sacramento (95838) (P-16062)
Mekanism Inc (PA) — E — 415 908-4000
570 Pacific Ave San Francisco (94133) (P-11770)
Mel Rapton Inc — C — 916 514-4050
2329 Fulton Ave Sacramento (95825) (P-14764)
Mel Rapton Honda, Sacramento Also called Mel Rapton Inc (P-14764)
Meldisco K-M Rancho Cordova CA — E — 916 635-3400
2344 Sunrise Blvd Gold River (95670) (P-19572)
Mele Enterprises Inc — E — 530 674-7900
399 State Highway 99 Yuba City (95993) (P-14578)
Melgar Facility Maint LLC (PA) — B — 408 657-0110
6980 Santa Teresa Blvd San Jose (95119) (P-11970)
Melgar Janitorial Solutions, San Jose Also called Melgar Facility Maint LLC (P-11970)
Melin Enterprises Inc — D — 209 726-9182
812 W 18th St Merced (95340) (P-11971)
Melissa & Doug LLC — D — 209 830-7900
4718 Newcastle Rd Stockton (95215) (P-9169)
Melissa Bradley RE Inc — E — 707 258-3900
3249 Browns Valley Rd NAPA (94558) (P-10617)
Melissa Bradley RE Inc — E — 707 536-0888
1401 4th St Santa Rosa (95404) (P-10618)
Melissa Bradley RE Inc — E — 415 435-2705
1690 Tiburon Blvd Belvedere Tiburon (94920) (P-10619)
Melissa Bradley RE Inc — E — 415 209-1000
1701 Novato Blvd Ste 100 Novato (94947) (P-10620)
Melissa Bradley RE Inc — E — 415 455-1080
850 Sir Frncis Drake Blvd San Anselmo (94960) (P-10621)
Melita Group, The, San Jose Also called Melita-Mcdonald Insur Svcs Inc (P-10314)
Melita-Mcdonald Insur Svcs Inc — E — 408 882-0800
75 E Santa Clara St # 1200 San Jose (95113) (P-10314)
Melkonian Enterprises Inc — E — 559 217-0749
2730 S De Wolf Ave Sanger (93657) (P-2263)
Mellanox Technologies Inc — F — 408 970-3400
2530 Zanker Rd San Jose (95131) (P-6197)
Mellanox Technologies Inc (HQ) — A — 408 970-3400
2530 Zanker Rd San Jose (95131) (P-6198)
Mellon Capital Management, San Francisco Also called Mellon Global Oprtnty Fund LLC (P-10765)
Mellon Global Oprtnty Fund LLC — E — 415 546-6056
50 Fremont St Ste 3900 San Francisco (94105) (P-10765)
Melo Machine & Mfg Inc — F — 209 892-2661
1707 Magnolia Ave Patterson (95363) (P-9123)
Melon Holdings LLC — D — 530 742-7311
1617 Ramirez St Marysville (95901) (P-16063)
Melrose Metal Products Inc — E — 510 657-8771
44533 S Grimmer Blvd Fremont (94538) (P-4786)
Melrose Nameplate Label Co Inc (PA) — E — 510 732-3100
26575 Corporate Ave Hayward (94545) (P-4938)
Meltwater News US Inc (HQ) — D — 415 829-5900
465 California St Fl 11 San Francisco (94104) (P-14156)
Members 1st Credit Union (PA) — E — 530 222-6060
4710 Mountain Lakes Blvd Redding (96003) (P-9794)
Membership Assction-Non-Profit, San Francisco Also called Interntnal Assn Bus Cmmncators (P-18307)
Membrane Technology & RES Inc (PA) — E — 650 328-2228
39630 Eureka Dr Newark (94560) (P-19088)
Memorial Medical Center, Modesto Also called Sutter Central Vly Hospitals (P-16575)
Memorial Medical Center, Modesto Also called Sutter Central Vly Hospitals (P-16576)
Memverge Inc — D — 408 605-0841
1525 Mccarthy Blvd # 218 Milpitas (95035) (P-12602)

Menasha Packaging Company LLC — E — 951 660-5361
1550 N Chrisman Rd Tracy (95304) (P-3359)
Mencarini & Jarwin Inc — E — 916 383-1660
5950 88th St Sacramento (95828) (P-4912)
Mendicino Wine Company, Ukiah Also called Parducci Wine Estates LLC (P-2678)
Mendocino Brewing Company Inc (HQ) — D — 707 463-2627
1601 Airport Rd Ukiah (95482) (P-2486)
Mendocino Cast Botanical Grdns, Fort Bragg Also called Mendocino Cast Btncal Grdns Co (P-18293)
Mendocino Cast Btncal Grdns Co — E — 707 964-4352
18220 N Highway 1 Fort Bragg (95437) (P-18293)
Mendocino Cmnty Hlth Clnic Inc (PA) — C — 707 468-1010
333 Laws Ave Ukiah (95482) (P-15529)
Mendocino Cmnty Hlth Clnic Inc — C — 707 456-9600
45 Hazel St Willits (95490) (P-15530)
Mendocino Coast Clinics Inc — D — 707 964-1251
205 South St Fort Bragg (95437) (P-17039)
Mendocino Coast District Hosp (PA) — B — 707 961-1234
700 River Dr Fort Bragg (95437) (P-16455)
Mendocino Forest Pdts Co LLC — C — 707 468-1431
850 Kunzler Ranch Rd Ukiah (95482) (P-8590)
Mendocino Forest Pdts Co LLC — B — 707 620-2961
3700 Old Redwood Hwy # 200 Santa Rosa (95403) (P-8591)
Mendocino Forest Pdts Co LLC — E — 707 485-6800
6375 N State St Calpella (95418) (P-8592)
Mendocino Forest Pdts Co LLC — E — 707 620-2961
1360 19th Hole Dr Ste 200 Windsor (95492) (P-8593)
Mendocino Hotel & Grdn Suites, Mendocino Also called Mendocino Hotel & Resort Corp (P-11294)
Mendocino Hotel & Resort Corp — D — 707 937-0511
45080 Main St Mendocino (95460) (P-11294)
Mendocino Land Company Inc (HQ) — D — 510 286-2000
383 4th St Ste 400 Oakland (94607) (P-65)
Mendocino Onsen Corportation — E — 707 462-6277
13201 Orr Springs Rd Ukiah (95482) (P-11295)
Mendocino Railway — D — 707 964-6371
100 W Laurel St Fort Bragg (95437) (P-7847)
Mendocino Redwood Company LLC (PA) — E — 707 463-5110
850 Kunzler Ranch Rd Ukiah (95482) (P-8594)
Mendocino Transit Authority (PA) — E — 707 462-3881
241 Plant Rd Ukiah (95482) (P-7341)
Mendoza & Associates (PA) — E — 415 644-0180
1390 Market St Ste 200 San Francisco (94102) (P-19370)
Menezes Hay Co — F — 209 394-3111
5030 Dwight Way Livingston (95334) (P-2348)
Menke & Associates Inc (PA) — E — 415 362-5200
1 Kaiser Plz Ste 505 Oakland (94612) (P-19818)
Menlo Circus Club — D — 650 322-4616
190 Park Ln Atherton (94027) (P-15109)
Menlo Country Club — D — 650 369-2342
2300 Woodside Rd Woodside (94062) (P-15110)
Menlo Gateway Inc — D — 650 356-2900
303 Vintage Park Dr # 250 Foster City (94404) (P-10472)
Menlo Industries Inc — D — 510 770-2350
44060 Old Warm Sprng Blvd Fremont (94538) (P-6453)
Menlo Park Surgical Hospital, Burlingame Also called Suttercare Corporation (P-16683)
Menlo Park VA Medical Center, Menlo Park Also called Veterans Health Administration (P-15804)
Menlo Prk-Thrton Edcatn Fndtio (PA) — E — 650 325-0100
181 Encinal Ave Atherton (94027) (P-18580)
Menlo Security Inc (PA) — D — 650 614-1705
800 W El Cmino Real Ste 2 Mountain View (94040) (P-12603)
Mens Wearhouse — E — 510 657-9821
6100 Stevenson Blvd Fremont (94538) (P-2989)
MENTAL HEALTH ASSOCIATION OF A, Oakland Also called Alameda Cnty Mental Hlth Assn (P-16984)
Mental Health Department, Oakland Also called La Clinica De La Raza Inc (P-15500)
Mental Health Services, Stockton Also called County of San Joaquin (P-17008)
Mental Health Services, San Jose Also called Santa Clara County of (P-17068)
Mental Hlth Assn San Francisco — E — 415 421-2926
870 Market St Ste 928 San Francisco (94102) (P-17040)
Mental Hlth Dpt-Administration, San Jose Also called Santa Clara County of (P-17066)
Mentis — E — 707 255-0966
709 Franklin St NAPA (94559) (P-17647)
Mentor Tchnical Group Intl LLC — E — 787 743-0897
601 Gateway Blvd Ste 1210 South San Francisco (94080) (P-19573)
Mentzer Electronics — E — 650 697-2642
858 Stanton Rd Burlingame (94010) (P-7113)
Mepco Label Systems — D — 209 946-0201
1313 S Stockton St Lodi (95240) (P-3742)
Meraki LLC (HQ) — B — 415 632-5800
500 Terry A Francois Blvd San Francisco (94158) (P-13935)
Meraqi Medical Inc — B — 669 222-7710
47225 Fremont Blvd Fremont (94538) (P-7006)
Mercado Latino Inc — E — 415 282-5563
2006 Jerrold Ave San Francisco (94124) (P-9417)
Mercado Latino Inc — C — 510 475-5500
33430 Western Ave Union City (94587) (P-9280)
Merced A Park California LP — E — 209 334-6565
2020 W Kettleman Ln Lodi (95242) (P-10449)
Merced City School District — D — 209 385-6364
2736 Franklin Rd Merced (95348) (P-17973)
Merced County Assn Governments — E — 209 723-3153
369 W 18th St Merced (95340) (P-19819)
Merced Faculty Associates (PA) — E — 209 723-3704
220 E 13th St Ste B Merced (95341) (P-15531)
Merced Irrigation District (PA) — E — 209 722-5761
744 W 20th St Merced (95340) (P-8123)

Merced Irrigation District ....D....209 722-2719
3321 Franklin Rd Merced (95348) ***(P-8414)***
Merced Irrigation District ....D....209 378-2421
9188 Village Dr Snelling (95369) ***(P-8124)***
Merced Medical Clinic Inc ....E....209 722-8047
650 W Olive Ave Merced (95348) ***(P-15532)***
Merced Orthopedic Med Group ....D....209 722-8161
123 W North Bear Creek Dr Merced (95348) ***(P-15533)***
Merced Schl Emplyees Fdral Cr (PA) ....**D....209 383-5550**
1021 Olivewood Dr Merced (95348) ***(P-9795)***
Merced Screw Products Inc ....E....209 723-7706
1861 Grogan Ave Merced (95341) ***(P-4867)***
Merced Transportation Company ....D....209 384-2575
300 Grogan Ave Merced (95341) ***(P-7441)***
Merced Urology Med Group Inc ....E....209 723-2122
2517 Canal St Ste 1 Merced (95340) ***(P-15534)***
Merceds-Benz RES Dev N Amer In (HQ) ....**E....650 845-2500**
309 N Pastoria Ave Sunnyvale (94085) ***(P-19089)***
Mercer Consulting Group Inc ....E....415 743-8510
3 Embarkadero Ctr Oakland (94619) ***(P-10315)***
Mercer Foods LLC (HQ) ....**F....209 529-0150**
1836 Lapham Dr Modesto (95354) ***(P-2264)***
Merchant Services Inc (PA) ....**B....817 725-0900**
1 S Van Ness Ave Fl 5 San Francisco (94103) ***(P-13728)***
Merchant Valley Corp ....E....916 410-2021
1786 Jayne Ave Coalinga (93210) ***(P-11296)***
Merchant Valley Corporation ....C....916 786-7227
1808 Avondale Dr Roseville (95747) ***(P-18309)***
Merchants Bank of Commerce (HQ) ....**D....530 224-7355**
1951 Churn Creek Rd Redding (96002) ***(P-9739)***
Mercury, Tracy *Also called Tracy Ford* ***(P-14601)***
Mercury Air Cargo Inc ....E....650 588-5440
648 West Field Rd San Francisco (94128) ***(P-14813)***
Mercury Insurance Company ....B....916 353-4859
104 Woodmere Rd Folsom (95630) ***(P-10170)***
Mercury Insurance Group, Folsom *Also called Mercury Insurance Company* ***(P-10170)***
Mercury Systems Inc ....D....510 252-0870
47200 Bayside Pkwy Fremont (94538) ***(P-5260)***
Mercy Doctors Med Group Inc ....E....415 752-0100
1 Shrader St Ste 640 San Francisco (94117) ***(P-15535)***
Mercy Gen Radiation Oncology, Sacramento *Also called Sutter Health* ***(P-15722)***
Mercy HM Svcs A Cal Ltd Partnr (HQ) ....**A....530 225-6000**
2175 Rosaline Ave Ste A Redding (96001) ***(P-16456)***
MERCY MCMAHON TERRACE, Sacramento *Also called Senior Mercy Housing Inc* ***(P-18179)***
Mercy Medical, Red Bluff *Also called Lassen Medical Group Inc* ***(P-15503)***
Mercy Medical Center - Redding, Redding *Also called Mercy HM Svcs A Cal Ltd Partnr* ***(P-16456)***
MERCY MEDICAL CENTER MERCED, Merced *Also called Mater Misericordiae Hospital* ***(P-16453)***
Mercy Retirement and Care Ctr ....D....510 534-8540
3431 Foothill Blvd Oakland (94601) ***(P-18145)***
Mercy San Juan Medical Center, Carmichael *Also called Dignity Health* ***(P-16348)***
Mercy San Juan Surgery Center, Roseville *Also called Dignity Health* ***(P-15381)***
Mercy Services Corporation ....E....650 359-6161
903 Oceana Blvd Ofc Pacifica (94044) ***(P-17648)***
Mercy Surgery Center LP ....D....530 225-7400
2175 Rosaline Ave Ste A Redding (96001) ***(P-16457)***
Meredith Corporation ....D....415 249-2362
201 Mission St Fl 12 San Francisco (94105) ***(P-3538)***
Meredith Publishing, San Francisco *Also called Meredith Corporation* ***(P-3538)***
Meredith Vineyard Estate Inc ....F....707 823-7466
636 Gold Ridge Rd Sebastopol (95472) ***(P-2658)***
Mereo Biopharma 5 Inc ....D....650 995-8200
800 Chesapeake Dr Redwood City (94063) ***(P-3948)***
Meridian Gold Inc ....B....209 785-3222
4461 Rock Creek Rd Copperopolis (95228) ***(P-541)***
Meridian Growers Proc Inc ....F....559 458-7272
1625 Howard Rd Madera (93637) ***(P-2449)***
Meridian Knwldge Solutions LLC (HQ) ....**E....916 985-9625**
80 Iron Point Cir Ste 100 Folsom (95630) ***(P-19574)***
Meridian Management Group ....C....415 434-9700
1145 Bush St San Francisco (94109) ***(P-10622)***
Meridian Supply, Meridian *Also called Davis Machine Shop Inc* ***(P-5002)***
Meriliz Incorporated ....C....916 923-3663
2031 Dome Ln McClellan (95652) ***(P-3676)***
Mering Holdings (PA) ....**D....916 441-0571**
1700 I St Ste 210 Sacramento (95811) ***(P-11771)***
Merit Ends Inc., Pittsburg *Also called Pittsburg General Inc* ***(P-4805)***
Meritage Group LP ....A....415 399-5330
1 Ferry Building San Francisco (94111) ***(P-19371)***
Meritage Medical Network ....D....415 884-1840
4 Hamilton Landing # 100 Novato (94949) ***(P-12185)***
Meritage Resort LLC ....B....707 251-1900
875 Bordeaux Way NAPA (94558) ***(P-11297)***
Meritage Resort and Spa, The, NAPA *Also called Meritage Resort LLC* ***(P-11297)***
Meritronics Inc (PA) ....**E....408 969-0888**
500 Yosemite Dr Ste 108 Milpitas (95035) ***(P-5946)***
Meritronics Materials Inc ....F....408 390-5642
42660 Christy St Fremont (94538) ***(P-5947)***
Meriwest Credit Union (PA) ....**C....408 363-3200**
5615 Chesbro Ave Ste 100 San Jose (95123) ***(P-9796)***
Merlin Solar Technologies Inc (HQ) ....**E....650 740-1160**
5891 Rue Ferrari San Jose (95138) ***(P-6199)***
Merrill Lynch Pierce Fenner ....D....650 473-7888
333 Middlefield Rd Menlo Park (94025) ***(P-9980)***
Merrill Lynch Pierce Fenner ....D....408 260-6001
560 S Winchester Blvd San Jose (95128) ***(P-9981)***
Merrill Lynch Prce Fnner Smith, Sacramento *Also called Merrill Lynch Prce Fnner Smith* ***(P-9989)***
Merrill Lynch Prce Fnner Smith ....D....925 988-2113
150 Parker St Vacaville (95688) ***(P-9982)***
Merrill Lynch Prce Fnner Smith ....D....530 223-3005
292 Hemsted Dr Ste 100 Redding (96002) ***(P-9983)***
Merrill Lynch Prce Fnner Smith ....D....650 842-2440
3075b Hansen Way Palo Alto (94304) ***(P-9984)***
Merrill Lynch Prce Fnner Smith ....C....415 955-3700
555 California St Fl 9 San Francisco (94104) ***(P-9985)***
Merrill Lynch Prce Fnner Smith ....D....209 578-2600
801 10th St Fl 7-1 Modesto (95354) ***(P-9986)***
Merrill Lynch Prce Fnner Smith ....D....916 984-3200
2320 E Bidwell St Ste 100 Folsom (95630) ***(P-9987)***
Merrill Lynch Prce Fnner Smith ....D....408 283-3000
50 W San Fernando St 16 San Jose (95113) ***(P-9988)***
Merrill Lynch Prce Fnner Smith ....D....916 648-6200
555 Capitol Mall Sacramento (95814) ***(P-9989)***
Merrill Lynch Prce Fnner Smith ....D....925 227-6600
4900 Hopyard Rd Ste 140 Pleasanton (94588) ***(P-9990)***
Merrill Lynch Prce Fnner Smith ....C....415 676-2500
101 California St Fl 21 San Francisco (94111) ***(P-9685)***
Merrill Lynch Prce Fnner Smith ....D....209 472-3500
3255 W March Ln Ste 110 Stockton (95219) ***(P-9991)***
Merrill Lynch Prce Fnner Smith ....D....707 575-6374
90 S E St Frnt Santa Rosa (95404) ***(P-9992)***
Merrill Lynch Prce Fnner Smith ....D....925 945-4800
1331 N Calif Blvd Ste 400 Walnut Creek (94596) ***(P-9993)***
Merrill Lynch Prce Fnner Smith ....E....415 274-7000
101 California St Fl 24 San Francisco (94111) ***(P-9994)***
Merrill Lynch Prce Fnner Smith ....D....559 436-0919
5260 N Palm Ave Ste 100 Fresno (93704) ***(P-9995)***
Merrill Lynch Prce Fnner Smith ....D....650 579-3050
101 S Ellsworth Ave Fl 4 San Mateo (94401) ***(P-9996)***
Merrill Lynch Prce Fnner Smith ....D....415 289-8800
2 Belvedere Pl Ste 100 Mill Valley (94941) ***(P-9997)***
Merrill Lynch Wealth MGT, San Jose *Also called Merrill Lynch Pierce Fenner* ***(P-9981)***
Merrill's Packaging Supply, Burlingame *Also called Merrills Packaging Inc* ***(P-4231)***
Merrills Packaging Inc ....D....650 259-5959
1529 Rollins Rd Burlingame (94010) ***(P-4231)***
Merrimak Capital Company LLC ....E....415 475-4100
64 Digital Dr Novato (94949) ***(P-12054)***
Merry Edwards Wines, Sebastopol *Also called Meredith Vineyard Estate Inc* ***(P-2658)***
Merryvale Vineyards LLC ....E....707 963-2225
1000 Main St Saint Helena (94574) ***(P-2659)***
Meru Health Holding Inc ....E....760 841-8040
19 S B St San Mateo (94401) ***(P-17041)***
Meru Networks Inc (HQ) ....**B....408 215-5300**
894 Ross Dr Sunnyvale (94089) ***(P-5890)***
Mes Solutions ....E....916 920-1222
11010 White Rock Rd # 160 Rancho Cordova (95670) ***(P-17161)***
Mesa/Boogie Limited (HQ) ....**D....707 765-1805**
1317 Ross St Petaluma (94954) ***(P-5763)***
Mesmerize LLC ....C....415 374-8298
350 Frank H Ogawa Plz # 310 Oakland (94612) ***(P-19575)***
Messagesolution Inc ....D....925 833-8000
7080 Donlon Way Ste 216 Dublin (94568) ***(P-13936)***
Messer LLC ....F....916 381-1606
5858 88th St Sacramento (95828) ***(P-3775)***
Messer LLC ....E....408 496-1177
2041 Mission College Blvd Santa Clara (95054) ***(P-5177)***
Messer Logging Inc ....E....559 855-3160
32111 Rock Hill Ln Auberry (93602) ***(P-3072)***
Meta Platforms Inc (PA) ....**A....650 543-4800**
1601 Willow Rd Menlo Park (94025) ***(P-13800)***
Metabyte Inc ....D....510 494-9700
43238 Christy St Fremont (94538) ***(P-13937)***
Metadesign Inc ....E....415 627-0790
2001 The Embarcadero San Francisco (94133) ***(P-11869)***
Metal Fd Hhld Pdts Pckging Div, Oakdale *Also called Ball Corporation* ***(P-4597)***
Metal Improvement Company LLC ....E....925 960-1090
7655 Longard Rd Bldg A Livermore (94551) ***(P-4588)***
Metal Manufacturing Co Inc ....E....916 922-3484
2240 Evergreen St Sacramento (95815) ***(P-4705)***
Metal Sales Manufacturing Corp ....E....707 826-2653
1326 Paddock Pl Woodland (95776) ***(P-4787)***
Metal Works Supply, Oroville *Also called Smb Industries Inc* ***(P-4684)***
Metalfab, Santa Clara *Also called Sutter P Dahlglen Entps Inc* ***(P-5624)***
Metalfx, Willits *Also called Advanced Mfg & Dev Inc* ***(P-4738)***
Metals Direct Inc ....E....530 605-1931
6771 Eastside Rd Redding (96001) ***(P-4788)***
Metals USA Building Pdts LP ....E....916 635-2245
11340 White Rock Rd Ste B Rancho Cordova (95742) ***(P-4563)***
Metalset Inc ....E....510 233-9998
1200 Hensley St Richmond (94801) ***(P-4676)***
Metamining Inc ....F....650 212-7900
1065 E Hillsdale Blvd Foster City (94404) ***(P-544)***
Metaswitch Networks ....E....415 513-1500
1751 Harbor Bay Pkwy # 125 Alameda (94502) ***(P-12604)***
Metaverse Mod Squad, Sacramento *Also called Modsquad Inc* ***(P-19579)***
Methadone Treatment Center, San Francisco *Also called Westside Cmnty Mental Hlth Ctr* ***(P-17094)***
Method Home Products ....F....415 568-4600
631 Howard St Fl 5 San Francisco (94105) ***(P-3345)***
Method Studios, San Francisco *Also called Atomic Fiction Inc* ***(P-14800)***
Methodist Hospital Sacramento, Sacramento *Also called Dignity Health* ***(P-16349)***
Metlsaw Systems Inc ....E....707 746-6200
2950 Bay Vista Ct Benicia (94510) ***(P-5076)***

ALPHABETIC

Metra Biosystems Inc (HQ) ....E....**408 616-4300**
2981 Copper Rd Santa Clara (95051) ***(P-4024)***
Metreo Inc ....A....650 935-9400
3500 W Bayshore Rd Palo Alto (94303) ***(P-12605)***
Metric Equipment Sales Inc ....D....510 264-0887
25841 Industrial Blvd # 200 Hayward (94545) ***(P-8932)***
Metric Theory LLC ....C....415 659-8600
311 California St Ste 200 San Francisco (94104) ***(P-11772)***
Metricstream Inc (PA) ....C....**650 620-2955**
6201 America Center Dr # 240 San Jose (95002) ***(P-13306)***
Metricus Inc ....C....650 328-2500
P.O. Box 458 Palo Alto (94302) ***(P-14330)***
Metro Caseworks, Fremont *Also called Goldfire Corporation* ***(P-1739)***
Metro Poly Corporation ....E....510 357-9898
1651 Aurora Dr San Leandro (94577) ***(P-3385)***
Metro Publishing Inc ....E....707 527-1200
445 Center St Healdsburg (95448) ***(P-3460)***
Metro Unlimited Wireless, Elk Grove *Also called Unlimited R US Inc* ***(P-7917)***
Metro YMCA Leitch, Fremont *Also called Young MNS Chrstn Assn of E Bay* ***(P-18508)***
Metromile Inc (PA) ....C....**888 242-5204**
425 Market St Ste 700 San Francisco (94105) ***(P-9860)***
Metromile Operating Company (PA) ....D....**888 244-1702**
425 Market St Ste 700 San Francisco (94105) ***(P-10171)***
Metropcs-Modesto, Modesto *Also called T-Mobile Usa Inc* ***(P-7914)***
Metroplitan Oakland Intl Arprt, Oakland *Also called Port Dept of The Cy Oakland* ***(P-7781)***
Metropltan Pain MGT Cons Inc A ....E....916 568-8338
2288 Auburn Blvd Ste 106 Sacramento (95821) ***(P-15536)***
Metropolitan Club ....D....415 673-0600
640 Sutter St San Francisco (94102) ***(P-15111)***
Metropolitan Education Dst (PA) ....B....**408 723-6464**
760 Hillsdale Ave Bldg 6 San Jose (95136) ***(P-17822)***
Metropolitan Elec Cnstr Inc ....C....415 642-3000
2400 3rd St San Francisco (94107) ***(P-1544)***
Metropolitan Golf Links ....E....510 569-5555
10505 Doolittle Dr Oakland (94603) ***(P-15011)***
Metropolitan Pain Mgmt Cons, Sacramento *Also called Metropltan Pain MGT Cons Inc A* ***(P-15536)***
Metropolitan Trnsp Comm (PA) ....D....**415 778-6700**
375 Beale St Ste 800 San Francisco (94105) ***(P-7342)***
Metropolitan Van and Stor Inc (PA) ....E....**707 745-1150**
5400 Industrial Way Benicia (94510) ***(P-7568)***
Metrosa, Healdsburg *Also called Metro Publishing Inc* ***(P-3460)***
Metrotech Corporation (PA) ....D....**408 734-3880**
3251 Olcott St Santa Clara (95054) ***(P-6675)***
Mettler-Toledo Rainin LLC (HQ) ....C....**510 564-1600**
7500 Edgewater Dr Oakland (94621) ***(P-6910)***
Mexi, Santa Cruz *Also called Seltzer Revolutions Inc* ***(P-2778)***
Mexican Heritg Ctr Gallery Inc ....D....209 969-9306
111 S Sutter St Stockton (95202) ***(P-18275)***
Mexico Tortilla Factory & Deli ....F....510 792-9909
7015 Thornton Ave Newark (94560) ***(P-2922)***
Meyenburg Goat Milk Products, Turlock *Also called Jackson-Mitchell Inc* ***(P-2192)***
Meyer Corporation US (HQ) ....D....**707 551-2800**
1 Meyer Plz Vallejo (94590) ***(P-4886)***
Meyer Sound Laboratories Inc (PA) ....C....**510 486-1166**
2832 San Pablo Ave Berkeley (94702) ***(P-5764)***
Meyer Sound Labs, Berkeley *Also called Meyer Sound Laboratories Inc* ***(P-5764)***
Meyer Wines, Vallejo *Also called Meyer Corporation US* ***(P-4886)***
Meyers Earthwork Inc ....D....530 365-8858
4150 Fig Tree Ln Redding (96002) ***(P-1965)***
Meyers Nave A Prof Corp (PA) ....D....**510 351-4300**
1999 Harrison St Ste 900 Oakland (94612) ***(P-17332)***
Meyers Sheet Metal Box Inc ....E....650 873-8889
138 W Harris Ave South San Francisco (94080) ***(P-4789)***
Meyers+engineers ....E....415 282-4380
98 Battery St Ste 500 San Francisco (94111) ***(P-18766)***
Meyers+engineers ....D....415 713-0005
98 Battery St Ste 502 San Francisco (94111) ***(P-18767)***
Mg4 Manufacturing Inc ....D....925 295-9700
370 N Wiget Ln Ste 200 Walnut Creek (94598) ***(P-9520)***
Mgh Enterprises Inc ....E....530 894-2537
2540 Cactus Ave Chico (95973) ***(P-1545)***
MGM Brakes, Cloverdale *Also called Indian Head Industries Inc* ***(P-6582)***
MGM Brakes ....D....707 894-3333
1184 S Cloverdale Blvd Cloverdale (95425) ***(P-6588)***
MGM Drywall Inc ....D....408 292-4085
1050 Coml St Ste 102 San Jose (95112) ***(P-1691)***
MGM Holiday Inc ....E....415 690-0020
1004 S Claremont St San Mateo (94402) ***(P-11298)***
Mgp Ix Properties LLC (PA) ....E....**415 693-9000**
425 California St # 1000 San Francisco (94104) ***(P-10395)***
Mhb Group Inc ....F....408 744-1011
1240 Mtn View Alviso Rd S Sunnyvale (94089) ***(P-3508)***
Mhm Services Inc ....C....707 652-2688
155 Glen Cove Marina Rd E Vallejo (94591) ***(P-17042)***
Mhm Services Inc ....C....559 412-8121
6041 N 1st St Fresno (93710) ***(P-17043)***
Mhm Services Inc ....C....707 623-9080
2380 Professional Dr Santa Rosa (95403) ***(P-17044)***
Mhm Services Inc ....C....415 416-6992
350 Brannan St San Francisco (94107) ***(P-17045)***
Mhn Government Services LLC ....A....916 294-4941
2370 Kerner Blvd San Rafael (94901) ***(P-17649)***
Mhp Builders Inc ....E....209 951-6190
3202 W March Ln Stockton (95219) ***(P-674)***
MHS, Fresno *Also called Turn Behavioral Hlth Svcs Inc* ***(P-17082)***
MI Group Inc ....D....510 887-8200
25821 Industrial Blvd # 400 Hayward (94545) ***(P-7569)***
MI Rancho Tortilla Inc ....D....559 299-3183
801 Purvis Ave Clovis (93612) ***(P-2923)***
MI Rancho Tortilla Factory, Elk Grove *Also called Berber Food Manufacturing Inc* ***(P-2870)***
Mi9, Pleasanton *Also called Software Development Inc* ***(P-13451)***
Miasole ....B....408 919-5700
2590 Walsh Ave Santa Clara (95051) ***(P-6200)***
Miasole Hi-Tech Corp (HQ) ....C....**408 919-5700**
3211 Scott Blvd Ste 201 Santa Clara (95054) ***(P-6201)***
Michaael S Hensley ....C....650 692-7007
180 W Hill Pl Brisbane (94005) ***(P-11725)***
Michaans Auctions, Alameda *Also called Auctions By Bay Inc* ***(P-14207)***
Michael and Company, Lockeford *Also called Woodside Investment Inc* ***(P-4989)***
Michael Baker Intl Inc ....E....510 879-0950
1 Kaiser Plz Ste 1150 Oakland (94612) ***(P-18768)***
Michael Baker Intl Inc ....E....916 361-8384
2729 Prospect Park Dr # 220 Rancho Cordova (95670) ***(P-19820)***
Michael Baker Intl Inc ....E....530 894-3469
140 Independence Cir C Chico (95973) ***(P-19821)***
Michael Baker Intl Inc ....D....925 949-2452
500 Ygnacio Valley Rd # 300 Walnut Creek (94596) ***(P-18769)***
Michael Joseph Sturgeon Cnstr, Sacramento *Also called Sturgeon Construction Inc* ***(P-968)***
Michael Kors (usa) Inc ....E....707 535-0301
1071 Santa Rosa Plz Santa Rosa (95401) ***(P-9253)***
Michael Kors (usa) Inc ....E....408 362-9537
925 Blossom Hill Rd San Jose (95123) ***(P-9254)***
Michael R Minnick Roofing ....E....559 346-1770
2974 Phillip Ave Clovis (93612) ***(P-1820)***
Michael Telfer (PA) ....D....**925 228-1515**
211 Foster St Martinez (94553) ***(P-1059)***
Michaels Furniture Company Inc ....C....916 381-9086
15 Koch Rd Ste J Corte Madera (94925) ***(P-3282)***
Michaels Trnsp Svc Inc ....D....707 674-6013
140 Yolano Dr Vallejo (94589) ***(P-7417)***
Michel-Schlmberger Partners LP ....F....707 433-7427
4155 Wine Creek Rd Healdsburg (95448) ***(P-2660)***
Michel-Schlmbrger Fine Wine Es, Healdsburg *Also called Michel-Schlmberger Partners LP* ***(P-2660)***
Micheli Farms Inc ....D....530 695-9022
6005 Highway 99 Live Oak (95953) ***(P-108)***
Michels Pacific Energy Inc ....D....920 924-8725
2200 Laurelwood Rd Santa Clara (95054) ***(P-922)***
Michelsen Packaging California, Fresno *Also called Michelsen Packaging Co Cal* ***(P-3376)***
Michelsen Packaging Co Cal ....E....559 237-3819
4165 S Cherry Ave Fresno (93706) ***(P-3376)***
Micrel LLC ....A....408 944-0800
2180 Fortune Dr San Jose (95131) ***(P-6202)***
Micro Connectors Inc ....E....510 266-0299
2700 Mccone Ave Hayward (94545) ***(P-5399)***
Micro Focus LLC (HQ) ....B....**801 861-7000**
4555 Great America Pkwy Santa Clara (95054) ***(P-13729)***
Micro Holding Corp ....E....415 788-5111
1 Maritime Plz Fl 12 San Francisco (94111) ***(P-13730)***
Micro Lambda Wireless Inc ....E....510 770-9221
46515 Landing Pkwy Fremont (94538) ***(P-6454)***
Micro Lithography Inc ....C....408 747-1769
1247 Elko Dr Sunnyvale (94089) ***(P-6726)***
Micro Prcision Calibration Inc (PA) ....E....**530 268-1860**
22835 Industrial Pl Grass Valley (95949) ***(P-19279)***
Micro Precision Test Equipment, Grass Valley *Also called Micro Prcision Calibration Inc* ***(P-19279)***
Micro Tech Systems, Fremont *Also called Mt Systems Inc* ***(P-5159)***
Micro-Mechanics Inc ....E....408 779-2927
465 Woodview Ave Morgan Hill (95037) ***(P-8933)***
Micro-Metric Inc ....F....408 452-8505
1050 Commercial St San Jose (95112) ***(P-6911)***
Micro-Vu Corp California (PA) ....D....**707 838-6272**
7909 Conde Ln Windsor (95492) ***(P-6880)***
Microbar Inc ....B....510 659-9770
45473 Warm Springs Blvd Fremont (94539) ***(P-5158)***
Microchip Technology ....E....408 474-3640
1931 Fortune Dr San Jose (95131) ***(P-6203)***
Microdental Laboratories Inc ....E....800 229-0936
7475 Southfront Rd Livermore (94551) ***(P-7086)***
Microform Precision LLC ....D....916 419-0580
4244 S Market Ct Ste A Sacramento (95834) ***(P-4790)***
Microgenics Corporation (HQ) ....C....**510 979-9147**
46500 Kato Rd Fremont (94538) ***(P-6838)***
Microgenics Corporation ....A....510 979-5000
44660 Osgood Rd Fremont (94539) ***(P-6839)***
Microland Electronics Corp (PA) ....E....**408 441-1688**
1883 Ringwood Ave San Jose (95131) ***(P-8726)***
Microlease, Hayward *Also called Metric Equipment Sales Inc* ***(P-8932)***
Micromega Systems Inc ....F....415 924-4700
2 Fifer Ave Ste 120 Corte Madera (94925) ***(P-13307)***
Micromenders Inc (PA) ....E....**415 344-0917**
1388 Sutter St Ste 650 San Francisco (94109) ***(P-8727)***
Micromidas Inc ....E....916 231-9329
930 Riverside Pkwy Ste 10 West Sacramento (95605) ***(P-4054)***
Micron Consumer Pdts Group Inc (HQ) ....D....**669 226-3000**
540 Alder Dr Fremont (94538) ***(P-5300)***
Micron Technology Inc ....E....408 855-4000
570 Alder Dr Bldg 2 Milpitas (95035) ***(P-6204)***
Micropoint Bioscience Inc ....E....408 588-1682
3521 Leonard Ct Santa Clara (95054) ***(P-4025)***
Microsemi Corp - Anlog Mxed Sg ....E....408 643-6000
3850 N 1st St San Jose (95134) ***(P-6205)***
Microsemi Corporation ....D....408 240-4560
3295 Scott Blvd 150 Santa Clara (95054) ***(P-6206)***

Microsemi Crp- Rf Intgrted Slt (HQ) ....C....**916 850-8640**
105 Lake Forest Way Folsom (95630) **(P-6207)**
Microsemi Frequency Time Corp (HQ) ....C....**480 792-7200**
3870 N 1st St San Jose (95134) **(P-5684)**
Microsemi Frequency Time Corp ....E....408 433-0910
3870 N 1st St San Jose (95134) **(P-6208)**
Microsemi Rfis, Folsom *Also called Microsemi Crp- Rf Intgrted Slt* **(P-6207)**
Microsemi Semiconductor US Inc ....E....707 568-5900
3843 Brickway Blvd # 100 Santa Rosa (95403) **(P-6209)**
Microsemi Soc Corp (HQ) ....B....**408 643-6000**
3870 N 1st St San Jose (95134) **(P-6210)**
Microsemi Soc Corp ....E....650 318-4200
2051 Stierlin Ct Mountain View (94043) **(P-6211)**
Microsemi Stor Solutions Inc (HQ) ....A....**408 239-8000**
1380 Bordeaux Dr Sunnyvale (94089) **(P-6212)**
Microsoft Corporation ....D....650 964-7200
680 Vaqueros Ave Sunnyvale (94085) **(P-13308)**
Microtech International Inc (HQ) ....C....**510 360-0210**
466 Kato Ter Fremont (94539) **(P-5400)**
Microtech Systems Inc ....F....650 596-1900
1334 Brommer St Ste B6 Santa Cruz (95062) **(P-6503)**
Microwave Technology Inc (HQ) ....D....**510 651-6700**
4268 Solar Way Fremont (94538) **(P-6455)**
Micrus Endovascular LLC (HQ) ....C....**408 433-1400**
821 Fox Ln San Jose (95131) **(P-7007)**
Mid Labs, San Leandro *Also called Medical Instr Dev Labs Inc* **(P-7003)**
Mid State Steel Erection (PA) ....D....**209 464-9497**
1916 Cherokee Rd Stockton (95205) **(P-1927)**
Mid Valley AG Svcs Inc (PA) ....E....**209 931-7600**
16401 E Highway 26 Linden (95236) **(P-9606)**
Mid Valley Dairy, Turlock *Also called Super Store Industries* **(P-2183)**
Mid Valley Labor Services Inc ....E....559 661-6390
19358 Avenue 18 1/2 Madera (93637) **(P-12108)**
Mid Valley Mfg Inc ....E....559 864-9441
2039 W Superior Ave Caruthers (93609) **(P-5571)**
Mid Valley Nut Company Inc (PA) ....E....**209 883-4491**
2065 Geer Rd Hughson (95326) **(P-293)**
Mid Valley Packaging & Sup Co, Fowler *Also called Gahvejian Enterprises Inc* **(P-9213)**
Mid Valley Plastering Inc ....B....209 858-9766
15300 Mckinley Ave Lathrop (95330) **(P-1692)**
Mid Valley Title and Escrow Co (HQ) ....D....**530 893-5644**
601 Main St Chico (95928) **(P-10202)**
Mid Valley Title and Escrow Co ....E....530 533-6680
2295 Fther Rver Blvd Ste Oroville (95965) **(P-10693)**
Mid-Peninsula Roofing Inc ....D....650 375-7850
1326 Marsten Rd Burlingame (94010) **(P-1821)**
Mid-Placer Public Schools ....E....530 823-4820
13121 Bill Francis Dr Auburn (95603) **(P-7442)**
Mid-Valley Distributors Inc ....E....559 485-2660
3886 E Jensen Ave Fresno (93725) **(P-8988)**
Mid-Valley Tarp Service, Modesto *Also called Modesto Tent and Awning Inc* **(P-3040)**
Middle East Baking Co ....F....650 348-7200
1380 Marsten Rd Burlingame (94010) **(P-2395)**
Middle Way ....E....707 823-8755
1425 Corporate Cntr Pkwy Santa Rosa (95407) **(P-17823)**
Middle Way Landscaping Svcs, Santa Rosa *Also called Middle Way* **(P-17823)**
Midea Emerging Tech Co Ltd ....E....973 539-5330
250 W Tasman Dr San Jose (95134) **(P-19224)**
Midglen Studio Associates ....E....650 366-0314
831 Midglen Way Woodside (94062) **(P-923)**
MIDPEN HOUSING, Foster City *Also called Menlo Gateway Inc* **(P-10472)**
Midpen Housing Corporation ....B....650 356-2900
303 Vintage Park Dr # 250 Foster City (94404) **(P-10709)**
Midpen Property MGT Corp ....E....408 773-8014
174 Carroll St Ofc Sunnyvale (94086) **(P-11592)**
Midpennsula Rgnal Open Space D ....D....650 691-1200
330 Distel Cir Los Altos (94022) **(P-19912)**
Midstate Barrier Inc ....D....209 944-9565
3291 S Highway 99 Stockton (95215) **(P-1060)**
Midstate Construction Corp ....D....707 762-3200
1180 Holm Rd Ste A Petaluma (94954) **(P-675)**
Midvalley Recovery Facilities ....E....530 742-6670
430 Teegarden Ave Yuba City (95991) **(P-17046)**
Midway Games West Inc ....C....408 434-3700
675 Sycamore Dr Milpitas (95035) **(P-7299)**
Midwestern Pipeline Svcs Inc (PA) ....F....**707 557-6633**
160 Klamath Ct American Canyon (94503) **(P-4192)**
Mighty Buildings Inc ....E....415 583-5657
610 85th Ave Oakland (94621) **(P-676)**
Mighty Leaf Tea ....D....415 491-2650
100 Smith Ranch Rd # 120 San Rafael (94903) **(P-9465)**
Mightyhive Inc (HQ) ....D....**888 727-9742**
394 Pacific Ave Ste B100 San Francisco (94111) **(P-12606)**
Migo Money Inc ....D....415 906-4040
3739 Balboa St Ste 1101 San Francisco (94121) **(P-14331)**
Mike Brown Electric Co ....C....707 792-8100
561a Mercantile Dr Cotati (94931) **(P-1546)**
Mike Hudson Distributing, Petaluma *Also called Hdp Enterprises Inc* **(P-9340)**
Mike Jensen Farms LLC ....C....559 897-4192
13138 S Bethel Ave Kingsburg (93631) **(P-109)**
Mike McCall Landscape Inc ....C....925 363-8100
4749 Clayton Rd Concord (94521) **(P-486)**
Mike Murach & Associates ....E....559 440-9071
3730 W Swift Ave Fresno (93722) **(P-3539)**
Mike Roses Auto Body Inc (PA) ....E....**925 689-1739**
2260 Via De Mercados Concord (94520) **(P-14530)**
Mike Rovner Construction Inc ....C....408 453-6070
1758 Junction Ave Ste C San Jose (95112) **(P-677)**
Mike's Towing Service, Modesto *Also called Reeves Enterprises Inc* **(P-14674)**
Mikes Auto Body, Concord *Also called Mike Roses Auto Body Inc* **(P-14530)**
Mikes Sheet Metal Pdts Inc ....E....916 348-3800
3315 Elkhorn Blvd North Highlands (95660) **(P-4791)**
Mila Usa Inc ....E....415 734-8540
11 Laurel Ave Belvedere Tiburon (94920) **(P-5705)**
Milan Corporation ....E....510 656-6400
43230 Osgood Rd Fremont (94539) **(P-1822)**
Milano Restaurants Intl Corp (HQ) ....B....**559 432-0399**
6729 N Palm Ave Ste 200 Fresno (93704) **(P-10807)**
Mile Post Properties LLC ....D....415 673-4711
1050 Van Ness Ave San Francisco (94109) **(P-11299)**
Miles Sears Eanni A Prof Corp ....E....559 486-5200
2844 Fresno St Fresno (93721) **(P-17333)**
Milestone Internet Mktg Inc (PA) ....C....**408 492-9055**
3001 Oakmead Village Dr # 100 Santa Clara (95051) **(P-13731)**
Milestone Technologies Inc (PA) ....A....**510 651-2454**
3101 Skyway Ct Fremont (94539) **(P-13632)**
Milestones Development Inc ....E....707 644-0496
1 Florida St Vallejo (94590) **(P-16191)**
Milgard Manufacturing LLC ....C....916 387-0700
6050 88th St Sacramento (95828) **(P-8595)**
Milgard Windows, Sacramento *Also called Milgard Manufacturing LLC* **(P-8595)**
Military Advantage Inc (HQ) ....C....**415 820-3434**
799 Market St Fl 7 San Francisco (94103) **(P-11773)**
Military Aircraft Parts (PA) ....E....**916 635-8010**
116 Oxburough Dr Folsom (95630) **(P-5572)**
Military.com, San Francisco *Also called Military Advantage Inc* **(P-11773)**
Mill Valley Inn Inc ....E....415 389-6608
165 Throckmorton Ave Mill Valley (94941) **(P-11300)**
Mill Valley Refuse Service Inc ....D....415 457-2287
112 Front St San Rafael (94901) **(P-8345)**
Mill Yard, Arcata *Also called Bracut International Corp* **(P-3092)**
Millard Group Inc ....C....530 899-7299
1950 E 20th St Chico (95928) **(P-11972)**
Millbrae Serra Sanitarium ....C....650 697-8386
150 Serra Ave Millbrae (94030) **(P-16253)**
Millbrae Srra Cnvalescent Hosp, Millbrae *Also called Millbrae Serra Sanitarium* **(P-16253)**
Millbrae Wcp Hotel II LLC ....E....650 443-5500
401 E Millbrae Ave Millbrae (94030) **(P-11301)**
Millennial Brands LLC (PA) ....D....**866 938-4806**
2002 Diablo Rd Danville (94506) **(P-9260)**
Millennium Engrg Intgrtion LLC ....C....703 413-7750
350 N Akron Rd Moffett Field (94035) **(P-18770)**
Millennium Hotel Inc ....E....510 432-5665
30073 Skylark Ct Hayward (94544) **(P-11302)**
Millennium Management LLC ....B....415 844-4048
2 Embarcadero Ctr # 1640 San Francisco (94111) **(P-10780)**
Millennium Metalcraft Inc ....E....510 657-4700
3201 Osgood Cmn Fremont (94539) **(P-4792)**
Millennium Sports Club, Fairfield *Also called Salutary Sports Clubs Inc* **(P-14969)**
Millennium Termite & Pest ....E....707 673-1050
9900 Horn Rd Ste 5 Sacramento (95827) **(P-11904)**
Miller Cat Corporation ....E....408 510-5224
384 Laurelwood Rd Santa Clara (95054) **(P-5216)**
Miller Creek School District ....C....415 492-3776
121 Marinwood Ave San Rafael (94903) **(P-11973)**
Miller Hot Dogs, Lodi *Also called Miller Packing Company* **(P-2120)**
Miller Law Group A Prof Corp ....E....415 464-4300
101 Montgomery St # 1400 San Francisco (94104) **(P-17334)**
Miller Packing Company ....E....209 339-2310
1122 Industrial Way Lodi (95240) **(P-2120)**
Miller Starr Rglia A Prof Law (PA) ....D....**925 935-9400**
1331 N Calif Blvd Fl 5 Walnut Creek (94596) **(P-17335)**
Miller's Rent All, Pleasanton *Also called Rapid Value Solutions Inc* **(P-19386)**
Millerick Engineering Inc ....D....209 664-9111
735 E Main St Turlock (95380) **(P-18771)**
Millerton Builders Inc ....F....559 252-0490
4714 E Home Ave Fresno (93703) **(P-3332)**
Milliman Inc ....E....415 403-1333
650 California St Fl 21 San Francisco (94108) **(P-19913)**
Mills Building, San Francisco *Also called Swig Company LLC* **(P-19646)**
Mills-Peninsula Health HM Care, San Mateo *Also called Alliance Hospital Services* **(P-16842)**
Millwood Inn, Millbrae *Also called Arvee Bros Inc* **(P-10933)**
Millwork Div, Oroville *Also called Setzer Forest Products Inc* **(P-3105)**
Milners Anodizing ....E....707 584-1188
3330 Mcmaude Pl Santa Rosa (95407) **(P-4913)**
Milpitas Courtyard By Marriott ....E....408 719-1966
1480 Falcon Dr Milpitas (95035) **(P-11303)**
Milpitas Golfland, Milpitas *Also called Golfland Entrmt Ctrs Inc* **(P-15208)**
Milpitas Materials Company ....E....650 969-4401
1125 N Milpitas Blvd Milpitas (95035) **(P-8630)**
Milpitas Medical Offices, Milpitas *Also called Kaiser Foundation Hospitals* **(P-15475)**
Milpitas Optometric Group Inc ....E....408 263-2040
1301 E Calaveras Blvd Milpitas (95035) **(P-15871)**
Milpitas Unified School Dst ....D....408 635-2686
250a Roswell Dr Milpitas (95035) **(P-17974)**
Mina-Tree Signs Incorporated (PA) ....E....**209 941-2921**
1233 E Ronald St Stockton (95205) **(P-7244)**
Minami Tamaki LLP ....E....415 788-9000
360 Post St Fl 8 San Francisco (94108) **(P-17336)**
Minaris Medical America Inc ....C....800 233-6278
630 Clyde Ct Mountain View (94043) **(P-6696)**
Mind Garden Inc ....F....650 322-6300
707 Menlo Ave Ste 120 Menlo Park (94025) **(P-3582)**
Mindray Ds Usa Inc ....B....650 230-2800
2100 Gold St San Jose (95002) **(P-4026)**
Mindray Innvtion Ctr Slcon Vly, San Jose *Also called Mindray Ds Usa Inc* **(P-4026)**

A L P H A B E T I C

Mindshare Design Inc (PA) ...E ...**510 904-6900**
475 14th St Ste 250 Oakland (94612) ***(P-11870)***
Mindsnacks Inc ...E ...415 875-9817
1390 Market St Ste 200 San Francisco (94102) ***(P-13309)***
Mindsource Inc ...D ...650 314-6400
995 Montague Expy Ste 121 Milpitas (95035) ***(P-12607)***
Mindstrong Inc ...E ...650 850-7050
303 Bryant St Ste 300 Mountain View (94041) ***(P-19576)***
Mindstrong Health, Mountain View *Also called Mindstrong Inc* ***(P-19576)***
Mindteck USA, Pleasanton *Also called Mindware Pertech Inc* ***(P-13633)***
Mindtickle Inc (PA) ...E ...**973 400-1717**
115 Sansome St Ste 700 San Francisco (94104) ***(P-13310)***
Mindware Pertech Inc (HQ) ...E ...**925 251-1550**
5820 Stnrdge Mall Rd Ste Pleasanton (94588) ***(P-13633)***
Mineral King Minerals Inc (PA) ...F ...**559 582-9228**
7600 N Ingram Ave Ste 105 Fresno (93711) ***(P-4134)***
Minerva Networks Inc (PA) ...D ...**800 806-9594**
1600 Technology Dr Fl 8 San Jose (95110) ***(P-12608)***
Minerva Surgical Inc ...C ...855 646-7874
4255 Burton Dr Santa Clara (95054) ***(P-7008)***
Miniature Precision Inc ...E ...530 244-4131
4488 Mountain Lakes Blvd Redding (96003) ***(P-5573)***
Minimatics Inc (PA) ...E ...**650 969-5630**
3445 De La Cruz Blvd Santa Clara (95054) ***(P-8934)***
Minimlly Invsive Srgcal Sltons, San Jose *Also called Minimlly Invsive Srgcal Sltons* ***(P-15537)***
Minimlly Invsive Srgcal Sltons ...E ...408 750-4658
105 N Bascom Ave Ste 104 San Jose (95128) ***(P-15537)***
Minio Inc ...E ...844 356-4646
530 University Ave Ste B Palo Alto (94301) ***(P-12609)***
Ministry Services of The Daugh ...D ...650 917-4500
26000 Altamont Rd Los Altos Hills (94022) ***(P-10799)***
Minitrans Corporation (PA) ...E ...**415 970-8091**
2260 Palou Ave San Francisco (94124) ***(P-7418)***
Minority Veterans Coalition ...E ...559 647-3425
2377 S Attucks Ave Fresno (93706) ***(P-18242)***
Mint Grips, Benicia *Also called Gibbs Plastic & Rubber LLC* ***(P-4215)***
Mint Software Inc ...D ...650 944-6000
280 Hope St Mountain View (94041) ***(P-13311)***
Minted LLC (PA) ...A ...**415 399-1100**
747 Front St Ste 200 San Francisco (94111) ***(P-9208)***
Minton Door Company (PA) ...E ...**650 961-9800**
1150 Elko Dr Sunnyvale (94089) ***(P-8596)***
Minturn Huller Cooperative Inc ...D ...559 665-1185
9080 S Minturn Rd Chowchilla (93610) ***(P-9510)***
Minturn Nut Co Inc ...E ...559 665-8500
8800 Minturn Rd Le Grand (95333) ***(P-2857)***
Mio Technology USA Ltd ...E ...510 252-6900
47988 Fremont Blvd Fremont (94538) ***(P-8935)***
Mipox International Corp ...E ...650 638-9830
1065 E Hillsdale Blvd # 401 Foster City (94404) ***(P-4525)***
Mips Tech Inc (HQ) ...C ...**408 530-5000**
300 Orchard Cy Dr Ste 170 Campbell (95008) ***(P-6213)***
Miramar Hospitality Consulting ...E ...408 298-7373
55 Tully Rd San Jose (95122) ***(P-11304)***
Miranda, Grass Valley *Also called Grass Valley Inc* ***(P-5845)***
Mirapath Inc (PA) ...E ...**408 873-7883**
10950 N Blaney Ave Cupertino (95014) ***(P-8728)***
Mirda, Daniel P MD, NAPA *Also called Redwood Rgnal Med Group DRG LL* ***(P-15646)***
Mirion Technologies Inc (PA) ...C ...**925 543-0800**
3000 Executive Pkwy # 518 San Ramon (94583) ***(P-6912)***
Miro Software, San Francisco *Also called Realtimeboard Inc* ***(P-13968)***
Mirror Plus Technologies Inc ...D ...510 403-2400
45545 Northport Loop E Fremont (94538) ***(P-12610)***
Mirum Pharmaceuticals Inc (PA) ...D ...**650 667-4085**
950 Tower Ln Ste 1050 Foster City (94404) ***(P-3949)***
Mishi Apparel Inc (PA) ...E ...**707 525-1075**
201 Western Ave Petaluma (94952) ***(P-2977)***
Mishi Apparel Retail Store, Petaluma *Also called Mishi Apparel Inc* ***(P-2977)***
Mission AG Resources LLC ...E ...559 591-3333
6801 Avenue 430 Unit A Reedley (93654) ***(P-2164)***
Mission Bell Winery, Madera *Also called Constllion Brnds US Oprtons I* ***(P-9572)***
Mission Child Care Consort ...E ...415 586-6139
4750 Mission St San Francisco (94112) ***(P-17975)***
Mission Cliffs Rock Climbing, San Francisco *Also called Touchstone Climbing Inc* ***(P-15254)***
Mission Cncil Alchol Abuse Spn ...E ...415 826-6767
154a Capp St San Francisco (94110) ***(P-17650)***
Mission College, Santa Clara *Also called West Vlly-Mssion Cmnty Cllege* ***(P-19890)***
Mission Constructors Inc ...D ...415 282-8453
195 Bay Shore Blvd San Francisco (94124) ***(P-924)***
Mission Crmchael Hlthcare Ctr, Carmichael *Also called SSC Carmichael Operating Co LP* ***(P-16126)***
Mission De La Casa, San Jose *Also called Careage Inc* ***(P-15951)***
Mission Economic Dev Agcy ...E ...415 282-3334
2301 Mission St Ste 301 San Francisco (94110) ***(P-19577)***
Mission Electric Company, Fremont *Also called Kositch Enterprises Inc* ***(P-1532)***
Mission Hospice & HM Care Inc ...C ...650 554-1000
66 Bovet Rd Ste 100 San Mateo (94402) ***(P-16192)***
Mission Lane LLC (PA) ...D ...**408 505-3081**
101 2nd St Ste 350 San Francisco (94105) ***(P-14332)***
Mission Linen & Uniform Svc, Sacramento *Also called Mission Linen Supply* ***(P-11638)***
Mission Linen & Uniform Svc, Modesto *Also called Mission Linen Supply* ***(P-11639)***
Mission Linen & Uniform Svc, Fresno *Also called Mission Linen Supply* ***(P-11641)***
Mission Linen & Uniform Svc, Hayward *Also called Mission Linen Supply* ***(P-11642)***
Mission Linen & Uniform Svc, San Francisco *Also called Mission Linen Supply* ***(P-11643)***
Mission Linen & Uniform Svc, Chico *Also called Mission Linen Supply* ***(P-11644)***
Mission Linen & Uniform Svc, Sacramento *Also called Mission Linen Supply* ***(P-11664)***
Mission Linen Supply ...D ...916 423-3179
7520 Reese Rd Sacramento (95828) ***(P-11638)***
Mission Linen Supply ...D ...510 996-3416
6590 Central Ave Newark (94560) ***(P-11974)***
Mission Linen Supply ...D ...209 523-6758
136 Coyado Ave Modesto (95350) ***(P-11639)***
Mission Linen Supply ...D ...707 443-8681
1401 Summer St Eureka (95501) ***(P-11640)***
Mission Linen Supply ...D ...559 268-0647
2555 S Orange Ave Fresno (93725) ***(P-11641)***
Mission Linen Supply ...D ...510 401-5904
1001 Whipple Rd Hayward (94544) ***(P-11642)***
Mission Linen Supply ...C ...510 429-7305
550 Florida St San Francisco (94110) ***(P-11643)***
Mission Linen Supply ...D ...530 342-4110
1340 W 7th St Chico (95928) ***(P-11644)***
Mission Linen Supply ...D ...916 423-3135
7524 Reese Rd Sacramento (95828) ***(P-11664)***
Mission Linen Supply & Svcs, Eureka *Also called Mission Linen Supply* ***(P-11640)***
Mission Merced Incorporated ...D ...209 722-9269
644 W 20th St Merced (95340) ***(P-18243)***
Mission Neighborhood Ctrs Inc (PA) ...E ...**415 206-7752**
362 Capp St San Francisco (94110) ***(P-18439)***
Mission Neighborhood Ctrs Inc ...E ...415 206-7756
534 Precita Ave San Francisco (94110) ***(P-18440)***
Mission Neighborhood Hlth Ctr, San Francisco *Also called Mission Neighborhood Hlth Ctr* ***(P-15538)***
Mission Neighborhood Hlth Ctr (PA) ...C ...**415 552-3870**
240 Shotwell St San Francisco (94110) ***(P-15538)***
Mission Oaks Hospital, Los Gatos *Also called Good Samaritan Hospital LP* ***(P-16383)***
Mission Park Hotel LP ...E ...408 809-3838
1950 Wyatt Dr Santa Clara (95054) ***(P-3792)***
Mission Peak Orthopedics ...D ...510 797-3933
5924 Stoneridge Dr # 200 Pleasanton (94588) ***(P-15539)***
Mission Pets Inc ...E ...415 904-9914
986 Mission St Fl 5 San Francisco (94103) ***(P-9667)***
Mission Ranches Company LLC ...E ...831 206-0535
880 Lucy Brown Rd San Juan Bautista (95045) ***(P-248)***
Mission Skilled Nursing Home, Santa Clara *Also called Covenant Care California LLC* ***(P-15966)***
Mission Springs Conf Cntr, Scotts Valley *Also called Pacific Sthwest Cnfrnce of Eva* ***(P-10398)***
Mission Stuart Ht Partners LLC ...C ...415 278-3700
8 Mission St San Francisco (94105) ***(P-11305)***
Mission Tool and Mfg Co Inc ...E ...510 782-8383
3440 Arden Rd Hayward (94545) ***(P-5574)***
Mission Trail Wste Systems Inc ...D ...408 727-5365
1060 Richard Ave Santa Clara (95050) ***(P-7484)***
Mission Vly Ford Strlng Trcks, San Jose *Also called Mission Vly Ford Trck Sls Inc* ***(P-14471)***
Mission Vly Ford Trck Sls Inc ...D ...408 933-2300
780 E Brokaw Rd San Jose (95112) ***(P-14471)***
Mission YMCA, San Francisco *Also called Young MNS Chrstn Assn San Frnc* ***(P-18525)***
Mist Systems Inc ...C ...408 326-0346
1601 S De Anza Blvd # 248 Cupertino (95014) ***(P-13634)***
Mistral Software, Fremont *Also called Mistral Solutions Inc* ***(P-12611)***
Mistral Solutions Inc (HQ) ...D ...**408 705-2240**
43092 Christy St Fremont (94538) ***(P-12611)***
Mitac Information Systems ...E ...510 668-3679
39889 Eureka Dr Newark (94560) ***(P-5401)***
Mitac Information Systems Corp ...E ...510 668-3507
44131 Nobel Dr Fremont (94538) ***(P-5261)***
Mitac Information Systems Corp (HQ) ...C ...**510 284-3000**
39889 Eureka Dr Newark (94560) ***(P-5301)***
Mitchell Concrete, Rancho Cordova *Also called Mitchell Jones Concrete Inc* ***(P-1894)***
Mitchell Engineering ...E ...415 227-1040
1395 Evans Ave San Francisco (94124) ***(P-1966)***
Mitchell Jones Concrete Inc ...E ...916 638-6870
3187 Fitzgerald Rd Rancho Cordova (95742) ***(P-1894)***
Mitsubshi Chem Advnced Mtls In ...E ...209 464-2701
3837 Imperial Way Stockton (95215) ***(P-3806)***
Mitsubshi Chem Crbn Fibr Cmpst (HQ) ...C ...**916 386-1733**
5900 88th St Sacramento (95828) ***(P-5672)***
Mitzu Printing Inc ...F ...650 922-0500
434 9th St San Francisco (94103) ***(P-3677)***
Miwa Inc ...F ...510 261-5999
5733 San Leandro St Ofc Oakland (94621) ***(P-3283)***
Mixamo Inc ...E ...415 255-7455
2415 3rd St Ste 239 San Francisco (94107) ***(P-13312)***
Mixpanel Inc (PA) ...E ...**415 688-4001**
1 Front St Ste 2800 San Francisco (94111) ***(P-12612)***
Miyamoto International Inc (PA) ...D ...**916 373-1995**
1450 Halyard Dr Ste 1 West Sacramento (95691) ***(P-18772)***
Miyoko's Creamery, Petaluma *Also called Miyokos Kitchen* ***(P-2142)***
Miyokos Kitchen ...E ...415 521-5313
2086 Marina Ave Petaluma (94954) ***(P-2142)***
Mizkan America Inc ...D ...831 728-2061
46 Walker St Watsonville (95076) ***(P-2924)***
Mizuho Orthopedic Systems Inc (HQ) ...B ...**510 429-1500**
30031 Ahern Ave Union City (94587) ***(P-7009)***
Mizuho OSI, Union City *Also called Mizuho Orthopedic Systems Inc* ***(P-7009)***
Mjc International Group LLC (HQ) ...E ...**415 467-9500**
25 Park Pl Brisbane (94005) ***(P-9248)***
Mkm Customs, Roseville *Also called Sinister Mfg Company Inc* ***(P-6593)***
Mks Instruments Inc ...E ...408 750-0300
3625 Peterson Way Santa Clara (95054) ***(P-14765)***
Mlslistings Inc ...D ...408 874-0200
740 Kifer Rd Sunnyvale (94086) ***(P-19578)***

Mly Technix Corp ....E....650 384-1456
2005 De La Cruz Blvd Santa Clara (95050) **(P-13313)**
Mmi Realty Services Inc ....D....415 288-6888
260 California St Fl 4 San Francisco (94111) **(P-10396)**
Mng Newspapers, San Jose *Also called California Newspapers Partnr* **(P-3424)**
Moback Inc ....E....510 565-6672
226 Airport Pkwy Ste 320 San Jose (95110) **(P-12613)**
Mobica US Inc ....A....650 450-6654
2570 N 1st St Fl 2 San Jose (95131) **(P-13635)**
Mobile Application, Santa Clara *Also called Soundhound Inc* **(P-12808)**
Mobile Home Park Magazines, Sunnyvale *Also called Mhb Group Inc* **(P-3508)**
Mobile Modular, Livermore *Also called McGrath Rentcorp* **(P-9078)**
Mobiledgex Inc (HQ) ....**E....707 364-8830**
333 W San Carlos St # 600 San Jose (95110) **(P-12614)**
Mobilehome Communities America ....C....408 298-3230
2681 Monterey Hwy San Jose (95111) **(P-10473)**
Mobileum Inc (PA) ....**C....408 844-6600**
20813 Stevns Crk Blvd Cupertino (95014) **(P-8081)**
Mobillcash, San Francisco *Also called Boku Inc* **(P-12305)**
Mobilygen Corporation ....D....408 601-1000
160 Rio Robles San Jose (95134) **(P-6214)**
Mobitv Inc (PA) ....**D....510 981-1303**
1900 Powell St Ste 900 Emeryville (94608) **(P-7973)**
Mobiveil Inc ....F....408 791-2977
890 Hillview Ct Ste 250 Milpitas (95035) **(P-6215)**
Moc Products Company Inc ....D....510 635-1230
9840 Kitty Ln Oakland (94603) **(P-14665)**
Mocana Corporation ....D....415 617-0055
1735 N 1st St Ste 306 San Jose (95112) **(P-13732)**
Mockingbird Networks ....F....408 342-5300
10040 Bubb Rd Cupertino (95014) **(P-5262)**
Mocse Federal Credit Union ....E....209 572-3600
3600 Coffee Rd Modesto (95355) **(P-9797)**
Mod Zombie LLC (PA) ....**E....650 346-2047**
3499 E Bayshore Rd Spc 30 Redwood City (94063) **(P-2962)**
Model N, San Mateo *Also called N Model Inc* **(P-12626)**
Model Schl Cmprhnsive Hmnstic ....E....510 549-2711
2330 Prince St Berkeley (94705) **(P-17976)**
Modern Ceramics Mfg Inc ....E....408 383-0554
2240 Lundy Ave San Jose (95131) **(P-4375)**
Modern Custom Fabrication Inc ....E....559 264-4741
4922 E Jensen Ave Fresno (93725) **(P-4725)**
Modern Health, San Francisco *Also called Modern Life Inc* **(P-17047)**
Modern Life Inc (PA) ....**D....617 980-9633**
450 Sansome St Fl 12 San Francisco (94111) **(P-17047)**
Modern Luxury Media LLC (HQ) ....**E....404 443-0004**
243 Vallejo St San Francisco (94111) **(P-3509)**
Modern Method Roofg Cnstr Inc ....E....707 255-8090
180 Coombs St NAPA (94559) **(P-1823)**
Modern-Twist, Emeryville *Also called Stasher Inc* **(P-9219)**
Modesto Christian School, Modesto *Also called Modestos Neighborhood Church* **(P-17977)**
Modesto Dial-Ride, Modesto *Also called Storer Transit Systems* **(P-7406)**
Modesto Executive A Chrtr Inc ....D....209 577-4654
825 Airport Way Modesto (95354) **(P-7758)**
Modesto Fitness & Racquet, Modesto *Also called Turlock Hlth & Fitnes Ctr Inc* **(P-14983)**
Modesto Food Distributors Inc ....E....650 756-3603
7601 El Camino Real Colma (94014) **(P-9348)**
Modesto Hospitality LLC ....C....209 526-6000
1150 9th St Modesto (95354) **(P-11306)**
Modesto Hospitality Lessee LLC ....D....209 526-6000
1150 9th St Ste C Modesto (95354) **(P-11307)**
Modesto Imaging Center ....D....209 524-6800
157 E Coolidge Ave Modesto (95350) **(P-15540)**
Modesto Irrigation District ....D....209 526-7563
1231 11th St Modesto (95354) **(P-8125)**
Modesto Irrigation District (PA) ....**C....209 526-7337**
1231 11th St Modesto (95354) **(P-8126)**
Modesto Irrigation District ....D....209 526-7373
929 Woodland Ave Modesto (95351) **(P-8127)**
Modesto Medical Offices, Modesto *Also called Kaiser Foundation Hospitals* **(P-15461)**
Modesto Scion World, Modesto *Also called Stinson Enterprises Inc* **(P-14625)**
Modesto Tent and Awning Inc ....E....209 545-1607
4448 Sisk Rd Modesto (95356) **(P-3040)**
Modestos Neighborhood Church ....C....209 529-5510
5921 Stoddard Rd Modesto (95356) **(P-17977)**
Modis Inc ....C....800 467-4448
1750 Creekside Oaks Dr # 225 Sacramento (95833) **(P-12615)**
Modis Inc ....C....415 896-5566
135 Main St Ste 1040 San Francisco (94105) **(P-12616)**
Modis Inc ....C....408 441-7144
2055 Gateway Pl Ste 300 San Jose (95110) **(P-12617)**
Modoc Medical Center, Alturas *Also called Last Frontier Healthcare Dst* **(P-16425)**
Modsquad Inc (PA) ....**C....916 913-4465**
1300 S St Ste B Sacramento (95811) **(P-19579)**
Modsy, San Francisco *Also called Pencil and Pixel Inc* **(P-12676)**
Modular Power Solutions LLC (HQ) ....**E....408 321-2270**
880 Mabury Rd San Jose (95133) **(P-19822)**
Modus Advanced Inc ....D....925 960-8700
1575 Greenville Rd Livermore (94550) **(P-4218)**
Modutek Corp ....E....408 362-2000
6387 San Ignacio Ave San Jose (95119) **(P-6727)**
Moffitt H C Hospital ....C....415 476-1000
505 Parnassus Ave San Francisco (94143) **(P-16458)**
Mofo, San Francisco *Also called Morrison & Foerster LLP* **(P-17338)**
Mogan David Wine, Ripon *Also called Wine Group Inc* **(P-2765)**
Mohawk Land & Cattle Co Inc ....D....408 436-1800
1660 Old Bayshore Hwy San Jose (95112) **(P-2101)**
Mohin Inc ....E....925 798-5572
5040 Commercial Cir Ste A Concord (94520) **(P-4985)**
Mohr Davidow Ventures, Menlo Park *Also called Mdv Management Company LLC* **(P-10868)**
Mojio USA Inc ....E....604 868-0804
300 Orchard Cy Dr Ste 100 Campbell (95008) **(P-12618)**
Mojo Mobility Inc ....E....650 446-0004
3707 Heron Way Palo Alto (94303) **(P-5695)**
Mojo Networks Inc (PA) ....**C....650 961-1111**
5453 Great America Pkwy Santa Clara (95054) **(P-13314)**
Molaniki Distributor, Sunnyvale *Also called Wayne* **(P-2168)**
Molding Solutions Inc ....D....707 575-1218
3225 Regional Pkwy Santa Rosa (95403) **(P-4301)**
Molecular Databank, Burlingame *Also called Collabrative DRG Discovery Inc* **(P-13084)**
Molecular Devices LLC ....F....408 747-3546
47661 Fremont Blvd Fremont (94538) **(P-6840)**
Molecular Devices LLC (HQ) ....**C....408 747-1700**
3860 N 1st St San Jose (95134) **(P-6841)**
Molecule Labs Inc ....E....925 473-8200
524 Stone Rd Ste A Benicia (94510) **(P-4125)**
Molinas Pntg Wallcovering Inc ....D....925 228-7487
4285 Pacheco Blvd Martinez (94553) **(P-1421)**
Mollie Stone Market, Greenbrae *Also called Albeco Inc* **(P-2360)**
Mom Enterprises LLC ....E....415 694-3799
1003 W Cutting Blvd # 110 Richmond (94804) **(P-3950)**
Momentive Global Inc ....A....503 225-1202
3050 S Delaware St San Mateo (94403) **(P-12619)**
Momentive Global Inc (PA) ....**A....650 543-8400**
1 Curiosity Way San Mateo (94403) **(P-12620)**
Momentive Inc (HQ) ....**E....650 543-8400**
1 Curiosity Way San Mateo (94403) **(P-13733)**
Momentum For Health (PA) ....**E....408 254-6828**
1922 The Alameda San Jose (95126) **(P-17048)**
Monarch Dental Corp ....E....925 732-4648
5867 Lone Tree Way Antioch (94531) **(P-15892)**
Mongabayorg Corporation ....F....209 315-5573
37 W Summit Dr Emerald Hills (94062) **(P-3583)**
Monica Bruce Designs Inc ....F....707 938-0277
28913 Arnold Dr Sonoma (95476) **(P-3046)**
Monkeybrains, San Francisco *Also called Another Corporate Isp LLC* **(P-7925)**
Mono Wind Casino ....D....559 855-4350
37302 Rancheria Ln Auberry (93602) **(P-11308)**
Monogram Biosciences Inc ....B....650 635-1100
345 Oyster Point Blvd South San Francisco (94080) **(P-4027)**
Monolith Materials Inc ....E....650 933-4957
662 Laurel St Ste 201 San Carlos (94070) **(P-3793)**
Monolithic Power Systems Inc ....D....408 826-0600
79 Great Oaks Blvd San Jose (95119) **(P-6216)**
Monsoon Commerce Inc ....D....510 594-4500
1250 45th St Ste 100 Emeryville (94608) **(P-13938)**
Monster Inc (PA) ....**B....415 840-2000**
601 Gateway Blvd Ste 900 South San Francisco (94080) **(P-9199)**
Monster City Studios ....E....559 498-0540
411 S West Ave Fresno (93706) **(P-4244)**
Monster Mep Inc ....D....408 727-8362
1521 Terminal Ave San Jose (95112) **(P-1312)**
Monster Products, South San Francisco *Also called Monster Inc* **(P-9199)**
Montage Technology Inc ....F....408 982-2788
101 Metro Dr Ste 500 San Jose (95110) **(P-6217)**
Montague Company ....C....510 785-8822
1830 Stearman Ave Hayward (94545) **(P-5443)**
Montalvo Association ....D....408 961-5800
15400 Montalvo Rd Saratoga (95070) **(P-18294)**
Montana Investigation, San Francisco *Also called Black Bear Security Svcs Inc* **(P-14038)**
Montavista Software LLC (HQ) ....**D....408 572-8000**
2315 N 1st St Fl 4 San Jose (95131) **(P-13315)**
Montclair Hotels Mb LLC ....B....925 687-5500
1050 Burnett Ave Concord (94520) **(P-11309)**
Monte Vista Farming Company, Denair *Also called California Royale LLC* **(P-274)**
Montepoyon Camp, Aptos *Also called United Cmps Cnfrences Retreats* **(P-11614)**
Monterey Design Systems Inc ....F....408 747-7370
2171 Landings Dr Mountain View (94043) **(P-6504)**
Monterey Mechanical Co (PA) ....**E....510 632-3173**
8275 San Leandro St Oakland (94621) **(P-1168)**
Monterey Mushrooms Inc (PA) ....**E....831 763-5300**
260 Westgate Dr Watsonville (95076) **(P-144)**
Monterey Pine Apartments ....D....510 215-1926
680 S 37th St Richmond (94804) **(P-10450)**
Monterey Structural Steel Inc ....F....831 768-1277
404 W Beach St Watsonville (95076) **(P-4677)**
Montessori School Silicon Vly (PA) ....**E....408 586-8643**
630 S Main St Milpitas (95035) **(P-17978)**
Montetisea Framing, Denair *Also called J Crecelius Inc* **(P-170)**
Montevina Winery, Plymouth *Also called Sierra Sunrise Vineyard Inc* **(P-2715)**
Montez Glass Inc ....E....916 452-1288
7571 14th Ave Sacramento (95820) **(P-1938)**
Montgomery Center, Santa Rosa *Also called Santa Rosa Memorial Hospital* **(P-16515)**
Montgomery-Sansome LP ....E....650 689-5622
161 El Camino Real South San Francisco (94080) **(P-925)**
Monticello Child Development ....E....408 261-0494
3401 Monroe St Ste A Santa Clara (95051) **(P-17979)**
Monticello Hotel LLC ....E....415 392-8800
127 Ellis St San Francisco (94102) **(P-11310)**
Monticello Inn, San Francisco *Also called Kimpton Hotel & Rest Group LLC* **(P-11233)**
Montivista, Danville *Also called San Ramon Vly Unified Schl Dst* **(P-18463)**
Montoya & Jaramillo Inc ....F....408 727-5776
1161 Richard Ave Santa Clara (95050) **(P-4914)**
Montpelier Nut Company Inc ....E....209 874-5126
4931 S Montpelier Rd Denair (95316) **(P-294)**

A L P H A B E T I C

Montrose Environmental Corp......C......925 680-4300
2825 Verne Roberts Cir Antioch (94509) *(P-19823)*
Montvale Inc......E......408 739-5446
21060 Homestead Rd # 120 Cupertino (95014) *(P-16254)*
Monument Construction Inc......D......408 778-1350
16200 Vineyard Blvd # 100 Morgan Hill (95037) *(P-426)*
Monument Security Inc......C......510 430-3540
24301 Suthland Dr Ste 312 Hayward (94545) *(P-14076)*
Monument Security Inc (PA)......**C......916 564-4234**
4926 43rd St Ste 10 McClellan (95652) *(P-14077)*
Monumental Nutrition LLC......E......408 410-0890
2349 Stratford Dr San Jose (95124) *(P-4443)*
Mooney Farms......E......530 899-2661
1220 Fortress St Chico (95973) *(P-295)*
Moonlight Companies, Reedley *Also called Moonlight Packing Corporation (P-9418)*
Moonlight Packing Corporation......A......559 638-7799
1300 I St Reedley (93654) *(P-9327)*
Moonlight Packing Corporation......A......559 638-7799
17770 E Huntsman Ave Reedley (93654) *(P-7868)*
Moonlight Packing Corporation (PA)......**C......559 638-7799**
17719 E Huntsman Ave Reedley (93654) *(P-9418)*
Moonlight Sales Corporation......E......559 637-7799
17719 E Huntsman Ave Reedley (93654) *(P-296)*
Moonshine Ink LLC......F......530 587-3607
10137 Riverside Dr Truckee (96161) *(P-3461)*
Moore Iacofano Goltsman Inc (PA)......**D......510 845-7549**
800 Hearst Ave Berkeley (94710) *(P-19824)*
Moore Quality Galvanizing Inc......E......559 673-2822
3001 Falcon Dr Madera (93637) *(P-4939)*
Moore Quality Galvanizing LP......E......559 673-2822
3001 Falcon Dr Madera (93637) *(P-4940)*
Moore Twining Associates Inc (PA)......**D......559 268-7021**
2527 Fresno St Fresno (93721) *(P-19280)*
Moore William and Kay Mark DDS......E......510 525-5510
1396 Solano Ave Albany (94706) *(P-15849)*
Moorefield Construction Inc......E......916 614-7888
4080 Truxel Rd Ste 200 Sacramento (95834) *(P-926)*
Mooretown Rancheria......B......530 533-3885
3 Alverda Dr Oroville (95966) *(P-15038)*
Mooretown Rancheria (PA)......**E......530 533-3625**
1 Alverda Dr Oroville (95966) *(P-15220)*
Moose Boats Inc......F......707 778-9828
1175 Nimitz Ave Ste 150 Vallejo (94592) *(P-6645)*
Moose International Inc......C......510 791-2654
6940 Rich Ave Newark (94560) *(P-18441)*
Moquin Press Inc......D......650 592-0575
555 Harbor Blvd Belmont (94002) *(P-3678)*
Morada Produce Company LP......A......209 546-0426
500 N Jack Tone Rd Stockton (95215) *(P-9419)*
Moraga Cntry CLB Hmowners Assn......D......925 376-2200
1600 Saint Andrews Dr Moraga (94556) *(P-15112)*
MORE WORKSHOP, Placerville *Also called Mother Lode Rhbltion Entps In (P-18146)*
Moreflavor Inc (PA)......**E......800 600-0033**
701 Willow Pass Rd Pittsburg (94565) *(P-9081)*
Moreno & Associates Inc......D......408 924-0353
782 Auzerais Ave San Jose (95126) *(P-11975)*
Morgan Lewis & Bockius LLP (HQ)......**B......415 442-1000**
1 Market Spear St Tower San Francisco (94105) *(P-17337)*
Morgan Advanced Ceramics Inc......C......530 823-3401
13079 Earhart Ave Auburn (95602) *(P-3794)*
Morgan Hill Plastics Inc......E......408 842-1322
8118 Arroyo Cir Gilroy (95020) *(P-4302)*
Morgan Hl Chrysler Ddge Jeep R, Morgan Hill *Also called TSC Motors Inc (P-8433)*
Morgan Manufacturing Inc......F......707 763-6848
521 2nd St Petaluma (94952) *(P-4607)*
Morgan Stanley & Co LLC......E......510 538-5203
4309 Hacienda Dr Ste 200 Pleasanton (94588) *(P-9998)*
Morgan Stnley Smith Barney LLC......D......650 496-4200
1400 Page Mill Rd Palo Alto (94304) *(P-9999)*
Morgan Stnley Smith Barney LLC......C......650 316-6788
650 Castro St Mountain View (94041) *(P-10050)*
Morgan Stnley Smith Barney LLC......D......209 526-3700
1020 10th St Modesto (95354) *(P-10000)*
Morgan Stnley Smith Barney LLC......D......925 730-3800
4309 Hacienda Dr Ste 200 Pleasanton (94588) *(P-10001)*
Morgan Stnley Smith Barney LLC......D......408 346-0105
225 W Santa Clara St # 9 San Jose (95113) *(P-10002)*
Morgan Stnley Smith Barney LLC......D......559 431-5900
5250 N Palm Ave Fresno (93704) *(P-10003)*
Morgan Stnley Smith Barney LLC......D......831 440-5200
6004 La Madrona Dr Scotts Valley (95060) *(P-10004)*
Morgan Stnley Smith Barney LLC......D......415 984-6500
555 California St Fl 35 San Francisco (94104) *(P-10005)*
Morgan Stnley Smith Barney LLC......D......916 983-8888
2365 Iron Point Rd # 235 Folsom (95630) *(P-10006)*
Morgan Stnley Smith Barney LLC......D......707 443-3071
2421 Buhne St Eureka (95501) *(P-10051)*
Morgan Technical Ceramics Inc......E......510 491-1100
2425 Whipple Rd Hayward (94544) *(P-4537)*
Morgan's, San Ramon *Also called Rockins Equipment Company (P-12061)*
Morgenthaler Ventures, Menlo Park *Also called Morgenthler MGT Prtners VI LLC (P-10869)*
Morgenthler MGT Prtners VI LLC......A......650 388-7600
2710 Sand Hill Rd Ste 100 Menlo Park (94025) *(P-10869)*
Morning Star, Los Banos *Also called Liberty Packing Company LLC (P-14322)*
Morning Star Company......B......209 827-2724
13448 Volta Rd Los Banos (93635) *(P-2226)*
Morning Star Company The, Woodland *Also called Liberty Packing Company LLC (P-9414)*
Morning Star Packing, Los Banos *Also called Morning Star Company (P-2226)*
Morning Star Packing Co LP......E......209 826-8000
12045 Ingomar Grade Los Banos (93635) *(P-2227)*
Morning Star Packing Co LP......E......530 473-3642
2211 Old Highway 99 Williams (95987) *(P-2228)*
Morningstar Foods, Gustine *Also called Saputo Dairy Foods Usa LLC (P-2194)*
Morosin Enterprises Inc......D......408 354-0300
2275 Winchester Blvd Campbell (95008) *(P-11311)*
Morphics Technology Inc......D......408 369-7227
1730 N 1st St Ms-13305 San Jose (95112) *(P-18773)*
Morpho Detection LLC......D......510 739-2400
7151 Gateway Blvd Newark (94560) *(P-6676)*
Morrill Industries Inc......D......209 838-2550
24754 E River Rd Escalon (95320) *(P-4961)*
Morris Distributing......D......707 769-7294
3800a Lakeville Hwy Petaluma (94954) *(P-9557)*
Morris General Contracting Inc......E......559 842-9453
14451 W Whitesbridge Ave Kerman (93630) *(P-927)*
Morris Newspaper Corp Cal (HQ)......**D......209 249-3500**
531 E Yosemite Ave Manteca (95336) *(P-3462)*
Morris Publications (PA)......**E......209 847-3021**
122 S 3rd Ave Oakdale (95361) *(P-3463)*
Morris Welding Co Inc......E......707 987-1114
11210 Socrates Mine Rd Middletown (95461) *(P-14717)*
Morrison & Foerster LLP (PA)......**B......415 268-7000**
425 Market St Fl 32 San Francisco (94105) *(P-17338)*
Morrison Building Materials, Chico *Also called Sunset Moulding Co (P-3155)*
Morrison MGT Specialists, Fresno *Also called Morrison MGT Specialists Inc (P-17162)*
Morrison MGT Specialists Inc......C......559 459-6449
2823 Fresno St Fresno (93721) *(P-17162)*
Morrow Snowboards Inc......A......916 415-0645
599 Menlo Dr Ste 200 Rocklin (95765) *(P-6456)*
Morton & Pitalo Inc (PA)......**D......916 984-7621**
600 Coolidge Dr Ste 140 Folsom (95630) *(P-18774)*
Morton Bakar Center, Alameda *Also called Garfield Nursing Home Inc (P-16011)*
Morton Golf LLC......D......916 481-4653
3645 Fulton Ave Sacramento (95821) *(P-15012)*
Morton Golf Management LLC......D......916 481-4653
3645 Fulton Ave Sacramento (95821) *(P-15013)*
Mosaic, Santa Clara *Also called Ciasom LLC (P-11745)*
Mosaic Brands Inc......E......925 322-8700
3266 Buskirk Ave Pleasant Hill (94523) *(P-7300)*
Mosaic Global Transportation, San Jose *Also called Rm Executive Transportation (P-7400)*
MOSplastics Inc......F......408 944-9407
2308 Zanker Rd San Jose (95131) *(P-4303)*
Mosser Hotel, The, San Francisco *Also called Mosser Vctrian Ht Arts Mus Inc (P-11312)*
Mosser Vctrian Ht Arts Mus Inc (HQ)......**E......415 986-4400**
308 Jessie St San Francisco (94103) *(P-11312)*
Mosser Vctrian Ht Arts Mus Inc......C......415 777-1200
68 4th St San Francisco (94103) *(P-11313)*
Mosys Inc......E......408 418-7500
2309 Bering Dr San Jose (95131) *(P-6218)*
Mota Group Inc (PA)......**E......408 370-1248**
60 S Market St Ste 1100 San Jose (95113) *(P-6505)*
Motel Trees, Klamath *Also called Trees of Mystery (P-15256)*
MOTHER JONES MAGAZINE, San Francisco *Also called Foundation For Nat Progress (P-3499)*
Mother Lode Holding Co......D......916 624-8141
9085 Foothills Blvd Roseville (95747) *(P-10203)*
Mother Lode Holding Co (PA)......**D......530 887-2410**
189 Fulweiler Ave Auburn (95603) *(P-10204)*
Mother Lode Job Training......E......209 533-8211
197 Mono Way Ste B Sonora (95370) *(P-17824)*
Mother Lode Plas Molding Inc......E......209 532-5146
1905 N Macarthur Dr # 100 Tracy (95376) *(P-4304)*
Mother Lode Prtg & Pubg Co Inc......E......530 344-5030
2889 Ray Lawyer Dr Placerville (95667) *(P-3464)*
Mother Lode Rhbltion Entps In......C......530 622-4848
399 Placerville Dr Placerville (95667) *(P-18146)*
Mother Lode River Trips Ltd......E......530 626-4187
6280 State Highway 49 Lotus (95651) *(P-15221)*
Mother Olson's Inn, San Jose *Also called San Jose Residence Club Inc (P-11440)*
Motherlode Investors LLC......D......209 736-8112
711 Mccauley Ranch Rd Angels Camp (95222) *(P-15014)*
Motherly Inc......E......917 860-9926
1725 Oakdell Dr Menlo Park (94025) *(P-3584)*
Motif Inc (HQ)......**C......917 903-5485**
300 N Bayshore Blvd San Mateo (94401) *(P-13734)*
Motion Math Inc......A......415 590-2961
582 Market St Ste 511 San Francisco (94104) *(P-12621)*
Motion Pro Inc......E......650 594-9600
3171 Swetzer Rd Loomis (95650) *(P-8456)*
Motista LLC......D......650 204-7976
2 Embarcadero Ctr Fl 8 San Francisco (94111) *(P-19580)*
Motiv Design Group Inc......F......408 441-0611
430 Perrymont Ave San Jose (95125) *(P-5575)*
Motivate International Inc (HQ)......**E......347 916-0210**
185 Berry St Ste 5000 San Francisco (94107) *(P-19372)*
Motivemetrics......F......800 216-5207
425 Sherman Ave Ste 300 Palo Alto (94306) *(P-5779)*
Motor Body Company Inc......E......408 993-9555
455 Sunol St San Jose (95126) *(P-14666)*
Motor Warehouse, Sacramento *Also called Dana Motors Inc (P-8449)*
Motorola Solutions Inc......C......510 217-7400
1101 Marina Village Pkwy # 200 Alameda (94501) *(P-5856)*
Motorola Solutions Inc......E......510 420-7400
6001 Shellmound St Fl 4th Emeryville (94608) *(P-5335)*
Motschdler McHlides Wishon LLP......D......559 439-4000
1690 W Shaw Ave Ste 200 Fresno (93711) *(P-17339)*

Mount Hermon Association Inc (PA).....D.....**831 335-4466**
37 Conference Dr Mount Hermon (95041) ***(P-11609)***
Mount Madonna School.....C.....408 847-2717
491 Summit Rd Watsonville (95076) ***(P-17980)***
Mount Seven, Atwater *Also called Five Keys Inc* ***(P-2992)***
Mount Shasta Resort, Mount Shasta *Also called Siskiyou Lake Golf Resort Inc* ***(P-15027)***
Mountain Cascade Inc (PA).....E.....**925 373-8370**
555 Exchange Ct Livermore (94550) ***(P-1120)***
Mountain Cmmnties Hlth Care Ds (PA).....C.....**530 623-5541**
60 Easter Ave Weaverville (96093) ***(P-16459)***
Mountain Democrat, Placerville *Also called Mother Lode Prtg & Pubg Co Inc* ***(P-3464)***
Mountain F Enterprises Inc.....E.....530 626-4127
950 Iron Point Rd Ste 210 Folsom (95630) ***(P-3073)***
Mountain G Engineering, Folsom *Also called Mountain G Enterprises Inc* ***(P-1061)***
Mountain G Enterprises Inc.....C.....866 464-6351
950 Iron Point Rd Ste 190 Folsom (95630) ***(P-1061)***
Mountain Home Inn.....D.....415 381-9000
810 Panoramic Hwy Mill Valley (94941) ***(P-11314)***
Mountain Manor, Sacramento *Also called Ronald Vanderbeek* ***(P-16264)***
Mountain Resorts Inc.....E.....530 286-2205
1750 Trinity Alps Rd Trinity Center (96091) ***(P-11315)***
Mountain Retreat Incorporated.....D.....925 838-7780
111 Deerwood Rd Ste 100 San Ramon (94583) ***(P-10710)***
Mountain View Healthcare Ctr, Mountain View *Also called Balboa Enterprises Inc* ***(P-15922)***
Mountain View Voice.....F.....650 326-8210
450 Cambridge Ave Palo Alto (94306) ***(P-3465)***
Mountain Vly Child Fmly Svcs I.....C.....530 265-9057
24077 State Highway 49 Nevada City (95959) ***(P-16193)***
Mountain Winery, Saratoga *Also called Chateau Masson LLC* ***(P-2531)***
Mountanos Brothers Coffee Co (PA).....E.....**707 774-8800**
1331 Commerce St Petaluma (94954) ***(P-9466)***
Mountanos Family Coffee & Tea, Petaluma *Also called Mountanos Brothers Coffee Co* ***(P-9466)***
Mounting Systems Inc.....D.....916 374-8872
180 Promenade Cir Ste 300 Sacramento (95834) ***(P-1313)***
Mountz Inc (PA).....E.....**408 292-2214**
1080 N 11th St San Jose (95112) ***(P-6728)***
Movano Inc.....F.....415 651-3172
1652 Chestnut St San Francisco (94123) ***(P-7114)***
Move Inc (HQ).....B.....**408 558-7100**
3315 Scott Blvd Santa Clara (95054) ***(P-10623)***
Move Sales Inc (HQ).....D.....**805 557-2300**
3315 Scott Blvd Santa Clara (95054) ***(P-10624)***
Moveonorg Political Action.....E.....202 465-4234
1442 Walnut St Ste 358 Berkeley (94709) ***(P-18538)***
Movers Intl World Scope, Hayward *Also called Ml Group Inc* ***(P-7569)***
Moveworks Inc (PA).....C.....**408 435-5100**
1277 Terra Bella Ave Mountain View (94043) ***(P-13316)***
Moving Solutions Inc.....C.....408 920-0110
7093 Central Ave Newark (94560) ***(P-7627)***
Movocash Inc.....E.....650 722-3990
530 Lytton Ave Fl 2 Palo Alto (94301) ***(P-12622)***
Movoto LLC (HQ).....E.....**650 241-0910**
1900 S Norfolk St Ste 350 San Mateo (94403) ***(P-10625)***
Moz Designs, Oakland *Also called Ngo Metals Inc* ***(P-4837)***
Mozilla Corp (PA).....E.....**408 946-2311**
273 Pescadero Ct Milpitas (95035) ***(P-14333)***
Mozilla Corporation (HQ).....A.....**650 903-0800**
2 Harrison St Ste 175 San Francisco (94105) ***(P-13636)***
Mozilla Foundation (PA).....B.....**650 903-0800**
2 Harrison St Ste 175 San Francisco (94105) ***(P-12623)***
Mozingo Construction Inc.....E.....209 848-0160
751 Wakefield Ct Oakdale (95361) ***(P-1967)***
Mozio Inc (PA).....D.....**916 719-9213**
44 Tehama St Fl 4 San Francisco (94105) ***(P-7803)***
Mp Associates Inc.....C.....209 274-4715
6555 Jackson Valley Rd Ione (95640) ***(P-4152)***
Mp Holdings, McClellan *Also called McClellan Business Park LLC* ***(P-19569)***
Mp Nexlevel California Inc.....D.....650 486-1359
266 Industrial Rd Ste B San Carlos (94070) ***(P-1121)***
MPA Networks Inc.....E.....650 566-8800
9 Vasilakos Ct Menlo Park (94025) ***(P-13637)***
Mpi America Inc.....F.....408 770-3650
2360 Qume Dr Ste C San Jose (95131) ***(P-6219)***
Mpl Brands Inc (PA).....E.....**888 513-3022**
71 Liberty Ship Way Sausalito (94965) ***(P-2661)***
Mpower Electronics Inc.....D.....408 320-1266
3046 Scott Blvd Santa Clara (95054) ***(P-8869)***
MPS International Ltd.....A.....408 826-0600
79 Great Oaks Blvd San Jose (95119) ***(P-6220)***
Mpt Inc.....E.....559 673-1552
10842 Road 28 1/2 Madera (93637) ***(P-3226)***
Mr Cool, Fresno *Also called Donald P Dick AC Inc* ***(P-1251)***
Mr Gears Inc.....F.....650 364-7793
428 Stanford Ave Redwood City (94063) ***(P-5576)***
Mr Plastics.....E.....510 895-0774
844 Doolittle Dr San Leandro (94577) ***(P-9514)***
Mr S Leather.....E.....415 863-7764
385 8th St San Francisco (94103) ***(P-3018)***
Mroadie LLC.....E.....650 300-4320
721 Colorado Ave Ste 101 Palo Alto (94303) ***(P-12624)***
Mrs Grossmans Paper Company.....D.....707 763-1700
3810 Cypress Dr Petaluma (94954) ***(P-3399)***
MS Intertrade Inc (PA).....E.....**707 837-8057**
2221 Bluebell Dr Ste A Santa Rosa (95403) ***(P-2831)***
Msci Barra, Berkeley *Also called Barra LLC* ***(P-13009)***
MSEFCU, Merced *Also called Merced Schl Emplyees Fdral Cr* ***(P-9795)***

Mshift Inc.....E.....408 437-2740
39899 Balentine Dr # 235 Newark (94560) ***(P-12625)***
MSI Inventory Service, Citrus Heights *Also called Wbi Inventory Service Inc* ***(P-14461)***
Msquared, Fresno *Also called M2 Antenna Systems Inc* ***(P-6450)***
Msr Hotels & Resorts Inc.....B.....408 745-6000
1100 N Mathilda Ave Sunnyvale (94089) ***(P-11316)***
Msr Hotels & Resorts Inc.....D.....408 496-6400
2885 Lakeside Dr Santa Clara (95054) ***(P-10870)***
Msrcosmos LLC (PA).....E.....**925 218-6919**
5250 Claremont Ave # 249 Stockton (95207) ***(P-13939)***
Mssp, San Francisco *Also called Institute On Aging* ***(P-17616)***
Mt Dblo Resource Recovery LLC.....B.....925 682-9113
4080 Mallard Dr Concord (94520) ***(P-7485)***
Mt Diablo Adult Education, Concord *Also called Mt Diablo Unified School Dst* ***(P-17651)***
MT DIABLO CENTER ADULT DAY HEA, Pleasant Hill *Also called Choice In Aging* ***(P-16999)***
Mt Diablo Surgery Center.....E.....925 674-4740
2540 East St Fl A22 Concord (94520) ***(P-16460)***
Mt Diablo Unified School Dst.....D.....925 685-1011
1026 Mohr Ln Concord (94518) ***(P-19581)***
Mt Diablo Unified School Dst.....D.....925 685-7340
1266 San Carlos Ave Concord (94518) ***(P-17651)***
Mt Eden Floral Company LLC (PA).....E.....**408 213-5777**
2124 Bering Dr San Jose (95131) ***(P-9637)***
Mt Eden Nursery Co Inc (PA).....E.....**408 213-5777**
2124 Bering Dr San Jose (95131) ***(P-10483)***
Mt Lassen Trout Farms Inc.....E.....530 474-1900
20560 Lanes Valley Rd Paynes Creek (96075) ***(P-538)***
Mt Systems Inc.....F.....510 651-5277
49040 Milmont Dr Fremont (94538) ***(P-5159)***
Mtc Holdings (HQ).....E.....**912 651-4000**
3 Embarcadero Ctr Ste 550 San Francisco (94111) ***(P-7723)***
Mtc Resturant Group Inc.....E.....408 371-3806
1777 S Bascom Ave Ste D Campbell (95008) ***(P-19582)***
Mtech Inc.....F.....530 894-5091
1072 Marauder St Ste 210 Chico (95973) ***(P-4305)***
MTI Adventurewear, Arcata *Also called Wing Inflatables Inc* ***(P-4334)***
MTI Corporation.....E.....510 525-3070
860 S 19th St Richmond (94804) ***(P-6457)***
Mtna Inc.....E.....559 354-9639
2855 S Elm Ave Fresno (93706) ***(P-11976)***
Mtr Transportation Inc.....E.....415 928-3279
1524 Hyde St San Francisco (94109) ***(P-14334)***
Mud Puppy Inc.....E.....760 961-1160
38688 Kentucky Ave Woodland (95695) ***(P-569)***
Muehlhan Certifed Coatings Inc.....E.....707 639-4414
2320 Cordelia Rd Fairfield (94534) ***(P-2045)***
Muehlhan Marine, Fairfield *Also called Sipco Surface Protection Inc* ***(P-1433)***
Mufg Americas Holdings Corp.....C.....212 782-5911
1221 Broadway Fl 8 Oakland (94612) ***(P-9686)***
Mufg Union Bank National Assn (HQ).....A.....**415 705-7000**
400 California St Fl 14 San Francisco (94104) ***(P-9687)***
Muir John Mgntic Imging Ctr L.....D.....925 296-7156
1601 Ygnacio Valley Rd Walnut Creek (94598) ***(P-16461)***
Muir Dblo Occptnal Mdcine Med.....E.....925 685-7744
2231 Galaxy Ct Concord (94520) ***(P-15541)***
Muir Labs.....E.....925 947-3335
1601 Ygnacio Valley Rd Walnut Creek (94598) ***(P-16462)***
Muir Orthopedic Specialists.....C.....925 939-8585
2405 Shadelands Dr # 210 Walnut Creek (94598) ***(P-15542)***
Muir Orthopedics Inc.....D.....925 939-8585
2405 Shadelands Dr # 210 Walnut Creek (94598) ***(P-15543)***
Muir WD Adolescent & Fmly Svcs, San Rafael *Also called Muir Wood LLC* ***(P-17163)***
Muir Wood LLC.....E.....310 903-1155
55 Shaver St Ste 200 San Rafael (94901) ***(P-17163)***
Muirlab, Walnut Creek *Also called Muir Labs* ***(P-16462)***
Mulesoft Inc.....A.....415 229-2009
50 Fremont St Ste 300 San Francisco (94105) ***(P-13317)***
Mulholland Brothers (PA).....D.....**415 824-5995**
1710 4th St Berkeley (94710) ***(P-3291)***
Muller Ranch LLC.....D.....530 662-0105
15810 County Road 95 Woodland (95695) ***(P-1)***
Mullikin Medical Center, San Mateo *Also called Bay Area Pdatric Med Group Inc* ***(P-15289)***
Mullikin Medical Center, Stockton *Also called Caremark Rx LLC* ***(P-15327)***
Multani Logistics, Hayward *Also called Do Dine Inc* ***(P-13117)***
Multi Specialty Group Practice, Yuba City *Also called Sutter North Med Foundation* ***(P-15730)***
Multi- Services, San Francisco *Also called Walden House Inc* ***(P-18207)***
Multi-Color Napa/Sonama, NAPA *Also called Collotype Labels USA Inc* ***(P-3725)***
Multibeam Corporation.....E.....408 980-1800
3951 Burton Dr Santa Clara (95054) ***(P-5160)***
Multimek Inc.....E.....408 653-1300
357 Reed St Santa Clara (95050) ***(P-5948)***
Multiphy Inc.....F.....650 600-9194
125 University Ave # 200 Palo Alto (94301) ***(P-6221)***
Multiplier.....D.....415 421-3774
780 Glendome Cir Oakland (94602) ***(P-19825)***
Multitest Elctrnic Systems Inc (HQ).....B.....**408 988-6544**
3021 Kenneth St Santa Clara (95054) ***(P-6771)***
Multiven Inc.....E.....408 828-2715
303 Twin Dolphin Dr # 600 Redwood City (94065) ***(P-13940)***
Multivision Inc (HQ).....D.....**510 740-5600**
66 Franklin St Fl 3 Oakland (94607) ***(P-14335)***
Multivitamin Direct Inc.....E.....408 573-7292
2178 Paragon Dr San Jose (95131) ***(P-3818)***
Mum NAPA Valley.....C.....707 942-3425
8445 Silverado Trl NAPA (94558) ***(P-382)***
Mumm NAPA Valley, Rutherford *Also called Pernod Ricard Usa LLC* ***(P-2681)***

Munger Tolles Olson Foundation..........E......415 512-4000
560 Mission St Fl 27 San Francisco (94105) *(P-17340)*
Municipal Svcs Agency, Sacramento *Also called County of Sacramento (P-1081)*
Muniservices LLC (HQ)..........C......**800 800-8181**
7625 N Palm Ave Ste 108 Fresno (93711) *(P-19583)*
Munn & Perkins, Modesto *Also called Reed Group (P-1071)*
Munselle Vineyards LLC..........F......707 857-9988
3660 Highway 128 Geyserville (95441) *(P-2662)*
Mural, San Francisco *Also called Tactivos Inc (P-7996)*
Murdoc Technology LLC..........E......559 497-1580
5683 E Fountain Way Fresno (93727) *(P-6458)*
Murga Strange & Chalmers Inc..........E......707 643-9075
924 Lemon St Vallejo (94590) *(P-1895)*
Murphy Astin Adams Schnfeld LL..........E......916 446-2300
555 Capitol Mall Ste 800 Sacramento (95814) *(P-17341)*
Murphy HARtelius/M&h Uniforms (PA)..........E......**650 344-2997**
845 Stanton Rd Burlingame (94010) *(P-9249)*
Murphy McKay & Associates Inc..........E......925 283-9555
1990 N Calif Blvd Fl 8th Walnut Creek (94596) *(P-13941)*
Murphy Prson Brdley Fney Inc A (PA)..........D......**415 788-1900**
580 California St # 1100 San Francisco (94104) *(P-17342)*
Murphy's Market, Arcata *Also called Ramsey Marketing & MGT Co (P-19618)*
Murphy-True Inc..........D......707 576-7337
464 Kenwood Ct Ste B Santa Rosa (95407) *(P-928)*
Murphys Historic Hotel..........D......209 728-3444
457 Main St Murphys (95247) *(P-11317)*
Murray Biscuit Company LLC..........C......209 472-3718
5250 Claremont Ave Stockton (95207) *(P-2417)*
Murray Trailers, Stockton *Also called Harley Murray Inc (P-6602)*
Mursion Inc (PA)..........D......**415 746-9631**
1 California St Ste 1550 San Francisco (94111) *(P-13318)*
Musco Family Olive Co, Tracy *Also called Olive Musco Products Inc (P-2234)*
Muscolino Inventory Svc Inc..........E......209 576-8469
1620 N Carptr Rd Ste D50 Modesto (95351) *(P-14336)*
Muse Concrete Contractors Inc..........D......530 226-5151
8599 Commercial Way Redding (96002) *(P-1062)*
Museum of Art Hstory At McPhrs..........E......831 429-1964
705 Front St Santa Cruz (95060) *(P-18276)*
Music Circus, Sacramento *Also called Broadway Sacramento (P-14840)*
Mustang Survival Inc..........D......360 676-1782
3701 Mt Diablo Blvd # 100 Lafayette (94549) *(P-4219)*
Mutual Aid Response Svcs Inc..........E......866 627-7911
88 Emery Bay Dr Emeryville (94608) *(P-19826)*
Mutual Assstnce Ntwrk of Del P (PA)..........E......**916 927-7694**
811 Grand Ave Ste A Sacramento (95838) *(P-17652)*
Mux Inc (PA)..........F......**510 402-2257**
1182 Market St Ste 425 San Francisco (94102) *(P-13319)*
Mv Transportation Inc..........C......510 351-1603
1944 Williams St San Leandro (94577) *(P-7343)*
Mve Inc (PA)..........D......**209 526-4214**
1117 L St Modesto (95354) *(P-18775)*
Mvinix Corporation..........E......408 321-9109
1759 Mccarthy Blvd Milpitas (95035) *(P-5949)*
Mw McWong International Inc (PA)..........E......**916 371-8080**
1921 Arena Blvd Sacramento (95834) *(P-5747)*
Mxb Battery LP..........D......415 230-8000
717 Battery St San Francisco (94111) *(P-18442)*
Mxic, Milpitas *Also called Macronix America Inc (P-8930)*
My Ally Inc..........D......650 387-9118
1000 Elwell Ct Ste 105 Palo Alto (94303) *(P-13638)*
My Doctor Medical Group, San Francisco *Also called Paul D Abramson MD Inc (P-15587)*
My Goods Market, San Ramon *Also called Eagle Canyon Capital LLC (P-2830)*
My Points.com, San Francisco *Also called Mypointscom LLC (P-11774)*
My True Image Mfg Inc..........D......510 970-7990
999 Marina Way S Richmond (94804) *(P-8788)*
Mya Systems Inc (PA)..........E......**877 679-0952**
351 California St Fl Mezz San Francisco (94104) *(P-12109)*
Mydax Inc..........F......530 888-6662
12260 Shale Ridge Ln # 4 Auburn (95602) *(P-5434)*
Myenersave Inc..........F......408 464-6385
440 N Wolfe Rd Sunnyvale (94085) *(P-13320)*
Myers & Sons Construction LLC..........C......916 283-9950
4600 Northgate Blvd # 10 Sacramento (95834) *(P-1122)*
Myers & Sons Construction LP (HQ)..........C......**916 283-9950**
4600 Northgate Blvd # 10 Sacramento (95834) *(P-1063)*
Myers & Sons Hi-Way Safety Inc..........F......909 591-1781
9510 Jackson Rd Sacramento (95827) *(P-5891)*
Myers Container, Richmond *Also called Imacc Corporation (P-9119)*
Myers Restaurant Supply LLC..........C......707 570-1200
1599 Cleveland Ave Santa Rosa (95401) *(P-8767)*
Myers-Briggs Company (PA)..........D......**650 969-8901**
185 N Wolfe Rd Sunnyvale (94086) *(P-19584)*
Mygrant Glass Company Inc (PA)..........E......**510 785-4360**
3271 Arden Rd Hayward (94545) *(P-8457)*
Mymaskmovement.org/ My Mask, Stanford *Also called Youmask Inc (P-12932)*
Myntahl Corporation..........E......510 413-0002
48273 Lakeview Blvd Fremont (94538) *(P-6459)*
Myokardia Inc..........C......650 741-0900
1000 Sierra Point Pkwy Brisbane (94005) *(P-3951)*
Myome Inc (PA)..........E......**541 826-6778**
201 Industrial Rd Ste 410 San Carlos (94070) *(P-16789)*
Myovant Sciences Inc..........C......650 392-0222
2000 Sierra Point Pkwy # 9 Brisbane (94005) *(P-9233)*
Mypointscom LLC (HQ)..........D......**415 615-1100**
44 Montgomery St Ste 1050 San Francisco (94104) *(P-11774)*
Myriad Womens Health Inc..........B......888 268-6795
180 Kimball Way South San Francisco (94080) *(P-16790)*
Mythic Inc..........E......734 707-7339
805 Veterans Blvd Ste 228 Redwood City (94063) *(P-19585)*
Myvr.com, Corte Madera *Also called Jomu Mist Incorporated (P-13257)*
N & S Tractor Co (PA)..........D......**209 383-5888**
600 S St 59 Merced (95341) *(P-14766)*
N & T Digmore Inc..........D......530 241-2992
1525 Tahoe Ct Redding (96003) *(P-1123)*
N D E Inc..........E......408 727-3955
3301 Keller St Santa Clara (95054) *(P-5950)*
N G S, Sacramento *Also called New Generation Software Inc (P-13328)*
N I D, Grass Valley *Also called Nevada Irrigation District (P-8415)*
N J Kann Painting..........E......408 437-0220
662 Giguere Ct Ste B San Jose (95133) *(P-1422)*
N Model Inc (PA)..........B......**650 610-4600**
777 Mariners Island Blvd San Mateo (94404) *(P-12626)*
N V Cast Stone LLC..........E......707 261-6615
2003 Seville Dr NAPA (94559) *(P-4444)*
N V H, Concord *Also called N V Heathorn Inc (P-1314)*
N V Heathorn Inc..........D......510 569-9100
1980 Olivera Rd Ste C Concord (94520) *(P-1314)*
Nadalie USA, Calistoga *Also called Tonnellerie Francaise French C (P-3242)*
Nadhan Inc..........D......707 544-7750
850 Sonoma Ave Santa Rosa (95404) *(P-16064)*
Nady Systems Inc..........E......510 652-2411
3341 Vincent Rd Pleasant Hill (94523) *(P-5765)*
Nagarro Inc (HQ)..........A......**408 436-6170**
2001 Gateway Pl Ste 100w San Jose (95110) *(P-13942)*
Nagel Landscaping..........E......209 545-1696
5719 Mchenry Ave Modesto (95356) *(P-487)*
Nagra, San Francisco *Also called Opentv Inc (P-13344)*
Naia Inc..........E......510 724-2479
736 Alfred Nobel Dr Hercules (94547) *(P-2181)*
Nakagawa Manufacturing USA Inc..........E......510 782-0197
8652 Thornton Ave Newark (94560) *(P-3346)*
Nakoma Golf Resort, Clio *Also called Nakoma Resort LLC (P-14963)*
Nakoma Resort LLC..........E......530 832-5067
348 Bear Run Clio (96106) *(P-14963)*
Nan Fang Dist Group Inc..........D......510 297-5382
2100 Williams St San Leandro (94577) *(P-9082)*
Nan Ya Technology Corp USA..........E......408 961-4000
1735 Tech Dr Ste 400 San Jose (95110) *(P-8936)*
Nana Enterprises..........D......415 383-0340
707 Rdwood Hwy Frntage Rd Mill Valley (94941) *(P-11318)*
Nana Wall Systems Inc..........E......415 383-3148
100 Madowcreek Dr Ste 250 Corte Madera (94925) *(P-8597)*
Nancys Specialty Foods..........B......510 494-1100
2400 Olympic Blvd Ste 8 Lafayette (94595) *(P-2925)*
Nanez Mfg Inc..........E......408 830-9903
164 Commercial St Sunnyvale (94086) *(P-5577)*
Nanoscale Cmbntrial Synthsis I (PA)..........D......**408 987-2004**
3100 Central Expy Santa Clara (95051) *(P-19090)*
Nanosilicon Inc..........E......408 263-7341
2461 Autumnvale Dr San Jose (95131) *(P-6222)*
Nanosyn, Santa Clara *Also called Nanoscale Cmbntrial Synthsis I (P-19090)*
Nanosys Inc (PA)..........B......**408 240-6700**
233 S Hillview Dr Milpitas (95035) *(P-6223)*
Nanotech Energy Inc..........E......310 806-9202
311 Otterson Dr Ste 60 Chico (95928) *(P-6488)*
Nanotronics Automation, Hollister *Also called Nanotronics Imaging Inc (P-6533)*
Nanotronics Imaging Inc..........E......831 630-0700
777 Flynn Rd Hollister (95023) *(P-6533)*
Nanval Inc..........D......925 634-3200
613 1st St Brentwood (94513) *(P-10626)*
Nanya Technologies U S A, San Jose *Also called Nan Ya Technology Corp USA (P-8936)*
NAPA Auto Parts, Oakland *Also called General Auto Repair Inc (P-8452)*
NAPA Auto Parts, San Bruno *Also called Airport Auto Parts Inc (P-8436)*
NAPA Es Leasing LLC..........D......707 253-9540
1075 California Blvd NAPA (94559) *(P-11319)*
NAPA Golf Associates LLC..........D......707 257-1900
2555 Jameson Canyon Rd NAPA (94558) *(P-15113)*
NAPA Golf Course At Kennedy Pk, NAPA *Also called Courseco Inc (P-14993)*
NAPA Jet Center Inc..........D......707 224-0887
2030 Airport Rd NAPA (94558) *(P-7777)*
NAPA Mill LLC..........E......707 251-8500
500 Main St Ste 208 NAPA (94559) *(P-11320)*
NAPA Motel and Restaurant..........E......707 257-1930
100 Soscol Ave NAPA (94559) *(P-11321)*
NAPA Nissan Inc..........E......707 253-1551
510 Soscol Ave NAPA (94559) *(P-8458)*
NAPA Nursing Center Inc..........E......707 257-0931
3275 Villa Ln NAPA (94558) *(P-16065)*
NAPA Post Acute, NAPA *Also called Napaidence Opco LLC (P-16066)*
NAPA Register, NAPA *Also called NAPA Valley Publishing Co (P-3467)*
NAPA River Inn..........D......707 251-8500
500 Main St NAPA (94559) *(P-11322)*
NAPA Sanitation District..........E......707 254-9231
1515 Soscol Ferry Rd NAPA (94558) *(P-8286)*
NAPA Select Vineyard Servi..........F......707 294-2637
5 Financial Plz Ste 200 NAPA (94558) *(P-2663)*
NAPA Solano Cmnty Blood Ctr, Fairfield *Also called Vitalant Research Institute (P-17190)*
NAPA State Hospital, NAPA *Also called State Hospitals Cal Dept (P-16746)*
NAPA Valley Balloons Inc..........E......707 253-2224
4086 Byway E NAPA (94558) *(P-7819)*
NAPA Valley Brewing Co Inc..........D......707 942-4101
1250 Lincoln Ave Calistoga (94515) *(P-11323)*
NAPA Valley Cast Stone, NAPA *Also called N V Cast Stone LLC (P-4444)*
NAPA Valley Country Club..........D......707 252-1111
3385 Hagen Rd NAPA (94558) *(P-15114)*

NAPA Valley Lodge LP ....D....707 875-3525
103 Coast Highway 1 Bodega Bay (94923) *(P-11324)*
NAPA Valley Marriott, NAPA *Also called IA Lodging NAPA Solano Trs LLC (P-11185)*
NAPA Valley PSI Inc ....D....707 255-0177
651 Trabajo Ln NAPA (94559) *(P-17825)*
NAPA Valley Publishing Co ....D....707 226-3711
1615 Soscol Ave NAPA (94559) *(P-3466)*
NAPA Valley Publishing Co (PA)....E....707 226-3711
1615 Soscol Ave NAPA (94559) *(P-3467)*
NAPA Valley Railroad Co, NAPA *Also called NAPA Valley Wine Train LLC (P-15222)*
NAPA Valley Register, NAPA *Also called NAPA Valley Publishing Co (P-3466)*
NAPA Valley Reserve, The, Saint Helena *Also called Meadowood Associates LP (P-15219)*
NAPA Valley Unified School Dst ....E....707 253-3520
1616 Lincoln Ave NAPA (94558) *(P-11977)*
NAPA Valley Vintners ....D....707 963-3388
1475 Library Ln Saint Helena (94574) *(P-18310)*
NAPA Valley Wine Train LLC (HQ)....C....707 253-2160
1275 Mckinstry St NAPA (94559) *(P-15222)*
NAPA Vly Orthpdic Med Group In ....E....707 254-7117
3273 Claremont Way # 100 NAPA (94558) *(P-15544)*
NAPA West, Five Points *Also called ATI Machinery Inc (P-9031)*
NAPA Wine Company LLC ....E....707 944-8669
7830 St Helena Hwy 40 Oakville (94562) *(P-2664)*
Napaidence Opco LLC ....C....707 255-6060
705 Trancas St NAPA (94558) *(P-16066)*
Naptech Test Equipment Inc ....F....707 995-7145
9781 Pt Lkeview Rd Unit 3 Kelseyville (95451) *(P-6772)*
Naraghi Farms LLC ....E....209 577-5777
20001 Mchenry Ave Escalon (95320) *(P-183)*
Narda Microwave West, Folsom *Also called Stellant Systems Inc (P-5871)*
NASA Ames Research Center ....E....650 604-4620
Nasa Exch Lodge 19 Mccord St Nasa Exchange Lod Mountain View (94035) *(P-11325)*
Nassau-Sosnick Dist Co LLC (PA)....D....650 952-2226
258 Littlefield Ave South San Francisco (94080) *(P-9467)*
Natalie Dstiny Entps Ltd Lblty ....E....408 429-8665
42 W Campbell Ave Ste 101 Campbell (95008) *(P-17653)*
Nates Fine Foods LLC ....E....310 897-2690
8880 Industrial Ave # 100 Roseville (95678) *(P-2304)*
National 9 Motels Inc ....E....530 622-3884
1500 Broadway Placerville (95667) *(P-11326)*
National Auto Prts Whse - CA I (HQ)....E....510 786-3555
901 Arden Way Sacramento (95815) *(P-8459)*
National Automobile Club (PA)....E....650 294-7000
111 Anza Blvd Ste 109 Burlingame (94010) *(P-18581)*
National Bevpak, Hayward *Also called Shasta Beverages Inc (P-2814)*
National Cnstr Rentals Inc ....E....510 563-4000
1300 Business Center Dr San Leandro (94577) *(P-12055)*
NATIONAL CONSORTIUM FOR JUSTIC, Sacramento *Also called Search Group Incorporated (P-19235)*
National Ctr For Lsbian Rights ....E....415 392-6257
870 Market St Ste 370 San Francisco (94102) *(P-17343)*
National Data Funding LLC ....D....530 343-1605
462 Waterford Dr Chico (95973) *(P-9849)*
National Directory Services ....E....530 268-8636
19698 View Forever Ln Grass Valley (95945) *(P-3540)*
National Dispatching, Fresno *Also called Cal Valley Construction Inc (P-1152)*
National Distribution Agcy Inc (HQ)....D....510 487-6226
7025 Central Ave Newark (94560) *(P-7695)*
National Ewp Inc ....F....510 236-6282
1961 Meeker Ave Richmond (94804) *(P-542)*
National Express LLC ....D....209 201-9345
880 Thornton Rd Merced (95341) *(P-7391)*
National Financial Svcs LLC ....A....415 912-2805
44 Montgomery St Ste 1900 San Francisco (94104) *(P-10052)*
National Financial Svcs LLC ....A....650 343-6775
1411 Chapin Ave Burlingame (94010) *(P-10871)*
National Fncl Srvcs Cnsrtm LLC ....D....650 572-2872
3161 Los Prados St San Mateo (94403) *(P-19586)*
National Food Laboratory LLC ....D....925 828-1440
365 N Canyons Pkwy # 201 Livermore (94551) *(P-19225)*
National Glass Systems Inc ....E....408 835-5124
4778 Gertrude Dr Fremont (94536) *(P-1939)*
National Historic Rest Inc ....D....209 984-3446
18187 Main St Jamestown (95327) *(P-11327)*
National Home Health Svcs Inc ....E....408 786-1035
2880 Zanker Rd Ste 101 San Jose (95134) *(P-16914)*
National Hotel & Restaurant, Jamestown *Also called National Historic Rest Inc (P-11327)*
National Inds For Svrely Hndcp, San Ramon *Also called Sourceamerica (P-18250)*
National Insur Insptn Svcs Inc ....E....559 435-1117
1040 E Herndon Ave # 205 Fresno (93720) *(P-10316)*
National Metal Fabricators ....E....510 887-6231
28435 Century St Hayward (94545) *(P-4678)*
National Mortgage Insur Corp ....E....855 530-6642
2100 Powell St Fl 12 Emeryville (94608) *(P-9916)*
NATIONAL NURSES UNITED, Oakland *Also called California Nurses Association (P-18329)*
National Opinion Research Ctr ....D....415 315-2000
50 California St Ste 1500 San Francisco (94111) *(P-19171)*
National Opinion Research Ctr ....D....415 315-3800
1250 Borregas Ave Sunnyvale (94089) *(P-19172)*
National Pro Security Svcs Inc ....E....877 392-2340
9306 International Blvd Oakland (94603) *(P-14141)*
National Raisin Company, Fowler *Also called Sunshine Raisin Corporation (P-311)*
National Recycling Corporation ....E....510 268-1022
1312 Kirkham St Oakland (94607) *(P-3403)*
National Rent A Car, San Francisco *Also called Enterprise Rnt—car San Frncsc (P-14477)*
National Security Industries ....D....831 425-2052
501 Mission St Ste 1a Santa Cruz (95060) *(P-14078)*
National Security Industries (PA)....C....408 371-6505
940 Park Ave Frnt Frnt San Jose (95126) *(P-14079)*
National Security Santa Cruz, Santa Cruz *Also called National Security Industries (P-14078)*
National Security Tech LLC ....A....925 960-2500
161 S Vasco Rd Ste A Livermore (94551) *(P-18776)*
National Semiconductor Corp (HQ)....A....408 721-5000
2900 Semiconductor Dr Santa Clara (95051) *(P-6224)*
National Traffic Safety Inst, San Jose *Also called Ntsi Corporation (P-17828)*
National Transfer and Stor Inc ....E....916 383-8800
6350 Sky Creek Dr Ste 600 Sacramento (95828) *(P-7628)*
Nations First Capital LLC ....D....855 396-3600
516 Gibson Dr Ste 160 Roseville (95678) *(P-9888)*
Nations Roof West LLC ....E....559 252-1255
5463 E Hedges Ave Fresno (93727) *(P-1824)*
Nationwide, Fresno *Also called National Insur Insptn Svcs Inc (P-10316)*
Nationwide, Fresno *Also called Jagdeep Singh Insur Agcy Inc (P-10301)*
Nationwide, San Jose *Also called Archway Insurance Brokers LLC (P-10236)*
Nationwide, Rancho Cordova *Also called Strachota Insurance Agency (P-10355)*
Nationwide, Santa Rosa *Also called Northwest Insurance Agency Inc (P-10325)*
Nationwide, San Carlos *Also called Professional Insur Assoc Inc (P-10336)*
Nationwide, Eureka *Also called Shaw & Petersen Insurance Inc (P-10351)*
Nationwide, San Mateo *Also called Andreini & Company (P-10232)*
Nationwide, San Francisco *Also called AON Risk Insurance Svcs W Inc (P-10235)*
Nationwide, San Francisco *Also called Maroevich Oshea Cghlan Insur S (P-10310)*
Nationwide, Petaluma *Also called Don Ramatici Insurance Inc (P-10274)*
Nationwide, San Mateo *Also called Abd Insurance & Fincl Svcs Inc (P-10224)*
Nationwide, San Francisco *Also called Woodruff-Sawyer & Co (P-10372)*
Nationwide, San Francisco *Also called Hub Intrntional Insur Svcs Inc (P-10294)*
Nationwide, NAPA *Also called Sander Jcobs Cssyre Grffin Inc (P-10341)*
Nationwide, Sacramento *Also called Rielli Insur & Fincl Svcs LL (P-10338)*
Nationwide, San Francisco *Also called Embroker Insurance Svcs LLC (P-10278)*
Nationwide, San Jose *Also called Leavitt Pacific Insur Brks Inc (P-10308)*
Nationwide, Fresno *Also called James G Parker Insurance Assoc (P-10303)*
Nationwide, Fresno *Also called Walter R Reinhardt Insur Agcy (P-10366)*
Nationwide, Modesto *Also called Tsm Insurance & Fincl Svcs Inc (P-10362)*
Nationwide, Fresno *Also called Dibuduo Dfendis Insur Brks LLC (P-10272)*
Nationwide, San Francisco *Also called Pennbrook Insurance Service (P-10331)*
Nationwide, San Mateo *Also called Newfront Insurance Svcs LLC (P-10318)*
Nationwide, Roseville *Also called Interwest Insurance Svcs LLC (P-10300)*
Nationwide, Turlock *Also called Winton Irland Strom Green Insu (P-10369)*
Nationwide, San Ramon *Also called A D Bilich Inc (P-9889)*
Nationwide, Modesto *Also called Capax Management & Insur Svcs (P-10259)*
Nationwide, San Francisco *Also called Cal Insurance and Assoc Inc (P-10255)*
Nationwide, San Francisco *Also called Insurnce Svcs San Frncisco Inc (P-10297)*
Nationwide, Grass Valley *Also called Networked Insurance Agents LLC (P-10317)*
Nationwide, San Francisco *Also called Edgewood Partners Insur Ctr (P-10275)*
Nationwide Boiler Incorporated (PA)....E....510 490-7100
42400 Christy St Fremont (94538) *(P-4726)*
Nationwide Envmtl Cnstr Svcs I ....E....916 708-7445
4470 Yankee Hill Rd # 200 Rocklin (95677) *(P-18777)*
Nationwide Sun, Rocklin *Also called Nationwide Envmtl Cnstr Svcs I (P-18777)*
Native ....E....562 217-9338
201 California St Ste 450 San Francisco (94111) *(P-4091)*
Native American Health Ctr Inc (PA)....D....510 535-4400
2950 International Blvd Oakland (94601) *(P-15545)*
Native Deodorants, San Francisco *Also called Zenlen Inc (P-4100)*
Natomas Racquet Club, Sacramento *Also called Spare-Time Inc (P-14977)*
Natron Energy Inc ....D....408 498-5828
3542 Bassett St Santa Clara (95054) *(P-6489)*
Natural Orange Inc ....D....408 963-6868
434 Park Ave San Jose (95110) *(P-11905)*
Natural Std RES Collaboration ....E....617 591-3300
3120 W March Ln Fl 1 Stockton (95219) *(P-3541)*
Nature Care Landscape Inds, Sacramento *Also called Dean Moon (P-456)*
Nature Conservancy ....D....415 777-0487
201 Mission St Ste 400 San Francisco (94105) *(P-18443)*
Nature Expeditions Africa, Sacramento *Also called Accent Hospitality Group LLC (P-7812)*
Naturener Glacier Wind Energy ....E....415 217-5500
394 Pacific Ave Ste 300 San Francisco (94111) *(P-19914)*
Naturener USA LLC (HQ)....E....415 217-5500
435 Pacific Ave Fl 4 San Francisco (94133) *(P-5664)*
Natures Products Inc (HQ)....C....954 233-3300
1221 Broadway Oakland (94612) *(P-9234)*
Naturescapes Landscaping Corp ....E....408 294-4994
560 Newhall Dr San Jose (95110) *(P-488)*
Naturner Mont Wind Enrgy 2 LLC ....E....415 217-5508
394 Pacific Ave Ste 300 San Francisco (94111) *(P-1169)*
Natus Medical Incorporated (PA)....B....925 223-6700
6701 Koll Center Pkwy # 12 Pleasanton (94566) *(P-7115)*
Naumes Inc ....D....530 743-2055
3792 Feather River Blvd Olivehurst (95961) *(P-131)*
Nautilus Biotechnology Inc ....C....206 333-2001
201 Industrial Rd Ste 310 San Carlos (94070) *(P-19091)*
Navarro Vineyard, Philo *Also called Navarro Winery (P-2665)*
Navarro Winery ....E....707 895-3686
5601 Highway 128 Philo (95466) *(P-2665)*
Navis Corporation (PA)....B....510 267-5000
55 Harrison St Ste 600 Oakland (94607) *(P-19827)*
Navitas LLC ....E....415 883-8116
15 Pamaron Way Novato (94949) *(P-9468)*
Navitas Naturals, Novato *Also called Navitas LLC (P-9468)*
Nazareth House, San Rafael *Also called Sisters of Nazareth (P-16269)*

ALPHABETIC

Nca Laboratories Inc...F.......916 852-7029
11305 Sunrise Gold Cir Rancho Cordova (95742) *(P-5766)*
Ncc Group Inc (HQ)...**D.......415 268-9300**
123 Mission St Ste 1020 San Francisco (94105) *(P-13943)*
Ncc Group Security Svcs Inc (HQ)...**E.......415 293-0808**
650 California St # 2950 San Francisco (94108) *(P-13944)*
Nccrc, Oakland *Also called Northern Cal Crpnters Rgnal CN (P-18370)*
NCIRE, San Francisco *Also called Northern Cal Inst For RES Edca (P-18244)*
Ncoup Inc (PA)...**E.......510 739-4010**
825 Corporate Way Fremont (94539) *(P-13321)*
Ncpa, Roseville *Also called Northern California Power Agcy (P-8128)*
Ncsra Medical Corporation...E.......916 389-7100
2801 K St Ste 410 Sacramento (95816) *(P-15546)*
ND Systems Inc...E.......408 776-0085
5750 Hellyer Ave San Jose (95138) *(P-11814)*
Ndga, Santa Clara *Also called Bandai Namco Entrmt Amer Inc (P-9164)*
NDk America Inc...F.......408 428-0800
1551 Mccarthy Blvd Milpitas (95035) *(P-6225)*
Nds, Fresno *Also called Agrifim Irrigation Pdts Inc (P-4994)*
Ndsp Crp, San Jose *Also called Ndsp Delaware Inc (P-6226)*
Ndsp Delaware Inc...E.......408 626-1640
224 Airport Pkwy Ste 400 San Jose (95110) *(P-6226)*
Neato Robotics Inc (HQ)...**D.......510 795-1351**
50 Rio Robles San Jose (95134) *(P-5110)*
Nebia Inc...F.......203 570-6222
375 Alabama St Ste 200 San Francisco (94110) *(P-4220)*
Necsel Intllctual Property Inc (HQ)...**E.......408 246-7555**
801 Ames Ave Milpitas (95035) *(P-10397)*
Nedilijka Colma Inc (PA)...**E.......650 992-2727**
1560 Bryant St Daly City (94015) *(P-16067)*
Neeva Inc...D.......408 220-9086
100 View St Ste 204 Mountain View (94041) *(P-13801)*
Nefab Packaging Inc...D.......408 678-2500
8477 Central Ave Newark (94560) *(P-3216)*
Nefab Packaging West LLC...D.......408 678-2516
8477 Central Ave Newark (94560) *(P-14337)*
Nefeli Networks Inc...E.......510 859-4665
2150 Shattuck Ave # 1300 Berkeley (94704) *(P-7155)*
Neff Corporation...E.......510 276-3080
15740 Hesperian Blvd San Lorenzo (94580) *(P-12056)*
Nehemiah Construction Inc...E.......707 746-6815
12150 Tributary Ln P Rancho Cordova (95670) *(P-1064)*
Nehemiah Rebar Services Inc...C.......530 676-6310
4110 Business Dr Ste B Cameron Park (95682) *(P-1928)*
Neighborly Pest Management Inc...D.......916 782-3767
324 Riverside Ave Roseville (95678) *(P-11906)*
Neil Jones Food Company...E.......831 637-0573
711 Sally St Hollister (95023) *(P-2229)*
Neil Jones Food Company...E.......559 659-5100
2502 N St Firebaugh (93622) *(P-2230)*
Neil O Anderson Assoc Inc NA, Lodi *Also called Anderson Neil O and Assoc Inc (P-18624)*
Neillo Audi, Sacramento *Also called Niello Imports II Inc (P-14579)*
Neilmed Pharmaceuticals Inc...B.......707 525-3784
601 Aviation Blvd Santa Rosa (95403) *(P-3952)*
Neils Controlled Blasting LP...E.......916 663-2500
490 Main St Newcastle (95658) *(P-1170)*
Neilsen TV Ratings, Benicia *Also called Nielsen Company (us) LLC (P-19173)*
Nektar Therapeutics (PA)...**B.......415 482-5300**
455 Mssion Bay Blvd S Ste San Francisco (94158) *(P-3953)*
Nel Hydrogen Inc...E.......650 543-3180
2371 Verna Ct San Leandro (94577) *(P-3776)*
Nelson & Kennard Law Offices...E.......916 920-2295
5011 Dudlley Blvd Bldg 25 Newcastle (95658) *(P-17344)*
Nelson & Sons Electric Inc...E.......209 667-4343
401 N Walnut Rd Turlock (95380) *(P-1547)*
Nelson & Sons Inc...E.......707 462-3755
550 Nelson Ranch Rd Ukiah (95482) *(P-2666)*
Nelson Family Vineyard, Ukiah *Also called Nelson & Sons Inc (P-2666)*
Nelson Staffing Solutions, Sonoma *Also called Gary D Nelson Associates Inc (P-12091)*
Nelson/Nygard Cnslting Assoc I (PA)...**E.......415 284-1544**
2 Bryant St Ste 300 San Francisco (94105) *(P-19587)*
Neo Advisory Inc...E.......415 462-0569
2880 Zanker Rd Ste 203 San Jose (95134) *(P-7974)*
Neo Power Technology Inc...D.......415 830-6167
2330 W Covell Blvd Davis (95616) *(P-1124)*
Neoconix Inc...E.......408 530-9393
4020 Moorpark Ave Ste 108 San Jose (95117) *(P-6227)*
Neodora LLC...E.......650 283-3319
1545 Berger Dr San Jose (95112) *(P-4306)*
Neoit, San Jose *Also called Neo Advisory Inc (P-7974)*
Neonode Inc (PA)...**E.......408 496-6722**
2880 Zanker Rd San Jose (95134) *(P-6460)*
Neophotonics Corporation (PA)...**A.......408 232-9200**
3081 Zanker Rd San Jose (95134) *(P-6228)*
Neosem Technology Inc (HQ)...**E.......408 643-7000**
1965 Concourse Dr San Jose (95131) *(P-6773)*
Nephrology Group Inc (PA)...**D.......559 228-6600**
568 E Herndon Ave Fresno (93720) *(P-15547)*
Neptec Optical Solutions, Fremont *Also called Neptec Os Inc (P-4571)*
Neptec Optical Solutions Inc...E.......510 687-1101
48603 Warm Springs Blvd Fremont (94539) *(P-4376)*
Neptec Os Inc...E.......510 687-1101
48603 Warm Springs Blvd Fremont (94539) *(P-4571)*
Neptune Palace Hotel, Alameda *Also called Parco LLC (P-11353)*
Nes Financial Corp...E.......800 339-1031
50 W San Fernando St # 300 San Jose (95113) *(P-14338)*
Nes Health Care Group...E.......415 435-4591
39 Main St Belvedere Tiburon (94920) *(P-15548)*
Nest Labs Inc...D.......855 469-6378
3400 Hillview Ave Palo Alto (94304) *(P-8937)*
Nestgsv Silicon Valley LLC...F.......650 421-2000
2955 Campus Dr Ste 100 San Mateo (94403) *(P-13322)*
Nestle Confections Factory, Modesto *Also called Nestle Usa Inc (P-2166)*
Nestle Dsd, Fresno *Also called Nestle Usa Inc (P-2165)*
Nestle Usa Inc...C.......559 834-2554
4065 E Therese Ave Fresno (93725) *(P-2165)*
Nestle Usa Inc...C.......209 574-2000
736 Garner Rd Modesto (95357) *(P-2166)*
Net Optics Inc...D.......408 737-7777
5301 Stevens Creek Blvd Santa Clara (95051) *(P-13323)*
Netafim Irrigation Inc (HQ)...**C.......559 453-6800**
5470 E Home Ave Fresno (93727) *(P-9041)*
Netapp Inc (PA)...**A.......408 822-6000**
3060 Olsen Dr San Jose (95128) *(P-5302)*
Netbase Quid, Santa Clara *Also called Netbase Solutions Inc (P-12627)*
Netbase Solutions Inc (PA)...**C.......650 810-2100**
3945 Freedom Cir Ste 730 Santa Clara (95054) *(P-12627)*
Netenrich Inc (PA)...**C.......408 436-5900**
2590 N 1st St Ste 300 San Jose (95131) *(P-13945)*
Netflix Inc...A.......408 540-3700
121 Albright Way Los Gatos (95032) *(P-14832)*
Netflix Inc (PA)...**C.......408 540-3700**
100 Winchester Cir Los Gatos (95032) *(P-14833)*
Netflix Studios LLC (HQ)...**A.......408 540-3700**
100 Winchester Cir Los Gatos (95032) *(P-14802)*
Netgear Inc (PA)...**C.......408 907-8000**
350 E Plumeria Dr San Jose (95134) *(P-5801)*
Nethra Imaging Inc (PA)...**E.......408 257-5880**
2855 Bowers Ave Santa Clara (95051) *(P-6229)*
Netlify...E.......925 922-0921
610 22nd St Ste 315 San Francisco (94107) *(P-13324)*
Netline Corporation (PA)...**D.......408 340-2200**
900 E Hamilton Ave # 100 Campbell (95008) *(P-19588)*
Netlinx Publishing Solutions, Sacramento *Also called System Integrators Inc (P-13673)*
Netpace Inc...C.......925 543-7760
5000 Executive Pkwy # 530 San Ramon (94583) *(P-12110)*
Netpolarity Inc...C.......408 971-1100
900 E Campbell Ave Campbell (95008) *(P-12111)*
Netpulse Inc (PA)...**E.......415 643-0223**
560 Fletcher Dr Atherton (94027) *(P-12628)*
Netronix Integration Inc (PA)...**D.......408 573-1444**
2170 Paragon Dr San Jose (95131) *(P-1548)*
Netskope Inc (PA)...**A.......800 979-6988**
2445 Augustine Dr Fl 3 Santa Clara (95054) *(P-13325)*
Netsuite Inc (HQ)...**A.......650 627-1000**
2955 Campus Dr Ste 100 San Mateo (94403) *(P-13326)*
Netsuite Inc...F.......650 627-1000
500 Oracle Pkwy Redwood City (94065) *(P-13327)*
Network Conference Co Inc...E.......408 562-6205
5201 Great America Pkwy # 122 Santa Clara (95054) *(P-19589)*
Network Fcilty Svcs Group LLC...E.......510 256-6035
48273 Lakeview Blvd Fremont (94538) *(P-11978)*
Network Fsg, Fremont *Also called Network Fcilty Svcs Group LLC (P-11978)*
Network Management & Ctrl Corp...D.......319 483-1123
529 Rock Oak Rd Walnut Creek (94598) *(P-19373)*
Network Meeting Center, Santa Clara *Also called Network Conference Co Inc (P-19589)*
Network Real Estate, Grass Valley *Also called Papola Enterprises Inc (P-10642)*
Networked Energy Services Corp (HQ)...**D.......408 622-9900**
5215 Hellyer Ave Ste 150 San Jose (95138) *(P-6534)*
Networked Insurance Agents LLC...C.......800 682-8476
443 Crown Point Cir Ste A Grass Valley (95945) *(P-10317)*
Netxen Inc (HQ)...**B.......949 389-6000**
205 Ravendale Dr Mountain View (94043) *(P-6230)*
Neumiller Bardslee A Prof Corp...D.......209 948-8200
3121 W March Ln Ste 100 Stockton (95219) *(P-17345)*
Neumora Therapeutics Inc...D.......510 828-4062
8000 Marina Blvd Ste 700 Brisbane (94005) *(P-19226)*
Neuron Fuel Inc...E.......408 537-3966
280 Hope St Mountain View (94041) *(P-12629)*
Neurona Therapeutics Inc...E.......510 366-1177
170 Harbor Way Ste 200 South San Francisco (94080) *(P-19092)*
Neuropace Inc...C.......650 237-2700
455 Bernardo Ave Mountain View (94043) *(P-7010)*
Neurosrgcal Assoc Med Group In...D.......559 449-1100
7130 N Sharon Ave Ste 100 Fresno (93720) *(P-15549)*
Neurosurgery, Eureka *Also called St Joseph Hospital (P-16541)*
Neustar Inc...E.......510 500-1000
300 Lakeside Dr Ste 1500 Oakland (94612) *(P-12630)*
Neuvector Inc...E.......408 455-4034
2880 Zanker Rd Ste 100 San Jose (95134) *(P-7156)*
Nevada Backyard Stores, Rocklin *Also called California Backyard Inc (P-8508)*
Nevada Heat Treating LLC (PA)...**E.......510 790-2300**
37955 Central Ct Ste D Newark (94560) *(P-14718)*
Nevada Irrigation District (PA)...**C.......530 273-6185**
1036 W Main St Grass Valley (95945) *(P-8415)*
Nevada Republic Electric N Inc...E.......916 294-0140
11855 White Rock Rd Rancho Cordova (95742) *(P-1549)*
Nevada Truck & Trailer Repair, West Sacramento *Also called Fredericksen Tank Lines Inc (P-7541)*
Nevell Group Inc...B.......714 579-7501
179 Mason Cir Concord (94520) *(P-929)*
Never Boring Design Associates...E.......209 526-9136
1016 14th St Modesto (95354) *(P-11871)*
Nevocal Enterprises Inc...E.......559 277-0700
5320 N Barcus Ave Fresno (93722) *(P-596)*
Nevro Corp (PA)...**A.......650 251-0005**
1800 Bridge Pkwy Redwood City (94065) *(P-7011)*

New Age Electric Inc ....D.....408 279-8787
1085 N 11th St San Jose (95112) ***(P-1550)***
New Age Metal Finishing LLC ....E.....559 498-8585
2169 N Pleasant Ave Fresno (93705) ***(P-4915)***
New American Funding, Santa Rosa *Also called Broker Solutions Inc* ***(P-19461)***
New American Funding, San Jose *Also called Broker Solutions Inc* ***(P-9869)***
New Avenue Inc ....E.....510 621-8679
36 Panoramic Way Berkeley (94704) ***(P-3254)***
New Berry Trading, Hayward *Also called Win Woo Trading LLC* ***(P-9323)***
New Bridge Foundation Inc ....D.....510 548-7270
2323 Hearst Ave Berkeley (94709) ***(P-17049)***
New Cal Metals Inc ....F.....916 652-7424
3495 Swetzer Rd Granite Bay (95746) ***(P-4793)***
New Cch LLC (PA) ....D.....855 234-6493
1 Sansome St Ste 1500 San Francisco (94104) ***(P-13735)***
New Colusa Indian Bingo ....B.....530 458-8844
3770 State Highway 45 Colusa (95932) ***(P-15223)***
New Deal Design LLC ....E.....415 399-0405
1265 Battery St 5 San Francisco (94111) ***(P-13639)***
New Desserts Inc ....D.....415 780-6860
5000 Fulton Dr Fairfield (94534) ***(P-9469)***
New Dimension Electronics, Santa Clara *Also called N D E Inc* ***(P-5950)***
New England Shtmtl & Mech Co ....C.....559 268-7375
2731 S Cherry Ave Fresno (93706) ***(P-1315)***
New England Shtmtl Works Inc ....C.....559 268-7375
2731 S Cherry Ave Fresno (93706) ***(P-18778)***
New Enterprise Associates Inc ....E.....650 854-9499
2855 Sand Hill Rd Menlo Park (94025) ***(P-10872)***
New Generation Software Inc ....E.....916 920-2200
3835 N Freeway Blvd # 200 Sacramento (95834) ***(P-13328)***
NEW GENERATIONS INTERNATIONAL, San Jose *Also called Cityteam Ministries* ***(P-17804)***
New Harbinger Publications Inc (PA) ....E.....510 652-0215
5674 Shattuck Ave Oakland (94609) ***(P-3542)***
New Haven Home Health Svcs Inc ....E.....650 301-1660
333 Gellert Blvd Ste 249a Daly City (94015) ***(P-16915)***
New Hong Kong Noodle Co Inc ....E.....650 588-6425
360 Swift Ave Ste 22 South San Francisco (94080) ***(P-2864)***
New Horizon Foods Inc ....E.....510 489-8600
33440 Western Ave Union City (94587) ***(P-2926)***
New Horizon Mobile Homes, San Jose *Also called John Naimi Inc* ***(P-657)***
New Iem LLC ....C.....510 656-1600
48205 Warm Springs Blvd Fremont (94539) ***(P-5652)***
New Image Landscape Company ....D.....510 226-9191
3250 Darby Cmn Fremont (94539) ***(P-489)***
New Legend Inc ....B.....530 674-3100
1235 Oswald Rd Yuba City (95991) ***(P-7570)***
New Life Discovery Schools Inc (PA) ....E.....559 292-8687
4926 E Yale Ave Ste 101 Fresno (93727) ***(P-17981)***
NEW MORNING YOUTH & FAMILY COU, Placerville *Also called New Mrning Youth Fmly Svcs Inc* ***(P-17654)***
New Mrning Youth Fmly Svcs Inc ....E.....530 622-5551
6767 Green Valley Rd F Placerville (95667) ***(P-17654)***
New Paradigm Productions Inc (PA) ....D.....415 924-8000
39 Mesa St Ste 212 San Francisco (94129) ***(P-14794)***
New Parrott & Co ....C.....925 456-2300
5565 Tesla Rd Livermore (94550) ***(P-9582)***
New Path Landscape Svcs Inc ....D.....408 310-8476
16170 Vineyard Blvd # 180 Morgan Hill (95037) ***(P-427)***
New Prduct Intgrtion Sltons In (PA) ....D.....408 944-9178
685 Jarvis Dr Ste A Morgan Hill (95037) ***(P-4544)***
New Pride Corporation ....E.....636 937-5200
333 Hegenberger Rd # 307 Oakland (94621) ***(P-14538)***
New Relic Inc (PA) ....A.....650 777-7600
188 Spear St Fl 11 San Francisco (94105) ***(P-13329)***
New Resource Bank, San Francisco *Also called Amalgamated Bank* ***(P-9755)***
New Schools Venture Fund ....E.....415 615-6860
1616 Franklin St 2 Oakland (94612) ***(P-14339)***
New Solar Electric Inc (PA) ....D.....888 886-0103
200 Brown Rd Ste 114 Fremont (94539) ***(P-1551)***
New Source Technology LLC ....F.....925 462-6888
6678 Owens Dr Ste 105 Pleasanton (94588) ***(P-7116)***
New Star Lasers Inc ....E.....916 677-1900
8331 Sierra College Blvd # 204 Roseville (95661) ***(P-7117)***
New Start Rcvery Solutions Inc ....D.....530 854-4119
2167 Montgomery St Ste A Oroville (95965) ***(P-16768)***
New Start Recovery Solutions, Oroville *Also called Sierra Hlth Wellness Group LLC* ***(P-17073)***
New Tech Solutions Inc ....E.....510 353-4070
4179 Business Center Dr Fremont (94538) ***(P-8729)***
New Vavin Inc ....E.....707 963-5972
3222 Ehlers Ln Saint Helena (94574) ***(P-2667)***
New Vision Display Inc (HQ) ....E.....916 786-8111
1430 Blue Oaks Blvd # 100 Roseville (95747) ***(P-6461)***
New Wave Industries Ltd (PA) ....F.....800 882-8854
3315 Orange Grove Ave North Highlands (95660) ***(P-5444)***
New West Partitions ....C.....916 456-8365
2550 Sutterville Rd Sacramento (95820) ***(P-1693)***
New World Library, Novato *Also called Whatever Publishing Inc* ***(P-3550)***
New World Machining Inc ....E.....408 227-3810
2799 Aiello Dr San Jose (95111) ***(P-5578)***
New World Van Lines Inc ....D.....510 487-1091
33373 Lewis St Union City (94587) ***(P-7629)***
New Wrld Van Lnes San Frncisco, Union City *Also called New World Van Lines Inc* ***(P-7629)***
New York Machine Shop Inc ....F.....530 534-7965
2875 Feather River Blvd Oroville (95965) ***(P-5579)***
NEWARK CRISIS CENTER, Newark *Also called Second Chance Inc* ***(P-17723)***
Newfield Wireless Inc (HQ) ....D.....510 848-8248
2855 Telg Ave Ste 200 Berkeley (94705) ***(P-19828)***
Newfront Insurance Svcs LLC (HQ) ....D.....415 754-3635
777 Mariners Island Blvd # 250 San Mateo (94404) ***(P-10318)***
Newgistics Inc ....D.....415 465-0564
27 Maiden Ln Fl 4 San Francisco (94108) ***(P-7651)***
Newline Rubber Company ....E.....408 214-0359
13165 Monterey Hwy # 100 San Martin (95046) ***(P-4221)***
Newline Transport Inc ....E.....559 515-5000
4460 W Shaw Ave Ste 234 Fresno (93722) ***(P-7888)***
Newman Flange & Fitting Co, Newman *Also called Titan Newman Inc* ***(P-9138)***
Newmat Norcal Inc ....E.....415 884-4421
32 Pamaron Way Ste A Novato (94949) ***(P-1694)***
Newport Fish, South San Francisco *Also called Tardio Enterprises Inc* ***(P-2832)***
Newport Group Inc (PA) ....C.....925 328-4540
1350 Treat Blvd Ste 300 Walnut Creek (94597) ***(P-10319)***
Newport Meat Company, Fremont *Also called Newport Meat Northern Cal Inc* ***(P-9328)***
Newport Meat Northern Cal Inc (HQ) ....E.....800 535-6328
48811 Warm Springs Blvd Fremont (94539) ***(P-9328)***
Newport Television LLC ....B.....559 761-0243
4880 N 1st St Fresno (93726) ***(P-14852)***
Newsmarket Inc (HQ) ....E.....917 861-3797
75 Broadway Ste 202 San Francisco (94111) ***(P-13946)***
Newton Vineyard LLC (HQ) ....E.....707 204-7423
1040 Main St Ste 204 NAPA (94559) ***(P-2668)***
Nexcoil Steel LLC ....F.....209 900-1919
1265 Shaw Rd Stockton (95215) ***(P-4547)***
Nexenta By Ddn Inc ....E.....408 791-3300
2025 Gateway Pl Ste 160 San Jose (95110) ***(P-13330)***
Nexgate Inc ....E.....650 762-9890
433 Airport Blvd Ste 303 Burlingame (94010) ***(P-13331)***
Nexgen Container LLC ....E.....916 716-8962
10576 N Old Course Dr Fresno (93730) ***(P-3360)***
Nexgen Power Systems Inc ....E.....408 230-7698
3151 Jay St Ste 201 Santa Clara (95054) ***(P-6231)***
Nexient LLC (PA) ....B.....415 992-7277
8000 Jarvis Ave Ste 200 Newark (94560) ***(P-13947)***
Nexlogic Technologies Inc ....D.....408 436-8150
2085 Zanker Rd San Jose (95131) ***(P-5951)***
Nexsan Technologies Inc (HQ) ....E.....408 724-9809
1289 Anvilwood Ave Sunnyvale (94089) ***(P-5303)***
Nexsentio Inc ....D.....408 392-9249
1346 Ridder Park Dr San Jose (95131) ***(P-11979)***
Nexsteppe Inc ....F.....650 887-5700
400 E Jamie Ct Ste 202 South San Francisco (94080) ***(P-2349)***
Nexsteppe Seeds Inc ....E.....650 887-5700
400 E Jamie Ct Ste 202 South San Francisco (94080) ***(P-4126)***
Next Insurance Inc (PA) ....B.....855 222-5919
490 California Ave # 300 Palo Alto (94306) ***(P-10320)***
Next Phase Solar, Berkeley *Also called Sunsystem Technology LLC* ***(P-6318)***
Nextag Inc (PA) ....D.....650 645-4700
555 Twin Dolphin Dr # 370 Redwood City (94065) ***(P-3585)***
Nextdoorcom Inc (PA) ....D.....415 236-0000
875 Stevenson St Ste 100 San Francisco (94103) ***(P-13802)***
Nextest Systems Corporation ....C.....408 960-2400
875 Embedded Way San Jose (95138) ***(P-6774)***
Nextest Systems Teradyne Co, San Jose *Also called Nextest Systems Corporation* ***(P-6774)***
Nextflex ....E.....408 435-5523
2244 Blach Pl Ste 150 San Jose (95131) ***(P-18311)***
Nextinput Inc (HQ) ....E.....408 770-9293
980 Linda Vista Ave Mountain View (94043) ***(P-5685)***
Nextlabs Inc (PA) ....E.....650 577-9101
3 E 3rd Ave Ste 223 San Mateo (94401) ***(P-13948)***
Nextlesson Inc ....F.....415 968-9655
28 2nd St Ste 501 San Francisco (94105) ***(P-3586)***
Nextnav LLC ....E.....800 775-0982
484 Oakmead Pkwy Sunnyvale (94085) ***(P-19590)***
Nextracker Inc (HQ) ....C.....510 270-2500
6200 Paseo Padre Pkwy Fremont (94555) ***(P-9001)***
Nextroll Inc (PA) ....A.....877 723-7655
2300 Harrison St Fl 2 San Francisco (94110) ***(P-13332)***
Nexus Energy Systems Inc ....E.....866 334-6639
4025 S Golden State Blvd Fresno (93725) ***(P-1316)***
NFC Innovation Center, San Jose *Also called Ensurge Micropower Inc* ***(P-6425)***
Nflash Inc (PA) ....E.....408 350-0341
3080 Kenneth St Santa Clara (95054) ***(P-5304)***
Nfp Advisors, Lafayette *Also called D A Financial Group California* ***(P-10270)***
Ngcodec Inc ....E.....408 766-4382
440 N Wolfe Rd Ste 2187 Sunnyvale (94085) ***(P-6232)***
Ngcw Inc ....E.....415 621-7223
69 Duboce Ave San Francisco (94103) ***(P-14767)***
Ngdata Us Inc (PA) ....E.....415 655-6732
71 Stevenson St Ste 400 San Francisco (94105) ***(P-13736)***
NGK Electronics Usa Inc ....E.....408 330-6900
2520 Mission College Blvd # 104 Santa Clara (95054) ***(P-8938)***
Ngm Biopharmaceuticals Inc (PA) ....C.....650 243-5555
333 Oyster Point Blvd South San Francisco (94080) ***(P-3954)***
Ngmbio, South San Francisco *Also called Ngm Biopharmaceuticals Inc* ***(P-3954)***
Ngo Metals Inc ....E.....510 632-0853
711 Kevin Ct Oakland (94621) ***(P-4837)***
Nguyen, Myhanh MD, Sunnyvale *Also called Sutter Health* ***(P-16627)***
Nhs Inc ....D.....831 459-7800
104 Bronson St Ste 9 Santa Cruz (95062) ***(P-7199)***
Ni Microwave Components, Santa Clara *Also called Phase Matrix Inc* ***(P-8946)***
Nia Healthcare Services Inc (PA) ....E.....559 834-2519
8448 E Adams Ave Fowler (93625) ***(P-16068)***
Nia Healthcare Services Inc ....E.....559 896-4990
2108 Stillman St Selma (93662) ***(P-16069)***
Nia Healthcare Services Inc ....D.....559 834-2519
8448 E Adams Ave Fowler (93625) ***(P-16070)***

ALPHABETIC

Niacc-Avitech Technologies Inc (PA).......D.......**559 291-2500**
245 W Dakota Ave Clovis (93612) ***(P-14768)***
Nibbi Bros Associates Inc.......C.......415 863-1820
1000 Brannan St Ste 102 San Francisco (94103) ***(P-759)***
Nibbi Bros Concrete, San Francisco *Also called Nibbi Bros Associates Inc* ***(P-759)***
Nic USA Inc.......E.......925 944-1222
2478 Warren Ln B Walnut Creek (94597) ***(P-17655)***
Nichelini General Engrg Contrs.......E.......916 371-1300
4101 W Capitol Ave West Sacramento (95691) ***(P-1065)***
Nicholas K Corporation.......C.......510 352-2000
1111 Marina Blvd San Leandro (94577) ***(P-14493)***
Nichols Research, Fremont *Also called AMS Ventures Inc* ***(P-19444)***
Nick Sciabica & Sons A Corp.......E.......209 577-5067
2150 Yosemite Blvd Modesto (95354) ***(P-2466)***
Nickel and Nickel Inc.......F.......707 967-9600
8164 St Helena Hwy Oakville (94562) ***(P-66)***
Nicks Cove Inc.......D.......415 663-1033
23240 Ca 1 Marshall (94940) ***(P-11328)***
Nidec Motor Corporation.......B.......916 463-9200
11380 White Rock Rd Rancho Cordova (95742) ***(P-5047)***
Niebam-Cppola Estate Winery LP.......E.......415 291-1700
916 Kearny St San Francisco (94133) ***(P-2669)***
Niebam-Cppola Estate Winery LP (PA).......C.......**707 968-1100**
1991 St Helena Hwy Rutherford (94573) ***(P-2670)***
Nieco Corporation.......D.......707 838-3226
7950 Cameron Dr Windsor (95492) ***(P-5445)***
Niello Acura Porsche, Roseville *Also called Niello Imports* ***(P-14494)***
Niello Imports.......D.......916 334-6300
150 Automall Dr Roseville (95661) ***(P-14494)***
Niello Imports II Inc.......C.......916 480-2800
2350 Auburn Blvd Sacramento (95821) ***(P-14579)***
Nielsen Company (us) LLC.......E.......707 746-6905
1001 Madison St Fl 2 Benicia (94510) ***(P-19173)***
Nielsen Mobile LLC (HQ).......C.......**917 435-9301**
1010 Battery St San Francisco (94111) ***(P-19174)***
Night Optics Usa Inc.......E.......714 899-4475
605 Oro Dam Blvd E Oroville (95965) ***(P-5892)***
Nightingale Nursing, San Leandro *Also called RES-Care Inc* ***(P-16930)***
Nightshade Holdings LLC.......E.......707 462-1436
1162 S Dora St Ukiah (95482) ***(P-16071)***
Nigro Krlin Sgal Fldstein Blno.......B.......415 463-1300
1 Embarcadero Ctr # 3840 San Francisco (94111) ***(P-18980)***
Nikon Precision Inc (HQ).......C.......**650 508-4674**
1399 Shoreway Rd Belmont (94002) ***(P-9083)***
Nikon Research Corp America.......E.......800 446-4566
1399 Shoreway Rd Belmont (94002) ***(P-6775)***
Nilgiri Press, Tomales *Also called Blue Mtn Ctr of Meditation Inc* ***(P-3524)***
Nimble Storage Inc (HQ).......A.......**408 432-9600**
900 N Mccarthy Blvd Milpitas (95035) ***(P-5305)***
Nimbula Inc.......F.......800 633-0738
4230 Leonard Stocking Dr Santa Clara (95054) ***(P-13333)***
Nimsoft Inc (HQ).......E.......**408 796-3400**
3965 Freedom Cir Fl 6 Santa Clara (95054) ***(P-6233)***
Ning Inc.......E.......650 244-4000
2000 Sierra Point Pkwy # 10 Brisbane (94005) ***(P-7975)***
Ninja Credit Consultants LLC.......E.......888 646-5282
71 1st Ave Ste 662 Lewiston (96052) ***(P-19591)***
Ninthdecimal Inc (PA).......C.......**415 264-1849**
150 Post St Ste 500 San Francisco (94108) ***(P-12631)***
Nippon Industries Inc.......E.......707 427-3127
2430 S Watney Way Fairfield (94533) ***(P-2305)***
Nippon Trends Food Service Inc.......D.......408 479-0558
631 Giguere Ct Ste A1 San Jose (95133) ***(P-2927)***
Nish-Ko Inc.......E.......559 275-6653
713 N Valentine Ave Fresno (93706) ***(P-490)***
Nisum Technologies Inc.......A.......714 619-7989
71 Stevenson St Ste 446 San Francisco (94105) ***(P-12632)***
Nisum Technologies Inc.......A.......714 579-7979
46231 Landing Pkwy Fremont (94538) ***(P-12633)***
Nitinol Development Corp.......A.......510 683-2000
47533 Westinghouse Dr Fremont (94539) ***(P-7145)***
Nitinol Devices & Components, Fremont *Also called Nitinol Development Corp* ***(P-7145)***
Nitro Software Inc.......C.......415 632-4894
150 Spear St Ste 1850 San Francisco (94105) ***(P-12634)***
Nitto Americas Inc (HQ).......C.......**510 445-5400**
101 Metro Dr San Jose (95110) ***(P-3381)***
Nivagen Pharmaceuticals Inc (PA).......E.......**916 364-1662**
3050 Fite Cir Ste 100 Sacramento (95827) ***(P-3955)***
Nixel Inc.......E.......650 618-9516
2225 E Byshore Rd Ste 200 Palo Alto (94303) ***(P-12635)***
Nkarta Inc.......D.......415 582-4923
6000 Shoreline Ct Ste 102 South San Francisco (94080) ***(P-3956)***
Nl Inc (PA).......E.......**925 295-9300**
3240 Stone Valley Rd W Alamo (94507) ***(P-9917)***
NM Machining Inc.......E.......408 972-8978
175 Lewis Rd Ste 25 San Jose (95111) ***(P-5580)***
Nmi Holdings Inc.......B.......855 530-6642
2100 Powell St Fl 12th Emeryville (94608) ***(P-10193)***
Nmi Industrial Holdings Inc.......D.......916 635-7030
8503 Weyand Ave Sacramento (95828) ***(P-18779)***
NMN Construction Inc.......D.......707 763-6981
1077 Lakeville St Petaluma (94952) ***(P-1896)***
Nmwd, Novato *Also called North Marin Water District* ***(P-8254)***
Noah Concrete Corporation.......D.......408 842-7211
5900 Rossi Ln Gilroy (95020) ***(P-1897)***
Noah Medical Corporation.......D.......718 564-3717
1501 Industrial Rd San Carlos (94070) ***(P-6913)***
Noah Pharmaceuticals Inc.......E.......707 631-0921
1380 San Andreas Rd Watsonville (95076) ***(P-3819)***
Noah's, Los Gatos *Also called Einstein Noah Rest Group Inc* ***(P-2147)***
Noah's, San Francisco *Also called Einstein Noah Rest Group Inc* ***(P-2379)***
Noah's Bagels, Redwood City *Also called Einstein Noah Rest Group Inc* ***(P-2380)***
Nob Hill Properties Inc.......B.......415 474-5400
1075 California St San Francisco (94108) ***(P-11329)***
Noble Aew Vineyard Creek LLC.......E.......707 284-1234
170 Railroad St Santa Rosa (95401) ***(P-11330)***
Noble Brewer Beer Company.......E.......301 536-1934
4721 Tidewater Ave Ste C Oakland (94601) ***(P-2840)***
Noble Credit Union (PA).......E.......**559 252-5000**
2580 W Shaw Ln Frnt Fresno (93711) ***(P-9798)***
Noble Credit Union.......D.......559 252-5000
2580 W Shaw Ln Frnt Fresno (93711) ***(P-9799)***
Noble Movers Inc.......D.......415 260-1000
101 Creekside Ridge Ct # 2 Roseville (95678) ***(P-7571)***
Noble Outfitters, Modesto *Also called LLC Noble Rider* ***(P-9247)***
Noble Vineyard Management Inc.......E.......415 533-8642
5350 Old River Rd Ukiah (95482) ***(P-383)***
Noel Technologies, Campbell *Also called Semi Automation & Tech Inc* ***(P-6280)***
Noia Residential Services Inc.......D.......559 485-5555
606 E Belmont Ave Ste 101 Fresno (93701) ***(P-18147)***
Nok Nok Labs Inc.......F.......650 433-1300
2890 Zanker Rd Ste 203 San Jose (95134) ***(P-13334)***
Noll/Norwesco LLC.......C.......209 234-1600
1320 Performance Dr Stockton (95206) ***(P-4794)***
Nolo.......C.......510 549-1976
6801 Koll Center Pkwy # 300 Pleasanton (94566) ***(P-3543)***
Nolte Associates, Sacramento *Also called Nv5 Inc* ***(P-18781)***
Nominum Inc.......C.......650 381-6000
3355 Scott Blvd Fl 3 Santa Clara (95054) ***(P-13335)***
Nomis Solutions Inc (PA).......C.......**650 588-9800**
611 Gateway Blvd Fl 2 South San Francisco (94080) ***(P-12636)***
Nonprofits Insur Aliance Cal.......E.......831 459-0980
300 Panetta Ave Santa Cruz (95060) ***(P-10321)***
Noodle Analytics Inc.......D.......415 412-2139
115 Sansome St Fl 8 San Francisco (94104) ***(P-12637)***
Noodle.ai, San Francisco *Also called Noodle Analytics Inc* ***(P-12637)***
Noodles Fresh LLC.......F.......510 898-1710
48 Rincon Rd Kensington (94707) ***(P-2928)***
Noon Home Inc.......E.......650 242-7565
20400 Stevens Creek Blvd # 370 Cupertino (95014) ***(P-19093)***
Nor Cal Truck Sales & Mfg.......F.......925 787-9735
200 Industrial Way Benicia (94510) ***(P-5065)***
Nor Car Truck Sales, Benicia *Also called Nor Cal Truck Sales & Mfg* ***(P-5065)***
Nor-Cal Beverage Co Inc (PA).......B.......**916 372-0600**
2150 Stone Blvd West Sacramento (95691) ***(P-9558)***
Nor-Cal Beverage Co Inc.......E.......916 371-8219
1347 Shore St West Sacramento (95691) ***(P-9016)***
Nor-Cal Beverage Co Inc.......D.......916 372-1700
1375 Terminal St West Sacramento (95691) ***(P-2796)***
Nor-Cal Climate Control Inc (PA).......E.......**916 439-6534**
3963 Apple Blossom Way Carmichael (95608) ***(P-1317)***
Nor-Cal Controls Es Inc.......D.......916 836-0800
4790 Golden Foothill Pkwy # 110 El Dorado Hills (95762) ***(P-8217)***
Nor-Cal Fire Protection, Morgan Hill *Also called Northern Cal Fire Prtction Svc* ***(P-1318)***
Nor-Cal Metal Fabricators.......D.......510 350-0121
1121 3rd St Oakland (94607) ***(P-4795)***
Nor-Cal Moving Services (PA).......C.......**510 371-4942**
3129 Corporate Pl Hayward (94545) ***(P-7630)***
Nor-Cal Overhead Inc.......F.......925 240-5141
2145 Elkins Way Ste E Brentwood (94513) ***(P-4706)***
Nor-Cal Pipeline Services.......D.......916 442-5400
983 Reserve Dr Roseville (95678) ***(P-1125)***
Nor-Cal Produce Inc.......C.......916 373-0830
2995 Oates St West Sacramento (95691) ***(P-9420)***
Nor-Cal Products Inc (HQ).......C.......**530 842-4457**
1967 S Oregon St Yreka (96097) ***(P-4962)***
Nor-Cal Vans Inc.......F.......530 892-0150
1300 Nord Ave Chico (95926) ***(P-6567)***
Nor-Wall Inc.......E.......707 445-5445
3909 Walnut Dr Eureka (95503) ***(P-15115)***
Norcal Ambulance LLC.......E.......925 452-8300
6761 Sierra Ct Ste G Dublin (94568) ***(P-7392)***
Norcal Ambulance Services, Oakland *Also called North Star Emergency Svcs Inc* ***(P-7393)***
Norcal Building Materials, Santa Rosa *Also called Northern Cal Bldg Mtls Inc* ***(P-4500)***
Norcal Care Centers Inc.......D.......925 757-8787
1210 A St Antioch (94509) ***(P-16072)***
Norcal Geophysical Cons Inc.......D.......707 796-7170
321 Blodgett St Ste A Cotati (94931) ***(P-19915)***
Norcal Gold Inc.......E.......916 285-1000
2081 Arena Blvd Ste 100 Sacramento (95834) ***(P-10627)***
Norcal Gold Inc.......E.......916 984-8778
2365 Iron Point Rd # 200 Folsom (95630) ***(P-10628)***
Norcal Gphysical Cons Inc NS, Cotati *Also called Norcal Geophysical Cons Inc* ***(P-19915)***
Norcal Materials Inc.......E.......650 365-4811
941 Bransten Rd San Carlos (94070) ***(P-4499)***
Norcal Mutual Insurance Co (HQ).......B.......**415 735-2000**
575 Market St Fl 10 San Francisco (94105) ***(P-10322)***
Norcal Vocational Inc (PA).......D.......**415 206-9766**
77 Mark Dr Ste 20 San Rafael (94903) ***(P-17656)***
Norco Printing Inc.......F.......510 569-2200
4588 Grenadier Pl Castro Valley (94546) ***(P-3765)***
Nordby Construction Co.......E.......707 526-4500
1550 Airport Blvd Ste 101 Santa Rosa (95403) ***(P-930)***
Nordby Wine Caves, Santa Rosa *Also called Nordby Construction Co* ***(P-930)***
Norden Millimeter Inc.......E.......530 642-9123
5441 Merchant Cir Ste C Placerville (95667) ***(P-5857)***
Nordic Industries Inc.......D.......530 742-7124
1437 Furneaux Rd Olivehurst (95961) ***(P-1171)***

Nordic Naturals Inc (PA) ....C....**800 662-2544**
111 Jennings Way Watsonville (95076) ***(P-2458)***
Nordic Saw & Tool Mfrs Inc ....E....209 634-9015
2114 Divanian Dr Turlock (95382) ***(P-4611)***
Nordson Corporation ....E....925 827-1240
2470 Bates Ave Ste A Concord (94520) ***(P-8939)***
Nordson March Inc (HQ) ....E....**925 827-1240**
2470 Bates Ave Ste A Concord (94520) ***(P-5187)***
Nordstrom Inc ....C....925 930-7959
1200 Broadway Plz Walnut Creek (94596) ***(P-19374)***
Noredink Corp ....D....617 308-4549
118 2nd St Fl 3 San Francisco (94105) ***(P-12638)***
Norland Group Inc ....C....408 855-8255
3350 Scott Blvd Ste 6501 Santa Clara (95054) ***(P-13949)***
Norman S Wrght Mech Eqp Crprtn (PA) ....D....**415 467-7600**
99 S Hill Dr Ste A Brisbane (94005) ***(P-9011)***
Normans Nursery Inc ....C....209 887-2033
6250 N Escalon Bellota Rd Linden (95236) ***(P-9638)***
Norogachi Construction Inc/CA ....D....916 236-4201
600 Industrial Dr Ste 100 Galt (95632) ***(P-1695)***
Norpak, Hayward *Also called Norton Packaging Inc* ***(P-4307)***
Nortech Waste LLC ....C....916 645-5230
3033 Fiddyment Rd Roseville (95747) ***(P-8346)***
North American Asset Dev Corp (HQ) ....D....**925 935-5599**
1855 Gateway Blvd Ste 650 Concord (94520) ***(P-10205)***
North American Cinemas Inc ....B....707 571-1412
409 Aviation Blvd Santa Rosa (95403) ***(P-14814)***
North American Pest Management, North Highlands *Also called Business Industry & Envmt Inc* ***(P-11880)***
North American Title Co Inc ....D....925 935-0400
175 Lennon Ln Ste 100 Walnut Creek (94598) ***(P-10206)***
North American Van Lines, Newark *Also called Moving Solutions Inc* ***(P-7627)***
North Amrcn Specialty Pdts LLC ....C....209 365-7500
300 S Beckman Rd Lodi (95240) ***(P-3807)***
North Area Cmnty Mntal Hlth Ct, Sacramento *Also called Heartland Child & Family Svcs* ***(P-17600)***
North Area News (PA) ....E....**916 486-1248**
2612 El Camino Ave Sacramento (95821) ***(P-3468)***
North Atlantic Books, Berkeley *Also called Society For The Study Ntiv Art* ***(P-3545)***
North Bay Auto Auction, Fairfield *Also called Wind River Enterprises Inc* ***(P-8434)***
North Bay Childrens Center Inc (PA) ....D....**415 883-6222**
932 C St Novato (94949) ***(P-17982)***
North Bay Distribution Inc (PA) ....D....**707 452-9984**
2050 Cessna Dr Vacaville (95688) ***(P-7696)***
North Bay Dvlpmntal Dsblties S (PA) ....D....**707 256-1224**
10 Executive Ct Ste A NAPA (94558) ***(P-17826)***
North Bay Fire ....D....707 823-1084
4500 Hessel Rd Sebastopol (95472) ***(P-535)***
North Bay Industries, Rohnert Park *Also called North Bay Rhblitation Svcs Inc* ***(P-3052)***
North Bay Landscape Mgt Inc ....E....707 762-3850
444 Payran St Petaluma (94952) ***(P-491)***
North Bay Plywood Inc ....E....707 224-7849
510 Northbay Dr NAPA (94559) ***(P-3143)***
North Bay Post Acute LLC ....E....707 763-6887
300 Douglas St Petaluma (94952) ***(P-16073)***
NORTH BAY REGIONAL CENTER, NAPA *Also called North Bay Dvlpmntal Dsblties S* ***(P-17826)***
North Bay Regional Water, Fairfield *Also called City of Fairfield* ***(P-8228)***
North Bay Rhblitation Svcs Inc (PA) ....C....**707 585-1991**
649 Martin Ave Rohnert Park (94928) ***(P-3052)***
North Cal Wood Products Inc ....E....707 462-0686
700 Kunzler Ranch Rd Ukiah (95482) ***(P-3099)***
North Cast Srgical Specialists ....E....707 443-2248
2321 Harrison Ave Eureka (95501) ***(P-15550)***
North Cast Tile Stone Dsign In ....E....707 586-2064
3854 Santa Rosa Ave Santa Rosa (95407) ***(P-1716)***
North Coast Brewing Co Inc ....E....707 964-3400
444 N Main St Fort Bragg (95437) ***(P-2487)***
North Coast Brewing Co Inc (PA) ....E....**707 964-2739**
455 N Main St Fort Bragg (95437) ***(P-2488)***
North Coast Cleaning Svcs Inc ....E....707 269-0838
211 7th St Eureka (95501) ***(P-11980)***
North Coast Clinics Network (PA) ....E....**707 826-8610**
770 10th St Arcata (95521) ***(P-15551)***
North Coast Fabricators Inc ....E....707 822-4629
4801 West End Rd Arcata (95521) ***(P-803)***
North Coast Industries, Sausalito *Also called Tony Marterie & Associates Inc* ***(P-3003)***
North Coast Laboratories Ltd ....E....707 822-4649
5680 West End Rd Arcata (95521) ***(P-16791)***
North Coast Mercantile Co Inc (PA) ....E....**707 445-4910**
1115 W Del Norte St Eureka (95501) ***(P-9559)***
North Counties Drywall Inc ....E....707 996-0198
20563 Broadway Sonoma (95476) ***(P-1696)***
North Face, The, Alameda *Also called Vf Outdoor LLC* ***(P-2996)***
North Landscaping Inc ....E....707 827-7980
1550 Gravenstein Hwy S Sebastopol (95472) ***(P-428)***
North Marin Community Services (PA) ....E....**415 892-1643**
680 Wilson Ave Novato (94947) ***(P-17657)***
North Marin Water District (PA) ....E....**415 897-4133**
999 Rush Creek Pl Novato (94945) ***(P-8254)***
North Pt Hlth Wellness Ctr LLC ....D....559 320-2200
668 E Bullard Ave Fresno (93710) ***(P-16074)***
North Ridge Country Club ....D....916 967-5717
7600 Madison Ave Fair Oaks (95628) ***(P-15116)***
North San Jose Job Center, San Jose *Also called Work2future Foundation* ***(P-17847)***
North Shore Investment Inc ....D....707 464-6151
1280 Marshall St Crescent City (95531) ***(P-16075)***
North Sonoma County Hosp Dst ....C....707 431-6500
1375 University St Healdsburg (95448) ***(P-16463)***
North Star Cnstr & Engrg Inc (PA) ....E....**530 673-7080**
1850 Lassen Blvd Yuba City (95993) ***(P-931)***
North Star Emergency Svcs Inc ....D....510 452-3400
2537 Willow St Oakland (94607) ***(P-7393)***
North State Bldg Indust Assn ....D....916 677-5717
1536 Eureka Rd Roseville (95661) ***(P-18312)***
North State Elec Contrs Inc ....D....916 572-0571
11101 White Rock Rd Rancho Cordova (95670) ***(P-1552)***
North State Imaging, Chico *Also called North State Radiology* ***(P-15552)***
North State Manufacuring ....F....530 378-5750
8794 Airport Rd Redding (96002) ***(P-5581)***
North State Radiology ....E....530 898-0504
1702 Esplanade Chico (95926) ***(P-15552)***
North State Rendering Co Inc ....E....530 343-6076
15 Shippee Rd Oroville (95965) ***(P-2459)***
North State Resources Inc ....E....530 222-5347
376 Hartnell Ave Ste B Redding (96002) ***(P-19829)***
North State Solar Energy, Forest Ranch *Also called Remodelors Inc* ***(P-19387)***
North Tahoe P U D, Tahoe Vista *Also called North Tahoe Public Utility Dst* ***(P-8287)***
North Tahoe Public Utility Dst (PA) ....E....**530 546-4212**
875 National Ave Tahoe Vista (96148) ***(P-8287)***
North Valley Dermatology ....E....530 809-2127
251 Cohasset Rd Ste 240 Chico (95926) ***(P-15553)***
North Valley Fleet Svcs Inc (PA) ....F....**916 374-8850**
3115 Coke St West Sacramento (95691) ***(P-14580)***
North Valley Rain Gutters ....F....530 894-3347
27 Freight Ln Ste C Chico (95973) ***(P-4796)***
North Valley School, Lodi *Also called Victor Treatment Centers Inc* ***(P-18201)***
North Vly Dvlopmental Svcs Inc ....D....530 222-5633
2970 Innsbruck Dr Ste C Redding (96003) ***(P-16916)***
North Vly Orthpd Hand Srgery A ....D....530 671-2650
470 Plumas Blvd Ste 201 Yuba City (95991) ***(P-16464)***
North Wind Cnstr Svcs LLC ....D....916 333-3015
730 Howe Ave Ste 700 Sacramento (95825) ***(P-678)***
North Zone Fallers Inc (PA) ....E....**530 598-8518**
4705 Hartstrand Rd Etna (96027) ***(P-536)***
Northbay Healthcare Corp (PA) ....C....**707 646-5000**
1200 B Gale Wilson Blvd Fairfield (94533) ***(P-16465)***
Northbay Healthcare Group (HQ) ....A....**707 646-5000**
1200 B Gale Wilson Blvd Fairfield (94533) ***(P-16466)***
Northbay Healthcare Group ....B....707 446-4000
1000 Nut Tree Rd Vacaville (95687) ***(P-16467)***
Northbay Healthcare System, Fairfield *Also called Northbay Healthcare Corp* ***(P-16465)***
Northbay Medical Center, Fairfield *Also called Northbay Healthcare Group* ***(P-16466)***
Northbound LLC ....C....408 333-9780
961 E Arques Ave Sunnyvale (94085) ***(P-19592)***
Northbrook Healthcare Center, Willits *Also called Ensign Willits LLC* ***(P-15993)***
Northcast Horticulture Sup Inc (PA) ....E....**707 839-0245**
513 K St Arcata (95521) ***(P-9042)***
Northcoast Childrens Svcs Inc (PA) ....C....**707 822-7206**
1266 9th St Arcata (95521) ***(P-17983)***
Northcoast Hydroponics, Arcata *Also called Northcast Horticulture Sup Inc* ***(P-9042)***
Northcountry Clinic ....E....707 822-2481
785 18th St Arcata (95521) ***(P-15554)***
Northeastern Rur Hlth Clinics (PA) ....D....**530 251-5000**
1850 Spring Ridge Dr Susanville (96130) ***(P-15555)***
Northern Aggregates Inc ....E....707 459-3929
500 Cropley Ln Willits (95490) ***(P-577)***
Northern CA Retiredd Ofcrs ....C....707 432-1200
2600 Estates Dr Fairfield (94533) ***(P-18148)***
Northern Cal Bldg Mtls Inc (PA) ....E....**707 546-9422**
1534 Copperhill Pkwy Santa Rosa (95403) ***(P-4500)***
Northern Cal Child Dev Inc ....D....530 838-1034
617 Fig Ln Corning (96021) ***(P-17658)***
Northern Cal Crpnters Rgnal CN ....E....510 568-4788
265 Hegenberger Rd Oakland (94621) ***(P-18370)***
Northern Cal Ctr For Arts ....E....530 274-8384
314 W Main St Grass Valley (95945) ***(P-18582)***
Northern Cal Fire Prtction Svc ....E....408 776-1580
16840 Joleen Way Ste A Morgan Hill (95037) ***(P-1318)***
Northern Cal Inst For RES Edca ....B....415 750-6954
4150 Clement St San Francisco (94121) ***(P-18244)***
Northern Cal Med Assoc Inc (PA) ....E....**707 573-6925**
3536 Mendocino Ave # 200 Santa Rosa (95403) ***(P-15556)***
Northern Cal Rehabilitation, Redding *Also called Ocadian Care Centers LLC* ***(P-16081)***
Northern Cal Rhblttion Hosp LL ....C....530 246-9000
2801 Eureka Way Redding (96001) ***(P-16468)***
Northern Cal Rtina Vtrous Asso, San Jose *Also called Retina-Vitreous Assoc Inc* ***(P-15650)***
Northern Cal Yuth Fmly Prgrams (PA) ....D....**530 893-2316**
2577 California Park Dr Chico (95928) ***(P-18149)***
Northern California Inalliance ....D....530 633-9695
411 4th St Wheatland (95692) ***(P-17659)***
Northern California Inalliance (PA) ....C....**916 381-1300**
6950 21st Ave Sacramento (95820) ***(P-17660)***
Northern California Inalliance ....D....530 344-1244
660 Main St Placerville (95667) ***(P-17661)***
Northern California Power Agcy (PA) ....D....**916 781-3636**
651 Commerce Dr Roseville (95678) ***(P-8128)***
Northern California Presbyteri ....C....650 851-1501
501 Portola Rd Portola Valley (94028) ***(P-18150)***
Northern California Presbyteri ....C....415 922-9700
1400 Geary Blvd San Francisco (94109) ***(P-16076)***
Northern California Pub Media, Rohnert Park *Also called Rural Cal Brdcstg Corp Krcb Kp* ***(P-8033)***
Northern California Svc Leag (PA) ....E....**415 621-5661**
40 Boardman Pl San Francisco (94103) ***(P-17827)***

A L P H A B E T I C

Northern Cir Indian Hsing Auth..........E.......707 468-1336
694 Pinoleville Rd Ukiah (95482) *(P-760)*
Northern Hydro, Big Creek *Also called Southern California Edison Co (P-8201)*
Northern Queen Inc..........E.......530 265-4492
400 Railroad Ave Nevada City (95959) *(P-11331)*
Northern Queen Inn, Nevada City *Also called Northern Queen Inc (P-11331)*
Northern Rfrigerated Trnsp Inc (PA)..........C.......209 664-3800
2700 W Main St Turlock (95380) *(P-7572)*
Northern Vly Cthlic Scial Svc..........C.......530 241-0552
2400 Washington Ave Redding (96001) *(P-17662)*
Northern Vly Indian Hlth Inc..........E.......530 896-9400
845 W East Ave Chico (95926) *(P-15850)*
Northern Vly Indian Hlth Inc..........C.......530 661-4400
175 W Court St Woodland (95695) *(P-16744)*
Northern Vly Indian Hlth Inc..........E.......530 529-2567
2500 Main St Red Bluff (96080) *(P-15851)*
Northgate Branch, San Rafael *Also called Bank of Marin (P-9702)*
Northgate Care Center Inc..........D.......415 479-1230
40 Professional Ctr Pkwy San Rafael (94903) *(P-16255)*
Northgate Convalescent Hosp, San Rafael *Also called Independent Quality Care Inc (P-16245)*
Northgate Ter Cmnty Partner LP..........E.......510 465-9346
550 24th St Oakland (94612) *(P-10629)*
Northland Control Systems Inc (PA)..........C.......833 811-4185
1533 California Cir Milpitas (95035) *(P-2046)*
Northpinte Veterinary Hosp Inc..........E.......530 674-8670
1566 Springbrook Rd Walnut Creek (94597) *(P-331)*
Northpointe Healthcare Centre, Fresno *Also called North Pt Hlth Wellness Ctr LLC (P-16074)*
Northrop Grumman Info Tech, San Francisco *Also called Northrop Grumman Systems Corp (P-19830)*
Northrop Grumman Mar Systems, Sunnyvale *Also called Northrop Grumman Systems Corp (P-6617)*
Northrop Grumman Systems Corp..........B.......408 735-2241
401 E Hendy Ave Sunnyvale (94086) *(P-6616)*
Northrop Grumman Systems Corp..........E.......415 281-4600
49 Stevenson St Ste 1400 San Francisco (94105) *(P-19830)*
Northrop Grumman Systems Corp..........C.......703 968-1239
6379 San Ignacio Ave San Jose (95119) *(P-6677)*
Northrop Grumman Systems Corp..........C.......650 604-6056
P.O. Box 81 Moffett Field (94035) *(P-13640)*
Northrop Grumman Systems Corp..........C.......916 570-4454
5441 Luce Ave McClellan (95652) *(P-6678)*
Northrop Grumman Systems Corp..........C.......408 735-3011
401 E Hendy Ave Ms33-3 Sunnyvale (94086) *(P-6617)*
Northstar Community Svcs Dst..........E.......530 562-0747
900 Northstar Dr Truckee (96161) *(P-8255)*
Northstar Contg Group Inc..........C.......510 491-1330
2616 Barrington Ct Hayward (94545) *(P-2047)*
Northstar Contg Group Inc (HQ)..........D.......510 491-1330
2614-20 Barrington Ct Hayward (94545) *(P-2048)*
Northstar Risk MGT Insur Svcs..........E.......925 975-5900
1777 Botelho Dr Ste 360 Walnut Creek (94596) *(P-10323)*
Northstar Senior Living Inc..........A.......530 242-8300
2334 Washington Ave Ste A Redding (96001) *(P-19375)*
Northstar-At-Tahoe, Truckee *Also called Trimont Land Company (P-10676)*
Northstate Cardiology Cons..........E.......530 342-0123
198 Cohasset Rd Chico (95926) *(P-15557)*
Northwest Administrators Inc..........E.......650 570-7300
1000 Marina Blvd Ste 400 Brisbane (94005) *(P-10324)*
Northwest Church Fresno Cal..........D.......559 435-2200
5415 N West Ave Fresno (93711) *(P-17984)*
Northwest Exteriors Inc..........D.......559 456-1632
4404 N Knoll Ave Fresno (93722) *(P-1746)*
Northwest Exteriors Inc (PA)..........E.......916 851-1632
11200 Sun Center Dr Rancho Cordova (95670) *(P-1747)*
Northwest General Engineering..........D.......707 579-1163
5492 Old Redwood Hwy Santa Rosa (95403) *(P-1968)*
Northwest Insurance Agency Inc (PA)..........E.......707 573-1300
175 W College Ave Santa Rosa (95401) *(P-10325)*
Northwest Landscape Maint Co..........E.......408 298-6489
283 Kinney Dr San Jose (95112) *(P-492)*
Northwest Medical Group Inc..........E.......559 271-6302
7355 N Palm Ave Ste 100 Fresno (93711) *(P-15558)*
Northwest Physcans Med Group I (PA)..........D.......559 271-6300
7355 N Palm Ave Ste 100 Fresno (93711) *(P-15559)*
Northwest Protective Service (PA)..........D.......650 345-8500
1163 Chess Dr Ste I Foster City (94404) *(P-14080)*
Northwest Signs, Santa Cruz *Also called Jeff Frank (P-7237)*
Northwest Stffing Rsources Inc..........A.......916 960-2668
100 Howe Ave Sacramento (95825) *(P-12112)*
Northwood Design Partners Inc..........E.......510 731-6505
1550 Atlantic St Union City (94587) *(P-3308)*
Norton Packaging Inc (PA)..........D.......510 786-1922
20670 Corsair Blvd Hayward (94545) *(P-4307)*
Nortra Cables Inc..........D.......408 942-1106
570 Gibraltar Dr Milpitas (95035) *(P-6462)*
Nossaman LLP..........D.......415 398-3600
50 California St Ste 3400 San Francisco (94111) *(P-17346)*
Nossaman LLP..........D.......916 442-8888
915 L St Ste 1000 Sacramento (95814) *(P-17347)*
Nothwest Pipe Company, Tracy *Also called Nwpc LLC (P-4727)*
Nova, Redding *Also called North Vly Dvlopmental Svcs Inc (P-16916)*
Nova Care Home Health Services..........E.......925 240-2334
181 Sand Creek Rd Ste B Brentwood (94513) *(P-16917)*
Nova Commercial Company Inc (PA)..........C.......510 728-7000
24683 Oneil Ave Hayward (94544) *(P-11981)*
Nova Drilling Services Inc..........E.......408 732-6682
1500 Buckeye Dr Milpitas (95035) *(P-5952)*
Nova Equipment Leasing LLC..........E.......707 265-1116
185 Devlin Rd NAPA (94558) *(P-8768)*
Nova Eye Inc..........E.......510 291-1300
41316 Christy St Fremont (94538) *(P-7012)*
Nova Group Inc (HQ)..........C.......707 265-1100
185 Devlin Rd NAPA (94558) *(P-1126)*
Nova Measuring Instruments Inc..........E.......408 510-7400
3342 Gateway Blvd Fremont (94538) *(P-6776)*
Nova-Cpf Inc..........D.......707 257-3200
7411 Napa Vallejo Hwy NAPA (94558) *(P-1127)*
Nova/Tic Gvrnment Prjcts A Jin..........C.......707 257-3200
185 Devlin Rd NAPA (94558) *(P-1128)*
Novabay Pharmaceuticals Inc..........E.......510 899-8800
2000 Powell St Ste 1150 Emeryville (94608) *(P-3957)*
Novacart (HQ)..........E.......510 215-8999
512 W Ohio Ave Richmond (94804) *(P-3347)*
Novacart USA, Richmond *Also called Novacart (P-3347)*
Novariant Inc (PA)..........D.......510 933-4800
46610 Landing Pkwy Fremont (94538) *(P-18780)*
Novartis Bphrmctcal Oprtons -, Vacaville *Also called Novartis Pharmaceuticals Corp (P-4028)*
Novartis Corporation..........D.......510 879-9500
5300 Chiron Way Emeryville (94608) *(P-4144)*
Novartis Pharmaceuticals Corp..........B.......707 452-8081
2010 Cessna Dr Vacaville (95688) *(P-4028)*
Novato Advance Newspaper, Novato *Also called St Louis Post-Dispatch LLC (P-3482)*
Novato Community Hospital, Novato *Also called Sutter West Bay Hospitals (P-16681)*
Novato Disposal Service Inc (PA)..........E.......707 765-9995
3417 Standish Ave Santa Rosa (95407) *(P-8347)*
Novato Fire Protection Dist..........D.......415 878-2690
95 Rowland Way Novato (94945) *(P-14340)*
Novato Healthcare Center LLC..........C.......415 897-6161
1565 Hill Rd Novato (94947) *(P-16077)*
Novato Hearing Center, Novato *Also called Kaiser Foundation Hospitals (P-15891)*
Novato Management Group Inc..........D.......415 897-7111
8141 Redwood Blvd Novato (94945) *(P-11332)*
Novato Medical Offices, Novato *Also called Kaiser Foundation Hospitals (P-15479)*
Novato Travelodge..........E.......415 892-7500
7600 Redwood Blvd Novato (94945) *(P-11333)*
Novatorque Inc..........E.......510 933-2700
281 Greenoaks Dr Atherton (94027) *(P-5665)*
Novo Construction Inc (PA)..........D.......650 701-1500
1460 Obrien Dr Menlo Park (94025) *(P-932)*
Novo Masters Wholesale Inc..........E.......916 665-0390
2504 Mercantile Dr Rancho Cordova (95742) *(P-8885)*
Novo Nordisk Biotech, Davis *Also called Novozymes Inc (P-19175)*
Novodiax Inc..........E.......510 342-3043
3517 Breakwater Ave Hayward (94545) *(P-19094)*
Novonutrients, Sunnyvale *Also called Oakbio Inc (P-4127)*
Novozymes Inc (HQ)..........D.......530 757-8100
1445 Drew Ave Davis (95618) *(P-19175)*
Novvi LLC (PA)..........D.......281 488-0833
1600 Harbor Bay Pkwy # 200 Alameda (94502) *(P-4177)*
Noyo Vista Inc..........E.......707 964-4003
888 S Main St Fort Bragg (95437) *(P-11334)*
Nozomi Networks Inc (HQ)..........D.......800 314-6114
575 Market St Ste 3650 San Francisco (94105) *(P-14142)*
Npc Corp (PA)..........E.......415 578-2455
4040 Civic Center Dr # 200 San Rafael (94903) *(P-4232)*
Npc Pak, San Rafael *Also called Npc Corp (P-4232)*
Npi Solutions, Morgan Hill *Also called New Prduct Intgrtion Sltons In (P-4544)*
NRC Environmental Services Inc (HQ)..........D.......510 749-1390
1605 Ferry Pt Alameda (94501) *(P-8400)*
NRC Environmental Services Inc..........E.......916 371-7202
2450 Rice Ave West Sacramento (95691) *(P-8401)*
NRC Manufacturing Inc..........F.......510 438-9400
500 Yosemite Dr Ste 108 Milpitas (95035) *(P-6463)*
NRG California North LLC (HQ)..........C.......925 287-3133
1350 Treat Blvd Ste 500 Walnut Creek (94597) *(P-8129)*
NRG Energy, San Francisco *Also called Clearway Renew LLC (P-8093)*
NS Solution USA Corp..........E.......650 627-1500
2000 Almeda De Las Pulgas San Mateo (94403) *(P-13641)*
Nsa Wireless Inc (PA)..........E.......925 867-2817
12893 Alcosta Blvd Ste G San Ramon (94583) *(P-7908)*
Nsfocus Incorporated (HQ)..........E.......408 907-6638
2520 Mission College Blvd # 130 Santa Clara (95054) *(P-13950)*
Nsg Technology Inc..........B.......408 547-8770
1705 Junction Ct Ste 200 San Jose (95112) *(P-14702)*
Nss Enterprises..........E.......408 970-9200
3380 Viso Ct Santa Clara (95054) *(P-3679)*
Ntk Construction Inc..........E.......415 643-1900
501 Cesar Chavez Ste 115 San Francisco (94124) *(P-1172)*
NTL Precision Machining Inc..........F.......408 298-6650
1355 Vander Way San Jose (95112) *(P-5582)*
Ntm Consulting Services Inc..........E.......510 744-3901
39300 Civic Center Dr # 250 Fremont (94538) *(P-13951)*
NTS, Fremont *Also called New Tech Solutions Inc (P-8729)*
NTS Technical Systems..........E.......510 578-3500
41039 Boyce Rd Fremont (94538) *(P-19281)*
Ntsi Corporation..........E.......408 297-7200
275 N 4th St Fl 2 San Jose (95112) *(P-17828)*
Ntt Cloud Infrastructure Inc (HQ)..........D.......408 567-2000
5201 Great America Pkwy Santa Clara (95054) *(P-12639)*
Ntt Glbal Data Ctrs Amrcas Inc (HQ)..........B.......916 286-3000
1625 National Dr Sacramento (95834) *(P-13816)*
Ntt Scrity Appsec Slutions Inc (HQ)..........D.......408 343-8300
1741 Tech Dr Ste 300 San Jose (95110) *(P-13952)*

Nu Forest Products Inc ....D....707 433-3313
280 Asti Rd Cloverdale (95425) ***(P-8598)***
Nu Horizons Electronics Corp ....E....408 946-4154
890 N Mccarthy Blvd San Jose (95131) ***(P-8940)***
Nu Rev Communications Inc ....E....925 980-2799
2428 Research Dr Livermore (94550) ***(P-19831)***
Nu West Textile Group LLC ....E....925 676-1414
1910 Mark Ct 100 Concord (94520) ***(P-11665)***
Nucompass Mobility Svcs Inc (PA) ....E....925 734-3434
6800 Koll Center Pkwy # 10 Pleasanton (94566) ***(P-14341)***
Nuevacare LLC (PA) ....D....650 539-2000
1900 S Norfolk St Ste 350 San Mateo (94403) ***(P-16918)***
Nuevora ....E....925 967-2000
5000 Executive Pkwy # 515 San Ramon (94583) ***(P-19176)***
Nugate Group LLC (PA) ....C....408 278-9911
619 N 1st St San Jose (95112) ***(P-19705)***
Nugeneration Technologies LLC (PA) ....F....707 820-4080
1155 Park Ave Emeryville (94608) ***(P-4165)***
Nugentec, Emeryville *Also called Nugeneration Technologies LLC* ***(P-4165)***
Nulaid Foods Inc (PA) ....D....209 599-2121
200 W 5th St Ripon (95366) ***(P-9349)***
Numano Sake Company, Berkeley *Also called Takara Sake USA Inc* ***(P-2779)***
Numotion, Sacramento *Also called Atg-Wci Inc* ***(P-14738)***
Nuna Health, San Francisco *Also called Nuna Incorporated* ***(P-12640)***
Nuna Incorporated ....D....415 942-5200
370 Townsend St San Francisco (94107) ***(P-12640)***
Nunn Ranches, Brentwood *Also called San Andreas Farms Co* ***(P-11)***
Nuprodx Inc ....F....925 292-0866
161 S Vasco Rd Ste G Livermore (94551) ***(P-7076)***
Nurix Therapeutics Inc (PA) ....C....415 660-5320
1700 Owens St Ste 205 San Francisco (94158) ***(P-19095)***
Nuro Inc ....C....650 476-2687
1300 Terra Bella Ave # 100 Mountain View (94043) ***(P-5161)***
Nushake Inc ....D....209 239-8616
319 S Parallel Ave Ripon (95366) ***(P-1825)***
Nushake Roofing, Ripon *Also called Nushake Inc* ***(P-1825)***
Nutanix Inc (PA) ....A....408 216-8360
1740 Tech Dr Ste 150 San Jose (95110) ***(P-13336)***
Nutcracker Therapeutics Inc ....E....510 473-8478
5858 Horton St Ste 540 Emeryville (94608) ***(P-6842)***
Nutiva ....C....510 255-2700
213 W Cutting Blvd Richmond (94804) ***(P-2929)***
Nutra-Blend LLC ....E....559 661-6161
2140 W Industrial Ave Madera (93637) ***(P-2350)***
Nutra-Figs, Fresno *Also called San Joaquin Figs Inc* ***(P-307)***
Nutribiotic, Lakeport *Also called Globalridge LLC* ***(P-3816)***
Nutrition Parent LLC (HQ) ....D....650 321-4910
1950 University Ave # 350 East Palo Alto (94303) ***(P-10873)***
Nutrius LLC ....E....559 897-5862
39494 Clarkson Dr Kingsburg (93631) ***(P-2351)***
Nutstar Software LLC ....F....209 250-1324
1460 W 18th St Merced (95340) ***(P-13337)***
Nuvia Inc ....E....408 654-9696
2811 Mission College Blvd F Santa Clara (95054) ***(P-6234)***
Nuvolum Inc ....E....415 413-4999
1450 Tech Ln Ste 150 Petaluma (94954) ***(P-19593)***
Nuvoton Technology Corp Amer ....D....408 544-1718
2727 N 1st St San Jose (95134) ***(P-8941)***
Nuwest Milling LLC ....F....209 883-1163
4636 Geer Rd Hughson (95326) ***(P-2352)***
Nv5 Inc (HQ) ....D....916 641-9100
2525 Natomas Park Dr # 300 Sacramento (95833) ***(P-18781)***
Nvent Thermal LLC (HQ) ....B....650 474-7414
899 Broadway St Redwood City (94063) ***(P-6702)***
Nvidia, Menlo Park *Also called Swiftstack Inc* ***(P-13475)***
Nvidia Corporation (PA) ....B....408 486-2000
2788 San Tomas Expy Santa Clara (95051) ***(P-6235)***
Nvidia Intl Holdings Inc (HQ) ....D....408 486-2000
2788 San Tomas Expy Santa Clara (95051) ***(P-6236)***
Nvidia US Investment Company ....D....408 615-2500
2701 San Tomas Expy Santa Clara (95050) ***(P-5858)***
Nvision Laser Eye Centers Inc ....D....415 421-8667
711 Van Ness Ave Ste 320 San Francisco (94102) ***(P-15560)***
Nwe Technology Inc ....C....408 919-6100
1688 Richard Ave Santa Clara (95050) ***(P-5306)***
Nwpc LLC ....D....209 836-5050
10100 W Linne Rd Tracy (95377) ***(P-4727)***
Nxedge Inc ....E....208 362-7200
925 Lightpost Way Morgan Hill (95037) ***(P-8942)***
Nxedge Csl LLC ....D....408 727-0893
529 Aldo Ave Santa Clara (95054) ***(P-4916)***
Nxedge San Carlos LLC ....E....650 422-2269
1000 Commercial St San Carlos (94070) ***(P-6237)***
Nxp Usa Inc ....B....408 518-5500
411 E Plumeria Dr San Jose (95134) ***(P-6238)***
Nyack Inc ....E....530 389-8212
1 Nyack Rd Emigrant Gap (95715) ***(P-14342)***
Nyack Shell, Emigrant Gap *Also called Nyack Inc* ***(P-14342)***
Nyansa Inc ....E....650 446-7818
430 Cowper St Ste 250 Palo Alto (94301) ***(P-13338)***
Nyse Arca Inc ....C....415 393-4000
115 Sansome St San Francisco (94104) ***(P-10025)***
NZ Winery Direct LLC (PA) ....E....844 569-9463
235 Montgomery St Fl 30 San Francisco (94104) ***(P-2671)***
O C Jones & Sons Inc (PA) ....C....510 526-3424
1520 4th St Berkeley (94710) ***(P-1066)***
O C Jones & Sons Inc ....D....510 663-6911
155 Filbert St Ste 209 Oakland (94607) ***(P-19832)***
O C McDonald Co Inc ....C....408 295-2182
1150 W San Carlos St San Jose (95126) ***(P-1319)***
O G Packing Co ....E....209 931-4392
2097 Beyer Ln Stockton (95215) ***(P-9421)***
O H I Company ....E....209 466-8921
820 S Pershing Ave Stockton (95206) ***(P-5133)***
O Jay On PA, Chico *Also called North Valley Dermatology* ***(P-15553)***
O Nelson & Son, Woodside *Also called O Nelson & Son Inc* ***(P-1969)***
O Nelson & Son Inc ....E....650 851-3600
3345 Tripp Rd Woodside (94062) ***(P-1969)***
O'Conner Wound Care Clinic, San Jose *Also called OConnor Hospital* ***(P-15564)***
O'Connor Hosp Pdtric Ctr For L, San Jose *Also called OConnor Hospital* ***(P-16471)***
O'Connor Hospital, San Jose *Also called Verity Health System Cal Inc* ***(P-16711)***
O'Connor Wound Care Clinic, San Jose *Also called OConnor Hospital* ***(P-16472)***
O'Dell Printing Company, Rohnert Park *Also called Inaudr LLC* ***(P-3658)***
O'Neill Vintners & Distillers, Parlier *Also called ONeill Beverages Co LLC* ***(P-67)***
O'Neill Vintners & Distillers, Larkspur *Also called ONeill Beverages Co LLC* ***(P-68)***
O-G Packing & Cold Storage Co, Stockton *Also called O G Packing Co* ***(P-9421)***
O-I Owens Illinois Inc ....F....510 436-2000
3600 Alameda Ave Oakland (94601) ***(P-4367)***
O1 Communications Inc ....D....888 444-1111
4359 Town Center Blvd # 21 El Dorado Hills (95762) ***(P-7976)***
O2 Micro Inc ....D....408 987-5920
3118 Patrick Henry Dr Santa Clara (95054) ***(P-13642)***
Oagi Suntelco, San Jose *Also called Office Automation Group* ***(P-1555)***
Oak Creek Apartments ....C....650 327-1600
1600 Sand Hill Rd Palo Alto (94304) ***(P-10451)***
Oak Flat Golf Company LLC ....E....209 892-4653
9521 Morton Davis Dr Patterson (95363) ***(P-15117)***
Oak Hill Capital MGT LLC ....A....650 234-0500
2775 Sand Hill Rd Ste 220 Menlo Park (94025) ***(P-10874)***
Oak Hill Capital Partners, Menlo Park *Also called Oak Hill Capital MGT LLC* ***(P-10874)***
Oak Hill Capital Partners LP ....A....650 234-0500
2775 Sand Hill Rd Ste 220 Menlo Park (94025) ***(P-16919)***
Oak Knoll Convalescent Ctr Inc ....D....707 778-8686
450 Hayes Ln Petaluma (94952) ***(P-16078)***
Oak Ridge Winery LLC ....E....209 369-4768
6100 E Hwy 12 Victor Rd Lodi (95240) ***(P-2672)***
Oak River Insurance Company ....B....800 661-6029
1 California St Ste 600 San Francisco (94111) ***(P-10326)***
Oak River Rehabilitation ....C....530 365-0025
3300 Franklin St Anderson (96007) ***(P-16079)***
Oak Valley Hospital District ....D....209 869-8102
2603 Patterson Rd Ste 3 Riverbank (95367) ***(P-16469)***
Oak Valley Hospital District (PA) ....B....209 847-3011
350 S Oak Ave Oakdale (95361) ***(P-16470)***
Oak View Snoma Hlls Apartments, Rohnert Park *Also called Kisco Senior Living LLC* ***(P-10446)***
Oakbio Inc ....F....888 591-9413
1292 Anvilwood Ct Sunnyvale (94089) ***(P-4127)***
Oakdale Golf and Country Club ....D....209 847-2984
243 N Stearns Rd Oakdale (95361) ***(P-15118)***
Oakdale Irrgtion Dst Fing Corp ....D....209 847-0341
1205 E F St Oakdale (95361) ***(P-8256)***
Oakhill Star, Granite Bay *Also called Star Inc* ***(P-18033)***
Oakhurst Country Club, Clayton *Also called American Golf Corporation* ***(P-15051)***
Oakhurst Healthcare Center LLC ....D....559 683-2244
40131 Highway 49 Oakhurst (93644) ***(P-16194)***
Oakhurst Hlthcare Wllness Cntr, Oakhurst *Also called Oakhurst Sklled Nrsing Wllness* ***(P-16080)***
Oakhurst Industries Inc ....C....510 265-2400
3265 Investment Blvd Hayward (94545) ***(P-9281)***
Oakhurst Sklled Nrsing Wllness ....D....559 683-2244
40131 Highway 49 Oakhurst (93644) ***(P-16080)***
Oakland Athletics, Oakland *Also called Athletics Investment Group LLC* ***(P-14903)***
Oakland Business Office, Oakland *Also called East Bay Mncpl Utlity Dst Wtr* ***(P-8242)***
Oakland District Office, Oakland *Also called State Compensation Insur Fund* ***(P-10176)***
Oakland Hills Tennis Club Inc ....E....510 531-3300
5475 Redwood Rd Oakland (94619) ***(P-15119)***
Oakland Medical Center, Oakland *Also called Kaiser Foundation Hospitals* ***(P-15450)***
Oakland Medical Group Inc ....E....510 452-4824
3300 Webster St Ste 1000 Oakland (94609) ***(P-15561)***
Oakland Mltary Inst Cllege Prp ....E....510 594-3900
3877 Lusk St Emeryville (94608) ***(P-18341)***
Oakland Mrriott Hotels Resorts, Oakland *Also called Oakland Renaissance Associates* ***(P-11335)***
Oakland Museum of California ....D....510 318-8400
1000 Oak St Oakland (94607) ***(P-18277)***
Oakland Pallet Company Inc (PA) ....C....510 278-1291
2500 Grant Ave San Lorenzo (94580) ***(P-8599)***
Oakland Prvate Indust Cncil In ....E....510 768-4400
268 Grand Ave Oakland (94610) ***(P-17829)***
Oakland Public Education Fund ....D....510 221-6968
520 3rd St Ste 109 Oakland (94607) ***(P-10789)***
Oakland Renaissance Associates ....B....510 451-4000
1001 Broadway Oakland (94607) ***(P-11335)***
Oakland Shops/Annex, Oakland *Also called San Francisco Bay Area Rapid* ***(P-7348)***
Oakland Tribune Inc ....E....510 208-6300
600 Grand Ave 308 Oakland (94610) ***(P-3469)***
Oakland V A Outpatient Clinic, Oakland *Also called Veterans Health Administration* ***(P-15794)***
Oakland Zoo In Knowland Park, Oakland *Also called Conservation Society Cal* ***(P-18290)***
Oaklandidence Opco LLC ....D....510 832-3222
475 29th St Oakland (94609) ***(P-16195)***
Oakmead Prtg Reproduction Inc ....E....408 734-5505
233 E Weddell Dr Ste G Sunnyvale (94089) ***(P-3680)***

ALPHABETIC

Employee Codes: A=Over 500 employees, B=251-500
C=101-250, D=51-100, E=20-50 F=10-19
2022 Northern California Business Directory and Buyers Guide
© Mergent Inc. 1-800-342-5647
1035

Oakmont Golf Club Inc ALPHABETIC SECTION

Oakmont Golf Club Inc ....D.......707 538-2454
7025 Oakmont Dr Santa Rosa (95409) *(P-15015)*
Oakridge Care Center, Oakland *Also called A T Associates Inc (P-16214)*
Oaks, The, Petaluma *Also called Oak Knoll Convalescent Ctr Inc (P-16078)*
Oakville Produce Partners LLC ....C.......415 647-2991
453 Valley Dr Brisbane (94005) *(P-9422)*
Oakville Pump Service Inc ....E.......707 944-2471
2310 Laurel St Ste 1 NAPA (94559) *(P-1320)*
Oakwood Athletic Club, Lafayette *Also called Clubsport San Ramon LLC (P-14939)*
Oakwood Gardens Care Center, Fresno *Also called Lily Holdings LLC (P-16037)*
Oakwood Worldwide, Sacramento *Also called Worldwide Corporate Housing LP (P-11595)*
Oasis Foods Inc ....F.......209 382-0263
10881 Toews Ave Le Grand (95333) *(P-2231)*
Ob/Gyn Prtners For Hlth Med Gr ....E.......510 893-1700
365 Hawthorne Ave Ste 301 Oakland (94609) *(P-15562)*
Obayashi Canada Ltd ....E.......650 952-4910
577 Airport Blvd Ste 600 Burlingame (94010) *(P-1067)*
Obayashi Usa LLC (HQ) ....**C.......650 952-4910**
577 Airport Blvd Ste 600 Burlingame (94010) *(P-10630)*
Oberon Co ....F.......408 227-3730
7216 Via Colina San Jose (95139) *(P-6464)*
Oberon Design and Mfg LLC ....E.......415 865-5440
1076 Illinois St San Francisco (94107) *(P-8517)*
Oberon Media Inc (PA) ....**D.......646 367-2020**
1100 La Avenida St Ste A Mountain View (94043) *(P-12641)*
Oberti Wholesales Foods Inc ....F.......510 357-8600
14471 Griffith St San Leandro (94577) *(P-2102)*
Objective Systems Integrators (HQ) ....**E.......916 467-1500**
2365 Iron Point Rd # 170 Folsom (95630) *(P-12642)*
OBrien Mechanical Inc ....E.......415 695-1800
1515 Galvez Ave San Francisco (94124) *(P-1321)*
OBrien Watters & Davis LLP ....E.......707 545-7010
3510 Unocal Pl Ste 200 Santa Rosa (95403) *(P-17348)*
Obstetrix Med Group Cal A Prof (HQ) ....**E.......800 463-6628**
900 E Hamilton Ave # 220 Campbell (95008) *(P-15563)*
Oc Acquisition LLC (HQ) ....**D.......650 506-7000**
500 Oracle Pkwy Redwood City (94065) *(P-12643)*
OC Sailing Club Inc ....D.......510 843-4200
1 Spinnaker Way Berkeley (94710) *(P-15224)*
Ocadian Care Centers LLC ....B.......530 246-9000
2801 Eureka Way Redding (96001) *(P-16081)*
Ocadian Care Centers LLC ....B.......510 832-3222
475 29th St Oakland (94609) *(P-16082)*
Ocadian Care Centers LLC ....B.......510 204-5801
2450 Ashby Ave Berkeley (94705) *(P-16083)*
Ocadian Care Centers LLC ....B.......415 461-9700
1220 S Eliseo Dr Greenbrae (94904) *(P-16084)*
Ocadian Care Centers LLC ....B.......415 499-1000
1550 Silveira Pkwy San Rafael (94903) *(P-16085)*
Ocadian Care Centers LLC ....B.......408 295-2665
75 N 13th St San Jose (95112) *(P-16086)*
Occidental Power Solar Co., San Francisco *Also called Oxypower Inc (P-1330)*
Occidental Union Hotel Inc ....E.......707 874-3444
3731 Main St Occidental (95465) *(P-11336)*
Occupational Health Clinic, San Francisco *Also called University Cal San Francisco (P-16699)*
Oce Dsplay Grphics Systems Inc ....D.......773 714-8500
2811 Orchard Pkwy San Jose (95134) *(P-5122)*
Oce USA, Sacramento *Also called Canon Financial Services Inc (P-8680)*
Ocean Colony Partners LLC ....C.......650 726-5764
2450 Cabrillo Hwy S # 200 Half Moon Bay (94019) *(P-10711)*
Ocean Fresh LLC (PA) ....**E.......707 964-1389**
344 N Franklin St Fort Bragg (95437) *(P-2827)*
Ocean Fresh Seafood Products, Fort Bragg *Also called Ocean Fresh LLC (P-2827)*
Ocean Pacific Lodge, Santa Cruz *Also called Ocean PCF Invstors A Cal Ltd P (P-11337)*
Ocean PCF Invstors A Cal Ltd P ....E.......831 457-1234
301 Pacific Ave Santa Cruz (95060) *(P-11337)*
Ocean Shore Brokerage Inc (PA) ....**E.......650 726-1100**
248 Main St Half Moon Bay (94019) *(P-10631)*
Oceana Terrace Senior Housing, Pacifica *Also called Mercy Services Corporation (P-17648)*
Oceanic, San Leandro *Also called American Underwater Products (P-7186)*
Oclaro Inc (HQ) ....**B.......408 383-1400**
400 N Mccarthy Blvd Milpitas (95035) *(P-6239)*
Oclaro (north America) Inc ....A.......408 383-1400
252 Charcot Ave San Jose (95131) *(P-5802)*
Oclaro Fiber Optics Inc (HQ) ....**C.......408 383-1400**
400 N Mccarthy Blvd Milpitas (95035) *(P-6240)*
Oclaro Subsystems Inc ....C.......408 383-1400
400 N Mccarthy Blvd Milpitas (95035) *(P-5803)*
Oclaro Technology Inc ....A.......408 383-1400
400 N Mccarthy Blvd Milpitas (95035) *(P-6881)*
Ocli, Santa Rosa *Also called Optical Coating Laboratory LLC (P-4941)*
OConner Woods A California ....E.......209 956-3400
3400 Wagner Heights Rd Stockton (95209) *(P-10452)*
OConnor Hospital ....C.......408 947-2929
2039 Forest Ave San Jose (95128) *(P-16471)*
OConnor Hospital ....D.......408 947-2804
2105 Forest Ave San Jose (95128) *(P-15564)*
OConnor Hospital (HQ) ....**A.......408 947-2500**
2105 Forest Ave San Jose (95128) *(P-16472)*
OConnor Woods Housing Corp ....D.......209 956-3400
3400 Wagner Heights Rd Stockton (95209) *(P-10453)*
Ocsi.co, Oakland *Also called Outsource Consulting Svcs Inc (P-12115)*
Octave Health Group Inc ....D.......415 360-3833
575 Market St Ste 600 San Francisco (94105) *(P-17050)*
Oculeve Inc ....F.......415 745-3784
4410 Rosewood Dr Pleasanton (94588) *(P-3958)*
Od Signs, Hayward *Also called Oki Doki Signs (P-7245)*

Odc Theater ....D.......415 863-6606
351 Shotwell St San Francisco (94110) *(P-14853)*
Odd Fellow-Rebekah Chld HM Cal (PA) ....**C.......408 846-2100**
290 I O O F Ave Gilroy (95020) *(P-18151)*
Odd Fellows Home California ....B.......408 741-7100
14500 Fruitvale Ave # 3000 Saratoga (95070) *(P-18152)*
Odoo Inc ....E.......650 691-3277
250 Executive Park Blvd # 3400 San Francisco (94134) *(P-12644)*
Odwalla Inc ....E.......510 559-6840
2996 Alvarado St F San Leandro (94577) *(P-11815)*
Odyssey Environmental Services, Lodi *Also called Odyssey Landscaping Co Inc (P-1898)*
Odyssey Landscaping Co Inc ....D.......209 369-6197
5400 W Highway 12 Lodi (95242) *(P-1898)*
Odyssey Learning Centers Inc ....E.......916 988-0258
7150 Santa Juanita Ave Orangevale (95662) *(P-17985)*
Oeg Inc ....D.......408 909-9399
602 Charcot Ave San Jose (95131) *(P-1553)*
Oepic Semiconductors Inc ....E.......408 747-0388
1231 Bordeaux Dr Sunnyvale (94089) *(P-6241)*
Office Automation Group ....E.......408 292-0308
6910 Santa Teresa Blvd San Jose (95119) *(P-1554)*
Office Automation Group (PA) ....**E.......408 554-6244**
1066 Elm St San Jose (95126) *(P-1555)*
Office Depot Inc ....E.......559 255-1711
5405 E Home Ave Ste 109 Fresno (93727) *(P-8653)*
Office Libations, Oakland *Also called Noble Brewer Beer Company (P-2840)*
Office of District Attorney, Marysville *Also called County of Yuba (P-17240)*
Office of Technology, Rancho Cordova *Also called Technology Services Cal Dept (P-13992)*
Office Team, San Ramon *Also called Robert Half International Inc (P-12130)*
OfficeMax North America Inc ....E.......559 298-0164
1465 Shaw Ave Clovis (93611) *(P-11848)*
OfficeMax North America Inc ....D.......209 551-9700
1800 Oakdale Rd Ste B Modesto (95355) *(P-9209)*
OfficeMax North America Inc ....E.......916 388-0120
2800 Power Inn Rd Sacramento (95826) *(P-8654)*
Officeworks Inc ....D.......510 444-2161
300 Frank H Ste 269 Oakland (94612) *(P-12113)*
Ogilvy Pub Rlations World Wide ....C.......650 324-7015
800 El Camino Real Menlo Park (94025) *(P-19692)*
Ogilvy Pub Rltons Wrldwide LLC ....E.......916 231-7700
1530 J St Sacramento (95814) *(P-11775)*
Ogletree's, Saint Helena *Also called Ronald F Ogletree Inc (P-4813)*
OGrady Paving Inc ....C.......650 966-1926
2513 Wyandotte St Mountain View (94043) *(P-1068)*
OHagin Manufacturing LLC ....E.......707 872-3620
210 Classic Ct Ste 100 Rohnert Park (94928) *(P-1322)*
OHagins Inc ....D.......707 303-3660
210 Classic Ct Ste 100 Rohnert Park (94928) *(P-1323)*
Ohana Partners Inc (PA) ....**D.......408 856-3232**
454 S Abbott Ave Milpitas (95035) *(P-12057)*
OHara Metal Products ....E.......707 863-9090
4949 Fulton Dr Ste E Fairfield (94534) *(P-4957)*
Ohio Inc ....E.......415 647-6446
630 Treat Ave San Francisco (94110) *(P-3309)*
Ohmnilabs Inc ....E.......408 675-9565
2367 Bering Dr San Jose (95131) *(P-5111)*
Oil Changer Inc ....D.......650 494-8353
780 San Antonio Rd Palo Alto (94303) *(P-14667)*
Oil Changer Inc ....D.......650 355-7233
2880 Skyline Dr Pacifica (94044) *(P-14668)*
Oil Changer Inc ....D.......925 447-3346
1247 Portola Ave Livermore (94551) *(P-14669)*
Oil Changer 303, Pacifica *Also called Oil Changer Inc (P-14668)*
Oil Changer 304, Livermore *Also called Oil Changer Inc (P-14669)*
Ojo De Agua Produce, Dos Palos *Also called C&S Global Foods Inc (P-2876)*
OK Produce, Fresno *Also called Charles Matoian Entps Inc (P-7685)*
Okabe International Inc (PA) ....**E.......415 921-0808**
1739 Buchanan St Ste B San Francisco (94115) *(P-7820)*
OKeeffes Inc ....C.......209 388-9072
220 S R St Merced (95341) *(P-4797)*
Oki Doki Signs ....F.......510 940-7446
3490 Depot Rd Hayward (94545) *(P-7245)*
Oki Graphics Inc ....F.......408 451-9294
2148 Zanker Rd San Jose (95131) *(P-3743)*
Okta Inc (PA) ....**A.......888 722-7871**
100 1st St Ste 600 San Francisco (94105) *(P-13339)*
Ol' Smokey, Fresno *Also called Specialty Branded Products Inc (P-9380)*
Olam Americas Inc (HQ) ....**A.......559 447-1390**
205 E River Park Cir # 310 Fresno (93720) *(P-297)*
Olam Edible Nuts, Fresno *Also called Olam Americas Inc (P-297)*
Olam Farming Inc ....D.......559 446-6446
205 E River Park Cir Fresno (93720) *(P-184)*
Olam LLC ....E.......559 446-6420
205 E Rver Pk Cir Ste 310 Fresno (93720) *(P-10)*
Olam Spces Vgtable Ingredients, Fresno *Also called Olam West Coast Inc (P-299)*
Olam Spices & Vegetables Inc (PA) ....**D.......408 846-3200**
1350 Pacheco Pass Hwy Gilroy (95020) *(P-298)*
Olam Spices and Vegetables, Woodland *Also called Olam West Coast Inc (P-2233)*
Olam Tomato Processors Inc (HQ) ....**D.......559 447-1390**
205 E River Park Cir # 310 Fresno (93720) *(P-2232)*
Olam West Coast Inc (HQ) ....**A.......559 256-6224**
205 E Rver Pk Cir Ste 310 Fresno (93720) *(P-299)*
Olam West Coast Inc ....E.......530 473-4290
1400 Churchill Downs Ave Woodland (95776) *(P-2233)*
Olander Company Inc ....E.......408 735-1850
144 Commercial St Sunnyvale (94086) *(P-9124)*
Old Country Roofing, Vacaville *Also called Vaca Valley Roofing Inc (P-1843)*

Old Durham Wood Inc ....E....530 342-7381
1156 Oroville Chico Hwy Durham (95938) *(P-519)*
Old English Rancho Inc ....E....559 787-3020
461 N Piedra Rd Sanger (93657) *(P-202)*
Old Oak Ranch, Sonora *Also called Interntnal Ch of Frsqare Gospl (P-11605)*
Old Republic HM Protection Inc ....B....925 866-1500
2 Annabel Ln Ste 112 San Ramon (94583) *(P-10327)*
Old Republic Nat Title Insur ....E....510 286-7798
555 12th St Oakland (94607) *(P-10207)*
Old Republic Title Company (HQ) ....E....415 421-3500
275 Battery St Ste 1500 San Francisco (94111) *(P-10208)*
Old Rpblic Title Info Concepts ....C....916 781-4100
524 Gibson Dr Roseville (95678) *(P-10209)*
Olde World Corporation ....E....209 384-1337
360 Grogan Ave Merced (95341) *(P-3317)*
Older Adults Care MGT Inc (PA) ....C....650 329-1411
881 Fremont Ave Ste A2 Los Altos (94024) *(P-17663)*
Ole Health ....D....707 254-1770
1141 Pear Tree Ln Ste 100 NAPA (94558) *(P-15565)*
Oleander Holdings LLC ....D....916 331-4590
5255 Hemlock St Sacramento (95841) *(P-16087)*
Oliso Inc ....F....415 864-7600
1200 Harbour Way S 215 Richmond (94804) *(P-5706)*
Olivarez Honey Bees Inc ....D....530 865-0298
6398 County Road 20 Orland (95963) *(P-243)*
Olive Branch School, Granite Bay *Also called Eureka Un Schl Dst Fing Corp (P-17932)*
Olive Corto L P ....F....209 888-8100
10201 Live Oak Rd Stockton (95212) *(P-2467)*
Olive Musco Products Inc (PA) ....C....209 836-4600
17950 Via Nicolo Tracy (95377) *(P-2234)*
Olive Musco Products Inc ....E....530 865-4111
Swift & 5th St # 5 Orland (95963) *(P-2283)*
Olive Oil Factory LLC ....E....707 426-3400
770 Chadbourne Rd Fairfield (94534) *(P-2468)*
Olive Pit LLC ....F....530 824-4667
2156 Solano St Corning (96021) *(P-2235)*
Oliveira-Lucas Enterprises Inc ....E....209 667-2851
1025 S Kilroy Rd Turlock (95380) *(P-1556)*
Oliver & Company Inc ....D....510 412-9090
1300 S 51st St Richmond (94804) *(P-933)*
Oliver De Silva Inc (PA) ....E....925 829-9220
11555 Dublin Blvd Dublin (94568) *(P-580)*
Olivera Egg Ranch LLC ....D....408 258-8074
3315 Sierra Rd San Jose (95132) *(P-2137)*
Olivera Foods, San Jose *Also called Olivera Egg Ranch LLC (P-2137)*
Olivia Companies LLC ....E....415 962-5700
434 Brannan St San Francisco (94107) *(P-7821)*
Olivia Cruises & Resorts, San Francisco *Also called Olivia Companies LLC (P-7821)*
Olly Public Benefit Corp ....C....415 412-0812
415 Jackson St Fl 2 San Francisco (94111) *(P-9470)*
Olsen & Fielding Moving Svcs, Sacramento *Also called National Transfer and Stor Inc (P-7628)*
Olson and Co Steel ....C....559 224-7811
3488 W Ashlan Ave Fresno (93722) *(P-4679)*
Olson and Co Steel (PA) ....C....510 489-4680
1941 Davis St San Leandro (94577) *(P-4838)*
Olson Hagel Fishburn LLC ....E....916 442-2952
555 Capitol Mall Ste 400 Sacramento (95814) *(P-17349)*
Olson Meat Company ....E....530 865-8111
7301 Cutler Ave Orland (95963) *(P-2103)*
Olt Solar, San Jose *Also called Orbotech Lt Solar LLC (P-6248)*
Oly, Berkeley *Also called Art of Muse LLC (P-3273)*
Olympic Cascade Publishing (HQ) ....C....916 321-1000
2100 Q St Sacramento (95816) *(P-3470)*
Olympic Circle Sailing Club, Berkeley *Also called OC Sailing Club Inc (P-15224)*
Olympic Club ....C....415 676-1412
665 Sutter St San Francisco (94102) *(P-15120)*
Olympic Club (PA) ....C....415 345-5100
524 Post St San Francisco (94102) *(P-18444)*
Olympic Club ....D....415 404-4300
599 Skyline Dr Daly City (94015) *(P-18445)*
Olympic Village Inn, Olympic Valley *Also called Village Inn Owners Association (P-11559)*
Omada Health Inc ....B....888 987-8337
500 Sansome St Ste 200 San Francisco (94111) *(P-16920)*
Omar Orozco ....D....530 723-0849
816 Gibson Rd Woodland (95695) *(P-361)*
Omar Orozco's Contracting, Woodland *Also called Omar Orozco (P-361)*
Ombudsman Patients Advocate, Modesto *Also called Catholic Chrties of The Dcese (P-17466)*
Omega Electronic Mfg Svcs, San Jose *Also called Omega Ems (P-8943)*
Omega Ems (PA) ....D....408 206-4260
5400 Hellyer Ave San Jose (95138) *(P-8943)*
Omega Industrial Supply Inc ....E....707 864-8164
101 Grobric Ct Fairfield (94534) *(P-4076)*
Omega Management Services, Corning *Also called Omega Waste Management Inc (P-19594)*
Omega Products Corp (HQ) ....D....916 635-3335
8111 Fruitridge Rd Sacramento (95826) *(P-4538)*
Omega Products International, Sacramento *Also called Omega Products Corp (P-4538)*
Omega Turnstiles, Benicia *Also called Gunnebo Entrance Control Inc (P-6904)*
Omega Walnut Inc ....E....530 865-0136
7233 County Road 24 Orland (95963) *(P-300)*
Omega Waste Management Inc ....D....530 824-1890
957 Colusa St Corning (96021) *(P-19594)*
Omex Agrifluids Inc ....F....559 661-6138
1675 Dockery Ave Selma (93662) *(P-4135)*
Omic USA Inc California ....E....916 285-8700
1984 Del Paso Rd Ste 166 Sacramento (95834) *(P-14343)*

Omics Group Inc ....B....650 268-9744
731 Gull Ave Foster City (94404) *(P-3510)*
Omni Duct Systems, West Sacramento *Also called ECB Corp (P-4758)*
Omni Hotels Corporation ....D....415 677-9494
500 California St San Francisco (94104) *(P-11338)*
Omni Ipa/Medcore Medical Group, Stockton *Also called Medcore Medical Group (P-18340)*
Omni Mechanical Solution (PA) ....D....925 784-4726
6712 Preston Ave Livermore (94551) *(P-679)*
Omni Womens Hlth Med Group Inc (PA) ....D....559 495-3120
3812 N 1st St Fresno (93726) *(P-15566)*
Omnicell Inc (PA) ....B....650 251-6100
590 E Middlefield Rd Mountain View (94043) *(P-5263)*
Omnicell Inc ....E....650 251-6100
1201 Charleston Rd Mountain View (94043) *(P-5264)*
Omnicell International Inc (HQ) ....E....650 251-6100
590 E Middlefield Rd Mountain View (94043) *(P-5265)*
Omnisci Inc (PA) ....D....415 997-2814
100 Montgomery St Ste 500 San Francisco (94104) *(P-13340)*
Omnitrol Networks Inc ....E....408 919-1100
4580 Auto Mall Pkwy Ste 1 Fremont (94538) *(P-13643)*
Omnivision Technologies Inc (PA) ....A....408 567-3000
4275 Burton Dr Santa Clara (95054) *(P-6242)*
Omniyig Inc ....E....408 988-0843
3350 Scott Blvd Bldg 66 Santa Clara (95054) *(P-6465)*
Omron Robotics Safety Tech Inc (HQ) ....C....925 245-3400
4550 Norris Canyon Rd # 150 San Ramon (94583) *(P-5053)*
On Lok Inc ....D....415 292-8888
1333 Bush St San Francisco (94109) *(P-15567)*
ON LOK LIFEWAYS, San Francisco *Also called On Lok Senior Health Services (P-10147)*
On Lok Senior Health Services (PA) ....A....415 292-8888
1333 Bush St San Francisco (94109) *(P-10147)*
On Semcndctor Cnnctvity Sltons (HQ) ....B....669 209-5500
1704 Automation Pkwy San Jose (95131) *(P-6243)*
On Semiconductor, Santa Clara *Also called Semicndctor Cmponents Inds LLC (P-6282)*
On Semiconductor, Sunnyvale *Also called Fairchild Semicdtr Intl Inc (P-6119)*
On Target Marketing ....E....209 723-1691
429 Grogan Ave Merced (95341) *(P-11872)*
On The Move, Oakland *Also called Escue and Associates Inc (P-2030)*
On The Spot Transportation LLC ....E....317 379-6692
10277 Jennick Way Elk Grove (95757) *(P-14344)*
On-Site Manager Inc (HQ) ....E....866 266-7483
307 Orchard Cy Dr Ste 110 Campbell (95008) *(P-14345)*
On-Time AC & Htg LLC ....E....916 229-6370
4430 Yankee Hill Rd Rocklin (95677) *(P-1324)*
On-Time AC & Htg LLC ....D....408 279-5843
2161 Del Franco St San Jose (95131) *(P-1325)*
On-Time AC & Htg LLC ....D....925 566-2422
200 Mason Cir Ste 200 # 200 Concord (94520) *(P-1326)*
On-Time AC & Htg LLC ....D....925 800-5804
96 Rickenbacker Cir Livermore (94551) *(P-1327)*
On-Time AC & Htg LLC (HQ) ....D....925 598-1911
7020 Commerce Dr Pleasanton (94588) *(P-1328)*
On24 Inc (PA) ....B....415 369-8000
50 Beale St Fl 8 San Francisco (94105) *(P-13341)*
Onanon Inc ....E....408 262-8990
720 S Milpitas Blvd Milpitas (95035) *(P-6394)*
Onboardiq Inc ....D....480 433-1197
275 Sacramento St Ste 300 San Francisco (94111) *(P-12645)*
Oncology Group Practice, Greenbrae *Also called Marin Cancer Care Inc (P-15517)*
Oncology Svcs Med Group Inc ....E....925 952-8700
1445 Livorna Rd Alamo (94507) *(P-17164)*
Oncore Consulting LLC ....E....916 461-3584
3100 Zinfandel Dr Ste 250 Rancho Cordova (95670) *(P-13644)*
Oncore Manufacturing LLC ....D....510 516-5488
6600 Stevenson Blvd Fremont (94538) *(P-5953)*
Ondot Systems Inc ....E....408 316-2379
1731 Tech Dr Ste 700 San Jose (95110) *(P-12646)*
One Inc Software Corporation (PA) ....C....866 343-6940
620 Coolidge Dr Ste 200 Folsom (95630) *(P-12647)*
One Bella Casa Inc ....E....707 746-8300
101 Lucas Valley Rd # 130 San Rafael (94903) *(P-3029)*
One Block Off Grid Inc ....D....530 304-3969
164 S Park St San Francisco (94107) *(P-9002)*
One Diversified LLC ....D....408 969-1972
3275 Edward Ave Santa Clara (95054) *(P-19833)*
One Hat One Hand LLC ....E....415 822-2020
1335 Yosemite Ave San Francisco (94124) *(P-3014)*
One Medical, San Francisco *Also called 1life Healthcare Inc (P-15266)*
One Nob Hill Associates LLC ....D....415 392-3434
999 California St San Francisco (94108) *(P-11339)*
One Planet Ops Inc (PA) ....C....925 983-2800
1820 Bonanza St Walnut Creek (94596) *(P-11776)*
One Putt ....E....559 497-5118
1415 Fulton St Fresno (93721) *(P-11804)*
One Putt Broadcasting, Fresno *Also called One Putt (P-11804)*
One True Vine LLC (PA) ....E....707 967-9398
1050 Adams St Ste A Saint Helena (94574) *(P-2673)*
One Workplace L Ferrari, San Francisco *Also called One Workplace L Ferrari LLC (P-8501)*
One Workplace L Ferrari LLC ....E....415 357-2200
475 Brannan St San Francisco (94107) *(P-8501)*
One Workplace L Ferrari LLC ....E....916 553-5900
1780 N Market Blvd Sacramento (95834) *(P-2049)*
One World Montessori School ....E....408 723-5140
1170 Foxworthy Ave San Jose (95118) *(P-17986)*
One10 LLC ....D....415 398-3534
180 Montgomery St San Francisco (94104) *(P-19595)*
One10 LLC ....D....415 844-2200
735 Battery St Fl 1 San Francisco (94111) *(P-19596)*

A L P H A B E T I C

Employee Codes: A=Over 500 employees, B=251-500
C=101-250, D=51-100, E=20-50 F=10-19
2022 Northern California Business
Directory and Buyers Guide
© Mergent Inc. 1-800-342-5647
1037

ONeill Beverages Co LLC ALPHABETIC SECTION

ONeill Beverages Co LLC......C......559 638-3544
8418 S Lac Jac Ave Parlier (93648) ***(P-67)***
ONeill Beverages Co LLC (PA)......**D......844 825-6600**
101 Larkspur Landing Cir Larkspur (94939) ***(P-68)***
ONeill Wetsuits LLC (PA)......**D......831 475-7500**
1071 41st Ave Santa Cruz (95062) ***(P-4222)***
Onelogin Inc (HQ)......**C......415 645-6830**
848 Bttery St San Frncsco San Francisco San Francisco (94111) ***(P-13342)***
Onepointone Inc......D......855 346-5964
1185 Campbell Ave Unit G1 San Jose (95126) ***(P-19096)***
Onesignal Inc......D......408 506-0701
2850 S Delaware St # 201 San Mateo (94403) ***(P-13343)***
Oneto Manufacturing Co Inc......E......650 875-1710
146 S Maple Ave South San Francisco (94080) ***(P-4798)***
Onevalley Inc......E......650 421-2000
2955 Campus Dr Ste 110 San Mateo (94403) ***(P-19597)***
Onfido Inc......D......844 663-4366
995 Market St Fl 2 San Francisco (94103) ***(P-19598)***
Onfleet Inc......D......650 283-7547
703 Market St Fl 20 San Francisco (94103) ***(P-12648)***
Onfulfillment Inc......E......510 793-3009
8678 Thornton Ave Newark (94560) ***(P-7697)***
Online Game Services Inc......E......408 333-9663
100 W San Fernando St # 365 San Jose (95113) ***(P-7977)***
Online Technical Services Inc (PA)......**E......408 378-1100**
1901 S Bascom Ave # 1460 Campbell (95008) ***(P-12114)***
Onmycare Home Health, Fremont *Also called Onmycare LLC* ***(P-16921)***
Onmycare LLC......D......510 858-2273
39159 Pseo Ptre Prkwy Ste Fremont (94538) ***(P-16921)***
Onq Solutions Inc (PA)......**E......650 262-4150**
24540 Clawiter Rd Hayward (94545) ***(P-3328)***
Onsite Health Inc......D......888 411-2290
6610 Goodyear Rd Benicia (94510) ***(P-17165)***
Onspec Technology Partners Inc......E......408 654-7627
975 Comstock St Santa Clara (95054) ***(P-6244)***
Ontario Airport Hotel Corp......C......408 562-6709
4949 Great America Pkwy Santa Clara (95054) ***(P-11340)***
Ontel Security Services Inc......D......209 521-0200
2125 Wylie Dr Ste 11 Modesto (95355) ***(P-14081)***
Ontellus, San Jose *Also called Quest Discovery Services Inc* ***(P-17359)***
Ontera Inc......C......831 222-2193
2161 Delaware Ave Ste B Santa Cruz (95060) ***(P-6245)***
Ontrac, Fresno *Also called Express Messenger Systems Inc* ***(P-7645)***
Onyx, South San Francisco *Also called Gino Morena Enterprises LLC* ***(P-11682)***
Onyx Optics Inc......F......925 833-1969
6551 Sierra Ln Dublin (94568) ***(P-6882)***
Ooma Inc (PA)......**B......650 566-6600**
525 Almanor Ave Ste 200 Sunnyvale (94085) ***(P-13737)***
Oomnitza Inc (PA)......**D......415 525-3949**
414 Brannan St San Francisco (94107) ***(P-12649)***
Oorja Corporation......E......510 659-1899
45473 Warm Springs Blvd Fremont (94539) ***(P-6246)***
Ooshirts Inc (PA)......**B......866 660-8667**
39899 Balentine Dr # 220 Newark (94560) ***(P-3744)***
Ooyala Inc (HQ)......**B......650 961-3400**
2099 Gateway Pl Ste 600 San Jose (95110) ***(P-12650)***
Opal Moon Winery LLC......F......707 996-0420
21660 8th St E Ste A Sonoma (95476) ***(P-2674)***
Opal Soft Inc......D......408 267-2211
1288 Kifer Rd Ste 201 Sunnyvale (94086) ***(P-13953)***
Opalsoft, Sunnyvale *Also called Opal Soft Inc* ***(P-13953)***
Open Door Community Hlth Ctrs......E......707 822-1385
3800 Janes Rd Arcata (95521) ***(P-15568)***
Open Door Community Hlth Ctrs......E......707 826-8636
685 11th St Arcata (95521) ***(P-15569)***
Open Door Community Hlth Ctrs (PA)......**D......707 826-8642**
670 9th St Ste 203cfo Arcata (95521) ***(P-17051)***
Open Text Inc (HQ)......**C......650 645-3000**
2950 S Delaware St # 400 San Mateo (94403) ***(P-12651)***
Open-Silicon Inc (HQ)......**E......408 240-5700**
490 N Mccarthy Blvd # 220 Milpitas (95035) ***(P-6247)***
Openai Inc......E......650 387-6701
3180 18th St Ste 100 San Francisco (94110) ***(P-19227)***
Opendoor Labs Inc......D......888 352-7075
8880 Cal Center Dr # 400 Sacramento (95826) ***(P-10632)***
Opendoor Property, Sacramento *Also called Opendoor Labs Inc* ***(P-10632)***
Openfive, Milpitas *Also called Open-Silicon Inc* ***(P-6247)***
Opengov Inc (PA)......**E......650 336-7167**
6525 Crown Blvd # 41340 San Jose (95160) ***(P-7978)***
Openmind Technologies Inc (PA)......**D......866 536-2324**
3984 Washington Blvd # 183 Fremont (94538) ***(P-12652)***
Opentable Inc (HQ)......**A......415 344-4200**
1 Montgomery St Ste 700 San Francisco (94104) ***(P-14346)***
Opentv Inc (HQ)......**C......415 962-5000**
275 Sacramento St San Francisco (94111) ***(P-13344)***
Openwave Mobility Inc (HQ)......**D......650 480-7200**
400 Seaport Ct Ste 104 Redwood City (94063) ***(P-13345)***
Opera San Jose Inc......D......408 437-4450
2149 Paragon Dr San Jose (95131) ***(P-14854)***
Opera Software Americas LLC......D......650 625-1262
1875 S Grant St Ste 750 San Mateo (94402) ***(P-13346)***
Operating Engineers JAC......D......916 354-2029
14738 Cantova Way Rancho Murieta (95683) ***(P-17830)***
Operating Engineers Loca......E......408 782-9803
325 Digital Dr Morgan Hill (95037) ***(P-18782)***
Operating Engneers Local Un 3 (PA)......**E......925 454-4000**
250 N Canyons Pkwy Livermore (94551) ***(P-9800)***
Operating Engners Lcal Un No 3, Alameda *Also called Interntnal Un Oper Engners Lca* ***(P-18367)***
Operating Engners Lcal Un No 3 (PA)......**C......510 748-7400**
1620 S Loop Rd Alameda (94502) ***(P-18371)***
Operation Dignity Inc......E......510 287-8465
3850 San Pablo Ave # 102 Emeryville (94608) ***(P-17664)***
Operations Management Intl Inc......E......408 848-0480
1500 Southside Dr Gilroy (95020) ***(P-8257)***
Ophelia Quinones......E......408 757-1718
223 S 22nd St San Jose (95116) ***(P-12186)***
Opi Commercial Builders Inc (PA)......**D......408 377-4800**
1202 Lincoln Ave Ste 10 San Jose (95125) ***(P-680)***
Opinr Inc......D......646 207-3000
20824 Pamela Way Saratoga (95070) ***(P-12653)***
Oplink Communications LLC (HQ)......**A......510 933-7200**
46360 Fremont Blvd Fremont (94538) ***(P-8082)***
Oportun Financial Corporation (PA)......**A......650 810-8823**
2 Circle Star Way San Carlos (94070) ***(P-9861)***
Opportnity For Indpendence Inc......D......415 721-7772
20 H St San Rafael (94901) ***(P-17665)***
Ops1, Los Altos *Also called Organztonal Prfmce Systems Inc* ***(P-12656)***
Opscruise Inc......E......916 204-4369
5255 Stevens Creek Blvd Santa Clara (95051) ***(P-13347)***
Opshub Inc......E......650 701-1800
1000 Elwell Ct Ste 101 Palo Alto (94303) ***(P-12654)***
Opsmatic LLC......F......650 777-7600
188 Spear St Ste 1200 San Francisco (94105) ***(P-13348)***
Opsveda Inc......E......408 628-0461
4030 Moorpark Ave Ste 107 San Jose (95117) ***(P-13349)***
Opsware Inc......E......408 744-7517
599 N Mathilda Ave Sunnyvale (94085) ***(P-5780)***
Optibase Inc (HQ)......**E......800 451-5101**
931 Benecia Ave Sunnyvale (94085) ***(P-5402)***
Optical Coating Laboratory LLC (HQ)......**B......707 545-6440**
2789 Northpoint Pkwy Santa Rosa (95407) ***(P-4941)***
Optim, Pleasanton *Also called Unchained Labs* ***(P-16811)***
Optima Building Services Maint......D......707 586-6640
210 Mountain View Ave Santa Rosa (95407) ***(P-11982)***
Optima Ldscp Sacramento Inc......E......916 541-5796
9350 Eagle Springs Pl Roseville (95747) ***(P-429)***
Optimal Hospice Care, Santa Clara *Also called Bristol Hospice Foundation Cal* ***(P-16861)***
Optimas Oe Solutions LLC......E......559 492-4441
5940 E Shields Ave # 102 Fresno (93727) ***(P-8870)***
Optimas Oe Solutions LLC......E......408 934-1001
1931 Lundy Ave San Jose (95131) ***(P-8871)***
Optimedica Corporation......C......408 850-8600
510 Cottonwood Dr Milpitas (95035) ***(P-7013)***
Optimum Solutions Group LLC......E......415 954-7100
419 Ponderosa Ct Lafayette (94549) ***(P-13350)***
Optio Solutions LLC......B......800 360-2827
1444 N Mcdowell Blvd Petaluma (94954) ***(P-11826)***
Optiworks Inc (PA)......**D......510 438-4560**
47211 Bayside Pkwy Fremont (94538) ***(P-4377)***
Optofidelity Inc......E......669 241-8383
20863 Stevns Crk Blvd Cupertino (95014) ***(P-18783)***
Optoma Technology Inc......C......510 897-8600
47697 Westinghouse Dr Fremont (94539) ***(P-7157)***
Optoplex Corporation......B......510 490-9930
48500 Kato Rd Fremont (94538) ***(P-5804)***
Optovue Inc (PA)......**D......510 623-8868**
2800 Bayview Dr Fremont (94538) ***(P-7014)***
Opus 2 International Inc......E......888 960-3117
100 Pine St Ste 775 San Francisco (94111) ***(P-14347)***
Opus One Winery LLC (PA)......**D......707 944-9442**
7900 St Helena Hwy Oakville (94562) ***(P-2675)***
Opya Inc......D......650 931-6300
1720 S Amphlett Blvd # 110 San Mateo (94402) ***(P-17052)***
Oracle, San Mateo *Also called Netsuite Inc* ***(P-13326)***
Oracle America Inc (HQ)......**A......650 506-7000**
500 Oracle Pkwy Redwood City (94065) ***(P-5266)***
Oracle America Inc......F......303 272-6473
1001 Sunset Blvd Rocklin (95765) ***(P-13351)***
Oracle America Inc......D......800 633-0584
500 Oracle Pkwy Redwood City (94065) ***(P-8730)***
Oracle Corporation......B......916 315-3500
1001 Sunset Blvd Rocklin (95765) ***(P-13352)***
Oracle Corporation......C......415 541-9462
75 Hawthorne St Ste 2000 San Francisco (94105) ***(P-12655)***
Oracle Credit Corporation (HQ)......**C......650 506-7000**
500 Oracle Pkwy Fl 1 Redwood City (94065) ***(P-9872)***
Oracle International Corp (HQ)......**E......650 506-7000**
500 Oracle Pkwy Redwood City (94065) ***(P-13353)***
Oracle Systems Corporation (HQ)......**A......650 506-7000**
500 Oracle Pkwy Redwood City (94065) ***(P-13954)***
Oracle Taiwan LLC (HQ)......**E......650 506-7000**
500 Oracle Pkwy Redwood City (94065) ***(P-13354)***
Oracle Taleo LLC (HQ)......**D......925 452-3000**
4140 Dublin Blvd Ste 400 Dublin (94568) ***(P-13355)***
Orange Silicon Valley......D......415 243-1500
60 Spear St Ste 1100 San Francisco (94105) ***(P-19834)***
Orange Silicon Valley LLC......D......415 284-9765
60 Spear St Ste 1100 San Francisco (94105) ***(P-19177)***
Orangeburg Medical Group......D......209 343-8126
1448 Florida Ave Modesto (95350) ***(P-15570)***
Oratec Interventions Inc (HQ)......**D......901 396-2121**
3696 Haven Ave Redwood City (94063) ***(P-7118)***
Oraya Therapeutics Inc......E......510 456-3700
3 Twin Dolphin Dr Ste 175 Redwood City (94065) ***(P-6883)***
Orb Enterprises Inc......D......669 281-9994
320 Crscent Vlg Cir Unit San Jose (95134) ***(P-13955)***
Orb Intelligence Inc......E......650 391-4298
1900 Camden Ave San Jose (95124) ***(P-13356)***

Orba Financial & Inter SEC, Rancho Cordova *Also called Orba Insurance Services Inc (P-10328)*
Orba Insurance Services Inc ....D.......916 858-1222
2339 Gold Mdal Way Ste 20 Rancho Cordova (95670) *(P-10328)*
Orban, San Leandro *Also called Crl Systems Inc (P-5836)*
Orbis Bioaid, Santa Rosa *Also called Orbis Wheels Inc (P-7015)*
Orbis Wheels Inc ....F.......415 548-4160
3200 Dutton Ave Santa Rosa (95407) *(P-7015)*
Orbit Industries, Grass Valley *Also called Countis Industries Inc (P-4407)*
Orbotech Lt Solar LLC ....E.......408 414-3777
5970 Optical Ct San Jose (95138) *(P-6248)*
Orca Heating and Rfrgn Inc ....E.......707 464-9529
250 Michigan Rd Crescent City (95531) *(P-1329)*
Orchard Dental Group ....E.......916 961-6810
11121 Fair Oaks Blvd Fair Oaks (95628) *(P-15852)*
Orchard Harvest, Yuba City *Also called Orchard Machinery Corp Disc (P-5015)*
Orchard Hospital ....C.......530 846-9000
240 Spruce St Gridley (95948) *(P-16473)*
Orchard Hotel, San Francisco *Also called Orchard Intl Group Inc (P-11341)*
Orchard Intl Group Inc (PA) ....D.......415 362-8878
665 Bush St San Francisco (94108) *(P-11341)*
Orchard Machinery Corp Disc (PA) ....D.......530 673-2822
2700 Colusa Hwy Yuba City (95993) *(P-5015)*
Orchard Park, Clovis *Also called Regent Assisted Living Inc (P-18168)*
Orcon Aerospace, Union City *Also called Lamart Corporation (P-4526)*
Orcon Aerospace ....D.......510 489-8100
2600 Central Ave Ste E Union City (94587) *(P-6636)*
Oregon PCF Bldg Pdts Calif Inc ....D.......916 381-8051
8185 Signal Ct Ste A Sacramento (95824) *(P-8600)*
OReilly Alphatech Ventures II ....E.......707 827-7000
101a Clay St San Francisco (94111) *(P-13357)*
OReilly Media Inc (PA) ....C.......707 827-7000
1005 Gravenstein Hwy N Sebastopol (95472) *(P-3587)*
Orepac Building Products, Sacramento *Also called Oregon PCF Bldg Pdts Calif Inc (P-8600)*
Organic Spices (PA) ....E.......510 440-1044
4180 Business Center Dr Fremont (94538) *(P-2930)*
Organztonal Prfmce Systems Inc ....E.......650 968-7032
1393 Oak Ave Los Altos (94024) *(P-12656)*
Oric Pharmaceuticals Inc ....D.......650 388-5600
240 E Grand Ave Fl 2 South San Francisco (94080) *(P-3959)*
Oridus Inc ....E.......510 796-1111
46335 Landing Pkwy Fremont (94538) *(P-12657)*
Orient & Flume Art Glass ....F.......530 893-0373
2161 Park Ave Chico (95928) *(P-4378)*
Orient Bancorporation (PA) ....C.......415 567-1554
100 Pine St Ste 600 San Francisco (94111) *(P-9740)*
Orientex Foods, Pittsburg *Also called Ramar International Corp (P-2182)*
Origaudio, Danville *Also called Forty Four Group LLC (P-11754)*
Origin Systems Inc ....B.......650 628-1500
209 Redwood Shores Pkwy Redwood City (94065) *(P-12658)*
Original Glass Design, San Jose *Also called Beveled Edge Inc (P-4384)*
Orinda Country Club ....D.......925 254-4313
315 Camino Sobrante Orinda (94563) *(P-15121)*
Orinda Pre School ....E.......925 254-2551
10 Irwin Way Orinda (94563) *(P-17987)*
Orion Group World LLC ....C.......415 602-5233
143 Seminary Dr Apt Q Mill Valley (94941) *(P-8822)*
Orion Manufacturing Inc ....F.......408 955-9001
5550 Hellyer Ave San Jose (95138) *(P-5954)*
Orion Security Patrol Inc ....B.......408 287-4411
675 E Gish Rd San Jose (95112) *(P-14082)*
Oro Loma Ranch LLC (PA) ....E.......209 364-0070
44474 W Nees Ave Firebaugh (93622) *(P-32)*
Oro Loma Sanitary District ....E.......510 276-4700
2655 Grant Ave San Lorenzo (94580) *(P-8402)*
Orohealth Corporation ....A.......530 534-9183
900 Oro Dam Blvd E Oroville (95965) *(P-15571)*
ORourke Electric Inc ....E.......707 528-8539
3347 Industrial Dr Ste 4 Santa Rosa (95403) *(P-1557)*
Oroville Hosp Post Acute Ctr, Oroville *Also called 1000 Executive Parkway LLC (P-15903)*
Oroville Hospital, Oroville *Also called Orohealth Corporation (P-15571)*
Oroville Hospital (PA) ....A.......530 533-8500
2767 Olive Hwy Oroville (95966) *(P-16474)*
Oroville Hospital ....C.......530 538-8700
2353 Myers St Ste B Oroville (95966) *(P-15893)*
Oroville Hospital ....B.......530 532-8697
2170 Bird St Oroville (95965) *(P-16475)*
Oroville Intrnal Mdcine Med Gr ....E.......530 538-3171
2721 Olive Hwy Ste 12 Oroville (95966) *(P-15572)*
Orphan Medical Inc ....D.......650 496-3777
3180 Porter Dr Palo Alto (94304) *(P-3960)*
Orr Hot Springs, Ukiah *Also called Mendocino Onsen Corportation (P-11295)*
Orrick Hrringtn Sut Foundtn ....E.......916 329-7928
400 Capitol Mall Ste 3000 Sacramento (95814) *(P-17350)*
Orrick Hrrington Sutcliffe LLP (PA) ....A.......415 773-5700
405 Howard St San Francisco (94105) *(P-17351)*
Orrick Hrrington Sutcliffe LLP ....C.......650 614-7400
1000 Marsh Rd Menlo Park (94025) *(P-17352)*
Ortech Inc ....F.......916 549-9696
6760 Folsom Blvd 100 Sacramento (95819) *(P-4401)*
Ortech Advanced Ceramics, Sacramento *Also called Ortech Inc (P-4401)*
Orthaheel, San Rafael *Also called Vionic Group LLC (P-4343)*
Orthocad, San Jose *Also called Cadent Inc (P-13562)*
Orthofix Medical Inc ....A.......214 937-2000
501 Mercury Dr Sunnyvale (94085) *(P-7016)*
Orthogroup Inc ....F.......916 859-0881
11280 Sanders Dr Ste A Rancho Cordova (95742) *(P-7017)*
Orthonorcal Inc ....E.......408 356-0464
340 Dardanelli Ln Ste 10 Los Gatos (95032) *(P-15573)*
Orthopedic Assoc Nthrn Cal ....E.......530 897-4500
131 Raley Blvd Chico (95928) *(P-15574)*
Orthopedic Assoc Nthrn Califo, Chico *Also called Orthopedic Assoc Nthrn Cal (P-15574)*
Oryx Advanced Materials Inc (PA) ....E.......510 249-1158
46458 Fremont Blvd Fremont (94538) *(P-5307)*
Oscar Printing, San Francisco *Also called La Brothers Enterprise Inc (P-3668)*
Osher Ctr For Intgrtive Mdcine, San Francisco *Also called University Cal San Francisco (P-15760)*
Oshman Family Jewish Cmnty Ctr ....C.......650 223-8700
3921 Fabian Way Palo Alto (94303) *(P-17666)*
OSI, Folsom *Also called Objective Systems Integrators (P-12642)*
OSI Engineering Inc ....C.......408 550-2800
901 Campisi Way Ste 160 Campbell (95008) *(P-18784)*
OSI Software, San Leandro *Also called Osisoft LLC (P-12659)*
Osisoft LLC (HQ) ....B.......510 297-5800
1600 Alvarado St San Leandro (94577) *(P-12659)*
Oski Technology Inc (PA) ....E.......408 216-7728
2099 Gateway Pl Ste 560 San Jose (95110) *(P-13956)*
Osram Opto Semiconductors Inc (HQ) ....E.......408 962-3736
1150 Kifer Rd Ste 100 Sunnyvale (94086) *(P-8944)*
Osram Sylvania Inc ....E.......408 922-7200
651 River Oaks Pkwy San Jose (95134) *(P-8872)*
Osseon LLC ....E.......707 636-5940
2301 Circadian Way # 300 Santa Rosa (95407) *(P-7018)*
Osterhout Design Group, San Francisco *Also called Osterhout Group Inc (P-14348)*
Osterhout Group Inc ....E.......415 644-4000
200 Brannan St Apt 326 San Francisco (94107) *(P-14348)*
Osterweis Capital MGT Inc ....E.......415 434-4441
1 Maritime Plz Ste 800 San Francisco (94111) *(P-10053)*
OT Precision Machining Inc ....E.......408 435-8818
1450 Seareel Ln San Jose (95131) *(P-5583)*
Oti Engineering Cons Inc ....E.......209 586-1022
24926 State Highway 108 Ml Wuk Village (95346) *(P-5859)*
Otis McAllister Inc (PA) ....E.......415 421-6010
300 Frank H Ogawa Plz Oakland (94612) *(P-9471)*
Oto Analytics Inc ....B.......310 683-0000
548 Market St Ste 73871 San Francisco (94104) *(P-13645)*
Otr Global Holdings II Inc ....D.......415 675-7660
155 Montgomery St Ste 501 San Francisco (94104) *(P-19178)*
Otterai Inc ....E.......650 250-6322
800 W El Cmino Real Ste 1 Mountain View (94040) *(P-12660)*
OTTO CONSTRUCTION, Sacramento *Also called John F Otto Inc (P-904)*
Otto Frei-Jules Borel Inc (PA) ....E.......800 772-3456
126 2nd St Oakland (94607) *(P-9184)*
Our Huse Rsdntial Care Ctr Inc ....E.......559 674-8670
109 E Central Ave Madera (93638) *(P-16256)*
Our Lady Fatima Villa Inc ....D.......408 741-2950
20400 Srtoga Los Gatos Rd Saratoga (95070) *(P-16088)*
Ouraring Inc ....D.......734 660-5566
60 Francisco St San Francisco (94133) *(P-14349)*
Ouster Inc (PA) ....D.......415 949-0108
350 Treat Ave Ste 1 San Francisco (94110) *(P-6914)*
Outback Construction Inc ....E.......530 528-2225
13660 State Highway 36 E Red Bluff (96080) *(P-1129)*
Outback Contractors Inc ....C.......530 528-2225
13670 State Highway 36 E Red Bluff (96080) *(P-1069)*
Outcast Agency LLC ....C.......415 392-8282
100 Montgomery St # 1201 San Francisco (94104) *(P-19693)*
Outfront Media LLC ....E.......209 466-5021
2512 River Plaza Dr Sacramento (95833) *(P-11797)*
Outlaw Beverage Inc ....F.......310 424-5077
3945 Freedom Cir Ste 560 Santa Clara (95054) *(P-2489)*
Outreach & Escort Inc (PA) ....D.......408 678-8585
2221 Oakland Rd Ste 200 San Jose (95131) *(P-17667)*
Outreach Corporation ....F.......888 938-7356
600 California St Fl 7 San Francisco (94108) *(P-13358)*
Outright Inc ....A.......918 926-6578
100 Mathilda Pl Ste 100 # 100 Sunnyvale (94086) *(P-12661)*
Outset Medical Inc ....B.......669 231-8200
3052 Orchard Dr San Jose (95134) *(P-7119)*
Outsource Consulting Svcs Inc (PA) ....E.......510 986-0686
7901 Okport St N Bldg Ste Oakland (94621) *(P-12115)*
Outspark Inc ....E.......415 495-1905
434 Brannan St 1 San Francisco (94107) *(P-7979)*
Oven Fresh Bakery Incorporated ....F.......650 366-9201
23188 Foley St Hayward (94545) *(P-2396)*
OVER 60 HEALTH CENTER, Berkeley *Also called Lifelong Medical Care (P-15505)*
Overaa Construction, Richmond *Also called C Overaa & Co (P-845)*
Overhead Door Santa Clara Vly, Sunnyvale *Also called Overhead Door Snta Clara Vly I (P-1748)*
Overhead Door Snta Clara Vly I ....E.......408 734-8010
1266 Lawrence Station Rd Sunnyvale (94089) *(P-1748)*
Overland Storage Inc (HQ) ....B.......408 283-4700
2633 Camino Ramon Ste 325 San Ramon (94583) *(P-5308)*
Overland-Tandberg, San Ramon *Also called Overland Storage Inc (P-5308)*
Overmiller Inc ....D.......925 798-2122
195 Mason Cir Concord (94520) *(P-14769)*
Overops Inc ....E.......415 767-1250
44 Montgomery St Ste 1050 San Francisco (94104) *(P-12662)*
Overton Security Services Inc ....C.......510 791-7380
39300 Civic Center Dr # 370 Fremont (94538) *(P-14083)*
Owen & Company ....D.......916 993-2700
1455 Response Rd Ste 260 Sacramento (95815) *(P-10329)*
Owens Corning Sales LLC ....B.......408 235-1351
960 Central Expy Santa Clara (95050) *(P-8640)*

A L P H A B E T I C

Owens Design Incorporated ..... E 510 659-1800
47427 Fremont Blvd Fremont (94538) *(P-5584)*
Oxbase Inc ..... E 707 824-2560
3500 N Laughlin Rd 100 Santa Rosa (95403) *(P-4353)*
Oxbow Landscape Contrs Inc ..... E 707 339-6001
2400 Oak St A NAPA (94559) *(P-430)*
Oxbow Pool & Landscape Contrs, NAPA *Also called Oxbow Landscape Contrs Inc (P-430)*
Oxford Instrs X-Ray Tech Inc ..... D 831 439-9729
360 El Pueblo Rd Scotts Valley (95066) *(P-6466)*
Oxypower Inc (PA) ..... D 415 681-8861
5982 Mission St San Francisco (94112) *(P-1330)*
Ozeki Sake (usa) Inc (HQ) ..... E 831 637-9217
249 Hillcrest Rd Hollister (95023) *(P-2676)*
Ozig LLC ..... E 510 588-7952
490 43rd St Ste 206 Oakland (94609) *(P-4622)*
Ozotech Inc ..... F 530 842-4189
1015 S Main St Yreka (96097) *(P-5446)*
P & F Metals, Turlock *Also called Turlock Sheet Metal & Wldg Inc (P-18841)*
P & L Concrete Products Inc ..... E 209 838-1448
1900 Roosevelt Ave Escalon (95320) *(P-4501)*
P & L Specialties ..... F 707 573-3141
1650 Almar Pkwy Santa Rosa (95403) *(P-5162)*
P A C, San Rafael *Also called Packaging Aids Corporation (P-5201)*
P B M, Chico *Also called PBM Supply & Mfg (P-9126)*
P C A, Livermore *Also called Pen-Cal Administrators Inc (P-19381)*
P C S, Concord *Also called Patriot Contract Services LLC (P-7711)*
P C S, Hollister *Also called Pride Conveyance Systems Inc (P-5054)*
P H I, South San Francisco *Also called Peking Handicraft Inc (P-8518)*
P H Ranch Inc ..... E 209 358-5111
6335 Oakdale Rd Winton (95388) *(P-218)*
P J'S Construction Supplies, Fremont *Also called PJs Lumber Inc (P-8603)*
P K B Investments Inc ..... C 559 243-1224
745 E Locust Ave Ste 105 Fresno (93720) *(P-19599)*
P L D S, Milpitas *Also called Philips Lt-On Dgtal Sltons USA (P-5309)*
P M S D Inc (PA) ..... C 408 988-5235
3411 Leonard Ct Santa Clara (95054) *(P-5585)*
P M S D Inc ..... E 408 727-5322
3411 Leonard Ct Santa Clara (95054) *(P-5586)*
P S C Manufacturing Inc ..... E 408 988-5115
3424 De La Cruz Blvd Santa Clara (95054) *(P-4308)*
P V M, Windsor *Also called Patin Vineyard Management Inc (P-384)*
P W Pipe, Shingle Springs *Also called Pw Eagle Inc (P-4235)*
P&P International Inc ..... F 559 891-9888
2014 2nd St Selma (93662) *(P-9216)*
P.J.'s Rebar, Turlock *Also called PJs Lumber Inc (P-1929)*
Paar Hospitality Inc ..... D 510 828-3585
500 W A St Hayward (94541) *(P-11342)*
Pabco Building Products LLC ..... D 510 792-9555
37851 Cherry St Newark (94560) *(P-4512)*
Pabco Building Products LLC ..... D 510 792-1577
37849 Cherry St Newark (94560) *(P-4513)*
Pabco Building Products LLC (HQ) ..... E 510 792-1577
10600 White Rock Rd Ste 1 Rancho Cordova (95670) *(P-4514)*
Pabco Building Products LLC ..... D 916 645-3341
601 7th St Lincoln (95648) *(P-4405)*
Pabco Clay Products LLC ..... C 916 645-3341
601 7th St Lincoln (95648) *(P-4399)*
Pabco Clay Products LLC ..... E 916 645-8937
1500 Shridan Lincoln Blvd Lincoln (95648) *(P-4531)*
Pabco Clay Products LLC ..... E 916 859-6320
4875 Bradshaw Rd Sacramento (95827) *(P-4400)*
Pabco Gypsum, Newark *Also called Pabco Building Products LLC (P-4512)*
Pac Trim, Rocklin *Also called Pacific Mdf Products Inc (P-3145)*
Pac-12 Enteprises LLC ..... E 415 580-4200
360 3rd St Ste 300 San Francisco (94107) *(P-11805)*
Pacatte Construction Co Inc ..... E 707 527-5983
5560 Skylane Blvd Ste A Santa Rosa (95403) *(P-934)*
Pacbell, San Francisco *Also called Pacific Bell Telephone Company (P-7980)*
PACE, Santa Clara *Also called Pacific Autism Ctr For Educatn (P-18153)*
Pace Solano ..... E 707 427-1731
350 Chadbourne Rd Fairfield (94534) *(P-18245)*
Pace Solano ..... D 707 426-6932
1955 W Texas St Fairfield (94533) *(P-17831)*
Pace Supply Corp (PA) ..... D 707 755-2499
6000 State Farm Dr # 200 Rohnert Park (94928) *(P-9003)*
Pacesetter Inc ..... C 925 730-4171
6035 Stoneridge Dr Pleasanton (94588) *(P-7120)*
Pachama Inc ..... E 650 338-9394
2261 Market St Ste 4303 San Francisco (94114) *(P-12663)*
Pacheco Brothers Gardening Inc ..... E 510 487-3580
6344 Bridgehead Rd Oakley (94561) *(P-520)*
Pacheco Brothers Gardening Inc (PA) ..... E 510 732-6330
20973 Cabot Blvd Hayward (94545) *(P-431)*
Pacific AG & Vineyard Inc ..... E 209 365-7222
21282 N Ray Rd Lodi (95242) *(P-362)*
Pacific AG Services, Firebaugh *Also called Robinson Agspray (P-256)*
PACIFIC ANALOGIX SEMICONDUCTOR, Santa Clara *Also called Analogix Semiconductor Inc (P-6037)*
Pacific Athletic Club, San Francisco *Also called Bay Club America Inc (P-15054)*
Pacific Autism Ctr For Educatn ..... C 408 245-3400
1880 Pruneridge Ave Santa Clara (95050) *(P-18153)*
Pacific Avenue Bowl ..... E 209 477-0267
5939 Pacific Ave Stockton (95207) *(P-14896)*
Pacific Aviation Corporation ..... C 650 821-1190
P.O. Box 250758 San Francisco (94125) *(P-7778)*
Pacific Beach House LLC (PA) ..... E 650 712-0220
4100 Cabrillo Hwy N Half Moon Bay (94019) *(P-11343)*

Pacific Bell Telephone Company ..... A 650 572-6807
262 19th Ave San Mateo (94403) *(P-7909)*
Pacific Bell Telephone Company (HQ) ..... A 415 542-9000
430 Bush St Fl 3 San Francisco (94108) *(P-7980)*
Pacific Bell Telephone Company ..... A 415 978-0881
2040 Polk St 267 San Francisco (94109) *(P-7910)*
Pacific Biosciences Cal Inc (PA) ..... B 650 521-8000
1305 Obrien Dr Menlo Park (94025) *(P-6843)*
Pacific Boring Incorporated ..... E 559 864-9444
1985 W Mountain View Ave Caruthers (93609) *(P-1130)*
Pacific Cast Crdiac Vsclar Srg ..... E 650 366-0225
2900 Whipple Ave Ste 225 Redwood City (94062) *(P-16476)*
Pacific Catch Inc ..... E 415 504-6905
770 Tamalpais Dr Ste 210 Corte Madera (94925) *(P-2353)*
Pacific Ceramics Inc ..... E 408 747-4600
3524 Bassett St Santa Clara (95054) *(P-4402)*
Pacific Cheese Co Inc (PA) ..... C 510 784-8800
21090 Cabot Blvd Hayward (94545) *(P-9341)*
Pacific Choice Brands Inc (PA) ..... C 559 892-5365
4652 E Date Ave Fresno (93725) *(P-2284)*
Pacific Cities Management Inc (PA) ..... D 916 348-1188
6056 Rutland Dr Ste 1 Carmichael (95608) *(P-10633)*
Pacific Civil & Strl Cons LLC ..... E 916 421-1000
7415 Greenhaven Dr # 100 Sacramento (95831) *(P-18785)*
Pacific Clears, Eureka *Also called Schmidbauer Lumber Inc (P-3103)*
Pacific Coast Bankers Bank ..... D 415 399-1900
1676 N Calif Blvd Ste 300 Walnut Creek (94596) *(P-9741)*
Pacific Coast Companies Inc ..... C 916 631-6500
10600 White Rock Rd # 100 Rancho Cordova (95670) *(P-14350)*
Pacific Coast Container Inc (PA) ..... C 510 346-6100
432 Estudillo Ave Ste 1 San Leandro (94577) *(P-7889)*
Pacific Coast Contg Spc Inc ..... D 916 929-3100
946 N Market Blvd Sacramento (95834) *(P-8601)*
Pacific Coast Fire Inc ..... E 408 370-1234
470 Division St Campbell (95008) *(P-1301)*
Pacific Coast Gen Engrg Inc ..... E 925 252-0214
12 Industry Rd Pittsburg (94565) *(P-18786)*
Pacific Coast Ingredients (PA) ..... F 831 316-7137
170 Technology Cir Scotts Valley (95066) *(P-2820)*
Pacific Coast Laboratories ..... E 510 351-2770
2100 Orchard Ave San Leandro (94577) *(P-7077)*
Pacific Coast Ldscp MGT Inc ..... D 925 513-2310
3960 Holway Dr Byron (94514) *(P-432)*
Pacific Coast Manor, Capitola *Also called Covenant Care LLC (P-15963)*
Pacific Coast Optics LLC ..... F 916 789-0111
10604 Industrial Ave # 100 Roseville (95678) *(P-5163)*
Pacific Coast Producers ..... D 209 334-3352
741 S Stockton St Lodi (95240) *(P-2236)*
Pacific Coast Producers (PA) ..... B 209 367-8800
631 N Cluff Ave Lodi (95240) *(P-2237)*
Pacific Coast Producers ..... D 530 533-4311
1601 Mitchell Ave Oroville (95965) *(P-2238)*
Pacific Coast Producers ..... D 530 662-8661
1376 Lemen Ave Woodland (95776) *(P-2239)*
Pacific Coast Producers ..... D 530 695-1126
6005 Highway 99 Live Oak (95953) *(P-2240)*
Pacific Coast Products LLC ..... E 831 316-7137
200 Technology Cir Scotts Valley (95066) *(P-2821)*
Pacific Coast Sales & Svc Inc ..... E 408 437-0390
890 Service St Ste A San Jose (95112) *(P-9012)*
Pacific Coast Services Inc ..... A 209 956-2532
3202 W March Ln Ste D Stockton (95219) *(P-16922)*
Pacific Coast Signs Inc (PA) ..... E 650 520-0724
1754 Hempstead Pl Redwood City (94061) *(P-7246)*
Pacific Coast Stage Lighting ..... F 916 765-4396
10774 Melody Rd Smartsville (95977) *(P-5748)*
Pacific Coast Supply LLC (HQ) ..... B 916 971-2301
4290 Roseville Rd North Highlands (95660) *(P-8602)*
Pacific Coast Supply LLC ..... F 916 339-8100
5550 Roseville Rd North Highlands (95660) *(P-3213)*
Pacific Coast Warehouse Co, Newark *Also called National Distribution Agcy Inc (P-7695)*
Pacific Cookie Company Inc (PA) ..... E 831 429-9709
303 Potrero St Ste 40 Santa Cruz (95060) *(P-9472)*
Pacific Copy and Print ..... E 916 928-8434
1700 N Market Blvd # 107 Sacramento (95834) *(P-11849)*
Pacific Corrugated Pipe Co LLC ..... E 916 383-4891
5999 Power Inn Rd Sacramento (95824) *(P-4445)*
Pacific Crown Partners LLC ..... E 559 900-1451
1100 W Shaw Ave Ste 116 Fresno (93711) *(P-9473)*
Pacific Die Cut Industries ..... D 510 732-8103
3399 Arden Rd Hayward (94545) *(P-4204)*
Pacific Door & Cabinet Company ..... E 559 439-3822
7050 N Harrison Ave Pinedale (93650) *(P-3144)*
Pacific Door Products Inc ..... E 707 795-7777
470 Aaron St Cotati (94931) *(P-1749)*
Pacific Earthscape, McKinleyville *Also called Ford Logging Inc (P-3060)*
Pacific Energy Fuels Company ..... A 415 973-8200
77 Beale St Ste 100 San Francisco (94105) *(P-8210)*
Pacific Environmental Group ..... D 408 453-7500
1921 Ringwood Ave San Jose (95131) *(P-18787)*
Pacific Eye Associated Inc ..... C 415 923-3007
2100 Webster St Ste 214 San Francisco (94115) *(P-15575)*
Pacific Farms and Orchards Inc ..... D 530 385-1475
22880 Gerber Rd Gerber (96035) *(P-110)*
Pacific Foundation Svcs LLC ..... D 415 561-6540
1660 Bush St 300 San Francisco (94109) *(P-19376)*
Pacific Fresh Seafood, Sacramento *Also called Pacific Sfood - Sacramento LLC (P-9329)*
Pacific Galvanizing Inc ..... E 510 261-7331
715 46th Ave Oakland (94601) *(P-4942)*
Pacific Gardens, Santa Clara *Also called Community Home Partners LLC (P-16177)*

Pacific Gardens Hlth Care Ctr, Fresno *Also called Covenant Care California LLC* ***(P-15968)***
Pacific Gas and Electric Co ....C....415 973-7000
425 Beck Ave Fairfield (94533) ***(P-8130)***
Pacific Gas and Electric Co (HQ) ....**A....415 973-7000**
77 Beale St San Francisco (94105) ***(P-8131)***
Pacific Gas and Electric Co ....C....916 375-5005
885 Embarcadero Dr West Sacramento (95605) ***(P-8132)***
Pacific Gas and Electric Co ....C....209 932-6550
P.O. Box 930 Stockton (95201) ***(P-8133)***
Pacific Gas and Electric Co ....C....209 726-7650
8 E River Park Pl W Fresno (93720) ***(P-8134)***
Pacific Gas and Electric Co ....C....916 923-7007
2730 Gateway Oaks Dr # 220 Sacramento (95833) ***(P-8135)***
Pacific Gas and Electric Co ....C....530 258-6215
350 Salem St Chico (95928) ***(P-8136)***
Pacific Gas and Electric Co ....C....510 450-5744
4525 Hollis St Oakland (94608) ***(P-8137)***
Pacific Gas and Electric Co ....C....510 784-3253
24300 Clawiter Rd Hayward (94545) ***(P-8211)***
Pacific Gas and Electric Co ....C....707 446-7381
4940 Allison Pkwy Vacaville (95688) ***(P-8138)***
Pacific Gas and Electric Co ....C....650 592-9411
1970 Industrial Way Belmont (94002) ***(P-8139)***
Pacific Gas and Electric Co ....C....209 726-7623
4400 E State Highway 140 Merced (95340) ***(P-1558)***
Pacific Gas and Electric Co ....C....209 223-5259
12626 Jackson Gate Rd Jackson (95642) ***(P-8140)***
Pacific Gas and Electric Co ....C....707 579-6337
3965 Occidental Rd Santa Rosa (95401) ***(P-8141)***
Pacific Gas and Electric Co ....C....510 437-2222
6537 Foothill Blvd Oakland (94605) ***(P-8142)***
Pacific Gas and Electric Co ....C....650 513-0700
3400 Crow Canyon Rd San Ramon (94583) ***(P-8143)***
Pacific Gas and Electric Co ....C....925 757-2000
777 Railroad Ave Pittsburg (94565) ***(P-8144)***
Pacific Gas and Electric Co ....C....800 743-5000
1220 Andersen Dr San Rafael (94901) ***(P-8145)***
Pacific Gas and Electric Co ....C....559 263-7361
650 O St Fresno (93721) ***(P-8146)***
Pacific Gas and Electric Co ....C....209 942-5142
3955 Arch Rd Ste 100 Stockton (95215) ***(P-8147)***
Pacific Gas and Electric Co ....C....707 765-5118
210 Corona Rd Petaluma (94954) ***(P-8148)***
Pacific Gas and Electric Co ....C....530 229-4164
631 N Colusa St Willows (95988) ***(P-8149)***
Pacific Gas and Electric Co ....C....800 756-7243
111 Stony Cir Santa Rosa (95401) ***(P-8150)***
Pacific Gas and Electric Co ....C....916 904-9035
14550 Tuolumne Rd Sonora (95370) ***(P-8151)***
Pacific Gas and Electric Co ....C....530 894-4739
460 Rio Lindo Ave Chico (95926) ***(P-8212)***
Pacific Gas and Electric Co ....C....925 676-0948
4690 Evora Rd Concord (94520) ***(P-8152)***
Pacific Gas and Electric Co ....C....800 684-4648
160 Peabody Rd 166 Vacaville (95687) ***(P-8153)***
Pacific Gas and Electric Co ....C....800 743-5000
2-98 7th St Marysville (95901) ***(P-8154)***
Pacific Gas and Electric Co ....C....800 684-4648
235 Industrial Rd San Carlos (94070) ***(P-8155)***
Pacific Gas and Electric Co ....C....800 684-4648
3050 Geneva Ave Daly City (94014) ***(P-8156)***
Pacific Gas and Electric Co ....C....800 684-4648
624 W 15th St Merced (95340) ***(P-8157)***
Pacific Gas and Electric Co ....C....559 891-2143
1745 2nd St Selma (93662) ***(P-8158)***
Pacific Gas and Electric Co ....C....530 621-7237
4636 Missouri Flat Rd Placerville (95667) ***(P-8159)***
Pacific Gas and Electric Co ....C....530 532-4093
1567 Huntoon St Oroville (95965) ***(P-8160)***
Pacific Gas and Electric Co ....C....530 389-2202
33995 Alta Bonny Nook Rd Alta (95701) ***(P-8161)***
Pacific Gas and Electric Co ....C....530 365-7672
3600 Meadow View Dr Redding (96002) ***(P-8162)***
Pacific Gas and Electric Co ....C....530 474-3333
31295 Manton Viola Rd Manton (96059) ***(P-8163)***
Pacific Gas and Electric Co ....C....707 577-7283
3395 Mcmaude Pl Santa Rosa (95407) ***(P-8164)***
Pacific Gas and Electric Co ....C....530 889-3102
12840 Bill Clark Way Auburn (95602) ***(P-8165)***
Pacific Gas and Electric Co ....D....925 674-6305
1850 Gateway Blvd Ste 800 Concord (94520) ***(P-8166)***
Pacific Gas and Electric Co ....C....530 327-7633
202 Pearson Rd Paradise (95969) ***(P-8167)***
Pacific Gas and Electric Co ....C....209 942-1523
4040 West Ln Stockton (95204) ***(P-8168)***
Pacific Gas and Electric Co ....C....530 629-2128
Hwy 299 Willow Creek (95573) ***(P-8169)***
Pacific Gas and Electric Co ....C....510 770-2025
42105 Boyce Rd Fremont (94538) ***(P-8170)***
Pacific Gas and Electric Co ....C....707 444-0700
1000 King Salmon Ave Eureka (95503) ***(P-8171)***
Pacific Gas and Electric Co ....C....559 855-6112
33755 Old Mill Rd Auberry (93602) ***(P-8172)***
Pacific Gas and Electric Co ....C....209 826-5131
1028 6th St Los Banos (93635) ***(P-8173)***
Pacific Gas and Electric Co ....C....650 755-1236
450 Eastmoor Ave Daly City (94015) ***(P-8174)***
Pacific Gas and Electric Co ....C....209 576-6636
1524 N Carpenter Rd Modesto (95351) ***(P-8175)***
Pacific Gas and Electric Co ....C....800 743-5000
811 W J St Oakdale (95361) ***(P-8176)***
Pacific Gas and Electric Co ....C....209 942-1787
3136 Boeing Way Fl 2 Stockton (95206) ***(P-8177)***
Pacific Gas and Electric Co ....C....559 263-7152
2221 S Orange Ave Fresno (93725) ***(P-8178)***
Pacific Gas and Electric Co ....C....707 452-1983
5221 Quinn Rd Vacaville (95688) ***(P-8179)***
Pacific Gas and Electric Co ....C....916 275-2763
5555 Florin Perkins Rd Sacramento (95826) ***(P-8180)***
Pacific Gas and Electric Co ....C....530 896-4318
11239 Midway Chico (95928) ***(P-8181)***
Pacific Gas and Electric Co ....C....559 263-5438
502 E Grant Line Rd Tracy (95376) ***(P-8182)***
Pacific Gas and Electric Co ....C....925 373-2623
3797 1st St Livermore (94551) ***(P-8183)***
Pacific Gas and Electric Co ....C....530 757-5803
316 L St Davis (95616) ***(P-8184)***
Pacific Gas and Electric Co ....C....925 779-7745
2111 Hillcrest Ave Antioch (94509) ***(P-8185)***
Pacific Gas and Electric Co ....C....415 695-3513
2180 Harrison St San Francisco (94110) ***(P-8186)***
Pacific Gas and Electric Co ....C....408 945-6215
66 Ranch Dr Milpitas (95035) ***(P-8187)***
Pacific Gas and Electric Co ....C....209 295-2651
28570 Tiger Creek Rd Pioneer (95666) ***(P-8188)***
Pacific Gold Marketing Inc ....E....559 272-8168
745 Broadway St Fresno (93721) ***(P-1970)***
Pacific Grain & Foods LLC (PA) ....**C....559 276-2580**
4067 W Shaw Ave Ste 116 Fresno (93722) ***(P-9503)***
Pacific Grain and Foods, Fresno *Also called Pacific Grain & Foods LLC* ***(P-9503)***
Pacific Groservice Inc ....B....408 727-4826
567 Cinnabar St San Jose (95110) ***(P-9643)***
Pacific Hart Vscular Med Group ....E....209 464-3615
1801 E March Ln Ste D400 Stockton (95210) ***(P-15576)***
Pacific Harvest Seafoods Inc ....E....408 295-2455
800 Salinas Rd San Juan Bautista (95045) ***(P-9368)***
Pacific Harvest Trading, San Juan Bautista *Also called Pacific Harvest Seafoods Inc* ***(P-9368)***
Pacific Health Advantage (HQ) ....**E....415 281-8660**
221 Main St Ste 1500 San Francisco (94105) ***(P-18342)***
Pacific Heights Asset MGT LLC (PA) ....**E....415 398-8000**
600 Montgomery St # 1700 San Francisco (94111) ***(P-10766)***
Pacific Hmtlogy Oncology Assoc ....D....415 923-3012
2100 Webster St Ste 225 San Francisco (94115) ***(P-15577)***
Pacific Home Health, San Jose *Also called Support Staff Services Inc* ***(P-16950)***
Pacific Homecare Services, Stockton *Also called Pacific Coast Services Inc* ***(P-16922)***
Pacific Hotel Dev Ventr LP ....C....650 347-8260
625 El Camino Real Palo Alto (94301) ***(P-11344)***
Pacific Hotel Management LLC ....C....510 791-7700
39270 Cedar Blvd Newark (94560) ***(P-11345)***
Pacific Hotel Management LLC ....C....510 547-7888
1603 Powell St Emeryville (94608) ***(P-11346)***
Pacific Hotel Management LLC ....C....510 262-0700
3150 Garrity Way Richmond (94806) ***(P-11347)***
Pacific Hotel Management LLC ....C....650 328-2800
625 El Camino Real Palo Alto (94301) ***(P-11348)***
Pacific Housing Group LLC ....D....559 651-1133
1356 S Buttonwillow Ave Reedley (93654) ***(P-2050)***
Pacific Imaging Consultants, San Leandro *Also called San Leandro Imaging Ctr A Cal* ***(P-15664)***
Pacific Inptient Med Group Inc ....E....415 485-8824
9 Jeffrey Ct Novato (94945) ***(P-15578)***
Pacific Instruments Inc ....E....925 827-9010
4080 Pike Ln Concord (94520) ***(P-6915)***
Pacific Intl Rice Mills, Woodland *Also called Farmers Rice Cooperative* ***(P-9502)***
Pacific Intrlock Pvngstone Inc (PA) ....**F....831 637-9163**
1895 San Felipe Rd Hollister (95023) ***(P-4446)***
Pacific Intrnal Medicine Assoc ....D....415 923-3050
2100 Webster St Ste 423 San Francisco (94115) ***(P-15579)***
Pacific Landscapes Inc (PA) ....**E....707 829-8064**
2833 Old Gravenstein Hwy Sebastopol (95472) ***(P-433)***
Pacific Legal Foundation (PA) ....**E....916 419-7111**
930 G St Sacramento (95814) ***(P-17353)***
Pacific Leisure Management, San Francisco *Also called Okabe International Inc* ***(P-7820)***
Pacific Lighting & Electrical, Sacramento *Also called Mw McWong International Inc* ***(P-5747)***
Pacific Lodging Group ....E....707 875-2217
521 Hwy 1 Bodega (94922) ***(P-11349)***
Pacific Market International (PA) ....**D....650 238-1059**
395 Oyster Point Blvd # 225 South San Francisco (94080) ***(P-19600)***
Pacific Mdf Products Inc (PA) ....**E....916 660-1882**
4312 Anthony Ct Ste A Rocklin (95677) ***(P-3145)***
Pacific Medical Inc (PA) ....**C....800 726-9180**
1700 N Chrisman Rd Tracy (95304) ***(P-14351)***
Pacific Metal Buildings Inc ....F....530 438-2777
270 Old Highway 99 Maxwell (95955) ***(P-4854)***
Pacific Metro Electric Inc ....D....209 939-3222
3150 E Fremont St Stockton (95205) ***(P-1559)***
Pacific Metro LLC (PA) ....**B....408 201-5000**
18715 Madrone Pkwy Morgan Hill (95037) ***(P-18278)***
Pacific Modern Homes Inc ....E....916 685-9514
9723 Railroad St Elk Grove (95624) ***(P-4799)***
Pacific Mortgage Resources, Walnut Creek *Also called Diablo Realty* ***(P-10537)***
Pacific Mtl Hdlg Solutions Inc ....E....209 524-5194
2242 Hoover Ave Modesto (95354) ***(P-9084)***
Pacific Neon ....E....916 927-0527
2939 Academy Way Sacramento (95815) ***(P-7247)***
Pacific Netsoft Inc (PA) ....**E....800 330-6558**
910 E Hamilton Ave # 400 Campbell (95008) ***(P-12116)***
Pacific Northwest Pubg Co Inc ....B....916 321-1828
2100 Q St Sacramento (95816) ***(P-3471)***

ALPHABETIC

Pacific Nurseries, Colma *Also called Baldocchi and Sons Inc* ***(P-9625)***
Pacific Paper Tube Inc (PA) .... **E** **510 562-8823**
4343 E Fremont St Stockton (95215) ***(P-3368)***
Pacific Park Management .... D 415 440-4840
1300 Fillmore St San Francisco (94115) ***(P-19377)***
Pacific Park Management Inc .... D 510 836-7730
989 Franklin St Oakland (94607) ***(P-14514)***
Pacific Partners MGT Svcs Inc .... D 650 358-5804
1051 E Hillsdale Blvd Foster City (94404) ***(P-19378)***
Pacific Partners MSI, Foster City *Also called Pacific Partners MGT Svcs Inc* ***(P-19378)***
Pacific Plaza Imports Inc (PA) .... **F** **925 349-4000**
3018 Willow Pass Rd # 102 Concord (94519) ***(P-2828)***
Pacific Powder Coating Inc .... E 916 381-1154
8637 23rd Ave Sacramento (95826) ***(P-4943)***
Pacific Power & Systems Inc .... E 707 437-2300
4970 Peabody Rd Fairfield (94533) ***(P-1560)***
Pacific Press Corporation .... F 408 292-3422
2350 S 10th St San Jose (95112) ***(P-3472)***
Pacific Pride, Hollister *Also called Dassels Petroleum Inc* ***(P-9532)***
Pacific Pulmonary Services Co, Petaluma *Also called Braden Prtners LP A Cal Ltd PR* ***(P-8776)***
Pacific Racing Association .... C 510 559-7300
1100 Eastshore Hwy Albany (94710) ***(P-14917)***
Pacific Redwood Medical Group .... D 707 462-7900
275 Hospital Dr Ukiah (95482) ***(P-15580)***
Pacific Res Inst For Pub Plicy (PA) .... **F** **415 989-0833**
1 Embarcadero Ctr Ste 350 San Francisco (94111) ***(P-19179)***
Pacific Restoration Inc .... E 707 588-8226
373 Blodgett St Cotati (94931) ***(P-11983)***
Pacific Retirement Svcs Inc .... D 530 753-1450
1515 Shasta Dr Ofc Davis (95616) ***(P-18154)***
Pacific Ridge Builders Inc .... E 408 627-4765
1500 Wyatt Dr Ste 14 Santa Clara (95054) ***(P-935)***
Pacific Rim Plumbing .... E 925 443-3333
2283 Research Dr Livermore (94550) ***(P-1332)***
Pacific Roller Die Co Inc .... F 510 244-7286
1321 W Winton Ave Hayward (94545) ***(P-5587)***
Pacific Rubber & Packing Inc (PA) .... **E** **650 595-5888**
1160 Industrial Rd Ste 3 San Carlos (94070) ***(P-9125)***
Pacific Sanitation, Windsor *Also called M & M Services Inc* ***(P-8339)***
Pacific Scientific Energetic (HQ) .... **B** **831 637-3731**
3601 Union Rd Hollister (95023) ***(P-4166)***
Pacific Screw Products Inc .... D 650 583-9682
1331 Old County Rd Ste C Belmont (94002) ***(P-5588)***
Pacific Secured Equities Inc .... B 916 677-2500
6020 West Oaks Blvd # 100 Rocklin (95765) ***(P-19601)***
Pacific Service Credit Union (PA) .... **D** **888 858-6878**
3000 Clayton Rd Concord (94519) ***(P-9801)***
Pacific Sfood - Sacramento LLC .... C 916 419-5500
1420 National Dr Sacramento (95834) ***(P-9329)***
Pacific Shoring Products LLC (PA) .... **D** **707 575-9014**
265 Roberts Ave Santa Rosa (95407) ***(P-4944)***
Pacific Southwest Cont LLC (PA) .... **B** **209 526-0444**
4530 Leckron Rd Modesto (95357) ***(P-3377)***
Pacific Southwest Cont LLC .... E 209 526-0444
568 S Riverside Dr Modesto (95354) ***(P-7698)***
Pacific Southwest Cont LLC .... E 209 526-0444
671 Mariposa Rd Modesto (95354) ***(P-3378)***
Pacific Standard Print, Sacramento *Also called American Lithographers Inc* ***(P-3619)***
Pacific State Bank (PA) .... **E** **209 870-3200**
115 James Dr W Ste 140 Stockton (95207) ***(P-9742)***
Pacific States Felt Mfg Co Inc .... F 510 783-2357
23850 Clawiter Rd Ste 20 Hayward (94545) ***(P-4205)***
Pacific Steel Group .... E 707 669-3136
2301 Napa Vallejo Hwy NAPA (94558) ***(P-4858)***
Pacific Steel Group .... D 858 251-1100
355 S Vasco Rd Livermore (94550) ***(P-4859)***
Pacific Sthwest Cnfrnce of Eva .... C 831 335-9133
1050 Lockhart Gulch Rd Scotts Valley (95066) ***(P-10398)***
Pacific Stone Inc .... E 925 680-8741
1375 Franquette Ave Ste F Concord (94520) ***(P-1717)***
Pacific Structures Sc Inc (PA) .... **C** **415 970-5434**
457 Minna St San Francisco (94103) ***(P-1899)***
Pacific Sttes Envmtl Cntrs Inc .... E 925 803-4333
11555 Dublin Blvd Dublin (94568) ***(P-936)***
Pacific Sun .... F 415 488-8100
445 Center St Healdsburg (95448) ***(P-3511)***
Pacific Supply, North Highlands *Also called Pacific Coast Supply LLC* ***(P-3213)***
Pacific Surfacing .... E 510 440-9494
2066 Warm Springs Ct Fremont (94539) ***(P-1900)***
Pacific Tech Products Ontario, Union City *Also called California Performance Packg* ***(P-4239)***
Pacific Telemanagement Svcs, San Ramon *Also called Jaroth Inc* ***(P-1525)***
Pacific Towing, Stockton *Also called Covey Auto Express Inc* ***(P-14659)***
Pacific Truck Tank Inc .... E 916 379-9280
7029 Flrin Prkins Rd Ste Sacramento (95828) ***(P-6568)***
Pacific Union Club .... D 415 775-1234
1000 California St San Francisco (94108) ***(P-18446)***
Pacific Union Co .... D 415 789-8686
1550 Tiburon Blvd Ste U Belvedere (94920) ***(P-10634)***
Pacific Union Co .... D 925 258-0090
51 Moraga Way Ste 1 Orinda (94563) ***(P-10635)***
Pacific Union Co .... D 415 474-6600
1699 Van Ness Ave San Francisco (94109) ***(P-10636)***
Pacific Union Homes Inc (PA) .... **D** **925 314-3800**
675 Hartz Ave Ste 300 Danville (94526) ***(P-10712)***
Pacific Union Intl Inc .... D 415 461-8686
23 Ross Cmn Ross (94957) ***(P-10637)***
Pacific Union Intl Inc .... D 707 934-2300
135 W Napa St Ste 200 Sonoma (95476) ***(P-9944)***
Pacific Union Intl Inc .... D 510 338-1379
1900 Mountain Blvd # 102 Oakland (94611) ***(P-10638)***
Pacific Union Intl Inc (PA) .... **B** **415 929-7100**
1 Letterman Dr Bldg C San Francisco (94129) ***(P-10639)***
Pacific Union RE Group (HQ) .... **D** **415 929-7100**
1699 Van Ness Ave 2 San Francisco (94109) ***(P-10640)***
Pacific Union Residental Brkg .... E 510 339-6460
1900 Mountain Blvd # 102 Oakland (94611) ***(P-10641)***
Pacific Union Residential Brkg, Orinda *Also called Pacific Union Co* ***(P-10635)***
Pacific West Forest Products .... F 530 899-7313
13434 Browns Valley Dr Chico (95973) ***(P-4860)***
Pacific West Security Inc .... D 801 748-1034
1587 Schallenberger Rd San Jose (95131) ***(P-14143)***
Pacific Western Systems Inc (PA) .... **E** **650 961-8855**
505 E Evelyn Ave Mountain View (94041) ***(P-6777)***
Pacific Ygnacio Corporation .... C 925 939-3275
201 California St Ste 500 San Francisco (94111) ***(P-10484)***
Pacifica Care Center .... D 650 355-5622
385 Esplanade Ave Pacifica (94044) ***(P-16089)***
Pacifica Hotel Company .... E 650 726-9000
2400 Cabrillo Hwy S Half Moon Bay (94019) ***(P-11350)***
Pacifica Linda Mar Inc .... D 650 359-4800
751 San Pedro Terrace Rd Pacifica (94044) ***(P-16090)***
Pacifica Nursing & Rehab Ctr, Pacifica *Also called Pacifica Care Center* ***(P-16089)***
Pacificare, Sacramento *Also called United Behavioral Health* ***(P-17084)***
Pacira Cryotech Inc .... E 800 442-0989
46400 Fremont Blvd Fremont (94538) ***(P-19835)***
Packageone Inc (PA) .... **E** **559 662-1910**
401 S Granada Dr Ste 100 Madera (93637) ***(P-3361)***
Packaging Aids Corporation (PA) .... **E** **415 454-4868**
25 Tiburon St San Rafael (94901) ***(P-5201)***
Packaging America - Sacramento, McClellan *Also called PCA Central Cal Corrugated LLC* ***(P-3363)***
Packaging Equity Holdings LLC .... B 209 404-9553
2334 M St Ste 2893 Merced (95340) ***(P-3369)***
Packaging Innovators LLC .... D 925 371-2000
6850 Brisa St Livermore (94550) ***(P-9217)***
Packaging Plus .... E 209 858-9200
3816 S Willow Ave Ste 102 Fresno (93725) ***(P-3362)***
Packard Childrens Hlth Aliance .... D 650 497-8000
725 Welch Rd Palo Alto (94304) ***(P-15581)***
Packet Fusion Inc (PA) .... **E** **650 292-6000**
4301 Hacienda Dr Ste 400 Pleasanton (94588) ***(P-19836)***
Packlane Inc .... E 855 289-7687
548 Market St 90143 San Francisco (94104) ***(P-14352)***
Pacon Mfg Inc .... E 925 961-0445
4777 Bennett Dr Ste H Livermore (94551) ***(P-5589)***
Pactech, San Jose *Also called Saco Enterprises Inc* ***(P-8066)***
Pactron .... D 408 329-5500
3000 Patrick Henry Dr Santa Clara (95054) ***(P-5955)***
Pactum Ai Inc .... E 669 289-9041
800 W El Cmino Real Ste 1 Mountain View (94040) ***(P-13359)***
Pacwood, Cottonwood *Also called Plum Valley Inc* ***(P-3100)***
Paddack Almond Hlling Shelling, Escalon *Also called Paddack Enterprises* ***(P-2450)***
Paddack Enterprises .... F 209 838-1536
27052 State Highway 120 Escalon (95320) ***(P-2450)***
Padilla, David A MD, Roseville *Also called Sutter Valley Med Foundation* ***(P-19406)***
Paganini Companies, San Francisco *Also called Paganini Electric Corporation* ***(P-1561)***
Paganini Electric Corporation .... C 415 575-3900
190 Hubbell St Ste 200 San Francisco (94107) ***(P-1561)***
Page One Automotive (PA) .... **E** **415 467-1000**
211 S Hill Dr Ste D Brisbane (94005) ***(P-14472)***
Pagebites Inc .... E 650 353-0546
395 Page Mill Rd Palo Alto (94306) ***(P-12664)***
Pagerduty Inc (PA) .... **A** **844 800-3889**
600 Townsend St Ste 200 San Francisco (94103) ***(P-13360)***
Paige LLC .... E 415 660-2970
2237 Fillmore St San Francisco (94115) ***(P-2964)***
Paige Denim, San Francisco *Also called Paige LLC* ***(P-2964)***
Paige Price & Co .... D 559 299-9540
570 N Magnolia Ave # 100 Clovis (93611) ***(P-18981)***
Pain Diagnstc & Trtmnt Ctr LLP .... E 916 231-8755
2805 J St Ste 200 Sacramento (95816) ***(P-15582)***
Pajaro Vly Prvntion Stdnt Asss .... D 831 728-6445
335 E Lake Ave Watsonville (95076) ***(P-17668)***
Pak Inc .... D 916 944-1428
6108 Lincoln Ave Carmichael (95608) ***(P-9668)***
Palace Business Solutions, Santa Cruz *Also called Trowbridge Enterprises* ***(P-9211)***
Paladin Private Security, Sacramento *Also called Paladin Prtction Spcalists Inc* ***(P-14084)***
Paladin Prtction Spcalists Inc .... C 916 331-3175
320 Commerce Cir Sacramento (95815) ***(P-14084)***
Palamida Inc .... E 415 777-9400
215 2nd St Lbby 2 San Francisco (94105) ***(P-8731)***
Palantir Technologies Inc Pac .... D 650 833-9460
100 Hamilton Ave Ste 300 Palo Alto (94301) ***(P-12665)***
Palantir Usg Inc (HQ) .... **E** **650 815-0200**
635 Waverley St Palo Alto (94301) ***(P-12666)***
Palcare Inc .... E 650 340-1289
945 California Dr Burlingame (94010) ***(P-17988)***
Palecek Imports Inc (PA) .... **D** **510 236-7730**
601 Parr Blvd Richmond (94801) ***(P-8502)***
Palex Metals Inc .... E 408 496-6111
3601 Thomas Rd Santa Clara (95054) ***(P-4800)***
Palio D'Asti, San Francisco *Also called Ristoranti Piemontesi Inc* ***(P-11729)***
Pallets Unlimited Inc .... F 916 408-1914
2390 Athens Ave Lincoln (95648) ***(P-3227)***

Palm Inc (HQ) ....B....408 617-7000
950 W Maude Ave Sunnyvale (94085) *(P-5860)*
Palm Drive Healthcare District, Sebastopol *Also called County of Sonoma (P-16340)*
Palm Haven Care Center, Manteca *Also called Palm Haven Nursing & Rehab LLC (P-16091)*
Palm Haven Nursing & Rehab LLC ....C....209 823-1788
469 E North St Manteca (95336) *(P-16091)*
Palm Latin America Inc ....E....650 857-1501
1501 Page Mill Rd Palo Alto (94304) *(P-5267)*
Palmaz Vineyards, NAPA *Also called Cedar Knoll Vineyards Inc (P-2527)*
Palo Alpo Medical Foudation, Palo Alto *Also called Sutter Health (P-16629)*
Palo Alto Community Child Care ....D....650 855-9828
890 Escondido Rd Stanford (94305) *(P-17989)*
Palo Alto Egg and Food Svc Co ....E....510 456-2420
6691 Clark Ave Newark (94560) *(P-9282)*
Palo Alto Food Company, Newark *Also called Palo Alto Egg and Food Svc Co (P-9282)*
Palo Alto Hlls Golf Cntry CLB ....D....650 948-1800
3000 Alexis Dr Palo Alto (94304) *(P-11726)*
Palo Alto Inn ....D....650 493-4222
4238 El Camino Real Palo Alto (94306) *(P-11351)*
Palo Alto Med Fndtion For Hlth, Palo Alto *Also called Sutter Bay Medical Foundation (P-15709)*
Palo Alto Med Fndtion For Hlth, Santa Cruz *Also called Visiting Nrse Assn of Snta Cru (P-16965)*
Palo Alto Networks Inc (PA) ....B....408 753-4000
3000 Tannery Way Santa Clara (95054) *(P-5403)*
Palo Alto Nursing Center, Palo Alto *Also called Covenant Care California LLC (P-15965)*
Palo Alto Research Center Inc ....C....650 812-4000
3333 Coyote Hill Rd Palo Alto (94304) *(P-19097)*
Palo Alto VA Medical Center, Palo Alto *Also called Veterans Health Administration (P-15792)*
Palo Alto Vineyard MGT LLC ....D....707 996-7725
50 Adobe Canyon Rd Kenwood (95452) *(P-363)*
Palo Alto Vterans Inst For RES ....C....650 858-3970
3801 Miranda Ave 101a Palo Alto (94304) *(P-19228)*
Palpilot International Corp (PA) ....E....408 855-8866
500 Yosemite Dr Milpitas (95035) *(P-5956)*
Pamelas Product Inc ....E....707 462-6605
1924 4th St San Rafael (94901) *(P-2397)*
Pamf - PA Division, Santa Clara *Also called Sutter Bay Medical Foundation (P-15710)*
Pan American Body Shop Inc (PA) ....E....408 289-8745
555 Burke St San Jose (95112) *(P-14531)*
Pan Magna Group ....E....707 433-5508
1141 Grant Ave Healdsburg (95448) *(P-2677)*
Pan Pacific Plastics Mfg Inc ....E....510 785-6888
26551 Danti Ct Hayward (94545) *(P-4309)*
Pan Pacific Rv Centers Inc (PA) ....E....209 234-2000
252 Yettner Rd French Camp (95231) *(P-14581)*
Pan Pennsylvania LLC (HQ) ....D....415 903-2100
225 Bush St Ste 1800 San Francisco (94104) *(P-10808)*
Pan Washington LLC (HQ) ....E....415 903-2100
225 Bush St Ste 1800 San Francisco (94104) *(P-10809)*
Pan-Cal Investment Company Inc ....E....408 248-6600
4125 Blackford Ave # 200 San Jose (95117) *(P-784)*
Pan-O-Rama Baking Inc ....E....415 522-5500
500 Florida St San Francisco (94110) *(P-2398)*
Pan-Pacific Mechanical LLC ....B....650 561-8810
48363 Fremont Blvd Fremont (94538) *(P-1333)*
Pana-Pacific, Fresno *Also called Brix Group Inc (P-8898)*
Pana-Pacific Corporation (HQ) ....C....559 457-4700
838 N Laverne Ave Fresno (93727) *(P-6589)*
Panalpina Inc ....E....650 825-3036
400 Oyster Point Blvd # 300 South San Francisco (94080) *(P-7848)*
Panapacific Shipping, Fresno *Also called Brix Group Inc (P-6509)*
Panasas Inc (PA) ....D....408 215-6800
2680 N 1st St Ste 150 San Jose (95134) *(P-12667)*
Pandora Data Systems Inc ....D....831 429-8900
10 Victor Sq Ste 250 Scotts Valley (95066) *(P-13361)*
Pandora Media LLC (HQ) ....A....510 451-4100
2100 Franklin St Ste 700 Oakland (94612) *(P-8030)*
Panelized Solar, Modesto *Also called Panelized Structures Inc (P-1826)*
Panelized Solar Inc ....E....209 343-8600
5731 Stoddard Rd Modesto (95356) *(P-1334)*
Panelized Structures Inc (PA) ....E....480 969-4447
5731 Stoddard Rd Modesto (95356) *(P-1826)*
Panera Bread, San Francisco *Also called Pan Washington LLC (P-10809)*
Panera Bread, San Francisco *Also called Pan Pennsylvania LLC (P-10808)*
Pannaway, Fremont *Also called Enablence Systems Inc (P-13141)*
Pano Logic Inc ....E....650 743-1773
1100 La Avenida St Ste A Mountain View (94043) *(P-5404)*
Panoche Water District ....E....209 364-6136
52027 W Althea Ave Firebaugh (93622) *(P-8258)*
Pantheon Systems Inc (PA) ....D....855 927-9387
717 California St San Francisco (94108) *(P-12668)*
Pantronix Corporation ....C....510 656-5898
2710 Lakeview Ct Fremont (94538) *(P-6249)*
Panzura LLC ....C....408 457-8504
2880 Stevens Creek Blvd San Jose (95128) *(P-13646)*
Pape Material Handling Inc ....D....510 659-4100
47132 Kato Rd Fremont (94538) *(P-9085)*
Pape Trucks Inc ....D....559 268-4344
2892 E Jensen Ave Fresno (93706) *(P-14582)*
Pape' Kenworth, Fresno *Also called Pape Trucks Inc (P-14582)*
Paper Pulp & Film ....E....559 233-1151
2822 S Maple Ave Fresno (93725) *(P-3404)*
Paper Culture LLC ....E....650 249-0800
475 El Cmino Real Ste 202 Millbrae (94030) *(P-9210)*
Papola Enterprises Inc ....D....530 272-8885
167 S Auburn St Grass Valley (95945) *(P-10642)*
Pappas Telecasting Company, Fresno *Also called Kmph Fox 26 (P-8048)*
Pappy's Fine Foods, Fresno *Also called Pappys Meat Company Inc (P-2931)*
Pappys Meat Company Inc ....E....559 291-0218
5663 E Fountain Way Fresno (93727) *(P-2931)*
Para & Palli Inc ....D....209 826-0790
931 Idaho Ave Los Banos (93635) *(P-16092)*
Paracor Medical Inc ....F....408 207-1050
19200 Stevns Crk Blvd Cupertino (95014) *(P-7121)*
Paracorp Incorporated (PA) ....D....916 576-7000
2804 Gateway Oaks Dr # 100 Sacramento (95833) *(P-17354)*
Paracosma Inc ....D....650 924-9896
2081 Norris Rd Walnut Creek (94596) *(P-12669)*
Parade Technologies Inc ....D....408 329-5540
2720 Orchard Pkwy San Jose (95134) *(P-8945)*
Paradigm Staffing Solutions ....E....510 663-7860
1970 Broadway Ste 615 Oakland (94612) *(P-12117)*
Paradise Ambulance Service, Chico *Also called First Responder Ems Inc (P-7383)*
Paradise Medical Group Inc ....E....530 877-3951
6470 Pentz Rd Ste A Paradise (95969) *(P-15583)*
Paradise Police Dept, Paradise *Also called Town of Paradise (P-17382)*
PARADISE RIDGE FAMILY RESOURCE, Paradise *Also called Youth For Change (P-17791)*
PARADISE VALLEY ESTATES, Fairfield *Also called Northern CA Retiredd Ofcrs (P-18148)*
Paradiso Mechanical Inc ....E....510 614-8390
2600 Williams St San Leandro (94577) *(P-2051)*
Paragon Controls Incorporated ....F....707 579-1424
2371 Circadian Way Santa Rosa (95407) *(P-6703)*
Paragon Health & Rehab CT ....E....559 638-3578
1090 E Dinuba Ave Reedley (93654) *(P-17053)*
Paragon Heating & AC, Stockton *Also called Paragon Ventures Inc (P-1335)*
Paragon Industries Inc (PA) ....D....559 275-5000
4285 N Golden State Blvd Fresno (93722) *(P-4519)*
Paragon Industries II Inc ....C....559 275-5000
4285 N Golden State Blvd Fresno (93722) *(P-4520)*
Paragon Label, Petaluma *Also called Mrs Grossmans Paper Company (P-3399)*
Paragon Machine Works Inc ....D....510 232-3223
253 S 25th St Richmond (94804) *(P-5590)*
Paragon Products Limited LLC (PA) ....E....916 941-9717
4475 Golden Foothill Pkwy El Dorado Hills (95762) *(P-9086)*
Paragon Swiss ....E....408 748-1617
545 Aldo Ave Ste 1 Santa Clara (95054) *(P-5591)*
Paragon Ventures Inc ....E....209 466-3530
1722 E Flora St Stockton (95205) *(P-1335)*
Parallax Incorporated ....E....916 624-8333
599 Menlo Dr Ste 100 Rocklin (95765) *(P-5268)*
Parallax Research, Rocklin *Also called Parallax Incorporated (P-5268)*
Parallel Advisors LLC ....D....866 627-6984
150 Spear St Ste 950 San Francisco (94105) *(P-10054)*
Parallel Machines Inc ....E....669 467-2638
2445 Augustine Dr Ste 150 Santa Clara (95054) *(P-13362)*
Parallelm, Santa Clara *Also called Parallel Machines Inc (P-13362)*
Parametric Manufacturing Inc ....F....408 654-9845
3465 Edward Ave Santa Clara (95054) *(P-5592)*
Paramit Corporation (PA) ....C....408 782-5600
18735 Madrone Pkwy Morgan Hill (95037) *(P-5957)*
Paramount Equity, Roseville *Also called Loanpal LLC (P-9914)*
Paramount Food Processing, Del Rey *Also called Del Rey Juice Co (P-2291)*
Paramount Investigations, San Jose *Also called Yosh Enterprises Inc (P-14112)*
Paramount Theatre of Arts Inc ....D....510 893-2300
2025 Broadway Oakland (94612) *(P-14855)*
Parasec, Sacramento *Also called Paracorp Incorporated (P-17354)*
Paratransit Incorporated (PA) ....C....916 429-2009
2501 Florin Rd Sacramento (95822) *(P-7394)*
Parc, Palo Alto *Also called Palo Alto Research Center Inc (P-19097)*
Parc 55 Hotel, San Francisco *Also called Rp/Kinetic Parc 55 Owner LLC (P-11422)*
Parc 55 Lessee LLC ....D....415 392-8000
55 Cyril Magnin St San Francisco (94102) *(P-11352)*
Parc Management LLC ....E....925 609-1364
1950 Waterworld Pkwy Concord (94520) *(P-15225)*
Parc Specialty Contractors ....D....916 992-5405
1400 Vinci Ave Sacramento (95838) *(P-2052)*
Parc Waterworld LLC ....B....925 609-1364
1950 Waterworld Pkwy Concord (94520) *(P-15044)*
Parca, Burlingame *Also called Partners Advctes For Rmrkble C (P-17669)*
Parco LLC ....E....510 865-0100
1546 Webster St Alameda (94501) *(P-11353)*
Parducci Wine Estates LLC ....E....707 463-5350
501 Parducci Rd Ukiah (95482) *(P-2678)*
Parentals Place Parent Educatn, San Rafael *Also called Jewish Family and Chld Svcs (P-17627)*
Parents & Friends Inc ....E....707 964-4940
306 E Redwood Ave Fort Bragg (95437) *(P-18155)*
Parents Place, Palo Alto *Also called Jewish Family and Chld Svcs (P-17626)*
Pareto Networks Inc ....D....877 727-8020
1183 Bordeaux Dr Ste 22 Sunnyvale (94089) *(P-7981)*
Parex Usa Inc ....F....510 444-2497
111290 S Vallejo Ct French Camp (95231) *(P-8631)*
Paribas Asset Management Inc ....C....415 772-1300
1 Front St Fl 23 San Francisco (94111) *(P-9837)*
Paribas Asset Management Inc ....C....415 772-1300
1 Front St Fl 23 San Francisco (94111) *(P-9838)*
Park Avenue Cleaners Inc ....E....209 914-1265
2529 N Tracy Blvd Tracy (95376) *(P-11629)*
Park Avenue Turf Inc ....E....707 823-8899
3075 Old Gravenstein Hwy Sebastopol (95472) *(P-493)*
Park Central Ht San Francisco, San Francisco *Also called Viva Soma Lessee Inc (P-19419)*
Park Cntl Care Rhblitation Ctr ....E....510 797-5300
2100 Parkside Dr Fremont (94536) *(P-16093)*

ALPHABETIC

Park DDS MPH Inc (PA) ....E.......**209 744-0463**
1067 C St Ste 125 Galt (95632) ***(P-15853)***
Park Greenhouses ....E.......209 599-7545
12813 W Ripon Rd Ripon (95366) ***(P-132)***
Park Hotels & Resorts Inc ....C.......510 635-5000
1 Hegenberger Rd Oakland (94621) ***(P-11354)***
Park Management Corp ....C.......707 643-6722
1001 Fairgrounds Dr Vallejo (94589) ***(P-15045)***
Park Merced LLC (PA) ....E.......**209 722-3944**
3144 G St Merced (95340) ***(P-16094)***
Park n Fly Llc ....E.......650 877-8438
101 Terminal Ct South San Francisco (94080) ***(P-14515)***
Park Plaza Hotel ....E.......510 635-5300
150 Hegenberger Rd Oakland (94621) ***(P-11355)***
Park Plaza San Jose Arprt LLC ....E.......408 453-5340
1355 N 4th St San Jose (95112) ***(P-11356)***
Park Shadelands Medical Offs, Walnut Creek *Also called Kaiser Foundation Hospitals* ***(P-16398)***
Park US Lessee Holdings LLC ....D.......707 887-7838
1 Doubletree Dr Rohnert Park (94928) ***(P-11357)***
Park View Gardens, Santa Rosa *Also called Ensign Group Inc* ***(P-15990)***
Park West Landscape Inc ....D.......925 560-9390
836 Jury Ct Ste 10 San Jose (95112) ***(P-494)***
Park's Prtg & Lithographic Co, Modesto *Also called Village Instant Printing Inc* ***(P-3709)***
Parker Kern Nard Wnzel Prof Co ....D.......559 449-2558
7112 N Fresno St Ste 300 Fresno (93720) ***(P-17355)***
Parker Landscape Dev Inc ....E.......916 383-4071
6011 Franklin Blvd Sacramento (95824) ***(P-434)***
Parker Plastics Inc ....E.......707 994-6363
12762 Highway 29 Lower Lake (95457) ***(P-4310)***
Parker Powis Inc ....D.......510 848-2463
2929 5th St Berkeley (94710) ***(P-5425)***
Parker-Hannifin Corporation ....A.......209 521-7860
1640 Cummins Dr Modesto (95358) ***(P-5230)***
Parkhurst Terrace ....D.......831 685-0800
100 Parkhurst Cir Aptos (95003) ***(P-761)***
Parkmerced Investors LLC ....E.......877 243-5544
3711 19th Ave San Francisco (94132) ***(P-12058)***
Parks and Recreation Dept, Carmichael *Also called County of Sacramento* ***(P-14992)***
Parks Silverwood, Sebastopol *Also called Silverwood Management Inc* ***(P-10460)***
Parkside Lending LLC ....D.......415 771-3700
180 Redwood St Ste 250 San Francisco (94102) ***(P-9918)***
Parkview Healthcare Center, Hayward *Also called Mariner Health Care Inc* ***(P-16049)***
Parliament Inc (PA) ....E.......**415 702-0624**
1307 El Centro Ave Oakland (94602) ***(P-11358)***
Parma Floors Inc ....F.......408 638-0247
2079 Hartog Ave S San Jose (95131) ***(P-7265)***
Parmar Ashok ....D.......559 661-1131
1855 W Cleveland Ave Madera (93637) ***(P-11359)***
Parmatech Corporation ....D.......707 778-2266
2221 Pine View Way Petaluma (94954) ***(P-4590)***
Parmeter Logging and Excav Inc ....E.......707 632-5610
6040 Cazadero Hwy Cazadero (95421) ***(P-1971)***
Parrott Investment Company Inc ....E.......530 342-4505
8369 Hugh Baber Ln Chico (95928) ***(P-185)***
Parsable Inc (PA) ....C.......**888 681-2119**
115 Sansome St Ste 500 San Francisco (94104) ***(P-12670)***
Parthenon Capital LLC ....A.......415 913-3900
4 Embarcadero Ctr # 2500 San Francisco (94111) ***(P-10875)***
Particle Industries Inc ....D.......415 316-1024
126 Post St Fl 4 San Francisco (94108) ***(P-12671)***
Partition Specialties, Novato *Also called Psi3g Inc* ***(P-8520)***
Partition Specialties, Hayward *Also called PSI Management Team Inc* ***(P-8769)***
Partners Advctes For Rmrkble C ....D.......650 312-0730
800 Airport Blvd Ste 320 Burlingame (94010) ***(P-17669)***
Partners In School Innovation ....D.......415 824-6196
1060 Tennessee St San Francisco (94107) ***(P-19837)***
Partnership Health Plan Cal ....B.......707 863-4100
4665 Business Center Dr Fairfield (94534) ***(P-10148)***
Partsflex Inc ....E.......408 677-7121
1775 Park St Ste 77 Selma (93662) ***(P-3047)***
Partyaid, Santa Cruz *Also called Anomalies International Inc* ***(P-2782)***
Paryroll Department, Redwood City *Also called Verity Health System Cal Inc* ***(P-16712)***
Pas Livermore, Livermore *Also called Performance Abatement Svcs Inc* ***(P-2055)***
Pasadena Hotel Dev Ventr LP ....D.......650 347-8260
400 S El Camino Real # 200 San Mateo (94402) ***(P-11360)***
Pasadena Newspapers Inc ....C.......707 442-1711
930 6th St Eureka (95501) ***(P-3473)***
Pasatiempo III Investments ....D.......831 423-5000
555 Highway 17 Santa Cruz (95060) ***(P-11361)***
Pascal Systems, West Sacramento *Also called Heco Inc* ***(P-5213)***
Pasha Freight, San Rafael *Also called Pasha Group* ***(P-7849)***
Pasha Group (PA) ....B.......**415 927-6400**
4040 Civic Center Dr # 350 San Rafael (94903) ***(P-7849)***
Pasha Hawaii Trnspt Lines LLC ....D.......510 271-1400
1425 Maritime St Oakland (94607) ***(P-7714)***
Paskenta Band Nomlaki Indians ....B.......530 528-3538
2655 Everett Freeman Way Corning (96021) ***(P-18246)***
Pass Laboratories Inc ....F.......530 878-5350
13395 New Arprt Rd Ste G Auburn (95602) ***(P-5767)***
Passages Adult Research Center, Chico *Also called Aging California Department* ***(P-17409)***
Passport Health LLC ....E.......925 239-8794
3478 Buskirk Ave Ste 1000 Pleasant Hill (94523) ***(P-15584)***
Passport Hlth Plsant Hl Trvl C, Pleasant Hill *Also called Passport Health LLC* ***(P-15584)***
Pasta Prima, Benicia *Also called Valley Fine Foods Company Inc* ***(P-2312)***
Pasta Shop (PA) ....D.......**510 250-6005**
5655 College Ave Ste 201 Oakland (94618) ***(P-9474)***
Pasta Sonoma LLC ....E.......707 584-0800
640 Martin Ave Ste 1 Rohnert Park (94928) ***(P-2865)***
Patel Plliam Hbli A Prof Med C ....E.......209 832-8984
644 W 12th St Tracy (95376) ***(P-15585)***
Patelco Credit Union (PA) ....C.......**800 358-8228**
3 Park Pl Dublin (94568) ***(P-9802)***
Patent and Trademark Office US ....D.......831 332-7127
26 S 4th St San Jose (95112) ***(P-9759)***
Pathfinder Services, Folsom *Also called Location Services LLC* ***(P-7887)***
Pathgroup San Francisco LLC (HQ) ....E.......**415 898-7649**
1615 Hill Rd Ste B Novato (94947) ***(P-15586)***
Pathology Associates ....C.......559 326-2800
305 Park Creek Dr Clovis (93611) ***(P-16769)***
Pathwater Inc ....E.......510 518-0014
44137 Fremont Blvd Fremont (94538) ***(P-2797)***
Pathway To Choices Inc ....E.......510 724-9044
751 Belmont Way Pinole (94564) ***(P-17670)***
PATHWAYS, Yuba City *Also called Midvalley Recovery Facilities* ***(P-17046)***
Pathways, Oakland *Also called Hospice & Home Health of E Bay* ***(P-16894)***
Pathways Home Health ....E.......650 634-0133
395 Oyster Point Blvd # 12 South San Francisco (94080) ***(P-17166)***
Patient Accounting, Sunnyvale *Also called Sutter Bay Medical Foundation* ***(P-15711)***
Patient Home Monitoring Inc (HQ) ....D.......**415 693-9690**
550 Kearny St Ste 300 San Francisco (94108) ***(P-16923)***
Patients Hospital ....D.......530 225-8700
2900 Eureka Way Redding (96001) ***(P-16477)***
Patientsafe Solutions Inc (PA) ....D.......**858 746-3100**
525 Race St Ste 150 San Jose (95126) ***(P-12672)***
Patin Vineyard Management Inc ....E.......707 838-6665
1601 Sanders Rd Windsor (95492) ***(P-384)***
Patio Espanol Restaurant, San Francisco *Also called Iberia Catering Inc* ***(P-11720)***
Patra Corporation (PA) ....C.......**415 595-9987**
1107 Inv Blvd Ste 100 El Dorado Hills (95762) ***(P-10078)***
Patreon Inc (PA) ....C.......**415 967-2735**
600 Townsend St Ste 500 San Francisco (94103) ***(P-12673)***
Patrick Baginski ....E.......530 544-8873
828 Eloise Ave South Lake Tahoe (96150) ***(P-495)***
Patrick J Ruane Inc ....D.......650 616-7676
283 Wattis Way South San Francisco (94080) ***(P-1697)***
Patrick K Willis and Co Inc ....B.......800 398-6480
5118 Rbert J Mathews Pkwy El Dorado Hills (95762) ***(P-14353)***
Patrick L Roetzer DDS Inc ....E.......707 745-8002
142 E D St Benicia (94510) ***(P-15854)***
Patrick Rynearson Rulin ....F.......209 943-2705
5320 Section Ave Stockton (95215) ***(P-6535)***
Patricks Construction Clean-Up ....D.......916 452-5495
7851 14th Ave Sacramento (95826) ***(P-1173)***
Patriot Contract Services LLC ....B.......925 296-2000
1320 Willow Pass Rd # 485 Concord (94520) ***(P-7711)***
Patriot Memory Inc (PA) ....C.......**510 979-1021**
47027 Benicia St Fremont (94538) ***(P-6250)***
Patrol Solutions LLC ....C.......916 919-6079
6060 Sunrise Vista Dr # 1 Citrus Heights (95610) ***(P-14085)***
Patsons Media Group, Santa Clara *Also called Patsons Press* ***(P-3681)***
Patsons Press ....E.......408 567-0911
3000 Scott Blvd Ste 101 Santa Clara (95054) ***(P-3681)***
Pattar Trans Inc ....E.......209 634-3849
4325 W Taylor Rd Turlock (95380) ***(P-7890)***
Pattar Transport, Turlock *Also called Pattar Trans Inc* ***(P-7890)***
Patten Christian Schools, Oakland *Also called Christian Evang Chrches Amer I* ***(P-14845)***
Pattern Energy Group One LP (PA) ....D.......**415 283-4000**
1088 Sansome St San Francisco (94111) ***(P-8189)***
Pattern Panhandle Wind LLC ....E.......415 283-4000
1088 Sansome St San Francisco (94111) ***(P-8190)***
Pattern Renewables 2 LP (HQ) ....C.......**415 283-4000**
1088 Sansome St San Francisco (94111) ***(P-1336)***
Pattern Tap LLC ....D.......408 341-0600
55 N 3rd St Campbell (95008) ***(P-13957)***
Pattern US Finance Company LLC ....E.......415 283-4000
1088 Sansome St San Francisco (94111) ***(P-8191)***
Patterson Dental Supply Inc ....F.......925 603-6350
5087 Commercial Cir Concord (94520) ***(P-7087)***
Patterson Frozen Foods Inc ....E.......209 892-5060
10 S 3rd St Patterson (95363) ***(P-2295)***
Patterson Travel Agency ....E.......916 929-5555
1750 Howe Ave Ste 320 Sacramento (95825) ***(P-7804)***
Patti Roscoe & Associates Inc (PA) ....E.......**760 496-0540**
508 Gibson Dr Ste 120 Roseville (95678) ***(P-14354)***
Patton Air Conditioning, Fresno *Also called Patton Sheet Metal Works Inc* ***(P-1827)***
Patton Music Co Inc (PA) ....E.......**209 574-1101**
1512 Princeton Ave Modesto (95350) ***(P-9644)***
Patton Sheet Metal Works Inc ....E.......559 486-5222
272 N Palm Ave Fresno (93701) ***(P-1827)***
Patton Vending, Modesto *Also called Patton Music Co Inc* ***(P-9644)***
Paul Baker Printing Inc ....E.......916 969-8317
4251 Gateway Park Blvd Sacramento (95834) ***(P-3682)***
Paul D Abramson MD Inc (PA) ....E.......**415 963-4431**
450 Sutter St Rm 840 San Francisco (94108) ***(P-15587)***
Paul Graham Drilling & Svc Co ....C.......707 374-5123
2500 Airport Rd Rio Vista (94571) ***(P-556)***
Paul Loewen ....F.......707 263-0452
900f Sky Park Rd Lakeport (95453) ***(P-7779)***
Paul M Zagaris Realtor Inc ....E.......209 527-2010
1230 E Orangeburg Ave A Modesto (95350) ***(P-10643)***
Paul Mitchell School Fresno, Fresno *Also called Pmca Bakersfield LLC* ***(P-11694)***
Paul Ryan Associates ....D.......415 861-3085
200 Gate 5 Rd Ste 113 Sausalito (94965) ***(P-681)***
Paul Trucking, Watsonville *Also called Amar Transportation Inc* ***(P-7503)***

Pauli Systems Inc ....E....707 429-2434
1820 Walters Ct Fairfield (94533) *(P-5593)*
Pavestone LLC ....F....530 795-4400
27600 County Road 90 Winters (95694) *(P-4521)*
Pavex Construction Company, Redwood City *Also called Granite Rock Co (P-1050)*
Pavilions, Pleasanton *Also called Vons Companies Inc (P-2195)*
Pavilions Management LLC (PA) ....**E....916 782-8822**
8450 Wood Thrush Way Granite Bay (95746) *(P-19379)*
PAVIR, Palo Alto *Also called Palo Alto Vterans Inst For RES (P-19228)*
Pax Labs Inc ....D....415 829-2336
660 Alabama St Ste 2 San Francisco (94110) *(P-18)*
Pax Water Technologies Inc ....E....866 729-6493
550 Sycamore Dr Milpitas (95035) *(P-19098)*
Paxata Inc ....D....650 542-7897
1800 Seaport Blvd 1 Redwood City (94063) *(P-13363)*
Pay Certify, Los Gatos *Also called Payment Reservations Inc (P-14355)*
Paychex Inc ....D....916 983-0303
50 Iron Point Cir Ste 200 Folsom (95630) *(P-18982)*
Paycycle Inc ....D....650 852-9650
210 Portage Ave Palo Alto (94306) *(P-7982)*
Payjoy Inc (PA) ....**D....888 632-1922**
655 4th St San Francisco (94107) *(P-13364)*
Payment Reservations Inc ....E....480 770-9064
59 N Santa Cruz Ave Ste Q Los Gatos (95030) *(P-14355)*
Payne Brothers Ranches ....D....530 662-2354
13330 County Road 102 Woodland (95776) *(P-33)*
Paypal Inc ....B....408 967-3256
18930 Newsom Ave Cupertino (95014) *(P-14356)*
Paypal Inc ....B....877 434-2894
1895 El Camino Real Palo Alto (94306) *(P-14357)*
Paypal Inc ....B....415 947-0834
123 Townsend St Fl 6 San Francisco (94107) *(P-14358)*
Paypal Inc ....B....855 449-3737
123 Townsend St Fl 6 San Francisco (94107) *(P-14359)*
Paypal Inc (HQ) ....**A....877 981-2163**
2211 N 1st St San Jose (95131) *(P-14360)*
Paypal Data Services Inc ....E....408 376-7400
2211 N 1st St San Jose (95131) *(P-14361)*
Paypal Global Holdings Inc (HQ) ....**A....408 967-1000**
303 Bryant St Mountain View (94041) *(P-13738)*
Paypal Holdings Inc (PA) ....**A....408 967-1000**
2211 N 1st St San Jose (95131) *(P-14362)*
Payroll Dept., Chico *Also called Enloe Medical Center (P-16366)*
Paysonic, Union City *Also called Spacesonics Incorporated (P-4820)*
Paystack Inc ....D....415 941-8102
201 Spear St Ste 1100 San Francisco (94105) *(P-12674)*
Payyourpeople LLC ....E....415 914-7110
303 2nd St Towe Ste 401 San Francisco (94107) *(P-13739)*
Pbc Enterprises ....E....916 415-9966
4760 Rocklin Rd Rocklin (95677) *(P-682)*
PBM Supply & Mfg ....E....530 345-1334
324 Meyers St Chico (95928) *(P-9126)*
Pbs Paymaster Sales & Service, Santa Rosa *Also called Protective Business & Health (P-13746)*
PC World Online, San Francisco *Also called Idg Consumer & Smb Inc (P-3503)*
PCA, Santa Clara *Also called Polishing Corporation America (P-6252)*
PCA Central Cal Corrugated LLC ....E....916 614-0580
4841 Urbani Ave McClellan (95652) *(P-3363)*
PCC Northwest, San Leandro *Also called Pacific Coast Container Inc (P-7889)*
PCC Structurals Inc ....C....510 568-6400
414 Hester St San Leandro (94577) *(P-4586)*
PCC Structurals-San Leandro, San Leandro *Also called PCC Structurals Inc (P-4586)*
Pcg Technology Solutions LLC ....C....916 565-8090
2150 River Plaza Dr # 380 Sacramento (95833) *(P-13958)*
Pch Innovation Hub, San Francisco *Also called Pch Labs Inc (P-18789)*
Pch International USA Inc ....E....415 643-5463
135 Mississippi St San Francisco (94107) *(P-18788)*
Pch Labs Inc ....E....415 643-5463
135 Mississippi St San Francisco (94107) *(P-18789)*
Pch Lime Lab, San Francisco *Also called Pch International USA Inc (P-18788)*
Pcha, Palo Alto *Also called Packard Childrens Hlth Aliance (P-15581)*
PCI, Santa Rosa *Also called Paragon Controls Incorporated (P-6703)*
PCI, Rancho Cordova *Also called Power Constructors Inc (P-18792)*
PCI Bay Area Interior, Alameda *Also called Performance Contracting Inc (P-1698)*
PCL Communications, San Leandro *Also called Pacific Coast Laboratories (P-7077)*
Pcs Concrete & Masonry, Atwater *Also called Esau Concrete Inc DBA Pcs Con (P-779)*
Pcs Mobile Solutions LLC ....D....408 229-8900
888 Blossom Hill Rd San Jose (95123) *(P-19838)*
PDC Logistics Inc (PA) ....**E....925 583-0200**
6383 Las Positas Rd Livermore (94551) *(P-7699)*
Pdf Solutions Inc (PA) ....**B....408 280-7900**
2858 De La Cruz Blvd Santa Clara (95050) *(P-13365)*
Pdi, San Carlos *Also called Precision Design Inc (P-5959)*
PDM Steel Service Centers Inc ....F....408 988-3000
3500 Bassett St Santa Clara (95054) *(P-8823)*
PDM Steel Service Centers Inc (HQ) ....**D....209 943-0555**
3535 E Myrtle St Stockton (95205) *(P-8824)*
PDM Steel Service Centers Inc ....C....916 513-4548
9245 Laguna Springs Dr # 350 Elk Grove (95758) *(P-8825)*
PDQ Automatic Transm Parts Inc ....D....916 681-7701
8380 Tiogawoods Dr Sacramento (95828) *(P-14541)*
Pds Tech Inc ....C....408 916-4848
1798 Tech Dr Ste 130 San Jose (95110) *(P-12118)*
Peace Action West (PA) ....**E....510 830-3600**
2201 Broadway Ste 321 Oakland (94612) *(P-18539)*
Peace Out Inc ....E....305 297-8017
666 Natoma St San Francisco (94103) *(P-4092)*
Peach Tree Healthcare ....D....530 749-3242
5730 Packard Ave Ste 500 Marysville (95901) *(P-15588)*
Peachpit Press ....F....415 336-6831
1301 Sansome St San Francisco (94111) *(P-3588)*
Peachwood Med Group Clovis Inc ....D....559 324-6200
275 W Herndon Ave Clovis (93612) *(P-15589)*
Peak Attractions LLC (PA) ....**E....415 981-6300**
350 Bay St Ste 370 San Francisco (94133) *(P-15226)*
Peak Plastics, San Jose *Also called Peak Technology Entps Inc (P-9515)*
Peak Property Management Sftwr, Berkeley *Also called I Manageproperty Inc (P-13220)*
Peak Technical Services Inc ....C....855 650-7325
1885 De La Cruz Blvd Santa Clara (95050) *(P-12119)*
Peak Technology Entps Inc ....E....408 748-1102
6951 Via Del Oro San Jose (95119) *(P-9515)*
Peak Travel Group ....E....408 286-2633
1723 Hamilton Ave Ste A San Jose (95125) *(P-7805)*
Peanut Shell, Union City *Also called Farallon Brands Inc (P-3025)*
Pearl Black Inc ....E....415 640-4987
100 Pine St Ste 475 San Francisco (94111) *(P-12675)*
Pearl Crop Inc (PA) ....**D....209 808-7575**
1550 Industrial Dr Stockton (95206) *(P-301)*
Pearl Crop Inc ....E....209 887-3731
8452 Demartini Ln Linden (95236) *(P-2932)*
Pearl Crop Inc ....E....209 982-9933
17641 French Camp Rd Ripon (95366) *(P-2454)*
Pearl Electric Co, Stockton *Also called Patrick Rynearson Rulin (P-6535)*
Pearl Law Group, Palo Alto *Also called Julie Pearl A Prof Corp (P-17300)*
Pearl Management Group Inc (PA) ....**D....818 383-0095**
2150 Bluebell Dr Santa Rosa (95403) *(P-19380)*
Pearson Realty One LLC (PA) ....**E....559 432-6200**
7480 N Palm Ave Ste 101 Fresno (93711) *(P-10644)*
Pebble Technology Corp ....E....888 224-5820
900 Middlefield Rd Ste 5 Redwood City (94063) *(P-7162)*
Peck & Hiller Company ....D....707 258-8800
870 Napa Vly Corp Way Ste NAPA (94558) *(P-1901)*
Peco Inspx ....F....209 576-3345
1616 Culpepper Ave Ste A Modesto (95351) *(P-5686)*
Pedersen Media Group Inc ....E....415 512-9800
1115 3rd St San Rafael (94901) *(P-19694)*
Pediatric Anesthesia Assoc Med ....D....559 449-4350
6235 N Fresno St Ste 103 Fresno (93710) *(P-16478)*
Pedro McCrcken Dsign Group Inc (PA) ....**E....916 415-5358**
6930 Destiny Dr Ste 100 Rocklin (95677) *(P-18903)*
Peer Services Inc ....E....559 970-1240
1396 W Sequoia Cir Reedley (93654) *(P-19602)*
Peerles Coffee and Tea, Oakland *Also called Peerless Coffee Company Inc (P-2841)*
Peerless Coffee Company Inc ....D....510 763-1763
260 Oak St Oakland (94607) *(P-2841)*
Peets Coffee Inc (HQ) ....**D....510 594-2100**
1400 Park Ave Emeryville (94608) *(P-2842)*
Peets Coffee & Tea LLC (HQ) ....**A....510 594-2100**
1400 Park Ave Emeryville (94608) *(P-2843)*
Peets Coffee & Tea LLC ....E....408 558-9535
1875 S Bascom Ave Campbell (95008) *(P-2844)*
Pega Precision Inc ....E....408 776-3700
18800 Adams Ct Morgan Hill (95037) *(P-4801)*
Pegasus Risk Management Inc (PA) ....**D....209 574-2800**
642 Galaxy Way Modesto (95356) *(P-10330)*
Pegasus Solar Inc ....E....510 210-3797
506 W Ohio Ave Richmond (94804) *(P-4632)*
Pegatron Usa Inc (HQ) ....**D....510 580-4276**
800 Corporate Way B Fremont (94539) *(P-13740)*
Peggy S Lane Inc ....D....510 483-1202
2701 Merced St San Leandro (94577) *(P-4251)*
Pei Placer Electric Inc (PA) ....**E....916 338-4400**
5439 Stationers Way Sacramento (95842) *(P-1562)*
Peju Province Winery A CA Ltd ....D....800 446-7358
8466 Saint Helena Hwy Rutherford (94573) *(P-2679)*
Peking Handicraft Inc (PA) ....**C....650 871-3788**
1388 San Mateo Ave South San Francisco (94080) *(P-8518)*
Pel Wholesale Inc ....E....925 373-3628
6818 Patterson Pass Rd H Livermore (94550) *(P-9200)*
Pelagic Pressure Systems Corp ....D....510 569-3100
480 Mccormick St San Leandro (94577) *(P-5098)*
Pelican Inn ....D....415 383-6000
10 Pacific Way Muir Beach (94965) *(P-11362)*
Pelican Sign Service Inc ....E....408 246-3833
391 Bundy Ave San Jose (95117) *(P-7248)*
Pelicantunes Inc ....F....925 838-8484
3950 Valley Ave Ste A Pleasanton (94566) *(P-15039)*
Pellenc America Inc (HQ) ....**E....707 568-7286**
3171 Guerneville Rd Santa Rosa (95401) *(P-5016)*
Peltier Winery, Acampo *Also called R & G Schatz Farms Inc (P-69)*
Pelton-Shepherd Industries Inc (PA) ....**E....209 460-0893**
812 W Luce St Ste B Stockton (95203) *(P-2861)*
Pen-Cal Administrators Inc ....D....925 251-3400
7633 Suthfront Rd Ste 120 Livermore (94551) *(P-19381)*
Pencil and Pixel Inc ....C....510 422-5036
340 Brannan St Ste 500 San Francisco (94107) *(P-12676)*
Pencom/Accuracy Inc ....D....510 785-5022
1300 Industrial Rd Ste 21 San Carlos (94070) *(P-4868)*
Pencom/Duall Thermo Products ....D....650 593-3288
1300 Industrial Rd Ste 21 San Carlos (94070) *(P-9504)*
Pendulum Instruments Inc ....E....866 644-1230
1123 Madison Ave Redwood City (94061) *(P-6536)*
Pendulum Therapeutics Inc ....D....844 912-2256
2001 Bryant St San Francisco (94110) *(P-19099)*
Penfield Products Inc ....E....916 635-0231
11300 Trade Center Dr A Rancho Cordova (95742) *(P-4802)*

ALPHABETIC

Penguin Computing Inc   **ALPHABETIC SECTION**

Penguin Computing Inc (HQ)..........D.......415 954-2800
   45800 Northport Loop W Fremont (94538) *(P-8732)*
Penhall Company..........E......408 970-9494
   696 Walsh Ave Santa Clara (95050) *(P-2053)*
Penhall Company..........E......916 386-1589
   8416 Specialty Cir Sacramento (95828) *(P-2054)*
Penhall Sacramento 151, Sacramento *Also called Penhall Company* *(P-2054)*
Penhall Santa Clara 152, Santa Clara *Also called Penhall Company* *(P-2053)*
Peninou French Ldry & Clrs Inc (PA)..........D......800 392-2532
   101 S Maple Ave South San Francisco (94080) *(P-11671)*
Peninsula Crrdor Jint Pwers Bd..........C.......650 508-6200
   1250 San Carlos Ave San Carlos (94070) *(P-7344)*
Peninsula Custom Homes Inc..........D.......650 574-0241
   1401 Old County Rd San Carlos (94070) *(P-683)*
Peninsula Family Service (PA)..........E.......650 403-4300
   24 2nd Ave San Mateo (94401) *(P-17990)*
Peninsula Family Service..........D.......650 403-4300
   2635 N 1st St San Jose (95134) *(P-17991)*
Peninsula Family Service..........D.......650 952-6848
   1200 Miller Ave South San Francisco (94080) *(P-17671)*
Peninsula Floors Inc..........E.......650 593-5825
   1070 Sixth Ave Ste 150 Belmont (94002) *(P-14363)*
Peninsula Hlthcare Cnnction In (PA)..........D.......650 853-0321
   33 Encina Ave Ste 103 Palo Alto (94301) *(P-15590)*
Peninsula Humane Soc & Spca..........D.......650 340-7022
   1450 Rollins Rd Burlingame (94010) *(P-18583)*
Peninsula Jewish Community Ctr..........D.......650 212-7522
   800 Foster City Blvd Foster City (94404) *(P-17672)*
Peninsula Metal Fabrication, San Jose *Also called I & A Inc* *(P-4771)*
Peninsula Metal Fabrication, San Jose *Also called Hardcraft Industries Inc* *(P-4768)*
Peninsula Ophthalmology Group, Burlingame *Also called Gilbert Smolin MD Inc* *(P-15415)*
Peninsula Pathology Associates, South San Francisco *Also called Pennisula Pthlogists Med Group* *(P-16792)*
Peninsula Post-Acute..........E.......650 443-2600
   1609 Trousdale Dr Burlingame (94010) *(P-18343)*
Peninsula Regent, The, San Mateo *Also called Bay Area Senior Services Inc* *(P-17441)*
Peninsula Sanitary Service Inc..........E.......650 321-4236
   339 Bonair Siding Rd Stanford (94305) *(P-8348)*
Peninsula School Ltd..........D.......650 325-1584
   920 Peninsula Way Menlo Park (94025) *(P-17992)*
Peninsula South Bay, Millbrae *Also called Vitalant Research Institute* *(P-17188)*
Peninsula Spring Corporation..........F.......408 848-3361
   6750 Silacci Way Gilroy (95020) *(P-4965)*
Peninsula Temple Beth El..........E.......650 341-7701
   1700 Almeda De Las Pulgas San Mateo (94403) *(P-17993)*
Peninsula Volunteer Prpts Inc (PA)..........E.......650 326-2025
   800 Middle Ave Menlo Park (94025) *(P-10454)*
Peninsula YMCA, San Mateo *Also called Young MNS Chrstn Assn San Frnc* *(P-18514)*
Penitencia Water Trtmnt Plant, San Jose *Also called Santa Clara Vly Wtr Dst Pub Fc* *(P-8268)*
Pennacchio Tile Inc..........D.......707 586-8858
   655 Carlson Ct Rohnert Park (94928) *(P-1718)*
Pennbrook Insurance Service..........E.......415 820-2200
   300 Montgomery St Ste 450 San Francisco (94104) *(P-10331)*
Penney Opco LLC..........D......916 564-0315
   1695 Arden Way Sacramento (95815) *(P-11691)*
Penney Opco LLC..........D.......209 951-1110
   4915 Claremont Ave Stockton (95207) *(P-11692)*
Penney Opco LLC..........D.......530 899-8160
   1932 E 20th St Chico (95928) *(P-11693)*
Pennisula Pthlogists Med Group..........C.......650 616-2940
   393 E Grand Ave Ste I South San Francisco (94080) *(P-16792)*
Penny Ice Creamery, The, Santa Cruz *Also called Glass Jar Inc* *(P-2175)*
Penny Newman Grain Co (PA)..........E.......559 448-8800
   2691 S Cedar Ave Fresno (93725) *(P-9505)*
Pennys Guest Home LLC (PA)..........E.......925 286-0424
   990 Rosehedge Ct Concord (94521) *(P-16257)*
Penrose Studios Inc..........F.......703 354-1801
   223 Mississippi St Ste 3 San Francisco (94107) *(P-3589)*
Pensando Systems Inc..........D.......408 451-9012
   570 Alder Dr Milpitas (95035) *(P-6729)*
Pensco LLC (PA)..........E.......415 274-5600
   275 Battery St Ste 1220 San Francisco (94111) *(P-10217)*
Pensco Trust Company NH, San Francisco *Also called Pensco LLC* *(P-10217)*
Penumbra Inc (PA)..........A.......510 748-3200
   1 Penumbra Alameda (94502) *(P-7019)*
People Center Inc..........E.......415 737-5780
   2443 Fillmore St 380-7 San Francisco (94115) *(P-13366)*
People Data Labs Inc..........D.......415 568-8415
   455 Market St Ste 1670 San Francisco (94105) *(P-13741)*
People Sciences Inc..........E.......888 924-1004
   951 Mrners Lsland Blvd St San Mateo (94404) *(P-12120)*
People Services Inc (PA)..........E.......707 263-3810
   4195 Lakeshore Blvd Lakeport (95453) *(P-18156)*
Peopleai Inc..........D.......888 997-3675
   475 Brannan St Ste 320 San Francisco (94107) *(P-12677)*
Peoplefinders Ngt Por Priof..........F.......916 341-0227
   1915 21st St Sacramento (95811) *(P-3590)*
Pep Boys Manny Moe Jack of Cal..........E.......916 331-4880
   5135 Auburn Blvd Sacramento (95841) *(P-14670)*
Pep Boys Manny Moe Jack of Cal..........E.......916 638-4808
   10899 Folsom Blvd Rancho Cordova (95670) *(P-14671)*
Pep Boys Manny Moe Jack of Cal..........E.......559 276-7501
   4490 W Shaw Ave Fresno (93722) *(P-14616)*
Pepper Plant, The, Gilroy *Also called Blossom Valley Foods Inc* *(P-2819)*
Pepper Tree Inn..........D.......530 583-3711
   645 N Lake Blvd Tahoe City (96145) *(P-11363)*
Pepsi Co, Oakland *Also called Svc Mfg Inc A Corp* *(P-2816)*
Pepsi-Cola, Fresno *Also called Roger Enrico* *(P-2809)*
Pepsico, Redding *Also called John Fitzpatrick & Sons* *(P-2794)*
Perazza Prints LLC (PA)..........E.......925 681-2458
   25 Crescent Dr Ste A349 Pleasant Hill (94523) *(P-3683)*
Perceptimed Inc..........E.......650 941-7000
   365 San Antonio Rd Mountain View (94040) *(P-5164)*
Percolata Corporation..........E.......650 308-4980
   3630 El Camino Real Palo Alto (94306) *(P-13647)*
Pereira & ODell LLC (PA)..........D.......415 284-9916
   1265 Battery St Fl 4 San Francisco (94111) *(P-11777)*
Pereira Indus Cnstr Maint Inc..........E.......209 835-2393
   15355 W Grant Line Rd Tracy (95304) *(P-684)*
Perennial Landscape and Nurs..........E.......530 546-7383
   6891 N Lake Blvd Tahoe Vista (96148) *(P-496)*
Perez Distributing Fresno Inc (PA)..........E.......800 638-3512
   103 S Academy Ave Sanger (93657) *(P-3961)*
Perez Farms LP..........E.......209 837-4701
   22001 E St Crows Landing (95313) *(P-10485)*
PERFECT DAY INC..........E.......203 848-8633
   1485 Park Ave Emeryville (94608) *(P-2193)*
Perfect Puree of NAPA Vly LLC..........F.......707 261-5100
   2700 Napa Valley Corp Dr NAPA (94558) *(P-2296)*
Perfect Shine Housekeeping, San Jose *Also called JMEKM Enterprises* *(P-11965)*
Perfect World Entrmt Inc..........C.......650 590-7700
   100 Redwood Shores Pkwy # 200 Redwood City (94065) *(P-12678)*
Performance Abatement Svcs Inc..........E.......925 273-3800
   1943 Rutan Dr Livermore (94551) *(P-2055)*
Performance Chevrolet Inc..........C.......916 338-7300
   8757 Auburn Folsom Rd Granite Bay (95746) *(P-14583)*
Performance Coatings Inc..........E.......707 462-3023
   360 Lake Mendocino Dr Ukiah (95482) *(P-4108)*
Performance Contracting Inc..........E.......925 273-3800
   7085 Las Positas Rd Ste E Livermore (94551) *(P-804)*
Performance Contracting Inc..........E.......510 214-1444
   1080 Marina Village Pkwy # 300 Alameda (94501) *(P-1698)*
Performance Food Group Inc..........C.......831 462-4400
   1047 17th Ave Santa Cruz (95062) *(P-9283)*
Performance Grp of Nrthn CA..........E.......510 923-9123
   4701 Doyle St Ste 510 Emeryville (94608) *(P-7806)*
Performance Matters LLC (HQ)..........E.......801 453-0136
   150 Parkshore Dr Folsom (95630) *(P-13367)*
Performance Polymer Tech LLC..........E.......916 677-1414
   8801 Washington Blvd # 109 Roseville (95678) *(P-4209)*
Performance Tech Partners LLC..........C.......800 787-4143
   500 Capitol Mall Ste 2350 Sacramento (95814) *(P-13959)*
Performance Trailer Inc..........E.......559 673-6300
   2901 Falcon Dr Madera (93637) *(P-6605)*
Performant Financial Corp (PA)..........B.......925 960-4800
   333 N Canyons Pkwy # 100 Livermore (94551) *(P-13803)*
Performant Recovery Inc..........C.......209 858-3500
   17080 S Harlan Rd Lathrop (95330) *(P-11827)*
Performant Recovery Inc (HQ)..........B.......209 858-3994
   333 N Canyons Pkwy # 100 Livermore (94551) *(P-11828)*
Performex Machining Inc..........E.......650 595-2228
   963 Terminal Way San Carlos (94070) *(P-5594)*
Performnce First Bldg Svcs Inc (PA)..........D.......408 441-4632
   789 E Brokaw Rd San Jose (95112) *(P-11984)*
Performnce Foodservice-Ledyard, Santa Cruz *Also called Performance Food Group Inc* *(P-9283)*
Perfumer's Apprentice, Scotts Valley *Also called Pacific Coast Ingredients* *(P-2820)*
Perfumer's Apprentice, Scotts Valley *Also called Pacific Coast Products LLC* *(P-2821)*
Peri & Sons Farms Cal LLC (PA)..........E.......775 463-4444
   48845 W Nees Ave Firebaugh (93622) *(P-9423)*
Pericom Semiconductor Corp (HQ)..........A.......408 232-9100
   1545 Barber Ln Milpitas (95035) *(P-6778)*
Peridot Corporation..........D.......925 461-8830
   1072 Serpentine Ln Pleasanton (94566) *(P-4887)*
Perkins & Will, San Francisco *Also called Perkins + Will Inc* *(P-18904)*
Perkins + Will Inc..........D.......415 856-3000
   2 Bryant St Ste 300 San Francisco (94105) *(P-18904)*
Perkville Inc..........E.......510 808-5668
   344 Thomas L Berkley Way # 111 Oakland (94612) *(P-13368)*
Permacel-Automotive, San Jose *Also called Nitto Americas Inc* *(P-3381)*
Permanente Federation LLC..........D.......510 625-6920
   1 Kaiser Plz Fl 27 Oakland (94612) *(P-19603)*
Permanente Kaiser Intl (HQ)..........D.......510 271-5910
   1 Kaiser Plz Oakland (94612) *(P-10149)*
Permanente Medical Group, Mountain View *Also called Kaiser Foundation Hospitals* *(P-16410)*
Permanente Medical Group Inc..........A.......650 301-5800
   395 Hickey Blvd Fl 2 Daly City (94015) *(P-15591)*
Permanente Medical Group Inc..........A.......707 765-3930
   1617 Broadway St Vallejo (94590) *(P-15592)*
Permanente Medical Group Inc..........A.......510 625-6262
   1800 Harrison St Fl 7th Oakland (94612) *(P-15593)*
Permanente Medical Group Inc..........A.......559 448-4500
   7300 N Fresno St Fresno (93720) *(P-15594)*
Permanente Medical Group Inc..........A.......916 688-2055
   6600 Bruceville Rd Sacramento (95823) *(P-15595)*
Permanente Medical Group Inc..........A.......650 742-2100
   901 El Camino Real San Bruno (94066) *(P-15596)*
Permanente Medical Group Inc..........A.......707 393-4000
   3558 Round Barn Blvd Santa Rosa (95403) *(P-15597)*
Permanente Medical Group Inc..........A.......415 833-2000
   2425 Geary Blvd San Francisco (94115) *(P-15598)*
Permanente Medical Group Inc..........A.......408 972-6883
   275 Hospital Pkwy Ste 470 San Jose (95119) *(P-15599)*
Permanente Medical Group Inc..........A.......925 372-1000
   200 Muir Rd Martinez (94553) *(P-15600)*

Permanente Medical Group Inc.......A.......510 752-1000
3779 Piedmont Ave Oakland (94611) ***(P-15601)***
Permanente Medical Group Inc.......A.......510 248-3000
39400 Paseo Padre Pkwy Fremont (94538) ***(P-15602)***
Permanente Medical Group Inc.......A.......510 752-1190
235 W Macarthur Blvd Oakland (94611) ***(P-15603)***
Permanente Medical Group Inc.......A.......408 945-2900
770 E Calaveras Blvd Milpitas (95035) ***(P-15604)***
Permanente Medical Group Inc.......A.......925 813-6149
4501 Sand Creek Rd Antioch (94531) ***(P-15605)***
Permanente Medical Group Inc.......B.......650 827-6500
220 Oyster Point Blvd South San Francisco (94080) ***(P-10150)***
Permanente Medical Group Inc.......A.......650 299-2000
1150 Veterans Blvd Redwood City (94063) ***(P-15606)***
Permanente Medical Group Inc.......A.......650 299-2015
910 Marshall St Redwood City (94063) ***(P-15607)***
Permanente Medical Group Inc.......A.......510 231-5406
914 Marina Way S Richmond (94804) ***(P-15608)***
Permanente Medical Group Inc.......A.......916 486-5686
3184 Arden Way Sacramento (95825) ***(P-15609)***
Permanente Medical Group Inc.......A.......510 454-1000
2500 Merced St San Leandro (94577) ***(P-15610)***
Permanente Medical Group Inc.......B.......650 598-2852
900 Veterans Blvd Ste 400 Redwood City (94063) ***(P-10151)***
Permanente Medical Group Inc (HQ).......**B.......866 858-2226**
1950 Franklin St Fl 18th Oakland (94612) ***(P-17167)***
Permanente Medical Group Inc.......A.......415 444-2000
99 Montecillo Rd San Rafael (94903) ***(P-15611)***
Permanente Medical Group Inc.......A.......925 906-2000
320 Lennon Ln Walnut Creek (94598) ***(P-15612)***
Permanente Medical Group Inc.......A.......415 209-2444
100 Rowland Way Ste 125 Novato (94945) ***(P-15613)***
Permanente Medical Group Inc.......A.......415 899-7400
97 San Marin Dr Novato (94945) ***(P-15614)***
Permanente Medical Group Inc.......B.......510 559-5119
1725 Eastshore Hwy Berkeley (94710) ***(P-10152)***
Permanente Medical Group Inc.......A.......916 784-4000
1600 Eureka Rd Roseville (95661) ***(P-15615)***
Permanente Medical Group Inc.......A.......209 476-3737
7373 West Ln Stockton (95210) ***(P-15616)***
Permanente Medical Group Inc.......A.......415 833-2000
2238 Geary Blvd San Francisco (94115) ***(P-15617)***
Permanente Medical Group Inc.......A.......510 559-5338
1750 2nd St Berkeley (94710) ***(P-15618)***
Permanente Medical Group Inc.......A.......707 765-3900
3900 Lakeville Hwy Petaluma (94954) ***(P-15619)***
Permanente Medical Group Inc.......A.......707 427-4000
1550 Gateway Blvd Fairfield (94533) ***(P-16479)***
Permanente Medical Group Inc.......A.......209 476-2000
1305 Tommydon St Stockton (95210) ***(P-15620)***
Permanente Medical Group Inc.......B.......510 675-4010
3555 Whipple Rd Union City (94587) ***(P-10153)***
Permanente Medical Group Inc.......A.......925 243-2600
3000 Las Positas Rd Livermore (94551) ***(P-15621)***
Permanente Medical Group Inc.......A.......916 631-3000
10725 International Dr Rancho Cordova (95670) ***(P-15622)***
Permanente Medical Group Inc.......A.......650 301-5860
395 Hickey Blvd Fl 1 Daly City (94015) ***(P-15623)***
Permanente Medical Group Inc.......A.......650 358-7000
1000 Franklin Pkwy San Mateo (94403) ***(P-15624)***
Permanente Medical Group Inc.......A.......209 735-5000
4601 Dale Rd Modesto (95356) ***(P-15625)***
Permanentee Medical Group, Roseville *Also called Kaiser Foundation Hospitals* ***(P-15481)***
Permira Advisers LLC.......B.......650 681-4701
3000 Sand Hill Rd 1-170 Menlo Park (94025) ***(P-10055)***
Pernixdata Inc.......D.......408 724-8413
1740 Tech Dr Ste 150 San Jose (95110) ***(P-12679)***
Pernod Ricard Usa LLC.......D.......707 833-5891
9592 Sonoma Hwy Kenwood (95452) ***(P-2680)***
Pernod Ricard Usa LLC.......D.......707 967-7770
8445 Silverado Trl Rutherford (94573) ***(P-2681)***
Perry Tool & Research Inc.......E.......510 782-9226
3415 Enterprise Ave Hayward (94545) ***(P-4591)***
Perry-Smith LLP.......E.......916 441-1000
400 Capitol Mall Ste 1400 Sacramento (95814) ***(P-18983)***
Perrys Custom Chopping LLC.......F.......209 667-8777
21365 Williams Ave Hilmar (95324) ***(P-5017)***
Perseid Therapeutics LLC.......E.......650 298-5800
515 Galveston Dr Redwood City (94063) ***(P-19100)***
Persistent Systems, Santa Clara *Also called Persistent Tlcom Solutions Inc* ***(P-12681)***
Persistent Systems Inc (HQ).......**D.......408 216-7010**
2055 Laurelwood Rd # 210 Santa Clara (95054) ***(P-12680)***
Persistent Tlcom Solutions Inc.......E.......408 216-7010
2055 Laurelwood Rd # 210 Santa Clara (95054) ***(P-12681)***
Personagraph Corporation.......D.......408 616-1600
920 Stewart Dr Ste 100 Sunnyvale (94085) ***(P-12682)***
Personal Mortgage Group LLC (HQ).......**D.......415 396-0560**
420 Montgomery St San Francisco (94104) ***(P-9919)***
Personal Protective Svcs Inc (PA).......**D.......650 344-3302**
398 Beach Rd Fl 2 Burlingame (94010) ***(P-14086)***
Personalis Inc (PA).......**C.......650 752-1300**
1330 Obrien Dr Menlo Park (94025) ***(P-16793)***
Persson Inc.......E.......559 683-3000
40077 Enterprise Dr Oakhurst (93644) ***(P-1070)***
Pescadero Conservation Aliance.......E.......650 879-1441
4100 Cabrillo Hwy Pescadero (94060) ***(P-18447)***
Pescatore, San Francisco *Also called Kimpton Hotel & Rest Group LLC* ***(P-11234)***
Pesenti Winery, Saint Helena *Also called Turley Wine Cellars Inc* ***(P-2749)***
Pestec Exterminator Co, San Francisco *Also called Luis A Agurto* ***(P-11901)***
Pet Emergency Treatment Svc.......E.......510 548-6684
1048 University Ave Berkeley (94710) ***(P-332)***
PET POURRI, Milpitas *Also called Humane Society Silicon Valley* ***(P-18573)***
Petalon Landscape MGT Inc.......D.......408 453-3998
1766 Rogers Ave San Jose (95112) ***(P-435)***
Petaluma Acquisitions LLC.......A.......707 763-1904
2700 Lakeville Hwy Petaluma (94954) ***(P-2138)***
Petaluma By Products.......E.......707 763-9181
84 Corona Rd Petaluma (94952) ***(P-2455)***
Petaluma Care, Petaluma *Also called Petaluma Post-Acute Rehab* ***(P-16095)***
Petaluma Cinemas LLC.......E.......707 762-0990
515 E Washington St Petaluma (94952) ***(P-14815)***
Petaluma Farms Inc.......E.......707 763-0921
700 Cavanaugh Ln Petaluma (94952) ***(P-231)***
Petaluma Golf and Country Club.......D.......707 762-7041
1500 Country Club Dr Petaluma (94952) ***(P-15122)***
Petaluma Health Center Inc.......B.......707 559-7500
1179 N Mcdowell Blvd A Petaluma (94954) ***(P-15626)***
Petaluma Medical Offices, Petaluma *Also called Kaiser Foundation Hospitals* ***(P-15478)***
Petaluma Post-Acute Rehab.......E.......707 765-3030
1115 B St Petaluma (94952) ***(P-16095)***
Petaluma Properties Inc.......D.......707 763-0994
200 S Mcdowell Blvd Petaluma (94954) ***(P-11364)***
Petaluma Valley Hospital, Petaluma *Also called Srm Alliance Hospital Services* ***(P-16534)***
Petaluma Valley Hospital Aux.......D.......707 778-1111
400 N Mcdowell Blvd Petaluma (94954) ***(P-16480)***
Petalumaidence Opco LLC.......C.......707 763-4109
101 Monroe St Petaluma (94954) ***(P-2682)***
Petasense Inc.......E.......650 336-0480
860 Hillview Ct Ste 150 Milpitas (95035) ***(P-6916)***
Petcube Inc (PA).......**E.......424 302-6107**
555 De Haro St Ste 280a San Francisco (94107) ***(P-5768)***
Pete Moffat Construction Inc.......E.......650 493-8899
947 Industrial Ave Palo Alto (94303) ***(P-685)***
Peter.......E.......916 588-9954
2850 Gateway Oaks Dr Sacramento (95833) ***(P-3391)***
Peter A Kuzinich.......E.......408 292-3686
328 S Bascom Ave San Jose (95128) ***(P-14856)***
Peter Castillo Md PA.......C.......408 236-6400
700 Lawrence Expy Santa Clara (95051) ***(P-15627)***
Peter H Mattson & Co Inc.......D.......650 356-2500
343 Hatch Dr Foster City (94404) ***(P-19101)***
Peter Michael Winery, Calistoga *Also called Sugarloaf Farming Corporation* ***(P-2733)***
Peter Walker & Partners, Berkeley *Also called Peter Wlker Prtners Ldscp Arch* ***(P-436)***
Peter Wlker Prtners Ldscp Arch.......D.......510 849-9494
739 Allston Way Berkeley (94710) ***(P-436)***
Peters Roofing Inc.......E.......559 876-1615
2529 Keiser Ave Sanger (93657) ***(P-1828)***
Petersen Precision Engrg LLC.......C.......650 365-4373
611 Broadway St Redwood City (94063) ***(P-5595)***
Petersen-Dean Commercial Inc.......D.......707 469-7470
1705 Enterprise Dr Fairfield (94533) ***(P-1829)***
Petersendean, Fairfield *Also called Petersen-Dean Commercial Inc* ***(P-1829)***
Peterson Cat, San Leandro *Also called Peterson Machinery Co* ***(P-9025)***
Peterson Family Inc.......D.......559 897-5064
38694 Road 16 Kingsburg (93631) ***(P-111)***
Peterson Machinery Co (PA).......**A.......541 302-9199**
955 Marina Blvd San Leandro (94577) ***(P-9025)***
Peterson Painting Inc.......B.......925 455-5864
5750 La Ribera St Livermore (94550) ***(P-1423)***
Peterson Sheet Metal Inc.......E.......925 830-1766
12925 Alcosta Blvd Ste 2 San Ramon (94583) ***(P-4803)***
Peterson Sheetmetal, San Ramon *Also called Peterson Sheet Metal Inc* ***(P-4803)***
Petit Pot Inc.......E.......650 488-7432
4221 Horton St Emeryville (94608) ***(P-2933)***
Petits Pains & Co LP.......F.......650 692-6000
1730 Gilbreth Rd Burlingame (94010) ***(P-2399)***
Petkus Brothers and Company, Rocklin *Also called Pbc Enterprises* ***(P-682)***
Petrinovich Pugh & Company, San Jose *Also called Petrinovich Pugh & Company* ***(P-18984)***
Petrinovich Pugh & Company.......E.......408 287-7911
333 W Santa Clara St # 830 San Jose (95113) ***(P-18984)***
Petro-Chem Industries Inc.......D.......707 644-7455
2300 Clayton Rd Concord (94520) ***(P-1699)***
Petro-Chem Insulation, Concord *Also called Petro-Chem Industries Inc* ***(P-1699)***
Petrochem Insulation Inc.......D.......707 645-1121
945 Teal Dr Benicia (94510) ***(P-1700)***
Petroleum Sales Inc.......E.......415 256-1600
2066 Redwood Hwy Greenbrae (94904) ***(P-548)***
Petroleum Sales Inc (PA).......**C.......415 256-1600**
1475 2nd St San Rafael (94901) ***(P-14651)***
Pets Choice Inc.......E.......916 229-9587
8732 La Riviera Dr Sacramento (95826) ***(P-15628)***
Pets Unlimited.......E.......415 563-6700
2343 Fillmore St San Francisco (94115) ***(P-18584)***
Pezzi King Vineyards, Healdsburg *Also called Strategic Capital Incorporated* ***(P-19643)***
Pfeiffer Electric Co Inc.......E.......408 436-8523
448 Queens Ln San Jose (95112) ***(P-1563)***
PG Emminger Inc.......E.......925 313-5830
4036 Pacheco Blvd A Martinez (94553) ***(P-3318)***
PG&e, Fairfield *Also called Pacific Gas and Electric Co* ***(P-8130)***
PG&E, San Francisco *Also called Pacific Gas and Electric Co* ***(P-8131)***
PG&e, West Sacramento *Also called Pacific Gas and Electric Co* ***(P-8132)***
PG&e, Stockton *Also called Pacific Gas and Electric Co* ***(P-8133)***
PG&e, Fresno *Also called Pacific Gas and Electric Co* ***(P-8134)***
PG&e, Sacramento *Also called Pacific Gas and Electric Co* ***(P-8135)***
PG&e, Chico *Also called Pacific Gas and Electric Co* ***(P-8136)***
PG&e, Hayward *Also called Pacific Gas and Electric Co* ***(P-8211)***

ALPHABETIC

PG&e, Vacaville *Also called Pacific Gas and Electric Co* ***(P-8138)***
PG&e, Jackson *Also called Pacific Gas and Electric Co* ***(P-8140)***
PG&e, Santa Rosa *Also called Pacific Gas and Electric Co* ***(P-8141)***
PG&e, Oakland *Also called Pacific Gas and Electric Co* ***(P-8142)***
PG&e, Pittsburg *Also called Pacific Gas and Electric Co* ***(P-8144)***
PG&e, San Rafael *Also called Pacific Gas and Electric Co* ***(P-8145)***
PG&e, Fresno *Also called Pacific Gas and Electric Co* ***(P-8146)***
PG&e, Stockton *Also called Pacific Gas and Electric Co* ***(P-8147)***
PG&e, Petaluma *Also called Pacific Gas and Electric Co* ***(P-8148)***
PG&e, Willows *Also called Pacific Gas and Electric Co* ***(P-8149)***
PG&e, Sonora *Also called Pacific Gas and Electric Co* ***(P-8151)***
PG&e, Chico *Also called Pacific Gas and Electric Co* ***(P-8212)***
PG&e, Concord *Also called Pacific Gas and Electric Co* ***(P-8152)***
PG&e, Vacaville *Also called Pacific Gas and Electric Co* ***(P-8153)***
PG&e, Marysville *Also called Pacific Gas and Electric Co* ***(P-8154)***
PG&e, San Carlos *Also called Pacific Gas and Electric Co* ***(P-8155)***
PG&e, Daly City *Also called Pacific Gas and Electric Co* ***(P-8156)***
PG&e, Merced *Also called Pacific Gas and Electric Co* ***(P-8157)***
PG&e, Selma *Also called Pacific Gas and Electric Co* ***(P-8158)***
PG&e, Placerville *Also called Pacific Gas and Electric Co* ***(P-8159)***
PG&e, Oroville *Also called Pacific Gas and Electric Co* ***(P-8160)***
PG&e, Alta *Also called Pacific Gas and Electric Co* ***(P-8161)***
PG&e, Redding *Also called Pacific Gas and Electric Co* ***(P-8162)***
PG&e, Manton *Also called Pacific Gas and Electric Co* ***(P-8163)***
PG&e, Santa Rosa *Also called Pacific Gas and Electric Co* ***(P-8164)***
PG&e, Auburn *Also called Pacific Gas and Electric Co* ***(P-8165)***
PG&e, Concord *Also called Pacific Gas and Electric Co* ***(P-8166)***
PG&e, Paradise *Also called Pacific Gas and Electric Co* ***(P-8167)***
PG&e, Stockton *Also called Pacific Gas and Electric Co* ***(P-8168)***
PG&e, Willow Creek *Also called Pacific Gas and Electric Co* ***(P-8169)***
PG&e, San Francisco *Also called Pacific Energy Fuels Company* ***(P-8210)***
PG&e, Fremont *Also called Pacific Gas and Electric Co* ***(P-8170)***
PG&e, Eureka *Also called Pacific Gas and Electric Co* ***(P-8171)***
PG&e, Auberry *Also called Pacific Gas and Electric Co* ***(P-8172)***
PG&e, Los Banos *Also called Pacific Gas and Electric Co* ***(P-8173)***
PG&e, Daly City *Also called Pacific Gas and Electric Co* ***(P-8174)***
PG&e, Modesto *Also called Pacific Gas and Electric Co* ***(P-8175)***
PG&e, Oakdale *Also called Pacific Gas and Electric Co* ***(P-8176)***
PG&e, Stockton *Also called Pacific Gas and Electric Co* ***(P-8177)***
PG&e, Fresno *Also called Pacific Gas and Electric Co* ***(P-8178)***
PG&e, Vacaville *Also called Pacific Gas and Electric Co* ***(P-8179)***
PG&e, Sacramento *Also called Pacific Gas and Electric Co* ***(P-8180)***
PG&e, Chico *Also called Pacific Gas and Electric Co* ***(P-8181)***
PG&e, Tracy *Also called Pacific Gas and Electric Co* ***(P-8182)***
PG&e, Livermore *Also called Pacific Gas and Electric Co* ***(P-8183)***
PG&e, Davis *Also called Pacific Gas and Electric Co* ***(P-8184)***
PG&e, Antioch *Also called Pacific Gas and Electric Co* ***(P-8185)***
PG&e, San Francisco *Also called Pacific Gas and Electric Co* ***(P-8186)***
PG&e, Milpitas *Also called Pacific Gas and Electric Co* ***(P-8187)***
PG&e, Pioneer *Also called Pacific Gas and Electric Co* ***(P-8188)***
PG&e Capital LLC ....B.......415 321-4600
1 Market St San Francisco (94105) ***(P-19604)***
PG&e Corporation ....D.......559 263-5303
705 P St Fresno (93721) ***(P-8192)***
PG&e Recovery Funding LLC ....C.......415 973-1000
77 Beale St San Francisco (94105) ***(P-8215)***
Pgh Wong Engineering (PA) ....**E.......415 284-0800**
182 2nd St Fl 5 San Francisco (94105) ***(P-18790)***
Pgp International Inc (HQ) ....**C.......530 662-5056**
351 Hanson Way Woodland (95776) ***(P-2934)***
Phamtec Inc (PA) ....**E.......408 210-4606**
1526 Centre Pointe Dr Milpitas (95035) ***(P-4572)***
Phantom Auto Inc ....E.......510 284-9898
601 Dna Way Unit C South San Francisco (94080) ***(P-18791)***
Phantom Cyber Corporation ....E.......650 208-5151
2479 E Byshore Rd Ste 185 Palo Alto (94303) ***(P-13369)***
Pharmacy At Cares, The, Sacramento *Also called Cares Community Health* ***(P-15329)***
Pharmacyclics LLC (HQ) ....**A.......408 215-3000**
1000 Gateway Blvd South San Francisco (94080) ***(P-3962)***
Pharmatech Associates Inc ....E.......510 732-0177
22320 Fthill Blvd Ste 330 Hayward (94541) ***(P-19102)***
Phase 3 Communications Inc (PA) ....**D.......408 946-9011**
1355 Felipe Ave San Jose (95122) ***(P-1564)***
Phase Matrix Inc ....E.......954 490-9429
4600 Patrick Henry Dr Santa Clara (95054) ***(P-8946)***
PHF Ruby LLC ....C.......415 885-4700
2620 Jones St San Francisco (94133) ***(P-11365)***
Phihong USA Corp (HQ) ....**D.......510 445-0100**
47800 Fremont Blvd Fremont (94538) ***(P-8733)***
Philbrick Inc ....E.......707 964-2277
32180 Airport Rd Fort Bragg (95437) ***(P-3074)***
Philbrick Logging & Trucking, Fort Bragg *Also called Philbrick Inc* ***(P-3074)***
Philip A Stitt Agency ....E.......916 451-2801
3900 Stockton Blvd Sacramento (95820) ***(P-3041)***
Philippines Today LLC ....F.......650 872-3200
6454 Mission St Daly City (94014) ***(P-3474)***
Philips Consumer Electronics, San Jose *Also called Philips North America LLC* ***(P-14681)***
Philips Hlthcare Infrmtics Inc (HQ) ....**E.......650 293-2300**
4430 Rosewood Dr Ste 200 Pleasanton (94588) ***(P-12683)***
Philips Lt-On Dgtal Sltons USA (HQ) ....**E.......510 687-1800**
720 S Hillview Dr Milpitas (95035) ***(P-5309)***
Philips North America LLC ....E.......408 436-8566
681 E Brokaw Rd San Jose (95112) ***(P-14681)***
Phillips 66 Spectrum Corp ....D.......707 745-6100
6100 Egret Ct Benicia (94510) ***(P-4196)***
Phillips Academy, The, Alameda *Also called Institute Humn Bhvior RES Edca* ***(P-17956)***
Philon Pappas Co ....E.......559 655-4282
181 Naples St Mendota (93640) ***(P-302)***
PHOEBE HEARST PRE SCHOOL, San Francisco *Also called Golden Gate Kindergarten Assn* ***(P-17942)***
Phoebus Co Inc ....F.......415 550-0770
2800 3rd St San Francisco (94107) ***(P-14857)***
Phoebus Lighting, San Francisco *Also called Phoebus Co Inc* ***(P-14857)***
Phoenix Amercn Fincl Svcs Inc (HQ) ....**E.......415 485-4500**
2401 Kerner Blvd San Rafael (94901) ***(P-14364)***
Phoenix American Incorporated (PA) ....**D.......415 485-4500**
2401 Kerner Blvd San Rafael (94901) ***(P-19605)***
Phoenix Day Inc ....F.......415 822-4414
3431 Regatta Blvd Richmond (94804) ***(P-5724)***
Phoenix Deventures Inc ....E.......408 782-6240
18655 Madrone Pkwy # 180 Morgan Hill (95037) ***(P-7020)***
Phoenix Hotel, San Francisco *Also called Joie De Vivre Hospitality LLC* ***(P-11219)***
Phoenix Inn, The, San Francisco *Also called Joie De Vivre Hotels* ***(P-11223)***
Phoenix Pharmaceuticals Inc ....E.......650 558-8898
330 Beach Rd Burlingame (94010) ***(P-3963)***
Phoenix Preschools, The, Sacramento *Also called Phoenix Schools Inc* ***(P-17998)***
Phoenix Schools Inc ....D.......916 415-0780
2820 Theona Way Rocklin (95765) ***(P-17994)***
Phoenix Schools Inc ....D.......916 725-0302
4110 Skyland Ct Antelope (95843) ***(P-17995)***
Phoenix Schools Inc ....D.......916 983-0224
76 Clarksville Rd Folsom (95630) ***(P-17996)***
Phoenix Schools Inc ....D.......916 442-0722
600 I St Sacramento (95814) ***(P-17997)***
Phoenix Schools Inc ....D.......916 452-5150
1820 Alhambra Blvd Sacramento (95816) ***(P-17998)***
Phoenix Schools Inc ....D.......916 723-2633
7998 Old Auburn Rd Citrus Heights (95610) ***(P-17999)***
Phoenix Schools Inc ....D.......916 353-1031
650 Willard Dr Folsom (95630) ***(P-18000)***
Phoenix Systems Exchange Inc ....E.......415 485-4500
2401 Kerner Blvd San Rafael (94901) ***(P-8734)***
PHOTO CENTRAL GALLERY DARK ROO, Hayward *Also called Hayward Area Recreation & Park* ***(P-11673)***
Photon Inc ....F.......408 226-1000
1671 Dell Ave Ste 208 Campbell (95008) ***(P-6730)***
Photon Dynamics Inc ....C.......408 723-7118
5970 Optical Ct San Jose (95138) ***(P-6779)***
Photon Dynamics Inc (HQ) ....**C.......408 226-9900**
5970 Optical Ct San Jose (95138) ***(P-6780)***
Photon Dynamics Inc ....C.......408 226-9900
17 Great Oaks Blvd San Jose (95119) ***(P-6781)***
Photon Infotech Inc ....D.......408 417-0600
100 Century Center Ct # 502 San Jose (95112) ***(P-12684)***
Photoworks Inc ....E.......415 626-6800
2077 Market St San Francisco (94114) ***(P-14181)***
Phynexus, San Jose *Also called Bab Acquisition Corp* ***(P-6813)***
Physical Rehabilitation Netwrk ....E.......408 570-0510
2833 Junction Ave Ste 206 San Jose (95134) ***(P-15894)***
Physicans Med Group Santa Cruz ....E.......831 465-7800
100 Enterprise Way Scotts Valley (95066) ***(P-18344)***
Physician Services, Scotts Valley *Also called Physicans Med Group Santa Cruz* ***(P-18344)***
Physicians Clinical Lab, Sacramento *Also called Unilab Corporation* ***(P-16816)***
Piano Disc, Sacramento *Also called Burgett Incorporated* ***(P-9192)***
Picarro Inc (PA) ....**C.......408 962-3900**
3105 Patrick Henry Dr Santa Clara (95054) ***(P-6844)***
Piccadilly Hospitality LLC ....E.......559 348-5520
2305 W Shaw Ave Fresno (93711) ***(P-11366)***
Piccadilly Inn Airport, Fresno *Also called Art Piccadilly Shaw LLC* ***(P-10931)***
Piccadilly Inn Airport ....E.......559 375-7760
5115 E Mckinley Ave Fresno (93727) ***(P-11367)***
Piccadilly Inn Shaw, Fresno *Also called Art Piccadilly Shaw LLC* ***(P-10930)***
Piccadilly Inn Shaw, Fresno *Also called Piccadilly Hospitality LLC* ***(P-11366)***
Pick Pull Auto Dismantling Inc ....E.......530 221-6184
19919 Viking Way Redding (96003) ***(P-8483)***
Pick Pull Auto Dismantling Inc ....E.......559 233-3881
3230 E Jensen Ave Fresno (93706) ***(P-8484)***
Pick Pull Auto Dismantling Inc ....E.......707 838-4691
10475 Old Redwood Hwy Windsor (95492) ***(P-8485)***
Pick Pull Auto Dismantling Inc ....E.......707 425-1044
4659 Air Base Pkwy Fairfield (94533) ***(P-8486)***
Pick Pull Auto Dismantling Inc (HQ) ....**E.......916 689-2000**
10850 Gold Center Dr # 325 Rancho Cordova (95670) ***(P-8487)***
Pick Pull Auto Dismantling Inc ....E.......916 784-6350
6355 Pacific St Rocklin (95677) ***(P-8488)***
Pick Pull Auto Dismantling Inc ....E.......510 742-2277
7400 Mowry Ave Newark (94560) ***(P-8489)***
Pickering Laboratories Inc ....E.......650 694-6700
1280 Space Park Way Mountain View (94043) ***(P-3795)***
Pickwick Hotel The, San Francisco *Also called Yhb San Francisco LLC* ***(P-11585)***
Picnic Basket, The, Santa Cruz *Also called Glass Jar Inc* ***(P-2174)***
Piedmont Airlines Inc ....C.......559 269-5694
5175 E Clinton Way Fresno (93727) ***(P-7739)***
Pier 39 Limited Partnership (PA) ....**D.......415 705-5500**
Beach Embarcadero Level 3 San Francisco (94133) ***(P-10399)***
Pier Restaurant, San Francisco *Also called Blue and Gold Fleet* ***(P-7718)***
Piercey Hm LLC ....E.......408 324-7400
920 Thompson St Milpitas (95035) ***(P-14672)***

Piercey Honda, Milpitas *Also called Piercey Hm LLC* ***(P-14672)***
Piercey North Inc ... C ... 408 240-1400
950 Thompson St Milpitas (95035) ***(P-8460)***
Piercey Toyota, Milpitas *Also called Piercey North Inc* ***(P-8460)***
Pilgrim Haven Retirement Home, Los Altos *Also called Humangood Norcal* ***(P-16242)***
Pillar Data Systems Inc ... B ... 408 503-4000
2840 Junction Ave San Jose (95134) ***(P-13370)***
Pillsbury Winthrop Shaw ... C ... 415 983-1000
4 Embarcadero Ctr Fl 22 San Francisco (94111) ***(P-17356)***
Pillsbury Winthrop Shaw ... B ... 415 983-1075
50 Fremont St Ste 522 San Francisco (94105) ***(P-17357)***
Pina Vineyard Management LLC ... E ... 707 944-2229
7960 Silverado Trl NAPA (94558) ***(P-385)***
Pinasco Mechinical, Stockton *Also called Pinasco Plumbing & Heating Inc* ***(P-1337)***
Pinasco Plumbing & Heating Inc ... D ... 209 463-7793
2145 E Taylor St Stockton (95205) ***(P-1337)***
Pine & Powell Partners LLC ... D ... 415 989-3500
905 California St San Francisco (94108) ***(P-11368)***
Pine Grove Group Inc ... E ... 209 295-7733
25500 State Highway 88 Pioneer (95666) ***(P-6537)***
Pine Mountain Lake Association (PA) ... **C ... 209 962-4080**
19228 Pine Mountain Dr Groveland (95321) ***(P-18448)***
Pine Ridge Vineyards, NAPA *Also called Pine Ridge Winery LLC* ***(P-2683)***
Pine Ridge Winery LLC (HQ) ... **D ... 707 253-7500**
5901 Silverado Trl NAPA (94558) ***(P-2683)***
Pine Ridge Winery LLC ... E ... 707 260-0330
700 Grove St Healdsburg (95448) ***(P-2684)***
Pine View Center, Paradise *Also called Sunbrdge Prdise Rhblttion Ctr* ***(P-16135)***
Pinecrest Lake Resort ... E ... 209 965-3411
421 Pinecrest Lake Rd Pinecrest (95364) ***(P-11369)***
Pinedridge Care Ctr, San Rafael *Also called Mariner Health Care Inc* ***(P-16055)***
Piner's Medical Supply, NAPA *Also called Piners Nursing Home Inc* ***(P-16096)***
Piners Nursing Home Inc ... D ... 707 224-7925
1800 Pueblo Ave NAPA (94558) ***(P-16096)***
Pines At Plcrvlle Hlthcare Ctr, Placerville *Also called Gladiolus Holdings LLC* ***(P-16013)***
Pines Resorts of California (PA) ... **C ... 559 642-3121**
54449 Road 432 Bass Lake (93604) ***(P-11370)***
Pink Poodle, San Jose *Also called Peter A Kuzinich* ***(P-14856)***
Pinnacle Builders Inc ... B ... 916 372-5000
1911 Douglas Blvd Ste 85 Roseville (95661) ***(P-686)***
Pinnacle Diversified Inc ... F ... 510 400-7929
1248 San Luis Obispo St Hayward (94544) ***(P-3684)***
Pinnacle Manufacturing Corp ... E ... 408 778-6100
17680 Bttrfeld Blvd Ste 1 Morgan Hill (95037) ***(P-4804)***
Pinnacle Press, Hayward *Also called Pinnacle Diversified Inc* ***(P-3684)***
Pinnacle Solutions Inc ... D ... 209 523-8300
1700 Mchenry Ave Ste 45 Modesto (95350) ***(P-14365)***
Pinney Insurance Center Inc ... E ... 916 773-3800
2266 Lava Ridge Ct # 200 Roseville (95661) ***(P-10332)***
Pinole Medical Offices, Pinole *Also called Kaiser Foundation Hospitals* ***(P-15463)***
Pinsetters Inc ... D ... 916 488-7545
2600 Watt Ave Sacramento (95821) ***(P-14897)***
Pinterest Inc (PA) ... **A ... 415 762-7100**
505 Brannan St San Francisco (94107) ***(P-13742)***
Pioneer Electric & Telecom Inc ... E ... 707 838-4057
7975 Cameron Dr Ste 1500 Windsor (95492) ***(P-1565)***
Pioneer Electric and Telcom, Windsor *Also called Pioneer Electric & Telecom Inc* ***(P-1565)***
Pioneer House, Sacramento *Also called Cathedral Pioneer Church Homes* ***(P-15954)***
Pionetics Corporation ... F ... 650 551-0250
151 Old County Rd Ste H San Carlos (94070) ***(P-4311)***
Pionyr Immunotherapeutics Inc ... E ... 415 226-7503
2 Tower Pl 8 South San Francisco (94080) ***(P-3964)***
Pipe and Plant Solutions Inc ... E ... 888 978-8264
225 3rd St Oakland (94607) ***(P-14366)***
Pipe Trades J A T C, San Jose *Also called Plumbing Indust Apprenticeship* ***(P-17832)***
Piranha Ems Inc ... E ... 408 520-3963
2681 Zanker Rd San Jose (95134) ***(P-5269)***
Piranha Pipe & Precast Inc ... E ... 559 665-7473
16000 Avenue 25 Chowchilla (93610) ***(P-4447)***
Pisor Industries Inc ... E ... 916 944-2851
7201 32nd St North Highlands (95660) ***(P-5596)***
Pistoresi Amblnce Svc of Mdera ... D ... 559 673-8004
113 N R St Madera (93637) ***(P-7395)***
Pit River Health Service Inc (PA) ... **D ... 530 335-3651**
36977 Park Ave Burney (96013) ***(P-17168)***
Pit River Health Services, Burney *Also called Pit River Tribal Council* ***(P-15629)***
Pit River Tribal Council ... E ... 530 335-5421
36970 Park Ave Burney (96013) ***(P-17673)***
Pit River Tribal Council ... D ... 530 335-3651
36977 Park Ave Burney (96013) ***(P-15629)***
Pit Rivr Indian Trib Chld Welf, Burney *Also called Pit River Tribal Council* ***(P-17673)***
Pitco, Brisbane *Also called Pittsburg Wholesale Groc Inc* ***(P-9284)***
Pitco Foods, San Jose *Also called Pacific Groservice Inc* ***(P-9643)***
Pitco Foods, West Sacramento *Also called Pittsburg Wholesale Groc Inc* ***(P-9286)***
Pitco Foods, San Leandro *Also called Pittsburg Wholesale Groc Inc* ***(P-9287)***
Pitman Farms (PA) ... **E ... 559 875-9300**
1075 North Ave Sanger (93657) ***(P-238)***
Pittsburg Care Center Inc ... D ... 925 432-3831
535 School St Pittsburg (94565) ***(P-16097)***
Pittsburg General Inc ... E ... 800 445-6374
620 Clark Ave Pittsburg (94565) ***(P-4805)***
Pittsburg Skilled Nursing Ctr, Pittsburg *Also called Pittsburg Care Center Inc* ***(P-16097)***
Pittsburg Wholesale Groc Inc ... E ... 415 865-0404
385 Valley Dr Brisbane (94005) ***(P-9284)***
Pittsburg Wholesale Groc Inc ... E ... 408 701-7326
1800 Merced St San Leandro (94577) ***(P-9285)***
Pittsburg Wholesale Groc Inc ... E ... 916 372-7772
3575 Ramos Dr West Sacramento (95691) ***(P-9286)***
Pittsburg Wholesale Groc Inc ... E ... 510 533-3444
1800 Merced St San Leandro (94577) ***(P-9287)***
Pittsburgh Health Center, Pittsburg *Also called CC Co Health Cntr Information* ***(P-15332)***
Pivot Interiors Inc (PA) ... **C ... 408 432-5600**
3355 Scott Blvd Ste 110 Santa Clara (95054) ***(P-14367)***
Pivotal Connections ... E ... 408 484-6200
75 E Santa Clara St # 14 San Jose (95113) ***(P-14368)***
Pivotal Labs, San Francisco *Also called Pivotal Software Inc* ***(P-12685)***
Pivotal Software Inc (HQ) ... **A ... 415 777-4868**
875 Howard St Fl 5 San Francisco (94103) ***(P-12685)***
Pivotal Systems Corporation ... E ... 510 770-9125
48389 Fremont Blvd # 100 Fremont (94538) ***(P-5687)***
Pixar (HQ) ... **A ... 510 922-3000**
1200 Park Ave Emeryville (94608) ***(P-14795)***
Pixar Animation Studios, Emeryville *Also called Pixar* ***(P-14795)***
Pixelworks Inc (PA) ... **C ... 408 200-9200**
226 Airport Pkwy Ste 595 San Jose (95110) ***(P-6251)***
Pixim Inc ... D ... 650 934-0550
1730 N 1st St San Jose (95112) ***(P-13648)***
Pixlee Inc ... E ... 718 753-5307
625 Market St Ste 900 San Francisco (94105) ***(P-12686)***
Pjk Winery LLC ... E ... 707 431-8333
4900 W Dry Creek Rd Healdsburg (95448) ***(P-2685)***
PJs Lumber Inc ... D ... 209 850-9444
250 D St Turlock (95380) ***(P-1929)***
PJs Lumber Inc ... C ... 510 743-5300
45055 Fremont Blvd Fremont (94538) ***(P-8603)***
Pjs Rebar Inc ... D ... 510 490-0321
45055 Fremont Blvd Fremont (94538) ***(P-8826)***
PK Kinder Co Inc ... E ... 925 939-7242
245 Ygnacio Valley Rd # 200 Walnut Creek (94596) ***(P-9288)***
Pk1 Inc (HQ) ... **D ... 916 858-1300**
4225 Pell Dr Sacramento (95838) ***(P-3364)***
Place Asian Amrcn Rcovery Svcs, San Jose *Also called Asian Amercn Recovery Svcs Inc* ***(P-16751)***
Placer Co Bar Association (PA) ... **C ... 916 557-9181**
P.O. Box 4598 Auburn (95604) ***(P-18345)***
Placer County Water Agency ... D ... 530 367-6701
24625 Harrison St Foresthill (95631) ***(P-8193)***
Placer County Water Agency (PA) ... **D ... 530 823-4850**
144 Ferguson Rd Auburn (95603) ***(P-8194)***
Placer Drmtlogy Skin Care Ctr (PA) ... **E ... 916 784-3376**
9285 Sierra College Blvd Roseville (95661) ***(P-15630)***
Placer Waterworks Inc ... E ... 530 742-9675
1325 Furneaux Rd Plumas Lake (95961) ***(P-4680)***
Placerville Physical Therapy, Diamond Springs *Also called Burger Physcl Therapy Svcs Inc* ***(P-15886)***
Placervlle Pnes Cnvlscent Hosp ... E ... 530 622-3400
1040 Marshall Way Placerville (95667) ***(P-16258)***
Plaid Inc (PA) ... **C ... 415 799-1354**
1098 Harrison St San Francisco (94103) ***(P-13804)***
Plainsight, San Francisco *Also called Sixgill LLC* ***(P-13665)***
Plan Design Consultants Inc ... E ... 650 341-3322
1111 Triton Dr Ste 201 Foster City (94404) ***(P-14369)***
Planchon Roofing Inc ... E ... 510 235-4056
2207 Emeric Ave San Pablo (94806) ***(P-1830)***
Planet Labs Inc (PA) ... **B ... 415 829-3313**
645 Harrison St Fl 4 San Francisco (94107) ***(P-13743)***
Planet One Products Inc (PA) ... **E ... 707 794-8000**
1445 N Mcdowell Blvd Petaluma (94954) ***(P-3319)***
Planet Orange, San Jose *Also called Natural Orange Inc* ***(P-11905)***
Planetout Inc (HQ) ... **D ... 415 834-6500**
795 Folsom St Fl 1 San Francisco (94107) ***(P-7983)***
Planful Inc (HQ) ... **C ... 650 249-7100**
555 Twin Dolphin Dr # 40 Redwood City (94065) ***(P-13371)***
Plangrid Inc (HQ) ... **D ... 800 646-0796**
2111 Mission St Ste 400 San Francisco (94110) ***(P-13372)***
PLANNED PARENTHOOD NORTHERN CA, Concord *Also called Planned Prnthod Shst-Dblo Inc* ***(P-17054)***
Planned Parenthood Nthrn Cal, San Francisco *Also called Planned Prnthod Shst-Dblo Inc* ***(P-17055)***
Planned Prnthod Shst-Dblo Inc (PA) ... **E ... 925 676-0300**
2185 Pacheco St Concord (94520) ***(P-17054)***
Planned Prnthod Shst-Dblo Inc ... E ... 415 821-1282
1522 Bush St San Francisco (94109) ***(P-17055)***
Planned Prnthod Mar Monte Inc (PA) ... **D ... 408 287-7532**
1691 The Alameda San Jose (95126) ***(P-17056)***
Planned Prnthood of Santa Cruz (PA) ... **E ... 831 426-5550**
1119 Pacific Ave Ste 210 Santa Cruz (95060) ***(P-17057)***
Planprescriber Inc ... C ... 650 584-2700
440 E Middlefield Rd Mountain View (94043) ***(P-10333)***
Plant 04, Reedley *Also called Moonlight Packing Corporation* ***(P-7868)***
Plant 1, North Highlands *Also called Livingstons Concrete Svc Inc* ***(P-4494)***
Plant 3, Lincoln *Also called Livingstons Concrete Svc Inc* ***(P-4495)***
Plant Maintenance Inc ... D ... 925 228-3285
1330 Arnold Dr Ste 147 Martinez (94553) ***(P-12187)***
Plant Sciences Inc (PA) ... **E ... 831 728-7771**
342 Green Valley Rd Watsonville (95076) ***(P-19103)***
Plant/Allison Corporation ... F ... 415 285-0500
300 Newhall St San Francisco (94124) ***(P-3146)***
Plantation Farm Camp, Cazadero *Also called Joplin Inc* ***(P-11607)***
Plantronics Inc (PA) ... **A ... 831 420-3002**
345 Encinal St Santa Cruz (95060) ***(P-5805)***
Plasma Rggedized Solutions Inc (PA) ... **D ... 408 954-8405**
2284 Ringwood Ave Ste A San Jose (95131) ***(P-4945)***
Plastic Service Center, Santa Clara *Also called P S C Manufacturing Inc* ***(P-4308)***

Plastic Surgery Center LLC ....E....650 322-6291
1515 El Camino Real Ste A Palo Alto (94306) *(P-17058)*
Plastic Surgery Center, The, Sacramento *Also called Sacramnto Plstic Rcnstrctive S (P-15658)*
Plastikon Industries (PA) ....**B....510 400-1010**
688 Sandoval Way Hayward (94544) *(P-4312)*
Plath & Company Inc ....E....415 460-1575
1575 Francisco Blvd E San Rafael (94901) *(P-937)*
Platinum Builders Inc ....E....408 456-0300
948 N 8th St San Jose (95112) *(P-687)*
Plato Hq, San Francisco *Also called Birdly Inc (P-19456)*
Plaxo Inc ....D....408 900-8701
1050 Enterprise Way # 200 Sunnyvale (94089) *(P-8064)*
Play and Learn School ....E....925 947-2820
1898 Pleasant Hill Rd Pleasant Hill (94523) *(P-18001)*
Play N Learn Pre School ....E....408 269-2338
3800 Narvaez Ave San Jose (95136) *(P-18002)*
Play-I, San Mateo *Also called Wonder Workshop Inc (P-12926)*
Player In Game Inc (PA) ....**E....559 905-6217**
1625 E Shaw Ave Ste 122 Fresno (93710) *(P-19606)*
Playfirst Inc ....E....415 738-4600
160 Spear St Fl 13 San Francisco (94105) *(P-13373)*
Playgrounds Unlimited, Santa Clara *Also called MAK Associates Inc (P-2043)*
Playphone Inc ....D....408 261-6200
3031 Tisch Way Ste 110pw San Jose (95128) *(P-12687)*
Playspan LLC ....D....408 617-9155
2900 Gordon Ave Ste 201 Santa Clara (95051) *(P-9873)*
Playworks Education Energized ....D....510 893-4180
380 Washington St Oakland (94607) *(P-15227)*
Playworks Education Energized (PA) ....**E....510 893-4180**
638 3rd St Oakland (94607) *(P-15228)*
Playwrights Foundation Inc ....D....415 626-2176
1616 16th St Ste 350 San Francisco (94103) *(P-14858)*
Plaza 7, Sacramento *Also called Century Theatres Inc (P-14821)*
Plaze De Caviar, Concord *Also called Pacific Plaza Imports Inc (P-2828)*
Plc LLC ....F....707 462-2423
2350 Mcnab Ranch Rd Ukiah (95482) *(P-2686)*
Pleasant Canyon Hotel Inc ....E....925 847-0535
11920 Dublin Canyon Rd Pleasanton (94588) *(P-11371)*
Pleasant Grove Farms, Pleasant Grove *Also called Sills Farms Inc (P-190)*
Pleasanton Hilton Hotel, Pleasanton *Also called American Property Management (P-10922)*
Pleasanton Project Owner LLC ....E....925 847-7592
11950 Dublin Canyon Rd Pleasanton (94588) *(P-11372)*
Pleasanton Ready Mix Con Inc ....F....925 846-3226
3400 Boulder St Pleasanton (94566) *(P-4502)*
Pleasanton Readymix Concrete, Pleasanton *Also called Pleasanton Ready Mix Con Inc (P-4502)*
Pleasanton Tool & Mfg Inc ....E....925 426-0500
1181 Quarry Ln Ste 450 Pleasanton (94566) *(P-5597)*
Pleats Plus, Oakland *Also called South Park Pleating Inc (P-14411)*
Plenty Unlimited Inc (PA) ....**C....650 735-3737**
570 Eccles Ave South San Francisco (94080) *(P-186)*
Plexus Corp ....C....510 668-9000
431 Kato Ter Fremont (94539) *(P-5958)*
Plexus Optix Inc ....C....800 852-7600
3333 Quality Dr Rancho Cordova (95670) *(P-4379)*
Plexxikon Inc ....E....510 647-4000
329 Oyster Point Blvd South San Francisco (94080) *(P-3965)*
Plug & Play LLC (PA) ....**D....408 524-1400**
440 N Wolfe Rd Sunnyvale (94085) *(P-10876)*
Plugandplaytechcenter.com, Sunnyvale *Also called Plug & Play LLC (P-10876)*
Plum Valley Inc ....E....530 262-6262
3308 Cyclone Ct Cottonwood (96022) *(P-3100)*
Plumas Bank (HQ) ....**E....530 283-7305**
35 S Lindan Ave Quincy (95971) *(P-9743)*
Plumas Hospital District (PA) ....**C....530 283-2121**
1065 Bucks Lake Rd Quincy (95971) *(P-16481)*
Plumas Lake Golf and Cntry CLB ....E....530 742-3201
1551 Country Club Rd Marysville (95901) *(P-15123)*
Plumas Rural Services ....E....530 283-2725
711 E Main St Quincy (95971) *(P-17674)*
Plumas-Sierra Rural Elc Coop (PA) ....**E....530 832-4261**
73233 State Route 70 Portola (96122) *(P-8195)*
Plumbers Stmftters Lcal Un 342, Concord *Also called United Association Local 342 (P-18381)*
Plumbing Enterprises, Rancho Cordova *Also called Lek Enterprises Inc (P-1304)*
Plumbing Indust Apprenticeship ....D....408 453-6330
780 Commercial St San Jose (95112) *(P-17832)*
Plume Design Inc ....D....408 498-5512
290 California Ave # 200 Palo Alto (94306) *(P-13649)*
Plume Wifi, Palo Alto *Also called Plume Design Inc (P-13649)*
Plumpjack The, Olympic Valley *Also called Cncml A California Ltd Partnr (P-11019)*
Pluribus Networks Inc (PA) ....**D....650 289-4717**
5201 Great America Pkwy # 422 Santa Clara (95054) *(P-8083)*
Pluris Inc ....C....408 863-9920
10455 Bandley Dr Cupertino (95014) *(P-13650)*
Plus Group Inc ....B....209 342-9022
3300 Tully Rd Ste B1 Modesto (95350) *(P-12188)*
Plus Group Inc ....B....925 831-8551
2551 San Ramon Valley Blv San Ramon (94583) *(P-12189)*
Plusai Inc ....D....408 508-4758
20401 Stevens Creek Blvd Cupertino (95014) *(P-13374)*
Plushcare Inc ....D....415 231-5333
650 5th St Ste 405 San Francisco (94107) *(P-15631)*
Plutoshift Inc ....F....213 400-2104
530 Lytton Ave Fl 2 Palo Alto (94301) *(P-13375)*
Plymouth Square, Stockton *Also called Stockton Congregational Home (P-18185)*

PM Design Group, Rocklin *Also called Pedro McCrcken Dsign Group Inc (P-18903)*
PM Entertainment Corp ....E....408 732-2121
146 S Murphy Ave Sunnyvale (94086) *(P-14874)*
Pmc Inc ....E....562 905-3101
345 Saratoga Ave Santa Clara (95050) *(P-4245)*
Pmca Bakersfield LLC ....E....559 224-2700
5091 N Fresno St Ste 104 Fresno (93710) *(P-11694)*
Pmdsoft Inc ....D....800 587-4989
345 California St Ste 600 San Francisco (94104) *(P-12688)*
PMI, San Carlos *Also called Precincal Mdvice Innvtions LLC (P-16794)*
PMI, San Jose *Also called Precision Measurements Inc (P-14703)*
PMI San Fran Export, South San Francisco *Also called Pacific Market International (P-19600)*
Pml Estates Division, San Mateo *Also called Pml Management Corporation (P-10645)*
Pml Management Corporation ....E....650 349-9113
655 Mariners Island Blvd San Mateo (94404) *(P-10645)*
Pmn Design Electric Inc (PA) ....**D....925 846-0650**
39 Wyoming St Pleasanton (94566) *(P-1566)*
Pmp Family, Modesto *Also called Scenic Faculty Med Group Inc (P-15676)*
Pmz Real Estate, Modesto *Also called Lily Development Inc (P-10601)*
PNC, San Francisco *Also called Esurance Insurance Svcs Inc (P-10281)*
PNC Multifamily Finance Inc (HQ) ....**D....415 733-1500**
575 Market St Ste 2800 San Francisco (94105) *(P-9920)*
Pneumatic Conveying & Mfg Pcm, Red Bluff *Also called Cascade Filtration Inc (P-1991)*
Pni Sensor, Santa Rosa *Also called Protonex LLC (P-6260)*
Pnm Company ....E....559 291-1986
2547 N Business Park Ave Fresno (93727) *(P-5598)*
Pocket, San Francisco *Also called Read It Later Inc (P-13400)*
Pocket Gems Inc ....C....415 371-1333
220 Montgomery St Ste 750 San Francisco (94104) *(P-7181)*
Poco Dolce Chocolates ....F....415 255-1443
2419 3rd St San Francisco (94107) *(P-2439)*
Pods of San Francisco LLC (HQ) ....**D....510 780-1654**
21001 Cabot Blvd Hayward (94545) *(P-7631)*
Point Blue Cnservation Science, Petaluma *Also called Point Reyes Bird Observator (P-18449)*
Point Blue Cnservation Science, Petaluma *Also called Point Reyes Bird Observatory (P-19229)*
Point Digital Finance Inc ....E....650 460-8668
635 High St Palo Alto (94301) *(P-10007)*
Point One Elec Systems Inc ....D....925 667-2935
6751 Southfront Rd Livermore (94551) *(P-1567)*
Point Pacific Drilling, Petaluma *Also called CLY Incorporated (P-1029)*
Point Reyes Bird Observator ....E....415 868-0371
3820 Cypress Dr Ste 11 Petaluma (94954) *(P-18449)*
Point Reyes Bird Observatory ....D....707 781-2555
3820 Cypress Dr Ste 11 Petaluma (94954) *(P-19229)*
Pokka Beverages, American Canyon *Also called Amcan Beverages Inc (P-2781)*
Polar Service Center ....E....916 643-4689
4432 Winters Ave McClellan (95652) *(P-5080)*
Polarion Software Inc ....D....877 572-4005
1001 Marina Village Pkwy # 403 Alameda (94501) *(P-13376)*
Polaris Building Maint Inc ....D....650 964-9400
2580 Wyandotte St Ste E Mountain View (94043) *(P-11985)*
Polaris Home Care LLC ....D....408 400-7020
830 Stewart Dr Ste 211 Sunnyvale (94085) *(P-16924)*
Polaris Networks Incorporated ....D....408 625-7273
14856 Holden Way San Jose (95124) *(P-12689)*
Polaris Wireless Inc ....E....408 492-8900
301 N Whisman Rd Mountain View (94043) *(P-12690)*
Police Credit Union of Cal (PA) ....**D....415 242-2142**
1250 Grundy Ln San Bruno (94066) *(P-9803)*
Police Officers Assn Lodi ....D....209 333-6886
215 W Elm St Lodi (95240) *(P-18450)*
Policeone Academy, San Francisco *Also called Praetorian Group (P-13961)*
Polishing Corporation America ....E....888 892-3377
442 Martin Ave Santa Clara (95050) *(P-6252)*
Poll Everywhere Inc ....D....800 388-2039
639 Howard St San Francisco (94105) *(P-18247)*
Polsinelli LLP, Palo Alto *Also called Polsinelli PC (P-17358)*
Polsinelli PC ....E....650 461-7700
1661 Page Mill Rd Ste A Palo Alto (94304) *(P-17358)*
Poly Processing Company LLC ....D....209 982-4904
8055 Ash St French Camp (95231) *(P-3808)*
Poly-Seal Industries ....F....510 843-9722
725 Channing Way Berkeley (94710) *(P-4223)*
Polycom Inc (HQ) ....**A....831 426-5858**
6001 America Center Dr San Jose (95002) *(P-5806)*
Polycomp Administrative Svcs ....E....916 773-3480
3000 Lava Ridge Ct # 130 Roseville (95661) *(P-10334)*
Polyfuel Inc ....E....650 429-4700
1245 Terra Bella Ave Mountain View (94043) *(P-19104)*
Polymer Technology Group, The, Berkeley *Also called DSM Biomedical Inc (P-19053)*
Polymeric Technology Inc ....E....510 895-6001
1900 Marina Blvd San Leandro (94577) *(P-4224)*
Polytec Products Corporation ....E....650 322-7555
3390 Valley Square Ln San Jose (95117) *(P-5599)*
Polyvore Inc ....D....650 968-1195
701 First Ave Sunnyvale (94089) *(P-9669)*
Pomeroy Rcrtion Rhbltation Ctr (PA) ....**C....415 665-4100**
207 Skyline Blvd San Francisco (94132) *(P-17675)*
Pometta's, Sonoma *Also called Sonoma Gourmet Inc (P-2286)*
Pomwonderful LLC ....D....310 966-5800
900 Airport Blvd Mendota (93640) *(P-9475)*
Ponder Environmental Svcs Inc (PA) ....**E....707 748-7775**
4563 E 2nd St Benicia (94510) *(P-19839)*

Ponderosa Garden Motel Inc..........D.......888 727-3423
7010 Skyway Paradise (95969) *(P-11373)*
Ponderosa Telephone Co (PA)..........**E.......559 868-6000**
47034 Rd 201 O Neals (93645) *(P-7984)*
Ponyai Inc..........B.......510 906-8868
3501 Gateway Blvd Fremont (94538) *(P-12691)*
Pool Covers Inc..........E.......707 864-6674
4925 Fulton Dr Fairfield (94534) *(P-9159)*
Pool Water Products..........F.......925 827-4300
1940 Arnold Industrial Pl Concord (94520) *(P-9160)*
Poolmaster Inc..........D.......916 567-9800
770 Del Paso Rd Sacramento (95834) *(P-7182)*
Popcorn Design LLC..........E.......707 321-7982
824a Healdsburg Ave Healdsburg (95448) *(P-9583)*
Popcorn Wine Group, Healdsburg *Also called Popcorn Design LLC (P-9583)*
Popout Inc..........D.......415 691-7447
731 Market St Ste 200 San Francisco (94103) *(P-13377)*
Poppy Bank (HQ)..........**D.......707 636-9000**
438 1st St Ste 100 Santa Rosa (95401) *(P-9744)*
Poppy Ridge Inc..........E.......925 456-8229
4280 Greenville Rd Livermore (94550) *(P-15016)*
Poppy Ridge Golf Course, Livermore *Also called Poppy Ridge Inc (P-15016)*
Poppy State Express Inc..........D.......209 664-3950
2700 W Main St Turlock (95380) *(P-7573)*
Poppycolor LLC..........E.......916 549-6209
4028 Adelheid Way Sacramento (95821) *(P-3685)*
Popsugar Inc (PA)..........**C.......415 391-7576**
111 Sutter St Fl 16 San Francisco (94104) *(P-3591)*
Populus Technologies Inc..........E.......415 364-8048
177 Post St Ste 200 San Francisco (94108) *(P-13378)*
Porrey Pines Bank Inc..........C.......510 899-7500
1951 Webster St Oakland (94612) *(P-9688)*
Port Dept City of Oakland (PA)..........**B.......510 627-1100**
530 Water St Fl 3 Oakland (94607) *(P-7724)*
Port Dept City of Oakland..........D.......510 563-3697
9532 Earhart Rd Ste 205 Oakland (94621) *(P-7780)*
Port Dept of The Cy Oakland..........D.......510 563-3300
1 Airport Dr Ste 45 Oakland (94621) *(P-7781)*
Port of Oakland, Oakland *Also called Port Dept City of Oakland (P-7724)*
Port of Sacramento, West Sacramento *Also called Sacramnt-Yolo Port Dst Fing Co (P-7725)*
PORT OF STOCKTON, Stockton *Also called Stockton Port District (P-7726)*
Porta-Bote International, Mountain View *Also called Kaye Sandy Enterprises Inc (P-6643)*
Portco Inc..........D.......415 771-5200
496 Jefferson St San Francisco (94109) *(P-9161)*
Portlock International Ltd..........E.......209 274-0167
1000 Castle Oaks Dr Ione (95640) *(P-15017)*
Portola Pharmaceuticals Inc (HQ)..........**B.......650 246-7300**
270 E Grand Ave South San Francisco (94080) *(P-19105)*
Portsmouth Financial Services..........E.......415 543-8500
601 Montgomery St # 1950 San Francisco (94111) *(P-10008)*
Portworx Inc..........D.......650 386-0766
650 Castro St Ste 400 Mountain View (94041) *(P-12692)*
Pos Portal Inc (HQ)..........**E.......530 695-3005**
180 Promenade Cir Ste 215 Sacramento (95834) *(P-5423)*
Poshmark Inc (PA)..........**B.......650 262-4771**
203 Rdwood Shres Pkwy Fl Flr 8 Redwood City (94065) *(P-13379)*
Posiflex Business Machines Inc..........E.......510 429-7097
30689 Huntwood Ave Hayward (94544) *(P-8735)*
Position2 Inc (PA)..........**E.......650 618-8900**
333 W Maude Ave Ste 207 Sunnyvale (94085) *(P-19607)*
Positive Option Family Service (PA)..........**E.......916 973-2838**
2400 Glendale Ln Ste H Sacramento (95825) *(P-17676)*
Positronics Incorporated..........F.......925 931-0211
173 Spring St Ste 120 Pleasanton (94566) *(P-5112)*
Post St Rnssnce Prtners A Cal..........A.......415 563-0303
545 Post St San Francisco (94102) *(P-11374)*
Poster Compliance Center, Walnut Creek *Also called Employerware LLC (P-3569)*
Postini Inc (PA)..........**E.......650 482-5130**
510 Veterans Blvd Redwood City (94063) *(P-13744)*
Postman Inc..........D.......415 796-6470
55 2nd St Ste 300 San Francisco (94105) *(P-12693)*
Postmates Inc (HQ)..........**B.......800 882-6106**
950 23rd St San Francisco (94107) *(P-7891)*
Postx Corporation..........E.......408 861-3500
3 Results Way Cupertino (95014) *(P-12694)*
Potawot Health Clinic, Arcata *Also called United Indian Health Svcs Inc (P-15751)*
Potrero Hills Landfill Inc..........E.......707 429-9600
3675 Potrero Hills Ln Suisun City (94585) *(P-8349)*
Potrero Medical..........D.......888 635-7280
26142 Eden Landing Rd Hayward (94545) *(P-7021)*
Pottery World LLC..........D.......916 358-8788
1006 White Rock Rd El Dorado Hills (95762) *(P-8519)*
Poumtjack Hotels, NAPA *Also called Carneros Inn LLC (P-10990)*
Power Automation Systems, Lathrop *Also called California Natural Products (P-2878)*
Power Business Technology LLC..........E.......844 769-3729
1020 Winding Creek Rd Roseville (95678) *(P-13960)*
Power Constructors Inc..........B.......916 858-8601
2934 Gold Pan Ct Ste 4 Rancho Cordova (95670) *(P-18792)*
Power Engineers Incorporated..........D.......925 372-9284
218 Loreto Ct Martinez (94553) *(P-18793)*
Power Factor Electric Inc..........E.......916 435-8838
4011 Alvis Ct Ste 4 Rocklin (95677) *(P-1568)*
Power Factors LLC (PA)..........**E.......415 299-7448**
135 Main St Ste 1750 San Francisco (94105) *(P-8736)*
Power Integrations Inc (PA)..........**A.......408 414-9200**
5245 Hellyer Ave San Jose (95138) *(P-6253)*
Power Intgrtons Intl Hldngs In..........D.......408 414-8528
5245 Hellyer Ave San Jose (95138) *(P-6254)*
Power One, Santa Clara *Also called Bel Power Solutions Inc (P-6377)*
Power Standards Lab Inc..........E.......510 522-4400
980 Atlantic Ave Ste 100 Alameda (94501) *(P-6782)*
Power Systems Division, Foresthill *Also called Placer County Water Agency (P-8193)*
Powercords, Santa Clara *Also called Volex Inc (P-4331)*
Powerflex Systems LLC..........E.......650 469-3392
392 1st St Los Altos (94022) *(P-5666)*
Powerhouse Engineering Inc..........F.......650 226-3560
101 Industrial Way Ste 13 Belmont (94002) *(P-7301)*
Powerlift Dumbwaiters Inc..........F.......800 409-5438
2444 Georgia Slide Rd Georgetown (95634) *(P-5048)*
Powerlight, Richmond *Also called Sunpower Corporation Systems (P-1368)*
Powers and Company, Rocklin *Also called Brown Brown Insur Brks Scrmnto (P-10251)*
Powerschool Group LLC (HQ)..........**C.......916 288-1588**
150 Parkshore Dr Folsom (95630) *(P-13380)*
Powerschool Holdings Inc..........A.......877 873-1550
150 Parkshore Dr Folsom (95630) *(P-13381)*
Powerside, Alameda *Also called Power Standards Lab Inc (P-6782)*
Powervision Inc..........E.......650 620-9948
298 Harbor Blvd Belmont (94002) *(P-14834)*
Powwow Inc..........E.......877 800-4381
71 Stevenson St Ste 400 San Francisco (94105) *(P-13382)*
Poynt Co..........E.......650 600-8849
4151 Middlefield Rd 2 Palo Alto (94303) *(P-12695)*
PPIC, San Francisco *Also called Public Policy Institute Cal (P-18313)*
Ppm Products Inc..........E.......408 946-4710
1538 Gladding Ct Milpitas (95035) *(P-5600)*
Pps Packaging Company..........D.......559 834-1641
3189 E Manning Ave Fowler (93625) *(P-3348)*
PR Rancho Hotel LLC..........D.......916 638-4141
11260 Point East Dr Rancho Cordova (95742) *(P-11375)*
PRA Destination Mangement, Roseville *Also called Patti Roscoe & Associates Inc (P-14354)*
Practice Wares Inc..........E.......916 526-2674
2377 Gold Meadow Way Gold River (95670) *(P-8789)*
Practicewares Dental Supply, Gold River *Also called Practice Wares Inc (P-8789)*
Praetorian Event Services, Windsor *Also called Praetorian USA (P-11727)*
Praetorian Group (PA)..........**E.......415 962-8310**
200 Green St Ste 200 # 200 San Francisco (94111) *(P-13961)*
Praetorian USA..........E.......707 780-3018
228 Windsor River Rd Windsor (95492) *(P-11727)*
Prairie City Commons LLC..........D.......916 458-0303
645 Willard Dr Folsom (95630) *(P-16196)*
Prairie City Landing, Folsom *Also called Prairie City Commons LLC (P-16196)*
Pratt & Whitney..........F.......650 634-3122
800 S Airport Blvd San Francisco (94128) *(P-6621)*
Pratt Industries Inc..........C.......770 922-0117
2131 E Louise Ave Lathrop (95330) *(P-3349)*
Pratt Lathrop Corrugating LLC..........E.......209 670-0900
2131 E Louise Ave Lathrop (95330) *(P-3365)*
Praxair, Oakland *Also called Linde Inc (P-3773)*
Praxair, San Pablo *Also called Linde Inc (P-3774)*
Praxair, Turlock *Also called Linde Gas & Equipment Inc (P-3772)*
Praxis Associates Inc..........E.......707 551-8200
332 Georgia St Vallejo (94590) *(P-14370)*
PRC..........D.......415 777-0333
170 9th St San Francisco (94103) *(P-18248)*
Prd Company, Hayward *Also called Pacific Roller Die Co Inc (P-5587)*
Pre-Employcom Inc..........D.......800 300-1821
3655 Meadow View Dr Redding (96002) *(P-14087)*
Pre-Insulated Metal Tech Inc (HQ)..........**E.......707 359-2280**
929 Aldridge Rd Vacaville (95688) *(P-4855)*
Pre-Peeled Potato Co Inc..........E.......209 469-6911
1585 S Union St Stockton (95206) *(P-2935)*
Pre/Plastics Inc..........E.......530 823-1820
12600 Locksley Ln Ste 100 Auburn (95602) *(P-4313)*
Prealize Health Inc..........E.......650 690-5300
745 Emerson St Palo Alto (94301) *(P-19608)*
Precast Con Tech Unlimited LLC..........D.......530 749-6501
1260 Furneaux Rd Olivehurst (95961) *(P-4448)*
Precious Enterprises Inc..........D.......408 265-2226
14130 Douglass Ln Saratoga (95070) *(P-18003)*
Precision Cnc LLC..........E.......209 277-2082
16818 Sycamore Ave Patterson (95363) *(P-5601)*
Precision Contacts Inc..........E.......916 939-4147
990 Suncast Ln El Dorado Hills (95762) *(P-5861)*
Precision Design Inc..........E.......650 508-8041
1160 Industrial Rd Ste 16 San Carlos (94070) *(P-5959)*
Precision Die Cutting Inc..........E.......510 636-9654
150 Doolittle Dr San Leandro (94577) *(P-6590)*
Precision Emprise LLC..........E.......866 792-8006
417 Harrison St Oakland (94607) *(P-1902)*
Precision Film & Tape, San Leandro *Also called Precision Die Cutting Inc (P-6590)*
Precision Fluid Controls Inc..........D.......916 626-3029
3860 Cincinnati Ave Rocklin (95765) *(P-9127)*
Precision Graphics, Redwood City *Also called Tilley Manufacturing Co Inc (P-4207)*
Precision Home Care LLC..........D.......916 749-4051
2365 Iron Point Rd # 270 Folsom (95630) *(P-17677)*
Precision Identity Corporation..........F.......408 374-2346
804 Camden Ave Campbell (95008) *(P-5602)*
Precision Ideo Inc..........B.......650 688-3400
780 High St Palo Alto (94301) *(P-14371)*
Precision Measurements Inc..........E.......408 733-8600
1630 Zanker Rd San Jose (95112) *(P-14703)*
Precision Medical Products Inc..........E.......888 963-6265
2217 Plaza Dr Rocklin (95765) *(P-8790)*
Precision Medical Products Inc..........D.......573 474-9302
2217 Plaza Dr Rocklin (95765) *(P-15632)*
Precision Printers, Grass Valley *Also called Igraphics (P-3738)*

ALPHABETIC

PRECITA VALLEY COMMUNITY CENTE, San Francisco *Also called Mission Neighborhood Ctrs Inc* ***(P-18439)***
Precita Valley Community Ctr, San Francisco *Also called Mission Neighborhood Ctrs Inc* ***(P-18440)***
Precincal Mdvice Innvtions LLC....E....510 704-0140
1031 Bing St San Carlos (94070) ***(P-16794)***
Precor Home Fitness, Roseville *Also called Precor Incorporated* ***(P-14964)***
Precor Incorporated....D....916 788-8334
1164 Galleria Blvd Roseville (95678) ***(P-14964)***
Predicine Inc....E....650 300-2188
3555 Arden Rd Hayward (94545) ***(P-15633)***
Predictspring Inc....E....650 917-9052
447 Rinconada Ct Los Altos (94022) ***(P-13383)***
Predii Inc....E....415 269-1146
283 Margarita Ave Palo Alto (94306) ***(P-13384)***
Preferred Corporate Svcs Inc....D....559 765-6755
1769 E El Paso Ave Fresno (93720) ***(P-10455)***
Preferred Mfg Svcs Inc (PA)....D....530 677-2675
4261 Business Dr Cameron Park (95682) ***(P-5603)***
Preferred Plumbing, Watsonville *Also called Tubular Flow Inc* ***(P-1386)***
Preferred Plumbing & Drain, North Highlands *Also called Graves 6 Inc* ***(P-1273)***
Premier Coatings Inc....D....209 982-5585
7910 Longe St Stockton (95206) ***(P-4946)***
Premier Eyecare San Francisco....E....415 648-3600
2480 Mission St Ste 212 San Francisco (94110) ***(P-15634)***
Premier Financial Group Inc....E....707 443-2741
725 6th St Eureka (95501) ***(P-10009)***
Premier Finishing, Stockton *Also called Premier Coatings Inc* ***(P-4946)***
Premier Floor Care Inc (PA)....D....925 679-4901
390 Carrol Ct Ste C Brentwood (94513) ***(P-11986)***
Premier Global Logistics LLC....E....877 671-0254
1656 Germano Way Pleasanton (94566) ***(P-7850)***
Premier Mushrooms LP (PA)....C....530 458-2700
2880 Niagara Ave Colusa (95932) ***(P-9424)***
Premier Pools and Spas Lp (PA)....D....916 852-0223
11250 Pyrites Way Gold River (95670) ***(P-2056)***
Premier Print & Mail Inc....F....916 503-5300
2615 Del Monte St West Sacramento (95691) ***(P-3745)***
Premier Properties Inc....E....707 467-0300
461 Beltrami Dr Ukiah (95482) ***(P-10646)***
Premier Senior Living LLC (PA)....D....707 778-6719
206 G St Ste 1 Petaluma (94952) ***(P-18157)***
Premier Source LLC....D....415 349-2010
999 Bayhill Dr Fl 3 San Bruno (94066) ***(P-19230)***
Premier Staffing Inc (PA)....D....415 362-2211
3595 Mt Diablo Blvd # 340 Lafayette (94549) ***(P-12121)***
Premier Surgery Center LP....E....925 691-5000
2222 East St Ste 200 Concord (94520) ***(P-15635)***
Premier Talent Partners, Lafayette *Also called Premier Staffing Inc* ***(P-12121)***
Premier Valley Bank (HQ)....D....559 438-2002
255 E River Park Cir # 180 Fresno (93720) ***(P-9760)***
Premier Valley Inc A Cal Corp....E....209 667-6111
1351 Geer Rd Ste 103 Turlock (95380) ***(P-10647)***
Premier Woodworking LLC....E....916 289-4058
2290 Dale Ave Sacramento (95815) ***(P-3147)***
Premiere Cinemas....E....831 638-1800
641 Mccray St Hollister (95023) ***(P-14816)***
Premiere Credit North Amer LLC....C....844 897-2901
17054 S Harlan Rd Lathrop (95330) ***(P-11829)***
Premiere Recycle Co....E....408 297-7910
348 Phelan Ave San Jose (95112) ***(P-4728)***
Premium Outlet Partners LP....D....916 985-0312
13000 Folsom Blvd Ste 309 Folsom (95630) ***(P-10400)***
Premium Outlet Partners LP....D....707 448-3661
321 Nut Tree Rd Ste 2 Vacaville (95687) ***(P-10401)***
Premium Outlet Partners LP....D....408 842-3729
681 Leavesley Rd Gilroy (95020) ***(P-10402)***
Prenav Inc....E....650 264-7279
1909 Lyon Ave Belmont (94002) ***(P-6679)***
Preplastics, Auburn *Also called Pre/Plastics Inc* ***(P-4313)***
Presbyterian Church USA, Lafayette *Also called Lafayette Orinda Presbt Ch* ***(P-17962)***
Prescott Hotel, The, San Francisco *Also called Post St Rnssnce Prtners A Cal* ***(P-11374)***
Presentertek Inc....E....916 251-7190
3710 N Lakeshore Blvd Loomis (95650) ***(P-5893)***
President James Monroe Manor, Sacramento *Also called Eskaton Properties Inc* ***(P-18107)***
Presidio Community YMCA, San Francisco *Also called Young MNS Chrstn Assn San Frnc* ***(P-18512)***
Presidio Gate Apartments (PA)....D....925 956-7400
2185 N Calif Blvd Ste 215 Walnut Creek (94596) ***(P-18158)***
Presidio Gate Apartments....D....415 567-1050
2770 Lombard St San Francisco (94123) ***(P-10456)***
Presidio Hill School....C....415 213-8600
3839 Washington St San Francisco (94118) ***(P-18004)***
Presidio Hotel Group LLC....C....916 631-7500
10713 White Rock Rd Rancho Cordova (95670) ***(P-11376)***
Presidio Surgery Center LLC....E....415 346-1218
1635 Divisadero St # 200 San Francisco (94115) ***(P-16482)***
Presidio Systems Inc (PA)....E....925 362-8400
159 Wright Brothers Ave Livermore (94551) ***(P-1569)***
Presido YMCA, San Francisco *Also called Young MNS Chrstn Assn San Frnc* ***(P-18513)***
Press Democrat, The, Santa Rosa *Also called Santa Rosa Press Democrat Inc* ***(P-3477)***
Pressed Juicery Inc....F....559 777-8900
3530 E Church Ave Fresno (93725) ***(P-9476)***
Pressure Cast Products Corp....E....510 532-7310
4210 E 12th St Oakland (94601) ***(P-4581)***
Prestige Protection, San Ramon *Also called Universal Protection Svc LP* ***(P-14105)***
Preston Pipelines Inc (PA)....C....408 262-1418
133 Bothelo Ave Milpitas (95035) ***(P-1131)***
Preston Vineyards Inc....F....707 433-3372
9282 W Dry Creek Rd Healdsburg (95448) ***(P-2687)***
Preston Vineyards & Winery, Healdsburg *Also called Preston Vineyards Inc* ***(P-2687)***
Prevent Life Safety Svcs Inc....E....925 667-2088
448 Commerce Way Ste B Livermore (94551) ***(P-14372)***
Prevention Institute....D....510 444-4133
221 Oak St Ste A Oakland (94607) ***(P-19609)***
Prevost Car (us) Inc....E....951 202-2064
28702 Hall Rd Hayward (94545) ***(P-6554)***
Prezi Inc (PA)....E....415 398-8012
450 Bryant St San Francisco (94107) ***(P-13385)***
Pribuss Engineering Inc....D....650 588-0447
523 Mayfair Ave South San Francisco (94080) ***(P-14688)***
Price Rubber Company Inc....E....209 239-7478
17760 Ideal Pkwy Manteca (95336) ***(P-4200)***
Price-Simms Ford LLC....D....707 421-3300
3050 Auto Mall Ct Fairfield (94534) ***(P-14584)***
Pricewaterhousecoopers LLP....A....408 817-3700
488 Almaden Blvd Ste 1800 San Jose (95110) ***(P-18985)***
Pride Conveyance Systems Inc....D....831 637-1787
1700 Shelton Dr Hollister (95023) ***(P-5054)***
Pride Industries (PA)....C....916 788-2100
10030 Foothills Blvd Roseville (95747) ***(P-7709)***
Pride Industries One Inc....A....916 788-2100
10030 Foothills Blvd Roseville (95747) ***(P-7302)***
Pride Line Products, Stockton *Also called Value Products Inc* ***(P-4065)***
Prima Fleur Botanicals Inc....F....415 455-0957
84 Galli Dr Novato (94949) ***(P-4093)***
Prima Noce Packing Inc....E....209 932-8800
16461 E Comstock Rd Linden (95236) ***(P-14373)***
Primal Pet Foods Inc....E....415 642-7400
2045 Mckinnon Ave San Francisco (94124) ***(P-9477)***
Primal Pet Foods Inc....D....415 642-7400
535 Watt Dr Ste B Fairfield (94534) ***(P-2335)***
Primark Benefits....E....650 692-2043
1810 Gateway Dr Ste 230 San Mateo (94404) ***(P-10335)***
Primary Diagnostics Inc....E....619 356-3701
595 Pacific Ave Fl 4 San Francisco (94133) ***(P-12696)***
Primary Eyecare Network, Alameda *Also called Abb/Con-Cise Optical Group LLC* ***(P-8797)***
Primarydata Inc (PA)....E....650 422-3800
4300 El Camino Realste100 Los Altos (94022) ***(P-12697)***
Prime Engineering, Fresno *Also called Axiom Industries Inc* ***(P-7066)***
Prime Finance Partners I LP (PA)....E....415 986-2415
600 Montgomery St # 1700 San Francisco (94111) ***(P-14374)***
Prime Hlthcare Svcs - Shsta LL....A....530 244-5400
1100 Butte St Redding (96001) ***(P-16483)***
Prime Solutions Inc (PA)....D....510 490-2255
4261 Business Center Dr Fremont (94538) ***(P-6255)***
Prime Time Athletic Club Inc....C....650 204-3662
1730 Rollins Rd Burlingame (94010) ***(P-14965)***
Primed MGT Consulting Svcs Inc....B....925 327-6710
2409 Camino Ramon San Ramon (94583) ***(P-19382)***
Primeflight Aviation Svcs Inc....C....650 877-1560
612 Mcdonald Rd Ste 100 San Francisco (94128) ***(P-7782)***
Primenano Inc....F....650 300-5115
4701 Patrick Henry Dr # 8 Santa Clara (95054) ***(P-6256)***
Primetek Field Solutions Inc....E....619 271-4555
605 Rialto Dr Vacaville (95687) ***(P-1570)***
Primex, Vacaville *Also called McC Controls LLC* ***(P-5442)***
Primitive Logic Inc....D....415 391-8080
130 Battery St Fl 3 San Francisco (94111) ***(P-13962)***
Primrose Alzheimers Living Inc (PA)....E....707 568-4355
726 College Ave Santa Rosa (95404) ***(P-18159)***
Primus Power Corporation....E....510 342-7600
3967 Trust Way Hayward (94545) ***(P-6496)***
Prince Peace Enterprises Inc (PA)....E....925 292-3888
751 N Canyons Pkwy Livermore (94551) ***(P-9478)***
Prince Peace Lutheran Church....D....510 797-8186
38451 Fremont Blvd Fremont (94536) ***(P-18005)***
Prince Peace Lutheran School, Fremont *Also called Prince Peace Lutheran Church* ***(P-18005)***
Principal Builders Inc....E....415 434-1500
616 Minna St San Francisco (94103) ***(P-688)***
Principal Svc Solutions Inc....C....209 408-1982
4285 Spyres Way Ste 2 Modesto (95356) ***(P-18794)***
Principia Biopharma Inc (HQ)....D....650 416-7700
220 E Grand Ave South San Francisco (94080) ***(P-3966)***
Prinsco Inc....E....559 485-5542
2839 S Cherry Ave Fresno (93706) ***(P-4234)***
Print Ink Inc....E....925 829-3950
6918 Sierra Ct Dublin (94568) ***(P-3746)***
Printed Image, The, Chico *Also called Srl Apparel Inc* ***(P-2978)***
Printerprezz Inc....F....510 225-8412
47929 Fremont Blvd Fremont (94538) ***(P-7022)***
Printpack Inc....D....925 469-0601
5870 Stnrdge Mall Rd Ste Pleasanton (94588) ***(P-3386)***
Printworx Inc....F....831 722-7147
195 Aviation Way Ste 201 Watsonville (95076) ***(P-5405)***
Priority Roofing Solutions Inc....E....408 532-8020
2928 Stanhope Dr San Jose (95121) ***(P-1831)***
Prism Electronics Corp (PA)....E....408 778-7050
900 Lightpost Way 100 Morgan Hill (95037) ***(P-8947)***
Privacera Inc....D....510 413-7300
39300 Civic Center Dr # 140 Fremont (94538) ***(P-12698)***
Private Eyes Inc (PA)....E....925 927-3333
2700 Ygnacio Valley Rd # 10 Walnut Creek (94598) ***(P-14088)***
Private Industry Cncl Slno Cty (PA)....E....707 864-3370
500 Chadbourne Rd Fairfield (94534) ***(P-12122)***

Private Mortgage Advisors LLC ....E....408 754-1610
390 Diablo Rd Ste 100 Danville (94526) ***(P-9921)***
Priyo Inc ....E....408 248-2507
605 Tumbleweed Cmn Fremont (94539) ***(P-12699)***
Pro Foods Solutions, Richmond *Also called Richmond Wholesale Meat LLC **(P-9379)***
Pro Pacific Fresh, Durham *Also called Chico Produce Inc **(P-9393)***
Pro Star Auto Service Inc ....E....408 942-3330
355 Sango Ct Milpitas (95035) ***(P-14617)***
Pro Unlimited Inc (PA) ....D....**561 994-9500**
1 Post St Ste 375 San Francisco (94104) ***(P-13386)***
Pro-Cision Machining, Morgan Hill *Also called KDF Inc **(P-5552)***
Pro-Form Laboratories, Benicia *Also called Pro-Form Manufacturing LLC **(P-19282)***
Pro-Form Manufacturing LLC ....C....707 752-9010
5001 Industrial Way Benicia (94510) ***(P-19282)***
Pro-Groom Inc ....E....916 782-4172
935 Roseville Pkwy # 100 Roseville (95678) ***(P-356)***
Pro-Tech Fire Prtction Systems ....D....916 388-0255
8880 Cal Center Dr # 400 Sacramento (95826) ***(P-1338)***
Pro-Tek Manufacturing Inc ....E....925 454-8100
4849 Southfront Rd Livermore (94551) ***(P-4806)***
Proactive Bus Solutions Inc ....C....510 302-0120
410 7th St 205 Oakland (94607) ***(P-19383)***
Proactive Technical Svcs Inc (HQ) ....E....**408 531-6040**
2350 Mission College Blvd # 246 Santa Clara (95054) ***(P-12700)***
Probation Dept, Modesto *Also called County of Stanislaus **(P-17515)***
Probation Dept, Palo Alto *Also called Santa Clara County of **(P-17721)***
Probe Information Services Inc ....C....916 676-1826
3835 N Freeway Blvd # 228 Sacramento (95834) ***(P-14089)***
Probe-Logic Inc ....E....408 416-0777
1885 Lundy Ave Ste 101 San Jose (95131) ***(P-6257)***
Procept Biorobotics Corp (PA) ....C....**650 232-7200**
900 Island Dr Ste 170 Redwood City (94065) ***(P-7023)***
Process Specialties Inc ....E....209 832-1344
1660 W Linne Rd Ste A Tracy (95377) ***(P-6258)***
Process Stainless Lab Inc (PA) ....E....**408 980-0535**
1280 Memorex Dr Santa Clara (95050) ***(P-4917)***
Processweaver Inc ....F....510 648-1420
5201 Great America Pkwy # 300 Santa Clara (95054) ***(P-13387)***
Procida Landscape Inc ....C....916 387-5296
8465 Specialty Cir Sacramento (95828) ***(P-497)***
Proco Products Inc (PA) ....E....**209 943-6088**
2431 Wigwam Dr Stockton (95205) ***(P-4225)***
Procter & Gamble Mfg Co ....C....916 383-3800
8201 Fruitridge Rd Sacramento (95826) ***(P-4064)***
Proctoru Inc ....C....205 870-8122
3687 Old Sta Pleasanton (94588) ***(P-13805)***
Procureability Inc ....E....904 432-7001
11260 Donner Pass Rd C Truckee (96161) ***(P-19610)***
Procurement Div, West Sacramento *Also called General Services Cal Dept **(P-12092)***
Prodigy Surface Tech Inc ....E....408 492-9390
807 Aldo Ave Ste 103 Santa Clara (95054) ***(P-4918)***
Produce Exchange Incorporated (HQ) ....D....**925 454-8700**
7407 Southfront Rd Livermore (94551) ***(P-9425)***
Produce World Inc ....D....510 441-1449
30611 San Antonio St Hayward (94544) ***(P-2936)***
Producers Dairy Foods Inc (PA) ....C....**559 264-6583**
250 E Belmont Ave Fresno (93701) ***(P-9330)***
Produces Dairy, Fresno *Also called L A S Transportation Inc **(P-7560)***
Productboard Inc (PA) ....C....**844 472-6273**
612 Howard St Fl 4 San Francisco (94105) ***(P-5066)***
Production Framing Systems Inc (PA) ....C....**916 978-2888**
2000 Opportunity Dr # 140 Roseville (95678) ***(P-1750)***
Professional Assn Svcs Inc ....E....510 683-8614
42612 Christy St Fremont (94538) ***(P-18451)***
Professional Bureau of Collect ....C....916 685-3399
9675 Elk Grove Florin Rd Elk Grove (95624) ***(P-11830)***
Professional Exchange Svc ....E....559 229-6249
4747 N 1st St Ste 140 Fresno (93726) ***(P-14375)***
Professional Finishing Inc ....D....510 233-7629
770 Market Ave Richmond (94801) ***(P-4947)***
Professional Healthcare At HM, Campbell *Also called Kindred Healthcare LLC **(P-16905)***
Professional Healthcare At HM ....E....415 492-8400
185 N Redwood Dr Ste 150 San Rafael (94903) ***(P-16925)***
Professional Insur Assoc Inc (PA) ....E....**650 592-7333**
1100 Industrial Rd Ste 3 San Carlos (94070) ***(P-10336)***
Professional Lumper Svc Inc ....E....209 613-5397
1943 Alex Way Turlock (95382) ***(P-5067)***
Professional Print & Mail Inc ....E....559 237-7468
2818 E Hamilton Ave Fresno (93721) ***(P-3686)***
Professional Retirement Svcs, San Mateo *Also called Primark Benefits **(P-10335)***
Professional Tree Care, Berkeley *Also called Arboricultural Specialties Inc **(P-512)***
Professnal Blling MGT Svcs Inc ....E....209 579-5628
220 Standiford Ave Ste F Modesto (95350) ***(P-18986)***
Professnal Fincl Investors Inc ....E....415 382-6001
350 Ignacio Blvd Ste 300 Novato (94949) ***(P-10648)***
Professnal Halthcare At HM LLC ....D....510 450-0422
395 Taylor Blvd Ste 118 Pleasant Hill (94523) ***(P-16926)***
Professnal Halthcare At HM LLC (PA) ....D....**925 849-1160**
395 Taylor Blvd Ste 118 Pleasant Hill (94523) ***(P-16927)***
Professnal Ldscp Solutions Inc ....E....916 424-3815
6108 27th St Ste C Sacramento (95822) ***(P-437)***
Professnal Tchncal SEC Svcs In (PA) ....B....**415 243-2100**
625 Market St Fl 9 San Francisco (94105) ***(P-14090)***
Professnal Tchncal SEC Svcs In ....C....510 645-9200
1970 Broadway Ste 840 Oakland (94612) ***(P-14091)***
Progistics Distribution Inc ....A....415 369-8845
480 Roland Way Ste 103 Oakland (94621) ***(P-7851)***
Program Plg Professionals Inc ....C....415 692-5870
71 Stevenson St Ste 825 San Francisco (94105) ***(P-14376)***
Progress Glass Co Inc (PA) ....C....**415 824-7040**
25 Patterson St San Francisco (94124) ***(P-1940)***
Progress Investment MGT Co LLC ....E....415 512-3480
33 New Montgomery St # 19 San Francisco (94105) ***(P-10056)***
Progressive Roofing, Stockton *Also called Progressive Services Inc **(P-1832)***
Progressive Services Inc ....E....209 824-2837
3832 S Highway 99 Ste A Stockton (95215) ***(P-1832)***
Progressive Solutions, San Jose *Also called Sarpa-Feldman Enterprises Inc **(P-14398)***
Progressive Sub-Acute Care ....D....408 378-8875
13425 Sousa Ln Saratoga (95070) ***(P-16484)***
Progressive Technology Inc ....E....916 632-6715
4130 Citrus Ave Ste 17 Rocklin (95677) ***(P-4403)***
Progrip Cargo Control, Lodi *Also called USA Products Group **(P-7202)***
Progrssive Employment Concepts (PA) ....E....**916 723-3112**
6060 Sunrise Vista Dr # 1 Citrus Heights (95610) ***(P-17833)***
Proguard Security Services ....E....415 672-0786
300 Montgomery St Ste 813 San Francisco (94104) ***(P-14144)***
Project Affinity, San Francisco *Also called Affinity Inc **(P-12234)***
Project Affinity Inc ....D....415 606-7649
170 Columbus Ave San Francisco (94133) ***(P-12701)***
Project Frog Inc ....C....415 814-8500
99 Green St Ste 200 San Francisco (94111) ***(P-762)***
Project Go Incorporated ....E....916 782-3443
801 Vernon St Roseville (95678) ***(P-2057)***
Project Hired (PA) ....D....**408 557-0880**
2505 Eaton Ave San Carlos (94070) ***(P-12190)***
Project Open Hand (PA) ....D....**415 292-3400**
730 Polk St Fl 3 San Francisco (94109) ***(P-17678)***
Project Partners LLC (PA) ....E....**650 712-6200**
520 Purissima St Half Moon Bay (94019) ***(P-13963)***
Project Sentinel Inc (PA) ....E....**650 321-6291**
1490 El Camino Real Santa Clara (95050) ***(P-19840)***
Projector Is Inc ....E....917 972-5553
130 11th Ave San Francisco (94118) ***(P-13388)***
Projistics, San Jose *Also called Nagarro Inc **(P-13942)***
Prolab Orthotics Inc ....E....707 257-4400
575 Airpark Rd NAPA (94558) ***(P-4226)***
Prologis Inc (PA) ....B....**415 394-9000**
Bay 1 Pier 1 San Francisco (94111) ***(P-10822)***
Prologis LP (HQ) ....B....**415 394-9000**
Bay 1 Pier 1 San Francisco (94111) ***(P-10823)***
Promab Biotechnologies Inc ....D....510 860-4615
2600 Hilltop Dr San Pablo (94806) ***(P-19106)***
Promega Bsystems Sunnyvale Inc ....E....408 636-2400
3945 Freedom Cir Ste 200 Santa Clara (95054) ***(P-6917)***
Promerio Inc (PA) ....D....**925 240-2400**
1240 Central Blvd Ste B Brentwood (94513) ***(P-18987)***
Promesa Behavioral Health (PA) ....C....**559 439-5437**
7120 N Marks Ave Fresno (93711) ***(P-18160)***
Promesys Division, Santa Clara *Also called KLA Corporation **(P-6172)***
Prometheus RE Group Inc (PA) ....C....**650 931-3400**
1900 S Norfolk St Ste 150 San Mateo (94403) ***(P-10649)***
Promex Industries Incorporated (PA) ....D....**408 496-0222**
3075 Oakmead Village Dr Santa Clara (95051) ***(P-6259)***
Promise Energy Inc ....E....707 938-7207
3558 Round Barn Blvd # 200 Santa Rosa (95403) ***(P-1339)***
Promise Network Inc ....E....877 717-7664
436 14th St Ste 920 Oakland (94612) ***(P-12702)***
Promise Technology Inc ....D....408 228-1400
3241 Keller St Santa Clara (95054) ***(P-8737)***
Promotion Xpress Prtg Graphics, San Leandro *Also called Akido Printing Inc **(P-3617)***
Prompt Precision Metals Inc ....E....209 531-1210
1649 E Whitmore Ave Ceres (95307) ***(P-4807)***
Proof of Concept Poc Lab, Sunnyvale *Also called Juniper Networks Inc **(P-13616)***
Proofpoint Inc (PA) ....A....**408 517-4710**
925 W Maude Ave Sunnyvale (94085) ***(P-13745)***
Proov Inc ....E....847 715-8218
2345 Yale St Fl 1 Palo Alto (94306) ***(P-12703)***
Propak Logistics Inc ....E....479 478-7828
2650 Industrial Blvd B West Sacramento (95691) ***(P-14770)***
Propane Cnstr & Meter Svcs (PA) ....C....**866 587-7411**
1262 Dupont Ct Manteca (95336) ***(P-9535)***
Propelplm Inc ....D....408 755-3780
451 El Camino Real # 110 Santa Clara (95050) ***(P-12704)***
Property Maintenance Company (PA) ....C....**408 297-7849**
255 W Julian St Ste 301 San Jose (95110) ***(P-11987)***
Property Sciences Group Inc (PA) ....E....**925 246-7300**
395 Taylor Blvd Ste 250 Pleasant Hill (94523) ***(P-10650)***
Prophet Brand Strategy (PA) ....E....**415 677-0909**
1 Bush St Fl 7 San Francisco (94104) ***(P-19611)***
Proplus Design Solutions Inc (PA) ....C....**408 459-6128**
2025 Gateway Pl Ste 130 San Jose (95110) ***(P-14377)***
Prosight Specity Insur Grp Inc ....D....707 324-5000
1425 N Mcdowell Blvd # 213 Petaluma (94954) ***(P-10337)***
Prospance Inc (PA) ....D....**925 415-2394**
4221 Bus Ctr Dr Ste 1 Fremont (94538) ***(P-12705)***
Prosper Funding LLC (HQ) ....D....**415 593-5400**
101 2nd St Fl 15 San Francisco (94105) ***(P-9874)***
Prosper Marketplace Inc (PA) ....B....**415 593-5400**
221 Main St Fl 3 San Francisco (94105) ***(P-9945)***
Prosurg Inc ....E....408 945-4040
2195 Trade Zone Blvd San Jose (95131) ***(P-7024)***
Protagonist Technology LLC (PA) ....E....**415 967-5530**
345 California St Ste 600 San Francisco (94104) ***(P-19612)***
Protagonist Therapeutics Inc ....D....510 474-0170
7707 Gateway Blvd Ste 140 Newark (94560) ***(P-3967)***
Protec, Hercules *Also called Mega Creation Inc **(P-4090)***
Protech, San Francisco *Also called Professnal Tchncal SEC Svcs In **(P-14090)***

ALPHABETIC

Protech Materials Inc ALPHABETIC SECTION

Protech Materials Inc ....F....510 887-5870
20919 Cabot Blvd Hayward (94545) *(P-4582)*
Protective Business & Health ....D....845 354-5372
3785 Brickway Blvd # 200 Santa Rosa (95403) *(P-13746)*
Protein Research, Livermore *Also called Berkeley Nutritional Mfg Corp (P-19153)*
Proteinsimple (HQ) ....E....**408 510-5500**
3001 Orchard Pkwy San Jose (95134) *(P-19107)*
Proterra Inc (PA) ....C....**864 438-0000**
1815 Rollins Rd Burlingame (94010) *(P-6555)*
Proterra Operating Company Inc (HQ) ....C....**864 438-0000**
1815 Rollins Rd Burlingame (94010) *(P-6556)*
Proteus Digital Health Inc (PA) ....C....**650 632-4031**
2600 Bridge Pkwy Redwood City (94065) *(P-4055)*
Proteus Industries Inc ....E....650 964-4163
340 Pioneer Way Mountain View (94041) *(P-6731)*
Prothena Biosciences Inc ....E....650 837-8550
331 Oyster Point Blvd South San Francisco (94080) *(P-19231)*
Prothena Corp Pub Ltd Co ....E....650 837-8550
331 Oyster Point Blvd South San Francisco (94080) *(P-3820)*
Protiviti Inc (HQ) ....D....**650 234-6000**
2884 Sand Hill Rd Ste 200 Menlo Park (94025) *(P-19613)*
Protominds Inc ....E....408 684-6363
1551 Mccarthy Blvd # 103 Milpitas (95035) *(P-12706)*
Protonex LLC ....F....707 566-2260
2331 Circadian Way Santa Rosa (95407) *(P-6260)*
Prototek California LLC ....E....408 730-5035
215 Devcon Dr San Jose (95112) *(P-5084)*
Protransport-1 LLC (HQ) ....A....**707 975-2386**
720 Portal St Cotati (94931) *(P-7396)*
Provac Sales Inc ....E....831 462-8900
3131 Soquel Dr Ste A Soquel (95073) *(P-5178)*
Provectus It Inc ....A....650 787-3207
125 University Ave # 290 Palo Alto (94301) *(P-12707)*
Proven Termite Solution, San Jose *Also called Weed Enterprises Inc (P-11910)*
Provena Foods Inc ....C....209 858-5555
251 Darcy Pkwy Lathrop (95330) *(P-2121)*
Provenance Vineyards ....E....707 968-3633
1695 Saint Helena Hwy S Saint Helena (94574) *(P-2688)*
Provide Inc ....E....877 341-0617
268 Bush St 2921 San Francisco (94104) *(P-13389)*
Providence Health & Svcs - Ore ....C....510 444-0839
540 23rd St Oakland (94612) *(P-16485)*
Providence Horticulture Inc ....D....559 251-7907
6931 E Belmont Ave Fresno (93727) *(P-521)*
Providence Place Inc ....E....415 359-9700
2456 Geary Blvd San Francisco (94115) *(P-18161)*
Providence Publications LLC ....E....916 774-4000
1620 Santa Roseville (95661) *(P-3592)*
Providence Veterinary Clinic W, Alameda *Also called Providence Veterinary Hospital (P-333)*
Providence Veterinary Hospital ....E....510 521-6608
2304 Pacific Ave Alameda (94501) *(P-333)*
Provident Care Inc ....C....209 578-1210
1025 14th St Modesto (95354) *(P-16928)*
Provident Credit Union (PA) ....C....**650 508-0300**
303 Twin Dolphin Dr # 303 Redwood City (94065) *(P-9835)*
Provident Funding Assoc LP ....E....707 568-2420
1235 N Dutton Ave Ste A Santa Rosa (95401) *(P-9922)*
Provident Funding Assoc LP (PA) ....E....**650 652-1300**
851 Traeger Ave Ste 100 San Bruno (94066) *(P-9923)*
Proxim Wireless Corporation (PA) ....D....**408 383-7600**
2114 Ringwood Ave San Jose (95131) *(P-5894)*
Proximex Corporation ....E....408 215-9000
300 Santana Row Ste 200 San Jose (95128) *(P-13390)*
Prozyme Inc ....E....510 638-6900
3832 Bay Center Pl Hayward (94545) *(P-19108)*
Prs/Roebbelen JV ....E....916 641-0324
4811 Tunis Rd Sacramento (95835) *(P-938)*
Prudential, San Bruno *Also called Trotter-Vogel Realty Inc (P-10678)*
Prudential California Realty ....E....415 664-9400
677 Portola Dr San Francisco (94127) *(P-10651)*
Prudential Cleanroom Services, Milpitas *Also called Prudential Overall Supply (P-11667)*
Prudential Norcal Realty, Carmichael *Also called Diez & Leis RE Group Inc (P-10539)*
Prudential Overall Supply ....C....408 263-3464
1429 N Milpitas Blvd Milpitas (95035) *(P-11666)*
Prudential Overall Supply ....E....408 719-0886
1437 N Milpitas Blvd Milpitas (95035) *(P-11667)*
Prudential Overall Supply ....E....559 264-8231
1260 E North Ave Fresno (93725) *(P-11668)*
Prudential Overall Supply ....E....916 372-7466
545 Jefferson Blvd Ste 5 West Sacramento (95605) *(P-11669)*
Prx Inc ....E....408 287-1700
991 W Hedding St Ste 201 San Jose (95126) *(P-19695)*
Prysm Inc (PA) ....D....**408 586-1127**
513 Fairview Way Milpitas (95035) *(P-7303)*
Przm LLC ....E....415 380-0400
555 Rdwood Hwy Frntage Rd Mill Valley (94941) *(P-11377)*
PS Bajwa Inc ....E....209 334-2011
5400 W Highway 12 Lodi (95242) *(P-7710)*
PS Print, LLC, Oakland *Also called TYT LLC (P-3706)*
Ps24 Inc ....D....415 834-5105
65 Division St San Francisco (94103) *(P-19384)*
Psas Inc ....E....559 896-1443
3400 Mccall Ave Ste 100 Selma (93662) *(P-11378)*
Psc LLC ....B....408 295-0607
189 Stauffer Blvd San Jose (95125) *(P-8350)*
PSG Fencing Corporation (PA) ....C....**831 726-2002**
6630 Monterey Rd Gilroy (95020) *(P-2058)*
PSI Management Team Inc ....D....510 266-0076
20996 Cabot Blvd Hayward (94545) *(P-8769)*
PSI Water Technologies Inc ....E....408 819-3043
550 Sycamore Dr Milpitas (95035) *(P-6732)*
Psi3g Inc (PA) ....D....**415 493-3854**
505 San Marin Dr Ste A120 Novato (94945) *(P-8520)*
Psiquantum Corp (PA) ....E....**650 427-0000**
700 Hansen Way Palo Alto (94304) *(P-19109)*
PSR West Coast Builders, Walnut Creek *Also called Advanced Ti Inc (P-734)*
Psynergy Programs Inc ....D....415 590-0579
18225 Hale Ave Morgan Hill (95037) *(P-18162)*
Pt Systems Inc ....E....925 676-0709
2350 Whitman Rd Ste B Concord (94518) *(P-18795)*
Pt Welding Inc ....F....530 406-0267
1960 E Main St Woodland (95776) *(P-14719)*
Pta Congress, Elk Grove *Also called Ptac Hlen Carr Cstllo Cal Cngr (P-18452)*
Ptac Hlen Carr Cstllo Cal Cngr ....E....916 686-1725
9850 Fire Poppy Dr Elk Grove (95757) *(P-18452)*
Ptec Solutions Inc (PA) ....D....**510 358-3578**
48633 Warm Springs Blvd Fremont (94539) *(P-5604)*
Ptr Manufacturing Inc ....E....510 477-9654
33390 Transit Ave Union City (94587) *(P-5605)*
Ptr Sheet Metal & Fabrication, Union City *Also called Ptr Manufacturing Inc (P-5605)*
Pts Communications Inc ....E....925 553-3609
2001 Crow Canyon Rd # 200 San Ramon (94583) *(P-1571)*
Pts Diagnostics California Inc ....C....877 870-5610
510 Oakmead Pkwy Sunnyvale (94085) *(P-16795)*
Pts Providers Inc ....E....925 553-3763
3130 Crow Canyon Pl # 210 San Ramon (94583) *(P-11728)*
Public Employees Retirement ....B....916 795-3400
400 Q St Sacramento (95811) *(P-10218)*
Public Health Dept, San Jose *Also called Santa Clara County of (P-17065)*
Public Health Institute ....C....916 285-1231
1825 Bell St Ste 203 Sacramento (95825) *(P-17169)*
Public Health Institute (PA) ....D....**510 285-5500**
555 12th St Ste 290 Oakland (94607) *(P-19232)*
Public Health Institute ....D....510 285-5500
1683 Shattuck Ave Ste B Berkeley (94709) *(P-19233)*
Public Health Laboratory, The, Vallejo *Also called County of Solano (P-16778)*
Public Health Nursing Service, Sacramento *Also called County of Sacramento (P-15962)*
Public Library of Science ....C....415 624-1200
1265 Battery St Ste 200 San Francisco (94111) *(P-3593)*
Public Policy Institute Cal (PA) ....D....**415 291-4400**
500 Washington St Ste 600 San Francisco (94111) *(P-18313)*
Public Works and Highway Dept, Burlingame *Also called City of Burlingame (P-1028)*
Public Works-Garage, Santa Rosa *Also called Santa Rosa City of (P-14590)*
Pubmatic Inc (PA) ....B....**650 331-3485**
3 Lagoon Dr Ste 180 Redwood City (94065) *(P-12708)*
Pubnub Inc (PA) ....C....**415 223-7552**
60 Francisco St San Francisco (94133) *(P-12709)*
Pulmonary Prctice At Parnassus, San Francisco *Also called University Cal San Francisco (P-15767)*
Pulmonary Sleep Disorders Ctr, Fresno *Also called Central Cal Fclty Med Group In (P-15338)*
Pulmuone USA Inc ....B....714 361-0806
5755 Rossi Ln Gilroy (95020) *(P-9479)*
Pulsar Vascular Inc ....F....408 246-4300
47709 Fremont Blvd Fremont (94538) *(P-7025)*
Pulse Biosciences Inc ....D....510 906-4600
3957 Point Eden Way Hayward (94545) *(P-19110)*
Pulse Q&A Inc ....E....215 908-0199
795 Folsom St Ste 1104 San Francisco (94107) *(P-19180)*
Pulse Secure LLC (HQ) ....D....**408 372-9600**
2700 Zanker Rd Ste 200 San Jose (95134) *(P-12710)*
Pulse Systems Inc (HQ) ....D....**316 636-5900**
438 Listowe Dr Folsom (95630) *(P-12711)*
Pulse Systems LLC ....D....925 798-4080
4090 Nelson Ave Concord (94520) *(P-7078)*
Punchh Inc ....D....415 623-4466
1875 S Grant St Ste 810 San Mateo (94402) *(P-13391)*
Punctus Temporis Translations ....E....510 309-0888
5201 Great America Pkwy Santa Clara (95054) *(P-14378)*
Pur-Clean Pressure Car Wash, North Highlands *Also called New Wave Industries Ltd (P-5444)*
Purcell-Murray Company Inc (PA) ....D....**415 468-6620**
235 Kansas St Fl 1 San Francisco (94103) *(P-9004)*
Pure Luxury Limousine Service ....C....800 626-5466
4246 Petaluma Blvd N Petaluma (94952) *(P-7397)*
Pure Luxury Worldwide Trnsp, Petaluma *Also called Pure Luxury Limousine Service (P-7397)*
Pure Nature Foods LLC ....E....530 723-5269
700 Santa Anita Dr Ste A Woodland (95776) *(P-2858)*
Pure Nightclub, Sunnyvale *Also called PM Entertainment Corp (P-14874)*
Pure Storage Inc (PA) ....A....**800 379-7873**
650 Castro St Ste 400 Mountain View (94041) *(P-13392)*
Pure Water Pool Service, Fresno *Also called B M D Enterprises Inc (P-5439)*
Pureline Oralcare Inc ....F....831 662-9500
804 Estates Dr Ste 104 Aptos (95003) *(P-7088)*
Purity Organic LLC ....E....415 440-7777
405 14th St Ste 1000 Oakland (94612) *(P-2297)*
Purls Sheet Metal & AC ....E....559 674-2774
232 S Schnoor Ave Madera (93637) *(P-1340)*
Purolator Liquid Process Inc ....E....916 689-2328
8314 Tiogawoods Dr Sacramento (95828) *(P-5231)*
Puronics Incorporated (HQ) ....D....**925 456-7000**
5775 Las Positas Rd Livermore (94551) *(P-5447)*
Purple Spirits, Petaluma *Also called Graton Spirits Company LLC (P-2771)*
Purple Wine Company ....C....707 829-6100
625 2nd St Petaluma (94952) *(P-2689)*

Purple Wines, Petaluma *Also called Purple Wine Company* ***(P-2689)***
Purveyors Kitchen ... E ... 530 823-8527
2043 Airpark Ct Ste 30 Auburn (95602) ***(P-2241)***
Push Inc ... E ... 209 257-1100
757 N Main St Jackson (95642) ***(P-13651)***
Putah Creek Cafe, Winters *Also called Buckhorn Cafe Inc* ***(P-2113)***
Putnam Lexus, Redwood City *Also called Putnam Motors Inc* ***(P-14618)***
Putnam Motors Inc ... D ... 650 381-3152
390 Convention Way Redwood City (94063) ***(P-14618)***
Putt-Putt of Modesto Inc (PA) ... **D ... 209 578-4386**
4307 Coffee Rd Modesto (95357) ***(P-15229)***
Puyallup Herald, Sacramento *Also called Olympic Cascade Publishing* ***(P-3470)***
PV SOLAR CONTRACTOR, Ripon *Also called Califrnia Solar Innovators Inc* ***(P-1228)***
Pw Eagle Inc ... D ... 530 677-2286
3500 Robin Ln Shingle Springs (95682) ***(P-4235)***
Pw Fund B LP ... D ... 916 379-3852
7585 Longe St Stockton (95206) ***(P-10767)***
Pyramid Alternatives Inc (PA) ... **E ... 650 355-8787**
480 Manor Pl Pacifica (94044) ***(P-17059)***
Pyramid Graphics ... E ... 650 871-0290
325 Harbor Way South San Francisco (94080) ***(P-3687)***
Pyramid Painting Inc ... E ... 650 903-9791
2925 Bayview Dr Fremont (94538) ***(P-1424)***
Pyramid Printing and Graphics, South San Francisco *Also called Pyramid Graphics* ***(P-3687)***
Q Analysts LLC (PA) ... **D ... 408 907-8500**
4320 Stevens Creek Blvd San Jose (95129) ***(P-19614)***
Q B Internationial, San Rafael *Also called Qb3 LLC* ***(P-19616)***
Q Bio Inc ... E ... 415 967-7622
1411 Industrial Rd San Carlos (94070) ***(P-19111)***
Q C A, San Jose *Also called Quality Circuit Assembly Inc* ***(P-5963)***
Q M S, Emeryville *Also called Quantitative Med Systems Inc* ***(P-12716)***
Q S I, South San Francisco *Also called Quality Systems Instlltons Ltd* ***(P-2059)***
Q Technology Inc ... E ... 925 373-3456
336 Lindbergh Ave Livermore (94551) ***(P-5749)***
Qantel Technologies Inc ... F ... 510 731-2080
9812 Vasquez Cir Loomis (95650) ***(P-5270)***
Qatalyst Group LP (PA) ... **E ... 415 844-7700**
1 Maritime Plz Fl 24 San Francisco (94111) ***(P-10877)***
Qb3 LLC ... E ... 415 515-3595
29 Hunter Crk Fairfax (94930) ***(P-19615)***
Qb3 LLC (PA) ... **E ... 415 459-7459**
824 E St San Rafael (94901) ***(P-19616)***
Qct LLC ... A ... 510 270-6111
1010 Rincon Cir San Jose (95131) ***(P-8738)***
Qg LLC ... D ... 209 384-0444
2201 Cooper Ave Merced (95348) ***(P-3688)***
Qmat Inc ... F ... 408 228-5880
2424 Walsh Ave Santa Clara (95051) ***(P-6261)***
Qmetry Inc ... C ... 408 727-1101
3200 Patrick Henry Dr # 2 Santa Clara (95054) ***(P-19841)***
Qolsys Inc (HQ) ... **C ... 855 476-5797**
1900 The Alameda San Jose (95126) ***(P-13652)***
Qor LLC ... F ... 707 658-1941
775 Baywood Dr Ste 312 Petaluma (94954) ***(P-2995)***
Qostronics Inc ... E ... 408 719-1286
2044 Corporate Ct San Jose (95131) ***(P-5960)***
Qrs Corporation (HQ) ... **D ... 510 215-5000**
1400 Marina Way S Richmond (94804) ***(P-12712)***
Qsolv Inc ... C ... 408 429-0918
440 N Wolfe Rd Ste 26 Sunnyvale (94085) ***(P-13653)***
Qt Company ... E ... 408 906-8400
2350 Mission College Blvd # 1020 Santa Clara (95054) ***(P-13964)***
Qtcom Helsinki Nasdaq, Santa Clara *Also called Qt Company* ***(P-13964)***
Quadco Printing Inc ... F ... 530 894-4061
2535 Zanella Way Chico (95928) ***(P-3689)***
Quadriga Inc ... D ... 650 270-6326
1 Sansome St Ste 3500 San Francisco (94104) ***(P-12713)***
Quady LLC (PA) ... **E ... 559 673-8068**
13181 Road 24 Madera (93637) ***(P-2690)***
Quady Winery Inc ... F ... 559 673-8068
13181 Road 24 Madera (93637) ***(P-2691)***
Quail H Farms LLC ... A ... 209 394-8001
5301 Robin Ave Livingston (95334) ***(P-19)***
Quail Hill Investments Inc ... C ... 408 978-9000
1124 Meridian Ave San Jose (95125) ***(P-10824)***
Quail Ridge Senior Living, Grass Valley *Also called Grass Valley LLC* ***(P-18124)***
Quaker Oats Company ... C ... 510 261-5800
5625 International Blvd Oakland (94621) ***(P-2822)***
Quaker Pet Group Inc ... D ... 415 721-7400
160 Mitchell Blvd San Rafael (94903) ***(P-9670)***
Qualcomm Atheros Inc (HQ) ... **A ... 408 773-5200**
1700 Technology Dr San Jose (95110) ***(P-6262)***
Qualia Collection Services, Petaluma *Also called Optio Solutions LLC* ***(P-11826)***
Qualia Labs Inc ... C ... 440 477-5625
201 Mission St Ste 1800 San Francisco (94105) ***(P-19842)***
Qualified Digital LLC ... E ... 518 727-3997
813 Folger Ave Unit 8 Berkeley (94710) ***(P-14379)***
Qualio Inc ... E ... 415 795-7331
268 Bush St San Francisco (94104) ***(P-13393)***
Qualitau Incorporated (PA) ... **D ... 408 675-3034**
5303 Betsy Ross Dr Santa Clara (95054) ***(P-6783)***
Qualitek Inc (HQ) ... **D ... 408 734-8686**
1116 Elko Dr Sunnyvale (94089) ***(P-5961)***
Qualitek Inc ... D ... 408 752-8422
1272 Forgewood Ave Sunnyvale (94089) ***(P-5962)***
Quality Circuit Assembly Inc ... D ... 408 441-1001
1709 Junction Ct Ste 380 San Jose (95112) ***(P-5963)***
Quality Cylinder Head Repair ... E ... 916 371-4302
2434 Evergreen Ave West Sacramento (95691) ***(P-14585)***
Quality Dentistry, Modesto *Also called Rickey & Wong DDS Inc* ***(P-15856)***
Quality Diesel, West Sacramento *Also called Quality Cylinder Head Repair* ***(P-14585)***
Quality Door & Trim, Stockton *Also called J & J Quality Door Inc* ***(P-3137)***
Quality Doors & Trim, Lakeport *Also called Young & Family Inc* ***(P-3164)***
Quality Erectors Cnstr Co Inc ... D ... 707 746-1233
3130 Bayshore Rd Benicia (94510) ***(P-1930)***
Quality First Home Imprv Inc (PA) ... **C ... 877 663-6707**
6545 Sunrise Blvd Ste 202 Citrus Heights (95610) ***(P-689)***
Quality Group Homes Inc ... C ... 916 930-0066
4928 E Clinton Way # 108 Fresno (93727) ***(P-690)***
Quality Inn, Petaluma *Also called Lok Redwood Empire Prpts Inc* ***(P-11267)***
Quality Inn and Suites ... D ... 806 335-1561
2315 Pentland Way San Jose (95148) ***(P-11379)***
Quality Inv Prpts Scrmento LLC ... D ... 916 679-2100
1100 N Market Blvd Sacramento (95834) ***(P-13747)***
Quality Life Insurance Agency, San Ramon *Also called Gateway Financial Advisors Inc* ***(P-19519)***
Quality Machine Engrg Inc ... E ... 707 528-1900
2559 Grosse Ave Santa Rosa (95404) ***(P-5606)***
Quality Machining & Design Inc ... E ... 408 224-7976
2857 Aiello Dr San Jose (95111) ***(P-5165)***
Quality Management, Stanford *Also called Stanford Health Care* ***(P-16554)***
Quality Metal Fabrication LLC ... E ... 530 887-7388
2350 Wilbur Way Auburn (95602) ***(P-4808)***
Quality Metal Spinning and ... E ... 650 858-2491
4047 Transport St Palo Alto (94303) ***(P-4888)***
Quality Motor Cars Stockton ... D ... 209 476-1640
2222 E Hammer Ln Stockton (95210) ***(P-14619)***
Quality Planning Corporation ... D ... 415 369-0707
388 Market St Ste 750 San Francisco (94111) ***(P-19617)***
Quality Sound, Stockton *Also called Bi-Jamar Inc* ***(P-1465)***
Quality Systems Instlltons Ltd ... D ... 650 875-9000
212 Shaw Rd Ste 3 South San Francisco (94080) ***(P-2059)***
Quality Tech Svcs Sacramento, Sacramento *Also called Quality Inv Prpts Scrmento LLC* ***(P-13747)***
Quality Techniques Engrg Cnstr, Rocklin *Also called Quality Telecom Cons Inc* ***(P-1132)***
Quality Telecom Cons Inc (PA) ... **D ... 916 315-0500**
3740 Cincinnati Ave Rocklin (95765) ***(P-1132)***
Quality Transformer & Elec ... E ... 408 935-0231
963 Ames Ave Milpitas (95035) ***(P-5647)***
Quality Transformer & Elec Co, Milpitas *Also called Quality Transformer & Elec* ***(P-5647)***
Qualium Corp (PA) ... **D ... 408 402-3697**
14981 National Ave Ste 1 Los Gatos (95032) ***(P-15636)***
Qualys Inc (PA) ... **A ... 650 801-6100**
919 E Hillsdale Blvd Fl 4 Foster City (94404) ***(P-12714)***
Quanergy Systems Inc (PA) ... **C ... 408 245-9500**
433 Lakeside Dr Sunnyvale (94085) ***(P-6680)***
Quanex Screens LLC ... F ... 916 386-8728
5901 88th St Sacramento (95828) ***(P-4707)***
Quanta Computer Usa Inc (HQ) ... **B ... 510 226-1000**
45630 Northport Loop E Fremont (94538) ***(P-8739)***
Quanta Service Incorporation (HQ) ... **D ... 510 226-1000**
45630 Northport Loop E Fremont (94538) ***(P-8740)***
Quantal International Inc ... E ... 415 644-0754
455 Market St Ste 1200 San Francisco (94105) ***(P-13394)***
Quantcast Corporation (PA) ... **D ... 800 293-5706**
795 Folsom St Fl 5 San Francisco (94107) ***(P-12715)***
Quantela Inc (PA) ... **D ... 650 479-3700**
691 S Milpitas Blvd # 217 Milpitas (95035) ***(P-13654)***
Quanticel Pharmacueticals Inc (PA) ... **E ... 415 358-7609**
1500 Owens St Ste 500 San Francisco (94158) ***(P-19112)***
Quantifind Inc ... E ... 650 561-4937
444 High St Ste 101 Palo Alto (94301) ***(P-13965)***
Quantitative Med Systems Inc (HQ) ... **E ... 510 654-9200**
1900 Powell St Ste 810 Emeryville (94608) ***(P-12716)***
Quantum Corporation (PA) ... **B ... 408 944-4000**
224 Airport Pkwy Ste 550 San Jose (95110) ***(P-5310)***
Quantum Global Tech LLC (HQ) ... **C ... 215 892-9300**
26462 Corporate Ave Hayward (94545) ***(P-4077)***
Quantum Government Inc ... E ... 408 944-4000
224 Airport Pkwy Ste 550 San Jose (95110) ***(P-5311)***
Quantum Hlthcare Med Assoc Inc (PA) ... **E ... 925 924-1600**
5000 Hopyard Rd Ste 100 Pleasanton (94588) ***(P-15637)***
Quantum Precision Inc ... E ... 908 928-1115
1307 66th St Emeryville (94608) ***(P-8873)***
Quantum3d Inc (PA) ... **F ... 408 600-2500**
920 Hillview Ct Ste 145 Milpitas (95035) ***(P-6681)***
Quantum3d Government Systems, Milpitas *Also called Cg2 Inc* ***(P-19207)***
Quantumclean, Hayward *Also called Quantum Global Tech LLC* ***(P-4077)***
Quantumscape Battery Inc ... C ... 408 452-2000
1730 Technology Dr San Jose (95110) ***(P-6263)***
Quantumscape Corporation (PA) ... **D ... 408 452-2000**
1730 Technology Dr San Jose (95110) ***(P-6264)***
Quark Pharmaceuticals Inc (HQ) ... **E ... 510 402-4020**
495 N Whisman Rd Ste 100 Mountain View (94043) ***(P-3968)***
Quarterwave Corp ... E ... 707 793-9105
1500 Valley House Dr # 100 Rohnert Park (94928) ***(P-19843)***
Quartz Hill Post Acute, Redding *Also called Honolua Bay Holdings LLC* ***(P-10737)***
Quartzy Inc ... D ... 855 782-7899
28321 Industrial Blvd Hayward (94545) ***(P-8802)***
Quasar Engineering Inc ... D ... 650 508-6600
1301 Shoreway Rd Ste 425 Belmont (94002) ***(P-18796)***
Quattrocchi Kwok Architects ... E ... 707 576-0829
636 5th St Santa Rosa (95404) ***(P-18905)***
Queen of The Valley Hospital, NAPA *Also called Work Health* ***(P-19671)***

Queen of Vly Med Ctr Fundation (HQ).......A.......**707 252-4411**
1000 Trancas St NAPA (94558) ***(P-16486)***
Queen of Vly Med Ctr Fundation.......B.......707 251-2000
3448 Villa Ln Ste 102 NAPA (94558) ***(P-16487)***
Quellan Inc.......E.......408 546-3487
1001 Murphy Ranch Rd Milpitas (95035) ***(P-6265)***
Quenta Material, Santa Clara *Also called Qmat Inc* ***(P-6261)***
Quercus Ranch, Kelseyville *Also called BT Holdings Inc* ***(P-97)***
Quest Dgnstics Clncal Labs Inc.......D.......408 975-1015
2369 Bering Dr San Jose (95131) ***(P-16796)***
Quest Dgnstics Clncal Labs Inc.......D.......559 299-5074
7075 N Maple Ave Ste 104 Fresno (93720) ***(P-16797)***
Quest Dgnstics Clncal Labs Inc.......D.......209 951-5831
2291 W March Ln Ste F145 Stockton (95207) ***(P-16798)***
Quest Dgnstics Clncal Labs Inc.......D.......408 259-6806
155 N Jackson Ave Ste 102 San Jose (95116) ***(P-16799)***
Quest Diagnostics, Roseville *Also called Unilab Corporation* ***(P-16813)***
Quest Discovery Services Inc (PA).......C.......**408 441-7000**
981 Ridder Park Dr San Jose (95131) ***(P-17359)***
Quest Inds - Stockton Plant, Stockton *Also called By Quest LLC* ***(P-3723)***
Quest Media & Supplies Inc (PA).......D.......**916 338-7070**
9000 Fthills Blvd Ste 100 Roseville (95747) ***(P-13966)***
Questcor Pharmaceuticals.......E.......510 400-0700
26118 Research Pl Hayward (94545) ***(P-9235)***
Questivity Inc.......F.......408 615-1781
1680 Civic Center Dr # 209 Santa Clara (95050) ***(P-13395)***
Questra Corporation (PA).......E.......**650 632-4011**
3200 Bridge Pkwy Ste 101 Redwood City (94065) ***(P-12717)***
Quetzal Group Inc.......E.......415 673-4181
1234 Polk St San Francisco (94109) ***(P-2845)***
Quick Lane, Manteca *Also called Manteca Ford-Mercury Inc* ***(P-14577)***
Quick Lane, Stockton *Also called Big Valley Ford Inc* ***(P-14549)***
Quick Mount Pv, Walnut Creek *Also called Wencon Development Inc* ***(P-1398)***
Quick-N-Ezee Indian Foods, Hayward *Also called Jagpreet Enterprises LLC* ***(P-9458)***
Quickbooks Capital, Mountain View *Also called Intuit Financing Inc* ***(P-13244)***
Quicken Inc.......C.......650 564-3399
3760 Haven Ave Ste C Menlo Park (94025) ***(P-12718)***
Quicklogic Corporation (PA).......E.......**408 990-4000**
2220 Lundy Ave San Jose (95131) ***(P-6266)***
Quicksilver Delivery Inc.......D.......415 431-1600
129 Kissling St San Francisco (94103) ***(P-7398)***
Quicksilver Delivery Service, San Francisco *Also called Quicksilver Delivery Inc* ***(P-7398)***
Quid LLC (PA).......C.......**415 813-5300**
3960 Freedom Cir Ste 200 Santa Clara (95054) ***(P-12719)***
Quiet Ride Solutions LLC.......F.......209 942-4777
1122 S Wilson Way Ste 1 Stockton (95205) ***(P-6591)***
Quietrock, Rancho Cordova *Also called Pabco Building Products LLC* ***(P-4514)***
Quincy Engineering Inc (PA).......E.......**916 368-9181**
11017 Cobblerock Dr # 100 Rancho Cordova (95670) ***(P-18797)***
Quinn Lift Inc (HQ).......E.......**559 896-4040**
10273 S Golden State Blvd Selma (93662) ***(P-9026)***
Quinoa Corporation.......E.......707 462-6605
1 Carousel Ln Ste D Ukiah (95482) ***(P-2400)***
Quinstreet Inc (PA).......E.......**650 578-7700**
950 Tower Ln Ste 600 Foster City (94404) ***(P-14380)***
Quintel Corporation.......E.......408 776-5190
685 Jarvis Dr Ste A Morgan Hill (95037) ***(P-5123)***
Quintessa Vinyards, NAPA *Also called Huneeus Vintners LLC* ***(P-2618)***
Quip Inc.......E.......877 544-7847
50 Fremont St Ste 300 San Francisco (94105) ***(P-12720)***
Quiring Corporation.......D.......559 432-2800
5118 E Clinton Way # 201 Fresno (93727) ***(P-939)***
Quiring General LLC.......D.......559 432-2800
5118 E Clinton Way # 201 Fresno (93727) ***(P-940)***
Quivira Vineyards, Healdsburg *Also called Pjk Winery LLC* ***(P-2685)***
Qumu Inc (HQ).......E.......**650 396-8530**
1100 Grundy Ln Ste 110 San Bruno (94066) ***(P-13396)***
Quoori Inc (PA).......E.......**707 393-8305**
44 Montgomery St Ste 3150 San Francisco (94104) ***(P-12721)***
Quora Inc.......E.......650 485-2464
650 Castro St Ste 450 Mountain View (94041) ***(P-13806)***
Quorumlabs Inc.......E.......408 708-4500
2870 Zanker Rd Ste 130 San Jose (95134) ***(P-8741)***
Quotient Technology Inc (PA).......A.......**650 605-4600**
400 Logue Ave Mountain View (94043) ***(P-11778)***
Quova Inc.......D.......650 965-2898
401 Castro St Fl 3 Mountain View (94041) ***(P-19844)***
Qurasense Inc (PA).......D.......**415 702-8935**
3517 Edison Way Ste A Menlo Park (94025) ***(P-19113)***
Quri Inc.......E.......415 413-0100
655 Montgomery St Lbby 1 San Francisco (94111) ***(P-19181)***
Qwilt Inc.......E.......866 824-8009
275 Shoreline Dr Ste 510 Redwood City (94065) ***(P-13397)***
Qxq Inc.......E.......510 252-1522
44113 S Grimmer Blvd Fremont (94538) ***(P-6784)***
R & A Painting Inc.......D.......916 688-3955
11730 Sheldon Lake Dr Elk Grove (95624) ***(P-1425)***
R & D Mfg Services, San Jose *Also called R Stephenson & D Cram Mfg Inc* ***(P-5608)***
R & D Partners, Redwood City *Also called R&D Consulting Group Inc* ***(P-12123)***
R & D Tech, Milpitas *Also called Hytek R&D Inc* ***(P-5939)***
R & G Schatz Farms Inc.......F.......209 367-4881
22150 N Kennefick Rd Acampo (95220) ***(P-69)***
R & J Joy Inc.......E.......530 832-4435
190 Industrial Way Portola (96129) ***(P-1972)***
R & K Industrial Products Co.......E.......510 234-7212
1945 7th St Richmond (94801) ***(P-4986)***
R & L Brosamer Inc (HQ).......E.......**925 627-1700**
1390 Willow Pass Rd # 95 Concord (94520) ***(P-941)***
R & L Enterprises Inc.......E.......559 233-1608
1955 S Mary St Fresno (93721) ***(P-5607)***
R & M Painting Inc.......F.......209 576-2576
2928 Yosemite Blvd Modesto (95354) ***(P-1426)***
R & R Maher Construction Co.......E.......707 552-0330
1324 Lemon St Vallejo (94590) ***(P-1903)***
R & R Marcuccia/C Htg & Shtmtl, Redwood City *Also called Marcucci Heating and AC Inc* ***(P-1309)***
R & R Pacific Construction.......E.......530 668-7525
619 1/2 Main St Ste 7 Woodland (95695) ***(P-18798)***
R & S Erection N Peninsula Inc.......E.......415 467-5630
133 S Linden Ave South San Francisco (94080) ***(P-1751)***
R & S Investments LLC.......D.......415 591-2700
1 Bush St Fl 9 San Francisco (94104) ***(P-10057)***
R & S Manufacturing Inc (HQ).......E.......**510 429-1788**
33955 7th St Union City (94587) ***(P-4708)***
R & S Rolling Door Products, Union City *Also called R & S Manufacturing Inc* ***(P-4708)***
R A Jenson Manufacturing Co.......F.......415 822-2732
102 Heather Dr Atherton (94027) ***(P-3187)***
R and R Labor Inc.......B.......831 638-0290
710 Kirkpatric Ct Ste A Hollister (95023) ***(P-364)***
R B Spencer Inc.......D.......530 674-8307
1188 Hassett Ave Yuba City (95991) ***(P-1341)***
R C H, San Francisco *Also called Pomeroy Rcrtion Rhbltation Ctr* ***(P-17675)***
R C Roberts & Co (PA).......C.......**415 456-8600**
801 A St San Rafael (94901) ***(P-10474)***
R C S, Rancho Cordova *Also called Residential Ctrl Systems Inc* ***(P-6704)***
R E Maher Inc.......D.......707 642-3907
4545 Hess Rd American Canyon (94503) ***(P-1904)***
R Emigh Livestock.......D.......707 374-5585
30 S 2nd St Rio Vista (94571) ***(P-9506)***
R F I Security Inc (HQ).......D.......**408 298-5400**
360 Turtle Creek Ct San Jose (95125) ***(P-1572)***
R F Macdonald Co (PA).......C.......**510 784-0110**
25920 Eden Landing Rd Hayward (94545) ***(P-9087)***
R Fellen Inc.......D.......559 233-6248
2939 S Peach Ave Fresno (93725) ***(P-16098)***
R H Kiggins Construction Inc.......E.......559 251-8661
4735 E Floradora Ave Fresno (93703) ***(P-1652)***
R I M, Santa Clara *Also called Rimnetics Inc* ***(P-4318)***
R J Dailey Construction Co.......D.......650 948-5196
401 1st St Los Altos (94022) ***(P-691)***
R J M Enterprises Inc.......E.......209 599-1186
18700 E River Rd Ripon (95366) ***(P-70)***
R J McGlennon Company Inc (PA).......E.......**415 552-0311**
198 Utah St San Francisco (94103) ***(P-4109)***
R J R Technologies Inc (PA).......D.......**480 800-2300**
7875 Edgewater Dr Oakland (94621) ***(P-6538)***
R Joy Inc.......D.......530 832-5760
1584 Wolf Meadows Ln Portola (96122) ***(P-18799)***
R K I, Union City *Also called Rki Instruments Inc* ***(P-9090)***
R K Larrabee Company Inc.......D.......925 828-9420
7800 Las Positas Rd Livermore (94551) ***(P-5667)***
R L T, Redding *Also called Redding Lumber Transport Inc* ***(P-7632)***
R Lance & Sons Co Inc.......E.......925 245-8884
6776 Patterson Pass Rd Livermore (94550) ***(P-14673)***
R M Harris Company Inc.......D.......925 335-3000
1000 Howe Rd Ste 200 Martinez (94553) ***(P-1085)***
R Millennium Transport, Turlock *Also called R Millennium Transport Inc* ***(P-7892)***
R Millennium Transport Inc.......E.......209 668-9700
1670 Fulkerth Rd Turlock (95380) ***(P-7892)***
R Montanez Farms LLC.......E.......831 761-5982
121 Hall Rd Royal Oaks (95076) ***(P-187)***
R S Software India Limited.......D.......408 382-1200
1900 Mccarthy Blvd # 103 Milpitas (95035) ***(P-13967)***
R Scott Foster MD.......E.......209 952-3700
36 W Yokuts Ave Ste 1 Stockton (95207) ***(P-15638)***
R Stephenson & D Cram Mfg Inc.......E.......408 452-0882
800 Faulstich Ct San Jose (95112) ***(P-5608)***
R Systems Inc (HQ).......D.......**916 939-9696**
5000 Windplay Dr Ste 5 El Dorado Hills (95762) ***(P-13655)***
R T I, Morgan Hill *Also called Robson Technologies Inc* ***(P-5614)***
R T I, Sunnyvale *Also called Real-Time Innovations Inc* ***(P-12729)***
R Thunder Inc (PA).......E.......**559 974-2203**
15711 Watts Valley Rd Sanger (93657) ***(P-14966)***
R Torre & Company Inc (PA).......C.......**800 775-1925**
2000 Marina Blvd San Leandro (94577) ***(P-2823)***
R Torre & Company Inc.......E.......650 624-2830
2000 Marina Ct San Leandro (94577) ***(P-2824)***
R V Cloud Co.......E.......408 378-7943
3000 Winchester Blvd Campbell (95008) ***(P-9005)***
R V Karls Inc.......E.......916 992-9703
1470 Vinci Ave Sacramento (95838) ***(P-8461)***
R V Stich Construction Inc.......E.......510 412-9070
769 S 13th St Richmond (94804) ***(P-1973)***
R W Garcia Co Inc (PA).......E.......**408 287-4616**
100 Enterprise Way C230 Scotts Valley (95066) ***(P-9356)***
R W Information Technologies, Auburn *Also called Rw3 Technologies Inc* ***(P-19391)***
R&B Protective Coatings Inc.......E.......209 887-2030
19968 E Highway 26 Linden (95236) ***(P-1427)***
R&D Altanova Inc.......E.......408 225-7011
6389 San Ignacio Ave San Jose (95119) ***(P-5964)***
R&D Consulting Group Inc.......C.......415 697-2585
920 Main St Redwood City (94063) ***(P-12123)***
R&D Educational Systems Inc.......F.......916 934-6223
9719 Village Center Dr # 125 Granite Bay (95746) ***(P-7304)***
R&K Industrial Wheels, Richmond *Also called R & K Industrial Products Co* ***(P-4986)***

R&L Carriers Shared Svcs LLC ....E....510 258-0547
15651 Worthley Dr San Lorenzo (94580) *(P-7574)*
R&M USA Inc ....D....408 945-6626
840 Yosemite Way Milpitas (95035) *(P-8948)*
R&R Security Solutions Inc ....E....925 494-9000
1975 Diamond Blvd E160 Concord (94520) *(P-14381)*
R-Bros Painting Inc ....E....408 291-6820
707 W Hedding St San Jose (95110) *(P-1428)*
R-Quest Technologies LLC ....F....530 621-9916
4710 Oak Hill Rd Placerville (95667) *(P-13398)*
R/GA Media Group Inc ....D....415 913-7531
35 Park St San Francisco (94110) *(P-19696)*
R/GA Media Group Inc ....D....415 624-2000
55 Marinero Cir Apt 204 Belvedere Tiburon (94920) *(P-13748)*
R2 Semiconductor Inc ....F....408 745-7400
3600 W Byshore Rd Ste 205 Palo Alto (94303) *(P-6267)*
R2g Enterprises Inc ....D....510 489-6218
31154 San Benito St Hayward (94544) *(P-1833)*
RABBIT HAVEN THE, Scotts Valley *Also called Ava The Rabbit Haven Inc (P-19724)*
Rabin Worldwide Inc ....D....415 522-5700
21 Locust Ave 2a Mill Valley (94941) *(P-14382)*
Race Street Partners Inc (PA) ....**D....408 294-6161**
967 W Hedding St San Jose (95126) *(P-9350)*
Race Telecommunications Inc (PA) ....**D....650 246-8900**
601 Gateway Blvd Ste 280 South San Francisco (94080) *(P-7985)*
Rack & Riddle, Healdsburg *Also called RB Wine Associates LLC (P-2693)*
Rackley Company Inc ....E....530 865-9619
3772 County Road 99w Orland (95963) *(P-805)*
Rackspace Hosting Inc ....B....201 792-1918
650 Castro St Ste 270 Mountain View (94041) *(P-13749)*
Rackspace Hosting Inc ....B....201 792-1918
150 S 1st St Ste 289 San Jose (95113) *(P-13750)*
Raco Manufacturing & Engrg Co ....E....510 658-6713
1400 62nd St Emeryville (94608) *(P-6539)*
Radian Heat Sinks, Santa Clara *Also called Radian Thermal Products Inc (P-4587)*
Radian Thermal Products Inc ....D....408 988-6200
2160 Walsh Ave Santa Clara (95050) *(P-4587)*
Radiant Logic Inc (HQ) ....**C....415 209-6800**
75 Rowland Way Ste 300 Novato (94945) *(P-13399)*
Radiation Oncology Center, Roseville *Also called Sutter Health (P-16620)*
Radio Time, San Francisco *Also called Tunein Inc (P-8035)*
Radisson Inn, Berkeley *Also called Boykin Mgt Co Ltd Lblty Co (P-10969)*
Radisson Inn, Sunnyvale *Also called S R H H Inc (P-11424)*
Raditek Inc (PA) ....**D....408 266-7404**
1702 Meridian Ave Ste L San Jose (95125) *(P-5862)*
Radonich Corp ....E....408 275-8888
886 Faulstich Ct San Jose (95112) *(P-1573)*
Radonich Enterprises Inc ....D....408 295-6507
890 Faulstich Ct San Jose (95112) *(P-1834)*
Radware Inc ....D....650 627-4672
100 Mathilda Pl Ste 170 Sunnyvale (94086) *(P-19114)*
Rae Systems Inc (HQ) ....**A....408 952-8200**
1349 Moffett Park Dr Sunnyvale (94089) *(P-6918)*
Rael Bernstein DDS A Prof Corp (PA) ....**E....707 575-0600**
2180 Northpoint Pkwy Santa Rosa (95407) *(P-15855)*
Rafael Convalescent Hospital ....D....415 479-3450
234 N San Pedro Rd San Rafael (94903) *(P-16259)*
Rafael Racquet & Swim Club, San Rafael *Also called Rafael Racquet Club Inc (P-15124)*
Rafael Racquet Club Inc ....E....415 456-5522
95 Racquet Club Dr San Rafael (94901) *(P-15124)*
Rafael Sandoval ....E....209 858-4173
16175 Mckinley Ave Lathrop (95330) *(P-3101)*
Ragers Recreational Entps ....E....209 522-2452
2301 Yosemite Blvd Modesto (95354) *(P-14898)*
Raging Wire, Sacramento *Also called Ntt Glbal Data Ctrs Amrcas Inc (P-13816)*
Rago & Son Inc ....D....510 536-5700
1029 51st Ave Oakland (94601) *(P-4889)*
Rago Neon Inc ....F....510 537-1903
235 Laurel Ave Hayward (94541) *(P-7249)*
Rahi Systems Inc (PA) ....**B....510 651-2205**
48303 Fremont Blvd Fremont (94538) *(P-19845)*
Rai Care Ctrs Nthrn Cal I LLC ....C....209 943-0854
2350 N California St Stockton (95204) *(P-16976)*
Rai Care Ctrs Nthrn Cal I LLC ....C....707 434-9088
490 Chadbourne Rd Ste D Fairfield (94534) *(P-16977)*
Rai Care Ctrs Nthrn Cal II LLC ....E....415 406-1090
1738 Ocean Ave San Francisco (94112) *(P-16978)*
Rai Technology Incorporated ....E....415 252-9393
4104 24th St 385 San Francisco (94114) *(P-12722)*
Rai-Chadbourne-Fairfield, Fairfield *Also called Rai Care Ctrs Nthrn Cal I LLC (P-16977)*
Railroad Park Inc ....E....530 235-2300
100 Railroad Park Rd Dunsmuir (96025) *(P-11380)*
Railway Distributing Inc ....E....408 280-7625
675 Emory St San Jose (95110) *(P-8632)*
Rainbow - Brite Indus Svcs LLC ....A....559 925-2580
463 E Salmon River Dr Fresno (93730) *(P-11988)*
Rainbow Agricultural Services, Ukiah *Also called Mayfield Equipment Company (P-9605)*
Rainbow Farms, Denair *Also called Valley Fresh Foods Inc (P-234)*
Rainbow Fin Company Inc ....F....831 728-2998
677 Beach Dr Watsonville (95076) *(P-7200)*
Rainbow Light ....E....831 429-9089
125 Mcpherson St Santa Cruz (95060) *(P-3821)*
Rainbow Orchards Inc ....F....530 644-1594
2569 Larsen Dr Camino (95709) *(P-2798)*
Rainbow Wtrprofing Restoration ....C....415 641-1578
600 Treat Ave San Francisco (94110) *(P-2060)*
Raindance Technologies Inc ....E....978 495-3300
5731 W Las Positas Blvd Pleasanton (94588) *(P-6845)*
Rainforest Qa Inc ....C....650 866-1407
5675 W Cog Hill Ter Dublin (94568) *(P-12723)*
Rainforth Grau Architects ....E....916 368-7990
2101 Capitol Ave Ste 100 Sacramento (95816) *(P-18906)*
Raiser Senior Services LLC ....D....650 342-4106
601 Laurel Ave Apt 903 San Mateo (94401) *(P-16099)*
Raisin ADM Committee ....E....559 225-0520
2445 Capitol St Ste 200 Fresno (93721) *(P-19385)*
Raison D'Etre Bakery, South San Francisco *Also called Ashbury Market Inc (P-9438)*
Raj Sharma ....E....530 633-2057
4750 Bear River Dr Rio Oso (95674) *(P-90)*
Rajappan Myer Cnslting Engners (PA) ....**E....408 280-2772**
1038 Leigh Ave Ste 100 San Jose (95126) *(P-18800)*
Rakuten Usa Inc (HQ) ....**D....617 491-5252**
800 Concar Dr Ste 175 San Mateo (94402) *(P-7986)*
RAL Builders ....E....916 960-4889
500 Giuseppe Ct Ste 1 Roseville (95678) *(P-692)*
Rally Health Inc ....E....408 821-5414
665 3rd St Ste 200 San Francisco (94107) *(P-17170)*
Ralphs-Pugh Co Inc ....D....707 745-6222
3931 Oregon St Benicia (94510) *(P-5055)*
Ram Commercial Enterprises Inc ....E....916 429-1205
5896 S Land Park Dr Sacramento (95822) *(P-10652)*
Ram Mechanical Inc ....D....209 531-9155
3506 Moore Rd Ceres (95307) *(P-1342)*
Ramada Inn, Redding *Also called Ramada Limited (P-11381)*
Ramada Inn, Alamo *Also called Sawhney Properties LP (P-11446)*
Ramada Inn Silicon Valley, Sunnyvale *Also called Executive Inn Inc (P-11088)*
Ramada Limited ....E....530 246-2222
1286 Twin View Blvd Redding (96003) *(P-11381)*
Ramar International Corp (PA) ....**E....925 439-9009**
1101 Railroad Ave Pittsburg (94565) *(P-2182)*
Rambus Inc (PA) ....**B....408 462-8000**
4453 N 1st St Ste 100 San Jose (95134) *(P-6268)*
Ramco Enterprises LP ....A....831 722-3370
585 Auto Center Dr Watsonville (95076) *(P-12124)*
Ramkabir LLC ....C....650 952-3200
1390 El Camino Real Millbrae (94030) *(P-11382)*
Ramos Oil Co Inc (PA) ....**D....916 371-2570**
1515 S River Rd West Sacramento (95691) *(P-9536)*
Ramp Restaurant , The, San Francisco *Also called St Francis Marine Center Inc (P-7733)*
Rams Gate Winery LLC ....E....707 721-8700
28700 Arnold Dr Sonoma (95476) *(P-2692)*
Ramsey Marketing & MGT Co (PA) ....**D....707 822-7665**
785 Bayside Rd Arcata (95521) *(P-19618)*
Ranch At Little Hills, The, San Ramon *Also called Concessionaires Urban Park (P-15199)*
Rancher Labs Inc (HQ) ....**D....650 521-6902**
10050 N Wolfe Rd Sw127 Cupertino (95014) *(P-12724)*
Rancho Cordova Medical Offices, Rancho Cordova *Also called Kaiser Foundation Hospitals (P-16409)*
Rancho Del Rey Golf Club Inc ....E....209 358-7131
5250 Green Sands Ave Atwater (95301) *(P-15018)*
Rancho Murieta Cmnty Svcs Dst ....E....916 354-3700
15160 Jackson Rd Sloughhouse (95683) *(P-8259)*
Rancho Murieta Country Club ....D....916 354-2400
7000 Alameda Dr Rancho Murieta (95683) *(P-15125)*
Rancho San Antnio Rtrment Hsin ....B....650 265-2637
23500 Cristo Rey Dr Cupertino (95014) *(P-18163)*
Ranchwood Contractors Inc ....D....209 826-6200
923 E Pacheco Blvd Los Banos (93635) *(P-942)*
Rand Machine Works, Fresno *Also called R & L Enterprises Inc (P-5607)*
Randal Optimal Nutrients LLC ....E....707 528-1800
1595 Hampton Way Santa Rosa (95407) *(P-3969)*
Randall Horton Associates Inc (PA) ....**E....408 490-3300**
4353 N 1st St Ste 100 San Jose (95134) *(P-8503)*
Randall-Bold Wtr Trtmnt Plant, Oakley *Also called Contra Costa Water District (P-8232)*
Randell C Towne ....D....510 483-1635
14558 Wicks Blvd San Leandro (94577) *(P-1574)*
Rando AAA Hvac Inc ....E....408 293-4717
1712 Stone Ave Ste 1 San Jose (95125) *(P-1343)*
Randstad Finance & Accounting, Burlingame *Also called Randstad Professionals Us LLC (P-12125)*
Randstad Professionals Us LLC ....D....650 343-5111
111 Anza Blvd Ste 202 Burlingame (94010) *(P-12125)*
Randstad Professionals Us LLC ....D....408 573-1111
2033 Gateway Pl Ste 120 San Jose (95110) *(P-12126)*
Randtron Antenna Systems, Menlo Park *Also called L3 Technologies Inc (P-5852)*
Randy Peters Catrg & Event Plg, Roseville *Also called Think Outside Box Inc (P-11732)*
Raney Planning & MGT Inc ....E....916 372-6100
1501 Sports Dr Sacramento (95834) *(P-19846)*
Rangeme USA LLC ....F....510 688-0995
821 Folsom St San Francisco (94107) *(P-3594)*
Ranger Pipelines Incorporated ....C....415 822-3700
1790 Yosemite Ave San Francisco (94124) *(P-1133)*
Rani Therapeutics LLC ....D....408 457-3700
2051 Ringwood Ave San Jose (95131) *(P-3970)*
Rani Therapeutics Holdings Inc (PA) ....**F....408 457-3700**
2051 Ringwood Ave San Jose (95131) *(P-3971)*
Rank Technology Corp ....E....408 737-1488
1190 Miraloma Way Ste Q Sunnyvale (94085) *(P-5312)*
Rankin and Rankin, Olivehurst *Also called Lhl Construction Inc (P-1926)*
Ransome Company ....E....510 686-9900
1933 Williams St San Leandro (94577) *(P-943)*
Ransome Manufacturing, Fresno *Also called Meeder Equipment Company (P-5157)*
Rap Investors LP ....E....707 964-2402
1111 N Main St Fort Bragg (95437) *(P-11383)*
Raphael Hse San Francisco Inc ....C....415 345-7200
1065 Sutter St San Francisco (94109) *(P-17679)*

ALPHABETIC

Rapid Accu-Form Inc ....F....707 745-1879
3825 Sprig Dr Benicia (94510) ***(P-4314)***
Rapid Courier & Freight Inc ....E....916 387-5505
8760 Younger Creek Dr Sacramento (95828) ***(P-7575)***
Rapid Displays Inc ....F....510 471-6955
33195 Lewis St Union City (94587) ***(P-7250)***
Rapid First Plumbing, McClellan *Also called Rov Enterprises Inc* ***(P-1351)***
Rapid Lasergraphics, San Francisco *Also called Rapid Typographers Company* ***(P-3767)***
Rapid Lasergraphics (HQ)....E....415 957-5840
836 Harrison St San Francisco (94107) ***(P-3766)***
Rapid Precision Mfg Inc ....E....408 617-0771
1516 Montague Expy San Jose (95131) ***(P-5609)***
Rapid Typographers Company (PA)....F....415 957-5840
836 Harrison St San Francisco (94107) ***(P-3767)***
Rapid Value Solutions Inc ....E....925 398-3344
7901 Stoneridge Dr # 225 Pleasanton (94588) ***(P-19386)***
Rapidapi ....D....650 575-7633
2 Shaw Aly Fl 4 San Francisco (94105) ***(P-12725)***
Rapidbizappscom LLC ....E....408 647-3050
1525 Mccarthy Blvd # 110 Milpitas (95035) ***(P-12726)***
Rapidwerks Incorporated ....F....925 417-0124
1257 Quarry Ln Ste 140 Pleasanton (94566) ***(P-4315)***
Rapiscan Laboratories Inc (HQ)....D....408 961-9700
46718 Fremont Blvd Fremont (94538) ***(P-7093)***
Raps Dublin LLC ....E....925 828-9393
6275 Dublin Blvd Dublin (94568) ***(P-11384)***
Raps Hospitality Group ....C....510 795-7995
5977 Mowry Ave Newark (94560) ***(P-11385)***
Rapt Therapeutics Inc ....D....650 489-9000
561 Eccles Ave South San Francisco (94080) ***(P-3972)***
Rare Barrel LLC ....E....510 984-6585
940 Parker St Berkeley (94710) ***(P-2490)***
Rare Breed Distilling LLC (HQ)....E....415 315-8060
55 Francisco St Ste 100 San Francisco (94133) ***(P-2776)***
Ras Management Inc (PA)....E....510 727-1800
4545 Crow Canyon Pl Castro Valley (94552) ***(P-7700)***
Rascal Therapeutics Inc ....E....650 770-0192
3000 El Cmino Real Bldg 4 Palo Alto (94306) ***(P-3973)***
Rash Curtis & Associates, Vacaville *Also called K B R Inc* ***(P-11825)***
Rasilient Systems Inc (PA)....E....408 730-2568
3281 Kifer Rd Santa Clara (95051) ***(P-5313)***
Rastergraf Inc (PA)....E....510 849-4801
7145 Marlborough Ter Berkeley (94705) ***(P-5965)***
Ratcliff Architects ....D....510 899-6400
5856 Doyle St Emeryville (94608) ***(P-18907)***
Ratermann Manufacturing Inc (PA)....E....800 264-7793
601 Pinnacle Pl Livermore (94550) ***(P-4316)***
Ratnakar & Sons (PA)....E....510 236-6280
2145 Rumrill Blvd Ste A San Pablo (94806) ***(P-11655)***
Raven Biotechnologies Inc ....C....650 624-2600
1 Corporate Dr South San Francisco (94080) ***(P-19115)***
RAVENSWOOD FAMILY HEALTH CENTE, East Palo Alto *Also called South Cnty Cmnty Hlth Ctr Inc* ***(P-15696)***
Ravenswood Solutions Inc (HQ)....D....650 241-3661
3065 Skyway Ct Fremont (94539) ***(P-13656)***
Ravenswood Winery, Sonoma *Also called Franciscan Vineyards Inc* ***(P-2580)***
Ravig Inc ....D....925 526-1234
510 Garcia Ave Ste E Pittsburg (94565) ***(P-8742)***
Ravioli Factory, NAPA *Also called Dominics Orgnal Gnova Deli Inc* ***(P-2376)***
Ravix Financial Inc ....E....408 216-0656
226 Airport Pkwy Ste 400 San Jose (95110) ***(P-19619)***
Ravix Group, San Jose *Also called Ravix Financial Inc* ***(P-19619)***
Raw Farm LLC ....E....559 846-9732
7221 S Jameson Ave Fresno (93706) ***(P-219)***
Rawitser Golf Shop Mike ....E....408 441-4653
1560 Oakland Rd San Jose (95131) ***(P-15019)***
Rawson Custom Cabinets Inc ....E....408 779-9838
1115 Holly Oak Cir San Jose (95120) ***(P-3188)***
Raxium Inc ....D....510 296-9935
1250 Reliance Way Fremont (94539) ***(P-18801)***
Ray Moles Farms Inc ....D....559 444-0324
9503 S Hughes Ave Fresno (93706) ***(P-2265)***
Ray Scheidts Electric Inc ....E....408 292-8715
1055 N 7th St San Jose (95112) ***(P-1575)***
Ray Stone Incorporated ....E....916 482-2363
6017 Winding Way Carmichael (95608) ***(P-17680)***
Ray Stone Incorporated ....E....530 272-5274
131 Eureka St Grass Valley (95945) ***(P-17681)***
Ray's Electric, Oakland *Also called Gruendl Inc* ***(P-1509)***
Raya6 Investments Inc (PA)....D....408 529-1269
1860 The Alameda San Jose (95126) ***(P-10058)***
Raybern Foods LLC ....E....925 302-7800
3170 Crow Canyon Pl # 200 San Ramon (94583) ***(P-9480)***
Raybern Quality Foods, San Ramon *Also called Raybern Foods LLC* ***(P-9480)***
Raydiance Inc ....E....408 764-4000
1100 La Avenida St Mountain View (94043) ***(P-19182)***
Raydiant ....D....888 966-5188
1 Letterman Dr 3500 San Francisco (94129) ***(P-12727)***
Raymar Information Tech Inc (PA)....E....916 783-1951
7325 Roseville Rd Sacramento (95842) ***(P-5807)***
Raymond - Northern Cal Inc ....D....925 602-4910
4589 Pacheco Blvd Martinez (94553) ***(P-1701)***
Raymond Brown Company, San Francisco *Also called Walter E McGuire RE Inc* ***(P-10682)***
Raymond Handling Concepts Corp (HQ)....D....510 745-7500
41400 Boyce Rd Fremont (94538) ***(P-14771)***
Raymond Interior Systems, Martinez *Also called Raymond - Northern Cal Inc* ***(P-1701)***
Raymond Vineyard & Cellar Inc ....E....707 963-3141
849 Zinfandel Ln Saint Helena (94574) ***(P-71)***
Raymonds Little Print Shop Inc ....B....510 353-3608
41454 Christy St Fremont (94538) ***(P-3690)***
Raymus Development & Sales Inc (PA)....E....209 823-3148
544 E Yosemite Ave Manteca (95336) ***(P-10713)***
Rayner Equipment Systems, Sacramento *Also called California Pavement Maint Inc* ***(P-1022)***
Raytheon Applied Sgnal Tech In (HQ)....B....408 749-1888
460 W California Ave Sunnyvale (94086) ***(P-5863)***
Razvi Inc ....E....925 242-1200
824 La Gonda Way Danville (94526) ***(P-13751)***
RB Wine Associates LLC ....D....707 433-8400
499 Moore Ln Healdsburg (95448) ***(P-2693)***
RC Readymix Co Inc ....E....925 449-7785
1227 Greenville Rd Livermore (94550) ***(P-4503)***
Rcac, West Sacramento *Also called Rural Cmnty Assistance Corp* ***(P-17696)***
Rcb Corporation (PA)....D....916 567-2600
2485 Natomas Park Dr # 100 Sacramento (95833) ***(P-9745)***
Rcca Dutra Place, Manteca *Also called RES-Care Inc* ***(P-16199)***
Rcca Gatewood Drvie Home, Modesto *Also called RES-Care Inc* ***(P-18171)***
Rcd Engineering Inc ....D....530 292-3133
17100 Salmon Mine Rd Nevada City (95959) ***(P-5688)***
RCEB, San Leandro *Also called Regional Center of E Bay Inc* ***(P-17687)***
Rceb, Concord *Also called Regional Center of E Bay Inc* ***(P-17688)***
Rcg Auto Logistics, Sacramento *Also called Rcg Logistics LLC* ***(P-7576)***
Rcg Logistics LLC ....D....916 999-1234
9300 Tech Center Dr # 190 Sacramento (95826) ***(P-7576)***
Rch Associates Inc ....E....510 657-7846
6111 Southfront Rd Ste C Livermore (94551) ***(P-5166)***
Rci Associates ....E....866 668-4732
5030 Business Center Dr # 280 Fairfield (94534) ***(P-14092)***
Rci Plumbing, Rio Linda *Also called Risse Construction Inc* ***(P-1347)***
RCP Construction Inc ....E....916 358-9530
5180 Gldn Fthl Pkwy # 110 El Dorado Hills (95762) ***(P-944)***
Rdc Machine Inc ....E....408 970-0721
2011 Stone Ave San Jose (95125) ***(P-5610)***
Rdi Finishing ....E....707 829-1226
350 Morris St Ste F Sebastopol (95472) ***(P-3189)***
RDM Express Inc (PA)....D....415 642-4916
750 La Playa St San Francisco (94121) ***(P-7486)***
RDm Industrial Products Inc ....F....408 945-8400
1652 Watson Ct Milpitas (95035) ***(P-3311)***
Rdo Construction Equipment Co ....E....925 454-3100
7650 Hawthorne Ave Ste 1 Livermore (94550) ***(P-9043)***
Rdr Builders LP ....D....209 368-7561
1806 W Kettleman Ln Ste F Lodi (95242) ***(P-763)***
Rdr Production Builders, Lodi *Also called Rdr Builders LP* ***(P-763)***
RE Infolink, Sunnyvale *Also called Mlslistings Inc* ***(P-19578)***
RE La Mesa LLC ....D....415 675-1500
300 California St Fl 8 San Francisco (94104) ***(P-1174)***
RE Milano Plumbing Corp ....E....925 500-1372
280 Arthur Rd B Martinez (94553) ***(P-1344)***
RE Tranquillity 8 LLC ....E....415 675-1500
300 California St Fl 7 San Francisco (94104) ***(P-4633)***
Re/Max, Folsom *Also called Norcal Gold Inc* ***(P-10628)***
Re/Max Gold-Natomas, Sacramento *Also called Norcal Gold Inc* ***(P-10627)***
Reach Air Medical Services LLC (HQ)....E....707 324-2400
8880 Cal Center Dr 125 Sacramento (95826) ***(P-7399)***
Reach Medical Holdings LLC (PA)....E....707 324-2400
2360 Becker Blvd Santa Rosa (95403) ***(P-7759)***
Reaction Search Intl Inc (PA)....D....925 275-0727
5000 Executive Pkwy # 450 San Ramon (94583) ***(P-12127)***
Reaction Technology Inc (HQ)....E....408 970-9601
3400 Bassett St Santa Clara (95054) ***(P-6269)***
Read It Later Inc ....E....415 692-6111
233 Sansome St Ste 1200 San Francisco (94104) ***(P-13400)***
Readcoor Inc ....D....617 453-2660
6230 Stoneridge Mall Rd Pleasanton (94588) ***(P-16800)***
Reading and Beyond ....E....559 840-1068
4670 E Butler Ave Fresno (93702) ***(P-18453)***
Reading International Inc ....E....916 442-0985
2508 Land Park Dr Sacramento (95818) ***(P-14817)***
Ready Pac Foods Inc ....B....925 552-0400
125 Railroad Ave Ste 203 Danville (94526) ***(P-9426)***
Ready Price LLC ....A....408 357-0931
5671 Santa Teresa Blvd San Jose (95123) ***(P-12728)***
Readymix - Cordelia R/M, Suisun City *Also called Cemex Cnstr Mtls PCF LLC* ***(P-4423)***
Readymix - Union City Rm, Union City *Also called Cemex Cnstr Mtls PCF LLC* ***(P-4468)***
Readymix -Newman Rm, Newman *Also called Cemex Cnstr Mtls PCF LLC* ***(P-4467)***
Readymix- Lodi Rm, Lodi *Also called Cemex Cnstr Mtls PCF LLC* ***(P-4469)***
Real Estate & Mortgage Broker, Fresno *Also called Xander Mortgage & Real Estate* ***(P-10689)***
Real Estate America Inc ....D....510 594-3100
2000 Powell St Ste 100 Emeryville (94608) ***(P-10653)***
Real Estate Equity Exchange ....D....415 992-4200
650 California St Fl 1800 San Francisco (94108) ***(P-9924)***
Real Intent ....E....408 830-0700
932 Hamlin Ct Sunnyvale (94089) ***(P-8743)***
Real Time Information Svcs Inc ....E....559 222-6456
191 W Shaw Ave Ste 106 Fresno (93704) ***(P-12191)***
Real-Time Innovations Inc (PA)....D....408 990-7400
232 E Java Dr Sunnyvale (94089) ***(P-12729)***
Real-Time Staffing Services, Fresno *Also called Real Time Information Svcs Inc* ***(P-12191)***
Realm, Palo Alto *Also called Tightdb Inc* ***(P-12866)***
Realm, Milpitas *Also called R&M USA Inc* ***(P-8948)***
Realscout Inc ....F....650 397-6500
480 Ellis St Ste 203 Mountain View (94043) ***(P-13401)***
Realsuite SM, Santa Clara *Also called Move Inc* ***(P-10623)***

Realtimeboard Inc (PA)..........C.......**415 669-8098**
201 Spear St Ste 1100 San Francisco (94105) ***(P-13968)***
Realty Concepts, Fresno *Also called JMS Realtors Ltd* ***(P-10584)***
REBEKAH CHILDREN'S SERVICES, Gilroy *Also called Odd Fellow-Rebekah Chld HM Cal* ***(P-18151)***
Rebel Girls Inc..........E.......808 398-2258
421 Elm Ave Larkspur (94939) ***(P-13657)***
Recall Management Inc..........E.......877 386-8186
2610 Crow Canyon Rd # 120 San Ramon (94583) ***(P-12730)***
Recall Masters Inc..........E.......650 434-5211
740 Tunbridge Rd Danville (94526) ***(P-11840)***
Reciprocity Inc..........E.......415 851-8667
548 Market St 73905 San Francisco (94104) ***(P-12731)***
Reclamation District 108..........E.......530 437-2221
975 Wilson Bend Rd Grimes (95950) ***(P-8260)***
Recoating-West Inc (PA)..........E.......**916 652-8290**
4170 Douglas Blvd Ste 120 Granite Bay (95746) ***(P-4809)***
Recognition Products Mfg, San Jose *Also called Stryker Enterprises Inc* ***(P-4987)***
Recology Inc (PA)..........D.......**415 875-1000**
50 California St Ste 2400 San Francisco (94111) ***(P-8351)***
Recology Inc..........D.......916 379-3300
245 N 1st St Dixon (95620) ***(P-8352)***
Recology Sonoma Marin..........B.......707 586-8261
3400 Standish Ave Santa Rosa (95407) ***(P-8353)***
Recology South Valley (HQ)..........D.......**408 842-3358**
1351 Pacheco Pass Hwy Gilroy (95020) ***(P-8354)***
Recology Sunset Scavenger, San Francisco *Also called Sunset Scavenger Company* ***(P-8365)***
Recology Vallejo (HQ)..........C.......**707 552-3110**
2021 Broadway St Vallejo (94589) ***(P-8355)***
Recology Yuba-Sutter..........D.......530 743-6933
3001 N Levee Rd Marysville (95901) ***(P-8356)***
Recommind Inc (HQ)..........D.......**415 394-7899**
550 Kearny St Ste 700 San Francisco (94108) ***(P-6506)***
Record The, Stockton *Also called Dow Jones Lmg Stockton Inc* ***(P-3433)***
Recore Growth Investments Inc..........E.......916 813-3798
1116 Mcclaren Dr Carmichael (95608) ***(P-10878)***
Recp/Wndsor Scramento Ventr LP..........E.......916 455-6800
4422 Y St Sacramento (95817) ***(P-11386)***
Recreation & Pk Dst Orangevale..........E.......916 988-4373
6826 Hazel Ave Orangevale (95662) ***(P-15230)***
Recruitment Alley LLC..........E.......559 614-5024
2505 W Shaw Ave Ste 150 Fresno (93711) ***(P-17171)***
Recruitment Service, Sacramento *Also called Sutter Hlth Scrmnto Sierra Reg* ***(P-16666)***
Recurrent Energy LLC (HQ)..........D.......**415 956-3168**
123 Mission St Ste 1800 San Francisco (94105) ***(P-1345)***
Recurrent Enrgy Dev Hldngs LLC (HQ)..........D.......**415 675-1501**
3000 Oak Rd Ste 300 Walnut Creek (94597) ***(P-10879)***
Recycle Waste, Santa Clara *Also called Mission Trail Wste Systems Inc* ***(P-7484)***
Recycled Spaces Inc..........F.......530 587-3394
10191 Donner Pass Rd # 1 Truckee (96161) ***(P-3299)***
Recycling Industries Inc..........D.......916 452-3961
4741 Watt Ave North Highlands (95660) ***(P-8357)***
Red and White Fleet, San Francisco *Also called Golden Gate Scnic Stmship Corp* ***(P-7720)***
Red Bay Coffee Company Inc..........E.......510 409-1076
3098 E 10th St Oakland (94601) ***(P-2846)***
Red Bear Inc..........E.......925 846-8802
807 Main St Pleasanton (94566) ***(P-11387)***
Red Carpet Car Wash, Clovis *Also called Bowie Enterprises* ***(P-14632)***
Red Condor Inc..........E.......707 569-7419
1300 Valley House Dr # 115 Rohnert Park (94928) ***(P-12732)***
Red Door Catering, The, Oakland *Also called Red Door Group* ***(P-19620)***
Red Door Group..........E.......510 339-2320
2925 Adeline St Oakland (94608) ***(P-19620)***
Red Eagle Ventures Inc..........E.......415 773-1800
338 Main St Unit 26b San Francisco (94105) ***(P-10880)***
Red Fox Casino..........E.......707 984-6800
200 Cahto Dr Laytonville (95454) ***(P-11388)***
Red Hawk Casino, Placerville *Also called Shingle Sprng Trbal Gming Auth* ***(P-11472)***
Red Line Synthetic Oil, Benicia *Also called Phillips 66 Spectrum Corp* ***(P-4196)***
Red Lion Hotel Eureka, Eureka *Also called Jjk Hotels LP* ***(P-11211)***
Red Lion Hotel Redding, Redding *Also called Kaidan Hospitality LP* ***(P-11227)***
Red River Consulting Svcs Inc (HQ)..........E.......**916 383-9005**
1030 R St Sacramento (95811) ***(P-12733)***
Red River Lumber Co..........E.......707 963-1251
2959 Saint Helena Hwy N Saint Helena (94574) ***(P-3239)***
Red Rock Ranch Inc..........E.......559 884-4201
15671 W Oakland Ave Five Points (93624) ***(P-188)***
Red Top Rice Growers..........D.......530 868-5975
3200 8th St Biggs (95917) ***(P-303)***
Redacted Inc..........D.......415 858-2719
350 Rhode Island St # 240 San Francisco (94103) ***(P-12734)***
Redding Aero Enterprises Inc..........D.......530 224-2300
3775 Flight Ave Ste 100 Redding (96002) ***(P-7345)***
Redding Distributing Company..........E.......530 226-5700
6450 Lockheed Dr Redding (96002) ***(P-9560)***
Redding District Office, Redding *Also called State Compensation Insur Fund* ***(P-10178)***
Redding Drmtlogy Med Group Inc..........E.......530 241-1111
2107 Airpark Dr Redding (96001) ***(P-15639)***
Redding Freightliner Inc..........E.......530 241-4412
4991 Caterpillar Rd Redding (96003) ***(P-8427)***
Redding Jet Center, Redding *Also called Redding Aero Enterprises Inc* ***(P-7345)***
Redding Lumber Transport Inc..........D.......530 241-8193
4301 Eastside Rd Redding (96001) ***(P-7632)***
Redding Medical Home Care, Redding *Also called Tenet Healthsystem Medical Inc* ***(P-16960)***
Redding Metal Crafters Inc..........E.......530 222-4400
3871 Rancho Rd Redding (96002) ***(P-4810)***
Redding Pathologists Lab (PA)..........C.......**530 225-8000**
1725 Gold St Redding (96001) ***(P-15640)***
Redding Pathologists Lab..........D.......530 225-8050
2036 Railroad Ave Redding (96001) ***(P-16801)***
Redding Printing Co Inc (PA)..........E.......**530 243-0525**
1130 Continental St Redding (96001) ***(P-3691)***
Redding Produce, Durham *Also called Chico Produce Inc* ***(P-9394)***
Redding Rancheria..........D.......530 245-9161
2100 Redding Rancheria Rd Redding (96001) ***(P-11389)***
Redding Rancheria (PA)..........D.......**530 225-8979**
2000 Redding Rancheria Rd Redding (96001) ***(P-11390)***
Redding Rnchria Ecnmic Dev Cor..........B.......530 243-3377
2100 Redding Rancheria Rd Redding (96001) ***(P-11391)***
Redding Super 8 Motel Inc..........D.......530 221-8881
5175 Churn Creek Rd Redding (96002) ***(P-11392)***
Redding V A Outpatient Clinic, Redding *Also called Veterans Health Administration* ***(P-15791)***
Reddit Inc (PA)..........C.......**415 666-2330**
548 Market St Ste 16093 San Francisco (94104) ***(P-3595)***
Redevelopment Agency of The Ci..........D.......707 421-7309
701 Civic Center Blvd Suisun City (94585) ***(P-19847)***
Redf..........E.......415 561-6677
2526 Piedmont Ave Berkeley (94704) ***(P-17682)***
Redfern Integrated Optics Inc..........E.......408 970-3500
3350 Scott Blvd Bldg 1 Santa Clara (95054) ***(P-6884)***
Redfern Ranches..........E.......209 392-2426
14664 Brannon Ave Dos Palos (93620) ***(P-203)***
Redhorse Constructors Inc..........D.......415 492-2020
36 Professional Ctr Pkwy San Rafael (94903) ***(P-693)***
Redi-Gro Corporation..........E.......916 381-6063
8909 Elder Creek Rd Sacramento (95828) ***(P-9607)***
Redis Inc..........B.......415 930-9666
700 E El Cmino Real Ste 1 Mountain View (94040) ***(P-12735)***
Redmont Cnstr & Inv Co Inc..........D.......650 306-9344
881 Hurlingame Ave Redwood City (94063) ***(P-694)***
Redrocks Fumigation, San Jose *Also called Homeguard Incorporated* ***(P-11900)***
Redrover, Sacramento *Also called United Animal Nations* ***(P-18604)***
Redseal Inc..........C.......408 641-2200
1600 Technology Dr Fl 4 San Jose (95110) ***(P-13402)***
Redstone Print & Mail Inc..........C.......925 335-9090
2830 Howe Rd Ste B Martinez (94553) ***(P-3692)***
Redstone Print & Mail Inc..........D.......916 318-6450
910 Riverside Pkwy Ste 40 West Sacramento (95605) ***(P-19621)***
Redtail Technology Inc..........D.......800 206-5030
3131 Fite Cir Sacramento (95827) ***(P-12736)***
Redwood City School District..........E.......650 568-3820
3600 Middlefield Rd Menlo Park (94025) ***(P-17683)***
Redwood Coast Medical Svcs Inc (PA)..........E.......**707 884-1721**
46900 Ocean Dr Gualala (95445) ***(P-15641)***
Redwood Coast Seniors Inc..........E.......707 964-0443
490 N Harold St Fort Bragg (95437) ***(P-17684)***
Redwood Community Services Inc..........D.......707 472-2922
350 E Gobbi St Ukiah (95482) ***(P-17685)***
Redwood Convalescent Hospital..........E.......510 537-8848
22103 Redwood Rd Castro Valley (94546) ***(P-16260)***
Redwood Cove Healthcare Center, Ukiah *Also called Nightshade Holdings LLC* ***(P-16071)***
Redwood Credit Union..........E.......800 479-7928
1129 S Cloverdale Blvd A Cloverdale (95425) ***(P-9804)***
Redwood Credit Union (PA)..........C.......**707 545-4000**
3033 Cleveland Ave # 100 Santa Rosa (95403) ***(P-9805)***
Redwood Credit Union..........E.......800 479-7928
1390 Market St San Francisco (94102) ***(P-9806)***
Redwood Credit Union..........E.......415 861-7928
100 Van Ness Ave Fl 10 San Francisco (94102) ***(P-9807)***
Redwood Electric Group Inc (PA)..........A.......**707 451-7348**
2775 Northwestern Pkwy Santa Clara (95051) ***(P-1576)***
Redwood Empire Addctons Prgram, Santa Rosa *Also called Drug Abuse Alternatives Center* ***(P-17015)***
Redwood Empire Food Bank..........E.......707 523-7900
3990 Brickway Blvd Santa Rosa (95403) ***(P-17686)***
Redwood Empire Golf Cntry CLB..........D.......707 725-5194
352 Country Club Dr Fortuna (95540) ***(P-15126)***
Redwood Empire Gymnastics, Petaluma *Also called Steven I Klotz* ***(P-15246)***
Redwood Empire Ice Oprtons LLC (PA)..........D.......**707 546-7147**
1667 W Steele Ln Santa Rosa (95403) ***(P-15231)***
Redwood Empire Stereocasters..........E.......707 528-4434
3392 Mendocino Ave Fl 2 Santa Rosa (95403) ***(P-8031)***
Redwood Empire Vinyrd MGT Inc..........D.......707 857-3401
22000 Geyserville Ave Geyserville (95441) ***(P-386)***
Redwood Fmly Drmtlogy Med Asso..........E.......707 545-4537
2725 Mendocino Ave Santa Rosa (95403) ***(P-15642)***
Redwood General Tire Svc Co..........E.......650 369-0351
1630 Broadway St Redwood City (94063) ***(P-14586)***
Redwood Health Club (PA)..........D.......**707 468-0441**
3101 S State St Ukiah (95482) ***(P-14967)***
Redwood Hill Farm & Crmry Inc (HQ)..........D.......**707 823-8250**
2064 Gravenstein Hwy N # 130 Sebastopol (95472) ***(P-220)***
Redwood Landfill Inc..........C.......415 892-2851
8950 Redwood Hwy Novato (94945) ***(P-8358)***
Redwood Memorial Hosp Fortuna (PA)..........C.......**707 725-7327**
3300 Renner Dr Fortuna (95540) ***(P-16488)***
Redwood Orthpdic Surgery Assoc..........E.......707 544-3400
208 Concourse Blvd Ste 1 Santa Rosa (95403) ***(P-15643)***
Redwood Painting Co Inc..........C.......925 432-4500
620 W 10th St Pittsburg (94565) ***(P-1429)***
Redwood Regional Hematology..........E.......707 528-1050
3555 Round Barn Cir 100 Santa Rosa (95403) ***(P-15644)***
Redwood Regional Medical Group, Santa Rosa *Also called Sotoyome Medical Building LLC* ***(P-10409)***

ALPHABETIC

Redwood Regional Medical Group....E....707 463-3636
1165 S Dora St Bldg H Ukiah (95482) *(P-15645)*
Redwood Regional Medical Group (PA)....D....**707 525-4080**
990 Sonoma Ave Ste 15 Santa Rosa (95404) *(P-16802)*
Redwood Regional Oncology Ctr, Santa Rosa *Also called Redwood Regional Medical Group (P-16802)*
Redwood Rgnal Med Group DRG LL....E....707 262-3060
5150 Hill Rd E Ste F Lakeport (95453) *(P-16803)*
Redwood Rgnal Med Group DRG LL....E....707 253-7161
1100 Trancas St Ste 256 NAPA (94558) *(P-15646)*
Redwood Security Systems Inc....E....415 388-5355
160 Almonte Blvd Mill Valley (94941) *(P-1577)*
Redwood Services Inc....E....650 872-2310
350 Lang Rd Burlingame (94010) *(P-8359)*
Redwood Toxicology Lab Inc....C....707 577-7958
3650 Westwind Blvd Santa Rosa (95403) *(P-16804)*
Redwood Trust Inc (PA)....C....**415 389-7373**
1 Belvedere Pl Ste 300 Mill Valley (94941) *(P-10825)*
Redwood Valley Gravel Pdts Inc....E....707 485-8585
11200 East Rd Redwood Valley (95470) *(P-4449)*
Redwoods....E....415 383-1600
40 Camino Alto Ofc Mill Valley (94941) *(P-18164)*
Redwoods Rural Health Ctr Inc....E....707 923-2783
101 Westcoast Rd Redway (95560) *(P-15647)*
REDWOODS, THE, Mill Valley *Also called The Redwoods A Cmnty Seniors (P-18192)*
Reeces Fantasies Inc (HQ)....D....**408 298-5400**
360 Turtle Creek Ct San Jose (95125) *(P-1578)*
Reed & Graham Inc (PA)....E....**408 287-1400**
690 Sunol St San Jose (95126) *(P-4178)*
Reed & Graham Inc....E....888 381-0800
26 Light Sky Ct Sacramento (95828) *(P-4189)*
Reed Brothers Security, San Leandro *Also called Security Central Inc (P-14775)*
Reed Group (HQ)....E....**209 521-7423**
928 12th St Ste 700 Modesto (95354) *(P-1071)*
Reed International (HQ)....F....**209 874-2357**
13024 Lake Rd Hickman (95323) *(P-5043)*
Reed Manufacturing Inc....E....831 637-5641
205 Apollo Way Ste A Hollister (95023) *(P-4552)*
Reed Mariculture Inc....F....408 377-1065
900 E Hamilton Ave # 100 Campbell (95008) *(P-2354)*
Reed Smith LLP....C....415 543-8700
101 2nd St Ste 1800 San Francisco (94105) *(P-17360)*
Reedley Community Hospital....D....559 638-8155
372 W Cypress Ave Reedley (93654) *(P-16489)*
Reedley Irrigation & Supply, Reedley *Also called Fortier & Fortier Inc (P-9037)*
Reeve Trucking Company Inc (PA)....D....**209 948-4061**
5050 Carpenter Rd Stockton (95215) *(P-7577)*
Reeve-Knight Construction Inc....D....916 786-5112
128 Ascot Dr Roseville (95661) *(P-945)*
Reeves Enterprises Inc....E....209 529-5698
229 Bangs Ave Modesto (95356) *(P-14674)*
Refactored Materials, Emeryville *Also called Bolt Threads Inc (P-19036)*
Refficiency Holdings LLC....A....408 347-3400
1601 Las Plumas Ave San Jose (95133) *(P-1579)*
Refinitiv US LLC....C....415 344-6000
50 California St San Francisco (94111) *(P-3512)*
Reflektion Inc (PA)....E....**650 293-0800**
1825 S Grant St Ste 900 San Mateo (94402) *(P-12737)*
Reflektive Inc....C....203 886-9240
123 Townsend St Ste 300 San Francisco (94107) *(P-12738)*
Reflex Photonics Inc....E....408 501-8886
1250 Oakmead Pkwy Sunnyvale (94085) *(P-6270)*
Reflexion Medical Inc....C....650 239-9070
25841 Industrial Blvd # 275 Hayward (94545) *(P-7122)*
Reforestation Tech Intl, Gilroy *Also called Sierra Reforestation Company (P-9610)*
Regal Electronics Inc (PA)....E....**408 988-2288**
820 Charcot Ave San Jose (95131) *(P-6467)*
Regal III LLC....D....707 836-2100
421 Aviation Blvd Santa Rosa (95403) *(P-9584)*
Regal Wine Co, Santa Rosa *Also called Regal III LLC (P-9584)*
Regency General Contrs Inc (PA)....D....**408 946-7100**
4400 Auto Mall Pkwy Fremont (94538) *(P-764)*
Regent Assisted Living Inc....E....916 722-2800
7241 Canelo Hills Dr Ofc Citrus Heights (95610) *(P-18165)*
Regent Assisted Living Inc....E....209 491-0800
2325 St Pauls Way Modesto (95355) *(P-18166)*
Regent Assisted Living Inc....E....831 459-8400
80 Front St Santa Cruz (95060) *(P-18167)*
Regent Assisted Living Inc....E....559 325-8400
675 W Alluvial Ave Ofc Clovis (93611) *(P-18168)*
Regent Court, Modesto *Also called Regent Assisted Living Inc (P-18166)*
Regents of The Univ of Cal....E....510 987-0043
1111 Franklin St Fl 10 Oakland (94607) *(P-19116)*
Regional Builders Inc (PA)....E....**916 717-2669**
3941 Park Dr Ste 20 El Dorado Hills (95762) *(P-695)*
Regional Burn Center, Sacramento *Also called Burn Unit Ucd Medical Center (P-16752)*
Regional Cardiology Associate (PA)....E....**916 564-3040**
8120 Timberlake Way # 108 Sacramento (95823) *(P-15648)*
Regional Center, Chico *Also called Far Nrthern Crdnting Cncil On (P-17567)*
Regional Center of E Bay Inc (PA)....C....**510 618-6100**
500 Davis St Ste 100 San Leandro (94577) *(P-17687)*
Regional Center of E Bay Inc....D....925 691-2300
1320 Willow Pass Rd # 300 Concord (94520) *(P-17688)*
Regional Medical Ctr San Jose, San Jose *Also called San Jose Healthcare System LP (P-16504)*
Regulus Intgrted Solutions LLC....E....707 254-4000
860 Latour Ct NAPA (94558) *(P-3693)*
Regusci Vineyard MGT Inc....E....707 254-0403
5584 Silverado Trl NAPA (94558) *(P-2694)*
Regusci Winery, NAPA *Also called Regusci Vineyard MGT Inc (P-2694)*
Rehabilitation Center, Lodi *Also called Lodi Memorial Hosp Assn Inc (P-15508)*
Rehabilitation Services, Sonora *Also called Adventist Health System/West (P-16300)*
Rehabltion Ctr At San Jquin G, French Camp *Also called County of San Joaquin (P-17007)*
Reichardt Duck Farm Inc....D....707 762-6314
3770 Middle Two Rock Rd Petaluma (94952) *(P-241)*
Reichs Pharmacy and Med Sup, Tracy *Also called Harold Reichs Pharmacy (P-6982)*
Relationalai Inc....F....650 307-8776
2120 University Ave Berkeley (94704) *(P-13403)*
Relationship Skills Center....E....916 362-1900
9719 Lincoln Sacramento (95827) *(P-17689)*
Relay2 Inc (PA)....D....**408 380-0031**
1525 Mccrthy Bllvard Ste Milpitas (95035) *(P-7987)*
Release On Rcgnznce For Prvate, Redwood City *Also called San Mateo County Bar Assn (P-18348)*
Relectric Inc....E....408 467-2222
2390 Zanker Rd San Jose (95131) *(P-5653)*
Reliable Concepts Corporation....E....408 271-6655
636 Newhall Dr San Jose (95110) *(P-806)*
Reliable Crane & Rigging, Petaluma *Also called Marin Storage & Trucking Inc (P-7625)*
Reliable Pntiac Cdllac Bick GM, Roseville *Also called Westrup-Sadler Inc (P-14496)*
Reliable Robotics Corporation....E....650 336-0608
950 N Rengstorff Ave E Mountain View (94043) *(P-9088)*
Reliance Computer Corp....C....408 492-1915
2451 Mission College Blvd Santa Clara (95054) *(P-6271)*
Reliance Intermodal Inc....D....209 946-0200
1919 Mrtin Lther King Ste Stockton (95210) *(P-7578)*
Reliance Machine Products Inc....E....510 438-6760
4265 Solar Way Fremont (94538) *(P-5611)*
Reliance Steel & Aluminum Co....D....510 476-4400
33201 Western Ave Union City (94587) *(P-8827)*
Reliant Ems, Fremont *Also called Reliant Engrg & Mfg Svcs Inc (P-18802)*
Reliant Engrg & Mfg Svcs Inc....E....510 252-1973
47366 Fremont Blvd Fremont (94538) *(P-18802)*
Rels Foods....E....916 927-7677
3001 Academy Way Sacramento (95815) *(P-9481)*
Reltio Inc (PA)....C....**855 360-3282**
100 Marine Pkwy Ste 275 Redwood City (94065) *(P-12739)*
Remax Accord, Pleasanton *Also called S&J Stadtler Inc (P-10656)*
Remax Gold Elite....D....707 422-4411
455 Lopes Rd Ste D Fairfield (94534) *(P-10654)*
Remax Value Properties, San Jose *Also called Quail Hill Investments Inc (P-10824)*
Remco, Stockton *Also called Rock Engineered McHy Co Inc (P-4179)*
Remedly Inc....F....650 265-8449
407 Sansome St Fl 4 San Francisco (94111) *(P-13404)*
Remel Inc....A....916 425-2651
46500 Kato Rd Fremont (94538) *(P-6846)*
Remi Vista Inc....D....530 222-4561
3191 Churn Creek Rd Redding (96002) *(P-18169)*
Remi Vista Inc....D....707 464-4349
370 9th St Crescent City (95531) *(P-18170)*
Remi Vista Transitional Hsing, Redding *Also called Remi Vista Inc (P-18169)*
Remick Associates Db Inc....E....415 896-9500
1230 Howard St 2 San Francisco (94103) *(P-696)*
Remington Ldging Hsptality LLC....D....877 932-5333
6526 Yount St Yountville (94599) *(P-11393)*
Remix Software Inc....D....415 900-4332
1128 Howard St San Francisco (94103) *(P-12740)*
Remodelors Inc....E....530 893-4741
15523 Nopel Ave Forest Ranch (95942) *(P-19387)*
Renaissance Clubsport, Walnut Creek *Also called Leisure Sports Inc (P-11260)*
Renaissance Construction, Grass Valley *Also called Manuel Bros Inc (P-1117)*
Renaissance Food Group LLC (HQ)....E....**916 638-8825**
11020 White Rock Rd Ste 1 Rancho Cordova (95670) *(P-2937)*
Renaissance Hotel Holdings Inc....E....707 935-6600
1325 Broadway Sonoma (95476) *(P-11394)*
Renaissance Hotel Operating Co....C....415 989-3500
905 California St San Francisco (94108) *(P-11395)*
Renaissance School....E....510 531-8566
3668 Dimond Ave Oakland (94602) *(P-18006)*
Renesas Electronics Amer Inc (HQ)....A....**408 432-8888**
6024 Silver Creek Vly Rd San Jose (95138) *(P-6272)*
Renesas Electronics Amer Inc....A....408 588-6750
240a Lawrence Ave South San Francisco (94080) *(P-6273)*
Reneson Hotels Inc (PA)....D....**650 449-5353**
2700 Junipero Serra Blvd Daly City (94015) *(P-11396)*
Reneson Hotels Inc....C....415 621-7001
112 7th St San Francisco (94103) *(P-11397)*
Renew Financial Corp II....C....610 433-7486
555 12th St Ste 1650 Oakland (94607) *(P-9925)*
Renew Financial Group LLC....E....888 996-0523
555 12th St Ste 1650 Oakland (94607) *(P-14383)*
Renn Transportation Inc....D....408 842-3545
8845 Forest St Gilroy (95020) *(P-7579)*
Renne Sloan Holtzman Sakai LLP (PA)....E....**415 678-3800**
555 Capitol Mall Ste 600 Sacramento (95814) *(P-17361)*
Reno News & Review, Chico *Also called Chico Community Publishing (P-3427)*
Renos Floor Covering Inc....E....415 459-1403
1515 Solano Ave Vallejo (94590) *(P-7266)*
Renovite Technologies Inc (PA)....D....**510 771-9200**
39785 Paseo Padre Pkwy Fremont (94538) *(P-19622)*
Renovorx Inc....F....650 284-4433
4546 El Cmino Real Ste B1 Los Altos (94022) *(P-7026)*
Rental Radar High-End, San Francisco *Also called Gavin Atwood Coombs (P-10557)*
Rentokil North America Inc....E....510 265-1949
3481 Arden Rd Hayward (94545) *(P-12059)*

Rentpayment.com, Walnut Creek *Also called Yapstone Inc* ***(P-14465)***
Renzenberger Inc A 530 283-3314
2096 E Main St Quincy (95971) ***(P-6569)***
Replicon Software Inc (PA) **E 650 286-9200**
3 Lagoon Dr Ste 130 Redwood City (94065) ***(P-12741)***
Reporter D 707 448-6401
916 Cotting Ln Vacaville (95688) ***(P-3475)***
Represent Development E 510 944-1938
650 University Ave Unit 3 Berkeley (94710) ***(P-12742)***
Reproductive Science Center D 925 867-1800
100 Park Pl Ste 200 San Ramon (94583) ***(P-15649)***
Reproductive Science Ctr Bay, San Ramon *Also called Reproductive Science Center* ***(P-15649)***
Repsco Inc E 303 294-0364
5300 Claus Rd Ste 3 Modesto (95357) ***(P-4317)***
Republic Document Management E 925 551-4747
6377 Clark Ave Ste 250 Dublin (94568) ***(P-19388)***
Republic Electric Inc C 916 294-0140
3820 Happy Ln Sacramento (95827) ***(P-1580)***
Republic Electric West Inc D 916 294-0140
3820 Happy Ln Sacramento (95827) ***(P-1581)***
Republic Indemnity Co Amer D 415 981-3200
100 Pine St Fl 14 San Francisco (94111) ***(P-10172)***
Republic Intelligent D 916 515-0855
1513 Sports Dr Ste 250 Sacramento (95834) ***(P-1582)***
Republic Svcs Vsco Rd Landfill E 925 447-0491
4001 N Vasco Rd Livermore (94551) ***(P-8360)***
Reputationcom Inc (PA) **B 800 888-0924**
1400 A Sport Blvd Ste 401 Redwood City (94063) ***(P-13405)***
Reputationdefender LLC (HQ) **D 888 851-9609**
1400a Saport Blvd Ste 401 Redwood City (94063) ***(P-19183)***
RES-Care Inc E 916 487-7497
3315 Green Park Ln Carmichael (95608) ***(P-16929)***
RES-Care Inc D 209 473-1202
5250 Claremont Ave Stockton (95207) ***(P-16197)***
RES-Care Inc D 916 567-1244
1485 Response Rd Sacramento (95815) ***(P-16198)***
RES-Care Inc E 209 578-1385
3408 Gatewood Dr Modesto (95355) ***(P-18171)***
RES-Care Inc D 800 866-0860
545 Dutra Pl Manteca (95337) ***(P-16199)***
RES-Care Inc E 510 357-4222
101 Callan Ave Ste 208 San Leandro (94577) ***(P-16930)***
RES-Care Inc E 916 307-3737
5346 Madison Ave Ste E Sacramento (95841) ***(P-16931)***
RES-Care Inc E 530 823-6475
4090 Truxel Rd Ste 250 Sacramento (95834) ***(P-16932)***
RES-Care Inc E 530 755-3027
1775 Augusta Ln Yuba City (95993) ***(P-16933)***
RES-Care Inc E 209 227-4568
55 S Highway 26 Ste 3 Valley Springs (95252) ***(P-16934)***
RES-Care Inc E 925 283-5076
18540 Gateway Blvd 280 Concord (94521) ***(P-16935)***
RES-Care Inc E 530 888-6580
11960 Heritage Oak Pl # 10 Auburn (95603) ***(P-16936)***
RES-Care Inc E 925 283-5076
3732 Mt Diablo Blvd # 286 Lafayette (94549) ***(P-16937)***
RES-Care Inc D 530 406-8603
618 Court St Ste D Woodland (95695) ***(P-16200)***
RES-Care Inc E 209 523-9130
1101 Sylvan Ave Modesto (95350) ***(P-16938)***
Rescale Inc D 855 737-2253
33 New Montgomery St # 950 San Francisco (94105) ***(P-13406)***
Rescue 42 Inc F 530 891-3473
370 Ryan Ave Ste 120 Chico (95973) ***(P-5232)***
Rescue Children Inc E 559 268-1123
335 G St Fresno (93706) ***(P-17690)***
Rescue Concrete Inc D 916 852-2400
9275 Beatty Dr Sacramento (95826) ***(P-1905)***
Rescue Rooter Bay East, San Leandro *Also called American Rsdntial Svcs Ind Inc* ***(P-1200)***
Research & Dev GL Pdts &, Berkeley *Also called Research Dev GL Pdts & Eqp Inc* ***(P-4392)***
Research Dev GL Pdts & Eqp Inc F 510 547-6464
1808 Harmon St Berkeley (94703) ***(P-4392)***
Research Institute, Palo Alto *Also called Dave Drunker* ***(P-16779)***
Resers Fine Foods Inc D 503 643-6431
1540 Giuntoli Ln Arcata (95521) ***(P-9289)***
Resers Fine Foods Inc D 503 643-6431
5800 Airport Rd Redding (96002) ***(P-9290)***
Resers Fine Foods Inc E 503 643-6431
15100 Jack Tone Rd Manteca (95336) ***(P-2938)***
Reservation Bureau, South Lake Tahoe *Also called Tahoe Keys Resort* ***(P-10668)***
Reservation Ranch (PA) **E 707 487-3516**
356 Sarina Rd N Smith River (95567) ***(P-11398)***
Residence Inn By Marriott, San Jose *Also called Island Hospitality MGT LLC* ***(P-11198)***
Residence Inn By Marriott, Pleasanton *Also called Pleasant Canyon Hotel Inc* ***(P-11371)***
Residence Inn By Marriott, Roseville *Also called Rl Heritg Inn Roseville LLC* ***(P-11407)***
Residence Inn By Marriott, San Mateo *Also called Island Hospitality MGT LLC* ***(P-11200)***
Residence Inn By Marriott, Los Altos *Also called Los Altos Hotel Associates LLC* ***(P-11269)***
Residence Inn By Marriott D 559 222-8900
5322 N Diana St Fresno (93710) ***(P-11399)***
Residence Inn By Marriott LLC E 650 637-5500
800 E San Carlos Ave San Carlos (94070) ***(P-11400)***
Residence Inn By Marriott LLC E 888 484-1695
1850 Freedom Way Roseville (95678) ***(P-11401)***
Residence Inn By Marriott LLC E 510 739-6000
35466 Dumbarton Ct Newark (94560) ***(P-11402)***
Residence Inn By Marriott LLC E 650 837-9000
1350 Veterans Blvd South San Francisco (94080) ***(P-11403)***
Residence Inn By Marriott LLC E 925 689-1010
700 Ellinwood Way Pleasant Hill (94523) ***(P-11404)***
Residence Inn Chico, Chico *Also called Chico Lodging LLC* ***(P-11005)***
Residence Inn San Jose Airport, San Jose *Also called San Jose Hhg Hotel Dev LP* ***(P-11438)***
Residential Ctrl Systems Inc E 916 635-6784
11481 Sunrise Gold Cir # 1 Rancho Cordova (95742) ***(P-6704)***
Residential Pacific Mortgage, Alamo *Also called Nl Inc* ***(P-9917)***
Residential Plumbing, San Jose *Also called Aqualine Piping Inc* ***(P-1204)***
Resideo Buoy, Santa Cruz *Also called Buoy Labs Inc* ***(P-13039)***
Residnce Inn By Mrriot Brkeley, Berkeley *Also called Berkeley Downtown Ht Owner LLC* ***(P-10953)***
Residnce Inn By Mrrott Nwark S, Newark *Also called Residence Inn By Marriott LLC* ***(P-11402)***
Residnce Inn By Mrrott Stckton, Stockton *Also called Castlehill Properties Inc* ***(P-10995)***
Residnce Inn Palo Alto Mtn Vie, Mountain View *Also called Island Hospitality MGT LLC* ***(P-11203)***
Residnce Inn San Frncsco Arprt, South San Francisco *Also called Residence Inn By Marriott LLC* ***(P-11403)***
Residnce Inn San Jose Nrth/SLC E 408 758-9550
656 America Center Ct San Jose (95002) ***(P-11405)***
Residntial Care Fclty For Eldr, Concord *Also called Pennys Guest Home LLC* ***(P-16257)***
Resolve Systems LLC (PA) **D 949 325-0120**
300 Orchard Cy Dr Ste 110 Campbell (95008) ***(P-12743)***
Resonate I Inc (PA) **C 408 545-5500**
90 Great Oaks Blvd Ste 20 San Jose (95119) ***(P-12744)***
Resort At Indian Springs LLC C 707 709-2434
1712 Lincoln Ave Calistoga (94515) ***(P-11406)***
Resort At Squaw Creek, Alpine Meadows *Also called Squaw Creek Associates LLC* ***(P-11496)***
Resource Cementing LLC E 707 374-3350
2500 Airport Rd Rio Vista (94571) ***(P-570)***
Resource Cnnction of Amdor Clv (PA) **C 209 754-3114**
444 E Saint Charles St San Andreas (95249) ***(P-17691)***
Resource Connection, San Andreas *Also called H R C Calaveras Head Srt State* ***(P-17947)***
RESOURCE CONNECTION, THE, San Andreas *Also called Resource Cnnction of Amdor Clv* ***(P-17691)***
Resource Design Interiors, San Francisco *Also called Ibex Enterprises* ***(P-8495)***
Resource Innovations Inc (HQ) **D 415 369-1000**
719 Main St Half Moon Bay (94019) ***(P-19848)***
Resource Label Group LLC E 510 477-0707
39611 Eureka Dr Newark (94560) ***(P-3747)***
Resource Staffing Group, Sacramento *Also called Northwest Stffing Rsources Inc* ***(P-12112)***
Resources For Ind Living Inc D 916 446-3074
420 I St Ste 3 Sacramento (95814) ***(P-17692)***
Responsible Metal Fab Inc E 408 734-0713
1256 Lawrence Station Rd Sunnyvale (94089) ***(P-4811)***
Responsys Inc (HQ) **A 650 745-1700**
1100 Grundy Ln Ste 300 San Bruno (94066) ***(P-12745)***
Responsys.com, San Bruno *Also called Responsys Inc* ***(P-12745)***
Resq Manufacturing E 916 638-6786
11430 White Rock Rd Rancho Cordova (95742) ***(P-7305)***
Restaurant Assets & Design Inc (PA) **E 916 532-1377**
3031 Stanford Ranch Rd Rocklin (95765) ***(P-14384)***
Restec Contractors Inc D 510 670-0100
22955 Kidder St Hayward (94545) ***(P-2061)***
Restoration Clean Up Co Inc (PA) **E 800 500-4310**
198 Harbor Ct Pittsburg (94565) ***(P-11989)***
Restoration Management Company, Hayward *Also called Jon K Takata Corporation* ***(P-17629)***
Restoration Resources, Rocklin *Also called Sierra View Landscape Inc* ***(P-502)***
Results Radio Licensee, Santa Rosa *Also called Results Radio LLC* ***(P-8032)***
Results Radio LLC (PA) **D 707 546-9185**
1355 N Dutton Ave Ste 225 Santa Rosa (95401) ***(P-8032)***
Retail Content Service Inc E 415 890-2097
440 N Wolfe Rd Sunnyvale (94085) ***(P-3596)***
Retail Pro International LLC (PA) **D 916 605-7200**
400 Plaza Dr Ste 200 Folsom (95630) ***(P-12746)***
Retail Pro Software, Folsom *Also called Retail Pro International LLC* ***(P-12746)***
Retail Radio Inc E 916 415-9446
7921 Kingswood Dr Ste A3 Citrus Heights (95610) ***(P-11779)***
Retail Realm Distribution Inc (PA) **D 707 996-5400**
454 W Napa St B Sonoma (95476) ***(P-9291)***
Retail Search Group, Grass Valley *Also called Managment Rcrters Grass Vly In* ***(P-12105)***
Retail Solutions Incorporated (HQ) **E 650 390-6100**
100 Century Center Ct # 800 San Jose (95112) ***(P-13407)***
Retail Zipline Inc D 510 390-4904
2370 Market St Ste 436 San Francisco (94114) ***(P-13408)***
Retailnext Inc (PA) **C 408 884-2162**
60 S Market St Ste 310 San Jose (95113) ***(P-12747)***
Retina Communications, Burlingame *Also called Transiris Corporation* ***(P-19652)***
Retina-Vitreous Assoc Inc E 408 402-3239
2512 Samaritan Ct Ste A San Jose (95124) ***(P-15650)***
Retinal Consultants Inc (PA) **D 916 454-4861**
3939 J St Ste 106 Sacramento (95819) ***(P-15651)***
Retronyms Inc (PA) **C 614 589-3121**
595 Pacific Ave Fl 4 San Francisco (94133) ***(P-8744)***
Reuben Junius & Rose LLP E 415 567-9000
1 Bush St Ste 600 San Francisco (94104) ***(P-17362)***
Reuben Borg Fence, Pleasanton *Also called Reuben J Borg* ***(P-2062)***
Reuben J Borg E 925 931-0570
3300 Busch Rd Pleasanton (94566) ***(P-2062)***
Reuse People of America Inc E 510 383-1983
9235 San Leandro St Oakland (94603) ***(P-8361)***
Reuse People, The, Oakland *Also called Reuse People of America Inc* ***(P-8361)***

ALPHABETIC

Reuser Inc ALPHABETIC SECTION

Reuser Inc........F.......707 894-4224
370 Santana Dr Cloverdale (95425) *(P-3102)*
Reutlinger Community........C.......925 964-2062
4000 Camino Tassajara Danville (94506) *(P-17693)*
REUTLINGER COMMUNITY FOR JEWIS, Danville *Also called Reutlinger Community (P-17693)*
Revance Therapeutics Inc........D.......510 742-3400
Rm 144 Mffett Blvd Bldg 2 Moffett Field (94035) *(P-7701)*
Revance Therapeutics Inc........D.......615 724-7755
7555 Gateway Blvd Newark (94560) *(P-3974)*
Revel Arch & Design Inc (PA)........**D.......415 230-7010**
417 Montgomery St San Francisco (94104) *(P-18908)*
Revel Gatherings Inc (PA)........**D.......909 323-0994**
450 Townsend St Ste 225 San Francisco (94107) *(P-18454)*
Revenue Solutions Inc........B.......916 780-8741
2995 Fthills Blvd Ste 110 Roseville (95747) *(P-13752)*
Revera Incorporated........E.......408 510-7400
3090 Oakmead Village Dr Santa Clara (95051) *(P-5406)*
Revinate Inc........D.......415 671-4703
1 Letterman Dr Bldg C San Francisco (94129) *(P-12748)*
Revivermx Inc........E.......916 580-3495
4170 Douglas Blvd Ste 200 Granite Bay (95746) *(P-5864)*
Revjet........C.......650 508-2215
981 Industrial Rd Ste D San Carlos (94070) *(P-13409)*
Revolan Systems, San Jose *Also called Tera-Lite Inc (P-1777)*
Revolution Medicines Inc (PA)........**D.......650 481-6801**
700 Saginaw Dr Redwood City (94063) *(P-19117)*
Revup Software Inc........E.......415 231-2315
101 Redwood Shores Pkwy # 125 Redwood City (94065) *(P-13410)*
Rex Moore Group Inc........B.......916 372-1300
6001 Outfall Cir Sacramento (95828) *(P-1583)*
Rex More Elec Cntrs Engners In (PA)........**B.......916 372-1300**
6001 Outfall Cir Sacramento (95828) *(P-1584)*
Rex More Elec Cntrs Engners In........C.......559 294-1300
5803 E Harvard Ave Fresno (93727) *(P-1585)*
Rexel Usa Inc........E.......510 476-3400
2301 Armstrong St Ste 205 Livermore (94551) *(P-8874)*
Reyes Coca-Cola Bottling LLC........D.......408 436-3700
1555 Old Bayshore Hwy San Jose (95112) *(P-2799)*
Reyes Coca-Cola Bottling LLC........D.......510 476-7000
2025 Pike Ave San Leandro (94577) *(P-2800)*
Reyes Coca-Cola Bottling LLC........C.......510 667-6300
14655 Wicks Blvd San Leandro (94577) *(P-2801)*
Reyes Coca-Cola Bottling LLC........D.......559 264-4631
3220 E Malaga Ave Fresno (93725) *(P-2802)*
Reyes Coca-Cola Bottling LLC........D.......209 466-9501
1467 El Pinal Dr Stockton (95205) *(P-2803)*
Reyes Coca-Cola Bottling LLC........D.......408 483-4259
1510 Rollins Rd Burlingame (94010) *(P-2804)*
Reyes Coca-Cola Bottling LLC........D.......530 241-4315
1580 Beltline Rd Redding (96003) *(P-2805)*
Reyes Coca-Cola Bottling LLC........D.......530 743-6533
1430 Melody Rd Marysville (95901) *(P-2806)*
Reyes Coca-Cola Bottling LLC........D.......707 747-2000
530 Getty Ct Benicia (94510) *(P-2807)*
Reyes Coca-Cola Bottling LLC........D.......925 830-6500
2633 Camino Ramon Ste 300 San Ramon (94583) *(P-2808)*
Reyes Group Enterprises Inc (PA)........**E.......415 524-5909**
1975 Mendocino Ave Santa Rosa (95401) *(P-14385)*
Reyes Holdings LLC........C.......831 761-6400
1729 Seabright Ave Ste A Santa Cruz (95062) *(P-9561)*
Reynen & Bardis Cnstr LLC (PA)........**C.......916 366-3665**
10630 Mather Blvd Mather (95655) *(P-697)*
Rezolute Inc (PA)........**E.......650 206-4507**
201 Rdwood Shres Pkwy Ste Redwood City (94065) *(P-3975)*
Rfgen Software, El Dorado Hills *Also called Datamax Software Group Inc (P-12372)*
RFI Communications SEC Systems, San Jose *Also called RFI Enterprises Inc (P-1586)*
RFI Enterprises Inc (PA)........**D.......408 298-5400**
360 Turtle Creek Ct San Jose (95125) *(P-1586)*
RFI Logistics Warehouse, Sacramento *Also called Rapid Courier & Freight Inc (P-7575)*
Rfid Corporation........C.......925 473-9978
701 Willow Pass Rd Ste 10 Pittsburg (94565) *(P-11645)*
Rfid4u, Concord *Also called Esmart Source Inc (P-13149)*
RFJ Corporation........D.......415 824-6890
930 Innes Ave San Francisco (94124) *(P-1702)*
Rfj Meiswinkel, San Francisco *Also called RFJ Corporation (P-1702)*
Rfmw, San Jose *Also called Tti Inc (P-8967)*
Rfxcel Corporation (PA)........**D.......925 824-0300**
12667 Alcosta Blvd # 375 San Ramon (94583) *(P-8745)*
Rgb Display Corporation........F.......530 268-2222
22525 Kingston Ln Grass Valley (95949) *(P-5336)*
Rgb Spectrum........D.......510 814-7000
1101 Marina Village Pkwy # 101 Alameda (94501) *(P-5407)*
Rgis LLC........D.......408 243-9141
4320 Stevens Creek Blvd San Jose (95129) *(P-14386)*
Rgis LLC........D.......530 898-1015
20 Landing Cir Ste 100 Chico (95973) *(P-14387)*
Rgm Products Inc........B.......559 499-2222
3301 Navone Rd Stockton (95215) *(P-4193)*
Rgs Industries, Santa Clara *Also called Rockys Gasket Shop Inc (P-4206)*
Rgw Equipment Sales LLC........E.......925 606-2456
550 Greenville Rd Livermore (94550) *(P-9027)*
Rh, Alamo *Also called Round Hill Country Club (P-15131)*
Rh Community Builders LP........D.......559 492-1373
2550 W Clinton Ave B-142 Fresno (93705) *(P-18314)*
Rh USA Inc........E.......925 245-7900
455 N Canyons Pkwy Ste B Livermore (94551) *(P-7027)*
Rhcc, Fremont *Also called Raymond Handling Concepts Corp (P-14771)*
Rhi, Santa Rosa *Also called Richard Hancock Inc (P-1752)*
RHODA GOLDMAN PLAZA, San Francisco *Also called Scott St Snior Hsing Cmplex In (P-16113)*
Rhp Soft Inc........E.......925 353-1629
5700 Stnrdge Mall Rd Ste Pleasanton (94588) *(P-12749)*
Rhumbix Inc........D.......435 764-3014
1169 Howard St San Francisco (94103) *(P-14388)*
Rhyne Design Cabinets Showroom, Sebastopol *Also called Rdi Finishing (P-3189)*
Rhys Vineyards LLC........E.......650 419-2050
11715 Skyline Blvd Los Gatos (95033) *(P-2695)*
Rhythmone LLC........D.......650 961-9024
800 W El Camino Real Mountain View (94040) *(P-12750)*
RI, Santa Clara *Also called Roos Instruments Inc (P-6787)*
RI Heritg Inn Roseville LLC........E.......916 780-1850
1850 Freedom Way Roseville (95678) *(P-11407)*
Rice Corporation (PA)........**E.......916 784-7745**
11140 Fair Oaks Blvd Fair Oaks (95628) *(P-2326)*
Rice Experiment Station, Biggs *Also called Califrnia Coop Rice RES Fndtio (P-19039)*
Rich Harvest Inc........D.......559 252-8000
3515 N Sabre Dr Fresno (93727) *(P-112)*
Richard Avlar Assoc A Cal Corp........E.......510 893-5501
590 Ygnacio Valley Rd # 200 Walnut Creek (94596) *(P-18909)*
Richard C Shebelut Inc........E.......559 439-1835
6215 N Fresno St Ste 108 Fresno (93710) *(P-15652)*
Richard H Vila, Richmond *Also called Vila Construction Co (P-981)*
Richard Hancock Inc........E.......707 528-4900
1029 3rd St Santa Rosa (95404) *(P-1752)*
Richard Iest Dairy, Madera *Also called Iest Family Farms (P-214)*
Richard Iest Dairy Inc........D.......559 673-2635
13507 Road 17 Madera (93637) *(P-20)*
Richard Joy Engineering, Portola *Also called R Joy Inc (P-18799)*
Richard K Gould Inc........E.......916 371-5943
788 Northport Dr West Sacramento (95691) *(P-4167)*
Richards Machining Co Inc........F.......408 526-9219
382 Martin Ave Santa Clara (95050) *(P-5612)*
Richardson Camp Resort Inc (PA)........**E.......530 542-6570**
1900 Jameson Beach Rd South Lake Tahoe (96150) *(P-11593)*
Richie Iest Farms Inc........E.......559 675-8658
14676 Avenue 14 Madera (93637) *(P-221)*
Richmond Area Mlt-Services Inc........D.......415 579-3021
1282 Market St San Francisco (94102) *(P-17060)*
Richmond Area Mlt-Services Inc (PA)........**D.......415 800-0699**
4355 Geary Blvd San Francisco (94118) *(P-17061)*
Richmond Country Club........D.......510 231-2241
1 Markovich Ln Richmond (94806) *(P-15127)*
Richmond District YMCA, San Francisco *Also called Young MNS Chrstn Assn San Frnc (P-18518)*
Richmond Dst Neighborhood Ctr (PA)........**D.......415 751-6600**
741 30th Ave San Francisco (94121) *(P-17694)*
Richmond Hotels LLC........D.......510 237-3000
915 W Cutting Blvd Richmond (94804) *(P-11408)*
Richmond Post Acute Care LLC........D.......510 237-5182
955 23rd St Richmond (94804) *(P-17172)*
Richmond Sanitary Service Inc (HQ)........**C.......510 262-7100**
3260 Blume Dr Ste 100 Richmond (94806) *(P-14772)*
Richmond Wholesale Meat LLC (PA)........**D.......510 233-5111**
2920 Regatta Blvd Richmond (94804) *(P-9379)*
Richter Bros Inc........E.......530 735-6721
22474 Karnak Rd Knights Landing (95645) *(P-34)*
Richwood Meat Company Inc........D.......209 722-8171
2751 N Santa Fe Ave Merced (95348) *(P-2104)*
Rick Carsey Trucking & Cnstr........E.......559 834-5385
3181 E Manning Ave Fowler (93625) *(P-765)*
Rickey & Wong DDS Inc........E.......209 577-0777
3608 Dale Rd Modesto (95356) *(P-15856)*
Rickshaw Bagworks Inc........F.......415 904-8368
904 22nd St San Francisco (94107) *(P-3032)*
Riddle Ranches Inc........E.......209 874-9784
12013 El Pomar Ave Waterford (95386) *(P-91)*
Rideout Memorial Hospital (HQ)........**A.......530 749-4416**
726 4th St Marysville (95901) *(P-16490)*
Ridge Cast Metals, San Leandro *Also called Ridge Foundry (P-4551)*
Ridge Communications Inc........E.......925 498-2340
12919 Alcosta Blvd Ste 1 San Ramon (94583) *(P-19849)*
Ridge Foundry........E.......510 352-0551
1554 Doolittle Dr San Leandro (94577) *(P-4551)*
Ridge Golf Course LLC........D.......530 888-7122
2020 Golf Course Rd Auburn (95602) *(P-15020)*
Ridgeline, Stockton *Also called Rgm Products Inc (P-4193)*
Ridgeway Swim Center, Santa Rosa *Also called Santa Rosa City of (P-15238)*
Ridi Home Care Inc........E.......209 579-9445
611 Scenic Dr Ste A Modesto (95350) *(P-16939)*
Riebe's Auto Parts, Loomis *Also called Bi Warehousing Inc (P-8444)*
Riebe's Auto Parts, Rocklin *Also called Bi Warehousing Inc (P-8445)*
Riebes Auto Parts, Yuba City *Also called Bi Warehousing Inc (P-8446)*
Rieke Corporation........C.......707 238-9250
1200 Valley House Dr # 100 Rohnert Park (94928) *(P-4878)*
Riekes Ctr For Humn Enhncement........D.......650 364-2509
3455 Edison Way Menlo Park (94025) *(P-14968)*
Rielli Insur & Fincl Svcs LL (PA)........**E.......916 234-1490**
100 Howe Ave Sacramento (95825) *(P-10338)*
Rigel Pharmaceuticals Inc (PA)........**C.......650 624-1100**
1180 Veterans Blvd South San Francisco (94080) *(P-3976)*
Riggs Distributing Inc (PA)........**E.......650 240-3000**
1755 Rollins Rd Burlingame (94010) *(P-8886)*
Right At Home Modesto, Modesto *Also called Ridi Home Care Inc (P-16939)*
Right Away Concrete Pmpg Inc........E.......510 536-1900
401 Kennedy St Oakland (94606) *(P-4504)*

Right Now Air ....E....707 447-3063
821 Eubanks Dr Ste C Vacaville (95688) ***(P-1346)***
Rightware Inc ....D....408 502-1017
470 Ramona St Palo Alto (94301) ***(P-12751)***
Riivos Inc ....D....415 813-1840
101 California St # 1500 San Francisco (94111) ***(P-1587)***
Ril, Sacramento *Also called Resources For Ind Living Inc* ***(P-17692)***
Rimnetics Inc ....F....650 969-6590
3445 De La Cruz Blvd Santa Clara (95054) ***(P-4318)***
Rinaldi Tile & Marble, Royal Oaks *Also called Gino Rinaldi Inc* ***(P-1715)***
Rinat Neuroscience Corp ....E....650 615-7300
230 E Grand Ave South San Francisco (94080) ***(P-3977)***
Ring2 Communications LLC ....E....415 829-2952
282 2nd St Ste 200 San Francisco (94105) ***(P-8084)***
Ringcentral Inc (PA) ....D....650 472-4100
20 Davis Dr Belmont (94002) ***(P-13753)***
Rio Del Oro Racquet Club, Sacramento *Also called Spare-Time Inc* ***(P-14978)***
Rio Mesa Farms LLC ....E....831 728-1965
75 Sakata Ln Watsonville (95076) ***(P-41)***
Rio Pluma Company LLC (HQ) ....E....530 846-5200
1900 Highway 99 Gridley (95948) ***(P-2242)***
RIO VISTA DELTA BREEZE, Rio Vista *Also called City of Rio Vista* ***(P-7328)***
Rios-Lovell Estate Winery ....E....925 443-0434
6500 Tesla Rd Livermore (94550) ***(P-2696)***
Rios-Lovell Winery, Livermore *Also called Rios-Lovell Estate Winery* ***(P-2696)***
Rip-Tie Inc ....F....510 577-0200
883 San Leandro Blvd San Leandro (94577) ***(P-2982)***
Ripcord Inc ....D....408 838-7446
30955 Huntwood Ave Hayward (94544) ***(P-18803)***
Ripon Mfg Co ....E....209 599-2148
652 S Stockton Ave Ripon (95366) ***(P-5134)***
Ripon Milling LLC ....E....209 599-4269
30636 E Carter Rd Farmington (95230) ***(P-2355)***
Ripple Foods Pbc ....D....510 269-2563
901 Gilman St Ste A Berkeley (94710) ***(P-19118)***
Rippling, San Francisco *Also called People Center Inc* ***(P-13366)***
Rising Star Montessori Assoc ....E....510 865-4536
1421 High St Alameda (94501) ***(P-18007)***
Risk Administration & MGT, Concord *Also called Inspro Corporation* ***(P-10296)***
Risk Management Solutions Inc (HQ) ....C....510 505-2500
7575 Gateway Blvd Ste 300 Newark (94560) ***(P-10810)***
Riskalyze Inc (PA) ....C....530 748-1660
470 Nevada St Ste 110 Auburn (95603) ***(P-13969)***
Risse Construction Inc ....E....916 991-2700
651 M St Rio Linda (95673) ***(P-1347)***
Ristoranti Piemontesi Inc ....D....415 395-9800
640 Sacramento St San Francisco (94111) ***(P-11729)***
Rita Christiana-Santa Farms ....E....209 387-4578
16035 Indiana Rd Dos Palos (93620) ***(P-387)***
Rite Track Equipment Svcs Inc ....F....408 432-0131
2151 Otoole Ave Ste 40 San Jose (95131) ***(P-5167)***
Ritescreen Inc ....F....800 949-4174
33444 Western Ave Union City (94587) ***(P-3148)***
Ritter Manufacturing Inc ....F....925 757-7296
321 Eastgate Ln Martinez (94553) ***(P-9089)***
Ritz-Carlton San Francisco ....D....415 296-7465
600 Stockton St San Francisco (94108) ***(P-11409)***
Ritz-Carlton Hotel Company LLC ....B....415 773-6168
600 Stockton St San Francisco (94108) ***(P-11410)***
Ritz-Carlton Lake Tahoe, The, Truckee *Also called Bhr Trs Tahoe LLC* ***(P-10961)***
Ritz-Carlton San Francisco, San Francisco *Also called Ritz-Carlton Hotel Company LLC* ***(P-11410)***
River Bend Holdings LLC ....C....916 371-1890
2215 Oakmont Way West Sacramento (95691) ***(P-16100)***
River Bend Nursing Center, West Sacramento *Also called River Bend Holdings LLC* ***(P-16100)***
River City ....E....707 253-1111
505 Lincoln Ave NAPA (94558) ***(P-3338)***
River City Auto Recovery Inc ....D....916 851-1100
3401 Fitzgerald Rd Rancho Cordova (95742) ***(P-14389)***
River City Bank, Sacramento *Also called Rcb Corporation* ***(P-9745)***
River City Bank (HQ) ....D....916 567-2600
2485 Natomas Park Dr # 100 Sacramento (95833) ***(P-9746)***
River City Millwork Inc ....E....916 364-8981
3045 Fite Cir Sacramento (95827) ***(P-3149)***
River City Printers LLC ....E....916 638-8400
4251 Gateway Park Blvd Sacramento (95834) ***(P-3694)***
River City Restaurant, NAPA *Also called River City* ***(P-3338)***
River City Staffing Inc ....E....916 485-1588
3301 Watt Ave Ste 100 Sacramento (95821) ***(P-12128)***
River Maid Land Co A Cal Ll (PA) ....E....209 369-3586
6011 E Pine St Lodi (95240) ***(P-304)***
River Oak Center For Children (PA) ....C....916 609-5100
5445 Laurel Hills Dr Sacramento (95841) ***(P-17062)***
River Oak Center For Children ....D....916 550-5600
5445 Laurel Hills Dr Sacramento (95841) ***(P-16261)***
River Parkway Trust, Fresno *Also called San Jquin Rver Pkwy Cnsrvtion* ***(P-18462)***
River Ranch ....D....530 583-4264
2285 River Rd Tahoe City (96145) ***(P-11411)***
River Ranch Raisins Inc ....E....559 843-2294
4087 N Howard Ave Kerman (93630) ***(P-2266)***
River Ready Mix, Forestville *Also called Canyon Rock Co Inc* ***(P-592)***
River Rock Casino, Geyserville *Also called River Rock Entertainment Auth* ***(P-11412)***
River Rock Entertainment Auth ....A....707 857-2777
3250 Highway 128 Geyserville (95441) ***(P-11412)***
River Valley Care Center ....D....530 695-8020
9000 Larkin Rd Live Oak (95953) ***(P-16101)***
River Vista Farms LLC ....E....530 458-2550
3536 State Highway 45 Colusa (95932) ***(P-2)***
Riverbank Health Center, Riverbank *Also called Oak Valley Hospital District* ***(P-16469)***
Riverbed Technology Inc (HQ) ....D....415 247-8800
680 Folsom St Ste 600 San Francisco (94107) ***(P-8746)***
Riverbend Rice Mill Inc ....F....530 458-8561
234 Main St Colusa (95932) ***(P-2327)***
Rivermeadow Software Inc ....F....408 217-6498
2107 N 1st St Ste 660 San Jose (95131) ***(P-13411)***
Riverpoint, NAPA *Also called California Vacation Club* ***(P-10983)***
Riverside Ltd ....E....916 777-6076
14400 Andrus Island Rd Isleton (95641) ***(P-7676)***
Riverside Cnvalescent Hosp Inc ....D....530 343-5595
375 Cohasset Rd Chico (95926) ***(P-16262)***
Riverside Elevators, Isleton *Also called Riverside Ltd* ***(P-7676)***
Riverside Golf Course, Fresno *Also called Ebit-Golf Inc* ***(P-15000)***
Riverside Health Care Corp (PA) ....D....530 897-5100
1469 Humboldt Rd Ste 175 Chico (95928) ***(P-16263)***
Riverview Golf and Country CLB ....D....530 224-2254
4200 Bechelli Ln Redding (96002) ***(P-15128)***
Riverview Intl Trcks LLC (PA) ....D....916 372-8541
2445 Evergreen Ave West Sacramento (95691) ***(P-14587)***
Riverview Systems Group Inc ....E....408 347-3700
1101 Cadillac Ct Milpitas (95035) ***(P-12060)***
Riviera Partners LLC (PA) ....D....877 748-4372
1 Blackfield Dr Ste 2 Belvedere Tiburon (94920) ***(P-12129)***
Rivos Inc ....E....408 663-6746
2811 Mission College Blvd F Santa Clara (95054) ***(P-5168)***
Rizal Community Center, Sacramento *Also called Southgate Recreation & Pk Dst* ***(P-15244)***
Rizo Lopez Foods Inc ....B....800 626-5587
201 S Mcclure Rd Modesto (95357) ***(P-2153)***
RJ Locicero Corp ....E....916 781-2004
503 Giuseppe Ct Ste 3 Roseville (95678) ***(P-1753)***
Rjms Corporation (PA) ....D....510 675-0500
6999 Southfront Rd Livermore (94551) ***(P-9128)***
Rjp Framing Inc ....C....916 941-3934
1139 Sibley St Ste 100 Folsom (95630) ***(P-1754)***
RJS & Associates Inc ....C....510 670-9111
1675 Sabre St Hayward (94545) ***(P-1906)***
RK Electric Inc ....C....510 772-4125
49211 Milmont Dr Fremont (94538) ***(P-1588)***
Rk Logistics Group Inc ....E....510 298-5128
44951 Industrial Dr Fremont (94538) ***(P-7852)***
Rk Logistics Group Inc (PA) ....C....408 942-8107
41707 Christy St Fremont (94538) ***(P-19623)***
Rki Instruments Inc (PA) ....D....510 441-5656
33248 Central Ave Union City (94587) ***(P-9090)***
RL Fuller Inc ....E....707 207-0100
5130 Fulton Dr Ste K Fairfield (94534) ***(P-1348)***
Rl Liquidators LLC ....E....916 747-7762
221 Richards Blvd Sacramento (95811) ***(P-14390)***
Rlj C San Francisco Lessee LP ....E....415 346-3800
761 Post St San Francisco (94109) ***(P-11413)***
Rljhgn Emeryville Lessee LP ....D....510 658-9300
1800 Powell St Emeryville (94608) ***(P-11414)***
Rlw Properties LLC ....D....925 418-5668
1771 Castellina Dr Brentwood (94513) ***(P-10403)***
Rm Executive Transportation ....E....650 260-1240
525 Sunol St San Jose (95126) ***(P-7400)***
Rm Pallets Inc ....F....209 632-9887
2512 Paulson Rd Turlock (95380) ***(P-3228)***
RMC, Ripon *Also called Ripon Mfg Co* ***(P-5134)***
RMC Constructors, Fresno *Also called Roberts Managing Contrs Inc* ***(P-947)***
RMC Engineering Co Inc (PA) ....E....408 842-2525
255 Mayock Rd Gilroy (95020) ***(P-5613)***
RMC Pacific Materials LLC (PA) ....C....925 426-8787
6601 Koll Center Pkwy # 30 Pleasanton (94566) ***(P-4397)***
RMC Water and Environment ....E....415 321-3400
101 Montgomery St # 1850 San Francisco (94104) ***(P-18804)***
Rmf Salt Holdings LLC ....F....510 477-9600
2217 S Shore Ctr 200 Alameda (94501) ***(P-4094)***
Rmi, Livermore *Also called Ratermann Manufacturing Inc* ***(P-4316)***
RMR Construction Company ....C....415 647-0884
2424 Oakdale Ave San Francisco (94124) ***(P-946)***
RMS, Newark *Also called Risk Management Solutions Inc* ***(P-10810)***
Rmt Landscape Contractors Inc ....E....510 568-3208
421 Pendleton Way Oakland (94621) ***(P-498)***
Rmtc Training Center, Rancho Murieta *Also called Operating Engineers JAC* ***(P-17830)***
Rmw Architecture & Interiors, San Francisco *Also called Robinson Mills + Williams* ***(P-18910)***
Roach Bros Inc ....D....707 964-9240
23550 Shady Ln Fort Bragg (95437) ***(P-3075)***
Road Runner Delivery LLC ....E....312 468-6940
530 Chestnut St Apt 17 San Carlos (94070) ***(P-7652)***
Road Safety Inc ....C....916 543-4600
4335 Pacific St Ste A Rocklin (95677) ***(P-14391)***
Roadrunner Tow Inc ....E....707 434-9560
1950 Walters Ct Fairfield (94533) ***(P-14675)***
Roadrunner Towing, Fairfield *Also called Roadrunner Tow Inc* ***(P-14675)***
Roadstar Trucking Inc ....D....510 487-2404
30527 San Antonio St Hayward (94544) ***(P-7580)***
Roadster Inc ....A....833 568-5968
300 De Haro St Ste 334 San Francisco (94103) ***(P-12752)***
Robb-Jack Corporation (PA) ....D....916 645-6045
3300 Nicolaus Rd Ste 1 Lincoln (95648) ***(P-5077)***
Robecks Wldg & Fabrication Inc ....E....408 287-0202
1150 Mabury Rd Ste 1 San Jose (95133) ***(P-4681)***

ALPHABETIC

Employee Codes: A=Over 500 employees, B=251-500
C=101-250, D=51-100, E=20-50 F=10-19
2022 Northern California Business
Directory and Buyers Guide
© Mergent Inc. 1-800-342-5647
1063

Robert A Bothman Inc (PA)..........C.......408 279-2277
2690 Scott Blvd Santa Clara (95050) ***(P-1907)***
Robert Alves Farms Inc..........D.......559 896-3309
10642 E Dinuba Ave Selma (93662) ***(P-72)***
Robert Half International Inc (PA)..........D.......650 234-6000
2884 Sand Hill Rd Ste 200 Menlo Park (94025) ***(P-12192)***
Robert Half International Inc..........E.......925 913-1000
2613 Camino Ramon San Ramon (94583) ***(P-12130)***
Robert J Alandt & Sons..........E.......559 275-1391
4692 N Brawley Ave Fresno (93722) ***(P-4682)***
Robert L Brown Cnstr Inc..........E.......925 228-4944
4878 Sunrise Dr Martinez (94553) ***(P-698)***
Robert Mondavi Corporation (HQ)..........D.......707 967-2100
166 Gateway Rd E NAPA (94558) ***(P-2697)***
Robert Mondavi Corporation..........A.......209 365-2995
770 N Guild Ave Lodi (95240) ***(P-2698)***
Robert Mondavi Winery..........E.......707 738-5727
7801 St Helena Hwy Oakville (94562) ***(P-2699)***
Robert R Wix Inc (PA)..........E.......209 537-4561
2140 Pine St Ceres (95307) ***(P-3748)***
Robert Sinskey Vineyards, NAPA *Also called Sinskey Vineyards Inc* ***(P-2720)***
Robert V Jensen Inc (PA)..........D.......559 485-8210
4029 S Maple Ave Fresno (93725) ***(P-9537)***
Robert W Baird & Co Inc..........E.......530 271-3000
360 Sierra College Dr # 200 Grass Valley (95945) ***(P-10220)***
Robert W Cameron & Co Inc..........E.......707 769-1617
149 Kentucky St Ste 7 Petaluma (94952) ***(P-3544)***
Robert Young Family Ltd Partnr..........E.......707 433-3228
4950 Red Winery Rd Geyserville (95441) ***(P-2700)***
Robert Young Vineyards, Geyserville *Also called Robert Young Family Ltd Partnr* ***(P-2700)***
Roberts Electric Co Inc..........E.......510 834-6161
480 23rd St Oakland (94612) ***(P-1589)***
Roberts Managing Contrs Inc..........E.......559 252-6000
5045 E Mckinley Ave Fresno (93727) ***(P-947)***
Robertson Precision Inc..........E.......408 230-3044
2971 Spring St Redwood City (94063) ***(P-6274)***
Robertson Stphens Wlth MGT LLC (PA)..........D.......415 500-6810
455 Market St Ste 1600 San Francisco (94105) ***(P-19389)***
Robinhood Markets Inc (PA)..........A.......844 428-5411
85 Willow Rd Menlo Park (94025) ***(P-10010)***
Robinhood Securities LLC..........C.......650 294-4857
85 Willow Rd Menlo Park (94025) ***(P-10011)***
Robinson Agspray..........E.......559 659-3015
915 10th St Firebaugh (93622) ***(P-256)***
Robinson Farms Feed Company..........E.......209 466-7915
7000 S Inland Dr Stockton (95206) ***(P-2356)***
Robinson Mills + Williams (PA)..........E.......415 781-9800
160 Pine St Ste 400 San Francisco (94111) ***(P-18910)***
Robles Bros Inc (PA)..........E.......408 436-5551
1700 Rogers Ave San Jose (95112) ***(P-2939)***
Roblox Corporation (PA)..........A.......888 858-2569
970 Park Pl San Mateo (94403) ***(P-13412)***
Robomart Inc..........F.......669 350-4463
555 California St # 4925 San Francisco (94104) ***(P-6557)***
Robotlab Inc..........E.......415 702-3033
1981 N Broadway Ste 322 Walnut Creek (94596) ***(P-5408)***
Robotslab US, Walnut Creek *Also called Robotlab Inc* ***(P-5408)***
Robson Technologies Inc..........E.......408 779-8008
135 E Main Ave Ste 130 Morgan Hill (95037) ***(P-5614)***
Rocha Transportation, Modesto *Also called Ed Rocha Livestock Trnsp Inc* ***(P-7529)***
Rochas Drywall Inc..........E.......408 842-4188
575 Southside Dr Ste C Gilroy (95020) ***(P-1703)***
Roche Diagnostics Corporation..........C.......650 491-7251
1 Dna Way South San Francisco (94080) ***(P-3978)***
Roche Molecular Systems Inc..........D.......650 225-1000
1 Dna Way South San Francisco (94080) ***(P-19119)***
Roche Molecular Systems Inc..........D.......925 523-8099
2821 Scott Blvd Santa Clara (95050) ***(P-19120)***
Roche Molecular Systems Inc (HQ)..........B.......925 730-8000
4300 Hacienda Dr Pleasanton (94588) ***(P-19121)***
Roche Nimblegen Inc..........C.......608 316-3890
4300 Hacienda Dr Pleasanton (94588) ***(P-19122)***
Roche Pharmaceuticals..........F.......908 635-5692
4300 Hacienda Dr Pleasanton (94588) ***(P-3979)***
Rock Engineered McHy Co Inc..........F.......925 447-0805
1627 Army Ct Ste 1 Stockton (95206) ***(P-4179)***
Rock Systems, Red Bluff *Also called Tedon Specialties A Cal Corp* ***(P-5627)***
Rock Wall Wine Company Inc..........E.......510 522-5700
2301 Monarch St Alameda (94501) ***(P-2701)***
Rocket Dog Brands, Danville *Also called Millennial Brands LLC* ***(P-9260)***
Rocket Ems Inc..........C.......408 727-3700
2950 Patrick Henry Dr Santa Clara (95054) ***(P-5966)***
Rocket Farms Inc (PA)..........C.......800 227-5229
2651 Cabrillo Hwy N Half Moon Bay (94019) ***(P-133)***
Rocket Fuel, San Francisco *Also called Sizmek Dsp Inc* ***(P-11786)***
Rocket Shop, Folsom *Also called Aerojet Rocketdyne Inc* ***(P-6627)***
Rockins Equipment Company..........E.......925 837-7296
2233 San Ramon Vly Blvd San Ramon (94583) ***(P-12061)***
Rockley Photonics Inc..........F.......408 579-9210
333 W San Carlos St # 850 San Jose (95110) ***(P-6275)***
Rocklin Lodging Group LLC..........D.......916 761-7500
6664 Lonetree Blvd Rocklin (95765) ***(P-11415)***
Rocklin Physical Therapy PC..........C.......916 435-3500
2217 Sunset Blvd Ste 711 Rocklin (95765) ***(P-15895)***
Rockwell Automation Inc..........D.......408 443-5425
111 N Market St Ste 200 San Jose (95113) ***(P-5689)***
Rocky Mountain Eggs Inc..........E.......209 254-2200
720 S Stockton Ave Ripon (95366) ***(P-9351)***
Rocky Mountain Home Care, Jackson *Also called Amador Home Care Service* ***(P-16845)***
Rockys Gasket Shop Inc..........E.......408 980-9190
445 Laurelwood Rd Santa Clara (95054) ***(P-4206)***
Rodan Builders Inc..........E.......650 508-1700
3486 Investment Blvd B Hayward (94545) ***(P-807)***
Rodda Electric Inc (PA)..........C.......925 240-6024
380 Carrol Ct Ste L Brentwood (94513) ***(P-1590)***
Rodeway Inn, Tahoe City *Also called Pepper Tree Inn* ***(P-11363)***
Rodgers Trucking Co, Alameda *Also called Frank Ghiglione Inc* ***(P-7466)***
Rodgz Farm Labor Contg LLC..........D.......530 329-8403
4422 College Way Olivehurst (95961) ***(P-365)***
Rodney Strong Vineyards, Healdsburg *Also called Klein Foods Inc* ***(P-61)***
Rodoni Dairy Farms..........D.......209 826-2978
Center & Copa De Ora Los Banos (93635) ***(P-222)***
Roebbelen Construction Inc..........D.......916 939-4000
1241 Hawks Flight Ct El Dorado Hills (95762) ***(P-948)***
Roebbelen Contracting Inc..........B.......916 939-4000
1241 Hawks Flight Ct El Dorado Hills (95762) ***(P-949)***
Roger Enrico..........C.......559 485-5050
1150 E North Ave Fresno (93725) ***(P-2809)***
Rogers Helicopters Inc..........D.......559 299-4903
5508 E Aircorp Way Fresno (93727) ***(P-7760)***
Rogers Joseph ODonnell A Pro (PA)..........D.......415 956-2828
311 California St Fl 10 San Francisco (94104) ***(P-17363)***
Rogers Trucking, San Leandro *Also called Frank Ghiglione Inc* ***(P-7467)***
Rohde & Schwarz Usa Inc..........F.......818 846-3600
409 Dixon Landing Rd Milpitas (95035) ***(P-6785)***
Rohlffs Memorial Manor (PA)..........E.......707 255-9555
2400 Fair Dr NAPA (94558) ***(P-18172)***
Rohnert Park Housing Fing Auth..........E.......707 588-2226
30 Avram Ave Rohnert Park (94928) ***(P-19624)***
Rohrer Bros Inc..........E.......916 443-5921
200 N 16th St Ste 600 Sacramento (95811) ***(P-9427)***
Roi Communications Inc (PA)..........D.......831 430-0170
5274 Scotts Valley Dr # 107 Scotts Valley (95066) ***(P-19625)***
Roi Dna Inc..........E.......831 238-2514
156 Cascade Dr Fairfax (94930) ***(P-11806)***
Roku Inc (PA)..........C.......408 556-9040
1155 Coleman Ave San Jose (95110) ***(P-8065)***
Roku Holdings Inc (HQ)..........D.......408 556-9391
1701 Junction Ct Ste 100 San Jose (95112) ***(P-12753)***
Roland Construction Inc..........E.......209 462-2687
3269 Tomahawk Dr Stockton (95205) ***(P-808)***
Roll Technology West, Pittsburg *Also called Chrome Deposit Corp* ***(P-4901)***
Rollapp Inc (PA)..........E.......650 617-3372
530 Lytton Ave Fl 2 Palo Alto (94301) ***(P-13413)***
Rollbar Inc (PA)..........D.......415 366-3254
665 3rd St Ste 150 San Francisco (94107) ***(P-13754)***
Rollin J. Lobaugh, Belmont *Also called Pacific Screw Products Inc* ***(P-5588)***
Rollin Valley Farm, Riverdale *Also called Sweet Haven Dairy* ***(P-224)***
Rolling Hills Casino..........C.......530 528-3500
2655 Everett Freeman Way Corning (96021) ***(P-11416)***
Rolling Hills Club, Novato *Also called Tennis Everyone Incorporated* ***(P-14981)***
Rolling Hills Club Inc..........E.......415 897-2185
351 San Andreas Dr Novato (94945) ***(P-15129)***
Rollins Road Acquisition Co (HQ)..........D.......415 937-7836
100 Rollins Rd Millbrae (94030) ***(P-6786)***
Rolls-Royce Corporation..........B.......510 635-1500
7200 Earhart Rd Oakland (94621) ***(P-4992)***
Roma Bakery Inc..........D.......408 294-0123
655 S Almaden Ave San Jose (95110) ***(P-2401)***
Roman Cathlic Bishp Sacramento..........D.......707 556-9317
125 Corporate Pl Vallejo (94590) ***(P-17695)***
Roman Spa Hot Sprng Resort LLC..........E.......707 942-4441
1300 Washington St Calistoga (94515) ***(P-11417)***
Rombauer Vineyards Inc (PA)..........D.......707 963-5170
3522 Silverado Trl N Saint Helena (94574) ***(P-2702)***
Romeo Packing Company..........E.......650 728-3393
106 Princeton Ave Half Moon Bay (94019) ***(P-3392)***
Ron Filice Enterprises Inc..........D.......408 294-0477
738 N 1st St Ste 202 San Jose (95112) ***(P-10339)***
Ron Nunes Enterprises LLC..........E.......925 371-0220
7703 Las Positas Rd Livermore (94551) ***(P-4812)***
Ron Nurss Inc..........D.......916 631-9761
11290 Sunrise Park Dr B Rancho Cordova (95742) ***(P-1908)***
Ronald F Ogletree Inc..........E.......707 963-3537
935 Vintage Ave Saint Helena (94574) ***(P-4813)***
Ronald Vanderbeek (PA)..........E.......916 481-9240
2100 Butano Dr Sacramento (95825) ***(P-16264)***
Ronald Vanderbeek..........E.......916 488-7211
6101 Fair Oaks Blvd Carmichael (95608) ***(P-16201)***
Ronbow Corporation..........E.......510 713-1188
7150 Patterson Pass Rd F Livermore (94550) ***(P-8604)***
Roofing Constructors Inc..........C.......415 648-6472
15002 Wicks Blvd San Leandro (94577) ***(P-1835)***
Roofline Builders Inc..........E.......925 201-1924
1807 Santa Rita Rd Pleasanton (94566) ***(P-699)***
Roos Instruments Inc..........E.......408 748-8589
2285 Martin Ave Santa Clara (95050) ***(P-6787)***
Roost, Sausalito *Also called Gate Five Group LLC* ***(P-8512)***
Rooster Run Golf Club Inc..........E.......707 778-1211
2301 E Washington St Petaluma (94954) ***(P-15021)***
Roostify Inc..........E.......888 908-2470
180 Howard St Ste 100 San Francisco (94105) ***(P-9946)***
Rootlieb Inc..........E.......209 632-2203
815 S Soderquist Rd Turlock (95380) ***(P-4877)***
Rootmusic, San Bruno *Also called Bandpage Inc* ***(P-13851)***
Rope Partner Inc..........D.......831 460-9448
125 Mcpherson St Ste B Santa Cruz (95060) ***(P-9129)***

ALPHABETIC SECTION Rudolph and Sletten Inc

Ropers Majeski A Prof Corp (PA) ....D....**650 364-8200**
1001 Marshall St Fl 5 Redwood City (94063) ***(P-17364)***

Roplast Industries Inc ....C....530 532-9500
3155 S 5th Ave Oroville (95965) ***(P-3387)***

Roppong-Thoe LP A Cal Ltd Prtn ....C....530 544-5400
4130 Lake Tahoe Blvd South Lake Tahoe (96150) ***(P-11418)***

Rose Child Development Center, Milpitas *Also called Milpitas Unified School Dst* ***(P-17974)***

Rose Electronics Distrg Co LLC ....E....408 943-0200
2030 Ringwood Ave San Jose (95131) ***(P-8949)***

Rose Fmly Crtive Empwrment Ctr ....D....916 376-7916
7000 Franklin Blvd # 100 Sacramento (95823) ***(P-18455)***

Rose Garden Inn, Berkeley *Also called Rose Grammas Garden Inn* ***(P-11419)***

Rose Grammas Garden Inn ....E....510 549-2145
2740 Telegraph Ave Berkeley (94705) ***(P-11419)***

Rose Hotel, Pleasanton *Also called Red Bear Inc* ***(P-11387)***

Rose International Inc ....C....636 812-4000
5000 Executive Pkwy # 430 San Ramon (94583) ***(P-19850)***

Rose Joaquin Inc ....E....209 632-0616
410 S Golden State Blvd Turlock (95380) ***(P-9091)***

Rosedale Medical, Fremont *Also called Intuity Medical Inc* ***(P-6988)***

Rosen Bien Galvan Grunfeld LLP ....E....415 433-6830
101 Mission St Ste 600 San Francisco (94105) ***(P-17365)***

Rosendin Electric Inc (PA) ....A....**408 286-2800**
880 Mabury Rd San Jose (95133) ***(P-1591)***

Rosendin Electric Inc ....A....408 321-2200
2698 Orchard Pkwy San Jose (95134) ***(P-1592)***

Roseryan Inc ....D....510 456-3056
35473 Dumbarton Ct Newark (94560) ***(P-18988)***

Roseville Care Center, Roseville *Also called Crocus Holdings LLC* ***(P-15977)***

Roseville Carpet One, Roseville *Also called Roseville Flooring Inc* ***(P-1775)***

Roseville Flooring Inc ....E....916 945-2015
1109 Smith Ln Roseville (95661) ***(P-1775)***

Roseville Golfland Ltd Partnr ....D....916 784-1273
1893 Taylor Rd Roseville (95661) ***(P-15232)***

Roseville Home Healthcare, Roseville *Also called Maxim Healthcare Services Inc* ***(P-12183)***

Roseville Imaging, Roseville *Also called Sutter Health* ***(P-16808)***

Roseville Rocklin Electric Inc ....E....916 772-2698
910 Pleasant Grove Blvd Roseville (95678) ***(P-1593)***

Roseville Sportworld ....E....916 783-8550
1009 Orlando Ave Roseville (95661) ***(P-15233)***

Roseville Toyota, Livermore *Also called John L Sllivan Investments Inc* ***(P-14574)***

Roseville Med Cntr-Rdtion Onclo, Roseville *Also called Kaiser Foundation Hospitals* ***(P-15444)***

Rosewood Convalescent Hospital, Pleasant Hill *Also called Dreamctchers Empwerment Netwrk* ***(P-18100)***

Rosewood Gardens, Livermore *Also called Watermark Rtrment Cmmnties Inc* ***(P-18208)***

Rosewood Hotels & Resorts LLC ....B....650 561-1500
2825 Sand Hill Rd Menlo Park (94025) ***(P-11420)***

Rosewood Rehabilitation, Carmichael *Also called Carmichael Care Inc* ***(P-15952)***

Rosewood Sand Hill Hotel, Menlo Park *Also called Rosewood Hotels & Resorts LLC* ***(P-11420)***

Ross & Christopher, Fresno *Also called Ross & Sons Rfrgn & Cnstr Inc* ***(P-1349)***

Ross & Sons Rfrgn & Cnstr Inc ....E....559 834-5947
7828 S Maple Ave Fresno (93725) ***(P-1349)***

Ross F Carroll Inc ....E....209 848-5959
8873 Warnerville Rd Oakdale (95361) ***(P-18805)***

Ross Periodicals, Novato *Also called Excellence Magazine Inc* ***(P-3498)***

Ross Valley Homes Inc ....D....415 461-2300
501 Via Casitas Greenbrae (94904) ***(P-18173)***

Ross Valley Sanitary District, San Rafael *Also called Sanitary Dst 1 Marin Cnty* ***(P-8406)***

Rossmoor, Walnut Creek *Also called Golden Rain Foundation* ***(P-10561)***

Rossmoor Realty ....E....925 932-1162
1641 Tice Valley Blvd Walnut Creek (94595) ***(P-10655)***

Rotary Club, Palo Cedro *Also called Rotary International* ***(P-18456)***

Rotary International ....D....530 547-5272
9839 Meadowlark Way Palo Cedro (96073) ***(P-18456)***

Rotating Equipment Specialist, Benicia *Also called Alfred Conhagen Inc California* ***(P-9109)***

Roth Wood Products Ltd ....E....408 723-8888
2260 Canoas Garden Ave San Jose (95125) ***(P-3339)***

Roto Rooter Service ....D....415 656-2130
3840 Bayshore Blvd Brisbane (94005) ***(P-14773)***

Roto-Rooter, Concord *Also called Overmiller Inc* ***(P-14769)***

Roto-Rooter, Brisbane *Also called Roto Rooter Service* ***(P-14773)***

Round Hill Cellars ....D....707 968-3200
1680 Silverado Trl S Saint Helena (94574) ***(P-2703)***

Round Hill Country Club ....C....925 934-8211
3169 Roundhill Rd Alamo (94507) ***(P-15130)***

Round Hill Country Club ....E....925 934-8211
3169 Roundhill Rd Alamo (94507) ***(P-15131)***

Round Table Pizza, Folsom *Also called Ejs Pizza Co* ***(P-11715)***

Round Table Pizza Inc (HQ) ....D....**925 969-3900**
1390 Willow Pass Rd # 300 Concord (94520) ***(P-10811)***

Round Vly Indian Hlth Ctr Inc ....D....707 983-6182
Hwy 162 Biggar Ln Covelo (95428) ***(P-15653)***

Rounds Logging Company ....E....530 247-0517
4350 Lynbrook Loop Apt 1 Redding (96003) ***(P-3076)***

Rountree Plumbing and Htg Inc ....D....650 298-0300
1624 Santa Clara Dr # 120 Roseville (95661) ***(P-1350)***

Route 40 Ventures Inc ....F....650 743-0051
717 San Miguel Ln Foster City (94404) ***(P-9482)***

Rov Enterprises Inc ....E....916 448-2672
5013 Roberts Ave Ste B McClellan (95652) ***(P-1351)***

Row Hotel, The, San Jose *Also called Stay Cal San Jose LLC* ***(P-11507)***

Rowar Corporation ....E....916 626-3030
4025 Cincinnati Ave Sacramento (94203) ***(P-2063)***

Roy C Shannon MD, Oroville *Also called Oroville Intrnal Mdcine Med Gr* ***(P-15572)***

Roy Carrington Inc ....D....530 893-2100
13804 Bosc Dr Chico (95973) ***(P-12131)***

Royal Ambulance Inc ....C....877 995-6161
14472 Wicks Blvd San Leandro (94577) ***(P-7401)***

Royal Circuit Solutions Inc (PA) ....E....**831 636-7789**
21 Hamilton Ct Hollister (95023) ***(P-5967)***

Royal Coach Tours (PA) ....C....**408 279-4801**
630 Stockton Ave San Jose (95126) ***(P-7422)***

Royal Express Inc (PA) ....C....**559 272-3500**
3545 E Date Ave Fresno (93725) ***(P-7633)***

Royal Glass Company Inc ....D....408 969-0444
3200 De La Cruz Blvd Santa Clara (95054) ***(P-1941)***

Royal Gorge Nordic Ski Resort (PA) ....C....**530 426-3871**
9411 Hillside Rd Soda Springs (95728) ***(P-11421)***

Royal Grge Cross Cntry Ski Rso, Soda Springs *Also called Royal Gorge Nordic Ski Resort* ***(P-11421)***

Royal Laundry, South San Francisco *Also called American Etc Inc* ***(P-11626)***

Royal Mountain King, Copperopolis *Also called Meridian Gold Inc* ***(P-541)***

Royal Plywood Company LLC ....D....916 426-3292
6003 88th St Ste 100 Sacramento (95828) ***(P-8605)***

Royal Trucking, Concord *Also called Lemore Transportation Inc* ***(P-7561)***

Royce Corporation (PA) ....D....**209 545-0789**
4970 Salida Blvd Salida (95368) ***(P-11907)***

Rp/Kinetic Parc 55 Owner LLC ....C....415 392-8000
55 Cyril Magnin St San Francisco (94102) ***(P-11422)***

Rpd Electrical Service Co Inc ....E....408 265-2850
3550 Charter Park Dr San Jose (95136) ***(P-1594)***

RPM Luxury Auto Sales Inc ....C....916 783-9111
300 Automall Dr Roseville (95661) ***(P-14620)***

RPM Mortgage, Alamo *Also called Lendusa LLC* ***(P-9912)***

RPM Services, Fresno *Also called Westco Equities Inc* ***(P-10685)***

Rpx Corporation (HQ) ....C....**866 779-7641**
4 Embarcadero Ctr Fl 40 San Francisco (94111) ***(P-10812)***

Rs Calibration Services Inc ....E....925 462-4217
1047 Serpentine Ln # 500 Pleasanton (94566) ***(P-14774)***

RS Hughes Company Inc (PA) ....E....**408 739-3211**
1162 Sonora Ct Sunnyvale (94086) ***(P-9130)***

Rs Investment Management Inc ....D....415 591-2700
1 Bush St Fl 9 San Francisco (94104) ***(P-10768)***

Rs Investments, San Francisco *Also called Rs Investment Management Inc* ***(P-10768)***

RS Technical Services Inc (PA) ....D....**707 778-1974**
1327 Clegg St Petaluma (94954) ***(P-6847)***

Rse, Sacramento *Also called Runyon Saltzman Inc* ***(P-11780)***

RSF SOCIAL FINANCE, San Francisco *Also called Rudolf Steiner Foundation Inc* ***(P-18585)***

Rsj Ventures LLC ....E....212 905-8666
117 W Napa St Ste A Sonoma (95476) ***(P-2122)***

RSM US LLP ....D....408 572-4440
100 W San Fernando St San Jose (95113) ***(P-18989)***

Rt Peak Travel Group, San Jose *Also called Peak Travel Group* ***(P-7805)***

Rt Western Inc ....E....415 677-9202
160 Mendell St San Francisco (94124) ***(P-2064)***

Rt Western Construction Svcs, San Francisco *Also called Rt Western Inc* ***(P-2064)***

Rtec-Instruments Inc ....E....408 456-0801
1810 Oakland Rd Ste B San Jose (95131) ***(P-6848)***

Ruan ....C....209 634-4928
830 W Glenwood Ave Turlock (95380) ***(P-7487)***

Ruan Transport Corporation ....E....209 599-5000
830 W Glenwood Ave Turlock (95380) ***(P-7581)***

Ruan Transport Corporation ....E....209 634-2768
475 S Tegner Rd Turlock (95380) ***(P-7582)***

Ruan Transport Corporation ....E....510 758-7383
6035 Giant Rd Richmond (94806) ***(P-7583)***

Ruan Transport Corporation ....E....925 427-3983
2000 Loveridge Rd Pittsburg (94565) ***(P-7584)***

Rubber Dust Inc (PA) ....E....**510 237-6344**
533 S 13th St Richmond (94804) ***(P-14539)***

Rubecon Builders, San Francisco *Also called Rubecon General Contg Inc* ***(P-950)***

Rubecon General Contg Inc ....E....415 206-7740
3450 3rd St Ste 1b San Francisco (94124) ***(P-950)***

Rubicon Enterprises Inc ....E....510 235-1516
2500 Bissell Ave Richmond (94804) ***(P-11990)***

RUBICON PROGRAMS, Richmond *Also called Rubicon Enterprises Inc* ***(P-11990)***

Rubicon Programs Incorporated (PA) ....D....**510 235-1516**
2500 Bissell Ave Richmond (94804) ***(P-11991)***

Rubrik Inc (PA) ....A....**650 300-5862**
3495 Deer Creek Rd Palo Alto (94304) ***(P-13755)***

Ruby Burma Investment LLC ....D....650 590-0545
612 El Camino Real San Carlos (94070) ***(P-19390)***

Ruby Hill Golf Club LLC ....D....925 417-5840
3400 W Ruby Hill Dr Pleasanton (94566) ***(P-15022)***

Ruby Ribbon ....E....650 525-4141
856 Mitten Rd Ste 101 Burlingame (94010) ***(P-9255)***

Rucker & Kolls Inc (PA) ....E....**408 934-9875**
1064 Yosemite Dr Milpitas (95035) ***(P-5169)***

Rucker Mill & Cab Works Inc ....F....530 621-0236
5828 Mother Lode Dr Placerville (95667) ***(P-3190)***

Ruckus Networks, Sunnyvale *Also called Ruckus Wireless Inc* ***(P-5865)***

Ruckus Wireless Inc (HQ) ....A....**650 265-4200**
350 W Java Dr Sunnyvale (94089) ***(P-5865)***

Rudd Winery, Oakville *Also called Rudd Wines Inc* ***(P-2704)***

Rudd Wines Inc (PA) ....E....**707 944-8577**
500 Oakville Xrd Oakville (94562) ***(P-2704)***

Rudolf Steiner Foundation Inc ....E....415 561-3900
1002 Oreilly Ave San Francisco (94129) ***(P-18585)***

Rudolph and Sletten Inc (HQ) ....D....**650 216-3600**
2 Circle Star Way Fl 4 San Carlos (94070) ***(P-951)***

Rudolph and Sletten Inc ....E....209 941-1040
3614 Zephyr Ct Stockton (95206) ***(P-952)***

ALPHABETIC

Rudolph and Sletten Inc E 916 781-8001
1504 Eureka Rd Ste 200 Roseville (95661) ***(P-953)***
Rudy, Exelrod, Zieff, & True, San Francisco *Also called Law Offces Rudy Exlrod Zeff LL* ***(P-17311)***
Ruffstuff Inc F 916 600-1945
3237 Rippey Rd Ste 200 Loomis (95650) ***(P-6592)***
Ruggeri-Jensen-Azar & Assoc E 925 227-9100
4690 Chabot Dr Ste 200 Pleasanton (94588) ***(P-18806)***
Rumble Entertainment Inc E 650 316-8819
2121 S El Cmino Real Ste San Mateo (94403) ***(P-7183)***
Rumble Games, San Mateo *Also called Rumble Entertainment Inc* ***(P-7183)***
Rumiano Cheese Co (PA) C **530 934-5438**
1629 County Road E Willows (95988) ***(P-2154)***
Rumiano Cheese Co E 707 465-1535
511 9th St Crescent City (95531) ***(P-2155)***
Runa Inc E 508 253-5000
2 W 5th Ave Ste 300 San Mateo (94402) ***(P-13414)***
Running Creek Casino C 707 275-9209
635 E State Highway 20 Upper Lake (95485) ***(P-11423)***
Runyon Saltzman Inc D 916 446-9900
2020 L St Ste 100 Sacramento (95811) ***(P-11780)***
Rupert Gibbon & Spider Inc E 800 442-0455
1147 Healdsburg Ave Healdsburg (95448) ***(P-4110)***
Rural Cal Brdcstg Corp Krcb Kp E 707 584-2062
5850 Labath Ave Rohnert Park (94928) ***(P-8033)***
Rural Cmmnities Hsing Dev Corp (PA) D **707 463-1975**
499 Leslie St Ukiah (95482) ***(P-10457)***
Rural Cmnty Assistance Corp (PA) D **916 447-2854**
3120 Freeboard Dr Ste 201 West Sacramento (95691) ***(P-17696)***
Rural County Rep Cal E 916 447-4806
1215 K St Ste 1650 Sacramento (95814) ***(P-19697)***
Rural Human Services (PA) E **707 464-7441**
286 M St Ste A Crescent City (95531) ***(P-17697)***
Rural/Metro Corporation C 510 266-0885
2364 W Winton Ave Hayward (94545) ***(P-7402)***
Rush Advertising Specialties, Fresno *Also called Kenneth Allen Rush* ***(P-9665)***
Rush Order Inc (PA) E **408 848-3525**
6600 Silacci Way Gilroy (95020) ***(P-7702)***
Russell Mechanical Inc D 916 635-2522
3251 Monier Cir Ste A Rancho Cordova (95742) ***(P-1352)***
Russell Sigler Inc D 916 387-3000
8615 23rd Ave Sacramento (95826) ***(P-9013)***
Russell Sigler Inc D 925 726-0141
1920 Mark Ct Concord (94520) ***(P-9014)***
Russell Wayne Lester E 530 795-4619
5430 Putah Creek Rd Winters (95694) ***(P-113)***
Russian River Vineyards, Forestville *Also called Topolos At Rssian River Vinyrd* ***(P-77)***
Russian River Winery Inc E 707 824-2005
2191 Laguna Rd Santa Rosa (95401) ***(P-2705)***
Russo Brothers Transport Inc D 916 519-1334
6108 Hedge Ave Sacramento (95829) ***(P-7893)***
Rutherford Wine Company, Saint Helena *Also called Round Hill Cellars* ***(P-2703)***
Rutter Armey Inc E 559 237-1866
2684 S Cherry Ave Fresno (93706) ***(P-14621)***
Rvision Inc E 408 437-5777
2365 Paragon Dr Ste D San Jose (95131) ***(P-6885)***
Rvj, Fresno *Also called Robert V Jensen Inc* ***(P-9537)***
Rvm Davis Housing Corporation C 530 747-7095
1501 Shasta Dr Davis (95616) ***(P-18174)***
Rw3 Technologies Inc (PA) E **925 743-7703**
1601 Cornell Way Auburn (95603) ***(P-19391)***
Rwi, Granite Bay *Also called Recoating-West Inc* ***(P-4809)***
RWS Life Sciences Inc E 415 981-5890
555 Montgomery St Ste 720 San Francisco (94111) ***(P-14392)***
Rxd Nova Pharmaceuticals Inc F 610 952-7242
2010 Cessna Dr Vacaville (95688) ***(P-3980)***
Ryan Partnership LLC (PA) B **415 289-1110**
100 Montgomery St # 1500 San Francisco (94104) ***(P-11781)***
Ryko Solutions Inc E 916 372-8815
3939 W Capitol Ave Ste D West Sacramento (95691) ***(P-5448)***
Ryland Custom Welding Inc E 408 781-2509
1815 Monterey Hwy San Jose (95112) ***(P-14720)***
Rypple F 888 479-7753
577 Howard St Fl 3 San Francisco (94105) ***(P-13415)***
Rysaw Painting Inc E 916 817-2393
1713 Stone Canyon Dr Roseville (95661) ***(P-1430)***
Rysigo Technologies Corp (PA) E **408 621-9274**
119 Lyon St Apt A San Francisco (94117) ***(P-13416)***
S & C Siding Inc E 916 491-0715
8733 Flute Cir Elk Grove (95757) ***(P-766)***
S & H Welding Inc F 916 386-8921
8604 Elder Creek Rd Sacramento (95828) ***(P-4729)***
S & J Ranches LLC D 559 437-2600
6715 N Palm Ave Ste 212 Fresno (93704) ***(P-305)***
S & J Royal Inc E 530 682-5861
2599 Reed Rd Yuba City (95993) ***(P-1993)***
S & M Moving Systems D 510 497-2300
48551 Warm Springs Blvd Fremont (94539) ***(P-7585)***
S & S Drywall Inc (PA) C **408 294-4393**
202 N 27th St San Jose (95116) ***(P-1704)***
S & S Ranch Inc D 559 655-3491
904 S Lyon Ave Mendota (93640) ***(P-257)***
S & S Supplies and Solutions, Fairfield *Also called S & S Tool & Supply Inc* ***(P-9131)***
S & S Tool & Supply Inc (HQ) D **800 430-8665**
2700 Maxwell Way Fairfield (94534) ***(P-9131)***
S & W Fine Foods Inc E 800 252-7033
P.O. Box 193575 San Francisco (94119) ***(P-2206)***
S A S, Concord *Also called Bay Alarm Company* ***(P-1458)***
S and L Food Sales, Chico *Also called S and L Meat Sales Company* ***(P-9292)***
S and L Meat Sales Company E 530 343-7953
2 Bellarmine Ct Chico (95928) ***(P-9292)***
S B M, McClellan *Also called Sbm Site Services LLC* ***(P-11995)***
S C Management, San Bruno *Also called Clay Sherman & Co* ***(P-10511)***
S C S, North Highlands *Also called Security Contractor Svcs Inc* ***(P-8646)***
S E Labs, Santa Clara *Also called SE Laboratories Inc* ***(P-19283)***
S E M, Fremont *Also called Streamline Electronics Mfg Inc* ***(P-5981)***
S F Auto Parts Whse Inc D 415 255-0115
6000 3rd St San Francisco (94124) ***(P-8462)***
S F Enterprises Incorporated F 650 455-3223
707 Warrington Ave Redwood City (94063) ***(P-5615)***
S J Amoroso Cnstr Co LLC (PA) B **650 654-1900**
390 Bridge Pkwy Redwood City (94065) ***(P-954)***
S J S Products, Loomis *Also called Jamcor Corporation* ***(P-8986)***
S J W, San Jose *Also called San Jose Water Company* ***(P-8264)***
S K S Enterprises Inc (PA) E **209 599-4095**
11830 French Camp Rd Manteca (95336) ***(P-232)***
S M C, Hayward *Also called Suarez & Munoz Cnstr Inc* ***(P-711)***
S M S Briners Inc E 209 941-8515
17750 E Highway 4 Stockton (95215) ***(P-2285)***
S M U D, Sacramento *Also called Sacramento Municpl Utility Dst* ***(P-8196)***
S Martinelli & Company (PA) C **831 724-1126**
735 W Beach St Watsonville (95076) ***(P-2940)***
S P S Inc D 650 685-5913
245 Medio Ave Half Moon Bay (94019) ***(P-19626)***
S R H H Inc E 408 247-0800
1085 E El Camino Real Sunnyvale (94087) ***(P-11424)***
S S 8, Milpitas *Also called Ss8 Networks Inc* ***(P-8085)***
S S F, South San Francisco *Also called Ssf Imported Auto Parts LLC* ***(P-8470)***
S Stamoules Inc A 559 655-9777
904 S Lyon Ave Mendota (93640) ***(P-306)***
S T L, Sacramento *Also called Sacramento Theatrical Ltg Ltd* ***(P-14860)***
S W G, Union City *Also called Smart Wires Inc* ***(P-6384)***
S&F Management Company Inc A 209 846-9744
2030 Evergreen Ave Modesto (95350) ***(P-16102)***
S&F Management Company LLC C 310 385-1088
25919 Gading Rd Hayward (94544) ***(P-17173)***
S&F Management Company LLC A 916 922-8855
501 Jessie Ave Sacramento (95838) ***(P-16103)***
S&F Management Company LLC A 209 466-0456
442 E Hampton St Stockton (95204) ***(P-16104)***
S&J Stadtler Inc B 925 847-8900
5980 Stoneridge Dr # 122 Pleasanton (94588) ***(P-10656)***
S-K-F County Sanitation Dist, Kingsburg *Also called Selma-Kngsburg-Fowler Cnty Stn* ***(P-8289)***
S-Mart, Modesto *Also called Save Mart Supermarkets Disc* ***(P-9296)***
S-Matrix Corporation E 707 441-0404
1594 Myrtle Ave Eureka (95501) ***(P-13417)***
S.T. Johnson Company, Fairfield *Also called Innovative Combustion Tech* ***(P-4630)***
S2c Inc F 408 213-8818
1754 Tech Dr Ste 206 San Jose (95110) ***(P-13418)***
S3 Graphics Inc C 510 687-4900
940 Mission Ct Fremont (94539) ***(P-6276)***
S4 LLC F 415 979-9640
601 California St Ste 100 San Francisco (94108) ***(P-9092)***
SA Photonics Inc C 408 560-3500
120 Knowles Dr Los Gatos (95032) ***(P-19851)***
Saa Sierra Programs LLC D 530 541-1244
130 Fallen Leaf Rd South Lake Tahoe (96150) ***(P-18457)***
Saags Products LLC D 510 678-3412
1799 Factor Ave San Leandro (94577) ***(P-2123)***
Saama Technologies Inc (PA) C **408 371-1900**
900 E Hamilton Ave # 200 Campbell (95008) ***(P-12754)***
Saarman Construction Ltd C 415 749-2700
683 Mcallister St San Francisco (94102) ***(P-767)***
Saba Decor Rentals LLC (PA) E **510 449-4890**
4451 Vincente St Fremont (94536) ***(P-12062)***
Saba Software Inc (HQ) D **877 722-2101**
4120 Dublin Blvd Ste 200 Dublin (94568) ***(P-13419)***
Sabah International Inc (HQ) D **925 463-0431**
5925 Stoneridge Dr Pleasanton (94588) ***(P-1595)***
Sabel Engineering Corporation E 707 938-4771
1579 N Castle Rd Sonoma (95476) ***(P-5202)***
Sable Computer Inc E 510 403-7500
48383 Fremont Blvd # 122 Fremont (94538) ***(P-13658)***
Sac City Blue Inc E 916 454-0800
620 Sunbeam Ave Sacramento (95811) ***(P-11850)***
Sac EDM & Waterjet, Rancho Cordova *Also called E D M Sacramento Inc* ***(P-5513)***
Sac River Water Treatment Plan E 916 808-3101
301 Water St Sacramento (95811) ***(P-8261)***
Saccani Distributing Company D 916 441-0213
2600 5th St Sacramento (95818) ***(P-9562)***
Sachs Industries Inc F 631 242-9000
801 Kate Ln Woodland (95776) ***(P-3405)***
Saco Enterprises Inc F 408 526-9363
2260 Trade Zone Blvd San Jose (95131) ***(P-8066)***
Sacramento 1st Mortgage Inc E 916 486-6500
3626 Fair Oaks Blvd # 100 Sacramento (95864) ***(P-9947)***
Sacramento 49er Travel Plaza C 916 927-4774
2828 El Centro Rd Sacramento (95833) ***(P-11425)***
Sacramento Animal Hospital Inc E 916 451-7213
5701 H St Sacramento (95819) ***(P-334)***
Sacramento Area Emerg Housing D 916 455-2160
4516 Parker Ave Sacramento (95820) ***(P-17698)***
Sacramento Area Sewer District (PA) B **916 876-6000**
10060 Goethe Rd Sacramento (95827) ***(P-8362)***
Sacramento Baking Co Inc E 916 361-2000
9221 Beatty Dr Sacramento (95826) ***(P-2402)***

ALPHABETIC SECTION Sagepoint Financial Inc

Sacramento Bee, Sacramento *Also called McClatchy Newspapers Inc (P-3456)*

Sacramento Childrens Home (PA) ....C....**916 452-3981**
2750 Sutterville Rd Sacramento (95820) ***(P-18175)***

Sacramento Coca-Cola Btlg Inc (HQ) ....B....**916 928-2300**
4101 Gateway Park Blvd Sacramento (95834) ***(P-2810)***

Sacramento Coca-Cola Btlg Inc ....D....209 541-3200
1733 Morgan Rd Ste 200 Modesto (95358) ***(P-2811)***

Sacramento Community Clinic, Sacramento *Also called Health Lf Orgnization Inc Halo (P-17152)*

Sacramento Control Systems Inc ....D....916 638-0788
11249 Sunco Dr Ste 3 Rancho Cordova (95742) ***(P-14145)***

Sacramento Cooling Systems Inc (PA) ....E....**916 677-1000**
2530 Warren Dr Rocklin (95677) ***(P-1596)***

Sacramento Cooling Systems Inc ....F....559 253-9660
5466 E Lamona Ave # 1022 Fresno (93727) ***(P-6919)***

Sacramento Credit Union (PA) ....D....**916 444-6070**
800 H St Ste 100 Sacramento (95814) ***(P-9836)***

Sacramento Cy Unified Schl Dst (PA) ....B....**916 643-7400**
5735 47th Ave Sacramento (95824) ***(P-18458)***

Sacramento Cy Unified Schl Dst ....D....916 277-6277
2930 21st Ave Sacramento (95820) ***(P-18008)***

Sacramento Cy Unified Schl Dst ....D....916 277-6263
5735 47th Ave Sacramento (95824) ***(P-18009)***

Sacramento Cy Unified Schl Dst ....D....916 264-4186
530 18th St Sacramento (95811) ***(P-18010)***

Sacramento Cy Unified Schl Dst ....D....916 277-6259
1901 60th Ave Sacramento (95822) ***(P-18011)***

Sacramento District Office, Sacramento *Also called State Compensation Insur Fund (P-10184)*

Sacramento Drive In, Sacramento *Also called Century Theatres Inc (P-14831)*

Sacramento Ear Nose & Throat (PA) ....D....**916 736-3399**
1111 Expo Blvd Bldg 700 Sacramento (95815) ***(P-15654)***

Sacramento Employement & Train (PA) ....C....**916 263-3800**
925 Del Paso Blvd Ste 100 Sacramento (95815) ***(P-17834)***

Sacramento Engineering Cons ....E....916 368-4468
10555 Old Placerville Rd Sacramento (95827) ***(P-18807)***

Sacramento Golf Course, Sacramento *Also called County of Sacramento (P-14991)*

Sacramento Harness Association ....D....916 239-4040
1600 Exposition Blvd Sacramento (95815) ***(P-18315)***

Sacramento Heart and Cardiovas (PA) ....E....**916 830-2000**
500 University Ave # 100 Sacramento (95825) ***(P-15655)***

Sacramento Housing Dev Corp (PA) ....D....**916 440-1333**
801 12th St Sacramento (95814) ***(P-19852)***

Sacramento Intl Jet Ctr Inc ....D....916 428-8292
6133 Freeport Blvd Sacramento (95822) ***(P-9538)***

Sacramento Job Corp ....E....916 391-1016
3100 Meadowview Rd Sacramento (95832) ***(P-17835)***

Sacramento Kings Ltd Partnr ....E....916 928-0000
1 Sports Pkwy Sacramento (95834) ***(P-14911)***

Sacramento Laundry Company Inc ....E....916 930-0330
3750 Pell Cir Sacramento (95838) ***(P-11650)***

Sacramento Loaves & Fishes (PA) ....D....**916 446-0874**
1351 N C St Ste 22 Sacramento (95811) ***(P-17699)***

Sacramento Memorial Lawn ....E....916 421-1171
6100 Stockton Blvd Sacramento (95824) ***(P-11700)***

Sacramento Mental Hlth Clinic, Mather *Also called Veterans Health Administration (P-15788)*

Sacramento Municpl Utility Dst (PA) ....A....**916 452-3211**
6201 S St Sacramento (95817) ***(P-8196)***

Sacramento Municpl Utility Dst ....B....916 452-3211
6201 S St Sacramento (95817) ***(P-8197)***

Sacramento Municpl Utility Dst ....D....916 732-5155
6301 S St Sacramento (95817) ***(P-8198)***

Sacramento Municpl Utility Dst ....B....916 732-5616
6201 S St Sacramento (95817) ***(P-8199)***

Sacramento Municpl Utility Dst ....B....916 732-5743
14295 Clay East Rd Herald (95638) ***(P-14393)***

Sacramento News & Review, Sacramento *Also called Chico Community Publishing (P-3428)*

Sacramento Operating Co LP ....C....916 422-4825
7400 24th St Sacramento (95822) ***(P-16105)***

Sacramento Packing Inc ....B....530 671-4488
833 Tudor Rd Yuba City (95991) ***(P-2267)***

Sacramento Post-Acute, Sacramento *Also called Oleander Holdings LLC (P-16087)*

Sacramento Rebar Inc (PA) ....E....**916 447-9700**
6415 Hedge Ave Sacramento (95829) ***(P-1931)***

Sacramento Reg Co Sanit Dist (PA) ....C....**916 876-6000**
10060 Goethe Rd Sacramento (95827) ***(P-8403)***

Sacramento Reg Co Sanit Dist ....B....916 875-9000
8521 Laguna Station Rd Elk Grove (95758) ***(P-8288)***

Sacramento Regional Trnst Dist (PA) ....A....**916 726-2877**
1400 29th St Sacramento (95816) ***(P-7346)***

Sacramento Regional Trnst Dist ....E....916 362-9490
1400 29th St Sacramento (95816) ***(P-7347)***

Sacramento Rendering Co, Sacramento *Also called SRC Milling Co LLC (P-2460)*

Sacramento Staffing, Sacramento *Also called Maxim Healthcare Services Inc (P-12180)*

SACRAMENTO STATE SPONSORED RES, Sacramento *Also called University Enterprises Inc (P-19414)*

Sacramento Stucco Co ....E....916 372-7442
1550 Parkway Blvd West Sacramento (95691) ***(P-8633)***

Sacramento Suburban Water Dst ....D....916 972-7171
3701 Marconi Ave Ste 100 Sacramento (95821) ***(P-8262)***

Sacramento Suburban Water Dst ....D....916 972-7171
3701 Marconi Ave Ste 100 Sacramento (95821) ***(P-8263)***

Sacramento Television Stns Inc (HQ) ....C....**916 374-1452**
2713 Kovr Dr West Sacramento (95605) ***(P-8054)***

Sacramento Theatre Company ....D....916 446-7501
1419 H St Sacramento (95814) ***(P-14859)***

Sacramento Theatrical Ltg Ltd ....D....916 447-3258
410 N 10th St Sacramento (95811) ***(P-14860)***

Sacramento Tree Foundation ....E....916 924-8733
191 Lathrop Way Ste D Sacramento (95815) ***(P-18459)***

SACRAMENTO URBAN LEAGUE, Sacramento *Also called Greater Sacramento Urban Leag (P-18230)*

Sacramento V A Medical Center, Mather *Also called Veterans Health Administration (P-15802)*

Sacramento Yolo Cnty Mosquito ....D....916 685-1022
8631 Bond Rd Elk Grove (95624) ***(P-8404)***

Sacramento Zoological Society ....E....916 808-5888
3930 W Land Park Dr Sacramento (95822) ***(P-18295)***

Sacramnt-Yolo Port Dst Fing Co ....D....916 371-8000
1110 W Capitol Ave West Sacramento (95691) ***(P-7725)***

Sacramnto Chnese Cmnty Svcs CT ....C....916 442-4228
420 I St Ste 5 Sacramento (95814) ***(P-17700)***

Sacramnto Cmnty Cble Fundation ....E....916 456-8600
4623 T St Ste A Sacramento (95819) ***(P-19916)***

Sacramnto Emplyment Trning AGC ....C....916 263-3800
925 Del Paso Blvd Ste 100 Sacramento (95815) ***(P-17836)***

Sacramnto Grdn Chapel Mortuary, Sacramento *Also called Sacramento Memorial Lawn (P-11700)*

Sacramnto Gstrntrlogy Med Grou ....D....916 454-0655
3941 J St Ste 450 Sacramento (95819) ***(P-15656)***

Sacramnto Hsing Rdvlpment Agcy ....D....916 440-1376
630 I St Fl 3 Sacramento (95814) ***(P-10340)***

Sacramnto Hsing Rdvlpment Agcy ....D....916 440-1399
801 12th St Sacramento (95814) ***(P-10657)***

Sacramnto Mdtown Endoscopy Ctr ....D....916 733-6940
3941 J St Ste 460 Sacramento (95819) ***(P-17063)***

Sacramnto Mtro A Qulty MGT Dst ....D....916 874-4800
777 12th St Ste 300 Sacramento (95814) ***(P-19853)***

Sacramnto Ntiv Amercn Hlth Ctr ....C....916 341-0575
2020 J St Sacramento (95811) ***(P-15657)***

Sacramnto Plstic Rcnstrctive S ....D....916 929-1833
95 Scripps Dr Sacramento (95825) ***(P-15658)***

Sacramnto Rver Cats Bsbal CLB ....E....916 376-4700
400 Ball Park Dr West Sacramento (95691) ***(P-14912)***

Sacramnto Soc For The Prvntion ....D....916 383-7387
6201 Florin Perkins Rd Sacramento (95828) ***(P-18586)***

Sacramnto Vly Alarm SEC Sys In ....E....916 452-1481
5933 Folsom Blvd Sacramento (95819) ***(P-1597)***

Sacred Heart Community Service ....E....408 278-2160
1381 S 1st St San Jose (95110) ***(P-17701)***

Sacred Heart Pre-School, Turlock *Also called Diocese Stockton Eductl Off (P-17923)*

Sadra Medical Inc ....D....408 370-1550
160 Knowles Dr Los Gatos (95032) ***(P-7028)***

Saf West, Redding *Also called Southern Alum Finshg Co Inc (P-4564)*

Saf-T-Cab Inc (PA) ....D....**559 268-5541**
3241 S Parkway Dr Fresno (93725) ***(P-6570)***

Safari Books Online LLC (PA) ....D....**707 827-7000**
1003 Gravenstein Hwy N Sebastopol (95472) ***(P-3597)***

Safari Kid Inc (PA) ....E....**510 739-1511**
34899 Newark Blvd Newark (94560) ***(P-18012)***

Safe & Sound ....E....415 668-0494
1757 Waller St San Francisco (94117) ***(P-17702)***

Safe Credit Union (PA) ....C....**916 979-7233**
2295 Iron Point Rd # 100 Folsom (95630) ***(P-9808)***

Safe Path Products, Chico *Also called Van Duerr Industries Inc (P-8649)*

Safe Securities Inc ....C....650 398-3669
3000 El Cmino Real Bldg 4 Palo Alto (94306) ***(P-12755)***

Safeamerica Credit Union (PA) ....E....**925 734-4111**
6001 Gibraltar Dr Pleasanton (94588) ***(P-9809)***

Safebreach Inc ....E....408 743-5279
111 W Evelyn Ave Ste 117 Sunnyvale (94086) ***(P-14146)***

Safeco Door & Hardware Inc ....D....510 429-4768
31054 San Antonio St Hayward (94544) ***(P-1942)***

Safeco Glass, Hayward *Also called Safeco Door & Hardware Inc (P-1942)*

Safety Ntwrk Traffic Signs Inc ....E....559 291-8000
1345 N Rabe Ave Fresno (93727) ***(P-5895)***

Safetychain Software Inc (PA) ....E....**415 233-9474**
7599 Redwood Blvd Ste 205 Novato (94945) ***(P-13420)***

Safetymax Corporation ....E....415 626-4650
2256 Palou Ave San Francisco (94124) ***(P-9201)***

Safeway Corporate Inc ....A....925 467-3000
5918 Stoneridge Mall Rd Pleasanton (94588) ***(P-9236)***

Safeway Inc ....A....415 661-3220
1200 Irving St Ste 2 San Francisco (94122) ***(P-2825)***

Safexai Inc (PA) ....F....**650 425-6376**
833 Main St Redwood City (94063) ***(P-13421)***

Safti, Merced *Also called OKeeffes Inc (P-4797)*

Safway Services LP ....E....650 652-9255
1660 Gilbreth Rd Burlingame (94010) ***(P-9028)***

Sage Group ....D....415 512-8200
33 Falmouth St San Francisco (94107) ***(P-12132)***

Sage Hospitality Resources LLC ....C....650 589-1600
2000 Shoreline Ct Brisbane (94005) ***(P-11426)***

Sage Instruments Inc ....D....831 761-1000
240 Airport Blvd Freedom (95019) ***(P-6788)***

Sage Intacct Inc (HQ) ....E....**408 878-0900**
300 Park Ave Ste 1400 San Jose (95110) ***(P-13970)***

Sage Microelectronics Corp ....F....408 680-0060
910 Campisi Way Ste 2a Campbell (95008) ***(P-13422)***

Sage Project Inc ....D....415 905-5050
68 12th St San Francisco (94103) ***(P-17703)***

Sage Veterinary Centers LP ....B....925 288-4856
1410 Monument Blvd Concord (94520) ***(P-335)***

Sagepoint Financial Inc ....D....209 825-8888
903 W Center St Manteca (95337) ***(P-10059)***

Sagepoint Financial Inc ....E....408 374-4787
4950 Hamilton Ave Ste 107 San Jose (95130) ***(P-10012)***

ALPHABETIC

Saia Inc D 916 483-8331
1508 Wyant Way Sacramento (95864) ***(P-7586)***
Saia Motor Freight Line LLC D 916 690-8417
9119 Elkmont Dr Elk Grove (95624) ***(P-7587)***
Saia Motor Freight Line LLC D 530 243-5540
1095 N Court St Redding (96001) ***(P-7588)***
Saia Motor Freight Line LLC D 510 347-6890
1755 Aurora Dr San Leandro (94577) ***(P-7589)***
Saia Motor Freight Line LLC D 559 499-6970
2575 S Sunland Ave Fresno (93725) ***(P-7590)***
Saia Motor Freight Line LLC E 408 487-1740
1705 Rogers Ave San Jose (95112) ***(P-7488)***
Saia S Reno Barbara K, Sacramento *Also called Saia Inc* ***(P-7586)***
Saic Innovation Center LLC D 408 614-9391
2680 Zanker Rd Ste 100 San Jose (95134) ***(P-8463)***
Saildrone Inc F 415 670-9700
1050 W Tower Ave Alameda (94501) ***(P-5113)***
Sailgp, San Francisco *Also called F50 League LLC* ***(P-18566)***
Saint Agnes Med Providers Inc D 559 435-2630
1379 E Herndon Ave Fresno (93720) ***(P-16491)***
Saint Agnes Med Providers Inc D 559 450-2300
6121 N Thesta St Ste 303 Fresno (93710) ***(P-16492)***
Saint Agnes Med Prviders Obgyn, Fresno *Also called Saint Agnes Med Providers Inc* ***(P-16492)***
Saint Agnes Medical Center (HQ) **A 559 450-3000**
1303 E Herndon Ave Fresno (93720) ***(P-16493)***
Saint Claires Nursing Ctr LLC C 916 392-4440
6248 66th Ave Sacramento (95823) ***(P-16106)***
Saint Francis Memorial Hosp (HQ) **A 415 353-6000**
900 Hyde St San Francisco (94109) ***(P-16494)***
Saint Francis Memorial Hosp E 415 353-6000
900 Hide St San Francisco (94120) ***(P-16495)***
Saint Francis Memorial Hosp E 415 353-6000
900 High St Ste 1201 San Francisco (94109) ***(P-16496)***
Saint Francis Memorial Hosp E 415 673-1317
909 Hyde St San Francisco (94109) ***(P-16497)***
Saint Francis Memorial Hosp E 415 353-6600
900 Hyde St San Francisco (94109) ***(P-16498)***
Saint Francis Memorial Hosp E 415 353-6420
900 Hyde St San Francisco (94109) ***(P-16499)***
Saint Francis Memorial Hosp E 415 353-6464
1199 Bush St Ste 300 San Francisco (94109) ***(P-16500)***
Saint Frncis Winery Tasting Rm, Santa Rosa *Also called Saint Frncis Winery Tasting Rm* ***(P-2706)***
Saint Frncis Winery Tasting Rm E 707 833-4666
500 Pythian Rd Santa Rosa (95409) ***(P-2706)***
Saint Germain Foundation (PA) **F 530 235-2994**
1120 Stonehedge Dr Dunsmuir (96025) ***(P-3513)***
Saint Helena Hosp Clearlake, Clearlake *Also called Adventist Hlth Clrlake Hosp In* ***(P-16303)***
Saint John Krnstadt Cnvlscent, Castro Valley *Also called Saint John Krnstadt HM For Age* ***(P-16107)***
Saint John Krnstadt HM For Age E 510 889-7000
4432 James Ave Castro Valley (94546) ***(P-16107)***
Saint Louise Hospital B 408 848-2000
9400 N Name Uno Gilroy (95020) ***(P-16501)***
Saint Orres Corporation E 707 884-3335
36601 S Highway 1 Gualala (95445) ***(P-11427)***
Saint Vincents Day Home E 510 832-8324
1086 8th St Oakland (94607) ***(P-18013)***
Sainte Claire, The, San Jose *Also called Larkspur Hsptality Dev MGT LLC* ***(P-11254)***
Saints Capital Dakota LLC (PA) **D 415 395-2897**
2020 Union St San Francisco (94123) ***(P-19854)***
Saints Management LLC (PA) **E 415 773-2080**
475 Sansome St Ste 1850 San Francisco (94111) ***(P-10881)***
Saintsbury LLC F 707 252-0592
1500 Los Carneros Ave NAPA (94559) ***(P-2707)***
Saitech Inc F 510 440-0256
42640 Christy St Fremont (94538) ***(P-8655)***
Sak Brand Group F 415 486-1200
400 Alabama St San Francisco (94110) ***(P-9256)***
Sak Construction LLC E 916 644-1400
4253 Duluth Ave Rocklin (95765) ***(P-700)***
Sak Hospitality Inc D 707 554-9655
1596 Fairgrounds Dr Vallejo (94589) ***(P-11428)***
Sakata Seed America Inc (HQ) **D 408 778-7758**
18095 Serene Dr Morgan Hill (95037) ***(P-9608)***
Saklan Valley School E 925 376-7900
1678 School St Moraga (94556) ***(P-18014)***
Sal J Acsta Sheetmetal Mfg Inc D 408 275-6370
930 Remillard Ct San Jose (95122) ***(P-4814)***
Salaber Associates Inc E 707 693-8800
180 S 1st St Ste 10 Dixon (95620) ***(P-19855)***
Salad Cosmo USA Corp E 707 678-6633
5944 Dixon Ave W Dixon (95620) ***(P-2941)***
Saladino Sausage Company, Fresno *Also called Choice Food Products Inc* ***(P-2114)***
Saladinos Inc D 559 271-3700
3045 Mulvany Pl West Sacramento (95691) ***(P-9293)***
Saladinos Inc (PA) **C 559 271-3700**
3325 W Figarden Dr Fresno (93711) ***(P-9294)***
Salas OBrien LLC (PA) **D 408 282-1500**
305 S 11th St San Jose (95112) ***(P-19392)***
Salas OBrien Engineers Inc (PA) **E 408 282-1500**
305 S 11th St San Jose (95112) ***(P-18808)***
Sale 121 Corp (PA) **D 888 233-7667**
1467 68th Ave Sacramento (95822) ***(P-5314)***
Sale Family Orchards LLC E 530 527-4854
425 Brearcliffe Dr Red Bluff (96080) ***(P-92)***
Salem Engineering Group Inc (PA) **E 559 271-9700**
4729 W Jacquelyn Ave Fresno (93722) ***(P-18809)***
Sales & Marketing, San Francisco *Also called Outreach Corporation* ***(P-13358)***
Sales Mkt Mfg Smart Dining Sys, Redwood City *Also called E La Carte Inc* ***(P-12409)***
Salesforcecom Inc (PA) **A 415 901-7000**
415 Mission St Fl 3 San Francisco (94105) ***(P-13423)***
Salesforcecom/Foundation C 800 667-6389
The Landmark One St The Landma San Francisco (94105) ***(P-17704)***
Salexo Software, Los Gatos *Also called Splash Data Inc* ***(P-12810)***
Salient Global Technologies, Pittsburg *Also called Ravig Inc* ***(P-8742)***
Salon Media Group Inc (PA) **E 415 870-7566**
870 Market St Ste 442 San Francisco (94102) ***(P-13807)***
Salt Lake Hotel Associates LP (PA) **C 415 397-5572**
222 Kearny St Ste 200 San Francisco (94108) ***(P-11429)***
Salt Security Inc D 650 254-6580
3921 Fabian Way Palo Alto (94303) ***(P-12756)***
Salters Distributing Inc D 559 825-3220
711 S 3rd St Chowchilla (93610) ***(P-9170)***
Saltmine USA Inc E 408 464-3631
601 California St Fl 4 San Francisco (94108) ***(P-12757)***
Salu Beauty Inc D 916 475-1400
11344 Coloma Rd Ste 725 Gold River (95670) ***(P-18346)***
Salu.net, Gold River *Also called Salu Beauty Inc* ***(P-18346)***
Salud Para La Gente C 831 728-0222
195 Aviation Way Ste 200 Watsonville (95076) ***(P-15659)***
Salud Para La Gnte Hlth Clinic, Watsonville *Also called Salud Para La Gente* ***(P-15659)***
Salutary Sports Clubs Inc E 707 438-2582
3250 Rncho Slano Pkwy Ste Fairfield (94534) ***(P-14969)***
Salutary Sports Clubs Inc E 530 677-5705
4242 Sports Club Dr Shingle Springs (95682) ***(P-14970)***
Salutron Incorporated (PA) **E 510 795-2876**
8371 Central Ave Ste A Newark (94560) ***(P-7123)***
Salvation Army Glden State Div (PA) **D 415 553-3500**
832 Folsom St Fl 6 San Francisco (94107) ***(P-17705)***
Sam Bennion D 650 341-3461
477 E Hillsdale Blvd San Mateo (94403) ***(P-11430)***
Sam Trans, South San Francisco *Also called San Mateo County Transit Dst* ***(P-7352)***
Sam Trans, San Carlos *Also called San Mateo County Transit Dst* ***(P-7445)***
Sam's Super Market, Fresno *Also called Sams Italian Deli & Mkt Inc* ***(P-2207)***
Samaritan Family Practice E 408 358-1911
15425 Los Gatos Blvd # 120 Los Gatos (95032) ***(P-15660)***
Samaritan Medical Care, San Jose *Also called Medamerica Inc* ***(P-15525)***
Samaritan Village Inc C 209 883-3212
7700 Fox Rd Hughson (95326) ***(P-17706)***
Samartan Intrnal Mdcine Med Gr E 408 371-9010
2410 Samaritan Dr Ste 201 San Jose (95124) ***(P-16502)***
Samax Precision Inc E 408 245-9555
926 W Evelyn Ave Sunnyvale (94086) ***(P-5616)***
Samba TV, San Francisco *Also called Free Stream Media Corp* ***(P-9659)***
Sambrailo Packaging (PA) **E 831 724-7581**
800 Walker St Watsonville (95076) ***(P-9218)***
Samil Power US Ltd E 925 930-3924
3478 Buskirk Ave Ste 1000 Pleasant Hill (94523) ***(P-6277)***
Samirian Chemicals Inc E 408 558-8282
1999 S Bascom Ave Ste 515 Campbell (95008) ***(P-9521)***
Sams Italian Deli & Mkt Inc E 559 229-9333
2415 N 1st St Fresno (93703) ***(P-2207)***
Samsara Inc (PA) **A 415 985-2400**
350 Rhode Island St # 400 San Francisco (94103) ***(P-13659)***
Samsung Electronics Amer Inc A 650 210-1000
665 Clyde Ave Mountain View (94043) ***(P-8950)***
Samsung Pay Inc E 617 279-0520
665 Clyde Ave Mountain View (94043) ***(P-14394)***
Samsung Research America Inc (HQ) **A 650 210-1001**
665 Clyde Ave Mountain View (94043) ***(P-19123)***
Samsung SDS America Inc D 408 638-8800
2665 N 1st St Ste 110 San Jose (95134) ***(P-12758)***
Samsung Semiconductor Inc (HQ) **C 408 544-4000**
3655 N 1st St San Jose (95134) ***(P-8951)***
SAMTRANS, San Carlos *Also called San Mateo County Transit Dst* ***(P-7351)***
Samuel Hale LLC A 916 235-1477
2365 Iron Point Rd # 190 Folsom (95630) ***(P-12133)***
San Andreas Farms Co E 925 634-1717
741 Sunset Rd Brentwood (94513) ***(P-11)***
San Andreas Regional Center (PA) **C 408 374-9960**
6203 San Ignacio Ave # 200 San Jose (95119) ***(P-17707)***
San Benito Health Foundation E 831 637-6871
351 Felice Dr Hollister (95023) ***(P-15661)***
San Benito House Inc E 650 726-3425
445 Main St Half Moon Bay (94019) ***(P-11431)***
San Benito Htg & Shtmtl Inc D 831 637-1112
1771 San Felipe Rd Hollister (95023) ***(P-1353)***
San Benito Supply (PA) **C 831 637-5526**
1060 Nash Rd Hollister (95023) ***(P-4450)***
San Bernabe Vineyards LLC F 209 824-3501
12001 S Highway 99 Manteca (95336) ***(P-2708)***
San Bernandina Steel, Stockton *Also called Herrick Corporation* ***(P-4666)***
San Bnito Cnty Cmnty Svcs Dev E 831 636-5524
1101 San Felipe Rd Hollister (95023) ***(P-11594)***
San Bruno Skilled Nursing Hosp, San Bruno *Also called Independent Quality Care Inc* ***(P-16246)***
San Francisco 49ers, Santa Clara *Also called Forty Niners Football Co LLC* ***(P-14905)***
San Francisco Aids Foundation (PA) **D 415 487-3000**
1035 Market St Ste 400 San Francisco (94103) ***(P-17708)***
San Francisco Aids Foundation E 415 581-7077
1035 Market St Ste 400 San Francisco (94103) ***(P-17709)***
San Francisco Ballet Assn C 415 865-2000
455 Franklin St San Francisco (94102) ***(P-14861)***
San Francisco Bath Salt Co, Alameda *Also called Rmf Salt Holdings LLC* ***(P-4094)***

ALPHABETIC SECTION San Jose Mailing Inc

San Francisco Bay AR Tran Assn ... C ... 510 501-5318
915 San Antonio Ave Alameda (94501) ***(P-18587)***

SAN FRANCISCO BAY AREA COUNCIL, San Leandro *Also called San Frncsc-Bay Area Cncil Boy* ***(P-18460)***

San Francisco Bay Area Rapid ... A ... 510 286-2893
601 E 8th St Oakland (94606) ***(P-7348)***

San Francisco Bay Brand Inc (PA) ... **E ... 510 792-7200**
8239 Enterprise Dr Newark (94560) ***(P-2357)***

San Francisco Bay Coffee Co, Lincoln *Also called Jbr Inc* ***(P-2907)***

San Francisco Bay Guardian, San Francisco *Also called Bay Guardian Company* ***(P-3416)***

San Francisco C & C Inc ... E ... 415 673-4711
1050 Van Ness Ave San Francisco (94109) ***(P-11432)***

San Francisco City & County ... C ... 415 550-4600
200 Paul Ave B San Francisco (94124) ***(P-14622)***

San Francisco Cmnty Hlth Ctr, San Francisco *Also called Asian PCF Islnder Wllness Ctr* ***(P-17433)***

San Francisco Critical Care ... D ... 415 923-3421
2351 Clay St Ste 501 San Francisco (94115) ***(P-15662)***

San Francisco Elev Svcs Inc ... E ... 925 829-5400
6517 Sierra Ln Dublin (94568) ***(P-9093)***

San Francisco Envelope, Fremont *Also called Cleansmart Solutions Inc* ***(P-3397)***

San Francisco Estuary Inst ... E ... 510 746-7334
4911 Central Ave Richmond (94804) ***(P-19234)***

San Francisco Federal Cr Un (PA) ... **D ... 415 775-5377**
770 Golden Gate Ave Fl 1 San Francisco (94102) ***(P-9810)***

San Francisco Film Society ... E ... 415 561-5000
39 Mesa St Ste 110 San Francisco (94129) ***(P-18588)***

San Francisco Fire Credit Un (PA) ... **E ... 415 674-4800**
3201 California St San Francisco (94118) ***(P-9811)***

San Francisco Food Bank ... D ... 415 282-1900
900 Pennsylvania Ave San Francisco (94107) ***(P-17710)***

San Francisco Foods Inc ... D ... 510 357-7343
14054 Catalina St San Leandro (94577) ***(P-2306)***

San Francisco Forty Niners (PA) ... **C ... 408 562-4949**
4949 Mrie P Debartolo Way Santa Clara (95054) ***(P-14913)***

San Francisco Foundation ... D ... 415 733-8500
1 Embarcadero Ctr # 1400 San Francisco (94111) ***(P-14395)***

San Francisco General Hospital, San Francisco *Also called Gastroenterology Division* ***(P-15414)***

San Francisco General Hospital, San Francisco *Also called City & County of San Francisco* ***(P-16332)***

San Francisco General Hospital, San Francisco *Also called University Cal San Francisco* ***(P-16749)***

San Francisco Golf Club ... E ... 415 469-4104
1310 Junipero Serra Blvd San Francisco (94132) ***(P-15132)***

San Francisco Health Authority (PA) ... **D ... 415 615-4407**
50 Beale St Fl 12 San Francisco (94105) ***(P-18347)***

San Francisco Hotel Associates ... E ... 415 392-4666
650 Bush St San Francisco (94108) ***(P-11433)***

San Francisco Hotel Group LLC ... C ... 415 276-9888
222 Sansome St San Francisco (94104) ***(P-11434)***

San Francisco Intl Arprt, San Francisco *Also called San Francisco Intl Arprt Corp* ***(P-7784)***

San Francisco Intl Arprt ... E ... 650 821-6700
670 W Field Rd San Francisco (94128) ***(P-7783)***

San Francisco Intl Arprt Corp ... E ... 650 616-2400
780 S Airport Blvd San Francisco (94128) ***(P-7784)***

SAN FRANCISCO LGBT COMMUNITY C, San Francisco *Also called San Frncsco Lsbian Gay Bsxual* ***(P-17711)***

San Francisco Museum Modrn Art (PA) ... **B ... 415 357-4035**
151 3rd St San Francisco (94103) ***(P-18279)***

San Francisco Opera Assn ... A ... 415 861-4008
301 Van Ness Ave San Francisco (94102) ***(P-14862)***

San Francisco Performances Inc ... E ... 415 398-6449
500 Sutter St Ste 710 San Francisco (94102) ***(P-14875)***

San Francisco Performing Arts ... E ... 415 621-6600
893 Folsom St San Francisco (94107) ***(P-15234)***

San Francisco Post Acute, San Francisco *Also called San Franciscoidence Opco LLC* ***(P-16265)***

San Francisco Print Media Co (PA) ... **D ... 415 487-2594**
835 Market St Ste 550 San Francisco (94103) ***(P-3695)***

San Francisco Radio Assets LLC (HQ) ... **C ... 415 216-1300**
750 Battery St Fl 2 San Francisco (94111) ***(P-8034)***

SAN FRANCISCO RESIDENTIAL CARE, San Francisco *Also called Self-Help For Elderly* ***(P-17728)***

San Francisco School ... D ... 415 239-5065
300 Gaven St San Francisco (94134) ***(P-18015)***

San Francisco Surgery Ctr LP ... D ... 415 393-9600
450 Sutter St Rm 500 San Francisco (94108) ***(P-15663)***

San Francisco Symphony (PA) ... **C ... 415 552-8000**
201 Van Ness Ave San Francisco (94102) ***(P-14876)***

San Francisco Tennis Club ... D ... 415 777-9000
645 5th St San Francisco (94107) ***(P-14971)***

San Francisco Towers, San Francisco *Also called Covia Communities* ***(P-18090)***

San Francisco Travel Assn ... D ... 415 974-6900
1 Front St Ste 2900 San Francisco (94111) ***(P-14396)***

San Francisco Unified Schl Dst (PA) ... **C ... 415 241-6000**
555 Franklin St San Francisco (94102) ***(P-19393)***

San Francisco Vamc, San Francisco *Also called Veterans Health Administration* ***(P-15795)***

San Francisco Yacht Club ... E ... 415 435-9133
98 Beach Rd Belvedere Tiburon (94920) ***(P-15133)***

San Francisco Zoological Soc ... C ... 415 753-7080
1 Zoo Rd San Francisco (94132) ***(P-15235)***

San Franciscoidence Opco LLC ... D ... 415 584-3294
5767 Mission St San Francisco (94112) ***(P-16265)***

San Franciso Adult Day Svcs, San Francisco *Also called Catholic Chrties Cyo of The AR* ***(P-17463)***

San Franstitchco Inc ... F ... 707 795-6891
624 Portal St Cotati (94931) ***(P-3043)***

San Frnciso Intl Youth Hostel, San Francisco *Also called Golden Gate Cncil Amrcn Yuth H* ***(P-11115)***

San Frnciso Staffing Staffing, Emeryville *Also called Maxim Healthcare Services Inc* ***(P-12181)***

San Frncsc-Bay Area Cncil Boy ... E ... 510 577-9000
1001 Davis St San Leandro (94577) ***(P-18460)***

San Frncsco Bar Plots Bnvlent ... D ... 415 362-5436
9 Pier Ste 119a San Francisco (94111) ***(P-18316)***

San Frncsco Bay Area Rpid Trns (PA) ... **B ... 510 464-6000**
2150 Webster St Oakland (94612) ***(P-7349)***

San Frncsco Bay Bird Obsrvtory ... E ... 408 946-6548
524 Valley Way Milpitas (95035) ***(P-18461)***

San Frncsco Bay Cmpssnate Cmnt, San Francisco *Also called Charolais Care V Inc* ***(P-16870)***

San Frncsco Cmnty Clnic Cnsrti ... D ... 415 355-2222
2720 Taylor St Ste 430 San Francisco (94133) ***(P-19394)***

San Frncsco Cnservatory of Mus ... C ... 415 864-7326
50 Oak St San Francisco (94102) ***(P-14877)***

San Frncsco Gen Hosp Fundation ... C ... 415 206-4478
2789 25th St Ste 2028 San Francisco (94110) ***(P-18249)***

San Frncsco Intl Film Festival, San Francisco *Also called San Francisco Film Society* ***(P-18588)***

San Frncsco Ldies Prtction Rli ... C ... 415 931-3136
3400 Laguna St San Francisco (94123) ***(P-18176)***

San Frncsco Lsbian Gay Bsxual ... E ... 415 865-5649
1800 Market St San Francisco (94102) ***(P-17711)***

San Frncsco North/Petaluma KOA ... E ... 707 763-1492
20 Rainsville Rd Petaluma (94952) ***(P-11620)***

San Frncsco Prtclar Cncil of T ... D ... 415 255-3525
525 5th St San Francisco (94107) ***(P-17712)***

San Frncsco Scide Prvntion Inc ... E ... 415 984-1900
230 8th St San Francisco (94103) ***(P-17713)***

San Frncsco Sport Spine Physcl (PA) ... **D ... 415 593-2532**
100 Bush St Ste 800 San Francisco (94104) ***(P-15896)***

San Joaquin Cnty Aging & Commu ... C ... 209 468-9455
102 S San Joaquin St Stockton (95202) ***(P-17714)***

San Joaquin Country Club ... D ... 559 439-3483
3484 W Bluff Ave Fresno (93711) ***(P-15134)***

San Joaquin Electric Inc ... E ... 209 952-9980
2342 Teepee Dr Stockton (95205) ***(P-1598)***

San Joaquin Figs Inc ... E ... 559 224-4492
3564 N Hazel Ave Fresno (93722) ***(P-307)***

San Joaquin General Hospital (PA) ... **A ... 209 468-6000**
500 W Hospital Rd French Camp (95231) ***(P-16503)***

San Joaquin Glass Inc ... E ... 559 268-7646
2150 E Mckinley Ave Fresno (93703) ***(P-1943)***

San Joaquin Hydraulic Inc (PA) ... **F ... 559 264-7325**
530 Van Ness Ave Fresno (93721) ***(P-9132)***

San Joaquin Regional Trnst Dst ... C ... 209 948-5566
421 E Weber Ave Stockton (95202) ***(P-7350)***

San Joaquin Val UNI Air Pol (PA) ... **C ... 559 230-6000**
1990 E Gettysburg Ave Fresno (93726) ***(P-19856)***

San Joaquin Valley Dairymen, Turlock *Also called California Dairies Inc* ***(P-2141)***

San Joaquin Valley Rehabili (HQ) ... **B ... 559 436-3600**
7173 N Sharon Ave Fresno (93720) ***(P-17064)***

San Joaquinn Vly Draing Auth, Los Banos *Also called San Luis Dlta-Mendota Wtr Auth* ***(P-8417)***

San Jose Air Conditioning Inc ... E ... 408 457-7936
5725 Winfield Blvd Ste 5 San Jose (95123) ***(P-1354)***

San Jose Airport Garden Hotel ... D ... 408 793-3300
1740 N 1st St San Jose (95112) ***(P-11435)***

San Jose Airport Hotel LLC ... C ... 408 793-3939
1740 N 1st St San Jose (95112) ***(P-11436)***

San Jose Arena Management LLC (PA) ... **C ... 408 287-7070**
525 W Santa Clara St San Jose (95113) ***(P-19395)***

San Jose Awning Company Inc ... E ... 408 350-7000
755 Chestnut St Ste E San Jose (95110) ***(P-3042)***

San Jose Bluprt Svc & Sup Co ... C ... 408 295-5770
821 Martin Ave Santa Clara (95050) ***(P-11851)***

San Jose Chld Discovery Museum ... D ... 408 298-5437
180 Woz Way San Jose (95110) ***(P-18280)***

San Jose Conservation Corps ... D ... 408 283-7171
2650 Senter Rd San Jose (95111) ***(P-17837)***

San Jose Country Club ... D ... 408 258-4901
15571 Alum Rock Ave San Jose (95127) ***(P-15135)***

San Jose Delta Associates Inc ... E ... 408 727-1448
482 Sapena Ct Santa Clara (95054) ***(P-4408)***

San Jose Die Casting Corp ... E ... 408 262-6500
600 Business Park Dr # 100 Lincoln (95648) ***(P-4579)***

San Jose Earthquakes MGT LLC ... D ... 408 556-7700
451 El Cmino Real Ste 220 Santa Clara (95050) ***(P-19396)***

San Jose Healthcare System LP ... A ... 408 259-5000
225 N Jackson Ave San Jose (95116) ***(P-16504)***

San Jose Hhg Hotel Dev LP ... E ... 408 650-0590
10 Skyport Dr San Jose (95110) ***(P-11437)***

San Jose Hhg Hotel Dev LP ... E ... 650 868-4911
10 Skyport Dr San Jose (95110) ***(P-11438)***

San Jose Hlthcare Wellness Ctr, San Jose *Also called San Jose Hlthcare Wllness Ctr* ***(P-16108)***

San Jose Hlthcare Wllness Ctr ... D ... 408 295-2665
75 N 13th St San Jose (95112) ***(P-16108)***

San Jose Lessee LLC ... D ... 408 453-4000
2050 Gateway Pl San Jose (95110) ***(P-11439)***

San Jose Mailing Inc ... E ... 408 971-1911
1445 Monterey Hwy San Jose (95110) ***(P-11841)***

ALPHABETIC

Employee Codes: A=Over 500 employees, B=251-500
C=101-250, D=51-100, E=20-50 F=10-19

2022 Northern California Business
Directory and Buyers Guide

© Mergent Inc. 1-800-342-5647
1069

San Jose Mercury-News LLC (HQ)....A....408 920-5000
4 N 2nd St Fl 8 San Jose (95113) *(P-3476)*
San Jose Municipal Golf Course, San Jose *Also called Rawitser Golf Shop Mike (P-15019)*
San Jose Museum of Art Assn....D....408 271-6840
110 S Market St San Jose (95113) *(P-18281)*
San Jose Office, Santa Clara *Also called McCarthy Bldg Companies Inc (P-920)*
San Jose Office, San Jose *Also called Lg Innotek Usa Inc (P-6674)*
San Jose Police Officers Assn....E....408 298-1133
1151 N 4th St San Jose (95112) *(P-18589)*
San Jose Redevelopment Agency....C....408 535-8500
200 E Santa Clara St 14th San Jose (95113) *(P-19857)*
San Jose Residence Club Inc....E....408 998-0223
72 N 5th St San Jose (95112) *(P-11440)*
San Jose Sharks LLC (PA)....C....408 999-6810
525 W Santa Clara St San Jose (95113) *(P-14914)*
San Jose Slcon Vly Chmber Cmmr....E....408 291-5250
101 W Santa Clara St San Jose (95113) *(P-18317)*
San Jose Surgical Supply Inc (PA)....E....408 293-9033
902 S Bascom Ave San Jose (95128) *(P-8791)*
San Jose Water Company (HQ)....C....408 288-5314
110 W Taylor St San Jose (95110) *(P-8264)*
San Jose Water Company....C....408 298-0364
1221 S Bascom Ave San Jose (95128) *(P-8265)*
San Jquin Cnty Off Sbstnce Abu, Stockton *Also called County of San Joaquin (P-17511)*
San Jquin Gen Hosp Fndtion A C....A....209 468-6000
500 W Hospital Rd French Camp (95231) *(P-16505)*
San Jquin Orthtics Prsthtics C....F....209 932-0170
2211 N California St Stockton (95204) *(P-7079)*
San Jquin Rver Pkwy Cnsrvtion....E....559 248-8480
11605 Old Friant Rd Fresno (93730) *(P-18462)*
San Jquin Vly Rhbltion Hosp A....C....559 658-6490
40232 Junction Dr Oakhurst (93644) *(P-15897)*
San Juan Oaks LLC....D....831 636-6113
3825 Union Rd Hollister (95023) *(P-15023)*
San Juan Oaks Golf Club, Hollister *Also called San Juan Oaks LLC (P-15023)*
San Juan Soccer Club....E....916 365-2801
11151 Trade Center Dr # 20 Rancho Cordova (95670) *(P-15136)*
San Juan Water District....E....916 791-0115
9935 Auburn Folsom Rd Granite Bay (95746) *(P-8266)*
San Leandro Healthcare Center....D....510 357-4015
368 Juana Ave San Leandro (94577) *(P-16109)*
San Leandro Hospital LP....B....510 357-6500
13855 E 14th St San Leandro (94578) *(P-16506)*
San Leandro Imaging Ctr A Cal....E....510 351-7734
2450 Washington Ave # 120 San Leandro (94577) *(P-15664)*
San Lndro Srgery Ctr Ltd A Cal....D....510 276-2800
15035 E 14th St San Leandro (94578) *(P-15665)*
San Lorenzo Village Shopg Ctr, San Mateo *Also called David D Bohannon Organization (P-10385)*
San Luis Care Center, Newman *Also called Avalon Care Ctr - Newman LLC (P-15918)*
San Luis Dlta-Mendota Wtr Auth....E....209 835-2593
15990 Kelso Rd Byron (94514) *(P-8416)*
San Luis Dlta-Mendota Wtr Auth (PA)....E....209 826-9696
842 6th St Los Banos (93635) *(P-8417)*
San Mar Properties Inc (PA)....E....559 439-5500
6356 N Fresno St Ste 101 Fresno (93710) *(P-10658)*
San Mateo Cnty Expo Fair Assn....E....650 574-3247
2495 S Delaware St San Mateo (94403) *(P-15236)*
San Mateo County Bar Assn....E....650 298-4000
333 Bradford St Ste 150 Redwood City (94063) *(P-18348)*
San Mateo County Expo Center, San Mateo *Also called San Mateo Cnty Expo Fair Assn (P-15236)*
San Mateo County Harbor Dst....E....650 583-4400
504 Avenue Alhambra Fl 2 El Granada (94018) *(P-7732)*
San Mateo County Transit Dst (PA)....C....650 508-6200
1250 San Carlos Ave San Carlos (94070) *(P-7351)*
San Mateo County Transit Dst....B....650 588-4860
301 N Access Rd South San Francisco (94080) *(P-7352)*
San Mateo County Transit Dst....C....650 508-6412
501 Pico Blvd San Carlos (94070) *(P-7445)*
San Mateo Credit Union....D....650 363-1725
525 Middlefield Rd Redwood City (94063) *(P-9812)*
San Mateo Credit Union (PA)....D....650 363-1725
350 Convention Way # 300 Redwood City (94063) *(P-9813)*
San Mateo Credit Union....C....650 363-1725
1515 S El Cmino Real Ste San Mateo (94402) *(P-9814)*
San Mateo Fish Market, San Mateo *Also called Fish Mkt Rstrants- San Jose LP (P-9366)*
SAN MATEO HEAD START PROGRAM, San Mateo *Also called Institute For Humn Social Dev (P-17955)*
San Mateo Health Commission....C....650 616-0050
801 Gateway Blvd Ste 100 South San Francisco (94080) *(P-17174)*
San Mateo Marriott, San Mateo *Also called Atrium Plaza LLC (P-10937)*
San Mateo Medical Center, San Mateo *Also called County of San Mateo (P-15370)*
San Mateo Sport Club, Burlingame *Also called 24 Hour Fitness Usa Inc (P-14921)*
San Mateo Staffing, San Mateo *Also called Maxim Healthcare Services Inc (P-12184)*
San Mateo Times, San Mateo *Also called Alameda Newspapers Inc (P-3412)*
San Miguel Villa, Concord *Also called Tranquility Incorporated (P-16280)*
San Mteo Cnty Msqito Vctor Ctr....E....650 344-8592
1351 Rollins Rd Burlingame (94010) *(P-8405)*
San Rafael Hillcrest LLC....D....415 479-8800
1010 Northgate Dr San Rafael (94903) *(P-11441)*
San Rafael Rock Quarry Inc....E....510 970-7700
961 Western Dr Richmond (94801) *(P-4190)*
San Rafael Rock Quarry Inc (HQ)....D....415 459-7740
2350 Kerner Blvd Ste 200 San Rafael (94901) *(P-581)*
San Ramon Endoscopy Center Inc....E....925 275-9910
5801 Norris Canyon Rd # 100 San Ramon (94583) *(P-16507)*
San Ramon Medical Offices, San Ramon *Also called Kaiser Foundation Hospitals (P-10118)*
San Ramon Regional Med Ctr LLC....A....925 275-9200
6001 Norris Canyon Rd San Ramon (94583) *(P-16508)*
San Ramon Vly Unified Schl Dst....D....925 552-2880
3131 Stone Valley Rd Danville (94526) *(P-18463)*
San Rfael Hlthcare Wllness Ctr....E....415 456-7170
1601 5th Ave San Rafael (94901) *(P-16110)*
San Tomas Convalescent Hosp, San Jose *Also called Aquinas Corporation (P-15910)*
San Tomo Inc....D....209 948-0792
11292 N Alpine Rd Stockton (95212) *(P-189)*
San-I-Pak Pacific Inc....E....209 836-2310
23535 S Bird Rd Tracy (95304) *(P-4730)*
Sanborn Chevrolet Inc....D....209 334-5000
1210 S Cherokee Ln Lodi (95240) *(P-14588)*
Sanborn Collison Center, Lodi *Also called Sanborn Chevrolet Inc (P-14588)*
Sanchez Business Inc....E....415 282-2400
250 Napoleon St Ste M San Francisco (94124) *(P-2208)*
Sanco Pipelines Incorporated....E....408 377-2793
727 University Ave Los Gatos (95032) *(P-1134)*
Sanctuary....E....559 498-8543
2336 Calaveras St Fresno (93721) *(P-17715)*
Sandbar Solar and Electric, Santa Cruz *Also called Santa Cruz Westside Elc Inc (P-1355)*
Sander Jcobs Cssyre Grffin Inc....E....707 252-8822
3200 Villa Ln NAPA (94558) *(P-10341)*
Sanderlings, Aptos *Also called Seascape Rsort Ltd A Cal Ltd P (P-11452)*
Sanders Contracting Inc....D....925 308-7305
P.O. Box 492 Byron (94514) *(P-955)*
Sanders Prcsion Tmber Flling I (PA)....E....530 938-4120
9509 N Old Stage Rd Weed (96094) *(P-3077)*
Sandis Civil Engineers (PA)....D....408 636-0900
1700 Winchester Blvd Campbell (95008) *(P-18925)*
Sandisk LLC (HQ)....C....408 801-1000
951 Sandisk Dr Milpitas (95035) *(P-5315)*
Sandman Inc (PA)....D....408 947-0669
1404 S 7th St San Jose (95112) *(P-4451)*
Sands Rv Resort, San Rafael *Also called R C Roberts & Co (P-10474)*
Sandys Drapery Inc (PA)....E....510 445-0112
48374 Milmont Dr Bldg A Fremont (94538) *(P-3022)*
Sangamo Therapeutics Inc (PA)....B....510 970-6000
7000 Marina Blvd Brisbane (94005) *(P-4056)*
Sanger Head Start Center, Sanger *Also called Fresno Cnty Ecnmic Opprtnties (P-17938)*
Sangiacomo Vineyards, Sonoma *Also called V Sangiacomo & Sons (P-80)*
Sangraf International Inc....E....216 800-9999
3171 Independence Dr Livermore (94551) *(P-5673)*
Sanhyd Inc....D....510 483-6200
524 Callan Ave San Leandro (94577) *(P-16266)*
Sanhyd Inc....D....510 843-2131
2131 Carleton St Berkeley (94704) *(P-16111)*
Sanitary Dst 1 Marin Cnty....E....415 259-2949
2960 Kerner Blvd San Rafael (94901) *(P-8406)*
Sanitation Process Control LLC....E....510 909-4910
24 W Jamestown St Apt 307 Stockton (95207) *(P-11992)*
Sankalp Semiconductor, Palo Alto *Also called Sankalp Usa Inc (P-6278)*
Sankalp Usa Inc....E....408 372-6090
2225 E Bayshore Rd 200 Palo Alto (94303) *(P-6278)*
Sanmina Corporation....E....408 964-3500
2700 N 1st St San Jose (95134) *(P-5968)*
Sanmina Corporation....B....408 964-6400
2050 Bering Dr San Jose (95131) *(P-5969)*
Sanmina Corporation....B....510 897-2000
42735 Christy St Fremont (94538) *(P-5970)*
Sanmina Corporation (PA)....B....408 964-3500
2700 N 1st St San Jose (95134) *(P-5971)*
Sanmina Corporation....C....510 494-2421
8455 Cabot Ct Newark (94560) *(P-4869)*
Sanmina-Sci Usa Inc....E....408 964-3500
30 E Plumeria Dr San Jose (95134) *(P-5972)*
Sano Intelligence Inc....D....408 483-6518
1155 Bryant St San Francisco (94103) *(P-12759)*
Sanofi US Services Inc....C....415 856-5000
185 Berry St San Francisco (94107) *(P-3981)*
Sanovas Inc....E....415 729-9391
2597 Kerner Blvd San Rafael (94901) *(P-7029)*
Sansa Technology LLC....E....866 204-3710
6990 Village Pkwy Dublin (94568) *(P-19124)*
Sansei Gardens Inc....C....510 226-9191
3250 Darby Cmn Fremont (94539) *(P-499)*
Santa Clara County of....D....408 885-5000
751 S Bascom Ave San Jose (95128) *(P-15666)*
Santa Clara County of....E....408 435-2000
2600 N 1st St San Jose (95134) *(P-17716)*
Santa Clara County of....D....408 362-9817
6201 San Ignacio Ave San Jose (95119) *(P-17175)*
Santa Clara County of....C....408 885-7470
2325 Enborg Ln 2h260 San Jose (95128) *(P-16509)*
Santa Clara County of....D....408 885-6666
751 S Bascom Ave Fl 4 San Jose (95128) *(P-15667)*
Santa Clara County of....C....408 885-5451
2325 Enborg Ln Fl 4 San Jose (95128) *(P-16510)*
Santa Clara County of....C....408 848-2000
9400 N Name Uno Gilroy (95020) *(P-16511)*
Santa Clara County of....E....408 573-3050
15555 Sanborn Rd Saratoga (95070) *(P-2065)*
Santa Clara Arques Med Offs, Sunnyvale *Also called Kaiser Foundation Hospitals (P-15466)*
Santa Clara Cnty Fair Grnds Mg....D....408 494-3100
344 Tully Rd San Jose (95111) *(P-15237)*
Santa Clara Cnty Fderal Cr Un....D....408 282-0700
1641 N 1st St Ste 170 San Jose (95112) *(P-9815)*

ALPHABETIC SECTION **Sap Labs LLC**

Santa Clara Cnty Fderal Cr Un (PA)....**D**....**408 282-0700**
1641 N 1st St Ste 245 San Jose (95112) ***(P-9816)***

Santa Clara Convention Center....C....408 748-7000
5001 Great America Pkwy Santa Clara (95054) ***(P-14397)***

Santa Clara County FMC, San Jose *Also called Santa Clara Cnty Fair Grnds Mg* ***(P-15237)***

Santa Clara County Health Auth....E....408 376-2000
210 E Hacienda Ave Campbell (95008) ***(P-10086)***

Santa Clara County of....D....408 792-5020
976 Lenzen Ave Ste 1800 San Jose (95126) ***(P-17065)***

Santa Clara County of....D....408 885-5770
828 S Bascom Ave Ste 100 San Jose (95128) ***(P-17066)***

Santa Clara County of....D....408 918-7755
231 Grant Ave Palo Alto (94306) ***(P-17067)***

Santa Clara County of....E....408 299-5437
333 W Julian St Ste 100 San Jose (95110) ***(P-17717)***

Santa Clara County of....E....408 686-3800
90 Highland Ave San Martin (95046) ***(P-17718)***

Santa Clara County of....E....408 846-5000
90 Highland Ave San Martin (95046) ***(P-17719)***

Santa Clara County of....E....408 573-2400
101 Skyport Dr San Jose (95110) ***(P-8407)***

Santa Clara County of....E....408 758-3500
1879 Senter Rd San Jose (95112) ***(P-17720)***

Santa Clara County of....E....650 324-6500
270 Grant Ave Ste 303 Palo Alto (94306) ***(P-17721)***

Santa Clara County of....E....408 792-5030
976 Lenzen Ave Ste 1800 San Jose (95126) ***(P-17722)***

Santa Clara County of....E....408 885-6818
2325 Enborg Ln Ste 380 San Jose (95128) ***(P-16512)***

Santa Clara County of....E....408 224-7476
6980 Santa Teresa Blvd San Jose (95119) ***(P-18464)***

Santa Clara County of....D....408 494-1561
614 Tully Rd Ste A San Jose (95111) ***(P-17068)***

Santa Clara County of....D....408 885-5920
2400 Moorpark Ave Ste 118 San Jose (95128) ***(P-17069)***

Santa Clara Facility, Santa Clara *Also called Summit Interconnect Inc* ***(P-5983)***

Santa Clara Family Health, San Jose *Also called Santa Clara County of* ***(P-17175)***

Santa Clara Hilton, The, Santa Clara *Also called Hostmark Investors Ltd Partnr* ***(P-19351)***

Santa Clara Imported Cars Inc....D....408 247-2550
4590 Stevens Creek Blvd San Jose (95129) ***(P-14589)***

Santa Clara Medical Center, San Jose *Also called Santa Clara County of* ***(P-17069)***

Santa Clara Plating Co Inc....D....408 727-9315
1773 Grant St Santa Clara (95050) ***(P-4919)***

Santa Clara Suites LP....E....408 241-6444
2455 El Camino Real Santa Clara (95051) ***(P-11442)***

Santa Clara Valley Corporation....D....408 947-1100
715 N 1st St Ste 27 San Jose (95112) ***(P-11993)***

Santa Clara Valley Health & Ho, San Jose *Also called Santa Clara County of* ***(P-16512)***

Santa Clara Valley Medica....D....408 885-6839
P.O. Box 5460 San Jose (95150) ***(P-17176)***

Santa Clara Valley Medical Ctr....E....408 885-6300
2400 Moorpark Ave San Jose (95128) ***(P-15668)***

Santa Clara Valley Medical Ctr....E....408 792-5586
976 Lenzen Ave San Jose (95126) ***(P-15669)***

Santa Clara Valley Medical Ctr....E....408 885-5730
2220 Moorpark Ave San Jose (95128) ***(P-17177)***

Santa Clara Valley Medical Ctr (PA)....**B**....**408 885-5000**
751 S Bascom Ave San Jose (95128) ***(P-16513)***

Santa Clara Valley Trnsp Auth (PA)....**A**....**408 321-2300**
3331 N 1st St San Jose (95134) ***(P-7353)***

Santa Clara Valley Trnsp Auth....D....408 321-5559
3331 N 1st St Bldg B San Jose (95134) ***(P-7354)***

Santa Clara Valley Water (PA)....**C**....**408 265-2600**
5750 Almaden Expy San Jose (95118) ***(P-8267)***

Santa Clara Vanguard, Santa Clara *Also called Vanguard Music and Prfrmg Arts* ***(P-18478)***

Santa Clara Vlly Hlth & Hsptl, San Jose *Also called Santa Clara County of* ***(P-16509)***

Santa Clara Vly Hlth Hosp Sys, San Jose *Also called Santa Clara County of* ***(P-16510)***

Santa Clara Vly Wtr Dst Pub Fc....C....408 630-2560
3959 Whitman Way San Jose (95132) ***(P-8268)***

Santa Clara Vly Wtr Dst Pub Fc....C....408 395-8121
400 More Ave Los Gatos (95032) ***(P-8269)***

Santa Croce LLC....F....707 227-7834
1097 Nimitz Ave Vallejo (94592) ***(P-2777)***

Santa Cruz Bicycles LLC....D....831 459-7560
2841 Mission St Santa Cruz (95060) ***(P-6654)***

Santa Cruz Bikes, Santa Cruz *Also called Santa Cruz Bicycles LLC* ***(P-6654)***

Santa Cruz City of....E....831 420-5200
212 Locust St Ste D Santa Cruz (95060) ***(P-8270)***

Santa Cruz Cmnty Cnselling Ctr, Watsonville *Also called Santa Cruz Co Head Start* ***(P-18016)***

Santa Cruz Cnty Rgnal Trnsp Co....E....831 460-3200
1523 Pacific Ave Santa Cruz (95060) ***(P-7403)***

Santa Cruz Co Head Start....E....831 724-3885
408 E Lake Ave Watsonville (95076) ***(P-18016)***

Santa Cruz Community Credit Un (PA)....**E**....**831 425-7708**
324 Front St Santa Cruz (95060) ***(P-9817)***

Santa Cruz Compost Company Inc....E....831 728-0113
71 Elkhorn Rd Royal Oaks (95076) ***(P-9609)***

Santa Cruz Guitar Corporation....E....831 425-0999
151 Harvey West Blvd C Santa Cruz (95060) ***(P-7173)***

Santa Cruz Ht Assoc A Cal Ltd....D....831 426-4330
175 W Cliff Dr Santa Cruz (95060) ***(P-11443)***

Santa Cruz Medical Foundation (HQ)....**E**....**831 458-5537**
2025 Soquel Ave Santa Cruz (95062) ***(P-15670)***

Santa Cruz Medical Foundation....A....831 477-2375
2915 Chanticleer Ave Santa Cruz (95065) ***(P-15671)***

Santa Cruz Medical Foundation....A....831 477-2325
2900 Chanticleer Ave Santa Cruz (95065) ***(P-15672)***

Santa Cruz Metro Trnst Dst....D....831 429-5455
138 Golf Club Dr Santa Cruz (95060) ***(P-7355)***

Santa Cruz Metro Trnst Dst....D....831 469-1954
110 Vernon St Ste B Santa Cruz (95060) ***(P-7356)***

Santa Cruz Metro Trnst Dst....D....831 426-6080
135 Aviation Way Ste 2 Watsonville (95076) ***(P-7357)***

Santa Cruz Montessori School....E....831 476-1646
6230 Soquel Dr Aptos (95003) ***(P-18017)***

Santa Cruz Nutritionals (PA)....**B**....**831 457-3200**
2200 Delaware Ave Santa Cruz (95060) ***(P-3982)***

Santa Cruz Seaside Company (PA)....**B**....**831 423-5590**
400 Beach St Santa Cruz (95060) ***(P-15046)***

Santa Cruz Seaside Company....A....831 427-3400
201 W Cliff Dr Santa Cruz (95060) ***(P-11444)***

Santa Cruz Skateboards, Santa Cruz *Also called Nhs Inc* ***(P-7199)***

Santa Cruz Surgery....E....831 462-5512
3003 Paul Sweet Rd Santa Cruz (95065) ***(P-15673)***

Santa Cruz Westside Elc Inc....D....831 469-8888
2656 Mission St Santa Cruz (95060) ***(P-1355)***

Santa Fe Aggregates Inc (HQ)....**F**....**209 358-3303**
11650 Shaffer Rd Winton (95388) ***(P-597)***

Santa Rosa City of....E....707 543-3421
455 Ridgway Ave Santa Rosa (95401) ***(P-15238)***

Santa Rosa City of....E....707 543-3882
55 Stony Point Rd Santa Rosa (95401) ***(P-14590)***

Santa Rosa & Sonoma Co Real Es....E....707 524-1124
1057 College Ave Santa Rosa (95404) ***(P-10659)***

Santa Rosa Ansthesia Med Group, Santa Rosa *Also called Anesthsia Anlgsia Med Group In* ***(P-15279)***

Santa Rosa Bus Lines....D....707 543-3333
45 Stony Point Rd Santa Rosa (95401) ***(P-7416)***

Santa Rosa Chrnic Pain Endcrnl, Santa Rosa *Also called Kaiser Foundation Hospitals* ***(P-16395)***

Santa Rosa City of, Santa Rosa *Also called Santa Rosa Bus Lines* ***(P-7416)***

Santa Rosa Clinic, Santa Rosa *Also called Veterans Health Administration* ***(P-15799)***

Santa Rosa Community Hlth Ctrs (PA)....**C**....**707 547-2222**
3569 Round Barn Cir Santa Rosa (95403) ***(P-15674)***

Santa Rosa Dental Group....E....707 545-0944
80 Doctors Park Dr Santa Rosa (95405) ***(P-15857)***

Santa Rosa Fire Eqp Svc Inc....E....707 546-0797
595a Portal St Cotati (94931) ***(P-9146)***

Santa Rosa Hardware Co Inc....F....707 795-2500
489 Portal St Cotati (94931) ***(P-8989)***

Santa Rosa Indian Cmnty of Snt, Fresno *Also called Rainbow - Brite Indus Svcs LLC* ***(P-11988)***

Santa Rosa Jet Center, Santa Rosa *Also called Kaiserair Inc* ***(P-7774)***

Santa Rosa Memorial Hospital, Santa Rosa *Also called St Joseph Hlth Nthrn Cal LLC* ***(P-16537)***

Santa Rosa Memorial Hospital....D....707 547-2221
751 Lombardi Ct Santa Rosa (95407) ***(P-16514)***

Santa Rosa Memorial Hospital....D....707 542-4704
1170 Montgomery Dr Santa Rosa (95405) ***(P-16515)***

Santa Rosa Memorial Hospital....D....707 525-5300
2700 Dolbeer St Eureka (95501) ***(P-16516)***

Santa Rosa Memorial Hospital....E....707 584-0672
1450 Medical Center Dr # 1 Rohnert Park (94928) ***(P-17070)***

Santa Rosa Orthpdics Med Group....C....707 546-1922
1405 Montgomery Dr Santa Rosa (95405) ***(P-15675)***

Santa Rosa Post Acute, Santa Rosa *Also called Santa Rosaidence Opco LLC* ***(P-16112)***

Santa Rosa Press Democrat Inc (HQ)....**B**....**707 546-2020**
427 Mendocino Ave Santa Rosa (95401) ***(P-3477)***

Santa Rosa Radiology Med Group (PA)....**E**....**707 546-4062**
121 Sotoyome St Santa Rosa (95405) ***(P-16805)***

Santa Rosa Stain....E....707 544-7777
1400 Airport Blvd Santa Rosa (95403) ***(P-6657)***

Santa Rosa Surgery Center LP....E....707 575-5831
1111 Sonoma Ave Ste 214 Santa Rosa (95405) ***(P-16517)***

Santa Rosaidence Opco LLC....C....707 546-0471
4650 Hoen Ave Santa Rosa (95405) ***(P-16112)***

Santa Teresa Golf Center, San Jose *Also called Santa Teresa Golf Club LP* ***(P-15024)***

Santa Teresa Golf Club LP....E....408 225-2650
260 Bernal Rd San Jose (95119) ***(P-15024)***

Santana Row, San Jose *Also called Federal Realty Investment Tr* ***(P-10818)***

Santana Row Hotel Partners LP....C....408 551-0010
355 Santana Row San Jose (95128) ***(P-11445)***

Sante Community Physicians, Fresno *Also called Sante Health System Inc* ***(P-10087)***

Sante Health System Inc (PA)....**C**....**559 228-5400**
7370 N Palm Ave Ste 101 Fresno (93711) ***(P-10087)***

Sante Specialty Foods, Santa Clara *Also called Aharoni & Steele Inc* ***(P-2441)***

Santen Incorporated....D....415 268-9100
6401 Hollis St Ste 125 Emeryville (94608) ***(P-15872)***

Santini Fine Wines, San Lorenzo *Also called Santini Foods Inc* ***(P-2167)***

Santini Foods Inc....C....510 317-8888
16505 Worthley Dr San Lorenzo (94580) ***(P-2167)***

Santos Ford Inc....E....209 826-4921
617 W Pacheco Blvd Los Banos (93635) ***(P-8464)***

Santos Legacy Builders LLC....D....916 439-2777
2829 Watt Ave 101 Sacramento (95821) ***(P-701)***

Santronics, Sunnyvale *Also called Ahn Enterprises LLC* ***(P-6375)***

Santur Corporation (HQ)....**C**....**510 933-4100**
40931 Encyclopedia Cir Fremont (94538) ***(P-5170)***

Sap AG....C....650 849-4000
3410 Hillview Ave Palo Alto (94304) ***(P-5316)***

Sap Labs LLC....D....650 849-4000
3475 Deer Creek Rd Palo Alto (94304) ***(P-12760)***

Sap Labs LLC (HQ)....**B**....**650 849-4000**
3410 Hillview Ave Palo Alto (94304) ***(P-13424)***

ALPHABETIC

Sapar Usa Inc ALPHABETIC SECTION

Sapar Usa Inc (HQ).....E.....**510 441-9500**
1610 Delta Ct Unit 1 Hayward (94544) ***(P-2124)***
Saputo Cheese USA Inc.....D.....262 307-6738
691 Inyo Ave Newman (95360) ***(P-2156)***
Saputo Dairy Foods Usa LLC.....C.....209 854-6461
299 5th Ave Gustine (95322) ***(P-2194)***
Saqqara Systems Inc.....E.....408 325-8241
2833 Junction Ave Ste 100 San Jose (95134) ***(P-13425)***
Sarabian Farms, Sanger *Also called Virginia Sarabian* ***(P-81)***
Saramark Inc.....E.....408 971-3881
15660 Mckinley Ave Lathrop (95330) ***(P-4856)***
Saratoga Country Club Inc.....D.....408 253-0340
21990 Prospect Rd Saratoga (95070) ***(P-15137)***
Saratoga Retirement Community, Saratoga *Also called Odd Fellows Home California* ***(P-18152)***
Sardee Corporation California.....F.....209 466-1526
2731 E Myrtle St Stockton (95205) ***(P-5056)***
Sardee Industries Inc.....E.....209 466-1526
2731 E Myrtle St Stockton (95205) ***(P-5203)***
Sarpa-Feldman Enterprises Inc.....D.....408 982-1790
650 N King Rd San Jose (95133) ***(P-14398)***
Sars Software Products Inc.....F.....415 226-0040
3589 Jerald Ct Castro Valley (94546) ***(P-13426)***
Sasco.....B.....916 565-4120
2400 Del Paso Rd Ste 200 Sacramento (95834) ***(P-19858)***
Sasco Electric Inc.....B.....408 970-8300
598 Gibraltar Dr Milpitas (95035) ***(P-1599)***
Sasco Valley Electric, Milpitas *Also called Sasco Electric Inc* ***(P-1599)***
Sass Labs Inc.....E.....404 731-7284
121 W Washington Ave # 209 Sunnyvale (94086) ***(P-13427)***
Sat, Sacramento *Also called Lpa Insurance Agency Inc* ***(P-13284)***
Sat Corporation (HQ).....D.....**402 208-9200**
3200 Patrick Henry Dr # 1 Santa Clara (95054) ***(P-12761)***
Satco Products of California.....D.....510 487-4822
31288 San Benito St Hayward (94544) ***(P-8875)***
Satellite Av LLC.....E.....916 677-0720
4021 Alvis Ct Ste 5 Rocklin (95677) ***(P-5866)***
Satellite Dialysis, South San Francisco *Also called Satellite Healthcare Inc* ***(P-16981)***
SATELLITE DIALYSIS CENTERS, San Jose *Also called Satellite Healthcare Inc* ***(P-16979)***
Satellite First Communities LP (PA).....D.....**510 647-0700**
1835 Alcatraz Ave Berkeley (94703) ***(P-10458)***
Satellite Healthcare Inc (PA).....D.....**650 404-3600**
300 Santana Row Ste 300 # 300 San Jose (95128) ***(P-16979)***
Satellite Healthcare Inc.....E.....650 566-0180
927 Hamilton Ave Menlo Park (94025) ***(P-16980)***
Satellite Healthcare Inc.....E.....650 377-0888
205 Kenwood Way South San Francisco (94080) ***(P-16981)***
Satellite Telework Centers Inc (PA).....D.....**831 222-2100**
6265 Highway 9 Felton (95018) ***(P-6789)***
Satmetrix Systems Inc.....C.....650 227-8300
555 Twin Dolphin Dr # 36 Redwood City (94065) ***(P-12762)***
Sauce Labs Inc (PA).....D.....**855 677-0011**
116 New Montgomery St # 3 San Francisco (94105) ***(P-13660)***
Saunco Air Technologies, Hickman *Also called Reed International* ***(P-5043)***
Saunders, Sunnyvale *Also called RS Hughes Company Inc* ***(P-9130)***
Sausalito Construction Inc.....E.....415 889-5281
75 Pelican Way Ste B San Rafael (94901) ***(P-768)***
Savage & Cooke, Vallejo *Also called Santa Croce LLC* ***(P-2777)***
Savage Industries.....E.....415 845-6264
48 Linda St San Francisco (94110) ***(P-7306)***
Savannah Chanelle Vineyards.....E.....301 758-2338
23600 Big Basin Way Saratoga (95070) ***(P-2709)***
Save Mart, Tracy *Also called Lucky Stores II LLC* ***(P-9229)***
Save Mart Supermarkets.....D.....916 348-3425
8065 Watt Ave Antelope (95843) ***(P-2403)***
Save Mart Supermarkets.....D.....916 989-3915
8839 Greenback Ln Orangevale (95662) ***(P-9295)***
Save Mart Supermarkets Disc (PA).....C.....**209 577-1600**
1800 Standiford Ave Modesto (95350) ***(P-9296)***
Save Mart Supermarkets Disc.....D.....530 222-6740
1330 Churn Creek Rd Redding (96003) ***(P-2404)***
Save Mart Supermarkets Disc.....D.....559 261-4123
6797 N Milburn Ave Fresno (93722) ***(P-11816)***
Save Mart Supermarkets Disc.....D.....559 253-1220
5671 E Kings Canyon Rd Fresno (93727) ***(P-9297)***
Save Mart Supermarkets Disc.....D.....209 863-1480
2237 Claribel Rd Riverbank (95367) ***(P-9298)***
Save Mart Supermarkets Disc.....D.....530 583-5231
100 River Rd Tahoe City (96145) ***(P-9299)***
Save Mart Supermarkets Disc.....D.....530 587-5522
11399 Deerfield Dr Truckee (96161) ***(P-9300)***
Save Mart Supermarkets Disc.....D.....916 723-2446
6982 Sunrise Blvd Citrus Heights (95610) ***(P-9301)***
Save Redwoods League.....E.....415 362-2352
111 Sutter St Fl 11 San Francisco (94104) ***(P-18465)***
Saviano Company Inc.....E.....650 948-3274
1784 Smith Ave San Jose (95112) ***(P-1175)***
Savicom, Oakland *Also called Mindshare Design Inc* ***(P-11870)***
Savills Inc.....E.....415 421-5900
150 California St Fl 14 San Francisco (94111) ***(P-10660)***
Savings Bank Mendocino County (PA).....C.....**707 462-6613**
200 N School St Ukiah (95482) ***(P-9747)***
Savnik & Company.....F.....510 568-4628
21698 Gail Dr Castro Valley (94546) ***(P-2979)***
Sawbirds Inc (PA).....E.....**415 861-0644**
721 Brannan St San Francisco (94103) ***(P-4612)***
Sawhney Properties LP (PA).....E.....**925 837-0932**
156 Las Quebradas Alamo (94507) ***(P-11446)***
Sawmill, Ukiah *Also called Mendocino Forest Pdts Co LLC* ***(P-8590)***
Saylor Lane Healthcare Center, Sacramento *Also called SLHCC Inc* ***(P-16123)***
Sb Architects (PA).....E.....**415 673-8990**
415 Jackson St Ste 100 San Francisco (94111) ***(P-18911)***
Sb Energy Devco (us) Inc.....E.....650 731-3262
1 Circle Star Way San Carlos (94070) ***(P-1176)***
SBC, San Jose *Also called AT&T Services Inc* ***(P-7930)***
SBC Long Distance LLC.....E.....314 505-0582
5850 W Las Positas Blvd Pleasanton (94588) ***(P-7911)***
Sbi Builders Inc (PA).....E.....**408 549-1300**
710 W Julian St San Jose (95126) ***(P-769)***
Sbm Management Services LP.....B.....866 855-2211
5241 Arnold Ave McClellan (95652) ***(P-11994)***
Sbm Site Services LLC (PA).....D.....**916 922-7600**
5241 Arnold Ave McClellan (95652) ***(P-11995)***
Sbmc, Ukiah *Also called Savings Bank Mendocino County* ***(P-9747)***
Sbragia Family Vineyards LLC.....E.....707 473-2992
9990 Dry Creek Rd Geyserville (95441) ***(P-2710)***
Sbrpstc, San Jose *Also called South Bay Regl Public Safety T* ***(P-17840)***
SBS, Fremont *Also called South Bay Solutions Inc* ***(P-5621)***
SBSA, Redwood City *Also called Silicon Valley Clean Water* ***(P-8290)***
SC Builders Inc (PA).....D.....**408 328-0688**
910 Thompson Pl Sunnyvale (94085) ***(P-956)***
SC Hockey Franchise Corp.....D.....209 373-1500
248 W Fremont St Stockton (95203) ***(P-14915)***
SC Hotel Partners LLC.....D.....415 775-5000
550 Geary St San Francisco (94102) ***(P-11447)***
Scafco Corporation.....E.....559 256-9911
2443 Foundry Park Ave Fresno (93706) ***(P-4592)***
Scalable Press.....F.....877 752-9060
41454 Christy St Fremont (94538) ***(P-3478)***
Scale Ai Inc (PA).....C.....**650 294-8644**
155 5th St Fl 6 San Francisco (94103) ***(P-12763)***
Scaleflux Inc.....D.....408 628-2291
97 E Brokaw Rd Ste 260 San Jose (95112) ***(P-13661)***
Scalio LLC.....E.....408 835-0640
548 Market St Pmb 21933 San Francisco (94104) ***(P-12764)***
Scality Inc.....E.....650 356-8500
149 New Montgomery St # 4 San Francisco (94105) ***(P-5317)***
Scan-Vino LLC (PA).....D.....**209 931-3570**
5463 Cherokee Rd Stockton (95215) ***(P-7591)***
Scandia Family Fun Center, Sacramento *Also called Scandia Sports Inc* ***(P-15239)***
Scandia Sports Inc.....E.....916 331-5757
5070 Hillsdale Blvd Sacramento (95842) ***(P-15239)***
Scandinavian Galleries LLC.....E.....650 862-8432
4127 Dry Creek Rd NAPA (94558) ***(P-14399)***
Scapes Inc.....E.....650 712-4460
12344 San Mateo Rd Half Moon Bay (94019) ***(P-500)***
Scarborough Lbr & Bldg Sup Inc (PA).....E.....**831 438-0331**
20 El Pueblo Rd Scotts Valley (95066) ***(P-8606)***
Scates Construction Inc.....E.....408 293-9050
1769 Park Ave Ste 200 San Jose (95126) ***(P-957)***
SCC ESA Dept of Risk Mgmt.....D.....408 441-4207
2310 N 1st St Ste 202 San Jose (95131) ***(P-10342)***
SCC Open Space Authority, San Jose *Also called Santa Clara County of* ***(P-18464)***
SCDS, Santa Rosa *Also called Sonoma Country Day School* ***(P-18023)***
Scenic Faculty Med Group Inc.....E.....209 558-7248
830 Scenic Dr Modesto (95350) ***(P-15676)***
Schakel, Mark E II MD, Santa Rosa *Also called Santa Rosa Orthpdics Med Group* ***(P-15675)***
Schalich Brothers Cnstr Inc.....E.....415 382-7733
85 Galli Dr Ste J Novato (94949) ***(P-702)***
Schaper Construction Inc (PA).....D.....**408 437-0337**
1177 N 15th St San Jose (95112) ***(P-1431)***
Scheid Vineyards Inc.....C.....707 433-1858
373 Healdsburg Ave Healdsburg (95448) ***(P-73)***
Schell & Kampeter Inc.....C.....209 983-4900
250 Roth Rd Lathrop (95330) ***(P-2336)***
Schetter Electric Inc (PA).....D.....**916 446-2521**
471 Bannon St Sacramento (95811) ***(P-1600)***
Schetter Electric Inc.....C.....925 228-2424
737 Arnold Dr Ste D Martinez (94553) ***(P-1601)***
Schetter Electric LLC.....D.....916 446-2521
471 Bannon St Sacramento (95811) ***(P-1602)***
Schindler Elevator Corporation.....E.....510 382-2075
555 Mccormick St San Leandro (94577) ***(P-5049)***
Schmeiser Farm Equipment, Fresno *Also called T G Schmeiser Co Inc* ***(P-4621)***
Schmid Thermal Systems Inc.....C.....831 763-0113
200 Westridge Dr Watsonville (95076) ***(P-5217)***
Schmidbauer Lumber Inc (PA).....C.....**707 443-7024**
1099 W Waterfront Dr Eureka (95501) ***(P-3103)***
Schmidbauer Lumber Inc.....D.....707 822-7607
1017 Samoa Blvd Arcata (95521) ***(P-3104)***
Schmitt Superior Classics, Redding *Also called William R Schmitt* ***(P-3087)***
Schnabel Foundation Company.....D.....925 947-1881
3075 Citrus Cir Ste 150 Walnut Creek (94598) ***(P-1974)***
Schneder Elc Bldngs Amrcas Inc.....E.....925 463-7100
5735 W Las Psts Blvd Pleasanton (94588) ***(P-6540)***
Schneider Electric.....F.....615 691-2586
200 W Pontiac Way Clovis (93612) ***(P-6541)***
Schnitzer Fresno Inc.....C.....559 233-3211
2727 S Chestnut Ave Fresno (93725) ***(P-9176)***
Schoenstein & Co.....E.....707 747-5858
4001 Industrial Way Benicia (94510) ***(P-7174)***
Scholastic Book Fairs Inc.....D.....510 771-1700
42001 Christy St Fremont (94538) ***(P-9619)***
Scholle Ipn Packaging Inc.....E.....209 384-3100
2500 Cooper Ave Merced (95348) ***(P-4319)***
Scholten Surgical Instrs Inc.....F.....209 365-1393
170 Commerce St Ste 101 Lodi (95240) ***(P-7030)***

School Apparel Inc (PA) ....C....**650 777-4500**
838 Mitten Rd Burlingame (94010) ***(P-3006)***
School Innovations Achievement (PA) ....D....**916 933-2290**
5200 Golden Foothill Pkwy El Dorado Hills (95762) ***(P-13428)***
School Innvations Advocacy, El Dorado Hills *Also called School Innvtons Achevement Inc* ***(P-19627)***
School Innvtons Achevement Inc ....E....800 487-9234
5200 Golden Foothill Pkwy El Dorado Hills (95762) ***(P-19627)***
School of Veterinary Medicine, Davis *Also called University California Davis* ***(P-16700)***
School Services California Inc ....E....916 446-7517
1121 L St Ste 1060 Sacramento (95814) ***(P-19628)***
Schoolcity Inc ....E....408 638-8438
462 Joshua Way Sunnyvale (94086) ***(P-12765)***
Schools Financial Credit Union (PA) ....C....**916 569-5400**
1485 Response Rd Ste 126 Sacramento (95815) ***(P-9818)***
Schramsberg Vineyards Company ....E....707 942-4558
1400 Schramsberg Rd Calistoga (94515) ***(P-74)***
Schuering Zimmerman & Scully ....E....916 567-0400
400 University Ave Sacramento (95825) ***(P-17366)***
Schuff Steel Company ....D....209 938-0869
10100 Trinity Pkwy # 400 Stockton (95219) ***(P-1932)***
Schwager Davis Inc ....C....408 281-9300
198 Hillsdale Ave San Jose (95136) ***(P-1177)***
Schwan's Home Service, Elk Grove *Also called Cygnus Home Service LLC* ***(P-2170)***
Schwin and Tran Mill & Bakery, Berkeley *Also called Vital Vittles Bakery Inc* ***(P-2410)***
Sciabica's, Modesto *Also called Nick Sciabica & Sons A Corp* ***(P-2466)***
Scientific Hardware Systems, Gilroy *Also called Technical Reps Intl Inc* ***(P-972)***
Scientific Learning Corp ....E....510 444-3500
300 Frank H Ogawa Plz # 600 Oakland (94612) ***(P-13429)***
Scientific Metal Finishing Inc ....E....408 970-9011
3180 Molinaro St Santa Clara (95054) ***(P-4948)***
Scientific Molding Corp Ltd ....D....707 303-3041
3250 Brickway Blvd Santa Rosa (95403) ***(P-4320)***
Scientific Specialties Inc ....D....209 333-2120
1310 Thurman St Lodi (95240) ***(P-4233)***
SCIHP, Santa Rosa *Also called Sonoma Cnty Indian Hlth Prj In* ***(P-15693)***
Scilex Pharmaceuticals Inc ....E....650 430-3238
960 San Antonio Rd Palo Alto (94303) ***(P-3983)***
Scimage Inc ....E....650 694-4858
4916 El Cmino Real Ste 20 Los Altos (94022) ***(P-12766)***
Scintera Networks Inc ....E....408 636-2600
160 Rio Robles San Jose (95134) ***(P-6279)***
Scio Technologies Inc ....E....408 203-0518
2650 Birch St Ste 150 Palo Alto (94306) ***(P-12767)***
Sciton Inc ....D....650 493-9155
925 Commercial St Palo Alto (94303) ***(P-7031)***
Scms, Aptos *Also called Santa Cruz Montessori School* ***(P-18017)***
Scoggan Co Inc (PA) ....E....**916 371-3984**
704 Houston St West Sacramento (95691) ***(P-8465)***
Sconza Candy Company ....D....209 845-3700
1 Sconza Candy Ln Oakdale (95361) ***(P-2432)***
Scope Technologies US Inc (PA) ....E....**855 207-2673**
575 Market St Fl 4 San Francisco (94105) ***(P-13430)***
Scott A Porter Prof Corp ....D....916 929-1481
350 University Ave # 200 Sacramento (95825) ***(P-17367)***
Scott Ag LLC ....F....707 545-4519
1275 N Dutton Ave Santa Rosa (95401) ***(P-7251)***
Scott Architectural, Fairfield *Also called Scott Lamp Company Inc* ***(P-5738)***
Scott Baldwin Cpas A Prof Corp ....E....916 722-2524
990 Reserve Dr Ste 120 Roseville (95678) ***(P-18990)***
Scott Lamp Company Inc ....D....707 864-2066
355 Watt Dr Fairfield (94534) ***(P-5738)***
Scott Shaw Entrprises Inc ....D....916 920-2273
11160 Sun Center Dr Rancho Cordova (95670) ***(P-16940)***
Scott St Snior Hsing Cmplex In ....C....415 345-5083
2180 Post St San Francisco (94115) ***(P-16113)***
Scott Vly Swimming Tennis CLB ....D....415 383-3483
50 Underhill Rd Mill Valley (94941) ***(P-15138)***
Scott's Seafood Grill & Bar, Oakland *Also called Food Specialists Inc* ***(P-10480)***
Scotts Valley Fire District, Scotts Valley *Also called Scotts Vly Fire Protection Dst* ***(P-14400)***
Scotts Valley Magnetics Inc ....E....831 438-3600
300 El Pueblo Rd Ste 107 Scotts Valley (95066) ***(P-6383)***
Scotts Valley Medical Clinic ....E....831 438-1430
2890 El Rancho Dr Santa Cruz (95060) ***(P-16518)***
Scotts Vly Fire Protection Dst ....D....831 438-0211
7 Erba Ln Scotts Valley (95066) ***(P-14400)***
Scotts- Hyponex, Linden *Also called Hyponex Corporation* ***(P-4132)***
Scp Distributors LLC ....E....925 687-9500
2051 Commerce Ave Concord (94520) ***(P-9162)***
Screen Machine, San Jose *Also called Lights Fantastic* ***(P-3673)***
Screen Spe Usa LLC (HQ) ....C....**408 523-9140**
820 Kifer Rd Ste B Sunnyvale (94086) ***(P-14704)***
Screen Tech Inc ....D....408 885-9750
4754 Bennett Dr Livermore (94551) ***(P-4815)***
Screenbeam Inc (PA) ....D....**800 752-7820**
220 Devcon Dr San Jose (95112) ***(P-12768)***
Screenmeet.com, San Francisco *Also called Projector Is Inc* ***(P-13388)***
Scribd Inc (PA) ....D....**415 896-9890**
460 Bryant St Fl 1 San Francisco (94107) ***(P-13808)***
Scribner Engineering Inc ....E....916 638-1515
11455 Hydraulics Dr Rancho Cordova (95742) ***(P-4321)***
Scribner Plastics ....F....916 638-1515
11455 Hydraulics Dr Rancho Cordova (95742) ***(P-4322)***
Scuderia West, San Francisco *Also called Ngcw Inc* ***(P-14767)***
Scusd ....E....916 277-6705
3101 Redding Ave Sacramento (95820) ***(P-7894)***
Scuttlebugs Child Dev Ctr, San Jose *Also called Childcare Foundry* ***(P-17895)***
Scvmc, San Jose *Also called Santa Clara Valley Medical Ctr* ***(P-16513)***

SD Deacon Corp California ....D....916 969-0900
7745 Greenback Ln Ste 250 Citrus Heights (95610) ***(P-958)***
Sdg Architects Inc ....E....925 634-7000
3361 Walnut Blvd Ste 120 Brentwood (94513) ***(P-18912)***
SE Laboratories Inc ....D....408 727-3286
1065 Comstock St Santa Clara (95054) ***(P-19283)***
SE Scher Corporation ....A....408 844-0772
1585 The Alameda San Jose (95126) ***(P-12193)***
SE Scher Corporation ....A....916 632-1363
6731 Five Star Blvd Ste C Rocklin (95677) ***(P-12134)***
Sea & Sand Inn, Santa Cruz *Also called Santa Cruz Seaside Company* ***(P-11444)***
Sea-Logix Llc ....D....510 271-1400
1425 Maritime St Oakland (94607) ***(P-7592)***
Sea-Logix Llc (HQ) ....E....**415 927-6400**
4040 Civic Center Dr # 350 San Rafael (94903) ***(P-7593)***
Seaca Packaging Inc ....E....559 813-9030
3194 E Manning Ave Ste 2 Fowler (93625) ***(P-14401)***
Seacastle Inc ....C....925 480-3000
4000 Executive Pkwy # 240 San Ramon (94583) ***(P-12063)***
Seacliff Inn Inc ....D....831 661-4671
7500 Old Dominion Ct Aptos (95003) ***(P-11448)***
Seagate Systems (us) Inc (HQ) ....D....**510 687-5200**
46831 Lakeview Blvd Fremont (94538) ***(P-5318)***
Seagate Technology LLC (HQ) ....A....**800 732-4283**
47488 Kato Rd Fremont (94538) ***(P-5319)***
Seagate US LLC ....E....408 658-1000
10200 S De Anza Blvd Cupertino (95014) ***(P-5320)***
Seagull Solutions Inc ....F....408 778-1127
15105 Concord Cir Ste 100 Morgan Hill (95037) ***(P-6790)***
Seal San Leandro LLC ....E....510 343-8105
510 Lewelling Blvd San Leandro (94579) ***(P-11449)***
Seal Software Incorporated (HQ) ....F....**650 938-7325**
1990 N Calif Blvd Ste 500 Walnut Creek (94596) ***(P-13431)***
Seaman Nurseries Inc ....D....559 665-1860
336 Robertson Blvd Ste A Chowchilla (93610) ***(P-258)***
Seaport Stainless, Richmond *Also called Andrus Sheet Metal Inc* ***(P-4741)***
Search Group Incorporated ....D....916 392-2550
1900 Point West Way # 161 Sacramento (95815) ***(P-19235)***
Sears, Benicia *Also called Innovel Solutions Inc* ***(P-7839)***
Sears Roebuck and Co ....C....408 864-6600
5540 Winfield Blvd San Jose (95123) ***(P-4620)***
Sears 1468, San Jose *Also called Sears Roebuck and Co* ***(P-4620)***
Sears Home Imprv Pdts Inc ....C....650 645-9974
1155 Veterans Blvd Redwood City (94063) ***(P-703)***
Sears Home Imprv Pdts Inc ....C....831 245-0062
491 Tres Pinos Rd Hollister (95023) ***(P-704)***
Seascape Beach Association ....E....831 688-6800
1 Seascape Resort Dr Aptos (95003) ***(P-11450)***
Seascape Lamps Inc ....F....831 728-5699
125a Lee Rd Watsonville (95076) ***(P-5725)***
Seascape Resort Owners Assn ....D....831 688-6800
1 Seascape Resort Dr Aptos (95003) ***(P-11451)***
Seascape Rsort Ltd A Cal Ltd P ....C....831 662-7120
19 Seascape Vlg Aptos (95003) ***(P-11452)***
Seasholtz John ....C....559 659-3805
1355 M St Firebaugh (93622) ***(P-35)***
Seaside Rfrigerated Trnspt Inc (PA) ....E....**510 732-0472**
7041 Las Positas Rd Ste H Livermore (94551) ***(P-7594)***
Searchin. Io., San Francisco *Also called Algolia Inc* ***(P-12971)***
Seaview Hlthcare Rhblttion Ctr ....E....707 443-5668
6400 Purdue Dr Eureka (95503) ***(P-18177)***
Seayu Enterprises ....F....415 566-9677
236 West Portal Ave 399 San Francisco (94127) ***(P-9522)***
Sebastian, Fresno *Also called Kertel Communications Inc* ***(P-1530)***
Sebastiani Vineyards Inc ....D....707 933-3200
389 4th St E Sonoma (95476) ***(P-2711)***
Sebastiani Vineyards & Winery, Sonoma *Also called Sebastiani Vineyards Inc* ***(P-2711)***
Sebring-West Automotive ....E....559 266-9378
1744 N Blackstone Ave Fresno (93703) ***(P-14591)***
Seco Manufacturing Company Inc ....C....530 225-8155
4155 Oasis Rd Redding (96003) ***(P-6920)***
Second Chance Inc (PA) ....E....**510 792-4357**
6330 Thornton Ave Ste B Newark (94560) ***(P-17723)***
Second Harvest Silicon Valley (PA) ....E....**408 266-8866**
750 Curtner Ave San Jose (95125) ***(P-17724)***
Second Home Inc ....E....559 298-0699
1797 San Jose Ave Clovis (93611) ***(P-18178)***
Second Hrvest Fd Bnk Srving Sn ....E....831 722-7110
800 Ohlone Pkwy Watsonville (95076) ***(P-17725)***
Secpod Technologies ....E....405 385-9890
303 Twin Dolphin Dr Fl 6 Redwood City (94065) ***(P-13432)***
Secugen Corporation ....E....408 834-7712
2065 Martin Ave Ste 102 Santa Clara (95050) ***(P-5409)***
Secure Computing Corporation (HQ) ....E....**408 979-2020**
3965 Freedom Cir 4 Santa Clara (95054) ***(P-13433)***
Securecom Inc ....D....916 638-2855
4822 Gldn Fthl Pkwy # 4 El Dorado Hills (95762) ***(P-1603)***
Securelion Security, Tracy *Also called Courtesy Security Inc* ***(P-14047)***
Securitas SEC Svcs USA Inc ....C....510 568-6818
505 Montgomery St San Francisco (94111) ***(P-14093)***
Securiti Inc ....C....408 401-1160
3031 Tisch Way Ste 502 San Jose (95128) ***(P-12769)***
Security Alarm Fing Entps Inc ....D....925 830-4786
2440 Camino Ramon Ste 200 San Ramon (94583) ***(P-14147)***
Security Central Inc ....E....510 652-2477
2950 Alvarado St Ste D San Leandro (94577) ***(P-14775)***
Security Classification Inc ....E....707 301-6052
2339 Gold Meadow Way Gold River (95670) ***(P-14402)***

ALPHABETIC

Security Contractor Svcs Inc (PA) ....D....**916 338-4200**
5339 Jackson St North Highlands (95660) ***(P-8646)***
Security Indust Spcialists Inc ....C....408 247-0100
2880 Stevens Creek Blvd San Jose (95128) ***(P-14094)***
Security MGT Group Intl Inc ....E....925 521-1500
3353 Alder Canyon Way Antelope (95843) ***(P-14095)***
Security Nat Mstr Holdg Co LLC (PA) ....C....**707 442-2818**
323 5th St Eureka (95501) ***(P-9926)***
Security Nat Prpts Holdg LLC (HQ) ....E....**707 476-2702**
323 5th St Eureka (95501) ***(P-10404)***
Security National Funding Tr, Eureka *Also called Security Nat Prpts Holdg LLC* ***(P-10404)***
Security Pacific Real Estate ....E....510 222-9772
3223 Blume Dr Ste 227 Richmond (94806) ***(P-10661)***
Security People Inc ....E....707 766-6000
9 Willowbrook Ct Petaluma (94954) ***(P-6468)***
Securly Inc (HQ) ....D....**855 732-8759**
111 N Market St Ste 400 San Jose (95113) ***(P-13434)***
Sedgwick Claims MGT Svcs Inc ....D....916 771-2900
1410 Rocky Ridge Dr Ste 3 Roseville (95661) ***(P-10343)***
Sedgwick Claims MGT Svcs Inc ....D....925 988-1536
1600 Riviera Ave Ste 405 Walnut Creek (94596) ***(P-10344)***
Sedgwick Claims MGT Svcs Inc ....D....510 302-3000
2101 Webster St Oakland (94612) ***(P-10345)***
Sedgwick Claims MGT Svcs Inc ....D....916 568-7394
1851 Heritage Ln Sacramento (95815) ***(P-10346)***
See's Candies, South San Francisco *Also called Sees Candy Shops Incorporated* ***(P-2433)***
Seed Factory Northwest Inc (PA) ....E....**209 634-8522**
4319 Jessup Rd Ceres (95307) ***(P-2358)***
Seedif Inc ....E....408 930-3446
85 Tamalpais Ave Mill Valley (94941) ***(P-12135)***
Seeds of Awareness Inc ....E....510 788-0876
2501 Harrison St Oakland (94612) ***(P-17071)***
Seeger's Printing, Turlock *Also called Seegers Industries Inc* ***(P-3696)***
Seegers Industries Inc ....E....209 667-2750
210 N Center St Turlock (95380) ***(P-3696)***
Seer Inc ....D....650 453-0000
3800 Bridge Pkwy Ste 102 Redwood City (94065) ***(P-6849)***
Sees Candy Shops Incorporated (HQ) ....E....**650 761-2490**
210 El Camino Real South San Francisco (94080) ***(P-2433)***
Segale Bros Wood Products Inc ....E....510 300-1170
1705 Sabre St Hayward (94545) ***(P-1755)***
Seghesio Family Vineyards, Healdsburg *Also called Pine Ridge Winery LLC* ***(P-2684)***
Seghesio Wineries Inc ....E....707 433-3579
700 Grove St Healdsburg (95448) ***(P-2712)***
Seghesio Winery, Healdsburg *Also called Seghesio Wineries Inc* ***(P-2712)***
Segmentio Inc ....B....844 611-0621
101 Spear St Fl 1 San Francisco (94105) ***(P-5410)***
Seguin Moreau NAPA Cooperage, NAPA *Also called Seguin Moreau USA Holdings Inc* ***(P-3240)***
Seguin Moreau USA Holdings Inc (HQ) ....E....**707 252-3408**
151 Camino Dorado NAPA (94558) ***(P-3240)***
Seguin Mreau NAPA Coperage Inc ....D....707 252-3408
151 Camino Dorado NAPA (94558) ***(P-9133)***
Segundo Metal Products Inc ....D....925 667-2009
7855 Southfront Rd Livermore (94551) ***(P-4816)***
Seiler LLP (PA) ....C....**650 365-4646**
3 Lagoon Dr Ste 400 Redwood City (94065) ***(P-18991)***
Seiler LLP ....D....415 392-2123
220 Montgomery St Ste 300 San Francisco (94104) ***(P-18992)***
Seirra Telephone, Oakhurst *Also called Sierra Tel Cmmunications Group* ***(P-7989)***
SEIU Local 1021 ....D....510 350-9811
447 29th St Oakland (94609) ***(P-18372)***
Seiu Uhw West, San Francisco *Also called Seiu Untd Hlthcare Wrkrs-West* ***(P-18375)***
Seiu Uhw-W & Joint Employer Ed (PA) ....E....**510 250-6800**
1000 Broadway Ste 675 Oakland (94607) ***(P-10790)***
Seiu Uhw-West, Sacramento *Also called Seiu Untd Hlthcare Wrkrs-West* ***(P-18374)***
Seiu Uhw-West, San Jose *Also called Seiu Untd Hlthcare Wrkrs-West* ***(P-18376)***
Seiu United Healthcare Workers (PA) ....C....**510 251-1250**
560 Thomas L Berkley Way Oakland (94612) ***(P-18373)***
Seiu Untd Hlthcare Wrkrs-West ....E....916 326-5850
1911 F St Sacramento (95811) ***(P-18374)***
Seiu Untd Hlthcare Wrkrs-West ....E....415 441-2500
47 Kearny St Fl 4 San Francisco (94108) ***(P-18375)***
Seiu Untd Hlthcare Wrkrs-West ....E....408 557-2835
2995 Moorpark Ave San Jose (95128) ***(P-18376)***
Select Communications Inc ....E....650 948-9000
138 Main St Los Altos (94022) ***(P-3514)***
Select Harvest Usa LLC (PA) ....C....**209 668-2471**
14827 W Harding Rd Turlock (95380) ***(P-9511)***
Select Hotels Group LLC ....E....925 743-1882
2323 San Ramon Vly Blvd San Ramon (94583) ***(P-11453)***
Select Hotels Group LLC ....E....510 601-5880
5800 Shellmound St Emeryville (94608) ***(P-11454)***
Select Hotels Group LLC ....E....510 623-6000
3101 W Warren Ave Fremont (94538) ***(P-11455)***
Select Hotels Group LLC ....E....408 486-0800
3915 Rivermark Plz Santa Clara (95054) ***(P-11456)***
Select Hotels Group LLC ....E....916 638-4141
11260 Point East Dr Rancho Cordova (95742) ***(P-11457)***
Select Hotels Group LLC ....E....916 781-6400
220 Conference Center Dr Roseville (95678) ***(P-11458)***
Select Hotels Group LLC ....E....408 324-1155
75 Headquarters Dr San Jose (95134) ***(P-11459)***
Selectiva Systems Inc ....E....408 297-1336
2051 Junction Ave Ste 225 San Jose (95131) ***(P-12770)***
Selectquote Insurance Services (HQ) ....C....**415 543-7338**
1440 Broadway Ste 1000 Oakland (94612) ***(P-10347)***
Selex Inc (PA) ....D....**707 836-8836**
442 Longfellow St Livermore (94550) ***(P-2066)***
Self-Dscvery Thrptic Exprnce P ....E....650 303-7365
14976 Swenson St San Leandro (94579) ***(P-17726)***
Self-Help For Elderly ....D....415 391-3843
777 Stockton St Ste 110 San Francisco (94108) ***(P-17727)***
Self-Help For Elderly (PA) ....C....**415 677-7600**
731 Sansome St Ste 100 San Francisco (94111) ***(P-17728)***
Self-Help For Elderly ....D....415 677-7581
1483 Mason St San Francisco (94133) ***(P-15240)***
Self-Help For The Elderly, San Francisco *Also called Sustainable San Mateo County* ***(P-18600)***
Selig Construction Corp ....E....530 893-5898
337 Huss Dr Chico (95928) ***(P-705)***
Selland's Market Cafe, Sacramento *Also called Sellands Broadway Inc* ***(P-19629)***
Sellands Broadway Inc ....E....916 732-3390
915 Broadway Ste 300 Sacramento (95818) ***(P-19629)***
Selligent Inc (HQ) ....C....**650 421-4255**
1300 Island Dr Ste 200 Redwood City (94065) ***(P-13662)***
Selma Convalescent Hospital, Selma *Also called Nia Healthcare Services Inc* ***(P-16069)***
Selma Pallet Inc ....E....559 896-7171
1651 Pacific St Selma (93662) ***(P-3229)***
Selma-Kngsburg-Fowler Cnty Stn ....E....559 897-6500
11301 E Conejo Ave Kingsburg (93631) ***(P-8289)***
Seltzer Revolutions Inc ....F....604 765-9966
2911 Branciforte Dr Santa Cruz (95065) ***(P-2778)***
Selvi-Vidovich LP ....D....408 720-8500
865 W El Camino Real Sunnyvale (94087) ***(P-11460)***
Selway Machine Tool Co Inc (PA) ....E....**510 487-9291**
29250 Union City Blvd Union City (94587) ***(P-9094)***
Semano Inc ....E....510 489-2360
31757 Knapp St Hayward (94544) ***(P-4920)***
Semi (PA) ....C....**408 943-6900**
673 S Milpitas Blvd Milpitas (95035) ***(P-18318)***
Semi Automation & Tech Inc ....E....408 374-9549
1510 Dell Ave Ste C Campbell (95008) ***(P-6280)***
Semicat Inc (PA) ....E....**408 514-6900**
47900 Fremont Blvd Fremont (94538) ***(P-6281)***
Semicndctor Cmponents Inds LLC ....E....408 660-2699
3001 Stender Way Santa Clara (95054) ***(P-6282)***
Semicndctor Cmponents Inds LLC ....C....408 542-1051
3001 Stender Way Santa Clara (95054) ***(P-6373)***
Semifab Inc ....D....408 414-5928
2027 Otoole Ave San Jose (95131) ***(P-6733)***
Semifreddi's Bakery, Alameda *Also called Semifreddis Inc* ***(P-9483)***
Semifreddis Inc (PA) ....C....**510 596-9930**
1980 N Loop Rd Alameda (94502) ***(P-9483)***
Seminet Inc ....E....408 754-8537
150 Great Oaks Blvd San Jose (95119) ***(P-6283)***
Semler Scientific Inc (PA) ....D....**877 774-4211**
2340-2348 Wlsh Ave Ste 23 Santa Clara (95051) ***(P-7032)***
Semotus Inc ....E....408 667-2046
20 S Santa Cruz Ave # 300 Los Gatos (95030) ***(P-13435)***
Semotus Solutions Inc ....F....408 367-1745
20 S Santa Cruz Ave # 300 Los Gatos (95030) ***(P-13436)***
Semprex Corporation ....E....408 379-3230
782 Camden Ave Campbell (95008) ***(P-6791)***
Sender Inc ....D....888 717-3287
447 Battery St Ste 200 San Francisco (94111) ***(P-17178)***
Sendmail Inc ....C....510 594-5400
892 Ross Dr Sunnyvale (94089) ***(P-7988)***
Sendoso, San Francisco *Also called Sender Inc* ***(P-17178)***
Seneca Center, Oakland *Also called Seneca Family of Agencies* ***(P-17729)***
SENECA CENTER, Oakland *Also called Seneca Family of Agencies* ***(P-17730)***
Seneca Family of Agencies ....B....510 317-1444
8945 Golf Links Rd Oakland (94605) ***(P-17729)***
Seneca Family of Agencies (PA) ....E....**510 317-1444**
8945 Golf Links Rd Oakland (94605) ***(P-17730)***
Seneca Family of Agencies ....B....707 429-4440
1234 Empire St Fairfield (94533) ***(P-17731)***
Seneca Family of Agencies ....B....510 434-7990
3695 High St Oakland (94619) ***(P-17732)***
Seneca Healthcare District (PA) ....C....**530 258-2151**
130 Brentwood Dr Chester (96020) ***(P-16519)***
Senetrics International, Berkeley *Also called Sensys Networks Inc* ***(P-5896)***
Senior Asssted Lving Cmnty Cht, Pleasant Hill *Also called Carlton Senior Living Inc* ***(P-18067)***
Senior Companions At Home LLC ....E....650 364-1265
650 El Camino Real Ste E Redwood City (94063) ***(P-16941)***
Senior Helpers, Cameron Park *Also called Dnt In Home Care Inc* ***(P-16879)***
Senior Living Solutions LLC ....C....408 385-1835
1725 S Bascom Ave Apt 105 Campbell (95008) ***(P-16202)***
Senior Mercy Housing Inc ....D....916 733-6510
3865 J St Sacramento (95816) ***(P-18179)***
Senior Nutrition, Fort Bragg *Also called Redwood Coast Seniors Inc* ***(P-17684)***
Seniors At Home, Palo Alto *Also called Jewish Family and Chld Svcs* ***(P-17624)***
Senju Comtek Corp ....F....408 792-3830
1171 N 4th St Ste 80 San Jose (95112) ***(P-4593)***
Senor Sisig ....D....415 608-5048
2277 Shafter Ave San Francisco (94124) ***(P-15241)***
Sensbey Inc (PA) ....F....**650 697-2032**
833 Mahler Rd Ste 3 Burlingame (94010) ***(P-5105)***
Sense Talent Labs Inc (PA) ....E....**408 674-5180**
225 Bush St Ste 1350 San Francisco (94104) ***(P-19630)***
Sensiba San Filippo LLP (PA) ....E....**925 271-8700**
5960 Inglewood Dr Ste 201 Pleasanton (94588) ***(P-18993)***
Sensient Dehydrated Flavors, Turlock *Also called Sensient Ntral Ingredients LLC* ***(P-2942)***
Sensient Ntral Ingredients LLC (HQ) ....E....**209 667-2777**
151 S Walnut Rd Turlock (95380) ***(P-2942)***

Sensity Systems Inc (HQ)....E....408 841-4200
1237 E Arques Ave Sunnyvale (94085) *(P-19859)*
Sensor Concepts LLC....D....925 443-9001
7950 National Dr Livermore (94550) *(P-18810)*
Sensory Inc (PA)....D....408 625-3302
4701 Patrick Henry Dr # 7 Santa Clara (95054) *(P-12771)*
Sensys Networks Inc (HQ)....D....510 548-4620
1608 4th St Ste 110 Berkeley (94710) *(P-5896)*
Sentient Technologies USA LLC....E....415 422-9886
611 Mission St Fl 6 San Francisco (94105) *(P-12772)*
Sentinelone Inc (PA)....A....855 868-3733
444 Castro St Ste 400 Mountain View (94041) *(P-13437)*
Sentons Usa Inc....E....408 732-9000
627 River Oaks Pkwy San Jose (95134) *(P-6284)*
Sentry Life Insurance Company....C....925 370-7339
535 Main St Fl 2 Martinez (94553) *(P-10348)*
Sepasoft Inc....E....916 939-1684
1262 Hawks Flight Ct # 190 El Dorado Hills (95762) *(P-13438)*
Sepragen Corporation....E....510 475-0650
33470 Western Ave Union City (94587) *(P-6850)*
Sequent Software Inc....F....650 419-2713
4699 Old Ironsides Dr # 470 Santa Clara (95054) *(P-13439)*
Sequenta LLC....E....650 243-3900
329 Oyster Point Blvd South San Francisco (94080) *(P-4029)*
Sequoia Bnefits Insur Svcs LLC (PA)....D....650 369-0200
1850 Gateway Dr Ste 600 San Mateo (94404) *(P-10349)*
Sequoia Capital Operations LLC (PA)....D....650 854-3927
2800 Sand Hill Rd Ste 101 Menlo Park (94025) *(P-10882)*
Sequoia Elementary School Pta....E....916 228-5850
3333 Rosemont Dr Sacramento (95826) *(P-18466)*
Sequoia Health Services (HQ)....A....650 369-5811
170 Alameda De Las Pulgas Redwood City (94062) *(P-16520)*
Sequoia Hospital, Redwood City *Also called Sequoia Health Services (P-16520)*
Sequoia Insurance Company....D....916 933-9524
P.O. Box 1510 Monterey (93942) *(P-10350)*
Sequoia Landscape MGT Inc....E....408 277-6390
1071 N 13th St San Jose (95112) *(P-438)*
Sequoia Living Inc....C....415 351-7956
1400 Geary Blvd San Francisco (94109) *(P-16267)*
Sequoia Living Inc....C....415 464-1767
501 Via Casitas Ofc Greenbrae (94904) *(P-16268)*
Sequoia Living Inc....E....415 776-0114
711 Eddy St Ofc San Francisco (94109) *(P-18180)*
Sequoia Living Health Services, San Francisco *Also called Sequoia Living Inc (P-16267)*
Sequoia Medical Associates, Redwood City *Also called Sequoia Medical Clinic (P-15677)*
Sequoia Medical Clinic (PA)....D....650 261-2300
2900 Whipple Ave Ste 130 Redwood City (94062) *(P-15677)*
Sequoia Residential Funding....D....415 389-7373
1 Belvedere Pl Ste 330 Mill Valley (94941) *(P-9875)*
Sequoia Safety Council Inc....E....559 638-9995
500 E 11th St Reedley (93654) *(P-7404)*
Sequoia Senior Solutions Inc....D....707 263-3070
825 S Main St Lakeport (95453) *(P-16942)*
Sequoia Senior Solutions Inc (PA)....C....707 763-6600
1372 N Mcdowell Blvd S Petaluma (94954) *(P-16943)*
Sequoia Steel and Supply Co....F....559 485-4100
1407 N Clark St Fresno (93703) *(P-8634)*
Sequoia Surgical Center LP....E....925 935-6700
2405 Shadelands Dr # 200 Walnut Creek (94598) *(P-16521)*
Sequoia Surgical Pavilion, Walnut Creek *Also called Sequoia Surgical Center LP (P-16521)*
Sequoia Wood Country Club....D....209 795-1000
1000 Cypress Point Dr Arnold (95223) *(P-15139)*
Sequoia YMCA, Redwood City *Also called Young MNS Chrstn Assn Slcon Vl (P-18530)*
Sequoias, The, Portola Valley *Also called Northern California Presbyteri (P-18150)*
Sequos-San Frncsco Residential, San Francisco *Also called Northern California Presbyteri (P-16076)*
Sequoyah Country Club....C....510 632-2900
4550 Heafey Rd Oakland (94605) *(P-15140)*
Sequoyah Golf Shop, Oakland *Also called Sequoyah Country Club (P-15140)*
Ser-Jobs For Prgress Inc - San (PA)....D....559 452-0881
255 N Fulton St Ste 106 Fresno (93701) *(P-17733)*
Seradyn Inc....D....317 610-3800
46360 Fremont Blvd Fremont (94538) *(P-6851)*
Serendipity School, San Mateo *Also called Clearview Quest Corporation (P-17909)*
Serenity Knolls....D....415 488-0400
145 Tamal Rd Forest Knolls (94933) *(P-17072)*
Serenity Now Lessee Inc....E....415 885-2500
405 Taylor St San Francisco (94102) *(P-11461)*
Serenity Spprted Lving Svc LLC (PA)....E....650 773-2762
813 Harbor Blvd West Sacramento (95691) *(P-17734)*
Seres Inc....C....214 585-3356
3303 Scott Blvd Santa Clara (95054) *(P-6498)*
Serpico Landscaping Inc....E....510 293-0341
1764 National Ave Hayward (94545) *(P-439)*
Serra Bowl Inc (PA)....E....415 626-2626
701 Price St Daly City (94014) *(P-14899)*
Serra Systems Inc (HQ)....F....707 433-5104
126 Mill St Healdsburg (95448) *(P-13440)*
Serra Yellow Cab Daly City Inc....E....650 333-9598
195 87th St Ste D Daly City (94015) *(P-7414)*
Serrano Associates LLC....D....916 939-3333
5005 Serrano Pkwy El Dorado Hills (95762) *(P-15141)*
Serrano Country Club, El Dorado Hills *Also called Serrano Associates LLC (P-15141)*
Serrano Country Club Inc....C....916 933-5005
5005 Serrano Pkwy P El Dorado Hills (95762) *(P-15142)*
Serrano Electric Inc....E....408 986-1570
15920 Concord Cir Morgan Hill (95037) *(P-1604)*
Serrano Hotel, San Francisco *Also called Kimpton Hotel & Rest Group LLC (P-11230)*
Serrato-Mcdermott Inc....D....510 656-6233
43815 S Grimmer Blvd Fremont (94538) *(P-8466)*
Servalan Enterprises Inc....E....415 899-1880
261 Wilson Ave Novato (94947) *(P-13971)*
Serve Robotics Inc....D....415 590-0160
1050 Noriega St San Francisco (94122) *(P-7653)*
Servi-Tech Controls Inc (PA)....D....559 264-6679
470 W Warwick Ave Clovis (93619) *(P-1356)*
Service By Medallion....A....650 625-1010
411 Clyde Ave Mountain View (94043) *(P-11996)*
Service Champions, Rocklin *Also called On-Time AC & Htg LLC (P-1324)*
Service Champions, San Jose *Also called On-Time AC & Htg LLC (P-1325)*
Service Champions, Concord *Also called On-Time AC & Htg LLC (P-1326)*
Service Champions, Livermore *Also called On-Time AC & Htg LLC (P-1327)*
Service Champions, Pleasanton *Also called On-Time AC & Htg LLC (P-1328)*
Service Emplyees Intl Un Lcal, San Jose *Also called Service Workers Local 715 (P-18377)*
Service Express Inc....E....559 495-4790
3619 S Fowler Ave Fresno (93725) *(P-3598)*
Service Hospitality LLC....D....925 566-8820
1050 Burnett Ave Concord (94520) *(P-11462)*
Service League San Mateo Cnty....E....650 364-4664
727 Middlefield Rd Redwood City (94063) *(P-17735)*
Service Opprtunity For Seniors....E....510 582-1263
2235 Polvorosa Ave # 260 San Leandro (94577) *(P-17736)*
Service Printing Co, San Leandro *Also called Edelstein Printing Co (P-3642)*
Service Station Systems Inc....E....408 971-2445
680 Quinn Ave San Jose (95112) *(P-2067)*
Service Workers Local 715 (PA)....E....408 678-3300
2302 Zanker Rd San Jose (95131) *(P-18377)*
Serviceaide Inc (PA)....E....650 206-8988
1762 Tech Dr Ste 116 San Jose (95110) *(P-13441)*
ServiceMaster, South San Francisco *Also called Cephas Enterprises Inc (P-11934)*
ServiceMaster, Merced *Also called Melin Enterprises Inc (P-11971)*
ServiceMaster, Grass Valley *Also called M & C Restoration Inc (P-11969)*
Servicemax Inc (PA)....C....925 965-7859
4450 Rosewood Dr Ste 200 Pleasanton (94588) *(P-12773)*
Servicenow Inc (PA)....E....408 501-8550
2225 Lawson Ln Santa Clara (95054) *(P-13972)*
Servicenow Delaware LLC (HQ)....A....408 501-8550
2225 Lawson Ln Santa Clara (95054) *(P-13973)*
SERVPRO Belmont / San Carlos, Stockton *Also called Cleanair Image Inc (P-11936)*
SERVPRO of Mendocino....E....707 462-3848
3001 S State St Ste 5 Ukiah (95482) *(P-11997)*
SERVPRO OF PETALUMA ROHNERT PA, Cotati *Also called Pacific Restoration Inc (P-11983)*
Sesame Software Inc (PA)....E....408 550-7999
5201 Great America Pkwy Santa Clara (95054) *(P-13442)*
Set A Head Start Westside, Sacramento *Also called Sacramnto Emplyment Trning AGC (P-17836)*
Seta, Sacramento *Also called Sacramento Employement & Train (P-17834)*
Sethi Conglomerate LLC....E....559 275-2374
5455 W Shaw Ave Fresno (93722) *(P-11463)*
Seti Institute....C....650 961-6633
339 Bernardo Ave Ste 200 Mountain View (94043) *(P-19236)*
Seti Institute, The, Mountain View *Also called Seti Institute (P-19236)*
Seton Medical Center (HQ)....A....650 992-4000
1900 Sullivan Ave Daly City (94015) *(P-16522)*
Seton Medical Center....C....650 563-7100
600 Marine Blvd Moss Beach (94038) *(P-16523)*
Seton Medical Center....D....650 992-4000
1784 Sullivan Ave Ste 200 Daly City (94015) *(P-16524)*
Seton Medical Center Coastside, Moss Beach *Also called Seton Medical Center (P-16523)*
Setzer Forest Products Inc (PA)....C....916 442-2555
2555 3rd St Ste 200 Sacramento (95818) *(P-3150)*
Setzer Forest Products Inc....C....530 534-8100
1980 Kusel Rd Oroville (95966) *(P-3105)*
Seva Foundation....D....510 845-7382
1786 5th St Berkeley (94710) *(P-17179)*
Seven Up Bottling, Sacramento *Also called Capitol Beverage Packers (P-2785)*
Seven Up Btlg Co San Francisco (HQ)....C....925 938-8777
2875 Prune Ave Fremont (94539) *(P-2812)*
Seven Up Btlg Co San Francisco....C....916 929-7777
2670 Land Ave Sacramento (95815) *(P-2813)*
Seven-Up Bottling, Fremont *Also called Seven Up Btlg Co San Francisco (P-2812)*
Seven-Up Bottling, Sacramento *Also called Seven Up Btlg Co San Francisco (P-2813)*
Seventh Heaven Inc....E....408 287-8945
1025 S 5th St San Jose (95112) *(P-3053)*
Severson & Werson A Prof Corp....C....415 398-3344
1 Embarcadero Ctr Ste 260 San Francisco (94111) *(P-17368)*
Seville Landscape Construction, Sunnyvale *Also called Seville Maintenance Inc (P-501)*
Seville Maintenance Inc....E....650 966-1091
214 Commercial St Sunnyvale (94085) *(P-501)*
Sew-Eurodrive Inc....E....510 487-3560
30599 San Antonio St Hayward (94544) *(P-5214)*
Sewer Maintenance, Stockton *Also called County of San Joaquin (P-1094)*
Seyfarth Shaw LLP....D....415 397-2823
560 Mission St Fl 31 San Francisco (94105) *(P-17369)*
Seyfarth Shaw LLP....C....916 448-0159
400 Capitol Mall Ste 2350 Sacramento (95814) *(P-17370)*
SF Marriott Marquis....E....415 896-1600
780 Mission St San Francisco (94103) *(P-11464)*
SF Mini Bus, San Francisco *Also called Minitrans Corporation (P-7418)*
SF Motors Inc (HQ)....C....408 617-7878
3303 Scott Blvd Santa Clara (95054) *(P-6558)*
SF Sierra Co Inc....E....415 752-2850
3112 Geary Blvd San Francisco (94118) *(P-1605)*

ALPHABETIC

SF Tube Inc...E.......510 785-9148
23099 Connecticut St Hayward (94545) *(P-4977)*
SF-MARIN FOOD BANK, San Francisco *Also called San Francisco Food Bank (P-17710)*
SFCCC, San Francisco *Also called San Frncsco Cmnty Clnic Cnsrti (P-19394)*
SFCM, San Francisco *Also called San Frncsco Cnservatory of Mus (P-14877)*
SFCU, Palo Alto *Also called Stanford Federal Credit Union (P-9821)*
Sfd Partners LLC...B.......415 392-7755
450 Powell St San Francisco (94102) *(P-11465)*
Sfdph...E.......415 554-2686
1424 18th Ave San Francisco (94122) *(P-18467)*
Sff, Sacramento *Also called Sierra Forever Families (P-17744)*
SFFCU, San Francisco *Also called San Francisco Fire Credit Un (P-9811)*
Sffi Company Inc (PA)...**C.......323 586-0000**
11020 White Rock Rd Ste 1 Rancho Cordova (95670) *(P-9428)*
SFMOMA MUSEUM STORE, San Francisco *Also called San Francisco Museum Modrn Art (P-18279)*
Sfn Group Inc...A.......650 348-4967
919 E Hillsdale Blvd Foster City (94404) *(P-12194)*
Sfn Group Inc...A.......408 526-0115
401 River Oaks Pkwy San Jose (95134) *(P-12195)*
Sfn Group Inc...A.......530 222-3434
3050 Bictor Ave Ste A Redding (96002) *(P-12196)*
Sfn Group Inc...A.......925 847-8500
3825 Hopyard Rd Ste 270 Pleasanton (94588) *(P-12197)*
Sfn Group Inc...A.......408 452-4845
2150 N 1st St Ste 230 San Jose (95131) *(P-12198)*
Sfn Group Inc...A.......707 551-2719
1 Meyer Plz Vallejo (94590) *(P-12199)*
Sfny Group Inc...E.......510 646-1360
1901 Harrison St Ste 1100 Oakland (94612) *(P-19397)*
Sfo, San Francisco *Also called San Francisco Intl Arprt (P-7783)*
Sfo Airporter Inc (PA)...**D.......650 246-2734**
1535 S 10th St San Jose (95112) *(P-7358)*
Sfo Airporter Inc...D.......415 495-3909
325 5th St San Francisco (94107) *(P-7359)*
Sfo Apparel...C.......415 468-8816
41 Park Pl 43 Brisbane (94005) *(P-3013)*
Sfo-3 - San Francisco Full Svc, Brisbane *Also called Expeditors Intl Wash Inc (P-7833)*
Sg Downtown LLC...E.......916 545-7100
500 J St Fl 4 Sacramento (95814) *(P-11466)*
Sgm Inc...E.......559 665-4462
9521 Morton Davis Dr Patterson (95363) *(P-15025)*
SGS Forensic Laboratories, Hayward *Also called SGS SA (P-19284)*
SGS SA...D.......800 827-3274
3777 Depot Rd Ste 409 Hayward (94545) *(P-19284)*
Sgws of CA, Union City *Also called Southern Glzers Wine Sprits WA (P-9585)*
Shafer Vineyards...F.......707 944-2877
6154 Silverado Trl NAPA (94558) *(P-2713)*
Shai, San Mateo *Also called Stottler Henke Associates Inc (P-13982)*
Shaker Cabinet Co (PA)...**E.......925 286-6066**
535 Palms Dr Martinez (94553) *(P-3191)*
Shalley-Dibble Incorporated...E.......510 769-7600
1305 Marina Village Pkwy # 1 Alameda (94501) *(P-18811)*
Shames Construction Co Ltd...E.......925 606-3000
5826 Brisa St Livermore (94550) *(P-959)*
Shamrock Foods Company...B.......602 819-1654
856 National Dr Sacramento (95834) *(P-9484)*
Shamrock Materials Inc (PA)...**E.......707 781-9000**
181 Lynch Creek Way # 201 Petaluma (94954) *(P-4505)*
Shamrock Materials of Novato...D.......415 892-1571
7552 Redwood Blvd Novato (94945) *(P-4506)*
Shandi Inc...D.......209 847-5951
11536 Cleveland Ave Oakdale (95361) *(P-336)*
Shane Alxander Cstm Tile Stone...E.......916 652-0250
1415 Nichols Dr Rocklin (95765) *(P-1719)*
Shannon Pump Co...E.......209 723-3904
275 S State Highway 59 Merced (95341) *(P-9095)*
Shannon Ranches Inc...C.......707 998-9656
12601 E Highway 20 Clearlake Oaks (95423) *(P-19631)*
Shannon Ridge Inc...E.......707 994-9656
13888 Point Lakeview Rd Lower Lake (95457) *(P-2714)*
Shannon Side Welding Inc (PA)...**E.......415 408-3219**
214 Shaw Rd Ste I South San Francisco (94080) *(P-14721)*
Shapco Inc...D.......559 834-1342
5220 S Peach Ave Fresno (93725) *(P-4978)*
Shape Memory Applications, San Jose *Also called Johnson Matthey Inc (P-6993)*
Shape Products, Oakland *Also called Vulpine Inc (P-4169)*
Shape Security Inc (HQ)...**C.......650 399-0400**
800 W El Cmino Real Ste 2 Mountain View (94040) *(P-12774)*
Sharcar Enterprises Inc...E.......209 531-2200
201 Winmoore Way Modesto (95358) *(P-4522)*
Sharehlder Rprsnttive Svcs LLC (PA)...**E.......303 648-4085**
601 Montgomery St Ste 750 San Francisco (94111) *(P-19398)*
Sharethis Inc (PA)...**E.......650 641-0191**
3000 El Cmino Real Ste 5 Palo Alto (94306) *(P-11782)*
Sharethrough Inc (PA)...**E.......415 644-0054**
170 Columbus Ave Ste 280 San Francisco (94133) *(P-11817)*
Sharks Sports & Entrmt LLC...A.......408 287-7070
525 W Santa Clara St San Jose (95113) *(P-14916)*
Sharp Dimension Inc...E.......510 656-8938
4240 Business Center Dr Fremont (94538) *(P-5617)*
Sharpswitch Inc...D.......866 633-6944
2655 Hill Park Dr San Jose (95124) *(P-12775)*
Shartsis Friese LLP...C.......415 421-6500
1 Maritime Plz Fl 18 San Francisco (94111) *(P-17371)*
Shascade Community Svcs Inc...D.......530 247-8324
900 Twin View Blvd Redding (96003) *(P-17737)*
Shascade Community Svcs Inc...D.......530 243-1653
1319 Sacramento St Redding (96001) *(P-17738)*
Shasta Beverages Inc (HQ)...**D.......954 581-0922**
26901 Indl Blvd Hayward (94545) *(P-2814)*
Shasta Blood Center, San Francisco *Also called Vitalant Research Institute (P-17189)*
Shasta County Head Start Child (PA)...**E.......530 241-1036**
375 Lake Blvd Ste 100 Redding (96003) *(P-18018)*
Shasta County Office Education...E.......530 225-0285
1644 Magnolia Ave Redding (96001) *(P-11610)*
Shasta County Women S Refuge...E.......530 244-0117
2280 Benton Dr Ste A Redding (96003) *(P-17739)*
Shasta County YMCA...E.......530 605-3330
1155 N Court St Redding (96001) *(P-18468)*
Shasta Electronic Mfg Svcs Inc...F.......408 436-1267
525 E Brokaw Rd San Jose (95112) *(P-5271)*
Shasta Ems, San Jose *Also called Shasta Electronic Mfg Svcs Inc (P-5271)*
Shasta Eye Medical Group Inc (PA)...**D.......530 226-5966**
3190 Churn Creek Rd Redding (96002) *(P-15678)*
Shasta Family, The, Redding *Also called Shasta County YMCA (P-18468)*
Shasta Forest Products Inc...E.......530 842-2787
1423 Montague Rd Yreka (96097) *(P-3271)*
Shasta Green Inc...E.......530 335-4924
35586a State Hwy 299 E Burney (96013) *(P-3078)*
Shasta Linen Supply Inc...E.......916 443-5966
1931 E St Sacramento (95811) *(P-11646)*
Shasta Orthpedics Spt Medicine...E.......530 246-2467
1255 Liberty St Redding (96001) *(P-15679)*
Shasta Point Retirement Cmnty, Davis *Also called Rvm Davis Housing Corporation (P-18174)*
Shasta Produce Co, South San Francisco *Also called Andrighetto Produce Inc (P-9386)*
Shasta Regional Med Ctr Srmc, Redding *Also called Prime Hlthcare Svcs - Shsta LL (P-16483)*
Shasta Senior Ntrtn Program (HQ)...**E.......530 226-3059**
200 Mercy Oaks Dr Redding (96003) *(P-17740)*
Shasta Services Inc...E.......530 926-4093
624 S Mount Shasta Blvd Mount Shasta (96067) *(P-960)*
Shasta.com, Redding *Also called Inter Star Inc (P-7964)*
Shattuck Health Care Inc...D.......510 665-2800
2829 Shattuck Ave Berkeley (94705) *(P-16114)*
Shaw & Petersen Insurance Inc...E.......707 443-0845
1313 5th St Eureka (95501) *(P-10351)*
Shaw Bakers LLC...C.......650 273-1440
320b Shaw Rd Ste B South San Francisco (94080) *(P-9485)*
Shaw Construction, Fresno *Also called Shaws Strctures Unlimited Inc (P-809)*
Shaws Strctures Unlimited Inc...E.......559 275-3475
2435 N Grantland Ave Fresno (93723) *(P-809)*
Shc Reference Laboratory, Palo Alto *Also called Stanford Health Care (P-16558)*
SHD, Chester *Also called Seneca Healthcare District (P-16519)*
Shea Lbagh Dbbrstein Crtif Pub (PA)...**E.......415 308-1368**
44 Montgomery St Ste 3200 San Francisco (94104) *(P-18994)*
Sheathing Technologies Inc...E.......408 782-2720
675 Jarvis Dr Ste A Morgan Hill (95037) *(P-7033)*
Sheeba Duleep...E.......267 250-9106
28850 Dixon St Apt 408 Hayward (94544) *(P-12776)*
Sheedy Drayage Co (PA)...**D.......415 648-7171**
1215 Michigan St San Francisco (94107) *(P-12022)*
Sheehan Construction Inc...D.......707 603-2610
477 Devlin Rd Ste 108 NAPA (94558) *(P-706)*
Sheet Metal Training Center...D.......510 483-9035
1700 Marina Blvd San Leandro (94577) *(P-18590)*
Sheet Mtal Fabrication Sup Inc...D.......916 641-6884
2020 Railroad Dr Sacramento (95815) *(P-4817)*
Shell Vacations Club, San Francisco *Also called Inn At Opera A Cal Ltd Partnr (P-11190)*
Shellpro Inc...E.......209 334-2081
18378 Atkins Rd Lodi (95240) *(P-7307)*
Shelter Inc (PA)...**D.......925 335-0698**
1333 Willow Pass Rd # 206 Concord (94520) *(P-17741)*
Shelter Solano Inc...D.......925 957-7576
1333 Willow Pass Rd # 20 Concord (94520) *(P-17742)*
Sheng-Kee Bakery, San Francisco *Also called Sheng-Kee of California Inc (P-9486)*
Sheng-Kee of California Inc (PA)...**E.......415 564-4800**
1941 Irving St San Francisco (94122) *(P-9486)*
Sheplace Design Center, San Francisco *Also called Bay West Shwplace Invstors LLC (P-10377)*
Sheppard Mllin Rchter Hmpton L...D.......415 434-9100
4 Embarcadero Ctr # 1700 San Francisco (94111) *(P-17372)*
Sheraton, Sunnyvale *Also called Msr Hotels & Resorts Inc (P-11316)*
Sheraton, Pleasanton *Also called Wh Pleasanton Hotel LP (P-11575)*
Sheraton, Emeryville *Also called Pacific Hotel Management LLC (P-11346)*
Sheraton, Palo Alto *Also called Pacific Hotel Management LLC (P-11348)*
Sheraton LLC...D.......415 362-5500
2500 Mason St San Francisco (94133) *(P-11467)*
Sheraton LLC...D.......831 438-1500
5030 Scotts Valley Dr Scotts Valley (95066) *(P-11468)*
Sheraton LLC...D.......916 447-1700
1230 J St 13th Sacramento (95814) *(P-11469)*
Sheraton Palo Alto, Palo Alto *Also called Pacific Hotel Dev Ventr LP (P-11344)*
Sheraton Pasadena, San Mateo *Also called Pasadena Hotel Dev Ventr LP (P-11360)*
Sheraton Rdding Ht At Sndial B...D.......530 364-2800
820 Sundial Bridge Dr Redding (96001) *(P-11470)*
Sheraton Sonoma Cnty Petaluma, Petaluma *Also called Sonoma Hotel Partners LP (P-11492)*
Sheriff's Dept, Carmichael *Also called County of Sacramento (P-17239)*
Shermn-Lehr Cstm Tile Wrks Inc...D.......916 386-0417
5691 Power Inn Rd Ste A Sacramento (95824) *(P-1720)*

Sherwood Forest Golf Club Inc............E......559 787-2611
79 N Frankwood Ave Sanger (93657) *(P-15026)*

Sherwood Healthcare Center, Sacramento *Also called H C C S Inc (P-16016)*

Sherwood Oaks Enterprises Inc............D......707 964-6333
130 Dana St Fort Bragg (95437) *(P-16115)*

Sherwood Oaks Health Center, Fort Bragg *Also called Sherwood Oaks Enterprises Inc (P-16115)*

Sherwood Valley Rancheria............D......707 459-7330
100 Kawi Pl Willits (95490) *(P-11471)*

Sherwood VIlley Rnchria Casino, Willits *Also called Sherwood Valley Rancheria (P-11471)*

Shi-III Prrie Cy Lnding Owner (PA)............E......916 458-0303
645 Willard Dr Folsom (95630) *(P-18181)*

Shibata Floral Company (PA)............E......415 495-8611
620 Brannan St San Francisco (94107) *(P-9639)*

Shield Commercial Inc (PA)............D......916 684-9093
7311 Greenhaven Dr # 100 Sacramento (95831) *(P-9948)*

Shields Nursing Centers Inc (PA)............C......510 724-9911
606 Alfred Nobel Dr Hercules (94547) *(P-16116)*

Shifamed LLC............E......408 560-2500
590 Division St Campbell (95008) *(P-15680)*

Shifamed LLC............E......408 364-1242
745 Camden Ave Ste A Campbell (95008) *(P-12200)*

Shift Finance LLC............A......541 335-9245
2500 Market St San Francisco (94114) *(P-12777)*

Shift3 Technologies LLC............E......559 560-3300
700 Van Ness Ave Fresno (93721) *(P-12778)*

Shih Yu-Lang Central YMCA, San Francisco *Also called Young MNS Chrstn Assn San Frnc (P-18520)*

Shikai Products, Santa Rosa *Also called Trans-India Products Inc (P-4097)*

Shimmick Construction Co Inc (PA)............A......510 777-5000
8201 Edgewater Dr Ste 202 Oakland (94621) *(P-1178)*

Shimmick Construction/Obayash (PA)............D......510 293-1100
24200 Clawiter Rd Hayward (94545) *(P-1179)*

Shimmick Nicholson Cnstr JV............C......510 777-5000
8201 Edgewater Dr Ste 202 Oakland (94621) *(P-961)*

Shine A Lght Cunseling Ctr Inc............E......530 748-8098
809 N Branciforte Ave Santa Cruz (95062) *(P-17743)*

Shine Facility Services, San Francisco *Also called Green Living Planet LLC (P-11958)*

Shine Logistics LLC............C......916 518-9393
9012 Pebble Field Way Sacramento (95829) *(P-7853)*

Shing Tai Corporation............E......415 986-2944
1160 Battery St San Francisco (94111) *(P-14532)*

Shingle Sprng Trbal Gming Auth............A......530 677-7000
1 Red Hawk Pkwy Placerville (95667) *(P-11472)*

Shining Star Preschool, Fresno *Also called Northwest Church Fresno Cal (P-17984)*

Shinko Electric America Inc (HQ)............E......408 232-0499
1280 E Arques Ave Sunnyvale (94085) *(P-8952)*

Ship Smart Inc............E......831 661-4841
783 Rio Del Mar Blvd Frnt # 9 Aptos (95003) *(P-3379)*

Shippo, San Francisco *Also called Popout Inc (P-13377)*

Shipt............A......408 592-1029
701 Pine St Apt 43 San Francisco (94108) *(P-13756)*

Shiva Enterprises Inc............C......650 366-2000
2834 El Camino Real Redwood City (94061) *(P-11473)*

Shlbao Distributors, Sacramento *Also called Peter (P-3391)*

Shn Cnslting Engners Glgsts In (PA)............D......707 441-8855
812 W Wabash Ave Eureka (95501) *(P-18812)*

Shockwave Medical Inc (PA)............C......510 279-4262
5403 Betsy Ross Dr Santa Clara (95054) *(P-7034)*

Shoei Foods (usa) Inc............D......530 742-7866
1900 Feather River Blvd Olivehurst (95961) *(P-9302)*

Shokawah Casino............E......707 744-1395
13101 Nokomis Rd Hopland (95449) *(P-11474)*

Shook & Waller Cnstr Inc............D......707 578-3933
7677 Bell Rd Ste 101 Windsor (95492) *(P-1756)*

Shook Hardy & Bacon LLP............C......415 544-1900
1 Montgomery St Ste 2700 San Francisco (94104) *(P-17373)*

Shooter & Butts Inc............E......925 460-5155
3768 Old Santa Rita Rd Pleasanton (94588) *(P-440)*

Shop -Ncal Rmx Fixed Maint Sho, Fairfield *Also called Cemex Cnstr Mtls PCF LLC (P-4466)*

Shopalyst Inc (PA)............D......949 583-0507
38350 Fremont Blvd # 203 Fremont (94536) *(P-19632)*

Shopify (usa) Inc............D......415 944-7572
33 New Montgomery St # 75 San Francisco (94105) *(P-12779)*

Shopkick Inc............D......650 763-8727
273a S Railroad Ave San Mateo (94401) *(P-12780)*

Shoppingcom Inc............C......650 616-6500
199 Fremont St Fl 4 San Francisco (94105) *(P-13757)*

Shopstyle Inc (HQ)............C......415 908-2200
160 Spear St Ste 1900 San Francisco (94105) *(P-12781)*

Shoreline Labs Inc............E......415 630-6212
315 Montgomery St San Francisco (94104) *(P-12782)*

Shorenstein Company LLC............E......415 772-7000
235 Montgomery St Fl 15 San Francisco (94104) *(P-10405)*

Shorenstein Properties LLC (PA)............C......415 772-7000
235 Montgomery St Fl 16 San Francisco (94104) *(P-10406)*

Shotspotter Inc............C......510 794-3100
7979 Gateway Blvd Ste 210 Newark (94560) *(P-13443)*

Showa Denko Materials Amer Inc (HQ)............E......408 873-2200
2150 N 1st St Ste 350 San Jose (95131) *(P-8876)*

Showare Ticketing, Fresno *Also called Visionone Inc (P-12908)*

Shower Glass & Mirror Co, Santa Clara *Also called South Bay Showers Inc (P-1945)*

Showpad Inc (HQ)............C......415 800-2033
301 Howard St Ste 500 San Francisco (94105) *(P-13974)*

Shred-It, Concord *Also called Stericycle Inc (P-14414)*

Shriners Hspitals For Children............B......916 453-2050
2425 Stockton Blvd Sacramento (95817) *(P-16525)*

Shuler, Kurt MD, Davis *Also called Sutter Health (P-16657)*

Shums Coda Associates Inc............D......925 463-0651
5776 Stnrdge Mall Rd Ste Pleasanton (94588) *(P-14403)*

Shusters Logging Inc............E......707 459-4131
750 E Valley St Willits (95490) *(P-3079)*

Shute Mihaly & Weinberger............E......415 552-7272
396 Hayes St San Francisco (94102) *(P-17374)*

Shutterfly LLC (HQ)............B......650 610-5200
2800 Bridge Pkwy Ste 100 Redwood City (94065) *(P-14182)*

Shyam Lodging Group II LLC............E......650 755-7500
2700 Junipero Serra Blvd Daly City (94015) *(P-11475)*

Shyft Group Inc............E......916 921-2639
4242 Forcum Ave B-640 McClellan (95652) *(P-6559)*

Sia Security Services, Sacramento *Also called Hg Holdings Inc (P-14068)*

Siblings Investment Inc............E......510 668-0368
43951 Boscell Rd Fremont (94538) *(P-8747)*

SICK CHILD CARE CENTER, THE, San Jose *Also called Sjb Child Development Centers (P-18021)*

Sidco Labelling Systems, Santa Clara *Also called Context Engineering Co (P-4880)*

Side Inc............E......650 930-0873
466 Brannan St San Francisco (94107) *(P-10662)*

Sideman & Bancroft LLP............D......415 392-1960
1 Embarcadero Ctr Fl 22 San Francisco (94111) *(P-17375)*

Sidemark Corporate Furniture, San Jose *Also called Randall Horton Associates Inc (P-8503)*

Sidjon Corporation............D......925 606-6135
3571 1st St Livermore (94551) *(P-11476)*

Siegel & Gale LLC............E......415 955-1250
650 California St Fl 10 San Francisco (94108) *(P-11783)*

Siemens............E......510 263-0367
1001 Marina Village Pkwy Alameda (94501) *(P-8877)*

Siemens Energy Inc............D......916 391-2993
3215 47th Ave Sacramento (95824) *(P-8200)*

Siemens Industry Inc............C......916 681-3000
7464 French Rd Sacramento (95828) *(P-6705)*

Siemens Industry Software Inc............E......510 445-1836
46871 Bayside Pkwy Fremont (94538) *(P-18813)*

Siemens Med Solutions USA Inc............B......650 694-5747
685 E Middlefield Rd Mountain View (94043) *(P-15681)*

Siemens Mobility Inc............D......916 621-2700
5301 Price Ave McClellan (95652) *(P-14592)*

Siemens Mobility Inc............A......916 681-3000
7464 French Rd Sacramento (95828) *(P-6560)*

Sienna Corporation Inc............E......510 440-0200
41350 Christy St Fremont (94538) *(P-6542)*

Sierra At Taho Ski Resorts............C......530 659-7519
1111 Sierra At Tahoe Rd Twin Bridges (95735) *(P-11477)*

Sierra Bancorp............D......559 449-8145
7029 N Ingram Ave Ste 101 Fresno (93650) *(P-9748)*

Sierra Central Credit Union (PA)............D......530 671-3009
1351 Harter Pkwy Yuba City (95993) *(P-9819)*

Sierra Chemical Company, West Sacramento *Also called Richard K Gould Inc (P-4167)*

Sierra Chevrolet Inc............D......530 346-8313
1624 S Canyon Way Colfax (95713) *(P-14623)*

Sierra Circuits Inc............C......408 735-7137
1108 W Evelyn Ave Sunnyvale (94086) *(P-5973)*

Sierra Club (PA)............C......415 977-5500
2101 Webster St Ste 1300 Oakland (94612) *(P-18469)*

SIERRA CLUB BOOKS, Oakland *Also called Sierra Club (P-18469)*

Sierra Cscade Aggrgate Asp PDT............E......530 258-4555
6600 Old Ski Rd Chester (96020) *(P-598)*

Sierra Cscade Fmly Opprtnities (PA)............D......530 283-1242
424 N Mill Creek Rd Quincy (95971) *(P-18019)*

Sierra Design Mfg Inc (PA)............E......925 443-3140
2602 Superior Dr Livermore (94550) *(P-5740)*

Sierra Disposal Service, South Lake Tahoe *Also called South Tahoe Refuse Co (P-8364)*

Sierra Electric Co, San Francisco *Also called SF Sierra Co Inc (P-1605)*

Sierra Endcrine Assoc Med Grou, Fresno *Also called Joseph B Hawkins Jr MD Inc (P-15442)*

Sierra Entertainment............E......530 666-9646
341 Industrial Way Woodland (95776) *(P-7319)*

Sierra Eye Tissue Donor, West Sacramento *Also called DCI Donor Services Inc (P-17132)*

Sierra Family Med Clinic Inc (PA)............E......530 292-3478
15301 Tyler Foote Rd Nevada City (95959) *(P-15682)*

Sierra Feeds, Reedley *Also called Mission AG Resources LLC (P-2164)*

Sierra Forever Families............E......916 368-5114
8912 Volunteer Ln Sacramento (95826) *(P-17744)*

Sierra Fthlls Otpatient Clinic, Auburn *Also called Veterans Health Administration (P-15793)*

Sierra Gardens Medical Offices, Roseville *Also called Kaiser Foundation Hospitals (P-10798)*

Sierra Gold Nurseries Inc............D......530 674-1145
5320 Garden Hwy Yuba City (95991) *(P-134)*

Sierra Health Services LLC............E......209 956-7725
2423 W March Ln Ste 100 Stockton (95207) *(P-10154)*

Sierra Hills Care Center Inc............D......916 782-7007
1139 Cirby Way Roseville (95661) *(P-16117)*

Sierra Hlth Wellness Ctrs LLC............D......530 854-4119
2167 Montgomery St Ste A Oroville (95965) *(P-17180)*

Sierra Hlth Wellness Group LLC............C......530 854-4119
2167 Montgomery St Ste A Oroville (95965) *(P-17073)*

Sierra Imging Assoc Med Group............C......559 297-0300
231 W Fir Ave Clovis (93611) *(P-15683)*

Sierra Intrnal Mdcine Med Grou............C......209 536-3738
680 Guzzi Ln Ste 201 Sonora (95370) *(P-15684)*

Sierra Landscape & Maint Inc............D......530 895-0263
546 Hickory St Chico (95928) *(P-441)*

Sierra Lumber & Decking, San Jose *Also called Sierra Lumber Co (P-1757)*

Sierra Lumber and Fence Co, San Jose *Also called Sierra Lumber and Fence PSI (P-2068)*

Sierra Lumber and Fence PSI............E......707 769-0345
1711 Senter Rd San Jose (95112) *(P-2068)*

Sierra Lumber and Fence PSI (HQ)............E......408 286-7071
1711 Senter Rd San Jose (95112) *(P-2069)*

ALPHABETIC

Employee Codes: A=Over 500 employees, B=251-500
C=101-250, D=51-100, E=20-50 F=10-19

2022 Northern California Business Directory and Buyers Guide

© Mergent Inc. 1-800-342-5647
1077

Sierra Lumber Co ALPHABETIC SECTION

Sierra Lumber Co......C......408 286-7071
1711 Senter Rd San Jose (95112) *(P-1757)*
Sierra Manor Apts, Chico *Also called Hignell Incorporated (P-10437)*
Sierra Metal Fabricators Inc......E......530 265-4591
529 Searls Ave Nevada City (95959) *(P-4683)*
Sierra Metalk Fabricators, Nevada City *Also called Sierra Metal Fabricators Inc (P-4683)*
Sierra Monitor Corporation (HQ)......D......408 262-6611
1991 Tarob Ct Milpitas (95035) *(P-6921)*
Sierra Motors, Jamestown *Also called Jamestown Motor Corporation (P-14663)*
Sierra Mountain Cnstr Inc......D......209 928-1900
13919 Mono Way Sonora (95370) *(P-17745)*
Sierra Nev Mmorial-Miners Hosp (HQ)......E......530 274-6000
155 Glasson Way Grass Valley (95945) *(P-16526)*
Sierra Nevada Brewing Co (PA)......B......530 893-3520
1075 E 20th St Chico (95928) *(P-2491)*
Sierra Nevada Cheese Co Inc......D......530 934-8660
6505 County Road 39 Willows (95988) *(P-2157)*
Sierra Nevada Corp......F......775 331-0222
3034 Gold Canal Dr Rancho Cordova (95670) *(P-6682)*
Sierra Nevada Corporation......E......408 395-2004
985 University Ave Ste 4 Los Gatos (95032) *(P-6683)*
Sierra Nevada Corporation......E......510 446-8400
39465 Paseo Padre Pkwy # 2900 Fremont (94538) *(P-5867)*
Sierra Nevada Corporation......E......916 985-8799
145 Parkshore Dr Folsom (95630) *(P-6684)*
Sierra Nevada Home Care, Grass Valley *Also called Sierra Nevada Mem HM Care Inc (P-16944)*
Sierra Nevada Lodge......D......760 934-2515
164 Old Mammoth Rd Mammoth Lakes (93546) *(P-11478)*
Sierra Nevada Mem HM Care Inc......C......530 274-6350
1020 Mccourtney Rd Ste A Grass Valley (95949) *(P-16944)*
Sierra Nevada Memorial Hosp, Grass Valley *Also called Sierra Nev Mmorial-Miners Hosp (P-16526)*
Sierra Office Supply & Prtg, Sacramento *Also called Sierra Office Systems Pdts Inc (P-3697)*
Sierra Office Systems Pdts Inc (PA)......D......916 369-0491
9950 Horn Rd Ste 5 Sacramento (95827) *(P-3697)*
Sierra Oncology Inc (PA)......E......650 376-8679
1820 Gateway Dr Ste 110 San Mateo (94404) *(P-3984)*
Sierra Pacific Htg & Air-Solar, Rancho Cordova *Also called Sierra PCF HM & Comfort Inc (P-9015)*
Sierra Pacific Industries......E......530 226-5181
2771 Bechelli Ln Redding (96002) *(P-3106)*
Sierra Pacific Industries......C......530 283-2820
1538 Lee Rd Quincy (95971) *(P-3107)*
Sierra Pacific Industries (PA)......D......530 378-8000
19794 Riverside Ave Anderson (96007) *(P-3108)*
Sierra Pacific Industries......E......530 378-8301
14980 Camage Ave Sonora (95370) *(P-3109)*
Sierra Pacific Industries......E......530 378-8301
36336 Hwy 299 E Burney (96013) *(P-3110)*
Sierra Pacific Industries......E......530 335-3681
Hwy 299 E Burney (96013) *(P-3111)*
Sierra Pacific Industries......D......530 824-2474
Alameda Rd Corning (96021) *(P-3151)*
Sierra Pacific Industries......E......530 275-8851
3735 El Cajon Ave Shasta Lake (96019) *(P-3112)*
Sierra Pacific Industries......E......530 365-3721
19758 Riverside Ave Anderson (96007) *(P-3113)*
Sierra Pacific Industries......E......530 644-2311
3950 Carson Rd Camino (95709) *(P-3114)*
Sierra Pacific Industries......E......916 645-1631
1440 Lincoln Blvd Lincoln (95648) *(P-3115)*
Sierra Pacific Industries......B......530 527-9620
11605 Reading Rd Red Bluff (96080) *(P-3116)*
Sierra Pacific Machining Inc......E......408 924-0281
530 Parrott St San Jose (95112) *(P-5618)*
Sierra Pacific Mortgage Co Inc (PA)......A......916 932-1700
1180 Iron Point Rd # 200 Folsom (95630) *(P-9927)*
Sierra Pacific Packaging, Oroville *Also called Graphic Packaging Intl LLC (P-3734)*
Sierra Pacific Surgery Ctr LLC......E......559 256-5200
1630 E Herndon Ave # 100 Fresno (93720) *(P-15685)*
Sierra PCF HM & Comfort Inc......D......916 638-0543
2550 Mercantile Dr Ste D Rancho Cordova (95742) *(P-9015)*
Sierra PCF Hotels & Resorts......D......530 583-5500
201 Squaw Peak Rd Olympic Valley (96146) *(P-11479)*
Sierra PCF Orthpdic Ctr Med Gr......C......559 256-5200
1630 E Herndon Ave Fresno (93720) *(P-15686)*
Sierra Precast Inc......C......408 779-1000
1 Live Oak Ave Morgan Hill (95037) *(P-4452)*
Sierra Precision Optics Inc......E......530 885-6979
12830 Earhart Ave Auburn (95602) *(P-6886)*
Sierra Proto Express, Sunnyvale *Also called Sierra Circuits Inc (P-5973)*
Sierra Pt Lbr & Plywd Co Inc (PA)......D......415 468-1000
601 Tunnel Ave Brisbane (94005) *(P-8607)*
Sierra Reforestation Company......E......408 848-9604
5355 Monterey Frontage Rd Gilroy (95020) *(P-9610)*
Sierra Repertory Theatre Inc......E......209 532-0502
13891 Mono Way Sonora (95370) *(P-14863)*
Sierra Resource Management Inc......E......209 984-1146
12015 La Grange Rd Jamestown (95327) *(P-3080)*
Sierra Select Distributors Inc......D......916 483-9295
4320 Roseville Rd North Highlands (95660) *(P-8887)*
Sierra Single Ply Inc (PA)......E......916 640-0123
1812 Main Ave Ste 130 Sacramento (95838) *(P-1836)*
Sierra Summit Inc......A......559 233-2500
59265 Hwy 168 Lakeshore (93634) *(P-11480)*
Sierra Sunrise Vineyard Inc......E......209 245-6942
20680 Shenandoah Schl Rd Plymouth (95669) *(P-2715)*
Sierra Tel Cmmunications Group (PA)......E......559 683-4611
49150 Road 426 Oakhurst (93644) *(P-7989)*
Sierra Telephone Company Inc......C......559 683-4611
49150 Road 426 Oakhurst (93644) *(P-7990)*
Sierra Trim Inc......E......916 259-2966
3137 Swetzer Rd Ste B Loomis (95650) *(P-1758)*
Sierra Valley Almonds LLC......E......559 662-8900
850 Commerce Dr Madera (93637) *(P-93)*
Sierra Ventures Management LLC......E......650 854-1000
1400 Fashion Island Blvd San Mateo (94404) *(P-10883)*
Sierra View Country Club......D......916 782-3741
105 Alta Vista Ave Roseville (95678) *(P-15143)*
Sierra View Homes......C......559 637-2256
1155 E Springfield Ave Reedley (93654) *(P-16118)*
SIERRA VIEW HOMES RESIDENTIAL, Reedley *Also called Sierra View Homes (P-16118)*
Sierra View Landscape Inc......E......916 408-2990
3888 Cincinnati Ave Rocklin (95765) *(P-502)*
Sierra View Medical Eye Inc......D......530 272-3411
400 Sierra College Dr A Grass Valley (95945) *(P-15687)*
Sierra Vista Hospital, Sacramento *Also called Willow Springs LLC (P-15816)*
Sierra Waldorf School Inc......E......209 984-0454
19234 Rawhide Rd Jamestown (95327) *(P-18020)*
Sierra Weatherization Co Inc......E......408 354-1900
43 E Main St Ste B Los Gatos (95030) *(P-11784)*
Sierra-Cascade Nursery Inc (PA)......B......530 254-6867
472-715 Johnson Rd Susanville (96130) *(P-135)*
Sierra-Tahoe Ready Mix Inc......E......530 541-1877
1526 Emerald Bay Rd South Lake Tahoe (96150) *(P-4507)*
Sierraware LLC......E......408 337-6400
1042 Westchester Dr Sunnyvale (94087) *(P-12783)*
Sift Science Inc (PA)......D......855 981-7438
123 Mission St Ste 2000 San Francisco (94105) *(P-12784)*
Sig Structured Products Lllp......E......415 951-3533
425 California St # 2450 San Francisco (94104) *(P-10013)*
Sight Machine Inc......D......888 461-5739
243 Vallejo St San Francisco (94111) *(P-13444)*
Sight Sciences Inc (PA)......C......650 352-4400
4040 Campbell Ave Ste 100 Menlo Park (94025) *(P-7035)*
Sigma Mfg & Logistics LLC......E......916 781-3052
10050 Fthlls Blvd Ste 100 Roseville (95747) *(P-5272)*
Sigmaways Inc......D......510 573-4208
39737 Paseo Padre Pkwy C1 Fremont (94538) *(P-19633)*
Sign Designs Inc......E......209 524-4484
204 Campus Way Modesto (95350) *(P-7252)*
Sign Technology Inc......E......916 372-1200
1700 Entp Blvd Ste F West Sacramento (95691) *(P-7253)*
Sign-A-Rama, Redding *Also called Jar Ventures Inc (P-7236)*
Signa Chemistry Inc......E......212 933-4101
720 Olive Dr Ste Cd Davis (95616) *(P-3796)*
Signal 88 SEC Contra Costa, Concord *Also called R&R Security Solutions Inc (P-14381)*
Signalfx Inc (HQ)......E......888 958-5950
3098 Olsen Dr San Jose (95128) *(P-13758)*
Signature Building Maint Inc......D......408 377-8066
4005 Clipper Ct Fremont (94538) *(P-11998)*
Signature Homes Inc......D......925 463-1122
4670 Willow Rd Ste 200 Pleasanton (94588) *(P-707)*
Signature Painting & Cnstr Inc......E......925 287-0444
1559 3rd Ave Walnut Creek (94597) *(P-1432)*
Signature Properties Inc......E......925 463-1122
4670 Willow Rd Ste 200 Pleasanton (94588) *(P-10714)*
Signature Reprographics, Sacramento *Also called Sac City Blue Inc (P-11850)*
Signet Testing Labs Inc......D......916 374-0754
498 N 3rd St Sacramento (95811) *(P-14404)*
Signet Testing Labs Inc (HQ)......E......510 887-8484
3526 Breakwater Ct Hayward (94545) *(P-19285)*
Significant Cleaning Svcs LLC......C......408 559-5959
148 E Virginia St Ste 1 San Jose (95112) *(P-11999)*
Signtech, West Sacramento *Also called Sign Technology Inc (P-7253)*
Sigona's Farmers Market, Redwood City *Also called Brothers Pride Produce Inc (P-2253)*
Sigos LLC (HQ)......E......650 535-0599
20813 Stevns Crk Blvd # 200 Cupertino (95014) *(P-14405)*
Sigray Inc......E......925 207-0925
5750 Imhoff Dr Ste I Concord (94520) *(P-6852)*
Sila Nanotechnologies Inc......C......707 901-7452
2450 Mariner Square Loop Alameda (94501) *(P-6490)*
Silara Medtech (PA)......E......707 757-5750
451 Aviation Blvd 107a Santa Rosa (95403) *(P-7036)*
Silenus Vintners......F......707 299-3930
5225 Solano Ave NAPA (94558) *(P-2716)*
Silgan Containers Mfg Corp......E......209 521-6469
4000 Yosemite Blvd Modesto (95357) *(P-4599)*
Silgan Containers Mfg Corp......E......925 778-8000
2200 Wilbur Ave Antioch (94509) *(P-4600)*
Silgan Containers Mfg Corp......E......209 869-3637
6180 Roselle Ave Riverbank (95367) *(P-4601)*
Silgan Containers Mfg Corp......E......209 869-3601
3250 Patterson Rd Riverbank (95367) *(P-4602)*
Silica Engineering Group, Santa Clara *Also called Superior Quartz Inc (P-4555)*
Silicon Genesis Corporation......E......408 228-5885
46816 Lakeview Blvd Fremont (94538) *(P-6285)*
Silicon Graphics Intl Corp (HQ)......A......669 900-8000
940 N Mccarthy Blvd Milpitas (95035) *(P-5411)*
Silicon Image Inc (HQ)......A......408 616-4000
2115 Onel Dr San Jose (95131) *(P-6286)*
Silicon Laboratories, San Jose *Also called Silicon Labs Integration Inc (P-6287)*
Silicon Labs Integration Inc (HQ)......E......408 702-1400
2708 Orchard Pkwy 30 San Jose (95134) *(P-6287)*
Silicon Light Machines Corp (HQ)......F......408 240-4700
820 Kifer Rd Ste B Sunnyvale (94086) *(P-6288)*

Silicon Microstructures Inc......D......408 473-9700
1701 Mccarthy Blvd Milpitas (95035) ***(P-5690)***
Silicon Motion Inc......D......408 501-5300
690 N Mccarthy Blvd # 200 Milpitas (95035) ***(P-6289)***
Silicon Standard Corp......E......408 234-6964
4701 Patrick Henry Dr # 16 Santa Clara (95054) ***(P-6290)***
Silicon Storage Technology Inc (HQ)......B......408 735-9110
1020 Kifer Rd Sunnyvale (94086) ***(P-6291)***
Silicon Turnkey Solutions Inc (HQ)......F......408 904-0200
1804 Mccarthy Blvd Milpitas (95035) ***(P-6292)***
Silicon Valley Ambulance Inc......D......408 225-2262
181 Martinvale Ln San Jose (95119) ***(P-7405)***
Silicon Valley Bank (HQ)......A......408 654-7400
3003 Tasman Dr Santa Clara (95054) ***(P-9761)***
Silicon Valley Capital (HQ)......D......408 971-9300
50 W San Fernando St Bsmt San Jose (95113) ***(P-15144)***
Silicon Valley Capital Club, San Jose *Also called Silicon Valley Capital* ***(P-15144)***
Silicon Valley Clean Water......D......650 591-7121
1400 Radio Rd Redwood City (94065) ***(P-8290)***
Silicon Valley Commerce LLC......D......888 507-8266
16 Jessie St San Francisco (94105) ***(P-12785)***
Silicon Valley Crane Inc......F......408 452-1537
10700 Bigge St San Leandro (94577) ***(P-5037)***
Silicon Valley Elite Mfg......F......408 654-9534
460 Aldo Ave Santa Clara (95054) ***(P-5619)***
Silicon Valley Glass Inc (PA)......E......408 778-7786
18695 Madrone Pkwy Morgan Hill (95037) ***(P-1944)***
Silicon Valley Mechanical Inc......B......408 943-0380
2115 Ringwood Ave San Jose (95131) ***(P-1357)***
Silicon Valley Mfg Inc......F......510 791-9450
6520 Central Ave Newark (94560) ***(P-4545)***
Silicon Valley Monterey Bay Co......D......209 965-3432
29211 Highway 108 Long Barn (95335) ***(P-18470)***
Silicon Valley Optics Tech......E......510 623-1161
44141 S Grimmer Blvd Fremont (94538) ***(P-8803)***
Silicon Valley Paving Inc......E......408 286-9101
1050 Coml St Ste 101 San Jose (95112) ***(P-1072)***
Silicon Valley Precision Mch, San Jose *Also called Hiep Nguyen Corporation* ***(P-5536)***
Silicon Valley Sftwr Group LLC......E......844 946-7874
74 Tehama St San Francisco (94105) ***(P-12786)***
Silicon Vly Aba Cnsulting Svcs......E......408 913-5019
1295 E Dunne Ave Morgan Hill (95037) ***(P-19860)***
Silicon Vly Cmnty Foundation (PA)......C......650 450-5400
2440 W El Cmino Real Ste Mountain View (94040) ***(P-18471)***
Silicon Vly Eye Care Optmtry C......E......408 296-0511
770 Scott Blvd Santa Clara (95050) ***(P-15873)***
Silicon Vly Law Group A Law Co......E......408 573-5700
1 N Market St 200 San Jose (95113) ***(P-17376)***
Silicon Vly McRelectronics Inc......E......408 844-7100
2985 Kifer Rd Santa Clara (95051) ***(P-6293)***
Silicon Vly SEC & Patrol Inc (PA)......C......408 267-1539
1131 Luchessi Dr Ste 2 San Jose (95118) ***(P-14096)***
Silicon Vly Technical Staffing (PA)......E......510 923-9898
2336 Harrison St Oakland (94612) ***(P-12136)***
Silicon Vly World Trade Corp......E......408 945-6355
1474 Gladding Ct Milpitas (95035) ***(P-5654)***
Siliconcore Technology Inc......E......408 946-8185
890 Hillview Ct Ste 120 Milpitas (95035) ***(P-6294)***
Siliconindia Inc......D......510 440-8249
46560 Fremont Blvd # 413 Fremont (94538) ***(P-3599)***
Siliconix Incorporated (HQ)......A......408 988-8000
2585 Junction Ave San Jose (95134) ***(P-6295)***
Siliconix Semiconductor Inc......D......408 988-8000
2201 Laurelwood Rd Santa Clara (95054) ***(P-6296)***
Siliconsage Construction Inc......C......408 916-3205
560 S Mathilda Ave Sunnyvale (94086) ***(P-770)***
Siliconware Usa Inc (HQ)......E......408 573-5500
1735 Tech Dr Ste 300 Fl 3 San Jose (95110) ***(P-8953)***
Silitronics Inc......E......408 605-1148
1957 Concourse Dr San Jose (95131) ***(P-6469)***
Silk Road Medical Inc......C......408 720-9002
1213 Innsbruck Dr Sunnyvale (94089) ***(P-7037)***
Sillajen Biotherapeutics Inc......E......415 281-8886
450 Sansome St Ste 650 San Francisco (94111) ***(P-19125)***
Siller and Siller Construction......F......916 893-3462
13286 Vineyard Ln Penn Valley (95946) ***(P-12023)***
Siller Aviation, Yuba City *Also called Siller Brothers Inc* ***(P-3081)***
Siller Brothers Inc (PA)......D......530 673-0734
1250 Smith Rd Yuba City (95991) ***(P-3081)***
Siller Helicopters Inc......E......530 674-9460
1250 Smith Rd Yuba City (95991) ***(P-7761)***
Sills Farms Inc......D......916 655-3391
5072 Pacific Ave Pleasant Grove (95668) ***(P-190)***
Silman Construction, San Leandro *Also called Silman Venture Corporation* ***(P-962)***
Silman Venture Corporation (PA)......C......510 347-4800
1600 Factor Ave San Leandro (94577) ***(P-962)***
Silray Inc......E......650 331-1117
1245 S Winchester Blvd # 301 San Jose (95128) ***(P-1358)***
Siluria Technologies Inc......E......415 978-2170
409 Illinois St San Francisco (94158) ***(P-549)***
Silva Trucking......E......209 982-1114
36 W Mathews Rd French Camp (95231) ***(P-7489)***
Silvaco Inc (PA)......C......408 567-1000
2811 Mission College Blvd # 6 Santa Clara (95054) ***(P-13663)***
Silveira Ranch, Atwater *Also called Edward Silveira* ***(P-17)***
Silver Creek Ftnes Physcl Thra......E......408 238-1552
4205 San Felipe Rd # 100 San Jose (95135) ***(P-15898)***
Silver Creek Vly Cntry CLB Inc......C......408 239-5775
5460 Country Club Pkwy San Jose (95138) ***(P-15145)***
Silver Lake Financial, San Francisco *Also called Silver Lake Partners II LP* ***(P-10783)***

Silver Lake Partners LP (PA)......D......650 233-8120
2775 Sand Hill Rd Ste 100 Menlo Park (94025) ***(P-10781)***
Silver Lake Partners II LP......E......408 454-4732
10080 N Wolfe Rd Sw3190 Cupertino (95014) ***(P-10782)***
Silver Lake Partners II LP......E......415 293-4355
1 Market Plz San Francisco (94105) ***(P-10783)***
Silver Lake Tech Assoc LLC (HQ)......D......650 233-8120
2725 Sand Hill Rd Ste 150 Menlo Park (94025) ***(P-10784)***
Silver Oak Health Services......E......925 447-2280
788 Holmes St Livermore (94550) ***(P-16119)***
Silver Oak Manor, Livermore *Also called Silver Oak Health Services* ***(P-16119)***
Silver Oak Wine Cellars LLC......E......707 942-7082
7300 Highway 128 Healdsburg (95448) ***(P-2717)***
Silver Oak Wine Cellars LLC (PA)......F......707 942-7022
915 Oakville Cross Rd Oakville (94562) ***(P-2718)***
Silver Peak Systems Inc (HQ)......C......408 935-1800
2860 De La Cruz Blvd Santa Clara (95050) ***(P-6297)***
Silver Service, San Andreas *Also called Mark Twain Medical Center* ***(P-16441)***
Silver Spur Christian Camp......E......209 928-4248
17301 Silver Spur Dr Tuolumne (95379) ***(P-11611)***
Silver Terrace Nurseries Inc......D......650 879-2110
501 North St Pescadero (94060) ***(P-136)***
Silverado Building Mtls Inc (PA)......E......916 361-7374
9297 Jackson Rd Sacramento (95826) ***(P-8608)***
Silverado Contractors Inc (PA)......D......510 658-9960
2855 Mandela Pkwy Fl 2 Oakland (94608) ***(P-1988)***
Silverado NAPA Corp (HQ)......D......707 226-1325
1600 Atlas Peak Rd NAPA (94558) ***(P-708)***
Silverado Orchards LLC (PA)......D......707 963-1461
601 Pope St Ofc Saint Helena (94574) ***(P-10459)***
Silverado Resort and Spa......A......707 257-0200
1600 Atlas Peak Rd NAPA (94558) ***(P-15146)***
Silverado Rsort Svcs Group LLC......B......707 257-0200
1600 Atlas Peak Rd NAPA (94558) ***(P-11481)***
Silverado Senior Living Inc......D......650 226-8017
1301 Ralston Ave Ste A Belmont (94002) ***(P-16120)***
Silverado Senior Living Inc......D......650 264-9020
1301 Ralston Ave Ste A Belmont (94002) ***(P-16121)***
Silverado Senior Living Inc......D......650 226-4152
1000 Marina Blvd Ste 200 Brisbane (94005) ***(P-16203)***
Silverado Veterinary Hosp Inc......E......707 224-7953
2035 Silverado Trl NAPA (94558) ***(P-337)***
Silverado Vineyards......E......707 257-1770
6121 Silverado Trl NAPA (94558) ***(P-2719)***
Silverthorn Resort Assoc LP......E......530 275-1571
16250 Silverthorn Rd Redding (96003) ***(P-15242)***
Silverton Rsrt-Mrina-Bar Grill, Redding *Also called Silverthorn Resort Assoc LP* ***(P-15242)***
Silverwood Management Inc (PA)......D......703 777-8322
5150 Douglas Ln Sebastopol (95472) ***(P-10460)***
Simas Floor Co Inc (PA)......C......916 452-4933
3550 Power Inn Rd Sacramento (95826) ***(P-1776)***
Simas Floor Co Design Center, Sacramento *Also called Simas Floor Co Inc* ***(P-1776)***
Simbe Robotics Inc......E......415 625-8555
385 Oyster Point Blvd # 2 South San Francisco (94080) ***(P-19634)***
Simbol Inc......D......925 226-7400
6920 Koll Center Pkwy # 216 Pleasanton (94566) ***(P-19126)***
Simbol Materials, Pleasanton *Also called Simbol Inc* ***(P-19126)***
Simco Electronics (PA)......D......408 734-9750
3131 Jay St Ste 100 Santa Clara (95054) ***(P-14705)***
Simco Foods Inc......D......415 982-5872
39 Pier Ste A202 San Francisco (94133) ***(P-9303)***
Simco-Ion Technology Group (PA)......C......510 217-0600
1601 Harbor Bay Pkwy # 150 Alameda (94502) ***(P-8954)***
Simi Winery, Healdsburg *Also called Franciscan Vinyards Inc* ***(P-2583)***
Simility LLC......D......650 351-7592
2211 N 1st St San Jose (95131) ***(P-13975)***
Simmba/Grm, Fremont *Also called Grm Infrmtion MGT Svcs San Frn* ***(P-14291)***
Simmons Stairways Inc......E......408 920-0105
255 Apollo Way B Hollister (95023) ***(P-3152)***
Simonian Brothers Inc (PA)......C......559 834-5921
511 N 7th St Fowler (93625) ***(P-308)***
Simonian Fruit, Fowler *Also called Simonian Brothers Inc* ***(P-308)***
Simonton Windows, Vacaville *Also called Fortune Brands Windows Inc* ***(P-4282)***
Simplex Filler Inc......F......707 265-6801
640 Airpark Rd Ste A NAPA (94558) ***(P-5204)***
Simplex Filler Co, NAPA *Also called Simplex Filler Inc* ***(P-5204)***
Simplify Medical Inc......F......650 946-2025
685 N Pastoria Ave Sunnyvale (94085) ***(P-7038)***
Simply Asia Foods LLC......E......800 967-8424
2342 Shattuck Ave Berkeley (94704) ***(P-2943)***
Simply Country Inc......F......530 615-0565
10110 Harvest Ln Rough and Ready (95975) ***(P-5018)***
Simply Fresh Fruit, Rancho Cordova *Also called Sffi Company Inc* ***(P-9428)***
Simply Fresh Fruit Inc......D......323 586-0000
11020 White Rock Rd # 100 Rancho Cordova (95670) ***(P-9429)***
Simply Smashing Inc......F......559 658-2367
4790 W Jacquelyn Ave Fresno (93722) ***(P-7254)***
Simpplr Inc......C......650 396-2646
3 Twin Dolphin Dr Ste 160 Redwood City (94065) ***(P-13445)***
Simpson & Simpson Inc......E......530 885-4354
10001 Ophir Rd Newcastle (95658) ***(P-1073)***
Simpson Coatings Group Inc......E......650 873-5990
401 S Canal St A South San Francisco (94080) ***(P-4111)***
Simpson Manufacturing Co Inc (PA)......C......925 560-9000
5956 W Las Positas Blvd Pleasanton (94588) ***(P-4594)***
Simpson Sheet Metal Inc......E......707 576-1500
2833 Dowd Dr Ste C Santa Rosa (95407) ***(P-1359)***
Simpson Strong-Tie Company Inc (HQ)......C......925 560-9000
5956 W Las Positas Blvd Pleasanton (94588) ***(P-4861)***

ALPHABETIC

Simpson Strong-Tie Company Inc ....D....209 234-7775
5151 S Airport Way Stockton (95206) ***(P-4862)***
Simpson Strong-Tie Intl Inc (HQ) ....**D....925 560-9000**
5956 W Las Positas Blvd Pleasanton (94588) ***(P-4863)***
Simpson, J H Co, Stockton *Also called J H Simpson Company Inc* ***(P-1289)***
Sims Group USA Corporation (HQ) ....**D....510 412-5300**
600 S 4th St Richmond (94804) ***(P-9177)***
Simsmetal America, Richmond *Also called Sims Group USA Corporation* ***(P-9177)***
Sinclair & Valentine, Watsonville *Also called Smith & Vandiver Corporation* ***(P-9238)***
Sinclair Companies ....D....559 997-3617
5792 N Palm Ave Fresno (93704) ***(P-4180)***
Sinclair Companies ....D....559 351-1916
1703 W Olive Ave Fresno (93728) ***(P-4181)***
Sinclair Concrete ....D....916 663-0303
7205 Church St Penryn (95663) ***(P-1909)***
Sing Seng Hing Co Ltd ....E....415 781-2220
1020 Clement St San Francisco (94118) ***(P-11482)***
Sing Tao Daily, Burlingame *Also called Sing Tao Newspapers* ***(P-3479)***
Sing Tao Newspapers (HQ) ....**D....650 808-8800**
1818 Gilbreth Rd Ste 108 Burlingame (94010) ***(P-3479)***
Singha North America Inc ....F....714 206-5097
303 Twin Dolphin Dr # 600 Redwood City (94065) ***(P-2492)***
Singlestore Inc (PA) ....**E....855 463-6775**
534 4th St San Francisco (94107) ***(P-12787)***
Singley Enterprises (PA) ....**E....916 375-0575**
2901 Duluth St West Sacramento (95691) ***(P-1759)***
Singtel Enterprise SEC US Inc (HQ) ....**E....650 508-6800**
901 Marshall St Ste 125 Redwood City (94063) ***(P-13664)***
Singular Labs Inc (PA) ....**E....415 999-8368**
2345 Yale St Fl 1 Palo Alto (94306) ***(P-12788)***
Sinister Mfg Company Inc ....E....916 772-9253
2025 Opportunity Dr Ste 7 Roseville (95678) ***(P-6593)***
Sinosource Intl Co Inc ....F....650 697-6668
230 Adrian Rd Millbrae (94030) ***(P-4523)***
Sinskey Vineyards Inc ....E....707 944-9090
6320 Silverado Trl NAPA (94558) ***(P-2720)***
Sintex Security Services Inc ....D....209 543-9044
501 Bangs Ave Ste D Modesto (95356) ***(P-14097)***
Sipco Surface Protection Inc (HQ) ....**D....707 639-4414**
2320 Cordelia Rd Fairfield (94534) ***(P-1433)***
Sipes, Mike K, Newcastle *Also called Nelson & Kennard Law Offices* ***(P-17344)***
Sipex Corporation (HQ) ....**C....669 265-6100**
48720 Kato Rd Fremont (94538) ***(P-6298)***
Sir Francis Drake Hotel, San Francisco *Also called Huskies Lessee LLC* ***(P-11177)***
Sir Francis Drake Hotel, San Francisco *Also called Sfd Partners LLC* ***(P-11465)***
Sirf Technology Holdings Inc ....A....408 523-6500
1060 Rincon Cir San Jose (95131) ***(P-6299)***
Sirna Therapeutics Inc ....D....415 512-7200
1700 Owens St San Francisco (94158) ***(P-3985)***
Sirona Medical Inc ....E....415 729-7301
703 Market St Ste 1900 San Francisco (94103) ***(P-16945)***
SIS, Walnut Creek *Also called Systems Intgrtion Slutions Inc* ***(P-13986)***
Sisa, Mountain View *Also called Samsung Research America Inc* ***(P-19123)***
Siskiyou County Family Plng R, Mount Shasta *Also called Sousa Ready Mix LLC* ***(P-4508)***
Siskiyou Daily News, Yreka *Also called Gatehouse Media LLC* ***(P-3439)***
Siskiyou Development Company ....D....530 938-2731
88 S Weed Blvd Edgewood (96094) ***(P-11483)***
Siskiyou Forest Products (PA) ....**E....530 378-6980**
6275 State Highway 273 Anderson (96007) ***(P-3153)***
Siskiyou Hospital Inc ....D....530 841-6211
475 Bruce St Ste 200 Yreka (96097) ***(P-15688)***
Siskiyou Hospital Inc ....B....530 842-4121
444 Bruce St Yreka (96097) ***(P-16527)***
Siskiyou Lake Golf Resort Inc ....D....530 926-3030
1000 Siskiyou Lake Blvd Mount Shasta (96067) ***(P-15027)***
Siskiyou Opportunity Center ....E....530 842-4110
321 N Gold St Yreka (96097) ***(P-12137)***
Siskiyou Opportunity Center (PA) ....**D....530 926-4698**
1516 S Mount Shasta Blvd Mount Shasta (96067) ***(P-17838)***
Sistema US Inc ....E....707 773-2200
775 Southpoint Blvd Petaluma (94954) ***(P-4323)***
Sisters of Nazareth ....D....415 479-8282
245 Nova Albion Way San Rafael (94903) ***(P-16269)***
Sisters of St Joseph Orange ....A....747 206-9124
111 Sonoma Ave Ste 308 Santa Rosa (95405) ***(P-16946)***
Sisters of St Joseph Orange ....A....707 443-9332
2127 Harrison Ave Ste 3 Eureka (95501) ***(P-16947)***
Sisters of St Joseph Orange ....A....707 431-1135
205 East St Healdsburg (95448) ***(P-16528)***
Sit Funding Corporation ....E....510 656-3333
44201 Nobel Dr Fremont (94538) ***(P-9876)***
Sita Ram LLC ....E....209 223-0211
200 S State Highway 49 Jackson (95642) ***(P-11484)***
Site 204, Manteca *Also called Forward Inc* ***(P-8332)***
Site 211, Martinez *Also called Browning-Ferris Inds Cal Inc* ***(P-8312)***
Site 212, Bay Point *Also called Keller Canyon Landfill Company* ***(P-8338)***
Site 915, Milpitas *Also called BFI Waste Systems N Amer Inc* ***(P-7452)***
Site L71, Half Moon Bay *Also called Browning-Ferris Inds Cal Inc* ***(P-8311)***
Sitek Process Solutions ....F....916 797-9000
233 Technology Way Ste 3 Rocklin (95765) ***(P-6300)***
Sitime Corporation ....C....408 328-4400
5451 Patrick Henry Dr Santa Clara (95054) ***(P-6301)***
Situne Corporation ....E....408 712-3350
2216 Ringwood Ave San Jose (95131) ***(P-5868)***
Sius Products and Distr Inc (PA) ....**F....510 382-1700**
700 Kevin Ct Oakland (94621) ***(P-3388)***
Siwibi Wholesale ....E....650 448-1041
625 Ellis St Mountain View (94043) ***(P-5648)***

Six Apart Ltd (HQ) ....**E....415 738-5100**
180 Townsend St Fl 3 San Francisco (94107) ***(P-12789)***
Six Continents Hotels Inc ....D....559 272-7840
2819 E Hamilton Ave Fresno (93721) ***(P-11485)***
Six Continents Hotels Inc ....C....415 626-6103
50 8th St San Francisco (94103) ***(P-11486)***
Six CS Enterprises Inc ....E....530 926-3101
111 Morgan Way Mount Shasta (96067) ***(P-11487)***
Six Rivers National Bank (HQ) ....**D....707 443-8400**
402 F St Eureka (95501) ***(P-9689)***
Six Sigma, Milpitas *Also called Winslow Automation Inc* ***(P-6356)***
Six3 Advanced Systems Inc ....E....408 878-4920
2933 Bunker Hill Ln Santa Clara (95054) ***(P-18814)***
Sixgill LLC (PA) ....**E....424 322-2009**
548 Market St 22409 San Francisco (94104) ***(P-13665)***
Sizmek Dsp Inc (PA) ....**E....650 595-1300**
1900 Seaport Blvd Redwood City (94063) ***(P-11785)***
Sizmek Dsp Inc (HQ) ....**A....650 595-1300**
2000 Seaport Blvd Ste 400 Redwood City (94063) ***(P-13976)***
Sizmek Dsp Inc ....D....415 757-2300
1455 Market St Ste 2100 San Francisco (94103) ***(P-11786)***
Sj 1st Street Hotel LLC ....E....408 453-6200
1350 N 1st St San Jose (95112) ***(P-11488)***
SJ Cimino Electric Inc ....E....707 542-6231
3267 Dutton Ave Santa Rosa (95407) ***(P-1606)***
SJ Distributors Inc (PA) ....**D....888 988-2328**
625 Vista Way Milpitas (95035) ***(P-9369)***
Sj Lighting, West Sacramento *Also called All Phase Security Inc* ***(P-14027)***
Sj Valley Plating Inc ....E....408 988-5502
491 Perry Ct Santa Clara (95054) ***(P-4921)***
Sjb Child Development Centers (PA) ....**D....408 538-0200**
1400 Parkmoor Ave Ste 220 San Jose (95126) ***(P-18021)***
Sjrtd, Stockton *Also called San Joaquin Regional Trnst Dst* ***(P-7350)***
SJW Group (PA) ....**B....408 279-7800**
110 W Taylor St San Jose (95110) ***(P-8271)***
Sk Hynix America Inc (HQ) ....**D....408 232-8000**
3101 N 1st St San Jose (95134) ***(P-8748)***
Sk Hynix Memory Solutions Inc ....B....408 514-3500
3103 N 1st St San Jose (95134) ***(P-6302)***
Sk Pharmteco Inc ....E....888 330-2232
12460 Akron St Ste 100 Rancho Cordova (95742) ***(P-3986)***
Sk Telecom Americas Inc ....E....408 328-2900
100 Mathilda Pl Ste 230 Sunnyvale (94086) ***(P-19184)***
Skael Inc ....D....415 653-9433
535 Mission St Fl 14 San Francisco (94105) ***(P-13759)***
Skalli Vineyards, Rutherford *Also called St Supery Inc* ***(P-2723)***
Skatetown, Roseville *Also called Roseville Sportworld* ***(P-15233)***
Skava, San Francisco *Also called Kallidus Inc* ***(P-12555)***
Ski Air Conditioning Company ....E....530 626-4010
5528 Merchant Cir Placerville (95667) ***(P-1360)***
Skidmore Owings & Merrill LLP ....C....415 981-1555
1 Maritime Plz Fl 5 San Francisco (94111) ***(P-18913)***
Skill Nurse ....E....209 394-2440
13435 Peach Ave Livingston (95334) ***(P-16122)***
Skilled Nursing, Folsom *Also called Folsom Care Center* ***(P-17148)***
Skilled Nursing Facility, Oakhurst *Also called Oakhurst Healthcare Center LLC* ***(P-16194)***
Skilled Nursing Facility, Oakland *Also called Summit Medical Center* ***(P-16562)***
Skillnet Solutions Inc (PA) ....**D....408 522-3600**
1901 S Bascom Ave Ste 600 Campbell (95008) ***(P-12790)***
Skippy's Wholesales, Petaluma *Also called Petaluma Farms Inc* ***(P-231)***
Skire Inc ....E....650 289-2600
500 Oracle Pkwy Redwood City (94065) ***(P-12791)***
Skitch, Redwood City *Also called Evernote Corporation* ***(P-12433)***
Skoll Foundation ....E....650 331-1031
250 University Ave # 200 Palo Alto (94301) ***(P-18591)***
Sks Die Cast & Machining Inc (PA) ....**D....510 523-2541**
1849 Oak St Alameda (94501) ***(P-4580)***
Skunk Train, The, Fort Bragg *Also called Mendocino Railway* ***(P-7847)***
Skupos Inc (PA) ....**C....303 718-4805**
1462 Pine St San Francisco (94109) ***(P-12792)***
Sky Park Gardens Assisted ....D....916 422-5650
5510 Sky Pkwy Ofc Sacramento (95823) ***(P-18182)***
Sky Trek Aviation, Modesto *Also called Modesto Executive A Chrtr Inc* ***(P-7758)***
Skybox Security Inc (PA) ....**D....408 441-8060**
2077 Gateway Pl Ste 200 San Jose (95110) ***(P-12793)***
Skycatch Inc ....E....415 504-3929
38350 Fremont Blvd # 203 Fremont (94536) ***(P-12794)***
Skydio Inc (PA) ....**D....855 463-5902**
114 Hazel Ave Redwood City (94061) ***(P-6618)***
Skyera, San Jose *Also called Hgst Inc* ***(P-5290)***
Skyhigh Networks Inc ....D....408 564-0278
900 E Hamilton Ave # 400 Campbell (95008) ***(P-14148)***
Skylawn Memorial Park, Redwood City *Also called Chapel of Chimes* ***(P-10725)***
Skylight Tools Inc ....E....800 961-2580
2797 Bryant St San Francisco (94110) ***(P-5620)***
Skyline Alterations Inc (PA) ....**E....530 549-4010**
10771 Cheshire Way Palo Cedro (96073) ***(P-3082)***
Skyline Commercial Interiors (PA) ....**D....415 908-1020**
505 Sansome St Fl 7 San Francisco (94111) ***(P-963)***
Skyline Construction, San Francisco *Also called Skyline Commercial Interiors* ***(P-963)***
Skyline Financial Services (PA) ....**D....818 995-1700**
2355 Gold Meadow Way # 160 Gold River (95670) ***(P-9928)***
Skyline Health Care Center, San Jose *Also called Mariner Health Care Inc* ***(P-16047)***
Skyline Scaffold Inc ....D....916 391-8929
3131 52nd Ave Sacramento (95823) ***(P-2070)***
Skyline Solar Inc ....E....650 864-9770
185 E Dana St Mountain View (94041) ***(P-4634)***

Skyline Tree Enterprise Inc E 530 736-9327
3650 Westhaven St Cottonwood (96022) *(P-309)*

Skylite Networks D 403 934-9349
761 Mabury Rd Ste 75 San Jose (95133) *(P-12795)*

Skyloom Global Corp E 415 696-4894
1901 Poplar St Oakland (94607) *(P-5808)*

Skypark, San Mateo *Also called Airport Parking Service Inc (P-14507)*

Skype Inc D 650 493-7900
1 Microsoft Way Redmond Palo Alto (94304) *(P-7991)*

Skyslope Inc D 916 833-2390
825 K St Fl 2 Sacramento (95814) *(P-13977)*

Skywalker Properties Ltd LLC (PA) **D 415 746-5059**
1 Letterman Dr Bldg B San Francisco (94129) *(P-10407)*

Skywalker Sound E 415 662-1000
1110 Gorgas Ave San Francisco (94129) *(P-1607)*

Skywest Airlines Inc B 559 252-3400
Fresno Air Terminal Fresno (93727) *(P-7740)*

SL One Global Inc (PA) **D 916 993-4100**
4211 Norwood Ave Sacramento (95838) *(P-9304)*

Sla LLC (PA) **E 650 322-2600**
245 Lytton Ave Ste 150 Palo Alto (94301) *(P-10408)*

Slack Technologies LLC (HQ) **A 415 902-5526**
500 Howard St Ste 100 San Francisco (94105) *(P-13446)*

Slalom LLC C 415 593-3450
100 Pine St Ste 2500 San Francisco (94111) *(P-19635)*

Slam Specialties LLC F 559 348-9038
5837 E Brown Ave Fresno (93727) *(P-6594)*

Slashsupport Inc (HQ) **C 408 985-4377**
75 E Santa Clara St # 900 San Jose (95113) *(P-7992)*

Slatter Construction Inc E 831 425-5425
126 Fern St Santa Cruz (95060) *(P-964)*

Slauson Transmission Parts E 310 768-2099
9675 Oconnell Rd Sebastopol (95472) *(P-14542)*

Slawomira Sobczyk, Milpitas *Also called Yuhas Tooling & Machining Inc (P-5644)*

SLC, Truckee *Also called Software Licensing Consultants (P-13452)*

Sleepio, San Francisco *Also called Big Health Inc (P-16170)*

Sleepmed Incorporated E 707 864-1869
4735 Mangels Blvd Fairfield (94534) *(P-15689)*

SLHCC Inc E 916 457-6521
3500 Folsom Blvd Sacramento (95816) *(P-16123)*

SLI Systems Inc D 408 255-2487
333 W San Carlos St # 1250 San Jose (95110) *(P-12796)*

Sliderule Labs Inc (PA) **C 646 748-0378**
22 Battery St Ste 1100 San Francisco (94111) *(P-12797)*

Sling Media LLC C 650 293-8000
1051 E Hillsdale Blvd # 500 Foster City (94404) *(P-7912)*

Slouber Enterprises Inc (PA) **E 530 273-2080**
11885 Sunrise Ln Grass Valley (95945) *(P-6853)*

Slow Sculpture E 707 537-7024
5715 Monte Verde Dr Santa Rosa (95409) *(P-18183)*

SM International, Fremont *Also called S & M Moving Systems (P-7585)*

SMA America, Rocklin *Also called SMA Solar Technology Amer LLC (P-8955)*

SMA America Production LLC C 720 347-6000
6020 West Oaks Blvd # 300 Rocklin (95765) *(P-4635)*

SMA Solar Technology Amer LLC (HQ) **C 916 625-0870**
6020 West Oaks Blvd Rocklin (95765) *(P-8955)*

Small Hand Foods, Hayward *Also called Still Room LLC (P-2826)*

Small Precision Tools Inc D 707 765-4545
1330 Clegg St Petaluma (94954) *(P-6303)*

Small Talk Pediatric Svcs Inc (PA) **E 530 226-8255**
2526 Goodwater Ave Ste A Redding (96002) *(P-15690)*

Small World Trading Co C 415 945-1900
90 Windward Way San Rafael (94901) *(P-9237)*

Smarsh Inc C 650 631-6300
900 Veterans Blvd Fl 5 Redwood City (94063) *(P-13447)*

Smart & Final Stores Inc C 916 486-6315
7223 Fair Oaks Blvd Carmichael (95608) *(P-9305)*

Smart & Final Stores Inc C 408 251-0109
1180 S King Rd San Jose (95122) *(P-9306)*

Smart & Final Stores Inc C 530 823-1205
2825 Grass Valley Hwy Auburn (95603) *(P-9307)*

Smart & Final Stores Inc C 559 229-2944
2425 N Blackstone Ave Fresno (93703) *(P-9308)*

Smart & Final Stores Inc C 408 941-9642
401 Jacklin Rd Milpitas (95035) *(P-9309)*

Smart & Final Stores Inc C 559 297-9376
790 W Shaw Ave Clovis (93612) *(P-9310)*

Smart Business Resource Center E 530 246-7911
1201 Placer St Redding (96001) *(P-17839)*

Smart Erp Solutions Inc (PA) **D 925 271-0200**
3875 Hopyard Rd Ste 180 Pleasanton (94588) *(P-12798)*

Smart Global Holdings Inc (PA) **B 510 623-1231**
39870 Eureka Dr Newark (94560) *(P-6304)*

Smart Machines Inc E 510 661-5000
46702 Bayside Pkwy Fremont (94538) *(P-5057)*

Smart Modular Tech De Inc (HQ) **D 510 623-1231**
45800 Northport Loop W Fremont (94538) *(P-6305)*

Smart Modular Technologies Inc (HQ) **A 510 623-1231**
39870 Eureka Dr Newark (94560) *(P-6306)*

Smart Sftwr Tstg Solutions Inc D 833 778-7872
2450 Peralta Blvd Ste 202 Fremont (94536) *(P-19861)*

Smart Spectrometer, Fremont *Also called Atonarp Us Inc (P-6811)*

Smart Storage Systems Inc (HQ) **E 510 623-1231**
39672 Eureka Dr Newark (94560) *(P-5321)*

Smart TV & Sound, Chico *Also called Videomaker Inc (P-3518)*

Smart Wires Inc (PA) **D 415 800-5555**
3292 Whipple Rd Union City (94587) *(P-6384)*

Smart World LLC E 510 933-9700
48225 Lakeview Blvd Fremont (94538) *(P-14406)*

Smartek21 LLC B 650 617-3221
530 Lytton Ave Fl 2 Palo Alto (94301) *(P-13978)*

Smartlogic Semaphore Inc E 408 213-9500
111 N Market St Ste 365 San Jose (95113) *(P-13448)*

Smartnews International Inc D 628 444-3000
144 2nd St San Francisco (94105) *(P-12799)*

Smartrecruiters Inc (PA) **B 415 659-9130**
225 Bush St Ste 300 San Francisco (94104) *(P-12800)*

Smartrevenuecom Inc B 203 733-9156
101 Cooper St Ste 205 Santa Cruz (95060) *(P-19185)*

Smartthings Inc (PA) **C 757 633-2308**
665 Clyde Ave Mountain View (94043) *(P-5218)*

Smartzip Analytics Inc D 855 661-1064
6200 Stnrdge Mall Rd Ste Pleasanton (94588) *(P-19636)*

Smb Industries Inc (PA) **D 530 534-6266**
550 Georgia Pacific Way Oroville (95965) *(P-4684)*

Smcmad, Burlingame *Also called San Mteo Cnty Msqito Vctor Ctr (P-8405)*

Smg B 209 937-7433
3445 S El Dorado St Stockton (95206) *(P-19706)*

Smg Stockton, Stockton *Also called Smg (P-19706)*

Smic Americas E 408 550-8888
1732 N 1st St Ste 200 San Jose (95112) *(P-9096)*

Smit's Heating & AC, Diamond Springs *Also called Smits Sheet Metal Inc (P-1361)*

Smith & Vandiver Corporation D 831 722-9526
480 Airport Blvd Watsonville (95076) *(P-9238)*

Smith Barney, San Jose *Also called Citigroup Global Markets Inc (P-9964)*

Smith News Company Inc E 415 861-4900
460 9th St San Francisco (94103) *(P-9671)*

Smith Novelty Company, San Francisco *Also called Smith News Company Inc (P-9671)*

Smith River Lucky 7 Casino C 707 487-7777
350 N Indian Rd Smith River (95567) *(P-11489)*

Smith Rnch Hmes Hmeowners Assn D 415 492-4900
500 Deer Valley Rd San Rafael (94903) *(P-10461)*

Smith Sons Wldg & Fabrication F 707 437-3027
2216 Cement Hill Rd Fairfield (94533) *(P-14722)*

Smith-Emery San Francisco Inc E 415 642-7326
1940 Oakdale Ave San Francisco (94124) *(P-14407)*

Smithgroup Inc C 313 442-8351
301 Battery St Fl 7 San Francisco (94111) *(P-18914)*

Smithgroupjjr, San Francisco *Also called Smithgroup Inc (P-18914)*

Smiths Detection Inc A 410 612-2625
7151 Gateway Blvd Newark (94560) *(P-6685)*

Smits Sheet Metal Inc E 530 622-8446
6205 Enterprise Dr Ste A Diamond Springs (95619) *(P-1361)*

Smoothie Operator Inc F 916 773-9541
8690 Sierra College Blvd Roseville (95661) *(P-2298)*

Smss, Foster City *Also called Sony Interactive Entrmt LLC (P-14410)*

Smtc Corporation (HQ) **D 510 737-0700**
431 Kato Ter Fremont (94539) *(P-5974)*

Smtc Manufacturing Corp Cal A 408 934-7100
431 Kato Ter Fremont (94539) *(P-5975)*

Smtc Mex Holdings Inc (HQ) **D 915 849-6752**
431 Kato Ter Fremont (94539) *(P-8956)*

Smtc Mex Holdings Inc C 510 737-0729
431 Kato Ter Fremont (94539) *(P-8957)*

Smucker Natural Foods Inc (HQ) **C 530 899-5000**
37 Speedway Ave Chico (95928) *(P-2815)*

Smud Energy Services, Sacramento *Also called Sacramento Municpl Utility Dst (P-8198)*

Smud Financing Authority, Herald *Also called Sacramento Municpl Utility Dst (P-14393)*

Sn Servicing Corporation E 916 779-2200
1484 Haddington Dr Folsom (95630) *(P-9929)*

Sn Servicing Corporation E 707 445-9883
323 5th St Eureka (95501) *(P-9930)*

Sna Electronics Inc E 510 656-3903
3249 Laurelview Ct Fremont (94538) *(P-5976)*

Snap Pack Mail, Oakdale *Also called Media Print Services Inc (P-11868)*

Snap Travel, San Francisco *Also called Snapcommerce Inc (P-7807)*

Snapcommerce Inc C 917 704-4588
18 Bartol St San Francisco (94133) *(P-7807)*

Snapdocs Inc E 415 967-0136
100 Montgomery St # 2400 San Francisco (94104) *(P-12801)*

Snapfish LLC (HQ) **D 415 979-3703**
100 Montgomery St # 1430 San Francisco (94104) *(P-14183)*

Snaplogic Inc (PA) **C 888 494-1570**
1825 S Grant St Ste 550 San Mateo (94402) *(P-13449)*

Snapwiz Inc C 510 328-3277
39300 Civic Center Dr # 310 Fremont (94538) *(P-13450)*

Snoopy's Galary and Gift Shop, Santa Rosa *Also called Redwood Empire Ice Oprtons LLC (P-15231)*

Snoozie Shavings Inc (PA) **D 707 464-6186**
525 Elk Valley Rd Crescent City (95531) *(P-7595)*

Snow Cleaners Inc (PA) **E 209 547-1454**
38 W Sonora St Stockton (95203) *(P-11656)*

Snow Creek Resort, Mammoth Lakes *Also called Snowcreek Property Management (P-10663)*

Snowcreek Property Management E 760 934-3333
1254 Old Mammoth Rd Mammoth Lakes (93546) *(P-10663)*

Snowflake Designs E 559 291-6234
2893 Larkin Ave Clovis (93612) *(P-2973)*

Snowline Engineering, Cameron Park *Also called Preferred Mfg Svcs Inc (P-5603)*

Snowline Hspice El Dorado Cnty C 530 621-7820
6520 Pleasant Valley Rd Diamond Springs (95619) *(P-16204)*

Snowline Hspice of El Drado CN C 916 817-2338
6520 Pleasant Valley Rd Diamond Springs (95619) *(P-16205)*

Snowshoe Brewing Co LLC (PA) **E 209 795-2272**
2050 Hwy 4 Arnold (95223) *(P-2493)*

Snyder Industries LLC D 559 665-7611
800 Commerce Dr Chowchilla (93610) *(P-4324)*

ALPHABETIC

Soaprojects Inc (PA)......D......**650 960-9900**
495 N Whisman Rd Ste 100 Mountain View (94043) ***(P-13979)***
Soares Dairy Farms Inc......D......209 826-3414
14515 Badger Flat Rd Los Banos (93635) ***(P-223)***
Soares Lumber Company, Gilroy *Also called PSG Fencing Corporation* ***(P-2058)***
Social Advocates For Youth, Santa Rosa *Also called Individuals Now* ***(P-17613)***
Social Brands LLC......E......415 728-1761
6575 Simson St Oakland (94605) ***(P-7308)***
Social Finance Inc (HQ)......C......**415 930-4467**
234 1st St San Francisco (94105) ***(P-9949)***
Social Finance Inc......B......707 473-9889
375 Healdsburg Ave # 280 Healdsburg (95448) ***(P-9950)***
Social Imprints LLC......E......510 610-6511
2500 Marin St San Francisco (94124) ***(P-3698)***
Social Interest Solutions, Sacramento *Also called Center To Prmote Hlthcare Acce* ***(P-17118)***
SOCIAL INTEREST SOLUTIONS, Oakland *Also called Center To Prmote Hlthcare Acce* ***(P-17119)***
Social Service Agency, San Jose *Also called Santa Clara County of* ***(P-17717)***
Social Service Agency, San Martin *Also called Santa Clara County of* ***(P-17718)***
Social Service Agency, San Jose *Also called Santa Clara County of* ***(P-17720)***
Social Services Agency, San Martin *Also called Santa Clara County of* ***(P-17719)***
Social Services Cal Dept......D......559 248-8400
1330 E Shaw Ave Fresno (93710) ***(P-17746)***
Social Services Cal Dept......D......530 889-7610
11519 B Ave Auburn (95603) ***(P-17747)***
Social Services Cal Dept......D......916 657-2346
744 P St Sacramento (95814) ***(P-17748)***
Social Vocational Services Inc......E......510 797-1916
37400 Cedar Blvd Ste A Newark (94560) ***(P-17074)***
Socialight, The, Campbell *Also called Afn Services LLC* ***(P-3334)***
Society For Blind......E......916 452-8271
1238 S St Sacramento (95811) ***(P-18592)***
Society For San Francisco......C......415 554-3000
201 Alabama St San Francisco (94103) ***(P-18593)***
Society For The Study Ntiv Art......E......510 549-4270
2526 Mrtin Lther King Jr Berkeley (94704) ***(P-3545)***
Society of St Vncent De Paul A (PA)......D......**510 638-7600**
2272 San Pablo Ave Oakland (94612) ***(P-18594)***
Society of St Vncent De Paul D......E......415 454-3303
822 B St San Rafael (94901) ***(P-17749)***
Society of St Vncent De Paul P (PA)......D......**650 373-0622**
134 N Claremont St San Mateo (94401) ***(P-18595)***
Socket Mobile Inc......E......510 933-3000
39700 Eureka Dr Newark (94560) ***(P-5869)***
Socksmith Design Inc (PA)......E......**831 426-6416**
1515 Pacific Ave Santa Cruz (95060) ***(P-2972)***
Socratic Technologies Inc (PA)......E......**415 430-2200**
245 N Main St Sebastopol (95472) ***(P-19186)***
Sodexo Management Inc......B......925 325-9657
851 Howard St San Francisco (94103) ***(P-19399)***
Sodexo Management Inc......B......209 667-3634
1 University Cir Turlock (95382) ***(P-19400)***
Sof-Tek Integrators Inc......E......530 242-0527
4712 Mtn Lakes Blvd # 200 Redding (96003) ***(P-18815)***
Sofa Holdco Dev LLC......D......847 713-0680
470 S Market St San Jose (95113) ***(P-12802)***
Sofar Ocean Technologies Inc (PA)......E......**415 230-2299**
Shed B Blkhead Of Pier 50 St Pier San Francisco (94158) ***(P-19127)***
Sofi, San Francisco *Also called Social Finance Inc* ***(P-9949)***
Sofi Technologies Inc (PA)......D......**855 456-7634**
234 1st St San Francisco (94105) ***(P-9931)***
Softgear Technologies, San Mateo *Also called Logigear Corporation* ***(P-12580)***
Softsol Resources Inc (HQ)......D......**510 824-2000**
42808 Christy St Ste 100 Fremont (94538) ***(P-12803)***
Software Dev & Technical Svc, San Jose *Also called Sofa Holdco Dev LLC* ***(P-12802)***
Software Development Inc......E......925 847-8823
5000 Hopyard Rd Ste 160 Pleasanton (94588) ***(P-13451)***
Software Licensing Consultants......E......925 371-1277
12030 Donner Pass Rd # 1 Truckee (96161) ***(P-13452)***
Soha Engineers (PA)......E......**415 989-9900**
48 Colin P Kelly Jr St San Francisco (94107) ***(P-18816)***
Soiree Valet Parking Service......D......415 284-9700
1470 Howard St San Francisco (94103) ***(P-11730)***
Soladigm, Milpitas *Also called View Operating Corporation* ***(P-4363)***
Solairus Aviation, Petaluma *Also called Sunset Aviation LLC* ***(P-7785)***
Solano Athletic Clubs Inc (PA)......E......**707 422-2858**
3006 Hillside Ct Fairfield (94533) ***(P-15147)***
Solano Collission Inc......E......707 644-4044
3267 Sonoma Blvd Vallejo (94590) ***(P-14533)***
Solano County Fair Association......D......707 551-2000
900 Fairgrounds Dr Vallejo (94589) ***(P-15243)***
Solano Diagnostics Imaging......E......707 646-4646
1101 B Gale Wilson Blvd # 100 Fairfield (94533) ***(P-6922)***
SOLANO FAMILY & CHILDREN'S SER, Fairfield *Also called Solano Fmly & Chld Council Inc* ***(P-18022)***
Solano First Federal Credit Un......E......707 422-9626
1000 Union Ave Fairfield (94533) ***(P-9820)***
Solano Fmly & Chld Council Inc......D......707 863-3950
421 Executive Ct N Fairfield (94534) ***(P-18022)***
Solano Gateway Realty Inc (PA)......E......**707 422-1725**
2420 Martin Rd Ste 100 Fairfield (94534) ***(P-10664)***
Solano Hematology/Oncology LLC......E......707 551-3300
100 Hospital Dr Ste 110 Vallejo (94589) ***(P-15691)***
Solano Irrigation District......D......707 448-6847
810 Vaca Valley Pkwy # 201 Vacaville (95688) ***(P-8418)***
Solano Juvenile Institution, Fairfield *Also called County of Solano* ***(P-17512)***
Solar 4 America, Livermore *Also called Solarjuice American Inc* ***(P-5038)***
Solar Company Inc......D......510 888-9488
20861 Wilbeam Ave Ste 1 Castro Valley (94546) ***(P-1362)***
Solar Energy Collective, Stockton *Also called Landmark Capital Inc* ***(P-1301)***
Solar Industries Inc......E......916 567-9650
731 N Market Blvd Ste J Sacramento (95834) ***(P-4636)***
Solarbos (HQ)......D......**925 456-7744**
2019 Elkins Way Ste A Brentwood (94513) ***(P-5655)***
Solarcraft Services Inc (PA)......E......**415 382-7717**
8 Digital Dr Ste 101 Novato (94949) ***(P-1608)***
Solaredge Technologies Inc (PA)......B......**510 498-3200**
700 Tasman Dr Milpitas (95035) ***(P-5696)***
Solari Ranch, Stockton *Also called Casa Del Rios Hbilitation Svcs* ***(P-18072)***
Solarjuice American Inc......B......925 474-8821
6950 Preston Ave Livermore (94551) ***(P-5038)***
Solarroofs.com, Carmichael *Also called ACR Solar International Corp* ***(P-4624)***
Solarroofscom Inc......F......916 481-7200
5840 Gibbons Dr Ste H Carmichael (95608) ***(P-4637)***
Solcom Inc......B......510 940-2490
24801 Huntwood Ave Hayward (94544) ***(P-1135)***
Solcom Communications Inc, Hayward *Also called Solcom Inc* ***(P-1135)***
Solecon Industrial Contrs Inc......D......209 572-7390
1401 Mcwilliams Way Modesto (95351) ***(P-1363)***
Soleeva Energy Inc......D......408 396-4954
1938 Junction Ave San Jose (95131) ***(P-1364)***
Solflower Computer Inc......E......408 733-8100
3337 Kifer Rd Santa Clara (95051) ***(P-5412)***
Solid Data Systems Inc......F......408 845-5700
3542 Bassett St Santa Clara (95054) ***(P-5322)***
Solid Gold Inc......D......415 536-0300
650 Howard St San Francisco (94105) ***(P-14878)***
Solid Solutions 24/7 Inc......D......916 800-1847
7700 14th Ave Sacramento (95820) ***(P-14408)***
Solid State Stor Tech USA Corp......D......510 687-1800
726 S Hillview Dr Milpitas (95035) ***(P-8749)***
Solidcore Systems Inc (HQ)......D......**408 387-8400**
3965 Freedom Cir Santa Clara (95054) ***(P-13453)***
Soligent Distribution LLC (HQ)......C......**707 992-3100**
1400 N Mcdowell Blvd # 201 Petaluma (94954) ***(P-8958)***
Soliman Hisham M D Inc......E......916 351-9400
510 Plaza Dr Ste 170 Folsom (95630) ***(P-15692)***
Solitude Lake Management, Benicia *Also called Aquatic Environments Inc* ***(P-1147)***
Solix Technologies Inc (PA)......D......**408 654-6405**
4701 Patrick Henry Dr # 2001 Santa Clara (95054) ***(P-12804)***
Solmetric Corporation......D......707 823-4600
117 Morris St Ste 100 Sebastopol (95472) ***(P-6923)***
Solopoint Solutions Inc (PA)......D......**408 246-5945**
3350 Scott Blvd Bldg 2 Santa Clara (95054) ***(P-19637)***
Solta Medical Inc (HQ)......D......**510 786-6946**
7031 Koll Center Pkwy # 260 Pleasanton (94566) ***(P-7039)***
Solta Medical Inc......C......510 782-2286
25901 Industrial Blvd Hayward (94545) ***(P-7124)***
Solutionsati Consulting Inc......E......408 655-0224
19925 Stevns Crk Blvd Cupertino (95014) ***(P-19862)***
Solvvy Inc......E......650 246-9685
1200 Park Pl Ste 350 San Mateo (94403) ***(P-12805)***
Somam Inc......E......559 436-0881
6011 N Fresno St Ste 130 Fresno (93710) ***(P-14409)***
Sombrero Time, Granite Bay *Also called R&D Educational Systems Inc* ***(P-7304)***
Somerford Place, Fresno *Also called Fresno Heritage Partners* ***(P-18118)***
Somerford Place Fresno, Fresno *Also called Five Star Quality Care Inc* ***(P-16004)***
Sonata Software North Amer Inc (HQ)......D......**510 791-7220**
39300 Civic Center Dr # 270 Fremont (94538) ***(P-12806)***
Sonesta Intl Hotels Corp......B......415 929-2393
495 Geary St San Francisco (94102) ***(P-11490)***
Sonia Corina Inc......E......707 644-4491
1100 Rose Dr Ste 140 Benicia (94510) ***(P-17181)***
Sonic Manufacturing Tech Inc......E......510 580-8551
47931 Westinghouse Dr Fremont (94539) ***(P-5977)***
Sonic Manufacturing Tech Inc......B......510 580-8500
47951 Westinghouse Dr Fremont (94539) ***(P-5978)***
Sonic Technology Products Inc......E......530 272-4607
108 Boulder St Nevada City (95959) ***(P-6307)***
Sonicwall Inc (PA)......A......**888 557-6642**
1033 Mccarthy Blvd Milpitas (95035) ***(P-13666)***
Sonitrol, San Jose *Also called Pacific West Security Inc* ***(P-14143)***
Sonitrol of Sacramento LLC......E......916 724-1170
1334 Blue Oaks Blvd Roseville (95678) ***(P-14149)***
Sonitrol Security Systems, Fresno *Also called Kimberlite Corporation* ***(P-14138)***
Sonnikson and Stordahl Cnstr......E......925 229-4028
4858 Sunrise Dr Martinez (94553) ***(P-1365)***
Sonoco Prtective Solutions Inc......D......510 785-0220
3466 Enterprise Ave Hayward (94545) ***(P-3366)***
Sonoma Access Ctrl Systems Inc......E......707 935-3458
21600 8th St E Sonoma (95476) ***(P-4839)***
Sonoma Acres Convalescent Inc......E......707 996-2161
765 Donald St Sonoma (95476) ***(P-16124)***
Sonoma Beverage Company LLC (PA)......F......**707 431-1099**
2710 Giffen Ave Santa Rosa (95407) ***(P-2299)***
Sonoma Canopy Tours, Occidental *Also called Alliance Rdwods Cnfrnce Grunds* ***(P-11597)***
Sonoma Cnty Indian Hlth Prj In (PA)......C......**707 521-4545**
144 Stony Point Rd Santa Rosa (95401) ***(P-15693)***
Sonoma Country Day School......C......707 284-3200
4400 Day School Pl Santa Rosa (95403) ***(P-18023)***
Sonoma County Airport Ex Inc......B......707 837-8700
5807 Old Redwood Hwy Santa Rosa (95403) ***(P-7360)***
Sonoma County Regional Parks......D......707 527-2041
2300 County Center Dr A120 Santa Rosa (95403) ***(P-11621)***
Sonoma County Water Agency......C......707 526-5370
404 Aviation Blvd Ste 0 Santa Rosa (95403) ***(P-8272)***

Sonoma Development Center, Eldridge *Also called Developmental Svcs Cal Dept (P-16756)*
Sonoma Foods, Santa Rosa *Also called MS Intertrade Inc (P-2831)*
Sonoma Gourmet, Sonoma *Also called Sonoma Specialty Foods Inc (P-9487)*
Sonoma Gourmet Inc....E....707 939-3700
21684 8th St E Ste 100 Sonoma (95476) **(P-2286)**
Sonoma Hotel Operator Inc....B....707 938-9000
100 Boyes Blvd Sonoma (95476) **(P-11491)**
Sonoma Hotel Partners LP....D....707 283-2888
745 Baywood Dr Petaluma (94954) **(P-11492)**
Sonoma Index-Tribune....E....707 938-2111
117 W Napa St Ste A Sonoma (95476) **(P-3480)**
Sonoma Media Investments LLC (PA)....D....707 526-8563
427 Mendocino Ave Santa Rosa (95401) **(P-3481)**
Sonoma Metal Products Inc....E....707 484-9876
601 Aviation Blvd Santa Rosa (95403) **(P-4818)**
Sonoma National Golf Club....D....707 939-4100
17700 Arnold Dr Sonoma (95476) **(P-15148)**
Sonoma Orthopedic Products Inc....F....847 807-4378
50 W San Fernando St Fl 5 San Jose (95113) **(P-7040)**
Sonoma Photonics Inc....E....707 568-1202
1750 Northpoint Pkwy C Santa Rosa (95407) **(P-6385)**
Sonoma Pins Etc Corporation....E....707 996-9956
841 W Napa St Sonoma (95476) **(P-3749)**
Sonoma Post Acute, Sonoma *Also called Sonomaidence Opco LLC (P-16206)*
Sonoma Promotional Solutions, Sonoma *Also called Sonoma Pins Etc Corporation (P-3749)*
Sonoma Specialty Foods Inc....E....707 939-3700
21684 8th St E Ste 100 Sonoma (95476) **(P-9487)**
Sonoma Stainless....F....707 546-3945
170 Todd Rd Ste 100 Santa Rosa (95407) **(P-4731)**
Sonoma Technology Inc....D....707 665-9900
1450 N Mcdowell Blvd # 2 Petaluma (94954) **(P-19863)**
Sonoma Tilemakers Inc (HQ)....D....707 837-8177
7750 Bell Rd Windsor (95492) **(P-1721)**
Sonoma Valley Cmnty Hlth Ctr....E....707 939-6070
19270 Highway 12 Sonoma (95476) **(P-15694)**
Sonoma Valley Health Care Dst (PA)....B....707 935-5000
347 Andrieux St Sonoma (95476) **(P-16529)**
Sonoma Valley Hospital, Sonoma *Also called Sonoma Valley Health Care Dst (P-16529)*
Sonoma Valley Publishing, Sonoma *Also called Sonoma Index-Tribune (P-3480)*
Sonoma Valley Unified Schl Dst....D....707 935-4291
18751 Railroad Ave Sonoma (95476) **(P-12000)**
Sonoma Wine Hardware Inc....E....650 866-3020
360 Swift Ave Ste 34 South San Francisco (94080) **(P-2721)**
Sonoma-Cutrer Vineyards Inc (HQ)....C....707 528-1181
4401 Slusser Rd Windsor (95492) **(P-75)**
Sonomaidence Opco LLC....D....707 938-1096
678 2nd St W Sonoma (95476) **(P-16206)**
Sonora Community Hospital....C....209 536-5012
1000 Greenley Rd Sonora (95370) **(P-15695)**
Sonora Eye Surgery Center, Sonora *Also called Donaldson Arthur M D Inc (P-15383)*
Sonora Sport & Fitnes Ctr Inc (PA)....E....209 532-1202
13760 Mono Way Sonora (95370) **(P-14972)**
Sonoran Roofing Inc....C....916 624-1080
4161 Citrus Ave Rocklin (95677) **(P-1837)**
Sontesta Select San Jose Arprt....E....408 441-6111
1727 Technology Dr San Jose (95110) **(P-11493)**
Sony Biotechnology Inc....E....408 352-4257
1730 N 1st St Fl 2 San Jose (95112) **(P-19128)**
Sony Biotechnology Inc....D....800 275-5963
1730 N 1st St Fl 2 San Jose (95112) **(P-13454)**
Sony Corporation of America....C....650 655-8000
2207 Bridgepointe Pkwy Foster City (94404) **(P-12807)**
Sony Interactive Entrmt LLC....D....650 655-8000
2207 Brindgepointe Pkwy San Mateo (94404) **(P-14879)**
Sony Interactive Entrmt LLC (HQ)....B....310 981-1500
2207 Bridgepointe Pkwy Foster City (94404) **(P-14410)**
Sony MBL Cmmunications USA Inc....C....866 766-9374
2207 Bridgepoint Pkwy San Mateo (94404) **(P-5870)**
Soojians Inc....E....559 875-5511
89 Academy Ave Sanger (93657) **(P-2418)**
Soper-Wheeler Company LLC (PA)....E....530 675-2343
100 N Pine St Unit B Nevada City (95959) **(P-3083)**
Soquel Creek Water District....E....831 475-0195
5180 Soquel Dr Soquel (95073) **(P-8273)**
Soraa Inc (HQ)....D....510 456-2200
6500 Kaiser Dr Ste 110 Fremont (94555) **(P-6308)**
Sorrento Networks Corporation (HQ)....F....510 577-1400
7195 Oakport St Oakland (94621) **(P-5809)**
SOS, Belvedere Tiburon *Also called System Operation Services Inc (P-19871)*
SOS Security Incorporated....D....510 782-4900
26250 Industrial Blvd # 48 Hayward (94545) **(P-14098)**
Sosa Granite & Marble Inc....E....925 373-7675
7701 Marathon Dr Livermore (94550) **(P-1722)**
Sosa Tile Co, Livermore *Also called Sosa Granite & Marble Inc (P-1722)*
Sotcher Measurement Inc....E....408 574-0112
115 Phelan Ave Ste 10 San Jose (95112) **(P-6792)**
Sotoyome Medical Building LLC....D....707 525-4000
990 Sonoma Ave Ste 15 Santa Rosa (95404) **(P-10409)**
Soul Machines Inc....D....649 283-0863
44 Tehama St Ste 411 San Francisco (94105) **(P-13667)**
Soundhound Inc (PA)....D....408 441-3200
5400 Betsy Ross Dr Santa Clara (95054) **(P-12808)**
Soundstream Technologies Mfg....E....916 635-3011
11365 Sunrise Park Dr Rancho Cordova (95742) **(P-5769)**
Sourceamerica....D....925 543-5100
2633 Camino Ramon Ste 450 San Ramon (94583) **(P-18250)**
Sourcecorp Bps Nthrn Cal Inc....D....530 893-7900
900 Fortress St Chico (95973) **(P-8656)**
Sourcewise....D....408 350-3200
3100 De La Cruz Blvd # 310 Santa Clara (95054) **(P-17750)**
Sourcing Group LLC....E....510 471-4749
1672 Delta Ct Hayward (94544) **(P-3699)**
Sousa Ready Mix LLC....F....530 926-4485
100 Upton Rd Mount Shasta (96067) **(P-4508)**
South Bay Circuits Inc....C....408 978-8992
210 Hillsdale Ave San Jose (95136) **(P-6470)**
South Bay Construction Company, Campbell *Also called B C C S Inc (P-614)*
South Bay Diversfd Systems Inc....F....510 784-3094
1841 National Ave Hayward (94545) **(P-4819)**
South Bay Marble Inc (PA)....E....650 594-4251
1770 Old Bayshore Hwy San Jose (95112) **(P-4524)**
South Bay Regl Public Safety T....E....408 270-6494
560 Bailey Ave San Jose (95141) **(P-17840)**
South Bay Showers Inc....E....408 988-3484
540 Martin Ave Santa Clara (95050) **(P-1945)**
South Bay Solutions Inc (PA)....E....650 843-1800
37399 Centralmont Pl Fremont (94536) **(P-5621)**
South Bay Solutions Texas LLC....F....936 494-0180
37399 Centralmont Pl Fremont (94536) **(P-5697)**
South Cnty Chrysler-Jeep-Dodge....E....408 842-8244
455 Automall Dr Gilroy (95020) **(P-14593)**
South Cnty Cmnty Hlth Ctr Inc (PA)....D....650 330-7407
1885 Bay Rd East Palo Alto (94303) **(P-15696)**
South Coast Medical Center (PA)....A....916 781-2000
2100 Douglas Blvd Roseville (95661) **(P-16530)**
South County Chrysler Dodge, Gilroy *Also called South Cnty Chrysler-Jeep-Dodge (P-14593)*
South County Fire, Tracy *Also called South San Jquin Cnty Fire Auth (P-8275)*
South County Housing Corp (PA)....E....510 582-1460
16500 Monterey St Ste 120 Morgan Hill (95037) **(P-10665)**
South County Housing Corp....D....408 842-9181
9015 Murray Ave Ste 100 Gilroy (95020) **(P-785)**
South County Property MGT, Gilroy *Also called South County Housing Corp (P-785)*
South E Bay Pdtric Med Group I....E....510 792-4373
2191 Mowry Ave Ste 600c Fremont (94538) **(P-15697)**
South Feather Water & Pwr Agcy (PA)....E....530 533-4578
2310 Oro Quincy Hwy Oroville (95966) **(P-8274)**
South Gate Brewing Company....E....559 692-2739
40233 Enterprise Dr Oakhurst (93644) **(P-965)**
South Imaging Center, Sacramento *Also called Sutter Health (P-15718)*
South Market Child Care Inc (PA)....E....415 820-3500
790 Folsom St San Francisco (94107) **(P-18024)**
South Park Pleating Inc....E....510 625-8050
867 Isabella St Oakland (94607) **(P-14411)**
South Plcer Fire Prtection Dst, Granite Bay *Also called County of Placer (P-17510)*
South Pninsula Hebrew Day Schl....D....408 738-3060
1030 Astoria Dr Sunnyvale (94087) **(P-18025)**
South San Frncsco Scvenger Inc....D....650 589-4020
500 E Jamie Ct South San Francisco (94080) **(P-8363)**
South San Jquin Cnty Fire Auth....D....209 831-6702
835 N Central Ave Tracy (95376) **(P-8275)**
South San Jquin Irrigation Dst....D....209 249-4600
11011 E Highway 120 Manteca (95336) **(P-8276)**
South Skyline Firefighters....F....408 354-0025
12900 Skyline Blvd Los Gatos (95033) **(P-5233)**
South Skyline Vlntr Fire Rscue, Los Gatos *Also called South Skyline Firefighters (P-5233)*
South Tahoe Public Utility Dst....C....530 544-6474
1275 Meadow Crest Dr South Lake Tahoe (96150) **(P-8291)**
South Tahoe Refuse Co....D....530 541-5105
2140 Ruth Ave South Lake Tahoe (96150) **(P-8364)**
South Valley Materials Inc (HQ)....D....559 277-7060
114 E Shaw Ave Ste 100 Fresno (93710) **(P-4509)**
South Yuba Club Inc....E....530 470-9100
130 W Berryhill Dr Grass Valley (95945) **(P-14973)**
Southbay Teen Challenge, Santa Clara *Also called Teen Challenge Norwestcal Nev (P-17766)*
Southbourne Inc....C....415 781-5555
340 Stockton St San Francisco (94108) **(P-11494)**
Southeast Fresno Rad LP....C....559 443-8400
4430 E Hamilton Ave Fresno (93702) **(P-19864)**
Southern Alum Finshg Co Inc....D....530 244-7518
4356 Caterpillar Rd Redding (96003) **(P-4564)**
Southern Bptst Jnness Pk Encmp, Long Barn *Also called Califrnia Sthern Bptst Cnvntio (P-11598)*
Southern Cal Disc Tire Co Inc....C....510 429-1977
34734 Alvarado Niles Rd Union City (94587) **(P-8478)**
Southern Cal Disc Tire Co Inc....C....916 638-2388
11127 Folsom Blvd Rancho Cordova (95670) **(P-8467)**
Southern Cal Disc Tire Co Inc....C....916 427-1961
6434 Florin Rd Sacramento (95823) **(P-8468)**
Southern Cal Disc Tire Co Inc....C....650 366-4003
1610 Broadway St Redwood City (94063) **(P-8479)**
Southern Cal Disc Tire Co Inc....C....650 988-9611
32 W El Camino Real Mountain View (94040) **(P-8480)**
Southern Cal Disc Tire Co Inc....C....408 377-5010
980 E Hamilton Ave Campbell (95008) **(P-8481)**
Southern Cal Disc Tire Co Inc....C....408 436-8274
536 E Brokaw Rd San Jose (95112) **(P-8482)**
Southern California Edison Co....C....559 893-3611
54205 Mt Poplar Ave Big Creek (93605) **(P-8201)**
Southern California Edison Co....C....559 893-2037
55481 Mt Poplar Big Creek (93605) **(P-8202)**
Southern California Rest Assn, Sacramento *Also called California Restaurant Assn (P-18401)*
Southern Glzers Wine Sprits WA....B....510 477-5500
33321 Dowe Ave Union City (94587) **(P-9585)**

ALPHABETIC

Southern Hmbldt Cmnty Dst Hosp.....D.....707 923-3921
733 Cedar St Garberville (95542) ***(P-16531)***
Southern Hmbldt Cmnty Hlth Car.....D.....707 923-3921
733 Cedar St Garberville (95542) ***(P-16532)***
Southern Humboldt Cmnty Clinic, Garberville *Also called Southern Hmbldt Cmnty Dst Hosp* ***(P-16531)***
Southern Mono Healthcare Dst.....B.....760 934-3311
85 Sierra Park Rd Mammoth Lakes (93546) ***(P-16533)***
Southern Oregon Goodwill Inds.....D.....530 842-6627
1202 S Main St Yreka (96097) ***(P-17841)***
Southerncarlson Inc.....F.....916 375-8322
801 Striker Ave Sacramento (95834) ***(P-8635)***
Southgate Glass & Screen Inc (PA).....**E.....916 476-8396**
6852 Franklin Blvd Sacramento (95823) ***(P-8647)***
Southgate Glass & Screen Inc.....E.....916 476-8396
6199 Warehouse Way Sacramento (95826) ***(P-8648)***
Southgate Recreation & Pk Dst.....D.....916 421-7275
7320 Florin Mall Dr Sacramento (95823) ***(P-15244)***
Southpnte Chrstn Ctr Scrmnto C.....E.....916 504-3370
7520 Stockton Blvd Sacramento (95823) ***(P-2965)***
Southwall Technologies Inc (HQ).....**C.....650 798-1285**
3788 Fabian Way Palo Alto (94303) ***(P-3809)***
Southwest Cnstr & Property Mgt.....E.....650 877-0717
1213 San Mateo Ave San Bruno (94066) ***(P-966)***
Southwest Fence and Sup Co Inc (PA).....**E.....209 892-9205**
18042 Sycamore Ave Patterson (95363) ***(P-2071)***
Southwest Logistics Services, Watsonville *Also called Southwest Truck Service* ***(P-7596)***
Southwest Products Corporation.....E.....209 745-6000
85 Enterprise Ct Ste B Galt (95632) ***(P-4993)***
Southwest Traders Incorporated.....C.....209 462-1607
4747 Frontier Way Stockton (95215) ***(P-9311)***
Southwest Truck Service.....E.....831 724-1041
50 Pine St Watsonville (95076) ***(P-7596)***
Southwest YMCA, Saratoga *Also called Young MNS Chrstn Assn Slcon Vl* ***(P-18609)***
Southwick Inc (PA).....**E.....510 845-2530**
2400 Shattuck Ave Berkeley (94704) ***(P-14624)***
Souvenir Coffee Corporation (PA).....**E.....510 919-2777**
2849 Garber St Berkeley (94705) ***(P-9202)***
Sovereign Gen Insur Svcs Inc.....E.....209 932-5200
501 W Weber Ave Ste 404 Stockton (95203) ***(P-10173)***
Sp Controls Inc.....F.....650 392-7880
930 Linden Ave South San Francisco (94080) ***(P-5413)***
SP McClenahan Co.....D.....650 326-8781
1 Arastradero Rd Portola Valley (94028) ***(P-522)***
Sp3 Diamond Technologies Inc.....F.....877 773-9940
1605 Wyatt Dr Santa Clara (95054) ***(P-5234)***
Spa At Club Sport, San Ramon *Also called Clubsport San Ramon LLC* ***(P-14940)***
Spa Fitness Center Inc.....D.....831 476-7373
1100 41st Ave Capitola (95010) ***(P-14974)***
Spa Fitness Center Inc.....D.....831 722-3895
25 Penny Ln Watsonville (95076) ***(P-14975)***
Spa Radiance Associates Inc.....E.....415 346-6281
3011 Fillmore St San Francisco (94123) ***(P-14976)***
Space Time Insight Inc (HQ).....**E.....650 513-8550**
1850 Gateway Dr Ste 125 San Mateo (94404) ***(P-13455)***
Spacer.com, Pleasant Hill *Also called 500 Startups Management Co LLC* ***(P-10827)***
Spacesonics Incorporated.....D.....650 610-0999
30300 Union City Blvd Union City (94587) ***(P-4820)***
Spacetone Acoustics Inc.....E.....925 931-0749
1051 Serpentine Ln # 300 Pleasanton (94566) ***(P-1705)***
Span Construction & Engrg Inc (PA).....**D.....559 661-1111**
1841 Howard Rd Madera (93637) ***(P-967)***
Span Digital Inc.....E.....415 484-9269
333 Bryant St Ste 140 San Francisco (94107) ***(P-18817)***
Spangler Concrete & Engrg Inc.....E.....408 830-0400
830 W Evelyn Ave Sunnyvale (94086) ***(P-1653)***
Spanish Spking Unity Cncil Alm (PA).....**E.....510 535-6900**
1900 Fruitvale Ave Ste 2a Oakland (94601) ***(P-17751)***
Spanish Spking Unity Cncil Alm.....C.....510 836-0543
1117 10th St Oakland (94607) ***(P-18251)***
Spanos Corporation (PA).....**E.....209 955-2550**
10100 Trinity Pkwy Fl 5 Stockton (95219) ***(P-771)***
Spansion LLC (HQ).....**B.....512 691-8500**
198 Champion Ct San Jose (95134) ***(P-6309)***
Spar Sausage Co.....F.....510 614-8100
688 Williams St San Leandro (94577) ***(P-2125)***
Spare-Time Inc.....D.....916 983-9180
820 Halidon Way Folsom (95630) ***(P-15149)***
Spare-Time Inc.....D.....209 334-4897
1900 S Hutchins St Lodi (95240) ***(P-15150)***
Spare-Time Inc.....D.....916 782-2600
2501 Eureka Rd Roseville (95661) ***(P-15151)***
Spare-Time Inc.....B.....209 371-0241
429 W Lockeford St Lodi (95240) ***(P-14900)***
Spare-Time Inc.....D.....916 638-7001
2201 Gold Rush Dr Gold River (95670) ***(P-15152)***
Spare-Time Inc.....D.....916 649-0909
2450 Natomas Park Dr Sacramento (95833) ***(P-14977)***
Spare-Time Inc.....D.....916 859-5910
9570 Racquet Ct Elk Grove (95758) ***(P-15153)***
Spare-Time Inc.....D.....916 488-8100
119 Scripps Dr Sacramento (95825) ***(P-14978)***
Spares & Strikes Bowling Sup, Stockton *Also called Pacific Avenue Bowl* ***(P-14896)***
Sparkcentral Inc (HQ).....**D.....866 559-6229**
535 Mission St Fl 14 San Francisco (94105) ***(P-3600)***
Sparqtron Corporation.....D.....510 657-7198
5079 Brandin Ct Fremont (94538) ***(P-5698)***
Sparrowk Livestock, Clements *Also called Jack Sparrowk* ***(P-201)***

Spartronics Milpitas Inc (HQ).....**C.....408 957-1300**
1940 Milmont Dr Milpitas (95035) ***(P-5979)***
Spatten West, South San Francisco *Also called Chrissa Imports Ltd* ***(P-9547)***
Spec Personnel LLC.....D.....408 727-8000
433 Airport Blvd Ste 310 Burlingame (94010) ***(P-12138)***
Spec Personnel LLC.....D.....408 727-8000
1900 La Fytte St Unit 125 Santa Clara (95050) ***(P-12139)***
Spec. Personnel, Burlingame *Also called Spec Personnel LLC* ***(P-12138)***
Special Events, Livermore *Also called High Summit LLC* ***(P-14612)***
Specialized Coating Services.....D.....510 226-8700
42680 Christy St Fremont (94538) ***(P-4949)***
Specialized Laundry Svcs Inc.....C.....510 487-8297
33485 Western Ave Union City (94587) ***(P-11670)***
Specialized Transport Inc.....E.....916 969-6300
9325 Viking Pl Roseville (95747) ***(P-7490)***
Specialty Baking Inc.....D.....408 298-6950
3134 Capelaw Ct San Jose (95135) ***(P-9488)***
Specialty Baking Co., San Jose *Also called Specialty Baking Inc* ***(P-9488)***
Specialty Branded Products Inc.....E.....559 222-8895
523 N Brawley Ave Fresno (93706) ***(P-9380)***
Specialty Clinic, Davis *Also called University California Davis* ***(P-15772)***
Specialty Granules LLC.....E.....209 274-5323
1900 State Hwy 104 Ione (95640) ***(P-4532)***
Specialty Graphics Inc.....F.....510 351-7705
18686 Walnut Rd Castro Valley (94546) ***(P-3762)***
Specialty Risk Services Inc.....D.....877 809-9478
6140 Stnrdge Mall Rd Ste Pleasanton (94588) ***(P-10352)***
Specialty Solid Waste & Recycl, Santa Clara *Also called Bay Counties Waste Svcs Inc* ***(P-8307)***
Specialty Steel Service, Stockton *Also called PDM Steel Service Centers Inc* ***(P-8824)***
Specialty Steel Service Co Inc.....E.....800 777-4258
1224 Coloma Way Ste 150 Roseville (95661) ***(P-8828)***
Specialty Steel Service Co Inc (HQ).....**D.....916 771-4737**
3300 Douglas Blvd Ste 128 Roseville (95661) ***(P-8829)***
Specialty Truck Parts Inc (PA).....**E.....408 998-7272**
7700 Arroyo Cir Gilroy (95020) ***(P-8469)***
Specific Diagnostics Inc.....E.....650 938-2030
855 Maude Ave Mountain View (94043) ***(P-7041)***
Specilized Packg Solutions Inc.....E.....510 494-5670
38505 Cherry St Ste H Newark (94560) ***(P-3241)***
Specilzed Packg Solutions-Wood, Newark *Also called Specilized Packg Solutions Inc* ***(P-3241)***
Speck Products, San Mateo *Also called Speculative Product Design LLC* ***(P-4349)***
Spectra, Santa Clara *Also called Spec Personnel LLC* ***(P-12139)***
Spectra Watermakers, Petaluma *Also called Katadyn Desalination LLC* ***(P-5704)***
Spectra-Physics Inc (HQ).....**A.....877 835-9620**
1565 Barber Ln Milpitas (95035) ***(P-6543)***
Spectral Dynamics Inc (PA).....**E.....760 761-0440**
2199 Zanker Rd San Jose (95131) ***(P-6924)***
Spectranetics Corporation.....D.....510 933-7964
5055 Brandin Ct Fremont (94538) ***(P-7042)***
Spectraprint Inc.....F.....415 460-1228
24 Moody Ct San Rafael (94901) ***(P-3750)***
Spectrum Label, Newark *Also called Resource Label Group LLC* ***(P-3747)***
Spectrum Lithograph Inc.....E.....510 438-9192
4300 Business Center Dr Fremont (94538) ***(P-3700)***
Spectrum Prsthtcs/Rthtics Rddi.....E.....530 243-4500
1844 South St Redding (96001) ***(P-7080)***
Spectrum Semiconductor Mtls.....F.....408 435-5555
155 Nicholson Ln San Jose (95134) ***(P-6310)***
Spectrum Services Group Inc.....D.....916 760-7913
3841 N Freeway Blvd # 120 Sacramento (95834) ***(P-19865)***
Spectrum Systems SF.....F.....415 361-2429
1585 Folsom St San Francisco (94103) ***(P-5726)***
Speculative Product Design LLC (HQ).....**D.....650 462-2040**
177 Bovet Rd Ste 200 San Mateo (94402) ***(P-4349)***
Speed Warehouse, Sacramento *Also called National Auto Prts Whse - CA I* ***(P-8459)***
Speedling Incorporated.....D.....813 645-3221
2640 San Juan Hwy San Juan Bautista (95045) ***(P-137)***
Speedway Copy Systems Inc.....E.....415 495-4330
275 E L St Benicia (94510) ***(P-11852)***
Speedway Digital Printing, Benicia *Also called Speedway Copy Systems Inc* ***(P-11852)***
Speedway Sonoma LLC.....D.....707 938-8448
Hwy 37 N Sonoma (95476) ***(P-14918)***
Spencer Building Maintenance.....B.....916 922-1900
10457 Old Placerville Rd # 10 Sacramento (95827) ***(P-12001)***
Spencer Enterprises Inc.....D.....559 252-4043
5286 E Home Ave Fresno (93727) ***(P-810)***
Sperasoft Inc.....B.....408 715-6615
2033 Gateway Pl Ste 500 San Jose (95110) ***(P-12809)***
SPHDS, Sunnyvale *Also called South Pninsula Hebrew Day Schl* ***(P-18025)***
Sphere Institute.....B.....650 558-3980
500 Airport Blvd Ste 340 Burlingame (94010) ***(P-19187)***
Spherion Hr Consulting, San Jose *Also called Sfn Group Inc* ***(P-12198)***
Spherion Staffing Group, Redding *Also called Sfn Group Inc* ***(P-12196)***
Spherion Technology Svcs Group, Pleasanton *Also called Sfn Group Inc* ***(P-12197)***
SPI Solar Inc.....A.....408 919-8000
4677 Old Ironsides Dr # 1 Santa Clara (95054) ***(P-4638)***
Spiceorb, San Jose *Also called Orb Enterprises Inc* ***(P-13955)***
Spidercloud Wireless Inc (HQ).....**E.....408 567-9165**
475 Sycamore Dr Milpitas (95035) ***(P-7913)***
Spin Memory Inc.....E.....510 933-8200
45500 Northport Loop W Fremont (94538) ***(P-6311)***
Spine View Inc.....D.....510 490-1753
110 Pioneer Way Ste A Mountain View (94041) ***(P-7043)***
Spinecare Med Group Inc A Prof.....D.....650 985-7500
455 Hickey Blvd Ste 310 Daly City (94015) ***(P-15698)***

Spire Global Subsidiary Inc (HQ) ....C....**415 356-3400**
251 Rhode Island St Ste 2 San Francisco (94103) ***(P-13809)***
Spire Manufacturing Inc ....E....510 226-1070
49016 Milmont Dr Fremont (94538) ***(P-5718)***
Spirent Communications Inc ....C....408 752-7100
2708 Orchard Pkwy Ste 20 San Jose (95134) ***(P-6793)***
Spirit Throws, Roseville *Also called Hudson & Company LLC* ***(P-3026)***
Splash Data Inc ....F....408 355-4508
155 N Santa Cruz Ave # 210 Los Gatos (95030) ***(P-12810)***
Splash Swim School Inc ....E....925 838-7946
2411 Old Crow Canyon Rd San Ramon (94583) ***(P-15245)***
Splashtop Inc (PA) ....E....**408 861-1088**
1054 S De Anza Blvd Ste 2 San Jose (95129) ***(P-12811)***
Splay Inc ....F....510 351-8230
2116 Farallon Dr San Leandro (94577) ***(P-4325)***
Splice Machine Inc (PA) ....C....**650 678-8985**
44 Tehama St San Francisco (94105) ***(P-12812)***
Split Software Inc (PA) ....C....**650 399-0005**
10 California St Redwood City (94063) ***(P-13760)***
Splunk Inc (PA) ....C....**415 848-8400**
270 Brannan St San Francisco (94107) ***(P-13456)***
Splunk Services Cayman Ltd (HQ) ....D....**415 848-8400**
270 Brannan St San Francisco (94107) ***(P-13457)***
Spoondrift Technologies, San Francisco *Also called Sofar Ocean Technologies Inc* ***(P-19127)***
Sport Boat Trailers Inc ....F....209 892-5388
430 C St Patterson (95363) ***(P-6659)***
Sporton International USA Inc ....F....732 407-8718
1175 Montague Expy Milpitas (95035) ***(P-571)***
Sports Club of El Dorado, Shingle Springs *Also called Salutary Sports Clubs Inc* ***(P-14970)***
Sports Medicine ....D....925 934-3536
1777 Botelho Dr Ste 110 Walnut Creek (94596) ***(P-15699)***
Sportsmobile West ....E....559 233-8267
3631 S Bagley Ave Fresno (93725) ***(P-14534)***
Spotinst Inc ....E....415 223-1333
600 California St Fl 11 San Francisco (94108) ***(P-13458)***
Spotlight Therapy Inc ....E....408 649-7349
600 Pnnsylvnia Ave Unit 3 Los Gatos (95030) ***(P-16948)***
Spotline Inc ....E....408 768-1664
226 Airport Pkwy Ste 450 San Jose (95110) ***(P-13668)***
Spoton Computing Inc ....E....650 293-7464
550 Sutter St San Francisco (94102) ***(P-13459)***
Spr Op Co Inc ....C....510 232-5030
70 W Ohio Ave Ste H Richmond (94804) ***(P-10740)***
Spraytronics Inc ....E....408 988-3636
6001 Butler Ln Ste 204 Scotts Valley (95066) ***(P-4950)***
Sprig Electric Co (HQ) ....C....**408 298-3134**
1860 S 10th St San Jose (95112) ***(P-1609)***
Spring Bioscience Corp ....A....925 474-8463
4300 Hacienda Dr Pleasanton (94588) ***(P-19129)***
Spring Creek Apartments, Santa Clara *Also called Acco Management Company* ***(P-10487)***
Spring Creek Golf & Cntry CLB ....E....209 599-3258
1580 Spring Creek Dr Ripon (95366) ***(P-15154)***
Spring Education Group Inc (PA) ....C....**408 973-7351**
1999 S Bascom Ave Ste 400 Campbell (95008) ***(P-18026)***
Spring Hills Golf Course ....E....831 724-1404
501 Spring Hills Dr Watsonville (95076) ***(P-15028)***
Spring Hills Golf Shop, Watsonville *Also called Spring Hills Golf Course* ***(P-15028)***
Spring Hl Mnor Cnvlescent Hosp, Grass Valley *Also called Spring Hl Mnor Cnvlscent Rhblt* ***(P-16125)***
Spring Hl Mnor Cnvlscent Rhblt ....E....530 273-7247
355 Joerschke Dr Grass Valley (95945) ***(P-16125)***
Spring Lake Village, Santa Rosa *Also called Covia Communities* ***(P-18089)***
Spring Mountain Hotel LLC (PA) ....C....**530 304-5619**
1485 Main St Ste 201 Saint Helena (94574) ***(P-11495)***
Spring Valley Golf Course Inc ....E....408 262-1722
3441 Calaveras Rd Milpitas (95035) ***(P-15029)***
Spring Valley Pro Shop, Milpitas *Also called Spring Valley Golf Course Inc* ***(P-15029)***
Springboard, San Francisco *Also called Sliderule Labs Inc* ***(P-12797)***
Springfield Montessori School ....E....925 944-0626
2780 Mitchell Dr Walnut Creek (94598) ***(P-18027)***
Springfield Place, Petaluma *Also called Leisure Care LLC* ***(P-18137)***
Springhill Stes San Jose Arprt, San Jose *Also called San Jose Hhg Hotel Dev LP* ***(P-11437)***
Springml Inc ....D....916 316-1566
6200 Stnrdge Mall Rd Ste Pleasanton (94588) ***(P-13980)***
Springs Jr Walter M Cnstr Co, Redwood City *Also called Redmont Cnstr & Inv Co Inc* ***(P-694)***
Springs Road Healthcare, Vallejo *Also called Evergreen At Springs Road LLC* ***(P-16000)***
Springsoft Usa Inc (HQ) ....E....**650 584-5000**
700 E Middlefield Rd Mountain View (94043) ***(P-12813)***
Sprinkler Irrgtion Specialists, San Jose *Also called United Green Mark Inc* ***(P-9046)***
Sprouts Farmers Market Inc ....D....209 527-7575
1700 Mchenry Ave Modesto (95350) ***(P-9312)***
Spruce Biosciences Inc ....F....415 294-1687
2001 Junipero Serra Blvd # 640 Daly City (94014) ***(P-3987)***
Spruce Multi Specialty Group ....E....559 229-2786
1275 W Spruce Ave Fresno (93650) ***(P-16806)***
Spt Microtechnologies USA Inc (PA) ....E....**408 571-1400**
5750 Hellyer Ave Ste 10 San Jose (95138) ***(P-5171)***
Spt Microtechnologies USA Inc ....F....408 571-1400
5750 Hellyer Ave San Jose (95138) ***(P-5205)***
Spur - San Frncsco Bay Area Pl (PA) ....D....**415 781-8726**
654 Mission St San Francisco (94105) ***(P-18472)***
Spycher Brothers, Turlock *Also called Select Harvest Usa LLC* ***(P-9511)***
Spyrus Inc (PA) ....E....**408 392-9131**
103 Bonaventura Dr San Jose (95134) ***(P-5414)***
Squab Producers Calif Inc ....D....209 537-4744
409 Primo Way Modesto (95358) ***(P-9352)***
Squaglia Manufacturing Company (PA) ....E....**650 965-9644**
275 Polaris Ave Mountain View (94043) ***(P-5622)***
Squar Milner Peterson ....E....415 781-2500
135 Main St Fl 9 San Francisco (94105) ***(P-18995)***
Square Inc (PA) ....E....**415 375-3176**
1455 Market St Ste 600 San Francisco (94103) ***(P-13460)***
Square Deal Mat Fctry & Uphl, Chico *Also called Square Deal Mattress Factory* ***(P-3297)***
Square Deal Mattress Factory ....E....530 342-2510
1354 Humboldt Ave Chico (95928) ***(P-3297)***
Squaretrade Inc (HQ) ....C....**415 541-1000**
600 Harrison St Ste 400 San Francisco (94107) ***(P-10221)***
Squaw Creek Associates LLC ....A....530 581-6624
400 Squaw Creek Rd Alpine Meadows (96146) ***(P-11496)***
Squaw Creek Transportation, Olympic Valley *Also called Lowe Enterprises* ***(P-11273)***
Squaw Valley Development Co (HQ) ....E....**530 452-6985**
1960 Squaw Valley Rd Olympic Valley (96146) ***(P-11497)***
Squaw Valley Lodge, Alpine Meadows *Also called Granite Peak Management* ***(P-10562)***
Squaw Valley Lodge, Olympic Valley *Also called Sierra PCF Hotels & Resorts* ***(P-11479)***
Squaw Valley Ski, Olympic Valley *Also called Squaw Valley Development Co* ***(P-11497)***
Squaw Valley Ski Corporation (HQ) ....C....**530 583-6985**
1960 Squaw Valley Rd Olympic Valley (96146) ***(P-11498)***
Squelch Inc ....E....650 241-2700
3945 Freedom Cir Ste 560 Santa Clara (95054) ***(P-13461)***
Squires, Sanders and Dempsey, San Francisco *Also called Graham & James LLP* ***(P-17280)***
SR Freeman Inc ....D....408 364-2200
2380 S Bascom Ave Ste 200 Campbell (95008) ***(P-1760)***
Sr Holdings LLC (HQ) ....F....**415 927-6400**
4040 Civic Center Dr San Rafael (94903) ***(P-18319)***
Sr Shroeder Inc ....F....707 693-8166
1150 N 1st St Dixon (95620) ***(P-8428)***
Sr. Thea Bowman Manor, Oakland *Also called Christian Church Homes* ***(P-10426)***
Sra Oss Inc ....D....408 855-8200
2114 Ringwood Ave San Jose (95131) ***(P-13462)***
SRC, Linden *Also called Stockton Rubber Mfgcoinc* ***(P-4227)***
SRC Milling Co LLC ....E....916 363-4821
11350 Kiefer Blvd Sacramento (95830) ***(P-2460)***
Srcsd, Sacramento *Also called Sacramento Reg Co Sanit Dist* ***(P-8403)***
SRI Golf Inc ....E....916 771-4649
5880 Woodcreek Oaks Blvd Roseville (95747) ***(P-15030)***
SRI International (PA) ....A....**650 859-2000**
333 Ravenswood Ave Menlo Park (94025) ***(P-19237)***
Srl Apparel Inc ....E....530 898-9525
2209 Park Ave Chico (95928) ***(P-2978)***
Srm Alliance Hospital Services (PA) ....B....**707 778-1111**
400 N Mcdowell Blvd Petaluma (94954) ***(P-16534)***
SRS, San Francisco *Also called Sharehlder Rprsnttive Svcs LLC* ***(P-19398)***
SRS, Sunnyvale *Also called Stanford Research Systems Inc* ***(P-6854)***
SRS Consulting Inc ....B....510 252-0625
39465 Paseo Padre Pkwy # 1100 Fremont (94538) ***(P-12814)***
Srss LLC ....F....707 544-7777
1400 Airport Blvd Santa Rosa (95403) ***(P-4864)***
Ss Skikos Incorporated ....D....707 575-3000
1289 Sebastopol Rd Santa Rosa (95407) ***(P-7634)***
Ss Travel, San Francisco *Also called San Francisco Travel Assn* ***(P-14396)***
SS&c Advent, San Francisco *Also called Advent Software Inc* ***(P-12232)***
Ss8 Networks Inc (PA) ....C....**408 894-8400**
750 Tasman Dr Milpitas (95035) ***(P-8085)***
SSC, Santa Clara *Also called Silicon Standard Corp* ***(P-6290)***
SSC Carmichael Operating Co LP ....C....916 485-4793
3630 Mission Ave Carmichael (95608) ***(P-16126)***
SSC Inc (HQ) ....D....**510 477-0008**
2910 Faber St Union City (94587) ***(P-9370)***
SSC Oakland Fruitvale Oper LP ....D....510 261-5613
3020 E 15th St Oakland (94601) ***(P-16270)***
SSC Pittsburg Operating Co LP ....C....925 427-4444
2351 Loveridge Rd Pittsburg (94565) ***(P-16271)***
SSC San Jose Operating Co LP ....B....408 249-0344
340 Northlake Dr San Jose (95117) ***(P-16127)***
SSE Merchandise, San Jose *Also called Sharks Sports & Entrmt LLC* ***(P-14916)***
Ssf Imported Auto Parts LLC (HQ) ....D....**800 203-9287**
466 Forbes Blvd South San Francisco (94080) ***(P-8470)***
Ssi, Stockton *Also called Super Store Industries* ***(P-9494)***
Ssi, Rocklin *Also called Survellnce Systems Intgrtion I* ***(P-8962)***
Ssi, Lodi *Also called Scientific Specialties Inc* ***(P-4233)***
Ssi G Debbas Chocolatier LLC ....E....559 294-2071
2794 N Larkin Ave Fresno (93727) ***(P-2440)***
Ssjid, Manteca *Also called South San Jquin Irrigation Dst* ***(P-8276)***
Ssmb Pacific Holding Co Inc (HQ) ....D....**510 836-6100**
1755 Adams Ave San Leandro (94577) ***(P-8429)***
Ssmb Pacific Holding Co Inc ....E....530 222-1212
20769 Industry Rd Anderson (96007) ***(P-8430)***
Ssmb Pacific Holding Co Inc ....E....408 500-3400
16715 Condit Rd Morgan Hill (95037) ***(P-8431)***
SSMC, Vallejo *Also called Sutter Solano Medical Center* ***(P-16675)***
Ssnp, Redding *Also called Shasta Senior Ntrtn Program* ***(P-17740)***
Sspca, Sacramento *Also called Sacramnto Soc For The Prvntion* ***(P-18586)***
Sst Construction LLC ....E....844 477-8787
2731 Citrus Rd Ste D Rancho Cordova (95742) ***(P-709)***
St Albans Country Day School ....D....916 782-3557
2312 Vernon St Roseville (95678) ***(P-18028)***
St Anne's Home, San Francisco *Also called Little Ssters of The Poor Okla* ***(P-18140)***
St Anthony Care Center Inc ....E....510 733-3877
553 Smalley Ave Hayward (94541) ***(P-16128)***
St Anthony Foundation (PA) ....E....**415 241-2600**
150 Golden Gate Ave San Francisco (94102) ***(P-17752)***
St Chrstpher Cnvlscent Hosp I ....E....510 537-4844
22822 Myrtle St Hayward (94541) ***(P-16129)***

ALPHABETIC

St Cyberlink Corporation ....E....510 623-9888
44063 Fremont Blvd Fremont (94538) ***(P-8750)***
St Elizabeth Community Hosp (HQ) ....**B....530 529-7760**
2550 Sster Mary Clumba Dr Red Bluff (96080) ***(P-16535)***
St Francis Electric Inc ....C....510 639-0639
975 Carden St San Leandro (94577) ***(P-1610)***
St Francis Electric LLC ....C....510 639-0639
975 Carden St San Leandro (94577) ***(P-1611)***
St Francis Extended Care Inc ....E....510 785-3630
718 Bartlett Ave Hayward (94541) ***(P-16272)***
St Francis Hts Convalescent ....D....650 755-9515
35 Escuela Dr Daly City (94015) ***(P-16273)***
St Francis Marine Center Inc ....E....415 621-2876
835 Terry A Francois Blvd San Francisco (94158) ***(P-7733)***
St Francis Medical Center, Redwood City *Also called Verity Health System Cal Inc* ***(P-16710)***
St Francis Memorial Hospital, San Francisco *Also called Saint Francis Memorial Hosp* ***(P-16499)***
St Francis Pavillion, Daly City *Also called Forte Enterprises Inc* ***(P-19337)***
St Francis Yacht Club ....C....415 563-6363
700 Marina Blvd San Francisco (94123) ***(P-15155)***
St George Spirits Inc ....E....510 769-1601
2601 Monarch St Alameda (94501) ***(P-2722)***
St Helena Hospital Clearlake, Clearlake *Also called Advintist Hlth Clearlake Hosp* ***(P-16318)***
St Helena Hospital (HQ) ....**A....707 963-3611**
10 Woodland Rd Saint Helena (94574) ***(P-16536)***
St Helena Hospital Clearlake, Clearlake *Also called Adventist Hlth Systm/West Corp* ***(P-16316)***
St Helena Montessori Schl Inc ....E....707 963-1527
880 College Ave Saint Helena (94574) ***(P-18029)***
St Johns Retirement Village ....C....530 662-9674
135 Woodland Ave Woodland (95695) ***(P-16274)***
ST Johnson Company LLC ....E....510 652-6000
5160 Fulton Dr Fairfield (94534) ***(P-4639)***
St Joseph Hlth Nthrn Cal LLC (HQ) ....**A....707 546-3210**
1165 Montgomery Dr Santa Rosa (95405) ***(P-16537)***
St Joseph Home Health Network (HQ) ....**D....714 712-9500**
441 College Ave Santa Rosa (95401) ***(P-16949)***
St Joseph Hospital (PA) ....**A....707 445-8121**
2700 Dolbeer St Eureka (95501) ***(P-16538)***
St Joseph Hospital ....E....707 445-8121
2700 Dolbeer St Eureka (95501) ***(P-16539)***
St Joseph Hospital ....E....707 445-8121
2700 Dolbeer St Eureka (95501) ***(P-16540)***
St Joseph Hospital ....E....707 268-0190
2752 Harrison Ave Ste A Eureka (95501) ***(P-16541)***
St Joseph Hospital ....E....707 445-8121
3645 E St Eureka (95503) ***(P-16542)***
St Joseph Hospital of Eureka ....B....707 445-8121
2700 Dolbeer St Eureka (95501) ***(P-16543)***
St Josephs Behavioral Hlth Ctr (HQ) ....**D....209 462-2826**
2510 N California St Stockton (95204) ***(P-16544)***
St Josephs Med Ctr Stockton ....A....209 943-2000
1800 N California St Stockton (95204) ***(P-16545)***
St Josephs Medical Center Inc ....C....209 943-2000
1800 N California St Stockton (95204) ***(P-16546)***
St Josephs Surgery Center LP ....D....209 467-6316
1800 N California St # 1 Stockton (95204) ***(P-15700)***
St Jsephs Regional Hsing Corp (PA) ....**C....209 956-3400**
3400 Wagner Heights Rd Stockton (95209) ***(P-10462)***
St Louis Post-Dispatch LLC ....D....415 892-1516
1068 Machin Ave Novato (94945) ***(P-3482)***
St Louis Post-Dispatch LLC ....D....707 762-4541
830 Petaluma Blvd N Petaluma (94952) ***(P-3483)***
St Lukes Health Care Center ....D....415 647-8600
1580 Valencia St Ste 506 San Francisco (94110) ***(P-16547)***
St Lukes Neighborhood Clinic, San Francisco *Also called St Lukes Health Care Center* ***(P-16547)***
St Marys Center ....E....510 923-9600
925 Brockhurst St Oakland (94608) ***(P-17753)***
St Marys Dining Room ....D....209 467-0703
545 W Sonora St Stockton (95203) ***(P-17754)***
St Marys Med Ctr Foundation ....C....415 668-1000
450 Stanyan St San Francisco (94117) ***(P-16548)***
St Marys Medical Center Inc ....A....415 668-1000
450 Stanyan St San Francisco (94117) ***(P-16549)***
St Matthews Episcopal Day Schl ....C....650 342-5436
16 Baldwin Ave San Mateo (94401) ***(P-18030)***
St Orres Restaurant & Inn, Gualala *Also called Saint Orres Corporation* ***(P-11427)***
St Paul's Towers, Oakland *Also called Covia Communities* ***(P-18087)***
St Philip School ....D....415 824-8467
665 Elizabeth St San Francisco (94114) ***(P-18031)***
St Philip The Apostle School, San Francisco *Also called St Philip School* ***(P-18031)***
St Regis Retirement Ctr Inc ....E....510 881-4240
23950 Mission Blvd Hayward (94544) ***(P-18184)***
St Regis San Francisco Ht LLC ....D....415 284-4000
125 3rd St San Francisco (94103) ***(P-11499)***
St Rose Hospital, Hayward *Also called Hayward Sisters Hospital* ***(P-16385)***
St Rose School ....E....707 545-0379
4300 Old Redwood Hwy Santa Rosa (95403) ***(P-18032)***
St Supery Inc (HQ) ....**E....707 963-4507**
8440 St Helena Hwy Rutherford (94573) ***(P-2723)***
St Vncent De Paul Bltmore Inc ....D....916 485-3482
3100 Norris Ave Sacramento (95821) ***(P-17755)***
St. Joseph Dental, Santa Rosa *Also called Santa Rosa Memorial Hospital* ***(P-16514)***
St. Joseph's Family Center, San Francisco *Also called Catholic Chrties Cyo of The AR* ***(P-17465)***
St. Louise Regional Hospital, Gilroy *Also called Santa Clara County of* ***(P-16511)***
St. Mary's Medical Center, San Francisco *Also called Dignity Health* ***(P-16350)***

STA Cruz Residential Care Svc, Santa Cruz *Also called Encompass Community Services* ***(P-17548)***
Stack Plastics Inc ....E....650 361-8600
3525 Haven Ave Menlo Park (94025) ***(P-4326)***
Stackla Inc ....D....415 789-3304
548 Market St San Francisco (94104) ***(P-13463)***
Stackrox Inc (PA) ....**E....650 489-6769**
100 View St Ste 204 Mountain View (94041) ***(P-13464)***
Staffing Industry Analysts Inc ....D....650 390-6200
1975 W El Cmino Real Ste Mountain View (94040) ***(P-3601)***
Staffing Industry Report, Mountain View *Also called Staffing Industry Analysts Inc* ***(P-3601)***
Stafford-King-Wiese Architects, Sacramento *Also called Coact Designworks* ***(P-18879)***
Stage 4 Solutions Incorporated ....E....408 868-9739
19200 Portos Dr Saratoga (95070) ***(P-19638)***
Stagnaro Brothers Seafood Inc ....D....831 423-1188
320 Washington St Santa Cruz (95060) ***(P-9371)***
Stags Leap Wine Cellars ....C....707 944-2020
5766 Silverado Trl NAPA (94558) ***(P-2724)***
Staidson Biopharma Inc ....F....800 345-1899
2600 Hilltop Dr Bldg A San Pablo (94806) ***(P-3988)***
Stailess Polishing Co., Oakland *Also called General Grinding Inc* ***(P-4907)***
Stair Service, Hollister *Also called Simmons Stairways Inc* ***(P-3152)***
Stalfab ....E....831 786-1600
131 Algen Ln Watsonville (95076) ***(P-5135)***
Stalker Software Inc ....E....415 569-2280
6 Tara View Rd Belvedere Tiburon (94920) ***(P-13465)***
Stamos Capital Partners LP ....D....650 233-5000
2498 Sand Hill Rd Menlo Park (94025) ***(P-10769)***
Stamoules Produce Co, Mendota *Also called S Stamoules Inc* ***(P-306)***
Stamoules Produce Company, Mendota *Also called S & S Ranch Inc* ***(P-257)***
Stampli Inc ....E....650 963-9429
191 Castro St Fl 2 Mountain View (94041) ***(P-18996)***
Stan Boyett & Son Inc (PA) ....**E....209 577-6000**
601 Mchenry Ave Modesto (95350) ***(P-9539)***
Stan Farm, Modesto *Also called Stanislaus Farm Supply Company* ***(P-9611)***
Stand For Fmlies Free Volence ....D....510 964-7109
3220 Blume Dr San Pablo (94806) ***(P-17756)***
Standard Cattle LLC ....D....559 693-1977
8105a S Lassen Ave San Joaquin (93660) ***(P-349)***
Standard Cognition Corp (PA) ....**D....415 324-4156**
965 Mission St Fl 7 San Francisco (94103) ***(P-13466)***
Standard Euler Inc ....E....954 261-6679
479 Jessie St San Francisco (94103) ***(P-12815)***
Standard Insurance Company ....E....925 947-3950
1600 Riviera Ave Ste 150 Walnut Creek (94596) ***(P-10353)***
Standard Iron & Metals Co ....E....510 535-0222
4525 San Leandro St Oakland (94601) ***(P-9178)***
Standard Pacific Capital LLC ....E....415 352-7100
101 California St Fl 36 San Francisco (94111) ***(P-10014)***
Standish Management LLC (PA) ....**D....415 391-7225**
750 Battery St Ste 600 San Francisco (94111) ***(P-19401)***
Stanford Alumni Association, Stanford *Also called Leland Stanford Junior Univ* ***(P-18437)***
Stanford Blood Center LLC (PA) ....**C....650 723-7994**
3373 Hillview Ave Palo Alto (94304) ***(P-15701)***
Stanford Cancer Center, Palo Alto *Also called Stanford Health Care* ***(P-17182)***
Stanford Cancer Center S Bay, San Jose *Also called Stanford Health Care* ***(P-16555)***
Stanford Court Hotel, San Francisco *Also called Pine & Powell Partners LLC* ***(P-11368)***
Stanford Equipment Company ....E....408 855-8040
1500 Wyatt Dr Ste 2 Santa Clara (95054) ***(P-8959)***
Stanford Federal Credit Union (PA) ....**D....650 725-1000**
1860 Embarcadero Rd # 200 Palo Alto (94303) ***(P-9821)***
Stanford Furniture Mfg Inc ....F....916 387-5300
3170 Orange Grove Ave North Highlands (95660) ***(P-3292)***
Stanford Health Care ....E....650 723-5171
1000 Welch Rd Ste 300 Palo Alto (94304) ***(P-16550)***
Stanford Health Care ....E....650 213-8360
1510 Page Mill Rd Ste 2 Palo Alto (94304) ***(P-16551)***
Stanford Health Care ....E....650 736-6661
300 Pasteur Dr Stanford (94305) ***(P-16552)***
Stanford Health Care ....E....650 497-8953
725 Welch Rd Palo Alto (94304) ***(P-16553)***
Stanford Health Care ....A....650 723-4000
300 Pasteur Dr Stanford (94305) ***(P-16554)***
Stanford Health Care ....E....408 426-4900
2589 Samaritan Dr San Jose (95124) ***(P-16555)***
Stanford Health Care ....E....925 847-3000
5555 W Las Positas Blvd Pleasanton (94588) ***(P-16556)***
Stanford Health Care ....E....650 723-8561
900 Blake Wilbur Dr Palo Alto (94304) ***(P-17182)***
Stanford Health Care (HQ) ....**A....650 723-4000**
300 Pasteur Dr Stanford (94305) ***(P-16557)***
Stanford Health Care ....E....650 736-7844
3375 Hillview Ave Palo Alto (94304) ***(P-16558)***
Stanford Health Care Advantage ....A....650 723-4000
300 Pasteur Dr Stanford (94305) ***(P-16559)***
Stanford Hlth Care-Valleycare, Livermore *Also called Hospi Comm For The L-P Area T* ***(P-19350)***
Stanford Hotels Corporation ....D....408 330-0001
4949 Great America Pkwy Santa Clara (95054) ***(P-11500)***
Stanford Hotels Corporation (PA) ....**E....415 398-3333**
433 California St Ste 700 San Francisco (94104) ***(P-11501)***
Stanford Investment Group ....E....650 941-1717
2570 W El Cmino Real Ste Mountain View (94040) ***(P-10060)***
Stanford Lthrop Mem HM For Frn, Sacramento *Also called Stanford Youth Solutions* ***(P-17759)***
STANFORD MEDICAL CENTER, Newark *Also called University Healthcare Alliance* ***(P-16962)***
Stanford Medical Center, Stanford *Also called Stanford Health Care* ***(P-16557)***

Stanford Park Hotel ....C....650 322-1234
100 El Camino Real Menlo Park (94025) ***(P-11502)***
Stanford Research Systems Inc....C....408 744-9040
1290 Reamwood Ave Ste D Sunnyvale (94089) ***(P-6854)***
Stanford Schl Mdcine Jay McHae, Palo Alto *Also called Stanford Health Care* ***(P-16550)***
Stanford Settlement Inc....E....916 927-1303
450 W El Camino Ave Sacramento (95833) ***(P-17757)***
Stanford Sierra Camp & Lodge, South Lake Tahoe *Also called Saa Sierra Programs LLC* ***(P-18457)***
Stanford Univ Frman Spgli Inst....C....650 723-8681
616 Jane Stanford Way Stanford (94305) ***(P-19238)***
Stanford Univ Med Ctr Aux....B....650 723-6636
300 Pasteur Dr Stanford (94305) ***(P-17758)***
Stanford University, Stanford *Also called Leland Stanford Junior Univ* ***(P-16763)***
Stanford University - Et, Redwood City *Also called Leland Stanford Junior Univ* ***(P-16764)***
Stanford Youth Solutions (PA)....D....916 344-0199
8912 Volunteer Ln Sacramento (95826) ***(P-17759)***
Stangenes Industries Inc (PA)....D....650 855-9926
1052 E Meadow Cir Palo Alto (94303) ***(P-6386)***
Staniflaus Cardiology....E....209 521-9661
3621 Forest Glenn Dr Modesto (95355) ***(P-15702)***
Stanislaus Cnty Tobacco Fundng....C....209 525-6376
1010 10th St Ste 6400 Modesto (95354) ***(P-9877)***
Stanislaus Consol Fire Prot (PA)....E....209 869-7470
3324 Topeka St Riverbank (95367) ***(P-14412)***
Stanislaus County Hsa....E....209 558-7094
830 Scenic Dr A Modesto (95350) ***(P-15703)***
Stanislaus Distributing, Modesto *Also called Varni Brothers Corporation* ***(P-9586)***
Stanislaus Distributing Co, Modesto *Also called Varni Brothers Corporation* ***(P-9564)***
Stanislaus Farm Supply Company (PA)....D....209 538-7070
624 E Service Rd Modesto (95358) ***(P-9611)***
Stanislaus Food Products Co (PA)....C....209 548-3537
1202 D St Modesto (95354) ***(P-2243)***
Stanislaus Health Svcs Agcy, Modesto *Also called County of Stanislaus* ***(P-15371)***
Stanislaus Medical Center, Modesto *Also called County of Stanislaus* ***(P-16341)***
STANISLAUS SURGICAL CENTER, Modesto *Also called Stanislaus Surgical Hosp LLC* ***(P-16560)***
Stanislaus Surgical Hosp LLC (PA)....C....209 572-2700
1421 Oakdale Rd Modesto (95355) ***(P-16560)***
Stanisluas County Mental Hlth, Modesto *Also called County of Stanislaus* ***(P-17010)***
Stanlee R Gatti Designs....E....415 558-8884
1208 Howard St San Francisco (94103) ***(P-14413)***
Stanley Access Tech LLC....E....209 221-4066
1312 Dupont Ct Manteca (95336) ***(P-4608)***
Stanley Electric Motor Co Inc....E....209 464-7321
222 N Wilson Way Stockton (95205) ***(P-14730)***
Stanley Produce Co Inc....E....415 282-7510
2088 Jerrold Ave San Francisco (94124) ***(P-9430)***
Stansbury Hm Preservation Assn....E....530 895-3848
307 W 5th St Chico (95928) ***(P-18282)***
Stantec Architecture Inc....C....415 882-9500
100 California St # 1000 San Francisco (94111) ***(P-18818)***
Stantec Architecture Inc....C....707 765-1660
1383 N Mcdowell Blvd # 25 Petaluma (94954) ***(P-18915)***
Stantec Consulting Svcs Inc....C....925 627-4500
1340 Treat Blvd Ste 300 Walnut Creek (94597) ***(P-18819)***
Stantec Energy & Resources Inc....C....925 627-4508
1340 Treat Blvd Ste 300 Walnut Creek (94597) ***(P-18926)***
Stanza, San Francisco *Also called Spoton Computing Inc* ***(P-13459)***
Stapleton - Spence Packing Co (PA)....D....408 297-8815
1900 State Highway 99 Gridley (95948) ***(P-2244)***
Star Inc....A....916 791-8442
9233 Twin School Rd # 505 Granite Bay (95746) ***(P-18033)***
Star Building Products, Fresno *Also called E-Z Haul Ready Mix Inc* ***(P-4479)***
Star Concrete, San Jose *Also called Sandman Inc* ***(P-4451)***
Star Energy Management Inc....E....530 532-9250
6120 Lincoln Blvd Ste G Oroville (95966) ***(P-1612)***
Star Finishes Inc....E....559 261-1076
40429 Brickyard Dr Madera (93636) ***(P-4951)***
Star H-R....B....707 265-9911
1822 Jefferson St NAPA (94559) ***(P-12140)***
Star H-R....B....707 894-4404
105 E 1st St Cloverdale (95425) ***(P-12141)***
Star H-R (PA)....A....707 762-4447
3820 Cypress Dr Ste 2 Petaluma (94954) ***(P-12142)***
Star Industries, Sacramento *Also called Barbara-Hoffman Inc* ***(P-11924)***
Star Microwave Service Corp....E....510 651-8096
41458 Christy St Fremont (94538) ***(P-14706)***
Star One Credit Union (PA)....C....408 543-5202
1306 Bordeaux Dr Sunnyvale (94089) ***(P-9822)***
Star Protection Agency CA, Oakland *Also called Star Protection Agency LLC* ***(P-14099)***
Star Protection Agency LLC....D....510 635-1732
8201 Edgewater Dr Ste 102 Oakland (94621) ***(P-14099)***
Star Staffing, Petaluma *Also called Star H-R* ***(P-12142)***
Star Transport LLC....E....559 834-3021
9500 S De Wolf Ave Selma (93662) ***(P-7895)***
Starlight Room Harry Dentons....E....415 392-7755
191 Sutter St San Francisco (94104) ***(P-11503)***
Starlite Electric Inc....E....415 648-8888
1465 Carroll Ave San Francisco (94124) ***(P-1613)***
Starmont Winery, Saint Helena *Also called Merryvale Vineyards LLC* ***(P-2659)***
Stars, San Leandro *Also called Subacute Trtmnt Adolescnt Reha* ***(P-17076)***
Stars Agency, The, San Francisco *Also called Alpha Agency Inc* ***(P-12074)***
Stars Recreation Center LP....E....707 455-7827
155 Browns Valley Pkwy Vacaville (95688) ***(P-14901)***
Starship Technologies Inc....E....844 445-5333
535 Mission St Fl 19 San Francisco (94105) ***(P-12816)***
Startup Farms Intl LLC....B....510 440-0110
45690 Northport Loop E Fremont (94538) ***(P-12817)***
Starving Students Inc....E....916 927-7071
2150 Bell Ave Ste 110 Sacramento (95838) ***(P-7635)***
Starvista....C....650 591-9623
610 Elm St Ste 212 San Carlos (94070) ***(P-17760)***
Starwest Botanicals LLC (PA)....D....916 638-8100
161 Main Ave Sacramento (95838) ***(P-9489)***
Starwood Capital Group LLC....C....415 247-1220
100 Pine St Ste 3000 San Francisco (94111) ***(P-10884)***
Starwood Htls & Rsrts Wrldwde....B....415 397-7000
335 Powell St San Francisco (94102) ***(P-11504)***
Starwood Htls & Rsrts Wrldwde....C....415 512-1111
2 New Montgomery St San Francisco (94105) ***(P-11505)***
Stasher Inc....F....510 531-2100
1310 63rd St Emeryville (94608) ***(P-9219)***
Stat Delivery Service Inc....D....510 681-6125
14755 Catalina St San Leandro (94577) ***(P-7491)***
Stat Nursing Services Inc (PA)....B....415 673-9791
2740 Van Ness Ave Ste 210 San Francisco (94109) ***(P-12143)***
Statcomm Inc....E....408 734-0440
939 San Rafael Ave Ste C Mountain View (94043) ***(P-18820)***
State Bar of California (PA)....B....415 538-2000
180 Howard St Fl Grnd San Francisco (94105) ***(P-18349)***
State Center Cmnty College Dst....D....559 442-4600
1101 E University Ave Fresno (93741) ***(P-18997)***
State Compensation Insur Fund (PA)....D....888 782-8338
333 Bush St Fl 8 San Francisco (94104) ***(P-10174)***
State Compensation Insur Fund....D....415 565-1222
1030 Vaquero Cir Vacaville (95688) ***(P-10175)***
State Compensation Insur Fund....C....510 577-3000
2955 Peralta Oaks Ct Oakland (94605) ***(P-10176)***
State Compensation Insur Fund....D....408 656-7417
1533 Shumaker Way San Jose (95131) ***(P-10177)***
State Compensation Insur Fund....D....888 782-8338
364 Knollcrest Dr Redding (96002) ***(P-10178)***
State Compensation Insur Fund....D....707 455-9900
1020 Vaquero Cir Vacaville (95688) ***(P-10179)***
State Compensation Insur Fund....D....530 223-7000
1416 9th St Sacramento (95814) ***(P-10180)***
State Compensation Insur Fund....D....559 433-2700
10 E Rver Pk Pl E Ste 110 Fresno (93720) ***(P-10181)***
State Compensation Insur Fund....D....916 263-8102
2300 River Plaza Dr # 150 Sacramento (95833) ***(P-10182)***
State Compensation Insur Fund....D....888 782-8338
3247 W March Ln Ste 110 Stockton (95219) ***(P-10183)***
State Compensation Insur Fund....D....916 924-5100
2275 Gateway Oaks Dr Sacramento (95833) ***(P-10184)***
State Compensation Insur Fund....D....707 443-9721
800 W Harris St Ste 37 Eureka (95503) ***(P-10185)***
State Compensation Insur Fund....C....925 523-5000
5880 Owens Dr Pleasanton (94588) ***(P-10186)***
State Compensation Insur Fund....D....888 782-8338
5890 Owens Dr Pleasanton (94588) ***(P-10187)***
State Farm Insurance, Gold River *Also called State Farm Life Insurance Co* ***(P-10354)***
State Farm Life Insurance Co....E....916 852-9491
11230 Gold Express Dr Gold River (95670) ***(P-10354)***
State Fund, San Francisco *Also called State Compensation Insur Fund* ***(P-10174)***
State Fund, Vacaville *Also called State Compensation Insur Fund* ***(P-10179)***
State Hornet....C....916 278-6583
6000 J St Sacramento (95819) ***(P-3484)***
State Hospitals Cal Dept....C....415 255-3400
1380 Howard St Fl 5 San Francisco (94103) ***(P-17075)***
State Hospitals Cal Dept....B....559 935-4300
24511 W Jayne Ave Coalinga (93210) ***(P-16745)***
State Hospitals Cal Dept....B....707 253-5000
2100 Napa Vallejo Hwy NAPA (94558) ***(P-16746)***
State Hospitals Cal Dept....B....707 449-6504
1600 California Dr Vacaville (95696) ***(P-16747)***
State Preschool....E....925 473-4380
950 El Pueblo Ave Pittsburg (94565) ***(P-18034)***
State Roofing Systems Inc....D....510 317-1477
15444 Hesperian Blvd San Leandro (94578) ***(P-1838)***
Stateline Travelodge Inc....E....530 544-6000
4011 Lake Tahoe Blvd South Lake Tahoe (96150) ***(P-11506)***
Statewide, Sacramento *Also called Domus Construction & Design* ***(P-632)***
Statewide Cnstr Sweeping LLC....E....510 683-9584
45945 Warm Springs Blvd Fremont (94539) ***(P-8408)***
Statewide Roofing Inc....E....408 286-7828
5542 Monterey Hwy 201 San Jose (95138) ***(P-1839)***
Station Ktsf-TV, Brisbane *Also called Lincoln Brdcstg A Cal Ltd Prtn* ***(P-8053)***
Stations, San Jose *Also called Andrian* ***(P-2003)***
Stats Chippac Inc (HQ)....E....510 979-8000
880 N Mccarthy Blvd # 250 Milpitas (95035) ***(P-6312)***
Stats Chippac Test Svcs Inc (HQ)....F....510 979-8000
46429 Landing Pkwy Fremont (94538) ***(P-6313)***
Status Medical Management, Modesto *Also called Pegasus Risk Management Inc* ***(P-10330)***
Stay Cal San Jose LLC....D....408 275-2147
2404 Stevens Creek Blvd San Jose (95128) ***(P-11507)***
Stay Safe Solutions Inc....E....916 640-1300
3140 Peacekeeper Way 101a McClellan (95652) ***(P-12201)***
Staybridge Suites, Rocklin *Also called Rocklin Lodging Group LLC* ***(P-11415)***
Staybridge Suites....E....408 745-1515
900 Hamlin Ct Sunnyvale (94089) ***(P-11508)***
Staybridge Suites NAPA, Fairfield *Also called Hotel NAPA I Opco L P* ***(P-11168)***
Stearns Holdings LLC....B....916 358-9170
2600 E Bidwell St Ste 160 Folsom (95630) ***(P-9932)***
Stebbins Construction Corp....E....650 299-1488
1057 Wilmington Way Emerald Hills (94062) ***(P-710)***

ALPHABETIC

Employee Codes: A=Over 500 employees, B=251-500
C=101-250, D=51-100, E=20-50 F=10-19
2022 Northern California Business
Directory and Buyers Guide
© Mergent Inc. 1-800-342-5647
1087

Steel Structures Inc ....E....559 673-8021
28777 Avenue 15 1/2 Madera (93638) ***(P-4732)***
Steele Cis LLC ....B....415 692-5000
1 Sansome St Ste 3500 San Francisco (94104) ***(P-17377)***
Steele Corp SEC Advisory Svcs, San Francisco *Also called Firstcall* ***(P-14059)***
Steele Wines Inc ....E....707 279-9475
4350 Thomas Dr Kelseyville (95451) ***(P-2725)***
Steelrver Infrstrcture Fund N (HQ) ....**C....415 291-2200**
1 Letterman Dr Bldg D San Francisco (94129) ***(P-8213)***
Steelrver Infrstrcture Prtners, San Francisco *Also called Steelrver Infrstrcture Fund N* ***(P-8213)***
Steelrver Infrstrcture Prtners (PA) ....**C....415 512-1515**
1 Harbor Dr Ste 101 Sausalito (94965) ***(P-10741)***
Steelwave Inc (PA) ....**C....650 571-2200**
999 Baker Way Ste 200 San Mateo (94404) ***(P-10715)***
Steelwave LLC ....A....650 571-2200
999 Baker Way Ste 200 San Mateo (94404) ***(P-10716)***
Steep Hill Inc (PA) ....**C....510 562-7400**
2448 6th St Berkeley (94710) ***(P-19286)***
Stein & Lubin LLP ....E....415 981-0550
600 Montgomery St Fl 14 San Francisco (94111) ***(P-17378)***
Stein Roe Inv Counsel Inc ....E....415 433-5844
3 Embarcadero Ctr # 1600 San Francisco (94111) ***(P-10061)***
Steinbeck Brewing Company ....D....510 886-9823
1082 B St Hayward (94541) ***(P-2494)***
Stella Technology Incorporated ....D....402 350-1681
450 S Abel St Unit 360832 Milpitas (95036) ***(P-13981)***
Stellant Systems Inc ....C....916 351-4500
107 Woodmere Rd Folsom (95630) ***(P-5871)***
Stellar Distributing Inc ....B....559 664-8400
21801 Ave Ste 16 Madera (93637) ***(P-9431)***
Stellar Enterprise Assoc Inc ....E....510 662-3333
2300 Stanwell Dr Ste A Concord (94520) ***(P-19402)***
Stellar It Solutions LLC ....E....669 250-6837
1620 Oakland Rd Ste D200 San Jose (95131) ***(P-18350)***
Stellar Labs Inc ....E....818 578-4078
1325 Howard Ave Pmb 412 Burlingame (94010) ***(P-12818)***
Stellartech Research Corp (PA) ....**D....408 331-3134**
560 Cottonwood Dr Milpitas (95035) ***(P-19130)***
Stem Inc (PA) ....**D....415 937-7816**
100 Rollins Rd Millbrae (94030) ***(P-5668)***
Step, Sacramento *Also called Stratgies To Empwer People Inc* ***(P-16207)***
Step Mobile Inc ....E....203 913-9229
120 Hawthorne Ave Palo Alto (94301) ***(P-13467)***
Step One Nursery School ....E....510 527-9021
499 Spruce St Berkeley (94708) ***(P-18035)***
Step Tools Unlimited Inc ....D....408 988-8898
18434 Technology Dr Morgan Hill (95037) ***(P-5099)***
Steppechange LLC ....D....415 279-7638
900 Uccelli Dr Apt 9301 Redwood City (94063) ***(P-12819)***
Steri-Tek, Fremont *Also called Smart World LLC* ***(P-14406)***
Stericycle Inc ....E....650 212-2332
5060 Forni Dr Concord (94520) ***(P-14414)***
Sterling Brand, San Francisco *Also called Sterling Consulting Group LLC* ***(P-19639)***
Sterling Consulting Group LLC ....D....415 248-7900
600 California St Fl 8 San Francisco (94108) ***(P-19639)***
Sterling Hsa Inc ....E....800 617-4729
475 14th St Ste 120 Oakland (94612) ***(P-14415)***
Sterling International Group ....E....408 972-7800
399 Silicon Valley Blvd San Jose (95138) ***(P-10717)***
Sterling Mktg & Fincl Corp ....E....209 593-1140
4660 Spyres Way Ste 1 Modesto (95356) ***(P-19640)***
Sterling Stamos Acceleration ....E....650 233-5000
2498 Sand Hill Rd Menlo Park (94025) ***(P-19641)***
Sterling Vineyards Inc (PA) ....**E....707 942-3300**
1111 Dunaweal Ln Calistoga (94515) ***(P-2726)***
Sterling Vineyards Inc ....C....707 252-7410
1105 Oak Knoll Ave NAPA (94558) ***(P-2727)***
Steuart Street Venture LP ....D....415 882-1300
191 Sutter St San Francisco (94104) ***(P-11509)***
Steve Manning Construction Inc ....D....530 222-0810
5211 Churn Creek Rd Redding (96002) ***(P-1074)***
Steve Silva Plumbing Inc ....E....707 252-3941
901a Enterprise Way NAPA (94558) ***(P-1366)***
Steve Silva Plumbing Showroom, NAPA *Also called Steve Silva Plumbing Inc* ***(P-1366)***
Steve Silver Productions Inc ....D....415 421-4284
678 Green St Ste 2 San Francisco (94133) ***(P-14864)***
Steve Stymeist Auto Bdy & Pntg, Placerville *Also called Stymeist Auto Body Inc* ***(P-14535)***
Steven Engineering Inc (PA) ....**D....650 588-9200**
230 Ryan Way South San Francisco (94080) ***(P-8878)***
Steven I Klotz ....E....707 763-5010
434 Payran St Ste D Petaluma (94952) ***(P-15246)***
Steven K Olsen DDS Prof Corp ....E....415 398-4400
2 Embarcadero Ctr San Francisco (94111) ***(P-15858)***
Steven Kent LLC ....F....925 243-6442
5443 Tesla Rd Livermore (94550) ***(P-2728)***
Steven P Abelow MD ....D....530 544-8033
2311 Lake Tahoe Blvd South Lake Tahoe (96150) ***(P-15704)***
Stevenot Winery & Imports Inc (PA) ....**E....209 728-0638**
2690 San Domingo Rd Murphys (95247) ***(P-2729)***
Stevens Creek Quarry Inc (PA) ....**D....408 253-2512**
12100 Stevens Canyon Rd Cupertino (95014) ***(P-1075)***
Stevens Creek Toyota, San Jose *Also called Halrec Inc* ***(P-14611)***
Stevens Frrone Biley Engrg Inc (PA) ....**E....925 688-1001**
1600 Willow Pass Ct Concord (94520) ***(P-18821)***
Stevenson-Smith Enterprises ....E....408 286-9616
426 Perrymont Ave San Jose (95125) ***(P-503)***
Stewart & Jasper Marketing Inc (PA) ....**C....209 862-9600**
3500 Shiells Rd Newman (95360) ***(P-2451)***
Stewart & Jasper Orchards, Newman *Also called Stewart & Jasper Marketing Inc* ***(P-2451)***
Stewart Superior ....F....510 346-9811
14487 Griffith St San Leandro (94577) ***(P-9134)***
Stewart Title of Sacramento (PA) ....**E....916 484-6990**
6700 Fair Oaks Blvd Ste B Carmichael (95608) ***(P-10694)***
Stewart Tool Company ....D....916 635-8321
3647 Omec Cir Rancho Cordova (95742) ***(P-5100)***
Stewart/Walker Company, Tracy *Also called Altium Packaging LLC* ***(P-4256)***
Stg IV Gp LP (PA) ....**B....650 935-9500**
2475 Hanover St Palo Alto (94304) ***(P-10770)***
Stiles Custom Metal Inc ....D....209 538-3667
1885 Kinser Rd Ceres (95307) ***(P-4709)***
Still Room LLC ....E....510 847-1930
2624 Barrington Ct Hayward (94545) ***(P-2826)***
Stillwater Sciences, Berkeley *Also called Stillwter Ecsystem Wtrshed Rvr* ***(P-19866)***
Stillwter Ecsystem Wtrshed Rvr (PA) ....**D....510 848-8098**
2855 Telg Ave Ste 400 Berkeley (94705) ***(P-19866)***
Stinson Enterprises Inc ....C....209 529-2933
4513 Mchenry Ave Modesto (95356) ***(P-14625)***
Stitch Labs Inc ....E....415 323-0630
1455 Market St Ste 600 San Francisco (94103) ***(P-19403)***
Stmicroelectronics Inc ....C....408 452-8585
2755 Great America Way Santa Clara (95054) ***(P-8960)***
Stockham Construction Inc ....B....707 664-0945
475 Portal St Cotati (94931) ***(P-1761)***
Stockton, French Camp *Also called Granite Construction Company* ***(P-1049)***
Stockton Ambltory Srgery Ctr L ....D....209 944-9100
2388 N California St Stockton (95204) ***(P-15705)***
Stockton Ceramic Tile Inc ....E....209 464-1291
420 N Harrison St Stockton (95203) ***(P-1723)***
Stockton Congregational Home ....D....209 466-4341
1319 N Madison St Ofc Stockton (95202) ***(P-18185)***
Stockton Crdlgy Med Group Cmpl (PA) ....**E....209 994-5750**
415 E Harding Way Ste D Stockton (95204) ***(P-15706)***
Stockton Delta Resort LLC ....E....209 369-1041
14900 W Highway 12 Lodi (95242) ***(P-11622)***
Stockton District Office, Stockton *Also called State Compensation Insur Fund* ***(P-10183)***
Stockton Edson Healthcare Corp ....D....209 948-8762
1630 N Edison St Stockton (95204) ***(P-16275)***
Stockton Fics, Stockton *Also called Victor Cmnty Support Svcs Inc* ***(P-17088)***
Stockton Hotel Ltd ....D....209 957-9090
2323 Grand Canal Blvd Stockton (95207) ***(P-11510)***
Stockton Orthpd Med Group Inc ....D....209 948-1641
2545 W Hammer Ln Stockton (95209) ***(P-16561)***
Stockton Pipe & Supply, Fresno *Also called Fresno Pipe & Supply Inc* ***(P-8996)***
Stockton Port District ....D....209 946-0246
2201 W Washington St # 13 Stockton (95203) ***(P-7726)***
Stockton Rubber Mfgcoinc ....E....209 887-1172
5023 N Flood Rd Linden (95236) ***(P-4227)***
Stockton Thunder, Stockton *Also called SC Hockey Franchise Corp* ***(P-14915)***
Stockton Tri-Industries LLC ....E....209 948-9701
2141 E Anderson St Stockton (95205) ***(P-5058)***
Stoel Rives LLP (PA) ....**D....916 447-0700**
500 Capitol Mall Ste 1600 Sacramento (95814) ***(P-17379)***
Stokes Brothers Farms ....D....209 794-2380
7581 W Kile Rd Lodi (95242) ***(P-76)***
Stokes Vannoy Inc ....E....530 747-2026
1560 Drew Ave Davis (95618) ***(P-18822)***
Stollwood Convalescent Hosp, Woodland *Also called St Johns Retirement Village* ***(P-16274)***
Stommel Inc (PA) ....**E....916 646-6626**
631 N Market Blvd Ste N Sacramento (95834) ***(P-1614)***
Stomper Co Inc ....D....510 574-0570
3135 Diablo Ave Hayward (94545) ***(P-1989)***
Stone & Youngberg LLC (PA) ....**C....415 445-2300**
1 Ferry Plz San Francisco (94111) ***(P-10015)***
Stone Bridge Cellars Inc (PA) ....**E....707 963-2745**
200 Taplin Rd Saint Helena (94574) ***(P-2730)***
Stone Bros Management ....D....209 952-7500
5308 Sherwood Mall Stockton (95207) ***(P-10718)***
Stone Bros Security, Stockton *Also called Stone Bros Management* ***(P-10718)***
Stone Edge Farm, Sonoma *Also called Stone Edge Winery LLC* ***(P-2731)***
Stone Edge Winery LLC ....F....707 935-6520
19330 Carriger Rd Sonoma (95476) ***(P-2731)***
Stone Publishing Inc (PA) ....**C....408 450-7910**
2549 Scott Blvd Santa Clara (95050) ***(P-3602)***
Stonebrae LP ....E....510 728-7878
222 Country Club Dr Hayward (94542) ***(P-15156)***
Stonebrook Convalescent Center ....C....925 689-7457
4367 Concord Blvd Concord (94521) ***(P-16130)***
Stonebrook Health Care Center, Concord *Also called Stonebrook Convalescent Center* ***(P-16130)***
Stonecrop Technologies LLC ....F....781 659-0007
103 H St Ste B Petaluma (94952) ***(P-5872)***
Stonecushion Inc (PA) ....**E....707 433-1911**
1400 Lytton Springs Rd Healdsburg (95448) ***(P-2732)***
Stoneridge Creek Pleasanton, Pleasanton *Also called Contining Lf Cmmnties Plsnton* ***(P-18081)***
Stonesfair Financial Corp ....D....650 347-0442
577 Airport Blvd Ste 700 Burlingame (94010) ***(P-10463)***
Stonetree Golf LLC ....E....415 209-6744
9 Stonetree Ln Novato (94945) ***(P-15031)***
Stonetree Management, Novato *Also called Stonetree Golf LLC* ***(P-15031)***
Stop 'n' Save Liquors, Modesto *Also called C W Brower Inc* ***(P-9264)***
Storage Masters Self Storage, Santa Rosa *Also called Kandy Investments LLC* ***(P-7692)***
Store Intelligence Inc ....E....925 400-8499
6700 Koll Center Pkwy # 10 Pleasanton (94566) ***(P-6471)***
Storer Transit Systems (PA) ....**E....209 527-4900**
3519 Mcdonald Ave Modesto (95358) ***(P-7406)***

Storer Transportation Service (PA) ....B....**209 521-8250**
3519 Mcdonald Ave Modesto (95358) ***(P-7419)***
Storer Travel Service, Modesto *Also called Storer Transportation Service* ***(P-7419)***
Storm Wtr Insptn Mint Svcs Inc ....E....925 516-8966
3361 Walnut Blvd Ste 110 Brentwood (94513) ***(P-14416)***
Storm8 Inc ....F....650 596-8600
2400 Bridge Pkwy Ste 2 Redwood City (94065) ***(P-13468)***
Storm8 Entertainment, Redwood City *Also called Storm8 Inc* ***(P-13468)***
Stormgeo (HQ) ....C....**408 731-8600**
140 Kifer Ct Sunnyvale (94086) ***(P-19917)***
Story Dental Health Center ....E....408 272-0888
2454 Story Rd San Jose (95122) ***(P-15859)***
Stott Outdoor Advertising ....E....888 342-7868
700 Fortress St Chico (95973) ***(P-11787)***
Stottler Henke Associates Inc (PA) ....E....**650 931-2700**
1650 S Amphlett Blvd # 300 San Mateo (94402) ***(P-13982)***
Strachan Apiaries Inc ....E....530 674-3881
2522 Tierra Buena Rd Yuba City (95993) ***(P-244)***
Strachota Insurance Agency ....E....951 676-2229
2721 Citrus Rd Ste A Rancho Cordova (95742) ***(P-10355)***
Strahmcolor ....F....415 459-5409
3000 Kerner Blvd San Rafael (94901) ***(P-3701)***
Straight Edge Stvdore Svcs Inc (PA) ....D....**707 837-8564**
9769 Dawn Way Windsor (95492) ***(P-12144)***
Straight Line Roofing & Cnstr ....E....530 672-9995
3811 Dividend Dr Ste A Shingle Springs (95682) ***(P-1840)***
Strands Finance, San Mateo *Also called Strands Labs Inc* ***(P-12820)***
Strands Labs Inc ....E....415 398-4333
999 Baker Way Ste 430 San Mateo (94404) ***(P-12820)***
Stratamet Advanced Mtls Corp ....F....510 440-1697
2718 Prune Ave Fremont (94539) ***(P-4404)***
Stratedge Inc (PA) ....E....**925 236-2022**
2410 Camino Ramon Ste 235 San Ramon (94583) ***(P-12821)***
Strategic Bus Insights Inc (PA) ....D....**650 859-4600**
333 Ravenswood Ave Menlo Park (94025) ***(P-19642)***
Strategic Capital Incorporated ....E....707 473-4310
3225 W Dry Creek Rd Healdsburg (95448) ***(P-19643)***
Strategic Industry Inc ....E....559 419-9481
1440 Draper St Ste C Kingsburg (93631) ***(P-572)***
Strategic Materials Inc ....E....707 452-3362
299 Beck Ave Fairfield (94533) ***(P-11873)***
Strategic Mechanical Inc ....C....559 291-1952
4661 E Commerce Ave Fresno (93725) ***(P-1367)***
Strategic Threat MGT Inc ....E....925 775-4777
2504 Verne Roberts Cir # 1 Antioch (94509) ***(P-14100)***
Strateos Inc (PA) ....D....**650 763-8432**
3565 Haven Ave Ste 3 Menlo Park (94025) ***(P-19644)***
Stratford, San Mateo *Also called Raiser Senior Services LLC* ***(P-16099)***
Stratford School Inc ....D....408 973-7320
1999 S Bascom Ave Ste 400 Campbell (95008) ***(P-18036)***
Stratford School Inc (PA) ....E....**650 493-1151**
870 N California Ave Palo Alto (94303) ***(P-18037)***
Stratgies To Empwer People Inc (PA) ....B....**916 679-1527**
2330 Glendale Ln Sacramento (95825) ***(P-16207)***
Strathmoore Press Inc ....E....510 843-8888
2550 9th St Ste 103 Berkeley (94710) ***(P-14417)***
Straus Family Creamery Inc ....D....707 776-2887
1105 Industrial Ave # 200 Petaluma (94952) ***(P-2143)***
Strava Inc (PA) ....C....**415 374-7298**
208 Utah St Fl 2 San Francisco (94103) ***(P-7993)***
Strawberry Inn ....E....209 965-3662
31888 Hwy 108 Strawberry (95375) ***(P-11511)***
Streamguys Inc ....E....707 667-9479
2212 Jacoby Creek Rd Bayside (95524) ***(P-14418)***
Streamguys.com, Bayside *Also called Streamguys Inc* ***(P-14418)***
Streamline Circuits LLC ....B....415 279-8650
1410 Martin Ave Santa Clara (95050) ***(P-5980)***
Streamline Construction, Grass Valley *Also called JM Streamline Inc* ***(P-902)***
Streamline Development LLC ....E....415 499-3355
100 Smith Ranch Rd # 124 San Rafael (94903) ***(P-12822)***
Streamline Electronics Mfg Inc ....E....408 263-3600
4285 Technology Dr Fremont (94538) ***(P-5981)***
Streamline Irrigation Inc ....E....559 897-1516
3630 Avenue 384 Kingsburg (93631) ***(P-8419)***
Streamline Solutions, San Rafael *Also called Streamline Development LLC* ***(P-12822)***
Streamlio Inc ....F....949 701-9729
801 Middlefield Rd Apt 9 Palo Alto (94301) ***(P-5781)***
Streamray Inc (PA) ....D....**408 745-5449**
910 E Hamilton Ave Fl 6 Campbell (95008) ***(P-14880)***
Streamsets Inc (PA) ....E....**415 851-1018**
150 Spear St Ste 300 San Francisco (94105) ***(P-12823)***
Streamvector Inc (PA) ....C....**415 870-8395**
4701 Patrick Henry Dr # 2 Santa Clara (95054) ***(P-12824)***
Street Graphics Inc ....E....209 948-1713
1834 W Euclid Ave Stockton (95204) ***(P-7255)***
Streetline Inc (HQ) ....D....**650 242-3400**
393 Vintage Park Dr # 140 Foster City (94404) ***(P-13761)***
Streivor Inc ....F....925 960-9090
2150 Kitty Hawk Rd Livermore (94551) ***(P-7168)***
Streivor Air Systems, Livermore *Also called Streivor Inc* ***(P-7168)***
Striim Inc (PA) ....E....**425 894-1998**
575 Middlefield Rd Palo Alto (94301) ***(P-12825)***
Strikes Unlimited Inc ....D....916 626-3600
5681 Lonetree Blvd Rocklin (95765) ***(P-14902)***
Striking Distance Studios Inc ....E....925 355-5131
6111 Bollinger Canyon Rd # 150 San Ramon (94583) ***(P-14881)***
String Letter Publishing Inc ....E....510 215-0010
941 Marina Way S Ste E Richmond (94804) ***(P-3603)***
Stripe Inc (PA) ....B....**888 963-8955**
510 Townsend St San Francisco (94103) ***(P-12826)***
Stripe Heavy Industries Inc (HQ) ....E....**877 887-7815**
510 Townsend St San Francisco (94103) ***(P-13669)***
Stripe Payments Company, San Francisco *Also called Stripe Inc* ***(P-12826)***
Strivr Labs Inc ....C....650 656-9987
3520 Thomas Rd Ste C Santa Clara (95054) ***(P-12827)***
Stroer & Graff Inc ....E....925 778-0200
1830 Phillips Ln Antioch (94509) ***(P-1180)***
Stroppini Enterprises ....E....916 635-8181
2546 Mercantile Dr Ste A Rancho Cordova (95742) ***(P-5068)***
Strouss Bros Construction Inc ....E....408 267-3222
700 Comstock St Santa Clara (95054) ***(P-1910)***
Structionsite Inc ....E....510 340-9515
248 3rd St Oakland (94607) ***(P-12828)***
Structural Integrity Assoc Inc (PA) ....D....**408 978-8200**
5215 Hellyer Ave Ste 210 San Jose (95138) ***(P-18823)***
Stryder Corp (PA) ....D....**415 981-8400**
225 Bush St Fl 12 San Francisco (94104) ***(P-13469)***
Stryker Endoscopy, San Jose *Also called Stryker Sales LLC* ***(P-7081)***
Stryker Enterprises Inc ....F....408 295-6300
1358 E San Fernando St San Jose (95116) ***(P-4987)***
Stryker Neurovascular, Fremont *Also called Stryker Sales LLC* ***(P-7044)***
Stryker Sales LLC ....E....510 413-2500
47900 Bayside Pkwy Fremont (94538) ***(P-7044)***
Stryker Sales LLC ....E....800 624-4422
5900 Optical Ct San Jose (95138) ***(P-7081)***
Stuart Rental Company, Milpitas *Also called Ohana Partners Inc* ***(P-12057)***
Studebaker Brown Electric Inc ....E....916 678-4660
3237 Rippey Rd Ste 100 Loomis (95650) ***(P-1615)***
Student Un of San Jose State U ....E....408 924-6405
211 S. 9th Street San Jose (95192) ***(P-18596)***
Student Un of San Jose State U ....E....408 321-8510
2160 Lundy Ave Ste 250 San Jose (95131) ***(P-18597)***
Student Un of San Jose State U ....E....408 924-6371
290 S 7th St San Jose (95192) ***(P-18598)***
Student Union Building, San Jose *Also called Student Un of San Jose State U* ***(P-18596)***
Stuke Nursery Co Inc ....E....530 846-2378
1463 State Highway 99 Gridley (95948) ***(P-138)***
Sturdy Gun Safe Inc ....E....559 485-8361
2030 S Sarah St Fresno (93721) ***(P-4988)***
Sturdy Safe, Fresno *Also called Sturdy Gun Safe Inc* ***(P-4988)***
Sturgeon Construction Inc ....E....916 452-6108
8259 Alpine Ave Sacramento (95826) ***(P-968)***
Stv Incorporated ....D....510 763-1313
505 14th St Ste 1060 Oakland (94612) ***(P-18916)***
Stx Inc ....E....707 284-3549
412 Aviation Blvd Ste K Santa Rosa (95403) ***(P-7201)***
Style Media Group Inc ....E....916 988-9888
909 Mormon St Folsom (95630) ***(P-3515)***
Stymeist Auto Body Inc ....E....530 622-7588
3948 State Highway 49 Placerville (95667) ***(P-14535)***
Styra Inc ....E....415 200-8871
1800 Broadway St Ste 1 Redwood City (94063) ***(P-12829)***
Suarez & Munoz Cnstr Inc ....E....510 782-6065
2490 American Ave Hayward (94545) ***(P-711)***
Sub Sea Systems Inc ....E....530 626-0100
6524 Commerce Way Ste A Diamond Springs (95619) ***(P-15247)***
Sub St Francis Mem Hosp, Walnut Creek *Also called Sports Medicine* ***(P-15699)***
Sub Zero, Burlingame *Also called Riggs Distributing Inc* ***(P-8886)***
Sub-Acute Saratoga Hospital, Saratoga *Also called Progressive Sub-Acute Care* ***(P-16484)***
Suba Mfg Inc ....F....707 745-0358
921 Bayshore Rd Benicia (94510) ***(P-3320)***
Suba Technology Inc ....D....408 434-6500
46501 Landing Pkwy Fremont (94538) ***(P-5982)***
Subacute Trtmnt Adolescnt Reha (PA) ....D....**510 352-9200**
545 Estudillo Ave San Leandro (94577) ***(P-17076)***
Subdirect LLC (PA) ....C....**559 321-0449**
653 W Fllbrook Ave Ste 10 Fresno (93711) ***(P-3516)***
Subdynamic Locating Svcs Inc ....E....408 723-4191
274 Hillsdale Ave San Jose (95136) ***(P-18927)***
Sublimation Inc ....E....888 994-2726
2537 Willow St Unit 6 Oakland (94607) ***(P-7309)***
Sublime, Oakland *Also called Sublimation Inc* ***(P-7309)***
Sublime Machining Inc ....F....858 349-2445
2537 Willow St Oakland (94607) ***(P-7310)***
Subtle Medical Inc ....E....650 397-8709
883 Santa Cruz Ave # 205 Menlo Park (94025) ***(P-13470)***
Suburban Steel Inc (PA) ....E....**559 268-6281**
706 W California Ave Fresno (93706) ***(P-4685)***
Success Factors, Palo Alto *Also called Successfactors Inc* ***(P-13471)***
Successfactors Inc (HQ) ....A....**650 212-1296**
3410 Hillview Ave Palo Alto (94304) ***(P-13471)***
Successfactors Inc ....D....650 645-2000
1500 Fashion Island Blvd San Mateo (94404) ***(P-12830)***
Successful Altrntves For Addct ....D....510 247-8300
795 Fletcher Ln Hayward (94544) ***(P-17077)***
Successful Altrntves For Addct (HQ) ....E....**707 649-8300**
1628 Broadway St Vallejo (94590) ***(P-16770)***
Suddath Rlction Systems Nthrn ....E....904 858-1273
2020 S 10th St San Jose (95112) ***(P-7597)***
Suddath Rlction Systems Nthrn ....D....408 288-3030
2055 S 7th St San Jose (95112) ***(P-7598)***
Sudwerk Privatbrauerei Hubsch ....D....530 756-2739
2001 2nd St Davis (95618) ***(P-2495)***
Suffolk Construction Co Inc ....C....415 848-0500
525 Market St Ste 2850 San Francisco (94105) ***(P-712)***
Sufi, Fremont *Also called Startup Farms Intl LLC* ***(P-12817)***

ALPHABETIC

Sugar Bowl Bakery, Hayward *Also called Ly Brothers Corporation (P-2392)*
Sugar Bowl Corporation ....D....530 426-9000
629 Sugar Bowl Rd Norden (95724) *(P-11512)*
Sugar Bowl Ski Resort ....E....530 426-3651
629 Sugar Bowl Rd Norden (95724) *(P-11513)*
Sugarcrm Inc (PA) ....C....877 842-7276
10050 N Wolfe Rd Sw2130 Cupertino (95014) *(P-12831)*
Sugarloaf Farming Corporation ....E....707 942-4459
12400 Ida Clayton Rd Calistoga (94515) *(P-2733)*
Suisun City Hotel LLC ....E....707 429-0900
212 Sutter St Fl 3 San Francisco (94108) *(P-11514)*
SUISUN REDEVELOPMENT AGENCY, Suisun City *Also called Redevelopment Agency of The Ci (P-19847)*
Suiteamerica, El Dorado Hills *Also called California Suites (P-10477)*
Suki Ai Inc ....E....650 549-8959
1823 El Cmino Real Unit A Redwood City (94063) *(P-12832)*
Sullivan & Brampton, San Leandro *Also called Brampton Mthesen Fabr Pdts Inc (P-3037)*
Sullivan Counter Tops Inc ....E....510 652-2337
1189 65th St Oakland (94608) *(P-3321)*
Sullivan Ctr For Chldren A Psy ....D....559 271-1186
3443 W Shaw Ave Fresno (93711) *(P-15707)*
Sulzer Pump Solutions US Inc ....E....916 925-8508
1650 Bell Ave Ste 140 Sacramento (95838) *(P-5179)*
Suma Fruit Intl USA Inc ....D....559 875-5000
1810 Academy Ave Sanger (93657) *(P-310)*
Suma Landscaping Inc ....E....415 332-7862
2857 Chapman St Oakland (94601) *(P-504)*
Sumanos Bakery LLC ....E....831 722-5511
358 Locust St Watsonville (95076) *(P-9490)*
Sumitomo Elc DVC Innvtons USA ....D....408 232-9500
2355 Zanker Rd San Jose (95131) *(P-8961)*
Summer House Inc (PA) ....D....530 662-8493
206 5th St Woodland (95695) *(P-18186)*
Summerhill Construction Co ....E....925 244-7520
3000 Executive Pkwy # 450 San Ramon (94583) *(P-713)*
Summerhill Homes, San Ramon *Also called Summerhill Construction Co (P-713)*
Summerville At Hazel Creek LLC ....B....916 988-7901
6125 Hazel Ave Orangevale (95662) *(P-16131)*
Summerville Senior Living Inc ....E....510 235-5514
1900 Church Ln San Pablo (94806) *(P-16132)*
Summerville Senior Living Inc ....E....510 234-5200
6510 Gladys Ave El Cerrito (94530) *(P-16133)*
Summit Bank ....E....510 839-8800
2969 Broadway Oakland (94611) *(P-9690)*
Summit Bank Foundation (HQ) ....E....510 839-8800
2969 Broadway Oakland (94611) *(P-9749)*
Summit Building Services Inc ....D....925 827-9500
1128 Willow Pass Ct Concord (94520) *(P-12002)*
Summit Crane Inc ....E....707 448-6740
892 Aldridge Rd Vacaville (95688) *(P-12024)*
Summit Electric, Santa Rosa *Also called Summit Technology Group Inc (P-1617)*
Summit Electric Inc (PA) ....E....707 542-4773
2450 Bluebell Dr Ste C Santa Rosa (95403) *(P-1616)*
Summit Engineering Inc ....E....707 527-0775
463 Aviation Blvd Ste 200 Santa Rosa (95403) *(P-18824)*
Summit Funding Inc ....D....916 571-3000
2241 Harvard St Ste 200 Sacramento (95815) *(P-9933)*
Summit Hotel Trs 115 LLC (PA) ....C....650 624-3700
264 S Airport Blvd South San Francisco (94080) *(P-11515)*
Summit Interconnect Inc ....C....408 727-1418
1401 Martin Ave Santa Clara (95050) *(P-5983)*
Summit Intrconnect Santa Clara, Santa Clara *Also called Streamline Circuits LLC (P-5980)*
Summit Medical Center ....C....510 869-6758
3100 Summit St Oakland (94609) *(P-16562)*
Summit Partners LP ....A....650 614-6670
200 Middlefield Rd # 200 Menlo Park (94025) *(P-10885)*
Summit Steel Works Corporation ....E....408 510-5880
850 Faulstich Ct San Jose (95112) *(P-4686)*
Summit Surgical, Fresno *Also called Sierra Pacific Surgery Ctr LLC (P-15685)*
Summit Technology Group Inc ....E....707 542-4773
2450c Bluebell Dr Ste C Santa Rosa (95403) *(P-1617)*
Summit Wireless Tech Inc (PA) ....E....408 627-4716
6840 Via Del Oro Ste 280 San Jose (95119) *(P-6314)*
Summitview Child & Family Svcs ....D....530 644-2412
670 Placerville Dr Ste 2 Placerville (95667) *(P-17761)*
Sumo Logic Inc (PA) ....A....650 810-8700
305 Main St Fl 3 Redwood City (94063) *(P-12833)*
Sun Basket Inc ....C....408 669-4418
1 Clarence Pl Unit 14 San Francisco (94107) *(P-2944)*
Sun Basket Inc (PA) ....C....408 669-4418
1170 Olinder Ct San Jose (95122) *(P-2945)*
Sun City Rsvlle Cmnty Assn Inc (PA) ....C....916 774-3880
7050 Del Webb Blvd Roseville (95747) *(P-15032)*
Sun Deep Cosmetics, Hayward *Also called Sun Deep Inc (P-4095)*
Sun Deep Inc ....C....510 441-2525
31285 San Clemente St Hayward (94544) *(P-4095)*
Sun Frost, Arcata *Also called Larry Schlussler (P-5702)*
Sun Hing Foods Inc (PA) ....E....650 583-8188
271 Harbor Way South San Francisco (94080) *(P-9491)*
Sun Innovations Inc ....E....510 573-3913
43241 Osgood Rd Fremont (94539) *(P-19131)*
Sun Light & Power ....D....510 845-2997
1035 Folger Ave Berkeley (94710) *(P-14419)*
Sun Microsystems, Redwood City *Also called Oracle America Inc (P-5266)*
Sun Microsystems, Rocklin *Also called Oracle America Inc (P-13351)*
Sun Microsystems Intl Inc (HQ) ....B....650 506-7000
500 Oracle Pkwy Redwood City (94065) *(P-13472)*
Sun Mountain Inc ....E....415 852-2320
2 Henry Adams St Ste 150 San Francisco (94103) *(P-3154)*
Sun Oak Assisted Living, Citrus Heights *Also called Regent Assisted Living Inc (P-18165)*
Sun Oak Assisted Living, Citrus Heights *Also called Sun Oak Limited Partners (P-18187)*
Sun Oak Limited Partners ....D....916 722-2800
7241 Canelo Hills Dr Ofc Citrus Heights (95610) *(P-18187)*
Sun Oaks Racquet Club, Redding *Also called W C Garcia & Associates Inc (P-15166)*
Sun Oaks Tennis & Fitness, Redding *Also called Walsh Group Inc (P-14985)*
Sun Power Security Gates Inc ....F....209 722-3990
438 Tyler Rd Merced (95341) *(P-4546)*
Sun Sheetmetal Solutions Inc ....E....408 445-8047
3565 Charter Park Dr San Jose (95136) *(P-4821)*
Sun Tropics Inc ....F....925 202-2221
2420 Camino Ramon Ste 101 San Ramon (94583) *(P-2300)*
Sun Valley Floral Group LLC ....A....707 826-8700
3160 Upper Bay Rd Arcata (95521) *(P-7311)*
Sun Valley Group Inc (PA) ....B....707 822-2885
3160 Upper Bay Rd Arcata (95521) *(P-139)*
Sun Valley Rice Company LLC ....D....530 476-3000
7050 Eddy Rd Arbuckle (95912) *(P-2328)*
Sun-Maid Growers California (PA) ....A....559 896-8000
6795 N Palm Ave Ste 200 Fresno (93704) *(P-9492)*
Sunbelt Supply 9256, Livermore *Also called Sunbelt Supply LP (P-9135)*
Sunbelt Supply LP ....E....925 449-5900
4754 Bennett Dr Ste C Livermore (94551) *(P-9135)*
Sunborne Nursery, San Francisco *Also called Goldman Enterprises (P-124)*
Sunbrdge Brttany Rhbltion Ctr ....A....916 484-1393
3900 Garfield Ave Carmichael (95608) *(P-16134)*
Sunbrdge Prdise Rhbltion Ctr ....A....530 872-3200
8777 Skyway Paradise (95969) *(P-16135)*
Sunbridge Care Entps W LLC ....A....559 897-5881
1101 Stroud Ave Kingsburg (93631) *(P-16136)*
Sunbridge Care Entps W LLC ....C....559 897-5881
1101 Stroud Ave Kingsburg (93631) *(P-16137)*
Suncrest Nurseries Inc ....D....831 728-2595
400 Casserly Rd Watsonville (95076) *(P-9640)*
Sundial Restaurant ....E....209 524-0808
808 Mchenry Ave Modesto (95350) *(P-11516)*
Sundt Construction, Sacramento *Also called Halstead Partnership (P-884)*
Sunera Technologies Inc ....E....510 474-2616
691 S Milpitas Blvd Milpitas (95035) *(P-13983)*
Suneye, Sebastopol *Also called Solmetric Corporation (P-6923)*
Sunfoods LLC (HQ) ....D....530 661-1923
1620 E Kentucky Ave Woodland (95776) *(P-9313)*
Sungard Bi-Tech Inc (HQ) ....E....530 891-5281
890 Fortress St Chico (95973) *(P-12834)*
Sunhill Corp ....D....415 383-9100
147 Lomita Dr Ste G Mill Valley (94941) *(P-19404)*
Suning Cmmerce R D Ctr USA Inc ....D....650 834-9800
845 Page Mill Rd Palo Alto (94304) *(P-19188)*
Suning USA, Palo Alto *Also called Suning Cmmerce R D Ctr USA Inc (P-19188)*
Sunkist Enterprises ....D....650 347-3900
1308 Rollins Rd Burlingame (94010) *(P-8990)*
Sunland Insurance Agency ....A....559 251-7861
4961 E Kings Canyon Rd Fresno (93727) *(P-10356)*
Sunmar Corporation ....E....408 249-5100
474 E El Camino Real Sunnyvale (94087) *(P-10666)*
Sunny Retirement Home ....D....408 454-5600
22445 Cupertino Rd Cupertino (95014) *(P-16276)*
Sunnybrae Animal Clinic Inc ....E....707 822-5124
900 Buttermilk Ln Arcata (95521) *(P-338)*
Sunnyhills Apts, Milpitas *Also called J M K Investments Inc (P-10582)*
Sunnyside Convalescent Hosp, Fresno *Also called R Fellen Inc (P-16098)*
Sunnyside Country Club ....D....559 255-6871
5704 E Butler Ave Fresno (93727) *(P-15157)*
Sunnyside Gardens, Cupertino *Also called Montvale Inc (P-16254)*
Sunnyside Gardens ....E....408 730-4070
1025 Carson Dr Sunnyvale (94086) *(P-18188)*
Sunnyside Resort ....E....530 583-7200
1850 W Lake Blvd Tahoe City (96145) *(P-11517)*
Sunnytech ....F....408 943-8100
2243 Ringwood Ave San Jose (95131) *(P-5984)*
Sunnyvale Christian School, Sunnyvale *Also called First Baptist Church Crosswalk (P-17934)*
Sunnyvale Fluid Sys Tech Inc (PA) ....E....510 933-2500
3393 W Warren Ave Fremont (94538) *(P-9136)*
Sunnyvale Health Care, Sunnyvale *Also called Sunnyvale Healthcare Center (P-16138)*
Sunnyvale Healthcare Center ....C....408 245-8070
1291 S Bernardo Ave Sunnyvale (94087) *(P-16138)*
Sunnyvale Larkspur Landing, Sunnyvale *Also called LL Sunnyvale LP (P-11264)*
Sunnyvale Seafood, Union City *Also called SSC Inc (P-9370)*
Sunnyvalley Smoked Meats Inc ....C....209 825-0288
2475 W Yosemite Ave Manteca (95337) *(P-2126)*
Sunopta Food Solutions, Scotts Valley *Also called Sunopta Globl Orgnic Ingrdnts (P-2287)*
Sunopta Globl Orgnic Ingrdnts (HQ) ....E....831 685-6506
100 Enterprise Way B10 Scotts Valley (95066) *(P-2287)*
Sunoptics Prismatic Skylights, Sacramento *Also called Washoe Equipment Inc (P-5729)*
Sunpower Corporation (HQ) ....A....408 240-5500
51 Rio Robles San Jose (95134) *(P-6315)*
Sunpower Corporation Systems (HQ) ....D....510 260-8200
1414 Hrbour Way S Ste 190 Richmond (94804) *(P-1368)*
Sunpower USA, Union City *Also called Aei Electech Corp (P-6395)*
Sunpreme Inc ....E....408 419-9281
4701 Patrick Henry Dr # 25 Santa Clara (95054) *(P-6316)*
Sunridge Farms, Royal Oaks *Also called Falcon Trading Company (P-2891)*
Sunrise Bistro, Walnut Creek *Also called Joroda Inc (P-2389)*
Sunrise Farms LLC ....D....707 778-6450
395 Liberty Rd Petaluma (94952) *(P-9353)*
Sunrise Fresh Dried Fruit Co, Stockton *Also called Sunrise Fresh LLC (P-2268)*

ALPHABETIC SECTION **Surgery Center of Marin**

Sunrise Fresh LLC ....E....209 932-0192
237 N Golden Gate Ave Stockton (95205) ***(P-2268)***
Sunrise Hospitality Inc ....E....916 419-4440
2060 Freeway Dr Woodland (95776) ***(P-11518)***
Sunrise Medical (us) LLC ....E....559 292-2171
2842 N Business Park Ave Fresno (93727) ***(P-8792)***
Sunrise Mfg Inc (PA) ....E....916 635-6262
2665 Mercantile Dr Rancho Cordova (95742) ***(P-3406)***
Sunrise of Petaluma ....E....707 776-2885
815 Wood Sorrel Dr Petaluma (94954) ***(P-16139)***
Sunrise Orchards, Rio Oso *Also called Raj Sharma* ***(P-90)***
Sunrise Palace Inc ....E....707 469-2323
610 Orange Dr Vacaville (95687) ***(P-11519)***
Sunrise Shs Pedorthic Svc Corp ....F....916 368-7700
3127 Fite Cir Ste G Sacramento (95827) ***(P-4342)***
Sunrun Cllsto Issuer 2015-1 LL ....E....415 580-6900
595 Market St Fl 29 San Francisco (94105) ***(P-1369)***
Sunrun Installation Svcs Inc ....B....408 746-3062
575 Dado St San Jose (95131) ***(P-1370)***
Sunrun Installation Svcs Inc ....B....415 580-6900
595 Market St Fl 29 San Francisco (94105) ***(P-1371)***
Sunrun Installation Svcs Inc ....B....559 298-7652
4933 W Jennifer Ave # 101 Fresno (93722) ***(P-1372)***
Sunseri Construction Inc ....E....530 891-6444
48 Comanche Ct Chico (95928) ***(P-772)***
Sunset Aviation LLC (PA) ....E....707 775-2786
201 1st St Ste 307 Petaluma (94952) ***(P-7785)***
Sunset Development Company (PA) ....C....925 277-1700
2600 Camino Ramon Ste 201 San Ramon (94583) ***(P-10410)***
Sunset Disposal Service Inc ....E....209 466-5192
1145 W Charter Way Stockton (95206) ***(P-7492)***
Sunset Linen Service, Santa Rosa *Also called City Towel & Dust Service Inc* ***(P-11634)***
Sunset Magazine, Oakland *Also called Sunset Publishing Corporation* ***(P-3517)***
Sunset Moulding Co (PA) ....E....530 790-2700
2231 Paseo Rd Live Oak (95953) ***(P-3117)***
Sunset Moulding Co ....E....530 695-1000
1856 Skyway Chico (95928) ***(P-3155)***
Sunset Publishing Corporation (HQ) ....C....800 777-0117
55 Harrison St Ste 200 Oakland (94607) ***(P-3517)***
Sunset Scavenger Company ....B....415 330-1300
250 Executive Park Blvd # 2100 San Francisco (94134) ***(P-8365)***
Sunshine Raisin Corporation (PA) ....C....559 834-5981
626 S 5th St Fowler (93625) ***(P-311)***
Sunshine Villa Assisted Living, Santa Cruz *Also called Regent Assisted Living Inc* ***(P-18167)***
Sunsil Inc (PA) ....E....925 648-7779
3174 Danville Blvd Ste 1 Alamo (94507) ***(P-6317)***
Sunstone Construction Inc ....D....408 379-0592
176 Gilman Ave Campbell (95008) ***(P-1911)***
Sunstone Partners LLC ....D....650 289-4400
400 S El Cmino Real Ste 3 San Mateo (94402) ***(P-10886)***
Sunstone Partners MGT LLC ....D....650 289-4400
400 S El Cmino Real Ste 3 San Mateo (94402) ***(P-10887)***
Sunsweet Dryers ....C....530 824-5854
23760 Loleta Ave Corning (96021) ***(P-2269)***
Sunsweet Dryers ....C....530 846-5578
26 E Evans Reimer Rd Gridley (95948) ***(P-2270)***
Sunsweet Growers Inc (PA) ....A....800 417-2253
901 N Walton Ave Yuba City (95993) ***(P-2271)***
Sunsweet Growers Inc ....D....530 824-5376
23760 Loleta Ave Corning (96021) ***(P-9493)***
Sunsystem Technology LLC ....C....559 412-7870
2025 N Gateway Blvd # 112 Fresno (93727) ***(P-19132)***
Sunsystem Technology LLC (PA) ....D....916 671-3351
2731 Citrus Rd Ste D Rancho Cordova (95742) ***(P-19133)***
Sunsystem Technology LLC ....C....510 984-2027
2802 10th St Berkeley (94710) ***(P-6318)***
Suntech America Inc (PA) ....F....415 882-9922
2721 Shattuck Ave Berkeley (94705) ***(P-4640)***
Suntech Power, Berkeley *Also called Suntech America Inc* ***(P-4640)***
Sunvalleytek International Inc ....D....510 255-6101
160 E Tasman Dr San Jose (95134) ***(P-8751)***
Sunwest Fruit Co Inc ....E....559 646-4000
755 E Manning Ave Parlier (93648) ***(P-9432)***
Sunworks Inc (PA) ....D....916 409-6900
2270 Douglas Blvd Ste 216 Roseville (95661) ***(P-6319)***
Sunworks United Inc (HQ) ....D....916 409-6900
2270 Douglas Blvd Ste 216 Roseville (95661) ***(P-1373)***
Super 8 Motel, Fort Bragg *Also called Noyo Vista Inc* ***(P-11334)***
Super 8 Motel, Stockton *Also called Inncal Incorporated* ***(P-11193)***
Super 8 Motel, Madera *Also called Parmar Ashok* ***(P-11359)***
Super 8 Motel ....E....530 233-3545
511 N Main St Alturas (96101) ***(P-11520)***
Super Chef, Redwood City *Also called American Production Co Inc* ***(P-4596)***
Super Evil Mega Corp ....E....650 787-2505
119a S B St San Mateo (94401) ***(P-12835)***
Super Micro Computer Inc (PA) ....A....408 503-8000
980 Rock Ave San Jose (95131) ***(P-5273)***
Super Pallet Recycling Center, Elk Grove *Also called Super Pallet Recycling Corp* ***(P-8609)***
Super Pallet Recycling Corp (PA) ....D....916 686-1700
10401 Grant Line Rd Elk Grove (95624) ***(P-8609)***
Super Store Industries ....B....209 858-3365
2800 W March Ln Ste 210 Stockton (95219) ***(P-9494)***
Super Store Industries ....D....209 668-2100
2600 Spengler Way Turlock (95380) ***(P-2183)***
Super Talent Technology Corp ....A....408 957-8133
2077 N Capitol Ave San Jose (95132) ***(P-8752)***
Superb Hospitality LLC ....E....559 897-8840
216 W Ventura Ct Kingsburg (93631) ***(P-11521)***
Superboward LLC ....C....650 348-4881
1222 Broadway Burlingame (94010) ***(P-11695)***
Supercloset ....E....831 588-7829
3555 Airway Dr Santa Rosa (95403) ***(P-4609)***
Supercuts, Burlingame *Also called Superbroward LLC* ***(P-11695)***
Supercuts, Fresno *Also called Dybeck Inc* ***(P-11680)***
Supercuts, Patterson *Also called Groves/Eden Corporation* ***(P-11683)***
Supercuts, Walnut Creek *Also called J M D Enterprises* ***(P-11686)***
Superior Automatic Sprnklr Co ....D....408 946-7272
4378 Enterprise St Fremont (94538) ***(P-1374)***
Superior Body Shop, San Carlos *Also called Aho Enterprises Inc* ***(P-14516)***
Superior Buildings Svcs Inc ....E....707 429-3000
1070 Horizon Dr Ste I Fairfield (94533) ***(P-12003)***
Superior Equipment Company Inc ....E....707 256-3600
2301 Napa Vallejo Hwy NAPA (94558) ***(P-8409)***
Superior Farms, Dixon *Also called Transhumance Holding Co Inc* ***(P-2105)***
Superior Farms, Sacramento *Also called Ellensburg Lamb Company Inc* ***(P-2096)***
Superior Foods Inc ....D....831 728-3691
275 Westgate Dr Watsonville (95076) ***(P-9314)***
Superior Foods Companies, The, Watsonville *Also called Superior Foods Inc* ***(P-9314)***
Superior Kitchen Cabinets Inc ....E....209 247-0097
1703 Voumard Ranch Dr Turlock (95382) ***(P-3192)***
Superior Mechanical, Fairfield *Also called RL Fuller Inc* ***(P-1348)***
Superior Metals Inc ....F....408 938-3488
838 Jury Ct Ste B San Jose (95112) ***(P-4822)***
Superior Packing Co, Dixon *Also called Ellensburg Lamb Company Inc* ***(P-2095)***
Superior Quartz Inc ....F....408 844-9663
3370 Edward Ave Santa Clara (95054) ***(P-4555)***
Superior Sensor Technology Inc ....E....408 703-2950
103 Cooper Ct Los Gatos (95032) ***(P-6706)***
Superior Tbeppe Bnding Fbrctn, Hayward *Also called Superior Tube Pipe Bnding Fbco* ***(P-4979)***
Superior Tile & Marble Inc (PA) ....E....510 895-2700
2300 Polvorosa Ave San Leandro (94577) ***(P-1724)***
Superior Tile Co, San Leandro *Also called TRM Corporation* ***(P-1726)***
Superior Truck Lines Inc (PA) ....E....209 862-9430
1457 Main St Ste A Newman (95360) ***(P-7599)***
Superior Tube Pipe Bnding Fbco ....E....510 782-9311
2407 Industrial Pkwy W Hayward (94545) ***(P-4979)***
Superior Vision Services Inc (HQ) ....D....800 507-3800
11090 White Rock Rd Ste 1 Rancho Cordova (95670) ***(P-10155)***
Supermarket Associates LLC ....E....209 529-2639
533 Boherty Ave Modesto (95354) ***(P-9672)***
Supermicro, San Jose *Also called Super Micro Computer Inc* ***(P-5273)***
Supernutrition, Pacifica *Also called Forever Young* ***(P-2894)***
Supershuttle International Inc ....D....650 246-2786
323 S Canal St South San Francisco (94080) ***(P-7361)***
Supershuttle International Inc ....D....650 246-2704
160 S Linden Ave South San Francisco (94080) ***(P-7362)***
Supershuttle International Inc ....D....415 558-8500
700 16th St San Francisco (94158) ***(P-7363)***
Supersonic ADS Inc ....E....650 825-6010
17 Bluxome St San Francisco (94107) ***(P-7256)***
Supertex Inc (HQ) ....B....408 222-8888
1235 Bordeaux Dr Sunnyvale (94089) ***(P-6320)***
Superwinch LLC ....E....800 323-2031
3945 Freedom Cir Ste 560 Santa Clara (95054) ***(P-8471)***
Superwinch Holding LLC ....D....860 412-1476
3945 Freedom Cir Ste 560 Santa Clara (95054) ***(P-5039)***
Supherb Farms, Turlock *Also called Daregal Inc* ***(P-16)***
Supira Medical Inc ....E....408 560-2500
590 Division St Campbell (95008) ***(P-7045)***
Supply Change Services, Sacramento *Also called Sacramento Municpl Utility Dst* ***(P-8199)***
Supplyshift ....D....831 824-4326
215 River St Santa Cruz (95060) ***(P-13473)***
Support For Family LLC ....D....877 916-9111
1333 Howe Ave Ste 206 Sacramento (95825) ***(P-17762)***
Support For Fmlies Chldren Wit ....E....415 920-5040
1663 Mission St Ste 700 San Francisco (94103) ***(P-17763)***
Support For Home Inc ....E....530 792-8484
1333 Howe Ave Ste 206 Sacramento (95825) ***(P-714)***
Support Staff Services Inc ....E....408 258-5803
175 N Jackson Ave 103a San Jose (95116) ***(P-16950)***
Support Systems Intl Corp ....D....510 234-9090
136 S 2nd St Dept B Richmond (94804) ***(P-6472)***
Supportlogic Inc ....E....408 471-4710
2658 Gamblin Dr Santa Clara (95051) ***(P-18252)***
Supportpay, Mountain View *Also called Ittavi Inc* ***(P-13250)***
Sure Fire Protection Co Inc ....E....510 490-7873
4141 Pestana Pl Fremont (94538) ***(P-1375)***
Surecall, Fremont *Also called Cellphone-Mate Inc* ***(P-5830)***
Surestay, Richmond *Also called Richmond Hotels LLC* ***(P-11408)***
Surewest Broadband ....C....916 772-5000
5411 Lucey Ave Roseville (95661) ***(P-7994)***
Surface Art Engineering Inc ....E....408 433-4700
81 Bonaventura Dr San Jose (95134) ***(P-6321)***
Surface Engineering Spc ....E....408 734-8810
919 Hamlin Ct Sunnyvale (94089) ***(P-5114)***
Surface Manufacturing Inc ....E....530 885-0700
2025 Airpark Ct Ste 10 Auburn (95602) ***(P-5623)***
Surface Techniques Corporation (PA) ....E....510 887-6000
25673 Nickel Pl Hayward (94545) ***(P-3322)***
Surface Technology, Hayward *Also called Surface Techniques Corporation* ***(P-3322)***
Surgery Center of Health South, Oakland *Also called EBSC LP* ***(P-15387)***
Surgery Center of Marin ....E....415 925-7266
250 Bon Air Rd Greenbrae (94904) ***(P-16563)***

ALPHABETIC

Surgery Ctr of Alta Btes Smmit (HQ) ... **A ... 510 204-4444**
2450 Ashby Ave Berkeley (94705) ***(P-16564)***
Surgery Ctr of Alta Btes Smmit ... E ... 510 204-1880
5730 Telegraph Ave Oakland (94609) ***(P-16565)***
Surgery Ctr of Alta Btes Smmit ... E ... 510 204-1591
2001 Dwight Way Berkeley (94704) ***(P-16566)***
Surgery Department, San Francisco *Also called St Marys Medical Center Inc* ***(P-16549)***
Surgical Care Affiliate ... E ... 916 529-4590
2450 Venture Oaks Way # 120 Sacramento (95833) ***(P-18998)***
Surplus Line Association Cal ... E ... 415 434-4900
12667 Alcosta Blvd # 450 San Ramon (94583) ***(P-18320)***
Surprise Valley Hlth Care Dst ... D ... 530 279-6111
741 Main St Cedarville (96104) ***(P-16567)***
Surprise Vly Elctrfcation Corp ... E ... 530 233-3511
800 W 12th St Alturas (96101) ***(P-8203)***
Surrozen Inc (PA) ... **E ... 650 489-9000**
171 Oyster Point Blvd # 30 South San Francisco (94080) ***(P-4057)***
Surrozen Operating Inc ... E ... 650 918-8818
171 Oyster Point Blvd South San Francisco (94080) ***(P-3989)***
Surtec Inc ... E ... 209 820-3700
1880 N Macarthur Dr Tracy (95376) ***(P-4078)***
Surtec System , The, Tracy *Also called Surtec Inc* ***(P-4078)***
Survellnce Systems Intgrtion I ... E ... 800 508-6981
4465 Granite Dr Ste 700 Rocklin (95677) ***(P-8962)***
Surveymonkey, San Mateo *Also called Momentive Global Inc* ***(P-12620)***
Surveymonkey Inc., San Mateo *Also called Momentive Inc* ***(P-13733)***
Surveysparrow Inc ... D ... 800 481-0410
2345 Yale St Fl 1 Palo Alto (94306) ***(P-19189)***
Susan G Komen Breast Cancer ... E ... 650 409-2656
2520 Old Middlefield Way Mountain View (94043) ***(P-18599)***
Susanville Indian Rancheria (PA) ... **E ... 530 257-6264**
745 Joaquin St Susanville (96130) ***(P-17078)***
Suspender Factory Inc ... E ... 510 547-5400
1425 63rd St Emeryville (94608) ***(P-3020)***
Suspender Factory of S F, Emeryville *Also called Suspender Factory Inc* ***(P-3020)***
Suss McRtec Prcsion Phtmask In ... F ... 415 494-3113
821 San Antonio Rd Palo Alto (94303) ***(P-7158)***
Sustainable San Mateo County (PA) ... **E ... 415 677-7600**
731 Sansome St Ste 100 San Francisco (94111) ***(P-18600)***
Sustainable San Mateo County ... E ... 415 398-3250
848 Kearny St San Francisco (94108) ***(P-17764)***
Sutro Biopharma Inc (PA) ... **C ... 650 392-8412**
310 Utah Ave Ste 150 South San Francisco (94080) ***(P-4058)***
Sutter Alhambra Surgery Center, Elk Grove *Also called Sutter Health* ***(P-16599)***
Sutter Amador Hospital, Jackson *Also called Sutter Valley Hospitals* ***(P-16678)***
Sutter Amador Hospital Lab, Jackson *Also called Sutter Hlth Scrmnto Sierra Reg* ***(P-16661)***
Sutter Basin Corporation Ltd ... E ... 530 738-4456
10982 Knights Rd Robbins (95676) ***(P-21)***
Sutter Bay Hospitals (HQ) ... **A ... 415 600-6000**
475 Brannan St Ste 130 San Francisco (94107) ***(P-16568)***
Sutter Bay Hospitals ... D ... 510 869-6199
2420 Ashby Ave Berkeley (94705) ***(P-16569)***
Sutter Bay Hospitals ... D ... 415 600-2403
3801 Sacramento St Ste 61 San Francisco (94118) ***(P-16570)***
Sutter Bay Hospitals ... D ... 510 655-4000
350 Hawthorne Ave Oakland (94609) ***(P-16571)***
Sutter Bay Hospitals ... D ... 831 423-4111
2025 Soquel Ave Santa Cruz (95062) ***(P-16572)***
Sutter Bay Hospitals ... D ... 510 869-8377
3100 Summit St Oakland (94609) ***(P-16573)***
Sutter Bay Hospitals ... D ... 510 204-4444
2450 Ashby Ave Berkeley (94705) ***(P-16574)***
Sutter Bay Hospitals ... E ... 415 600-2632
3698 California St San Francisco (94118) ***(P-15708)***
Sutter Bay Hospitals ... E ... 707 263-7400
843 Parallel Dr Lakeport (95453) ***(P-16951)***
Sutter Bay Medical Foundation (HQ) ... **A ... 650 321-4121**
795 El Camino Real Palo Alto (94301) ***(P-15709)***
Sutter Bay Medical Foundation ... D ... 650 812-3751
2951 Gordon Ave Santa Clara (95051) ***(P-15710)***
Sutter Bay Medical Foundation ... C ... 408 730-4321
535 Oakmead Pkwy Sunnyvale (94085) ***(P-15711)***
Sutter Bay Medical Foundation ... D ... 650 934-7956
877 W Fremont Ave Ste N Sunnyvale (94087) ***(P-15712)***
Sutter Buttes Mfg, Gridley *Also called Sutter Buttes Mfg LLC* ***(P-2072)***
Sutter Buttes Mfg LLC ... E ... 530 846-9960
1221 Independence Pl Gridley (95948) ***(P-2072)***
Sutter Buttes Olive Oil, Yuba City *Also called California Olive and Vine LLC* ***(P-2463)***
SUTTER C H S, Emeryville *Also called Sutter Vsting Nrse Assn Hspice* ***(P-16956)***
SUTTER C H S, Sacramento *Also called Sutter Valley Hospitals* ***(P-16677)***
Sutter Cancer Ctr, Sacramento *Also called Sutter Health* ***(P-16807)***
Sutter Care & Home ... D ... 650 685-2800
700 S Claremont St # 220 San Mateo (94402) ***(P-16952)***
Sutter Center For Rehab, Elk Grove *Also called Sutter Health* ***(P-16654)***
Sutter Central Vly Hospitals ... A ... 209 572-5900
1200 Scenic Dr Ste 200 Modesto (95350) ***(P-16575)***
Sutter Central Vly Hospitals (HQ) ... **C ... 209 526-4500**
1700 Coffee Rd Modesto (95355) ***(P-16576)***
Sutter Central Vly Hospitals ... A ... 209 569-7544
1800 Coffee Rd Ste 30 Modesto (95355) ***(P-16577)***
Sutter Central Vly Hospitals ... A ... 209 526-4500
1700 Coffee Rd Modesto (95355) ***(P-16578)***
Sutter Central Vly Hospitals ... A ... 209 572-8270
1316 Celeste Dr Ste 104 Modesto (95355) ***(P-16579)***
Sutter Club ... D ... 916 442-0456
1220 9th St Sacramento (95814) ***(P-18473)***
Sutter Coast Hospital (HQ) ... **C ... 707 464-8511**
800 E Washington Blvd Crescent City (95531) ***(P-16580)***
Sutter Coast Hospital ... B ... 707 464-8741
983 3rd St Ste D Crescent City (95531) ***(P-16953)***
Sutter Connect LLC ... C ... 510 596-4700
2000 Powell St Ste 100 Emeryville (94608) ***(P-14420)***
Sutter Counseling Center, Sacramento *Also called Sutter Hlth Scrmnto Sierra Reg* ***(P-15727)***
Sutter Delta Medical Center ... C ... 925 779-7200
3901 Lone Tree Way Antioch (94509) ***(P-16581)***
Sutter Elk Grove Surgery Ctr, Elk Grove *Also called Sutter Health* ***(P-16604)***
Sutter Gould Med Foundation, Modesto *Also called Sutter Valley Med Foundation* ***(P-16679)***
Sutter Gould Med Foundation (PA) ... **E ... 209 948-5940**
600 Coffee Rd Modesto (95355) ***(P-15713)***
Sutter Health, Santa Rosa *Also called Santa Rosa Surgery Center LP* ***(P-16517)***
Sutter Health, Sacramento *Also called Sutter Medical Group Inc* ***(P-16670)***
Sutter Health ... C ... 530 747-0389
2068 John Jones Rd # 100 Davis (95616) ***(P-16582)***
Sutter Health ... C ... 916 733-1025
1625 Stockton Blvd # 207 Sacramento (95816) ***(P-16583)***
Sutter Health ... C ... 916 797-4725
2 Medical Plaza Dr Roseville (95661) ***(P-16584)***
Sutter Health ... D ... 925 371-3800
2950 Collier Canyon Rd Livermore (94551) ***(P-17183)***
Sutter Health ... C ... 415 600-7034
2395 Sacramento St San Francisco (94115) ***(P-16585)***
Sutter Health ... D ... 650 853-2975
795 El Camino Real Palo Alto (94301) ***(P-15714)***
Sutter Health ... C ... 916 733-9588
1020 29th St Ste 600 Sacramento (95816) ***(P-16586)***
Sutter Health ... C ... 408 524-5952
2734 El Camino Real Santa Clara (95051) ***(P-16587)***
Sutter Health ... C ... 925 779-7273
3901 Lone Tree Way Antioch (94509) ***(P-16588)***
Sutter Health ... C ... 415 345-0100
3468 California St San Francisco (94118) ***(P-16589)***
Sutter Health ... C ... 209 366-2007
1335 S Fairmont Ave Lodi (95240) ***(P-16590)***
Sutter Health ... C ... 209 223-5445
100 Mission Blvd Jackson (95642) ***(P-16591)***
Sutter Health ... C ... 415 731-6300
595 Buckingham Way # 515 San Francisco (94132) ***(P-16592)***
Sutter Health ... C ... 415 600-0110
1375 Sutter St Ste 406 San Francisco (94109) ***(P-16593)***
Sutter Health ... C ... 831 458-6310
1301 Mission St Santa Cruz (95060) ***(P-16594)***
Sutter Health ... C ... 916 797-4715
3 Medical Plaza Dr # 100 Roseville (95661) ***(P-16595)***
Sutter Health ... C ... 530 750-5904
2030 Sutter Pl Ste 1000 Davis (95616) ***(P-16596)***
Sutter Health ... C ... 916 691-5900
8170 Laguna Blvd Ste 210 Elk Grove (95758) ***(P-16597)***
Sutter Health ... C ... 707 535-5600
110 Stony Point Rd # 200 Santa Rosa (95401) ***(P-16598)***
Sutter Health ... C ... 916 455-8137
8170 Laguna Blvd Ste 103 Elk Grove (95758) ***(P-16599)***
Sutter Health ... C ... 415 600-1020
2340 Clay St Rm 121 San Francisco (94115) ***(P-16600)***
Sutter Health ... D ... 707 263-6885
5196 Hill Rd E Ste 300 Lakeport (95453) ***(P-15715)***
Sutter Health ... C ... 916 262-9400
2725 Capitol Ave Sacramento (95816) ***(P-16601)***
Sutter Health ... C ... 916 566-4819
2880 Gateway Oaks Dr # 200 Sacramento (95833) ***(P-16602)***
Sutter Health ... C ... 831 458-6272
2950 Research Park Dr Soquel (95073) ***(P-16603)***
Sutter Health ... C ... 916 544-5423
8200 Laguna Blvd Elk Grove (95758) ***(P-16604)***
Sutter Health ... C ... 209 827-4866
520 W I St Los Banos (93635) ***(P-16605)***
Sutter Health ... C ... 415 600-0140
1375 Sutter St Ste 208 San Francisco (94109) ***(P-16606)***
Sutter Health ... C ... 415 600-4280
2015 Steiner St Fl 1 San Francisco (94115) ***(P-16607)***
Sutter Health ... C ... 510 537-1234
20103 Lake Chabot Rd Castro Valley (94546) ***(P-16608)***
Sutter Health ... C ... 415 897-8495
100 Rowland Way Ste 210 Novato (94945) ***(P-16609)***
Sutter Health ... C ... 707 864-4660
4830 Bus Center Dr # 200 Fairfield (94534) ***(P-16610)***
Sutter Health ... C ... 916 262-9414
2725 Capitol Ave Dept 304 Sacramento (95816) ***(P-16611)***
Sutter Health ... C ... 530 750-5800
2030 Sutter Pl Ste 2000 Davis (95616) ***(P-16612)***
Sutter Health ... D ... 916 783-8114
1680 E Rsvlle Pkwy Ste 10 Roseville (95661) ***(P-15716)***
Sutter Health ... A ... 916 646-8300
1500 Expo Pkwy Sacramento (95815) ***(P-15717)***
Sutter Health ... C ... 510 547-2244
3875 Telegraph Ave Oakland (94609) ***(P-16613)***
Sutter Health ... D ... 916 681-8852
8118 Timberlake Way # 110 Sacramento (95823) ***(P-15718)***
Sutter Health ... C ... 510 869-8777
3000 Telegraph Ave Oakland (94609) ***(P-16614)***
Sutter Health ... C ... 916 878-2588
6 Medical Plaza Dr Roseville (95661) ***(P-16615)***
Sutter Health ... C ... 415 600-6000
1101 Van Ness Ave San Francisco (94109) ***(P-16616)***
Sutter Health (PA) ... **A ... 916 733-8800**
2200 River Plaza Dr Sacramento (95833) ***(P-16617)***
Sutter Health ... C ... 530 406-5600
475 Pioneer Ave Ste 400 Woodland (95776) ***(P-16618)***

Sutter Health ...C...916 297-9923
75 Encina Ave Palo Alto (94301) ***(P-16619)***
Sutter Health ...D...916 454-8200
3707 Schriever Ave Mather (95655) ***(P-16140)***
Sutter Health ...D...530 406-5600
3 Medical Plaza Dr # 100 Roseville (95661) ***(P-15719)***
Sutter Health ...C...916 781-1225
2 Medical Plaza Dr # 180 Roseville (95661) ***(P-16620)***
Sutter Health ...D...916 220-1927
1201 Alhambra Blvd # 210 Sacramento (95816) ***(P-17079)***
Sutter Health ...C...209 538-1733
2516 E Whitmore Ave Ceres (95307) ***(P-16621)***
Sutter Health ...C...209 522-0146
3612 Dale Rd Modesto (95356) ***(P-16622)***
Sutter Health ...C...916 691-5900
8170 Laguna Blvd Ste 220 Elk Grove (95758) ***(P-16623)***
Sutter Health ...C...650 262-4262
50 S San Mateo Dr Ste 470 San Mateo (94401) ***(P-16624)***
Sutter Health ...C...831 477-3600
2880 Soquel Ave Ste 10 Santa Cruz (95062) ***(P-16625)***
Sutter Health ...C...209 334-3333
999 S Fairmont Ave # 200 Lodi (95240) ***(P-16626)***
Sutter Health ...C...408 733-4380
325 N Mathilda Ave Sunnyvale (94085) ***(P-16627)***
Sutter Health ...C...707 263-6885
5196 Hill Rd E Ste 300 Lakeport (95453) ***(P-15720)***
Sutter Health ...C...707 545-2255
4702 Hoen Ave Santa Rosa (95405) ***(P-16628)***
Sutter Health ...C...650 853-2904
795 El Camino Real Palo Alto (94301) ***(P-16629)***
Sutter Health ...D...916 454-6600
2800 L St Ste 10 Sacramento (95816) ***(P-16807)***
Sutter Health ...D...916 784-2277
1640 E Rsvlle Pkwy Ste 10 Roseville (95661) ***(P-16808)***
Sutter Health ...D...916 451-3344
3161 L St Sacramento (95816) ***(P-15721)***
Sutter Health ...D...916 984-0739
1655 Creekside Dr Folsom (95630) ***(P-16809)***
Sutter Health ...C...916 453-5955
1020 29th St Ste 570b Sacramento (95816) ***(P-16630)***
Sutter Health ...D...916 453-4528
2800 L St Sacramento (95816) ***(P-15722)***
Sutter Health ...D...916 929-3393
2 Scripps Dr Ste 110 Sacramento (95825) ***(P-15723)***
Sutter Health ...C...510 450-8900
1900 Powell St Ste 140 Emeryville (94608) ***(P-16631)***
Sutter Health ...C...415 600-6000
1580 Valencia St Ste 237 San Francisco (94110) ***(P-16632)***
Sutter Health ...C...707 262-5000
5176 Hill Rd E Lakeport (95453) ***(P-16633)***
Sutter Health ...C...415 600-4325
2300 California St San Francisco (94115) ***(P-16634)***
Sutter Health ...C...530 741-1300
440 Plumas Blvd Yuba City (95991) ***(P-16635)***
Sutter Health ...C...510 618-5200
1651 Alvarado St San Leandro (94577) ***(P-16208)***
Sutter Health ...C...916 386-3000
7700 Folsom Blvd Sacramento (95826) ***(P-16636)***
Sutter Health ...C...415 600-1400
2200 Webster St San Francisco (94115) ***(P-16637)***
Sutter Health ...C...510 537-1234
20130 Lake Chabot Rd # 201 Castro Valley (94546) ***(P-16638)***
Sutter Health ...C...707 551-3400
100 Hospital Dr Vallejo (94589) ***(P-16639)***
Sutter Health ...C...530 749-3585
969 Plumas St Ste 103116 Yuba City (95991) ***(P-16640)***
Sutter Health ...C...415 600-6000
2333 Buchanan St San Francisco (94115) ***(P-16641)***
Sutter Health ...C...415 600-4280
1700 California St # 530 San Francisco (94109) ***(P-16642)***
Sutter Health ...C...415 600-1000
2340 Clay St Fl 4 San Francisco (94115) ***(P-16643)***
Sutter Health ...C...650 696-5838
1720 Carmelita Ave Ste 22 Burlingame (94010) ***(P-16644)***
Sutter Health ...C...707 432-2500
2700 Low Ct Fairfield (94534) ***(P-16645)***
Sutter Health ...C...510 204-6600
2000 Powell St Emeryville (94608) ***(P-16646)***
Sutter Health ...C...650 934-7000
701 E El Camino Real Mountain View (94040) ***(P-16647)***
Sutter Health ...C...510 204-1554
3030 Telegraph Ave Berkeley (94705) ***(P-16648)***
Sutter Health ...C...415 861-1110
115 Diamond St San Francisco (94114) ***(P-16649)***
Sutter Health ...C...916 731-5672
P.O. Box 160100 Sacramento (95816) ***(P-16650)***
Sutter Health ...C...916 453-9999
1020 29th St Ste 120 Sacramento (95816) ***(P-16651)***
Sutter Health ...C...916 961-4910
6620 Coyle Ave Ste 110 Carmichael (95608) ***(P-16652)***
Sutter Health ...C...916 797-4700
3 Medical Plaza Dr # 100 Roseville (95661) ***(P-16653)***
Sutter Health ...D...916 733-5051
2801 K St Ste 110 Sacramento (95816) ***(P-15724)***
Sutter Health ...C...916 731-7900
8170 Laguna Blvd Ste 103 Elk Grove (95758) ***(P-16654)***
Sutter Health ...C...707 523-7253
2449 Summerfield Rd Santa Rosa (95405) ***(P-16655)***
Sutter Health ...C...916 286-8267
633 Folsom St Fl 7 San Francisco (94107) ***(P-16656)***
Sutter Health ...D...916 262-9456
2725 Capitol Ave Dept 404 Sacramento (95816) ***(P-15725)***
Sutter Health ...C...530 750-5888
2030 Sutter Pl Ste 1300 Davis (95616) ***(P-16657)***
Sutter Health ...C...415 602-5380
100 Rowland Way Novato (94945) ***(P-16658)***
Sutter Health At Work ...E...916 565-8607
1014 N Market Blvd Ste 20 Sacramento (95834) ***(P-15726)***
Sutter Health Sacsierra Region, Sacramento *Also called Sutter Health* ***(P-16617)***
Sutter Hlth At Work - Natomas, Sacramento *Also called Sutter Health At Work* ***(P-15726)***
Sutter Hlth Rhabilitation Svcs ...D...916 733-3040
2801 L St Fl 3 Sacramento (95816) ***(P-16659)***
Sutter Hlth Scrmnto Sierra Reg ...B...530 747-5010
2030 Sutter Pl Ste 2000 Davis (95616) ***(P-16660)***
Sutter Hlth Scrmnto Sierra Reg ...B...209 223-7540
100 Mission Blvd Jackson (95642) ***(P-16661)***
Sutter Hlth Scrmnto Sierra Reg ...C...916 733-7080
701 Howe Ave Ste F20 Sacramento (95825) ***(P-17184)***
Sutter Hlth Scrmnto Sierra Reg (HQ) ...**B...916 733-8800**
2200 River Plaza Dr Sacramento (95833) ***(P-16662)***
Sutter Hlth Scrmnto Sierra Reg ...B...916 373-3400
1600 Cebrian St West Sacramento (95691) ***(P-16663)***
Sutter Hlth Scrmnto Sierra Reg ...B...916 454-2222
5151 F St Sacramento (95819) ***(P-16664)***
Sutter Hlth Scrmnto Sierra Reg ...B...916 446-3100
1234 U St Sacramento (95818) ***(P-16665)***
Sutter Hlth Scrmnto Sierra Reg ...B...916 924-7666
2700 Gateway Oaks Dr Sacramento (95833) ***(P-16666)***
Sutter Hlth Scrmnto Sierra Reg ...B...707 554-4444
300 Hospital Dr Vallejo (94589) ***(P-16667)***
Sutter Hlth Scrmnto Sierra Reg ...C...916 386-3000
7700 Folsom Blvd Sacramento (95826) ***(P-15727)***
Sutter Hlth Scrmnto Sierra Reg ...B...916 733-3095
2800 L St Sacramento (95816) ***(P-16668)***
Sutter Hlth Scrmnto Sierra Reg ...B...530 406-5616
475 Pioneer Ave Ste 100 Woodland (95776) ***(P-16669)***
Sutter Home Winery Inc (PA) ...**C...707 963-3104**
100 Saint Helena Hwy S Saint Helena (94574) ***(P-2734)***
Sutter Home Winery Inc ...C...209 368-4357
18667 Jacob Brack Rd Lodi (95242) ***(P-2735)***
Sutter Inc ...E...916 733-5097
1020 29th St Ste 480 Sacramento (95816) ***(P-15728)***
Sutter Lakeside Home Med Svcs, Lakeport *Also called Sutter Bay Hospitals* ***(P-16951)***
Sutter Lakeside Hospital, Lakeport *Also called Sutter West Bay Hospitals* ***(P-16682)***
Sutter Material Management, West Sacramento *Also called Sutter Hlth Scrmnto Sierra Reg* ***(P-16663)***
Sutter Maternity & Surgery, Santa Cruz *Also called Sutter Bay Hospitals* ***(P-16572)***
Sutter Med Group of Redwoods ...C...707 546-2788
3883 Airway Dr Ste 202 Santa Rosa (95403) ***(P-15729)***
Sutter Medical Center, Sacramento *Also called Sutter Hlth Scrmnto Sierra Reg* ***(P-16668)***
Sutter Medical Center, Woodland *Also called Sutter Hlth Scrmnto Sierra Reg* ***(P-16669)***
Sutter Medical Ctr Sacramento, Sacramento *Also called Sutter Hlth Rhabilitation Svcs* ***(P-16659)***
Sutter Medical Group Inc (PA) ...**E...916 733-5090**
1201 Alhambra Blvd # 330 Sacramento (95816) ***(P-16670)***
Sutter Medical Plaza Roseville, Roseville *Also called Sutter Valley Med Foundation* ***(P-15734)***
Sutter Memorial Hospital, Sacramento *Also called Sutter Hlth Scrmnto Sierra Reg* ***(P-16662)***
Sutter Memorial Hospital, Sacramento *Also called Sutter Hlth Scrmnto Sierra Reg* ***(P-16664)***
Sutter Mtrnty/Srgry Ctr-Snt Cr ...D...831 477-2200
2900 Chanticleer Ave Santa Cruz (95065) ***(P-16671)***
Sutter N Med Group A Prof Corp (PA) ...**D...530 749-3661**
969 Plumas St Ste 205 Yuba City (95991) ***(P-16672)***
Sutter North Med Foundation (PA) ...**C...530 741-1300**
969 Plumas St Yuba City (95991) ***(P-15730)***
Sutter Occupational Hlth Svcs, Roseville *Also called Sutter Health* ***(P-16653)***
Sutter P Dahlglen Entps Inc ...F...408 727-4640
1650 Grant St Santa Clara (95050) ***(P-5624)***
Sutter Pacific Med Foundation, San Francisco *Also called Sutter Health* ***(P-16593)***
Sutter Pacific Med Foundation, Lakeport *Also called Sutter Health* ***(P-15720)***
Sutter Pacific Med Foundation, Santa Rosa *Also called Sutter Health* ***(P-16628)***
Sutter Physician Services (HQ) ...**A...916 854-6600**
10470 Old Placerville Rd Sacramento (95827) ***(P-19645)***
Sutter Regional Med Foundation ...D...707 631-9423
2720 Low Ct Fairfield (94534) ***(P-15731)***
Sutter Regional Med Foundation (PA) ...**B...707 427-4900**
2702 Low Ct Fairfield (94534) ***(P-15732)***
Sutter Regional Med Foundation ...D...707 454-5800
770 Mason St Vacaville (95688) ***(P-15733)***
Sutter Roseville Medical Ctr ...A...916 781-1000
1 Medical Plaza Dr Roseville (95661) ***(P-16673)***
Sutter Rsvlle Med Ctr Fndation ...D...916 781-1000
1 Medical Plaza Dr Roseville (95661) ***(P-16674)***
Sutter Senior Care, Sacramento *Also called Sutter Hlth Scrmnto Sierra Reg* ***(P-16665)***
Sutter Solano Medical Center ...A...707 554-4444
300 Hospital Dr Vallejo (94589) ***(P-16675)***
Sutter Surgical Hospital N Vly ...C...530 749-5700
455 Plumas Blvd Yuba City (95991) ***(P-16676)***
Sutter Valley Hospitals (HQ) ...**B...916 733-8800**
2200 River Plaza Dr Sacramento (95833) ***(P-16677)***
Sutter Valley Hospitals ...B...209 223-7514
200 Mission Blvd Jackson (95642) ***(P-16678)***
Sutter Valley Med Foundation ...D...916 924-7764
1625 Stockton Blvd # 110 Sacramento (95816) ***(P-15899)***
Sutter Valley Med Foundation ...C...916 865-1140
3100 Douglas Blvd Roseville (95661) ***(P-15734)***

ALPHABETIC

Employee Codes: A=Over 500 employees, B=251-500
C=101-250, D=51-100, E=20-50 F=10-19
2022 Northern California Business
Directory and Buyers Guide

1093

Sutter Valley Med Foundation...B......209 524-1211
600 Coffee Rd Modesto (95355) *(P-16679)*
Sutter Valley Med Foundation...D......916 454-8449
3707 Schriever Ave Mather (95655) *(P-19405)*
Sutter Valley Med Foundation...D......916 865-1140
568 N Sunrise Ave Ste 250 Roseville (95661) *(P-19406)*
Sutter Vsiting Nurse Assn Hosp, Concord *Also called Sutter Vsting Nrse Assn Hspice (P-16958)*
Sutter Vsting Nrse Assn Hspice...C......415 600-6200
1625 Van Ness Ave San Francisco (94109) *(P-16954)*
Sutter Vsting Nrse Assn Hspice...C......510 895-4403
2953 Teagarden St San Leandro (94577) *(P-16955)*
Sutter Vsting Nrse Assn Hspice (HQ)...E......**866 652-9178**
1900 Powell St Ste 300 Emeryville (94608) *(P-16956)*
Sutter Vsting Nrse Assn Hspice...C......510 618-5277
1651 Alvarado St San Leandro (94577) *(P-16141)*
Sutter Vsting Nrse Assn Hspice...C......209 342-4048
1316 Celeste Dr Ste 140 Modesto (95355) *(P-16957)*
Sutter Vsting Nrse Assn Hspice...C......925 677-4250
5099 Coml Cir Ste 2059452 Concord (94520) *(P-16958)*
Sutter West Bay Hospitals...C......415 492-4800
100 Rowland Way Ste 310 Novato (94945) *(P-16680)*
Sutter West Bay Hospitals (HQ)...B......**415 209-1300**
180 Rowland Way Novato (94945) *(P-16681)*
Sutter West Bay Hospitals...B......707 262-5000
5176 Hill Rd E Lakeport (95453) *(P-16682)*
Sutter West Foundation, Davis *Also called Sutter Hlth Scrmnto Sierra Reg (P-16660)*
Sutter/Yuba B-Cnty Mntal Hlth...E......530 822-7200
1965 Live Oak Blvd Yuba City (95991) *(P-15735)*
Suttercare Corporation...A......650 696-5363
1601 Trousdale Dr Burlingame (94010) *(P-17080)*
Suttercare Corporation...A......650 853-8500
1501 Trousdale Dr Burlingame (94010) *(P-16683)*
Sutters Place Inc (PA)...A......**408 451-8888**
1801 Bering Dr San Jose (95112) *(P-15248)*
Sv Probe Inc...B......480 635-4700
6680 Via Del Oro San Jose (95119) *(P-6794)*
Svb Asset Management...E......408 654-7400
185 Berry St Ste 3000 San Francisco (94107) *(P-9762)*
Svb Financial Group (PA)...A......**408 654-7400**
3003 Tasman Dr Santa Clara (95054) *(P-9750)*
Svc Mfg Inc A Corp...F......510 261-5800
5625 International Blvd Oakland (94621) *(P-2816)*
SVCF, Mountain View *Also called Silicon Vly Cmnty Foundation (P-18471)*
Svendsen Enterprises LLC...E......510 522-2886
2900 Main St Alameda (94501) *(P-9152)*
Svi Healdsburg LLC...E......707 433-4000
110 Dry Creek Rd Healdsburg (95448) *(P-11522)*
Svm Machining Inc...E......510 791-9450
6520 Central Ave Newark (94560) *(P-4687)*
Svs Group, Oakland *Also called Silicon Vly Technical Staffing (P-12136)*
SW Safety Solutions Inc...E......510 429-8692
33278 Central Ave Ste 102 Union City (94587) *(P-2975)*
Swa Group (PA)...D......**415 332-5100**
2200 Bridgeway Sausalito (94965) *(P-442)*
Swa Services Group Inc...E......408 938-8678
64 Bonaventura Dr San Jose (95134) *(P-12004)*
Swagelok Northern California, Fremont *Also called Sunnyvale Fluid Sys Tech Inc (P-9136)*
Swan Associates Incorporated...E......707 746-1989
4680 E 2nd St Ste H Benicia (94510) *(P-14776)*
Swan Engineering Inc...D......916 474-5299
4470 Yankee Hill Rd # 130 Rocklin (95677) *(P-1975)*
Swander Pace Capital LLC (PA)...A......**415 477-8500**
101 Mission St Ste 1900 San Francisco (94105) *(P-10888)*
Swanson Farms...E......209 667-2002
5213 W Main St Turlock (95380) *(P-239)*
Swanson Vineyards and Winery (HQ)...E......**707 754-4018**
1271 Manley Ln Rutherford (94573) *(P-2736)*
Swartout Inc...D......559 252-4441
5594 E Belmont Ave Fresno (93727) *(P-14652)*
Sweco Products Inc (PA)...E......**530 673-8949**
8949 Colusa Hwy Sutter (95982) *(P-14777)*
Sweet Factory Express, Livermore *Also called Dsd Merchandisers Inc (P-2444)*
Sweet Haven Dairy...E......559 866-5414
10467 W Kamm Ave Riverdale (93656) *(P-224)*
Sweetie Pies LLC...F......707 257-7280
520 Main St NAPA (94559) *(P-2405)*
Sweetrush Inc...E......415 647-1956
363 Valencia St Apt 4 San Francisco (94103) *(P-13762)*
Swenson Developers and Contrs, San Jose *Also called Santa Clara Valley Corporation (P-11993)*
Swenson Group...E......650 655-4990
1620 S Amphlett Blvd San Mateo (94402) *(P-7159)*
Swenson Group Inc Xerox, San Mateo *Also called Swenson Group (P-7159)*
Swenson, Barry Builder, San Jose *Also called Green Valley Corporation (P-880)*
Swift Metal Finishing, Santa Clara *Also called Montoya & Jaramillo Inc (P-4914)*
Swift Navigation Inc (PA)...D......**415 484-9026**
201 Mission St Ste 2400 San Francisco (94105) *(P-5873)*
Swiftcomply US Opco Inc...F......650 430-4341
6701 Koll Center Pkwy # 25 Pleasanton (94566) *(P-13474)*
Swiftstack Inc (HQ)...D......**408 486-2000**
423 Central Ave Menlo Park (94025) *(P-13475)*
Swig Company LLC...E......415 291-1100
220 Montgomery St Ste 950 San Francisco (94104) *(P-19646)*
Swinerton, Concord *Also called Towill Inc (P-18928)*
Swinerton Builders Inc (HQ)...C......**415 421-2980**
2001 Clayton Rd Ste 700 Concord (94520) *(P-811)*
Swinerton Builders Inc...D......510 208-5800
1 Kaiser Plz Ste 701 Oakland (94612) *(P-812)*
Swinerton Builders Inc...D......415 984-1302
377 Oyster Point Blvd # 19 South San Francisco (94080) *(P-813)*
Swinerton Builders Hc...C......916 383-4825
15 Business Park Way # 101 Sacramento (95828) *(P-969)*
Swinerton Incorporated (PA)...C......**415 421-2980**
2001 Clayton Rd Fl 7 Flr 7 San Francisco (94107) *(P-970)*
Swinerton MGT & Consulting, Concord *Also called Swinerton Builders Inc (P-811)*
Swinerton MGT & Consulting Inc (HQ)...E......**415 984-1261**
260 Townsend St San Francisco (94107) *(P-19647)*
Swirl Inc...D......415 276-8300
1620 Montgomery St # 220 San Francisco (94111) *(P-11788)*
Swirl McGarrybowen, San Francisco *Also called Swirl Inc (P-11788)*
Swiss Hotel Group Inc...D......707 938-2884
18 W Spain St Sonoma (95476) *(P-11523)*
Swiss RE Solutions Holdg Corp...C......415 834-2200
111 Sutter St Ste 400 San Francisco (94104) *(P-10188)*
Swiss Screw Products Inc...E......408 748-8400
339 Mathew St Santa Clara (95050) *(P-5625)*
Swiss-Tech Machining LLC...E......916 797-6010
10564 Industrial Ave Roseville (95678) *(P-4870)*
Swisscom Cloud Lab Ltd...E......404 316-9160
675 Forest Ave Palo Alto (94301) *(P-13476)*
Swissport Usa Inc...D......650 821-6220
San Francisco Intl Arprt San Francisco (94128) *(P-7786)*
Swissport Usa Inc...D......571 214-7068
Delta Crgo Bldg 612 Rm 21 San Francisco (94128) *(P-7787)*
Switchboard Software Inc...F......415 425-3660
268 Bush St San Francisco (94104) *(P-13477)*
Swords To Plwshres Vtrans Rght (PA)...E......**415 252-4788**
1060 Howard St San Francisco (94103) *(P-18474)*
Swords To Plwshres Vtrans Rght...D......415 834-0341
1433 Halibut Ct San Francisco (94130) *(P-18475)*
Sybase Inc (HQ)...E......**925 236-5000**
1 Sybase Dr Dublin (94568) *(P-13478)*
Sybase 365 LLC...D......925 236-5000
1 Sybase Dr Dublin (94568) *(P-12836)*
Sycamore Hospitality Corp (PA)...E......**415 398-3333**
433 California St San Francisco (94104) *(P-11524)*
Sycle LLC (PA)...D......**888 881-7925**
480 Green St San Francisco (94133) *(P-13479)*
Sycomp A Technology Co Inc (PA)...E......**877 901-7416**
950 Tower Ln Ste 1785 Foster City (94404) *(P-13670)*
Sycomp Computer Services, Foster City *Also called Sycomp A Technology Co Inc (P-13670)*
Sygma Network Inc...C......209 932-5300
3741 Gold River Ln Stockton (95215) *(P-9315)*
Symantec Operating Corporation (HQ)...A......**650 527-8000**
350 Ellis St Mountain View (94043) *(P-12837)*
Symantec SEC Holdings I Inc...F......650 527-8000
350 Ellis St Mountain View (94043) *(P-6322)*
Symbiosys Inc (HQ)...A......**408 996-9700**
2055 Gateway Pl Ste 350 San Jose (95110) *(P-19867)*
Symed Corporation...E......707 255-3300
215 Gateway Rd W Ste 101 NAPA (94558) *(P-18999)*
Symphony Comm Svcs Hldings LLC (PA)...C......**650 733-6660**
640 W California Ave # 200 Sunnyvale (94086) *(P-14421)*
Symphony Metreo Inc...A......650 935-9500
2475 Hanover St Palo Alto (94304) *(P-12838)*
Symphony Technology Group LLC (PA)...A......**650 935-9500**
428 University Ave Palo Alto (94301) *(P-19868)*
Symprotek Co...E......408 956-0700
950 Yosemite Dr Milpitas (95035) *(P-5985)*
Synack Inc...C......855 796-2251
1600 Seaport Blvd Ste 170 Redwood City (94063) *(P-13984)*
Synactive Inc (PA)...E......**650 341-3310**
2253 Harbor Bay Pkwy Alameda (94502) *(P-12839)*
Synagro West LLC...D......650 652-6531
1499 Bayshore Hwy Ste 111 Burlingame (94010) *(P-19869)*
Synapse Design Automation Inc (HQ)...D......**408 850-9527**
2200 Laurelwood Rd Santa Clara (95054) *(P-13671)*
Synapsense Corporation...E......916 294-0110
340 Palladio Pkwy Ste 530 Folsom (95630) *(P-5323)*
Synaptics Incorporated...D......408 904-1100
1109 Mckay Dr San Jose (95131) *(P-5415)*
Synaptics Incorporated...D......408 454-5100
3120 Scott Blvd Santa Clara (95054) *(P-7995)*
Synaptics Incorporated (PA)...A......**408 904-1100**
1251 Mckay Dr San Jose (95131) *(P-5416)*
Synaptics International Inc...E......408 955-0783
1251 Mckay Dr San Jose (95131) *(P-5417)*
Synarc Inc (HQ)...C......**415 817-8900**
777 Mariners Island Blvd # 550 San Mateo (94404) *(P-12840)*
Sync Logistics LLC (PA)...E......**510 353-3749**
44308 Pcf Commons Blvd Fremont (94538) *(P-7654)*
Synchr Inc...D......720 893-2000
2201 Broadway Ste 701 Oakland (94612) *(P-17185)*
Synchronoss Technologies Inc...B......800 575-7606
60 S Market St Ste 700 San Jose (95113) *(P-1618)*
Synctruck LLC (PA)...C......**650 239-6231**
510 Eccles Ave South San Francisco (94080) *(P-7655)*
Synder Inc (PA)...E......**707 451-6060**
4941 Allison Pkwy Vacaville (95688) *(P-6387)*
Synder California Container, Chowchilla *Also called Central California Cont Mfg (P-4265)*
Synder Filtration, Vacaville *Also called Synder Inc (P-6387)*
Syndicate Corp...E......408 740-5565
350 N 2nd St Apt 131 San Jose (95112) *(P-14422)*
Synergex International Corp...D......916 635-7300
2355 Gold Meadow Way # 200 Gold River (95670) *(P-12841)*
Synergy Companies, Hayward *Also called Eagle Systems Intl Inc (P-1253)*

Synergy Environmental, Hayward *Also called American Synrgy Asb Rmval Svcs (P-2002)*
Synergy Health Companies Inc....D....209 577-4625
1521 N Carptr Rd Ste D1 Modesto (95351) *(P-17186)*
Synergy LLC (PA)....**E....415 252-1128**
601 Laguna St San Francisco (94102) *(P-18189)*
Synergy Machines LLC....E....408 676-9696
3152 San Gabriel Way Union City (94587) *(P-14423)*
Synophic Systems Inc....B....408 459-7676
19925 Stevens Creek Blvd Cupertino (95014) *(P-12842)*
Synopsys Inc (PA)....**B....650 584-5000**
690 E Middlefield Rd Mountain View (94043) *(P-13480)*
Synoptek Inc....C....415 651-4236
930 Alabama St San Francisco (94110) *(P-19648)*
Synova Interactive Group Inc....E....650 513-1058
1400 Marsten Rd Burlingame (94010) *(P-12843)*
Synplicity Inc (HQ)....**C....650 584-5000**
690 E Middlefield Rd Mountain View (94043) *(P-13481)*
Synqy Corporation....F....925 407-2601
3380 Vincent Rd Ste A Pleasant Hill (94523) *(P-13482)*
Synvasive Technology Inc....C....916 939-3913
4925 Robert J Mathews Pkw El Dorado Hills (95762) *(P-7046)*
Sypartners LLC (HQ)....**D....415 536-6600**
475 Brannan St Ste 100 San Francisco (94107) *(P-19870)*
Sysco Central California Inc....B....209 527-7700
136 Mariposa Rd Modesto (95354) *(P-9316)*
Sysco Labs, San Mateo *Also called Cake Corporation (P-12319)*
Sysco Sacramento Inc....B....916 275-2714
7062 Pacific Ave Pleasant Grove (95668) *(P-9317)*
Sysco San Francisco Inc....A....510 226-3000
5900 Stewart Ave Fremont (94538) *(P-9318)*
Sysdig Inc (PA)....**C....415 872-9473**
135 Main St Fl 21 San Francisco (94105) *(P-12844)*
Sysorex International Inc (PA)....**E....408 702-2167**
335 E Middlefield Rd Mountain View (94043) *(P-12845)*
Sysorex USA (HQ)....**E....415 389-7500**
101 Larkspur Landing Cir # 120 Larkspur (94939) *(P-13672)*
Systech Integrators Inc....D....408 441-2700
2050 Gateway Pl San Jose (95110) *(P-13985)*
System Integrators Inc (HQ)....**C....916 830-2400**
1740 N Market Blvd Sacramento (95834) *(P-13673)*
System Operation Services Inc (PA)....**D....800 699-7674**
200 Martinique Ave Belvedere Tiburon (94920) *(P-19871)*
System Studies Incorporated (PA)....**E....831 475-5777**
21340 E Cliff Dr Santa Cruz (95062) *(P-5810)*
System Studies Incorporated....E....831 475-5777
2900 Research Park Dr Soquel (95073) *(P-5811)*
Systems America Public Sector, Pleasanton *Also called Tryfacta Inc (P-12878)*
Systems Intgrtion Slutions Inc (PA)....**E....925 465-7400**
1255 Treat Blvd Ste 100 Walnut Creek (94597) *(P-13986)*
Systems Plus Lumber, Anderson *Also called Haisch Construction Co Inc (P-3206)*
Systron Donner Inertial, Walnut Creek *Also called Carros Sensors Systems Co LLC (P-6896)*
Systron Donner Inertial Inc....C....925 979-4400
2700 Systron Dr Concord (94518) *(P-6473)*
Syufy Century Corporation (PA)....**D....415 448-8300**
150 Pelican Way San Francisco (94102) *(P-14818)*
T & P Farms....C....530 476-3038
1241 Putnam Way Arbuckle (95912) *(P-3)*
T & T Trucking Inc (PA)....**C....800 692-3457**
11396 N Hwy 99 Lodi (95240) *(P-7600)*
T B B Inc....E....559 222-4100
3586 N Hazel Ave Fresno (93722) *(P-8753)*
T B C, Santa Rosa *Also called Barricade Co & Traffic Sup Inc (P-4981)*
T C B, San Jose *Also called Thermal Conductive Bonding Inc (P-6333)*
T C R, San Mateo *Also called Trammell Crow Residential Co (P-10464)*
T D R, Turlock *Also called Turlock Dairy & Rfrgn Inc (P-9045)*
T E R, Santa Clara *Also called E R T Inc (P-5514)*
T F Louderback Inc....C....510 965-6120
700 National Ct Richmond (94804) *(P-9563)*
T G Schmeiser Co Inc....E....559 486-4569
3160 E California Ave Fresno (93702) *(P-4621)*
T M C, Berkeley *Also called Terminal Manufacturing Co LLC (P-4689)*
T M Cobb Company....D....209 948-5358
2651 E Roosevelt St Stockton (95205) *(P-3156)*
T M I, Santa Clara *Also called Tool Makers International Inc (P-5086)*
T M S, Campbell *Also called Telecmmnctons MGT Slutions Inc (P-1619)*
T P G, Emeryville *Also called Performance Grp of Nrthn CA (P-7806)*
T R Manufacturing....F....510 657-3850
41938 Christy St Fremont (94538) *(P-6474)*
T Royal Management (PA)....**D....559 447-9887**
7419 N Cedar Ave Ste 102 Fresno (93720) *(P-10667)*
T T Miyasaka Inc (PA)....**C....831 722-3871**
209 Riverside Rd Watsonville (95076) *(P-42)*
T T S Construction Corporation....E....209 333-7788
1220 E Pine St Lodi (95240) *(P-1181)*
T U D, Sonora *Also called Tuolumne Utilities District (P-8277)*
T W I, Sunnyvale *Also called Thomas West Inc (P-3030)*
T Y Lin International (HQ)....**D....415 291-3700**
345 California St Fl 23 San Francisco (94104) *(P-18825)*
T&C Roofing Inc....D....925 513-8463
2155 Elkins Way Ste H Brentwood (94513) *(P-1841)*
T&S Manufacturing Tech LLC....F....408 441-0285
1530 Oakland Rd Ste 120 San Jose (95112) *(P-4688)*
T-Mobile Usa Inc....C....209 529-0539
2225 Plaza Pkwy Ste I1b Modesto (95350) *(P-7914)*
T-Ram Semiconductor Inc....F....408 597-3670
2109 Landings Dr Mountain View (94043) *(P-6323)*
T.C.A.H, Sonora *Also called Watch Resources Inc (P-17784)*
T3 Direct, Modesto *Also called Sterling Mktg & Fincl Corp (P-19640)*
T4 Manufacturing Inc (PA)....**F....707 689-3849**
51 Poppy House Rd Rio Vista (94571) *(P-7312)*
Tab Label Inc....F....510 638-4411
21 Hegenberger Ct Oakland (94621) *(P-3407)*
TABERNACLE CHRISTEN SCHOOL, Concord *Also called Christian Tabernacle School (P-17907)*
Table Bluff Brewing Inc (PA)....**E....707 445-4480**
617 4th St Eureka (95501) *(P-2496)*
Table Mountain Casino....A....559 822-7777
8184 Table Mountain Rd Friant (93626) *(P-11525)*
Table Mountain Golf Club Inc....E....530 533-3922
2700 Oro Dam Blvd W Oroville (95965) *(P-15158)*
Table Mountain Golf Course, Oroville *Also called Table Mountain Golf Club Inc (P-15158)*
Tabula Inc....D....408 986-9140
1100 La Avenida St Mountain View (94043) *(P-8963)*
TAC Rbo, Sacramento *Also called Surgical Care Affiliate (P-18998)*
TAC Yamas, Pleasanton *Also called Schneder Elc Bldngs Amrcas Inc (P-6540)*
Tacgicon Armament, Rancho Cordova *Also called Concealed Carrier LLC (P-4952)*
Tacit Knowledge Inc (HQ)....**D....415 694-4322**
5000 Executive Pkwy # 520 San Ramon (94583) *(P-13987)*
Tackett Volume Press Inc....E....916 374-8991
1348 Terminal St West Sacramento (95691) *(P-3702)*
Tactai Technologies Inc....E....844 439-8228
150 Mathilda Pl Ste 104 Sunnyvale (94086) *(P-12846)*
Tactical Telesolutions Inc....C....415 788-8808
2121 N Calif Blvd Ste 260 Walnut Creek (94596) *(P-14424)*
Tactivos Inc (PA)....**D....415 687-2501**
650 Clfrnia St Fl 7 Ste 1 Flr 7 San Francisco (94108) *(P-7996)*
Tactus Technology Inc....C....510 244-3968
47509 Seabridge Dr Fremont (94538) *(P-13988)*
Tactx Medical Inc (HQ)....**C....408 364-7100**
1353 Dell Ave Campbell (95008) *(P-7047)*
Taft Street Inc....E....707 823-2049
2030 Barlow Ln Sebastopol (95472) *(P-2737)*
Taft Street Winery, Sebastopol *Also called Taft Street Inc (P-2737)*
Taggle Systems LLC....E....800 619-2919
2804 Gateway Oaks Dr 10 Sacramento (95833) *(P-7915)*
Tagit Solutions Inc (PA)....**D....888 518-8710**
5201 Great America Pkwy Santa Clara (95054) *(P-19872)*
Tahoe Beach & Ski Club....D....530 541-6220
3601 Lake Tahoe Blvd South Lake Tahoe (96150) *(P-11526)*
Tahoe City Public Utility Dist....E....530 583-3796
221 Fairway Dr Tahoe City (96145) *(P-8292)*
Tahoe Crss-Cntry Ski Edcatn As....E....530 583-5475
925 Country Club Dr Tahoe City (96145) *(P-11527)*
Tahoe Forest Hospital District....E....530 582-7488
10710 Donner Pass Rd Truckee (96161) *(P-15736)*
Tahoe Forest Hospital District....D....530 582-3277
10956 Dnner Paca Rd Ste 2 Truckee (96161) *(P-16684)*
Tahoe Forest Hospital District (PA)....**B....530 587-6011**
10121 Pine Ave Truckee (96161) *(P-16685)*
Tahoe Forest Womens Center....E....530 587-1041
10175 Levone Ave Truckee (96161) *(P-15737)*
Tahoe House Inc....F....530 583-1377
625 W Lake Blvd Tahoe City (96145) *(P-2406)*
Tahoe Keys Resort....E....530 544-5397
599 Tahoe Keys Blvd B1 South Lake Tahoe (96150) *(P-10668)*
Tahoe Outdoor Living, South Lake Tahoe *Also called Patrick Baginski (P-495)*
Tahoe Rf Semiconductor Inc....E....530 823-9786
12834 Earhart Ave Auburn (95602) *(P-6324)*
Tahoe Seasons Resort Time Inte....C....530 541-6700
3901 Saddle Rd South Lake Tahoe (96150) *(P-10669)*
Tahoe Workx, Truckee *Also called Tahoe Forest Hospital District (P-16684)*
Tahoe-Truckee Sanitation Agcy....D....530 587-2525
13720 Butterfield Dr Truckee (96161) *(P-8293)*
Tai Seng Entertainment, South San Francisco *Also called U-2 Home Entertainment Inc (P-8968)*
Tailor Research, Walnut Creek *Also called Halfzeez LLC (P-19165)*
Tailored Living Choices LLC....C....707 259-0526
1957 Sierra Ave NAPA (94558) *(P-2073)*
Tait & Associates Inc....E....916 635-2444
2880 Sunrise Blvd Rancho Cordova (95742) *(P-18826)*
Taiwan Apple LLC (HQ)....**E....408 996-1010**
1 Apple Park Way Cupertino (95014) *(P-5874)*
Takao Nursery Inc....E....559 275-3844
2665 N Polk Ave Fresno (93722) *(P-140)*
Takara Bio Usa Inc (HQ)....**C....650 919-7300**
2560 Orchard Pkwy San Jose (95131) *(P-19134)*
Takara Sake USA Inc (HQ)....**E....510 540-8250**
708 Addison St Berkeley (94710) *(P-2779)*
Take It For Granite Inc....E....408 790-2812
345 Phelan Ave San Jose (95112) *(P-576)*
Takex America Inc....E....877 371-2727
1810 Oakland Rd Ste F San Jose (95131) *(P-6325)*
Takt Manufacturing Inc....F....408 250-4975
1300 E Victor Rd Lodi (95240) *(P-7313)*
Talamo Food Service Inc....E....408 612-8751
18675 Madrone Pkwy 100 Morgan Hill (95037) *(P-9319)*
Talamo Foods, Morgan Hill *Also called Talamo Food Service Inc (P-9319)*
Talari Networks Inc (HQ)....**D....408 689-0400**
4230 Leonard Stocking Dr Santa Clara (95054) *(P-12847)*
Talco Foam Inc (PA)....**F....916 492-8840**
1631 Entp Blvd Ste 30 West Sacramento (95691) *(P-4228)*
Talco Foam Products, West Sacramento *Also called Talco Foam Inc (P-4228)*
Talena Inc....F....408 649-6338
2860 Zanker Rd Ste 109 San Jose (95134) *(P-13483)*
Talend Inc (HQ)....**B....650 539-3200**
800 Bridge Pkwy Ste 200 Redwood City (94065) *(P-13674)*

ALPHABETIC

Employee Codes: A=Over 500 employees, B=251-500
C=101-250, D=51-100, E=20-50 F=10-19
2022 Northern California Business
Directory and Buyers Guide
© Mergent Inc. 1-800-342-5647
1095

Talent Space Inc....D....408 330-1900
1650 The Alameda San Jose (95126) *(P-12145)*
Talentburst Inc....D....415 813-4011
575 Market St Ste 3025 San Francisco (94105) *(P-14425)*
Talis Biomedical Corporation (PA)....**D....650 433-3000**
230 Constitution Dr Menlo Park (94025) *(P-6855)*
Talix Inc....D....628 220-3885
660 3rd St Ste 302 San Francisco (94107) *(P-13484)*
Talkdesk Inc (PA)....**A....864 642-5230**
388 Market St Ste 1300 San Francisco (94111) *(P-13485)*
Talkplus Inc....E....650 403-5800
1825 S Grant St Ste 400 San Mateo (94402) *(P-7997)*
Tall Tree Insurance Company....E....650 857-1501
1501 Page Mill Rd Palo Alto (94304) *(P-5274)*
Tallahassee Democrat, Inc, Sacramento *Also called Pacific Northwest Pubg Co Inc (P-3471)*
Taller Technologies, San Francisco *Also called Quadriga Inc (P-12713)*
Talley Oil Inc....E....559 673-9011
12483 Road 29 Madera (93638) *(P-1076)*
Talley Transportation....D....559 673-9013
12325 Road 29 Madera (93638) *(P-7493)*
Tally One Inc (PA)....**E....650 726-6361**
2651 Cabrillo Hwy N Half Moon Bay (94019) *(P-141)*
Talmadge & Talmadge Inc....D....415 703-9650
290 De Haro St San Francisco (94103) *(P-14979)*
Talmadge Construction Inc....E....831 689-9133
8070 Soquel Dr Aptos (95003) *(P-715)*
Talos Secure Group Inc....E....707 927-5432
110 Railroad Ave Ste B Suisun City (94585) *(P-14101)*
Talus Construction Inc....E....925 406-4756
311 Oak St Apt 114 Oakland (94607) *(P-1136)*
Talview Inc (PA)....**C....830 484-6221**
400 Concar Dr San Mateo (94402) *(P-13989)*
Tamaki Rice Corporation....E....530 473-2862
1701 Abel Rd Williams (95987) *(P-2329)*
Tamal Pais, Greenbrae *Also called Sequoia Living Inc (P-16268)*
Tamalpais, Greenbrae *Also called Ross Valley Homes Inc (P-18173)*
Tamalpais Coml Cabinetry Inc....E....510 231-6800
200 9th St Richmond (94801) *(P-3193)*
Tamalpais Community Svcs Dst....E....415 388-6393
305 Bell Ln Mill Valley (94941) *(P-8366)*
Tamarack Springs Mutual Wtr Co (PA)....**F....209 369-2761**
125 N Church St Lodi (95240) *(P-3485)*
Tamtron Corporation (HQ)....**D....408 323-3303**
6203 San Ignacio Ave # 110 San Jose (95119) *(P-12848)*
Tan Packaging LLC....E....800 237-1009
3527 Mt Diablo Blvd Ste 2 Lafayette (94549) *(P-3380)*
Tanco Inc....E....209 523-8365
2310 N Walnut Rd Turlock (95382) *(P-1376)*
Tandem Properties Incorporated (PA)....**E....530 756-5075**
3500 Anderson Rd Davis (95616) *(P-10670)*
Tanfield Engrg Systems US Inc....F....559 443-6602
2686 S Maple Ave Fresno (93725) *(P-5040)*
Tangent Computer Inc (PA)....**D....888 683-2881**
191 Airport Blvd Burlingame (94010) *(P-5275)*
Tanget Fastnet, Burlingame *Also called Tangent Computer Inc (P-5275)*
Tangible Play Inc (HQ)....**C....650 667-1693**
195 Page Mill Rd Ste 105 Palo Alto (94306) *(P-12849)*
Tangle Inc DBA Tangle Creat....E....703 478-0500
310 Littlefield Ave South San Francisco (94080) *(P-7184)*
Tanko Streetlighting Inc....E....415 254-7579
220 Bay Shore Blvd San Francisco (94124) *(P-5739)*
Tanko Streetlighting Services, San Francisco *Also called Tanko Streetlighting Inc (P-5739)*
Tanner Companies LLC (PA)....**C....925 463-9672**
4670 Willow Rd Ste 250 Pleasanton (94588) *(P-10079)*
Tanner Pacific Inc....E....650 585-4484
261 Oakview Dr San Carlos (94070) *(P-18827)*
Tanoshi Inc....F....949 677-5261
505 14th St Fl 9 Oakland (94612) *(P-13486)*
Tanox Inc (HQ)....**C....650 851-1607**
1 Dna Way South San Francisco (94080) *(P-3990)*
Tao Mechanical Ltd....E....925 447-5220
136 Wright Brothers Ave Livermore (94551) *(P-1377)*
Taos Mountain LLC (PA)....**B....408 324-2800**
121 Daggett Dr San Jose (95134) *(P-13990)*
Tap Plastics Inc A Cal Corp (PA)....**F....510 357-3755**
3011 Alvarado St Ste A San Leandro (94577) *(P-3810)*
Tap Plastics Inc A Cal Corp....E....510 357-3755
3011 Alvarado St San Leandro (94577) *(P-3811)*
Tapemation Machining Inc (PA)....**E....831 438-3069**
13 Janis Way Scotts Valley (95066) *(P-5626)*
Tapestry Family Services Inc....D....707 463-3300
169 Mason St Ste 300 Ukiah (95482) *(P-18190)*
Tapia Bros Company, Fresno *Also called Tapia Enterprises Inc (P-9320)*
Tapia Enterprises Inc....E....559 486-8347
2324 S Barton Ave Fresno (93725) *(P-9320)*
Tapingo Inc (HQ)....**D....415 283-5222**
39 Stillman St San Francisco (94107) *(P-13487)*
Tapjoy Inc (PA)....**E....415 766-6900**
353 Sacramento St Ste 600 San Francisco (94111) *(P-11789)*
Tapp Label, NAPA *Also called Ingenious Packaging Group (P-14302)*
Tapp Label Inc (HQ)....**E....707 252-8300**
161 S Vasco Rd L Livermore (94551) *(P-3408)*
Tapp Label Holding Company LLC (PA)....**D....707 252-8300**
580 Gateway Dr NAPA (94558) *(P-10357)*
Taracom Corporation....F....408 691-6655
1220 Memorex Dr Santa Clara (95050) *(P-5276)*
Tarana Wireless Inc (PA)....**F....408 365-8483**
590 Alder Dr Milpitas (95035) *(P-5875)*
Tarc Construction Inc (PA)....**E....408 224-2154**
3230 Darby Cmn Ste A Fremont (94539) *(P-716)*
Tardio Enterprises Inc....E....650 877-7200
457 S Canal St South San Francisco (94080) *(P-2832)*
Tariff Building Associates LP (PA)....**D....415 397-5572**
222 Kearny St Ste 200 San Francisco (94108) *(P-10411)*
Tarra Landscape, San Leandro *Also called Tree Sculpture Group (P-505)*
Tarrant Capital Ip LLC (PA)....**A....415 743-1500**
345 California St # 3300 San Francisco (94104) *(P-10062)*
Tart Collections, Concord *Also called JD Fine & Company Inc (P-9252)*
Tartine LP....E....415 487-2600
600 Guerrero St San Francisco (94110) *(P-2407)*
Tartine Bakery & Cafe, San Francisco *Also called Tartine LP (P-2407)*
Tascent Inc....F....650 799-4611
475 Alberto Way Ste 200 Los Gatos (95032) *(P-6544)*
Task Help LLC....D....833 229-0726
1390 Market St Ste 200 San Francisco (94102) *(P-12850)*
Tata America Intl Corp....D....916 803-5441
3115 Java Ct West Sacramento (95691) *(P-2074)*
Tata America Intl Corp....E....408 569-5845
5201 Great America Pkwy Santa Clara (95054) *(P-13991)*
Tata Consulting Services, Santa Clara *Also called Tata America Intl Corp (P-13991)*
Tata Elxsi Ltd (HQ)....**E....408 894-8282**
4677 Old Ironsides Dr # 315 Santa Clara (95054) *(P-13675)*
Tatung Telecom Corporation....D....650 961-2288
2660 Marine Way Mountain View (94043) *(P-5812)*
Taulia Inc (PA)....**C....415 376-8280**
95 3rd St San Francisco (94103) *(P-12851)*
Taurus Fabrication Inc....E....530 268-2650
22838 Industrial Pl Grass Valley (95949) *(P-4840)*
Tavant Technologies Inc (PA)....**A....408 519-5400**
3965 Freedom Cir Ste 750 Santa Clara (95054) *(P-12852)*
Taxaudit.com, Folsom *Also called Taxresources Inc (P-11703)*
Taxresources Inc (PA)....**C....877 369-7827**
600 Coolidge Dr Ste 300 Folsom (95630) *(P-11703)*
Taylor Brothers Farms Inc (PA)....**E....530 671-1505**
182 Wilkie Ave Yuba City (95991) *(P-94)*
Taylor Communications Inc....F....916 927-1891
1300 Ethan Way Ste 675 Sacramento (95825) *(P-3757)*
Taylor Communications Inc....F....916 340-0200
3885 Seaport Blvd Ste 40 West Sacramento (95691) *(P-3758)*
Taylor Communications Inc....F....916 368-1200
10390 Coloma Rd Ste 7 Rancho Cordova (95670) *(P-3759)*
Taylor Farms, San Juan Bautista *Also called Earthbound Farm LLC (P-281)*
Taylor Heavy Hauling, Roseville *Also called Specialized Transport Inc (P-7490)*
Taylor Investments LLC....E....530 273-4135
13355 Nevada City Ave Grass Valley (95945) *(P-5188)*
Taylor Maid Farms LLC....E....707 824-9110
6790 Mckinley Ave Sebastopol (95472) *(P-2847)*
Taylor Morrision Homes....E....916 355-8900
81 Blue Ravine Rd Ste 220 Folsom (95630) *(P-717)*
Taylor Motors Inc....E....530 222-1200
2525 Churn Creek Rd Redding (96002) *(P-14594)*
Taylor Packing Co, Yuba City *Also called Taylor Brothers Farms Inc (P-94)*
Taylor Wings Inc....E....916 851-9464
8392 Carbide Ct Sacramento (95828) *(P-4823)*
Tayman Park Golf Group Inc....E....707 433-4275
927 S Fitch Mountain Rd Healdsburg (95448) *(P-15033)*
Tbf Travel, Rocklin *Also called Total Body Fitness (P-15253)*
Tbi Construction Cnstr MGT Inc....E....408 246-3691
1960 The Alameda Ste 100 San Jose (95126) *(P-814)*
Tc Prprty MGT Ltd A Cal Ltd PR....E....530 666-5799
1723 Oak Ave Davis (95616) *(P-10889)*
TC Steel....F....707 773-2150
464 Sonoma Mountain Rd Petaluma (94954) *(P-14723)*
Tcb Industrial Inc (PA)....**D....209 571-0569**
2955 Farrar Ave Modesto (95354) *(P-815)*
Tcg Builders Inc....E....408 321-6450
890 N Mccarthy Blvd # 100 Milpitas (95035) *(P-971)*
TCI Aluminum/North Inc....D....510 786-3750
2353 Davis Ave Hayward (94545) *(P-8830)*
TCI International Inc (HQ)....**C....510 687-6100**
3541 Gateway Blvd Fremont (94538) *(P-5876)*
Tcmi Inc (PA)....**E....650 614-8200**
250 Middlefield Rd Menlo Park (94025) *(P-10890)*
Tcv Management 2004 LLC....E....650 614-8200
528 Ramona St Palo Alto (94301) *(P-19407)*
Td Synnex Corporation (PA)....**C....510 656-3333**
44201 Nobel Dr Fremont (94538) *(P-13676)*
Td Synnex Corporation....D....510 688-3507
44131 Nobel Dr Fremont (94538) *(P-14426)*
Tdc Convalescent Inc....C....559 321-0883
3034 E Herndon Ave Fresno (93720) *(P-16142)*
Tdic, Sacramento *Also called Dentists Insurance Company (P-10271)*
Tdic Insurance Solutions....E....800 733-0633
1201 K St Sacramento (95814) *(P-10358)*
Tdl Aero Enterprises Inc....F....209 722-7300
44 Macready Dr Merced (95341) *(P-6619)*
Tdw Construction Inc....E....925 455-5259
101 Greenville Rd Livermore (94551) *(P-1137)*
Te Circuit Protection, Fremont *Also called Te Connectivity Ltd (P-6475)*
Te Connectivity, Grass Valley *Also called Measurement Specialties Inc (P-6770)*
Te Connectivity Ltd....E....650 361-4923
6900 Paseo Padre Pkwy Fremont (94555) *(P-6475)*
Te Connectivity MOG Inc (HQ)....**A....650 361-5292**
501 Oakside Ave Redwood City (94063) *(P-4380)*
Te Tech LLC....F....510 770-8610
44380 Osgood Rd Fremont (94539) *(P-9137)*

Teach Inc ....D....530 233-3111
112 E 2nd St Alturas (96101) ***(P-17765)***
Teacher Training Organization, San Jose *Also called One World Montessori School* ***(P-17986)***
Teachers Curriculum Inst LLC (PA) ....**E....800 497-6138**
2440 W El Cmino Real Ste Mountain View (94040) ***(P-3546)***
Teal Bend Golf Club Inc ....D....916 922-5209
7200 Garden Hwy Sacramento (95837) ***(P-15159)***
Teale Data Center, Rancho Cordova *Also called California Department Tech* ***(P-13701)***
Team Allied Distribution, Benicia *Also called Allied Exhaust Systems Inc* ***(P-8438)***
Team Casing ....E....530 743-5424
5073 Arboga Rd Marysville (95901) ***(P-573)***
Team Fishel, Tracy *Also called Fishel Company* ***(P-1505)***
Team Ghilotti Inc ....E....707 763-8700
2531 Petaluma Blvd S Petaluma (94952) ***(P-1077)***
Team K9, Sacramento *Also called Confidential Canine Services* ***(P-353)***
Team San Jose ....A....408 295-9600
408 Almaden Blvd San Jose (95110) ***(P-14427)***
Team Superstores, Vallejo *Also called Teamross Inc* ***(P-14595)***
Teammate Builders Inc ....F....408 377-9000
281 E Mcglincy Ln Frnt Campbell (95008) ***(P-3329)***
Teamross Inc ....D....707 643-9000
301 Auto Mall Pkwy Vallejo (94591) ***(P-14595)***
Teamsable Inc ....E....408 452-8788
1911 Hartog Dr San Jose (95131) ***(P-8754)***
Teamsters Local 856, San Bruno *Also called Freight Chckers Clrcal Emplyee* ***(P-18358)***
Teamsters Local Union 70 ....E....510 569-9317
400 Roland Way Oakland (94621) ***(P-18378)***
Teamworks Inc (PA) ....**E....408 243-3970**
2398 Walsh Ave Santa Clara (95051) ***(P-19000)***
Teamwrkx Inc (PA) ....**E....408 287-2700**
1855 Park Ave San Jose (95126) ***(P-773)***
Teamwrkx Construction, San Jose *Also called Teamwrkx Inc* ***(P-773)***
Teasdale Quality Foods Inc ....A....209 356-5616
901 Packers St Atwater (95301) ***(P-2245)***
Tecan Systems Inc ....D....408 953-3100
2450 Zanker Rd San Jose (95131) ***(P-6697)***
Tech 2 U, Sacramento *Also called Tech Service 2 U Inc* ***(P-13823)***
Tech Interactive (PA) ....**C....408 795-6116**
201 S Market St San Jose (95113) ***(P-18283)***
Tech Service 2 U Inc ....E....888 931-0942
1590 Howe Ave Sacramento (95825) ***(P-13823)***
Tech West Vacuum Inc ....D....559 291-1650
2625 N Argyle Ave Fresno (93727) ***(P-7089)***
Techart, San Francisco *Also called Trans Pacific Digital Inc* ***(P-11874)***
Techcon, Morgan Hill *Also called Monument Construction Inc* ***(P-426)***
Techexcel Inc (PA) ....**D....925 871-3900**
3675 Mt Diablo Blvd # 330 Lafayette (94549) ***(P-12853)***
Technibuilders Iron Inc ....F....408 287-8797
1049 Felipe Ave San Jose (95122) ***(P-4841)***
Technical Instr San Francisco (PA) ....**E....650 651-3000**
1826 Rollins Rd Ste 100 Burlingame (94010) ***(P-8804)***
Technical Instrument SF, Burlingame *Also called Technical Instr San Francisco* ***(P-8804)***
Technical Reps Intl Inc ....F....408 848-8868
5770 Obata Way Ste B Gilroy (95020) ***(P-972)***
Technical Sales Intl LLC (HQ) ....**E....866 493-6337**
910 Pleasant Grove Blvd Roseville (95678) ***(P-13488)***
Technical Services, Mountain View *Also called Northrop Grumman Systems Corp* ***(P-13640)***
Technicolor Usa Inc ....A....530 478-3000
400 Providence Mine Rd Nevada City (95959) ***(P-5877)***
Technicon Engineering Svcs Inc ....E....559 276-9311
4539 N Brawley Ave # 108 Fresno (93722) ***(P-18828)***
Technique Gymnastics Inc ....E....916 635-7900
11345 Folsom Blvd Rancho Cordova (95742) ***(P-15249)***
Technology Credit Union (PA) ....**C....408 451-9111**
2010 N 1st St Ste 200 San Jose (95131) ***(P-9823)***
Technology Crossover Ventures, Menlo Park *Also called Tcmi Inc* ***(P-10890)***
Technology Services Cal Dept ....C....916 464-3747
3101 Gold Camp Dr Rancho Cordova (95670) ***(P-13992)***
Technoprobe America Inc ....E....408 573-9911
2526 Qume Dr Ste 27 San Jose (95131) ***(P-6326)***
Techsoup Global (PA) ....**C....800 659-3579**
435 Brannan St Ste 100 San Francisco (94107) ***(P-18476)***
Techstyles Sportswear LLC ....E....800 733-3629
2051 Alpine Way Hayward (94545) ***(P-9257)***
Techtron Products Inc ....E....510 293-3500
2694 W Winton Ave Hayward (94545) ***(P-5727)***
Tect Aerospace, San Francisco *Also called Turbine Eng Cmpnents Tech Corp* ***(P-6622)***
Tectonic Engrg Srvying Cons PC ....E....925 357-8236
2855 Mitchell Dr Ste 227 Walnut Creek (94598) ***(P-18829)***
Tectura Corporation (PA) ....**E....650 273-4249**
951 Old County Rd 2-317 Belmont (94002) ***(P-13993)***
Tectura Intl Holdings Inc ....D....650 585-5500
333 Twin Dolphin Dr # 750 Redwood City (94065) ***(P-13994)***
Ted Collwell ....E....530 666-2433
1224 Cottonwood St Ofc Woodland (95695) ***(P-18191)***
Ted Jacob Engrg Group Inc (PA) ....**E....510 763-4880**
1763 Broadway Oakland (94612) ***(P-18830)***
Ted Stevens Inc ....C....415 927-5664
5860 Paradise Dr Corte Madera (94925) ***(P-14495)***
Tedon Specialties A Cal Corp ....F....530 527-6600
1255 Vista Way Red Bluff (96080) ***(P-5627)***
Teeco Products Inc ....E....916 688-3535
7471 Reese Rd Sacramento (95828) ***(P-6595)***
Teecom ....D....510 337-2800
50 California St Ste 1500 San Francisco (94111) ***(P-18831)***
Teen Challenge Norwestcal Nev ....E....408 703-2001
390 Mathew St Santa Clara (95050) ***(P-17766)***
Teespring Inc (PA) ....**C....855 833-7774**
2430 3rd St San Francisco (94107) ***(P-14428)***
Tegile Systems Inc ....C....510 791-7900
7999 Gateway Blvd Ste 120 Newark (94560) ***(P-19135)***
Tegsco LLC (PA) ....**D....415 865-8200**
450 7th St San Francisco (94103) ***(P-14676)***
Tegtmeier Associates Inc ....D....530 872-7700
6701 Clark Rd Paradise (95969) ***(P-10412)***
Tehiyah Day School Inc ....D....510 233-4405
6402 Claremont Ave Richmond (94805) ***(P-18038)***
Teichert Inc (PA) ....**A....916 484-3011**
5200 Franklin Dr Ste 115 Pleasanton (94588) ***(P-4510)***
Teichert Aggregates, Truckee *Also called A Teichert & Son Inc* ***(P-582)***
Teichert Aggregates, Tracy *Also called A Teichert & Son Inc* ***(P-583)***
Teichert Aggregates, Esparto *Also called A Teichert & Son Inc* ***(P-584)***
Teichert Aggregates, Cool *Also called A Teichert & Son Inc* ***(P-585)***
Teichert Aggregates, Marysville *Also called A Teichert & Son Inc* ***(P-586)***
Teichert Aggregates, Marysville *Also called A Teichert & Son Inc* ***(P-587)***
Teichert Aggregates, Rancho Cordova *Also called A Teichert & Son Inc* ***(P-588)***
Teichert Aggregates, Sacramento *Also called A Teichert & Son Inc* ***(P-589)***
Teichert Construction, Stockton *Also called A Teichert & Son Inc* ***(P-997)***
Teichert Construction, Davis *Also called A Teichert & Son Inc* ***(P-998)***
Teichert Construction, Roseville *Also called A Teichert & Son Inc* ***(P-999)***
Teichert Construction, Pleasanton *Also called A Teichert & Son Inc* ***(P-8614)***
Teichert Construction, Fresno *Also called A Teichert & Son Inc* ***(P-1000)***
Teichert Construction, Stockton *Also called A Teichert & Son Inc* ***(P-1001)***
Teichert Readymix, Sacramento *Also called A Teichert & Son Inc* ***(P-4456)***
Teichert Readymix, Roseville *Also called A Teichert & Son Inc* ***(P-4457)***
Teijin Pharma USA LLC ....A....415 893-1518
1 Harbor Dr Ste 200 Sausalito (94965) ***(P-9242)***
Teikoku Pharma Usa Inc (HQ) ....**D....408 501-1800**
1718 Ringwood Ave San Jose (95131) ***(P-3991)***
Teixeira and Sons LLC (PA) ....**C....209 827-9800**
22759 S Mercey Springs Rd Los Banos (93635) ***(P-12)***
Teka Illumination Inc ....F....559 438-5800
40429 Brickyard Dr Madera (93636) ***(P-5750)***
Tekberry Inc ....B....707 313-5345
3763 Shillingford Pl Santa Rosa (95404) ***(P-12146)***
Tekion Corp ....C....925 399-5569
12647 Alcosta Blvd San Ramon (94583) ***(P-13995)***
Teknos Associates LLC ....E....650 330-8800
548 Market St San Francisco (94104) ***(P-19649)***
Tekreliance LLC ....E....732 829-7585
46560 Fremont Blvd # 302 Fremont (94538) ***(P-12854)***
Tekrevol LLC ....D....832 426-3532
39899 Balentine Dr # 200 Newark (94560) ***(P-12855)***
Tekvalley Corporation ....E....925 558-2275
4695 Chabot Dr Ste 200 Pleasanton (94588) ***(P-13996)***
Tela Innovations Inc ....E....408 558-6300
475 Alberto Way Ste 120 Los Gatos (95032) ***(P-6327)***
Tele-Direct Communications Inc ....E....916 348-2170
4741 Madison Ave Ste 200 Sacramento (95841) ***(P-14429)***
Telecare Corporation (PA) ....**A....510 337-7950**
1080 Marina Village Pkwy # 100 Alameda (94501) ***(P-16748)***
Telecmmnctons MGT Slutions Inc ....D....408 866-5495
570 Division St Campbell (95008) ***(P-1619)***
Telecom Inc ....D....510 873-8283
2201 Broadway Ste 103 Oakland (94612) ***(P-14430)***
Telecom Technology Svcs Inc ....C....925 224-7812
7901 Stoneridge Dr # 500 Pleasanton (94588) ***(P-19873)***
Telecommunications Designs, Santa Rosa *Also called Fonexperts Inc* ***(P-1506)***
Telecommunications Engrg Assoc ....E....650 590-1801
1160 Industrial Rd Ste 15 San Carlos (94070) ***(P-5878)***
Telecontact Resource Services, Riverbank *Also called Econtactlive Inc* ***(P-14259)***
Teledyne Defense Elec LLC ....C....408 737-0992
765 Sycamore Dr Milpitas (95035) ***(P-6328)***
Teledyne Defense Elec LLC ....C....916 638-3344
11361 Sunrise Park Dr Rancho Cordova (95742) ***(P-6476)***
Teledyne Defense Elec LLC (HQ) ....**E....650 691-9800**
1274 Terra Bella Ave Mountain View (94043) ***(P-6477)***
Teledyne Dgital Imaging US Inc ....F....408 736-6000
765 Sycamore Dr Milpitas (95035) ***(P-6925)***
Teledyne E2v Hirel Electronics, Milpitas *Also called Teledyne Defense Elec LLC* ***(P-6328)***
Teledyne E2v, Inc. ....E....408 737-0992
765 Sycamore Dr Milpitas (95035) ***(P-6329)***
Teledyne Hirel Electronics, Milpitas *Also called Teledyne E2v, Inc.* ***(P-6329)***
Teledyne Microwave, Santa Clara *Also called Teledyne Wireless Inc* ***(P-5701)***
Teledyne Microwave Solutions, Rancho Cordova *Also called Teledyne Defense Elec LLC* ***(P-6476)***
Teledyne Microwave Solutions, Mountain View *Also called Teledyne Defense Elec LLC* ***(P-6477)***
Teledyne RAD-Icon Imaging, Milpitas *Also called Teledyne Dgital Imaging US Inc* ***(P-6925)***
Teledyne Risi Inc (HQ) ....**E....925 456-9700**
32727 S Corral Hollow Rd Tracy (95377) ***(P-4153)***
Teledyne Wireless LLC ....C....916 638-3344
11361 Sunrise Park Dr Rancho Cordova (95742) ***(P-6478)***
Teledyne Wireless Inc ....C....408 986-5060
3236 Scott Blvd Santa Clara (95054) ***(P-5701)***
Telefunken Semiconductors Amer, Roseville *Also called Tsi Semiconductors America LLC* ***(P-6336)***
Telegraph Hill Nursery, San Francisco *Also called Telegraph Hl Neighborhood Ctr* ***(P-17767)***
Telegraph Hill Partners Invest (PA) ....**E....415 765-6980**
360 Post St Ste 601 San Francisco (94108) ***(P-19650)***
Telegraph Hl Neighborhood Ctr ....E....415 421-6443
660 Lombard St San Francisco (94133) ***(P-17767)***

A L P H A B E T I C

Telehealth Services USA....D....415 424-4266
10775 Pioneer Trl Ste 215 Truckee (96161) *(P-15738)*
Telemarketing, Fresno *Also called Fowler Packing Company Inc (P-284)*
Telemundo of Fresno LLC....E....559 252-5101
500 Media Pl Sacramento (95815) *(P-8055)*
Telenav Inc (PA)....A....**408 245-3800**
4655 Great America Pkwy Santa Clara (95054) *(P-6686)*
Telepathy Inc....E....408 306-8421
1202 Kifer Rd Sunnyvale (94086) *(P-5418)*
Teleplan Service Solutions Inc....D....916 677-4500
8875 Washington Blvd B Roseville (95678) *(P-13824)*
Telesis Onion Co....C....559 884-2441
21484 S Colusa Five Points (93624) *(P-312)*
Telestream LLC (PA)....C....**530 470-1300**
848 Gold Flat Rd Nevada City (95959) *(P-12856)*
Telewave Inc....E....408 929-4400
48421 Milmont Dr Fremont (94538) *(P-5879)*
Telirite Technical Svcs Inc....E....510 440-3888
2857 Lakeview Ct Fremont (94538) *(P-5986)*
Tellapart Inc (HQ)....D....**415 222-9670**
1355 Market St 5 San Francisco (94103) *(P-12857)*
Tellme Networks Inc....B....650 693-1009
1065 La Avenida St Mountain View (94043) *(P-3604)*
Tellus Solutions Inc....E....408 850-2942
3350 Scott Blvd Bldg 34a Santa Clara (95054) *(P-13489)*
Telmate LLC (HQ)....D....**866 516-0115**
20 California St Ste 600 San Francisco (94111) *(P-7998)*
Telstar Instruments (PA)....E....**925 671-2888**
1717 Solano Way Ste 34 Concord (94520) *(P-1620)*
Telstra Incorporated....E....415 243-3430
575 Market St Ste 1650 San Francisco (94105) *(P-13763)*
Tempest Technology Corporation....E....559 277-7577
4708 N Blythe Ave Fresno (93722) *(P-5192)*
Tempo Automation Inc....E....415 320-1261
2460 Alameda St San Francisco (94103) *(P-5987)*
Tempo Interactive Inc....E....415 964-2975
575 7th Ave San Francisco (94118) *(P-14980)*
Temporary Plant Cleaners, Martinez *Also called Plant Maintenance Inc (P-12187)*
Temujin Labs Inc....E....650 850-9037
444 High St Ste 300 Palo Alto (94301) *(P-12858)*
Ten 15 Inc....D....415 431-1200
1015 Folsom St San Francisco (94103) *(P-10413)*
Ten Lifestyle MGT USA Inc (HQ)....C....**415 625-1900**
33 New Montgomery St # 10 San Francisco (94105) *(P-11731)*
Tenaya Lodge, Fish Camp *Also called DNC Prks Resorts At Tenaya Inc (P-11054)*
Tencate Advanced Composite....D....707 359-3400
2450 Cordelia Rd Fairfield (94534) *(P-9612)*
Tencue Productions LLC....E....510 841-3000
1250 Addison St Ste 110 Berkeley (94702) *(P-14431)*
Tencue, An Opus Company, Berkeley *Also called Tencue Productions LLC (P-14431)*
Tend Insights Inc....E....510 619-9289
46567 Fremont Blvd Fremont (94538) *(P-13490)*
Tenddo Inc....E....415 295-4849
101 California St # 2710 San Francisco (94111) *(P-13677)*
Tender Loving Things Inc....F....510 300-1260
26203 Prod Ave Ste 4 Hayward (94545) *(P-4096)*
Tender Rose Home Care LLC....E....415 340-3990
2001 Junipero Serra Blvd # 520 Daly City (94014) *(P-16959)*
Tenderloin Housing Clinic Inc (PA)....C....**415 771-9850**
126 Hyde St San Francisco (94102) *(P-10671)*
Tenergy Corporation....D....510 687-0388
436 Kato Ter Fremont (94539) *(P-6491)*
Tenet Health System Hospital, Manteca *Also called Tenet Healthsystem Medical Inc (P-16686)*
Tenet Healthsystem Medical Inc....D....925 275-8303
414 Cliffside Dr Danville (94526) *(P-15739)*
Tenet Healthsystem Medical Inc....C....209 823-3111
1205 E North St Manteca (95336) *(P-16686)*
Tenet Healthsystem Medical Inc....D....530 222-1992
475 Knollcrest Dr Redding (96002) *(P-16960)*
Tenet Healthsystem Medical Inc....C....408 378-6131
815 Pollard Rd Los Gatos (95032) *(P-16687)*
Tenney A Norquist, Turlock *Also called Tanco Inc (P-1376)*
Tennis Everyone Incorporated....E....415 897-2185
351 San Andreas Dr Novato (94945) *(P-14981)*
Tennyson Electric Inc....E....925 606-1038
7275 National Dr Livermore (94550) *(P-1621)*
Tensilica Inc (HQ)....D....**408 986-8000**
3393 Octavius Dr Santa Clara (95054) *(P-10813)*
Tenter Enterprises Inc....E....530 680-9917
180 Redbud Dr Paradise (95969) *(P-7656)*
Teocal Transport Inc....E....510 569-3485
2101 Carden St San Leandro (94577) *(P-7636)*
Teohc California Inc....B....209 234-1600
1320 Performance Dr Stockton (95206) *(P-4824)*
Teqtron Inc....E....925 583-5411
256 Snider Ct Livermore (94550) *(P-13678)*
Tequilas Premium Inc....F....415 399-0496
470 Columbus Ave Ste 210 San Francisco (94133) *(P-2780)*
Tera Sahara Inc....E....530 223-1600
536 E Cypress Ave Redding (96002) *(P-11528)*
Tera-Lite Inc....E....408 288-8655
1631 S 10th St San Jose (95112) *(P-1777)*
Terarecon Inc....E....650 372-1100
93141 Civic Ct Dr Fremont (94538) *(P-5419)*
Teresi Trucking LLC (PA)....E....**209 368-2472**
900 1/2 E Victor Rd Lodi (95240) *(P-7494)*
Terix Computer Service, Santa Clara *Also called Tusa Inc (P-13825)*
Terminal Inc (PA)....D....**281 682-8294**
1 Letterman Dr Bldg C San Francisco (94129) *(P-18832)*
Terminal Manufacturing Co LLC....E....510 526-3071
707 Gilman St Berkeley (94710) *(P-4689)*
Terminix Company LLC....E....800 480-8439
5451 Industrial Way Benicia (94510) *(P-11908)*
Tern, Davis *Also called Electronic Resources Network (P-5363)*
Terns Pharmaceuticals Inc (PA)....E....**650 525-5535**
1065 E Hillsdale Blvd # 100 Foster City (94404) *(P-3992)*
Terra Millennium Corp....E....510 233-2500
1060 Hensley St Richmond (94801) *(P-4534)*
Terra Nova Counseling (PA)....D....**916 344-0249**
5750 Sunrise Blvd Ste 100 Citrus Heights (95610) *(P-17768)*
Terra Nova Industries....E....925 934-6133
1607 Tice Valley Blvd Walnut Creek (94595) *(P-973)*
TERRACES AT SQUAW PEAK, Pleasanton *Also called Humangood (P-16241)*
Terraces of Los Gatos Agei, Los Gatos *Also called Humangood Norcal (P-16243)*
Terraces of Roseville, The, Roseville *Also called Westmont Living Inc (P-18212)*
Terramai....E....530 964-2740
1104 Firenze St McCloud (96057) *(P-3118)*
Terranova Ranch Inc....E....559 866-5644
16729 W Floral Ave Helm (93627) *(P-191)*
Terrapin Energy LLC (PA)....E....**650 386-6180**
897 Independence Ave 2g Mountain View (94043) *(P-550)*
Terrasat Communications Inc....E....408 782-5911
315 Digital Dr Morgan Hill (95037) *(P-5880)*
Terre Du Soleil Ltd....B....707 963-1211
180 Rutherford Hill Rd Rutherford (94573) *(P-11529)*
Territory Designs Inc....E....530 836-2511
5000 Gold Lake Rd Blairsden (96103) *(P-11530)*
Terry Mechanical Inc....E....408 629-7822
6541 Via Del Oro Ste C San Jose (95119) *(P-1378)*
Terry Meyer....D....408 723-3300
1712 Meridian Ave Ste C San Jose (95125) *(P-10672)*
Terry Tuell Concrete Inc....D....559 431-0812
287 W Fllbrook Ave Ste 10 Fresno (93711) *(P-1912)*
Tescra....E....925 242-0100
3130 Crow Canyon Pl # 205 San Ramon (94583) *(P-12859)*
Tesla Inc (PA)....C....**650 681-5000**
3500 Deer Creek Rd Palo Alto (94304) *(P-6561)*
Tesla Energy Operations Inc (HQ)....A....**888 765-2489**
3055 Clearview Way San Mateo (94402) *(P-1379)*
Tesla Vineyards Lp....E....925 456-2500
4590 Tesla Rd Livermore (94550) *(P-2738)*
Teslarati LLC....F....323 405-7657
11040 Bollinger Canyon Rd San Ramon (94582) *(P-12860)*
Tesoro Golden Eagle Refin....E....925 370-3249
150 Solano Way Pacheco (94553) *(P-14432)*
Tessera Inc (HQ)....D....**408 321-6000**
3025 Orchard Pkwy San Jose (95134) *(P-6330)*
Tessera Technologies Inc (HQ)....C....**408 321-6000**
3025 Orchard Pkwy San Jose (95134) *(P-6331)*
Tessolve Dts, Saratoga *Also called Tessolve Services Inc (P-6856)*
Tessolve Services Inc (HQ)....D....**408 865-0873**
14567 Big Basin Way A3 Saratoga (95070) *(P-6856)*
Tessolvedts Inc (PA)....E....**408 865-0873**
226 Airport Pkwy Ste 300 San Jose (95110) *(P-18833)*
Test Enterprises Inc (PA)....E....**408 542-5900**
1288 Reamwood Ave Sunnyvale (94089) *(P-6734)*
Test-Um Inc....E....818 464-5021
430 N Mccarthy Blvd Milpitas (95035) *(P-6332)*
Testamerica Laboratories Inc....E....916 373-5600
880 Riverside Pkwy West Sacramento (95605) *(P-19287)*
Testarossa Vineyards LLC....E....408 354-6150
300 College Ave Ste A Los Gatos (95030) *(P-2739)*
Testarossa Winery, Los Gatos *Also called Testarossa Vineyards LLC (P-2739)*
Testing Engineers Incorporated (PA)....E....**510 835-3142**
2811 Teagarden St San Leandro (94577) *(P-18834)*
Testmetrix Inc....E....408 730-5511
1141 Ringwood Ct Ste 90 San Jose (95131) *(P-6795)*
Teter LLP (PA)....E....**559 437-0887**
7535 N Palm Ave Ste 201 Fresno (93711) *(P-18835)*
Tetra Tech Ec Inc....E....916 852-8300
3101 Zinfandel Dr Ste 200 Rancho Cordova (95670) *(P-19874)*
Tevelde Farms (PA)....E....**209 394-8008**
8632 Meadow Dr Winton (95388) *(P-225)*
Texaco Inc (HQ)....A....**925 842-1000**
6001 Bollinger Canyon Rd San Ramon (94583) *(P-552)*
Texaco Overseas Holdings Inc (HQ)....F....**510 242-5357**
6001 Bollinger Canyon Rd San Ramon (94583) *(P-4182)*
Texas Instruments Sunnyvale....E....408 541-9900
165 Gibraltar Ct Sunnyvale (94089) *(P-14433)*
Texchem Chemical, Sacramento *Also called Kds Nail Products (P-7291)*
Textainer Equipment Mgt US Ltd (HQ)....D....**415 434-0551**
650 California St Fl 16 San Francisco (94108) *(P-12064)*
Textainer Group Holdings Ltd (HQ)....D....**415 434-0551**
650 California St Fl 16 San Francisco (94108) *(P-19408)*
Textnow Inc....F....226 476-1578
1 Sutter St Ste 800 San Francisco (94104) *(P-7999)*
Tf Welch Enterprises Inc....F....916 645-4277
10556 Combie Rd 6528 Auburn (95602) *(P-1380)*
TFC Credit Corp California....D....800 832-5626
2010 Crow Canyon Pl # 300 San Ramon (94583) *(P-9862)*
TFC Tuition Financing, San Ramon *Also called TFC Credit Corp California (P-9862)*
TG Schmeiser Co Inc....F....559 268-8128
8135 E Dinuba Ave Selma (93662) *(P-5019)*
Tgcon Inc (HQ)....B....**925 449-5764**
50 Contractors St Livermore (94551) *(P-18836)*

TGIF Body Shop Inc ....E....510 490-1342
4595 Enterprise St Fremont (94538) *(P-14536)*
Thai Kitchen, Berkeley *Also called Simply Asia Foods LLC (P-2943)*
Thales Esecurity Inc (HQ) ....**D....408 433-6000**
2125 Zanker Rd San Jose (95131) *(P-13997)*
Thatcher's Gourmet Popcorn, San Francisco *Also called Gourmet Plus Inc (P-9354)*
Thawte Inc ....E....650 426-7400
405 Clyde Ave Mountain View (94043) *(P-5881)*
Thawte Consulting USA, Mountain View *Also called Thawte Inc (P-5881)*
The Broadmoore, San Francisco *Also called Broadmoor Hotel (P-10975)*
The Cameo Club, Stockton *Also called Lewis & Lewis Inc (P-15216)*
The Chanate, Santa Rosa *Also called Chanate Ldge Assoc A Cal Ltd P (P-10423)*
The Charles Schwab Trust Co (HQ) ....**E....415 371-0518**
425 Market St Fl 7 San Francisco (94105) *(P-10016)*
The Clearwater Company, Rancho Cordova *Also called Nca Laboratories Inc (P-5766)*
The David Lcile Pckard Fndtion ....D....650 917-7167
300 2nd St Los Altos (94022) *(P-18601)*
The Inn ....D....925 682-1601
3555 Clayton Rd Concord (94519) *(P-11531)*
The Linux Foundation (PA) ....**C....415 723-9709**
548 Market St Pmb 57274 San Francisco (94104) *(P-18477)*
The Origin Project Inc ....D....415 601-2409
2121 Vallejo St San Francisco (94123) *(P-18284)*
The Peddler, Modesto *Also called Vintage Car Wash Inc (P-14653)*
The Redwoods A Cmnty Seniors ....C....415 383-2741
40 Camino Alto Ofc Mill Valley (94941) *(P-18192)*
The Sterling Hotel, Sacramento *Also called Elizabethan Inn Associates LP (P-11077)*
The Villa Florence Hotel, San Francisco *Also called Florence Villa Hotel (P-11096)*
The Woodbridge Golf Cntry CLB ....D....209 369-2371
800 E Woodbridge Rd Woodbridge (95258) *(P-15160)*
Theatre Department, Fresno *Also called California State Univ Long Bch (P-14843)*
Theatreworks Silicon Valley ....E....650 517-5870
350 Twin Dolphin Dr Redwood City (94065) *(P-14865)*
Theodore E Staahl MD Inc (PA) ....**E....209 577-5700**
1329 Spanos Ct Ste A1 Modesto (95355) *(P-15740)*
Theraex Rehab Services Inc (PA) ....**C....510 239-9614**
211 Apollo Apt 6 Hercules (94547) *(P-16961)*
Theraex Staffing Services, Hercules *Also called Theraex Rehab Services Inc (P-16961)*
Theranos Inc (PA) ....**D....650 838-9292**
7373 Gateway Blvd Newark (94560) *(P-7048)*
Therapeutic RES Faculty LLC ....C....209 472-2240
3120 W March Ln Stockton (95219) *(P-3751)*
Theraputic Solutions Prof Corp ....E....530 899-3150
3255 Esplanade Chico (95973) *(P-15900)*
Therapydia Inc ....E....802 772-7801
18 E Blithedale Ave # 21 Mill Valley (94941) *(P-15901)*
Therasense Inc ....E....510 749-5400
1360 S Loop Rd Alameda (94502) *(P-7049)*
Theravance Biopharma Us Inc ....C....650 808-6000
901 Gateway Blvd South San Francisco (94080) *(P-3993)*
Theravnce Bphrma Antbotics Inc ....E....877 275-6930
901 Gateway Blvd South San Francisco (94080) *(P-3994)*
Therm-X of California Inc (HQ) ....**C....510 441-7566**
3200 Investment Blvd Hayward (94545) *(P-6926)*
Therma Holdings LLC (PA) ....**A....408 347-3400**
1601 Las Plumas Ave San Jose (95133) *(P-1622)*
Therma LLC ....A....408 347-3400
1601 Las Plumas Ave San Jose (95133) *(P-4825)*
Thermal Conductive Bonding Inc (PA) ....**E....408 920-0255**
19 Great Oaks Blvd Ste 20 San Jose (95119) *(P-6333)*
Thermal Mechanical ....D....408 988-8744
425 Aldo Ave Santa Clara (95054) *(P-1381)*
Thermcraft Inc ....F....916 363-9411
3762 Bradview Dr Sacramento (95827) *(P-3703)*
Thermionics Laboratory Inc ....D....510 786-0680
3118 Depot Rd Hayward (94545) *(P-4922)*
Thermionics Laboratory Inc ....E....530 272-3436
10230 Twin Pines Pl Grass Valley (95949) *(P-5449)*
Thermo Finnigan LLC (HQ) ....**B....408 965-6000**
355 River Oaks Pkwy San Jose (95134) *(P-6857)*
Thermo Fisher Scientific, Santa Clara *Also called Fiberlite Centrifuge LLC (P-6829)*
Thermo Fisher Scientific ....B....408 894-9835
355 River Oaks Pkwy San Jose (95134) *(P-6858)*
Thermo Fisher Scientific Inc ....E....408 731-5056
3380 Central Expy Santa Clara (95051) *(P-6859)*
Thermo Kevex X-Ray Inc ....D....831 438-5940
320 El Pueblo Rd Scotts Valley (95066) *(P-5904)*
Thermo King Fresno Inc (PA) ....**E....559 496-3500**
3247 E Annadale Ave Fresno (93725) *(P-9017)*
Thermofinnegan, San Jose *Also called Thermo Fisher Scientific (P-6858)*
Thermogenesis Holdings Inc (PA) ....**E....916 858-5100**
2711 Citrus Rd Rancho Cordova (95742) *(P-7050)*
Thermonics, Sunnyvale *Also called Test Enterprises Inc (P-6734)*
Thermoquest Corporation ....A....408 965-6000
355 River Oaks Pkwy San Jose (95134) *(P-6860)*
Thetos Advisors LLC ....E....415 917-0485
268 Bush St San Francisco (94104) *(P-10063)*
Thiele Technologies Inc ....E....559 638-8484
1949 E Manning Ave Reedley (93654) *(P-5206)*
Think Outside Box Inc ....E....916 726-2339
105 Vernon St Roseville (95678) *(P-11732)*
Think Social Publishing Inc ....E....408 557-8595
404 Saratoga Ave Ste 200 Santa Clara (95050) *(P-3605)*
Think Surgical Inc ....C....510 249-2300
47201 Lakeview Blvd Fremont (94538) *(P-7082)*
Thinkwave Inc ....F....707 824-6200
103 Morris St Ste F Sebastopol (95472) *(P-6507)*
Third Culture Food Group Inc ....E....650 479-4585
2701 8th St Berkeley (94710) *(P-2408)*
Third Pillar Systems Inc (PA) ....**E....650 346-3108**
703 Market St Ste 700 San Francisco (94103) *(P-12861)*
Thirsty Bear Brewing Co LLC ....E....415 974-0905
661 Howard St San Francisco (94105) *(P-2497)*
Thismoment Inc ....C....415 200-4730
690 Market St Unit 1101 San Francisco (94104) *(P-12862)*
Thistle Health Inc ....B....917 587-2341
1000 Van Ness Ave Ste 100 San Francisco (94109) *(P-2946)*
Thoits Insurance Service Inc ....D....408 792-5400
160 W Santa Clara St # 1200 San Jose (95113) *(P-10359)*
Thoits Love Herschberger & McL (PA) ....**E....650 330-7321**
285 Hamilton Ave Ste 300 Palo Alto (94301) *(P-17380)*
Thoits Love Herschberger & McL ....E....650 327-4200
400 Main St Ste 250 Los Altos (94022) *(P-17381)*
Thomas Dehlinger ....E....707 823-2378
4101 Ginehill Rd Sebastopol (95472) *(P-2740)*
Thomas Doll & Company, Walnut Creek *Also called Thomas Wirig Doll & Co Cpas (P-19001)*
Thomas Fogarty Winery LLC (PA) ....**E....650 851-6777**
3130 Alpine Rd Portola Valley (94028) *(P-2741)*
Thomas H Murphy Od ....E....916 929-1169
1689 Arden Way Ste 1091 Sacramento (95815) *(P-15874)*
Thomas Kinkade Company, The, Morgan Hill *Also called Pacific Metro LLC (P-18278)*
Thomas Leonardini ....F....707 963-9454
1563 Saint Helena Hwy S Saint Helena (94574) *(P-2742)*
Thomas Lundberg ....E....415 695-0110
2620 3rd St San Francisco (94107) *(P-3295)*
Thomas Manufacturing Co LLC ....F....530 893-8940
1308 W 8th Ave Chico (95926) *(P-14724)*
Thomas Mark & Company Inc (PA) ....**E....408 453-5373**
2833 Junction Ave Ste 110 San Jose (95134) *(P-18837)*
Thomas Products, Madera *Also called Nutra-Blend LLC (P-2350)*
Thomas Weisel Partners LLC (HQ) ....**B....415 364-2500**
1 Montgomery St Ste 3700 San Francisco (94104) *(P-10017)*
Thomas Welding & Machine Inc ....E....530 893-8940
1308 W 8th Ave Chico (95926) *(P-14725)*
Thomas West Inc (PA) ....**E....408 481-3850**
470 Mercury Dr Sunnyvale (94085) *(P-3030)*
Thomas Wirig Doll & Co Cpas ....D....925 939-2500
165 Lennon Ln Ste 200 Walnut Creek (94598) *(P-19001)*
Thomas Wsel Partners Group Inc (HQ) ....**D....415 364-2500**
1 Montgomery St Fl 36 San Francisco (94104) *(P-10018)*
Thomas-Swan Sign Company Inc ....E....415 621-1511
2717 Goodrick Ave Richmond (94801) *(P-7257)*
Thomason Tractor Co California ....E....559 659-2039
985 12th St Firebaugh (93622) *(P-9044)*
Thomes Creek Rock Co Inc ....E....530 824-0191
6069 99w Corning (96021) *(P-599)*
Thompson & Rich Crane Service ....E....209 465-3161
2373 E Mariposa Rd Stockton (95205) *(P-14434)*
Thompson Bldg Mtls Sacramento, Sacramento *Also called Silverado Building Mtls Inc (P-8608)*
Thompson Brooks Inc ....E....415 581-2600
151 Vermont St Ste 9 San Francisco (94103) *(P-718)*
Thompson Builders Corporation ....C....415 456-8972
5400 Hanna Ranch Rd Novato (94945) *(P-774)*
Thompsons Auto & Trck Ctr Inc (PA) ....**E....530 295-5700**
140 Forni Rd Placerville (95667) *(P-14596)*
Thomsen Farms Inc ....E....209 835-5442
2365 W Durham Ferry Rd Tracy (95304) *(P-22)*
Thomson and Thomson Fence Co, Oakland *Also called United Fence Contractors Inc (P-2081)*
Thoratec LLC (HQ) ....**C....925 847-8600**
6035 Stoneridge Dr Pleasanton (94588) *(P-7125)*
Thorpe Design Inc ....D....925 634-0787
410 Beatrice St Ct Ste A Brentwood (94513) *(P-1382)*
Thorsens Plumbing & AC, Turlock *Also called Thorsens-Norquist Inc (P-1842)*
Thorsens-Norquist Inc ....D....209 524-5296
2310 N Walnut Rd Turlock (95382) *(P-1842)*
Thorx Laboratories Inc ....F....510 240-6000
30831 Huntwood Ave Hayward (94544) *(P-3995)*
Thought Stream LLC ....E....650 567-4550
303 Twin Dolphin Dr Fl 6 Redwood City (94065) *(P-12863)*
Thoughtspot Inc (PA) ....**B....800 508-7008**
1900 Camden Ave Ste 101 San Jose (95124) *(P-13491)*
Thousandeyes LLC (HQ) ....**D....415 513-4526**
201 Mission St Ste 1700 San Francisco (94105) *(P-13492)*
Thousandeyes, Inc., San Francisco *Also called Thousandeyes LLC (P-13492)*
Thousandshores Inc ....F....510 477-0249
37707 Cherry St Newark (94560) *(P-5277)*
Threatmetrix Inc ....C....408 200-5700
160 W Santa Clara St # 1 San Jose (95113) *(P-12864)*
Three D Electric, Benicia *Also called Western Sun Enterprises Inc (P-1636)*
Three Marketeers Advertising, San Jose *Also called Three Mrkters Cmmnctons Group (P-11790)*
Three Mrkters Cmmnctons Group ....E....408 293-3233
6399 San Ignacio Ave San Jose (95119) *(P-11790)*
Three Sticks Wines LLC ....E....707 996-3328
21692 8th St E Ste 280 Sonoma (95476) *(P-2743)*
Three Twins Organic Ice Cream, San Francisco *Also called Three Twins Organic Inc (P-2184)*
Three Twins Organic Inc (PA) ....**E....707 763-8946**
600 California St Fl 6 San Francisco (94108) *(P-2184)*
Three Way Logistics Inc (PA) ....**D....408 748-3929**
42505 Christy St Fremont (94538) *(P-7854)*
Thresher Cmmnctons Prdctvity I ....D....408 780-3066
234 E Caribbean Dr Sunnyvale (94089) *(P-14796)*

Threshold Enterprises Ltd (PA).....B.....**831 438-6851**
23 Janis Way Scotts Valley (95066) ***(P-3822)***
Thriving Seniors LLC.....D.....707 317-1740
479 Mason St Ste 109 Vacaville (95688) ***(P-16277)***
Throughput Inc.....F.....215 606-8552
2100 Geng Rd Palo Alto (94303) ***(P-5782)***
Ths, Wilton *Also called Triple H Solutions Inc* ***(P-7657)***
Thunder Mountain Entps Inc (PA).....D.....**916 381-3400**
9335 Elder Creek Rd Sacramento (95829) ***(P-2075)***
Thunder Valley Casino, Lincoln *Also called United Auburn Indian Community* ***(P-11550)***
Thunderbolt Sales Inc.....F.....209 869-4561
3400 Patterson Rd Riverbank (95367) ***(P-3261)***
Thundrbird Ldge Frmont A Cal L.....E.....510 792-4300
5400 Mowry Ave Fremont (94538) ***(P-11532)***
Thurgood Mrshall Erly Head Sta, Oakland *Also called Spanish Spking Unity Cncil Alm* ***(P-18251)***
Thycoticcentrify, Redwood City *Also called Centrify Corporation* ***(P-12332)***
Thycoticcentrify Holdings Inc.....A.....669 444-5200
201 Rdwood Shres Pkwy St3 Redwood City (94065) ***(P-10742)***
Thyssenkrupp Indus Svcs NA Inc.....D.....209 395-9111
201 Discovery Dr Livermore (94551) ***(P-8831)***
Tibco Software Federal Inc.....E.....703 208-3900
3301 Hillview Ave Palo Alto (94304) ***(P-13493)***
Tibco Software Inc (HQ).....B.....**650 846-1000**
3307 Hillview Ave Palo Alto (94304) ***(P-12865)***
Tibit Communications Inc.....E.....707 664-5906
1465 N Mcdowell Blvd # 150 Petaluma (94954) ***(P-8086)***
Tiburcio Vasquez Hlth Ctr Inc (PA).....E.....**510 471-5880**
22211 Foothill Blvd Hayward (94541) ***(P-15741)***
Tiburon Hotel LLC.....E.....415 435-5996
1651 Tiburon Blvd Belvedere Tiburon (94920) ***(P-11533)***
Tiburon Lodge Ltd.....D.....415 435-3133
1651 Tiburon Blvd Belvedere Tiburon (94920) ***(P-11534)***
Tiburon Peninsula Club.....E.....415 789-7900
1600 Mar West St Belvedere Tiburon (94920) ***(P-15161)***
Ticketweb LLC.....E.....415 901-0210
685 Market St Ste 200 San Francisco (94105) ***(P-15250)***
Tico Construction Company Inc (PA).....E.....**408 487-0700**
1585 Terminal Ave San Jose (95112) ***(P-974)***
Ticomi Production Inc.....E.....925 399-5117
6350 Stoneridge Mall Rd Pleasanton (94588) ***(P-14797)***
Tides Inc (PA).....D.....**415 561-6400**
1012 Torney Ave San Francisco (94129) ***(P-18253)***
Tides Center.....B.....415 359-9401
124 Turk St San Francisco (94102) ***(P-11535)***
Tides Center (PA).....E.....**415 561-6400**
The Prsdio 1014 Trney Ave The Presidio San Francisco (94129) ***(P-18254)***
Tides Shared Spaces, San Francisco *Also called Tides Inc* ***(P-18253)***
Tiedemann Investment Group LLC.....E.....415 762-2541
101 California St San Francisco (94111) ***(P-10064)***
Tiedemann Wealth Management, San Francisco *Also called Tiedemann Investment Group LLC* ***(P-10064)***
Tiffany Motor Company.....E.....831 637-4461
300 Gateway Dr Hollister (95023) ***(P-14597)***
Tiger Analytics Inc (PA).....D.....**408 508-4430**
2350 Mission College Blvd # 495 Santa Clara (95054) ***(P-19190)***
Tiger Lines LLC (HQ).....D.....**209 334-4100**
927 Black Diamond Way Lodi (95240) ***(P-7601)***
Tiger-Sul Products LLC.....F.....209 451-2725
61 Stork Rd Stockton (95203) ***(P-3797)***
Tigergraph Inc (PA).....E.....**650 206-8888**
3 Twin Dolphin Dr Ste 160 Redwood City (94065) ***(P-13764)***
Tightdb Inc.....D.....415 766-2020
100 Forest Ave Palo Alto (94301) ***(P-12866)***
Tigo Energy Inc (PA).....E.....**408 402-0802**
655 Campbell Tech Pkwy # 150 Campbell (95008) ***(P-19136)***
Tile Inc.....C.....650 274-0676
1900 S Norfolk St Ste 310 San Mateo (94403) ***(P-8964)***
Tile West Inc (PA).....E.....**415 382-7550**
11 Hamilton Dr Novato (94949) ***(P-1725)***
Tilley Manufacturing Co Inc (PA).....D.....**650 365-3598**
2734 Spring St Redwood City (94063) ***(P-4207)***
Tilton Pacific Cnstr Inc.....E.....408 551-0492
940 Saratoga Ave Ste 105 San Jose (95129) ***(P-19409)***
Tim Lewis Communities.....E.....916 783-2300
3500 Douglas Blvd Ste 270 Roseville (95661) ***(P-719)***
Tim Mello Construction.....E.....530 205-8588
464 Lamarque Ct Grass Valley (95945) ***(P-720)***
Timber Cove Inn.....E.....707 847-3231
21780 N Coast Hwy 1 Jenner (95450) ***(P-11536)***
Timber Creek Golf Course, Roseville *Also called Sun City Rsvlle Cmnty Assn Inc* ***(P-15032)***
Timber Products Co Ltd Partnr.....F.....530 842-2310
130 N Phillipe Ln Yreka (96097) ***(P-3196)***
Timber Ridge At Eureka, Eureka *Also called Western Living Concepts Inc* ***(P-18211)***
Timber Works, Mount Shasta *Also called Shasta Services Inc* ***(P-960)***
Timberlake Cabinet, Rancho Cordova *Also called American Woodmark Corporation* ***(P-3166)***
Timberlake Corporation.....D.....916 423-2198
8322 Ferguson Ave Sacramento (95828) ***(P-12015)***
Timberlake Medical Gas Supply, Sacramento *Also called Timberlake Corporation* ***(P-12015)***
Timberlake-Forrest Inc (PA).....E.....**415 647-3117**
1133 S Van Ness Ave San Francisco (94110) ***(P-16278)***
Timberline Wall Systems.....E.....530 613-8070
5276 Cold Springs Dr Foresthill (95631) ***(P-721)***
Timbuk2 Designs Inc.....E.....800 865-2513
2031 Cessna Dr Vacaville (95688) ***(P-3033)***
Timbuk2 Designs Inc (PA).....C.....**415 252-4300**
400 Alabama St 201 San Francisco (94110) ***(P-3034)***
Time Warner Cable Entps LLC.....E.....408 747-7330
360 W Caribbean Dr Sunnyvale (94089) ***(P-8067)***
Timec Acquisitions Inc (HQ).....A.....**707 642-2222**
155 Corporate Pl Vallejo (94590) ***(P-1182)***
Timec Companies Inc (HQ).....B.....**707 642-2222**
155 Corporate Pl Vallejo (94590) ***(P-1183)***
Times Herald, Hayward *Also called Alameda Newspapers Inc* ***(P-3411)***
Times-Standard, Eureka *Also called Humboldt Newspaper Inc* ***(P-3447)***
Timmerman Starlite Trckg Inc.....D.....209 538-1706
3955 Starlite Dr Ceres (95307) ***(P-7602)***
Tini Aerospace Inc.....E.....415 524-2124
2505 Kerner Blvd San Rafael (94901) ***(P-6687)***
Tink Inc.....E.....530 895-0897
2361 Durham Dayton Hwy Durham (95938) ***(P-5041)***
Tintri Inc.....B.....650 810-8200
303 Ravendale Dr Mountain View (94043) ***(P-13810)***
Tinyco Inc.....C.....415 644-8101
225 Bush St Ste 1900 San Francisco (94104) ***(P-13494)***
Tipping Mar & Associates.....E.....510 549-1906
1906 Shattuck Ave Berkeley (94704) ***(P-18838)***
Tipping Point Community.....E.....415 348-1240
220 Montgomery St Ste 850 San Francisco (94104) ***(P-18602)***
Tire Store 40 Inc.....E.....530 662-9106
220 W Main St Woodland (95695) ***(P-14598)***
Titan Metal Products, Sacramento *Also called Tmp LLC* ***(P-4710)***
Titan Mfg & Distrg Inc.....D.....559 475-0882
480 E North Ave Ste 101 Fresno (93706) ***(P-9163)***
Titan Newman Inc.....D.....209 862-2977
1649 L St Newman (95360) ***(P-9138)***
Titan Pharmaceuticals Inc (PA).....E.....**650 244-4990**
400 Oyster Point Blvd # 505 South San Francisco (94080) ***(P-3996)***
Titan Photonics Inc.....E.....510 687-0488
1241 Quarry Ln Ste 140 Pleasanton (94566) ***(P-5813)***
Titus Industrial Supply, Concord *Also called Titus Mint Instlltion Svcs Inc* ***(P-8367)***
Titus Mint Instlltion Svcs Inc.....E.....909 357-3156
1430 Willow Pass Rd # 25 Concord (94520) ***(P-8367)***
Tivo Corporation (HQ).....A.....**408 519-9100**
2160 Gold St San Jose (95002) ***(P-10814)***
Tizeti Inc.....E.....281 377-6715
1437 Chilco St Menlo Park (94025) ***(P-8000)***
Tizona Therapeutics Inc.....E.....650 383-0800
4000 Shoreline Ct Ste 200 South San Francisco (94080) ***(P-19137)***
Tjd LLC.....C.....209 357-3420
1685 Shaffer Rd Atwater (95301) ***(P-16279)***
Tk Classics LLC.....E.....916 209-5500
3771 Channel Dr Ste 100 West Sacramento (95691) ***(P-3296)***
Tk Elevator Corporation.....D.....510 476-1900
14400 Catalina St San Leandro (94577) ***(P-9097)***
Tk Elevator Corporation.....D.....415 544-8150
520 Townsend St Fl 1 San Francisco (94103) ***(P-9098)***
Tk Elevator Corporation.....E.....510 476-1900
30984 Santana St Hayward (94544) ***(P-14778)***
Tk Elevator Corporation.....E.....916 376-8700
940 Riverside Pkwy Ste 20 West Sacramento (95605) ***(P-1994)***
Tk Elevator Corporation.....E.....408 392-0910
2140 Zanker Rd San Jose (95131) ***(P-14779)***
Tk Elevator Corporation.....D.....559 271-1238
3711 W Swift Ave Fresno (93722) ***(P-9099)***
Tks Wireless Inc.....C.....510 227-6440
3320 Foothill Blvd Oakland (94601) ***(P-7916)***
TLC Foods LLC.....E.....415 205-7111
4123 24th St San Francisco (94114) ***(P-816)***
TLC Insurance Administrators, Fremont *Also called Lipman Company Inc* ***(P-10309)***
TLC Machining Incorporated.....E.....408 321-9002
2571 Chant Ct San Jose (95122) ***(P-5101)***
TLC of Bay Area Inc.....D.....408 988-7667
991 Clyde Ave Santa Clara (95054) ***(P-16143)***
Tlcs Inc.....C.....916 441-0123
650 Howe Ave Ste 400-A Sacramento (95825) ***(P-17769)***
Tlg, Newark *Also called Lancashire Group Incorporated* ***(P-19554)***
Tli Enterprises Inc (PA).....E.....**510 538-3304**
3118 Depot Rd Hayward (94545) ***(P-6698)***
Tm Financial Forensics LLC (PA).....E.....**415 692-6350**
3595 Mt Diablo Blvd 250 Lafayette (94549) ***(P-19875)***
Tm Sleeves LLC.....D.....415 374-8210
475 14th St Ste 200 Oakland (94612) ***(P-11791)***
TMC Financing.....D.....415 989-8855
1720 Broadway Fl 3 Oakland (94612) ***(P-14435)***
TMI, San Jose *Also called Traffic Management Inc* ***(P-14438)***
Tmk Manufacturing.....D.....408 732-3200
2110 Oakland Rd San Jose (95131) ***(P-5085)***
Tmp LLC.....E.....916 920-2555
3011 Academy Way Sacramento (95815) ***(P-4710)***
Tmr Executive Interiors Inc.....E.....559 346-0631
1287 W Nielsen Ave Fresno (93706) ***(P-3157)***
Tmr Wine Company LLC.....E.....707 944-8100
1677 Sage Canyon Rd Saint Helena (94574) ***(P-2744)***
Tmt Enterprises Inc.....E.....408 432-9040
1996 Oakland Rd San Jose (95131) ***(P-7603)***
TNT Industrial Contractors Inc (PA).....E.....**916 395-8400**
3800 Happy Ln Sacramento (95827) ***(P-5042)***
Tobar Industries Inc.....D.....408 494-3530
912 Olinder Ct San Jose (95122) ***(P-5719)***
Todays Hotel Corporation.....E.....415 447-3005
835 Airport Blvd Ste 288 Burlingame (94010) ***(P-11537)***
Todays Hotel Corporation (PA).....C.....**415 441-4000**
1500 Van Ness Ave San Francisco (94109) ***(P-11538)***
Todd Dipietro Salon (PA).....E.....**415 397-0177**
520 Washington St San Francisco (94111) ***(P-11696)***

Tofu Shop Specialty Foods Inc .... F 707 822-7401
65 Frank Martin Ct Arcata (95521) *(P-2947)*
Together Labs Inc .... C 650 231-4688
1001 Marshall St Redwood City (94063) *(P-8001)*
Togo's and Baskin, Folsom *Also called Healthy Living Enterprise Inc (P-14295)*
Togo's Eatery, Campbell *Also called Mtc Resturant Group Inc (P-19582)*
Tok America, Milpitas *Also called Tokyo Ohka Kogyo America Inc (P-3798)*
Tokyo Ohka Kogyo America Inc .... E 408 956-9901
190 Topaz St Milpitas (95035) *(P-3798)*
Tollhouse Hotel, Los Gatos *Also called Trevi Partners A Calif LP (P-11540)*
Tom Corea Construction Inc .... E 559 292-9224
2696 Nfordham Ave Fresno (93727) *(P-1913)*
Tom Duffy Co .... D 800 479-5671
5200 Watt Ct Ste B Fairfield (94534) *(P-8521)*
Tom Lopes Distributing Inc (PA) .... **E 408 292-1041**
1790 S 10th St San Jose (95112) *(P-9540)*
Tom Sawyer Software Corp (PA) .... **E 510 208-4370**
1997 El Dorado Ave Berkeley (94707) *(P-12867)*
Toma Tek, Firebaugh *Also called Neil Jones Food Company (P-2230)*
Tomas Jewelry, Arcata *Also called Toucan Inc (P-9185)*
Tomato Press, Westley *Also called Just Tomatoes Inc (P-291)*
Tomotherapy Inc .... E 408 716-4600
1310 Chesapeake Ter Sunnyvale (94089) *(P-17081)*
Tomra Sorting Inc (HQ) .... **C 720 870-2240**
875 Embarcadero Dr West Sacramento (95605) *(P-8368)*
Tonal Systems Inc .... D 855 698-6625
617 Bryant St San Francisco (94107) *(P-15251)*
Tonicai Inc .... E 415 340-0330
548 Market St San Francisco (94104) *(P-12868)*
Tonnellerie Francaise French C .... F 707 942-9301
1401 Tubbs Ln Calistoga (94515) *(P-3242)*
Tonnellerie Radoux Usa Inc .... F 707 284-2888
480 Aviation Blvd Santa Rosa (95403) *(P-3243)*
Tony Lrssas Anmal Rscue Fndtio .... D 925 256-1273
2890 Mitchell Dr Walnut Creek (94598) *(P-339)*
Tony Marterie & Associates Inc .... E 415 331-7150
28 Liberty Ship Way Fl 2 Sausalito (94965) *(P-3003)*
Tonys Express Inc .... D 209 234-1000
4727 Fite Ct Ste C Stockton (95215) *(P-7604)*
Tonys Fine Foods (HQ) .... **B 916 374-4000**
3575 Reed Ave West Sacramento (95605) *(P-9342)*
Too Good Gourmet Inc (PA) .... **D 510 317-8150**
2380 Grant Ave San Lorenzo (94580) *(P-9495)*
Tool Makers International Inc .... E 408 980-8888
3390 Woodward Ave Santa Clara (95054) *(P-5086)*
Toolwire Inc .... D 925 227-8500
6754 Bernal Ave Ste 740 Pleasanton (94566) *(P-12869)*
Toolworks Inc .... E 510 649-1322
3075 Adeline St Ste 230 Berkeley (94703) *(P-17770)*
Toolworks Inc (PA) .... **B 415 733-0990**
25 Kearny St Ste 400 San Francisco (94108) *(P-17842)*
Top Dawg Modular Service, Fremont *Also called Lftm Inc (P-8500)*
Top Shelf Manufacturing LLC .... F 209 834-8185
1851 Paradise Rd Ste A Tracy (95304) *(P-7051)*
Topbuild Services Group Corp .... A 408 882-0411
1341 Old Oakland Rd San Jose (95112) *(P-2076)*
Topcon Med Laser Systems Inc .... E 888 760-8657
606 Enterprise Ct Livermore (94550) *(P-7126)*
Topcon Positioning Systems Inc (HQ) .... **C 925 245-8300**
7400 National Dr Livermore (94550) *(P-6927)*
Topdot Solar LLC .... E 800 731-5104
30930 Huntwood Ave Hayward (94544) *(P-1383)*
Topdown Consulting Inc .... D 888 644-8445
530 Divisadero St Ste 310 San Francisco (94117) *(P-19651)*
Topgolf Media LLC (HQ) .... **D 214 377-0615**
100 California St Ste 650 San Francisco (94111) *(P-15252)*
Topguest Inc .... E 646 415-9402
601 Montgomery St Fl 17 San Francisco (94111) *(P-13495)*
Topology Eyewear, San Francisco *Also called Bespoke Inc (P-7137)*
Topolos At Rssian River Vinyrd .... E 707 887-1575
5700 Gravenstein Hwy N Forestville (95436) *(P-77)*
TOPS, Orinda *Also called Orinda Pre School (P-17987)*
Toptal LLC .... B 888 604-3188
548 Market St Ste 36879 San Francisco (94104) *(P-13998)*
Torani Syrups & Flavors, San Leandro *Also called R Torre & Company Inc (P-2823)*
Toray Advnced Cmpsites ADS LLC .... E 707 359-3400
2450 Cordelia Rd Fairfield (94534) *(P-3812)*
Torn Ranch Inc (PA) .... **D 415 506-3000**
2198 S Mcdowell Blvd Ext Petaluma (94954) *(P-2434)*
Toro Engineering Inc .... E 916 238-4535
651 M St Rio Linda (95673) *(P-1138)*
Torr Industries Inc .... E 530 247-6909
4564 Caterpillar Rd Redding (96003) *(P-12870)*
Torres Community Shelter, Chico *Also called True North Housing Aliance Inc (P-17772)*
Torres Fence Co Inc .... E 559 237-4141
2357 S Orange Ave Fresno (93725) *(P-2077)*
Toscalito Enterprises Inc (PA) .... **E 415 456-2324**
668 Irwin St San Rafael (94901) *(P-14599)*
Toscalito Tire & Automotive, San Rafael *Also called Toscalito Enterprises Inc (P-14599)*
Toshiba America Inc .... C 212 596-0600
280 Utah Ave South San Francisco (94080) *(P-7127)*
Tosoh Bioscience Inc .... D 650 615-4970
6000 Shoreline Ct Ste 101 South San Francisco (94080) *(P-19138)*
Tosoh USA, South San Francisco *Also called Tosoh Bioscience Inc (P-19138)*
Total Airport Services LLC .... D 650 589-8560
900 N Access Rd San Francisco (94128) *(P-7788)*
Total Airport Services LLC .... D 650 358-0144
3537 Branson Dr San Mateo (94403) *(P-7789)*
Total Body Fitness .... E 916 202-3006
5209 Blaze Ct Rocklin (95677) *(P-15253)*
Total Concept Enterprises Inc .... F 559 485-8413
3745 E Jensen Ave Fresno (93725) *(P-7212)*
Total Monitoring Services Inc .... E 916 480-4828
2440 Glendale Ln Sacramento (95825) *(P-14150)*
Total Quality Maintenance Inc .... C 650 846-4700
895 Commercial St Palo Alto (94303) *(P-12005)*
Total Tire Recycling, Sacramento *Also called AAA Signs Inc (P-14537)*
Total Waste Systems, Santa Rosa *Also called Novato Disposal Service Inc (P-8347)*
Total-Western Inc .... F 707 747-5506
3985 Teal Ct Benicia (94510) *(P-574)*
Totalrewards Software Inc .... F 916 632-1000
2208 Plaza Dr Ste 100 Rocklin (95765) *(P-13496)*
Toucan Inc (PA) .... **D 707 822-6662**
824 L St Ste 6 Arcata (95521) *(P-9185)*
Toucaned Inc .... E 831 464-0508
1716 Brommer St Santa Cruz (95062) *(P-3606)*
Touchmark, Hayward *Also called Delphon Industries LLC (P-4274)*
Touchofmodern Inc .... C 888 868-1232
30063 Ahern Ave Union City (94587) *(P-14436)*
Touchstone Climbing Inc (PA) .... **D 415 550-0515**
2295 Harrison St San Francisco (94110) *(P-15254)*
Tournesol Siteworks LLC (PA) .... **D 800 542-2282**
2930 Faber St Union City (94587) *(P-2078)*
Tower Brew Co LLC .... F 916 606-3373
1210 66th St Sacramento (95819) *(P-2498)*
Tower Brewing, Sacramento *Also called Tower Brew Co LLC (P-2498)*
Tower Holdings Inc (HQ) .... **D 510 240-6000**
30831 Huntwood Ave Hayward (94544) *(P-3997)*
Tower Semiconductor Usa Inc .... F 408 770-1320
2570 N 1st St Ste 480 San Jose (95131) *(P-6334)*
Towill Inc (HQ) .... **E 925 682-6976**
2300 Clayton Rd Ste 1200 Concord (94520) *(P-18928)*
Town & Country Roofing, Brentwood *Also called T&C Roofing Inc (P-1841)*
Town of Danville .... E 925 314-3400
420 Front St Danville (94526) *(P-15255)*
Town of Paradise .... E 530 872-6241
5595 Black Olive Dr Paradise (95969) *(P-17382)*
Towne Electric Company, San Leandro *Also called Randell C Towne (P-1574)*
Towne Ford Sales, Redwood City *Also called Towne Motor Company (P-14626)*
Towne Motor Company .... C 650 366-5744
1601 El Camino Real Redwood City (94063) *(P-14626)*
Townsend & Schmidt Masonry .... E 916 383-5354
8788 Elder Creek Rd Sacramento (95828) *(P-1654)*
Toyota Material Hdlg Nthrn Cal, Livermore *Also called Rjms Corporation (P-9128)*
Toyota of Berkeley, Berkeley *Also called Southwick Inc (P-14624)*
Toyota of Santa Cruz, Capitola *Also called Capitola Imports Inc (P-14658)*
Toyota-Sunnyvale Inc (PA) .... **D 408 245-6640**
898 W El Camino Real Sunnyvale (94087) *(P-14600)*
Tp-Link Research Inst USA Corp .... F 408 618-5478
245 Charcot Ave San Jose (95131) *(P-13679)*
TPC Stonebrea, Hayward *Also called Stonebrae LP (P-15156)*
Tpg Growth, San Francisco *Also called Tpg Partners III LP (P-551)*
Tpg Growth, San Francisco *Also called Tarrant Capital Ip LLC (P-10062)*
Tpg Partners III LP (HQ) .... **E 415 743-1500**
345 California St # 3300 San Francisco (94104) *(P-551)*
Tpmg Laboratory Stockton .... D 209 476-3646
7373 West Ln Stockton (95210) *(P-16810)*
Tps Aviation Inc (PA) .... **D 510 475-1010**
1515 Crocker Ave Hayward (94544) *(P-8965)*
Tr Manufacturing LLC (HQ) .... **C 510 657-3850**
33210 Central Ave Union City (94587) *(P-6479)*
Trace Genomics Inc .... E 650 332-6661
303 Twin Dolphin Dr # 600 Redwood City (94065) *(P-19139)*
Traceable Inc .... E 855 346-7233
548 Market St Ste 83903 San Francisco (94104) *(P-12871)*
Tracpatch Health Inc .... D 916 355-7123
1115 Windfield Way # 100 El Dorado Hills (95762) *(P-8793)*
Traction Corporation .... E 415 962-5800
1349 Larkin St San Francisco (94109) *(P-11792)*
Tracy Auto LP .... D 209 834-1111
2895 Naglee Rd Tracy (95304) *(P-14490)*
Tracy Dlta Solid Waste Mgt Inc .... D 209 835-0601
30703 S Macarthur Dr Tracy (95377) *(P-8369)*
Tracy Ford .... E 209 879-4700
3500 Auto Plaza Way Tracy (95304) *(P-14601)*
Tracy Grading & Paving Inc .... E 209 839-6590
11 W 12th St Tracy (95376) *(P-1078)*
Tracy Medical Offices, Tracy *Also called Kaiser Foundation Hospitals (P-15456)*
Tracy Mtl Rcvery Slid Wste Trn .... E 209 832-2355
30703 S Macarthur Dr Tracy (95377) *(P-8370)*
Tracy Occupational Medical Ctr, Tracy *Also called Patel Plliam Hbli A Prof Med C (P-15585)*
Tracy Press Inc .... E 209 835-3030
145 W 10th St Tracy (95376) *(P-3486)*
Tracy Sutter Community Hosp .... B 209 835-1500
1420 N Tracy Blvd Tracy (95376) *(P-16688)*
Tracy Toyota, Tracy *Also called Tracy Auto LP (P-14490)*
Tracy Unified School District .... E 209 830-6054
2525 N Tracy Blvd Tracy (95376) *(P-18039)*
Trade Litho Inc .... F 510 965-6501
720 Harbour Way S Ste A Richmond (94804) *(P-3704)*
Trade Lithography, Richmond *Also called Trade Litho Inc (P-3704)*
Trade Shift APS, San Francisco *Also called Tradeshift Inc (P-13680)*
Tradebeam Inc .... D 650 653-4800
303 Twin Dolphin Dr # 600 Redwood City (94065) *(P-13999)*
Trader Vics .... D 510 653-3400
9 Anchor Dr Emeryville (94608) *(P-9147)*

ALPHABETIC

Tradeshift Holdings Inc (PA)..........D......**800 381-3585**
221 Main St Ste 250 San Francisco (94105) ***(P-10743)***
Tradeshift Inc (HQ)..........C......**800 381-3585**
612 Howard St Ste 100 San Francisco (94105) ***(P-13680)***
Tradewinds Lodge (PA)..........D......**707 964-4761**
400 S Main St Fort Bragg (95437) ***(P-11539)***
Tradin Organics USA LLC..........E......831 685-6565
100 Enterprise Way B10 Scotts Valley (95066) ***(P-2948)***
Traditional Medicinals Inc (PA)..........C......**707 823-8911**
4515 Ross Rd Sebastopol (95472) ***(P-2949)***
Traditional Medicinals Inc..........F......707 664-5801
1400 Valley House Dr # 120 Rohnert Park (94928) ***(P-2950)***
Traditions Golf LLC..........D......408 323-5200
23600 Mckean Rd San Jose (95141) ***(P-15034)***
Traffic Management Inc..........E......408 279-9900
1277 Old Bayshore Hwy San Jose (95112) ***(P-14437)***
Traffic Management Inc..........E......415 370-7916
8399 Edgewater Dr Oakland (94621) ***(P-19410)***
Traffic Management Inc..........E......916 394-2200
5806 Perrin Ave McClellan (95652) ***(P-19411)***
Traffic Management Inc..........E......877 763-5999
690 Quinn Ave San Jose (95112) ***(P-14438)***
Traffic Signal Maintenance, Fremont *Also called Econolite* ***(P-14258)***
Traform Inc..........E......650 387-5536
49016 Milmont Dr Fremont (94538) ***(P-12872)***
Traina Dried Fruit Inc..........C......209 892-5472
280 S 1st St Patterson (95363) ***(P-9496)***
Traina Dried Fruit Inc (PA)..........D......**209 892-5472**
337 Lemon Ave Patterson (95363) ***(P-9497)***
Traina Foods, Patterson *Also called Traina Dried Fruit Inc* ***(P-9496)***
Traina Foods, Patterson *Also called Traina Dried Fruit Inc* ***(P-9497)***
Training Toward Self Reliance..........E......916 442-8877
1007 7th St Fl 4 Sacramento (95814) ***(P-17771)***
Trainor Commercial Cnstr Inc (PA)..........E......**415 259-0200**
1925 Francisco Blvd E # 21 San Rafael (94901) ***(P-975)***
Trainor Fairbrook A Prof Corp..........E......916 929-7000
980 Fulton Ave Sacramento (95825) ***(P-17383)***
Trammell Crow Residential Co..........E......650 349-1224
1810 Gateway Dr Ste 100 San Mateo (94404) ***(P-10464)***
Tranpak Inc..........E......800 827-2474
1209 Victory Ln Madera (93637) ***(P-3230)***
Tranquility Incorporated..........C......925 825-4280
1050 San Miguel Rd Concord (94518) ***(P-16280)***
Tranquilmoney Inc..........D......800 979-6739
5823 Ruddy Duck Ct Stockton (95207) ***(P-8755)***
Trans Bay Steel Corporation (PA)..........E......**510 277-3756**
2801 Giant Rd Ste H San Pablo (94806) ***(P-4690)***
Trans Pacific Digital Inc..........F......415 362-1110
1629b Irving St San Francisco (94122) ***(P-11874)***
Trans Pacific Inc (PA)..........E......**408 445-4455**
1610 Blossom Hill Rd 7c San Jose (95124) ***(P-10673)***
Trans Valley Transport..........E......408 842-2188
450 E 9th St Gilroy (95020) ***(P-7605)***
Trans-India Products Inc..........E......707 544-0298
3330 Coffey Ln Ste A&B Santa Rosa (95403) ***(P-4097)***
Transamerica Cbo I Inc..........D......415 983-4000
600 Montgomery St Fl 16 San Francisco (94111) ***(P-10065)***
Transamerica Finance Corp (HQ)..........C......**415 983-4000**
600 Montgomery St Fl 16 San Francisco (94111) ***(P-10080)***
Transamerica Intl Holdings..........C......415 983-4000
600 Montgomery St Fl 16 San Francisco (94111) ***(P-10744)***
Transbay Fire Protection Inc (PA)..........E......**925 846-9484**
2182 Rheem Dr Pleasanton (94588) ***(P-1995)***
Transcense Inc (PA)..........E......**415 867-7230**
1864 Fell St San Francisco (94117) ***(P-12873)***
Transcontinental Nrthern CA 20..........C......510 580-7700
47540 Kato Rd Fremont (94538) ***(P-3752)***
Transcounty Title Co (PA)..........E......**209 383-4660**
635 W 19th St Merced (95340) ***(P-10210)***
Transdev Services Inc..........B......408 282-4706
2361 Airport Blvd San Jose (95110) ***(P-7407)***
Transfair USA..........C......510 663-5260
1901 Harrison St Ste 1700 Oakland (94612) ***(P-19239)***
Transforce Inc..........E......209 952-2573
965 E Yosemite Ave Ste 7 Manteca (95336) ***(P-12202)***
Transhumance Holding Co Inc..........C......707 693-2303
7390 Rio Dixon Rd Dixon (95620) ***(P-2105)***
Transhumance Holding Co Inc (PA)..........E......**530 758-3091**
2530 River Plaza Dr # 200 Sacramento (95833) ***(P-2106)***
Transiris Corporation..........D......650 303-3495
555 Airport Blvd Ste 325 Burlingame (94010) ***(P-19652)***
Transitamerica Services Inc..........E......408 961-4350
93 Cahill St San Jose (95110) ***(P-7364)***
Translarity Inc..........F......510 371-7900
46575 Fremont Blvd Fremont (94538) ***(P-6796)***
Translattice Inc (PA)..........E......**408 749-8478**
3398 Londonderry Dr Santa Clara (95050) ***(P-5278)***
Transpac, Vacaville *Also called Valyria LLC* ***(P-8523)***
Transpak Inc (PA)..........C......**408 254-0500**
520 Marburg Way San Jose (95133) ***(P-14439)***
Transportation, Lodi *Also called Lodi Unified School District* ***(P-7440)***
Transportation Department, Sacramento *Also called Elk Grove Unified School Dst* ***(P-7429)***
Transportation Service Dept, Davis *Also called University California Davis* ***(P-7792)***
Transportation Services, Davis *Also called University California Davis* ***(P-7443)***
Transsight LLC..........E......510 415-6301
7599 Balmoral Way San Ramon (94582) ***(P-19876)***
Transwstern Insur Admnistrator (PA)..........E......**559 499-0285**
955 N St Fresno (93721) ***(P-10360)***

Tranzeal Inc..........E......408 834-8711
2107 N 1st St Ste 500 San Jose (95131) ***(P-19653)***
Trashlogic LLC..........E......916 900-4008
5740 Windmill Way Ste 17 Carmichael (95608) ***(P-12006)***
Travelator Inc..........E......415 322-9265
2710 Gateway Oaks Dr # 150 Sacramento (95833) ***(P-14440)***
Travelbank, Sacramento *Also called Travelator Inc* ***(P-14440)***
Travelers Insurance, Walnut Creek *Also called Travelers Property Cslty Corp* ***(P-10361)***
Travelers Property Cslty Corp..........C......925 945-4000
401 Lennon Ln Walnut Creek (94598) ***(P-10361)***
Travelmasters Inc..........E......916 722-1648
8350 Auburn Blvd Ste 200 Citrus Heights (95610) ***(P-7808)***
Travelodge, Mill Valley *Also called Nana Enterprises* ***(P-11318)***
Travelodge By The Bay, San Francisco *Also called Esterle LLC* ***(P-11085)***
Travelzoo Inc..........D......650 316-6956
800 W El Camino Real Mountain View (94040) ***(P-11807)***
Travis Credit Union (PA)..........B......**707 449-4000**
1 Travis Way Vacaville (95687) ***(P-9824)***
Travis Flight Service Inc..........D......707 437-4900
2112 Adams Ave San Leandro (94577) ***(P-7790)***
Travis James Watts..........C......209 810-6159
646 Willowgreen Cir Galt (95632) ***(P-192)***
Tray Io Inc (PA)..........D......**415 418-3570**
25 Stillman St Ste 200 San Francisco (94107) ***(P-12874)***
Trayer Engineering Corporation..........D......415 285-7770
1569 Alvarado St San Leandro (94577) ***(P-5656)***
TRC Solutions..........C......916 962-7001
10680 White Rock Rd # 100 Rancho Cordova (95670) ***(P-19877)***
Treadwell & Rollo Inc (HQ)..........E......**415 955-9040**
555 Montgomery St # 1300 San Francisco (94111) ***(P-18839)***
Treaster Miles & Associates..........D......916 373-1800
1810 13th St Sacramento (95811) ***(P-2079)***
Treasure Data Inc (HQ)..........D......**866 899-5386**
800 W El Cmino Real Ste 1 Mountain View (94040) ***(P-12875)***
Treasury Wine Estates Americas (HQ)..........B......**707 259-4500**
555 Gateway Dr NAPA (94558) ***(P-2745)***
Treasury Wine Estates Americas..........D......707 963-7115
2000 Saint Helena Hwy N Saint Helena (94574) ***(P-2746)***
Treau Inc..........E......866 945-3514
375 Alabama St Ste 220 San Francisco (94110) ***(P-5435)***
Tree Doctorx, Fresno *Also called Providence Horticulture Inc* ***(P-521)***
Tree Movers, Fremont *Also called A To Z Tree Nursery Inc* ***(P-9621)***
Tree Nuts LLC..........E......209 669-6400
451 W F St Turlock (95380) ***(P-9357)***
Tree Sculpture Group..........D......510 562-4000
642 Mccormick St San Leandro (94577) ***(P-505)***
Tree Service, Folsom *Also called Mountain F Enterprises Inc* ***(P-3073)***
Tree Tech Services, Sacramento *Also called Tree Technology Inc* ***(P-523)***
Tree Technology Inc..........E......916 386-9416
8609 Weyand Ave Sacramento (95828) ***(P-523)***
Trees of Mystery..........E......707 482-2251
15500 Us Highway 101 N Klamath (95548) ***(P-15256)***
Trefethen Family Vineyards, NAPA *Also called Trefethen Vineyards Winery Inc* ***(P-2747)***
Trefethen Vineyards Winery Inc..........E......707 255-7700
1160 Oak Knoll Ave NAPA (94558) ***(P-2747)***
Tremont Group Incorporated..........F......530 662-5442
201 East St Woodland (95776) ***(P-9613)***
Trendsetter Solar Products Inc..........F......707 443-5652
818 Broadway Eureka (95501) ***(P-1384)***
Trent Construction Inc..........E......530 385-1778
8270 Truckee Ave Gerber (96035) ***(P-817)***
Tresco Paint Co..........E......510 887-7254
21595 Curtis St Hayward (94545) ***(P-4112)***
Tresl Inc (PA)..........E......**650 868-2862**
855 El Cmino Real Ste 125 Palo Alto (94301) ***(P-14000)***
Trestles Holdings LLC..........D......707 778-8686
450 Hayes Ln Petaluma (94952) ***(P-10745)***
Trevi Partners A Calif LP..........E......408 395-7070
140 S Santa Cruz Ave Los Gatos (95030) ***(P-11540)***
Trevi Partners A Calif LP (HQ)..........C......**925 828-7750**
6680 Regional St Dublin (94568) ***(P-11541)***
Trevi Partners A Calif LP..........E......650 347-2381
1250 Old Bayshore Hwy Burlingame (94010) ***(P-11542)***
Trevi Partners A Calif LP (PA)..........C......**925 225-4000**
5955 Coronado Ln Pleasanton (94588) ***(P-11543)***
Trevi Partners A Calif LP..........E......415 332-5700
160 Shoreline Hwy Mill Valley (94941) ***(P-11544)***
Trevi Systems Inc..........E......707 992-0567
1500 Valley House Dr # 130 Rohnert Park (94928) ***(P-19288)***
Trevis Berry Transportation..........D......408 842-8238
655 E Luchessa Ave Gilroy (95020) ***(P-7637)***
Tri Ced Community Recycling, Union City *Also called Tri-City Economic Dev Corp* ***(P-8371)***
Tri Commercial RE Svcs..........E......925 296-3300
1777 Oakland Blvd Ste 100 Walnut Creek (94596) ***(P-10674)***
Tri Commercial RE Svcs..........E......916 677-8000
2250 Douglas Blvd Ste 200 Roseville (95661) ***(P-10675)***
Tri Counties Bank (HQ)..........D......**530 898-0300**
63 Constitution Dr Chico (95973) ***(P-9763)***
Tri Counties Bank..........C......650 583-8450
975 El Camino Real South San Francisco (94080) ***(P-9764)***
Tri Delta Transit, Antioch *Also called Eastern Cntra Costa Trnst Auth* ***(P-7329)***
Tri Fab Associates Inc..........D......510 651-7628
48351 Lakeview Blvd Fremont (94538) ***(P-4826)***
Tri Pointe Homes Inc..........C......925 804-2220
2700 Camino Ramon Ste 130 San Ramon (94583) ***(P-775)***
Tri Tool Inc (HQ)..........C......**916 288-6100**
3041 Sunrise Blvd Rancho Cordova (95742) ***(P-9100)***
Tri Valley Haven..........E......925 449-1664
3663 Pacific Ave Livermore (94550) ***(P-18255)***

ALPHABETIC SECTION — True North

Company	Code	Phone
Tri Valley Home Health Care	D	209 957-0708
1231 W Robinhood Dr D5 Stockton (95207) *(P-16144)*		
Tri Valley Wholesale, Fremont *Also called Tri-Valley Supply Inc* *(P-8641)*		
Tri-C Manufacturing Inc	E	916 371-1700
517 Houston St West Sacramento (95691) *(P-5172)*		
Tri-City Economic Dev Corp	D	510 429-8030
33377 Western Ave Union City (94587) *(P-8371)*		
Tri-City Print & Mail, West Sacramento *Also called Premier Print & Mail Inc* *(P-3745)*		
Tri-Continent Scientific Inc	D	530 273-8888
12740 Earhart Ave Auburn (95602) *(P-6741)*		
Tri-Phase Inc	C	408 284-7700
6190 San Ignacio Ave San Jose (95119) *(P-5988)*		
Tri-Signal Integration Inc	D	916 933-3155
5007 Windplay Dr Ste 1 El Dorado Hills (95762) *(P-1623)*		
Tri-Signal Integration Inc	D	559 274-1299
4277 W Richert Ave # 105 Fresno (93722) *(P-1624)*		
Tri-State Enterprises Inc	E	650 210-0085
2133 Leghorn St Mountain View (94043) *(P-19412)*		
Tri-Valley Supply Inc (HQ)	D	510 494-9982
39300 Civic Center Dr # 300 Fremont (94538) *(P-8641)*		
Tri-Valley YMCA, Pleasanton *Also called Young MNS Chrstn Assn of E Bay* *(P-18504)*		
Triad Global Group, Acampo *Also called Global Wine Group* *(P-2595)*		
Triad Tool & Engineering Inc	E	408 436-8411
1750 Rogers Ave San Jose (95112) *(P-4327)*		
Triage Consulting Group LLC (PA)	B	415 512-9400
221 Main St Ste 1100 San Francisco (94105) *(P-19654)*		
Triangle Rock Product Inc	C	209 826-5066
22101 W Sunset Ave Los Banos (93635) *(P-8636)*		
Triangle Rock Products, Los Banos *Also called Triangle Rock Product Inc* *(P-8636)*		
Triangle T Ranch Inc	D	559 665-2964
4408 Hays Dr Chowchilla (93610) *(P-13)*		
Trianz LLC (HQ)	C	408 387-5800
2350 Mission College Blvd Santa Clara (95054) *(P-14001)*		
Trib3com Inc	D	415 562-5561
4 Embarcadero Ctr Ste 780 San Francisco (94111) *(P-13765)*		
Tribe Dynamics, San Francisco *Also called Trib3com Inc* *(P-13765)*		
Tribune, The, Oakland *Also called Oakland Tribune Inc* *(P-3469)*		
Trical Inc (PA)	E	831 637-0195
8100 Arroyo Cir Gilroy (95020) *(P-4145)*		
Trical Inc	E	831 637-0195
8770 Hwy 25 Hollister (95023) *(P-4146)*		
Tricentis USA Corp	B	650 383-8329
2570 W El Cmino Real Ste Mountain View (94040) *(P-13681)*		
Tricida Inc	D	415 429-7800
7000 Shoreline Ct Ste 201 South San Francisco (94080) *(P-3998)*		
Trick or Treat Stdios Hldngs L		831 713-9665
1005 17th Ave Santa Cruz (95062) *(P-7314)*		
Tricks Gymnastics Inc (PA)	E	916 791-4496
4070 Cavitt Stallman Rd Granite Bay (95746) *(P-15257)*		
Trico Bancshares	E	707 476-0981
2844 F St Eureka (95501) *(P-9765)*		
Trico Bancshares (PA)	D	530 898-0300
63 Constitution Dr Chico (95973) *(P-9751)*		
Trico Bancshares	E	530 221-8400
880 E Cypress Ave Redding (96002) *(P-9766)*		
Trico Bancshares	E	530 245-5930
1327 South St Redding (96001) *(P-9767)*		
Tricorp Group Inc (PA)	D	916 779-8010
2540 Warren Dr Ste A Rocklin (95677) *(P-976)*		
Tricorp Hearn Construction, Rocklin *Also called Tricorp Group Inc* *(P-976)*		
Tridecs Corporation	E	510 785-2620
3513 Arden Rd Hayward (94545) *(P-5628)*		
Triesten Technologies LLC (PA)	C	916 719-6150
320 Channing Way Apt 121 San Rafael (94903) *(P-12876)*		
Trifacta Inc (PA)	D	415 429-7570
575 Market St Ste 1100 San Francisco (94105) *(P-14002)*		
Triformix Inc	E	707 545-7645
487 Aviation Blvd Ste 100 Santa Rosa (95403) *(P-4328)*		
Trigild International Inc	D	530 223-1935
2731 Bechelli Ln Redding (96002) *(P-11545)*		
Trijicon Electro Optics, Auburn *Also called IRD Acquisitions LLC* *(P-7142)*		
Trilliant Networks Inc (PA)	D	650 204-5050
1100 Island Dr Ste 201 Redwood City (94065) *(P-14441)*		
Trillium Pump USA, Fresno *Also called Trillium Pumps Usa Inc* *(P-5180)*		
Trillium Pumps Usa Inc (HQ)		559 442-4000
2495 S Golden State Blvd Fresno (93706) *(P-5180)*		
Trilogy At Rio Vista	C	707 374-6871
1200 Clubhouse Dr Rio Vista (94571) *(P-722)*		
Trimac Trnsp Svcs Wstn Inc	E	707 745-5414
331 E Channel Rd Benicia (94510) *(P-7606)*		
Trimacs Maint Ldscp Cnstr Inc	E	510 569-9660
80 Hegenberger Loop Oakland (94621) *(P-506)*		
Trimark Associates Inc	D	916 357-5970
2365 Iron Point Rd # 100 Folsom (95630) *(P-19878)*		
Trimark Erf Inc	E	916 447-6600
415 Richards Blvd Sacramento (95811) *(P-8770)*		
Trimble Inc (PA)	A	408 481-8000
935 Stewart Dr Sunnyvale (94085) *(P-6928)*		
Trimble Military & Advnced Sys	D	408 481-8000
510 De Guigne Dr Sunnyvale (94085) *(P-6688)*		
Trimont Land Company (HQ)	B	530 562-1010
5001 Northstar Dr Truckee (96161) *(P-10676)*		
Trina Solar (us) Inc	E	800 696-7114
7100 Stevenson Blvd Fremont (94538) *(P-1385)*		
Trinchero Family Estates, Saint Helena *Also called Sutter Home Winery Inc* *(P-2734)*		
Trinet Communications Inc (PA)	F	925 294-1720
6567 Brisa St Livermore (94550) *(P-8966)*		
Trinet Group Inc (PA)	A	510 352-5000
1 Park Pl Ste 600 Dublin (94568) *(P-14442)*		
Trinet Usa Inc	D	510 352-5000
1 Park Pl Ste 600 Dublin (94568) *(P-12147)*		
Trinity Alps Resort, Trinity Center *Also called Mountain Resorts Inc* *(P-11315)*		
Trinity Building Services	D	650 873-2121
1071 Sneath Ln San Bruno (94066) *(P-12007)*		
Trinity Construction Entps Inc	E	559 313-9612
3604 W Gettysburg Ave Fresno (93722) *(P-723)*		
Trinity Engineering	E	707 585-2959
583 Martin Ave Rohnert Park (94928) *(P-18840)*		
Trinity Hospital, Weaverville *Also called Mountain Cmmnties Hlth Care Ds* *(P-16459)*		
Trinity Management Services	E	415 864-1111
1145 Market St Fl 12 San Francisco (94103) *(P-10677)*		
Trinity Packing Company Inc (PA)	B	559 433-3785
18700 E South Ave Reedley (93654) *(P-14443)*		
Trinity Packing Company Inc	B	559 743-3913
7612 S Reed Ave Reedley (93654) *(P-14444)*		
Trinity River Lumber Company (PA)	C	530 623-5561
1375 Main St Weaverville (96093) *(P-8610)*		
Trinity Technology Group Inc	D	916 779-0201
2015 J St Ste 105 Sacramento (95811) *(P-13682)*		
Tripactions Inc (PA)	A	888 505-8747
1501 Page Mill Rd Palo Alto (94304) *(P-7809)*		
Triple A Pallets Inc	F	559 313-7636
3555 S Academy Ave Sanger (93657) *(P-3231)*		
Triple Aught Design LLC	E	415 318-8252
660 22nd St San Francisco (94107) *(P-2974)*		
Triple C Foods Inc	E	510 357-8880
1465 Factor Ave San Leandro (94577) *(P-2419)*		
Triple Crown International, Fresno *Also called Pacific Crown Partners LLC* *(P-9473)*		
Triple H Solutions Inc	E	916 475-8367
9575 Stablegate Rd Wilton (95693) *(P-7657)*		
Triple Hs Inc (PA)	D	408 458-3200
983 University Ave Bldg D Los Gatos (95032) *(P-19918)*		
Triple Ring Technologies Inc	E	510 592-3000
39655 Eureka Dr Newark (94560) *(P-19655)*		
Triple S Metal Inc	E	925 449-3262
567 Exchange Ct Livermore (94550) *(P-8372)*		
Triquint Wj Inc	D	408 577-6200
3099 Orchard Dr San Jose (95134) *(P-5882)*		
Trireme Medical LLC	D	925 931-1300
7060 Koll Center Pkwy # 30 Pleasanton (94566) *(P-7052)*		
Triton Enterprises Inc	E	925 230-8395
5638 Wells Ln San Ramon (94582) *(P-19879)*		
Triton Tower Inc (PA)	D	916 375-8546
3200 Jefferson Blvd West Sacramento (95691) *(P-1139)*		
Triumph Protection Group Inc	C	800 224-0286
853 Cotting Ct Ste D Vacaville (95688) *(P-14102)*		
Trius Trucking Inc	D	559 834-4000
4692 E Lincoln Ave Fowler (93625) *(P-7607)*		
Trivad Inc	E	650 286-1086
1350 Bayshore Hwy Ste 799 Burlingame (94010) *(P-8756)*		
Trizic Inc	E	415 366-6583
60 E Sir Francis Drake Bl Larkspur (94939) *(P-13497)*		
TRM Corporation (PA)	D	510 895-2700
2378 Polvorosa Ave San Leandro (94577) *(P-1726)*		
Tronex Technology Incorporated	E	707 426-2550
2860 Cordelia Rd Ste 230 Fairfield (94534) *(P-4610)*		
Tronson Manufacturing Inc	E	408 533-0369
3421 Yale Way Fremont (94538) *(P-5629)*		
Tropian Inc	E	408 865-1300
20813 Stevens Creek Blvd Cupertino (95014) *(P-6335)*		
Tropos Technologies Inc	F	408 571-6104
16890 Church St Bldg 1a Morgan Hill (95037) *(P-6596)*		
Trotter-Vogel Realty Inc	D	650 589-1000
180 El Camino Real San Bruno (94066) *(P-10678)*		
Trov Inc (PA)	F	925 478-5500
347 Hartz Ave Danville (94526) *(P-13498)*		
Trove Recommerce Inc	C	925 726-3316
240 Valley Dr Brisbane (94005) *(P-19656)*		
Trowbridge Enterprises (PA)	E	831 476-3815
2606 Chanticleer Ave Santa Cruz (95065) *(P-9211)*		
Tru Machining	E	510 573-3408
45979 Warm Springs Blvd Fremont (94539) *(P-5630)*		
Tru-Fit Manufacturing, Lathrop *Also called Accurate Heating & Cooling Inc* *(P-4737)*		
Truckee Dnner Pub Utlity Dst F	D	530 587-3896
11570 Donner Pass Rd Truckee (96161) *(P-8204)*		
Truckee Dnner Rcreation Pk Dst	D	530 582-7720
10981 Truckee Way Truckee (96161) *(P-15258)*		
Truckee Donner Pud, Truckee *Also called Truckee Dnner Pub Utlity Dst F* *(P-8204)*		
Truckee River Ranch, Tahoe City *Also called River Ranch* *(P-11411)*		
Truckee Sanitary District	E	530 587-3804
12304 Joerger Dr Truckee (96161) *(P-8294)*		
Truckee Sourdough Co, Truckee *Also called L and C Cook Spcalty Foods Inc* *(P-9462)*		
Truckee-Tahoe Lumber Company (PA)	E	530 587-9211
10242 Church St Truckee (96161) *(P-8522)*		
Trucker Huss A Professional	E	415 788-3111
1 Embarcadero Ctr Fl 12 San Francisco (94111) *(P-17384)*		
True Botanicals Inc	F	415 420-0403
1 Lovell Ave Mill Valley (94941) *(P-4098)*		
True Health Inc	E	209 464-4743
2324 Lever Blvd Stockton (95206) *(P-18193)*		
True Leaf Farms LLC	B	831 623-4667
1275 San Justo Rd San Juan Bautista (95045) *(P-2272)*		
True Leaf Technologies, Cotati *Also called Biotherm Hydronic Inc* *(P-4626)*		
True Link Financial Inc (PA)	D	800 299-7646
47 Maiden Ln San Francisco (94108) *(P-14445)*		
True North	D	650 207-9800
8 Cadiz Cir Redwood City (94065) *(P-12877)*		

True North Ar LLC (HQ)....E....**800 700-0220**
100 Wood Hllow Dr Ste 200 Novato (94945) ***(P-11831)***
True North Housing Aliance Inc....E....530 891-9048
101 Silver Dollar Way Chico (95928) ***(P-17772)***
True Wrld Fods San Frncsco LLC....D....510 352-8140
1815 Williams St San Leandro (94577) ***(P-9372)***
Truebeck Construction Inc (PA)....D....**650 227-1957**
951 Mariners Island Blvd # 700 San Mateo (94404) ***(P-977)***
Truecar Inc....E....415 821-8270
2 Embarcadero Ctr Fl 8 San Francisco (94111) ***(P-8432)***
Truepill Inc (PA)....D....**510 388-0406**
1720 S Amphlett Blvd San Mateo (94402) ***(P-3999)***
Truepoint Solutions LLC (PA)....E....**916 259-1293**
3262 Penryn Rd Ste 100b Loomis (95650) ***(P-13683)***
Truett-Hurst Inc (PA)....E....**707 431-4423**
125 Foss Creek Cir Healdsburg (95448) ***(P-2748)***
Trufocus Corporation....F....831 761-9981
468 Westridge Dr Watsonville (95076) ***(P-7094)***
Trugreen, Rancho Cordova *Also called Landcare USA LLC* ***(P-477)***
Trugreen, San Jose *Also called Landcare USA LLC* ***(P-479)***
Trujillo Orlando Pntg Contr....E....650 579-0707
6 S Amphlett Blvd San Mateo (94401) ***(P-1434)***
Trulia Inc....A....415 648-4358
116 New Montgomery St San Francisco (94105) ***(P-10465)***
Trulia Inc (HQ)....B....**415 648-4358**
535 Mission St Fl 7 San Francisco (94105) ***(P-13766)***
Trumaker & Co., San Francisco *Also called Trumaker Inc* ***(P-2985)***
Trumaker Inc....E....415 662-3836
228 Grant Ave Fl 2 San Francisco (94108) ***(P-2985)***
Truroots Inc (HQ)....E....**925 218-2205**
6999 Southfront Rd Livermore (94551) ***(P-2951)***
Truss Engineering Inc....E....209 527-6387
477 Zeff Rd Modesto (95351) ***(P-3214)***
Trust For Hidden Villa....E....650 949-8650
26870 Moody Rd Los Altos Hills (94022) ***(P-11612)***
Trustarc Inc (HQ)....D....**415 520-3400**
2121 N Calif Blvd Ste 290 Walnut Creek (94596) ***(P-19657)***
Truste, Walnut Creek *Also called Trustarc Inc* ***(P-19657)***
Trustees of The Ilwu, San Francisco *Also called Trustees of The Intrntnl Lngsh* ***(P-18379)***
Trustees of The Intrntnl Lngsh (PA)....E....**415 673-8500**
1188 Franklin St Fl 3 San Francisco (94109) ***(P-18379)***
Truteam of California Inc....D....916 826-3194
2400 Rockefeller Dr Ceres (95307) ***(P-1706)***
Trux Transport....D....650 244-0200
237 Harbor Way South San Francisco (94080) ***(P-7791)***
TRY VALLEY MONTESSORI SCHOOL, Livermore *Also called Valley Montessori School* ***(P-18043)***
Tryfacta Inc....B....408 419-9200
4637 Chabot Dr Ste 100 Pleasanton (94588) ***(P-12878)***
TS Logging....E....707 895-3751
18121 Rays Rd Philo (95466) ***(P-3084)***
TSC Motors Inc....E....408 580-0410
17085 Condit Rd Morgan Hill (95037) ***(P-8433)***
Tshirtguyscom (PA)....D....**619 793-4635**
11264 Chula Vista Ave San Jose (95127) ***(P-3048)***
Tsi Semiconductors America LLC (PA)....C....**916 786-3900**
7501 Foothills Blvd Roseville (95747) ***(P-6336)***
Tsm Insurance & Fincl Svcs Inc....D....209 524-6366
1317 Oakdale Rd Ste 910 Modesto (95355) ***(P-10362)***
Tsmc North America (HQ)....A....**408 382-8000**
2851 Junction Ave San Jose (95134) ***(P-19658)***
Tsmc Technology Inc....D....408 382-8052
2851 Junction Ave San Jose (95134) ***(P-6337)***
TSS Link Inc....E....408 745-7875
2099 Gateway Pl Ste 310 San Jose (95110) ***(P-14003)***
Tsu/Tree Service Unlimited Inc....E....530 626-8733
5531 Silver Lode Dr Placerville (95667) ***(P-524)***
Tti Inc....D....408 414-1450
188 Martinvale Ln San Jose (95119) ***(P-8967)***
Ttm Printed Circuit Group Inc....E....408 486-3100
407 Mathew St Santa Clara (95050) ***(P-5989)***
Ttm Technologies Inc....B....408 486-3100
407 Mathew St Santa Clara (95050) ***(P-5990)***
Ttm Technologies Inc....C....408 280-0422
355 Turtle Creek Ct San Jose (95125) ***(P-5991)***
Tts, Pleasanton *Also called Telecom Technology Svcs Inc* ***(P-19873)***
Ttsa, Truckee *Also called Tahoe-Truckee Sanitation Agcy* ***(P-8293)***
Ttsr, Sacramento *Also called Training Toward Self Reliance* ***(P-17771)***
TTT-Cubed Inc....D....510 656-2325
1120 Auburn St Fremont (94538) ***(P-6797)***
Tty-Deaf Hndcppd-Cmmnction Ctr, Chico *Also called Enloe Medical Center* ***(P-7382)***
Tubemogul Inc....A....510 653-0126
1250 53rd St Ste 1 Emeryville (94608) ***(P-13499)***
Tubi Inc....E....415 504-3505
315 Montgomery St Fl 16 San Francisco (94104) ***(P-11818)***
Tubit Enterprises Inc....E....530 335-5085
21640 S Vallejo St Burney (96013) ***(P-3085)***
Tubitv, San Francisco *Also called Tubi Inc* ***(P-11818)***
Tubular Flow Inc....D....831 761-0644
317 W Beach St Watsonville (95076) ***(P-1386)***
Tuck Aire Heating & AC Corp....D....650 873-7000
407 Cabot Rd South San Francisco (94080) ***(P-1387)***
Tucker Technology Inc (PA)....E....**510 836-0422**
300 Frank H Ogawa Plz Oakland (94612) ***(P-1625)***
Tudor Cnstr & Restoration, Elk Grove *Also called Bennathon Corp* ***(P-831)***
Tula Technology Inc (PA)....D....**408 383-9447**
2460 Zanker Rd San Jose (95131) ***(P-14677)***
Tulip Pubg & Graphics Inc....E....510 898-0000
1003 Canal Blvd Richmond (94804) ***(P-3705)***
Tullys Coffee Co Inc (HQ)....E....**415 929-8808**
2455 Fillmore St San Francisco (94115) ***(P-2848)***
Tullys Coffee Co Inc....E....415 213-8791
1509 Sloat Blvd San Francisco (94132) ***(P-2849)***
Tumelo Inc....E....707 523-4411
420 Tesconi Cir Ste B Santa Rosa (95401) ***(P-4168)***
Tunein Inc....C....650 319-7100
210 King St Fl 3 San Francisco (94107) ***(P-8035)***
Tuolomne Cnty Bhvral Hlth Rcve, Sonora *Also called Kingsview Corp* ***(P-17032)***
Tuolumne M-Wuk Indian Hlth Ctr....D....209 928-5400
18880 Cherry Valley Blvd Tuolumne (95379) ***(P-15742)***
TUOLUMNE MEWUK INDIAN HEALTH, Tuolumne *Also called Tuolumne M-Wuk Indian Hlth Ctr* ***(P-15742)***
Tuolumne Utilities District....D....209 532-5536
18885 Nugget Blvd Sonora (95370) ***(P-8277)***
Tupaz Day Care Services Inc....D....408 377-1622
3015 Union Ave San Jose (95124) ***(P-17773)***
Tupaz Homes LLC....D....408 377-1622
2038 Biarritz Pl San Jose (95138) ***(P-724)***
Turbine Eng Cmpnents Tech Corp....B....415 626-2000
1211 Old Albany Rd San Francisco (94103) ***(P-6622)***
Turbosand, Anderson *Also called Voorwood Company* ***(P-5116)***
Turing Video....D....877 730-8222
1730 S El Cmino Real Ste San Mateo (94402) ***(P-12879)***
Turingsense Inc (PA)....E....**408 887-7833**
4675 Stevens Creek Blvd # 101 Santa Clara (95051) ***(P-12880)***
Turkhan Nuts, Ripon *Also called Pearl Crop Inc* ***(P-2454)***
Turley Wine Cellars Inc....D....707 968-2700
3358 Saint Helena Hwy N Saint Helena (94574) ***(P-2749)***
Turlock Christian School (PA)....D....**209 632-2337**
1619 E Monte Vista Ave Turlock (95382) ***(P-18040)***
Turlock Dairy & Rfrgn Inc....D....209 667-6455
1819 S Walnut Rd Turlock (95380) ***(P-9045)***
Turlock Fruit Co (PA)....E....**209 634-7207**
500 S Tully Rd Turlock (95380) ***(P-9433)***
Turlock Golf and Country Club (PA)....E....**209 634-5471**
10532 Golf Rd Turlock (95380) ***(P-15162)***
Turlock Hlth & Fitnes Ctr Inc....E....209 826-6011
1520 Racquet Club Dr Los Banos (93635) ***(P-14982)***
Turlock Hlth & Fitnes Ctr Inc....E....209 571-2582
200 Norwegian Ave Modesto (95350) ***(P-14983)***
Turlock Hospitality LLC....E....209 250-1501
1000 Powers Ct Turlock (95380) ***(P-11546)***
Turlock Irrgtion Dst Emplyees (PA)....C....**209 883-8222**
333 E Canal Dr Turlock (95380) ***(P-8205)***
Turlock Machine Works....E....209 632-2275
1240 S 1st St Turlock (95380) ***(P-5453)***
Turlock Nrsing Rhabilation Ctr, Turlock *Also called Covenant Care California LLC* ***(P-15970)***
Turlock Petroleum Inc....F....209 634-8432
2219 Lander Ave Turlock (95380) ***(P-4183)***
Turlock Plant, Turlock *Also called Evergreen Packaging LLC* ***(P-9657)***
Turlock Poker Room, Turlock *Also called Central Valley Gaming LLC* ***(P-15190)***
Turlock Rsidential Care Fcilty, Turlock *Also called Covenant Care California LLC* ***(P-16180)***
Turlock Scavenger Company....E....209 668-7274
1200 S Walnut Rd Turlock (95380) ***(P-8373)***
Turlock Sheet Metal & Wldg Inc....E....209 667-4716
301 S Broadway Turlock (95380) ***(P-18841)***
Turn Behavioral Hlth Svcs Inc....E....559 264-7521
2550 W Clinton Ave Fresno (93705) ***(P-17082)***
Turn Inc (HQ)....B....**650 353-4399**
901 Marshall St Ste 200 Redwood City (94063) ***(P-11819)***
Turncare Inc....F....203 437-6768
2225 E Byshore Rd Ste 200 Palo Alto (94303) ***(P-7128)***
Turner Camera SEC Systems Inc....C....559 486-3466
120 W Shields Ave Fresno (93705) ***(P-14151)***
Turner Construction Company....D....916 444-4421
2500 Venture Oaks Way # 200 Sacramento (95833) ***(P-978)***
Turner Construction Company....E....510 267-8100
300 Frank H Ogawa Plz # 510 Oakland (94612) ***(P-979)***
Turner Designs Inc....E....408 749-0994
1995 N 1st St San Jose (95112) ***(P-6861)***
Turner Dsgns Hydrcrbon Instrs....E....559 253-1414
2023 N Gateway Blvd # 101 Fresno (93727) ***(P-6545)***
Turner Manufacturing Company....F....559 251-1918
2677 S Chestnut Ave Fresno (93725) ***(P-2080)***
Turning Point Central Cal Inc....E....559 638-8588
1311 11th St Reedley (93654) ***(P-15743)***
Turning Point Cmnty Programs (PA)....D....**916 364-8395**
10850 Gold Center Dr # 325 Rancho Cordova (95670) ***(P-17083)***
Turnongreen Inc....E....510 657-2635
1635 S Main St Milpitas (95035) ***(P-6798)***
Turnure Medical Group Inc....E....916 300-1188
6805 Five Star Blvd Ste 1 Rocklin (95677) ***(P-15744)***
Turtle Bay Exploration Park....E....530 242-3186
1335 Arboretum Dr Ste A Redding (96003) ***(P-18285)***
Tusa Inc (PA)....C....**888 848-3749**
986 Walsh Ave Santa Clara (95050) ***(P-13825)***
Tuscan Inn, San Francisco *Also called Kms Fishermans Wharf LP* ***(P-11237)***
Tuscan Inn, San Francisco *Also called Kimpton Hotel & Rest Group LLC* ***(P-11232)***
Tuscan Inn, San Francisco *Also called 425 North Point Street LLC* ***(P-10904)***
Tusco Casting Corporation....E....209 368-5137
934 E Victor Rd Lodi (95240) ***(P-4553)***
Tusker Medical Inc....E....650 223-6900
155 Jefferson Dr Menlo Park (94025) ***(P-7129)***
Tvia Inc (PA)....E....**408 982-8591**
4800 Great America Pkwy Santa Clara (95054) ***(P-6338)***

ALPHABETIC SECTION
Ukiah Adventist Hospital

Twelveacres Inc.....E.....408 341-0400
286 E Hamilton Ave Ste F Campbell (95008) *(P-18194)*
Twenty First District AG Assn (HQ).....E.....559 650-3247
1121 S Chance Ave Fresno (93702) *(P-15259)*
Twenty Twenty Therapeutics LLC.....E.....208 696-2020
259 E Grand Ave South San Francisco (94080) *(P-7130)*
Twilight Haven.....D.....559 251-8417
1717 S Winery Ave Fresno (93727) *(P-16145)*
Twilio Inc (PA).....A.....415 390-2337
101 Spear St Fl 1 San Francisco (94105) *(P-13500)*
Twin Arbors LLC.....E.....209 334-4897
1900 S Hutchins St Lodi (95240) *(P-14984)*
Twin Arbors Athletic Club, Lodi *Also called Spare-Time Inc (P-15150)*
Twin Bridges Technologies LLC.....F.....707 591-4500
30286 Oakbrook Rd Hayward (94544) *(P-8757)*
Twin Creeks Sunnyvale Inc.....D.....408 734-0888
969 E Caribbean Dr Sunnyvale (94089) *(P-15260)*
Twin Creeks Vineyard Company.....E.....707 224-4575
1000 Wooden Vly Cross Rd NAPA (94558) *(P-78)*
Twin Health Inc.....E.....970 215-8300
2525 Charleston Rd # 104 Mountain View (94043) *(P-12881)*
Twin Industries Inc.....F.....925 866-8946
2303 Camino Ramon Ste 106 San Ramon (94583) *(P-5992)*
Twin Lakes Baptist Church.....D.....831 465-3302
2701 Cabrillo College Dr Aptos (95003) *(P-18041)*
Twin Lakes Resort.....E.....760 932-7751
10316 Twin Lakes Rd Bridgeport (93517) *(P-11547)*
Twin Oaks Nrsing Rhblttion Ctr, Chico *Also called Evergreen At Chico LLC (P-15996)*
Twin Peaks Winery Inc.....E.....707 945-0855
1473 Yountville Cross Rd Yountville (94599) *(P-2750)*
Twin Pine Casino & Hotel.....D.....707 987-0197
22223 Rancheria Rd Hwy 29 Middletown (95461) *(P-11548)*
Twin Teaks Winery.....E.....707 944-8642
1473 Yountville Cross Rd Yountville (94599) *(P-79)*
Twin Termite and Pest Ctrl Inc.....E.....916 344-8946
3720 Madison Ave Ste 100 North Highlands (95660) *(P-11909)*
Twist Bioscience Corporation (PA).....B.....800 719-0671
681 Gateway Blvd South San Francisco (94080) *(P-19140)*
Twisted Oak Winery LLC (PA).....F.....209 728-3000
4280 Red Hill Rd Vallecito (95251) *(P-2751)*
Twitch Interactive Inc.....A.....415 919-5000
350 Bush St Fl 2 San Francisco (94104) *(P-3607)*
Two Lines A Journal.....F.....415 512-8812
582 Market St Ste 700 San Francisco (94104) *(P-3608)*
Two Rivers Demolition Inc.....D.....916 638-6775
2620 Mercantile Dr 100 Rancho Cordova (95742) *(P-1990)*
Tyche Medtech Inc.....F.....408 919-0098
3022 Scott Blvd Santa Clara (95054) *(P-7053)*
Tyler House, Watsonville *Also called Encompass Community Services (P-16757)*
TYlin Intl Group Ltd (PA).....C.....415 291-3700
345 California St Fl 23 San Francisco (94104) *(P-18842)*
Tyme Maidu Tribe-Berry Creek.....A.....530 538-4560
4020 Olive Hwy Oroville (95966) *(P-11549)*
Tynker, Mountain View *Also called Neuron Fuel Inc (P-12629)*
Typekit Inc.....E.....415 596-6319
601 Townsend St San Francisco (94103) *(P-13501)*
TYT LLC (HQ).....C.....510 444-3933
2861 Mandela Pkwy Oakland (94608) *(P-3706)*
U C P-UNITED CEREBAL PALSY ASS, Fresno *Also called United Crbral Plsy Cntl Cal In (P-18257)*
U C S F Frtlity Ctr For Rprdct, San Francisco *Also called Ucsf Fertility Group (P-15749)*
U C S F Medical Center, San Francisco *Also called Devron H Char MD (P-15377)*
U C San Francisco Gynecology.....D.....415 885-7788
2356 Sutter St San Francisco (94115) *(P-15745)*
U Haul Co of Sacramento Inc (HQ).....E.....916 929-2215
1650 El Camino Ave Sacramento (95815) *(P-14473)*
U P C Inc.....C.....650 462-2010
165 Channing Ave Palo Alto (94301) *(P-11733)*
U S Enterprise Corporation.....E.....510 487-8877
30560 San Antonio St Hayward (94544) *(P-2288)*
U S Fabrications, Hayward *Also called South Bay Diversfd Systems Inc (P-4819)*
U S GOVERNMENT, Tulelake *Also called Lava Beds National Monuments (P-18577)*
U S I, Saratoga *Also called United Supertek Inc (P-5993)*
U S Perma Inc.....E.....408 436-0600
1696 Rogers Ave San Jose (95112) *(P-1727)*
U S R, Stockton *Also called Universal Service Recycl Inc (P-8374)*
U S Technical Ceramics Inc.....E.....408 779-0303
15400 Concord Cir Morgan Hill (95037) *(P-8637)*
U-2 Home Entertainment Inc.....E.....650 871-8118
170 S Spruce Ave Ste 200 South San Francisco (94080) *(P-8968)*
U-C Components Inc (PA).....E.....408 782-1929
18700 Adams Ct Morgan Hill (95037) *(P-4873)*
U-Haul, Sacramento *Also called U Haul Co of Sacramento Inc (P-14473)*
U-Haul Co of California (HQ).....C.....800 528-0463
44511 S Grimmer Blvd Fremont (94538) *(P-14474)*
U.S. Concrete Precast Group, Morgan Hill *Also called Sierra Precast Inc (P-4452)*
U.S. Trading Company, Hayward *Also called Ustov Inc (P-9322)*
UAS Management Inc.....D.....209 580-3400
1390 E Yosemite Ave Ste B Merced (95340) *(P-16689)*
Ub Inc.....E.....916 374-8899
1115 Shore St West Sacramento (95691) *(P-9498)*
Uber.....D.....866 440-6700
101 Jefferson Dr Menlo Park (94025) *(P-7810)*
Uber Technologies Inc (PA).....A.....415 612-8582
1515 3rd St San Francisco (94158) *(P-14446)*
Ubertal Inc.....E.....650 542-8100
1730 S Amphlett Blvd # 250 San Mateo (94402) *(P-12882)*
Ubertal Technology, San Mateo *Also called Ubertal Inc (P-12882)*
Ubet.com, San Francisco *Also called Igt Interactive Inc (P-15211)*
Ubi Soft Entertainment.....D.....415 547-4000
625 3rd St Fl 3 San Francisco (94107) *(P-14882)*
Ubicom Inc.....D.....408 433-3330
195 Baypointe Pkwy San Jose (95134) *(P-6339)*
Ubicom Inc (PA).....E.....408 523-7800
635 Clyde Ave Mountain View (94043) *(P-6340)*
Ubics Inc.....C.....415 289-1400
1050 Bridgeway Sausalito (94965) *(P-12883)*
Ubiquiti Networks Inc.....D.....408 942-3085
2580 Orchard Pkwy San Jose (95131) *(P-13684)*
Ubiquity, San Francisco *Also called Decimal Inc (P-14248)*
Ubisoft Inc (HQ).....A.....415 547-4000
625 3rd St San Francisco (94107) *(P-12884)*
Uc Davis Alzhimers Disease Ctr, Martinez *Also called Ucd Ncadc (P-15747)*
Uc Davis Children's Hospital, Sacramento *Also called University California Davis (P-15774)*
Uc Davis Hlth Sys Fclties Dsig.....E.....916 734-7024
4800 2nd Ave Ste 3010 Sacramento (95817) *(P-15746)*
Uc Davis Medical Center, Sacramento *Also called Uc Davis Hlth Sys Fclties Dsig (P-15746)*
Uc Davis Medical Center, Sacramento *Also called University California Davis (P-16702)*
Uc Davis Shared Services Ctr.....E.....530 754-4772
260 Cousteau Pl Ste 150 Davis (95618) *(P-19002)*
Uc Hastings Foundation.....D.....415 565-4704
200 Mcallister St San Francisco (94102) *(P-18603)*
Ucc Guide Inc.....F.....800 345-3822
225 Cabrillo Hwy S 200c Half Moon Bay (94019) *(P-3609)*
Uccr, Petaluma *Also called United Cmps Cnfrences Retreats (P-11613)*
Ucd Ncadc.....D.....925 372-2485
150 Muir Rd Ste 127a Martinez (94553) *(P-15747)*
Uclass Inc.....F.....630 520-8553
901 Mission St Ste 105 San Francisco (94103) *(P-13502)*
Ucs Limo LLC.....E.....866 345-5640
1710 S Amphlett Blvd San Mateo (94402) *(P-7408)*
Ucs Worldwide, San Mateo *Also called Ucs Limo LLC (P-7408)*
UCSF BENIOFF CHILDREN'S HOSPIT, Oakland *Also called Childrens Hosp RES Ctr At Okla (P-16329)*
Ucsf Btty Irene Moore Wns Hosp (HQ).....E.....415 476-1000
1855 4th St San Francisco (94143) *(P-16146)*
Ucsf Cardiovascular Care.....D.....415 353-2873
535 Mission Bay Blvd S San Francisco (94143) *(P-15748)*
Ucsf Center On Deafness, San Francisco *Also called University Cal San Frncsco Fnd (P-18195)*
Ucsf Dental Center-Buchanan, San Francisco *Also called University Cal San Francisco (P-15861)*
Ucsf Design Construction, San Francisco *Also called University Cal San Francisco (P-15756)*
Ucsf East Bay Surgery Program (PA).....E.....510 437-4800
1411 E 31st St Oakland (94602) *(P-16690)*
Ucsf Fertility Group.....E.....415 353-2667
2356 Sutter St San Francisco (94115) *(P-15749)*
Ucsf Medical Center, San Francisco *Also called Ucsf Btty Irene Moore Wns Hosp (P-16146)*
Ucsf Medical Center At Mt Zion, San Francisco *Also called University Cal San Francisco (P-16698)*
Ucsf Mmory Clnic Alzhimers Ctr, San Francisco *Also called University Cal San Francisco (P-15763)*
Ucsf Mount Zion Cancer Center, San Francisco *Also called University Cal San Francisco (P-15768)*
Ucsf Neuro Epidemiology Lab, San Francisco *Also called University Cal San Francisco (P-19242)*
Ucsf Orthpdic Srgery Fclty Prc, San Francisco *Also called University Cal San Francisco (P-15753)*
Ucsf Otlrynglogy - Head Neck S, San Francisco *Also called University Cal San Francisco (P-15754)*
Ucsf Pdiatric Pulmonary Clinic, Pleasanton *Also called University Cal San Francisco (P-15759)*
Ucsf Plstic Rcnstrctive Srgery, San Francisco *Also called University Cal San Francisco (P-15766)*
Ucsf Sports Medicine Center, San Francisco *Also called University Cal San Francisco (P-15758)*
Ucsf/Div Behv & Dev Pediatrics, San Francisco *Also called University Cal San Francisco (P-15762)*
Ucsf/Mz Neurosurgery Abic, San Francisco *Also called University Cal San Francisco (P-15764)*
Ucsf/Obgyn Oncology, San Francisco *Also called University Cal San Francisco (P-15765)*
Uct, Hayward *Also called Ultra Clean Tech Systems Svc I (P-6342)*
Udelv Inc.....E.....650 376-3785
1826 Rollins Rd Ste 100 Burlingame (94010) *(P-12885)*
Ufcw & Employers Trust LLC (PA).....C.....800 552-2400
1000 Burnett Ave Ste 110 Concord (94520) *(P-10800)*
Ufcw & Employers Trust LLC.....D.....916 782-1618
2200 Prfcional Dr Ste 190 Roseville (95661) *(P-18380)*
Ufcw 5, San Jose *Also called United Fd Coml Wkrs Un Local 5 (P-18383)*
Ufcw 8 Golden State, Roseville *Also called United Fd Coml Wkrs Un Lcal 8 (P-18382)*
Uhuru Network LLC.....E.....415 745-3616
100 Pine St Ste 1250 San Francisco (94111) *(P-11793)*
Uhv Sputtering Inc.....E.....408 779-2826
275 Digital Dr Morgan Hill (95037) *(P-6341)*
Ujet Inc.....C.....855 242-8538
201 3rd St Ste 950 San Francisco (94103) *(P-13503)*
Ukiah Adventist Hospital.....D.....707 462-8855
1165 S Dora St Ste C2 Ukiah (95482) *(P-16691)*
Ukiah Adventist Hospital (HQ).....B.....707 462-3111
275 Hospital Dr Ukiah (95482) *(P-16692)*

ALPHABETIC

Ukiah Adventist Hospital ALPHABETIC SECTION

Ukiah Adventist Hospital ....D....707 463-7587
245 Hospital Dr Ukiah (95482) *(P-16693)*

Ukiah Adventist Hospital ....D....707 462-3111
1120 S Dora St Ukiah (95482) *(P-16694)*

Ukiah Convalescent Hospital, Ukiah *Also called Berryman Health Inc (P-15946)*

Ukiah Post Acute, Ukiah *Also called Ensign Pleasanton LLC (P-15991)*

Ukiah V A Outpatient Clinic, Ukiah *Also called Veterans Health Administration (P-15801)*

Ukiah Valley Medical Center, Ukiah *Also called Ukiah Adventist Hospital (P-16692)*

Ulab Systems Inc (PA) ....E....**866 900-8522**
1820 Gateway Dr Ste 300 San Mateo (94404) *(P-15860)*

Ultima Genomics Inc ....E....650 861-1194
7979 Gateway Blvd Ste 101 Newark (94560) *(P-19141)*

Ultimate Creations LLC ....D....559 221-4936
516 W Shaw Ave Ste 200 Fresno (93704) *(P-10891)*

Ultimatum Records LLC ....F....925 353-5202
4695 Chabot Dr Ste 200 Pleasanton (94588) *(P-5770)*

Ultimo Software Solutions Inc ....C....408 943-1490
33268 Central Ave 2 Union City (94587) *(P-12886)*

Ultra Clean Tech Systems Svc I (HQ) ....C....**510 576-4400**
26462 Corporate Ave Hayward (94545) *(P-6342)*

Ultra Glass ....F....916 338-3911
4001 Vista Park Ct Ste 1 Sacramento (95834) *(P-4393)*

Ultracell Corporation (PA) ....F....**925 292-4226**
399 Lindbergh Ave Livermore (94551) *(P-5699)*

Ultraex Inc ....E....800 882-1000
2633 Barrington Ct Hayward (94545) *(P-7751)*

Ultragenyx Pharmaceutical Inc (PA) ....A....**415 483-8800**
60 Leveroni Ct Novato (94949) *(P-4000)*

Ultrasense Systems Inc (PA) ....E....**408 391-5734**
2025 Gateway Pl Ste 156 San Jose (95110) *(P-12887)*

Ultrasil LLC ....E....510 266-3700
3527 Breakwater Ave Hayward (94545) *(P-6343)*

Ultratech Inc (HQ) ....C....**408 321-8835**
3050 Zanker Rd San Jose (95134) *(P-5173)*

Umba Inc ....E....914 426-1771
1714 Stockton St San Francisco (94133) *(P-14447)*

Umc Group (usa) ....D....408 523-7800
488 De Guigne Dr Sunnyvale (94085) *(P-6344)*

Umec, Union City *Also called United Mech Met Fbricators Inc (P-4827)*

Umo Steel, Union City *Also called United Misc & Orna Stl Inc (P-4691)*

Umspe, Fresno *Also called University Cal San Francisco (P-10486)*

Unbound Renewable Energy Inc ....D....800 472-1142
412 N Mount Shasta Blvd Mount Shasta (96067) *(P-1388)*

Unchained Labs (PA) ....C....**925 587-9800**
6870 Koll Center Pkwy Pleasanton (94566) *(P-16811)*

Uncle Credit Union (PA) ....D....**925 447-5001**
2100 Las Positas Ct Livermore (94551) *(P-9825)*

Uncountable Inc (PA) ....E....**650 208-5949**
300 Kansas St San Francisco (94103) *(P-13504)*

Undc, Sacramento *Also called Universal Network Dev Corp (P-19880)*

Underground Cnstr Co Inc ....C....707 746-8800
5145 Industrial Way Benicia (94510) *(P-8216)*

Undergrund Svc Alert Nthrn Cal ....E....800 640-5137
4005 Port Chicago Hwy Concord (94520) *(P-19659)*

Underwriters Laboratories Inc ....C....408 754-6500
4510 Riding Club Ct Hayward (94542) *(P-19289)*

Unfi, Rocklin *Also called United Natural Foods West Inc (P-7703)*

UNI Poly Inc ....F....510 357-9898
2040 Williams St San Leandro (94577) *(P-3389)*

UNI-Pixel Displays Inc ....D....281 825-4500
4699 Old Ironsides Dr # 3 Santa Clara (95054) *(P-5337)*

Unico Engineering Inc ....E....916 293-8953
110 Blue Ravine Rd Folsom (95630) *(P-18843)*

Unico Mechanical Corp ....D....707 745-4540
1209 Polk St Benicia (94510) *(P-9101)*

Unicorn Group, Novato *Also called Forest Investment Group Inc (P-3649)*

Unifi Software Inc ....E....732 614-9522
1810 Gateway Dr Ste 380 San Mateo (94404) *(P-13505)*

Unilab Corporation ....A....916 927-9900
3714 Northgate Blvd Sacramento (95834) *(P-16812)*

Unilab Corporation ....A....916 781-3031
51 N Sunrise Ave Ste 515 Roseville (95661) *(P-16813)*

Unilab Corporation ....A....510 444-5213
470 27th St Oakland (94612) *(P-16814)*

Unilab Corporation ....A....408 927-8331
6475 Camden Ave Ste 104 San Jose (95120) *(P-16815)*

Unilab Corporation ....A....916 733-3330
3160 Folsom Blvd Sacramento (95816) *(P-16816)*

Unilab Corporation ....A....559 225-5076
5325 N Fresno St Ste 106 Fresno (93710) *(P-16817)*

Unilever United States Inc ....A....209 466-9580
1400 Waterloo Rd Stockton (95205) *(P-193)*

Union City Medical Offices, Union City *Also called Kaiser Foundation Hospitals (P-15457)*

Union Landing Dental Center, Union City *Also called Del Rosario Rene DMD (P-15831)*

Union Sanitary District ....C....510 477-7500
5072 Benson Rd Union City (94587) *(P-8295)*

Unionbancal Mortgage Corp ....D....415 705-7350
400 California St San Francisco (94104) *(P-9691)*

Uniproducts, North Highlands *Also called Mikes Sheet Metal Pdts Inc (P-4791)*

Unique Scaffold, Concord *Also called Ernie & Sons Scaffolding (P-2029)*

Uniquify Inc ....E....408 235-8810
2030 Fortune Dr Ste 200 San Jose (95131) *(P-6480)*

Unison, San Francisco *Also called Real Estate Equity Exchange (P-9924)*

Unisource Packaging Inc ....C....925 227-6000
4225 Hacienda Dr Ste A Pleasanton (94588) *(P-9220)*

Unitech Tool & Machine Inc ....F....408 566-0333
3025 Stender Way Santa Clara (95054) *(P-5631)*

United Administrative Services, San Jose *Also called Chelbay Schuler & Chelbay (P-10214)*

United Animal Nations ....E....916 429-2457
3800 J St Ste 100 Sacramento (95816) *(P-18604)*

United Association Local 342 ....D....925 686-5880
935 Detroit Ave Concord (94518) *(P-18381)*

United Auburn Indian Community ....A....916 408-7777
1200 Athens Ave Lincoln (95648) *(P-11550)*

United Bakery and Company, West Sacramento *Also called Ub Inc (P-9498)*

United Behavioral Health (HQ) ....C....**415 547-1403**
425 Market St Fl 18 San Francisco (94105) *(P-19413)*

United Behavioral Health ....E....916 927-0606
8880 Cal Center Dr # 300 Sacramento (95826) *(P-17084)*

United Building Maint Inc ....C....916 772-8101
8211 Sierra College Blvd Roseville (95661) *(P-12008)*

United California Glass & Door ....D....415 824-8500
745 Cesar Chavez San Francisco (94124) *(P-14780)*

United Cerebral Palsy Assoc (PA) ....C....**209 956-0290**
333 W Benjamin Holt Dr # 1 Stockton (95207) *(P-18351)*

United Chrisitan Schools, Stockton *Also called Christian Brookside Schools (P-17903)*

United Cmps Cnfrences Retreats (PA) ....E....**707 762-3220**
1304 Sthpint Blvd Ste 200 Petaluma (94954) *(P-11613)*

United Cmps Cnfrences Retreats ....E....831 684-0148
220 Cloister Ln Aptos (95003) *(P-11614)*

United Com Serve ....C....530 790-3000
1260 Williams Way Yuba City (95991) *(P-16147)*

United Compost & Organics Inc ....E....707 443-4369
2200 Bendixsen St Samoa (95564) *(P-9614)*

United Compost & Organics Inc ....E....707 443-4369
1900 Bendixsen St Samoa (95564) *(P-4136)*

United Contract Services Inc ....E....408 577-0105
1161 Ringwood Ct Ste 170 San Jose (95131) *(P-12009)*

United Craftsmen Priniting ....E....408 224-6464
2526 Qume Dr Ste 20 San Jose (95131) *(P-3707)*

United Crbral Plsy Assn San Jq ....D....209 239-3066
134 S Pacific Rd Manteca (95337) *(P-18256)*

United Crbral Plsy Cntl Cal In (PA) ....E....**559 221-8272**
4224 N Cedar Ave Fresno (93726) *(P-18257)*

United Distlrs Vintners N Amer, San Francisco *Also called Diageo North America Inc (P-2550)*

United Emrgncy Anmal Clnic Inc (PA) ....E....**408 371-6252**
905 Dell Ave Campbell (95008) *(P-340)*

United Engrg Resources Inc (PA) ....D....**916 375-6700**
498 N 3rd St Sacramento (95811) *(P-19660)*

United Fd Coml Wkrs Un Lcal 8 ....D....916 786-0588
2200 Prfcional Dr Ste 100 Roseville (95661) *(P-18382)*

United Fd Coml Wkrs Un Local 5 ....E....408 998-0428
240 S Market St San Jose (95113) *(P-18383)*

United Fence Contractors Inc (PA) ....E....**510 276-8350**
515 23rd Ave Oakland (94606) *(P-2081)*

United Foods Intl USA Inc (HQ) ....E....**510 264-5850**
23447 Cabot Blvd Hayward (94545) *(P-2952)*

United Gran Cab Ctr Cbnets Cnt, Richmond *Also called United Granite & Cabinets LLC (P-3194)*

United Granite & Cabinets LLC ....F....510 558-8999
5225 Central Ave Richmond (94804) *(P-3194)*

United Green Mark Inc ....D....408 295-3376
1145 N 13th St San Jose (95112) *(P-9046)*

United Health Systems Inc ....C....530 662-9161
124 Walnut St Woodland (95695) *(P-16148)*

United Hlth Ctrs of San Jquin (PA) ....D....**559 646-6618**
3875 W Beechwood Ave Fresno (93711) *(P-15750)*

United Indian Health Svcs Inc (PA) ....C....**707 825-5000**
1600 Weeot Way Arcata (95521) *(P-15751)*

United Innovation Services Inc ....D....831 334-0673
950 Tower Ln Foster City (94404) *(P-19661)*

United International, Novato *Also called Cellmark Inc (P-9193)*

United Landscape Resource Inc ....E....530 671-1029
5411 Colusa Hwy Yuba City (95993) *(P-507)*

United Marble & Granite Inc ....D....408 347-3300
2163 Martin Ave Santa Clara (95050) *(P-2082)*

United Mech Met Fbricators Inc ....E....510 537-4744
33353 Lewis St Union City (94587) *(P-4827)*

United Mfg Assembly Inc ....D....510 490-4680
44169 Fremont Blvd Fremont (94538) *(P-19290)*

United Misc & Orna Stl Inc ....E....510 429-8755
4700 Horner St Union City (94587) *(P-4691)*

United Natural Foods West Inc (HQ) ....B....**916 625-4100**
1101 Sunset Blvd Rocklin (95765) *(P-7703)*

United Pallet Services Inc ....C....209 538-5844
4043 Crows Landing Rd Modesto (95358) *(P-3232)*

United Parcel Service Inc ....D....678 339-3171
3331 Industrial Dr Ste C Santa Rosa (95403) *(P-14448)*

United Parcel Service Inc ....C....510 262-2338
1601 Atlas Rd Richmond (94806) *(P-7658)*

United Parcel Service Inc ....C....530 365-7850
6845 Eastside Rd Anderson (96007) *(P-7659)*

United Parcel Service Inc ....C....707 864-8200
5000 W Cordelia Rd Fairfield (94534) *(P-7660)*

United Parcel Service Inc ....C....800 742-5877
1400 Hil Mor Dr Ceres (95307) *(P-7661)*

United Parcel Service Inc ....C....916 373-4076
1380 Shore St West Sacramento (95691) *(P-7662)*

United Parcel Service Inc ....C....707 224-1205
2531 Napa Valley Corp Dr NAPA (94558) *(P-7663)*

United Parcel Service Inc ....C....916 373-4089
128 Shore St Sacramento (95829) *(P-7664)*

United Parcel Service Inc ....C....559 442-2950
1601 W Mckinley Ave Fresno (93728) *(P-7495)*

United Parcel Service Inc ....C....408 291-2942
1999 S 7th St San Jose (95112) *(P-7665)*

United Parcel Service Inc...C...415 252-4564
2222 17th St San Francisco (94103) ***(P-7666)***
United Parcel Service Inc...C...707 252-4560
1012 Sterling St Vallejo (94591) ***(P-7667)***
United Parcel Service Inc...D...415 837-1929
222 Mason St San Francisco (94102) ***(P-14449)***
United Parcel Service Inc...D...510 264-8880
26557 Danti Ct Fl 1 Hayward (94545) ***(P-7741)***
United Parcel Service Inc...D...916 231-0814
10295 Truemper Way Mather (95655) ***(P-7742)***
United Parcel Service Inc...C...510 813-5662
8400 Pardee Dr Oakland (94621) ***(P-7668)***
United Parcel Service Inc...D...800 742-5877
1746 D St South Lake Tahoe (96150) ***(P-14450)***
United Parcel Service Inc...C...707 468-5481
259 Cherry St Ukiah (95482) ***(P-7669)***
United Parcel Service Inc...C...209 736-0878
2342 Gun Club Rd Angels Camp (95222) ***(P-7670)***
United Parcel Service Inc...C...916 632-4826
2275 Sierra Meadows Dr Rocklin (95677) ***(P-7671)***
United Parcel Service Inc...C...831 425-1054
251 Sylvania Ave Santa Cruz (95060) ***(P-7672)***
United Parcel Service Inc...C...800 833-9943
4500 Norris Canyon Rd San Ramon (94583) ***(P-7673)***
United Parcel Service Inc...D...800 742-5877
48921 Warm Springs Blvd Fremont (94539) ***(P-14451)***
United Parcel Service Inc...C...916 857-0311
3930 Kristi Ct Sacramento (95827) ***(P-7674)***
United Reporting Pubg Corp...F...916 542-7501
1835 Iron Point Rd # 100 Folsom (95630) ***(P-3610)***
United SEC Specialists Inc (PA)...C...408 431-0691
275 Saratoga Ave Ste 200 Santa Clara (95050) ***(P-14103)***
United SEC Specialists Inc...E...408 878-5120
2010 El Camino Real Santa Clara (95050) ***(P-14104)***
United Sign Systems, Modesto *Also called Johnson United Inc* ***(P-7238)***
United Site Services Cal Inc...C...408 295-2263
3408 Hillcap Ave San Jose (95136) ***(P-12065)***
United Sportsmen Incorporated...E...925 676-1963
4700 Evora Rd Concord (94520) ***(P-15261)***
United States Cold Storage Inc...E...916 640-2800
3936 Dudley Blvd McClellan (95652) ***(P-2862)***
United States Cold Storage Inc...E...916 392-9160
4233 Rosecrest Way Sacramento (95826) ***(P-2863)***
United States Dept of Energy...A...510 486-4000
1 Cyclotron Rd Berkeley (94720) ***(P-19240)***
United States Dept of Energy...A...510 486-4936
1 Cyclotron Rd Berkeley (94720) ***(P-19142)***
United States Dept of Energy...A...925 422-1100
7000 East Ave Livermore (94550) ***(P-19143)***
United States Enrgy Foundation...D...415 561-6700
301 Battery St Fl 5 San Francisco (94111) ***(P-18605)***
United States Fire Insur Co...D...415 541-3249
1 Front St Ste 300 San Francisco (94111) ***(P-10189)***
United States Gypsum Company...C...408 279-3001
2049 Senter Rd San Jose (95112) ***(P-8638)***
United States Info Systems Inc...C...845 353-9224
7621 Galilee Rd Roseville (95678) ***(P-1626)***
United Sttes Intrmdal Svcs LLC...D...209 341-4045
502 E Whitmore Ave Modesto (95358) ***(P-7855)***
United Sttes Thrmlctric Cnsrti...E...530 345-8000
13267 Contrs Dr Ste D Chico (95973) ***(P-6735)***
United Supertek Inc...F...408 922-0730
14930 Vintner Ct Saratoga (95070) ***(P-5993)***
United Temp Services Inc...D...408 472-4309
694 Albanese Cir San Jose (95111) ***(P-12148)***
United Way Cal Capitl Reg...E...916 368-3000
10389 Old Placerville Rd Sacramento (95827) ***(P-17774)***
United Way of Bay Area (PA)...D...415 808-4300
550 Kearny St Ste 1000 San Francisco (94108) ***(P-17775)***
United Way Santa Cruz County...E...831 465-2204
4450 Capitola Rd Ste 106 Capitola (95010) ***(P-18258)***
United Way Silicon Valley...E...408 260-3915
1400 Parkmoor Ave Ste 250 San Jose (95126) ***(P-17776)***
UNITED WAY, THE, San Francisco *Also called United Way of Bay Area* ***(P-17775)***
United Western Industries Inc...E...559 226-7236
3515 N Hazel Ave Fresno (93722) ***(P-5632)***
Unitek Inc...D...510 623-8544
41350 Christy St Fremont (94538) ***(P-13685)***
Unitek Miyachi International, San Jose *Also called Directed Light Inc* ***(P-9063)***
UNItogether Inc...D...707 208-7602
1253 Gray Hawk Ln Suisun City (94585) ***(P-18606)***
Unitrans International Corp (HQ)...E...650 588-1233
351 Swift Ave South San Francisco (94080) ***(P-7856)***
Unitrin Direct Insurance Co (HQ)...D...760 603-3276
80 Blue Ravine Rd Ste 200 Folsom (95630) ***(P-10222)***
Unity Biotechnology Inc...C...650 416-1192
285 E Grand Ave South San Francisco (94080) ***(P-19144)***
Unity Care Group...D...408 971-9822
1400 Parkmoor Ave Ste 115 San Jose (95126) ***(P-17777)***
Unity Courier Service Inc...C...916 246-0390
1645 Parkway Blvd Ste A West Sacramento (95691) ***(P-14452)***
Unity Courier Service Inc...B...510 568-8890
1132 Beecher St San Leandro (94577) ***(P-7675)***
Unity Forest Products Inc...E...530 671-7152
1162 Putman Ave Yuba City (95991) ***(P-3158)***
Unity Software Inc (PA)...B...415 539-3162
30 3rd St San Francisco (94103) ***(P-12888)***
Universal Bldg Svcs & Sup Co...D...707 781-7434
1318 Ross St Petaluma (94954) ***(P-12010)***
Universal Bldg Svcs & Sup Co (PA)...C...510 527-1078
3120 Pierce St Richmond (94804) ***(P-12011)***
Universal Bldg Svcs & Sup Co...D...925 934-5533
421 N Buchanan Cir Pacheco (94553) ***(P-12012)***
Universal Bldg Svcs & Sup Co...D...408 995-5111
430 Roberson Ln San Jose (95112) ***(P-12013)***
Universal Building Svc & Sup, Petaluma *Also called Universal Bldg Svcs & Sup Co* ***(P-12010)***
Universal Custom Design, Elk Grove *Also called Universal Custom Display* ***(P-7258)***
Universal Custom Display...C...916 714-2505
9104 Elkmont Dr Ste 100 Elk Grove (95624) ***(P-7258)***
Universal Custom Farming Co, Tranquillity *Also called Don Gragnani Farms* ***(P-159)***
Universal Janitorial Maint, San Jose *Also called Full Service Janitorial Inc* ***(P-11955)***
Universal Limousine & Trnsp Co...D...916 361-5466
9944 Mills Station Rd C Sacramento (95827) ***(P-7409)***
Universal Maintenance, San Jose *Also called Full Service Maintenance Inc* ***(P-11956)***
Universal McLoud USA Corp...F...613 222-5904
580 California St San Francisco (94104) ***(P-13506)***
Universal Meditech Inc...E...559 366-7798
1320 E Fortune Ave # 102 Fresno (93725) ***(P-7264)***
Universal Network Dev Corp (PA)...C...916 475-1200
2555 3rd St Ste 112 Sacramento (95818) ***(P-19880)***
Universal Plant Svcs Nthrn Cal (HQ)...E...707 864-0100
505 Lopes Rd Ste D Fairfield (94534) ***(P-14781)***
Universal Plastics Inc...E...916 787-0541
1020 Winding Creek Rd Roseville (95678) ***(P-1435)***
Universal Protection Svc LP...D...805 496-4401
2415 San Ramon Vly Blvd San Ramon (94583) ***(P-14105)***
Universal Service Recycl Inc (PA)...E...209 944-9555
3200 S El Dorado St Stockton (95206) ***(P-8374)***
Universal Services America LP...A...408 993-1965
777 N 1st St Ste 150 San Jose (95112) ***(P-14106)***
Universal Site Services Inc (PA)...C...800 647-9337
760 E Capitol Ave Milpitas (95035) ***(P-12014)***
Universal Svc Rcycl Merced Inc (PA)...D...209 944-9555
3200 S El Dorado St Stockton (95206) ***(P-8375)***
University Art Center Inc (PA)...D...650 328-3500
2550 El Camino Real Redwood City (94061) ***(P-14782)***
University Cal Press Fundation (PA)...D...510 642-4247
155 Grand Ave Ste 400 Oakland (94612) ***(P-3547)***
University Cal Press Fundation...E...510 642-4247
2000 Center St Ste 303 Berkeley (94704) ***(P-3548)***
University Cal San Francisco...D...415 476-9000
500 Parnassus Ave San Francisco (94143) ***(P-19241)***
University Cal San Francisco...C...415 353-7900
1545 Divisadero St San Francisco (94143) ***(P-15752)***
University Cal San Francisco...C...415 353-1915
1500 Owens St San Francisco (94158) ***(P-15753)***
University Cal San Francisco...C...415 353-2757
2380 Sutter St Fl 3 San Francisco (94115) ***(P-15754)***
University Cal San Francisco...C...415 989-5339
311 California St Ste 410 San Francisco (94104) ***(P-15755)***
University Cal San Francisco...C...415 885-7257
3333 California St # 115 San Francisco (94118) ***(P-15756)***
University Cal San Francisco...B...415 476-7000
401 Parnassus Ave San Francisco (94143) ***(P-16695)***
University Cal San Francisco...E...559 251-3033
2120 N Winery Ave Ste 102 Fresno (93703) ***(P-10486)***
University Cal San Francisco...B...415 476-1611
400 Parnassus Ave A633 San Francisco (94143) ***(P-16696)***
University Cal San Francisco...C...415 353-2383
400 Parnassus Ave San Francisco (94143) ***(P-15757)***
University Cal San Francisco...D...415 476-9323
1450 3rd St St230 San Francisco (94143) ***(P-19242)***
University Cal San Francisco...C...415 353-7576
1701 Divisadero St # 240 San Francisco (94115) ***(P-15758)***
University Cal San Francisco...D...510 987-0700
616 Forbes Blvd South San Francisco (94080) ***(P-7704)***
University Cal San Francisco...C...925 598-3500
5565 W Las Psts Blvd Pleasanton (94588) ***(P-15759)***
University Cal San Francisco...C...415 476-3016
521 Parnassus Ave Rm C152 San Francisco (94143) ***(P-16697)***
University Cal San Francisco...B...415 567-6600
1600 Divisadero St San Francisco (94143) ***(P-16698)***
University Cal San Francisco...B...415 206-8812
2550 23rd St Rm 10 San Francisco (94110) ***(P-16699)***
University Cal San Francisco...D...415 476-5608
100 Buchanan St San Francisco (94102) ***(P-15861)***
University Cal San Francisco...C...415 353-7700
1545 Divisadero St Fl 4 San Francisco (94143) ***(P-15760)***
University Cal San Francisco...C...415 597-8047
982 Mission St San Francisco (94103) ***(P-17085)***
University Cal San Francisco...C...415 353-7300
1701 Divisadero St San Francisco (94115) ***(P-15761)***
University Cal San Francisco...C...415 206-8430
1001 Potrero Ave Ste 7m San Francisco (94110) ***(P-16749)***
University Cal San Francisco...C...415 476-4575
400 Parnassus Ave Fl 2 San Francisco (94143) ***(P-15762)***
University Cal San Francisco...C...415 885-3668
1500 Owens St Ste 320 San Francisco (94158) ***(P-15763)***
University Cal San Francisco...C...415 885-7495
2233 Post St Ste 303 San Francisco (94115) ***(P-15764)***
University Cal San Francisco...C...415 885-3610
2356 Sutter St Fl 3 San Francisco (94115) ***(P-15765)***
University Cal San Francisco...C...415 476-3061
350 Parnassus Ave Ste 509 San Francisco (94117) ***(P-15766)***
University Cal San Francisco...C...415 353-2961
400 Parnassus Ave Fl 5 San Francisco (94143) ***(P-15767)***
University Cal San Francisco...C...415 885-7478
2356 Sutter St San Francisco (94115) ***(P-15768)***

University Cal San Frncsco Fnd.....D.....415 775-2111
3333 California St Ste 10 San Francisco (94118) ***(P-18195)***
University California Davis.....D.....916 734-8514
4150 V St Sacramento (95817) ***(P-15769)***
University California Davis.....D.....530 752-1653
4112a Tupper Hl Davis (95616) ***(P-16700)***
University California Davis.....D.....916 295-5700
550 W Ranch View Dr # 20 Rocklin (95765) ***(P-15770)***
University California Davis.....E.....530 750-1313
2801 2nd St Davis (95618) ***(P-19145)***
University California Davis.....D.....916 985-9300
251 Turn Pike Dr Folsom (95630) ***(P-15771)***
University California Davis.....D.....530 747-3000
2660 W Covell Blvd Davis (95616) ***(P-15772)***
University California Davis.....D.....530 752-2314
980 Old Davis Rd Davis (95616) ***(P-16818)***
University California Davis.....D.....916 734-3574
4430 V St Sacramento (95817) ***(P-15773)***
University California Davis.....D.....916 734-2846
2315 Stockton Blvd # 6309 Sacramento (95817) ***(P-15774)***
University California Davis.....D.....530 752-8277
1 Shields Ave Davis (95616) ***(P-7443)***
University California Davis.....C.....916 734-3141
4400 V St Sacramento (95817) ***(P-16701)***
University California Davis.....D.....916 734-3588
4860 Y St Sacramento (95817) ***(P-15775)***
University California Davis.....D.....530 885-5618
3200 Bell Rd Auburn (95603) ***(P-15776)***
University California Davis.....D.....916 734-2105
2521 Stockton Blvd Sacramento (95817) ***(P-15777)***
University California Davis.....D.....530 752-4167
Rm Tb 128 Old Davis Rd Davis (95616) ***(P-15778)***
University California Davis.....D.....530 752-2300
Student Hse Ctr Univ Of C Davis (95616) ***(P-15779)***
University California Davis.....C.....916 734-2011
2315 Stockton Blvd Sacramento (95817) ***(P-16702)***
University California Davis.....D.....916 734-6280
4860 Y St Ste 3700 Sacramento (95817) ***(P-15780)***
University California Davis.....D.....916 442-1011
500 University Ave # 220 Sacramento (95825) ***(P-15781)***
University California Davis.....D.....530 752-2330
501 Oak Ave Davis (95616) ***(P-15782)***
University California Davis.....C.....916 734-5113
4150 V St Ste 1200 Sacramento (95817) ***(P-16703)***
University California Davis.....C.....530 752-5435
1 Shields Ave Davis (95616) ***(P-7792)***
University California Berkeley.....E.....510 642-4247
155 Grand Ave Ste 400 Oakland (94612) ***(P-3549)***
University Club of Sf LLC.....E.....415 781-0900
800 Powell St San Francisco (94108) ***(P-15163)***
University Corp Advncd Internt.....E.....510 858-0881
6001 Shellmound St # 850 Emeryville (94608) ***(P-18321)***
University East-West Medicine.....E.....408 992-0218
595 Lawrence Expy Sunnyvale (94085) ***(P-19662)***
University Enterprises Inc.....A.....916 278-7001
6000 J St Sacramento (95819) ***(P-19414)***
University Fndtion Cal State U.....D.....530 898-5936
400 W 1st St Chico (95929) ***(P-10791)***
University Healthcare Alliance.....A.....510 974-8281
7999 Gateway Blvd Ste 200 Newark (94560) ***(P-16962)***
University Honda, Davis *Also called Envirnmental Trnsp Specialists* ***(P-14560)***
University of California.....D.....530 752-0503
1 Shields Ave Davis (95616) ***(P-19415)***
University of California Press, Oakland *Also called University California Berkeley* ***(P-3549)***
University Plating Co, San Jose *Also called Hane and Hane Inc* ***(P-4910)***
University Retirement Cmnty, Davis *Also called Pacific Retirement Svcs Inc* ***(P-18154)***
University Sequoia, Fresno *Also called Sunnyside Country Club* ***(P-15157)***
University Srgcal Diagnstc Ctr, Merced *Also called UAS Management Inc* ***(P-16689)***
University Surgical Associates, Fresno *Also called Central Cal Fclty Med Group In* ***(P-15335)***
Uniwell Corporation.....C.....559 268-1000
2233 Ventura St Fresno (93721) ***(P-10719)***
Uniwell Fresno Hotel LLC.....D.....559 268-1000
2233 Ventura St Fresno (93721) ***(P-11551)***
Unixsurplus Inc.....E.....408 844-0082
3060 Raymond St Santa Clara (95054) ***(P-8758)***
Unknown, San Rafael *Also called Kaiser Foundation Hospitals* ***(P-15452)***
Unknown, Roseville *Also called Kaiser Foundation Hospitals* ***(P-15472)***
Unknown, Reedley *Also called Adventist Health System/West* ***(P-15880)***
Unknown, Susanville *Also called Golden 1 Credit Union* ***(P-9833)***
Unlimited R US Inc (PA).....**E.....916 509-4496**
10535 E Stockton Blvd F Elk Grove (95624) ***(P-7917)***
Unorth, San Jose *Also called Mota Group Inc* ***(P-6505)***
Unshackled, Palo Alto *Also called Level Labs LP* ***(P-13277)***
Unspun Inc.....E.....207 577-8745
371 10th St San Francisco (94103) ***(P-2988)***
Untangle Holdings Inc (PA).....**E.....408 598-4299**
25 Metro Dr Ste 210 San Jose (95110) ***(P-13507)***
Upgrade Inc (PA).....**B.....347 776-1730**
275 Battery St Ste 2300 San Francisco (94111) ***(P-9863)***
Upguard Inc (PA).....**E.....888 882-3223**
723 N Shoreline Blvd Mountain View (94043) ***(P-13508)***
Uplift Inc.....D.....408 396-3374
440 N Wolfe Rd Sunnyvale (94085) ***(P-12889)***
Uplift Family Services (PA).....**D.....408 379-3790**
251 Llewellyn Ave Campbell (95008) ***(P-17778)***
Upper Valley Disposal Service (PA).....**E.....707 963-7988**
1285 Whitehall Ln Saint Helena (94574) ***(P-8376)***
Upright, Fresno *Also called Tanfield Engrg Systems US Inc* ***(P-5040)***

UPS, Santa Rosa *Also called United Parcel Service Inc* ***(P-14448)***
UPS, Richmond *Also called United Parcel Service Inc* ***(P-7658)***
UPS, Anderson *Also called United Parcel Service Inc* ***(P-7659)***
UPS, Fairfield *Also called United Parcel Service Inc* ***(P-7660)***
UPS, Ceres *Also called United Parcel Service Inc* ***(P-7661)***
UPS, West Sacramento *Also called United Parcel Service Inc* ***(P-7662)***
UPS, NAPA *Also called United Parcel Service Inc* ***(P-7663)***
UPS, Sacramento *Also called United Parcel Service Inc* ***(P-7664)***
UPS, Fresno *Also called United Parcel Service Inc* ***(P-7495)***
UPS, San Jose *Also called United Parcel Service Inc* ***(P-7665)***
UPS, Vallejo *Also called United Parcel Service Inc* ***(P-7667)***
UPS, San Francisco *Also called United Parcel Service Inc* ***(P-14449)***
UPS, Hayward *Also called United Parcel Service Inc* ***(P-7741)***
UPS, Mather *Also called United Parcel Service Inc* ***(P-7742)***
UPS, Oakland *Also called United Parcel Service Inc* ***(P-7668)***
UPS, South Lake Tahoe *Also called United Parcel Service Inc* ***(P-14450)***
UPS, Ukiah *Also called United Parcel Service Inc* ***(P-7669)***
UPS, Sacramento *Also called Mailboxes and Bus Svcs Inc* ***(P-14327)***
UPS, Angels Camp *Also called United Parcel Service Inc* ***(P-7670)***
UPS, Rocklin *Also called United Parcel Service Inc* ***(P-7671)***
UPS, Santa Cruz *Also called United Parcel Service Inc* ***(P-7672)***
UPS, San Ramon *Also called United Parcel Service Inc* ***(P-7673)***
UPS, Fremont *Also called United Parcel Service Inc* ***(P-14451)***
UPS, Sacramento *Also called United Parcel Service Inc* ***(P-7674)***
UPS Ground Freight Inc.....D.....408 400-0595
925 Morse Ave Sunnyvale (94089) ***(P-7608)***
UPS Ground Freight Inc.....D.....916 371-9101
900 E St West Sacramento (95605) ***(P-7609)***
UPS Supply Chain Solutions Inc.....D.....209 319-4116
1150 E Arbor Ave Ste 101 Tracy (95304) ***(P-7857)***
Upscale Construction Inc.....D.....415 563-7550
2151 Union St 1 San Francisco (94123) ***(P-776)***
Upside Foods Inc.....E.....510 746-1198
804 Heinz Ave Ste 200 Berkeley (94710) ***(P-2953)***
Upstart Holdings Inc (PA).....**B.....650 204-1000**
2950 S Del St Ste 300 San Mateo (94403) ***(P-9934)***
Upstart Network Inc.....D.....650 204-1000
2950 S Del St Ste 300 San Mateo (94403) ***(P-9864)***
Uptima Inc.....E.....408 933-9505
55 E Empire St San Jose (95112) ***(P-12890)***
Uptown Theatre.....D.....707 259-0123
1350 Third St NAPA (94559) ***(P-14866)***
Upwork Global Inc (HQ).....**E.....650 316-7500**
655 Montgomery St Ste 490 San Francisco (94111) ***(P-12891)***
Upwork Inc (PA).....**C.....650 316-7500**
2625 Augustine Dr Fl 6th Santa Clara (95054) ***(P-12149)***
Urata & Sons Concrete Inc.....C.....916 638-5364
3430 Luyung Dr Rancho Cordova (95742) ***(P-1914)***
Urata & Sons Concrete LLC.....D.....916 638-5364
3430 Luyung Dr Rancho Cordova (95742) ***(P-1915)***
Urban Farmer Store Inc (PA).....**E.....415 661-2204**
2833 Vicente St San Francisco (94116) ***(P-9047)***
Urban Painting Inc.....D.....415 485-1130
40 Lisbon St San Rafael (94901) ***(P-1436)***
Urban Services Eastlake YMCA, Oakland *Also called Young MNS Chrstn Assn of E Bay* ***(P-18505)***
Urban Services YMCA, Oakland *Also called Young MNS Chrstn Assn of E Bay* ***(P-18487)***
Urbanbcn Worldwide, South San Francisco *Also called Black Car Network LLC* ***(P-7325)***
Urbanbcn Worldwide.....E.....415 494-8122
1184 San Mateo Ave South San Francisco (94080) ***(P-7410)***
Urgent Care-Selma Dst Hosp, Selma *Also called Adventist Health Selma* ***(P-16286)***
Urgent Upfits, Rancho Cordova *Also called Form & Fusion Mfg Inc* ***(P-4883)***
Uri Tech Inc.....F.....408 456-0115
1670 Santa Lucia Dr San Jose (95125) ***(P-5994)***
Urology Associates Central Cal.....D.....559 321-2800
7014 N Whitney Ave Ste A Fresno (93720) ***(P-15783)***
URS Alaska LLC (HQ).....**E.....415 774-2700**
600 Montgomery St Fl 25 San Francisco (94111) ***(P-18844)***
URS Corporation (HQ).....**E.....213 593-8100**
300 California St Fl 4 San Francisco (94104) ***(P-18845)***
URS Corporation.....E.....510 893-3600
300 Lakeside Dr Ste 400 Oakland (94612) ***(P-18846)***
URS Group Inc.....D.....510 893-3600
300 Lakeside Dr Ste 400 Oakland (94612) ***(P-18847)***
URS Group Inc.....D.....925 446-3800
300 Lakeside Dr Ste 400 Oakland (94612) ***(P-18848)***
URS Group Inc.....D.....408 297-9585
4 N 2nd St San Jose (95113) ***(P-18849)***
URS Group Inc.....D.....559 255-2541
1360 E Spruce Ave Ste 101 Fresno (93720) ***(P-18850)***
URS Group Inc.....D.....530 893-9675
1550 Humboldt Rd Ste 2 Chico (95928) ***(P-19243)***
URS Holdings Inc (HQ).....**B.....415 774-2700**
600 Montgomery St Fl 25 San Francisco (94111) ***(P-18851)***
US Carenet Services LLC.....C.....408 871-9860
901 Campisi Way Ste 205 Campbell (95008) ***(P-16963)***
US Carenet Services LLC.....C.....408 378-6131
815 Pollard Rd Los Gatos (95032) ***(P-16964)***
US Dies Inc (PA).....**E.....209 664-1402**
1992 Rockefeller Dr # 300 Ceres (95307) ***(P-5087)***
US Foods Inc.....B.....925 606-3525
300 Lawrence Dr Frnt Livermore (94551) ***(P-9321)***
US Glass Inc.....E.....916 376-8801
1745 Enterprise Blvd West Sacramento (95691) ***(P-1946)***

ALPHABETIC SECTION Valley Health Plan

US Interactive Delaware (PA) ....C....**408 863-7500**
1270 Oakmead Pkwy Ste 318 Sunnyvale (94085) ***(P-18852)***
US Machining, San Jose *Also called TLC Machining Incorporated* ***(P-5101)***
US Pipe Fabrication LLC ....E....530 742-5171
3387 Plumas Arboga Rd Marysville (95901) ***(P-4236)***
US Power, Vacaville *Also called MCS Opco LLC* ***(P-8868)***
US Script Inc (HQ) ....E....**559 244-3700**
5 E River Park Pl E # 210 Fresno (93720) ***(P-10363)***
Us1com Inc ....F....707 781-2560
715 Southpoint Blvd Ste D Petaluma (94954) ***(P-3753)***
USA Multifamily Management Inc ....C....916 773-6060
3200 Douglas Blvd Ste 200 Roseville (95661) ***(P-10679)***
USA North 811, Concord *Also called Undergrund Svc Alert Nthrn Cal* ***(P-19659)***
USA Products Group (PA) ....E....**209 334-1460**
1300 E Vine St Lodi (95240) ***(P-7202)***
USA Properties Fund Inc (PA) ....C....**916 773-6060**
3200 Douglas Blvd Ste 200 Roseville (95661) ***(P-10720)***
USA Seller Co LLC ....B....209 656-7085
2840 Countryside Dr Turlock (95380) ***(P-357)***
USA Waste of California Inc (HQ) ....E....**916 387-1400**
11931 Foundation Pl # 200 Gold River (95670) ***(P-8377)***
Uscf Advisers LLC ....B....510 522-9600
1999 Harrison St Ste 1530 Oakland (94612) ***(P-10066)***
Uscf Caps Department Medicine, San Francisco *Also called University Cal San Francisco* ***(P-19241)***
USD, Union City *Also called Union Sanitary District* ***(P-8295)***
Used Pellet Co, Fresno *Also called JJ Charles Inc* ***(P-3260)***
User Zoom Inc ....D....408 533-8619
10 Almaden Blvd Ste 250 San Jose (95113) ***(P-12892)***
Usertesting Inc (PA) ....D....**650 567-5616**
144 Townsend St San Francisco (94107) ***(P-13509)***
USG, West Sacramento *Also called US Glass Inc* ***(P-1946)***
USG Interiors LLC ....B....209 466-4636
2575 Loomis Rd Stockton (95205) ***(P-8611)***
USI Insrnce Svcs Nthrn Cal Inc (HQ) ....E....**209 954-3900**
2021 W March Ln Ste 3 Stockton (95207) ***(P-10364)***
USI Insurance Services Nat Inc ....D....914 749-8500
39899 Balentine Dr # 200 Newark (94560) ***(P-9692)***
USI Insurance Services Nat Inc ....D....925 988-1700
1001 Galaxy Way Ste 300 Concord (94520) ***(P-9693)***
USI Manufacturing Services Inc ....E....408 636-9600
1255 E Arques Ave Sunnyvale (94085) ***(P-5420)***
Usk Manufacturing Inc ....E....510 471-7555
720 Zwissig Way Union City (94587) ***(P-4828)***
Usko Expedite Inc (PA) ....E....**916 233-4455**
11290 Point East Dr # 110 Rancho Cordova (95742) ***(P-7858)***
Usko Express Inc ....D....916 515-8065
11290 Point East Dr # 200 Rancho Cordova (95742) ***(P-7680)***
Ustc, Chico *Also called United Sttes Thrmlctric Cnsrti* ***(P-6735)***
Ustov Inc ....E....510 781-1818
21118 Cabot Blvd Hayward (94545) ***(P-9322)***
Ustream Inc ....D....415 489-9400
410 Townsend St Fl 4 San Francisco (94107) ***(P-8002)***
Utap Printing Co Inc ....E....650 588-2818
1423 San Mateo Ave South San Francisco (94080) ***(P-3708)***
Utility Tree Service LLC (HQ) ....E....**530 226-0330**
1884 Keystone Ct Ste A Redding (96003) ***(P-525)***
Utility Tree Service, Inc., Redding *Also called Utility Tree Service LLC* ***(P-525)***
Utstarcom Inc (HQ) ....C....**408 791-6168**
2635 N 1st St Ste 148 San Jose (95134) ***(P-5814)***
Uxreactor Inc ....E....888 897-3228
5870 Stnrdge Mall Rd Ste Pleasanton (94588) ***(P-13686)***
V A Anderson Enterprises Inc ....D....925 866-6150
2680 Bishop Dr Ste 140 San Ramon (94583) ***(P-11853)***
V and V Farms, Lodi *Also called Jose Vramontes* ***(P-176)***
V B Glass Co Inc ....E....209 984-4111
10002 Victoria Way Jamestown (95327) ***(P-1947)***
V C A Almaden Vly Animal Hosp, San Jose *Also called VCA Almaden Valley Hospital* ***(P-341)***
V C A Animal Hosp Santa Cruz, Santa Cruz *Also called Animal Clinic of Santa Cruz* ***(P-320)***
V C A Blossom Hill Animal Hosp, San Jose *Also called HB Animal Clinics Inc* ***(P-326)***
V S S, West Sacramento *Also called Vss International Inc* ***(P-1079)***
V Sangiacomo & Sons ....E....707 938-5503
21543 Broadway Sonoma (95476) ***(P-80)***
V Sattui Winery ....D....707 963-7774
1111 White Ln Saint Helena (94574) ***(P-2752)***
V Tech, Sunnyvale *Also called V-Tech Manufacturing Inc* ***(P-5633)***
V-Tech Manufacturing Inc ....F....408 730-9200
1140 W Evelyn Ave Sunnyvale (94086) ***(P-5633)***
V2solutions Inc (PA) ....C....**408 550-2340**
2340 Walsh Ave Santa Clara (95051) ***(P-19881)***
V3 Electric Inc ....C....916 597-2627
4925 Robert J Mathews Pkw El Dorado Hills (95762) ***(P-8206)***
V3 Systems Scrtyautomation Inc ....E....916 543-1543
4925 Robert J Matthews Pa El Dorado Hills (95762) ***(P-14453)***
VA Fremont Clinic, Fremont *Also called Veterans Health Administration* ***(P-15789)***
VA Hospital, Fresno *Also called Veterans Health Administration* ***(P-16713)***
VA Palo Alto Healthcare System, Palo Alto *Also called Veterans Health Administration* ***(P-19417)***
Vaca Valley Hospital, Vacaville *Also called Northbay Healthcare Group* ***(P-16467)***
Vaca Valley Inn ....D....707 446-8888
1050 Orange Dr Vacaville (95687) ***(P-11552)***
Vaca Valley Roofing Inc (PA) ....E....**707 469-7470**
21 Town Sq Uppr Vacaville (95688) ***(P-1843)***
Vacaville Condolescent and Reh ....C....707 449-8000
585 Nut Tree Ct Vacaville (95687) ***(P-12203)***
Vacaville Fruit Co Inc (PA) ....E....**707 448-5292**
2055 Cessna Dr Ste 200 Vacaville (95688) ***(P-2273)***
Vacaville Medical Center, Vacaville *Also called Kaiser Foundation Hospitals* ***(P-15455)***
Vacaville Psychiatric Program, Vacaville *Also called State Hospitals Cal Dept* ***(P-16747)***
Vacavlle Cnvalescent Rehab Ctr ....D....707 449-8000
585 Nut Tree Ct Vacaville (95687) ***(P-16281)***
Vacuum Engrg & Mtls Co Inc ....E....408 871-9900
390 Reed St Santa Clara (95050) ***(P-3799)***
Vacuum Process Engineering Inc ....D....916 925-6100
150 Commerce Cir Sacramento (95815) ***(P-19146)***
Vagaro Inc ....D....800 919-0157
4120 Dublin Blvd Ste 250 Dublin (94568) ***(P-12893)***
Valassis Direct Mail Inc ....D....510 505-6500
6955 Mowry Ave Newark (94560) ***(P-11842)***
Valassis Direct Mail Inc ....D....916 923-2398
1601 Response Rd Ste 100 Sacramento (95815) ***(P-11843)***
Valdor Fiber Optics Inc (PA) ....F....**510 293-1212**
1838 D St Hayward (94541) ***(P-6799)***
Vale Healthcare Center, San Pablo *Also called Mariner Health Care Inc* ***(P-16050)***
Vale Healthcare Center, San Pablo *Also called Vale Operating Company LP* ***(P-16149)***
Vale Operating Company LP ....A....510 232-5945
13484 San Pablo Ave San Pablo (94806) ***(P-16149)***
Valent Dublin Laboratories, San Ramon *Also called Valent USA LLC* ***(P-4147)***
Valent USA LLC ....E....925 256-2700
4600 Norris Canyon Rd San Ramon (94583) ***(P-4147)***
Valentine Corporation ....E....415 453-3732
111 Pelican Way San Rafael (94901) ***(P-2083)***
Valero Energy Corporation ....B....707 745-7011
3400 E 2nd St Benicia (94510) ***(P-4184)***
Valero Ref Company-California ....A....707 745-7011
3400 E 2nd St Benicia (94510) ***(P-4185)***
Valgenesis Inc (PA) ....D....**510 445-0505**
395 Oyster Point Blvd # 228 South San Francisco (94080) ***(P-8759)***
Valiantica Inc (PA) ....E....**408 694-3803**
940 Saratoga Ave Ste 290 San Jose (95129) ***(P-13510)***
Validant, San Francisco *Also called Kinsale Holdings Inc* ***(P-19550)***
Valimet Inc (PA) ....D....**209 444-1600**
431 Sperry Rd Stockton (95206) ***(P-4595)***
Valin Corporation (PA) ....D....**408 730-9850**
5225 Hellyer Ave Ste 250 San Jose (95138) ***(P-9102)***
Valine Court Senior Care Inc ....D....916 394-9400
966 43rd Ave Sacramento (95831) ***(P-18196)***
Vallejo City Unified Schl Dst ....D....707 556-8694
1155 Capitol St Vallejo (94590) ***(P-18042)***
Vallejo Flood & Wastewater Dst ....D....707 644-8949
450 Ryder St Vallejo (94590) ***(P-19882)***
Vallejo Flood Wstwter Dst Fing ....D....707 644-8949
450 Ryder St Vallejo (94590) ***(P-19883)***
Vallejo Garbage & Recycling, Vallejo *Also called Recology Vallejo* ***(P-8355)***
Vallejo Nissan Inc ....E....707 643-8291
3287 Sonoma Blvd Vallejo (94590) ***(P-8472)***
Vallejo Plice Dept Plg RES Uni, Vallejo *Also called City of Vallejo* ***(P-17229)***
Valley AC & Repr Inc ....E....559 237-3188
1350 F St Fresno (93706) ***(P-1389)***
Valley AC Engrg Inc ....E....209 524-7756
1313 Lone Palm Ave Modesto (95351) ***(P-1390)***
Valley Air District, Fresno *Also called San Joaquin Val UNI Air Pol* ***(P-19856)***
Valley Care Health System, The, Pleasanton *Also called Hospi Comm For The L-P Area T* ***(P-19349)***
Valley Childrens Hospital ....C....559 353-6425
9300 Valley Childrens Pl Madera (93636) ***(P-16704)***
Valley Childrens Hospital (PA) ....A....**559 353-3000**
9300 Valley Childrens Pl Madera (93636) ***(P-16705)***
Valley Childrens Hospital ....C....559 353-7442
5085 E Mckinley Ave Fresno (93727) ***(P-16706)***
Valley Childrens Medical Group ....D....559 353-6241
9300 Valley Childrens Pl Sc61 Madera (93636) ***(P-16771)***
Valley Chld Hlthcare Fundation ....A....559 353-3000
9300 Valley Childrens Pl Madera (93636) ***(P-15784)***
Valley Chrome Plating Inc ....D....559 298-8094
1028 Hoblitt Ave Clovis (93612) ***(P-4923)***
Valley Clerks Trust Fund, Roseville *Also called Ufcw & Employers Trust LLC* ***(P-18380)***
Valley Communications Inc (PA) ....D....**916 349-7300**
6921 Roseville Rd Sacramento (95842) ***(P-1627)***
Valley Controls Inc ....F....559 638-5115
583 E Dinuba Ave Reedley (93654) ***(P-6736)***
Valley Convalescent Hospital, Watsonville *Also called West Coast Hospitals Inc* ***(P-16156)***
Valley Decorating Company ....E....559 495-1100
2829 E Hamilton Ave Fresno (93721) ***(P-4329)***
Valley Fig Growers ....E....559 349-1686
2028 S 3rd St Fresno (93702) ***(P-313)***
Valley Fine Foods Company Inc ....D....530 671-7200
300 Epley Dr Yuba City (95991) ***(P-2954)***
Valley Fine Foods Company Inc (PA) ....D....**707 746-6888**
3909 Park Rd Ste H Benicia (94510) ***(P-2312)***
Valley First Credit Union (PA) ....D....**209 549-8511**
1419 J St Modesto (95354) ***(P-9826)***
Valley Forklift ....F....916 371-6165
3834 Commerce Dr West Sacramento (95691) ***(P-5069)***
Valley Fresh Inc (HQ) ....E....**209 943-5411**
1404 S Fresno Ave Stockton (95206) ***(P-2139)***
Valley Fresh Foods Inc ....E....209 669-5600
3600 E Linwood Ave Turlock (95380) ***(P-233)***
Valley Fresh Foods Inc ....E....209 669-5510
1220 Hall Rd Denair (95316) ***(P-234)***
Valley Garlic Inc ....E....559 934-1763
500 Enterprise Pkwy Coalinga (93210) ***(P-2289)***
Valley Health Care Systems Inc ....C....916 505-4112
1300 National Dr Ste 140 Sacramento (95834) ***(P-12150)***
Valley Health Plan ....B....408 885-4760
2480 N 1st St Ste 160 San Jose (95131) ***(P-10156)***

ALPHABETIC

Valley Health Team, Kerman *Also called Valley Optometric Center* ***(P-15875)***
Valley Healthcare Center LLC..........D.......559 251-7161
4840 E Tulare Ave Fresno (93727) ***(P-16150)***
Valley Healthcare Staffing, Sacramento *Also called Valley Health Care Systems Inc* ***(P-12150)***
Valley Heights Senior Cmnty..........E.......831 722-4884
925 Freedom Blvd Watsonville (95076) ***(P-18197)***
Valley House Care Center, Santa Clara *Also called TLC of Bay Area Inc* ***(P-16143)***
Valley Images LLC..........F.......408 279-6777
1925 Kyle Park Ct San Jose (95125) ***(P-3754)***
Valley Inventory Service Inc..........D.......707 422-6050
1180 Horizon Dr Ste B Fairfield (94533) ***(P-14454)***
Valley Iron Works Inc..........E.......209 368-7037
127 E Harney Ln Lodi (95240) ***(P-1933)***
Valley Lahvosh Baking Co Inc..........E.......559 485-2700
502 M St Fresno (93721) ***(P-2409)***
Valley Landscaping & Maint Inc..........C.......209 334-3659
12900 N Lwer Scramento Rd Lodi (95242) ***(P-508)***
Valley Milk LLC..........D.......209 410-6701
400 N Washington Rd Turlock (95380) ***(P-226)***
Valley Montessori School..........D.......925 455-8021
1273 N Livermore Ave Livermore (94551) ***(P-18043)***
Valley Northamerican, Concord *Also called Valley Rlction Stor Nthrn Cal* ***(P-7638)***
Valley Northamerican, West Sacramento *Also called Valley Rlction Stor Nthrn Cal* ***(P-7639)***
Valley Northamerican, Milpitas *Also called Valley Rlction Stor Nthrn Cal* ***(P-7640)***
Valley Oak Dental Group..........E.......209 823-9341
1507 W Yosemite Ave Manteca (95337) ***(P-15862)***
Valley of California, Inc., Concord *Also called Coldwell Bnkr Residential Brkg* ***(P-10515)***
Valley of Moon Winery..........F.......707 939-4500
134 Church St Sonoma (95476) ***(P-2753)***
Valley Oil Co, Mountain View *Also called Bosco Oil Inc* ***(P-9523)***
Valley Optometric Center..........E.......559 846-5252
449 S Madera Ave Kerman (93630) ***(P-15875)***
Valley Pacific Petro Svcs Inc (PA)..........**E.......209 948-9412**
152 Frank West Cir # 100 Stockton (95206) ***(P-9541)***
Valley Packline Solutions..........E.......559 638-7821
5259 Avenue 408 Reedley (93654) ***(P-5136)***
Valley Peterbilt, Stockton *Also called Interstate Truck Center LLC* ***(P-8426)***
Valley Pinte Nursing Rehab Ctr..........E.......510 538-8464
20090 Stanton Ave Castro Valley (94546) ***(P-18198)***
Valley Power Systems Inc..........F.......510 635-8991
2070 Farallon Dr San Leandro (94577) ***(P-9103)***
Valley Printing, Ceres *Also called Robert R Wix Inc* ***(P-3748)***
Valley Protein LLC..........D.......559 498-7115
1828 E Hedges Ave Fresno (93703) ***(P-2127)***
Valley Public Radio, Clovis *Also called White Ash Broadcasting Inc* ***(P-8037)***
Valley Public Television Inc..........D.......559 266-1800
1544 Van Ness Ave Fresno (93721) ***(P-8056)***
Valley Rgnal Occptnal Programs..........D.......559 876-2122
1305 Q St Sanger (93657) ***(P-17843)***
Valley Rlction Stor Nthrn Cal (PA)..........**E.......925 230-2025**
5000 Marsh Dr Concord (94520) ***(P-7638)***
Valley Rlction Stor Nthrn Cal..........D.......916 375-0001
3230 Reed Ave West Sacramento (95605) ***(P-7639)***
Valley Rlction Stor Nthrn Cal..........D.......408 938-3672
835 Sinclair Frontage Rd Milpitas (95035) ***(P-7640)***
Valley Rock Lndscpe Material..........E.......916 652-7209
4018 Taylor Rd Loomis (95650) ***(P-4415)***
Valley Rubber & Gasket, Sacramento *Also called Eriks North America Inc* ***(P-9117)***
Valley Services Electronics, San Jose *Also called Tri-Phase Inc* ***(P-5988)***
Valley Sheet Metal, South San Francisco *Also called Frank M Booth Inc* ***(P-1267)***
Valley Sheet Metal Co, Marysville *Also called Frank M Booth Inc* ***(P-1266)***
Valley Stairway Inc..........F.......559 299-0151
5684 E Shields Ave Fresno (93727) ***(P-4842)***
Valley Sun Products of Cali..........E.......209 862-1200
3324 Orestimba Rd Newman (95360) ***(P-2955)***
Valley Surgical Center..........E.......925 734-3360
5555 W Las Positas Blvd Pleasanton (94588) ***(P-16707)***
Valley Tech Systems Inc..........E.......916 760-1025
160 Blue Ravine Rd Ste A Folsom (95630) ***(P-18853)***
Valley Teen Ranch..........D.......559 437-1144
2610 W Shaw Ln Ste 105 Fresno (93711) ***(P-18199)***
Valley Tire and Brake of Santa (PA)..........**E.......707 544-3420**
1688 Piner Rd Santa Rosa (95403) ***(P-14627)***
Valley Tool & Mfg Co Inc..........E.......209 883-4093
2507 Tully Rd Hughson (95326) ***(P-5634)***
Valley Toxicology Service Inc..........E.......916 371-5440
2401 Port St West Sacramento (95691) ***(P-16819)***
Valley Transportation Inc (PA)..........**D.......559 266-6674**
2837 S East Ave Fresno (93725) ***(P-7496)***
Valley Truck and Tractor Inc..........D.......530 738-4421
Hwy 113 Robbins (95676) ***(P-9048)***
Valley Unique Electric Inc..........D.......559 237-4795
75 Park Creek Dr Ste 101 Clovis (93611) ***(P-1628)***
Valley Vascular Surgery Assoc..........E.......559 431-6226
1247 E Alluvial Ave # 101 Fresno (93720) ***(P-15785)***
Valley View Care Center, Riverbank *Also called Valley West Health Care Inc* ***(P-16151)***
Valley View Foods Inc..........D.......530 673-7356
7547 Sawtelle Ave Yuba City (95991) ***(P-2246)***
Valley Village, Santa Clara *Also called Church of Vly Rtrment Hmes Inc* ***(P-18077)***
Valley Waterproofing Inc..........D.......408 985-7701
825 Civic Center Dr Ste 6 Santa Clara (95050) ***(P-2084)***
Valley Welding & Machine Works, Fresno *Also called Garabedian Bros Inc* ***(P-5529)***
Valley West Care Center, Williams *Also called Valley West Health Care Inc* ***(P-16282)***
Valley West Health Care Inc (PA)..........**D.......530 473-5321**
1224 E St Williams (95987) ***(P-16282)***
Valley West Health Care Inc..........E.......209 869-2569
2649 Topeka St Riverbank (95367) ***(P-16151)***
Valley Wholesale Drug Co LLC..........D.......209 466-0131
1401 W Fremont St Stockton (95203) ***(P-9239)***
Valley Wide Beverage Company, Fresno *Also called Fresno Beverage Company Inc* ***(P-9551)***
Valley Yellow Pages, Fresno *Also called Agi Publishing Inc* ***(P-11738)***
Valley-HI Country Club..........C.......916 684-2120
9595 Franklin Blvd Elk Grove (95758) ***(P-15164)***
Valley-Mntain Regional Ctr Inc (PA)..........**C.......209 473-0951**
702 N Aurora St Stockton (95202) ***(P-17779)***
Valley-Mntain Regional Ctr Inc..........D.......209 955-3207
Cummins Dr MODESTO (95350) ***(P-17780)***
Valleycare Health, Livermore *Also called Valleycare Hospital Corp* ***(P-16709)***
Valleycare Hospital Corp..........C.......925 447-7000
1119 E Stanley Blvd Livermore (94550) ***(P-16708)***
Valleycare Hospital Corp (HQ)..........**A.......925 447-7000**
1111 E Stanley Blvd Livermore (94550) ***(P-16709)***
VALLEYPBS, Fresno *Also called Valley Public Television Inc* ***(P-8056)***
Valleywide Maintenance, Fresno *Also called San Mar Properties Inc* ***(P-10658)***
Valor Compounding Pharmacy Inc..........E.......510 548-8777
2461 Shattuck Ave Berkeley (94704) ***(P-4001)***
Valtox Laboratories, West Sacramento *Also called Valley Toxicology Service Inc* ***(P-16819)***
Value Place Hotel..........D.......916 688-1330
550 Hawkcrest Cir Sacramento (95835) ***(P-11553)***
Value Products Inc..........E.......209 345-3817
2128 Industrial Dr Stockton (95206) ***(P-4065)***
Valueact Capital Management LP..........E.......415 249-1232
1 Letterman Dr Bldg D4th San Francisco (94129) ***(P-10771)***
Valyria LLC (HQ)..........**D.......707 452-0600**
1050 Aviator Dr Vacaville (95688) ***(P-8523)***
Vampire Penguin LLC (PA)..........**F.......916 553-4197**
907 K St Sacramento (95814) ***(P-2185)***
Van Acker Cnstr Assoc Inc..........C.......415 383-5589
1060 Rdwood Hwy Frntage R Mill Valley (94941) ***(P-725)***
Van Beurden Insurance Svcs Inc (PA)..........**D.......559 634-7125**
1600 Draper St Kingsburg (93631) ***(P-10365)***
Van De Poel Levy & Allen LLP..........E.......925 274-7650
1600 S Main St Ste 325 Walnut Creek (94596) ***(P-17385)***
Van De Pol Enterprises Inc (PA)..........**D.......209 465-3421**
4895 S Airport Way Stockton (95206) ***(P-9542)***
Van Der Hout Brggiano Nghtngal..........E.......415 981-3000
180 Sutter St Fl 5 San Francisco (94104) ***(P-17386)***
Van Duerr Industries Inc..........E.......530 893-1596
21 Valley Ct Chico (95973) ***(P-8649)***
Van Dykes Rice Dryer Inc..........E.......916 655-3171
4036 Pleasant Grove Rd Pleasant Grove (95668) ***(P-314)***
Van Groningen & Sons Inc..........B.......209 982-5248
15100 Jack Tone Rd Manteca (95336) ***(P-194)***
Van Midde & Son Concrete..........D.......415 459-2530
490 B St San Rafael (94901) ***(P-1916)***
Van Ness Hotel Inc..........D.......415 673-4711
1050 Van Ness Ave San Francisco (94109) ***(P-11554)***
Van Sark Inc (PA)..........**C.......510 635-1111**
410 Harriet St San Francisco (94103) ***(P-3293)***
Van Winden Landscaping Inc..........E.......707 224-1367
3101 California Blvd NAPA (94558) ***(P-443)***
Van Wolfs LLC..........E.......916 372-6464
8130 Berry Ave Ste 100 Sacramento (95828) ***(P-9331)***
Vander Lans & Sons Inc (PA)..........**E.......209 334-4115**
1320 S Sacramento St Lodi (95240) ***(P-5450)***
Vander-Bend Manufacturing Inc (PA)..........**B.......408 245-5150**
2701 Orchard Pkwy San Jose (95134) ***(P-6481)***
Vander-Bend Manufacturing Inc..........C.......916 631-6375
3510 Luyung Dr Rancho Cordova (95742) ***(P-5635)***
Vanderhulst Associates Inc..........E.......408 727-1313
3300 Victor Ct Santa Clara (95054) ***(P-5636)***
Vanguard Marketing, Scotts Valley *Also called Threshold Enterprises Ltd* ***(P-3822)***
Vanguard Music and Prfrmg Arts..........D.......408 727-5532
1795 Space Park Dr Santa Clara (95054) ***(P-18478)***
Vanir Construction MGT Inc (PA)..........**D.......916 444-3700**
4540 Duckhorn Dr Ste 300 Sacramento (95834) ***(P-19416)***
Vanir Development Company Inc..........E.......916 419-2400
4540 Duckhorn Dr Ste 100 Sacramento (95834) ***(P-980)***
Vanmali Inc..........E.......650 576-9134
251 El Camino Real San Carlos (94070) ***(P-11555)***
Vann Brothers..........C.......530 473-2607
365 Ruggieri Way Williams (95987) ***(P-36)***
Vann Family LLC..........C.......530 473-3317
6141 Abel Rd Williams (95987) ***(P-114)***
Vann Family Orchard, Williams *Also called Vann Family LLC* ***(P-114)***
Vannelli Foods LLC..........F.......916 412-1204
4031 Alvis Ct Rocklin (95677) ***(P-2956)***
Vantage Data Ctrs MGT Co LLC (PA)..........**E.......408 748-9830**
2820 Northwestern Pkwy Santa Clara (95051) ***(P-10826)***
Vantagepoint Capital Partners, San Bruno *Also called Vantagepoint Management Inc* ***(P-10893)***
Vantagepoint Capital Partners (PA)..........**D.......650 866-3100**
1111 Bayhill Dr Ste 220 San Bruno (94066) ***(P-10892)***
Vantagepoint Management Inc (PA)..........**D.......650 866-3100**
1111 Bayhill Dr Ste 220 San Bruno (94066) ***(P-10893)***
Vantec Thermal Technologies, Fremont *Also called Siblings Investment Inc* ***(P-8747)***
Vaquero Farms Inc..........D.......559 659-2790
43405 W Panoche Rd Firebaugh (93622) ***(P-195)***
Varex Imaging West LLC (HQ)..........**C.......408 565-0850**
2175 Mission College Blvd Santa Clara (95054) ***(P-7095)***
Varian Associates Limited..........E.......650 493-4000
3100 Hansen Way Palo Alto (94304) ***(P-7054)***

Varian Medical Systems Inc (HQ)....A....**650 493-4000**
3100 Hansen Way Palo Alto (94304) ***(P-7131)***
Varian Medical Systems Inc....E....650 213-8000
3120 Hansen Way Palo Alto (94304) ***(P-7055)***
Varian Medical Systems Inc....C....408 321-9400
660 N Mccarthy Blvd Milpitas (95035) ***(P-7056)***
Various Technologies Inc....E....408 972-4460
2720 Aiello Dr Ste C San Jose (95111) ***(P-5691)***
Varis LLC....D....916 294-0860
3915 Security Park Dr B Rancho Cordova (95742) ***(P-19663)***
Varis LLC (PA)....E....**916 294-0860**
9245 Sierra College Blvd Roseville (95661) ***(P-19664)***
Varite Inc (PA)....E....**408 977-0700**
111 N Market St Ste 730 San Jose (95113) ***(P-12894)***
Varmour Networks Inc (PA)....D....**650 564-5100**
270 3rd St Los Altos (94022) ***(P-13511)***
Varni Brothers Corporation (PA)....D....**209 521-1777**
400 Hosmer Ave Modesto (95351) ***(P-9564)***
Varni Brothers Corporation....D....209 526-5513
416 Hosmer Ave Modesto (95351) ***(P-9586)***
Varni Brothers Corporation....D....209 464-7778
1109 W Anderson St Stockton (95206) ***(P-2817)***
Vascular and Varicose Vein Ctr, Roseville *Also called Sutter Health* ***(P-15716)***
Vasko Electric Inc....D....916 568-7700
4300 Astoria St Sacramento (95838) ***(P-1629)***
Vasona Management Inc....D....510 352-8728
13949 Doolittle Dr San Leandro (94577) ***(P-10466)***
Vasona Management Inc....B....510 413-0091
37390 Central Mont Pl Fremont (94538) ***(P-726)***
Vasonic Construction, Fremont *Also called Vasona Management Inc* ***(P-726)***
Vast Systems Technology Corp....E....650 584-5000
700 E Middlefield Rd Mountain View (94043) ***(P-12895)***
Vasto Valle Farms, Huron *Also called Dick Anderson & Sons Farming* ***(P-158)***
Vat Incorporated (HQ)....E....**800 935-1446**
655 River Oaks Pkwy San Jose (95134) ***(P-9139)***
Vave Health Inc....F....650 387-7059
2350 Mission College Blvd # 1200 Santa Clara (95054) ***(P-7132)***
Vavrinek Trine Day & Co, Fresno *Also called Eide Bailly LLP* ***(P-18954)***
Vaxaville Medical Offices, Vacaville *Also called Kaiser Foundation Hospitals* ***(P-10120)***
Vaxcyte Inc (PA)....D....**650 837-0111**
353 Hatch Dr Foster City (94404) ***(P-4059)***
Vb Golf LLC....E....650 573-7888
2401 E 3rd Ave Foster City (94404) ***(P-15035)***
Vbp Orange, San Francisco *Also called Venables/Bell & Partners LLC* ***(P-11794)***
VCA Almaden Valley Hospital....D....408 268-3550
15790 Almaden Expy San Jose (95120) ***(P-341)***
VCA Animal Hospitals Inc....E....650 631-7400
501 Laurel St San Carlos (94070) ***(P-342)***
VCA Holly Street, San Carlos *Also called VCA Animal Hospitals Inc* ***(P-342)***
Vcinity Inc (PA)....E....**408 841-4700**
2055 Gateway Pl Ste 650 San Jose (95110) ***(P-14004)***
Vcinity Ultimate Access, San Jose *Also called Vcinity Inc* ***(P-14004)***
Vcognition Technologies Inc....E....415 374-0189
230 42nd Ave San Mateo (94403) ***(P-13512)***
Vcom, Pleasanton *Also called Avanquest Publishing Usa Inc* ***(P-12291)***
Vcomply Technologies Inc....D....650 319-8842
75 E Santa Clara St Fl 6 San Jose (95113) ***(P-12896)***
Vector Capital Management LP (PA)....B....**415 293-5000**
1 Market St Ste 2300 San Francisco (94105) ***(P-10019)***
Vector Data LLC....D....408 933-3266
801 Addison St Berkeley (94710) ***(P-5279)***
Vector Fabrication Inc (PA)....F....**408 942-9800**
1629 Watson Ct Milpitas (95035) ***(P-5995)***
Vector Laboratories Inc (HQ)....D....**650 697-3600**
30 Ingold Rd Burlingame (94010) ***(P-4060)***
Vector Stealth Holdings II LLC (PA)....E....**415 293-5000**
456 Montgomery St Fl 19 San Francisco (94104) ***(P-14005)***
Vectra AI Inc (PA)....E....**408 326-2020**
550 S Wnchester Blvd # 200 San Jose (95128) ***(P-14152)***
Veear Projects....D....415 827-1671
4695 Chabot Dr Ste 108 Pleasanton (94588) ***(P-12897)***
Veeco C V C, Santa Clara *Also called Veeco Instruments Inc* ***(P-6345)***
Veeco Instruments Inc....E....510 657-8523
3100 Laurelview Ct Santa Clara (95054) ***(P-6345)***
Veer Incorporated (PA)....D....**877 297-7900**
690 Airpark Rd NAPA (94558) ***(P-11855)***
Veev Group Inc....C....650 292-0752
777 Mariners Island Blvd # 15 San Mateo (94404) ***(P-10020)***
Veeva Systems Inc (PA)....A....**925 452-6500**
4280 Hacienda Dr Pleasanton (94588) ***(P-13513)***
Veex Inc....F....510 651-0500
2827 Lakeview Ct Fremont (94538) ***(P-6737)***
Vega Economic Consulting....E....510 280-5520
2040 Bancroft Way Ste 200 Berkeley (94704) ***(P-19884)***
Vega Economics, Berkeley *Also called Vega Economic Consulting* ***(P-19884)***
Vegiworks Inc....D....415 643-8686
6 Viewmont Ter South San Francisco (94080) ***(P-9434)***
Vehicle Recycling Services LLC....E....916 870-4383
2274 E Muscat Ave Fresno (93725) ***(P-8378)***
Veldhuis Dairy, Winton *Also called P H Ranch Inc* ***(P-218)***
Velociti Partners Inc....E....866 300-2925
712 Bancroft Rd 124 Walnut Creek (94598) ***(P-19665)***
Velodyne Acoustics Inc....D....408 465-2800
850 Tanglewood Dr Lafayette (94549) ***(P-5771)***
Velodyne Lidar Inc (PA)....C....**669 275-2251**
5521 Hellyer Ave San Jose (95138) ***(P-13514)***
Velodyne Lidar Usa Inc (HQ)....C....**408 465-2800**
5521 Hellyer Ave San Jose (95138) ***(P-6689)***
Venable LLP....E....415 653-3750
101 California St # 3800 San Francisco (94111) ***(P-17387)***
Venables/Bell & Partners LLC....C....415 288-3300
201 Post St Fl 2 San Francisco (94108) ***(P-11794)***
Vendini Inc (PA)....D....**415 693-9611**
201 1st St Ste 111 Petaluma (94952) ***(P-12898)***
Vendio Services Inc (PA)....D....**650 293-3500**
1510 Fashion Island Blvd San Mateo (94404) ***(P-12899)***
Venice Team, The, Alamo *Also called Lendus LLC* ***(P-9911)***
Ventek International, Petaluma *Also called Caracal Enterprises LLC* ***(P-5426)***
Ventex Corp....E....408 436-2929
2153 Otoole Ave Ste 10 San Jose (95131) ***(P-14783)***
Ventur Hospitality LLC (PA)....D....**415 279-8688**
855 Burnett Ave Apt 7 San Francisco (94131) ***(P-11556)***
Venture Electronics Intl Inc....E....510 744-3720
6701 Mowry Ave Newark (94560) ***(P-5996)***
Venture Lending & Lsg Ix Inc....E....650 234-4300
104 La Mesa Dr Ste 102 Portola Valley (94028) ***(P-9951)***
Venus Concept Inc....D....855 882-7827
128 Baytech Dr San Jose (95134) ***(P-7057)***
Vep Healthcare Inc....C....925 482-2839
1001 Galaxy Way Ste 400 Concord (94520) ***(P-15786)***
Veracyte Inc (PA)....C....**650 243-6300**
6000 Shoreline Ct Ste 300 South San Francisco (94080) ***(P-16820)***
Verana Health Inc....E....415 215-4440
600 Harrison St Ste 250 San Francisco (94107) ***(P-13515)***
Veranda Luxe Cinema, Concord *Also called Concord Veranda Cinema LLC* ***(P-14787)***
Verb Surgical Inc....D....408 438-3363
5490 Great America Pkwy Santa Clara (95054) ***(P-7058)***
Verge Genomics....E....312 489-7455
2 Tower Pl Ste 950 South San Francisco (94080) ***(P-4030)***
Vericool Inc....E....925 337-0808
7066 Las Positas Rd Ste C Livermore (94551) ***(P-5207)***
Verifone Intrmdate Hldings Inc....D....408 232-7800
2099 Gateway Pl San Jose (95110) ***(P-5424)***
Verinata Health Inc....D....650 632-1680
200 Lincoln Centre Dr Foster City (94404) ***(P-19147)***
Verint, Santa Clara *Also called Kana Software Inc* ***(P-13259)***
Veripic, Sunnyvale *Also called Kwan Software Engineering Inc* ***(P-13270)***
Verisilicon Inc (HQ)....F....**408 844-8560**
2150 Gold St Ste 200 San Jose (95002) ***(P-6346)***
Veritable Vegetable Inc....D....415 641-3500
1100 Cesar Chavez San Francisco (94124) ***(P-9435)***
Veritas Media Group LLC....E....510 867-4699
1111 Broadway Ste 300 Oakland (94607) ***(P-19666)***
Veritas Software Global LLC....F....650 335-8000
1600 Plymouth St Mountain View (94043) ***(P-13516)***
Veritas Technologies LLC (HQ)....C....**866 837-4827**
2625 Augustine Dr Santa Clara (95054) ***(P-12900)***
Veritas US Inc....C....650 933-1000
2625 Augustine Dr Santa Clara (95054) ***(P-12901)***
Veritiv Operating Company....D....559 268-0467
4395 S Minnewawa Ave # 101 Fresno (93725) ***(P-9221)***
Verity Health System Cal Inc....B....310 900-8900
203 Redwood Shores Pkwy Redwood City (94065) ***(P-16710)***
Verity Health System Cal Inc....A....408 947-2500
2105 Forest Ave San Jose (95128) ***(P-16711)***
Verity Health System Cal Inc....C....650 551-6507
203 Redwood Shores Pkwy # 700 Redwood City (94065) ***(P-16712)***
Verizon, Manteca *Also called Frontier California Inc* ***(P-7951)***
Verizon, Folsom *Also called Frontier California Inc* ***(P-7952)***
Verizon Business Global LLC....E....415 328-1020
6023 Jqn Murieta Ave Newark (94560) ***(P-8003)***
Verizon Media Inc....A....310 907-3016
701 First Ave Sunnyvale (94089) ***(P-19919)***
Verizon Sourcing, San Jose *Also called Blue Jeans Network Inc* ***(P-8071)***
Verizon Wireless, Grass Valley *Also called Cellco Partnership* ***(P-7899)***
Verizon Wireless, Sacramento *Also called Cellco Partnership* ***(P-7900)***
Verizon Wireless, Clovis *Also called Cellco Partnership* ***(P-7901)***
Verizon Wireless, Stockton *Also called Cellco Partnership* ***(P-7903)***
Verizon Wreless Authorized Ret, Campbell *Also called Clickaway Corporation* ***(P-13819)***
Verkada Inc (PA)....B....**833 837-5232**
405 E 4th Ave San Mateo (94401) ***(P-14153)***
Vernon Transportation Company, Stockton *Also called John Aguilar & Company Inc* ***(P-7476)***
Veronica Foods Company....E....510 535-6833
1991 Dennison St Oakland (94606) ***(P-2469)***
Versa Engineering & Tech Inc (PA)....D....**925 405-4505**
1320 Willow Pass Rd S500 Concord (94520) ***(P-18854)***
Versa Networks Inc (PA)....B....**408 385-7660**
6001 America Center Dr # 400 San Jose (95002) ***(P-12902)***
Versaco Manufacturing Inc....F....408 848-2880
550 E Luchessa Ave Gilroy (95020) ***(P-5137)***
Versant Corporation (HQ)....D....**650 232-2400**
500 Arguello St Ste 200 Redwood City (94063) ***(P-13517)***
Versant Health, Rancho Cordova *Also called Superior Vision Services Inc* ***(P-10155)***
Versatile Power Inc....E....408 341-4600
743 Camden Ave Ste B Campbell (95008) ***(P-7059)***
Verseon Corporation (PA)....E....**510 225-9000**
47071 Bayside Pkwy Fremont (94538) ***(P-4002)***
Vertical Communication (HQ)....D....**408 969-9600**
3979 Freedom Cir Ste 400 Santa Clara (95054) ***(P-8087)***
Vertisystem Inc....C....510 794-8099
39300 Civic Center Dr # 160 Fremont (94538) ***(P-13687)***
Verve Group Inc....D....760 536-8350
350 Marine Pkwy Ste 220 Redwood City (94065) ***(P-11820)***
Vestek Systems Inc (HQ)....D....**415 344-6000**
425 Market St Fl 6 San Francisco (94105) ***(P-13811)***

ALPHABETIC

Veterans Health Administration ....C....707 562-8200
Walnut Ave Bldg 201 Vallejo (94589) ***(P-15787)***
Veterans Health Administration ....C....559 225-6100
2615 E Clinton Ave Fresno (93703) ***(P-16713)***
Veterans Health Administration ....C....916 366-5427
10535 Hospital Way Mather (95655) ***(P-15788)***
Veterans Health Administration ....C....510 791-4000
39199 Liberty St Fremont (94538) ***(P-15789)***
Veterans Health Administration ....E....650 493-5000
3801 Miranda Ave Palo Alto (94304) ***(P-19417)***
Veterans Health Administration ....C....559 225-6100
2615 E Clinton Ave Fresno (93703) ***(P-15790)***
Veterans Health Administration ....C....530 226-7555
351 Hartnell Ave Redding (96002) ***(P-15791)***
Veterans Health Administration ....C....650 493-5000
3801 Miranda Ave Bldg 101 Palo Alto (94304) ***(P-15792)***
Veterans Health Administration ....C....530 889-0872
3123 Professional Dr Auburn (95603) ***(P-15793)***
Veterans Health Administration ....C....510 267-7820
2221 Mrtin Lther King Jr Oakland (94612) ***(P-15794)***
Veterans Health Administration ....C....415 750-2009
4150 Clement St Bldg 6 San Francisco (94121) ***(P-15795)***
Veterans Health Administration ....C....925 372-2000
150 Muir Rd Martinez (94553) ***(P-15796)***
Veterans Health Administration ....C....530 879-5000
280 Cohasset Rd Chico (95926) ***(P-15797)***
Veterans Health Administration ....C....707 437-1800
103 Bodin Cir Fairfield (94535) ***(P-15798)***
Veterans Health Administration ....C....707 570-3800
3315 Chanate Rd Santa Rosa (95404) ***(P-15799)***
Veterans Health Administration ....C....702 341-3020
40597 Westlake Dr Oakhurst (93644) ***(P-15800)***
Veterans Health Administration ....C....707 468-7700
630 Kings Ct Ukiah (95482) ***(P-15801)***
Veterans Health Administration ....C....916 843-7000
10535 Hospital Way Mather (95655) ***(P-15802)***
Veterans Health Administration ....C....925 447-2560
4951 Arroyo Rd Livermore (94550) ***(P-15803)***
Veterans Health Administration ....C....650 614-9997
795 Willow Rd Menlo Park (94025) ***(P-15804)***
Veterans Health Administration ....C....925 680-4526
1333 Willow Pass Rd # 10 Concord (94520) ***(P-15805)***
Veterans Health Administration ....C....925 372-2076
150 Muir Rd 90c Martinez (94553) ***(P-15806)***
Veterinary Emergency Service ....E....559 486-0520
1639 N Fresno St Fresno (93703) ***(P-343)***
Veterinary Genetics Laboratory, Davis *Also called University California Davis* ***(P-16818)***
Veterinary Information Network (PA) ....**E....530 756-4881**
777 W Covell Blvd Davis (95616) ***(P-344)***
Veterinary Medical Associates ....E....209 527-5855
204 W Granger Ave Modesto (95350) ***(P-345)***
Veterinary Service Inc ....E....209 722-7600
4048 Strolling Ct Merced (95340) ***(P-8794)***
Veterinary Surgical Associates ....D....650 696-8196
251 N Amphlett Blvd San Mateo (94401) ***(P-15807)***
Veterinary Surgical Associates (PA) ....**E....925 827-1777**
1410 Monu Blvd Ste 100 Concord (94520) ***(P-346)***
Vetted, Saratoga *Also called Opinr Inc* ***(P-12653)***
Vexillum Inc (PA) ....**C....408 541-4245**
1250 Birchwood Dr Sunnyvale (94089) ***(P-1630)***
Vf Marketing Corp ....E....530 473-2607
365 Ruggieri Way Williams (95987) ***(P-9512)***
Vf Outdoor LLC (HQ) ....**C....855 500-8639**
2701 Harbor Bay Pkwy Alameda (94502) ***(P-2996)***
Vl At Palo Alto, Palo Alto *Also called Cc-Palo Alto Inc* ***(P-16175)***
Via Adventures Inc (PA) ....**E....209 384-1315**
300 Grogan Ave Merced (95341) ***(P-7423)***
Via Charter Lines, Merced *Also called Via Adventures Inc* ***(P-7423)***
Via Embedded Store, Fremont *Also called Via Technologies Inc* ***(P-6347)***
Via Technologies Inc ....C....510 683-3300
940 Mission Ct Fremont (94539) ***(P-6347)***
Vian Enterprises Inc ....D....530 885-1997
2120 Precision Pl Auburn (95603) ***(P-5637)***
Viansa Winery & Italian Mkt Pl, Sonoma *Also called 360 Viansa LLC* ***(P-11704)***
Viant Medical LLC ....D....510 657-5800
45581 Northport Loop W Fremont (94538) ***(P-4330)***
Viavi Solutions Inc ....C....707 545-6440
2789 Northpoint Pkwy Santa Rosa (95407) ***(P-6546)***
Viavi Solutions Inc ....C....408 546-5000
430 N Mccarthy Blvd Milpitas (95035) ***(P-6862)***
Vibra Healthcare LLC ....E....559 325-5601
1315 Shaw Ave Ste 102 Clovis (93612) ***(P-16714)***
Vibra Healthcare LLC ....E....530 246-9000
2801 Eureka Way Redding (96001) ***(P-16715)***
Vibra Healthcare LLC ....E....559 436-3600
7173 N Sharon Ave Fresno (93720) ***(P-16716)***
Vibra Healthcare LLC ....D....415 853-9499
1125 Sir Frncis Drake Blv Kentfield (94904) ***(P-16717)***
Vibra Healthcare LLC ....E....559 431-2635
7033 N Fresno St Ste 101 Fresno (93720) ***(P-16718)***
Vibra Hospital Northern Cal, Redding *Also called Vibra Healthcare LLC* ***(P-16715)***
Vibra Hospital Sacramento LLC ....C....916 351-9151
330 Montrose Dr Folsom (95630) ***(P-16719)***
Vibrant Care Pharmacy Inc ....E....510 638-9851
7400 Macarthur Blvd Ste B Oakland (94605) ***(P-4003)***
Vibrant Sciences LLC ....C....408 203-9383
1021 Howard Ave Ste B San Carlos (94070) ***(P-6863)***
Vibrantcare Outpatient Rehab (PA) ....**D....916 782-1212**
2270 Douglas Blvd Ste 216 Roseville (95661) ***(P-17086)***
Vibrynt Inc ....E....650 362-6100
2570 W El Camino Real # 310 Mountain View (94040) ***(P-7133)***
Vicarious Fpc Inc ....E....415 604-3278
1320 Decoto Rd Ste 200 Union City (94587) ***(P-8760)***
Vicolo Pizza, Hayward *Also called Vicolo Wholesale LLC* ***(P-2313)***
Vicolo Wholesale LLC (PA) ....**E....510 475-6019**
31112 San Clemente St Hayward (94544) ***(P-2313)***
Vicom Systems Inc ....E....408 588-1286
2336 Walsh Ave Ste H Santa Clara (95051) ***(P-5324)***
Vics Trader Restaurants Inc ....D....510 653-3400
9 Anchor Dr Emeryville (94608) ***(P-11734)***
Victims Services Center, Madera *Also called Community Action Prtnr Mdera C* ***(P-18227)***
Victor Cmnty Support Svcs Inc ....C....530 273-2244
900 E Main St Ste 201 Grass Valley (95945) ***(P-17087)***
Victor Cmnty Support Svcs Inc ....C....209 465-1080
2495 W March Ln Ste 125 Stockton (95207) ***(P-17088)***
Victor Cmnty Support Svcs Inc ....C....530 267-1710
1360 E Lassen Ave Chico (95973) ***(P-17089)***
Victor Packing Inc ....E....559 673-5908
11687 Road 27 1/2 Madera (93637) ***(P-2274)***
Victor Treatment Centers Inc ....E....707 360-1509
341 Irwin Ln Santa Rosa (95401) ***(P-18200)***
Victor Treatment Centers Inc ....C....209 465-1080
12755 N Highway 88 Lodi (95240) ***(P-18201)***
Victoria Island LP ....E....209 465-5600
16021 W Highway 4 Holt (95234) ***(P-37)***
Victorian Post Acute, San Francisco *Also called Golden Gateidence Opco LLC* ***(P-16184)***
Victus Group Inc ....C....559 429-8080
2377 W Shaw Ave Ste 201 Fresno (93711) ***(P-19418)***
Vida Health Inc ....D....415 989-1017
100 Montgomery St Ste 750 San Francisco (94104) ***(P-12903)***
Videomaker Inc ....E....530 891-8410
645 Mangrove Ave Chico (95926) ***(P-3518)***
Vidhwan Inc (PA) ....**A....408 289-8200**
2 N Market St Ste 400 San Jose (95113) ***(P-12151)***
Vie-Del Company (PA) ....**D....559 834-2525**
11903 S Chestnut Ave Fresno (93725) ***(P-2247)***
Vie-Del Company ....E....559 896-3065
13363 S Indianola Ave Kingsburg (93631) ***(P-2754)***
Vieira Agricultural Entps LLC ....E....209 394-2771
3978 Sultana Ave Atwater (95301) ***(P-23)***
Vieiras Resort ....E....916 777-6661
15476 State Highway 160 Isleton (95641) ***(P-11557)***
Vienna Convalescent Hosp Inc ....C....209 368-7141
800 S Ham Ln Lodi (95242) ***(P-16152)***
Viet Nam Daily Newspaper, San Jose *Also called Pacific Press Corporation* ***(P-3472)***
Vietnam Daily News LLC ....F....408 292-3422
510 Parrott St Ste 1 San Jose (95112) ***(P-3487)***
View Inc (PA) ....**B....408 263-9200**
195 S Milpitas Blvd Milpitas (95035) ***(P-4362)***
View Operating Corporation (HQ) ....**D....408 263-9200**
195 S Milpitas Blvd Milpitas (95035) ***(P-4363)***
View Rite Manufacturing ....E....415 468-3856
455 Allan St Daly City (94014) ***(P-3323)***
Viewpint Gvrnment Slutions Inc ....E....617 577-9000
955 Charter St Redwood City (94063) ***(P-13688)***
Viewray Technologies Inc ....D....650 252-0920
815 E Middlefield Rd Mountain View (94043) ***(P-8795)***
Vifor Pharma Inc ....B....650 421-9500
200 Cardinal Way 200-B Redwood City (94063) ***(P-4004)***
Vigilant Private Security ....D....559 800-7233
2100 N Winery Ave Ste 102 Fresno (93703) ***(P-14107)***
Vigilent Corporation (PA) ....**E....888 305-4451**
1111 Broadway Fl 3 Oakland (94607) ***(P-6707)***
Vignette Winery LLC (PA) ....**E....707 637-8821**
45 Enterprise Ct NAPA (94558) ***(P-2755)***
Viking Processing Corporation (PA) ....**E....925 427-2518**
620 Clark Ave Pittsburg (94565) ***(P-8832)***
Vila Construction Co ....D....510 236-9111
590 S 33rd St Richmond (94804) ***(P-981)***
Villa Amorosa ....D....707 942-8200
4045 Saint Helena Hwy Calistoga (94515) ***(P-2756)***
Villa At San Mateo, San Mateo *Also called Elder Care Alliance San Mateo* ***(P-15981)***
Villa Del Rey ....D....707 252-3333
3255 Villa Ln NAPA (94558) ***(P-16153)***
Villa Florence Hotel, San Francisco *Also called Let It Flho Lessee Inc* ***(P-11261)***
Villa Inn ....E....415 456-4975
1600 Lincoln Ave San Rafael (94901) ***(P-11558)***
Villa Marin Homeowners Assn ....C....415 499-8711
100 Thorndale Dr San Rafael (94903) ***(P-18479)***
VILLA MONTALVO, Saratoga *Also called Montalvo Association* ***(P-18294)***
Villa Mrin Rtrement Residences, San Rafael *Also called Villa Marin Homeowners Assn* ***(P-18479)***
Villa Real Inc ....E....209 460-5069
421 S El Dorado St Unit D Stockton (95203) ***(P-19885)***
Villa Siena ....D....650 961-6484
1855 Miramonte Ave 117 Mountain View (94040) ***(P-18202)***
Villa Sport Athletic CLB & Spa, San Rafael *Also called Villasport LLC* ***(P-18607)***
Villa Toscano Winery ....E....209 245-3800
10600 Shenandoah Rd Plymouth (95669) ***(P-2757)***
Village At Granite Bay ....D....916 789-0326
8550 Barton Rd Granite Bay (95746) ***(P-18203)***
Village Inn Owners Association ....D....530 581-6000
1909 Chamonix Pl Olympic Valley (96146) ***(P-11559)***
Village Instant Printing Inc ....E....209 576-2568
1515 10th St Modesto (95354) ***(P-3709)***
Village Nurseries Whl LLC ....B....916 993-2292
6901 Bradshaw Rd Sacramento (95829) ***(P-9641)***

Village Voice Media ... E ... 510 879-3700
537 Crofton Ave Oakland (94610) *(P-3488)*
Villages Golf and Country Club ... C ... 408 274-4400
5000 Cribari Ln San Jose (95135) *(P-15165)*
Villages, The, San Jose *Also called Villages Golf and Country Club (P-15165)*
Villara Corporation (PA) ... **B ... 916 646-2700**
4700 Lang Ave McClellan (95652) *(P-1391)*
Villara Corporation ... E ... 707 863-8222
5005 Fulton Dr Ste F Fairfield (94534) *(P-1844)*
Villara Corporation ... E ... 209 824-1082
332 E Wetmore St Manteca (95337) *(P-1392)*
Villasport LLC (PA) ... **D ... 415 448-8300**
150 Pelican Way San Rafael (94901) *(P-18607)*
Vim Inc ... D ... 844 843-5381
548 Market St Pmb 84904 San Francisco (94104) *(P-12904)*
Vimark Inc ... D ... 707 857-3588
19500 Geyserville Ave Geyserville (95441) *(P-388)*
Vimark Vineyards, Geyserville *Also called Vimark Inc (P-388)*
Vimco, Santa Rosa *Also called Randal Optimal Nutrients LLC (P-3969)*
Vimo Inc (PA) ... **B ... 650 618-4600**
1305 Terra Bella Ave Mountain View (94043) *(P-19886)*
Vin, Davis *Also called Veterinary Information Network (P-344)*
Vin Lux LLC ... E ... 707 265-4100
1200 Green Island Rd American Canyon (94503) *(P-7641)*
Vin-Max, San Leandro *Also called MArs Engineering Company Inc (P-5565)*
Vincent Electic Motor Company, Oakland *Also called Vincent Electric Company (P-14731)*
Vincent Electric Company (PA) ... **E ... 510 639-4500**
8383 Baldwin St Oakland (94621) *(P-14731)*
Vincerx Pharma Inc (PA) ... **E ... 650 800-6676**
260 Sheridan Ave Ste 400 Palo Alto (94306) *(P-4005)*
Vinces Shellfish Co Inc ... E ... 650 589-5385
1063 Montgomery Ave San Bruno (94066) *(P-9373)*
Vindicia Inc ... C ... 650 264-4700
2988 Campus Dr Ste 300 San Mateo (94403) *(P-13518)*
Vindra Inc ... D ... 707 994-7738
3805 Dexter Ln Clearlake (95422) *(P-16154)*
Vine Village Inc ... E ... 707 255-4006
4059 Old Sonoma Rd NAPA (94559) *(P-18204)*
Vineburg Wine Company Inc (PA) ... **E ... 707 938-5277**
2000 Denmark St Sonoma (95476) *(P-2758)*
Vineti Inc ... D ... 415 704-8730
633 Howard St San Francisco (94105) *(P-12905)*
Vineyard Post Acute, Petaluma *Also called Petalumaidence Opco LLC (P-2682)*
Vineyards and Winery, Sebastopol *Also called Iron Horse Vineyards (P-2621)*
Vineyards of Monterey, Santa Rosa *Also called Jackson Family Wines Inc (P-2628)*
Vino Farms Inc (PA) ... **E ... 209 334-6975**
1377 E Lodi Ave Lodi (95240) *(P-389)*
Vino Farms Inc ... C ... 707 433-8241
10651 Eastside Rd Healdsburg (95448) *(P-390)*
Vino Farms Inc ... C ... 916 775-4095
51375 S Netherlands Rd Clarksburg (95612) *(P-196)*
Vino Farms LLC ... A ... 209 334-6975
1377 E Lodi Ave Lodi (95240) *(P-9587)*
Vinotheque Wine Cellars ... F ... 209 466-9463
1738 E Alpine Ave Stockton (95205) *(P-5436)*
Vinsuite, NAPA *Also called Diamond Touch Inc (P-12388)*
Vintage 99 Label Mfg Inc (PA) ... **E ... 925 294-5270**
611 Enterprise Ct Livermore (94550) *(P-3382)*
Vintage Car Wash Inc ... E ... 209 572-1215
1801 Standiford Ave Modesto (95350) *(P-14653)*
Vintage Fire Nrsing Rhbltion C, Modesto *Also called Covenant Care California LLC (P-16228)*
VINTAGE GARDENS, Fresno *Also called Central Cal Nikkei Foundation (P-18073)*
Vintage Senior Management Inc ... E ... 707 595-0009
91 Napa Rd Sonoma (95476) *(P-10467)*
Vintellus Inc ... F ... 510 972-4710
19918 Wellington Ct Saratoga (95070) *(P-13519)*
Vintners Inn ... D ... 707 575-7350
4350 Barnes Rd Santa Rosa (95403) *(P-11560)*
Vinyl Specialties, Fresno *Also called Millerton Builders Inc (P-3332)*
Vionic Group LLC ... D ... 415 526-6932
4040 Civic Center Dr # 430 San Rafael (94903) *(P-4343)*
Vionic International LLC (HQ) ... **D ... 888 882-7954**
4040 Civic Center Dr # 430 San Rafael (94903) *(P-4344)*
Vioptix Inc ... F ... 510 226-5860
39655 Eureka Dr Newark (94560) *(P-19244)*
VIP, Folsom *Also called Visionary Intgrtion Prfssnals (P-10746)*
VIP Manufacturing & Engrg Corp ... D ... 408 727-6545
1084 Martin Ave Santa Clara (95050) *(P-6623)*
VIP Mfg & Engr, Santa Clara *Also called VIP Manufacturing & Engrg Corp (P-6623)*
Vipa Hospitality Inc ... E ... 209 544-2000
2025 W Orangeburg Ave Modesto (95350) *(P-11561)*
Vir Biotechnology Inc (PA) ... **C ... 415 906-4324**
499 Illinois St Ste 500 San Francisco (94158) *(P-19148)*
Virage Logic Corporation (HQ) ... **B ... 650 584-5000**
700 E Middlefield Rd Mountain View (94043) *(P-6348)*
Virga Investment Property ... C ... 530 755-4409
430 S George Wash Blvd Yuba City (95993) *(P-10414)*
Virgin America Crisis Fund (PA) ... **E ... 650 762-7000**
555 Airport Blvd Burlingame (94010) *(P-7743)*
Virgin America Inc (HQ) ... **A ... 877 359-8474**
555 Airport Blvd Burlingame (94010) *(P-7744)*
Virgin Htels San Francisco LLC ... E ... 415 534-6500
250 4th St San Francisco (94103) *(P-11562)*
Virginia Sarabian ... E ... 559 493-2900
2816 S Leonard Ave Sanger (93657) *(P-81)*
Virgo Investment Group LLC ... E ... 650 453-3627
555 Twin Dolphin Dr # 61 Redwood City (94065) *(P-10894)*
Virident Systems Inc ... C ... 408 573-5000
1745 Tech Dr Ste 700 San Jose (95110) *(P-19149)*
Virta Health Corp ... D ... 844 847-8216
501 Folsom St Fl 1 San Francisco (94105) *(P-17187)*
Virtana, San Jose *Also called Virtual Instruments Corp (P-12906)*
Virtual Instruments Corp (PA) ... **D ... 408 579-4000**
2363 Bering Dr San Jose (95131) *(P-12906)*
Virtual Technologies Inc ... E ... 408 597-3400
1380 Piper Dr Milpitas (95035) *(P-7315)*
Virtunet LLC ... D ... 650 847-8633
1900 S Norfolk St Ste 300 San Mateo (94403) *(P-12907)*
Virtunet Systems, San Mateo *Also called Virtunet LLC (P-12907)*
Virtuoz Inc (HQ) ... **E ... 415 202-5709**
6001 Shellmound St # 500 Emeryville (94608) *(P-19887)*
Vis Tech, Modesto *Also called Vistech Mfg Solutions LLC (P-5208)*
Visa Commerce Solutions Inc ... E ... 650 432-3200
900 Metro Center Blvd Foster City (94404) *(P-14006)*
Visa Inc ... E ... 415 805-4000
1 Market St Ste 600 San Francisco (94105) *(P-11735)*
Visa Inc (PA) ... **A ... 650 432-3200**
900 Metro Center Blvd Foster City (94404) *(P-14455)*
Visa Tech & Operations LLC (HQ) ... **C ... 650 432-3200**
900 Metro Center Blvd Foster City (94404) *(P-14456)*
Visby Medical Inc ... D ... 408 650-8878
3010 N 1st St San Jose (95134) *(P-6929)*
Viscira LLC ... D ... 415 848-8010
360 3rd St Ste 500 San Francisco (94107) *(P-8761)*
Visger Precision Inc ... F ... 408 988-0184
1815 Russell Ave Santa Clara (95054) *(P-5638)*
Vishay Siliconix LLC ... A ... 408 988-8000
2585 Junction Ave San Jose (95134) *(P-6349)*
Vishnu Hotel LLC ... E ... 650 508-1800
25921 Industrial Blvd Hayward (94545) *(P-11563)*
Vision Care Center Central Cal, Fresno *Also called Vision Care Ctr A Med Group In (P-15808)*
Vision Care Ctr A Med Group In (PA) ... **D ... 559 486-2000**
7075 N Sharon Ave Fresno (93720) *(P-15808)*
Vision Design Studio, Calistoga *Also called Vision Publications Inc (P-3611)*
Vision Publications Inc ... E ... 562 597-4000
109 Wappo Ave Calistoga (94515) *(P-3611)*
Vision Service Plan Inc (PA) ... **A ... 916 851-5000**
3333 Quality Dr Rancho Cordova (95670) *(P-10157)*
Visionary Electronics Inc ... F ... 415 751-8811
141 Parker Ave San Francisco (94118) *(P-6350)*
Visionary Intgrtion Prfssnals (HQ) ... **D ... 916 985-9625**
80 Iron Point Cir Ste 100 Folsom (95630) *(P-14007)*
Visionary Intgrtion Prfssnals (PA) ... **D ... 916 985-9625**
80 Iron Point Cir Ste 100 Folsom (95630) *(P-10746)*
Visionary Intgrtion Prfssonals, Folsom *Also called Visionary Intgrtion Prfssnals (P-14007)*
Visionary Nutrition LLC ... C ... 510 567-1200
9957 Medford Ave Ste 4 Oakland (94603) *(P-818)*
Visioncare Devices Inc ... E ... 530 364-2271
6100 Bellevue Ln Anderson (96007) *(P-8796)*
Visioneer Inc (HQ) ... **E ... 925 251-6300**
5696 Stewart Ave Fremont (94538) *(P-5421)*
Visionone Inc (PA) ... **E ... 559 432-8000**
5260 N Palm Ave Ste 229 Fresno (93704) *(P-12908)*
Visions Paint Recycling, Sacramento *Also called Visions Recycling Inc (P-8379)*
Visions Recycling Inc ... E ... 916 564-9121
4105 S Market Ct Ste A Sacramento (95834) *(P-8379)*
Visions Unlimited (PA) ... **D ... 916 394-0800**
6833 Stockton Blvd # 485 Sacramento (95823) *(P-17090)*
Visistat Inc ... E ... 408 725-9370
2290 N 1st St Ste 102 San Jose (95131) *(P-12909)*
Visit California, Sacramento *Also called California Trvl & Tourism Comm (P-7794)*
Visit Healthcare Inc ... E ... 408 890-6648
20 S Santa Cruz Ave # 30 Los Gatos (95030) *(P-4061)*
Visiting Angels, Redding *Also called Vonhof Enterprises Inc (P-16966)*
Visiting Nrse Assn of Snta Cru (HQ) ... **D ... 831 477-2600**
2880 Soquel Ave Ste 10 Santa Cruz (95062) *(P-16965)*
Visiworks Software, El Dorado Hills *Also called Dorado Software Inc (P-12399)*
Vista Cmplete Care Inc A Prof ... E ... 530 885-3951
13555 Bowman Rd Ste 100 Auburn (95603) *(P-15809)*
Vista Eqity Prtners Fund III L (HQ) ... **A ... 415 765-6500**
4 Embarcadero Ctr # 2000 San Francisco (94111) *(P-10895)*
Vista Eqity Prtners Fund VI LP (PA) ... **E ... 415 765-6500**
4 Embarcadero Ctr Lbby 2 San Francisco (94111) *(P-10067)*
Vista Equity Partners Fund III, San Francisco *Also called Amber Holdings Inc (P-12246)*
Vista Livestock Co New (PA) ... **E ... 209 874-9446**
22323 E Monte Vista Ave Denair (95316) *(P-227)*
Vista Way Corporation ... E ... 408 586-8107
472 Vista Way Milpitas (95035) *(P-3710)*
Vistech Mfg Solutions LLC (HQ) ... **D ... 209 544-9333**
1156 Scenic Dr Ste 120 Modesto (95350) *(P-5208)*
Visual Concepts Entertainment ... D ... 415 479-3634
10 Hamilton Landing Novato (94949) *(P-12910)*
Visual Supply Company (PA) ... **D ... 847 721-9285**
1500 Broadway Ste 300 Oakland (94612) *(P-12911)*
Visualon Inc ... E ... 408 645-6618
1475 S Bascom Ave Ste 103 Campbell (95008) *(P-13520)*
Vita-Pakt Citrus Products Co ... F ... 559 233-4452
8898 E Central Ave Del Rey (93616) *(P-2248)*
Vital Connect Inc ... E ... 408 963-4600
224 Airport Pkwy Ste 300 San Jose (95110) *(P-7134)*
Vital Farmland Holdings LLC ... D ... 415 465-2400
3 Corte Las Casas Belvedere Tiburon (94920) *(P-14457)*
Vital Vittles Bakery Inc ... E ... 510 644-2022
2810 San Pablo Ave Berkeley (94702) *(P-2410)*

ALPHABETIC

Vitalant Research Institute............E......650 697-4034
111 Rollins Rd Millbrae (94030) ***(P-17188)***
Vitalant Research Institute (PA)............**C......415 567-6400**
270 Masonic Ave San Francisco (94118) ***(P-17189)***
Vitalant Research Institute............E......707 428-6001
1325 Gateway Blvd Ste C1 Fairfield (94533) ***(P-17190)***
Vitalant Research Institute............E......530 221-0600
2680 Larkspur Ln Redding (96002) ***(P-17191)***
Vitalant Research Institute............E......415 454-2700
570 Price Ave Ste 100 San Rafael (94901) ***(P-17192)***
Vitas Healthcare Corp Cal............E......408 964-6800
670 N Mccarthy Blvd # 22 Milpitas (95035) ***(P-16209)***
Vitas Healthcare Corp Cal............E......925 930-9373
355 Lennon Ln Ste 150 Walnut Creek (94598) ***(P-16210)***
Vitas Healthcare Corporation............D......415 874-4400
1388 Sutter St Ste 700 San Francisco (94109) ***(P-16211)***
Vitas Innovative Hospice Care, Milpitas *Also called Vitas Healthcare Corp Cal* ***(P-16209)***
Vitek Mortgage Group, Rancho Cordova *Also called Vitek RE Inds Group Inc* ***(P-9935)***
Vitek RE Inds Group Inc (PA)............**E......916 486-6400**
2882 Prospect Park Dr # 10 Rancho Cordova (95670) ***(P-9935)***
Vitesse LLC............A......650 543-4800
1601 Willow Rd Menlo Park (94025) ***(P-13767)***
Vitisystems Inc............E......707 258-4000
1885 N Kelly Rd NAPA (94558) ***(P-19291)***
Vito Trucking LLC............D......209 342-5104
1415 Sandpoint Dr Ceres (95307) ***(P-7610)***
Vitrico Corp............E......510 652-6731
2181 Williams St San Leandro (94577) ***(P-4381)***
Vitro Flat Glass LLC............C......559 485-4660
3333 S Peach Ave Fresno (93725) ***(P-4364)***
Vitron Electronic Services Inc............D......408 251-1600
5400 Hellyer Ave San Jose (95138) ***(P-5997)***
Vitron Electronics Mfg & Svcs, San Jose *Also called Vitron Electronic Services Inc* ***(P-5997)***
Vituity, Emeryville *Also called Cep America LLC* ***(P-15345)***
Viv Labs Inc............E......650 268-9837
60 S Market St Ste 900 San Jose (95113) ***(P-13521)***
Viva International, Belvedere Tiburon *Also called Marcolin USA Inc* ***(P-8799)***
Viva Soma Lessee Inc............A......415 974-6400
50 3rd St San Francisco (94103) ***(P-19419)***
Vivalon............D......415 454-0964
930 Tamalpais Ave San Rafael (94901) ***(P-17781)***
Vivax-Metrotech, Santa Clara *Also called Metrotech Corporation* ***(P-6675)***
Vivid Inc............E......408 982-9101
180 E Sunnyoaks Ave Campbell (95008) ***(P-4113)***
Vivido Labs Inc (PA)............**C......408 692-5002**
3350 Scott Blvd Bldg 201 Santa Clara (95054) ***(P-12912)***
Vivio Health Inc............E......925 365-6600
1933 Davis St Ste 274 San Leandro (94577) ***(P-10158)***
Vivo Capital LLC (PA)............**D......650 688-0818**
192 Lytton Ave Palo Alto (94301) ***(P-10021)***
Vivotek Usa Inc............E......408 773-8686
2050 Ringwood Ave San Jose (95131) ***(P-8969)***
Vivus Inc (PA)............**E......650 934-5200**
900 E Hamilton Ave # 550 Campbell (95008) ***(P-4006)***
Viz Media LLC............C......415 546-7073
1355 Market St Ste 200 San Francisco (94103) ***(P-3519)***
Viz Media Music, San Francisco *Also called Viz Media LLC* ***(P-3519)***
Vizu Corporation (HQ)............**D......415 362-8498**
1010 Battery St San Francisco (94111) ***(P-19191)***
Vlot Brothers, Chowchilla *Also called Case Vlott Cattle* ***(P-207)***
Vlsi Standards Inc............E......408 428-1800
5 Technology Dr Milpitas (95035) ***(P-6800)***
Vly Air Cond & RPR............D......559 237-2123
825 S Topeka Ave Fresno (93721) ***(P-14689)***
Vm Services Inc (HQ)............**C......510 744-3720**
1621 Barber Ln Milpitas (95035) ***(P-12913)***
Vm Services Inc............D......510 744-3720
6723 Mowry Ave Newark (94560) ***(P-12914)***
Vmware Inc (PA)............**A......650 427-5000**
3401 Hillview Ave Palo Alto (94304) ***(P-13522)***
Vnomic Inc............E......408 641-3810
19925 Stevns Crk Blvd # 100 Cupertino (95014) ***(P-13523)***
Vnus Medical Technologies Inc............C......408 360-7200
5799 Fontanoso Way San Jose (95138) ***(P-7060)***
Vocality Community Credit Un............E......707 923-2012
757 Redwood Dr Garberville (95542) ***(P-9827)***
Vocation Plus Inc............C......559 221-8019
3985 N Fresno St Ste 106 Fresno (93726) ***(P-17844)***
Voce Communications Inc............E......415 975-2200
550 3rd St San Francisco (94107) ***(P-19698)***
Vocera Communications Inc (PA)............**A......408 882-5100**
525 Race St Ste 150 San Jose (95126) ***(P-5897)***
Vode Lighting LLC............F......707 996-9898
21684 8th St E Ste 700 Sonoma (95476) ***(P-5728)***
Voiceai, San Francisco *Also called Dialpad Inc* ***(P-8693)***
Voicebase Inc (PA)............**E......415 886-7799**
2081 Center St Berkeley (94704) ***(P-13768)***
Volcano Communications Company (PA)............**D......209 296-7502**
20000 State Highway 88 Pine Grove (95665) ***(P-8004)***
Volcano Telephone Co., Pine Grove *Also called Volcano Vision Inc* ***(P-8068)***
Volcano Telephone Company, Pine Grove *Also called Volcano Communications Company* ***(P-8004)***
Volcano Vision Inc............E......209 296-2288
20000 State Highway 88 Pine Grove (95665) ***(P-8068)***
Volex Inc (HQ)............**E......669 444-1740**
3110 Coronado Dr Santa Clara (95054) ***(P-4331)***
Volk Enterprises Inc............D......209 632-3826
618 S Kilroy Rd Turlock (95380) ***(P-4972)***
Volkman Seed Company Inc............E......209 669-3040
4319 Jessup Rd Ceres (95307) ***(P-9673)***
Voloagri Inc............C......805 547-9391
41970 E Main St Woodland (95776) ***(P-9615)***
Volpe Chiu Abel Sternberg............E......415 668-0411
3838 California St Rm 616 San Francisco (94118) ***(P-15810)***
Volt Management Corp............D......559 435-1255
7330 N Palm Ave Ste 105 Fresno (93711) ***(P-12204)***
Volt Management Corp............D......916 923-0454
1544 Eureka Rd Ste 150 Roseville (95661) ***(P-12205)***
Volt Management Corp............D......209 952-5627
3558 Deer Park Dr 2 Stockton (95219) ***(P-12206)***
Volt Management Corp............D......707 547-1660
3700 Old Redwood Hwy # 1 Santa Rosa (95403) ***(P-12207)***
Volt Workforce Solutions, Fresno *Also called Volt Management Corp* ***(P-12204)***
Volt Workforce Solutions, Roseville *Also called Volt Management Corp* ***(P-12205)***
Volt Workforce Solutions, Stockton *Also called Volt Management Corp* ***(P-12206)***
Volt Workforce Solutions, Santa Rosa *Also called Volt Management Corp* ***(P-12207)***
Volta Charging LLC............D......415 735-5169
155 De Haro St San Francisco (94103) ***(P-11798)***
Volta Industries Inc (HQ)............**D......415 583-3805**
155 De Haro St San Francisco (94103) ***(P-7316)***
Volterra Semiconductor LLC (HQ)............**D......408 601-1000**
160 Rio Robles San Jose (95134) ***(P-6351)***
Volterra Semiconductor LLC............C......510 743-1200
3839 Spinnaker Ct Fremont (94538) ***(P-6352)***
Voltus Inc............E......415 617-9602
542b Presidio Blvd San Francisco (94129) ***(P-6708)***
Volume Services Inc............C......415 972-1500
24 Willie Mays Plz San Francisco (94107) ***(P-15262)***
Volume Snacks............E......530 662-3500
1948 Hays Ln Woodland (95776) ***(P-9381)***
Volumetric Bldg Companies LLC............E......623 236-5322
2302 Paradise Rd Tracy (95304) ***(P-3215)***
Volunteer Center Sonoma County (PA)............**E......707 573-3399**
153 Stony Cir Ste 100 Santa Rosa (95401) ***(P-17782)***
Volunteer Referral Service, Santa Rosa *Also called Volunteer Center Sonoma County* ***(P-17782)***
Volunters Amer Nthrn Cal Nthrn (PA)............**B......916 265-3400**
3434 Marconi Ave Sacramento (95821) ***(P-17783)***
Volvo, Chico *Also called Courtesy Motors Auto Ctr Inc* ***(P-14555)***
Volvo, Stockton *Also called Berberian Bros Inc* ***(P-14548)***
Vomela Specialty Company............E......650 877-8000
1342 San Mateo Ave South San Francisco (94080) ***(P-7259)***
Vonhof Enterprises Inc............E......530 223-2400
3050 Victor Ave Ste B Redding (96002) ***(P-16966)***
Vons Companies Inc (HQ)............**A......925 467-3000**
5918 Stoneridge Mall Rd Pleasanton (94588) ***(P-2195)***
Voorwood Company............E......530 365-3311
2350 Barney Rd Anderson (96007) ***(P-5116)***
Vortex Marine Construction Inc............E......510 261-2400
1 Maritime Way Antioch (94509) ***(P-1184)***
Vossloh Signaling LLC............E......530 272-8194
12799 Loma Rica Dr Grass Valley (95945) ***(P-12915)***
Vox Network Solutions Inc............C......650 989-1000
130 Produce Ave Ste C South San Francisco (94080) ***(P-5815)***
Vps Companies Inc (PA)............**E......831 724-7551**
310 Walker St Watsonville (95076) ***(P-9332)***
VSC Sports Inc............D......415 820-3525
750 Folsom St San Francisco (94107) ***(P-19888)***
Vsco, Oakland *Also called Visual Supply Company* ***(P-12911)***
Vsp Labs Inc (PA)............**B......866 569-8800**
3333 Quality Dr Rancho Cordova (95670) ***(P-6887)***
Vsp Optical Group Inc (PA)............**B......916 851-4682**
3333 Quality Dr Rancho Cordova (95670) ***(P-10159)***
Vsp Products Inc............D......209 862-1200
3324 Orestimba Rd Newman (95360) ***(P-2275)***
Vsp Retail Inc............F......800 852-7600
3333 Quality Dr Rancho Cordova (95670) ***(P-7146)***
Vsp Vntres Optmtric Sltons LLC (HQ)............**E......916 858-5656**
3333 Quality Dr Rancho Cordova (95670) ***(P-15876)***
Vspone, Rancho Cordova *Also called Vsp Labs Inc* ***(P-6887)***
Vss International Inc (HQ)............**D......916 373-1500**
3785 Channel Dr West Sacramento (95691) ***(P-1079)***
Vss Monitoring Inc (HQ)............**C......408 585-6800**
178 E Tasman Dr San Jose (95134) ***(P-8005)***
Vta Telephone Information............D......408 321-7127
3331 N 1st St San Jose (95134) ***(P-8006)***
Vuclip Inc............E......408 649-2240
1551 Mccarthy Blvd # 214 Milpitas (95035) ***(P-8007)***
Vucovich Inc (PA)............**D......559 486-8020**
4288 S Bagley Ave Fresno (93725) ***(P-9049)***
Vudu Inc............D......408 492-1010
600 W California Ave Sunnyvale (94086) ***(P-5772)***
Vulcan Cnstr & Maint Inc............E......559 443-1607
1010 W Whites Bridge Ave Fresno (93706) ***(P-1140)***
Vulcan Construction Mtls LLC............E......408 213-4270
346 Mathew St Santa Clara (95050) ***(P-600)***
Vulpine Inc............E......510 534-1186
1127 57th Ave Oakland (94621) ***(P-4169)***
Vumedi Inc............D......650 450-2603
555 12th St Ste 500 Oakland (94607) ***(P-14798)***
Vungle Inc (PA)............**C......415 800-1400**
1255 Battery St Ste 500 San Francisco (94111) ***(P-11795)***
Vwi Concord LLC............C......925 827-2000
1970 Diamond Blvd Concord (94520) ***(P-11564)***
W A Call Manufacturing Co Inc............E......408 436-1450
1710 Rogers Ave San Jose (95112) ***(P-4829)***
W A M S, Santa Clara *Also called Wide Area Management Svcs Inc* ***(P-13527)***

W B Mason Co Inc....E....888 926-2766
4100 Whipple Rd Union City (94587) ***(P-3711)***
W Banks Moore Inc....E....559 485-3456
2403 E Belmont Ave Fresno (93701) ***(P-2085)***
W Bradley Electric Inc....C....650 701-1502
501 Seaport Ct Ste 103a Redwood City (94063) ***(P-1631)***
W Bradley Electric Inc (PA)....**E....415 898-1400**
90 Hill Rd Novato (94945) ***(P-1632)***
W C Garcia & Associates Inc....E....530 221-4405
3452 Argyle Rd Redding (96002) ***(P-15166)***
W C I, Hollister *Also called Woltcom Inc* ***(P-1640)***
W C Q, Fremont *Also called West Coast Quartz Corporation* ***(P-4382)***
W E Plemons McHy Svcs Inc....E....559 646-6630
13479 E Industrial Dr Parlier (93648) ***(P-5209)***
W Fs Financial Inc....E....209 955-7800
10100 Trinity Pkwy # 400 Stockton (95219) ***(P-9865)***
W I C Program, Modesto *Also called County of Stanislaus* ***(P-17129)***
W L Butler Construction Inc (PA)....**E....650 361-1270**
1629 Main St Redwood City (94063) ***(P-982)***
W L Gore & Associates Inc....C....928 864-2705
2890 De La Cruz Blvd Santa Clara (95050) ***(P-7061)***
W L Hickey Sons Inc....C....408 736-4938
930 E California Ave Sunnyvale (94085) ***(P-1393)***
W M Lyles Co (HQ)....**B....559 441-1900**
525 W Alluvial Ave Fresno (93711) ***(P-1141)***
W R E Colortech, Berkeley *Also called Western Roto Engravers Inc* ***(P-3755)***
W R Grace & Co....C....209 839-2800
252 W Larch Rd Ste H Tracy (95304) ***(P-3800)***
W R Hambrecht Co Inc (PA)....**D....415 551-8600**
Bay 3 Pier 1 San Francisco (94111) ***(P-10022)***
W S B & Associates Inc....D....510 444-6266
150 Executive Park Blvd # 4700 San Francisco (94134) ***(P-14108)***
W S B & Associates Inc....C....415 864-3510
150 Executive Park Blvd # 4700 San Francisco (94134) ***(P-14109)***
W S West, Fresno *Also called Gea Farm Technologies Inc* ***(P-4074)***
W-Neweb Corporation....E....408 457-6800
1525 Mccarthy Blvd # 206 Milpitas (95035) ***(P-8970)***
W-Star Investments Inc....E....408 821-7678
2130 Ringwood Ave San Jose (95131) ***(P-9952)***
W2 Optronics Inc (PA)....**F....510 207-8320**
5500 Stewart Ave Fremont (94538) ***(P-6353)***
W3ll People Inc....F....800 790-1563
570 10th St 3 Oakland (94607) ***(P-4099)***
Wabash National Trlr Ctrs Inc....E....916 371-6921
3600 W Capitol Ave West Sacramento (95691) ***(P-8473)***
Wade Casey....D....916 395-9996
1648 Kathleen Ave Ste A Sacramento (95815) ***(P-14110)***
Wade Metal Products Inc....F....559 237-9233
1818 Los Angeles St Fresno (93721) ***(P-4692)***
Wafer Process Systems Inc....F....408 445-3010
3641 Charter Park Dr San Jose (95136) ***(P-6354)***
Wafernet Inc....F....408 437-9747
2142 Paragon Dr San Jose (95131) ***(P-6355)***
Wagan Corporation....E....510 471-9221
31088 San Clemente St Hayward (94544) ***(P-8474)***
Wageworks Inc (HQ)....**C....650 577-5200**
1100 Park Pl Fl 4 San Mateo (94403) ***(P-19667)***
Waggl Inc (PA)....**D....415 399-9949**
1750 Bridgeway Ste B103 Sausalito (94965) ***(P-13524)***
Wagner Hts Nrsing Rhbltion Ct, Stockton *Also called Covenant Care California LLC* ***(P-15964)***
Wagner Krkmn Blne Klmp & Ymns (PA)....**E....916 920-5286**
10640 Mather Blvd Ste 200 Mather (95655) ***(P-17388)***
Waitwhile Inc....E....888 983-0869
1407 Funston Ave San Francisco (94122) ***(P-12916)***
Wal-Martcom Usa LLC (HQ)....**E....650 837-5000**
850 Cherry Ave San Bruno (94066) ***(P-9674)***
Walashek Industrial & Mar Inc....E....206 624-2880
2826 8th St Berkeley (94710) ***(P-6640)***
Walden Capital Partnership....E....415 391-7225
750 Battery St Ste 700 San Francisco (94111) ***(P-10896)***
Walden House Inc (PA)....**E....415 554-1100**
520 Townsend St San Francisco (94103) ***(P-18205)***
Walden House Inc....C....415 554-1480
214 Haight St San Francisco (94102) ***(P-18206)***
Walden House Inc....C....415 554-1131
1735 Mission St San Francisco (94103) ***(P-18207)***
Walden House Adolescent, San Francisco *Also called Walden House Inc* ***(P-18206)***
Walden Vc, San Francisco *Also called Walden Capital Partnership* ***(P-10896)***
Waldorf School of Mendocino....E....707 485-8719
6280 3rd St Calpella (95418) ***(P-18044)***
WALDORF SCHOOL OF MENDOCINO CO, Calpella *Also called Waldorf School of Mendocino* ***(P-18044)***
Walgreen Co....E....415 558-8749
1979 Mission St San Francisco (94103) ***(P-14184)***
Walgreens, San Francisco *Also called Walgreen Co* ***(P-14184)***
Walk Through Video, McClellan *Also called Villara Corporation* ***(P-1391)***
Walker Bags, San Francisco *Also called Walker/Dunham Corp* ***(P-4350)***
Walker Communications Inc....E....707 421-1300
521 Railroad Ave Suisun City (94585) ***(P-1633)***
Walker Lithograph....E....530 527-2142
20869 Walnut St Red Bluff (96080) ***(P-3712)***
Walker Printing, Red Bluff *Also called Walker Lithograph* ***(P-3712)***
Walker/Dunham Corp....E....415 821-3070
445 Barneveld Ave San Francisco (94124) ***(P-4350)***
Walkme Inc (PA)....**D....855 492-5563**
71 Stevenson St Ste 2000 San Francisco (94105) ***(P-12917)***
Walkup Law Office, San Francisco *Also called Walkup Mldia Klly Schnbrger A* ***(P-17389)***
Walkup Mldia Klly Schnbrger A....E....415 981-7210
650 California St Fl 26 San Francisco (94108) ***(P-17389)***
Wallace-Kuhl Investments LLC....E....209 234-7722
3422 W Hammer Ln Ste G Stockton (95219) ***(P-18855)***
Wallace-Kuhl Investments LLC (PA)....**D....916 372-1434**
3050 Industrial Blvd West Sacramento (95691) ***(P-18856)***
Wallis Fashions Inc....C....510 763-8018
1100 8th Ave Oakland (94606) ***(P-14458)***
Wally's Natural Products, Auburn *Also called Wallys Natural* ***(P-9675)***
Wallys Natural....E....530 887-0396
11837 Kemper Rd Ste 5 Auburn (95603) ***(P-9675)***
Walmart, San Bruno *Also called Wal-Martcom Usa LLC* ***(P-9674)***
Walmart Inc....F....209 368-6658
1601 S Lwer Sacramento Rd Lodi (95242) ***(P-3713)***
Walnut Country, Concord *Also called Cowell Homeowners Assn Inc* ***(P-18411)***
Walnut Creek Associates 2 Inc....D....925 934-0530
1707 N Main St Walnut Creek (94596) ***(P-14602)***
Walnut Creek Honda, Walnut Creek *Also called Walnut Creek Associates 2 Inc* ***(P-14602)***
Walnut Creek Sklled Nrsing Rhb, Walnut Creek *Also called Life Gnerations Healthcare LLC* ***(P-16036)***
Walnut Whtney Convalecent Hosp, Carmichael *Also called Horizon West Inc* ***(P-16025)***
Walschon Fire Protection Inc....E....650 594-1588
2178 Rheem Dr Ste A Pleasanton (94588) ***(P-1394)***
Walsh Group Inc....D....530 221-4405
3135 Agassi Ln Redding (96002) ***(P-14985)***
Walsh Vineyards Management Inc....C....707 255-1650
1125 Golden Gate Dr NAPA (94558) ***(P-10680)***
Walt Disney Company....D....916 780-1470
8265 Sierra College Blvd # 21 Roseville (95661) ***(P-8036)***
Walt Disney Family Museum....D....415 345-6800
104 Montgomery St San Francisco (94129) ***(P-18286)***
Walt Oxley Enterprises Inc....E....408 278-0370
663 Walnut St San Jose (95110) ***(P-983)***
Walter & Wolf, Fremont *Also called Walters & Wolf Glass Company* ***(P-1948)***
Walter C Voigt Inc....E....559 233-3055
2479 S Orange Ave Fresno (93725) ***(P-9499)***
Walter E Mc Guire RE Inc (PA)....**E....415 929-1500**
2001 Lombard St San Francisco (94123) ***(P-10681)***
Walter E McGuire RE Inc....E....415 296-0123
17 Bluxome St San Francisco (94107) ***(P-10682)***
Walter R Reinhardt Insur Agcy....E....559 226-4700
499 W Shaw Ave Ste 130 Fresno (93704) ***(P-10366)***
Walters & Wolf Glass Company (PA)....**C....510 490-1115**
41450 Boscell Rd Fremont (94538) ***(P-1948)***
Walters & Wolf Glass Company....E....510 226-9800
41450 Cowbell Rd Fremont (94538) ***(P-4453)***
Walters & Wolf Interiors (PA)....**D....415 243-9400**
41450 Boscell Rd Fremont (94538) ***(P-1762)***
Walters & Wolf Precast....C....510 226-9800
41450 Boscell Rd Fremont (94538) ***(P-4454)***
Walton Engineering Inc....D....916 372-1888
3900 Commerce Dr West Sacramento (95691) ***(P-2086)***
Walton Industries Inc....E....559 495-4004
1220 E North Ave Fresno (93725) ***(P-4114)***
Wandera Inc....E....408 667-5489
220 Sansome St Fl 14 San Francisco (94104) ***(P-13769)***
Wanderlust LLC (PA)....**F....209 404-0716**
2401 E Orangeburg Ave # 6 Modesto (95355) ***(P-2499)***
Waneshear Technologies LLC....E....707 462-4761
3471 N State St Ukiah (95482) ***(P-5117)***
Wang Nmr Inc....E....925 443-0212
550 N Canyons Pkwy Livermore (94551) ***(P-7062)***
Wanger Jones Helsley PC....E....559 233-4800
265 E Rver Pk Cir Ste 310 Fresno (93720) ***(P-17390)***
Wantz Equipment Company Inc....E....916 372-1792
3300 W Capitol Ave West Sacramento (95691) ***(P-4733)***
Warbritton & Assoc Impairment (PA)....**D....510 251-8851**
300 Frank H Ogawa Plz Oakland (94612) ***(P-17193)***
Ward, E B, Brisbane *Also called Edward B Ward & Company Inc* ***(P-9009)***
Ward/Davis Associates Inc....E....408 213-1090
1155 N 1st St Ste 205 San Jose (95112) ***(P-8971)***
Warden Security Associates Inc....D....408 722-6463
353 E 10th St Ste 730 Gilroy (95020) ***(P-14111)***
Wardley Industrial Inc....E....209 932-1088
907 Stokes Ave Stockton (95215) ***(P-4246)***
Wardrobe and Bath Specialties, Modesto *Also called Dons Mobile Glass Inc* ***(P-8643)***
Warmboard Inc....E....831 685-9276
100 Enterprise Way G300 Scotts Valley (95066) ***(P-5219)***
Warmington Homes....C....925 866-6700
4160 Dublin Blvd Ste 130 Dublin (94568) ***(P-786)***
Warmington Residental, Dublin *Also called Warmington Homes* ***(P-786)***
Warner Enterprises Inc....E....530 241-4000
1577 Beltline Rd Redding (96003) ***(P-3086)***
Warner Walker Architects....E....415 318-8900
353 Folsom St Fl 1 San Francisco (94105) ***(P-18917)***
Warnock Food Products Inc....D....559 661-4845
20237 Masa St Madera (93638) ***(P-2859)***
Warren Cnsulting Engineers Inc....E....916 985-1870
1117 Windfield Way # 110 El Dorado Hills (95762) ***(P-18857)***
Warren Knox Roofing, Santa Cruz *Also called Forever Firewood Inc* ***(P-1804)***
Warren Resorts Inc....D....707 251-8687
195 Main St Saint Helena (94574) ***(P-11565)***
Warren, Lewis R, Santa Rosa *Also called Abbey Wtznberg Wrren Emery A P* ***(P-17197)***
Warwick California Corporation....C....415 992-3809
490 Geary St San Francisco (94102) ***(P-11566)***
Warwick Hotel San Francisco, San Francisco *Also called Warwick California Corporation* ***(P-11566)***
Warwick, Mal & Associates, Berkeley *Also called Strathmoore Press Inc* ***(P-14417)***

ALPHABETIC

Wasco Hardfacing Co D 559 485-5860
4585 E Citron Fresno (93725) ***(P-5020)***
Wash Mltfmily Ldry Systems LLC F 559 233-0595
1104 S Parallel Ave Fresno (93702) ***(P-11651)***
Washington Center D 510 352-2211
14766 Washington Ave San Leandro (94578) ***(P-16720)***
Washington Children's Center, Sacramento *Also called Sacramento Cy Unified Schl Dst* ***(P-18010)***
Washington Hosp Healthcare Sys A 510 797-3342
2000 Mowry Ave Fremont (94538) ***(P-16721)***
Washington Inn Associates D 510 452-1776
495 10th St Oakland (94607) ***(P-11567)***
Washington Otptent Srgery Ctr D 510 791-5374
2299 Mowry Ave Fl 1 Fremont (94538) ***(P-16722)***
Washington Otptent Surgery Ctr, Fremont *Also called Washington Otptent Srgery Ctr* ***(P-16722)***
Washington Rdologist Med Group E 510 797-1111
2000 Mowry Ave Fremont (94538) ***(P-16723)***
Washington Unified School Dst E 916 375-7720
508 Poplar Ave West Sacramento (95691) ***(P-18045)***
Washoe Equipment Inc D 916 395-4700
6201 27th St Sacramento (95822) ***(P-5729)***
Waste Connections Cal Inc (HQ) **C 408 282-4400**
1333 Oakland Rd San Jose (95112) ***(P-8380)***
Waste Management, Gold River *Also called USA Waste of California Inc* ***(P-8377)***
Waste Management Cal Inc C 408 779-2206
910 Coyote Creek Golf Dr Morgan Hill (95037) ***(P-8381)***
Waste Management Wisconsin Inc E 530 283-2065
1166 Industrial Way Quincy (95971) ***(P-8382)***
Waste Managment, Corning *Also called Andersncttonwood Disposal Svcs* ***(P-7450)***
Waste MGT Alameda Cnty Inc (HQ) **A 510 613-8710**
172 98th Ave Oakland (94603) ***(P-8383)***
Waste MGT Collectn Recycl Inc C 925 935-8900
2658 N Main St Walnut Creek (94597) ***(P-7497)***
Waste MGT Collectn Recycl Inc D 707 964-9172
219 Pudding Creek Rd Fort Bragg (95437) ***(P-8384)***
Waste MGT Collectn Recycl Inc D 530 662-8748
1324 Paddock Pl Woodland (95776) ***(P-8385)***
Waste MGT Collectn Recycl Inc D 831 768-9505
1340 W Beach St Watsonville (95076) ***(P-8386)***
Waste MGT Collectn Recycl Inc D 707 462-0210
219 Pudding Creek Rd Fort Bragg (95437) ***(P-8387)***
Waste MGT Collectn Recycl Inc D 707 462-0210
450 Orr Springs Rd Ukiah (95482) ***(P-8388)***
Wastexperts Incorporated D 925 484-1057
901 Howe Rd Martinez (94553) ***(P-19420)***
Watch Resources Inc (PA) **E 209 533-0510**
12801 Cabezut Rd Sonora (95370) ***(P-17784)***
Watchpoint Logistics Inc C 650 871-4747
50 Tanforan Ave South San Francisco (94080) ***(P-7859)***
Water Course Way, Palo Alto *Also called Watercourse Way* ***(P-11736)***
Water Division, Fresno *Also called City of Fresno* ***(P-8229)***
Water Heater Specialists Inc E 415 775-5100
23 28th Ave San Mateo (94403) ***(P-1395)***
Water Ink Technology F 707 426-9420
2350 S Watney Way Ste G Fairfield (94533) ***(P-4155)***
Water One Industries Inc (PA) **E 707 747-4300**
5410 Gateway Plaza Dr Benicia (94510) ***(P-5451)***
Water Resources Cal Dept D 916 574-1423
3310 El Cmino Ave Ste 200 Sacramento (95821) ***(P-19245)***
Water Resources Cal Dept E 916 651-9203
901 P St Lbby Sacramento (95814) ***(P-6738)***
Water Supply Division, Stockton *Also called East Bay Mncpl Utility Dst Wtr* ***(P-8241)***
Water Works Manufacturing, Marysville *Also called US Pipe Fabrication LLC* ***(P-4236)***
Watercourse Way C 650 462-2000
165 Channing Ave Palo Alto (94301) ***(P-11736)***
Waterfall F 866 251-1200
25 Division St Ste 205 San Francisco (94103) ***(P-13525)***
Waterford Almond Hller Sheller, Waterford *Also called Riddle Ranches Inc* ***(P-91)***
Watergate Community Assn (PA) **E 510 428-0118**
8 Captain Dr Emeryville (94608) ***(P-18480)***
Waterhouse Management Corp C 916 772-4918
500 Giuseppe Ct Ste 2 Roseville (95678) ***(P-10475)***
Waterleaf At Land Park, The, Sacramento *Also called Valine Court Senior Care Inc* ***(P-18196)***
Watermark Rtrment Cmmnties Inc D 925 344-5661
35 Fenton St Livermore (94550) ***(P-18208)***
Waters Edge Inc E 510 748-4300
2401 Blanding Ave Alameda (94501) ***(P-16155)***
Waters Edge Lodge E 510 769-6264
801 Island Dr Apt 267 Alameda (94502) ***(P-18209)***
Waters Edge Nursing Home, Alameda *Also called Waters Edge Inc* ***(P-16155)***
Waters Moving & Storage Inc D 925 372-0914
37 Bridgehead Rd Martinez (94553) ***(P-7498)***
WATERSHED CENTER, Hayfork *Also called Watershed Res & Training Ctr* ***(P-537)***
Watershed Res & Training Ctr E 530 628-4206
98 Clinic Ave Ste B Hayfork (96041) ***(P-537)***
Waterworks Park, Redding *Also called Yanaco Inc* ***(P-15047)***
Waterworld California, Concord *Also called Parc Waterworld LLC* ***(P-15044)***
Waterworld USA, Concord *Also called Parc Management LLC* ***(P-15225)***
Wathen-Castanos-Mazmanian Inc E 559 432-8181
2505 Alluvial Ave Clovis (93611) ***(P-727)***
Watlow Electric Mfg Co D 408 776-6646
6781 Via Del Oro San Jose (95119) ***(P-18858)***
Watry Design Inc (PA) **E 408 392-7900**
2099 Gateway Pl Ste 550 San Jose (95110) ***(P-18918)***
Watson Companies Inc E 916 481-6293
3185 Longview Dr Sacramento (95821) ***(P-1845)***
Watsonville Coast Produce Inc D 831 722-3851
275 Kearney Ext Frnt Watsonville (95076) ***(P-9436)***
Watsonville Community Hospital, Watsonville *Also called Halsen Healthcare LLC* ***(P-16384)***
Watt Stopper Inc (HQ) **E 408 988-5331**
2700 Zanker Rd Ste 168 San Jose (95134) ***(P-5720)***
Watt Stopper Inc F 408 988-5331
2800 De La Cruz Blvd Santa Clara (95050) ***(P-5898)***
Watt Stopper Le Grand, San Jose *Also called Watt Stopper Inc* ***(P-5720)***
Watts Equipment Company E 209 825-1700
17547 Comconex Rd Manteca (95336) ***(P-9104)***
Watts Machining Inc E 408 654-9300
3370 Victor Ct Santa Clara (95054) ***(P-5639)***
Wattzon, Mountain View *Also called Glyntai Inc* ***(P-13193)***
Wave Computing Inc (PA) **D 408 412-8645**
780 Montague Expy Ste 308 San Jose (95131) ***(P-14008)***
Wavelabs Technologies Inc (PA) **D 408 203-7670**
691 S Milpitas Blvd # 217 Milpitas (95035) ***(P-14459)***
Waverley Surgery Center LP (PA) **D 650 324-0600**
400 Forest Ave Palo Alto (94301) ***(P-15811)***
Wawona Frozen Foods (PA) **C 559 299-2901**
100 W Alluvial Ave Clovis (93611) ***(P-2957)***
Waxies Enterprises LLC E 925 454-2900
901 N Canyon Pkwy Livermore (94551) ***(P-9148)***
Wayne E 669 206-2179
640 W California Ave Sunnyvale (94086) ***(P-2168)***
Wayne E Swisher Cem Contr Inc D 925 757-3660
2620 E 18th St Antioch (94509) ***(P-1917)***
Wayne Maples Plumbing & Htg D 707 445-2500
317 W Cedar St Eureka (95501) ***(P-1396)***
Waypoint Building Group Inc D 415 738-4730
847 Sansome St Fl 3 San Francisco (94111) ***(P-19668)***
Wayside Lumber, Rancho Cordova *Also called M J&C Holding Inc* ***(P-8588)***
Wazuh Inc (PA) **C 844 349-2984**
1021 Lenor Way San Jose (95128) ***(P-14009)***
Wb Electric Inc D 408 842-7911
6790 Monterey Rd Gilroy (95020) ***(P-1634)***
Wb Machining & Mech Design E 408 453-5005
1670 Zanker Rd San Jose (95112) ***(P-5640)***
Wbb Management Company Inc E 415 456-8972
250 Bel Marin Keys Blvd A Novato (94949) ***(P-19421)***
Wbe Traffic Control Inc D 707 771-5870
5150 Fair Oaks Blvd Ste 1 Carmichael (95608) ***(P-14460)***
Wbi Inventory Service Inc (PA) **E 916 729-1147**
7609 Greenback Ln Citrus Heights (95610) ***(P-14461)***
Wc, Fairfield *Also called West-Com Nrse Call Systems Inc* ***(P-5883)***
Wc AG Services Inc A 209 538-3131
800 E Keyes Rd Ceres (95307) ***(P-391)***
WC Maloney Inc E 209 942-1129
4020 Newton Rd Stockton (95205) ***(P-1976)***
Wcg World, San Francisco *Also called Weisscomm Group Ltd* ***(P-19889)***
Wchs Inc E 877 706-0510
20400 Stevens Creek Blvd Cupertino (95014) ***(P-16967)***
WCIRB, Oakland *Also called Workers Cmpnstion Insur Rting* ***(P-10190)***
Wcr Incorporated E 559 266-8374
4636 E Drummond Ave Fresno (93725) ***(P-14784)***
WD, San Jose *Also called Western Digital Tech Inc* ***(P-5327)***
WD Media LLC B 408 576-2000
1710 Automation Pkwy San Jose (95131) ***(P-5325)***
Wdr Restoration Inc E 800 886-1801
2450 Alvarado St Ste 1 San Leandro (94577) ***(P-728)***
We're Organized Northern Cal, Rancho Cordova *Also called Garage Cabinet Warehouse Inc* ***(P-1738)***
Wealthfront Corporation E 650 249-4258
261 Hamilton Ave Palo Alto (94301) ***(P-10068)***
Weatherflow-Tempest Inc E 831 438-9742
108 Whispering Pines Dr Scotts Valley (95066) ***(P-19920)***
Weatherford BMW, Concord *Also called Weatherford Motors Inc* ***(P-14603)***
Weatherford Motors Inc C 510 654-8280
1967 Market St Concord (94520) ***(P-14603)***
Weatherly Aircraft Company E 916 640-0120
5000 Bailey Loop Bldg 360 McClellan (95652) ***(P-6620)***
Weave Inc (PA) **D 916 448-2321**
1900 K St Ste 200 Sacramento (95811) ***(P-12208)***
Weaver Crlson Mc Crtney Accntn E 925 447-2010
2117 4th St Livermore (94550) ***(P-19003)***
Weaver Schlenger and Mazel E 415 395-9331
550 Montgomery St Ste 650 San Francisco (94111) ***(P-17391)***
Web Traffic School, Oakland *Also called Interactive Solutions Inc* ***(P-13241)***
Webb Ranch Inc E 650 854-6334
2720 Alpine Rd Portola Valley (94028) ***(P-38)***
Webcor Builders, San Francisco *Also called Webcor Construction LP* ***(P-985)***
Webcor Builders Inc D 650 591-7400
850 N El Camino Real San Mateo (94401) ***(P-984)***
Webcor Construction LP (HQ) **D 415 978-1000**
207 King St Ste 300 San Francisco (94107) ***(P-985)***
Webcor Management Company, San Mateo *Also called Webcor Builders Inc* ***(P-984)***
Webenertia Inc E 408 246-0000
1570 The Alameda Ste 330 San Jose (95126) ***(P-13770)***
Weber Motors Fresno Inc D 559 447-6700
7171 N Palm Ave Fresno (93650) ***(P-14678)***
Webers Quality Meats Inc D 510 635-9892
990 Carden St San Leandro (94577) ***(P-9382)***
Webevents Global, Rocklin *Also called Webevents LLC* ***(P-12918)***
Webevents LLC E 916 784-9456
3706 Atherton Rd 100 Rocklin (95765) ***(P-12918)***
Webex.com, San Jose *Also called Cisco Webex LLC* ***(P-14226)***
Webgility Inc E 415 640-7906
575 Market St Ste 1900 San Francisco (94105) ***(P-13526)***

Webpass Inc ....D....415 233-4100
267 8th St San Francisco (94103) ***(P-8008)***
Webster Investment Management, San Francisco *Also called Forward Management LLC* ***(P-10044)***
Webster Orthpdc Med Grp A Prof ....E....925 362-2116
200 Porter Dr Ste 101 San Ramon (94583) ***(P-15812)***
Webster Surgery Center LP (PA) ....**D....510 451-0957**
80 Grand Ave Ste 250 Oakland (94612) ***(P-15813)***
Webtyme Design & Hosting, San Mateo *Also called D E M Enterprises Inc* ***(P-13706)***
Weco Aerospace Systems, Lincoln *Also called Gdsa-Lincoln Inc* ***(P-14699)***
Wedemeyer Bakery, South San Francisco *Also called Windmill Corporation* ***(P-2412)***
Wedgewood Connect ....E....855 321-3477
17 Great Oaks Blvd San Jose (95119) ***(P-4007)***
Wedriveu Inc ....E....650 645-6800
700 Airport Blvd Ste 250 Burlingame (94010) ***(P-7860)***
Wedriveu Holdings Inc (HQ) ....**E....650 579-5800**
700 Airport Blvd Ste 250 Burlingame (94010) ***(P-10747)***
Weed Enterprises Inc ....E....408 929-1992
662 Giguere Ct Ste F San Jose (95133) ***(P-11910)***
Weeks Drilling and Pump Co (PA) ....**E....707 823-3184**
6100 Sebastopol Ave Sebastopol (95472) ***(P-1397)***
Wehah Farm Inc ....B....530 538-3500
5311 Midway Richvale (95974) ***(P-2330)***
WEI Laboratories Inc ....E....408 970-8700
3002 Scott Blvd Santa Clara (95054) ***(P-2209)***
Weibel Champagne Vineyards, Lodi *Also called Weibel Incorporated* ***(P-2759)***
Weibel Incorporated ....E....209 365-9463
1 Winemaster Way Ste D Lodi (95240) ***(P-2759)***
Weidner Archtctral Sgng/Huse S ....D....800 561-7446
5001 24th St Sacramento (95822) ***(P-7260)***
WEIDNERCA, Sacramento *Also called Weidner Archtctral Sgng/Huse S* ***(P-7260)***
Weil Gotshal & Manges LLP ....C....650 802-3000
201 Rdwood Shres Pkwy Ste Redwood City (94065) ***(P-17392)***
Weiland, David S MD, San Pablo *Also called East Bay Cardiology Med Group* ***(P-15385)***
Weinberg Roger & Resenfeld (PA) ....**D....510 337-1001**
1001 Marina Village Pkwy # 200 Alameda (94501) ***(P-17393)***
Weintraub Tobin Chediak (PA) ....**E....916 558-6000**
400 Capitol Mall Fl 11 Sacramento (95814) ***(P-17394)***
Weiss Associates, Emeryville *Also called Aguatierra Associates Inc* ***(P-19700)***
Weiss-Mcnair LLC (HQ) ....**D....530 891-6214**
100 Loren Ave Chico (95928) ***(P-5021)***
Weisscomm Group Ltd (PA) ....**D....415 362-5018**
50 Francisco St Ste 400 San Francisco (94133) ***(P-19889)***
Welbe Health LLC (PA) ....**D....650 862-6371**
934 Santa Cruz Ave Ste B Menlo Park (94025) ***(P-16968)***
Welcome Group Inc ....D....916 920-5300
1780 Tribute Rd Sacramento (95815) ***(P-11568)***
Welcome Natomas LLC ....E....916 649-1300
2618 Gateway Oaks Dr Sacramento (95833) ***(P-11569)***
Weldway Inc ....E....209 847-8083
521 Hi Tech Pkwy Oakdale (95361) ***(P-4693)***
Welker Bros, Milpitas *Also called H V Welker Co Inc* ***(P-1771)***
Well Being Senior Solutions ....D....559 321-8295
55 Shaw Ave Ste 220 Clovis (93612) ***(P-16969)***
Wellex Corporation (PA) ....**C....510 743-1818**
551 Brown Rd Fremont (94539) ***(P-6482)***
Wellhead Electric Company Inc ....E....916 447-5171
650 Bercut Dr Ste C Sacramento (95811) ***(P-8207)***
Wellmade Products, Merced *Also called WLMD* ***(P-2089)***
Wells & Bennett Realtors (PA) ....**D....510 531-7000**
1451 Leimert Blvd Oakland (94602) ***(P-10683)***
Wells Capital Management Inc (HQ) ....**B....415 396-8000**
525 Market St Fl 10 San Francisco (94105) ***(P-10069)***
Wells Construction Inc ....E....916 257-6172
10648 Industrial Ave Roseville (95678) ***(P-986)***
Wells Dental Inc ....F....707 937-0521
5860 Flynn Creek Rd Comptche (95427) ***(P-7090)***
Wells Fargo & Company (PA) ....**A....866 249-3302**
420 Montgomery St San Francisco (94104) ***(P-9694)***
Wells Fargo Asset MGT Intl LLC ....D....415 396-8000
525 Market St Fl 10 San Francisco (94105) ***(P-10070)***
Wells Fargo Bank National Assn ....D....925 746-3718
1655 Grant St Concord (94520) ***(P-9695)***
Wells Fargo Coml Dist Fin LLC ....C....916 636-2020
3100 Zinfandel Dr Ste 255 Rancho Cordova (95670) ***(P-9878)***
Wells Fargo Dealer Services, Stockton *Also called W Fs Financial Inc* ***(P-9865)***
Wells Fargo Investments LLC (HQ) ....**B....415 396-7767**
420 Montgomery St Frnt San Francisco (94104) ***(P-9696)***
Wells Fargo Prime Services LLC ....D....415 848-0269
45 Fremont St Ste 3000 San Francisco (94105) ***(P-10023)***
Wells Precision Machining, Comptche *Also called Wells Dental Inc* ***(P-7090)***
Wellspace Health (PA) ....**D....916 325-5556**
1820 J St Sacramento (95811) ***(P-17091)***
Wellspring, Sacramento *Also called Positive Option Family Service* ***(P-17676)***
Wellspring Family Camp, Reedley *Also called Camp Wellspring LLC* ***(P-17454)***
Wemakeiot, Hayward *Also called Sheeba Duleep* ***(P-12776)***
Wencon Development Inc ....D....925 478-8269
2700 Mitchell Dr Ste 2 Walnut Creek (94598) ***(P-1398)***
Wendel Rosen LLP (PA) ....**C....510 834-6600**
1111 Broadway Ste 2400 Oakland (94607) ***(P-17395)***
Wendt Construction Co Inc ....E....707 725-5641
1660 Newburg Rd Fortuna (95540) ***(P-10721)***
Wendt Industries Inc ....E....209 836-4100
1875 N Macarthur Dr Tracy (95376) ***(P-19422)***
Wente Bros (PA) ....**D....925 456-2300**
5565 Tesla Rd Livermore (94550) ***(P-2760)***
Wente Bros ....E....925 456-2450
5050 Arroyo Rd Livermore (94550) ***(P-2761)***
Wente Vineyard Restaurant, Livermore *Also called Wente Bros* ***(P-2761)***
Wente Vineyards, Livermore *Also called Wente Bros* ***(P-2760)***
Wentworth Hauser & Violich Inc ....D....415 981-6911
301 Battery St Fl 4 San Francisco (94111) ***(P-10071)***
Wepay Inc ....E....855 469-3729
350 Convention Way # 200 Redwood City (94063) ***(P-13771)***
Weride Corp ....E....408 645-7118
2630 Orchard Pkwy San Jose (95134) ***(P-12919)***
Wes Manufacturing Inc ....E....408 727-0750
431 Greenwood Dr Santa Clara (95054) ***(P-5641)***
Wescam Sonoma Operations, Santa Rosa *Also called L-3 Cmmnications Sonoma Eo Inc* ***(P-7152)***
Wesley B Lasher Inv Corp (PA) ....**D....916 290-8500**
5800 Florin Rd Sacramento (95823) ***(P-14604)***
Wespac Plan Services LLC (HQ) ....**E....510 740-4163**
4 Orinda Way Ste 100b Orinda (94563) ***(P-10367)***
West Air Inc ....D....559 454-7843
5005 E Andersen Ave Fresno (93727) ***(P-7752)***
West Bay Builders, Novato *Also called Wbb Management Company Inc* ***(P-19421)***
West Cast Retina Med Group Inc ....E....415 972-4600
1445 Bush St San Francisco (94109) ***(P-15814)***
West Chester, San Francisco *Also called Ace Usa Inc* ***(P-10160)***
West Coast Arborists Inc ....C....559 275-2086
5424 N Barcus Ave Fresno (93722) ***(P-526)***
West Coast Arborists Inc ....D....408 855-8660
3625 Stevenson Ave Stockton (95205) ***(P-509)***
West Coast Contractors Inc ....E....214 281-3100
2320 Courage Dr Ste 111 Fairfield (94533) ***(P-987)***
West Coast Cryogenics Inc ....E....800 657-0545
503 W Larch Rd Ste K Tracy (95304) ***(P-5174)***
West Coast Cryogenics Services, Tracy *Also called West Coast Cryogenics Inc* ***(P-5174)***
West Coast Fab Inc ....F....510 529-0177
700 S 32nd St Richmond (94804) ***(P-4830)***
West Coast Garment Mfg Inc ....F....415 896-1772
70 Elmira St San Francisco (94124) ***(P-2990)***
West Coast Hospitals Inc ....E....831 722-3581
919 Freedom Blvd Watsonville (95076) ***(P-16156)***
West Coast Legal Service Inc ....E....408 938-6520
1925 Winchester Blvd # 20 Campbell (95008) ***(P-14462)***
West Coast Magnetics, Stockton *Also called Wjlp Company Inc* ***(P-6388)***
West Coast Novelty Corporation (PA) ....**E....510 748-4248**
2401 Monarch St Alameda (94501) ***(P-9203)***
West Coast Office & Dist Ctr, Rancho Cordova *Also called E-Filliate Inc* ***(P-8696)***
West Coast Pathology Lab ....D....510 662-5200
712 Alfred Nobel Dr Hercules (94547) ***(P-16821)***
West Coast Property Maint LLC ....E....415 885-6970
714 Van Ness Ave San Francisco (94102) ***(P-10684)***
West Coast Property Management ....D....408 263-5566
400 Valley Way Milpitas (95035) ***(P-11570)***
West Coast Quartz Corporation (HQ) ....**D....510 249-2160**
1000 Corporate Way Fremont (94539) ***(P-4382)***
West Coast Santa Cruz Hotel, Santa Cruz *Also called Santa Cruz Ht Assoc A Cal Ltd* ***(P-11443)***
West Coast Tree Care Inc ....E....408 260-2007
2845 Moorpark Ave Ste 205 San Jose (95128) ***(P-527)***
West Coast Venture Capital LLC (PA) ....**B....408 725-0700**
10050 Bandley Dr Cupertino (95014) ***(P-5816)***
West Contra Costa YMCA, Richmond *Also called Young MNS Chrstn Assn of E Bay* ***(P-18501)***
West County Health Centers Inc (PA) ....**D....707 869-1594**
16312 3rd St Guerneville (95446) ***(P-15815)***
West County Resource Recovery ....E....510 231-4200
101 Pittsburg Ave Richmond (94801) ***(P-8389)***
West County Trnsp Agcy ....C....707 206-9988
367 W Robles Ave Santa Rosa (95407) ***(P-7365)***
West County Wastewater Dst ....E....510 237-6603
2377 Garden Tract Rd Richmond (94801) ***(P-8296)***
West Hotel Partners LP ....C....408 947-4450
300 Almaden Blvd San Jose (95110) ***(P-11571)***
West Marine Inc (PA) ....**B....831 728-2700**
500 Westridge Dr Watsonville (95076) ***(P-9153)***
West Medions, San Leandro *Also called KMA Emergency Services Inc* ***(P-7384)***
WEST OAKLAND HEALTH CENTER, Oakland *Also called West Oakland Health Council* ***(P-17092)***
West Oakland Health Council (PA) ....**C....510 835-9610**
700 Adeline St Oakland (94607) ***(P-17092)***
West Prtal Ctr For After Schl (PA) ....**D....415 753-1113**
1560 Noriega St Ste 206 San Francisco (94122) ***(P-18046)***
West San Crlos Ht Partners LLC ....D....408 998-0400
282 Almaden Blvd San Jose (95113) ***(P-11572)***
West Side Cmnty Healthcare Dst ....E....209 862-2951
990 Tulare St Ste C Newman (95360) ***(P-17194)***
West Side Community Ambulance ....E....209 862-2951
151 State Highway 33 Newman (95360) ***(P-7411)***
West Star Industries, Stockton *Also called Hackett Industries Inc* ***(P-5131)***
West Valley Aviation Inc ....F....559 659-7378
1011 12th St Firebaugh (93622) ***(P-6637)***
West Valley Carpet Service ....E....408 946-2447
1291 Pintail Ct San Jose (95118) ***(P-1778)***
West Valley Cnstr - Stockton, Stockton *Also called West Valley Cnstr Co Inc* ***(P-1143)***
West Valley Cnstr Co Inc (PA) ....**C....408 371-5510**
580 E Mcglincy Ln Campbell (95008) ***(P-1142)***
West Valley Cnstr Co Inc ....E....209 943-6812
2655 E Miner Ave Ste A Stockton (95205) ***(P-1143)***
West Valley Cnstr Co Inc ....E....650 364-9464
809 Hurlingame Ave Redwood City (94063) ***(P-1144)***
West Valley Engineering Inc (PA) ....**A....408 735-1420**
390 Potrero Ave Sunnyvale (94085) ***(P-12209)***

West Valley Gymnastics School, Campbell *Also called Balanced Rock Inc* ***(P-15178)***
West Valley Staffing Group, Sunnyvale *Also called West Valley Engineering Inc* ***(P-12209)***
West Vlly-Mssion Cmnty Cllege ....B....408 988-2200
3000 Mission College Blvd Santa Clara (95054) ***(P-19890)***
West Yost & Associates Inc (PA) ....**D....530 756-5905**
2020 Res Pk Dr Ste 100 Davis (95618) ***(P-18859)***
West-Com Nrse Call Systems Inc (PA) ....**E....707 428-5900**
2200 Cordelia Rd Fairfield (94534) ***(P-5883)***
West-Mark, Ceres *Also called Certified Stainless Svc Inc* ***(P-4715)***
West-Mark, Atwater *Also called Certified Stainless Svc Inc* ***(P-4716)***
Westak, Sunnyvale *Also called Qualitek Inc* ***(P-5962)***
Westak Inc (PA) ....**D....408 734-8686**
1116 Elko Dr Sunnyvale (94089) ***(P-5998)***
Westak International Sales Inc (HQ) ....**C....408 734-8686**
1116 Elko Dr Sunnyvale (94089) ***(P-5999)***
Westamerica Bancorporation (PA) ....**C....707 863-6000**
1108 5th Ave San Rafael (94901) ***(P-9752)***
Westamerica Bank (HQ) ....**C....707 863-6113**
1108 5th Ave San Rafael (94901) ***(P-9753)***
Westar Marine Services, San Francisco *Also called Cross Link Inc* ***(P-7727)***
Westates Mechanical Corp Inc ....D....510 635-9830
2566 Barrington Ct Hayward (94545) ***(P-1399)***
Westbrdge Cpitl US Advsors LLC ....E....650 645-6220
400 S El Camino Real San Mateo (94402) ***(P-10772)***
Westbrook Enterprises Inc ....D....916 929-4680
1000 Arden Way Sacramento (95815) ***(P-14785)***
Westcal Management, Carmichael *Also called Pacific Cities Management Inc* ***(P-10633)***
Westcare California Inc (HQ) ....**C....559 251-4800**
1900 N Gateway Blvd 100 Fresno (93727) ***(P-18210)***
Westco Equities Inc (PA) ....**D....559 228-6788**
1625 E Shaw Ave Ste 116 Fresno (93710) ***(P-10685)***
Westco Iron Works Inc (PA) ....**D....925 961-9152**
1080 Concannon Blvd # 110 Livermore (94550) ***(P-4694)***
Westcoast Childrens Clinic ....C....510 269-9030
3301 E 12th St Ste 259 Oakland (94601) ***(P-17093)***
Westcoast Precision Inc ....D....408 943-9998
2091 Fortune Dr San Jose (95131) ***(P-5175)***
Westcott Designs Inc ....E....510 367-7229
4455 Park Rd Benicia (94510) ***(P-3284)***
Westech Inv Advisors LLC (PA) ....**E....650 234-4300**
104 La Mesa Dr 102 Portola Valley (94028) ***(P-2307)***
Westech Systems Inc ....D....559 455-1720
827 Jefferson Ave Clovis (93612) ***(P-1635)***
Wested ....E....510 302-4200
300 Lakeside Dr Fl 25th Oakland (94612) ***(P-19246)***
Wested ....E....415 289-2300
180 Harbor Dr Ste 112 Sausalito (94965) ***(P-19247)***
Wested (PA) ....**C....415 565-3000**
730 Harrison St Ste 500 San Francisco (94107) ***(P-19248)***
Wested ....E....650 381-6400
400 Seaport Ct Ste 222 Redwood City (94063) ***(P-19249)***
Wested ....E....408 299-1700
1550 The Alameda Ste 201 San Jose (95126) ***(P-19250)***
Wested ....E....916 492-9999
1000 G St Ste 500 Sacramento (95814) ***(P-19891)***
Westek Electronics Inc ....E....831 740-6300
165 Westridge Dr Watsonville (95076) ***(P-8972)***
Western Alliance Bank, Oakland *Also called Porrey Pines Bank Inc* ***(P-9688)***
Western Alliance Bank ....D....408 423-8500
55 Almaden Blvd Ste 200 San Jose (95113) ***(P-9754)***
Western Allied Mechanical Inc ....C....650 326-8290
1180 Obrien Dr Menlo Park (94025) ***(P-1400)***
Western Blended Products, West Sacramento *Also called Sacramento Stucco Co* ***(P-8633)***
Western Building Materials Co (PA) ....**D....559 454-8500**
4620 E Olive Ave Fresno (93702) ***(P-1707)***
Western Buyers LLC (PA) ....**E....916 576-3042**
1030 Winding Creek Rd Roseville (95678) ***(P-8612)***
Western Camps Inc ....E....559 787-2551
6450 Elwood Rd Sanger (93657) ***(P-11615)***
Western Care Cnstr Co Inc ....E....916 624-6200
4020 Sierra College Blvd # 200 Rocklin (95677) ***(P-988)***
Western City Magazine, Sacramento *Also called League of California Cities* ***(P-19691)***
Western Concrete Products, Pleasanton *Also called Central Precast Concrete Inc* ***(P-4424)***
Western Digital, Milpitas *Also called Sandisk LLC* ***(P-5315)***
Western Digital Corporation (PA) ....**A....408 717-6000**
5601 Great Oaks Pkwy San Jose (95119) ***(P-5326)***
Western Digital Tech Inc (HQ) ....**A....408 717-6000**
5601 Great Oaks Pkwy San Jose (95119) ***(P-5327)***
Western Dovetail Incorporated ....E....707 556-3683
1101 Nimitz Ave Ste 209 Vallejo (94592) ***(P-3285)***
Western Drug Medical Supply, Stockton *Also called H and H Drug Stores Inc* ***(P-8781)***
Western Drywall Inc ....D....209 543-9361
4971 Salida Blvd Salida (95368) ***(P-1708)***
Western Flower Company, Arcata *Also called Endors Toi Pbc* ***(P-19500)***
Western Foam, Livermore *Also called Induspac California Inc* ***(P-3804)***
Western Foods LLC (HQ) ....**C....530 601-5991**
420 N Pioneer Ave Woodland (95776) ***(P-2958)***
Western Grinding Service Inc ....E....650 591-2635
2375 De La Cruz Blvd Santa Clara (95050) ***(P-5642)***
Western Health Advantage ....D....916 567-1950
2349 Gateway Oaks Dr # 100 Sacramento (95833) ***(P-10088)***
Western Health Resources ....D....707 459-1818
100 San Hedrin Cir Willits (95490) ***(P-19423)***
Western Living Concepts Inc (PA) ....**E....707 443-3000**
2740 Timber Ridge Ln Ofc Eureka (95503) ***(P-18211)***
Western Messenger Service Inc ....C....415 487-4229
75 Columbia Sq San Francisco (94103) ***(P-7499)***
Western Mountaineering, San Jose *Also called Seventh Heaven Inc* ***(P-3053)***
Western National Life Insur Co ....C....925 946-5100
1395 Creekside Dr Walnut Creek (94596) ***(P-10368)***
Western Nevada Supply Co ....C....530 582-5009
10990 Industrial Way A Truckee (96161) ***(P-9006)***
Western Oil & Spreading, Martinez *Also called Michael Telfer* ***(P-1059)***
Western Pacific Signal LLC ....F....510 276-6400
15890 Foothill Blvd San Leandro (94578) ***(P-5899)***
Western Real Estate News, South San Francisco *Also called Business Extension Bureau Ltd* ***(P-3492)***
Western Region, Milpitas *Also called Xcerra Corporation* ***(P-8974)***
Western Regional Office, Rancho Cordova *Also called Ducks Unlimited Inc* ***(P-18412)***
Western Roofing Service, San Leandro *Also called Roofing Constructors Inc* ***(P-1835)***
Western Roto Engravers Inc ....E....510 525-2950
1225 6th St Berkeley (94710) ***(P-3755)***
Western Sign Company Inc ....E....916 933-3765
6221a Enterprise Dr Ste A Diamond Springs (95619) ***(P-7261)***
Western Slope Health Care, Placerville *Also called Western Slope Health Center* ***(P-16157)***
Western Slope Health Center ....C....530 622-6842
3280 Washington St Placerville (95667) ***(P-16157)***
Western Square Industries Inc ....E....209 944-0921
1621 N Brdwy Stockton (95205) ***(P-4843)***
Western Stabilization, Dixon *Also called J & A Jeffery Inc* ***(P-7289)***
Western State Design Inc ....D....510 786-9271
2331 Tripaldi Way Hayward (94545) ***(P-5427)***
Western States Glass, Fremont *Also called Wsglass Holdings Inc* ***(P-4365)***
Western States Info Netwrk Inc ....D....916 263-1188
1825 Bell St Ste 205 Sacramento (95825) ***(P-19251)***
Western States Oil, San Jose *Also called Tom Lopes Distributing Inc* ***(P-9540)***
Western Sun Enterprises Inc ....E....707 748-2542
4690 E 2nd St Ste 4 Benicia (94510) ***(P-1636)***
Western Tree Nursery ....D....408 842-6800
3873 Hecker Pass Rd Gilroy (95020) ***(P-532)***
Western Water Features Inc ....E....916 939-1600
5088 Hillsdale Cir Ste A El Dorado Hills (95762) ***(P-2087)***
Western Waterproofing Co Inc ....E....510 875-2109
15061 Wicks Blvd San Leandro (94577) ***(P-2088)***
Western Web Inc ....E....707 444-6236
1900 Bendixsen St Ste 2 Samoa (95564) ***(P-3714)***
Western Wine Services Inc (PA) ....**D....800 999-8463**
880 Hanna Dr American Canyon (94503) ***(P-7705)***
Western Wood Treating, Woodland *Also called California Cascade-Woodland* ***(P-3257)***
Western Woods Inc (PA) ....**E....530 343-5821**
275 Sikorsky Ave Chico (95973) ***(P-8613)***
Westervelt Company ....E....916 646-3644
600 N Market Blvd Ste 3 Sacramento (95834) ***(P-19892)***
Westfab Manufacturing Inc ....E....408 727-0550
3370 Keller St Santa Clara (95054) ***(P-4831)***
Westfield Vlg Elementary Schl, West Sacramento *Also called Washington Unified School Dst* ***(P-18045)***
Westgate Cnstr & Maint Inc ....D....707 208-5763
5045 Fulton Dr Ste D Fairfield (94534) ***(P-989)***
Westgate Hardwoods Inc (PA) ....**E....530 892-0300**
9296 Midway Durham (95938) ***(P-3159)***
Westgate Rhab Spcalty Care Crt ....E....408 253-7502
1601 Petersen Ave San Jose (95129) ***(P-16158)***
Westin Monache ....E....760 934-0400
50 Hillside Dr Mammoth Lakes (93546) ***(P-11573)***
Westin Sacramento, Sacramento *Also called Eht Wsac LLC* ***(P-11074)***
Westin St. Francis, The, San Francisco *Also called Dtrs St Francis LLC* ***(P-11064)***
Westin Verasa NAPA, NAPA *Also called Intrawest NAPA Rvrbend Hsptlit* ***(P-11197)***
Westinghouse A Brake Tech Corp ....E....707 459-5563
452 E Hill Rd Willits (95490) ***(P-4406)***
Westlake Bakery Inc ....F....650 994-7741
7099 Mission St Daly City (94014) ***(P-2411)***
Westlake Christian Terrace, Oakland *Also called Christian Church Homes* ***(P-10425)***
Westlake Christian Terrace - E, Oakland *Also called Christian Church Homes* ***(P-10427)***
Westlake Development Group LLC (PA) ....**D....650 579-1010**
520 S El Camino Real # 900 San Mateo (94402) ***(P-10415)***
Westlake Development Group LLC ....E....650 579-1010
520 El Camino Real Fl 9 Belmont (94002) ***(P-19424)***
Westlake Development Group LLC ....C....707 447-7496
799 Yellowstone Dr Ofc Vacaville (95687) ***(P-16283)***
Westlake Realty Group Inc (PA) ....**D....650 579-1010**
520 S El Cmino Real 9th F San Mateo (94402) ***(P-10686)***
Westland Technologies Inc ....D....800 877-7734
107 S Riverside Dr Modesto (95354) ***(P-4210)***
Westland Trailer Mfg, Lodi *Also called Bjj Company LLC* ***(P-7513)***
Westmark, Atwater *Also called Certified Stainless Svc Inc* ***(P-4714)***
Westmed Ambulance ....D....510 401-5420
14275 Wicks Blvd San Leandro (94577) ***(P-7412)***
Westmont Living Inc ....D....916 786-3277
707 Sunrise Ave Roseville (95661) ***(P-18212)***
Westport Scandinavia, Watsonville *Also called Nordic Naturals Inc* ***(P-2458)***
Westpost Berkeley LLC ....E....510 548-7920
200 Marina Blvd Berkeley (94710) ***(P-11574)***
Westrup-Sadler Inc ....D....916 783-2077
400 Automall Dr Roseville (95661) ***(P-14496)***
Westside Building Materials, San Jose *Also called Central Concrete Supply Co Inc* ***(P-4475)***
Westside Cmnty Mental Hlth Ctr ....E....415 563-8200
1301 Pierce St San Francisco (94115) ***(P-17094)***
Westside Cmnty Mental Hlth Ctr ....E....415 355-0311
888 Turk St San Francisco (94102) ***(P-17095)***
Westside Community Crisis Ctr, San Francisco *Also called Westside Cmnty Mental Hlth Ctr* ***(P-17095)***
Westside Pallet Inc ....E....209 862-3941
2138 L St Newman (95360) ***(P-3233)***

Westside Research Inc ....F....530 330-0085
4293 County Road 99w Orland (95963) ***(P-3049)***
WESTWOOD FAMILY PRACTICE, Susanville *Also called Northeastern Rur Hlth Clinics* ***(P-15555)***
Wetherby Asset Management ....D....415 399-9159
580 California St Fl 8 San Francisco (94104) ***(P-10072)***
Wfc Holdings LLC (HQ) ....**C....415 396-7392**
420 Montgomery St San Francisco (94104) ***(P-9697)***
Wg Security Products Inc (PA) ....**E....408 241-8000**
591 W Hamilton Ave # 260 Campbell (95008) ***(P-6547)***
Wh Acquisitions Inc (HQ) ....**C....650 358-5000**
800 Concar Dr Ste 100 San Mateo (94402) ***(P-9105)***
Wh Pleasanton Hotel LP ....E....925 463-3330
5990 Stoneridge Mall Rd Pleasanton (94588) ***(P-11575)***
Wharf ....D....707 964-4283
32260 N Harbor Dr Fort Bragg (95437) ***(P-11576)***
Wharf Inn, The, San Francisco *Also called Wharf Motel Corp* ***(P-11577)***
Wharf Motel Corp ....D....415 673-7411
2601 Mason St San Francisco (94133) ***(P-11577)***
Wharf Restaurant & Anchr Lodge, Fort Bragg *Also called Wharf* ***(P-11576)***
Whatever Publishing Inc ....F....415 884-2100
14 Pamaron Way Ste 1 Novato (94949) ***(P-3550)***
Whatsapp LLC (HQ) ....**D....650 336-3079**
1601 Willow Rd Menlo Park (94025) ***(P-8088)***
Wheelabrator Lassen Inc (HQ) ....**D....530 365-9173**
20811 Industry Rd Anderson (96007) ***(P-8390)***
Wheeler and Company, Cupertino *Also called Max Sportsters Inc* ***(P-19368)***
Wheeler Auto Group Inc ....D....530 673-3765
350 Colusa Ave Yuba City (95991) ***(P-14605)***
Wheeler Chevrolet, Yuba City *Also called Wheeler Auto Group Inc* ***(P-14605)***
Wheeler Clyde Pipe Line, Oakdale *Also called Clyde Wheeler Pipeline Inc* ***(P-1093)***
Wheeler Winery Inc ....E....415 979-0630
9000 Windsor Rd Windsor (95492) ***(P-2762)***
Wheels, Livermore *Also called Livermore Amdor Vly Trnst Auth* ***(P-7339)***
Wheels and Deals, Redding *Also called Great Northern Wheels Deals* ***(P-3443)***
Whipple Industries Inc ....F....559 442-1261
3292 N Weber Ave Fresno (93722) ***(P-5193)***
Whipsaw Inc ....E....408 297-9771
434 S 1st St San Jose (95113) ***(P-18860)***
Whisperai Inc ....E....855 765-0088
260 8th St San Francisco (94103) ***(P-19425)***
Whisperkoll, Stockton *Also called Whisperkool Corporation* ***(P-2763)***
Whisperkool Corporation ....F....800 343-9463
1738 E Alpine Ave Stockton (95205) ***(P-2763)***
Whistlestop, San Rafael *Also called Vivalon* ***(P-17781)***
White Ash Broadcasting Inc ....D....559 862-2480
2589 Alluvial Ave Clovis (93611) ***(P-8037)***
White Gazelle Inc (PA) ....**E....916 718-0601**
1220 Melody Ln Ste 150 Roseville (95678) ***(P-10073)***
White House Sales, Sacramento *Also called Chem Quip Inc* ***(P-9154)***
White Mgic Clg Restoration Inc ....E....925 935-4449
1024 Shary Ct Concord (94518) ***(P-11662)***
White Oak Frozen Foods, Merced *Also called Jain Farm Fresh Foods Inc* ***(P-2260)***
White Oak Global Advisors LLC (PA) ....**E....415 644-4100**
3 Embarcadero Ctr Ste 550 San Francisco (94111) ***(P-19669)***
White Swan Inn, The, San Francisco *Also called Joie De Vivre Hospitality LLC* ***(P-11221)***
Whitehall Lane Winery, Saint Helena *Also called Thomas Leonardini* ***(P-2742)***
Whiterabbitai Inc ....D....408 215-8876
3930 Freedom Cir Ste 101 Santa Clara (95054) ***(P-12920)***
Whiteside Construction Corp ....E....510 234-6681
1151 Hensley St Richmond (94801) ***(P-1918)***
Whitethorn Construction Co ....E....707 986-7412
545 Shelter Cove Rd Whitethorn (95589) ***(P-10722)***
Whitevale Co Inc ....D....650 324-1882
180 Constitution Dr Ste 3 Menlo Park (94025) ***(P-10723)***
Whiting Fallon & Ross ....E....925 296-6000
101 Ygnacio Valley Rd # 250 Walnut Creek (94596) ***(P-17396)***
Whiting-Turner Contracting Co ....C....916 355-1355
800 R St Sacramento (95811) ***(P-990)***
Whitney Oaks Care Center ....D....916 488-8601
3529 Walnut Ave Carmichael (95608) ***(P-16159)***
Whits Painting Inc (PA) ....**E....925 429-2669**
150 Mason Cir Ste K Concord (94520) ***(P-1437)***
Whizz Systems Inc ....E....408 207-0400
3240 Scott Blvd Santa Clara (95054) ***(P-6000)***
Wholesale Art and Framing Inc ....F....916 851-0770
3068 Sunrise Blvd Ste E Rancho Cordova (95742) ***(P-3272)***
Wholesale Flooring Products, Fairfield *Also called Tom Duffy Co* ***(P-8521)***
Wholesale Olive Tree Nursery, Gridley *Also called Agromillora California* ***(P-9622)***
Wholesale Outlet Inc (PA) ....**E....916 338-2444**
4920 Raley Blvd Sacramento (95838) ***(P-8833)***
Wholesale Trailer Supply, Sacramento *Also called R V Karls Inc* ***(P-8461)***
Wi2wi Inc (PA) ....**E....408 416-4200**
1879 Lundy Ave Ste 218 San Jose (95131) ***(P-5884)***
Wic, Oakland *Also called La Clinica De La Raza Inc* ***(P-15497)***
Wic, San Jose *Also called Gardner Family Hlth Netwrk Inc* ***(P-15410)***
Wick Communications Co ....E....650 726-4424
714 Kelly St Half Moon Bay (94019) ***(P-3489)***
Wickland Pipelines LLC (PA) ....**E....916 978-2432**
8950 Cal Center Dr # 125 Sacramento (95826) ***(P-560)***
Wickman Development and Cnstr ....E....415 239-4500
5616 Mission St San Francisco (94112) ***(P-729)***
Wide Area Management Svcs Inc ....E....408 327-1260
3226 Scott Blvd Santa Clara (95054) ***(P-13527)***
Wideorbit LLC (PA) ....**D....415 675-6700**
1160 Battery St Ste 300 San Francisco (94111) ***(P-12921)***
Wiedeman, Geoffrey Jr MD, Sacramento *Also called Hand Surgery Associates* ***(P-15424)***
Wiegmann & Rose, Livermore *Also called Xchanger Manufacturing Corp* ***(P-4734)***
Wiggins Enterprises LLC (PA) ....**E....707 545-7869**
1370 Airport Blvd Santa Rosa (95403) ***(P-1637)***
Wikia, San Francisco *Also called Fandom Inc* ***(P-13790)***
Wikimedia Foundation Inc ....B....415 839-6885
1 Montgomery St Ste 1600 San Francisco (94104) ***(P-18608)***
Wilbur Packing Company Inc ....D....530 671-4911
1500 Eager Rd Live Oak (95953) ***(P-315)***
Wilbur-Ellis Company LLC ....D....559 442-1220
2903 S Cedar Ave Fresno (93725) ***(P-9616)***
Wilbur-Ellis Company LLC (HQ) ....**B....415 772-4000**
345 California St Fl 27 San Francisco (94104) ***(P-9617)***
Wilbur-Ellis Holdings II Inc (HQ) ....**D....415 772-4000**
345 California St Fl 27 San Francisco (94104) ***(P-9618)***
Wilcox AG Products, Walnut Grove *Also called Wilcox Brothers Inc* ***(P-5022)***
Wilcox Brothers Inc ....D....916 776-1784
14180 State Highway 160 Walnut Grove (95690) ***(P-5022)***
Wilcox Oaks Golf Club ....E....530 527-7087
20995 Wilcox Rd Red Bluff (96080) ***(P-15167)***
Wild Crter Tipton A Prof Corp ....E....559 224-2131
246 W Shaw Ave Fresno (93704) ***(P-17397)***
Wild Electric Incorporated ....D....559 251-7770
4626 E Olive Ave Fresno (93702) ***(P-1638)***
Wild Goose Storage Inc ....D....530 846-7350
2780 W Liberty Rd Gridley (95948) ***(P-8209)***
Wild Karma Inc ....B....510 639-9088
5275 Broadway Oakland (94618) ***(P-16160)***
Wild Palms Hotel & Bar, Sunnyvale *Also called Joie De Vivre Hospitality Inc* ***(P-11222)***
Wild Planet Entertainment Inc (HQ) ....**E....415 705-8300**
225 Bush St Fl 13 San Francisco (94104) ***(P-9171)***
Wild Planet Foods Inc (HQ) ....**D....707 840-9116**
1585 Heartwood Dr Ste F McKinleyville (95519) ***(P-9374)***
Wild Planet Toys, San Francisco *Also called Wild Planet Entertainment Inc* ***(P-9171)***
Wild Turkey Distillery, San Francisco *Also called Rare Breed Distilling LLC* ***(P-2776)***
Wild Type Inc ....F....408 669-5207
2325 3rd St Ste 209 San Francisco (94107) ***(P-2833)***
Wildbrine LLC (PA) ....**E....707 657-7607**
322 Bellevue Ave Santa Rosa (95407) ***(P-2249)***
Wildcare Trwllger Nture Edcatn ....D....415 453-1000
76 Albert Park Ln San Rafael (94901) ***(P-540)***
Wildcat Metals, San Jose *Also called Radonich Enterprises Inc* ***(P-1834)***
Wildenradt-Mcmurray Inc ....D....510 835-5500
568 7th St San Francisco (94103) ***(P-8991)***
Wildlife Control Tech Inc ....E....559 490-2262
2501 N Sunnyside Ave Fresno (93727) ***(P-11911)***
Wildlife Fur Dressing Inc ....F....209 538-2901
3415 Harold St Ceres (95307) ***(P-4338)***
Wildlife Health Center, Davis *Also called University California Davis* ***(P-15778)***
Wildlife International, Santa Clara *Also called Evans Analytical Group LLC* ***(P-19272)***
Wildlife Product, Fresno *Also called Wildlife Control Tech Inc* ***(P-11911)***
Wildtype, San Francisco *Also called Wild Type Inc* ***(P-2833)***
Wildwood Express ....E....559 805-3237
12416 Swanson Ave Kingsburg (93631) ***(P-7611)***
Wiley X Eyewear, Livermore *Also called Wiley X Inc* ***(P-7147)***
Wiley X Inc (PA) ....**C....925 243-9810**
7800 Patterson Pass Rd Livermore (94550) ***(P-7147)***
Wilkey Industries Inc ....E....209 656-0561
830 S Tegner Rd Turlock (95380) ***(P-1846)***
Wilkeys Construction Inc ....E....530 741-2233
4557 Skyway Dr Olivehurst (95961) ***(P-730)***
Wilkins Drlshgen Czshinski LLP ....E....559 438-2390
6785 N Willow Ave Fresno (93710) ***(P-17398)***
Will's Fresh Foods, San Leandro *Also called Woolery Enterprises Inc* ***(P-2960)***
Willamette Valley Trtmnt Ctr, Cupertino *Also called CRC Health Corporate* ***(P-17012)***
Willdan Engineering ....D....916 661-3520
9281 Office Park Cir # 10 Elk Grove (95758) ***(P-18861)***
Willdan Engineering ....D....916 924-7000
2240 Douglas Blvd Ste 270 Roseville (95661) ***(P-18862)***
Willey Printing Company (PA) ....**E....209 524-4811**
1405 10th St Modesto (95354) ***(P-3715)***
William D White Co Inc ....F....510 658-8167
3505 Magnolia St Oakland (94608) ***(P-1639)***
William Ho ....F....510 226-9089
40760 Encyclopedia Cir Fremont (94538) ***(P-6001)***
William Kreysler & Assoc Inc ....E....707 552-3500
501 Green Island Rd American Canyon (94503) ***(P-4332)***
William L Lyon & Assoc Inc (HQ) ....**E....916 978-4200**
3640 Amrcn Rver Dr Ste 10 Sacramento (95864) ***(P-19426)***
William L Lyon & Assoc Inc ....C....916 447-7878
2801 J St Sacramento (95816) ***(P-10687)***
William L Lyon & Assoc Inc ....C....916 535-0356
8814 Madison Ave Fair Oaks (95628) ***(P-10688)***
William R Ridgeway Family Rela, Sacramento *Also called County of Sacramento* ***(P-17916)***
William R Schmitt ....E....530 243-3069
18135 Clear Creek Rd Redding (96001) ***(P-3087)***
William Stucky & Assoc Inc ....E....415 788-2441
6059 Sycamore Ter Pleasanton (94566) ***(P-12922)***
Williams Adley & Company L L P (PA) ....**E....510 893-8114**
7677 Oakport St Ste 1000 Oakland (94621) ***(P-19004)***
Williams Scotsman Inc ....E....559 441-8181
2829 S Chestnut Ave Fresno (93725) ***(P-8650)***
Williams Scotsman - Fresno, Fresno *Also called Williams Scotsman Inc* ***(P-8650)***
Williams Tank Lines (PA) ....**D....209 944-5613**
1477 Tillie Lewis Dr Stockton (95206) ***(P-7612)***
Williams-Foster Group LLC ....E....317 786-3230
7475 N Palm Ave Ste 106 Fresno (93711) ***(P-16161)***
Willis Construction Co Inc ....C....831 623-2900
2261 San Juan Hwy San Juan Bautista (95045) ***(P-4455)***

ALPHABETIC

Employee Codes: A=Over 500 employees, B=251-500
C=101-250, D=51-100, E=20-50 F=10-19
2022 Northern California Business
Directory and Buyers Guide
© Mergent Inc. 1-800-342-5647
1119

Willis Hrh, San Francisco *Also called Hilb Rgal Hobbs Insur Svcs Inc* ***(P-10292)***
Willis Rebar Inc....E....707 419-5949
2333 Courage Dr Ste H9 Fairfield (94533) ***(P-8834)***
Willits Hospital Inc....B....707 459-6801
1 Marcela Dr Willits (95490) ***(P-16724)***
Willits Redwood Company Inc....E....707 459-4549
220 Franklin Ave Willits (95490) ***(P-3119)***
Willow, Mountain View *Also called Exploramed Nc7 Inc* ***(P-7105)***
Willow Cmty Day School, Tracy *Also called Tracy Unified School District* ***(P-18039)***
Willow Creek Alzheimer's, Castro Valley *Also called Altcare Willow Creek Inc* ***(P-18055)***
Willow Creek Center, Concord *Also called Mt Diablo Unified School Dst* ***(P-19581)***
Willow Creek Halthcare Ctr LLC....C....559 323-6200
650 W Alluvial Ave Clovis (93611) ***(P-16162)***
Willow Creek Treatment Center, Santa Rosa *Also called Victor Treatment Centers Inc* ***(P-18200)***
Willow Glen Villa A....D....408 266-1660
1660 Gaton Dr San Jose (95125) ***(P-10468)***
Willow Innovations Inc....C....650 472-0300
1975 W El Cmino Real Ste Mountain View (94040) ***(P-5181)***
Willow Pass Healthcare Center, Concord *Also called Kissito Health Case Inc* ***(P-16908)***
Willow Pass Hlth Care Ctr Inc....D....925 689-9222
3318 Willow Pass Rd Concord (94519) ***(P-16970)***
Willow Springs LLC....D....916 288-0300
8001 Bruceville Rd Sacramento (95823) ***(P-15816)***
Willow Springs LLC....C....916 489-3336
4250 Auburn Blvd Sacramento (95841) ***(P-16725)***
Willow Springs LLC....D....510 796-1100
39001 Sundale Dr Fremont (94538) ***(P-15817)***
Willow Sprng Alzhmers Spcial C....E....530 242-0654
191 Churn Creek Rd Redding (96003) ***(P-18213)***
Willow Tree Nursing Center, Oakland *Also called Covenant Care California LLC* ***(P-15967)***
Wilmar Oils Fats Stockton LLC....E....925 627-1600
2008 Port Road B Stockton (95203) ***(P-2456)***
Wilmor & Sons Plumbing & Cnstr....E....916 381-9114
8510 Thys Ct Sacramento (95828) ***(P-1401)***
Wilson Artisan Wineries, Healdsburg *Also called Stonecushion Inc* ***(P-2732)***
Wilson Elser Mskwitz Edlman DC....E....202 626-7660
525 Market St Fl 17 San Francisco (94105) ***(P-17399)***
Wilson Snsini Gdrich Rsati Pro (PA)....A....650 493-9300
650 Page Mill Rd Palo Alto (94304) ***(P-17400)***
Wilson Trophy Co California....F....916 927-9733
1724 Frienza Ave Sacramento (95815) ***(P-9186)***
Win Foods Corporation....D....510 487-8877
30560 San Antonio St Hayward (94544) ***(P-2959)***
Win River Hotel Corporation....B....530 226-5111
5050 Bechelli Ln Redding (96002) ***(P-11578)***
Win River Resort & Casino, Redding *Also called Redding Rancheria* ***(P-11389)***
Win Woo Trading LLC....E....510 259-1888
31056 Genstar Rd Hayward (94544) ***(P-9323)***
Win-Glo Window Coverings, San Jose *Also called Hunter Douglas Fabrications* ***(P-3331)***
Win-River Casino, Redding *Also called Redding Rnchria Ecnmic Dev Cor* ***(P-11391)***
Winbond Electronics Corp Amer....D....408 943-6666
2727 N 1st St San Jose (95134) ***(P-8973)***
Winchester Mystery House LLC....D....408 247-2101
525 S Winchester Blvd San Jose (95128) ***(P-15263)***
Winchster Interconnect Rf Corp....A....707 573-1900
5590 Skylane Blvd Santa Rosa (95403) ***(P-6483)***
Wind River Enterprises Inc....D....707 864-1040
250 Dittmer Rd Fairfield (94534) ***(P-8434)***
Wind River Systems Inc (HQ)....A....510 748-4100
500 Wind River Way Alameda (94501) ***(P-13528)***
Wind River Systems Intl Inc (HQ)....D....510 748-4100
500 Wind River Way Alameda (94501) ***(P-19670)***
Wind Youth Services Inc....E....916 532-5185
815 S St Fl 1 Sacramento (95811) ***(P-17785)***
Windmill Corporation....F....650 873-1000
314 Harbor Way South San Francisco (94080) ***(P-2412)***
Window Hardware Supply....F....510 463-0301
1717 Kirkham St Oakland (94607) ***(P-4333)***
Windows Hawaii, Rancho Cordova *Also called Northwest Exteriors Inc* ***(P-1747)***
Windsor Capital Holet Group, Sacramento *Also called Recp/Wndsor Scramento Ventr LP* ***(P-11386)***
Windsor Care Center Petaluma, Petaluma *Also called Windsor Care Ctr Petaluma LLC* ***(P-16163)***
Windsor Care Ctr Petaluma LLC....E....707 763-2457
523 Hayes Ln Petaluma (94952) ***(P-16163)***
Windsor Cnvlscent Rhblttion CT....C....925 689-2266
3806 Clayton Rd Concord (94521) ***(P-16164)***
Windsor Cnvlscent Rhblttion CT....D....510 793-7222
2400 Parkside Dr Fremont (94536) ***(P-16165)***
Windsor Foods, Hayward *Also called Ajinomoto Foods North Amer Inc* ***(P-2301)***
Windsor Gardens Healthcare C....C....510 582-4636
1628 B St Hayward (94541) ***(P-16284)***
Windsor Golf Club Inc....E....707 838-7888
1340 19th Hole Dr Windsor (95492) ***(P-15036)***
Windsor Mill, Willits *Also called Windsor Willits Company* ***(P-3161)***
Windsor Mnor Rhabilitation Ctr, Concord *Also called Windsor Cnvlscent Rhblttion CT* ***(P-16164)***
Windsor Oaks Vineyards LLP....E....707 433-4050
10810 Hillview Rd Windsor (95492) ***(P-2764)***
Windsor One, Petaluma *Also called Windsor Willits Company* ***(P-3160)***
Windsor Park Care Ctr Fremont, Fremont *Also called Windsor Cnvlscent Rhblttion CT* ***(P-16165)***
Windsor Post Acute Care Center, Hayward *Also called S&F Management Company LLC* ***(P-17173)***
Windsor Redding Care Ctr LLC....D....530 246-0600
2490 Court St Redding (96001) ***(P-16166)***
Windsor Sacramento Estates, Sacramento *Also called S&F Management Company LLC* ***(P-16103)***
Windsor Tea Room, The, San Francisco *Also called International Hotel Assoc LLC* ***(P-11195)***
Windsor Vallejo Care Center, Vallejo *Also called Helios Healthcare LLC* ***(P-16238)***
Windsor Willits Company (PA)....E....707 665-9663
737 Southpoint Blvd Ste H Petaluma (94954) ***(P-3160)***
Windsor Willits Company....D....707 459-8568
661 Railroad Ave Willits (95490) ***(P-3161)***
Windy Cy Wire Cble Tech Pdts L....C....510 284-3956
8024 Central Ave Newark (94560) ***(P-8879)***
Wine & Roses LLC....C....209 334-6988
2505 W Turner Rd Lodi (95242) ***(P-11579)***
Wine & Roses Hotel and Rest, Lodi *Also called Wine & Roses LLC* ***(P-11579)***
Wine Business Monthly, Sonoma *Also called Wine Communications Group* ***(P-3520)***
Wine Communications Group....F....707 939-0822
584 1st St E Sonoma (95476) ***(P-3520)***
Wine Country Care Center....E....209 334-3760
321 W Turner Rd Lodi (95240) ***(P-16167)***
Wine Country Cases Inc....D....707 967-4805
621 Airpark Rd NAPA (94558) ***(P-3244)***
Wine Country Pty & Events LLC (PA)....D....707 940-6060
22674 Broadway Ste A Sonoma (95476) ***(P-12066)***
Wine Foundry, NAPA *Also called Vignette Winery LLC* ***(P-2755)***
Wine Group Inc (HQ)....C....209 599-4111
17000 E State Highway 120 Ripon (95366) ***(P-2765)***
Wine Group, The, Ripon *Also called Franzia Winery LLC* ***(P-2585)***
Wine Mart Groups LLC....F....866 583-2312
766 Harrison St Unit 312 San Francisco (94107) ***(P-2766)***
Wine Warehouse, Richmond *Also called Ben Myerson Candy Co Inc* ***(P-9567)***
Winegard Energy Inc....E....559 441-0243
2885 S Chestnut Ave Fresno (93725) ***(P-1709)***
Winery Direct Distributors, Lodi *Also called Ah Wines Inc* ***(P-2503)***
Winery Exchange Inc (PA)....E....415 382-6900
500 Redwood Blvd Ste 200 Novato (94947) ***(P-9588)***
Winfield Design International....F....415 216-3169
3000 23rd St San Francisco (94110) ***(P-3409)***
Winfield International, San Francisco *Also called Winfield Design International* ***(P-3409)***
Wing Aviation LLC....C....650 224-1198
1600 Amphitheatre Pkwy Mountain View (94043) ***(P-7753)***
Wing Aviation LLC....D....650 260-8170
100 Mayfield Ave Mountain View (94043) ***(P-7754)***
Wing Inflatables Inc (HQ)....C....707 826-2887
1220 5th St Arcata (95521) ***(P-4334)***
Wing Master, Clovis *Also called Valley Chrome Plating Inc* ***(P-4923)***
Wing Nien Company, Hayward *Also called U S Enterprise Corporation* ***(P-2288)***
Wing Nien Foods, Hayward *Also called Win Foods Corporation* ***(P-2959)***
Winmax Systems Corporation....D....408 894-9000
1900 Mccarthy Blvd # 301 Milpitas (95035) ***(P-12923)***
Winnarainbow Inc (PA)....E....510 525-4304
1301 Henry St Berkeley (94709) ***(P-11616)***
Winner Chevrolet, Colfax *Also called Sierra Chevrolet Inc* ***(P-14623)***
Winnov Inc....E....888 315-9460
3945 Freedom Cir Ste 560 Santa Clara (95054) ***(P-5773)***
Winnresidential Ltd Partnr....C....559 435-3434
2350 W Shaw Ave Ste 148 Fresno (93711) ***(P-14475)***
Winnresidential Ltd Partnr....E....559 665-9600
255 Washington Rd Chowchilla (93610) ***(P-10469)***
Winslow Automation Inc....D....408 262-9004
905 Montague Expy Milpitas (95035) ***(P-6356)***
Winston & Strawn LLP....D....415 591-1000
101 California St # 3500 San Francisco (94111) ***(P-17401)***
Winstronics, Fremont *Also called Wintronics International Inc* ***(P-4573)***
Wintec Industries Inc (PA)....D....510 953-7440
8674 Thornton Ave Newark (94560) ***(P-6357)***
WINTER LODGE, Palo Alto *Also called Community Skating Inc* ***(P-15194)***
Winters Hlthcare Fundation Inc....E....530 795-4377
172 E Grant Ave Winters (95694) ***(P-17195)***
Winters Veterinary Clinic, Winters *Also called Ann Breznock* ***(P-19257)***
Winton Irland Strom Green Insu (PA)....D....209 667-0995
627 E Canal Dr Turlock (95380) ***(P-10369)***
Wintronics International Inc....E....510 226-7588
3817 Spinnaker Ct Fremont (94538) ***(P-4573)***
Winward International Inc (PA)....D....510 487-8686
42760 Albrae St Fremont (94538) ***(P-9642)***
Winward Silks, Fremont *Also called Winward International Inc* ***(P-9642)***
Winway Usa Inc....F....203 775-9311
1800 Wyatt Dr Ste 2 Santa Clara (95054) ***(P-6358)***
Wipeout Bar & Grill, San Francisco *Also called Simco Foods Inc* ***(P-9303)***
Wipro LLC....E....650 316-3555
425 National Ave Ste 200 Mountain View (94043) ***(P-13689)***
Wipro Technologies, Mountain View *Also called Wipro LLC* ***(P-13689)***
Wire Bonding Tools, Petaluma *Also called Small Precision Tools Inc* ***(P-6303)***
Wire US Inc....F....415 602-6260
650 Clfornia St Ste 6-129 San Francisco (94108) ***(P-13529)***
Wirex Systems....E....408 799-4498
100 S Murphy Ave Ste 200 Sunnyvale (94086) ***(P-13530)***
Wisdomtree Cnada Qlty Dvdend G....E....415 905-5448
50 Fremont St Ste 3900 San Francisco (94105) ***(P-10773)***
Wise Villa Winery LLC....F....916 543-0323
4226 Wise Rd Lincoln (95648) ***(P-2767)***
Wish, San Francisco *Also called Contextlogic Inc* ***(P-11812)***
Wisk Aero LLC (PA)....B....650 641-0920
2700 Broderick Way Mountain View (94043) ***(P-7366)***
Wit Group....E....530 243-4447
1822 Buenaventura Blvd # 101 Redding (96001) ***(P-2818)***

ALPHABETIC SECTION
Worldmark Club

Withrow Cattle....D.....916 780-0364
5301 Pleasant Grove Rd Pleasant Grove (95668) *(P-228)*
Withrow Dairy, Pleasant Grove *Also called Withrow Cattle (P-228)*
Withumsmith+brown PC....D.....415 434-3744
601 California St # 1800 San Francisco (94108) *(P-19005)*
Wittman Enterprises LLC....E.....916 381-6552
21 Blue Sky Ct Ste Ab Sacramento (95828) *(P-19006)*
Wixcom Inc....D.....415 329-4610
500 Terry A Francois Blvd # 600 San Francisco (94158) *(P-12924)*
Wizard Manufacturing Inc....E.....530 342-1861
2244 Ivy St Chico (95928) *(P-2452)*
Wizeline Inc (PA)....A.....888 386-9493
1 Market Plz Fl 36 San Francisco (94105) *(P-12925)*
Wjlp Company Inc....D.....800 628-1123
4848 Frontier Way Ste 100 Stockton (95215) *(P-6388)*
WKBk&y, Mather *Also called Wagner Krkmn Blne Klmp & Ymns (P-17388)*
Wkf (friedman Enterprises Inc (PA)....F.....925 673-9100
2334 Stagecoach Rd Ste B Stockton (95215) *(P-6624)*
WL Butler Inc....C.....650 361-1270
1629 Main St Redwood City (94063) *(P-991)*
WL Butler Inc....D.....650 361-1270
5666 La Ribera St Ste A Livermore (94550) *(P-731)*
WLMD....C.....209 723-9120
1715 Kibby Rd Merced (95341) *(P-2089)*
Wm, Grass Valley *Also called McCourtney Road Transfer Stn (P-8344)*
Wm B Saleh Co....D.....559 255-2046
1364 N Jackson Ave Fresno (93703) *(P-1438)*
WM LYLES CO, Fresno *Also called Lyles Services Co (P-19563)*
Wm Michael Stemler Inc (PA)....C.....209 948-8483
3244 Brookside Rd Ste 200 Stockton (95219) *(P-10370)*
Wm Michael Stemler Inc....D.....559 228-4144
7110 N Fresno St Ste 350 Fresno (93720) *(P-10371)*
Wm Oneill Lath and Plst Corp....E.....408 329-1413
1261 Birchwood Dr Sunnyvale (94089) *(P-1710)*
Wmh Corporation....E.....408 971-7300
55 S Market St Ste 1200 San Jose (95113) *(P-18863)*
Wo Hing LLC....F.....510 922-8778
78 4th St Oakland (94607) *(P-2107)*
Wohler Technologies Inc....E.....510 870-0810
1280 San Luis Obispo St Hayward (94544) *(P-5885)*
Wolfs Precision Works Inc....E.....650 364-1341
3549 Haven Ave Ste F Menlo Park (94025) *(P-5643)*
Wolfsen Incorporated....C.....209 827-7700
1269 W I St Los Banos (93635) *(P-14)*
Wolt Com Inc....C.....940 271-4703
2300 Tech Pkwy Ste 8 Hollister (95023) *(P-12152)*
Woltcom, Hollister *Also called Wolt Com Inc (P-12152)*
Woltcom Inc....D.....831 638-4900
2300 Tech Pkwy Ste 8 Hollister (95023) *(P-1640)*
Womack International Inc....F.....707 763-1800
3855 Cypress Dr Ste H Petaluma (94954) *(P-5235)*
Womankind, San Francisco *Also called Saint Francis Memorial Hosp (P-16495)*
Women Health Center....E.....707 537-1171
1442 Ethan Way Ste 200 Sacramento (95825) *(P-17096)*
Women's Heath Specialist, Sacramento *Also called Women Health Center (P-17096)*
Women's Imaging Center, Redding *Also called MD Imaging Inc A Prof Med Corp (P-15524)*
WOMEN'S REFUGE, Redding *Also called Shasta County Women S Refuge (P-17739)*
Womens Center-Youth Fmly Svcs (PA)....D.....209 941-2611
620 N San Joaquin St Stockton (95202) *(P-17786)*
Womens Community Clinic....D.....415 379-7800
1735 Mission St San Francisco (94103) *(P-17097)*
Womens Health Specialists....D.....510 248-1470
2299 Mowry Ave Ste 3c Fremont (94538) *(P-15818)*
Womens Rcvery Assn San Mteo CN....C.....650 348-6603
2015 Pioneer Ct San Mateo (94403) *(P-18352)*
Womens Recovery Association, San Mateo *Also called Womens Rcvery Assn San Mteo CN (P-18352)*
Womply, San Francisco *Also called Oto Analytics Inc (P-13645)*
Wonder Valley Resort, Sanger *Also called Western Camps Inc (P-11615)*
Wonder Workshop Inc (PA)....E.....408 785-7981
116c E 25th Ave San Mateo (94403) *(P-12926)*
Wonderful Union LLC....E.....916 526-0285
1909 H St Sacramento (95811) *(P-14883)*
Wondertreats Inc....B.....209 521-8881
2200 Lapham Dr Modesto (95354) *(P-9676)*
Wong Electric Inc....E.....650 813-9999
4067 Transport St Ste A Palo Alto (94303) *(P-1641)*
Wonolo Inc....D.....415 766-7692
535 Mission St Fl 14 San Francisco (94105) *(P-12153)*
Woocommerce, San Francisco *Also called Automattic Inc (P-7931)*
Wood AG Management Inc....E.....559 432-5164
652 W Cromwell Ave # 103 Fresno (93711) *(P-19427)*
Wood Connection Inc....E.....209 577-1044
4701 N Star Way Modesto (95356) *(P-3162)*
Wood Rodgers Inc (PA)....C.....916 341-7760
3301 C St Ste 100b Sacramento (95816) *(P-18864)*
Wood Tech Inc....D.....510 534-4930
4611 Malat St Oakland (94601) *(P-3286)*
Wood-N-Wood Products Cal Inc (PA)....E.....559 896-3636
2247 W Birch Ave Fresno (93711) *(P-3245)*
Wood-N-Wood Products Cal Inc....F.....559 896-3636
13598 S Golden State Blvd Selma (93662) *(P-3246)*
Woodbridge Medical Group, Lodi *Also called Community Medical Centers Inc (P-15362)*
Woodbridge Winery, Acampo *Also called Franciscan Vineyards Inc (P-2581)*
Woodcreek Golf Club, Roseville *Also called SRI Golf Inc (P-15030)*
Woodcrest Hotel, Santa Clara *Also called Yangs Brothers Intl Corp (P-11584)*
Wooden Valley Farms, Fairfield *Also called Lanza Vineyards Inc (P-63)*
Wooden Window Inc....E.....510 893-1157
849 29th St Oakland (94608) *(P-3163)*
Woodlake, The, Sacramento *Also called Lbn Leisure Care LLC (P-18135)*
Woodland Biomass Power Ltd....E.....530 661-6095
1786 E Kentucky Ave Woodland (95776) *(P-8208)*
Woodland Fire Department, Woodland *Also called City of Woodland (P-7275)*
Woodland Healthcare, Woodland *Also called Woodland Memorial Hospital (P-16730)*
Woodland Healthcare....C.....530 669-5680
261 California St Woodland (95695) *(P-16726)*
Woodland Healthcare....C.....530 756-2364
2660 W Covell Blvd Davis (95616) *(P-16727)*
Woodland Healthcare....C.....530 668-2600
1207 Fairchild Ct Woodland (95695) *(P-16728)*
Woodland Healthcare Home Hlth, Woodland *Also called Woodland Healthcare (P-16726)*
Woodland Lfyett Sklled Nursing, Lafayette *Also called Independent Quality Care Inc (P-16248)*
Woodland Lfytte Cnvlscent Hosp, San Ramon *Also called Independent Quality Care Inc (P-16244)*
Woodland Memorial Hospital (PA)....C.....530 669-5323
1325 Cottonwood St Woodland (95695) *(P-16729)*
Woodland Memorial Hospital....E.....530 669-5600
1321 Cottonwood St Woodland (95695) *(P-16730)*
Woodland Swim Team Bosters CLB....D.....530 662-9783
155 West St Woodland (95695) *(P-18481)*
Woodland Veterinary Hospital....E.....530 666-2461
445 Matmor Rd Woodland (95776) *(P-347)*
Woodline Cabinets, Fairfield *Also called Woodline Partners Inc (P-3195)*
Woodline Partners Inc....E.....707 864-5445
5165 Fulton Dr Fairfield (94534) *(P-3195)*
Woodmont Real Estate Svcs LP....E.....707 569-0582
3883 Airway Dr Santa Rosa (95403) *(P-19921)*
Woodmont Realty Advisors Inc....B.....650 592-3960
1050 Ralston Ave Belmont (94002) *(P-10219)*
Woodruff-Sawyer & Co (PA)....C.....415 391-2141
50 California St Fl 12 San Francisco (94111) *(P-10372)*
Woodside Investment Inc....D.....209 787-8040
12405 E Brandt Rd Lockeford (95237) *(P-4989)*
Woodspring Suites Sacramento....E.....916 688-1330
550 Hawkcrest Cir Sacramento (95835) *(P-11580)*
Woodward Drilling Company Inc....E.....707 374-4300
550 River Rd Rio Vista (94571) *(P-557)*
Woodys Poultry Supply....F.....209 634-2948
2900 E Monte Vista Ave Denair (95316) *(P-992)*
Woolery Enterprises Inc....E.....510 357-5700
1991 Republic Ave San Leandro (94577) *(P-2960)*
Woolf Enterprises, Huron *Also called California Valley Land Co Inc (P-250)*
Woolf Farming Co Cal Inc....A.....559 945-9292
7041 N Van Ness Blvd Fresno (93711) *(P-197)*
Work Health....D.....707 257-4084
3421 Villa Ln Ste 2a NAPA (94558) *(P-19671)*
Work Truck Solutions Inc....D.....855 987-4544
2485 Notre Dame Blvd # 3 Chico (95928) *(P-14010)*
Work2fture - Yuth Training Ctr, San Jose *Also called Work2future Foundation (P-17846)*
Work2future - Gilroy Job Ctr, Gilroy *Also called Work2future Foundation (P-17848)*
Work2future Foundation (PA)....B.....408 794-1100
38 N Almaden Blvd # 306 San Jose (95110) *(P-17845)*
Work2future Foundation....E.....408 794-1234
2072 Lucretia Ave San Jose (95122) *(P-17846)*
Work2future Foundation....E.....408 216-6202
1901 Zanker Rd San Jose (95112) *(P-17847)*
Work2future Foundation....E.....408 758-3477
379 Tomkins Ct Gilroy (95020) *(P-17848)*
Workboard Inc (PA)....C.....650 294-4480
487 Seaport Ct Ste 100 Redwood City (94063) *(P-13531)*
Workday Inc (PA)....A.....925 951-9000
6110 Stoneridge Mall Rd Pleasanton (94588) *(P-12927)*
Workers Cmpnstion Insur Rting (PA)....C.....888 229-2472
1221 Broadway Ste 900 Oakland (94612) *(P-10190)*
Workforce Dev Bd Solano Cnty, Fairfield *Also called Private Industry Cncl Slno Cty (P-12122)*
Working Assets Long Distance, San Francisco *Also called Credo Mobile Inc (P-7906)*
Workspot Inc (PA)....E.....888 426-8113
1901 S Bascom Ave Ste 900 Campbell (95008) *(P-13532)*
Workstream Technologies Inc....D.....415 767-1006
521 7th St San Francisco (94103) *(P-12928)*
World Centric....F.....707 241-9190
1400 Valley House Dr # 220 Rohnert Park (94928) *(P-3410)*
World Class Distribution Inc....D.....909 574-4140
2121 Boeing Way Stockton (95206) *(P-7706)*
World Financial Group (PA)....E.....408 941-1838
2099 Gold St Alviso (95002) *(P-19672)*
World Gym Fitness Centers, San Francisco *Also called Talmadge & Talmadge Inc (P-14979)*
World Journal Inc (PA)....D.....650 692-9936
231 Adrian Rd Millbrae (94030) *(P-3490)*
World of Change Inc....E.....352 495-3300
2941 Shadow Brook Ln Redding (96001) *(P-14463)*
World Projects Corporation....E.....707 556-5885
110 E D St Ste K Benicia (94510) *(P-7811)*
World Rlief Corp of Nat Assn E....D.....916 978-2650
4616 Roseville Rd Ste 107 North Highlands (95660) *(P-17787)*
World Textile and Bag Inc....E.....916 922-9222
4680 Pell Dr Ste B Sacramento (95838) *(P-3035)*
World Trade Network Inc (PA)....E.....713 358-5603
4635 Georgetown Pl Stockton (95207) *(P-8009)*
Worldmark Club....D.....707 274-0118
3927 E State Hwy 20 Nice (95464) *(P-11581)*
Worldmark Club....D.....559 642-6780
53134 Road 432 Bass Lake (93604) *(P-11582)*

ALPHABETIC

Worldmark Club At Bass Lake, Bass Lake *Also called Worldmark Club* ***(P-11582)***
Worldwide Corporate Housing LP ....C....916 631-3777
10183 Croydon Way Ste E Sacramento (95827) ***(P-11595)***
Worldwide Energy and Mfg USA (PA) ....A....**650 692-7788**
1675 Rollins Rd Ste F Burlingame (94010) ***(P-6359)***
Wpcs Intrntional-Suisun Cy Inc ....D....916 624-1300
2208 Srra Madows Dr Ste B Rocklin (95677) ***(P-1642)***
WR Forde Associates Inc ....D....510 215-9338
984 Hensley St Richmond (94801) ***(P-1080)***
Wrangler Topco LLC (HQ) ....D....**415 439-1400**
555 California St # 2900 San Francisco (94104) ***(P-8762)***
Wrc Huntington, San Francisco *Also called Hmb Investors LLC* ***(P-11146)***
Wrex Products Inc Chico ....D....530 895-3838
25 Wrex Ct Chico (95928) ***(P-4335)***
Wright Contracting Inc ....E....707 528-1172
3020 Dutton Ave Santa Rosa (95407) ***(P-777)***
Wright Contracting EPA, Santa Rosa *Also called Wright Contracting LLC* ***(P-993)***
Wright Contracting LLC ....D....707 528-1172
3020 Dutton Ave Santa Rosa (95407) ***(P-993)***
Wright Engineered Plastics Inc ....E....707 575-1218
3681 N Laughlin Rd Santa Rosa (95403) ***(P-5088)***
Wright Institute ....E....510 841-9230
2728 Durant Ave Berkeley (94704) ***(P-15902)***
Wright Pharma Inc ....E....209 549-9771
700 Kiernan Ave Ste A Modesto (95356) ***(P-4008)***
Wrightspeed Inc ....D....866 960-9482
650 W Tower Ave Alameda (94501) ***(P-6597)***
Wrns Studio (PA) ....E....**415 489-2224**
501 2nd St Ste 402 San Francisco (94107) ***(P-18919)***
Wsglass Holdings Inc (HQ) ....C....**510 623-5000**
3241 Darby Cmn Fremont (94539) ***(P-4365)***
Wso2 Inc (PA) ....E....**650 745-4499**
3080 Olcott St Ste C220 Santa Clara (95054) ***(P-12929)***
Wt.net, Stockton *Also called World Trade Network Inc* ***(P-8009)***
Wu Yee Childrens Services (PA) ....E....**415 230-7504**
827 Broadway San Francisco (94133) ***(P-18047)***
Wunder-Mold Inc ....E....707 448-2349
790 Eubanks Dr Vacaville (95688) ***(P-4336)***
Wurl Inc (PA) ....C....**662 649-8825**
591 Lytton Ave Palo Alto (94301) ***(P-19428)***
Wx Brands, Novato *Also called Winery Exchange Inc* ***(P-9588)***
Wycen Foods Inc (PA) ....F....**510 351-1987**
560 Estabrook St San Leandro (94577) ***(P-2128)***
Wylatti Resource MGT Inc ....E....707 983-8135
23601 Cemetery Ln Covelo (95428) ***(P-3088)***
Wymac Capital Inc (PA) ....E....**925 937-4300**
2700 Ygnacio Valley Rd # 260 Walnut Creek (94598) ***(P-9953)***
Wyman-Empires Fabric, Rancho Cordova *Also called Koehler Lefforge Inc* ***(P-8514)***
Wyndgate Technologies ....E....916 404-8400
4925 Robert J Mathews Pkw El Dorado Hills (95762) ***(P-14011)***
Wyndham Cntrbury At San Frncsc, San Francisco *Also called Canterbury Hotel Corp* ***(P-10987)***
Wyndham Garden Fresno Airport, Fresno *Also called Fresno Airport Hotels LLC* ***(P-11107)***
Wyndham Garden Silicon Valley, San Jose *Also called Sterling International Group* ***(P-10717)***
Wyre Inc ....E....415 374-7356
660 4th St Pmb 462 San Francisco (94107) ***(P-14464)***
X Therm ....F....510 441-7566
3325 Investment Blvd Hayward (94545) ***(P-6709)***
X-37 LLC ....F....650 273-5748
400 Oyster Point Blvd # 20 South San Francisco (94080) ***(P-4009)***
X-Ray Technology Group, Scotts Valley *Also called Oxford Instrs X-Ray Tech Inc* ***(P-6466)***
X-Scan Imaging Corporation ....E....408 432-9888
107 Bonaventura Dr San Jose (95134) ***(P-19292)***
X2nsat ....E....707 664-5700
1310 Redwood Way Ste C Petaluma (94954) ***(P-14012)***
X7/24 Corporation ....E....650 401-2300
433 Airport Blvd Ste 219 Burlingame (94010) ***(P-994)***
Xactly Corporation (HQ) ....B....**408 977-3132**
505 S Market St San Jose (95113) ***(P-12930)***
Xander Mortgage & Real Estate ....D....855 905-2575
2520 W Shaw Ln Ste 106 Fresno (93711) ***(P-10689)***
Xandex Inc ....E....707 763-7799
1360 Redwood Way Ste A Petaluma (94954) ***(P-6801)***
Xantrion Incorporated ....E....510 272-4701
651 Thomas L Berkley Way Oakland (94612) ***(P-14013)***
Xcelmobility Inc ....D....650 320-1728
2225 E Byshore Rd Ste 200 Palo Alto (94303) ***(P-13533)***
Xcerra Corporation ....C....408 635-4300
880 N Mccarthy Blvd # 100 Milpitas (95035) ***(P-8974)***
Xchanger Manufacturing Corp ....E....510 632-8828
263 S Vasco Rd Livermore (94551) ***(P-4734)***
Xcommerce Inc (HQ) ....A....**310 954-8012**
345 Park Ave San Jose (95110) ***(P-14014)***
Xerox International Partners (HQ) ....D....**408 953-2700**
2100 Geng Rd Ste 210 Palo Alto (94303) ***(P-5124)***
Xia LLC ....E....510 401-5760
2744 E 11th St Ste H2 Oakland (94601) ***(P-6864)***
Xiaomi USA Inc ....E....833 942-6648
97 E Brokaw Rd Ste 310 San Jose (95112) ***(P-5774)***
Xicato Inc (PA) ....E....**866 223-8395**
102 Cooper Ct Los Gatos (95032) ***(P-5730)***
Xilinx Inc (PA) ....A....**408 559-7778**
2100 All Programable San Jose (95124) ***(P-6002)***
Xilinx Development Corporation (HQ) ....D....**408 559-7778**
2100 All Programable San Jose (95124) ***(P-6360)***
Ximad Inc ....E....415 222-9909
21 Airport Blvd Ste B South San Francisco (94080) ***(P-13534)***
Ximed Medical Systems, San Jose *Also called Prosurg Inc* ***(P-7024)***
Xinet LLC (HQ) ....D....**510 845-0555**
2560 9th St Ste 312 Berkeley (94710) ***(P-13535)***
Xinlab, Milpitas *Also called Vuclip Inc* ***(P-8007)***
Xintec Corporation (PA) ....E....**510 832-2130**
1660 S Loop Rd Alameda (94502) ***(P-7135)***
Xiphos Corporation ....E....719 963-3948
2951 Sunrise Blvd Ste 150 Rancho Cordova (95742) ***(P-1643)***
Xl Construction Corporation ....D....916 282-2900
1810 13th St Ste 110 Sacramento (95811) ***(P-732)***
Xl Construction Corporation (PA) ....B....**408 240-6000**
851 Buckeye Ct Milpitas (95035) ***(P-995)***
Xl Specialty Insurance Company ....B....925 942-6142
1340 Treat Blvd Walnut Creek (94597) ***(P-10194)***
Xmotorsai Inc ....F....650 213-1359
850 N Shoreline Blvd Mountain View (94043) ***(P-6598)***
Xobee Networks Inc ....D....559 579-1300
7910 N Ingram Ave Ste 101 Fresno (93711) ***(P-8010)***
Xodus Manufacturing Inc ....F....510 413-7925
45999 Warm Springs Blvd Fremont (94539) ***(P-7317)***
Xoft Inc ....E....408 493-1500
101 Nicholson Ln San Jose (95134) ***(P-7063)***
Xojet Sales LLC ....E....877 599-6538
2000 Sierra Point Pkwy # 200 Brisbane (94005) ***(P-10897)***
Xolvio LLC ....F....415 857-1317
18 Bartol St San Francisco (94133) ***(P-13536)***
Xoom Corporation ....C....415 777-4800
425 Market St Ste 1200 San Francisco (94105) ***(P-9850)***
Xoriant Corporation (PA) ....C....**408 743-4400**
1248 Reamwood Ave Sunnyvale (94089) ***(P-14015)***
Xp Power LLC ....D....209 267-1630
11383 Prospect Dr Jackson (95642) ***(P-8975)***
Xp Power LLC (HQ) ....D....**408 732-7777**
990 Benecia Ave Sunnyvale (94085) ***(P-8976)***
Xpansiv Data Systems Inc ....E....415 915-5124
3041 Fulton St Berkeley (94705) ***(P-13537)***
Xperi Corporation (HQ) ....C....**408 321-6000**
3025 Orchard Pkwy San Jose (95134) ***(P-6361)***
Xpo Enterprise Services Inc ....C....916 399-8291
3810 Hill Rd Lakeport (95453) ***(P-7613)***
Xpo Logistics Freight Inc ....D....209 983-8285
5475 S Airport Way Stockton (95206) ***(P-7614)***
Xpo Logistics Freight Inc ....E....408 435-3876
2171 Otoole Ave San Jose (95131) ***(P-7861)***
Xpo Logistics Freight Inc ....E....559 485-1164
4195 E Central Ave Fresno (93725) ***(P-7862)***
Xpo Logistics Freight Inc ....D....916 399-8291
3516 Kiessig Ave Sacramento (95823) ***(P-7615)***
Xpo Logistics Freight Inc ....D....707 584-0211
4095 S Moorland Ave Santa Rosa (95407) ***(P-7616)***
Xpo Logistics Freight Inc ....E....530 243-6175
2201 Branstetter Ln Redding (96001) ***(P-7863)***
Xpo Logistics Freight Inc ....D....510 785-6920
2200 Claremont Ct Hayward (94545) ***(P-7617)***
Xtandi, San Francisco *Also called Medivation Inc* ***(P-3947)***
Xtime Inc ....E....650 508-4300
1400 Bridge Pkwy Ste 200 Redwood City (94065) ***(P-4337)***
Xtraplus Corporation ....E....510 897-1890
39889 Eureka Dr Newark (94560) ***(P-8763)***
Xulu Inc ....E....800 975-7199
505 Howard St Fl 4 San Francisco (94105) ***(P-10074)***
Xyratex, Fremont *Also called Seagate Systems (us) Inc* ***(P-5318)***
Xythos Software Inc ....D....415 248-3800
655 Montgomery St Fl 16 San Francisco (94111) ***(P-12931)***
XYZ Graphics Inc (PA) ....E....**415 227-9972**
190 Lombard St San Francisco (94111) ***(P-3756)***
Y & Y Property Management Inc ....E....559 226-2110
3110 N Blackstone Ave Fresno (93703) ***(P-11583)***
Y Combinator Management LLC ....E....775 287-3519
335 Pioneer Way Mountain View (94041) ***(P-10898)***
Y M C A, Berkeley *Also called Young MNS Chrstn Assn of E Bay* ***(P-18499)***
Y M C A Metro Clinic, Berkeley *Also called Young MNS Chrstn Assn of E Bay* ***(P-18493)***
Yaana Technologies LLC ....E....650 996-2927
542 Gibraltar Dr Milpitas (95035) ***(P-14016)***
Yadav Technology Inc ....F....510 438-0148
48371 Fremont Blvd # 101 Fremont (94538) ***(P-6362)***
Yageo America Corporation ....E....408 240-6200
2550 N 1st St Ste 480 San Jose (95131) ***(P-6374)***
Yagi Brothers Produce LLC, Livingston *Also called Ybp Holdings LLC* ***(P-2961)***
Yahoo Cv LLC (HQ) ....B....**408 349-3300**
701 First Ave Sunnyvale (94089) ***(P-13772)***
Yaley Enterprises Inc ....F....530 365-5252
7664 Avianca Dr Redding (96002) ***(P-9204)***
Yamaichi Electronics USA Inc (HQ) ....E....**408 435-9800**
475 Holger Way San Jose (95134) ***(P-8977)***
Yammer Inc ....C....415 796-7400
410 Townsend St San Francisco (94107) ***(P-14017)***
Yanaco Inc ....C....530 246-9550
151 N Boulder Dr Redding (96003) ***(P-15047)***
Yancey Roofing, Sacramento *Also called Gudgel Roofing Inc* ***(P-1809)***
Yanfeng US Auto Intr Systems I ....E....616 886-3622
30559 San Antonio St Hayward (94544) ***(P-6599)***
Yangs Brothers Intl Corp ....C....408 446-9636
5415 Stevens Creek Blvd Santa Clara (95051) ***(P-11584)***
Yanka Industries Inc ....D....855 981-8208
660 4th St Ste 443 San Francisco (94107) ***(P-14884)***
Yapstone Inc (PA) ....C....**866 289-5977**
2121 N Calif Blvd Ste 400 Walnut Creek (94596) ***(P-14465)***
Yara North America Inc ....E....916 375-1109
3961 Channel Dr West Sacramento (95691) ***(P-4148)***

Yard & Garden Ldscp Maint Inc E 209 369-9071
802 N Cluff Ave Lodi (95240) ***(P-444)***
Yard House Restaurants LLC C 925 602-0523
2005 Diamond Blvd Concord (94520) ***(P-15264)***
Yates Gear Inc D 530 222-4606
2608 Hartnell Ave Ste 6 Redding (96002) ***(P-4354)***
Yb Media LLC E 310 467-5804
1534 Plaza Ln 146 Burlingame (94010) ***(P-3612)***
Ybp Holdings LLC E 209 394-7311
5614 Lincoln Blvd Livingston (95334) ***(P-2961)***
YC Cable Usa Inc (HQ) **D 510 824-2788**
44061 Nobel Dr Fremont (94538) ***(P-14466)***
Ycusd, Yuba City *Also called Yuba City Unified School* ***(P-18259)***
Ydesign Group LLC (HQ) **E 866 842-6209**
2020 L St Ste Ll10 Sacramento (95811) ***(P-8880)***
Yefllow Shttle Vtrans Sdan Svc, San Leandro *Also called A-Para Transit Corp* ***(P-7320)***
Yellich Steel & Klein D 831 475-0221
1663 Dominican Way # 112 Santa Cruz (95065) ***(P-15863)***
Yellow Cab Company, San Jose *Also called Yellow Checker Cab Company Inc* ***(P-7415)***
Yellow Checker Cab Company Inc E 408 286-3400
646 N King Rd Ste A San Jose (95133) ***(P-7415)***
Yellowbrick Data Inc (PA) **B 877 492-3282**
250 Cambridge Ave Ste 301 Palo Alto (94306) ***(P-13773)***
Yelp Inc (PA) **D 415 908-3801**
140 New Montgomery St # 900 San Francisco (94105) ***(P-13812)***
Yerba Buena Children's Center, San Jose *Also called Eastside Union High School Dst* ***(P-17928)***
Yerba Buena Engrg & Cnstr Inc (PA) **E 415 822-4400**
1340 Egbert Ave San Francisco (94124) ***(P-18865)***
Yertleworks LLC E 408 916-4121
5470 Great America Pkwy Santa Clara (95054) ***(P-13538)***
Yes Videocom Inc (PA) **C 408 907-7600**
2805 Bowers Ave Ste 230 Santa Clara (95051) ***(P-14799)***
Yesco, Sacramento *Also called Young Electric Sign Company* ***(P-7262)***
Yesco, Fremont *Also called Young Electric Sign Company* ***(P-7263)***
Yhb San Francisco LLC C 415 421-7500
85 5th St San Francisco (94103) ***(P-11585)***
Yield Engineering Systems Inc D 510 954-6889
3178 Laurelview Ct Fremont (94538) ***(P-6363)***
Yiheng Capital LLC (PA) **D 415 875-5600**
1 Montgomery St Ste 3450 San Francisco (94104) ***(P-10899)***
Yliving, Sacramento *Also called Ydesign Group LLC* ***(P-8880)***
YMCA, South San Francisco *Also called Young MNS Chrstn Assn San Frnc* ***(P-17790)***
YMCA, San Francisco *Also called Young MNS Chrstn Assn San Frnc* ***(P-18519)***
YMCA, Berkeley *Also called Young MNS Chrstn Assn of E Bay* ***(P-18509)***
YMCA, Berkeley *Also called Young MNS Chrstn Assn of E Bay* ***(P-18511)***
YMCA After School-Olinda, Richmond *Also called Young MNS Chrstn Assn of E Bay* ***(P-18510)***
YMCA Child Care Chadbourne, Fremont *Also called Young MNS Chrstn Assn of E Bay* ***(P-18500)***
YMCA Elementary School, Mountain View *Also called Young MNS Chrstn Assn of E Bay* ***(P-18498)***
YMCA Head Start, Berkeley *Also called Young MNS Chrstn Assn of E Bay* ***(P-18494)***
YMCA NAPA Slano N Bay Gymnstic, Vallejo *Also called Young MNS Chrstn Assn San Frnc* ***(P-18522)***
YMCA of East Bay, Oakland *Also called Young MNS Chrstn Assn of E Bay* ***(P-18491)***
YMCA of Mid-Peninsula B 650 493-9622
1922 The Alameda Ste 300 San Jose (95126) ***(P-18482)***
YMCA of Redwoods, Boulder Creek *Also called Young MNS Chrstn Assn Slcon Vl* ***(P-18533)***
YMCA OF SAN FRANCISCO, San Francisco *Also called Young MNS Chrstn Assn San Frnc* ***(P-18516)***
YMCA of San Joaquin County E 209 472-9622
2105 W March Ln Ste 1 Stockton (95207) ***(P-18483)***
YMCA of Santa Clara Valley, San Jose *Also called Young MNS Chrstn Assn Slcon Vl* ***(P-18531)***
YMCA of Santa Clara Valley, San Jose *Also called Young MNS Chrstn Assn Slcon Vl* ***(P-18532)***
YMCA Pre School Hillview, Richmond *Also called Young MNS Chrstn Assn of E Bay* ***(P-18496)***
YMCA Pt Bnita Otdoor Cnfrnce C, Sausalito *Also called Young MNS Chrstn Assn San Frnc* ***(P-18521)***
YMCA San Benito County, Hollister *Also called Central Coast YMCA* ***(P-18405)***
YMCA Sch Age Pgrm Durham, Fremont *Also called Young MNS Chrstn Assn of E Bay* ***(P-18507)***
Ymcasf, San Rafael *Also called Young MNS Chrstn Assn San Frnc* ***(P-18523)***
Yodlee Inc (HQ) **C 650 980-3600**
999 Baker Way Ste 100 San Mateo (94404) ***(P-19673)***
Yoga Source Partners LLC D 408 402-9642
16185 Los Gatos Blvd Los Gatos (95032) ***(P-15265)***
Yogasource, Los Gatos *Also called Yoga Source Partners LLC* ***(P-15265)***
Yolo Co Office of Education (PA) **E 530 668-6700**
1280 Santa Anita Ct # 10 Woodland (95776) ***(P-18048)***
Yolo County Childrens Alliance E 530 757-5558
600 A St Ste Y Davis (95616) ***(P-10801)***
Yolo County Sherrfs Anml, Woodland *Also called City of Woodland* ***(P-352)***
YOLO COUNTY SUPERINTENDENT OF, Woodland *Also called Yolo Co Office of Education* ***(P-18048)***
Yolo Employment Services E 530 662-8616
660 6th St Woodland (95695) ***(P-17849)***
Yolo Federal Credit Union (PA) **E 530 668-2700**
266 W Main St Woodland (95695) ***(P-9828)***
Yolo Hospice Inc (PA) **D 530 758-5566**
1909 Galileo Ct Ste A Davis (95618) ***(P-16971)***

Yolo Ice & Creamery Inc F 530 662-7337
1462 Churchill Downs Ave Woodland (95776) ***(P-9343)***
Yorba Bena Ice Skting Bowl Ctr, San Francisco *Also called VSC Sports Inc* ***(P-19888)***
York Hotel Group LLC E 415 885-6800
940 Sutter St San Francisco (94109) ***(P-11586)***
York Insur Srvcs Group - CA E 916 783-0100
1101 Creekside Ridge Dr Roseville (95678) ***(P-10373)***
York Label, El Dorado Hills *Also called Cameo Crafts* ***(P-3724)***
Yosemite Church E 209 383-5038
2230 E Yosemite Ave Merced (95340) ***(P-17788)***
Yosemite Concession Services, Yosemite Ntpk *Also called DNC Prks Rsrts At Yosemite Inc* ***(P-11055)***
YOSEMITE CONSERVANCY, San Francisco *Also called Yosemite Foundation* ***(P-18484)***
Yosemite Farm Credit Aca (PA) **D 209 667-2366**
806 W Monte Vista Ave Turlock (95382) ***(P-9853)***
Yosemite Farms E 209 383-3411
2341 N St Merced (95340) ***(P-2453)***
Yosemite Foods Inc C 209 990-5400
4221 E Mariposa Rd Stockton (95215) ***(P-9383)***
Yosemite Foundation (PA) **D 415 434-1782**
101 Montgomery St # 1700 San Francisco (94104) ***(P-18484)***
Yosemite Lakes Owners Assn D 559 658-7466
30250 Yosemite Springs Pk Coarsegold (93614) ***(P-18485)***
Yosemite Lanes, Modesto *Also called Ragers Recreational Entps* ***(P-14898)***
Yosemite Linen Supply Inc E 559 233-2654
3330 E Church Ave Fresno (93725) ***(P-11647)***
Yosemite Meat Company Inc D 209 524-5117
601 Zeff Rd Modesto (95351) ***(P-9384)***
Yosemite Pthlogy Med Group Inc (PA) **E 209 577-1200**
4301 N Star Way Modesto (95356) ***(P-16822)***
Yosemite Vly Beef Pkg Co Inc E 626 435-0170
970 E Sandy Mush Rd Merced (95341) ***(P-2108)***
Yosemite Welding & Mfg Inc F 209 874-6140
647 Galaxy Way Modesto (95356) ***(P-14726)***
Yosh Enterprises Inc (PA) **C 408 287-4411**
675 E Gish Rd San Jose (95112) ***(P-14112)***
Yosh For Hair (PA) **E 415 989-7704**
173 Maiden Ln San Francisco (94108) ***(P-11697)***
Yosh For Hair Gina Khan, San Francisco *Also called Yosh For Hair* ***(P-11697)***
Youappi Inc D 646 854-3390
2 Embarcadero Ctr # 2310 San Francisco (94111) ***(P-19674)***
Youmask Inc E 818 282-2496
730 Serra St Apt 408 Stanford (94305) ***(P-12932)***
Young & Burton Inc E 925 820-4953
1947 San Ramon Valley Blv San Ramon (94583) ***(P-733)***
Young & Family Inc E 707 263-8877
64 Soda Bay Rd Lakeport (95453) ***(P-3164)***
Young & Rubicam LLC C 650 287-4000
100 Pine St Ste 2300 San Francisco (94111) ***(P-19699)***
Young & Rubicam LLC C 415 365-1700
1001 Front St San Francisco (94111) ***(P-11875)***
Young Brdcstg of San Francisco D 415 441-4444
900 Front St San Francisco (94111) ***(P-8057)***
Young Communications, San Francisco *Also called Young Electric Co* ***(P-1644)***
Young Community Developers E 415 822-3491
1715 Yosemite Ave San Francisco (94124) ***(P-17789)***
Young Electric Co C 415 648-3355
195 Erie St San Francisco (94103) ***(P-1644)***
Young Electric Sign Company E 916 419-8101
875 National Dr Ste 107 Sacramento (95834) ***(P-7262)***
Young Electric Sign Company E 510 877-7815
46750 Fremont Blvd # 101 Fremont (94538) ***(P-7263)***
Young Mens Christian Assoc SF D 415 883-9622
3 Hamilton Landing # 140 Novato (94949) ***(P-18486)***
Young Mens Christn Assocation, San Jose *Also called Young MNS Chrstn Assn Slcon Vl* ***(P-18527)***
Young Minney & Corr LLP E 916 646-1400
655 University Ave # 150 Sacramento (95825) ***(P-17402)***
Young MNS Chrstn Assn of E Bay B 510 654-9622
3265 Market St Oakland (94608) ***(P-18487)***
Young MNS Chrstn Assn of E Bay B 510 412-5644
200 Lake Ave Rodeo (94572) ***(P-18488)***
Young MNS Chrstn Assn of E Bay B 510 412-5640
1250 23rd St Richmond (94804) ***(P-18489)***
Young MNS Chrstn Assn of E Bay B 925 609-7971
1705 Thornwood Dr Concord (94521) ***(P-18490)***
Young MNS Chrstn Assn of E Bay A 510 451-8039
2350 Broadway Oakland (94612) ***(P-18491)***
Young MNS Chrstn Assn of E Bay B 510 601-8674
4727 San Pablo Ave Emeryville (94608) ***(P-18492)***
Young MNS Chrstn Assn of E Bay B 510 486-8400
2111 Mrtin Lther King Jr Berkeley (94704) ***(P-18493)***
Young MNS Chrstn Assn of E Bay B 510 848-9092
2009 10th St Berkeley (94710) ***(P-18494)***
Young MNS Chrstn Assn of E Bay B 510 848-9622
2001 Allston Way Berkeley (94704) ***(P-18495)***
Young MNS Chrstn Assn of E Bay B 510 223-7070
3800 Clark Rd Richmond (94803) ***(P-18496)***
Young MNS Chrstn Assn of E Bay B 510 526-2146
1130 Oxford St Berkeley (94707) ***(P-18497)***
Young MNS Chrstn Assn of E Bay B 650 526-3500
505 Escuela Ave Mountain View (94040) ***(P-18498)***
Young MNS Chrstn Assn of E Bay B 510 644-6290
2241 Russell St Berkeley (94705) ***(P-18499)***
Young MNS Chrstn Assn of E Bay B 510 656-7243
801 Plymouth Ave Fremont (94539) ***(P-18500)***
Young MNS Chrstn Assn of E Bay B 510 222-9622
4300 Lakeside Dr Ste 150 Richmond (94806) ***(P-18501)***

A L P H A B E T I C

Young MNS Chrstn Assn of E Bay B 510 412-5647
263 S 20th St Richmond (94804) ***(P-18502)***

Young MNS Chrstn Assn of E Bay B 510 222-9622
4300 Lakeside Dr Richmond (94806) ***(P-18503)***

Young MNS Chrstn Assn of E Bay B 925 475-6100
5000 Pleasanton Ave # 200 Pleasanton (94566) ***(P-18504)***

Young MNS Chrstn Assn of E Bay B 510 534-7441
1612 45th Ave Oakland (94601) ***(P-18505)***

Young MNS Chrstn Assn of E Bay B 510 683-9165
41811 Blacow Rd Fremont (94538) ***(P-18506)***

Young MNS Chrstn Assn of E Bay B 510 683-9107
40292 Leslie St 402 Fremont (94538) ***(P-18507)***

Young MNS Chrstn Assn of E Bay B 510 683-9147
47100 Fernald St 471 Fremont (94539) ***(P-18508)***

Young MNS Chrstn Assn of E Bay B 510 848-6800
2001 Allston Way Berkeley (94704) ***(P-18509)***

Young MNS Chrstn Assn of E Bay B 510 262-6588
5855 Olinda Rd Richmond (94803) ***(P-18510)***

Young MNS Chrstn Assn of E Bay B 510 559-2090
1422 San Pablo Ave Berkeley (94702) ***(P-18511)***

Young MNS Chrstn Assn San Frnc E 415 447-9602
57 Post St San Francisco (94104) ***(P-18512)***

Young MNS Chrstn Assn San Frnc E 415 447-9622
63 Funston Ave San Francisco (94129) ***(P-18513)***

Young MNS Chrstn Assn San Frnc E 650 286-9622
1877 S Grant St San Mateo (94402) ***(P-18514)***

Young MNS Chrstn Assn San Frnc E 650 747-1200
11000 Pescadero Creek Rd La Honda (94020) ***(P-18515)***

Young MNS Chrstn Assn San Frnc D 650 877-8642
1486 Huntington Ave # 100 South San Francisco (94080) ***(P-17790)***

Young MNS Chrstn Assn San Frnc (PA) **E 415 777-9622**
50 California St Ste 650 San Francisco (94111) ***(P-18516)***

Young MNS Chrstn Assn San Frnc E 415 931-9622
1530 Buchanan St San Francisco (94115) ***(P-18517)***

Young MNS Chrstn Assn San Frnc E 415 666-9622
360 18th Ave San Francisco (94121) ***(P-18518)***

Young MNS Chrstn Assn San Frnc E 415 957-9622
169 Steuart St San Francisco (94105) ***(P-18519)***

Young MNS Chrstn Assn San Frnc E 415 885-0460
246 Eddy St San Francisco (94102) ***(P-18520)***

Young MNS Chrstn Assn San Frnc E 415 331-9622
981 Fort Barry Ggnra Sausalito (94965) ***(P-18521)***

Young MNS Chrstn Assn San Frnc E 707 643-9622
415 Mississippi St Vallejo (94590) ***(P-18522)***

Young MNS Chrstn Assn San Frnc E 415 492-9622
1500 Los Gamos Dr San Rafael (94903) ***(P-18523)***

Young MNS Chrstn Assn San Frnc E 415 822-7728
1601 Lane St San Francisco (94124) ***(P-18524)***

Young MNS Chrstn Assn San Frnc E 415 586-6900
4080 Mission St San Francisco (94112) ***(P-18525)***

Young MNS Chrstn Assn Slcon Vl (PA) **D 408 351-6400**
80 Saratoga Ave Santa Clara (95051) ***(P-18526)***

Young MNS Chrstn Assn Slcon Vl C 650 493-9622
1922 The Alameda Ste 300 San Jose (95126) ***(P-18527)***

Young MNS Chrstn Assn Slcon Vl C 408 298-1717
1717 The Alameda San Jose (95126) ***(P-18528)***

Young MNS Chrstn Assn Slcon Vl C 650 969-9622
2400 Grant Rd Mountain View (94040) ***(P-18529)***

Young MNS Chrstn Assn Slcon Vl E 650 368-4168
1445 Hudson St Redwood City (94061) ***(P-18530)***

Young MNS Chrstn Assn Slcon Vl C 408 226-9622
5632 Santa Teresa Blvd San Jose (95123) ***(P-18531)***

Young MNS Chrstn Assn Slcon Vl C 408 370-1877
13500 Quito Rd Saratoga (95070) ***(P-18609)***

Young MNS Chrstn Assn Slcon Vl C 408 729-4223
1855 Majestic Way San Jose (95132) ***(P-18532)***

Young MNS Chrstn Assn Slcon Vl C 831 338-2128
16275 Highway 9 Boulder Creek (95006) ***(P-18533)***

Young Pecan Company, Stockton *Also called Kr Subsidiary Inc* ***(P-9508)***

Young Wns Chrstn Assn of Wtsnv E 831 724-6078
340 E Beach St Watsonville (95076) ***(P-18534)***

Youngdahl Consulting Group Inc E 916 933-0633
1234 Glenhaven Ct El Dorado Hills (95762) ***(P-18866)***

Youngs Market Company LLC D 408 782-3121
850 Jarvis Dr Morgan Hill (95037) ***(P-9589)***

Youngs Market Company LLC D 213 612-1216
1255 E Fortune Ave # 101 Fresno (93725) ***(P-9590)***

Youngs Market Company LLC D 707 584-5170
256 Sutton Pl Ste 106 Santa Rosa (95407) ***(P-9591)***

Youngs Market Company LLC D 916 617-4402
3620 Industrial Blvd # 10 West Sacramento (95691) ***(P-9592)***

Youngstown Grape Distrs Inc C 559 638-2271
1625 G St Reedley (93654) ***(P-316)***

Your Warm Friend Inc E 510 893-1343
1451 32nd St Oakland (94608) ***(P-1402)***

Yourmechanic Inc D 800 701-6230
20 Park Rd Ste H Burlingame (94010) ***(P-14606)***

Yourpeople Inc A 888 249-3263
50 Beale St San Francisco (94105) ***(P-13539)***

Youth Employment Partnr Inc D 510 533-3447
2300 International Blvd Oakland (94601) ***(P-17850)***

Youth For Change (PA) **C 530 877-8187**
5538 Skyway Paradise (95969) ***(P-17791)***

Youth Homes Incorporated E 925 933-2627
1159 Everett Ct Concord (94518) ***(P-18214)***

Youth Services, Watsonville *Also called Encompass Community Services* ***(P-17550)***

Youth Services North, Santa Cruz *Also called Encompass Community Services* ***(P-17549)***

Youth Uprising D 510 777-9909
8711 Macarthur Blvd Oakland (94605) ***(P-12210)***

Yreka Division, Yreka *Also called Timber Products Co Ltd Partnr* ***(P-3196)***

Yreka Employment Services, Yreka *Also called Siskiyou Opportunity Center* ***(P-12137)***

Yuba City Community Hosp Inc E 510 796-1100
39001 Sundale Dr Fremont (94538) ***(P-16750)***

Yuba City Honda, Yuba City *Also called Mele Enterprises Inc* ***(P-14578)***

Yuba City Manor LLC E 530 673-6051
1880 Live Oak Blvd Yuba City (95991) ***(P-18215)***

Yuba City Nursing & Rehab LLC D 530 671-0550
1220 Plumas St Yuba City (95991) ***(P-16168)***

Yuba City Post-Acute, Yuba City *Also called Guava Holdings LLC* ***(P-16759)***

Yuba City Racquet Club Inc E 530 673-6900
825 Jones Rd Yuba City (95991) ***(P-15168)***

Yuba City Residential Care, Yuba City *Also called Yuba City Manor LLC* ***(P-18215)***

Yuba City Steel Products Co E 530 673-4554
532 Crestmont Ave Yuba City (95991) ***(P-4695)***

Yuba City Unified School A 530 822-7601
750 N Palora Ave Yuba City (95991) ***(P-18259)***

Yuba Cnty Prbtion Chldren Fmli, Marysville *Also called County of Yuba* ***(P-17519)***

Yuba County Juvenile Hall, Marysville *Also called County of Yuba* ***(P-18084)***

Yuba County Probation Dept, Marysville *Also called County of Yuba* ***(P-17521)***

Yuba Cy Wste Wtr Trtmnt Fcilty E 530 822-7698
302 Burns Dr Yuba City (95991) ***(P-5452)***

Yuba Rver Mlding Mill Work Inc (PA) **E 530 742-2168**
3757 Feather River Blvd Olivehurst (95961) ***(P-3165)***

Yubico Inc C 408 774-4064
530 Lytton Ave Ste 301 Palo Alto (94301) ***(P-8657)***

Yuhas Tooling & Machining Inc E 408 934-9196
1031 Pecten Ct Milpitas (95035) ***(P-5644)***

Yuja Inc C 888 257-2278
84 W Santa Clara St # 690 San Jose (95113) ***(P-13540)***

Yume Inc (HQ) **B 650 591-9400**
601 Montgomery St # 1600 San Francisco (94111) ***(P-11796)***

Yupana Inc (PA) **E 925 482-0657**
4020 Nelson Ave Ste 200 Concord (94520) ***(P-18867)***

Yva.ai, Santa Clara *Also called Yvaai Inc* ***(P-12933)***

Yvaai Inc (PA) **D 650 704-5503**
2445 Augustine Dr Ste 150 Santa Clara (95054) ***(P-12933)***

YWCA Contra Costa/Sacramento (PA) **D 925 372-4213**
1320 Arnold Dr Ste 170 Martinez (94553) ***(P-17792)***

YWCA Golden Gate Silicon Vly D 408 295-4011
375 S 3rd St San Jose (95112) ***(P-18535)***

YWCA of Watsonville, Watsonville *Also called Young Wns Chrstn Assn of Wtsnv* ***(P-18534)***

Ywd Cartoners, Fresno *Also called Kodiak Cartoners Inc* ***(P-5200)***

Z Hotel Jack London Square, Alameda *Also called Inn At Jack London Square LLC* ***(P-11189)***

Z Logging LLC F 707 488-2151
403 Old State Hwy Orick (95555) ***(P-3089)***

Z-Axis Tech Solutions Inc (PA) **D 408 263-8038**
1754 Tech Dr Ste 224 San Jose (95110) ***(P-13690)***

Zacharias, Don M MD, Sacramento *Also called University California Davis* ***(P-15781)***

Zacky & Sons Poultry LLC (PA) **A 559 443-2700**
2020 S East Ave Fresno (93721) ***(P-2140)***

Zacky Farms, Fresno *Also called Zacky & Sons Poultry LLC* ***(P-2140)***

Zadaonet D 650 556-6377
685 Scofield Ave Apt 22 East Palo Alto (94303) ***(P-8011)***

Zag Technical Services Inc E 408 383-2000
645 River Oaks Pkwy San Jose (95134) ***(P-13817)***

Zanker Rd Rsrce MGT Ltd A Cal E 408 846-1575
980 State Highway 25 Gilroy (95020) ***(P-8391)***

Zanker Road Landfill, Gilroy *Also called Zanker Rd Rsrce MGT Ltd A Cal* ***(P-8391)***

Zanker Road Resource MGT Ltd E 916 738-9279
4201 Florin Perkins Rd Sacramento (95826) ***(P-8392)***

Zaplabs LLC (HQ) **D 510 735-2600**
2000 Powell St Ste 700 Emeryville (94608) ***(P-10690)***

Zazmic Inc (PA) **C 415 728-1621**
79 Coleridge St San Francisco (94110) ***(P-12934)***

Zealtech Inc E 510 797-7006
39111 Paseo Padre Pkwy Fremont (94538) ***(P-19893)***

Zededa Inc (PA) **D 408 550-5531**
160 W Santa Clara St # 775 San Jose (95113) ***(P-12935)***

Zeesoft Inc (PA) **E 408 247-2987**
14891 Vine St Saratoga (95070) ***(P-12936)***

Zeiter Eye Medical Group Inc (PA) **D 209 366-0446**
255 E Weber Ave Stockton (95202) ***(P-15819)***

Zeltiq Aesthetics Inc (HQ) **A 925 474-2500**
4410 Rosewood Dr Pleasanton (94588) ***(P-7064)***

Zenbooth Inc E 510 646-8368
650 University Ave # 10 Berkeley (94710) ***(P-3310)***

Zendar Inc (PA) **E 510 590-8060**
1110 Euclid Ave Berkeley (94708) ***(P-19675)***

Zenefits, San Francisco *Also called Yourpeople Inc* ***(P-13539)***

Zeniq Inc E 415 562-6367
47 Lusk St San Francisco (94107) ***(P-13774)***

Zenique Hotel Management LLC E 650 483-9968
800 Airport Blvd Ste 418 Burlingame (94010) ***(P-11587)***

Zenith Infotech Limited C 510 687-1943
39675 Cedar Blvd Ste 240b Newark (94560) ***(P-13691)***

Zenith Talent Corporation E 408 300-0531
6030 Hellyer Ave San Jose (95138) ***(P-12154)***

Zenlen Inc E 415 834-8238
201 California St San Francisco (94111) ***(P-4100)***

Zeno Group Inc D 650 801-7950
275 Shoreline Dr Ste 530 Redwood City (94065) ***(P-19922)***

Zenput Inc E 800 537-0227
548 Market St San Francisco (94104) ***(P-12937)***

Zenreach Inc (HQ) **C 415 612-1900**
1 Letterman Dr Bldg C San Francisco (94129) ***(P-11808)***

Zensar Technologies Inc A 408 469-5408
555 E El Camino Real Sunnyvale (94087) ***(P-12938)***

ALPHABETIC SECTION Zytek Ems, Milpitas

Zentera Systems Inc.....F.....408 436-4811
97 E Brokaw Rd Ste 360 San Jose (95112) ***(P-13541)***
Zep Solar Llc (HQ).....**E.....415 479-6900**
161 Mitchell Blvd Ste 104 San Rafael (94903) ***(P-6364)***
Zephyr Real Estate, San Francisco *Also called Dppm Inc* ***(P-10542)***
Zero Base, Fremont *Also called Zerobase Energy LLC* ***(P-6492)***
Zero Waste Solutions Inc.....C.....925 270-3339
1850 Gateway Blvd # 1030 Concord (94520) ***(P-19707)***
Zerobase Energy LLC.....E.....888 530-9376
46609 Fremont Blvd Fremont (94538) ***(P-6492)***
Zest Consulting LLC.....E.....415 361-5696
5000 Hopyard Rd Ste 165 Pleasanton (94588) ***(P-19894)***
Zest Labs Inc (HQ).....**E.....408 200-6500**
2349 Bering Dr San Jose (95131) ***(P-6365)***
Zeus Living, San Francisco *Also called Egomotion Corp* ***(P-10543)***
ZF Array Technology Inc.....E.....408 433-9920
2302 Trade Zone Blvd San Jose (95131) ***(P-6372)***
Zglobal Inc (PA).....**E.....916 985-9461**
604 Sutter St Ste 250 Folsom (95630) ***(P-19895)***
Zi Machine Manufacturing, El Dorado Hills *Also called 478826 Limited* ***(P-5455)***
Ziff Davis B2b Focus Inc (HQ).....**E.....415 696-5453**
625 2nd St San Francisco (94107) ***(P-19676)***
Zignal Labs Inc.....D.....415 683-7871
600 California St Fl 18 San Francisco (94108) ***(P-12939)***
Zilog Inc (HQ).....**D.....408 513-1500**
1590 Buckeye Dr Milpitas (95035) ***(P-6366)***
Zimad, South San Francisco *Also called Ximad Inc* ***(P-13534)***
Zimbio Inc (PA).....**D.....650 594-1723**
990 Industrial Rd Ste 204 San Carlos (94070) ***(P-3521)***
Zimmerman Roofing Inc.....D.....916 454-3667
3675 R St Sacramento (95816) ***(P-1847)***
Zinfi Technologies Inc.....E.....925 251-0332
6200 Stnrdge Mall Rd Ste Pleasanton (94588) ***(P-19150)***
Zinier Inc.....C.....787 504-4826
3182 Campus Dr Ste 333 San Mateo (94403) ***(P-14018)***
Zinus Inc (HQ).....**D.....925 417-2100**
1951 Fairway Dr Ste A San Leandro (94577) ***(P-3298)***
Ziontech Solutions Inc.....E.....408 434-6001
1900 Mccarthy Blvd # 100 Milpitas (95035) ***(P-14019)***
Zip-Chem Products, Morgan Hill *Also called Andpak Inc* ***(P-14201)***
Zipi Inc.....E.....424 444-6700
101 Creekside Ridge Ct # 2 Roseville (95678) ***(P-10691)***
Zipline International Inc.....C.....415 993-0604
333 Corey Way South San Francisco (94080) ***(P-19677)***
Zipline International Inc.....C.....508 340-3291
495 Pine Ave Half Moon Bay (94019) ***(P-12940)***
Zipline Medical Inc.....F.....408 412-7228
747 Camden Ave Ste A Campbell (95008) ***(P-7065)***
Zippedi Inc.....E.....858 353-9743
1633 Bayshore Hwy Ste 335 Burlingame (94010) ***(P-14020)***
Zipzoomfly, Newark *Also called Xtraplus Corporation* ***(P-8763)***
Zira Group Inc.....E.....650 701-7026
400 Concar Dr San Mateo (94402) ***(P-13542)***
Zircon Corporation (PA).....**E.....408 866-8600**
1580 Dell Ave Campbell (95008) ***(P-5103)***
Ziro Ride LLC.....E.....951 801-4981
201 Spear St Ste 1100 San Francisco (94105) ***(P-7822)***
Zl Technologies Inc (PA).....**D.....408 240-8989**
860 N Mccarthy Blvd # 10 Milpitas (95035) ***(P-12941)***
ZMC Hotels LLC (HQ).....**E.....925 933-4000**
1855 Olympic Blvd Ste 300 Walnut Creek (94596) ***(P-19429)***
Znshine Pv-Tech Inc.....E.....415 810-0861
400 Oyster Point Blvd # 326 South San Francisco (94080) ***(P-6367)***
Zoca Roseville Inc.....D.....916 788-0303
1182 Rsville Pkwy Ste 110 Roseville (95678) ***(P-14467)***
Zocalo, Roseville *Also called Zoca Roseville Inc* ***(P-14467)***
Zocalo.....D.....415 293-1600
1551 Bancroft Ave 1508 San Francisco (94124) ***(P-8504)***
Zocalo Coffee House.....F.....510 569-0102
659 Broadmoor Blvd San Leandro (94577) ***(P-2850)***
Zoe Holding Company Inc.....D.....916 646-3100
2143 Hurley Way Sacramento (95825) ***(P-12155)***
Zoe Holding Company Inc.....D.....415 421-4900
44 Montgomery St San Francisco (94104) ***(P-19923)***
Zogenix Inc (PA).....**E.....510 550-8300**
5959 Horton St Ste 500 Emeryville (94608) ***(P-4010)***
Zoho Corporation.....B.....925 924-9500
4900 Hopyard Rd Ste 310 Pleasanton (94588) ***(P-18868)***
Zoho Corporation.....B.....925 924-9500
4141 Hacienda Dr Pleasanton (94588) ***(P-19678)***
Zola Acai, San Jose *Also called Amazon Prsrvation Partners Inc* ***(P-2211)***
Zola Electric Labs Inc.....E.....650 542-6939
555 De Haro St Ste 220 San Francisco (94107) ***(P-6368)***
Zoll Circulation Inc.....C.....408 541-2140
2000 Ringwood Ave San Jose (95131) ***(P-7136)***
Zollner Electronics Inc.....E.....408 434-5400
575 Cottonwood Dr Milpitas (95035) ***(P-6003)***
Zonare Medical Systems Inc.....D.....650 230-2800
420 Bernardo Ave Mountain View (94043) ***(P-19252)***
Zonic Design & Imaging LLC.....E.....415 643-3700
875 Mahler Rd Ste 238 Burlingame (94010) ***(P-19679)***
Zonneveld Dairies Inc.....E.....559 923-4546
1560 Cerini Ave Laton (93242) ***(P-229)***
Zoom Video Communications Inc (PA).....**A.....888 799-9666**
55 Almaden Blvd Fl 6 San Jose (95113) ***(P-12942)***
Zoomifier Corporation (PA).....**B.....800 255-5303**
5776 Stnrdge Mall Rd Ste Pleasanton (94588) ***(P-13543)***
Zoosk Inc (HQ).....**E.....415 728-9543**
989 Market St Fl 5 San Francisco (94103) ***(P-8012)***
Zoox Inc (HQ).....**E.....650 539-9669**
1149 Chess Dr Foster City (94404) ***(P-6562)***
Zoox Labs, Foster City *Also called Zoox Inc* ***(P-6562)***
Zoran Corporation (HQ).....**A.....972 673-1600**
1060 Rincon Cir San Jose (95131) ***(P-6369)***
Zosano, Fremont *Also called Zp Opco Inc* ***(P-4012)***
Zosano Pharma Corporation (PA).....**E.....510 745-1200**
34790 Ardentech Ct Fremont (94555) ***(P-4011)***
Zp Opco Inc.....E.....510 745-1200
34790 Ardentech Ct Fremont (94555) ***(P-4012)***
Zs Pharma Inc.....E.....650 753-1823
1100 Park Pl Fl 3 San Mateo (94403) ***(P-4013)***
Zscaler Inc (PA).....**A.....408 533-0288**
120 Holger Way San Jose (95134) ***(P-12943)***
Zspace Inc (PA).....**D.....408 498-4050**
55 Nicholson Ln Ste 2 San Jose (95134) ***(P-8881)***
Zuca Inc.....E.....408 377-9822
320 S Milpitas Blvd Milpitas (95035) ***(P-4351)***
Zuckerman-Heritage Inc (PA).....**E.....209 444-1724**
111 N Zuckerman Rd Stockton (95206) ***(P-198)***
Zukes Landscape Inc.....E.....916 635-6502
3373 Luyung Dr Rancho Cordova (95742) ***(P-510)***
Zultys Inc.....E.....408 328-0450
785 Lucerne Dr Sunnyvale (94085) ***(P-14021)***
Zumwalt Construction Inc.....D.....559 252-1000
5520 E Lamona Ave Fresno (93727) ***(P-996)***
Zuo Modern Contemporary Inc (PA).....**E.....510 877-4087**
80 Swan Way Ste 150 Oakland (94621) ***(P-5731)***
Zuora Inc (PA).....**B.....800 425-1281**
101 Redwood Shores Pkwy # 100 Redwood City (94065) ***(P-13544)***
Zwicker & Associates PC.....D.....925 689-7070
1320 Wllow Paca Rd Ste 73 Concord (94520) ***(P-17403)***
Zyante Inc.....D.....510 541-4434
41 E Main St Los Gatos (95030) ***(P-9620)***
Zybooks, Los Gatos *Also called Zyante Inc* ***(P-9620)***
Zygo Epo.....F.....510 243-7592
3900 Lakeside Dr Richmond (94806) ***(P-6888)***
Zyme Solutions Inc (PA).....**D.....650 585-2258**
240 Twin Dolphin Dr Ste D Redwood City (94065) ***(P-13813)***
Zymergen Inc (PA).....**A.....415 801-8073**
5980 Horton St Ste 105 Emeryville (94608) ***(P-19151)***
Zynga Inc (PA).....**C.....855 449-9642**
699 8th St San Francisco (94103) ***(P-13775)***
Zyrion Inc.....D.....408 524-7424
440 N Wolfe Rd Sunnyvale (94085) ***(P-13545)***
Zytek Corp (PA).....**E.....408 520-4287**
1755 Mccarthy Blvd Milpitas (95035) ***(P-6004)***
Zytek Ems, Milpitas *Also called Zytek Corp* ***(P-6004)***

ALPHABETIC

COUNTY/CITY CROSS-REFERENCE INDEX

Alameda
Alameda
Albany
Berkeley
Castro Valley
Dublin
Emeryville
Fremont
Hayward
Kensington
Livermore
Newark
Oakland
Piedmont
Pleasanton
San Leandro
San Lorenzo
Sunol
Union City

Amador
Ione
Jackson
Martell
Pine Grove
Pioneer
Plymouth
Sutter Creek

Butte
Biggs
Chico
Durham
Forest Ranch
Gridley
Nelson
Oroville
Paradise
Richvale

Calaveras
Angels Camp
Arnold
Bear Valley
Copperopolis
Murphys
San Andreas
Vallecito
Valley Springs
West Point

Colusa
Arbuckle
Colusa
Grimes
Maxwell
Princeton
Williams

Contra Costa
Alamo
Antioch
Bay Point
Brentwood
Byron
Clayton
Concord
Crockett
Danville
Diablo
El Cerrito
El Sobrante
Hercules
Lafayette
Martinez
Moraga
Oakley
Orinda
Pacheco
Pinole
Pittsburg
Pleasant Hill
Point Richmond
Richmond
Rodeo
San Pablo
San Ramon
Walnut Creek

Del Norte
Crescent City
Klamath
Smith River

El Dorado
Cameron Park
Camino
Coloma
Cool
Diamond Springs
Echo Lake
El Dorado
El Dorado Hills
Garden Valley
Georgetown
Kelsey
Lotus
Pilot Hill
Placerville
Shingle Springs
South Lake Tahoe
Twin Bridges

Fresno
Auberry
Big Creek
Caruthers
Clovis
Coalinga
Del Rey
Firebaugh
Five Points
Fowler
Fresno
Friant
Helm
Huron
Kerman
Kingsburg
Lakeshore
Laton
Mendota
Miramonte
Orange Cove
Parlier
Pinedale
Reedley
Riverdale
San Joaquin
Sanger
Selma
Tollhouse
Tranquillity

Glenn
Glenn
Orland
Willows

Humboldt
Arcata
Bayside
Blue Lake
Eureka
Fields Landing
Fortuna
Garberville
Hoopa
Kneeland
Loleta
McKinleyville
Orick
Redway
Samoa
Scotia
Trinidad
Whitethorn
Willow Creek

Lake
Clearlake
Clearlake Oaks
Hidden Valley Lake
Kelseyville
Lakeport
Lower Lake
Middletown
Nice
Upper Lake

Lassen
Bieber
Susanville
Wendel
Westwood

Madera
Bass Lake
Chowchilla
Coarsegold
Madera
O Neals
Oakhurst

Marin
Belvedere
Belvedere Tiburon
Bolinas
Corte Madera
Dillon Beach
Fairfax
Forest Knolls
Greenbrae
Kentfield
Larkspur
Marshall
Mill Valley
Muir Beach
Nicasio
Novato
Ross
San Anselmo
San Rafael
Sausalito
Tomales

Mariposa
Fish Camp
Mariposa
Yosemite Ntpk

Mendocino
Albion
Boonville
Branscomb
Calpella
Comptche
Covelo
Fort Bragg
Gualala
Hopland
Laytonville
Little River
Mendocino
Philo
Point Arena
Potter Valley
Redwood Valley
Ukiah
Willits

Merced
Atwater
Ballico
Delhi
Dos Palos
El Nido
Gustine
Hilmar
Le Grand
Livingston
Los Banos
Merced
Snelling
South Dos Palos
Stevinson
Winton

Modoc
Alturas
Cedarville

Mono
Bridgeport
Crowley Lake
June Lake
Mammoth Lakes

Napa
American Canyon
Angwin
Calistoga
NAPA
Oakville
Rutherford
Saint Helena
Vallejo
Yountville

Nevada
Grass Valley
Nevada City
Norden
Penn Valley
Rough and Ready
Smartsville
Soda Springs
Truckee

Placer
Alpine Meadows
Alta
Auburn
Colfax
Emigrant Gap
Foresthill
Granite Bay
Homewood
Lincoln
Loomis
Newcastle
Olympic Valley
Penryn
Rocklin
Roseville
Tahoe City
Tahoe Vista

Plumas
Blairsden
Chester
Clio
Greenville
Portola
Quincy

Sacramento
Antelope
Carmichael
Citrus Heights
Elk Grove
Elverta
Fair Oaks
Folsom
Galt
Gold River
Herald
Isleton
Mather
McClellan
North Highlands
Orangevale
Rancho Cordova
Rancho Murieta
Rio Linda
Sacramento
Sloughhouse
Walnut Grove
Wilton

San Benito
Hollister
Paicines

COUNTY/CITY CROSS-REFERENCE

	ENTRY #	ENTRY #	ENTRY #	ENTRY #	ENTRY #

San Juan Bautista
San Francisco
San Francisco
San Joaquin
Acampo
Clements
Escalon
Farmington
French Camp
Holt
Lathrop
Linden
Lockeford
Lodi
Manteca
Ripon
Stockton
Tracy
Woodbridge
San Mateo
Atherton
Belmont
Brisbane
Burlingame
Colma
Daly City
El Granada
Emerald Hills
Foster City
Half Moon Bay
Hillsborough
La Honda
Menlo Park
Millbrae
Moss Beach
Pacifica
Pescadero
Portola Valley
Redwood City
San Bruno
San Carlos

San Francisco
San Gregorio
San Mateo
South San Francisco
Woodside
Santa Clara
Alviso
Campbell
Cupertino
E Palo Alto
East Palo Alto
Gilroy
Los Altos
Los Altos Hills
Los Gatos
Milpitas
Moffett Field
Monte Sereno
Morgan Hill
Mountain View
Palo Alto
San Jose
San Martin
Santa Clara
Saratoga
Stanford
Sunnyvale
Santa Cruz
Aptos
Ben Lomond
Boulder Creek
Brookdale
Capitola
Davenport
Felton
Freedom
Los Gatos
Mount Hermon
Royal Oaks
Santa Cruz
Scotts Valley

Soquel
Watsonville
Shasta
Anderson
Burney
Cottonwood
Hat Creek
Lakehead
Palo Cedro
Redding
Round Mountain
Shasta Lake
Sierra
Loyalton
Siskiyou
Dunsmuir
Edgewood
Etna
McCloud
Mount Shasta
Tulelake
Weed
Yreka
Solano
Benicia
Dixon
Fairfield
Rio Vista
Suisun City
Vacaville
Vallejo
Sonoma
Bodega
Bodega Bay
Cazadero
Cloverdale
Cotati
Duncans Mills
Eldridge
Forestville

Fulton
Geyserville
Glen Ellen
Graton
Guerneville
Healdsburg
Jenner
Kenwood
Occidental
Penngrove
Petaluma
Rohnert Park
Santa Rosa
Sebastopol
Sonoma
Windsor
Stanislaus
Ceres
Crows Landing
Denair
Hickman
Hughson
La Grange
Modesto
Newman
Oakdale
Patterson
Riverbank
Salida
Turlock
Waterford
Westley
Sutter
Live Oak
Meridian
Pleasant Grove
Rio Oso
Robbins
Sutter
Yuba City

Tehama
Corning
Gerber
Manton
Paynes Creek
Red Bluff
Vina
Trinity
Hayfork
Junction City
Lewiston
Trinity Center
Weaverville
Tuolumne
Columbia
Groveland
Jamestown
Long Barn
MI Wuk Village
Pinecrest
Sonora
Strawberry
Tuolumne
Twain Harte
Yolo
Brooks
Clarksburg
Davis
Dunnigan
El Macero
Esparto
Knights Landing
West Sacramento
Winters
Woodland
Yuba
Marysville
Olivehurst
Plumas Lake
Wheatland

GEOGRAPHIC SECTION

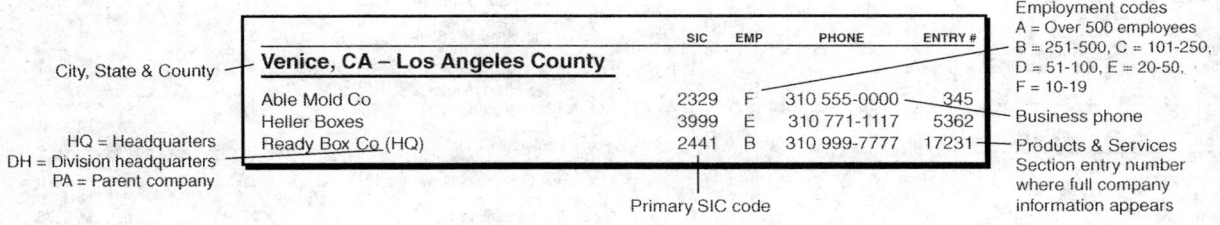

- Listings in this section are sorted alphabetically by city.
- Listings within each city are sorted alphabetically by company name.

ACAMPO, CA - San Joaquin County

Company	SIC	EMP	Phone	Entry #
Acampo Grape Harvesting LLC	0722	E	209 333-7072	259
California Concentrate Company	2037	E	209 334-9112	2290
Calva Products LLC (PA)	2048	E	800 328-9680	2338
Calva Products Co Inc	2048	E	209 339-1516	2339
Engineered Automation LLC	3599	F	209 368-6363	5520
Franciscan Vineyards Inc	2084	D	209 369-5861	2581
Global Wine Group	2084	D	209 340-8500	2595
JJ Rios Farm Services Inc	0761	D	209 333-7467	359
Langetwins Inc	2084	E	209 339-4055	2648
Langetwins Wine Company Inc	2084	D	209 334-9780	2649
Macchia Inc	2084	F	209 333-2600	2652
R & G Schatz Farms Inc	0172	F	209 367-4881	69

ALAMEDA, CA - Alameda County

Company	SIC	EMP	Phone	Entry #
ABB Inc	3612	D	510 987-7111	5645
Abb/Con-Cise Optical Group LLC	5048	D	800 852-8089	8797
Abb/Con-Cise Optical Group LLC	5048	C	510 483-9400	8798
Abbott Diabetes Care Inc (HQ)	2835	C	510 749-5400	4014
Abbott Diabetes Care Sls Corp	2834	C	510 749-5400	3824
Absolutdata Technologies Inc	7389	D	510 748-9922	14193
Adrienne Mattos Swim Schl Inc (PA)	7999	E	866 633-4147	15169
Alameda Alliance For Health	6324	C	510 747-4555	10090
Alameda Bureau Elec Imprv Corp (HQ)	4911	D	510 748-3902	8089
Alameda Family Services	8351	E	510 629-6300	17854
Alameda Hlthcare & Wellnss Ctr	8051	D	510 523-8857	15907
Alameda Hospitality LLC	7011	D	510 522-1000	10913
Allcells LLC	8731	D	510 521-2600	19016
Alveo Technologies Inc	8731	E	510 851-5314	19019
Alveo Technologies Inc	8731	D	510 749-4895	19020
American Cancer Soc Cal Div (PA)	8733	D	510 893-7900	19195
Aqua Metals Inc	3341	E	510 479-7635	4557
Asterias Biotherapeutics Inc	8731	D	510 456-3800	19031
Auctions By Bay Inc	7389	E	510 740-0220	14207
Balaji Alameda LLC	7011	E	510 521-4500	10943
Bay Marine & Indus Sup LLC	5099	E	510 337-9122	9188
Bay Maritime Corp (PA)	4482	E	510 337-9122	7717
Bay Ship & Yacht Co (PA)	3731	C	510 337-9122	6638
Bay View Rhbilitation Hosp LLC	8051	D	510 521-5600	15923
Berg Wlliam L Attorney At Law (PA)	8111	E	510 523-3200	17211
Bladium Inc (PA)	7991	D	510 814-4999	14930
Boost Healthcare Consulting LLC	8748	E	415 377-7589	19733
Bowlero Corp	7933	D	510 523-6767	14888
Business Recovery Services Inc	7374	D	510 522-9700	13700
Center For Cllbrtive Classroom	2731	D	510 533-0213	3527
Center For Social Dynamics LLC (PA)	8322	B	510 268-8120	17475
Centrro Inc (PA)	7375	D	510 891-7500	13781
Chipman Corporation (PA)	4213	E	510 748-8700	7519
City Alameda Health Care Corp	8062	A	510 522-3700	16333
Clear-Com LLC (HQ)	3663	A	510 337-6600	5831
Commodore Dining Cruises Inc	4489	D	510 337-9000	7719
Community Hlth For Asian Amrca	8093	E	925 778-1667	17002
Community of Harbor Bay Isle	8641	B	510 865-3363	18408
Continental Terminals Inc	4225	E	510 746-1100	7687
Coral Reef Motel LLC	7011	E	510 521-2330	11034
Delphi Productions Inc (PA)	7389	C	510 748-7494	14250
Dynamic Graphics Inc (PA)	7371	D	510 522-0700	12407
Elder Care Alliance San Mateo (HQ)	8361	D	510 769-2700	18103
Elder Care Alliance San Rafael	8051	E	510 769-2700	15982
Encinal Yacht Club	7997	D	510 522-3272	15089
Ettore Products Co	5087	B	510 748-4130	9142
Exelixis Inc	3824	C	650 837-7000	6740
Exelixis Inc	2834	C	650 837-7000	3896
Exelixis Inc (PA)	2836	D	650 837-7000	4047
Family Stations Inc (PA)	4832	C	510 568-6200	8024
First 5 Alameda County	8322	D	510 227-6900	17569
Fleenor Company Inc (PA)	2679	E	800 433-2531	3401
Fluxion Biosciences Inc	3841	E	650 241-4777	6973
Frank Ghiglione Inc (PA)	4212	E	510 483-7000	7466
G&R Almeda Healthcare Svcs LLC	8322	D	510 521-5765	17587
Gallagher & Lindsey Inc (PA)	6531	E	510 521-8181	10556
Garfield Nursing Home Inc	8051	C	510 582-7676	16011
Girl Scouts Northern Cal (PA)	8641	D	510 562-8470	18421
Global Grid For Learning Pbc (PA)	7372	F	888 904-9773	13191
Golden State Imports Intl Inc (PA)	5094	D	510 995-1320	9182
Golden West Envelope Corp	2677	E	510 452-5419	3398
Heliotrope Technologies Inc	3211	E	510 871-3980	4359
Icon Exhibits LLC	7389	E	260 482-8700	14300
Imprint Energy Inc	3672	F	510 847-7027	6495
Inn At Jack London Square LLC	7011	D	510 452-4565	11189
Institute Humn Bhvior RES Edca	8351	E	510 769-7100	17956
Interntnl Un Oper Engners Lca	8631	B	510 748-7400	18367
Kaiser Foundation Hospitals	8062	A	510 749-3021	16407
Kaiser Foundation Hospitals	8011	C	510 752-1190	15487
Lens C-C Inc (PA)	3851	D	800 772-3911	7143
Makani Technologies LLC (PA)	8742	E	503 939-5359	19565
Marina Garden Nursing Ctr Inc	8051	C	510 523-2363	16043
Mariner Square Athletic Inc	7991	D	510 523-8011	14962
Mbh Architects Inc	8712	C	510 865-8663	18902
McGuire and Hester (PA)	1623	B	510 632-7676	1119
Metaswitch Networks	7371	C	415 513-1500	12604
Motorola Solutions Inc	3663	C	510 217-7400	5856
Novvi LLC (PA)	2911	D	281 488-0833	4177
NRC Environmental Services Inc (DH)	4959	C	510 749-1390	8400
Operating Engnrs Lcal Un No 3 (PA)	8631	C	510 748-7400	18371
Parco LLC	7011	E	510 865-0100	11353
Penumbra Inc (PA)	3841	A	510 748-3200	7019
Performance Contracting Inc	1742	E	510 214-1444	1698
Polarion Software Inc	7372	D	877 572-4005	13376
Power Standards Lab Inc	3825	E	510 522-4400	6782
Providence Veterinary Hospital	0742	E	510 521-6608	333
Rgb Spectrum	3577	D	510 814-7000	5407
Rising Star Montessori Assoc	8351	E	510 865-4536	18007
Rmf Salt Holdings LLC	2844	F	510 477-9600	4094
Rock Wall Wine Company Inc	2084	D	510 522-5700	2701
Saildrone Inc	3549	F	415 670-9700	5113
San Francisco Bay AR Tran Assn	8699	C	510 501-5318	18587
Semifreddis Inc (PA)	5149	D	510 596-9930	9483
Shalley-Dibble Incorporated	8711	E	510 769-7600	18811
Siemens	5063	C	510 263-0367	8877
Sila Nanotechnologies Inc	3691	C	707 901-7452	6490
Simco-Ion Technology Group (PA)	5065	C	510 217-0600	8954
Sks Die Cast & Machining Inc (PA)	3363	D	510 523-2541	4580
St George Spirits Inc	2084	E	510 769-1601	2722
Svendsen Enterprises LLC	5088	E	510 522-2886	9152
Synactive Inc (PA)	7371	E	650 341-3310	12839
Telecare Corporation (PA)	8063	A	510 337-7950	16748
Therasense Inc	3841	E	510 749-5400	7049
Vf Outdoor LLC (HQ)	2329	C	855 500-8639	2996
Waters Edge Inc	8051	E	510 748-4300	16155
Waters Edge Lodge	8361	E	510 769-6264	18209
Weinberg Roger & Resenfeld (PA)	8111	D	510 337-1001	17393
West Coast Novelty Corporation (PA)	5099	E	510 748-4248	9203
Wind River Systems Inc (HQ)	7372	A	510 748-4100	13528
Wind River Systems Intl Inc (DH)	8742	D	510 748-4100	19670
Wrightspeed Inc	3714	D	866 960-9482	6597
Xintec Corporation (PA)	3845	E	510 832-2130	7135

ALAMO, CA - Contra Costa County

Company	SIC	EMP	Phone	Entry #
Beta Healthcare Group (PA)	6321	E	925 838-6070	10082
D W Young Cnstr Co Inc	1623	D	925 743-1536	1097
Gridbright Inc	7373	F	925 899-9025	13601
Heirloom Computing Inc	7372	E	510 709-7245	13208
Hospice and Palliative Care	8052	D	925 945-8924	16186
Insitesource Inc	7372	F	510 263-9157	13238
Lendus LLC	6162	A	925 295-9300	9911
Lendusa LLC (PA)	6162	D	925 295-9300	9912
NI Inc (PA)	6162	E	925 295-9300	9917
Oncology Svcs Med Group Inc	8099	D	925 952-8700	17164
Round Hill Country Club	7997	C	925 934-8211	15130
Round Hill Country Club	7997	E	925 934-8211	15131

Employment Codes: A=Over 500 employees, B=251-500, C=101-250, D=51-100, E=20-50 F=10-19

2022 Northern California Business Directory and Buyers Guide

© Mergent Inc. 1-800-342-5647

	SIC	EMP	PHONE	ENTRY #
Sawhney Properties LP **(PA)**	7011	E	925 837-0932	11446
Sunsil Inc **(PA)**	3674	E	925 648-7779	6317

ALBANY, CA - Alameda County

	SIC	EMP	PHONE	ENTRY #
Albany Ford Inc **(PA)**	7538	D	510 528-1244	14544
Energy Berkeley Office US Dept	8733	C	510 701-1089	19216
Moore William and Kay Mark DDS	8021	E	510 525-5510	15849
Pacific Racing Association	7948	C	510 559-7300	14917

ALBION, CA - Mendocino County

	SIC	EMP	PHONE	ENTRY #
Albion River Inn Incorporated	7011	D	707 937-1919	10914

ALPINE MEADOWS, CA - Placer County

	SIC	EMP	PHONE	ENTRY #
Alpine Meadows Ski Area	7011	E	530 583-4232	10918
Arcade Belts Inc **(PA)**	2387	D	530 580-8089	3019
Granite Peak Management **(PA)**	6531	E	530 583-7545	10562
Squaw Creek Associates LLC	7011	A	530 581-6624	11496

ALTA, CA - Placer County

	SIC	EMP	PHONE	ENTRY #
Pacific Gas and Electric Co	4911	C	530 389-2202	8161

ALTURAS, CA - Modoc County

	SIC	EMP	PHONE	ENTRY #
Califrnia Property Owners Assn	7011	E	530 233-5842	10984
Last Frontier Healthcare Dst	8062	C	530 708-8800	16425
Super 8 Motel	7011	E	530 233-3545	11520
Surprise Vly Elctrfcation Corp	4911	E	530 233-3511	8203
Teach Inc	8322	D	530 233-3111	17765

ALVISO, CA - Santa Clara County

	SIC	EMP	PHONE	ENTRY #
Acme Building Maint Co Inc **(DH)**	7349	D	408 263-5911	11913
Aloft Hotel Santa Clara	7011	C	408 263-3900	10915
Bayscape Management Inc	0781	D	408 288-2940	395
Colony Landscape & Maint Inc	0782	E	408 941-1090	454
Flextronics Corporation **(DH)**	3679	C	803 936-5200	6428
Gardner Family Hlth Netwrk Inc	8011	C	408 457-7100	15412
World Financial Group **(PA)**	8742	E	408 941-1838	19672

AMERICAN CANYON, CA - Napa County

	SIC	EMP	PHONE	ENTRY #
Alcan Packg Capsules Cal LLC	5085	E	707 257-6481	9108
Amcan Beverages Inc	2086	B	707 557-0500	2781
Amcor Flexibles LLC	2671	C	707 257-6481	3374
Barry Callebaut USA LLC	2066	C	707 642-8200	2435
Billet Transportation Inc **(PA)**	4213	E	707 649-9200	7512
Bvk Gaming Inc	7999	D	707 644-8853	15184
C Line Express	4213	E	707 553-6041	7516
Coast Lm Inc **(PA)**	0781	C	707 251-8872	408
Coca-Cola Company American Cyn	2086	F	707 556-1220	2788
DHR Construction Inc	1629	E	707 552-6500	1155
Eagle Vnes Vnyrds Golf CLB LLC	7992	D	707 257-4470	14999
Envirocare International Inc	3564	E	707 638-6800	5191
G L Mezzetta Inc	2033	D	707 648-1050	2215
Hess Collection Winery	2084	D	707 255-1144	2616
Madison Vineyard Holdings LLC	5182	E	707 254-8673	9580
Midwestern Pipeline Svcs Inc **(PA)**	2952	F	707 557-6633	4192
R E Maher Inc	1771	D	707 642-3907	1904
Vin Lux LLC	4214	E	707 265-4100	7641
Western Wine Services Inc **(PA)**	4225	D	800 999-8463	7705
William Kreysler & Assoc Inc	3089	E	707 552-3500	4332

ANDERSON, CA - Shasta County

	SIC	EMP	PHONE	ENTRY #
Apex Fence Co Inc	1799	E	530 365-3316	2004
Cascade Comfort Service Inc	1711	E	530 365-5350	1230
Checchi Enterprises Inc	2752	F	530 378-1207	3635
Davey Tree Surgery Company	0783	D	530 378-2674	516
Elizabeth Headrick	2411	E	530 247-8000	3059
Haisch Construction Co Inc	2439	F	530 378-6800	3206
Harbert Roofing Inc	1761	D	530 223-3251	1811
Linkus Enterprises LLC **(PA)**	1623	A	530 229-9197	1115
Oak River Rehabilitation	8051	C	530 365-0025	16079
Sierra Pacific Industries **(PA)**	2421	D	530 378-8000	3108
Sierra Pacific Industries	2421	E	530 365-3721	3113
Siskiyou Forest Products **(PA)**	2431	E	530 378-6980	3153
Ssmb Pacific Holding Co Inc	5012	E	530 222-1212	8430
United Parcel Service Inc	4215	C	530 365-7850	7659
Visioncare Devices Inc	5047	E	530 364-2271	8796
Voorwood Company	3553	E	530 365-3311	5116
Wheelabrator Lassen Inc **(DH)**	4953	D	530 365-9173	8390

ANGELS CAMP, CA - Calaveras County

	SIC	EMP	PHONE	ENTRY #
Greenhorn Creek Associates LP **(PA)**	7997	D	209 729-8111	15097
Motherlode Investors LLC	7992	D	209 736-8112	15014
United Parcel Service Inc	4215	C	209 736-0878	7670

ANGWIN, CA - Napa County

	SIC	EMP	PHONE	ENTRY #
Helmer and Sons Inc **(PA)**	1542	E	707 965-2425	889
Ladera Vineyards LLC	2084	D	707 965-2445	2644
Ladera Winery LLC	2084	E	707 965-2445	2645

ANTELOPE, CA - Sacramento County

	SIC	EMP	PHONE	ENTRY #
Magnatrans LLC	4212	E	916 969-6300	7481
Phoenix Schools Inc	8351	D	916 725-0302	17995
Save Mart Supermarkets	2051	D	916 348-3425	2403
Security MGT Group Intl Inc	7381	E	925 521-1500	14095

ANTIOCH, CA - Contra Costa County

	SIC	EMP	PHONE	ENTRY #
Aiken Underground Inc	1521	E	925 776-4600	605
Allied Container Systems Inc	3448	C	925 944-7600	4844
Antioch Public Golf Corp	7992	D	925 706-4220	14987
Antioch Rotary Club	7997	E	925 757-1800	15052
Banister Electrical Inc	1731	D	925 778-7801	1455
Black Diamond Electric Inc	1731	D	925 777-3440	1467
Bond Manufacturing Co Inc **(PA)**	3272	D	866 771-2663	4421
Delta Grinding Company Inc	1629	E	925 778-3939	1154
Dennis Zai MD Inc	8011	E	925 754-8710	15376
Eastern Cntra Costa Trnst Auth	4111	E	925 754-6622	7329
Ed Supports LLC	8322	D	201 478-8711	17538
Farwest Sanitation and Storage	7359	E	925 686-1625	12041
First Student Inc	4151	C	925 754-4878	7438
Freschi Air Systems Inc	1711	D	925 827-9761	1268
Kaiser Foundation Hospitals	8011	C	925 813-6500	15446
Kaiser Foundation Hospitals	8093	C	925 779-5000	17030
Kie-Con Inc	3272	D	925 754-9494	4440
Kilgore Enterprises Llc	1389	E	925 885-8999	567
Limitless Kitchen and Bath Inc	2541	F	925 238-0046	3316
Lone Tree Cnvalescent Hosp Inc	8051	C	925 754-0470	16038
Longs Drug Stores Cal Inc	7384	E	925 754-4600	14161
Lowes Home Centers LLC	5031	C	925 756-0370	8562
Lowes Home Centers LLC	5031	C	925 779-4560	8576
Marine & Industrial Svcs Inc	3498	F	925 757-8791	4976
Markstein Sales Company	5181	C	925 755-1919	9555
Mc Donald Sloan M DDS Rbrto J	8021	E	925 778-2100	15848
Monarch Dental Corp	8049	E	925 732-4648	15892
Montrose Environmental Corp	8748	C	925 680-4300	19823
Norcal Care Centers Inc	8051	D	925 757-8787	16072
Pacific Gas and Electric Co	4911	C	925 779-7745	8185
Permanente Medical Group Inc	8011	A	925 813-6149	15605
Silgan Containers Mfg Corp	3411	E	925 778-8000	4600
Strategic Threat MGT Inc	7381	E	925 775-4777	14100
Stroer & Graff Inc	1629	E	925 778-0200	1180
Sutter Delta Medical Center	8062	C	925 779-7200	16581
Sutter Health	8062	C	925 779-7273	16588
Vortex Marine Construction Inc	1629	E	510 261-2400	1184
Wayne E Swisher Cem Contr Inc	1771	D	925 757-3660	1917

APTOS, CA - Santa Cruz County

	SIC	EMP	PHONE	ENTRY #
Aegis Senior Communities LLC	8082	C	831 684-2700	16840
Allen Property Group Inc	6512	E	831 688-5100	10376
Cabrillo Cmnty Cllege Dst Fing **(PA)**	7922	A	831 479-6100	14841
Cabrillo College Children Ctr	8351	E	831 479-6352	17869
Cabrillo Fitness Club	7997	E	831 475-5979	15067
Coldwell Bnkr Residential Brkg	6531	E	831 462-9000	10517
Easter Seals Central Cal	8322	D	831 684-2166	17537
Enlighticare Inc	8069	D	831 750-3546	16758
First Alarm **(PA)**	7382	C	831 476-1111	14133
Parkhurst Terrace	1522	D	831 685-0800	761
Pureline Oralcare Inc	3843	F	831 662-9500	7088
Santa Cruz Montessori School	8351	E	831 476-1646	18017
Seacliff Inn Inc	7011	D	831 661-4671	11448
Seascape Beach Association	7011	E	831 688-6800	11450
Seascape Resort Owners Assn	7011	D	831 688-6800	11451
Seascape Rsort Ltd A Cal Ltd P	7011	C	831 662-7120	11452
Ship Smart Inc	2671	E	831 661-4841	3379
Talmadge Construction Inc	1521	E	831 689-9133	715
Twin Lakes Baptist Church	8351	D	831 465-3302	18041
United Cmps Cnfrences Retreats	7032	E	831 684-0148	11614

ARBUCKLE, CA - Colusa County

	SIC	EMP	PHONE	ENTRY #
Alsco - Geyer Irrigation Inc	5083	D	530 476-2253	9029
Cal Vsta Erosion Ctrl Pdts LLC	3531	E	530 476-0706	5026
California Family Foods LLC	2044	D	530 476-3326	2316
Conrad Wood Preserving Co	2491	F	530 476-2894	3258
Grindstone Wines LLC	2084	E	530 393-2162	2606
Sun Valley Rice Company LLC	2044	D	530 476-3000	2328
T & P Farms	0111	C	530 476-3038	3

ARCATA, CA - Humboldt County

	SIC	EMP	PHONE	ENTRY #
American Hospital Mgt Corp **(PA)**	8062	B	707 822-3621	16320
American Hospital Mgt Corp	8062	E	707 826-8420	16321
Aquatic Designing Inc	8711	E	707 822-4629	18626
Arcata Garbage Co	4953	E	707 822-0304	8303
Baywood Golf and Country Club	7997	D	707 822-3686	15057
Bettendorf Enterprises Inc **(PA)**	4213	E	707 822-0173	7509
Bracut International Corp	2421	E	707 826-9850	3092
Crestmark Millwork Inc	2431	E	707 822-4034	3127
Cypress Grove Chevre Inc	2022	D	707 825-1100	2145
Danco Builders	1522	D	707 822-9000	743
Desserts On Us Inc	2051	F	707 822-0160	2374
Emerald Triangle MGT Group Inc	3999	F	707 630-5040	7283
Endors Toi Pbc	8742	D	434 987-0919	19500
Healthsport Ltd A Ltd Partnr **(PA)**	7991	C	707 822-3488	14952
Holly Yashi Inc	3911	D	707 822-0389	7166
Humboldt State Univ Spnsred PR	8748	D	707 826-4189	19790
JR Stephens Company	2434	E	707 825-0100	3183
Kokatat Inc	2329	D	707 822-7621	2993
Larry Schlussler	3632	F	707 822-9095	5702
Los Bagels Inc **(PA)**	2051	E	707 822-3150	2391
McCullough Construction Inc	1611	D	707 825-1014	1057
North Coast Clinics Network **(PA)**	8011	E	707 826-8610	15551
North Coast Fabricators Inc	1541	E	707 822-4629	803
North Coast Laboratories Ltd	8071	E	707 822-4649	16791
Northcast Horticulture Sup Inc **(PA)**	5083	E	707 839-0245	9042
Northcoast Childrens Svcs Inc **(PA)**	8351	C	707 822-7206	17983
Northcountry Clinic	8011	E	707 822-2481	15554
Open Door Community Hlth Ctrs	8011	E	707 822-1385	15568
Open Door Community Hlth Ctrs	8011	E	707 826-8636	15569
Open Door Community Hlth Ctrs **(PA)**	8093	D	707 826-8642	17051
Ramsey Marketing & MGT Co **(PA)**	8742	D	707 822-7665	19618
Resers Fine Foods Inc	5141	D	503 643-6431	9289
Schmidbauer Lumber Inc	2421	D	707 822-7607	3104

Name	SIC	EMP	PHONE	ENTRY #
Sun Valley Floral Group LLC	3999	A	707 826-8700	7311
Sun Valley Group Inc (PA)	0181	B	707 822-2885	139
Sunnybrae Animal Clinic Inc	0742	E	707 822-5124	338
Tofu Shop Specialty Foods Inc	2099	F	707 822-7401	2947
Toucan Inc (PA)	5094	D	707 822-6662	9185
United Indian Health Svcs Inc (PA)	8011	C	707 825-5000	15751
Wing Inflatables Inc (HQ)	3089	C	707 826-2887	4334

ARNOLD, CA - Calaveras County

Name	SIC	EMP	PHONE	ENTRY #
Adventist Health Sonora	8062	E	209 795-1270	16291
Mark Twain Medical Center	8062	E	209 795-4193	16439
Market Force Information Inc	8742	E	209 795-0830	19566
Sequoia Wood Country Club	7997	D	209 795-1000	15139
Snowshoe Brewing Co LLC (PA)	2082	E	209 795-2272	2493

ATHERTON, CA - San Mateo County

Name	SIC	EMP	PHONE	ENTRY #
Menlo Circus Club	7997	D	650 322-4616	15109
Menlo Prk-Thrton Edcatn Fndtio (PA)	8699	E	650 325-0100	18580
Netpulse Inc (PA)	7371	E	415 643-0223	12628
Novatorque Inc	3621	E	510 933-2700	5665
R A Jenson Manufacturing Co	2434	F	415 822-2732	3187

ATWATER, CA - Merced County

Name	SIC	EMP	PHONE	ENTRY #
Anberry Physcl Rhblttion Ctr I	8049	D	209 357-5121	15881
Atwater Medical Group	8011	E	209 358-5611	15286
Castle Dental Surgery Centre	8021	E	209 381-2047	15826
Castle Family Health Ctrs Inc (PA)	8011	D	209 381-2000	15330
Central Counties	8734	D	209 356-0355	19262
Certified Stainless Svc Inc	3443	D	209 356-3300	4714
Certified Stainless Svc Inc	3443	D	209 537-4747	4716
Edward Silveira (PA)	0139	E	209 394-8656	17
Esau Concrete Inc DBA Pcs Con	1531	D	209 357-7601	779
Esparza Inc	7538	E	209 358-4944	14561
Five Keys Inc	2329	F	209 358-7971	2992
Gallo Cattle Co A Ltd Partnr	0241	B	209 394-7984	213
Gallo Global Nutrition LLC	2022	C	209 394-7984	2148
Gino/Giuseppe Inc	1771	C	209 358-0556	1873
Global Modular Inc (HQ)	2452	E	209 676-8029	3252
Green Valley Labor Inc	0761	E	209 358-2851	358
Hoffmans Electronic Systems	7382	D	209 723-2667	14136
Keney Manufacturing Co (PA)	2434	F	209 358-4715	3184
MB Sports Inc	3732	E	209 357-4153	6644
Rancho Del Rey Golf Club Inc	7992	E	209 358-7131	15018
Teasdale Quality Foods Inc	2033	A	209 356-5616	2245
Tjd LLC	8059	C	209 357-3420	16279
Vieira Agricultural Entps LLC	0139	E	209 394-2771	23

AUBERRY, CA - Fresno County

Name	SIC	EMP	PHONE	ENTRY #
Messer Logging Inc	2411	E	559 855-3160	3072
Mono Wind Casino	7011	D	559 855-4350	11308
Pacific Gas and Electric Co	4911	C	559 855-6112	8172

AUBURN, CA - Placer County

Name	SIC	EMP	PHONE	ENTRY #
Absinthe Group Inc	2033	E	530 823-8527	2210
Alpine Allrgy Asthma Assoc Inc	8011	E	530 888-1016	15275
Andregg Geomatics	8713	D	530 885-7072	18920
API Marketing	2752	F	916 632-1946	3620
Armstrong Mfg & Engrg Inc	8711	E	530 888-6262	18629
Armstrong Technology Sv Inc	3599	F	530 888-6262	5477
Auburn Alehouse LP	5181	E	530 885-2537	9543
Auburn Associates Inc	7538	D	530 823-7234	14546
Auburn Journal Inc (HQ)	2711	C	530 885-5656	3413
Auburn Oaks Care Center	8051	E	650 949-7777	15912
Auburn Otptent Srgery Dgnstc C	8062	E	530 888-8899	16322
Auburn Trader Inc (DH)	2711	E	530 888-7653	3414
Broach Masters Inc	3545	E	530 885-1939	5090
Burger Physcl Therapy Svcs Inc	8049	E	530 823-6835	15887
California Envmtl Systems Inc	8711	E	530 820-3693	18655
Century Commercial Service	5063	E	530 823-1004	8850
Chapa-De Indian Hlth Prgram In (PA)	8011	E	530 887-2800	15347
Congrgtnal Ch Retirement Cmnty	8361	D	530 823-6131	18080
Court House Athletic Club Inc	7991	E	530 885-1964	14941
D O Neronde Inc	7538	D	530 823-6591	14556
Darkhorse Golf Club	7992	E	530 269-7900	14997
Decker Landscaping Inc	0782	E	916 652-1780	457
Dimaxx Technologies LLC	3827	F	530 888-1942	6871
Early Childhood Education Svcs	8351	E	530 745-1380	17926
Emeritus Corporation	8052	E	530 653-1974	16181
Foothill Oaks Care Center Inc	8051	E	530 888-6257	16006
Gold Rush Chevrolet Inc	7538	D	530 885-0471	14567
Hyland LLC	7371	F	440 788-5045	12507
Intermotive Inc	8742	E	530 823-1048	19542
IRD Acquisitions LLC	3851	F	530 210-2966	7142
James Cunningham	8111	E	530 269-1515	17296
Kp Research Services Inc	7381	E	530 878-5390	14072
Lake of Pines Association	7992	E	530 268-1141	15006
Longs Drug Stores Cal Inc	7384	E	530 823-0922	14157
Longs Drug Stores Cal Inc	7384	E	530 885-8783	14169
M Rothrock Properties Inc	7011	E	530 885-8611	11277
M Tek Corporation	7699	E	530 888-9609	14761
Mid-Placer Public Schools	4151	E	530 823-4820	7442
Morgan Advanced Ceramics Inc	2819	C	530 823-3401	3794
Mother Lode Holding Co (PA)	6361	E	530 887-2410	10204
Mydax Inc	3585	F	530 888-6662	5434
Pacific Gas and Electric Co	4911	C	530 889-3102	8165
Pass Laboratories Inc	3651	F	530 878-5350	5767
Placer Co Bar Association (PA)	8621	C	916 557-9181	18345
Placer County Water Agency (PA)	4911	E	530 823-4850	8194
Pre/Plastics Inc	3089	E	530 823-1820	4313
Purveyors Kitchen	2033	E	530 823-8527	2241
Quality Metal Fabrication LLC	3444	E	530 887-7388	4808
RES-Care Inc	8082	E	530 888-6580	16936
Ridge Golf Course LLC	7992	D	530 888-7122	15020
Riskalyze Inc (PA)	7379	C	530 748-1660	13969
Rw3 Technologies Inc (PA)	8741	E	925 743-7703	19391
Sierra Precision Optics Inc	3827	E	530 885-6979	6886
Smart & Final Stores Inc	5141	C	530 823-1205	9307
Social Services Cal Dept	8322	D	530 889-7610	17747
Surface Manufacturing Inc	3599	E	530 885-0700	5623
Tahoe Rf Semiconductor Inc	3674	E	530 823-9786	6324
Tf Welch Enterprises Inc	1711	F	916 645-4277	1380
Tri-Continent Scientific Inc	3824	D	530 273-8888	6741
University California Davis	8011	D	530 885-5618	15776
Veterans Health Administration	8011	C	530 889-0872	15793
Vian Enterprises Inc	3599	D	530 885-1997	5637
Vista Cmplete Care Inc A Prof	8011	E	530 885-3951	15809
Wallys Natural	5199	E	530 887-0396	9675

BALLICO, CA - Merced County

Name	SIC	EMP	PHONE	ENTRY #
Hilltop Ranch Inc	0723	C	209 874-1875	289

BASS LAKE, CA - Madera County

Name	SIC	EMP	PHONE	ENTRY #
Home Away Inc	7011	D	559 642-3121	11158
Pines Resorts of California (PA)	7011	C	559 642-3121	11370
Worldmark Club	7011	E	559 642-6780	11582

BAY POINT, CA - Contra Costa County

Name	SIC	EMP	PHONE	ENTRY #
Ambrose Recreation & Park Dst	7999	E	925 458-1601	15172
Elite Security Group Inc	7382	E	925 597-8852	14130
Henkel US Operations Corp	8711	E	925 458-8086	18729
Kahn Rennaissance LLC	7213	C	510 260-3161	11635
Keller Canyon Landfill Company	4953	A	925 458-9800	8338

BAYSIDE, CA - Humboldt County

Name	SIC	EMP	PHONE	ENTRY #
Streamguys Inc	7389	E	707 667-9479	14418

BEAR VALLEY, CA - Calaveras County

Name	SIC	EMP	PHONE	ENTRY #
Bear Valley Ski Co	7999	B	209 753-2301	15182
Lodge At The Bear Valley Inc	7011	E	209 753-2325	11265

BELMONT, CA - San Mateo County

Name	SIC	EMP	PHONE	ENTRY #
Anita Borg Inst For Women Tech	8699	D	650 236-4756	18545
Belmont Oaks Academy	8351	E	650 593-6175	17858
Carlmont Gardens LLC	8059	D	650 591-9601	16226
Clark Pest Ctrl Stockton Inc	7342	E	650 596-1270	11891
Cutting Edge Machining Inc (PA)	3599	E	408 738-8677	5500
Fineline Carpentry Inc	2434	E	650 592-2442	3179
Folio3 Software Inc	7372	E	650 802-8668	13168
General Radar Corp	3812	E	626 319-5827	6670
Grand Prix Belmont LLC	7011	E	650 591-8600	11117
Immaculate Heart Mary School	8351	E	650 593-2344	17954
Island Hospitality MGT LLC	7011	E	650 591-8600	11202
James Electronics Limited	5065	D	650 592-6718	8922
JS Trade Bindery Services Inc	2789	E	650 486-1475	3761
Martin Ragno & Associates Inc	0782	E	650 325-4996	483
Moquin Press Inc	2752	D	650 592-0575	3678
Nikon Precision Inc (DH)	5084	C	650 508-4674	9083
Nikon Research Corp America	3825	E	800 446-4566	6775
Pacific Gas and Electric Co	4911	C	650 592-9411	8139
Pacific Screw Products Inc	3599	E	650 583-9682	5588
Peninsula Floors Inc	7389	E	650 593-5825	14363
Powerhouse Engineering Inc	3999	F	650 226-3560	7301
Powervision Inc	7841	E	650 620-9948	14834
Prenav Inc	3812	E	650 264-7279	6679
Quasar Engineering Inc	8711	D	650 508-6600	18796
Ringcentral Inc (PA)	7374	E	650 472-4100	13753
Silverado Senior Living Inc	8051	D	650 226-8017	16120
Silverado Senior Living Inc	8051	D	650 264-9020	16121
Tectura Corporation (PA)	7379	E	650 273-4249	13993
Westlake Development Group LLC	8741	E	650 579-1010	19424
Woodmont Realty Advisors Inc	6371	B	650 592-3960	10219

BELVEDERE, CA - Marin County

Name	SIC	EMP	PHONE	ENTRY #
Pacific Union Co	6531	D	415 789-8686	10634

BELVEDERE TIBURON, CA - Marin County

Name	SIC	EMP	PHONE	ENTRY #
1651 Tiburon Hotel LLC	7011	D	401 946-4600	10901
Angel Island-Tiburon Ferry Inc	4499	E	415 435-2131	7734
Digital Foundry Inc	7379	E	415 789-1600	13881
Higherring	7389	E	415 272-6948	14297
Magave Tequila Inc	5182	E	415 515-3536	9581
Marcolin USA Inc	5048	E	415 383-6348	8799
Marin Cnvlscent Rhblttion Hosp	8051	E	415 435-4554	16042
Melissa Bradley RE Inc	6531	E	415 435-2145	10619
Mila Usa Inc	3634	E	415 734-8540	5705
Nes Health Care Group	8011	E	415 435-4591	15548
R/GA Media Group Inc	7374	E	415 624-2000	13748
Riviera Partners LLC (PA)	7361	E	877 748-4372	12129
San Francisco Yacht Club	7997	E	415 435-9133	15133
Stalker Software Inc	7372	E	415 569-2281	13465
System Operation Services Inc (PA)	8748	E	800 699-7674	19871
Tiburon Hotel LLC	7011	E	415 435-5996	11533
Tiburon Lodge LLC	7011	E	415 435-3133	11534
Tiburon Peninsula Club	7997	E	415 789-7900	15161
Vital Farmland Holdings LLC	7389	D	415 465-2400	14457

BEN LOMOND, CA - Santa Cruz County

Name	SIC	EMP	PHONE	ENTRY #
Childrens Ctr of San Lrnzo Vly	8351	D	831 336-2857	17899

BENICIA, CA - Solano County

	SIC	EMP	PHONE	ENTRY #
1-800 Radiator & A/C **(DH)**	5013	D	707 747-7400	8435
Abb Inc	5063	D	808 497-7240	8836
Alfred Conhagen Inc California	5085	E	707 746-4848	9109
All-Points Petroleum LLC	5172	D	707 745-1116	9527
Allied Exhaust Systems Inc **(PA)**	5013	E	707 745-0506	8438
American Civil Const	1611	D	707 746-8028	1007
American Civil Constrs LLC	1629	D	707 746-8028	1145
Anthony Trevino	1752	D	707 747-4776	1764
Applied Sewing Resources Inc	2211	E	707 748-1614	2963
Aquatic Environments Inc	1629	E	925 521-0400	1147
Awt Construction Group Inc	1521	D	707 746-7500	613
Barrys Cultured Marble Inc	3281	F	707 745-3444	4516
Bay Vave Service & Engineering	7699	D	925 849-8600	14741
Benicia Fabrication & Mch Inc	3443	C	707 745-8111	4712
Benicia Plumbing Inc	1711	D	707 745-2930	1218
C E Toland & Son	1799	C	707 747-1000	2013
Califrnia Erctors Bay Area Inc	1791	C	707 746-1990	1923
Central Coast Wine Company **(DH)**	5182	C	707 745-8500	9570
Certifiedsafety Inc	8742	D	707 747-9400	19469
Clean Harbors Envmtl Svcs Inc	8748	D	707 747-6699	19744
Cork Supply Usa Inc	5199	E	707 746-0353	9652
Custom Coils Inc	3677	F	707 752-8633	6379
Delta Tech Service Inc **(PA)**	7349	E	707 745-2080	11943
Dunlop Manufacturing Inc **(PA)**	3931	D	707 745-2722	7171
Durkee Drayage Company	4214	D	510 970-7550	7620
Dusouth Industries	3823	E	707 745-5117	6716
East Bay Tire Co	3011	F	707 747-5613	4198
F3 and Associates Inc **(PA)**	8713	D	707 748-4300	18923
Flatiron Construction Corp	8741	B	707 742-6270	19335
Flatiron West Inc	1622	C	707 742-6000	1082
Frontline Envmtl Tech Group In	3823	E	707 745-1116	6720
Gibbs Plastic & Rubber LLC	3069	F	707 746-7300	4215
Gibson Printing & Pubg Inc	2711	E	707 745-0733	3441
Gold Rush Kettle Korn Llc	2064	E	707 747-6773	2428
Gunnebo Entrance Control Inc **(HQ)**	3829	F	707 748-0885	6904
Henry Wine Group LLC **(HQ)**	5182	B	707 745-8500	9579
High End Development Inc	1799	C	925 687-2540	2036
Innovel Solutions Inc	4731	A	707 748-1940	7839
J F Hillebrand Usa Inc	4731	E	707 996-5686	7840
Jae Properties Inc	6531	E	707 747-2861	10583
Kwik Bond Polymers LLC	2891	E	866 434-1772	4151
Lamassu Utility Services Inc	7699	E	707 750-5130	14759
Lane Safety Co Inc	7363	E	707 746-4820	12179
Lathrop Construction Assoc Inc **(PA)**	1542	D	707 746-8000	912
Metlsaw Systems Inc	3541	E	707 746-6200	5076
Metropolitan Van and Stor Inc **(PA)**	4213	E	707 745-1150	7568
Molecule Labs Inc	2869	E	925 473-8200	4125
Nielsen Company (us) LLC	8732	E	707 746-6905	19173
Nor Cal Truck Sales & Mfg	3537	F	925 787-9735	5065
Onsite Health Inc	8099	D	888 411-2290	17165
Patrick L Roetzer DDS Inc	8021	E	707 745-8002	15854
Petrochem Insulation Inc	1742	D	707 645-1121	1700
Phillips 66 Spectrum Corp	2992	D	707 745-6100	4196
Ponder Environmental Svcs Inc **(PA)**	8748	E	707 748-7775	19839
Pro-Form Manufacturing LLC	8734	C	707 752-9010	19282
Quality Erectors Cnstr Co Inc	1791	D	707 746-1233	1930
Ralphs-Pugh Co Inc	3535	D	707 745-6222	5055
Rapid Accu-Form Inc	3089	F	707 745-1879	4314
Reyes Coca-Cola Bottling LLC	2086	D	707 747-2000	2807
Schoenstein & Co	3931	E	707 747-5858	7174
Sonia Corina Inc	8099	E	707 644-4491	17181
Speedway Copy Systems Inc	7334	E	415 495-4330	11852
Suba Mfg Inc	2541	F	707 745-0358	3320
Swan Associates Incorporated	7699	E	707 746-1989	14776
Terminix Company LLC	7342	E	800 480-8439	11908
Total-Western Inc	1389	F	707 747-5506	574
Trimac Trnsp Svcs Wstn Inc	4213	E	707 745-5414	7606
Underground Cnstr Co Inc	4931	C	707 746-8800	8216
Unico Mechanical Corp	5084	D	707 745-4540	9101
Valero Energy Corporation	2911	B	707 745-7011	4184
Valero Ref Company-California	2911	A	707 745-7011	4185
Valley Fine Foods Company Inc **(PA)**	2041	D	707 746-6888	2312
Water One Industries Inc **(PA)**	3589	E	707 747-4300	5451
Westcott Designs Inc	2511	E	510 367-7229	3284
Western Sun Enterprises Inc	1731	E	707 748-2542	1636
World Projects Corporation	4724	E	707 556-5885	7811

BERKELEY, CA - Alameda County

	SIC	EMP	PHONE	ENTRY #
24 Hour Fitness Usa Inc	7991	E	510 524-4583	14922
3d Robotics Inc **(PA)**	3699	D	415 599-1404	6508
4d Sight Inc	7372	E	415 425-1321	12944
A Better Way Inc **(PA)**	8399	C	510 601-0203	18216
A T Associates Inc	8059	E	510 649-6670	16213
A3Geo-Ce&g Joint Venture	8711	E	510 705-1664	18610
Aduro Gvax Inc	2834	E	510 848-4400	3834
Agenus West LLC	2836	E	781 674-4400	4032
Ala Csta Ctr Prgram For The Dv **(PA)**	8351	E	510 527-2550	17853
Albert Nahman Plumbing & Htg	1711	E	510 843-6904	1195
Alderson Construction Inc	1522	E	510 841-7159	736
Alta Bates Summit Foundation	8011	D	510 204-1667	15276
Alward Construction Company	1521	E	510 527-6498	610
Alzheimers Svcs of East Bay **(PA)**	8322	E	510 644-3181	17420
American Assn Univ Women	8641	E	510 528-3284	18385
Andrew M Jordan Inc	1794	D	510 999-6000	1950
Annies Inc **(HQ)**	2099	C	510 558-7500	2867
Arboricultural Specialties Inc	0783	E	510 549-3954	512
Art of Muse LLC	2511	E	510 644-2100	3273
Ashby Lumber Company **(PA)**	7513	D	510 843-4832	14468
Assoc Students University CA **(PA)**	7999	C	510 642-5420	15176
Associed Stdnts of The Univ CA	2741	D	510 590-7874	3558
Assoction Asn/Pcfic Cmnty Hlth	8611	E	510 272-9536	18298
Attocube Systems Inc **(DH)**	8711	E	510 649-9245	18631
Autumn Press Inc	2752	E	510 654-4545	3623
Backroads **(PA)**	4725	D	510 527-1555	7815
Bancroft Club	7011	E	510 549-0152	10944
Barra LLC **(HQ)**	7372	B	510 548-5442	13009
Bay Area Hspano Inst For Advnc	8351	D	510 525-1463	17857
Bayer Healthcare LLC	2834	C	510 705-7545	3863
Bebop Sensors Inc **(PA)**	2296	E	503 875-4990	2980
Berkeley	7011	E	510 845-7300	10952
Berkeley Cement Inc	1771	C	510 525-8175	1853
Berkeley Communications Corp	7379	E	510 644-1599	13855
Berkeley Community Health Prj	8082	E	510 548-2570	16858
Berkeley Dog & Cat Hosp Inc	0742	D	510 848-5041	323
Berkeley Downtown Ht Owner LLC	7011	D	510 982-2100	10953
Berkeley Mllwk & Furn Co Inc	2511	E	510 549-2854	3275
Berkeley Montessori School Inc	8351	D	510 843-9374	17859
Berkeley Pediatric Med Group	8011	E	510 848-2566	15296
Berkeley Repertory Theatre **(PA)**	7922	D	510 204-8901	14837
Berkeley Student Coop Inc	7041	D	510 848-1936	11624
Berkeley Symphony Orchestra	7929	E	510 841-2800	14869
Berkeley Therapy Institute	8049	D	510 841-8484	15883
Berkeley Youth Alternatives **(PA)**	8322	D	510 845-9010	17442
Berkeleyside LLC	2711	F	510 671-0380	3417
Berkley Crdovascular Med Group	8011	E	510 204-1691	15297
Berkwood Hedge School	8351	D	510 883-6990	17860
Better Way Fster Fmly Adption	8322	E	510 601-0203	17444
Bierwith Forge & Tool Inc	3462	D	510 526-5034	4875
Bonsai Ai Inc	7372	E	510 900-1112	13032
Boykin Mgt Co Ltd Lblty Co	7011	D	510 548-7920	10969
C P Shades Inc	7389	C	510 647-9605	14221
Cancer Prevention Inst Cal	8733	E	510 608-5000	19204
Caribou Biosciences Inc	2836	D	510 982-6030	4041
Cellmobility Inc	3399	E	510 549-3300	4589
Cemex Corp	5032	C	800 992-3639	8623
Chaparral Foundation	8051	D	510 848-8774	15959
Claremont Hotel Properties LLC	7011	A	510 843-3000	11010
Clp Apg LLC	2731	C	510 528-1444	3530
Consolidated Printers Inc	2732	E	510 843-8524	3551
Core+data Corporation	4813	E	510 540-0168	7943
Curacubby Inc	7372	F	415 200-3373	13101
Design Community & Envmt Inc **(PA)**	8748	D	510 848-3815	19760
Direct Line Inc	7389	E	510 843-3900	14255
Direct Urgent Care Inc	8011	E	510 686-3621	15382
Doughtronics Inc **(PA)**	2051	E	510 524-1327	2377
Doughtronics Inc	2051	E	510 843-2978	2378
DSM Biomedical Inc	8731	C	510 841-8800	19053
Earth Island Institute Inc	8699	D	510 859-9100	18564
Easy Does It Emerg Svcs Progrm	8699	D	510 845-5513	18565
Emanio Inc **(PA)**	7371	C	510 849-9300	12420
Endsight	7379	D	510 280-2019	13887
Energy Berkeley Office US Dept	8733	C	510 486-4033	19217
Enthalpy Analytical Llc	8734	E	510 486-0900	19265
Ep Executive Press Inc	2741	F	925 685-5111	3570
Evolv Surfaces Inc	2542	C	415 767-4600	3324
Fadelli Concrete Pumping **(PA)**	1771	E	510 525-4111	1868
Fantasy Inc	3652	D	510 486-2038	5777
Four D Imaging	3829	F	510 290-3533	6902
Gatsby Inc	7371	E	650 468-0587	12470
Gobp Holdings Inc	6799	C	510 845-1999	10848
Graysix Company	3444	E	510 845-5936	4765
GTM Technologies LLC **(PA)**	3443	F	415 856-0570	4721
Gu	2834	F	510 527-4664	3922
Hanson Aggrgtes Md-Pacific Inc	3273	F	510 526-1611	4486
Harsch Investment Realty LLC	7011	C	510 843-3000	11130
Hasselgren Engineering Inc	8711	E	510 524-2485	18727
Hesperian Health Guides **(PA)**	2731	E	510 845-1447	3534
Holiday Inn Ex Ht & Suites	7011	E	510 548-1700	11149
Holophane Corporation	3646	C	510 540-0156	5736
Homeenergy Inc	1711	D	707 200-8287	1279
Hornblower Yachts LLC	4489	D	916 446-1185	7721
Hotel Durant A Ltd Partnership	7011	D	510 845-8981	11163
I Manageproperty Inc	7372	E	510 665-0665	13220
Indepndent Brkley Stdnt Pubg I	2711	D	510 548-8300	3448
Interaction Associates Inc **(PA)**	8742	E	617 234-2700	19541
International House	7021	C	510 642-9490	11591
International Society For	8732	E	510 680-6126	19167
Internet-Journals LLC	7379	D	510 665-1200	13918
Interntional Cmpt Science Inst	8733	E	510 643-9153	19222
Interntnal Child Rsrce Exch In **(PA)**	8399	C	510 644-1000	18234
ISI Inspection Services Inc **(PA)**	7389	D	510 900-2101	14311
Ivu Traffic Technologies Inc	3714	F	415 655-2200	6583
Janco Chemical Corporation	2851	E	510 527-9770	4105
Jewish Cmnty Fdrtion of Grter	8322	D	510 848-0237	17622
Jewish Community Ctr of E Bay	8322	D	510 848-0237	17623
Jewish Fmly & Cmnty Svcs E Bay **(PA)**	8322	E	510 704-7475	17628
Kaiser Foundation Hospitals	6324	C	510 559-5362	10121
L J Kruse Co	1711	D	510 644-0260	1299
Lead Genius	7311	E	415 969-2915	11766
Libby Laboratories Inc	2844	E	510 527-5400	4087
Lifelong Medical Care **(PA)**	8011	E	510 704-6010	15505
Malibu Compost LLC **(PA)**	2875	E	800 282-6676	4140
Mango Materials Inc	2821	F	650 440-0430	3805

	SIC	EMP	PHONE	ENTRY #
McCutcheon Construction Co Inc	1521	E	925 280-0083	672
McKesson Corporation	5122	D	510 666-0854	9230
Meyer Sound Laboratories Inc **(PA)**	3651	C	510 486-1166	5764
Model Schl Cmprhnsive Hmnstic	8351	E	510 549-2711	17976
Moore Iacofano Goltsman Inc **(PA)**	8748	D	510 845-7549	19824
Moveonorg Political Action	8651	E	202 465-4234	18538
Mulholland Brothers **(PA)**	2512	D	415 824-5995	3291
Nefeli Networks Inc	3861	E	510 859-4665	7155
New Avenue Inc	2452	E	510 621-8679	3254
New Bridge Foundation Inc	8093	D	510 548-7270	17049
Newfield Wireless Inc **(DH)**	8748	D	510 848-8248	19828
O C Jones & Sons Inc **(PA)**	1611	C	510 526-3424	1066
OC Sailing Club Inc	7999	D	510 843-4200	15224
Ocadian Care Centers LLC	8051	B	510 204-5801	16083
Parker Powis Inc	3579	D	510 848-2463	5425
Permanente Medical Group Inc	6324	B	510 559-5119	10152
Permanente Medical Group Inc	8011	A	510 559-5338	15618
Pet Emergency Treatment Svc	0742	E	510 548-6684	332
Peter Wlker Prtners Ldscp Arch	0781	D	510 849-9494	436
Poly-Seal Industries	3069	F	510 843-9722	4223
Public Health Institute	8733	D	510 285-5500	19233
Qualified Digital LLC	7389	E	518 727-3997	14379
Rare Barrel LLC	2082	E	510 984-6585	2490
Rastergraf Inc **(PA)**	3672	E	510 849-4801	5965
Redf	8322	E	415 561-6677	17682
Relationalai Inc	7372	F	650 307-8776	13403
Represent Development	7371	E	510 944-1938	12742
Research Dev GL Pdts & Eqp Inc	3231	F	510 547-6464	4392
Ripple Foods Pbc	8731	D	510 269-2563	19118
Rose Grammas Garden Inn	7011	E	510 549-2145	11419
Sanhyd Inc	8051	D	510 843-2131	16111
Satellite First Communities LP **(PA)**	6513	D	510 647-0700	10458
Sensys Networks Inc **(HQ)**	3669	D	510 548-4620	5896
Seva Foundation	8099	D	510 845-7382	17179
Shattuck Health Care Inc	8051	D	510 665-2800	16114
Simply Asia Foods LLC	2099	E	800 967-8424	2943
Society For The Study Ntiv Art	2731	E	510 549-4270	3545
Southwick Inc **(PA)**	7539	E	510 845-2530	14624
Souvenir Coffee Corporation **(PA)**	5099	E	510 919-2777	9202
Steep Hill Inc **(PA)**	8734	C	510 562-7400	19286
Step One Nursery School	8351	E	510 527-9021	18035
Stillwter Ecsystem Wtrshed Rvr **(PA)**	8748	D	510 848-8098	19866
Strathmoore Press Inc	7389	E	510 843-8888	14417
Sun Light & Power	7389	D	510 845-2997	14419
Sunsystem Technology LLC	3674	C	510 984-2027	6318
Suntech America Inc **(PA)**	3433	F	415 882-9922	4640
Surgery Ctr of Alta Btes Smmit **(HQ)**	8062	A	510 204-4444	16564
Surgery Ctr of Alta Btes Smmit	8062	E	510 204-1591	16566
Sutter Bay Hospitals	8062	D	510 869-6199	16569
Sutter Bay Hospitals	8062	D	510 204-4444	16574
Sutter Health	8062	C	510 204-1554	16648
Takara Sake USA Inc **(DH)**	2085	E	510 540-8250	2779
Tencue Productions LLC	7389	E	510 841-3000	14431
Terminal Manufacturing Co LLC	3441	E	510 526-3071	4689
Third Culture Food Group Inc	2051	E	650 479-4585	2408
Tipping Mar & Associates	8711	E	510 549-1906	18838
Tom Sawyer Software Corp **(PA)**	7371	E	510 208-4370	12867
Toolworks Inc	8322	E	510 649-1322	17770
United States Dept of Energy	8733	A	510 486-4000	19240
United States Dept of Energy	8731	A	510 486-4936	19142
University Cal Press Fundation	2731	E	510 642-4247	3548
Upside Foods Inc	2099	E	510 746-1198	2953
Valor Compounding Pharmacy Inc	2834	E	510 548-8777	4001
Vector Data LLC	3571	D	408 933-3266	5279
Vega Economic Consulting	8748	E	510 280-5520	19884
Vital Vittles Bakery Inc	2051	E	510 644-2022	2410
Voicebase Inc **(PA)**	7374	E	415 886-7799	13768
Walashek Industrial & Mar Inc	3731	E	206 624-2880	6640
Western Roto Engravers Inc	2759	E	510 525-2950	3755
Westpost Berkeley LLC	7011	E	510 548-7920	11574
Winnarainbow Inc **(PA)**	7032	E	510 525-4304	11616
Wright Institute	8049	E	510 841-9230	15902
Xinet LLC **(HQ)**	7372	D	510 845-0555	13535
Xpansiv Data Systems Inc	7372	E	415 915-5124	13537
Young MNS Chrstn Assn of E Bay	8641	B	510 486-8400	18493
Young MNS Chrstn Assn of E Bay	8641	B	510 848-9092	18494
Young MNS Chrstn Assn of E Bay	8641	B	510 848-9622	18495
Young MNS Chrstn Assn of E Bay	8641	B	510 526-2146	18497
Young MNS Chrstn Assn of E Bay	8641	B	510 644-6290	18499
Young MNS Chrstn Assn of E Bay	8641	B	510 848-6800	18509
Young MNS Chrstn Assn of E Bay	8641	B	510 559-2090	18511
Zenbooth Inc	2521	E	510 646-8368	3310
Zendar Inc **(PA)**	8742	E	510 590-8060	19675

BIEBER, CA - Lassen County

	SIC	EMP	PHONE	ENTRY #
Del Logging Inc	2411	F	530 294-5492	3058

BIG CREEK, CA - Fresno County

	SIC	EMP	PHONE	ENTRY #
Southern California Edison Co	4911	C	559 893-3611	8201
Southern California Edison Co	4911	C	559 893-2037	8202

BIGGS, CA - Butte County

	SIC	EMP	PHONE	ENTRY #
Califrnia Coop Rice RES Fndtio	8731	E	530 868-5481	19039
Chuck Jones Flying Service **(PA)**	0721	E	530 868-5798	251
Red Top Rice Growers	0723	D	530 868-5975	303

BLAIRSDEN, CA - Plumas County

	SIC	EMP	PHONE	ENTRY #
Territory Designs Inc	7011	E	530 836-2511	11530

BLUE LAKE, CA - Humboldt County

	SIC	EMP	PHONE	ENTRY #
Blue Lake Casino	7011	D	707 668-5101	10963
Mad River Brewing Company Inc	2082	E	707 668-4151	2484

BODEGA, CA - Sonoma County

	SIC	EMP	PHONE	ENTRY #
Pacific Lodging Group	7011	E	707 875-2217	11349

BODEGA BAY, CA - Sonoma County

	SIC	EMP	PHONE	ENTRY #
Bbcert	8742	E	480 220-3799	19453
Bodega Bay Associates	7011	D	650 330-8888	10965
Bodega Harbour Homeowners Assn	8641	D	707 875-3519	18393
NAPA Valley Lodge LP	7011	D	707 875-3525	11324

BOLINAS, CA - Marin County

	SIC	EMP	PHONE	ENTRY #
Commonweal	8322	D	415 868-0970	17492

BOONVILLE, CA - Mendocino County

	SIC	EMP	PHONE	ENTRY #
Anderson Valley Brewing Inc	2082	E	707 895-2337	2471

BOULDER CREEK, CA - Santa Cruz County

	SIC	EMP	PHONE	ENTRY #
Cortlandt Liquidating LLC	6531	D	831 338-4500	10526
Godfathers Exterminator Inc	7342	E	831 338-4800	11899
Heartmath LLC	6794	E	831 338-8700	10805
Institute of Heartmath	8733	E	831 338-8500	19220
Young MNS Chrstn Assn Slcon Vl	8641	C	831 338-2128	18533

BRANSCOMB, CA - Mendocino County

	SIC	EMP	PHONE	ENTRY #
Harwood Products	2431	C	707 984-1601	3135

BRENTWOOD, CA - Contra Costa County

	SIC	EMP	PHONE	ENTRY #
Assocted Vtrnary Practices Inc	0742	E	925 634-1177	322
Bay Standard Inc	5085	D	925 634-1181	9110
Bay Standard Manufacturing Inc **(PA)**	3452	E	925 634-1181	4871
Brentwood Press & Pubg Co LLC	2711	E	925 516-4757	3419
Caps Oak Street Bar and Grill	7299	E	925 634-1025	11710
Christian Education Dev Co	8351	E	925 240-5437	17905
Clark Pest Ctrl Stockton Inc	7342	E	209 483-4043	11882
Club Corp Incorporated	7991	D	925 240-2990	14937
Frank and Patricia Maggiore **(PA)**	0161	E	925 634-4176	30
Groundworks Inc	1771	D	925 513-0300	1878
Harvest Park Bowl	7933	D	925 516-1221	14895
Hot Line Construction Inc	1731	A	925 634-9333	1517
Hudson Excavation Inc	1794	E	925 250-1990	1962
Nanval Inc	6531	D	925 634-3200	10626
Nor-Cal Overhead Inc	3442	F	925 240-5141	4706
Nova Care Home Health Services	8082	E	925 240-2334	16917
Premier Floor Care Inc **(PA)**	7349	D	925 679-4901	11986
Promerio Inc **(PA)**	8721	D	925 240-2400	18987
Rlw Properties LLC	6512	D	925 418-5668	10403
Rodda Electric Inc **(PA)**	1731	C	925 240-6024	1590
San Andreas Farms Co	0131	E	925 634-1717	11
Sdg Architects Inc	8712	E	925 634-7000	18912
Solarbos **(HQ)**	3613	D	925 456-7744	5655
Storm Wtr Insptn Mint Svcs Inc	7389	E	925 516-8966	14416
T&C Roofing Inc	1761	D	925 513-8463	1841
Thorpe Design Inc	1711	D	925 634-0787	1382

BRIDGEPORT, CA - Mono County

	SIC	EMP	PHONE	ENTRY #
Twin Lakes Resort	7011	E	760 932-7751	11547

BRISBANE, CA - San Mateo County

	SIC	EMP	PHONE	ENTRY #
Aimmune Therapeutics Inc	2834	C	650 614-5220	3837
Aircargo Communities Inc	7374	E	650 952-9050	13692
Aircraft Technical Publishers **(PA)**	2741	E	415 330-9500	3553
Bi-Rite Restaurant Sup Co Inc	5141	B	415 656-0187	9262
Childcare Careers LLC	7363	A	650 372-0211	12162
Covenant Aviation Security LLC	7381	A	650 219-3473	14048
Cutera Inc **(PA)**	3845	B	415 657-5500	7102
Edward B Ward & Company Inc **(DH)**	5075	E	415 330-6600	9009
Expeditors Intl Wash Inc	4731	E	415 657-3600	7833
F W Spencer & Son Inc	1711	C	415 468-5000	1259
Faster Faster Inc	3714	E	323 839-0654	6579
Fedex Corporation	7389	E	415 657-0403	14271
Florian Industries Inc	3441	F	415 330-9000	4661
Fong Brothers Printing Inc **(PA)**	2752	C	415 467-1050	3647
Hyperion Therapeutics Inc	2834	E	650 492-1385	3924
Infoimage of California Inc **(PA)**	2759	D	650 473-6388	3739
Inxeption Corporation	7379	C	888 852-4783	13920
Leemah Corporation **(PA)**	3671	C	415 394-1288	5903
Lettieri & Co Ltd	5149	E	415 657-3392	9464
Lincoln Brdcstg A Cal Ltd Prtn **(PA)**	4833	D	415 508-1056	8053
Lyon Medical Construction Inc	1542	E	415 508-1970	917
Macrogenics West Inc	2834	E	650 624-2600	3944
Mammoth Biosciences Inc	8731	D	770 655-1937	19087
Maverick Therapeutics Inc	2834	E	650 684-7140	3945
Michaael S Hensley	7299	C	650 692-7007	11725
Mjc International Group LLC **(HQ)**	5136	E	415 467-9500	9248
Myokardia Inc	2834	C	650 741-0900	3951
Myovant Sciences Inc	5122	C	650 392-0222	9233
Neumora Therapeutics Inc	8733	D	510 828-4062	19226
Ning Inc	4813	E	650 244-4000	7975
Norman S Wrght Mech Eqp Crprtn **(PA)**	5075	D	415 467-7600	9011
Northwest Administrators Inc	6411	E	650 570-7300	10324
Oakville Produce Partners LLC	5148	C	415 647-2991	9422
Page One Automotive **(PA)**	7513	E	415 467-1000	14472
Pittsburg Wholesale Groc Inc	5141	E	415 865-0404	9284
Roto Rooter Service	7699	D	415 656-2130	14773
Sage Hospitality Resources LLC	7011	C	650 589-1600	11426
Sangamo Therapeutics Inc **(PA)**	2836	B	510 970-6000	4056

GEOGRAPHIC

Employment Codes: A=Over 500 employees, B=251-500, C=101-250, D=51-100, E=20-50 F=10-19
2022 Northern California Business Directory and Buyers Guide
© Mergent Inc. 1-800-342-5647
1133

	SIC	EMP	PHONE	ENTRY #
Sfo Apparel	2339	C	415 468-8816	3013
Sierra Pt Lbr & Plywd Co Inc **(PA)**	5031	D	415 468-1000	8607
Silverado Senior Living Inc	8052	D	650 226-4152	16203
Trove Recommerce Inc	8742	C	925 726-3316	19656
Xojet Sales LLC	6799	E	877 599-6538	10897

BROOKDALE, CA - Santa Cruz County

	SIC	EMP	PHONE	ENTRY #
Brookdale Inn and Spa	7011	D	831 588-6609	10979

BROOKS, CA - Yolo County

	SIC	EMP	PHONE	ENTRY #
Cache Creek Casino Resort	7011	A	530 796-3118	10982

BURLINGAME, CA - San Mateo County

	SIC	EMP	PHONE	ENTRY #
24 Hour Fitness Usa Inc	7991	E	650 343-7922	14921
24i Unit Media Inc	7371	C	818 802-9995	12212
765 Airport Boulevard Partnr	7011	E	650 347-7800	10907
Abx Engineering Inc	5065	D	650 552-2300	8888
Acumen LLC	7373	C	650 558-8882	13550
Advanced Components Mfg	3599	E	650 344-6272	5465
Airline Coach Service Inc **(PA)**	4111	E	650 697-7733	7323
Allen Drywall & Associates	1742	D	650 579-0664	1658
Alpha Pet Grooming Salon LLC	0752	E	650 271-4282	350
Amato Industries Incorporated	4119	E	650 697-5548	7367
American Carequest Inc **(PA)**	8082	E	415 885-9100	16846
AMS Relocation Incorporated	4212	D	650 697-3530	7448
Anza Parking Corporation	7521	E	650 348-8800	14508
Aperia Technologies Inc	3559	E	415 494-9624	5140
Ares Holding Corporation **(PA)**	8711	E	650 401-7100	18627
Ares Project Management LLC **(HQ)**	8711	D	650 401-7100	18628
Ares Technical Services Corp	8742	A	650 401-7100	19448
Asia America Enterprise Inc	2752	E	650 348-2333	3621
B & N Industries Inc **(PA)**	5046	D	650 593-4127	8764
Burlingame Htg Ventilation Inc	3444	E	650 697-9142	4745
BURLINGAME SENIOR CARE LLC	8361	E	650 692-3758	18064
Caban Systems Inc	3691	E	831 245-1608	6486
Cala Health Inc	3845	D	415 890-3961	7098
Calcpa Institute	8641	E	800 922-5272	18399
California Teachers Assn **(PA)**	8621	C	650 697-1400	18332
Califrnia Soc Crtif Pub Accntn **(PA)**	8621	E	650 522-3000	18335
Carbon Design Innovations Inc **(PA)**	3624	E	650 697-7070	5670
Cardivsclar Assoc of Peninsula	8011	E	650 652-8600	15326
Carr Mc Clellan Ingersoll Thom **(PA)**	8111	D	650 342-9600	17226
Century Theatres Inc	7833	E	650 340-1516	14827
Cielo House Inc **(HQ)**	8093	E	650 292-0253	17000
City of Burlingame	1611	E	650 558-7670	1028
Coastal Pacific Fd Distrs Inc	5141	D	650 692-8211	9267
Coit Services Inc	7217	D	650 697-6190	11660
Coldwell Bnkr Residential Brkg	6531	E	650 558-4200	10516
Collabrative DRG Discovery Inc	7372	E	650 204-3084	13084
Color Health Inc **(PA)**	5047	B	650 651-7116	8777
Community Rcnstrction Slutions	1522	E	650 692-3030	739
Corvus Pharmaceuticals Inc	2834	D	650 900-4520	3886
Cotchett Pitre & McCarthy LLP	8111	E	650 697-6000	17237
Crown Shtmtl & Skylights Inc	1761	F	415 467-5008	1793
Crystal Springs Golf Partners	7992	E	650 342-4188	14996
Devincenzi Metal Products Inc	3444	D	650 692-5800	4755
Disney Construction Inc	1611	D	650 689-5149	1033
Djont Operations LLC	7011	C	650 342-4600	11050
Drivewyze Inc	7371	E	888 988-1590	12404
Dyned International Inc **(PA)**	7371	D	650 375-7011	12408
Emmett W McCrkle Inc Insur Svc	6411	E	650 349-2364	10279
Environmental Chemical Corp **(PA)**	8711	D	650 347-1555	18705
Epitomics Inc **(HQ)**	8731	C	650 583-6688	19058
Foundation For Educational ADM	6732	E	916 444-3216	10788
Garratt-Callahan Company **(PA)**	2899	D	650 697-5811	4160
General Mortgage Capital Corp **(PA)**	6162	D	650 340-7800	9906
Gilbert Smolin MD Inc	8011	E	650 697-3200	15415
Greenough Consulting Group LLC	8742	E	650 548-6900	19522
Grm Byshore Property Owner LLC	7011	E	650 347-2381	11120
Guardsmark LLC	7381	C	650 652-9130	14066
Guittard Chocolate Holdings Co	2066	C	650 697-4427	2438
Hamilton Partners	8742	D	650 347-8800	19528
Hanergy Holding (america) LLC **(HQ)**	3674	C	650 288-3722	6140
Hanergy Holding America Inc	4911	B	650 288-3722	8115
Hcr Manorcare Inc	8051	D	419 252-5743	16019
Hotel Leger LLC	7011	E	209 286-1401	11166
Imply Data Inc **(PA)**	7372	C	415 685-8187	13225
Innowave Marketing Group LLC	8742	E	650 454-4952	19539
J J J & K Inc	1751	E	650 373-3900	1744
Jeremiah Phillips LLC	4111	D	650 697-7733	7337
July Systems Inc **(PA)**	3695	D	650 685-2460	6502
Kindred Biosciences Inc **(HQ)**	2834	C	650 701-7901	3936
Lahlouh Inc	2752	C	650 692-6600	3670
Loma Vista Medical Inc	3841	E	650 490-4747	6997
Lyra Health Inc	8011	C	650 477-2991	15514
Mentzer Electronics	3845	E	650 697-2642	7113
Merrills Packaging Inc	3081	D	650 259-5959	4231
Mid-Peninsula Roofing Inc	1761	D	650 375-7850	1821
Middle East Baking Co	2051	F	650 348-7200	2395
Murphy HARTelius/M&h Uniforms **(PA)**	5136	E	650 344-2997	9249
National Automobile Club **(PA)**	8699	E	650 294-7000	18581
National Financial Svcs LLC	6799	A	650 343-6775	10871
Nexgate Inc	7372	E	650 762-9890	13331
Obayashi Canada Ltd	1611	E	650 952-4910	1067
Obayashi Usa LLC **(HQ)**	6531	C	650 952-4910	10630
Palcare Inc	8351	E	650 340-1289	17988
Partners Advctes For Rmrkble C	8322	D	650 312-0730	17669
Peninsula Humane Soc & Spca	8699	D	650 340-7022	18583
Peninsula Post-Acute	8621	E	650 443-2600	18343
Personal Protective Svcs Inc **(PA)**	7381	D	650 344-3302	14086
Petits Pains & Co LP	2051	F	650 692-6000	2399
Phoenix Pharmaceuticals Inc	2834	E	650 558-8898	3963
Prime Time Athletic Club Inc	7991	C	650 204-3662	14965
Proterra Inc **(PA)**	3711	C	864 438-0000	6555
Proterra Operating Company Inc **(HQ)**	3711	C	864 438-0000	6556
Randstad Professionals Us LLC	7361	D	650 343-5111	12125
Redwood Services Inc	4953	E	650 872-2310	8359
Reyes Coca-Cola Bottling LLC	2086	D	408 483-4259	2804
Riggs Distributing Inc **(PA)**	5064	E	650 240-3000	8886
Ruby Ribbon	5137	E	650 525-4141	9255
Safway Services LP	5082	E	650 652-9255	9028
San Mteo Cnty Msqito Vctor Ctr	4959	E	650 344-8592	8405
School Apparel Inc **(PA)**	2337	C	650 777-4500	3006
Sensbey Inc **(PA)**	3548	F	650 697-2032	5105
Sing Tao Newspapers **(HQ)**	2711	D	650 808-8800	3479
Spec Personnel LLC	7361	D	408 727-8000	12138
Sphere Institute	8732	B	650 558-3980	19187
Stellar Labs Inc	7371	E	818 578-4078	12818
Stonesfair Financial Corp	6513	D	650 347-0442	10463
Sunkist Enterprises	5072	D	650 347-3900	8990
Superbroward LLC	7231	C	650 348-4881	11695
Sutter Health	8062	C	650 696-5838	16644
Suttercare Corporation	8093	A	650 696-5363	17080
Suttercare Corporation	8062	A	650 853-8500	16683
Synagro West LLC	8748	D	650 652-6531	19869
Synova Interactive Group Inc	7371	E	650 513-1058	12843
Tangent Computer Inc **(PA)**	3571	D	888 683-2881	5275
Technical Instr San Francisco **(PA)**	5049	E	650 651-3000	8804
Todays Hotel Corporation	7011	E	415 447-3005	11537
Transiris Corporation	8742	D	650 303-3495	19652
Trevi Partners A Calif LP	7011	E	650 347-2381	11542
Trivad Inc	5045	C	650 286-1086	8756
Udelv Inc	7371	E	650 376-3785	12885
Vector Laboratories Inc **(HQ)**	2836	D	650 697-3600	4060
Virgin America Crisis Fund **(PA)**	4512	E	650 762-7000	7743
Virgin America Inc **(HQ)**	4512	A	877 359-8474	7744
Wedriveu Inc	4731	E	650 645-6800	7860
Wedriveu Holdings Inc **(DH)**	6719	E	650 579-5800	10747
Worldwide Energy and Mfg USA **(PA)**	3674	A	650 692-7788	6359
X7/24 Corporation	1542	E	650 401-2300	994
Yb Media LLC	2741	E	310 467-5804	3612
Yourmechanic Inc	7538	D	800 701-6230	14606
Zenique Hotel Management LLC	7011	E	650 483-9968	11587
Zippedi Inc	7379	E	858 353-9743	14020
Zonic Design & Imaging LLC	8742	E	415 643-3700	19679

BURNEY, CA - Shasta County

	SIC	EMP	PHONE	ENTRY #
Dicalite Minerals Corp **(HQ)**	3295	E	530 335-5451	4528
Hat Creek Cnstr & Mtls Inc **(PA)**	1629	E	530 335-5501	1166
Pit River Health Service Inc **(PA)**	8099	D	530 335-3651	17168
Pit River Tribal Council	8322	E	530 335-5421	17673
Pit River Tribal Council	8011	D	530 335-3651	15629
Shasta Green Inc	2411	E	530 335-4924	3078
Sierra Pacific Industries	2421	E	530 378-8301	3110
Sierra Pacific Industries	2421	E	530 335-3681	3111
Tubit Enterprises Inc	2411	E	530 335-5085	3085

BYRON, CA - Contra Costa County

	SIC	EMP	PHONE	ENTRY #
Byron Bethany Irrigation Dst	4941	D	209 835-0375	8223
G3 Enterprises Inc	4731	E	209 341-3441	7836
Marin Food Specialties Inc	2032	E	925 634-6126	2205
Pacific Coast Ldscp MGT Inc	0781	D	925 513-2310	432
San Luis Dlta-Mendota Wtr Auth	4971	E	209 835-2593	8416
Sanders Contracting Inc	1542	D	925 308-7305	955

CALISTOGA, CA - Napa County

	SIC	EMP	PHONE	ENTRY #
Calistoga Spa Inc	7991	D	707 942-6269	14934
Chateau Montelena LLC	2084	E	707 942-5105	2532
Clos Pegase Winery Inc	2084	E	707 942-4981	2536
Duffys Myrtledale	8093	D	707 942-6888	17016
Jericho Canyon Vineyards LLC	2084	E	707 942-9665	2632
Kenefick Ranches LLC	2084	E	707 942-6175	2639
Lavender Hill Spa	7991	E	707 942-4495	14956
NAPA Valley Brewing Co Inc	7011	D	707 942-4101	11323
Resort At Indian Springs LLC	7011	C	707 709-2434	11406
Roman Spa Hot Sprng Resort LLC	7011	E	707 942-4441	11417
Schramsberg Vineyards Company	0172	E	707 942-4558	74
Sterling Vineyards Inc **(PA)**	2084	E	707 942-3300	2726
Sugarloaf Farming Corporation	2084	E	707 942-4459	2733
Tonnellerie Francaise French C	2449	F	707 942-9301	3242
Villa Amorosa	2084	D	707 942-8200	2756
Vision Publications Inc	2741	E	562 597-4000	3611

CALPELLA, CA - Mendocino County

	SIC	EMP	PHONE	ENTRY #
Mendocino Forest Pdts Co LLC	5031	E	707 485-6800	8592
Waldorf School of Mendocino	8351	E	707 485-8719	18044

CAMERON PARK, CA - El Dorado County

	SIC	EMP	PHONE	ENTRY #
Cameron Park Country Club Inc	7997	D	530 672-9840	15069
Cameron Park Firefighters Assn	7999	D	530 677-6190	15187
Carlton Engineering Inc **(PA)**	8711	E	916 932-7855	18661
Dnt In Home Care Inc	8082	E	530 556-4030	16879
Eskaton	8361	C	530 672-8900	18105
Eskaton Properties Inc	8361	D	530 677-5066	18109
Hawthorne Group Inc	7361	E	530 672-1330	12096
Hemington Landscape Svcs Inc	0781	D	530 677-9290	421
JEI	5065	F	530 677-3210	8923

Company	SIC	EMP	PHONE	ENTRY #
Jj Express Freight Inc	4789	E	916 914-3231	7886
Marshall Medical Center	8062	E	530 672-7040	16447
Marshall Medical Center	8062	E	530 672-7050	16452
McClone Construction Company	1521	C	559 431-9411	671
Nehemiah Rebar Services Inc	1791	C	530 676-6310	1928
Preferred Mfg Svcs Inc **(PA)**	3599	D	530 677-2675	5603

CAMINO, CA - El Dorado County

Company	SIC	EMP	PHONE	ENTRY #
Coastal Mountain Timber Inc	0783	D	530 303-3378	515
Crystal Basin Cellars	2084	F	530 303-3749	2541
Rainbow Orchards Inc	2086	F	530 644-1594	2798
Sierra Pacific Industries	2421	E	530 644-2311	3114

CAMPBELL, CA - Santa Clara County

Company	SIC	EMP	PHONE	ENTRY #
8x8 Inc **(PA)**	4813	A	408 727-1885	7921
A-Pro Pest Control Inc	7342	E	408 559-0933	11877
Accountble Hlthcare Stffing In	7361	C	408 377-9960	12069
Adorno Construction Inc	1771	D	408 369-8675	1848
Afn Services LLC	2599	E	408 364-1564	3334
Agc Inc	1711	D	408 369-6305	1189
Age Defy Dermatology Wellness	8011	E	408 559-0988	15270
Applied Systems Engrg Inc	7379	F	408 364-0500	13842
Argonaut Window & Door Inc	5031	D	408 376-4018	8528
Arteris Inc **(PA)**	3674	E	408 470-7300	6050
Arteris Holdings Inc	3674	E	408 470-7300	6051
Atmosic Technologies Inc	5065	E	650 678-7864	8893
B C C S Inc **(PA)**	1521	C	408 379-5500	614
Balanced Rock Inc	7999	D	408 374-8692	15178
Barracuda Networks Inc **(DH)**	7372	C	408 342-5400	13010
Barrera Adolfo DDS **(PA)**	8021	E	408 871-2885	15824
Bill Hamilton Roofing Inc	1761	E	408 379-1303	1790
Bluestack Systems Inc	7372	E	408 412-9439	13031
Bouton Construction Inc	5082	D	408 375-0829	9019
Campbell Christian School	7032	D	408 370-4900	11599
Campbell Hhg Hotel Dev LLP	7011	D	408 626-9590	10986
Centric Software Inc **(PA)**	8742	E	408 574-7802	19468
Cenzic Inc	5065	E	408 200-0700	8902
Chargepoint Inc **(PA)**	3629	A	408 841-4500	5693
Chargepoint Holdings Inc **(PA)**	3621	A	408 841-4500	5658
Charles Culberson Inc	1742	C	650 335-4730	1668
Chicago Title Insurance Co	6361	A	408 371-4100	10197
Childrens Recovery Ctr 1 LLC	8069	D	408 558-3640	16753
Clickaway Corporation	7378	E	408 626-9400	13819
Collimated Holes Inc	3827	E	408 374-5080	6868
Comglobal Systems Inc **(DH)**	7373	D	619 321-6000	13571
Community Intgrted Work Prgram	8331	E	408 871-9680	17806
Community Management Svcs Inc	6531	E	408 559-1977	10521
Concentric Power Inc	8748	D	888 321-0620	19749
Condeco Software Inc **(HQ)**	7372	F	917 677-7600	13089
Consoldted Hnge Mnfctured Pdts	3599	F	408 379-6550	5495
Content Guru Inc	7373	B	408 559-3988	13573
Cornami Inc	8742	E	408 337-0070	19482
CRC Health Group Inc	8093	D	408 866-8167	17013
Creganna Medical Devices Inc **(DH)**	3841	E	408 364-7100	6968
Crystalgraphics Inc	7371	F	800 394-0700	12364
Daleys Drywall and Taping Inc	1742	B	408 378-9500	1670
Dasher Technologies Inc **(HQ)**	7371	E	408 409-2607	12370
Douglas Ross Construction Inc	1522	D	408 429-7700	744
Emq Families First **(PA)**	8322	D	408 379-3790	17544
Eos Software Inc	7372	E	408 439-2903	13145
Family Eye Care Optometry Corp	8042	D	408 379-2020	15868
Fierce Wombat Games Inc	7374	E	408 745-5400	13713
Firetide Inc **(DH)**	3577	D	408 399-7771	5367
Gidel & Kocal Cnstr Co Inc	1542	E	408 370-0280	878
Groupware Technology Inc **(DH)**	7373	E	408 540-0090	13602
Harman Management Corporation **(PA)**	5046	B	650 941-5681	8765
Imperative Care Inc **(PA)**	3842	E	669 228-3814	7072
Implus LLC	3021	C	408 796-7739	4199
Internal Drive	7032	B	408 871-2227	11604
Italent Corporation **(PA)**	7379	C	408 496-6200	13922
Iwatt Inc **(DH)**	3674	E	408 374-4200	6167
Jay Nolan Community Svcs Inc	8322	C	408 293-5002	17619
Jessee Brothers Machine Sp Inc	3599	F	408 866-1755	5547
John A Hughes DDS Incorporated	8021	D	408 378-3489	15842
Kalila Medical Inc	3829	E	408 819-5175	6906
Kerrock Countertops Inc **(PA)**	2511	F	510 441-2300	3279
Kindred Healthcare LLC	8082	D	408 871-9860	16905
Largo Concrete Inc	1771	B	408 874-2500	1887
Lark Avenue Car Wash	7542	D	408 377-2525	14649
List Biological Labs Inc	2836	E	408 866-6363	4053
Liveworld Inc **(PA)**	4813	D	800 301-9507	7969
LLP Moss Adams	8721	D	408 369-2400	18971
Luidia Inc	8731	E	650 413-7500	19084
Martina Landscape Inc	0782	D	408 871-8800	484
Maxonic Inc	7379	D	408 739-4900	13933
Megachips LSI USA Corporation	3674	D	408 570-0555	6195
Mips Tech Inc **(HQ)**	3674	C	408 530-5000	6213
Mojio USA Inc	7371	E	604 868-0804	12618
Morosin Enterprises Inc	7011	D	408 354-0300	11311
Mtc Resturant Group Inc	8742	E	408 371-3806	19582
Natalie Dstiny Entps Ltd Lblty	8322	E	408 429-8665	17653
Netline Corporation **(PA)**	8742	D	408 340-2200	19588
Netpolarity Inc	7361	C	408 971-1100	12111
Obstetrix Med Group Cal A Prof **(HQ)**	8011	E	800 463-6628	15563
On-Site Manager Inc **(DH)**	7389	E	866 266-7483	14345
Online Technical Services Inc **(PA)**	7361	E	408 378-1100	12114
OSI Engineering Inc	8711	C	408 550-2800	18784
Pacific Coast Fire Inc	1711	E	408 370-1234	1331
Pacific Netsoft Inc **(PA)**	7361	E	800 330-6558	12116
Pattern Tap LLC	7379	D	408 341-0600	13957
Peets Coffee & Tea LLC	2095	E	408 558-9535	2844
Photon Inc	3823	F	408 226-1000	6730
Precision Identity Corporation	3599	F	408 374-2346	5602
R V Cloud Co	5074	E	408 378-7943	9005
Reed Mariculture Inc	2048	F	408 377-1065	2354
Resolve Systems LLC **(PA)**	7371	D	949 325-0120	12743
Saama Technologies Inc **(PA)**	7371	C	408 371-1900	12754
Sage Microelectronics Corp	7372	F	408 680-0060	13422
Samirian Chemicals Inc	5169	E	408 558-8282	9521
Sandis Civil Engineers **(PA)**	8713	D	408 636-0900	18925
Santa Clara County Health Auth	6321	E	408 376-2000	10086
Semi Automation & Tech Inc	3674	E	408 374-9549	6280
Semprex Corporation	3825	E	408 379-3230	6791
Senior Living Solutions LLC	8052	C	408 385-1835	16202
Shifamed LLC	8011	E	408 560-2500	15680
Shifamed LLC	7363	E	408 364-1242	12200
Skillnet Solutions Inc **(PA)**	7371	D	408 522-3600	12790
Skyhigh Networks Inc	7382	D	408 564-0278	14148
Southern Cal Disc Tire Co Inc	5014	C	408 377-5010	8481
Spring Education Group Inc **(PA)**	8351	C	408 973-7351	18026
SR Freeman Inc	1751	D	408 364-2200	1760
Stratford School Inc	8351	D	408 973-7320	18036
Streamray Inc **(PA)**	7929	D	408 745-5449	14880
Sunstone Construction Inc	1771	D	408 379-0592	1911
Supira Medical Inc	3841	E	408 560-2500	7045
Tactx Medical Inc **(DH)**	3841	C	408 364-7100	7047
Teammate Builders Inc	2542	F	408 377-9000	3329
Telecmmnctons MGT Slutions Inc	1731	D	408 866-5495	1619
Tigo Energy Inc **(PA)**	8731	E	408 402-0802	19136
Twelveacres Inc	8361	E	408 341-0400	18194
United Emrgncy Anmal Clnic Inc **(PA)**	0742	E	408 371-6252	340
Uplift Family Services **(PA)**	8322	D	408 379-3790	17778
US Carenet Services LLC	8082	C	408 871-9860	16963
Versatile Power Inc	3841	E	408 341-4600	7059
Visualon Inc	7372	E	408 645-6618	13520
Vivid Inc	2851	E	408 982-9101	4113
Vivus Inc **(PA)**	2834	E	650 934-5200	4006
West Coast Legal Service Inc	7389	E	408 938-6520	14462
West Valley Cnstr Co Inc **(PA)**	1623	C	408 371-5510	1142
Wg Security Products Inc **(PA)**	3699	E	408 241-8000	6547
Workspot Inc **(PA)**	7372	E	888 426-8113	13532
Zipline Medical Inc	3841	F	408 412-7228	7065
Zircon Corporation **(PA)**	3546	E	408 866-8600	5103

CAPITOLA, CA - Santa Cruz County

Company	SIC	EMP	PHONE	ENTRY #
Alpha Machine Company Inc	3599	F	831 462-7400	5469
Bay Federal Credit Union **(PA)**	6061	D	831 479-6000	9775
Campus Kids Connection Inc **(PA)**	8351	E	831 462-9822	17876
Capitola Imports Inc	7549	C	831 462-4200	14658
Commerce Home Mortgage LLC	6162	D	831 460-0202	9903
Covenant Care LLC	8051	D	831 476-0770	15963
Golden Age Cnvlescent Hosp Inc	8059	E	831 475-0722	16236
Inn At Depot Hill	7011	E	831 462-3376	11188
Spa Fitness Center Inc	7991	D	831 476-7373	14974
United Way Santa Cruz County	8399	E	831 465-2204	18258

CARMICHAEL, CA - Sacramento County

Company	SIC	EMP	PHONE	ENTRY #
Acct Holdings LLC	7389	A	916 971-1981	14194
ACR Solar International Corp	3433	E	916 481-7200	4624
AEgis of Carmichael	8361	E	916 972-1313	18051
Aegis Senior Communities LLC	8361	D	916 972-1313	18054
Blue Shield Cal Lf Hlth Insur	6324	A	800 660-3007	10093
Capital Eye Medical Group	8011	D	916 241-9378	15318
Capitol Intrventional Crdiolgy	8011	E	916 967-0115	15320
Carmichael Care Inc	8051	E	916 483-8103	15952
Carmichael Oaks Joint Venture	8361	D	916 944-1588	18069
Carmichael Recreation & Pk Dst	7999	D	916 485-5322	15189
County of Sacramento	8111	D	916 874-1953	17239
County of Sacramento	7992	E	916 482-9792	14992
Crestwood Behavioral Hlth Inc	8063	E	916 977-0949	16741
Diez & Leis RE Group Inc	6531	A	916 487-4287	10539
Dignity Health	8062	A	916 537-5000	16348
Donations With Care	8322	D	916 544-3080	17534
El Rancho School Inc	8351	E	916 482-8656	17931
Empire Golf Inc	7992	E	916 482-3284	15001
Eskaton **(PA)**	6512	D	916 334-0296	10386
Eskaton Properties Inc	8051	B	916 974-2060	15994
Eskaton Properties Inc	8361	D	916 331-8513	18108
Eskaton Properties Inc **(PA)**	8361	D	916 334-0810	18113
Eskaton Properties Inc	8322	C	916 334-0296	17554
Eskaton Properties Inc	8361	D	916 974-2000	18114
Fairwood Associates Apts	6513	D	916 944-0152	10435
Greater Secrement Pediatrics **(PA)**	8011	E	916 965-4612	15420
Helios Healthcare LLC	8051	D	916 482-0465	16021
Horizon West Inc	8051	E	916 488-8601	16025
Indian Rock Universal Inc	4812	E	916 696-6973	7907
International Building Inv Inc	1522	D	916 716-9565	749
Nor-Cal Climate Control Inc **(PA)**	1711	E	916 439-6534	1317
Pacific Cities Management Inc **(PA)**	6531	D	916 348-1188	10633
Pak Inc	5199	D	916 944-1428	9668
Ray Stone Incorporated	8322	E	916 482-2363	17680
Recore Growth Investments Inc	6799	E	916 813-3798	10878
RES-Care Inc	8082	E	916 487-7497	16929
Ronald Vanderbeek	8052	E	916 488-7211	16201
Smart & Final Stores Inc	5141	C	916 486-6315	9305
Solarroofscom Inc	3433	F	916 481-7200	4637

GEOGRAPHIC

Employment Codes: A=Over 500 employees, B=251-500, C=101-250, D=51-100, E=20-50 F=10-19

CARMICHAEL, CA **GEOGRAPHIC SECTION**

	SIC	EMP	PHONE	ENTRY #
SSC Carmichael Operating Co LP	8051	C	916 485-4793	16126
Stewart Title of Sacramento (PA)	6541	E	916 484-6990	10694
Sunbrdge Brttany Rhblttion Ctr	8051	A	916 484-1393	16134
Sutter Health	8062	C	916 961-4910	16652
Trashlogic LLC	7349	E	916 900-4008	12006
Wbe Traffic Control Inc	7389	D	707 771-5870	14460
Whitney Oaks Care Center	8051	D	916 488-8601	16159

CARUTHERS, CA - Fresno County

	SIC	EMP	PHONE	ENTRY #
Adventist Hlth Systm/West Corp	8062	D	559 864-3212	16311
Batth Dehydrator LLC	2034	E	559 864-3501	2252
Caruthers Raisin Pkg Co Inc (PA)	2034	E	559 864-9448	2256
Charanjit Singh Batth	0173	D	559 864-9421	85
H & R Gunlund Ranches Inc	0172	C	559 864-8186	55
Mid Valley Mfg Inc	3599	E	559 864-9441	5571
Pacific Boring Incorporated	1623	E	559 864-9444	1130

CASTRO VALLEY, CA - Alameda County

	SIC	EMP	PHONE	ENTRY #
Altcare Willow Creek Inc (PA)	8361	E	510 527-7282	18055
American Building Service Inc	7349	D	510 483-5120	11921
Bay Counties Investments Inc	7933	E	510 538-8100	14885
Baywood Court (PA)	8082	C	510 733-2102	16854
Bonetti Frank Plumbing Company	1711	E	510 582-0934	1224
Cardiovascular Cons Med Group	8011	E	510 537-3556	15324
Creative Dmnsions In Dentistry (PA)	8021	E	510 881-8010	15829
Dreamalliance Entrmt Inc (PA)	7929	E	510 270-8693	14871
Eden Labs Med Group Inc	8062	C	510 537-1234	16360
Edwards & Anderson Inc	7542	E	510 581-0230	14640
Fern Lodge Inc	8051	E	510 886-2448	16002
His Grwing Grove Child Care CT	8351	E	510 581-5088	17952
Lawyers Title Insurance Corp	6361	E	510 733-2250	10201
Norco Printing Inc	2791	F	510 569-2200	3765
Ras Management (PA)	4225	E	510 727-1800	7700
Redwood Convalescent Hospital	8059	E	510 537-8848	16260
Saint John Krnstadt HM For Age	8051	E	510 889-7000	16107
Sars Software Products Inc	7372	F	415 226-0040	13426
Savnik & Company	2273	E	510 568-4628	2979
Solar Company Inc	1711	D	510 888-9488	1362
Specialty Graphics Inc	2789	F	510 351-7705	3762
Sutter Health	8062	C	510 537-1234	16608
Sutter Health	8062	C	510 537-1234	16638
Valley Pinte Nursing Rehab Ctr	8361	E	510 538-8464	18198

CAZADERO, CA - Sonoma County

	SIC	EMP	PHONE	ENTRY #
Berrys Sawmill Inc	2421	E	707 865-2365	3090
Dharma Mudranalaya (PA)	2731	E	707 847-3380	3532
Flowers Vineyard & Winery LLC	2084	F	707 847-3661	2573
Joplin Inc (PA)	7032	E	707 847-3494	11607
Parmeter Logging and Excav Inc	1794	E	707 632-5610	1971

CEDARVILLE, CA - Modoc County

	SIC	EMP	PHONE	ENTRY #
Surprise Valley Hlth Care Dst	8062	D	530 279-6111	16567

CERES, CA - Stanislaus County

	SIC	EMP	PHONE	ENTRY #
Access To Power Inc	1731	E	209 577-1491	1444
Advanced Technology Distrs Inc	5045	E	209 541-1111	8661
Aemetis Advnced Fels Keyes Inc	2869	E	209 632-4511	4118
B & H Manufacturing Co Inc (PA)	3565	E	209 537-5785	5196
Certified Stainless Svc Inc (PA)	3443	E	209 537-4747	4715
Dan Avila & Sons Farms Inc	0161	D	209 495-3899	25
Dennis Design & Mfg Inc	5084	E	209 632-9956	9062
Elite Family Systems	8361	E	209 531-2088	18104
I C Refrigeration Svc Inc	1711	E	209 538-8271	1281
Klair Real Estate Inc	6531	C	209 484-8075	10597
Mark One Corporation	8059	E	209 537-4581	16251
McMillan - Hendryx Inc	3053	F	209 538-2300	4203
Prompt Precision Metals Inc	3444	E	209 531-1210	4807
Ram Mechanical Inc	1711	D	209 531-9155	1342
Robert R Wix Inc (PA)	2759	E	209 537-4561	3748
Seed Factory Northwest Inc (PA)	2048	E	209 634-8522	2358
Stiles Custom Metal Inc	3442	D	209 538-3667	4709
Sutter Health	8062	C	209 538-1733	16621
Timmerman Starlite Trckg Inc	4213	E	209 538-1706	7602
Truteam of California Inc	1742	C	916 826-3194	1706
United Parcel Service Inc	4215	C	800 742-5877	7661
US Dies Inc (PA)	3544	E	209 664-1402	5087
Vito Trucking LLC	4213	D	209 342-5104	7610
Volkman Seed Company Inc	5199	E	209 669-3040	9673
Wc AG Services Inc	0762	A	209 538-3131	391
Wildlife Fur Dressing Inc	3111	F	209 538-2901	4338

CHESTER, CA - Plumas County

	SIC	EMP	PHONE	ENTRY #
Collins Pine Company	2421	E	530 258-2111	3095
Collins Pine Company	2421	E	530 258-2131	3096
Seneca Healthcare District (PA)	8062	C	530 258-2151	16519
Sierra Cscade Aggrgate Asp PDT	1442	E	530 258-4555	598

CHICO, CA - Butte County

	SIC	EMP	PHONE	ENTRY #
11 Main Inc	4813	C	530 892-9191	7918
Addus Healthcare Inc	8082	D	530 566-0405	16833
Adventist Health System/West	8062	D	530 342-4576	16297
Aging California Department	8322	E	530 898-5923	17409
Allevity Hr Inc	8721	D	530 345-2486	18930
Alternative Energy Systems Inc	1711	D	530 345-6980	1198
ARC of Butte County (PA)	8322	C	530 891-5865	17430
Armed Guard Private SEC Inc	7381	D	530 751-3218	14031
Artic Aire of Chico Inc	1711	E	530 895-3330	1209
Associated Pension Cons Inc (PA)	6371	D	530 343-4233	10211
Assocted Stdnts Cal State Univ (PA)	7999	A	530 898-6815	15177
B A M I Inc	7991	D	530 343-5678	14927
Bailey Creek Invstors A Cal Lt (PA)	6552	E	530 891-6753	10695
Baldwin Contracting Co Inc (DH)	1611	E	530 891-6555	1013
BCM Construction Company Inc	1541	E	530 342-1722	789
Beaver Dam Health Care Center	8051	E	530 343-6084	15944
Bertagna Orchards Inc	0175	E	530 343-8014	96
Bidwell Senior Care Svcs Inc	8361	D	530 899-3585	18063
Bidwell Title and Escrow Co (PA)	6361	E	530 894-2612	10195
Bloodsource Inc	8099	E	530 893-5433	17109
Boys & Girls Clubs of N Vly	8641	D	530 899-0335	18397
Buildcom Inc	5074	B	800 375-3403	8993
Butte Home Health Inc	8082	D	530 895-0462	16862
Caliber Home Loans Inc	6162	E	530 894-6418	9895
California Olive Ranch Inc (PA)	2079	E	530 846-8000	2464
California Park Rehab Hos	8051	E	530 894-1010	15949
California Security Svcs Inc	7381	E	530 899-3751	14042
California Vocations Inc	8059	C	530 877-0937	16223
Caminar	8093	E	530 343-4421	16997
Catamunt Brdcstg Chc-Rdding In (PA)	4833	C	530 893-2424	8040
Ces Electric Inc	1731	E	530 636-4257	1475
Chico Area Recreation & Pk Dst (PA)	7999	C	530 895-4711	15192
Chico Community Publishing (PA)	2711	E	530 894-2300	3427
Chico Electric Inc	1731	D	530 891-1933	1476
Chico Immdate Care Med Ctr Inc (PA)	8011	E	530 891-1676	15348
Chico Lodging LLC	7011	E	318 635-8000	11004
Chico Lodging LLC	7011	E	530 894-5500	11005
Chico State Enterprises	8641	A	530 898-6811	18407
Chicoeco Inc	2393	E	530 342-4426	3031
City of Chico	4581	D	530 896-7699	7767
Cleanrite Inc	7217	C	800 870-0030	11658
Cloudpeople Global	7371	E	530 591-7028	12344
Community Hsing Imprv Prgram I (PA)	8748	E	530 891-6931	19748
Country House	8361	E	530 342-7002	18082
Courtesy Motors Auto Ctr Inc	7538	D	530 345-9444	14555
Cummings-Violich Inc	0762	E	530 894-5494	371
Dan Fitzgerald & Assoc Inc	7389	E	530 592-6500	14247
Davids Bridal Inc	2335	F	530 342-5914	3001
Deer Creek Broadcasting LLC	4832	E	530 345-0021	8017
Digital Path Inc	4813	E	800 676-7284	7946
Elite Biomechanical Design (PA)	3842	E	530 894-6913	7070
Emerald Investments Inc	7011	E	530 894-8600	11081
Enloe Hospt-Phys Thrpy (PA)	8062	B	530 891-7300	16363
Enloe Hospt-Phys Thrpy	8062	C	530 891-7300	16364
Enloe Medical Center	4119	C	530 891-7347	7382
Enloe Medical Center	8062	C	530 332-4111	16365
Enloe Medical Center	8062	C	530 332-7522	16366
Enloe Medical Center	8082	C	530 332-6050	16881
Enloe Medical Center	8049	D	530 332-6138	15890
Enloe Medical Center	8062	C	530 332-5520	16367
Enloe Medical Center	8062	C	530 332-6400	16368
Enloe Medical Center	8062	C	530 332-6000	16369
Estes Express Lines	4213	D	530 895-5123	7530
Evergreen At Chico LLC	8051	C	530 342-4885	15996
Fafco Inc (PA)	3433	E	530 332-2100	4628
Far Nrthern Crdnting Cncil On	8322	D	530 895-8633	17567
Farmers International Inc	0173	E	530 566-1405	88
Federal Land Bnk Assn Nthrn CA	6029	D	530 895-8698	9756
Ferguson & Brewer Inv Co (PA)	6531	E	530 872-1810	10548
Fifth Sun LLC	2339	D	530 343-8725	3010
First Responder Ems Inc	4119	D	530 897-6345	7383
Gas Transmission Systems Inc (HQ)	8711	D	530 893-6711	18716
Gatehouse Media LLC	2711	E	530 891-1234	3440
Gonzales Park LLC	5136	C	530 343-8725	9244
Guynn Inc (PA)	7549	E	530 566-9292	14660
Helios Healthcare LLC	8051	D	530 345-1306	16022
Hignell Incorporated	6552	D	530 342-0707	10704
Hignell Incorporated	6513	E	530 345-1965	10437
Hmclause Inc	0181	D	530 713-5838	128
Home Health Care MGT Inc	8082	D	530 343-0727	16892
Hr-Oakmont F/C 5212	8322	E	530 895-0123	17607
Hupp Signs & Lighting Inc	3993	F	530 345-7078	7232
IL Helth Buty Natural Oils Inc	2899	E	530 358-0222	4162
Jai Shri Ram Hospitali	7011	D	530 345-2491	11206
James Hazlehurst	8042	E	530 895-1727	15870
Jeff Stover Inc	7991	D	530 345-9427	14955
Jessee Heating & AC	1711	E	530 891-4926	1294
Joy Signal Technology LLC	3643	E	530 891-3551	5717
Klean Kanteen Inc	3411	E	530 592-4552	4598
Landacorp Inc	7371	E	530 891-0853	12567
Lares Research	3843	E	530 345-1767	7085
Lowes Home Centers LLC	5031	C	530 895-5130	8568
Mabrey Products Inc	2431	F	530 895-3799	3142
Mangrove Medical Group	8011	E	530 345-0064	15516
Mathews Ready Mix LLC	3273	E	530 893-8856	4497
Matrix Logic Corporation	7372	E	415 893-9897	13295
Mgh Enterprises Inc	1731	E	530 894-2537	1545
Michael Baker Intl Inc	8748	E	530 894-3469	19821
Mid Valley Title and Escrow Co (DH)	6361	D	530 893-5644	10202
Millard Group Inc	7349	C	530 899-7299	11972
Mission Linen Supply	7213	D	530 342-4110	11644
Mooney Farms	0723	E	530 899-2661	295
Mtech Inc	3089	E	530 894-5091	4305
Nanotech Energy Inc	3691	E	310 806-9202	6488
National Data Funding LLC	6099	D	530 343-1605	9849
Nor-Cal Vans Inc	3713	E	530 892-0150	6567
North State Radiology	8011	E	530 890-0504	15552
North Valley Dermatology	8011	E	530 809-2127	15553

GEOGRAPHIC SECTION CLOVIS, CA

	SIC	EMP	PHONE	ENTRY #
North Valley Rain Gutters	3444	F	530 894-3347	4796
Northern Cal Yuth Fmly Prgrams **(PA)**	8361	D	530 893-2316	18149
Northern Vly Indian Hlth Inc	8021	E	530 896-9400	15850
Northstate Cardiology Cons	8011	E	530 342-0123	15557
Orient & Flume Art Glass	3229	F	530 893-0373	4378
Orthopedic Assoc Nthrn Cal	8011	E	530 897-4500	15574
Pacific Gas and Electric Co	4911	C	530 258-6215	8136
Pacific Gas and Electric Co	4924	C	530 894-4739	8212
Pacific Gas and Electric Co	4911	C	530 896-4318	8181
Pacific West Forest Products	3449	F	530 899-7313	4860
Parrott Investment Company Inc	0191	E	530 342-4505	185
PBM Supply & Mfg	5085	E	530 345-1334	9126
Penney Opco LLC	7231	D	530 899-8160	11693
Quadco Printing Inc	2752	F	530 894-4061	3689
Rescue 42 Inc	3569	F	530 891-3473	5232
Rgis LLC	7389	D	530 898-1015	14387
Riverside Cnvalescent Hosp Inc	8059	D	530 343-5595	16262
Riverside Health Care Corp **(PA)**	8059	D	530 897-5100	16263
Roy Carrington Inc	7361	D	530 893-2100	12131
S and L Meat Sales Company	5141	E	530 343-7953	9292
Selig Construction Corp	1521	E	530 893-5898	705
Sierra Landscape & Maint Inc	0781	D	530 895-0263	441
Sierra Nevada Brewing Co **(PA)**	2082	B	530 893-3520	2491
Smucker Natural Foods Inc **(HQ)**	2086	C	530 899-5000	2815
Sourcecorp Bps Nthrn Cal Inc	5044	D	530 893-7900	8656
Square Deal Mattress Factory	2515	E	530 342-2510	3297
Srl Apparel Inc	2261	E	530 898-9525	2978
Stansbury Hm Preservation Assn	8412	E	530 895-3848	18282
Stott Outdoor Advertising	7311	E	888 342-7868	11787
Sungard Bi-Tech Inc **(DH)**	7371	E	530 891-5281	12834
Sunseri Construction Inc	1522	E	530 891-6444	772
Sunset Moulding Co	2431	E	530 695-1000	3155
Theraputic Solutions Prof Corp	8049	E	530 899-3150	15900
Thomas Manufacturing Co LLC	7692	F	530 893-8940	14724
Thomas Welding & Machine Inc	7692	E	530 893-8940	14725
Tri Counties Bank **(HQ)**	6029	D	530 898-0300	9763
Trico Bancshares **(PA)**	6022	D	530 898-0300	9751
True North Housing Aliance Inc	8322	E	530 891-9048	17772
United Sttes Thrmlctric Cnsrti	3823	E	530 345-8000	6735
University Fndtion Cal State U	6732	D	530 898-5936	10791
URS Group Inc	8733	D	530 893-9675	19243
Van Duerr Industries Inc	5039	E	530 893-1596	8649
Veterans Health Administration	8011	C	530 879-5000	15797
Victor Cmnty Support Svcs Inc	8093	C	530 267-1710	17089
Videomaker Inc	2721	E	530 891-8410	3518
Weiss-Mcnair LLC **(DH)**	3523	D	530 891-6214	5021
Western Woods Inc **(PA)**	5031	E	530 343-5821	8613
Wizard Manufacturing Inc	2068	E	530 342-1861	2452
Work Truck Solutions Inc	7379	D	855 987-4544	14010
Wrex Products Inc Chico	3089	D	530 895-3838	4335

CHOWCHILLA, CA - Madera County

	SIC	EMP	PHONE	ENTRY #
Almond Company	2068	E	559 665-4405	2442
Anderson Pump Company	4941	D	559 665-4477	8221
Avalon Care Ctr - Chwchlla LLC	8051	D	559 665-4826	15915
Blacks Irrigations Systems	3272	E	559 665-4891	4420
Case Vlott Cattle	0241	E	559 665-7399	207
Castle Distribution Svcs Inc	4225	E	559 665-3716	7683
Central California Cont Mfg	3089	E	559 665-7611	4265
Chowchilla Mem Hlth Care Dst **(PA)**	8051	D	559 665-3781	15960
Global Diversified Inds Inc **(PA)**	2452	E	559 665-5800	3251
J & R Debenedetto Orchards Inc	0175	E	559 665-1712	103
JRP Hospitality Inc	7011	E	408 569-2911	11224
Madera Community Hospital	8062	E	559 665-3768	16435
Madera Disposal Systems Inc **(DH)**	4953	D	559 665-3099	8340
Minturn Huller Cooperative Inc	5159	D	559 665-1185	9510
Piranha Pipe & Precast Inc	3272	E	559 665-7473	4447
Salters Distributing Inc	5092	D	559 825-3220	9170
Seaman Nurseries Inc	0721	D	559 665-1860	258
Snyder Industries LLC	3089	D	559 665-7611	4324
Triangle T Ranch Inc	0131	D	559 665-2964	13
Winnresidential Ltd Partnr	6513	E	559 665-9600	10469

CITRUS HEIGHTS, CA - Sacramento County

	SIC	EMP	PHONE	ENTRY #
Accountble Hlthcare Stffing In	7361	C	916 286-7667	12068
Always Home Nursing Svc Inc	8082	C	916 989-6420	16844
Citrus Heights Pre-School Inc **(PA)**	8351	D	916 726-1550	17908
Cort Yard Creamery Inc	5149	E	916 729-4021	9446
Crossroads Diversfd Svcs Inc	7361	D	916 676-2540	12081
Fireside Lanes Inc	7933	E	916 725-2101	14890
Fortune Senior Enterprises	8082	C	916 560-9100	16884
Golden 1 Credit Union	6062	D	916 732-2900	9829
Itc Srvice Group Acqstion LLC **(DH)**	8748	E	877 370-4482	19800
J R Roberts Corp **(HQ)**	1542	D	916 729-5600	897
J R Roberts Enterprises Inc	1542	C	916 729-5600	898
Longs Drug Stores Cal LLC	7384	C	916 726-4433	14176
Lowes Home Centers LLC	5031	C	916 728-7800	8571
Patrol Solutions LLC	7381	C	916 919-6079	14085
Phoenix Schools Inc	8351	D	916 723-2633	17999
Progrssive Employment Concepts **(PA)**	8331	E	916 723-3112	17833
Quality First Home Imprv Inc **(PA)**	1521	C	877 663-6707	689
Regent Assisted Living Inc	8361	E	916 722-2800	18165
Retail Radio Inc	7311	E	916 415-9446	11779
Save Mart Supermarkets Disc	5141	D	916 723-2446	9301
SD Deacon Corp California	1542	D	916 969-0900	958
Sun Oak Limited Partners	8361	D	916 722-2800	18187
Terra Nova Counseling **(PA)**	8322	D	916 344-0249	17768
Travelmasters Inc	4724	E	916 722-1648	7808

	SIC	EMP	PHONE	ENTRY #
Wbi Inventory Service Inc **(PA)**	7389	E	916 729-1147	14461

CLARKSBURG, CA - Yolo County

	SIC	EMP	PHONE	ENTRY #
Bogle Vineyards Inc	0172	E	916 744-1139	46
Vino Farms Inc	0191	C	916 775-4095	196

CLAYTON, CA - Contra Costa County

	SIC	EMP	PHONE	ENTRY #
American Golf Corporation	7997	D	925 672-9737	15051
Cemex Cnstr Mtls PCF LLC	5032	E	925 672-4900	8621
Comco Sheet Metal Company	3444	F	510 832-6433	4747

CLEARLAKE, CA - Lake County

	SIC	EMP	PHONE	ENTRY #
Adventist Hlth Clrlake Hosp In **(HQ)**	8062	B	707 994-6486	16303
Adventist Hlth Clrlake Hosp In	8062	C	707 994-6486	16304
Adventist Hlth Systm/West Corp	8062	D	707 995-4888	16309
Adventist Hlth Systm/West Corp	8062	D	707 995-4500	16312
Adventist Hlth Systm/West Corp	8062	D	707 994-6486	16316
Advintist Hlth Clearlake Hosp	8062	D	707 994-6486	16318
Bayberry Inc	8051	D	707 995-1643	15924
Highlands Water Company	4941	E	707 994-2393	8250
Lake Cnty Fire Protection Dst	8322	D	707 994-2170	17633
Vindra Inc	8051	D	707 994-7738	16154

CLEARLAKE OAKS, CA - Lake County

	SIC	EMP	PHONE	ENTRY #
Shannon Ranches Inc	8742	C	707 998-9656	19631

CLEMENTS, CA - San Joaquin County

	SIC	EMP	PHONE	ENTRY #
Jack Sparrowk	0212	E	209 759-3530	201

CLIO, CA - Plumas County

	SIC	EMP	PHONE	ENTRY #
Nakoma Resort LLC	7991	E	530 832-5067	14963

CLOVERDALE, CA - Sonoma County

	SIC	EMP	PHONE	ENTRY #
Classic Mill & Cabinet LLC	2434	E	707 894-9800	3175
Coppertower Family Medical Ctr	8011	E	707 894-4229	15366
Ensign Cloverdale LLC	8051	C	707 894-5201	15989
Indian Head Industries Inc	3714	D	707 894-3333	6582
MGM Brakes	3714	D	707 894-3333	6588
Nu Forest Products Inc	5031	D	707 433-3313	8598
Redwood Credit Union	6061	E	800 479-7928	9804
Reuser Inc	2421	F	707 894-4224	3102
Star H-R	7361	B	707 894-4404	12141

CLOVIS, CA - Fresno County

	SIC	EMP	PHONE	ENTRY #
Agri Technovation Inc	2873	C	559 931-3332	4128
Agrian Inc **(PA)**	7379	D	559 437-5700	13835
Agriclture Prrity Plltnts Labs **(PA)**	8734	E	559 275-2175	19254
Anlin Industries	2431	C	800 287-7996	3122
Anlin Windows & Doors	3442	C	800 287-7996	4696
Atmf Inc	3471	E	559 299-6836	4899
Beaver Dam Health Care Center	8051	E	559 299-2591	15937
Blair Ch Flynn Cnslting Engner **(PA)**	8711	C	559 326-1400	18642
Bowie Enterprises	7542	D	559 292-6565	14632
Brighten Academy Preschool Inc	8351	E	559 299-8100	17866
C2 Financial Corporation	6282	C	559 824-2300	10037
Calpine Containers Inc **(PA)**	5113	F	559 519-7199	9212
Cellco Partnership	4812	D	559 321-8116	7901
Central Valley Indian Hlth Inc **(PA)**	8011	D	559 299-2578	15340
Clovis Hotels Inc	7011	E	559 323-8080	11015
Drakaina Logistics	4789	D	559 765-1347	7879
Elite Landscaping Inc	0782	C	559 292-7760	461
Ember Industries	3672	F	310 490-8926	5928
FL Service Team Inc	7629	E	559 647-5120	14696
Floyd Johnston Cnstr Co Inc	1623	D	559 299-7373	1101
Fresenius Med Care Clovis LLC	8092	A	559 324-8023	16973
Fresno Cmnty Hosp & Med Ctr	8062	D	559 324-4000	16375
Generation Clovis LLC	8361	C	559 297-4900	18119
Graham Concrete Cnstr Inc	1771	D	559 292-6571	1876
Guarantee Real Estate Corp	6531	D	559 321-6040	10568
Hodges Electric Inc	1731	E	559 298-5533	1515
Holiday Inn Express & Suites	7011	D	559 297-0555	11154
Hydratech LLC **(HQ)**	7699	D	559 233-0876	14755
Jim Crawford Cnstr Co Inc	1611	E	559 299-0306	1052
Kaiser Foundation Hospitals	6324	C	559 324-5100	10124
Kemper Independence Insur Co	6411	E	559 326-2551	10306
Krazan & Associates **(PA)**	8748	D	559 348-2200	19808
Kw Automotive North Amer Inc	3714	E	800 445-3767	6585
Labor One Inc	0761	D	559 430-4202	360
Ladell Inc	1711	E	559 650-2000	1300
Live Action General Engrg Inc	1711	E	559 564-3444	1307
Lowes Home Centers LLC	5031	C	559 322-3000	8573
Lyons Transportation Inc **(PA)**	4213	E	559 299-0123	7563
MI Rancho Tortilla Inc	2099	D	559 299-3183	2923
Michael R Minnick Roofing	1761	E	559 346-1770	1820
Niacc-Avitech Technologies Inc **(PA)**	7699	D	559 291-2500	14768
OfficeMax North America Inc	7334	D	559 298-0164	11848
Paige Price & Co	8721	D	559 299-9540	18981
Pathology Associates	8069	C	559 326-2800	16769
Peachwood Med Group Clovis Inc	8011	D	559 324-6200	15589
Regent Assisted Living Inc	8361	E	559 325-8400	18168
Schneider Electric	3699	F	615 691-2586	6541
Second Home Inc	8361	E	559 298-0699	18178
Servi-Tech Controls Inc **(PA)**	1711	D	559 264-6679	1356
Sierra Imging Assoc Med Group	8011	C	559 297-0300	15683
Smart & Final Stores Inc	5141	C	559 297-9376	9310
Snowflake Designs	2253	E	559 291-6234	2973
Valley Chrome Plating Inc	3471	D	559 298-8094	4923
Valley Unique Electric Inc	1731	D	559 237-4795	1628
Vibra Healthcare LLC	8062	E	559 325-5601	16714
Wathen-Castanos-Mazmanian Inc	1521	E	559 432-8181	727

GEOGRAPHIC

Employment Codes: A=Over 500 employees, B=251-500, C=101-250, D=51-100, E=20-50 F=10-19
2022 Northern California Business Directory and Buyers Guide
© Mergent Inc. 1-800-342-5647
1137

	SIC	EMP	PHONE	ENTRY #
Wawona Frozen Foods **(PA)**	2099	C	559 299-2901	2957
Well Being Senior Solutions	8082	D	559 321-8295	16969
Westech Systems Inc	1731	D	559 455-1720	1635
White Ash Broadcasting Inc	4832	D	559 862-2480	8037
Willow Creek Halthcare Ctr LLC	8051	C	559 323-6200	16162

COALINGA, CA - Fresno County

	SIC	EMP	PHONE	ENTRY #
Aera Energy Services Company	3533	E	559 935-7418	5044
Coalinga Dstngished Cmnty Care	8051	D	559 935-5939	15961
Coalinga Feed Yard Inc	0211	D	559 935-0836	199
Coalinga Regional Med Ctr Aux	8062	C	559 935-6400	16334
Double D Farms **(PA)**	0191	E	559 573-7500	160
Fresno Cnty Ecnmic Opprtnties	8322	E	559 935-2058	17575
Harris Farms Inc	0191	B	559 935-0717	169
Harris Woolf Cal Almonds LLC	0723	C	559 884-2147	288
Merchant Valley Corp	7011	E	916 410-2021	11296
State Hospitals Cal Dept	8063	B	559 935-4300	16745
Valley Garlic Inc	2035	E	559 934-1763	2289

COARSEGOLD, CA - Madera County

	SIC	EMP	PHONE	ENTRY #
Charging Tree Corporation	1389	F	559 760-5473	562
Chukchansi Gold Resort Casino	7011	A	866 794-6946	11008
Kuykendall Solar Corporation	1711	E	559 658-2525	1298
Yosemite Lakes Owners Assn	8641	D	559 658-7466	18485

COLFAX, CA - Placer County

	SIC	EMP	PHONE	ENTRY #
Fox Barrel Cider Company Inc	2084	E	530 346-9699	2577
M B I Ready-Mix L L C	3273	F	530 346-2432	4496
Sierra Chevrolet Inc	7539	D	530 346-8313	14623

COLMA, CA - San Mateo County

	SIC	EMP	PHONE	ENTRY #
Baldocchi and Sons Inc	5193	E	650 755-2330	9625
Christy Vault Company **(PA)**	3272	E	650 994-1378	4426
Congregation Emanu-El	6531	C	650 755-4700	10522
Cypress Lawn Cemetery Assn	6553	C	650 755-0580	10726
Lucky Chances Inc	7011	A	650 758-2237	11275
Modesto Food Distributors Inc	5144	E	650 756-3603	9348

COLOMA, CA - El Dorado County

	SIC	EMP	PHONE	ENTRY #
American Whtwter Expdtions Inc	7999	E	530 642-0804	15173

COLUMBIA, CA - Tuolumne County

	SIC	EMP	PHONE	ENTRY #
Columbia City Hotel LLC	7011	E	209 532-5341	11026
Courtney Aviation Inc	0851	E	209 532-2345	534

COLUSA, CA - Colusa County

	SIC	EMP	PHONE	ENTRY #
American Carports Inc **(PA)**	3448	E	866 730-9865	4846
Colusa Indian Cmnty Council	8011	B	530 458-5787	15354
Colusa Indian Cmnty Council	8399	C	530 458-6572	18226
Colusa Indian Cmnty Council	8011	B	530 458-5501	15355
Farmers Rice Cooperative	0723	D	530 439-2244	283
Frederick L Richter & Son Inc	0119	E	530 458-3180	8
New Colusa Indian Bingo	7999	B	530 458-8844	15223
Premier Mushrooms LP **(PA)**	5148	C	530 458-2700	9424
River Vista Farms LLC	0111	E	530 458-2550	2
Riverbend Rice Mill Inc	2044	F	530 458-8561	2327

COMPTCHE, CA - Mendocino County

	SIC	EMP	PHONE	ENTRY #
Wells Dental Inc	3843	F	707 937-0521	7090

CONCORD, CA - Contra Costa County

	SIC	EMP	PHONE	ENTRY #
Acme Press Inc	2752	D	925 682-1111	3614
Addforce Inc **(PA)**	8748	E	415 738-6469	19713
Admiral Security Services Inc	7382	B	888 471-1128	14118
Aetna Health California Inc **(DH)**	6324	C	925 543-9223	10089
Airvapor LLC	2671	F	925 405-5582	3373
Albert D Seeno Cnstr Co Inc	1521	D	925 671-7711	607
Alvellan Inc	3599	E	925 689-2421	5472
American National Red Cross	8322	E	925 603-7400	17428
Aptim Federal Services LLC	1521	C	925 288-9898	612
Ascent Services Group Inc	7363	B	925 627-4900	12160
Assetmark Inc **(HQ)**	6282	E	925 521-1040	10029
Assetmark Financial Inc **(HQ)**	6282	B	925 521-2200	10030
Assetmark Fincl Holdings Inc **(PA)**	6282	D	925 521-2200	10031
Athens Insurance Service Inc	6411	C	925 826-1000	10243
Atlas Tree Service Inc	0783	E	925 687-3631	514
Ausenco Psi Inc **(HQ)**	8711	E	925 939-4420	18632
Avanta Inc **(HQ)**	7371	E	925 818-4760	12292
Bay Alarm Company **(PA)**	1731	D	925 935-1100	1458
Bay Area Motorcycle Training	7999	E	925 677-7408	15180
Bay Area Seating Service Inc	7999	B	925 671-4000	15181
Bay Area/Diablo Petroleum Co	5172	E	925 228-2222	9530
Bay Cities Pav & Grading Inc	1794	C	925 687-6666	1951
Bay Medic Transportation Inc	4119	D	800 689-9511	7374
Bayside Insulation & Cnstr Inc	1542	D	925 288-8960	828
Beko Radiator Cores LLC	3714	F	925 671-2975	6574
Biomicrolab Inc	3596	E	925 689-1200	5454
Bora Bora Residential Coml Cle	7349	E	925 243-5992	11928
Brenden Theatre Corporation **(PA)**	7832	C	925 677-0462	14806
Building Services/System Inc	7349	E	925 688-1234	11931
Building Srvcs/System Mint Inc	1542	D	925 688-1234	843
C Big Corporation	7991	D	925 671-2110	14933
C&T Publishing Inc	2741	E	925 677-0377	3561
Cal Ranch Inc **(PA)**	2034	D	925 429-2900	2254
Calex Mfg Co Inc	5065	E	925 687-4411	8899
California Lumber Company Inc	1799	E	925 939-2105	2015
Carlton Senior Living Inc **(PA)**	6531	E	925 338-2434	10503
Carlton Senior Living Inc	6552	E	925 935-1660	10700
Carone & Company Inc	1794	D	925 602-8800	1952
Cerus Corporation **(PA)**	2836	B	925 288-6000	4042
Christian Concord Center	8351	D	925 687-2020	17904
Christian Tabernacle School	8351	D	925 685-9169	17907
Clarion Inn	7011	E	925 566-8820	11012
Clark Pest Ctrl Stockton Inc	7342	E	925 935-5077	11886
Clark Pest Ctrl Stockton Inc	7342	E	925 757-5890	11894
Closet Innovation Inc	1799	E	925 687-5033	2021
Clyde Ned Construction Inc	1794	E	925 689-5411	1953
Cocokids Inc	8399	C	925 676-5442	18225
Coldwell Bnkr Residential Brkg **(DH)**	6531	D	925 275-3000	10515
Compumail Information Svcs Inc	7389	D	925 689-7100	14233
Conco Companies	1771	E	925 685-6799	1858
Concord Graphic Arts Inc	7336	E	925 682-9670	11858
Concord Hotel LLC	7011	D	925 521-3751	11031
Concord Veranda Cinema LLC	7812	C	707 762-0990	14787
Connealy Chiropractic Inc **(PA)**	8041	E	913 669-8023	15864
Connexsys Engineering Inc	8711	E	510 243-2050	18674
Consumer Cr Cnsling Svc San Fr **(PA)**	7299	D	888 456-2227	11713
Contra Costa County Employees	8641	E	925 521-3960	18409
Contra Costa Door Co	1751	E	925 671-7888	1734
Contra Costa Water District **(PA)**	4941	C	925 688-8000	8230
Contra Costa Water District	4941	E	925 688-8090	8231
Contra Csta Msqito Vctor Ctrl	4959	E	925 685-9301	8394
Cooper Vali & Associates Inc **(HQ)**	8711	D	510 446-8301	18676
Cowell Homeowners Assn Inc **(PA)**	8641	D	925 825-0250	18411
Creation Networks Inc	1731	F	925 446-4332	1487
D & K Leather Corporation	5199	D	415 433-9320	9654
D A McCosker Construction Co	1611	E	925 686-1780	1030
D C Taylor Co	1761	D	925 603-1100	1795
Daratel Ltd **(PA)**	7299	E	925 825-1443	11714
Dave Calhoun and Assoc LLC	7349	C	925 688-1234	11941
Delta Personnel Services Inc	7381	D	925 356-3034	14054
Denova Home Sales Inc	6531	D	925 852-0545	10536
Diablo Creek Information LLC	7375	E	925 330-3200	13784
Dianne Adair Day Care Centers **(PA)**	8351	D	925 580-9704	17922
E Z 8 Motels Inc	7011	E	925 674-0888	11065
Eichleay Inc **(PA)**	8711	C	925 689-7000	18699
Eichleay Engineers Inc	8711	D	925 689-7000	18700
Electric Tech Construction Inc	1623	D	925 849-5324	1100
Enterprise Roofing Service Inc	1761	D	925 689-8100	1801
Epic Holdings Inc **(PA)**	6411	D	650 295-4600	10280
Ernie & Sons Scaffolding	1799	C	925 446-4442	2029
Esmart Source Inc	7372	F	408 739-3500	13149
FAA Concord T Inc	7538	D	925 682-7131	14562
Fidelity Nat HM Warranty Co	6361	C	925 356-0194	10198
First Student Inc	4151	C	510 628-0014	7432
Fjellbo & Son Construction Inc	1521	E	925 363-3000	638
Future Ford of Concord LLC	7539	D	925 686-5000	14609
Futures Explored	8322	C	925 332-7183	17586
Gardelle Cnstr & Ldscp Inc	0782	E	925 680-6425	463
GGF Marble & Supply Inc	3281	E	925 676-8385	4517
Gilbane Aecom JV	8741	D	925 946-3100	19341
Gilbane Federal **(DH)**	8711	C	925 946-3100	18722
Gonsalves & Santucci Inc **(PA)**	1771	E	925 685-6799	1875
Graphic Reproduction **(PA)**	7334	D	925 674-0900	11847
Grappa Software Inc	7371	D	925 818-4760	12487
Groundlvel - Ovraa Joint Ventr	1542	D	925 446-6084	882
H R Options Inc	8742	E	800 777-8944	19526
Harris & Associates Inc **(PA)**	8711	C	925 827-4900	18726
Heritage Invstmnts Concord LLC	7011	E	925 686-4466	11135
Hnc Printing Services LLC	2752	F	925 771-2080	3655
Honor Technology Inc **(PA)**	7371	D	415 999-0555	12502
I Trovatori Opera Inc	7929	E	925 246-9360	14872
Indepndent Flr Tstg Insptn Inc	3272	F	925 676-7682	4438
Inspro Corporation	6411	D	925 685-1600	10296
Jacobs Engineering Group Inc	8711	D	925 356-3900	18742
James C Jenkins Insur Svc Inc	6411	C	925 798-3334	10302
Janus Corporation **(PA)**	1799	C	925 969-9200	2039
JD Fine & Company Inc	5137	E	925 521-3300	9252
John Muir Behavioral Hlth Ctr	8063	D	925 674-4100	16742
Jopari Solutions Inc	7389	D	925 459-5200	14314
Kainos Dental Technologies LLC **(PA)**	3841	E	800 331-4834	6994
Kissito Health Case Inc	8082	D	925 689-9222	16908
Land Home Financial Svcs Inc **(PA)**	6162	E	925 676-7038	9910
Laserbeam Software LLC	7372	F	925 459-2595	13272
Laughlin Falbo Levy Moresi LLP **(PA)**	8111	D	510 628-0496	17309
LD Strobel Co Inc	1799	E	925 686-3241	2042
Lehigh Southwest Cement Co **(DH)**	3241	F	972 653-5500	4396
Lemore Transportation Inc **(PA)**	4213	D	925 689-6444	7561
Lescure Company Inc	1711	D	925 283-2528	1305
Lettis Consultants Intl Inc **(PA)**	8748	E	925 482-0360	19811
Lloyds Custom Woodwork Inc	2431	E	925 680-6600	3140
Longs Drug Stores Cal Inc	7384	E	925 676-4700	14158
Longs Drug Stores Cal LLC	7384	C	925 672-0547	14180
Lowes Home Centers LLC	5031	C	925 566-9000	8587
Majestic Floors Inc	5023	E	925 825-0771	8516
Marvac Scientific Mfg Co	3821	F	925 825-4636	6695
Matson Logistics Inc	4731	E	925 887-6207	7846
McE Corporation **(PA)**	1611	D	925 803-4111	1058
Mdusd	8099	E	925 682-8000	17160
Mike McCall Landscape Inc	0782	C	925 363-8100	486
Mike Roses Auto Body Inc **(PA)**	7532	E	925 689-1739	14530
Mohin Inc	3499	E	925 798-5572	4985
Montclair Hotels Mb LLC	7011	B	925 687-5500	11309
Mt Dblo Resource Recovery LLC	4212	B	925 682-9113	7485
Mt Diablo Surgery Center	8062	E	925 674-4740	16460
Mt Diablo Unified School Dst	8742	D	925 685-1011	19581
Mt Diablo Unified School Dst	8322	D	925 685-7340	17651

(P-0000) Products & Services Section entry number
(PA)=Parent Co (HQ)=Headquarters (DH)=Div Headquarters

GEOGRAPHIC SECTION

	SIC	EMP	PHONE	ENTRY #
Muir Dblo Occptnal Mdcine Med	8011	E	925 685-7744	15541
N V Heathorn Inc	1711	D	510 569-9100	1314
Nevell Group Inc	1542	B	714 579-7501	929
Nordson Corporation	5065	E	925 827-1240	8939
Nordson March Inc (HQ)	3563	E	925 827-1240	5187
North American Asset Dev Corp (DH)	6361	D	925 935-5599	10205
Nu West Textile Group LLC	7218	E	925 676-1414	11665
On-Time AC & Htg LLC	1711	D	925 566-2422	1326
Overmiller Inc	7699	D	925 798-2122	14769
Pacific Gas and Electric Co	4911	C	925 676-0948	8152
Pacific Gas and Electric Co	4911	D	925 674-6305	8166
Pacific Instruments Inc	3829	E	925 827-9010	6915
Pacific Plaza Imports Inc (PA)	2091	F	925 349-4000	2828
Pacific Service Credit Union (PA)	6061	D	888 858-6878	9801
Pacific Stone Inc	1743	E	925 680-8741	1717
Parc Management LLC	7999	E	925 609-1364	15225
Parc Waterworld LLC	7996	B	925 609-1364	15044
Patriot Contract Services LLC	4412	B	925 296-2000	7711
Patterson Dental Supply Inc	3843	F	925 603-6350	7087
Pennys Guest Home LLC (PA)	8059	E	925 286-0424	16257
Petro-Chem Industries Inc	1742	D	707 644-7455	1699
Planned Prnthod Shst-Dblo Inc (PA)	8093	E	925 676-0300	17054
Pool Water Products	5091	F	925 827-4300	9160
Premier Surgery Center LP	8011	E	925 691-5000	15635
Pt Systems Inc	8711	E	925 676-0709	18795
Pulse Systems LLC	3842	D	925 798-4080	7078
R & L Brosamer Inc (HQ)	1542	E	925 627-1700	941
R&R Security Solutions Inc	7389	E	925 494-9000	14381
Regional Center of E Bay Inc	8322	D	925 691-2551	17688
RES-Care Inc	8082	E	925 283-5076	16935
Round Table Pizza Inc (DH)	6794	D	925 969-3900	10811
Russell Sigler Inc	5075	D	925 726-0141	9014
Sage Veterinary Centers LP	0742	B	925 288-4856	335
Scp Distributors LLC	5091	E	925 687-9500	9162
Service Hospitality LLC	7011	D	925 566-8820	11462
Shelter Inc (PA)	8322	E	925 335-0698	17741
Shelter Solano Inc	8322	E	925 957-7576	17742
Sigray Inc	3826	E	925 207-0925	6852
Stellar Enterprise Assoc Inc	8741	E	510 662-3333	19402
Stericycle Inc	7389	E	650 212-2332	14414
Stevens Frrone Biley Engrg Inc (PA)	8711	E	925 688-1001	18821
Stonebrook Convalescent Center	8051	C	925 689-7457	16130
Summit Building Services Inc	7349	E	925 827-9500	12002
Sutter Vsting Nrse Assn Hspice	8082	E	925 677-4250	16958
Swinerton Builders Inc (HQ)	1541	E	415 421-2980	811
Systron Donner Inertial Inc	3679	E	925 979-4400	6473
Telstar Instruments Inc	1731	E	925 671-2888	1620
The Inn	7011	D	925 682-1601	11531
Titus Mint Instlltion Svcs Llc	4953	E	909 357-3156	8367
Towill Inc (HQ)	8713	E	925 682-6976	18928
Tranquility Incorporated	8059	E	925 825-4280	16280
Ufcw & Employers Trust LLC (PA)	6733	C	800 552-2400	10800
Undergrund Svc Alert Nthrn Cal	8742	E	800 640-5137	19659
United Association Local 342	8631	D	925 686-5880	18381
United Sportsmen Incorporated	7999	E	925 676-1963	15261
USI Insurance Services Nat Inc	6021	D	925 988-1700	9693
Valley Rlction Stor Nthrn Cal (PA)	4214	E	925 230-2025	7638
Vep Healthcare Inc	8011	C	925 482-2839	15786
Versa Engineering & Tech Inc (PA)	8711	E	925 405-4505	18854
Veterans Health Administration	8011	C	925 680-4526	15805
Veterinary Surgical Associates (PA)	0742	E	925 827-1777	346
Vwi Concord LLC	7011	E	925 827-2000	11564
Weatherford Motors Inc	7538	C	510 654-8280	14603
Wells Fargo Bank National Assn	6021	B	925 746-3718	9695
White Mgic Clg Restoration Inc	7217	E	925 935-4449	11662
Whits Painting Inc (PA)	1721	E	925 429-2669	1437
Willow Pass Hlth Care Ctr Inc	8082	E	925 689-9222	16970
Windsor Cnvlscent Rhbltltion CT	8051	E	925 689-2266	16164
Yard House Restaurants LLC	7999	C	925 602-0523	15264
Young MNS Chrstn Assn of E Bay	8641	B	925 609-7971	18490
Youth Homes Incorporated	8361	E	925 933-2627	18214
Yupana Inc (PA)	8711	E	925 482-0657	18867
Zero Waste Solutions Inc	8744	C	925 270-3339	19707
Zwicker & Associates PC	8111	D	925 689-7070	17403

COOL, CA - El Dorado County

	SIC	EMP	PHONE	ENTRY #
A Teichert & Son Inc	1442	E	530 885-4244	585

COPPEROPOLIS, CA - Calaveras County

	SIC	EMP	PHONE	ENTRY #
Meridian Gold Inc	1041	B	209 785-3222	541

CORNING, CA - Tehama County

	SIC	EMP	PHONE	ENTRY #
Andersncttonwood Disposal Svcs	4212	D	530 824-4700	7450
Bell-Carter Foods LLC	2035	B	530 528-4820	2276
Blue Beacon USA LP	7542	E	530 824-0474	14629
Crane Mills	0173	D	530 824-5427	87
Eco-Shell Inc	3999	E	530 824-8794	7280
Jason Abel Construction Inc	1771	E	530 824-2022	1884
Northern Cal Child Dev Inc	8322	D	530 838-1034	17658
Olive Pit LLC	2033	F	530 824-4667	2235
Omega Waste Management Inc	8742	E	530 824-1890	19594
Paskenta Band Nomlaki Indians	8399	B	530 528-3538	18246
Rolling Hills Casino	7011	C	530 528-3500	11416
Sierra Pacific Industries	2431	D	530 824-2474	3151
Sunsweet Dryers	2034	E	530 824-5854	2269
Sunsweet Growers Inc	5149	D	530 824-5376	9493
Thomes Creek Rock Co Inc	1442	E	530 824-0191	599

CORTE MADERA, CA - Marin County

	SIC	EMP	PHONE	ENTRY #
Automted Mdia Proc Sltions Inc	4813	E	415 332-4343	7932
Brett V Crtis MD A Prof Corp I	8011	E	415 924-4525	15301
Century Theatres Inc	7833	E	415 924-6505	14828
Fifer Street Fitness Inc	7991	E	415 927-4653	14950
Golden Pppy Prschool Infant CT	8351	E	415 924-2828	17943
IL Fornaio (america) LLC (HQ)	5149	E	415 945-0500	9454
Jomu Mist Incorporated	7372	F	415 448-7273	13257
Marin Municipal Water District (PA)	4971	C	415 945-1455	8413
Marin Suites Hotel LLC	7011	D	415 924-3608	11284
Michaels Furniture Company Inc	2511	C	916 381-9086	3282
Micromega Systems Inc	7372	F	415 924-4900	13307
Nana Wall Systems Inc	5031	E	415 383-3148	8597
Pacific Catch Inc	2048	E	415 504-6905	2353
Ted Stevens Inc	7515	C	415 927-5664	14495

COTATI, CA - Sonoma County

	SIC	EMP	PHONE	ENTRY #
21st Century Health Club (PA)	8093	D	707 795-0400	16982
Barlow and Sons Printing Inc	2752	F	707 664-9773	3628
Beyond Pool Care Inc (PA)	7389	D	707 535-6463	14216
Biotherm Hydronic Inc	3433	F	707 794-9660	4626
Goode Printing and Mailing LLC	7331	E	707 588-8028	11837
J&M Manufacturing Inc	3679	E	707 795-8223	6438
Lowes Home Centers LLC	5031	C	707 242-5000	8578
Mike Brown Electric Co	1731	C	707 792-8100	1546
Norcal Geophysical Cons Inc	8999	D	707 796-7170	19915
Pacific Door Products Inc	1751	E	707 795-7777	1749
Pacific Restoration Inc	7349	E	707 588-8226	11983
Protransport-1 LLC (HQ)	4119	A	707 975-2386	7396
San Franstitchco Inc	2395	E	707 795-6891	3043
Santa Rosa Fire Eqp Svc Inc	5087	E	707 546-0797	9146
Santa Rosa Hardware Co Inc	5072	E	707 795-2500	8989
Stockham Construction Inc	1751	B	707 664-0945	1761

COTTONWOOD, CA - Shasta County

	SIC	EMP	PHONE	ENTRY #
All Pro Drywall	1742	E	530 722-5182	1657
Plum Valley Inc	2421	E	530 262-6262	3100
Skyline Tree Enterprise Inc	0723	E	530 736-9327	309

COVELO, CA - Mendocino County

	SIC	EMP	PHONE	ENTRY #
Round Vly Indian Hlth Ctr Inc	8011	D	707 983-6182	15653
Wylatti Resource MGT Inc	2411	E	707 983-8135	3088

CRESCENT CITY, CA - Del Norte County

	SIC	EMP	PHONE	ENTRY #
Del Norte Assoc For Dvlpmntl S	8331	E	707 464-8338	17811
Elk Valley Casino Inc	7011	C	707 464-1020	11078
North Shore Investment Inc	8051	D	707 464-6151	16075
Orca Heating and Rfrgn Inc	1711	E	707 464-9529	1329
Remi Vista Inc	8361	D	707 464-4349	18170
Rumiano Cheese Co	2022	E	707 465-1535	2155
Rural Human Services (PA)	8322	E	707 464-7441	17697
Snoozie Shavings Inc (PA)	4213	E	707 464-6186	7595
Sutter Coast Hospital (HQ)	8062	C	707 464-8511	16580
Sutter Coast Hospital	8082	B	707 464-8741	16953

CROCKETT, CA - Contra Costa County

	SIC	EMP	PHONE	ENTRY #
Bruce Carone Grading & Pav Inc	1611	D	510 787-4070	1018
C&H Sugar Company Inc	2063	A	510 787-2121	2423

CROWLEY LAKE, CA - Mono County

	SIC	EMP	PHONE	ENTRY #
Convict Lake Resort Inc	7011	E	760 934-3800	11033

CROWS LANDING, CA - Stanislaus County

	SIC	EMP	PHONE	ENTRY #
Covanta Stanislaus Inc	4953	E	209 837-4423	8321
Perez Farms LP	6519	E	209 837-4701	10485

CUPERTINO, CA - Santa Clara County

	SIC	EMP	PHONE	ENTRY #
AAC Technologies Holdings Inc (HQ)	5064	E	408 490-4263	8882
Abound Logic Inc	3674	E	408 873-3400	6006
Aemetis Inc (PA)	2869	F	408 213-0940	4117
Altia Systems Inc	3861	E	408 996-9710	7148
Amino Technologies (us) LLC (HQ)	3663	E	408 861-1400	5820
Anacom Inc	3663	E	408 519-2062	5821
Apple Inc (PA)	3663	A	408 996-1010	5823
Athelas Inc	3841	E	408 603-1954	6946
California Dental Arts LLC	8072	D	408 255-1020	16823
Celona Inc	7372	E	408 839-7625	13056
Ch Cupertino Owner LLC	7011	D	408 253-8900	11000
Chasen (Jay) Inc	6719	E	408 725-7571	10730
Claris International Inc (HQ)	7371	C	408 987-7000	12340
Codefast Inc	7372	E	408 687-4700	13082
Corinthian Intl Prkg Svcs Inc	7382	B	408 867-7275	14125
Courtyard Management Corp	7011	E	408 252-9100	11037
CRC Health Corporate (DH)	8093	D	408 367-0044	17012
CRC Health LLC (DH)	8069	D	877 272-8668	16754
Cupertino Dental Group	8021	D	408 257-3031	15830
Cupertino Healthcare	8051	D	408 253-9034	15978
Cupertino Hspitality Assoc LLC	7011	C	408 777-8787	11042
Cupertino Lessee LLC	7011	E	908 253-8900	11043
Digite Inc	7371	C	408 418-3834	12392
Durect Corporation (PA)	2834	D	408 777-1417	3894
Ecrio Inc	7372	E	408 973-7290	13130
Ewing-Foley Inc (PA)	5065	E	408 342-1201	8910
Falkonry Inc	7371	E	408 761-7108	12442
First Technology Federal Cr Un	6061	D	408 863-6240	9788
Forge-Vdvich Mtl Ltd Prtnr A C	7011	E	408 996-7700	11098
Forum Healthcare Center	8051	E	650 944-0200	16008
Gregory Associates Inc	3825	E	408 446-5725	6759
Hantronix Inc	3559	E	408 252-1100	5151

Employment Codes: A=Over 500 employees, B=251-500, C=101-250, D=51-100, E=20-50 F=10-19

CUPERTINO, CA GEOGRAPHIC SECTION

	SIC	EMP	PHONE	ENTRY #
Huawei Enterprise USA Inc	4813	D	408 394-4295	7959
Indium Software Inc	7372	E	408 501-8844	13228
Lehigh Southwest Cement Co	3241	F	408 996-4271	4395
Liberty Laboratories Inc	3825	E	408 262-6633	6765
Max Sportsters Inc	8741	E	408 446-8330	19368
Mirapath Inc **(PA)**	5045	E	408 873-7883	8728
Mist Systems Inc	7373	C	408 326-0346	13634
Mobileum Inc **(PA)**	4899	C	408 844-6600	8081
Mockingbird Networks	3571	F	408 342-5300	5262
Montvale Inc	8059	E	408 739-5446	16254
Noon Home Inc	8731	E	650 242-7565	19093
Optofidelity Inc	8711	E	669 241-8383	18783
Paracor Medical Inc	3845	F	408 207-1050	7121
Paypal Inc	7389	B	408 967-3256	14356
Pluris Inc	7373	C	408 863-9920	13650
Plusai Inc	7372	D	408 508-4758	13374
Postx Corporation	7371	E	408 861-3500	12694
Rancher Labs Inc **(DH)**	7371	D	650 521-6902	12724
Rancho San Antnio Rtrment Hsin	8361	B	650 265-2637	18163
Seagate US LLC	3572	E	408 658-1000	5320
Sigos LLC **(HQ)**	7389	E	650 535-0599	14405
Silver Lake Partners II LP	6726	E	408 454-4732	10782
Solutionsati Consulting Inc	8748	E	408 655-0224	19862
Stevens Creek Quarry Inc **(PA)**	1611	D	408 253-2512	1075
Sugarcrm Inc **(PA)**	7371	C	877 842-7276	12831
Sunny Retirement Home	8059	D	408 454-5600	16276
Synophic Systems Inc	7371	B	408 459-7676	12842
Taiwan Apple LLC **(HQ)**	3663	E	408 996-1010	5874
Tropian Inc	3674	E	408 865-1300	6335
Vnomic Inc	7372	E	408 641-3810	13523
Wchs Inc	8082	E	877 706-0510	16967
West Coast Venture Capital LLC **(PA)**	3661	B	408 725-0700	5816

DALY CITY, CA - San Mateo County

	SIC	EMP	PHONE	ENTRY #
Bay Area Obstetrics Gynecology	8011	E	650 756-2404	15288
Bdp Bowl Inc	7933	D	650 878-0300	14886
Catholic Chrties Cyo of The AR	4151	D	650 757-2110	7424
Creative Instructional Systems	8351	E	650 756-4737	17919
Duggans Serra Mortuary	7261	D	650 756-4500	11699
EKI Environment & Water Inc **(PA)**	8711	E	650 292-9100	18701
Forte Enterprises Inc **(PA)**	8741	C	650 994-3200	19337
Genesys Cloud Services Inc **(HQ)**	7372	B	650 466-1100	13187
Hillcrest Senior Housing Corp	6513	A	650 757-1737	10438
Kaiser Foundation Hospitals	6324	C	650 301-5860	10128
Lake Merced Golf Club	7997	D	650 755-2233	15104
Longs Drug Stores Cal LLC	7384	C	650 994-0752	14174
Nediljka Colma Inc **(PA)**	8051	E	650 992-2727	16067
New Haven Home Health Svcs Inc	8082	E	650 301-1660	16915
Olympic Club	8641	D	415 404-4300	18445
Pacific Gas and Electric Co	4911	C	800 684-4648	8156
Pacific Gas and Electric Co	4911	C	650 755-1236	8174
Permanente Medical Group Inc	8011	A	650 301-5800	15591
Permanente Medical Group Inc	8011	A	650 301-5860	15623
Philippines Today LLC	2711	F	650 872-3200	3474
Reneson Hotels Inc **(PA)**	7011	D	650 449-5353	11396
Serra Bowl Inc **(PA)**	7933	E	415 626-2626	14899
Serra Yellow Cab Daly City Inc	4121	E	650 333-9598	7414
Seton Medical Center **(HQ)**	8062	A	650 992-4000	16522
Seton Medical Center	8062	D	650 992-4000	16524
Shyam Lodging Group II LLC	7011	E	650 755-7500	11475
Spinecare Med Group Inc A Prof	8011	D	650 985-7500	15698
Spruce Biosciences Inc	2834	F	415 294-1687	3987
St Francis Hts Convalescent	8059	D	650 755-9515	16273
Tender Rose Home Care LLC	8082	E	415 340-3990	16959
View Rite Manufacturing	2541	E	415 468-3856	3323
Westlake Bakery Inc	2051	F	650 994-7741	2411

DANVILLE, CA - Contra Costa County

	SIC	EMP	PHONE	ENTRY #
Bara Infoware Inc **(PA)**	8711	D	925 790-0130	18636
Bay Valley Medical Group Inc **(PA)**	8011	D	510 785-5000	15293
Blackhawk Country Club	7997	C	925 736-6500	15062
Braddock & Logan Services Inc	1542	C	925 736-4000	836
Braddock Logan Ventr Group LP **(PA)**	1531	A	925 736-4000	778
Brookfeld Bay Area Hldings LLC	6552	D	925 743-8000	10697
Central Garden & Pet Company	5199	E	925 964-9879	9650
Choice Foodservices Inc	3365	D	925 837-0104	4583
Cleary Bros Landscape Inc	0781	C	925 838-2551	407
Community Presbt Ch Danville **(PA)**	8351	C	925 837-5525	17913
Cooke & Associates Inc **(PA)**	7381	E	408 842-0602	14046
Crow Canyon Management Corp	7997	D	925 735-5700	15080
Danville Long-Term Care Inc	8051	D	925 837-4566	15979
Discovery Cnsling Ctr of San R	8322	D	925 837-0505	17533
DW Morgan LLC	4789	D	925 460-2700	7880
Empire Realty Associates Inc	6531	A	925 217-5000	10544
Forty Four Group LLC **(PA)**	7311	D	949 407-6360	11754
Fremont Bank	6022	D	925 314-1420	9733
Grigsby & Associates Inc **(PA)**	6211	D	214 522-4664	9974
Hanson & Fitch Inc	7389	D	800 847-7037	14292
I Can Do That Theatre Company	7922	E	415 264-2518	14848
James E Roberts-Obayashi Corp	1522	C	925 820-0600	751
Millennial Brands LLC **(PA)**	5139	D	866 938-4806	9260
Pacific Union Homes Inc **(PA)**	6552	D	925 314-3800	10712
Private Mortgage Advisors LLC	6162	E	408 754-1610	9921
Razvi Inc	7374	E	925 242-1200	13751
Ready Pac Foods Inc	5148	B	925 552-0400	9426
Recall Masters Inc	7331	E	650 434-5211	11840
Reutlinger Community	8322	C	925 964-2062	17693
San Ramon Vly Unified Schl Dst	8641	D	925 552-2880	18463
Tenet Healthsystem Medical Inc	8011	D	925 275-8303	15739
Town of Danville	7999	E	925 314-3400	15255
Trov Inc **(PA)**	7372	F	925 478-5500	13498

DAVENPORT, CA - Santa Cruz County

	SIC	EMP	PHONE	ENTRY #
Big Creek Lumber Company **(PA)**	2421	D	831 457-5015	3091

DAVIS, CA - Yolo County

	SIC	EMP	PHONE	ENTRY #
A Teichert & Son Inc	1611	E	530 406-4200	998
Agrinos Inc **(PA)**	0723	D	888 706-9505	267
Antibodies Incorporated	2835	F	800 824-8540	4016
Chai DDS Inc	8021	C	909 810-7287	15827
Communicare Health Centers	8011	C	530 758-2060	15356
Covell Gardens	8361	D	530 756-0700	18086
Covenant Care Courtyard LLC	8051	C	530 756-1800	15973
Cvf Capital Partners Inc	6799	C	530 757-7004	10840
Davis Community Clinic **(PA)**	8011	D	530 758-2060	15373
Davis Community Meals Inc	8322	D	530 756-4008	17528
Davis Golf Course Inc	7992	E	530 756-0647	14998
Dmg Mori Digital Tech Lab Corp	3545	E	530 746-7400	5093
Dmg Mori Manufacturing USA Inc **(HQ)**	3541	C	530 746-7400	5073
Doug Arnold Real Estate Inc **(PA)**	6531	E	530 758-3080	10541
Electronic Resources Network	3577	E	530 758-0180	5363
Engage3 Inc	8742	E	530 231-5485	19502
Envirnmental Trnsp Specialists	7538	D	916 442-4971	14560
Expression Systems LLC **(PA)**	2836	E	877 877-7421	4048
Far Wstern Anthrplgcal RES Gro **(PA)**	8748	E	530 756-3941	19774
FPI Management Inc	6531	C	530 756-5332	10552
Frontier AG Co Inc **(PA)**	2048	E	530 297-1020	2344
Gold Standard Diagnostics Corp **(PA)**	5047	D	530 759-8000	8780
Greenvenus LLC	8731	E	530 648-9985	19064
Hmclause Inc **(DH)**	0181	C	800 320-4672	127
Ikes Landscaping & Maintenance	0782	D	530 758-1698	470
Interior United States Dept	8011	D	530 752-6745	15436
Kaiser Foundation Hospitals	8011	C	530 757-7100	15477
Mariner Health Care Inc	8051	E	530 756-1800	16051
Marrone Bio Innovations Inc **(PA)**	2879	C	530 750-2800	4143
McNaughton Newspapers	2711	D	530 756-0800	3457
Neo Power Technology Inc	1623	D	415 830-6167	1124
Novozymes Inc **(DH)**	8732	D	530 757-8100	19175
Pacific Gas and Electric Co	4911	C	530 757-5803	8184
Pacific Retirement Svcs Inc	8361	D	530 753-1450	18154
Rvm Davis Housing Corporation	8361	C	530 747-7095	18174
Signa Chemistry Inc	2819	E	212 933-4101	3796
Stokes Vannoy Inc	8711	E	530 747-2026	18822
Sudwerk Privatbrauerei Hubsch	2082	D	530 756-2739	2495
Sutter Health	8062	C	530 747-0389	16582
Sutter Health	8062	C	530 750-5904	16596
Sutter Health	8062	C	530 750-5800	16612
Sutter Health	8062	C	530 750-5888	16657
Sutter Hlth Scrmnto Sierra Reg	8062	B	530 747-5010	16660
Tandem Properties Incorporated **(PA)**	6531	E	530 756-5075	10670
Tc Prprty MGT Ltd A Cal Ltd PR	6799	E	530 666-5799	10889
Uc Davis Shared Services Ctr	8721	E	530 754-4772	19002
University California Davis	8062	D	530 752-1653	16700
University California Davis	8731	E	530 750-1313	19145
University California Davis	8011	D	530 747-3000	15772
University California Davis	8071	D	530 752-2314	16818
University California Davis	4151	D	530 752-8277	7443
University California Davis	8011	D	530 752-4167	15778
University California Davis	8011	D	530 752-2300	15779
University California Davis	8011	D	530 752-2330	15782
University California Davis	4581	C	530 752-5435	7792
University of California	8741	D	530 752-0503	19415
Veterinary Information Network **(PA)**	0742	E	530 756-4881	344
West Yost & Associates Inc **(PA)**	8711	D	530 756-5905	18859
Woodland Healthcare	8062	C	530 756-2364	16727
Yolo County Childrens Alliance	6733	E	530 757-5558	10801
Yolo Hospice Inc **(PA)**	8082	D	530 758-5566	16971

DEL REY, CA - Fresno County

	SIC	EMP	PHONE	ENTRY #
Chooljian & Sons Inc **(PA)**	0723	D	559 888-2031	279
Cy Truss	2439	E	559 888-2160	3204
Del Rey Juice Co	2037	D	559 888-8533	2291
Economy Stock Feed Company Inc	2048	E	559 888-2187	2340
Vita-Pakt Citrus Products Co	2033	F	559 233-4452	2248

DELHI, CA - Merced County

	SIC	EMP	PHONE	ENTRY #
Califrnia Psychtric Trnsitions	8011	D	209 667-9304	15316

DENAIR, CA - Stanislaus County

	SIC	EMP	PHONE	ENTRY #
California Royale LLC	0723	E	209 874-1866	274
Central Valley Concrete Inc	1711	D	209 667-0161	1232
J Crecelius Inc	0191	D	209 883-4826	170
Montpelier Nut Company Inc	0723	E	209 874-5126	294
Valley Fresh Foods Inc	0252	E	209 669-5510	234
Vista Livestock Co New **(PA)**	0241	E	209 874-9446	227
Woodys Poultry Supply	1542	F	209 634-2948	992

DIABLO, CA - Contra Costa County

	SIC	EMP	PHONE	ENTRY #
Diablo Country Club	7997	E	925 837-4221	15086

DIAMOND SPRINGS, CA - El Dorado County

	SIC	EMP	PHONE	ENTRY #
Burger Physcl Therapy Svcs Inc	8049	E	530 626-4734	15886
Cook Cabinets Inc	1751	E	530 621-0851	1735
Demtech Services Inc	3089	E	530 621-3200	4276
McDaniel Manufacturing Inc	3429	F	530 626-6336	4619
Smits Sheet Metal Inc	1711	E	530 622-8446	1361
Snowline Hspice El Dorado Cnty	8052	C	530 621-7820	16204

	SIC	EMP	PHONE	ENTRY #
Snowline Hspice of El Drado CN	8052	C	916 817-2338	16205
Sub Sea Systems Inc	7999	E	530 626-0100	15247
Western Sign Company Inc	3993	E	916 933-3765	7261

DILLON BEACH, CA - Marin County

	SIC	EMP	PHONE	ENTRY #
Lawsons Landing Inc	7033	E	707 878-2443	11619

DIXON, CA - Solano County

	SIC	EMP	PHONE	ENTRY #
Bellingham Marine Inds Inc	1629	E	707 678-2385	1150
Button Transportation Inc	4213	C	707 678-7434	7515
Bwdixon LLC **(PA)**	7011	E	707 678-1400	10981
Castlelite Block LLC **(PA)**	3271	E	707 678-3465	4412
Cemex Materials LLC	3273	D	707 678-4311	4470
Chavez & Sons Trucking LLC	3715	F	707 999-1409	6600
Community Medical Center	8011	E	209 944-4705	15357
Dependable Sheet Metal	1711	E	707 678-9600	1249
Ellensburg Lamb Company Inc	2011	D	707 678-3091	2095
First Northern Bank of Dixon **(HQ)**	6022	D	707 678-4422	9717
First Northern Cmnty Bancorp **(PA)**	6022	D	707 678-3041	9718
Fremouw Environmental Svcs Inc	8748	D	707 448-3700	19779
Fresenius Med Care Slano Cnty	8092	D	707 678-6433	16974
Gaelco Leasing Inc **(PA)**	6159	E	707 678-4404	9887
Global Rental Co Inc	7513	C	707 693-2520	14469
Greiner Htg - A - Slar Enrgy I	1711	E	707 678-1784	1274
Hemostat Laboratories Inc **(PA)**	2836	E	707 678-9594	4050
Isec Incorporated	1751	D	707 693-6555	1743
J & A Jeffery Inc	3999	E	707 678-0369	7289
John Stewart Company	6531	E	707 676-5660	10585
Recology Inc	4953	D	916 379-3300	8352
Salaber Associates Inc	8748	E	707 693-8800	19855
Salad Cosmo USA Corp	2099	E	707 678-6633	2941
Sr Shroeder Inc	5012	F	707 693-8166	8428
Transhumance Holding Co Inc	2011	C	707 693-2303	2105

DOS PALOS, CA - Merced County

	SIC	EMP	PHONE	ENTRY #
C&S Global Foods Inc	2099	F	209 392-2223	2876
Dos Palos Memorial Hosp Inc	8011	D	209 392-6121	15384
James Carollo & Co	0722	F	209 392-3737	264
Redfern Ranches	0212	E	209 392-2426	203
Rita Christiana-Santa Farms	0762	E	209 387-4578	387

DUBLIN, CA - Alameda County

	SIC	EMP	PHONE	ENTRY #
A A Label Inc **(PA)**	2679	E	925 803-5709	3400
Allyn James Inc	2752	F	925 828-5530	3618
AMS Electric Inc	1731	D	925 961-1600	1452
Astute Business Solutions	7371	C	925 997-3267	12279
Azure Biosystems Inc	8731	E	925 307-7127	19032
Bay Area News Group E Bay LLC **(HQ)**	7319	E	925 302-1683	11810
Carl Zeiss Meditec Inc **(DH)**	3827	B	925 557-4100	6867
Carl Zeiss Ophthalmic Systems	3841	E	925 557-4100	6960
Carl Ziss X-Ray Microscopy Inc	3844	D	925 701-3600	7091
CCM Partnership	7539	E	925 829-1950	14608
Challenge Dairy Products Inc **(HQ)**	5143	D	925 828-6160	9335
Cypress Green	0762	E	510 861-2214	372
Del Monte Electric Co Inc **(PA)**	1731	E	925 829-6000	1495
Desilva Gates Construction LP **(PA)**	1611	D	925 361-1380	1031
Dublin Hstrcal Prsrvation Assn	8412	D	925 785-2898	18270
Dublin San Ramon Services Dst **(PA)**	4941	C	925 875-2276	8233
Dublin Volkswagen	7538	D	925 829-0800	14558
Eg Systems LLC **(PA)**	3674	D	510 324-0126	6107
Epicor Software Corporation	7372	C	925 361-9900	13146
Franklin Tmpleton Inv Svcs LLC	6282	C	925 875-2619	10046
Gateway Landscape Cnstr Inc	0782	D	925 875-0000	466
Gettler-Ryan Inc **(PA)**	1799	D	925 551-7555	2034
Giga-Tronics Incorporated **(PA)**	3825	F	925 328-4650	6757
Harvey & Madding Inc	7538	D	925 828-8030	14570
Hdx International Inc **(PA)**	5065	E	925 922-1448	8916
Health Svcs Bneft Admnstrtors **(PA)**	6371	D	925 833-7300	10215
Hope Hospice Inc	7021	C	925 829-8770	11590
Immunoscience LLC **(PA)**	8731	E	925 460-8111	19071
Interntnal Ptro Pdts Addtves I	2992	F	925 556-5530	4194
Ipac Inc	2992	F	925 556-5530	4195
Itradenetwork Inc **(HQ)**	8742	E	925 660-1100	19546
Kensington Laboratories LLC **(PA)**	3625	F	510 324-0126	5682
Kms Technology Inc **(PA)**	7371	E	925 828-1906	12560
Lowes Home Centers LLC	5031	C	925 241-3082	8585
Lusardi Construction Co	1542	C	925 829-1114	916
Messagesolution Inc	7379	D	925 833-8000	13936
Norcal Ambulance LLC	4119	E	925 452-8300	7392
Oliver De Silva Inc **(PA)**	1429	E	925 829-9220	580
Onyx Optics Inc	3827	F	925 833-1969	6882
Oracle Taleo LLC **(HQ)**	7372	D	925 452-3000	13355
Pacific Sttes Envmtl Cntrs Inc	1542	E	925 803-4333	936
Patelco Credit Union **(PA)**	6061	C	800 358-8228	9802
Print Ink Inc	2759	E	925 829-3950	3746
Rainforest Qa Inc	7371	C	650 866-1407	12723
Raps Dublin LLC	7011	E	925 828-9393	11384
Republic Document Management	8741	E	925 551-4747	19388
Saba Software Inc **(DH)**	7372	D	877 722-2101	13419
San Francisco Elev Svcs Inc	5084	E	925 829-5400	9093
Sansa Technology LLC	8731	E	866 204-3710	19124
Sybase Inc **(DH)**	7372	E	925 236-5000	13478
Sybase 365 LLC	7371	D	925 236-5000	12836
Trevi Partners A Calif LP **(HQ)**	7011	C	925 828-7750	11541
Trinet Group Inc **(PA)**	7389	A	510 352-5000	14442
Trinet Usa Inc	7361	D	510 352-5000	12147
Vagaro Inc	7371	D	800 919-0157	12893
Warmington Homes	1531	C	925 866-6700	786

DUNCANS MILLS, CA - Sonoma County

	SIC	EMP	PHONE	ENTRY #
Casini Enterprises Inc	7033	E	707 865-2255	11617

DUNNIGAN, CA - Yolo County

	SIC	EMP	PHONE	ENTRY #
Ankoor Financial Llc	7011	E	530 724-3471	10925

DUNSMUIR, CA - Siskiyou County

	SIC	EMP	PHONE	ENTRY #
Castle Rock Spring Water Co	2086	E	530 678-4444	2786
Railroad Park Inc	7011	E	530 235-2300	11380
Saint Germain Foundation **(PA)**	2721	F	530 235-2994	3513

DURHAM, CA - Butte County

	SIC	EMP	PHONE	ENTRY #
Cal Custom Enterprises Inc	7692	F	530 774-2621	14711
Chico Produce Inc **(PA)**	5148	C	530 893-0596	9393
Chico Produce Inc	5148	E	530 241-1124	9394
Old Durham Wood Inc	0783	E	530 342-7381	519
Tink Inc	3531	E	530 895-0897	5041
Westgate Hardwoods Inc **(PA)**	2431	E	530 892-0300	3159

E PALO ALTO, CA - Santa Clara County

	SIC	EMP	PHONE	ENTRY #
Golden Bay Insulation Inc **(PA)**	1742	E	650 743-1628	1677

EAST PALO ALTO, CA - Santa Clara County

	SIC	EMP	PHONE	ENTRY #
Alston & Bird LLP	8111	D	650 838-2000	17200
Cal-Spray Inc	3479	F	650 325-0096	4929
Cintas Corporation No 3	7218	E	650 589-4300	11663
East Palo Alto Hotel Dev Inc	7011	C	650 566-1200	11070
Greenberg Traurig LLP	8111	D	650 328-8500	17282
Hggc LLC **(PA)**	6799	B	650 321-4910	10853
Incognia US Inc	7371	D	650 463-9280	12515
Machine Zone LLC	7372	D	650 320-1678	13286
Marvel Parent LLC **(HQ)**	7371	E	650 321-4910	12597
Nutrition Parent LLC **(DH)**	6799	D	650 321-4910	10873
South Cnty Cmnty Hlth Ctr Inc **(PA)**	8011	D	650 330-7407	15696
Zadaonet	4813	D	650 556-6377	8011

ECHO LAKE, CA - El Dorado County

	SIC	EMP	PHONE	ENTRY #
Echo Chalet Inc	7011	E	530 659-7207	11072

EDGEWOOD, CA - Siskiyou County

	SIC	EMP	PHONE	ENTRY #
Siskiyou Development Company	7011	D	530 938-2731	11483

EL CERRITO, CA - Contra Costa County

	SIC	EMP	PHONE	ENTRY #
Bay Area Cmnty Resources Inc	8322	E	510 559-3000	17436
Berkeley Country Club	7997	C	510 233-7550	15059
Borden Decal Company Inc	2759	F	415 431-1587	3722
Doulas By Bay LLC	8099	D	415 510-9736	17138
Marvin Gardens Real Property	6531	E	510 527-9111	10613
Summerville Senior Living Inc	8051	E	510 234-5200	16133

EL DORADO, CA - El Dorado County

	SIC	EMP	PHONE	ENTRY #
Conforti Plumbing Inc	1711	E	530 622-0202	1240
Hearthco Inc	3429	E	530 622-3877	4617

EL DORADO HILLS, CA - El Dorado County

	SIC	EMP	PHONE	ENTRY #
478826 Limited	3599	E	916 933-5280	5455
8minute Solar Energy LLC **(PA)**	1711	E	916 608-9060	1185
Access Systems Inc	3826	E	916 941-8099	6803
Aerometals Inc **(PA)**	3728	D	916 939-6888	6629
Almendariz Consulting Inc	8748	E	916 939-3392	19718
Alpha Research & Tech Inc	3571	D	916 431-9340	5239
Amdocs Bcs Inc	7371	B	916 934-7000	12247
Ampac Fine Chemicals LLC	2834	E	916 245-6500	3845
Bayshore Metals	5051	E	415 647-7981	8808
Bayview Engrg & Cnstr Co Inc	1711	D	916 939-8986	1215
Blaize Inc **(PA)**	3674	B	916 347-0050	6068
Bruder Industry	3599	D	916 939-6888	5484
California Suites **(PA)**	6519	E	916 941-7970	10477
Cameo Crafts	2759	D	513 381-1480	3724
Cason Engineering Inc	3599	E	916 939-9311	5490
CBS Maxpreps Inc	4813	E	530 676-6440	7938
Clear Image Inc **(PA)**	2673	E	916 933-4700	3383
Comerit Inc	7379	E	888 556-5990	13872
Datamax Software Group Inc	7371	E	916 939-4065	12372
Digital Doc LLC	5047	E	916 941-8010	8779
Dorado Software Inc	7371	D	916 673-1100	12399
Dst Output California Inc	7378	C	916 939-4617	13821
El Dorado Hills Cmnty Svcs Dst	7999	C	916 933-6624	15202
El Dorado Hills County Wtr Dst	4941	D	916 933-6623	8247
Enterprise Rnt—car Scrmnto LL	7514	C	916 934-0783	14484
Filtration Development Co LLC	3677	E	415 884-0555	6380
Frank Gates Service Company	8742	E	916 934-0812	19518
G3 Enterprises Inc	4225	E	209 341-8670	7690
Gold Rush Energy Solutions	1711	E	530 334-0676	1272
Hdd Co Inc	8742	E	530 676-5705	19532
Illinois Tool Works Inc	3674	D	916 939-4332	6148
Infinite Technologies Inc **(PA)**	8711	D	916 987-3261	18737
Jared G Dnielson DDS Dntl Corp **(PA)**	8021	D	916 230-8837	15840
Kdf Enterprises LLC	3531	C	803 928-7073	5035
Lyon Realty	6531	C	916 939-5300	10607
Marshall Medical Center	8062	E	530 344-5400	16443
Marshall Medical Center	8062	E	916 933-2273	16449
Maxar Space LLC	3663	A	916 605-5448	5854
McClone Construction Company	1771	C	916 358-5495	1893
Nor-Cal Controls Es Inc	4939	D	916 836-0800	8217
O1 Communications Inc	4813	D	888 444-1111	7976
Paragon Products Limited LLC **(PA)**	5084	E	916 941-9717	9086
Patra Corporation **(PA)**	6311	C	415 595-9987	10078
Patrick K Willis and Co Inc	7389	B	800 398-6480	14353
Pottery World LLC	5023	D	916 358-8788	8519

GEOGRAPHIC

Employment Codes: A=Over 500 employees, B=251-500, C=101-250, D=51-100, E=20-50 F=10-19

2022 Northern California Business Directory and Buyers Guide

© Mergent Inc. 1-800-342-5647

1141

	SIC	EMP	PHONE	ENTRY #
Precision Contacts Inc	3663	E	916 939-4147	5861
R Systems Inc **(HQ)**	7373	D	916 939-9696	13655
RCP Construction Inc	1542	E	916 358-9530	944
Regional Builders Inc **(PA)**	1521	E	916 717-2669	695
Roebbelen Construction Inc	1542	D	916 939-4000	948
Roebbelen Contracting Inc	1542	B	916 939-4000	949
School Innovations Achievement **(PA)**	7372	D	916 933-2290	13428
School Innvtons Achevement Inc	8742	E	800 487-9234	19627
Securecom Inc	1731	D	916 638-2855	1603
Sepasoft Inc	7372	E	916 939-1684	13438
Sequoia Insurance Company	6411	D	916 933-9524	10350
Serrano Associates LLC	7997	D	916 939-3333	15141
Serrano Country Club Inc	7997	C	916 933-5005	15142
Synvasive Technology Inc	3841	C	916 939-3913	7046
Tracpatch Health Inc	5047	D	916 355-7123	8793
Tri-Signal Integration Inc	1731	D	916 933-3155	1623
V3 Electric Inc	4911	C	916 597-2627	8206
V3 Systems Scrtyautomation Inc	7389	E	916 543-1543	14453
Warren Cnsulting Engineers Inc	8711	E	916 985-1870	18857
Western Water Features Inc	1799	E	916 939-1600	2087
Wyndgate Technologies	7379	E	916 404-8400	14011
Youngdahl Consulting Group Inc	8711	E	916 933-0633	18866

EL GRANADA, CA - San Mateo County

	SIC	EMP	PHONE	ENTRY #
Exclusive Fresh Inc	5146	E	650 728-7321	9365
San Mateo County Harbor Dst	4493	E	650 583-4400	7732

EL MACERO, CA - Yolo County

	SIC	EMP	PHONE	ENTRY #
El Macero Country Club Inc	7997	D	530 753-3363	15088

EL NIDO, CA - Merced County

	SIC	EMP	PHONE	ENTRY #
Double Diamond Dairy & Ranch	0241	D	209 722-8505	210
Frank Coelho & Sons LP	0241	E	209 722-6843	211

EL SOBRANTE, CA - Contra Costa County

	SIC	EMP	PHONE	ENTRY #
Central Assembly of God	8351	E	510 223-1966	17881
Falcon Critical Care Trans A	8099	E	510 223-1171	17147
Greenridge Senior Care	8361	C	510 758-9600	18125

ELDRIDGE, CA - Sonoma County

	SIC	EMP	PHONE	ENTRY #
Developmental Svcs Cal Dept	8069	A	707 938-6000	16756

ELK GROVE, CA - Sacramento County

	SIC	EMP	PHONE	ENTRY #
Aardvark Woodcraft Inc **(PA)**	2491	E	916 230-3518	3255
Airborne Security Patrol Inc **(PA)**	7381	D	916 394-2400	14026
Alldata LLC	7372	B	916 684-5200	12975
Apex Site Solutions Inc	8742	D	916 685-8619	19446
Bel Air Mart	6099	C	916 714-6996	9843
Bennathon Corp **(PA)**	1542	E	916 405-2100	831
Berber Food Manufacturing Inc	2099	C	510 553-0444	2870
Cal-Asia Truss Inc	2439	E	916 685-5648	3202
Carlton Senior Living Inc	6531	D	916 714-2404	10502
Century Theatres Inc	7833	C	916 683-5290	14819
Champion Installs Inc	2434	E	916 627-0929	3174
Citizens Telecom Co Cal Inc **(HQ)**	4813	B	317 208-3567	7939
Comprehensive SEC Svcs Inc **(PA)**	7381	D	916 683-3605	14044
Concrete North Inc	1771	D	209 745-7400	1859
Cosumnes Community Svcs Dst	7999	B	916 405-7150	15200
Cygnus Home Service LLC	2024	F	916 686-8662	2170
Decore-Ative Spc NC LLC	2431	C	916 686-4700	3128
Dominion International Inc	7011	E	916 683-9545	11057
Drd Hospitality Inc	7011	E	916 952-6552	11061
Eden Home Health Elk Grove LLC	8099	E	916 681-4949	17141
El & El Wood Products Corp	5031	E	916 685-1855	8544
Elk Grove Milling Inc	2048	E	916 684-2056	2341
Feist Cabinets & Woodworks Inc	1751	E	916 686-8230	1736
Future Energy Corporation **(PA)**	1742	C	800 985-0733	1675
G-Elk Grove LP	7011	D	916 478-9000	11110
Glacier Valley Ice Company LP **(PA)**	2097	E	916 394-2939	2860
GNB Corporation	3541	D	916 233-3543	5074
Grand Cabinets and Stone Inc **(PA)**	2434	F	916 270-7207	3180
Hanford Ready-Mix Inc	3273	E	916 405-1918	4484
Hayes Family Enterprises Inc	7532	D	916 686-8454	14526
Internal Revenue Service	8011	C	916 974-5678	15438
International Micro Design Inc	7371	E	888 216-6041	12534
Kaiser Foundation Hospitals	6324	C	916 478-5000	10111
Kaiser Foundation Hospitals	6324	C	916 544-6000	10116
Longs Drug Stores Cal LLC	7384	C	916 684-6811	14177
Lowes Home Centers LLC	5031	C	916 688-1922	8567
Matheson Fast Freight Inc **(HQ)**	4213	D	916 686-4600	7566
On The Spot Transportation LLC	7389	E	317 379-6692	14344
Pacific Modern Homes Inc	3444	E	916 685-9514	4799
PDM Steel Service Centers Inc	5051	C	916 513-4548	8825
Professional Bureau of Collect	7322	C	916 685-3399	11830
Ptac Hlen Carr Cstllo Cal Cngr	8641	E	916 686-1725	18452
R & A Painting Inc	1721	D	916 688-3955	1425
S & C Siding Inc	1522	E	916 491-0715	766
Sacramento Reg Co Sanit Dist	4952	B	916 875-9000	8288
Sacramento Yolo Cnty Mosquito	4959	D	916 685-1022	8404
Saia Motor Freight Line LLC	4213	D	916 690-8417	7587
Spare-Time Inc	7997	D	916 859-5910	15153
Super Pallet Recycling Corp **(PA)**	5031	D	916 686-1700	8609
Sutter Health	8062	C	916 691-5900	16597
Sutter Health	8062	C	916 455-8137	16599
Sutter Health	8062	C	916 544-5423	16604
Sutter Health	8062	C	916 691-5900	16623
Sutter Health	8062	C	916 731-7900	16654
Universal Custom Display	3993	C	916 714-2505	7258
Unlimited R US Inc **(PA)**	4812	E	916 509-4496	7917
Valley-HI Country Club	7997	C	916 684-2120	15164
Willdan Engineering	8711	D	916 661-3520	18861

ELVERTA, CA - Sacramento County

	SIC	EMP	PHONE	ENTRY #
Air Blown Concrete	1799	E	916 991-1738	1999

EMERALD HILLS, CA - San Mateo County

	SIC	EMP	PHONE	ENTRY #
Ernst Development Inc	1521	E	650 368-4539	636
Lakeview Lodge Inc	8361	E	650 369-7476	18133
Legion Industries	8641	E	650 743-6358	18436
Mongabayorg Corporation	2741	F	209 315-5573	3583
Stebbins Construction Corp	1521	E	650 299-1488	710

EMERYVILLE, CA - Alameda County

	SIC	EMP	PHONE	ENTRY #
4d Molecular Therapeutics Inc	8731	D	510 505-2680	19008
Adamas Pharmaceuticals Inc **(PA)**	2834	C	510 450-3500	3832
Aguatierra Associates Inc **(PA)**	8744	E	510 450-6000	19700
American Telesource Inc	5065	E	510 428-1111	8889
Amyris Inc **(PA)**	2869	A	510 450-0761	4120
Amyris Clean Beauty Inc	2844	E	510 450-0761	4080
Amyris Fuels LLC	5172	E	510 450-0761	9529
APM Terminals Pacific Ltd	4731	B	510 992-6430	7823
Armstrong Instllion Svc A Cal	1721	C	408 777-1234	1403
Art Supply Enterprises Inc **(PA)**	5199	E	800 289-9800	9646
Artcom Inc **(PA)**	8412	C	510 879-4700	18260
Assocted Intrnal Mdcine Med Gr **(PA)**	8011	E	510 465-6700	15285
Avg Technologies Usa Inc **(DH)**	7379	E	978 319-4460	13848
Bacchus Press Inc **(PA)**	2752	E	510 420-5800	3627
Barry Bishop	8111	D	510 596-0888	17207
Bayer Healthcare LLC	2834	C	510 597-6150	3862
Behavioral Intervention Assn	7363	E	510 652-7445	12161
Beigene Usa Inc	7389	D	619 733-1842	14213
Berkeley Lights Inc **(PA)**	3826	C	510 858-2855	6815
Bolt Threads Inc **(PA)**	8731	D	415 279-5585	19036
Broadmoor Hotel	7011	D	415 673-8445	10976
Califrnia Emrgncy Physcans Med	8011	E	510 350-2777	15314
Cell Design Labs Inc	2834	E	510 398-0501	3880
Center For Culinary Dev Inc	8731	D	415 693-8900	19041
Cep America - Anesthesia PC	8011	E	510 350-2842	15341
Cep America - Illinois LLP	8011	D	510 350-2777	15342
Cep America - Illinois Snf LLP	8051	E	510 350-2777	15955
Cep America - Intensivists PC	8011	E	510 350-2777	15343
Cep America - Kansas LLC	8011	E	510 350-2777	15344
Cep America LLC	8011	D	510 350-2691	15345
Cep Amrc-Llnois Hsptalists LLP	8011	E	510 350-2777	15346
Chiron Corporation	2834	A	510 655-8730	3883
Clark Richardson and Biskup	8711	E	510 907-2700	18671
Cleaire Advanced Emission **(PA)**	2911	E	510 347-6103	4174
Clear Skye Inc	7372	E	415 619-5001	13068
Clif Bar & Company **(PA)**	2064	A	510 596-6300	2427
Coulter Forge Technology Inc	3462	F	510 420-3500	4876
Cuberg Inc	8731	E	510 725-4200	19048
Dynavax Technologies Corp **(PA)**	2836	D	510 848-5100	4045
E2 Consulting Engineers Inc	8711	E	510 652-1164	18695
E2 Consulting Engineers Inc	8711	E	510 652-1164	18696
East Bay Endoscopy Center LP	8062	D	510 654-4554	16358
Engine World LLC	3714	E	510 653-4444	6577
Eureka Therapeutics Inc	8731	E	510 654-7045	19059
Folkmanis Inc	3999	E	510 658-7677	7285
Fort James Corporation	8741	A	510 594-4900	19336
FReal Foods LLC	2023	D	800 483-3218	2161
Geo M Martin Company **(PA)**	3554	D	510 652-2200	5118
Giampolini & Co	1721	C	415 673-1236	1415
Gracenote Inc **(DH)**	7371	B	510 428-7200	12486
Greenberg Inc **(PA)**	8732	E	510 446-8200	19164
Grid Alternative	1711	B	510 731-1310	1275
Gritstone Bio Inc **(PA)**	2836	C	510 871-6100	4049
Grocery Outlet Holding Corp **(PA)**	5141	B	510 845-1999	9272
Head Over Heels	7999	E	510 655-1265	15210
La Casa Ventures Inc	7359	E	415 272-3147	12051
Leapfrog Enterprises Inc **(HQ)**	3944	B	510 420-5000	7177
Ligand Pharmaceuticals Inc **(PA)**	2834	E	858 550-7500	3940
Lucira Health Inc	2835	D	510 350-8071	4023
Lumigrow Inc	3646	E	800 514-0487	5737
M Nexon Inc	7371	D	805 448-3351	12589
Maxim Healthcare Services Inc	7363	D	510 873-0700	12181
Mobitv Inc **(PA)**	4813	D	510 981-1303	7973
Monsoon Commerce Inc	7379	D	510 594-4500	13938
Motorola Solutions Inc	3575	E	510 420-7400	5335
Mutual Aid Response Svcs Inc	8748	E	866 627-7911	19826
National Mortgage Insur Corp	6162	E	855 530-6642	9916
Nmi Holdings Inc	6351	B	855 530-6642	10193
Novabay Pharmaceuticals Inc	2834	E	510 899-8800	3957
Novartis Corporation	2879	D	510 879-9500	4144
Nugeneration Technologies LLC **(PA)**	2899	F	707 820-4080	4165
Nutcracker Therapeutics Inc	3826	E	510 473-8478	6842
Oakland Mltary Inst Cllege Prp	8621	E	510 594-3900	18341
Operation Dignity Inc	8322	E	510 287-8465	17664
Pacific Hotel Management LLC	7011	C	510 547-7888	11346
Peets Coffee Inc **(DH)**	2095	D	510 594-2100	2842
Peets Coffee & Tea LLC **(DH)**	2095	A	510 594-2100	2843
PERFECT DAY INC	2026	E	203 848-8633	2193
Performance Grp of Nrthn CA	4724	E	510 923-9123	7806
Petit Pot Inc	2099	E	650 488-7432	2933
Pixar **(DH)**	7812	A	510 922-3000	14795
Quantitative Med Systems Inc **(DH)**	7371	E	510 654-9200	12716
Quantum Precision Inc	5063	E	908 928-1115	8873
Raco Manufacturing & Engrg Co	3699	E	510 658-6713	6539

	SIC	EMP	PHONE	ENTRY #
Ratcliff Architects	8712	D	510 899-6400	18907
Real Estate America Inc	6531	D	510 594-3100	10653
Rljhgn Emeryville Lessee LP	7011	D	510 658-9300	11414
Santen Incorporated	8042	D	415 268-9100	15872
Select Hotels Group LLC	7011	E	510 601-5880	11454
Stasher Inc	5113	F	510 531-2100	9219
Suspender Factory Inc	2389	E	510 547-5400	3020
Sutter Connect LLC	7389	C	510 596-4700	14420
Sutter Health	8062	C	510 450-8900	16631
Sutter Health	8062	C	510 204-6600	16646
Sutter Vsting Nrse Assn Hspice **(HQ)**	8082	E	866 652-9178	16956
Trader Vics	5087	D	510 653-3400	9147
Tubemogul Inc	7372	A	510 653-0126	13499
University Corp Advncd Internt	8611	E	510 858-0881	18321
Vics Trader Restaurants Inc	7299	D	510 653-3400	11734
Virtuoz Inc **(HQ)**	8748	E	415 202-5709	19887
Watergate Community Assn **(PA)**	8641	E	510 428-0118	18480
Young MNS Chrstn Assn of E Bay	8641	B	510 601-8674	18492
Zaplabs LLC **(DH)**	6531	D	510 735-2600	10690
Zogenix Inc **(PA)**	2834	E	510 550-8300	4010
Zymergen Inc **(PA)**	8731	A	415 801-8073	19151

EMIGRANT GAP, CA - Placer County

	SIC	EMP	PHONE	ENTRY #
Nyack Inc	7389	E	530 389-8212	14342

ESCALON, CA - San Joaquin County

	SIC	EMP	PHONE	ENTRY #
Barton Ranch Inc	0291	E	209 838-8930	245
Caron Compactor Co	3531	E	800 448-8236	5028
Dan R Costa Inc	0191	C	209 234-2004	154
De Ruosi Group LLC	0723	E	209 838-8307	280
Hogan Mfg Inc **(PA)**	3999	C	209 838-7323	7286
Hogan Mfg Inc	3999	C	209 838-2400	7287
Morrill Industries Inc	3494	D	209 838-2550	4961
Naraghi Farms LLC	0191	E	209 577-5777	183
P & L Concrete Products Inc	3273	E	209 838-1448	4501
Paddack Enterprises	2068	F	209 838-1536	2450

ESPARTO, CA - Yolo County

	SIC	EMP	PHONE	ENTRY #
A Teichert & Son Inc	1442	E	530 787-3468	584
Bz - Bee Pollination Inc	0721	E	530 787-3044	249

ETNA, CA - Siskiyou County

	SIC	EMP	PHONE	ENTRY #
North Zone Fallers Inc **(PA)**	0851	E	530 598-8518	536

EUREKA, CA - Humboldt County

	SIC	EMP	PHONE	ENTRY #
Adoption Clinical Services LLC	8322	E	405 476-1983	17407
Best Western Bayshore Inn	7011	E	707 268-8005	10954
Bien Padre Foods Inc	2032	F	707 442-4585	2196
Caliber Home Loans Inc	6162	E	707 834-6094	9897
California Department Trnsp	8748	E	707 445-6600	19737
Canon Solutions America Inc	5112	E	707 442-9397	9205
Carlson Wireless Tech Inc	3663	F	707 443-0100	5829
Carson House Inn	7011	E	707 443-1601	10991
Chance 4 Change Inc **(PA)**	8322	E	707 443-8601	17480
Clarion Resort	7011	E	707 442-3261	11013
Coast Central Credit Union **(PA)**	6061	D	707 445-8801	9777
County of Humboldt	4581	E	707 839-5402	7770
Crestwood Behavioral Hlth Inc	8059	E	707 442-5721	16230
E G Ayers Distributing Inc	5141	E	707 445-2077	9271
Eureka Rehab & Wellness Center	8051	D	707 445-3261	15995
Eureka Super 8 Motel	7011	E	707 443-3193	11086
Food For People Inc	8322	D	707 445-3166	17573
Hagadone Directories Inc	2741	C	707 444-0255	3575
Hilfiker Pipe Co	3272	E	707 443-5091	4437
Hospice of Humboldt Inc **(PA)**	8093	E	707 445-8443	17023
Humboldt Bay Fire Jint Pwers A	8099	D	707 441-4000	17154
Humboldt Bay Hbr Rcrtion Cnsrv	4493	D	707 443-0801	7730
Humboldt Cmnty Access Rsrce CT	8322	D	707 441-8625	17608
Humboldt Cmnty Access Rsrce CT	8322	D	707 443-7077	17609
Humboldt Commnty Accss Resrc **(PA)**	8322	C	707 443-7077	17610
Humboldt Community Service Dst	4941	E	707 443-4558	8251
Humboldt Dog Obedience Group	0752	E	707 444-3862	355
Humboldt Newspaper Inc	2711	D	707 442-1711	3447
Humboldt Senior Resource Ctr **(PA)**	8322	D	707 443-9747	17611
Institute For Wildlife Studies **(PA)**	8641	E	707 822-4258	18434
Jjk Hotels LP **(PA)**	7011	D	707 441-4721	11211
Laco Associates **(PA)**	8711	E	707 443-5054	18751
Marine Spill Response Corp	3826	E	707 442-6087	6835
Mark Carter	7011	E	707 444-8062	11285
Mission Linen Supply	7213	D	707 443-8681	11640
Morgan Stnley Smith Barney LLC	6282	D	707 443-3071	10051
Nor-Wall Inc	7997	E	707 445-5445	15115
North Cast Srgical Specialists	8011	E	707 443-2248	15550
North Coast Cleaning Svcs Inc	7349	E	707 269-0838	11980
North Coast Mercantile Co Inc **(PA)**	5181	E	707 445-4910	9559
Pacific Gas and Electric Co	4911	C	707 444-0700	8171
Pasadena Newspapers Inc	2711	C	707 442-1711	3473
Premier Financial Group Inc	6211	E	707 443-2741	10009
S-Matrix Corporation	7372	E	707 441-0404	13417
Santa Rosa Memorial Hospital	8062	D	707 525-5300	16516
Schmidbauer Lumber Inc **(PA)**	2421	C	707 443-7024	3103
Seaview Hlthcare Rhblttion Ctr	8361	E	707 443-5668	18177
Security Nat Mstr Holdg Co LLC **(PA)**	6162	C	707 442-2818	9926
Security Nat Prpts Holdg LLC **(HQ)**	6512	E	707 476-2702	10404
Shaw & Petersen Insurance Inc	6411	E	707 443-0845	10351
Shn Cnslting Engners Glgsts In **(PA)**	8711	D	707 441-8855	18812
Sisters of St Joseph Orange	8082	A	707 443-9332	16947
Six Rivers National Bank **(HQ)**	6021	D	707 443-8400	9689
Sn Servicing Corporation	6162	E	707 445-9883	9930
St Joseph Hospital **(PA)**	8062	A	707 445-8121	16538
St Joseph Hospital	8062	E	707 445-8121	16539
St Joseph Hospital	8062	E	707 445-8121	16540
St Joseph Hospital	8062	E	707 268-0190	16541
St Joseph Hospital	8062	E	707 445-8121	16542
St Joseph Hospital of Eureka	8062	B	707 445-8121	16543
State Compensation Insur Fund	6331	D	707 443-9721	10185
Table Bluff Brewing Inc **(PA)**	2082	E	707 445-4480	2496
Trendsetter Solar Products Inc	1711	F	707 443-5652	1384
Trico Bancshares	6029	E	707 476-0981	9765
Wayne Maples Plumbing & Htg	1711	D	707 445-2500	1396
Western Living Concepts Inc **(PA)**	8361	E	707 443-3000	18211

FAIR OAKS, CA - Sacramento County

	SIC	EMP	PHONE	ENTRY #
Atlaz Inc	7371	D	415 671-6142	12282
Carons Service Center Inc	7538	F	916 444-3713	14551
David Smith	1521	E	916 570-1460	630
Eskaton	8082	B	916 536-3750	16882
Eskaton Properties Inc	8361	D	916 965-4663	18111
Fair Oaks Water District	4941	E	916 967-5723	8249
Folsom Lake Appliance Inc	7629	D	916 985-3426	14697
Lyon Realty	6531	C	916 962-0111	10606
North Ridge Country Club	7997	D	916 967-5717	15116
Orchard Dental Group	8021	E	916 961-6810	15852
Rice Corporation **(PA)**	2044	E	916 784-7745	2326
William L Lyon & Assoc Inc	6531	C	916 535-0356	10688

FAIRFAX, CA - Marin County

	SIC	EMP	PHONE	ENTRY #
Fairfx-San Anslmo Children Ctr **(PA)**	8351	E	415 454-1811	17933
Meadow Club	7997	D	415 453-3274	15108
Qb3 LLC	8742	E	415 515-3595	19615
Roi Dna Inc	7313	E	831 238-2514	11806

FAIRFIELD, CA - Solano County

	SIC	EMP	PHONE	ENTRY #
Aanw Inc	7538	E	707 428-1623	14543
Abbott Nutrition	2834	F	707 399-1100	3825
Abbott Nutrition Mfg Inc **(HQ)**	2834	C	707 399-1100	3826
Abco Laboratories Inc **(PA)**	2834	D	707 432-2200	3828
Aldea Inc	8322	E	925 577-3102	17413
Amos & Andrews Inc	1711	E	707 422-4844	1201
Anheuser-Busch LLC	2082	B	707 429-7595	2472
B & F Logistics LLC **(PA)**	4789	E	707 720-6101	7875
Bay Area Underpinning Inc **(PA)**	1771	D	707 310-0602	1851
Bay-TEC Engineering **(PA)**	8711	D	714 257-1680	18637
Bruni Glass Packaging Inc	5099	E	707 752-6200	9191
Calbee North America LLC	5142	E	707 427-2500	9324
Caliber Home Loans Inc	6162	E	707 432-1000	9896
California Department Trnsp	1611	D	707 428-2031	1020
Cemex Cnstr Mtls PCF LLC	3273	E	707 422-2520	4466
Certified Coatings Company	1721	D	707 639-4414	1407
Child Start Inc	8351	E	707 423-4050	17893
City of Fairfield	4941	E	707 428-7680	8228
Clorox Manufacturing Company	2842	D	707 437-1051	4070
CMC Rebar West	5051	D	707 759-1400	8811
Compu Tech Lumber Products	2439	E	707 437-6683	3203
Cordelia Winery LLC **(PA)**	7389	E	707 286-1764	14235
County of Solano	8322	D	707 784-6570	17512
County of Solano	8052	D	707 784-2080	16179
Courage Production LLC	2013	D	707 422-6300	2117
Crestwood Behavioral Hlth Inc	8322	E	707 428-1131	17524
Crystal Geyser Water Company	2086	E	707 647-4410	2789
Dependable Plas & Pattern Inc	3089	E	707 863-4900	4277
Directv Group Inc	4841	C	707 452-7409	8061
Drake Enterprises Incorporated	2399	D	707 864-3077	3050
Edwards Theatres Circuit Inc	7832	D	707 432-2121	14810
Embassy Investments LLC	7011	D	707 422-4111	11080
Fabricated Glass Spc Inc	3231	E	707 429-6160	4386
Fairfield Health Care Inc	8051	C	707 425-0623	16001
Fairfield Rental Service Inc	7353	F	707 422-2270	12020
Fairfield-Suisun Sewer Dst	4952	D	707 429-8930	8282
Fairfld-Sisun Unified Schl Dst	7349	D	707 421-4253	11949
First Priority Financial Inc	6162	B	707 432-1000	9905
Frank-Lin Distillers Pdts Ltd **(PA)**	5182	C	408 259-8900	9577
Gaw Van Male Smith Myers	8111	D	707 425-1250	17271
Geovera Specialty Insurance Co	6411	D	707 863-3700	10287
Gillespies Carpet Center Inc	7216	E	707 427-3773	11653
Green Valley Country Club	7997	D	707 864-1101	15096
Halabi Inc **(PA)**	3281	C	707 402-1600	4518
Hotel NAPA I Opco L P	7011	D	707 863-0900	11168
Hotel NAPA II Opco LP	7011	E	707 863-0300	11169
Innovative Combustion Tech **(PA)**	3433	F	510 652-6000	4630
Jack Anthony Industries Inc	7542	E	707 426-2000	14643
Jsj Electrical Display Corp	3993	F	707 747-5595	7239
Kaiser Foundation Hospitals	8011	C	707 427-4000	15458
Kappel and Kappel Inc	6531	D	707 429-2922	10591
Kindred Healthcare LLC	8082	D	707 639-4155	16906
Lanza Vineyards Inc **(PA)**	0172	D	707 864-0730	63
LB Ford Painting Inc	1721	E	707 447-5274	1420
Lin Frank Distillers	2085	E	707 437-1092	2775
Lowes Home Centers LLC	5064	C	707 207-2070	8884
Lystek International Inc	3999	F	707 419-0084	7298
Macro Plastics Inc **(PA)**	3089	E	707 437-1200	4298
Mark Scott Construction Inc	1522	E	707 864-8880	757
McNaughton Newspapers Inc **(PA)**	2711	D	707 425-4646	3458
Medic Ambulance Service Inc	4119	E	916 564-9011	7388
Muehlhan Certifed Coatings Inc	1799	E	707 639-4414	2045
New Desserts Inc	5149	D	415 780-6860	9469
Nippon Industries Inc	2038	E	707 427-3127	2305

GEOGRAPHIC

Employment Codes: A=Over 500 employees, B=251-500, C=101-250, D=51-100, E=20-50 F=10-19

2022 Northern California Business Directory and Buyers Guide

1143

	SIC	EMP	PHONE	ENTRY #
Northbay Healthcare Corp **(PA)**	8062	C	707 646-5000	16465
Northbay Healthcare Group **(HQ)**	8062	A	707 646-5000	16466
Northern CA Retiredd Ofcrs	8361	C	707 432-1200	18148
OHara Metal Products	3493	E	707 863-9090	4957
Olive Oil Factory LLC	2079	E	707 426-3400	2468
Omega Industrial Supply Inc	2842	E	707 864-8164	4076
Pace Solano	8399	E	707 427-1731	18245
Pace Solano	8331	D	707 426-6932	17831
Pacific Gas and Electric Co	4911	C	415 973-7000	8130
Pacific Power & Systems Inc	1731	E	707 437-2300	1560
Partnership Health Plan Cal	6324	B	707 863-4100	10148
Pauli Systems Inc	3599	E	707 429-2434	5593
Permanente Medical Group Inc	8062	A	707 427-4000	16479
Petersen-Dean Commercial Inc	1761	D	707 469-7470	1829
Pick Pull Auto Dismantling Inc	5015	E	707 425-1044	8486
Pool Covers Inc	5091	E	707 864-6674	9159
Price-Simms Ford LLC	7538	D	707 421-3300	14584
Primal Pet Foods Inc	2047	D	415 642-7400	2335
Private Industry Cncl Slno Cty **(PA)**	7361	E	707 864-3370	12122
Rai Care Ctrs Nthrn Cal I LLC	8092	C	707 434-9088	16977
Rci Associates	7381	E	866 668-4732	14092
Remax Gold Elite	6531	D	707 422-4411	10654
RL Fuller Inc	1711	E	707 207-0100	1348
Roadrunner Tow Inc	7549	E	707 434-9560	14675
S & S Tool & Supply Inc **(HQ)**	5085	D	800 430-8665	9131
Salutary Sports Clubs Inc	7991	E	707 438-2582	14969
Scott Lamp Company Inc	3646	D	707 864-2066	5738
Seneca Family of Agencies	8322	B	707 429-4440	17731
Sipco Surface Protection Inc **(DH)**	1721	D	707 639-4414	1433
Sleepmed Incorporated	8011	E	707 864-1869	15689
Smith Sons Wldg & Fabrication	7692	F	707 437-3027	14722
Solano Athletic Clubs Inc **(PA)**	7997	E	707 422-2858	15147
Solano Diagnostics Imaging	3829	E	707 646-4646	6922
Solano First Federal Credit Un	6061	E	707 422-9626	9820
Solano Fmly & Chld Council Inc	8351	D	707 863-3950	18022
Solano Gateway Realty Inc **(PA)**	6531	E	707 422-1725	10664
ST Johnson Company LLC	3433	E	510 652-6000	4639
Strategic Materials Inc	7336	E	707 452-3362	11873
Superior Buildings Svcs Inc	7349	E	707 429-3000	12003
Sutter Health	8062	C	707 864-4660	16610
Sutter Health	8062	C	707 432-2500	16645
Sutter Regional Med Foundation	8011	D	707 631-9423	15731
Sutter Regional Med Foundation **(PA)**	8011	B	707 427-4900	15732
Tencate Advanced Composite	5191	D	707 359-3400	9612
Tom Duffy Co	5023	D	800 479-5671	8521
Toray Advnced Cmpsites ADS LLC	2821	E	707 359-3400	3812
Tronex Technology Incorporated	3423	E	707 426-2550	4610
United Parcel Service Inc	4215	C	707 864-8200	7660
Universal Plant Svcs Nthrn Cal **(HQ)**	7699	E	707 864-0100	14781
Valley Inventory Service Inc	7389	D	707 422-6050	14454
Veterans Health Administration	8011	C	707 437-1800	15798
Villara Corporation	1761	E	707 863-8222	1844
Vitalant Research Institute	8099	E	707 428-6001	17190
Water Ink Technology	2893	F	707 426-9420	4155
West Coast Contractors Inc	1542	E	214 281-3100	987
West-Com Nrse Call Systems Inc **(PA)**	3663	E	707 428-5900	5883
Westgate Cnstr & Maint Inc	1542	D	707 208-5763	989
Willis Rebar Inc	5051	E	707 419-5949	8834
Wind River Enterprises Inc	5012	D	707 864-1040	8434
Woodline Partners Inc	2434	E	707 864-5445	3195

FARMINGTON, CA - San Joaquin County

	SIC	EMP	PHONE	ENTRY #
Brightview Tree Company	0781	D	209 886-5511	406
Ripon Milling LLC	2048	E	209 599-4269	2355

FELTON, CA - Santa Cruz County

	SIC	EMP	PHONE	ENTRY #
Cupertino Electric Inc	1731	A	408 808-8260	1490
Exploring New Horizons Inc	7032	E	831 338-3013	11601
Satellite Telework Centers Inc **(PA)**	3825	D	831 222-2100	6789

FIELDS LANDING, CA - Humboldt County

	SIC	EMP	PHONE	ENTRY #
Environmental Technology Inc	2821	E	707 443-9323	3802

FIREBAUGH, CA - Fresno County

	SIC	EMP	PHONE	ENTRY #
Baker Farming	0172	E	559 659-3942	43
Blackburn Farming Company Inc	0762	E	559 659-3753	368
Cartel Transport LLC **(PA)**	4212	C	559 659-3981	7455
Davis Drier & Elevator N F	0191	E	559 659-3035	155
Empresas Del Bosque Inc	0191	B	209 364-6428	164
Hammonds Ranch Inc	0291	D	209 364-6185	247
Hiller Aircraft Corporation	3728	E	559 659-5959	6633
I S A Contracting Svcs Inc	0722	A	559 659-1080	262
JFB Ranch Inc	0191	E	209 364-6149	175
Neil Jones Food Company	2033	E	559 659-5100	2230
Oro Loma Ranch LLC **(PA)**	0161	E	209 364-0070	32
Panoche Water District	4941	E	209 364-6136	8258
Peri & Sons Farms Cal LLC **(PA)**	5148	E	775 463-4444	9423
Robinson Agspray	0721	E	559 659-3015	256
Seasholtz John	0161	C	559 659-3805	35
Thomason Tractor Co California	5083	E	559 659-2039	9044
Vaquero Farms Inc	0191	D	559 659-2790	195
West Valley Aviation Inc	3728	F	559 659-7378	6637

FISH CAMP, CA - Mariposa County

	SIC	EMP	PHONE	ENTRY #
DNC Prks Resorts At Tenaya Inc **(DH)**	7011	C	877 247-9241	11054

FIVE POINTS, CA - Fresno County

	SIC	EMP	PHONE	ENTRY #
ATI Machinery Inc	5083	E	559 884-2471	9031
Britz Fertilizers Inc	5191	E	559 884-2421	9596
Coelho West Custom Farming	0191	D	559 884-2566	152
Red Rock Ranch Inc	0191	E	559 884-4201	188
Telesis Onion Co	0723	C	559 884-2441	312

FOLSOM, CA - Sacramento County

	SIC	EMP	PHONE	ENTRY #
Aerojet Rocketdyne Inc	3728	E	916 355-4000	6627
Aerojet Rocketdyne Inc	3728	E	916 355-4000	6628
Agreeya Solutions Inc **(PA)**	8742	D	916 294-0075	19437
Altergy Systems	3629	E	916 458-8590	5692
American Concrete Washouts Inc **(PA)**	1771	C	916 990-0842	1849
Atcg Technology Solutions Inc **(HQ)**	7371	E	916 850-2620	12280
Benefit & Risk Management Svcs	6411	C	916 467-1200	10246
Biddle Consulting Group Inc	8748	E	916 294-4250	19730
Bre Select Hotels Oper LLC	7011	E	916 353-1717	10971
Burger Physcl Therapy Svcs Inc **(HQ)**	8049	C	916 983-5900	15885
Burger Rhblitation Systems Inc **(PA)**	8049	C	800 900-8491	15888
Calcerts Inc	8742	E	916 985-3400	19464
Califrnia Ind Sys Oprator Corp **(PA)**	4911	B	916 351-4400	8090
Care Innovations LLC	3845	E	800 450-0970	7099
Central Valley Community Bank	6022	E	916 985-8700	9714
City of Folsom	3669	D	916 355-7272	5886
City of Folsom	4111	C	916 355-8395	7326
Cni Thl Ops LLC	7011	E	916 984-7624	11025
Computer Power Sftwr Group Inc **(PA)**	7371	F	916 985-4445	12353
Csac Excess Insurance Auth	6411	D	916 850-7300	10269
Dokken Engineering **(PA)**	8711	D	916 858-0642	18692
Donahue & Davies LLP	8111	E	916 817-2900	17254
Ed Supports LLC	8322	D	201 478-8711	17539
Ejs Pizza Co	7299	D	916 989-1133	11715
Erepublic Inc **(PA)**	7389	C	916 932-1300	14267
Eurofins Air Toxics LLC	8734	D	916 985-1000	19266
First Step Housing	8748	D	916 769-8877	19775
Flt Inc	7538	C	916 355-1500	14563
Folsom Care Center	8099	E	916 985-3641	17148
Folsom Recreation Corp	7933	D	916 983-4411	14891
Folsom Surgery Center Inc	8011	D	916 673-1990	15407
FPI Management Inc **(PA)**	6531	E	916 357-5300	10553
Frontier California Inc	4813	B	212 395-1000	7952
Gekkeikan Sake USAinC	2084	E	916 985-3111	2592
General Dynmics Ots Vrstron In	3812	D	916 355-7700	6669
Green Acres Nursery & Sup LLC	5083	D	916 673-9720	9039
Healthy Living Enterprise Inc	7389	E	916 296-0228	14295
Home Depot USA Inc	7359	C	916 983-0401	12048
Hoonuit LLC **(DH)**	7372	E	320 631-5900	13211
Ifeatu Nnebe DDS Inc **(PA)**	8021	E	916 299-9487	15837
Inductive Automation LLC	8742	D	800 266-7798	19535
Ingram Entertainment Inc	5099	F	916 235-5400	9196
Intel Corporation	3674	D	916 356-8080	6161
Investment Retrievers Inc	7322	E	916 941-8851	11824
Ixerv Americas Inc	7379	E	786 542-9744	13925
Jac Logistics LLC	4789	E	954 881-2231	7884
Kaiser Foundation Hospitals	8011	C	916 986-4178	15459
Kaiser Foundation Hospitals	8011	C	916 817-5200	15483
Kaiser Foundation Hospitals	8071	C	916 817-5651	16787
Kioxia America Inc	8731	E	916 986-4707	19078
Lake Natoma Lodging LP	7011	D	916 351-1500	11243
Larkspur Hsptality Dev MGT LLC	7011	E	916 355-1616	11250
Liberty American Mortgage Corp **(PA)**	6163	D	916 780-3000	9943
Location Services LLC **(PA)**	4789	D	800 588-0097	7887
Lowes Home Centers LLC	5031	C	916 984-7979	8559
Mailcentro Inc	4813	C	916 985-4445	7972
Marvell Semiconductor Inc	3674	C	916 605-3700	6189
Matthew Burns	1542	D	209 676-4940	919
Mercury Insurance Company	6331	B	916 353-4859	10170
Meridian Knwldge Solutions LLC **(DH)**	8742	E	916 985-9625	19574
Merrill Lynch Prce Fnner Smith	6211	D	916 984-3200	9987
Microsemi Crp- Rf Intgrted Slt **(DH)**	3674	C	916 850-8640	6207
Military Aircraft Parts **(PA)**	3599	E	916 635-8010	5572
Morgan Stnley Smith Barney LLC	6211	D	916 983-8888	10006
Morton & Pitalo Inc **(PA)**	8711	D	916 984-7621	18774
Mountain F Enterprises Inc	2411	E	530 626-4127	3073
Mountain G Enterprises Inc	1611	C	866 464-6351	1061
Norcal Gold Inc	6531	E	916 984-8778	10628
Objective Systems Integrators **(HQ)**	7371	E	916 467-1500	12642
One Inc Software Corporation **(PA)**	7371	E	866 343-6940	12647
Paychex Inc	8721	D	916 983-0303	18982
Performance Matters LLC **(DH)**	7372	E	801 453-0136	13367
Phoenix Schools Inc	8351	D	916 983-0224	17996
Phoenix Schools Inc	8351	D	916 353-1031	18000
Powerschool Group LLC **(HQ)**	7372	C	916 288-1588	13380
Powerschool Holdings Inc	7372	A	877 873-1550	13381
Prairie City Commons LLC	8052	D	916 458-0303	16196
Precision Home Care LLC	8322	D	916 749-4051	17677
Premium Outlet Partners LP	6512	D	916 985-0312	10400
Pulse Systems Inc **(DH)**	7371	D	316 636-5900	12711
Retail Pro International LLC **(PA)**	7371	D	916 605-7200	12746
Rjp Framing Inc	1751	C	916 941-3934	1754
Safe Credit Union **(PA)**	6061	C	916 979-7233	9808
Samuel Hale LLC	7361	A	916 235-1477	12133
Shi-III Prrie Cy Lnding Owner **(PA)**	8361	E	916 458-0303	18181
Sierra Nevada Corporation	3812	E	916 985-8799	6684
Sierra Pacific Mortgage Co Inc **(PA)**	6162	A	916 932-1700	9927
Sn Servicing Corporation	6162	E	916 779-2200	9929
Soliman Hisham M D Inc	8011	E	916 351-9400	15692
Spare-Time Inc	7997	D	916 983-9180	15149
Stearns Holdings LLC	6162	B	916 358-9170	9932
Stellant Systems Inc	3663	C	916 351-4500	5871
Style Media Group Inc	2721	E	916 988-9888	3515

GEOGRAPHIC SECTION

FREMONT, CA

	SIC	EMP	PHONE	ENTRY #
Sutter Health	8071	D	916 984-0739	16809
Synapsense Corporation	3572	E	916 294-0110	5323
Taxresources Inc (PA)	7291	C	877 369-7827	11703
Taylor Morrision Homes	1521	E	916 355-8900	717
Trimark Associates Inc	8748	D	916 357-5970	19878
Unico Engineering Inc	8711	E	916 293-8953	18843
United Reporting Pubg Corp	2741	F	916 542-7501	3610
Unitrin Direct Insurance Co (HQ)	6399	D	760 603-3276	10222
University California Davis	8011	D	916 985-9300	15771
Valley Tech Systems Inc	8711	E	916 760-1025	18853
Vibra Hospital Sacramento LLC	8062	C	916 351-9151	16719
Visionary Intgrtion Prfssnals (HQ)	7379	D	916 985-9625	14007
Visionary Intgrtion Prfssnals (PA)	6719	C	916 985-9625	10746
Zglobal Inc (PA)	8748	E	916 985-9461	19895

FOREST KNOLLS, CA - Marin County

	SIC	EMP	PHONE	ENTRY #
Serenity Knolls	8093	E	415 488-0400	17072

FOREST RANCH, CA - Butte County

	SIC	EMP	PHONE	ENTRY #
Remodelors Inc	8741	E	530 893-4741	19387

FORESTHILL, CA - Placer County

	SIC	EMP	PHONE	ENTRY #
Placer County Water Agency	4911	D	530 367-6701	8193
Timberline Wall Systems	1521	E	530 613-8070	721

FORESTVILLE, CA - Sonoma County

	SIC	EMP	PHONE	ENTRY #
Canyon Rock Co Inc	1442	E	707 887-2207	592
Farmhouse Inn & Restaurant LLC	7011	E	707 887-3300	11092
Hartford Jackson LLC	2084	E	707 887-1756	2613
Kozlowski Farms A Corporation	2033	E	707 887-1587	2218
Topolos At Rssian River Vinyrd	0172	E	707 887-1575	77

FORT BRAGG, CA - Mendocino County

	SIC	EMP	PHONE	ENTRY #
Anderson Logging Inc	2411	D	707 964-2770	3055
Caito Fisheries Inc (PA)	5146	D	707 964-6368	9361
Cv Starr Community Center	8322	E	707 964-9446	17527
Epg Gym LLC	7991	E	707 964-6290	14947
Harbor Lite Lodge LLC	7011	E	707 964-0221	11128
Mendocino Cast Btncal Grdns Co	8422	E	707 964-4352	18293
Mendocino Coast Clinics Inc	8093	E	707 964-1251	17039
Mendocino Coast District Hosp (PA)	8062	B	707 961-1234	16455
Mendocino Railway	4731	E	707 964-6371	7847
North Coast Brewing Co Inc	2082	E	707 964-3400	2487
North Coast Brewing Co Inc (PA)	2082	E	707 964-2739	2488
Noyo Vista Inc	7011	E	707 964-4003	11334
Ocean Fresh LLC (PA)	2091	E	707 964-1389	2827
Parents & Friends Inc	8361	E	707 964-4940	18155
Philbrick Inc	2411	E	707 964-2277	3074
Rap Investors LP	7011	E	707 964-2402	11383
Redwood Coast Seniors Inc	8322	E	707 964-0443	17684
Roach Bros Inc	2411	D	707 964-9240	3075
Sherwood Oaks Enterprises Inc	8051	D	707 964-6333	16115
Tradewinds Lodge (PA)	7011	E	707 964-4761	11539
Waste MGT Collectn Recycl Inc	4953	D	707 964-9172	8384
Waste MGT Collectn Recycl Inc	4953	D	707 462-0210	8387
Wharf	7011	D	707 964-4283	11576

FORTUNA, CA - Humboldt County

	SIC	EMP	PHONE	ENTRY #
Eel River Brewing Co Inc (PA)	2082	E	707 725-2739	2477
Epic Hospitality Inc	7011	E	707 725-5500	11082
Fortuna Country Inn Corp	7011	E	707 725-6822	11099
Fortuna Rhbltition Wllness Ctr	8051	E	707 725-4467	16007
Foster Dairy Farms	2023	F	707 725-6182	2160
Huffman Logging Co Inc	2411	E	707 725-4335	3064
Humboldt Bottling LLC	2086	F	707 725-4119	2793
Leonardo Logging and Cnstr Inc	2411	E	707 725-1809	3068
Lewis Logging	2411	E	707 722-1975	3069
Redwood Empire Golf Cntry CLB	7997	D	707 725-5194	15126
Redwood Memorial Hosp Fortuna (PA)	8062	C	707 725-7327	16488
Wendt Construction Co Inc	6552	E	707 725-5641	10721

FOSTER CITY, CA - San Mateo County

	SIC	EMP	PHONE	ENTRY #
1st Chice HM Halthcare Hospice	8082	E	650 393-5936	16825
Agari Data Inc (DH)	7371	E	650 627-7667	12235
American Infrastructure Mlp Fu	8748	E	650 854-6000	19719
American Precision Gear Co	3566	E	650 627-8060	5210
Angad Corp	7371	E	650 743-0461	12254
Applied Biosystems Inc	7374	E	800 327-3002	13693
Bailard Inc (HQ)	6282	E	650 571-5800	10032
Bayshore Ambulance Inc (PA)	4119	D	650 525-9700	7375
Bertram Capital Management LLC (PA)	6799	C	650 358-5000	10835
Brightedge Technologies Inc (PA)	7371	E	800 578-8023	12309
Capnia Inc (PA)	2834	D	650 213-8444	3877
Central Business Forms Inc	2752	E	650 548-0918	3633
Cetec Automation Inc	7371	E	650 570-7557	12334
Conversica Inc (PA)	5045	F	650 290-7674	8683
Courtyard Management Corp	7011	E	650 377-0600	11040
Csg Consultants Inc (PA)	8711	E	650 522-2500	18679
Cybersource Corporation (HQ)	7374	A	650 432-7350	13705
D A Pope Incorporated	1542	E	650 349-5086	859
Ecker Consumer Recruiting Inc	8732	D	650 871-6800	19157
Emeter Corporation	7371	E	650 227-7770	12423
Emvco LLC	3679	E	650 432-3149	6424
Exabeam Inc (PA)	7382	E	844 392-2326	14132
Flyex Inc	7371	E	650 646-3339	12459
Forty Seven Inc (HQ)	2834	D	650 352-4150	3900
Founders Management II Corp	7011	B	650 570-5700	11100
Geron Corporation (PA)	2834	D	650 473-7700	3914
Gilead Colorado Inc	2834	D	650 574-3000	3915
Gilead Palo Alto Inc (HQ)	2834	B	650 384-8500	3916
Gilead Sciences Inc (PA)	2834	B	650 574-3000	3917
Gridgain Systems Inc	7372	C	650 241-2281	13199
Hilton Garden In San Mateo	7011	D	650 522-9000	11140
Inolux Corporation	3674	F	650 483-6227	6155
Legacy Prtners Residential Inc (PA)	8741	C	650 571-2250	19362
Logicbio Therapeutics Inc	2834	F	415 710-8265	3942
Matrixx Software Inc (PA)	7373	B	408 215-9344	13631
McCown De Leeuw & Co	6726	E	650 854-6000	10779
Menlo Gateway Inc	6514	E	650 356-2900	10472
Metamining Inc	1241	F	650 212-7900	544
Midpen Housing Corporation	6552	B	650 356-2900	10709
Mipox International Corp	3291	E	650 638-9830	4525
Mirum Pharmaceuticals Inc (PA)	2834	D	650 667-4085	3949
Northwest Protective Service (PA)	7381	D	650 345-8500	14080
Omics Group Inc	2721	B	650 268-9744	3510
Pacific Partners MGT Svcs Inc	8741	D	650 358-5804	19378
Peninsula Jewish Community Ctr	8322	E	650 212-7522	17672
Peter H Mattson & Co Inc	8731	D	650 356-2500	19101
Plan Design Consultants Inc	7389	E	650 341-3322	14369
Qualys Inc (PA)	7371	A	650 801-6100	12714
Quinstreet Inc (PA)	7389	E	650 578-7700	14380
Route 40 Ventures Inc	5149	F	650 743-0051	9482
Sfn Group Inc	7363	E	650 348-4967	12194
Sling Media LLC	4812	C	650 293-8000	7912
Sony Corporation of America	7371	C	650 655-8000	12807
Sony Interactive Entrmt LLC (HQ)	7389	A	310 981-1500	14410
Streetline Inc (DH)	7374	D	650 242-3400	13761
Sycomp A Technology Co Inc (PA)	7373	E	877 901-7416	13670
Terns Pharmaceuticals Inc (PA)	2834	E	650 525-5535	3992
United Innovation Services Inc	8742	D	831 334-0673	19661
Vaxcyte Inc (PA)	2836	D	650 837-0111	4059
Vb Golf LLC	7992	E	650 573-7888	15035
Verinata Health Inc	8731	E	650 632-1680	19147
Visa Commerce Solutions Inc	7379	E	650 432-3200	14006
Visa Inc (PA)	7389	A	650 432-3200	14455
Visa Tech & Operations LLC (DH)	7389	C	650 432-3200	14456
Zoox Inc (HQ)	3711	B	650 539-9669	6562

FOWLER, CA - Fresno County

	SIC	EMP	PHONE	ENTRY #
Adventist Hlth Systm/West Corp	8062	D	559 834-1614	16308
Beaver Dam Health Care Center	8051	E	559 834-2542	15925
Bobby Slzars Mxcan Fd Pdts Inc (PA)	2032	E	559 834-4787	2197
Boghosian Raisin Pkg Co Inc	0723	E	559 834-5348	273
Borga Stl Bldngs Cmponents Inc	3446	D	559 834-5375	4835
C D Simonian Insurance Inc	6411	E	559 834-5333	10254
Dale Brisco Inc	3444	F	559 834-5926	4752
Fowler Labor Service Inc	7361	B	559 834-3723	12090
Gahvejian Enterprises Inc	5113	E	559 834-5956	9213
J B Hunt Transport Svcs Inc	4213	A	559 834-3852	7555
Jacobsen Trailer Inc	3715	E	559 834-5971	6604
Kandarian Agri Enterprises	0172	E	559 834-1501	59
McWane Inc	3321	F	559 834-4630	4550
Nia Healthcare Services Inc (PA)	8051	D	559 834-2519	16068
Nia Healthcare Services Inc	8051	D	559 834-2519	16070
Pps Packaging Company	2621	E	559 834-1641	3348
Rick Carsey Trucking & Cnstr	1522	E	559 834-5385	765
Seaca Packaging Inc	7389	E	559 813-9030	14401
Simonian Brothers Inc (PA)	0723	C	559 834-5921	308
Sunshine Raisin Corporation (PA)	0723	C	559 834-5981	311
Trius Trucking Inc	4213	D	559 834-4000	7607

FREEDOM, CA - Santa Cruz County

	SIC	EMP	PHONE	ENTRY #
Sage Instruments Inc	3825	D	831 761-1000	6788

FREMONT, CA - Alameda County

	SIC	EMP	PHONE	ENTRY #
3dconnexion Inc	3577	D	510 713-6000	5338
3par Inc (HQ)	3571	C	510 445-1046	5236
A & D Precision Machining Inc	3599	E	510 657-6781	5456
A To Z Tree Nursery Inc (PA)	5193	C	510 651-9021	9621
Abgenix Inc (PA)	2834	C	510 608-6500	3829
Abjayon Inc	7371	C	510 824-3260	12222
Abode Services (PA)	8322	D	510 657-7409	17406
Access International Company (DH)	5045	E	510 226-1000	8658
Ace USA	6411	D	510 790-4695	10226
Acm Research Inc (PA)	3589	E	510 445-3700	5437
Acma Computers Inc	5045	E	510 497-8626	8659
Actelis Networks Inc (PA)	8748	E	510 545-1045	19712
Ad-In Incorporated	1742	E	510 656-6700	1655
Adroit Resources Inc (HQ)	7379	E	510 344-8797	13831
Aegis Asssted Living Prpts LLC	8361	C	510 739-1515	18050
Aegis Senior Communities LLC	8082	C	510 739-0909	16838
Aehr Test Systems (PA)	3825	D	510 623-9400	6743
Aer Electronics Inc (PA)	4953	E	510 300-0500	8298
AG Neovo Technology Corp	3575	F	408 321-8210	5329
Agama Solutions Inc	8742	E	510 796-9300	19436
Air Liquide Electronics US LP	2819	A	510 624-4338	3777
Alameda County Water District (PA)	4941	D	510 668-4200	8218
Alameda County Water District	4941	E	510 668-6631	8219
Alaniz Construction Inc	1611	E	510 770-5000	1004
Alertenterprise Inc	7372	C	510 440-0840	12969
All Quality & Services Inc	3672	C	510 249-5800	5908
All West Fabricators Inc	3441	F	510 623-1200	4643
All-Tech Machine & Engrg Inc	3599	E	510 353-2000	5468
Alom Technologies Corporation (PA)	7389	C	510 360-3600	14199
Alpha Ems Corporation	3672	C	510 498-8788	5909
Alphagem Bio Inc	3089	F	510 999-1153	4255
Alta Manufacturing Inc	3672	E	510 668-1870	5910

FREMONT, CA

GEOGRAPHIC SECTION

Company	SIC	EMP	PHONE	ENTRY #
Alterg Inc	3949	D	510 270-5900	7185
Amax Engineering Corporation (PA)	5045	C	510 651-8886	8665
American Air Liquide Inc (DH)	2813	D	510 624-4000	3770
American Bldg Maint Co of Ill	7349	B	510 573-1618	11918
American High Schl Booster CLB	8641	E	510 796-1776	18386
American Portwell Tech Inc	5045	D	510 403-3399	8666
Amprius Inc (PA)	8731	E	800 425-8803	19023
Amprius Technologies Inc	5063	E	800 425-8803	8842
Ampro Systems Inc	3672	E	510 624-9000	5912
AMS Ventures Inc	8742	D	301 980-5087	19444
Anaspec Inc (HQ)	8731	E	510 791-9560	19025
Apacer Memory America Inc	5065	E	408 518-8699	8890
Applied Ceramics Inc (PA)	3674	C	510 249-9700	6038
Applied Thin-Film Products (HQ)	3679	C	510 661-4287	6398
Applied Thin-Film Products	3679	C	510 661-4287	6399
Arcsoft Inc (PA)	7371	A	510 440-9901	12268
Ardelyx Inc	2834	C	510 745-1700	3853
Ardenbrook Inc	6531	D	510 794-1020	10492
Aries Research Inc	3577	E	925 818-1078	5343
Arrow Systems Integration Inc	4813	F	510 897-2900	7926
Arstasis Inc	3841	F	650 508-1549	6944
Aruba Networks Inc	3663	E	408 227-4500	5824
Asa Computers Inc	7373	E	650 230-8000	13555
Ashford Trs Fremont LLC	7011	C	510 413-3700	10934
Asi Computer Technologies Inc (PA)	5045	D	510 226-8000	8670
Asteel Flash USA Corp (DH)	3672	E	510 440-2840	5917
Asus Computer International	5045	C	510 739-3777	8671
Atonarp Us Inc	3826	E	650 714-6290	6811
Attivo Networks Inc (PA)	5045	C	510 623-1000	8672
Avalanche Technology Inc	3674	D	510 438-0148	6059
Aver Information Inc	5045	E	408 263-3828	8673
Avermedia Technologies Inc	3577	E	510 403-0006	5348
AVI Systems Inc	5065	D	415 915-2070	8894
Avp Technology LLC	3565	E	510 683-0157	5195
Axt Inc	3674	A	510 683-5900	6061
Axt Inc (PA)	3674	E	510 438-4700	6062
Axt-Tongmei Inc	3674	E	510 438-4700	6063
Ayantra Inc	3661	E	510 623-7526	5788
Azuga Inc (DH)	7373	B	888 790-0715	13558
B & G Precision Inc	3599	F	510 438-9785	5479
B2 Machining LLC	7699	E	510 668-1360	14739
Bace Manufacturing Inc	3089	E	510 657-5800	4262
Ball Screws & Actuators Co Inc (HQ)	3568	D	510 770-5932	5220
Bart Manufacturing Inc (PA)	3999	E	408 320-4373	7270
BASF Venture Capital Amer Inc	2869	E	510 445-6140	4121
Basic Solutions Corp	7379	C	510 573-3658	13852
Bay Area Circuits Inc	3672	E	510 933-9000	5918
Bay Area Community Health (PA)	8011	C	510 770-8040	15287
Bay Area Community Svcs Inc	8322	E	510 656-7742	17437
Bay Area Traffic Solutions Inc	7389	C	510 657-2543	14212
Bay Associates Wire Tech Corp (DH)	2298	A	510 988-3800	2981
Bay Equipment Co Inc	3462	E	510 226-8800	4874
Bay Polymers Corp	4953	E	510 490-1791	8308
Bayside Interiors Inc (PA)	1742	C	510 438-9171	1661
Bayview Plastic Solutions Inc	3089	E	510 360-0001	4263
Bema Electronic Mfg Inc	3672	D	510 490-7770	5920
Berkeley Design Automation Inc	3674	E	408 496-6600	6066
Berkshire Hathaway Inc	6531	E	510 651-6500	10494
Biogenex Laboratories (PA)	3841	E	510 824-1400	6956
Biokey Inc	2834	E	510 668-0881	3867
Biomedican Inc (PA)	8733	D	412 475-8886	19199
Bionova Scientific LLC	8731	E	510 305-8048	19035
Bipolarics Inc	3674	F	408 372-7574	6067
Bitmicro Networks Inc (PA)	3572	D	510 743-3124	5283
Bizlink Technology (HQ)	3643	D	510 252-0786	5710
Bjork Construction Company Inc (PA)	1542	C	510 656-4688	832
Blazer Exhibits & Graphics Inc	3993	F	408 263-7000	7220
Bold Data Technology Inc	3571	E	510 490-8296	5243
Braemac (ca) LLC	5065	E	510 687-1000	8897
Bridgelux Inc	3674	D	925 583-8400	6071
C & C Security Patrol Inc (PA)	7381	C	510 713-1260	14040
C J Health Services Inc	8051	E	510 793-3000	15948
C3-Ilex LLC (PA)	3822	E	510 659-8300	6700
Cable Connection Inc	3643	E	510 249-9000	5711
Cal Coast Financial Inc	6162	D	510 683-9850	9892
Cal-Sierra Technologies Inc	7371	E	510 742-9996	12320
Cal-Weld Inc	3499	C	510 226-0100	4984
Cali Food Company Inc (PA)	2032	E	408 515-3178	2198
Califrnia Crdvsclar Cons Med A (PA)	8011	D	510 796-0222	15313
Calogic (PA)	3825	E	510 656-2900	6747
Camtek Usa Inc	3674	E	510 624-9905	6079
Cancer Prevention Inst Cal (PA)	8733	C	510 608-5000	19205
Celestica LLC	3679	C	510 770-5100	6404
Celestica Prcsion McHining Ltd (PA)	3566	E	510 742-0500	5211
Celestica Prcsion McHining Ltd	3599	F	510 252-2100	5491
Cellphone-Mate Inc	3663	D	510 770-0469	5830
Centerville Presbyterian Ch	8351	E	510 793-3575	17880
Ceramic Tech Inc	3593	E	510 252-8500	5493
Ceterix Orthopaedics Inc	3841	E	650 241-1748	6961
Cfr Rinkens LLC	4225	E	310 297-8488	7684
Chart Inc	3443	E	408 371-3303	4717
Chayachitra Media LLC (PA)	4899	E	510 397-8344	8074
Chemetall US Inc	2842	E	408 387-5340	4067
China Custom Manufacturing Ltd	3089	A	510 979-1920	4268
Chinese Overseas Mktg Svc Corp	2741	D	626 280-8588	3563
Chrisp Company (PA)	1611	C	510 656-2840	1027
Citragen Pharmaceuticals Inc	2834	F	510 249-9066	3884
City Beach Inc	7032	E	408 654-9330	11600
Clean Hrbors Es Indus Svcs Inc	1799	E	510 979-9210	2019
Cleansmart Solutions Inc	2677	E	650 871-9123	3397
Cli Liquidating Corporation	3845	D	510 354-0300	7101
Cliosoft Inc	7372	E	510 790-4732	13072
Club Sport of Fremont	7991	E	510 226-8500	14938
Cmp I Fremont Owner LP	7011	D	510 656-1800	11018
Coagusense Inc	8733	E	510 270-5442	19210
Cofan Usa Inc	5085	D	510 490-7533	9113
Cognitiveclouds Software Inc	7371	D	415 234-3611	12350
Coldwell Bnkr Residential Brkg	6531	E	510 608-7600	10518
Colleen & Herb Enterprises Inc	3599	C	510 226-6083	5494
Comcore Technologies Inc	3827	E	408 623-9704	6869
Commercial Casework Inc (PA)	2431	C	510 657-7933	3125
Compass Components Inc (PA)	3679	D	510 656-4700	6409
Compressed A Benz Systems Inc (DH)	3563	D	510 413-5200	5182
Compugraphics USA Inc (HQ)	3674	D	510 249-2600	6084
Concentrix Corporation	7379	E	510 668-3717	13874
Concentrix Corporation (PA)	7389	A	800 747-0583	14234
Concessionaires Urban Park	7999	D	530 529-1596	15198
Content Management Corporation	2759	F	510 505-1100	3726
Corbin Willits Systems Inc	7371	F	510 979-5600	12355
Core Systems Incorporated	3674	D	510 933-2300	6088
Corsair Gaming Inc (PA)	3577	B	510 657-8747	5360
Corsair Memory Inc	3674	C	510 657-8747	6090
Corsair Memory Inc (HQ)	3674	C	510 657-8747	6091
Covidien Holding Inc	3841	C	510 456-1500	6966
Creative Shower Door Corp	3088	E	510 623-9000	4248
Crestwood Behavioral Hlth Inc	8361	B	510 651-1244	18095
Crestwood Behavioral Hlth Inc	8361	C	510 793-8383	18096
Cross Match Inc	7371	E	650 474-4000	12361
Crossing Automation Inc (HQ)	5084	A	510 661-5000	9061
CSC Covansys Corporation	7371	B	510 304-3430	12365
Custom Micro Machining Inc	3599	E	510 651-9434	5499
Cytek Biosciences Inc (PA)	3826	E	877 922-9835	6823
D&H Manufacturing Company	3999	E	510 770-5100	7279
Dawn VME Products	3679	E	510 657-4444	6415
Db Design Group Inc	8711	E	408 834-1400	18685
Dcm Technologies Inc	7371	E	510 494-2321	12376
Del Contes Landscaping Inc	0781	D	510 353-6030	412
Delta America Ltd (HQ)	5065	E	510 668-5100	8906
Delta Electronics Americas Ltd (DH)	8741	D	510 668-5100	19323
Dgn Technologies Inc	7371	D	510 252-0346	12387
Dhyan Infotech Inc	7379	E	510 589-7875	13880
Digital Nirvana Inc (PA)	8742	B	510 226-9000	19493
Discopylabs Inc	4731	E	510 651-5100	7832
Discopylabs	7379	E	510 651-5100	13883
Dixon Corp	7336	F	510 366-6697	11859
DMS Facility Services Inc	7349	A	510 656-9400	11944
Droisys Inc (PA)	7373	B	408 874-8333	13579
Dryco Construction Inc (PA)	1611	C	510 438-6500	1035
Duke Scientific Corporation	3826	D	650 424-1177	6826
E & E Co Ltd (PA)	5023	C	510 490-9788	8511
E-Base Technologies Inc (PA)	7371	E	510 790-2547	12410
E2e Mfg LLC	3469	E	925 862-2057	4882
East Private Holdings II LLC (PA)	2759	E	650 357-3500	3730
Econolite	7389	F	408 577-1733	14258
Edata Solutions Inc	7374	A	510 574-5380	13710
Electronics For Imaging Inc (HQ)	2759	E	650 357-3500	3731
Elma Electronic Inc (HQ)	3571	C	510 656-3400	5249
Emeritus Corporation	8051	E	510 797-4011	15984
Enablence Systems Inc (HQ)	7372	D	510 226-8900	13141
Enablence USA Components Inc	3661	B	510 226-8900	5794
Enervenue Inc	3356	E	408 664-0355	4565
Enexus Global Inc	7379	D	510 936-4044	13888
Enovix Corporation	3692	C	510 695-2350	6493
Enovix Corporation	3692	C	510 695-2399	6494
Enphase Energy Inc (PA)	3674	A	707 774-7000	6112
Epoch International Entps Inc (PA)	3559	D	510 556-1225	5149
Esg Consulting Inc (PA)	7379	E	408 970-8595	13891
Essai Inc (PA)	3825	C	510 580-1700	6751
Eurofins Discoverx Pdts LLC	8731	D	510 979-1415	19060
Everest Consulting Group Inc	7371	D	510 494-8440	12431
Evolve Manufacturing Tech Inc	3841	D	650 968-9292	6972
Excelfore Corporation (PA)	7373	C	510 868-2500	13586
Exxact Corporation	5045	D	510 226-7366	8704
Fabri-Tech Components Inc	3679	F	510 249-2000	6426
Famsoft Corporation	7372	C	510 683-3940	13159
Fei Efa Inc (DH)	3826	D	510 897-6800	6828
FM Industries Inc (DH)	3599	E	510 661-1900	5526
Formac Inc	7373	C	510 379-9027	13591
Free Flow Medical Inc (PA)	8062	D	717 669-2566	16370
Fremont Ambltory Srgery Ctr LP	8011	D	510 456-4600	15408
Fremont Amgen Inc (HQ)	2834	C	510 284-6500	3901
Fremont Bank (HQ)	6022	D	510 505-5226	9731
Fremont Marriott	7011	E	510 413-3700	11105
Fremont Sports Inc	7933	E	510 656-4411	14893
Garnett Signs LLC	3993	F	650 871-9518	7230
Genmark Automation (DH)	5084	D	510 897-3400	9068
Gigamat Technologies Inc	3674	F	510 770-8008	6128
Glenmoor Realty Inc	6531	E	510 793-4030	10560
Global Plating Inc	3471	E	510 659-8764	4908
Golden N-Life Diamite Intl Inc (PA)	5122	D	510 651-0405	9227
Golden State Assembly Inc (PA)	3353	C	510 226-8155	4559
Golden State Utility Co	1623	E	408 982-5420	1103
Goldfire Corporation	1751	F	510 354-3666	1739
Gooch & Housego Palo Alto LLC (HQ)	3679	D	650 856-7911	6431

GEOGRAPHIC SECTION — FREMONT, CA

Company	SIC	EMP	PHONE	ENTRY #
Good Shepherd Lutheran HM of W	8361	D	510 505-1244	18122
Gotion Inc	8732	E	510 249-5610	19163
Graphiant Inc (PA)	7389	E	510 676-5916	14290
Greatlink International Inc	5063	A	510 657-1667	8861
Green Wall Tech Inc	1742	E	510 252-1170	1678
Greenbriar Management Company	6531	D	510 497-8200	10564
Grm Information MGT Svcs Inc (PA)	4226	B	201 798-7100	7708
Grm Infrmtion MGT Svcs San Frn	7389	E	888 907-9687	14291
Hayward Quartz Technology Inc	3674	C	510 657-9605	6141
Headway Technologies Inc	7231	A	425 503-2131	11685
Helitek Company Ltd	3674	D	510 933-7688	6142
Henry Plastic Molding Inc	3089	C	510 490-7993	4288
Hid Global Safe Inc	7373	D	408 453-1008	13608
Highpoint Technologies Inc	3572	E	408 942-5800	5292
Homelegance Inc (PA)	5021	D	510 933-6888	8494
Hpe Government Llc	3575	D	916 435-9200	5332
HPM Incorporated	5045	D	510 353-0770	8710
Hurricane Electric LLC (PA)	7375	D	510 580-4100	13793
Ic Sensors Inc	3674	D	510 498-1570	6146
Ichor Holdings Ltd (PA)	8711	D	510 897-5200	18735
Ichor Systems Inc (HQ)	3674	E	510 897-5200	6147
Identiv Inc (PA)	3577	C	949 250-8888	5373
IMG Altair LLC	3559	D	650 508-8700	5152
Imtec Acculine LLC	3559	E	510 770-1800	5153
Imusti Inc (PA)	7371	D	510 453-1864	12513
Incal Technology Inc	3577	E	510 657-8405	5375
Incalus Inc	7379	E	510 209-4064	13909
Innodisk Usa Corporation	3674	E	510 770-9421	6153
Innovative Installers Inc	1799	E	510 651-9890	2037
Innovtive Intllgent Sltons LLC (PA)	8748	D	408 332-5736	19795
Inspur Systems Inc	3571	E	510 400-7599	5257
Instant Systems Inc	7371	E	510 657-8100	12526
Intuity Medical Inc	3841	D	408 530-1700	6988
Iron Systems Inc	5045	D	408 943-8000	8714
Iscience Interventional Corp	3841	E	650 421-2700	6992
ISE Labs Inc (DH)	8734	C	510 687-2500	19277
Isomedia LLC	3652	E	510 668-1656	5778
Ituner Networks Corporation	3577	F	510 573-0783	5389
Iyp Inc	7221	E	305 593-1211	11674
J M Fremont Motors LLC	7538	D	510 403-3700	14573
Ja Apparel Corp (HQ)	5136	C	877 986-9669	9245
Jabil Silver Creek Inc	7692	C	669 255-2900	14715
Jaton Corporation	3672	D	510 933-8888	5942
Jem America Corp	5065	E	510 683-9234	8924
Jiangsu Juwang Info Tech Co (PA)	7371	E	510 967-3729	12547
Johnson & Johnson	2676	A	650 237-4878	3395
Kaiser Foundation Hospitals	8011	C	510 248-3000	15486
Kal-Kustom Enterprises (PA)	5091	F	510 651-8400	9157
Kdr Holding Inc (PA)	6799	D	510 230-2777	10859
Kidango Inc (PA)	8351	D	510 897-6900	17958
Kidango Inc	8351	D	510 494-9601	17959
Kilam Inc	5136	C	510 943-4040	9246
Knight Roofing Co (PA)	1761	D	510 438-9077	1814
Knightsbridge Plastics Inc	3089	D	510 440-8444	4296
Kositch Enterprises Inc	1731	D	510 657-4460	1532
Kyocera Sld Laser Inc	3699	E	805 696-6999	6531
Lam Research Corporation (PA)	3674	A	510 572-0200	6175
Land Services Ldscp Contrs Inc	6552	D	510 656-8101	10706
Lanner Electronics Usa Inc	5045	E	510 979-0688	8719
Lees Imperial Welding Inc	3441	C	510 657-4900	4672
Legend Silicon Corp	3663	D	510 656-9888	5853
Leisure Sports Inc	7991	B	510 226-8500	14957
Leopard Imaging Inc (PA)	3861	D	408 263-0988	7153
Level-It Installations Group	1542	E	604 942-2022	914
Lftm Inc	5021	F	510 249-0900	8500
Linear Integrated Systems Inc	3674	E	510 490-9160	6179
Lipman Company Inc	6411	E	510 796-4676	10309
Lipman Insur Administrators Inc (PA)	6371	E	510 796-4676	10216
Loginext Solutions Inc	7372	D	339 244-0380	13280
Lowes Home Centers LLC	5031	C	510 344-4920	8575
Luca International Group LLC (PA)	1382	E	510 498-8829	559
Lumens Integration Inc	3861	E	510 657-8367	7154
Lyncean Technologies Inc	3844	F	650 320-8300	7092
M Construction & Design Inc	1623	E	510 651-6981	1116
Magnum Drywall Inc	1742	D	510 979-0420	1690
Mallar Industrial Finshg Inc	2851	F	510 651-6694	4107
Manufacturing Resource Corp	7389	E	510 438-9600	14328
Mariner Health Care Inc	8051	E	510 792-3743	16045
Mass Precision Inc	3444	C	408 954-0200	4784
Mattson Technology Inc (DH)	3674	B	510 657-5900	6192
Mecoptron Inc	3599	F	510 226-9966	5569
Medical Analysis Systems Inc (DH)	3826	C	510 979-5000	6837
Melrose Metal Products Inc	3444	E	510 657-8771	4786
Menlo Industries Inc	3679	D	510 770-2350	6453
Mens Wearhouse	2326	E	510 657-9821	2989
Meraqi Medical Inc	3841	B	669 222-7101	7006
Mercury Systems Inc	3571	E	510 252-0870	5260
Meritronics Materials Inc	3672	F	408 390-5642	5947
Metabyte Inc	7379	E	510 494-9700	13937
Micro Lambda Wireless Inc	3679	E	510 770-9221	6454
Microbar Inc	3559	B	510 659-9770	5158
Microgenics Corporation (HQ)	3826	C	510 979-9147	6838
Microgenics Corporation	3826	A	510 979-5000	6839
Micron Consumer Pdts Group Inc (HQ)	3572	D	669 226-3000	5300
Microtech International Inc (PA)	3577	C	510 360-0210	5400
Microwave Technology Inc (DH)	3679	D	510 651-6700	6455
Milan Corporation	1761	E	510 656-6400	1822
Milestone Technologies Inc (PA)	7373	A	510 651-2454	13632
Millennium Metalcraft Inc	3444	E	510 657-4700	4792
Mio Technology USA Ltd	5065	E	510 252-6900	8935
Mirror Plus Technologies Inc	7371	D	510 403-2400	12610
Mistral Solutions Inc (PA)	7371	D	408 705-2240	12611
Mitac Information Systems Corp	3571	E	510 668-3507	5261
Molecular Devices LLC	3826	F	408 747-3546	6840
Mt Systems Inc	3559	F	510 651-5277	5159
Myntahl Corporation	3679	E	510 413-0002	6459
National Glass Systems Inc	1793	E	408 835-5124	1939
Nationwide Boiler Incorporated (PA)	3443	E	510 490-7100	4726
Ncoop Inc (PA)	7372	E	510 739-4010	13321
Neptec Optical Solutions Inc	3229	E	510 687-1101	4376
Neptec Os Inc	3357	E	510 687-1101	4571
Network Fcilty Svcs Group LLC	7349	E	510 256-6035	11978
New Iem LLC	3613	C	510 656-1600	5652
New Image Landscape Company	0782	E	510 226-9191	489
New Solar Electric Inc (PA)	1731	D	888 886-0103	1551
New Tech Solutions Inc	5045	E	510 353-4070	8729
Newport Meat Northern Cal Inc (HQ)	5142	E	800 535-6328	9328
Nextracker Inc (DH)	5074	C	510 270-2500	9001
Nisum Technologies Inc	7371	A	714 579-7979	12633
Nitinol Development Corp	3851	A	510 683-2000	7145
Nova Eye Inc	3841	E	510 291-1300	7012
Nova Measuring Instruments Inc	3825	E	408 510-7400	6776
Novariant Inc (PA)	8711	D	510 933-4800	18780
Ntm Consulting Services Inc	7379	E	510 744-3901	13951
NTS Technical Systems	8734	E	510 578-3500	19281
Omnitrol Networks Inc	7373	E	408 919-1100	13643
Oncore Manufacturing LLC	3672	D	510 516-5488	5953
Onmycare LLC	8082	E	510 858-2273	16921
Oorja Corporation	3674	E	510 659-1899	6246
Openmind Technologies Inc (PA)	7371	D	866 536-2324	12652
Oplink Communications LLC (DH)	4899	A	510 933-7200	8082
Optiworks Inc	3229	D	510 438-4560	4377
Optoma Technology Inc	3861	C	510 897-8600	7157
Optoplex Corporation	3661	B	510 490-9930	5804
Optovue Inc (PA)	3841	D	510 623-8868	7014
Organic Spices (PA)	2099	E	510 440-1044	2930
Oridus Inc	7371	E	510 249-1158	12657
Oryx Advanced Materials Inc (PA)	3572	E	510 249-1158	5307
Overton Security Services Inc	7381	C	510 791-7380	14083
Owens Design Incorporated	3599	E	510 659-1800	5584
Pacific Gas and Electric Co	4911	C	510 770-2025	8170
Pacific Surfacing	1771	E	510 440-9494	1900
Pacira Cryotech Inc	8748	E	800 442-0989	19835
Pan-Pacific Mechanical LLC	1711	B	650 561-8810	1333
Pantronix Corporation	3674	C	510 656-5898	6249
Pape Material Handling Inc	5084	D	510 659-4100	9085
Park Cntl Care Rhblitation Ctr	8051	E	510 797-5300	16093
Pathwater Inc	2086	E	510 518-0014	2797
Patriot Memory Inc (PA)	3674	C	510 979-1021	6250
Pegatron Usa Inc (HQ)	7374	D	510 580-4276	13740
Penguin Computing Inc (DH)	5045	E	415 954-2800	8732
Permanente Medical Group Inc	8011	A	510 248-3000	15602
Phihong USA Corp (HQ)	5045	D	510 445-0100	8733
Pivotal Systems Corporation	3625	E	510 770-9125	5687
PJs Lumber Inc	5031	D	510 743-5300	8603
Pjs Rebar Inc	5051	D	510 490-0321	8826
Plexus Corp	3672	D	510 668-9000	5958
Ponyai Inc	7371	B	510 906-8868	12691
Prime Solutions Inc (PA)	3674	D	510 490-2255	6255
Prince Peace Lutheran Church	8351	D	510 797-8186	18005
Printerprezz Inc	3841	F	510 225-8412	7022
Privacera Inc	7371	D	510 413-7300	12698
Priyo Inc	7371	E	408 248-2507	12699
Professional Assn Svcs Inc	8641	E	510 683-8614	18451
Prospance Inc (PA)	7371	D	925 415-2394	12705
Ptec Solutions Inc (PA)	3599	D	510 358-3578	5604
Pulsar Vascular Inc	3841	F	408 246-4300	7025
Pyramid Painting Inc	1721	E	650 903-9791	1424
Quanta Computer Usa Inc (HQ)	5045	B	510 226-1000	8739
Quanta Service Incorporation (DH)	5045	D	510 226-1000	8740
Qxq Inc	3825	E	510 252-1522	6784
Rahi Systems Inc (PA)	8748	B	510 651-2205	19845
Rapiscan Laboratories Inc (HQ)	3844	D	408 961-9700	7093
Ravenswood Solutions Inc (HQ)	7373	D	650 241-3661	13656
Raxium Inc	8711	D	510 296-9935	18801
Raymond Handling Concepts Corp (DH)	7699	D	510 745-7500	14771
Raymonds Little Print Shop Inc	2752	B	510 353-3608	3690
Regency General Contrs Inc (PA)	1522	D	408 946-7100	764
Reliance Machine Products Inc	3599	E	510 438-6760	5611
Reliant Engrg & Mfg Svcs Inc	8711	E	510 252-1973	18802
Remel Inc	3826	A	916 425-2651	6846
Renovite Technologies Inc (PA)	8742	D	510 771-9200	19622
RK Electric Inc	1731	C	510 772-4125	1588
Rk Logistics Group Inc	4731	C	510 298-5128	7852
Rk Logistics Group Inc (PA)	8742	C	408 942-8107	19623
S & M Moving Systems	4213	D	510 497-2300	7585
S3 Graphics Inc	3674	C	510 687-4900	6276
Saba Decor Rentals LLC (PA)	7359	E	510 449-4890	12062
Sable Computer Inc	7373	D	510 403-7500	13658
Saitech Inc	5044	F	510 440-0256	8655
Sandys Drapery Inc (PA)	2391	E	510 445-0112	3022
Sanmina Corporation	3672	B	510 897-2000	5970
Sansei Gardens Inc	0782	E	510 226-9191	499
Santur Corporation (HQ)	3559	C	510 933-4100	5170

Employment Codes: A=Over 500 employees, B=251-500, C=101-250, D=51-100, E=20-50 F=10-19

FREMONT, CA GEOGRAPHIC SECTION

	SIC	EMP	PHONE	ENTRY #
Scalable Press	2711	F	877 752-9060	3478
Scholastic Book Fairs Inc	5192	D	510 771-1700	9619
Seagate Systems (us) Inc **(DH)**	3572	D	510 687-5200	5318
Seagate Technology LLC **(DH)**	3572	A	800 732-4283	5319
Select Hotels Group LLC	7011	E	510 623-6000	11455
Semicat Inc **(PA)**	3674	E	408 514-6900	6281
Seradyn Inc	3826	D	317 610-3800	6851
Serrato-Mcdermott Inc	5013	D	510 656-6233	8466
Seven Up Btlg Co San Francisco **(HQ)**	2086	C	925 938-8777	2812
Sharp Dimension Inc	3599	E	510 656-8938	5617
Shopalyst Inc **(PA)**	8742	D	949 583-0507	19632
Siblings Investment Inc	5045	E	510 668-0368	8747
Siemens Industry Software Inc	8711	E	510 445-1836	18813
Sienna Corporation Inc	3699	E	510 440-0200	6542
Sierra Nevada Corporation	3663	E	510 446-8400	5867
Sigmaways Inc	8742	D	510 573-4208	19633
Signature Building Maint Inc	7349	D	408 377-8066	11998
Silicon Genesis Corporation	3674	E	408 228-5885	6285
Silicon Valley Optics Tech	5049	E	510 623-1161	8803
Siliconindia Inc	2741	D	510 440-8249	3599
Sipex Corporation **(DH)**	3674	C	669 265-6100	6298
Sit Funding Corporation	6153	E	510 656-3333	9876
Skycatch Inc	7371	E	415 504-3929	12794
Smart Machines Inc	3535	E	510 661-5000	5057
Smart Modular Tech De Inc **(HQ)**	3674	D	510 623-1231	6305
Smart Sftwr Tstg Solutions Inc	8748	D	833 778-7872	19861
Smart World LLC	7389	E	510 933-9700	14406
Smtc Corporation **(HQ)**	3672	D	510 737-0700	5974
Smtc Manufacturing Corp Cal	3672	A	408 934-7100	5975
Smtc Mex Holdings Inc **(HQ)**	5065	D	915 849-6752	8956
Smtc Mex Holdings Inc	5065	C	510 737-0729	8957
Sna Electronics Inc	3672	E	510 656-3903	5976
Snapwiz Inc	7372	C	510 328-3277	13450
Softsol Resources Inc **(HQ)**	7371	D	510 824-2000	12803
Sonata Software North Amer Inc **(HQ)**	7371	D	510 791-7220	12806
Sonic Manufacturing Tech Inc	3672	E	510 580-8551	5977
Sonic Manufacturing Tech Inc	3672	B	510 580-8500	5978
Soraa Inc **(HQ)**	3674	D	510 456-2200	6308
South Bay Solutions Inc **(PA)**	3599	E	650 843-1800	5621
South Bay Solutions Texas LLC	3629	F	936 494-0180	5697
South E Bay Pdtric Med Group I	8011	E	510 792-4373	15697
Sparqtron Corporation	3629	D	510 657-7198	5698
Specialized Coating Services	3479	D	510 226-8700	4949
Spectranetics Corporation	3841	D	510 933-7964	7042
Spectrum Lithograph Inc	2752	E	510 438-9192	3700
Spin Memory Inc	3674	E	510 933-8200	6311
Spire Manufacturing Inc	3643	E	510 226-1070	5718
SRS Consulting Inc	7371	B	510 252-0625	12814
St Cyberlink Corporation	5045	E	510 623-9888	8750
Star Microwave Service Corp	7629	E	510 651-8096	14706
Startup Farms Intl LLC	7371	B	510 440-0110	12817
Statewide Cnstr Sweeping LLC	4959	E	510 683-9584	8408
Stats Chippac Test Svcs Inc **(DH)**	3674	F	510 979-8000	6313
Stratamet Advanced Mtls Corp	3253	F	510 440-1697	4404
Streamline Electronics Mfg Inc	3672	E	408 263-3600	5981
Stryker Sales LLC	3841	E	510 413-2500	7044
Suba Technology Inc	3672	D	408 434-6500	5982
Sun Innovations Inc	8731	E	510 573-3913	19131
Sunnyvale Fluid Sys Tech Inc **(PA)**	5085	E	510 933-2500	9136
Superior Automatic Sprnklr Co	1711	D	408 946-7272	1374
Sure Fire Protection Co Inc	1711	E	510 490-7873	1375
Sync Logistics LLC **(PA)**	4215	E	510 353-3749	7654
Sysco San Francisco Inc	5141	A	510 226-3000	9318
T R Manufacturing	3679	F	510 657-3850	6474
Tactus Technology Inc	7379	C	510 244-3968	13988
Tarc Construction Inc **(PA)**	1521	E	408 224-2154	716
TCI International Inc **(HQ)**	3663	C	510 687-6100	5876
Td Synnex Corporation **(PA)**	7373	C	510 656-3333	13676
Td Synnex Corporation	7389	D	510 688-3507	14426
Te Connectivity Ltd	3679	E	650 361-4923	6475
Te Tech LLC	5085	F	510 770-8610	9137
Tekreliance LLC	7371	E	732 829-7585	12854
Telewave Inc	3663	E	408 929-4400	5879
Telirite Technical Svcs Inc	3672	E	510 440-3888	5986
Tend Insights Inc	7372	E	510 619-9289	13490
Tenergy Corporation	3691	D	510 687-0388	6491
Terarecon Inc	3577	E	650 372-1100	5419
TGIF Body Shop Inc	7532	E	510 490-1342	14536
Think Surgical Inc	3842	C	510 249-2300	7082
Three Way Logistics Inc **(PA)**	4731	D	408 748-3929	7854
Thundrbird Ldge Frmont A Cal L	7011	E	510 792-4300	11532
Traform Inc	7371	E	650 387-5536	12872
Transcontinental Nrthern CA 20	2759	C	510 580-7700	3752
Translarity Inc	3825	F	510 371-7900	6796
Tri Fab Associates Inc	3444	D	510 651-7628	4826
Tri-Valley Supply Inc **(HQ)**	5033	D	510 494-9982	8641
Trina Solar (us) Inc	1711	E	800 696-7114	1385
Tronson Manufacturing Inc	3599	E	408 533-0369	5629
Tru Machining	3599	F	510 573-3408	5630
TTT-Cubed Inc	3825	D	510 656-2325	6797
U-Haul Co of California **(DH)**	7513	C	800 528-0463	14474
United Mfg Assembly Inc	8734	D	510 490-4680	19290
United Parcel Service Inc	7389	D	800 742-5877	14451
Unitek Inc	7373	D	510 623-8544	13685
Vasona Management Inc	1521	B	510 413-0091	726
Veex Inc	3823	F	510 651-0500	6737
Verseon Corporation **(PA)**	2834	E	510 225-9000	4002
Vertisystem Inc	7373	C	510 794-8099	13687
Veterans Health Administration	8011	C	510 791-4000	15789
Via Technologies Inc	3674	C	510 683-3300	6347
Viant Medical LLC	3089	D	510 657-5800	4330
Visioneer Inc **(HQ)**	3577	E	925 251-6300	5421
Volterra Semiconductor LLC	3674	C	510 743-1200	6352
W2 Optronics Inc **(PA)**	3674	F	510 207-8320	6353
Walters & Wolf Glass Company **(PA)**	1793	C	510 490-1115	1948
Walters & Wolf Glass Company	3272	E	510 226-9800	4453
Walters & Wolf Interiors **(PA)**	1751	D	415 243-9400	1762
Walters & Wolf Precast	3272	C	510 226-9800	4454
Washington Hosp Healthcare Sys	8062	A	510 797-3342	16721
Washington Otptent Srgery Ctr	8062	D	510 791-5374	16722
Washington Rdologist Med Group	8062	E	510 797-1111	16723
Wellex Corporation **(PA)**	3679	C	510 743-1818	6482
West Coast Quartz Corporation **(HQ)**	3229	D	510 249-2160	4382
William Ho	3672	F	510 226-9089	6001
Willow Springs LLC	8011	D	510 796-1100	15817
Windsor Cnvlscent Rhbltion CT	8051	D	510 793-7222	16165
Wintronics International Inc	3357	E	510 226-7588	4573
Winward International Inc **(PA)**	5193	D	510 487-8686	9642
Womens Health Specialists	8011	D	510 248-1470	15818
Wsglass Holdings Inc **(HQ)**	3211	C	510 623-5000	4365
Xodus Manufacturing Inc	3999	F	510 413-7925	7317
Yadav Technology Inc	3674	F	510 438-0148	6362
YC Cable Usa Inc **(HQ)**	7389	D	510 824-2788	14466
Yield Engineering Systems Inc	3674	D	510 954-6889	6363
Young Electric Sign Company	3993	E	510 877-7815	7263
Young MNS Chrstn Assn of E Bay	8641	B	510 656-7243	18500
Young MNS Chrstn Assn of E Bay	8641	B	510 683-9165	18506
Young MNS Chrstn Assn of E Bay	8641	B	510 683-9107	18507
Young MNS Chrstn Assn of E Bay	8641	B	510 683-9147	18508
Yuba City Community Hosp Inc	8063	E	510 796-1100	16750
Zealtech Inc	8748	E	510 797-7006	19893
Zerobase Energy LLC	3691	E	888 530-9376	6492
Zosano Pharma Corporation **(PA)**	2834	E	510 745-1200	4011
Zp Opco Inc	2834	E	510 745-1200	4012

FRENCH CAMP, CA - San Joaquin County

	SIC	EMP	PHONE	ENTRY #
American Hl Security Inc	1731	E	209 518-9207	1450
County of San Joaquin	8093	E	209 468-6280	17007
First Transit Inc	4111	C	866 244-6383	7332
Fresno Truck Center	5012	C	209 983-2400	8423
Granite Construction Company	1611	C	209 982-4750	1049
Health Plan of San Joaquin	6324	C	209 942-6300	10108
Interstate Con Pmpg Co Inc	1771	D	209 983-3092	1883
Jumbo Logistics LLC	4731	E	216 662-5420	7843
Pan Pacific Rv Centers Inc **(PA)**	7538	E	209 234-2000	14581
Parex Usa Inc	5032	F	510 444-2497	8631
Poly Processing Company LLC	2821	D	209 982-4904	3808
San Joaquin General Hospital **(PA)**	8062	A	209 468-6000	16503
San Jquin Gen Hosp Fndtion A C	8062	A	209 468-6000	16505
Silva Trucking	4212	E	209 982-1114	7489

FRESNO, CA - Fresno County

	SIC	EMP	PHONE	ENTRY #
1st Quality Produce Inc	5148	E	559 442-1932	9385
3 Ink Productions Inc	2221	E	559 275-4565	2966
4961 North Cdr LLC	7011	D	559 224-4200	10906
A J Excavation Inc	1794	C	559 408-5908	1949
A Plus Signs Inc	3993	E	559 275-0700	7213
A Teichert & Son Inc	1611	E	559 813-3100	1000
A-C Electric Company	1731	D	559 233-2208	1440
A-Mark T-Shirts Inc	2759	D	559 227-6370	3717
Aaron Dowling Incorporated	8111	D	559 432-4500	17196
Abelisk Inc **(PA)**	7371	E	559 227-1000	12221
Absolute Urethane	1761	E	877 471-3626	1779
Access Capital Services Inc **(PA)**	7322	D	559 627-5221	11821
Acclamation Insurance Mgt Svcs	6411	D	559 227-9891	10225
Agi Publishing Inc **(PA)**	7311	E	559 251-8888	11738
Agrifim Irrigation Pdts Inc	3523	F	559 443-6680	4994
Airport Specialty Products Inc	1521	E	559 439-9737	606
All Commercial Landscape Svc	0782	E	559 453-1670	445
Alliant International Univ Inc	8093	D	559 456-2777	16985
Allied Electric Motor Svc Inc **(PA)**	5063	D	559 486-4222	8840
Altapacific Inc	7371	E	559 439-5700	12245
Alw Enterprises Inc	1795	E	559 275-2828	1978
American Avk Co	3494	F	559 452-4305	4958
American Carrier Systems	3711	E	559 442-1500	6548
American Crier Eqp Trlr Sls LL	7549	E	559 442-1500	14655
American Grape Harvesters Inc	5083	E	559 277-7380	9030
American Paving Co	1611	E	559 268-9886	1009
Ameriguard Security Svcs Inc	7381	D	559 271-5984	14029
Anesthsia Cons of Frsno A Med	8011	D	559 436-0871	15280
Anthem Insurance Companies Inc	6324	B	559 230-6200	10091
Apco-Ettner Inc **(PA)**	8711	D	559 439-6766	18625
Appleby & Company Inc **(PA)**	7389	E	559 222-8402	14202
Applied Earthworks Inc **(PA)**	8733	E	559 229-1856	19196
ARC Fresno/Madera Counties **(PA)**	8331	C	559 226-6268	17793
Architectural Wood Design Inc	2434	E	559 292-9104	3167
Aries Industries Inc	4952	C	559 291-0383	8278
Arrow Electric Motor Service	7694	E	559 266-0104	14727
Art Piccadilly Shaw LLC **(PA)**	7011	C	559 348-5520	10930
Art Piccadilly Shaw LLC	7011	D	559 375-7760	10931
Art Piccadilly Shaw LLC	7011	D	559 224-4200	10932
Ashwood Construction Inc	1522	E	559 253-7240	737
Automated Bldg Components Inc	2439	E	559 485-8232	3200
Aweta-Autoline Inc **(DH)**	3523	E	559 244-8340	4996
Axiom Industries Inc	3842	E	559 276-1310	7066

GEOGRAPHIC SECTION FRESNO, CA

	SIC	EMP	PHONE	ENTRY #
B & L Mechanical Inc	1711	E	559 268-2727	1211
B M D Enterprises Inc	3589	F	559 291-7708	5439
Baggie Farms Express Inc	4213	E	559 486-7330	7506
Bailey Valve Inc	3491	E	559 434-2838	4954
Baker Manock & Jensen Pc	8111	D	559 432-5400	17206
Baloian Packing Co Inc **(PA)**	0161	C	559 485-9200	24
Barney & Co California LLC	2099	F	559 442-1752	2869
Barrier Spclty Rofg Ctings Inc	1761	E	559 233-1680	1787
Bbt Health LLC	8082	D	559 248-0131	16855
BCT Consulting Inc **(PA)**	7379	E	559 579-1400	13853
Beaver Dam Health Care Center	8051	E	559 275-4785	15927
Beaver Dam Health Care Center	8051	E	559 226-9401	15929
Beaver Dam Health Care Center	8051	E	559 222-4807	15936
Beaver Dam Health Care Center	8051	E	559 227-5383	15938
Bermad Inc **(PA)**	3494	E	877 577-4283	4959
Betts Company **(PA)**	3495	D	559 498-3304	4964
Betts Company	3713	F	559 498-8624	6564
Bimbo Bakeries Usa Inc	2051	F	559 498-3632	2371
Bio Behavioral Medical Clinics	8011	E	559 437-1111	15299
Biola Fresh Inc	8748	D	559 970-8881	19731
BNP Lodging LLC	7011	E	559 251-5200	10964
Bottling Group LLC	2086	A	559 485-5050	2783
Bottling Group LLC	2086	A	914 767-6000	2784
Bowie Enterprises **(PA)**	7542	D	559 227-6221	14631
Bowlero Corp	7933	D	201 797-5400	14887
Bradford Messenger Service	7389	D	559 252-0775	14218
Brix Group Inc	4812	E	800 726-2333	7898
Brix Group Inc **(PA)**	5065	D	559 457-4700	8898
Brix Group Inc	3699	E	559 457-4750	6509
Brix Group Inc	5064	E	559 457-4794	8883
Bronco Concrete Inc	1771	E	559 323-5005	1855
Brooks Home Health Care	8099	E	559 221-4800	17111
Brownie Baker Inc	2052	D	559 277-7070	2414
Brunos Iron & Metal LP	4953	E	559 233-6543	8313
BSK Associates	8711	E	559 277-6960	18649
BSK Associates	8711	E	559 497-2888	18650
BSK Associates	8711	E	559 256-2251	18652
Buckingham Property Management	7299	D	559 322-1105	11708
Builders Concrete Inc **(DH)**	3273	E	559 225-3667	4461
Business Journal	2721	E	559 490-3400	3493
Busseto Foods Inc **(PA)**	2099	C	559 485-9882	2875
C&S Wholesale Grocers Inc	5141	C	559 442-4700	9265
Cablecom LLC	7629	E	559 412-8720	14692
Cal Valley Construction Inc	1629	E	559 274-0300	1152
Calaveras Materials Inc	5032	E	559 233-2311	8620
Caliber Bodyworks Texas Inc	7532	E	559 435-9900	14522
Calif Stat Univ Fres Foun	8699	E	559 278-0850	18552
California Autism Center	8322	D	559 475-7860	17450
California Coml Solar Inc	1711	D	559 667-9200	1226
California Dairies Inc	2026	C	559 233-5154	2186
California Eye Institute	8011	C	559 449-5000	15309
California Hlth Collaborative **(PA)**	7389	D	559 221-6315	14223
California HM For The Aged Inc	8059	C	559 251-8414	16222
California Imaging Inst LLC **(PA)**	8733	E	559 325-5810	19202
California Industrial Rbr Co **(PA)**	5085	E	559 268-7321	9111
California Physicians Service	6324	D	559 440-4000	10100
California Sierra Express Inc	4512	E	559 441-1300	7738
California State Univ Long Bch	7922	C	559 278-2216	14843
California Tiny House Inc	2451	F	559 316-4500	3247
California Track & Engineering	3949	E	559 237-2590	7190
Califrnia Cncer Assoc For RES **(PA)**	8011	D	800 456-5860	15311
Cambridge Homes **(HQ)**	6552	D	559 447-3400	10699
Campos Family Farms LLC	0191	D	559 275-3000	149
Campus Pointe Cinemas Oper LLC	7832	E	213 805-5333	14807
Cardio Vascular Associates	8011	D	559 439-6808	15322
Cardiovascular Consultants Hea	8011	D	559 432-4303	15325
Cargill Meat Solutions Corp	2011	B	559 268-5586	2091
Caro Nut Company	2034	E	559 475-5400	2255
Carreys Care Center Inc	8361	D	559 444-0151	18070
Carrollco Inc	0782	E	559 396-3939	450
Caylym Technologies Intl LLC	7373	E	209 322-9596	13564
Cemex Materials LLC	3273	D	559 275-2241	4474
Central Cal Ear Nose Throat ME	8011	C	559 432-3724	15334
Central Cal Fclty Med Group In	8011	D	559 435-6600	15335
Central Cal Fclty Med Group In	8011	D	559 266-4100	15336
Central Cal Fclty Med Group In	8011	D	559 320-1090	15337
Central Cal Fclty Med Group In	8011	D	559 435-4700	15338
Central Cal Nikkei Foundation	8361	D	559 237-4006	18073
Central California Blood Ctr	8099	D	559 389-5433	17120
Central California Blood Ctr **(PA)**	8099	C	559 389-5433	17121
Central California Faculty Med **(PA)**	8011	D	559 453-5200	15339
Central California Food Bank	8399	E	559 237-3663	18224
Central Fish Inc	5146	D	559 237-2049	9364
Central Valley Cmnty Bancorp **(PA)**	6022	C	559 298-1775	9713
Central Valley Community Bank **(HQ)**	6022	C	800 298-1775	9715
Central Valley GMC **(PA)**	7538	D	559 334-3496	14552
Central Valley Machining Inc	3441	E	559 291-7749	4652
Central Valley Tank of Cal	3443	F	559 456-3500	4713
Central Valley Trlr Repr Inc	7538	D	559 233-8444	14553
Central Vly Assembly Packg Inc	3432	E	559 486-4260	4623
Central Vly Chld Svcs Netwrk	8322	D	559 456-1100	17478
Centro La Familia Advacasy Svc	8322	E	559 237-2961	17479
Certified Meat Products Inc	2011	D	559 256-1433	2092
Cerutti & Sons Trnsp Co	4212	E	559 275-6608	7458
Ch Industrial Technology Inc	3441	F	559 485-8011	4653
Champagne Landscape Nurs Inc	0782	D	559 277-8188	451
Charles Matoian Entps Inc **(PA)**	4225	C	559 445-8600	7685
Charles McMurray Co **(PA)**	5072	D	559 292-5751	8980
Chase Inc **(PA)**	6021	D	559 277-2828	9681
Choice Food Products Inc	2013	E	559 266-1674	2114
City of Fresno	4111	B	559 621-7433	7327
City of Fresno	4941	C	559 621-5300	8229
Clay Miranda Trucking Inc	4212	E	559 275-6250	7459
Clay Mix LLC **(PA)**	3273	E	559 485-0065	4476
Clinica Sierra Vista	8011	E	559 457-5200	15350
Clinica Sierra Vista	8011	E	559 457-5292	15351
Clinica Sierra Vista	8011	E	559 457-5500	15352
Club One Casino Inc	7011	B	559 497-3000	11016
Collins Electrical Company Inc	1731	E	559 454-8164	1481
Commercial Manufacturing	3556	E	559 237-1855	5127
Community Hospitals Centl Cal **(PA)**	8062	A	559 459-6000	16335
Community Hospitals Centl Cal	8062	A	559 459-6000	16336
Community Intgrted Work Prgram	8322	E	559 276-8564	17498
Community Medical Center	8062	C	559 222-7416	16337
Community Vocational Svcs LLC	8322	E	559 227-8287	17501
Comprhnsive Yuth Svcs Frsno In	8322	D	559 229-3561	17505
Conner Logistics Inc	4731	D	888 939-4637	7830
Consoldted Metal Fbrctng Coinc	5051	E	559 268-7887	8813
Construction Developers Inc	1542	E	559 277-4700	858
Contract Interiors San Diego	5021	D	559 276-0561	8492
Cooks Communications Corp	7629	E	559 233-8818	14694
Copper River Country Club LP **(PA)**	7997	E	559 434-5200	15077
Cosco Fire Protection Inc	1711	E	559 275-3795	1243
Counter Hospitality Group LLC	7372	D	559 228-9735	13094
Courtyard Management Corp	7011	D	559 221-6000	11038
Covenant Care California LLC	8051	D	559 251-8463	15968
Cox Enterprises Inc	4841	E	559 432-3947	8060
Craigo Investments Inc	3993	E	559 222-9293	7226
Cummins Pacific LLC	3714	E	559 277-6760	6575
Custom AG Formulators Inc **(PA)**	5191	D	559 435-1052	9597
Cve Contracting Group Inc	8748	E	559 222-1122	19756
Cwes Inc	8748	E	559 346-1251	19758
D&M Manufacturing Co LLC	3523	F	559 834-4668	5000
D-K-P Inc	3523	F	559 266-2695	5001
Dan On & Associates (usa) Ltd **(PA)**	2099	E	559 233-2828	2887
Dantel Inc	3661	E	559 292-1111	5792
Darden Architects Inc	8712	D	559 448-8051	18881
Dave J Mendrin Inc	0172	F	559 352-1700	49
David Knott Inc	1795	E	559 449-8935	1984
Demera Dmera Cmron An Accntncy	8721	E	559 226-9200	18950
Devine Organics LLC **(PA)**	0191	E	559 573-7500	157
Dhillon Bros Trucking Inc	4212	E	559 834-5600	7461
Diamond Learning Center Inc	8322	D	559 241-0580	17532
Dibuduo Dfendis Insur Brks LLC **(PA)**	6411	D	559 432-0222	10272
Digestive Disease Consultants	8011	E	559 440-0450	15380
Digital Prototype Systems Inc	3663	E	559 454-1600	5838
Donaghy Sales Inc	5181	A	559 486-0901	9550
Donald P Dick AC Inc **(PA)**	1711	E	559 255-1644	1251
Donor Network West	8099	E	510 418-0336	17135
Dri Clean & Restoration	1389	E	559 292-1100	563
Drisas Groom McCormick	8721	D	559 447-8484	18951
Dumont Printing Inc	2752	E	559 485-6311	3641
Duncan Enterprises **(HQ)**	2851	C	559 291-4444	4103
DV Kap Inc	2392	E	559 435-5575	3024
Dybeck Inc **(PA)**	7231	E	559 299-7696	11680
E&S Residential Care Svcs LLC	8361	E	559 275-3555	18101
E-Z Haul Ready Mix Inc	3273	E	559 233-6603	4479
Ebit-Golf Inc	7992	D	559 275-5900	15000
Educare Services Inc **(PA)**	8351	E	559 228-3232	17930
Educational Employees Cr Un **(PA)**	6061	C	559 437-7700	9782
Educational Employees Cr Un	6061	D	559 896-0222	9783
Educational Employees Cr Un	6061	D	559 437-7700	9784
Edward B Ward & Company Inc	5075	D	559 487-1860	9010
Eezer Products Inc	2821	E	559 255-4140	3801
Eide Bailly LLP	8721	E	559 248-0871	18954
Electric Motor Shop **(PA)**	5063	E	559 233-1153	8859
Electric Motor Shop	5063	C	559 233-1153	8860
Electrnic Rcyclers Intl - Ind	4953	D	317 522-1414	8324
Electrnic Rcyclers Intl - Wash	4953	E	253 736-2627	8325
Electronic Recyclers Intl Inc **(PA)**	4953	A	800 374-3473	8326
Elitecare Medical Staffing LLC	7361	D	559 438-7700	12086
Elliott Manufacturing Co Inc	3599	F	559 233-6235	5518
Emerzian Woodworking Inc	2541	E	559 292-2448	3314
Energy Star Construction Inc **(PA)**	1521	E	559 231-5998	635
Entercom Media Corp	4832	D	559 490-0106	8021
Envelope Products Co	2621	E	925 939-5173	3344
Environment Control	7349	E	559 456-9791	11946
Eric Ladenheim MD Inc	8011	E	559 446-1065	15391
Estes Express Lines	4213	D	559 441-0915	7531
Everyday Health Care Fresno	8011	E	559 225-4706	15392
Excel Restoration Inc	7389	D	559 903-8902	14268
Excelsior Inc	3441	E	559 346-0932	4658
Exceptnal Prents Unlimited Inc	8322	C	559 229-2000	17556
Expo Marketing & Services Inc	7389	E	559 495-3300	14269
Express Messenger Systems Inc	4215	D	559 277-4910	7645
Eye Medical Clinic Fresno Inc	8011	D	559 486-5000	15395
Eye Q Vision Care **(PA)**	8011	C	559 486-2000	15397
Family Plg Assoc Med Group	8011	E	559 233-8657	15403
Famous Software II LLC **(PA)**	7371	D	559 438-3600	12443
Fast AG Svcs Trnspt Inc **(PA)**	4789	E	559 233-0970	7881
Fedex Freight West Inc	4213	C	559 266-0732	7537
Fiore Di Pasta Inc	2099	D	559 457-0431	2892
Fire System Solutions Inc	7389	E	559 275-4894	14274
First Student Inc	4151	C	559 268-4077	7435

GEOGRAPHIC

Employment Codes: A=Over 500 employees, B=251-500, C=101-250, D=51-100, E=20-50 F=10-19

2022 Northern California Business Directory and Buyers Guide

© Mergent Inc. 1-800-342-5647

1149

FRESNO, CA GEOGRAPHIC SECTION

	SIC	EMP	PHONE	ENTRY #
Five Star Quality Care Inc	8051	E	559 446-6226	16004
Flake R Recycling	1629	E	559 233-9361	1161
Fort Wash Golf & Cntry CLB	7997	D	559 434-1702	15091
Foster Farms	0191	D	559 265-2000	168
Foster Poultry Farms	2015	B	559 265-2000	2134
Foster Poultry Farms	2015	B	559 442-3771	2135
Four CS Service Inc	1761	D	559 237-3990	1805
Fowler Packing Company Inc	0723	C	559 834-5911	284
Frank Toste	0241	E	559 233-4329	212
Freshko Produce Services Inc	5148	C	559 497-7000	9404
Fresn-Mdera Fdral Land Bnk Ass **(HQ)**	6111	E	559 277-7000	9852
Fresno Airport Hotels LLC	7011	D	559 252-3611	11107
FRESNO ART MUSEUM	8412	E	559 441-4221	18272
Fresno Auto Dealers Auction	5012	A	559 268-8051	8421
Fresno Baseball Club LLC	7997	E	559 320-4487	15093
Fresno Beverage Company Inc	5181	C	559 650-1500	9551
Fresno Chrysler Jeep Inc	7538	D	559 431-4000	14565
Fresno Cmnty Hosp & Med Ctr **(HQ)**	8062	A	559 459-3948	16376
Fresno Cnty Ecnmic Opprtnties	8322	E	559 486-6587	17574
Fresno Cnty Ecnmic Opprtnties	8351	D	559 263-1584	17937
Fresno Cnty Ecnmic Opprtnties	8322	E	559 263-1000	17576
Fresno Cnty Ecnmic Opprtnties **(PA)**	8322	A	559 263-1010	17577
Fresno Cnty Ecnmic Opprtnties	8322	E	559 485-3733	17580
Fresno Cnty Ecnmic Opprtnties	8322	E	559 263-1013	17581
Fresno Cnty Ecnmic Opprtnties	8322	E	559 485-3733	17582
Fresno Cnty Ecnmic Opprtnties	8322	E	559 266-3663	17583
Fresno Credit Bureau	7322	E	559 650-7177	11822
Fresno Distributing Co	3651	E	559 442-8800	5757
Fresno Ford Tractor Inc	3524	E	559 485-9090	5023
Fresno French Bread Bakery Inc	2051	E	559 268-7088	2384
Fresno Heart Hospital LLC	8062	B	559 433-8000	16377
Fresno Heritage Partners	8361	E	559 446-6226	18118
Fresno Imaging Center **(PA)**	8011	E	559 447-2600	15409
Fresno Irrigation District	4971	D	559 233-7161	8410
Fresno Metro Flood Ctrl Dst	7389	D	559 456-3292	14279
Fresno Oral Mxllfcial Srgery D	8021	E	559 226-2722	15834
Fresno Oxgn Wldg Suppliers Inc **(PA)**	5084	E	559 233-6684	9067
Fresno Pipe & Supply Inc **(PA)**	5074	E	559 233-0500	8996
Fresno Plumbing & Heating Inc **(PA)**	1711	C	559 294-0200	1269
Fresno Produce Inc	5148	E	559 495-0143	9406
Fresno Rescue Mission Inc **(PA)**	8322	E	559 268-0839	17584
Fresno Roofing Co Inc	1761	D	559 255-8377	1806
Fresno Skilled Nursing	8051	D	559 268-5361	16009
Fresno Surgery Center LP **(PA)**	8062	C	559 431-8000	16378
Fresno Truck Center	5012	D	559 486-4310	8422
Fresnos Chaffee Zoo Corp	8422	C	559 498-5910	18292
Full Circle Brewing Co Ltd LLC	2082	F	559 264-6323	2479
Future Fast Inc	7389	D	559 813-0113	14280
Garabedian Bros Inc **(PA)**	3599	E	559 268-5014	5529
Garcias Pallets Inc	2448	E	559 485-8182	3223
Gary McDonald Development Co	1521	E	559 436-1700	642
Gea Farm Technologies Inc	2842	E	559 497-5074	4074
Geil Enterprises Inc	7381	A	559 495-3000	14064
General Coatings Corporation	1721	D	559 495-4004	1413
Gerawan Farming Partners Inc	0721	D	559 787-8780	254
Gerawan Ranches **(PA)**	0175	E	559 787-8780	101
Gerawan Ranches	0175	C	559 787-8780	102
GK Transport Inc	4213	E	559 275-3628	7546
GLad Entertainment Inc **(PA)**	7999	D	559 292-9000	15206
Glaxosmthkline Cnsmr Hlthcare	2834	C	559 650-1550	3918
Glovefit International Corp	3089	F	559 243-1110	4284
GNA Industries Inc	3625	E	559 276-0953	5679
Go Express LLC	4212	E	559 274-0168	7471
Golden Gate Freightliner Inc	3537	B	559 486-4310	5062
Golden State Family Svcs Inc **(PA)**	8361	E	559 241-0955	18120
Good Shepherd Lutheran HM of W	8361	D	559 454-8514	18123
Graham-Prewett Inc	1761	E	559 291-3741	1808
Granville Homes Inc	1521	D	559 268-2000	648
Greater Frsno Area Chmber Cmmr	8611	E	559 495-4800	18306
Greyhound Lines Inc	4111	D	559 268-1829	7336
Gusmer Enterprises Inc	3569	D	908 301-1811	5229
Harley-Davidson Fresno Inc	7699	E	559 275-8586	14753
Harris Construction Co Inc	1542	C	559 251-0301	885
Havens For Total Security Inc	7699	E	559 432-7600	14754
Health Comp Administrators **(PA)**	6411	C	559 499-2450	10290
Healthcare Centre of Fresno	8069	C	559 268-5361	16760
Healthcomp	6411	B	559 499-2450	10291
Helados La Tapatia Inc	2024	E	559 441-1105	2176
Herndon Investors	8011	D	559 435-2630	15429
Herndon Recovery Center LLC **(PA)**	8093	E	559 472-3669	17022
Herndon Surgery Center Inc	8011	D	559 323-6611	15430
Hinds Hospice **(PA)**	8052	C	559 674-0407	16185
Hire Up Staffing Service	7361	B	559 579-1331	12097
Holiday Inn Suites	7011	E	559 277-5700	11157
Holt Lumber Inc **(PA)**	2439	E	559 233-3291	3208
Homwood Suites By Hilton	7011	D	559 440-0801	11161
Horizon Global Americas Inc	7549	C	559 266-9000	14661
Horizon Home Care LLC	8082	E	559 840-1559	16893
Howe Electric Inc **(PA)**	1731	E	559 255-8992	1518
Howe Electric Inc	1731	C	559 255-8992	1519
Howe Electric Construction Inc	1731	C	559 255-8992	1520
HP Water Systems Inc	3561	E	559 268-4751	5176
Hub Intrntional Insur Svcs Inc	6411	D	559 447-4600	10295
Hye Quality Bakery Inc	2052	E	559 445-1511	2415
Iheartcommunications Inc	4832	D	559 230-4300	8027
Inland Star Dist Ctrs Inc **(PA)**	4213	D	559 237-2052	7552
Innovative Integrated Hlth Inc	8099	C	949 228-5577	17155
Insul-Flow Inc	1771	D	559 456-1105	1882
International Glace Inc **(PA)**	2064	E	559 385-7675	2429
Interntnal Trque Cnverters Inc	7537	E	559 266-7471	14540
Irritec Usa Inc	3523	D	559 275-8825	5008
Island Water Park Inc	7996	E	559 277-6800	15043
J & D Meat Company	5149	C	559 445-1123	9456
J P Lamborn Co **(PA)**	3585	B	559 650-2120	5432
Jacks Car Wash 3	7542	D	559 438-8201	14645
Jagdeep Singh Insur Agcy Inc	6411	E	559 277-5580	10301
Jai Jai Mata Inc	7011	E	559 435-5650	11205
James G Parker Insurance Assoc **(PA)**	6411	D	559 222-7722	10303
Jensen & Pilegard **(PA)**	5083	E	559 268-9221	9040
Jerico Fire Protection Co Inc	1711	E	559 255-6446	1293
Jerrys Trenching Service Inc	1623	E	559 275-1520	1110
JJ Charles Inc	2491	E	559 264-6664	3260
JM Custom Cabinets & Furniture	2511	E	559 291-6638	3278
JMS Realtors Ltd **(PA)**	6531	C	559 490-1500	10584
Johanson Transportation Svc **(PA)**	4731	E	559 458-2200	7842
Johnston Industrial Supply Inc **(PA)**	5084	E	559 233-1822	9073
Jorgensen & Sons Inc **(PA)**	5099	D	559 268-6241	9198
Joseph B Hawkins Jr MD Inc	8011	E	559 431-6197	15442
Jpmorgan Chase Bank Nat Assn	6021	C	559 449-0632	9684
Justice United States Dept	7361	E	559 251-4040	12102
Justin Carey Enterprises Inc	1752	E	559 213-4731	1774
K B W Inc	3365	E	559 233-2591	4585
Kaiser Foundation Hospitals	6324	C	559 448-4620	10110
Kaiser Foundation Hospitals	6324	C	559 448-4555	10115
Kaiser Foundation Hospitals	6324	C	559 448-4500	10142
Kaiser Foundation Hospitals	8011	C	559 448-4500	15492
Karsyn Construction Inc	1542	D	559 271-2900	908
Kasco Fab Inc	3441	D	559 442-1018	4669
Kearneys Aluminum Foundry Inc **(PA)**	3363	E	559 233-2591	4578
Kearneys Metals Inc	5051	E	559 233-2591	8820
Keiser Corporation **(PA)**	3949	D	559 256-8000	7198
Kenneth Allen Rush	5199	E	559 224-3976	9665
Kenyon Construction Inc	1742	E	559 277-5645	1683
Kertel Communications Inc **(HQ)**	1731	D	559 432-5800	1530
Kfsn Television LLC	4833	C	559 442-1170	8047
Kimberlite Corporation **(PA)**	7382	D	559 264-9730	14138
Kings River Conservation Dst	8999	D	559 237-5567	19908
Kisco Senior Living LLC	6513	D	559 449-8070	10445
Klippenstein Corporation	3565	E	559 834-4258	5199
Kmph Fox 26	4833	C	559 255-2600	8048
Kochergen Farms Composting Inc **(PA)**	8748	D	559 498-0900	19807
Kodiak Cartoners Inc	3565	E	559 266-4844	5200
Krm Risk Management Svcs Inc	8741	E	559 277-4800	19360
Kroeger Eqp Sup Co A Cal Corp	5013	E	559 485-9900	8454
Kroeker Inc	1795	C	559 237-3764	1987
KS Trans Service Co	4213	D	559 264-5650	7559
KWPH Enterprises	4119	A	559 443-5900	7385
L A S Transportation Inc	4213	E	559 264-6583	7560
L J Inc	7532	E	559 485-1413	14529
La Boulangerie French Bky Cafe	2051	E	559 222-0555	2390
La Tapatia Tortilleria Inc	2099	C	559 441-1030	2911
Lakos Corporation	5084	D	559 255-1601	9075
Lang Richert & Patch	8111	E	559 228-6700	17308
Larry Fisher & Sons Ltd Partnr	5021	F	559 252-2575	8499
Lasar Underground Cnstr Inc	1623	E	559 291-1024	1113
Lehmans Manufacturing Co Inc	3441	F	559 486-1700	4673
Leisure Care LLC	8361	C	559 434-1237	18138
Lidestri Foods Inc	2033	D	559 251-1000	2221
Lily Holdings LLC	8051	E	559 222-4807	16037
Lincare Inc	8082	D	559 435-6379	16909
Linkus Enterprises LLC	1623	C	559 256-6600	1114
Lithia Mazda of Fresno	7538	E	559 256-0700	14576
Lithia Motors Inc	7515	C	559 435-8400	14492
LLC Lyons Magnus **(PA)**	2033	B	559 268-5966	2222
LLC Lyons Magnus	2033	F	559 268-5966	2223
Los Gatos Tomato Products LLC **(PA)**	2033	F	559 945-2700	2224
Louie Foods International	2099	E	559 264-2745	2917
Lowes Home Centers LLC	5031	C	559 436-6266	8556
Lozano Smith LLP	8111	C	559 431-5600	17322
Lozano Smith A Prof Corp **(PA)**	8111	D	559 431-5600	17323
Lyles Services Co	8742	D	559 441-1900	19563
M2 Antenna Systems Inc	3679	F	559 221-2271	6450
Macdonalds Restaurants	8748	E	559 440-9206	19815
Major Transportation Svcs Inc	4213	E	559 485-5949	7564
Malaga County Water District	4952	E	559 485-7353	8284
Manning Gardens Care Ctr Inc	8051	D	559 834-2586	16040
Matson Alarm Co Inc **(PA)**	7382	E	559 438-8000	14139
Maxim Healthcare Services Inc	7363	D	559 224-0299	12182
Maxim Healthcare Services Inc	8082	C	559 227-2250	16912
Mbtechnology	2952	E	559 233-2181	4191
McCalls Nurseries Inc	5193	E	559 255-7679	9636
McCormick Brstow Shppard Wyte **(PA)**	8111	C	559 433-1300	17329
McGrayel Company	2899	E	559 299-7660	4164
McV Group Inc **(PA)**	7379	E	559 431-3142	13934
McWealth Care Inc	8059	E	559 293-3174	16252
Meeder Equipment Company **(PA)**	3559	E	559 485-0979	5157
Merrill Lynch Prce Fnner Smith	6211	D	559 436-0919	9995
Mhm Services Inc	8093	C	559 412-8121	17043
Michelsen Packaging Co Cal	2671	E	559 237-3819	3376
Mid-Valley Distributors Inc	5072	E	559 485-2660	8988
Mike Murach & Associates	2731	E	559 440-9071	3539
Milano Restaurants Intl Corp **(HQ)**	6794	B	559 432-0399	10807
Miles Sears Eanni A Prof Corp	8111	E	559 486-5200	17333
Millerton Builders Inc	2591	F	559 252-0490	3332

GEOGRAPHIC SECTION **FRESNO, CA**

	SIC	EMP	PHONE	ENTRY #
Mineral King Minerals Inc **(PA)**	2873	F	559 582-9228	4134
Minority Veterans Coalition	8399	E	559 647-3425	18242
Mission Linen Supply	7213	D	559 268-0647	11641
Modern Custom Fabrication Inc	3443	E	559 264-4741	4725
Monster City Studios	3086	E	559 498-0540	4244
Moore Twining Associates Inc **(PA)**	8734	D	559 268-7021	19280
Morgan Stnley Smith Barney LLC	6211	D	559 431-5900	10003
Morrison MGT Specialists Inc	8099	C	559 459-6449	17162
Motschdler McHlides Wishon LLP	8111	D	559 439-4000	17339
Mtna Inc	7349	E	559 354-9639	11976
Muniservices LLC **(DH)**	8742	C	800 800-8181	19583
Murdoc Technology LLC	3679	E	559 497-1580	6458
National Insur Insptn Svcs Inc	6411	E	559 435-1117	10316
Nations Roof West LLC	1761	E	559 252-1255	1824
Nephrology Group Inc **(PA)**	8011	D	559 228-6600	15547
Nestle Usa Inc	2023	C	559 834-2554	2165
Netafim Irrigation Inc **(HQ)**	5083	C	559 453-6800	9041
Neurosrgcal Assoc Med Group In	8011	D	559 449-1100	15549
Nevocal Enterprises Inc	1442	E	559 277-0700	596
New Age Metal Finishing LLC	3471	E	559 498-8585	4915
New England Shtmtl & Mech Co	1711	C	559 268-7375	1315
New England Shtmtl Works Inc	8711	C	559 268-7375	18778
New Life Discovery Schools Inc **(PA)**	8351	E	559 292-8687	17981
Newline Transport Inc	4789	E	559 515-5000	7888
Newport Television LLC	7922	B	559 761-0243	14852
Nexgen Container LLC	2653	E	916 716-8962	3360
Nexus Energy Systems Inc	1711	E	866 334-6639	1316
Nish-Ko Inc	0782	E	559 275-6653	490
Noble Credit Union **(PA)**	6061	E	559 252-5000	9798
Noble Credit Union	6061	D	559 252-5000	9799
Noia Residential Services Inc	8361	D	559 485-5555	18147
North Pt Hlth Wellness Ctr LLC	8051	D	559 320-2200	16074
Northwest Church Fresno Cal	8351	D	559 435-2200	17984
Northwest Exteriors Inc	1751	D	559 456-1632	1746
Northwest Medical Group Inc	8011	E	559 271-6302	15558
Northwest Physcans Med Group I **(PA)**	8011	D	559 271-6300	15559
Office Depot Inc	5044	E	559 255-1711	8653
Olam Americas Inc **(DH)**	0723	A	559 447-1390	297
Olam Farming Inc	0191	D	559 446-6446	184
Olam LLC	0131	E	559 446-6420	10
Olam Tomato Processors Inc **(DH)**	2033	D	559 447-1390	2232
Olam West Coast Inc **(DH)**	0723	A	559 256-6224	299
Olson and Co Steel	3441	C	559 224-7811	4679
Omni Womens Hlth Med Group Inc **(PA)**	8011	D	559 495-3120	15566
One Putt	7313	E	559 497-5118	11804
Optimas Oe Solutions LLC	5063	E	559 492-4441	8870
P K B Investments Inc	8742	C	559 243-1224	19599
Pacific Choice Brands Inc **(PA)**	2035	C	559 892-5365	2284
Pacific Crown Partners LLC	5149	E	559 900-1451	9473
Pacific Gas and Electric Co	4911	C	209 726-7650	8134
Pacific Gas and Electric Co	4911	C	559 263-7361	8146
Pacific Gas and Electric Co	4911	C	559 263-7152	8178
Pacific Gold Marketing Inc	1794	E	559 272-8168	1970
Pacific Grain & Foods LLC **(PA)**	5153	C	559 276-2580	9503
Packaging Plus	2653	E	209 858-9200	3362
Pana-Pacific Corporation **(HQ)**	3714	C	559 457-4700	6589
Pape Trucks Inc	7538	D	559 268-4344	14582
Paper Pulp & Film	2679	E	559 233-1151	3404
Pappys Meat Company Inc	2099	E	559 291-0218	2931
Paragon Industries Inc **(PA)**	3281	D	559 275-5000	4519
Paragon Industries II Inc	3281	C	559 275-5000	4520
Parker Kern Nard Wnzel Prof Co	8111	D	559 449-2558	17355
Patton Sheet Metal Works Inc	1761	E	559 486-5222	1827
Pearson Realty One LLC **(PA)**	6531	E	559 432-6200	10644
Pediatric Anesthesia Assoc Med	8062	D	559 449-4350	16478
Penny Newman Grain Co **(PA)**	5153	E	559 448-8800	9505
Pep Boys Manny Moe Jack of Cal	7539	E	559 276-7501	14616
Permanente Medical Group Inc	8011	A	559 448-4500	15594
PG&e Corporation	4911	D	559 263-5303	8192
Piccadilly Hospitality LLC	7011	E	559 348-5520	11366
Piccadilly Inn Airport	7011	E	559 375-7760	11367
Pick Pull Auto Dismantling Inc	5015	E	559 233-3881	8484
Piedmont Airlines Inc	4512	C	559 269-5694	7739
Player In Game Inc **(PA)**	8742	E	559 905-6217	19606
Pmca Bakersfield LLC	7231	E	559 224-2700	11694
Pnm Company	3599	E	559 291-1986	5598
Preferred Corporate Svcs Inc	6513	D	559 765-6755	10455
Premier Valley Bank **(HQ)**	6029	D	559 438-2002	9760
Pressed Juicery Inc	5149	F	559 777-8900	9476
Prinsco Inc	3084	E	559 485-5542	4234
Producers Dairy Foods Inc **(PA)**	5142	C	559 264-6583	9330
Professional Exchange Svc	7389	E	559 229-6249	14375
Professional Print & Mail Inc	2752	E	559 237-7468	3686
Promesa Behavioral Health **(PA)**	8361	C	559 439-5437	18160
Providence Horticulture Inc	0783	D	559 251-7907	521
Prudential Overall Supply	7218	E	559 264-8231	11668
Quality Group Homes Inc	1521	C	916 930-0066	690
Quest Dgnstics Clncal Labs Inc	8071	D	559 299-5074	16797
Quiring Corporation	1542	D	559 432-2800	939
Quiring General LLC	1542	D	559 432-2800	940
R & L Enterprises Inc	3599	E	559 233-1608	5607
R Fellen Inc	8051	D	559 233-6248	16098
R H Kiggins Construction Inc	1741	E	559 251-8661	1652
Rainbow - Brite Indus Svcs LLC	7349	A	559 925-2580	11988
Raisin ADM Committee	8741	E	559 225-0520	19385
Raw Farm LLC	0241	E	559 846-9732	219
Ray Moles Farms Inc	2034	D	559 444-0324	2265

	SIC	EMP	PHONE	ENTRY #
Reading and Beyond	8641	E	559 840-1068	18453
Real Time Information Svcs Inc	7363	E	559 222-6456	12191
Recruitment Alley LLC	8099	E	559 614-5024	17171
Rescue Children Inc	8322	E	559 268-1123	17690
Residence Inn By Marriott	7011	D	559 222-8900	11399
Rex More Elec Cntrs Engners In	1731	C	559 294-1300	1585
Reyes Coca-Cola Bottling LLC	2086	D	559 264-4631	2802
Rh Community Builders LP	8611	D	559 492-1373	18314
Rich Harvest Inc	0175	D	559 252-8000	112
Richard C Shebelut Inc	8011	E	559 439-1835	15652
Robert J Alandt & Sons	3441	E	559 275-1391	4682
Robert V Jensen Inc **(PA)**	5172	D	559 485-8210	9537
Roberts Managing Contrs Inc	1542	E	559 252-6000	947
Roger Enrico	2086	C	559 485-5050	2809
Rogers Helicopters Inc	4522	D	559 299-4903	7760
Ross & Sons Rfrgn & Cnstr Inc	1711	E	559 834-5947	1349
Royal Express Inc **(PA)**	4214	C	559 272-3500	7633
Rutter Armey Inc	7539	E	559 237-1866	14621
S & J Ranches LLC	0723	D	559 437-2600	305
Sacramento Cooling Systems Inc	3829	F	559 253-9660	6919
Saf-T-Cab Inc **(PA)**	3713	D	559 268-5541	6570
Safety Ntwrk Traffic Signs Inc	3669	E	559 291-8000	5895
Saia Motor Freight Line LLC	4213	D	559 499-6970	7590
Saint Agnes Med Providers Inc	8062	D	559 435-2630	16491
Saint Agnes Med Providers Inc	8062	D	559 450-2300	16492
Saint Agnes Medical Center **(HQ)**	8062	A	559 450-3000	16493
Saladinos Inc **(PA)**	5141	C	559 271-3700	9294
Salem Engineering Group Inc **(PA)**	8711	E	559 271-9700	18809
Sams Italian Deli & Mkt Inc	2032	E	559 229-9333	2207
San Joaquin Country Club	7997	D	559 439-3483	15134
San Joaquin Figs Inc	0723	E	559 224-4492	307
San Joaquin Glass Inc	1793	E	559 268-7646	1943
San Joaquin Hydraulic Inc **(PA)**	5085	F	559 264-7325	9132
San Joaquin Val UNI Air Pol **(PA)**	8748	C	559 230-6000	19856
San Joaquin Valley Rehabili **(HQ)**	8093	B	559 436-3600	17064
San Jquin Rver Pkwy Cnsrvtion	8641	E	559 248-8480	18462
San Mar Properties Inc **(PA)**	6531	E	559 439-5500	10658
Sanctuary	8322	E	559 498-8543	17715
Sante Health System Inc **(PA)**	6321	C	559 228-5400	10087
Save Mart Supermarkets Disc	7319	D	559 261-4123	11816
Save Mart Supermarkets Disc	5141	D	559 253-1220	9297
Scafco Corporation	3399	E	559 256-9911	4592
Schnitzer Fresno Inc	5093	C	559 233-3211	9176
Sebring-West Automotive	7538	E	559 266-9378	14591
Sequoia Steel and Supply Co	5032	F	559 485-4100	8634
Ser-Jobs For Prgress Inc - San **(PA)**	8322	D	559 452-0881	17733
Service Express Inc	2741	E	559 495-4790	3598
Sethi Conglomerate LLC	7011	E	559 275-2374	11463
Shapco Inc	3498	D	559 834-1342	4978
Shaws Strctures Unlimited Inc	1541	E	559 275-3475	809
Shift3 Technologies LLC	7371	E	559 560-3300	12778
Sierra Bancorp	6022	D	559 449-8145	9748
Sierra Pacific Surgery Ctr LLC	8011	E	559 256-5200	15685
Sierra PCF Orthpdic Ctr Med Gr	8011	C	559 256-5200	15686
Simply Smashing Inc	3993	F	559 658-2367	7254
Sinclair Companies	2911	D	559 997-3617	4180
Sinclair Companies	2911	D	559 351-1916	4181
Six Continents Hotels Inc	7011	D	559 272-7840	11485
Skywest Airlines Inc	4512	B	559 252-3400	7740
Slam Specialties LLC	3714	F	559 348-9038	6594
Smart & Final Stores Inc	5141	C	559 229-2944	9308
Social Services Cal Dept	8322	D	559 248-8400	17746
Somam Inc	7389	E	559 436-0881	14409
South Valley Materials Inc **(DH)**	3273	D	559 277-7060	4509
Southeast Fresno Rad LP	8748	C	559 443-8400	19864
Specialty Branded Products Inc	5147	E	559 222-8895	9380
Spencer Enterprises Inc	1541	D	559 252-4043	810
Sportsmobile West	7532	E	559 233-8267	14534
Spruce Multi Specialty Group	8071	E	559 229-2786	16806
Ssi G Debbas Chocolatier LLC	2066	E	559 294-2071	2440
State Center Cmnty College Dst	8721	D	559 442-4600	18997
State Compensation Insur Fund	6331	D	559 433-2700	10181
Strategic Mechanical Inc	1711	C	559 291-1952	1367
Sturdy Gun Safe Inc	3499	E	559 485-8361	4988
Subdirect LLC **(PA)**	2721	C	559 321-0449	3516
Suburban Steel Inc **(PA)**	3441	E	559 268-6281	4685
Sullivan Ctr For Chldren A Psy	8011	D	559 271-1186	15707
Sun-Maid Growers California **(PA)**	5149	A	559 896-8000	9492
Sunland Insurance Agency	6411	A	559 251-7861	10356
Sunnyside Country Club	7997	D	559 255-6871	15157
Sunrise Medical (us) LLC	5047	E	559 292-2171	8792
Sunrun Installation Svcs Inc	1711	B	559 298-7652	1372
Sunsystem Technology LLC	8731	C	559 412-7870	19132
Swartout Inc	7542	D	559 252-4441	14652
T B B Inc	5045	E	559 222-4100	8753
T G Schmeiser Co Inc	3429	E	559 486-4569	4621
T Royal Management **(PA)**	6531	D	559 447-9887	10667
Takao Nursery Inc	0181	E	559 275-3844	140
Tanfield Engrg Systems US Inc	3531	F	559 443-6602	5040
Tapia Enterprises Inc	5141	E	559 486-8347	9320
Tdc Convalescent Inc	8051	C	559 321-0883	16142
Tech West Vacuum Inc	3843	D	559 291-1650	7089
Technicon Engineering Svcs Inc	8711	E	559 276-9311	18828
Tempest Technology Corporation	3564	E	559 277-7577	5192
Terry Tuell Concrete Inc	1771	D	559 431-0812	1912
Teter LLP **(PA)**	8711	E	559 437-0887	18835
Thermo King Fresno Inc **(PA)**	5078	E	559 496-3500	9017

GEOGRAPHIC

Employment Codes: A=Over 500 employees, B=251-500, C=101-250, D=51-100, E=20-50 F=10-19

2022 Northern California Business Directory and Buyers Guide

© Mergent Inc. 1-800-342-5647

1151

	SIC	EMP	PHONE	ENTRY #
Titan Mfg & Distrg Inc	5091	D	559 475-0882	9163
Tk Elevator Corporation	5084	D	559 271-1238	9099
Tmr Executive Interiors Inc	2431	E	559 346-0631	3157
Tom Corea Construction Inc	1771	E	559 292-9224	1913
Torres Fence Co Inc	1799	E	559 237-4141	2077
Total Concept Enterprises Inc	3965	F	559 485-8413	7212
Transwstern Insur Admnistrator **(PA)**	6411	E	559 499-0285	10360
Tri-Signal Integration Inc	1731	D	559 274-1299	1624
Trillium Pumps Usa Inc **(DH)**	3561	C	559 442-4000	5180
Trinity Construction Entps Inc	1521	E	559 313-9612	723
Turn Behavioral Hlth Svcs Inc	8093	E	559 264-7521	17082
Turner Camera SEC Systems Inc	7382	C	559 486-3466	14151
Turner Dsgns Hydrcrbon Instrs	3699	E	559 253-1414	6545
Turner Manufacturing Company	1799	F	559 251-1918	2080
Twenty First District AG Assn **(DH)**	7999	E	559 650-3247	15259
Twilight Haven	8051	D	559 251-8417	16145
Ultimate Creations LLC	6799	D	559 221-4936	10891
Unilab Corporation	8071	A	559 225-5076	16817
United Crbral Plsy Cntl Cal In **(PA)**	8399	E	559 221-8272	18257
United Hlth Ctrs of San Jquin **(PA)**	8011	D	559 646-6618	15750
United Parcel Service Inc	4212	C	559 442-2950	7495
United Western Industries Inc	3599	E	559 226-7236	5632
Universal Meditech Inc	3995	E	559 366-7798	7264
University Cal San Francisco	6519	E	559 251-3033	10486
Uniwell Corporation	6552	C	559 268-1000	10719
Uniwell Fresno Hotel LLC	7011	D	559 268-1000	11551
Urology Associates Central Cal	8011	D	559 321-2800	15783
URS Group Inc	8711	D	559 255-2541	18850
US Script Inc **(HQ)**	6411	E	559 244-3700	10363
Valley AC & Repr Inc	1711	E	559 237-3188	1389
Valley Childrens Hospital	8062	C	559 353-7442	16706
Valley Decorating Company	3089	E	559 495-1100	4329
Valley Fig Growers	0723	E	559 349-1686	313
Valley Healthcare Center LLC	8051	D	559 251-7161	16150
Valley Lahvosh Baking Co Inc	2051	E	559 485-2700	2409
Valley Protein LLC	2013	D	559 498-7115	2127
Valley Public Television Inc	4833	D	559 266-1800	8056
Valley Stairway Inc	3446	F	559 299-0151	4842
Valley Teen Ranch	8361	D	559 437-1144	18199
Valley Transportation Inc **(PA)**	4212	D	559 266-6674	7496
Valley Vascular Surgery Assoc	8011	E	559 431-6226	15785
Vehicle Recycling Services LLC	4953	E	916 870-4383	8378
Veritiv Operating Company	5113	D	559 268-0467	9221
Veterans Health Administration	8062	C	559 225-6100	16713
Veterans Health Administration	8011	C	559 225-6100	15790
Veterinary Emergency Service	0742	E	559 486-0520	343
Vibra Healthcare LLC	8062	E	559 436-3600	16716
Vibra Healthcare LLC	8062	E	559 431-2635	16718
Victus Group Inc	8741	C	559 429-8080	19418
Vie-Del Company **(PA)**	2033	D	559 834-2525	2247
Vigilant Private Security	7381	D	559 800-7233	14107
Vision Care Ctr A Med Group In **(PA)**	8011	D	559 486-2000	15808
Visionone Inc **(PA)**	7371	E	559 432-8000	12908
Vitro Flat Glass LLC	3211	C	559 485-4660	4364
Vly Air Cond & RPR	7623	D	559 237-2123	14689
Vocation Plus Inc	8331	C	559 221-8019	17844
Volt Management Corp	7363	D	559 435-1255	12204
Vucovich Inc **(PA)**	5083	D	559 486-8020	9049
Vulcan Cnstr & Maint Inc	1623	E	559 443-1607	1140
W Banks Moore Inc	1799	E	559 485-3456	2085
W M Lyles Co **(HQ)**	1623	B	559 441-1900	1141
Wade Metal Products Inc	3441	F	559 237-9233	4692
Walter C Voigt Inc	5149	E	559 233-3055	9499
Walter R Reinhardt Insur Agcy	6411	E	559 226-4700	10366
Walton Industries Inc	2851	E	559 495-4004	4114
Wanger Jones Helsley PC	8111	E	559 233-4800	17390
Wasco Hardfacing Co	3523	D	559 485-5860	5020
Wash Mltfmily Ldry Systems LLC	7215	F	559 233-0595	11651
Wcr Incorporated	7699	E	559 266-8374	14784
Weber Motors Fresno Inc	7549	D	559 447-6700	14678
West Air Inc	4513	D	559 454-7843	7752
West Coast Arborists Inc	0783	C	559 275-2086	526
Westcare California Inc **(HQ)**	8361	C	559 251-4800	18210
Westco Equities Inc **(PA)**	6531	D	559 228-6788	10685
Western Building Materials Co **(PA)**	1742	D	559 454-8500	1707
Whipple Industries Inc	3564	F	559 442-1261	5193
Wilbur-Ellis Company LLC	5191	D	559 442-1220	9616
Wild Crter Tipton A Prof Corp	8111	E	559 224-2131	17397
Wild Electric Incorporated	1731	D	559 251-7770	1638
Wildlife Control Tech Inc	7342	E	559 490-2262	11911
Wilkins Drlshgen Czshinski LLP	8111	E	559 438-2390	17398
Williams Scotsman Inc	5039	E	559 441-8181	8650
Williams-Foster Group LLC	8051	E	317 786-3230	16161
Winegard Energy Inc	1742	E	559 441-0243	1709
Winnresidential Ltd Partnr	7513	C	559 435-3434	14475
Wm B Saleh Co	1721	D	559 255-2046	1438
Wm Michael Stemler Inc	6411	D	559 228-4144	10371
Wood AG Management Inc	8741	E	559 432-5164	19427
Wood-N-Wood Products Cal Inc **(PA)**	2449	E	559 896-3636	3245
Woolf Farming Co Cal Inc	0191	A	559 945-9292	197
Xander Mortgage & Real Estate	6531	D	855 905-2575	10689
Xobee Networks Inc	4813	D	559 579-1300	8010
Xpo Logistics Freight Inc	4731	E	559 485-1164	7862
Y & Y Property Management Inc	7011	E	559 226-2110	11583
Yosemite Linen Supply Inc	7213	E	559 233-2654	11647
Youngs Market Company LLC	5182	D	213 612-1216	9590
Zacky & Sons Poultry LLC **(PA)**	2015	A	559 443-2700	2140
Zumwalt Construction Inc	1542	D	559 252-1000	996

FRIANT, CA - Fresno County

	SIC	EMP	PHONE	ENTRY #
Table Mountain Casino	7011	A	559 822-7777	11525

FULTON, CA - Sonoma County

	SIC	EMP	PHONE	ENTRY #
Kendall-Jackson Wine Center	0762	E	707 571-7500	378

GALT, CA - Sacramento County

	SIC	EMP	PHONE	ENTRY #
Building Material Distrs Inc **(PA)**	5031	C	209 745-3001	8532
Califrnia Wste Rcvery Systems	4953	E	209 369-6887	8316
Calstone Company	3271	E	209 745-2981	4411
Cardinal Glass Industries Inc	3211	C	209 744-8940	4355
Carsons Coatings Inc	3469	E	209 745-2387	4879
Herburger Publications Inc **(PA)**	2711	D	916 685-5533	3445
Norogachi Construction Inc/CA	1742	D	916 236-4201	1695
Park DDS MPH Inc **(PA)**	8021	E	209 744-0463	15853
Southwest Products Corporation	3519	E	209 745-6000	4993
Travis James Watts	0191	C	209 810-6159	192

GARBERVILLE, CA - Humboldt County

	SIC	EMP	PHONE	ENTRY #
Humboldt House Inn LLC	7011	E	707 923-2771	11176
Southern Hmbldt Cmnty Dst Hosp	8062	D	707 923-3921	16531
Southern Hmbldt Cmnty Hlth Car	8062	D	707 923-3921	16532
Vocality Community Credit Un	6061	E	707 923-2012	9827

GARDEN VALLEY, CA - El Dorado County

	SIC	EMP	PHONE	ENTRY #
Buckland Vineyard MGT Inc	8741	D	530 333-1534	19310

GEORGETOWN, CA - El Dorado County

	SIC	EMP	PHONE	ENTRY #
Georgetown Pre-Cast Inc	3272	F	530 333-4404	4435
Powerlift Dumbwaiters Inc	3534	F	800 409-5438	5048

GERBER, CA - Tehama County

	SIC	EMP	PHONE	ENTRY #
Dudleys Excavating Inc	1794	E	530 385-1445	1956
Pacific Farms and Orchards Inc	0175	D	530 385-1475	110
Trent Construction Inc	1541	E	530 385-1778	817

GEYSERVILLE, CA - Sonoma County

	SIC	EMP	PHONE	ENTRY #
Clos Du Bois Wines Inc	2084	E	707 857-1651	2533
County of Sonoma	8049	E	707 433-0728	15889
Dry Creek Rancheria	7011	E	707 857-1266	11063
Francis Coppola Winery LLC	2084	E	707 857-1400	2578
Francis Ford Cppola Prsnts LLC	2084	E	707 251-3200	2579
Gardenworks Inc	0782	D	707 857-2050	465
Iav Inc	7011	E	707 857-4343	11186
J Pedroncelli Winery	2084	E	707 857-3531	2624
Munselle Vineyards LLC	2084	F	707 857-9988	2662
Redwood Empire Vinyrd MGT Inc	0762	D	707 857-3401	386
River Rock Entertainment Auth	7011	A	707 857-2777	11412
Robert Young Family Ltd Partnr	2084	E	707 433-3228	2700
Sbragia Family Vineyards LLC	2084	E	707 473-2992	2710
Vimark Inc	0762	D	707 857-3588	388

GILROY, CA - Santa Clara County

	SIC	EMP	PHONE	ENTRY #
Accent Manufacturing Inc	2599	E	408 846-9993	3333
Advance Services Inc	7631	A	408 767-2797	14707
Amcs Inc	5014	E	408 846-9274	8475
American Steel & Stairways Inc	3446	E	408 848-2992	4833
Archictrai Fcdes Unlmited Inc	3272	D	408 846-5350	4417
Bert E Jessup Transportation	4213	D	408 848-3390	7507
Blossom Valley Foods Inc	2087	E	408 848-5520	2819
Chalgren Enterprises	3845	F	408 847-3994	7100
Chameleon Like Inc	2782	D	408 847-3661	3760
Christopher Ranch LLC **(PA)**	0139	C	408 847-1100	15
Community Sltons For Chldren F **(PA)**	8322	C	408 842-7138	17499
Containment Consultants Inc	3443	F	408 848-6998	4718
Countryside Mushrooms Inc	0182	E	408 683-2748	142
Covenant Care California LLC	8051	D	408 842-9311	15971
Crothall Services Group	7215	A	909 991-4887	11648
Daleo Inc	1623	D	408 846-9621	1098
Eagle Ridge Golf Cntry CLB LLC	7997	D	408 846-4531	15087
Edwards & Anderson Inc	3578	E	408 847-6770	5422
Enterprise Protective Svcs Inc **(PA)**	7381	E	408 840-2680	14055
G B Group Inc **(PA)**	1522	D	408 848-8118	747
Germains Seed Technology Inc	5191	E	408 848-8120	9599
Gilroy Dispatch	2711	F	408 842-6400	3442
Gilroy Gardens Family Theme Pk	7996	C	408 840-7100	15042
Gilroy Im Automotive LLC	7538	E	408 713-3200	14566
Gilroy Motorcycle Center Inc	3751	E	408 842-9955	6649
Hanaps Enterprises	3577	D	669 235-3810	5372
Hanson Drywall	1742	D	831 297-4581	1679
Headstart Nursery Inc **(PA)**	5193	D	408 842-3030	9634
Heart Wood Manufacturing Inc	2434	F	408 848-9750	3181
Hilton Garden Inns MGT LLC	7011	D	408 840-7000	11142
Infosoft Inc	8748	D	408 659-4326	19793
Kaiser Foundation Hospitals	6324	C	408 848-4600	10141
Learning Services Corporation	8093	E	408 848-4379	17034
Lowes Home Centers LLC	5031	C	408 413-6000	8570
Lucas/Signatone Corporation **(PA)**	3825	E	408 848-2851	6766
Mariner Health Care Inc	8051	E	408 842-9311	16046
Morgan Hill Plastics Inc	3089	E	408 842-1322	4302
Noah Concrete Corporation	1771	D	408 842-7211	1897
Odd Fellow-Rebekah Chld HM Cal **(PA)**	8361	C	408 846-2100	18151
Olam Spices & Vegetables Inc **(PA)**	0723	D	408 846-3200	298
Operations Management Intl Inc	4941	E	408 848-0480	8257
Peninsula Spring Corporation	3495	F	408 848-3361	4965
Premium Outlet Partners LP	6512	D	408 842-3729	10402
PSG Fencing Corporation **(PA)**	1799	C	831 726-2002	2058
Pulmuone USA Inc	5149	B	714 361-0806	9479

Company	SIC	EMP	PHONE	ENTRY #
Recology South Valley **(HQ)**	4953	D	408 842-3358	8354
Renn Transportation Inc	4213	D	408 842-3545	7579
RMC Engineering Co Inc **(PA)**	3599	E	408 842-2525	5613
Rochas Drywall Inc	1742	E	408 842-4188	1703
Rush Order Inc **(PA)**	4225	E	408 848-3525	7702
Saint Louise Hospital	8062	B	408 848-2000	16501
Santa Clara County of	8062	C	408 848-2000	16511
Sierra Reforestation Company	5191	E	408 848-9604	9610
South Cnty Chrysler-Jeep-Dodge	7538	E	408 842-8244	14593
South County Housing Corp	1531	D	408 842-9181	785
Specialty Truck Parts Inc **(PA)**	5013	E	408 998-7272	8469
Technical Reps Intl Inc	1542	F	408 848-8868	972
Trans Valley Transport	4213	E	408 842-2188	7605
Trevis Berry Transportation	4214	D	408 842-8238	7637
Trical Inc **(PA)**	2879	E	831 637-0195	4145
Versaco Manufacturing Inc	3556	F	408 848-2880	5137
Warden Security Associates Inc	7381	D	408 722-6463	14111
Wb Electric Inc	1731	D	408 842-7911	1634
Western Tree Nursery	0811	D	408 842-6800	532
Work2future Foundation	8331	E	408 758-3477	17848
Zanker Rd Rsrce MGT Ltd A Cal	4953	E	408 846-1575	8391

GLEN ELLEN, CA - Sonoma County

Company	SIC	EMP	PHONE	ENTRY #
Bfw Associates LLC **(HQ)**	2084	E	707 935-3000	2511
Blooms Wholesale Nursery Inc	5193	E	707 935-0606	9627

GLENN, CA - Glenn County

Company	SIC	EMP	PHONE	ENTRY #
Carriere Family Farms LLC	0173	E	530 934-8200	84
Carriere Farms LLC	0112	E	530 934-8200	4
Knight Farms	0119	E	530 934-9536	9

GOLD RIVER, CA - Sacramento County

Company	SIC	EMP	PHONE	ENTRY #
Adco/Grier Inc	1742	E	916 631-7010	1656
Berk Street Enterprises Inc	8082	D	916 370-6179	16857
Centene Corporation	6324	E	314 505-6689	10101
Cleanworld	3949	F	916 635-7300	7193
Cni Thl Ops LLC	7011	D	916 638-4800	11022
Creative Recrtl Systems Inc	5091	D	916 638-5375	9155
Cretelligent Inc	8742	E	916 288-8177	19486
Ehealthinsurance Services Inc	7371	C	916 608-6101	12414
Eskaton	8361	C	916 852-7900	18106
Firstservice Residential	8741	D	916 293-4740	19334
Goyette Ruano & Thompson Inc **(PA)**	8748	D	916 851-1900	19787
Itsago Builders Inc	1521	E	916 496-2316	654
Jts Communities Inc **(PA)**	1521	E	916 487-3434	658
Markes International Inc	3826	F	513 745-0241	6836
Meldisco K-M Rancho Cordova CA	8742	E	916 635-3400	19572
Practice Wares Inc	5047	E	916 526-2674	8789
Premier Pools and Spas Lp **(PA)**	1799	D	916 852-0223	2056
Salu Beauty Inc	8621	D	916 475-1400	18346
Security Classification Inc	7389	E	707 301-6052	14402
Skyline Financial Services **(PA)**	6162	D	818 995-1700	9928
Spare-Time Inc	7997	D	916 638-7001	15152
State Farm Life Insurance Co	6411	E	916 852-9491	10354
Synergex International Corp	7371	D	916 635-7300	12841
USA Waste of California Inc **(HQ)**	4953	E	916 387-1400	8377

GRANITE BAY, CA - Placer County

Company	SIC	EMP	PHONE	ENTRY #
Badass Brand Inc	5122	E	916 990-3873	9223
Bushnell Gardens	5193	D	916 791-4199	9628
County of Placer	8322	D	916 791-7059	17510
Eureka Un Schl Dst Fing Corp	8351	E	916 774-3437	17932
Fullstack Labs LLC **(PA)**	7371	E	415 609-2453	12466
Granite Bay Golf Club Inc	7997	D	916 791-5379	15095
New Cal Metals Inc	3444	F	916 652-7424	4793
Pavilions Management LLC **(PA)**	8741	E	916 782-8822	19379
Performance Chevrolet Inc	7538	C	916 338-7300	14583
R&D Educational Systems Inc	3999	F	916 934-6223	7304
Recoating-West Inc **(PA)**	3444	E	916 652-8290	4809
Revivermx Inc	3663	E	916 580-3495	5864
San Juan Water District	4941	E	916 791-0115	8266
Star Inc	8351	A	916 791-8442	18033
Tricks Gymnastics Inc **(PA)**	7999	E	916 791-4496	15257
Village At Granite Bay	8361	D	916 789-0326	18203

GRASS VALLEY, CA - Nevada County

Company	SIC	EMP	PHONE	ENTRY #
A & A AC Htg & Shtmtl	1711	E	530 273-1301	1186
Aja Video Systems Inc **(PA)**	3663	E	530 274-2048	5817
Alta Sierra Country Club Inc	7992	E	530 273-2041	14986
Applied Science Inc **(PA)**	3841	F	530 273-8299	6943
Autometrix Inc	3559	F	530 477-5065	5142
Beam Vacuums California Inc	1731	E	916 564-3279	1461
Benchmark Thermal Corporation	3433	D	530 477-5011	4625
Blue Eagle Contracting Inc	4212	D	530 272-0287	7453
Briarpatch Coop Nev Cnty Inc	8699	C	530 272-5333	18550
Byers Enterprises Inc	1761	D	530 272-7777	1791
Cellco Partnership	4812	D	530 477-8042	7899
Chapa-De Indian Hlth Prgram In	8021	D	530 477-8545	15828
Charis Youth Center	8322	E	530 477-9800	17481
Countis Industries Inc	3264	E	530 272-8334	4407
Durham School Services L P	4151	C	530 273-7282	7427
Ei Corp	3651	E	530 274-1240	5756
Farlows Scntfic Glssblwing Inc	3229	E	530 477-5513	4371
Ferguson Family Entps Inc	1731	E	530 273-0686	1503
Fowles Wine (usa) Inc	2084	F	703 975-8093	2576
FPI Management Inc	6531	C	530 272-5274	10554
Geologic Associates Inc	8711	D	530 272-2448	18720
Golden Empire Convalescent Hos	8062	C	530 273-1316	16380
Granite Wellness Centers	8093	C	530 878-5166	17020
Grass Roots Realty	6531	E	530 273-7293	10563
Grass Valley Inc	3663	C	530 478-3000	5844
Grass Valley Inc **(DH)**	3663	D	530 265-1000	5845
Grass Valley LLC	8361	E	530 272-1055	18124
Grass Valley Surgery Ctr LLC	8011	D	530 271-2282	15418
Grass Valley Usa LLC **(PA)**	3661	B	800 547-8949	5798
Hansen Bros Enterprises **(PA)**	1442	D	530 273-3100	594
Hills Flat Lumber Co **(PA)**	5031	D	530 273-6171	8550
Holbrooke Hotel LLC	7011	E	530 273-2300	11147
Hospice of Foothills **(PA)**	8082	D	530 272-5739	16895
Huntington Mechanical Labs Inc	3563	E	530 273-9533	5185
Igraphics **(PA)**	2759	E	530 273-2200	3738
JM Streamline Inc	1542	D	530 272-6806	902
Lifekind Products Inc	2841	F	530 477-5395	4063
Longs Drug Stores Cal Inc	7384	E	530 272-6611	14159
M & C Restoration Inc	7349	D	530 273-1957	11969
Maier Manufacturing Inc	3751	E	530 272-9036	6652
Managment Rcrters Grass Vly In	7361	E	530 432-1966	12105
Manuel Bros Inc	1623	D	530 272-4213	1117
Manufacturers Coml Fin LLC	3433	E	530 477-5011	4631
McCourtney Road Transfer Stn	4953	E	530 274-2215	8344
Measurement Specialties Inc	3825	D	530 273-4608	6770
Micro Prcision Calibration Inc **(PA)**	8734	E	530 268-1860	19279
National Directory Services	2731	E	530 268-8636	3540
Networked Insurance Agents LLC	6411	C	800 682-8476	10317
Nevada Irrigation District **(PA)**	4971	C	530 273-6185	8415
Northern Cal Ctr For Arts	8699	E	530 274-8384	18582
Papola Enterprises Inc	6531	D	530 272-8885	10642
Ray Stone Incorporated	8322	E	530 272-5274	17681
Rgb Display Corporation	3575	F	530 268-2222	5336
Robert W Baird & Co Inc	6399	E	530 271-3000	10220
Sierra Nev Mmorial-Miners Hosp **(DH)**	8062	E	530 274-6000	16526
Sierra Nevada Mem HM Care Inc	8082	C	530 274-6350	16944
Sierra View Medical Eye Inc	8011	D	530 272-3411	15687
Slouber Enterprises Inc **(PA)**	3826	E	530 273-2080	6853
South Yuba Club Inc	7991	E	530 470-9100	14973
Spring Hl Mnor Cnvlscent Rhblt	8051	E	530 273-7247	16125
Taurus Fabrication Inc	3446	E	530 268-2650	4840
Taylor Investments LLC	3563	E	530 273-4135	5188
Thermionics Laboratory Inc	3589	E	530 272-3436	5449
Tim Mello Construction	1521	E	530 205-8588	720
Victor Cmnty Support Svcs Inc	8093	C	530 273-2244	17087
Vossloh Signaling LLC	7371	E	530 272-8194	12915

GRATON, CA - Sonoma County

Company	SIC	EMP	PHONE	ENTRY #
Empire West Inc	3089	E	707 823-1190	4279

GREENBRAE, CA - Marin County

Company	SIC	EMP	PHONE	ENTRY #
Albeco Inc	2051	D	415 461-1164	2360
Califrnia Cncer Care A Med Gro	8011	D	415 925-5000	15312
Coldwell Bnkr Rsdntial RE Svcs	6531	B	415 461-2020	10519
Einstein Noah Rest Group Inc	2051	C	415 925-9971	2381
Giorgios Restaurant Italiano	2032	E	415 925-0808	2199
Greenbrae Management Inc **(PA)**	6513	E	415 461-0200	10436
Live2kite LLC **(PA)**	3944	E	415 924-9463	7180
Marin Cancer Care Inc	8011	E	415 925-5000	15517
Marin Healthcare District **(PA)**	8062	D	415 464-2090	16438
Ocadian Care Centers LLC	8051	B	415 461-9700	16084
Petroleum Sales Inc	1311	E	415 256-1600	548
Ross Valley Homes Inc	8361	D	415 461-2300	18173
Sequoia Living Inc	8059	C	415 464-1767	16268
Surgery Center of Marin	8062	E	415 925-7266	16563

GREENVILLE, CA - Plumas County

Company	SIC	EMP	PHONE	ENTRY #
Indian Valley Health Care Dist	8062	E	530 284-7191	16388

GRIDLEY, CA - Butte County

Company	SIC	EMP	PHONE	ENTRY #
Agromillora California	5193	E	530 846-0404	9622
California Industiral Mfg LLC **(PA)**	3999	F	530 846-9960	7273
Casa Lupe Inc **(PA)**	2099	D	530 846-3218	2879
Gridley Hlthcare & Wellnss Cen	8051	D	530 846-6266	16015
Orchard Hospital	8062	C	530 846-9000	16473
Rio Pluma Company LLC **(HQ)**	2033	E	530 846-5200	2242
Stapleton - Spence Packing Co **(PA)**	2033	D	408 297-8815	2244
Stuke Nursery Co Inc	0181	E	530 846-2378	138
Sunsweet Dryers	2034	C	530 846-5578	2270
Sutter Buttes Mfg LLC	1799	E	530 846-9960	2072
Wild Goose Storage Inc	4922	D	530 846-7350	8209

GRIMES, CA - Colusa County

Company	SIC	EMP	PHONE	ENTRY #
Reclamation District 108	4941	E	530 437-2221	8260

GROVELAND, CA - Tuolumne County

Company	SIC	EMP	PHONE	ENTRY #
Evergreen Dstntion Hldings LLC	7011	D	209 379-2606	11087
Pine Mountain Lake Association **(PA)**	8641	C	209 962-4080	18448

GUALALA, CA - Mendocino County

Company	SIC	EMP	PHONE	ENTRY #
Redwood Coast Medical Svcs Inc **(PA)**	8011	E	707 884-1721	15641
Saint Orres Corporation	7011	E	707 884-3335	11427

GUERNEVILLE, CA - Sonoma County

Company	SIC	EMP	PHONE	ENTRY #
F Korbel & Bros **(PA)**	2084	C	707 824-7000	2565
West County Health Centers Inc **(PA)**	8011	D	707 869-1594	15815

GUSTINE, CA - Merced County

Company	SIC	EMP	PHONE	ENTRY #
Agri-Comm Express Inc	4212	E	209 854-2474	7446
Andersen Nut Company	0723	E	209 854-6820	270
Growers Transplanting Inc	0181	E	209 854-3702	126
Holiday Inn Express	7011	E	209 826-8282	11153
John B Sanfilippo & Son Inc	2068	C	209 854-2455	2446

	SIC	EMP	PHONE	ENTRY #
Legacy Vulcan LLC	3272	F	209 854-3088	4442
Saputo Dairy Foods Usa LLC	2026	C	209 854-6461	2194

HALF MOON BAY, CA - San Mateo County

	SIC	EMP	PHONE	ENTRY #
Accurate Always Inc	3571	E	650 728-9428	5237
Allvia Inc	3674	E	408 234-8778	6024
Bay City Flower Co **(PA)**	5193	D	650 726-5535	9626
Brewery On Half Moon Bay Inc	2082	C	650 728-2739	2475
Browning-Ferris Inds Cal Inc	4953	E	650 726-1819	8311
Cameron & Lisa Palmer	6512	E	650 726-5705	10381
Genentech Inc	2834	F	650 438-7573	3912
Half Moon Bay Lodge	7011	D	650 726-9000	11123
La Petite Baleen **(PA)**	7999	E	650 726-7166	15215
Lesley Foundation	8748	D	650 726-4888	19810
Ocean Colony Partners LLC	6552	C	650 726-5764	10711
Ocean Shore Brokerage Inc **(PA)**	6531	E	650 726-1100	10631
Pacific Beach House LLC **(PA)**	7011	E	650 712-0220	11343
Pacifica Hotel Company	7011	E	650 726-9000	11350
Project Partners LLC **(PA)**	7379	E	650 712-6200	13963
Resource Innovations Inc **(HQ)**	8748	D	415 369-1000	19848
Rocket Farms Inc **(PA)**	0181	C	800 227-5229	133
Romeo Packing Company	2674	E	650 728-3393	3392
S P S Inc	8742	D	650 685-5913	19626
San Benito House Inc	7011	E	650 726-3425	11431
Scapes Inc	0782	E	650 712-4460	500
Tally One Inc **(PA)**	0181	E	650 726-6361	141
Ucc Guide Inc	2741	F	800 345-3822	3609
Wick Communications Co	2711	E	650 726-4424	3489
Zipline International Inc	7371	C	508 340-3291	12940

HAT CREEK, CA - Shasta County

	SIC	EMP	PHONE	ENTRY #
Hermsmeyer Painting Co Inc **(PA)**	1721	E	707 575-4549	1416

HAYFORK, CA - Trinity County

	SIC	EMP	PHONE	ENTRY #
Watershed Res & Training Ctr	0851	E	530 628-4206	537

HAYWARD, CA - Alameda County

	SIC	EMP	PHONE	ENTRY #
AAC Glass Inc	1793	E	909 214-4049	1934
Absl Construction	1611	E	510 727-0900	1003
Abundant Robotics	3569	F	510 274-5846	5223
Acelrx Pharmaceuticals Inc **(PA)**	2834	E	650 216-3500	3830
Acf Components & Fasteners Inc **(PA)**	5072	E	510 487-2100	8978
Action Gypsum Supply West LP **(PA)**	5085	E	510 259-1965	9106
Admail-Express Inc	2752	E	510 471-6200	3616
Advance Carbon Products Inc	3624	E	510 293-5930	5669
Advance Construction Tech Inc	1521	D	408 658-3682	604
Aeco Systems Inc	1731	E	510 342-0008	1445
Ajinomoto Foods North Amer Inc	2038	C	510 293-1838	2301
Akas Manufacturing Corporation	3444	E	510 786-3200	4740
Alameda Electric Supply **(HQ)**	5063	E	510 786-1400	8838
Alameda Newspapers Inc **(DH)**	2711	C	510 783-6111	3411
Alcal Industries Inc **(PA)**	5063	E	510 786-1400	8839
Alcatel-Lucent USA Inc	3661	E	510 475-5000	5786
All Bay Pallet Company Inc **(PA)**	2448	E	510 636-4131	3217
Allmodular Systems Inc	5044	E	510 887-9000	8651
Allstate Plastics LLC	3089	F	510 783-9600	4254
Allure Labs Inc	2844	E	510 489-8896	4079
Amedica Biotech Inc	3841	F	510 785-5980	6940
American Asp Repr Rsrfcing Inc **(PA)**	1611	D	510 723-0280	1006
American Blinds and Drap Inc	2391	E	510 487-3500	3021
American Poly-Foam Company Inc	3086	E	510 786-3626	4238
American Synrgy Asb Rmval Svcs	1799	E	510 444-2333	2002
Ameriflight LLC	4512	D	510 569-6000	7737
Ametek Inc	5045	E	510 431-6718	8667
Amity Home Health Care Inc	8082	E	510 785-9088	16847
Ampex Data Systems Corporation **(HQ)**	3572	D	650 367-2011	5281
Andrew Chekene Enterprises Inc	1521	C	650 588-1001	611
Anning-Johnson Company	1742	C	510 670-0100	1659
Applied Photon Technology Inc	3641	E	510 780-9500	5708
Applied Silver Inc	2499	F	888 939-4747	3264
Arborwell Inc **(PA)**	0783	C	510 881-4260	513
ARC of The East Bay **(PA)**	8322	E	510 357-3569	17431
Arch Foods Inc **(PA)**	3421	E	510 331-8352	4603
Arcus Biosciences Inc **(PA)**	8731	C	510 694-6200	19028
Armanino Foods Distinction Inc	2038	E	510 441-9300	2303
ATI Restoration LLC	1799	D	510 429-5000	2007
Autohaus Automotive Inc **(PA)**	5013	E	510 881-1915	8440
Automatic Control Engrg Corp	3829	E	510 293-6040	6894
Axis Services Inc	1522	C	510 732-6111	738
Azuma Foods Intl Inc USA **(HQ)**	2092	D	510 782-1112	2829
Bailey Fence Company Inc	1799	E	510 538-1175	2008
Bassard Cnvalescent Med HM Inc **(PA)**	8059	D	510 537-6700	16217
Bay Area Concrete LLC	4953	D	510 294-0220	8305
Bay Area Seafood Inc **(PA)**	5146	E	510 475-7100	9359
Beeline Group LLC	3993	D	510 477-5400	7219
Bel Aire Engineering Inc	5051	F	510 538-6950	8809
Bess Testlab Inc	1623	E	408 988-0101	1089
Best Choice LLC	7389	E	510 862-4989	14215
Bfl Transportation LLC **(PA)**	1611	E	510 727-0900	1016
Big Joe California North Inc **(PA)**	5084	C	510 785-6900	9054
Bigham Taylor Roofing Corp	1761	D	510 886-0197	1789
Biolog Inc	3826	E	510 785-2564	6818
Blue River Seafood Inc	5146	D	510 300-6800	9360
Boyett Construction Inc **(PA)**	1742	D	510 264-9100	1662
Brightview Landscape Svcs Inc	0781	C	510 487-4826	398
Buffalo Distribution Inc	3613	F	510 324-3800	5650
C&C Building Automation Co Inc	3829	E	650 292-7450	6895
C3 Nano Inc	8732	D	510 259-9650	19154
California Hydronics Corp **(PA)**	5075	E	510 293-1993	9007
California Sierra Express Inc	4731	E	510 786-9974	7828
California Trenchless Inc	1623	E	510 782-5335	1091
Califrnia State Univ E Bay Fnd	8741	E	510 885-2700	19313
Campanella Corporation	1795	E	510 536-4800	1982
Casa Sandoval LLC	6513	D	510 727-1700	10422
Casey-Fogli Con Contrs Inc **(PA)**	1771	D	510 887-0837	1857
Chapel of Chimes **(DH)**	6553	D	510 471-3363	10724
Chawk Technology Intl Inc **(PA)**	3089	C	510 330-5299	4266
Chrono Therapeutics Inc **(PA)**	8733	E	510 362-7788	19209
City of Hayward	4581	E	510 293-8678	7768
Clarmil Manufacturing Corp **(PA)**	2099	D	510 476-0700	2883
Cleveland Wrecking Company	1795	A	510 674-2600	1983
Closet Dimension **(PA)**	1799	E	650 594-1155	2020
Cnet Technology Corporation **(HQ)**	5065	C	408 392-9966	8903
Coastal Construction Svcs LLC	5039	E	510 785-9220	8642
Columbus Foods LLC	2011	B	510 921-3400	2094
Columbus Manufacturing Inc **(HQ)**	2013	D	510 921-3423	2115
Commercial Patterns Inc	3089	F	510 784-1014	4270
Community Child Care Crdnting **(PA)**	8351	E	510 582-2182	17911
Compass Group Usa Inc	7389	C	510 259-0416	14232
Computer Plastics	3544	E	510 785-3600	5082
Control Air North Inc	1711	D	510 441-1800	1241
Coram Halthcare Corp Nthrn Cal	8082	A	415 292-6811	16872
Core Diagnostics Inc	2835	F	650 561-4176	4019
Corporate Interior Solutions	1799	E	510 670-8800	2024
Corrugated Packaging Pdts Inc	2653	E	650 615-9180	3357
CPS Security Solutions Inc	7381	D	510 806-7227	14049
Crafton Carton	2657	E	510 441-5985	3370
Crescent Healthcare Inc	8082	D	510 264-5454	16875
Crown Management Services Inc	7011	E	510 537-8470	11041
Custom Label & Decal LLC	2759	E	510 876-0000	3727
CW Horton General Contr Inc	1521	E	510 780-0949	628
D W Nicholson Corporation **(PA)**	1711	C	510 887-0900	1246
Daily Review	2711	F	510 783-6111	3431
Dapper Tire Co Inc	3714	F	510 780-1616	6576
Davis Instruments Corporation	3812	D	510 732-9229	6666
Delphon Industries LLC **(PA)**	3089	C	510 576-2220	4274
Detention Device Systems	3599	E	510 783-0771	5507
Dhx-Dependable Hawaiian Ex Inc	4731	D	510 686-2600	7831
Die and Tool Products Inc	3469	F	415 822-2888	4881
Do Dine Inc	7372	F	510 583-7546	13117
Durham School Services L P	4151	C	510 887-6005	7426
Dynamic Security Tech Inc	5065	E	510 786-1121	8908
Eagle Systems Intl Inc	1711	B	510 259-1700	1253
Eden Area Rgnal Occptnal Prgra	8331	D	510 293-2900	17812
Eden Housing Inc **(PA)**	1522	C	510 582-1460	746
Eden Housing Resident Svcs Inc	6513	D	510 582-1460	10431
Ekc Technology Inc **(HQ)**	2819	C	510 784-9105	3784
Electro-Plating Spc Inc	3471	E	510 786-1881	4903
Environmental Remedies Inc	8999	D	925 461-3285	19900
Escueta Care Home 3 Inc **(PA)**	8059	D	510 785-0203	16232
Family Paths Inc	8322	E	510 582-0148	17562
Fante Inc **(PA)**	2096	E	650 697-7525	2855
Farasis Energy Usa Inc	3621	D	510 732-6600	5661
Fba Inc **(PA)**	8711	E	510 265-1888	18709
Felson Companies Inc	6531	D	510 538-1150	10547
First Impressions Printing Inc	2752	E	510 784-0811	3646
Flo Stor Engineering Inc **(PA)**	3535	E	510 887-7179	5051
Florence & New Itln Art Co Inc	3272	E	510 785-9674	4432
Fmw Machine Shop	3599	E	650 363-1313	5527
Foam Distributors Incorporated	5199	D	510 441-8377	9658
Folgergraphics Inc	2791	E	510 293-2294	3764
Four Dimensions Inc	3825	F	510 782-1843	6756
Fremont Bank	6022	D	510 512-1900	9732
Frontage Laboratories Inc	2834	E	510 626-9993	3902
Fulfillment Whsng Slutions Inc	4789	E	760 685-5388	7882
Gallo Sales Company Inc **(DH)**	2084	C	510 476-5000	2591
Gco Inc **(PA)**	5074	E	510 786-3333	8997
Gel Pak LLC	7336	D	510 576-2220	11863
Glazier Steel Inc	3441	D	510 471-5300	4665
Golden Bay Construction Inc	1771	E	510 783-2960	1874
Goldilocks Corporation Calif **(PA)**	2051	E	510 476-0700	2387
Gothic Landscaping Inc	0781	D	661 857-9020	417
Gymdoc Inc	7699	F	510 886-4321	14752
Haigs Delicacies LLC	2099	E	510 782-6285	2899
Halio Inc **(PA)**	3231	C	650 416-5200	4389
Hanford Hotels	7011	E	510 732-6300	11126
Hanson & Fitch Inc	7359	E	408 778-0499	12043
Hantel Technologies Inc	3841	E	510 400-1164	6981
Harvest Food Products Co Inc	2099	D	510 675-0383	2901
Hayward Area Recreation & Park	7221	E	510 881-6721	11673
Hayward Sisters Hospital **(HQ)**	8062	A	510 264-4000	16385
Hayward Unified School Dst	8641	E	510 723-3830	18430
Hayward Unified School Dst	8351	E	510 723-3170	17950
Hd Supply Facilities Maint Ltd	7359	D	510 783-4019	12044
HEs Transportation Svcs Inc	4731	E	510 783-6100	7838
Hester Fabrication Inc	7692	E	530 227-6867	14713
Hillsdale Group LP	8059	C	510 538-3866	16240
Hong Kong Evrgrn Trdg Co Inc	5149	E	510 476-1881	9453
Hsq Technology A Corporation	7373	E	510 259-1334	13609
IMT Precision Inc	3599	E	510 324-8926	5539
Infineon Tech N Amer Corp	3674	C	919 768-0315	6151
Inland Marine Industries Inc	3444	C	510 785-8555	4773
Integrated Flow Systems LLC **(HQ)**	3823	D	510 659-4900	6722
Integrity Technology Corp	3679	F	270 812-8867	6434
Internal Revenue Service	8011	C	510 576-7589	15437

GEOGRAPHIC SECTION HEALDSBURG, CA

	SIC	EMP	PHONE	ENTRY #
IROC	7389	E	510 706-8669	14310
Ironridge Inc **(DH)**	5074	E	800 227-9523	8999
Ita-Med Co	5047	E	510 200-9249	8783
J S Hckley Archtctral Sgnage	3993	E	510 940-2608	7235
J W Floor Covering Inc	2099	C	858 444-1214	2906
Jack James Tow Svc	7549	E	510 581-1950	14662
Jagpreet Enterprises LLC	5149	C	510 336-8376	9458
Jon K Takata Corporation **(PA)**	8322	D	510 315-5400	17629
Joong-Ang Daily News Cal Inc	2711	E	510 487-3333	3452
Jupiter Systems Inc	3575	E	510 675-1000	5333
Justipher Inc	3993	F	510 918-6800	7240
Kaiser Foundation Hospitals	6324	D	510 454-1000	10117
Kaiser Foundation Hospitals	8011	C	510 678-4000	15480
KLA Tencor	3568	E	510 887-2647	5222
Kosan Biosciences Incorporated	2834	D	650 995-7356	3938
Krug Associates Inc	1731	D	510 887-1117	1533
Kwan Wo Ironworks Inc	1791	C	415 822-9628	1925
La Tapatia - Norcal Inc	2099	F	510 783-2045	2910
Landavazo Bros Inc **(PA)**	1771	C	510 888-1043	1886
LBC Mundial Corporation **(DH)**	4513	D	650 873-0750	7750
Lea & Braze Engineering Inc **(PA)**	8711	D	510 887-4086	18752
Leggett & Platt Incorporated	7319	D	510 487-8063	11813
Longevity Global Inc	3548	F	877 566-4462	5104
Lonza Biologics Inc	2834	D	510 731-3500	3943
Ly Brothers Corporation **(PA)**	2051	C	510 782-2118	2392
Lyrical Foods Inc	2099	C	510 784-0955	2920
Macintyre Corp	3585	E	800 229-3560	5433
Magico LLc	3651	E	510 649-9700	5762
Maier Racing Enterprises Inc	3714	E	510 581-7600	6587
Mar Cor Purification Inc	3589	E	510 397-0025	5441
Marelich Mechanical Co Inc **(HQ)**	1711	D	510 785-5500	1310
Mariner Health Care Inc	8051	E	510 783-8150	16049
Mariner Health Care Inc	8051	E	510 538-4424	16053
Mariner Health Care Inc	8051	E	510 785-2880	16054
Mdc Vacuum Products LLC **(PA)**	3563	D	510 265-3500	5186
Mdc Vacuum Products LLC	3491	C	510 265-3500	4955
Melrose Nameplate Label Co Inc **(PA)**	3479	E	510 732-3100	4938
Metric Equipment Sales Inc	5065	D	510 264-0887	8932
Ml Group Inc	4213	D	510 887-8200	7569
Micro Connectors Inc	3577	E	510 266-0299	5399
Millennium Hotel Inc	7011	E	510 432-5665	11302
Mission Linen Supply	7213	D	510 401-5904	11642
Mission Tool and Mfg Co Inc	3599	E	510 782-8383	5574
Montague Company	3589	C	510 785-8822	5443
Monument Security Inc	7381	C	510 430-3540	14076
Morgan Technical Ceramics Inc	3299	E	510 491-1100	4537
Mygrant Glass Company Inc **(PA)**	5013	E	510 785-4360	8457
National Metal Fabricators	3441	E	510 887-6231	4678
Nor-Cal Moving Services **(PA)**	4214	C	510 371-4942	7630
Northstar Contg Group Inc	1799	C	510 491-1330	2047
Northstar Contg Group Inc **(DH)**	1799	D	510 491-1330	2048
Norton Packaging Inc **(PA)**	3089	D	510 786-1922	4307
Nova Commercial Company Inc **(PA)**	7349	C	510 728-7000	11981
Novodiax Inc	8731	E	510 342-3043	19094
Oakhurst Industries Inc	5141	C	510 265-2400	9281
Oki Doki Signs	3993	F	510 940-7446	7245
Onq Solutions Inc **(PA)**	2542	E	650 262-4150	3328
Oven Fresh Bakery Incorporated	2051	F	650 366-9201	2396
Paar Hospitality Inc	7011	D	510 828-3585	11342
Pacheco Brothers Gardening Inc **(PA)**	0781	E	510 732-6330	431
Pacific Cheese Co Inc **(PA)**	5143	C	510 784-8800	9341
Pacific Die Cut Industries	3053	D	510 732-8103	4204
Pacific Gas and Electric Co	4924	C	510 784-3253	8211
Pacific Roller Die Co Inc	3599	F	510 244-7286	5587
Pacific States Felt Mfg Co Inc	3053	F	510 783-2357	4205
Pan Pacific Plastics Mfg Inc	3089	E	510 785-6888	4309
Perry Tool & Research Inc	3399	E	510 782-9226	4591
Pharmatech Associates Inc	8731	E	510 732-0177	19102
Pinnacle Diversified Inc	2752	F	510 400-7929	3684
Plastikon Industries **(PA)**	3089	B	510 400-1010	4312
Pods of San Francisco LLC **(HQ)**	4214	D	510 780-1654	7631
Posiflex Business Machines Inc	5045	E	510 429-7097	8735
Potrero Medical	3841	D	888 635-7280	7021
Predicine Inc	8011	E	650 300-2188	15633
Prevost Car (us) Inc	3711	E	951 202-2064	6554
Primus Power Corporation	3692	E	510 342-7600	6496
Produce World Inc	2099	D	510 441-1449	2936
Protech Materials Inc	3364	F	510 887-5870	4582
Prozyme Inc	8731	E	510 638-6900	19108
PSI Management Team Inc	5046	D	510 266-0076	8769
Pulse Biosciences Inc	8731	D	510 906-4600	19110
Quantum Global Tech LLC **(HQ)**	2842	C	215 892-9300	4077
Quartzy Inc	5049	D	855 782-7899	8802
Questcor Pharmaceuticals	5122	E	510 400-0700	9235
R F Macdonald Co **(PA)**	5084	C	510 784-0110	9087
R2g Enterprises Inc	1761	D	510 489-6218	1833
Rago Neon Inc	3993	F	510 537-1903	7249
Reflexion Medical Inc	3845	C	650 239-9070	7122
Rentokil North America Inc	7359	E	510 265-1949	12059
Restec Contractors Inc	1799	D	510 670-0100	2061
Ripcord Inc	8711	D	408 838-7446	18803
RJS & Associates Inc	1771	C	510 670-9111	1906
Roadstar Trucking Inc	4213	D	510 487-2404	7580
Rodan Builders Inc	1541	E	650 508-1700	807
Rural/Metro Corporation	4119	C	510 266-0885	7402
S&F Management Company LLC	8099	C	310 385-1088	17173
Safeco Door & Hardware Inc	1793	D	510 429-4768	1942
Sapar Usa Inc **(HQ)**	2013	E	510 441-9500	2124
Satco Products of California	5063	D	510 487-4822	8875
Segale Bros Wood Products Inc	1751	E	510 300-1170	1755
Semano Inc	3471	E	510 489-2360	4920
Serpico Landscaping Inc	0781	E	510 293-0341	439
Sew-Eurodrive Inc	3566	E	510 487-3560	5214
SF Tube Inc	3498	E	510 785-9148	4977
SGS SA	8734	D	800 827-3274	19284
Shasta Beverages Inc **(DH)**	2086	D	954 581-0922	2814
Sheeba Duleep	7371	E	267 250-9106	12776
Shimmick Construction/Obayash **(PA)**	1629	D	510 293-1100	1179
Signet Testing Labs Inc **(HQ)**	8734	E	510 887-8484	19285
Solcom Inc	1623	B	510 940-2490	1135
Solta Medical Inc	3845	C	510 782-2286	7124
Sonoco Prtective Solutions Inc	2653	D	510 785-0220	3366
SOS Security Incorporated	7381	D	510 782-4900	14098
Sourcing Group LLC	2752	E	510 471-4749	3699
South Bay Diversfd Systems Inc	3444	F	510 784-3094	4819
St Anthony Care Center Inc	8051	E	510 733-3877	16128
St Chrstpher Cnvlscent Hosp I	8051	E	510 537-4844	16129
St Francis Extended Care Inc	8059	E	510 785-3630	16272
St Regis Retirement Ctr Inc	8361	E	510 881-4240	18184
Steinbeck Brewing Company	2082	D	510 886-9823	2494
Still Room LLC	2087	E	510 847-1930	2826
Stomper Co Inc	1795	D	510 574-0570	1989
Stonebrae LP	7997	E	510 728-7878	15156
Suarez & Munoz Cnstr Inc	1521	E	510 782-6065	711
Successful Altrntves For Addct	8093	D	510 247-8300	17077
Sun Deep Inc	2844	C	510 441-2525	4095
Superior Tube Pipe Bnding Fbco	3498	E	510 782-9311	4979
Surface Techniques Corporation **(PA)**	2541	E	510 887-6000	3322
TCI Aluminum/North Inc	5051	D	510 786-3750	8830
Techstyles Sportswear LLC	5137	E	800 733-3629	9257
Techtron Products Inc	3645	E	510 293-3500	5727
Tender Loving Things Inc	2844	F	510 300-1260	4096
Therm-X of California Inc **(HQ)**	3829	C	510 441-7566	6926
Thermionics Laboratory Inc	3471	D	510 786-0680	4922
Thorx Laboratories Inc	2834	F	510 240-6000	3995
Tiburcio Vasquez Hlth Ctr Inc **(PA)**	8011	E	510 471-5880	15741
Tk Elevator Corporation	7699	E	510 476-1900	14778
Tli Enterprises Inc **(PA)**	3821	E	510 538-3304	6698
Topdot Solar LLC	1711	E	800 731-5104	1383
Tower Holdings Inc **(DH)**	2834	D	510 240-6000	3997
Tps Aviation Inc **(PA)**	5065	D	510 475-1010	8965
Tresco Paint Co	2851	E	510 887-7254	4112
Tridecs Corporation	3599	E	510 785-2620	5628
Twin Bridges Technologies LLC	5045	F	707 591-4500	8757
U S Enterprise Corporation	2035	E	510 487-8877	2288
Ultra Clean Tech Systems Svc I **(HQ)**	3674	C	510 576-4400	6342
Ultraex Inc	4513	E	800 882-1000	7751
Ultrasil LLC	3674	E	510 266-3700	6343
Underwriters Laboratories Inc	8734	C	408 754-6500	19289
United Foods Intl USA Inc **(HQ)**	2099	E	510 264-5850	2952
United Parcel Service Inc	4512	D	510 264-8880	7741
Ustov Inc	5141	E	510 781-1818	9322
Valdor Fiber Optics Inc **(PA)**	3825	F	510 293-1212	6799
Vicolo Wholesale LLC **(PA)**	2041	E	510 475-6019	2313
Vishnu Hotel LLC	7011	E	650 508-1800	11563
Wagan Corporation	5013	E	510 471-9221	8474
Westates Mechanical Corp Inc	1711	D	510 635-9830	1399
Western State Design Inc	3582	D	510 786-9271	5427
Win Foods Corporation	2099	D	510 487-8877	2959
Win Woo Trading LLC	5141	E	510 259-1888	9323
Windsor Gardens Healthcare C	8059	C	510 582-4636	16284
Wohler Technologies Inc	3663	E	510 870-0810	5885
X Therm	3822	F	510 441-7566	6709
Xpo Logistics Freight Inc	4213	D	510 785-6920	7617
Yanfeng US Auto Intr Systems I	3714	E	616 886-3622	6599

HEALDSBURG, CA - Sonoma County

	SIC	EMP	PHONE	ENTRY #
Adams Winery LLC **(PA)**	2084	E	707 395-6126	2501
Adams Winery LLC	2084	E	508 648-2505	2502
Alexander Valley Gourmet LLC	2099	E	707 473-0116	2866
Alliance Medical Center Inc	8011	D	707 431-8234	15274
AVV Winery Co LLC	2084	E	707 433-7209	2507
Bells Haldsburg Ambulance Svc	4119	E	707 433-1114	7376
Bevill Vineyard Management LLC	0172	E	707 433-1101	45
Capital Lumber Company	5031	E	707 433-7070	8534
Chateau Diana LLC **(PA)**	2084	F	707 433-6992	2530
Cooling Tower Resources Inc **(PA)**	2499	E	707 433-3900	3267
Criveller California Corp	3556	F	707 431-2211	5128
DJ Grey Company Inc	3679	F	707 431-2779	6419
Dry Creek Inn Ltd Partnership	7011	D	707 433-0300	11062
Dry Creek Vineyard Inc	2084	E	707 433-1000	2554
E & M Electric and McHy Inc **(PA)**	5084	E	707 433-5578	9064
Eandm	7694	F	707 473-3137	14729
Ferrar-Crano Vnyrds Winery LLC **(PA)**	2084	C	707 433-6700	2567
Field Stone Winery Vinyrd Inc	2084	F	707 433-7266	2569
Finlink Inc **(PA)**	7371	C	888 999-5467	12452
Franciscan Vinyards Inc	2084	E	707 433-6981	2583
General Dynmics Ots Ncvlle Inc **(DH)**	3728	D	707 473-9200	6632
Haus Beverage Inc	2084	E	503 939-5298	2614
Healdsburg Lumber Company Inc	2431	D	707 431-9663	3136
Healdsburg Primary Care Inc	8011	E	707 433-3383	15427
Hotel Healdsburg LLC **(PA)**	7011	D	707 431-2800	11164
Jordan Vineyard & Winery LP	2084	E	707 431-5250	2634
Jvw Corporation	2084	D	707 431-5250	2636
Klein Foods Inc	0172	D	707 431-1533	61

GEOGRAPHIC

Employment Codes: A=Over 500 employees, B=251-500, C=101-250, D=51-100, E=20-50 F=10-19
2022 Northern California Business Directory and Buyers Guide
© Mergent Inc. 1-800-342-5647
1155

HEALDSBURG, CA

	SIC	EMP	PHONE	ENTRY #
L Foppiano Wine Co	2084	E	707 433-2736	2643
Madrona Mnor Wine Cntry Inn RE	7011	D	707 433-4231	11281
Max Machinery Inc	3823	E	707 433-2662	6725
Max Process Equipment LLC	5046	E	707 433-7281	8766
Metro Publishing Inc	2711	E	707 527-1200	3460
Michel-Schlmberger Partners LP	2084	F	707 433-7427	2660
North Sonoma County Hosp Dst	8062	C	707 431-6500	16463
Pacific Sun	2721	F	415 488-8100	3511
Pan Magna Group	2084	E	707 433-5508	2677
Pine Ridge Winery LLC	2084	E	707 260-0330	2684
Pjk Winery LLC	2084	E	707 431-8333	2685
Popcorn Design LLC	5182	E	707 321-7982	9583
Preston Vineyards Inc	2084	E	707 433-3372	2687
RB Wine Associates LLC	2084	D	707 433-8400	2693
Rupert Gibbon & Spider Inc	2851	E	800 442-0455	4110
Scheid Vineyards Inc	0172	C	707 433-1858	73
Seghesio Wineries Inc	2084	E	707 433-3579	2712
Serra Systems Inc (HQ)	7372	F	707 433-5104	13440
Silver Oak Wine Cellars LLC	2084	E	707 942-7082	2717
Sisters of St Joseph Orange	8062	A	707 431-1135	16528
Social Finance Inc	6163	B	707 473-9889	9950
Stonecushion Inc (PA)	2084	E	707 433-1911	2732
Strategic Capital Incorporated	8742	E	707 473-4310	19643
Svi Healdsburg LLC	7011	E	707 433-4000	11522
Tayman Park Golf Group Inc	7992	E	707 433-4275	15033
Truett-Hurst Inc (PA)	2084	E	707 431-4423	2748
Vino Farms Inc	0762	C	707 433-8241	390

HELM, CA - Fresno County

	SIC	EMP	PHONE	ENTRY #
Terranova Ranch Inc	0191	E	559 866-5644	191

HERALD, CA - Sacramento County

	SIC	EMP	PHONE	ENTRY #
Sacramento Municpl Utility Dst	7389	B	916 732-5743	14393

HERCULES, CA - Contra Costa County

	SIC	EMP	PHONE	ENTRY #
A & B Die Casting Co Inc	3363	E	877 708-0009	4574
Benda Tool & Model Works Inc	3544	E	510 741-3170	5081
Bio-RAD Laboratories Inc (PA)	3826	A	510 724-7000	6816
Bio-RAD Laboratories Inc	3826	A	510 741-6916	6817
Blize Healthcare Cal Inc	8082	D	800 343-2549	16860
Bridger Technologies Inc	3826	E	406 556-0300	6819
City Mechanical Inc	7623	D	510 724-9088	14685
Eurofins Eag Agroscience LLC	8734	E	510 741-3000	19267
In Front Enterprises	7371	E	510 799-9018	12514
Mega Creation Inc	2844	E	510 741-9998	4090
Naia Inc	2024	E	510 724-2479	2181
Shields Nursing Centers Inc (PA)	8051	C	510 724-9911	16116
Theraex Rehab Services Inc (PA)	8082	C	510 239-9614	16961
West Coast Pathology Lab	8071	D	510 662-5200	16821

HICKMAN, CA - Stanislaus County

	SIC	EMP	PHONE	ENTRY #
Dave Wilson Nursery (PA)	0181	E	209 874-1821	118
Frantz Wholesale Nursery LLC	0181	C	209 874-1459	122
Reed International (HQ)	3532	F	209 874-2357	5043

HIDDEN VALLEY LAKE, CA - Lake County

	SIC	EMP	PHONE	ENTRY #
Adventist Health System/West	8062	D	707 987-8344	16298
Hidden Valley Lake Association (PA)	8641	D	707 987-3146	18431
Hidden Vly Lk Cmnty Svcs Dst	4952	E	707 987-9201	8283

HILLSBOROUGH, CA - San Mateo County

	SIC	EMP	PHONE	ENTRY #
Algo Technologies Inc	7372	F	608 332-9716	12970
Burlingame Country Club	7997	D	650 696-8100	15066
John Plane Construction Inc	1542	C	415 468-0555	905
Manticore Games Inc	7372	E	650 799-6145	13290

HILMAR, CA - Merced County

	SIC	EMP	PHONE	ENTRY #
Americore Inc	3448	E	209 632-5679	4847
Hilmar Cheese Company Inc (PA)	2022	A	209 667-6076	2150
Hilmar Lumber Inc	5031	E	209 668-8123	8551
Hilmar Oaks LLC	2241	E	209 668-0867	2969
Hilmar Whey Protein Inc (PA)	2023	B	209 667-6076	2163
Perrys Custom Chopping LLC	3523	F	209 667-8777	5017

HOLLISTER, CA - San Benito County

	SIC	EMP	PHONE	ENTRY #
A & R Doors Inc	2431	E	831 637-8139	3121
Advantage Truss Company LLC	2439	E	831 635-0377	3198
Alpha Teknova Inc	2836	C	831 637-1100	4034
Associated R V Ent Inc	5013	E	831 636-9566	8439
B & R Farms LLC	2034	E	831 637-9168	2250
Bhandal Bros Inc	4213	E	831 728-2691	7510
Bhandal Bros Trucking Inc	4213	D	831 728-2691	7511
Brent Redmond Trnsp Inc	4213	E	831 637-5342	7514
Central Coast YMCA	8641	C	831 637-8600	18405
Chamberlains Children Ctr Inc	8361	D	831 636-2121	18074
Dassels Petroleum Inc (PA)	5172	C	831 636-5100	9532
Food Equipment Mfg Co	3556	E	831 637-1624	5130
Goodwill Silicon Valley LLC	7363	A	831 634-0960	12174
Guerra Nut Shelling Company	0723	C	831 637-4471	287
Hazel Hawkins Memorial Hosp	8011	C	831 636-2664	15426
Hazel Hawkins Memorial Hosp (PA)	8062	B	831 637-5711	16386
Hollister Landscape Supply Inc	3273	D	831 636-8750	4488
International Hort Tech LLC	3523	E	831 637-1800	5007
Mandego Inc	2261	E	831 637-5241	2976
Marich Confectionery Co Inc	2064	C	831 634-4700	2431
Mark Nicholson Inc	1611	D	831 637-5728	1054
Mc Electronics LLC	3672	B	831 637-1651	5945
Nanotronics Imaging Inc	3699	E	831 630-0700	6533
Neil Jones Food Company	2033	E	831 637-0573	2229
Ozeki Sake (usa) Inc (HQ)	2084	E	831 637-9217	2676

	SIC	EMP	PHONE	ENTRY #
Pacific Intrlock Pvngstone Inc (PA)	3272	F	831 637-9163	4446
Pacific Scientific Energetic (HQ)	2899	B	831 637-3731	4166
Premiere Cinemas	7832	E	831 638-1800	14816
Pride Conveyance Systems Inc	3535	D	831 637-1787	5054
R and R Labor Inc	0761	B	831 638-0290	364
Reed Manufacturing Inc	3324	E	831 637-5641	4552
Royal Circuit Solutions Inc (PA)	3672	E	831 636-7789	5967
San Benito Health Foundation	8011	E	831 637-6871	15661
San Benito Htg & Shtmtl Inc	1711	D	831 637-1112	1353
San Benito Supply (PA)	3272	C	831 637-5526	4450
San Bnito Cnty Cmnty Svcs Dev	7021	E	831 636-5524	11594
San Juan Oaks LLC	7992	D	831 636-6113	15023
Sears Home Imprv Pdts Inc	1521	C	831 245-0062	704
Simmons Stairways Inc	2431	E	408 920-0105	3152
Tiffany Motor Company	7538	E	831 637-4461	14597
Trical Inc	2879	E	831 637-0195	4146
Wolt Com Inc	7361	C	940 271-4703	12152
Woltcom Inc	1731	E	831 638-4900	1640

HOLT, CA - San Joaquin County

	SIC	EMP	PHONE	ENTRY #
Victoria Island LP	0161	E	209 465-5600	37

HOMEWOOD, CA - Placer County

	SIC	EMP	PHONE	ENTRY #
Homewood Village Resorts LLC	7011	E	530 525-2992	11160

HOOPA, CA - Humboldt County

	SIC	EMP	PHONE	ENTRY #
Hoopa Forest Industries	2411	E	530 625-4281	3063
Hoopa Modular Building Entp (PA)	1531	E	530 625-4551	782
Klma W Medical Center	8093	D	530 625-4114	17031
Lucky Bear Casino	7011	E	530 625-5198	11274

HOPLAND, CA - Mendocino County

	SIC	EMP	PHONE	ENTRY #
Brutocao Vineyards	2084	E	707 744-1320	2517
Fetzer Vineyards (HQ)	2084	E	707 744-1250	2568
Golden Cellars LLC	2084	E	707 528-8500	2597
Hopland Band Pomo Indians Inc (PA)	8699	C	707 472-2100	18572
Shokawah Casino	7011	E	707 744-1395	11474

HUGHSON, CA - Stanislaus County

	SIC	EMP	PHONE	ENTRY #
Alpine Pacific Nut Co Inc	0722	E	209 667-8688	260
Bella Viva Orchards Inc	0191	F	209 883-9015	147
Calaveras Materials Inc (DH)	3273	E	209 883-0448	4464
Duarte Nursery Inc (PA)	0181	E	209 531-0351	120
Grossi Fabrication Inc	3496	F	209 883-2817	4970
Grower Direct Nut Company Inc	0723	E	209 883-4890	286
Hughson Nut Inc (HQ)	2068	B	209 883-0403	2445
Mid Valley Nut Company Inc (PA)	0723	E	209 883-4491	293
Nuwest Milling LLC	2048	E	209 883-1163	2352
Samaritan Village Inc	8322	C	209 883-3212	17706
Valley Tool & Mfg Co Inc	3599	E	209 883-4093	5634

HURON, CA - Fresno County

	SIC	EMP	PHONE	ENTRY #
California Valley Land Co Inc (PA)	0721	D	559 945-9292	250
Dick Anderson & Sons Farming	0191	E	559 945-2511	158
Dresick Farms Inc (PA)	0161	C	559 945-2513	28

IONE, CA - Amador County

	SIC	EMP	PHONE	ENTRY #
Aces Waste Services Inc	4953	E	209 274-2237	8297
Amador Disposal Service Inc	4953	E	209 274-4095	8302
Buena Vista Gaming Authority	7011	B	866 915-0777	10980
Concessionaires Urban Park	7999	D	209 763-5121	15196
Concessionaires Urban Park	7999	E	209 763-5166	15197
Gambrel Companies Inc	3273	F	209 274-0150	4483
Indian Hill Processing	1499	F	209 274-9164	603
Isp Granule Products Inc	3295	E	209 274-2930	4530
Lodi Memorial Hosp Assn Inc	8062	D	209 274-2183	16429
Mp Associates Inc	2892	C	209 274-4715	4152
Portlock International Ltd	7992	E	209 274-0167	15017
Specialty Granules LLC	3295	E	209 274-5323	4532

ISLETON, CA - Sacramento County

	SIC	EMP	PHONE	ENTRY #
B & W Resort Marina	7011	E	916 777-6161	10940
Bureau of Reclamation	8322	E	916 777-6992	17449
Kay Dix Inc	0175	E	916 776-1701	106
Ken & Laura Scheidegger	4493	E	916 777-6462	7731
Riverside Ltd	4221	E	916 777-6076	7676
Vieiras Resort	7011	E	916 777-6661	11557

JACKSON, CA - Amador County

	SIC	EMP	PHONE	ENTRY #
Amador Home Care Service	8082	E	209 223-3866	16845
Amador Residential Care Inc	8361	E	209 223-4444	18056
Amador Tlmne Cmnty Action Agcy (PA)	8399	C	209 296-2785	18218
Happy Team Inc	7011	E	209 257-1500	11127
Jackson Creek Dental Group	8021	E	209 223-2712	15839
K&B Pichette Enterprises Inc	8082	D	209 452-5999	16901
Kit Carson Nursing & Rehab	8051	E	209 223-2231	16033
Lowes Home Centers LLC	5031	C	209 223-6140	8579
Pacific Gas and Electric Co	4911	C	209 223-5259	8140
Push Inc	7373	E	209 257-1100	13651
Sita Ram LLC	7011	E	209 223-0211	11484
Sutter Health	8062	C	209 223-5445	16591
Sutter Hlth Scrmnto Sierra Reg	8062	B	209 223-7540	16661
Sutter Valley Hospitals	8062	B	209 223-7514	16678
Xp Power LLC	5065	D	209 267-1630	8975

JAMESTOWN, CA - Tuolumne County

	SIC	EMP	PHONE	ENTRY #
Chicken Rnch Economic Dev Corp	2711	E	209 984-9066	3426
Condor Earth Technologies Inc	8711	E	209 984-4593	18673
Diestel Turkey Ranch	0253	E	209 984-0826	235
Fray Logging	2411	E	209 984-5968	3062

GEOGRAPHIC SECTION

LATHROP, CA

	SIC	EMP	PHONE	ENTRY #
Jamestown Motor Corporation	7549	E	209 984-5272	14663
National Historic Rest Inc	7011	D	209 984-3446	11327
Sierra Resource Management Inc	2411	E	209 984-1146	3080
Sierra Waldorf School Inc	8351	E	209 984-0454	18020
V B Glass Co Inc	1793	E	209 984-4111	1947

JENNER, CA - Sonoma County
| Timber Cove Inn | 7011 | E | 707 847-3231 | 11536 |

JUNCTION CITY, CA - Trinity County
| Eagle Rock Incorporated | 3531 | F | 530 623-4444 | 5031 |

JUNE LAKE, CA - Mono County
| Double Eagle Resort | 7011 | E | 760 648-7004 | 11059 |

KELSEY, CA - El Dorado County
| Califrnia Frnsic Med Group Inc | 8099 | D | 530 573-3035 | 17114 |

KELSEYVILLE, CA - Lake County
BT Holdings Inc	0175	E	707 279-4317	97
Girl Scouts Northern Cal	8641	E	707 279-4689	18420
Lake County Walnut Inc	2068	F	707 279-1200	2448
Naptech Test Equipment Inc	3825	E	707 995-7145	6772
Steele Wines Inc	2084	E	707 279-9475	2725

KENSINGTON, CA - Alameda County
| Noodles Fresh LLC | 2099 | F | 510 898-1710 | 2928 |

KENTFIELD, CA - Marin County
1125 Sir Frncis Drake Blvd Ope	8062	C	415 456-9680	16285
Marin Community College Dst	8351	E	415 457-8811	17969
Marin Community College Dst	8351	D	415 485-9468	17970
Marin General Hospital	8062	A	415 925-7000	16437
Vibra Healthcare LLC	8062	D	415 853-9499	16717

KENWOOD, CA - Sonoma County
Arthur Kunde & Sons Inc	0762	E	707 833-5501	367
Kunde Enterprises Inc	2084	D	707 833-5501	2642
Palo Alto Vineyard MGT LLC	0761	E	707 996-7725	363
Pernod Ricard Usa LLC	2084	D	707 833-5891	2680

KERMAN, CA - Fresno County
Acemij Farms Inc	0191	E	559 842-7766	145
Actagro LLC (HQ)	5191	E	559 369-2222	9593
Adventist Hlth Systm/West Corp	8062	D	559 846-9370	16313
Baker Commodities Inc	2077	E	559 237-4320	2457
Bar 20 Dairy LLC	0241	D	559 846-7095	205
California Mfg & Engrg Co LLC	3531	C	559 842-1500	5027
Central Cal Almond Grwers Assn (PA)	0723	E	559 846-5377	275
Dole Food Company Inc	2034	C	559 843-2504	2259
Hall Management Corp	8741	A	559 846-7382	19346
Helena Industries LLC	2875	C	559 846-5303	4139
Macs Equip Repair	7699	E	559 846-6534	14762
Morris General Contracting Inc	1542	E	559 842-9453	927
River Ranch Raisins Inc	2034	E	559 843-2294	2266
Valley Optometric Center	8042	E	559 846-5252	15875

KINGSBURG, CA - Fresno County
Cencal Cnc Inc	3599	E	559 897-8706	5492
Cheema Logistics	4449	D	559 702-1444	7715
Cheema Transport Inc	4789	E	559 634-9109	7877
Crestwood Behavioral Hlth Inc	8059	D	559 238-6981	16229
Crinklaw Farm Services Inc	0721	E	559 897-1077	252
Design Machine and Mfg	7699	E	559 897-7374	14744
Dfa of California	8741	E	559 233-7249	19325
Don Berry Construction Inc	1611	D	559 896-5700	1034
Foster Commodities	2048	E	559 897-1081	2342
Foster Farms LLC	2015	E	559 897-1081	2129
Guardian Industries LLC	3211	B	559 891-8867	4356
Guardian Industries Corp	3211	D	559 891-8867	4357
Guardian Industries Corp	3211	D	559 638-3588	4358
Guss Automation LLC	3523	F	559 897-0245	5005
In Home Services LLC	8082	E	559 897-5161	16899
Kap LP	0175	D	559 897-5132	105
Kingsburg Apple Packers Inc	5148	B	559 897-5132	9412
Kingsburg Cultivator Inc	3523	E	559 897-3662	5012
Kingsburg Orchards	5148	E	559 897-2986	9413
Longs Drug Stores Cal Inc	7384	E	559 897-0116	14163
Mike Jensen Farms LLC	0175	C	559 897-4192	109
Nutrius LLC	2048	E	559 897-5862	2351
Peterson Family Inc	0175	D	559 897-5064	111
Selma-Kngsburg-Fowler Cnty Stn	4952	E	559 897-6500	8289
Strategic Industry Inc	1389	E	559 419-9481	572
Streamline Irrigation Inc	4971	E	559 897-1516	8419
Sunbridge Care Entps W LLC	8051	A	559 897-5881	16136
Sunbridge Care Entps W LLC	8051	E	559 897-5881	16137
Superb Hospitality LLC	7011	E	559 897-8840	11521
Van Beurden Insurance Svcs Inc (PA)	6411	D	559 634-7125	10365
Vie-Del Company	2084	E	559 896-3065	2754
Wildwood Express	4213	E	559 805-3237	7611

KLAMATH, CA - Del Norte County
| Trees of Mystery | 7999 | E | 707 482-2251 | 15256 |

KNEELAND, CA - Humboldt County
| J & S Stakes Inc | 2499 | F | 707 668-5647 | 3269 |

KNIGHTS LANDING, CA - Yolo County
| Matteoli Brothers | 0191 | E | 530 738-4201 | 182 |
| Richter Bros Inc | 0161 | E | 530 735-6721 | 34 |

	SIC	EMP	PHONE	ENTRY #

LA GRANGE, CA - Stanislaus County
| Green Tree Nursery | 5193 | E | 209 874-9100 | 9633 |

LA HONDA, CA - San Mateo County
| Young MNS Chrstn Assn San Frnc | 8641 | E | 650 747-1200 | 18515 |

LAFAYETTE, CA - Contra Costa County
Acp Ventures	2752	F	925 297-0100	3615
Cbem LLC Corporate Office (PA)	8322	D	925 283-9000	17470
Civicactions Inc	7379	D	510 408-7510	13865
Clubsport San Ramon LLC	7991	D	925 283-4000	14939
Compass Marketing Inc	7311	E	925 299-7878	11747
D A Financial Group California	6411	D	925 254-7100	10270
Diablo Vly Montessori Schl Inc	8351	E	925 283-4456	17921
Dolans Pinole Lbr Bldg Mtls Co	5031	E	925 927-4662	8542
East Bay Municipl Utility Distr	4941	E	866 403-2683	8243
Econoday Inc	2741	F	925 299-5350	3568
Edtuit Inc (PA)	4899	E	415 269-4471	8075
Franz Inc	7372	E	510 452-2000	13179
Helix Re Inc (PA)	2899	D	415 254-2724	4161
Independent Quality Care Inc	8059	E	925 284-5544	16248
Lafayette Orinda Presbt Ch	8351	D	925 283-8722	17962
Lafayette Park Hotel Corp	7011	E	925 283-3700	11242
Longs Drug Stores Cal Inc	7384	E	925 284-7177	14170
Lumen Technologies Inc	4813	E	925 974-0200	7971
Mustang Survival Inc	3069	D	360 676-1782	4219
Nancys Specialty Foods	2099	B	510 494-1100	2925
Optimum Solutions Group LLC	7372	E	415 954-7100	13350
Premier Staffing Inc (PA)	7361	E	415 362-2211	12121
RES-Care Inc	8082	E	925 283-5076	16937
Tan Packaging LLC	2671	E	800 237-1009	3380
Techexcel Inc (PA)	7371	E	925 871-3900	12853
Tm Financial Forensics LLC (PA)	8748	E	415 692-6350	19875
Velodyne Acoustics Inc	3651	D	408 465-2800	5771

LAKEHEAD, CA - Shasta County
| Holiday Harbor Inc (PA) | 4493 | E | 530 238-2383 | 7729 |

LAKEPORT, CA - Lake County
California Tribal Tanf Partnr (PA)	8322	D	707 262-4404	17451
Evergreen At Lakeport LLC (PA)	8051	D	707 263-6382	15998
Globalridge LLC	2833	F	800 225-4345	3816
Hospice Services Lake County	8052	E	707 263-6222	16187
Konocti Vista Casino (PA)	7999	C	707 262-1900	15214
Lake Cnty Trbal Hlth Cnsrtium	8021	E	707 263-8382	15845
Lake County Office Education (PA)	8611	E	707 262-4102	18308
Lakeport Post Acute LLC	8052	D	707 263-6382	16188
Paul Loewen	4581	F	707 263-0452	7779
People Services Inc (PA)	8361	E	707 263-3810	18156
Redwood Rgnal Med Group DRG LL	8071	D	707 262-3600	16803
Sequoia Senior Solutions Inc	8082	D	707 263-3070	16942
Sutter Bay Hospitals	8082	E	707 263-7400	16951
Sutter Health	8011	D	707 263-6885	15715
Sutter Health	8011	C	707 263-6885	15720
Sutter Health	8062	C	707 262-5000	16633
Sutter West Bay Hospitals	8062	B	707 262-5000	16682
Xpo Enterprise Services Inc	4213	C	916 399-8291	7613
Young & Family Inc	2431	E	707 263-8877	3164

LAKESHORE, CA - Fresno County
China Peak Mountain Resort LLC	7011	D	559 233-2500	11006
Lakeshore Resort	7011	D	559 893-3193	11244
Sierra Summit Inc	7011	A	559 233-2500	11480

LARKSPUR, CA - Marin County
Answerlab LLC (PA)	8732	E	415 814-9910	19152
Blackwater Cellular Corp	4812	C	415 526-2200	7897
By The Bay Health (PA)	8082	C	415 927-2273	16863
Courtyard Management Corp	7011	E	415 925-1800	11039
Evolva Nutrition Inc	2099	F	415 374-0785	2890
Golden Gate Brdge Hwy Trnsp Ds	4785	D	415 455-2000	7871
Lark Creek Inn Prtners L P A C	7299	E	415 924-7767	11724
Larkspur Hspitality Dev MGT LLC (PA)	7011	E	415 945-5000	11256
Lilien LLC (HQ)	7373	E	415 389-7500	13626
Marin Brewing Co Inc	2082	E	415 461-4677	2485
Marin Primary & Middle School (PA)	8351	E	415 924-2608	17972
ONeill Beverages Co LLC (PA)	0172	D	844 825-6600	68
Rebel Girls Inc	7373	E	808 398-2258	13657
Sysorex USA (HQ)	7373	E	415 389-7500	13672
Trizic Inc	7372	E	415 366-6583	13497

LATHROP, CA - San Joaquin County
Accurate Heating & Cooling Inc	3444	E	209 858-4125	4737
Allied Janitorial Maint Inc	7349	E	209 992-6687	11915
Boise Cascade Company	2621	E	209 983-4114	3342
California Natural Products	2099	B	209 858-2525	2878
Capstone Logistics LLC	4789	A	209 858-1401	7876
Captive Plastics LLC	3089	D	209 858-9188	4264
Cbc Steel Buildings LLC	3448	C	209 858-2425	4849
Cen Cal Plastering Inc	1742	D	209 981-5265	1667
Clorox Manufacturing Company	2812	E	925 425-6040	3769
Con-Fab California Corporation (PA)	3272	F	209 249-4700	4427
Crosslink Prof Tax Sltions LLC (PA)	7371	D	209 835-2720	12363
Cunha Draying Inc	4213	D	209 858-7445	7522
Diamond Pet Fd Prcssors Cal LL	2047	D	209 983-4900	2334
Eclipse Metal Fabrication Inc	3444	E	650 298-8731	4759
Global Building Services Inc	8999	C	209 858-9501	19902
Horizon Snack Foods Inc	2053	D	925 373-7700	2422
Icon Design and Display Inc	2521	E	707 416-0230	3304

Employment Codes: A=Over 500 employees, B=251-500, C=101-250, D=51-100, E=20-50 F=10-19

LATHROP, CA

Company	SIC	EMP	PHONE	ENTRY #
Mid Valley Plastering Inc	1742	B	209 858-9766	1692
Performant Recovery Inc	7322	C	209 858-3500	11827
Pratt Industries Inc	2621	C	770 922-0117	3349
Pratt Lathrop Corrugating LLC	2653	C	209 670-0900	3365
Premiere Credit North Amer LLC	7322	C	844 897-2901	11829
Provena Foods Inc	2013	E	209 858-5555	2121
Rafael Sandoval	2421	E	209 858-4173	3101
Saramark Inc	3448	E	408 971-3881	4856
Schell & Kampeter Inc	2047	E	209 983-4900	2336

LATON, CA - Fresno County

Company	SIC	EMP	PHONE	ENTRY #
Zonneveld Dairies Inc	0241	E	559 923-4546	229

LAYTONVILLE, CA - Mendocino County

Company	SIC	EMP	PHONE	ENTRY #
Long Valley Health Center	8011	E	707 984-6131	15509
Red Fox Casino	7011	E	707 984-6800	11388

LE GRAND, CA - Merced County

Company	SIC	EMP	PHONE	ENTRY #
J Marchini & Son Inc	0191	D	559 665-2944	172
Minturn Nut Co Inc	2096	E	559 665-8500	2857
Oasis Foods Inc	2033	F	209 382-0263	2231

LEWISTON, CA - Trinity County

Company	SIC	EMP	PHONE	ENTRY #
EH Suda Inc	3599	E	530 778-9830	5516
Ninja Credit Consultants LLC	8742	E	888 646-5282	19591

LINCOLN, CA - Placer County

Company	SIC	EMP	PHONE	ENTRY #
Alpha Dyno Nobel (PA)	5169	E	916 645-3377	9516
American Hard Bag LLC	3751	F	707 484-1283	6647
B Z Plumbing Company Inc	1711	E	916 645-1600	1213
Catta Verdera Country Club LLC	7997	D	916 645-7200	15071
Ctc Services Inc	7389	E	916 434-0195	14242
Gary Beebe Industries Inc	4212	E	916 645-6073	7468
Gc Products Inc	3272	E	916 645-3870	4434
Gdas-Lincoln Inc	3721	E	916 645-8961	6610
Gdsa-Lincoln Inc (PA)	7629	D	916 645-8961	14699
Global Defense Group LLC	7381	D	530 510-5204	14065
J D Pasquetti Engineering	8711	E	916 543-9401	18741
Jbr Inc (PA)	2099	C	916 258-8000	2907
Kaiser Foundation Hospitals	8011	C	916 543-5153	15460
Lincoln Hills Golf Club	7992	E	916 543-9200	15008
Livingstons Concrete Svc Inc	3273	E	916 334-4313	4495
Longs Drug Stores Cal Inc	7384	E	916 408-0209	14160
Pabco Building Products LLC	3259	D	916 645-3341	4405
Pabco Clay Products LLC	3251	C	916 645-3341	4399
Pabco Clay Products LLC	3295	E	916 645-8937	4531
Pallets Unlimited Inc	2448	F	916 408-1914	3227
Robb-Jack Corporation (PA)	3541	D	916 645-6045	5077
San Jose Die Casting Corp	3363	E	408 262-6500	4579
Sierra Pacific Industries	2421	E	916 645-1631	3115
United Auburn Indian Community	7011	A	916 408-7777	11550
Wise Villa Winery LLC	2084	E	916 543-0323	2767

LINDEN, CA - San Joaquin County

Company	SIC	EMP	PHONE	ENTRY #
BWC Weststeyn Dairy LP	0241	E	209 886-5334	206
Duarte Nursery Inc	0181	B	209 887-3409	119
Hyponex Corporation	2873	E	209 887-3845	4132
Mid Valley AG Svcs Inc (PA)	5191	E	209 931-7600	9606
Normans Nursery Inc	5193	C	209 887-2033	9638
Pearl Crop Inc	2099	E	209 887-3731	2932
Prima Noce Packing Inc	7389	E	209 932-8800	14373
R&B Protective Coatings Inc	1721	E	209 887-2030	1427
Stockton Rubber Mfgcoinc	3069	E	209 887-1172	4227

LITTLE RIVER, CA - Mendocino County

Company	SIC	EMP	PHONE	ENTRY #
Little River Inn Inc	7011	C	707 937-5942	11263

LIVE OAK, CA - Sutter County

Company	SIC	EMP	PHONE	ENTRY #
Cal Nor Trucking Inc (PA)	4213	D	530 695-9219	7517
Coe Orchard Equipment Inc	3523	E	530 695-5121	4999
Micheli Farms Inc	0175	D	530 695-9022	108
Pacific Coast Producers	2033	D	530 695-1126	2240
River Valley Care Center	8051	E	530 695-8020	16101
Sunset Moulding Co (PA)	2421	E	530 790-2700	3117
Wilbur Packing Company Inc	0723	D	530 671-4911	315

LIVERMORE, CA - Alameda County

Company	SIC	EMP	PHONE	ENTRY #
Adams Label Company LLC (PA)	2759	E	925 371-5393	3720
Admedes Inc (DH)	5047	E	925 417-0778	8771
Aero Precision Holdings LP	3728	C	925 455-9900	6626
Aero Precision Industries LLC (PA)	5088	C	424 252-8294	9149
Aerospace Composite Products (PA)	3728	F	925 443-5900	6630
Air Factors Inc	3564	F	925 579-0040	5189
Akira Seiki USA Inc	3541	E	925 443-1200	5071
All American Fence Corporation	1799	E	925 275-5110	2000
All Guard Alarm Systems Inc (PA)	1731	D	800 255-4273	1447
Altamont Manufacturing Inc	3599	E	925 371-5401	5470
American Wholesale Ltg Inc	5063	D	510 252-1088	8841
Amerimade Technology Inc	3089	E	925 243-9090	4257
Amsnet Inc (PA)	7373	E	925 245-6100	13552
Aqua Gunite Inc	1799	E	408 271-2782	2005
Aragon Commercial Ldscpg Inc	0782	C	408 998-0600	446
Architectural GL & Alum Co Inc (PA)	5051	C	925 583-2460	8806
Aria Technologies Inc	3357	E	925 292-1616	4567
Assay Technology Inc	7389	E	925 461-8880	14204
Baycorr Packaging LLC (PA)	2653	C	925 449-1148	3353
Bayview General Engrg Inc	1611	E	925 447-6600	1015
Berkeley Nutritional Mfg Corp	8732	E	925 243-6300	19153
Bmf - Baktek Metal Fabrication	3499	F	925 245-0200	4983
Bolb Inc	3674	F	925 453-6293	6070
Bonner Processing Inc	3471	E	925 455-3833	4900
Boole Inc	5045	E	408 368-2515	8677
Brightview Landscape Svcs Inc	0781	C	925 243-0288	402
Brock LLC (PA)	4731	E	925 371-2184	7826
Byer California	2331	D	925 245-0184	2998
C D International Tech Inc	3679	F	408 986-0725	6403
Cable Wholesalecom Inc (PA)	5045	E	925 455-0800	8679
Caledonian Building Svcs Inc	7349	E	925 803-3500	11932
Califrnias Gnite Pool Plst Inc	1799	E	925 960-9500	2017
Cape Inc	8351	D	925 443-3434	17877
Cbx Technologies Inc	7379	E	510 729-7130	13861
Cha Industries Inc	3559	E	510 683-8554	5143
Clark Pest Ctrl Stockton Inc	7342	E	925 449-6203	11893
Clfrn/Clrd/Flrd/rgon I Comcast	4812	C	925 424-0273	7904
Cooling Source Inc	3363	C	925 292-1293	4575
Cornerstone Select Bldrs Inc	1521	E	510 490-7911	627
Cosco Fire Protection Inc	1731	D	925 455-2751	1486
Country Builders Inc	1522	E	925 373-1020	740
Coventina-Gse Jv LLC	1623	E	813 509-0669	1095
Cresta Blanca Golf LLC	7992	D	925 456-2475	14995
Custom Product Dev Corp	1761	E	925 960-0577	1794
D M Jepsen Inc	1731	E	925 455-0872	1493
Darcie Kent Vineyards	2084	E	925 243-9040	2543
Darcie Kent Winery LLC	5182	E	925 443-5368	9573
Davey Tree Surgery Company (HQ)	0783	A	925 443-1723	517
Dryden Construction Inc	1522	E	925 243-8750	745
DS Baxley Inc	1752	E	925 371-3950	1768
Dsd Merchandisers Inc	2068	E	925 449-2044	2444
Durham School Services L P	4151	C	925 606-0871	7425
Emerald Landscape Company Inc (HQ)	0781	E	925 449-4743	414
Eurofins Fd Chmstry Tstg Mdson	8734	A	609 452-4440	19270
Fabco Holdings Inc	3714	E	925 454-9500	6578
Fault Line Plumbing Inc	1711	E	925 443-6450	1262
Fbd Vanguard Construction Inc	1771	C	925 245-1300	1869
Formfactor Inc (PA)	3674	E	925 290-4000	6122
Fred Matter Inc	3599	E	925 371-1234	5528
Fusion Coatings Inc	3479	F	925 443-8083	4933
Gdca Inc	3577	E	925 456-9900	5370
Gillig LLC (HQ)	3713	A	510 264-5000	6566
Gmr Northern California LLC	7699	E	925 294-9074	14750
Goodfellow Bros California LLC	1521	B	925 245-2111	646
Granada Bowl Inc	7933	E	925 447-5600	14894
GS Cosmeceutical Usa Inc	2844	D	925 371-5000	4083
GSe Construction Company Inc (PA)	1623	E	925 447-0292	1106
Harris Rebar Northern Cal Inc	1791	C	925 373-0733	1924
High Summit LLC	7539	E	925 605-2900	14612
Hilton Garden Inns MGT LLC	7011	D	925 292-2000	11143
Homesite Svcs Inc A Cal Corp (PA)	5023	E	925 237-3050	8513
Hoskin & Muir Inc	5031	E	925 373-1135	8552
Hospi Comm For The L-P Area T	8741	A	925 447-7000	19350
IMG Companies LLC (PA)	3599	D	925 273-1100	5538
Individual Software Inc	7372	E	925 734-6767	13229
Induspac California Inc (HQ)	2821	E	510 324-3626	3804
Inland Valley Publishing Co	2711	E	925 243-8000	3450
Inphenix Inc	3674	E	925 606-8809	6156
J & M Inc	1623	E	925 724-0300	1108
J M ONeill Inc	1541	E	925 225-1200	798
J Redfern Inc	0782	D	925 371-3300	471
Jamie G Watt	3531	F	925 580-2805	5034
Jifco Inc (PA)	3498	D	925 449-4665	4974
John L Sllivan Investments Inc (PA)	7538	C	916 969-5911	14574
Jpa Landscape & Cnstr Inc	0782	E	925 960-9602	475
Kaiser Foundation Hospitals	8011	C	925 432-6000	15490
Karm Inc	8711	E	650 741-5276	18746
Kenyon Construction Inc	1742	E	800 949-4319	1682
Kier Wrght Cvil Engners Srvyor	8713	E	925 245-8788	18924
Kinetics Mechanical Svc Inc	1711	D	925 245-6200	1297
Laco Inc	3678	E	775 461-2960	6393
Lam Research Corporation	3674	E	510 572-8400	6176
Lam Research Corporation	3674	E	209 597-2194	6177
Lanlogic Inc (HQ)	7373	E	925 273-2300	13624
Lazestar Inc	2431	E	925 443-5293	3138
Leisure Care LLC	8361	C	925 371-2300	18136
Livermore Amdor Vly Trnst Auth	4111	E	925 455-7555	7339
Livermore Area Rcration Pk Dst (PA)	7999	B	925 373-5700	15218
Livermore Pediatrics	8011	E	925 455-5050	15506
Livermore Snior Lving Assoc LP	6513	E	925 371-2300	10448
Livermore Software Tech LLC (HQ)	7371	D	925 449-2500	12577
Livermore Valley Tennis Club	7991	D	925 443-7700	14960
LJ Walch Co Inc	5088	E	925 449-9252	9151
Lowes Home Centers LLC	5031	C	925 245-2440	8566
Maas Brothers Inc	3479	D	925 294-8200	4937
Macpherson Wstn Tl Sup Co LLC (PA)	5085	E	925 443-8665	9122
Marshall Brothers Entps Inc	1611	E	925 449-4020	1055
McGrath Rentcorp	5084	C	877 221-2813	9078
McGrath Rentcorp (PA)	5084	B	925 606-9200	9079
Mch Electric Inc (PA)	1731	E	925 453-5041	1539
Medallion Industries Inc	5031	F	925 449-9040	8589
Metal Improvement Company LLC	3398	E	925 960-1090	4588
Microdental Laboratories Inc	3843	E	800 229-0936	7086
Modus Advanced Inc	3069	E	925 960-8700	4218
Mountain Cascade Inc (PA)	1623	E	925 373-8370	1120
National Food Laboratory LLC	8733	D	925 828-1440	19225
National Security Tech LLC	8711	A	925 960-2500	18776
New Parrott & Co	5182	C	925 456-2300	9582
Nu Rev Communications Inc	8748	E	925 980-2799	19831
Nuprodx Inc	3842	F	925 292-0866	7076

GEOGRAPHIC SECTION LODI, CA

	SIC	EMP	PHONE	ENTRY #
Oil Changer Inc	7549	D	925 447-3346	14669
Omni Mechanical Solution **(PA)**	1521	D	925 784-4726	679
On-Time AC & Htg LLC	1711	D	925 800-5804	1327
Operating Engineers Local Un 3 **(PA)**	6061	E	925 454-4000	9800
Pacific Gas and Electric Co	4911	C	925 373-2623	8183
Pacific Rim Plumbing	1711	E	925 443-3333	1332
Pacific Steel Group	3449	D	858 251-1100	4859
Packaging Innovators LLC	5113	D	925 371-2000	9217
Pacon Mfg Inc	3599	E	925 961-0445	5589
PDC Logistics Inc **(PA)**	4225	E	925 583-0200	7699
Pel Wholesale Inc	5099	E	925 373-3628	9200
Pen-Cal Administrators Inc	8741	D	925 251-3400	19381
Performance Abatement Svcs Inc	1799	E	925 273-3800	2055
Performance Contracting Inc	1541	E	925 273-3800	804
Performant Financial Corp **(PA)**	7375	B	925 960-4800	13803
Performant Recovery Inc **(HQ)**	7322	B	209 858-3994	11828
Permanente Medical Group Inc	8011	A	925 243-2600	15621
Peterson Painting Inc	1721	B	925 455-5864	1423
Point One Elec Systems Inc	1731	D	925 667-2930	1567
Poppy Ridge Inc	7992	E	925 456-8229	15016
Presidio Systems Inc **(PA)**	1731	E	925 362-8400	1569
Prevent Life Safety Svcs Inc	7389	E	925 667-2088	14372
Prince Peace Enterprises Inc **(PA)**	5149	E	925 292-3888	9478
Pro-Tek Manufacturing Inc	3444	E	925 454-8100	4806
Produce Exchange Incorporated **(DH)**	5148	D	925 454-8700	9425
Puronics Incorporated **(HQ)**	3589	D	925 456-7000	5447
Q Technology Inc	3648	E	925 373-3456	5749
R K Larrabee Company Inc	3621	D	925 828-9420	5667
R Lance & Sons Co Inc	7549	E	925 245-8884	14673
Ratermann Manufacturing Inc **(PA)**	3089	E	800 264-7793	4316
RC Readymix Co Inc	3273	E	925 449-7785	4503
Rch Associates Inc	3559	E	510 657-7846	5166
Rdo Construction Equipment Co	5083	E	925 454-3100	9043
Republic Svcs Vsco Rd Landfill	4953	E	925 447-0491	8360
Rexel Usa Inc	5063	E	510 476-3400	8874
Rgw Equipment Sales LLC	5082	E	925 606-2456	9027
Rh USA Inc	3841	E	925 245-7900	7027
Rios-Lovell Estate Winery	2084	E	925 443-0434	2696
Rjms Corporation **(PA)**	5085	D	510 675-0500	9128
Ron Nunes Enterprises LLC	3444	E	925 371-0220	4812
Ronbow Corporation	5031	E	510 713-1188	8604
Sangraf International Inc	3624	E	216 800-9999	5673
Screen Tech Inc	3444	D	408 885-9750	4815
Seaside Rfrigerated Trnspt Inc **(PA)**	4213	E	510 732-0472	7594
Segundo Metal Products Inc	3444	D	925 667-2009	4816
Selex Inc **(PA)**	1799	D	707 836-8836	2066
Sensor Concepts LLC	8711	D	925 443-9001	18810
Shames Construction Co Ltd	1542	E	925 606-3000	959
Sidjon Corporation	7011	D	925 606-6135	11476
Sierra Design Mfg Inc **(PA)**	3647	E	925 443-3140	5740
Silver Oak Health Services	8051	E	925 447-2280	16119
Solarjuice American Inc	3531	B	925 474-8821	5038
Sosa Granite & Marble Inc	1743	E	925 373-7675	1722
Steven Kent LLC	2084	F	925 243-6442	2728
Streivor Inc	3914	F	925 960-9090	7168
Sunbelt Supply LP	5085	E	925 449-5900	9135
Sutter Health	8099	D	925 371-3800	17183
Tao Mechanical Ltd	1711	E	925 447-5220	1377
Tapp Label Inc **(HQ)**	2679	E	707 252-8300	3408
Tdw Construction Inc	1623	E	925 455-5259	1137
Tennyson Electric Inc	1731	E	925 606-1038	1621
Teqtron Inc	7373	E	925 583-5411	13678
Tesla Vineyards Lp	2084	E	925 456-2500	2738
Tgcon Inc **(HQ)**	8711	B	925 449-5764	18836
Thyssenkrupp Indus Svcs NA Inc	5051	D	209 395-9111	8831
Topcon Med Laser Systems Inc	3845	E	888 760-8657	7126
Topcon Positioning Systems Inc **(DH)**	3829	C	925 245-8300	6927
Tri Valley Haven	8399	E	925 449-1664	18255
Trinet Communications Inc **(PA)**	5065	F	925 294-1720	8966
Triple S Metal Inc	4953	E	925 449-3262	8372
Truroots Inc **(HQ)**	2099	E	925 218-2205	2951
Ultracell Corporation **(PA)**	3629	F	925 292-4226	5699
Uncle Credit Union **(PA)**	6061	D	925 447-5001	9825
United States Dept of Energy	8731	A	925 422-1100	19143
US Foods Inc	5141	B	925 606-3525	9321
Valley Montessori School	8351	D	925 455-8021	18043
Valleycare Hospital Corp	8062	C	925 447-7000	16708
Valleycare Hospital Corp **(DH)**	8062	A	925 447-7000	16709
Vericool Inc	3565	E	925 337-0808	5207
Veterans Health Administration	8011	C	925 447-2560	15803
Vintage 99 Label Mfg Inc **(PA)**	2672	E	925 294-5270	3382
Wang Nmr Inc	3841	E	925 443-0212	7062
Watermark Rtrment Cmmnties Inc	8361	D	925 344-5661	18208
Waxies Enterprises LLC	5087	E	925 454-2900	9148
Weaver Crlson Mc Crtney Accntn	8721	E	925 447-2010	19003
Wente Bros **(PA)**	2084	D	925 456-2300	2760
Wente Bros	2084	E	925 456-2450	2761
Westco Iron Works Inc **(PA)**	3441	D	925 961-9152	4694
Wiley X Inc **(PA)**	3851	C	925 243-9810	7147
WL Butler Inc	1521	D	650 361-1270	731
Xchanger Manufacturing Corp	3443	E	510 632-8828	4734

LIVINGSTON, CA - Merced County

	SIC	EMP	PHONE	ENTRY #
Foster Poultry Farms **(PA)**	2015	C	209 394-7901	2130
Foster Poultry Farms	2015	B	209 394-7901	2132
Foster Poultry Farms	2048	C	209 394-7950	2343
Foster Poultry Farms	0254	C	209 394-7901	240
Foster Turkey Products	0253	A	209 394-7901	237
Hughson Nut Inc	2099	F	209 394-6005	2902
Livingston Community Health **(PA)**	8011	D	209 394-7913	15507
Livingston Farmers Association	5148	E	209 394-7941	9415
Menezes Hay Co	2048	F	209 394-3111	2348
Quail H Farms LLC	0139	A	209 394-8001	19
Skill Nurse	8051	E	209 394-2440	16122
Ybp Holdings LLC	2099	E	209 394-7311	2961

LOCKEFORD, CA - San Joaquin County

	SIC	EMP	PHONE	ENTRY #
Elements By Grapevine Inc	2511	F	209 727-3711	3277
Kellogg Supply Inc	2873	E	209 727-3130	4133
Lomelis Statuary Inc **(PA)**	3299	E	209 367-1131	4536
McLaughlin Waste Equipment Inc **(PA)**	5084	D	209 367-8810	9080
Woodside Investment Inc	3499	D	209 787-8040	4989

LODI, CA - San Joaquin County

	SIC	EMP	PHONE	ENTRY #
Ah Wines Inc	2084	F	209 625-8170	2503
American Mstr Tech Scntfic Inc	3841	C	209 368-4031	6941
Anderson Neil O and Assoc Inc **(DH)**	8711	E	209 367-3701	18624
Baywood Cellars Inc	2084	E	415 606-4640	2510
Beaver Dam Health Care Center	8051	E	209 368-0693	15930
Belco Cabinets Inc	3442	F	209 334-5437	4699
Best Supplement Guide LLC **(PA)**	7991	E	209 366-2800	14929
Bjj Company LLC **(PA)**	4213	D	209 941-8361	7513
Boething Treeland Farms Inc	0811	D	209 727-3741	529
Bull Outdoor Products Inc	3631	E	909 770-8626	5700
Buy 4 Less	5063	D	209 368-3614	8846
California Fruit Exchange LLC **(PA)**	5148	C	209 334-2988	9389
Campbell Grinding Inc	3599	E	209 339-8838	5489
Castelanelli Brothers	0241	E	209 369-9218	208
Cemex Cnstr Mtls PCF LLC	3273	E	855 292-8453	4469
Cen-Cal Fire Systems Inc	1711	E	209 334-9166	1231
Century Assembly Inc **(PA)**	8351	D	209 334-3230	17882
Century Assembly Inc	8351	E	209 334-3230	17883
Chancellor Hlth Care of Cal IV	8051	B	209 367-8870	15958
City of Lodi **(PA)**	7389	D	209 333-6700	14227
Clark Pest Ctrl Stockton Inc **(HQ)**	7342	D	209 368-7152	11883
Community Medical Centers Inc	8011	E	209 331-8019	15360
Community Medical Centers Inc	8011	E	209 368-2212	15362
Csn Winddown Inc	0181	C	209 369-3018	117
Dart Container Corp California	3086	D	209 333-8088	4242
Del Castillo Foods Inc	2099	E	209 369-2877	2888
Delta Radiology Medical Group	8011	D	209 334-4416	15375
Delu Vineyards Inc	0172	D	209 334-6660	50
Dependable Precision Mfg Inc	3444	F	209 369-1055	4754
Design Woodworking Inc **(PA)**	2431	E	209 334-6674	3129
Diede Construction Inc	1542	D	209 369-8255	863
East Bay Mncpl Utlty Dst Wtr	4941	E	209 333-2095	8238
F & H Construction **(PA)**	1542	D	209 931-3738	870
Farmers & Merchants Bancorp **(PA)**	6022	B	209 367-2300	9716
Farwest Safety Inc	1611	E	209 339-8085	1039
Ford Construction Company Inc	1629	D	209 333-1116	1162
Frank C Alegre Trucking Inc **(PA)**	4213	C	209 334-2112	7540
Frontier Performance Lubr Inc	5172	E	209 334-6353	9533
FTg Construction Mtls Inc	4213	C	209 334-4038	7542
General Mills Inc	2043	E	209 334-7061	2314
George Kishida Inc	4212	D	209 368-0603	7469
Goldstone Land Company LLC	2084	E	209 368-3113	2602
Greg H Carpenter Concrete Inc	1771	E	209 367-4224	1877
Hanot Foundation Inc **(PA)**	8361	E	209 334-6454	18127
Holz Rubber Company Inc	3069	C	209 368-7171	4216
Horn Electric	1731	E	209 339-4278	1516
Jessies Grove Winery	2084	E	209 368-0880	2633
John H Kautz Farms	0721	E	209 334-4786	255
Jose Vramontes	0191	E	209 810-5384	176
Joseph Bui Dmd Inc **(PA)**	8021	E	209 224-8104	15844
Kautz Vineyards Inc	2084	E	209 369-1911	2637
KG Vineyard Management LLC	0762	E	209 367-8996	380
Larry Mthvin Installations Inc	3231	D	209 368-2105	4390
LLC Merritt West	2431	F	209 334-6674	3139
Lodi Iron Works Inc **(PA)**	3321	E	209 368-5395	4548
Lodi Memorial Hosp Assn Inc	8062	D	209 339-7441	16426
Lodi Memorial Hosp Assn Inc **(HQ)**	8062	A	209 334-3411	16427
Lodi Memorial Hosp Assn Inc	8062	D	209 339-7583	16428
Lodi Memorial Hosp Assn Inc	8011	E	209 333-3100	15508
Lodi News Sentinel	2711	E	209 369-2761	3455
Lodi Nut Company Inc	5159	E	209 334-2081	9509
Lodi Regional Hlth Systems Inc **(PA)**	8062	D	800 323-3360	16430
Lodi Unified School District	4151	E	209 331-7169	7440
Lowes Home Centers LLC	5031	C	209 339-2600	8574
LTS Rentals LLC **(PA)**	7513	E	209 334-4100	14470
Lustre-Cal LLC	2759	D	206 370-1600	3740
Lustre-Cal Nameplate Corp	2759	D	209 370-1600	3741
Mechanical Analysis/Repair Inc	7699	E	209 333-8478	14763
Mepco Label Systems	2759	D	209 946-0201	3742
Merced A Park California LP	6513	E	209 334-6565	10449
Miller Packing Company	2013	E	209 339-2310	2120
North Amrcn Specialty Pdts LLC	2821	C	209 365-7500	3807
Oak Ridge Winery LLC	2084	E	209 369-4768	2672
Odyssey Landscaping Co Inc	1771	D	209 369-6197	1898
Pacific AG & Vineyard Inc	0761	E	209 365-7222	362
Pacific Coast Producers	2033	D	209 334-3352	2236
Pacific Coast Producers **(PA)**	2033	B	209 367-8800	2237
Police Officers Assn Lodi	8641	D	209 333-6886	18450
PS Bajwa Inc	4231	E	209 334-2011	7710
Rdr Builders LP	1522	D	209 368-7561	763
River Maid Land Co A Cal Ll **(PA)**	0723	E	209 369-3586	304
Robert Mondavi Corporation	2084	A	209 365-2995	2698

GEOGRAPHIC

Employment Codes: A=Over 500 employees, B=251-500, C=101-250, D=51-100, E=20-50 F=10-19
2022 Northern California Business Directory and Buyers Guide
© Mergent Inc. 1-800-342-5647
1159

LODI, CA

Company	SIC	EMP	PHONE	ENTRY #
Sanborn Chevrolet Inc	7538	D	209 334-5000	14588
Scholten Surgical Instrs Inc	3841	F	209 365-1393	7030
Scientific Specialties Inc	3081	D	209 333-2120	4233
Shellpro Inc	3999	E	209 334-2081	7307
Spare-Time Inc	7997	D	209 334-4897	15150
Spare-Time Inc	7933	B	209 371-0241	14900
Stockton Delta Resort LLC	7033	D	209 369-1041	11622
Stokes Brothers Farms	0172	D	209 794-2380	76
Sutter Health	8062	C	209 366-2007	16590
Sutter Health	8062	C	209 334-3333	16626
Sutter Home Winery Inc	2084	C	209 368-4357	2735
T & T Trucking Inc (PA)	4213	E	800 692-3457	7600
T T S Construction Corporation	1629	E	209 333-7788	1181
Takt Manufacturing Inc	3999	F	408 250-4975	7313
Tamarack Springs Mutual Wtr Co (PA)	2711	F	209 369-2761	3485
Teresi Trucking LLC (PA)	4212	E	209 368-2472	7494
Tiger Lines LLC (HQ)	4213	D	209 334-4100	7601
Tusco Casting Corporation	3325	E	209 368-5137	4553
Twin Arbors LLC	7991	E	209 334-4897	14984
USA Products Group (PA)	3949	E	209 334-1460	7202
Valley Iron Works Inc	1791	E	209 368-7037	1933
Valley Landscaping & Maint Inc	0782	C	209 334-3659	508
Vander Lans & Sons Inc (PA)	3589	E	209 334-4115	5450
Victor Treatment Centers Inc	8361	C	209 465-1080	18201
Vienna Convalescent Hosp Inc	8051	C	209 368-7141	16152
Vino Farms Inc (PA)	0762	E	209 334-6975	389
Vino Farms LLC	5182	A	209 334-6975	9587
Walmart Inc	2752	F	209 368-6658	3713
Weibel Incorporated	2084	E	209 365-9463	2759
Wine & Roses LLC	7011	C	209 334-6988	11579
Wine Country Care Center	8051	E	209 334-3760	16167
Yard & Garden Ldscp Maint Inc	0781	E	209 369-9071	444

LOLETA, CA - Humboldt County

Company	SIC	EMP	PHONE	ENTRY #
Bear River Casino	7011	C	707 733-9644	10946
Bear River Casino (PA)	7011	D	707 733-9644	10947

LONG BARN, CA - Tuolumne County

Company	SIC	EMP	PHONE	ENTRY #
Califrnia Sthern Bptst Cnvntio	7032	D	209 965-3735	11598
Silicon Valley Monterey Bay Co	8641	D	209 965-3432	18470

LOOMIS, CA - Placer County

Company	SIC	EMP	PHONE	ENTRY #
Abshear Landscape Development	0781	E	916 660-1617	392
Bi Warehousing Inc	5013	D	916 652-4433	8444
DFI Technologies LLC	5045	D	916 378-4166	8692
Energy Saving Pros LLC	1711	E	916 259-2501	1255
Fletcher Plumbing Inc	1711	E	916 652-9769	1263
Gary Doupnik Manufacturing Inc	2452	E	916 652-9291	3250
High Ranch Nursery Inc	5193	E	916 652-9261	9635
Jamcor Corporation	5072	E	916 652-7713	8986
Jls Environmental Services Inc	8744	D	916 660-1525	19703
Js Contracting Services Inc	1522	E	916 625-1690	752
Knisley Welding Inc	7692	E	916 652-5891	14716
Leeman Brothers Drywall Inc	1742	E	916 652-9019	1688
Level 1 Roofing Inc	1761	E	888 505-0878	1817
Lobo Services Ltd	1522	E	916 660-9909	755
Loomis Bsin Vtrnary Clinic Inc	0742	E	916 652-5816	328
Motion Pro Inc	5013	E	650 594-9600	8456
Presentertek Inc	3669	E	916 251-7190	5893
Qantel Technologies Inc	3571	F	510 731-2080	5270
Ruffstuff Inc	3714	F	916 600-1945	6592
Sierra Trim Inc	1751	E	916 259-2966	1758
Studebaker Brown Electric Inc	1731	E	916 678-4660	1615
Truepoint Solutions LLC (PA)	7373	E	916 259-1293	13683
Valley Rock Lndscpe Material	3271	E	916 652-7209	4415

LOS ALTOS, CA - Santa Clara County

Company	SIC	EMP	PHONE	ENTRY #
Aae Systems Inc	7373	F	408 732-1710	13548
Adobe Animal Hospital	0742	D	650 948-9661	319
Altos Pedia Assoc A Prof Corp	8011	E	650 941-0550	15277
Attackiq Inc (PA)	7379	C	858 228-0864	13847
Childrens House of Los Altos	8351	E	650 968-9052	17901
Cohesity Inc	6733	B	650 968-4470	10793
Comity Designs Inc	7379	D	415 967-1530	13873
Cothera Biopharma Inc	2834	E	510 364-4913	3887
Covenant Care California LLC	8051	D	650 941-5255	15972
Creative Lrng Ctr Preschool	8351	E	650 823-1496	17920
Epicurean Group	8741	B	650 947-6800	19328
Hirsch Machine Inc	3599	E	408 738-8844	5537
Humangood Norcal	8059	D	650 948-8291	16242
Jemstep Inc	7372	E	650 966-6500	13252
JP Research Inc	8748	D	650 559-5999	19801
Kisco Senior Living LLC	6513	E	650 948-7337	10447
Los Altos Golf and Country CLB	7997	D	650 947-3100	15105
Los Altos Hotel Associates LLC	7011	D	650 559-7890	11269
Markov Corporation	8732	E	650 207-9445	19169
Maxval Group Inc (PA)	8748	D	650 472-0644	19817
Midpennsula Rgnal Open Space D	8999	D	650 691-1200	19912
Older Adults Care MGT Inc (PA)	8322	C	650 329-1411	17663
Organztonal Prfmce Systems Inc	7371	E	650 968-7032	12656
Powerflex Systems LLC	3621	E	650 469-3392	5666
Predictspring Inc	7372	E	650 917-9052	13383
Primarydata (PA)	7371	E	650 422-3800	12697
R J Dailey Construction Co	1521	E	650 948-5196	691
Renovorx Inc	3841	F	650 284-4433	7026
Scimage Inc	7371	E	650 694-4858	12766
Select Communications Inc	2721	E	650 948-9000	3514
The David Lcile Pckard Fndtion	8699	D	650 917-7167	18601
Thoits Love Herschberger & McL	8111	E	650 327-4200	17381
Varmour Networks Inc (PA)	7372	D	650 564-5100	13511

LOS ALTOS HILLS, CA - Santa Clara County

Company	SIC	EMP	PHONE	ENTRY #
First Baptist Church Los Altos	8351	D	650 948-3738	17935
Foothll-De Anza Cmnty Cllege D	4832	B	650 949-7260	8025
Fremont Hills Country Club	7997	E	650 948-8261	15092
Idea Travel Company	4724	A	650 948-0207	7801
Impact Destinations & Events	7299	D	415 766-4170	11721
Ministry Services of The Daugh	6733	D	650 917-4500	10799
Trust For Hidden Villa	7032	E	650 949-8650	11612

LOS BANOS, CA - Merced County

Company	SIC	EMP	PHONE	ENTRY #
A Rpac Ltd Liability Company	0723	E	209 826-0272	266
Azusa Rock LLC	3273	E	209 826-5066	4459
Bowles Farming Company Inc	0191	D	209 827-3000	148
Cemex Corp	5032	E	800 992-3639	8622
Cheese Administrative Corp Inc	2022	E	209 826-3744	2144
Espanas Mexican Restaurant	7011	D	209 826-4041	11084
Ingomar Packing Company LLC (PA)	2033	E	209 826-9494	2216
JN Restaurants Inc (PA)	5087	B	209 710-8385	9144
Kagome Inc (HQ)	2033	C	209 826-8850	2217
Karthikeya Devireddy MD Inc	8011	E	209 826-2222	15494
Liberty Packing Company LLC	7389	E	209 826-7100	14322
Los Banos Abattoir Co	2011	E	209 826-2212	2100
Los Banos Veterinary Clinic	0741	E	209 826-5860	317
McElvany Inc	1623	D	209 826-1102	1118
Morning Star Company	2033	B	209 827-2724	2226
Morning Star Packing Co LP	2033	E	209 826-8000	2227
Pacific Gas and Electric Co	4911	C	209 826-5131	8173
Para & Palli Inc	8051	E	209 826-0790	16092
Ranchwood Contractors Inc	1542	D	209 826-6200	942
Rodoni Dairy Farms	0241	D	209 826-2978	222
San Luis Dlta-Mendota Wtr Auth (PA)	4971	E	209 826-9696	8417
Santos Ford Inc	5013	E	209 826-4921	8464
Soares Dairy Farms Inc	0241	D	209 826-3414	223
Sutter Health	8062	C	209 827-4866	16605
Teixeira and Sons LLC (PA)	0131	C	209 827-9800	12
Triangle Rock Product Inc	5032	E	209 826-5066	8636
Turlock Hlth & Fitnes Ctr Inc	7991	E	209 826-6011	14982
Wolfsen Incorporated	0131	C	209 827-7700	14

LOS GATOS, CA - Santa Clara County

Company	SIC	EMP	PHONE	ENTRY #
Adaptive Insights LLC	2323	D	408 656-4229	2986
Adara Power Inc	3691	F	844 223-2969	6485
Addappt Inc	7372	F	408 402-5468	12953
Addisn-Pnzak Jwish Cmnty Ctr S	7991	C	408 358-3636	14923
Aridis Pharmaceuticals Inc	2834	E	408 385-1742	3854
Assembly Systems (PA)	3423	E	408 395-5313	4604
Associated Pathology Med Group	8071	D	408 399-5010	16773
Auto World Car Wash LLC	7542	A	408 345-6532	14628
Bainbridge and Associates Inc	1521	E	408 356-5040	615
Beaver Dam Health Care Center	8051	E	408 356-8136	15928
Beaver Dam Health Care Center	8051	E	408 356-9151	15941
Bona Furtuna LLC (PA)	5199	D	800 380-8819	9647
Brightsign LLC	3993	E	408 852-9263	7221
Calvary Church Los Gatos Cal (PA)	8351	D	408 358-8871	17873
Calvary Church Los Gatos Cal	8351	E	408 356-6776	17874
Calvary Church Los Gatos Cal	8351	E	408 356-5126	17875
Cirtec Medical Corp	3841	E	408 395-0443	6962
Courtside Tennis Club	7997	E	408 395-7111	15079
Covia Communities	8361	C	408 354-0211	18088
Cryptic Studios Inc	3944	E	408 399-1969	7175
D Carlson Construction Inc (PA)	1521	E	408 354-2893	629
Depuy Synthes Products Inc	3841	F	408 246-4300	6969
Dicom Systems Inc	7371	F	415 684-8790	12389
E-Fuel Corporation	3699	E	408 267-2667	6515
Ebreastimaging LLC (PA)	8071	E	408 800-5247	16780
Einstein Noah Rest Group Inc	2022	C	408 358-5895	2147
Emq Familiesfirst	8322	E	408 354-0149	17545
Facilitron Inc (PA)	7372	E	800 272-2962	13157
Foodlink Online LLC	7372	E	408 395-7280	13169
Funding Pace Group LLC	6153	D	844 873-7223	9871
Good Samaritan Hospital LP	8062	C	408 358-8414	16382
Good Samaritan Hospital LP	8062	C	408 356-4111	16383
Humangood Norcal	8059	D	408 357-1100	16243
I Merit Inc (PA)	7374	E	650 777-7857	13720
Infogain Corporation (PA)	7379	C	408 355-6000	13911
Jennifer Lee MD Inc (PA)	8011	D	408 866-1135	15440
Joie De Vivre Hospitality LLC	7011	D	408 335-1700	11212
La Rinconada Country Club Inc (PA)	7997	D	408 395-4181	15101
Lark Avenue Car Wash	7542	D	408 356-2525	14647
Los Gatos Dog & Cat Hospital	0742	E	408 354-6474	329
Los Gatos Imaging Center Ltd	8011	D	408 374-8897	15510
Los Gatos Saratoga Dept of Com	8351	C	408 354-8700	17967
Los Gatos Swim and Racquet CLB	7991	D	408 356-2136	14961
Los Olivos Wns Med Group Inc (PA)	8011	E	408 356-0431	15511
Lrimg Inc	8011	D	408 358-2479	15512
Mark/Space Inc (PA)	7372	E	408 399-5300	13292
McCarthy Ranch	2452	F	408 356-2300	3253
Mehus Construction Inc	1521	E	408 395-2388	673
Netflix Inc	7841	A	408 540-3700	14832
Netflix Inc (PA)	7841	A	408 540-3700	14833
Netflix Studios LLC (HQ)	7819	A	408 540-3700	14802
Orthonorcal Inc	8011	E	408 356-0464	15573
Payment Reservations Inc	7389	E	480 770-9064	14355
Qualium Corp (PA)	8011	D	408 402-3697	15636
SA Photonics Inc	8748	C	408 560-3500	19851

	SIC	EMP	PHONE	ENTRY #
Sadra Medical Inc	3841	D	408 370-1550	7028
Samaritan Family Practice	8011	E	408 358-1911	15660
Sanco Pipelines Incorporated	1623	E	408 377-2793	1134
Santa Clara Vly Wtr Dst Pub Fc	4941	C	408 395-8121	8269
Semotus Inc	7372	E	408 667-2046	13435
Semotus Solutions Inc	7372	F	408 367-1745	13436
Sierra Nevada Corporation	3812	E	408 395-2004	6683
Sierra Weatherization Co Inc	7311	E	408 354-1900	11784
Splash Data Inc	7371	F	408 355-4508	12810
Spotlight Therapy Inc	8082	E	408 649-7349	16948
Superior Sensor Technology Inc	3822	E	408 703-2950	6706
Tascent Inc	3699	F	650 799-4611	6544
Tela Innovations Inc	3674	E	408 558-6300	6327
Tenet Healthsystem Medical Inc	8062	C	408 378-6131	16687
Testarossa Vineyards LLC	2084	E	408 354-6150	2739
Trevi Partners A Calif LP	7011	E	408 395-7070	11540
Triple Hs Inc **(PA)**	8999	D	408 458-3200	19918
US Carenet Services LLC	8082	C	408 378-6131	16964
Visit Healthcare Inc	2836	E	408 890-6648	4061
Xicato Inc **(PA)**	3645	E	866 223-8395	5730
Yoga Source Partners LLC	7999	D	408 402-9642	15265
Zyante Inc	5192	D	510 541-4434	9620
Automation & Entertainment Inc	3491	E	408 353-4223	4953
David Bruce Winery Inc	2084	F	408 354-4214	2545
Rhys Vineyards LLC	2084	E	650 419-2050	2695
South Skyline Firefighters	3569	F	408 354-0025	5233

LOTUS, CA - El Dorado County

	SIC	EMP	PHONE	ENTRY #
Mother Lode River Trips Ltd	7999	E	530 626-4187	15221

LOWER LAKE, CA - Lake County

	SIC	EMP	PHONE	ENTRY #
Aloha Bay	3999	E	707 994-3267	7268
Epidendio Construction Inc	1771	E	707 994-5100	1867
Jim Jonas Inc	5171	E	707 994-5911	9526
Parker Plastics Inc	3089	E	707 994-6363	4310
Shannon Ridge Inc	2084	E	707 994-9656	2714

LOYALTON, CA - Sierra County

	SIC	EMP	PHONE	ENTRY #
Eastern Plumas Health Care	8051	D	530 993-1225	15980

MADERA, CA - Madera County

	SIC	EMP	PHONE	ENTRY #
Adventist Hlth Systm/West Corp	8062	D	559 645-4191	16307
B & C Chandler Trucking Inc	4212	E	559 674-7181	7451
B-K Lighting Inc	3645	D	559 438-5800	5723
Baker Custom Cabinets Inc	2434	F	559 675-1395	3168
Baltimore Aircoil Company Inc	3585	C	559 673-9231	5429
Beaver Dam Health Care Center	8051	E	559 673-9278	15934
Benton Enterprises LLC	0173	E	559 664-0800	83
Better Cleaning Systems Inc	3635	E	559 673-5700	5707
California Custom Proc LLC	1541	E	559 416-5122	791
Camarena Health **(PA)**	8011	C	559 664-4000	15317
Canandaigua Wine Company Inc	5182	C	559 673-7071	9569
Carris Reels California Inc **(HQ)**	2499	E	802 733-9111	3266
Community Action Prtnr Mdera C **(PA)**	8351	C	559 673-9173	17910
Community Action Prtnr Mdera C	8399	D	559 661-1000	18227
Community Intgrted Work Prgram	8331	E	559 673-5174	17807
Constllation Brnds US Oprtons I	5182	A	559 485-0141	9572
Costa View Farms	0241	E	559 675-3131	209
Cosyns Farms	0173	E	559 674-6283	86
County of Los Angeles	8322	E	559 675-7739	17509
Creekside Farming Company	0762	E	559 674-9999	370
Darrell Herzog Enterprises	1761	E	559 307-4566	1797
Design Industries Inc	3272	D	559 675-3535	4430
Diamond Communications Inc	7382	E	559 673-5925	14128
Domries Enterprises Inc	3523	E	559 485-4306	5003
Eurodrip USA Inc	5083	D	559 674-2670	9035
Eye Q Vision Care	8011	E	559 673-8055	15396
Farmland Management Services	0762	E	559 674-4305	375
First Student Inc	4151	C	559 661-7433	7439
Fitzgrald Alvrez Cmmo A Prof L	8111	E	559 674-4696	17267
Florestone Products Co **(PA)**	3088	E	559 661-4171	4250
Gardner Family Ltd Partnership	3429	E	559 675-8149	4616
Golden Vly Grape Jice Wine LLC **(PA)**	2084	E	559 661-4657	2601
Herman Produce Sales LLC	5148	D	559 661-8253	9410
Herman Produce Sales LLC **(PA)**	5148	E	559 871-3161	9411
Horn Machine Tools Inc **(PA)**	3542	E	559 431-4131	5079
Hulling Company	0723	E	559 674-1896	290
Iest Family Farms	0241	D	559 674-9417	214
Innovtive Rttional Molding Inc	3089	E	559 673-4764	4291
John Bean Technologies Corp	3556	C	559 661-3200	5132
Kings View	7929	E	559 673-0167	14873
Lamanuzzi & Pantaleo LLC **(PA)**	0172	D	559 432-3170	62
Lees Concrete Materials Inc	3273	D	559 486-2440	4492
Lion Raisins Inc	0191	C	559 662-8686	179
Lowes Home Centers LLC	5031	C	559 416-4000	8586
Madera Cmnty Hosp Foundation	8062	D	559 673-5101	16433
Madera Cnty Msqito Vctor Ctrl	7342	E	559 662-8880	11902
Madera Community Hospital	8062	E	559 675-5530	16434
Madera Community Hospital **(PA)**	8062	A	559 675-5555	16436
Madera Convalescent Hosp Inc **(PA)**	8051	C	559 673-9228	16039
Madera Family Med Group Inc	8011	D	559 673-3000	15515
Madera Irrigation District	4941	E	559 673-3514	8252
Meridian Growers Proc Inc	2068	F	559 458-7272	2449
Mid Valley Labor Services Inc	7361	E	559 661-6390	12108
Moore Quality Galvanizing Inc	3479	E	559 673-2822	4939
Moore Quality Galvanizing LP	3479	E	559 673-2822	4940
Mpt Inc	2448	E	559 673-1552	3226
Nutra-Blend LLC	2048	E	559 661-6161	2350
Our Huse Rsdntial Care Ctr Inc	8059	E	559 674-8670	16256
Packageone Inc **(PA)**	2653	E	559 662-1910	3361
Parmar Ashok	7011	D	559 661-1131	11359
Performance Trailer Inc	3715	E	559 673-6300	6605
Pistoresi Amblnce Svc of Mdera	4119	D	559 673-8004	7395
Purls Sheet Metal & AC	1711	E	559 674-2774	1340
Quady LLC **(PA)**	2084	E	559 673-8068	2690
Quady Winery Inc	2084	F	559 673-8068	2691
Richard Iest Dairy Inc	0139	D	559 673-2635	20
Richie Iest Farms Inc	0241	E	559 675-8658	221
Sierra Valley Almonds LLC	0173	E	559 662-8900	93
Span Construction & Engrg Inc **(PA)**	1542	D	559 661-1111	967
Star Finishes Inc	3479	E	559 261-1076	4951
Steel Structures Inc	3443	E	559 673-8021	4732
Stellar Distributing Inc	5148	B	559 664-8400	9431
Talley Oil Inc	1611	E	559 673-9011	1076
Talley Transportation	4212	D	559 673-9013	7493
Teka Illumination Inc	3648	F	559 438-5800	5750
Tranpak Inc	2448	E	800 827-2474	3230
Valley Childrens Hospital	8062	C	559 353-6425	16704
Valley Childrens Hospital **(PA)**	8062	A	559 353-3000	16705
Valley Childrens Medical Group	8069	D	559 353-6241	16771
Valley Chld Hlthcare Fundation	8011	A	559 353-3000	15784
Victor Packing Inc	2034	E	559 673-5908	2274
Warnock Food Products Inc	2096	D	559 661-4845	2859

MAMMOTH LAKES, CA - Mono County

	SIC	EMP	PHONE	ENTRY #
1849 Homeowners Association	7041	E	760 934-7525	11623
Fluidix Inc **(PA)**	3567	E	760 935-2016	5215
Footloose Incorporated	7999	E	760 934-2400	15204
Horizon Cal Publications Inc	2711	E	760 934-3929	3446
Horizons 4 Condominiums Inc	8641	D	760 934-6779	18432
Mammoth Community Water Dst	4941	E	760 934-2596	8253
Mammoth Disposal Company	4953	D	760 934-2201	8341
Mammoth Mountain Ski Area LLC **(DH)**	7011	B	760 934-2571	11282
Sierra Nevada Lodge	7011	D	760 934-2515	11478
Snowcreek Property Management	6531	E	760 934-3333	10663
Southern Mono Healthcare Dst	8062	B	760 934-3311	16533
Westin Monache	7011	E	760 934-0400	11573

MANTECA, CA - San Joaquin County

	SIC	EMP	PHONE	ENTRY #
1st Light Energy Inc **(PA)**	1799	E	209 824-5500	1996
A C Trucking Inc	4213	E	209 823-3224	7501
American Crane Rental Inc	7353	D	209 838-8815	12016
American Modular Systems Inc	2452	D	209 825-1921	3248
B R Funsten & Co	5023	D	209 825-5375	8506
Bay Area Cnstr Framers Inc	1751	C	925 454-8514	1731
Bbva USA	6022	C	209 239-1381	9708
Betts Company	3493	D	209 599-1824	4956
Bimbo Bakeries Usa Inc	2051	F	209 825-8647	2370
C&N Reinforcing Inc	1791	E	209 399-2022	1922
Cal-West Concrete Cutting Inc	1771	C	209 823-2236	1856
California Stl Stair Rail Mfr	3312	E	209 824-1785	4540
Casino Real Inc	7011	E	209 239-1455	10994
Cen Cal Plastering Inc **(PA)**	1742	B	209 858-1045	1666
Clearpath Workforce MGT Inc	7363	C	209 239-8700	12164
Cynthia Dunlap Dutra	0781	E	209 456-1531	410
Delicato Vineyards LLC **(PA)**	2084	C	209 824-3600	2548
Dkw Precision Machining Inc	3599	E	209 824-7899	5509
Doctors Hospital Manteca Inc	8062	B	209 823-3111	16356
Drd Hospitality Inc	7011	E	916 952-6552	11060
E-M Manufacturing Inc	3444	F	209 825-1800	4757
Eckert Cold Storage Company	4222	C	209 823-3181	7678
Forward Inc	4953	C	209 982-4298	8332
Frontier California Inc	4813	B	209 239-4128	7951
H Lima Company Inc	1499	E	209 239-6787	602
Heritage Estates Inc	8361	D	209 823-6061	18130
J M Equipment Company Inc **(PA)**	7359	D	209 522-3271	12050
Kaiser Foundation Hospitals	6324	C	209 825-3700	10138
Karma Inc	8051	C	209 239-1222	16030
Lee Jennings Target Ex Inc	4731	D	209 823-0071	7845
Linden Steel & Cnstr Inc	1389	E	209 239-2160	568
Lowery-Pena Cnstr Co Inc	1522	E	209 328-2050	756
Manteca Ford-Mercury Inc	7538	E	209 239-3561	14577
Manteca Hampton Inn & Suites	7011	E	209 823-1926	11283
Manteca Unified School Dst	8351	E	209 239-3689	17968
McLane Foodservice Dist Inc	5141	C	209 823-7157	9278
Morris Newspaper Corp Cal **(HQ)**	2711	D	209 249-3500	3462
Palm Haven Nursing & Rehab LLC	8051	C	209 823-1788	16091
Price Rubber Company Inc	3052	E	209 239-7478	4200
Propane Cnstr & Meter Svcs **(PA)**	5172	C	866 587-7411	9535
Raymus Development & Sales Inc **(PA)**	6552	E	209 823-3148	10713
RES-Care Inc	8052	D	800 866-0860	16199
Resers Fine Foods Inc	2099	E	503 643-6431	2938
S K S Enterprises Inc **(PA)**	0252	E	209 599-4095	232
Sagepoint Financial Inc	6282	D	209 825-8888	10059
San Bernabe Vineyards LLC	2084	F	209 824-3501	2708
South San Jquin Irrigation Dst	4941	D	209 249-4600	8276
Stanley Access Tech LLC	3423	E	209 221-4066	4608
Sunnyvalley Smoked Meats Inc	2013	C	209 825-0288	2126
Tenet Healthsystem Medical Inc	8062	C	209 823-3111	16686
Transforce Inc	7363	E	209 952-2573	12202
United Crbral Plsy Assn San Jq	8399	D	209 239-3066	18256
Valley Oak Dental Group	8021	E	209 823-9341	15862
Van Groningen & Sons Inc	0191	B	209 982-5248	194
Villara Corporation	1711	E	209 824-1082	1392
Watts Equipment Company	5084	E	209 825-1700	9104

GEOGRAPHIC

Employment Codes: A=Over 500 employees, B=251-500, C=101-250, D=51-100, E=20-50 F=10-19

2022 Northern California Business Directory and Buyers Guide
© Mergent Inc. 1-800-342-5647
1161

MANTON, CA — GEOGRAPHIC SECTION

	SIC	EMP	PHONE	ENTRY #
MANTON, CA - Tehama County				
Pacific Gas and Electric Co	4911	C	530 474-3333	8163
MARIPOSA, CA - Mariposa County				
35-A District AG Assn	7389	E	209 966-2432	14187
Haztech Systems Inc	2865	E	209 966-8088	4116
John C Fremont Healthcare Dst	8062	B	209 966-3631	16389
John C Fremont Hosp Foundation	8062	E	209 966-0850	16390
MARSHALL, CA - Marin County				
Nicks Cove Inc	7011	D	415 663-1033	11328
MARTELL, CA - Amador County				
Ampine LLC (HQ)	2436	F	209 223-6091	3197
MARTINEZ, CA - Contra Costa County				
Baja Construction Co Inc (PA)	1791	D	925 229-0732	1921
Bridgestone Americas	7538	D	925 372-9056	14550
Brightview Landscape Svcs Inc	0781	C	925 957-8831	400
Browning-Ferris Inds Cal Inc	4953	E	925 313-8901	8312
Careonsite Inc	8011	D	562 437-0381	15328
Central Contra Costa Sani Dst	4952	E	925 228-9500	8279
Contra Costa County	4812	C	925 313-1323	7905
Contra Costa Federal Inc (DH)	1731	B	925 229-4250	1485
Contra Costa Federal Credit Un (PA)	6061	E	925 228-7550	9781
Contra Csta Rgonal Med Ctr Aux	8011	D	925 370-5000	15365
County of Contra Costa	8062	C	925 370-5000	16339
County of Contra Costa	8099	E	510 463-7325	17127
County Quarry Products	4953	E	925 682-0707	8320
Document Proc Solutions Inc	2621	E	925 839-1182	3343
Eco Services Operations Corp	2819	E	925 313-8224	3783
Enginrrg/Rmdtion Rsrces Group (PA)	4959	D	925 839-2200	8398
Euv Tech Inc	3826	F	925 229-4388	6827
Hamilton Tree Service Inc	0783	E	925 228-1010	518
Harmony Home Associated	8361	E	925 256-6303	18128
Kaiser Foundation Hospitals	6733	D	925 372-1000	10796
Legacy and Nursing Rehab	8051	D	925 228-8383	16035
Longs Drug Stores Cal Inc	7384	E	925 370-8075	14168
Mason Bpp Inc	1521	E	925 256-1092	669
Michael Telfer (PA)	1611	D	925 228-1515	1059
Molinas Pntg Wallcovering Inc	1721	D	925 228-7487	1421
Permanente Medical Group Inc	8011	A	925 372-1000	15600
PG Emminger Inc	2541	E	925 313-5830	3318
Plant Maintenance Inc	7363	D	925 228-3285	12187
Power Engineers Incorporated	8711	D	925 372-9284	18793
R M Harris Company Inc	1622	D	925 335-3000	1085
Raymond - Northern Cal Inc	1742	D	925 602-4910	1701
RE Milano Plumbing Corp	1711	E	925 500-1372	1344
Redstone Print & Mail Inc	2752	C	925 335-9090	3692
Ritter Manufacturing Inc	5084	F	925 757-7296	9089
Robert L Brown Cnstr Inc	1521	E	925 228-4944	698
Schetter Electric Inc	1731	C	925 228-2424	1601
Sentry Life Insurance Company	6411	E	925 370-7339	10348
Shaker Cabinet Co (PA)	2434	E	925 286-6066	3191
Sonnikson and Stordahl Cnstr	1711	E	925 229-4028	1365
Ucd Ncadc	8011	E	925 372-2485	15747
Veterans Health Administration	8011	C	925 372-2000	15796
Veterans Health Administration	8011	C	925 372-2076	15806
Wastexperts Incorporated	8741	D	925 484-1057	19420
Waters Moving & Storage Inc	4212	D	925 372-0914	7498
YWCA Contra Costa/Sacramento (PA)	8322	E	925 372-4213	17792
MARYSVILLE, CA - Yuba County				
A Teichert & Son Inc	1442	E	530 749-1230	586
A Teichert & Son Inc	1442	E	530 743-6111	587
Advantage Framing Solutions	1542	E	530 742-7660	820
Childrens Protective Services	8322	D	530 749-6311	17487
County of Yuba	8322	D	530 741-6275	17519
County of Yuba	8322	E	530 749-6471	17520
County of Yuba	8322	E	530 749-7550	17521
County of Yuba	8361	D	530 741-6371	18084
County of Yuba	8111	D	530 749-7770	17240
Ecmd Inc	2431	E	530 741-0769	3131
Frank M Booth Inc (PA)	1711	D	530 742-7134	1266
Freemont Rideout Health Group	8062	D	530 751-4270	16371
Fremont Hospital	8062	C	530 751-4000	16373
Gino Morena Enterprises LLC	7241	B	530 788-0053	11698
Homewood Components Inc	2439	E	530 743-8855	3209
Hust Brothers Inc (PA)	6531	E	530 743-1561	10578
Mariani Packing Co Inc	2034	E	530 749-6565	2262
Melon Holdings LLC	8051	E	530 742-7311	16063
Pacific Gas and Electric Co	4911	C	800 743-5000	8154
Peach Tree Healthcare	8011	E	530 749-3242	15588
Plumas Lake Golf and Cntry CLB	7997	E	530 742-3201	15123
Recology Yuba-Sutter	4953	D	530 743-6933	8356
Reyes Coca-Cola Bottling LLC	2086	D	530 743-6533	2806
Rideout Memorial Hospital (HQ)	8062	A	530 749-4416	16490
Team Casing	1389	E	530 742-5425	573
US Pipe Fabrication LLC	3084	E	530 742-5171	4236
MATHER, CA - Sacramento County				
Bloodsource Inc (PA)	8099	B	916 456-1500	17106
Califrnia Elctrnic Asset Rcver	4953	E	916 388-1777	8315
Construction Innovations LLC	3699	C	855 725-9555	6511
Mather Aviation LLC (PA)	4581	E	916 364-4711	7775
Mather Community Campus (PA)	8361	D	916 228-3100	18144
Reynen & Bardis Cnstr LLC (PA)	1521	E	916 366-3665	697
Sutter Health	8051	D	916 454-8200	16140
Sutter Valley Med Foundation	8741	D	916 454-8449	19405
United Parcel Service Inc	4512	D	916 231-0814	7742
Veterans Health Administration	8011	C	916 366-5427	15788
Veterans Health Administration	8011	C	916 843-7000	15802
Wagner Krkmn Blne Klmp & Ymns (PA)	8111	E	916 920-5286	17388
MAXWELL, CA - Colusa County				
American Rice Inc	2044	D	530 438-2265	2315
California Heritage Mills Inc	2044	E	530 438-2100	2317
Emerald Farms LLC	0191	E	530 438-2133	163
Pacific Metal Buildings Inc	3448	F	530 438-2777	4854
MCCLELLAN, CA - Sacramento County				
Aviate Enterprises Inc	3585	D	916 993-4000	5428
Berger Steel Corporation	3441	E	916 640-8778	4646
Cablecom LLC	7629	E	916 891-2400	14691
California Shock Truma A Rescue (PA)	4119	D	916 921-4000	7379
Enterprise Rnt—car Scrmnto LL	7514	E	916 648-1725	14485
Faneuil Inc	7361	B	757 722-4095	12087
Gmj Air Shuttle LLC	4111	D	916 884-2001	7335
Lionsgate Ht & Conference Ctr	7011	D	916 643-6222	11262
Luxer Corporation	2521	C	415 390-0123	3307
McClellan Business Park LLC	8742	D	916 965-7100	19569
McClellan Hospitality Svcs LLC	7011	D	916 965-7100	11292
McClellan Realty LLC	6531	E	916 965-7100	10616
Meriliz Incorporated	2752	E	916 923-3663	3676
Monument Security Inc (PA)	7381	C	916 564-4234	14077
Northrop Grumman Systems Corp	3812	E	916 570-4454	6678
PCA Central Cal Corrugated LLC	2653	E	916 614-0580	3363
Polar Service Center	3542	E	916 643-4689	5080
Rov Enterprises Inc	1711	E	916 448-2672	1351
Sbm Management Services LP	7349	B	866 855-2211	11994
Sbm Site Services LLC (PA)	7349	D	916 922-7600	11995
Shyft Group Inc	3711	E	916 921-2639	6559
Siemens Mobility Inc	7538	E	916 621-2700	14592
Stay Safe Solutions Inc	7363	E	916 640-1300	12201
Traffic Management Inc	8741	E	916 394-2200	19411
United States Cold Storage Inc	2097	E	916 640-2800	2862
Villara Corporation (PA)	1711	B	916 646-2700	1391
Weatherly Aircraft Company	3721	E	916 640-0120	6620
MCCLOUD, CA - Siskiyou County				
Terramai	2421	E	530 964-2740	3118
MCKINLEYVILLE, CA - Humboldt County				
Beau Pre Corporation	7997	E	707 839-2342	15058
Cabinets By Andy Inc	2434	F	707 839-9425	3171
Coast Central Credit Union	6061	E	707 445-8801	9778
Doors Unlimited	5031	E	707 822-5959	8543
Ford Logging Inc	2411	E	707 840-9442	3060
Humboldt Sanitation Co	4212	D	707 839-3285	7474
Kernen Construction	1541	D	707 826-8686	800
McKinleyville Cmnty Svcs Dst	4952	E	707 839-3251	8285
Wild Planet Foods Inc (DH)	5146	D	707 840-9116	9374
MENDOCINO, CA - Mendocino County				
Big River Ltd-Design	7011	D	707 937-5615	10962
Hill House Associates	7011	E	707 937-0554	11136
Maccallum House Restaurant	7011	E	707 937-0289	11280
Mendocino Hotel & Resort Corp	7011	D	707 937-0511	11294
MENDOTA, CA - Fresno County				
Philon Pappas Co	0723	E	559 655-4282	302
Pomwonderful LLC	5149	D	310 966-5800	9475
S & S Ranch Inc	0721	D	559 655-3491	257
S Stamoules Inc	0723	A	559 655-9777	306
MENLO PARK, CA - San Mateo County				
3jam Inc	3661	F	415 867-1339	5783
A-A Lock & Alarm Inc (PA)	5087	E	650 326-9020	9140
Accel-KKR Capitl Partners V LP (PA)	6799	B	650 289-2460	10829
Accel-KKR Company LLC (PA)	6799	E	650 289-2460	10830
Aegea Medical Inc	3841	E	650 701-1125	6936
Ah Parallel Fund V LP	6799	E	650 798-3900	10831
Aha Labs Inc	7372	D	650 575-1425	12964
Allay Therapeutics Inc	3841	E	650 514-6284	6938
Alto International School	8351	E	650 324-8617	17855
Astero Bio Corporation	3841	E	800 749-0898	6945
Avitas Systems Inc	7389	D	650 233-3900	14210
Baynetwork Inc (PA)	5045	D	650 561-8120	8674
Billiontoone Inc	8071	E	650 666-6443	16774
Boys & Girls CLB of Peninsula	7997	E	650 322-6255	15063
Brightview Landscape Svcs Inc	0781	C	650 289-9324	401
Burr Pilger Mayer Inc	8721	E	650 855-6800	18941
Cal Care Inc	8741	E	650 325-8600	19312
Care Indeed Inc (PA)	8082	D	650 800-7645	16867
Carr & Ferrell LLP (PA)	8111	E	650 812-3400	17225
Cataphora Inc (PA)	7371	D	650 622-9840	12331
Century Pk Capitl Partners LLC	6799	D	650 324-1956	10838
Cfkba Inc (PA)	3357	E	650 847-3900	4568
Continuumglobal Inc (PA)	8742	A	415 685-3302	19479
Corcept Therapeutics Inc	2834	C	650 327-3270	3885
Cornerstone Research Inc (PA)	8748	D	650 853-1660	19754
Countrymain Associates Inc	3651	F	650 364-9988	5753
Coyne & Blanchard Inc	2721	D	650 326-6040	3495
Credence Medsystems Inc	3841	F	844 263-3797	6967
Critchfield Mechanical Inc	1711	B	650 321-7801	1244
Crosslink Capital Inc	6799	E	415 617-1800	10839
D E Shaw Valence LLC	6799	C	650 926-9460	10841
Davis Polk & Wardwell LLP	8111	D	650 752-2000	17248

GEOGRAPHIC SECTION MILL VALLEY, CA

	SIC	EMP	PHONE	ENTRY #
Dcm Management Inc	6726	E	650 233-1400	10776
Dermira Inc	2834	B	650 421-7200	3891
Dfj Management LLC	6799	E	650 233-9000	10842
Diageo North America Inc	2085	E	650 329-3220	2770
Drivescale Inc	7372	E	408 849-4651	13126
Encore Technical Staffing LLC **(PA)**	7363	E	541 396-1885	12169
Ensighten Inc **(HQ)**	8742	C	650 249-4712	19503
Evalve Inc	3494	D	650 330-8100	4960
Exponent Inc **(PA)**	8711	B	650 326-9400	18708
Facebook	7375	D	650 823-7128	13788
Fcl Tech Inc	8734	E	650 656-7570	19273
Finsix Corporation	7373	E	650 285-6400	13588
First Republic Bank	6022	D	650 233-8880	9721
First Republic Bank	6022	D	650 470-8888	9729
Gachina Landscape MGT Inc	0781	B	650 853-0400	416
Garda CL West Inc	7381	E	650 617-4548	14063
Gauss Surgical Inc	3841	E	650 949-4153	6976
GE Ventures Inc	3841	F	650 233-3900	6977
Global Meddata Inc **(PA)**	8099	D	650 369-9734	17149
Grail LLC **(HQ)**	2834	B	833 694-2553	3920
Guy Plumbing & Heating Inc	1711	E	650 323-8415	1276
Hewlett Wlliam Flora Fndation	8699	D	650 234-4500	18570
Hines Interests Ltd Partnr	6531	C	650 518-6139	10576
Hogan Lovells US LLP	8111	D	650 463-4000	17292
Ideal Aerosmith Inc	8734	F	650 353-3641	19275
Insignia Environmental	8748	D	650 321-6787	19796
Institutional Ventr MGT X LLC	7389	E	650 854-0132	14305
Intersect Ent Inc **(PA)**	3841	B	650 641-2100	6985
Jasper Ridge Partners	6726	E	650 494-4800	10778
Jobtrain Inc	8331	E	650 330-6429	17820
Jorgensen Sgel Mc Clure Flgel	8111	E	650 324-9300	17299
Khosla Ventures LLC	6799	E	650 376-8500	10860
Kind Homecare Inc	8082	D	888 885-5463	16904
Kintara Therapeutics Inc	2834	F	650 269-1984	3937
Kleiner Prkins Cfeld Byers LLC **(PA)**	6799	E	650 233-2750	10862
Knob Hill Oil & Gas Co	0191	E	650 328-0820	178
Kohlberg Kravis Roberts Co LP	6799	D	650 233-6560	10863
Kpcb Holdings Inc **(PA)**	6799	E	650 233-2750	10864
L3 Technologies Inc	3663	C	650 326-9500	5852
Lattice Data Inc	7372	E	650 800-7262	13274
Lifemoves **(PA)**	8699	E	650 685-5880	18578
Lovazzano Mechanical Inc	1711	D	650 367-6216	1308
Makena Capital Management LLC	6799	D	650 926-0510	10866
Maxar Space LLC	4225	A	650 852-4000	7694
Mayfield Fund	6799	E	650 854-5560	10867
Mc Graw Commercial Insur Svc **(PA)**	6411	D	650 780-4800	10311
Mdv Management Company LLC	6799	E	650 233-9301	10868
Merrill Lynch Pierce Fenner	6211	D	650 473-7888	9980
Meta Platforms Inc **(PA)**	7375	A	650 543-4800	13800
Mind Garden Inc	2741	F	650 322-6300	3582
Morgenthler MGT Prtners VI LLC	6799	A	650 388-7600	10869
Motherly Inc	2741	E	917 860-9926	3584
MPA Networks Inc	7373	E	650 566-8800	13637
New Enterprise Associates Inc	6799	E	650 854-9499	10872
Novo Construction Inc **(PA)**	1542	D	650 701-1500	932
Oak Hill Capital MGT LLC	6799	A	650 234-0500	10874
Oak Hill Capital Partners LP	8082	A	650 234-0500	16919
Ogilvy Pub Rlations World Wide	8743	C	650 324-7015	19692
Orrick Hrrington Sutcliffe LLP	8111	C	650 614-7400	17352
Pacific Biosciences Cal Inc **(PA)**	3826	B	650 521-8000	6843
Peninsula School Ltd	8351	D	650 325-1584	17992
Peninsula Volunteer Prpts Inc **(PA)**	6513	E	650 326-2025	10454
Permira Advisers LLC	6282	B	650 681-4701	10055
Personalis Inc **(PA)**	8071	C	650 752-1300	16793
Protiviti Inc **(HQ)**	8742	D	650 234-6000	19613
Quicken Inc	7371	C	650 564-3399	12718
Qurasense Inc **(PA)**	8731	D	415 702-8935	19113
Redwood City School District	8322	E	650 568-3820	17683
Riekes Ctr For Humn Enhncement	7991	D	650 364-2509	14968
Robert Half International Inc **(PA)**	7363	D	650 234-6000	12192
Robinhood Markets Inc **(PA)**	6211	A	844 428-5411	10010
Robinhood Securities LLC	6211	C	650 294-4857	10011
Rosewood Hotels & Resorts LLC	7011	B	650 561-1500	11420
Satellite Healthcare Inc	8092	E	650 566-0180	16980
Sequoia Capital Operations LLC **(PA)**	6799	D	650 854-3927	10882
Sight Sciences Inc **(PA)**	3841	C	650 352-4400	7035
Silver Lake Partners LP **(PA)**	6726	D	650 233-8120	10781
Silver Lake Tech Assoc LLC **(HQ)**	6726	D	650 233-8120	10784
SRI International **(PA)**	8733	A	650 859-2000	19237
Stack Plastics Inc	3089	E	650 361-8600	4326
Stamos Capital Partners LP	6722	D	650 233-5000	10769
Stanford Park Hotel	7011	C	650 322-1234	11502
Sterling Stamos Acceleration	8742	E	650 233-5000	19641
Strategic Bus Insights Inc **(PA)**	8742	D	650 859-4600	19642
Strateos Inc **(PA)**	8742	D	650 763-8432	19644
Subtle Medical Inc	7372	E	650 397-8709	13470
Summit Partners LP	6799	A	650 614-6670	10885
Swiftstack Inc **(HQ)**	7372	D	408 486-2000	13475
Talis Biomedical Corporation **(PA)**	3826	D	650 433-3000	6855
Tcmi Inc **(PA)**	6799	E	650 614-8200	10890
Tizeti Inc	4813	E	281 377-6715	8000
Tusker Medical Inc	3845	E	650 223-6900	7129
Uber	4724	D	866 440-6700	7810
Veterans Health Administration	8011	C	650 614-9997	15804
Vitesse LLC	7374	A	650 543-4800	13767
Welbe Health LLC **(PA)**	8082	D	650 862-6371	16968
Western Allied Mechanical Inc	1711	C	650 326-8290	1400
Whatsapp LLC **(HQ)**	4899	D	650 336-3079	8088
Whitevale Co Inc	6552	D	650 324-1882	10723
Wolfs Precision Works Inc	3599	E	650 364-1341	5643

MERCED, CA - Merced County

	SIC	EMP	PHONE	ENTRY #
A Ccess **(PA)**	8351	D	209 383-7147	17851
Avalon Care Cen	8051	E	209 723-1056	15913
Avalon Care Ctr - Mrced Frncsc	8051	D	209 722-6231	15917
Berliner Cohen LLP	8111	E	209 385-0700	17212
Bestco Electric Inc	1731	E	209 723-2061	1464
Bloodsource Inc	8099	E	209 724-0428	17107
Builders Concrete Inc **(DH)**	3273	F	209 388-0183	4462
Central Irrigation Inc	3523	E	209 262-3723	4998
Central Valley Concrete Inc **(PA)**	4212	C	209 723-8846	7457
CF Merced La Sierra LLC	8051	D	209 723-4224	15956
Chw Mrcy Mrced Cmnty Hosp Kids	8062	E	209 564-4500	16331
Clark Pest Ctrl Stockton Inc	7342	E	209 826-6051	11881
Community Intgrted Work Prgram	8322	E	209 723-4025	17497
Country Villa Service Corp	8322	D	209 723-2911	17508
Dedicated Management Group LLC	7389	C	209 385-0694	14249
Fineline Industries Inc **(PA)**	3732	D	209 384-0255	6642
First Transit Inc	4111	C	209 385-1226	7330
Fortis Solutions Group LLC	2759	E	800 388-1990	3733
Golden Valley Health Centers **(PA)**	8011	C	209 383-1848	15417
Holiday Inn Express Merced	7011	D	209 383-0333	11155
Jain Farm Fresh Foods Inc **(DH)**	2034	E	541 481-2522	2260
Kirby Manufacturing Inc **(PA)**	3523	D	209 723-0778	5013
Label Technology Inc	2679	E	209 384-1000	3402
Laird Mfg LLC **(PA)**	3523	E	209 722-4145	5014
Longs Drug Stores Cal LLC	7384	C	209 723-3292	14175
Lowes Home Centers LLC	5031	C	209 385-5000	8572
M A D Inc **(PA)**	6531	E	209 383-6475	10609
M Nunes Inc	0191	E	209 722-7943	180
Mater Misericordiae Hospital **(PA)**	8062	A	209 564-5000	16453
Maxs Partnership A Gen Partnr	7011	E	209 725-1221	11290
McLane/Pacific Inc	5141	B	209 725-2500	9279
Melin Enterprises Inc	7349	D	209 726-9182	11971
Merced City School District	8351	D	209 385-6364	17973
Merced County Assn Governments	8748	E	209 723-3153	19819
Merced Faculty Associates **(PA)**	8011	E	209 723-3704	15531
Merced Irrigation District **(PA)**	4911	E	209 722-5761	8123
Merced Irrigation District	4971	D	209 722-2719	8414
Merced Medical Clinic Inc	8011	E	209 722-8047	15532
Merced Orthopedic Med Group	8011	D	209 722-8161	15533
Merced Schl Emplyees Fdral Cr **(PA)**	6061	D	209 383-5550	9795
Merced Screw Products Inc	3451	E	209 723-7706	4867
Merced Transportation Company	4151	D	209 384-2575	7441
Merced Urology Med Group Inc	8011	E	209 723-2122	15534
Mission Merced Incorporated	8399	D	209 722-9269	18243
N & S Tractor Co **(PA)**	7699	D	209 383-5888	14766
National Express LLC	4119	D	209 201-9345	7391
Nutstar Software LLC	7372	F	209 250-1324	13337
OKeeffes Inc	3444	C	209 388-9072	4797
Olde World Corporation	2541	E	209 384-1337	3317
On Target Marketing	7336	E	209 723-1691	11872
Pacific Gas and Electric Co	1731	C	209 726-7623	1558
Pacific Gas and Electric Co	4911	C	800 684-4648	8157
Packaging Equity Holdings LLC	2656	B	209 404-9553	3369
Park Merced LLC **(PA)**	8051	E	209 722-3944	16094
Qg LLC	2752	D	209 384-0444	3688
Richwood Meat Company Inc	2011	D	209 722-8171	2104
Scholle Ipn Packaging Inc	3089	E	209 384-3100	4319
Shannon Pump Co	5084	E	209 723-3904	9095
Sun Power Security Gates Inc	3315	F	209 722-3990	4546
Tdl Aero Enterprises Inc	3721	F	209 722-7300	6619
Transcounty Title Co **(PA)**	6361	E	209 383-4660	10210
UAS Management Inc	8062	D	209 580-3400	16689
Veterinary Service Inc	5047	E	209 722-7600	8794
Via Adventures Inc **(PA)**	4142	E	209 384-1315	7423
WLMD	1799	C	209 723-9120	2089
Yosemite Church	8322	E	209 383-5038	17788
Yosemite Farms	2068	E	209 383-3411	2453
Yosemite Vly Beef Pkg Co Inc	2011	E	626 435-0170	2108

MERIDIAN, CA - Sutter County

	SIC	EMP	PHONE	ENTRY #
Colusa Produce Corporation	5149	D	530 696-0121	9445
Davis Machine Shop Inc	3523	E	530 696-2577	5002

MI WUK VILLAGE, CA - Tuolumne County

	SIC	EMP	PHONE	ENTRY #
Oti Engineering Cons Inc	3663	E	209 586-1022	5859

MIDDLETOWN, CA - Lake County

	SIC	EMP	PHONE	ENTRY #
Geysers Power Company LLC	4911	E	707 431-6000	8113
Heart Consciousness Church Inc **(PA)**	7041	C	707 987-2477	11625
Langtry Farms LLC	2084	F	707 987-2772	2650
Morris Welding Co Inc	7692	E	707 987-1114	14717
Twin Pine Casino & Hotel	7011	D	707 987-0197	11548

MILL VALLEY, CA - Marin County

	SIC	EMP	PHONE	ENTRY #
Advantis Global Inc **(PA)**	7379	C	415 612-3338	13833
Adventres Rlling Cross-Country	7032	E	415 332-5075	11596
Alice Gray	6531	E	415 388-5060	10488
Allianz Technology America Inc	7379	C	415 899-4110	13837
Chouinard & Myhre Inc	7373	E	415 480-3636	13567
Cliff View Terrace Inc	8361	D	415 388-9526	18078
Fingerprint Digital Inc	2752	E	415 497-2611	3645
First Republic Bank	6022	D	415 389-0880	9719
Four Corners Property Tr Inc **(PA)**	6798	C	415 965-8030	10819
General Lgstics Systems US Inc	4215	C	415 492-1112	7649

GEOGRAPHIC

MILL VALLEY, CA

	SIC	EMP	PHONE	ENTRY #
Joie De Vivre Hospitality LLC	7011	D	415 380-0400	11216
Jungsten Construction	1521	E	415 381-3162	659
Liz Palacios Designs Ltd	3961	F	628 444-3339	7210
Marin Horizon School Inc	8351	E	415 388-8408	17971
Merrill Lynch Prce Fnner Smith	6211	D	415 289-8800	9997
Mill Valley Inn Inc	7011	E	415 389-6608	11300
Mountain Home Inn	7011	D	415 381-9000	11314
Nana Enterprises	7011	D	415 383-0340	11318
Orion Group World LLC	5051	C	415 602-5233	8822
Przm LLC	7011	D	415 380-0400	11377
Rabin Worldwide Inc	7389	D	415 522-5700	14382
Redwood Security Systems Inc	1731	E	415 388-5355	1577
Redwood Trust Inc (PA)	6798	C	415 389-7373	10825
Redwoods	8361	E	415 383-1600	18164
Scott Vly Swimming Tennis CLB	7997	D	415 383-3483	15138
Seedif Inc	7361	E	408 930-3446	12135
Sequoia Residential Funding	6153	D	415 389-7373	9875
Sunhill Corp	8741	D	415 383-9100	19404
Tamalpais Community Svcs Dst	4953	E	415 388-6393	8366
The Redwoods A Cmnty Seniors	8361	E	415 383-2741	18192
Therapydia Inc	8049	E	802 772-7801	15901
Trevi Partners A Calif LP	7011	E	415 332-5700	11544
True Botanicals Inc	2844	F	415 420-0403	4098
Van Acker Cnstr Assoc Inc	1521	C	415 383-5589	725

MILLBRAE, CA - San Mateo County

	SIC	EMP	PHONE	ENTRY #
Aloft Ht San Francisco Arprt	7011	D	650 443-5500	10916
Arvee Bros Inc	7011	D	650 583-3935	10933
Cycle Shack	3751	F	650 583-7014	6648
El Rancho Motel Inc	7011	C	650 588-8500	11076
Hillsdale Group LP	8059	C	650 742-9150	16239
Jiseki Health Inc	7372	E	408 763-7264	13255
Magnolia of Millbrae Inc	8361	D	650 697-7700	18141
Millbrae Serra Sanitarium	8059	E	650 697-8386	16253
Millbrae Wcp Hotel II LLC	7011	E	650 443-5500	11301
Paper Culture LLC	5112	E	650 249-0800	9210
Ramkabir LLC	7011	E	650 952-3200	11382
Rollins Road Acquisition Co (HQ)	3825	D	415 937-7836	6786
Sinosource Intl Co Inc	3281	F	650 697-6668	4523
Stem Inc (PA)	3621	E	415 937-7816	5668
Vitalant Research Institute	8099	E	650 697-4034	17188
World Journal Inc (PA)	2711	D	650 692-9936	3490

MILPITAS, CA - Santa Clara County

	SIC	EMP	PHONE	ENTRY #
22 Miles Inc	7375	E	408 933-3000	13776
3k Technologies LLC	7371	C	408 716-5900	12215
3s Communications	1731	E	408 505-9517	1439
Abbyy USA Software House Inc (DH)	7371	C	408 457-9777	12220
ABC Printing Inc	2752	F	408 263-1118	3613
Abzooba Inc (DH)	7371	C	650 453-8760	12223
Advantech Corporation (HQ)	7371	B	408 519-3800	12231
Aerohive Networks Inc (HQ)	7373	A	408 510-6100	13551
Airgard Inc (PA)	3564	E	408 573-0701	5190
Alps Group Inc	7011	E	760 500-4490	10919
Altigen Communications Inc	3661	C	408 597-9000	5787
Ambios Technology Inc (PA)	3674	E	831 427-1160	6032
Applied Stemcell Inc	8731	E	408 773-8007	19026
Appsroi Inc	7372	D	510 470-0095	8669
Aras Power Technologies (PA)	3677	E	408 935-8877	6376
Arena Stuart Rentals Inc	7359	C	408 856-3232	12029
B H R Operations Inc	7011	A	408 321-9500	10941
B T Mancini Co Inc (PA)	1752	D	408 942-7900	1765
Balch Petro Contrs & Bldrs Inc	1623	D	408 942-8686	1088
Bar-S Foods Co	2013	D	408 941-9958	2112
Bestek Manufacturing Inc	3577	E	408 321-8834	5350
BFI Waste Systems N Amer Inc	4212	E	408 432-1234	7452
Blue Ring Stencils LLC	3953	F	866 763-3873	7204
Blue Sky Research Incorporated (PA)	3827	E	408 941-6068	6866
Bottomley Distributing Co Inc	5181	D	408 945-0660	9545
Bounce A Rama Inc	7929	D	510 754-8799	14870
Boys & Girls Club Silicon Vly	8641	D	408 957-9685	18396
Brandt Electronics Inc	3679	E	408 240-0004	6402
C N C Solutions (PA)	5084	E	408 586-8236	9058
Centerra Solutions Inc	7379	E	408 791-6188	13862
Century Theatres Inc	7833	C	408 942-7441	14820
Cetecom Inc	8748	C	408 586-6200	19742
Cg2 Inc	8733	D	407 737-8800	19207
Clarizen Inc	8741	E	866 502-9813	19316
Cnc Solutions Inc	7699	E	408 586-8236	14743
Comba Telecom Inc	5065	F	408 526-0180	8904
Comfort Energy Inc	1711	E	408 263-3100	1239
Composite Software LLC (DH)	7372	C	800 553-6387	13087
Continuum Electro-Optics Inc	3826	D	408 727-3240	6822
Contract Sweeping Services LLC	4959	E	408 828-5280	8395
Cordova Printed Circuits Inc	3672	F	408 942-1100	5924
Crain Cutter Company Inc	3429	D	408 946-6100	4615
Creative Labs Inc (DH)	5045	D	408 428-6600	8685
Custom Drywall Inc	1742	D	408 263-1616	1669
Cyral Inc	7371	E	310 689-8512	12369
Daystar Technologies Inc	3674	D	408 582-7100	6098
Decision Minds	7374	C	408 309-8051	13707
Devcon Construction Inc (PA)	1542	B	408 942-8200	862
Dga Services Inc (PA)	4214	D	408 232-4800	7619
Djont Operations LLC	7011	C	408 942-0400	11051
Duran & Venables Inc	1794	E	408 741-9883	1957
EDS Manufacturing	3999	E	408 982-3688	7281
Elo Touch Solutions Inc (HQ)	5045	B	408 597-8000	8699
Enquero Inc	7373	D	408 406-3203	13583
Envision Peripherals Inc (PA)	5045	E	510 770-9988	8701
Estuate Inc	7371	D	408 946-0002	12429
Eurofins Nanolab Tech Inc (PA)	8734	D	408 433-3320	19271
Extron Contract Mfg Inc	3944	E	510 353-0177	7176
FAI Electronics Corp	5065	E	408 434-0369	8912
Fireeye International LLC (HQ)	7373	D	408 321-6300	13589
First Call Nursing Svcs Inc	7361	D	408 262-1533	12088
Flex Interconnect Tech Inc	3672	E	408 956-8204	5930
Floor Seal Technology Inc (PA)	1752	D	408 436-8181	1770
Fluid Industrial Mfg Inc	3585	F	408 782-9900	5430
Forsys Inc	7374	D	408 409-2567	13715
Frontier Semiconductor (PA)	3674	D	408 432-8338	6124
Gateway Precision Inc	3599	F	408 855-8849	5530
Golden Altos Corporation	3825	E	408 956-1010	6758
Golfland Entrmt Ctrs Inc	7999	C	408 263-4330	15208
Gyrfalcon Technology Inc (PA)	3674	E	408 944-9219	6138
H V Welker Co Inc	1752	D	408 263-4400	1771
Hansen Adkins Auto Trnspt Inc	4213	B	408 514-2345	7549
Headway Technologies Inc	7359	B	408 934-5660	12045
Headway Technologies Inc	3572	A	408 935-1020	5286
Headway Technologies Inc (HQ)	3572	A	408 934-5300	5287
Headway Technologies Inc	3572	A	408 934-5300	5288
Headway Technologies Inc	3572	A	408 934-3262	5289
HI Relblity McRelectronics Inc	3674	D	408 764-5500	6144
Hitachi Metals America Ltd	5051	D	408 467-8900	8819
Home First	8322	E	408 539-2125	17601
Homefrst Svcs Santa Clara Cnty	8322	C	408 539-2100	17603
Hoya Holdings Inc (HQ)	3861	C	408 654-2300	7151
Humane Society Silicon Valley	8699	D	408 262-2133	18573
Huntford Printing	2752	E	408 957-5000	3656
Hytek R&D Inc (PA)	3672	E	408 761-5266	5939
Ice Consulting Inc (PA)	7379	D	408 701-5700	13908
Idc Technologies Inc (PA)	7361	C	408 376-0212	12098
Igenex Inc	8071	E	650 424-1191	16785
Incube Labs LLC	6799	E	847 565-9506	10856
Infineon Tech Americas Corp	3674	A	866 951-9519	6149
Infineon Tech N Amer Corp (DH)	3674	B	408 503-2642	6150
Infineon Tech US Holdco Inc (HQ)	3674	D	866 951-9519	6152
Innomedia Inc	7371	E	408 943-8604	12520
Innovative Machining Inc	3599	D	408 262-2270	5540
Inspur Systems Inc (HQ)	3571	E	800 697-5893	5256
Integra Tech Silicon Vly LLC (DH)	3674	C	408 618-8700	6158
Integrated Mfg Tech Inc	7692	E	510 659-9770	14714
Integrated Mfg Tech Inc	3599	F	510 366-8793	5541
Integrted Silicon Solution Inc (PA)	3674	A	408 969-6600	6159
Isolink Inc	3672	E	408 946-1968	6436
Ixys LLC (HQ)	3674	B	408 457-9000	6168
J M K Investments Inc	6531	E	408 263-2626	10582
Jensen Corporate Holdings Inc (PA)	0782	C	408 446-1118	473
JIC Industrial Co Inc	3679	E	408 935-9880	6441
Jit Transportation Inc	4789	B	408 232-4800	7885
Kaiser Foundation Hospitals	8011	A	408 945-2900	15475
Kelytech Corporation	3679	E	408 935-0888	6442
Ketos Inc	7373	D	408 550-2162	13619
Khuus Inc	3599	D	408 522-8000	5553
KLA Corporation (PA)	3827	B	408 875-3000	6878
KLA-Tencor Asia-Pac Dist Corp	3674	E	408 875-4144	6173
Krish Compusoft Services Inc	7371	C	855 527-7890	12564
Larson Packaging Company LLC	2421	E	408 946-4971	3098
Lifescan Products LLC (HQ)	3841	B	408 719-8443	6996
Lightwaves 2020 Inc	8731	E	408 503-8888	19082
Linear Technology LLC (HQ)	3674	A	408 432-1900	6180
Lion Trading Company LLC (PA)	5023	D	408 946-0888	8515
Lite-On Inc (HQ)	5065	E	408 946-4873	8929
Lite-On Technology Intl Inc (HQ)	3577	D	408 945-0222	5392
Lite-On Trading Usa Inc (PA)	5045	E	408 946-4873	8721
Lre Silicon Services	3674	F	408 262-8725	6181
Lucid Vr Inc (PA)	7371	D	408 391-0506	12584
Lumasense Technologies Inc (HQ)	3845	D	408 727-1600	7111
Lumentum Inc	3669	E	408 546-5483	5889
Luminostics Inc	3841	E	760 709-2230	7000
Luxshare-Ict Inc	3999	E	408 957-0535	7297
Macronix America Inc (HQ)	5065	D	408 262-8887	8930
Mandiant Inc (PA)	3577	A	408 321-6300	5396
Manutronics Inc	3679	F	408 262-6579	6452
Marburg Technology Inc	3577	D	408 262-8400	5397
Marketshare Inc (PA)	3993	D	408 262-0677	7242
Memverge Inc	7371	D	408 605-0841	12602
Meritronics Inc (PA)	3672	E	408 969-0888	5946
Micron Technology Inc	3674	E	408 855-4000	6204
Midway Games West Inc	3999	C	408 434-3700	7299
Milpitas Courtyard By Marriott	7011	E	408 719-1966	11303
Milpitas Materials Company	5032	E	650 969-4401	8630
Milpitas Optometric Group Inc	8042	E	408 263-2040	15871
Milpitas Unified School Dst	8351	D	408 635-2686	17974
Mindsource Inc	7371	D	650 314-6400	12607
Mobiveil Inc	3674	F	408 791-2977	6215
Montessori School Silicon Vly (PA)	8351	E	408 586-8643	17978
Mozilla Corp (PA)	7389	E	408 946-2311	14333
Mvinix Corporation	3672	E	408 321-9109	5949
Nanosys Inc (PA)	3674	B	408 240-6700	6223
NDk America Inc	3674	F	408 428-0800	6225
Necsel Intllctual Property Inc (DH)	6512	E	408 246-7555	10397
Nimble Storage Inc (HQ)	3572	A	408 432-9600	5305
Northland Control Systems Inc (PA)	1799	C	833 811-4185	2046
Nortra Cables Inc	3679	E	408 942-1106	6462
Nova Drilling Services Inc	3672	E	408 732-6682	5952

	SIC	EMP	PHONE	ENTRY #
NRC Manufacturing Inc	3679	F	510 438-9400	6463
Oclaro Inc **(HQ)**	3674	B	408 383-1400	6239
Oclaro Fiber Optics Inc **(DH)**	3674	C	408 383-1400	6240
Oclaro Subsystems Inc	3661	C	408 383-1400	5803
Oclaro Technology Inc	3827	A	408 383-1400	6881
Ohana Partners Inc **(PA)**	7359	D	408 856-3232	12057
Onanon Inc	3678	E	408 262-8990	6394
Open-Silicon Inc **(DH)**	3674	E	408 240-5700	6247
Optimedica Corporation	3841	C	408 850-8600	7013
Pacific Gas and Electric Co	4911	C	408 945-6215	8187
Palpilot International Corp **(PA)**	3672	E	408 855-8866	5956
Pax Water Technologies Inc	8731	E	866 729-6493	19098
Pensando Systems Inc	3823	D	408 451-9012	6729
Pericom Semiconductor Corp **(HQ)**	3825	A	408 232-9100	6778
Permanente Medical Group Inc	8011	A	408 945-2900	15604
Petasense Inc	3829	E	650 336-0480	6916
Phamtec Inc **(PA)**	3357	E	408 210-4606	4572
Philips Lt-On Dgtal Sltons USA **(DH)**	3572	E	510 687-1800	5309
Piercey Hm LLC	7549	E	408 324-7400	14672
Piercey North Inc	5013	C	408 240-1400	8460
Ppm Products Inc	3599	E	408 946-4710	5600
Preston Pipelines Inc **(PA)**	1623	C	408 262-1418	1131
Pro Star Auto Service Inc	7539	E	408 942-3330	14617
Protominds Inc	7371	E	408 684-6363	12706
Prudential Overall Supply	7218	C	408 263-3464	11666
Prudential Overall Supply	7218	E	408 719-0886	11667
Prysm Inc **(PA)**	3999	D	408 586-1127	7303
PSI Water Technologies Inc	3823	E	408 819-3043	6732
Quality Transformer & Elec	3612	E	408 935-0231	5647
Quantela Inc **(PA)**	7373	D	650 479-3700	13654
Quantum3d Inc **(PA)**	3812	F	408 600-2500	6681
Quellan Inc	3674	E	408 546-3487	6265
R S Software India Limited	7379	D	408 382-1200	13967
R&M USA Inc	5065	D	408 945-6626	8948
Rapidbizappscom LLC	7371	E	408 647-3050	12726
RDm Industrial Products Inc	2522	F	408 945-8400	3311
Relay2 Inc **(PA)**	4813	D	408 380-0031	7987
Riverview Systems Group Inc	7359	E	408 347-3700	12060
Rohde & Schwarz Usa Inc	3825	F	818 846-3600	6785
Rucker & Kolls Inc **(PA)**	3559	E	408 934-9875	5169
San Frncsco Bay Bird Obsrvtory	8641	E	408 946-6548	18461
Sandisk LLC **(DH)**	3572	C	408 801-1000	5315
Sasco Electric Inc	1731	B	408 970-8300	1599
Semi **(PA)**	8611	C	408 943-6900	18318
Sierra Monitor Corporation **(HQ)**	3829	D	408 262-6611	6921
Silicon Graphics Intl Corp **(HQ)**	3577	A	669 900-8000	5411
Silicon Microstructures Inc	3625	D	408 473-9700	5690
Silicon Motion Inc	3674	D	408 501-5300	6289
Silicon Turnkey Solutions Inc **(HQ)**	3674	F	408 904-0200	6292
Silicon Vly World Trade Corp	3613	E	408 945-6355	5654
Siliconcore Technology Inc	3674	E	408 946-8185	6294
SJ Distributors Inc **(PA)**	5146	D	888 988-2328	9369
Smart & Final Stores Inc	5141	C	408 941-9642	9309
Solaredge Technologies Inc **(PA)**	3629	B	510 498-3200	5696
Solid State Stor Tech USA Corp	5045	D	510 687-1800	8749
Sonicwall Inc **(PA)**	7373	A	888 557-6642	13666
Spartronics Milpitas Inc **(DH)**	3672	C	408 957-1300	5979
Spectra-Physics Inc **(DH)**	3699	A	877 835-9620	6543
Spidercloud Wireless Inc **(HQ)**	4812	E	408 567-9165	7913
Sporton International USA Inc	1389	F	732 407-8718	571
Spring Valley Golf Course Inc	7992	E	408 262-1722	15029
Ss8 Networks Inc **(PA)**	4899	C	408 894-8400	8085
Stats Chippac Inc **(DH)**	3674	E	510 979-8000	6312
Stella Technology Incorporated	7379	D	402 350-1681	13981
Stellartech Research Corp **(PA)**	8731	D	408 331-3134	19130
Sunera Technologies Inc	7379	E	510 474-2616	13983
Symprotek Co	3672	E	408 956-0700	5985
Tarana Wireless Inc **(PA)**	3663	F	408 365-8483	5875
Tcg Builders Inc	1542	E	408 321-6450	971
Teledyne Defense Elec LLC	3674	C	408 737-0992	6328
Teledyne Dgital Imaging US Inc	3829	F	408 736-6000	6925
Teledyne E2v, Inc.	3674	E	408 737-0992	6329
Test-Um Inc	3674	E	818 464-5021	6332
Tokyo Ohka Kogyo America Inc	2819	E	408 956-9901	3798
Turnongreen Inc	3825	E	510 657-2635	6798
Universal Site Services Inc **(PA)**	7349	C	800 647-9337	12014
Valley Rlction Stor Nthrn Cal	4214	D	408 938-3672	7640
Varian Medical Systems Inc	3841	C	408 321-9400	7056
Vector Fabrication Inc **(PA)**	3672	F	408 942-9800	5995
Viavi Solutions Inc	3826	C	408 546-5000	6862
View Inc **(PA)**	3211	B	408 263-9200	4362
View Operating Corporation **(HQ)**	3211	D	408 263-9200	4363
Virtual Technologies Inc	3999	E	408 597-3400	7315
Vista Way Corporation	2752	E	408 586-8107	3710
Vitas Healthcare Corp Cal	8052	E	408 964-6800	16209
Vlsi Standards Inc	3825	E	408 428-1800	6800
Vm Services Inc **(DH)**	7371	C	510 744-3720	12913
Vuclip Inc	4813	E	408 649-2240	8007
W-Neweb Corporation	5065	E	408 457-6800	8970
Wavelabs Technologies Inc **(PA)**	7389	D	408 203-7670	14459
West Coast Property Management	7011	D	408 263-5566	11570
Winmax Systems Corporation	7371	D	408 894-9000	12923
Winslow Automation Inc	3674	D	408 262-9004	6356
Xcerra Corporation	5065	C	408 635-4300	8974
Xl Construction Corporation **(PA)**	1542	B	408 240-6000	995
Yaana Technologies LLC	7379	E	650 996-2927	14016
Yuhas Tooling & Machining Inc	3599	E	408 934-9196	5644
Zilog Inc **(DH)**	3674	D	408 513-1500	6366
Ziontech Solutions Inc	7379	E	408 434-6001	14019
Zl Technologies Inc **(PA)**	7371	D	408 240-8989	12941
Zollner Electronics Inc	3672	E	408 434-5400	6003
Zuca Inc	3161	E	408 377-9822	4351
Zytek Corp **(PA)**	3672	E	408 520-4287	6004

MIRAMONTE, CA - Fresno County

	SIC	EMP	PHONE	ENTRY #
Hume Lake Christian Camps Inc	7032	E	559 305-7770	11603

MODESTO, CA - Stanislaus County

	SIC	EMP	PHONE	ENTRY #
A & A Portables Inc	7359	E	209 524-0401	12026
ABS Direct Inc	7331	E	209 545-6090	11834
Acme Construction Company Inc	1541	E	209 523-2674	787
Addus Healthcare Inc	8082	D	209 526-8451	16832
Addus Homecare Corporation **(HQ)**	8082	E	209 526-8451	16835
Allcare Hsptlist Med Group Inc	8741	E	209 550-5200	19295
Allied Concrete and Supply Co	3273	E	209 524-3177	4458
Almond Board of California	8611	E	209 549-8262	18296
Altium Packaging LLC	3085	F	209 531-9180	4237
Amcor Manufacturing Inc	2819	F	209 581-9687	3778
American Financial Network Inc	6282	E	209 238-3210	10028
American Pavement Systems Inc	1611	E	209 522-2277	1008
Architecture Plus Inc	8712	E	209 577-4661	18871
Arete Hotels LLC	7011	D	209 602-7952	10928
Avalon Care Center - Modesto	8051	C	209 526-1775	15914
Avalon Care Ctr - Modesto LLC	8051	D	209 529-0516	15916
Bambacigno Steel Company	3312	E	209 524-9681	4539
Bank America National Assn	6021	E	209 578-6006	9679
Barton Overhead Door Inc	1751	E	209 571-3667	1730
Basic Resources Inc **(PA)**	1611	E	209 521-9771	1014
Batchlder Bus Cmmnications Inc	2752	E	209 577-2222	3629
Beaver Dam Health Care Center	8051	E	209 548-0318	15940
Behavral Edctl Strtgies Trning	8748	E	209 579-9444	19728
Bell-Carter Foods Inc	2033	E	209 549-5939	2212
Berliner Cohen LLP	8111	E	209 576-1197	17213
Bertolotti Disposal Inc	4953	E	209 537-1500	8309
Bestco Electric Inc **(PA)**	1731	E	209 569-0120	1463
Bethel Rtrment Cmnty A Cal Ltd	8059	E	209 577-1901	16219
Big Valley Grace Cmnty Ch Inc **(PA)**	8351	C	209 577-1604	17862
Billington Welding & Mfg Inc	3556	D	209 526-0846	5125
BJs Restaurants Inc	5094	E	209 526-8850	9179
Blue Diamond Growers	0723	C	209 545-6221	271
Brenden Theatre Corporation	7832	D	209 491-7770	14805
Bright Development	1521	E	209 526-8242	623
Bristol Hospice Foundation Cal	8052	D	209 338-3000	16172
Bunge Oils Inc	2079	D	209 574-9981	2462
C & S Draperies Inc	7217	C	209 466-5371	11657
C L S Woodside Mgt Group **(PA)**	6531	E	209 577-4181	10500
C W Brower Inc **(PA)**	5141	D	209 523-1828	9264
Cal-Sign Wholesale Inc	3993	F	209 523-7446	7222
California Stl Fabricators Inc	3441	E	209 566-0629	4649
Califrnia Frnsic Med Group Inc	8011	C	209 525-5670	15315
Califrnia High Rach Eqp Rntl I	7353	E	209 577-0515	12018
Capax Management & Insur Svcs **(DH)**	6411	E	209 526-3110	10259
Careone HM Hlth & Hospice Inc	8052	E	209 632-8888	16174
Catholic Chrties of The Dcese	8322	D	209 529-3784	17466
Center For Human Services **(PA)**	8322	C	209 526-1476	17473
Central Sanitary Supply LLC **(DH)**	5087	E	209 523-3002	9141
Central Valley AG Trnspt Inc	4741	E	209 544-9246	7864
Central Valley Electric Inc	1731	E	209 531-2470	1474
Central Valley Injured **(PA)**	8111	D	209 522-2777	17228
Central Valley Party Supply	7359	E	209 569-0399	12034
Central Vly Ctr For Arts Inc **(PA)**	7922	E	209 338-2100	14844
Central Vly Specialty Hosp Inc	8062	C	209 248-7700	16328
Champion Industrial Contrs Inc **(PA)**	1711	E	209 524-6601	1233
Champion Industrial Contrs Inc	1711	E	209 579-5478	1234
Charles Fenley Enterprises **(PA)**	7542	E	209 576-0381	14636
Charles Fenley Enterprises	7542	E	209 523-2832	14637
Charles Fenley Enterprises	7542	E	209 576-0381	14638
Childrens Crsis Ctr Stnslaus C	8322	E	209 577-4413	17484
Citizen Corporation	1731	E	209 537-6334	1478
Clark Pest Ctrl Stockton Inc	7342	E	209 524-6384	11885
Community Hospice Inc **(PA)**	8052	C	209 578-6300	16178
County of Stanislaus	8062	C	209 525-7000	16341
County of Stanislaus	4959	E	209 522-4098	8397
County of Stanislaus	8322	E	209 558-8828	17514
County of Stanislaus	8322	E	209 567-4120	17515
County of Stanislaus	8322	E	209 558-7377	17516
County of Stanislaus	8099	D	209 558-7377	17129
County of Stanislaus	8322	E	209 558-9675	17517
County of Stanislaus	8011	D	209 558-5312	15371
County of Stanislaus	8093	D	209 525-7423	17010
County of Stanislaus	8322	C	209 558-2500	17518
County of Stanislaus	8331	E	209 558-2100	17810
County of Stanislaus	7363	E	209 558-8118	12168
County of Stanislaus	8361	E	209 525-5400	18083
Covenant Care California LLC	8059	E	209 521-2094	16228
Crestwood Behavioral Hlth Inc	8063	B	209 526-8050	16734
Crown Painting Inc	1721	D	209 322-3275	1409
Curtis Lgal Group A Prof Law C	8111	E	209 521-1800	17243
D C Vient Inc **(PA)**	1721	D	209 578-1224	1410
Damrell Nelson Schrimp Pall **(PA)**	8111	E	209 526-3500	17244
Davis Guest Home Inc	8361	E	209 538-1496	18097
Del Rio Golf & Country Club	7997	C	209 341-2414	15085
Deloitte Consulting LLP	8742	E	212 492-4000	19491
Deltatrak Inc	3829	E	209 579-5343	6898
Dependable Highway Express Inc	4213	D	209 342-0184	7523

GEOGRAPHIC

Employment Codes: A=Over 500 employees, B=251-500, C=101-250, D=51-100, E=20-50 F=10-19

2022 Northern California Business Directory and Buyers Guide

© Mergent Inc. 1-800-342-5647

1165

	SIC	EMP	PHONE	ENTRY #
Dons Mobile Glass Inc **(PA)**	5039	D	209 548-7000	8643
DOT Foods Inc	5141	C	209 581-9090	9270
E & J Gallo Winery **(PA)**	2084	A	209 341-3111	2558
E & S Precision Machine Inc	3599	F	209 545-6161	5512
Eastside Management Co Inc	0762	C	209 578-9852	373
Eastside Management Co Inc **(PA)**	0762	C	209 578-9852	374
Ed Rocha Livestock Trnsp Inc	4213	D	209 538-1302	7529
English Oaks Convalescent	8051	D	209 577-1001	15988
Entekra LLC	2452	E	209 624-1630	3249
Enviro Tech Chemical Svcs Inc **(PA)**	5169	C	209 581-9576	9518
Exact Corp	5083	E	209 544-8600	9036
Fabricated Extrusion Co LLC **(PA)**	3089	E	209 529-9200	4281
Fabritec Precision Inc	3444	E	209 529-8504	4763
Family Health Care Med Group	8011	E	209 527-6900	15398
Family Plg Assoc Med Group	8011	E	209 578-0443	15404
Fellowship Homes Inc	8361	C	209 529-4950	18115
Fig Holdings LLC	8051	D	209 524-4817	16003
First Tactical LLC	2311	A	855 665-3410	2984
Fiscalini Cheese Company LP	2026	F	209 346-0384	2188
Fisher Graphic Inds A Cal Corp	3555	E	209 577-0181	5119
Fisher Nut Company	2099	F	209 527-0108	2893
Flowers Baking Co Modesto LLC **(HQ)**	2051	D	209 857-4600	2382
Foster Dairy Farms **(PA)**	5143	A	209 576-3400	9338
Foster Dairy Farms	2026	F	209 576-2300	2189
Foster Dairy Products Distrg **(PA)**	5143	E	209 576-3400	9339
Four Star Recovery Inc	7389	E	209 524-2854	14277
Frito-Lay North America Inc	2096	B	209 544-5400	2856
G Pallets Inc	2448	E	209 814-2250	3222
G3 Enterprises Inc **(PA)**	4225	C	209 341-7515	7689
G3 Enterprises Inc	4731	E	209 341-4045	7837
G3 Enterprises Inc	7336	E	209 341-5265	11862
Gallo Glass Company **(HQ)**	3221	A	209 341-3710	4366
General Petroleum Corporation	5171	D	209 537-1056	9524
George Reed Inc **(HQ)**	1771	E	877 823-2305	1872
Gianelli & Associates	8111	E	209 521-6260	17273
Gilwin Company	3442	E	209 522-9775	4704
Global Healthcare Services LLC	8082	D	209 549-9875	16886
Golden Valley & Associates Inc	3537	E	209 549-1549	5063
Golden Valley Industries Inc	2011	E	209 939-3370	2097
Greater Mdsto Med Srgcal Assoc **(HQ)**	8011	E	209 577-3388	15419
Grimbleby Clman Crtif Pub Accn	8721	D	209 527-4220	18960
Grover Landscape Services Inc	0181	D	209 545-4401	125
Hamilton and Dillon Elc Inc	1731	D	209 529-6292	1512
Haven Wns Ctr Stanislaus Cnty	8322	E	209 524-4331	17598
House Modesto **(PA)**	8351	C	209 529-7346	17953
Houston Mfg & Installation Inc	5084	E	209 556-0163	9071
Howard Prep **(PA)**	8331	E	209 538-2431	17817
Howard Prep	8331	E	209 521-9877	17818
Howk Well & Equipment Co Inc	1623	E	209 529-4110	1107
Hoya Optical Inc **(PA)**	3851	D	209 579-7739	7141
Hsi Mechanical Inc	3444	E	209 408-0183	4770
Industrial Automtn Group LLC	8711	D	209 579-7527	18736
Iron Works Enterprises Inc	3715	E	209 572-7450	6603
J S West and Company **(PA)**	5172	C	209 577-3221	9534
J S West Milling Co Inc	2048	E	209 529-4232	2345
J&T Crenshaw Inc	7991	E	209 606-8256	14954
Jackrabbit	3523	F	209 521-9325	5010
JM Huber Corporation	2819	D	209 549-9771	3790
Johnson United Inc **(PA)**	3993	E	209 543-1320	7238
JR Daniels Commercial Bldrs	3449	E	209 545-6040	4857
K Darpinian & Sons Inc	0175	D	209 524-4442	104
Kaiser Foundation Hospitals	8011	C	209 735-5000	15461
Kaiser Foundation Hospitals	8011	C	209 735-5000	15462
Kaiser Foundation Hospitals	6324	C	855 268-4096	10134
Kaiser Foundation Hospitals	6324	C	209 557-1000	10143
Kingspan Insulated Panels Inc	3448	D	209 531-9091	4852
Kissito Healthcare Inc	8051	E	209 524-4817	16032
La Pachanga Foods Inc	2011	E	209 522-2222	2099
Lamar Tool & Die Casting Inc	3312	E	209 545-5525	4543
Lily Development Inc **(PA)**	6531	E	209 527-2010	10601
LLC Noble Rider **(PA)**	5136	D	209 566-7800	9247
Loandepotcom LLC	6162	A	209 846-6400	9913
Longs Drug Stores Cal LLC	7384	C	209 522-1047	14179
Lowes Home Centers LLC	5031	C	209 545-7676	8557
LTI Boyd	3549	A	800 554-0200	5109
Matson Navigation Company	4424	E	209 577-1081	7712
McHenry Medical Group Inc	8011	D	209 577-3388	15523
Medamerica Billing Svcs Inc **(HQ)**	8721	B	209 491-7710	18979
Mercer Foods LLC **(HQ)**	2034	F	209 529-0150	2264
Merrill Lynch Prce Fnner Smith	6211	D	209 578-2600	9986
Mission Linen Supply	7213	D	209 523-6758	11639
Mocse Federal Credit Union	6061	E	209 572-3600	9797
Modesto Executive A Chrtr Inc	4522	D	209 577-4654	7758
Modesto Hospitality LLC	7011	C	209 526-6000	11306
Modesto Hospitality Lessee LLC	7011	D	209 526-6000	11307
Modesto Imaging Center	8011	D	209 524-6800	15540
Modesto Irrigation District	4911	D	209 526-7563	8125
Modesto Irrigation District **(PA)**	4911	C	209 526-7337	8126
Modesto Irrigation District	4911	D	209 526-7373	8127
Modesto Tent and Awning Inc	2394	E	209 545-1607	3040
Modestos Neighborhood Church	8351	C	209 529-5510	17977
Morgan Stnley Smith Barney LLC	6211	D	209 526-3700	10000
Muscolino Inventory Svc Inc	7389	E	209 576-8469	14336
Mve Inc **(PA)**	8711	D	209 526-4214	18775
Nagel Landscaping	0782	E	209 545-1696	487
Nestle Usa Inc	2023	C	209 574-2000	2166
Never Boring Design Associates	7336	E	209 526-9136	11871
Nick Sciabica & Sons A Corp	2079	E	209 577-5067	2466
OfficeMax North America Inc	5112	D	209 551-9700	9209
Ontel Security Services Inc	7381	D	209 521-0200	14081
Orangeburg Medical Group	8011	D	209 343-8126	15570
Pacific Gas and Electric Co	4911	C	209 576-6636	8175
Pacific Mtl Hdlg Solutions Inc	5084	E	209 524-5194	9084
Pacific Southwest Cont LLC **(PA)**	2671	B	209 526-0444	3377
Pacific Southwest Cont LLC	4225	E	209 526-0444	7698
Pacific Southwest Cont LLC	2671	E	209 526-0444	3378
Panelized Solar Inc	1711	E	209 343-8600	1334
Panelized Structures Inc **(PA)**	1761	E	480 969-4447	1826
Parker-Hannifin Corporation	3569	A	209 521-7860	5230
Patton Music Co Inc **(PA)**	5194	E	209 574-1101	9644
Paul M Zagaris Realtor Inc	6531	E	209 527-2010	10643
Peco Inspx	3625	F	209 576-3345	5686
Pegasus Risk Management Inc **(PA)**	6411	D	209 574-2800	10330
Permanente Medical Group Inc	8011	A	209 735-5000	15625
Pinnacle Solutions Inc	7389	D	209 523-8300	14365
Plus Group Inc	7363	B	209 342-9022	12188
Principal Svc Solutions Inc	8711	C	209 408-1982	18794
Professnal Blling MGT Svcs Inc	8721	E	209 579-5628	18986
Provident Care Inc	8082	C	209 578-1210	16928
Putt-Putt of Modesto Inc **(PA)**	7999	D	209 578-4386	15229
R & M Painting Inc	1721	F	209 576-2576	1426
Ragers Recreational Entps	7933	E	209 522-2452	14898
Reed Group **(HQ)**	1611	E	209 521-7423	1071
Reeves Enterprises Inc	7549	E	209 529-5698	14674
Regent Assisted Living Inc	8361	E	209 491-0800	18166
Repsco Inc	3089	E	303 294-0364	4317
RES-Care Inc	8361	E	209 578-1385	18171
RES-Care Inc	8082	E	209 523-9130	16938
Rickey & Wong DDS Inc	8021	E	209 577-0777	15856
Ridi Home Care Inc	8082	E	209 579-9445	16939
Rizo Lopez Foods Inc	2022	B	800 626-5587	2153
S&F Management Company Inc	8051	A	209 846-9744	16102
Sacramento Coca-Cola Btlg Inc	2086	D	209 541-3200	2811
Save Mart Supermarkets Disc **(PA)**	5141	C	209 577-1600	9296
Scenic Faculty Med Group Inc	8011	E	209 558-7248	15676
Sharcar Enterprises Inc	3281	E	209 531-2200	4522
Sign Designs Inc	3993	E	209 524-4484	7252
Silgan Containers Mfg Corp	3411	E	209 521-6469	4599
Sintex Security Services Inc	7381	D	209 543-9044	14097
Solecon Industrial Contrs Inc	1711	D	209 572-7390	1363
Sprouts Farmers Market Inc	5141	D	209 527-7575	9312
Squab Producers Calif Inc	5144	D	209 537-4744	9352
Stan Boyett & Son Inc **(PA)**	5172	E	209 577-6000	9539
Staniflaus Cardiology	8011	E	209 521-9661	15702
Stanislaus Cnty Tobacco Fundng	6153	C	209 525-6376	9877
Stanislaus County Hsa	8011	E	209 558-7094	15703
Stanislaus Farm Supply Company **(PA)**	5191	D	209 538-7070	9611
Stanislaus Food Products Co **(PA)**	2033	C	209 548-3537	2243
Stanislaus Surgical Hosp LLC **(PA)**	8062	C	209 572-2700	16560
Sterling Mktg & Fincl Corp	8742	E	209 593-1140	19640
Stinson Enterprises Inc	7539	C	209 529-2933	14625
Storer Transit Systems **(PA)**	4119	E	209 527-4900	7406
Storer Transportation Service **(PA)**	4141	B	209 521-8250	7419
Sundial Restaurant	7011	E	209 524-0808	11516
Supermarket Associates LLC	5199	E	209 529-2639	9672
Sutter Central Vly Hospitals	8062	A	209 572-5900	16575
Sutter Central Vly Hospitals **(HQ)**	8062	C	209 526-4500	16576
Sutter Central Vly Hospitals	8062	A	209 569-7544	16577
Sutter Central Vly Hospitals	8062	A	209 526-4500	16578
Sutter Central Vly Hospitals	8062	A	209 572-8270	16579
Sutter Gould Med Foundation **(PA)**	8011	E	209 948-5940	15713
Sutter Health	8062	C	209 522-0146	16622
Sutter Valley Med Foundation	8062	B	209 524-1211	16679
Sutter Vsting Nrse Assn Hspice	8082	C	209 342-4048	16957
Synergy Health Companies Inc	8099	D	209 577-4625	17186
Sysco Central California Inc	5141	B	209 527-7700	9316
T-Mobile Usa Inc	4812	C	209 529-0539	7914
Tcb Industrial Inc **(PA)**	1541	D	209 571-0569	815
Theodore E Staahl MD Inc **(PA)**	8011	E	209 577-5700	15740
Truss Engineering Inc	2439	E	209 527-6387	3214
Tsm Insurance & Fincl Svcs Inc	6411	D	209 524-6366	10362
Turlock Hlth & Fitnes Ctr Inc	7991	E	209 571-2582	14983
United Pallet Services Inc	2448	C	209 538-5844	3232
United Sttes Intrmdal Svcs LLC	4731	D	209 341-4045	7855
Valley AC Engrg Inc	1711	E	209 524-7756	1390
Valley First Credit Union **(PA)**	6061	D	209 549-8511	9826

MODESTO, CA - Stanislaus County

	SIC	EMP	PHONE	ENTRY #
Valley-Mntain Regional Ctr Inc	8322	D	209 955-3207	17780

MODESTO, CA - Stanislaus County

	SIC	EMP	PHONE	ENTRY #
Varni Brothers Corporation **(PA)**	5181	D	209 521-1777	9564
Varni Brothers Corporation	5182	D	209 526-5513	9586
Veterinary Medical Associates	0742	E	209 527-5855	345
Village Instant Printing Inc	2752	E	209 576-2568	3709
Vintage Car Wash Inc	7542	E	209 572-1215	14653
Vipa Hospitality Inc	7011	E	209 544-2000	11561
Vistech Mfg Solutions LLC **(HQ)**	3565	D	209 544-9333	5208
Wanderlust LLC **(PA)**	2082	F	209 404-0716	2499
Westland Technologies Inc	3061	D	800 877-7734	4210
Willey Printing Company **(PA)**	2752	E	209 524-4811	3715
Wondertreats Inc	5199	B	209 521-8881	9676
Wood Connection Inc	2431	E	209 577-1044	3162
Wright Pharma Inc	2834	E	209 549-9771	4008
Yosemite Meat Company Inc	5147	D	209 524-5117	9384

GEOGRAPHIC SECTION MOUNTAIN VIEW, CA

	SIC	EMP	PHONE	ENTRY #
Yosemite Pthlogy Med Group Inc **(PA)**	8071	E	209 577-1200	16822
Yosemite Welding & Mfg Inc	7692	F	209 874-6140	14726

MOFFETT FIELD, CA - Santa Clara County

	SIC	EMP	PHONE	ENTRY #
Bay Area Envmtl Res Inst	8733	E	707 938-9387	19198
Intrinsyx Technologies Corp	7371	E	650 210-9220	12537
Millennium Engrg Intgrtion LLC	8711	C	703 413-7750	18770
Revance Therapeutics Inc	4225	D	510 742-3400	7701

MONTE SERENO, CA - Santa Clara County

	SIC	EMP	PHONE	ENTRY #
El Camino Surgery Center LLC	8062	D	650 961-1200	16361

MORAGA, CA - Contra Costa County

	SIC	EMP	PHONE	ENTRY #
Aegis Senior Communities LLC	8361	D	925 377-7900	18052
Bergerson Group	8742	D	925 948-8110	19454
Goodwill Cntl Southern Ind Inc	8322	E	925 631-0148	17593
Moraga Cntry CLB Hmowners Assn	7997	D	925 376-2200	15112
Saklan Valley School	8351	E	925 376-7900	18014

MORGAN HILL, CA - Santa Clara County

	SIC	EMP	PHONE	ENTRY #
A H K Electronic Shtmtl Inc	3444	E	408 778-3901	4736
Accu-Image Inc	7371	E	408 736-9066	12225
Admi Inc	7372	E	408 776-0060	12954
Advanced McHning Tchniques Inc	3599	E	408 778-4500	5466
Aircraft Covers Inc	2394	E	408 738-3959	3036
Airtronics Metal Products Inc **(PA)**	3444	C	408 977-7800	4739
All Sensors Corporation	3674	E	408 776-9434	6022
Allied Lube Inc	7549	D	408 779-8969	14654
Amtech Microelectronics Inc	3672	E	408 612-8888	5913
Andpak Inc **(PA)**	7389	E	408 776-1072	14201
Anritsu Americas Sales Company	5084	A	408 778-2000	9051
Anritsu Company **(DH)**	3663	B	800 267-4878	5822
Anritsu US Holding Inc **(HQ)**	3825	B	408 778-2000	6746
Applied Wireless Identific **(PA)**	5065	E	408 779-1929	8891
Aragen Bioscience Inc	8731	E	408 779-1700	19027
Art Brand Studios LLC **(PA)**	2741	E	408 201-5000	3556
Assurx Inc	7371	D	408 778-1376	12278
Babylon Printing Inc	2752	E	408 519-5000	3626
California Kit Cab Door Corp **(PA)**	2434	B	408 782-5700	3173
Catalyst Family Inc **(PA)**	8351	D	408 556-7300	17879
Child Development Incorporated **(PA)**	8351	E	408 556-7300	17890
Cni Thl Ops LLC	7011	D	408 782-6034	11023
Collaris LLC	3679	D	510 825-9995	6408
Condit Inn GP LLC	7011	E	408 779-7666	11032
Coyote Creek Consulting Inc	7379	E	408 383-9200	13875
Coyote Creek Golf Club	7992	E	408 463-1400	14994
Creative Mfg Solutions Inc	3444	E	408 327-0600	4751
Custom Chrome Manufacturing	5013	B	408 825-5000	8448
D & J Lumber Co Inc **(PA)**	5031	D	408 778-1550	8540
Dcpm Inc	3599	E	408 928-2510	5504
Don Vito Ozuna Foods Corp	2096	E	408 465-2010	2854
Elmech Inc	3679	F	408 782-2990	6423
Emilio Guglielmo Winery Inc	2084	F	408 779-2145	2562
Emtec Engineering	3444	E	408 779-5800	4761
Ford Store Morgan Hill Inc	7515	D	408 782-8201	14491
Fresh Pick Produce	5099	E	408 315-4612	9195
George Chiala Farms Inc	0161	C	408 778-0562	31
Global Motorsport Parts Inc	3751	C	408 778-0500	6650
Golden State Assembly Inc	3353	F	408 438-0314	4558
Gryphon Financial Group Inc	8721	E	408 825-2500	18961
Guglielmo Emilo Winery Inc	0172	F	408 779-2145	54
Hillview Convalescent Hospital	8051	E	408 779-3633	16024
Italix Company Inc	3479	F	408 988-2487	4935
K R Anderson Inc **(PA)**	5169	D	408 825-1800	9519
Kal Machining Inc	3599	E	408 782-8989	5550
Kalman Manufacturing Inc	3599	E	408 776-7664	5551
Kawahara Nursery Inc	0181	C	408 779-2400	129
KDF Inc	3599	E	408 779-3731	5552
Kycon Inc	5065	E	408 494-0330	8926
Lin Engineering Inc	3621	C	408 919-0200	5663
Lusamerica Foods Inc **(PA)**	5146	C	408 778-7200	9367
M & L Precision Machining Inc **(PA)**	3599	E	408 436-3955	5563
Marki Microwave Inc	5065	E	408 778-4200	8931
Marutiz Inc	7011	E	408 778-3400	11288
Medallion Landscape MGT Inc **(PA)**	0781	D	408 782-7500	425
Micro-Mechanics Inc	5065	E	408 779-2927	8933
Monument Construction Inc	0781	D	408 778-1350	426
New Path Landscape Svcs Inc	0781	D	408 310-8476	427
New Prduct Intgrtion Sltons In **(PA)**	3315	D	408 944-9178	4544
Northern Cal Fire Prtction Svc	1711	E	408 776-1580	1318
Nxedge Inc	5065	E	208 362-7200	8942
Operating Engineers Loca	8711	E	408 782-9803	18782
Pacific Metro LLC **(PA)**	8412	B	408 201-5000	18278
Paramit Corporation **(PA)**	3672	C	408 782-5600	5957
Pega Precision Inc	3444	E	408 776-3700	4801
Phoenix Deventures Inc	3841	E	408 782-6240	7020
Pinnacle Manufacturing Corp	3444	E	408 778-6100	4804
Prism Electronics Corp **(PA)**	5065	E	408 778-7050	8947
Psynergy Programs Inc	8361	D	415 590-0579	18162
Quintel Corporation	3555	E	408 776-5190	5123
Robson Technologies Inc	3599	E	408 779-8008	5614
Sakata Seed America Inc **(HQ)**	5191	D	408 778-7758	9608
Seagull Solutions Inc	3825	F	408 778-1127	6790
Serrano Electric Inc	1731	E	408 986-1570	1604
Sheathing Technologies Inc	3841	E	408 782-2720	7033
Sierra Precast Inc	3272	C	408 779-1000	4452
Silicon Valley Glass Inc **(PA)**	1793	E	408 778-7786	1944
Silicon Vly Aba Cnsulting Svcs	8748	E	408 913-5019	19860
South County Housing Corp **(PA)**	6531	E	510 582-1460	10665
Ssmb Pacific Holding Co Inc	5012	E	408 500-3400	8431
Step Tools Unlimited Inc	3545	D	408 988-8898	5099
Talamo Food Service Inc	5141	E	408 612-8751	9319
Terrasat Communications Inc	3663	E	408 782-5911	5880
Tropos Technologies Inc	3714	F	408 571-6104	6596
TSC Motors Inc	5012	E	408 580-0410	8433
U S Technical Ceramics Inc	5032	E	408 779-0303	8637
U-C Components Inc **(PA)**	3452	E	408 782-1929	4873
Uhv Sputtering Inc	3674	E	408 779-2826	6341
Waste Management Cal Inc	4953	C	408 779-2206	8381
Youngs Market Company LLC	5182	D	408 782-3121	9589

MOSS BEACH, CA - San Mateo County

	SIC	EMP	PHONE	ENTRY #
Biz Performance Solutions Inc	7372	F	408 844-4284	13022
Seton Medical Center	8062	C	650 563-7100	16523

MOUNT HERMON, CA - Santa Cruz County

	SIC	EMP	PHONE	ENTRY #
Mount Hermon Association Inc **(PA)**	7032	D	831 335-4466	11609

MOUNT SHASTA, CA - Siskiyou County

	SIC	EMP	PHONE	ENTRY #
Shasta Services Inc	1542	E	530 926-4093	960
Siskiyou Lake Golf Resort Inc	7992	D	530 926-3030	15027
Siskiyou Opportunity Center **(PA)**	8331	D	530 926-4698	17838
Six CS Enterprises Inc	7011	E	530 926-3101	11487
Sousa Ready Mix LLC	3273	F	530 926-4485	4508
Unbound Renewable Energy Inc	1711	D	800 472-1142	1388

MOUNTAIN VIEW, CA - Santa Clara County

	SIC	EMP	PHONE	ENTRY #
8181 LLC	6512	E	303 779-3053	10375
Achievo Corporation **(PA)**	7371	D	925 498-8864	12226
Addepar Inc **(PA)**	7371	D	855 464-6268	12228
Advanced Crdvsclar Spclsts Inc	8011	E	650 962-4690	15269
Aera Technology Inc **(PA)**	7371	C	408 524-2222	12233
Aeva Technologies Inc **(PA)**	3714	E	650 481-7070	6571
Agilepoint Inc **(PA)**	7372	C	650 968-6789	12962
Ahntech Inc **(PA)**	8711	D	650 861-3987	18622
Alcatel-Lucent USA Inc	3661	D	650 623-3300	5785
Alexza Pharmaceuticals Inc **(HQ)**	2834	E	650 944-7000	3839
Alivecor Inc **(PA)**	7372	D	650 396-8650	12973
Alphabet Inc **(PA)**	7371	A	650 253-0000	12243
Alphonso Inc **(PA)**	7371	E	415 223-2112	12244
Alza Corporation	3826	A	650 564-5000	6806
Apigee Corporation	7371	B	408 343-7300	12258
Applied Intuition Inc **(PA)**	7371	E	630 935-8986	12262
Applied Physics Systems **(PA)**	3829	C	650 965-0500	6892
Apteligent Inc	7371	D	415 371-1402	12265
Asrc Aerospace Corp	3812	C	650 604-5946	6662
At-Bay Inc **(PA)**	6411	E	888 338-9522	10242
Atrenta Inc **(HQ)**	7371	D	408 453-3333	12284
Attainia Inc	7372	F	866 288-2464	12991
Aurora Operations Inc **(PA)**	7372	A	888 583-9506	12995
Auto-Chlor System NY Cy Inc **(PA)**	3589	C	650 967-3085	5438
Avicenatech Corp **(PA)**	7389	D	919 376-6258	14209
Avid Systems Inc **(HQ)**	3663	C	650 526-1600	5827
Balboa Enterprises Inc	8051	C	650 961-6161	15922
Bank America National Assn	6021	E	650 960-4701	9678
Bella Terra Technologies Inc	4899	D	650 316-6660	8070
Bioelectron Technology Corp **(PA)**	2834	F	650 641-9200	3866
Bionetics Corporation	8731	D	650 604-5327	19034
Bloomreach Inc **(PA)**	4813	C	650 964-1541	7935
Blue Coat LLC	7372	A	408 220-2200	13027
Bosco Oil Inc	5171	E	650 967-2253	9523
Bossa Nova Robotics Inc	5099	C	415 234-5136	9190
Camino Real Group LLC	7011	E	650 964-1700	10985
Capella Photonics Inc	3695	E	408 360-4240	6500
Centrl Inc	7372	E	650 641-7092	13058
Century Theatres Inc	7833	C	650 961-3828	14826
Chay & Harris Pntg Contrs Inc	1721	E	650 966-1472	1408
Childrens Crative Lrng Ctr Inc	8351	B	650 968-2600	17897
Chronicle LLC **(HQ)**	7382	D	650 214-5199	14124
Clearpath Management Group Inc	7363	E	650 691-4140	12163
Clearwell Systems Inc	7372	C	877 253-2793	13070
Cloudjee Inc	7372	E	866 660-6099	13078
Cloudsimple Inc	7372	D	412 568-3487	13080
Cobalt Power Systems Inc	1711	E	650 938-9574	1237
Cobalt Technologies Inc	8731	E	650 230-0722	19043
Community Hlth Awrness Council	8322	E	650 965-2020	17496
Community Svcs Agcy Mtn View L	8322	C	650 968-0836	17500
Compex Legal Services LLC	7334	C	650 833-0460	11845
Computer History Museum	8412	D	650 810-1010	18266
Confluent Inc **(PA)**	7372	A	800 439-3207	13090
Core Mobility Inc **(PA)**	7371	E	650 603-6600	12356
Coursera Inc **(PA)**	7372	A	650 963-9884	13096
Covenant Care California LLC	8062	D	650 964-0543	16342
Cumulus Networks Inc **(PA)**	7372	C	650 383-6700	13100
Datavisor Inc	7372	D	408 331-9886	13109
Dg Architects Inc **(PA)**	8712	E	650 943-1660	18883
Dome9 Security Inc	5045	E	831 212-2353	8694
Drishti Technologies Inc	7371	C	669 273-9090	12403
Driveai Inc	7372	C	408 693-0765	13124
Ebrary	7375	D	650 475-8700	13787
Edcast Inc **(PA)**	7372	E	650 823-3511	13131
El Camino Hospital Auxiliary	8082	A	650 940-7214	16880
El Camino Hospital District RE **(PA)**	6733	C	650 940-7000	10794
Enfabrica Corporation	3674	E	650 206-8533	6111
Esperanto Technologies Inc **(PA)**	3674	D	650 319-7357	6115
Euphonix Inc **(HQ)**	3663	D	650 526-1600	5843

GEOGRAPHIC

Employment Codes: A=Over 500 employees, B=251-500, C=101-250, D=51-100, E=20-50 F=10-19

2022 Northern California Business Directory and Buyers Guide

1167

MOUNTAIN VIEW, CA

Company	SIC	EMP	PHONE	ENTRY #
Everest Networks Inc	3577	F	408 300-9236	5366
Everflow Technologies Inc	7373	E	408 479-9405	13585
Exploramed Nc7 Inc	3845	C	650 559-5805	7105
Eyefluence Inc	3851	E	408 586-8632	7139
Fenwick & West LLP (PA)	8111	B	650 988-8500	17264
Fernqvist Retail Systems Inc (HQ)	2754	F	650 428-0330	3716
First Republic Bank	6022	D	650 383-2888	9728
Fortanix Inc	7372	C	650 943-2484	13174
Gca Law Partners LLP	8111	E	650 428-3900	17272
Global Automation Inc (PA)	7379	E	650 316-5900	13900
Global Testing Corporation	3674	E	408 745-0718	6130
Glyntai Inc	7372	F	650 386-6932	13193
Gold Star Gymnastics	7991	E	650 694-7827	14951
Google LLC (HQ)	7372	C	650 253-0000	12484
Google Payment Corp	7389	E	650 253-0000	14287
Greystar LP	8741	D	650 386-6438	19345
Groq Inc	7371	C	650 521-9007	12491
Group Avantica Inc	7371	E	650 248-9678	12492
Guardian Analytics Inc	7372	E	650 383-9200	13200
Guidant Sales LLC	3841	B	650 965-2634	6979
Guy Chaddock & Company (PA)	2512	C	408 907-9200	3287
Guzik Technical Enterprises (PA)	3825	E	650 625-8000	6761
H2oai Inc	7371	C	650 429-8337	12494
Hansen Medical Inc	3841	E	650 404-5800	6980
Harman Cnncted Svcs Holdg Corp (DH)	7373	A	650 623-9400	13604
Harman Connected Services Inc (DH)	7373	E	650 623-9400	13605
Health Iq	8099	D	917 770-2190	17151
Healthpocket Inc	6321	C	800 984-8015	10085
Healthtap Inc	8011	D	650 268-9806	15428
Humu Inc (PA)	7371	D	669 241-4868	12505
Hytrust Inc (PA)	7372	D	650 681-8100	12509
Igm Biosciences Inc	8731	E	650 965-7873	19070
Inmage Systems Inc	7372	D	408 200-3840	13237
Intellisync Corporation (HQ)	7371	C	650 625-2185	12531
Intuit Financing Inc	7372	E	605 944-6000	13244
Intuit Inc (PA)	7372	D	650 944-6000	13245
Intuit Inc	7372	C	650 944-6000	13246
Iridex Corporation (PA)	3845	D	650 940-4700	7108
Iris Medical Instruments Inc	3845	E	650 940-4700	7109
Island Hospitality MGT LLC	7011	E	650 940-1300	11203
Ittavi Inc	7372	E	866 246-4408	13250
Jigsaw Operations LLC (PA)	4813	E	212 565-8046	7967
Joie De Vivre Hospitality LLC	7011	D	650 940-1000	11220
Jumio Software & Dev LLC	7372	E	650 388-0264	13258
Kaiser Foundation Hospitals	8062	A	650 903-3000	16410
Kaye Sandy Enterprises Inc	3732	E	650 961-5334	6643
Kelly Computer Systems Inc	3577	E	650 960-1010	5391
Khan Academy Inc	7372	D	650 336-5426	13264
Kirosh Inc	7011	E	650 595-2847	11236
Knightscope Inc	3699	D	650 924-1025	6530
Kodiak Robotics Inc	8711	E	781 626-2729	18749
Lark Technologies Inc	7371	E	650 300-1750	12568
Lenz Precision Technology Inc	3599	E	650 966-1784	5560
Livongo Health Inc (HQ)	8069	E	866 435-5643	16765
Loon LLC	7389	C	310 625-3449	14323
Lozano Inc	7542	C	650 941-0590	14650
Marketmile Inc	8721	E	650 903-5600	18976
Matternet Inc (PA)	3728	E	650 260-2727	6635
Maxiscale Inc	8741	F	408 962-6000	19369
Menlo Security Inc (PA)	7371	D	650 614-1705	12603
Microsemi Soc Corp	3674	E	650 318-4200	6211
Minaris Medical America Inc	3821	C	800 233-6278	6696
Mindstrong Inc	8742	E	650 850-7050	19576
Mint Software Inc	7372	D	650 944-6000	13311
Monterey Design Systems Inc	3695	F	408 747-7370	6504
Morgan Stnley Smith Barney LLC	6282	C	650 316-6788	10050
Moveworks Inc (PA)	7372	C	408 435-5100	13316
NASA Ames Research Center	7011	E	650 604-4620	11325
Neeva Inc	7375	D	408 220-9086	13801
Netxen Inc (DH)	3674	B	949 389-6000	6230
Neuron Fuel Inc	7371	E	408 537-3966	12629
Neuropace Inc	3841	C	650 237-2700	7010
Nextinput Inc (HQ)	3625	E	408 770-9293	5685
Northrop Grumman Systems Corp	7373	C	650 604-6056	13640
Nuro Inc	3559	C	650 476-2687	5161
Oberon Media Inc (PA)	7371	D	646 367-2020	12641
OGrady Paving Inc	1611	C	650 966-1926	1068
Omnicell (PA)	3571	B	650 251-6100	5263
Omnicell Inc	3571	B	650 251-6100	5264
Omnicell International Inc (HQ)	3571	E	650 251-6100	5265
Otterai Inc	7371	E	650 250-6322	12660
Pacific Western Systems Inc (PA)	3825	E	650 961-8855	6777
Pactum Ai Inc	7372	E	669 289-9041	13359
Pano Logic Inc	3577	E	650 743-1773	5404
Paypal Global Holdings Inc (HQ)	7374	A	408 967-1000	13738
Perceptimed Inc	3559	E	650 941-7000	5164
Pickering Laboratories Inc	2819	E	650 694-6700	3795
Planprescriber Inc	6411	C	650 584-2700	10333
Polaris Building Maint Inc	7349	D	650 964-9400	11985
Polaris Wireless Inc	7371	E	408 492-8900	12690
Polyfuel Inc	8731	E	650 429-4700	19104
Portworx Inc	7371	D	650 386-0766	12692
Proteus Industries Inc	3823	E	650 964-4163	6731
Pure Storage Inc	7372	A	800 379-7873	13392
Quark Pharmaceuticals Inc (DH)	2834	E	510 402-4020	3968
Quora Inc	7375	E	650 485-2464	13806
Quotient Technology Inc (PA)	7311	A	650 605-4600	11778
Quova Inc	8748	D	650 965-2898	19844
Rackspace Hosting Inc	7374	B	201 792-1918	13749
Raydiance Inc	8732	E	408 764-4000	19182
Realscout Inc	7372	F	650 397-6500	13401
Redis Inc	7371	B	415 930-9666	12735
Reliable Robotics Corporation	5084	E	650 336-0608	9088
Rhythmone LLC	7371	D	650 961-9024	12750
Samsung Electronics Amer Inc	5065	A	650 210-1000	8950
Samsung Pay Inc	7389	E	617 279-0520	14394
Samsung Research America Inc (DH)	8731	A	650 210-1001	19123
Sentinelone Inc (PA)	7372	A	855 868-3733	13437
Service By Medallion	7349	E	650 625-1010	11996
Seti Institute	8733	C	650 961-6633	19236
Shape Security Inc (HQ)	7371	C	650 399-0400	12774
Siemens Med Solutions USA Inc	8011	B	650 694-5747	15681
Silicon Vly Cmnty Foundation (PA)	8641	C	650 450-5400	18471
Siwibi Wholesale	3612	E	650 541-1007	5648
Skyline Solar Inc	3433	E	650 864-9770	4634
Smartthings Inc (PA)	3567	C	757 633-2308	5218
Soaprojects Inc (PA)	7379	D	650 960-9900	13979
Southern Cal Disc Tire Co Inc	5014	C	650 988-9611	8480
Specific Diagnostics Inc	3841	E	650 938-2030	7041
Spine View Inc	3841	D	510 490-1753	7043
Springsoft Usa Inc (HQ)	7371	E	650 584-5000	12813
Squaglia Manufacturing Company (PA)	3599	E	650 965-9644	5622
Stackrox Inc	7372	E	650 489-6769	13464
Staffing Industry Analysts Inc	2741	D	650 390-6200	3601
Stampli Inc	8721	E	650 963-9429	18996
Stanford Investment Group	6282	E	650 941-1717	10060
Statcomm Inc	8711	E	408 734-0440	18820
Susan G Komen Breast Cancer	8699	E	650 409-2656	18599
Sutter Health	8062	C	650 934-7000	16647
Symantec Operating Corporation (HQ)	7371	A	650 527-8000	12837
Symantec SEC Holdings I Inc	3674	B	650 527-8000	6322
Synopsys Inc	7372	E	650 584-5000	13480
Synplicity Inc (HQ)	7372	C	650 584-5000	13481
Sysorex International Inc (PA)	7371	E	408 702-2167	12845
T-Ram Semiconductor Inc	3674	F	408 597-3670	6323
Tabula Inc	5065	D	408 986-9140	8963
Tatung Telecom Corporation	3661	D	650 961-2288	5812
Teachers Curriculum Inst LLC (PA)	2731	E	800 497-6138	3546
Teledyne Defense Elec LLC (HQ)	3679	E	650 691-9800	6477
Tellme Networks Inc	2741	B	650 693-1009	3604
Terrapin Energy LLC (PA)	1311	E	650 386-6180	550
Thawte Inc	3663	E	650 426-7400	5881
Tintri Inc	7375	B	650 810-8200	13810
Travelzoo Inc	7313	D	650 316-6956	11807
Treasure Data Inc (HQ)	7371	D	866 899-5386	12875
Tri-State Enterprises Inc	8741	D	650 210-0085	19412
Tricentis USA Corp	7373	B	650 383-8329	13681
Twin Health Inc	7371	E	970 215-8300	12881
Ubicom Inc (PA)	3674	E	408 523-7800	6340
Upguard Inc (PA)	7372	E	888 882-3223	13508
Vast Systems Technology Corp	7371	E	650 584-5000	12895
Veritas Software Global LLC	7372	F	650 335-8000	13516
Vibrynt Inc	3845	E	650 362-6100	7133
Vieway Technologies Inc	5047	D	650 252-0920	8795
Villa Siena	8361	E	650 961-6484	18202
Vimo Inc (PA)	8748	B	650 618-4600	19886
Virage Logic Corporation (HQ)	3674	E	650 584-5000	6348
Willow Innovations Inc	3561	C	650 472-0300	5181
Wing Aviation LLC	4513	C	650 224-1198	7753
Wing Aviation LLC	4513	C	650 260-8170	7754
Wipro LLC	7373	E	650 316-3555	13689
Wisk Aero LLC (PA)	4111	B	650 641-0920	7366
Xmotorsai Inc	3714	F	650 213-1359	6598
Y Combinator Management LLC	6799	E	775 287-3519	10898
Young MNS Chrstn Assn of E Bay	8641	B	650 526-3500	18498
Young MNS Chrstn Assn Slcon Vl	8641	C	650 969-9622	18529
Zonare Medical Systems Inc	8733	D	650 230-2800	19252

MUIR BEACH, CA - Marin County

Company	SIC	EMP	PHONE	ENTRY #
Pelican Inn	7011	D	415 383-6000	11362

MURPHYS, CA - Calaveras County

Company	SIC	EMP	PHONE	ENTRY #
Alchemy Cafe Inc	7378	E	925 825-8400	13818
Kaiser Enterprises Inc	3498	D	209 728-2091	4975
Kautz Vineyards Inc (PA)	0172	D	209 728-1251	60
Murphys Historic Hotel	7011	D	209 728-3444	11317
Stevenot Winery & Imports Inc (PA)	2084	E	209 728-0638	2729

NAPA, CA - Napa County

Company	SIC	EMP	PHONE	ENTRY #
Adanta Inc	8999	D	707 709-8894	19896
Advanced Pressure Technology	3823	D	707 259-0102	6711
Aegis Senior Communities LLC	8361	E	707 927-3981	18053
Allworth Financial LP	6282	D	888 577-2489	10026
Amadeus Spa NAPA Vly Marriott	7991	E	707 254-3330	14925
Antinori California	2084	E	707 265-8866	2505
Asl Print Fx	2752	F	707 927-3096	3622
Audio Visual MGT Solutions	3651	E	707 254-3395	5751
AUL Corp (PA)	7694	E	707 257-9700	14728
Back Street Fitness Inc	7991	E	707 254-7200	14928
Balloons Above Valley Ltd	7999	E	707 253-2222	15179
Barbour Vineyards LLC	2084	E	707 257-1829	2508
Barrel Ten Qarter Cir Land Inc	2084	F	209 538-3131	2509
Bell Products Inc	1711	D	707 255-1811	1217
Benchmark Wine Group Inc	5182	E	707 255-3500	9568
Bert Williams and Sons Inc	5013	E	707 255-7003	8442

	SIC	EMP	PHONE	ENTRY #
Blacktalon Industries Inc	3496	F	707 256-1812	4966
Bnnv LLC	7922	E	707 880-2300	14838
Bouchaine Vineyards Inc	2084	F	707 252-9065	2515
Boys & Girls Club NAPA Valley	8641	E	707 255-8866	18395
Bruce Tucker Construction Inc	1542	E	707 255-1587	839
Buoncristiani Wine Co LLC	2084	F	707 259-1681	2519
Byer California	5137	C	707 259-1225	9251
Cal Land Title	6411	E	707 361-5760	10256
Caldwell Vineyard LLC	2084	F	707 255-1294	2524
California Physicians Service	6324	D	949 859-6303	10098
California Vacation Club	7011	E	707 252-4200	10983
Califrnia Odd Fllows Hsing Nap **(PA)**	6513	D	707 257-7885	10420
Califrnia Odd Fllows Hsing Nap	6513	D	707 257-7885	10421
Carneros Inn LLC	7011	B	707 299-4880	10990
Carneros Ranching Inc	2084	F	707 253-9464	2525
Cedar Knoll Vineyards Inc	2084	E	707 226-5587	2527
Cello & Maudru Cnstr Co Inc	1542	E	707 257-0454	851
Cemex Materials LLC	3273	D	707 255-3035	4473
Chambers & Chambers Inc **(PA)**	5182	E	415 642-5500	9571
Chardonnay/ Club Shakespeare	7997	E	707 257-1900	15072
Chaudhary & Associates	8711	E	707 255-2729	18668
Child Start Inc **(PA)**	8351	E	707 252-8931	17894
Clean Power Research LLC	7379	E	707 258-2765	13866
Clos Du Val Wine Company Ltd	2084	E	707 259-2200	2534
CMC Rebar West	1541	C	707 863-3933	792
Codorniu Napa Inc	2084	D	707 254-2148	2537
Collabria Care	8082	D	707 258-9080	16871
Collotype Labels USA Inc **(DH)**	2759	D	707 603-2500	3725
Copia The Amrcn Ctr For Wine F	8412	E	707 259-1600	18267
Courseco Inc	7992	B	707 255-4333	14993
Crimson Wine Group Ltd **(PA)**	2084	C	800 486-0503	2540
Crop Care Associates Inc	0721	E	707 258-2998	253
Cultured Stone Corporation **(PA)**	3272	A	707 255-1727	4429
Cup4cup LLC **(PA)**	2096	E	707 754-4263	2853
Darioush Khaledi Winery LLC	2084	E	707 257-2345	2544
Decrevel Incorporated	3544	E	707 258-8065	5083
Delicato Vineyards	2084	E	707 265-1700	2547
Demptos NAPA Cooperage **(HQ)**	2449	E	707 257-2628	3235
Dexta Corporation	3843	D	707 255-2454	7084
Diamond Touch Inc	7371	D	707 253-7450	12388
Dickenson Ptman Fgrty Inc A PR **(PA)**	8111	E	707 252-7122	17250
Doctors Company Foundation	6321	A	800 421-2368	10084
Doctors Company Insurance Svcs	6351	B	707 226-0100	10192
Doctors Management Company **(HQ)**	6411	C	707 226-0100	10273
Domaine Carneros Ltd	0172	D	707 257-0101	51
Dominics Orgnal Gnova Deli Inc	2051	D	707 253-8686	2376
Don Sbstani Sons Intl Wine Ngc	2084	E	707 337-1961	2553
Dry Farm Wines Inc **(PA)**	2084	D	707 944-1500	2555
Essex National Securities LLC	8742	C	707 258-5000	19508
Etude Wines Inc	2084	E	707 299-3057	2563
Fior Di Sole LLC	2084	C	707 259-1477	2570
Fior Di Sole LLC	2084	E	707 259-1477	2571
First American Title Co NAPA **(PA)**	6541	E	707 254-4500	10692
Folio Wine Company LLC **(PA)**	5182	E	707 256-2700	9575
Folio Wine Company LLC	5182	D	707 256-2757	9576
Fortis Solutions Group LLC	2759	E	707 256-6343	3732
Franks Janitorial Service	7349	E	707 226-1848	11954
Fryes Printing Inc	7334	E	707 253-1114	11846
GD Long Electric Company	1731	E	707 252-3512	1507
GD Nielson Construction Inc	1623	D	707 253-8774	1102
Geyser Peak Winery	2084	E	707 857-9463	2593
GF Carneros Tenant LLC	7231	E	707 299-4900	11681
Golden State Vintners	2084	E	707 254-1985	2599
H De V LLC	2084	E	541 386-9119	2608
Hagafen Cellars Inc	2084	F	707 252-0781	2609
Hayward Enterprises Inc	2037	E	707 261-5100	2294
Hedgeside Vintners	2084	E	707 963-2134	2615
Hess Collection Winery **(DH)**	2084	E	707 255-1144	2617
Huneeus Vintners LLC **(PA)**	2084	E	707 286-2724	2618
IA Lodging NAPA Solano Trs LLC	7011	C	707 253-8600	11185
Ingenious Packaging Group **(HQ)**	7389	E	707 252-8300	14302
Intrawest NAPA Rvrbend Hsptlit	7011	D	408 829-4141	11197
Jarvis	2084	E	707 255-5280	2630
Joes Dwntwn Brewry & Rest Inc	2082	E	707 258-2337	2482
Kaiser Foundation Hospitals	6733	D	707 258-2500	10797
Kaufman Building & MGT Inc	1442	F	707 732-3770	595
Kenzo Estate Inc	0762	E	707 254-7572	379
Kieu Hoang Winery LLC	2084	F	707 253-1615	2640
Laird Family Estate LLC **(PA)**	2084	E	707 257-0360	2647
Le Belge Chocolatier Inc	2064	E	707 258-9200	2430
Lixit Corporation **(PA)**	3999	C	800 358-8254	7296
Lodgeworks LP	7011	D	707 690-9800	11266
Melissa Bradley RE Inc	6531	E	707 258-3900	10617
Mentis	8322	E	707 255-0966	17647
Meritage Resort LLC	7011	B	707 251-1900	11297
Modern Method Roofg Cnstr Inc	1761	E	707 255-8090	1823
Mum NAPA Valley	0762	C	707 942-3425	382
N V Cast Stone LLC	3272	E	707 261-6615	4444
NAPA Es Leasing LLC	7011	D	707 253-9540	11319
NAPA Golf Associates LLC	7997	D	707 257-1900	15113
NAPA Jet Center Inc	4581	D	707 224-0887	7777
NAPA Mill LLC	7011	E	707 251-8500	11320
NAPA Motel and Restaurant	7011	E	707 257-1930	11321
NAPA Nissan Inc	5013	E	707 253-1551	8458
NAPA Nursing Center Inc	8051	E	707 257-0931	16065
NAPA River Inn	7011	D	707 251-8500	11322
NAPA Sanitation District	4952	E	707 254-9231	8286
NAPA Select Vineyard Servi	2084	F	707 294-2637	2663
NAPA Valley Balloons Inc	4725	E	707 253-2224	7819
NAPA Valley Country Club	7997	D	707 252-1111	15114
NAPA Valley PSI Inc	8331	D	707 255-0177	17825
NAPA Valley Publishing Co	2711	D	707 226-3711	3466
NAPA Valley Publishing Co **(PA)**	2711	E	707 226-3711	3467
NAPA Valley Unified School Dst	7349	E	707 253-3520	11977
NAPA Valley Wine Train LLC **(HQ)**	7999	C	707 253-2160	15222
NAPA Vly Orthpdic Med Group In	8011	E	707 254-7117	15544
Napaidence Opco LLC	8051	C	707 255-6060	16066
Newton Vineyard LLC **(DH)**	2084	E	707 204-7423	2668
North Bay Dvlpmntal Dsblties S **(PA)**	8331	D	707 256-1224	17826
North Bay Plywood Inc	2431	E	707 224-7849	3143
Nova Equipment Leasing LLC	5046	E	707 265-1116	8768
Nova Group Inc **(HQ)**	1623	C	707 265-1100	1126
Nova-Cpf Inc	1623	D	707 257-3200	1127
Nova/Tic Gvrnment Prjcts A Jin	1623	C	707 257-3200	1128
Oakville Pump Service Inc	1711	E	707 944-2471	1320
Ole Health	8011	D	707 254-1770	15565
Oxbow Landscape Contrs Inc	0781	E	707 339-6001	430
Pacific Steel Group	3449	E	707 669-3136	4858
Peck & Hiller Company	1771	D	707 258-8800	1901
Perfect Puree of NAPA Vly LLC	2037	F	707 261-5100	2296
Pina Vineyard Management LLC	0762	E	707 944-2229	385
Pine Ridge Winery LLC **(HQ)**	2084	D	707 253-7500	2683
Piners Nursing Home Inc	8051	D	707 224-7925	16096
Prolab Orthotics Inc	3069	E	707 257-4400	4226
Queen of Vly Med Ctr Fundation **(DH)**	8062	A	707 252-4411	16486
Queen of Vly Med Ctr Fundation	8062	B	707 251-2000	16487
Redwood Rgnal Med Group DRG LL	8011	E	707 253-7161	15646
Regulus Intgrted Solutions LLC	2752	E	707 254-4000	3693
Regusci Vineyard MGT Inc	2084	E	707 254-0403	2694
River City	2599	E	707 253-1111	3338
Robert Mondavi Corporation **(HQ)**	2084	D	707 967-2100	2697
Rohlffs Memorial Manor **(PA)**	8361	E	707 255-9555	18172
Saintsbury LLC	2084	F	707 252-0592	2707
Sander Jcobs Cssyre Grffin Inc	6411	E	707 252-8822	10341
Scandinavian Galleries LLC	7389	E	650 862-8432	14399
Seguin Moreau USA Holdings Inc **(HQ)**	2449	E	707 252-3408	3240
Seguin Mreau NAPA Coperage Inc	5085	D	707 252-3408	9133
Shafer Vineyards	2084	F	707 944-2877	2713
Sheehan Construction Inc	1521	D	707 603-2610	706
Silenus Vintners	2084	F	707 299-3930	2716
Silverado NAPA Corp **(HQ)**	1521	D	707 226-1325	708
Silverado Resort and Spa	7997	A	707 257-0200	15146
Silverado Rsort Svcs Group LLC	7011	B	707 257-0200	11481
Silverado Veterinary Hosp Inc	0742	E	707 224-7953	337
Silverado Vineyards	2084	E	707 257-1770	2719
Simplex Filler Inc	3565	F	707 265-6801	5204
Sinskey Vineyards Inc	2084	E	707 944-9090	2720
Stags Leap Wine Cellars	2084	C	707 944-2020	2724
Star H-R	7361	B	707 265-9911	12140
State Hospitals Cal Dept	8063	B	707 253-5000	16746
Sterling Vineyards Inc	2084	C	707 252-7410	2727
Steve Silva Plumbing Inc	1711	E	707 252-3941	1366
Superior Equipment Company Inc	4959	E	707 256-3600	8409
Sweetie Pies LLC	2051	F	707 257-7280	2405
Symed Corporation	8721	E	707 255-3300	18999
Tailored Living Choices LLC	1799	C	707 259-0526	2073
Tapp Label Holding Company LLC **(PA)**	6411	D	707 252-8300	10357
Treasury Wine Estates Americas **(HQ)**	2084	B	707 259-4500	2745
Trefethen Vineyards Winery Inc	2084	E	707 255-7700	2747
Twin Creeks Vineyard Company	0172	E	707 224-4575	78
United Parcel Service Inc	4215	C	707 224-1205	7663
Uptown Theatre	7922	D	707 259-0123	14866
Van Winden Landscaping Inc	0781	E	707 224-1367	443
Veer Incorporated **(PA)**	7335	D	877 297-7900	11855
Vignette Winery LLC **(PA)**	2084	E	707 637-8821	2755
Villa Del Rey	8051	D	707 252-3333	16153
Vine Village Inc	8361	E	707 255-4006	18204
Vitisystems Inc	8734	E	707 258-4000	19291
Walsh Vineyards Management Inc	6531	C	707 255-1650	10680
Wine Country Cases Inc	2449	D	707 967-4805	3244
Work Health	8742	D	707 257-4084	19671

NELSON, CA - Butte County

	SIC	EMP	PHONE	ENTRY #
Far West Rice Inc	2044	E	530 891-1339	2319

NEVADA CITY, CA - Nevada County

	SIC	EMP	PHONE	ENTRY #
Ananda Church of Self-Realztn **(PA)**	2731	D	530 478-7560	3522
Anderson Physical Therapy	8049	E	530 265-8100	15882
Best Sanitizers Inc	2842	D	530 265-1800	4066
C & D Contractors Inc	1521	E	530 264-7074	625
Dylern Incorporated	3599	E	530 470-8785	5511
Holdrege Kull Cnslting Engners	8711	D	530 478-1305	18733
Mountain Vly Child Fmly Svcs I	8052	C	530 265-9057	16193
Northern Queen Inc	7011	E	530 265-4492	11331
Rcd Engineering Inc	3625	D	530 292-3133	5688
Sierra Family Med Clinic Inc **(PA)**	8011	E	530 292-3478	15682
Sierra Metal Fabricators Inc	3441	E	530 265-4591	4683
Sonic Technology Products Inc	3674	E	530 272-4607	6307
Soper-Wheeler Company LLC **(PA)**	2411	E	530 675-2343	3083
Technicolor Usa Inc	3663	A	530 478-3000	5877
Telestream LLC **(PA)**	7371	C	530 470-1300	12856

NEWARK, CA - Alameda County

	SIC	EMP	PHONE	ENTRY #
Accurate Tube Bending Inc	3498	E	510 790-6500	4973
Adonai Enterprises Inc **(PA)**	7699	E	510 475-9950	14733

GEOGRAPHIC

	SIC	EMP	PHONE	ENTRY #
Advanced Cell Diagnostics Inc	8731	D	510 576-8800	19011
Advantek Taping Systems Inc **(DH)**	5085	D	510 623-1877	9107
Aloft Silicon Valley	7011	D	510 494-8800	10917
Apn Software Services Inc **(PA)**	7379	C	510 623-5050	13840
Aspire Bakeries LLC	5149	D	510 494-1700	9439
Bay Advanced Technologies LLC	5084	E	510 857-0900	9052
Cellotape Inc **(HQ)**	3993	C	510 651-5551	7223
Central Business Solutions Inc	7379	D	510 573-5500	13863
Challenger Schools	8351	D	510 770-1771	17886
Cloudwick Technologies Inc **(PA)**	7379	D	650 346-5788	13871
Crown Mfg Co Inc	3089	E	510 742-8800	4271
Cymabay Therapeutics Inc **(PA)**	2834	E	510 293-8800	3888
Dna Twopointo Inc	8731	D	650 853-8347	19051
Drishticon Inc **(PA)**	8748	E	510 402-4515	19762
E Z 8 Motels Inc	7011	E	510 794-7775	11066
Elitegroup Cmpt Systems Inc	3577	C	510 226-7333	5365
Elitegroup Computer Systems Ho	5045	C	510 794-2952	8698
Envia Systems Inc	3699	E	510 509-1367	6517
Etm—Electromatic Inc **(PA)**	3663	D	510 797-1100	5842
Etouch Systems Corp	7379	A	510 795-4800	13892
Everest Silicon Valley MGT LP	8741	D	510 494-8800	19331
Evergreen Envmtl Svcs Inc	4953	C	510 795-4400	8328
Ferma Corporation	1795	C	510 794-0414	1985
Fine Line Sawing & Drlg Inc	1771	E	510 793-6700	1870
Five Star Lumber Company LLC **(PA)**	2448	E	510 795-7204	3221
Foot Locker Retail Inc	3149	E	510 797-5750	4345
Fremont Paving Company Inc	1611	D	510 797-3553	1042
Fullbloom Baking Company Inc	2051	A	510 456-3638	2385
Holo Inc	3825	E	510 221-4177	6762
IMS - Insurance Med Svcs Inc	8731	C	510 490-6211	19072
Incarda Therapeutics Inc	2834	E	510 422-5522	3928
Innovated Packaging Co Inc	4783	D	510 745-8180	7866
Integrated Pkg & Crating Svcs	4783	E	510 745-8180	7867
Intelliswift Software Inc **(PA)**	7371	C	510 490-9240	12530
Intime Infotech Inc	7371	E	650 396-4319	12536
Itrenew Inc **(HQ)**	7379	E	408 744-9600	13924
J & S Operations LLC	7538	D	510 360-7165	14572
Javelin Logistics Company Inc	4731	C	800 577-1060	7841
Javelin Logistics Corporation **(PA)**	4214	E	510 795-7287	7623
Jri Inc	3444	E	510 494-5300	4774
Kaiam Corp	1731	D	650 344-2231	1529
Kateeva Inc	3663	C	800 385-7802	5850
Knt Inc	3599	C	510 651-7163	5555
Knt Manufacturing Inc	3999	D	510 896-1699	7294
Kpi Partners Inc	7371	E	510 818-9480	12563
Kwj Engineering Inc **(PA)**	3829	E	510 794-4296	6907
Lancashire Group Incorporated	8742	E	510 792-9384	19554
Logitech Inc **(HQ)**	3577	B	510 795-8500	5393
Logitech Latin America Inc	3577	F	510 795-8500	5394
Logitech Streaming Media Inc	3577	D	510 795-8500	5395
Lucid Group Inc **(PA)**	3711	E	510 648-3553	6552
Lucid Usa Inc **(HQ)**	3711	C	510 648-3553	6553
Massingham & Assoc MGT Inc **(PA)**	6531	E	510 896-2634	10615
Membrane Technology & RES Inc **(PA)**	8731	D	650 328-2228	19088
Mexico Tortilla Factory & Deli	2099	F	510 792-9909	2922
Mission Linen Supply	7349	D	510 996-3416	11974
Mitac Information Systems	3577	E	510 668-3679	5401
Mitac Information Systems Corp **(DH)**	3572	C	510 284-3000	5301
Moose International Inc	8641	C	510 791-2654	18441
Morpho Detection LLC	3812	D	510 739-2400	6676
Moving Solutions Inc	4214	C	408 920-0110	7627
Mshift Inc	7371	E	408 437-2740	12625
Nakagawa Manufacturing USA Inc	2621	E	510 782-0197	3346
National Distribution Agcy Inc **(HQ)**	4225	D	510 487-6226	7695
Nefab Packaging Inc	2441	D	408 678-2500	3216
Nefab Packaging West LLC	7389	D	408 678-2516	14337
Nevada Heat Treating LLC **(PA)**	7692	E	510 790-2300	14718
Nexient LLC **(PA)**	7379	B	415 992-7277	13947
Onfulfillment Inc	4225	E	510 793-3009	7697
Ooshirts Inc **(PA)**	2759	B	866 660-8667	3744
Pabco Building Products LLC	3275	D	510 792-9555	4512
Pabco Building Products LLC	3275	D	510 792-1577	4513
Pacific Hotel Management LLC	7011	C	510 791-7700	11345
Palo Alto Egg and Food Svc Co	5141	E	510 456-2420	9282
Pick Pull Auto Dismantling Inc	5015	E	510 742-2277	8489
Protagonist Therapeutics Inc	2834	D	510 474-0170	3967
Raps Hospitality Group	7011	C	510 795-7995	11385
Residence Inn By Marriott LLC	7011	E	510 739-6000	11402
Resource Label Group LLC	2759	E	510 477-0707	3747
Revance Therapeutics Inc	2834	D	615 724-7755	3974
Risk Management Solutions Inc **(HQ)**	6794	C	510 505-2500	10810
Roseryan Inc	8721	D	510 456-3056	18988
Safari Kid Inc **(PA)**	8351	E	510 739-1511	18012
Salutron Incorporated **(PA)**	3845	E	510 795-2876	7123
San Francisco Bay Brand Inc **(PA)**	2048	E	510 792-7200	2357
Sanmina Corporation	3451	C	510 494-2421	4869
Second Chance Inc **(PA)**	8322	E	510 792-4357	17723
Shotspotter Inc	7372	C	510 794-3100	13443
Silicon Valley Mfg Inc	3315	F	510 791-9450	4545
Smart Global Holdings Inc **(PA)**	3674	B	510 623-1231	6304
Smart Modular Technologies Inc **(HQ)**	3674	A	510 623-1231	6306
Smart Storage Systems Inc **(DH)**	3572	E	510 623-1231	5321
Smiths Detection Inc	3812	A	410 612-2625	6685
Social Vocational Services Inc	8093	E	510 797-1916	17074
Socket Mobile Inc	3663	E	510 933-3000	5869
Specilized Packg Solutions Inc	2449	E	510 494-5670	3241
Svm Machining Inc	3441	E	510 791-9450	4687
Tegile Systems Inc	8731	C	510 791-7900	19135
Tekrevol LLC	7371	D	832 426-3532	12855
Theranos Inc **(PA)**	3841	D	650 838-9292	7048
Thousandshores Inc	3571	F	510 477-0249	5277
Triple Ring Technologies Inc	8742	E	510 592-3000	19655
Ultima Genomics Inc	8731	E	650 861-1194	19141
University Healthcare Alliance	8082	A	510 974-8281	16962
USI Insurance Services Nat Inc	6021	D	914 749-8500	9692
Valassis Direct Mail Inc	7331	D	510 505-6500	11842
Venture Electronics Intl Inc	3672	E	510 744-3720	5996
Verizon Business Global LLC	4813	E	415 328-1020	8003
Vioptix Inc	8733	F	510 226-5860	19244
Vm Services Inc	7371	D	510 744-3720	12914
Windy Cy Wire Cble Tech Pdts L	5063	C	510 284-3956	8879
Wintec Industries Inc **(PA)**	3674	D	510 953-7440	6357
Xtraplus Corporation	5045	E	510 897-1890	8763
Zenith Infotech Limited	7373	C	510 687-1943	13691

NEWCASTLE, CA - Placer County

	SIC	EMP	PHONE	ENTRY #
A & A Stepping Stone Mfg Inc **(PA)**	3272	E	530 885-7481	4416
J Ginger Masonry LP	1741	E	209 229-1581	1648
Jim Dobbas Inc **(PA)**	7389	E	916 663-3363	14313
Neils Controlled Blasting LP	1629	E	916 663-2500	1170
Nelson & Kennard Law Offices	8111	E	916 920-2295	17344
Simpson & Simpson Inc	1611	E	530 885-4354	1073

NEWMAN, CA - Stanislaus County

	SIC	EMP	PHONE	ENTRY #
Avalon Care Ctr - Newman LLC	8051	D	209 862-2862	15918
Beaver Dam Health Care Center	8051	E	209 862-2862	15945
Cemex Cnstr Mtls PCF LLC	3273	E	209 862-0182	4467
Dimare Enterprises Inc **(PA)**	0161	C	209 827-2900	26
Saputo Cheese USA Inc	2022	D	262 307-6738	2156
Stewart & Jasper Marketing Inc **(PA)**	2068	C	209 862-9600	2451
Superior Truck Lines Inc **(PA)**	4213	E	209 862-9430	7599
Titan Newman Inc	5085	D	209 862-2977	9138
Valley Sun Products of Cali	2099	E	209 862-1200	2955
Vsp Products Inc	2034	D	209 862-1200	2275
West Side Cmnty Healthcare Dst	8099	E	209 862-2951	17194
West Side Community Ambulance	4119	E	209 862-2951	7411
Westside Pallet Inc	2448	E	209 862-3941	3233

NICASIO, CA - Marin County

	SIC	EMP	PHONE	ENTRY #
Lucas Learning Ltd	7371	E	415 662-1927	12583

NICE, CA - Lake County

	SIC	EMP	PHONE	ENTRY #
Worldmark Club	7011	D	707 274-0118	11581

NORDEN, CA - Nevada County

	SIC	EMP	PHONE	ENTRY #
Sugar Bowl Corporation	7011	D	530 426-9000	11512
Sugar Bowl Ski Resort	7011	E	530 426-3651	11513

NORTH HIGHLANDS, CA - Sacramento County

	SIC	EMP	PHONE	ENTRY #
Acertus	4789	E	916 331-2355	7873
BMC Stock Holdings Inc	5031	B	916 481-5030	8531
Business Industry & Envmt Inc	7342	D	916 481-0268	11880
Capital City Drywall Inc	1742	D	916 331-9200	1665
Child Abuse Prvntion Cncil SCR	8322	E	916 244-1900	17482
Construction Tstg & Engrg Inc	8734	E	916 331-6030	19263
Graves 6 Inc **(PA)**	1711	D	916 348-3098	1273
Harris Lorenzo	7349	E	916 993-5863	11960
Heritage 1 Window and Building	5031	C	916 481-5030	8548
Heritage Interests LLC **(PA)**	1751	D	916 481-5030	1740
Heritage One Door Crpentry LLC	5031	D	916 481-5030	8549
Homeq Servicing Corporation **(DH)**	6162	A	916 339-6192	9909
Kenyon Construction Inc	1742	E	916 514-9502	1684
Livingstons Concrete Svc Inc **(PA)**	3273	E	916 334-4313	4493
Livingstons Concrete Svc Inc	3273	E	916 334-4313	4494
Lund Construction Co	8711	C	916 344-5800	18756
MCM Construction Inc **(PA)**	1622	D	916 334-1221	1084
Mikes Sheet Metal Pdts Inc	3444	E	916 348-3800	4791
New Wave Industries Ltd **(PA)**	3589	F	800 882-8854	5444
Pacific Coast Supply LLC **(HQ)**	5031	B	916 971-2301	8602
Pacific Coast Supply LLC	2439	F	916 339-8100	3213
Pisor Industries Inc	3599	E	916 944-2851	5596
Recycling Industries Inc	4953	D	916 452-3961	8357
Security Contractor Svcs Inc **(PA)**	5039	D	916 338-4200	8646
Sierra Select Distributors Inc	5064	D	916 483-9295	8887
Stanford Furniture Mfg Inc	2512	F	916 387-5300	3292
Twin Termite and Pest Ctrl Inc	7342	E	916 344-8946	11909
World Rlief Corp of Nat Assn E	8322	D	916 978-2650	17787

NOVATO, CA - Marin County

	SIC	EMP	PHONE	ENTRY #
2k Marin Inc	7371	E	646 536-2898	12213
ADS Solutions	7372	F	415 897-3700	12958
Advisorycloud Inc	8748	C	415 289-7115	19714
Anchor Brewers & Distlrs LLC **(HQ)**	2082	D	415 892-4569	2470
Arena Press	2741	F	415 883-3314	3555
Automatic Data Processing Inc	7374	C	415 899-7300	13694
Bank of Marin Bancorp **(PA)**	6022	C	415 763-4520	9703
Barbier Security Group	7381	C	415 747-8473	14036
Bear Flag Marketing Corp	8082	C	415 899-8466	16856
Birkenstock Usa Lp **(DH)**	5139	E	415 884-3200	9258
Bodies In Motion	7991	E	415 897-2185	14931
Body Kinetics **(PA)**	7991	E	415 895-5965	14932
Brayton Purcell	8111	E	801 521-1712	17220
Brayton Purcell APC **(PA)**	8111	C	415 898-1555	17221
Buck Inst For RES On Aging **(PA)**	8733	C	415 209-2000	19200
Buckelew Programs **(PA)**	8093	C	415 457-6964	16996
California Advncd Imaging Med	8099	E	415 884-3413	17112

GEOGRAPHIC SECTION

OAKLAND, CA

	SIC	EMP	PHONE	ENTRY #
California Newspapers Inc	2711	A	415 883-8600	3423
Cellmark Inc (DH)	5099	D	415 927-1700	9193
Cg Roxane LLC	2086	E	415 339-9521	2787
Charming Trim & Packaging	5131	A	415 302-7021	9241
Comet Building Maintenance Inc	0781	D	415 382-1150	409
Conservation Corps N Bay Inc	8331	E	415 454-4554	17808
Cricket Company LLC	3069	E	415 475-4150	4214
Crittenden Publishing Inc (HQ)	2741	D	415 475-1522	3565
Csw/Stbr-Stroeh Engrg Group In (PA)	8711	E	415 883-9850	18680
Drivesavers Inc	7375	D	415 382-2000	13786
EDG Interior Arch & Design Inc (PA)	7389	D	415 454-2277	14260
Et Water Systems LLC	3829	E	415 945-9383	6900
Excellence Magazine Inc	2721	F	415 382-0582	3498
Fibres International Inc	4953	E	425 455-9811	8329
Fibres International Inc	4953	E	425 455-9811	8330
Forest Investment Group Inc	2752	F	415 459-2330	3649
George Family Enterprises	1742	E	415 884-0399	1676
Good Shepherd Lutheran School	8351	E	415 897-2510	17944
Heart Humanity Health Svcs Inc (PA)	8082	E	415 898-4278	16887
Hired Hands Inc (PA)	8082	E	415 884-4343	16890
Indian Valley Golf Club Inc	7992	E	415 897-1118	15004
Jaylaneentertainment Corp	7313	D	707 820-2773	11803
Kaiser Foundation Hospitals	8049	E	415 209-2444	15891
Kaiser Foundation Hospitals	8011	C	415 899-7400	15479
Kelleher Corporation	5031	E	415 898-8440	8555
L & L Logic and Logistics LP	5139	E	707 795-2475	9259
Marin Airporter Inc	4111	D	415 884-2878	7340
Marin Community Clinic	8011	D	415 448-1500	15518
Marin Country Club Inc	7997	D	415 382-6700	15106
Marin County Sart Program	8063	E	415 892-1628	16743
Marin Humane Society	8699	D	415 883-4621	18579
Marin Med Prctice Concepts Inc	8741	E	415 493-3300	19365
McInnis Park Golf Center Ltd (PA)	7992	E	415 492-1800	15010
Melissa Bradley RE Inc	6531	E	415 209-1000	10620
Meritage Medical Network	7363	D	415 884-1840	12185
Merrimak Capital Company LLC	7359	E	415 475-4100	12054
Navitas LLC	5149	E	415 883-8116	9468
Newmat Norcal Inc	1742	E	415 884-4421	1694
North Bay Childrens Center Inc (PA)	8351	D	415 883-6222	17982
North Marin Community Services (PA)	8322	E	415 892-1643	17657
North Marin Water District (PA)	4941	E	415 897-4133	8254
Novato Fire Protection Dist	7389	E	415 878-2690	14340
Novato Healthcare Center LLC	8051	C	415 897-6161	16077
Novato Management Group Inc	7011	D	415 897-7111	11332
Novato Travelodge	7011	E	415 892-7500	11333
Pacific Inptient Med Group Inc	8011	E	415 485-8824	15578
Pathgroup San Francisco LLC (HQ)	8011	E	415 898-7649	15586
Permanente Medical Group Inc	8011	A	415 209-2444	15613
Permanente Medical Group Inc	8011	E	415 899-7400	15614
Prima Fleur Botanicals Inc	2844	F	415 455-0957	4093
Professnal Fincl Investors Inc	6531	E	415 382-6001	10648
Psi3g Inc (PA)	5023	D	415 493-3854	8520
Radiant Logic Inc (HQ)	7372	C	415 209-6800	13399
Redwood Landfill Inc	4953	C	415 892-2851	8358
Rolling Hills Club Inc	7997	E	415 897-2185	15129
Safetychain Software Inc (PA)	7372	E	415 233-9474	13420
Schalich Brothers Cnstr Inc	1521	E	415 382-7733	702
Servalan Enterprises Inc	7379	E	415 899-1880	13971
Shamrock Materials of Novato	3273	D	415 892-1571	4506
Solarcraft Services Inc (PA)	1731	E	415 382-7717	1608
St Louis Post-Dispatch LLC	2711	D	415 892-1516	3482
Stonetree Golf LLC	7992	E	415 209-6744	15031
Sutter Health	8062	C	415 897-8495	16609
Sutter Health	8062	C	415 602-5380	16658
Sutter West Bay Hospitals	8062	C	415 492-4800	16680
Sutter West Bay Hospitals (HQ)	8062	B	415 209-1300	16681
Tennis Everyone Incorporated	7991	E	415 897-2185	14981
Thompson Builders Corporation	1522	E	415 456-8972	774
Tile West Inc (PA)	1743	E	415 382-7550	1725
True North Ar LLC (DH)	7322	E	800 700-0220	11831
Ultragenyx Pharmaceutical Inc (PA)	2834	A	415 483-8800	4000
Visual Concepts Entertainment	7371	D	415 479-3634	12910
W Bradley Electric Inc (PA)	1731	E	415 898-1400	1632
Wbb Management Company Inc	8741	E	415 456-8972	19421
Whatever Publishing Inc	2731	F	415 884-2100	3550
Winery Exchange Inc (PA)	5182	E	415 382-6900	9588
Young Mens Christian Assoc SF	8641	E	415 883-9622	18486

O NEALS, CA - Madera County

	SIC	EMP	PHONE	ENTRY #
Ponderosa Telephone Co (PA)	4813	E	559 868-6000	7984

OAKDALE, CA - Stanislaus County

	SIC	EMP	PHONE	ENTRY #
Accu-Swiss Inc (PA)	3451	F	209 847-1016	4865
Alldrin Brothers Inc	0723	E	855 667-4231	268
Amerine Systems Incorporated	0781	E	209 847-5968	393
Ball Corporation	3411	B	209 848-6500	4597
Brichetto Bros	3999	E	209 847-2775	7271
Central Valley AG Grinding Inc (PA)	0723	E	209 869-1721	276
Central Valley AG Trnspt Inc	0723	D	209 544-9246	277
Clyde Wheeler Pipeline Inc	1623	D	209 848-0809	1093
D A Wood Construction Inc	8711	D	209 491-4970	18684
Fishbio Environmental LLC (PA)	8748	E	209 847-6300	19776
Formulation Technology Inc	2834	E	209 847-0331	3899
Gcu Trucking Inc	4213	D	209 845-2117	7544
Gilton Rsrce Rcvery Trnsf Fclt (PA)	4953	D	209 527-3781	8333
Gilton Solid Waste MGT Inc	4953	C	209 527-3781	8334
Haeger Incorporated (DH)	3549	E	209 848-4000	5108
Heighten America Inc	3599	E	209 845-0455	5535
Infinity Sports Inc	0971	E	209 845-3940	539
Inter-Muntain Truss Girder Inc	2439	E	209 847-9184	3211
J L G Enterprises Inc	0751	E	209 847-4797	348
Lent Burden Farming Company	0762	E	209 847-3276	381
Media Print Services Inc	7336	F	866 935-5077	11868
Morris Publications (PA)	2711	E	209 847-3021	3463
Mozingo Construction Inc	1794	E	209 848-0160	1967
Oak Valley Hospital District (PA)	8062	B	209 847-3011	16470
Oakdale Golf and Country Club	7997	D	209 847-2984	15118
Oakdale Irrgtion Dst Fing Corp	4941	E	209 847-0341	8256
Pacific Gas and Electric Co	4911	C	800 743-5000	8176
Ross F Carroll Inc	8711	E	209 848-5959	18805
Sconza Candy Company	2064	D	209 845-3700	2432
Shandi Inc	0742	D	209 847-5951	336
Weldway Inc	3441	E	209 847-8083	4693

OAKHURST, CA - Madera County

	SIC	EMP	PHONE	ENTRY #
Kaiser Foundation Hospitals	6324	C	559 658-8388	10127
Kings View	8069	E	559 641-2805	16762
Oakhurst Healthcare Center LLC	8052	D	559 683-2244	16194
Oakhurst Sklled Nrsing Wllness	8051	E	559 683-2244	16080
Persson Inc	1611	E	559 683-3000	1070
San Jquin Vly Rhblttion Hosp A	8049	E	559 658-6490	15897
Sierra Tel Cmmunications Group (PA)	4813	C	559 683-4611	7989
Sierra Telephone Company Inc	4813	C	559 683-4611	7990
South Gate Brewing Company	1542	E	559 692-2739	965
Veterans Health Administration	8011	C	702 341-3020	15800

OAKLAND, CA - Alameda County

	SIC	EMP	PHONE	ENTRY #
16500 Sixteen Five Hundred	5063	E	510 208-5005	8835
3vr Security Inc	7382	D	415 513-4577	14114
643 Capital Management Inc (PA)	6211	E	650 759-0599	9954
99designs Inc	7336	E	415 539-1088	11856
A T Associates Inc	8059	D	510 261-8564	16214
A&M Products Manufacturing Co (HQ)	3295	D	510 271-7000	4527
A3 Labs LLC (PA)	8731	E	925 274-8503	19009
ABC Imaging of Washington	2759	F	202 429-8870	3718
ABC Security Service Inc (PA)	7381	C	510 436-0666	14025
Able Metal Plating Inc	3471	E	510 569-6539	4892
Ace Parking Management Inc	7521	D	510 589-2313	14498
Ace Parking Management Inc	7521	D	510 251-0509	14501
Advance Day Care Center Inc	8351	E	510 434-9288	17852
Advanced Grinding Incorporated	3479	D	510 536-3465	4925
Aecom-TSE Joint Venture	8711	D	510 285-6639	18620
Afscme Local 3299 (PA)	8631	D	510 844-1160	18353
Agribag Inc	2299	D	510 533-2388	2983
Agriculture Bag Mfg USA Inc (PA)	2221	E	510 632-5637	2967
Ahoy-Hoy Inc (PA)	7372	E	415 669-6902	12965
AJW Construction	2951	E	510 568-2300	4186
Al Stockwell Inc	7371	E	510 269-7423	12237
Al Tabase Summit Hospital	8093	D	510 869-6600	16983
Alameda Cnty Cmnty Fd Bnk Inc	8322	D	510 635-3663	17411
Alameda Cnty Emplyees Rtrment	6411	D	510 628-3000	10227
Alameda Cnty Mental Hlth Assn	8093	D	510 835-5010	16984
Alameda County Bar Association	8621	E	510 302-2222	18322
Alameda Health System	8399	B	510 437-4800	18217
Alameda-Contra Costa Trnst Dst (PA)	4111	C	510 891-4777	7324
Alameda-Contra Costa Trnst Dst	4173	A	510 577-8816	7444
Alarcon Bohm Corp	1795	E	510 893-4405	1977
Alliance For Safety & Justice	8699	D	209 507-6882	18541
Allied Fire Protection	1711	E	510 533-5516	1197
Alpha Delta PHI International	8641	E	415 704-1879	18384
AM & S Transportation Co	4213	E	510 208-0271	7502
American Cylinder Head Repr Exc	3714	E	510 516-1764	6573
American National Red Cross	8322	E	510 594-5100	17422
American National Red Cross	8322	E	510 595-4400	17423
Americas Best Beverage Inc	2095	E	800 723-8808	2834
Amin-Oakland LLC	7011	E	510 568-1500	10923
Ani Private SEC & Patrol Inc	7381	E	510 652-6833	14030
Ankar Cycles Inc	7699	D	510 657-7200	14736
Aperian Global Inc (PA)	8742	E	628 222-3773	19445
Arrow Sign Co (PA)	3993	E	209 931-5522	7216
Art Craft Statuary Inc	3281	E	510 633-1411	4515
Art Sign Company	7389	E	510 632-6353	14203
Asbestos MGT Group of Cal	1799	E	510 654-8441	2006
Asia Network Pacific Home Care (PA)	8082	E	510 268-1118	16850
Asian Community Mental Hlth Bd	8093	D	510 869-6003	16988
Asian Health Services (PA)	8011	C	510 986-6600	15282
Ask Media Group LLC	2741	F	510 985-7400	3557
Associated Lighting Rep Inc (PA)	5063	E	510 638-3800	8844
Astound Commerce Corporation (HQ)	7379	B	800 591-4710	13846
Asylum Access	8699	E	510 891-8700	18548
Athletics Investment Group LLC (PA)	7941	C	510 638-4900	14903
Autocom Power LLC	3089	F	510 350-1030	4261
B&C Transit Inc (HQ)	8711	D	510 483-3560	18634
Babette (PA)	2339	E	510 625-8500	3007
Backbone Software Inc	7373	E	415 993-2468	13559
Bananas Incorporated	8399	E	510 658-7353	18221
Bay Area Community Svcs Inc (PA)	8322	E	510 613-0330	17438
Bay Area Community Svcs Inc	8322	D	510 601-1074	17439
Bay Area Healthcare Center	8099	D	510 536-6512	17103
Bay Area Indus Filtration Inc	3569	E	510 562-6373	5225
Bay Area Legal Aid (PA)	8111	D	510 663-4755	17209
Bay Bolt Inc	5072	F	510 532-1188	8979
Baychildrens Physicians	8011	E	510 428-3460	15294
Bayview Demolition Svcs Inc	1795	D	510 544-5270	1979
Bayview Environmental Svcs Inc	1799	C	510 562-6181	2010
Bayview Services Inc (PA)	1795	E	510 562-6181	1980

Employment Codes: A=Over 500 employees, B=251-500, C=101-250, D=51-100, E=20-50 F=10-19

	SIC	EMP	PHONE	ENTRY #
Beezwax Datatools Inc	7371	E	510 835-4483	12300
Belcampo Group Inc **(PA)**	0279	D	510 250-7810	242
Bellevue Club	8641	D	510 451-1000	18392
Berrett-Koehler Publishers Inc **(PA)**	2731	F	510 817-2277	3523
Better Business Bureau Inc	8611	E	510 844-2000	18300
Beyond Emancipation	8361	E	510 667-7694	18062
Binti Inc	7372	E	844 424-6844	13020
Blue Skies For Children	8351	E	510 261-1076	17864
Bme Electrical Construction	1731	E	510 208-1967	1468
Bonita House Inc	8322	D	510 923-0180	17446
Brightside Health Inc	8099	E	415 662-8618	17110
Brita Products Company	5074	D	510 271-7000	8992
Brite Industries Inc	3999	D	510 250-9330	7272
Brite Media LLC **(PA)**	7311	C	877 479-7777	11742
Broadly Inc	7372	E	510 400-6039	13037
Broadway Mech - Contrs Inc	1711	C	510 746-4000	1225
Brown Tland Physcn Svcs Orgnzt **(HQ)**	8011	C	415 972-4162	15306
Build It Green	8621	E	510 590-3360	18325
Building Robotics Inc	5084	D	510 972-9709	9057
Bulldog Reporter	2711	F	510 596-9300	3420
Burnham Brown A Prof Corp	8111	C	510 444-6800	17222
C R Martin Auctioneers Inc	7389	E	510 428-0100	14222
Cable Moore Inc **(PA)**	3496	E	510 436-8000	4967
Calidad Industries Inc	8331	B	510 698-7200	17796
California Cereal Products Inc **(PA)**	5153	D	510 452-4500	9501
California Nurses Association **(PA)**	8621	D	510 273-2200	18329
California Physicians Service **(PA)**	6324	A	510 607-2000	10096
Califrnia Assn Pub Hsptals HLT	8743	E	510 874-7100	19684
Califrnia Child Care Rsrce Rfr	8322	E	510 658-0381	17452
Califrnia Leag Cnsrvtion Vters **(PA)**	8641	E	510 271-0900	18403
Califrnia-Nevada Methdst Homes	8059	C	510 835-5511	16224
Callisto Media Inc	2731	D	510 253-0500	3526
Carpenter Fnds Admnstrtive Off	6733	D	510 633-0333	10792
Carter & Burgess Inc	8712	D	510 457-0027	18876
Cass Inc **(PA)**	5093	D	510 893-6476	9174
Catamorphic Co **(PA)**	7371	C	415 579-3275	12330
Catholic Chrties of The Dcese **(PA)**	8322	D	510 768-3100	17467
Center For Care Innvations Inc **(PA)**	8621	E	415 561-6393	18337
Center For Elders Independence	6324	C	510 433-1150	10102
Center To Prmote Hlthcare Acce **(PA)**	8099	D	510 273-4651	17119
Central Parking Corporation	7521	D	510 832-7227	14509
Chabot Space Scnce Ctr Fndtion **(PA)**	8412	E	510 336-7300	18263
Changelab Solutions	8699	E	510 302-3380	18558
Channel Systems Inc	3272	E	510 568-7170	4425
Charles Pnkow Bldrs Ltd A Cal	1542	B	510 893-5170	853
Chevron Federal Credit Union **(PA)**	6061	D	888 884-4630	9776
Child Family Health Inter **(PA)**	8099	D	415 957-9000	17123
Childrens Hosp RES Ctr At Okla **(PA)**	8062	A	510 428-3000	16329
Chiodo Candy Co	2064	F	510 464-2977	2426
Christian Church Homes **(PA)**	6513	E	510 632-6712	10425
Christian Church Homes	6513	E	510 420-8802	10426
Christian Church Homes	6513	E	510 893-2998	10427
Christian Evang Chrches Amer I	7922	E	510 533-8300	14845
Christopher Ransom LLC	6531	D	510 345-9144	10509
Cim/Oakland City Center LLC	7011	D	510 451-4000	11009
Civicorps	4953	E	510 992-7800	8319
Civicsolar Inc **(PA)**	5074	E	800 409-2257	8995
Clamp Swing Pricing Co Inc	3999	E	510 567-1600	7276
Claremont Country Club	7997	D	510 653-6789	15074
Clark Harry Plumbing & Heating	1711	E	510 444-1776	1235
Clorox Company **(PA)**	2842	A	510 271-7000	4068
Clorox International Company **(HQ)**	2879	D	510 271-7000	4142
Clorox Manufacturing Company **(HQ)**	2842	C	510 271-7000	4071
Clorox Services Company **(HQ)**	2842	D	510 271-7000	4072
Cloud9 Charts Inc	7372	F	510 507-3661	13074
Cnc Noodle Corporation	2099	F	510 835-2269	2885
Cohen Ventures Inc **(PA)**	8748	D	510 482-4420	19746
College Track	8742	C	510 834-3295	19473
Commercial Energy Montana Inc	1311	F	510 567-2700	547
Common Counsel Foundation	8699	E	510 834-2995	18561
Compass Container Group Inc **(PA)**	5085	E	510 839-7500	9114
Condon-Johnson & Assoc Inc **(PA)**	1771	E	510 636-2100	1860
Conservation Society Cal	8422	C	510 632-9525	18290
Consumer Hlth Interactive LLC	8742	E	415 537-0735	19477
Corelogic Inc	7389	E	925 676-0225	14236
County of Alameda	8111	D	510 272-6222	17238
County of Alameda	8082	D	510 437-4190	16873
Courtyard By Marriott	7011	E	510 568-7600	11035
Covenant Care California LLC	8051	D	510 261-2628	15967
Covia Communities	8361	C	510 835-4700	18087
Creative Energy Foods Inc	5149	D	510 638-8668	9447
Creative Wood Products Inc	2521	C	510 635-5399	3302
Credence Id LLC	3663	E	888 243-5452	5835
Credit Karma LLC **(HQ)**	7389	A	415 510-5059	14239
Crisis Spport Svcs Almeda Cnty	7389	E	510 420-2460	14241
Crucible	8322	C	510 444-0919	17525
CSC Corporation	1731	E	510 430-0399	1489
Cushman & Wakefield Cal Inc	6531	A	510 763-4900	10529
Custom Alloy Scrap Sales Inc **(HQ)**	5093	E	510 893-6476	9175
Cy Oakland Operator LLC	7011	E	510 625-8282	11044
Cygna Group Inc	8711	C	510 419-5000	18682
D Zelinsky & Sons Inc	1721	E	510 215-5253	1411
Dado Inc	7372	E	510 364-6263	13106
Darcoid Company of California	5085	E	510 836-2449	9116
David Darroch	8111	E	510 835-9100	17247
Deem Inc **(DH)**	7372	D	415 590-8300	13112
Degenkolb Engineers	8711	E	510 272-9040	18687
Destiny Arts Center	7999	E	510 597-1619	15201
Diamond Tool and Die Inc	3599	E	510 534-7050	5508
Digicom Electronics Inc	3672	E	510 639-7003	5926
Diligence Security Group	1731	C	510 710-5806	1496
Donahue Fitzgerald LLP	8111	E	510 451-3300	17255
Donahue Gallager Woods LLP **(PA)**	8111	D	415 381-4161	17256
Dorado Network Systems Corp	7372	C	650 227-7300	13122
Dreisbach Enterprises Inc	6519	E	510 533-6600	10478
Dreyers Grand Ice Cream Inc **(DH)**	2024	C	510 594-9466	2171
Dreyers Grand Ice Cream Inc	2024	A	510 652-8187	2172
Dreyers Grnd Ice Cream Hldngs **(DH)**	5143	C	510 652-8187	9337
Dura Chemicals Inc **(PA)**	2899	E	510 658-1987	4159
E T Horn Company	5169	C	510 532-8689	9517
Earth Tech	8711	C	510 419-6000	18697
East Bay Agency For Children	8351	E	510 655-4896	17927
East Bay Asian Local Dev Corp	6513	C	510 267-1917	10430
East Bay Asian Youth Center **(PA)**	8322	E	510 533-1092	17535
East Bay Asian Youth Center	8322	D	510 533-1092	17536
East Bay Clarklift Inc **(PA)**	5084	E	510 534-6566	9065
East Bay Community Foundation	8641	D	510 836-3223	18413
East Bay Fixture Company	2491	E	510 652-4421	3259
East Bay Fmly Prctice Med Grou	8062	E	510 645-9900	16359
East Bay Mncpl Utlty Dst Wstw **(HQ)**	4952	E	866 403-2683	8281
East Bay Mncpl Utlty Dst Wtr **(PA)**	4941	A	866 403-2683	8236
East Bay Mncpl Utlty Dst Wtr	4941	E	866 403-2683	8237
East Bay Mncpl Utlty Dst Wtr	4941	E	510 287-0600	8242
East Bay Municipl Utilty Distr	4941	E	866 403-2683	8244
East Bay Municipl Utilty Distr	4953	E	866 403-2683	8322
East Bay Municipl Utilty Distr	4941	D	866 403-2683	8246
East Bay Pump & Equipment Co	5084	F	510 532-1800	9066
EBSC LP	8011	D	510 547-2244	15387
Ecms Inc **(HQ)**	7212	E	510 986-0131	11627
Ed Supports LLC	8093	D	201 478-8711	17019
Education For Change **(PA)**	8741	E	510 568-7936	19326
Eko Devices Inc	3845	D	844 356-3384	7104
ELF Beauty Inc **(PA)**	2844	C	510 210-8602	4082
Enerparc Ca3 LLC	3674	F	844 367-7272	6110
Engie Services US Inc **(HQ)**	8711	D	844 678-3772	18703
Enterprise Rnt—car San Frncsc	7514	E	510 271-4160	14480
Environmental Science Assoc	8731	D	510 839-5066	19056
Eqecat Inc **(DH)**	8742	D	415 817-3100	19506
Erg Aerospace Corporation	2819	D	510 658-9785	3787
Escue and Associates Inc	1799	E	510 924-7422	2030
Everett Graphics Inc	2657	D	510 577-6777	3371
Exponential Interactive Inc **(HQ)**	8742	D	510 250-5500	19512
Family Bridges Inc	8322	C	510 839-2270	17559
Family Support Services **(PA)**	8322	E	510 834-2443	17564
Federal Express Corporation	4215	B	510 382-2344	7647
Federal Express Corporation	4513	C	510 465-5209	7748
Feeney Inc	3496	E	510 893-9473	4969
Fidelity Roof Company **(PA)**	1761	D	510 547-6330	1802
First Place For Youth **(PA)**	8322	E	510 272-0979	17571
First Transit Inc	4111	C	510 437-8990	7333
Fitzgrald Abbott Beardsley LLP	8111	E	510 451-3300	17266
Five Flavors Herbs Inc	2023	F	510 923-0178	2159
Flipcause Inc	7372	F	800 523-1950	13166
Fluid Inc **(DH)**	7371	D	877 343-3240	12457
Flurish Inc	6141	D	855 253-6387	9857
Food Specialists Inc	6519	B	510 444-3456	10480
Foresight Analytics LLC	8742	D	510 893-1760	19517
Fox Rent A Car Inc	7514	D	408 210-2208	14488
Gaffar Enterprise Inc	8059	E	510 834-9880	16234
Galileo Learning LLC **(PA)**	7032	E	510 595-7293	11602
Gallagher Properties Inc **(PA)**	1794	E	510 261-0466	1960
Gazzalis Supermarket Inc	5148	E	510 569-8159	9408
General Auto Repair Inc	5013	E	510 533-3333	8452
General Grinding Inc	3471	E	510 261-5557	4907
General Lgstics Systems US Inc	4215	C	800 322-5555	7648
George E Masker Inc	1721	D	510 568-1206	1414
Gill Grove Electric Company	1731	E	510 451-2929	1508
Glad Products Company **(HQ)**	3081	C	510 271-7000	4230
Global Steel Products Corp	2542	E	510 652-2060	3326
GM Associates Inc	3679	D	510 430-0806	6430
Golden Gate Freightliner Inc **(HQ)**	7538	C	559 486-4310	14568
Golden Plastics Corporation	3089	E	510 569-6465	4285
Goldfarb & Lipman LLP **(PA)**	8111	E	510 836-6336	17275
Goldstein Dmchak Bller Brgen D	8111	E	510 763-9800	17276
Goodwill Inds of Grter E Bay I **(PA)**	8331	D	510 698-7200	17813
Gordon Rees Scully Mansukhani	8111	E	510 463-8600	17278
Grand Lake Montessori	8351	E	510 836-4313	17946
Grubb Co Inc	6531	D	510 339-0400	10566
Gruendl Inc	1731	E	510 577-7700	1509
GSC Logistics Inc **(PA)**	4214	C	510 844-3700	7622
Gt Nexus Inc **(DH)**	7371	D	510 808-2222	12493
H V Food Products Company	2035	B	510 271-7612	2280
Hakomi Institute of Cal LLC	8733	E	415 839-6788	19218
Hanna Brphy McLean Mcleer Jnse **(PA)**	8111	E	510 839-1180	17286
Hapag-Lloyd (america) LLC	8742	D	510 286-1940	19529
Harmless Harvest Inc **(PA)**	2099	E	347 688-6286	2900
Health Care Workers Union **(PA)**	6512	D	510 251-1250	10392
Health Ventures Inc **(DH)**	8071	E	510 869-6703	16783
HGH Electric Inc	1731	E	510 923-1859	1514
Highcom Security Services	7381	D	510 893-7600	14069
Higher One Payments Inc	7372	C	510 769-9888	13210
Hntb Corporation	8711	D	510 208-4599	18732
Hoffman/Lewis **(PA)**	7311	E	415 434-8500	11760
Home Depot USA Inc	7359	C	510 533-7379	12047

Mergent email: customerrelations@mergent.com
1172
2022 Northern California Business Directory and Buyers Guide
(P-0000) Products & Services Section entry number
(PA)=Parent Co (HQ)=Headquarters (DH)=Div Headquarters

GEOGRAPHIC SECTION

OAKLAND, CA

	SIC	EMP	PHONE	ENTRY #
Homewood Suites Management LLC	7011	E	510 663-2700	11159
Hospice & Home Health of E Bay	8082	E	510 632-4390	16894
Humanstic Altrntves To Addctio	8093	E	510 875-2300	17025
Hydrapak Inc	3949	E	510 632-8318	7197
IAC Publishing LLC	4813	D	510 985-7400	7960
IAC Search & Media Inc **(HQ)**	7375	C	510 985-7400	13794
Independent Quality Care Inc	8059	D	510 836-3677	16247
Industrial Relations Cal Dept	4789	D	510 286-7000	7883
Industrial Wiper & Supply Inc	2241	F	408 286-4752	2971
Integral Group Inc	8711	C	510 663-2070	18739
Inter-City Printing Co Inc	2752	F	510 451-4775	3660
Interactive Solutions Inc **(DH)**	7372	D	510 214-9002	13241
Iris Environmental	8748	E	510 834-4747	19799
Jalaram Investment LLC	7011	E	510 568-1880	11207
Jaqui Foundation Inc	8999	E	510 562-4721	19907
Jewish Cmnty Fdrtion of Grter **(PA)**	8322	E	510 839-2900	17621
Jewish Vctnal Creer Cnsling Sv	8331	D	415 391-3600	17819
Jiff Inc	7375	C	510 844-4139	13797
Jt2 Integrated Resources **(PA)**	8741	D	925 556-7012	19356
K G O T V News Bureau	4832	D	510 451-4772	8028
Kadiant LLC	8748	E	209 521-4791	19803
Kaiser Foundation Hospitals	8011	A	510 752-1000	15450
Kaiser Foundation Hospitals **(HQ)**	8062	C	510 271-6611	16400
Kaiser Foundation Hospitals	8062	A	510 752-1000	16402
Kaiser Foundation Hospitals	6324	C	510 752-7864	10114
Kaiser Foundation Hospitals	5047	C	510 752-6808	8785
Kaiser Foundation Hospitals	8011	C	510 752-1000	15467
Kaiser Foundation Hospitals	8011	A	510 987-1000	15476
Kaiser Foundation Hospitals	6324	C	510 891-3400	10122
Kaiser Foundation Hospitals	8062	E	510 625-3431	16413
Kaiser Foundation Hospitals	6324	C	510 251-0121	10136
Kaiser Foundation Hospitals	8062	A	510 434-5835	16416
Kaiser Fundation Hlth Plan Inc **(PA)**	8011	B	510 271-5800	15493
Kaiser Group Holdings Inc	8711	D	510 419-6000	18745
Kaiser Hlth Plan Asset MGT Inc	8741	E	510 271-5910	19357
Kaiser Permanente	8062	E	510 450-2109	16421
Kaiserair Inc **(PA)**	4522	C	510 569-9622	7757
Kay Chesterfield Inc	2512	E	510 533-5565	3289
Kazan McClain Sttrley Grnwood	8111	C	877 995-6372	17302
Kemeera LLC **(PA)**	5045	E	510 281-9000	8718
Kids Overcoming LLC	8082	D	415 748-8052	16903
Kingsford Manufacturing Co	2842	F	510 271-7000	4075
Kingsford Products Company LLC **(HQ)**	2861	D	510 271-7000	4115
Kitanica LLC	3999	F	707 272-7286	7292
Kiva Manufacturing Inc	3999	E	510 780-0777	7293
Ktvu Partnership Inc	4833	C	510 834-1212	8050
La Cascada Inc	2032	F	510 452-3663	2204
La Clinica De La Raza Inc	8011	C	510 535-6300	15495
La Clinica De La Raza Inc	8099	C	510 535-3500	17158
La Clinica De La Raza Inc	8011	C	510 535-4110	15497
La Clinica De La Raza Inc	8099	C	510 535-4130	17159
La Clinica De La Raza Inc **(PA)**	8011	E	510 535-4000	15498
La Clinica De La Raza Inc	8011	C	510 535-4700	15499
La Clinica De La Raza Inc	8011	C	510 535-6200	15500
La Quinta Inn	7011	D	510 632-8900	11241
Label Art - HM Es-E Stik Lbels	2752	E	510 465-1125	3669
Lake Mrritt Healthcare Ctr LLC	8741	D	510 227-1806	19361
Lapham Company Inc	6531	D	510 531-6000	10598
Lennar Mltfmily Cmmunities LLC	1531	A	415 975-4980	783
Levine Arthur Lansky & Assoc **(PA)**	3423	F	415 234-6020	4606
Lewis John Glass Studio	3229	E	510 635-4607	4373
Lincoln **(PA)**	8093	C	510 273-4700	17035
Linde Inc	2813	C	510 451-4100	3773
Linoleum Sales Co Inc **(PA)**	3211	C	510 652-1032	4361
Live Journal Inc	2711	E	415 230-3600	3454
Lombardi Loper & Conant LLP	8111	E	510 433-2600	17319
Loss Prevention Group Inc	7381	E	510 836-6011	14074
Lucid Design Group Inc	7373	D	510 907-0400	13628
Lumedx Corporation **(PA)**	7371	F	510 419-1000	12586
M Arthur Gensler Jr Assoc Inc	8712	C	510 625-7400	18900
Mack & Reiss Inc	2369	D	510 434-9122	3016
Mad Oak Bar and Yard	2599	F	510 924-2047	3337
Magnetic Imaging Affilates	8071	E	510 204-1820	16788
Mariner Health Care Inc	8051	E	510 261-5200	16057
Marqeta Inc	7372	A	888 462-7738	13293
Mathematica Inc	8732	D	510 830-3700	19170
Matson Alaska Inc	4499	E	704 973-7000	7735
Matson Navigation Co Alsk LLC	4499	D	510 628-4000	7736
Matson Navigation Company Inc **(HQ)**	4424	C	510 628-4000	7713
McInerney & Dillon PC	8111	E	510 465-7100	17330
McWane Inc	3321	C	510 632-3467	4549
Medical Insurance Exchange Cal	6411	D	510 596-4935	10312
Medical Underwriters Cal Inc **(PA)**	6411	D	510 428-9411	10313
Mendocino Land Company Inc **(DH)**	0172	D	510 286-2000	65
Menke & Associates Inc **(PA)**	8748	E	415 362-5200	19818
Mercer Consulting Group Inc	6411	E	415 743-8510	10315
Mercy Retirement and Care Ctr	8361	D	510 534-8540	18145
Mesmerize LLC	8742	C	415 374-8298	19575
Metropolitan Golf Links	7992	E	510 569-5555	15011
Mettler-Toledo Rainin LLC **(HQ)**	3829	C	510 564-1600	6910
Meyers Nave A Prof Corp **(PA)**	8111	D	510 351-4300	17332
Michael Baker Intl Inc	8711	E	510 879-0950	18768
Mighty Buildings Inc	1521	E	415 583-5657	676
Mindshare Design Inc **(PA)**	7336	E	510 904-6900	11870
Miwa Inc	2511	F	510 261-5999	3283
Moc Products Company Inc	7549	D	510 635-1230	14665
Monterey Mechanical Co **(PA)**	1629	E	510 632-3173	1168

	SIC	EMP	PHONE	ENTRY #
Mufg Americas Holdings Corp	6021	C	212 782-5911	9686
Multiplier	8748	D	415 421-3774	19825
Multivision Inc **(DH)**	7389	D	510 740-5600	14335
National Pro Security Svcs Inc	7382	E	877 392-2340	14141
National Recycling Corporation	2679	E	510 268-1022	3403
Native American Health Ctr Inc **(PA)**	8011	D	510 535-4400	15545
Natures Products Inc **(DH)**	5122	C	954 233-3300	9234
Navis Corporation **(PA)**	8748	B	510 267-5000	19827
Neustar Inc	7371	E	510 500-1000	12630
New Harbinger Publications Inc **(PA)**	2731	E	510 652-0215	3542
New Pride Corporation	7534	E	636 937-5200	14538
New Schools Venture Fund	7389	E	415 615-6860	14339
Ngo Metals Inc	3446	E	510 632-0853	4837
Noble Brewer Beer Company	2095	E	301 536-1934	2840
Nor-Cal Metal Fabricators	3444	D	510 350-0121	4795
North Star Emergency Svcs Inc	4119	D	510 452-3400	7393
Northern Cal Crpnters Rgnal CN	8631	E	510 568-4788	18370
Northgate Ter Cmnty Partner LP	6531	E	510 465-9346	10629
O C Jones & Sons Inc	8748	D	510 663-6911	19832
O-I Owens Illinois Inc	3221	F	510 436-2000	4367
Oakland Hills Tennis Club Inc	7997	E	510 531-3300	15119
Oakland Medical Group Inc	8011	E	510 452-4824	15561
Oakland Museum of California	8412	D	510 318-8400	18277
Oakland Prvate Indust Cncil In	8331	E	510 768-4400	17829
Oakland Public Education Fund	6732	D	510 221-6968	10789
Oakland Renaissance Associates	7011	B	510 451-4000	11335
Oakland Tribune Inc	2711	E	510 208-6300	3469
Oaklandidence Opco LLC	8052	D	510 832-3222	16195
Ob/Gyn Prtners For Hlth Med Gr	8011	E	510 893-1700	15562
Ocadian Care Centers LLC	8051	B	510 832-3222	16082
Officeworks Inc	7361	D	510 444-2161	12113
Old Republic Nat Title Insur	6361	E	510 286-7798	10207
Otis McAllister Inc **(PA)**	5149	E	415 421-6010	9471
Otto Frei-Jules Borel Inc **(PA)**	5094	E	800 772-3456	9184
Outsource Consulting Svcs Inc **(PA)**	7361	E	510 986-0686	12115
Ozig LLC	3431	E	510 588-7952	4622
Pacific Galvanizing Inc	3479	E	510 261-7331	4942
Pacific Gas and Electric Co	4911	C	510 450-5744	8137
Pacific Gas and Electric Co	4911	C	510 437-2222	8142
Pacific Park Management Inc	7521	D	510 836-7730	14514
Pacific Union Intl Inc	6531	D	510 338-1379	10638
Pacific Union Residental Brkg	6531	E	510 339-6460	10641
Pandora Media LLC **(DH)**	4832	A	510 451-4100	8030
Paradigm Staffing Solutions	7361	E	510 663-7860	12117
Paramount Theatre of Arts Inc	7922	D	510 893-2300	14855
Park Hotels & Resorts Inc	7011	C	510 635-5000	11354
Park Plaza Hotel	7011	E	510 635-5300	11355
Parliament Inc **(PA)**	7011	E	415 702-0624	11358
Pasha Hawaii Trnspt Lines LLC	4424	D	510 271-1400	7714
Pasta Shop **(PA)**	5149	D	510 250-6005	9474
Peace Action West **(PA)**	8651	E	510 830-3600	18539
Peerless Coffee Company Inc	2095	D	510 763-1763	2841
Perkville Inc	7372	E	510 808-5668	13368
Permanente Federation LLC	8742	D	510 625-6920	19603
Permanente Kaiser Intl **(HQ)**	6324	D	510 271-5910	10149
Permanente Medical Group Inc	8011	A	510 625-6262	15593
Permanente Medical Group Inc	8011	A	510 752-1000	15601
Permanente Medical Group Inc	8011	A	510 752-1190	15603
Permanente Medical Group Inc **(DH)**	8099	B	866 858-2226	17167
Pipe and Plant Solutions Inc	7389	E	888 978-8264	14366
Playworks Education Energized	7999	D	510 893-4180	15227
Playworks Education Energized **(PA)**	7999	E	510 893-4180	15228
Porrey Pines Bank Inc	6021	C	510 899-7500	9688
Port Dept City of Oakland **(PA)**	4491	B	510 627-1100	7724
Port Dept City of Oakland	4581	D	510 563-3697	7780
Port Dept of The Cy Oakland	4581	D	510 563-3300	7781
Precision Emprise LLC	1771	E	866 792-8006	1902
Pressure Cast Products Corp	3364	E	510 532-7310	4581
Prevention Institute	8742	D	510 444-4133	19609
Proactive Bus Solutions Inc	8741	C	510 302-0120	19383
Professnal Tchncal SEC Svcs In	7381	C	510 645-9200	14091
Progistics Distribution Inc	4731	A	415 369-8845	7851
Promise Network Inc	7371	E	877 717-7664	12702
Providence Health & Svcs - Ore	8062	C	510 444-0839	16485
Public Health Institute **(PA)**	8733	D	510 285-5500	19232
Purity Organic LLC	2037	E	415 440-7777	2297
Quaker Oats Company	2087	C	510 261-5800	2822
R J R Technologies Inc **(PA)**	3699	D	480 800-2300	6538
Rago & Son Inc	3469	D	510 536-5700	4889
Red Bay Coffee Company Inc	2095	E	510 409-1076	2846
Red Door Group	8742	E	510 339-2320	19620
Regents of The Univ of Cal	8731	E	510 987-0043	19116
Renaissance School	8351	E	510 531-8566	18006
Renew Financial Corp II	6162	C	610 433-7486	9925
Renew Financial Group LLC	7389	E	888 996-0523	14383
Reuse People of America Inc	4953	E	510 383-1983	8361
Right Away Concrete Pmpg Inc	3273	E	510 536-1900	4504
Rmt Landscape Contractors Inc	0782	E	510 568-3208	498
Roberts Electric Co Inc	1731	E	510 834-6161	1589
Rolls-Royce Corporation	3519	B	510 635-1500	4992
Saint Vincents Day Home	8351	E	510 832-8324	18013
San Francisco Bay Area Rapid	4111	A	510 286-2893	7348
San Frncsco Bay Area Rpid Trns **(PA)**	4111	B	510 464-6000	7349
Scientific Learning Corp	7372	E	510 444-3500	13429
Sea-Logix Llc	4213	D	510 271-1400	7592
Sedgwick Claims MGT Svcs Inc	6411	D	510 302-3000	10345
Seeds of Awareness Inc	8093	E	510 788-0876	17071

GEOGRAPHIC

Employment Codes: A=Over 500 employees, B=251-500, C=101-250, D=51-100, E=20-50 F=10-19

2022 Northern California Business Directory and Buyers Guide

© Mergent Inc. 1-800-342-5647

1173

	SIC	EMP	PHONE	ENTRY #
SEIU Local 1021	8631	D	510 350-9811	18372
Seiu Uhw-W & Joint Employer Ed **(PA)**	6732	E	510 250-6800	10790
Seiu United Healthcare Workers **(PA)**	8631	C	510 251-1250	18373
Selectquote Insurance Services **(HQ)**	6411	C	415 543-7338	10347
Seneca Family of Agencies	8322	B	510 317-1444	17729
Seneca Family of Agencies **(PA)**	8322	E	510 317-1444	17730
Seneca Family of Agencies	8322	B	510 434-7990	17732
Sequoyah Country Club	7997	C	510 632-2900	15140
Sfny Group Inc	8741	E	510 646-1360	19397
Shimmick Construction Co Inc **(PA)**	1629	A	510 777-5000	1178
Shimmick Nicholson Cnstr JV	1542	C	510 777-5000	961
Sierra Club **(PA)**	8641	C	415 977-5500	18469
Silicon Vly Technical Staffing **(PA)**	7361	E	510 923-9898	12136
Silverado Contractors Inc **(PA)**	1795	D	510 658-9960	1988
Sius Products and Distr Inc **(PA)**	2673	F	510 382-1700	3388
Skyloom Global Corp	3661	E	415 696-4894	5808
Social Brands LLC	3999	E	415 728-1761	7308
Society of St Vncent De Paul A **(PA)**	8699	D	510 638-7600	18594
Sorrento Networks Corporation **(HQ)**	3661	F	510 577-1400	5809
South Park Pleating Inc	7389	E	510 625-8050	14411
Spanish Spking Unity Cncil Alm **(PA)**	8322	E	510 535-6900	17751
Spanish Spking Unity Cncil Alm	8399	C	510 836-0543	18251
SSC Oakland Fruitvale Oper LP	8059	D	510 261-5613	16270
St Marys Center	8322	E	510 923-9600	17753
Standard Iron & Metals Co	5093	E	510 535-0222	9178
Star Protection Agency LLC	7381	D	510 635-1732	14099
State Compensation Insur Fund	6331	C	510 577-3000	10176
Sterling Hsa Inc	7389	E	800 617-4729	14415
Structionsite Inc	7371	E	510 340-9515	12828
Stv Incorporated	8712	D	510 763-1313	18916
Sublimation Inc	3999	E	888 994-2726	7309
Sublime Machining Inc	3999	F	858 349-2445	7310
Sullivan Counter Tops Inc	2541	E	510 652-2337	3321
Suma Landscaping Inc	0782	E	415 332-7862	504
Summit Bank	6021	E	510 839-8800	9690
Summit Bank Foundation **(HQ)**	6022	E	510 839-8800	9749
Summit Medical Center	8062	C	510 869-6758	16562
Sunset Publishing Corporation **(HQ)**	2721	C	800 777-0117	3517
Surgery Ctr of Alta Btes Smmit	8062	E	510 204-1880	16565
Sutter Bay Hospitals	8062	D	510 655-4000	16571
Sutter Bay Hospitals	8062	D	510 869-8377	16573
Sutter Health	8062	C	510 547-2244	16613
Sutter Health	8062	C	510 869-8777	16614
Svc Mfg Inc A Corp	2086	F	510 261-5800	2816
Swinerton Builders Inc	1541	D	510 208-5800	812
Synchr Inc	8099	D	720 893-2000	17185
Tab Label Inc	2679	F	510 638-4411	3407
Talus Construction Inc	1623	E	925 406-4756	1136
Tanoshi Inc	7372	F	949 677-5261	13486
Teamsters Local Union 70	8631	E	510 569-9317	18378
Ted Jacob Engrg Group Inc **(PA)**	8711	E	510 763-4880	18830
Telecom Inc	7389	D	510 873-8283	14430
Tks Wireless Inc	4812	C	510 227-6440	7916
Tm Sleeves LLC	7311	D	415 374-8210	11791
TMC Financing	7389	D	415 989-8855	14435
Traffic Management Inc	8741	E	415 370-7916	19410
Transfair USA	8733	C	510 663-5260	19239
Trimacs Maint Ldscp Cnstr Inc	0782	E	510 569-9660	506
Tucker Technology Inc **(PA)**	1731	E	510 836-0422	1625
Turner Construction Company	1542	E	510 267-8100	979
TYT LLC **(HQ)**	2752	C	510 444-3933	3706
Ucsf East Bay Surgery Program **(PA)**	8062	E	510 437-4800	16690
Unilab Corporation	8071	A	510 444-5213	16814
United Fence Contractors Inc **(PA)**	1799	E	510 276-8350	2081
United Parcel Service Inc	4215	C	510 813-5662	7668
University Cal Press Fundation **(PA)**	2731	D	510 642-4247	3547
University California Berkeley	2731	E	510 642-4247	3549
URS Corporation	8711	E	510 893-3600	18846
URS Group Inc	8711	D	510 893-3600	18847
URS Group Inc	8711	D	925 446-3800	18848
Uscf Advisers LLC	6282	B	510 522-9600	10066
Veritas Media Group LLC	8742	E	510 867-4699	19666
Veronica Foods Company	2079	E	510 535-6833	2469
Veterans Health Administration	8011	C	510 267-7820	15794
Vibrant Care Pharmacy Inc	2834	E	510 638-9851	4003
Vigilent Corporation **(PA)**	3822	E	888 305-4451	6707
Village Voice Media	2711	E	510 879-3700	3488
Vincent Electric Company **(PA)**	7694	E	510 639-4500	14731
Visionary Nutrition LLC	1541	C	510 567-1200	818
Visual Supply Company **(PA)**	7371	D	847 721-9285	12911
Vulpine Inc	2899	E	510 534-1186	4169
Vumedi Inc	7812	D	650 450-2603	14798
W3ll People Inc	2844	F	800 790-1563	4099
Wallis Fashions Inc	7389	C	510 763-8018	14458
Warbritton & Assoc Impairment **(PA)**	8099	D	510 251-8851	17193
Washington Inn Associates	7011	D	510 452-1776	11567
Waste MGT Alameda Cnty Inc **(HQ)**	4953	A	510 613-8710	8383
Webster Surgery Center LP **(PA)**	8011	D	510 451-0957	15813
Wells & Bennett Realtors **(PA)**	6531	D	510 531-7000	10683
Wendel Rosen LLP **(PA)**	8111	C	510 834-6600	17395
West Oakland Health Council **(PA)**	8093	C	510 835-9610	17092
Westcoast Childrens Clinic	8093	C	510 269-9030	17093
Wested	8733	E	510 302-4200	19246
Wild Karma Inc	8051	B	510 639-9088	16160
William D White Co Inc	1731	F	510 658-8167	1639
Williams Adley & Company L L P **(PA)**	8721	E	510 893-8114	19004
Window Hardware Supply	3089	F	510 463-0301	4333
Wo Hing LLC	2011	F	510 922-8778	2107
Wood Tech Inc	2511	D	510 534-4930	3286
Wooden Window Inc	2431	E	510 893-1157	3163
Workers Cmpnstion Insur Rting **(PA)**	6331	C	888 229-2472	10190
Xantrion Incorporated	7379	E	510 272-4701	14013
Xia LLC	3826	E	510 401-5760	6864
Young MNS Chrstn Assn of E Bay	8641	B	510 654-9622	18487
Young MNS Chrstn Assn of E Bay	8641	A	510 451-8039	18491
Young MNS Chrstn Assn of E Bay	8641	B	510 534-7441	18505
Your Warm Friend Inc	1711	E	510 893-1343	1402
Youth Employment Partnr Inc	8331	D	510 533-3447	17850
Youth Uprising	7363	D	510 777-9909	12210
Zuo Modern Contemporary Inc **(PA)**	3645	E	510 877-4087	5731

OAKLEY, CA - Contra Costa County

	SIC	EMP	PHONE	ENTRY #
Coldwell Bnkr Amral Assoc Rlto	6531	D	925 439-7400	10514
Contra Costa Water District	4941	E	925 383-2576	8232
Cowboy Concrete Pumping LLC **(PA)**	1771	E	925 350-2700	1861
Foundation Constructors Inc **(PA)**	1629	D	925 754-6633	1163
Pacheco Brothers Gardening Inc	0783	E	510 487-3580	520

OAKVILLE, CA - Napa County

	SIC	EMP	PHONE	ENTRY #
Far Niente Winery Inc	2084	D	707 944-2861	2566
Groth Vineyards and Winery	0172	E	707 944-0290	53
NAPA Wine Company LLC	2084	E	707 944-8669	2664
Nickel and Nickel Inc	0172	F	707 967-9600	66
Opus One Winery LLC **(PA)**	2084	D	707 944-9442	2675
Robert Mondavi Winery	2084	E	707 738-5727	2699
Rudd Wines Inc **(PA)**	2084	E	707 944-8577	2704
Silver Oak Wine Cellars LLC **(PA)**	2084	F	707 942-7022	2718

OCCIDENTAL, CA - Sonoma County

	SIC	EMP	PHONE	ENTRY #
Alliance Rdwods Cnfrnce Grunds	7032	C	707 874-3507	11597
Occidental Union Hotel Inc	7011	E	707 874-3444	11336

OLIVEHURST, CA - Yuba County

	SIC	EMP	PHONE	ENTRY #
Ace Composites Inc	3089	E	530 743-1885	4252
California Security Svcs Inc **(PA)**	7381	E	530 749-0280	14041
D & D Cbnets - Svage Dsgns Inc	2434	E	530 634-9713	3177
Hanson Truss Components Inc	2439	D	530 740-7750	3207
Lhl Construction Inc	1791	E	916 782-9001	1926
Naumes Inc	0181	D	530 743-2055	131
Nordic Industries Inc	1629	D	530 742-7124	1171
Precast Con Tech Unlimited LLC	3272	D	530 749-6501	4448
Rodgz Farm Labor Contg LLC	0761	D	530 329-8403	365
Shoei Foods (usa) Inc	5141	D	530 742-7866	9302
Wilkeys Construction Inc	1521	E	530 741-2233	730
Yuba Rver Mlding Mill Work Inc **(PA)**	2431	E	530 742-2168	3165

OLYMPIC VALLEY, CA - Placer County

	SIC	EMP	PHONE	ENTRY #
Alpenglow Expeditions LLC	7999	E	877 873-5376	15171
Cncml A California Ltd Partnr	7011	D	530 583-1578	11019
Lowe Enterprises	7011	E	530 581-6628	11273
Sierra PCF Hotels & Resorts	7011	D	530 583-5500	11479
Squaw Valley Development Co **(HQ)**	7011	E	530 452-6985	11497
Squaw Valley Ski Corporation **(DH)**	7011	C	530 583-6985	11498
Village Inn Owners Association	7011	D	530 581-6000	11559

ORANGE COVE, CA - Fresno County

	SIC	EMP	PHONE	ENTRY #
Adventist Health System/West	8062	D	559 626-0882	16299
Booth Ranches LLC **(PA)**	0291	C	559 626-4732	246
Cecelia Packing Corporation	5148	C	559 626-5000	9392
Family Healthcare Network	8011	C	559 528-2804	15399
M Park Inc	7389	E	559 626-5057	14326

ORANGEVALE, CA - Sacramento County

	SIC	EMP	PHONE	ENTRY #
Albano Dale Dunn & Lewis Insur	6411	E	916 988-0214	10228
Fountainwood Residential Care	8361	E	916 988-2200	18117
Longs Drug Stores Cal Inc	7384	E	916 989-2212	14171
MA Steiner Construction Inc	1541	D	916 988-6300	802
Odyssey Learning Centers Inc	8351	E	916 988-0258	17985
Recreation & Pk Dst Orangevale	7999	E	916 988-4373	15230
Save Mart Supermarkets	5411	D	916 989-3915	9295
Summerville At Hazel Creek LLC	8051	B	916 988-7901	16131

ORICK, CA - Humboldt County

	SIC	EMP	PHONE	ENTRY #
Z Logging LLC	2411	F	707 488-2151	3089

ORINDA, CA - Contra Costa County

	SIC	EMP	PHONE	ENTRY #
Advanced Software Design Inc	7371	D	925 457-8540	12229
Agemark Corporation **(PA)**	8051	C	925 257-4671	15906
California Shakespeare Theater **(PA)**	7922	C	510 548-3422	14842
East Bay Mncpl Utlty Dst Wtr	4941	E	925 254-3778	8239
First Republic Bank	6022	D	925 254-8993	9724
Orinda Country Club	7997	D	925 254-4313	15121
Orinda Pre School	8351	E	925 254-2551	17987
Pacific Union Co	6531	D	925 258-0090	10635
Wespac Plan Services LLC **(DH)**	6411	E	510 740-4163	10367

ORLAND, CA - Glenn County

	SIC	EMP	PHONE	ENTRY #
Baldwin-Minkler Farms	0173	E	530 865-7676	82
Glenn County Office Education	8351	E	530 865-1145	17940
Jensen Enterprises Inc	3272	E	530 865-4277	4439
Kraemer & Co Mfg Inc	3448	E	530 865-7982	4853
Land OLakes Inc	2022	E	530 865-7626	2151
Olivarez Honey Bees Inc	0279	D	530 865-0298	243
Olive Musco Products Inc	2035	E	530 865-4111	2283
Olson Meat Company	2011	E	530 865-8111	2103
Omega Walnut Inc	0723	E	530 865-0136	300
Rackley Company Inc	1541	E	530 865-9619	805

GEOGRAPHIC SECTION — PALO ALTO, CA

Company	SIC	EMP	PHONE	ENTRY #
Westside Research Inc	2396	F	530 330-0085	3049

OROVILLE, CA - Butte County

Company	SIC	EMP	PHONE	ENTRY #
1000 Executive Parkway LLC	8051	C	530 533-7335	15903
Ames 1 LLC	1542	E	907 344-0067	823
Bains Woodward Insur Svcs Inc	6411	D	530 534-6600	10244
Ball Rig Welding LLC	7692	E	530 990-5795	14710
Better Builders Cnstr Inc	1521	E	530 589-2574	617
Compass Equipment Inc (PA)	3535	E	530 533-7284	5050
Conners Oro-Cal Mfg Co	3911	E	530 533-5065	7165
Country Connection Inc (PA)	2449	F	530 589-5176	3234
Elijah House SLe	8322	E	530 370-8386	17542
Endeavor Homes Inc	3531	E	530 534-0300	5032
Feather River Recreation Pk Dst	7999	D	530 533-2011	15203
Graphic Packaging Intl LLC	2759	C	530 533-1058	3734
J W Bamford Inc	2411	F	530 533-0732	3066
Mid Valley Title and Escrow Co	6541	E	530 533-6680	10693
Mooretown Rancheria	7993	B	530 533-3885	15038
Mooretown Rancheria (PA)	7999	E	530 533-3625	15220
New Start Rcvery Solutions Inc	8069	D	530 854-4119	16768
New York Machine Shop Inc	3599	F	530 534-7965	5579
Night Optics Usa Inc	3669	E	714 899-4475	5892
North State Rendering Co Inc	2077	A	530 343-6076	2459
Orohealth Corporation	8011	A	530 534-9183	15571
Oroville Hospital (PA)	8062	A	530 533-8500	16474
Oroville Hospital	8049	C	530 538-8700	15893
Oroville Hospital	8062	B	530 532-8697	16475
Oroville Intrnal Mdcine Med Gr	8011	E	530 538-3171	15572
Pacific Coast Producers	2033	D	530 533-4311	2238
Pacific Gas and Electric Co	4911	C	530 532-4093	8160
Roplast Industries Inc	2673	C	530 532-9500	3387
Setzer Forest Products Inc	2421	E	530 534-8100	3105
Sierra Hlth Wellness Ctrs LLC	8099	D	530 854-4119	17180
Sierra Hlth Wellness Group LLC	8093	D	530 854-4119	17073
Smb Industries Inc (PA)	3441	D	530 534-6266	4684
South Feather Water & Pwr Agcy (PA)	4941	E	530 534-4578	8274
Star Energy Management Inc	1731	E	530 532-9250	1612
Table Mountain Golf Club Inc	7997	D	530 533-3922	15158
Tyme Maidu Tribe-Berry Creek	7011	A	530 538-4560	11549

PACHECO, CA - Contra Costa County

Company	SIC	EMP	PHONE	ENTRY #
Biocare Medical LLC	3841	C	925 603-8000	6954
California Grand Casino	7999	D	925 685-8397	15186
Martinez Cogen Ltd Partnership	4911	D	925 313-0800	8122
Tesoro Golden Eagle Refin	7389	C	925 370-3249	14432
Universal Bldg Svcs & Sup Co	7349	D	925 934-5533	12012

PACIFICA, CA - San Mateo County

Company	SIC	EMP	PHONE	ENTRY #
Cal-Pacific Construction Inc	1542	E	650 557-1238	849
Centurioni Industries Inc	3999	F	858 213-7433	7274
Forever Young	2099	E	650 355-5481	2894
Kibblwhite Prcsion McHning Inc	3751	E	650 359-4704	6651
Little Giant Bldg Maint Inc	7349	C	415 508-0282	11968
Mercy Services Corporation	8322	E	650 359-6161	17648
Oil Changer Inc	7549	D	650 355-7233	14668
Pacifica Care Center	8051	D	650 355-5622	16089
Pacifica Linda Mar Inc	8051	D	650 359-4800	16090
Pyramid Alternatives Inc (PA)	8093	E	650 355-8787	17059

PAICINES, CA - San Benito County

Company	SIC	EMP	PHONE	ENTRY #
County of San Benito	3569	D	831 389-4591	5227

PALO ALTO, CA - Santa Clara County

Company	SIC	EMP	PHONE	ENTRY #
24hr Homecare LLC	8082	D	650 209-3295	16826
4290 El Camino Properties LP	7011	C	650 857-0787	10905
Abaqus Inc	7372	E	415 496-9436	12945
Accellion Inc	7379	C	650 485-4300	13828
Acme Bioscience Inc	8731	C	650 969-8000	19010
Activewire Inc (PA)	3577	E	650 969-4000	5340
Adaptive Insights LLC (HQ)	7372	C	650 528-7500	12951
Adara Inc (PA)	7372	C	408 876-6360	12952
Adrenas Therapeutics Inc	8049	E	408 899-9018	15879
Affymax Research Institute	8733	D	650 812-8700	19194
Aisera Inc	7371	D	650 667-4308	12236
Altamont Capital Partners LLC (PA)	6799	B	650 264-7750	10833
Altep California LLC (DH)	4813	C	650 691-4500	7924
Altrubio Inc (PA)	2834	E	650 453-3462	3841
American Hotel Inc	7011	E	650 323-5101	10921
Anacor Pharmaceuticals Inc	2834	A	650 543-7500	3846
Applied Expert Systems Inc	7372	E	650 617-2400	12980
Applovin Corporation (PA)	7372	B	800 839-9646	12981
Apporto Corporation	7372	E	650 326-0920	12982
Aquera Inc	7371	E	650 618-6442	12266
Archer Aviation Inc (PA)	3721	C	650 272-3233	6607
Archer Aviation Operating Corp	3721	C	650 272-3233	6608
Ardor Learning Inc (PA)	8999	E	650 245-6300	19897
Ariba Inc (DH)	7372	E	650 849-4000	12987
Arundo Analytics Inc (PA)	3569	E	713 256-7584	5224
Ascendis Pharma Inc	2834	F	650 352-8389	3856
Ascension Labs Inc	7371	E	650 898-9798	12277
Assured Insurance Technologies	6411	D	424 781-7123	10240
Atempo Americas Inc (DH)	7371	E	650 494-2600	12281
Autonomic LLC (PA)	7371	E	650 823-1806	12289
Avenidas Inc	8322	E	650 289-5600	17434
Baker & McKenzie LLP	8111	C	650 856-2400	17205
Bay Systems Consulting Inc (PA)	7373	E	650 960-3310	13560
Beauty Bazar Inc	7231	E	650 326-8522	11675
Beneficent Technology Inc	7389	E	650 644-3400	14214
Billcom LLC (HQ)	7372	C	650 353-3301	13018
Birdeye Inc (PA)	2741	C	800 561-3357	3560
Blameless Inc	7372	E	425 749-8859	13024
Bpr Properties Berkeley LLC	6512	C	650 424-1400	10378
Bridgebio Pharma Inc (PA)	2834	C	650 391-9740	3873
Bridgebio Services Inc	8731	D	650 438-1302	19037
Broadrach Cpitl Prtners Fund I	6722	A	650 331-2500	10751
Broadreach Capitl Partners LLC (PA)	6799	D	650 331-2500	10836
Callsign Inc (PA)	7371	E	650 320-1710	12322
Calmar Optcom Inc	3661	E	408 733-7800	5790
Cambridge Cm Inc	8741	E	650 543-3030	19314
Capital Asset Exch & Trdg LLC (PA)	5084	E	650 326-3313	9059
Caspian Networks Inc	3577	E	408 382-5200	5356
Caw Architects Inc	8712	D	650 328-1818	18877
Cc-Palo Alto Inc	8052	D	650 853-5000	16175
Cetas Inc	7372	F	847 530-5785	13060
Challenger Schools	8351	D	650 213-8245	17885
Channing House	8059	D	650 327-0950	16227
Childrens Crative Lrng Ctr Inc	8351	B	650 473-1100	17898
Childrens Hlth Cncil of The MD	8322	C	650 326-5530	17486
Citicorp Select Investments	6282	E	650 353-2765	10039
Citigate Cunningham Inc (PA)	8743	E	650 858-3700	19685
Cobalt Robotics Inc	3571	D	650 781-3626	5245
Communications & Pwr Inds LLC	3663	A	650 846-3729	5832
Communications & Pwr Inds LLC (HQ)	3671	A	650 846-2900	5900
Community Housing Inc	8361	D	650 328-3300	18079
Community Skating Inc	7999	E	650 493-4566	15194
Convrgd Data Tech Inc	5045	C	650 461-4488	8684
Cooley LLP (PA)	8111	B	650 843-5000	17235
Covenant Care California LLC	8051	D	415 327-0511	15965
CPI International Holding Corp	3679	C	650 846-2900	6411
CPI International Holding LLC	3679	D	650 846-2900	6412
CPI Subsidiary Holdings LLC (DH)	3679	D	650 846-2900	6413
Danisco US Inc (HQ)	2835	C	650 846-7500	4020
Dave Drunker	8071	E	650 853-4827	16779
Declara Inc	7379	D	877 216-0604	13878
Deleon Realty Inc	6531	E	650 543-8500	10535
Demand Known Inc	3652	F	310 929-5930	5776
Denodo Technologies Inc (PA)	7371	D	650 566-8833	12382
Dinahs Garden Hotel Inc	7011	C	650 493-2844	11049
Dlight Design Inc	1711	A	415 872-6136	1250
Docker Inc (PA)	7371	B	800 764-4847	12398
Docomo Innovations Inc	8731	E	650 493-9600	19052
Duda Mobile Inc	7372	D	855 790-0003	13129
Eiger Biopharmaceuticals Inc (PA)	2836	C	650 272-6138	4046
Electric Power RES Inst Inc (PA)	8733	A	650 855-2000	19214
Embarcadero Publishing Company (PA)	2711	D	650 964-6300	3435
Emerson Collective LLC	7371	C	650 422-2152	12422
End To End Analytics LLC	8748	E	650 331-9659	19765
Enjoy Technology Inc (PA)	7379	B	650 488-7676	13889
Entco Holdings Inc	7372	E	650 687-5817	13144
Essential Products Inc	7371	E	650 300-0000	12428
Essex Management Corporation (HQ)	6513	D	650 494-3700	10433
Eton Corporation	3699	E	650 903-3866	6520
F-Secure Inc (HQ)	5045	E	888 432-8233	8705
Family & Children Services	8322	D	650 326-6576	17558
Fiorano Software Inc	7372	E	650 326-1136	13160
Fisher House Palo Alto	8641	E	650 858-3903	18414
Fono Unlimited (PA)	2024	E	650 322-4664	2173
Foundation Capital LLC	6799	E	650 614-0500	10845
Fujifilm Bi Intrntnal Oprtons	5045	E	650 240-3740	8707
Function Engineering Inc (PA)	8711	E	650 326-8834	18714
Fx Palo Alto Laboratory Inc	8732	E	650 842-4800	19159
Gator Bio Inc	8732	D	650 800-7651	19160
Genpact LLC	8748	E	203 690-9308	19783
Gentle Dental	8021	A	650 341-8008	15835
Globality Inc	8741	E	650 352-8900	19342
Gobig Inc	7373	E	415 513-3029	13599
Gongio Inc	7371	E	415 412-0214	12481
Gordon Betty Moore Foundation	8641	D	650 213-3000	18428
Gordon E Btty I More Fundation	8748	D	650 213-3000	19786
Hammon Plating Corporation	3471	E	650 494-2691	4909
Handle Inc	2499	E	650 863-6113	3268
Harrell Remodeling Inc	1521	E	650 230-2900	651
Harris Mycfo Inc	8742	D	480 348-7725	19531
Hds Mercury Inc	8742	E	650 800-7701	19533
Health Gorilla Inc (PA)	7372	C	844 446-7455	13206
Hewlett Packard	7371	A	650 857-1501	12500
Hippo Analytics Inc (PA)	6411	E	925 895-9184	10293
Houzz Inc (PA)	7371	D	650 326-3000	12503
HP Hewlett Packard Group LLC	7374	D	650 857-1501	13719
HP Inc (PA)	3571	A	650 857-1501	5251
HP R&D Holding LLC (HQ)	3571	D	650 857-1501	5252
Hpi Cchgpii LLC	7372	E	650 687-5817	13215
Hpi Federal LLC (HQ)	3571	E	650 857-1501	5253
Hypergrid Inc	7371	D	650 316-5524	12508
Ideo LP (PA)	7336	C	650 289-3400	11865
Ideo Partners LLC	8748	E	650 289-3400	19791
Indigo America Inc	3571	C	650 857-1501	5254
Infoworksio Inc	7371	E	408 899-4687	12518
Inpixon Inc	7379	E	408 702-2167	13916
Inscopix Inc	3827	F	650 600-3886	6876
Instabug Inc	7371	E	650 422-9555	12525
Institute For Future	8733	E	650 854-6322	19219
Insulation Sources Inc (PA)	5063	E	650 856-6378	8863
Intapp Us Inc (HQ)	7371	E	650 852-0400	12528
Integrated Archive Systems Inc (PA)	8742	E	650 390-9995	19540
Interntional Ht Assoc No 3 LLC	7011	D	650 493-2411	11196

Employment Codes: A=Over 500 employees, B=251-500, C=101-250, D=51-100, E=20-50 F=10-19

PALO ALTO, CA

Company	SIC	EMP	PHONE	ENTRY #
Issuu Inc (PA)	2741	D	844 477-8800	3578
Jazz Pharmaceuticals Inc (HQ)	2834	A	650 496-3777	3934
Jewish Family and Chld Svcs	8322	C	650 931-1860	17624
Jewish Family and Chld Svcs	8322	C	650 688-3030	17626
Jive Software Inc	7372	F	503 295-3700	13256
Joguru Inc	4725	D	855 526-4332	7818
Julie Pearl A Prof Corp	8111	D	415 771-7500	17300
Jumio Corporation (HQ)	7371	E	650 424-8545	12551
Juut Midwest Inc	7231	D	650 328-4067	11688
KUDos&co Inc	2741	F	650 799-9104	3581
Ladder Financial Inc	7371	E	844 533-7206	12566
Lastline Inc (PA)	7372	C	877 671-3239	13273
Leena Ai Inc	4822	C	332 232-9740	8014
Level Labs LP	7372	F	408 499-6839	13277
Liveaction Inc (PA)	7372	E	415 837-3303	13278
Lucile Packard Childrens Hosp	8062	D	650 321-2545	16432
Lucile Pckard Fndtion For Chld (PA)	8322	E	650 497-8365	17638
Lucile Slter Pckard Chld Hosp (HQ)	8069	A	650 497-8000	16766
Lunar Design Incorporated (HQ)	7389	E	415 252-4388	14325
M10 Dev LLC (PA)	7011	C	650 424-8991	11278
M10 Dev LLC	7011	D	650 565-8100	11279
Maana Inc (PA)	7371	D	888 956-2262	12590
Machine Zone Inc (HQ)	7371	D	650 320-1678	12591
Magnet Systems Inc	7372	E	650 329-5904	13287
Map Energy LLC	6211	D	650 324-9095	9979
Map Royalty Inc (PA)	6792	C	650 324-9095	10802
Marcus Millichap Corp RE Svcs (HQ)	6531	E	650 391-1700	10610
Marcus Mllchap RE Inv Svcs Inc	6531	E	650 494-8900	10611
Mashgin Inc	3575	E	650 847-8050	5334
Mattermost Inc (PA)	7371	C	650 667-8512	12598
Maxar Space LLC	4899	D	650 852-4000	8080
Maximus Holdings Inc	7372	A	650 935-9500	13297
Mayview Community Hlth Ctr Inc (PA)	8011	E	650 327-8717	15522
Mda Cmmunications Holdings LLC	8741	E	650 842-4000	5855
Merrill Lynch Prce Fnner Smith	6211	D	650 842-2440	9984
Metreo Inc	7371	A	650 935-9400	12605
Metricus Inc	7389	C	650 328-2500	14330
Minio Inc	7371	E	844 356-4646	12609
Mojo Mobility Inc	3629	E	650 446-0004	5695
Morgan Stnley Smith Barney LLC	6211	D	650 496-4200	9999
Motivemetrics	3652	F	800 216-5207	5779
Mountain View Voice	2711	F	650 326-8210	3465
Movocash Inc	7371	E	650 722-3990	12622
Mroadie LLC	7371	E	650 300-4320	12624
Multiphy Inc	3674	F	650 600-9194	6221
My Ally Inc	7373	E	650 387-9118	13638
Nest Labs Inc	5065	D	855 469-6378	8937
Next Insurance Inc (PA)	6411	B	855 222-5919	10320
Nixel Inc	7371	E	650 618-9516	12635
Nyansa Inc	7372	E	650 446-7818	13338
Oak Creek Apartments	6513	C	650 327-1600	10451
Oil Changer Inc	7549	D	650 494-8353	14667
Opshub Inc	7371	E	650 701-1800	12654
Orphan Medical Inc	2834	D	650 496-3777	3960
Oshman Family Jewish Cmnty Ctr	8322	C	650 223-8700	17666
Pacific Hotel Dev Ventr LP	7011	C	650 347-8260	11344
Pacific Hotel Management LLC	7011	C	650 328-2800	11348
Packard Childrens Hlth Aliance	8011	D	650 497-8000	15581
Pagebites Inc	7371	E	650 353-0546	12664
Palantir Technologies Inc Pac	7371	D	650 833-9460	12665
Palantir Usg Inc (HQ)	7371	E	650 815-0200	12666
Palm Latin America Inc	3571	E	650 857-1501	5267
Palo Alto Hlls Golf Cntry CLB	7299	D	650 948-1800	11726
Palo Alto Inn	7011	D	650 493-4222	11351
Palo Alto Research Center Inc	8731	C	650 812-4000	19097
Palo Alto Vterans Inst For RES	8733	E	650 858-3970	19228
Paycycle Inc	4813	D	650 852-9650	7982
Paypal Inc	7389	B	877 434-2894	14357
Peninsula Hlthcare Cnnction In (PA)	8011	E	650 853-0321	15590
Percolata Corporation	7373	E	650 308-4980	13647
Pete Moffat Construction Inc	1521	E	650 493-8899	685
Phantom Cyber Corporation	7372	E	650 208-5151	13369
Plastic Surgery Center LLC	8093	E	650 322-6291	17058
Plume Design Inc	7373	D	408 498-5512	13649
Plutoshift Inc	7372	F	213 400-2104	13375
Point Digital Finance Inc	6211	E	650 460-8668	10007
Polsinelli PC	8111	E	650 461-7700	17358
Poynt Co	7371	E	650 600-8849	12695
Prealize Health Inc	8742	E	650 690-5300	19608
Precision Ideo Inc	7389	B	650 688-3400	14371
Predii Inc	7372	E	415 269-1146	13384
Proov Inc	7371	E	847 715-8218	12703
Provectus It Inc	7371	A	650 787-3207	12707
Psiquantum Corp (PA)	8731	E	650 427-0000	19109
Quality Metal Spinning and	3469	E	650 828-2491	4888
Quantifind Inc	7379	E	650 561-4937	13965
R2 Semiconductor Inc	3674	F	408 745-7400	6267
Rascal Therapeutics Inc	2834	E	650 770-0192	3973
Rightware Inc	7371	E	408 502-1017	12751
Rollapp Inc (PA)	7372	E	650 617-3372	13413
Rubrik Inc (PA)	7374	A	650 300-5862	13755
Safe Securities Inc	7371	E	650 398-3669	12755
Salt Security Inc	7371	E	650 254-6580	12756
Sankalp USA Inc	3674	E	408 372-6090	6278
Santa Clara County of	8093	D	408 918-7755	17067
Santa Clara County of	8322	E	650 324-6500	17721
Sap AG	3572	C	650 849-4000	5316
Sap Labs LLC	7371	D	650 849-4000	12760
Sap Labs LLC (DH)	7372	B	650 849-4000	13424
Scilex Pharmaceuticals Inc	2834	E	650 430-3238	3983
Scio Technologies Inc	7371	E	408 203-0518	12767
Sciton Inc	3841	D	650 493-9155	7031
Sharethis Inc (PA)	7311	D	650 641-0191	11782
Singular Labs Inc (PA)	7371	E	415 999-8368	12788
Skoll Foundation	8699	E	650 331-1031	18591
Skype Inc	4813	D	650 493-7900	7991
Sla LLC (PA)	6512	E	650 322-2600	10408
Smartek21 LLC	7379	B	650 617-3221	13978
Southwall Technologies Inc (DH)	2821	E	650 798-1285	3809
Stanford Blood Center LLC (PA)	8011	C	650 723-7994	15701
Stanford Federal Credit Union (PA)	6061	D	650 725-1000	9821
Stanford Health Care	8062	E	650 723-5171	16550
Stanford Health Care	8062	E	650 213-8360	16551
Stanford Health Care	8062	E	650 497-8953	16553
Stanford Health Care	8099	E	650 723-8561	17182
Stanford Health Care	8062	E	650 736-7844	16558
Stangenes Industries Inc (PA)	3677	D	650 855-9926	6386
Step Mobile Inc	7372	E	203 913-9229	13467
Stg IV Gp LP (PA)	6722	B	650 935-9500	10770
Stratford School Inc (PA)	8351	E	650 493-1151	18037
Streamlio Inc	3652	F	949 701-9729	5781
Striim Inc (PA)	7371	E	425 894-1998	12825
Successfactors Inc (DH)	7372	A	650 212-1296	13471
Suning Cmmerce R D Ctr USA Inc	8732	D	650 834-9800	19188
Surveysparrow Inc	8732	D	800 481-0410	19189
Suss McRtec Prcsion Phtmask In	3861	F	415 494-3113	7158
Sutter Bay Medical Foundation (HQ)	8011	A	650 321-4121	15709
Sutter Health	8011	D	650 853-2975	15714
Sutter Health	8062	C	916 297-9923	16619
Sutter Health	8062	C	650 853-2904	16629
Swisscom Cloud Lab Ltd	7372	E	404 316-9160	13476
Symphony Metreo Inc	7371	A	650 935-9500	12838
Symphony Technology Group LLC (PA)	8748	A	650 935-9500	19868
Tall Tree Insurance Company	3571	E	650 857-1501	5274
Tangible Play Inc (HQ)	7371	E	650 667-1693	12849
Tcv Management 2004 LLC	8741	E	650 614-8200	19407
Temujin Labs Inc	7371	C	650 850-9037	12858
Tesla Inc (PA)	3711	C	650 681-5000	6561
Thoits Love Herschberger & McL (PA)	8111	E	650 330-7321	17380
Throughput Inc	3652	F	215 606-8552	5782
Tibco Software Federal Inc	7372	E	703 208-3900	13493
Tibco Software Inc (HQ)	7371	B	650 846-1000	12865
Tightdb Inc	7371	D	415 766-2020	12866
Total Quality Maintenance Inc	7349	C	650 846-4700	12005
Tresl Inc (PA)	7379	E	650 868-2862	14000
Tripactions Inc (PA)	4724	A	888 505-8747	7809
Turncare Inc	3845	F	203 437-6768	7128
U P C Inc	7299	C	650 462-2010	11733
Varian Associates Limited	3841	E	650 493-4000	7054
Varian Medical Systems Inc (DH)	3845	A	650 493-4000	7131
Varian Medical Systems Inc	3841	E	650 213-8000	7055
Veterans Health Administration	8741	E	650 493-5000	19417
Veterans Health Administration	8011	C	650 493-5000	15792
Vincerx Pharma Inc (PA)	2834	E	650 800-6676	4005
Vivo Capital LLC (PA)	6211	D	650 688-0818	10021
Vmware Inc (PA)	7372	A	650 427-5000	13522
Watercourse Way	7299	E	650 462-2000	11736
Waverley Surgery Center LP (PA)	8011	D	650 324-0600	15811
Wealthfront Corporation	6282	E	650 249-4258	10068
Wilson Snsini Gdrich Rsati Pro (PA)	8111	A	650 493-9300	17400
Wong Electric Inc	1731	E	650 813-9999	1641
Wurl Inc (PA)	8741	C	662 649-8825	19428
Xcelmobility Inc	7372	E	650 320-1728	13533
Xerox International Partners (DH)	3555	D	408 953-2700	5124
Yellowbrick Data Inc (PA)	7374	B	877 492-3282	13773
Yubico Inc	5044	C	408 774-4064	8657

PALO CEDRO, CA - Shasta County

Company	SIC	EMP	PHONE	ENTRY #
Rotary International	8641	D	530 547-5272	18456
Skyline Alterations Inc (PA)	2411	E	530 549-4010	3082

PARADISE, CA - Butte County

Company	SIC	EMP	PHONE	ENTRY #
Califrnia Nwspapers Ltd Partnr	2711	C	530 877-4413	3425
Compac Engineering Inc	3822	E	530 872-2042	6701
Pacific Gas and Electric Co	4911	C	530 327-7633	8167
Paradise Medical Group Inc	8011	E	530 877-3951	15583
Ponderosa Garden Motel Inc	7011	D	888 727-3423	11373
Sunbrdge Prdise Rhbltion Ctr	8051	A	530 872-3200	16135
Tegtmeier Associates Inc	6512	D	530 872-7700	10412
Tenter Enterprises Inc	4215	D	530 680-9917	7656
Town of Paradise	8111	E	530 872-6241	17382
Youth For Change (PA)	8322	C	530 877-8187	17791

PARLIER, CA - Fresno County

Company	SIC	EMP	PHONE	ENTRY #
Adventist Hlth Systm/West Corp	8062	D	559 646-1200	16306
Custom Produce Sales (PA)	5148	C	559 254-5800	9396
John Daniel Gonzalez	2449	E	559 646-6621	3237
Kozuki Farming Inc	0175	D	559 646-2652	107
Maxco Supply Inc (PA)	5113	E	559 646-8449	9215
ONeill Beverages Co LLC	0172	C	559 638-3544	67
Sunwest Fruit Co Inc	5148	E	559 646-4000	9432
W E Plemons McHy Svcs Inc	3565	E	559 646-6630	5209

PATTERSON, CA - Stanislaus County

Company	SIC	EMP	PHONE	ENTRY #
Cartel Transport LLC	4212	E	209 892-3880	7456

	SIC	EMP	PHONE	ENTRY #
Del Mar Farms Partners Ltd **(PA)**	0191	E	209 894-5555	156
Del Puerto Health Care Dst	8011	D	209 892-9100	15374
Designed MBL Systems Inds Inc	1542	F	209 892-6298	861
DK Enterprises Inc	1761	E	209 892-3386	1799
Global Valley Networks Inc	4813	E	209 892-4100	7955
Groves/Eden Corporation **(PA)**	7231	C	209 894-2481	11683
Hpl Contract Inc	2521	F	209 892-1717	3303
Longs Drug Stores Cal LLC	4225	C	209 895-7839	7693
Lrg Builder Services Inc	1541	E	209 894-7100	801
Melo Machine & Mfg Inc	5085	F	209 892-2661	9123
Oak Flat Golf Company LLC	7997	E	209 892-4653	15117
Patterson Frozen Foods Inc	2037	E	209 892-5060	2295
Precision Cnc LLC	3599	E	209 277-2082	5601
Sgm Inc	7992	E	559 665-4462	15025
Southwest Fence and Sup Co Inc **(PA)**	1799	E	209 892-9205	2071
Sport Boat Trailers Inc	3799	F	209 892-5388	6659
Traina Dried Fruit Inc	5149	C	209 892-5472	9496
Traina Dried Fruit Inc **(PA)**	5149	D	209 892-5472	9497

PAYNES CREEK, CA - Tehama County

	SIC	EMP	PHONE	ENTRY #
Mt Lassen Trout Farms Inc	0921	E	530 474-1900	538

PENN VALLEY, CA - Nevada County

	SIC	EMP	PHONE	ENTRY #
Lake Wildwood Association	8641	C	530 432-1152	18435
Siller and Siller Construction	7353	F	916 893-3462	12023

PENNGROVE, CA - Sonoma County

	SIC	EMP	PHONE	ENTRY #
Kbi Painting Inc	1721	E	707 795-4955	1419

PENRYN, CA - Placer County

	SIC	EMP	PHONE	ENTRY #
Loomis Bsin Equine Med Ctr Inc	0742	E	916 652-7645	327
Sinclair Concrete	1771	D	916 663-0303	1909

PESCADERO, CA - San Mateo County

	SIC	EMP	PHONE	ENTRY #
Atmos Engineering Inc	3829	F	650 879-1674	6893
King-Reynolds Ventures LLC	7389	D	650 879-2136	14317
Pescadero Conservation Aliance	8641	E	650 879-1441	18447
Silver Terrace Nurseries Inc	0181	D	650 879-2110	136

PETALUMA, CA - Sonoma County

	SIC	EMP	PHONE	ENTRY #
101mfg Llc	8742	E	415 828-9015	19430
205 Kentucky Street LLC	7011	E	707 559-3393	10902
Accountmate Software Corp **(PA)**	7372	E	707 774-7500	12950
Ace Products Enterprises Inc	3161	E	707 765-1500	4346
All-American Prtg Svcs Corp **(PA)**	7334	E	707 762-2500	11844
Allianz Globl Risks US Insur	6331	B	415 899-3758	10161
Allianz Reinsurance Amer Inc	6321	A	415 899-2000	10081
Amys Kitchen Inc **(PA)**	2038	A	707 578-7188	2302
Architectural Plastics Inc	3089	E	707 765-9898	4259
Arntz Builders Inc	1541	E	415 382-1188	788
Associated Indemnity Corp	6311	C	415 899-2000	10076
Bausch Health Americas Inc	2834	C	707 793-2600	3861
Beaver Dam Health Care Center	8051	E	707 763-4109	15933
Bibbero Systems Inc **(HQ)**	2752	E	800 242-2376	3631
Biosearch Technologies Inc **(DH)**	2836	C	415 883-8400	4040
Braden Prtners LP A Cal Ltd PR **(HQ)**	5047	D	415 893-1518	8776
California Department Trnsp	1611	D	707 762-6641	1019
Camelbak Acquisition Corp	3949	E	707 792-9700	7191
Camelbak Products LLC **(HQ)**	3949	D	707 792-9700	7192
Caracal Enterprises LLC	3581	E	707 773-3373	5426
Clover-Stornetta Farms Inc **(PA)**	5149	C	707 769-3282	9444
CLY Incorporated	1611	E	707 763-5591	1029
Colter & Peterson Microsystems	3823	E	707 776-4500	6714
Colvin-Friedman LLC	3089	E	707 769-4488	4269
Committee On Shelterless	8322	E	707 765-6530	17491
County Engineers Assn Cal	8711	D	707 762-3492	18677
Deweyl Tool Co Inc	3545	E	707 765-5779	5092
Don Ramatici Insurance Inc	6411	E	707 782-9200	10274
Donal Machine Inc	3599	E	707 763-6625	5510
Empire Shower Doors Inc	3231	E	707 773-2898	4385
Evergreen At Petaluma LLC	8051	D	707 763-6887	15999
Express Messenger Systems Inc	4215	E	707 773-1564	7643
Federal Express Corporation	4513	D	800 463-3339	7746
Fedex Freight West Inc	4213	E	707 778-3191	7538
G C Micro Corporation	5045	E	707 789-0600	8708
Gefen LLC	3699	E	818 772-9100	6523
Gmpc LLC	3993	F	707 766-1702	7231
Goebel Construction Inc	1611	E	707 763-0088	1044
Graton Spirits Company LLC **(PA)**	2085	E	707 829-6100	2771
Harris Company Concrete Cnstr	1771	E	707 246-5697	1880
Hdp Enterprises Inc	5143	E	707 763-7388	9340
Henris Supply Inc	1761	E	707 763-1535	1812
Hunt & Behrens Inc	5191	E	707 762-4594	9600
Hydrofarm LLC **(HQ)**	3648	E	707 765-9990	5743
Hydropoint Data Systems Inc	3523	E	707 769-9696	5006
Incom Mechanical Inc	1711	D	707 586-0511	1283
Institute of Noetic Sciences	8733	E	707 775-3500	19221
James Furuli Investment Co	7349	D	707 778-7102	11963
Kaiser Foundation Hospitals	8011	C	707 765-3900	15478
Katadyn Desalination LLC	3634	E	415 526-2780	5704
Kval Inc	3553	C	707 762-4363	5115
Labcon North America	3089	C	707 766-2100	4297
Lace House Ldry & Lin Sup Inc	7213	E	707 763-1515	11636
Legacy Marketing Group **(PA)**	8742	C	707 778-8638	19557
Leisure Care LLC	8361	C	707 769-3300	18137
Lind Marine Inc **(PA)**	2048	E	707 762-7251	2347
Lok Redwood Empire Prpts Inc	7011	D	707 584-8280	11267
Marin Mountain Bikes **(PA)**	5091	F	415 382-6000	9158
Marin Storage & Trucking Inc **(PA)**	4214	E	707 778-8313	7625
Marr B Olsen Inc	1771	E	707 763-9707	1892
McEvoy of Marin LLC	2079	E	707 778-2307	2465
Mesa/Boogie Limited **(HQ)**	3651	D	707 765-1805	5763
Midstate Construction Corp	1521	D	707 762-3200	675
Mishi Apparel Inc **(PA)**	2261	E	707 525-1075	2977
Miyokos Kitchen	2021	E	415 521-5313	2142
Morgan Manufacturing Inc	3423	F	707 763-6848	4607
Morris Distributing	5181	D	707 769-7294	9557
Mountanos Brothers Coffee Co **(PA)**	5149	E	707 774-8800	9466
Mrs Grossmans Paper Company	2678	D	707 763-1700	3399
NMN Construction Inc	1771	D	707 763-6981	1896
North Bay Landscape Mgt Inc	0782	E	707 762-3850	491
North Bay Post Acute LLC	8051	E	707 763-6887	16073
Nuvolum Inc	8742	E	415 413-4999	19593
Oak Knoll Convalescent Ctr Inc	8051	D	707 778-8686	16078
Optio Solutions LLC	7322	B	800 360-2827	11826
Pacific Gas and Electric Co	4911	C	707 765-5118	8148
Parmatech Corporation	3399	D	707 778-2266	4590
Permanente Medical Group Inc	8011	A	707 765-3900	15619
Petaluma Acquisitions LLC	2015	A	707 763-1904	2138
Petaluma By Products	2076	E	707 763-9181	2455
Petaluma Cinemas LLC	7832	E	707 762-0990	14815
Petaluma Farms Inc	0252	E	707 763-0921	231
Petaluma Golf and Country Club	7997	D	707 762-7041	15122
Petaluma Health Center Inc	8011	B	707 559-7500	15626
Petaluma Post-Acute Rehab	8051	E	707 765-3030	16095
Petaluma Properties Inc	7011	D	707 763-0994	11364
Petaluma Valley Hospital Aux	8062	D	707 778-1111	16480
Petalumaidence Opco LLC	2084	C	707 763-4109	2682
Planet One Products Inc **(PA)**	2541	E	707 794-8000	3319
Point Reyes Bird Observator	8641	E	415 868-0371	18449
Point Reyes Bird Observatory	8733	D	707 781-2555	19229
Premier Senior Living LLC **(PA)**	8361	D	707 778-6719	18157
Prosight Specity Insur Grp Inc	6411	D	707 324-5000	10337
Pure Luxury Limousine Service	4119	C	800 626-5466	7397
Purple Wine Company	2084	C	707 829-6100	2689
Qor LLC	2329	F	707 658-1941	2995
Reichardt Duck Farm Inc	0259	D	707 762-6314	241
Robert W Cameron & Co Inc	2731	E	707 769-1617	3544
Rooster Run Golf Club Inc	7992	E	707 778-1211	15021
RS Technical Services Inc **(PA)**	3826	D	707 778-1974	6847
San Frncsco North/Petaluma KOA	7033	E	707 763-1492	11620
Security People Inc	3679	E	707 766-6000	6468
Sequoia Senior Solutions Inc **(PA)**	8082	C	707 763-6600	16943
Shamrock Materials Inc **(PA)**	3273	E	707 781-9000	4505
Sistema US Inc	3089	E	707 773-2200	4323
Small Precision Tools Inc	3674	D	707 765-4545	6303
Soligent Distribution LLC **(HQ)**	5065	C	707 992-3100	8958
Sonoma Hotel Partners LP	7011	D	707 283-2888	11492
Sonoma Technology Inc	8748	D	707 665-9900	19863
Srm Alliance Hospital Services **(PA)**	8062	B	707 778-1111	16534
St Louis Post-Dispatch LLC	2711	D	707 762-4541	3483
Stantec Architecture Inc	8712	C	707 765-1660	18915
Star H-R **(PA)**	7361	A	707 762-4447	12142
Steven I Klotz	7999	E	707 763-5010	15246
Stonecrop Technologies LLC	3663	F	781 659-0007	5872
Straus Family Creamery Inc	2021	D	707 776-2887	2143
Sunrise Farms LLC	5144	D	707 778-6450	9353
Sunrise of Petaluma	8051	E	707 776-2885	16139
Sunset Aviation LLC **(PA)**	4581	E	707 775-2786	7785
TC Steel	7692	F	707 773-2150	14723
Team Ghilotti Inc	1611	E	707 763-8700	1077
Tibit Communications Inc	4899	E	707 664-5906	8086
Torn Ranch Inc **(PA)**	2064	D	415 506-3000	2434
Trestles Holdings LLC	6719	D	707 778-8686	10745
United Cmps Cnfrences Retreats **(PA)**	7032	E	707 762-3220	11613
Universal Bldg Svcs & Sup Co	7349	D	707 781-7434	12010
Us1com Inc	2759	F	707 781-2560	3753
Vendini Inc **(PA)**	7371	D	415 693-9611	12898
Windsor Care Ctr Petaluma LLC	8051	E	707 763-2457	16163
Windsor Willits Company **(PA)**	2431	E	707 665-9663	3160
Womack International Inc	3569	F	707 763-1800	5235
X2nsat	7379	E	707 664-5700	14012
Xandex Inc	3825	E	707 763-7799	6801

PHILO, CA - Mendocino County

	SIC	EMP	PHONE	ENTRY #
Handley Cellars Ltd	2084	E	707 895-3876	2611
Husch Vineyards Inc **(PA)**	2084	E	707 895-3216	2619
I & E Lath Mill	2421	E	707 895-3380	3097
James Taylor Roberts Inc	7389	E	707 895-2500	14312
Navarro Winery	2084	E	707 895-3686	2665
TS Logging	2411	E	707 895-3751	3084

PIEDMONT, CA - Alameda County

	SIC	EMP	PHONE	ENTRY #
Avoy Corp	2752	E	510 295-8055	3624
Evb LLC	7311	E	415 281-3950	11753
M F A Incorporated **(PA)**	3651	D	510 547-8444	5761

PILOT HILL, CA - El Dorado County

	SIC	EMP	PHONE	ENTRY #
Ao Sky Corporation	3812	F	415 717-9901	6661
Dirt Dggers N Mtrcycle CLB Inc	8699	E	916 640-7328	18563

PINE GROVE, CA - Amador County

	SIC	EMP	PHONE	ENTRY #
Volcano Communications Company **(PA)**	4813	D	209 296-7502	8004
Volcano Vision Inc	4841	E	209 296-2288	8068

PINECREST, CA - Tuolumne County

	SIC	EMP	PHONE	ENTRY #
Dodge Ridge Corporation	7011	B	209 536-5300	11056
Pinecrest Lake Resort	7011	E	209 965-3411	11369

GEOGRAPHIC

Employment Codes: A=Over 500 employees, B=251-500, C=101-250, D=51-100, E=20-50 F=10-19

2022 Northern California Business Directory and Buyers Guide

1177

PINEDALE, CA

	SIC	EMP	PHONE	ENTRY #

PINEDALE, CA - Fresno County
Pacific Door & Cabinet Company	2431	E	559 439-3822	3144

PINOLE, CA - Contra Costa County
Already	8699	E	510 322-4988	18543
Califrnia Atism Foundation Inc	8399	D	510 724-1751	18222
Jarvis & Jarvis Inc	7539	E	510 222-0431	14614
Kaiser Foundation Hospitals	8011	C	510 243-4000	15463
Pathway To Choices Inc	8322	E	510 724-9044	17670

PIONEER, CA - Amador County
Bear River Lake Resort Inc	7011	E	209 295-4868	10948
Mace Meadow Golf Cntry CLB Inc	7992	E	209 295-7020	15009
Pacific Gas and Electric Co	4911	C	209 295-2651	8188
Pine Grove Group Inc	3699	E	209 295-7733	6537

PITTSBURG, CA - Contra Costa County
A T Associates Inc (PA)	8059	D	925 808-6540	16215
Allied Crane Inc	7699	E	925 427-9200	14735
Antioch Building Materials Co (PA)	5032	E	925 432-0171	8617
Apollo Graph Inc	7371	E	206 225-9488	12259
Aquamatic Fire Protection Inc (PA)	1711	E	925 753-0420	1205
Bishop-Wisecarver Corporation (PA)	3499	D	925 439-8272	4982
California Expanded Met Pdts	3448	F	925 473-9340	4848
CC Co Health Cntr Information	8011	D	925 431-2300	15332
Centen AG LLC	2879	E	925 432-5000	4141
Chrome Deposit Corp	3471	E	925 432-4507	4901
Cintas Corporation No 3	7213	C	925 692-5860	11633
Concord Iron Works Inc	3441	C	925 432-0136	4654
Diverse Steel Sales Inc (PA)	5051	F	925 756-0555	8815
Durham School Services L P	4151	D	925 686-3391	7428
First Baptist Head Start	8351	E	925 473-2000	17936
Frase Enterprises	3644	E	510 856-3600	5721
Granberg Pump and Meter Ltd	3546	F	707 562-2099	5102
Hammond Enterprises Inc	3599	E	925 432-3537	5534
Hospital Systems Inc	3845	C	925 427-7800	7107
K2 Pure Slutions Nocal Salt LP	2899	E	925 297-4901	4163
La Clinica De La Raza Inc	8011	C	925 431-1250	15501
Levmar Inc	3444	E	925 680-8723	4777
LLC Baker Cummins	2844	E	925 732-9338	4088
Longs Drug Stores Cal Inc	7384	E	925 439-7288	14167
Masterank Wax Incorporated (PA)	2911	F	925 998-2186	4176
Maya Pittsburg Cinemas LLC	7832	E	213 805-5333	14812
McCampbell Analytical Inc	8734	E	925 252-9262	19278
Moreflavor Inc (PA)	5084	E	800 600-0033	9081
Pacific Coast Gen Engrg Inc	8711	E	925 252-0214	18786
Pacific Gas and Electric Co	4911	D	925 757-2000	8144
Pittsburg Care Center Inc	8051	D	925 432-3831	16097
Pittsburg General Inc	3444	E	800 445-6374	4805
Ramar International Corp (PA)	2024	E	925 439-9009	2182
Ravig Inc	5045	D	925 526-1234	8742
Redwood Painting Co Inc	1721	C	925 432-4500	1429
Restoration Clean Up Co Inc (PA)	7349	E	800 500-4310	11989
Rfid Corporation	7213	C	925 473-9978	11645
Ruan Transport Corporation	4213	E	925 427-3983	7584
SSC Pittsburg Operating Co LP	8059	C	925 427-4444	16271
State Preschool	8351	E	925 473-4380	18034
Viking Processing Corporation (PA)	5051	E	925 427-2518	8832

PLACERVILLE, CA - El Dorado County
Advanced Gases and Eqp Inc	5084	D	530 344-0771	9050
Applied Control Electronics	3625	F	530 626-5181	5676
Boeger Winery Inc	2084	E	530 622-8094	2512
Chili Bar LLC	1429	E	530 622-3325	578
Coastal PVA Opco LLC	3571	F	530 406-3303	5244
Cold Springs Golf & Cntry CLB	7997	E	530 622-4567	15075
El Dorado County Health Dept	8011	D	530 621-6100	15388
El Dorado Irrigation District	4941	B	530 622-4513	8248
El Dorado Savings Bank (PA)	6035	D	530 622-1492	9770
El Dorado Truss Co Inc	2439	C	530 622-1264	3205
Elder Options (PA)	8322	E	530 626-6939	17541
Gist Inc	3965	D	530 644-8000	7211
Gladiolus Holdings LLC	8051	E	530 622-3400	16013
Gold Country Health Center Inc (PA)	8051	C	530 621-1100	16014
Health and Humn Svcs Agcy Hhsa	8011	E	530 621-5834	11134
Innovative Education MGT Inc (PA)	8741	D	530 295-3566	19354
Lava Springs Inc	2084	E	530 621-0175	2651
Lyon Realty	6519	C	530 295-4444	10481
Marshall Medical Center	8062	E	530 626-3682	16442
Marshall Medical Center	8062	E	530 626-2900	16444
Marshall Medical Center	8062	E	530 626-2616	16445
Marshall Medical Center	8062	E	530 344-5470	16446
Marshall Medical Center	8062	E	530 621-3600	16448
Marshall Medical Center	8062	E	530 626-2920	16450
Marshall Medical Center (PA)	8062	A	530 622-1441	16451
Mother Lode Prtg & Pubg Co Inc	2711	E	530 344-5030	3464
Mother Lode Rhbltition Entps In	8361	C	530 622-4848	18146
National 9 Motels Inc	7011	E	530 622-3884	11326
New Mrning Youth Fmly Svcs Inc	8322	E	530 622-5551	17654
Norden Millimeter Inc	3663	E	530 642-9123	5857
Northern California Inalliance	8322	D	530 344-1244	17661
Pacific Gas and Electric Co	4911	E	530 621-7237	8159
Placervlle Pnes Cnvlscent Hosp	8059	E	530 622-3400	16258
R-Quest Technologies LLC	7372	F	530 621-9916	13398
Rucker Mill & Cab Works Inc	2434	E	530 621-0236	3190
Shingle Sprng Trbal Gming Auth	7011	A	530 677-7000	11472
Ski Air Conditioning Company	1711	E	530 626-4010	1360
Stymiest Auto Body Inc	7532	E	530 622-7588	14535
Summitview Child & Family Svcs	8322	D	530 644-2412	17761
Thompsons Auto & Trck Ctr Inc (PA)	7538	E	530 295-5700	14596
Tsu/Tree Service Unlimited Inc	0783	E	530 626-8733	524
Western Slope Health Center	8051	C	530 622-6842	16157

PLEASANT GROVE, CA - Sutter County
Hoc Holdings Inc (PA)	5082	C	916 921-8950	9021
Holt of California (HQ)	5082	C	916 991-8200	9022
Holt Rental Services	5082	D	916 921-8800	9024
Sills Farms Inc	0191	D	916 655-3391	190
Sysco Sacramento Inc	5141	B	916 275-2714	9317
Van Dykes Rice Dryer Inc	0723	C	916 655-3171	314
Withrow Cattle	0241	D	916 780-0364	228

PLEASANT HILL, CA - Contra Costa County
500 Startups Management Co LLC	6799	C	650 743-4738	10827
Aegis Senior Communities LLC	8082	D	925 588-7030	16839
American National Red Cross	8322	E	925 602-1460	17421
Argo Insurance Brokers Inc (HQ)	6411	E	925 682-7001	10237
Carlton Senior Living Inc	8361	E	925 935-1001	18067
Cbiz Inc	6411	E	925 956-0505	10260
Century Theatres Inc	7833	E	925 681-2000	14824
Chemsw Inc	7372	F	707 864-0845	13062
Choice In Aging (PA)	8093	D	925 682-6330	16999
Contra Costa Cnty Off Educatn (PA)	8741	B	925 942-3388	19319
Contra Costa Country Club	7997	D	925 798-7135	15076
Crestwood Behavioral Hlth Inc	8051	E	925 938-8051	15976
Diablo Vly College Foundation (PA)	7389	A	925 685-1230	14254
Dreamctchers Empwerment Netwrk	8361	C	925 935-6630	18100
El Charro Mexican Dining	7299	E	925 283-2345	11716
Elson Electric Holdings Inc	1731	E	925 464-7461	1502
Etic (PA)	8748	E	925 602-4710	19771
Interim Asssted Care E Bay Inc	8082	E	925 944-5779	16900
Mark Scott Construction Inc	1522	E	209 982-0502	758
Mark Scott Construction Inc (PA)	1542	E	925 944-0502	918
Maze & Assoc Accounting Corp	8721	D	925 930-0902	18977
Mc Namara Dodge Ney Beatt (PA)	8111	E	925 939-5330	17328
Mosaic Brands Inc	3999	E	925 322-8700	7300
Nady Systems Inc	3651	E	510 652-2411	5765
Passport Health LLC	8011	E	925 239-8794	15584
Perazza Prints LLC (PA)	2752	E	925 681-2458	3683
Play and Learn School	8351	E	925 947-2820	18001
Professnal Healthcare At HM LLC	8082	D	510 450-0422	16926
Professnal Healthcare At HM LLC (PA)	8082	D	925 849-1160	16927
Property Sciences Group Inc (PA)	6531	E	925 246-7300	10650
Residence Inn By Marriott LLC	7011	E	925 689-1010	11404
Samil Power US Ltd	3674	E	925 930-3924	6277
Synqy Corporation	7372	F	925 407-2601	13482

PLEASANTON, CA - Alameda County
10x Genomics Inc (PA)	8731	B	925 401-7300	19007
1st United Credit Union (PA)	6061	D	800 649-0193	9774
2dream Inc	7389	C	650 943-2366	14186
314e Corporation (PA)	7371	C	510 371-6736	12214
4leaf Inc (PA)	7389	C	925 462-5959	14188
A B Boyd Co (PA)	3069	A	888 244-6931	4211
A Teichert & Son Inc (HQ)	5032	A	916 484-3011	8614
ABM Elctrcal Ltg Solutions Inc	7349	D	408 399-3030	11912
Accurate Firestop Inc	7389	C	510 886-1169	14195
Accusplit (PA)	3873	F	925 290-1900	7160
Advanced Digital Solutions Intl	5045	E	510 490-6667	8660
Advantage Sales & Marketing	5141	E	925 463-5600	9261
Aegis Fire Systems LLC	1711	E	925 417-5550	1188
Akshaya Inc (PA)	7379	C	925 914-7395	13836
Alameda County AG Fair Assn	7999	E	925 426-7600	15170
Alliance Info Tech Cmpt Sftwr (PA)	7371	F	925 462-9787	12241
American National Red Cross	8322	A	800 733-2767	17426
American Property Management	7011	C	925 463-8000	10922
Anixter Inc	5063	E	925 469-8500	8843
AOC Technologies Inc	5051	B	925 875-0808	8805
Archeyy & Friends LLC	2047	E	703 579-7649	2332
Ascendify Corporation	7371	E	415 528-5503	12276
Astex Pharmaceuticals Inc (DH)	2834	C	925 560-0100	3858
Avanquest Publishing Usa Inc (HQ)	7371	D	925 474-1700	12291
Avatier Corporation (PA)	7372	E	925 217-5170	13002
Axis Community Health Inc	8093	D	925 462-1755	16990
B & B Travelware LLC	3161	F	408 564-7569	4347
Bay East Assn Rltors Fundation	8641	E	925 730-4600	18391
Bay Vista Senior Housing	6513	A	925 924-7100	10418
Bayone Solutions	7371	C	408 930-1600	12298
BB&T Insurance Svcs Cal Inc (DH)	6411	E	925 463-9672	10245
Berlogar Geotechnical Cons	8711	D	925 484-0220	18639
Big-D Pacific Builders LP	1521	D	925 460-3232	618
Bkf Engineers	8713	E	925 396-7700	18921
Black Tie Transportation LLC	4119	C	925 847-0747	7378
Blackhawk Engagement Solution	7375	D	925 226-9990	13780
Blackhawk Network Inc (DH)	6099	A	925 226-9990	9844
Blackhawk Network Holdings Inc (HQ)	6099	B	925 226-9990	9845
Blackrock Logistics Inc (PA)	4731	C	925 523-3878	7825
Blocka Construction Inc	1711	D	510 657-3686	1221
Blueline Associates Inc	1542	E	925 462-2200	834
Bon Appetit Management Co	8741	C	925 730-3653	19304
Boresha International Inc	2095	E	925 676-1400	2836
Boyd Corporation (HQ)	2891	A	209 236-1111	4150
Brightview Landscape Dev Inc	1629	E	925 463-0700	1151
Brightview Landscape Svcs Inc	0781	C	925 924-8900	405
Brown Brown Insur Svcs Cal Inc	6411	E	925 416-1692	10252
Bvrp America Inc	7372	E	303 450-1139	13041

	SIC	EMP	PHONE	ENTRY #
Select Hotels Group LLC	7011	E	916 638-4141	11457
Sffi Company Inc **(PA)**	5148	C	323 586-0000	9428
Sierra Nevada Corp	3812	F	775 331-0222	6682
Sierra PCF HM & Comfort Inc	5075	D	916 638-0543	9015
Simply Fresh Fruit Inc	5148	D	323 586-0000	9429
Sk Pharmteco Inc	2834	E	888 330-2232	3986
Soundstream Technologies Mfg	3651	E	916 635-3011	5769
Southern Cal Disc Tire Co Inc	5013	C	916 638-2388	8467
Sst Construction LLC	1521	E	844 477-8787	709
Stewart Tool Company	3545	D	916 635-8321	5100
Strachota Insurance Agency	6411	E	951 676-2229	10355
Stroppini Enterprises	3537	E	916 635-8181	5068
Sunrise Mfg Inc **(PA)**	2679	E	916 635-6262	3406
Sunsystem Technology LLC **(PA)**	8731	D	916 671-3351	19133
Superior Vision Services Inc **(DH)**	6324	D	800 507-3800	10155
Tait & Associates Inc	8711	E	916 635-2444	18826
Taylor Communications Inc	2761	F	916 368-1200	3759
Technique Gymnastics Inc	7999	E	916 635-7900	15249
Technology Services Cal Dept	7379	C	916 464-3747	13992
Teledyne Defense Elec LLC	3679	C	916 638-3344	6476
Teledyne Wireless LLC	3679	C	916 638-3344	6478
Tetra Tech Ec Inc	8748	E	916 852-8300	19874
Thermogenesis Holdings Inc **(PA)**	3841	E	916 858-5100	7050
TRC Solutions	8748	C	916 962-7001	19877
Tri Tool Inc **(HQ)**	5084	C	916 288-6100	9100
Turning Point Cmnty Programs **(PA)**	8093	D	916 364-8395	17083
Two Rivers Demolition Inc	1795	D	916 638-6775	1990
Urata & Sons Concrete Inc	1771	C	916 638-5364	1914
Urata & Sons Concrete LLC	1771	D	916 638-5364	1915
Usko Expedite Inc **(PA)**	4731	E	916 233-4455	7858
Usko Express Inc	4222	D	916 515-8065	7680
Vander-Bend Manufacturing Inc	3599	C	916 631-6375	5635
Varis LLC	8742	D	916 294-0860	19663
Vision Service Plan Inc **(PA)**	6324	A	916 851-5000	10157
Vitek RE Inds Group Inc **(PA)**	6162	E	916 486-6400	9935
Vsp Labs Inc **(PA)**	3827	B	866 569-8800	6887
Vsp Optical Group Inc **(PA)**	6324	B	916 851-4682	10159
Vsp Retail Inc	3851	F	800 852-7600	7146
Vsp Vntres Optmtric Sltons LLC **(HQ)**	8042	E	916 858-5656	15876
Wells Fargo Coml Dist Fin LLC	6153	C	916 636-2020	9878
Wholesale Art and Framing Inc	2499	F	916 851-0770	3272
Xiphos Corporation	1731	E	719 963-3948	1643
Zukes Landscape Inc	0782	E	916 635-6502	510

RANCHO MURIETA, CA - Sacramento County

	SIC	EMP	PHONE	ENTRY #
Operating Engineers JAC	8331	D	916 354-2029	17830
Rancho Murieta Country Club	7997	D	916 354-2400	15125

RED BLUFF, CA - Tehama County

	SIC	EMP	PHONE	ENTRY #
Adobe Road Investment Group	7011	E	530 529-4178	10910
Brentwood Sklled Nrsing Rhbltt	8059	D	530 527-2046	16221
Cascade Filtration Inc	1796	E	530 529-1212	1991
Cedar Creek Corporation	1623	D	530 364-2143	1092
Concessionaires Urban Park **(PA)**	7999	B	530 529-1512	15195
Electro Star Indus Coating Inc	3479	F	530 527-5400	4932
F C Bickert Company Inc	1742	E	530 529-3575	1674
Foothill Ready Mix Inc	3273	F	530 527-2565	4482
John Wheeler Logging Inc	2411	C	530 527-2993	3067
Lassen Forest Products Inc	2439	E	530 527-7677	3212
Lassen Hse Assisted Living LLC	8361	D	530 529-2900	18134
Lassen Medical Group Inc **(PA)**	8011	E	530 527-0414	15503
Northern Vly Indian Hlth Inc	8021	E	530 529-2567	15851
Outback Construction Inc	1623	E	530 528-2225	1129
Outback Contractors Inc	1611	C	530 528-2225	1069
Sale Family Orchards LLC	0173	E	530 527-4854	92
Sierra Pacific Industries	2421	B	530 527-9620	3116
St Elizabeth Community Hosp **(DH)**	8062	B	530 529-7760	16535
Tedon Specialties A Cal Corp	3599	F	530 527-6600	5627
Walker Lithograph	2752	E	530 527-2142	3712
Wilcox Oaks Golf Club	7997	E	530 527-7087	15167

REDDING, CA - Shasta County

	SIC	EMP	PHONE	ENTRY #
Absolute Machine Inc	3599	F	530 242-6840	5460
Addus Healthcare Inc	8049	E	530 247-0858	15878
Alpine Land Info Svcs Inc **(PA)**	0851	E	530 222-8100	533
Altexsoft Inc	7379	C	877 777-9097	13838
Ambr Inc **(PA)**	6411	E	530 221-4759	10229
American Med Rspnse Inland Emp	4119	B	530 246-9111	7369
Andersncttonwood Disposal Svcs **(PA)**	4212	E	530 221-6510	7449
Art Hild Body and Frame Inc	7532	E	530 222-6828	14518
Asphalt Cowboys of Reddin	8699	E	530 244-1117	18546
Automobile Accessories Company	5013	E	530 223-1561	8441
Bank America National Assn	6021	E	530 226-6172	9680
Best Value Textbooks LLC	2741	E	800 646-7782	3559
Big Lgue Dreams Consulting LLC	7997	C	530 223-1177	15060
Bill Sharp Electrical Contr	1731	E	530 338-1735	1466
Bridge Bay Resort & Marina	7011	D	530 275-3021	10973
Builder Inc	1542	E	530 691-4354	842
Bundy and Sons Inc	2411	F	530 246-3868	3057
California Oregon Broadcasting **(HQ)**	4833	D	530 243-7777	8039
California Physicians Service	6324	D	530 351-6115	10097
Cameron International Corp	3533	D	530 242-6965	5045
Captive-Aire Systems Inc	3444	C	530 351-7150	4746
Care Optons MGT Plans Spprtive **(PA)**	8082	C	530 242-8580	16868
Cdg Technology LLC	3624	E	530 243-4451	5671
City of Redding **(PA)**	8999	A	530 225-4079	19899
Class Act Hair & Nail Salon	7231	D	530 223-3442	11679
Cleanrite Inc	7217	E	530 246-4886	11659
Commerce Home Mortgage LLC	6162	D	530 282-1166	9904
Cook Concrete Products Inc	3272	E	530 243-2562	4428
Court Street Surgery Center	8011	E	530 246-4444	15372
Cox & Cox Construction Inc	1623	E	530 243-6016	1096
Creekside Counseling Ctr Inc	8322	E	530 722-9957	17523
Crestwood Behavioral Hlth Inc	8361	C	530 221-0976	18094
David Beard	2434	F	530 244-1248	3178
Denham Sj Inc **(PA)**	7532	E	530 241-1756	14524
Donor Network West	8099	E	510 418-0336	17137
Dunamis Center Inc	8093	D	530 338-0087	17017
Eagle Paving & Grading	1611	E	530 221-4194	1036
Electric Innovations Inc	1731	D	530 222-3366	1499
Enterprise Rnt—car Scrmnto LL	7514	C	530 223-0700	14487
Executive Scheduling Assoc	8741	C	877 315-3689	19332
Far Nrthern Crdnting Cncil On **(PA)**	8322	D	530 222-4791	17568
Ferrosaur Inc	3441	E	530 246-7843	4659
Fife Metal Fabricating Inc	3441	E	530 243-4696	4660
Franklin Logging Inc	2411	D	530 549-4924	3061
Gbk Corporation **(PA)**	7215	E	530 241-2337	11649
Gerlinger Fndry Mch Works Inc **(PA)**	3441	E	530 243-1053	4664
Good News Rescue Mission	8361	E	530 241-5754	18121
Great Northern Wheels Deals	2711	E	530 533-2134	3443
Guitons Pool Center Inc	1799	E	530 221-6656	2035
Hanes Floor Incorporated	1752	E	530 221-6544	1772
Harbor Distributing LLC	5181	D	530 691-5811	9553
Hilltop Inn Redding LLC	7011	D	530 221-6100	11139
Honolua Bay Holdings LLC	6719	E	530 243-6317	10737
I-5 Rentals Inc	7359	E	530 226-8081	12049
Inter Star Inc	4813	D	530 224-6866	7964
J W Wood Co Inc **(PA)**	5074	E	530 894-1325	9000
Jar Ventures Inc	3993	F	530 224-9655	7236
JF Shea Construction Inc	1521	D	530 246-4292	655
John Fitzpatrick & Sons	2086	E	530 241-3216	2794
K&I International Trade Inc	5021	E	320 228-2788	8498
Kaidan Hospitality LP	7011	D	530 221-8700	11227
Kennie C Knowles Trucking	4212	E	530 243-1366	7479
Kirkwood Asssted Lving Rsdence	8051	E	530 241-2900	16031
Ku Kyoung	8051	C	510 582-2765	16034
Larkspur Group LLC	7011	D	530 223-9344	11246
Larkspur Group LLC **(PA)**	7011	D	530 224-1001	11247
Lassen Canyon Nursery Inc **(PA)**	5141	C	530 223-1075	9275
Lowes Home Centers LLC	5031	C	530 351-0181	8581
Marquis Companies I Inc	8051	E	530 222-3630	16059
McConnell Foundation	8399	E	530 226-6200	18240
McEntire Landscaping Inc	0782	E	530 245-4590	485
MD Imaging Inc A Prof Med Corp	8011	D	530 243-1249	15524
Medical Home Specialists Inc	8082	D	530 226-5577	16913
Members 1st Credit Union **(PA)**	6061	E	530 222-6060	9794
Merchants Bank of Commerce **(HQ)**	6022	D	530 224-7355	9739
Mercy HM Svcs A Cal Ltd Partnr **(DH)**	8062	A	530 225-6000	16456
Mercy Surgery Center LP	8062	E	530 225-7400	16457
Merrill Lynch Prce Fnner Smith	6211	D	530 223-3005	9983
Metals Direct Inc	3444	E	530 605-1931	4788
Meyers Earthwork Inc	1794	D	530 365-8858	1965
Miniature Precision Inc	3599	E	530 244-4131	5573
Muse Concrete Contractors Inc	1611	D	530 226-5151	1062
N & T Digmore Inc	1623	D	530 241-2992	1123
North State Manufacuring	3599	F	530 378-5750	5581
North State Resources Inc	8748	E	530 222-5347	19829
North Vly Dvlopmental Svcs Inc	8082	D	530 222-5633	16916
Northern Cal Rhbltion Hosp LL	8062	C	530 246-9000	16468
Northern Vly Cthlic Scial Svc	8322	C	530 241-0552	17662
Northstar Senior Living Inc	8741	A	530 242-8300	19375
Ocadian Care Centers LLC	8051	B	530 246-9000	16081
Pacific Gas and Electric Co	4911	C	530 365-7672	8162
Patients Hospital	8062	D	530 225-8700	16477
Pick Pull Auto Dismantling Inc	5015	E	530 221-6184	8483
Pre-Employcom Inc	7381	D	800 300-1821	14087
Prime Hlthcare Svcs - Shsta LL	8062	A	530 244-5400	16483
Ramada Limited	7011	E	530 246-2222	11381
Redding Aero Enterprises Inc	4111	D	530 224-2300	7345
Redding Distributing Company	5181	E	530 226-5700	9560
Redding Drmtlogy Med Group Inc	8011	E	530 241-1111	15639
Redding Freightliner Inc	5012	E	530 241-4412	8427
Redding Lumber Transport Inc	4214	D	530 241-8193	7632
Redding Metal Crafters Inc	3444	E	530 222-4400	4810
Redding Pathologists Lab **(PA)**	8011	C	530 225-8000	15640
Redding Pathologists Lab	8071	D	530 225-8050	16801
Redding Printing Co Inc **(PA)**	2752	E	530 243-0525	3691
Redding Rancheria	7011	D	530 245-9161	11389
Redding Rancheria **(PA)**	7011	D	530 225-8979	11390
Redding Rnchria Ecnmic Dev Cor	7011	B	530 243-3377	11391
Redding Super 8 Motel Inc	7011	D	530 221-8881	11392
Remi Vista Inc	8361	D	530 222-4561	18169
Resers Fine Foods Inc	5141	D	503 643-6431	9290
Reyes Coca-Cola Bottling LLC	2086	D	530 241-4315	2805
Riverview Golf and Country CLB	7997	D	530 224-2254	15128
Rounds Logging Company	2411	E	530 247-0517	3076
Saia Motor Freight Line LLC	4213	D	530 243-5540	7588
Save Mart Supermarkets Disc	2051	D	530 222-6740	2404
Seco Manufacturing Company Inc	3829	C	530 225-8155	6920
Sfn Group Inc	7363	A	530 222-3434	12196
Shascade Community Svcs Inc	8322	D	530 247-8324	17737
Shascade Community Svcs Inc	8322	D	530 243-1653	17738
Shasta County Head Start Child **(PA)**	8351	E	530 241-1036	18018
Shasta County Office Education	7032	E	530 225-0285	11610
Shasta County Women S Refuge	8322	E	530 244-0117	17739

GEOGRAPHIC

REDDING, CA

	SIC	EMP	PHONE	ENTRY #
Shasta County YMCA	8641	E	530 605-3330	18468
Shasta Eye Medical Group Inc (PA)	8011	D	530 226-5966	15678
Shasta Orthpedics Spt Medicine	8011	E	530 246-2467	15679
Shasta Senior Ntrtn Program (DH)	8322	E	530 226-3059	17740
Sheraton Rdding Ht At Sndial B	7011	D	530 364-2800	11470
Sierra Pacific Industries	2421	E	530 226-5181	3106
Silverthorn Resort Assoc LP	7999	E	530 275-1571	15242
Small Talk Pediatric Svcs Inc (PA)	8011	E	530 226-8255	15690
Smart Business Resource Center	8331	E	530 246-7911	17839
Sof-Tek Integrators Inc	8711	E	530 242-0527	18815
Southern Alum Finshg Co Inc	3355	D	530 244-7518	4564
Spectrum Prsthtcs/Rthtics Rddi	3842	E	530 243-4500	7080
State Compensation Insur Fund	6331	D	888 782-8338	10178
Steve Manning Construction Inc.	1611	E	530 220-0810	1074
Taylor Motors Inc	7538	D	530 222-1200	14594
Tenet Healthsystem Medical Inc	8082	D	530 222-1992	16960
Tera Sahara Inc	7011	E	530 223-1600	11528
Torr Industries Inc.	7371	E	530 247-6909	12870
Trico Bancshares	6029	E	530 221-8400	9766
Trico Bancshares	6029	E	530 245-5930	15245
Trigild International Inc	7011	D	530 223-1935	11545
Turtle Bay Exploration Park	8412	E	530 242-3186	18285
Utility Tree Service LLC (DH)	0783	E	530 226-0330	525
Veterans Health Administration	8011	C	530 226-7555	15791
Vibra Healthcare LLC	8062	E	530 246-9000	16715
Vitalant Research Institute	8099	E	530 221-0600	17191
Vonhof Enterprises Inc	8082	E	530 223-2400	16966
W C Garcia & Associates Inc	7997	E	530 221-4405	15166
Walsh Group Inc	7991	D	530 221-4405	14985
Warner Enterprises Inc	2411	E	530 241-4000	3086
William R Schmitt	2411	E	530 243-3069	3087
Willow Sprng Alzhmers Spcial C	8361	E	530 242-0654	18213
Win River Hotel Corporation	7011	B	530 226-5111	11578
Windsor Redding Care Ctr LLC	8051	D	530 246-0600	16166
Wit Group	2086	E	530 243-4447	2818
World of Change Inc	7389	E	352 495-3300	14463
Xpo Logistics Freight Inc	4731	E	530 243-6175	7863
Yaley Enterprises Inc	5099	F	530 365-5252	9204
Yanaco Inc	7996	C	530 246-9550	15047
Yates Gear Inc	3199	D	530 222-4606	4354

REDWAY, CA - Humboldt County

	SIC	EMP	PHONE	ENTRY #
Redwoods Rural Health Ctr Inc	8011	E	707 923-2783	15647

REDWOOD CITY, CA - San Mateo County

	SIC	EMP	PHONE	ENTRY #
AB Sciex LLC (HQ)	3826	D	877 740-2129	6802
Abbvie Biotherapeutics Inc	2834	D	650 454-1000	3827
ABC Bus Inc	5012	D	650 368-3364	8420
Abilitypath	8322	C	650 259-8500	17404
Abilitypath Housing (PA)	8322	D	650 494-0550	17405
Accelerance Inc	7372	F	650 472-3785	12947
Actiance Inc	3446	E	650 631-6300	4832
Adaptive Spctrum Sgnal Algnmt (PA)	4813	F	650 654-3400	7922
Advanced Circuits Inc	3672	F	415 602-6834	5907
Adverum Biotechnologies Inc	2836	D	650 656-9323	4031
Aea Pharmaceuticals Inc	2834	D	650 996-5895	3835
Agiloft Inc	7372	E	650 587-8615	12963
Ai Industries LLC (PA)	3471	D	650 366-4099	4894
Aire Sheet Metal Inc	1711	E	650 364-8081	1194
Alation Inc (PA)	7372	D	650 779-4440	12968
Alcatraz Ai Inc	7382	C	650 600-0197	14119
All Fence Company Inc	1799	E	650 369-4556	2001
Allakos Inc	8731	E	650 597-5002	19015
Alliances MGT Consulting Inc	8748	E	650 780-0466	19717
Altos Labs Inc (PA)	8731	E	650 438-7055	19018
American Production Co Inc	3411	E	650 368-5334	4596
Amobee Inc (DH)	7311	B	650 353-4399	11739
Anomali Incorporated	7382	D	408 800-4050	14121
Applied Process Equipment	3599	E	650 365-6895	5475
Aricent US Inc	7371	C	650 632-4310	12273
Armo Biosciences Inc	2834	E	650 779-5075	3855
Art of Yoga Project	7999	E	650 924-9222	15174
Ascend Clinical LLC (PA)	8071	E	800 800-5655	16772
Assocted Lrng Lngage Spcialist (PA)	8748	E	650 631-9999	19722
Assured Relocation Inc	4289	E	888 670-9700	14205
Astrazeneca Pharmaceuticals LP	2834	E	650 305-2600	3860
Auris Health Inc (DH)	3841	D	650 610-0750	6947
Autogrid Systems Inc (PA)	7372	F	650 461-9038	13000
Avinger Inc	3841	E	650 241-7900	6950
Aviso Inc	8742	D	650 567-5470	19452
Azumio Inc (PA)	7372	C	719 310-3774	12294
Badgeville Inc	7372	E	650 323-6668	13007
Balsam Brands Inc (PA)	3999	D	877 442-2572	7269
Barnard Bessac Joint Venture	1629	D	650 212-8957	1149
Bay Club Peninsula LLC	7997	E	650 593-2800	15056
Bay Precision Machining Inc	3599	E	650 365-3010	5482
Baysport Inc	8011	C	650 593-2800	15295
Biocentury Inc (PA)	2711	E	650 595-5333	3418
Biointellisense Inc	3845	E	650 481-8140	7097
Biotricity Inc	3841	E	650 832-1626	6957
Bkf Engineers (PA)	8711	D	650 482-6300	18641
Bluevine Capital Inc	6163	B	888 216-9619	9936
Bolt Biotherapeutics Inc	2834	E	650 260-9295	3872
Box Inc (PA)	7372	A	877 729-4269	13033
Branch Metrics Inc (PA)	7374	B	650 209-6491	13699
Brantner Holding LLC (DH)	3678	D	650 361-5292	6389
Brava Home Inc	3634	E	408 675-2569	5703
Breakthrough Behavioral Inc	8322	C	888 282-2522	17447

GEOGRAPHIC SECTION

	SIC	EMP	PHONE	ENTRY #
Bristol-Myers Squibb Company	2834	D	800 332-2056	3875
Brothers Pride Produce Inc (PA)	2034	E	650 368-6993	2253
Buildingminds Inc (PA)	7371	E	973 397-6510	12314
C3 Delaware Inc	7372	F	650 503-2200	13042
C3AI INC (PA)	7372	C	650 503-2200	13043
Carbon Inc	3577	C	650 285-6307	5355
Cardivsclar Mdcine Crnary Intr	8062	E	650 306-2300	16326
Care 2	8699	E	650 622-0860	18556
Centrify Corporation (PA)	7371	A	669 444-5200	12332
Century Theatres Inc	7833	C	866 322-4547	14822
Cfkba Inc	3357	F	650 302-6331	4569
Chapel of Chimes	6553	E	650 349-4411	10725
Clustrix Inc	7371	E	415 501-9560	12345
Coddington Hcks Dnfrth A Prof	8111	E	650 592-5400	17232
Codexis Inc (PA)	2819	C	650 421-8100	3782
Coherus Biosciences Inc (PA)	8731	C	650 649-3530	19045
Concept Hotels LLC	7011	E	650 600-8257	11030
Congrgtion Beth Jcob Irving Lv	8351	E	650 366-8481	17915
Coraid Inc (PA)	3572	D	650 517-9300	5284
Crystal Dynamics Inc (DH)	7372	C	650 421-7600	13099
Cyara Inc (PA)	7372	C	650 549-8522	13102
Cyara Solutions Corp	5045	C	650 549-8522	8686
D N G Cummings Inc	3993	F	650 593-8974	7227
Deep North Inc (PA)	7371	D	650 781-1550	12378
Delphix Corp (PA)	7371	E	650 494-1645	12379
Des Architects Engineers Inc	8712	C	650 364-6453	18882
Digital Insight Corporation (HQ)	7375	D	818 879-1010	13785
Dpr Construction Inc	1542	A	650 474-1450	864
Dpr Construction A Gen Partnr (HQ)	1542	A	650 474-1450	867
Dpr Skanska A Joint Venture	1542	E	650 306-7671	868
E A Davidovits & Co Inc	3089	D	650 366-6068	869
E La Carte Inc	7371	D	650 468-0680	12409
Einstein Noah Rest Group Inc	2051	D	650 299-9050	2380
Elastic Beam LLC	7371	E	925 963-8122	12416
Electronic Arts Inc (PA)	7372	B	650 628-1500	13138
Electronic Arts Redwood Inc (HQ)	3695	A	650 628-1500	6501
Energy Experts International (PA)	8742	C	650 593-4261	19501
Epic Creations Inc	7371	E	650 918-7327	12426
Equilar Inc	7389	C	877 441-6090	14266
Equinix Inc (PA)	7374	C	650 598-6000	13711
Equinix (us) Enterprises Inc (HQ)	4899	D	650 598-6363	8076
Equinix Pacific LLC (HQ)	4813	B	650 598-6000	7948
Equinix Professional Svcs Inc	4813	E	800 322-9280	7949
Evernote Corporation (PA)	7371	B	650 216-7700	12433
Fintan Partners LLC	6211	E	650 687-3400	9968
Flywheel Software Inc	7372	C	650 260-1700	13167
Fortex Technologies Inc (PA)	7371	D	650 591-8822	12461
French Redwood Inc	7011	C	650 598-9000	11106
Genelabs Technologies Inc (HQ)	2834	D	415 297-2901	3904
Genentech Inc	2834	C	650 216-2900	3909
Genomic Health Inc (HQ)	8071	A	650 556-9300	16781
Glasslab Inc	7372	C	415 244-5584	13190
Granite Rock Co	2951	E	650 482-3800	4187
Granite Rock Co	1611	E	650 869-3370	1050
Graybug Vision Inc (PA)	2834	E	650 487-2800	3921
Guardant Health Inc (PA)	8071	B	855 698-8887	16782
Gunderson Dettmer Stough Ville (PA)	8111	C	650 321-2400	17285
H N Lockwood Inc	3089	E	650 366-9557	4287
Heartflow Inc (PA)	7373	D	650 241-1221	13607
Holt Tool & Machine Inc	3312	E	650 364-2547	4542
Hopkins Manor	8361	E	650 368-5656	18131
I2c Inc	5045	B	650 593-5400	8712
Icracked Inc (DH)	7629	E	877 700-0349	14700
Imidomics Inc	2834	F	415 652-4963	3927
Impossible Foods Inc (PA)	2099	B	650 461-4385	2905
Incline Therapeutics Inc	2834	E	650 241-6800	3929
Inevit Inc	3691	C	650 298-6001	6487
Inflection Risk Solutions LLC	7374	C	650 618-9910	13722
Inflectioncom Inc (PA)	8748	C	650 618-9910	19792
Informatica Holdco Inc	7372	A	650 385-5000	13231
Informatica Inc	7372	A	650 385-5000	13232
Informatica International Inc (DH)	7372	A	650 385-5000	13233
Informatica LLC (DH)	7372	A	650 385-5000	13234
Invoice 2go LLC (DH)	7372	C	650 300-5180	13247
Ipass Inc (HQ)	4813	C	650 232-4100	7966
Isheriff Inc	7371	C	650 412-4300	12542
Itco Solutions Inc	7379	B	650 367-0514	13923
Ivalua Inc (HQ)	7371	E	650 930-9710	12543
Joveo Inc (PA)	7371	D	408 896-9030	12550
Kainos HM Trning Ctr For Dvlpm	8322	E	650 361-1355	17630
Kaiser Foundation Hospitals	8062	A	650 299-2234	16399
Kaiser Foundation Hospitals	8011	C	650 299-2000	15470
Karius Inc	8731	D	866 452-7857	19077
Kaspick & Co LLC (DH)	6411	D	650 585-4100	10305
Klutz	2731	E	650 687-2650	3536
Kriya Therapeutics Inc	2836	E	833 574-9289	4052
Kyo Autism Therapy LLC	8742	D	877 264-6747	19551
La Estrellita Tizapan Mercado (PA)	2099	E	650 369-3877	2908
Leland Stanford Junior Univ	8069	A	650 935-5365	16764
Lencioni Construction Co Inc	1521	E	650 216-9900	663
Lensa Inc	7361	E	415 528-8467	12104
Light Labs Inc	3827	D	650 257-8100	6879
Lydia C Gonzalez	8322	E	650 299-4707	17639
Mad Apparel Inc	2329	E	650 503-3386	2994
Marcucci Heating and AC Inc	1711	E	650 556-1882	1309
Master of Code Global	7372	F	650 200-8490	13294
Mereo Biopharma 5 Inc	2834	D	650 995-8200	3948

GEOGRAPHIC SECTION

RICHMOND, CA

Company	SIC	EMP	PHONE	ENTRY #
Mod Zombie LLC (PA)	2131	E	650 346-2047	2962
Mr Gears Inc	3599	F	650 364-7793	5576
Multiven Inc	7379	E	408 828-2715	13940
Mythic Inc	8742	E	734 707-7339	19585
Netsuite Inc	7372	F	650 627-1000	13327
Nevro Corp	3841	A	650 251-0005	7011
Nextag Inc (PA)	2741	D	650 645-4700	3585
Nvent Thermal LLC	3822	B	650 474-7414	6702
Oc Acquisition LLC (HQ)	7371	E	650 506-7000	12643
Openwave Mobility Inc (DH)	7372	D	650 480-7200	13345
Oracle America Inc (HQ)	3571	A	650 506-7000	5266
Oracle America Inc	5045	D	800 633-0584	8730
Oracle Credit Corporation (DH)	6153	C	650 506-7000	9872
Oracle International Corp (HQ)	7372	E	650 506-7000	13353
Oracle Systems Corporation (HQ)	7379	E	650 506-7000	13954
Oracle Taiwan LLC (HQ)	7372	E	650 506-7000	13354
Oratec Interventions Inc (DH)	3845	E	901 396-2121	7118
Oraya Therapeutics Inc	3827	E	510 456-3700	6883
Origin Systems Inc	7371	B	650 628-1500	12658
Pacific Cast Crdiac Vsclar Srg	8062	E	650 366-0225	16476
Pacific Coast Signs Inc (PA)	3993	E	650 520-0724	7246
Paxata Inc	7372	D	650 542-7897	13363
Pebble Technology Corp	3873	E	888 224-5820	7162
Pendulum Instruments Inc	3699	E	866 644-1230	6536
Perfect World Entrmt Inc	7371	C	650 590-7700	12678
Permanente Medical Group Inc	8011	A	650 299-2000	15606
Permanente Medical Group Inc	8011	A	650 299-2015	15607
Permanente Medical Group Inc	6324	B	650 598-2852	10151
Perseid Therapeutics LLC	8731	E	650 298-5600	19100
Petersen Precision Engrg LLC	3599	C	650 365-4373	5595
Planful (HQ)	7372	C	650 249-7100	13371
Poshmark Inc (PA)	7372	B	650 262-4771	13379
Postini Inc (PA)	7374	D	650 482-5130	13744
Procept Biorobotics Corp	3841	C	650 232-7200	7023
Proteus Digital Health Inc (PA)	2836	C	650 632-4031	4055
Provident Credit Union (PA)	6062	C	650 508-0300	9835
Pubmatic Inc (PA)	7371	C	650 331-3485	12708
Putnam Motors Inc	7539	C	650 381-3152	14618
Questra Corporation (PA)	7371	E	650 632-4011	12717
Qwilt Inc	7372	C	866 824-8009	13397
R&D Consulting Group Inc	7361	C	415 697-2585	12123
Redmont Cnstr & Inv Co Inc	1521	D	650 306-9344	694
Redwood General Tire Svc Co	7538	E	650 369-0351	14586
Reltio Inc (PA)	7371	E	855 360-3282	12739
Replicon Software Inc (PA)	7371	E	650 286-9200	12741
Reputationcom Inc (PA)	7372	B	800 888-0924	13405
Reputationdefender LLC (HQ)	8732	E	888 851-9609	19183
Revolution Medicines Inc (PA)	8731	D	650 481-6801	19117
Revup Software Inc	7372	E	415 231-2315	13410
Rezolute Inc (PA)	2834	E	650 206-4507	3975
Robertson Precision Inc	3674	E	408 230-3044	6274
Ropers Majeski A Prof Corp (PA)	8111	C	650 364-8200	17364
S F Enterprises Incorporated	3599	F	650 455-3223	5615
S J Amoroso Cnstr Co LLC (PA)	1542	B	650 654-1900	954
Safexai Inc (PA)	7372	F	650 425-6376	13421
San Mateo County Bar Assn	8621	E	650 298-4000	18348
San Mateo Credit Union	6061	D	650 363-1725	9812
San Mateo Credit Union (PA)	6061	D	650 363-1725	9813
Satmetrix Systems Inc	7371	C	650 227-8300	12762
Sears Home Imprv Pdts Inc	1521	C	650 645-9974	703
Secpod Technologies	7372	E	405 385-9890	13432
Seer Inc	3826	E	650 453-0000	6849
Seiler LLP (PA)	8721	C	650 365-4646	18991
Selligent Inc (HQ)	7373	C	650 421-4255	13662
Senior Companions At Home LLC	8082	E	650 364-1265	16941
Sequoia Health Services (DH)	8062	A	650 369-5811	16520
Sequoia Medical Clinic (PA)	8011	E	650 261-2300	15677
Service League San Mateo Cnty	8322	E	650 364-4664	17735
Shiva Enterprises Inc	7011	C	650 366-2000	11473
Shutterfly LLC (HQ)	7384	B	650 610-5200	14182
Silicon Valley Clean Water	4952	E	650 591-7121	8290
Simplr Inc	7372	C	650 396-2646	13445
Singha North America Inc	2082	F	714 206-5097	2492
Singtel Enterprise SEC US Inc (HQ)	7373	E	650 508-6800	13664
Sizmek Dsp Inc (PA)	7311	E	650 595-1300	11785
Sizmek Dsp Inc (HQ)	7379	E	650 595-1300	13976
Skire Inc	7371	E	650 289-2600	12791
Skydio Inc (PA)	3721	D	855 463-5902	6618
Smarsh Inc	7372	C	650 631-6300	13447
Southern Cal Disc Tire Co Inc	5014	E	650 366-4003	8479
Split Software Inc (PA)	7374	C	650 399-0005	13760
Steppechange LLC	7371	D	415 279-7638	12819
Storm8 Inc (PA)	7372	F	650 596-8600	13468
Styra Inc	7371	E	415 200-8871	12829
Suki Ai Inc	7371	E	650 549-8959	12832
Sumo Logic Inc (PA)	7371	A	650 810-8700	12833
Sun Microsystems Intl Inc (HQ)	7372	A	650 506-7000	13472
Synack Inc	7379	C	855 796-2251	13984
Talend (HQ)	7373	A	650 539-3200	13674
Te Connectivity MOG Inc (HQ)	3229	A	650 361-5292	4380
Tectura Intl Holdings Inc	7379	D	650 585-5500	13994
Theatreworks Silicon Valley	7922	E	650 517-5870	14865
Thought Stream LLC	7371	E	650 567-4550	12863
Thycoticcentrify Holdings Inc	6719	A	669 444-5200	10742
Tigergraph Inc	7374	C	650 206-8888	13764
Tilley Manufacturing Co Inc (PA)	3053	D	650 365-3598	4207
Together Labs Inc	4813	C	650 231-4688	8001
Towne Motor Company	7539	C	650 366-5744	14626
Trace Genomics Inc	8731	E	650 332-6661	19139
Tradebeam Inc	7379	D	650 653-4800	13999
Trilliant Networks Inc (PA)	7389	D	650 204-5050	14441
True North	7371	D	650 207-9800	12877
Turn Inc (DH)	7319	B	650 353-4399	11819
University Art Center Inc (PA)	7699	D	650 328-3500	14782
Verity Health System Cal Inc	8062	A	310 900-8900	16710
Verity Health System Cal Inc	8062	C	650 551-6507	16712
Versant Corporation (DH)	7372	A	650 232-2400	13517
Verve Group Inc	7319	E	760 536-8350	11820
Viewpint Gvrnment Slutions Inc	7373	E	617 577-9000	13688
Vifor Pharma Inc	2834	B	650 421-9500	4004
Virgo Investment Group LLC	6799	E	650 453-3627	10894
W Bradley Electric Inc	1731	C	650 701-1502	1631
W L Butler Construction Inc (PA)	1542	E	650 361-1270	982
Weil Gotshal & Manges LLP	8111	A	650 802-3000	17392
Wepay Inc	7374	E	855 469-3729	13771
West Valley Cnstr Co Inc	1623	E	650 364-9464	1144
Wested	8733	E	650 381-6400	19249
WL Butler Inc	1542	E	650 361-1270	991
Workboard Inc (PA)	7372	C	650 294-4480	13531
Xtime Inc	3089	E	650 508-4300	4337
Young MNS Chrstn Assn Slcon Vl	8641	E	650 368-4168	18530
Zeno Group Inc	8999	D	650 801-7950	19922
Zuora Inc (PA)	7372	B	800 425-1281	13544
Zyme Solutions Inc (PA)	7375	D	650 585-2258	13813

REDWOOD VALLEY, CA - Mendocino County

Company	SIC	EMP	PHONE	ENTRY #
Burgess Lumber	2421	E	707 485-8072	3094
Consoldted Tribal Hlth Prj Inc	8093	D	707 485-5115	17004
Frey Vineyards Ltd	2084	F	707 485-5177	2589
Redwood Valley Gravel Pdts Inc	3272	E	707 485-8585	4449

REEDLEY, CA - Fresno County

Company	SIC	EMP	PHONE	ENTRY #
Adventist Health System/West	8049	E	559 638-2154	15880
Al Lamm Ranch Inc	0212	E	559 638-3204	200
Beaver Dam Health Care Center	8051	E	559 638-3577	15939
Bw Integrated Systems	3565	F	559 638-8484	5198
Cal Packing & Storage LP	4222	E	559 638-2929	7677
Camp Wellspring LLC (DH)	8322	E	559 638-5374	17454
Family Tree Farms Mktg LLC	5148	E	559 591-6280	9401
Fortier & Fortier Inc	5083	E	559 638-5774	9037
Fresno Cnty Ecnmic Opprtnties	8322	E	559 638-0025	17578
Gerawan Farming LLC	0175	D	559 638-9281	100
Maxco Supply Inc	2631	E	559 638-8449	3351
Mission AG Resources LLC	2023	E	559 591-3333	2164
Moonlight Packing Corporation	5142	A	559 638-7799	9327
Moonlight Packing Corporation	4783	A	559 638-7799	7868
Moonlight Packing Corporation (PA)	5148	C	559 638-7799	9418
Moonlight Sales Corporation	0723	E	559 637-7799	296
Pacific Housing Group LLC	1799	D	559 651-1133	2050
Paragon Health & Rehab CT	8093	E	559 638-7555	17053
Peer Services Inc	8742	E	559 970-1240	19602
Reedley Community Hospital	8062	D	559 638-8155	16489
Sequoia Safety Council Inc	4119	E	559 638-9995	7404
Sierra View Homes	8051	E	559 637-2256	16118
Thiele Technologies Inc	3565	E	559 638-8484	5206
Trinity Packing Company Inc (PA)	7389	B	559 433-3785	14443
Trinity Packing Company Inc	7389	B	559 743-3913	14444
Turning Point Central Cal Inc	8011	E	559 638-8588	15743
Valley Controls Inc	3823	F	559 638-5115	6736
Valley Packline Solutions	3556	E	559 638-7821	5136
Youngstown Grape Distrs Inc	0723	C	559 638-2271	316

RICHMOND, CA - Contra Costa County

Company	SIC	EMP	PHONE	ENTRY #
AA Portable Power Corporation	3691	E	510 525-2328	6484
ACS Instrumentation Valves Inc	3823	D	510 262-1880	6710
Alion Energy Inc	3674	E	510 965-0868	6021
All West Coast Shipping Inc (PA)	4212	E	510 236-3008	7447
Alsco Inc	7213	E	510 237-9634	11630
Alten Construction Inc	1521	D	510 234-4200	609
Amt Metal Fabricators Inc	3441	E	510 236-1414	4644
Andrus Sheet Metal Inc	3444	E	510 232-8687	4741
Annies Annuals Perennials LLC	5193	E	510 215-3301	9623
Bay Area Distributing Coinc	5181	E	510 232-8554	9544
Bay Area Rescue Mission (PA)	8322	D	510 215-4555	17440
Bay Cities Crane & Rigging Inc (PA)	7359	E	510 232-7222	12031
Bay Cities Refuse Service Inc	4953	D	510 237-4614	8306
Bay City Mechanical Inc (PA)	1711	C	510 233-7000	1214
Bay Marine Boatworks Inc	7699	E	510 237-0140	14740
Ben Myerson Candy Co Inc	5182	E	510 236-2233	9567
Black Diamond Video Inc	3577	D	510 439-4500	5351
Black Point Products Inc	3661	E	510 232-7723	5789
Brighter Beginnings (PA)	8322	E	510 903-7503	17448
C Overaa & Co (PA)	1542	B	510 234-0926	845
California Closet Company Inc (DH)	1799	E	510 763-2033	2014
California Dept of Pub Hlth	8011	D	510 231-7408	15307
Cemex Materials LLC	3273	D	510 234-3616	4472
Century Theatres Inc	7833	C	510 758-9626	14823
Champion Scaffold Services Inc	1799	E	510 788-4731	2018
Chevron USA Inc	2911	D	510 242-3000	4172
Cirimele Electrical Works Inc	1731	E	510 620-1150	1477
Concentra Medical Center	8011	C	909 558-2273	15364
Dahl-Beck Electric Co	5063	D	510 237-2325	8856
Dicon Fiberoptics Inc (PA)	3679	A	510 620-5000	6418
East Bay Brass Foundry Inc	3363	E	510 233-7171	4576
East Bay Mncpl Utlity Dst Wtr	4941	E	866 403-2683	8235

Employment Codes: A=Over 500 employees, B=251-500, C=101-250, D=51-100, E=20-50 F=10-19

RICHMOND, CA

Company	SIC	EMP	PHONE	ENTRY #
Ekso Bionics Inc (PA)	3559	D	510 984-1761	5146
Ekso Bionics Holdings Inc	3842	D	510 984-1761	7069
Enterprise Rnt—car San Frncsc	7514	E	510 223-6444	14479
Estes Commercial Rfrgn Inc	7623	E	510 232-5464	14687
First Student Inc	4151	C	510 237-6677	7430
Galaxy Desserts	2051	C	510 439-3160	2386
Gardeners Guild Inc	0782	E	415 457-0400	464
Golden Gate Meat Company Inc (PA)	5147	E	415 861-3800	9378
Hero Arts Rubber Stamps Inc	3953	D	510 232-4200	7206
Hood Exhibits	7389	E	510 965-9999	14298
Imacc Corporation	5085	E	510 233-4865	9119
International Group Inc	2911	E	510 232-8704	4175
Ironies	2521	E	510 644-2100	3305
Kaiser Foundation Hospitals	8011	E	510 307-1500	15454
Kodiak Precision Inc (PA)	3599	F	510 234-4165	5556
Levin-Richmond Terminal Corp	4491	E	510 232-4422	7722
M & M Bakery Products Inc	2051	D	510 235-0274	2393
Manson Construction Co	1629	E	510 232-6319	1167
Metalset Inc	3441	E	510 233-9998	4676
Mom Enterprises LLC	2834	E	415 694-3799	3950
Monterey Pine Apartments	6513	E	510 215-1926	10450
MTI Corporation	3679	E	510 525-3070	6457
My True Image Mfg Inc	5047	D	510 970-7990	8788
National Ewp Inc	1081	F	510 236-6282	542
Novacart (DH)	2621	E	510 215-8999	3347
Nutiva	2099	C	510 255-2700	2929
Oliso Inc	3634	E	415 864-7600	5706
Oliver & Company Inc	1542	D	510 412-9090	933
Pacific Hotel Management LLC	7011	D	510 262-0700	11347
Palecek Imports Inc (PA)	5021	E	510 236-7730	8502
Paragon Machine Works Inc	3599	E	510 232-3223	5590
Pegasus Solar Inc	3433	E	510 210-3797	4632
Permanente Medical Group Inc	8011	A	510 231-5406	15608
Phoenix Day Inc	3645	F	415 822-4414	5724
Professional Finishing Inc	3479	E	510 233-7629	4947
Qrs Corporation (DH)	7371	D	510 215-5000	12712
R & K Industrial Products Co	3499	E	510 234-7212	4986
R V Stich Construction Inc	1794	E	510 412-9070	1973
Richmond Country Club	7997	D	510 231-2241	15127
Richmond Hotels LLC	7011	D	510 237-3000	11408
Richmond Post Acute Care LLC	8099	E	510 237-5182	17172
Richmond Sanitary Service Inc (HQ)	7699	C	510 262-7100	14772
Richmond Wholesale Meat LLC (PA)	5147	E	510 233-5111	9379
Ruan Transport Corporation	4213	E	510 758-7383	7583
Rubber Dust Inc (PA)	7534	E	510 237-6344	14539
Rubicon Enterprises Inc	7349	E	510 235-1516	11990
Rubicon Programs Incorporated (PA)	7349	D	510 235-1516	11991
San Francisco Estuary Inst	8733	E	510 746-7334	19234
San Rafael Rock Quarry Inc	2951	E	510 970-7700	4190
Security Pacific Real Estate	6531	E	510 222-9772	10661
Sims Group USA Corporation (DH)	5093	D	510 412-5300	9177
Spr Op Co Inc	6719	C	510 232-5030	10740
String Letter Publishing Inc	2741	E	510 215-0010	3603
Sunpower Corporation Systems (DH)	1711	D	510 260-8200	1368
Support Systems Intl Corp	3679	E	510 234-9090	6472
T F Louderback Inc	5181	C	510 965-6120	9563
Tamalpais Coml Cabinetry Inc	2434	E	510 231-6800	3193
Tehiyah Day School Inc	8351	E	510 233-4405	18038
Terra Millennium Corp	3297	E	510 233-2500	4534
Thomas-Swan Sign Company Inc	3993	E	415 621-1511	7257
Trade Litho Inc	2752	F	510 965-6501	3704
Tulip Pubg & Graphics Inc	2752	E	510 898-0000	3705
United Granite & Cabinets LLC	2434	E	510 558-8999	3194
United Parcel Service Inc	4215	C	510 262-2338	7658
Universal Bldg Svcs & Sup Co (PA)	7349	C	510 527-1078	12011
Vila Construction Co	1542	D	510 236-9111	981
West Coast Fab Inc	3444	F	510 529-0177	4830
West County Resource Recovery	4953	E	510 231-4200	8389
West County Wastewater Dst	4952	E	510 237-6603	8296
Whiteside Construction Corp	1771	E	510 234-6681	1918
WR Forde Associates Inc	1611	E	510 215-9338	1080
Young MNS Chrstn Assn of E Bay	8641	B	510 412-5640	18489
Young MNS Chrstn Assn of E Bay	8641	B	510 223-7070	18496
Young MNS Chrstn Assn of E Bay	8641	B	510 222-9622	18501
Young MNS Chrstn Assn of E Bay	8641	B	510 412-5647	18502
Young MNS Chrstn Assn of E Bay	8641	B	510 222-9622	18503
Young MNS Chrstn Assn of E Bay	8641	B	510 262-6588	18510
Zygo Epo	3827	F	510 243-7592	6888

RICHVALE, CA - Butte County

Company	SIC	EMP	PHONE	ENTRY #
Bianchi AG Services Inc (PA)	5083	C	530 882-4575	9032
Wehah Farm Inc	2044	B	530 538-3500	2330

RIO LINDA, CA - Sacramento County

Company	SIC	EMP	PHONE	ENTRY #
John Taylor Fertilizers Co (DH)	5191	B	916 991-9840	9601
Marques Gen Engrg Inc A Cal Co	8711	B	916 923-3434	18762
Martinez Pallets Inc	2448	F	916 238-4548	3225
Risse Construction Inc	1711	B	916 991-2700	1347
Toro Engineering Inc	1623	E	916 238-4535	1138

RIO OSO, CA - Sutter County

Company	SIC	EMP	PHONE	ENTRY #
Raj Sharma	0173	E	530 633-2057	90

RIO VISTA, CA - Solano County

Company	SIC	EMP	PHONE	ENTRY #
Asta Construction Inc (PA)	1381	E	707 374-6472	554
Birds Lnding Hnting Prsrve Inc	7997	E	707 374-5092	15061
California Vegetable Spc Inc	5148	D	707 374-2111	9390
City of Rio Vista	4111	E	707 374-5337	7328
Coughran Mechanical Svcs Inc	3599	E	707 374-2100	5496
Delta Marina Yacht Harbor	4493	E	707 374-2315	7728
Dick Brown Technical Services	1381	F	707 374-2133	555
Dolk Tractor Company	7699	E	707 374-6438	14745
Dry Vac Environmental Inc (PA)	3826	E	707 374-7500	6825
Dutra Dredging Company	1629	E	707 374-5127	1159
Paul Graham Drilling & Svc Co	1381	C	707 374-5123	556
R Emigh Livestock	5154	D	707 374-5585	9506
Resource Cementing LLC	1389	E	707 374-3350	570
T4 Manufacturing Inc (PA)	3999	F	707 689-3849	7312
Trilogy At Rio Vista	1521	C	707 374-6871	722
Woodward Drilling Company Inc	1381	E	707 374-4300	557

RIPON, CA - San Joaquin County

Company	SIC	EMP	PHONE	ENTRY #
Bethany HM Soc San Jquin Cnty	8051	D	209 599-7670	15947
Better Built Truss Inc	2439	E	209 869-4545	3201
Brocchini Farms Inc	0172	E	209 599-4229	47
California Nuggets Inc	2096	E	209 599-7131	2852
California Rock Crushers	1629	E	209 599-9941	1153
Califrnia Solar Innovators Inc	1711	D	209 596-0350	1228
Ducttesters Inc	8748	E	209 579-5000	19763
Fishers Nursery	5193	D	209 599-3412	9632
Franzia Winery LP	2084	F	209 599-4111	2584
Franzia Winery LLC	2084	E	209 599-4111	2585
Franzia/Sanger Winery	2084	D	209 599-4111	2586
Gate-Or-Door Inc	7372	F	209 751-4881	13184
Guntert Sales Div Inc	5051	E	209 599-6131	8817
Guntert Zmmerman Const Div Inc	3531	E	209 599-0066	5033
Jackrabbit (PA)	3523	D	209 599-6118	5009
John Sikkema Construction Inc	1542	D	209 599-1573	906
Kamper Fabrication Inc	3523	E	209 599-7137	5011
Maxim Equipment Inc	2951	F	209 649-7225	4188
McManis Family Vineyards Inc	2084	E	209 599-1186	2656
Nulaid Foods Inc (PA)	5144	D	209 599-2121	9349
Nushake Inc	1761	D	209 239-8616	1825
Park Greenhouses	0181	E	209 599-7545	132
Pearl Crop Inc	2076	E	209 982-9933	2454
R J M Enterprises Inc	0172	E	209 599-1186	70
Ripon Mfg Co	3556	E	209 599-2148	5134
Rocky Mountain Eggs Inc	5144	E	209 254-2200	9351
Spring Creek Golf & Cntry CLB	7997	E	209 599-3258	15154
Wine Group Inc (HQ)	2084	C	209 599-4111	2765

RIVERBANK, CA - Stanislaus County

Company	SIC	EMP	PHONE	ENTRY #
Econtactlive Inc	7389	D	209 548-4300	14259
Galaxy Patterson Road LLC	6512	D	209 863-9012	10389
LMC West Inc	5084	E	209 869-0144	9076
Oak Valley Hospital District	8062	E	209 869-8102	16469
Save Mart Supermarkets Disc	5141	E	209 863-1480	9298
Silgan Containers Mfg Corp	3411	E	209 869-3637	4601
Silgan Containers Mfg Corp	3411	E	209 869-3601	4602
Stanislaus Consol Fire Prot (PA)	7389	E	209 869-7470	14412
Thunderbolt Sales Inc	2491	E	209 869-4561	3261
Valley West Health Care Inc	8051	E	209 869-2569	16151

RIVERDALE, CA - Fresno County

Company	SIC	EMP	PHONE	ENTRY #
C Case Company Inc	1389	E	559 867-3912	561
Errotabere Ranches	0191	D	559 867-4461	166
Linda Terra Farms (PA)	0213	C	559 867-3473	204
Maddox Dairy LLC	0241	D	559 866-5308	216
Maddox Dairy A Ltd Partnership (PA)	0241	D	559 867-3545	217
Maddox Farms LLC	0191	E	559 866-5308	181
Sweet Haven Dairy	0241	D	559 866-5414	224

ROBBINS, CA - Sutter County

Company	SIC	EMP	PHONE	ENTRY #
Sutter Basin Corporation Ltd	0139	E	530 738-4456	21
Valley Truck and Tractor Inc	5083	D	530 738-4421	9048

ROCKLIN, CA - Placer County

Company	SIC	EMP	PHONE	ENTRY #
American Hlthcare ADM Svcs Inc	8099	B	916 773-7227	17100
Asa Corporation	3826	F	530 305-3720	6810
Bi Warehousing Inc (PA)	5013	E	916 624-0654	8443
Bi Warehousing Inc	5013	E	916 624-0654	8445
Brightview Landscape Svcs Inc	0781	C	916 415-1004	399
Brower Mechanical Inc	7623	E	530 749-0808	14683
Brown Brown Insur Brks Scrmnto	6411	E	916 630-8643	10251
Builders & Tradesmens	6411	E	916 772-9200	10253
Builders & Tradesmens Insur	6311	E	916 772-9200	10077
California Backyard Inc (PA)	5023	E	916 543-1900	8508
Cell Marque Corporation	2835	E	916 746-8900	4017
Cmor Manufacturing Inc	3643	D	916 626-3100	5713
Cosco Fire Protection Inc	1711	D	916 652-7100	1242
Ecorp Consulting Inc (PA)	8742	D	916 782-9100	19496
Educational Media Foundation (PA)	4832	C	916 251-1600	8018
Emf Broadcasting	4832	E	601 992-6988	8019
Financial Pacific Insur Group (DH)	6411	E	916 630-5000	10283
First Technology Federal Cr Un	6061	D	855 855-8805	9790
Foothill Fire Protection Inc (PA)	1711	E	916 663-3582	1265
Forgen LLC (PA)	8748	D	916 462-6400	19777
Galil Motion Control Inc	3823	E	800 377-6329	6721
Global Blue Dvbe Inc	7376	D	916 632-2583	13814
Golden Eagle Distributing Corp	5084	C	916 645-6600	9070
Horizon West Inc (PA)	8051	E	916 624-6230	16027
Horizon West Healthcare Inc (HQ)	8051	E	916 624-6230	16028
Hugin Components Inc	3469	E	916 652-1070	4884
Infinity Energy Inc	1711	C	916 474-4723	1284
Iron Oak Plumbing Inc	1711	E	916 782-9565	1287
J Bender Company	1542	F	916 462-7900	896
Jad Construction Inc	1522	E	916 408-6850	750

GEOGRAPHIC SECTION ROSEVILLE, CA

	SIC	EMP	PHONE	ENTRY #
Jkf Auto Service Inc	7542	D	916 315-0555	14646
Joseph Systems Inc	7373	E	916 303-7200	13615
Jostens Inc	3911	E	916 408-2295	7167
Journey Inc	6411	E	916 780-7000	10304
JR Perce Plbg Inc Sacramento	1711	C	916 434-9554	1296
Longs Drug Stores Cal Inc	7384	E	916 624-8288	14166
Marksys LLC	8742	D	916 745-4883	19567
Marksys Holdings LLC	8742	D	916 745-4883	19568
Matric Absence Management	8741	E	916 773-5737	19366
Morrow Snowboards Inc	3679	A	916 415-0645	6456
Nationwide Envmtl Cnstr Svcs I	8711	E	916 708-7445	18777
On-Time AC & Htg LLC	1711	E	916 229-6370	1324
Oracle America Inc	7372	F	303 272-6473	13351
Oracle Corporation	7372	B	916 315-3500	13352
Pacific Mdf Products Inc **(PA)**	2431	E	916 660-1882	3145
Pacific Secured Equities Inc	8742	B	916 677-2500	19601
Parallax Incorporated	3571	E	916 624-8333	5268
Pbc Enterprises	1521	E	916 415-9966	682
Pedro McCrcken Dsign Group Inc **(PA)**	8712	E	916 415-5358	18903
Phoenix Schools Inc	8351	D	916 415-0780	17994
Pick Pull Auto Dismantling Inc	5015	E	916 784-6350	8488
Power Factor Electric Inc	1731	E	916 435-8838	1568
Precision Fluid Controls Inc	5085	D	916 626-3029	9127
Precision Medical Products Inc	5047	E	888 963-6265	8790
Precision Medical Products Inc	8011	D	573 474-9302	15632
Progressive Technology Inc	3253	E	916 632-6715	4403
Quality Telecom Cons Inc **(PA)**	1623	D	916 315-0500	1132
Restaurant Assets & Design Inc **(PA)**	7389	E	916 532-1377	14384
Road Safety Inc	7389	C	916 543-4600	14391
Rocklin Lodging Group LLC	7011	D	916 761-7500	11415
Rocklin Physical Therapy PC	8049	C	916 435-3500	15895
Sacramento Cooling Systems Inc **(PA)**	1731	E	916 677-1000	1596
Sak Construction LLC	1521	E	916 644-1400	700
Satellite Av LLC	3663	E	916 677-0720	5866
SE Scher Corporation	7361	A	916 632-1363	12134
Shane Alxander Cstm Tile Stone	1743	E	916 652-0250	1719
Sierra View Landscape Inc	0782	E	916 408-2990	502
Sitek Process Solutions	3674	F	916 797-9000	6300
SMA America Production LLC	3433	C	720 347-6000	4635
SMA Solar Technology Amer LLC **(HQ)**	5065	C	916 625-0870	8955
Sonoran Roofing Inc	1761	C	916 624-1080	1837
Strikes Unlimited Inc	7933	D	916 626-3600	14902
Survellnce Systems Intgrtion I	5065	E	800 508-6981	8962
Swan Engineering Inc	1794	D	916 474-5299	1975
Total Body Fitness	7999	E	916 202-3006	15253
Totalrewards Software Inc	7372	F	916 632-1000	13496
Tricorp Group Inc **(PA)**	1542	D	916 779-8010	976
Turnure Medical Group Inc	8011	E	916 300-1188	15744
United Natural Foods West Inc **(HQ)**	4225	B	916 625-4100	7703
United Parcel Service Inc	4215	C	916 632-4826	7671
University California Davis	8011	D	916 295-5700	15770
Vannelli Foods LLC	2099	F	916 412-1204	2956
Webevents LLC	7371	E	916 784-9456	12918
Western Care Cnstr Co Inc	1542	E	916 624-6200	988
Wpcs Intrntional-Suisun Cy Inc	1731	D	916 624-1300	1642

RODEO, CA - Contra Costa County

	SIC	EMP	PHONE	ENTRY #
Young MNS Chrstn Assn of E Bay	8641	B	510 412-5644	18488

ROHNERT PARK, CA - Sonoma County

	SIC	EMP	PHONE	ENTRY #
Alembic Inc	3931	F	707 523-2611	7169
Asm Precision Inc	3444	F	707 584-7950	4743
Associated Students of S S U	8641	E	707 664-2815	18388
Chick-Fil-A Inc	8741	D	707 585-7462	19315
Codding Enterprises LP **(PA)**	6512	E	707 795-3550	10383
Cve Nb Contracting Group Inc	8748	E	707 584-1900	19757
Designit Global LLC	8711	E	707 584-4000	18689
Double Decker Corporation	7933	E	707 585-0226	14889
Estes Express Lines	4213	D	707 585-7961	7532
Eugene Burger Management Corp **(PA)**	6531	E	707 584-5123	10546
Federted Indans Grton Rncheria	7011	D	707 588-7100	11093
Flip Hospitality & Entrmt LLC **(PA)**	5087	D	707 584-1405	9143
Fox Tail Golf Course	7992	D	707 584-7766	15003
Harold A Steuber Entps Inc	7389	E	707 586-5205	14293
Idex Health & Science LLC **(HQ)**	3821	D	707 588-2000	6693
Inaudr LLC **(PA)**	2752	E	707 585-2718	3658
Innovative Molding **(HQ)**	3089	D	707 238-9250	4290
Kaiser Foundation Hospitals	6324	C	707 206-3000	10135
Kalkai Advance Mfg Inc	3672	E	707 588-9906	5943
KG Technologies Inc	3679	F	888 513-1874	6443
Kisco Senior Living LLC	6513	D	707 585-1800	10446
Lemo USA Inc	5065	D	707 206-3700	8927
North Bay Rhblitation Svcs Inc **(PA)**	2399	C	707 585-1991	3052
OHagin Manufacturing LLC	1711	E	707 872-3620	1322
OHagins Inc	1711	D	707 303-3660	1323
Pace Supply Corp **(PA)**	5074	D	707 755-2499	9003
Park US Lessee Holdings LLC	7011	D	707 887-7838	11357
Pasta Sonoma LLC	2098	E	707 584-0800	2865
Pennacchio Tile Inc	1743	D	707 586-8858	1718
Quarterwave Corp	8748	E	707 793-9105	19843
Red Condor Inc	7371	E	707 569-7419	12732
Rieke Corporation	3466	C	707 238-9250	4878
Rohnert Park Housing Fing Auth	8742	E	707 588-2226	19624
Rural Cal Brdcstg Corp Krcb Kp	4832	E	707 584-2062	8033
Santa Rosa Memorial Hospital	8093	E	707 584-0672	17070
Traditional Medicinals Inc	2099	F	707 664-5801	2950
Trevi Systems Inc	8734	E	707 992-0567	19288
Trinity Engineering	8711	E	707 585-2959	18840
World Centric	2679	F	707 241-9190	3410

ROSEVILLE, CA - Placer County

	SIC	EMP	PHONE	ENTRY #
10up Inc **(PA)**	7373	D	888 571-7130	13547
A & S Motorcycle Parts Inc	7699	E	916 726-7334	14732
A Teichert & Son Inc	1611	E	916 645-4800	999
A Teichert & Son Inc	3273	E	916 783-7132	4457
Abcsp LLC	8082	C	855 470-2273	16830
Advanced Ipm	7342	E	916 759-1570	11878
Advanced Metal Finishing LLC	3471	E	530 888-7772	4893
Adventist Hlth Systm/West Corp **(PA)**	8062	B	844 574-5686	16310
Aesyntix Health Inc **(HQ)**	8099	D	916 791-9500	17098
Aim Higher Incorporated **(PA)**	8322	D	916 786-0351	17410
Alta Cal Regional Ctr Inc	8322	C	916 786-8110	17416
Altus Health Inc	8082	C	916 781-6500	16843
Amazing Facts International	4832	D	916 434-3880	8015
American Pacific Mortgage Corp **(PA)**	6162	C	916 960-1325	9890
Arizona Tile LLC	5032	E	916 782-3200	8619
Arrive Technologies Inc	3674	F	916 715-9775	6049
Asset Preservation Inc **(DH)**	8742	E	916 791-5991	19450
Assoc CA Wtr AGC/Jt Pw Ins	6411	E	916 786-5742	10239
Associates In Womens Hlth Care	8011	E	916 782-2229	15284
Axcess Financial Services Inc	6099	E	916 783-0173	9842
Barbee Elc	8082	D	916 884-1983	16853
Basalite Building Products LLC **(HQ)**	3272	E	707 678-1901	4418
Bel Air Mart	2051	C	916 786-6101	2366
Beyond Security Inc	5065	D	279 201-7150	8896
Bianco Landscape Management	0782	D	916 521-1314	448
Blue Oak Dental Group	8021	E	916 786-6777	15825
Bre Select Hotels Oper LLC	7011	E	916 773-7171	10970
Bristol Hspice - Scramento LLC	8052	D	916 782-5511	16173
Burrell Consulting Group Inc	8711	E	916 783-8898	18654
Cal Consoldated Communications	4813	B	916 786-6141	7936
California Sun Inc	7299	D	916 789-1034	11709
California Waterfowl Assn	8641	E	916 648-1406	18402
Califrnia Rur Indian Hlth Bd I	8399	D	916 437-0104	18223
Castle Medical Center	8011	E	808 263-5182	15331
Catalyst Mortgage	6162	E	916 283-9922	9899
Cattlemens	7299	D	916 782-5587	11711
Central Valley Engrg & Asp Inc	1611	E	916 791-1609	1026
Certent Inc **(HQ)**	7371	E	925 730-4300	12333
CJS Lighting Inc	5063	E	916 774-6888	8854
Claims Management Inc	6411	E	916 631-1250	10262
Clark & Sullivan Constrs Inc	1542	C	916 338-7707	856
Clark Sllvan Bldrs Inc DBA Clr	1542	C	916 338-7707	857
CLC Incorporated **(PA)**	7361	E	916 789-7600	12080
Clearcaptions LLC	4813	E	866 868-8695	7940
Cliftonlarsonallen LLP	8721	B	916 784-7800	18945
Clp Resources Inc	7363	D	916 788-0300	12165
Cmd Products	3086	F	916 434-0228	4240
Cni Thl Ops LLC	7011	D	916 772-3500	11020
Cni Thl Ops LLC	7011	E	916 772-3404	11024
Cobeal	8748	E	916 622-7330	19745
Cokeva Inc	7378	C	916 462-6001	13820
Coleman Chavez & Assoc LLP	8111	D	916 787-2310	17233
Collette Foods LLC	2035	D	209 487-1260	2278
Cooks Truck Body Mfg Inc	3713	E	916 784-3220	6565
Coors Brewing Company	2082	E	916 786-2666	2476
Crocus Holdings LLC	8051	D	916 782-1238	15977
D Augustine & Associates	7311	D	916 774-9600	11748
Denios Rsvlle Frmrs Mkt Actn I	7389	C	916 782-2704	14251
Dick James & Associates Inc	6531	C	916 332-7430	10538
Dignity Health	8011	E	916 965-1936	15381
Directapps Inc **(PA)**	7379	C	916 787-2200	13882
Dwayne Nash Industries Inc	1761	C	916 253-1900	1800
Dynamic Staffing Inc **(PA)**	7361	C	916 773-3900	12085
Eisneramper LLP	8721	C	916 563-7790	18956
Empire Paper Corporation	5112	E	510 534-2700	9207
Enterprise Rnt—car Scrmnto LL **(DH)**	7514	E	916 787-4500	14486
Eskaton Properties Inc	8361	D	916 334-0810	18110
Esl Technologies Inc	7378	B	916 677-4500	13822
Fire Recovery Usa LLC	7389	D	916 200-3999	14273
Flexcare LLC	7361	A	866 564-3589	12089
Flint Builders Inc	1542	D	916 757-1000	874
Garner Products Inc	3812	F	916 784-0200	6668
Gateway Residential Programs	8322	E	916 782-1111	17588
Global Touchpoints Inc	7371	D	916 878-5954	12478
Golden 1 Credit Union	6062	D	916 784-9226	9834
Granite Payment Alliance LLC **(PA)**	7389	E	916 580-6285	14289
Guaranteed Rate Inc	6162	C	916 501-3919	9908
Gutterglove Inc	1761	D	916 624-5000	1810
Harris & Bruno Machine Co Inc **(PA)**	3555	D	916 781-7676	5121
Hudson & Company LLC	2392	F	916 774-6465	3026
Industrial Cont Svcs - CA N LL	5085	D	916 781-2775	9120
Infinite Solutions Inc **(PA)**	7373	E	916 641-0500	13611
Inn Ventures Inc	7011	D	916 773-7171	11192
Innerscope Hearing Tech Inc	3842	F	916 218-4100	7073
Intech Mechanical Company LLC	1711	C	916 797-4900	1285
Inter-Tribal Council Cal Inc **(PA)**	8322	E	916 973-9581	17618
Intercare Spclty Risk Insur Sv **(PA)**	6411	E	916 757-1200	10298
Interwest Insurance Svcs LLC	6411	D	916 784-1008	10300
Iosafe Inc	3572	F	888 984-6723	5296
Iptor Supply Chain Systems USA **(DH)**	7371	C	916 542-2820	12538
Jewelry Supply Inc	5094	E	916 780-9610	9183
Jfc Electric Inc	1731	E	916 789-9311	1526
John L Sullivan Chevrolet Inc	7539	C	916 782-1243	14615
Jts Sports Services Inc	7999	E	916 390-0829	15212
Kaiser Foundation Hospitals	8062	A	916 746-3937	16397

GEOGRAPHIC

	SIC	EMP	PHONE	ENTRY #
Kaiser Foundation Hospitals	8011	C	916 771-2871	15444
Kaiser Foundation Hospitals	8011	C	916 614-4350	15472
Kaiser Foundation Hospitals	8011	C	916 784-4000	15481
Kaiser Foundation Hospitals	6324	C	916 784-4050	10125
Kaiser Foundation Hospitals	6733	D	916 784-5081	10798
Kaiser Foundation Hospitals	8062	A	916 784-4000	16417
Kenco Engineering Inc	3531	E	916 782-8494	5036
Kkp - Roseville Inc	2752	E	916 786-8573	3664
Kyles Rock & Redi-Mix Inc	3273	F	916 681-4848	4489
Lancaster Burns Cnstr Inc	1742	C	916 624-8404	1687
Landscape & Tree Company Inc **(HQ)**	0781	D	916 246-9987	423
Larkspur Hsptality Dev MGT LLC	7011	E	916 773-1717	11248
Larkspur Hsptality Dev MGT LLC	7011	E	916 773-7171	11249
Life Time Inc	7991	C	916 472-2000	14958
Loanpal LLC **(PA)**	6162	B	916 290-9999	9914
Longs Drug Stores Cal Inc	7384	E	916 783-1350	14172
Lowes Home Centers LLC	5031	C	916 771-7111	8565
Lumen Tech Gvrnment Sltons Inc	4813	A	916 781-7772	7970
Lyon Realty	6531	C	916 784-1500	10603
Lyon Realty	6531	C	916 787-7700	10605
Matrix Absence Management Inc	8741	D	916 773-5737	19367
Maxim Healthcare Services Inc	7363	D	916 771-7444	12183
Med-Data Incorporated	8721	D	916 771-1362	18978
Merchant Valley Corporation	8611	C	916 786-7227	18309
Mother Lode Holding Co	6361	D	916 624-8141	10203
Nates Fine Foods LLC	2038	E	310 897-2690	2304
Nations First Capital LLC	6159	D	855 396-3600	9888
Neighborly Pest Management Inc	7342	D	916 782-3767	11906
New Star Lasers Inc	3845	E	916 677-1900	7117
New Vision Display Inc **(DH)**	3679	E	916 786-8111	6461
Niello Imports	7515	D	916 334-6300	14494
Noble Movers Inc	4213	D	415 260-1000	7571
Nor-Cal Pipeline Services	1623	D	916 442-5400	1125
Nortech Waste LLC	4953	C	916 645-5230	8346
North State Bldg Indust Assn	8611	D	916 677-5717	18312
Northern California Power Agcy **(PA)**	4911	D	916 781-3636	8128
Old Rpblic Title Info Concepts	6361	C	916 781-4100	10209
Optima Ldscp Sacramento Inc	0781	E	916 541-5796	429
Pacific Coast Optics LLC	3559	F	916 789-0111	5163
Patti Roscoe & Associates Inc **(PA)**	7389	E	760 496-0540	14354
Performance Polymer Tech LLC	3061	E	916 677-1414	4209
Permanente Medical Group Inc	8011	A	916 784-4000	15615
Pinnacle Builders Inc	1521	B	916 372-5000	686
Pinney Insurance Center Inc	6411	E	916 773-3800	10332
Placer Drmtlogy Skin Care Ctr **(PA)**	8011	E	916 784-3376	15630
Polycomp Administrative Svcs	6411	E	916 773-3480	10334
Power Business Technology LLC	7379	E	844 769-3729	13960
Precor Incorporated	7991	D	916 788-8334	14964
Pride Industries **(PA)**	4226	C	916 788-2100	7709
Pride Industries One Inc	3999	A	916 788-2100	7302
Pro-Groom Inc	0752	E	916 782-4172	356
Production Framing Systems Inc **(PA)**	1751	C	916 978-2888	1750
Project Go Incorporated	1799	E	916 782-3443	2057
Providence Publications LLC	2741	E	916 774-4000	3592
Quest Media & Supplies Inc **(PA)**	7379	D	916 338-7070	13966
RAL Builders	1521	E	916 960-4889	692
Reeve-Knight Construction Inc	1542	D	916 786-5112	945
Residence Inn By Marriott LLC	7011	E	888 484-1695	11401
Revenue Solutions Inc	7374	B	916 780-8741	13752
RI Herltg Inn Roseville LLC	7011	E	916 780-1850	11407
RJ Locicero Corp	1751	E	916 781-2004	1753
Roseville Flooring Inc	1752	E	916 945-2015	1775
Roseville Golfland Ltd Partnr	7999	D	916 784-1273	15232
Roseville Rocklin Electric Inc	1731	E	916 772-2698	1593
Roseville Sportworld	7999	E	916 783-8550	15233
Rountree Plumbing and Htg Inc	1711	D	650 298-0300	1350
RPM Luxury Auto Sales Inc	7539	C	916 783-9111	14620
Rudolph and Sletten Inc	1542	E	916 781-8001	953
Rysaw Painting Inc	1721	E	916 817-2393	1430
Scott Baldwin Cpas A Prof Corp	8721	E	916 722-2524	18990
Sedgwick Claims MGT Svcs Inc	6411	D	916 771-2900	10343
Select Hotels Group LLC	7011	E	916 781-6400	11458
Sierra Hills Care Center Inc	8051	D	916 782-7007	16117
Sierra View Country Club	7997	D	916 782-3741	15143
Sigma Mfg & Logistics LLC	3571	E	916 781-3052	5272
Sinister Mfg Company Inc	3714	E	916 772-9253	6593
Smoothie Operator Inc	2037	F	916 773-9541	2298
Sonitrol of Sacramento LLC	7382	E	916 724-1170	14149
South Coast Medical Center **(PA)**	8062	A	916 781-2000	16530
Spare-Time Inc	7997	D	916 782-2600	15151
Specialized Transport Inc	4212	E	916 969-6300	7490
Specialty Steel Service Co Inc	5051	E	800 777-4258	8828
Specialty Steel Service Co Inc **(HQ)**	5051	D	916 771-4737	8829
SRI Golf Inc	7992	E	916 771-4649	15030
St Albans Country Day School	8351	D	916 782-3557	18028
Sun City Rsvlle Cmnty Assn Inc **(PA)**	7992	C	916 774-3880	15032
Sunworks Inc **(PA)**	3674	D	916 409-6900	6319
Sunworks United Inc **(HQ)**	1711	D	916 409-6900	1373
Surewest Broadband	4813	C	916 772-5000	7994
Sutter Health	8062	C	916 797-4725	16584
Sutter Health	8062	C	916 797-4715	16595
Sutter Health	8011	D	916 783-8114	15716
Sutter Health	8062	C	916 878-2588	16615
Sutter Health	8011	D	530 406-5600	15719
Sutter Health	8062	C	916 781-1225	16620
Sutter Health	8071	D	916 784-2277	16808
Sutter Health	8062	C	916 797-4700	16653

	SIC	EMP	PHONE	ENTRY #
Sutter Roseville Medical Ctr	8062	A	916 781-1000	16673
Sutter Rsvlle Med Ctr Fndation	8062	D	916 781-1000	16674
Sutter Valley Med Foundation	8011	C	916 865-1140	15734
Sutter Valley Med Foundation	8741	D	916 865-1140	19406
Swiss-Tech Machining LLC	3451	E	916 797-6010	4870
Technical Sales Intl LLC **(HQ)**	7372	E	866 493-6337	13488
Teleplan Service Solutions Inc	7378	D	916 677-4500	13824
Think Outside Box Inc	7299	E	916 726-2339	11732
Tim Lewis Communities	1521	E	916 783-2300	719
Tri Commercial RE Svcs	6531	E	916 677-8000	10675
Tsi Semiconductors America LLC **(PA)**	3674	C	916 786-3900	6336
Ufcw & Employers Trust LLC	8631	D	916 782-1618	18380
Unilab Corporation	8071	A	916 781-3031	16813
United Building Maint Inc	7349	C	916 772-8101	12008
United Fd Coml Wkrs Un Lcal 8	8631	D	916 786-0588	18382
United States Info Systems Inc	1731	C	845 353-9224	1626
Universal Plastics Inc	1721	E	916 787-0541	1435
USA Multifamily Management Inc	6531	C	916 773-6060	10679
USA Properties Fund Inc **(PA)**	6552	C	916 773-6060	10720
Varis LLC **(PA)**	8742	E	916 294-0860	19664
Vibrantcare Outpatient Rehab **(PA)**	8093	D	916 782-1212	17086
Volt Management Corp	7363	D	916 923-0454	12205
Walt Disney Company	4832	D	916 780-1470	8036
Waterhouse Management Corp	6515	C	916 772-4918	10475
Wells Construction Inc	1542	E	916 257-6172	986
Western Buyers LLC **(PA)**	5031	E	916 576-3042	8612
Westmont Living Inc	8361	D	916 786-3277	18212
Westrup-Sadler Inc	7515	D	916 783-2077	14496
White Gazelle Inc **(PA)**	6282	E	916 718-0601	10073
Willdan Engineering	8711	D	916 924-7000	18862
York Insur Srvcs Group - CA	6411	E	916 783-0100	10373
Zipi Inc	6531	E	424 444-6700	10691
Zoca Roseville Inc	7389	D	916 788-0303	14467

ROSS, CA - Marin County

	SIC	EMP	PHONE	ENTRY #
Cedars of Marin **(PA)**	8052	D	415 454-5310	16176
Pacific Union Intl Inc	6531	D	415 461-8686	10637

ROUGH AND READY, CA - Nevada County

	SIC	EMP	PHONE	ENTRY #
Simply Country Inc	3523	F	530 615-0565	5018

ROUND MOUNTAIN, CA - Shasta County

	SIC	EMP	PHONE	ENTRY #
Hill Country Community Clinic	8011	E	530 337-6243	15431

ROYAL OAKS, CA - Santa Cruz County

	SIC	EMP	PHONE	ENTRY #
Cal Southern Seafood Inc **(PA)**	5146	D	805 698-8262	9362
Classic Salads LLC	2099	E	831 763-4520	2884
Falcon Trading Company **(PA)**	2099	C	831 786-7000	2891
Faurot Ranch LLC	0161	E	831 722-1346	29
Gino Rinaldi Inc	1743	D	831 761-0195	1715
Hildebrand & Sons Trucking Inc **(PA)**	4212	D	831 722-3006	7473
Kristich-Monterey Pipe Co Inc	3272	E	831 724-4186	4441
R Montanez Farms LLC	0191	E	831 761-5982	187
Santa Cruz Compost Company Inc	5191	E	831 728-0113	9609

RUTHERFORD, CA - Napa County

	SIC	EMP	PHONE	ENTRY #
Cakebread Cellars	2084	D	707 963-5221	2523
Colinas Farming Company	0762	E	707 963-2053	369
Diageo North America Inc	2085	D	707 967-5200	2768
Frogs Leap Winery	2084	E	707 963-4704	2590
Grgich Hills Cellar	2084	E	707 963-2784	2605
Honig Vineyard and Winery LLC	0172	E	707 963-5618	56
Inglenook	2084	E	707 968-1100	2620
Niebam-Cppola Estate Winery LP **(PA)**	2084	C	707 968-1100	2670
Peju Province Winery A CA Ltd	2084	D	800 446-7358	2679
Pernod Ricard Usa LLC	2084	D	707 967-7770	2681
St Supery Inc **(DH)**	2084	E	707 963-4507	2723
Swanson Vineyards and Winery **(DH)**	2084	E	707 754-4018	2736
Terre Du Soleil Ltd	7011	B	707 963-1211	11529

SACRAMENTO, CA - Sacramento County

	SIC	EMP	PHONE	ENTRY #
15th & L Investors LLC	7011	D	916 267-6805	10900
A Teichert & Son Inc	3273	E	916 386-6974	4456
A Teichert & Son Inc	1442	E	916 386-6900	589
A&A Metal Finishing Entps LLC	3471	E	916 442-1063	4891
A-1 Advantage Asphalt Inc	1611	D	916 388-2020	1002
A1 Protective Services LLC	7381	E	916 421-3000	14023
A29 Funding LLC	7011	C	916 446-0100	10908
AAA Signs Inc	7534	D	916 568-3456	14537
Abacus Service Corporation	7371	B	916 288-8948	12219
ABM Industry Groups LLC	7521	E	916 443-9094	14497
Accent Hospitality Group LLC	4725	C	415 286-2867	7812
Ace Parking Management Inc	7521	D	916 497-0222	14500
ADM Associates Incorporated	8711	C	916 363-8383	18615
ADM Garage Doors **(PA)**	1751	E	916 595-5355	1728
Admail West Inc	2655	D	916 554-5755	3367
Administrative Systems Inc	7389	D	916 563-1121	14196
Advanced Bus Integrators Inc	7379	E	916 381-3809	13832
Advanced Home Health Inc	8082	D	916 978-0744	16836
Advanced Roof Design Inc **(PA)**	1761	E	916 381-2266	1780
Aee Solar Inc	5063	D	800 777-6609	8837
Ainor Signs Inc	3993	E	916 348-4370	7215
Air & Lube Systems Inc **(PA)**	1799	E	916 381-5588	1998
Air Systems Service & Cnstr	1711	C	916 368-0336	1191
Airco Commercial Services Inc **(HQ)**	1711	E	866 731-4458	1192
Airco Mechanical Inc **(PA)**	1711	C	916 381-4523	1193
Alcal Specialty Contg Inc **(DH)**	1761	B	916 929-3100	1782
Alccon General Engineering	1611	E	916 381-4600	1005
Aldetec Inc	3663	E	916 453-3382	5818

	SIC	EMP	PHONE	ENTRY #
All Weather Inc	3829	D	916 928-1000	6891
Allied Aviation Fueling Co Inc	4581	D	916 924-1002	7765
ALS Interiors Inc	1521	E	916 344-2942	608
Alston Construction Co Inc **(PA)**	1542	D	916 340-2400	822
Altamedix Corporation	8322	D	916 648-3999	17418
Aluminum Coating Tech Inc	3471	E	916 442-1063	4895
Amador Stage Lines Inc	4142	D	916 444-7880	7420
AMD Metal Works Inc	1761	E	916 465-8185	1785
American Building Supply Inc	8741	D	916 387-4101	19296
American Building Supply Inc **(HQ)**	5031	C	916 503-4100	8524
American Building Supply Inc	5031	D	916 387-4101	8525
American Building Supply Inc	5031	D	916 503-4100	8527
American Lithographers Inc	2752	D	916 441-5392	3619
American Med Rspnse Inland Emp	4119	B	916 563-0600	7368
American National Red Cross	8322	E	800 733-2767	17427
American River Bank **(PA)**	6022	E	916 565-6100	9698
American River Hospice Svcs	8052	E	229 255-4609	16169
Amerisourcebergen Drug Corp	5122	C	916 830-4500	9222
Ames-Grenz Insurance Svcs Inc	6411	E	916 486-2900	10230
Angelo Kilday & Kilduff	8111	D	916 564-6100	17202
Anrak Corporation	1611	E	916 383-5030	1010
Apexcare Inc **(PA)**	8082	A	916 924-9111	16849
Aramark Unf & Career AP LLC	7213	D	916 286-4100	11631
Archerhall LLC **(PA)**	7379	E	916 449-2820	13844
Architectural Blomberg LLC	3442	E	916 428-8060	4697
Arden Hills Country Club Inc	7991	D	916 482-6111	14926
Arden Little League Snack Bar **(PA)**	7997	E	916 359-6379	15053
Arleen Logistics Inc **(PA)**	4789	D	916 514-9746	7874
Armor Brer Protective Svcs Inc	7381	E	833 692-2774	14032
Arraycon Inc	1711	D	916 925-0201	1207
Arraycon LLC **(PA)**	1711	E	916 925-0201	1208
Arreolas Complete Ldscp Svc	0782	D	916 387-6777	447
Arrow Drillers Inc **(PA)**	1623	E	916 640-0600	1087
Asbury Pk Nrsing Rhblttion Ctr	8059	C	916 649-2000	16216
Ashen Company Ltd **(PA)**	8021	D	916 487-0117	15822
Asian Community Center of Sac	8051	E	916 393-9020	15911
Asomeo Envmtl Rstrtion Indust	5082	D	530 434-6869	9018
Associated Fmly Physicians Inc	8011	D	916 689-4111	15283
Association Cal Wtr Agencies **(PA)**	8611	E	916 441-4545	18297
Assuredpartners Inc	6411	D	916 443-0200	10241
Atg-Wci Inc **(DH)**	7699	C	916 489-3651	14738
Atkinson Youth Services Inc	8361	E	916 977-3790	18059
Atlas Specialties Corporation **(PA)**	3231	E	503 636-8182	4383
Atrium Finance I LP	7011	B	916 446-0100	10936
Attainit	7349	E	916 325-7800	11922
Atv Video Center Inc	7812	E	916 973-9100	14786
Auburn Constructors LLC	1629	D	916 924-0344	1148
Aurrera Health Group LLC	8742	E	916 662-7930	19451
Axcess Financial Services Inc	6099	E	916 424-4180	9841
Azalea Holdings LLC	8051	D	916 452-3592	15921
B T Mancini Co Inc	5023	C	916 381-3660	8507
Baco Realty Corporation	7381	D	916 974-9898	14035
Bagatelos Glass Systems Inc **(PA)**	1793	D	916 364-3600	1935
Bancorp Financial Services Inc **(HQ)**	6159	D	916 641-2000	9885
Barbara-Hoffman Inc	7349	D	916 635-9767	11924
Bargas Envmtl Consulting LLC	8748	E	916 993-9218	19726
Barnum & Celillo Electric Inc **(PA)**	1731	C	916 646-4661	1456
Bayer Protective Services Inc	7381	C	916 486-5800	14037
Bdg Innovations LLC **(PA)**	8711	E	855 725-9555	18638
Beauty Craft Furniture Corp	2511	E	916 428-2238	3274
Bel Air Mart	2051	C	916 739-8647	2367
Bel Air Mart	2051	C	916 920-2493	2368
Bel Air Mart	2052	C	916 972-0555	2413
Benetech Inc **(PA)**	6411	D	916 484-6811	10248
Bennetts Baking Company	2053	F	916 481-3349	2420
Berke Door & Hardware Inc	5031	F	916 452-7331	8529
BEST Consulting Inc	8748	E	916 448-2050	19729
Bickmore and Associates Inc **(DH)**	6411	D	916 244-1100	10250
Big Hairy Dog Info Systems	5045	E	916 368-3939	8675
Bioware Sacramento **(HQ)**	5092	E	916 403-3500	9165
BJ Jrdan Child Care Prgrams **(PA)**	8351	E	916 344-6259	17863
Blomberg Building Materials **(PA)**	3442	D	916 428-8060	4700
Bloodsource Inc	8099	E	916 488-1701	17108
Blue Diamond Growers	2099	C	916 446-8464	2871
BM Lynn Painting Inc	1721	E	916 920-4000	1404
Bohm Law Group Inc **(PA)**	8111	E	916 927-5574	17216
Borge Construction Inc **(PA)**	1521	E	916 927-4800	621
Bradford & Barthel LLP **(PA)**	8111	E	916 569-0790	17218
Brewer Brewer Lofgren LLP **(PA)**	2099	E	916 550-1482	2873
Bridgstone Amrcas Tire Oprtons	5014	D	916 447-4220	8476
Brightview Landscape Dev Inc	0781	C	916 386-4875	397
Brightview Landscape Svcs Inc	0781	C	916 381-2800	404
Broadway Sacramento	6512	C	916 446-5880	10379
Broadway Sacramento **(PA)**	7922	C	916 446-5880	14840
Buehler Engineering Inc **(PA)**	8711	E	916 443-0303	18653
Burgett Incorporated **(PA)**	5099	D	916 567-9999	9192
Burn Unit Ucd Medical Center	8069	E	916 734-3637	16752
Burnett Sons Planing Mill Lbr	2434	E	916 442-0493	3170
Buzz Oates Management Services	6531	E	916 381-3843	10499
C W A District Nine **(HQ)**	8631	E	916 921-4500	18354
C&S Wholesale Grocers Inc	4225	D	916 383-5275	7682
California Apartment Assn	8611	E	916 447-7881	18301
California Cab & Store Fix	2431	E	916 386-1340	3123
California Cabinet & Str Fixs	2434	E	916 681-0901	3172
California Cascade Industries	2491	C	916 736-3353	3256
California Chamber Commerce **(PA)**	8611	D	916 444-6670	18302
California Cmplte CNT Cnsus	8733	D	916 852-2020	19201

	SIC	EMP	PHONE	ENTRY #
California Dental Association **(PA)**	8621	C	916 443-0505	18326
California Department Tech **(DH)**	7379	C	916 319-9223	13859
California Fire Fghtrs Apprent	8331	E	916 648-1717	17797
California Health Benefit Exch	8621	D	916 228-8210	18327
California Medical Association **(PA)**	8621	D	916 444-5532	18328
California Pavement Maint Inc	1611	C	916 381-8033	1022
California Primary Care Assn	8621	E	916 440-8170	18330
California Restaurant Assn	8641	E	916 447-5793	18401
California Rural Water Assn	8611	E	916 553-4900	18303
California Trvl & Tourism Comm	4724	E	916 444-4429	7794
California-American Water Co	4941	E	916 568-4216	8227
Califrnia Assn Hlth Facilities **(PA)**	8611	E	916 441-6400	18304
Califrnia Assn Hsptals Hlth Sy **(PA)**	8621	D	916 443-7401	18333
Califrnia Chldren Fmilies Comm	8699	E	916 263-1050	18553
Califrnia High Speed Rail Auth	4011	D	916 324-1541	7318
Califrnia Indian Mnpwer Cnsrti **(PA)**	8331	E	916 920-0285	17800
Califrnia Mantel Fireplace Inc **(PA)**	2431	E	916 925-5775	3124
Califrnia Prson Hlthcare Rcvrs	8082	D	916 691-6721	16865
Califrnia Pub Emplyees Rtrment **(DH)**	6371	A	916 795-3000	10212
Califrnia Srvying Drftg Sup In **(PA)**	7353	E	916 344-0232	12019
Califrnia State Employees Assn **(PA)**	8631	D	916 444-8134	18357
Califrnia State Tchers Rtrment	8721	E	916 445-0211	18942
Califrnia Yuth Soccer Assn Inc	8699	D	925 426-5437	18554
Calpo Hom Dong Architects Inc	8712	D	916 446-7741	18875
Calvada Sales Company **(PA)**	5147	E	916 441-6290	9376
Calvary Chrstn Ch Ctr of Scrmn	8351	E	916 921-9303	17872
Calvey Incorporated	5199	D	916 681-4800	9648
Cambria Solutions Inc **(PA)**	8748	C	916 326-4446	19738
Canon Financial Services Inc	5045	E	916 368-7610	8680
Capital Athletic Club Inc	7991	E	916 442-3927	14935
Capital Christian Center	8351	E	916 722-6169	17878
Capital Corrugated LLC	2653	D	916 388-7848	3355
Capital Lumber	5031	F	916 922-8861	8533
Capital Obgyn **(PA)**	8011	D	916 920-2082	15319
Capital Public Radio Inc	4832	E	916 278-8900	8016
Capitol Barricade Inc **(PA)**	5084	D	916 451-5176	9060
Capitol Beverage Packers	2086	E	916 929-7777	2785
Capitol Builders Hardware Inc **(HQ)**	1751	D	916 451-2821	1732
Capitol Casino	7999	C	916 446-0700	15188
Capitol Corporate Services Inc **(PA)**	8732	D	916 444-6787	19155
Capitol Iron Works Inc	3441	E	916 381-1554	4650
Capitol Regency LLC	7011	B	916 443-1234	10988
Capitol Services Inc	8742	C	916 443-0657	19465
Capitol Steel Company	5051	E	916 924-3195	8810
Capitol Store Fixtures	2521	E	916 646-9096	3301
Capitol Valley Electric Inc	1731	E	916 686-3244	1473
Caravali Coffees Inc **(DH)**	5149	D	916 565-5500	9442
Cardiac Surgery West Med Corp	8011	E	916 733-6850	15321
Cares Community Health	8011	C	916 443-3299	15329
Carlton Senior Living Inc	8361	D	916 971-4800	18068
Carrier Corporation	7623	E	916 928-9500	14684
Case Dealer Holding Co LLC **(DH)**	5082	D	916 649-0096	9020
Cathedral Pioneer Church Homes **(PA)**	8051	D	916 442-4906	15954
CB&i Government Solutions Inc	8711	E	916 928-3300	18665
Cbre Inc	6531	D	916 446-6800	10506
Ccapp Education Institute	8699	D	916 338-9460	18557
Cccs Inc	1611	E	916 457-6111	1024
Cda Holding Company Inc **(PA)**	8621	D	916 442-2462	18336
Cellco Partnership	4812	D	916 838-9525	7900
Cemex California Cement LLC	3241	B	760 381-7616	4394
Cenpatico Behavioral Hlth LLC	8099	C	877 858-3855	17116
Center For Fathers & Families	8322	E	916 568-3237	17472
Center To Prmote Hlthcare Acce	8099	D	916 563-4004	17118
Central Ansthsia Svc Exch Med	8011	D	916 481-6800	15333
Central Parking System Inc	7521	D	916 441-1074	14510
Century Theatres Inc	7833	E	916 442-7000	14821
Century Theatres Inc	7833	C	916 332-2622	14829
Century Theatres Inc	7833	C	916 363-6572	14831
CFM Equipment Distributors Inc **(PA)**	5075	E	916 447-7022	9008
Cgl Companies LLC	8712	D	916 678-7890	18878
Channel 40 Inc	4833	C	916 454-4422	8041
Charles McMurray Co	5072	E	916 929-9560	8981
Chem Quip Inc	5091	D	800 821-1678	9154
Chico Community Publishing	2711	C	916 498-1234	3428
Child Action Inc	8351	E	916 921-5345	17888
Child Action Inc	8351	D	916 369-0191	17889
Childrens Recvg Hm Sacramento	8322	C	916 482-2370	17488
Christian Bradshaw School **(PA)**	8351	D	916 688-0521	17902
Christie Bryant Inc	8742	E	916 492-7062	19470
City of Sacramento	4953	E	916 808-4949	8318
Clark Pest Ctrl Stockton Inc	7342	E	916 925-7000	11887
Clas Information Services	8732	D	916 564-7800	19156
Class a Powdercoat Inc	3479	E	916 681-7474	4930
Cleanrite Inc	7342	E	916 381-1321	11897
Coact Designworks	8712	E	916 930-5900	18879
Coffee Works Inc	2095	F	916 452-1086	2838
Coit Services Inc	7217	D	916 731-7006	11661
Colonial Van & Storage Inc **(PA)**	4213	E	916 546-3600	7520
Community College Foundation **(PA)**	8748	D	916 418-5100	19747
Composite Technology Intl Inc	2431	E	916 551-1850	3126
Comstock Publishing Inc	2721	F	916 364-1000	3494
Comtech Communications Inc	7622	E	800 377-7422	14679
Confidential Canine Services	0752	E	800 574-5545	353
Connected Cannabis	3999	E	916 308-4175	7277
Consol	8742	E	209 474-8446	19476
Consoldted Protective Svcs Inc	7381	E	916 483-2500	14045
Consolidated Pallet Company	5031	F	916 381-8123	8538

Employment Codes: A=Over 500 employees, B=251-500, C=101-250, D=51-100, E=20-50 F=10-19

2022 Northern California Business Directory and Buyers Guide

© Mergent Inc. 1-800-342-5647

1187

	SIC	EMP	PHONE	ENTRY #
Consultnts In Edctl Per Skills **(PA)**	8322	D	916 348-1890	17506
Cook Realty Inc	6531	E	916 451-6702	10523
Cooperative Personnel Services **(PA)**	8742	C	916 263-3600	19481
Countertop Designs Inc	1799	D	916 929-4562	2025
County of Sacramento	8351	E	916 875-3412	17916
County of Sacramento	8099	E	916 874-9670	17128
County of Sacramento	1622	D	916 875-2711	1081
County of Sacramento	8051	C	916 875-0900	15962
County of Sacramento	8011	E	916 875-5701	15367
County of Sacramento	7992	E	916 575-4653	14991
County of Sacramento	4581	D	916 874-0912	7772
Covenant Care California LLC	8051	D	916 391-6011	15969
CRC Roofing Inc	1761	E	916 362-4373	1792
Creative Design Interiors Inc **(PA)**	1752	D	916 641-1121	1767
Crestwood Behavioral Hlth Inc **(PA)**	8063	D	510 651-1244	16735
Crestwood Behavioral Hlth Inc	8063	D	916 452-1431	16736
Crestwood Behavioral Hlth Inc	8063	D	916 452-1431	16737
Crocker Art Museum Association	8699	D	916 808-7000	18562
Crown Building Maintenance Co	7349	B	916 920-9556	11938
Crown Building Maintenance Co	7349	B	415 546-6534	11940
Crystal Cream & Butter Co **(HQ)**	2026	D	916 444-7200	2187
Csus	8742	D	916 278-4489	19487
Cumming Management Group Inc	8741	D	916 779-7140	19322
Cuneo Black Ward Missler A Law	8111	E	916 363-8822	17242
Cvc Construction Corp **(HQ)**	1771	B	916 852-6030	1862
Cy Sac Operator LLC	7011	D	916 455-6800	11045
D & J Plumbing Inc	1711	E	916 922-4888	1245
D & T Fiberglass Inc	3089	E	916 383-9012	4272
Dana Motors Inc **(PA)**	5013	F	916 920-0150	8449
Danoc Manufacturing Corp Inc	2337	F	916 455-2876	3005
Dave Gross Enterprises Inc	1799	D	916 388-2000	2028
David Allen & Associates **(PA)**	8111	E	916 455-4800	17246
Davis Uc Medical Center	8062	B	916 734-2011	16345
Davison Iron Works Inc	3441	E	916 381-2121	4656
Dealertrack Clltral MGT Svcs I	7371	C	916 368-5300	12377
Dean Moon	0782	E	916 387-1339	456
Del Norte Club Inc	7997	E	916 483-5111	15083
Del Paso Country Club	7997	C	916 489-3681	15084
Delegata Corporation	7373	D	916 609-5400	13576
Delta Dental of California	6324	E	916 853-7373	10104
Delta Dental of California	6324	E	916 381-4054	10105
Delta Web Printing Inc	2759	E	916 375-0044	3729
Dentists Insurance Company **(HQ)**	6411	C	916 443-4567	10271
Dentists Supply Company	3843	E	888 253-1223	7083
Develop Disabilities Svc Org	8322	D	916 973-1951	17530
Develpmntal Dsblties Svc Orgnz **(PA)**	8322	D	916 456-5166	17531
Dhm Enterprises Inc	3799	F	916 688-7767	6658
Diepenbrock Elkin LLP	8111	E	916 492-5000	17251
Dignity Health	8062	C	916 423-5940	16349
Dignity Health Med Foundation	8062	D	916 450-2600	16353
Disability Rights California **(PA)**	8111	D	916 488-9950	17253
Dja-Mge JV LLC	8711	E	916 421-1000	18691
Dominguez Landscape Svcs Inc	0782	D	916 381-8855	459
Domus Construction & Design	1521	D	916 381-7500	632
Dongalen Enterprises Inc **(PA)**	5162	E	916 422-3110	9513
Dorris Lumber and Moulding Co **(PA)**	2431	D	916 452-7531	3130
Downey Brand LLP **(PA)**	8111	C	916 444-1000	17257
Dpr Construction A Gen Partnr	1542	C	916 568-3434	866
Dreyer Bbich Bccola Cllham LLP	8111	D	916 379-3500	17258
Dreyer Bbich Bccola WD Cmpora **(PA)**	8111	D	916 379-3500	17259
Dupont Market Inc **(PA)**	5147	D	510 562-3593	9377
Dura-Metrics Inc **(PA)**	8072	D	707 546-5138	16824
Dvbe Technology Group	7379	E	916 565-7610	13884
Eagle Trs 4 LLC	7011	E	916 443-8400	11069
East Lawn Inc **(PA)**	6553	E	916 732-2000	10727
Easter Seal Soc Superior Cal **(PA)**	8099	D	916 485-6711	17139
Easun Inc	7011	E	916 929-8855	11071
Ebara Technologies Inc **(DH)**	3563	D	916 920-5451	5183
Econo Lodge	7011	E	916 443-6631	11073
Ehealthwirecom Inc	8099	C	916 924-8092	17142
Eht Wsac LLC	7011	E	916 443-8400	11074
Eide Bailly LLP	8721	E	916 570-1880	18952
El Dorado Newspapers **(DH)**	2711	C	916 321-1826	3434
Eldorado Air LLC	4522	D	916 391-5000	7756
Elegant Surfaces	5032	E	209 823-9388	8625
Elevator Industries Inc	3534	F	916 921-1495	5046
Elica Health Centers	8011	E	916 454-2345	15389
Elite Power Inc	1731	D	916 739-1580	1501
Elite Ready-Mix LLC	3273	E	916 366-4627	4480
Elite Service Experts Inc **(PA)**	3559	D	916 568-1400	5147
Elizabethan Inn Associates LP	7011	E	916 448-1300	11077
Elk Grove Unified School Dst	4151	E	916 686-7733	7429
Ellensburg Lamb Company Inc **(HQ)**	2011	F	530 758-3091	2096
Elliott Benson	8732	E	916 325-1670	19158
Emerald Site Services Inc	1794	D	916 685-7211	1958
Emilykate LLC	7371	F	916 761-6261	12424
Energy Performance Intl	7699	E	916 995-1511	14746
Energy Salvage Inc	8741	E	916 737-8640	19327
Ensher Alexander & Barsoom Inc **(PA)**	0191	E	916 443-6875	165
Entercom Communications Corp	4832	C	916 766-5000	8020
Entercom Media Corp	4832	D	916 923-6800	8023
Enterprise Rnt—car Scrmnto LL	7514	C	916 576-3164	14483
Envirnmntal Cmpliance Pros Inc	2842	E	916 953-9006	4073
Environmental Science Assoc	8748	D	916 564-4500	19769
Epn Enterprises Inc	7363	D	888 788-5424	12170
Eriks North America Inc	5085	D	916 366-9340	9117
Eskaton	6512	C	916 395-1722	10387
Eskaton Properties Inc	8361	D	916 441-1015	18107
Eskaton Properties Inc	8361	D	916 393-2550	18112
Estrada Consulting Inc	8748	E	916 473-7493	19770
Ethan Conrad Properties Inc **(PA)**	6531	D	916 779-1000	10545
Evergreen Co	6552	E	916 923-9000	10702
Evergreen Paper and Energy LLC **(PA)**	2611	D	802 357-1003	3341
Excel Managed Care Disa	8742	C	916 944-7185	19510
Experian Health Inc	7373	D	415 716-6633	13587
Express Messenger Systems Inc	4215	D	916 921-6016	7644
Fairytale Town Inc	7996	D	916 808-7462	15041
Famand Inc **(PA)**	1711	E	916 988-8808	1261
Farmers Rice Cooperative **(PA)**	2044	E	916 923-5100	2320
Farmers Rice Cooperative	2044	D	916 373-5549	2321
Federal Express Corporation	4513	D	916 361-5500	7749
Fencecorp Inc	1799	D	916 388-0887	2031
First US Community Credit Un **(PA)**	6061	E	916 576-5700	9791
Fischer Tile and Marble Inc	1743	C	916 452-1426	1714
Fluid Tech Hydraulics Inc	7699	E	916 681-0888	14749
Fni International Inc	8742	D	916 643-1400	19516
Fong Fong Prtrs Lthgrphers Inc	2752	E	916 739-1313	3648
Forterra Pipe & Precast LLC	3272	E	916 379-9695	4433
Frank Carson Ldscp & Maint Inc	0781	C	916 856-5400	415
Freeport Bakery Inc	2051	F	916 442-4256	2383
Fremont Package Express	3537	F	916 541-1812	5061
Fresno Precision Plastics Inc	3089	D	916 689-5284	4283
Fruitridge Prtg Lithograph Inc **(PA)**	2752	E	916 452-9213	3651
Fusion Real Estate Network Inc	6531	D	916 448-3174	10555
G B Commercial LLC	7011	D	916 263-9000	11109
Gallagher Bassett Services Inc	6411	E	916 929-7581	10284
Gat - Arln Ground Support Inc	4581	B	916 923-2349	7773
Geico General Insurance Co	6411	B	916 923-5050	10285
General Prod A Cal Ltd Partnr **(PA)**	5148	C	916 441-6431	9409
General Services Cal Dept	1542	E	916 322-3880	877
Gh Foods Ca LLC **(DH)**	2099	B	916 844-1140	2895
Gilbert Associates Inc	8721	E	916 646-6464	18959
Girl Scouts Heart Central Cal	8641	C	916 452-9181	18419
Glocol Inc	4111	E	650 224-2108	7334
Gluware Inc **(PA)**	7373	E	916 877-8224	13598
Golden 1 Credit Union	6062	D	916 732-2900	9830
Golden 1 Credit Union **(PA)**	6062	B	916 732-2900	9832
Golden Coast Cnstr Restoration	1521	D	916 955-7461	645
Golden Empire Mortgage Inc	6162	E	916 576-7919	9907
Golden Pacific Bank Nat Assn **(DH)**	6022	E	916 288-1069	9734
Golden State Fire Appratus Inc	3711	F	916 330-1638	6551
Golden State Utility Co	1623	E	916 387-6255	1104
Goodwin-Cole Company Inc	7359	E	916 381-8888	12042
Gordon and Schwenkmeyer Inc	7389	C	916 569-1740	14288
Gordon Rees Scully Mansukhani	8111	E	916 830-6900	17277
Government App Solutions Inc	7371	E	833 538-2220	12485
Greater Sacramento Sur	8093	D	916 929-7229	17021
Greater Sacramento Urban Leag	8399	E	916 286-8600	18230
Greenleaf Power LLC **(PA)**	4911	E	916 596-2500	8114
Griffin & Reed A Medical Corp	3851	F	916 483-2525	7140
Growing Company Inc	0782	D	916 379-9088	468
Grutzmacher & Lewis Med Corp	8011	E	916 649-1515	15421
Gsl Fine Lithographers	2752	E	916 231-1410	3653
Gudgel Roofing Inc	1761	E	916 387-6900	1809
Gupta Technologies LLC	5045	D	916 928-6400	8709
H & D Electric	1731	B	916 332-0794	1510
H C C S Inc	8051	D	916 454-5752	16016
Halstead Partnership	1542	D	916 830-8000	884
Hand Biomechanics Lab Inc	3842	F	916 923-5073	7071
Hand Surgery Associates	8011	E	916 457-4263	15424
Hank Fisher Properties Inc	8361	E	916 447-4444	18126
Hank Fisher Properties Inc	8059	C	916 921-1970	16237
Hansford Industries Inc **(PA)**	5051	E	916 379-0210	8818
Harold E Nutter Inc	1731	E	916 334-4343	1513
Harris & Sloan Consulting	8748	E	916 921-2800	19788
Hawthorn Suites	7011	E	916 441-1200	11132
HDR Engineering Inc	8711	D	916 564-4214	18728
Health Lf Orgnization Inc Halo	8099	D	916 428-3788	17152
Hearst Stations Inc	4833	C	916 446-3333	8044
Hearst Stations Inc	4833	C	916 447-5858	8045
Hearst Stations Inc **(DH)**	4833	D	916 446-3333	8046
Heartland Child & Family Svcs	8322	D	916 922-9868	17600
Helping Hearts Foundation Inc	8082	D	916 368-7200	16889
Hendrickson Truck Lines Inc	4213	C	916 387-9614	7550
Hendrickson Trucking Inc	4213	B	916 387-9614	7551
Henwood Energy Services Inc **(DH)**	8711	C	916 955-6031	18730
Heritage Community Credit Un **(PA)**	6061	E	916 364-1700	9792
Hg Holdings Inc	7381	E	916 944-2828	14068
Hill Top Hospitality LLC	7011	E	530 888-7441	11137
Hironaka Promotions LLC	2759	E	916 631-8470	3736
Hmr Architects Inc	8712	E	916 736-2724	18890
Hoppy Brewing Co Inc	2085	E	916 451-4677	2772
Horizon West Inc	8051	E	916 331-4590	16026
HP Hood LLC	2026	B	916 379-9266	2191
Huhtamaki Inc	5199	D	916 688-4938	9661
Human Resource Consultants	8093	E	916 485-6500	17024
Humboldt Dev LLC	7379	D	213 295-2890	13907
Hunt & Sons Inc **(PA)**	5171	E	916 383-4868	9525
Hurley Construction Inc	1522	D	916 446-7599	748
Hydroscience Engineers Inc **(PA)**	8711	E	916 364-1490	18734
Hylton Security Inc	7381	E	916 442-1000	14070
Iab Brands Inc	3999	F	844 426-2634	7288
Illuminated Creations Inc	3993	E	916 924-1936	7233
Imperial Die Cutting Inc	2675	E	916 443-6142	3394

	SIC	EMP	PHONE	ENTRY #
Inland Business Machines Inc **(DH)**	7699	D	916 928-0770	14756
Intake Screens Inc	3496	F	916 665-2727	4971
Interior Specialists Inc	7389	E	916 779-1666	14307
Interntional Un Oper Engineers **(PA)**	8631	D	916 444-6880	18363
Interpress Technologies Inc **(HQ)**	5199	E	916 929-9771	9663
Interwest Insurance Svcs LLC **(PA)**	6411	C	916 488-3100	10299
Introlligent Inc **(PA)**	7379	E	916 436-8889	13919
Ips Printing Inc	2752	F	916 442-8961	3661
Iron Mechanical Inc **(PA)**	1711	D	916 341-3530	1286
Is Inc	7373	E	916 920-1700	13614
ITW Blding Cmponents Group Inc	3443	E	916 387-0116	4722
Iunlimited Incorporated	7381	C	916 218-6198	14071
Iuoe Sttonary Engineers Lcl 39	8631	E	916 928-0399	18368
J B Company	1542	D	916 929-3003	895
Jackson Construction **(PA)**	1541	E	916 381-8113	799
Jackson Laboratory	8733	E	916 373-5905	19223
Jampro Antennas Inc	3663	D	916 383-1177	5849
Java City **(HQ)**	5149	D	916 565-5500	9459
Jck Legacy Company **(HQ)**	2711	C	916 321-1844	3451
Jensen Enterprises Inc	5039	D	916 992-8301	8645
Jj Pfister Distilling Co LLC	2085	F	503 939-9535	2774
JJR Enterprises Inc **(HQ)**	7629	D	916 363-2666	14701
John Boyd Enterprises Inc **(PA)**	3714	C	916 381-4790	6584
John C Destefano	2434	E	916 276-4056	3182
John F Otto Inc	1542	C	916 441-6870	904
John Jackson Masonry	1741	D	916 381-8021	1649
John Stewart Company	6531	E	916 561-0323	10586
John Zink Company LLC	3823	E	918 234-1884	6723
Johnson Schchter Lwis A Prof L	8111	E	916 921-5800	17297
Jts Engineering Cons Inc	8711	E	916 441-6708	18744
Kaiser Foundation Hospitals	8093	C	916 482-1132	17027
Kaiser Foundation Hospitals	8093	C	916 525-6790	17029
Kaiser Foundation Hospitals	8062	A	916 558-6520	16403
Kaiser Foundation Hospitals	8742	A	916 974-6211	19548
Kaiser Foundation Hospitals	8062	A	916 973-5000	16408
Kaiser Foundation Hospitals	8011	A	916 688-2000	15485
Kaiser Foundation Hospitals	6324	C	916 973-5000	10139
Kaiser Foundation Hospitals	8062	A	916 525-6300	16418
Kds Nail Products	3999	E	916 381-9358	7291
Kelleher Corporation	5031	E	916 561-2860	8554
Key Business Solutions Inc **(PA)**	7371	E	916 646-2080	12559
Keystone Door & Bldg Sup Inc	1751	E	916 623-8100	1745
Khanna Entps - II Ltd Partnr	7011	E	916 338-5800	11228
Kimmel Construction Inc	1542	D	916 927-3118	909
Kings Arena Ltd Partnership	7941	D	916 928-0000	14909
Kitchens Now Inc	2434	E	916 229-8222	3185
Kleary Masonry Inc	1741	C	916 869-6835	1651
Kratos Unmnned Arial Systems I **(HQ)**	8711	B	916 431-7977	18750
Kronick Mskvitz Tdmann Grard A **(PA)**	8111	C	916 321-4500	17306
Kvie Inc **(PA)**	4833	D	916 929-5843	8051
Kxtv Inc	4833	C	916 441-2345	8052
La Familia Counseling Ctr Inc	8322	D	916 452-3601	17632
Landmark Healthcare Svcs Inc **(DH)**	8041	C	800 638-4557	15865
Langills General Machine Inc	3599	E	916 452-0167	5559
Larkspur Hsptality Dev MGT LLC	7011	E	916 646-1212	11252
Laser Recharge Inc **(PA)**	3955	E	916 813-2717	7207
Laser Skin Srgery Med Group In	8011	E	916 456-0400	15502
Lawson Mechanical Contractors **(PA)**	1711	D	916 381-5000	1302
Lbn Leisure Care LLC	8361	A	916 604-3780	18135
League of California Cities **(PA)**	8743	D	916 658-8200	19691
League of Women Voters Cal **(PA)**	8651	F	916 442-7215	18537
Legal Services Northern Cal **(PA)**	8111	E	916 551-2150	17313
Levan Import-Export Inc	5013	E	916 381-5712	8455
Lewis S Bliss MD	8011	E	916 863-3143	15504
Lexisnexis Courtlink Inc	8621	D	425 974-5000	18339
Licap Technologies Inc	2819	D	916 329-8099	3791
Lifeline SEC & Automtn Inc	3699	D	916 285-9078	6532
Limelight Bar and Cafe LLC	7999	E	916 446-2208	15217
Lionakis **(PA)**	8712	C	916 558-1901	18895
Little Blssom Mntssori Schl In	8351	E	916 515-0550	17965
Longs Drug Stores Cal Inc	7384	E	916 334-7170	14164
Longs Drug Stores Cal Inc	7384	D	916 391-1200	14165
Lotus Bed Solutions LLC	2511	F	415 756-5099	3281
Lpa Insurance Agency Inc	7372	D	916 286-7850	13284
Lpas Inc	8712	D	916 443-0335	18897
Lr Leasing Inc	4213	E	916 438-0888	7562
Lumens LLC **(DH)**	5063	E	916 444-5585	8866
Lupton Excavation Inc	1794	D	916 387-1104	1963
Lyon Realty	6531	C	916 481-3840	10604
Lyon Realty **(PA)**	6531	D	916 574-8800	10608
M Neils Engineering Inc	8711	D	916 923-4400	18757
Macias Gini & OConnell LLP **(PA)**	8721	D	916 928-4600	18973
Madsen Roofg Waterproofing Inc	1761	E	916 361-3327	1818
Mailboxes and Bus Svcs Inc	7389	E	916 971-4957	14327
Mariner Health Care Inc	8051	E	916 481-5500	16044
Mariner Health Care Inc	8051	E	916 422-4825	16048
Mark III Construction Inc **(PA)**	1731	D	916 381-8080	1535
Marketone Builders Inc	1521	E	916 928-7474	668
Markstein Bev Co Sacramento	5181	C	916 920-3911	9554
Marquee Fire Protection LLC **(PA)**	1711	E	916 641-7997	1311
Marticus Electric Inc	1731	E	916 368-2186	1536
Martin Brothers Cnstr LLC **(PA)**	1611	D	916 386-1600	1056
Mary Anns Baking Co Inc	2051	C	916 681-7444	2394
Matheny Sars Linkert Jaime LLP	8111	D	916 978-3434	17326
Matheson Fast Freight Inc	4213	B	209 342-0184	7565
Matheson Trucking Inc **(PA)**	4213	E	916 685-2330	7567
Matsudas By Green Acres LLC	0181	C	916 673-9290	130
Matterhorn Ice Cream Inc	2024	F	208 287-8916	2179
Maxim Healthcare Services Inc	7363	D	916 614-9539	12180
May-Han Electric Inc	1731	D	916 929-0150	1537
MBK Engineers	8711	E	916 456-4400	18764
McClatchy Company	8999	A	916 321-1941	19911
McClatchy Newspapers Inc **(DH)**	2711	A	916 321-1855	3456
Meals On Wheels By ACC	8322	E	916 444-9533	17643
Medical Vision Technology Inc **(PA)**	8011	E	916 731-8040	15528
Meditab Software Inc	7372	D	510 201-0130	13304
Medmark Trtmnt Ctrs - Scrmnto	8093	E	916 391-4293	17038
Medstar LLC	4119	D	916 669-0550	7389
Mek Norwood Pines LLC	8051	D	916 922-7177	16062
Mel Rapton Inc	7699	C	916 514-4050	14764
Mencarini & Jarwin Inc	3471	E	916 383-1660	4912
Mering Holdings **(PA)**	7311	D	916 441-0571	11771
Merrill Lynch Prce Fnner Smith	6211	D	916 648-6200	9989
Messer LLC	2813	F	916 381-1606	3775
Metal Manufacturing Co Inc	3442	E	916 922-3484	4705
Metropltan Pain MGT Cons Inc A	8011	E	916 568-8338	15536
Microform Precision LLC	3444	D	916 419-0580	4790
Milgard Manufacturing LLC	5031	C	916 387-0700	8595
Millennium Termite & Pest	7342	E	707 673-1050	11904
Mission Linen Supply	7213	D	916 423-3179	11638
Mission Linen Supply	7218	D	916 423-3135	11664
Mitsubshi Chem Crbn Fibr Cmpst **(DH)**	3624	C	916 386-1733	5672
Modis Inc	7371	C	800 467-4448	12615
Modsquad Inc **(PA)**	8742	C	916 913-4465	19579
Montez Glass Inc	1793	E	916 452-1288	1938
Moorefield Construction Inc	1542	E	916 614-7888	926
Morton Golf LLC	7992	D	916 481-4653	15012
Morton Golf Management LLC	7992	D	916 481-4653	15013
Mounting Systems Inc	1711	D	916 374-8872	1313
Murphy Astin Adams Schnfeld LL	8111	E	916 446-2300	17341
Mutual Assstnce Ntwrk of Del P **(PA)**	8322	E	916 927-7694	17652
Mw McWong International Inc **(PA)**	3648	E	916 371-8080	5747
Myers & Sons Construction LLC	1623	C	916 283-9950	1122
Myers & Sons Construction LP **(HQ)**	1611	C	916 283-9950	1063
Myers & Sons Hi-Way Safety Inc	3669	F	909 591-1781	5891
National Auto Prts Whse - CA I **(HQ)**	5013	E	510 786-3555	8459
National Transfer and Stor Inc	4214	E	916 383-8800	7628
Ncsra Medical Corporation	8011	E	916 389-7100	15546
New Generation Software Inc	7372	E	916 920-2200	13328
New West Partitions	1742	C	916 456-8365	1693
Niello Imports II Inc	7538	C	916 480-2800	14579
Nivagen Pharmaceuticals Inc **(PA)**	2834	E	916 364-1662	3955
Nmi Industrial Holdings Inc	8711	D	916 635-7030	18779
Norcal Gold Inc	6531	E	916 285-1000	10627
North Area News **(PA)**	2711	E	916 486-1248	3468
North Wind Cnstr Svcs LLC	1521	D	916 333-3015	678
Northern California Inalliance **(PA)**	8322	C	916 381-1300	17660
Northwest Stffing Rsources Inc	7361	A	916 960-2668	12112
Nossaman LLP	8111	D	916 442-8888	17347
Ntt Glbal Data Ctrs Amrcas Inc **(DH)**	7376	B	916 286-3000	13816
Nv5 Inc **(DH)**	8711	D	916 641-9100	18781
OfficeMax North America Inc	5044	E	916 388-0120	8654
Ogilvy Pub Rltons Wrldwide LLC	7311	E	916 231-7700	11775
Oleander Holdings LLC	8051	D	916 331-4590	16087
Olson Hagel Fishburn LLC	8111	E	916 442-2952	17349
Olympic Cascade Publishing **(DH)**	2711	C	916 321-1000	3470
Omega Products Corp **(HQ)**	3299	D	916 635-3335	4538
Omic USA Inc California	7389	E	916 285-8700	14343
One Workplace L Ferrari LLC	1799	E	916 553-5900	2049
Opendoor Labs Inc	6531	D	888 352-7075	10632
Oregon PCF Bldg Pdts Calif Inc	5031	D	916 381-8051	8600
Orrick Hrringtn Sut Foundtn	8111	E	916 329-7928	17350
Ortech Inc	3253	F	916 549-9696	4401
Outfront Media LLC	7312	E	209 466-5021	11797
Owen & Company	6411	D	916 993-2700	10329
Pabco Clay Products LLC	3251	E	916 859-6320	4400
Pacific Civil & Strl Cons LLC	8711	E	916 421-1000	18785
Pacific Coast Contg Spc Inc	5031	D	916 929-3100	8601
Pacific Copy and Print	7334	E	916 928-8434	11849
Pacific Corrugated Pipe Co LLC	3272	E	916 383-4891	4445
Pacific Gas and Electric Co	4911	C	916 923-7007	8135
Pacific Gas and Electric Co	4911	C	916 275-2763	8180
Pacific Legal Foundation **(PA)**	8111	E	916 419-7111	17353
Pacific Neon	3993	E	916 927-0527	7247
Pacific Northwest Pubg Co Inc	2711	B	916 321-1828	3471
Pacific Powder Coating Inc	3479	E	916 381-1154	4943
Pacific Sfood - Sacramento LLC	5142	C	916 419-5500	9329
Pacific Truck Tank Inc	3713	E	916 379-9280	6568
Pain Diagnstc & Trtmnt Ctr LLP	8011	E	916 231-8755	15582
Paladin Prtction Spcalists Inc	7381	C	916 331-3175	14084
Paracorp Incorporated **(PA)**	8111	D	916 576-7000	17354
Paratransit Incorporated **(PA)**	4119	C	916 429-2009	7394
Parc Specialty Contractors	1799	D	916 992-5405	2052
Parker Landscape Dev Inc	0781	E	916 383-4071	434
Patricks Construction Clean-Up	1629	D	916 452-5495	1173
Patterson Travel Agency	4724	E	916 929-5555	7804
Paul Baker Printing Inc	2752	E	916 969-8317	3682
Pcg Technology Solutions LLC	7379	C	916 565-8090	13958
PDQ Automatic Transm Parts Inc	7537	D	916 681-7701	14541
Pei Placer Electric Inc **(PA)**	1731	E	916 338-4400	1562
Penhall Company	1799	E	916 386-1589	2054
Penney Opco LLC	7231	D	916 564-0315	11691
Peoplefinders Ngt Por Priof	2741	F	916 341-0227	3590
Pep Boys Manny Moe Jack of Cal	7549	E	916 331-4880	14670

GEOGRAPHIC

Employment Codes: A=Over 500 employees, B=251-500, C=101-250, D=51-100, E=20-50 F=10-19

SACRAMENTO, CA GEOGRAPHIC SECTION

	SIC	EMP	PHONE	ENTRY #
Performance Tech Partners LLC	7379	C	800 787-4143	13959
Permanente Medical Group Inc	8011	A	916 688-2055	15595
Permanente Medical Group Inc	8011	A	916 486-5686	15609
Perry-Smith LLP	8721	E	916 441-1000	18983
Peter	2674	E	916 588-9954	3391
Pets Choice Inc	8011	E	916 229-9587	15628
Philip A Stitt Agency	2394	E	916 451-2801	3041
Phoenix Schools Inc	8351	D	916 442-0722	17997
Phoenix Schools Inc	8351	D	916 452-5150	17998
Pinsetters Inc	7933	D	916 488-7545	14897
Pk1 Inc **(HQ)**	2653	D	916 858-1300	3364
Poolmaster Inc	3944	D	916 567-9800	7182
Poppycolor LLC	2752	E	916 549-6209	3685
Pos Portal Inc **(HQ)**	3578	E	530 695-3005	5423
Positive Option Family Service **(PA)**	8322	E	916 973-2838	17676
Premier Woodworking LLC	2431	E	916 289-4058	3147
Pro-Tech Fire Prtction Systems	1711	D	916 388-0255	1338
Probe Information Services Inc	7381	C	916 676-1826	14089
Procida Landscape Inc	0782	C	916 387-5296	497
Procter & Gamble Mfg Co	2841	C	916 383-3800	4064
Professnal Ldscp Solutions Inc	0781	E	916 424-3815	437
Prs/Roebbelen JV	1542	E	916 641-0324	938
Public Employees Retirement	6371	B	916 795-3400	10218
Public Health Institute	8099	C	916 285-1231	17169
Purolator Liquid Process Inc	3569	E	916 689-2328	5231
Quality Inv Prpts Scrmento LLC	7374	D	916 679-2100	13747
Quanex Screens LLC	3442	F	916 386-8728	4707
R V Karls Inc	5013	E	916 992-9703	8461
Rainforth Grau Architects	8712	E	916 368-7990	18906
Ram Commercial Enterprises Inc	6531	E	916 429-1205	10652
Raney Planning & MGT Inc	8748	E	916 372-6100	19846
Rapid Courier & Freight Inc	4213	E	916 387-5505	7575
Raymar Information Tech Inc **(PA)**	3661	E	916 783-1951	5807
Rcb Corporation **(PA)**	6022	D	916 567-2600	9745
Rcg Logistics LLC	4213	D	916 999-1234	7576
Reach Air Medical Services LLC **(HQ)**	4119	E	707 324-2400	7399
Reading International Inc	7832	E	916 442-0985	14817
Recp/Wndsor Scramento Ventr LP	7011	E	916 455-6800	11386
Red River Consulting Svcs Inc **(HQ)**	7371	E	916 383-9005	12733
Redi-Gro Corporation	5191	E	916 381-6063	9607
Redtail Technology Inc	7371	D	800 206-5030	12736
Reed & Graham Inc	2951	E	888 381-0800	4189
Regional Cardiology Associate **(PA)**	8011	E	916 564-3040	15648
Relationship Skills Center	8322	E	916 362-1900	17689
Rels Foods	5149	E	916 927-7677	9481
Renne Sloan Holtzman Sakai LLP **(PA)**	8111	E	415 678-3800	17361
Republic Electric Inc	1731	C	916 294-0140	1580
Republic Electric West Inc	1731	D	916 294-0140	1581
Republic Intelligent	1731	D	916 515-0855	1582
RES-Care Inc	8052	D	916 567-1244	16198
RES-Care Inc	8082	E	916 307-3737	16931
RES-Care Inc	8082	E	530 823-6475	16932
Rescue Concrete Inc	1771	D	916 852-2400	1905
Resources For Ind Living Inc	8322	D	916 446-3074	17692
Retinal Consultants Inc **(PA)**	8011	D	916 454-4861	15651
Rex Moore Group Inc	1731	B	916 372-1300	1583
Rex More Elec Cntrs Engners In **(PA)**	1731	B	916 372-1300	1584
Rielli Insur & Fincl Svcs LL **(PA)**	6411	E	916 234-1490	10338
River City Bank **(HQ)**	6022	D	916 567-2600	9746
River City Millwork Inc	2431	E	916 364-8981	3149
River City Printers LLC	2752	E	916 638-8400	3694
River City Staffing Inc	7361	E	916 485-1588	12128
River Oak Center For Children **(PA)**	8093	C	916 609-5100	17062
River Oak Center For Children	8059	D	916 550-5600	16261
Rl Liquidators LLC	7389	E	916 747-7762	14390
Rohrer Bros Inc	5148	E	916 443-5921	9427
Ronald Vanderbeek **(PA)**	8059	E	916 481-9240	16264
Rose Fmly Crtive Empwrment Ctr	8641	D	916 376-7916	18455
Rowar Corporation	1799	E	916 626-3030	2063
Royal Plywood Company LLC	5031	D	916 426-3292	8605
Runyon Saltzman Inc	7311	D	916 446-9900	11780
Rural County Rep Cal	8743	E	916 447-4806	19697
Russell Sigler Inc	5075	D	916 387-3000	9013
Russo Brothers Transport Inc	4789	D	916 519-1334	7893
S & H Welding Inc	3443	F	916 386-8921	4729
S&F Management Company LLC	8051	A	916 922-8855	16103
Sac City Blue Inc	7334	E	916 454-0800	11850
Sac River Water Treatment Plan	4941	E	916 808-3101	8261
Saccani Distributing Company	5181	D	916 441-0213	9562
Sacramento 1st Mortgage Inc	6163	E	916 486-6500	9947
Sacramento 49er Travel Plaza	7011	C	916 927-4774	11425
Sacramento Animal Hospital Inc	0742	E	916 451-7213	334
Sacramento Area Emerg Housing	8322	D	916 455-2160	17698
Sacramento Area Sewer District **(PA)**	4953	B	916 876-6000	8362
Sacramento Baking Co Inc	2051	E	916 361-2000	2402
Sacramento Childrens Home **(PA)**	8361	C	916 452-3981	18175
Sacramento Coca-Cola Btlg Inc **(HQ)**	2086	B	916 928-2300	2810
Sacramento Credit Union **(PA)**	6062	D	916 444-6070	9836
Sacramento Cy Unified Schl Dst **(PA)**	8641	B	916 643-7400	18458
Sacramento Cy Unified Schl Dst	8351	D	916 277-6277	18008
Sacramento Cy Unified Schl Dst	8351	D	916 277-6263	18009
Sacramento Cy Unified Schl Dst	8351	D	916 264-4186	18010
Sacramento Cy Unified Schl Dst	8351	D	916 277-6259	18011
Sacramento Ear Nose & Throat **(PA)**	8011	D	916 736-3399	15654
Sacramento Employement & Train **(PA)**	8331	C	916 263-3800	17834
Sacramento Engineering Cons	8711	E	916 368-4468	18807
Sacramento Harness Association	8611	D	916 239-4040	18315
Sacramento Heart and Cardiovas **(PA)**	8011	E	916 830-2000	15655
Sacramento Housing Dev Corp **(PA)**	8748	D	916 440-1333	19852
Sacramento Intl Jet Ctr Inc	5172	D	916 428-8292	9538
Sacramento Job Corp	8331	E	916 391-1016	17835
Sacramento Kings Ltd Partnr	7941	E	916 928-0000	14911
Sacramento Laundry Company Inc	7215	E	916 930-0330	11650
Sacramento Loaves & Fishes **(PA)**	8322	D	916 446-0874	17699
Sacramento Memorial Lawn	7261	E	916 421-1171	11700
Sacramento Municpl Utility Dst **(PA)**	4911	A	916 452-3211	8196
Sacramento Municpl Utility Dst	4911	B	916 452-3211	8197
Sacramento Municpl Utility Dst	4911	D	916 732-5155	8198
Sacramento Municpl Utility Dst	4911	B	916 732-5616	8199
Sacramento Operating Co LP	8051	C	916 422-4825	16105
Sacramento Rebar Inc **(PA)**	1791	E	916 447-9700	1931
Sacramento Reg Co Sanit Dist **(PA)**	4959	C	916 876-6000	8403
Sacramento Regional Trnst Dist **(PA)**	4111	A	916 726-2877	7346
Sacramento Regional Trnst Dist	4111	E	916 362-9490	7347
Sacramento Suburban Water Dst	4941	D	916 972-7171	8262
Sacramento Suburban Water Dst	4941	D	916 972-7171	8263
Sacramento Theatre Company	7922	D	916 446-7501	14859
Sacramento Theatrical Ltg Ltd	7922	D	916 447-3258	14860
Sacramento Tree Foundation	8641	E	916 924-8733	18459
Sacramento Zoological Society	8422	E	916 808-5888	18295
Sacramnto Chnese Cmnty Svcs CT	8322	C	916 442-4228	17700
Sacramnto Cmnty Cble Fundation	8999	E	916 456-8600	19916
Sacramnto Emplyment Trning AGC	8331	C	916 263-3800	17836
Sacramnto Gstrntrlogy Med Grou	8011	D	916 454-0655	15656
Sacramnto Hsing Rdvlpment Agcy	6411	D	916 440-1376	10340
Sacramnto Hsing Rdvlpment Agcy	6531	D	916 440-1399	10657
Sacramnto Mdtown Endoscopy Ctr	8093	D	916 733-6940	17063
Sacramnto Mtro A Qulty MGT Dst	8748	D	916 874-4800	19853
Sacramnto Ntiv Amercn Hlth Ctr	8011	C	916 341-0575	15657
Sacramnto Plstic Rcnstrctive S	8011	D	916 929-1833	15658
Sacramnto Soc For The Prvntion	8699	D	916 383-7387	18586
Sacramnto Vly Alarm SEC Sys In	1731	E	916 452-1481	1597
Saia Inc	4213	D	916 483-8331	7586
Saint Claires Nursing Ctr LLC	8051	C	916 392-4440	16106
Sale 121 Corp **(PA)**	3572	D	888 233-7667	5314
Santos Legacy Builders LLC	1521	D	916 439-2777	701
Sasco	8748	B	916 565-4120	19858
Scandia Sports Inc	7999	E	916 331-5757	15239
Schetter Electric Inc **(PA)**	1731	D	916 446-2521	1600
Schetter Electric LLC	1731	D	916 446-2521	1602
School Services California Inc	8742	E	916 446-7517	19628
Schools Financial Credit Union **(PA)**	6061	C	916 569-5400	9818
Schuering Zimmerman & Scully	8111	E	916 567-0400	17366
Scott A Porter Prof Corp	8111	D	916 929-1481	17367
Scusd	4789	E	916 277-6705	7894
Search Group Incorporated	8733	D	916 392-2550	19235
Sedgwick Claims MGT Svcs Inc	6411	D	916 568-7394	10346
Seiu Untd Hlthcare Wrkrs-West	8631	E	916 326-5850	18374
Sellands Broadway Inc	8742	E	916 732-3390	19629
Senior Mercy Housing Inc	8361	D	916 733-6510	18179
Sequoia Elementary School Pta	8641	E	916 228-5850	18466
Setzer Forest Products Inc **(PA)**	2431	C	916 442-2555	3150
Seven Up Btlg Co San Francisco	2086	C	916 929-7777	2813
Seyfarth Shaw LLP	8111	C	916 448-0159	17370
Sg Downtown LLC	7011	E	916 545-7100	11466
Shamrock Foods Company	5149	B	602 819-1654	9484
Shasta Linen Supply Inc	7213	E	916 443-5966	11646
Sheet Mtal Fabrication Sup Inc	3444	D	916 641-6884	4817
Sheraton LLC	7011	D	916 447-1700	11469
Shermn-Lehr Cstm Tile Wrks Inc	1743	D	916 386-0417	1720
Shield Commercial Inc **(PA)**	6163	D	916 684-9093	9948
Shine Logistics LLC	4731	C	916 518-9393	7853
Shriners Hspitals For Children	8062	B	916 453-2050	16525
Siemens Energy Inc	4911	D	916 391-2993	8200
Siemens Industry Inc	3822	C	916 681-3000	6705
Siemens Mobility Inc	3711	A	916 681-3000	6560
Sierra Forever Families	8322	E	916 368-5114	17744
Sierra Office Systems Pdts Inc **(PA)**	2752	D	916 369-0491	3697
Sierra Single Ply Inc **(PA)**	1761	E	916 640-0123	1836
Signet Testing Labs Inc	7389	D	916 374-0754	14404
Silverado Building Mtls Inc **(PA)**	5031	E	916 361-7374	8608
Simas Floor Co Inc **(PA)**	1752	C	916 452-4933	1776
Sky Park Gardens Assisted	8361	D	916 422-5650	18182
Skyline Scaffold Inc	1799	D	916 391-8929	2070
Skyslope Inc	7379	D	916 833-2390	13977
SL One Global Inc **(PA)**	5141	D	916 993-4100	9304
SLHCC Inc	8051	E	916 457-6521	16123
Social Services Cal Dept	8322	D	916 657-2346	17748
Society For Blind	8699	E	916 452-8271	18592
Solar Industries Inc	3433	E	916 567-9650	4636
Solid Solutions 24/7 Inc	7389	D	916 800-1847	14408
Southern Cal Disc Tire Co Inc	5013	C	916 427-1961	8468
Southerncarlson Inc	5032	F	916 375-8322	8635
Southgate Glass & Screen Inc **(PA)**	5039	E	916 476-8396	8647
Southgate Glass & Screen Inc	5039	E	916 476-8396	8648
Southgate Recreation & Pk Dst	7999	D	916 421-7275	15244
Southpnte Chrstn Ctr Scrmnto C	2211	E	916 504-3370	2965
Spare-Time Inc	7991	D	916 649-0909	14977
Spare-Time Inc	7991	D	916 488-8100	14978
Spectrum Services Group Inc	8748	D	916 760-7913	19865
Spencer Building Maintenance	7349	B	916 922-1900	12001
SRC Milling Co LLC	2077	E	916 363-4821	2460
St Vncent De Paul Bltmore Inc	8322	D	916 485-3482	17755
Stanford Settlement Inc	8322	E	916 927-1303	17757

	SIC	EMP	PHONE	ENTRY #
Stanford Youth Solutions **(PA)**	8322	D	916 344-0199	17759
Starving Students Inc	4214	E	916 927-7071	7635
Starwest Botanicals LLC **(PA)**	5149	D	916 638-8100	9489
State Compensation Insur Fund	6331	D	530 223-7000	10180
State Compensation Insur Fund	6331	D	916 263-8102	10182
State Compensation Insur Fund	6331	D	916 924-5100	10184
State Hornet	2711	C	916 278-6583	3484
Stoel Rives LLP **(PA)**	8111	D	916 447-0700	17379
Stommel Inc **(PA)**	1731	E	916 646-6626	1614
Stratgies To Empwer People Inc **(PA)**	8052	B	916 679-1527	16207
Sturgeon Construction Inc	1542	E	916 452-6108	968
Sulzer Pump Solutions US Inc	3561	E	916 925-8508	5179
Summit Funding Inc	6162	D	916 571-3000	9933
Sunrise Shs Pedorthic Svc Corp	3143	F	916 368-7700	4342
Support For Family LLC	8322	D	877 916-9111	17762
Support For Home Inc	1521	E	530 792-8484	714
Surgical Care Affiliate	8721	E	916 529-4590	18998
Sutter Club	8641	D	916 442-0456	18473
Sutter Health	8062	C	916 733-1025	16583
Sutter Health	8062	C	916 733-9588	16586
Sutter Health	8062	C	916 262-9400	16601
Sutter Health	8062	C	916 566-4819	16602
Sutter Health	8062	C	916 262-9414	16611
Sutter Health	8011	A	916 646-8300	15717
Sutter Health	8011	D	916 681-8852	15718
Sutter Health **(PA)**	8062	A	916 733-8800	16617
Sutter Health	8093	D	916 220-1927	17079
Sutter Health	8071	D	916 454-6600	16807
Sutter Health	8011	D	916 451-3344	15721
Sutter Health	8062	C	916 453-5955	16630
Sutter Health	8011	D	916 453-4528	15722
Sutter Health	8011	D	916 929-3393	15723
Sutter Health	8062	C	916 386-3000	16636
Sutter Health	8062	C	916 731-5672	16650
Sutter Health	8062	C	916 453-9999	16651
Sutter Health	8011	D	916 733-5051	15724
Sutter Health	8011	D	916 262-9456	15725
Sutter Health At Work	8011	E	916 565-8607	15726
Sutter Hlth Rhabilitation Svcs	8062	D	916 733-3040	16659
Sutter Hlth Scrmnto Sierra Reg	8099	C	916 733-7080	17184
Sutter Hlth Scrmnto Sierra Reg **(HQ)**	8062	B	916 733-8800	16662
Sutter Hlth Scrmnto Sierra Reg	8062	B	916 454-2222	16664
Sutter Hlth Scrmnto Sierra Reg	8062	B	916 446-3100	16665
Sutter Hlth Scrmnto Sierra Reg	8062	B	916 924-7666	16666
Sutter Hlth Scrmnto Sierra Reg	8011	C	916 386-3000	15727
Sutter Hlth Scrmnto Sierra Reg	8062	B	916 733-3095	16668
Sutter Inc	8011	E	916 733-5097	15728
Sutter Medical Group Inc **(PA)**	8062	E	916 733-5090	16670
Sutter Physician Services **(HQ)**	8742	A	916 854-6600	19645
Sutter Valley Hospitals **(HQ)**	8062	B	916 733-8800	16677
Sutter Valley Med Foundation	8049	D	916 924-7764	15899
Swinerton Builders Hc	1542	C	916 383-4825	969
System Integrators Inc **(HQ)**	7373	C	916 830-2400	13673
Taggle Systems LLC	4812	E	800 619-2919	7915
Taylor Communications Inc	2761	F	916 927-1891	3757
Taylor Wings Inc	3444	E	916 851-9464	4823
Tdic Insurance Solutions	6411	E	800 733-0633	10358
Teal Bend Golf Club Inc	7997	D	916 922-5209	15159
Tech Service 2 U Inc	7378	E	888 931-0942	13823
Teeco Products Inc	3714	E	916 688-3535	6595
Tele-Direct Communications Inc	7389	E	916 348-2170	14429
Telemundo of Fresno LLC	4833	E	559 252-5101	8055
Thermcraft Inc	2752	F	916 363-9411	3703
Thomas H Murphy Od	8042	E	916 929-1169	15874
Thunder Mountain Entps Inc **(PA)**	1799	D	916 381-3400	2075
Timberlake Corporation	7352	D	916 423-2198	12015
Tlcs Inc	8322	C	916 441-0123	17769
Tmp LLC	3442	E	916 920-2555	4710
TNT Industrial Contractors Inc **(PA)**	3531	E	916 395-8400	5042
Total Monitoring Services Inc	7382	E	916 480-4828	14150
Tower Brew Co LLC	2082	F	916 606-3373	2498
Townsend & Schmidt Masonry	1741	E	916 383-5354	1654
Training Toward Self Reliance	8322	E	916 442-8877	17771
Trainor Fairbrook A Prof Corp	8111	E	916 929-7000	17383
Transhumance Holding Co Inc **(PA)**	2011	E	530 758-3091	2106
Travelator Inc	7389	E	415 322-9265	14440
Treaster Miles & Associates	1799	D	916 373-1800	2079
Tree Technology Inc	0783	E	916 386-9416	523
Trimark Erf Inc	5046	E	916 447-6600	8770
Trinity Technology Group Inc	7373	D	916 779-0201	13682
Turner Construction Company	1542	D	916 444-4421	978
U Haul Co of Sacramento Inc **(HQ)**	7513	E	916 929-2215	14473
Uc Davis Hlth Sys Fclties Dsig	8011	E	916 734-7024	15746
Ultra Glass	3231	F	916 338-3911	4393
Unilab Corporation	8071	A	916 927-9900	16812
Unilab Corporation	8071	A	916 733-3330	16816
United Animal Nations	8699	E	916 429-2457	18604
United Behavioral Health	8093	E	916 927-0606	17084
United Engrg Resources Inc **(PA)**	8742	D	916 375-6700	19660
United Parcel Service Inc	4215	C	916 373-4089	7664
United Parcel Service Inc	4215	C	916 857-0311	7674
United States Cold Storage Inc	2097	E	916 392-9160	2863
United Way Cal Capitl Reg	8322	E	916 368-3000	17774
Universal Limousine & Trnsp Co	4119	D	916 361-5466	7409
Universal Network Dev Corp **(PA)**	8748	C	916 475-1200	19880
University California Davis	8011	D	916 734-8514	15769
University California Davis	8011	D	916 734-3574	15773
University California Davis	8011	D	916 734-2846	15774
University California Davis	8062	C	916 734-3141	16701
University California Davis	8011	D	916 734-3588	15775
University California Davis	8011	D	916 734-2105	15777
University California Davis	8062	C	916 734-2011	16702
University California Davis	8011	D	916 734-6280	15780
University California Davis	8011	D	916 442-1011	15781
University California Davis	8062	C	916 734-5113	16703
University Enterprises Inc	8741	A	916 278-7001	19414
Vacuum Process Engineering Inc	8731	D	916 925-6100	19146
Valassis Direct Mail Inc	7331	D	916 923-2398	11843
Valine Court Senior Care Inc	8361	D	916 394-9400	18196
Valley Communications Inc **(PA)**	1731	D	916 349-7300	1627
Valley Health Care Systems Inc	7361	C	916 505-4112	12150
Value Place Hotel	7011	D	916 688-1330	11553
Vampire Penguin LLC **(PA)**	2024	F	916 553-4197	2185
Van Wolfs LLC	5142	E	916 372-6464	9331
Vanir Construction MGT Inc **(PA)**	8741	D	916 444-3700	19416
Vanir Development Company Inc	1542	E	916 419-2400	980
Vasko Electric Inc	1731	D	916 568-7700	1629
Village Nurseries Whl LLC	5193	B	916 993-2292	9641
Visions Recycling Inc	4953	E	916 564-9121	8379
Visions Unlimited **(PA)**	8093	D	916 394-0800	17090
Volunters Amer Nthrn Cal Nthrn **(PA)**	8322	B	916 265-3400	17783
Wade Casey	7381	D	916 395-9996	14110
Washoe Equipment Inc	3645	D	916 395-4700	5729
Water Resources Cal Dept	8733	D	916 574-1423	19245
Water Resources Cal Dept	3823	E	916 651-9203	6738
Watson Companies Inc	1761	E	916 481-6293	1845
Weave Inc **(PA)**	7363	D	916 448-2321	12208
Weidner Archtctral Sgng/Huse S	3993	D	800 561-7446	7260
Weintraub Tobin Chediak **(PA)**	8111	E	916 558-6000	17394
Welcome Group Inc	7011	D	916 920-5300	11568
Welcome Natomas LLC	7011	E	916 649-1300	11569
Wellhead Electric Company Inc	4911	E	916 447-5171	8207
Wellspace Health **(PA)**	8093	D	916 325-5556	17091
Wesley B Lasher Inv Corp **(PA)**	7538	D	916 290-8500	14604
Westbrook Enterprises Inc	7699	D	916 929-4680	14785
Wested	8748	E	916 492-9999	19891
Western Health Advantage	6321	D	916 567-1950	10088
Western States Info Netwrk Inc	8733	D	916 263-1188	19251
Westervelt Company	8748	E	916 646-3644	19892
Whiting-Turner Contracting Co	1542	C	916 355-1355	990
Wholesale Outlet Inc **(PA)**	5051	E	916 338-2444	8833
Wickland Pipelines LLC **(PA)**	1382	E	916 978-2432	560
William L Lyon & Assoc Inc **(HQ)**	8741	E	916 978-4200	19426
William L Lyon & Assoc Inc	6531	C	916 447-7878	10687
Willow Springs LLC	8011	D	916 288-0300	15816
Willow Springs LLC	8062	C	916 489-3336	16725
Wilmor & Sons Plumbing & Cnstr	1711	E	916 381-9114	1401
Wilson Trophy Co California	5094	F	916 927-9733	9186
Wind Youth Services Inc	8322	E	916 532-5185	17785
Wittman Enterprises LLC	8721	E	916 381-6552	19006
Women Health Center	8093	E	707 537-1171	17096
Wonderful Union LLC	7929	E	916 526-0285	14883
Wood Rodgers Inc **(PA)**	8711	C	916 341-7760	18864
Woodspring Suites Sacramento	7011	E	916 688-1330	11580
World Textile and Bag Inc	2393	E	916 922-9222	3035
Worldwide Corporate Housing LP	7021	C	916 631-3777	11595
Xl Construction Corporation	1521	D	916 282-2900	732
Xpo Logistics Freight Inc	4213	D	916 399-8291	7615
Ydesign Group LLC **(DH)**	5063	E	866 842-6209	8880
Young Electric Sign Company	3993	E	916 419-8101	7262
Young Minney & Corr LLP	8111	E	916 646-1400	17402
Zanker Road Resource MGT Ltd	4953	E	916 738-9279	8392
Zimmerman Roofing Inc	1761	D	916 454-3667	1847
Zoe Holding Company Inc	7361	D	916 646-3100	12155

SAINT HELENA, CA - Napa County

	SIC	EMP	PHONE	ENTRY #
Apriori Cellar LLC **(PA)**	2084	F	707 512-0606	2506
Brown Estate Vineyards LLC **(PA)**	2084	E	707 963-2435	2516
Bryant Estate	2084	E	707 963-0483	2518
Burgess Cellars Inc	2084	E	707 963-4766	2520
C Mondavi & Family **(PA)**	2084	D	707 967-2200	2522
Central Valley Builders Supply	5083	E	707 963-3622	9033
Chappellet Vineyard	2084	E	707 286-4219	2528
Chappellet Winery Inc **(PA)**	2084	E	707 286-4268	2529
Dana Estates Inc **(PA)**	2084	E	707 963-4365	2542
Duckhorn Portfolio Inc **(HQ)**	2084	C	707 302-2658	2556
Duckhorn Wine Company **(HQ)**	2084	E	707 963-7108	2557
E & J Gallo Winery	2084	E	707 963-2736	2559
Ehren Jordan Wine Cellars LLC	2084	F	707 963-0530	2560
Flora Springs Wine Company	2084	F	707 963-5711	2572
Franciscan Vineyards Inc **(HQ)**	2084	D	707 963-7111	2582
Freemark Abbey Wnery Ltd Prtnr	2084	E	707 963-9694	2587
Gotts Partners LP	7372	E	415 213-2992	13196
Hall Wines LLC	2084	E	707 967-2626	2610
Harold Smith & Son Inc	1629	E	707 963-7977	1165
Harvest Inn Investors I LLC	7011	D	707 963-9463	11131
Herdell Prtg & Lithography Inc	2752	E	707 963-3634	3654
Jack Neal & Son Inc	0172	C	707 963-7303	58
Joseph Phelps Vineyards LLC	2084	D	707 963-2745	2635
Las Alcobas Hotel	7011	E	707 963-7000	11257
Long Meadow Ranch Partners LP	7011	E	707 963-4555	11268
Mallard Holdco LLC **(PA)**	2084	E	707 302-2658	2654
Meadowood Assoc A Ltd Partnr **(PA)**	7011	C	707 963-3646	11293
Meadowood Associates LP	7999	D	707 968-3190	15219
Merryvale Vineyards LLC	2084	E	707 963-2225	2659

SAINT HELENA, CA GEOGRAPHIC SECTION

	SIC	EMP	PHONE	ENTRY #
NAPA Valley Vintners	8611	D	707 963-3388	18310
New Vavin Inc	2084	E	707 963-5972	2667
One True Vine LLC **(PA)**	2084	E	707 967-9398	2673
Provenance Vineyards	2084	E	707 968-3633	2688
Raymond Vineyard & Cellar Inc	0172	E	707 963-3141	71
Red River Lumber Co	2449	E	707 963-1251	3239
Rombauer Vineyards Inc **(PA)**	2084	D	707 963-5170	2702
Ronald F Ogletree Inc	3444	E	707 963-3537	4813
Round Hill Cellars	2084	D	707 968-3200	2703
Silverado Orchards LLC **(PA)**	6513	D	707 963-1461	10459
Spring Mountain Hotel LLC **(PA)**	7011	C	530 304-5619	11495
St Helena Hospital **(HQ)**	8062	A	707 963-3611	16536
St Helena Montessori Schl Inc	8351	E	707 963-1527	18029
Stone Bridge Cellars Inc **(PA)**	2084	E	707 963-2745	2730
Sutter Home Winery Inc **(PA)**	2084	C	707 963-3104	2734
Thomas Leonardini	2084	F	707 963-9454	2742
Tmr Wine Company LLC	2084	E	707 944-8100	2744
Treasury Wine Estates Americas	2084	D	707 963-7115	2746
Turley Wine Cellars Inc	2084	D	707 968-2700	2749
Upper Valley Disposal Service **(PA)**	4953	E	707 963-7988	8376
V Sattui Winery	2084	D	707 963-7774	2752
Warren Resorts Inc	7011	D	707 251-8687	11565

SALIDA, CA - Stanislaus County

	SIC	EMP	PHONE	ENTRY #
Flory Industries	3523	D	209 545-1167	5004
JL Bray & Son Inc	1542	D	209 545-2856	900
Medical Ambassadors Intl	8399	E	209 543-7500	18241
Royce Corporation **(PA)**	7342	D	209 545-0789	11907
Western Drywall Inc	1742	D	209 543-9361	1708

SAMOA, CA - Humboldt County

	SIC	EMP	PHONE	ENTRY #
United Compost & Organics Inc	5191	E	707 443-4369	9614
United Compost & Organics Inc	2873	E	707 443-4369	4136
Western Web Inc	2752	E	707 444-6236	3714

SAN ANDREAS, CA - Calaveras County

	SIC	EMP	PHONE	ENTRY #
Avalon Care Ctr - San Andreas	8051	C	209 754-3823	15919
Calaveras County Water Dst	4941	D	209 754-3543	8224
Calaveras First Co Inc	2711	E	209 754-3861	3422
H R C Calaveras Head Srt State **(PA)**	8351	E	209 772-3980	17947
K W Emerson Inc	1623	E	209 754-3839	1112
Krisalis Precision Machining	3599	F	209 296-6866	5557
Mark Twain Medical Center **(DH)**	8062	C	209 754-3521	16440
Mark Twain Medical Center	8062	E	209 754-1487	16441
Resource Cnnction of Amdor Clv **(PA)**	8322	C	209 754-3114	17691

SAN ANSELMO, CA - Marin County

	SIC	EMP	PHONE	ENTRY #
Bright Path Therapists Inc	8049	E	415 689-1700	15884
Direct Commerce Inc	7374	E	415 288-9700	13708
Kleinfelder Inc	8711	C	415 458-5803	18748
Melissa Bradley RE Inc	6531	E	415 455-1080	10621

SAN BRUNO, CA - San Mateo County

	SIC	EMP	PHONE	ENTRY #
Airport Auto Parts Inc	5013	F	650 952-1135	8436
Artichoke Joes	7999	B	650 589-8812	15175
Associated Trucking Inc	4213	E	650 652-3960	7504
Bandpage Inc	7379	E	415 800-6614	13851
Calvary Cross Ch of Highlands **(PA)**	8322	C	650 873-4095	17453
Clay Sherman & Co **(PA)**	6531	E	650 952-2300	10511
Cord Blood Donor Foundation	8641	E	650 635-1420	18410
Dynamic Signal Inc **(PA)**	7374	B	650 231-2550	13709
Epixel Solutions	8742	D	650 616-4488	19505
Freight Chckers Clrcal Emplyee	8631	E	650 635-0111	18358
Freshdesk Inc **(HQ)**	7379	E	866 832-3090	13898
Happy Hall Preschool	8351	E	650 583-7370	17949
Independent Quality Care Inc	8059	E	650 583-7768	16246
Integrted Rsrce Sltons Group L	8748	E	650 726-7628	19798
Kaiser Foundation Hospitals	6324	C	650 742-2100	10131
Ksi Corp **(PA)**	4731	D	650 952-0815	7844
Lash Group LLC	8399	C	800 788-9637	18239
Latino Comm On Alchol DRG Abus **(PA)**	8093	E	650 244-1444	17033
Longs Drug Stores Cal Inc	7384	D	650 873-9363	14162
Lowes Home Centers LLC	5031	C	650 616-7800	8564
Permanente Medical Group Inc	8011	A	650 742-2100	15596
Police Credit Union of Cal **(PA)**	6061	D	415 242-2142	9803
Premier Source LLC	8733	D	415 349-2010	19230
Provident Funding Assoc LP **(PA)**	6162	E	650 652-1300	9923
Qumu Inc **(DH)**	7372	E	650 396-8530	13396
Responsys Inc **(DH)**	7371	A	650 745-1700	12745
Southwest Cnstr & Property Mgt	1542	E	650 877-0717	966
Trinity Building Services	7349	D	650 873-2121	12007
Trotter-Vogel Realty Inc	6531	D	650 589-1000	10678
Vantagepoint Capital Partners **(PA)**	6799	D	650 866-3100	10892
Vantagepoint Management Inc **(PA)**	6799	D	650 866-3100	10893
Vinces Shellfish Co Inc	5146	E	650 589-5385	9373
Wal-Martcom Usa LLC **(HQ)**	5199	E	650 837-5000	9674

SAN CARLOS, CA - San Mateo County

	SIC	EMP	PHONE	ENTRY #
Aho Enterprises Inc	7532	E	650 593-1019	14516
Alkahest Inc	8731	D	650 801-0474	19014
Alpine Biomed Corp	3841	D	650 802-0400	6939
Apex Die Corporation	2675	D	650 592-6350	3393
Apexigen Inc	2834	E	650 931-6236	3850
AT&T Mobility LLC	4899	C	650 638-1188	8069
Atreca Inc	2836	D	650 595-2595	4037
Bayview Villa	8361	E	650 596-3489	18061
Begovic Industries Inc	3599	E	650 594-2861	5483
Britannia Construction Inc	1521	E	650 742-6490	624
Cellink Corporation	3679	E	650 799-3018	6405
Check Point Software Tech Inc **(HQ)**	7372	C	650 628-2000	13061
Chemocentryx Inc **(PA)**	2834	D	650 210-2900	3882
Colabo Inc	7372	E	650 288-6649	13083
Coldwell Banker	6411	D	650 596-5400	10265
Commercial Mechanical Svc Inc **(PA)**	7623	E	650 610-8440	14686
D & J Tile Company Inc	1743	D	650 632-4000	1712
Daniel Larratt Plumbing Inc	1711	E	415 553-6011	1248
Dees-Hennessey Inc	1541	E	650 595-8933	793
Dishcraft Robotics Inc	8733	D	888 231-3318	19213
Duckys Car Wash **(PA)**	7542	E	650 637-1301	14639
Edgewood Ctr For Chldren Fmlie	8351	D	650 832-6900	17929
EH Suda Inc **(PA)**	3599	F	650 622-9700	5515
Emagined Security Inc	7382	E	415 944-2977	14131
Fbn Inputs LLC	0762	D	844 200-3276	376
First Student Inc	4151	C	650 685-8245	7433
Gala Therapeutics Inc **(PA)**	3841	C	628 800-1154	6974
Galaxy Medical Inc	3841	E	510 847-5189	6975
Gmw Associates	5084	F	650 802-8292	9069
Gmw Associates	3812	E	650 802-8292	6671
Hayes Scott Bnino Ellngson McL	8111	E	650 551-8929	17289
Helix Holdings I LLC	8731	D	415 805-3360	19066
House of Bagels Inc **(PA)**	2051	F	650 595-4700	2388
Hy-Tech Plating Inc	3471	F	650 593-4566	4911
Intermountain Electric Company	1731	E	650 591-7118	1524
International Process Solution	8734	D	310 432-0665	19276
Iovance Biotherapeutics Inc **(PA)**	2834	C	650 260-7120	3931
Ira Services Trust Company	6733	E	650 591-3335	10795
Iron Ox Inc	5099	E	281 381-0409	9197
J & L Digital Precision Inc	3679	F	650 592-0170	6437
Jim Walters Construction Inc **(PA)**	1542	D	650 596-9751	899
Kelly-Moore Paint Company Inc **(PA)**	2851	C	650 592-8337	4106
Kinetic Farm Inc	7372	F	650 503-3279	13265
Lawyers Title Insurance Corp	6361	C	650 445-6300	10200
Level 5 Drywall Inc	1742	D	650 486-1657	1689
Life Street Corporation	7311	E	415 757-0497	11767
Lifestreet Corporation	5199	D	650 508-2220	9666
Lindeburg & Co	3961	E	650 592-6275	7209
Liveleaf Inc **(PA)**	8731	E	650 722-2984	19083
Lyngso Garden Materials Inc	5032	E	650 364-1730	8629
Magnitude Electronics LLC	3679	F	650 551-1850	6451
Marklogic Corporation **(PA)**	7371	B	650 655-2300	12596
Maxx Metals Inc	5051	D	650 654-1500	8821
Monolith Materials Inc	2819	E	650 933-4957	3793
Mp Nexlevel California Inc	1623	D	650 486-1359	1121
Myome Inc **(PA)**	8071	E	541 826-6778	16789
Nautilus Biotechnology Inc	8731	C	206 333-2001	19091
Noah Medical Corporation	3829	D	718 564-3717	6913
Norcal Materials Inc	3273	E	650 365-4811	4499
Nxedge San Carlos LLC	3674	E	650 422-2269	6237
Oportun Financial Corporation **(PA)**	6141	A	650 810-8823	9861
Pacific Gas and Electric Co	4911	C	800 684-4648	8155
Pacific Rubber & Packing Inc **(PA)**	5085	E	650 595-5888	9125
Pencom/Accuracy Inc	3451	D	510 785-5022	4868
Pencom/Duall Thermo Products	5153	D	650 593-3288	9504
Peninsula Crrdor Jint Pwers Bd	4111	C	650 508-6200	7344
Peninsula Custom Homes Inc	1521	D	650 574-0241	683
Performex Machining Inc	3599	E	650 595-2228	5594
Pionetics Corporation	3089	F	650 551-0250	4311
Precision Design Inc	3672	E	650 508-8041	5959
Preclncal Mdvice Innvtions LLC	8071	E	510 704-0140	16794
Professional Insur Assoc Inc **(PA)**	6411	E	650 592-7333	10336
Project Hired **(PA)**	7363	D	408 557-0880	12190
Q Bio Inc	8731	E	415 967-7622	19111
Residence Inn By Marriott LLC	7011	E	650 637-5500	11400
Revjet	7372	C	650 508-2215	13409
Road Runner Delivery LLC	4215	E	312 468-6940	7652
Ruby Burma Investment LLC	8741	D	650 590-0545	19390
Rudolph and Sletten Inc **(HQ)**	1542	D	650 216-3600	951
San Mateo County Transit Dst **(PA)**	4111	C	650 508-6200	7351
San Mateo County Transit Dst	4173	C	650 508-6412	7445
Sb Energy Devco (us) Inc	1629	E	650 731-3262	1176
Starvista	8322	C	650 591-9623	17760
Tanner Pacific Inc	8711	E	650 585-4484	18827
Telecommunications Engrg Assoc	3663	E	650 590-1801	5878
Vanmali Inc	7011	E	650 576-9134	11555
VCA Animal Hospitals Inc	0742	E	650 631-7400	342
Vibrant Sciences LLC	3826	C	408 203-9383	6863
Zimbio Inc **(PA)**	2721	D	650 594-1723	3521

SAN FRANCISCO, CA - San Francisco County

	SIC	EMP	PHONE	ENTRY #
1000 Sansome Associates LLC	7373	E	415 233-8357	13546
150 The Tunnel Center For Reha	8051	E	415 673-8405	15904
18 Rabbits Inc **(PA)**	2064	F	415 922-6006	2424
1919 Investment Counsel LLC	3131	E	415 500-6707	4339
1healthio Inc	4813	E	208 681-4058	7919
1life Healthcare Inc **(PA)**	8011	B	415 814-0927	15266
28 Sasf Owner LLC	7011	E	415 276-9888	10903
280 Capmarkets LLC **(PA)**	7389	E	628 231-2390	14185
3degrees Group Inc **(PA)**	8748	E	415 561-6852	19708
3scale Inc **(PA)**	7382	E	415 349-5187	14113
425 North Point Street LLC	7011	E	800 648-4626	10904
4505 Meats Inc	2096	E	415 255-3094	2851
4th & Folsom Associates LP	6513	B	415 417-3086	10416
89bio Inc	2834	E	415 500-4614	3823
A Ruiz Cnstr Co & Assoc Inc	1542	E	415 647-4010	819
A1 Protective Services Inc	7381	D	415 467-7200	14022
AAA California State Auto Assn **(PA)**	8699	C	415 773-1900	18540
Abacus Information Tech LLC **(HQ)**	8742	D	415 517-8005	19431

GEOGRAPHIC SECTION

SAN FRANCISCO, CA

Company	SIC	EMP	PHONE	ENTRY #
Abbett Electric Corporation	1731	E	415 864-7500	1442
ABC Cable Networks Group	4833	C	415 954-7911	8038
ABC Imaging of Washington	7336	E	415 869-1669	11857
ABC Imaging of Washington	2759	F	415 525-3874	3719
Able Services Inc (PA)	8711	D	800 461-9577	18611
ABS Capital Partners III LP	6799	B	415 617-2800	10828
Access Public Relations LLC	8743	D	415 904-7070	19681
Accor Services US LLC (HQ)	7011	A	415 772-5000	10909
Ace Mailing & Data Processing	7331	E	415 863-4223	11835
Ace Parking Management Inc	7521	D	415 398-1900	14499
Ace Parking Management Inc	7521	D	415 749-1949	14502
Ace Parking Management Inc	7521	D	415 674-1799	14503
Ace Parking Management Inc	7521	D	415 421-8800	14505
Ace Usa Inc	6331	E	415 773-6500	10160
Action Property Management Inc	8742	E	800 400-2284	19433
Active Wellness LLC	8741	A	415 741-3300	19294
Ad Art Inc	3993	D	415 869-6460	7214
Adivo Associates LLC	8742	E	415 992-1449	19434
Adler & Colvin A Law Corp	8111	E	415 421-7555	17198
Adobe	2741	E	415 832-7791	3552
Adobe Macromedia Software LLC (HQ)	7372	A	415 832-2000	12957
Advanced McRgrid Solutions Inc	8731	D	415 638-6146	19012
Advantage Workforce Svcs LLC	7363	C	415 212-6464	12157
Advent Software Inc (HQ)	7371	A	415 543-7696	12232
Aechelon Technology Inc (PA)	3571	C	415 255-0120	5238
Aecom	8711	E	415 796-8100	18617
Aecom	8711	D	415 908-6135	18618
Aecom International Inc (DH)	8711	C	415 716-8100	18619
Aerial Topco LP (PA)	7375	E	415 983-2700	13778
Aero Technologies Inc (PA)	4111	E	415 314-7479	7321
Affiliated Engineers W Inc (HQ)	8711	D	415 546-3120	18621
Affinity Inc	7371	E	650 380-9305	12234
Affirm Inc (HQ)	6153	E	415 984-0490	9866
Affirm Holdings Inc (PA)	6153	E	415 984-0490	9867
Afresh Technologies Inc	7372	D	805 551-9245	12960
Agent Iq Inc	5045	E	844 243-6847	8662
Airbnb Inc (PA)	7389	A	415 510-4027	14197
Airbnb Payments Inc	6099	E	415 861-2325	9840
Airline Coach Service Inc	4111	E	650 697-7733	7322
Akash Systems Inc (PA)	3679	F	408 887-6682	6397
Aki Technologies Inc	8742	E	415 462-4254	19438
Akoonu Inc	7372	F	844 425-6668	12966
Akqa Inc (PA)	8742	B	415 645-9400	19439
Aktana Inc (PA)	7372	B	888 707-3125	12967
Alcatraz Cruises LLC	4725	D	415 981-7625	7813
Algolia Inc	7372	C	415 366-9672	12971
All Turtles Corporation (PA)	7371	E	609 352-3172	12239
Allbirds Inc	3143	A	628 225-4848	4340
Allens Press Clipping Bureau (PA)	7389	E	415 392-2353	14198
Allied Administrators Inc	8742	E	415 989-7443	19441
Alloy Technologies Inc (PA)	5045	E	415 990-5140	8664
Allstripes Research Inc	2834	F	415 404-9287	3840
Aloha Seafood Inc	5146	E	415 441-4484	9358
Alois LLC	7361	C	215 297-4492	12073
Alpha Agency Inc	7361	E	415 421-6272	12074
Alston & Bird LLP	8111	D	415 243-3440	17199
Alta Partners Management Corp	6799	E	415 362-4022	10832
Alterra Spcalty Insur Svcs Ltd	6311	D	415 490-4615	10075
Always Be Learning Inc	8351	E	650 450-2603	17856
Amalgamated Bank	6029	E	415 995-8157	9755
Amaranth Medical Inc	8011	E	650 965-3830	15278
Amber Holdings Inc	7371	E	415 765-6500	12246
American Acdemy Ophthlmlogy In (PA)	8621	C	415 561-8500	18323
American Bldg Maint Co-West (HQ)	7349	D	415 733-4000	11919
American Building Maint Co NY	7349	D	415 733-4000	11920
American Clg Trdtnl Chnse Mdcn (PA)	8093	D	415 282-0156	16987
American Cnsrvtory Thtre Fndti (PA)	7922	D	415 834-3200	14835
American Conservatory Theater (PA)	7299	C	415 749-2228	11705
American Civil Lbrties Un Fndti	8699	D	415 621-2488	18544
American Marketing Systems Inc	6531	D	800 747-7784	10489
American Med Rspnse Inland Emp	4119	B	415 922-9400	7370
American National Red Cross	8322	E	415 371-1740	17425
American Scence Tech As T Corp (PA)	3721	E	415 251-2800	6606
American Securities Company	6799	D	415 396-4566	10834
Americom Central Station Inc	7382	D	415 550-7100	14120
Ammunition LLC	8742	E	415 632-1170	19443
Amour Vert Inc	5137	E	650 388-4284	9250
Ampac Technology Corporation	3674	F	415 912-2838	6035
Ample Inc	7389	D	617 504-3557	14200
Amplitude Inc (PA)	7371	B	650 988-5131	12250
Amzn Mobile LLC	7371	B	925 348-4580	12251
Anaplan Inc (PA)	7379	A	415 742-8199	13839
Anchor Distilling Company	2084	E	415 863-8350	2504
Anderson Rowe & Buckley Inc	1711	C	415 282-1625	1203
Andre-Boudin Bakeries Inc	2051	E	415 283-1230	2362
Andrews Hotel (PA)	7011	E	415 563-6877	10924
Andytown LLC (PA)	2095	E	415 702-9859	2835
Anfield Insurance Service	6411	D	415 439-5750	10233
Angaza Design Inc	7371	E	415 993-5595	12255
Angotti & Reilly Inc	1542	E	415 575-3700	824
Animoto LLC	7371	E	415 987-3139	12256
Another Corporate Isp LLC	4813	E	415 974-1313	7925
Anthem Insurance Companies Inc	6324	B	415 617-1700	10092
Antipodean Pharmaceuticals Inc (PA)	2834	E	866 749-3338	3848
Anvil Builders Inc	1611	E	415 285-5000	1011
AON Consulting & Insur Svcs	6411	C	415 486-7500	10234
AON Risk Insurance Svcs W Inc (DH)	6411	E	415 486-7000	10235
APA Family Support Services	8322	E	415 617-0061	17429
Apartment List Inc	6514	E	415 817-1068	10470
Apellis Pharmaceuticals Inc	2834	E	415 872-9970	3849
App Annie Inc (DH)	7371	B	844 277-2664	12260
Appdirect Inc (PA)	7372	D	415 852-3924	12978
Appdynamics LLC (HQ)	7371	A	415 442-8400	12261
Appodeal Inc (PA)	5199	E	415 996-6877	9645
Appsflyer Inc	7371	E	408 367-9938	12264
Appsflyer Ltd	7313	D	415 636-9430	11801
April Six Inc	8742	E	415 363-6070	19447
Aquarium of Bay (HQ)	8422	E	415 623-5300	18287
Aradigm Corporation	2834	E	510 265-9000	3852
Arangodb Inc	7372	E	415 992-7801	12985
ARC San Francisco (PA)	8331	C	415 255-7200	17794
Arcbyt Inc (PA)	3531	E	415 449-4852	5024
Arceo Labs Inc (PA)	8734	D	628 222-3622	19258
Archipelago Analytics Holdings (PA)	7371	E	415 696-4896	12267
Architctral Rsources Group Inc (PA)	8712	E	415 421-1680	18870
Arcline Elvtion Svcs Hldngs LL	7699	A	860 805-2025	14737
Arcline Investment MGT LP (PA)	2824	F	415 801-4570	3815
Arctouch LLC	7371	E	415 944-2000	12269
Arden Wood Inc	8361	D	415 681-5500	18057
Argonaut Hotel	7011	E	415 563-0800	10929
Arguello Pet Hospital Inc	0742	E	415 751-3242	321
Aria Systems Inc (PA)	7371	C	415 852-7250	12270
Arista Networks	7372	F	408 547-5725	12988
Arkose Labs Holdings Inc (PA)	7382	E	415 917-8701	14122
Armin Maier and Associates Inc (PA)	5023	E	415 332-6467	8505
Arnold & Porter PC	8111	B	415 434-1600	17203
Arnold Palmer Golf MGT LLC	8741	E	415 561-4670	19299
Arriba Juntos (PA)	8331	E	415 487-3240	17795
Arterys Inc	5047	D	650 319-7230	8773
Artisan Partners Ltd Partnr	6221	E	415 283-2444	10024
Arup North America Limited (DH)	8711	C	415 957-9445	18630
Arxan Technologies Inc	7371	E	301 968-4290	12275
Asana Inc (PA)	7379	A	415 525-3888	13845
Asia Foundation (PA)	8733	E	415 982-4640	19197
Asian Inc (PA)	8399	E	415 928-5910	18219
Asian Art Mseum Fndtion San Fr	8412	C	415 581-3500	18261
Asian PCF Islnder Wllness Ctr	8322	E	415 292-3400	17433
Aspen Apts I	6513	E	415 673-5879	10417
Aspireiq Inc	8742	D	415 445-3567	19449
Associated Building Entp Inc	1542	E	415 285-6200	825
Associated Materials Inc	3089	A	415 788-5111	4260
Astranis Space Tech Corp	3663	C	415 854-0586	5826
Astronomical Soc of The PCF	8699	E	415 337-1100	18547
AT&T Services Inc	4813	C	415 545-9051	7928
AT&T Services Inc	4813	D	415 545-9058	7929
Atel 12 LLC	6159	C	415 989-8800	9880
Atel 14 LLC	6159	D	415 989-8800	9881
Atel Associates 14 LLC (PA)	6159	D	415 989-8800	9882
Atel Capital Group (PA)	6159	D	800 543-2835	9883
Atel Corporation	7389	D	415 989-8800	14206
Atel Financial Services LLC (DH)	6159	D	415 989-8800	9884
Athleta LLC	2329	E	707 559-2200	2991
Athletic Media Company (PA)	7319	B	415 891-7354	11809
Atlassian Inc (DH)	7372	D	415 701-1110	12990
Atomic Fiction Inc (HQ)	7819	E	510 488-6641	14800
Atomic Labs LLC (PA)	6726	D	415 896-4148	10774
Atomic Public Relations (HQ)	8743	D	415 402-0230	19683
Audentes Therapeutics Inc (DH)	2836	D	415 818-1001	4038
Augmedix Inc (PA)	7372	A	888 669-4885	12993
Augmedix Operating Corporation	7389	D	855 720-2929	14208
August Home Inc	3429	E	415 891-0866	4614
Aurora Innovation Inc	7372	D	646 725-4999	12994
Authentica Solutions LLC (PA)	7372	F	614 296-6479	12996
Auto Ex Towing & Recovery LLC	7549	E	415 846-2262	14657
Autodesk Inc	7372	D	415 356-0700	12997
Automattic Inc	4813	A	877 273-3049	7931
Automotivemastermind Inc	7371	D	646 679-3441	12288
Autonomy Inc (PA)	7372	E	415 243-9955	13001
Ava Food Labs Inc	8734	E	415 806-3914	19259
Axiom Inc	7011	E	415 392-9466	10939
Ayoob & Peery Plumbing Co Inc	1711	D	415 641-6700	1210
Ayusa International	8699	D	888 552-9872	18549
Azulworks Inc	4941	C	415 558-1507	8222
B F C Inc	1731	C	415 495-3085	1454
B44 Catalan Bistro	2024	E	415 986-6287	2169
Ba Leasing & Capital Corp (DH)	7359	E	415 765-1804	12030
Baart Behavioral Hlth Svcs Inc (HQ)	8093	E	415 552-7914	16991
Babcock Brown Rnwble Hldngs In (DH)	8711	E	415 512-1515	18635
Babycenter LLC (DH)	7299	D	415 537-0900	11706
Badger Maps Inc	7372	E	415 592-5909	13006
Baker & McKenzie LLP	8111	E	415 576-3000	17204
Baker Avenue Asset MGT LP (PA)	6282	D	415 986-1110	10033
Baker Places Inc	8093	D	415 503-3137	16992
Baker Places Inc	8322	E	415 387-2275	17435
Banc America Lsg & Capitl LLC (DH)	6021	C	415 765-7349	9677
Bancwest Corporation	6022	A	415 765-4800	9701
Bank of Orient Foundation (HQ)	6022	E	415 338-0668	9704
Bank of San Francisco	6022	E	415 744-6700	9705
BANK OF THE WEST (HQ)	6022	A	415 765-4800	9707
Bankamerica Financial Inc	6153	E	415 622-3521	9868
Bar Architects	8712	D	415 293-5970	18872
Bar Asscation of San Francisco (PA)	8621	E	415 982-1600	18324
Bar Media Inc	2711	E	415 861-5019	3415
Barebottle Brewing Company Inc	2082	F	415 926-8617	2474

Employment Codes: A=Over 500 employees, B=251-500, C=101-250, D=51-100, E=20-50 F=10-19

SAN FRANCISCO, CA

Name	SIC	EMP	PHONE	ENTRY #
Barrett SF	7311	E	415 986-2960	11740
Barri Electric Company Inc	1731	E	415 468-6477	1457
Bartko Zankel Tarrant & Mil	8111	D	415 956-1900	17208
Basis Science Inc	5047	E	415 367-7477	8774
Bauers Intelligent Trnsp Inc (PA)	4119	C	415 263-4020	7373
Baum Thornley Architects	8712	D	415 503-1411	18873
Bay Area Air Quality (PA)	8748	E	415 749-4900	19727
Bay Area Air Quality MGT Dst	8741	B	415 749-4900	19301
Bay Area Video Coalition Inc	7819	D	415 861-3282	14801
Bay Bread LLC	5149	D	415 440-0356	9440
Bay Club America Inc	7997	C	415 781-1874	15054
Bay Club Golden Gateway LLC	7997	E	415 616-8800	15055
Bay Grove Capital Group LLC (PA)	6722	E	415 229-7953	10748
Bay Guardian Company	2711	E	415 255-3100	3416
Bay West Shwplace Invstors LLC (PA)	6512	E	415 490-5800	10377
Baylands Soil Processing LLC (PA)	2875	E	415 956-4157	4137
Bayorg	8422	D	415 623-5300	18288
Bayview Hnters Pt Fndtion For	8093	E	415 822-8200	16994
Bbam US LP	6211	B	415 267-1600	9957
Bcci Construction LLC (HQ)	1542	C	415 817-5100	829
Beamery Inc (PA)	7372	E	866 473-7136	13011
Beats Music LLC	7372	D	415 590-5104	13012
Bechtel Capital MGT Corp	8741	D	415 768-1234	19302
Becks Motor Lodge	7011	D	415 621-8212	10949
Bee Content Design Inc	7372	D	888 962-4587	13013
Beezy Inc (PA)	7373	D	510 567-7110	13561
Behaviosec USA Inc	7372	E	833 248-6732	13014
Bella Circus	7922	E	415 205-8355	14836
Bellabeat Inc	3961	E	415 317-6153	7208
Benefit Cosmetics LLC (DH)	5122	E	415 781-8153	9224
Bento Technologies Inc	7372	E	415 887-2028	13016
Beresford Corporation	7011	E	415 673-9900	10951
Berkel & Company Contrs Inc	1771	D	415 495-3627	1852
Berkshire Hathaway Homestates (HQ)	6411	C	415 433-1650	10249
Bespoke Inc	3851	E	612 201-6800	7137
Best Western Civic Ctr Mtr Inn	7011	E	415 621-2826	10955
Best Western Hotel Tomo	7011	E	415 921-4000	10956
Betawave Corporation (PA)	7374	E	415 738-8706	13696
Better Therapeutics Inc	2834	E	415 887-2311	3865
Betterup Inc (PA)	8742	B	415 862-0708	19455
Betty K Ng	8011	E	415 364-7600	15298
Beyondid Inc	7379	D	415 878-6210	13856
Bhr Operations LLC	7011	C	415 771-9000	10960
Big Health Inc	8052	E	415 867-3473	16170
Big Heart Pet Brands Inc (HQ)	2047	B	415 247-3000	2333
Bigstepcom	4813	C	415 229-8500	7934
Billing Services Plus DBA Apex	7349	E	415 604-3515	11926
Binbin Windows Inc (PA)	5031	D	415 282-1688	8530
Biomaas Inc	8748	E	415 255-8077	19732
Bioq Pharma Incorporated (PA)	2834	F	415 336-6496	3869
Birdly Inc	8742	E	650 942-9388	19456
Birst Inc	7371	B	415 766-4800	12302
Bitalign Inc	7371	D	415 395-9525	12303
Bite Communications LLC (HQ)	8742	D	415 365-0222	19457
Bittorrent Inc	7371	E	408 641-4219	12304
Black Bear Security Svcs Inc	7381	E	415 559-5159	14038
Black Knight Infoserv LLC	7389	E	415 989-9800	14217
Blackrock Global Investors	6722	A	415 670-2000	10749
Blackrock Instnl Tr Nat Assn (HQ)	6722	A	415 597-2000	10750
Blackstone Technology Group (PA)	6211	D	415 837-1400	9958
Blackthorn Therapeutics Inc	2834	E	415 548-5401	3870
Bleacher Report Inc	7374	D	415 777-5505	13697
Bleacher Report Inc	7822	E	415 777-5505	14803
Bledsoe Cthcart Dstel Peterson	8111	D	415 981-5411	17215
Blend Insurance Agency Inc	6162	C	650 550-4810	9891
Blend Labs Inc	7372	A	650 550-4810	13025
Bliss World LLC	5094	D	415 217-7047	9180
Blockfreight Inc	7372	E	415 815-3924	13026
Bloomlife Inc	3841	E	415 215-4251	6958
Blue and Gold Fleet	4489	D	415 705-8200	7718
Blue Cedar Networks Inc	3577	E	415 329-0401	5352
Blueshift Labs Inc	7372	C	844 258-3735	13030
Blum Capital Partners T LP	6282	E	415 645-0092	10035
Blurb Inc	2731	D	415 364-6300	3525
Bohemian Club (PA)	8641	D	415 885-2440	18394
Boku Inc (PA)	7371	D	415 375-3160	12305
Boldt Company	1542	C	415 762-8300	835
Bolton Rsnbaum Brnsten Pdtric	8011	D	415 666-1860	15300
Bongmi Inc	5047	E	415 823-8595	8775
Bospar LLC	8742	E	415 913-7528	19458
Bossa Nova Robotics Inc (HQ)	5099	D	415 234-5136	9189
Boston Properties Ltd Partnr	6552	D	415 772-0700	10696
Bourdolan 25 Lusk LLC	7011	E	415 495-5875	10968
Boutique Air Inc (PA)	4522	B	415 449-0505	7755
Bpaz Holdings 18 LLC	6719	D	972 354-6250	10728
Bpaz Holdings 2 LLC	6531	E	972 354-6250	10495
Bpaz Holdings 6 LLC	6719	D	415 295-8080	10729
Bpm LLP (PA)	8721	E	415 421-5757	18936
Brandwatch LLC	8742	E	415 429-5800	19459
Braunhagey & Borden LLP	8111	D	415 599-0210	17219
Bre/Japantown Owner LLC	7011	E	415 922-3000	10972
Breaktime Studios Inc (PA)	7372	E	415 290-4900	13034
Brereton Architects Inc	8712	E	415 546-1212	18874
Brex Inc (PA)	7389	B	650 250-6428	14219
Bridge Economic Dev Corp (PA)	1521	D	415 989-1111	622
Bridge Housing Corporation (PA)	8699	D	415 989-1111	18551
Bridgecrew Inc	3577	E	510 304-4622	5353

Name	SIC	EMP	PHONE	ENTRY #
Brience Inc (DH)	7371	D	415 974-5300	12308
Bright Machines Inc (PA)	3549	B	415 867-4402	5107
Brighterion Inc	7371	E	415 986-5600	12310
Brightidea Incorporated	7372	E	415 814-1387	13035
Brightmark LLC (PA)	1311	C	415 964-4411	545
Brighttalk Inc (PA)	7371	E	415 625-1500	12311
Brilliant Worldwide Inc	7372	E	650 468-2966	13036
Brite Media Group LLC (PA)	7313	E	877 479-7777	11802
Broadmoor Hotel (PA)	7011	D	415 776-7034	10975
Broadmoor Hotel	7011	D	415 673-2511	10977
Broadreach Capitl Partners LLC	6799	A	415 354-4640	10837
Brondell Inc	5122	E	415 315-9000	9225
Brown & Toland Medical Group	8011	C	415 923-3015	15304
Brown & Toland Medical Group	8011	C	415 752-8038	15305
Btig LLC (PA)	6211	D	415 248-2200	9959
Bugcrowd Inc (PA)	7379	C	650 260-8443	13858
Bugsnag Inc	7372	E	415 484-8664	13038
Build Group Inc (PA)	1542	C	415 367-9399	840
Builtio LLC	7371	E	415 255-5955	12315
Bumblebee Spaces Inc (PA)	7389	E	415 624-3785	14220
Bungalow Living Inc	6531	E	415 501-0981	10498
Burr Pilger Mayer Inc (PA)	8721	C	415 421-5757	18938
Business For Scial Rspnsbility (PA)	8742	E	415 984-3200	19462
Business Services Network	7331	E	415 282-8161	11836
Buycoins Inc	7371	E	650 278-7402	12316
By The Bay Health	8082	E	415 626-5900	16864
Byer California (PA)	2331	A	415 626-7844	2997
Bynd LLC	7371	D	415 944-2293	12317
C 5 Children School	8351	E	415 626-4880	17867
C 5 Childrens School	8351	D	415 703-1277	17868
Cable Car Partners LLC (PA)	7999	E	415 922-2425	15185
Cahill Contractors Inc (PA)	1542	E	415 986-0600	846
Cahill Contractors LLC	1542	C	415 986-0600	847
Cai Insurance Inc	7359	E	415 788-0100	12033
Cal Insurance and Assoc Inc	6411	D	415 661-6500	10255
California Academy Sciences (PA)	8422	A	415 379-8000	18289
California Appellate Project	8111	E	415 495-0500	17223
California Parking Company (PA)	6519	D	415 781-4896	10476
California School of Mech Arts	6512	D	415 333-4021	10380
California Shellfish Co Inc	5146	C	707 542-9490	9363
Califrnia Integrated Media Inc	2752	F	415 627-8310	3632
Callan LLC (PA)	6282	C	415 974-5060	10038
Calmcom Inc (PA)	7372	E	415 284-0991	13046
Cammisa Wipf Cnslting Engineers	8711	E	415 863-5740	18656
Campaign Monitor USA Inc (DH)	7371	D	888 533-8098	12324
Canaccord Genuity LLC	6211	D	415 229-7171	9960
Canadian American Oil Co Inc (PA)	6512	E	415 621-8676	10382
Canadian American Oil Co Inc	7542	E	510 644-8229	14633
Canadian American Oil Co Inc	7542	E	415 621-8676	14634
Canary Technologies Corp	7372	E	415 578-1414	13048
Candle3 LLC	5063	E	415 365-9679	8848
Canterbury Hotel Corp	7011	D	415 345-3200	10987
Canto Inc	7372	E	415 495-6545	13049
Capcom Entertainment Inc	5092	C	650 350-6500	9167
Capcom U S A Inc (HQ)	5092	C	650 350-6500	9168
Capella Space Corp	5063	D	650 334-7734	8849
Capgemini America Inc	7379	A	415 796-6777	13860
Capitol Communications Inc	1731	E	415 861-1727	1472
Cappstone Inc	7349	C	415 821-6757	11933
Captivateiq Inc	7371	C	650 930-0619	12325
Carbon Health Technologies Inc	8742	D	415 223-2858	19466
Carbon Lighthouse Inc	8711	E	415 787-3550	18658
Carbonfive Incorporated	7371	D	415 546-0500	12326
Cardno Chemrisk LLC (DH)	8748	E	415 896-2400	19739
Care At Home Inc	8082	E	408 379-3990	16866
Care Zone Inc	7372	E	206 707-9127	13050
Career Group Inc	7361	C	415 781-8188	12079
Caritas Management Corporation	6531	D	415 647-7191	10501
Carlton Ht Prpts A Cal Ltd Prt	7011	E	415 673-0242	10989
Carpenter Group (PA)	3536	E	415 285-1954	5059
Carroll Burdick Mc Donough LLP (PA)	8111	C	415 989-5900	17227
Cartwright Hotel	7011	E	415 421-2865	10992
Casetext Inc	7371	E	317 407-0790	12328
Casey Securities Inc (PA)	6211	D	415 544-5030	9961
Cassidy Trly Prop MGT Sn Frncs	6531	E	415 781-8100	10505
Castle Global Inc	7371	C	401 523-9531	12329
Castlight Health Inc (PA)	7374	B	415 829-1400	13702
Catholic Chrties Cyo of The AR	8322	E	415 743-0017	17456
Catholic Chrties Cyo of The AR	8322	E	415 405-2000	17457
Catholic Chrties Cyo of The AR	8322	E	415 861-1141	17458
Catholic Chrties Cyo of The AR	8322	E	415 334-5550	17459
Catholic Chrties Cyo of The AR	8322	E	415 553-8700	17460
Catholic Chrties Cyo of The AR	8322	E	415 452-3500	17463
Catholic Chrties Cyo of The AR	8322	E	415 668-9543	17464
Catholic Chrties Cyo of The AR	8322	E	415 206-1467	17465
CB Engineers (PA)	8711	E	415 477-7330	18664
CB Mill Inc	2511	F	415 386-5309	3276
Cb-1 Hotel	7011	D	415 633-3838	10998
CBS Interactive Inc (DH)	7319	A	415 344-2000	11811
Cdc San Francisco LLC	7011	r	415 616-6512	10999
Celerity Consulting Group Inc (PA)	8742	D	415 986-8850	19467
Celo Labs Inc (PA)	8734	E	415 942-4178	19261
Center For Youth Wellness	8099	E	415 684-9520	17117
Central City Hospitality House	8322	E	415 749-2100	17477
Century Theatres Inc	7833	C	415 776-2388	14825
Century Theatres Inc	7833	C	415 661-2539	14830
Cenveo Worldwide Limited	2752	C	415 821-7171	3634

	SIC	EMP	PHONE	ENTRY #
Certain Inc **(PA)**	7372	E	415 353-5330	13059
Chan Zuckerberg Biohub Inc	8733	D	628 200-3246	19208
Chancellor Hotel Associates A	7011	E	415 362-2004	11002
Changeorg Inc **(PA)**	7375	C	415 817-1840	13782
Changing Future Outcome	7231	E	415 901-7000	11677
Charles Hlen Schwab Foundation	8699	E	415 795-4920	18559
Charles M Salter Associates **(PA)**	8711	E	415 470-5461	18667
Charles Schwab & Co Inc **(HQ)**	6211	B	415 636-7000	9962
Charles Schwab Corporation **(PA)**	6211	A	415 667-7000	9963
Charolais Care V Inc	8082	E	415 921-5038	16870
Chartboost Inc **(HQ)**	7371	C	415 493-0727	12335
Chase Manhattan Mortgage Corp	6162	C	858 605-3300	9900
Chatterbug Inc **(PA)**	7371	E	415 957-9000	12336
Checkr Inc	7323	C	844 824-3257	11832
Chesapeake Lodging Trust	7011	C	415 296-2900	11003
CHI West LLC **(DH)**	3621	D	415 608-8757	5659
Chia Network Inc	7372	F	628 222-5925	13063
Childrens Creativity Museum	8412	D	415 820-3320	18264
Childrens Cuncil San Francisco **(PA)**	8322	D	415 343-3378	17485
Childrens Day School	8351	E	415 861-5432	17900
Chinatown Cmnty Dev Ctr Inc **(PA)**	6513	E	415 984-1450	10424
Chinese Community Health Plan	8011	E	415 955-8800	15349
Chinese For Affirmative Action	8651	E	415 274-6750	18536
Chinese Hospital Association **(PA)**	8062	B	415 982-2400	16330
Chinese-American Bio Phrm Soc	8699	E	650 892-6283	18560
Christian Church Homes	8361	C	415 814-2670	18076
Chronicle Books LLC **(HQ)**	2731	C	415 537-4200	3528
Chronicle Broadcasting Co	4833	B	415 561-8000	8042
Chronicled Inc	5045	E	415 355-4681	8681
Chsp Trs Fisherman Wharf LLC	7011	B	415 563-1234	11007
Cinta Salon Inc	7231	E	415 989-1000	11678
Circle Internet Services Inc **(PA)**	7372	E	707 731-4912	13066
Circosta Iron and Metal Co Inc	4953	E	415 282-8568	8317
Circus Center	7999	E	415 759-8123	15193
Citibank FSB **(HQ)**	6021	B	415 627-6000	9682
Citibank FSB	6035	C	415 817-9111	9769
Citibank FSB	6021	C	415 649-6971	9683
Citicorp Select Investments	6282	E	415 658-4468	10040
Citiscape Prprty MGT Group LLC	6531	D	415 401-2000	10510
City & County of San Francisco	8412	D	415 581-3500	18265
City & County of San Francisco	8062	A	415 206-8000	16332
City and County of San Francis	8322	E	415 557-5000	17490
City Club LLC	7997	E	415 362-2480	15073
City Lights Books	2731	E	415 362-8193	3529
City Lights Lighting Showroom	5063	E	415 863-2020	8853
City View At Metreon	7941	E	415 369-6142	14904
Claude Lambert	7011	D	415 421-3154	11014
Cleantech Group Inc **(PA)**	6282	D	415 684-1020	10041
Clearslide Inc **(DH)**	7372	D	877 360-3366	13069
Clearway Energy Group LLC **(PA)**	4911	B	415 627-1600	8092
Clearway Renew LLC **(HQ)**	4911	E	415 627-1600	8093
Clearxchange LLC	7389	D	415 813-4801	14229
Cleasby Manufacturing Co Inc **(PA)**	3531	E	415 822-6565	5029
Click Labs Inc	7371	E	415 658-5227	12341
Clicktale Inc **(PA)**	7374	D	800 807-2117	13703
Climate Corporation **(DH)**	7372	E	415 363-0500	13071
Climb Real Estate **(DH)**	6531	D	415 431-8888	10513
Cloudflare Inc **(PA)**	7372	A	888 993-5273	13077
Cloudpassage Inc	7371	D	800 838-4098	12343
Clover Health Labs LLC	8099	E	415 548-6456	17124
Clovis Oncology Inc	8011	D	415 409-5440	15353
Club Donatello Owners Assn	3873	E	415 474-7333	7161
Club Quarters San Francisco	7011	E	415 268-3606	11017
Cnet Networks Inc	7373	A	415 344-2000	13569
Coalition Inc **(PA)**	6411	D	833 866-1337	10264
Cobalt Labs Inc **(PA)**	7372	F	415 651-7028	13081
Cobaltix LLC	8742	E	415 322-1025	19471
Coblentz Patch Duffy Bass LLP	8111	D	510 655-4598	17231
Code For America Labs Inc	8742	D	415 816-1286	19472
Codility US Inc	7371	C	415 568-5055	12348
Cognician Inc **(HQ)**	7371	E	858 997-6732	12349
Cognifit Inc	8331	D	646 340-1740	17805
Collabrus Inc	8721	C	415 288-1826	18946
Collectivehealth Inc	6411	B	650 376-3804	10266
Collier Warehouse Inc	5031	E	415 920-9720	8536
Colliers International	6531	D	415 788-3100	10520
Columbia Hospitality Inc	7011	D	415 362-8878	11027
Comcast Sprtsnet Bay Area Hldn	4833	E	415 896-2557	8043
Comfort California Inc	7011	C	415 928-5000	11028
Community Forward Sf Inc **(PA)**	8322	D	415 241-1199	17495
Community Partners Intl	6732	C	510 225-9676	10787
Commure Inc **(PA)**	7371	D	415 741-1114	12352
Compass Family Services **(PA)**	8322	E	415 644-0504	17502
Compass Family Services	8351	D	415 644-0504	17914
Compass Family Services	8322	D	415 644-0504	17503
Compass Family Services	8322	D	415 644-0504	17504
Compassionate Health Options **(PA)**	8099	D	415 255-1200	17126
Con-Quest Contractors Inc	8711	E	415 206-0524	18672
Concord Worldwide Inc	7371	D	415 689-5488	12354
Condor Trading LP	6719	A	415 248-2200	10732
Conduent State Lcal Sltons Inc	7373	A	415 486-2409	13572
Conifer Financial Services LLC **(HQ)**	6211	D	415 677-1500	9965
Conifer Fund Services LLC	6211	E	415 677-5979	9966
Contentstack LLC	8742	E	415 255-5955	19478
Contextlogic Inc **(PA)**	7319	B	415 795-8061	11812
Continuumglobal Inc	8742	C	415 685-3301	19480
Cooley LLP	8111	D	415 693-2000	17234
Cooper White & Cooper LLP **(PA)**	8111	C	415 433-1900	17236
Coordnted Rsrces Inc San Frncs	5021	E	415 989-0773	8493
Corelogic Inc	6531	E	714 250-6400	10524
Coreos LLC	7371	D	888 733-4281	12357
Cornerstone Cnsulting Tech Inc	8748	E	415 705-7800	19752
Cornerstone Concilium Inc	8742	E	415 705-7800	19483
Cornerstone Hotel Management **(DH)**	8741	D	415 397-5572	19320
Cornerstone Research Inc	8748	E	617 927-3000	19753
Cornerstone Research Inc	8748	D	415 229-8100	19755
Corovan	7389	E	415 934-1600	14237
Corporatecouch	3674	E	415 312-6078	6089
Corportion of Fine Arts Mseums **(PA)**	8412	A	415 750-3600	18268
Coveo Software Corp	7371	D	800 635-5476	12359
Coverity LLC **(HQ)**	7371	D	415 321-5200	12360
Covia Communities	8361	C	415 776-0500	18090
Cox Wtton Grffin Hnsen Plos LL	8111	D	415 438-4600	17241
CP Employer Inc **(PA)**	1522	C	415 273-2900	741
CP Multifamily Cnstr Cal Inc	1522	C	415 273-2900	742
CPM Associates Inc	8741	E	415 543-6515	19321
Crane Acquisition Inc	7342	A	415 922-1666	11898
Credo Mobile Inc	4812	D	415 369-2000	7906
Crestwood Behavioral Hlth Inc	8059	D	415 213-7993	16231
Crimson Sv LLC **(PA)**	6726	D	415 970-5800	10775
Cross Link Inc	4492	D	415 495-3191	7727
Crossinstall Inc	7371	E	415 425-5929	12362
Crown Building Maintenance Co	7349	B	303 680-3713	11939
Crown Electric Inc **(PA)**	1731	E	415 559-7432	1488
Cruise LLC	3711	D	415 787-2346	6550
Cruise LLC **(HQ)**	4119	D	415 335-4097	7380
Crunch LLC	7991	D	415 346-0222	14942
Crunch LLC	7991	D	415 543-1110	14944
Crunch LLC	7991	D	415 495-1939	14945
Crux Informatics Inc **(PA)**	7374	E	415 614-4400	13704
Cumming Management Group Inc	8711	D	415 748-3080	18681
Cupertino Electric Inc	1731	A	415 970-3400	1492
Curated Inc	7371	D	415 855-1825	12366
Curebase Inc	7371	E	248 978-3541	12367
Curology Inc **(PA)**	8099	B	858 859-1188	17130
Current Tv LLC	7389	C	415 995-8328	14245
Curry Senior Center **(PA)**	8322	E	415 885-2274	17526
Cushman & Wakefield Cal Inc **(DH)**	6531	C	408 275-6730	10527
Cushman & Wakefield Cal Inc	6531	A	415 828-1923	10533
Cut Loose **(PA)**	2339	D	415 822-2031	3009
Cutler Group LP	7389	E	415 645-6745	14246
Cvpartners Inc **(HQ)**	7361	C	415 543-8600	12082
CVS Health Corporation	8099	B	415 348-1814	17131
Cybernet Entertainment LLC **(PA)**	7812	C	415 865-0230	14788
Cypress Creek Renewables LLC	4911	D	415 306-5300	8094
Cypress Private Security LP **(DH)**	7381	B	866 345-1277	14052
D F P F Corporation	1542	E	415 512-7677	860
Dacast	7812	E	510 619-4857	14789
Daggett Solar Power 3 LLC	1711	C	415 627-1600	1247
Dannis Wlver Klley A Prof Corp **(PA)**	8111	D	415 543-4111	17245
Darktrace Inc **(PA)**	7373	D	415 229-9100	13574
Data Advantage Group Inc	7372	F	415 947-0400	13107
Database Specialists Inc **(DH)**	7375	D	415 344-0500	13783
Databricks Inc **(PA)**	7371	D	415 494-7672	12371
Datafox Intelligence Inc	7372	F	415 969-2144	13108
Datameer Inc **(PA)**	7371	C	650 286-9100	12373
Datasafe Inc **(PA)**	4226	E	650 875-3800	7707
Dav-El Reservations System Inc	4119	D	415 206-7950	7381
Davis Wright Tremaine LLP	8111	D	415 276-6500	17249
Days Inn By Wyndham San Frncsc	7011	D	415 766-0678	11047
Dco Environmental & Recycl LLC	3089	F	573 204-3844	4273
DDB Worldwide	7311	C	415 732-3600	11749
Deans & Homer **(PA)**	6331	E	415 421-8332	10167
Decentral TV Corporation	4813	D	415 480-6800	7945
Decimal Inc	7389	D	855 980-6612	14248
Deep Labs Inc **(PA)**	7372	E	877 504-4544	13113
Degenkolb Engineers **(PA)**	8711	D	415 392-6952	18686
Del Monte Corporation **(PA)**	2099	C	415 247-3000	2889
Delancey Street Foundation **(PA)**	8361	B	415 957-9800	18098
Delegat Usa Inc	2084	D	415 538-7988	2546
Deloitte Consulting LLP	8742	E	510 251-4400	19489
Deloitte Tax LLP	8721	B	415 783-4000	18949
Delta Dental of California **(PA)**	6324	B	415 972-8300	10103
Demandbase Inc **(PA)**	7372	C	415 683-2660	13114
Demandforce Inc	7371	E	800 246-9853	12380
Density Inc	7371	E	888 990-2253	12383
Dental Bneft Providers Cal Inc	8021	E	415 778-3800	15832
Derco Inc	5094	E	415 626-7442	9181
Designit North America Inc	7371	E	415 267-3500	12384
Detecon Inc	8748	E	415 549-6999	19761
Devonway Inc **(PA)**	7371	D	415 904-4000	12386
Devron H Char MD	8011	D	415 522-0700	15377
Dewolf Realty Co Inc	8741	D	415 221-2032	19324
Dhl Express (usa) Inc	4513	D	415 826-7338	7745
Diageo North America Inc	2084	E	415 835-7300	2550
Dialpad Inc	5045	B	760 648-3282	8693
Dietrich Post Co Inc	5112	E	510 596-0080	9206
Digital Japan LLC **(HQ)**	6798	D	415 738-6500	10816
Digital Mania Inc	2752	E	415 896-0500	3640
Digital Shadows Inc **(PA)**	7382	C	888 889-4143	14129
Digitalthink Inc **(DH)**	8742	C	415 625-4000	19494
Digits Financial Inc	7372	E	814 634-4487	13116
Dignity Community Care **(PA)**	8062	E	415 438-5500	16346
Dignity Health **(HQ)**	8062	C	415 438-5500	16347

GEOGRAPHIC

Employment Codes: A=Over 500 employees, B=251-500, C=101-250, D=51-100, E=20-50 F=10-19
2022 Northern California Business Directory and Buyers Guide
© Mergent Inc. 1-800-342-5647
1195

SAN FRANCISCO, CA

GEOGRAPHIC SECTION

Company	SIC	EMP	PHONE	ENTRY #
Dignity Health	8062	A	415 668-1000	16350
Dillingham & Murphy LLP (PA)	8111	E	415 397-2700	17252
Directly Inc	7371	D	650 714-7334	12393
Discord Inc	7371	C	650 389-2453	12394
Discount Builders Supply	5031	D	415 285-2800	8541
Dispatcher Newspaper	2711	F	415 775-0533	3432
Dissmeyer Corporation	1761	B	415 587-5869	1798
Divco West Acquisitions LLC (PA)	6722	E	415 284-5700	10752
Divco West RE Svcs Inc	6531	E	415 284-5700	10540
Divisadero 500 LLC	2599	E	415 572-6062	3335
Diy Co	3699	F	844 564-6349	6512
Docsend Inc	7372	D	888 258-5951	13118
Docusign Inc (PA)	7372	B	415 489-4940	13119
Dodge & Cox	6722	C	415 981-1710	10753
Dolby Laboratories Inc (PA)	3651	A	415 558-0200	5754
Dolby Labs Licensing Corp	3651	B	415 558-0200	5755
Domino Data Lab Inc (PA)	7372	C	415 570-2425	13121
Doremus & Company	7311	B	415 273-7800	11750
Doubledutch Inc (DH)	7372	C	800 748-9024	13123
Doximity Inc	7371	A	650 549-4330	12400
Dpp Tech Inc	7371	E	415 754-9170	12401
Dppm Inc	6531	D	415 695-7707	10542
Dreams Duvets & Bed Linens Inc	2392	F	415 543-1800	3023
Driver Inc	7372	D	415 999-4960	13125
Dropbox Inc (PA)	7372	A	415 857-6800	13127
Dtrs St Francis LLC	7011	D	415 397-7000	11064
Duetto Research Inc	7371	D	415 968-9389	12406
Durie Tangri LLP	8111	E	415 362-6666	17260
Dwell Life Inc	2741	F	212 382-2010	3567
Dwell Life Inc (PA)	2721	E	415 373-5100	3497
Earls Organic	5148	D	415 824-7419	9400
Eat Just Inc (PA)	2035	D	844 423-6637	2279
Eco Bay Services Inc	8748	D	415 643-7777	19764
Edaw Inc (HQ)	6552	E	415 955-2800	10701
Eden Technologies Inc	7371	D	800 754-3166	12412
Edge Electronics Corporation	3443	E	510 614-7988	4720
Edgewood Ctr For Chldren Fmlie (PA)	8361	C	415 681-3211	18102
Edgewood Partners Insur Ctr (HQ)	6411	D	415 356-3900	10275
Edward W Scott Electric Co Inc	4911	E	415 206-7120	8095
Eero LLC	3873	E	415 738-7972	13580
Efront Financial Solutions Inc	7371	D	415 653-3239	12413
Egomotion Corp (PA)	6531	E	415 849-4662	10543
Eidos Therapeutics Inc	8731	E	415 887-1471	19054
Eileen Nottoli	8111	E	415 837-1515	17261
Einstein Noah Rest Group Inc	2051	D	415 731-1700	2379
Eis Group Inc	7372	C	415 402-2622	13137
Eisneramper LLP	8721	E	415 974-6000	18955
EJ Weber Electric Co Inc	1731	E	415 641-9300	1497
Elastic Projects Inc	7371	D	415 857-1593	12417
Elation Health Inc	7389	D	415 213-5164	14261
Elder Care Alnce San Francisco	8051	A	415 337-1339	15983
Element Analytics Inc	7373	A	415 483-0310	13581
Element Science Inc	8733	E	415 872-6500	19215
Elevate Labs LLC	7371	E	415 875-9817	13140
Eleven Inc	7311	C	415 707-1111	11752
Ellation LLC (DH)	7371	C	415 796-3560	12419
Embarcadero Inn Associates	7011	D	415 495-2100	11079
Embark Trucks Inc	4212	E	765 409-4499	7462
Embassador Private Securities	6211	D	415 822-8811	9967
Embroker Insurance Svcs LLC (PA)	6411	C	844 436-2765	10278
Emburse LLC	7389	E	415 766-2012	14263
End Timey Industries LLC (PA)	3999	F	202 550-7570	7284
Engine No 1 LP	7389	E	628 251-1222	14264
Enovity Inc (DH)	8711	E	415 974-0390	18704
Entercom Media Corp	4832	D	415 765-4097	8022
Enterprise Rent-A-Car Co	7514	E	415 330-0290	14476
Enterprise Rnt—car San Frncsc	7514	E	415 882-9440	14477
Environmental Science Assoc (PA)	8731	E	415 896-5900	19057
Envoy Inc (PA)	7371	E	415 787-7871	12425
Epignosis LLC	7372	E	646 797-2799	13147
Episcpl Cmnty Svcs San Frncsc (PA)	8322	E	415 487-3300	17553
Epocrates (DH)	8099	B	650 227-1700	17143
Epstein Becker & Green PC	8111	D	415 398-3500	17262
Equal Rights Advocates Inc	8111	E	415 621-0672	17263
Equilibrium Management LLC	8742	E	415 516-2930	19507
Equinox Hotel Management Inc	7011	D	415 668-6887	11083
Equinox-76th Street Inc	7991	D	415 398-0747	14948
Eride Inc	7372	F	415 848-7800	13148
Ermico Enterprises Inc	3949	D	415 822-6776	7194
Ernst & Young LLP	8721	A	415 894-8000	18958
Escrowcom Inc	6099	E	949 635-3800	9847
Eshares Inc	8741	D	650 669-8381	19329
Esquivel Grading & Paving Inc	1711	E	415 822-5400	1037
Esterle LLC	7011	E	415 673-0691	11085
Esurance Insurance Svcs Inc (HQ)	6411	C	415 875-4500	10281
Etech-360 Inc	7371	A	714 900-3486	12430
Eventbrite Inc (PA)	7379	B	415 692-7779	13893
Eventbrite International Inc (PA)	7379	E	415 692-7779	13894
Events Management Inc	7299	B	415 487-9114	11717
Eventure Cpitl Partners II LLC	6799	E	415 869-5200	10843
Everest Wtrprfing Rstrtion Inc	7299	D	415 282-9800	11718
Eviction Def Cllbrtive Inc A C	3812	E	415 947-0797	6667
Evolent Health Inc	8099	B	571 389-6000	17145
Evolv Technology Solutions Inc (PA)	7372	E	415 444-9040	13152
Exacttarget LLC (HQ)	7372	E	415 901-7000	13154
Executives Outlet Inc	7991	D	415 433-6044	14949
Exigen (usa) Inc (PA)	7371	B	415 402-2600	12437
Exin LLC	2711	F	415 359-2600	3436
Expanse LLC	7371	C	415 590-0129	12438
Exploratorium	8412	B	415 528-4462	18271
Exponent Partners	8742	E	800 918-2917	19511
Express Messenger Systems Inc	4215	D	415 495-7300	7646
Extend Inc (PA)	7379	E	650 270-9184	13895
Extole Inc	8742	E	415 625-0411	19514
F50 League LLC	8699	E	415 939-4076	18566
Facebook Park Tower	7375	A	949 725-8637	13789
Faces SF Fmly Child Empwrmnt	8322	E	415 567-2357	17557
Fairmont Hrtig Pl Ghrrdelli Sq	7011	C	415 268-9900	11091
Family Caregiver Alliance	8322	E	415 434-3388	17560
Family House Inc (PA)	8322	E	415 476-8321	17561
Fandom Inc (PA)	7375	D	415 762-0780	13790
Farallon Capital Partners LP (PA)	6722	D	415 421-2132	10754
Fastly Inc (PA)	7371	A	844 432-7859	12444
Fastsigns	3993	E	415 537-6900	7229
Federal Hm Ln Bnk San Frncisco (PA)	6111	E	415 616-1000	9851
Felcor Union Square Lessee LLC	7011	D	415 398-8900	11094
Felton Institute (PA)	7363	D	415 474-7310	12172
Fenwick & West LLP	8111	E	415 875-2300	17265
Ffl Partners LLC (PA)	6726	D	415 402-2100	10777
Fibrogen Inc (PA)	2834	A	415 978-1200	3897
Fictiv Inc	7371	E	415 580-2509	12447
Field Construction Inc (PA)	1542	E	415 648-8140	871
Field Paoli Architects PC	8712	E	415 788-6606	18884
Fieldwirelabs Inc	7371	E	415 234-3050	12448
Figma Inc (PA)	7371	D	888 236-4310	12449
Figure Eight Technologies Inc	7374	D	415 471-1920	13714
Figure Technologies Inc (PA)	7389	B	888 819-6388	14272
Financialforcecom Inc (DH)	7371	A	866 743-2220	12451
Finastra Merchant Services Inc (PA)	6099	D	415 277-9900	9848
Fine Line Group Inc	1542	E	415 777-4070	872
Firewood Marketing Inc	8742	E	415 872-5132	19515
First Last & Always Inc	1752	E	415 541-7978	1769
First Advntage Tlent MGT Svcs	7372	E	415 446-3930	13161
First Orleans Hotel Assoc LP	7011	C	415 397-5572	11095
First Republic Bank	6022	E	415 392-3888	9720
First Republic Bank	6022	E	415 561-2988	9722
First Republic Bank	6022	D	415 564-8881	9725
First Republic Bank	6022	D	415 487-0888	9726
First Republic Bank	6022	D	415 975-3877	9727
First Republic Bank (PA)	6029	B	415 392-1400	9757
First Republic Inv MGT Inc	6022	E	415 296-5727	9730
First Round Capital LLC	6799	E	415 646-0072	10844
First Student Inc	4151	C	415 778-7779	7436
Firstcall (PA)	7381	E	415 781-4300	14059
Firstup Inc (PA)	7372	C	415 655-2700	13162
Fisher Development Inc	1542	E	415 228-3060	873
Fitbit LLC (DH)	3829	A	415 513-1000	6901
Fitstar Inc	7372	E	415 409-8348	13163
Five Keys Schools and Programs	8322	E	415 734-3310	17572
Five Point Holdings LLC	6531	E	415 344-8865	10549
Flexport Inc (PA)	7372	A	415 231-5252	13165
Flickr Inc	7371	E	650 265-0396	12455
Flock Is Inc	7371	E	415 851-2376	12456
Florence Villa Hotel	7011	C	415 397-7700	11096
Florence Villa Hotel LLC	7011	E	415 397-7700	11097
Fluxx Labs Inc	7371	D	408 981-7080	12458
Flynn Properties Inc	6531	E	415 765-6500	10551
Fong & Chan Architect Inc	7389	E	415 931-8600	14275
Forager Project LLC (PA)	2037	D	855 729-5253	2293
Forethought Technologies Inc	3231	E	415 994-9706	4388
Forge Architecture	8712	E	415 434-0320	18885
Forge Global Inc (PA)	7372	C	415 881-1612	13171
Forgerock Inc (PA)	5045	A	415 599-1100	8706
Forgerock Us Inc (HQ)	7372	E	415 599-1100	13172
Form & Fiction LLC (PA)	7336	E	415 802-2000	11860
Formation Inc	7372	D	650 257-2277	13173
Fort Mason Center	8999	E	415 345-7500	19901
Fort Point Beer Company (PA)	2082	C	415 336-3596	2478
Fortezza Iridium Holdings Inc	7372	A	415 765-6500	13175
Forward Management LLC	6282	E	415 869-6300	10044
Fotowtio Rnewable Ventures Inc	8711	E	415 986-8038	18711
Found Health Inc	8734	E	415 854-3296	19274
Foundation For Nat Progress	2721	E	415 321-1700	3499
Founders Fund LLC	7389	E	415 359-1922	14276
Foundtion For Stdnts Rsing ABO	8641	D	415 333-4222	18416
Four Seasons Hotel Inc	7011	C	415 633-3441	11103
Fox Rothschild LLP	8111	E	415 539-3336	17268
Foxpass Inc	7372	F	415 805-6350	13177
Framehawk Inc	7372	F	415 371-9110	13178
Francis Ford Coppola Inc	7812	B	415 788-7500	14791
Francisca Club	8641	E	415 781-1200	18417
Francisco Partners Agility LP (PA)	6722	C	415 418-2900	10755
Francisco Partners GP III LP (HQ)	7373	D	415 418-2900	13592
Francisco Partners Iv-A LP	6722	E	415 418-2900	10756
Francisco Partners MGT LP (PA)	6799	E	415 418-2900	10846
Francisco Partners Vi LP (PA)	7389	C	415 418-2900	14278
Francsco Prtners III Cayman LP	8748	E	415 418-2900	19778
Free Stream Media Corp (PA)	5199	E	415 854-0073	9659
Freedom of Press Foundation	2721	F	510 995-0780	3501
Fremont Group LLC (PA)	6282	E	415 284-8500	10047
Fremont Mutual Funds Inc	6211	D	800 548-4539	9971
Fremont Properties Inc	6512	E	415 284-8500	10388
Frog Design Inc (DH)	7336	B	415 442-4804	11861
Frontapp Inc	7372	D	415 680-3048	13181

GEOGRAPHIC SECTION

SAN FRANCISCO, CA

Company	SIC	EMP	PHONE	ENTRY #
Fti Consulting Inc	8748	D	415 283-4200	19780
Ftv Management Company LP (PA)	6722	C	415 229-3000	10761
Fullcontact Inc	7371	E	415 366-6587	12464
Fun To Stay Lessee Inc	7011	E	415 882-1300	11108
Funding Circle Usa Inc	6153	D	855 385-5356	9870
Fundx Investment Group LLC	2741	F	415 986-7979	3572
Fuse Project LLC	8748	D	415 908-1492	19782
Future State	7379	C	925 956-4200	13899
Fuzebox Software Corporation (HQ)	7372	D	415 692-4800	13183
Gainsight Inc	7371	B	888 623-8562	12469
Galindo Instlltion Mvg Svcs In	2542	F	415 861-4230	3325
Galleria Park Associates LLC	7011	E	415 781-3060	11111
Gameplay Inc	7993	E	415 617-1550	15037
Gasna 10p LLC	4911	E	775 562-4104	8097
Gasna 36p LLC	4911	E	775 562-4104	8098
Gasna 38p LLC	4911	E	775 562-4104	8099
Gasna 39p LLC	4911	E	415 230-5601	8100
Gasna 44p LLC	4911	E	415 230-5601	8101
Gasna 45p LLC	4911	E	415 230-5601	8102
Gasna 57p LLC	4911	E	415 230-5601	8103
Gasna 60p LLC	4911	E	415 230-5601	8104
Gasna 61p LLC	4911	E	415 230-5601	8105
Gasna 65p LLC	4911	E	775 562-4104	8106
Gasna 69p LLC	4911	E	415 230-5601	8107
Gasna 75p LLC	4911	E	775 562-4104	8108
Gasna 76p LLC	4911	E	775 562-4104	8109
Gasna 78p LLC	4911	E	415 230-5601	8110
Gasna 79p LLC	4911	E	415 230-5601	8111
Gasna 81p LLC	4911	E	775 562-4104	8112
Gastroenterology Division	8011	D	415 206-8823	15414
Gavin Atwood Coombs (PA)	6531	D	415 292-2384	10557
Gayner Engineers	8711	E	415 474-9500	18718
Gb Sport Sf LLC	2386	E	415 863-6171	3017
Gci Inc	1542	D	415 978-2790	876
GCI General Contractors	1799	D	415 978-2790	2033
Gcl Solar Energy Inc	1711	D	415 362-2601	1270
Geary Darling Lessee Inc	7011	C	415 292-0100	11113
Gelfland Partners Architects	8712	E	415 346-4040	18886
General RE Corporation	6331	D	415 781-1700	10169
Generate Capital Inc	6799	D	415 360-3063	10847
Gensler Asscts/Ntrnational Ltd (HQ)	8712	B	415 433-3700	18887
Genstar Capital LLC (PA)	6211	E	415 834-2350	9972
Genstar Capital Partners Ix LP	6722	E	415 834-2350	10762
Geographic Expeditions Inc	4724	D	415 922-0448	7797
German Motors Corporation (PA)	7532	C	415 590-3773	14525
Getaround (PA)	7514	C	866 438-2768	14489
Gfk Custom Research LLC	8732	D	415 398-2812	19161
Ggc Administration LLC	6719	A	415 983-2700	10736
GI GP IV LLC (PA)	6211	E	415 688-4800	9973
Giant Creative Strategy Llc	7311	E	415 655-5200	11755
Gic Real Estate Inc	6798	E	415 229-1800	10820
Gic Real Estate Inc (DH)	6531	E	415 229-1800	10558
Giga Omni Media Inc	7383	D	415 974-6355	14154
Gigster Inc	7371	D	941 888-4447	12474
Gingerio Inc	7371	D	408 455-0574	12475
Gitlab Inc (PA)	7372	F	415 829-2854	13189
Gladly Software Inc	7371	D	650 387-8485	12476
Gladstone Foundation	8641	E	415 734-2000	18425
Glass Lewis & Co LLC (HQ)	8732	D	415 678-4110	19162
Glassdoor Inc (HQ)	7361	C	415 275-7411	12093
Global Fund For Women Inc	8399	E	415 248-4800	18229
Global Innovation Partners LLC	7389	D	650 233-3600	14284
Globant LLC (HQ)	7371	A	877 215-5230	12480
Glodow Nead Communications LLC	8743	E	415 394-6500	19686
Glp	8351	C	415 777-9696	17941
Glu Mobile Inc (PA)	7372	B	415 800-6100	13192
Glumac International (PA)	8711	E	415 398-7667	18723
Gmr Marketing LLC	8743	E	415 229-7733	19687
Go West Holdings LLC	7389	C	888 670-0080	14285
Gobble Inc	2099	C	650 847-1258	2897
Godfrey Dadich Partners LLC	7311	E	415 217-2800	11756
Golden Gate Brdge Hwy Trnsp Ds (PA)	4785	C	415 921-5858	7870
Golden Gate Cncil Amrcn Yuth H	7011	E	415 474-5721	11114
Golden Gate Cncil Amrcn Yuth H	7011	E	415 771-7277	11115
Golden Gate Debris Box Service (HQ)	5113	E	415 626-4000	9214
Golden Gate Kindergarten Assn	8351	E	415 931-1018	17942
Golden Gate Nat Prks Cnsrvancy	8999	C	415 440-4068	19903
Golden Gate Nat Prks Cnsrvancy	8641	D	415 933-6760	18426
Golden Gate Nat Prks Cnsrvancy (PA)	8999	E	415 561-3000	19905
Golden Gate Private Equity Inc (PA)	6799	A	415 983-2706	10850
Golden Gate Regional Ctr Inc (PA)	8322	C	415 546-9222	17589
Golden Gate Scnic Stmship Corp	4489	E	415 901-5249	7720
Golden Gate Urology Inc (PA)	8011	D	415 543-2830	15416
Golden Gateidence Opco LLC	8052	E	415 922-5085	16184
Golden State Warriors LLC	7941	D	415 388-0100	14907
Goldenspear LLC	7389	E	415 643-0100	14286
Goldman Enterprises	0181	E	415 821-7726	124
Good Smritan Fmly Resource Ctr	8322	E	415 401-4253	17592
Goodby Slverstein Partners Inc	7311	C	392 920-0669	11757
Goodwill Inds San Frncsco San (PA)	8331	B	415 575-2101	17815
Google LLC	7371	E	415 546-3149	12483
Gordon Rees Scully Mansukhani (PA)	8111	B	415 986-5900	17279
Gourmet Plus Inc	5145	E	415 643-9945	9354
Goyard Miami LLC	3161	E	415 398-1110	4348
Graham & James LLP	8111	A	415 954-0200	17280
Grammarly Inc (PA)	7373	C	888 318-6146	13600
Grand Hyatt Sf LLC	7011	E	415 398-1234	11116
Grand Rounds Inc (PA)	8099	C	800 929-0926	17150
Granite Solutions Groupe Inc (PA)	7361	C	415 963-3999	12094
Gree International Inc	7371	C	415 409-5200	12488
Gree International Entrmt Inc	7371	C	415 409-5200	12489
Green Catalysts Inc (PA)	2819	D	415 271-0675	3789
Green Living Planet LLC	7349	D	415 715-4718	11958
Greene Rdvsky Maloney Share LP	8111	E	415 981-1400	17283
Greenoaks Opportunity I LLC	8742	E	415 805-8922	19521
Greentree Property MGT Inc	6512	E	415 347-8600	10391
Greyline Partners LLC (PA)	8742	E	415 604-9527	19523
Grid Net Inc (PA)	7371	E	415 419-6632	12490
Grosvenor Inv MGT US Inc	6411	D	415 773-0275	10289
Grosvenor Properties Ltd (PA)	7011	E	415 421-5940	11121
Grosvenor Properties Ltd	6531	B	415 421-1899	10565
Ground Control Inc	3663	E	415 508-8589	5846
Gryphon Investors Inc (PA)	6799	A	415 217-7400	10852
Guadalupe Associates Inc (PA)	2741	F	415 387-2324	3574
Gum Moon Residence Hall	7021	E	415 421-8827	11589
Gum Sun Times Inc (PA)	2711	E	415 379-6788	3444
Gumas Advertising LLC	7311	E	415 621-7575	11759
Gupshup Inc (PA)	7372	B	415 506-9095	13203
Gusto Inc (PA)	7372	C	800 936-0383	13204
Guzzardo and Associates Inc	0781	E	510 923-1677	418
H&Gbygiselleco	0782	F	415 829-3867	469
H&H Catering LP	8742	E	408 354-1964	19527
H2o Plus LLC	7231	E	415 964-5100	11684
H2o Plus LLC (PA)	2844	D	800 242-2284	4084
Haas Jr Evelyn & Walter Fund	8699	D	415 856-1400	18567
Habitat For Hmnity Grter San F	8399	E	415 625-1000	18231
Hackerearth Inc	7371	C	650 461-4192	12495
Hackerone Inc (PA)	7379	B	415 891-0777	13904
Hall Capital Partners LLC (PA)	6722	E	415 288-0544	10763
Halo Neuro Inc	3845	F	415 851-3338	7106
Hamilton Families	8322	D	415 409-2100	17597
Hamlin Hotel LP	7011	E	415 984-1450	11124
Handley Hotels Inc	7011	C	415 781-7800	11125
Handpick Inc (PA)	7371	E	415 859-8955	12496
Hands-On Mobile Inc (PA)	7373	E	415 580-6400	13603
Hanson Bridgett LLP (PA)	8111	B	415 543-2055	17287
Harrison Drywall Inc	1742	E	415 821-9584	1680
Harsch Investment Realty LLC	7521	E	415 673-6757	14512
Hart Howerton Ltd (PA)	0781	D	415 439-2200	419
Hartle Media Ventures LLC	2721	E	415 362-7797	3502
Haseeb Al-Mufti MD Inc (PA)	8011	E	510 604-6012	15425
Hashicorp Inc (PA)	7371	A	415 301-3250	12497
Hashicorp Federal Inc	7371	A	415 672-0721	12498
Hassard Bonnington LLP (PA)	8111	E	415 288-9800	17288
Hasura Inc	7373	E	833 690-2124	13606
Hathaway Dinwiddie Cnstr Co	1542	B	415 986-2718	887
Hathaway Dinwiddie Cnstr Group (PA)	1542	E	415 986-2718	888
Hawthrn/Stone RE Invstmnts Inc	6531	E	415 441-8400	10571
Hayes Convalescent Hospital	8051	E	415 931-8806	16017
Health Evolution Partners (PA)	8741	D	415 362-5800	19347
Healthline Media Inc (PA)	2741	B	415 281-3100	3576
Healthline Networks Inc	7375	E	415 281-3100	13791
Hearsay Social Inc (PA)	7372	C	888 399-2280	13207
Heath Ceramics Ltd	5032	E	415 399-9284	8628
Heath Ceramics Ltd	3269	E	415 361-5552	4409
Hebrew Home For Aged Disabled	8051	A	415 334-2500	16020
Heights Capital Management Inc	6211	D	415 403-6500	9975
Helix Medical Comm LLC (DH)	5047	E	650 357-0958	8782
Hellmuth Obata & Kassabaum Inc (DH)	8712	C	415 243-0555	18888
Helpware Inc (PA)	7371	E	949 273-2824	12499
Henry Broadcasting Co	4832	E	415 285-1133	8026
Henry J Kaiser Fmly Foundation (PA)	8699	C	650 854-9400	18569
Herman Coliver Locus Arch	8712	E	415 495-1776	18889
Hero Digital LLC (PA)	8748	C	415 230-0724	19789
Heroku Inc	7372	E	650 704-6107	13209
Herrero Builders Incorporated (PA)	1541	C	415 824-7675	796
Highland Technology	3829	E	415 551-1700	6905
Highmark Capital MGT Inc	6282	D	800 582-4734	10048
Highwire Public Relations Inc (HQ)	8743	D	415 963-4174	19688
Hilb Rgal Hobbs Insur Svcs Inc (DH)	6411	E	212 915-8084	10292
Hill & Co Real Estate Inc (HQ)	6531	E	415 921-6000	10575
Hilton San Francisco Fincl Dst	7011	D	415 433-6600	11144
Hims Inc (HQ)	2844	D	415 851-0195	4085
Hims & Hers Health Inc (PA)	2834	E	415 851-0195	3923
Hinge Health Inc (PA)	8099	A	855 902-7777	17153
Hint Inc	2086	E	415 513-4051	2792
Hipcamp Inc	4724	C	242 377-8982	7798
Hmb Investors LLC	7011	E	415 474-5400	11146
HMw and Jk Enterprises Inc (PA)	6163	E	415 731-3100	9941
Hoefer & Arnett Inc (PA)	6211	E	415 538-5700	9976
Hogan Lovells US LLP	8111	D	415 374-2300	17291
Hollins Consulting Inc	8741	E	415 238-1300	19348
Holzmueller Corporation	7359	E	415 826-8383	12046
Homebridge Inc	8322	B	415 255-2079	17602
Homeless Childrens Network	8699	E	415 437-3990	18571
Homeless Prenatal Program	8322	E	415 546-6756	17604
Homelssness Spprtive Hsing Dep	8399	C	628 652-7700	18233
Homestar Systems Inc	7379	D	415 323-4008	13906
Honeybook Inc	7371	D	770 403-9234	12501
Hood & Strong LLP (PA)	8721	E	415 781-0793	18962
Hootsuite Media US Inc	7375	E	206 519-5705	13792
Horizons Unlmted San Frncsco I	8322	E	415 487-6700	17605
Horn Group Inc	7311	E	415 905-4000	11761
Hornberger Worstell Assoc Inc	8712	E	415 391-1080	18891

Employment Codes: A=Over 500 employees, B=251-500, C=101-250, D=51-100, E=20-50 F=10-19

SAN FRANCISCO, CA

GEOGRAPHIC SECTION

Company	SIC	EMP	PHONE	ENTRY #
Hornblower Energy LLC	2813	F	415 788-7020	3771
Hornblower Group Inc (PA)	4724	B	415 635-2210	7799
Hornblower Yachts LLC (PA)	4724	C	415 788-8866	7800
Horsley Bridge Partners Inc (PA)	6799	E	415 986-7733	10854
Horsley Bridge Partners LLC	6799	D	415 986-7733	10855
Hotaling & Co LLC (PA)	2085	E	415 630-5910	2773
Hotel Emplyee Rest Emplyee Un	8631	E	415 864-8770	18359
Hotel Nikko San Francisco Inc	7011	B	415 394-1111	11170
Hotel Tonight Inc (PA)	7011	B	800 208-2949	11172
Hotel Tonight LLC (PA)	7011	C	248 525-3814	11173
Hotel Whitcomb	7011	D	415 626-8000	11174
Hotwire Inc	4813	C	415 343-8400	7958
Housecanary Inc (PA)	7374	B	866 729-7770	13718
Howard Hughes Medical Inst	8731	D	415 476-9668	19069
Hp Inc	3571	E	415 979-3700	5250
Hub Intrntional Insur Svcs Inc	6411	E	415 512-2100	10294
Huey Construction MGT Co Inc	1521	E	415 558-9806	652
Humangear Inc	3089	F	415 580-7553	4289
Huntsman Architectural Group (PA)	8712	D	415 394-1212	18892
Huskies Lessee LLC (PA)	7011	C	415 392-7755	11177
Hustle Inc	7371	E	415 851-4878	12506
Hvr Software Inc (PA)	7372	E	415 655-6361	13218
Hvr Software Usa Inc	7372	D	415 489-3427	13219
Hvsf Transition LLC	7311	D	415 477-1999	11762
Hyatt Corporation	7011	B	415 848-6050	11180
Hyatt Corporation	7011	A	415 788-1234	11183
Iberia Catering Inc	7299	E	415 587-5117	11720
Ibex Enterprises	5021	E	415 777-0202	8495
Icon Internet Ventures Inc	8742	E	415 874-3397	19534
Ideoorg	8641	D	415 426-7080	18433
Idg Consumer & Smb Inc (DH)	2721	C	415 243-0500	3503
Ifwe Inc (HQ)	7372	E	415 946-1850	13223
Igt Interactive Inc (DH)	7999	E	415 625-8300	15211
Ihms (sf) LLC	7011	C	415 781-5555	11187
Ijk & Co Inc	3699	E	415 826-8899	6525
Imagine H20 Inc	8741	E	415 828-6344	19353
Immersion Corporation (PA)	3577	E	408 467-1900	5374
Immigration Inst of Bay Area (PA)	8322	A	415 538-8100	17612
Imperfect Foods Inc (PA)	2099	A	415 829-2262	2904
Imperial Parking (us) LLC	7521	A	415 495-3909	14513
Incountry Inc	7372	A	415 323-0322	13227
Indepndnt Online Dstribution (PA)	7389	D	415 777-4632	14301
Indiegogo Inc	4813	C	866 641-4646	7961
Indus Corporation	7371	D	415 202-1830	12516
Industrial Grwth Partners V LP	6719	C	415 882-4550	10738
Industrial Lght Mgic Vncver LL	7812	C	415 292-4671	14792
Industrial Relations Cal Dept	8631	E	415 703-5133	18361
Industry Ventures LLC (PA)	6799	D	415 273-4201	10857
Influxdata Inc	7371	C	415 295-1901	12517
Infotech Consulting LLC	7361	E	415 986-5400	12100
Infotech Sourcing	7379	E	415 986-5400	13913
Infovie Inc	7379	E	551 214-8745	13914
Infoworld Media Group Inc (DH)	2721	C	415 243-4344	3504
Ingenio Inc	4813	C	415 248-4000	7962
Ingenio LLC	8742	D	415 992-8218	19537
Inkling Systems Inc	8742	D	415 975-4420	19538
Inmobi Inc (HQ)	7311	D	650 269-5173	11763
Inn At Opera A Cal Ltd Partnr	7011	E	415 863-8400	11190
Innovaccer Inc (PA)	7371	B	650 479-4891	12523
Inpowered Inc	4813	E	415 796-7800	11764
Insideview Technologies Inc	5045	C	415 728-9309	8713
Insignia	7373	E	415 777-0320	13612
Insignia/Esg Ht Partners Inc	6531	B	415 772-0123	10580
Instabase Inc (PA)	7389	D	213 453-0488	14304
Instagis Inc (PA)	7372	F	415 527-6636	13239
Institute On Aging	8322	D	415 600-2690	17615
Institute On Aging (PA)	8322	E	415 750-4101	17616
Institutional Venture Partners	6799	E	415 432-4660	10858
Instituto Familiar De La Raza	8099	D	415 229-0500	17156
Insurnce Svcs San Frncisco Inc	6411	E	415 788-9810	10297
Integrated Digital Media (PA)	2752	D	415 986-4091	3659
Intercntnntal Htels San Frncsc	7011	C	415 616-6500	11194
Intercom Inc	7371	B	831 920-7088	12532
International Bus Mchs Corp	5044	C	415 545-4747	8652
International Hotel Assoc LLC	7011	E	415 283-4832	11195
International Transport Federa	8631	E	415 440-7043	18362
Internet Archive	7375	C	415 561-6767	13795
Internet Escrow Services Inc	6531	E	888 511-8600	10581
Interntnal Assn Bus Cmmncators	8611	D	415 544-4711	18307
Interntnal Brthd Elec Wkrs Lca	8631	E	415 861-5752	18365
Interpacific Group Inc	8721	A	415 442-0711	18963
Intershop Communications Inc	7372	E	415 844-1500	13243
Invitae Corporation (PA)	8071	D	415 374-7782	16786
Invuity Inc	3841	C	415 665-2100	6989
Ionetix Corporation (PA)	3699	F	415 944-1440	6528
Ip Portfolio I LLC	4911	E	510 260-2192	8117
Iqvia Inc	8732	D	415 692-9898	19168
Irhythm Technologies Inc (PA)	3841	E	415 632-5700	6991
Ironclad Inc (PA)	7371	C	855 999-4766	12540
Ishares Inc (PA)	6722	A	415 597-2000	10764
Isolation Network Inc (PA)	3651	E	415 489-7000	5759
Isrs/Aao	8011	E	415 447-0369	15439
J Flores Construction Co Inc	1623	E	415 337-2934	1109
Jack Plump Inc	7011	E	415 346-5712	11204
Jackson & Hertogs LLP	8111	E	415 986-4559	17295
Jaguar Health Inc (PA)	2834	E	415 371-8300	3932
Jame Hotel Corporation	7011	D	415 885-2500	11208
Japanese Cltral Cmnty N Cali C	6512	E	415 567-5505	10393
Japanese Cmnty Youth Council (PA)	8399	D	415 202-7905	18235
Jasper Hall LLC	7299	D	415 872-5745	11722
Jbear Associates LLC	7011	E	415 673-2332	11209
JC Metal Specialists Inc (PA)	3441	F	415 822-3878	4668
Jeremiahs Pick Coffee Company	2095	F	415 206-9900	2839
Jessica McClintock Inc (PA)	2361	D	415 553-8200	3015
Jewish Cmnty Ctr San Francisco (PA)	7032	D	415 292-1200	11606
Jewish Cmnty Fdrtion of San Fr (PA)	8399	D	415 777-0411	18236
Jewish Family and Chld Svcs (PA)	8322	D	415 449-1200	17625
Jewish Senior Living Group	6513	D	415 562-2600	10442
Jiff Inc (PA)	7371	B	415 829-1400	12548
Jinkosolar (us) Holding Inc (PA)	1711	C	415 402-0502	1295
Jinkosolar (us) Inc	3674	D	415 402-0502	6170
Jmp Group Inc (HQ)	6211	D	415 835-8900	9977
Jmp Securities LLC (DH)	6211	C	415 835-8900	9978
Jn Projects Inc	7299	D	415 766-0273	11723
John Paul USA (PA)	7363	D	415 905-6088	12177
John Stewart Company (PA)	6531	D	415 345-4400	10588
John Stewart Company	6531	E	415 621-6258	10589
Joie De Vivre Hospitality LLC (PA)	7011	E	415 922-6000	11213
Joie De Vivre Hospitality LLC	7011	D	415 278-3700	11214
Joie De Vivre Hospitality LLC	7011	D	415 567-8467	11215
Joie De Vivre Hospitality LLC	7011	D	415 441-2700	11217
Joie De Vivre Hospitality LLC	7011	B	415 921-5520	11218
Joie De Vivre Hospitality LLC	7011	E	415 776-1380	11219
Joie De Vivre Hospitality LLC	7011	E	415 775-1755	11221
Joie De Vivre Hotels	7011	E	415 776-1380	11223
Jones Hall A Prof Law Corp	8111	E	415 391-5780	17298
Joseph Cozza Salon Inc (PA)	7231	E	415 433-3030	11687
Joyent Inc	7379	C	415 400-0600	13927
JR Watkins LLC	2392	E	415 477-8500	3027
Jumpshot Inc	7371	D	415 212-9250	12552
Jumpstart Digital Mktg Inc (DH)	8742	D	415 844-6336	19547
June Sf LLC	2082	E	415 906-4021	2483
Juniper Square Inc	5045	B	415 841-2722	8717
Justanswer LLC	4813	E	800 785-2305	7968
Justice Dvrsity Ctr of The Bar	8111	C	415 575-3130	17301
Juul Labs Inc (PA)	3999	B	415 829-2336	7290
K J Woods Construction Inc	1623	E	415 759-0506	1511
Kabam Inc (HQ)	7371	A	604 256-0054	12553
Kai Ming Inc (PA)	8699	E	415 982-4777	18575
Kaise Perma San Franc Medic Ce	3842	E	415 833-2000	7075
Kaiser Foundation Hospitals	8011	C	415 833-2616	15447
Kaiser Foundation Hospitals	8011	A	415 833-2000	15451
Kaiser Foundation Hospitals	8062	A	415 833-2200	16401
Kaiser Foundation Hospitals	8011	A	415 216-5853	15469
Kaiser Foundation Hospitals	8011	C	415 833-9688	15473
Kaiser Foundation Hospitals	8011	C	415 833-3450	15482
Kaiser Foundation Hospitals	8011	A	415 833-2000	15489
Kaiser Foundation Hospitals	8011	C	415 833-3780	15491
Kaizen Technology Partners LLC	7371	E	415 515-1909	12554
Kallidus Inc	7371	D	877 554-2176	12555
Kas Direct LLC	2676	E	516 934-0541	3396
Kba2 Inc	7372	E	415 528-5500	13260
Keep Truckin Inc (PA)	7371	E	855 434-3564	12558
Keker Van Nest & Peters LLP	8111	D	415 391-5400	17303
Ken Fulk Inc	7389	E	415 285-1164	14316
Kendo Holdings Inc (HQ)	5122	B	415 284-6000	9228
Kennedy/Jenks Consultants Inc (PA)	8711	D	415 243-2150	18747
Kenshoo Inc (HQ)	8742	E	877 536-7462	19549
Ketchum Incorporated	8743	E	415 984-6100	19690
Kevala Inc	7372	E	415 712-7829	13263
Keystone Strategy LLC	8748	E	877 419-2623	19805
Khp III SF Sutter LLC (PA)	7011	D	415 921-4000	11229
Kidder Mathews California Inc (HQ)	6531	E	415 229-8888	10594
Kidder Mathews Inc	6531	E	415 229-8888	10596
Kikkoman Sales Usa Inc (HQ)	5149	E	415 956-7750	9461
Kimpton Hotel & Rest Group LLC	7011	C	415 885-2500	11230
Kimpton Hotel & Rest Group LLC (HQ)	7011	E	415 397-5572	11231
Kimpton Hotel & Rest Group LLC	7011	C	415 561-1100	11232
Kimpton Hotel & Rest Group LLC	7011	C	415 392-8800	11233
Kimpton Hotel & Rest Group LLC	7011	C	415 561-1111	11234
Kimpton Hotel & Rest Group LLC	7011	C	415 292-0100	11235
Kinesso LLC	7311	E	415 262-5900	11765
Kinetix Technology Svcs LLC	7379	E	650 454-8850	13929
Kingfish Group Inc (PA)	6799	D	650 980-0200	10861
Kings Asian Gourmet Inc	2032	E	415 222-6100	2203
Kinsa Inc	8082	D	347 405-4315	16907
Kinsale Holdings Inc (PA)	8742	C	415 400-2600	19550
Kipp Foundation	8399	E	415 399-1556	18238
Kirkland & Ellis LLP	8111	C	415 439-1400	17304
Kisco Senior Living LLC	8741	C	415 664-6264	19359
KKR Financial Corporation (DH)	6798	D	415 315-3620	10821
Klingstubbins Inc	8999	D	415 356-2040	19909
KMD Architects (PA)	8712	D	415 398-5191	18894
Kms Fishermans Wharf LP	7011	D	415 561-1100	11237
Knobbe Martens Olson Bear LLP	8111	E	415 954-4114	17305
Kong Inc	7371	E	415 754-9283	12561
Kong Inc	7371	E	415 754-9283	12562
Kountable Inc (PA)	7389	D	310 613-5481	14318
Kpisoft Inc	7372	E	415 439-5228	13268
Kpmg Llp	8721	E	415 963-5100	18964
Kqed Inc (PA)	4833	B	415 864-2000	8049
Krueger Bros Builders Inc	1521	E	415 863-5846	660
Kyo Autism Therapy LLC (PA)	8742	B	877 264-6747	19553
L Y Z Ltd (PA)	2335	F	415 445-9505	3002

	SIC	EMP	PHONE	ENTRY #
L-O Soma Hotel Inc	7011	A	415 974-6400	11240
La Brothers Enterprise Inc	2752	E	415 626-8818	3668
La Casa De Las Madres	8322	E	415 503-0500	17631
La Raza Centro Legal SF	8111	E	415 575-3500	17307
Labelbox Inc **(PA)**	7372	E	415 294-0791	13271
Lambdatest Inc	7373	C	866 430-7087	13623
Landmark Worldwide LLC **(PA)**	8742	C	415 981-8850	19555
Landor LLC	7389	D	415 365-1700	14319
Landor Associates Intl Ltd **(DH)**	7336	C	415 365-1700	11866
Larkin Street Youth Services	8322	D	415 567-1020	17634
Latch So Chropractic Prof Corp	8041	E	415 775-4204	15866
Law Offces Rudy Exlrod Zeff LL	8111	E	415 434-9800	17311
Law Office Robert B Jobe PC	8111	D	415 956-5513	17312
Lawson Roofing Co Inc	1761	D	415 285-1661	1815
Lcr-Dixon Corporation	7372	F	404 307-1695	13275
Leadspace Inc **(DH)**	7379	E	855 532-3772	13930
Leapyear Technologies Inc	7371	E	510 542-9193	12572
Leemah Electronics Inc	4911	E	415 394-1288	8119
Leewood Press Inc	2752	E	415 896-0513	3671
Legion Corporation **(PA)**	7381	D	800 750-0062	14073
Leighfisher Inc **(HQ)**	8742	D	650 579-7722	19558
Leland Prchini Stnberg Mtzger	8111	E	415 957-1800	17315
Lembi Group Inc **(PA)**	6531	D	415 861-1111	10600
Lendingclub Corporation **(PA)**	6141	A	415 632-5600	9859
Lendlease US Construction Inc	8741	E	415 512-0586	19363
Lendup Card Services Inc	7389	C	855 253-6387	14320
Let It Flho Lessee Inc	7011	E	415 397-7700	11261
Letterman Digital Arts Ltd	8351	D	415 746-5044	17964
Level-It Installations Ltd	1542	E	604 942-2022	915
Lever Inc	7371	D	415 458-2731	12573
Levi Strauss & Co **(PA)**	2325	A	415 501-6000	2987
Lewis & Taylor LLC	7349	C	415 781-3496	11966
Lewis Brsbois Bsgard Smith LLP	8111	D	415 362-2580	17316
Lieff Cbrser Hmann Brnstein LL **(PA)**	8111	C	415 788-0245	17317
Lifi Labs Inc **(PA)**	3229	E	650 739-5563	4374
Liftopia Inc **(PA)**	8742	D	415 728-0444	19560
Lightbend Inc	7371	D	877 989-7372	12574
Lighthuse For Blind Vslly Impr **(PA)**	8322	E	415 431-1481	17636
Lilt Inc **(PA)**	7371	D	650 530-7180	12575
Lime Light Crm Inc	3274	E	800 455-9645	4511
Linardos Enterprises Inc	8742	D	415 644-0827	19561
Linden Research Inc	7371	B	415 243-9000	12576
Lindquist Von Husen & Joyce	8721	E	415 957-9999	18966
Line2 Inc	8999	E	415 223-5811	19910
Linqia Inc	8742	D	415 913-7179	19562
Linux Foundation Japan LLC **(PA)**	8641	C	415 723-9709	18438
Little Giant Bldg Maint Inc **(PA)**	7349	D	415 508-0282	11967
Little Passports Inc	3944	E	415 874-9577	7179
Little Ssters of The Poor Okla	8361	D	415 751-6510	18140
Littler Mendelson PC **(PA)**	8111	B	415 433-1940	17318
Littlethings Inc	7379	D	917 364-9277	13931
Live Fit Gym Inc **(PA)**	7991	D	415 525-4364	14959
Liveramp Holdings Inc **(PA)**	7374	B	866 352-3267	13724
Livevox Inc **(PA)**	8748	C	415 671-6000	19812
LLP Moss Adams	8721	D	415 956-1500	18970
Loc-Aid Technologies Inc **(PA)**	7371	E	415 666-2370	12578
Localmind Corp	7371	A	858 382-4809	12579
Logans Gap B Member LLC **(DH)**	4931	D	415 283-4000	8214
Logik Systems Inc **(PA)**	7375	D	844 363-3347	13799
Long & Levit LLP	8111	D	415 397-2222	17320
Lookout Inc **(PA)**	7373	B	650 241-2358	13627
Loopnet Inc **(HQ)**	6531	C	415 243-4200	10602
Lopezgarcia Group Inc **(DH)**	8711	C	415 796-8100	18754
Low Ball & Lynch A Prof Corp **(PA)**	8111	D	415 981-6630	17321
Lowes Home Centers LLC	5031	C	415 486-8611	8558
Lowpensky Moulding	2431	F	415 822-7422	3141
Loyal3 Holdings Inc	7389	D	415 981-0700	14324
Lucasfilm Ltd **(DH)**	7812	C	415 623-1000	14793
Lucidworks Inc **(PA)**	7373	B	415 329-6515	13629
Luis A Agurto	7342	E	925 238-0744	11901
Lukes Local Inc **(PA)**	2099	D	415 643-4510	2919
Lumetra Healthcare Solutions	8748	E	415 677-2000	19813
Lundi Inc	7374	E	415 735-0101	13725
Luxor Cabs Inc	4121	E	415 282-4141	7413
Lyft Inc **(PA)**	4119	A	844 250-2773	7386
Lynch Gilardi & Grummer LLP	8111	E	415 397-2800	17324
Lyon-Martin Wns Hlth Svcs Inc	8011	E	415 565-7667	15513
M & H Realty Partners LP	6799	D	415 693-9000	10865
M Arthur Gensler Jr Assoc Inc **(PA)**	8712	B	415 433-3700	18899
M/H Vccp LLC **(HQ)**	7311	E	415 255-6363	11768
Mac Publishing LLC **(DH)**	2721	E	415 243-0505	3505
Macarthur Trnst Cmnty Prtners	1521	D	415 989-1111	664
Macqurie Arcft Lsg Svcs US Inc	7359	D	415 829-6600	12053
Macys Inc	7231	D	415 951-5700	11689
Madison Reed Inc	2844	E	415 225-0872	4089
Maitri Compassionate Care	8069	E	415 558-3000	16767
Makersights Inc	7371	E	415 658-7709	12593
Malcolm Drilling Company Inc **(PA)**	1799	A	415 901-4400	2044
Maltby Electric Supply Co Inc **(PA)**	5063	E	415 863-5000	8867
Mapbox Inc	7372	E	202 250-3633	13291
Maplebear Inc **(PA)**	4212	A	888 246-7822	7482
Marco Fine Furniture Inc	2512	E	415 285-3235	3290
Marcum LLP	8721	E	415 432-6200	18975
Margaret OLeary Inc **(PA)**	2339	D	415 354-6663	3012
Mariadb Usa Inc	5045	E	847 562-9000	8724
Marin Software Incorporated **(PA)**	7374	C	415 399-2580	13727
Marina Security Services Inc	7381	C	415 773-2300	14075

	SIC	EMP	PHONE	ENTRY #
Marinship Dev Interest LLC **(PA)**	6552	E	415 282-5160	10707
Marketwatch Inc **(DH)**	7383	D	415 439-6400	14155
Markmonitor (all-D) Inc	8111	D	415 278-8400	17325
Maroevich Oshea Cghlan Insur S	6411	D	415 957-0600	10310
Marriott Downtown	7011	E	415 896-1600	11287
Martinelli Envmtl Graphics	3993	F	415 468-4000	7243
Mason Street Opco LLC	7011	A	415 772-5000	11289
Masonic Homes of California **(PA)**	8361	B	415 776-7000	18142
Massdrop Inc **(PA)**	7389	D	415 340-2999	14329
Matarzzi / Pelsinger Bldrs Inc	1521	E	415 285-6930	670
Matrix Resources Inc	7361	D	415 644-0642	12107
Matter LLC	7336	E	415 589-7036	11867
Maximus Real Estate Partners	6519	D	415 584-4832	10482
Mazzetti Inc **(PA)**	8711	E	615 579-4375	18763
MC Metal Inc	3446	F	415 822-2288	4836
McCann-Erickson Corporation **(HQ)**	7311	D	415 348-5600	11769
McEvoy Properties LLC	2731	F	415 537-4200	3537
McKee and Company Electric	1731	D	415 724-2738	1540
McKesson Medical-Surgical Inc	5122	D	415 983-8300	9231
McKesson Spclty Hlth Tech Pdts **(HQ)**	5122	E	415 983-8300	9232
McKinsey & Company Inc	8742	B	415 981-0250	19571
McMillan Data Cmmnications Inc	1731	D	415 992-6582	1541
McMillan Electric	1731	B	415 826-5100	1542
McMillen Jacobs Associates Inc **(PA)**	8711	D	415 434-1822	18765
Meals On Whels San Frncsco Inc	8322	E	415 920-1111	17645
Meany Wilson L P	6552	E	415 905-5300	10708
Medallia Inc **(PA)**	7372	C	650 321-3000	13303
Medivation Inc	2834	F	415 812-6345	3946
Medivation Inc **(HQ)**	2834	A	415 543-3470	3947
Medrio Inc **(PA)**	7372	C	415 963-3700	13305
Mega Herbal Products Inc	2833	E	516 996-7770	3817
Mekanism Inc **(PA)**	7311	E	415 908-4000	11770
Mellon Global Oprtnty Fund LLC	6722	E	415 546-6056	10765
Meltwater News US Inc **(DH)**	7383	D	415 829-5900	14156
Mendoza & Associates **(PA)**	8741	E	415 644-0180	19370
Mental Hlth Assn San Francisco	8093	E	415 421-2926	17040
Meraki LLC **(HQ)**	7379	B	415 632-5800	13935
Mercado Latino Inc	5148	E	415 282-5563	9417
Merchant Services Inc **(PA)**	7374	B	817 725-0900	13728
Mercy Doctors Med Group Inc	8011	E	415 752-0100	15535
Meredith Corporation	2731	D	415 249-2362	3538
Meridian Management Group	6531	C	415 434-9700	10622
Meritage Group LP	8741	A	415 399-5330	19371
Merrill Lynch Prce Fnner Smith	6211	C	415 955-3700	9985
Merrill Lynch Prce Fnner Smith	6021	C	415 676-2500	9685
Merrill Lynch Prce Fnner Smith	6211	E	415 274-7000	9994
Metadesign Inc	7336	E	415 627-0790	11869
Method Home Products	2621	F	415 568-4600	3345
Metric Theory LLC	7311	C	415 659-8600	11772
Metromile Inc **(PA)**	6141	C	888 242-5204	9860
Metromile Operating Company **(PA)**	6331	D	888 244-1702	10171
Metropolitan Club	7997	D	415 673-0600	15111
Metropolitan Elec Cnstr Inc	1731	C	415 642-3000	1544
Metropolitan Trnsp Comm **(PA)**	4111	D	415 778-6700	7342
Meyers+engineers	8711	E	415 282-4380	18766
Meyers+engineers	8711	D	415 713-0005	18767
Mgp Ix Properties LLC **(PA)**	6512	E	415 693-9000	10395
Mhm Services Inc	8093	C	415 416-6992	17045
Micro Holding Corp	7374	E	415 788-5111	13730
Micromenders Inc **(PA)**	5045	E	415 344-0917	8727
Mightyhive Inc **(HQ)**	7371	D	888 727-9742	12606
Migo Money Inc	7389	D	415 906-4040	14331
Mile Post Properties LLC	7011	D	415 673-4711	11299
Military Advantage Inc **(DH)**	7311	C	415 820-3434	11773
Millennium Management LLC	6726	B	415 844-4048	10780
Miller Law Group A Prof Corp	8111	E	415 464-4300	17334
Milliman Inc	8999	E	415 403-1333	19913
Minami Tamaki LLP	8111	E	415 788-9000	17336
Mindsnacks Inc	7372	E	415 875-9817	13309
Mindtickle Inc **(PA)**	7372	E	973 400-1717	13310
Minitrans Corporation **(PA)**	4141	E	415 970-8091	7418
Minted LLC **(PA)**	5112	A	415 399-1100	9208
Mission Child Care Consort	8351	E	415 586-6139	17975
Mission Cncil Alchol Abuse Spn	8322	E	415 826-6767	17650
Mission Constructors Inc	1542	D	415 282-8453	924
Mission Economic Dev Agcy	8742	E	415 282-3334	19577
Mission Lane LLC **(PA)**	7389	D	408 505-3081	14332
Mission Linen Supply	7213	C	510 429-7305	11643
Mission Neighborhood Ctrs Inc **(PA)**	8641	E	415 206-7752	18439
Mission Neighborhood Ctrs Inc	8641	E	415 206-7756	18440
Mission Neighborhood Hlth Ctr **(PA)**	8011	C	415 552-3870	15538
Mission Pets Inc	5199	E	415 904-9914	9667
Mission Stuart Ht Partners LLC	7011	C	415 278-3700	11305
Mitchell Engineering	1794	E	415 227-1040	1966
Mitzu Printing Inc	2752	F	650 922-0500	3677
Mixamo Inc	7372	E	415 255-7455	13312
Mixpanel Inc **(PA)**	7371	E	415 688-4001	12612
Mmi Realty Services Inc	6512	D	415 288-6888	10396
Modern Life Inc **(PA)**	8093	D	617 980-9633	17047
Modern Luxury Media LLC **(HQ)**	2721	E	404 443-0004	3509
Modis Inc	7371	C	415 896-5566	12616
Moffitt H C Hospital	8062	C	415 476-1000	16458
Monticello Hotel LLC	7011	E	415 392-8800	11310
Morgan Lewis & Bockius LLP **(HQ)**	8111	B	415 442-1000	17337
Morgan Stnley Smith Barney LLC	6211	D	415 984-6500	10005
Morrison & Foerster LLP **(PA)**	8111	B	415 268-7000	17338
Mosser Vctrian Ht Arts Mus Inc **(HQ)**	7011	E	415 986-4400	11312

Employment Codes: A=Over 500 employees, B=251-500, C=101-250, D=51-100, E=20-50 F=10-19

2022 Northern California Business Directory and Buyers Guide

© Mergent Inc. 1-800-342-5647

1199

SAN FRANCISCO, CA

Company	SIC	EMP	PHONE	ENTRY #
Mosser Vctrian Ht Arts Mus Inc	7011	C	415 777-1200	11313
Motion Math Inc	7371	A	415 590-2961	12621
Motista LLC	8742	D	650 204-7976	19580
Motivate International Inc **(HQ)**	8741	E	347 916-0210	19372
Movano Inc	3845	F	415 651-3172	7114
Mozilla Corporation **(HQ)**	7373	A	650 903-0800	13636
Mozilla Foundation **(PA)**	7371	B	650 903-0800	12623
Mozio Inc **(PA)**	4724	D	916 719-9213	7803
Mr S Leather	2386	E	415 863-7764	3018
Mtc Holdings **(DH)**	4491	B	912 651-4000	7723
Mtr Transportation Inc	7389	E	415 928-3279	14334
Mufg Union Bank National Assn **(DH)**	6021	A	415 705-7000	9687
Mulesoft Inc	7372	A	415 229-2009	13317
Munger Tolles Olson Foundation	8111	E	415 512-4000	17340
Murphy Prson Brdley Fney Inc A **(PA)**	8111	E	415 788-1900	17342
Mursion Inc **(PA)**	7372	D	415 746-9631	13318
Mux Inc **(PA)**	7372	F	510 402-2257	13319
Mxb Battery LP	8641	D	415 230-8000	18442
Mya Systems Inc **(PA)**	7361	E	877 679-0952	12109
Mypointscom LLC **(HQ)**	7371	D	415 615-1100	11774
National Ctr For Lsbian Rights	8111	E	415 392-6257	17343
National Financial Svcs LLC	6282	A	415 912-2805	10052
National Opinion Research Ctr	8732	D	415 315-2000	19171
Native	2844	E	562 217-9338	4091
Nature Conservancy	8641	D	415 777-0487	18443
Naturener Glacier Wind Energy	8999	D	415 217-5500	19914
Naturener USA LLC **(HQ)**	3621	E	415 217-5500	5664
Naturner Mont Wind Enrgy 2 LLC	1629	E	415 217-5508	1169
Ncc Group Inc **(PA)**	7379	D	415 268-9300	13943
Ncc Group Security Svcs Inc **(DH)**	7379	E	415 293-0808	13944
Nebia Inc	3069	F	203 570-6222	4220
Nektar Therapeutics **(PA)**	2834	B	415 482-5300	3953
Nelson/Nygard Cnslting Assoc I **(PA)**	8742	E	415 284-1544	19587
Netlify	7372	E	925 922-0921	13324
New Cch LLC **(PA)**	7374	E	855 234-6493	13735
New Deal Design LLC	7373	D	415 399-0405	13639
New Paradigm Productions Inc **(PA)**	7812	D	415 924-8000	14794
New Relic Inc **(PA)**	7372	A	650 777-7600	13329
Newgistics Inc	4215	D	415 465-0564	7651
Newsmarket Inc **(DH)**	7379	E	917 861-3797	13946
Nextdoorcom Inc **(PA)**	7375	D	415 236-0000	13802
Nextlesson Inc	2741	F	415 968-9655	3586
Nextroll Inc **(PA)**	7372	A	877 723-7655	13332
Ngcw Inc	7699	E	415 621-7223	14767
Ngdata Us Inc **(PA)**	7374	E	415 655-6732	13736
Nibbi Bros Associates Inc	1522	C	415 863-1820	759
Niebam-Cppola Estate Winery LP	2084	E	415 291-1700	2669
Nielsen Mobile LLC **(DH)**	8732	C	917 435-9301	19174
Nigro Krlin Sgal Fldstein Blno	8721	B	415 463-1300	18980
Ninthdecimal Inc	7371	D	415 264-1849	12631
Nisum Technologies Inc	7371	A	714 619-7989	12632
Nitro Software Inc	7371	C	415 632-4894	12634
Nob Hill Properties Inc	7011	B	415 474-5400	11329
Noodle Analytics Inc	7371	D	415 412-2139	12637
Norcal Mutual Insurance Co **(HQ)**	6411	E	415 735-2000	10322
Noredink Corp	7371	D	617 308-4549	12638
Northern Cal Inst For RES Edca	8399	B	415 750-6954	18244
Northern California Presbyteri	8051	A	415 922-9700	16076
Northern California Svc Leag **(PA)**	8331	E	415 621-5661	17827
Northrop Grumman Systems Corp	8748	E	415 281-4600	19830
Nossaman LLP	8111	D	415 398-3600	17346
Nozomi Networks Inc **(HQ)**	7382	D	800 314-6114	14142
Ntk Construction Inc	1629	E	415 643-1900	1172
Nuna Incorporated	7371	D	415 942-5200	12640
Nurix Therapeutics Inc **(PA)**	8731	C	415 660-5320	19095
Nvision Laser Eye Centers Inc	8011	D	415 421-8667	15560
Nyse Arca Inc	6231	C	415 393-4000	10025
NZ Winery Direct LLC **(PA)**	2084	E	844 569-9463	2671
Oak River Insurance Company	6411	B	800 661-6029	10326
Oberon Design and Mfg LLC	5023	E	415 865-5440	8517
OBrien Mechanical Inc	1711	E	415 695-1800	1321
Octave Health Group Inc	8093	D	415 360-3833	17050
Odc Theater	7922	D	415 863-6606	14853
Odoo Inc	7371	E	650 691-3277	12644
Ohio Inc	2521	D	415 647-6446	3309
Okabe International Inc **(PA)**	4725	E	415 921-0808	7820
Okta Inc **(PA)**	7372	A	888 722-7871	13339
Old Republic Title Company **(DH)**	6361	E	415 421-3500	10208
Olivia Companies LLC	4725	E	415 962-5700	7821
Olly Public Benefit Corp	5149	C	415 412-0812	9470
Olympic Club	7997	E	415 676-1412	15120
Olympic Club **(PA)**	8641	C	415 345-5100	18444
Omada Health Inc	8082	B	888 987-8337	16920
Omni Hotels Corporation	7011	E	415 677-9494	11338
Omnisci Inc **(PA)**	7372	D	415 997-2814	13340
On Lok Inc	8011	E	415 292-8888	15567
On Lok Senior Health Services **(PA)**	6324	A	415 292-8888	10147
On24 Inc **(PA)**	7372	B	415 369-8000	13341
Onboardiq Inc	7371	D	480 433-1197	12645
One Block Off Grid Inc	5074	D	530 304-3969	9002
One Hat One Hand LLC	2353	E	415 822-2020	3014
One Nob Hill Associates LLC	7011	E	415 392-3434	11339
One Workplace L Ferrari LLC	5021	E	415 357-2200	8501
One10 LLC	8742	D	415 398-3534	19595
One10 LLC	8742	D	415 844-2200	19596
Onelogin Inc **(DH)**	7372	C	415 645-6830	13342
Onfido Inc	8742	D	844 663-4366	19598
Onfleet Inc	7371	D	650 283-7547	12648
Oomnitza Inc **(PA)**	7371	D	415 525-3949	12649
Openai Inc	8733	E	650 387-6701	19227
Opentable Inc **(HQ)**	7389	A	415 344-4200	14346
Opentv Inc **(DH)**	7372	C	415 962-5000	13344
Opsmatic LLC	7372	F	650 777-7600	13348
Opus 2 International Inc	7389	E	888 960-3117	14347
Oracle Corporation	7371	C	415 541-9462	12655
Orange Silicon Valley	8748	D	415 243-1500	19834
Orange Silicon Valley LLC	8732	E	415 284-9765	19177
Orchard Intl Group Inc **(PA)**	7011	D	415 362-8878	11341
OReilly Alphatech Ventures II	7372	E	707 827-7000	13357
Orient Bancorporation **(PA)**	6022	C	415 567-1554	9740
Orrick Hrrington Sutcliffe LLP **(PA)**	8111	A	415 773-5700	17351
Osterhout Group Inc	7389	E	415 644-4000	14348
Osterweis Capital MGT Inc	6282	E	415 434-4441	10053
Oto Analytics Inc	7373	B	310 683-0000	13645
Otr Global Holdings II Inc	8732	E	415 675-7660	19178
Ouraring Inc	7389	D	734 660-5566	14349
Ouster Inc **(PA)**	3829	D	415 949-0108	6914
Outcast Agency LLC	8743	C	415 392-8282	19693
Outreach Corporation	7372	F	888 938-7356	13358
Outspark Inc	4813	E	415 495-1905	7979
Overops Inc	7371	E	415 767-1250	12662
Oxypower Inc **(PA)**	1711	D	415 681-8861	1330
Pac-12 Enteprises LLC	7313	C	415 580-4200	11805
Pachama Inc	7371	E	650 338-9394	12663
Pacific Aviation Corporation	4581	C	650 821-1190	7778
Pacific Bell Telephone Company **(HQ)**	4813	A	415 542-9000	7980
Pacific Bell Telephone Company	4812	B	415 978-0881	7910
Pacific Energy Fuels Company	4924	A	415 973-8200	8210
Pacific Eye Associated Inc	8011	C	415 923-3007	15575
Pacific Foundation Svcs LLC	8741	E	415 561-6540	19376
Pacific Gas and Electric Co **(HQ)**	4911	A	415 973-7000	8131
Pacific Gas and Electric Co	4911	C	415 695-3513	8186
Pacific Health Advantage **(HQ)**	8621	E	415 281-8660	18342
Pacific Heights Asset MGT LLC **(PA)**	6722	E	415 398-8000	10766
Pacific Hmtlogy Oncology Assoc	8011	D	415 923-3012	15577
Pacific Intrnal Medicine Assoc	8011	D	415 923-3050	15579
Pacific Park Management	8741	E	415 923-1900	19377
Pacific Res Inst For Pub Plicy **(PA)**	8732	F	415 989-0833	19179
Pacific Structures Sc Inc **(PA)**	1771	C	415 970-5434	1899
Pacific Union Club	8641	D	415 775-1234	18446
Pacific Union Co	6531	D	415 474-6600	10636
Pacific Union Intl Inc **(PA)**	6531	B	415 929-7100	10639
Pacific Union RE Group **(DH)**	6531	D	415 929-7100	10640
Pacific Ygnacio Corporation	6519	C	925 939-3275	10484
Packlane Inc	7389	E	855 289-7687	14352
Paganini Electric Corporation	1731	C	415 575-3900	1561
Pagerduty Inc **(PA)**	7372	A	844 800-3889	13360
Paige LLC	2211	E	415 660-2970	2964
Palamida Inc	5045	E	415 777-9400	8731
Pan Pennsylvania LLC **(HQ)**	6794	D	415 903-2100	10808
Pan Washington LLC **(HQ)**	6794	D	415 903-2100	10809
Pan-O-Rama Baking Inc	2051	E	415 522-5500	2398
Pantheon Systems Inc **(PA)**	7371	D	855 927-9387	12668
Parallel Advisors LLC	6282	D	866 627-6984	10054
Parc 55 Lessee LLC	7011	E	415 392-8000	11352
Paribas Asset Management Inc	6081	C	415 772-1300	9837
Paribas Asset Management Inc	6082	C	415 772-1300	9838
Parkmerced Investors LLC	7359	E	877 243-5544	12058
Parkside Lending LLC	6162	E	415 771-3700	9918
Parsable Inc	7371	C	888 681-2119	12670
Parthenon Capital LLC	6799	A	415 913-3900	10875
Particle Industries Inc	7371	D	415 316-1024	12671
Partners In School Innovation	8748	D	415 824-6196	19837
Patient Home Monitoring Inc **(DH)**	8082	D	415 693-9690	16923
Patreon Inc **(PA)**	7371	C	415 967-2735	12673
Pattern Energy Group One LP **(PA)**	4911	D	415 283-4000	8189
Pattern Panhandle Wind LLC	4911	E	415 283-4000	8190
Pattern Renewables 2 LP **(DH)**	1711	C	415 283-4000	1336
Pattern US Finance Company LLC	4911	E	415 283-4000	8191
Paul D Abramson MD Inc **(PA)**	8011	E	415 963-4431	15587
Pax Labs Inc	0139	D	415 829-2336	18
Payjoy Inc **(PA)**	7372	D	888 632-1922	13364
Paypal Inc	7389	B	415 947-0834	14358
Paypal Inc	7389	B	855 449-3737	14359
Paystack Inc	7371	E	415 941-8102	12674
Payyourpeople LLC	7374	E	415 914-7110	13739
Pch International USA Inc	8711	E	415 643-5463	18788
Pch Labs Inc	8711	E	415 643-5463	18789
Peace Out Inc	2844	E	305 297-8017	4092
Peachpit Press	2741	F	415 336-6831	3588
Peak Attractions LLC **(PA)**	7999	E	415 981-6300	15226
Pearl Black Inc	7371	E	415 640-4987	12675
Pencil and Pixel Inc	7371	C	510 422-5036	12676
Pendulum Therapeutics Inc	8731	E	844 912-2256	19099
Pennbrook Insurance Service	6411	E	415 820-2200	10331
Penrose Studios Inc	2741	F	703 354-1801	3589
Pensco LLC **(PA)**	6371	E	415 274-5600	10217
People Center Inc	7372	E	415 737-5780	13366
People Data Labs Inc	7374	D	415 568-6415	13741
Peopleai Inc	7371	D	888 997-3675	12677
Pereira & ODell LLC **(PA)**	7311	D	415 284-9916	11777
Perkins + Will Inc	8712	D	415 856-3000	18904
Permanente Medical Group Inc	8011	A	415 833-2000	15598
Permanente Medical Group Inc	8011	A	415 833-2000	15617

GEOGRAPHIC SECTION
SAN FRANCISCO, CA

	SIC	EMP	PHONE	ENTRY #
Personal Mortgage Group LLC (HQ)	6162	D	415 396-0560	9919
Petcube Inc (PA)	3651	E	424 302-6107	5768
Pets Unlimited	8699	E	415 563-6700	18584
PG&e Capital LLC	8742	B	415 321-4600	19604
PG&e Recovery Funding LLC	4931	C	415 973-1000	8215
Pgh Wong Engineering (PA)	8711	E	415 284-0800	18790
PHF Ruby LLC	7011	C	415 885-4700	11365
Phoebus Co Inc	7922	F	415 550-0770	14857
Photoworks Inc	7384	E	415 626-6800	14181
Pier 39 Limited Partnership (PA)	6512	D	415 705-5500	10399
Pillsbury Winthrop Shaw	8111	C	415 983-1000	17356
Pillsbury Winthrop Shaw	8111	B	415 983-1075	17357
Pine & Powell Partners LLC	7011	D	415 989-3500	11368
Pinterest Inc (PA)	7374	A	415 762-7100	13742
Pivotal Software Inc (HQ)	7371	A	415 777-4868	12685
Pixlee Inc	7371	E	718 753-5307	12686
Plaid Inc (PA)	7375	C	415 799-1354	13804
Planet Labs Inc (PA)	7374	B	415 829-3313	13743
Planetout Inc (HQ)	4813	D	415 834-6500	7983
Plangrid Inc (HQ)	7372	D	800 646-0796	13372
Planned Prnthod Shst-Dblo Inc	8093	E	415 821-1282	17055
Plant/Allison Corporation	2431	F	415 285-0500	3146
Playfirst Inc	7372	E	415 738-4600	13373
Playwrights Foundation Inc	7922	D	415 626-2176	14858
Plushcare Inc	8011	D	415 231-5333	15631
Pmdsoft Inc	7371	E	800 587-4989	12688
PNC Multifamily Finance Inc (DH)	6162	E	415 733-1500	9920
Pocket Gems Inc	3944	C	415 371-1333	7181
Poco Dolce Chocolates	2066	F	415 255-1443	2439
Poll Everywhere Inc	8399	D	800 388-2039	18247
Pomeroy Rcrtion Rhbltation Ctr (PA)	8322	C	415 665-4100	17675
Popout Inc	7372	E	415 691-7447	13377
Popsugar Inc (PA)	2741	C	415 391-7576	3591
Populus Technologies Inc	7372	E	415 364-8048	13378
Portco Inc	5091	C	415 771-5200	9161
Portsmouth Financial Services	6211	E	415 543-8500	10008
Post St Rnssnce Prtners A Cal	7011	A	415 563-0303	11374
Postman Inc	7371	E	415 796-6470	12693
Postmates Inc (HQ)	4789	B	800 882-6106	7891
Power Factors LLC (PA)	5045	E	415 299-7448	8736
Powwow Inc	7372	E	877 800-4381	13382
Praetorian Group (PA)	7379	E	415 962-8310	13961
PRC	8399	E	415 777-0333	18248
Premier Eyecare San Francisco	8011	E	415 648-3600	15634
Presidio Gate Apartments	6513	D	415 567-1050	10456
Presidio Hill School	8351	C	415 213-8600	18004
Presidio Surgery Center LLC	8062	E	415 346-1218	16482
Prezi Inc (PA)	7372	E	415 398-8012	13385
Primal Pet Foods Inc	5149	E	415 642-7400	9477
Primary Diagnostics Inc	7371	E	619 356-3701	12696
Prime Finance Partners I LP (PA)	7389	E	415 986-2415	14374
Primitive Logic Inc	7379	D	415 391-8080	13962
Principal Builders Inc	1521	E	415 434-1500	688
Pro Unlimited Inc (PA)	7372	D	561 994-9500	13386
Productboard Inc	3537	C	844 472-6273	5066
Professnal Tchncal SEC Svcs In (PA)	7381	B	415 243-2100	14090
Program Plg Professionals Inc	7389	E	415 692-5870	14376
Progress Glass Co Inc (PA)	1793	C	415 824-7040	1940
Progress Investment MGT Co LLC	6282	C	415 512-3480	10056
Proguard Security Services	7382	E	415 672-0786	14144
Project Affinity Inc	7371	D	415 606-7649	12701
Project Frog Inc	1522	E	415 814-8500	762
Project Open Hand (PA)	8322	A	415 292-3400	17678
Projector Is Inc	7372	E	917 972-5553	13388
Prologis Inc (PA)	6798	B	415 394-9000	10822
Prologis LP (HQ)	6798	B	415 394-9000	10823
Prophet Brand Strategy (PA)	8742	E	415 677-0909	19611
Prosper Funding LLC (HQ)	6153	D	415 593-5400	9874
Prosper Marketplace Inc (PA)	6163	B	415 593-5400	9945
Protagonist Technology LLC (PA)	8742	E	415 967-5530	19612
Provide Inc	7372	E	877 341-0617	13389
Providence Place Inc	8361	E	415 359-9700	18161
Prudential California Realty	6531	E	415 664-9400	10651
Ps24 Inc	8741	D	415 834-5105	19384
Public Library of Science	2741	C	415 624-1200	3593
Public Policy Institute Cal (PA)	8611	D	415 291-4400	18313
Pubnub Inc (PA)	7371	C	415 223-7552	12709
Pulse Q&A Inc	8732	E	215 908-0199	19180
Purcell-Murray Company Inc (PA)	5074	E	415 468-6620	9004
Qatalyst Group LP (PA)	6799	E	415 844-7700	10877
Quadriga	7371	E	650 270-6326	12713
Qualia Labs Inc	8748	C	440 477-5625	19842
Qualio Inc	7372	E	415 795-7331	13393
Quality Planning Corporation	8742	D	415 369-0707	19617
Quantal International Inc	7372	E	415 644-0754	13394
Quantcast Corporation (PA)	7371	E	800 293-5706	12715
Quanticel Pharmaceuticals Inc (PA)	8731	E	415 358-7609	19112
Quetzal Group Inc	2095	E	415 673-4181	2845
Quicksilver Delivery Inc	4119	D	415 431-1600	7398
Quip Inc	7371	E	877 544-7847	12720
Quoori Inc (PA)	7371	E	707 393-8305	12721
Quri Inc	8732	E	415 413-0100	19181
R & S Investments LLC	6282	D	415 591-2700	10057
R J McGlennon Company Inc (PA)	2851	E	415 552-0311	4109
R/GA Media Group Inc	8743	E	415 913-7531	19696
Rai Care Ctrs Nthrn Cal II LLC	8092	E	415 406-1090	16978
Rai Technology Incorporated	7371	E	415 252-9393	12722
Rainbow Wtrprofing Restoration	1799	C	415 641-1578	2060
Rally Health Inc	8099	E	408 821-5414	17170
Rangeme USA LLC	2741	F	510 688-0995	3594
Ranger Pipelines Incorporated	1623	C	415 822-3700	1133
Raphael Hse San Francisco Inc	8322	C	415 345-7200	17679
Rapid Lasergraphics (HQ)	2791	F	415 957-5840	3766
Rapid Typographers Company (PA)	2791	F	415 957-5840	3767
Rapidapi Inc	7371	D	650 575-7633	12725
Rare Breed Distilling LLC (DH)	2085	E	415 315-8060	2776
Raydiant	7371	D	888 966-5188	12727
RDM Express Inc (PA)	4212	D	415 642-4916	7486
RE La Mesa LLC	1629	D	415 675-1500	1174
RE Tranquillity 8 LLC	3433	E	415 675-1500	4633
Read It Later Inc	7372	E	415 692-6111	13400
Real Estate Equity Exchange	6162	D	415 992-4200	9924
Realtimeboard Inc (PA)	7379	E	415 669-8098	13968
Reciprocity Inc	7371	E	415 851-8667	12731
Recology Inc (PA)	4953	D	415 875-1000	8351
Recommind Inc (HQ)	3695	E	415 394-7899	6506
Recurrent Energy LLC (HQ)	1711	D	415 956-3168	1345
Red Eagle Ventures Inc	6799	E	415 773-1800	10880
Redacted Inc	7371	E	415 858-2719	12734
Reddit Inc (PA)	2741	C	415 666-2330	3595
Redwood Credit Union	6061	E	800 479-7928	9806
Redwood Credit Union	6061	E	415 861-7928	9807
Reed Smith LLP	8111	E	415 543-8700	17360
Refinitiv US LLC	2721	C	415 344-6000	3512
Reflektive Inc	7371	C	203 886-9240	12738
Remedly Inc	7372	F	650 265-8449	13404
Remick Associates Db Inc	1521	E	415 896-9500	696
Remix Software Inc	7371	D	415 900-4332	12740
Renaissance Hotel Operating Co	7011	C	415 989-3500	11395
Reneson Hotels Inc	7011	E	415 621-7001	11397
Republic Indemnity Co Amer	6331	D	415 981-3200	10172
Rescale Inc	7372	D	855 737-2253	13406
Retail Zipline Inc	7372	E	510 390-4904	13408
Retronyms Inc (PA)	5045	C	614 589-3121	8744
Reuben Junius & Rose LLP	8111	E	415 567-9000	17362
Revel Arch & Design Inc (PA)	8712	E	415 230-7010	18908
Revel Gatherings Inc (PA)	8641	E	909 323-0994	18454
Revinate Inc	7371	E	415 671-4703	12748
RFJ Corporation	1742	D	415 824-6890	1702
Rhumbix Inc	7389	F	435 764-3014	14388
Richmond Area Mlt-Services Inc	8093	E	415 579-3021	17060
Richmond Area Mlt-Services Inc (PA)	8093	E	415 800-0699	17061
Richmond Dst Neighborhood Ctr (PA)	8322	E	415 751-6600	17694
Rickshaw Bagworks Inc	2393	F	415 904-8368	3032
Riivos Inc	1731	D	415 813-1840	1587
Ring2 Communications LLC	4899	E	415 829-2952	8084
Ristoranti Piemontesi Inc	7299	E	415 395-9800	11729
Ritz-Carlton San Francisco	7011	D	415 296-7465	11409
Ritz-Carlton Hotel Company LLC	7011	B	415 773-6168	11410
Riverbed Technology Inc (HQ)	5045	D	415 247-8800	8746
Rlj C San Francisco Lessee LP	7011	E	415 346-3800	11413
RMC Water and Environment	8711	D	415 321-3400	18804
RMR Construction Company	1542	C	415 647-0884	946
Roadster Inc	7371	A	833 568-5968	12752
Robertson Stphens Wlth MGT LLC (PA)	8741	D	415 500-6810	19389
Robinson Mills + Williams (PA)	8712	E	415 781-9800	18910
Robomart Inc	3711	F	669 350-4463	6557
Rogers Joseph ODonnell A Pro (PA)	8111	E	415 956-2828	17363
Rollbar Inc (PA)	7374	D	415 366-3254	13754
Roostify Inc	6163	E	888 908-2470	9946
Rosen Bien Galvan Grunfeld LLP	8111	E	415 433-6830	17365
Rp/Kinetic Parc 55 Owner LLC	7011	C	415 392-8000	11422
Rpx Corporation (PA)	6794	C	866 779-7641	10812
Rs Investment Management Inc	6722	D	415 591-2700	10768
Rt Western Inc	1799	E	415 677-9202	2064
Rubecon General Contg Inc	1542	E	415 206-7740	950
Rudolf Steiner Foundation Inc	8699	E	415 561-3900	18585
RWS Life Sciences Inc	7389	E	415 981-5890	14392
Ryan Partnership LLC (PA)	7311	B	415 289-1110	11781
Rypple	7372	F	888 479-7753	13415
Rysigo Technologies Corp (PA)	7372	E	408 621-9274	13416
S & W Fine Foods Inc	2032	C	800 252-7033	2206
S F Auto Parts Whse Inc	5013	D	415 255-0115	8462
S4 LLC	5084	F	415 979-9640	9092
Saarman Construction Ltd	1522	C	415 749-2700	767
Safe & Sound	8322	E	415 668-0494	17702
Safetymax Corporation	5099	E	415 626-4650	9201
Safeway Inc	2087	A	415 661-3220	2825
Sage Group	7361	E	415 512-8200	12132
Sage Project Inc	8322	D	415 905-5050	17703
Saint Francis Memorial Hosp (DH)	8062	A	415 353-6000	16494
Saint Francis Memorial Hosp	8062	A	415 353-6000	16495
Saint Francis Memorial Hosp	8062	E	415 353-6000	16496
Saint Francis Memorial Hosp	8062	E	415 673-1317	16497
Saint Francis Memorial Hosp	8062	E	415 353-6600	16498
Saint Francis Memorial Hosp	8062	E	415 353-6363	16499
Saint Francis Memorial Hosp	8062	E	415 353-6464	16500
Saints Capital Dakota LLC (PA)	8748	D	415 395-2897	19854
Saints Management LLC (PA)	6799	E	415 773-2080	10881
Sak Brand Group	5137	F	415 486-1200	9256
Salesforcecom Inc (PA)	7372	A	415 901-7000	13423
Salesforcecom/Foundation	8322	E	800 667-6389	17704
Salon Media Group Inc (PA)	7375	E	415 870-7566	13807
Salt Lake Hotel Associates LP (PA)	7011	C	415 397-5572	11429

Employment Codes: A=Over 500 employees, B=251-500, C=101-250, D=51-100, E=20-50 F=10-19

SAN FRANCISCO, CA GEOGRAPHIC SECTION

	SIC	EMP	PHONE	ENTRY #
Saltmine USA Inc	7371	E	408 464-3631	12757
Salvation Army Glden State Div **(PA)**	8322	D	415 553-3500	17705
Samsara Inc **(PA)**	7373	A	415 985-2400	13659
San Francisco Aids Foundation **(PA)**	8322	D	415 487-3000	17708
San Francisco Aids Foundation	8322	D	415 581-7077	17709
San Francisco Ballet Assn	7922	C	415 865-2000	14861
San Francisco C & C Inc	7011	E	415 673-4711	11432
San Francisco City & County	7539	C	415 550-4600	14622
San Francisco Critical Care	8011	D	415 923-3421	15662
San Francisco Federal Cr Un **(PA)**	6061	D	415 775-5377	9810
San Francisco Film Society	8699	E	415 561-5000	18588
San Francisco Fire Credit Un **(PA)**	6061	E	415 674-4800	9811
San Francisco Food Bank	8322	D	415 282-1900	17710
San Francisco Foundation	7389	D	415 733-8500	14395
San Francisco Golf Club	7997	E	415 469-4104	15132
San Francisco Health Authority **(PA)**	8621	D	415 615-4407	18347
San Francisco Hotel Associates	7011	E	415 392-4666	11433
San Francisco Hotel Group LLC	7011	C	415 276-9888	11434
San Francisco Museum Modrn Art **(PA)**	8412	B	415 357-4035	18279
San Francisco Opera Assn	7922	A	415 861-4008	14862
San Francisco Performances Inc	7929	E	415 398-6449	14875
San Francisco Performing Arts	7999	E	415 621-6600	15234
San Francisco Print Media Co **(PA)**	2752	D	415 487-2594	3695
San Francisco Radio Assets LLC **(DH)**	4832	C	415 216-1300	8034
San Francisco School	8351	D	415 239-5065	18015
San Francisco Surgery Ctr LP	8011	D	415 393-9600	15663
San Francisco Symphony **(PA)**	7929	C	415 552-8000	14876
San Francisco Tennis Club	7991	D	415 777-9000	14971
San Francisco Travel Assn	7389	D	415 974-6900	14396
San Francisco Unified Schl Dst **(PA)**	8741	C	415 241-6000	19393
San Francisco Zoological Soc	7999	C	415 753-7080	15235
San Franciscoidence Opco LLC	8059	D	415 584-3294	16265
San Frncsco Bar Plots Bnvlent	8611	D	415 362-5436	18316
San Frncsco Cmnty Clnic Cnsrti	8741	D	415 355-2222	19394
San Frncsco Cnservatory of Mus	7929	C	415 864-7326	14877
San Frncsco Gen Hosp Fundation	8399	C	415 206-4478	18249
San Frncsco Ldies Prtction Rli	8361	C	415 931-3136	18176
San Frncsco Lsbian Gay Bsxual	8322	E	415 865-5649	17711
San Frncsco Prtclar Cncil of T	8322	D	415 255-3525	17712
San Frncsco Scide Prvntion Inc	8322	E	415 984-1900	17713
San Frncsco Sport Spine Physcl **(PA)**	8049	D	415 593-2532	15896
Sanchez Business Inc	2032	E	415 282-2400	2208
Sano Intelligence Inc	7371	D	408 483-6518	12759
Sanofi US Services Inc	2834	C	415 856-5000	3981
Sauce Labs Inc **(PA)**	7373	D	855 677-0011	13660
Savage Industries	3999	E	415 845-6264	7306
Save Redwoods League	8641	E	415 362-2352	18465
Savills Inc	6531	E	415 421-5900	10660
Sawbirds Inc **(PA)**	3425	E	415 861-0644	4612
Sb Architects **(PA)**	8712	E	415 673-8990	18911
SC Hotel Partners LLC	7011	D	415 775-5000	11447
Scale Ai Inc **(PA)**	7371	C	650 294-8644	12763
Scalio LLC	7371	E	408 835-0640	12764
Scality Inc	3572	E	650 356-8500	5317
Scope Technologies US Inc **(PA)**	7372	E	855 207-2673	13430
Scott St Snior Hsing Cmplex In	8051	C	415 345-5083	16113
Scribd Inc **(PA)**	7375	D	415 896-9890	13808
Seayu Enterprises	5169	F	415 566-9677	9522
Securitas SEC Svcs USA Inc	7381	C	510 568-6818	14093
Segmentio Inc	3577	B	844 611-0621	5410
Seiler LLP	8721	D	415 392-2123	18992
Seiu Untd Hlthcare Wrkrs-West	8631	E	415 441-2500	18375
Self-Help For Elderly	8322	D	415 391-3843	17727
Self-Help For Elderly **(PA)**	8322	C	415 677-7600	17728
Self-Help For Elderly	7999	C	415 677-7581	15240
Sender Inc	8099	D	888 717-3287	17178
Senor Sisig	7999	D	415 608-5048	15241
Sense Talent Labs Inc **(PA)**	8742	E	408 674-5180	19630
Sentient Technologies USA LLC	7371	E	415 422-9886	12772
Sequoia Living Inc	8059	C	415 351-7956	16267
Sequoia Living Inc	8361	E	415 776-0114	18180
Serenity Now Lessee Inc	7011	E	415 885-2500	11461
Serve Robotics Inc	4215	D	415 590-0160	7653
Severson & Werson A Prof Corp	8111	C	415 398-3344	17368
Seyfarth Shaw LLP	8111	D	415 397-2823	17369
SF Marriott Marquis	7011	E	415 896-1600	11464
SF Sierra Co Inc	1731	E	415 752-2850	1605
Sfd Partners LLC	7011	B	415 392-7755	11465
Sfdph	8641	E	415 554-2686	18467
Sfo Airporter Inc	4111	D	415 495-3909	7359
Sharehlder Rprsnttive Svcs LLC **(PA)**	8741	E	303 648-4085	19398
Sharethrough Inc **(PA)**	7319	E	415 644-0054	11817
Shartsis Friese LLP	8111	C	415 421-6500	17371
Shea Lbagh Dbbrstein Crtif Pub **(PA)**	8721	E	415 308-1368	18994
Sheedy Drayage Co **(PA)**	7353	D	415 648-7171	12022
Sheng-Kee of California Inc **(PA)**	5149	E	415 564-4800	9486
Sheppard Mllin Rchter Hmpton L	8111	D	415 434-9100	17372
Sheraton LLC	7011	D	415 362-5500	11467
Shibata Floral Company **(PA)**	5193	E	415 495-8611	9639
Shift Finance LLC	7371	A	541 335-9245	12777
Shing Tai Corporation	7532	E	415 986-2944	14532
Shipt	7374	A	408 592-1029	13756
Shook Hardy & Bacon LLP	8111	C	415 544-1900	17373
Shopify (usa) Inc	7371	D	415 944-7572	12779
Shoppingcom Inc	7374	C	650 616-6500	13757
Shopstyle Inc **(DH)**	7371	C	415 908-2200	12781
Shoreline Labs Inc	7371	E	415 630-6212	12782

	SIC	EMP	PHONE	ENTRY #
Shorenstein Company LLC	6512	E	415 772-7000	10405
Shorenstein Properties LLC **(PA)**	6512	E	415 772-7000	10406
Showpad Inc **(HQ)**	7379	C	415 800-2033	13974
Shute Mihaly & Weinberger	8111	E	415 552-7272	17374
Side Inc	6531	E	650 930-0873	10662
Sideman & Bancroft LLP	8111	D	415 392-1960	17375
Siegel & Gale LLC	7311	E	415 955-1250	11783
Sift Science Inc **(PA)**	7371	D	855 981-7438	12784
Sig Structured Products Lllp	6211	E	415 951-3533	10013
Sight Machine Inc	7372	D	888 461-5739	13444
Silicon Valley Commerce LLC	7371	D	888 507-8266	12785
Silicon Valley Sftwr Group LLC	7371	E	844 946-7874	12786
Sillajen Biotherapeutics Inc	8731	E	415 281-8886	19125
Siluria Technologies Inc	1311	E	415 978-2170	549
Silver Lake Partners II LP	6726	E	415 293-4355	10783
Simco Foods Inc	5141	D	415 982-5872	9303
Sing Seng Hing Co Ltd	7011	E	415 781-2220	11482
Singlestore Inc **(PA)**	7371	E	855 463-6775	12787
Sirna Therapeutics Inc	2834	D	415 512-7200	3985
Sirona Medical Inc	8082	E	415 729-7301	16945
Six Apart Ltd **(HQ)**	7371	E	415 738-5100	12789
Six Continents Hotels Inc	7011	C	415 626-6103	11486
Sixgill LLC **(PA)**	7373	E	424 322-2009	13665
Sizmek Dsp Inc	7311	D	415 757-2300	11786
Skael Inc	7374	D	415 653-9433	13759
Skidmore Owings & Merrill LLP	8712	C	415 981-1555	18913
Skupos Inc **(PA)**	7371	C	303 718-4805	12792
Skylight Tools Inc	3599	E	800 961-2580	5620
Skyline Commercial Interiors **(PA)**	1542	D	415 908-1020	963
Skywalker Properties Ltd LLC **(PA)**	6512	D	415 746-5059	10407
Skywalker Sound	1731	E	415 662-1000	1607
Slack Technologies LLC **(HQ)**	7372	A	415 902-5526	13446
Slalom LLC	8742	C	415 593-3450	19635
Sliderule Labs Inc **(PA)**	7371	C	646 748-0378	12797
Smartnews International Inc	7371	D	628 444-3000	12799
Smartrecruiters Inc **(PA)**	7371	B	415 659-9130	12800
Smith News Company Inc	5199	E	415 861-4900	9671
Smith-Emery San Francisco Inc	7389	E	415 642-7326	14407
Smithgroup Inc	8712	C	313 442-8351	18914
Snapcommerce Inc	4724	C	917 704-4588	7807
Snapdocs Inc	7371	E	415 967-0136	12801
Snapfish LLC **(HQ)**	7384	D	415 979-3703	14183
Social Finance Inc **(HQ)**	6163	C	415 930-4467	9949
Social Imprints LLC	2752	E	510 610-6511	3698
Society For San Francisco	8699	C	415 554-3000	18593
Sodexo Management Inc	8741	B	925 325-9657	19399
Sofar Ocean Technologies Inc **(PA)**	8731	E	415 230-2299	19127
Sofi Technologies Inc **(PA)**	6162	D	855 456-7634	9931
Soha Engineers **(PA)**	8711	E	415 989-9900	18816
Soiree Valet Parking Service	7299	D	415 284-9700	11730
Solid Gold Inc	7929	D	415 536-0300	14878
Sonesta Intl Hotels Corp	7011	B	415 929-2393	11490
Soul Machines Inc	7373	D	649 283-0863	13667
South Market Child Care Inc **(PA)**	8351	E	415 820-3500	18024
Southbourne Inc	7011	C	415 781-5555	11494
Spa Radiance Associates Inc	7991	E	415 346-6281	14976
Span Digital Inc	8711	E	415 484-9269	18817
Sparkcentral Inc **(HQ)**	2741	D	866 559-6229	3600
Spectrum Systems SF	3645	F	415 361-2429	5726
Spire Global Subsidiary Inc **(HQ)**	7375	C	415 356-3400	13809
Splice Machine Inc **(PA)**	7371	C	650 678-8985	12812
Splunk Inc **(PA)**	7372	C	415 848-8400	13456
Splunk Services Cayman Ltd **(HQ)**	7372	D	415 848-8400	13457
Spotinst Inc	7372	E	415 223-1333	13458
Spoton Computing Inc	7372	E	650 293-7464	13459
Spur - San Frncsco Bay Area Pl **(PA)**	8641	D	415 781-8726	18472
Squar Milner Peterson	8721	E	415 781-2500	18995
Square Inc **(PA)**	7372	E	415 375-3176	13460
Squaretrade Inc **(DH)**	6399	C	415 541-1000	10221
St Anthony Foundation **(PA)**	8322	E	415 241-2600	17752
St Francis Marine Center Inc	4493	E	415 621-2876	7733
St Francis Yacht Club	7997	C	415 563-6363	15155
St Lukes Health Care Center	8062	D	415 647-8600	16547
St Marys Med Ctr Foundation	8062	C	415 668-1000	16548
St Marys Medical Center Inc	8062	A	415 668-1000	16549
St Philip School	8351	D	415 824-8467	18031
St Regis San Francisco Ht LLC	7011	D	415 284-4000	11499
Stackla Inc	7372	D	415 789-3304	13463
Standard Cognition Corp **(PA)**	7372	D	415 324-4156	13466
Standard Euler Inc	7371	E	954 261-6679	12815
Standard Pacific Capital LLC	6211	E	415 352-7100	10014
Standish Management LLC **(PA)**	8741	D	415 391-7225	19401
Stanford Hotels Corporation **(PA)**	7011	E	415 398-3333	11501
Stanlee R Gatti Designs	7389	E	415 558-8884	14413
Stanley Produce Co Inc	5148	E	415 282-7510	9430
Stantec Architecture Inc	8711	C	415 882-9500	18818
Starlight Room Harry Dentons	7011	E	415 392-7755	11503
Starlite Electric Inc	1731	E	415 648-8888	1613
Starship Technologies Inc	7371	E	844 445-5333	12816
Starwood Capital Group LLC	6799	C	415 247-1220	10884
Starwood Htls & Rsrts Wrldwde	7011	B	415 397-7000	11504
Starwood Htls & Rsrts Wrldwde	7011	C	415 512-1111	11505
Stat Nursing Services Inc **(PA)**	7361	B	415 673-9791	12143
State Bar of California **(PA)**	8621	B	415 538-2000	18349
State Compensation Insur Fund **(PA)**	6331	D	888 782-8338	10174
State Hospitals Cal Dept	8093	C	415 255-3400	17075
Steele Cis LLC	8111	B	415 692-5000	17377

GEOGRAPHIC SECTION — SAN FRANCISCO, CA

Company	SIC	EMP	PHONE	ENTRY #
Steelrver Infrstrcture Fund N (HQ)	4924	C	415 291-2200	8213
Stein & Lubin LLP	8111	E	415 981-0550	17378
Stein Roe Inv Counsel Inc	6282	E	415 433-5844	10061
Sterling Consulting Group LLC	8742	D	415 248-7900	19639
Steuart Street Venture LP	7011	D	415 882-1300	11509
Steve Silver Productions Inc	7922	D	415 421-4284	14864
Steven K Olsen DDS Prof Corp	8021	E	415 398-4400	15858
Stitch Labs Inc	8741	E	415 323-0630	19403
Stone & Youngberg LLC (PA)	6211	E	415 445-2300	10015
Strava Inc (PA)	4813	C	415 374-7298	7993
Streamsets Inc (PA)	7371	E	415 851-1018	12823
Stripe Inc	7371	B	888 963-8955	12826
Stripe Heavy Industries Inc (HQ)	7373	B	877 887-7815	13669
Stryder Corp (PA)	7372	E	415 981-8400	13469
Suffolk Construction Co Inc	1521	C	415 848-0500	712
Suisun City Hotel LLC	7011	E	707 429-0900	11514
Sun Basket Inc	2099	C	408 669-4418	2944
Sun Mountain Inc	2431	E	415 852-2320	3154
Sunrun Cllsto Issuer 2015-1 LL	1711	E	415 580-6900	1369
Sunrun Installation Svcs Inc	1711	B	415 580-6900	1371
Sunset Scavenger Company	4953	B	415 330-1300	8365
Supershuttle International Inc	4111	D	415 558-8500	7363
Supersonic ADS Inc	3993	E	650 825-6010	7256
Support For Fmlies Chldren Wit	8322	E	415 920-5040	17763
Sustainable San Mateo County (PA)	8699	E	415 677-7600	18600
Sustainable San Mateo County	8322	E	415 398-3250	17764
Sutter Bay Hospitals (HQ)	8062	A	415 600-6000	16568
Sutter Bay Hospitals	8062	D	415 600-2403	16570
Sutter Bay Hospitals	8011	E	415 600-2632	15708
Sutter Health	8062	C	415 600-7034	16585
Sutter Health	8062	C	415 345-0100	16589
Sutter Health	8062	C	415 731-6300	16592
Sutter Health	8062	C	415 600-0110	16593
Sutter Health	8062	C	415 600-1020	16600
Sutter Health	8062	C	415 600-0140	16606
Sutter Health	8062	C	415 600-4280	16607
Sutter Health	8062	C	415 600-6000	16616
Sutter Health	8062	C	415 600-6000	16632
Sutter Health	8062	C	415 600-4325	16634
Sutter Health	8062	C	415 600-1400	16637
Sutter Health	8062	C	415 600-6000	16641
Sutter Health	8062	C	415 600-4280	16642
Sutter Health (HQ)	8062	C	415 600-1000	16643
Sutter Health	8062	C	415 861-1110	16649
Sutter Health	8062	C	916 286-8267	16656
Sutter Vsting Nrse Assn Hspice	8082	E	415 600-6200	16954
Svb Asset Management	6029	E	408 654-7400	9762
Swander Pace Capital LLC (PA)	6799	A	415 477-8500	10888
Sweetrush Inc	7374	E	415 647-1956	13762
Swift Navigation Inc (PA)	3663	D	415 484-9026	5873
Swig Company LLC	8742	E	415 291-1100	19646
Swinerton Incorporated (PA)	1542	C	415 421-2980	970
Swinerton MGT & Consulting Inc (HQ)	8742	E	415 984-1261	19647
Swirl Inc	7311	E	415 276-8300	11788
Swiss RE Solutions Holdg Corp	6331	C	415 834-2200	10188
Switchboard Software Inc	7372	F	415 425-3660	13477
Swords To Plwshres Vtrans Rght	8641	E	415 252-4788	18474
Swords To Plwshres Vtrans Rght	8641	E	415 834-0341	18475
Sycamore Hospitality Corp (PA)	7011	E	415 398-3333	11524
Sycle LLC (PA)	7372	C	888 881-7925	13479
Synergy LLC (PA)	8361	E	415 252-1128	18189
Synoptek Inc	8742	E	415 651-4236	19648
Sypartners LLC (HQ)	8748	D	415 536-6600	19870
Sysdig Inc (PA)	7371	C	415 872-9473	12844
Syufy Century Corporation (PA)	7832	D	415 448-8300	14818
T Y Lin International (HQ)	8711	E	415 291-3700	18825
Tactivos Inc (PA)	4813	C	415 687-2501	7996
Talentburst Inc	7389	E	415 813-4011	14425
Talix Inc	7372	E	628 220-3885	13484
Talkdesk Inc (PA)	7372	A	864 642-5230	13485
Talmadge & Talmadge Inc	7991	D	415 703-9650	14979
Tanko Streetlighting Inc	3646	E	415 254-7579	5739
Tapingo Inc (DH)	7372	E	415 283-5222	13487
Tapjoy Inc (PA)	7311	E	415 766-6900	11789
Tariff Building Associates LP (PA)	6512	E	415 397-5572	10411
Tarrant Capital lp LLC (PA)	6282	A	415 743-1500	10062
Tartine LP	2051	E	415 487-2600	2407
Task Help LLC	7371	E	833 229-0726	12850
Taulia Inc (PA)	7371	C	415 376-8280	12851
Techsoup Global (PA)	8641	C	800 659-3579	18476
Teecom	8711	E	510 337-2800	18831
Teespring Inc (PA)	7389	C	855 833-7774	14428
Tegsco Inc (PA)	7549	D	415 865-8200	14676
Teknos Associates LLC	8742	E	650 330-8800	19649
Telegraph Hill Partners Invest (PA)	8742	E	415 765-6980	19650
Telegraph Hl Neighborhood Ctr	8322	E	415 421-6443	17767
Tellapart (HQ)	7371	E	415 222-9670	12857
Telmate LLC (DH)	4813	D	866 516-0115	7998
Telstra Incorporated	7374	E	415 243-3430	13763
Tempo Automation Inc	3672	E	415 320-1261	5987
Tempo Interactive Inc	7991	E	415 964-2975	14980
Ten 15 Inc	6512	E	415 431-1200	10413
Ten Lifestyle MGT USA Inc (DH)	7299	C	415 625-1900	11731
Tenddo Inc	7373	E	415 295-4849	13677
Tenderloin Housing Clinic Inc (PA)	6531	C	415 771-9850	10671
Tequilas Premium Inc	2085	F	415 399-0496	2780
Terminal Inc (PA)	8711	D	281 682-8294	18832
Textainer Equipment Mgt US Ltd (DH)	7359	D	415 434-0551	12064
Textainer Group Holdings Ltd (DH)	8741	E	415 434-0551	19408
Textnow Inc	4813	F	226 476-1971	7999
The Charles Schwab Trust Co (HQ)	6211	E	415 371-0518	10016
The Linux Foundation (PA)	8641	C	415 723-9709	18477
The Origin Project Inc	8412	D	415 601-2409	18284
Thetos Advisors LLC	6282	E	415 917-0485	10063
Third Pillar Systems Inc (PA)	7371	E	650 346-3108	12861
Thirsty Bear Brewing Co LLC	2082	E	415 974-0905	2497
Thismoment Inc	7371	C	415 200-4730	12862
Thistle Health Inc	2099	B	917 587-2341	2946
Thomas Lundberg	2514	E	415 695-0110	3295
Thomas Weisel Partners LLC (DH)	6211	B	415 364-2500	10017
Thomas Wsel Partners Group Inc (HQ)	6211	B	415 364-2500	10018
Thompson Brooks Inc	1521	E	415 581-2600	718
Thousandeyes LLC (HQ)	7372	B	415 513-4526	13492
Three Twins Organic Inc (PA)	2024	E	707 763-8946	2184
Ticketweb LLC	7999	E	415 901-0210	15250
Tides Inc (PA)	8399	D	415 561-6400	18253
Tides Center	7011	B	415 359-9401	11535
Tides Center (PA)	8399	E	415 561-6400	18254
Tiedemann Investment Group LLC	6282	E	415 762-2541	10064
Timberlake-Forrest Inc (PA)	8059	E	415 647-3117	16278
Timbuk2 Designs Inc (PA)	2393	C	415 252-4300	3034
Tinyco Inc	7372	C	415 644-8101	13494
Tipping Point Community	8699	E	415 348-1260	18602
Tk Elevator Corporation	5084	D	415 544-8150	9098
TLC Foods LLC	1541	E	415 205-7111	816
Todays Hotel Corporation (PA)	7011	C	415 441-4000	11538
Todd Dipietro Salon (PA)	7231	E	415 397-0177	11696
Tonal Systems Inc	7999	D	855 698-6625	15251
Tonicai Inc	7371	E	415 340-0330	12886
Toolworks Inc (PA)	8331	B	415 733-0990	17842
Topdown Consulting Inc	8742	D	888 648-8445	19651
Topgolf Media LLC (DH)	7999	E	214 377-0615	15252
Topguest Inc	7372	E	646 415-9402	13495
Toptal LLC	7379	B	888 604-3188	13998
Touchstone Climbing Inc (PA)	7999	D	415 550-0515	15254
Tpg Partners III LP (HQ)	1311	E	415 743-1500	551
Traceable Inc	7371	E	855 346-7233	12871
Traction Corporation	7311	E	415 962-5800	11792
Tradeshift Holdings Inc (PA)	6719	D	800 381-3585	10743
Tradeshift Inc (HQ)	7373	E	800 381-3585	13680
Trans Pacific Digital Inc	7336	F	415 362-1110	11874
Transamerica Cbo I Inc	6282	D	415 983-4000	10065
Transamerica Finance Corp (DH)	6311	C	415 983-4000	10080
Transamerica Intl Holdings	6719	E	415 983-4000	10744
Transcense Inc (PA)	7371	E	415 867-7230	12873
Tray Io Inc (PA)	7371	E	415 418-3570	12874
Treadwell & Rollo Inc (DH)	8711	E	415 955-9040	18839
Treau Inc	3585	E	866 945-3514	5435
Triage Consulting Group LLC (PA)	8742	B	415 512-9400	19654
Trib3com Inc (PA)	7374	E	415 562-5561	13765
Trifacta Inc (PA)	7379	D	415 429-7570	14002
Trinity Management Services	6531	E	415 864-1111	10677
Triple Aught Design LLC	2253	E	415 318-8252	2974
Trucker Huss A Professional	8111	D	415 788-3111	17384
True Link Financial Inc (PA)	7389	E	800 299-7646	14445
Truecar Inc	5012	E	415 821-8270	8432
Trulia Inc	6513	A	415 648-4358	10465
Trulia Inc (HQ)	7374	E	415 648-4358	13766
Trumaker Inc	2311	E	415 662-3836	2985
Trustees of The Intrntnl Lngsh (PA)	8631	E	415 673-8500	18379
Tubi Inc	7319	E	415 504-3505	11818
Tullys Coffee Co Inc (HQ)	2095	E	415 929-8808	2848
Tullys Coffee Co Inc	2095	E	415 213-8791	2849
Tunein Inc	4832	C	650 319-7100	8035
Turbine Eng Cmpnents Tech Corp	3724	B	415 626-2000	6622
Twilio Inc (PA)	7372	A	415 390-2337	13500
Twitch Interactive Inc	2741	A	415 919-5000	3607
Two Lines A Journal	2741	F	415 512-8812	3608
TYlin Intl Group Ltd (PA)	8711	E	415 291-3700	18842
Typekit Inc	7372	E	415 596-6319	13501
U C San Francisco Gynecology	8011	D	415 885-7788	15745
Uber Technologies Inc (PA)	7389	A	415 612-8582	14446
Ubi Soft Entertainment	7929	E	415 547-4000	14882
Ubisoft Inc (DH)	7371	D	415 547-4000	12884
Uc Hastings Foundation	8699	D	415 565-4704	18603
Uclass Inc	7372	F	630 520-8553	13502
Ucsf Btty Irene Moore Wns Hosp (HQ)	8051	E	415 476-1000	16146
Ucsf Cardiovascular Care	8011	E	415 353-2873	15748
Ucsf Fertility Group	8011	E	415 353-2667	15749
Uhuru Network LLC	7311	E	415 745-3616	11793
Ujet Inc	7372	C	855 242-8538	13503
Umba Inc	7389	E	914 426-1771	14447
Uncountable Inc (PA)	7372	E	650 208-5949	13504
Unionbancal Mortgage Corp	6021	D	415 705-7350	9691
United Behavioral Health (HQ)	8741	C	415 547-1403	19413
United California Glass & Door	7699	D	415 824-8500	14780
United Parcel Service Inc	4215	C	415 252-4564	7666
United Parcel Service Inc	7389	D	415 837-1929	14449
United States Enrgy Foundation	8699	C	415 561-6700	18605
United States Fire Insur Co	6331	C	415 541-3249	10189
United Way of Bay Area (PA)	8322	D	415 808-4300	17775
Unity Software Inc (PA)	7371	B	415 539-3162	12888
Universal McLoud USA Corp	7372	E	613 222-5904	13506
University Cal San Francisco	8733	D	415 476-9000	19241

Employment Codes: A=Over 500 employees, B=251-500, C=101-250, D=51-100, E=20-50 F=10-19

SAN FRANCISCO, CA

Company	SIC	EMP	PHONE	ENTRY #
University Cal San Francisco	8011	C	415 353-7900	15752
University Cal San Francisco	8011	C	415 353-1915	15753
University Cal San Francisco	8011	C	415 353-2757	15754
University Cal San Francisco	8011	C	415 989-5339	15755
University Cal San Francisco	8011	C	415 885-7257	15756
University Cal San Francisco	8062	B	415 476-7000	16695
University Cal San Francisco	8062	B	415 476-1611	16696
University Cal San Francisco	8011	C	415 353-2383	15757
University Cal San Francisco	8733	D	415 476-9323	19242
University Cal San Francisco	8011	C	415 353-7576	15758
University Cal San Francisco	8062	C	415 476-3016	16697
University Cal San Francisco	8062	B	415 567-6600	16698
University Cal San Francisco	8062	B	415 206-8812	16699
University Cal San Francisco	8021	C	415 476-5608	15861
University Cal San Francisco	8011	C	415 353-7700	15760
University Cal San Francisco	8093	C	415 597-8047	17085
University Cal San Francisco	8011	C	415 353-7300	15761
University Cal San Francisco	8063	C	415 206-8430	16749
University Cal San Francisco	8011	C	415 476-4575	15762
University Cal San Francisco	8011	C	415 885-3668	15763
University Cal San Francisco	8011	C	415 885-7495	15764
University Cal San Francisco	8011	C	415 885-3610	15765
University Cal San Francisco	8011	C	415 476-3061	15766
University Cal San Francisco	8011	C	415 353-2961	15767
University Cal San Francisco	8011	C	415 885-7478	15768
University Cal San Frncsco Fnd	8361	D	415 775-2111	18195
University Club of Sf LLC	7997	E	415 781-0900	15163
Unspun Inc	2325	E	207 577-8745	2988
Upgrade Inc (PA)	6141	B	347 776-1730	9863
Upscale Construction Inc	1522	D	415 563-7550	776
Upwork Global Inc (HQ)	7371	E	650 316-7500	12891
Urban Farmer Store Inc (PA)	5083	E	415 661-2204	9047
URS Alaska LLC (HQ)	8711	D	415 774-2700	18844
URS Corporation (HQ)	8711	E	213 593-8100	18845
URS Holdings Inc (DH)	8711	E	415 774-2700	18851
Usertesting Inc (PA)	7372	D	650 567-5616	13509
Ustream Inc	4813	D	415 489-9400	8002
Valueact Capital Management LP	6722	E	415 249-1232	10771
Van Der Hout Brgglano Nghtngal	8111	E	415 981-3000	17386
Van Ness Hotel Inc	7011	D	415 673-4711	11554
Van Sark Inc (PA)	2512	C	510 635-1111	3293
Vector Capital Management LP (PA)	6211	B	415 293-5000	10019
Vector Stealth Holdings II LLC (PA)	7379	E	415 293-5000	14005
Venable LLP	8111	E	415 653-3750	17387
Venables/Bell & Partners LLC	7311	C	415 288-3300	11794
Ventur Hospitality LLC (PA)	7011	E	415 279-8688	11556
Verana Health Inc	7372	E	415 215-4440	13515
Veritable Vegetable Inc	5148	D	415 641-3500	9435
Vestek Systems Inc (DH)	7375	D	415 344-6000	13811
Veterans Health Administration	8011	E	415 750-2009	15795
Vida Health Inc	7371	D	415 989-1017	12903
Vim Inc	7371	E	844 843-5381	12904
Vineti Inc	7371	D	415 704-8730	12905
Vir Biotechnology Inc (PA)	8731	C	415 906-4324	19148
Virgin Htels San Francisco LLC	7011	E	415 534-6500	11562
Virta Health Corp	8099	D	844 847-8216	17187
Visa Inc	7299	E	415 805-4000	11735
Viscira LLC	5045	D	415 848-8010	8761
Visionary Electronics Inc	3674	F	415 751-8811	6350
Vista Eqity Prtners Fund III L (DH)	6799	A	415 765-6500	10895
Vista Eqity Prtners Fund VI LP (PA)	6282	E	415 765-6500	10067
Vitalant Research Institute (PA)	8099	C	415 567-6400	17189
Vitas Healthcare Corporation	8052	E	415 874-4400	16211
Viva Soma Lessee Inc	8741	A	415 974-6400	19419
Viz Media LLC	2721	C	415 546-7073	3519
Vizu Corporation (DH)	8732	E	415 362-8498	19191
Voce Communications Inc	8743	E	415 975-2200	19698
Volpe Chiu Abel Sternberg	8111	E	415 668-0411	15810
Volta Charging LLC	7312	D	415 735-5169	11798
Volta Industries Inc (HQ)	3999	D	415 583-3805	7316
Voltus Inc	3822	E	415 617-9602	6708
Volume Services Inc	7999	C	415 972-1500	15262
VSC Sports Inc	8748	C	415 820-3525	19888
Vungle Inc	7311	C	415 800-1400	11795
W R Hambrecht Co Inc (PA)	6211	B	415 551-8600	10022
W S B & Associates Inc	7381	D	510 444-6266	14108
W S B & Associates Inc	7381	C	415 864-3510	14109
Waitwhile Inc	7371	E	888 983-0869	12916
Walden Capital Partnership	6799	E	415 391-7225	10896
Walden House Inc (PA)	8361	E	415 554-1100	18205
Walden House Inc	8361	C	415 554-1480	18206
Walden House Inc	8361	C	415 554-1131	18207
Walgreen Co	7384	E	415 558-8749	14184
Walker/Dunham Corp	3161	E	415 821-3070	4350
Walkme Inc (PA)	7371	D	855 492-5563	12917
Walkup Mldia Klly Schnbrger A	8111	E	415 981-7210	17389
Walt Disney Family Museum	8412	E	415 345-6800	18286
Walter E Mc Guire RE Inc (PA)	6531	E	415 929-1500	10681
Walter E McGuire RE Inc	6531	E	415 296-0123	10682
Wandera Inc	7374	E	408 667-5489	13769
Warner Walker Architects	8712	E	415 318-8900	18917
Warwick California Corporation	7011	E	415 992-3809	11566
Waterfall	7372	F	866 251-1200	13525
Waypoint Building Group Inc	1522	D	415 738-4730	19668
Weaver Schlenger and Mazel	8111	E	415 395-9331	17391
Webcor Construction LP (DH)	1542	D	415 978-1000	985
Webgility Inc	7372	E	415 640-7906	13526
Webpass Inc	4813	D	415 233-4100	8008
Weisscomm Group Ltd (PA)	8748	D	415 362-5018	19889
Wells Capital Management Inc (DH)	6282	B	415 396-8000	10069
Wells Fargo & Company (PA)	6021	A	866 249-3302	9694
Wells Fargo Asset MGT Intl LLC	6282	D	415 396-8000	10070
Wells Fargo Investments LLC (DH)	6021	B	415 396-7767	9696
Wells Fargo Prime Services LLC	6211	D	415 848-0269	10023
Wentworth Hauser & Violich Inc	6282	D	415 981-6911	10071
West Cast Retina Med Group Inc	8011	E	415 972-4600	15814
West Coast Garment Mfg Inc	2326	F	415 896-1772	2990
West Coast Property Maint LLC	6531	E	415 885-6970	10684
West Prtal Ctr For After Schl (PA)	8351	D	415 753-1113	18046
Wested (PA)	8733	C	415 565-3000	19248
Western Messenger Service Inc	4212	C	415 487-4229	7499
Westside Cmnty Mental Hlth Ctr	8093	C	415 563-8200	17094
Westside Cmnty Mental Hlth Ctr	8093	E	415 355-0311	17095
Wetherby Asset Management	6282	C	415 399-9159	10072
Wfc Holdings LLC (HQ)	6021	D	415 396-7392	9697
Wharf Motel Corp	7011	D	415 673-7411	11577
Whisperai Inc	8741	E	855 765-0088	19425
White Oak Global Advisors LLC (PA)	8742	E	415 644-4100	19669
Wickman Development and Cnstr	1521	E	415 239-4500	729
Wideorbit LLC (PA)	7371	D	415 675-6700	12921
Wikimedia Foundation Inc	8699	B	415 839-6885	18608
Wilbur-Ellis Company LLC (DH)	5191	E	415 772-4000	9617
Wilbur-Ellis Holdings II Inc (HQ)	5191	E	415 772-4000	9618
Wild Planet Entertainment Inc (DH)	5092	E	415 705-8300	9171
Wild Type Inc	2092	F	408 669-5207	2833
Wildenradt-Mcmurray Inc	5072	D	510 835-5500	8991
Wilson Elser Mskwitz Edlman DC	8111	E	202 626-7660	17399
Wine Mart Groups LLC	2084	F	866 583-2312	2766
Winfield Design International	2679	F	415 216-3169	3409
Winston & Strawn LLP	8111	E	415 591-1000	17401
Wire US Inc	7372	F	415 602-6260	13529
Wisdomtree Cnada Qlty Dvdend G	6722	E	415 905-5448	10773
Withumsmith+brown PC	8721	D	415 434-3744	19005
Wixcom Inc	7371	E	415 329-4610	12924
Wizeline Inc (PA)	7371	A	888 386-9493	12925
Womens Community Clinic	8093	D	415 379-7800	17097
Wonolo Inc	7361	E	415 766-7692	12153
Woodruff-Sawyer & Co (PA)	6411	C	415 391-2141	10372
Workstream Technologies Inc	7371	D	415 767-1006	12928
Wrangler Topco LLC (HQ)	5045	D	415 439-1400	8762
Wrns Studio (PA)	8712	E	415 489-2224	18919
Wu Yee Childrens Services (PA)	8351	E	415 230-7504	18047
Wyre Inc	7389	E	415 374-7356	14464
Xolvio LLC	7372	F	415 857-1317	13536
Xoom Corporation	6099	C	415 777-4800	9850
Xulu Inc	6282	E	800 975-7199	10074
Xythos Software Inc	7371	E	415 248-3800	12931
XYZ Graphics Inc (PA)	2759	E	415 227-9972	3756
Yammer Inc	7379	E	415 796-7400	14017
Yanka Industries Inc	7929	E	855 981-8208	14884
Yelp Inc (PA)	7375	D	415 908-3801	13812
Yerba Buena Engrg & Cnstr Inc (PA)	8711	E	415 822-4400	18865
Yhb San Francisco LLC	7011	C	415 421-7500	11585
Yiheng Capital LLC (PA)	6799	D	415 875-5600	10899
York Hotel Group LLC	7011	E	415 885-6800	11586
Yosemite Foundation (PA)	8641	D	415 434-1782	18484
Yosh For Hair (PA)	7231	E	415 989-7704	11697
Youappi Inc	8742	D	646 854-3390	19674
Young & Rubicam LLC	8743	E	650 287-4000	19699
Young & Rubicam LLC	7336	C	415 365-1700	11875
Young Brdcstg of San Francisco	4833	D	415 441-4444	8057
Young Community Developers	8322	E	415 822-3491	17789
Young Electric Co	1731	C	415 648-3355	1644
Young MNS Chrstn Assn San Frnc	8641	E	415 447-9602	18512
Young MNS Chrstn Assn San Frnc	8641	E	415 447-9622	18513
Young MNS Chrstn Assn San Frnc (PA)	8641	E	415 777-9622	18516
Young MNS Chrstn Assn San Frnc	8641	E	415 931-9622	18517
Young MNS Chrstn Assn San Frnc	8641	E	415 666-9622	18518
Young MNS Chrstn Assn San Frnc	8641	E	415 957-9622	18519
Young MNS Chrstn Assn San Frnc	8641	E	415 885-0460	18520
Young MNS Chrstn Assn San Frnc	8641	E	415 822-7728	18524
Young MNS Chrstn Assn San Frnc	8641	E	415 586-6900	18525
Yourpeople Inc	7372	A	888 249-3263	13539
Yume Inc (HQ)	7311	B	650 591-9400	11796
Zazmic Inc (PA)	7371	C	415 728-1621	12934
Zeniq Inc	7374	E	415 562-6367	13774
Zenlen Inc	2844	E	833 834-8238	4100
Zenput Inc	7371	E	800 537-0227	12937
Zenreach Inc (HQ)	7313	C	415 612-1900	11808
Ziff Davis B2b Focus Inc (DH)	8742	E	415 696-5453	19676
Zignal Labs Inc	7371	D	415 683-7871	12939
Ziro Ride LLC	4729	E	951 801-4981	7822
Zocalo	5021	D	415 293-1600	8504
Zoe Holding Company Inc	8999	D	415 421-4900	19923
Zola Electric Labs Inc	3674	E	650 542-6939	6368
Zoosk Inc (HQ)	4813	E	415 728-9543	8012
Zynga Inc (PA)	7374	C	855 449-9642	13775
Alliance Ground Intl LLC	4581	C	650 821-0855	7764
Enterprise Rnt—car San Frncsc	7514	E	650 697-9200	14481
Hyatt Corporation	7011	C	650 452-1234	11182
Mercury Air Cargo Inc	7832	E	650 588-5440	14813
Pratt & Whitney	3724	F	650 634-3122	6621
Primeflight Aviation Svcs Inc	4581	E	650 877-1560	7782
San Francisco Intl Arprt	4581	E	650 821-6700	7783

GEOGRAPHIC SECTION

SAN JOSE, CA

Company	SIC	EMP	PHONE	ENTRY #
San Francisco Intl Arprt Corp	4581	E	650 616-2400	7784
Swissport Usa Inc	4581	D	650 821-6220	7786
Swissport Usa Inc	4581	D	571 214-7068	7787
Total Airport Services LLC	4581	D	650 589-8560	7788

SAN GREGORIO, CA - San Mateo County

Company	SIC	EMP	PHONE	ENTRY #
Cybernetic Micro Systems Inc	3575	E	650 726-3000	5330

SAN JOAQUIN, CA - Fresno County

Company	SIC	EMP	PHONE	ENTRY #
Standard Cattle LLC	0751	D	559 693-1977	349

SAN JOSE, CA - Santa Clara County

Company	SIC	EMP	PHONE	ENTRY #
2150 N Frst Nvel Coworking LLC	6512	D	312 283-3683	10374
22nd Century Technologies Inc	7371	B	866 537-9191	12211
24 Hour Fitness Usa Inc	7991	E	408 923-2639	14920
247ai Inc (PA)	7379	A	650 385-2247	13826
2crsi Corporation	3572	F	408 598-3176	5280
40 Hrs Inc	7361	A	408 414-0158	12067
4d Inc	7371	C	408 557-4600	12216
4info Inc	7313	E	650 350-4800	11799
501(c Insurance Programs Inc	6411	E	408 216-9796	10223
A & E Anodizing Inc	3471	E	408 297-5910	4890
A & J Precision Sheetmetal Inc	3444	D	408 885-9134	4735
A Is For Apple Inc	8049	D	877 991-0009	15877
A&T Precision Machining	3599	E	408 363-1198	5457
A-1 Jays Machining Inc (PA)	3599	D	408 262-1845	5458
A-1 Ruiz & Sons Inc	2721	E	408 293-0909	3491
A10 Networks Inc (PA)	7379	A	408 325-8668	13827
ABB Enterprise Software Inc	5049	D	408 770-8968	8800
Abbott Strngham Lynch A Prof A	8721	D	408 377-8700	18929
Acacia Communications Inc	3674	D	212 331-8417	6007
Acceldata Inc	7382	C	650 450-3423	14117
Access Telecomm Systems Inc	1731	E	800 342-4439	1443
Accordent Technologies Inc	7372	F	310 374-7491	12949
Ace Parking Management Inc	7521	D	408 437-2185	14504
Acer America Corporation (DH)	7379	D	408 533-7700	13830
Acer American Holdings Corp (DH)	3577	A	408 533-7700	5339
Acer Cloud Technology Inc	8711	A	408 830-9809	18612
Acfn Franchised Inc	6099	E	888 794-2236	9839
Achievement Engineering Corp	8711	E	408 217-9174	18613
Aci Alloys Inc	3479	F	408 259-7337	4924
Acronics Systems Inc	8711	C	408 432-0888	18614
Action Urgent Care Inc (PA)	8011	D	408 440-8335	15268
Activevideo Networks LLC (DH)	7373	D	408 931-9200	13549
Addison Technology Inc	3672	E	408 749-1000	5906
Adobe Inc	7372	A	408 536-6000	12955
Adobe Inc (PA)	7372	A	408 536-6000	12956
Advance Modular Technology Inc	3577	E	408 453-9880	5341
Advanced Analogic Tech Inc	3674	C	408 330-1400	6011
Advanced Industrial Ceramics	3559	E	408 955-9990	5139
Advancedcath Technologies LLC (HQ)	3841	E	408 433-9505	6935
Advantest America Inc (HQ)	3674	A	408 456-3600	6015
Advent Group Ministries Inc	8361	D	408 281-0708	18049
Advolife Inc (HQ)	8082	D	408 879-1835	16837
Aecom Usa Inc	8748	C	408 392-0670	19715
Aeris Communications Inc (PA)	4813	C	408 557-1900	7923
Ahead Magnetics Inc	3679	D	408 226-9800	6396
Air Systems Inc	1711	B	408 280-1666	1190
Airdrome Orchards Inc (PA)	0174	E	408 297-6461	95
Airfield Supply Co	5099	D	408 320-0230	9187
Airmagnet Inc	5045	E	408 571-5000	8663
Ajilon LLC	7363	C	408 367-2592	12158
Akm Semiconductor Inc	3674	E	408 436-8580	6017
Akon Incorporated	3999	E	408 432-8039	7267
Akribis Systems Incorporated	3621	F	408 913-1300	5657
Alacritech Inc	3674	E	408 867-3809	6020
Alfa Tech Cnslting Engners Inc (PA)	8711	D	408 487-1200	18623
Alien Technology LLC	7371	D	408 782-3900	12238
Alien Technology LLC (PA)	3663	E	408 782-3900	5819
Aligntech	7538	E	714 605-7114	14545
All Bay Mechanical Inc	1711	E	408 280-5558	1196
All Fab Prcsion Sheetmetal Inc	1761	D	408 279-1099	1783
All Klin Construction Inc (PA)	5013	E	408 327-1000	8437
Alldragon International Inc	7371	E	408 410-6248	12240
Allergy Asthma Assoc Snta Clar (PA)	8011	D	408 243-2700	15273
Alliant Tchsystems Oprtons LLC	3812	E	408 513-3271	6660
Allied Telesis Inc	3577	E	408 519-8700	5342
Almaden Golf & Country Club	7997	D	408 323-4812	15049
Almaden Valley Athletic Club	7991	D	408 445-4900	14924
Almaden Vly Counseling Svc Inc	8322	E	408 997-0200	17414
Alpha Innotech Corp (DH)	5047	C	510 483-9620	8772
Altera Corporation (HQ)	3674	A	408 544-7000	6027
Altest Corporation	3599	E	408 436-9900	5471
Altierre Corporation	3674	E	408 435-7343	6028
Alum Rock Counseling Ctr Inc (PA)	8322	E	408 240-0070	17419
Alumawall Inc	3448	D	408 275-7165	4845
Alzeta Corporation	8731	F	408 727-8282	19021
AM and S Mfg Inc	3443	F	408 396-3027	4711
Amazon Prsrvation Partners Inc	2033	E	415 775-6355	2211
Amberwood Gardens	8093	D	408 253-7502	16986
Amphenol DC Electronics Inc	3643	B	408 947-4500	5709
Ampro Adlink Technology Inc	3571	D	408 360-0200	5240
Amtek Electronic Inc	3571	D	408 971-8787	5241
Amtel Inc	8748	E	408 615-0522	19720
Anatomage Inc (PA)	7371	E	408 885-1474	12253
Andapt Inc	7372	E	408 931-4898	12976
Anderson Brule Architects Inc	8712	E	408 298-1885	18869
Andrian	1799	E	408 434-0730	2003
Angular Machining Inc	3599	E	408 954-8326	5473
Aopen America Incorporated	5045	D	408 586-1200	8668
Apache Design Inc (HQ)	7371	C	408 457-2000	12257
Apex Healthcare Services LLC	8082	D	925 922-3525	16848
Apex Machining Inc	3599	E	408 441-1335	5474
Apolent Corporation (PA)	7379	E	408 203-6828	13841
Aporeto Inc	7372	D	408 472-7648	12977
Appex Networks Corporation	7372	E	408 973-7898	12979
Applied Anodize Inc	3471	E	408 435-9191	4897
Appro International Inc (DH)	3572	D	408 941-8100	5282
Aptiv Digital LLC	7372	D	818 295-6789	12984
Apx Inc (PA)	8748	E	408 517-2100	19721
Aqualine Piping Inc	1711	D	408 745-7100	1204
Aquatek Plumbing Inc	1711	E	408 354-5885	1206
Aquinas Corporation	8051	D	408 248-7100	15910
Aramark Spt & Entrmt Group LLC	7929	B	408 999-5735	14867
Archway Insurance Brokers LLC	6411	E	408 441-2000	10236
Ardent Systems Inc	3672	E	408 526-0100	5916
Arh Recovery Homes Inc (PA)	8361	D	408 281-6570	18058
Ariosa Diagnostics Inc	8731	C	408 229-7500	19029
Arm Inc (HQ)	3674	B	408 576-1500	6048
Armanino LLP	8721	E	408 200-6400	18931
Armanino LLP	8721	E	408 200-6400	18933
Arrcus Inc	7371	E	408 884-1965	12274
Asante Technologies Inc (PA)	3577	E	408 435-8388	5347
Ascent Technology Inc	3444	F	408 213-1080	4742
Asian Amercn Recovery Svcs Inc	8069	C	408 271-3900	16751
Asian Amrcans For Cmnty Invlvm (PA)	8399	C	408 975-2730	18220
Asic Advantage Inc	3674	D	408 541-8686	6052
Asm America Inc	7629	C	408 451-0830	14690
Associated Students S J S U	8641	E	408 924-6240	18389
Assured Care Enterprises Inc	8099	E	408 379-7000	17101
AT&T Services Inc	4813	C	408 554-3335	7930
Atlantic Aviation Svc	4581	D	408 297-7552	7766
Atlas Private Security Inc	7381	E	408 613-0668	14034
Atp Electronics Inc	3674	E	408 732-5000	6053
Automated Solutions Group Inc	3822	E	408 432-0300	6699
Automation Anywhere Inc (PA)	7371	B	888 484-3535	12286
Automation Technology Inc	7371	E	408 350-7020	12287
Autowest Collision Repairs Inc	7532	E	408 392-1200	14519
Autox Technologies Inc	7371	E	650 492-8869	12290
Auxin Solar Inc	3674	E	408 225-4380	6054
Avago Tech Wreless USA Mfg LLC	3674	E	800 433-8778	6055
Avago Technologies US Inc	3674	D	408 433-4068	6056
Avago Technologies US Inc	3674	F	408 435-7400	6057
Avago Technologies US Inc (HQ)	3674	B	800 433-8778	6058
Avantis Medical Systems Inc	3845	E	408 733-1901	7096
Avaya Inc	4813	E	408 437-2504	7933
Avidbank (PA)	6022	E	408 200-7390	9699
Avidbank Holdings Inc	6022	C	408 200-7390	9700
Avr San Jose Downtown Ht LLC	7011	D	408 924-0900	10938
Ayehu Inc (HQ)	7372	D	800 652-5601	13004
Azazie Inc	2335	E	650 963-9420	3000
B R Printers Inc (PA)	2752	D	408 278-7711	3625
B W Padilla Inc	7692	E	408 275-9834	14709
B&Z Manufacturing Company Inc	3599	E	408 943-1117	5480
Bab Acquisition Corp	3826	F	408 267-7214	6813
Babbitt Bearing Co Inc	3599	E	408 298-1101	5481
Bad Boys Bail Bonds Inc (PA)	7389	D	408 298-3333	14211
Bae Systems Imging Sltions Inc	3674	D	408 433-2500	6065
Bae Systems Land Armaments LP	3812	B	408 289-0111	6664
Balbix Inc	7371	D	866 936-3180	12296
Bam Advisor Services LLC	6282	D	800 366-7266	10034
Banh An Binh	3679	E	408 935-8950	6400
Banksia Landscape	0781	E	408 617-7100	394
Bay Dynamics Inc	7371	E	415 912-3130	12297
Bay Elctrnc Spport Trnics Inc	3672	C	408 432-3222	5919
Bay Print Solutions Inc	2752	F	408 579-6640	3630
Bayspec Inc	3826	E	408 512-5928	6814
Baytech Webs Inc	7374	E	408 533-8519	13695
Bd Biscnces Systems Rgents Inc	2819	C	408 518-5024	3781
Bea Systems Inc (HQ)	7371	A	650 506-7000	12299
Beaver Dam Health Care Center	8051	E	408 366-6510	15932
Beaver Dam Health Care Center	8051	E	408 923-7232	15935
Becton Dickinson and Company	3841	B	408 432-9475	6952
Behavior Frontiers LLC	8093	E	310 856-0800	16995
Bellavista Landscape Svcs Inc (PA)	0781	D	408 410-6000	396
Belmont Bruns Construction Inc	1542	E	408 977-1708	830
Benchmark Elec Mfg Sltions Inc (HQ)	3672	E	805 222-1303	5921
Bentek Corporation	3679	D	408 954-9600	6401
Bestronics Holdings Inc (PA)	3675	D	408 385-7777	6370
Bethel Church of San Jose	8351	D	408 246-6790	17861
Beveled Edge Inc	3231	F	408 467-9900	4384
Bhatnagar Law Office	8111	E	408 564-8051	17214
Bhogart LLC	5084	E	855 553-3887	9053
Biarca Inc (PA)	7379	D	408 564-4465	13857
Biggs Cardosa Associates Inc (PA)	8711	E	408 296-5515	18640
Bill Brown Construction Co	1521	E	408 297-3738	619
Billcom Holdings Inc (PA)	7372	B	650 621-7700	13019
Bio-Ved Pharmaceuticals Inc	8731	E	408 432-4020	19033
Blach Construction Company (PA)	1541	D	408 244-7100	790
Blackstone Gaming LLC	5092	D	424 488-0505	9166
Blackwell Engrg Inc	1623	E	408 441-1120	1090
Bloom Energy Corporation (PA)	3674	B	408 543-1500	6069
Blossom Valley Cnstr Inc	0782	D	408 993-0766	449
Blue Jeans Network Inc (HQ)	4899	C	408 550-2828	8071
Blum Construction Co Inc	3442	F	408 629-3740	4701

Employment Codes: A=Over 500 employees, B=251-500, C=101-250, D=51-100, E=20-50 F=10-19

SAN JOSE, CA — GEOGRAPHIC SECTION

Company	SIC	EMP	PHONE	ENTRY #
Boston Scientific Corporation	3842	C	408 935-3400	7067
Boundless Care Inc	8059	E	408 363-8900	16220
Bpm LLP	8721	D	408 961-6300	18935
Brandvia Alliance Inc (PA)	7311	E	408 955-0500	11741
Breakfast Club At Midtown	7997	E	408 280-0688	15064
Bridgene Biosciences	2834	F	626 632-3188	3874
Brightview Landscape Svcs Inc	0781	D	408 453-5904	403
Brilliant General Maint Inc (PA)	7349	C	408 287-6708	11929
Bristlecone Incorporated	7371	A	650 386-4000	12313
Bristol Hotel	7011	F	408 559-3330	10974
Britelab Inc	3824	D	650 961-0671	6739
Broadcom Corporation	3674	E	408 922-7000	6072
Broadcom Corporation (HQ)	3674	A	408 433-8000	6073
Broadcom Inc (HQ)	3674	B	408 433-8000	6074
Broadcom Technologies Inc (HQ)	3674	E	408 433-8000	6075
Brocade Cmmnctions Systems Inc	8748	D	408 333-4300	19735
Brocade Cmmnctions Systems LLC (DH)	3577	A	408 333-8000	5354
Broker Solutions Inc	6153	E	408 429-2085	9869
BSI Services & Solutions W Inc (DH)	8711	E	408 790-9200	18648
Buckingham Strategic Partners	8741	E	800 366-7266	19309
Buena Vista Business Svcs LP	7231	D	908 452-9002	11676
Burke Industries Delaware Inc (HQ)	3069	C	408 297-3500	4213
Burr Pilger Mayer Inc	8721	D	408 961-6300	18940
Business Jrnl Publications Inc	2711	B	408 295-3800	3421
C & D Semiconductor Svcs Inc (PA)	3674	E	408 383-1888	6077
C & J Contracting Inc	1542	E	408 374-6025	844
C & O Painting Inc	1721	C	408 279-8011	1405
C H Reynolds Electric Inc	1731	B	408 436-9280	1471
C L Hann Industries Inc	3599	F	408 293-4800	5485
C R S Drywall Inc	1742	C	408 998-4360	1663
Ca Inc	3674	D	408 433-8000	6078
Cabrera Painting Inc	1721	E	408 998-4789	1406
Cade Corporation	2899	D	310 539-2508	4156
Cadence Design Systems Inc (PA)	7372	A	408 943-1234	13045
Cadent Inc	7373	C	408 470-1000	13562
Cadent Tech Inc (HQ)	7371	D	408 642-6400	12318
Cafe Chromatic	2095	E	510 220-1341	2837
Caliber Bodyworks Texas Inc	7532	D	408 972-0300	14521
California Drywall Co (PA)	1742	C	408 292-7500	1664
California Newspapers Partnr (PA)	2711	E	408 920-5333	3424
California Schl Employees Assn (PA)	8631	A	408 473-1000	18355
California Skin Institute	8011	D	650 969-5600	15310
California United Mech Inc (PA)	1711	B	408 232-9000	1227
California Waste Solutions Inc (PA)	4953	D	510 832-8111	8314
California Water Service Co (HQ)	4941	C	408 367-8200	8225
California Water Service Group (PA)	4941	C	408 367-8200	8226
Calix Inc (PA)	4899	A	408 514-3000	8073
Calsoft Labs Inc (HQ)	7373	C	408 755-3000	13563
Calvac Inc	1611	E	408 262-1162	1023
Calypto Design Systems Inc	7372	E	408 850-2300	13047
Calyx Technology Inc (PA)	7371	E	408 997-5525	12323
Cambrian School District	8699	E	408 377-3882	18555
Canary Communications Inc	3663	F	408 365-0609	5828
Canyon Springs Post-Acute	8051	E	408 259-8700	15950
Cardinal Paint and Powder Inc	2851	D	408 452-8522	4102
Care2com Inc	8641	E	650 622-0860	18404
Careage Inc	8051	E	408 238-9751	15951
Caremore Health Plan	8062	E	408 963-2400	16327
Carlton Senior Living Inc	8361	D	408 972-1400	18066
Carter & Burgess Inc	8711	E	408 428-2010	18663
Casavina Foundation Corp	8051	E	408 238-9751	15953
Catholic Chrties Snta Clara CN	8322	E	408 282-8600	17468
Catholic Chrties Snta Clara CN (PA)	8322	E	408 468-0100	17469
Cato Networks Inc	7372	E	646 975-9243	13053
Cavendish Kinetics Inc	5065	E	408 627-4504	8901
Cavium Networks Intl Inc (DH)	3674	D	650 625-7000	6081
Ccintegration Inc (PA)	8731	E	408 228-1314	19040
Cellfusion Inc (PA)	7372	E	650 347-4000	13055
Center For Employment Training (PA)	8331	D	408 287-7924	17801
Central Concrete Supply Co Inc (DH)	3273	D	408 293-6272	4475
Central Tech Inc	3699	E	408 955-0919	6510
Century Theatres Inc	7832	E	408 226-2251	14809
Cerium Systems Inc	7379	D	408 623-0787	13864
Cernex Inc	3679	E	408 541-9226	6406
Challenger Schools	8351	D	408 723-0111	17884
Checkpoint Technologies LLC	8731	E	408 321-9780	19042
Chelbay Schuler & Chelbay (PA)	6371	D	408 288-4400	10214
Chemical Safety Technology Inc	3089	D	408 263-0984	4267
Chester C Lehmann Co Inc (PA)	5063	D	408 293-5818	8851
Chicago Title Company	6531	C	408 292-4212	10196
Childcare Foundry	8351	E	408 564-5356	17895
Childrens Crative Lrng Ctr Inc	8351	B	408 978-1500	17896
Chilisin America Ltd	3677	E	408 954-7389	6378
Chip Arasan Systems Inc	6531	D	408 282-1616	10508
Chip Estimate Corporation	7372	E	408 943-1234	13064
Christian Milpitas School (PA)	8351	D	408 945-6530	17906
Chrontel Inc (PA)	3674	D	408 383-9328	6082
Ciphercloud Inc (HQ)	7372	D	408 687-4350	13065
Circus Ice Cream	5143	E	408 977-1134	9336
Cisco Systems Inc (PA)	3577	A	408 526-4000	5357
Cisco Systems Capital Corp (HQ)	7389	A	610 386-5870	14225
Cisco Systems LLC (PA)	7372	B	650 989-6500	13067
Cisco Technology Inc (HQ)	3577	A	408 526-4000	5358
Cisco Webex LLC (HQ)	7389	A	408 435-7000	14226
Citcon USA LLC (PA)	6099	E	888 254-4887	9846
Citigroup Global Markets Inc	6211	D	408 947-2200	9964
City Canvas	2394	E	408 287-2688	3038
City II Enterprises Inc	0782	E	408 275-1200	453
City of San Jose	4581	D	650 965-4156	7769
City San Jose Animal Care Ctr	0742	E	408 794-7297	325
Cityteam Ministries (PA)	8331	E	408 885-8080	17804
Civil Engineering Assoc Inc	8711	E	408 453-1066	18670
Clarion Hotel San Jose Airport	7011	E	408 453-5340	11011
Clark Pest Ctrl Stockton Inc	7342	E	408 866-2278	11892
Classic Custom Vacations Inc	4724	D	800 221-3949	7795
Classic Parking Inc	7521	E	408 278-1444	14511
Classic Vacations LLC	4725	C	408 287-4550	7817
Clean Roofing	7699	E	408 472-7378	14742
Clear Shape Technologies Inc	3629	F	408 943-1234	5694
Clear View LLC	3442	F	408 271-2734	4702
Clearedge Solutions Inc	3229	F	408 262-2800	4370
Clearist Inc	3993	F	408 835-8620	7224
Cloudcar Inc	7372	E	650 946-1236	13075
Cloudely Inc (PA)	7371	E	800 797-8608	12342
Cloudious LLC (PA)	7379	C	732 666-2468	13869
Cloudradiant Corp	5199	A	408 256-1527	9651
Cnex Labs Inc (PA)	3674	E	408 695-1045	6083
Coast Engraving Companies Inc	2796	E	408 297-2555	3768
Cobham Adv Elec Sol Inc	3812	B	408 624-3000	6665
Cog Group LLC (PA)	5021	D	408 213-1790	8490
Cohesity Inc (PA)	7371	E	855 926-4374	12351
Comet Technologies USA Inc	3829	C	408 325-8770	6897
Common Ground Ldscp MGT Inc	0782	E	408 278-9807	455
Commonwealth Central Credit Un (PA)	6061	D	408 531-3100	9779
Community Health Partnr Inc	8099	E	408 556-6605	17125
Compensia Inc	8742	E	408 876-4025	19474
Complete Genomics Inc	8733	B	408 648-2560	19212
Concentric Software Inc	7372	E	408 816-7068	13088
Concept Part Solutions Inc	3545	E	408 748-1244	5091
Concept Systems Mfg Inc	3674	E	408 855-8595	6085
Concrete Ready Mix Inc	3273	E	408 224-2452	4478
Conklin Bros San Jose Inc (PA)	5023	E	408 266-2250	8509
Continntal Intllgent Trnsp Sys	3011	E	408 391-9008	4197
Coraltree Inc	7372	E	408 215-1441	13093
Cortec Precision Shtmtl Inc (PA)	3444	C	408 278-8540	4750
County Building Materials Inc	5031	D	408 274-4920	8539
Cpacket Networks Inc	3577	E	650 969-9500	5361
CPI Satcom & Antenna Tech Inc	3663	D	408 955-1900	5834
Cpk Manufacturing Inc	3599	F	408 971-4019	5497
Crawford Communications Group	8742	E	408 343-0200	19485
Createpros LLC	5065	C	844 752-7328	8905
Creative Metal Products Corp	3599	E	408 281-0797	5498
Creative Plant Design Inc	5193	F	408 452-1444	9630
Creative Security Company Inc	7381	E	408 295-2600	14050
Credo Semiconductor Inc	7389	E	408 664-9329	14240
Crestwood Behavioral Hlth Inc	8361	C	408 275-1067	18093
Crestwood Behavioral Hlth Inc	8063	E	408 275-1067	16738
Crunch LLC	7991	D	650 257-8000	14943
Cryptography Research Inc	7379	E	408 462-8000	13877
Csr Technology Inc (DH)	3679	B	408 523-6500	6414
CTT Inc (PA)	3663	D	408 541-0596	5837
Cubeware Inc	7389	E	650 847-8345	14243
Cupertino Electric Inc (PA)	1731	B	408 808-8000	1491
Cushman & Wakefield Cal Inc	6531	A	408 572-4134	10528
Cushman & Wakefield Cal Inc	6531	A	408 436-5500	10530
Cushman & Wakefield Cal Inc	6531	A	415 397-1700	10532
Customer Service Realty (PA)	6531	E	408 558-5000	10534
Cws Utility Services Corp	8611	C	408 367-8200	18305
Cybernet Software Systems Inc	7371	B	972 792-7597	12368
Cymmetrik Usa Inc	2759	E	408 205-1114	3728
Cyoptics Inc	3674	F	408 433-7343	6094
Cypress Envirosystems Inc	8711	E	800 544-5411	18683
Cypress Semiconductor Corp (HQ)	3674	E	408 943-2600	6095
Cypress Semiconductor Intl Inc (DH)	3674	C	408 943-2600	6096
D & F Standler Inc	3599	E	408 226-8188	5501
Dale Grove Corporation	3556	F	408 251-7220	5129
Datacare Corporation	8742	E	866 834-2334	19488
Dataendure	5045	E	408 734-3339	8690
DC Electronics Inc	3643	D	408 947-4531	5714
De Anza Cupertino Aquatics	7997	E	408 446-5600	15082
De Mattei Construction Inc	1521	D	408 295-7516	631
Deep Ocean Engineering Inc	3732	F	408 436-1102	6641
Delave Inc (PA)	5199	D	408 293-7200	9655
Deliverimates LLC	4789	D	857 445-7736	7878
Della Maggiore Tile Inc	1743	D	408 286-3991	1713
Deloitte & Touche LLP	8721	B	408 704-4000	18948
Deloitte Consulting LLP	8742	E	212 492-4000	19490
Delta Matrix Inc	3599	E	408 955-9140	5506
Denali Software Inc (HQ)	7372	E	408 943-1234	13115
Denron Inc	3679	E	408 435-8588	6417
Dfine Inc (HQ)	3841	C	408 321-9999	6970
DH Smith Company Inc	1742	D	408 532-7617	1672
Diablo Landscape Inc	0782	E	408 487-9620	458
Diamanti Inc (PA)	3575	E	408 645-5111	5331
Diamond Sales & Services Inc	7538	E	408 263-8997	14557
Dicar Inc	3357	E	408 295-1106	4570
Digital Onus Inc (PA)	7371	C	408 228-3490	12391
Directed Light Inc	5084	E	408 321-8500	9063
Displaylink Corp (HQ)	7371	F	650 838-0481	12395
Ditech Networks Inc (HQ)	3661	D	408 883-3636	5793
Dnfcs Inc (PA)	7371	E	510 201-9809	12396
Dolphin Technology Inc	3674	E	408 392-0012	6100
Doudell Trucking Company (PA)	4213	D	408 263-7300	7527
Dpr Construction A Gen Partnr	1542	C	408 370-2322	865

	SIC	EMP	PHONE	ENTRY #
Dreambig Semiconductor Inc	3674	D	408 839-1232	6101
Dsb Inc	5023	E	408 228-3000	8510
Dsp Group Inc **(PA)**	3674	D	408 986-4300	6102
Dten Inc **(PA)**	3577	E	866 936-3836	5362
Du-All Anodizing Inc	3471	E	408 275-6694	4902
Duel Systems Inc	3678	D	408 453-9500	6391
Dunan Sensing LLC	3699	E	408 613-1015	6514
Dynamic Intgrted Solutions LLC	3674	F	408 727-3400	6104
Eah Elena Gardens LP	6513	D	415 295-8840	10429
Eargo Inc **(PA)**	3842	D	650 351-7700	7068
Eastside Union High School Dst	8351	E	408 347-4700	17928
Eclipse Microwave Inc	3679	F	408 806-8938	6421
Ecolab	2841	F	408 928-8100	4062
Econosoft Inc	7371	D	408 442-3663	12411
Ed Supports LLC	8093	D	201 478-8711	17018
Edc-Biosystems Inc **(PA)**	3823	E	510 257-1500	6718
Edges Electrical Group LLC **(HQ)**	5063	D	408 293-5818	8858
Edgewater Networks Inc	7379	D	408 351-7200	13885
Einfochips Inc **(HQ)**	7371	C	408 496-1882	12415
Ek Health Services Inc **(PA)**	8742	C	408 973-0888	19498
Elcon Inc	3679	E	408 292-7800	6422
Elcon Precision LLC	3545	E	408 292-7800	5096
Electric Cloud Inc **(HQ)**	5045	C	408 419-4300	8697
Electromax Inc	3672	E	408 428-9474	5927
Electronic Interface Co Inc	3699	D	408 286-2134	6516
Elementcxi	3674	E	408 935-8090	6108
Eli Kiselman	1389	E	832 886-3743	565
Eligius Manufacturing Inc	3441	E	408 437-0337	4657
Elisity Inc	3577	F	408 839-3971	5364
Elite Metal Fabrication Inc	3599	F	408 433-9926	5517
Empress Care Center LLC	8051	E	408 287-0616	15987
Encore Industries	3444	E	408 416-0501	4762
Endodontics Associates	8021	E	408 294-4149	15833
Endwave Corporation **(DH)**	3663	B	408 522-3100	5839
Endwave Defense Systems Inc **(DH)**	3674	D	408 522-3180	6109
Energous Corporation	3663	D	408 963-0200	5840
Engeo Incorporated	8711	D	408 574-4900	18702
Ensurge Micropower Inc	3679	D	408 503-7300	6425
Enterprise Rnt—car San Frncsc	7514	E	408 450-6000	14482
Envestment Management Inc **(HQ)**	6282	E	408 962-7878	10043
Environ-Clean Technology Inc	3674	F	408 487-1770	6113
Eoplex Inc	3699	E	408 638-5100	6518
Eoplex Technologies Inc	3699	E	408 638-5100	6519
Epmware Inc	5045	E	408 614-0442	8702
Epson Research and Dev Inc **(DH)**	7373	D	408 952-6000	13584
Eric Electronics Inc	5065	E	408 432-1111	8909
Eric Stark Interiors Inc	1742	D	408 441-6136	1673
Ericsson Inc	3663	E	408 970-2000	5841
Ess Technology Holdings Inc **(HQ)**	3674	E	408 643-8818	6116
Estes Express Lines	4213	D	408 286-3894	7533
Eugenus Inc **(HQ)**	3825	D	669 235-8244	6752
European Paving Designs Inc	1721	D	408 283-5230	1412
Everycaronline Inc	7374	E	650 284-0497	13712
Exar Corporation **(HQ)**	3674	C	669 265-6100	6117
Exatron Inc	3825	E	408 629-7600	6754
Excite Credit Union **(PA)**	6061	D	800 232-8669	9785
Exclusive Networks Usa Inc	5045	E	408 943-9193	8703
Exis Inc	5065	E	408 944-4600	8911
Expedite Precision Works Inc	3599	E	408 437-1893	5523
Expert Dry Wall Systems Inc	5031	D	408 271-5044	8545
Extreme Networks Inc **(PA)**	3661	B	408 579-2800	5795
Extreme Precision Inc	3599	F	408 275-8365	5524
Eye Mdcal Clnic Snta Clara Vly	8011	D	408 869-3400	15394
Fab-9 Corporation	7379	D	408 667-2448	13896
Facility Masters Inc **(PA)**	7349	C	408 436-9090	11948
FAI Electronics Corp	5065	E	408 829-7581	8913
Fair Isaac Corporation **(PA)**	7389	C	408 535-1500	14270
Fairmont Hotel Guest)	7011	D	615 578-2670	11090
Familiar Srrndings HM Care LLC	8082	E	408 979-9990	16883
Family and Children Services	8748	E	408 292-9353	19773
Fastrak Manufacturing Svcs Inc	3679	E	408 298-6414	6427
Fcs Software Solutions Limited	7371	C	408 324-1203	12445
Federal Realty Investment Tr	6798	E	408 551-4600	10818
Fertility Physicians Northe **(PA)**	8011	D	408 356-5000	15406
Fime USA Inc	7371	E	408 228-4040	12450
First 5 Santa Clara County	8322	E	408 260-3700	17570
First Alarm SEC & Patrol Inc **(PA)**	7381	C	408 866-1111	14058
First Student Inc	4151	C	408 971-3466	7437
First Technology Federal Cr Un **(PA)**	6061	D	855 855-8805	9789
Fixstream Networks Inc	7371	E	408 921-0200	12453
Flagship Airport Services Inc **(HQ)**	7349	B	408 977-0155	11950
Flagship Enterprises Holdg Inc **(PA)**	7349	C	408 977-0155	11951
Flagship Sweeping Services Inc **(HQ)**	4959	E	408 977-0155	8399
Flea Market Inc	6519	E	408 453-1110	10479
Fleetpride Inc	5013	E	408 286-9200	8451
Flextronics America LLC **(DH)**	3672	C	408 576-7000	5931
Flextronics Intl USA Inc	3672	A	408 576-7000	5932
Flextronics Intl USA Inc **(HQ)**	3672	A	408 576-7000	5933
Flextronics Logistics USA Inc **(DH)**	3672	B	408 576-7000	5934
Flextronics Semiconductor **(DH)**	3674	E	408 576-7000	6120
Fluor Facility & Plant Svcs	7349	C	408 256-1333	11953
Flytbase Inc	4724	E	805 470-8985	7796
Fonseca/Mcelroy Grinding Inc	1611	E	408 573-9364	1040
Force10 Networks Global Inc	7373	A	800 289-3355	13590
Foreal Spectrum Inc	3827	E	408 923-1675	6873
Forescout Technologies Inc **(PA)**	7371	A	408 213-3191	12460
Fortrend Engineering Corp	3823	E	408 734-9311	6719

	SIC	EMP	PHONE	ENTRY #
Fotonation Corporation **(PA)**	3679	D	650 843-9025	6429
Foundtion For Hispanic Educatn **(PA)**	8641	E	408 585-5022	18415
Four Points San Jose Downtown	7011	E	408 282-8800	11102
Fourth Street Bowl Inc	7933	E	408 453-5555	14892
FPI Management Inc	8741	C	408 267-3952	19339
Franchise Update Inc	2721	F	408 402-5681	3500
Frt of America LLC	3545	F	408 261-2632	5097
Full Service Janitorial Inc	7349	E	408 227-0600	11955
Full Service Maintenance Inc	7349	E	408 227-2400	11956
Fusionone Inc	7371	E	408 282-1200	12467
G D M Electronic Assembly Inc	3643	D	408 945-4100	5715
Galante Brothers Gen Engrg Inc	1611	D	408 291-0100	1043
Galli Produce Company	5148	D	408 436-6100	9407
Garage Doors Incorporated	2431	E	408 293-7443	3133
Garden City Inc	7011	A	408 244-3333	11112
Garden City Construction Inc	1542	E	408 289-8807	875
Gardner Family Hlth Netwrk Inc	8011	C	408 254-5197	15410
Gardner Family Hlth Netwrk Inc **(PA)**	8011	E	408 457-7100	15411
Gct Semiconductor Inc **(PA)**	3674	E	408 434-6040	6125
Gemtech Sales Corp	3433	E	408 432-9900	4629
General Dynamics Mission	3669	B	408 908-7300	5887
General Elec Assembly Inc	3672	E	408 980-8819	5935
Genesys Logic America Inc	3674	E	408 435-8899	6126
Gentec Manufacturing Inc	3599	F	408 432-6220	5532
Geo Semiconductor Inc **(PA)**	3674	D	408 638-0400	6127
Geometrics Inc	3829	D	408 428-4244	6903
George Bianchi Cnstr Inc	1741	E	408 453-3037	1647
George M Robinson & Co **(PA)**	1711	E	510 632-7017	1271
Ghangor Cloud Inc	3699	D	408 713-3303	6524
Ghd Inc	8711	E	408 451-9615	18721
Gigpeak Inc **(DH)**	3674	C	408 546-3316	6129
Girl Scouts Northern Cal	8641	E	408 287-4170	18422
Girl Scouts Santa Clara County **(PA)**	8641	E	408 287-4170	18424
Glasforms Inc	2821	F	408 297-9300	3803
Glassbeam Inc	7371	D	408 740-4600	12477
Glasshouse Sj LLC	7999	E	408 606-8148	15207
Glenrock Group	7997	E	408 323-9900	15094
Global Information Dist Inc	3861	F	408 232-5500	7149
Global Infotech Corporation	8748	A	408 567-0600	19785
Global Technology Services Inc	7379	E	408 333-9639	13902
Global Upside Inc **(PA)**	6141	E	650 964-4820	9858
Globallogic Inc **(HQ)**	7371	C	408 273-8900	12479
Goalsr Inc	7372	F	650 453-5844	13195
Gogrid LLC	4813	C	415 869-7444	7956
Gold Technologies Inc	3643	E	408 321-9568	5716
Gonzalez Pallets Inc **(PA)**	2448	E	408 999-0280	3224
Good Samaritan Hospital LP **(DH)**	8062	A	408 559-2011	16381
Goodwill Silicon Valley LLC **(PA)**	7363	D	408 998-5774	12173
Goodwill Silicon Valley LLC	7363	E	408 281-1449	12175
Gordon Biersch Brewing Company	2082	D	408 792-1546	2480
Gordon Biersch Brewing Company **(PA)**	2082	F	408 278-1008	2481
Gorilla Circuits **(PA)**	3672	C	408 294-9897	5936
Graham Contractors Inc	1611	E	408 293-9516	1045
Granite Rick Co	6799	C	831 768-2000	10851
Great American Plumbing Co Inc	7699	E	408 279-1515	14751
Green Circuits Inc	3672	C	408 526-1700	5937
Green Valley Corporation **(PA)**	1542	E	408 287-0246	880
Greenwaste Recovery Inc	3089	E	408 283-4800	4286
Gremlin Inc	7372	E	408 214-9885	13197
Grinding & Dicing Services Inc	3674	E	408 451-2000	6134
Group Manufacturing Svcs Inc **(PA)**	3444	D	408 436-1040	4766
Guavus Inc **(HQ)**	7372	D	650 243-3400	13201
Guidetech Inc	3825	E	408 733-6555	6760
H M H Engineers	8711	D	408 487-2200	18725
H&H Resolution LLC	7322	D	408 362-2293	11823
Hagensen Pacific Cnstr Inc	1542	E	408 961-8656	883
Haig Precision Mfg Corp	3599	D	408 378-4920	5533
Halrec Inc	7539	C	408 984-1234	14611
Hamilton Avenue Med Group Inc	8011	D	408 279-0548	15423
Hane and Hane Inc	3471	E	408 292-2140	4910
Hardcraft Industries Inc	3444	D	408 432-8340	4768
Harding Mktg Cmmunications Inc **(PA)**	7336	D	408 345-4545	11864
Hardwoods Specialty Pdts US LP	5031	D	408 275-1990	8547
Harmonic Drive LLC	3566	F	800 921-3332	5212
Harmonic Inc **(PA)**	3663	A	408 542-2500	5847
Hayes Mansion Conference Ctr	7011	C	408 226-3200	11133
HB Animal Clinics Inc	0742	E	408 227-3717	326
Health Trust **(PA)**	8621	C	408 513-8700	18338
Health Trust	8322	D	408 513-8700	17599
Healthier Kids Foundation Inc	8399	E	408 564-5114	18232
Heavenly Construction Inc	0781	D	408 723-4954	420
Heritage Bank of Commerce **(HQ)**	6022	C	408 947-6900	9735
Heritage Commerce Corp **(PA)**	6022	D	408 947-6900	9736
Herman Sanitarium	8051	D	408 269-0701	16023
Hermes-Microvision Inc	3674	E	408 597-8600	6143
Herotek Inc	3663	E	408 941-8399	5848
Hgst Inc	3572	E	408 954-8100	5290
Hgst Inc **(DH)**	3572	A	408 717-6000	5291
Hickman Plrmo Trong Becker LLP	8111	E	408 414-1080	17290
Hiep Nguyen Corporation	3599	E	408 451-9042	5536
Hillhouse Construction Co Inc	1541	E	408 467-1000	797
History San Jose	8412	D	408 287-2290	18273
Hitech Global Distribution LLC	3674	E	408 781-8043	6145
HLT San Jose LLC	7011	E	408 437-2103	11145
Hntb Corporation	8711	D	408 451-7300	18731
Hoffman Agency **(PA)**	8743	E	408 286-2611	19689
Holder Corporation	1542	D	408 516-4401	892

GEOGRAPHIC

Employment Codes: A=Over 500 employees, B=251-500, C=101-250, D=51-100, E=20-50 F=10-19
2022 Northern California Business Directory and Buyers Guide
© Mergent Inc. 1-800-342-5647
1207

SAN JOSE, CA — GEOGRAPHIC SECTION

Company	SIC	EMP	PHONE	ENTRY #
Homeguard Incorporated (PA)	7342	D	408 993-1900	11900
Hoopla Software Inc	7372	E	408 498-9600	13212
Hope Services (PA)	8331	E	408 284-2849	17816
Hopkins & Carley A Law Corp (PA)	8111	E	408 286-9800	17293
Horizon Services Incorporated	8361	E	408 283-8555	18132
Hospice of Valley (PA)	8082	E	408 947-1233	16898
Host International Inc	7011	C	408 294-1702	11162
Hpe Enterprises LLC (HQ)	7372	A	650 857-5817	13214
Hti Turnkey Manufacturing Svcs	3679	E	408 955-0807	6433
Hula Networks Inc (PA)	5045	F	866 485-2638	8711
Hunter Douglas Fabrications	2591	C	408 435-8844	3331
Hwang LLC	7011	D	408 435-8800	11179
I & A Inc	3444	E	408 432-8340	4771
Icom Mechanical Inc	1711	C	408 292-4968	1282
Ics Integrated Comm Systems	1731	D	408 491-6000	1521
Icu Medical Inc	3841	E	408 284-7064	6983
Iguard Security Services Inc (PA)	7382	E	650 714-1884	14137
Iitjobs Inc	7361	D	510 509-9368	12099
Imax Corporation	7832	D	408 294-8324	14811
Imerys Filtration Minerals Inc (DH)	3295	E	805 562-0200	4529
Impossible Aerospace Corp	3721	F	707 293-9367	6611
Indian Hlth Ctr Snta Clara Vly	8011	D	408 445-3400	15433
Industrial Metal Recycling Inc	4953	E	408 294-2334	8337
Indusys Technology Inc	7373	E	408 321-2888	13610
Infinera Corporation (PA)	3661	B	408 572-5200	5799
Infiniti Solutions Usa Inc (PA)	3672	C	408 923-7300	5940
Infobahn Softworld Inc (PA)	7379	E	408 855-9610	13910
Infrrd Inc	7371	E	844 446-3773	12519
Ingrasys Technology USA Inc	3825	F	863 271-8266	6764
Innogrit Corporation	3674	E	408 785-3678	6154
Innolux Optoelectronic Inc	7349	D	408 573-8438	11962
Innominds Software Inc	7371	E	408 434-6463	12521
Innovative Circuits Engrg Inc	8748	E	408 955-9505	19794
Invision Way Home	8322	E	408 271-5160	17614
Ino-Tech Laser Processing Inc	3699	C	408 262-1845	6526
Inphi Corporation (HQ)	3674	C	408 217-7300	6157
Insieme Networks LLC	3661	E	408 424-1227	5800
Insignia/Esg Ht Partners Inc	6531	B	408 288-2900	10579
Insite Digestive Health Care	8011	E	408 471-2222	15434
Inspira Inc	7371	E	408 247-9500	12524
Institute On Aging	8059	C	510 536-3377	16249
Insync Software Inc	7372	E	408 352-0600	13240
Intel Corporation	3577	A	408 544-7000	5380
Intelligent Energy Inc	3429	E	562 997-3600	4618
Intelligent Storage Solution	3572	E	408 428-0105	5295
Interface Masters Inc	3577	F	408 441-9341	5388
Interface Masters Tech Inc	3679	E	408 441-9341	6435
Interior Plant Design	7389	E	408 286-1367	14306
Intermolecular Inc	3674	C	408 582-5700	6165
International Bus Mchs Corp	7371	A	408 463-2000	12533
International Bus Mchs Corp	8731	B	408 927-1080	19075
Invensense Inc (HQ)	3812	A	408 501-2200	6672
Iogyn Inc	3841	E	408 996-2517	6990
Iron Construction Inc	1521	E	408 282-1080	653
Irvine APT Communities LP	6513	C	408 943-1595	10441
Iscs Inc	7371	C	408 362-3000	12541
Island Hospitality MGT LLC	7011	E	408 226-7676	11198
Itron Networked Solutions Inc (HQ)	4899	B	669 770-4000	8079
Itsj Group Inc	3599	E	408 609-6392	5543
ITW Semisystems Inc	3353	E	408 350-0244	4560
Ixsystems Inc (PA)	7371	D	408 943-4100	12545
J & J Air Conditioning Inc	1711	D	408 920-0662	1288
J Lohr Winery Corporation (PA)	2084	E	408 288-5057	2622
J Lohr Winery Corporation	2084	D	408 293-1345	2623
J&N Engineering Inc	3541	E	408 680-1810	5075
Jabil Inc	3672	B	408 361-3200	5941
Jacobs Engineering Group Inc	8711	D	408 436-4936	18743
Jade Global Inc (PA)	7379	D	408 899-7200	13926
Jai Inc	5065	D	408 383-0300	8921
Jarka Enterprises Inc (PA)	1799	E	408 325-5700	2040
Jarvis Manufacturing Inc	3599	F	408 226-2600	5545
Javad Ems Inc	3679	E	408 770-1700	6439
Jay Nolan Community Svcs Inc	8322	C	408 293-5002	17620
Jdi Display America Inc (PA)	3679	E	408 501-3720	6440
Jennings Technology Co LLC (DH)	3675	D	408 292-4025	6371
Jensen Corp Landscape Contr	0782	C	408 446-4881	472
Jensen Landscape Services Inc	0782	C	408 446-1118	474
Jeppesen Dataplan Inc	7375	A	408 961-2825	13796
Jessie Steele Inc	2399	F	510 204-0991	3051
Jetstream Software Inc	7371	E	408 766-1775	12546
JMEKM Enterprises	7349	E	866 370-0419	11965
John Naimi Inc	1521	E	408 280-7433	657
Johnson Matthey Inc	3841	E	408 727-2221	6993
Johnson Service Group Inc	6512	A	408 728-9510	10394
Jonna Corp Inc	3443	E	408 297-7910	4723
Josephines Prof Staffing Inc (PA)	7361	C	408 943-0111	12101
Jts Corporation	3572	E	408 468-1800	5297
K B M Office Equipment Inc (PA)	5021	D	408 351-7100	8497
Kaiser Foundation Hospitals	8082	B	408 361-2100	16902
Kaiser Foundation Hospitals	8011	E	408 439-6808	15449
Kaiser Foundation Hospitals	8062	A	408 972-6010	16404
Kaiser Foundation Hospitals	8011	C	408 972-7000	15468
Kaiser Foundation Hospitals	8011	C	408 972-3000	15488
Kaiser Foundation Hospitals	6324	C	408 972-3376	10140
Kaiser Foundation Hospitals	8062	A	408 972-6700	16415
Kanrad Technologies Inc	7371	E	408 615-8880	12556
KC Metal Products Inc (PA)	3441	D	408 436-8754	4670
Kennerley-Spratling Inc	3089	C	408 944-9407	4295
Keri Systems Inc (PA)	3699	D	408 435-8400	6529
Kerio Technologies Inc	7372	F	409 880-7011	13261
Ketera Technologies Inc (DH)	7372	E	408 572-9500	13262
Kidango Inc	8351	D	408 258-9129	17957
Kidder Mathews Inc	6531	E	408 970-9400	10595
Kids Haven	8351	E	408 274-8766	17960
Kids Haven (PA)	8351	C	408 274-8766	17961
Kimball Electronics Ind Inc	3672	E	669 234-1110	5944
Kindred Healthcare LLC	8062	E	408 261-6943	16423
Kion Technology Inc	3479	E	408 435-3008	4936
Kioxia America Inc (PA)	5065	E	408 526-2400	8925
Kloves Inc (PA)	7373	E	408 768-5966	13621
Kmic Technology Inc	3663	D	408 240-3600	5851
Koning & Associates Inc (PA)	6411	E	408 265-3800	10307
Kranem Corporation	7372	C	650 319-6743	13269
Ksm Corp	3674	D	408 514-2400	6174
Kuprion Inc	2893	E	650 223-1600	4154
Kyma Medical Technologies Inc	3845	F	650 386-5089	7110
L & B Laboratories Inc	3999	E	408 251-7888	7295
L & D Construction Co Inc	1521	E	408 292-0128	661
L & H Iron Inc	3441	E	408 287-8797	4671
L & T Precision Engrg Inc	3599	E	408 441-1890	5558
Lab-Gistics LLC	8731	C	650 309-2627	19080
Labcyte Inc (DH)	8731	D	408 747-2000	19081
Lacework Inc (PA)	7373	B	888 292-5027	13622
Lanai Garden Corporation	7011	E	408 929-8100	11245
Landcare USA LLC	0782	D	408 727-4099	479
Landmark Technology Inc	3679	E	408 435-8890	6446
Laptalo Enterprises Inc	3444	E	408 727-6633	4776
Lark Avenue Car Wash	7542	E	408 371-2565	14648
Larkspur Hsptality Dev MGT LLC	7011	E	408 885-1234	11254
Larson Automation Inc	7371	E	408 432-4800	12569
Laser Reference Inc	3821	E	408 361-0220	6694
Lasertec USA Inc (HQ)	7699	E	408 437-1441	14760
Latentview Analytics Corp	8742	E	408 493-6653	19556
Lattice Semiconductor Corp	3674	B	408 826-6000	6178
Law Foundation Silicon Valley	8111	E	408 293-4790	17310
Learningstar Inc (PA)	8351	E	408 221-4067	17963
Leavitt Pacific Insur Brks Inc	6411	E	408 288-6262	10308
Lee Bros Foodservices Inc (PA)	5141	D	408 275-0700	9276
Lee Brothers	2035	E	650 964-9650	2282
Lees Sandwiches Intl Inc	6794	E	408 280-1595	10806
Leeyo Software Inc (HQ)	7372	E	408 988-5800	13276
Legacy Roofg Waterproofing Inc (PA)	1761	E	408 451-9785	1816
Legacy Transportation Svcs Inc (PA)	4214	C	408 294-9800	7624
Lemtech USA Inc	3469	F	408 824-5352	4885
Lenovo (united States) Inc	3571	D	510 813-3331	5258
Lensvector Inc	3851	E	408 542-0300	7144
Leotek Electronics USA LLC	3993	E	408 380-1788	7241
Lg Display America Inc (HQ)	5065	D	408 350-0190	8928
Lg Innotek Usa Inc	3812	E	408 234-6316	6674
Lg Innotek Usa Inc (HQ)	3679	C	408 955-0364	6447
Lights Fantastic	2752	F	408 266-2787	3673
Lincoln Glen Manor LLC	8361	C	408 267-1492	18139
Lita & Ava Inc	8082	C	408 241-3844	16910
Litmus Automation Inc	5045	E	765 418-7405	8722
Live Oak Adult Day Services	8322	E	408 971-9363	17637
Loayzas Ldscpg Pools Spas Inc	0782	E	408 297-5555	480
Lobob Laboratories Inc	2834	F	408 243-0313	3941
Lockheed Martin Corporation	3721	B	408 742-5219	6615
Lowes Home Centers LLC	5031	C	408 518-4165	8560
Loyalty Juggernaut Inc	7372	F	650 283-5081	13283
LSI Corporation (DH)	3674	A	408 433-8000	6182
Lucero Cables Inc	3679	C	408 536-0340	6449
Lumenis Be Inc	3841	C	408 764-3000	6998
Lumenis Inc (DH)	3841	C	408 764-3000	6999
Lumentum Holdings Inc (PA)	3669	A	408 546-5483	5888
Lumewave Inc (DH)	1731	E	916 400-3535	1534
Lumileds LLC (HQ)	3825	E	408 964-2900	6767
Lumina Networks Inc (PA)	7371	E	800 430-7321	12588
Lynx Software Technologies Inc (PA)	7372	D	408 979-3900	13285
Lyric Recovery Services Inc	8093	E	408 219-4681	17036
M Arthur Gensler Jr Assoc Inc	8712	E	408 885-8100	18898
M C I Manufacturing Inc	3444	E	408 456-2700	4781
M-Pulse Microwave Inc	3674	E	408 432-1480	6183
Mac Cal Company	3444	D	408 441-1435	4783
Mackin Consultancy LLC	8748	C	828 755-4073	19816
Macquarie Electronics Inc	3674	E	408 965-3860	6185
Magma Design Automation Inc (HQ)	7371	B	408 565-7500	12592
Magma Design Automation Inc	5045	E	408 432-7288	8723
Magnum Semiconductor Inc	3674	C	408 934-3700	6186
MAI Construction Inc	1521	C	408 434-9880	666
Maintenancenet LLC	7374	D	408 526-4000	13726
Managed Fclities Solutions LLC	8741	E	408 920-0110	19364
Maniglia Landscape Inc	0781	E	408 487-9620	424
Manufctring Engrg Exclince Inc	8711	E	408 382-1900	18761
Marcum LLP	8721	E	408 918-0900	18974
Mariner Health Care Inc	8051	E	408 298-3950	16047
Mariner Health Care Inc	8051	E	408 377-9275	16056
Marquez Brothers Intl Inc (PA)	5141	C	408 960-2700	9277
Mass Precision Inc	1761	D	408 786-0378	1819
Mass Precision Inc (PA)	3444	E	408 954-0200	4785
Maternal Cnnctons El Cmino Hos	8062	E	650 988-8287	16454
Mavens Creamery LLC	2024	E	408 216-9270	2180
Maxim Healthcare Services Inc	8082	C	408 914-7478	16911
Maxim Integrated Products Inc (HQ)	3674	A	408 601-1000	6193

GEOGRAPHIC SECTION — SAN JOSE, CA

Company	SIC	EMP	PHONE	ENTRY #
Mbkt Corp.	1731	E	408 212-0230	1538
McAfee LLC (HQ)	7372	A	888 847-8766	13298
McAfee Corp (PA)	7372	B	866 622-3911	13299
McAfee Public Sector LLC (DH)	7382	E	888 847-8766	14140
McClelland Aviation Inc	4581	E	408 258-4075	7776
McLarney Construction Inc	1542	E	408 246-8600	921
McManis Faulkner A Prof Corp	8111	E	408 279-8700	17331
McNeal Enterprises Inc	3089	D	408 922-7290	4300
McUbe (PA)	3674	D	408 637-5503	6194
Medamerica Inc	8011	E	408 281-2772	15525
Medianews Group Inc	2711	B	408 920-5713	3459
Mediatek USA Inc (PA)	3571	C	408 526-1899	5259
Mega Force Corporation	3577	E	408 956-9989	5398
Meivac Incorporated	3674	E	408 362-1000	6196
Melgar Facility Maint LLC (PA)	7349	B	408 657-0110	11970
Melita-Mcdonald Insur Svcs Inc	6411	E	408 882-0800	10314
Mellanox Technologies Inc	3674	E	408 970-3400	6197
Mellanox Technologies Inc (DH)	3674	A	408 970-3400	6198
Meriwest Credit Union (PA)	6061	C	408 363-3200	9796
Merlin Solar Technologies Inc (HQ)	3674	E	650 740-1160	6199
Merrill Lynch Pierce Fenner	6211	D	408 260-6001	9981
Merrill Lynch Prce Fnner Smith	6211	D	408 283-3000	9988
Metricstream Inc (PA)	7372	C	650 620-2911	13306
Metropolitan Education Dst (PA)	8331	B	408 723-6464	17822
MGM Drywall Inc	1742	D	408 292-4085	1691
Michael Kors (usa) Inc	5137	E	408 362-9537	9254
Micrel LLC	3674	A	408 944-0800	6202
Micro-Metric Inc	3829	F	408 452-8505	6911
Microchip Technology	3674	E	408 474-3640	6203
Microland Electronics Corp (PA)	5045	E	408 441-1688	8726
Microsemi Corp - Anlog Mxed Sg	3674	E	408 643-6000	6205
Microsemi Frequency Time Corp	3625	C	480 792-7200	5684
Microsemi Frequency Time Corp (DH)	3674	E	408 433-0910	6208
Microsemi Soc Corp (DH)	3674	E	408 643-6000	6210
Micrus Endovascular LLC (HQ)	3841	C	408 433-1400	7007
Midea Emerging Tech Co Ltd	8733	E	973 539-5330	19224
Mike Rovner Construction Inc	1521	C	408 453-6070	677
Mindray Ds Usa Inc	2835	B	650 230-2800	4026
Minerva Networks Inc (PA)	7371	D	800 806-9594	12608
Minimlly Invsive Srgcal Sltons	8011	E	408 750-4658	15537
Miramar Hospitality Consulting	7011	E	408 298-7373	11304
Mission Vly Ford Trck Sls Inc	7513	D	408 933-2300	14471
Moback Inc	7371	E	510 565-6672	12613
Mobica US Inc	7373	A	650 450-6654	13635
Mobiledgex Inc (HQ)	7371	E	707 364-8830	12614
Mobilehome Communities America	6515	C	408 298-3230	10473
Mobilygen Corporation	3674	E	408 601-1000	6214
Mocana Corporation	7374	D	415 617-0055	13732
Modern Ceramics Mfg Inc	3229	E	408 383-0554	4375
Modis Inc	7371	C	408 441-7144	12617
Modular Power Solutions LLC (HQ)	8748	E	408 321-2270	19822
Modutek Corp	3823	E	408 362-2000	6727
Mohawk Land & Cattle Co Inc	2011	D	408 436-1800	2101
Molecular Devices LLC (HQ)	3826	C	408 747-1700	6841
Momentum For Health (PA)	8093	E	408 254-6828	17048
Monolithic Power Systems Inc	3674	D	408 826-0600	6216
Monster Mep Inc	1711	D	408 727-8362	1312
Montage Technology Inc	3674	F	408 982-2788	6217
Montavista Software LLC (DH)	7372	D	408 572-8000	13315
Monumental Nutrition LLC	3272	E	408 410-0890	4443
Moreno & Associates Inc	7349	D	408 924-0353	11975
Morgan Stnley Smith Barney LLC	6211	D	408 346-0105	10002
Morphics Technology Inc	8711	B	408 369-7227	18773
MOSplastics Inc	3089	F	408 944-9407	4303
Mosys Inc	3674	E	408 418-7500	6218
Mota Group Inc (PA)	3695	E	408 370-1248	6505
Motiv Design Group Inc	3599	F	408 441-0611	5575
Motor Body Company Inc	7549	E	408 993-9555	14666
Mountz Inc (PA)	3823	E	408 292-2214	6728
Mpi America Inc	3674	F	408 770-3650	6219
MPS International Ltd	3674	A	408 826-0600	6220
Mt Eden Floral Company LLC (PA)	5193	E	408 213-5777	9637
Mt Eden Nursery Co Inc (PA)	6519	E	408 213-5777	10483
Multivitamin Direct Inc	2833	E	408 573-7292	3818
N J Kann Painting	1721	E	408 437-0220	1422
Nagarro Inc (HQ)	7379	A	408 436-6170	13942
Nan Ya Technology Corp USA	5065	E	408 961-4000	8936
Nanosilicon Inc	3674	E	408 263-7341	6222
National Home Health Svcs Inc	8082	E	408 786-1035	16914
National Security Industries (PA)	7381	C	408 371-6505	14079
Natural Orange Inc	7342	D	408 963-6868	11905
Naturescapes Landscaping Corp	0782	E	408 294-4994	488
ND Systems Inc	7319	E	408 776-0085	11814
Ndsp Delaware Inc	3674	E	408 626-1640	6226
Neato Robotics Inc (HQ)	3549	D	510 795-1351	5110
Neo Advisory Inc	4813	E	415 462-0569	7974
Neoconix Inc	3674	E	408 530-9393	6227
Neodora LLC	3089	E	650 283-3319	4306
Neonode Inc	3679	E	408 496-6722	6460
Neophotonics Corporation (PA)	3674	A	408 232-9200	6228
Neosem Technology Inc (DH)	3825	E	408 643-6000	6773
Nes Financial Corp	7389	E	800 339-1031	14338
Netapp Inc (HQ)	3572	A	408 822-6000	5302
Netenrich Inc (PA)	7379	C	408 436-5900	13945
Netgear Inc (PA)	3661	B	408 907-8000	5801
Netronix Integration Inc (PA)	1731	D	408 573-1444	1548
Networked Energy Services Corp (HQ)	3699	D	408 622-9900	6534
Neuvector Inc	3861	E	408 455-4034	7156
New Age Electric Inc	1731	D	408 279-8787	1550
New World Machining Inc	3599	E	408 227-3810	5578
Nexenta By Ddn Inc	7372	E	408 791-3300	13330
Nexlogic Technologies Inc	3672	D	408 436-8150	5951
Nexsentio Inc	7349	E	408 392-9249	11979
Nextest Systems Corporation	3825	C	408 960-2400	6774
Nextflex	8611	E	408 435-5523	18311
Nippon Trends Food Service Inc	2099	D	408 479-0558	2927
Nitto Americas Inc (HQ)	2672	C	510 445-5400	3381
NM Machining Inc	3599	E	408 972-8978	5580
Nok Nok Labs Inc	7372	F	650 433-1300	13334
Northrop Grumman Systems Corp	3812	C	703 968-1239	6677
Northwest Landscape Maint Co	0782	E	408 298-6489	492
Nsg Technology Inc	7629	B	408 547-8770	14702
NTL Precision Machining Inc	3599	E	408 298-6650	5582
Ntsi Corporation	8331	E	408 297-7200	17828
Ntt Scrity Appsec Slutions Inc (DH)	7379	D	408 343-8300	13952
Nu Horizons Electronics Corp	5065	E	408 946-4154	8940
Nugate Group LLC (PA)	8744	E	408 278-9911	19705
Nutanix Inc (PA)	7372	A	408 216-8360	13336
Nuvoton Technology Corp Amer	5065	D	408 544-1718	8941
Nxp Usa Inc	3674	B	408 518-5500	6238
O C McDonald Co Inc	1711	D	408 295-2182	1319
Oberon Co	3679	F	408 227-3730	6464
Ocadian Care Centers LLC	8051	B	408 295-2665	16086
Oce Dsplay Grphics Systems Inc	3555	D	773 714-8500	5122
Oclaro (north America) Inc	3661	A	408 383-1400	5802
OConnor Hospital	8062	C	408 947-2929	16471
OConnor Hospital	8011	E	408 947-2804	15564
OConnor Hospital (HQ)	8062	A	408 947-2500	16472
Oeg Inc	1731	D	408 909-9399	1553
Office Automation Group	1731	E	408 292-0308	1554
Office Automation Group (PA)	1731	E	408 554-6244	1555
Ohmnilabs Inc	3549	E	408 675-9565	5111
Oki Graphics Inc	2759	F	408 451-9294	3743
Olivera Egg Ranch LLC	2015	D	408 258-8074	2137
Omega Ems Inc	5065	D	408 206-4260	8943
On Semcndctor Cnnctvty Sltons (HQ)	3674	E	669 209-5500	6243
On-Time AC & Htg LLC	1711	D	408 279-5843	1325
Ondot Systems Inc	7371	E	408 316-2379	12646
One World Montessori School	8351	E	408 723-5140	17986
Onepointone Inc	8731	D	855 346-5964	19096
Online Game Services Inc	4813	D	408 333-9663	7977
Ooyala Inc (HQ)	7371	B	650 961-3400	12650
Opengov Inc	4813	E	650 336-7167	7978
Opera San Jose Inc	7922	D	408 437-4450	14854
Ophelia Quinones	7363	E	408 757-1718	12186
Opi Commercial Builders Inc (PA)	1521	D	408 377-4800	680
Opsveda Inc	7372	E	408 628-0461	13349
Optimas Oe Solutions LLC	5063	E	408 934-1001	8871
Orb Enterprises Inc	7379	D	669 281-9994	13955
Orb Intelligence Inc	7372	E	650 391-4298	13356
Orbotech Lt Solar LLC	3674	E	408 414-3777	6248
Orion Manufacturing Inc	3672	F	408 955-9001	5954
Orion Security Patrol Inc	7381	B	408 287-4411	14082
Oski Technology Inc (PA)	7379	E	408 216-7728	13956
Osram Sylvania Inc	5063	E	408 922-7200	8872
OT Precision Machining Inc	3599	E	408 435-8818	5583
Outreach & Escort Inc (PA)	8322	E	408 678-8585	17667
Outset Medical Inc	3845	B	669 231-8200	7119
Pacific Coast Sales & Svc Inc	5075	E	408 437-0390	9012
Pacific Environmental Group	8711	B	408 453-7500	18787
Pacific Groservice Inc	5194	B	408 727-4826	9643
Pacific Press Corporation	2711	F	408 292-3422	3472
Pacific West Security Inc	7382	E	801 748-1034	14143
Pan American Body Shop Inc (PA)	7532	E	408 289-8745	14531
Pan-Cal Investment Company Inc	1531	E	408 248-6600	784
Panasas Inc (PA)	7371	D	408 215-6800	12667
Panzura LLC	7373	C	408 457-8504	13646
Parade Technologies Inc	5065	D	408 329-5540	8945
Park Plaza San Jose Arprt LLC	7011	B	408 453-5340	11356
Park West Landscape Inc	0782	D	925 560-9390	494
Parma Floors Inc	3996	F	408 638-0247	7265
Patent and Trademark Office US	6029	D	831 332-7127	9759
Patientsafe Solutions Inc (PA)	7371	D	858 746-3100	12672
Paypal (HQ)	7389	A	877 981-2163	14360
Paypal Data Services Inc	7389	E	408 376-7400	14361
Paypal Holdings Inc (PA)	7389	A	408 967-1000	14362
Pcs Mobile Solutions LLC	8748	D	408 229-8900	19838
Pds Tech Inc	7361	C	408 916-4848	12118
Peak Technology Entps Inc	5162	E	408 748-1102	9515
Peak Travel Group	4724	E	408 286-2633	7805
Pelican Sign Service Inc	3993	E	408 246-3833	7248
Peninsula Family Service	8351	D	650 403-4300	17991
Performnce First Bldg Svcs Inc (PA)	7011	E	408 441-4632	11984
Permanente Medical Group Inc	8011	A	408 972-6883	15599
Pernixdata Inc	7371	D	408 724-8413	12679
Petalon Landscape MGT Inc	0781	D	408 453-3998	413
Peter A Kuzinich	7922	E	408 292-3686	14856
Petrinovich Pugh & Company	8721	E	408 287-7911	18984
Pfeiffer Electric Co Inc	1731	E	408 436-8523	1563
Phase 3 Communications Inc	1731	D	408 946-9011	1564
Philips North America LLC	7622	E	408 436-8566	14681
Photon Dynamics Inc	3825	E	408 723-7118	6779
Photon Dynamics Inc (HQ)	3825	B	408 226-9900	6780
Photon Dynamics Inc	3825	C	408 226-9900	6781

Employment Codes: A=Over 500 employees, B=251-500, C=101-250, D=51-100, E=20-50 F=10-19

SAN JOSE, CA GEOGRAPHIC SECTION

	SIC	EMP	PHONE	ENTRY #
Photon Infotech Inc	7371	D	408 417-0600	12684
Physical Rehabilitation Netwrk	8049	E	408 570-0510	15894
Pillar Data Systems Inc	7372	B	408 503-4000	13370
Piranha Ems Inc	3571	E	408 520-3963	5269
Pivotal Connections	7389	E	408 484-6200	14368
Pixelworks Inc **(PA)**	3674	C	408 200-9200	6251
Pixim Inc	7373	D	650 934-0550	13648
Planned Prnthood Mar Monte Inc **(PA)**	8093	D	408 287-7532	17056
Plasma Rggedized Solutions Inc **(PA)**	3479	D	408 954-8405	4945
Platinum Builders Inc	1521	E	408 456-0300	687
Play N Learn Pre School	8351	E	408 269-2338	18002
Playphone Inc	7371	D	408 261-6200	12687
Plumbing Indust Apprenticeship	8331	D	408 453-6330	17832
Polaris Networks Incorporated	7371	D	408 625-7273	12689
Polycom Inc **(HQ)**	3661	A	831 426-5858	5806
Polytec Products Corporation	3599	E	650 322-7555	5599
Power Integrations Inc **(PA)**	3674	A	408 414-9200	6253
Power Intgrtons Intl Hldngs In	3674	D	408 414-8528	6254
Precision Measurements Inc	7629	E	408 733-8600	14703
Premiere Recycle Co	3443	E	408 297-7910	4728
Pricewaterhousecoopers LLP	8721	A	408 817-3700	18985
Priority Roofing Solutions Inc	1761	E	408 532-8020	1831
Probe-Logic Inc	3674	E	408 416-0777	6257
Property Maintenance Company **(PA)**	7349	C	408 297-7849	11987
Proplus Design Solutions Inc **(PA)**	7389	C	408 459-6128	14377
Prosurg Inc	3841	E	408 945-4040	7024
Proteinsimple **(HQ)**	8731	E	408 510-5500	19107
Prototek California LLC	3544	E	408 730-5035	5084
Proxim Wireless Corporation **(PA)**	3669	D	408 383-7600	5894
Proximex Corporation	7372	E	408 215-9000	13390
Prx Inc	8743	E	408 287-1700	19695
Psc LLC	4953	B	408 295-0607	8350
Pulse Secure LLC **(DH)**	7371	D	408 372-9600	12710
Q Analysts LLC **(PA)**	8742	D	408 907-8500	19614
Qct LLC	5045	A	510 270-6111	8738
Qolsys Inc **(HQ)**	7373	C	855 476-5797	13652
Qostronics Inc	3672	E	408 719-1286	5960
Quail Hill Investments Inc	6798	C	408 978-9000	10824
Qualcomm Atheros Inc **(HQ)**	3674	A	408 773-5200	6262
Quality Circuit Assembly Inc	3672	D	408 441-1001	5963
Quality Inn and Suites	7011	D	806 335-1561	11379
Quality Machining & Design Inc	3559	E	408 224-7976	5165
Quantum Corporation **(PA)**	3572	B	408 944-4000	5310
Quantum Government Inc	3572	E	408 944-4000	5311
Quantumscape Battery Inc	3674	C	408 452-2000	6263
Quantumscape Corporation **(PA)**	3674	D	408 452-2000	6264
Quest Dgnstics Clncal Labs Inc	8071	D	408 975-1015	16796
Quest Dgnstics Clncal Labs Inc	8071	D	408 259-6806	16799
Quest Discovery Services Inc **(PA)**	8111	C	408 441-7000	17359
Quicklogic Corporation **(PA)**	3674	E	408 990-4000	6266
Quorumlabs Inc	5045	E	408 708-4500	8741
R F I Security Inc **(HQ)**	1731	D	408 298-5400	1572
R Stephenson & D Cram Mfg Inc	3599	E	408 452-0882	5608
R&D Altanova Inc	3672	E	408 225-7011	5964
R-Bros Painting Inc	1721	E	408 291-6820	1428
Race Street Partners Inc **(PA)**	5144	D	408 294-6161	9350
Rackspace Hosting Inc	7374	B	201 792-1918	13750
Raditek Inc **(PA)**	3663	D	408 266-7404	5862
Radonich Corp	1731	E	408 275-8888	1573
Radonich Enterprises Inc	1761	D	408 295-6507	1834
Railway Distributing Inc	5032	E	408 280-7625	8632
Rajappan Myer Cnslting Engners **(PA)**	8711	E	408 280-2772	18800
Rambus Inc **(PA)**	3674	B	408 462-8000	6268
Randall Horton Associates Inc **(PA)**	5021	E	408 490-3300	8503
Rando AAA Hvac Inc	1711	E	408 293-4717	1343
Randstad Professionals Us LLC	7361	D	408 573-1111	12126
Rani Therapeutics LLC	2834	D	408 457-3700	3970
Rani Therapeutics Holdings Inc **(PA)**	2834	F	408 457-3700	3971
Rapid Precision Mfg Inc	3599	E	408 617-0771	5609
Ravix Financial Inc	8742	E	408 216-0656	19619
Rawitser Golf Shop Mike	7992	E	408 441-4653	15019
Rawson Custom Cabinets Inc	2434	E	408 779-9838	3188
Ray Scheidts Electric Inc	1731	E	408 292-8715	1575
Raya6 Investments Inc **(PA)**	6282	D	408 529-1269	10058
Rdc Machine Inc	3599	E	408 970-0721	5610
Ready Price LLC	7371	A	408 357-0931	12728
Redseal Inc	7372	C	408 641-2200	13402
Reeces Fantasies Inc **(HQ)**	1731	D	408 298-5400	1578
Reed & Graham Inc **(PA)**	2911	E	408 287-1400	4178
Refficiency Holdings LLC	1731	A	408 347-3400	1579
Regal Electronics Inc **(PA)**	3679	E	408 988-2288	6467
Relectric Inc	3613	E	408 467-2222	5653
Reliable Concepts Corporation	1541	E	408 271-6655	806
Renesas Electronics Amer Inc **(HQ)**	3674	A	408 432-8888	6272
Residnce Inn San Jose Nrth/SLC	7011	E	408 758-9550	11405
Resonate I Inc **(PA)**	7371	C	408 545-5500	12744
Retail Solutions Incorporated **(HQ)**	7372	E	650 390-6100	13407
Retailnext Inc **(PA)**	7371	C	408 884-2162	12747
Retina-Vitreous Assoc Inc	8011	E	408 402-3239	15650
Reyes Coca-Cola Bottling LLC	2086	D	408 436-3700	2799
RFI Enterprises Inc **(PA)**	1731	D	408 298-5400	1586
Rgis LLC	7389	D	408 243-9141	14386
Rite Track Equipment Svcs Inc	3559	F	408 432-0131	5167
Rivermeadow Software Inc	7372	F	408 217-6498	13411
Rm Executive Transportation	4119	E	650 260-1240	7400
Robecks Wldg & Fabrication Inc	3441	E	408 287-0202	4681
Robles Bros Inc **(PA)**	2099	E	408 436-5551	2939
Rockley Photonics Inc	3674	F	408 579-9210	6275
Rockwell Automation Inc	3625	D	408 443-5425	5689
Roku Inc **(PA)**	4841	C	408 556-9040	8065
Roku Holdings Inc **(HQ)**	7371	D	408 556-9391	12753
Roma Bakery Inc	2051	D	408 294-0123	2401
Ron Filice Enterprises Inc	6411	D	408 294-0477	10339
Rose Electronics Distrg Co LLC	5065	E	408 943-0200	8949
Rosendin Electric Inc **(PA)**	1731	A	408 286-2800	1591
Rosendin Electric Inc	1731	A	408 321-2200	1592
Roth Wood Products Ltd	2599	E	408 723-8888	3339
Royal Coach Tours **(PA)**	4142	C	408 279-4801	7422
Rpd Electrical Service Co Inc	1731	E	408 265-2850	1594
RSM US LLP	8721	D	408 572-4440	18989
Rtec-Instruments Inc	3826	E	408 456-0801	6848
Rvision Inc	3827	E	408 437-5777	6885
Ryland Custom Welding Inc	7692	E	408 781-2509	14720
S & S Drywall Inc **(PA)**	1742	C	408 294-4393	1704
S2c Inc	7372	F	408 213-8818	13418
Saco Enterprises Inc	4841	F	408 526-9363	8066
Sacred Heart Community Service	8322	E	408 278-2160	17701
Sage Intacct Inc **(HQ)**	7379	E	408 878-0900	13970
Sagepoint Financial Inc	6211	E	408 374-4787	10012
Saia Motor Freight Line LLC	4212	E	408 487-1740	7488
Saic Innovation Center LLC	5013	D	408 614-9391	8463
Sal J Acsta Sheetmetal Mfg Inc	3444	D	408 275-6370	4814
Salas OBrien LLC **(PA)**	8741	D	408 282-1500	19392
Salas OBrien Engineers Inc **(PA)**	8711	E	408 282-1500	18808
Samartan Intrnal Mdcine Med Gr	8062	E	408 371-9010	16502
Samsung SDS America Inc	7371	D	408 638-8800	12758
Samsung Semiconductor Inc **(DH)**	5065	C	408 544-4000	8951
San Andreas Regional Center **(PA)**	8322	C	408 374-9960	17707
San Jose Air Conditioning Inc	1711	E	408 457-7936	1354
San Jose Airport Garden Hotel	7011	D	408 793-3300	11435
San Jose Airport Hotel LLC	7011	C	408 793-3939	11436
San Jose Arena Management LLC **(PA)**	8741	C	408 287-7070	19395
San Jose Awning Company Inc	2394	E	408 350-7000	3042
San Jose Chld Discovery Museum	8412	D	408 298-5437	18280
San Jose Conservation Corps	8331	D	408 283-7171	17837
San Jose Country Club	7997	D	408 258-4901	15135
San Jose Healthcare System LP	8062	A	408 259-5000	16504
San Jose Hhg Hotel Dev LP	7011	E	408 650-0590	11437
San Jose Hhg Hotel Dev LP	7011	E	650 868-4911	11438
San Jose Hlthcare Wllness Ctr	8051	D	408 295-2665	16108
San Jose Lessee LLC	7011	D	408 453-4000	11439
San Jose Mailing Inc	7331	E	408 971-1911	11841
San Jose Mercury-News LLC **(DH)**	2711	A	408 920-5000	3476
San Jose Museum of Art Assn	8412	D	408 271-6840	18281
San Jose Police Officers Assn	8699	E	408 298-1133	18589
San Jose Redevelopment Agency	8748	C	408 535-8500	19857
San Jose Residence Club Inc	7011	E	408 998-0223	11440
San Jose Sharks LLC **(PA)**	7941	C	408 999-6810	14914
San Jose Slcon Vly Chmber Cmmr	8611	E	408 291-5250	18317
San Jose Surgical Supply Inc **(PA)**	5047	E	408 293-9033	8791
San Jose Water Company **(HQ)**	4941	C	408 288-5314	8264
San Jose Water Company	4941	C	408 298-0364	8265
Sandman Inc **(PA)**	3272	D	408 947-0669	4451
Sanmina Corporation	3672	E	408 964-3500	5968
Sanmina Corporation	3672	B	408 964-6400	5969
Sanmina Corporation **(PA)**	3672	B	408 964-3500	5971
Sanmina-Sci Usa Inc	3672	E	408 964-3500	5972
Santa Clara County of	8011	D	408 885-5000	15666
Santa Clara County of	8322	E	408 435-2000	17716
Santa Clara County of	8099	D	408 362-9817	17175
Santa Clara County of	8062	C	408 885-7470	16509
Santa Clara County of	8011	D	408 885-6666	15667
Santa Clara County of	8062	C	408 885-5451	16510
Santa Clara Cnty Fair Grnds Mg	7999	D	408 494-3100	15237
Santa Clara Cnty Fderal Cr Un	6061	D	408 282-0700	9815
Santa Clara Cnty Fderal Cr Un **(PA)**	6061	D	408 282-0700	9816
Santa Clara County of	8093	D	408 792-5020	17065
Santa Clara County of	8093	D	408 885-5770	17066
Santa Clara County of	8322	E	408 299-5437	17717
Santa Clara County of	4959	E	650 573-2400	8407
Santa Clara County of	8322	E	408 758-3500	17720
Santa Clara County of	8322	E	408 792-5030	17722
Santa Clara County of	8062	E	408 885-6818	16512
Santa Clara County of	8641	E	408 224-7476	18464
Santa Clara County of	8093	D	408 494-1561	17068
Santa Clara County of	8093	D	408 885-5920	17069
Santa Clara Imported Cars Inc	7538	D	408 247-2550	14589
Santa Clara Valley Corporation	7349	D	408 947-1100	11993
Santa Clara Valley Medica	8099	D	408 885-6839	17176
Santa Clara Valley Medical Ctr	8011	E	408 885-6300	15668
Santa Clara Valley Medical Ctr	8011	E	408 792-5586	15669
Santa Clara Valley Medical Ctr	8099	E	408 885-5730	17177
Santa Clara Valley Medical Ctr **(PA)**	8062	B	408 885-5000	16513
Santa Clara Valley Trnsp Auth **(PA)**	4111	A	408 321-2300	7353
Santa Clara Valley Trnsp Auth	4111	D	408 321-5559	7354
Santa Clara Valley Water **(PA)**	4941	C	408 265-2600	8267
Santa Clara Vly Wtr Dst Pub Fc	4941	C	408 630-2560	8268
Santa Teresa Golf Club LP	7992	E	408 225-2650	15024
Santana Row Hotel Partners LP	7011	C	408 551-0010	11445
Saqqara Systems Inc	7372	E	408 325-8241	13425
Sarpa-Feldman Enterprises Inc	7389	D	408 982-1790	14398
Satellite Healthcare Inc **(PA)**	8092	D	650 404-3600	16979
Saviano Company Inc	1629	E	650 948-3274	1175
Sbi Builders Inc **(PA)**	1522	E	408 549-1300	769

	SIC	EMP	PHONE	ENTRY #
Scaleflux Inc	7373	D	408 628-2291	13661
Scates Construction Inc	1542	E	408 293-9050	957
SCC ESA Dept of Risk Mgmt	6411	D	408 441-4207	10342
Schaper Construction Inc **(PA)**	1721	D	408 437-0337	1431
Schwager Davis Inc	1629	C	408 281-9300	1177
Scintera Networks Inc	3674	E	408 636-2600	6279
Screenbeam Inc **(PA)**	7371	D	800 752-7820	12768
SE Scher Corporation	7363	A	408 844-0772	12193
Sears Roebuck and Co	3429	C	408 864-6600	4620
Second Harvest Silicon Valley **(PA)**	8322	E	408 266-8866	17724
Securiti Inc	7371	C	408 401-1160	12769
Security Indust Spcialists Inc	7381	C	408 247-0100	14094
Securly Inc **(HQ)**	7372	D	855 732-8759	13434
Seiu Untd Hlthcare Wrkrs-West	8631	E	408 557-2835	18376
Select Hotels Group LLC	7011	E	408 324-1155	11459
Selectiva Systems Inc	7371	E	408 297-1336	12770
Semifab Inc	3823	D	408 414-5928	6733
Seminet Inc	3674	E	408 754-8537	6283
Senju Comtek Corp	3399	F	408 792-3830	4593
Sentons Usa Inc	3674	E	408 732-9000	6284
Sequoia Landscape MGT Inc	0781	E	408 277-6390	438
Service Station Systems Inc	1799	E	408 971-2445	2067
Service Workers Local 715 **(PA)**	8631	E	408 678-3300	18377
Serviceaide Inc **(PA)**	7372	E	650 206-8988	13441
Seventh Heaven Inc	2399	E	408 287-8945	3053
Sfn Group Inc	7363	A	408 526-0115	12195
Sfn Group Inc	7363	A	408 452-4845	12198
Sfo Airporter Inc **(PA)**	4111	D	650 246-2734	7358
Sharks Sports & Entrmt LLC	7941	A	408 287-7070	14916
Sharpswitch Inc	7371	D	866 633-6944	12775
Shasta Electronic Mfg Svcs Inc	3571	F	408 436-1267	5271
Showa Denko Materials Amer Inc **(DH)**	5063	E	408 873-2200	8876
Sierra Lumber and Fence PSI	1799	E	707 769-0345	2068
Sierra Lumber and Fence PSI **(HQ)**	1799	E	408 286-7071	2069
Sierra Lumber Co	1751	C	408 286-7071	1757
Sierra Pacific Machining Inc	3599	E	408 924-0281	5618
Signalfx Inc **(HQ)**	7374	E	888 958-5950	13758
Significant Cleaning Svcs LLC	7349	C	408 559-5959	11999
Silicon Image Inc **(HQ)**	3674	A	408 616-4000	6286
Silicon Labs Integration Inc **(HQ)**	3674	E	408 702-1400	6287
Silicon Valley Ambulance Inc	4119	D	408 225-2262	7405
Silicon Valley Capital **(DH)**	7997	D	408 971-9300	15144
Silicon Valley Mechanical Inc	1711	B	408 943-0380	1357
Silicon Valley Paving Inc	1611	E	408 286-9101	1072
Silicon Vly Law Group A Law Co	8111	E	408 573-5700	17376
Silicon Vly SEC & Patrol Inc **(PA)**	7381	C	408 267-1539	14096
Siliconix Incorporated **(HQ)**	3674	A	408 988-8000	6295
Siliconware Usa Inc **(DH)**	5065	E	408 573-5500	8953
Silitronics Inc	3679	E	408 605-1148	6469
Silray Inc	1711	E	650 331-1117	1358
Silver Creek Ftnes Physcl Thra	8049	E	408 238-1552	15898
Silver Creek Vly Cntry CLB Inc	7997	C	408 239-5775	15145
Simility LLC	7379	D	650 351-7592	13975
Sirf Technology Holdings Inc	3674	A	408 523-6500	6299
Situne Corporation	3663	E	408 712-3350	5868
Sj 1st Street Hotel LLC	7011	E	408 453-6200	11488
Sjb Child Development Centers **(PA)**	8351	D	408 538-0200	18021
SJW Group **(PA)**	4941	B	408 279-7800	8271
Sk Hynix America Inc **(HQ)**	5045	D	408 232-8000	8748
Sk Hynix Memory Solutions Inc	3674	B	408 514-3500	6302
Skybox Security Inc **(PA)**	7371	D	408 441-8060	12793
Skylite Networks	7371	D	403 934-9349	12795
Slashsupport Inc **(HQ)**	4813	C	408 985-4377	7992
SLI Systems Inc	7371	D	408 255-2487	12796
Smart & Final Stores Inc	5141	C	408 251-0109	9306
Smartlogic Semaphore Inc	7372	E	408 213-9500	13448
Smic Americas	5084	E	408 550-8888	9096
Sofa Holdco Dev LLC	7371	D	847 713-0680	12802
Soleeva Energy Inc	1711	D	408 396-4954	1364
Sonoma Orthopedic Products Inc	3841	F	847 807-4378	7040
Sontesta Select San Jose Arprt	7011	E	408 441-6111	11493
Sony Biotechnology Inc	8731	E	408 352-4257	19128
Sony Biotechnology Inc	7372	D	800 275-5963	13454
Sotcher Measurement Inc	3825	E	408 574-0112	6792
South Bay Circuits Inc	3679	C	408 978-8992	6470
South Bay Marble Inc **(PA)**	3281	E	650 594-4251	4524
South Bay Regl Public Safety T	8331	E	408 270-6494	17840
Southern Cal Disc Tire Co Inc	5014	C	408 436-8274	8482
Spansion LLC **(DH)**	3674	B	512 691-8500	6309
Specialty Baking Inc	5149	D	408 298-6950	9488
Spectral Dynamics Inc **(PA)**	3829	E	760 761-0440	6924
Spectrum Semiconductor Mtls	3674	F	408 435-5555	6310
Sperasoft Inc	7371	B	408 715-6615	12809
Spirent Communications Inc	3825	C	408 752-7100	6793
Splashtop Inc **(PA)**	7371	E	408 861-1088	12811
Spotline Inc	7373	E	408 768-1664	13668
Sprig Electric Co **(HQ)**	1731	C	408 298-3134	1609
Spt Microtechnologies USA Inc **(PA)**	3559	E	408 571-1400	5171
Spt Microtechnologies USA Inc	3565	F	408 571-1400	5205
Spyrus Inc **(PA)**	3577	E	408 392-9131	5414
Sra Oss Inc	7372	D	408 855-8200	13462
SSC San Jose Operating Co LP	8051	B	408 249-0344	16127
Stanford Health Care	8062	E	408 426-4900	16555
State Compensation Insur Fund	6331	D	408 656-7417	10177
Statewide Roofing Inc	1761	E	408 286-7828	1839
Stay Cal San Jose LLC	7011	D	408 275-2147	11507
Stellar It Solutions LLC	8621	E	669 250-6837	18350

	SIC	EMP	PHONE	ENTRY #
Sterling International Group	6552	E	408 972-7800	10717
Stevenson-Smith Enterprises	0782	E	408 286-9616	503
Story Dental Health Center	8021	E	408 272-0888	15859
Structural Integrity Assoc Inc **(PA)**	8711	D	408 978-8200	18823
Stryker Enterprises Inc	3499	F	408 295-6300	4987
Stryker Sales LLC	3842	E	800 624-4422	7081
Student Un of San Jose State U	8699	E	408 924-6405	18596
Student Un of San Jose State U	8699	E	408 321-8510	18597
Student Un of San Jose State U	8699	E	408 924-6371	18598
Subdynamic Locating Svcs Inc	8713	E	408 723-4191	18927
Suddath Rlction Systems Nthrn	4213	E	904 858-1273	7597
Suddath Rlction Systems Nthrn	4213	D	408 288-3030	7598
Sumitomo Elc DVC Innvtons USA	5065	D	408 232-9500	8961
Summit Steel Works Corporation	3441	E	408 510-5880	4686
Summit Wireless Tech Inc **(PA)**	3674	E	408 627-4716	6314
Sun Basket Inc **(PA)**	2099	C	408 669-4418	2945
Sun Sheetmetal Solutions Inc	3444	E	408 445-8047	4821
Sunnytech	3672	F	408 943-8100	5984
Sunpower Corporation **(DH)**	3674	A	408 240-5500	6315
Sunrun Installation Svcs Inc	1711	B	408 746-3062	1370
Sunvalleytek International Inc	5045	D	510 255-6101	8751
Super Micro Computer Inc **(PA)**	3571	A	408 503-8000	5273
Super Talent Technology Corp	5045	A	408 957-8133	8752
Superior Metals Inc	3444	F	408 938-3488	4822
Support Staff Services Inc	8082	E	408 258-5803	16950
Surface Art Engineering Inc	3674	E	408 433-4700	6321
Sutters Place Inc **(PA)**	7999	A	408 451-8888	15248
Sv Probe Inc	3825	B	480 635-4700	6794
Swa Services Group Inc	7349	E	408 938-8678	12004
Symbiosys Inc **(HQ)**	8748	A	408 996-9700	19867
Synaptics Incorporated	3577	D	408 904-1100	5415
Synaptics Incorporated **(PA)**	3577	A	408 904-1100	5416
Synaptics International Inc	3577	E	408 955-0783	5417
Synchronoss Technologies Inc	1731	B	800 575-7606	1618
Syndicate Corp	7389	E	408 740-5565	14422
Systech Integrators Inc	7379	D	408 441-2700	13985
T&S Manufacturing Tech LLC	3441	F	408 441-0285	4688
Takara Bio Usa Inc **(DH)**	8731	C	650 919-7300	19134
Take It For Granite Inc	1411	E	408 790-2812	576
Takex America Inc	3674	E	877 371-2727	6325
Talena Inc	7372	F	408 649-6338	13483
Talent Space Inc	7361	D	408 330-1900	12145
Tamtron Corporation **(DH)**	7371	D	408 323-3303	12848
Taos Mountain LLC **(PA)**	7379	B	408 324-2800	13990
Tbi Construction Cnstr MGT Inc	1541	E	408 246-3691	814
Team San Jose	7389	A	408 295-9600	14427
Teamsable Inc	5045	E	408 452-8788	8754
Teamwrkx Inc **(PA)**	1522	E	408 287-2700	773
Tecan Systems Inc	3821	D	408 953-3100	6697
Tech Interactive **(PA)**	8412	C	408 795-6116	18283
Technibuilders Iron Inc	3446	F	408 287-8797	4841
Technology Credit Union **(PA)**	6061	C	408 451-9111	9823
Technoprobe America Inc	3674	E	408 573-9911	6326
Teikoku Pharma Usa Inc **(HQ)**	2834	D	408 501-1800	3991
Tera-Lite Inc	1752	E	408 288-8655	1777
Terry Mechanical Inc	1711	E	408 629-7822	1378
Terry Meyer	6531	D	408 723-3300	10672
Tessera Inc **(DH)**	3674	D	408 321-6000	6330
Tessera Technologies Inc **(DH)**	3674	C	408 321-6000	6331
Tessolvedts Inc **(PA)**	8711	E	408 865-0873	18833
Testmetrix Inc	3825	E	408 730-5511	6795
Thales Esecurity Inc **(HQ)**	7379	D	408 433-6000	13997
Therma Holdings LLC **(PA)**	1731	A	408 347-3400	1622
Therma LLC	3444	A	408 347-3400	4825
Thermal Conductive Bonding Inc **(PA)**	3674	E	408 920-0255	6333
Thermo Finnigan LLC **(HQ)**	3826	B	408 965-6000	6857
Thermo Fisher Scientific	3826	B	408 894-9835	6858
Thermoquest Corporation	3826	A	408 965-6000	6860
Thoits Insurance Service Inc	6411	D	408 792-5400	10359
Thomas Mark & Company Inc **(PA)**	8711	E	408 453-5373	18837
Thoughtspot Inc **(PA)**	7372	B	800 508-7008	13491
Threatmetrix Inc	7371	C	408 200-5700	12864
Three Mrkters Cmmnctons Group	7311	E	408 293-3233	11790
Tico Construction Company Inc **(PA)**	1542	E	408 487-0700	974
Tilton Pacific Cnstr Inc	8741	E	408 551-0492	19409
Tivo Corporation **(HQ)**	6794	A	408 519-9100	10814
Tk Elevator Corporation	7699	E	408 392-0910	14779
TLC Machining Incorporated	3545	E	408 321-9002	5101
Tmk Manufacturing	3544	D	408 732-3200	5085
Tmt Enterprises Inc	4213	E	408 432-9040	7603
Tobar Industries Inc	3643	D	408 494-3530	5719
Tom Lopes Distributing Inc **(PA)**	5172	E	408 292-1041	9540
Topbuild Services Group Corp	1799	A	408 882-0411	2076
Tower Semiconductor Usa Inc	3674	F	408 770-1320	6334
Tp-Link Research Inst USA Corp	7373	F	408 618-5478	13679
Traditions Golf LLC	7992	D	408 323-5200	15034
Traffic Management Inc	7389	E	408 279-9900	14437
Traffic Management Inc	7389	E	877 763-5999	14438
Trans Pacific Inc **(PA)**	6531	E	408 445-4455	10673
Transdev Services Inc	4119	B	408 282-4706	7407
Transitamerica Services Inc	4111	E	408 961-4350	7364
Transpak Inc **(PA)**	7389	C	408 254-0500	14439
Tranzeal Inc	8742	E	408 834-8711	19653
Tri-Phase Inc	3672	C	408 284-7700	5988
Triad Tool & Engineering Inc	3089	E	408 436-8411	4327
Triquint Wj Inc	3663	D	408 577-6200	5882
Tshirtguyscom **(PA)**	2396	D	619 793-4635	3048

SAN JOSE, CA

Company	SIC	EMP	PHONE	ENTRY #
Tsmc North America (HQ)	8742	A	408 382-8000	19658
Tsmc Technology Inc	3674	D	408 382-8052	6337
TSS Link Inc	7379	E	408 745-7875	14003
Tti Inc	5065	D	408 414-1450	8967
Ttm Technologies Inc	3672	C	408 280-0422	5991
Tula Technology Inc	7549	D	408 383-9447	14677
Tupaz Day Care Services Inc	8322	E	408 377-1622	17773
Tupaz Homes LLC	1521	D	408 377-1622	724
Turner Designs Inc	3826	E	408 749-0994	6861
U S Perma Inc	1743	E	408 436-0600	1727
Ubicom Inc	3674	D	408 433-3330	6339
Ubiquiti Networks Inc	7373	E	408 942-3085	13684
Ultrasense Systems Inc (PA)	7371	E	408 391-5734	12887
Ultratech Inc (HQ)	3559	C	408 321-8835	5173
Unilab Corporation	8071	A	408 927-8331	16815
Uniquify Inc	3679	E	408 235-8810	6480
United Contract Services Inc	7349	E	408 577-0105	12009
United Craftsmen Prinitng	2752	E	408 224-6464	3707
United Fd Coml Wkrs Un Local 5	8631	E	408 998-0428	18383
United Green Mark Inc	5083	D	408 295-3376	9046
United Parcel Service Inc	4215	E	408 291-2942	7665
United Site Services Cal Inc	7359	C	408 295-2263	12065
United States Gypsum Company	5032	C	408 279-3001	8638
United Temp Services Inc	7361	E	408 472-4309	12148
United Way Silicon Valley	8322	E	408 260-3915	17776
Unity Care Group	8322	D	408 971-9812	17777
Universal Bldg Svcs & Sup Co	7349	E	408 995-5111	12013
Universal Services America LP	7381	A	408 993-1965	14106
Untangle Holdings Inc (PA)	7372	E	408 598-4299	13507
Uptima Inc	7371	E	408 933-9505	12890
Uri Tech Inc	3672	F	408 456-0115	5994
URS Group Inc	8711	D	408 297-9585	18849
User Zoom Inc	7371	E	408 533-8619	12892
Utstarcom Inc (HQ)	3661	C	408 791-6168	5814
Valiantica Inc (PA)	7372	E	408 694-3803	13510
Valin Corporation (PA)	5084	D	408 730-9850	9102
Valley Health Plan	6324	B	408 885-4760	10156
Valley Images LLC	2759	F	408 279-6777	3754
Vander-Bend Manufacturing Inc (PA)	3679	B	408 245-5150	6481
Various Technologies Inc	3625	E	408 972-4460	5691
Varite Inc (PA)	7371	E	408 977-0700	12894
Vat Incorporated (DH)	5085	E	800 935-1446	9139
VCA Almaden Valley Hospital	0742	D	408 268-3550	341
Vcinity Inc (PA)	7379	E	408 841-4700	14004
Vcomply Technologies Inc	7371	D	650 319-9842	12896
Vectra AI Inc (PA)	7382	E	408 326-2020	14152
Velodyne Lidar Inc (PA)	7372	C	669 275-2251	13514
Velodyne Lidar Usa Inc (HQ)	3812	C	408 465-2800	6689
Ventex Corp	7699	E	408 436-2929	14783
Venus Concept Inc	3841	D	855 882-7827	7057
Verifone Intrmdate Hldings Inc	3578	D	408 232-7800	5424
Verisilicon (HQ)	3674	E	408 844-8560	6346
Verity Health System Cal Inc	8062	A	408 947-2500	16711
Versa Networks Inc	7371	B	408 385-7660	12902
Vidhwan Inc (PA)	7361	E	408 289-8200	12151
Vietnam Daily News LLC	2711	F	408 292-3422	3487
Villages Golf and Country Club	7997	E	408 274-4400	15165
Virident Systems Inc	8731	E	408 573-5000	19149
Virtual Instruments Corp (PA)	7371	D	408 579-4000	12906
Visby Medical Inc	3829	E	408 650-8874	6929
Vishay Siliconix LLC	3674	A	408 988-8000	6349
Visistat Inc	7371	E	408 725-9370	12909
Vital Connect Inc	3845	E	408 963-4600	7134
Vitron Electronic Services Inc	3672	E	408 251-1600	5997
Viv Labs Inc	7372	E	650 268-9837	13521
Vivotek Usa Inc	5065	E	408 773-8686	8969
Vnus Medical Technologies Inc	3841	C	408 360-7200	7060
Vocera Communications Inc (PA)	3669	A	408 882-5100	5897
Volterra Semiconductor LLC (DH)	3674	E	408 601-1000	6351
Vss Monitoring Inc (HQ)	4813	C	408 585-6800	8005
Vta Telephone Information	4813	E	408 321-7127	8006
W A Call Manufacturing Co Inc	3444	E	408 436-1450	4829
W-Star Investments Inc	6163	E	408 821-7678	9952
Wafer Process Systems Inc	3674	E	408 445-3010	6354
Wafernet Inc	3674	F	408 437-9747	6355
Walt Oxley Enterprises Inc	1542	E	408 278-0370	983
Ward/Davis Associates Inc	5065	C	408 213-1090	8971
Waste Connections Cal Inc (DH)	4953	A	408 282-4400	8380
Watlow Electric Mfg Co	8711	D	408 776-6646	18858
Watry Design Inc (PA)	8712	E	408 392-7900	18918
Watt Stopper Inc (DH)	3643	D	408 988-5331	5720
Wave Computing Inc (PA)	7379	D	408 412-8645	14008
Wazuh Inc	7379	C	844 349-2984	14009
Wb Machining & Mech Design	3599	E	408 453-5005	5640
WD Media LLC	3572	B	408 576-2000	5325
Webenertia Inc	7374	E	408 246-0000	13770
Wedgewood Connect	2834	E	855 321-3477	4007
Weed Enterprises Inc	7342	E	408 929-1992	11910
Weride Corp	7371	E	408 645-7118	12919
West Coast Tree Care Inc	0783	E	408 260-2007	527
West Hotel Partners LP	7011	C	408 947-4450	11571
West San Crlos Ht Partners LLC	7011	E	408 998-0400	11572
West Valley Carpet Service	1752	E	408 946-2447	1778
Westcoast Precision Inc	3559	D	408 943-9998	5175
Wested	8733	E	408 299-1700	19250
Western Alliance Bank	6022	D	408 423-8500	9754
Western Digital Corporation (PA)	3572	A	408 717-6000	5326
Western Digital Tech Inc (HQ)	3572	A	408 717-6000	5327
Westgate Rhab Spcalty Care Crt	8051	E	408 253-7502	16158
Whipsaw Inc	8711	E	408 297-9771	18860
Wi2wi Inc (PA)	3663	E	408 416-4200	5884
Willow Glen Villa A	6513	D	408 266-1660	10468
Winbond Electronics Corp Amer	5065	D	408 943-6666	8973
Winchester Mystery House LLC	7999	E	408 247-2101	15263
Wmh Corporation	8711	E	408 971-7300	18863
Work2future Foundation (PA)	8331	B	408 794-1100	17845
Work2future Foundation	8331	E	408 794-1234	17846
Work2future Foundation	8331	E	408 216-6202	17847
X-Scan Imaging Corporation	8734	E	408 432-9888	19292
Xactly Corporation (HQ)	7371	B	408 977-3132	12930
Xcommerce Inc (HQ)	7379	A	310 954-8012	14014
Xiaomi USA Inc	3651	E	833 942-6648	5774
Xilinx Inc (PA)	3672	A	408 559-7778	6002
Xilinx Development Corporation (HQ)	3674	D	408 559-7778	6360
Xoft Inc	3841	E	408 493-1500	7063
Xperi Corporation (HQ)	3674	C	408 321-6000	6361
Xpo Logistics Freight Inc	4731	E	408 435-3876	7861
Yageo America Corporation	3676	E	408 240-6200	6374
Yamaichi Electronics USA Inc (HQ)	5065	E	408 435-9800	8977
Yellow Checker Cab Company Inc	4121	E	408 286-3400	7415
YMCA of Mid-Peninsula	8641	B	650 493-9622	18482
Yosh Enterprises Inc	7381	C	408 287-4411	14112
Young MNS Chrstn Assn Slcon Vl	8641	C	650 493-9622	18527
Young MNS Chrstn Assn Slcon Vl	8641	C	408 298-1717	18528
Young MNS Chrstn Assn Slcon Vl	8641	C	408 226-9622	18531
Young MNS Chrstn Assn Slcon Vl	8641	C	408 729-4223	18532
Yuja Inc	7372	C	888 257-2278	13540
YWCA Golden Gate Silicon Vly	8641	D	408 295-4011	18535
Z-Axis Tech Solutions Inc (PA)	7373	E	408 263-8038	13690
Zag Technical Services Inc	7376	E	408 383-2000	13817
Zededa Inc (PA)	7371	E	408 550-5531	12935
Zenith Talent Corporation	7361	E	408 300-0531	12154
Zentera Systems Inc	7372	F	408 436-4811	13541
Zest Labs Inc (HQ)	3674	E	408 200-6500	6365
ZF Array Technology Inc	3675	E	408 403-9920	6372
Zoll Circulation Inc	3845	E	408 541-2140	7136
Zoom Video Communications Inc (PA)	7371	A	888 799-9666	12942
Zoran Corporation (DH)	3674	E	972 673-1600	6369
Zscaler Inc (PA)	7371	A	408 533-0288	12943
Zspace Inc (PA)	5063	D	408 498-4050	8881

SAN JUAN BAUTISTA, CA - San Benito County

Company	SIC	EMP	PHONE	ENTRY #
Durden Construction Inc	1521	E	831 623-1200	633
Earthbound Farm LLC (PA)	0723	A	831 623-7880	281
Eb Sav Inc	0723	E	303 635-4500	282
Ftg Builders Inc (PA)	1521	E	408 564-1534	640
Mission Ranches Company LLC	0291	E	831 206-0535	248
Pacific Harvest Seafoods Inc	5146	E	408 295-2455	9368
Speedling Incorporated	0181	D	813 645-3221	137
True Leaf Farms LLC	2034	B	831 623-4667	2272
Willis Construction Co Inc	3272	E	831 623-2900	4455

SAN LEANDRO, CA - Alameda County

Company	SIC	EMP	PHONE	ENTRY #
14766 Wash Ave Operations LLC	8059	D	510 352-2211	16212
A-1 Modular Inc	7641	E	408 393-8808	14708
A-1 Roof MGT & Cnstr Inc	8741	E	510 347-5400	19293
A-Para Transit Corp	4111	C	510 562-5500	7320
Aa/Acme Locksmiths Inc	1731	E	510 483-6584	1441
Acco Engineered Systems Inc	1711	C	510 346-4300	1187
Airspace Systems Inc	3625	E	415 226-7779	5674
Akido Printing Inc	2752	F	510 357-0238	3617
Akzo Nobel Coatings Inc	2851	E	510 562-8812	4101
Alameda County Industries Inc	4953	E	510 357-7282	8299
Alco Iron & Metal Co (PA)	5093	D	510 562-1107	9172
Alco Iron & Metal Co	4953	E	510 562-1107	8300
Alemeda County Industries LLC	4953	D	510 357-7282	8301
All Saintsidence Opco LLC	8051	E	510 481-3200	15908
Alpha Granite & Marble Inc	5032	E	303 373-4911	8616
American Emperor Inc	3429	E	713 478-5973	4613
American Medical Response Inc	4119	C	415 794-9224	7372
American Rsdntial Svcs Ind Inc	1711	C	650 409-1986	1200
American Underwater Products (HQ)	3949	D	800 435-3483	7186
Andys Roofing Co Inc	1761	E	510 777-1100	1786
Apple Inns Inc	7011	E	510 895-1311	10926
Artisan Brewers LLC	2082	E	510 567-4926	2473
Asa Eden LLC	5193	E	510 653-7227	9624
Bae Systems Srra Dtroit Desl A (HQ)	7538	D	510 635-8991	14547
Bay Area Installations Inc (PA)	1799	D	510 895-8196	2009
Bay Point Control Inc	7623	E	510 614-3500	14682
Bayfab Metals Inc	3442	E	510 568-8950	4698
Bestliving Care LLC	8082	D	510 862-3508	16859
Bluewater Envmntl Svcs Inc	1795	E	510 346-8800	1981
Bobs Iron Inc	3441	E	510 567-8983	4648
Borden Lighting	3646	E	510 567-0171	5732
Brampton Mthesen Fabr Pdts Inc	2394	E	510 483-7771	3037
Buckeye Fire Equipment Company	5084	B	510 483-1815	9055
California Government Trnsp	4785	E	510 614-5942	7869
Carlton Senior Living Inc	6531	D	510 636-0660	10504
Cintas Corporation No 3	7299	D	510 352-6330	11712
Columbia Cosmetics Mfrs Inc (PA)	2844	D	510 562-5900	4081
Columbia Electric Inc	1731	E	510 430-9505	1482
Concreteworks Studio Inc	5051	E	510 534-7141	8812
Contech Solutions Incorporated	3674	E	510 357-7900	6087
Continental Sales & Mktg Inc (PA)	5063	E	510 895-1881	8855
Continental Western Corp (PA)	5085	E	510 352-3133	9115

GEOGRAPHIC SECTION SAN MATEO, CA

	SIC	EMP	PHONE	ENTRY #
Copper Harbor Company Inc	2899	F	510 639-4670	4158
County of Alameda	8063	E	510 346-1300	16732
County of Alameda	8062	D	510 895-4200	16338
Crl Systems Inc	3663	C	510 351-3500	5836
Crossroad Services Inc	5199	B	714 728-3915	9653
Crown Worldwide Mvg & Stor LLC **(PA)**	4213	E	510 895-8050	7521
Custom Paper Products LP	2652	D	510 352-6880	3352
Dakota Press Inc	2752	F	510 895-1300	3639
Davis Street Community Center **(PA)**	8322	D	510 347-4620	17529
Dependable Highway Express Inc	4213	D	510 357-2223	7524
Dependable Highway Express Inc	4213	D	510 357-2223	7525
Direct Stone Tool Supply Inc **(PA)**	3423	F	510 747-9720	4605
East Bay Innovations	7389	D	510 618-1580	14257
Edelstein Printing Co	2752	E	510 352-7890	3642
Eden Lodge LP **(HQ)**	6513	E	510 352-7008	10432
Electriq Power Inc	3825	F	833 462-2883	6750
Energy Recovery Inc **(PA)**	3559	C	510 483-7370	5148
Environmental Sampling Sup Inc	3089	C	510 465-4988	4280
Epac Technologies Inc **(PA)**	2752	C	510 317-7979	3643
Estes Express Lines	4213	D	510 635-0165	7534
Family Med Group San Leandro	8011	D	510 351-2100	15400
Farmers Insurance Exchange	6411	B	510 895-6000	10282
Federal Express Corporation	4513	C	510 347-2430	7747
Fedex Freight West Inc	4213	D	650 244-9522	7536
Floor & Decor Outlets Amer Inc	1771	D	510 394-9976	1871
Flory Construction Inc	1541	E	510 483-6860	795
Frank Ghiglione Inc	4212	D	510 483-2063	7467
Freewire Technologies Inc	3621	E	415 779-5515	5662
Friant & Associates LLC **(PA)**	1799	D	510 535-5113	2032
Fxi Inc	3086	D	510 357-2600	4243
G4s Tchnology Holdings USA Inc	7381	B	510 633-1300	14061
Galena Equipment Rental LLC	7353	D	510 638-8100	12021
General Foundry Service Corp	3365	D	510 297-5040	4584
Ghirardelli Chocolate Co **(DH)**	2066	B	510 483-6970	2437
Glesby Building Mtls Co Inc	5031	E	510 639-9350	8546
Goodman Manufacturing Co LP	3585	B	510 265-1212	5431
H A Bowen Electric Inc	1731	D	510 483-0500	1511
Hayward Ford Inc	7538	E	510 352-2000	14571
Heathorn & Assoc Contrs Inc	1711	E	510 351-7578	1277
Hilton Garden Inn	7011	D	510 346-5533	11141
IMT Associates	8111	E	510 352-6000	17294
Independent Electric Sup Inc **(DH)**	5063	C	510 877-9850	8862
India-West Publications Inc **(PA)**	2711	E	510 383-1140	3449
Innovative Pathways Inc	8093	D	510 346-7100	17026
Italian American Corp	5199	E	510 877-9000	9664
J R Pierce Plumbing Company	1711	E	510 483-5473	1290
Japan Engine Inc	3694	F	510 532-7878	6497
Kae Properties **(PA)**	6513	E	510 276-2635	10443
Kaiser Foundation Hospitals	8011	C	510 454-1000	15465
Karcher Environmental Inc	1799	D	510 297-0180	2041
Kennerley-Spratling Inc **(PA)**	3089	C	510 351-8230	4294
Kindred Healthcare Oper LLC	8062	B	510 357-8300	16424
KMA Emergency Services Inc	4119	D	510 614-1420	7384
Koffler Elec Mech Apprtus Repr	5063	D	510 567-0630	8864
Kone Inc	7699	E	510 351-5141	14757
Kp LLC **(PA)**	2752	D	510 346-0729	3665
Kp LLC	2752	E	510 346-0729	3666
L3 Applied Technologies Inc	8731	C	510 577-7100	19079
Landmark Event Staffing	7363	A	510 632-9000	12178
Lightech Fiberoptic Inc	3679	F	510 567-8700	6448
Loco Ventures Inc	2024	E	510 351-0405	2177
Lyru Engineering Inc	3599	E	510 357-5951	5562
M-T Metal Fabrications Inc	3444	E	510 357-5262	4782
Malik Dental Corp **(PA)**	8021	E	925 692-2010	15847
Marathon Products Incorporated	3829	E	510 562-6450	6909
MArs Engineering Company Inc	3599	E	510 483-0541	5565
Marymount Villa LLC	8052	D	510 895-5007	16190
McIntyre	8742	D	510 614-5890	19570
Medical Instr Dev Labs Inc	3841	E	510 357-3952	7003
Metro Poly Corporation	2673	E	510 357-9898	3385
Mr Plastics	5162	E	510 895-0774	9514
Mv Transportation Inc	4111	C	510 351-1603	7343
Nan Fang Dist Group Inc	5084	D	510 297-5382	9082
National Cnstr Rentals Inc	7359	E	510 563-4000	12055
Nel Hydrogen Inc	2813	E	650 543-3180	3776
Nicholas K Corporation	7515	C	510 352-2000	14493
Oberti Wholesales Foods Inc	2011	F	510 357-8600	2102
Odwalla Inc	7319	E	510 559-6840	11815
Olson and Co Steel **(PA)**	3446	C	510 489-4680	4838
Osisoft LLC **(HQ)**	7371	B	510 297-5800	12659
Pacific Coast Container Inc **(PA)**	4789	C	510 346-6100	7889
Pacific Coast Laboratories	3842	E	510 351-2770	7077
Paradiso Mechanical Inc	1799	E	510 614-8390	2051
PCC Structurals Inc	3369	C	510 568-6400	4586
Peggy S Lane Inc	3088	D	510 483-1202	4251
Pelagic Pressure Systems Corp	3545	D	510 569-3100	5098
Permanente Medical Group Inc	8011	A	510 454-1000	15610
Peterson Machinery Co **(PA)**	5082	A	541 302-9199	9025
Pittsburg Wholesale Groc Inc	5141	E	408 701-7326	9285
Pittsburg Wholesale Groc Inc	5141	E	510 533-3444	9287
Polymeric Technology Inc	3069	E	510 895-6001	4224
Precision Die Cutting Inc	3714	E	510 636-9654	6590
R Torre & Company Inc **(PA)**	2087	C	800 775-1925	2823
R Torre & Company Inc	2087	E	650 624-2830	2824
Randell C Towne	1731	D	510 483-1635	1574
Ransome Company	1542	E	510 686-9900	943
Regional Center of E Bay Inc **(PA)**	8322	C	510 618-6100	17687
RES-Care Inc	8082	E	510 357-4222	16930
Reyes Coca-Cola Bottling LLC	2086	D	510 476-7000	2800
Reyes Coca-Cola Bottling LLC	2086	C	510 667-6300	2801
Ridge Foundry	3321	E	510 352-0551	4551
Rip-Tie Inc	2298	F	510 577-0200	2982
Roofing Constructors Inc	1761	C	415 648-6472	1835
Royal Ambulance Inc	4119	C	877 995-6161	7401
Saags Products LLC	2013	D	510 678-3412	2123
Saia Motor Freight Line LLC	4213	D	510 347-6890	7589
San Francisco Foods Inc	2038	D	510 357-7343	2306
San Frncsc-Bay Area Cncil Boy	8641	E	510 577-9000	18460
San Leandro Healthcare Center	8051	D	510 357-4015	16109
San Leandro Hospital LP	8062	B	510 357-6500	16506
San Leandro Imaging Ctr A Cal	8011	E	510 351-7734	15664
San Lndro Srgery Ctr Ltd A Cal	8011	D	510 276-2800	15665
Sanhyd Inc	8059	D	510 483-6200	16266
Schindler Elevator Corporation	3534	E	510 382-2075	5049
Seal San Leandro LLC	7011	E	510 343-8105	11449
Security Central Inc	7699	E	510 652-2477	14775
Self-Dscvery Thrptic Exprnce P	8322	E	650 303-7365	17726
Service Opprtunity For Seniors	8322	E	510 582-1263	17736
Sheet Metal Training Center	8699	E	510 483-9035	18590
Silicon Valley Crane Inc	3531	F	408 452-1537	5037
Silman Venture Corporation **(PA)**	1542	C	510 347-4800	962
Spar Sausage Co	2013	F	510 614-8100	2125
Splay Inc	3089	F	510 351-8230	4325
Ssmb Pacific Holding Co Inc **(HQ)**	5012	D	510 836-6100	8429
St Francis Electric Inc	1731	C	510 639-0639	1610
St Francis Electric LLC	1731	C	510 639-0639	1611
Stat Delivery Service Inc	4212	D	510 681-6125	7491
State Roofing Systems Inc	1761	D	510 317-1477	1838
Stewart Superior	5085	F	510 346-9811	9134
Subacute Trtmnt Adolescnt Reha **(PA)**	8093	D	510 352-9200	17076
Superior Tile & Marble Inc **(PA)**	1743	E	510 895-2700	1724
Sutter Health	8052	C	510 618-5200	16208
Sutter Vsting Nrse Assn Hspice	8082	C	510 895-4403	16955
Sutter Vsting Nrse Assn Hspice	8051	C	510 618-5277	16141
Tap Plastics Inc A Cal Corp **(PA)**	2821	F	510 357-3755	3810
Tap Plastics Inc A Cal Corp	2821	E	510 357-3755	3811
Teocal Transport Inc	4214	E	510 569-3485	7636
Testing Engineers Incorporated **(PA)**	8711	E	510 835-3142	18834
Tk Elevator Corporation	5084	D	510 476-1900	9097
Travis Flight Service Inc	4581	D	707 437-4900	7790
Trayer Engineering Corporation	3613	D	415 285-7770	5656
Tree Sculpture Group	0782	D	510 562-4000	505
Triple C Foods Inc	2052	E	510 357-8880	2419
TRM Corporation **(PA)**	1743	D	510 895-2700	1726
True Wrld Fods San Frncsco LLC	5146	D	510 352-8140	9372
UNI Poly Inc	2673	F	510 357-9898	3389
Unity Courier Service Inc	4215	B	510 568-8890	7675
Valley Power Systems Inc	5084	F	510 635-8991	9103
Vasona Management Inc	6513	D	510 352-8728	10466
Vitrico Corp	3229	E	510 652-6731	4381
Vivio Health Inc	6324	E	925 365-6600	10158
Washington Center	8062	D	510 352-2211	16720
Wdr Restoration Inc	1521	E	800 886-1801	728
Webers Quality Meats Inc	5147	D	510 635-9892	9382
Western Pacific Signal LLC	3669	F	510 276-6400	5899
Western Waterproofing Co Inc	1799	E	510 875-2109	2088
Westmed Ambulance	4119	D	510 401-5420	7412
Woolery Enterprises Inc	2099	E	510 357-5700	2960
Wycen Foods Inc **(PA)**	2013	F	510 351-1987	2128
Zinus Inc **(HQ)**	2515	D	925 417-2100	3298
Zocalo Coffee House	2095	F	510 569-0102	2850

SAN LORENZO, CA - Alameda County

	SIC	EMP	PHONE	ENTRY #
Aidells Sausage Company Inc	2013	A	510 614-5450	2109
Custom Freight Systems Inc **(PA)**	4214	E	510 728-7515	7618
Directv Group Inc	4841	C	510 481-1324	8062
Fanfa Inc	1611	E	510 278-8410	1038
Golden W Ppr Converting Corp	2657	E	510 317-0646	3372
Hutchs Car Washes Inc	7542	E	510 538-9274	14641
Lewis Rents Inc	7359	E	510 276-3080	12052
Neff Corporation	7359	E	510 276-3080	12056
Oakland Pallet Company Inc **(PA)**	5031	C	510 278-1291	8599
Oro Loma Sanitary District	4959	E	510 276-4700	8402
R&L Carriers Shared Svcs LLC	4213	E	510 258-0547	7574
Santini Foods Inc	2023	C	510 317-8888	2167
Too Good Gourmet Inc **(PA)**	5149	D	510 317-8150	9495

SAN MARTIN, CA - Santa Clara County

	SIC	EMP	PHONE	ENTRY #
Calstone Company	3271	E	408 686-9627	4410
Clos La Chance Wines Inc	2084	E	408 686-1050	2535
Cordevalle Golf Club LLC	7997	A	408 695-4500	15078
Lone Star Landscape Inc	0782	E	408 682-0100	481
Newline Rubber Company	3069	E	408 214-0359	4221
Santa Clara County of	8322	E	408 686-3800	17718
Santa Clara County of	8322	E	408 846-5000	17719

SAN MATEO, CA - San Mateo County

	SIC	EMP	PHONE	ENTRY #
24hr Homecare LLC	8082	D	650 209-3248	16827
3q Digital Inc **(HQ)**	7311	C	650 539-4124	11737
5 Palms LLC	7389	C	650 457-0539	14189
A B C Pediatrics	8011	E	650 579-6500	15267
Abd Insurance & Fincl Svcs Inc **(PA)**	6411	D	650 488-8565	10224
Acco Brands USA LLC	3575	D	650 572-2700	5328
Accrualify Inc	3652	F	650 437-7225	5775
Actuate Corporation **(HQ)**	7371	B	650 645-3000	12227

GEOGRAPHIC

Employment Codes: A=Over 500 employees, B=251-500, C=101-250, D=51-100, E=20-50 F=10-19
2022 Northern California Business Directory and Buyers Guide

1213

SAN MATEO, CA — GEOGRAPHIC SECTION

Company	SIC	EMP	PHONE	ENTRY #
Addus Healthcare Inc	8082	D	650 638-7943	16834
Adswizz Inc (DH)	7313	D	408 674-4355	11800
Airport Parking Service Inc	7521	D	650 875-6655	14507
Alameda Newspapers Inc	2711	C	650 348-4321	3412
Alexa Alborzi DDS Mds Inc (PA)	8011	E	650 342-4171	15271
Alienvault LLC (DH)	7372	B	650 713-3333	12972
Alliance Hospital Services	8082	B	650 697-6900	16842
Alphadetail Inc	8742	E	650 581-3100	19442
Amwins Connect Insur Svcs LLC (PA)	6411	D	650 348-4131	10231
Andersen Tax LLC	7291	D	650 289-5700	11701
Andreini & Company (PA)	6411	D	650 573-1111	10232
Applied Extracts Inc	2836	F	415 260-9786	4035
Applitools Inc	7371	E	650 680-1000	12263
Apttus Corporation (PA)	7373	A	650 445-7700	13553
Archives Management Corp (PA)	8741	C	650 544-2200	19298
Area 1 Security Inc	7372	E	650 924-1637	12986
Aryaka Networks Inc (PA)	7373	B	888 692-7925	13554
Atrium Plaza LLC	7011	B	650 653-6000	10937
Avegant Corp	7371	E	800 270-0760	12293
Avistar Communications Corp (PA)	3577	E	650 525-3300	5349
Backblaze Inc	7375	C	650 352-3738	13779
Barkerblue Inc	2791	E	650 696-2100	3763
Barrett Business Services Inc	7361	A	650 653-7588	12077
Bay Area Pdatric Med Group Inc	8011	E	650 343-4200	15289
Bay Area Senior Services Inc	8322	C	650 579-5500	17441
Bay Meadows Racing Association	8611	C	650 573-4500	18299
Bears For Humanity Inc	2869	E	866 325-1668	4122
Beigene Usa Inc	2834	D	877 828-5568	3864
Big Oak Hardwood Floor Co Inc	1752	D	650 591-8651	1766
Blackwell Solar Park LLC	1711	D	650 539-3380	1220
Brain Technologies Inc	7371	B	650 918-2245	12307
Brilliant Home Technology Inc	3613	E	650 539-5320	5649
Building & Facilities Svcs LLC (PA)	7349	C	650 458-9083	11930
Cake Corporation	7371	D	650 215-7777	12319
California Casualty Mgt Co (HQ)	6331	C	650 574-4000	10162
California Cslty Fire Insur Co	6331	E	650 574-4000	10163
California Cslty Gen Insur Co (DH)	6331	E	650 574-4000	10164
Califrnia CPA Edcatn Fundation	8621	E	800 922-5272	18334
Califrnia Cslty Indemnity Exch (PA)	6331	E	650 574-4000	10165
Calysta Inc (PA)	2869	F	650 492-6880	4123
Camico Mutual Insurance Co (PA)	6411	D	650 378-6874	10258
Camico Services Inc	6141	D	800 652-1772	9854
Celigo Inc (PA)	7372	C	650 579-0210	13054
Center For Lrng Atism Spport S	8322	B	800 538-8365	17474
Centra Software Inc	7372	E	650 378-1363	13057
City Building Inc	1542	E	415 285-1711	855
Clearview Quest Corporation	8351	E	650 574-7400	17909
Cloudian Inc	7373	E	650 227-2380	13568
Cobalt Robotics Inc	7371	D	650 315-4314	12346
Coen Company Inc (DH)	3433	E	650 522-2100	4627
Compose Inc	7372	F	415 574-7038	13086
Contract Wrangler Inc	7372	E	408 472-6898	13092
Contrctor Cmpliance Monitoring (PA)	1799	E	650 522-4403	2023
Cora Cmnty Ovrcming Rltnship A	8322	E	650 652-0800	17507
County of San Mateo	8011	A	650 208-3480	15370
Coupa Software Incorporated (PA)	7372	A	650 931-3200	13095
Cprime (HQ)	8742	D	650 931-1650	19484
Crowdcircle Inc	7372	E	206 853-7560	13097
Culligan Partners Ltd Partnrs	7389	E	650 573-1500	14244
Curiodyssey	8412	E	650 342-7755	18269
D E M Enterprises Inc	7374	E	650 401-6200	13706
David D Bohannon Organization (PA)	6512	D	650 345-8222	10385
David Powell Inc (PA)	7361	D	650 357-6000	12083
Delta Project Management Inc	8711	D	415 590-3202	18688
Demandtec LLC	7371	B	914 499-1900	12381
Device Anywhere	7371	D	650 655-6400	12385
Digital Chocolate Inc	7371	E	650 372-1600	12390
Eagle Trs 3 LLC	7011	E	650 418-2444	11068
Edmodo (DH)	7372	E	310 614-6868	13132
Edmodo Inc	7372	E	202 489-8129	13133
Eide Bailly LLP	8721	E	650 462-0400	18953
Elder Care Alliance San Mateo	8051	D	650 212-4400	15981
Endorse Corp	5045	E	617 470-8332	8700
Engagio Inc	7372	E	650 265-2264	13143
Essex Portfolio LP (HQ)	6798	B	650 655-7800	10817
Essex Property Trust Inc (PA)	6513	E	650 655-7800	10434
Evidation Health (PA)	8099	C	833 234-7048	17144
Evidation Health Inc	7371	B	650 727-5557	12434
Feedzai Inc	7371	B	650 649-9486	12446
Fish Mkt Rstrants- San Jose LP	5146	E	650 349-3474	9366
Fortasa Memory Systems Inc	3572	E	888 367-8588	5285
Franklin Advisers Inc (HQ)	6722	A	650 312-2000	10757
Franklin Resources Inc	6282	A	650 312-2000	10045
Franklin Templeton Instnl LLC (HQ)	6722	D	650 312-2000	10758
Franklin Templeton Svcs LLC	6722	A	650 312-3000	10759
Freedom Financial Network LLC (PA)	7299	D	650 393-6619	11719
Freshworks (PA)	7372	E	650 513-0514	13180
Genesis Building Services Inc	7349	D	650 375-5935	11957
Gengo Inc	7389	C	650 585-4390	14282
Genium Inc	7371	E	415 935-3593	12472
Getfeedback Inc	7371	D	888 684-8821	12473
Glenborough LLC (PA)	6531	D	650 343-9300	10559
Golden Gate Regional Ctr Inc	8322	E	650 574-9232	17590
Good View Future Group Inc	2099	F	408 834-5698	2898
Gopro Inc	3861	B	650 332-7600	7150
Green Rush Group Inc	7311	D	650 762-5474	11758
Guidewire Software Inc (PA)	7372	A	650 357-9100	13202
Hazelcast Inc (PA)	7372	D	650 521-5453	13205
HE Inc	6531	D	650 794-1128	10573
Helix Opco LLC	8731	C	415 805-3360	19067
Heritage Realty	6531	D	650 349-9300	10574
Hulft Inc (PA)	7372	D	650 393-4930	13216
Humanapi Inc	7371	D	650 542-9800	12504
Imperva Inc (HQ)	7371	A	650 345-9000	12512
Inclin Inc (PA)	8731	D	650 961-3422	19073
Infogroup Inc	7331	D	650 389-0700	11838
Institute For Humn Social Dev (PA)	8351	D	650 871-5613	17955
Intelpeer Cloud Cmmnctions LLC	4899	C	650 525-9200	8078
Ip International Inc	7379	E	650 403-7800	13921
Island Hospitality MGT LLC	7011	E	650 574-4700	11200
Itouchless Housewares Pdts Inc	3089	E	650 578-0578	4292
Jaunt Inc	7372	E	650 618-6579	13251
Jetlore LLC	7372	E	650 485-1822	13253
Jigsaw Data Corporation	2741	E	650 235-8400	3579
Jivox Corporation (HQ)	5045	D	650 412-1125	8716
John Gore Organization Inc	7922	D	650 340-0469	14849
Jump Associates LLC (PA)	8748	E	650 373-7200	19802
Jupiter Intelligence Inc	1731	E	650 255-7122	1528
Kaiser Foundation Hospitals	8011	C	650 358-7000	15464
Kotobuki-Ya Inc	4111	D	650 344-9955	7338
Kronos Bio Inc (PA)	2834	E	650 781-5200	3939
Kurt Meiswinkel Inc	1742	E	650 344-7200	1686
Kyndi Inc	8748	E	917 304-5531	19809
Lattice Engines Inc (DH)	7373	C	877 460-0010	13625
Lending Express Inc	8742	E	838 800-0644	19559
Lindstrom Co	1711	E	650 343-4542	1306
Logictier Inc	7379	C	650 235-6600	13932
Logigear Corporation (PA)	7371	A	650 572-1400	12580
Lohika Systems Inc	7371	D	636 636-6993	12581
Loral Landscaping	0782	E	650 340-6940	482
Luma Health Inc	7371	E	415 741-3377	12585
Lumiata Inc	8731	E	916 607-2442	19085
Lumity Inc	6324	D	844 258-6489	10145
Magnetic Michigan (PA)	8742	E	650 544-2400	19564
Marketo Inc (DH)	7371	A	650 376-2300	12595
Maxim Healthcare Services Inc	7363	D	410 910-1500	12184
Merrill Lynch Prce Fnner Smith	6211	D	650 579-3050	9996
Meru Health Holding Inc	8093	E	760 841-8040	17041
MGM Holiday Inc	7011	E	415 690-0020	11298
Mission Hospice & HM Care Inc	8052	C	650 554-1000	16192
Momentive Global Inc	7371	E	503 225-1202	12619
Momentive Global Inc (PA)	7371	A	650 543-8400	12620
Momentive Inc (HQ)	7374	E	650 543-8400	13733
Motif Inc (DH)	7374	C	917 903-5485	13734
Movoto LLC (HQ)	6531	E	650 241-0910	10625
N Model Inc (PA)	7371	B	650 610-4600	12626
National Fncl Srvcs Cnsrtm LLC	8742	C	650 572-2872	19586
Nestgsv Silicon Valley LLC	7372	F	650 421-2000	13322
Netsuite Inc	7372	A	650 627-1000	13326
Newfront Insurance Svcs LLC (HQ)	6411	C	415 754-3635	10318
Nextlabs Inc (PA)	7379	E	650 577-9101	13948
NS Solution USA Corp	7373	C	650 627-1500	13641
Nuevacare LLC (PA)	8082	C	650 539-2000	16918
Onesignal Inc	7372	E	408 506-0701	13343
Onevalley Inc	8742	E	650 421-2000	19597
Open Text Inc (HQ)	7371	C	650 645-3000	12651
Opera Software Americas LLC	7372	E	650 625-1262	13346
Opya Inc	8093	D	650 931-6300	17052
Pacific Bell Telephone Company	4812	A	650 572-6807	7909
Pasadena Hotel Dev Ventr LP	7011	D	650 347-8260	11360
Peninsula Family Service (PA)	8351	D	650 403-4300	17990
Peninsula Temple Beth El	8351	E	650 341-7701	17993
People Sciences Inc	7361	E	888 924-1004	12120
Permanente Medical Group Inc	8011	A	650 358-7000	15624
Pml Management Corporation	6531	E	650 349-9113	10645
Primark Benefits	6411	E	650 692-2043	10335
Prometheus RE Group Inc (PA)	6531	C	650 931-3400	10649
Punchh Inc	7372	D	415 623-4466	13391
Raiser Senior Services LLC	8051	E	650 344-4106	16099
Rakuten Usa Inc (HQ)	4813	D	617 491-5252	7986
Reflektion Inc (PA)	7371	E	650 293-0800	12737
Roblox Corporation (PA)	7372	A	888 858-2569	13412
Rumble Entertainment Inc	3944	E	650 316-8819	7183
Runa Inc	7372	E	508 253-5000	13414
Sam Bennion	7011	E	650 341-3461	11430
San Mateo Cnty Expo Fair Assn	7999	E	650 574-3247	15236
San Mateo Credit Union	6061	C	650 363-1725	9814
Sequoia Bnefits Insur Svcs LLC (PA)	6411	C	650 369-0200	10349
Shopkick Inc	7371	D	650 763-8727	12780
Sierra Oncology Inc (PA)	2834	E	650 376-8679	3984
Sierra Ventures Management LLC	6799	E	650 854-1000	10883
Snaplogic Inc (PA)	7372	C	888 494-1570	13449
Society of St Vincent De Paul P (PA)	8699	D	650 373-0622	18595
Solvvy Inc	7371	E	650 246-9685	12805
Sony Interactive Entrmt LLC	7929	D	650 655-8000	14879
Sony MBL Cmmunications USA Inc	3663	C	866 766-9374	5870
Space Time Insight Inc (HQ)	7372	E	650 513-8550	13455
Speculative Product Design LLC (DH)	3161	D	650 462-2040	4349
St Matthews Episcopal Day Schl	8351	C	650 342-5436	18030
Steelwave Inc (PA)	6552	E	650 571-2200	10715
Steelwave LLC	6552	A	650 571-2200	10716
Stottler Henke Associates Inc (PA)	7379	E	650 931-2700	13982
Strands Labs Inc	7371	E	415 398-4333	12820
Successfactors Inc	7371	D	650 645-2000	12830

Mergent email: customerrelations@mergent.com
2022 Northern California Business Directory and Buyers Guide
(P-0000) Products & Services Section entry number
(PA)=Parent Co (HQ)=Headquarters (DH)=Div Headquarters

	SIC	EMP	PHONE	ENTRY #
Sunstone Partners LLC	6799	D	650 289-4400	10886
Sunstone Partners MGT LLC	6799	D	650 289-4400	10887
Super Evil Mega Corp	7371	E	650 787-2505	12835
Sutter Care & Home	8082	D	650 685-2800	16952
Sutter Health	8062	C	650 262-4262	16624
Swenson Group	3861	E	650 655-4990	7159
Synarc Inc **(DH)**	7371	C	415 817-8900	12840
Talkplus Inc	4813	E	650 403-5800	7997
Talview Inc **(PA)**	7379	C	830 484-6221	13989
Tesla Energy Operations Inc **(HQ)**	1711	A	888 765-2489	1379
Tile Inc	5065	C	650 274-0676	8964
Total Airport Services LLC	4581	D	650 358-0144	7789
Trammell Crow Residential Co	6513	E	650 349-1224	10464
Truebeck Construction Inc **(PA)**	1542	D	650 227-1957	977
Truepill Inc **(PA)**	2834	D	510 388-0406	3999
Trujillo Orlando Pntg Contr	1721	E	650 579-0707	1434
Turing Video	7371	D	877 730-8222	12879
Ubertal Inc	7371	E	650 542-8100	12882
Ucs Limo LLC	4119	E	866 345-5640	7408
Ulab Systems Inc **(PA)**	8021	E	866 900-8522	15860
Unifi Software Inc	7372	E	732 614-9522	13505
Upstart Holdings Inc **(PA)**	6162	B	650 204-1000	9934
Upstart Network Inc	6141	D	650 204-1000	9864
Vcognition Technologies Inc	7372	E	415 374-0189	13512
Veev Group Inc	6211	C	650 292-0752	10020
Vendio Services Inc **(PA)**	7371	D	650 293-3500	12899
Verkada Inc **(PA)**	7382	B	833 837-5232	14153
Veterinary Surgical Associates	8011	D	650 696-8196	15807
Vindicia Inc	7372	C	650 264-4700	13518
Virtunet LLC	7371	D	650 847-8633	12907
Wageworks Inc **(HQ)**	8742	C	650 577-5200	19667
Water Heater Specialists Inc	1711	E	415 775-5100	1395
Webcor Builders Inc	1542	D	650 591-7400	984
Westbrdge Cpitl US Advsors LLC	6722	E	650 645-6220	10772
Westlake Development Group LLC **(PA)**	6512	D	650 579-1010	10415
Westlake Realty Group Inc **(PA)**	6531	D	650 579-1010	10686
Wh Acquisitions Inc **(HQ)**	5084	C	650 358-5000	9105
Womens Rcvery Assn San Mteo CN	8621	C	650 348-6603	18352
Wonder Workshop Inc **(PA)**	7371	E	408 785-7981	12926
Yodlee Inc **(HQ)**	8742	C	650 980-3600	19673
Young MNS Chrstn Assn San Frnc	8641	E	650 286-9622	18514
Zinier Inc	7379	C	787 504-4826	14018
Zira Group Inc	7372	E	650 701-7026	13542
Zs Pharma Inc	2834	E	650 753-1823	4013

SAN PABLO, CA - Contra Costa County

	SIC	EMP	PHONE	ENTRY #
Analytcal Scentific Instrs Inc	3826	E	510 669-2250	6808
Brookside Cmnty Hlth Ctr Inc **(PA)**	8011	D	510 215-9092	15303
Contra Costa Newspapers Inc	2711	D	510 758-8400	3430
Creekside Healthcare Ctr	8051	E	510 235-5514	15975
Davita Inc	8092	E	510 234-0835	16972
East Bay Cardiology Med Group	8011	E	510 233-9300	15385
East Bay Nephrology	8011	E	510 235-1057	15386
Linde Inc	2813	E	510 223-9593	3774
Lotus Hotels Inc	7011	D	510 965-1900	11271
Lytton Rancheria	7011	A	510 215-7888	11276
Mariner Health Care Inc	8051	E	510 232-5945	16050
Planchon Roofing Inc	1761	E	510 235-4056	1830
Promab Biotechnologies Inc	8731	D	510 860-4615	19106
Ratnakar & Sons **(PA)**	7216	E	510 236-6280	11655
Staidson Biopharma Inc	2834	F	800 345-1899	3988
Stand For Fmlies Free Volence	8322	D	510 964-7109	17756
Summerville Senior Living Inc	8051	E	510 235-5514	16132
Trans Bay Steel Corporation **(PA)**	3441	E	510 277-3756	4690
Vale Operating Company LP	8051	A	510 232-5945	16149

SAN RAFAEL, CA - Marin County

	SIC	EMP	PHONE	ENTRY #
A Pet Emrgncy & Specialty Ctr	0742	E	415 456-7372	318
Ann Lilli Corp **(PA)**	2337	D	415 482-9444	3004
Anthonys Auto Craft Inc **(PA)**	7532	D	415 456-7591	14517
Arcadia Services Inc	7363	E	248 352-7530	12159
Autodesk Inc **(PA)**	7372	B	415 507-5000	12998
Autodesk Global Inc **(HQ)**	7372	B	415 507-5000	12999
Axis Appraisal MGT Solutions **(PA)**	8741	D	888 806-2947	19300
Bank of Marin	6022	D	415 472-2265	9702
Bernard Osher Mrin Jwish Cmnty	8322	C	415 444-8000	17443
Biomarin Pharmaceutical Inc **(PA)**	2834	B	415 506-6700	3868
Bluewave Express LLC **(PA)**	7542	E	877 503-0008	14630
Bordenaves Marin Baking	5149	D	415 453-2957	9441
California Mrtg Advisors Inc	6162	E	415 451-4888	9898
Canal Alliance	8111	D	415 485-3074	17224
Casa Allegra Community Svcs	8361	E	415 499-1116	18071
Casa Allegra Community Svcs	8322	D	415 499-1116	17455
Catholic Chrties Cyo of The AR **(PA)**	8322	D	415 972-1200	17461
Catholic Chrties Cyo of The AR	8322	E	415 507-2000	17462
Center For Domestic Peace	8322	E	415 457-2464	17471
Center Point Inc **(PA)**	8322	C	415 492-4444	17476
Central Marin Sanitation Agcy	4959	E	415 459-1455	8393
Christensen Advertising	7311	E	415 924-8575	11744
Clp Resources Inc	7363	E	415 446-7000	12166
Comcast California Ix Inc	4841	E	215 286-3345	8059
Community Action Marin	8093	C	415 459-6330	17001
Do Arellanes Holdings	7361	E	415 472-5700	12084
Dostal Studio	3952	F	415 721-7080	7203
Dutra Construction Co Inc **(HQ)**	1629	D	415 258-6876	1157
Dutra Dredging Company **(HQ)**	1629	D	415 721-2131	1158
Dutra Group **(PA)**	1629	D	415 258-6876	1160
Eah Inc **(PA)**	6514	D	415 258-1800	10471
Elsa L Inc	5099	E	415 472-8388	9194
Enterprise Events Group Inc	8742	C	415 499-4444	19504
Eo Products LLC	5122	C	415 945-1900	9226
Etrac Inc	8713	E	415 462-0421	18922
Fair Isaac International Corp **(HQ)**	7372	A	415 446-6000	13158
Family Svcs Agcy Marin Cnty **(PA)**	8322	D	415 491-5700	17566
Fcsi Inc	7212	E	415 457-8000	11628
First Student Inc	4151	C	415 455-9098	7431
Ghilotti Bros Inc	1794	B	415 454-7011	1961
Ghilotti Brothers Cnstr Inc	1521	D	415 454-7011	643
Gilardi & Co LLC	8741	D	415 798-5900	19340
Glass & Sash Inc **(PA)**	5039	E	415 456-2240	8644
Goff Investment Group LLC	2741	E	415 456-2934	3573
Golden Gate Bridge High	4785	A	415 457-3110	7872
Golden Gate Nat Prks Cnsrvancy	8999	C	415 785-4787	19904
Golden Gate Regional Ctr Inc	8322	E	415 446-3000	17591
Guide Dogs For Blind Inc **(PA)**	0752	C	415 499-4000	354
Herbs Pool Service Inc	7389	D	415 479-4040	14296
Hotel McInnis Marin LLC	7011	D	415 499-9222	11167
Idex Global Services Inc	1731	C	415 482-4242	1522
Independent Quality Care Inc	8059	D	415 479-1230	16245
Infrastructureworld LLC	3826	E	415 699-1543	6833
Insight Editions LP	2731	D	415 526-1370	3535
Installtion Dgtal Trnsmssons I	1799	F	415 226-0020	2038
Integrated Community Services	8322	D	415 455-8481	17617
Interctive Med Specialists Inc	7363	D	415 472-4204	12176
Jack L Hunt Inc	7539	E	415 453-1611	14613
Jacksons Hardware Inc	5072	D	415 870-4083	8985
Jeff Burgess & Associates Inc **(DH)**	3651	E	415 256-2800	5760
Jerry Thompson & Sons Pntg Inc	1721	C	415 454-1500	1418
Jewish Family and Chld Svcs	8322	C	415 449-3862	17627
Johnson & Daly Moving & Strg	4213	E	415 435-1192	7557
Kaiser Foundation Hospitals	8011	C	415 491-1164	15452
Kaiser Foundation Hospitals	8011	A	415 444-2000	15453
Kaiser Foundation Hospitals	6324	C	415 444-3522	10113
Kaiser Foundation Hospitals	6324	C	415 482-6800	10126
Kisco Senior Living LLC	6513	D	415 491-1935	10444
Kyo Autism Therapy LLC	8742	D	877 264-6747	19552
L P McNear Brick Co Inc	3271	D	415 453-7702	4414
Lamperti Associates	1521	E	415 454-1623	662
Laurent Culinary Service	2099	F	415 485-1122	2915
Lifehouse Inc **(PA)**	8322	B	415 472-2373	17635
Lithos Energy Inc	2752	E	415 944-5482	3674
Lucas Digital Ltd **(DH)**	7922	B	415 258-2000	14850
Managed Health Network **(DH)**	6324	B	415 460-8168	10146
Marin Beauty Company **(PA)**	7231	E	415 454-4500	11690
Marin Clean Energy	4911	D	415 464-6028	8121
Marin Community Food Bank	8322	E	415 883-1302	17641
Marin County Office Education **(PA)**	8331	B	415 472-4110	17821
Marin Manufacturing Inc	3441	E	415 453-1825	4675
Marin Ophthlmic Cons A Med Cor	8011	D	415 454-5565	15519
Marin Sanitary Service **(PA)**	4953	D	415 456-2601	8342
Marin Sanitary Service	4953	D	415 485-5646	8343
Marin Treatment Center	8093	D	415 457-3755	17037
Mariner Health Care Inc	8051	E	415 479-3610	16055
Megacycle Engineering Inc	3751	E	415 472-3195	6653
Mhn Government Services LLC	8322	A	916 294-4941	17649
Mighty Leaf Tea	5149	D	415 491-2650	9465
Mill Valley Refuse Service Inc	4953	D	415 457-2287	8345
Miller Creek School District	7349	C	415 492-3776	11973
Muir Wood LLC	8099	E	310 903-1155	17163
Norcal Vocational Inc **(PA)**	8322	D	415 206-9766	17656
Northgate Care Center Inc	8059	D	415 479-1230	16255
Npc Corp **(PA)**	3081	E	415 578-2455	4232
Ocadian Care Centers LLC	8051	B	415 499-1000	16085
One Bella Casa Inc	2392	E	707 746-8300	3029
Opportnity For Indpendence Inc	8322	D	415 721-7772	17665
Pacific Gas and Electric Co	4911	C	800 743-5000	8145
Packaging Aids Corporation **(PA)**	3565	E	415 454-4868	5201
Pamelas Product Inc	2051	E	707 462-6605	2397
Pasha Group **(PA)**	4731	B	415 927-6400	7849
Pedersen Media Group Inc	8743	E	415 512-9800	19694
Permanente Medical Group Inc	8011	A	415 444-2000	15611
Petroleum Sales Inc **(PA)**	7542	C	415 256-1600	14651
Phoenix Amercn Fincl Svcs Inc **(HQ)**	7389	E	415 485-4500	14364
Phoenix American Incorporated **(PA)**	8742	D	415 485-4500	19605
Phoenix Systems Exchange Inc	5045	E	415 485-4500	8734
Plath & Company Inc	1542	E	415 460-1575	937
Professional Healthcare At HM	8082	E	415 492-8400	16925
Qb3 LLC **(PA)**	8742	E	415 459-7459	19616
Quaker Pet Group Inc	5199	D	415 721-7400	9670
R C Roberts & Co **(PA)**	6515	C	415 456-8600	10474
Rafael Convalescent Hospital	8059	D	415 479-3450	16259
Rafael Racquet Club Inc	7997	E	415 456-5522	15124
Redhorse Constructors Inc	1521	D	415 492-2020	693
San Rafael Hillcrest LLC	7011	D	415 479-8800	11441
San Rafael Rock Quarry Inc **(HQ)**	1429	D	415 459-7740	581
San Rfael Hlthcare Wllness Ctr	8051	E	415 456-7170	16110
Sanitary Dst 1 Marin Cnty	4959	E	415 259-2949	8406
Sanovas Inc	3841	E	415 729-9391	7029
Sausalito Construction Inc	1522	E	415 889-5281	768
Sea-Logix Llc **(HQ)**	4213	E	415 927-6400	7593
Sisters of Nazareth	8059	D	415 479-8282	16269
Small World Trading Co	5122	C	415 945-1900	9237
Smith Rnch Hmes Hmeowners Assn	6513	D	415 492-4900	10461
Society of St Vncent De Paul D	8322	E	415 454-3303	17749
Spectraprint Inc	2759	F	415 460-1228	3750

GEOGRAPHIC

Employment Codes: A=Over 500 employees, B=251-500, C=101-250, D=51-100, E=20-50 F=10-19
2022 Northern California Business Directory and Buyers Guide

1215

	SIC	EMP	PHONE	ENTRY #
Sr Holdings LLC **(HQ)**	8611	F	415 927-6400	18319
Strahmcolor	2752	F	415 459-5409	3701
Streamline Development LLC	7371	E	415 499-3355	12822
Tini Aerospace Inc	3812	E	415 524-2124	6687
Toscalito Enterprises Inc **(PA)**	7538	E	415 456-2324	14599
Trainor Commercial Cnstr Inc **(PA)**	1542	E	415 259-0200	975
Triesten Technologies LLC **(PA)**	7371	C	916 719-6150	12876
Urban Painting Inc	1721	D	415 485-1130	1436
Valentine Corporation	1799	E	415 453-3732	2083
Van Midde & Son Concrete	1771	D	415 459-2530	1916
Villa Inn	7011	E	415 456-4975	11558
Villa Marin Homeowners Assn	8641	C	415 499-8711	18479
Villasport LLC **(PA)**	8699	D	415 448-8300	18607
Vionic Group LLC	3143	D	415 526-6932	4343
Vionic International LLC **(HQ)**	3143	D	888 882-7954	4344
Vitalant Research Institute	8099	E	415 454-2700	17192
Vivalon	8322	D	415 454-0964	17781
Westamerica Bancorporation **(PA)**	6022	C	707 863-6000	9752
Westamerica Bank **(HQ)**	6022	C	707 863-6113	9753
Wildcare Trwllger Nture Edcatn	0971	D	415 453-1000	540
Young MNS Chrstn Assn San Frnc	8641	E	415 492-9622	18523
Zep Solar Llc **(DH)**	3674	E	415 479-6900	6364

SAN RAMON, CA - Contra Costa County

	SIC	EMP	PHONE	ENTRY #
A D Bilich Inc	6162	D	925 820-5557	9889
A3 Smart Home LP	7381	D	925 830-4777	14024
Accela Inc **(PA)**	7372	C	925 659-3200	12946
Accountnow Inc	8742	D	925 498-1800	19432
Advent Engineering Svcs Inc **(PA)**	8711	E	925 830-4700	18616
AG & Associates Inc **(PA)**	8742	E	925 327-0804	19435
Allteq Industries Inc	3674	F	925 833-7666	6023
AMF Media Group	8743	E	925 790-2662	19682
Amick Brown LLC **(PA)**	7371	D	925 820-2000	12248
AMP Technologies LLC	7371	C	877 442-2824	12249
AMR Appraisals Inc	6531	D	925 400-6066	10491
ARC Document Solutions Inc **(PA)**	7335	E	925 949-5100	11854
Arctic Express Norcal LLC	5143	E	925 553-3681	9333
Armanino LLP **(PA)**	8721	C	925 790-2600	18932
Ascor Inc **(HQ)**	3625	D	925 328-4650	5677
AT&T Corp	4812	B	925 823-6949	7896
Athoc Inc **(DH)**	7372	D	925 242-5660	12989
Atlas Lift Tech Inc	8099	C	415 283-1804	17102
Atlas Technical Cons LLC	8748	B	925 314-7100	19723
Baco Realty Corporation	4225	D	925 275-0100	7681
Bay Area Techworkers **(PA)**	7361	A	925 359-2200	12078
Benefitstreet Inc	6411	D	925 831-0800	10247
Berkeley Emrgncy Med Group Inc	8099	D	925 962-1067	17104
Bishop Ranch Veterinary Center **(PA)**	0742	D	925 743-9300	324
Blackberry Corporation **(HQ)**	7372	A	972 650-6126	13023
Brass Engineering Intl	4619	C	925 867-1000	7793
Bridges At Gale Ranch LLC	7992	D	925 735-4253	14989
Broadway Management Co Inc	6531	E	925 820-7292	10496
Buxton Consulting	8748	D	925 467-0700	19736
Buyersroad Inc	7372	F	937 313-4466	13040
Caitcon LLC	7353	A	925 314-7100	12017
California Coastal Insurance **(PA)**	6411	E	925 866-7050	10257
California Security Alarms Inc **(PA)**	7382	E	800 669-7779	14123
Califrnia Archtectural Ltg Inc **(PA)**	5063	E	925 242-0111	8847
Callidus Software Inc **(DH)**	7371	A	925 251-2200	12321
Cardiovascular Cons Med Group	8011	E	925 277-1900	15323
Carlson Barbee & Gibson Inc	8711	D	925 866-0322	18660
Casahl Technology Inc	7371	E	925 328-2828	12327
Castro Valley Health Inc	8082	C	510 690-1930	16869
Cellco Partnership	4812	D	925 743-9327	7902
Chevron Corporation **(PA)**	2911	A	925 842-1000	4170
Chevron Global Energy Inc **(HQ)**	2911	D	925 842-1000	4171
Chevron Global Tech Svcs Co	8711	E	925 842-1000	18669
Chevron Munaigas Inc **(HQ)**	1311	D	925 842-1000	546
Chevron Oronite Company LLC **(DH)**	2899	E	925 842-1000	4157
Chevron Shipping Company LLC	4731	D	925 842-1000	7829
Chevron Stations Inc	5144	C	925 328-0292	9346
Chevron Trading LLC **(HQ)**	5172	C	925 842-1000	9531
Chevron USA Inc	2911	D	925 842-0855	4173
Claims Services Group LLC **(DH)**	6411	D	925 866-1100	10263
Clever Girls Collective Inc	7311	E	408 676-6428	11746
Cloud Destinations Inc	7379	E	510 715-7044	13867
Clubsport San Ramon LLC **(PA)**	7991	C	925 735-1182	14940
Cmg Financial Services	6162	C	925 983-3073	9902
Cmg Mortgage Inc **(PA)**	6163	B	619 554-1327	9938
Concessionaires Urban Park	7999	D	530 529-1513	15199
Cooper Companies Inc **(PA)**	3851	A	925 460-3600	7138
Courtyard By Marriott	7011	C	925 866-2900	11036
Cti-Controltech Inc	3625	F	925 208-4250	5678
Cvh Care	8082	E	650 393-5657	16877
Cyber Inc	7372	F	925 242-0777	13103
Cyberinc Corporation **(HQ)**	7372	E	925 242-0777	13104
Cylance Inc **(DH)**	7372	A	949 375-3380	13105
Devil Mountain Whl Nurs LLC **(PA)**	5193	D	925 829-6006	9631
Donor Network West **(PA)**	8099	C	925 480-3100	17136
Dorris Eatons School	8351	D	925 930-9000	17924
Eagle Canyon Capital LLC **(PA)**	2092	A	925 884-0800	2830
Enclipse Corp	7379	E	866 261-3503	13886
Enpower Management Corp	4911	D	925 244-1100	8096
Ets-Esc Holdings LLC	6719	B	925 314-7100	10733
Evolphin Software Inc **(PA)**	7372	E	888 386-4114	13151
Express System Intermodal Inc	4731	E	801 302-6625	7834
Expressworks International LLC **(PA)**	8742	D	925 244-0900	19513
Federal Solutions Group	7338	E	510 775-9068	11876
Five9 Inc **(PA)**	7372	A	925 201-2000	13164
Flyleaf Windows Inc	3231	E	925 344-1181	4387
Fujitsu America Inc	7371	E	925 327-0050	12463
G4s Secure Solutions (usa)	7381	C	925 543-0008	14060
Gateway Financial Advisors Inc **(PA)**	8742	D	925 999-8699	19519
GE Digital LLC **(HQ)**	7372	B	925 242-6200	13185
GE Digital LLC	7372	E	925 242-6200	13186
Good Technology Corporation **(HQ)**	7371	C	408 352-9102	12482
Greenan Pffer Sllnder Llly LLP	8111	E	925 866-1000	17281
Grid Dynamics Holdings Inc **(PA)**	7372	C	650 523-5000	13198
Grid Dynamics Intl LLC **(HQ)**	7379	B	650 523-5000	13903
Hanson Lehigh Inc	3273	E	972 653-5603	4487
Hexaware Technologies Inc	7379	B	609 409-6950	13905
Hill Physicians Med Group Inc **(PA)**	8011	B	800 445-5747	15432
Homegaincom Inc	6531	D	925 983-2852	10577
Hotan Corp	5065	E	925 290-1000	8918
Hyatt Corporation	7011	B	925 743-1882	11181
Independent Quality Care Inc **(PA)**	8059	D	925 855-0881	16244
Insight Wealth Strategies LLC	6282	E	925 659-0251	10049
Integrated Bldg Solutions Inc	8748	F	925 244-1900	19797
Interform Commercial Interiors	5021	E	925 867-1001	8496
Iron Horse Ventures LLC	8742	E	925 415-6141	19544
J B Hunt Transport Inc	4213	C	866 759-1127	7554
Japonesque LLC	2844	F	925 866-6670	4086
Jaroth Inc	1731	C	925 553-3650	1525
Kaiser Foundation Hospitals	6324	C	925 244-7600	10118
KB Home South Bay Inc	1522	C	925 983-2500	754
Kraft Heinz Foods Company	2033	F	925 242-4504	2219
Legacy Mech & Enrgy Svcs Inc	1711	D	925 820-6938	1303
Leica Geosystems Hds LLC	3829	D	925 790-2300	6908
Lindquist LLP **(PA)**	8721	D	925 277-9100	18965
Lumin Digital LLC	7371	D	727 561-2227	12587
Macdonald Mott LLC **(HQ)**	8711	E	925 469-8010	18759
Mason McDuffie Mortgage Corp **(PA)**	6162	D	925 242-4400	9915
Mirion Technologies Inc **(PA)**	3829	C	925 543-0800	6912
Mountain Retreat Incorporated	6552	D	925 838-7780	10710
Netpace Inc	7361	C	925 543-7760	12110
Nsa Wireless Inc **(PA)**	4812	E	925 867-2817	7908
Nuevora	8732	E	925 967-2000	19176
Old Republic HM Protection Inc	6411	B	925 866-1500	10327
Omron Robotics Safety Tech Inc **(HQ)**	3535	C	925 245-3400	5053
Overland Storage Inc **(HQ)**	3572	B	408 283-4700	5308
Pacific Gas and Electric Co	4911	C	650 513-0700	8143
Peterson Sheet Metal Inc	3444	E	925 830-1766	4803
Plus Group Inc	7363	B	925 831-8551	12189
Primed MGT Consulting Svcs Inc	8741	B	925 327-6710	19382
Pts Communications Inc	1731	E	925 553-3609	1571
Pts Providers Inc	7299	E	925 553-3763	11728
Raybern Foods LLC	5149	E	925 302-7800	9480
Reaction Search Intl Inc **(PA)**	7361	D	925 275-0727	12127
Recall Management Inc	7371	E	877 386-8186	12730
Reproductive Science Center	8011	D	925 867-1800	15649
Reyes Coca-Cola Bottling LLC	2086	D	925 830-6500	2808
Rfxcel Corporation **(PA)**	5045	D	925 824-0300	8745
Ridge Communications Inc	8748	E	925 498-2340	19849
Robert Half International Inc	7361	E	925 913-1000	12130
Rockins Equipment Company	7359	E	925 837-7296	12061
Rose International Inc	8748	C	636 812-4000	19850
San Ramon Endoscopy Center Inc	8062	E	925 275-9910	16507
San Ramon Regional Med Ctr LLC	8062	A	925 275-9200	16508
Seacastle Inc	7359	C	925 480-3000	12063
Security Alarm Fing Entps Inc	7382	D	925 830-4786	14147
Select Hotels Group LLC	7011	E	925 743-1882	11453
Sourceamerica	8399	D	925 543-5100	18250
Splash Swim School Inc	7999	E	925 838-7946	15245
Stratedge Inc **(PA)**	7371	E	925 236-2022	12821
Striking Distance Studios Inc	7929	E	925 355-5131	14881
Summerhill Construction Co	1521	E	925 244-7520	713
Sun Tropics Inc	2037	F	925 202-2221	2300
Sunset Development Company **(PA)**	6512	C	925 277-1700	10410
Surplus Line Association Cal	8611	E	415 434-4900	18320
Tacit Knowledge Inc **(HQ)**	7379	D	415 694-4322	13987
Tekion Corp	7379	C	925 399-5569	13995
Tescra	7371	E	925 242-0100	12859
Teslarati LLC	7371	F	323 405-7657	12860
Texaco Inc **(HQ)**	1321	A	925 842-1000	552
Texaco Overseas Holdings Inc **(DH)**	2911	F	510 242-5357	4182
TFC Credit Corp California	6141	D	800 832-5626	9862
Transsight LLC	8748	E	510 415-6301	19876
Tri Pointe Homes Inc	1522	C	925 804-2220	775
Triton Enterprises LLC	8748	E	925 230-8395	19879
Twin Industries Inc	3672	F	925 866-8946	5992
United Parcel Service Inc	4215	C	800 833-9943	7673
Universal Protection Svc LP	7381	D	805 496-4401	14105
V A Anderson Enterprises Inc	7334	D	925 866-6150	11853
Valent USA LLC	2879	E	925 256-2700	4147
Webster Orthpdc Med Grp A Prof	8011	E	925 362-2116	15812
Young & Burton Inc	1521	E	925 820-4953	733

SANGER, CA - Fresno County

	SIC	EMP	PHONE	ENTRY #
Adco Manufacturing	3565	C	559 875-5563	5194
Adventist Hlth Systm/West Corp	8062	D	559 875-6900	16314
Algonquin Power Sanger LLC	3612	E	559 875-0800	5646
Blue Diamond Growers	0723	C	559 251-4044	272
Builders Concrete Inc	3273	E	559 787-3117	4463
Cal Custom Tile	1743	D	559 875-1460	1711
Cargill Meat Solutions Corp	2011	B	559 875-2232	2090
Chooljian Bros Packing Co Inc	5149	E	559 875-5501	9443

GEOGRAPHIC SECTION

SANTA CLARA, CA

	SIC	EMP	PHONE	ENTRY #
Dole Packaged Foods LLC	2037	B	559 875-3354	2292
Fresno Cnty Ecnmic Opprtnties	8351	D	559 875-2581	17938
Fresno Fab-Tech Inc	3441	E	559 875-9800	4662
Gibson Wine Company	2084	E	559 875-2505	2594
Gongs Market of Sanger Inc (PA)	6512	E	559 875-5576	10390
If Copack LLC	2032	E	559 875-3354	2201
If Holding Inc (PA)	2099	C	559 875-3354	2903
Initiative Foods LLC	2032	C	559 875-3354	2202
Kings River Casting Inc	2531	E	559 875-8250	3312
Kings River Packing LP	0191	E	559 787-2056	177
Melkonian Enterprises Inc	2034	E	559 217-0749	2263
Old English Rancho Inc	0212	E	559 787-3020	202
Perez Distributing Fresno Inc (PA)	2834	E	800 638-3512	3961
Peters Roofing Inc	1761	E	559 876-1615	1828
Pitman Farms (PA)	0253	E	559 875-9300	238
R Thunder Inc (PA)	7991	E	559 974-2203	14966
Sherwood Forest Golf Club Inc	7992	E	559 787-2611	15026
Soojians Inc	2052	E	559 875-5511	2418
Suma Fruit Intl USA Inc	0723	D	559 875-5000	310
Triple A Pallets Inc	2448	F	559 313-7636	3231
Valley Rgnal Occptnal Programs	8331	E	559 876-2122	17843
Virginia Sarabian	0172	E	559 493-2900	81
Western Camps Inc	7032	E	559 787-2551	11615

SANTA CLARA, CA - Santa Clara County

	SIC	EMP	PHONE	ENTRY #
24hr Homecare LLC	8082	D	408 550-8295	16828
2wire Inc (DH)	4813	C	408 235-5500	7920
5-Stars Engineering Associates	3549	E	408 380-4849	5106
6wind Usa Inc	7371	D	408 816-1366	12217
A-1 Machine Manufacturing Inc (PA)	3599	C	408 727-0880	5459
Abbott Laboratories	3841	B	408 330-0057	6930
Abbott Laboratories	3841	A	408 845-3000	6931
Abbott Vascular Inc (HQ)	3841	A	408 845-3000	6932
Absolute Turnkey Services Inc	3672	E	408 850-7530	5905
AC Photonics Inc	3559	E	408 986-9838	5138
Acalvio Technologies Inc	7382	D	408 931-6160	14116
Accel Manufacturing Inc	3541	F	408 727-5883	5070
Accelerite (PA)	7372	C	408 216-7010	12948
Access Closure Inc	3841	B	408 610-6500	6933
Access Systems Americas Inc	7371	D	408 400-3000	12224
Accion Labs Us Inc	8734	C	408 970-9809	19253
Acco Management Company	6531	C	408 241-3000	10487
Accrete Solutions LLC	7379	B	877 849-5838	13829
Achronix Semiconductor Corp	3674	D	408 889-4100	6008
Actsolar Inc	3674	E	408 721-5000	6009
Adem LLC	3599	E	408 727-8955	5464
Adesto Technologies Corp (HQ)	3674	C	408 400-0578	6010
Advance Staffing Inc	7361	B	408 205-6154	12070
Advanced Component Labs Inc	3674	E	408 327-0200	6012
Advanced Micro Devices Inc (PA)	3674	A	408 749-4000	6014
Advanced Microtechnology	3825	F	408 945-9191	6742
Affymetrix Inc (HQ)	3826	A	408 731-5000	6804
Agilent Tech Foundation	3825	A	408 345-8886	6744
Agilent Tech World Trade Inc (HQ)	3825	A	408 345-8886	6745
Agilent Technologies Inc (PA)	3826	A	800 227-9770	6805
Aharoni & Steele Inc	2068	F	408 451-9585	2441
Aixtron Inc	3674	C	669 228-3759	6016
Akraya Inc	7361	E	408 907-6400	12071
Akt America Inc (HQ)	3674	B	408 563-5455	6018
Akt America Inc	3674	B	408 563-5455	6019
Alkira Inc	7372	F	408 654-9696	12974
All Metals Inc (PA)	3341	E	408 200-7000	4556
Alliance Roofing Company Inc	1761	E	800 579-2595	1784
Alpha Net Consulting Llc	7371	D	408 330-0896	12242
Altaflex	3672	E	408 727-6614	5911
Amat	3674	F	408 563-5385	6029
Ambarella Inc (PA)	3674	A	408 734-8888	6030
Ambarella Corporation	3674	E	408 734-8888	6031
American Precision Spring Corp	3495	E	408 986-1020	4963
Amex Plating Incorporated	3471	E	408 986-8222	4896
Amlogic Inc	3674	E	408 850-9688	6034
Analogix Semiconductor Inc	3674	E	408 988-8848	6037
Ancora Heart Inc	3841	E	408 727-1105	6942
Anderson PCF Engrg Cnstr Inc	1629	D	408 970-9900	1146
Andros Incorporated	3823	F	510 837-3525	6713
Anglepoint Group Inc (PA)	8741	C	855 512-6453	19297
Apct Inc (HQ)	3672	C	408 727-6442	5914
Apct Holdings LLC (PA)	3672	E	408 727-6442	5915
Applied Cells Inc	3821	C	800 960-3004	6690
Applied Films Corporation	3674	C	408 727-5555	6039
Applied Materials Inc (PA)	3559	A	408 727-5555	5141
Applied Materials Inc	3674	C	408 727-5555	6040
Applied Materials (holdings) (HQ)	3674	C	408 727-5555	6043
Applied Mfr Group Inc	3674	E	408 855-8857	6044
Applied Micro Circuits Corp (HQ)	3674	B	408 542-8600	6045
Applied Mtls Asia-Pacific LLC (HQ)	3674	E	408 727-5555	6046
Appvance Inc	7372	E	408 871-0122	12983
Aquantia Corp (DH)	3674	B	408 228-8300	6047
Aramark Spt & Entrmt Group LLC	7929	B	408 748-7030	14868
Aricent NA Inc (DH)	7371	B	408 324-1800	12271
Aricent US Inc (DH)	7371	E	408 329-7400	12272
Aruba Networks Inc (HQ)	3577	B	408 227-4500	5345
Asiainfo-Linkage Inc	4813	A	408 970-9788	7927
Astro Digital US Inc	3812	E	650 804-3210	6663
Atac (PA)	7373	D	408 736-2822	13557
Atoptech Inc	7371	E	408 550-2600	12283
Atr International Inc (PA)	7361	E	408 328-8000	12075
Atypon Systems LLC (PA)	7372	D	408 988-1240	12992
Automated Bldg Solutions Inc (PA)	8711	E	408 380-8518	18633
Avail Medsystems Inc	3841	E	650 772-1529	6948
Aviatrix Systems Inc	7379	D	844 262-3100	13849
Awake Security Inc	7372	E	833 292-5348	13003
Axiad Ids Inc (HQ)	5065	E	408 841-4670	8895
Ayar Labs Inc (PA)	3571	E	650 963-7200	5242
B R & F Spray Inc	3479	E	408 988-7582	4928
Baffle Inc	7372	E	408 663-6737	13008
Bandai Namco Entrmt Amer Inc	5092	C	408 235-2000	9164
Bandmerch LLC	2396	E	818 736-4800	3045
Bay Area Builders Inc	1521	E	408 648-4500	616
Bay Counties Waste Svcs Inc	4953	D	408 565-9900	8307
Beam Dynamics Inc	3545	E	408 764-4805	5089
Beam On Technology Corporation	3569	E	408 982-0161	5226
Beechwood Computing Limited (PA)	7379	E	408 496-2900	13854
Bel Power Solutions Inc	3677	A	866 513-2839	6377
Bell Electrical Supply Inc (PA)	5063	E	408 727-2355	8845
Big Switch Networks LLC	7372	C	650 322-6510	13017
Bill Wilson Center (PA)	8322	D	408 243-0222	17445
Bitzer Mobile Inc	7372	E	866 603-8392	13021
Bizcom Electronics Inc (HQ)	5045	C	408 262-7877	8676
Bluedata Software Inc	7372	F	650 450-4067	13029
Bon Appetit Management Co	8741	C	408 554-2728	19305
Bon Appetit Management Co	8741	C	408 554-5771	19307
Borqs International Holdg Corp	3695	E	619 363-3168	6499
Bramasol Inc	5045	B	408 831-0046	8678
Brillio LLC	7371	A	800 317-0575	12312
Bristol Hospice Foundation Cal	8082	E	408 207-9222	16861
Broadlight Inc	3674	D	408 982-4210	6076
Buckles-Smith Electric Company (PA)	5084	D	408 280-7777	9056
Build Group Inc	1542	D	408 986-8711	841
Burdick Painting	1799	D	408 567-1330	2012
Bytemobile Inc (DH)	4899	B	408 327-7788	8072
Byton North America Corp	3711	C	408 966-5078	6549
Ca Inc	7372	C	800 225-5224	13044
Cadatasoft Inc (PA)	8742	D	214 935-1355	19463
Cal-West Precision Solutions	3541	F	408 988-8069	5072
California Eastern Labs Inc (PA)	5065	D	408 919-2500	8900
Calmax Technology Inc	3599	E	408 748-8600	5486
Calmax Technology Inc	3599	F	408 506-2035	5487
Calmax Technology Inc	3599	E	408 748-8660	5488
Calstar Products Inc	3251	F	262 752-9131	4398
Carbonic Service	5085	C	408 727-8835	9112
Cardiva Medical Inc	3841	C	408 470-7100	6959
Casemaker Inc	7372	F	408 261-8265	13051
Cavisson Systems Inc	8748	B	800 701-6125	19740
Cavium LLC (DH)	3674	B	408 222-2500	6080
Cedar Fair LP	7996	C	408 988-1776	15040
Church of Vly Rtrment Hmes Inc	8361	D	408 241-7100	18077
Ciasom LLC (PA)	7311	E	408 560-2990	11745
Cirexx Corporation	3672	E	408 988-3980	5922
Cirexx International Inc (PA)	3672	E	408 988-3980	5923
Citrix Systems Inc	7371	D	408 790-8000	12338
Cleanpartset Inc	3559	C	408 886-3300	5144
Cli-Metrics Inc	1711	B	408 886-3800	1236
Cloudera Inc (PA)	7372	A	650 362-0488	13076
Cloudinary Inc	7379	D	650 772-1833	13868
Cloudphysics Inc	7379	E	650 646-4616	13870
Coast Personnel Services Inc (PA)	7363	A	408 653-2100	12167
Cohere Technologies Inc	8731	E	408 246-1277	19044
Coherent Inc (PA)	3826	A	408 764-4000	6821
Coherent Asia Inc	3679	E	408 764-4000	6407
Colfax International	3571	E	408 730-2275	5246
Colortokens Inc (PA)	7372	E	408 341-6030	13085
Commercial Sting Spcalists Inc	5021	E	408 453-8983	8491
Community Home Partners LLC	8052	D	408 985-5252	16177
Community Recreation Center	7033	E	408 615-3140	11618
Compass Innovations Inc	3081	C	408 418-3985	4229
Complete Millwork Services Inc	5031	E	408 567-9664	8537
Computer Access Tech Corp	3571	D	408 727-6600	5247
Computer Performance Inc	5045	E	408 330-5599	8682
Comtech Stllite Ntwrk Tech Inc	3663	C	408 213-3000	5833
Condor Reliability Svcs Inc	3674	E	408 486-9600	6086
Console (PA)	4813	E	855 858-5497	7942
Context Engineering Co	3469	E	408 748-9112	4880
Convergent Manufacturing Tech	3577	E	408 987-2770	5359
Cordis Corporation	3841	E	408 273-3700	6964
Corporate Sign Systems Inc	3993	E	408 292-1600	7225
Cortina Systems Inc (DH)	3674	C	408 481-2300	6092
Couchbase Inc (PA)	7371	A	650 417-7500	12358
Covenant Care California LLC	8051	D	408 248-3736	15966
Creation Tech Santa Clara Inc	3672	D	408 235-7500	5925
Crossbar Inc	3674	E	408 884-0281	6093
Custom Pad and Partition Inc	2653	E	408 970-9711	3358
Cybercsi Inc	5045	D	408 727-2900	8687
D & T Machining Inc	3599	F	408 486-6035	5502
D and T Foods Inc	5142	E	408 727-8331	9325
D-Tek Manufacturing	3674	E	408 588-1574	6097
Dahlhauser Mfg Co Inc	3496	E	408 988-3717	4968
Darko Precision Inc	3599	D	408 988-6133	5503
Data Domain LLC	7373	A	408 980-4800	13575
Data Physics Corporation (PA)	5045	F	408 437-0100	8689
Dataself Corp	7371	E	888 910-9802	12374
Datastax Inc (PA)	7371	A	650 389-6000	12375
Datera Inc	7372	D	844 432-8372	13110
Decathlon Club Inc	7991	E	408 738-2582	14946
Delong Manufacturing Co Inc	3599	F	408 727-3348	5505

Employment Codes: A=Over 500 employees, B=251-500, C=101-250, D=51-100, E=20-50 F=10-19

SANTA CLARA, CA

Company	SIC	EMP	PHONE	ENTRY #
Dialog Semiconductor Inc (DH)	3674	C	408 845-8500	6099
Dialog Semiconductor Inc	5065	C	408 327-8800	8907
Digital Loggers Inc	3613	E	408 330-5599	5651
Diligente Technologies LLC	7373	B	510 304-0852	13578
Dlive Inc	2741	E	650 491-9555	3566
Dolan Concrete Construction	1771	D	408 869-3250	1866
Dpss Lasers Inc	3699	E	408 988-4300	6513
Dremio Corporation (PA)	7371	E	408 882-3569	12402
Dynamic Intgrted Solutions LLC (PA)	3674	E	408 727-3400	6105
E R T Inc	3599	E	408 986-9920	5514
E Z 8 Motels Inc	7011	E	408 246-3119	11067
E-Fab Inc	3479	E	408 727-5218	4931
Eag Holdings LLC	8734	A	408 530-3500	19264
Earthpro Inc	3271	E	408 294-1920	4413
Echelon Corporation (DH)	3825	D	408 938-5200	6748
Edgeq Inc	3674	E	408 209-0368	6106
EDS Mfg Inc	3999	F	408 900-8941	7282
Edwards Vacuum LLC (PA)	3563	E	978 658-5410	5184
Ehealth Inc (PA)	6411	C	650 584-2700	10276
Ehealthinsurance Services Inc (HQ)	6411	D	650 584-2700	10277
Eightfold Ai Inc (PA)	7372	E	650 265-7380	13136
Ej Plumbing	1711	E	650 520-8718	1254
Elance Inc (HQ)	7311	C	650 316-7500	11751
Elcor Electric Inc	1731	E	408 986-1320	1498
Electric USA	1731	E	800 921-1151	1500
Electronic Cooling Solutions	3571	F	408 738-8331	5248
Element Six Tech US Corp	2819	E	408 986-8184	3785
Elite E/M Inc	3444	E	408 988-3505	4760
Emagia Corporation	7389	E	408 654-6575	14262
Eme Technologies Inc	3599	E	408 720-8817	5519
Emergent Payments Inc	7371	D	646 867-7200	12421
Enki Technology Inc	2819	E	408 383-9034	3786
Enlighted Inc	3646	D	650 964-1094	5734
Enterprise Solutions Inc	8748	B	408 727-3627	19767
Envirnmntal Systems Inc Nthrn (PA)	1711	E	408 980-1711	1256
Envivio Inc	4813	C	650 243-2700	7947
Ericsson Inc	4813	A	408 750-5000	7950
Esilicon Corporation (DH)	3674	C	408 217-7300	6114
Espressive Inc	7372	E	408 753-8766	13150
Eurofins Eag Engrg Science LLC (DH)	8734	D	408 588-0050	19268
Eva Automation Inc	8742	B	650 513-6875	19509
Evans Analytical Group LLC	8734	D	408 454-4600	19272
Everactive Inc	3825	D	517 256-0679	6753
Evolveware Inc	7371	E	408 748-8301	12436
Excel Cnc Machining Inc	3599	E	408 970-9460	5522
Excel Precision Corp USA	3825	E	408 727-4260	6755
Exclara Inc	3674	F	408 329-9319	6118
Expandable Software Inc (PA)	7372	E	408 261-7880	13156
Extreme Networks Inc	7371	D	630 288-3665	12440
Eyecarelive Inc	7371	E	415 329-7848	12441
F M G Enterprises	7699	E	408 982-0110	14748
Fabrinet West Inc	3672	C	408 748-0900	5929
Family Christian Stores LLC (PA)	8741	D	616 554-8700	19333
Fast Pro Inc	5013	E	408 566-0200	8450
Ferrotec (usa) Corporation (HQ)	3568	D	408 964-7700	5221
Fiberlite Centrifuge LLC	3826	D	408 492-1109	6829
Fja Industries Inc	3569	F	408 727-0100	5228
Flair Building Services Inc	7349	E	408 987-4040	11952
Forest Park Cabana Club	7997	E	408 244-1884	15090
Fortemedia Inc (PA)	3674	E	408 716-8028	6123
Fortify Infrstructure Svcs Inc (DH)	7379	D	408 850-3119	13897
Forty Niners Football Co LLC	7941	D	408 562-4949	14905
Forty Niners SC Stadium Co LLC	7941	E	408 562-4949	14906
Forty Niners Stadium MGT LLC	8741	E	408 562-4949	19338
Forward Networks Inc	7372	D	844 393-6389	13176
Four D Metal Finishing	3471	E	408 730-5722	4906
Frontier Ford (PA)	5012	C	408 241-1800	8424
Fujifilm Dimatix Inc (DH)	3577	A	408 565-9150	5369
Fujifilm Dimatix Inc	8731	D	408 565-0670	19061
Fungible Inc	8748	D	669 292-5522	19781
Futurewei Technologies Inc	4813	C	469 277-5700	7954
Gamus LLC	5199	E	408 441-0170	9660
Genia Technologies Inc	8731	E	650 300-5970	19063
Gigamon Inc (HQ)	3577	A	408 831-4000	5371
Gilbert Spray Coat Inc	3479	E	408 988-0747	4934
Ginsberg Holdco Inc	7372	B	408 831-4000	13188
Glf Integrated Power Inc (PA)	7389	E	408 239-4326	14283
Globalfoundries US Inc (DH)	3671	D	408 462-3900	5901
Glodyne Technoserve Inc (PA)	7373	A	408 340-5017	13597
Gogreen Roofing Corporation (PA)	1761	D	408 343-8495	1807
Golden Optical Corporation	8042	E	408 246-4500	15869
Greenliant Systems Inc	3674	C	408 217-7400	6133
Gsi Technology Inc	3674	E	408 980-8388	6135
H&M Precision Machining	3451	F	408 982-9184	4866
H-Square Corporation	3674	E	408 732-1240	6139
Hana Microelectronics Inc	5065	E	408 452-7474	8915
Harbor Electronics Inc (PA)	3672	C	408 988-6544	5938
Hathaway Dinwiddie Cnstr Co	1542	D	415 986-2718	886
Hcr Manorcare Inc	8051	D	408 450-7850	16018
Heliovolt Corporation	3679	E	512 767-6079	6432
Hewlett Packard Enterprise Co	7374	A	408 914-2390	13717
Hill Manufacturing Company LLC	3444	E	408 988-4744	4769
Hitachi Vantara Corporation (DH)	3572	B	408 970-1000	5293
Holiday Inn Great America	7011	B	408 235-8900	11156
Hortonworks Inc (HQ)	7372	A	408 916-4121	13213
Hostmark Investors Ltd Partnr	8741	E	408 330-0001	19351
Hyatt Regency Santa Clara	7011	D	408 200-1234	11184
Imagine Easy Solutions LLC (HQ)	8732	E	212 675-6738	19166
Impact Marketing Displays LLC	3993	F	408 217-6850	7234
Impakt Holdings LLC	3444	E	408 727-0880	4772
Impec Group Inc (PA)	7349	C	408 330-9350	11961
Ineda Systems Inc (PA)	3572	E	408 400-7375	5294
Infoblox International Inc (DH)	3577	B	408 986-4000	5376
Infor500 LLC	8742	D	408 209-6837	19536
Information Scan Tech Inc	3825	F	408 988-1908	6763
Infostretch Corporation (PA)	7379	E	408 727-1100	13912
Innova Solutions Inc	7379	A	408 889-2020	13915
Innovate Concrete Inc	8711	E	408 497-2000	18738
Innovative Silicon Inc	7389	D	408 532-8700	14303
Innowi Inc	3571	E	408 609-9404	5255
Instart Logic Inc	7371	E	888 576-3166	12527
Integrated Optical Svcs Corp	2851	E	408 982-9510	4104
Intel Americas Inc (HQ)	3577	C	408 765-8080	5377
INTEL Corporation	3577	E	408 765-2508	5378
Intel Corporation (PA)	3674	A	408 765-8080	6160
Intel Corporation	3577	C	408 425-8398	5379
Intel International Inc	3577	E	408 765-8080	5381
INTEL International Limited (HQ)	3674	F	408 765-8080	6162
Intel McRoelectronics Asia Ltd (HQ)	3577	D	408 765-8080	5382
Intel Media Inc	4841	B	408 765-0063	8063
Intel Overseas Corporation	3577	F	408 765-8080	5383
Intel Phils Holding LLC (HQ)	3577	B	408 765-8080	5384
INTEL Puerto Rico Inc	3577	D	408 765-8080	6163
INTEL Resale Corporation	3577	E	408 765-8080	5385
Intel Semiconductor (us) LLC (HQ)	3674	D	408 765-8080	6164
Intel Services LLC (HQ)	3577	A	408 765-8080	5386
Intel Technologies Inc (HQ)	3577	E	408 765-8080	5387
Intellipro Group Inc	7379	B	408 200-9891	13917
Interctive Fitnes Holdings LLC	6719	E	888 528-8589	10739
Interntnal Elctrnic Cmpnnts US (PA)	5065	F	408 477-2755	8920
Intevac Inc (PA)	3559	C	408 986-9888	5154
Intevac Photonics Inc (HQ)	3827	D	408 986-9888	6877
Invecas Inc (PA)	3674	E	408 758-5636	6166
Ip Infusion Inc (HQ)	7373	D	408 400-1900	13613
Irdeto Usa Inc (DH)	7371	D	818 508-2313	12539
It Management Corp	8742	E	408 739-1100	19545
Itapp Inc	7372	F	415 786-3455	13249
J & J Acoustics Inc	1742	C	408 275-9255	1681
J P Graphics Inc	2752	E	408 235-8821	3662
Jasper Display Corp	3559	E	408 831-5788	5155
Jighi Inc	7371	E	408 332-1262	12549
Joseph J Albanese Inc	1771	A	408 727-5700	1885
JWP Manufacturing LLC	3599	E	408 970-0641	5549
Kaiser Foundation Hospitals	8062	A	408 235-4005	16406
Kaiser Foundation Hospitals	8062	A	408 851-1000	16420
Kana Software Inc (HQ)	7372	D	650 614-8300	13259
Kazeon Systems Inc	7371	E	650 641-8100	12557
Kenna Security Inc (HQ)	7379	C	855 474-7546	13928
Keypoint Credit Union (PA)	6061	C	408 731-4100	9793
Keyssa Inc (PA)	3674	E	408 637-2300	6171
KG Oldco Inc (HQ)	7373	E	408 980-8550	13620
KLA Corporation	3674	F	408 986-5600	6172
Kno Inc	7372	D	408 844-8120	13267
L P Glassblowing Inc	3679	E	408 988-7561	6445
Laird Technologies Inc	3625	F	408 726-5329	5683
Landec Corporation (PA)	2033	C	650 306-1650	2220
Laxmi Group Inc	7371	D	408 329-7733	12570
Leandata Inc	5045	D	669 600-5676	8720
Leantaas Inc	7371	E	650 409-3501	12571
Level 5 Inc	1611	E	669 263-6292	1053
Levi Stadium	7941	E	408 757-1156	14910
Lin-Zhi International Inc	5047	D	408 970-8811	8787
Logicool Inc	7372	E	408 907-1344	13279
Lombardo Diamnd Core Drlg Inc	1771	D	408 727-7922	1888
Lor-Van Manufacturing LLC	3444	E	408 980-1045	4778
Lotusflare Inc	7372	E	626 695-5634	13282
Lunas Sheet Metal Inc	3444	F	408 492-1260	4779
Macaulay Brown Inc	8711	A	937 426-3421	18758
Macom Cnnctivity Solutions LLC	3674	E	408 542-8686	6184
Magnetic Rcrding Solutions Inc	3825	F	408 970-8266	6768
MAK Associates Inc	1799	E	408 244-9848	2043
Malwarebytes Inc	7372	A	408 852-4336	13289
Marseille Inc	3674	B	408 855-9003	6187
Marvell Semiconductor Inc	3825	E	408 855-8839	6769
Marvell Semiconductor Inc (DH)	3674	A	408 222-2500	6190
Marvell Technology Group Ltd	3674	D	408 222-2500	6191
Marx Digital Mfg Inc (PA)	3599	A	408 748-1783	5566
Master Precision Machining	3599	E	408 727-0185	5567
McAfee Finance 1 LLC (DH)	7372	E	888 847-8766	13300
McAfee Finance 2 LLC	7372	A	888 847-8766	13301
McAfee Security LLC	7372	E	866 622-3911	13302
McCarthy Bldg Companies Inc	1542	D	408 908-7005	920
McKenzie Machining Inc	3599	F	408 748-8885	5568
Mecpro Inc	3599	E	408 727-9757	5570
Medconx Inc	3069	D	408 330-0003	4217
Messer Inc	3561	E	408 496-1177	5177
Metra Biosystems Inc (HQ)	2835	E	408 616-4300	4024
Metrotech Corporation (PA)	3812	D	408 734-3880	6675
Miasole	3674	B	408 919-5700	6200
Miasole Hi-Tech Corp (DH)	3674	C	408 919-5700	6201
Michels Pacific Energy Inc	1542	D	920 924-8725	922
Micro Focus LLC (DH)	7374	B	801 861-7000	13729
Micropoint Bioscience Inc	2835	E	408 588-1682	4025
Microsemi Corporation	3674	D	408 240-4560	6206

SANTA CLARA, CA

Company	SIC	EMP	PHONE	ENTRY #
Milestone Internet Mktg Inc (PA)	7374	C	408 492-9055	13731
Miller Cat Corporation	3567	E	408 510-5224	5216
Minerva Surgical Inc	3841	C	855 646-7874	7008
Minimatics Inc (PA)	5065	E	650 969-5630	8934
Mission Park Hotel LP	2819	E	408 809-3838	3792
Mission Trail Wste Systems Inc	4212	D	408 727-5365	7484
Mks Instruments Inc	7699	E	408 750-0300	14765
Mly Technix Corp	7372	E	650 384-1456	13313
Mojo Networks Inc (PA)	7372	C	650 961-1111	13314
Monticello Child Development	8351	E	408 261-0494	17979
Montoya & Jaramillo Inc	3471	F	408 727-5776	4914
Move (HQ)	6531	B	408 558-7100	10623
Move Sales Inc (DH)	6531	D	805 557-2300	10624
Mpower Electronics Inc	5063	D	408 320-1266	8869
Msr Hotels & Resorts Inc	6799	D	408 496-6400	10870
Multibeam Corporation	3559	E	408 980-1800	5160
Multimek Inc	3672	E	408 653-1300	5948
Multitest Elctrnic Systems Inc (DH)	3825	B	408 988-6544	6771
N D E Inc	3672	E	408 727-3955	5950
Nanoscale Cmbntrial Synthsis I (PA)	8731	D	408 987-2004	19090
National Semiconductor Corp (HQ)	3674	A	408 721-5000	6224
Natron Energy Inc	3691	D	408 498-5828	6489
Net Optics Inc	7372	D	408 737-7777	13323
Netbase Solutions Inc (PA)	7371	C	650 810-2100	12627
Nethra Imaging Inc (PA)	3674	E	408 257-5880	6229
Netskope Inc (PA)	7372	A	800 979-6988	13325
Network Conference Co Inc	8742	E	408 562-6205	19589
Nexgen Power Systems Inc	3674	E	408 230-7698	6231
Nflash Inc	3572	E	408 350-0341	5304
NGK Electronics Usa Inc	5065	E	408 330-6900	8938
Nimbula Inc	7372	F	800 633-0738	13333
Nimsoft Inc (DH)	3674	E	408 796-3400	6233
Nominum Inc	7372	C	650 381-6000	13335
Norland Group Inc	7379	C	408 855-8255	13949
Nsfocus Incorporated (HQ)	7372	E	408 907-6638	13950
Nss Enterprises	2752	E	408 970-9200	3679
Ntt Cloud Infrastructure Inc (DH)	7371	E	408 567-2000	12639
Nuvia Inc	3674	E	408 654-9696	6234
Nvidia Corporation (PA)	3674	B	408 486-2000	6235
Nvidia Intl Holdings Inc (HQ)	3674	E	408 486-2000	6236
Nvidia US Investment Company	3663	D	408 615-2500	5858
Nwe Technology Inc	3572	C	408 919-6100	5306
Nxedge Csl LLC	3471	D	408 727-0893	4916
O2 Micro Inc	7373	D	408 987-5920	13642
Omnivision Technologies Inc (PA)	3674	A	408 567-3000	6242
Omniyig Inc	3679	E	408 988-0843	6465
One Diversified LLC	8748	D	408 969-1972	19833
Onspec Technology Partners Inc	3674	E	408 654-7627	6244
Ontario Airport Hotel Corp	7011	C	408 562-6709	11340
Opscruise Inc	7372	E	916 204-4369	13347
Outlaw Beverage Inc	2082	F	310 424-5077	2489
Owens Corning Sales LLC	5033	B	408 235-1351	8640
P M S D Inc (PA)	3599	E	408 988-5235	5585
P M S D Inc	3599	E	408 727-5322	5586
P S C Manufacturing Inc	3089	E	408 988-5115	4308
Pacific Autism Ctr For Educatn	8361	C	408 245-3400	18153
Pacific Ceramics Inc	3253	E	408 747-4600	4402
Pacific Ridge Builders Inc	1542	E	408 627-4765	935
Pactron	3672	D	408 329-5500	5955
Palex Metals Inc	3444	E	408 496-6111	4800
Palo Alto Networks Inc (PA)	3577	B	408 753-4000	5403
Paragon Swiss	3599	E	408 748-1617	5591
Parallel Machines Inc	7372	E	669 467-2638	13362
Parametric Manufacturing Inc	3599	F	408 654-9845	5592
Patsons Press	2752	E	408 567-0911	3681
Pdf Solutions Inc (PA)	7372	E	408 280-7900	13365
PDM Steel Service Centers Inc	5051	F	408 988-3000	8823
Peak Technical Services Inc	7361	C	855 650-7325	12119
Penhall Company	1799	E	408 970-9494	2053
Persistent Systems Inc (HQ)	7371	D	408 216-7010	12680
Persistent Tlcom Solutions Inc	7371	E	408 216-7010	12681
Peter Castillo Md PA	8011	C	408 236-6400	15627
Phase Matrix Inc	5065	E	954 490-9429	8946
Picarro Inc (PA)	3826	C	408 962-3900	6844
Pivot Interiors Inc (PA)	7389	C	408 432-5600	14367
Playspan LLC	6153	D	408 617-9155	9873
Pluribus Networks Inc (PA)	4899	E	650 289-4717	8083
Pmc Inc	3086	E	562 905-3101	4245
Polishing Corporation America	3674	E	888 892-3377	6252
Primenano Inc	3674	F	650 300-5115	6256
Proactive Technical Svcs Inc (HQ)	7371	E	408 531-6040	12700
Process Stainless Lab Inc (PA)	3471	E	408 980-0535	4917
Processweaver Inc	7372	F	510 648-1420	13387
Prodigy Surface Tech Inc	3471	E	408 492-9390	4918
Project Sentinel Inc (PA)	8748	E	650 321-6291	19840
Promega Bsystems Sunnyvale Inc	3829	E	408 636-2400	6917
Promex Industries Incorporated (PA)	3674	E	408 496-0222	6259
Promise Technology Inc	5045	D	408 228-1400	8737
Propelplm Inc	7371	E	408 755-3780	12704
Punctus Temporis Translations	7389	E	510 309-0888	14378
Qmat Inc	3674	F	408 228-5880	6261
Qmetry Inc	8748	C	408 727-1101	19841
Qt Company	7379	E	408 906-8400	13964
Qualitau Incorporated (PA)	3825	E	408 675-3034	6783
Questivity Inc	7372	F	408 615-1781	13395
Quid LLC (PA)	7371	C	415 813-5300	12719
Radian Thermal Products Inc	3369	D	408 988-6200	4587

Company	SIC	EMP	PHONE	ENTRY #
Rasilient Systems Inc (PA)	3572	E	408 730-2568	5313
Reaction Technology Inc (HQ)	3674	E	408 970-9601	6269
Redfern Integrated Optics Inc	3827	E	408 970-3500	6884
Redwood Electric Group Inc (PA)	1731	A	707 451-7348	1576
Reliance Computer Corp	3674	C	408 492-1915	6271
Revera Incorporated	3577	E	408 510-7400	5406
Richards Machining Co Inc	3599	F	408 526-9219	5612
Rimnetics Inc	3089	F	650 969-6590	4318
Rivos Inc	3559	E	408 663-6746	5168
Robert A Bothman Inc (PA)	1771	C	408 279-2277	1907
Roche Molecular Systems Inc	8731	D	925 523-8099	19120
Rocket Ems Inc	3672	C	408 727-3700	5966
Rockys Gasket Shop Inc	3053	E	408 980-9190	4206
Roos Instruments Inc	3825	E	408 748-8589	6787
Royal Glass Company Inc	1793	D	408 969-0444	1941
San Francisco Forty Niners (PA)	7941	E	408 562-4949	14913
San Jose Bluprt Svc & Sup Co	7334	C	408 295-5770	11851
San Jose Delta Associates Inc	3264	E	408 727-1448	4408
San Jose Earthquakes MGT LLC	8741	E	408 556-7700	19396
Santa Clara Convention Center	7389	C	408 748-7000	14397
Santa Clara Plating Co Inc	3471	D	408 727-9315	4919
Santa Clara Suites LP	7011	E	408 241-6444	11442
Sat Corporation (PA)	7371	D	402 208-9200	12761
Scientific Metal Finishing Inc	3479	E	408 970-9011	4948
SE Laboratories Inc	8734	D	408 727-3286	19283
Secugen Corporation	3577	E	408 834-7712	5409
Secure Computing Corporation (DH)	7372	E	408 979-2020	13433
Select Hotels Group LLC	7011	E	408 486-0800	11456
Semicndctor Cmponents Inds LLC	3674	E	408 660-2699	6282
Semicndctor Cmponents Inds LLC	3676	C	408 542-1051	6373
Semler Scientific Inc (PA)	3841	D	877 774-4211	7032
Sensory Inc (PA)	7371	E	408 625-3302	12771
Sequent Software Inc	7372	F	650 419-2713	13439
Seres Inc	3694	C	214 585-3356	6498
Servicenow Inc (PA)	7379	E	408 501-8550	13972
Servicenow Delaware LLC (HQ)	7379	A	408 501-8550	13973
Sesame Software Inc (PA)	7372	E	408 550-7999	13442
SF Motors Inc (DH)	3711	C	408 617-7878	6558
Shockwave Medical Inc (PA)	3841	C	510 279-4262	7034
Silicon Standard Corp	3674	E	408 234-6964	6290
Silicon Valley Bank (HQ)	6029	A	408 654-7400	9761
Silicon Valley Elite Mfg	3599	F	408 654-9534	5619
Silicon Vly Eye Care Optmtry C	8042	E	408 296-0511	15873
Silicon Vly McRelectronics Inc	3674	E	408 844-7100	6293
Siliconix Semiconductor Inc	3674	D	408 988-8000	6296
Silvaco Inc (PA)	7372	C	408 567-1000	13663
Silver Peak Systems Inc (HQ)	3674	E	408 935-1800	6297
Simco Electronics (PA)	7629	D	408 734-9750	14705
Sitime Corporation	3674	C	408 328-4400	6301
Six3 Advanced Systems Inc	8711	E	408 878-4920	18814
Sj Valley Plating Inc	3471	E	408 988-5502	4921
Solflower Computer Inc	3577	E	408 733-8100	5412
Solid Data Systems Inc	3572	F	408 845-5700	5322
Solidcore Systems Inc (DH)	7372	D	408 387-8400	13453
Solix Technologies Inc (PA)	7371	E	408 654-6405	12804
Solopoint Solutions Inc (PA)	8742	D	408 246-5945	19637
Soundhound Inc (PA)	7371	E	408 441-3200	12808
Sourcewise	8322	E	408 350-3200	17750
South Bay Showers Inc	1793	E	408 988-3484	1945
Sp3 Diamond Technologies Inc	3569	F	877 773-9940	5234
Spec Personnel LLC	7361	E	408 727-8000	12139
SPI Solar Inc	3433	A	408 919-8000	4638
Squelch Inc	7372	E	650 241-2700	13461
Stanford Equipment Company	5065	E	408 855-8040	8959
Stanford Hotels Corporation	7011	D	408 330-0001	11500
Stmicroelectronics Inc	5065	C	408 452-8585	8960
Stone Publishing Inc (PA)	2741	E	408 450-7910	3602
Streamline Circuits LLC	3672	B	415 279-8650	5980
Streamvector Inc (PA)	7371	E	415 870-8395	12824
Strivr Labs Inc	7371	C	650 656-9987	12827
Strouss Bros Construction Inc	1771	E	408 267-3222	1910
Summit Interconnect Inc	3672	C	408 727-1418	5983
Sunpreme Inc	3674	E	408 419-9281	6316
Superior Quartz Inc	3339	F	408 844-9663	4555
Superwinch LLC	5013	E	800 323-2031	8471
Superwinch Holding LLC	3531	D	860 412-1476	5039
Supportlogic Inc	8399	E	408 471-4710	18252
Sutter Bay Medical Foundation	8011	E	650 812-3751	15710
Sutter Health	8062	C	408 524-5952	16587
Sutter P Dahlglen Entps Inc	3599	F	408 727-4640	5624
Svb Financial Group (PA)	6022	A	408 654-7400	9750
Swiss Screw Products Inc	3599	E	408 748-8400	5625
Synapse Design Automation Inc (DH)	7373	D	408 850-9527	13671
Synaptics Incorporated	4813	D	408 454-5100	7995
Tagit Solutions Inc (PA)	8748	D	888 518-8710	19872
Talari Networks Inc (HQ)	7371	D	408 689-0400	12847
Taracom Corporation	3571	F	408 691-6655	5276
Tata America Intl Corp	7379	E	408 569-5845	13991
Tata Elxsi Ltd (HQ)	7373	E	408 894-8282	13675
Tavant Technologies Inc (PA)	7371	A	408 519-5400	12852
Teamworks Inc (PA)	8721	E	408 243-3970	19000
Teen Challenge Norwestcal Nev	8322	E	408 703-2001	17766
Teledyne Wireless Inc	3631	C	408 986-5060	5701
Telenav Inc (PA)	3812	A	408 245-3800	6686
Tellus Solutions Inc	7372	E	408 850-2942	13489
Tensilica Inc (HQ)	6794	D	408 986-8000	10813
Thermal Mechanical	1711	D	408 988-8744	1381

	SIC	EMP	PHONE	ENTRY #
Thermo Fisher Scientific Inc	3826	E	408 731-5056	6859
Think Social Publishing Inc	2741	E	408 557-8595	3605
Tiger Analytics Inc **(PA)**	8732	D	408 508-4430	19190
TLC of Bay Area Inc	8051	D	408 988-7667	16143
Tool Makers International Inc	3544	E	408 980-8888	5086
Translattice Inc **(PA)**	3571	E	408 749-8478	5278
Trianz LLC **(HQ)**	7379	C	408 387-5800	14001
Ttm Printed Circuit Group Inc	3672	E	408 486-3100	5989
Ttm Technologies Inc	3672	B	408 486-3100	5990
Turingsense Inc **(PA)**	7371	E	408 887-7833	12880
Tusa Inc **(PA)**	7378	C	888 848-3749	13825
Tvia Inc **(PA)**	3674	E	408 982-8591	6338
Tyche Medtech Inc	3841	F	408 919-0098	7053
UNI-Pixel Displays Inc	3575	D	281 825-4500	5337
Unitech Tool & Machine Inc	3599	F	408 566-0333	5631
United Marble & Granite Inc	1799	D	408 347-3300	2082
United SEC Specialists Inc **(PA)**	7381	C	408 431-0691	14103
United SEC Specialists Inc	7381	E	408 878-5120	14104
Unixsurplus Inc	5045	E	408 844-0082	8758
Upwork Inc **(PA)**	7361	C	650 316-7500	12149
V2solutions Inc **(PA)**	8748	C	408 550-2340	19881
Vacuum Engrg & Mtls Co Inc	2819	E	408 871-9900	3799
Valley Waterproofing Inc	1799	D	408 985-7701	2084
Vanderhulst Associates Inc	3599	E	408 727-1313	5636
Vanguard Music and Prfrmg Arts	8641	D	408 727-5532	18478
Vantage Data Ctrs MGT Co LLC **(PA)**	6798	E	408 748-9830	10826
Varex Imaging West LLC **(HQ)**	3844	C	408 565-0850	7095
Vave Health Inc	3845	F	650 387-7059	7132
Veeco Instruments Inc	3674	E	510 657-8523	6345
Verb Surgical Inc	3841	D	408 438-3363	7058
Veritas Technologies LLC **(DH)**	7371	C	866 837-4827	12900
Veritas US Inc	7371	C	650 933-1000	12901
Vertical Communication **(HQ)**	4899	D	408 969-9600	8087
Vicom Systems Inc	3572	E	408 588-1286	5324
VIP Manufacturing & Engrg Corp	3724	D	408 727-6545	6623
Visger Precision Inc	3599	F	408 988-0184	5638
Vivido Labs Inc **(PA)**	7371	C	408 692-5002	12912
Volex Inc **(HQ)**	3089	E	669 444-1740	4331
Vulcan Construction Mtls LLC	1442	E	408 213-4270	600
W L Gore & Associates Inc	3841	C	928 864-2705	7061
Watt Stopper Inc	3669	F	408 988-5331	5898
Watts Machining Inc	3599	E	408 654-9300	5639
WEI Laboratories Inc	2032	E	408 970-8700	2209
Wes Manufacturing Inc	3599	E	408 727-0750	5641
West Vlly-Mssion Cmnty Cllege	8748	B	408 988-2200	19890
Western Grinding Service Inc	3599	E	650 591-2635	5642
Westfab Manufacturing Inc	3444	E	408 727-0550	4831
Whiterabbitai Inc	7371	D	408 215-8876	12920
Whizz Systems Inc	3672	E	408 207-0400	6000
Wide Area Management Svcs Inc	7372	E	408 327-1260	13527
Winnov Inc	3651	E	888 315-9460	5773
Winway Usa Inc	3674	F	203 775-9311	6358
Wso2 Inc **(PA)**	7371	E	650 745-4499	12929
Yangs Brothers Intl Corp	7011	C	408 446-9636	11584
Yertleworks LLC	7372	E	408 916-4121	13538
Yes Videocom Inc **(PA)**	7812	C	408 907-7600	14799
Young MNS Chrstn Assn Slcon Vl **(PA)**	8641	D	408 351-6400	18526
Yvaai Inc **(PA)**	7371	D	650 704-5503	12933

SANTA CRUZ, CA - Santa Cruz County

	SIC	EMP	PHONE	ENTRY #
(a) Tool Shed Inc **(PA)**	7359	E	831 477-7133	12025
7th Avenue Center LLC	8063	E	831 476-1700	16731
Alliance Member Services Inc	8699	D	831 459-0980	18542
Alvarez Industries	7349	E	831 423-5515	11916
American Leisure Company **(PA)**	3645	F	831 427-4270	5722
American Med Rspnse Inland Emp	4119	B	831 423-7030	7371
Anatometal Inc	3911	E	831 454-9880	7164
Animal Clinic of Santa Cruz	0742	E	831 427-3345	320
Anomalies International Inc	2086	D	800 855-1113	2782
Arrow Surf Products **(PA)**	3949	F	831 462-2791	7187
Bagelry Inc **(PA)**	2051	E	831 429-8049	2364
Beckmanns Old World Bakery Ltd	2051	D	831 423-9242	2365
Bogner Sheet Metal	1711	E	831 423-4322	1223
Bonny Doon Vineyard **(PA)**	2084	E	831 425-3625	2513
Bonny Doon Winery Inc	2084	F	831 425-3625	2514
Boys Grls Clubs Snta Cruz Cnty	8641	E	831 423-3138	18398
Buoy Labs Inc	7372	F	855 481-7112	13039
Canyon View Capital Inc	6798	D	831 480-6335	10815
Chaminade Ltd	7011	C	831 475-5600	11001
Community Printers Inc	2752	E	831 426-4682	3638
Dignity Health Med Foundation	8062	D	831 475-8834	16351
Dignity Health Med Foundation	8062	D	831 475-1111	16355
Dominican Hospital Foundation	8361	C	831 457-7057	18099
Dominican Hospital Foundation **(DH)**	8062	C	831 462-7700	16357
Dominican Oaks Corporation	6513	D	831 462-6257	10428
Dtj Inc	5149	E	831 423-8956	9449
Duke Empirical Inc	3841	D	831 420-1104	6971
Elements Manufacturing Inc	2541	E	831 421-9440	3313
Encompass Community Services	8322	E	831 479-9494	17546
Encompass Community Services	8322	E	831 423-2003	17547
Encompass Community Services	8322	E	831 423-3890	17548
Encompass Community Services	8322	E	831 425-0771	17549
Encompass Community Services	8322	E	831 459-6644	17552
Family Svc Agcy of Centl Coast	8322	D	831 423-9444	17565
Fiber Systems Inc	3661	E	831 430-0700	5796
First American Title Insur Co **(HQ)**	6361	A	714 250-3109	10199
First Transit Inc	4111	C	831 460-9911	7331
Forever Firewood Inc **(PA)**	1761	E	831 461-0634	1804
Friends Santa Cruz State Parks	8641	D	831 429-1840	18418
Front St Inc	8059	C	831 420-0120	16233
Fullpower Technologies Inc	7371	E	831 459-0447	12465
Glass Jar Inc	2024	F	831 427-9946	2174
Glass Jar Inc **(PA)**	2024	D	831 227-2247	2175
Granite Rock Co	5032	E	831 471-3440	8626
Green Valley Corporation	1521	D	831 475-7100	649
Grey Bears	4953	E	831 479-1055	8336
Happily Ever Laughter LLC	8351	E	831 346-0002	17948
Holiday Inn Express	7011	D	888 803-5176	11152
Hotel Prdox Autograph Collectn	7011	E	831 425-7100	11171
Housing Matters	8322	D	831 458-6020	17606
Internet Store Inc	8999	E	831 459-6301	19906
Island Conservation	8699	E	831 359-4787	18574
Jacobs Farm/Del Cabo Inc	0191	D	831 421-9171	173
Jane Technologies Inc	5045	D	617 285-2466	8715
Janus of Santa Cruz	8069	D	831 462-1060	16761
JC Heating & AC Inc **(PA)**	1711	E	831 475-6538	1292
Jeff Frank	3993	F	831 469-8208	7237
Joby Aviation Inc	3721	A	831 426-3733	6612
Journeyworks Publishing	2741	F	831 423-1400	3580
Karssli Corporation	4215	E	831 420-8900	7650
Krafts Body Shop	7532	E	831 476-2440	14528
Lackey Woodworking Inc	2434	E	831 462-0528	3186
Larsens Inc	2394	F	831 476-3009	3039
Las Animas Con & Bldg Sup Inc	3273	E	831 425-4084	4491
Lifeaid Beverage Company LLC **(PA)**	2086	D	888 558-1113	2795
Looker Data Sciences Inc **(DH)**	7371	D	831 244-0340	12582
Mariannes Ice Cream LLC **(PA)**	2024	E	831 457-1447	2178
Mariner Health Care Inc	8051	E	831 475-6323	16052
Microtech Systems Inc	3695	F	650 596-1900	6503
Museum of Art Hstory At McPhrs	8412	E	831 429-1964	18276
National Security Industries	7381	D	831 425-2052	14078
Nhs Inc	3949	D	831 459-7800	7199
Nonprofits Insur Aliance Cal	6411	E	831 459-0980	10321
Ocean PCF Invstors A Cal Ltd P	7011	E	831 457-1234	11337
ONeill Wetsuits LLC **(PA)**	3069	D	831 475-7500	4222
Ontera Inc	3674	C	831 222-2193	6245
Pacific Cookie Company Inc **(PA)**	5149	E	831 429-9709	9472
Pasatiempo III Investments	7011	D	831 423-5000	11361
Performance Food Group Inc	5141	C	831 462-4400	9283
Planned Prnthood of Santa Cruz **(PA)**	8093	E	831 426-5550	17057
Plantronics Inc **(PA)**	3661	A	831 420-3002	5805
Rainbow Light	2833	E	831 429-9089	3821
Regent Assisted Living Inc	8361	E	831 459-8400	18167
Reyes Holdings LLC	5181	C	831 761-6400	9561
Rope Partner Inc	5085	D	831 460-9448	9129
Santa Cruz Bicycles LLC	3751	D	831 459-7560	6654
Santa Cruz City of	4941	E	831 420-5200	8270
Santa Cruz Cnty Rgnal Trnsp Co	4119	E	831 460-3200	7403
Santa Cruz Community Credit Un **(PA)**	6061	E	831 425-7708	9817
Santa Cruz Guitar Corporation	3931	E	831 425-0999	7173
Santa Cruz Ht Assoc A Cal Ltd	7011	D	831 426-4330	11443
Santa Cruz Medical Foundation **(HQ)**	8011	E	831 458-5537	15670
Santa Cruz Medical Foundation	8011	A	831 477-2375	15671
Santa Cruz Medical Foundation	8011	A	831 477-2325	15672
Santa Cruz Metro Trnst Dst	4111	D	831 429-5455	7355
Santa Cruz Metro Trnst Dst	4111	D	831 469-1954	7356
Santa Cruz Nutritionals **(PA)**	2834	B	831 457-3200	3982
Santa Cruz Seaside Company **(PA)**	7996	B	831 423-5590	15046
Santa Cruz Seaside Company	7011	A	831 427-3400	11444
Santa Cruz Surgery	8011	E	831 462-5512	15673
Santa Cruz Westside Elc Inc	1711	D	831 469-8888	1355
Scotts Valley Medical Clinic	8062	E	831 438-1430	16518
Seltzer Revolutions Inc	2085	F	604 765-9966	2778
Shine A Lght Cunseling Ctr Inc	8322	E	530 748-8098	17743
Slatter Construction Inc	1542	E	831 425-5425	964
Smartrevenuecom Inc	8732	B	203 733-9156	19185
Socksmith Design Inc **(PA)**	2252	E	831 426-6416	2972
Stagnaro Brothers Seafood Inc	5146	D	831 423-1188	9371
Supplyshift	7372	D	831 824-4326	13473
Sutter Bay Hospitals	8062	D	831 423-4111	16572
Sutter Health	8062	C	831 458-6310	16594
Sutter Health	8062	C	831 477-3600	16625
Sutter Mtrnty/Srgry Ctr-Snt Cr	8062	D	831 477-2200	16671
System Studies Incorporated **(PA)**	3661	E	831 475-5777	5810
Toucaned Inc	2741	E	831 464-0508	3606
Trick or Treat Stdios Hldngs L	3999	E	831 713-9665	7314
Trowbridge Enterprises **(PA)**	5112	E	831 476-3815	9211
United Parcel Service Inc	4215	C	831 425-1054	7672
Visiting Nrse Assn of Snta Cru **(DH)**	8082	D	831 477-2600	16965
Yellich Steel & Klein	8021	D	831 475-0221	15863

SANTA ROSA, CA - Sonoma County

	SIC	EMP	PHONE	ENTRY #
Abbey Wtznberg Wrren Emery A P	8111	E	415 986-3103	17197
AEG Industries Inc	3728	E	707 575-0697	6625
Ahlborn Fence & Steel Inc **(PA)**	1799	E	707 573-0742	1997
Ahlborn Structural Steel Inc	3441	E	707 573-0742	4642
Air Monitor Corporation **(PA)**	3823	D	707 544-2706	6712
Airport Club	7997	D	707 528-2582	15048
Aluma USA Inc	3911	E	707 545-9344	7163
American Agcredit Flca **(PA)**	6159	D	707 545-1200	9879
Anderson Zeigler Disharoon **(PA)**	8111	E	707 545-4910	17201
Anesthsia Anlgsia Med Group In	8011	E	707 522-1800	15279
Argonaut Constructors Inc	1611	C	707 542-4862	1012
Atech Logistics Inc	4731	C	707 526-1910	7824
Atech Warehousing & Dist Inc **(PA)**	4213	D	707 526-1910	7505
Aurora Bhvral Hlthcare - STA R	8093	D	707 800-7700	16989

GEOGRAPHIC SECTION SANTA ROSA, CA

	SIC	EMP	PHONE	ENTRY #
Avalon At Brush Creek LLC	8361	E	707 538-2590	18060
Bana Solomon LLC	8082	E	707 867-1770	16852
Barricade Co & Traffic Sup Inc **(PA)**	3499	F	707 523-2350	4981
Bavarian Lion Company Cal **(PA)**	7011	C	707 545-8530	10945
Bcj Sand and Rock Inc	1446	F	707 544-0303	601
Beaver Dam Health Care Center	8051	E	707 546-0471	15931
Bellevue Un Elmentary Schl Dst **(PA)**	8741	E	707 542-5197	19303
Big Poppy Holdings Inc	6022	C	707 636-9020	9711
Blentech Corporation	3556	D	707 523-5949	5126
Blood Bank of Redwoods **(PA)**	8099	C	707 545-1222	17105
Bo Dean Co Inc **(PA)**	1411	E	707 576-8205	575
Bohan Cnlis - Astin Creek Rdym	3273	D	707 632-5296	4460
Brelje and Race Labs Inc	8734	E	707 544-8807	19260
Brelje Race Cnslting Engineers	8711	E	707 576-1322	18645
Broker Solutions Inc	8742	D	707 392-4254	19461
Bromley Properties Inc	7011	D	707 546-4031	10978
Burbank Housing Dev Corp **(PA)**	6552	C	707 526-9782	10698
Burgess Lumber **(PA)**	2421	F	707 542-5091	3093
Burr Pilger Mayer Inc	8721	D	707 544-4078	18937
C and C Wine Services Inc	2084	E	707 546-5712	2521
Calculex	3678	E	707 578-2307	6390
Calico Hardwoods Inc	2426	D	707 546-4045	3120
California Human Dev Corp **(PA)**	8331	C	707 523-1155	17798
California Parenting Institute	8351	D	707 585-6108	17870
Canine Cmpnons For Indpendence **(PA)**	0752	D	707 577-1700	351
Care At Home	8059	E	707 579-6822	16225
Carlilemacy Inc	8711	E	707 542-6451	18659
Cfarms Inc **(PA)**	2099	E	916 375-3000	2882
Chanate Ldge Assoc A Cal Ltd P	6513	E	707 575-7503	10423
Change Lending LLC	6163	D	707 596-5111	9937
Chase Manhattan Mortgage Corp	6162	C	707 525-5060	9901
Childrens Vlg of Sonoma Cnty	8322	E	707 566-7044	17489
City Electric Supply	5063	E	707 523-4600	8852
City Towel & Dust Service Inc	7213	D	707 542-0391	11634
Clark Pest Ctrl Stockton Inc	7342	E	707 571-0414	11896
Community Action Prtnr Snoma C	8399	D	707 544-0120	18228
Community Chld Cre Cncl Sonoma **(PA)**	8351	D	707 522-1413	17912
Community First Credit Union **(PA)**	6061	C	707 546-6000	9780
Conetech Custom Services LLC	2084	F	707 823-2404	2538
County of Sonoma	8082	E	707 565-4963	16874
County of Sonoma	8322	D	707 565-4711	17513
County of Sonoma	8063	D	707 565-4850	16733
Covia Communities	8361	C	707 538-8400	18089
CPI International	5049	D	707 521-6327	8801
Creekside Cnvalescent Hosp Inc	8051	E	707 544-7750	15974
Creekside Rhbltion Bhvral HLT	8093	D	707 524-7030	17014
Crescent Healthcare Inc	8082	D	707 543-5822	16876
Dana Kitchens & Associates Inc	1742	E	707 571-8326	1671
DCs Asphalt Maintenance	7349	E	415 577-6705	11942
Deposition Sciences Inc	8731	D	707 573-6700	19049
Devincenzi Concrete Cnstr	1771	E	707 568-4370	1865
Dr Pepper/Seven Up Inc	2086	F	707 545-7797	2790
Drug Abuse Alternatives Center	8093	C	707 571-2233	17015
Dynamic Pre-Cast Co Inc	3272	E	707 573-1110	4431
Dynatex International	3545	E	707 542-4227	5095
Eagle Transportation Co Inc	4213	E	707 586-9766	7528
Eco Farm Holdings Pbc	0191	E	707 485-3035	161
Emeritus Corporation	8052	C	707 324-7087	16183
Emg Inc	3931	D	707 525-9941	7172
Endrun Technologies LLC	3821	F	707 573-8633	6692
Ensign Group Inc	8051	D	707 525-1250	15990
Epic Ventures Inc **(PA)**	5182	E	844 824-0422	9574
Ernest Ongaro & Sons Inc	1711	E	707 579-3511	1258
Exchange Bank **(PA)**	6036	C	707 524-3000	9771
Eye Care Institute	8011	D	707 546-9800	15393
Fairweather & Associates Inc	1521	E	707 829-2922	637
Famand Inc	1711	D	707 255-9295	1260
First Alarm SEC & Patrol Inc	7381	B	707 584-1110	14057
Fischl Tibor **(HQ)**	5149	E	707 529-9350	9451
Fixture-Pro Inc	1751	E	707 545-3901	1737
Flashco Manufacturing Inc **(PA)**	3356	E	707 824-4448	4566
Flex Products Inc	3827	C	707 525-9200	6872
Foley Family Wines Inc **(HQ)**	2084	D	707 708-7600	2574
Foley Fmly Wines Holdings Inc **(PA)**	2084	D	707 708-7600	2575
Fonexperts Inc	1731	E	707 303-8200	1506
Fountain Grove Golf & Athc CLB	7992	D	707 701-3050	15002
Fountaingrove Inn LLC	7011	D	707 578-6101	11101
Freeman Motors Inc	7538	E	707 542-1791	14564
Friedmans Home Improvement	5072	D	707 584-7811	8983
Gaddis Nursery Inc	0181	E	707 542-2202	123
Garda CL West Inc	7381	E	707 591-0282	14062
Gco Inc	5085	E	707 584-3333	9118
Gentiva Health Services Inc	8082	D	707 545-7114	16885
Ghilotti Construction Co Inc **(PA)**	1629	B	707 585-1221	1164
Girl Scouts Northern Cal	8641	E	707 544-5472	18423
Goodwill Inds of Rdwood Empire	8322	E	707 546-4481	17594
Goodwill Inds of Rdwood Empire **(PA)**	8331	D	707 523-0550	17814
Grape Links Inc	2084	E	707 524-8000	2604
Green Lake Investors LLC	3953	E	707 577-1301	7205
Growthpoint Tech Partners LLC **(PA)**	8742	D	650 322-2500	19525
Ham Delles Company Inc **(PA)**	6531	E	707 578-8840	10569
Hansel - Prestige Inc	5013	E	707 578-4717	8453
Hawthorne Hydroponics LLC	2873	E	800 221-1760	4131
Hdc Business Development Inc **(HQ)**	6531	D	707 523-1155	10572
Hillside Inn Inc	7011	E	707 546-9353	11138
Hotel La Rose	7011	D	707 284-2879	11165
Immecor	7371	E	707 636-2550	12511
Individuals Now	8322	D	707 544-3299	17613
Industrial Wste Dbris Box Rnta	4212	E	707 585-0511	7475
Inoxpa Usa Inc	5084	B	707 585-3900	9072
Intelenex Inc **(HQ)**	7371	E	415 367-4871	12529
Interdent Service Corporation	8021	C	707 528-7000	15838
Iron Dog Fabrication Inc	3441	F	707 579-7831	4667
ITT LLC	3625	C	707 523-2300	5680
Jackson Family Farms LLC **(PA)**	2084	C	707 837-1000	2625
Jackson Family Farms LLC	2084	D	707 836-2047	2626
Jackson Family Wines Inc	2084	E	707 836-2035	2627
Jackson Family Wines Inc **(PA)**	2084	D	707 544-4000	2628
James L Hall Co Incorporated	3677	D	707 544-2436	6381
Jl Construction Inc	1542	E	707 527-5788	901
Joe Lunardi Electric Inc	1731	D	707 545-4755	1527
Johns Formica Inc	2542	E	707 544-8585	3327
K G Walters Cnstr Co Inc	1542	D	707 527-9968	907
K9 Activity Club Inc **(PA)**	7997	E	707 569-1394	15100
Kaiser Foundation Hospitals	8062	A	707 393-4633	16395
Kaiser Foundation Hospitals	8011	C	707 393-4000	15445
Kaiser Foundation Hospitals	6324	C	707 571-3835	10132
Kaiser Foundation Hospitals	6324	C	707 393-4033	10133
Kaiserair Inc	4581	E	707 528-7400	7774
Kandy Investments LLC	4225	E	707 584-8363	7692
Keegan & Coppin Company Inc **(PA)**	6531	E	707 528-1400	10593
Kendall-Jackson Wine Estates **(HQ)**	2084	B	707 544-4000	2638
Kenyon Construction Inc	7532	D	707 528-1906	14527
Keysight Technologies Inc **(PA)**	3823	A	800 829-4444	6724
Klh Consulting Inc	8748	D	707 575-9986	19806
L-3 Cmmnications Sonoma Eo Inc	3861	C	707 568-3000	7152
L-3 Communications Wescam	3812	D	707 568-3000	6673
La Tortilla Factory Inc **(PA)**	5149	B	707 586-4000	9463
La Tortilla Factory Inc	2099	E	707 586-4000	2913
Laguna Oaks Vnyards Winery Inc	2084	E	707 568-2455	2646
Linkenhmer LLT Cpas Advsors LL	8721	E	707 546-0272	18967
LLP Moss Adams	8721	D	707 527-0800	18972
Loring Smart Roast Inc	5084	D	707 526-7215	9077
Luther Burbank Corporation **(PA)**	6029	D	844 446-8201	9758
Luther Burbank Mem Foundation	7922	D	707 546-3600	14851
Luther Burbank Savings **(HQ)**	6036	E	707 578-9216	9772
Mac Thin Films Inc	3231	E	707 791-1656	4391
Make Community LLC	2721	E	707 200-3714	3506
Making It Big Inc	2331	F	707 795-1995	2999
Marathon Business Group Inc	4212	D	707 575-8252	7483
Mark E Jacobson M D	8011	D	707 571-4022	15520
Matanzas Creek Winery	2084	F	707 528-6464	2655
Mayacama Golf Club LLC	7997	C	707 569-2900	15107
MB Hosptlity Srosa AC 2018 LLC	7011	E	707 527-1075	11291
Mc Leas Tire Service Inc **(PA)**	5014	E	707 542-0363	8477
Medtronic Inc	3841	E	707 541-3144	7004
Melissa Bradley RE Inc	6531	E	707 536-0888	10618
Mendocino Forest Pdts Co LLC **(PA)**	5031	B	707 620-2961	8591
Merrill Lynch Prce Fnner Smith	6211	D	707 575-6374	9992
Mhm Services Inc	8093	C	707 623-9080	17044
Michael Kors (usa) Inc	5137	E	707 535-0301	9253
Microsemi Semiconductor US Inc	3674	E	707 568-5900	6209
Middle Way	8331	E	707 823-8755	17823
Milners Anodizing	3471	E	707 584-1188	4913
Molding Solutions Inc	3089	D	707 575-1218	4301
MS Intertrade Inc **(PA)**	2092	E	707 837-8057	2831
Murphy-True Inc	1542	D	707 576-7337	928
Myers Restaurant Supply LLC	5046	C	707 570-1200	8767
Nadhan Inc	8051	D	707 544-7750	16064
Neilmed Pharmaceuticals Inc	2834	B	707 525-3784	3952
Noble Aew Vineyard Creek LLC	7011	E	707 284-1234	11330
Nordby Construction Co	1542	E	707 526-4500	930
North American Cinemas Inc	7832	B	707 571-1412	14814
North Cast Tile Stone Dsign In	1743	E	707 586-2064	1716
Northern Cal Bldg Mtls Inc **(PA)**	3273	E	707 546-9422	4500
Northern Cal Med Assoc Inc **(PA)**	8011	E	707 573-6925	15556
Northwest General Engineering	1794	D	707 579-1163	1968
Northwest Insurance Agency Inc **(PA)**	6411	E	707 573-1300	10325
Novato Disposal Service Inc **(PA)**	4953	E	707 765-9995	8347
Oakmont Golf Club Inc	7992	D	707 538-2454	15015
OBrien Watters & Davis LLP	8111	E	707 545-7010	17348
Optical Coating Laboratory LLC **(HQ)**	3479	B	707 545-6440	4941
Optima Building Services Maint	7349	D	707 586-6640	11982
Orbis Wheels Inc	3841	F	415 548-4160	7015
ORourke Electric Inc	1731	E	707 528-8539	1557
Osseon LLC	3841	E	707 636-5940	7018
Oxbase Inc	3199	E	707 824-2560	4353
P & L Specialties	3559	F	707 573-3141	5162
Pacatte Construction Co Inc	1542	E	707 527-5983	934
Pacific Gas and Electric Co	4911	C	707 579-6337	8141
Pacific Gas and Electric Co	4911	C	800 756-7243	8150
Pacific Gas and Electric Co	4911	C	707 577-7283	8164
Pacific Shoring Products LLC **(PA)**	3479	D	707 575-9014	4944
Paragon Controls Incorporated	3822	F	707 579-1424	6703
Pearl Management Group Inc **(PA)**	8741	D	818 383-0095	19380
Pellenc America Inc **(DH)**	3523	E	707 568-7286	5016
Permanente Medical Group Inc	8011	A	707 393-4000	15597
Poppy Bank **(HQ)**	6022	D	707 636-9000	9744
Primrose Alzheimers Living Inc **(PA)**	8361	E	707 568-4355	18159
Promise Energy Inc	1711	E	707 938-7207	1339
Protective Business & Health	7374	D	845 354-5372	13746
Protonex LLC	3674	F	707 566-2260	6260
Provident Funding Assoc LP	6162	E	707 568-2420	9922
Quality Machine Engrg Inc	3599	E	707 528-1900	5606

GEOGRAPHIC

Employment Codes: A=Over 500 employees, B=251-500, C=101-250, D=51-100, E=20-50 F=10-19
2022 Northern California Business Directory and Buyers Guide

1221

	SIC	EMP	PHONE	ENTRY #
Quattrocchi Kwok Architects	8712	E	707 576-0829	18905
Rael Bernstein DDS A Prof Corp **(PA)**	8021	E	707 575-0600	15855
Randal Optimal Nutrients LLC	2834	E	707 528-1800	3969
Reach Medical Holdings LLC **(PA)**	4522	E	707 324-2400	7759
Recology Sonoma Marin	4953	B	707 586-8261	8353
Redwood Credit Union **(PA)**	6061	C	707 545-4000	9805
Redwood Empire Food Bank	8322	E	707 523-7900	17686
Redwood Empire Ice Oprtons LLC **(PA)**	7999	D	707 546-7147	15231
Redwood Empire Stereocasters	4832	E	707 528-4434	8031
Redwood Fmly Drmtlogy Med Asso	8011	E	707 545-4537	15642
Redwood Orthpdic Surgery Assoc	8011	E	707 544-3400	15643
Redwood Regional Hematology	8011	E	707 528-1050	15644
Redwood Regional Medical Group **(PA)**	8071	D	707 525-4080	16802
Redwood Toxicology Lab Inc	8071	C	707 577-7958	16804
Regal III LLC	5182	D	707 836-2100	9584
Results Radio LLC **(PA)**	4832	D	707 546-9185	8032
Reyes Group Enterprises Inc **(PA)**	7389	E	415 524-5909	14385
Richard Hancock Inc	1751	E	707 528-4900	1752
Russian River Winery Inc	2084	E	707 824-2005	2705
Saint Frncis Winery Tasting Rm	2084	E	707 833-4666	2706
Santa Rosa City of	7999	E	707 543-3421	15238
Santa Rosa City of	7538	E	707 543-3882	14590
Santa Rosa & Sonoma Co Real Es	6531	E	707 524-1124	10659
Santa Rosa Bus Lines	4131	D	707 543-3333	7416
Santa Rosa Community Hlth Ctrs **(PA)**	8011	C	707 547-2222	15674
Santa Rosa Dental Group	8021	E	707 545-0944	15857
Santa Rosa Memorial Hospital	8062	D	707 547-2221	16514
Santa Rosa Memorial Hospital	8062	D	707 542-4704	16515
Santa Rosa Orthpdics Med Group	8011	C	707 546-1922	15675
Santa Rosa Press Democrat Inc **(HQ)**	2711	B	707 546-2020	3477
Santa Rosa Radiology Med Group **(PA)**	8071	E	707 546-4062	16805
Santa Rosa Stain	3795	E	707 544-7777	6657
Santa Rosa Surgery Center LP	8062	E	707 575-5831	16517
Santa Rosaidence Opco LLC	8051	C	707 546-0471	16112
Scientific Molding Corp Ltd	3089	D	707 303-3041	4320
Scott Ag LLC	3993	F	707 545-4519	7251
Silara Medtech **(PA)**	3841	E	707 757-5750	7036
Simpson Sheet Metal Inc	1711	E	707 576-1500	1359
Sisters of St Joseph Orange	8082	A	747 206-9124	16946
SJ Cimino Electric Inc	1731	E	707 542-6231	1606
Slow Sculpture	8361	E	707 537-7024	18183
Sonoma Beverage Company LLC **(PA)**	2037	F	707 431-1099	2299
Sonoma Cnty Indian Hlth Prj In **(PA)**	8011	C	707 521-4545	15693
Sonoma Country Day School	8351	C	707 284-3200	18023
Sonoma County Airport Ex Inc	4111	B	707 837-8700	7360
Sonoma County Regional Parks	7033	D	707 527-2041	11621
Sonoma County Water Agency	4941	C	707 526-5370	8272
Sonoma Media Investments LLC **(PA)**	2711	D	707 526-8563	3481
Sonoma Metal Products Inc	3444	E	707 484-9876	4818
Sonoma Photonics Inc	3677	E	707 568-1202	6385
Sonoma Stainless	3443	F	707 546-3945	4731
Sotoyome Medical Building LLC	6512	D	707 525-4000	10409
Srss LLC	3449	F	707 544-7777	4864
Ss Skikos Incorporated	4214	D	707 575-3000	7634
St Joseph Hlth Nthrn Cal LLC **(DH)**	8062	A	707 546-3210	16537
St Joseph Home Health Network **(DH)**	8082	D	714 712-9500	16949
St Rose School	8351	E	707 545-0379	18032
Stx Inc	3949	E	707 284-3549	7201
Summit Electric Inc **(PA)**	1731	E	707 542-4773	1616
Summit Engineering Inc	8711	E	707 527-0775	18824
Summit Technology Group Inc	1731	E	707 542-4773	1617
Supercloset	3423	E	831 588-7829	4609
Sutter Health	8062	C	707 535-5600	16598
Sutter Health	8062	C	707 545-2255	16628
Sutter Health	8062	C	707 523-7253	16655
Sutter Med Group of Redwoods	8011	C	707 546-2788	15729
Tekberry Inc	7361	B	707 313-5345	12146
Tonnellerie Radoux Usa Inc	2449	F	707 284-2888	3243
Trans-India Products Inc	2844	E	707 544-0298	4097
Triformix Inc	3089	E	707 545-7645	4328
Tumelo Inc	2899	E	707 523-4411	4168
United Parcel Service Inc	7389	D	678 339-3171	14448
Valley Tire and Brake of Santa **(PA)**	7539	E	707 544-3420	14627
Veterans Health Administration	8011	C	707 570-3800	15799
Viavi Solutions Inc	3699	C	707 545-6440	6546
Victor Treatment Centers Inc	8361	E	707 360-1509	18200
Vintners Inn	7011	D	707 575-7350	11560
Volt Management Corp	7363	D	707 547-1660	12207
Volunteer Center Sonoma County **(PA)**	8322	E	707 573-3399	17782
West County Trnsp Agcy	4111	C	707 206-9988	7365
Wiggins Enterprises LLC **(PA)**	1731	E	707 545-7869	1637
Wildbrine LLC **(PA)**	2033	E	707 657-7607	2249
Winchster Interconnect Rf Corp	3679	A	707 573-1900	6483
Woodmont Real Estate Svcs LP	8999	E	707 569-0582	19921
Wright Contracting Inc	1522	E	707 528-1172	777
Wright Contracting LLC	1542	D	707 528-1172	993
Wright Engineered Plastics Inc	3544	E	707 575-1218	5088
Xpo Logistics Freight Inc	4213	D	707 584-0211	7616
Youngs Market Company LLC	5182	D	707 584-5170	9591

SARATOGA, CA - Santa Clara County

	SIC	EMP	PHONE	ENTRY #
3plus1 Technology Inc	3674	E	408 374-1111	6005
Aleyegn Inc **(PA)**	3841	D	301 758-2949	6937
Chateau Masson LLC	2084	E	408 741-7002	2531
Club At Los Gatos Inc	7991	D	408 867-5110	14936
Distinctive Corporation	7389	E	408 568-5598	14256
Dtex Systems Inc	7371	E	408 418-3786	12405
Help & Care LLC **(PA)**	8082	D	408 384-4412	16888
I Merit Inc	7374	A	504 226-2427	13721
Kasra Investments LLC	7389	E	408 464-0074	14315
Montalvo Association	8422	D	408 961-5800	18294
Odd Fellows Home California	8361	B	408 741-7100	18152
Opinr Inc	7371	D	646 207-3000	12653
Our Lady Fatima Villa Inc	8051	D	408 741-2950	16088
Precious Enterprises Inc	8351	D	408 265-2226	18003
Progressive Sub-Acute Care	8062	D	408 378-8875	16484
Santa Clara County of	1799	E	408 573-3050	2065
Saratoga Country Club Inc	7997	D	408 253-0340	15137
Savannah Chanelle Vineyards	2084	E	301 758-2338	2709
Stage 4 Solutions Incorporated	8742	E	408 868-9739	19638
Tessolve Services Inc **(DH)**	3826	D	408 865-0873	6856
United Supertek Inc	3672	F	408 922-0730	5993
Vintellus Inc	7372	F	510 972-4710	13519
Young MNS Chrstn Assn Slcon Vl	8699	C	408 370-1877	18609
Zeesoft Inc **(PA)**	7371	E	408 247-2987	12936

SAUSALITO, CA - Marin County

	SIC	EMP	PHONE	ENTRY #
Alta Mira Recovery Ctrs LLC	7011	D	415 332-1350	10920
American Media Corp	2741	F	800 652-0778	3554
Bay Area Discovery Museum	8412	E	415 339-3900	18262
Bay City Capital MGT LLC **(PA)**	6211	C	415 676-3830	9956
Boyd Lighting Fixture Company **(PA)**	3646	E	415 778-4300	5733
Butler Shine Stern Prtners LLC	7311	C	415 331-6049	11743
C P Shades Inc **(PA)**	2339	F	415 331-4581	3008
Casa Madrona Hotel and Spa LLC	7011	A	415 332-0502	10993
Cavallo Point LLC **(PA)**	7011	D	415 339-4700	10997
Coastal Intl Holdings LLC **(PA)**	7389	C	415 339-1700	14231
Cthulhu Ventures LLC **(PA)**	6282	E	415 444-9602	10042
Do Big Things LLC	7371	E	415 806-3423	12397
Gate Five Group LLC	5023	E	415 339-9500	8512
Headlands Center For Arts	8699	E	415 331-2787	18568
Humanconcepts LLC	7372	E	650 581-2500	13217
Marin Magazine Inc	2721	E	415 332-4800	3507
Marine Mammal Center **(PA)**	0742	E	415 339-0430	330
Mpl Brands Inc **(PA)**	2084	E	888 513-3022	2661
Paul Ryan Associates	1521	D	415 861-3085	681
Steelrver Infrstrcture Prtners **(PA)**	6719	C	415 512-1515	10741
Swa Group **(PA)**	0781	D	415 332-5100	442
Teijin Pharma USA LLC	5131	A	415 893-1518	9242
Tony Marterie & Associates Inc	2335	E	415 331-7150	3003
Ubics Inc	7371	C	415 289-1400	12883
Waggl Inc **(PA)**	7372	D	415 399-9949	13524
Wested	8733	E	415 289-2300	19247
Young MNS Chrstn Assn San Frnc	8641	E	415 331-9622	18521

SCOTIA, CA - Humboldt County

	SIC	EMP	PHONE	ENTRY #
Humboldt Redwood Company LLC **(HQ)**	5031	C	707 764-4472	8553

SCOTTS VALLEY, CA - Santa Cruz County

	SIC	EMP	PHONE	ENTRY #
AV Now Inc	3651	E	831 425-2500	5752
Ava The Rabbit Haven Inc	8748	D	831 600-7479	19724
Bell Sports Inc **(HQ)**	3949	D	469 417-6600	7188
Best Western Inn Inc	7011	E	831 438-6666	10957
Bfp Fire Protection Inc	1711	D	831 461-1100	1219
Canepa Group Inc	7532	E	831 430-9940	14523
Digital Dynamics Inc	3823	E	831 438-4444	6715
Education Training & RES Assoc **(PA)**	2731	D	831 438-4060	3533
Ert Operating Company	7371	A	412 390-3000	12427
Etr Associates Inc	8322	D	831 438-4060	17555
Expert Semiconductor Tech Inc	3559	E	831 439-9300	5150
Extraview Corporation	7371	E	831 461-7100	12439
Fox Factory Inc	3714	E	831 274-6545	6581
Hospice of Santa Cruz County **(PA)**	8082	C	831 430-3000	16896
Inn At Scotts Valley LLC	7011	D	831 440-1000	11191
Intrado Interactive Svcs Corp	4822	D	888 527-5225	8013
J A-Co Machine Works LLC	3599	E	877 429-8175	5544
John Stewart Company	6531	E	831 438-5725	10587
Kaiser Foundation Hospitals	8011	C	831 430-2700	15474
Maxtor Corporation **(DH)**	3572	D	831 438-6550	5299
Morgan Stnley Smith Barney LLC	6211	D	831 440-5200	10004
Oxford Instrs X-Ray Tech Inc	3679	D	831 439-9729	6466
Pacific Coast Ingredients **(PA)**	2087	F	831 316-7137	2820
Pacific Coast Products LLC	2087	E	831 316-7137	2821
Pacific Sthwest Cnfrnce of Eva	6512	C	831 335-9133	10398
Pandora Data Systems Inc	7372	D	831 429-8900	13361
Physicans Med Group Santa Cruz	8621	E	831 465-7800	18344
R W Garcia Co Inc **(PA)**	5145	E	408 287-4616	9356
Roi Communications Inc **(PA)**	8742	D	831 430-0170	19625
Scarborough Lbr & Bldg Sup Inc **(PA)**	5031	D	831 438-0331	8606
Scotts Valley Magnetics Inc	3677	E	831 438-3600	6383
Scotts Vly Fire Protection Dst	7389	D	831 438-0211	14400
Sheraton LLC	7011	D	831 438-1500	11468
Spraytronics Inc	3479	E	408 988-3636	4950
Sunopta Globl Orgnic Ingrdnts **(DH)**	2035	E	831 685-6506	2287
Tapemation Machining Inc **(PA)**	3599	E	831 438-3069	5626
Thermo Kevex X-Ray Inc	3671	D	831 438-5940	5904
Threshold Enterprises Ltd **(PA)**	2833	B	831 438-6851	3822
Tradin Organics USA LLC	2099	E	831 685-6565	2948
Warmboard Inc	3567	E	831 685-9276	5219
Weatherflow-Tempest Inc	8999	E	831 438-9742	19920

SEBASTOPOL, CA - Sonoma County

	SIC	EMP	PHONE	ENTRY #
Alasco Rubber & Plastics Corp	3069	F	707 823-5270	4212
Andys Produce Market Inc	5148	E	707 823-8661	9387
Apple Vly Cnvalescent Hosp Inc	8051	D	707 823-7675	15909
Catherine-Elizabeth Inc **(PA)**	2084	E	707 827-1655	2526

	SIC	EMP	PHONE	ENTRY #
Copperfields Books Inc **(PA)**	6512	E	707 823-8991	10384
County of Sonoma	8062	C	707 823-8511	16340
Dutton Ranch Corp	0175	D	707 823-0448	99
Guayaki Sstnble Rnfrest Pdts I **(PA)**	5149	E	888 482-9254	9452
Integrity Cnstr Maint Inc	1542	E	707 829-5300	893
Iron Horse Ranch & Vineyard	0172	E	707 887-1507	57
Iron Horse Vineyards	2084	E	707 887-1909	2621
Kone Inc	7699	E	707 778-2247	14758
Kosta Browne Wines LLC	2084	E	707 823-7430	2641
Magito & Company LLC	2084	F	707 567-1521	2653
Manzana Products Co Inc	2033	E	707 823-5313	2225
Meredith Vineyard Estate Inc	2084	F	707 823-7466	2658
North Bay Fire	0851	D	707 823-1084	535
North Landscaping Inc	0781	E	707 827-7980	428
OReilly Media Inc **(PA)**	2741	C	707 827-7000	3587
Pacific Landscapes Inc **(PA)**	0781	E	707 829-8064	433
Park Avenue Turf Inc	0782	E	707 823-8899	493
Rdi Finishing	2434	E	707 829-1226	3189
Redwood Hill Farm & Crmry Inc **(DH)**	0241	D	707 823-8250	220
Safari Books Online LLC **(PA)**	2741	D	707 827-7000	3597
Silverwood Management Inc **(PA)**	6513	D	703 777-8322	10460
Slauson Transmission Parts	7537	E	310 768-2099	14542
Socratic Technologies Inc **(PA)**	8732	E	415 430-2200	19186
Solmetric Corporation	3829	D	707 823-4600	6923
Taft Street Inc	2084	E	707 823-2049	2737
Taylor Maid Farms LLC	2095	E	707 824-9110	2847
Thinkwave Inc	3695	F	707 824-6200	6507
Thomas Dehlinger	2084	E	707 823-2378	2740
Traditional Medicinals Inc **(PA)**	2099	C	707 823-8911	2949
Weeks Drilling and Pump Co **(PA)**	1711	E	707 823-3184	1397

SELMA, CA - Fresno County

	SIC	EMP	PHONE	ENTRY #
Adventist Health Selma	8062	B	559 891-1000	16286
Adventist Hlth Systm/West Corp	8062	D	559 856-6110	16305
Adventist Hlth Systm/West Corp	8062	D	559 856-6090	16315
Bethel Lutheran Home Inc	8059	D	559 896-4900	16218
Circle K Ranch **(PA)**	0175	D	559 834-1571	98
F R O Inc	8748	E	559 891-0237	19772
Fresno Cnty Ecnmic Opprtnties	8322	E	559 896-0142	17579
Fresno Valves & Castings Inc **(PA)**	4971	C	559 834-2511	8411
Golden State Utility Co	1623	E	559 896-6690	1105
Harris Ranch Beef Company	2011	A	559 896-3081	2098
Imperial Western Products Inc	5159	D	559 891-2600	9507
Kaiser Foundation Hospitals	6324	C	559 898-6000	10137
Khalsa Transportation Inc	4213	E	559 697-6557	7558
Lion Raisins Inc **(PA)**	2034	C	559 834-6677	2261
Nia Healthcare Services Inc	8051	E	559 896-4990	16069
Omex Agrifluids Inc	2873	F	559 661-6138	4135
P&P International Inc	5113	F	559 891-9888	9216
Pacific Gas and Electric Co	4911	C	559 891-2143	8158
Partsflex Inc	2396	E	408 677-7121	3047
Psas Inc	7011	E	559 896-1443	11378
Quinn Lift Inc **(HQ)**	5082	E	559 896-4040	9026
Robert Alves Farms Inc	0172	D	559 896-3309	72
Selma Pallet Inc	2448	E	559 896-7171	3229
Star Transport LLC	4789	E	559 834-3021	7895
TG Schmeiser Co Inc	3523	F	559 268-8128	5019
Wood-N-Wood Products Cal Inc	2449	F	559 896-3636	3246

SHASTA LAKE, CA - Shasta County

	SIC	EMP	PHONE	ENTRY #
Knauf Insulation Inc	3296	C	530 275-9665	4533
Sierra Pacific Industries	2421	E	530 275-8851	3112

SHINGLE SPRINGS, CA - El Dorado County

	SIC	EMP	PHONE	ENTRY #
Calnet Inc	4813	D	530 672-1078	7937
Harpers Model Home Services	7349	E	916 335-0282	11959
M & W Engineering Inc	3599	E	530 676-7185	5564
Pw Eagle Inc	3084	D	530 677-2286	4235
Salutary Sports Clubs Inc	7991	E	530 677-5705	14970
Straight Line Roofing & Cnstr	1761	E	530 672-9995	1840

SLOUGHHOUSE, CA - Sacramento County

	SIC	EMP	PHONE	ENTRY #
Rancho Murieta Cmnty Svcs Dst	4941	E	916 354-3700	8259

SMARTSVILLE, CA - Nevada County

	SIC	EMP	PHONE	ENTRY #
Pacific Coast Stage Lighting	3648	F	916 765-4396	5748

SMITH RIVER, CA - Del Norte County

	SIC	EMP	PHONE	ENTRY #
Reservation Ranch **(PA)**	7011	E	707 487-3516	11398
Smith River Lucky 7 Casino	7011	C	707 487-7777	11489

SNELLING, CA - Merced County

	SIC	EMP	PHONE	ENTRY #
JS Homen Trucking Inc	4212	D	209 723-9559	7477
Merced Irrigation District	4911	D	209 378-2421	8124

SODA SPRINGS, CA - Nevada County

	SIC	EMP	PHONE	ENTRY #
Boreal Ridge Corporation	7011	C	530 426-1012	10967
Royal Gorge Nordic Ski Resort **(PA)**	7011	C	530 426-3871	11421

SONOMA, CA - Sonoma County

	SIC	EMP	PHONE	ENTRY #
3 Badge Beverage Corporation	2084	F	707 343-1167	2500
360 Viansa LLC	7299	E	707 935-4700	11704
After-Party2 Inc	7359	D	408 457-1187	12028
All-Truss Inc	2439	E	707 938-5595	3199
Appellation Tours Inc	4725	E	707 938-8001	7814
Arbor Fence Inc	3446	E	707 938-3133	4834
Arrowhead Mountain Winery Corp **(PA)**	5182	E	707 938-3254	9565
Artisan Bakers	5149	D	707 939-1765	9437
AV Brands Inc	5182	E	410 884-9463	9566
Beaver Dam Health Care Center	8051	E	707 938-1096	15943
Bookheaded Learning LLC	8351	D	707 996-3427	17865
Bright Event Rentals LLC	7359	D	310 202-0011	12032
Broderick General Engineering	1611	E	707 996-7809	1017
Broderick General Engineering	3531	D	707 996-7809	5025
Carneros Vintners Inc	0722	F	707 933-9349	261
CP Opco LLC	7359	D	707 253-2332	12037
CP Opco LLC	7359	D	650 652-0300	12038
CP Opco LLC	7359	E	916 444-6120	12039
Diageo North America Inc	2084	D	707 939-6200	2549
El Pueblo Motel Inc	7011	D	707 996-3651	11075
Emeritus Corporation	8052	C	707 996-7101	16182
Ensign Sonoma LLC	8051	C	707 938-8406	15992
Enterprise Vineyards Inc	0172	E	707 996-6513	52
Evehrtay LLC **(PA)**	2084	E	707 293-3033	2564
Fastening Systems Intl	5072	E	707 935-1170	8982
Four Sisters Inns	7011	D	707 939-1340	11104
Franciscan Vineyards Inc	2084	D	707 933-2332	2580
Freixenet Sonoma Caves Inc	2084	E	707 996-4981	2588
Freixenet Usa Inc	5182	D	707 996-7256	9578
Gary D Nelson Associates Inc **(PA)**	7361	E	707 935-6113	12091
Groskopf Warehouse & Logistics	2084	E	707 939-3100	2607
Hanzell Vineyards	2084	F	707 996-3860	2612
Innerstave LLC	2449	E	707 996-8781	3236
Jacuzzi Family Vineyards LLC	2084	E	707 931-7500	2629
Krave Pure Foods Inc	2013	D	707 939-9176	2119
LAuberge De Sonoma LLC	7011	C	707 938-2929	11258
Longs Drug Stores Cal LLC	7384	C	707 938-4734	14173
Monica Bruce Designs Inc	2396	F	707 938-0277	3046
North Counties Drywall Inc	1742	E	707 996-0198	1696
Opal Moon Winery LLC	2084	F	707 996-0420	2674
Pacific Union Intl Inc	6163	D	707 934-2300	9944
Rams Gate Winery LLC	2084	E	707 721-8700	2692
Renaissance Hotel Holdings Inc	7011	E	707 935-6600	11394
Retail Realm Distribution Inc **(PA)**	5141	D	707 996-5400	9291
Rsj Ventures LLC	2013	E	212 905-8666	2122
Sabel Engineering Corporation	3565	E	707 938-4771	5202
Sebastiani Vineyards Inc	2084	D	707 933-3200	2711
Sonoma Access Ctrl Systems Inc	3446	E	707 935-3458	4839
Sonoma Acres Convalescent Inc	8051	E	707 996-2161	16124
Sonoma Gourmet Inc	2035	E	707 939-3700	2286
Sonoma Hotel Operator Inc	7011	B	707 938-9000	11491
Sonoma Index-Tribune	2711	E	707 938-2111	3480
Sonoma National Golf Club	7997	D	707 939-4100	15148
Sonoma Pins Etc Corporation	2759	E	707 996-9956	3749
Sonoma Specialty Foods Inc	5149	E	707 939-3700	9487
Sonoma Valley Cmnty Hlth Ctr	8011	E	707 939-6070	15694
Sonoma Valley Health Care Dst **(PA)**	8062	B	707 935-5000	16529
Sonoma Valley Unified Schl Dst	7349	D	707 935-4291	12000
Sonomaidence Opco LLC	8052	D	707 938-1096	16206
Speedway Sonoma LLC	7948	D	707 938-8448	14918
Stone Edge Winery LLC	2084	F	707 935-6520	2731
Swiss Hotel Group Inc	7011	D	707 938-2884	11523
Three Sticks Wines LLC	2084	E	707 996-3328	2743
V Sangiacomo & Sons	0172	E	707 938-5503	80
Valley of Moon Winery	2084	F	707 939-4500	2753
Vineburg Wine Company Inc **(PA)**	2084	E	707 938-5277	2758
Vintage Senior Management Inc	6513	E	707 595-0009	10467
Vode Lighting LLC	3645	F	707 996-9898	5728
Wine Communications Group	2721	F	707 939-0822	3520
Wine Country Pty & Events LLC **(PA)**	7359	D	707 940-6060	12066

SONORA, CA - Tuolumne County

	SIC	EMP	PHONE	ENTRY #
Adventist Health Sonora	8062	E	209 536-5000	16287
Adventist Health Sonora	8062	E	209 536-5070	16288
Adventist Health Sonora	8062	E	209 532-0126	16289
Adventist Health Sonora	8062	E	209 532-3167	16290
Adventist Health Sonora **(HQ)**	8062	A	209 532-5000	16292
Adventist Health Sonora	8062	E	209 536-5770	16293
Adventist Health Sonora	8062	E	209 536-3900	16294
Adventist Health Sonora	8062	E	209 536-5060	16295
Adventist Health Sonora	8062	E	209 536-2665	16296
Adventist Health System/West	8062	D	209 532-3161	16300
Adventist Health System/West	8062	D	209 536-5043	16302
Adventist Hlth Systm/West Corp	8062	D	209 536-5700	16317
Alderman Timber Company Inc	2411	E	209 532-9636	3054
American National Red Cross	8322	E	209 533-1513	17424
Avalon Care Ctr - Sonora LLC	8051	C	209 533-2500	15920
Brandelli Arts Inc	3299	E	714 537-0969	4535
California Gold Dev Corp	1542	E	209 533-3333	850
Clark Pest Ctrl Stockton Inc	7342	E	209 532-3464	11889
Diestel Turkey Ranch **(PA)**	0253	C	209 532-4950	236
Donaldson Arthur M D Inc	8011	D	209 532-0966	15383
Front Porch Inc **(PA)**	7371	D	209 288-5500	12462
Interntnal Ch of Frsqare Gospl	7032	E	209 532-4295	11605
Kanthal Thermal Process Inc	3559	D	209 533-1990	5156
Kinematic Automation Inc	3841	D	209 532-3200	6995
Kingsview Corp	8093	E	209 533-6245	17032
L K Lehman Trucking	3273	E	209 532-5586	4490
Leslie Heavy Haul LLC	7389	E	209 840-1664	14321
Mother Lode Job Training	8331	E	209 533-8211	17824
Pacific Gas and Electric Co	4911	C	916 904-9035	8151
Sierra Intrnal Mdcine Med Grou	8011	C	209 536-3738	15684
Sierra Mountain Cnstr Inc	8322	D	209 928-1900	17745
Sierra Pacific Industries	2421	E	530 378-8301	3109
Sierra Repertory Theatre Inc	7922	E	209 532-0502	14863
Sonora Community Hospital	8011	C	209 536-5012	15695
Sonora Sport & Fitnes Ctr Inc **(PA)**	7991	E	209 532-1202	14972
Tuolumne Utilities District	4941	D	209 532-5536	8277

GEOGRAPHIC

Employment Codes: A=Over 500 employees, B=251-500, C=101-250, D=51-100, E=20-50 F=10-19
2022 Northern California Business Directory and Buyers Guide
© Mergent Inc. 1-800-342-5647
1223

SONORA, CA

	SIC	EMP	PHONE	ENTRY #
Watch Resources Inc (PA)	8322	E	209 533-0510	17784

SOQUEL, CA - Santa Cruz County

	SIC	EMP	PHONE	ENTRY #
Bay Photo Inc	7221	C	831 475-6090	11672
Bowman & Williams A Cal Corp	8711	D	831 426-3560	18644
Design Octaves	3089	E	831 464-8500	4278
Junopacific Inc	3089	C	831 462-1141	4293
Kennolyn Camp Inc	7032	E	831 479-6714	11608
Provac Sales Inc	3561	E	831 462-8900	5178
Soquel Creek Water District	4941	E	831 475-0195	8273
Sutter Health	8062	C	831 458-6272	16603
System Studies Incorporated	3661	E	831 475-5777	5811

SOUTH DOS PALOS, CA - Merced County

	SIC	EMP	PHONE	ENTRY #
Koda Farms Inc	2044	E	209 392-2191	2325

SOUTH LAKE TAHOE, CA - El Dorado County

	SIC	EMP	PHONE	ENTRY #
Alpine Carpets Corporation (PA)	1752	D	530 541-6171	1763
Americana Vacation Resorts Inc (PA)	6531	E	530 544-8463	10490
Barton Memorial Hospital (HQ)	8062	A	530 541-3420	16325
Belmont Corporation	7011	D	530 542-1101	10950
California Tahoe Conservancy	8999	E	530 542-5580	19898
Cha-Dor Realty LLC	5031	E	530 544-2237	8535
Environmental Incentives LLC (PA)	8748	D	530 541-2980	19768
Healthcare Barton System (PA)	8062	A	530 541-3420	16387
Holiday Inn Express	7011	E	530 544-5900	11151
Kemper & Sons Masonry Inc	1741	E	530 600-3697	1650
Lake Tahoe Historical Society	8699	E	530 541-5458	18576
Lcof Lake Tahoe Operating LLC	7011	E	530 541-6722	11259
Liberty Utlties Clpeco Elc LLC	4911	D	800 782-2506	8120
Marriots Tmber Ldge At Lk Thoe	7011	D	530 542-8416	11286
Patrick Baginski	0782	E	530 544-8873	495
Richardson Camp Resort Inc (PA)	7021	E	530 542-6570	11593
Roppong-Thoe LP A Cal Ltd Prtn	7011	E	530 544-5400	11418
Saa Sierra Programs LLC	8641	D	530 541-1244	18457
Sierra-Tahoe Ready Mix Inc	3273	E	530 541-1877	4507
South Tahoe Public Utility Dst	4952	C	530 544-6474	8291
South Tahoe Refuse Co	4953	D	530 541-5105	8364
Stateline Travelodge Inc	7011	E	530 544-6000	11506
Steven P Abelow MD	8011	E	530 544-8033	15704
Tahoe Beach & Ski Club	7011	D	530 541-6220	11526
Tahoe Keys Resort	6531	E	530 544-5459	10668
Tahoe Seasons Resort Time Inte	6531	E	530 541-6700	10669
United Parcel Service Inc	7389	D	800 742-5877	14450

SOUTH SAN FRANCISCO, CA - San Mateo County

	SIC	EMP	PHONE	ENTRY #
4into1 Inc	3751	C	650 741-6175	6646
Abbvie Stemcentrx LLC	8733	C	415 298-9242	19193
ABM Aviation Inc	4581	D	650 872-5400	7762
ABS-Cbn International (DH)	4841	C	800 527-2820	8058
Achaogen Inc	2834	C	650 800-3636	3831
Aclara Biosciences Inc	3829	E	800 297-2728	6890
Acme Bread Co	2051	F	650 938-2978	2359
Aegis Senior Communities LLC	8082	E	650 952-6100	16841
Aeroground Inc (DH)	4581	A	650 266-6965	7763
Akero Therapeutics Inc (PA)	2834	F	650 487-6488	3838
Alector LLC (HQ)	8731	C	415 231-5660	19013
Aligos Therapeutics Inc (PA)	2836	D	800 466-6059	4033
Allogene Therapeutics Inc	8731	C	650 457-2700	19017
Alpha Rstoration Waterproofing	1542	E	650 875-7500	821
Alvah Contractors Inc	1731	B	650 741-6785	1448
Alx Oncology Holdings Inc (PA)	2834	C	650 466-7125	3842
Ambys Medicines Inc	8731	E	650 481-7662	19022
American Etc Inc	7211	B	650 873-5353	11626
American Tech Netwrk Corp (PA)	3827	E	800 910-2862	6865
Amgen Inc	2834	E	650 244-2000	3844
Amunix Pharmaceutical Inc	8731	E	650 428-1800	19024
Andrighetto Produce Inc (PA)	5148	C	650 588-0930	9386
Annexon Inc (PA)	2834	E	650 822-5500	3847
Apple Six Hospitality MGT	7011	E	650 872-1515	10927
Applied Molecular Trnspt Inc	2834	D	650 392-0420	3851
Arsenal Biosciences Inc	8731	D	858 945-3091	19030
Ashbury Market Inc	5149	E	650 952-8889	9438
Assembly Biosciences Inc (PA)	2834	E	833 509-4583	3857
Astrazeneca LP	2834	E	650 634-0103	3859
Atara Biotherapeutics Inc (PA)	2836	C	650 278-8930	4036
Audentes Therapeutics Inc	2836	E	415 818-1001	4039
Axl Musical Instruments Co Ltd (PA)	3931	E	415 508-1398	7170
B Metal Fabrication Inc	3441	E	650 615-7705	4645
B&R Maintenance Inc	7349	E	650 589-0331	11923
Balliet Bros Construction Corp	1542	E	650 871-9000	827
Bay Area Herbs & Spc LLC	5148	E	650 583-0857	9388
Bay Area Systems Solutions Inc	1731	E	650 295-1600	1460
Bay Contract Maintenance Inc	7349	E	650 737-5902	11925
Berlin Food & Lab Equipment Co	3821	E	650 589-4231	6691
Bertetta Tanklines Inc	4213	E	650 872-2900	7508
Biocheck Inc (HQ)	3841	D	650 573-1968	6955
Black Car Network LLC (PA)	4111	E	877 277-0208	7325
Blade Therapeutics Inc	2834	E	650 334-2079	3871
Blue Bus Tours LLC	4725	C	415 353-5310	7816
Blue Line Transfer Inc	4953	E	650 589-5511	8310
Bon Appetit Management Co	8741	C	650 467-3767	19306
Boosted Inc (PA)	3949	E	650 933-5151	7189
Box Lunch Company Inc	5141	E	650 589-1886	9263
Brightseed Bio	8071	E	415 965-7778	16775
Business Extension Bureau Ltd	2721	E	650 737-5700	3492
Calico Life Sciences LLC	8731	D	650 754-6200	19038
California Cryobank Inc	8099	B	650 635-1420	17113
Califrnia Golf CLB San Frncsco	7997	D	650 588-9021	15068
Calithera Biosciences Inc	2834	D	650 870-1000	3876
Calpico Inc	3643	E	650 588-2241	5712
Caredx Inc (PA)	8071	B	415 287-2300	16776
Catalyst Bio Inc (HQ)	2834	F	650 871-0761	3878
Catalyst Biosciences Inc (PA)	2834	F	650 871-0761	3879
Cedarlane Natural Foods North	2099	E	650 742-0444	2880
Centra Freight Services Inc (PA)	4783	D	650 873-8147	7865
Centrix Builders Inc	1521	D	650 876-9400	626
Cephas Enterprises Inc	7349	E	650 244-0310	11934
Chrissa Imports Ltd	5181	E	650 877-8460	9547
City Baking Company	2051	D	650 332-8730	2373
Clara Foods Co	2034	E	415 570-1535	2257
Clic LLC	2752	E	415 421-2900	3636
Coleman Company Inc	3086	C	650 837-9178	4241
Comentis Inc	8733	E	650 869-7600	19211
Comfort Suites	7011	E	650 589-7100	11029
Comparenetworks Inc (PA)	8731	D	650 873-9031	19046
Contractors Scaffold Sup Inc	7359	E	650 871-8190	12036
Corbion Biotech Inc (HQ)	2099	E	650 780-4777	2886
Cortexyme Inc (PA)	2836	F	415 910-5717	4043
Crown Energy Services Inc	8711	A	415 546-6534	18678
Cytokinetics Incorporated (PA)	2834	C	650 624-3000	3889
Cytomx Therapeutics Inc	2834	D	650 515-3185	3890
D P Nicoli Inc	5051	F	650 873-2999	8814
Dbi Beverage San Francisco	5181	C	415 643-9900	9549
Denali Therapeutics Inc (PA)	2836	D	650 866-8548	4044
Dice Molecules Sv Inc	2834	F	650 566-1402	3893
Digitalist USA Ltd	7373	A	949 278-1354	13577
Djont/Cmb Ssf Leasing LLC	7011	E	650 589-3400	11052
Djont/Cmb Ssf Leasing LLC	7011	D	650 589-3400	11053
Dpw Inc	1711	E	650 588-8482	1252
Education Elements Inc	7372	E	650 440-7860	13134
Electroneek Robotics Inc	7371	D	650 600-9550	12418
Emerald Cloud Lab Inc	8731	C	650 257-7554	19055
Epibiome Inc (HQ)	2835	F	650 825-1600	4021
Essence Printing Inc (PA)	2752	E	650 952-5072	3644
Exelixis Inc	2834	C	650 837-8254	3895
Fern Electric & Control Inc	1731	E	650 952-3203	1504
First Databank Inc (DH)	2741	D	800 633-3453	3571
Five Prime Therapeutics Inc	2834	F	415 365-5600	3898
Fluidigm Corporation (PA)	3826	A	650 266-6000	6830
Fluidigm Sciences Inc	3826	E	408 900-7205	6831
Fly With Y LLC	6531	E	844 435-9948	10550
Fonco Inc	1761	F	650 873-4585	1803
Frank M Booth Inc	1711	C	650 871-8292	1267
Freenome Holdings Inc	2835	E	650 446-6630	4022
Friends To Parents	8351	E	650 588-8212	17939
Frontier Medicines	2834	E	650 457-1005	3903
Fusion Ranch Inc	2013	E	650 589-8899	2118
Gamut Smart Media From Cox LLC	4899	E	650 392-6238	8077
Genentech Inc	2834	E	650 225-2911	3906
Genentech Inc (DH)	2834	A	650 225-1000	3907
Genentech Inc	2834	C	408 963-8759	3908
Genentech Inc	2834	C	650 225-3214	3910
Genentech Inc	2834	C	650 225-1000	3911
Genentech Usa Inc	2834	A	650 225-1000	3913
Genmark Diagnostics Inc (DH)	3841	A	650 225-1000	6978
Giannini Garden Ornaments Inc	3272	E	650 873-4493	4436
Giant Horse Printing Inc	2752	F	650 875-7137	3652
Gino Morena Enterprises LLC (PA)	7231	E	800 227-6905	11682
Giustos Specialty Foods LLC (PA)	2041	E	650 873-6566	2311
Global Blood Therapeutics Inc (PA)	2834	B	650 741-7700	3919
Graphic Sportswear LLC	2759	E	415 206-7200	3735
Grosvenor Properties Ltd	7011	C	650 873-3200	11122
Harpoon Therapeutics Inc	8731	E	650 443-7400	19065
Hoem & Associates Inc	1752	E	650 871-5194	1773
Homestead Ravioli Company	2032	F	910 755-6802	2200
Ideaya Biosciences Inc	2834	D	650 443-6209	3925
Ignyta Inc (HQ)	2834	E	858 255-5959	3926
Insitro Inc	8731	D	650 488-1789	19074
Inter-City Cleaners	7216	D	650 875-9200	11654
Intermune Inc (DH)	2834	E	415 466-4383	3930
Interstate Grading and Pav Inc	1611	E	650 952-7333	1051
Isec Incorporated	1751	E	650 872-1391	1741
Italfoods Inc	5141	D	650 877-0724	9274
J F Fitzgerald Company Inc	2512	E	415 648-6161	3288
Jacobs Farm/Del Cabo Inc	0191	D	650 827-1133	174
Janssen Alzheimer Immunothera	8731	D	650 794-2500	19076
Janssen Biopharma Inc	2834	E	650 635-5500	3933
Japanese Weekend Inc (PA)	2339	E	415 621-0555	3011
JMB Construction Inc	1542	E	650 267-5300	903
Junk King (PA)	4212	C	888 888-5865	7478
Kaiser Foundation Hospitals	8011	C	650 742-2000	15484
Kezar Life Sciences Inc	2834	E	650 822-5600	3935
L B C Holdings U S A Corp (PA)	4724	C	650 873-0750	7802
Larkspur Hsptality Dev MGT LLC	7011	E	650 827-1515	11251
Larkspur Hsptality Dev MGT LLC	7011	E	650 872-1515	11255
Leadstack Inc	7361	D	628 200-3063	12103
Legalmatchcom (PA)	8111	E	415 946-0800	17314
Lehar Sales Co	5144	D	510 465-3255	9347
Lenaco Corporation	5085	E	650 873-3500	9121
Liberty Bank (PA)	6022	E	650 871-2400	9737
Lithotype Company Inc (PA)	2752	D	650 871-1750	3675
Lotus Hospitality Inc	7011	E	650 737-5700	11270
Lyell Immunopharma Inc (PA)	8731	C	650 695-0677	19086
Mad Dog Express Inc (PA)	4212	D	650 588-1900	7480

	SIC	EMP	PHONE	ENTRY #
Magnolia Lane Soft HM Furn Inc	2392	E	650 624-0700	3028
Matagrano Inc	5181	C	650 829-4829	9556
Medical Care Professionals Inc	8051	E	650 583-9898	16061
Medical Linen Service Inc	7213	D	650 873-1221	11637
Mentor Tchnical Group Intl LLC	8742	E	787 743-0897	19573
Meyers Sheet Metal Box Inc	3444	E	650 873-8889	4789
Monogram Biosciences Inc	2835	B	650 635-1100	4027
Monster Inc **(PA)**	5099	B	415 840-2000	9199
Montgomery-Sansome LP	1542	E	650 689-5622	925
Myriad Womens Health Inc	8071	B	888 268-6795	16790
Nassau-Sosnick Dist Co LLC **(PA)**	5149	D	650 952-2226	9467
Neurona Therapeutics Inc	8731	E	510 366-1177	19092
New Hong Kong Noodle Co Inc	2098	E	650 588-6425	2864
Nexsteppe Inc	2048	F	650 887-5700	2349
Nexsteppe Seeds Inc	2869	E	650 887-5700	4126
Ngm Biopharmaceuticals Inc **(PA)**	2834	C	650 243-5555	3954
Nkarta Inc	2834	D	415 582-4923	3956
Nomis Solutions Inc **(PA)**	7371	C	650 588-9800	12636
Oneto Manufacturing Co Inc	3444	E	650 875-1710	4798
Oric Pharmaceuticals Inc	2834	D	650 388-5600	3959
Pacific Market International **(PA)**	8742	D	650 238-1059	19600
Panalpina Inc	4731	E	650 825-3036	7848
Park n Fly Llc	7521	E	650 877-8438	14515
Pathways Home Health	8099	E	650 634-0133	17166
Patrick J Ruane Inc	1742	D	650 616-7676	1697
Peking Handicraft Inc **(PA)**	5023	C	650 871-3788	8518
Peninou French Ldry & Clrs Inc **(PA)**	7219	D	800 392-2532	11671
Peninsula Family Service	8322	D	650 952-6848	17671
Pennisula Pthlogists Med Group	8071	C	650 616-2940	16792
Permanente Medical Group Inc	6324	B	650 827-6500	10150
Phantom Auto Inc	8711	E	510 284-9898	18791
Pharmacyclics LLC **(HQ)**	2834	A	408 215-3000	3962
Pionyr Immunotherapeutics Inc	2834	E	415 226-7503	3964
Plenty Unlimited Inc **(PA)**	0191	C	650 735-3737	186
Plexxikon Inc	2834	E	510 647-4000	3965
Portola Pharmaceuticals Inc **(DH)**	8731	B	650 246-7300	19105
Pribuss Engineering Inc	7623	D	650 588-0447	14688
Principia Biopharma Inc **(HQ)**	2834	D	650 416-7700	3966
Prothena Biosciences Inc	8733	E	650 837-8550	19231
Prothena Corp Pub Ltd Co	2833	E	650 837-8550	3820
Pyramid Graphics	2752	E	650 871-0290	3687
Quality Systems Instlltons Ltd	1799	D	650 875-9000	2059
R & S Erection N Peninsula Inc	1751	E	415 467-5630	1751
Race Telecommunications Inc **(PA)**	4813	D	650 246-8900	7985
Rapt Therapeutics Inc	2834	D	650 489-9000	3972
Raven Biotechnologies Inc	8731	C	650 624-2600	19115
Renesas Electronics Amer Inc	3674	A	408 588-6750	6273
Residence Inn By Marriott LLC	7011	E	650 837-9000	11403
Rigel Pharmaceuticals Inc **(PA)**	2834	C	650 624-1100	3976
Rinat Neuroscience Corp	2834	E	650 615-7300	3977
Roche Diagnostics Corporation	2834	C	650 491-7251	3978
Roche Molecular Systems Inc	8731	D	650 225-1000	19119
San Mateo County Transit Dst	4111	B	650 588-4860	7352
San Mateo Health Commission	8099	C	650 616-0050	17174
Satellite Healthcare Inc	8092	E	650 377-0888	16981
Sees Candy Shops Incorporated **(HQ)**	2064	E	650 761-2490	2433
Sequenta LLC	2835	E	650 243-3900	4029
Shannon Side Welding Inc **(PA)**	7692	E	415 408-3219	14721
Shaw Bakers LLC	5149	C	650 273-1440	9485
Simbe Robotics Inc	8742	E	415 625-8555	19634
Simpson Coatings Group Inc	2851	E	650 873-5990	4111
Sonoma Wine Hardware Inc	2084	E	650 866-3020	2721
South San Frncsco Scvenger Inc	4953	D	650 589-4020	8363
Sp Controls Inc	3577	F	650 392-7880	5413
Ssf Imported Auto Parts LLC **(DH)**	5013	D	800 203-9287	8470
Steven Engineering Inc **(PA)**	5063	D	650 588-9200	8878
Summit Hotel Trs 115 LLC **(PA)**	7011	C	650 624-3700	11515
Sun Hing Foods Inc **(PA)**	5149	E	650 583-8188	9491
Supershuttle International Inc	4111	D	650 246-2786	7361
Supershuttle International Inc	4111	D	650 246-2704	7362
Surrozen Inc **(PA)**	2836	E	650 489-9000	4057
Surrozen Operating Inc	2834	E	650 918-8818	3989
Sutro Biopharma Inc **(PA)**	2836	C	650 392-8412	4058
Swinerton Builders Inc	1541	D	415 984-1302	813
Synctruck LLC **(PA)**	4215	C	650 239-6231	7655
Tangle Inc DBA Tangle Creat	3944	E	703 478-0500	7184
Tanox Inc **(DH)**	2834	C	650 851-1607	3990
Tardio Enterprises Inc	2092	E	650 877-7200	2832
Theravance Biopharma Us Inc	2834	C	650 808-6000	3993
Theravnce Bphrma Antbotics Inc	2834	E	877 275-6930	3994
Titan Pharmaceuticals Inc **(PA)**	2834	E	650 244-4990	3996
Tizona Therapeutics Inc	8731	E	650 383-0800	19137
Toshiba America Inc	3845	C	212 596-0600	7127
Tosoh Bioscience Inc	8731	D	650 615-4970	19138
Tri Counties Bank	6029	C	650 583-8450	9764
Tricida Inc	2834	D	415 429-7800	3998
Trux Transport	4581	D	650 244-0200	7791
Tuck Aire Heating & AC Corp	1711	D	650 873-7000	1387
Twenty Twenty Therapeutics LLC	3845	E	208 696-2020	7130
Twist Bioscience Corporation **(PA)**	8731	B	800 719-0671	19140
U-2 Home Entertainment Inc	5065	E	650 871-8118	8968
Unitrans International Corp **(HQ)**	4731	E	650 588-1233	7856
Unity Biotechnology Inc	8731	C	650 416-1192	19144
University Cal San Francisco	4225	D	510 987-0700	7704
Urbanbcn Worldwide	4119	E	415 494-8122	7410
Utap Printing Co Inc	2752	E	650 588-2818	3708
Valgenesis Inc **(PA)**	5045	D	510 445-0505	8759
Vegiworks Inc	5148	D	415 643-8686	9434
Veracyte Inc **(PA)**	8071	C	650 243-6300	16820
Verge Genomics	2835	E	312 489-7455	4030
Vomela Specialty Company	3993	E	650 877-8000	7259
Vox Network Solutions Inc	3661	C	650 989-1000	5815
Watchpoint Logistics Inc	4731	C	650 871-4747	7859
Windmill Corporation	2051	F	650 873-1000	2412
X-37 LLC	2834	F	650 273-5748	4009
Ximad Inc	7372	E	415 222-9909	13534
Young MNS Chrstn Assn San Frnc	8322	D	650 877-8642	17790
Zipline International Inc	8742	C	415 993-0604	19677
Znshine Pv-Tech Inc	3674	E	415 810-0861	6367

STANFORD, CA - Santa Clara County

	SIC	EMP	PHONE	ENTRY #
Associated Students Stanford **(PA)**	8641	D	650 723-4331	18390
Carnegie Institution Wash	8733	D	650 319-8904	19206
Event and Labor Services	7812	C	650 723-2285	14790
Hoover Institution	7389	C	650 723-0603	14299
Howard Hughes Medical Inst	8731	D	650 725-8252	19068
Leland Stanford Junior Univ **(PA)**	8069	C	650 723-2300	16763
Leland Stanford Junior Univ	8641	C	650 723-2021	18437
Palo Alto Community Child Care	8351	D	650 855-9828	17989
Peninsula Sanitary Service Inc	4953	E	650 321-4236	8348
Stanford Health Care	8062	E	650 736-6661	16552
Stanford Health Care	8062	A	650 723-4000	16554
Stanford Health Care **(HQ)**	8062	A	650 723-4000	16557
Stanford Health Care Advantage	8062	A	650 723-4000	16559
Stanford Univ Frman Spgli Inst	8733	C	650 723-8681	19238
Stanford Univ Med Ctr Aux	8322	B	650 723-6636	17758
Youmask Inc	7371	E	818 282-2496	12932

STEVINSON, CA - Merced County

	SIC	EMP	PHONE	ENTRY #
James J Stevinson A Corp **(PA)**	0241	E	209 632-1681	215
Machado Backhoe Inc	1794	E	209 634-4836	1964

STOCKTON, CA - San Joaquin County

	SIC	EMP	PHONE	ENTRY #
24 Hour Fitness Usa Inc	7991	E	209 951-5999	14919
A & D Rubber Products Co Inc **(PA)**	3053	E	209 941-0100	4201
A Teichert & Son Inc	1611	E	209 983-2300	997
A Teichert & Son Inc	1611	E	209 461-3700	1001
AC Square Inc	8748	C	650 293-2730	19709
Acrt Pacific LLC	8748	B	330 945-7500	19711
Adecco Employment Services	7363	D	209 474-0443	12156
Advanced Indus Coatings Inc	3479	D	209 234-2700	4926
Aegis Treatment Centers	8322	E	209 565-5982	17408
Aero Turbine Inc	3511	D	209 983-1112	4990
AG Spanos Companies **(PA)**	1522	D	209 478-7954	735
Alsha Academy	7021	D	310 908-1962	11588
Aisin Electronics Inc	3714	C	209 983-4988	6572
Al Kramp Specialties	3648	F	209 464-7539	5741
Alcohol DRG Awareness Program	8322	E	209 870-6500	17412
All Good Pallets Inc	2448	E	209 467-7000	3218
All-American Lumping LLC	3537	D	209 715-0309	5060
Alpine Meats Inc	2013	E	209 477-2691	2110
American Biodiesel Inc	2869	F	209 466-4823	4119
American Building Supply Inc	5031	D	209 941-8852	8526
American Cstm Private SEC Inc	7381	E	209 369-1200	14028
AMS Heating Inc	1711	E	209 466-6692	1202
Anand Software Inc	7371	D	209 287-1708	12252
Anderson Moulds Incorporated	3089	F	209 943-1145	4258
Applied Arospc Structures Corp **(PA)**	3728	C	209 982-0160	6631
Arandas Tortilla Company Inc	2099	E	209 464-8675	2868
Ardent Mills LLC	2041	F	209 983-6551	2308
Area Wide Exterminators Inc	7342	E	209 464-4731	11879
Arrow Sign Co	3993	E	209 931-7852	7217
Aspire Bakeries LLC	2051	D	209 469-4920	2363
Atharwa Investments LLC	7011	E	209 474-3301	10935
B & C Painting Solutions Inc	3479	E	209 982-0422	4927
B T Automotive Inc	5093	E	209 462-4444	9173
Balance Staffing Workforce LLC	7361	E	209 215-4188	12076
Baldwin Contracting Co Inc	1442	F	209 460-3785	590
Bank of Stockton **(HQ)**	6022	C	209 929-1600	9706
Bay Alarm Company	1731	E	209 465-1986	1459
Bbva USA	6022	C	209 473-6925	9709
Bbva USA	6022	C	209 939-3288	9710
Beaver Dam Health Care Center	8051	E	707 546-0471	15926
Beaver Dam Health Care Center	8051	E	209 466-3522	15942
Berberian Bros Inc	7538	D	209 944-5514	14548
Best Express Foods Inc	2051	B	209 490-2612	2369
Best Western Plus-Heritage Inn	7011	D	209 474-3301	10958
Bi-Jamar Inc	1731	E	209 948-2104	1465
Big Valley Ford Inc	7538	C	209 870-4400	14549
Bockmon & Woody Elc Co Inc	1731	C	209 464-4878	1469
Borgens & Borgens Inc	7381	E	209 547-2980	14039
Bowman & Co LLP	8721	E	209 473-1040	18934
Bristol Hospice Foundation Cal	8052	D	661 670-8000	16171
Brookside Country Club	7997	D	209 956-6200	15065
Brookside Optometric Group	8042	E	209 951-0820	15867
Burlingame Industries Inc	5033	C	209 464-9001	8639
Buzz Converting Inc	2631	E	209 948-1341	3350
By Quest LLC	2759	F	209 234-0202	3723
Cal Sheets LLC	2653	D	209 234-3300	3354
Calchef Foods LLC	2035	E	888 638-7083	2277
California Bulk Inc	4213	C	209 983-1069	7518
California Cedar Products Co **(PA)**	2499	E	209 932-5002	3265
California Concrete Pipe Corp	3272	D	209 466-4212	4422
California Materials Inc	4212	E	209 472-7422	7454
Canepas Car Wash	7542	E	209 478-5516	14635

GEOGRAPHIC

Employment Codes: A=Over 500 employees, B=251-500, C=101-250, D=51-100, E=20-50 F=10-19

STOCKTON, CA GEOGRAPHIC SECTION

	SIC	EMP	PHONE	ENTRY #
Carando Technologies Inc	3542	E	209 948-6500	5078
Caremark Rx LLC	8011	E	209 957-7050	15327
Casa Del Rios Hbilitation Svcs	8361	E	209 931-1027	18072
Castlehill Properties Inc **(PA)**	7011	D	209 472-9800	10995
Castlehill Properties Inc	7011	E	209 472-9700	10996
Cellco Partnership	4812	D	209 474-9071	7903
Cencal Recycling LLC	2611	F	209 546-8000	3340
Center State Pipe and Sup Co	5074	F	209 466-0871	8994
Chase Chevrolet Co Inc	7538	D	209 475-6600	14554
CHi Doors Holdings Inc	1751	C	209 229-5663	1733
Childrens Home of Stockton	8361	C	209 466-0853	18075
Chinchiolo Stemilt Cal LLC	0723	C	209 931-7000	278
Christian Brookside Schools	8351	D	209 954-7656	17903
Cintas Corporation No 3	7213	C	209 922-0500	11632
Clark Pest Ctrl Stockton Inc	7342	E	209 474-3204	11890
Cleanair Image Inc	7349	D	510 352-2480	11936
Coastal Pacific Fd Distrs Inc **(PA)**	5141	C	909 947-2066	9266
Collins Electrical Company Inc **(PA)**	1731	C	209 466-3691	1479
Comfort Air Inc	1711	D	209 466-4601	1238
Community Medical Centers Inc	8011	E	209 944-4700	15358
Community Medical Centers Inc	8011	E	209 940-5600	15359
Community Medical Centers Inc **(PA)**	8093	D	209 373-2800	17003
Community Medical Centers Inc	8011	E	209 373-2800	15363
Con J Franke Electric Inc	1731	D	209 462-0717	1484
Concrete Inc **(DH)**	3273	D	209 933-6999	4477
Condor Earth Technologies Inc	8748	E	209 388-9601	19750
Conrad Corporation	5047	E	209 942-2654	8778
Contract Sweeping Services LLC	4959	E	408 828-5280	8396
Corn Products Development Inc **(HQ)**	2046	A	209 982-1920	2331
County of San Joaquin	8071	E	209 468-3460	16777
County of San Joaquin	8093	E	209 468-8750	17008
County of San Joaquin	7389	D	209 468-3123	14238
County of San Joaquin	8322	D	209 468-3720	17511
County of San Joaquin	7349	D	209 468-3357	11937
County of San Joaquin	1623	D	209 468-3090	1094
County of San Joaquin	8011	E	209 468-2385	15368
County of San Joaquin	8331	C	209 468-3500	17809
County of San Joaquin	8011	E	209 468-3983	15369
County of San Joaquin	8093	D	209 948-3612	17009
Covenant Care California LLC	8051	D	209 477-5252	15964
Covey Auto Express Inc **(PA)**	7549	C	253 826-0461	14659
Cozad Trailer Sales LLC	3715	D	209 931-3000	6601
Creative Child Care Inc	8351	B	209 462-2282	17917
Creative Child Care Inc **(PA)**	8351	E	209 941-9100	17918
Crestwood Behavioral Hlth Inc	8063	D	209 478-5291	16740
Custom Building Products Inc	3531	E	209 983-8322	5030
Cutter Lumber Products	2448	E	209 982-4477	3219
Dameron Hospital Association **(HQ)**	8062	A	209 944-5550	16344
De Gregori Gormsen Ringer LLP	8721	E	209 944-0740	18947
De La Cruz Lath and Plaster Co	1771	E	209 368-8658	1863
Deck West Inc	3444	E	209 939-9700	4753
Del Rio West Pallets	2448	E	209 983-8215	3220
Delta Blood Bank LLC **(HQ)**	8099	D	800 244-6794	17134
Delta Charter Service Inc	4142	E	209 465-1053	7421
Delta Hawkeye Security Inc	7381	D	209 957-3333	14053
Delta Specialties Inc	1793	F	209 937-9650	1936
Delta Wireless Inc	7622	E	209 948-9611	14680
Dentonis Welding Works Inc **(PA)**	7692	E	209 464-4930	14712
Dfa of California	7389	D	209 465-2289	14253
Diamond Foods LLC **(PA)**	2068	A	209 467-6000	2443
Dietrich Industries Inc	3312	D	209 547-9066	4541
Dignity Health	8082	E	209 943-4663	16878
Dirt Movers	1794	E	209 461-7111	1955
DK Express Cargo Inc	4213	E	209 954-9354	7526
Dorfman-Pacific Co **(HQ)**	5136	C	209 982-1400	9243
Dow Jones Lmg Stockton Inc	2711	A	209 943-6397	3433
DTE Stockton LLC	1389	E	209 467-3838	564
Dynamex Inc	4215	D	209 464-7008	7642
E & S Westcoast LLC **(PA)**	5063	E	209 870-1900	8857
East Bay Mncpl Utlity Dst Wtr	4941	E	209 946-8000	8241
El Concilio California **(PA)**	8322	C	209 644-2600	17540
Enviroplex Inc	3448	D	209 466-8000	4851
ES West Coast LLC	3621	E	209 870-1900	5660
Estes Express Lines	4213	D	209 982-1841	7535
Exactacator Inc **(PA)**	3949	E	209 464-8979	7195
Family Resource & Referral Ctr	8322	D	209 948-1553	17563
Financial Center Credit Union	6061	E	209 462-2807	9786
Financial Center Credit Union **(PA)**	6061	E	209 948-6024	9787
First Alarm SEC & Patrol Inc	7382	B	209 473-1110	14134
First Student Inc	4151	C	209 466-7737	7434
Five Star Qulty Care-CA II LLC	8051	C	209 466-2066	16005
Foodliner Inc	4213	D	209 941-8361	7539
Forward Inc **(DH)**	4953	E	209 466-4482	8331
Freeman D Aiuto Prof Law Corp	8111	D	209 474-1818	17269
Fresh Innovations Cal LLC	5148	C	209 983-9700	9403
Friends Outside	8322	D	209 955-0701	17585
Frontier Land Companies	1521	E	209 957-8112	639
Fsq Rio Las Palmas Business Tr	8051	C	209 957-4711	16010
Fuel Delivery Services Inc	4213	D	209 751-2185	7543
G and L Brock Cnstr Co Inc	1794	E	209 931-3626	1959
G2 Metal Fab	3441	E	925 443-7903	4663
Gallien Technology Inc **(PA)**	3651	D	209 234-7300	5758
Gary M Alegre MD	8011	E	209 946-7162	15413
Geiger Manufacturing Inc	3599	F	209 464-7746	5531
General Trailer Inc	7539	E	209 948-6090	14610
Genesis Healthcare LLC	8051	C	209 478-6488	16012
Gillies Trucking Inc	4212	E	209 948-6268	7470
Gillson Trucking Inc	4213	C	925 400-9094	7545
GLS US Freight Inc **(PA)**	4213	D	209 823-2168	7547
Gnekow Family Winery LLC	2084	E	209 463-0697	2596
Golden 85 Investments Corp	6799	E	209 242-2916	10849
Golden State Restaurant Group	8742	E	209 478-0234	19520
Goodwill Inds San Jquin Vly FN **(PA)**	8322	D	209 466-2311	17595
Gospel Ctr Rescue Mission Inc	8322	D	209 466-2138	17596
Gregory B Bragg & Associates	6411	E	209 956-2119	10288
Grimaud Farms California Inc **(DH)**	2015	E	209 466-3200	2136
Grupe Commercial Company	6552	D	209 473-6000	10703
Grupe Company **(PA)**	6531	D	209 473-6000	10567
Grupe Dev Companynorthern Cal	1531	D	209 473-6000	780
Guard Force Inc	7382	E	951 233-0206	14135
Gymstars Gymnastics Inc **(PA)**	7941	E	209 955-7595	14908
H and H Drug Stores Inc	5047	D	209 931-5200	8781
Hackett Industries Inc	3556	E	209 955-8220	5131
Haggerty Construction Inc	1521	E	209 475-9898	650
Harley Murray Inc	3715	E	209 466-0266	6602
Harrison Home	8361	E	209 955-2277	18129
Head Start Child Dev Cncil Inc	8351	D	209 464-9542	17951
Healthcare Clinical Labs **(PA)**	8071	D	209 467-6330	16784
Herrick Corporation **(PA)**	3441	E	209 956-4751	4666
Highland Wholesale Foods Inc	5141	D	209 933-0580	9273
Hoover Little League Stockt	7997	D	209 467-7271	15099
Hospice of San Joaquin	8051	D	209 957-3888	16029
IC Ink Image Co Inc	2759	E	209 931-3040	3737
In-Shape Health Clubs LLC **(PA)**	7991	E	209 472-2231	14953
Inland Valley Truss Inc	2439	F	209 943-4710	3210
Inncal Incorporated	7011	D	209 477-5576	11193
Inreach Internet LLC **(HQ)**	4813	D	888 467-3224	7963
Interntnal Lngshrmens Wrhsmen	8631	E	209 464-1827	18366
Interstate Truck Center LLC **(PA)**	5012	D	209 944-5821	8426
Iris Usa Inc	5149	C	209 982-9100	9455
J & J Quality Door Inc	2431	E	209 948-5013	3137
J B Hunt Transport Inc	4213	C	209 235-1371	7553
J H Simpson Company Inc	1711	D	209 466-1477	1289
J Milano Co Inc	5072	F	209 944-0902	8984
Jack Klein Trust Partnership	0722	E	209 956-8800	263
John Aguilar & Company Inc	4212	D	209 546-0171	7476
Kaiser Foundation Hospitals	8062	A	209 476-3101	16419
Kehe Distributors LLC	5149	E	209 467-1962	9460
Kenyon Construction Inc	1742	E	209 462-4060	1685
Kindred Healthcare LLC	8062	C	209 474-7884	16422
Klein Bros Holdings Ltd	2068	E	209 465-5033	2447
Kp LLC	2752	E	209 466-6761	3667
Kr Subsidiary Inc **(DH)**	5159	E	915 320-7033	9508
Kruger Foods Inc	2035	C	209 941-8518	2281
Landmark Capital Inc	1711	E	209 242-8880	1301
Lawleys Inc	2048	E	209 337-1170	2346
Lee & Associates Central Vly	6531	E	209 983-1111	10599
Lewis & Lewis Inc	7999	E	209 474-1777	15216
Linden Unified School District	8744	D	209 946-0707	19704
Lineage Logistics Holdings LLC	4222	D	209 942-2323	7679
LLP Moss Adams	8721	D	209 955-6100	18969
Lodi Farming Inc	0172	E	209 948-4022	64
Lodi Regional Hlth Systems Inc	8062	C	209 948-0808	16431
Lodi Unified School District	8351	D	209 331-7127	17966
Lowes Home Centers LLC	5031	C	209 956-7200	8569
Lowes Home Centers LLC	5031	C	209 513-9843	8577
M Calosso & Son	5191	E	209 466-8994	9604
Mariner Health Care Inc	8051	E	209 466-2066	16058
Mark H Nishiki MD	8011	D	209 465-6221	15521
Mayall Hrley Kntsen Smith Gree	8111	E	209 465-8733	17327
Meadowood Hlth Rehabilitation	8051	E	209 956-3444	16060
Medcore Medical Group	8621	D	209 320-2600	18340
Melissa & Doug LLC	5092	D	209 830-7900	9169
Merrill Lynch Prce Fnner Smith	6211	D	209 472-3500	9991
Mexican Heritg Ctr Gallery Inc	8412	D	209 969-9306	18275
Mhp Builders Inc	1521	E	209 951-6190	674
Mid State Steel Erection **(PA)**	1791	D	209 464-9497	1927
Midstate Barrier Inc	1611	D	209 944-9565	1060
Mina-Tree Signs Incorporated **(PA)**	3993	E	209 941-2921	7244
Mitsubshi Chem Advnced Mtls In	2821	E	209 464-2701	3806
Morada Produce Company LP	5148	A	209 546-0426	9419
Msrcosmos LLC **(PA)**	7379	E	925 218-6919	13939
Murray Biscuit Company LLC	2052	C	209 472-3718	2417
Natural Std RES Collaboration	2731	E	617 591-3300	3541
Neumiller Bardslee A Prof Corp	8111	D	209 948-8200	17345
Nexcoil Steel LLC	3316	F	209 900-1919	4547
Noll/Norwesco LLC	3444	C	209 234-1600	4794
O G Packing Co	5148	E	209 931-4392	9421
O H I Company	3556	E	209 466-8921	5133
OConner Woods A California	6513	E	209 956-3400	10452
OConnor Woods Housing Corp	6513	D	209 956-3400	10453
Olive Corto L P	2079	F	209 888-8100	2467
Pacific Avenue Bowl	7933	E	209 477-0267	14896
Pacific Coast Services Inc	8082	A	209 956-2532	16922
Pacific Gas and Electric Co	4911	C	209 932-6550	8133
Pacific Gas and Electric Co	4911	C	209 942-5142	8147
Pacific Gas and Electric Co	4911	C	209 942-1523	8168
Pacific Gas and Electric Co	4911	C	209 942-1787	8177
Pacific Hart Vscular Med Group	8011	E	209 464-3615	15576
Pacific Metro Electric Inc	1731	D	209 939-3222	1559
Pacific Paper Tube Inc **(PA)**	2655	E	510 562-8823	3368
Pacific State Bank **(PA)**	6022	E	209 870-3200	9742
Paragon Ventures Inc	1711	E	209 466-3530	1335
Patrick Rynearson Rulin	3699	F	209 943-2705	6535

	SIC	EMP	PHONE	ENTRY #
PDM Steel Service Centers Inc **(HQ)**	5051	D	209 943-0555	8824
Pearl Crop Inc **(PA)**	0723	D	209 808-7575	301
Pelton-Shepherd Industries Inc **(PA)**	2097	E	209 460-0893	2861
Penney Opco LLC	7231	D	209 951-1110	11692
Permanente Medical Group Inc	8011	A	209 476-3737	15616
Permanente Medical Group Inc	8011	A	209 476-2000	15620
Pinasco Plumbing & Heating Inc	1711	D	209 463-7793	1337
Pre-Peeled Potato Co Inc	2099	E	209 469-6911	2935
Premier Coatings Inc	3479	D	209 982-5585	4946
Proco Products Inc **(PA)**	3069	E	209 943-6088	4225
Progressive Services Inc	1761	E	209 824-2837	1832
Pw Fund B LP	6722	D	916 379-3852	10767
Quality Motor Cars Stockton	7539	D	209 476-1640	14619
Quest Dgnstics Clncal Labs Inc	8071	D	209 951-5831	16798
Quiet Ride Solutions LLC	3714	F	209 942-4777	6591
R Scott Foster MD	8011	E	209 952-3700	15638
Rai Care Ctrs Nthrn Cal I LLC	8092	C	209 943-0854	16976
Reeve Trucking Company Inc **(PA)**	4213	D	209 948-4061	7577
Reliance Intermodal Inc	4213	D	209 946-0200	7578
RES-Care Inc	8052	D	209 473-1202	16197
Reyes Coca-Cola Bottling LLC	2086	D	209 466-9501	2803
Rgm Products Inc	2952	B	559 499-2222	4193
Robinson Farms Feed Company	2048	E	209 466-7915	2356
Rock Engineered McHy Co Inc	2911	F	925 447-0805	4179
Roland Construction Inc	1541	E	209 462-2687	808
Rudolph and Sletten Inc	1542	E	209 941-1040	952
S M S Briners Inc	2035	E	209 941-8515	2285
S&F Management Company LLC	8051	A	209 466-0456	16104
San Joaquin Cnty Aging & Commu	8322	C	209 468-9455	17714
San Joaquin Electric Inc	1731	E	209 952-9980	1598
San Joaquin Regional Trnst Dst	4111	C	209 948-5566	7350
San Jquin Orthtics Prsthtics C	3842	F	209 932-0170	7079
San Tomo Inc	0191	D	209 948-0792	189
Sanitation Process Control LLC	7349	E	510 909-4910	11992
Sardee Corporation California	3535	F	209 466-1526	5056
Sardee Industries Inc	3565	E	209 466-1526	5203
SC Hockey Franchise Corp	7941	D	209 373-1500	14915
Scan-Vino LLC **(PA)**	4213	D	209 931-3570	7591
Schuff Steel Company	1791	D	209 938-0869	1932
Sierra Health Services LLC	6324	E	209 956-7725	10154
Simpson Strong-Tie Company Inc	3449	D	209 234-7775	4862
Smg	8744	B	209 937-7433	19706
Snow Cleaners Inc **(PA)**	7216	E	209 547-1454	11656
Southwest Traders Incorporated	5141	C	209 462-1607	9311
Sovereign Gen Insur Svcs Inc	6331	E	209 932-5200	10173
Spanos Corporation **(PA)**	1522	E	209 955-2550	771
St Josephs Behavioral Hlth Ctr **(DH)**	8062	D	209 462-2826	16544
St Josephs Med Ctr Stockton	8062	A	209 943-2000	16545
St Josephs Medical Center Inc	8062	C	209 943-2000	16546
St Josephs Surgery Center LP	8011	D	209 467-6316	15700
St Jsephs Regional Hsing Corp **(PA)**	6513	C	209 956-3400	10462
St Marys Dining Room	8322	D	209 467-0703	17754
Stanley Electric Motor Co Inc	7694	E	209 464-7321	14730
State Compensation Insur Fund	6331	D	888 782-8338	10183
Stockton Ambltory Srgery Ctr L	8011	D	209 944-9100	15705
Stockton Ceramic Tile Inc	1743	E	209 464-1291	1723
Stockton Congregational Home	8361	D	209 466-4341	18185
Stockton Crdlgy Med Group Cmpl **(PA)**	8011	E	209 994-5750	15706
Stockton Edson Healthcare Corp	8059	D	209 948-8762	16275
Stockton Hotel Ltd	7011	D	209 957-9090	11510
Stockton Orthpd Med Group Inc	8062	D	209 948-1641	16561
Stockton Port District	4491	D	209 946-0246	7726
Stockton Tri-Industries LLC	3535	E	209 948-9701	5058
Stone Bros Management	6552	D	209 952-7500	10718
Street Graphics Inc	3993	E	209 948-1713	7255
Sunrise Fresh LLC	2034	E	209 932-0192	2268
Sunset Disposal Service Inc	4212	E	209 466-5192	7492
Super Store Industries	5149	B	209 858-3365	9494
Sygma Network Inc	5141	C	209 932-5300	9315
T M Cobb Company	2431	D	209 948-5358	3156
Teohc California Inc	3444	B	209 234-1600	4824
Therapeutic RES Faculty LLC	2759	C	209 472-2240	3751
Thompson & Rich Crane Service	7389	E	209 465-3161	14434
Tiger-Sul Products LLC	2819	F	209 451-2725	3797
Tonys Express Inc	4213	D	209 234-1000	7604
Tpmg Laboratory Stockton	8071	D	209 476-3646	16810
Tranquilmoney Inc	5045	D	800 979-6739	8755
Tri Valley Home Health Care	8051	D	209 957-0708	16144
True Health Inc	8361	E	209 464-4743	18193
Unilever United States Inc	0191	A	209 466-9580	193
United Cerebral Palsy Assoc **(PA)**	8621	C	209 956-0290	18351
Universal Service Recycl Inc **(PA)**	4953	E	209 944-9555	8374
Universal Svc Rcycl Merced Inc **(PA)**	4953	D	209 944-9555	8375
USG Interiors LLC	5031	B	209 466-4636	8611
USI Insrnce Svcs Nthrn Cal Inc **(DH)**	6411	E	209 954-3900	10364
Valimet Inc **(PA)**	3399	D	209 444-1600	4595
Valley Fresh Inc **(HQ)**	2015	E	209 943-5411	2139
Valley Pacific Petro Svcs Inc **(PA)**	5172	E	209 948-9412	9541
Valley Wholesale Drug Co LLC	5122	D	209 466-0131	9239
Valley-Mntain Regional Ctr Inc **(PA)**	8322	C	209 473-0951	17779
Value Products Inc	2841	E	209 345-3817	4065
Van De Pol Enterprises Inc **(PA)**	5172	D	209 465-3421	9542
Varni Brothers Corporation	2086	D	209 464-7778	2817
Victor Cmnty Support Svcs Inc	8093	C	209 465-1080	17088
Villa Real Inc	8748	E	209 460-5069	19885
Vinotheque Wine Cellars	3585	F	209 466-9463	5436
Volt Management Corp	7363	D	209 952-5627	12206
W Fs Financial Inc	6141	E	209 955-7800	9865
Wallace-Kuhl Investments LLC	8711	E	209 234-7722	18855
Wardley Industrial Inc	3086	E	209 932-1088	4246
WC Maloney Inc	1794	E	209 942-1129	1976
West Coast Arborists Inc	0782	D	408 855-8660	509
West Valley Cnstr Co Inc	1623	E	209 943-6812	1143
Western Square Industries Inc	3446	E	209 944-0921	4843
Whisperkool Corporation	2084	F	800 343-9463	2763
Williams Tank Lines **(PA)**	4213	D	209 944-5613	7612
Wilmar Oils Fats Stockton LLC	2076	E	925 627-1600	2456
Wjlp Company Inc	3677	D	800 628-1123	6388
Wkf (friedman Enterprises Inc **(PA)**	3724	F	925 673-9100	6624
Wm Michael Stemler Inc **(PA)**	6411	C	209 948-8483	10370
Womens Center-Youth Fmly Svcs **(PA)**	8322	D	209 941-2611	17786
World Class Distribution Inc	4225	D	909 574-4140	7706
World Trade Network Inc **(PA)**	4813	E	713 358-5603	8009
Xpo Logistics Freight Inc	4213	D	209 983-8285	7614
YMCA of San Joaquin County	8641	E	209 472-9622	18483
Yosemite Foods Inc	5147	C	209 990-5400	9383
Zeiter Eye Medical Group Inc **(PA)**	8011	D	209 366-0446	15819
Zuckerman-Heritage Inc **(PA)**	0191	E	209 444-1724	198

STRAWBERRY, CA - Tuolumne County

	SIC	EMP	PHONE	ENTRY #
Strawberry Inn	7011	E	209 965-3662	11511

SUISUN CITY, CA - Solano County

	SIC	EMP	PHONE	ENTRY #
Cemex Cnstr Mtls PCF LLC	3272	E	800 992-3639	4423
E B Stone & Son Inc	5191	D	707 426-2500	9598
Hal-Mar-Jac Enterprises	7381	C	415 467-1470	14067
Meals On Whels Solano Cnty Inc	8322	D	707 426-3079	17646
Potrero Hills Landfill Inc	4953	E	707 429-9600	8349
Redevelopment Agency of The Ci	8748	D	707 421-7309	19847
Talos Secure Group Inc	7381	E	707 927-5432	14101
UNItogether Inc	8699	D	707 208-7602	18606
Walker Communications Inc	1731	E	707 421-1300	1633

SUNNYVALE, CA - Santa Clara County

	SIC	EMP	PHONE	ENTRY #
23andme Inc **(HQ)**	7375	B	650 961-7152	13777
A 3 By Airbus LLC	8733	D	650 660-5809	19192
Aarki Inc **(PA)**	7371	C	408 382-1180	12218
Accurate Technology Mfg Inc	3599	D	408 733-4344	5461
Accuray Incorporated **(PA)**	3841	C	408 716-4600	6934
Adaps Photonics Inc **(PA)**	3661	D	650 521-3925	5784
Addlife	7359	E	650 556-9430	12027
Adeza Biomedical Corporation	2835	A	408 745-6491	4015
Adiana Inc	2834	B	650 421-2900	3833
Adswood Trs LLC	7011	E	408 247-0800	10911
Advanced Linear Dvcs RES Inc	3674	E	408 747-1155	6013
Agiliance Inc **(PA)**	7379	E	408 200-0400	13834
Ahn Enterprises LLC	3677	F	408 734-1878	6375
Al-Tar Services Inc	7699	D	866 522-3499	14734
Algomedica Inc **(PA)**	8011	E	650 857-0116	15272
Alibabacom US LLC **(DH)**	8742	C	408 785-5580	19440
Alliance Fiber Optic Pdts Inc	3229	A	408 736-6900	4368
Alpha and Omega Semicdtr Inc **(HQ)**	3674	C	408 789-0008	6025
Alta Devices Inc	3674	C	408 988-8600	6026
Amazon	8734	E	510 676-6906	19256
AMD Far East Ltd **(HQ)**	3674	B	408 749-4000	6033
Analog Bits	3674	E	650 279-9323	6036
Applied Materials Inc	3674	E	408 727-5555	6042
Apstra Inc **(HQ)**	7379	D	650 307-3245	13843
ARA Technology	3471	E	408 734-8131	4898
Armstrong Technology Sv Inc	3599	F	408 734-4434	5476
Art Robbins Instruments LLC	3826	E	408 734-8400	6809
Aruba Networks Inc	3577	A	408 227-4500	5344
Aruba Networks Inc	3577	A	408 227-4500	5346
Aruba Networks Inc	3663	A	408 227-4500	5825
Arvi Manufacturing Inc	3499	E	408 734-4776	4980
Ase (us)inc **(DH)**	5065	D	408 636-9500	8892
Avantec Vascular Corporation	3841	E	408 329-5400	6949
Azul Systems Inc **(PA)**	7372	C	650 230-6500	13005
Baidu USA LLC	7379	C	669 224-6400	13850
Barrx Medical Inc	3841	D	408 328-7300	6951
Belkasoft LLC	7372	E	650 272-0384	13015
Best Western Silicon Vly Inn	7011	E	408 735-7800	10959
Blue Coat Systems LLC **(HQ)**	7372	A	650 527-8000	13028
Bmi Imaging Systems Inc **(PA)**	7374	E	916 924-6666	13698
Bondline Elctrnic Adhsive Corp	2891	D	408 830-9200	4149
Borderx Lab Inc **(PA)**	7371	D	408 746-5462	12306
California Young World Center	8351	E	408 245-7285	17871
Cambrios Technologies Corp	8733	E	408 738-7400	19203
Canyon House Resthomes Inc **(PA)**	8361	E	408 730-4004	18065
Cashedge Inc	7389	D	408 541-3900	14224
Caspio Inc **(PA)**	7372	E	650 691-0900	13052
Cepheid	2835	F	408 548-9104	4018
Cepheid **(HQ)**	3826	A	408 541-4191	6820
Cerebras Systems Inc	7373	C	650 933-4980	13566
Chelsio Communications Inc	7371	C	408 962-3600	12337
Cloudknox Security Inc	7381	E	408 647-5515	14043
Cloudshield Technologies LLC	7372	C	408 331-6640	13079
Clover Network Inc	4813	D	650 210-7888	7941
Coadna Holdings Inc	6719	D	408 736-1100	10731
Coadna Photonics Inc **(HQ)**	3661	D	408 736-1100	5791
Code Green Networks Inc	7371	E	408 498-8413	12347
Comtel Systems Technology Inc	1731	D	408 543-5600	1483
Contactual Inc	7372	D	650 292-4408	13091
Covidien Holding Inc	3841	C	408 585-7700	6965
Cpp Inc	2731	F	650 969-8901	3531

SUNNYVALE, CA — GEOGRAPHIC SECTION

Company	SIC	EMP	PHONE	ENTRY #
Crazy Maple Studio Inc (PA)	2741	E	972 757-1283	3564
Crowdstrike Inc (HQ)	7379	C	888 512-8906	13876
Crowdstrike Holdings Inc (PA)	7372	C	888 512-8906	13098
D2m Inc	8748	E	650 567-9995	19759
Datrium Inc	5045	D	650 485-2165	8691
Days Inn	7011	E	408 737-1177	11046
Dcatalog Inc	7372	E	408 824-5648	13111
De Anza Manufacturing Svcs Inc	3679	D	408 734-2020	6416
Digilens Inc	3827	E	408 734-0219	6870
Dionex Corporation (HQ)	3826	E	408 737-0700	6824
Drawbridge Inc	8742	D	650 513-2323	19495
Drobo (HQ)	5045	D	408 454-4200	8695
Druva Inc (HQ)	7372	E	650 241-3501	13128
Ebr Systems Inc (PA)	3845	E	408 720-1906	7103
Edelman Financial Engines LLC (HQ)	8742	C	408 498-6000	19497
Egain Corporation	7372	E	408 636-4500	13135
Elekta Inc	7372	E	408 830-8000	13139
ERC Concepts Co Inc	3599	E	408 734-5345	5521
Eurofins Eag Mtls Science LLC (DH)	8734	E	408 454-4600	19269
Evergent Technologies Inc	7371	B	877 897-1240	12432
Exablox Corporation	7372	E	408 773-8477	13153
Executive Inn Inc	7011	D	408 245-5330	11088
Fairchild Semicdtr Intl Inc (HQ)	3674	A	408 822-2000	6119
Finisar Corporation (HQ)	3661	E	408 548-1000	5797
First Baptist Church Crosswalk	8351	D	408 736-3120	17934
Focus Enhancements Inc (DH)	3674	E	650 230-2400	6121
Fortinet Inc (PA)	3577	A	408 235-7700	5368
Fujitsu Components America Inc (DH)	5065	E	408 745-4900	8914
Fujitsu Computer Pdts Amer Inc (HQ)	7373	B	800 626-4686	13593
Fujitsu Consulting (canada) (PA)	7373	C	732 549-4100	13594
Fujitsu Consulting LLC (DH)	7373	D	408 746-6000	13595
Fujitsu Electronics Amer Inc (DH)	8711	D	408 737-5600	18713
Fujitsu Research America Inc (HQ)	8731	A	408 530-4500	19062
Fujitsu Retirement MGT Inc (DH)	7373	B	408 746-6000	13596
Fujitsu Tech & Bus Amer Inc	3229	E	408 746-6000	4372
Future Dial Incorporated	7371	E	408 245-8880	12468
Gener8 LLC (PA)	8711	C	650 940-9898	18719
General Motors LLC	7371	E	408 529-6794	12471
Ghc of Sunnyvale LLC	8059	C	408 738-4880	16235
Glint Inc	7374	D	650 817-7240	13716
Globalfoundries Dresden	3674	A	408 462-3900	6131
Globalfoundries US Inc	3674	D	408 462-3900	6132
Go Risk Vision	7372	F	925 271-8227	13194
Gordon Prill Inc	1542	E	408 745-7164	879
Gordon-Prill-Drapes Inc	8711	E	650 335-1990	18724
Graphics Microsystems Inc (HQ)	3555	D	408 731-2000	5120
Gsi Technology Inc (PA)	3674	E	408 331-8800	6136
Gulshan International Corp	3674	E	408 745-6090	6137
Hardrock Concrete Inc	1771	E	408 481-4990	1879
Hcl America Inc (DH)	7376	C	408 733-0480	13815
High Connection Density Inc	3678	E	408 743-9700	6392
Hyatt Die Cast Engrg Corp - S	3363	E	408 523-7000	4577
I G S Inc	3211	E	408 733-4621	4360
I T M Software Corp	7372	F	650 864-2500	13221
Idec Corporation (HQ)	5065	D	408 747-0550	8919
Illumio Inc	7371	E	669 800-5000	12510
Impac Medical Systems Inc (HQ)	7372	E	408 830-8000	13224
Inbenta Technologies Inc (PA)	7372	E	408 213-8771	13226
Inko Industrial Corporation	7374	D	408 830-1040	13723
Inktomi Corporation (HQ)	7372	E	408 653-2800	13236
Innovalight Inc	3648	E	408 419-4400	5744
Intella Interventional Systems	3841	D	650 269-1375	6984
Intergen Inc	3699	F	408 245-2737	6527
Intermdia Cloud Cmmnctions Inc	7372	E	650 641-4000	13242
Intermedia Communications Inc (DH)	4813	C	800 940-0011	7965
Intertrust Technologies Corp (PA)	7371	E	408 616-1600	12535
Intuitive Srgcal Oprations Inc (HQ)	3841	A	408 523-2100	6986
Intuitive Srgical Holdings LLC (HQ)	3841	D	408 523-2100	6987
Intuitive Surgical Inc (PA)	3842	C	408 523-2100	7074
Ipolipo Inc	7372	E	408 916-5290	13248
Island Hospitality MGT LLC	7011	E	408 720-1000	11199
Island Hospitality MGT LLC	7011	E	408 720-8893	11201
Ix Layer Inc	7371	E	408 594-7586	12544
Jdj Semiconductor LLC	3674	E	408 542-9430	6169
Jeffrey Hung-Yip Lee DDS Inc (PA)	8021	E	650 325-2496	15841
Jfrog Ltd (PA)	7372	D	408 329-1540	13254
John Vellequette DDS	8021	E	408 245-7500	15843
Joie De Vivre Hospitality Inc	7011	E	408 738-0500	11222
Jsl Partners Inc	2752	E	408 747-9000	3663
Jsr Micro Inc (HQ)	2869	C	408 543-8800	4124
Jsr North America Holdings Inc	8741	D	408 543-8800	19355
Juniper Networks Inc.	7373	A	408 745-2000	13616
Juniper Networks Inc (HQ)	3577	B	408 745-2000	5390
Juniper Networks (us) Inc (HQ)	7373	E	408 745-2000	13617
Juniper Networks Intl LLC	7373	F	408 745-2000	13618
K3 Dev LLC	7011	D	408 733-7950	11225
K3 Dev LLC	7011	E	408 733-7950	11226
Kaiser Foundation Hospitals	8011	C	408 851-1000	15466
Kloudgin Inc	7372	C	877 256-8303	13266
Krytar Inc	3679	E	408 734-5999	6444
Ksm Vacuum Products Inc	3443	F	408 514-2400	4724
Kwan Software Engineering Inc	7372	E	408 496-1200	13270
Larry Hopkins Inc	7538	D	408 720-1888	14575
Learning Squared Inc (PA)	3944	C	650 567-9995	7178
Level 10 Construction LP	1542	E	408 747-5000	913
Lge Electrical Sales Inc	5063	C	408 992-4145	8865
Linkedin Corporation (HQ)	7375	A	650 687-3600	13798
Liquid Robotics Inc (HQ)	3714	D	408 636-4200	6586
LL Sunnyvale LP	7011	E	408 733-1212	11264
Lockheed Martin	3721	D	408 834-9741	6613
Lora H Costa DDS Inc (PA)	8021	E	408 774-1200	15846
Lore Io Inc	7372	E	415 691-9680	13281
Lowes Home Centers LLC	5031	C	408 470-1680	8580
Luminus Inc (HQ)	3648	D	408 708-7000	5745
Luminus Devices Inc	3648	C	978 528-8000	5746
Manor Care Sunnyvale Ca LLC	8051	C	408 735-7200	16041
Maplelabs Inc	7371	C	408 743-4414	12594
Marvell Semiconductor	3674	E	408 222-2500	6188
Mass Microsystems Inc	3572	F	408 522-1200	5298
Matterport Inc (PA)	7372	E	650 641-2241	13296
Matterport Operating LLC (HQ)	5045	C	650 641-2241	8725
Mc Liquidation Inc	3845	D	408 636-1020	7112
MDE Electric Company Inc	1731	E	408 738-8600	1543
Medeonbio Inc	3841	E	650 397-5100	7002
Medtronic Spine LLC	3841	A	408 548-6500	7005
Mercedes-Benz RES Dev N Amer In (DH)	8731	E	650 845-2500	19089
Meru Networks Inc (HQ)	3669	B	408 215-5300	5890
Mhb Group Inc	2721	F	408 744-1011	3508
Micro Lithography Inc	3823	E	408 747-1769	6726
Microsemi Stor Solutions Inc (DH)	3674	A	408 239-8000	6212
Microsoft Corporation	7372	D	650 964-7200	13308
Midpen Property MGT Corp	7021	E	408 773-8014	11592
Minton Door Company (PA)	5031	E	650 961-9800	8596
Mlslistings Inc	8742	D	408 874-0200	19578
Msr Hotels & Resorts Inc	7011	B	408 745-6000	11316
Myenersave Inc	7372	F	408 464-6385	13320
Myers-Briggs Company (PA)	8742	E	650 969-8901	19584
Nanez Mfg Inc	3599	E	408 830-9903	5577
National Opinion Research Ctr	8732	D	415 315-3800	19172
Nexsan Technologies Inc (HQ)	3572	E	408 724-9809	5303
Nextnav LLC	8742	E	800 775-0982	19590
Ngcodec Inc	3674	E	408 766-4382	6232
Northbound LLC	8742	C	408 333-9780	19592
Northrop Grumman Systems Corp	3721	B	408 735-2241	6616
Northrop Grumman Systems Corp	3721	E	408 735-3011	6617
Oakbio Inc	2869	F	888 591-9413	4127
Oakmead Prtg Reproduction Inc	2752	E	408 734-5505	3680
Oepic Semiconductors Inc	3674	E	408 747-0388	6241
Olander Company Inc	5085	E	408 735-1850	9124
Ooma Inc (PA)	7374	B	650 566-6600	13737
Opal Soft Inc	7379	D	408 267-2211	13953
Opsware Inc	3652	E	408 744-7517	5780
Optibase Inc (HQ)	3577	E	800 451-5101	5402
Orthofix Medical Inc	3841	A	214 937-2000	7016
Osram Opto Semiconductors Inc (DH)	5065	E	408 962-3736	8944
Outright Inc	7371	A	918 926-6578	12661
Overhead Door Snta Clara Vly I	1751	E	408 734-8010	1748
Palm Inc (HQ)	3663	B	408 617-7000	5860
Pareto Networks Inc	4813	D	877 727-8020	7981
Personagraph Corporation	7371	B	408 616-1600	12682
Plaxo Inc	4841	D	408 900-8701	8064
Plug & Play LLC (PA)	6799	D	408 524-1400	10876
PM Entertainment Corp	7929	E	408 732-2121	14874
Polaris Home Care LLC	8082	D	408 400-7020	16924
Polyvore Inc	5199	D	650 968-1195	9669
Position2 Inc (PA)	8742	E	650 618-8900	19607
Proofpoint Inc (PA)	7374	A	408 517-4710	13745
Pts Diagnostics California Inc	8071	C	877 870-5610	16795
Qsolv Inc	7373	C	408 429-0918	13653
Qualitek Inc (HQ)	3672	D	408 734-8686	5961
Qualitek Inc	3672	D	408 752-8422	5962
Quanergy Systems Inc (PA)	3812	C	408 245-9500	6680
Radware Inc	8731	E	650 627-4672	19114
Rae Systems Inc (DH)	3829	A	408 952-8200	6918
Rank Technology Corp	3572	E	408 737-1488	5312
Raytheon Applied Sgnal Tech In (DH)	3663	B	408 749-1888	5863
Real Intent	5045	E	408 830-0700	8743
Real-Time Innovations Inc (PA)	7371	D	408 990-7400	12729
Reflex Photonics Inc	3674	E	408 501-8886	6270
Responsible Metal Fab Inc	3444	E	408 734-0713	4811
Retail Content Service Inc	2741	E	415 890-2097	3596
RS Hughes Company Inc (PA)	5085	E	408 739-3211	9130
Ruckus Wireless Inc (DH)	3663	A	650 265-4200	5865
S R H H Inc	7011	E	408 247-0800	11424
Safebreach Inc	7382	E	408 743-5279	14146
Samax Precision Inc	3599	E	408 245-9555	5616
Sass Labs Inc	7372	E	404 731-7284	13427
SC Builders Inc (PA)	1542	D	408 328-0688	956
Schoolcity Inc	7371	E	408 638-8438	12765
Screen Spe Usa LLC (DH)	7629	C	408 523-9140	14704
Selvi-Vidovich LP	7011	E	408 720-8500	11460
Sendmail Inc	4813	C	510 594-5400	7988
Sensity Systems Inc (HQ)	8748	E	408 841-4200	19859
Seville Maintenance Inc	0782	E	650 966-1091	501
Shinko Electric America Inc (DH)	5065	E	408 232-0499	8952
Sierra Circuits Inc	3672	C	408 735-7137	5973
Sierraware LLC	7371	E	408 337-6400	12783
Silicon Light Machines Corp (DH)	3674	F	408 240-4700	6288
Silicon Storage Technology Inc (HQ)	3674	B	408 735-9110	6291
Siliconsage Construction Inc	1522	C	408 916-3205	770
Silk Road Medical Inc	3841	C	408 720-9002	7037
Simplify Medical Inc	3841	F	650 946-2025	7038
Sk Telecom Americas Inc	8732	E	408 328-2900	19184
South Pninsula Hebrew Day Schl	8351	D	408 738-3060	18025

GEOGRAPHIC SECTION TRUCKEE, CA

Company	SIC	EMP	PHONE	ENTRY #
Spangler Concrete & Engrg Inc	1741	E	408 830-0400	1653
Stanford Research Systems Inc	3826	C	408 744-9040	6854
Star One Credit Union **(PA)**	6061	C	408 543-5202	9822
Staybridge Suites	7011	E	408 745-1515	11508
Stormgeo **(DH)**	8999	C	408 731-8600	19917
Sunmar Corporation	6531	E	408 249-5100	10666
Sunnyside Gardens	8361	E	408 730-4070	18188
Sunnyvale Healthcare Center	8051	C	408 245-8070	16138
Supertex Inc **(HQ)**	3674	B	408 222-8888	6320
Surface Engineering Spc	3552	E	408 734-8810	5114
Sutter Bay Medical Foundation	8011	C	408 730-4321	15711
Sutter Bay Medical Foundation	8011	D	650 934-7956	15712
Sutter Health	8062	C	408 733-4380	16627
Symphony Comm Svcs Hldings LLC **(PA)**	7389	C	650 733-6660	14421
Tactai Technologies Inc	7371	E	844 439-8228	12846
Telepathy Inc	3577	E	408 306-8421	5418
Test Enterprises Inc **(PA)**	3823	E	408 542-5900	6734
Texas Instruments Sunnyvale	7389	E	408 541-9900	14433
Thomas West Inc **(PA)**	2392	E	408 481-3850	3030
Thresher Cmmnctons Prdctvity I	7812	D	408 780-3066	14796
Time Warner Cable Entps LLC	4841	E	408 747-7330	8067
Tomotherapy Inc	8093	E	408 716-4600	17081
Toyota-Sunnyvale Inc **(PA)**	7538	D	408 245-6640	14600
Trimble Inc **(PA)**	3829	A	408 481-8000	6928
Trimble Military & Advnced Sys	3812	D	408 481-8000	6688
Twin Creeks Sunnyvale Inc	7999	D	408 734-0888	15260
Umc Group (usa)	3674	D	408 523-7800	6344
University East-West Medicine	8742	E	408 992-0218	19662
Uplift Inc	7371	D	408 396-3374	12889
UPS Ground Freight Inc	4213	D	408 400-0595	7608
US Interactive Delaware **(PA)**	8711	C	408 863-7500	18852
USI Manufacturing Services Inc	3577	E	408 636-9600	5420
V-Tech Manufacturing Inc	3599	F	408 730-9200	5633
Verizon Media Inc	8999	A	310 907-3016	19919
Vexillum Inc **(PA)**	1731	C	408 541-4245	1630
Vudu Inc	3651	D	408 492-1010	5772
W L Hickey Sons Inc	1711	C	408 736-4938	1393
Wayne	2023	E	669 206-2179	2168
West Valley Engineering Inc **(PA)**	7363	A	408 735-1420	12209
Westak Inc **(PA)**	3672	D	408 734-8686	5998
Westak International Sales Inc **(HQ)**	3672	C	408 734-8686	5999
Wirex Systems	7372	E	408 799-4498	13530
Wm Oneill Lath and Plst Corp	1742	E	408 329-1413	1710
Xoriant Corporation **(PA)**	7379	C	408 743-4400	14015
Xp Power LLC **(HQ)**	5065	D	408 732-7777	8976
Yahoo Cv LLC **(HQ)**	7374	B	408 349-3300	13772
Zensar Technologies Inc	7371	A	408 469-5408	12938
Zultys Inc	7379	E	408 328-0450	14021
Zyrion Inc	7372	D	408 524-7424	13545

SUNOL, CA - Alameda County

Company	SIC	EMP	PHONE	ENTRY #
Brightview Tree Company	0811	D	925 862-2485	530
Elliston Vineyards Inc	2084	D	925 862-2377	2561
Ge-Hitachi Nuclear Energy	2819	D	925 862-4382	3788
Hanson Aggrgtes Md-Pacific Inc	3273	F	925 862-2236	4485

SUSANVILLE, CA - Lassen County

Company	SIC	EMP	PHONE	ENTRY #
Banner Health	8062	C	530 251-3147	16323
Banner Lssen Med Ctr Fndtion I	8062	C	530 252-2000	16324
CF Susanville LLC	8051	D	530 257-5341	15957
Diamond Mountain Casino	7011	C	530 252-1100	11048
Four Tribes Enterprises LLC	1611	E	530 317-2500	1041
Golden 1 Credit Union	6062	D	530 251-0205	9833
Lassen Municipal Utility Dst	4911	E	530 257-4174	8118
Northeastern Rur Hlth Clinics **(PA)**	8011	D	530 251-5000	15555
Sierra-Cascade Nursery Inc **(PA)**	0181	B	530 254-6867	135
Susanville Indian Rancheria **(PA)**	8093	E	530 257-6264	17078

SUTTER, CA - Sutter County

Company	SIC	EMP	PHONE	ENTRY #
Butte Sand and Gravel	1442	E	530 755-0225	591
Sweco Products Inc **(PA)**	7699	E	530 673-8949	14777

SUTTER CREEK, CA - Amador County

Company	SIC	EMP	PHONE	ENTRY #
Amador Water Agency	4941	D	209 223-3018	8220
American Legion Ambulance Svc	8641	E	209 223-2963	18387
Ampine LLC	2521	D	209 223-1690	3300
Fuller Manufacturing Inc	3699	F	209 267-5071	6522

TAHOE CITY, CA - Placer County

Company	SIC	EMP	PHONE	ENTRY #
Granlibakken Management Co Ltd	7011	D	800 543-3221	11118
Pepper Tree Inn	7011	D	530 583-3711	11363
River Ranch	7011	D	530 583-4264	11411
Save Mart Supermarkets Disc	5141	D	530 583-5231	9299
Sunnyside Resort	7011	E	530 583-7200	11517
Tahoe City Public Utility Dist	4952	E	530 583-3796	8292
Tahoe Crss-Cntry Ski Edcatn As	7011	E	530 583-5475	11527
Tahoe House Inc	2051	F	530 583-1377	2406

TAHOE VISTA, CA - Placer County

Company	SIC	EMP	PHONE	ENTRY #
North Tahoe Public Utility Dst **(PA)**	4952	E	530 546-4212	8287
Perennial Landscape and Nurs	0782	E	530 546-7383	496

TOLLHOUSE, CA - Fresno County

Company	SIC	EMP	PHONE	ENTRY #
Duleys Landscape Inc	0782	E	559 855-5090	460

TOMALES, CA - Marin County

Company	SIC	EMP	PHONE	ENTRY #
Blue Mtn Ctr of Meditation Inc	2731	E	707 878-2369	3524

TRACY, CA - San Joaquin County

Company	SIC	EMP	PHONE	ENTRY #
A Teichert & Son Inc	1442	E	209 832-4150	583
All-In Machining LLC	3599	E	209 839-8672	5467
Altium Packaging LLC	3089	F	209 820-1700	4256
Amador Vly Med Group Ltd A CA	8062	D	925 828-9211	16319
American Custom Meats LLC	2013	D	209 839-8800	2111
American Engrg Contrs Inc	1731	C	209 229-1591	1449
American Pwr & Communications	1731	E	209 833-1369	1451
American Trck Trlr Bdy Co Inc **(PA)**	3713	E	209 836-8985	6563
AP Unlimited Corporation	5131	F	209 834-0287	9240
Applied Materials Inc	3674	E	408 679-2925	6041
Arnaudo Bros Transport Inc **(PA)**	0191	D	209 835-0406	146
Ashok N Veeranki DDS A Pro **(PA)**	8021	D	209 836-3870	15823
Aubin Industries Inc	3087	F	800 324-0051	4247
Barbosa Cabinets Inc	2434	B	209 836-2501	3169
Bescal Inc	3272	E	209 836-3492	4419
Chevron Stations Inc	5144	C	209 830-0370	9345
CJ Logistics America LLC	4225	D	209 362-2232	7686
Clonetab Inc	7372	E	209 292-5663	13073
Contract Metal Products Inc	3444	E	510 979-0000	4749
Controller Consulting Svcs Inc	8748	C	408 221-2492	19751
Costco Wholesale Corporation	4225	B	209 835-5222	7688
Courtesy Security Inc	7381	D	888 572-5545	14047
Drilling & Trenching Sup Inc **(PA)**	3545	F	510 895-1650	5094
Dynatect Ro-Lab Inc	3061	E	262 786-1500	4208
Feral Productions LLC	3599	E	510 791-5392	5525
Finis Inc **(PA)**	3949	E	925 454-0111	7196
First Class Svc Trckg Co Inc	4212	E	209 832-4669	7464
Fishel Company	1731	E	209 207-9068	1505
Frontier Transportation Inc	4214	E	209 836-0251	7621
Glassfab Tempering Svcs Inc **(PA)**	8748	D	209 229-1060	19784
Gloriann Farms Inc **(PA)**	0723	C	209 834-0010	285
Golden State Vintners **(PA)**	2084	F	707 254-4900	2598
Goodland Landscape Cnstr Inc	0782	E	209 835-9956	467
Green Valley Trnsp Corp	4213	E	209 836-5192	7548
Hand Crfted Dutchman Doors Inc	2431	E	209 833-7378	3134
Harold Reichs Pharmacy	3841	F	209 835-1832	6982
Industrial Relations Cal Dept	8631	E	209 830-7200	18360
Kaiser Foundation Hospitals	8011	C	209 839-3200	15456
Kaiser Foundation Hospitals	6324	C	209 832-6339	10130
Keebler Company	2052	C	209 836-0302	2416
Leprino Foods Company	2022	B	209 835-8340	2152
Lockheed Martin Corporation	3721	B	408 756-3008	6614
Lucky Stores II LLC	5122	D	209 830-1977	9229
Lynx Enterprises Inc	3444	D	209 833-3400	4780
Madruga Iron Works Inc	3441	E	209 832-7003	4674
Menasha Packaging Company LLC	2653	E	951 660-5361	3359
Mother Lode Plas Molding Inc	3089	E	209 532-5146	4304
Nwpc LLC	3443	D	209 836-5050	4727
Olive Musco Products Inc **(PA)**	2033	C	209 836-4600	2234
Pacific Gas and Electric Co	4911	C	559 263-5438	8182
Pacific Medical Inc **(PA)**	7389	C	800 726-9180	14351
Park Avenue Cleaners Inc	7212	E	209 914-1265	11629
Patel Plliam Hbli A Prof Med C	8011	E	209 832-8984	15585
Pereira Indus Cnstr Maint Inc	1521	E	209 835-2393	684
Process Specialties Inc	3674	E	209 832-1344	6258
San-I-Pak Pacific Inc	3443	E	209 836-2310	4730
South San Jquin Cnty Fire Auth	4941	D	209 831-6702	8275
Surtec Inc	2842	E	209 820-3700	4078
Teledyne Risi Inc **(HQ)**	2892	E	925 456-9700	4153
Thomsen Farms Inc	0139	E	209 835-5442	22
Top Shelf Manufacturing LLC	3841	F	209 834-8185	7051
Tracy Auto LP	7514	D	209 834-1111	14490
Tracy Dlta Solid Waste Mgt Inc	4953	D	209 835-0601	8369
Tracy Ford	7538	E	209 879-4700	14601
Tracy Grading & Paving Inc	1611	E	209 839-6590	1078
Tracy Mtl Rcvery Slid Wste Trn	4953	E	209 832-2355	8370
Tracy Press Inc	2711	E	209 835-3030	3486
Tracy Sutter Community Hosp	8062	B	209 835-1500	16688
Tracy Unified School District	8351	E	209 830-6054	18039
UPS Supply Chain Solutions Inc	4731	D	209 319-4116	7857
Volumetric Bldg Companies LLC	2439	E	623 236-5322	3215
W R Grace & Co	2819	C	209 839-2800	3800
Wendt Industries Inc	8741	E	209 836-4100	19422
West Coast Cryogenics Inc	3559	E	800 657-0545	5174

TRANQUILLITY, CA - Fresno County

Company	SIC	EMP	PHONE	ENTRY #
Don Gragnani Farms	0191	D	559 693-4352	159

TRINIDAD, CA - Humboldt County

Company	SIC	EMP	PHONE	ENTRY #
Cher-Ae Heights Indian Cmnty	7999	C	707 677-3611	15191

TRINITY CENTER, CA - Trinity County

Company	SIC	EMP	PHONE	ENTRY #
Mountain Resorts Inc	7011	E	530 286-2205	11315

TRUCKEE, CA - Nevada County

Company	SIC	EMP	PHONE	ENTRY #
A Teichert & Son Inc	1442	E	530 587-3811	582
Advanced Companies Inc	5032	E	530 582-0800	8615
Bhr Trs Tahoe LLC	7011	C	530 562-3045	10961
Clearcapitalcom Inc	6531	C	530 550-2500	10512
Donner Lake Village Resort	7011	D	530 587-6081	11058
Elements Mountain Company	7349	E	530 582-0300	11945
Epic Tech Inc **(PA)**	7389	D	877 627-2215	14265
Gallagher Inc	1521	E	530 414-0267	641
Gla Morris Construction Inc	1521	E	530 448-1613	644
Horvath Holdings Inc	2241	F	530 587-4700	2970
Isbell Construction Inc	1542	D	530 587-0230	894
Kelly & Stone Architects Inc	8712	E	530 214-8896	18893
L and C Cook Spcalty Foods Inc	5149	E	530 587-3939	9462
Lahontan Golf Club	7997	C	530 550-2400	15103

GEOGRAPHIC

TRUCKEE, CA GEOGRAPHIC SECTION

	SIC	EMP	PHONE	ENTRY #
Lahontan LLC	6552	D	530 550-2990	10705
Mark Tanner Construction Inc	1521	E	530 587-4000	667
Martis Camp Club	8322	B	530 550-6000	17642
Moonshine Ink LLC	2711	F	530 587-3607	3461
Northstar Community Svcs Dst	4941	E	530 562-0747	8255
Procureability Inc	8742	E	904 432-7001	19610
Recycled Spaces Inc	2519	F	530 587-3394	3299
Save Mart Supermarkets Disc	5141	D	530 587-5522	9300
Software Licensing Consultants	7372	E	925 371-1277	13452
Tahoe Forest Hospital District	8011	E	530 582-7488	15736
Tahoe Forest Hospital District	8062	D	530 582-3277	16684
Tahoe Forest Hospital District **(PA)**	8062	B	530 587-6011	16685
Tahoe Forest Womens Center	8011	E	530 587-1041	15737
Tahoe-Truckee Sanitation Agcy	4952	D	530 587-2525	8293
Telehealth Services USA	8011	D	415 424-4266	15738
Trimont Land Company **(DH)**	6531	B	530 562-1010	10676
Truckee Dnner Pub Utlty Dst F	4911	D	530 587-3896	8204
Truckee Dnner Rcreation Pk Dst	7999	D	530 582-7720	15258
Truckee Sanitary District	4952	E	530 587-3804	8294
Truckee-Tahoe Lumber Company **(PA)**	5023	E	530 587-9211	8522
Western Nevada Supply Co	5074	C	530 582-5009	9006

TULELAKE, CA - Siskiyou County

	SIC	EMP	PHONE	ENTRY #
Lava Beds National Monuments	8699	E	530 667-2282	18577

TUOLUMNE, CA - Tuolumne County

	SIC	EMP	PHONE	ENTRY #
Black Oak Casino	7999	D	209 928-9300	15183
Silver Spur Christian Camp	7032	E	209 928-4248	11611
Tuolumne M-Wuk Indian Hlth Ctr	8011	D	209 928-5400	15742

TURLOCK, CA - Stanislaus County

	SIC	EMP	PHONE	ENTRY #
Adtek Inc	3441	E	209 634-0300	4641
Advantage Route Systems Inc	7371	E	209 632-1122	12230
Alan J Vallarine DDS Inc	8021	E	209 669-8120	15820
Aspiranet	8082	E	209 669-2583	16851
Associated Feed & Supply Co **(PA)**	5191	C	209 667-2708	9594
Blue Diamond Growers	2099	C	209 604-1501	2872
Bonander Pontiac Inc **(PA)**	7539	D	209 632-8871	14607
Cal-Coast Dairy Systems Inc	3523	E	209 634-9026	4997
California Dairies Inc	2021	C	209 656-1942	2141
Central Cal Dar Cnstr Inc	1542	C	209 667-0381	852
Central California Faculty Med	8099	D	209 620-6937	17122
Central Valley Cheese Inc	5143	D	209 664-1080	9334
Central Valley Gaming LLC	7999	F	209 668-1010	15190
Central Valley Pizza LLC	6794	E	209 589-9633	10804
Clausen Meat Company Inc	2011	E	209 667-8690	2093
County of Stanislaus	8093	D	209 664-8044	17011
Covenant Care California LLC	8052	D	209 667-8409	16180
Covenant Care California LLC	8051	D	209 632-3821	15970
Covenant Living West	8062	D	209 667-5600	16343
Creative Alternatives	8361	C	209 668-9361	18091
Crimetek Security	7381	D	209 668-6208	14051
Dairy Farmers America Inc	2022	D	209 667-9627	2146
Daregal Inc	0139	C	209 633-3600	16
Diocese Stockton Eductl Off	8351	C	209 634-8578	17923
Emanuel Medical Center Inc **(DH)**	8062	A	209 667-4200	16362
Evergreen Packaging LLC	5199	C	209 664-3426	9657
Family Medical Group	8011	D	209 668-4101	15401
Fletcher Dors Windows Trim Inc	2431	F	209 632-3610	3132
Formax LLC	7629	E	800 800-1822	14698
Formax Technologies Inc	3699	F	209 668-1001	6521
Foster Poultry Farms	2015	D	209 668-5922	2133
Freshpoint Central California	5148	C	209 216-0200	9405
Funtopia Inc	7999	D	510 246-3098	15205
Garton Tractor Inc **(PA)**	5083	D	209 632-3931	9038
Gemperle Enterprises	0252	D	209 667-2651	230
Golden State Mixing Inc	2026	E	209 632-3656	2190
Grewal Bros Trucking Inc	4212	E	209 678-2557	7472
Hilmar Cheese Company Inc	2022	D	209 667-6076	2149
Humphrey Plumbing Inc	1711	D	209 634-4626	1280
Jackson-Mitchell Inc **(PA)**	2026	E	209 667-0786	2192
Jkb Homes Corp	1521	E	209 668-5303	656
Js Trucking Inc	3537	E	209 252-0007	5064
La Follette Enterprises Inc	0722	E	209 632-1385	265
Linde Gas & Equipment Inc	2813	E	800 225-8247	3772
Lock-N-Stitch Inc	3599	E	209 632-2345	5561
Lowes Home Centers LLC	5031	C	209 656-3020	8583
M4 Concrete and Drywall Inc **(PA)**	1771	D	209 850-9250	1890
M4 Concrete and Drywall Inc	1771	E	209 850-9250	1891
Machado & Sons Cnstr Inc	1521	E	209 632-5260	665
Mark One Corporation	8059	C	209 667-2484	16250
Millerick Engineering Inc	8711	D	209 664-9111	18771
Nelson & Sons Electric Inc	1731	E	209 667-4343	1547
Nordic Saw & Tool Mfrs Inc	3425	E	209 634-9015	4611
Northern Rfrigerated Trnsp Inc **(PA)**	4213	C	209 664-3800	7572
Oliveira-Lucas Enterprises Inc	1731	E	209 667-2851	1556
Pattar Trans Inc	4789	E	209 634-3849	7890
PJs Lumber Inc	1791	D	209 850-9444	1929
Poppy State Express Inc	4213	D	209 664-3950	7573
Premier Valley Inc A Cal Corp	6531	E	209 667-6111	10647
Professional Lumper Svc Inc	3537	E	209 613-5397	5067
R Millennium Transport Inc	4789	E	209 668-9700	7892
Rm Pallets Inc	2448	F	209 632-9887	3228
Rootlieb Inc	3465	E	209 632-2203	4877
Rose Joaquin Inc	5084	E	209 632-0616	9091
Ruan	4212	C	209 634-4928	7487
Ruan Transport Corporation	4213	E	209 599-5000	7581
Ruan Transport Corporation	4213	E	209 634-2768	7582
Seegers Industries Inc	2752	E	209 667-2750	3696
Select Harvest Usa LLC **(PA)**	5159	C	209 668-2471	9511
Sensient Ntral Ingredients LLC **(HQ)**	2099	E	209 667-2777	2942
Sodexo Management Inc	8741	B	209 667-3634	19400
Super Store Industries	2024	D	209 668-2100	2183
Superior Kitchen Cabinets Inc	2434	E	209 247-0097	3192
Swanson Farms	0253	E	209 667-2002	239
Tanco Inc	1711	E	209 523-8365	1376
Thorsens-Norquist Inc	1761	D	209 524-5296	1842
Tree Nuts LLC	5145	E	209 669-6400	9357
Turlock Christian School **(PA)**	8351	D	209 632-2337	18040
Turlock Dairy & Rfrgn Inc	5083	D	209 667-6455	9045
Turlock Fruit Co **(PA)**	5148	E	209 634-7207	9433
Turlock Golf and Country Club **(PA)**	7997	E	209 634-5471	15162
Turlock Hospitality LLC	7011	E	209 250-1501	11546
Turlock Irrgtion Dst Emplyees **(PA)**	4911	C	209 883-8222	8205
Turlock Machine Works	3593	E	209 632-2275	5453
Turlock Petroleum Inc	2911	F	209 634-8432	4183
Turlock Scavenger Company	4953	E	209 668-7274	8373
Turlock Sheet Metal & Wldg Inc	8711	E	209 667-4716	18841
USA Seller Co LLC	0752	B	209 656-7085	357
Valley Fresh Foods Inc	0252	E	209 669-5600	233
Valley Milk LLC	0241	D	209 410-6701	226
Volk Enterprises Inc	3496	D	209 632-3826	4972
Wilkey Industries Inc	1761	E	209 656-0561	1846
Winton Irland Strom Green Insu **(PA)**	6411	D	209 667-0995	10369
Yosemite Farm Credit Aca **(PA)**	6111	D	209 667-2366	9853

TWAIN HARTE, CA - Tuolumne County

	SIC	EMP	PHONE	ENTRY #
Century 21 Wildwood Properties	6531	E	209 586-3258	10507
M E Prigmore & Co **(PA)**	7291	E	530 223-6672	11702

TWIN BRIDGES, CA - El Dorado County

	SIC	EMP	PHONE	ENTRY #
Sierra At Taho Ski Resorts	7011	C	530 659-7519	11477

UKIAH, CA - Mendocino County

	SIC	EMP	PHONE	ENTRY #
AJPJ II LLC	7011	C	707 972-9563	10912
Alpha Analytical Labs Inc **(PA)**	8734	D	707 468-0401	19255
Berryman Health Inc	8051	E	707 462-8864	15946
Cold Creek Compost Inc	2875	E	707 485-5966	4138
County of Mendocino	4581	E	707 463-4363	7771
County of Mendocino	8093	C	707 463-4396	17006
Empire Waste Management	4953	D	707 462-2063	8327
Ensign Pleasanton LLC	8051	C	707 462-8864	15991
Enterprise Rnt—car San Frncsc	7514	E	707 462-2200	14478
Ford Street Project Inc	8361	E	707 462-1934	18116
Gatehouse Media LLC	2711	E	707 964-5642	3438
Jepson Vineyard Ltd	2084	F	707 468-8936	2631
Lake County Publishing Co Inc **(DH)**	2711	D	707 263-5636	3453
Maverick Enterprises Inc	3353	C	707 463-5591	4561
Mayfield Equipment Company **(PA)**	5191	E	707 462-2404	9605
McNab Ridge Winery LLC	2084	F	707 462-2423	2657
Medstar Amblnce Mndcino Cnty I	4119	E	707 462-3808	7390
Mendocino Brewing Company Inc **(HQ)**	2082	D	707 463-2627	2486
Mendocino Cmnty Hlth Clnic Inc **(PA)**	8011	C	707 468-1010	15529
Mendocino Forest Pdts Co LLC	5031	C	707 468-1431	8590
Mendocino Onsen Corportation	7011	E	707 462-6277	11295
Mendocino Redwood Company LLC **(PA)**	5031	E	707 463-5110	8594
Mendocino Transit Authority **(PA)**	4111	E	707 462-3881	7341
Nelson & Sons Inc	2084	E	707 462-3755	2666
Nightshade Holdings LLC	8051	E	707 462-1436	16071
Noble Vineyard Management Inc	0762	E	415 533-8642	383
North Cal Wood Products Inc	2421	E	707 462-0686	3099
Northern Cir Indian Hsing Auth	1522	E	707 468-1336	760
Pacific Redwood Medical Group	8011	D	707 462-7900	15580
Parducci Wine Estates LLC	2084	E	707 463-5350	2678
Performance Coatings Inc	2851	E	707 462-3023	4108
Plc LLC	2084	F	707 462-2423	2686
Premier Properties Inc	6531	E	707 467-0300	10646
Quinoa Corporation	2051	E	707 462-6605	2400
Redwood Community Services Inc	8322	D	707 472-2922	17685
Redwood Health Club **(PA)**	7991	D	707 468-0441	14967
Redwood Regional Medical Group	8011	E	707 463-3636	15645
Rural Cmmnities Hsing Dev Corp **(PA)**	6513	D	707 463-1975	10457
Savings Bank Mendocino County **(PA)**	6022	C	707 462-6613	9747
SERVPRO of Mendocino	7349	E	707 462-3848	11997
Tapestry Family Services Inc	8361	D	707 463-3300	18190
Ukiah Adventist Hospital	8062	D	707 462-8855	16691
Ukiah Adventist Hospital **(HQ)**	8062	B	707 462-3111	16692
Ukiah Adventist Hospital	8062	D	707 463-7587	16693
Ukiah Adventist Hospital	8062	D	707 462-3111	16694
United Parcel Service Inc	4215	C	707 468-5481	7669
Veterans Health Administration	8011	C	707 468-7700	15801
Waneshear Technologies LLC	3553	E	707 462-4761	5117
Waste MGT Collectn Recycl Inc	4953	D	707 462-0210	8388

UNION CITY, CA - Alameda County

	SIC	EMP	PHONE	ENTRY #
AAA Restaurant Fire Ctrl Inc	7389	D	510 786-9555	14191
Abaxis Inc **(HQ)**	3829	C	510 675-6500	6889
Aei Electech Corp	3679	F	510 489-5088	6395
Ajax - Untd Pttrns & Molds Inc	3089	C	510 476-8000	4253
American Licorice Company	2064	B	510 487-5500	2425
Animus Inc **(PA)**	8011	C	800 306-7910	15281
Ariat International Inc **(PA)**	3199	C	510 477-7000	4352
Axis Group Inc	3674	E	510 487-7393	6060
Axygen Inc **(HQ)**	3826	C	510 494-8900	6812
Azimuth Industrial Co Inc	3674	E	510 441-6000	6064
Basquez Tiburcio Health Center	8093	E	510 471-5907	16993

Company	SIC	EMP	PHONE	ENTRY #
Best Contracting Services Inc	1761	D	510 886-7240	1788
Blc Wc Inc	3565	E	510 489-5400	5197
Blommer Chocolate Company Cal	2066	C	510 471-4300	2436
California Performance Packg	3086	D	909 390-4422	4239
Caravan Bakery Inc	2051	F	510 487-2600	2372
Caravan Foods II Inc	2053	F	510 487-2600	2421
Celltheon Corporation	2834	F	650 743-3672	3881
Cemex Cnstr Mtls PCF LLC	3273	E	855 292-8453	4468
Child Family & Cmnty Svcs Inc	8351	C	510 796-9512	17892
Chinese Overseas Mktg Svc Corp	2741	E	510 476-0880	3562
Cmy Image Corporation	2752	F	510 516-6668	3637
Coast Citrus Distributors	5148	E	213 955-3448	9395
Compactor Management Co LLC	3444	E	510 623-2323	4748
Compro Packaging LLC	2653	E	510 475-0118	3356
Conklin & Conklin Incorporated	3452	E	510 489-5500	4872
Corinthian Realty LLC	6531	D	510 487-8653	10525
Datalogix Texas Inc	1731	E	510 475-8787	1494
Daylight Foods Inc	5148	C	510 931-4207	9397
Del Rosario Rene DMD **(PA)**	8021	E	510 324-2000	15831
Delta Yimin Technologies Inc	3089	E	510 487-4411	4275
Dust Networks Inc	3674	D	510 400-2900	6103
E-3 Systems	1541	E	510 487-9195	794
Electrochem Solutions Inc	3471	B	510 476-1840	4904
Electrochem Solutions LLC	3471	E	510 476-1840	4905
Emerald Packaging Inc	5199	C	510 429-5700	9656
EMR Cpr LLC	7373	B	408 471-6804	13582
Envise	1711	C	510 447-3300	1257
Farallon Brands Inc **(PA)**	2392	F	510 550-4299	3025
Finelite Inc **(PA)**	3646	C	510 441-1100	5735
Forward Air Inc	4731	E	415 570-6040	7835
Fricke-Parks Press Inc	2752	E	510 489-6543	3650
Gcm Holding Corporation	6719	B	510 475-0404	10735
Gcm Medical & Oem Inc **(PA)**	3444	D	510 475-0404	4764
Genesis Logistics Inc	4225	E	510 476-0790	7691
Harsch Investment Realty LLC	6531	E	510 475-0755	10570
Heco-Pacific Manufacturing Inc	3535	E	510 487-1155	5052
Jenson Mechanical Inc	3599	E	510 429-8078	5546
Kaiser Foundation Hospitals	6324	C	510 675-5777	10109
Kaiser Foundation Hospitals	8093	C	510 675-2377	17028
Kaiser Foundation Hospitals	8011	C	510 675-4010	15457
Kaiser Foundation Hospitals	6324	C	510 675-2170	10129
Kba Docusys Inc **(PA)**	5084	E	510 214-4040	9074
Kinwai USA Inc	2511	E	510 780-9388	3280
La Terra Fina Usa Inc	2099	D	510 404-5888	2912
Lamart Corporation	3292	C	510 489-8100	4526
Lane International Trading Inc **(PA)**	3143	D	510 489-7364	4341
Lotus Hotels - Union City LLC	7011	E	510 475-0600	11272
Lowes Home Centers LLC	5031	C	510 476-0600	8563
Masonic Homes of California	8361	B	510 441-3700	18143
Mercado Latino Inc	5141	C	510 475-5500	9280
Mizuho Orthopedic Systems Inc **(HQ)**	3841	B	510 429-1500	7009
New Horizon Foods Inc	2099	E	510 489-8600	2926
New World Van Lines Inc	4214	D	510 487-1091	7629
Northwood Design Partners Inc	2521	E	510 731-6505	3308
Orcon Aerospace	3728	D	510 489-8100	6636
Permanente Medical Group Inc	6324	B	510 675-4010	10153
Ptr Manufacturing Inc	3599	E	510 477-9654	5605
R & S Manufacturing Inc **(HQ)**	3442	E	510 429-1788	4708
Rapid Displays Inc	3993	F	510 471-6955	7250
Reliance Steel & Aluminum Co	5051	D	510 476-4400	8827
Ritescreen Inc	2431	F	800 949-4174	3148
Rki Instruments Inc **(PA)**	5084	D	510 441-5656	9090
Selway Machine Tool Co Inc **(PA)**	5084	E	510 487-9291	9094
Sepragen Corporation	3826	E	510 475-0650	6850
Smart Wires Inc **(PA)**	3677	D	415 800-5555	6384
Southern Cal Disc Tire Co Inc	5014	C	510 429-1977	8478
Southern Glzers Wine Sprits WA	5182	B	510 477-5500	9585
Spacesonics Incorporated	3444	D	650 610-0999	4820
Specialized Laundry Svcs Inc	7218	C	510 487-8297	11670
SSC Inc **(HQ)**	5146	D	510 477-0008	9370
SW Safety Solutions Inc	2259	E	510 429-8692	2975
Synergy Machines LLC	7389	E	408 676-9696	14423
Touchofmodern Inc	7389	C	888 868-1232	14436
Tournesol Siteworks LLC **(PA)**	1799	D	800 542-2282	2078
Tr Manufacturing LLC **(HQ)**	3679	C	510 657-3850	6479
Tri-City Economic Dev Corp	4953	D	510 429-8030	8371
Ultimo Software Solutions Inc	7371	C	408 943-1490	12886
Union Sanitary District	4952	C	510 477-7500	8295
United Mech Met Fbricators Inc	3444	E	510 537-4744	4827
United Misc & Orna Stl Inc	3441	E	510 429-8755	4691
Usk Manufacturing Inc	3444	E	510 471-7555	4828
Vicarious Fpc Inc	5045	E	415 604-3278	8760
W B Mason Co Inc	2752	E	888 926-2766	3711

UPPER LAKE, CA - Lake County

Company	SIC	EMP	PHONE	ENTRY #
Running Creek Casino	7011	C	707 275-9209	11423

VACAVILLE, CA - Solano County

Company	SIC	EMP	PHONE	ENTRY #
Ad Spcial TS EMB Scrnprnting I	2396	F	707 452-7272	3044
Allied Framers Inc	1751	C	707 452-7050	1729
Alza Corporation **(HQ)**	2834	A	707 453-6400	3843
Alza Corporation	3826	A	707 453-6400	6807
B K D Holdings	7011	E	650 704-3454	10942
Backyard Unlimited	1542	E	707 447-7433	826
Blue Mountain Cnstr Svcs Inc	1711	C	800 889-2085	1222
Bouwman Engineering Inc	8711	F	707 447-5414	18643
Brenden Theatre Corporation	7832	D	707 469-0180	14804
Cal Inc	1542	E	707 446-7996	848
Clark Pest Ctrl Stockton Inc	7342	E	707 446-9748	11888
Community Medical Centers Inc	8011	E	707 359-1800	15361
Dr Earth Inc	2873	F	707 448-4676	4130
Duravent Inc **(DH)**	3444	B	800 835-4429	4756
Fairfeld Inn By Mrrott Vcville	7011	D	707 469-0800	11089
Fortune Brands Windows Inc	3089	C	707 446-7600	4282
Genentech Inc	2834	E	707 454-1000	3905
Icon Aircraft Inc **(PA)**	3728	C	707 564-4000	6634
Integration Banks Group LLC	8711	E	707 451-1100	18740
Interntnal Brthd Elc Wkr Lcal **(PA)**	8631	D	707 452-2700	18364
Jack Anthony Industries Inc	7542	E	707 448-0104	14642
Jaj Roofing **(PA)**	1761	B	707 446-5500	1813
Jbr Associates Inc	7011	D	707 451-3500	11210
K B R Inc **(PA)**	7322	D	707 454-2000	11825
Kaiser Foundation Hospitals	8062	A	707 624-4000	16396
Kaiser Foundation Hospitals	8011	C	707 624-4000	15455
Kaiser Foundation Hospitals	6324	C	707 624-4000	10120
Kappel and Kappel Inc **(PA)**	6531	E	707 446-0600	10590
Kuic Inc	4832	D	707 446-0200	8029
Lowes Home Centers LLC	5031	C	707 455-4400	8561
Mariani Packing Co Inc **(PA)**	0723	B	707 452-2800	292
Mariani Packing Partnership LP	2671	E	707 452-2864	3375
Master Plastics Incorporated	3089	E	707 451-3168	4299
McC Controls LLC	3589	E	218 847-1317	5442
McKenzie Hardware Inc	5072	E	707 448-2978	8987
MCS Opco LLC	5063	E	203 740-4236	8868
Merrill Lynch Prce Fnner Smith	6211	D	925 988-2113	9982
North Bay Distribution Inc **(PA)**	4225	D	707 452-9984	7696
Northbay Healthcare Group	8062	E	707 446-4000	16467
Novartis Pharmaceuticals Corp	2835	B	707 452-8081	4028
Pacific Gas and Electric Co	4911	C	707 446-7381	8138
Pacific Gas and Electric Co	4911	C	800 684-4648	8153
Pacific Gas and Electric Co	4911	C	707 452-1983	8179
Pre-Insulated Metal Tech Inc **(HQ)**	3448	E	707 359-2280	4855
Premium Outlet Partners LP	6512	D	707 448-3661	10401
Primetek Field Solutions Inc	1731	E	619 271-4555	1570
Reporter	2711	D	707 448-6401	3475
Right Now Air	1711	E	707 447-3063	1346
Rxd Nova Pharmaceuticals Inc	2834	F	610 952-7242	3980
Solano Irrigation District	4971	D	707 448-6847	8418
Stars Recreation Center LP	7933	E	707 455-7827	14901
State Compensation Insur Fund	6331	D	415 565-1222	10175
State Compensation Insur Fund	6331	D	707 455-9900	10179
State Hospitals Cal Dept	8063	B	707 449-6504	16747
Summit Crane Inc	7353	E	707 448-6740	12024
Sunrise Palace Inc	7011	E	707 469-2323	11519
Sutter Regional Med Foundation	8011	D	707 454-5800	15733
Synder Inc **(PA)**	3677	E	707 451-6060	6387
Thriving Seniors LLC	8059	D	707 317-1740	16277
Timbuk2 Designs Inc	2393	E	800 865-2513	3033
Travis Credit Union **(PA)**	6061	B	707 449-4000	9824
Triumph Protection Group Inc	7381	C	800 224-0286	14102
Vaca Valley Inn	7011	D	707 446-8888	11552
Vaca Valley Roofing Inc **(PA)**	1761	E	707 469-7470	1843
Vacaville Condolescent and Reh	7363	C	707 449-8000	12203
Vacaville Fruit Co Inc **(PA)**	2034	E	707 448-5292	2273
Vacavlle Cnvalescent Rehab Ctr	8059	D	707 449-8000	16281
Valyria LLC **(HQ)**	5023	D	707 452-0600	8523
Westlake Development Group LLC	8059	C	707 447-7496	16283
Wunder-Mold Inc	3089	E	707 448-2349	4336

VALLECITO, CA - Calaveras County

Company	SIC	EMP	PHONE	ENTRY #
Chalcedon Inc	6732	F	209 736-4365	10786
Twisted Oak Winery LLC **(PA)**	2084	F	209 728-3000	2751

VALLEJO, CA - Napa County

Company	SIC	EMP	PHONE	ENTRY #
Golden State Vintners	2084	E	707 553-6480	2600
1st Pacific Credit Union **(PA)**	6061	E	707 552-4550	9773
Blu Homes Inc **(PA)**	1521	C	866 887-7997	620
Broadspectrum Americas Inc	8742	E	707 642-2222	19460
Califrnia Mrtime Acdemy Fndtio	6732	C	707 654-1000	10785
Caminar	8093	E	707 648-8121	16998
Century Theatres Inc	7832	C	707 648-3456	14808
City of Vallejo	8111	E	707 648-4361	17229
County of Solano	8071	E	707 553-5029	16778
Crestwood Behavioral Hlth Inc	8063	D	707 234-2222	16739
Dreamctchers Empwerment Netwrk	3679	E	707 558-1775	6420
Earthquake Protection Systems	8711	D	707 644-5993	18698
Emeritus Corporation	8051	C	707 552-3336	15985
Empres Financial Services LLC	8051	A	707 643-2793	15986
Evergreen At Heartwood Ave LLC	8051	E	707 643-2267	15997
Evergreen At Springs Road LLC	8051	D	360 892-6628	16000
Getright Ventures Inc	6163	D	510 402-4816	9940
Ghiringhlli Spcialty Foods Inc	2099	C	707 561-7670	2896
Greater Vallejo Recreation Dst	7999	D	707 648-4600	15209
Greenflds Intrmdate Care Fclty	8741	E	707 553-2935	19344
Helios Healthcare LLC	8059	E	707 644-7401	16238
Hiddenbrook Golf Club **(PA)**	7997	D	707 558-0330	15098
Jack Anthony Industries Inc	7542	E	707 557-5353	14644
Jbe Inc	2541	F	707 552-6800	3315
Jeffco Painting & Coating Inc	1721	D	707 562-1900	1417
Kaiser Foundation Hospitals	6324	C	707 645-2720	10112
Kaiser Foundation Hospitals	6324	C	707 651-2311	10119
Kaiser Foundation Hospitals	8062	A	707 651-1000	16414
Keystone NPS LLC	8399	C	510 206-8463	18237
La Clinica De La Raza Inc	8011	C	707 556-8100	15496
M F Maher Inc	1771	D	707 552-2774	1889
Mare Island Dry Dock LLC	3731	D	707 652-7356	6639

GEOGRAPHIC

Employment Codes: A=Over 500 employees, B=251-500, C=101-250, D=51-100, E=20-50 F=10-19
2022 Northern California Business Directory and Buyers Guide

1231

	SIC	EMP	PHONE	ENTRY #
Medic Ambulance Service Inc **(PA)**	4119	C	707 644-1761	7387
Meyer Corporation US **(HQ)**	3469	D	707 551-2800	4886
Mhm Services Inc	8093	C	707 652-2688	17042
Michaels Trnsp Svc Inc	4141	D	707 674-6013	7417
Milestones Development Inc	8052	E	707 644-0496	16191
Moose Boats Inc	3732	F	707 778-9828	6645
Murga Strange & Chalmers Inc	1771	E	707 643-9075	1895
Park Management Corp	7996	C	707 643-6722	15045
Permanente Medical Group Inc	8011	A	707 765-3930	15592
Praxis Associates Inc	7389	E	707 551-8200	14370
R & R Maher Construction Co	1771	E	707 552-0330	1903
Recology Vallejo **(HQ)**	4953	C	707 552-3110	8355
Renos Floor Covering Inc	3996	E	415 459-1403	7266
Roman Cathlic Bishp Sacramento	8322	D	707 556-9317	17695
Sak Hospitality Inc	7011	D	707 554-9655	11428
Santa Croce LLC	2085	F	707 227-7834	2777
Sfn Group Inc	7363	A	707 551-2719	12199
Solano Collission Inc	7532	E	707 644-4044	14533
Solano County Fair Association	7999	D	707 551-2000	15243
Solano Hematology/Oncology LLC	8011	E	707 551-3300	15691
Successful Altrntves For Addct **(HQ)**	8069	E	707 649-8300	16770
Sutter Health	8062	C	707 551-3400	16639
Sutter Hlth Scrmnto Sierra Reg	8062	B	707 554-4444	16667
Sutter Solano Medical Center	8062	A	707 554-4444	16675
Teamross Inc	7538	D	707 643-9000	14595
Timec Acquisitions Inc **(DH)**	1629	A	707 642-2222	1182
Timec Companies Inc **(DH)**	1629	B	707 642-2222	1183
United Parcel Service Inc	4215	C	707 252-4560	7667
Vallejo City Unified Schl Dst	8351	D	707 556-8694	18042
Vallejo Flood & Wastewater Dst	8748	D	707 644-8949	19882
Vallejo Flood Wstwter Dst Fing	8748	D	707 644-8949	19883
Vallejo Nissan Inc	5013	E	707 643-8291	8472
Veterans Health Administration	8011	C	707 562-8200	15787
Western Dovetail Incorporated	2511	E	707 556-3683	3285
Young MNS Chrstn Assn San Frnc	8641	E	707 643-9622	18522

VALLEY SPRINGS, CA - Calaveras County

	SIC	EMP	PHONE	ENTRY #
Dirt Dynasty Inc	1611	E	209 623-1141	1032
East Bay Mncpl Utlity Dst Wstw	4941	C	209 772-8204	8234
East Bay Mncpl Utlity Dst Wtr	4941	E	209 772-8200	8240
Fisk Demolition Inc **(PA)**	1795	E	209 323-8999	1986
La Contenta Investors Ltd	7992	E	209 772-1081	15005
RES-Care Inc	8082	E	209 227-4568	16934

VINA, CA - Tehama County

	SIC	EMP	PHONE	ENTRY #
Andersen & Sons Shelling Inc	0723	D	530 839-2236	269

WALNUT CREEK, CA - Contra Costa County

	SIC	EMP	PHONE	ENTRY #
10 Fold Communications Inc	8743	E	925 271-8205	19680
24hr Homecare LLC	8082	D	925 322-8627	16829
A F Evans Company Inc	7389	D	925 937-1700	14190
Ace Parking Management Inc	7521	D	925 295-3283	14506
Advanced Ti Inc	1522	E	925 299-0515	734
Advisor Software Inc **(PA)**	7372	E	925 299-7782	12959
Alamo Capital	6211	E	925 472-5700	9955
All Environmental Inc **(PA)**	8748	E	925 746-6000	19716
Amen Clinics Inc A Med Corp	8099	E	650 416-7830	17099
American Financial Network Inc	6282	D	925 705-7710	10027
American Mechanical Inc	1711	E	925 946-9101	1199
American Reprographics Co LLC **(HQ)**	8744	E	925 949-5100	19701
Amerit Fleet Solutions Inc **(HQ)**	7549	D	877 512-6374	14656
Amerit Fleet Solutions Inc	8744	C	877 512-6374	19702
Andre-Boudin Bakeries Inc	2051	E	925 935-4375	2361
Arch US MI Holdings Inc **(HQ)**	6351	C	800 909-4264	10191
Argonaut Kensington Associates	8322	E	925 943-1121	17432
Asd Global Inc	7373	E	925 975-0690	13556
Auto Clerk Inc	7371	E	925 284-1005	12285
Axiom Global Technologies Inc	8748	C	925 393-5800	19725
Barcelon Associates MGT Corp	6531	C	925 627-7000	10493
Basic American Inc **(PA)**	2034	D	925 472-4438	2251
Bay Area Srgcal Spclsts Inc A	8011	C	925 350-4044	15290
Bay Imaging Cons Med Group Inc **(PA)**	8011	D	925 296-7150	15291
Bay Medical Management LLC	8011	C	925 296-7150	15292
Bb Franchising LLC	6794	D	510 817-2786	10803
Bbva USA	6035	C	925 947-3434	9768
BDS Plumbing Inc	1711	E	925 939-1004	1216
Bell-Carter Foods LLC **(PA)**	2033	B	209 549-5939	2213
Bentley Systems Incorporated	7371	D	925 933-2525	12301
Berding & Weil LLP **(PA)**	8111	D	925 838-2090	17210
Blanding Boyer & Rockwell LLP	6513	E	925 954-0113	10419
Bohannan Concrete Inc	1771	E	925 932-2192	1854
Bowles & Verna	8111	E	925 935-3300	17217
Bpg Storage Solutions Inc	8741	E	562 467-2000	19308
Bpo Systems Inc **(PA)**	8748	E	925 478-4299	19734
Brian D Hopkins MD	8011	E	925 378-4517	15302
Broadway By Bay	7922	C	650 579-5565	14839
Brosamer & Wall Inc	8711	C	925 932-7900	18646
Brosamer & Wall LLC	6531	E	925 932-7900	10497
Brown and Caldwell **(PA)**	8711	C	925 937-9010	18647
Burr Pilger Mayer Inc	8721	D	925 296-1040	18939
C2 Financial Corporation	6282	C	925 938-1300	10036
California Physicians Service	6324	D	925 927-7419	10094
Carollo Engineers Inc **(PA)**	8711	D	925 932-1710	18662
Carros Sensors Systems Co LLC	3829	B	925 979-4400	6896
Central Garden & Pet Company **(PA)**	5199	E	925 948-4000	9649
Cherry Bekaert LLP	8721	E	925 954-0100	18944
Civil Svc Employees Insur Co **(PA)**	6411	E	800 282-6848	10261
Compwest Insurance Company	6331	C	415 593-5100	10166
Concord Jet Service Inc	7359	E	925 825-2980	12035
Contra Costa Newspapers Inc **(DH)**	2711	A	925 935-2525	3429
Covello Group Inc	4952	E	925 933-2300	8280
Covia Affordable Communities	8322	C	925 956-7400	17522
Csaa Insurance Exchange **(PA)**	6411	A	925 279-2300	10267
Csaa Insurance Services Inc **(HQ)**	6411	D	925 279-3153	10268
Cushman & Wakefield Cal Inc	6531	A	925 935-0770	10531
Cytosport Inc	2023	C	707 751-3942	2158
David L Gates & Associates Inc	0781	D	925 736-8176	411
Del Monte Foods Inc **(HQ)**	5149	C	925 949-2772	9448
Denalect Inc	7382	D	925 935-2680	14127
Deplabs Inc	7379	D	415 456-5600	13879
Derouen Enterprises LLC	7389	D	925 360-5743	14252
Diablo Ballet	7922	E	925 943-1775	14846
Diablo Clinical Research Inc	2834	E	925 930-7267	3892
Diablo Country Magazine Inc	2721	E	925 943-1111	3496
Diablo Crdiolgy Med Group Inc	8011	E	925 933-6981	15378
Diablo Realty	6531	E	925 933-9300	10537
Diablo Valley Eye Medical Ctr	8011	E	925 934-6300	15379
Domico Software	7372	F	510 841-4155	13120
E E S Corp	8711	E	925 947-6880	18693
East Bay Municipl Utilty Distr	4941	E	866 403-2683	8245
Employerware LLC	2741	E	925 283-9735	3569
Engineered Soil Repairs Inc **(PA)**	1741	D	408 297-2150	1646
Erin Engineering and RES Inc **(HQ)**	8711	E	925 943-7077	18706
Erm-West Inc **(DH)**	8711	C	925 946-0455	18707
Ernest J Wintter	8721	E	925 933-2626	18957
Exadel Inc **(PA)**	7372	C	925 363-9510	13155
Fashion Cleaners **(PA)**	7216	E	925 672-5505	11652
Fehr & Peers **(PA)**	8711	D	925 977-3200	18710
First Alarm SEC & Patrol Inc	7381	B	925 295-1260	14056
Forensic Logic Inc	7372	E	415 810-2114	13170
Fugro William Lettis Assoc Inc **(DH)**	8711	E	925 256-6070	18712
Galloway Lucchese Everson	8111	E	925 930-9090	17270
Gas Transmission Systems Inc	8711	E	925 478-8530	18715
General Plumbing Supply Co Inc **(PA)**	5074	E	925 939-4622	8998
Glaspy & Glaspy A Prof Corp	8111	E	408 279-8844	17274
Gmp Manufacturing Inc	2023	E	707 751-3942	2162
Golden Rain Foundation **(PA)**	6531	B	925 988-7700	10561
Golden Rain Foundation	8641	E	925 988-7800	18427
Halfzeez LLC	8732	E	833 824-5675	19165
Harvest Technical Service Inc	7361	C	925 937-4874	12095
Hofmann Construction Co **(PA)**	1531	E	925 478-2000	781
Holiday Garden Wc Corp	7011	E	925 932-3332	11148
Home Care Assistance LLC **(PA)**	8082	A	650 462-9501	16891
Innosys Incorporated	7371	E	510 594-1034	12522
Insignia Capital Partners LP **(PA)**	5145	D	925 399-8900	9355
Institutional Real Estate Inc **(PA)**	2741	E	925 933-4040	3577
Integrated Pain Management	8011	D	925 691-9806	15435
Interpet Usa LLC **(HQ)**	5199	E	925 948-4000	9662
Izt Mortgage Inc **(PA)**	6163	E	925 946-1858	9942
J M D Enterprises **(PA)**	7231	D	925 935-4780	11686
John Muir Diabetes Cntr Walnut	8062	E	925 952-2944	16391
John Muir Health **(HQ)**	8062	A	925 947-4449	16392
John Muir Health	8062	A	925 939-3000	16393
John Muir Physician Network	8011	E	925 988-7580	15441
John Muir Physician Network **(PA)**	8062	A	925 296-9700	16394
Joroda Inc **(PA)**	2051	E	925 930-0122	2389
Kaiser Foundation Hospitals	8062	A	925 906-2380	16398
Kaiser Foundation Hospitals	8011	C	925 295-4145	15448
Kaiser Foundation Hospitals	8011	C	925 295-4000	15471
Kaiser Foundation Hospitals	8062	A	925 906-2000	16411
Kaiser Foundation Hospitals	6324	D	925 926-3000	10123
Kcctech LLC	8748	C	628 400-2420	19804
Kelleyamerit Holdings Inc **(PA)**	8741	A	877 512-6374	19358
Kimco Staffing Services Inc	8099	A	925 945-1444	17157
Kugga Inc	7371	D	925 639-0721	12565
Leisure Sports Inc	7011	B	925 938-3058	11260
Leland Saylor & Associates Inc	8711	E	415 291-3200	18753
Life Gnerations Healthcare LLC	8051	E	925 937-7450	16036
Lindsay Wildlife Museum	8412	D	925 935-1978	18274
Lithia of Walnut Creek Inc	7549	E	925 937-6900	14664
LN Curtis and Sons **(PA)**	5087	D	510 839-5111	9145
Longs Drug Stores Cal LLC	7384	C	925 938-7616	14178
Loving Campos Associates **(PA)**	8712	E	925 944-1626	18896
Mackevision LLC	7373	C	248 656-6566	13630
Malikco LLC	7372	E	925 974-3555	13288
Marquez & Associates RE Inc	6531	E	510 863-0081	10612
Mason-Mcduffie Real Estate Inc **(PA)**	6531	E	925 924-4600	10614
Maximum Games Inc **(PA)**	7371	E	925 708-3242	12599
Meals On Wheels Diablo Region **(PA)**	8322	E	925 937-8311	17644
Mechanics Bank **(DH)**	6022	C	800 797-6324	9738
Mediajel Inc **(PA)**	7371	E	925 393-0444	12601
Medical Anesthesia Cons LLC	8011	C	925 287-1505	15526
Medical Anesthesia Cons LLC **(DH)**	8011	E	925 543-0140	15527
Merrill Lynch Prce Fnner Smith	6211	D	925 945-4800	9993
Mg4 Manufacturing Inc	5169	D	925 295-9700	9520
Michael Baker Intl Inc	8711	D	925 949-2452	18769
Miller Starr Rglia A Prof Law **(PA)**	8111	D	925 935-9400	17335
Muir John Mgntic Imging Ctr L	8062	D	925 296-7156	16461
Muir Labs	8062	E	925 947-3335	16462
Muir Orthopedic Specialists	8011	C	925 939-8585	15542
Muir Orthopedics Inc	8011	D	925 939-8585	15543
Murphy McKay & Associates Inc	7379	E	925 283-9555	13941
Network Management & Ctrl Corp	8741	D	319 483-1123	19373
Newport Group Inc **(PA)**	6411	C	925 328-4540	10319
Nic USA Inc	8322	E	925 944-1222	17655

GEOGRAPHIC SECTION WEST SACRAMENTO, CA

	SIC	EMP	PHONE	ENTRY #
Nordstrom Inc	8741	C	925 930-7959	19374
North American Title Co Inc	6361	D	925 935-0400	10206
Northpinte Veterinary Hosp Inc	0742	E	530 674-8670	331
Northstar Risk MGT Insur Svcs	6411	E	925 975-5900	10323
NRG California North LLC **(HQ)**	4911	C	925 287-3133	8129
One Planet Ops Inc **(PA)**	7311	C	925 983-2800	11776
Pacific Coast Bankers Bank	6022	D	415 399-1900	9741
Paracosma Inc	7371	D	650 924-9896	12669
Permanente Medical Group Inc	8011	A	925 906-2000	15612
PK Kinder Co Inc	5141	E	925 939-7242	9288
Presidio Gate Apartments **(PA)**	8361	D	925 956-7400	18158
Private Eyes Inc **(PA)**	7381	E	925 927-3333	14088
Recurrent Enrgy Dev Hldngs LLC **(DH)**	6799	D	415 675-1501	10879
Richard Avlar Assoc A Cal Corp	8712	E	510 893-5501	18909
Robotlab Inc	3577	E	415 702-3033	5408
Rossmoor Realty	6531	E	925 932-1162	10655
Schnabel Foundation Company	1794	D	925 947-1881	1974
Seal Software Incorporated **(HQ)**	7372	F	650 938-7325	13431
Sedgwick Claims MGT Svcs Inc	6411	D	925 988-1536	10344
Sequoia Surgical Center LP	8062	E	925 935-6700	16521
Signature Painting & Cnstr Inc	1721	E	925 287-0444	1432
Sports Medicine	8011	D	925 934-3536	15699
Springfield Montessori School	8351	E	925 944-0626	18027
Standard Insurance Company	6411	E	925 947-3950	10353
Stantec Consulting Svcs Inc	8711	C	925 627-4500	18819
Stantec Energy & Resources Inc	8713	C	925 627-4508	18926
Systems Intgrtion Slutions Inc **(PA)**	7379	E	925 465-7400	13986
Tactical Telesolutions Inc	7389	C	415 788-8808	14424
Tectonic Engrg Srvying Cons PC	8711	E	925 357-8236	18829
Terra Nova Industries	1542	E	925 934-6133	973
Thomas Wirig Doll & Co Cpas	8721	D	925 939-2500	19001
Tony Lrssas Anmal Rscue Fndtio	0742	D	925 256-1273	339
Travelers Property Cslty Corp	6411	C	925 945-4000	10361
Tri Commercial RE Svcs	6531	E	925 296-3300	10674
Trustarc Inc **(HQ)**	8742	D	415 520-3400	19657
Van De Poel Levy & Allen LLP	8111	E	925 274-7650	17385
Velociti Partners Inc	8742	E	866 300-2925	19665
Vitas Healthcare Corp Cal	8052	E	925 930-9373	16210
Walnut Creek Associates 2 Inc	7538	D	925 934-0530	14602
Waste MGT Collectn Recycl Inc	4212	C	925 935-8900	7497
Wencon Development Inc	1711	D	925 478-8269	1398
Western National Life Insur Co	6411	C	925 946-5100	10368
Whiting Fallon & Ross	8111	E	925 296-6000	17396
Wymac Capital Inc **(PA)**	6163	E	925 937-4300	9953
Xl Specialty Insurance Company	6351	B	925 942-6142	10194
Yapstone Inc **(PA)**	7389	C	866 289-5977	14465
ZMC Hotels LLC **(HQ)**	8741	E	925 933-4000	19429

WALNUT GROVE, CA - Sacramento County

	SIC	EMP	PHONE	ENTRY #
Wilcox Brothers Inc	3523	D	916 776-1784	5022

WATERFORD, CA - Stanislaus County

	SIC	EMP	PHONE	ENTRY #
Foster Poultry Farms	2015	B	209 394-7901	2131
Frazier Nut Farms Inc	0173	E	209 522-1406	89
Riddle Ranches Inc	0173	E	209 874-9784	91

WATSONVILLE, CA - Santa Cruz County

	SIC	EMP	PHONE	ENTRY #
3-Way Farms **(PA)**	0181	E	831 722-0748	115
A & I Trucking Inc **(PA)**	4213	E	831 763-7805	7500
Aggrigator Inc	7372	E	831 728-2824	12961
Amar Transportation Inc **(PA)**	4213	C	831 728-8209	7503
Ameri-Kleen	7349	C	831 722-8888	11917
Annieglass Inc **(PA)**	3229	F	831 761-2041	4369
Bonnie Plants Inc	5191	B	541 441-2847	9595
Boyer Inc	2873	E	831 724-0123	4129
California Pajarosa Floral	0181	E	831 722-6374	116
Camflor Inc	5193	C	831 726-1330	9629
CBS Farms LLC	0171	E	831 724-0700	39
Central Coast YMCA	8641	C	831 728-9622	18406
Coastwide Envmtl Tech Inc	1799	E	831 761-5511	2022
Colleen Strawberries Inc **(PA)**	0171	E	831 724-0700	40
Community Bridges **(PA)**	8322	E	831 688-8840	17493
Community Bridges	8322	D	831 724-2024	17494
Consolidated Training LLC	3999	E	831 768-8888	7278
Corralitos Market & Sausage Co	2013	E	831 722-2633	2116
Couch Distributing Company Inc	5181	C	831 724-0649	9548
Cryowest Inc	3443	E	831 786-9721	4719
Del Mar Food Products Corp	2033	B	831 722-3516	2214
DLa Colmena Inc	2051	E	831 724-4544	2375
Driscolls Inc **(PA)**	5148	D	831 424-0506	9398
Driscolls Inc	5148	D	800 871-3333	9399
E & B Marine Inc **(HQ)**	5088	D	831 728-2700	9150
Eagle Tech Manufacturing Inc	3823	E	831 768-7467	6717
Elecraft Incorporated	3825	E	831 763-4211	6749
Elkhorn Berry Farms LLC	0191	E	831 722-2472	162
Encompass Community Services	8069	D	831 688-6293	16757
Encompass Community Services	8322	E	831 728-2226	17550
Encompass Community Services	8322	E	831 724-3885	17551
Ernst Benary of America Inc	0181	E	831 288-2803	121
Field Fresh Farms LLC	5148	D	831 722-1422	9402
Fitz Fresh Inc	0182	D	831 763-4440	143
Fox Factory Inc **(HQ)**	3714	C	831 274-6500	6580
Granit-Bayashi 3 A Joint Ventr	1611	E	831 724-1011	1046
Granite Cnstr Northeast Inc	1611	E	831 724-1011	1047
Granite Construction Co Guam **(DH)**	1521	D	831 724-1011	647
Granite Construction Company **(HQ)**	1611	C	831 724-1011	1048
Granite Construction Inc **(PA)**	1622	A	831 724-1011	1083
Granite Power Inc	8741	B	831 724-1011	19343
Granite Rock Co **(PA)**	1442	D	831 768-2000	593
Granite Rock Co	5032	E	831 724-3847	8627
Greenhouse System USA	1542	E	831 722-1188	881
Greenwaste Recovery Inc **(PA)**	4953	D	408 283-4800	8335
Grunsky Ebey Farrar & Howel	8111	E	831 688-1180	17284
HA Rider & Sons Inc	2086	E	831 722-3882	2791
Halsen Healthcare LLC	8062	A	831 724-4741	16384
Hanuman Fellowship **(PA)**	8641	E	408 847-0406	18429
Heatwave Labs Inc	3671	F	831 722-9081	5902
Hospice of Santa Cruz County	8082	D	831 430-3000	16897
K & D Landscaping Inc	0781	D	831 728-4018	422
La Rosa Tortilla Factory Inc	2099	C	831 728-5332	2909
Laselva Beach Spice Co Inc	2099	F	831 724-4500	2914
Maggiora Bros Drilling Inc **(PA)**	1781	E	831 724-1338	1920
Martinlli Orchrd Oprations LLC	2099	E	831 724-1126	2921
Mizkan America Inc	2099	D	831 728-2061	2924
Monterey Mushrooms Inc **(PA)**	0182	E	831 763-5300	144
Monterey Structural Steel Inc	3441	F	831 768-1277	4677
Mount Madonna School	8351	C	408 847-2717	17980
Noah Pharmaceuticals Inc	2833	E	707 631-0921	3819
Nordic Naturals Inc **(PA)**	2077	C	800 662-2544	2458
Pajaro Vly Prvntion Stdnt Asss	8322	D	831 728-6445	17668
Plant Sciences Inc **(PA)**	8731	E	831 728-7771	19103
Printworx Inc	3577	F	831 722-7147	5405
Rainbow Fin Company Inc	3949	F	831 728-2998	7200
Ramco Enterprises LP	7361	A	831 722-3370	12124
Rio Mesa Farms LLC	0171	E	831 728-1965	41
S Martinelli & Company **(PA)**	2099	C	831 724-1126	2940
Salud Para La Gente	8011	C	831 728-0222	15659
Sambrailo Packaging **(PA)**	5113	E	831 724-7581	9218
Santa Cruz Co Head Start	8351	E	831 724-3885	18016
Santa Cruz Metro Trnst Dst	4111	D	831 426-6080	7357
Schmid Thermal Systems Inc	3567	C	831 763-0113	5217
Seascape Lamps Inc	3645	F	831 728-5699	5725
Second Hrvest Fd Bnk Srving Sn	8322	E	831 722-7110	17725
Smith & Vandiver Corporation	5122	D	831 722-9526	9238
Southwest Truck Service	4213	E	831 724-1041	7596
Spa Fitness Center Inc	7991	D	831 722-3895	14975
Spring Hills Golf Course	7992	E	831 724-1404	15028
Stalfab	3556	E	831 786-1600	5135
Sumanos Bakery LLC	5149	E	831 722-5511	9490
Suncrest Nurseries Inc	5193	D	831 728-2595	9640
Superior Foods Inc	5141	D	831 728-3691	9314
T T Miyasaka Inc **(PA)**	0171	C	831 722-3871	42
Trufocus Corporation	3844	F	831 761-9981	7094
Tubular Flow Inc	1711	D	831 761-0644	1386
Valley Heights Senior Cmnty	8361	E	831 722-4884	18197
Vps Companies Inc **(PA)**	5142	E	831 724-7551	9332
Waste MGT Collectn Recycl Inc	4953	D	831 768-9505	8386
Watsonville Coast Produce Inc	5148	D	831 722-3851	9436
West Coast Hospitals Inc	8051	E	831 722-3581	16156
West Marine Inc **(PA)**	5088	B	831 728-2700	9153
Westek Electronics Inc	5065	E	831 740-6300	8972
Young Wns Chrstn Assn of Wtsnv	8641	E	831 724-6078	18534

WEAVERVILLE, CA - Trinity County

	SIC	EMP	PHONE	ENTRY #
Emerald Kingdom Greenhouse LLC **(PA)**	3448	E	530 215-5670	4850
Mountain Cmmnties Hlth Care Ds **(PA)**	8062	C	530 623-5541	16459
Trinity River Lumber Company **(PA)**	5031	C	530 623-5561	8610

WEED, CA - Siskiyou County

	SIC	EMP	PHONE	ENTRY #
Lake Shstina Golf Cntry CLB In	7992	D	530 938-3201	15007
Sanders Prcsion Tmber Flling I **(PA)**	2411	E	530 938-4120	3077

WENDEL, CA - Lassen County

	SIC	EMP	PHONE	ENTRY #
Hl Power Company	4911	E	530 254-6161	8116

WEST POINT, CA - Calaveras County

	SIC	EMP	PHONE	ENTRY #
Martin Fischer Logging Co Inc	2411	F	209 293-4847	3070

WEST SACRAMENTO, CA - Yolo County

	SIC	EMP	PHONE	ENTRY #
3stonedeggs Inc	5144	E	541 225-7491	9344
ABM Security Services Inc	7382	D	916 614-9571	14115
AEP Span Inc	1761	C	916 372-0933	1781
Agraquest Inc **(DH)**	2834	C	866 992-2937	3836
Ahtna Facility Services Inc	7349	C	916 375-0199	11914
All Phase Security Inc	7381	D	916 919-3859	14027
Anthonys Industrial Rents	1382	F	916 373-5320	558
Arcadia Inc	3355	E	916 375-1478	4562
ASC Profiles LLC **(DH)**	5051	D	916 376-2800	8807
Aus Decking Inc	1771	D	916 373-5320	1850
Bassian Farms Inc	5147	E	408 286-6262	9375
Big Valley Metals LP	3441	F	916 372-2383	4647
Blazona Concrete Cnstr Inc	1542	D	916 375-8337	833
Brown Construction Inc	1542	D	916 374-8616	838
Bytheways Manufacturing Inc	2591	D	916 453-1212	3330
California School Boards Assn	8621	D	800 266-3382	18331
California Sierra Express Inc	4731	E	916 375-7070	7827
Califrnia Crrctnal Pace Offcer **(PA)**	8631	D	916 372-6060	18356
Califrnia State Tchers Rtrment **(DH)**	6371	B	800 228-5453	10213
Capay Incorporated **(PA)**	5148	D	530 796-0730	9391
Capital Beverage Company **(PA)**	5181	C	916 371-8164	9546
Capitol Clutch & Brake Inc	5013	E	916 371-5970	8447
Carter Group **(PA)**	3441	E	916 373-0148	4651
Cirks Construction Inc	1542	C	916 362-5460	854
Clark - Pacific Corporation **(PA)**	5032	B	916 371-0305	8624
Collins Electrical Company Inc	1731	E	209 466-3691	1480
Core Medical Clinic Inc	8093	E	916 796-0020	17005
Core-Mark Holding Company Inc	5141	E	866 791-4210	9268

GEOGRAPHIC

Employment Codes: A=Over 500 employees, B=251-500, C=101-250, D=51-100, E=20-50 F=10-19

2022 Northern California Business Directory and Buyers Guide

1233

WEST SACRAMENTO, CA

	SIC	EMP	PHONE	ENTRY #
Cosmo Import & Export LLC	2514	E	916 209-5500	3294
Creative Living Options Inc	8361	C	916 372-2102	18092
Cummins Pacific LLC	3519	F	916 371-0630	4991
Davis Community Clinic	8069	E	916 403-2970	16755
DCI Donor Services Inc	8099	D	877 401-2546	17132
DCI Donor Services Inc	8099	D	916 567-1600	17133
Del Monte Capitol Meat Co LLC (HQ)	5141	E	916 927-0595	9269
Dennis Blazona Construction	1771	E	916 375-8337	1864
Dependable Highway Express Inc	4212	E	916 374-0782	7460
Devine & Son Trucking Co Inc (PA)	4449	C	559 486-7440	7716
ECB Corp	3444	E	916 492-8900	4758
Elica Health Centers	8011	E	916 275-3747	15390
Farm Fresh To You LLC (PA)	0191	C	916 303-7145	167
Farmers Rice Cooperative	2044	D	916 373-5500	2323
Fredericksen Tank Lines Inc (PA)	4213	E	916 371-4960	7541
General Services Cal Dept	7361	E	916 376-5330	12092
Global Diving & Salvage Inc	1389	F	707 561-6810	566
Goodyear Coml Tire & Svc Ctrs	7538	C	479 788-6400	14569
Harbor Distributing LLC	5181	B	916 373-5700	9552
Heco Inc	3566	E	916 372-5411	5213
Holt of California	5082	C	916 373-4100	9023
Horizon Contract Glazing Inc	1793	E	916 373-9900	1937
Icon Apparel Group LLC	2231	E	916 372-4266	2968
Jacmar Ddc LLC	5149	D	916 372-9795	9457
Jamestown Hlth Med Sup Co LLC (PA)	5047	E	916 431-8046	8784
Jj Barn Transport Inc	4213	E	916 371-5800	7556
Krw Enterprises	1542	E	916 372-8600	910
Marathon Staffing Solutions	7361	D	978 649-6230	12106
McKesson Corporation	3841	F	916 372-4600	7001
Micromidas Inc	2836	E	916 231-9329	4054
Miyamoto International Inc (PA)	8711	D	916 373-1995	18772
Nichelini General Engrg Contrs	1611	E	916 371-1300	1065
Nor-Cal Beverage Co Inc (PA)	5181	E	916 372-0600	9558
Nor-Cal Beverage Co Inc	5078	E	916 371-8219	9016
Nor-Cal Beverage Co Inc	2086	D	916 372-1700	2796
Nor-Cal Produce Inc	5148	C	916 373-0830	9420
North Valley Fleet Svcs Inc (PA)	7538	F	916 374-8850	14580
NRC Environmental Services Inc	4959	E	916 371-7202	8401
Pacific Gas and Electric Co	4911	C	916 375-5005	8132
Pittsburg Wholesale Groc Inc	5141	E	916 372-7772	9286
Premier Print & Mail Inc	2759	F	916 503-5300	3745
Propak Logistics Inc	7699	E	479 478-7828	14770
Prudential Overall Supply	7218	E	916 372-7466	11669
Quality Cylinder Head Repair	7538	E	916 371-4302	14585
Ramos Oil Co Inc (PA)	5172	D	916 371-2570	9536
Redstone Print & Mail Inc	8742	E	916 318-6450	19621
Richard K Gould Inc	2899	E	916 371-5943	4167
River Bend Holdings LLC	8051	C	916 371-1890	16100
Riverview Intl Trcks LLC (PA)	7538	D	916 372-8541	14587
Rural Cmnty Assistance Corp (PA)	8322	E	916 447-2854	17696
Ryko Solutions Inc	3589	E	916 372-8815	5448
Sacramento Stucco Co	5032	E	916 372-7442	8633
Sacramento Television Stns Inc (DH)	4833	C	916 374-1452	8054
Sacramnt-Yolo Port Dst Fing Co	4491	D	916 371-8000	7725
Sacramnto Rver Cats Bsbal CLB	7941	D	916 376-4700	14912
Saladinos Inc	5141	D	559 271-3700	9293
Scoggan Co Inc (PA)	5013	E	916 371-3984	8465
Serenity Spprted Lving Svc LLC (PA)	8322	E	650 773-2762	17734
Sign Technology Inc	3993	E	916 372-1200	7253
Singley Enterprises (PA)	1751	E	916 375-0575	1759
Sutter Hlth Scrmnto Sierra Reg	8062	B	916 373-3400	16663
Tackett Volume Press Inc	2752	E	916 374-8991	3702
Talco Foam Inc (PA)	3069	F	916 492-8840	4228
Tata America Intl Corp	1799	D	916 803-5441	2074
Taylor Communications Inc	2761	E	916 340-0200	3758
Testamerica Laboratories Inc	8734	E	916 373-5600	19287
Tk Classics LLC	2514	E	916 209-5500	3296
Tk Elevator Corporation	1796	E	916 376-8700	1994
Tomra Sorting Inc (DH)	4953	C	720 870-2240	8368
Tonys Fine Foods (HQ)	5143	B	916 374-4000	9342
Tri-C Manufacturing Inc	3559	E	916 371-1700	5172
Triton Tower Inc (PA)	1623	D	916 375-8546	1139
Ub Inc	5149	E	916 374-8899	9498
United Parcel Service Inc	4215	C	916 373-4076	7662
Unity Courier Service Inc	7389	C	916 246-0390	14452
UPS Ground Freight Inc	4213	E	916 371-9101	7609
US Glass Inc	1793	E	916 376-8801	1946
Valley Forklift	3537	F	916 371-6165	5069
Valley Rlction Stor Nthrn Cal	4214	E	916 375-0001	7639
Valley Toxicology Service Inc	8071	E	916 371-5440	16819
Vss International Inc (HQ)	1611	E	916 373-1500	1079
Wabash National Trlr Ctrs Inc	5013	E	916 371-6921	8473
Wallace-Kuhl Investments LLC (PA)	8711	D	916 372-1434	18856
Walton Engineering Inc	1799	E	916 372-1888	2086
Wantz Equipment Company Inc	3443	E	916 372-1792	4733
Washington Unified School Dst	8351	E	916 375-7720	18045
Yara North America Inc	2879	E	916 375-1109	4148
Youngs Market Company LLC	5182	E	916 617-4402	9592

WESTLEY, CA - Stanislaus County

	SIC	EMP	PHONE	ENTRY #
Cox & Perez	0191	E	209 894-3741	153
Holiday Inn Express	7011	E	650 863-8771	11150
Just Tomatoes Inc	0723	D	209 894-5371	291

WESTWOOD, CA - Lassen County

	SIC	EMP	PHONE	ENTRY #
Bailey Creek Investors A Cali	7992	E	530 259-4653	14988
Brett Lee Womack (PA)	1799	E	530 596-3358	2011

WHEATLAND, CA - Yuba County

	SIC	EMP	PHONE	ENTRY #
Hard Rock Cafe Intl Inc	7011	D	530 633-6938	11129
Northern California Inalliance	8322	D	530 633-9695	17659

WHITETHORN, CA - Humboldt County

	SIC	EMP	PHONE	ENTRY #
Whitethorn Construction Co	6552	E	707 986-7412	10722

WILLIAMS, CA - Colusa County

	SIC	EMP	PHONE	ENTRY #
ACC-Gwg LLC	8748	D	530 473-2827	19710
Adventist Health System/West	8062	D	530 473-5641	16301
Kosmadi Brothers	7011	D	530 473-5120	11238
Morning Star Packing Co LP	2033	E	530 473-3642	2228
Tamaki Rice Corporation	2044	E	530 473-2862	2329
Valley West Health Care Inc (PA)	8059	E	530 473-5321	16282
Vann Brothers	0161	C	530 473-2607	36
Vann Family LLC	0175	D	530 473-3317	114
Vf Marketing Corp	5159	E	530 473-2607	9512

WILLITS, CA - Mendocino County

	SIC	EMP	PHONE	ENTRY #
Advanced Mfg & Dev Inc	3444	C	707 459-9451	4738
Brooktrails Resort Golf Course	7992	E	707 459-6761	14990
Dripworks Inc	5083	E	707 459-6323	9034
Ensign Willits LLC	8051	C	707 459-5592	15993
Magnetic Coils Inc	3677	E	707 459-5994	6382
Mariposa Natural Foods	5148	E	707 459-9630	9416
Mendocino Cmnty Hlth Clnic Inc	8011	C	707 456-9600	15530
Northern Aggregates Inc	1422	E	707 459-3929	577
Sherwood Valley Rancheria	7011	D	707 459-7330	11471
Shusters Logging Inc	2411	E	707 459-4131	3079
Western Health Resources	8741	E	707 459-1818	19423
Westinghouse A Brake Tech Corp	3261	E	707 459-5563	4406
Willits Hospital Inc	8062	B	707 459-6801	16724
Willits Redwood Company Inc	2421	E	707 459-4549	3119
Windsor Willits Company	2431	D	707 459-8568	3161

WILLOW CREEK, CA - Humboldt County

	SIC	EMP	PHONE	ENTRY #
Pacific Gas and Electric Co	4911	C	530 629-2128	8169

WILLOWS, CA - Glenn County

	SIC	EMP	PHONE	ENTRY #
A L Gilbert Company	2048	F	530 934-2157	2337
Calplant I LLC	2493	E	530 361-0003	3262
Calplant I Holdco LLC (PA)	2493	E	530 570-0542	3263
Glenn Medical Center Inc	8062	D	530 934-4681	16379
Glenn-Colusa Irrigation Dst (PA)	4971	E	530 934-8881	8412
Kumar Hotels Inc (PA)	7011	C	530 934-8900	11239
Pacific Gas and Electric Co	4911	C	530 229-4164	8149
Rumiano Cheese Co (PA)	2022	E	530 934-5438	2154
Sierra Nevada Cheese Co Inc	2022	D	530 934-8660	2157

WILTON, CA - Sacramento County

	SIC	EMP	PHONE	ENTRY #
Triple H Solutions Inc	4215	E	916 475-8367	7657

WINDSOR, CA - Sonoma County

	SIC	EMP	PHONE	ENTRY #
Advanced Viticulture Inc	0762	E	707 838-3805	366
Armorous	7381	D	707 387-4400	14033
Big Poppy Holdings Inc	6022	C	707 836-1588	9712
Cali Calmecac Language Academy	8641	D	707 837-7747	18400
Enartis Usa Inc (PA)	5149	E	707 838-6312	9450
Encore Events Rentals Inc	7359	D	707 431-3500	12040
Henry Mechanical Inc	1711	E	707 838-3311	1278
Knights Electric Incorporated	1731	E	707 433-6931	1531
Landcare USA LLC	0782	C	707 836-1460	476
Luthiers Mercantile Intl Inc	2499	F	707 433-1823	3270
M & M Services Inc (PA)	4953	E	707 838-2597	8339
Mendocino Forest Pdts Co LLC	5031	E	707 620-2961	8593
Micro-Vu Corp California (PA)	3827	E	707 838-6272	6880
Nieco Corporation	3589	D	707 838-3226	5445
Patin Vineyard Management Inc	0762	E	707 838-6665	384
Pick Pull Auto Dismantling Inc	5015	E	707 838-4691	8485
Pioneer Electric & Telecom Inc	1731	E	707 838-4057	1565
Praetorian USA	7299	E	707 780-3018	11727
Shook & Waller Cnstr Inc	1751	E	707 578-3933	1756
Sonoma Tilemakers Inc (DH)	1743	D	707 837-8177	1721
Sonoma-Cutrer Vineyards Inc (HQ)	0172	C	707 528-1181	75
Straight Edge Stvdore Svcs Inc (PA)	7361	E	707 837-8564	12144
Wheeler Winery Inc	2084	E	415 979-0630	2762
Windsor Golf Club Inc	7992	E	707 838-7888	15036
Windsor Oaks Vineyards LLP	2084	E	707 433-4050	2764

WINTERS, CA - Yolo County

	SIC	EMP	PHONE	ENTRY #
Ann Breznock	8734	E	530 795-2356	19257
Buckhorn Cafe Inc (PA)	2013	D	530 795-1319	2113
Martinez Ranches Inc	0811	E	530 795-2957	531
Pavestone LLC	3281	F	530 795-4400	4521
Russell Wayne Lester	0175	E	530 795-4619	113
Winters Hlthcare Fundation Inc	8099	E	530 795-4377	17195

WINTON, CA - Merced County

	SIC	EMP	PHONE	ENTRY #
Carl J Kruppa	0191	E	209 358-1759	150
Cederlind Farms LP	0172	D	209 606-8586	48
Central Valley Oprtnty Ctr Inc (PA)	8331	D	209 357-0062	17802
P H Ranch Inc	0241	E	209 358-5111	218
Santa Fe Aggregates Inc (HQ)	1442	F	209 358-3303	597
Tevelde Farms (PA)	0241	E	209 394-8008	225

WOODBRIDGE, CA - San Joaquin County

	SIC	EMP	PHONE	ENTRY #
City Rise LLC	7389	D	209 334-2703	14228
The Woodbridge Golf Cntry CLB	7997	D	209 369-2371	15160

WOODLAND, CA - Yolo County

Name	SIC	EMP	PHONE	ENTRY #
Acme Bag Co Inc **(PA)**	2674	F	530 662-6130	3390
Alta Cal Regional Ctr Inc	8322	C	530 666-3391	17415
American International Mfg Co	3523	D	530 666-2446	4995
Ames Fire Waterworks	3625	D	530 666-2493	5675
B Js Heating & AC Inc	1711	E	530 662-8601	1212
Bay State Milling Company	2041	E	530 666-6565	2309
Bentec Medical Opco LLC	3841	E	530 406-3333	6953
Boundary Bend Inc	2079	E	844 626-2726	2461
Bright People Foods Inc **(PA)**	2099	E	530 669-6870	2874
Broward Builders Inc	1542	D	530 666-5635	837
Bunge Milling Inc	5153	D	530 666-1691	9500
Butterfield Electric Inc	1731	C	530 666-2116	1470
Cache Creek Foods LLC	2099	F	530 662-1764	2877
California Cascade-Woodland	2491	E	530 666-1261	3257
California Physicians Service	6324	D	530 668-2986	10095
Califrnia PCF Rice Mil A CA LP	2044	E	530 661-1923	2318
Certified Foods Inc	2041	E	530 666-6565	2310
Cfarms Inc	2099	E	916 375-3000	2881
Child Development Incorporated	8351	B	530 666-4822	17891
Circle G Ranch Inc	0191	D	530 666-0979	151
City of Woodland	0752	D	530 668-5287	352
City of Woodland	3999	E	530 661-5860	7275
Communications & Pwr Inds LLC	7629	D	530 662-7553	14693
Crist Group Inc	3559	E	530 661-0700	5145
Culinary Farms Inc	2034	E	916 375-3000	2258
Dfc Inc	3721	E	530 669-7115	6609
Donald W Beeman	0161	E	530 662-3012	27
E & E Co Ltd	1521	B	530 669-5991	634
Eaton Drilling Co Inc	1781	E	530 402-1143	1919
Elm Ford Inc **(PA)**	7538	C	530 662-2817	14559
Empower Yolo Inc	8322	E	530 662-1133	17543
Farmers Rice Cooperative	2044	D	530 666-1691	2322
Farmers Rice Cooperative	5153	D	530 666-1691	9502
Four Wheel Campers Inc	3792	E	530 666-1442	6656
Fresenius Med Care Wdlnd Cal L	8092	D	530 668-4503	16975
Gerlirger Fndry Mch Works Inc	5051	F	530 243-1053	8816
Gold River Mills LLC **(PA)**	2044	D	530 661-1923	2324
Grow West LLC **(PA)**	8742	D	530 662-5442	19524
Half Moon Fruit & Produce Co **(PA)**	0112	E	530 662-1727	5
Harrison Con Ctng Inc A Cal Co	1771	E	530 662-2185	1881
Hygieia Biological Labs	2836	E	530 661-1442	4051
Interpac Technologies Inc	7389	D	530 662-6363	14309
J H Meek & Sons Inc	0191	E	530 662-1106	171
Joe Heidrick Enterprises Inc	0115	E	530 662-2339	7
Johnstons Trading Post Inc	2449	E	530 661-6152	3238
Kimzey Welding Works	3599	F	530 662-9331	5554
Liberty Packing Company LLC **(PA)**	5148	E	209 826-7100	9414
Limagrain Sunflowers Inc	5191	C	530 661-0756	9602
Luhdorff Sclmnini Cnslting Eng	8711	D	530 661-0109	18755
Lyman Group Inc **(PA)**	5191	E	530 662-5442	9603
Metal Sales Manufacturing Corp	3444	E	707 826-2653	4787
Mud Puppy Inc	1389	E	760 961-1160	569
Muller Ranch LLC	0111	D	530 662-0105	1
Northern Vly Indian Hlth Inc	8063	C	530 661-4400	16744
Olam West Coast Inc	2033	E	530 473-4290	2233
Omar Orozco	0761	D	530 723-0849	361
Pacific Coast Producers	2033	E	530 662-8661	2239
Payne Brothers Ranches	0161	D	530 662-2354	33
Pgp International Inc **(DH)**	2099	C	530 662-5056	2934
Pt Welding Inc	7692	E	530 406-0267	14719
Pure Nature Foods LLC	2096	E	530 723-5269	2858
R & R Pacific Construction	8711	E	530 668-7525	18798
RES-Care Inc	8052	D	530 406-8603	16200
Sachs Industries Inc	2679	F	631 242-9000	3405
Sierra Entertainment	4011	E	530 666-9646	7319
St Johns Retirement Village	8059	C	530 662-9674	16274
Summer House Inc LLC	8361	E	530 662-8493	18186
Sunfoods LLC **(HQ)**	5141	E	530 661-1923	9313
Sunrise Hospitality Inc	7011	E	916 419-4440	11518
Sutter Health	8062	C	530 406-5600	16618
Sutter Hlth Scrmnto Sierra Reg	8062	B	530 406-5616	16669
Ted Collwell	8361	E	530 666-2433	18191
Tire Store 40 Inc	7538	E	530 662-9106	14598
Tremont Group Incorporated	5191	F	530 662-5442	9613
United Health Systems Inc	8051	E	530 662-9161	16148
Voloagri Inc	5191	C	805 547-9391	9615
Volume Snacks	5147	E	530 662-3500	9381
Waste MGT Collectn Recycl Inc	4953	D	530 662-8748	8385
Western Foods LLC **(DH)**	2099	C	530 601-5991	2958
Woodland Biomass Power Ltd	4911	E	530 661-6095	8208
Woodland Healthcare	8062	C	530 669-5680	16726
Woodland Healthcare	8062	C	530 668-2600	16728
Woodland Memorial Hospital **(PA)**	8062	D	530 669-5323	16729
Woodland Memorial Hospital	8062	E	530 669-5600	16730
Woodland Swim Team Bosters CLB	8641	D	530 662-9783	18481
Woodland Veterinary Hospital	0742	E	530 666-2461	347
Yolo Co Office of Education **(PA)**	8351	E	530 668-6700	18048
Yolo Employment Services	8331	E	530 662-8616	17849
Yolo Federal Credit Union **(PA)**	6061	D	530 668-2700	9828
Yolo Ice & Creamery Inc	5143	F	530 662-7337	9343

WOODSIDE, CA - San Mateo County

Name	SIC	EMP	PHONE	ENTRY #
Ecullet Inc	4953	D	650 493-7300	8323
Filoli Center	8422	E	650 364-8300	18291
Fox Paine & Company LLC **(PA)**	6211	C	650 235-2075	9969
Langley Hill Quarry	1429	E	650 851-0179	579
Menlo Country Club	7997	D	650 369-2342	15110
Midglen Studio Associates	1542	E	650 366-0314	923
O Nelson & Son Inc	1794	E	650 851-3600	1969

YOSEMITE NTPK, CA - Mariposa County

Name	SIC	EMP	PHONE	ENTRY #
DNC Prks Rsrts At Yosemite Inc	7011	A	209 372-1001	11055

YOUNTVILLE, CA - Napa County

Name	SIC	EMP	PHONE	ENTRY #
Cosentino Signature Wineries	2084	E	707 921-2809	2539
Domaine Chandon Inc **(DH)**	2084	D	707 944-8844	2551
Dominus Estate Corporation	2084	F	707 944-8954	2552
Goosecross Cellars A Cal Corp	2084	E	707 944-1986	2603
Hotel Yountville LLC	7011	E	707 967-7900	11175
Kapcsandy Family LLC	0762	F	707 948-3100	377
Remington Ldging Hsptality LLC	7011	D	877 932-5333	11393
Twin Peaks Winery Inc	2084	E	707 945-0855	2750
Twin Teaks Winery	0172	E	707 944-8642	79

YREKA, CA - Siskiyou County

Name	SIC	EMP	PHONE	ENTRY #
Belcampo Group Inc	7299	D	530 842-5200	11707
California Department Trnsp	1611	D	530 842-2723	1021
Custom Crushing Industries Inc	1221	E	530 842-5544	543
Fairchild Med Ctr Fndation Inc	8099	D	530 842-4121	17146
Gatehouse Media LLC	2711	E	530 842-5777	3439
Madrone Hospice Inc **(PA)**	8052	D	530 842-3160	16189
Nor-Cal Products Inc **(DH)**	3494	C	530 842-4457	4962
Ozotech Inc **(PA)**	3589	F	530 842-4189	5446
Shasta Forest Products Inc	2499	E	530 842-2787	3271
Siskiyou Hospital Inc	8011	D	530 841-6211	15688
Siskiyou Hospital Inc	8062	B	530 842-6491	16527
Siskiyou Opportunity Center	7361	E	530 842-4110	12137
Southern Oregon Goodwill Inds	8331	D	530 842-6627	17841
Timber Products Co Ltd Partnr	2435	F	530 842-2310	3196

YUBA CITY, CA - Sutter County

Name	SIC	EMP	PHONE	ENTRY #
A & E Arborists Tree Care Inc	0783	C	530 790-5312	511
Alta Cal Regional Ctr Inc	8322	C	530 674-3070	17417
Amcor Flexibles LLC	2759	D	530 671-9000	3721
Ampla Health **(PA)**	8021	C	530 674-4261	15821
Bi Warehousing Inc	5013	E	530 671-8787	8446
Bi-County Ambulance Svc Inc	4119	E	530 674-2060	7377
Big Hill Logging & Rd Building **(PA)**	2411	E	530 673-4155	3056
Bonanza Inn Magnuson Grand Ht	7011	D	530 674-8824	10966
Butte Basin Management Co	8741	E	530 674-2060	19311
California Industrial Rbr Co	2822	D	530 674-2444	3813
California Olive and Vine LLC	2079	F	530 763-7921	2463
Calpine Corporation	4911	E	530 821-2075	8091
Citifinancial Credit Company	6141	C	530 671-7970	9855
City of Yuba City	8331	D	530 822-4601	17803
Clark Pest Ctrl Stockton Inc	7342	E	530 235-6101	11884
Courtyard	8361	D	530 790-3050	18085
E Center	8351	C	530 634-1200	17925
Express Personnel Services	7363	E	530 671-9202	12171
Family Physcans Inc A Med Corp	8011	E	530 671-2020	15402
Farm Credit West	6159	C	530 671-1420	9886
Feather River Surgery Center	8011	C	530 751-4800	15405
Five River Trucking Inc	4212	E	530 212-4477	7465
Fletchers Plumbing & Contg Inc **(PA)**	1711	E	530 673-2489	1264
Freemont Rideout Health Group	8062	D	530 671-2883	16372
Fremont Rideout Comp Clinic	8062	D	530 749-4411	16374
Golden 1 Credit Union	6062	D	877 465-3361	9831
Grace Baptist Church Inc	8351	E	530 673-6847	17945
Guava Holdings LLC	8069	E	530 671-0550	16759
Hilbers Inc	1542	D	530 673-2947	891
Lamon Construction Company Inc	1542	E	530 671-1370	911
Lowes Home Centers LLC	5031	C	530 844-5000	8582
Mathews Ready Mix LLC	3273	D	530 671-2400	4498
Mele Enterprises Inc	7538	E	530 674-7900	14578
Midvalley Recovery Facilities	8093	E	530 742-6670	17046
New Legend Inc	4213	B	530 674-3100	7570
North Star Cnstr & Engrg Inc **(PA)**	1542	E	530 673-7080	931
North Vly Orthpd Hand Srgery A	8062	D	530 671-2650	16464
Orchard Machinery Corp Disc **(PA)**	3523	D	530 673-2822	5015
R B Spencer Inc	1711	D	530 674-8307	1341
RES-Care Inc	8082	E	530 755-3027	16933
S & J Royal Inc	1796	D	530 682-5861	1993
Sacramento Packing Inc	2034	B	530 671-4488	2267
Sierra Central Credit Union **(PA)**	6061	D	530 671-3009	9819
Sierra Gold Nurseries Inc	0181	E	530 674-1145	134
Siller Brothers Inc **(PA)**	2411	E	530 673-0734	3081
Siller Helicopters Inc	4522	E	530 674-9460	7761
Strachan Apiaries Inc	0279	E	530 674-3881	244
Sunsweet Growers Inc **(PA)**	2034	A	800 417-2253	2271
Sutter Health	8062	C	530 741-1300	16635
Sutter Health	8062	C	530 749-3585	16640
Sutter N Med Group A Prof Corp **(PA)**	8062	D	530 749-3661	16672
Sutter North Med Foundation **(PA)**	8011	C	530 741-1300	15730
Sutter Surgical Hospital N Vly	8062	D	530 749-5700	16676
Sutter/Yuba B-Cnty Mntal Hlth	8011	E	530 822-7200	15735
Taylor Brothers Farms Inc **(PA)**	0173	C	530 671-5585	94
United Com Serve	8051	C	530 790-3000	16147
United Landscape Resource Inc	0782	E	530 671-1029	507
Unity Forest Products Inc	2431	E	530 671-7152	3158
Valley Fine Foods Company Inc	2099	E	530 671-7200	2954
Valley View Foods Inc	2033	D	530 673-7356	2246
Virga Investment Property	6512	E	530 755-4409	10414
Wheeler Auto Group Inc	7538	D	530 673-3765	14605
Yuba City Manor LLC	8361	E	530 673-6051	18215

YUBA CITY, CA

GEOGRAPHIC SECTION

Company	SIC	EMP	PHONE	ENTRY #
Yuba City Nursing & Rehab LLC	8051	D	530 671-0550	16168
Yuba City Racquet Club Inc	7997	E	530 673-6900	15168
Yuba City Steel Products Co	3441	E	530 673-4554	4695
Yuba City Unified School	8399	A	530 822-7601	18259
Yuba Cy Wste Wtr Trtmnt Fcilty	3589	E	530 822-7698	5452